D1325362

WHITAKER'S ALMANACK
2004

A & C BLACK

LONDON

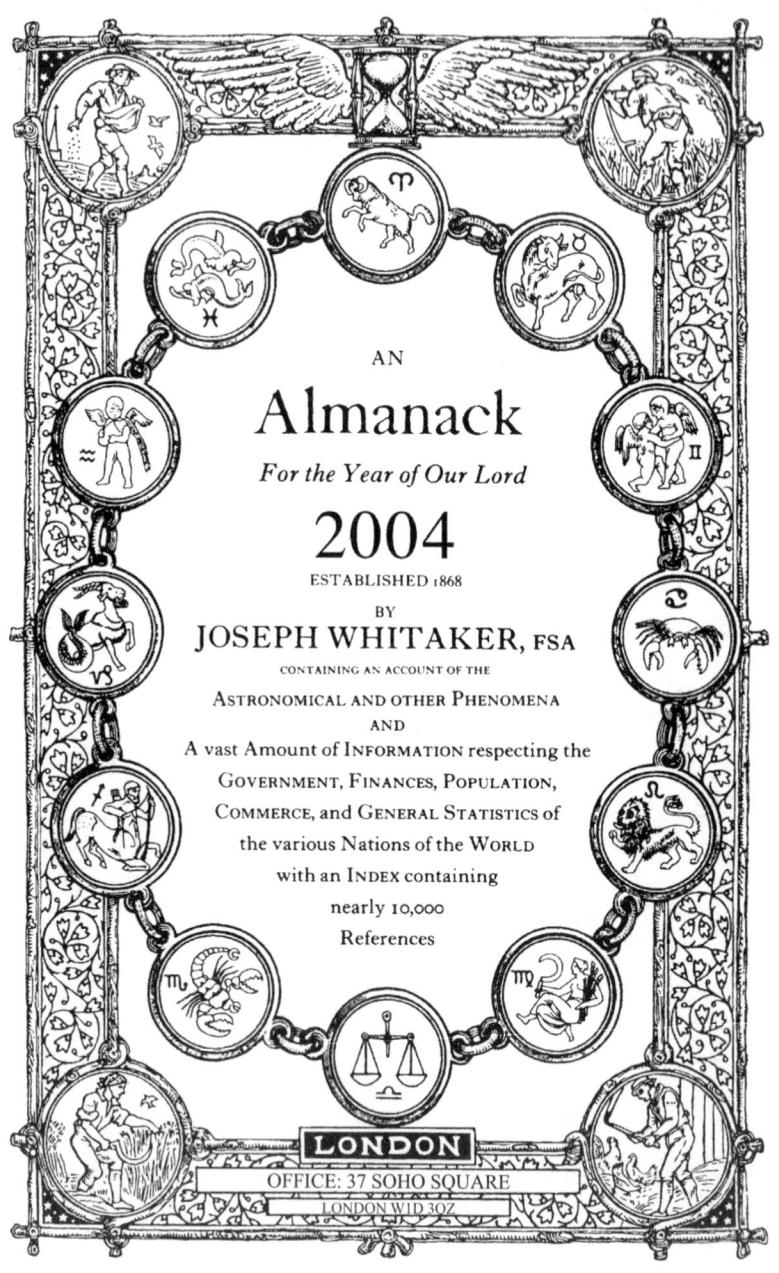

AN

Almanack

For the Year of Our Lord

2004

ESTABLISHED 1868

BY

JOSEPH WHITAKER, FSA

CONTAINING AN ACCOUNT OF THE

ASTRONOMICAL AND OTHER PHENOMENA

AND

A vast Amount of INFORMATION respecting the

GOVERNMENT, FINANCES, POPULATION,

COMMERCE, and GENERAL STATISTICS of

the various Nations of the WORLD

with an INDEX containing

nearly 10,000

References

LONDON

OFFICE: 37 SOHO SQUARE

LONDON W1D 3QZ

The traditional design of the title page for Whitaker's Almanack which has appeared in each edition since 1868

WHITAKER'S ALMANACK
2004

A & C BLACK

LONDON

A&C BLACK (PUBLISHERS) LTD
37 Soho Square, London W1D 3QZ

Whitaker's Almanack published annually since 1868
© 136th edition A & C Black (Publishers) Ltd

STANDARD EDITION
Cloth covers 0-7136-6721-4
TSP edition CN 121634

Designed by: Fiona Pike
Jacket photographs: © Corbis; Reuters/Popperfoto.com;
  Getty Images
Typeset in the EU by: Parliamentary Press,
  The Stationery Office, London
Printed and bound in the EU by: William Clowes Ltd,
  Beccles, Suffolk

Whitaker's Almanack was compiled with the assistance
of: Christian Research; *Flagmaster*, the quarterly
publication of the Flag Institute; Military Balance 2002-3
published by Oxford University Press; People in Power ©
Cambridge International Reference on Current Affairs
(CIRCA); The Diplomatic List © Crown Copyright;
World Bank Atlas © International Bank for
Reconstruction and Development/World Bank; UN
Statistical Division © United Nations; UK Hydrographic
Office; The Met Office; Oxford Cartographers; The
Police and Constabulary Almanac 2003 © R. Hazell &
Co.; International Statistics Year Book © International
Monetary Fund; Parliamentary Monitoring Services; *The
Business* © Bloomsbury Publishing; Guide to
Independent Schools 2004.

EDITORIAL STAFF
Editor-in-Chief: Lauren Simpson
Editor: Inna Ward
UK Project Editors: Ruth Northey, Anna Collishaw
International Project Editor: Lindsay Brown

CONTRIBUTORS
Vanessa White, Hilary Marsden, Jo Pearce (Editorial);
Elizabeth Holmes (Education); Gordon Taylor
(Astronomy); Hemant Kanitkar (Hindu calendar); Norris
McWhirter (World Geographical Statistics); Karen
Kenning (Mobile Communications); Karen Harries-Rees
(Environment); Martin Miller (Information Technology);
Clive Longhurst (Insurance); Roger Merrick (Mutual
Societies); Duncan Murray, Victoria Parkin (Legal Notes);
Ken Tingley (Taxation); Ian Robertson (Archaeology);
Ossian Ward (Art); Steve Clarke (Broadcasting); Peter
Marren, Matthew Saunders (Conservation); Bridie
Macmahon (Dance); Tom Charity (Film); Jon Ashworth
(Business and Finance); Nicolette Jones (Literature); Pippa
Murphy, Peter Nelson (Music); Elizabeth Forbes (Opera);
Patrick Robathan (Parliament); Erica Stary (Public Acts);
Neil Bone (Science); Jane Edwardes (Theatre); Edward
Gibbes, Stan Greenberg (Sport).

INDEX
Colin Izat, Fiona Smith – IndX Ltd

CONTENTS

6

PREFACE

TO THE 136TH ANNUAL EDITION

Welcome to the 2004 edition of *Whitaker's Almanack*. As ever, putting pen to paper to write a preface to a book that spans an entire year is exceedingly difficult. Where does one start? The conflict with Iraq dominated column inches during the early part of 2003 not least because of concerns over the legitimacy of the war and demonstrations of public opposition to the attacks on Saddam Hussein's regime. Long after the bombs had stopped falling, however, the 'dodgy dossier' debates continued and boxing matches between the media and the government ensued.

The outbreak of Severe Acute Respiratory Syndrome (SARS) in China, which reached epidemic proportions and claimed victims as far away as Canada, was also front page news for several months in the first half of 2003. Fearing for their health, many international travellers postponed travel to affected regions, however, a feeling of 'business as usual' was witnessed as travellers continued with their journeys, looking the same as always albeit for the wearing of face masks.

Low interest rates, cabinet reshuffles, royal pregnancies, controversy over gay bishops, proposals to reform the GCSE and A-level system, regional elections and, of course, a summer spent being saturated with the goings-on in the world of reality TV (whether you are interested or not) are just a snapshot of the diverse events which make current affairs so compelling.

In our fast-moving world it is essential that we are kept informed not just of those issues which make headline news. It is of equal importance for us to know which people and institutions make our world tick; how Britain's infrastructure works; how science and the arts continue to enrich the fabric of our society – and that's where a publication like *Whitaker's Almanack* is invaluable.

Updated annually, *Whitaker's Almanack* is the ultimate single-volume reference source packed with authoritative information on a wide range of subjects from politics to sport, astronomy to geography and film to science – essential for helping you keep your finger on the global pulse.

Regular readers will notice that this edition heralds a change of page design for *Whitaker's Almanack*. I very much hope that the larger, clearer headings and more modern fonts give the pages a 'fresher' look, and I welcome any comments you may have regarding the new style. On this point, tucked inside this edition you will find a Readership Survey. While we welcome readers' comments and suggestions all year round, we hope that you will find the time to respond to these specific questions about *Whitaker's Almanack*, its content and how we present reference material in the future.

As ever, the compilation of *Whitaker's Almanack* would not have been possible without the help and support of the many hundreds of organisations and individuals that assist with our research and editorial processes. Many thanks to all of you.

Lastly, I regret to announce that Ian Robertson, the archaeology contributor to *Whitaker's Almanack* for over twenty years, died suddenly on 1 August 2003. Director of the National Army Museum since 1988 and keen historian, Ian's comprehensive, informative and lively articles will be greatly missed. I would like to extend my sympathies, and those of the Whitaker's team, to all Ian's family and friends.

Lauren Simpson
Editor-in-Chief

Whitaker's Almanack
A&C Black Publishers Ltd
37 Soho Square, London, W1D 3QZ
Tel: 020-7287 5385
Fax: 020-7734 6856
Email: whitakers@acblack.com
Web: www.acblack.com

THE YEAR 2004

CHRONOLOGICAL CYCLES AND ERAS

Dominical Letter	DC
Golden Number (Lunar Cycle)	X
Julian Period	6717
Roman Indiction	12
Solar Cycle	25

	Beginning
Japanese year Heisei 16	1 January
Chinese year of the Monkey	22 January
Regnal year 53	6 February
Hindu new year	21 March
Indian (Saka) year 1926	21 March
Muslim year AH 1425	22 February
Sikh new year	13 April
Jewish year AM 5765	16 September
Roman year 2757 AUC	

RELIGIOUS CALENDARS

CHRISTIAN

Epiphany	6 January
Presentation of Christ in the Temple	2 February
Ash Wednesday	25 February
The Annunciation	25 March
Maundy Thursday	8 April
Good Friday	9 April
Easter Day (western churches)	11 April
Easter Day (Eastern Orthodox)	11 April
Rogation Sunday	16 May
Ascension Day	20 May
Pentecost (Whit Sunday)	30 May
Trinity Sunday	6 June
Corpus Christi	10 June
All Saints' Day	1 November
Advent Sunday	28 November
Christmas Day	25 December

HINDU

Makara Sankranti	15 January
Vasant Panchami (Sarasvati-puja)	26 January
Mahashivaratri	18 February
Holi	6 March
Chaitra (Hindu new year)	21 March
Ramanavami	30 March
Raksha-bandhan	29 August
Janmashtami	6 September
Ganesh Chaturthi, first day	18 September
Ganesh festival, last day	27 September
Durga-puja	14 October
Navaratri festival, first day	14 October
Sarasvati-puja	20 October
Dasara	22 October
Diwali, first day	10 November
Diwali, last day	14 November

JEWISH

Purim,	7 March
Passover, first day	6 April
Feast of Weeks, first day	26 May
Jewish new year, first day	16 September
Yom Kippur (Day of Atonement)	25 September
Feast of Tabernacles, first day	30 September
Chanucah, first day	8 December

MUSLIM

Muslim new year	22 February
Ramadan, first day	15 October

SIKH

Birthday of Guru Gobind Singh Ji	5 January
Baisakhi Mela (Sikh new year)	13 April
Martyrdom of Guru Arjan Dev Ji	16 June
Birthday of Guru Nanak Dev Ji	26 November
Martyrdom of Guru Tegh Bahadur Ji	24 November

CIVIL CALENDAR

Accession of Queen Elizabeth II	6 February
Duke of York's birthday	19 February
St David's Day	1 March
Earl of Wessex birthday	10 March
Commonwealth Day	8 March
St Patrick's Day	17 March
Birthday of Queen Elizabeth II	21 April
St George's Day	23 April
Europe Day	9 May
Coronation of Queen Elizabeth II	2 June
Duke of Edinburgh's birthday	10 June
The Queen's Official Birthday	12 June
Princess Royal's birthday	15 August
Lord Mayor's Day	13 November
Remembrance Sunday	14 November
Prince of Wales's birthday	14 November
Wedding Day of Queen Elizabeth II	20 November
St Andrew's Day	30 November

LEGAL CALENDAR

LAW TERMS

Hilary Term	12 January to 7 April
Easter Term	20 April to 28 May
Trinity Term	8 June to 31 July
Michaelmas Term	1 October to 21 December

QUARTER DAYS

England, Wales and Northern Ireland

Lady	25 March
Midsummer	24 June
Michaelmas	29 September
Christmas	25 December

TERM DAYS

Scotland

Candlemas	28 February
Whitsunday	28 May
Lammas	28 August
Martinmas	28 November
Removal Terms	28 May, 28 November

2004

JANUARY

Sunday		4	11	18	25
Monday		5	12	19	26
Tuesday		6	13	20	27
Wednesday		7	14	21	28
Thursday	1	8	15	22	29
Friday	2	9	16	23	30
Saturday	3	10	17	24	31

FEBRUARY

Sunday	1	8	15	22	29
Monday	2	9	16	23	
Tuesday	3	10	17	24	
Wednesday	4	11	18	25	
Thursday	5	12	19	26	
Friday	6	13	20	27	
Saturday	7	14	21	28	

MARCH

Sunday		7	14	21	28
Monday	1	8	15	22	29
Tuesday	2	9	16	23	30
Wednesday	3	10	17	24	31
Thursday	4	11	18	25	
Friday	5	12	19	26	
Saturday	6	13	20	27	

APRIL

Sunday		4	11	18	25
Monday		5	12	19	26
Tuesday		6	13	20	27
Wednesday		7	14	21	28
Thursday	1	8	15	22	29
Friday	2	9	16	23	30
Saturday	3	10	17	24	

MAY

Sunday		2	9	16	23	30
Monday		3	10	17	24	31
Tuesday		4	11	18	25	
Wednesday		5	12	19	26	
Thursday		6	13	20	27	
Friday		7	14	21	28	
Saturday	1	8	15	22	29	

JUNE

Sunday		6	13	20	27
Monday		7	14	21	28
Tuesday	1	8	15	22	29
Wednesday	2	9	16	23	30
Thursday	3	10	17	24	
Friday	4	11	18	25	
Saturday	5	12	19	26	

JULY

Sunday		4	11	18	25
Monday		5	12	19	26
Tuesday		6	13	20	27
Wednesday		7	14	21	28
Thursday	1	8	15	22	29
Friday	2	9	16	23	30
Saturday	3	10	17	24	31

AUGUST

Sunday	1	8	15	22	29
Monday	2	9	16	23	30
Tuesday	3	10	17	24	31
Wednesday	4	11	18	25	
Thursday	5	12	19	26	
Friday	6	13	20	27	
Saturday	7	14	21	28	

SEPTEMBER

Sunday		5	12	19	26
Monday		6	13	20	27
Tuesday		7	14	21	28
Wednesday	1	8	15	22	29
Thursday	2	9	16	23	30
Friday	3	10	17	24	
Saturday	4	11	18	25	

OCTOBER

Sunday		3	10	17	24	31
Monday		4	11	18	25	
Tuesday		5	12	19	26	
Wednesday		6	13	20	27	
Thursday		7	14	21	28	
Friday	1	8	15	22	29	
Saturday	2	9	16	23	30	

NOVEMBER

Sunday		7	14	21	28
Monday	1	8	15	22	29
Tuesday	2	9	16	23	30
Wednesday	3	10	17	24	
Thursday	4	11	18	25	
Friday	5	12	19	26	
Saturday	6	13	20	27	

DECEMBER

Sunday		5	12	19	26
Monday		6	13	20	27
Tuesday		7	14	21	28
Wednesday	1	8	15	22	29
Thursday	2	9	16	23	30
Friday	3	10	17	24	31
Saturday	4	11	18	25	

PUBLIC HOLIDAYS

	England and Wales	*Scotland*	*Northern Ireland*
New Year	† 1 January	1, †2 January	† 1 January
St Patrick's Day	–	–	‡ 17 March
'Good Friday	9 April	9 April	9 April
Easter Monday	12 April	–	12 April
Early May	† 3 May	3 May	† 3 May
Spring	31 May	† 31 May	31 May
Battle of the Boyne	–	–	‡ 12 July
Summer	30 August	2 August	30 August
'Christmas	25, 26 December	25, †26 December	25, 26 December
	27, 28 taken in lieu	27, 28 taken in lieu	27, 28 taken in lieu

'In England, Wales and Northern Ireland, Christmas Day and Good Friday are common law holidays
In the Channel Islands, Liberation Day is a bank and public holiday
† Subject to royal proclamation
‡ Subject to proclamation by the Secretary of State for Northern Ireland

2005

JANUARY						
Sunday		2	9	16	23	30
Monday		3	10	17	24	31
Tuesday		4	11	18	25	
Wednesday		5	12	19	26	
Thursday		6	13	20	27	
Friday		7	14	21	28	
Saturday	1	8	15	22	29	

FEBRUARY					
Sunday		6	13	20	27
Monday		7	14	21	28
Tuesday	1	8	15	22	
Wednesday	2	9	16	23	
Thursday	3	10	17	24	
Friday	4	11	18	25	
Saturday	5	12	19	26	

MARCH					
Sunday		6	13	20	27
Monday		7	14	21	28
Tuesday	1	8	15	22	29
Wednesday	2	9	16	23	30
Thursday	3	10	17	24	31
Friday	4	11	18	25	
Saturday	5	12	19	26	

APRIL					
Sunday		3	10	17	24
Monday		4	11	18	25
Tuesday		5	12	19	26
Wednesday		6	13	20	27
Thursday		7	14	21	28
Friday	1	8	15	22	29
Saturday	2	9	16	23	30

MAY					
Sunday	1	8	15	22	29
Monday	2	9	16	23	30
Tuesday	3	10	17	24	31
Wednesday	4	11	18	25	
Thursday	5	12	19	26	
Friday	6	13	20	27	
Saturday	7	14	21	28	

JUNE					
Sunday		5	12	19	26
Monday		6	13	20	27
Tuesday		7	14	21	28
Wednesday	1	8	15	22	29
Thursday	2	9	16	23	30
Friday	3	10	17	24	
Saturday	4	11	18	25	

JULY						
Sunday		3	10	17	24	31
Monday		4	11	18	25	
Tuesday		5	12	19	26	
Wednesday		6	13	20	27	
Thursday		7	14	21	28	
Friday	1	8	15	22	29	
Saturday	2	9	16	23	30	

AUGUST					
Sunday		7	14	21	28
Monday	1	8	15	22	29
Tuesday	2	9	16	23	30
Wednesday	3	10	17	24	31
Thursday	4	11	18	25	
Friday	5	12	19	26	
Saturday	6	13	20	27	

SEPTEMBER					
Sunday		4	11	18	25
Monday		5	12	19	26
Tuesday		6	13	20	27
Wednesday		7	14	21	28
Thursday	1	8	15	22	29
Friday	2	9	16	23	30
Saturday	3	10	17	24	

OCTOBER						
Sunday		2	9	16	23	30
Monday		3	10	17	24	31
Tuesday		4	11	18	25	
Wednesday		5	12	19	26	
Thursday		6	13	20	27	
Friday		7	14	21	28	
Saturday	1	8	15	22	29	

NOVEMBER					
Sunday		6	13	20	27
Monday		7	14	21	28
Tuesday	1	8	15	22	29
Wednesday	2	9	16	23	30
Thursday	3	10	17	24	
Friday	4	11	18	25	
Saturday	5	12	19	26	

DECEMBER					
Sunday		4	11	18	25
Monday		5	12	19	26
Tuesday		6	13	20	27
Wednesday		7	14	21	28
Thursday	1	8	15	22	29
Friday	2	9	16	23	30
Saturday	3	10	17	24	31

PUBLIC HOLIDAYS

	England and Wales	Scotland	Northern Ireland
New Year	† 3 January	3, †4 January	† 3 January
St Patrick's Day	–	–	‡ 17 March
*Good Friday	25 March	25 March	25 March
Easter Monday	28 March	–	28 March
Early May	† 2 May	2 May	† 2 May
Spring	30 May	† 30 May	30 May
Battle of the Boyne	–	–	‡ 12 July
Summer	29 August	1 August	29 August
*Christmas	25, 26 December	25, †26 December	25, 26 December
	27 taken in lieu	27 taken in lieu	27 taken in lieu

*In England, Wales and Northern Ireland, Christmas Day and Good Friday are common law holidays
In the Channel Islands, Liberation Day is a bank and public holiday
† Subject to royal proclamation
‡ Subject to proclamation by the Secretary of State for Northern Ireland

FORTHCOMING EVENTS 2004

*Provisional dates
†Venue not confirmed

JANUARY

8–18	London International Boat Show, Earls Court, London
10–25	London International Mime Festival
14–18	London Art Fair, Business Design Centre, London
22	Chinese New Year Celebrations, London

FEBRUARY

| 28–7 March | Bath Literature Festival |

MARCH

4–7	Crufts Dog Show, NEC, Birmingham
4	World Book Day
10–4 April	Ideal Home Exhibition, Earls Court, London
12–21	National Science Week
14–16	London Book Fair
19–21	Liberal Democrat Party Spring Conference, Southport

APRIL

31–16 October	Pitlochry Festival Theatre season
22–25	Chelsea Art Fair, Chelsea Old Town Hall
April–October	Chichester Festival Theatre season, Tayside

MAY

20–29 August	Glyndebourne Festival Opera season
21–6 June	Bath International Music Festival
27–28	Chelsea Flower Show, Royal Hospital, Chelsea
28–6 June	The Hay Festival, Hay-on-Wye, Hereford

JUNE

8–16 August	Royal Academy of Arts Summer Exhibition
10	London Mayoral Election
11–27	The Aldeburgh Festival
12	Trooping the Colour, Horseguards Parade, London
22–24	Wisley Flower Show, RHS Garden, Wisley

JULY

2–10	York Early Music Festival
2–18	Cheltenham International Festival of Music
4–7	The Royal Show, National Agricultural Centre, Stoneleigh Park
6–11	Hampton Court Palace Flower Show, Surrey
10–25	Buxton Festival, Derbyshire
15–24	The Welsh Proms, St David's Hall, Cardiff
16–11 September	BBC Promenade Concerts, Royal Albert Hall, London

| 21–25 | RHS Flower Show, Tatton Park, Cheshire |
| 31–7 August | Royal National Eisteddfod of Wales, Meifod, Powys |

AUGUST

6–28	Edinburgh Military Tattoo, Edinburgh Castle
7–14	Three Choirs Festival, Gloucester
15–4 September	Edinburgh International Festival
17–19	Wisley Flower Show, RHS Garden, Wisley
*29–30	Notting Hill Carnival, Notting Hill, London
28–30	Town and Country Festival, National Agricultural Centre, Stoneleigh Park

SEPTEMBER

3–7 November	Blackpool Illuminations, Promenade
4	Braemar Royal Highland Gathering, Aberdeenshire
13–16	TUC Annual Congress, Brighton
19–23	Liberal Democrat Party Conference, Bournemouth
26–30	Labour Party Conference, Brighton

OCTOBER

5–8	Conservative Party Conference, Bournemouth
14	National Poetry Day
29–4 January	Turner Prize Exhibition

NOVEMBER

7	London to Brighton Veteran Car Run
13	Lord Mayor's Procession and Show, City of London
19–28	Huddersfield Contemporary Music Festival
*6–21 November	London Film Festival, NFT and other venues

SPORTS EVENTS

FEBRUARY

1–8	Snooker: Benson and Hedges Masters, Wembley Conference Centre
14	Rugby Union: Six Nations Championship, France v. Ireland, Stade de France
14	Rugby Union: Six Nations Championship, Wales v. Scotland, Millennium Stadium, Cardiff
15	Rugby Union: Six Nations Championship, Italy v. England, Rome
21	Rugby Union: Six Nations Championship, France v. Italy, Stade de France
21	Rugby Union: Six Nations Championship, Scotland v. England, Murrayfield
22	Rugby Union: Six Nations Championship, Ireland v. Wales, Lansdowne Road

MARCH

6	Rugby Union: Six Nations Championship, England v. Ireland, Twickenham
6	Rugby Union: Six Nations Championship, Italy v. Scotland, Rome
7	Rugby Union: Six Nations Championship, Wales v. France, Millennium Stadium, Cardiff
20	Rugby Union: Six Nations Championship, England v. Wales, Twickenham
20	Rugby Union: Six Nations Championship, Ireland v. Italy, Lansdowne Road
21	Rugby Union: Six Nations Championship, Scotland v. France, Murrayfield
27	Rugby Union: Six Nations Championship, France v. England, Stade de France
27	Rugby Union: Six Nations Championship, Ireland v. Scotland, Lansdowne Road
27	Rugby Union: Six Nations Championship, Wales v. Italy, Millennium Stadium, Cardiff
28	Oxford and Cambridge Boat Race, Putney to Mortlake, London

APRIL

17–3 May	Snooker: Embassy World Championship, Crucible Theatre, Sheffield
18	Athletics: Flora London Marathon
29–2 May	Badminton Horse Trials, Badminton

MAY

9	Welsh FA Cup Final[†]
12–16	Royal Windsor Horse Show, Home Park, Windsor
15	Rugby League: Challenge Cup Final, Millennium Stadium, Cardiff
22	The FA Cup Final, Millennium Stadium, Cardiff
22	Scottish FA Cup Final, Hampden Park, Glasgow
29–11 June	TT Motorcycle Races, Isle of Man
31–5 June	British Amateur Golf Championship, St Andrews Golf Club

JUNE

12–4 July	European Football Championship, Portugal
21–4 July	Tennis: Wimbledon Championship, All England Lawn Tennis Club, Wimbledon
30–4 July	Rowing: Henley Royal Regatta, Henley-on-Thames

JULY

5–24	Shooting: NRA Imperial Meeting, Bisley Camp, Surrey
15–18	Golf: The Open, Royal Troon Golf Club
[*]11	British Formula 1 Grand Prix, Silverstone, Northants
21–1 August	Sailing: Commodores' Cup, Royal Ocean Racing Club

AUGUST

7–14	Sailing: Cowes Week

SEPTEMBER

2–5	Burghley Horse Trials, Burghley Park, Lincolnshire
17–19 September	The Ryder Cup, Michigan, USA

OCTOBER

6–10	Horse of the Year Show, NEC, Birmingham

HORSE-RACING

27 March	Lincoln Handicap
1–3 April	Grand National, Aintree, Liverpool
[*]1 May	Two Thousand Guineas, Newmarket
[*]2 May	One Thousand Guineas, Newmarket
4 June	The Oaks, Epsom
4 June	Coronation Cup, Epsom
5 June	The Derby, Epsom
15–19 June	Royal Ascot
26 July	King George VI and Queen Elizabeth Diamond Stakes
11 September	St Leger, Doncaster
[*]2 October	Cambridgeshire Handicap, Newmarket
[*]16 October	Cesarewitch, Newmarket

CRICKET

Npower Test Match Series

20–24 May	England v. New Zealand, 1st, Lord's
3–7 June	England v. New Zealand, 2nd, Headingley
10–14 June	England v. New Zealand, 3rd, Trent Bridge, Nottingham
22–26 July	England v. West Indies, 1st, Lord's
29 July–2 August	England v. West Indies, 2nd, Edgbaston
12–16 August	England v. West Indies, 3rd, Old Trafford, Manchester
19–23 August	England v. West Indies, 4th, The Oval

NatWest Series

24 June	England v. New Zealand, Old Trafford, Manchester
26 June	New Zealand v. West Indies, Edgbaston
27 June	England v. West Indies, Trent Bridge, Nottingham
29 June	England v. New Zealand, Chester-le-Street
1 July	England v. West Indies, Headingley[†]
3 July	New Zealand v. West Indies, Cardiff
4 July	England v. New Zealand, Bristol
6 July	England v. West Indies, Lord's
8 July	New Zealand v. West Indies, Southampton
10 July	The Final, Lord's
11 July	Reserve Day

CENTENARIES OF 2004

1204
13 December Moses Maimonides, philosopher, jurist and physician, died

1304
18/19 July Francesco Petrarch, scholar and poet, born

1604
29 February John Whitgift, Archbishop of Canterbury, died

1704
28 October John Locke, philosopher and founder of philosophical Liberalism, died

1804
6 February Joseph Priestley, physicist, political theorist and clergyman, died
12 February Immanuel Kant, philosopher, died
14 March Johann Strauss, composer, born
1 June Mikhail Glinka, composer, born
3 June Richard Cobden, economist and politician, born
1 July George Sand, novelist, born
4 July Nathaniel Hawthorne, novelist and short story writer, born
21 December Earl of Beaconsfield, Benjamin Disraeli, Prime Minister February–December 1868, 1874–80, born

1904
14 January Sir Cecil Beaton, photographer; designer for theatre and film, born
18 January Cary Grant, actor, born
22 January George Balanchine, choreographer, born
14 April Sir John Gielgud, actor, born
16 April Samuel Smiles, Scottish social reformer and author, died
22 April Robert Oppenheimer, nuclear physicist, born
24 April Willem de Kooning, painter, born
27 April Cecil Day-Lewis, poet laureate from 1968-72, born
1 May Antonin Dvořák, composer, died

2 May Bing Crosby, singer and actor, born
10 May Sir Henry Stanley, explorer of Africa; rescued missionary and explorer David Livingstone, died
11 May Salvador Dalí, painter, principal artist of the Surrealist movement, born
26 May George Formby, comedian and actor, born
10 June Frederick Loewe, composer, teacher and singer, born
2 July René Lacoste, tennis player, born
3 July Theodor Herzl, Zionist leader, died
5 July Sir Harold Acton, aesthete, born
12 July Pablo Neruda, poet and diplomat; won Nobel prize for Literature in 1971, born
14 July Isaac Bashevis, singer, author, born
14 July (Stephen J.) Paul Kruger, president of the South African Republic 1883–1902, died
15 July Anton Chekhov, playwright, died
27 July Sir Anton Dolin, dancer, choreographer and director, born
21 August William Basie, pianist, band-leader and composer, born
22 August Xiaoping Deng, statesman and politician, born
25 August Henri Fantin-Latour, painter and lithographer, died
26 August Christopher Isherwood, novelist and playwright, born
17 September Sir Frederick Ashton, choreographer, born
2 October Graham Greene, novelist, born
20 October Dame Anna Neagle, actress and dancer, born
14 November Harold Larwood, cricketer, bowler at the centre of 'Bodyline' controversy, born
14 November Baron Ramsey, Archbishop of Canterbury, 1961–74, born
27 December Marlene Dietrich, actress, born

CENTENARIES OF 2005

1605
13 April Boris Godunov, tsar of Russia 1598-1605, died

1705
17 January John Ray, naturalist, died
13 July Titus Oates, Anglican priest, fabricated the Popish Plot in 1678, died
17 November Ninon de l'Enclos, French courtesan, died

1805
27 January Samuel Palmer, painter, born
2 April Hans Christian Andersen, novelist and writer of fairy tales, born
9 May Johann von Schiller, dramatist, died
28 May Luigi Boccherini, composer, died
21 October Lord Horatio Nelson, naval commander, died
23 October John Bartlett, lexicographer, born

1905
2 January Sir Michael Tippett, composer, born
21 January Christian Dior, dress designer and couturier, born

24 March Jules Verne, writer, died
26 April Jean Vigo, film director, born
16 May Henry Fonda, film actor, born
16 May H. E. Bates, novelist and playwright and short story writer, born
21 June Jean-Paul Sartre, writer, born
25 July Elias Canetti, novelist and playwright; won Nobel Prize for Literature in 1981, born
5 September Arthur Koestler, political refugee and prisoner, born
18 September Agnes de Mille, dancer and choreographer, born
18 September Greta Garbo, film actress, born
19 September Thomas Barnardo, founder of the Barnardo's children's homes, died
23 October Felix Bloch, physicist, Nobel prize winner 1952, born
21 December Anthony Powell, writer, born
24 December Howard Hughes, industrialist, pilot, film producer, born
31 December Jule Styne, composer, born

THE UNITED KINGDOM

THE UNITED KINGDOM

The United Kingdom comprises Great Britain (England, Wales and Scotland) and Northern Ireland. The Isle of Man and the Channel Islands are Crown dependencies with their own legislative systems, and not a part of the United Kingdom.

AREA (2000)

	Land miles²	km²
United Kingdom	93,787	242,910
England	50,356	130,422
Wales	8,023	20,779
Scotland	30,167	78,133
Northern Ireland	5,242	13,576
Isle of Man*	221	572
Channel Islands*	75	194

*1981 data.

POPULATION

The first official census of population in England, Wales and Scotland was taken in 1801 and a census has been taken every ten years since, except in 1941 when there was no census because of war. The last official census in the United Kingdom was taken on 29 April 2001 and the next is due in April 2011.

The first official census of population in Ireland was taken in 1841. However, all figures given below refer only to the area which is now Northern Ireland. Figures for Northern Ireland in 1921 and 1931 are estimates based on the censuses taken in 1926 and 1937 respectively.

Estimates of the population of England before 1801, calculated from the number of baptisms, burials and marriages, are:

1570	4,160,221	1670	5,773,646
1600	4,811,718	1700	6,045,008
1630	5,600,517	1750	6,517,035

For further details see www.statistics.gov.uk

CENSUS RESULTS 1801–2001

	United Kingdom			England and Wales			Scotland			Northern Ireland		
Thousands	Total	Male	Female	Total	Male	Female	Total	Male	Female	Total	Male	Female
1801	—	—	—	8,893	4,255	4,638	1,608	739	869	—	—	—
1811	13,368	6,368	7,000	10,165	4,874	5,291	1,806	826	980	—	—	—
1821	15,472	7,498	7,974	12,000	5,850	6,150	2,092	983	1,109	—	—	—
1831	17,835	8,647	9,188	13,897	6,771	7,126	2,364	1,114	1,250	—	—	—
1841	20,183	9,819	10,364	15,914	7,778	8,137	2,620	1,242	1,378	1,649	800	849
1851	22,259	10,855	11,404	17,928	8,781	9,146	2,889	1,376	1,513	1,443	698	745
1861	24,525	11,894	12,631	20,066	9,776	10,290	3,062	1,450	1,612	1,396	668	728
1871	27,431	13,309	14,122	22,712	11,059	11,653	3,360	1,603	1,757	1,359	647	712
1881	31,015	15,060	15,955	25,974	12,640	13,335	3,736	1,799	1,936	1,305	621	684
1891	34,264	16,593	17,671	29,003	14,060	14,942	4,026	1,943	2,083	1,236	590	646
1901	38,237	18,492	19,745	32,528	15,729	16,799	4,472	2,174	2,298	1,237	590	647
1911	42,082	20,357	21,725	36,070	17,446	18,625	4,761	2,309	2,452	1,251	603	648
1921	44,027	21,033	22,994	37,887	18,075	19,811	4,882	2,348	2,535	1,258	610	648
1931	46,038	22,060	23,978	39,952	19,133	20,819	4,843	2,326	2,517	1,243	601	642
1951	50,225	24,118	26,107	43,758	21,016	22,742	5,096	2,434	2,662	1,371	668	703
1961	52,709	25,481	27,228	46,105	22,304	23,801	5,179	2,483	2,697	1,425	694	731
1971	55,515	26,952	28,562	48,750	23,683	25,067	5,229	2,515	2,714	1,536	755	781
1981	55,848	27,104	28,742	49,155	23,873	25,281	5,131	2,466	2,664	*1,533	750	783
1991	56,467	27,344	29,123	49,890	24,182	25,707	4,999	2,392	2,607	1,578	769	809
2001	58,789	28,581	30,208	52,042	25,327	26,715	5,062	2,432	2,630	1,685	821	864

*Figure includes 44,500 non-enumerated persons.

Source: ONS-Census reports (Crown Copyright)

†RESIDENT POPULATION: 2001 ESTIMATES AND FUTURE PROJECTIONS (MID-YEAR)

Thousands	United Kingdom			England and Wales			Scotland			Northern Ireland		
	Total	Male	Female	Total	Male	Female	Total	Male	Female	Total	Male	Female
§ 2001	58,837	28,611	30,225	52,084	25,355	26,730	5,064	2,434	2,630	1,689	824	865
2006	59,657	29,053	30,604	52,920	25,798	27,122	5,023	2,418	2,605	1,714	837	877
2011	60,524	29,487	31,037	53,806	26,241	27,565	4,983	2,398	2,585	1,735	847	888
2021	62,386	30,316	32,070	55,722	27,109	28,614	4,895	2,346	2,549	1,769	862	907
2026	63,156	30,609	32,547	56,553	27,442	29,112	4,828	2,305	2,523	1,775	862	912

† Projections are 2001 based.
§ Estimates are based on the 2001 Census
Source: The Stationery Office – Annual Abstract of Statistics 2003

ISLANDS: CENSUS RESULTS 1901–2001

	Isle of Man			Jersey			*Guernsey		
	Total	Male	Female	Total	Male	Female	Total	Male	Female
1901	54,752	25,496	29,256	52,576	23,940	28,636	40,446	19,652	20,794
1911	52,016	23,937	28,079	51,898	24,014	27,884	41,858	20,661	21,197
1921	60,284	27,329	32,955	49,701	22,438	27,263	38,315	18,246	20,069
1931	49,308	22,443	26,865	50,462	23,424	27,038	40,643	19,659	20,984
1951	55,123	25,749	29,464	57,296	27,282	30,014	43,652	21,221	22,431
1961	48,151	22,060	26,091	57,200	27,200	30,000	45,068	21,671	23,397
1971	56,289	26,461	29,828	72,532	35,423	37,109	51,458	24,792	26,666
1981	64,679	30,901	33,778	77,000	37,000	40,000	53,313	25,701	27,612
1991	69,788	33,693	36,095	84,082	40,862	43,220	58,867	28,297	30,570
2001	76,315	37,372	38,943	87,186	42,485	44,701	59,807	29,138	30,669

* Population of Guernsey, Herm, Jethou and Lithou.
Figures for 1901–71 record all persons present on census night; census figures for 1981–2001 record all persons resident in the islands on census night. The 2001 population census also recorded the population of Alderney as 2,294 and an informal census of Sark gave their population as 591.
Source: Census 2001 (Crown copyright).

RESIDENT POPULATION

BY AGE AND SEX 2001
Thousands

Age Range	Males	Females
0–4	1,786	1,700
5–9	1,915	1,823
10–14	1,988	1,893
15–19	1,871	1,793
20–24	1,765	1,781
25–29	1,896	1,972
30–34	2,200	2,294
35–39	2,278	2,348
40–44	2,057	2,095
45–49	1,851	1,885
50–54	2,003	2,037
55–59	1,651	1,687
60–64	1,410	1,470
65–69	1,241	1,355
70–74	1,059	1,280
75–79	818	1,149
80–84	483	831
85–89	227	526
90 and over	83	288

Source: Census 2001 (Crown copyright).

BY ETHNIC GROUP AVERAGE SPRING 2001–WINTER 2001/2*

Ethnic group	Estimated population (thousands)
White	
British	51,312
Other	1,690
Mixed	
White and Black Caribbean	271
White and Black African	65
White and Asian	145
Other Mixed	30
Asian	
Indian	956
Pakistani	728
Bangladeshi	261
Other Asian	250
Black	
Black Caribbean	618
Black African	506
Black Other	72
Chinese	180
Other	282
All†	59,139

* These are Labour Force Survey (LFS) estimates which have not been seasonally adjusted or adjusted to take account of the Census 2001 results.
† Includes ethnic groups not stated.
Source: The Stationery Office – Annual Abstract of Statistics 2003 (Crown copyright).

IMMIGRATION 2001

ACCEPTANCE FOR SETTLEMENT IN THE UK BY
NATIONALITY

Region	Number of persons	
	2000	2001
Europe*	15,105	13,795
Americas: total	11,520	11,895
USA	4,580	4,385
Canada	1,325	1,320
Africa: total	44,460	31,430
Asia: total	47,540	43,340
Indian sub-continent	22,735	22,860
Middle East	7,090	4,595
Oceania: total	4,900	5,450
British Overseas Citizens	630	515
Stateless	930	385
Total	125,090	106,820

* Excluding European Economic Area nationals
Source: The Stationery Office – Annual Abstract of Statistics 2003
(Crown copyright).

BIRTHS 2001

	Live births	Male	Female	Birth rate*
United Kingdom	669,000	343,000	326,000	11.4
England and Wales	595,000	305,000	290,000	11.4
Scotland	53,000	27,000	26,000	10.4
Northern Ireland	22,000	11,000	11,000	13.0

* Live births per 1,000 population
Source: The Stationery Office – Annual Abstract of Statistics 2003
(Crown copyright).

CONCEPTIONS BY OUTCOME

		Percentages
England and Wales	1991	2000
Conceptions leading to:		
Maternities	81	77
Legal Abortions	19	23
Total Number of		
Conceptions (=100%)	854,000	767,000

Source: The Stationery Office – Social Trends 2003
(Crown copyright).

MARRIAGE AND DIVORCE 2001

	Marriages	Divorces
United Kingdom	286,129	156,814
England and Wales	249,227	143,818
Scotland	29,621	10,631
Northern Ireland	7,281	2,365

Source: The Stationery Office – Annual Abstract of Statistics 2003
(Crown copyright).

HOUSEHOLDS 2002

BY TYPE OF HOUSEHOLD AND FAMILY IN
GREAT BRITAIN

Percentages	2002
One Person	
Under state pension age	15
Over state pension age	14
Two or more unrelated adults	3
One family households	
Couple	
No children	29
1–2 dependent children	19
3 or more dependent children	4
non-dependent children only	6
Lone parent	
Dependent children	6
Non-dependent children only	3
Multi-family households	1

Source: The Stationery Office – Social Trends 2003
(Crown copyright).

HOUSEHOLDS BY SIZE

Percentages	2002
One person	29
Two people	35
Three people	16
Four people	14
Five people	5
Six or more people	2
All households (=100%) (millions)	24.4
Average household size (number of people)	2.4

Source: The Stationery Office – Social Trends 2003
(Crown copyright).

DEATHS 2001

Males	Deaths	Death Rate*
United Kingdom	286,760	10.0
England and Wales	252,426	
Scotland	27,324	
Northern Ireland	7,010	
Females		
United Kingdom	315,508	10.4
England and Wales	277,947	
Scotland	30,058	
Northern Ireland	7,503	

* Death rate per 1,000 population
Sources: The Stationery Office – Annual Abstract of Statistics 2003
(Crown copyright).

INFANT MORTALITY 2001

Deaths of infants under 1 year of age per 1,000 live births

	Number
United Kingdom	5.5
England and Wales	5.4
Scotland	5.5
Northern Ireland	6.1

Source: The Stationery Office – Annual Abstract of Statistics 2003
(Crown copyright).

HEALTH

DEATHS ANALYSED BY CAUSE 2001

	England and Wales	Scotland	N. Ireland
TOTAL DEATHS	530,373	57,382	14,513
Deaths from natural causes	511,667	54,961	13,968
Infectious and parasitic diseases	4,253	558	117
Neoplasms	139,135	15,475	3,802
Diseases of blood and blood-forming organs and certain disorders involving the immune mechanism	1,000	124	32
Endocrine, nutritional and metabolic diseases	7,711	891	200
Mental and behavioural disorders	14,143	2,425	381
Diseases of the nervous system and sense organs	14,732	1,243	467
Diseases of the circulatory system	211,842	22,666	5,829
Diseases of the respiratory system	67,391	6,435	1,975
Diseases of the digestive system	23,386	3,063	556
Diseases of the skin and subcutaneous tissue	1,291	90	24
Diseases of the musculo-skeletal system and connective tissue	4,588	357	94
Diseases of the genito-urinary system	7,682	969	278
Complications of pregnancy, childbirth and the puerperium	42	6	2
Certain conditions originating in the perinatal period	200	167	63
Congenital malformations, deformations and chromasomal abnormalities	1,280	172	83
Symptons, signs and abnormal findings not classified elsewhere	13,351	320	65
Deaths from external causes	16,569	2,421	545

Source: The Stationery Office – *Annual Abstract of Statistics 2003* (Crown copyright).

NOTIFICATIONS OF INFECTIOUS DISEASES UK 2001

Measles	2,661
Mumps	3,433
Rubella	1,782
Whooping cough	1,059
Scarlet fever	2,320
Dysentery	1,495
Food poisoning	95,752
Typhoid and paratyphoid fevers	254
Hepatitis	4,419
Tuberculosis	7,231
Malaria	1,118

Source: The Stationery Office – *Annual Abstract of Statistics 2003* (Crown copyright).

AVERAGE WEEKLY ALCOHOL CONSUMPTION BY GENDER AND SOCIO-ECONOMIC GROUP (GREAT BRITAIN) 2000

*units of alcohol**

	Males	Females
Professional	17.9	8.6
Employers and managers	18.0	7.9
Intermediate non-manual	18.1	7.9
Junior non-manual	16.3	6.6
Skilled manual	17.3	6.9
Semi-skilled manual	16.2	5.9
Unskilled manual	17.1	4.3
All aged 16 and over	17.4	7.1

* A unit of alcohol is 8 grams by weight or 10ml by volume of pure alcohol, i.e. the amount contained in half a pint of ordinary strength beer or lager, a single pub measure of spirits or a small glass of ordinary strength wine.

Source: The Stationery Office – *Social Trends 2003* (Crown copyright).

PREVALENCE OF CIGARETTE SMOKING BY GENDER AND SOCIO-ECONOMIC GROUP (GREAT BRITAIN) 2000

Percentages

	Males	Females
Professional	17	14
Employers and managers	23	20
Intermediate/junior non-manual	27	26
Skilled manual	33	26
Semi-skilled manual	36	32
Unskilled manual	39	35
All non-manual	23	22
All manual	34	29
All aged 16 and over	29	25

Source: The Stationery Office – *Social Trends 2003* (Crown copyright).

BODY MASS* BY GENDER (ENGLAND) 2001

Percentages

	Males	Females
Underweight	4	6
Desirable	28	38
Overweight	47	33
Obese	21	23

*The Body Mass Index (BMI) standardised weight for height and is calculated as weight (kg)/height (m)^2. Underweight is defined as a BMI of 20 or less, desirable 20-25, overweight 25-30 and obese over 30.

Source: The Stationery Office – *Social Trends 2003* (Crown copyright).

THE NATIONAL FLAG

The national flag of the United Kingdom is the Union Flag, generally known as the Union Jack.

The Union Flag is a combination of the cross of St George, patron saint of England, the cross of St Andrew, patron saint of Scotland, and a cross similar to that of St Patrick, patron saint of Ireland.

Cross of St George: cross Gules in a field Argent (red cross on a white ground)

Cross of St Andrew: saltire Argent in a field Azure (white diagonal cross on a blue ground)

Cross of St Patrick: saltire Gules in a field Argent (red diagonal cross on a white ground)

The Union Flag was first introduced in 1606 after the union of the kingdoms of England and Scotland under one sovereign. The cross of St Patrick was added in 1801 after the union of Great Britain and Ireland.

FLYING THE UNION FLAG

The correct orientation of the Union Flag when flying is with the broader diagonal band of white uppermost in the hoist (i.e. near the pole) and the narrower diagonal band of white uppermost in the fly (i.e. furthest from the pole).

It is the practice to fly the Union Flag daily on some customs houses. In all other cases, flags are flown on government buildings by command of The Queen. It is now customary for the Union Flag to be flown at Buckingham Palace, Windsor Castle and Sandringham when the Queen is not in residence.

The flying of the Union Flag on public buildings is decided by the Department for Culture, Media and Sport at The Queen's command. On the days appointed, the Union Flag is flown on government buildings in the United Kingdom from 8 a.m. to sunset.

FLAGS AT HALF-MAST

Flags are flown at half-mast (i.e. two-thirds up between the top and bottom of the flagstaff) on the following occasions:

(a) From the announcement of the death up to the funeral of the Sovereign, except on Proclamation Day, when flags are hoisted right up from 11 a.m. to sunset
(b) The funerals of members of the royal family, subject to special commands from The Queen in each case
(c) The funerals of foreign rulers, subject to special commands from The Queen in each case
(d) The funerals of prime ministers and ex-prime ministers of the UK, subject to special commands from The Queen in each case
(e) Other occasions by special command of The Queen

On occasions when days for flying flags coincide with days for flying flags at half-mast, the following rules are observed. Flags are flown:
(a) although a member of the royal family, or a near relative of the royal family, may be lying dead, unless special commands are received from The Queen to the contrary

(b) although it may be the day of the funeral of a foreign ruler

If the body of a very distinguished subject is lying at a government office, the flag may fly at half-mast on that office until the body has left (provided it is a day on which the flag would fly) and then the flag is to be hoisted right up. On all other government buildings the flag will fly as usual.

THE ROYAL STANDARD

The Royal Standard is hoisted only when The Queen is actually present in the building, and never when Her Majesty is passing in procession.

DAYS FOR FLYING FLAGS

Birthday of The Countess of Wessex	20 January
The Queen's Accession	6 February
Birthday of The Duke of York	19 February
*St David's Day (in Wales only)	1 March
**Commonwealth Day (2004)	8 March
Birthday of The Earl of Wessex	10 March
Birthday of The Queen	21 April
*St George's Day (in England only)	23 April
†Europe Day	9 May
Coronation Day	2 June
Birthday of The Duke of Edinburgh	10 June
The Queen's Official Birthday (2004)	12 June
Birthday of The Princess Royal	15 August
Remembrance Sunday (2004)	14 November
Birthday of The Prince of Wales	14 November
The Queen's Wedding Day	20 November
*St Andrew's Day (in Scotland only)	30 November
‡The opening of Parliament by The Queen	
‡The prorogation of Parliament by The Queen	

*Where a building has two or more flagstaffs, the appropriate national flag may be flown in addition to the Union Flag, but not in a superior position
**Commonwealth Day is always the second Monday in March
†The Union Flag should fly alongside the European flag. On government buildings that have only one flagpole, the Union Flag should take precedence
‡Flags are flown whether or not The Queen performs the ceremony in person. Flags are flown only in the Greater London area

THE ROYAL FAMILY

THE SOVEREIGN

ELIZABETH II, by the Grace of God, of the United Kingdom of Great Britain and Northern Ireland and of her other Realms and Territories Queen, Head of the Commonwealth, Defender of the Faith
Her Majesty Elizabeth Alexandra Mary of Windsor, elder daughter of King George VI and of HM Queen Elizabeth the Queen Mother
Born 21 April 1926, at 17 Bruton Street, London W1
Ascended the throne 6 February 1952
Crowned 2 June 1953, at Westminster Abbey
Married 20 November 1947, in Westminster Abbey, HRH The Prince Philip, Duke of Edinburgh
Official residences: Buckingham Palace, London SW1A 1AA; Windsor Castle, Berks; Palace of Holyroodhouse, Edinburgh
Private residences: Sandringham, Norfolk; Balmoral Castle, Aberdeenshire

HUSBAND OF THE QUEEN

HRH THE PRINCE PHILIP, DUKE OF EDINBURGH, KG, KT, OM, GBE, AC, QSO, PC, Ranger of Windsor Park
Born 10 June 1921, son of Prince and Princess Andrew of Greece and Denmark, naturalised a British subject 1947, created Duke of Edinburgh, Earl of Merioneth and Baron Greenwich 1947

CHILDREN OF THE QUEEN

HRH THE PRINCE OF WALES (Prince Charles Philip Arthur George), KG, KT, GCB, OM and Great Master of the Order of the Bath, AK, QSO, PC, ADC(P)
Born 14 November 1948, created Prince of Wales and Earl of Chester 1958, succeeded as Duke of Cornwall, Duke of Rothesay, Earl of Carrick and Baron Renfrew, Lord of the Isles and Great Steward of Scotland 1952
Married 29 July 1981 Lady Diana Frances Spencer (Diana, Princess of Wales (1961–97), youngest daughter of the 8th Earl Spencer and the Hon. Mrs Shand Kydd), marriage dissolved 1996
Issue:
(1) HRH Prince William of Wales (Prince William Arthur Philip Louis), *born* 21 June 1982
(2) HRH Prince Henry of Wales (Prince Henry Charles Albert David), *born* 15 September 1984
Residences of the Prince of Wales: St James's Palace, London SW1A 1BS; Highgrove, Doughton, Tetbury, Glos GL8 8TN

HRH THE PRINCESS ROYAL (Princess Anne Elizabeth Alice Louise), KG, GCVO
Born 15 August 1950, declared The Princess Royal 1987
Married (1) 14 November 1973 Captain Mark Anthony Peter Phillips, CVO (*born* 22 September 1948); marriage dissolved 1992; (2) 12 December 1992 Captain Timothy James Hamilton Laurence, MVO, RN (*born* 1 March 1955)
Issue:
(1) Peter Mark Andrew Phillips, *born* 15 November 1977

(2) Zara Anne Elizabeth Phillips, *born* 15 May 1981
Residence: Gatcombe Park, Minchinhampton, Glos

HRH THE DUKE OF YORK (Prince Andrew Albert Christian Edward), KCVO, ADC(P)
Born 19 February 1960, created Duke of York, Earl of Inverness and Baron Killyleagh 1986
Married 23 July 1986 Sarah Margaret Ferguson, now Sarah, Duchess of York (*born* 15 October 1959, younger daughter of Major Ronald Ferguson and Mrs Hector Barrantes), marriage dissolved 1996
Issue:
(1) HRH Princess Beatrice of York (Princess Beatrice Elizabeth Mary), *born* 8 August 1988
(2) HRH Princess Eugenie of York (Princess Eugenie Victoria Helena), *born* 23 March 1990
Residences: Buckingham Palace, London SW1A 1AA; Sunninghill Park, Ascot, Berks

HRH THE EARL OF WESSEX (Prince Edward Antony Richard Louis), KCVO
Born 10 March 1964, created Earl of Wessex, Viscount Severn 1999
Married 19 June 1999 Sophie Helen Rhys-Jones, now HRH The Countess of Wessex (*born* 20 January 1965, daughter of Mr and Mrs Christopher Rhys-Jones)
Residence: Bagshot Park, Bagshot, Surrey GU19 5HS

NEPHEW OF THE QUEEN

DAVID ALBERT CHARLES ARMSTRONG-JONES, VISCOUNT LINLEY, *born* 3 November 1961, *married* 8 October 1993 the Hon. Serena Stanhope, and has issue, Hon. Charles Patrick Inigo Armstrong-Jones, *born* 1 July 1999; Hon. Margarita Elizabeth Alleyne Armstrong-Jones, *born* May 14 2002

NIECE OF THE QUEEN

LADY SARAH CHATTO (Sarah Frances Elizabeth), *born* 1 May 1964, *married* 14 July 1994 Daniel Chatto, and has issue, Samuel David Benedict Chatto, *born* 28 July 1996; Arthur Robert Nathaniel Chatto, *born* 5 February 1999
Residence: Kensington Palace, London W8 4PU

AUNT OF THE QUEEN

HRH PRINCESS ALICE, DUCHESS OF GLOUCESTER (Alice Christabel), GCB, CI, GCVO, GBE, Grand Cordon of Al Kamal
Born 25 December 1901, third daughter of the 7th Duke of Buccleuch and Queensberry
Married 6 November 1935 (as Lady Alice Montagu-Douglas-Scott) Prince Henry, Duke of Gloucester, third son of King George V
Residence: Kensington Palace, London W8 4PU

COUSINS OF THE QUEEN

HRH THE DUKE OF GLOUCESTER (Prince Richard Alexander Walter George), KG, GCVO, Grand Prior of the Order of St John of Jerusalem
Born 26 August 1944
Married 8 July 1972 Birgitte Eva van Deurs, now HRH The Duchess of Gloucester, GCVO (*born* 20 June 1946, daughter of Asger Henriksen and Vivian van Deurs)
Issue:
(1) Earl of Ulster (Alexander Patrick Gregers Richard), *born* 24 October 1974
(2) Lady Davina Windsor (Davina Elizabeth Alice Benedikte), *born* 19 November 1977
(3) Lady Rose Windsor (Rose Victoria Birgitte Louise), *born* 1 March 1980
Residence: Kensington Palace, London W8 4PU

HRH THE DUKE OF KENT (Prince Edward George Nicholas Paul Patrick), KG, GCMG, GCVO, ADC(P)
Born 9 October 1935
Married 8 June 1961 Katharine Lucy Mary Worsley, now HRH The Duchess of Kent, GCVO (*born* 22 February 1933, daughter of Sir William Worsley, Bt.)
Issue:
(1) Earl of St Andrews (George Philip Nicholas), *born* 26 June 1962, *married* 9 January 1988 Sylvana Tomaselli, and has issue, Edward Edmund Maximilian George, Baron Downpatrick, *born* 2 December 1988; Lady Marina Charlotte Alexandra Katharine Windsor, *born* 30 September 1992; Lady Amelia Sophia Theodora Mary Margaret Windsor, *born* 24 August 1995
(2) Lady Helen Taylor (Helen Marina Lucy), *born* 28 April 1964, *married* 18 July 1992 Timothy Taylor, and has issue, Columbus George Donald Taylor, *born* 6 August 1994; Cassius Edward Taylor, *born* 26 December 1996; daughter Eloise Taylor, *born* 3 March 2003
(3) Lord Nicholas Windsor (Nicholas Charles Edward Jonathan), *born* 25 July 1970
Residence: Wren House, Palace Green, London W8 4PY

HRH PRINCESS ALEXANDRA, THE HON. LADY OGILVY (Princess Alexandra Helen Elizabeth Olga Christabel), KG GCVO
Born 25 December 1936
Married 24 April 1963 The Rt. Hon. Sir Angus Ogilvy, KCVO (*born* 14 September 1928, second son of 12th Earl of Airlie)
Issue:
(1) James Robert Bruce Ogilvy, *born* 29 February 1964, *married* 30 July 1988 Julia Rawlinson, and has issue, Flora Alexandra Ogilvy, *born* 15 December 1994; Alexander Charles Ogilvy, *born* 12 November 1996
(2) Marina Victoria Alexandra, Mrs Mowatt, *born* 31 July 1966, *married* 2 February 1990 Paul Mowatt (marriage dissolved 1997), and has issue, Zenouska May Mowatt, *born* 26 May 1990; Christian Alexander Mowatt, *born* 4 June 1993
Residence: Thatched House Lodge, Richmond Park, Surrey

HRH PRINCE MICHAEL OF KENT (Prince Michael George Charles Franklin), GCVO
Born 4 July 1942
Married 30 June 1978 Baroness Marie-Christine Agnes Hedwig Ida von Reibnitz, now HRH Princess Michael of Kent (*born* 15 January 1945, daughter of Baron Gunther von Reibnitz)
Issue:
(1) Lord Frederick Windsor (Frederick Michael George David Louis), *born* 6 April 1979
(2) Lady Gabriella Windsor (Gabriella Marina Alexandra Ophelia), *born* 23 April 1981
Residences: Kensington Palace, London W8 4PU; Nether Lypiatt Manor, Stroud, Glos GL6 7LS

ORDER OF SUCCESSION

1 HRH The Prince of Wales
2 HRH Prince William of Wales
3 HRH Prince Henry of Wales
4 HRH The Duke of York
5 HRH Princess Beatrice of York
6 HRH Princess Eugenie of York
7 HRH The Earl of Wessex
8 HRH The Princess Royal
9 Peter Phillips
10 Zara Phillips
11 Viscount Linley
12 Hon. Charles Armstrong-Jones
13 Hon. Margarita Armstrong-Jones
14 Lady Sarah Chatto
15 Samuel Chatto
16 Arthur Chatto
17 HRH The Duke of Gloucester
18 Earl of Ulster
19 Lady Davina Windsor
20 Lady Rose Windsor
21 HRH The Duke of Kent
22 Baron Downpatrick
23 Lady Marina Charlotte Windsor
24 Lady Amelia Windsor
25 Lady Helen Taylor
26 Columbus Taylor
27 Cassius Taylor
28 Eloise Taylor
29 Lord Frederick Windsor
30 Lady Gabriella Windsor
31 HRH Princess Alexandra, the Hon. Lady Ogilvy
32 James Ogilvy
33 Alexander Ogilvy
34 Flora Ogilvy
35 Marina, Mrs Paul Mowatt
36 Christian Mowatt
37 Zenouska Mowatt

HRH Prince Michael of Kent, and The Earl of St Andrews both lost the right of succession to the throne through marriage to a Roman Catholic. Lord Nicholas Windsor renounced his rights to the throne on converting to Roman Catholicism in 2001. Their children remain in succession provided that they are in communion with the Church of England.

PRIVATE SECRETARIES TO THE ROYAL FAMILY

THE QUEEN

Office: Buckingham Palace, London SW1A 1AA
Tel: 020-7930 4832
Web: www.royal.gov.uk
Private Secretary to The Queen, The Rt. Hon. Sir Robin Janvrin, KCVO, CB

PRINCE PHILIP, THE DUKE OF EDINBURGH

Office: Buckingham Palace, London SW1A 1AA
Tel: 020-7930 4832
Private Secretary, Brig. M. Hunt-Davis, CVO, CBE

THE PRINCE OF WALES

Office: Clarence House, London SW1A 1BA
Tel: 020-7930 4832
Private Secretary, Sir Michael Peat, KCVO

THE DUKE OF YORK

Office: Buckingham Palace, London SW1A 1AA
Tel: 020-7930 4832
Private Secretary, Miss C. Manley, OBE

THE EARL AND COUNTESS OF WESSEX

Office: The Old Stables, Bagshot Park, Surrey GU19 5PJ
Tel: 01276-700 843/022
Private Secretary, Brigadier J. Smedley

THE PRINCESS ROYAL

Office: Buckingham Palace, London SW1A 1AA
Tel: 020-7930 4832
Private Secretary, N. Wright

PRINCESS ALICE, DUCHESS OF GLOUCESTER AND THE DUKE AND DUCHESS OF GLOUCESTER

Office: Kensington Palace, London W8 4PU
Tel: 020-7937 6374
Private Secretary, Maj. N. Barne, LVO

THE DUKE OF KENT

Office: St James's Palace, London, SW1A 1BQ
Tel: 020-7930 4872
Private Secretary, N. Adamson, LVO, OBE

THE DUCHESS OF KENT

Office: Wren House, Palace Green, London, W8 4PY
Tel: 020-7937 2730
Personal Secretary, Miss V. Utley

PRINCE AND PRINCESS MICHAEL OF KENT

Office: Kensington Palace, London W8 4PU
Tel: 020-7938 3519
Private Secretary, N. Chance

PRINCESS ALEXANDRA, THE HON. LADY OGILVY

Office: Buckingham Palace, London SW1A 1AA
Tel: 020-7024 4270
Private Secretary, Lt.-Col. R. Macfarlane

OFFICES OF THE ROYAL HOUSEHOLD

PRIVATE SECRETARY'S OFFICE
The Private Secretary, assisted by the two Assistant Private Secretaries, is responsible for:

– Informing and advising The Queen on constitutional, governmental and political matters in the UK, her other Realms and the wider Commonwealth, including communications with the Prime Minister and Government Departments.
– Organising The Queen's domestic and overseas official programme, including the Presentation of Credentials by incoming foreign ambassadors from overseas countries.
– The Queen's speeches and messages, The Queen's patronage, The Queen's photographs and official presents, portraits of The Queen and dedications and congratulatory messages.
– Communications in connection with the role of the Royal Family and other members of the Royal Family and their households.
– Dealing with correspondence to The Queen from members of the public.
– Organising and co-ordinating Royal travel through the Royal Travel Office.
– Co-ordinating and initiating research to support engagements by members of the Royal Family through the Co-ordination and Research Unit.

The Private Secretary is also responsible for communications and media affairs. The Press Secretary is in charge of Buckingham Palace Press Office and reports to the Private Secretary. Assisted by the Deputy Press Secretary and three Assistant Press Secretaries, the Press Secretary is responsible for:

– Developing communications strategies to enhance the public understanding of the role of the Monarchy, including an education strategy, encompassing website development and other multi-media initiatives.
– Briefing the British and international media on the role and duties of The Queen and issues relating to the royal family.
– Responding to media enquiries.
– Arranging media facilities in the United Kingdom and overseas to support royal functions and engagements.
– The management of the Royal website.

The Private Secretary is Keeper of the Royal Archives and is responsible for the care of the records of the Sovereign and the Royal Household from previous reigns. These papers are preserved in the Royal Archives at Windsor, where they are managed by the Registrar, reporting to the Assistant Keeper, and made available for historical research. As Keeper, it is the Private Secretary's responsibility to ensure the proper management of the records of the present reign with a view to their transfer to the archives as and when appropriate.

The Private Secretary is an *ex officio* trustee of the Royal Collection Trust.

PRIVY PURSE AND TREASURER'S OFFICE
The Keeper of the Privy Purse and Treasurer to The Queen, assisted by the Deputy Treasurer and the Deputy Keeper of the Privy Purse, is responsible for:

- The Queen's Civil List, which is the money paid from the Government's Consolidated Fund to meet official expenditure relating to The Queen's duties as Head of State and Head of the Commonwealth.
- Through the Director of Personnel, the identification, planning and management of personnel policy across the Household, the administration of all pension schemes provided for the Household and Private Estates employees, and the allocation of employee and pensioner housing.
- Information technology systems for the Household.
- Internal audit services.
- All insurance matters.
- The Privy Purse, which is mainly financed by the net income of the Duchy of Lancaster, and which meets both official expenditure incurred by The Queen as Sovereign and private expenditure.
- Liaison with other Members of the Royal Family and their Households on financial matters.
- The Queen's private estates at Sandringham and Balmoral, The Queen's Racing Establishment and the Royal Studs and liaison with the Ascot Authority.
- The Home Park at Windsor and liaison with the Crown Estate Commissioners concerning the Home Park and the Great Park at Windsor.
- The Royal Philatelic Collection, which is managed by the Keeper of the Royal Philatelic Collection.
- Administrative aspects of the Military Knights of Windsor and the Royal Almonry.
- Administration of the Royal Victorian Order, of which the Keeper of the Privy Purse is Secretary, Long and Faithful Service Medals, and the Queen's Cups, Medals and Prizes, and policy on Commemorative Medals.

The Keeper of the Privy Purse is one of three Royal Trustees (in respect of his responsibilities for the Civil List) and is Receiver General of the Duchy of Lancaster and a member of the Duchy's Council.

The Keeper of the Privy Purse is also responsible for property services for the Occupied Royal Palaces in England, which comprise Buckingham Palace, St James's Palace and Clarence House, Marlborough House Mews, the residential, office and general areas of Kensington Palace, Windsor Castle and related areas and buildings, Frogmore House, and Hampton Court Mews and Paddocks. The costs of property services for the Occupied Royal Palaces are met from a Grant-in-aid from the Department for Culture, Media and Sport.

The Director of Property Services, assisted by the Deputy Treasurer has day-to-day responsibility for the Royal Household's Property Section, which is responsible for:

- Fire, health and safety issues.
- Repairs and refurbishment of buildings and new buildings work.
- Utilities and telecommunications.
- Putting up stages, tents and other work in connection with ceremonial occasions and garden parties and other official functions.

The Property Section is also responsible, in effect on a sub-contract basis from the Department for Culture, Media and Sport, for the maintenance of Marlborough House (which is occupied by the Commonwealth Secretariat).

The Keeper of the Privy Purse, assisted by the Deputy Treasurer, also oversees Royal Communications and Information expenditure, which is met from the Property Services Grant-in-aid.

The Keeper of the Privy Purse is responsible for the financial aspects of Royal travel, which are overseen on a day-to-day basis by the Deputy Treasurer. The costs of official Royal travel by aeroplane and train are met from a Grant-in-aid provided by the Department for Transport.

The Keeper of the Privy Purse is an *ex officio* trustee of the Royal Collection Trust and is also chairman of its trading subsidiary Royal Collection Enterprises Limited. He is also an *ex officio* trustee of the Historic Royal Palaces Trust.

The Queen's Civil List and the Grants-in-aid for property services and Royal travel are provided by the Government in return for the surrender by the Sovereign of the net surplus from the Crown Estate and other hereditary revenues.

MASTER OF THE HOUSEHOLD'S DEPARTMENT
The Master of the Household, assisted by two Deputy Masters of the Household (one of whom is also Equerry to the Queen), is responsible for the staff and domestic arrangements at Buckingham Palace, Windsor Castle and the Palace of Holyroodhouse and at Balmoral Castle and Sandringham House when The Queen is in residence. These arrangements include:

- The provision of meals for The Queen and other members of the Royal Family, their guests and Royal Household employees.
- Service by liveried staff at meals, receptions and other events.
- Travel arrangements for employees and the movement of baggage between the Royal residences.
- Cleaning and laundry.
- Furnishings and the internal decorative appearance of the Occupied Royal Palaces in collaboration with the Director of the Royal Collection.
- Liaison with the Royalty and Diplomatic Protection Department of the Metropolitan Police concerning security procedures at the Occupied Royal Palaces.

The Master of the Household is responsible for The Queen's official entertaining, both at home and overseas, including preparation of guest lists, invitations and seating plans, and overseeing aspects of The Queen's private entertaining.

LORD CHAMBERLAIN'S OFFICE

The Comptroller, Lord Chamberlain's Office, assisted by the Deputy Comptroller and the Assistant Comptroller, is responsible for:

- The organisation of all ceremonial engagements, including state visits to The Queen in the United Kingdom, royal weddings and royal funerals, the state opening of Parliament, Guards of Honour at Buckingham Palace, Investitures, and the Garter and Thistle ceremonies.
- Garden Parties at Buckingham Palace and Palace at Holyroodhouse (except for catering and tents).
- The Crown Jewels, which are part of the Royal Collection, when they are in use on state occasions.
- Co-ordination of the arrangements for The Queen to be represented at funerals and memorial services and at the arrival and departure of visiting Heads of State.
- Advising on matters of precedence, style and titles, dress, flying of flags, gun salutes, mourning and other ceremonial questions.
- Supervising the applications from tradesmen for Royal Warrants of Appointment.
- Advising on the commercial use of royal emblems and contemporary royal photographs.
- The Ecclesiastical Household, the Medical Household, the Body Guards and certain ceremonial appointments such as Gentlemen Ushers and Pages of Honour.
- The Lords in Waiting, who represent The Queen on various occasions and escort the visiting Head of State during incoming state visits.
- The Queen's Bargemaster and Watermen and The Queen's Swans.

The Comptroller, Lord Chamberlain's Office is also responsible for the Royal Mews, assisted by the Crown Equerry, who has day-to-day responsibility for:

- The provision of carriage processions for the State Opening of Parliament, State Visits, Trooping of the Colour, Royal Ascot, the Garter Ceremony, the Thistle Service, the Presentation of credentials to The Queen by incoming foreign Ambassadors and High Commissioners, and other state and ceremonial occasions.
- The provision of chauffeur-driven cars.
- Co-ordinating the travelling and transport arrangements by road in respect of The Queen's official engagements.
- Supervision and administration of the Royal Mews at Buckingham Palace, Windsor Castle, Hampton Court and the Palace of Holyroodhouse.

The Comptroller, Lord Chamberlain's Office also has overall responsibility for the Marshal of the Diplomatic Corps, who is responsible for the relationship between the Royal Household and the Diplomatic Heads of Mission in London; and the Secretary of the Central Chancery of the Orders of Knighthood, who administers the Orders of Chivalry and their records, makes arrangements for the recipients at Investitures and the distribution of insignia, and ensures the proper public notification of awards through the London Gazette. The Secretary of the Central Chancery is also the Assistant Comptroller.

ROYAL COLLECTION DEPARTMENT

The Royal Collection, which contains a large number of works of art of all kinds, is held by The Queen as Sovereign in trust for her successors and the nation and is not owned by her as an individual. The administration, conservation and presentation of the Royal Collection are funded by the Royal Collection Trust solely from income from visitors to Windsor Castle, Buckingham Palace and the Palace of Holyroodhouse in Edinburgh. The Royal Collection Trust is chaired by the Prince of Wales. The Lord Chamberlain, the Private Secretary and the Keeper of the Privy Purse are *ex officio* trustees and there are three external trustees appointed by The Queen.

The Director of the Royal Collection is responsible for:

- The administration and custodial control of the Royal Collection in all royal residences.
- The care, display, conservation and restoration of items in the Collection.
- Initiating and assisting research into the Collection and publishing catalogues and books on the Collection.
- Making the Collection accessible to the public by display in places open to the public (including the unoccupied palaces), The Queen's Gallery at Buckingham Palace and the Queen's Gallery at the Palace of Holyroodhouse, by travelling exhibitions organised by museums and galleries in the United Kingdom and abroad.
- Educating and informing the public about the Collection.

The Director of the Royal Collection, who is at present also the Surveyor of The Queen's Works of Art, is assisted by the Surveyor of the Queen's Pictures, the Royal Librarian, the Deputy Surveyor of The Queen's Works of Art, the Managing Director, Royal Collection Enterprises, and the Finance Director, Royal Collection.

The Surveyor of the Queen's Pictures is responsible for pictures and miniatures, the Royal Librarian is responsible for all the books, manuscripts, coins and medals, insignia and works of art on paper including the watercolours, prints and drawings in the Print Room at Windsor Castle, and the Surveyor of the Queen's Works of art is responsible for furniture, ceramics and the other decorative arts in the Collection.

The Director of the Royal Collection has overall responsibility for the trading activities that fund the Royal Collection Department. These are administered by Royal Collection Enterprises Limited, the trading subsidiary of The Royal Collection Trust, which is run by the Managing Director, Royal Collection Enterprises. The company, whose chairman is the Keeper of the Privy Purse, is responsible for:

- Managing access by the public to Windsor Castle (including Frogmore House), Buckingham Palace (including the Royal Mews and The Queen's Gallery) and the Palace of Holyroodhouse.
- Running shops at each location.
- Managing the images and intellectual property rights of the Royal Collection.

The Director of the Royal Collection is also an ex officio trustee of the Historic Royal Palaces Trust.

ROYAL SALUTES

ENGLAND

The basic Royal Salute is 21 rounds with 41 rounds fired at Hyde Park because it is a Royal park. At the Tower of London 62 rounds are fired on Royal anniversaries (21 plus a further 20 because the Tower is a Royal Palace and a further 21 'for the city of London'). Gun salutes occur on the following Royal anniversaries:

– Accession Day
– The Queen's Birthday
– Coronation Day
– The birthday of the Duke of Edinburgh
– The Queen's official birthday
– State Opening of Parliament

Gun salutes also occur when Parliament is prorogued by the Sovereign, on Royal births and when a visiting Head of State meets the Sovereign in London, Windsor or Edinburgh.

In London, salutes are fired at Hyde Park and The Tower of London although on some occassions (State visits, State Opening of Parliament and The Queen's Birthday Parade) Green Park is used instead.

Constable of the Royal Palace and Fortress of London, Gen. Sir Roger Wheeler, GCB, CBE
Lieutenant of the Tower of London, Lt.-Gen. Sir Roderick Cordy-Simpson, KBE, CB
Resident Governor and Keeper of the Jewel House, Maj.-Gen. Geoffrey Field, CB, OBE
Master Gunner of St James's Park, Gen. Sir Alex Harley, KBE, CB
Master Gunner within the Tower, Col. George Clarke, TD

SCOTLAND

Royal salutes are authorised at Edinburgh Castle and Stirling Castle, although in practice Edinburgh Castle is the only operating saluting station in Scotland.

A salute of 21 guns is fired on the following occasions:
– the anniversaries of the birth, accession and coronation of the Sovereign
– the anniversary of the birth of HRH Prince Philip, Duke of Edinburgh

A salute of 21 guns is fired in Edinburgh on the occasion of the opening of the General Assembly of the Church of Scotland.

A salute of 21 guns may also be fired in Edinburgh on the arrival of HM The Queen or a member of the royal family who is a Royal Highness on an official visit.

Other Military saluting stations are at Cardiff and Belfast.

ROYAL FINANCES

FUNDING

THE CIVIL LIST

The Civil List dates back to the late 17th century. It was originally used by the sovereign to supplement hereditary revenues for paying the salaries of judges, ambassadors and other government officers as well as the expenses of the royal household. In 1760 on the accession of George III it was decided that the Civil List would be provided by Parliament to cover all relevant expenditure in return for the King surrendering the hereditary revenues of the Crown. At that time Parliament undertook to pay the salaries of judges, ambassadors, etc. In 1831 Parliament agreed also to meet the costs of the royal palaces in return for a reduction in the Civil List. Each sovereign has agreed to continue this arrangement.

The Civil List paid to The Queen is charged on the Consolidated Fund. Until 1972, the amount of money allocated annually under the Civil List was set for the duration of a reign. The system was then altered to a fixed annual payment for ten years but from 1975 high inflation made an annual review necessary. The system of payments reverted to the practice of a fixed annual payment of £7.9m for ten years from 1 January 1991. In 2001 the payments were further fixed until 31 December 2010. In June 2002 the annual accounts for the Civil List were published for the first time and are to continue to be published annually instead of at 10 yearly intervals.

The Civil List Acts provide for other members of the royal family to receive parliamentary annuities from government funds to meet the expenses of carrying out their official duties. Since 1975 The Queen has reimbursed the Treasury for the annuities paid to the Duke of Gloucester, the Duke of Kent and Princess Alexandra. Since 1993 The Queen has reimbursed all the annuities except those paid to herself, the late Queen

Elizabeth the Queen Mother and the Duke of Edinburgh.

The Prince of Wales does not receive a parliamentary annuity. He derives his income from the revenues of the Duchy of Cornwall and these monies meet the official and private expenses of the Prince of Wales and his family.

The annual payments for the years 2001–11:

The Queen	£7,900,000
The Duke of Edinburgh	359,000
*The Duke of York	249,000
*†The Earl of Wessex	141,000
*The Princess Royal	228,000
*Princess Alice, Duchess of Gloucester	87,000
*The Duke and Duchess of Gloucester	175,000
*The Duke and Duchess of Kent	236,000
*Princess Alexandra	225,000
	9,600,000
*Refunded to the Treasury	1,341,000
Total	8,259,000

†The Earl of Wessex's annuity was increased from £96,000 upon his marriage in June 1999

GRANTS-IN-AID

The royal household receives grants-in-aid from two government departments to meet various official expenses. The Department for Culture, Media and Sport provides grant-in-aid to pay for the upkeep of English occupied royal palaces, the maintenance of Marlborough House and to meet the cost of royal media and information services. The Royal Travel grant-in-aid is provided by the Department for Transport to meet the cost of official royal travel by air and rail, using mainly aircraft from 32 (The Royal) Squadron, chartered commercial aircraft for major overseas state visits and the Royal Train.

Grants-in-aid 2002–3:
Property Services, Royal Communications and
   Information and Maintenance
   of Marlborough House   £16,507,000
Royal Travel   £5,400,000

THE PRIVY PURSE

The funds received by the Privy Purse pay for official
expenses incurred by The Queen as head of state and for
some of The Queen's private expenditure. The revenues
of the Duchy of Lancaster are the principal source of
income for the Privy Purse. The revenues of the Duchy
were retained by George III in 1760 when the hereditary
revenues were surrendered in exchange for the Civil List.

PERSONAL INCOME

The Queen's personal income derives mostly from
investments, and is used to meet private expenditure.

DEPARTMENTAL VOTES

Items of expenditure connected with the official duties of
the royal family which fall directly on votes of
government departments include:

Ministry of Defence – equerries
Foreign and Commonwealth Office – Marshal of the
   Diplomatic Corps; costs (other than travel costs)
   associated with overseas visits at the request of
   government departments
HM Treasury – Central Chancery of the Orders of
   Knighthood
The Post Office – postal services

TAXATION

The sovereign is not legally liable to pay income tax or
capital gains tax. After income tax was reintroduced in
1842, some income tax was paid voluntarily by the
sovereign but over a long period these payments were
phased out. In 1992 The Queen offered to pay tax on a
voluntary basis from 6 April 1993, and the Prince of
Wales offered to pay tax on a voluntary basis on his
income from the Duchy of Cornwall. (He was already
taxed in all other respects.)

The main provisions for The Queen and the Prince of
Wales to pay tax, set out in a Memorandum of
Understanding on Royal Taxation presented to
Parliament on 11 February 1993, are that The Queen
will pay income tax and capital gains tax in respect of her
private income and assets, and on the proportion of the
income and capital gains of the Privy Purse used for
private purposes. Inheritance tax will be paid on The
Queen's assets, except for those which pass to the next
sovereign, whether automatically or by gift or bequest.
The Prince of Wales will pay income tax on income from
the Duchy of Cornwall used for private purposes.

The Prince of Wales has confirmed that he intends to
pay tax on the same basis following his accession to the
throne.

Other members of the royal family are subject to tax as
for any taxpayer.

MILITARY RANKS AND TITLES

THE QUEEN

ROYAL NAVY
Lord High Admiral of the United Kingdom

ARMY
Colonel-in-Chief
   The Life Guards; The Blues and Royals (Royal Horse
   Guards and 1st Dragoons); The Royal Scots Dragoon
   Guards (Carabiniers and Greys); The Queen's Royal
   Lancers; Royal Tank Regiment; Corps of Royal
   Engineers; Grenadier Guards; Coldstream Guards;
   Scots Guards; Irish Guards; Welsh Guards; The Royal
   Welch Fusiliers; The Queen's Lancashire Regiment;
   The Argyll and Sutherland Highlanders (Princess
   Louise's); The Royal Green Jackets; Adjutant General's
   Corps; The Royal Mercian and Lancastrian Yeomanry;
   The Governor General's Horse Guards (of Canada);
   The King's Own Calgary Regiment (Royal Canadian
   Armoured Corps); Canadian Forces Military Engineers
   Branch; Royal 22e Regiment (of Canada); Governor-
   General's Foot Guards (of Canada); The Canadian
   Grenadier Guards; Le Regiment de la Chaudiere (of
   Canada); 2nd Battalion Royal New Brunswick
   Regiment (North Shore); The 48th Highlanders of
   Canada; The Argyll and Sutherland Highlanders of
   Canada (Princess Louise's); The Calgary Highlanders;
   Royal Australian Engineers; Royal Australian Infantry
   Corps; Royal Australian Army Ordnance Corps; Royal
   Australian Army Nursing Corps; The Corps of Royal
   New Zealand Engineers; Royal New Zealand Infantry
   Regiment; The Malawi Rifles; The Royal Malta
   Artillery

Affiliated Colonel-in-Chief
   The Queen's Gurkha Engineers

Captain General
   Royal Regiment of Artillery; The Honourable Artillery
   Company; Combined Cadet Force; Royal Regiment of
   Canadian Artillery; Royal Regiment of Australian
   Artillery; Royal Regiment of New Zealand Artillery;
   Royal New Zealand Armoured Corps

Patron
   Royal Army Chaplains' Department

ROYAL AIR FORCE
Air Commodore-in-Chief
   Royal Auxiliary Air Force; Royal Air Force Regiment;
   Air Reserve of Canada; Royal Australian Air Force
   Reserve; Territorial Air Force (of New Zealand)

Commandant-in-Chief
   Royal Air Force College, Cranwell

Royal Hon. Air Commodore
   Royal Air Force Marham; 603 (City of Edinburgh)
   Squadron Royal Auxiliary Air Force

HRH THE PRINCE PHILIP, DUKE OF EDINBURGH

ROYAL NAVY
Admiral of the Fleet
Admiral of the Fleet, Royal Australian Navy
Admiral of the Fleet, Royal New Zealand Navy
Admiral of the Royal Canadian Sea Cadets

ROYAL MARINES
Captain General, Royal Marines

ARMY
Field Marshal
Field Marshal, Australian Military Forces
Field Marshal, New Zealand Army

Colonel-in-Chief
The Queen's Royal Hussars (Queen's Own and Royal Irish); The Royal Gloucestershire, Berkshire and Wiltshire Regiment; The Highlanders (Seaforth, Gordons and Camerons); Corps of Royal Electrical and Mechanical Engineers; Intelligence Corps; Army Cadet Force Association; The Royal Canadian Regiment; The Royal Hamilton Light Infantry (Wentworth Regiment of Canada); The Cameron Highlanders of Ottawa; The Queen's Own Cameron Highlanders of Canada; The Seaforth Highlanders of Canada; The Royal Canadian Army Cadets; The Royal Australian Corps of Electrical and Mechanical Engineers; The Australian Army Cadet Corps

Colonel
Grenadier Guards

Royal Hon. Colonel
City of Edinburgh University Officers' Training Corps; The Trinidad and Tobago Regiment

Member
Honourable Artillery Company

ROYAL AIR FORCE
Marshal of the Royal Air Force
Marshal of the Royal Australian Air Force
Marshal of the Royal New Zealand Air Force

Air Commodore-in-Chief
Air Training Corps; Royal Canadian Air Cadets

Royal Hon. Air Commodore
Royal Air Force Kinloss

HRH THE PRINCE OF WALES

ROYAL NAVY
Vice Admiral

ARMY
Lieutenant-General

Colonel-in-Chief
The Royal Dragoon Guards; The Cheshire (22nd) Regiment; The Royal Regiment of Wales (24th/41st Foot); The Parachute Regiment; The Royal Gurkha Rifles; Army Air Corps; The Royal Canadian Dragoons; Lord Strathcona's Horse (Royal Canadians); Royal Regiment of Canada (10th Royal Grenadiers);

Royal Winnipeg Rifles; Royal Australian Armoured Corps; The Royal Pacific Islands Regiment

Deputy Colonel-in-Chief
The Highlanders (Seaforth, Gordons and Camerons)

Colonel
Welsh Guards

Royal Hon. Colonel
The Queen's Own Yeomanry

ROYAL AIR FORCE
Air Vice-Marshal

Hon. Air Commodore
Royal Air Force Valley

Air Commodore-in-Chief
Royal New Zealand Air Force

Colonel-in-Chief
Air Reserve Group of Air Command (of Canada)

HRH THE DUKE OF YORK

ROYAL NAVY
Commander
Admiral of the Sea Cadet Corps

ARMY
Colonel-in-Chief
The Staffordshire Regiment (The Prince of Wales's); The Royal Irish Regiment (27th (Inniskilling), 83rd, 87th and The Ulster Defence Regiment); The Queen's York Rangers (First Americans); Royal New Zealand Army Logistics Regiment

ROYAL AIR FORCE
Royal Hon. Air Commodore
Royal Air Force Lossiemouth

HRH THE PRINCESS ROYAL

ROYAL NAVY
Rear Admiral Chief Commandant for Women in the Royal Nav

ARMY
Colonel-in-Chief
The King's Royal Hussars; Royal Corps of Signals; Royal Logistic Corps; The Worcestershire and Sherwood Foresters Regiment (29th/45th Foot); The Royal Scots (The Royal Regiment); 8th Canadian Hussars (Princess Louise's); Royal Newfoundland Regiment; Canadian Forces Communications and Electronics Branch; The Grey and Simcoe Foresters (Royal Canadian Armoured Corps); The Royal Regina Rifle Regiment; Royal Australian Corps of Signals; Royal New Zealand Corps of Signals; Royal New Zealand Nursing Corps

Affiliated Colonel-in-Chief
The Queen's Gurkha Signals; The Queen's Own Gurkha Transport Regiment

Colonel
The Blues and Royals (Royal Horse Guards and 1st Dragoons)

Royal Hon. Colonel
University of London Officers' Training Corps

Commandant
First Aid Nursing Yeomanry (Princess Royal's Volunteer Corps)

ROYAL AIR FORCE
Royal Hon. Air Commodore
Royal Air Force Lyneham; University of London Air Squadron

HRH PRINCESS ALICE, DUCHESS OF GLOUCESTER

ARMY
Colonel-in-Chief
The King's Own Scottish Borderers; The Royal Anglian Regiment; Royal Australian Corps of Transport

Deputy Colonel-in-Chief
The King's Royal Hussars

ROYAL AIR FORCE
Air Chief Marshal

Air Chief Commandant
Women, Royal Air Force

HRH THE DUKE OF GLOUCESTER

ARMY
Deputy Colonel-in-Chief
The Royal Gloucestershire, Berkshire and Wiltshire Regiment; The Royal Logistic Corps

Royal Hon. Colonel
Royal Monmouthshire Royal Engineers (Militia)

ROYAL AIR FORCE
Hon. Air Marshal

Royal Hon. Air Commodore
Royal Air Force Odiham; No 501 (County of Gloucester) Squadron Royal Auxiliary Air Force

HRH THE DUCHESS OF GLOUCESTER

ARMY
Colonel-in-Chief
Royal Army Dental Corps; Royal Australian Army Educational Corps; Royal New Zealand Army Educational Corps

Deputy Colonel-in-Chief
Adjutant-General's Corps

HRH THE DUKE OF KENT

ARMY
Field Marshal

Colonel-in-Chief
The Royal Regiment of Fusiliers; The Devonshire and Dorset Regiment; Lorne Scots (Peel, Dufferin and Hamilton Regiment)

Deputy Colonel-in-Chief
The Royal Scots Dragoon Guards (Carabiniers and Greys)

Colonel
Scots Guards

ROYAL AIR FORCE
Hon. Air Chief Marshal

Royal Hon. Air Commodore
Royal Air Force Leuchars

HRH THE DUCHESS OF KENT

ARMY
Hon. Major-General

Colonel-in-Chief
The Prince of Wales's Own Regiment of Yorkshire

Deputy Colonel-in-Chief
The Royal Dragoon Guards; Adjutant-General's Corps; The Royal Logistic Corps

HRH PRINCE MICHAEL OF KENT

ROYAL NAVY
Hon. Commodore Royal Naval Reserve

ARMY
Major (retd), The Royal Hussars (Prince of Wales's Own)

Colonel-in-Chief
Essex and Kent Scottish Regiment (Ontario)

ROYAL AIR FORCE
Royal Hon. Air Commodore
RAF Benson

HRH PRINCESS ALEXANDRA, THE HON. LADY OGILVY

ROYAL NAVY
Patron
Queen Alexandra's Royal Naval Nursing Service

ARMY
Colonel-in-Chief
The King's Own Royal Border Regiment; The Light Infantry; The Queen's Own Rifles of Canada; The Canadian Scottish Regiment (Princess Mary's)

Deputy Colonel-in-Chief
The Queen's Royal Lancers

Royal Hon. Colonel
The Royal Yeomanry

ROYAL AIR FORCE
Patron and Air Chief Commandant
Princess Mary's Royal Air Force Nursing Service

Royal Hon. Air Commodore
Royal Air Force Cottesmore

THE HOUSE OF WINDSOR

King George V assumed by royal proclamation (17 July 1917) for his House and family, as well as for all descendants in the male line of Queen Victoria who are subjects of these realms, the name of Windsor.

KING GEORGE V

(George Frederick Ernest Albert), second son of King Edward VII, *born* 3 June 1865; *married* 6 July 1893 HSH Princess Victoria Mary Augusta Louise Olga Pauline Claudine Agnes of Teck (Queen Mary, *born* 26 May 1867; *died* 24 March 1953); *succeeded* to the throne 6 May 1910; *died* 20 January 1936. *Issue:*

1. HRH PRINCE EDWARD Albert Christian George Andrew Patrick David, *born* 23 June 1894, *succeeded* to the throne as King Edward VIII, *born* 23 June 1894, *succeeded* to the throne as King Edward VIII, *abdicated* 11 December 1936; *created Duke of Windsor* 1937; *married* 3 June 1937, Mrs Wallis Simpson (Her Grace The Duchess of Windsor, *born* 19 June 1896; *died* 24 April 1986), *died* 28 May 1972.

2. HRH PRINCE ALBERT Frederick Arthur George, *born* 14 December 1895, *created* Duke of York 1920; *married* 26 April 1923, Lady Elizabeth Bowes-Lyon, youngest daughter of the 14th Earl of Strathmore and Kinghorne (HM Queen Elizabeth the Queen Mother, *born* 4 August 1900; *died* 30 March 2002), *succeeded* to the throne as King George VI, 11 December 1936; *died* 6 February 1952, having had issue

3. HRH PRINCESS (Victoria Alexandra Alice) MARY, *born* 25 April 1897, *created* Princess Royal 1932; *married* 28 February 1922, Viscount Lascelles, later the 6th Earl of Harewood (1882–1947), *died* 28 March 1965. *Issue:*
(1) George Henry Hubert Lascelles, 7th Earl of Harewood, KBE, *born* 7 February 1923; *married* (1) 1949, Maria (Marion) Stein (marriage dissolved 1967); *issue, (a)* David Henry George, Viscount

Lascelles, *born* 1950; *(b)* James Edward, *born* 1953; *(c)* (Robert) Jeremy Hugh, *born* 1955; (2) 1967, Mrs Patricia Tuckwell; *issue, (d)* Mark Hubert, *born* 1964
(2) Gerald David Lascelles (1924–98), *married* (1) 1952, Miss Angela Dowding (marriage dissolved 1978); *issue, (a)* Henry Ulick, *born* 1953; (2) 1978, Mrs Elizabeth Colvin; *issue, (b)* Martin David, *born* 1962

4. HRH PRINCE HENRY William Frederick Albert, *born* 31 March 1900, *created* Duke of Gloucester, Earl of Ulster and Baron Culloden 1928, *married* 6 November 1935, Lady Alice Christabel Montagu-Douglas-Scott, daughter of the 7th Duke of Buccleuch (HRH Princess Alice, Duchess of Gloucester); *died* 10 June 1974. *Issue:*
(1) HRH Prince William Henry Andrew Frederick, *born* 18 December 1941; *accidentally killed* 28 August 1972
(2) HRH Prince Richard Alexander Walter George (HRH The Duke of Gloucester)

5. HRH PRINCE GEORGE Edward Alexander Edmund, *born* 20 December 1902, *created* Duke of Kent, Earl of St Andrews and Baron Downpatrick 1934, *married* 29 November 1934, HRH Princess Marina of Greece and Denmark (*born* 30 November, 1906; *died* 27 August 1968); *killed on active service,* 25 August 1942. *Issue:*
(1) HRH Prince Edward George Nicholas Paul Patrick (HRH The Duke of Kent)
(2) HRH Princess Alexandra Helen Elizabeth Olga Christabel (HRH Princess Alexandra, the Hon. Lady Ogilvy)
(3) HRH Prince Michael George Charles Franklin (HRH Prince Michael of Kent)

6. HRH PRINCE JOHN Charles Francis, *born* 12 July 1905; *died* 18 January 1919

DESCENDANTS OF QUEEN VICTORIA

QUEEN VICTORIA (Alexandrina Victoria), *born* 24 May 1819; *succeeded* to the throne 20 June 1837; *married* 10 February 1840 (Francis) Albert Augustus Charles Emmanuel, Duke of Saxony, Prince of Saxe-Coburg and Gotha (HRH Albert, Prince Consort, *born* 26 August 1819, *died* 14 December 1861); *died* 22 January 1901. *Issue:*

1. HRH PRINCESS VICTORIA Adelaide Mary Louisa (Princess Royal) (1840–1901), *m.* 1858, Friedrich III (1831–88), German Emperor March–June 1888. *Issue:*
(1) HIM Wilhelm II (1859–1941), German Emperor 1888–1918, *m.* (1) 1881 Princess Augusta Victoria of Schleswig-Holstein-Sonderburg-Augustenburg (1858–1921);
(2) 1922 Princess Hermine of Reuss (1887–1947). *Issue:*
  (a) Prince Wilhelm (1882–1951), *Crown Prince* 1888–1918, m. 1905 Duchess Cecilie of Mecklenburg-Schwerin; *Issue:* Prince Wilhelm (1906–40); Prince Louis Ferdinand (1907–94), *m.* 1938 Grand Duchess Kira, Prince Hubertus (1909–50); Prince Friedrich Georg (1911–66); Princess Alexandrine Irene (1915–80); Princess Cecilie (1917–75)
  (b) Prince Eitel-Friedrich (1883–1942), m. 1906 Duchess Sophie of Oldenburg (marriage dissolved 1926)
  (c) Prince Adalbert (1884–1948), m. 1914 Princess Adelheid of Saxe-Meiningen. *Issue:* Princess Victoria Marina (1917–81); Prince Wilhelm Victor (1919–89)
  (d) Prince August Wilhelm (1887–1949), m. 1908 Princess Alexandra of Schleswig-Holstein-Sonderburg-Glücksburg (marriage dissolved 1920). *Issue:* Prince Alexander (1912–85)
  (e) Prince Oskar (1888–1958), m. 1914 Countess von Ruppin; *Issue:* Prince Oskar (1915–39); Prince Burchard

(1917–88); Princess Herzeleide (1918–89); Prince Wilhelm-Karl (b. 1922)
  (f) Prince Joachim (1890–1920), m. 1916 Princess Marie of Anhalt; *Issue:* Prince (Karl) Franz Joseph (1916–75), and has issue
  (g) Princess Viktoria Luise (1892–1980), m. 1913 Ernst, Duke of Brunswick 1913–18 (1887–1953); *Issue:* Prince Ernst (1914–87); Prince Georg (b. 1915), m. 1946 Princess Sophie of Greece and has issue (two sons, one daughter); Princess Frederika (1917–81), m. 1938 Paul I, King of the Hellenes; Prince Christian (1919–81); Prince Welf Heinrich (1923–97)
(2) Princess Charlotte (1860–1919), m. 1878 Bernhard, Duke of Saxe-Meiningen 1914 (1851–1928). *Issue:* Princess Feodora (1879–1945), m. 1898 Prince Heinrich XXX of Reuss
(3) Prince Heinrich (1862–1929), m. 1888 Princess Irene of Hesse. *Issue:*
  (a) Prince Waldemar (1889–1945), m. Princess Calixta Agnes of Lippe
  (b) Prince Sigismund (1896–1978), m. 1919 Princess Charlotte of Saxe-Altenburg. *Issue:* Princess Barbara (1920–94); Prince Alfred (b. 1924)
  (c) Prince Heinrich (1900–4)
(4) Prince Sigismund (1864–6)
(5) Princess Victoria (1866–1929), m. (1) 1890, Prince Adolf of Schaumburg-Lippe (1859–1916); (2) 1927, Alexander Zubkov (1900–36)
(6) Prince Waldemar (1868–79)
(7) Princess Sophie (1870–1932), m. 1889 Constantine I (1868–1923), King of the Hellenes 1913–17, 1920–3. *Issue:*
  (a) George II (1890–1947), King of the Hellenes 1923–4 and

1935–47, *m.* 1921 Princess Elisabeth of Roumania (marriage dissolved 1935)
(b) Alexander I (1893–1920), King of the Hellenes 1917–20, *m.* 1919 Aspasia Manos. *Issue:* Princess Alexandra (1921–93), *m.* 1944 King Petar II of Yugoslavia
(c) Princess Helena (1896–1982), *m.* 1921 King Carol of Roumania, (marriage dissolved 1928)
(d) Paul I (1901–64), King of the Hellenes 1947–64, *m.* 1938 Princess Frederika of Brunswick. *Issue:* King Constantine II (*b.* 1940), *m.* 1964 Princess Anne-Marie of Denmark, and has issue (three sons, two daughters); Princess Sophie (1938–2002), *m.* 1962 Juan Carlos I of Spain; Princess Irene (*b.* 1942)
(e) Princess Irene (1904–74), *m.* 1939 4th Duke of Aosta. *Issue:* Prince Amedeo, 5th Duke of Aosta (*b.* 1943)
(f) Princess Katherine (Lady Katherine Brandram) (*b.* 1913), *m.* 1947 Major R. C. A. Brandram, MC, TD. *Issue:* R. Paul G. A. Brandram (*b.* 1948)
(8) Princess Margarethe (1872–1954), *m.* 1893 Prince Friedrich Karl of Hesse (1868–1940). *Issue:*
(a) Prince Friedrich Wilhelm (1893–1916)
(b) Prince Maximilian (1894–1914)
(c) Prince Philipp (1896–1980), *m.* 1925 Princess Mafalda of Italy. *Issue:* Prince Moritz (*b.* 1926); Prince Heinrich (1927-99); Prince Otto (1937–98); Princess Elisabeth (*b.* 1940)
(d) Prince Wolfgang (1896–1989), *m.* (1) 1924 Princess Marie Alexandra of Baden; (2) 1948 Ottilie Möller
(e) Prince Richard (1901–69)
(f) Prince Christoph (1901–43), *m.* 1930 Princess Sophie of Greece (see below) and has issue (two sons, three daughters)

2. HRH PRINCE ALBERT EDWARD (HM KING EDWARD VII), *b.* 9 November 1841, *m.* 1863 HRH Princess Alexandra of Denmark (1844–1925), *succeeded* to the throne 22 January 1901, *d.* 6 May 1910. *Issue:*
(1) Albert Victor, Duke of Clarence and Avondale (1864–92)
(2) George (HM KING GEORGE V) (1865–1936)
(3) Louise (1867–1931) Princess Royal 1905–31, *m.* 1889 1st Duke of Fife (1849–1912). *Issue:*
(a) Princess Alexandra, Duchess of Fife (1891–1959), *m.* 1913 Prince Arthur of Connaught *(b)* Princess Maud (1893–1945), *m.* 1923 11th Earl of Southesk (1893–1992). *Issue:* The Duke of Fife (*b.* 1929)
(4) Victoria (1868–1935)
(5) Maud (1869–1938), *m.* 1896 Prince Carl of Denmark (1872–1957), later King Haakon VII of Norway 1905–57. *Issue:*
(a) Olav V (1903–91), King of Norway 1957–91, *m.* 1929 Princess Märtha of Sweden (1901–54). *Issue:* Princess Ragnhild (*b.* 1930); Princess Astrid (*b.* 1932); Harald V, King of Norway (*b.* 1937)
(6) Alexander (6–7 April 1871)

3. HRH PRINCESS ALICE Maud Mary (1843–78), *m.* 1862 Prince Ludwig (1837–92), Grand Duke of Hesse 1877–92. *Issue:*
(1) Victoria (1863–1950), *m.* 1884 *Admiral of the Fleet* Prince Louis of Battenberg (1854–1921), *cr.* 1st Marquess of Milford Haven 1917. *Issue:*
(a) Alice (1885–1969), *m.* 1903 Prince Andrew of Greece (1882–1944). *Issue:* Princess Margarita (1905–81), *m.* 1931 Prince Gottfried of Hohenlohe-Langenburg (see below); Princess Theodora (1906–69), *m.* Prince Berthold of Baden (1906–63) and has issue (two sons, one daughter); Princess Cecilie (1911–37), *m.* George, Grand Duke of Hesse (see below); Princess Sophie (1914–2001), *m.* (1) 1930 Prince Christoph of Hesse (see above); (2) 1946 Prince Georg of Hanover; Prince Philip, Duke of Edinburgh (*b.* 1921)
(b) Louise (1889–1965), *m.* 1923 Gustaf VI Adolf (1882–1973), King of Sweden 1950–73
(c) George, 2nd Marquess of Milford Haven (1892–1938), *m.* 1916 Countess Nadejda, daughter of Grand Duke Michael of Russia. *Issue:* Lady Tatiana (1917–88); David Michael, 3rd Marquess (1919–70)
(d) Louis, 1st Earl Mountbatten of Burma (1900–79), *m.* 1922 Edwina Ashley, daughter of Lord Mount Temple. *Issue:* Patricia,

Countess Mountbatten of Burma (*b.* 1924), Pamela (*b.* 1929)
(2) Elizabeth (1864–1918), *m.* 1884 Grand Duke Sergius of Russia (1857–1905)
(3) Irene (1866–1953), *m.* 1888 Prince Heinrich of Prussia (4) Ernst Ludwig (1868–1937), Grand Duke of Hesse 1892–1918, *m.* (1) 1894 Princess Victoria Melita of Saxe-Coburg (see below) (marriage dissolved 1901); (2) 1905 Princess Eleonore of Solms-Hohensolmslich. *Issue:*
(a) Princess Elizabeth (1895–1903)
(b) George, Hereditary Grand Duke of Hesse (1906–37), *m.* Princess Cecilie of Greece (see above), and had issue, two sons, accidentally killed with parents, 1937
(c) Ludwig, Prince of Hesse (1908–68), *m.* 1937 Margaret, daughter of 1st Lord Geddes
(5) Frederick William (1870–3)
(6) Alix (Tsaritsa of Russia) (1872–1918), *m.* 1894 Nicholas II (1868–1918) Tsar of All the Russias 1894–1917, assassinated 16 July 1918. *Issue:*
(a) Grand Duchess Olga (1895–1918)
(b) Grand Duchess Tatiana (1897–1918)
(c) Grand Duchess Marie (1899–1918)
(d) Grand Duchess Anastasia (1901–18)
(e) Alexis, Tsarevich of Russia (1904–18)
(7) Marie (1874–8)

4. HRH PRINCE ALFRED Ernest Albert, Duke of Edinburgh, *Admiral of the Fleet* (1844–1900), *m.* 1874 Grand Duchess Marie Alexandrovna of Russia (1853–1920); succeeded as Duke of Saxe-Coburg and Gotha 22 August 1893. *Issue:*
(1) Alfred, Prince of Saxe-Coburg (1874–99)
(2) Marie (1875–1938), *m.* 1893 Ferdinand (1865–1927), King of Roumania 1914–27. *Issue:*
(a) Carol II (1893–1953), King of Roumania 1930–40, m. (2) 1921 Princess Helena of Greece (see above) (marriage dissolved 1928). *Issue:* Michael (*b.* 1921), King of Roumania 1927–30, 1940–7, *m.* 1948 Princess Anne of Bourbon-Parma, and has issue (five daughters)
(b) Elisabeth (1894–1956), *m.* 1921 George II, King of the Hellenes
(c) Marie (1900–61), *m.* 1922 Alexander (1888–1934), King of Yugoslavia 1921–34. *Issue:* Petar II (1923–70), King of Yugoslavia 1934–45, *m.* 1944 Princess Alexandra of Greece (see above) and has issue (Crown Prince Alexander, *b.* 1945); Prince Tomislav (1928–2000), *m.* (1) 1957 Princess Margarita of Baden (daughter of Princess Theodora of Greece and Prince Berthold of Baden, see above); (2) 1982 Linda Bonney; and has issue (three sons, one daughter); Prince Andrej (1929–90), *m.* (1) 1956 Princess Christina of Hesse (daughter of Prince Christoph of Hesse and Princess Sophie of Greece, see above); (2) 1963 Princess Kira-Melita of Leiningen (see below); and has issue (three sons, two daughters)
(d) Prince Nicolas (1903–78)
(e) Princess Ileana (1909–91), *m.* (1) 1931 Archduke Anton of Austria; (2) 1954 Dr Stefan Issarescu. *Issue:* Archduke Stefan (1932–98); Archduchess Maria Ileana (1933–59); Archduchess Alexandra (*b.* 1935); Archduke Dominic (*b.* 1937); Archduchess Maria Magdalena (*b.* 1939); Archduchess Elisabeth (*b.* 1942)
(f) Prince Mircea (1913–16)
(3) Victoria Melita (1876–1936), *m.* (1) 1894 Grand Duke Ernst Ludwig of Hesse (see above) (marriage dissolved 1901); (2) 1905 the Grand Duke Kirill of Russia (1876–1938). *Issue:*
(a) Marie Kirillovna (1907–51), *m.* 1925 Prince Friedrich Karl of Leiningen. *Issue:* Prince Emich (1926–91); Prince Karl (1928–90); Princess Kira-Melita (*b.* 1930), *m.* Prince Andrej of Yugoslavia (see above); Princess Margarita (1932–96); Princess Mechtilde (*b.* 1936); Prince Friedrich (1938–98)
(b) Kira Kirillovna (1909–67), *m.* 1938 Prince Louis Ferdinand of Prussia. *Issue:* Prince Friedrich Wilhelm (*b.* 1939); Prince Michael (*b.* 1940); Princess Marie (*b.* 1942); Princess Kira (*b.* 1943); Prince Louis Ferdinand (1944–77); Prince Christian (*b.* 1946); Princess Xenia (1949–92)
(c) Vladimir Kirillovich (1917–92), *m.* 1948 Princess Leonida Bagration-Mukhransky. *Issue:* Grand Duchess Maria (*b.* 1953), and has issue

(4) Alexandra (1878–1942), *m.* 1896 Ernst, Prince of Hohenlohe Langenburg. *Issue:*
(a) Gottfried (1897–1960), *m.* 1931 Princess Margarita of Greece (*see above*). *Issue:* Prince Kraft (*b.* 1935), Princess Beatrice (1936–97), Prince Georg Andreas (*b.* 1938), Prince Ruprecht (1944–76); Prince Albrecht (1944–92)
(b) Maria (1899–1967), *m.* 1916 Prince Friedrich of Schleswig-Holstein-Sonderburg-Glücksburg. *Issue:* Prince Peter (1922–80); Princess Marie (1927–2000)
(c) Princess Alexandra (1901–63)
(d) Princess Irma (1902–86)
(5) Princess Beatrice (1884–1966), *m.* 1909 Alfonso of Orleans, Infante of Spain. *Issue:*
(a) Prince Alvaro (1910–97), *m.* 1937 Carla Parodi-Delfino. *Issue:* Doña Gerarda (*b.* 1939); Don Alonso (1941–75); Doña Beatriz (*b.* 1943); Don Alvaro (*b.* 1947)
(b) Prince Alonso (1912–36)
(c) Prince Ataulfo (1913–74)

5. HRH PRINCESS HELENA Augusta Victoria (1846–1923), *m.* 1866 Prince Christian of Schleswig-Holstein-Sonderburg-Augustenburg (1831–1917). *Issue:*
(1) Prince Christian Victor (1867–1900)
(2) Prince Albert (1869–1931), Duke of Schleswig-Holstein 1921–31
(3) Princess Helena (1870–1948)
(4) Princess Marie Louise (1872–1956), *m.* 1891 Prince Aribert of Anhalt (marriage dissolved 1900)
(5) Prince Harold (12–20 May 1876)

6. HRH PRINCESS LOUISE Caroline Alberta (1848–1939), *m.* 1871 the Marquess of Lorne, afterwards 9th Duke of Argyll (1845–1914); without issue

7. HRH PRINCE ARTHUR William Patrick Albert, Duke of Connaught, *Field Marshal* (1850–1942), *m.* 1879 Princess Louisa of Prussia (1860–1917). *Issue:*
(1) Margaret (1882–1920), *m.* 1905 Crown Prince Gustaf Adolf (1882–1973), afterwards King of Sweden 1950–73. *Issue:*
(a) Gustaf Adolf, Duke of Västerbotten (1906–47), *m.* 1932 Princess Sibylla of Saxe-Coburg-Gotha (*see below*). *Issue:* Princess Margaretha (*b.* 1934); Princess Birgitta (*b.* 1937); Princess Désirée (*b.* 1938); Princess Christina (*b.* 1943); Carl XVI Gustaf, King of Sweden (*b.* 1946)
(b) Count Sigvard Bernadotte (1907–2002), *m.* (1) 1934 Erika Patzeck; (2) 1943 Sonja Robbert; (3) 1961 Marianne Lindberg. *Issue:* Count Michael (*b.* 1944)
(c) Princess Ingrid (Queen Mother of Denmark) (1910–2000), *m.* 1935 Frederick IX (1899–1972), King of Denmark 1947–72. *Issue:* Margrethe II, Queen of Denmark (*b.* 1940); Princess Benedikte (*b.* 1944); Princess Anne-Marie (*b.* 1946), *m.* 1964 Constantine II of Greece

(d) Prince Bertil, Duke of Halland (1912–97), *m.* 1976 Mrs Lilian Craig
(e) Count Carl Bernadotte (1916–2003), *m.* (1) 1946 Mrs Kerstin Johnson; (2) 1988 Countess Gunnila Bussler
(2) Arthur (1883–1938), *m.* 1913 HH the Duchess of Fife. *Issue:* Alastair Arthur, 2nd Duke of Connaught (1914–43)
(3) (Victoria) Patricia (1886–1974), *m.* 1919 Adm. Hon. Sir Alexander Ramsay. *Issue:*
(a) Alexander Ramsay of Mar (1919–2000), *m.* 1956 Hon. Flora Fraser (Lady Saltoun)

8. HRH PRINCE LEOPOLD George Duncan Albert, Duke of Albany (1853–84), *m.* 1882 Princess Helena of Waldeck (1861–1922). *Issue:*
(1) Alice (1883–1981), *m.* 1904 Prince Alexander of Teck (1874–1957), *cr.* 1st Earl of Athlone 1917. *Issue:*
(a) Lady May (1906–94), *m.* 1931 Sir Henry Abel-Smith, KCMG, KCVO, DSO. *Issue:* Anne (*b.* 1932); Richard (*b.* 1933); Elizabeth (*b.* 1936)
(b) Rupert, Viscount Trematon (1907–28)
(c) Prince Maurice (March–September 1910)
(2) Charles Edward (1884–1954), Duke of Albany 1884 until title suspended 1917, Duke of Saxe-Coburg-Gotha 1900–18, *m.* 1905 Princess Victoria Adelheid of Schleswig-Holstein-Sonderburg-Glücksburg. *Issue:*
(a) Prince Johann Leopold (1906–72), and has issue
(b) Princess Sibylla (1908–72), *m.* 1932 Prince Gustav Adolf of Sweden (*see above*)
(c) Prince Dietmar Hubertus (1909–43)
(d) Princess Caroline (1912–83), and has issue
(e) Prince Friedrich Josias (1918–98), and has issue

9. HRH PRINCESS BEATRICE Mary Victoria Feodore (1857–1944), *m.* 1885 Prince Henry of Battenberg (1858–96). *Issue:*
(1) Alexander, 1st Marquess of Carisbrooke (1886–1960), *m.* 1917 Lady Irene Denison. *Issue:*
Lady Iris Mountbatten (1920–82), *m. Issue:* Robin A. Bryan (*b.* 1957)
(2) Victoria Eugénie (1887–1969), *m.* 1906 Alfonso XIII (1886–1941) King of Spain 1886–1931. *Issue:*
(a) Prince Alfonso (1907–38)
(b) Prince Jaime (1908–75), and has issue
(c) Princess Beatriz (1909–2002), and has issue
(d) Princess Maria (1911–96), and has issue
(e) Prince Juan (1913–93), Count of Barcelona. *Issue:* Princess Maria (*b.* 1936); Juan Carlos I, King of Spain (*b.* 1938), *m.* 1962 Princess Sophie of Greece and has issue (one son, two daughters); Princess Margarita (*b.* 1939)
(f) Prince Gonzalo (1914–34)
(3) Major Lord Leopold Mountbatten (1889–1922)
(4) Maurice (1891–1914), died of wounds received in action

KINGS AND QUEENS

ENGLISH KINGS AND QUEENS 927 TO 1603

HOUSES OF CERDIC AND DENMARK
Reign

927–939 ÆTHELSTAN
Son of Edward the Elder, by Ecgwynn, and Grandson of Alfred Acceded to Wessex and Mercia *c.*924, established direct rule over Northumbria 927, effectively creating the Kingdom of England
Reigned 15 years

939–946 EDMUND I
Born 921, son of Edward the Elder, by Eadgifu
Married (1) Ælfgifu (2) Æthelflæd
Killed aged 25, *reigned* 6 years

946–955 EADRED
Son of Edward the Elder, by Eadgifu
Reigned 9 years

955–959 EADWIG
Born before 943, son of Edmund and Ælfgifu
Married Ælfgifu
Reigned 3 years

959–975 EDGAR I
Born 943, son of Edmund and Ælfgifu
Married (1) Æthelflæd (2) Wulfthryth (3) Ælfthryth
Died aged 32, *reigned* 15 years

975–978 EDWARD I (the Martyr)
*Born c.*962, son of Edgar and Æthelflæd
Assassinated aged *c.*16, *reigned* 2 years

978–1016 ÆTHELRED (the Unready)
*Born c.*968/969, son of Edgar and Ælfthryth
Married (1) Ælfgifu (2) Emma, daughter of Richard I, Count of Normandy 1013–14 dispossessed of kingdom by Swegn Forkbeard (King of Denmark 987–1014)
Died aged *c.*47, *reigned* 38 years

1016 EDMUND II (Ironside)
Born before 993, son of Æthelred and Ælfgifu
Married Ealdgyth

Died aged over 23, *reigned* 7 months (April–November)

1016–1035 CNUT (Canute)
Born c.995, son of Swegn Forkbeard, King of Denmark, and Gunhild
Married (1) Ælfgifu (2) Emma, widow of Æthelred the Unready
Gained submission of West Saxons 1015, Northumbrians 1016, Mercia 1016, King of all England after Edmund's death
King of Denmark 1019–35, King of Norway 1028—35
Died aged c.40, *reigned* 19 years

1035–1040 HAROLD I (Harefoot)
Born c.1016/17, son of Cnut and Ælfgifu
Married Ælfgifu
1035 recognised as regent for himself and his brother Harthacnut; 1037 recognised as king
Died aged c.23, *reigned* 4 years

1040–1042 HARTHACNUT
Born c.1018, son of Cnut and Emma
Titular king of Denmark from 1028
Acknowledged King of England 1035–7 with Harold I as regent; effective king after Harold's death
Died aged c.24, *reigned* 2 years

1042–1066 EDWARD II (the Confessor)
Born between 1002 and 1005, son of Æthelred the Unready and Emma
Married Eadgyth, daughter of Godwine, Earl of Wessex
Died aged over 60, *reigned* 23 years

1066 HAROLD II (Godwinesson)
Born c.1020, son of Godwine, Earl of Wessex, and Gytha
Married (1) Eadgyth (2) Ealdgyth
Killed in battle aged c.46, *reigned* 10 months (January – October)

THE HOUSE OF NORMANDY

1066–1087 WILLIAM I (the Conqueror)
Born 1027/8, son of Robert I, Duke of Normandy; obtained the Crown by conquest
Married Matilda, daughter of Baldwin, Count of Flanders
Died aged c.60, *reigned* 20 years

1087–1100 WILLIAM II (Rufus)
Born between 1056 and 1060, third son of William I; succeeded his father in England only
Killed aged c.40, *reigned* 12 years

1100–1135 HENRY I (Beauclerk)
Born 1068, fourth son of William I
Married (1) Edith or Matilda, daughter of Malcolm III of Scotland (2) Adela, daughter of Godfrey, count of Louvain
Died aged 67, *reigned* 35 years

1135–1154 STEPHEN
Born not later than 1100, third son of Adela, daughter of William I, and Stephen, Count of Blois
Married Matilda, daughter of Eustace, Count of Boulogne
1141 (February – November) held captive by adherents of Matilda, daughter of Henry I, who contested the crown until 1153
Died aged over 53, *reigned* 18 years

THE HOUSE OF ANJOU (PLANTAGENETS)

1154–1189 HENRY II (Curtmantle)
Born 1133, son of Matilda, daughter of Henry I, and Geoffrey, Count of Anjou
Married Eleanor, daughter of William, Duke of Aquitaine, and divorced queen of Louis VII of France
Died aged 56, *reigned* 34 years

1189–1199 RICHARD I (Coeur de Lion)
Born 1157, third son of Henry II
Married Berengaria, daughter of Sancho VI, King of Navarre
Died aged 42, *reigned* 9 years

1199–1216 JOHN (Lackland)
Born 1167, fifth son of Henry II
Married (1) Isabella or Avisa, daughter of William, Earl of Gloucester (divorced) (2) Isabella, daughter of Aymer, Count of Angoulême
Died aged 48, *reigned* 17 years

1216–1272 HENRY III
Born 1207, son of John and Isabella of Angoulême
Married Eleanor, daughter of Raymond, Count of Provence
Died aged 65, *reigned* 56 years

1272–1307 EDWARD I (Longshanks)
Born 1239, eldest son of Henry III
Married (1) Eleanor, daughter of Ferdinand III, King of Castile (2) Margaret, daughter of Philip III of France
Died aged 68, *reigned* 34 years

1307–1327 EDWARD II
Born 1284, eldest surviving son of Edward I and Eleanor
Married Isabella, daughter of Philip IV of France
Deposed January 1327, *killed* September 1327 aged 43, *reigned* 19 years

1327–1377 EDWARD III
Born 1312, eldest son of Edward II
Married Philippa, daughter of William, Count of Hainault
Died aged 64, *reigned* 50 years

1377–1399 RICHARD II
Born 1367, son of Edward (the Black Prince), eldest son of Edward III
Married (1) Anne, daughter of Emperor Charles IV (2) Isabelle, daughter of Charles VI of France
Deposed September 1399, *killed* February 1400 aged 33, *reigned* 22 years

THE HOUSE OF LANCASTER

1399–1413 HENRY IV
Born 1366, son of John of Gaunt, fourth son of Edward III, and Blanche, daughter of Henry, Duke of Lancaster
Married (1) Mary, daughter of Humphrey, Earl of Hereford (2) Joan, daughter of Charles, King of Navarre, and widow of John, Duke of Brittany
Died aged c.47, *reigned* 13 years

1413–1422 HENRY V
Born 1387, eldest surviving son of Henry IV and Mary
Married Catherine, daughter of Charles VI of France
Died aged 34, *reigned* 9 years

1422–1471 HENRY VI
Born 1421, son of Henry V
Married Margaret, daughter of René, Duke of Anjou and Count of Provence
Deposed March 1461, *restored* October 1470
Deposed April 1471, *killed* May 1471 aged 49, *reigned* 39 years

THE HOUSE OF YORK

1461–1483 EDWARD IV
Born 1442, eldest son of Richard of York (grandson of Edmund, fifth son of Edward III, and son of Anne, great-granddaughter of Lionel, third son of Edward III)
Married Elizabeth Woodville, daughter of Richard, Lord Rivers, and widow of Sir John Grey
Acceded March 1461, *deposed* October 1470, *restored* April 1471
Died aged 40, *reigned* 21 years

1483 EDWARD V
Born 1470, eldest son of Edward IV
Deposed June 1483, died probably July – September
1483, aged 12, reigned 2 months (April – June)

1483–1485 RICHARD III
Born 1452, fourth son of Richard of York
Married Anne Neville, daughter of Richard, Earl of
Warwick, and widow of Edward, Prince of Wales,
son of Henry VI
Killed in battle aged 32, reigned 2 years

THE HOUSE OF TUDOR

1485–1509 HENRY VII
Born 1457, son of Margaret Beaufort (great
granddaughter of John of Gaunt, fourth son of
Edward III) and Edmund Tudor, Earl of Richmond
Married Elizabeth, daughter of Edward IV
Died aged 52, reigned 23 years

1509–1547 HENRY VIII
Born 1491, second son of Henry VII
Married (1) Catherine, daughter of Ferdinand II,
King of Aragon, and widow of his elder brother
Arthur (divorced) (2) Anne, daughter of Sir Thomas
Boleyn (executed) (3) Jane, daughter of Sir John
Seymour (died in childbirth) (4) Anne, daughter of
John, Duke of Cleves (divorced) (5) Catherine
Howard, niece of the Duke of Norfolk (executed) (6)
Catherine, daughter of Sir Thomas Parr and widow
of Lord Latimer
Died aged 55, reigned 37 years

1547–1553 EDWARD VI
Born 1537, son of Henry VIII and Jane Seymour
Died aged 15, reigned 6 years

1553 JANE
Born 1537, daughter of Frances (daughter of Mary
Tudor, the younger daughter of Henry VII) and
Henry Grey, Duke of Suffolk
Married Lord Guildford Dudley, son of the Duke of
Northumberland
Deposed July 1553, executed February 1554 aged 16,
reigned 14 days

1553–1558 MARY I
Born 1516, daughter of Henry VIII and Catherine of
Aragon
Married Philip II of Spain
Died aged 42, reigned 5 years

1558–1603 ELIZABETH I
Born 1533, daughter of Henry VIII and Anne Boleyn
Died aged 69, reigned 44 years

BRITISH KINGS AND QUEENS SINCE 1603

THE HOUSE OF STUART

Reign

1603–1625 JAMES I (VI OF SCOTLAND)
Born 1566, son of Mary, Queen of Scots
(granddaughter of Margaret Tudor, elder daughter of
Henry VII), and Henry Stewart, Lord Darnley
Married Anne, daughter of Frederick II of Denmark
Died aged 58, reigned 22 years

1625–1649 CHARLES I
Born 1600, second son of James I
Married Henrietta Maria, daughter of Henry IV of
France
Executed 1649 aged 48, reigned 23 years

COMMONWEALTH DECLARED
19 May 1649
1649–53 Government by a council of state
1653–8 Oliver Cromwell, Lord Protector
1658–9 Richard Cromwell, Lord Protector

1660–1685 CHARLES II
Born 1630, eldest son of Charles I
Married Catherine, daughter of John IV of Portugal
Died aged 54, reigned 24 years

1685–1688 JAMES II (VII of Scotland)
Born 1633, second son of Charles I
Married (1) Lady Anne Hyde, daughter of Edward,
Earl of Clarendon (2) Mary, daughter of Alphonso,
Duke of Modena
Reign ended with flight from kingdom December
1688
Died 1701 aged 67, reigned 3 years

INTERREGNUM
11 December 1688 to 12 February 1689

1689–1702 WILLIAM III
Born 1650, son of William II, Prince of Orange, and
Mary Stuart, daughter of Charles I
Married Mary, elder daughter of James II
Died aged 51, reigned 13 years

and

1689–1694 MARY II
Born 1662, elder daughter of James II and Anne
Died aged 32, reigned 5 years

1702–1714 ANNE
Born 1665, younger daughter of James II and Anne
Married Prince George of Denmark, son of Frederick
III of Denmark
Died aged 49, reigned 12 years

THE HOUSE OF HANOVER

1714–1727 GEORGE I (Elector of Hanover)
Born 1660, son of Sophia (daughter of Frederick,
Elector Palatine, and Elizabeth Stuart, daughter of
James I) and Ernest Augustus, Elector of Hanover
Married Sophia Dorothea, daughter of George
William, Duke of Lüneburg-Celle
Died aged 67, reigned 12 years

1727–1760 GEORGE II
Born 1683, son of George I
Married Caroline, daughter of John Frederick,
Margrave of Brandenburg-Anspach
Died aged 76, reigned 33 years

1760–1820 GEORGE III
Born 1738, son of Frederick, eldest son of George II
Married Charlotte, daughter of Charles Louis, Duke
of Mecklenburg-Strelitz
Died aged 81, reigned 59 years

REGENCY 1811–20
Prince of Wales regent owing to the insanity of
George III

1820–1830 GEORGE IV
Born 1762, eldest son of George III
Married Caroline, daughter of Charles, Duke of
Brunswick-Wolfenbüttel
Died aged 67, reigned 10 years

1830–1837 WILLIAM IV
Born 1765, third son of George III
Married Adelaide, daughter of George, Duke of
Saxe-Meiningen
Died aged 71, reigned 7 years

1837–1901 VICTORIA
Born 1819, daughter of Edward, fourth son of
George III
Married Prince Albert of Saxe-Coburg and Gotha
Died aged 81, reigned 63 years

THE HOUSE OF SAXE-COBURG AND GOTHA

1901–1910 EDWARD VII
> Born 1841, eldest son of Victoria and Albert
> Married Alexandra, daughter of Christian IX of
> Denmark
> Died aged 68, reigned 9 years

THE HOUSE OF WINDSOR

1910–1936 GEORGE V
> Born 1865, second son of Edward VII
> Married Victoria Mary, daughter of Francis, Duke of
> Teck
> Died aged 70, reigned 25 years

1936 EDWARD VIII
> Born 1894, eldest son of George V
> Married (1937) Mrs Wallis Simpson
> Abdicated 1936, died 1972 aged 77, reigned 10
> months (20 January to 11 December)

1936–1952 GEORGE VI
> Born 1895, second son of George V
> Married Lady Elizabeth Bowes-Lyon, daughter of
> 14th Earl of Strathmore and Kinghorne
> Died aged 56, reigned 15 years

1952– ELIZABETH II
> Born 1926, elder daughter of George VI
> Married Philip, son of Prince Andrew of Greece

KINGS AND QUEENS OF SCOTS 1016 TO 1603

Reign
1016–1034 MALCOLM II
> Born c.954, son of Kenneth II
> Acceded to Alba 1005, secured Lothian c.1016,
> obtained Strathclyde for his grandson Duncan
> c.1016, thus reigning over an area approximately the
> same as that governed by later rulers of Scotland
> Died aged c.80, reigned 18 years

THE HOUSE OF ATHOLL

1034–1040 DUNCAN I
> Son of Bethoc, daughter of Malcolm II, and Crinan,
> Mormaer of Atholl
> Married a cousin of Siward, Earl of Northumbria
> Reigned 5 years

1040–1057 MACBETH
> Born c.1005, son of a daughter of Malcolm II and
> Finlaec, Mormaer of Moray
> Married Gruoch, granddaughter of Kenneth III
> Killed aged c.52, reigned 17 years

1057–1058 LULACH
> Born c.1032, son of Gillacomgan, Mormaer of
> Moray, and Gruoch (and stepson of Macbeth)
> Died aged c.26, reigned 7 months (August–March)

1058–1093 MALCOLM III (CANMORE)
> Born c.1031, elder son of Duncan I
> Married (1) Ingibiorg (2) Margaret (St Margaret),
> granddaughter of Edmund II of England
> Killed in battle aged c.62, reigned 35 years

1093–1097 DONALD III BÁN
> Born c.1033, second son of Duncan I
> Deposed May 1094, restored November 1094, deposed
> October 1097, reigned 3 years

1094 DUNCAN II
> Born c.1060, elder son of Malcolm III and Ingibiorg
> Married Octreda of Dunbar
> Killed aged c.34, reigned 6 months (May
> November)

1097–1107 EDGAR
> Born c.1074, second son of Malcolm III and Margaret
> Died aged c.32, reigned 9 years

1107–1124 ALEXANDER I (THE FIERCE)
> Born c.1077, fifth son of Malcolm III and Margaret
> Married Sybilla, illegitimate daughter of Henry I of
> England
> Died aged c.47, reigned 17 years

1124–1153 DAVID I (THE SAINT)
> Born c.1085, sixth son of Malcolm III and Margaret
> Married Matilda, daughter of Waltheof, Earl of
> Huntingdon
> Died aged c.68, reigned 29 years

1153–1165 MALCOLM IV (THE MAIDEN)
> Born c.1141, son of Henry, Earl of Huntingdon,
> second son of David I
> Died aged c.24, reigned 12 years

1165–1214 WILLIAM I (THE LION)
> Born c.1142, brother of Malcolm IV
> Married Ermengarde, daughter of Richard, Viscount
> of Beaumont
> Died aged c.72, reigned 49 years

1214–1249 ALEXANDER II
> Born 1198, son of William I
> Married (1) Joan, daughter of John, King of
> England (2) Marie, daughter of Ingelram de Coucy
> Died aged 50, reigned 34 years

1249–1286 ALEXANDER III
> Born 1241, son of Alexander II and Marie
> Married (1) Margaret, daughter of Henry III of
> England (2) Yolande, daughter of the Count of
> Dreux
> Killed accidentally aged 44, reigned 36 years

1286–1290 MARGARET (The Maid of Norway)
> Born 1283, daughter of Margaret (daughter of
> Alexander III) and Eric II of Norway
> Died aged 7, reigned 4 years

FIRST INTERREGNUM 1290–2
Throne disputed by 13 competitors. Crown awarded
to John Balliol by adjudication of Edward I of
England

THE HOUSE OF BALLIOL

1292–1296 JOHN (Balliol)
> Born c.1250, son of Dervorguilla, great-great
> granddaughter of David I, and John de Balliol
> Married Isabella, daughter of John, Earl of Surrey
> Abdicated 1296, died 1313 aged c.63, reigned 3 years

SECOND INTERREGNUM 1296–1306
Edward I of England declared John Balliol to have
forfeited the throne for contumacy in 1296 and took
the government of Scotland into his own hands

THE HOUSE OF BRUCE

1306–1329 ROBERT I (Bruce)
> Born 1274, son of Robert Bruce and Marjorie,
> countess of Carrick, and great-grandson of the
> second daughter of David, Earl of Huntingdon,
> brother of William I
> Married (1) Isabella, daughter of Donald, Earl of Mar
> (2) Elizabeth, daughter of Richard, Earl of Ulster
> Died aged 54, reigned 23 years

1329–1371 DAVID II
> Born 1324, son of Robert I and Elizabeth
> Married (1) Joanna, daughter of Edward II of
> England (2) Margaret Drummond, widow of Sir
> John Logie (divorced)
> Died aged 46, reigned 41 years
> 1332 Edward Balliol, son of John Balliol, crowned
> King of Scots September, expelled December
> 1333–6 Edward Balliol restored as King of Scots

THE HOUSE OF STEWART

1371–1390 ROBERT II (Stewart)
Born 1316, son of Marjorie (daughter of Robert I)
and Walter, High Steward of Scotland
Married (1) Elizabeth, daughter of Sir Robert Mure
of Rowallan (2) Euphemia, daughter of Hugh, Earl
of Ross
Died aged 74, *reigned* 19 years

1390–1406 ROBERT III
*Born c.*1337, son of Robert II and Elizabeth
Married Annabella, daughter of Sir John Drummond
of Stobhall
Died aged *c.*69, *reigned* 16 years

1406–1437 JAMES I
Born 1394, son of Robert III
Married Joan Beaufort, daughter of John, Earl of
Somerset
Assassinated aged 42, *reigned* 30 years

1437–1460 JAMES II
Born 1430, son of James I
Married Mary, daughter of Arnold, Duke of Gueldres
Killed accidentally aged 29, *reigned* 23 years

1460–1488 JAMES III
Born 1452, son of James II
Married Margaret, daughter of Christian I of Denmark
Assassinated aged 36, *reigned* 27 years

1488–1513 JAMES IV
Born 1473, son of James III
Married Margaret Tudor, daughter of Henry VII of
England
Killed in battle aged 40, *reigned* 25 years

1513–1542 JAMES V
Born 1512, son of James IV
Married (1) Madeleine, daughter of Francis I of
France (2) Mary of Lorraine, daughter of the Duc de
Guise
Died aged 30, *reigned* 29 years

1542–1567 MARY
Born 1542, daughter of James V and Mary
Married (1) the Dauphin, afterwards Francis II of
France (2) Henry Stewart, Lord Darnley (3) James
Hepburn, Earl of Bothwell
Abdicated 1567, prisoner in England from 1568,
executed 1587, *reigned* 24 years

1567–1625 JAMES VI (and I of England)
Born 1566, son of Mary, Queen of Scots, and Henry,
Lord Darnley
Acceded 1567 to the Scottish throne, *reigned* 58 years
Succeeded 1603 to the English throne, so joining
the English and Scottish crowns in one person. The
two kingdoms remained distinct until 1707 when
the parliaments of the kingdoms became conjoined

WELSH SOVEREIGNS AND PRINCES

Wales was ruled by sovereign princes from the earliest times until the
death of Llywelyn in 1282. The first English Prince of Wales was
the son of Edward I, who was born in Caernarvon town on 25 April
1284. According to a discredited legend, he was presented to the
Welsh chieftains as their prince, in fulfilment of a promise that they
should have a prince who 'could not speak a word of English' and
should be native born. This son, who afterwards became Edward II,
was created 'Prince of Wales and Earl of Chester' at the Lincoln
Parliament on 7 February 1301.
The title Prince of Wales is borne after individual conferment and is
not inherited at birth, though some Princes have been declared and
styled Prince of Wales but never formally so created (*s*). The title was
conferred on Prince Charles by The Queen on 26 July 1958. He was
invested at Caernarvon on 1 July 1969.

INDEPENDENT PRINCES AD 844 TO 1282

844–878	Rhodri the Great
878–916	Anarawd, son of Rhodri
916–950	Hywel Dda, the Good
950–979	Iago ab Idwal (or Ieuaf)
979–985	Hywel ab Ieuaf, the Bad
985–986	Cadwallon, his brother
986–999	Maredudd ab Owain ap Hywel Dda
999–1008	Cynan ap Hywel ab Ieuaf
1018–1023	Llywelyn ap Seisyll
1023–1039	Iago ab Idwal ap Meurig
1039–1063	Gruffydd ap Llywelyn ap Seisyll
1063–1075	Bleddyn ap Cynfyn
1075–1081	Trahaern ap Caradog
1081–1137	Gruffydd ap Cynan ab Iago
1137–1170	Owain Gwynedd
1170–1194	Dafydd ab Owain Gwynedd
1194–1240	Llywelyn Fawr, the Great
1240–1246	Dafydd ap Llywelyn
1246–1282	Llywelyn ap Gruffydd ap Llywelyn

ENGLISH PRINCES SINCE 1301

1301	Edward (Edward II)
1343	Edward the Black Prince, son of Edward III
1376	Richard (Richard II), son of the Black Prince
1399	Henry of Monmouth (Henry V)
1454	Edward of Westminster, son of Henry VI
1471	Edward of Westminster (Edward V)
1483	Edward, son of Richard III (*d.* 1484)
1489	Arthur Tudor, son of Henry VII
1504	Henry Tudor (Henry VIII)
1610	Henry Stuart, son of James I (*d.* 1612)
1616	Charles Stuart (Charles I)
c.1638 (s.)	Charles Stuart (Charles II)
1688 (s.)	James Francis Edward Stuart (The Old Pretender), son of James II (*d.* 1766)
1714	George Augustus (George II)
1729	Frederick Lewis, son of George II (*d.* 1751)
1751	George William Frederick (George III)
1762	George Augustus Frederick (George IV)
1841	Albert Edward (Edward VII)
1901	George (George V)
1910	Edward (Edward VIII)
1958	Charles, son of Elizabeth II

PRINCESSES ROYAL

The style Princess Royal is conferred at the Sovereign's discretion on
his or her eldest daughter. It is an honorary title, held for life, and
cannot be inherited or passed on. It was first conferred on Princess
Mary, daughter of Charles I, in approximately 1642.

c.1642	Princess Mary (1631–60), daughter of Charles I
1727	Princess Anne (1709–59), daughter of George II
1766	Princess Charlotte (1766–1828), daughter of George III
1840	Princess Victoria (1840–1901), daughter of Victoria
1905	Princess Louise (1867–1931), daughter of Edward VII
1932	Princess Mary (1897–1965), daughter of George V
1987	Princess Anne (b. 1950), daughter of Elizabeth II

PRECEDENCE

ENGLAND AND WALES

The Sovereign
The Prince Philip, Duke of
 Edinburgh
The Prince of Wales
The Sovereign's younger sons
The Sovereign's grandsons
The Sovereign's cousins
Archbishop of Canterbury
Lord High Chancellor
Archbishop of York
The Prime Minister
Lord President of the Council
Speaker of the House of Commons
Lord Privy Seal
Ambassadors and High
 Commissioners
Lord Great Chamberlain
Earl Marshal
Lord Chamberlain of the Household
Lord Steward of the Household
Master of the Horse
Dukes, according to their patent of
 creation:
 (1) of England
 (2) of Scotland
 (3) of Great Britain
 (4) of Ireland
 (5) those created since the Union
Eldest sons of Dukes of the Blood
 Royal
Marquesses, according to their patent
 of creation:
 (1) of England
 (2) of Scotland
 (3) of Great Britain
 (4) of Ireland
 (5) those created since the Union
Dukes' eldest sons
Earls, according to their patent of
 creation:
 (1) of England
 (2) of Scotland
 (3) of Great Britain
 (4) of Ireland
 (5) those created since the Union
Younger sons of Dukes of Blood
 Royal
Marquesses' eldest sons
Dukes' younger sons
Viscounts, according to their patent
 of creation:
 (1) of England
 (2) of Scotland
 (3) of Great Britain
 (4) of Ireland
 (5) those created since the Union
Earls' eldest sons
Marquesses' younger sons
Bishop of London
Bishop of Durham
Bishop of Winchester
Other English Diocesan Bishops,
 according to seniority of
 consecration
Suffragan Bishops, according to
 seniority of consecration
Secretaries of State, if of the degree
 of a Baron
Barons, according to their patent of
 creation:

(1) of England
(2) of Scotland
(3) of Great Britain
(4) of Ireland
(5) those created since the Union,
 including Life Barons
Treasurer of the Household
Comptroller of the Household
Vice-Chamberlain of the Household
Secretaries of State under the degree
 of Baron
Viscounts' eldest sons
Earls' younger sons
Barons' eldest sons
Knights of the Garter
Privy Counsellors
Chancellor of the Exchequer
Chancellor of the Duchy of
 Lancaster
Lord Chief Justice of England
Master of the Rolls
President of the Family Division
Vice-Chancellor
Lords Justices of Appeal, according
 to seniority of appointment
Judges of the High Court, according
 to seniority of appointment
Viscounts' younger sons
Barons' younger sons
Sons of Life Peers and Lords of
 Appeal in Ordinary
Baronets, according to date of patent
Knights of the Thistle
Knights Grand Cross of the Bath
Knights Grand Commanders of the
 Star of India
Knights Grand Cross of St Michael
 and St George
Knights Grand Commanders of the
 Indian Empire
Knights Grand Cross of the Royal
 Victorian Order
Knights Grand Cross of the British
 Empire
Knights Commanders of the Bath
Knights Commanders of the Star of
 India
Knights Commanders of St Michael
 and St George
Knights Commanders of the Indian
 Empire
Knights Commanders of the Royal
 Victorian Order
Knights Commanders of the British
 Empire
Knights Bachelor
Vice-Chancellor of the County
 Palatine of Lancaster
Circuit Judges who held office as
 Official Referees to Supreme
 Court (immediately before 1
 January 1972)
Recorder of London
Recorders of Liverpool and
 Manchester, according to priority
 of appointment
Common Serjeant
Circuit Judges who held office
 immediately before 1 January
 1972, according to priority of
 appointment
Other Circuit Judges according to

priority or order of their
 respective appointments
Companions of the Bath
Companions of the Star of India
Companions of St Michael and St
 George
Companions of the Indian Empire
Commanders of the Royal Victorian
 Order
Commanders of the British Empire
Companions of the Distinguished
 Service Order
Lieutenants of the Royal Victorian
 Order
Officers of the British Empire
Companions of the Imperial Service
 Order
Eldest sons of younger sons of Peers
Baronets' eldest sons
Eldest sons of Knights, in the same
 order as their fathers
Members of the Royal Victorian
 Order
Members of the British Empire
Younger sons of Baronets
Younger sons of Knights, in the same
 order as their fathers
Esquires
Gentlemen

SCOTLAND

The Sovereign
The Prince Philip, Duke of
 Edinburgh
The Lord High Commissioner to the
 General Assembly of the Church
 of Scotland (while that Assembly
 is sitting)
The Duke of Rothesay (eldest son of
 the Sovereign)
The Sovereign's younger sons
Grandsons of the Sovereign
The Sovereign's cousins
Lord-Lieutenants
Lord Provosts of Cities being *ex
 officio* Lord-Lieutenants of those
 Cities during their term of office
Sheriffs Principal, successively,
 within their own localities and
 during holding of office
Lord Chancellor of Great Britain
Moderator of the General Assembly
 of the Church of Scotland
Keeper of the Great Seal of Scotland
 (the First Minister)
The Presiding Officer
The Secretary of State for Scotland
Hereditary High Constable of
 Scotland
Hereditary Master of the Household
 in Scotland
Dukes, in same order as in England
Eldest sons of Dukes of the Blood
 Royal
Marquesses, as in England
Eldest sons of Dukes
Earls, as in England
Younger sons of Dukes of Blood
 Royal
Eldest sons of Marquesses

Dukes' younger sons
Lord Justice General
Lord Clerk Register
Lord Advocate
The Advocate-General
Lord Justice Clerk
Viscounts, as in England
Eldest sons of Earls
Marquesses' younger sons
Lord-Barons, as in England
Eldest sons of Viscounts
Earls' younger sons
Lord-Barons' eldest sons
Knights of the Garter
Knights of the Thistle
Privy Counsellors
Senators of College of Justice (Lords
   of Session)
Viscounts' younger sons
Lord-Barons' younger sons
Baronets
Knights Grand Cross and Knights
   Grand Commanders of Orders, as
   in England
Knights Commanders of Orders, as
   in England
Solicitor-General for Scotland
Lord Lyon King of Arms
Sheriffs Principal, when not within
   own county
Knights Bachelor
Sheriffs
Companions of Orders, as in
   England
Commanders of the Royal Victorian
   Order
Commanders of the British Empire
Companions of the Distinguished
   Service Order
Lieutenants of the Royal Victorian
   Order
Officers of the British Empire
Companions of the Imperial Service
   Order
Eldest sons of younger sons of Peers
Eldest sons of Baronets
Eldest sons of Knights, as in
   England
Members of the Royal Victorian
   Order
Members of the British Empire
Baronets' younger sons
Knights' younger sons
Esquires
Gentlemen

WOMEN

Women take the same rank as their husbands or as their brothers; but the daughter of a peer marrying a commoner retains her title as Lady or Honourable. Daughters of peers rank next immediately after the wives of their elder brothers, and before their younger brothers' wives. Daughters of peers marrying peers of lower degree take the same order of precedence as that of their husbands; thus the daughter of a Duke marrying a Baron becomes of the rank of Baroness only, while her sisters married to commoners retain their rank and take precedence of the Baroness. Merely official rank on the husband's part does not give any similar precedence to the wife.

Peeresses in their own right take the same precedence as peers of the same rank, i.e. from their date of creation.

LOCAL PRECEDENCE

Scotland

The Lord Provosts of the city districts of Aberdeen, Dundee, Edinburgh and Glasgow are Lord Lieutenants for those districts *ex officio* and take precedence as such.

FORMS OF ADDRESS

It is only possible to cover here the forms of address for peers, baronets and knights, their wife and children, and Privy Counsellors. Greater detail should be sought in one of the publications devoted to the subject.

Both formal and social forms of address are given where usage differs; nowadays, the social form is generally preferred to the formal, which increasingly is used only for official documents and on very formal occasions.

F_ represents forename
S_ represents surname

BARON – *Envelope (formal)*, The Right Hon. Lord _; *(social)*, The Lord _. *Letter (formal)*, My Lord; *(social)*, Dear Lord _. *Spoken, Lord _.

BARON'S WIFE – *Envelope (formal)*, The Right Hon. Lady _; *(social)*, The Lady _. *Letter (formal)*, My Lady; *(social)*, Dear Lady _. *Spoken*, Lady _.

BARON'S CHILDREN – *Envelope*, The Hon. F_ S_. *Letter*, Dear Mr/Miss/Mrs S_. *Spoken*, Mr/Miss/Mrs S_.

BARONESS IN OWN RIGHT – *Envelope*, may be addressed in same way as a Baron's wife or, if she prefers *(formal)*, The Right Hon. the Baroness _; *(social)*, The Baroness _. Otherwise as for a Baron's wife.

BARONET – *Envelope*, Sir F_ S_, Bt. *Letter (formal)*, Dear Sir; *(social)*, Dear Sir F_. *Spoken*, Sir F_.

BARONET'S WIFE – *Envelope*, Lady S_. *Letter (formal)*, Dear Madam; *(social)*, Dear Lady S_. *Spoken*, Lady S.

COUNTESS IN OWN RIGHT – As for an Earl's wife.

COURTESY TITLES – The heir apparent to a Duke, Marquess or Earl uses the highest of his father's other titles as a courtesy title. (For a list, *see* the Peerage section.) The holder of a courtesy title is not styled The Most Hon. or The Right Hon., and in correspondence 'The' is omitted before the title. The heir apparent to a Scottish title may use the title 'Master' *(see* below).

DAME – *Envelope*, Dame F_ S_, followed by appropriate post-nominal letters. *Letter (formal)*, Dear Madam; *(social)*, Dear Dame F_. *Spoken*, Dame F_.

DUKE – *Envelope (formal)*, His Grace the Duke of _; *(social)*, The Duke of _. *Letter (formal)*, My Lord Duke; *(social)*, Dear Duke. *Spoken (formal)*, Your Grace; *(social)*, Duke.

DUKE'S WIFE – *Envelope (formal)*, Her Grace the Duchess of _; *(social)*, The Duchess of _. *Letter (formal)*, Dear Madam; *(social)*, Dear Duchess. *Spoken*, Duchess.

DUKE'S ELDEST SON – *see* Courtesy titles.

DUKE'S YOUNGER SONS – *Envelope*, Lord F_ S_. *Letter (formal)*, My Lord; *(social)*, Dear Lord F_. *Spoken (formal)*, My Lord; *(social)*, Lord F_.

DUKE'S DAUGHTER – *Envelope*, Lady F_ S_. *Letter (formal)*, Dear Madam; *(social)*, Dear Lady F_. *Spoken*, Lady F_.

EARL – *Envelope (formal)*, The Right Hon. the Earl (of) _; *(social)*, The Earl (of) _. *Letter (formal)*, My Lord; *(social)*, Dear Lord _. *Spoken (formal)*, My Lord; *(social)*, Lord _.

EARL'S WIFE – *Envelope (formal)*, The Right Hon. the Countess (of) _; *(social)*, The Countess (of) _. *Letter (formal)*, Madam; *(social)*, Lady _. *Spoken (formal)*, Madam; *(social)*, Lady _.

EARL'S CHILDREN – Eldest son, *see* Courtesy Titles. Younger sons, The Hon. F_ S_ (for forms of address, *see* Baron's children). Daughters, Lady F_ S_ (for forms of address, *see* Duke's daughter).

KNIGHT (BACHELOR) – *Envelope*, Sir F_ S_. *Letter (formal)*, Dear Sir; *(social)*, Dear Sir F_. *Spoken*, Sir F_.

KNIGHT (ORDERS OF CHIVALRY) – *Envelope*, Sir F_ S_, followed by appropriate post-nominal letters. Otherwise as for Knight Bachelor.

KNIGHT'S WIFE – As for Baronet's wife.

LIFE PEER – As for Baron/Baroness in own right.

LIFE PEER'S WIFE – As for Baron's wife.

LIFE PEER'S CHILDREN – As for Baron's children.

MARQUESS – *Envelope (formal)*, The Most Hon. the Marquess of _; *(social)*, The Marquess of _. *Letter (formal)*, My Lord; *(social)*, Dear Lord _. *Spoken (formal)*, My Lord; *(social)*, Lord _.

MARQUESS'S WIFE – *Envelope (formal)*, The Most Hon. the Marchioness of _; *(social)*, The Marchioness of _. *Letter (formal)*, Madam; *(social)*, Dear Lady _. *Spoken*, Lady _.

MARQUESS'S CHILDREN – Eldest son, *see* Courtesy titles. Younger sons, Lord F_ S_; (for forms of address, *see* Duke's younger sons). Daughters, Lady F_ S_ (for forms of address, *see* Duke's daughter).

MASTER – The title is used by the heir apparent to a Scottish peerage, though usually the heir apparent to a Duke, Marquess or Earl uses his courtesy title rather than 'Master'. *Envelope*, The Master of _. *Letter (formal)*, Dear Sir; *(social)*, Dear Master of _. *Spoken (formal)*, Master, or Sir; *(social)*, Master, or Mr S_.

MASTER'S WIFE – Addressed as for the wife of the appropriate peerage style, otherwise as Mrs S_.

PRIVY COUNSELLOR – *Envelope*, The Right (or Rt.) Hon. F_ S_. *Letter*, Dear Mr/Miss/Mrs S_. *Spoken*, Mr/Miss/Mrs S_. It is incorrect to use the letters PC after the name in conjunction with the prefix The Right Hon., unless the Privy Counsellor is a peer below the rank of Marquess and so is styled The Right Hon. because of his rank. In this case only, the post-nominal letters may be used in conjunction with the prefix The Right Hon.

VISCOUNT – *Envelope (formal)*, The Right Hon. the Viscount _; *(social)*, The Viscount _. *Letter (formal)*, My Lord; *(social)*, Dear Lord _. *Spoken*, Lord _.

VISCOUNT'S WIFE – *Envelope (formal)*, The Right Hon. the Viscountess _; *(social)*, The Viscountess _. *Letter (formal)*, Madam; *(social)*, Dear Lady _. *Spoken*, Lady _.

VISCOUNT'S CHILDREN – As for Baron's children.

THE PEERAGE

AND MEMBERS OF THE HOUSE OF LORDS

The rules which govern the creation and succession of peerages are extremely complicated. There are, technically, five separate peerages, the Peerage of England, of Scotland, of Ireland, of Great Britain, and of the United Kingdom. The Peerage of Great Britain dates from 1707 when an Act of Union combined the two kingdoms of England and Scotland and separate peerages were discontinued. The Peerage of the United Kingdom dates from 1801 when Great Britain and Ireland were combined under an Act of Union. Some Scottish peers have received additional peerages of Great Britain or of the United Kingdom since 1707, and some Irish peers additional peerages of the United Kingdom since 1801.

The Peerage of Ireland was not entirely discontinued from 1801 but holders of Irish peerages, whether pre-dating or created subsequent to the Union of 1801, were not entitled to sit in the House of Lords if they had no additional English, Scottish, Great Britain or United Kingdom peerage. However, they are eligible for election to the House of Commons and to vote in parliamentary elections. An Irish peer holding a peerage of a lower grade which enabled him to sit in the House of Lords was introduced there by the title which enabled him to sit, though for all other purposes he was known by his higher title.

In the Peerage of Scotland there is no rank of Baron; the equivalent rank is Lord of Parliament, abbreviated to 'Lord' (the female equivalent is 'Lady'). All peers of England, Scotland, Great Britain or the United Kingdom who are 21 years or over, and of British, Irish or Commonwealth nationality were entitled to sit in the House of Lords until the House of Lords Act 1999, when hereditary peers lost the right to sit. Ninety-two hereditaries are to remain in the House of Lords for a transitional period. In the list below, these peers are indicated by **. Ten hereditary peers received Life Peerages in 1999 enabling them to remain in the reformed chamber, and two further hereditary peers reverted to sitting by virtue of the Life Peerages they already held.

HEREDITARY WOMEN PEERS

Most hereditary peerages pass on death to the nearest male heir, but there are exceptions, and several are held by women.

A woman peer in her own right retains her title after marriage, and if her husband's rank is the superior she is designated by the two titles jointly, the inferior one second. Her hereditary claim still holds good in spite of any marriage whether higher or lower. No rank held by a woman can confer any title or even precedence upon her husband but the rank of a hereditary woman peer in her own right is inherited by her eldest son (or in some cases daughter).

After the Peerage Act 1963, hereditary women peers in their own right were entitled to sit in the House of Lords, subject to the same qualifications as men, until the House of Lords Act 1999.

LIFE PEERS

Since 1876 non-hereditary or life peerages have been conferred on certain eminent judges to enable the judicial functions of the House of Lords to be carried out. These Lords are known as Lords of Appeal or law lords and, to date, such appointments have all been male.

Since 1958 life peerages have been conferred upon distinguished men and women from all walks of life, giving them seats in the House of Lords in the degree of Baron or Baroness. They are addressed in the same way as hereditary Lords and Barons, and their children have similar courtesy titles.

PEERAGES EXTINCT SINCE THE LAST EDITION

VISCOUNTCIES: Greenwood (cr. 1937)
LIFE PEERAGES: Boardman (cr. 1980); Butterworth (cr. 1985); Dacre of Glanton (cr. 1979); Emslie (cr. 1980); Gladwin of Clee (cr. 1994); Hambro (cr. 1994); Haslam (cr. 1990); Hylton-Foster (cr. 1965); Jenkins of Hillhead (cr. 1987); Perry of Walton (cr. 1979); Porter of Luddenham (cr. 1990); Ryder of Eaton Hastings (cr. 1975); Serota (cr. 1967); Shawcross (cr. 1959); Stodart of Leaston (cr. 1981); Wilberforce (cr. 1964); Williams of Mostyn (cr. 1992); Younger of Prestwick (cr. 1992);

DISCLAIMER OF PEERAGES

The Peerage Act 1963 enables peers to disclaim their peerages for life. Peers alive in 1963 could disclaim within twelve months after the passing of the Act (31 July 1963); a person subsequently succeeding to a peerage may disclaim within 12 months (one month if an MP) after the date of succession, or of reaching 21, if later. The disclaimer is irrevocable but does not affect the descent of the peerage after the disclaimant's death, and children of a disclaimed peer may, if they wish, retain their precedence and any courtesy titles and styles borne as children of a peer. The disclaimer permitted the disclaimant to sit in the House of Commons if elected as an MP. As the House of Lords Act 1999 removed hereditary peers from the House of Lords, they are now entitled to sit in the House of Commons without having to disclaim their titles.

The following peerages are currently disclaimed:

EARLDOMS: Durham (1970); Selkirk (1994)
VISCOUNTCIES: Stansgate (1963)
BARONIES: Merthyr (1977); Reith (1972); Sanderson of Ayot (1971)

PEERS WHO ARE MINORS (ie: under 21 years of age)
EARLS: Craven (b. 1989); Cottenham (b. 1983)
VISCOUNTS: Selby (b. 1993)

CONTRACTIONS AND SYMBOLS

S. Scottish title
I. Irish title
* The peer holds also an Imperial title, specified after the name by Eng., Brit. or UK
** Hereditary peer remaining in the House of Lords for a transitional period
° there is no 'of' in the title
b. Born
s. Succeeded
m. Married
w. widower or widow
M. Minor
† heir not ascertained at time of going to press

HEREDITARY PEERS

PEERS OF THE BLOOD ROYAL

Style, His Royal Highness The Duke of __/His Royal Highness the Earl of__
Style of address (formal) May it please your Royal Highness; *(informal)* Sir

Created	Title, order of succession, name, etc.	Heir
	Dukes	
1337	*Cornwall,* Charles, Prince of Wales, *s.* 1952	‡
1398 S.	*Rothesay,* Charles, Prince of Wales, *s.* 1952	‡
1986	*York* (1st), The Prince Andrew, Duke of York	None
1928	*Gloucester* (2nd), Prince Richard, Duke of Gloucester, *s.* 1974	Earl of Ulster
1934	*Kent* (2nd), Prince Edward, Duke of Kent, *s.* 1942	Earl of St Andrews
	Earl	
1999	*Wessex* (1st), The Prince Edward, Earl of Wessex	None

‡ The title is not hereditary but is held by the Sovereign's eldest son from the moment of his birth or the Sovereign's accession

DUKES

Coronet, Eight strawberry leaves
Style, His Grace the Duke of _
Wife's style, Her Grace the Duchess of _
Eldest son's style, Takes his father's second title as a courtesy title
Younger sons' style, 'Lord' before forename and family name
Daughters' style, 'Lady' before forename and family name
For forms of address, *see* page 40

Created	Title, order of succession, name, etc.	Heir
1868 I.	*Abercorn (5th),* James Hamilton, KG, *b.* 1934, *s.* 1979, *m., Lord Steward*	Marquess of Hamilton, *b.* 1969
1701 S.*	*Argyll (13th) and 6th UK Duke Argyll,* 1892, Torquhil Ian Campbell, *b.* 1968, *s.* 2001	Lord Colin I. C., *b.* 1946
1703 S.	*Atholl (11th),* John Murray, *b.* 1929, *s.* 1996, *m.*	Marquess of Tullibardine, *b.* 1960
1682	*Beaufort (11th),* David Robert Somerset, *b.* 1928, *s.* 1984, *w.,*	Marquess of Worcester, *b.* 1952
1694	*Bedford (15th),* Andrew Ian, Henry Russell, *b.* 1962, *s.* 2003, *m.* 14th Duke of Bedford died in June 2003 after succeding father in October 2002.	Lord Robin L. H. R., *b.* 1963
1663 S.*	*Buccleuch (9th) and Queensberry (11th) (S. 1684) and 8th Eng. Earl, Doncaster,* 1662, Walter Francis John Montagu Douglas Scott, KT, VRD, *b.* 1923, *s.* 1973, *m.*	Earl of Dalkeith, *b.* 1954
1694	*Devonshire (11th),* Andrew Robert Buxton Cavendish, KG, MC, PC, *b.* 1920, *s.* 1950, *m.*	Marquess of Hartington, CBE, *b.* 1944
1947	*Edinburgh (1st),* HRH The Prince Philip, Duke of Edinburgh, *(see* page 22)	The Prince of Wales §
1900	*Fife (3rd) and 12th Scott. Earl, Southesk,* 1633, (S. 1992), James George Alexander Bannerman Carnegie, b. 1929, *s.* 1959,	Earl of Southesk, *b.* 1961
1675	*Grafton (11th),* Hugh Denis Charles FitzRoy, KG, *b.* 1919, *s.* 1970, *m.*	Earl of Euston, b. 1947
1643 S.*	*Hamilton (15th) and Brandon (12th) (Brit. 1711),* Angus Alan Douglas Douglas-Hamilton, *b.* 1938, *s.* 1973, *Premier Peer of Scotland*	Marquess of Douglas and Clydesdale, *b.* 1978
1766 I.*	*Leinster (8th) and 8th Brit. Visct., Leinster,* 1747, Gerald FitzGerald, *b.* 1914, *s.* 1976, *m., Premier Duke and Marquess of Ireland*	Marquess of Kildare, *b.* 1948
1719	*Manchester (13th),* Alexander Charles David Drogo Montagu, *b.* 1962, *s.* 2002, *m.*	Viscount Mandeville, *b.* 1993
1702	*Marlborough (11th),* John George Vanderbilt Henry Spencer-Churchill, *b.* 1926, *s.* 1972, *m.*	Marquess of Blandford, *b.* 1955
1707 S. * **	*Montrose (8th) and 6th Brit. Earl,* Graham, 1722, James Graham, *b.* 1935, *s.* 1992, *m.*	Marquess of Graham, *b.* 1973

§In June 1999, Buckingham Palace revealed that the current Earl of Wessex will succeed to the Dukedom of Edinburgh after the title has returned to the crown. The Prince of Wales will only be able to confer the Dukedom on the Earl of Wessex when he succeeds his mother as King.

Created	Title, order of succession, name, etc.	Heir
1483	** *Norfolk (18th) and 13th Eng. Baron, Beaumont 1309, and 5th UK Baron, Howard of Glossop* 1869, Edward Wiliam Fitzalan-Howard, *b.* 1956, *s.* 2002, *m., Premier Duke and Earl Marshal 1987*	Earl of Arundel and Surrey, *b.* 1987
1766	*Northumberland (12th),* Ralph George Algernon Percy, *b.* 1956, *s.* 1995, *m.*	Earl Percy, *b.* 1984
1675	*Richmond (10th) and Gordon (5th) (UK 1876) and Scott. Duke Lennox (10th),* Charles Henry Gordon Lennox, *b.* 1929, *s.* 1989, *m.*	Earl of March and Kinrara, *b.* 1955
1707 S.*	*Roxburghe (10th) and 5th UK Earl, Innes,* 1837, Guy David Innes-Ker, *b.* 1954, *s.* 1974, *m., Premier Baronet of Scotland*	Marquess of Bowmont and Cessford, *b.* 1981
1703	*Rutland (11th),* David Charles Robert Manners, *b.* 1959, *s.* 1999, *m.*	Marquess of Granby, *b.* 1999
1684	*St Albans (14th),* Murray de Vere Beauclerk, *b.* 1939, *s.* 1988, *m.*	Earl of Burford, *b.* 1965
1547	*Somerset (19th),* John Michael Edward Seymour, *b.* 1952, *s.* 1984, *m.*	Lord Seymour, *b.* 1982
1833	*Sutherland (7th) and 6th UK Earl, Ellesmere,* 1846, Francis Ronald Egerton, *b.* 1940, *s.* 2000, *m.*	Marquess of Stafford, *b.* 1975
1814	*Wellington (8th) and 9th Irish Earl, Mornington,* 1760, Arthur Valerian Wellesley, KG, LVO, OBE, MC, *b.* 1915, *s.* 1972, *m.*	Marquess of Douro, *b.* 1945
1874	*Westminster (6th),* Gerald Cavendish Grosvenor, KG, OBE, *b.* 1951, *s.* 1979, *m.*	Earl Grosvenor, *b.* 1991

MARQUESSES

Coronet, Four strawberry leaves alternating with four silver balls
Style, The Most Hon. the Marquess (of) _. In Scotland the spelling 'Marquis' is preferred for pre-Union creations
Wife's style, The Most Hon. the Marchioness (of)_
Eldest son's style, Takes his father's second title as a courtesy title
Younger sons' style, 'Lord' before forename and family name
Daughters' style, 'Lady' before forename and family name
For forms of address, *see* page 40

Created	Title, order of succession, name, etc.	Heir
1916	*Aberdeen and Temair (7th) and Scott. Earl, Aberdeen* (1682), Alexander George Gordon, *b.* 1955, *s.* 2002, *m.*	Earl of Haddo, *b.* 1983
1876	*Abergavenny (6th),* Christopher George Charles Nevill, *b.* 1955, *s.* 2000, *m.*	To the Earldom David M. R. N., *b.* 1941
1821	*Ailesbury (8th),* Michael Sidney Cedric Brudenell-Bruce, *b.* 1926, *s.* 1974	Earl of Cardigan, *b.* 1952
1831	*Ailsa (8th) and 20th Scott. Earl, Cassillis,* 1509, Archibald Angus Charles Kennedy, *b.* 1956, *s.* 1994	Lord David Kennedy, *b.* 1958
1815	*Anglesey (7th),* George Charles Henry Victor Paget, *b.* 1922, *s.* 1947, *m.*	Earl of Uxbridge, *b.* 1950
1789	*Bath (7th),* Alexander George Thynn, *b.* 1932, *s.* 1992, *m.*	Viscount Weymouth, *b.* 1974
1826	*Bristol (8th),* Frederick William Augustus Hervey, *b.* 1979, *s.* 1999, *m.*	Timothy H. H., *b.* 1960
1796	*Bute (7th),* John Colum Crichton-Stuart, *b.* 1958, *s.* 1993, *m.*	Lord Mount Stuart, *b.* 1989
1812	° *Camden (6th),* David George Edward Henry Pratt, *b.* 1930, *s.* 1983	Earl of Brecknock, *b.* 1965
1815	** *Cholmondeley (7th) and 11th Irish Visct., Cholmondeley,* 1661, David George Philip Cholmondeley, *b.* 1960, *s.* 1990, *Lord Great Chamberlain*	Charles G. C., *b.* 1959
1816	° *Conyngham (7th) and 7th UK Baron, Minster,* 1821, Frederick William Henry Francis Conyngham, *b.* 1924, *s.* 1974, *m.*	Earl of Mount Charles, *b.* 1951
1791 I.*	*Donegall (7th) and 7th Brit. Baron, Fisherwick, 1970 and 6th Brit. Baron Templemore,* 1831, S. 1953, Dermot Richard Claud Chichester, LVO, *b.* 1916, *s.* 1975, *w.*	Earl of Belfast, *b.* 1952
1789 I.*	*Downshire (8th) and 8th Brit. Earl, Hillsborough,* 1772, (Arthur) Robin Ian Hill, *b.* 1929, *s.* 1989, *w.*	Earl of Hillsborough, *b.* 1959
1801 I.*	*Ely (8th) and 8th UK Baron, Loftus,* 1801, Charles John Tottenham, *b.* 1913, *s.* 1969, *w.*	Viscount Loftus, *b.* 1943
1801	*Exeter (8th),* (William) Michael Anthony Cecil, *b.* 1935, *s.* 1988, *m.,*	Lord Burghley, *b.* 1970
1800 I.*	*Headfort (6th) and 4th UK Baron, Kenlis,* 1831, Thomas Geoffrey Charles Michael Taylour, *b.* 1932, *s.* 1960, *m.*	Earl of Bective, *b.* 1959

Created	Title, order of succession, name, etc.	Heir
1793	Hertford (9th) and 10th Irish Baron, Conway, 1712, Henry Jocelyn Seymour, b. 1958, s. 1997, m.	Earl of Yarmouth, b. 1993
1599 S.*	Huntly (13th) and 5th UK Baron, Meldrum, 1815, Granville Charles Gomer Gordon, b. 1944, s. 1987, m., Premier Marquess of Scotland	Earl of Aboyne, b. 1973
1784	Lansdowne (9th) and 9th Irish Earl, Kerry, 1723, Charles Maurice Mercer Nairne Petty-Fitzmaurice, b. 1941, s. 1999, m.	Earl of Shelburne, b. 1970
1902	Linlithgow (4th) and 10th Scott. Earl, Hopetoun, 1703, Adrian John Charles Hope, b. 1946, s. 1987, m.	Earl of Hopetoun, b. 1969
1816 I.*	Londonderry (9th) and 6th UK Earl, Vane, 1823, Alexander Charles Robert Vane-Tempest-Stewart, b. 1937, s. 1955, m.	Viscount Castlereagh, b. 1972
1701 S.*	Lothian (12th) and 6th UK Baron, Kerr, 1821, Peter Francis Walter Kerr, KCVO, b. 1922, s. 1940, m.	Earl of Ancram, PC, MP, b. 1945
1917	Milford Haven (4th), George Ivar Louis Mountbatten, b. 1961, s. 1970, m.	Earl of Medina, b. 1991
1838	Normanby (5th) and 9th Irish Baron, Mulgrave, 1767, Constantine Edmund Walter Phipps, b. 1954, s. 1994, m.	Earl of Mulgrave, b. 1994
1812	Northampton (7th), Spencer Douglas David Compton, b. 1946, s. 1978, m.	Earl Compton, b. 1973
1682 S.	Queensberry (12th), David Harrington Angus Douglas, b. 1929, s. 1954,	Viscount Drumlanrig, b. 1967
1926	Reading (4th), Simon Charles Henry Rufus Isaacs, b. 1942, s. 1980, m.	Viscount Erleigh, b. 1986
1789	Salisbury (7th), and Baron Gascoyne-Cecil (life peerage, 1999) Robert Michael James Gascoyne-Cecil, PC b. 1946, s. 2003, m. Received a Writ in Acceleration in the Barony of Cecil (1603) to enable him to sit in the House of Lords prior to his father's death.	Viscount Cranborne b. 1970
1800 I.*	Sligo (11th) and 11th UK Baron, Monteagle, 1806, Jeremy Ulick Browne, b. 1939, s. 1991, m.	Sebastian U. B., b. 1964
1787	° Townshend (7th), George John Patrick Dominic Townshend, b. 1916, s. 1921, w.	Viscount Raynham, b. 1945
1694	° Tweeddale (13th) and 4th UK Baron Tweeddale, 1881, Edward Douglas John Hay, b. 1947, s. 1979	Lord Charles D. M. H., b. 1947
1789 I.*	Waterford (8th) and 8th Brit. Baron Tyrone, 1786, John Hubert de la Poer Beresford, b. 1933, s. 1934, m.	Earl of Tyrone, b. 1958
1551	Winchester (18th), Nigel George Paulet, b. 1941, s. 1968, m., Premier Marquess of England	Earl of Wiltshire, b. 1969
1892	Zetland (4th) and 6th UK Earl, Zetland, 1838 and 7th Brit. Baron Dundas, 1794, Lawrence Mark Dundas, b. 1937, s. 1989, m.	Earl of Ronaldshay, b. 1965

EARLS

Coronet, Eight silver balls on stalks alternating with eight gold strawberry leaves
Style, The Right Hon. the Earl (of) _
Wife's style, The Right Hon. the Countess (of)_
Eldest son's style, Takes his father's second title as a courtesy title
Younger sons' style, 'The Hon.' before forename and family name
Daughters' style, 'Lady' before forename and family name
For forms of address, see page 40

Created	Title, order of succession, name, etc.	Heir
1639 S.	Airlie (13th), David George Coke Patrick Ogilvy, KT, GCVO, PC, Royal Victorian, b. 1926, s. 1968, m.	Lord Ogilvy, b. 1958
1696	Albemarle (10th), Rufus Arnold Alexis Keppel, b. 1965, s. 1979, m.	Crispian W. J. K., b. 1948
1952	° Alexander of Tunis (2nd), Shane William Desmond Alexander, b. 1935, s. 1969, m.	Hon. Brian J. A., b. 1939
1662	Annandale and Hartfell (11th), Patrick Andrew Wentworth Hope Johnstone, b. 1941, s. 1983, m., claim established 1985	Lord Johnstone, b. 1971
1789	° Annesley (11th), Philip Harrison Annesley, b. 1927, s. 2001, m.	Hon. Michael R. A., b. 1933
1785	Antrim (9th), Alexander Randal Mark McDonnell, b. 1935, s. 1977, m.	Viscount Dunluce, b. 1967
1762	** Arran (9th) and 5th UK Baron Sudley, 1884, Arthur Desmond Colquhoun Gore, b. 1938, s. 1983, m.	Paul A. G., CMG, CVO, b. 1921
1955	° ** Attlee (3rd), John Richard Attlee, b. 1956, s. 1991, m.	None
1714	Aylesford (11th), Charles Ian Finch-Knightley, b. 1918, s. 1958, w.	Lord Guernsey, b. 1947

Created	Title, order of succession, name, etc.	Heir
1937	° ** *Baldwin of Bewdley (4th)*, Edward Alfred Alexander Baldwin, *b.* 1938, *s.* 1976, *w.*	Viscount Corvedale, *b.* 1973
1922	*Balfour (5th)*, Roderick Francis Arthur Balfour, *b.* 1948, *s.* 2003, *m.*	Charles G. Y. B., *b.* 1951
1772	° *Bathurst (8th)*, Henry Allen John Bathurst, *b.* 1927, *s.* 1943, *m.*	Lord Apsley, *b.* 1961
1919	° *Beatty (3rd)*, David Beatty, *b.* 1946, *s.* 1972, *m.*	Viscount Borodale, *b.* 1973
1797	*Belmore (8th)*, John Armar Lowry-Corry, *b.* 1951, *s.* 1960, *m.*	Viscount Corry, *b.* 1985
1739 I.*	*Bessborough (12th) and 9th UK Baron Duncannon*, 1834, Myles Fitzhugh Longfield Ponsonby, *b.* 1941, *s.* 2002, *m.*	Viscount Duncannon, *b.* 1974
1815	*Bradford (7th)*, Richard Thomas Orlando Bridgeman, *b.* 1947, *s.* 1981, *m.*	Viscount Newport, *b.* 1980
1469	*Buchan (17th) and 8th UK Baron Erskine*, 1806, Malcolm Harry Erskine, *b.* 1930, *s.* 1984, *m.*	Lord Cardross, *b.* 1960
1746	*Buckinghamshire (10th)*, (George) Miles Hobart-Hampden, *b.* 1944, *s.* 1983, *m.*	Sir John Hobart, Bt., *b.* 1945
1800	° *Cadogan (8th)*, Charles Gerald John Cadogan, *b.* 1937, *s.* 1997, *m.*	Viscount Chelsea, *b.* 1966
1878	° *Cairns (6th)*, Simon Dallas Cairns, CVO, CBE, *b.* 1939, *s.* 1989, *m.*	Viscount Garmoyle, *b.* 1965
1455	** *Caithness (20th)*, Malcolm Ian Sinclair, PC, *b.* 1948, *s.* 1965, *w.*	Lord Berriedale, *b.* 1981
1800	*Caledon (7th)*, Nicholas James Alexander, *b.* 1955, *s.* 1980, *m.*	Viscount Alexander, *b.* 1990
1661	*Carlisle (13th) and 13th Scott. Baron Ruthven of Freeland*, 1651, George William Beaumont Howard, *b.* 1949, *s.* 1994	Hon. Philip C. W. H., *b.* 1963
1793	*Carnarvon (8th)*, George Reginald Oliver Molyneux Herbert, *b.* 1956, *s.* 2001, *m.*	Lord Porchester, *b.* 1992
1748 I.*	*Carrick (10th) and 4th UK Baron Butler*, 1912, David James Theobald Somerset Butler, *b.* 1953, *s.* 1992, *m.*	Viscount Ikerrin, *b.* 1975
1800 I.	° *Castle Stewart (8th)*, Arthur Patrick Avondale Stuart, *b.* 1928, *s.* 1961, *m.*	Viscount Stuart, *b.* 1953
1814	° *Cathcart (7th) and 16th Scott. Baron Cathcart*, 1447, Charles Alan Andrew Cathcart, *b.* 1952, *s.* 1999, *m.*	Lord Greenock, *b.* 1986
1647	*Cavan*, The 12th Earl died in 1988. Heir had not established his claim to the title at the time of going to press	Roger C. Lambart, *b.* 1944
1827	° *Cawdor (7th)*, Colin Robert Vaughan Campbell, *b.* 1962, *s.* 1993, *m.*	Viscount Emlyn, *b.* 1998
1801	*Chichester (9th)*, John Nicholas Pelham, *b.* 1944, *s.* 1944, *m.*	Richard A. H. P., *b.* 1952
1803 I.	*Clancarty (9th) and 8th UK Visct. Clancarty*, 1823, Nicholas Power Richard Le Poer Trench, *b.* 1952, *s.* 1995	None
1776 I.	*Clanwilliam (7th) and 5th UK Baron Clanwilliam*, 1828, John Herbert Meade, *b.* 1919, *s.* 1989, *m.*	Lord Gillford, *b.* 1960
1776	*Clarendon (7th)*, George Frederick Laurence Hyde Villiers, *b.* 1933, *s.* 1955, *m.*	Lord Hyde, *b.* 1976
1620 I.	*Cork and Orrery (14th) (I. 1660) and 10th Brit. Baron Boyle of Marston*, 1711, John William Boyle, DSC, *b.* 1916, *s.* 1995, *m.*	Viscount Dungarvan, *b.* 1945
1850 M.	*Cottenham (9th)*, Mark John Henry Pepys, *b.* 1983, *s.* 2000,	Hon. Sam R. P., *b.* 1986
1762 I.	** *Courtown (9th) and 8th Brit. Baron Saltersford*, 1796, James Patrick Montagu Burgoyne Winthrop Stopford, *b.* 1954, *s.* 1975, *m.*	Viscount Stopford, *b.* 1988
1697	*Coventry (12th)*, Francis Henry Coventry, *b.* 1912, *s.* 2002, *m.*	Victor G. C., *b.* 1917
1857	° *Cowley (7th)*, Garret Graham Wellesley, *b.* 1934, *s.* 1975, *m.*	Viscount Dangan, *b.* 1965
1892	*Cranbrook (5th)*, Gathorne Gathorne-Hardy, *b.* 1933, *s.* 1978, *m.*	Lord Medway, *b.* 1968
1801 M.	*Craven (9th)*, Benjamin Robert Joseph Craven, *b.* 1989, *s.*	Rupert J. E. C., *b.* 1926
1398 S.*	*Crawford (29th) and Balcarres (12th) (S. 1651) and 5th UK Baron, Wigan, 1826 and Baron Balniel (life peerage, 1974)*, Robert Alexander Lindsay, KT, GCVO, PC, *b.* 1927, *s.* 1975, *m.*, Premier Earl on Union Roll	Lord Balniel, *b.* 1958
1861	*Cromartie (5th)*, John Ruaridh Blunt Grant Mackenzie, *b.* 1948, *s.* 1989, *m.*	Viscount Tarbat, *b.* 1987
1901	*Cromer (4th)*, Evelyn Rowland Esmond Baring, *b.* 1946, *s.* 1991, *m.*	Viscount Errington, *b.* 1994
1633 S.*	*Dalhousie (17th) and 5th UK Baron Ramsay*, 1875, James Hubert Ramsay, *b.* 1948, *s.* 1999, *m.*	Lord Ramsay, *b.* 1981
1725 I.	*Darnley (11th) and 20th Engl. Baron Clifton of Leighton Bromswold*, 1608, Adam Ivo Stuart Bligh, *b.* 1941, *s.* 1980, *m.*	Lord Clifton, *b.* 1968
1711	*Dartmouth (10th)*, William Legge, *b.* 1949, *s.* 1997	Hon. Rupert L., *b.* 1951
1761	° *De La Warr (11th)*, William Herbrand Sackville, *b.* 1948, *s.* 1988, *m.*	Lord Buckhurst, *b.* 1979
1622	*Denbigh (12th) and Desmond (11th) (I. 1622)*, Alexander Stephen Rudolph Feilding, *b.* 1970, *s.* 1995, *m.*	William D. F. *b.* 1939
1485	*Derby (19th)*, Edward Richard William Stanley, *b.* 1962, *s.* 1994, *m.*	Lord Stanley, *b.* 1998
1553	*Devon (18th)*, Hugh Rupert Courtenay, *b.* 1942, *s.* 1998, *m.*	Lord Courtenay, *b.* 1975
1800 I.*	*Donoughmore (8th) and 8th UK Visct. Hutchinson*, 1821, Richard Michael John Hely-Hutchinson, *b.* 1927, *s.* 1981, *w.*	Viscount Suirdale, *b.* 1952

Created	Title, order of succession, name, etc.	Heir
1661 I.*	*Drogheda (12th) and 3rd UK Baron Moore,* 1954, Henry Dermot Ponsonby Moore, *b.* 1937, *s.* 1989, *m.*	Viscount Moore, *b.* 1983
1837	*Ducie (7th),* David Leslie Moreton, *b.* 1951, *s.* 1991, *m.*	Lord Moreton, *b.* 1981
1860	*Dudley (4th),* William Humble David Ward, *b.* 1920, *s.* 1969, *m.*	Viscount Ednam, *b.* 1947
1660 S. * **	*Dundee (12th) and 2nd UK Baron Glassary,* 1954, Alexander Henry Scrymgeour, *b.* 1949, *s.* 1983, *m.*	Lord Scrymgeour, *b.* 1982
1669 S.	*Dundonald (15th),* Iain Alexander Douglas Blair Cochrane, *b.* 1961, *s.* 1986, *m.*	Lord Cochrane, *b.* 1991
1686 S.	*Dunmore (12th),* Malcolm Kenneth Murray, *b.* 1946, *s.* 1995, *m.*	Hon. Geoffrey C. M., *b.* 1949
1822 I.	*Dunraven and Mount-Earl (7th),* Thady Windham Thomas Wyndham-Quin, *b.* 1939, *s.* 1965, *m.*	None
1833	*Durham (6th),* Antony Claud Frederick Lambton, *b.* 1922, *s.* 1970, *m.,* Disclaimed for life 1970	Hon. Edward R. L. (Baron Durham), *b.* 1961
1837	*Effingham (7th) and 17th Eng. Baron Howard of Effingham,* 1554, David Mowbray Algernon Howard, *b.* 1939, *s.* 1996, *m.*	Lord Howard of Effingham, *b.* 1971
1507 S.*	*Eglinton (18th) and Winton (9th) and 6th UK Earl Winton,* 1859, Archibald George Montgomerie, *b.* 1939, *s.* 1966, *m.*	Lord Montgomerie, *b.* 1966
1733 I.*	*Egmont (12th) and 10th Brit. Baron Lovel and Holland,* 1762, Thomas Frederick Gerald Perceval, *b.* 1934, *s.* 2001, *m.*	Hon. Donald W. P. *b.* 1954
1821	*Eldon (5th),* John Joseph Nicholas Scott, *b.* 1937, *s.* 1976, *m.*	Viscount Encombe, *b.* 1962
1633 S.*	*Elgin (11th) and Kincardine (15th) (s. 1647) and 4th UK Baron, Elgin,* 1849, Andrew Douglas Alexander Thomas Bruce, KT, *b.* 1924, *s.* 1968, *m.*	Lord Bruce, *b.* 1961
1789 I.*	*Enniskillen (7th) and 5th UK Baron, Grinstead,* 1815, Andrew John Galbraith Cole, *b.* 1942, *s.* 1989, *m.*	Arthur G. C., *b.* 1920
1789 I.*	*Erne (6th) and 3rd UK Baron Fermanagh,* 1876, Henry George Victor John Crichton, *b.* 1937, *s.* 1940, *m.*	Viscount Crichton, *b.* 1971
1452 S. **	*Erroll (24th),* Merlin Sereld Victor Gilbert Hay, *b.* 1948, *s.* 1978, *m.,* *Hereditary Lord High Constable and Knight Marischal of Scotland*	Lord Hay, *b.* 1984
1661	*Essex (10th),* Robert Edward de Vere Capell, *b.* 1920, *s.* 1981, *m.*	Viscount Malden, *b.* 1944
1711 ° **	*Ferrers (13th),* Robert Washington Shirley, PC, *b.* 1929, *s.* 1954, *m.*	Viscount Tamworth, *b.* 1952
1789 °	*Fortescue (8th),* Charles Hugh Richard Fortescue, *b.* 1951, *s.* 1993, *m.*	Hon. Martin D. F., *b.* 1924
1841	*Gainsborough (5th),* Anthony Gerard Edward Noel, *b.* 1923, *s.* 1927, *m.*	Viscount Campden, *b.* 1950
1623 S.*	*Galloway (13th) and 6th Brit. Baron of Garlies,* 1796, Randolph Keith Reginald Stewart, *b.* 1928, *s.* 1978, *w.*	Andrew C. S., *b.* 1949
1703 S.*	*Glasgow (10th) and 4th UK Baron, Fairlie,* 1897, Patrick Robin Archibald Boyle, *b.* 1939, *s.* 1984, *m.*	Viscount of Kelburn, *b.* 1978
1806 I.*	*Gosford (7th) and 5th UK Baron, Worlingham,* 1835, Charles David Nicholas Alexander John Sparrow Acheson, *b.* 1942, *s.* 1966, *m.*	Hon. Patrick B. V. M. A., *b.* 1915
1945	*Gowrie (2nd) and 3rd UK Baron Ruthven of Gowrie,* 1919, Alexander Patric Greysteil Hore-Ruthven, PC, *b.* 1939, *s.* 1955, *m.*	Viscount Ruthven of Canberra, *b.* 1964
1684 I.*	*Granard (10th) and 5th UK Baron, Granard,* 1806, Peter Arthur Edward Hastings Forbes, *b.* 1957, *s.* 1992, *m.*	Viscount Forbes, *b.* 1981
1833 °	*Granville (6th),* Granville George Fergus Leveson-Gower, *b.* 1959, *s.* 1996, *m.*	Lord Leveson, *b.* 1999
1806 °	*Grey (6th),* Richard Fleming George Charles Grey, *b.* 1939, *s.* 1963, *m.*	Philip K. G., *b.* 1940
1752	*Guilford (10th),* Piers Edward Brownlow North, *b.* 1971, *s.* 1999, *m.*	Lord North, *b.* 2002
1619	*Haddington (13th),* John George Baillie-Hamilton, *b.* 1941, *s.* 1986, *m.*	Lord Binning, *b.* 1985
1919 °	*Haig (2nd),* George Alexander Eugene Douglas Haig, OBE, *b.* 1918, *s.* 1928, *m.*	Viscount Dawick, *b.* 1961
1944	*Halifax (3rd) and 5th UK Visct., Halifax,* 1866, Charles Edward Peter Neil Wood, *b.* 1944, *s.* 1980, *m.*	Lord Irwin, *b.* 1977
1898	*Halsbury (4th),* Adam Edward Giffard, *b.* 1934, *s.* 2000, *m.*	None
1754	*Hardwicke (10th),* Joseph Philip Sebastian Yorke, *b.* 1971, *s.* 1974,	Charles E. Y., *b.* 1951
1812	*Harewood (7th),* George Henry Hubert Lascelles, KBE, *b.* 1923, *s.* 1947, *m.*	Viscount Lascelles, *b.* 1950,
1742	*Harrington (11th) and 8th Brit. Visct. Stanhope of Mahon,* 1717, William Henry Leicester Stanhope, *b.* 1922, *s.* 1929, *m.*	Viscount Petersham, *b.* 1945
1809	*Harrowby (7th),* Dudley Danvers Granville Coutts Ryder, TD, *b.* 1922, *s.* 1987, *m.*	Viscount Sandon, *b.* 1951
1605 **	*Home (15th),* David Alexander Cospatrick Douglas-Home, CVO, CBE, *b.* 1943, *s.* 1995, *m.*	Lord Dunglass, *b.* 1987
1821 ° **	*Howe (7th),* Frederick Richard Penn Curzon, *b.* 1951, *s.* 1984, *m.*	Viscount Curzon, *b.* 1994
1529	*Huntingdon (16th),* William Edward Robin Hood Hastings Bass, LVO, *b.* 1948, *s.* 1990, *m.*	Hon. Simon A. R. H. H. B., *b.* 1950
1885	*Iddesleigh (4th),* Stafford Henry Northcote, *b.* 1932, *s.* 1970, *m.*	Viscount St Cyres, *b.* 1957

Created	Title, order of succession, name, etc.	Heir
1756	Ilchester (9th), Maurice Vivian de Touffreville Fox-Strangways, b. 1920, s. 1970, m.	Hon. Raymond G. F.-S., b. 1921
1929	Inchcape (4th), (Kenneth) Peter (Lyle) Mackay, b. 1943, s. 1994, m.	Viscount Glenapp, b. 1979
1919	Iveagh (4th), Arthur Edward Rory Guinness, b. 1969, s. 1992	Hon. Rory M. B. G., b. 1974
1925	° Jellicoe (2nd) and Baron Jellicoe of Southampton (life peerage, 1999), George Patrick John Rushworth Jellicoe, KBE, DSO, MC, PC, FRS, b. 1918, s. 1935, m.	Viscount Brocas, b. 1950
1697	Jersey (10th) and 13th Visct. Grandison, 1620, George Francis William Child Villiers, b. 1976, s. 1998	Hon. Jamie C. V., b. 1994
1822 I.	Kilmorey (6th), Richard Francis Needham, Kt., PC, b. 1942, s. 1977, m. (does not use title)	Viscount Newry and Morne, b. 1966
1866	Kimberley (5th), John Armine Wodehouse, b. 1951, s. 2002, m.	Lord Wodehouse, b.1978
1768 I.	Kingston (12th), Robert Charles Henry King-Tenison, b. 1969, s. 2002, m.	Viscount Kingsborough, b. 2000
1633 S.*	Kinnoull (15th) and 9th Brit. Baron Hay of Pedwardine, 1711, Arthur William George Patrick Hay, b. 1935, s. 1938, m.	Viscount Dupplin, b. 1962
1677 S.*	Kintore (13th) and 3rd UK Visct. Stonehaven, 1938, Michael Canning William John Keith, b. 1939, s. 1989, m.	Lord Inverurie, b. 1976
1914	° Kitchener of Khartoum (3rd), Henry Herbert Kitchener, TD, b. 1919, s. 1937	None
1624	Lauderdale (17th), Patrick Francis Maitland, b. 1911, s. 1968, w.	Viscount Maitland, b. 1937
1837	Leicester (7th), Edward Douglas Coke, b. 1936, s. 1994, m.	Viscount Coke, b. 1965
1641 S.*	Leven (14th) and Melville (13th) (s. 1690), Alexander Robert Leslie Melville, b. 1924, s. 1947, m.	Lord Balgonie, b. 1954
1831	Lichfield (5th), Thomas Patrick John Anson, b. 1939, s. 1960	Viscount Anson, b. 1978
1803 I.*	Limerick (7th) and 7th UK Baron Foxford, 1815, Edmund Christopher Pery, KBE, b. 1963, s. 2003, m.	Viscount Glentworth, b. 1991
1572	Lincoln (19th), Robert Edward Fiennes-Clinton, b. 1972, s. 2001	Hon. William R. F.-C., b. 1980
1633 S.	** Lindsay (16th), James Randolph Lindsay-Bethune, b. 1955, s. 1989, m.	Viscount Garnock, b. 1990
1626	Lindsey (14th) and Abingdon (9th) (1682), Richard Henry Rupert Bertie, b. 1931, s. 1963, m.	Lord Norreys, b. 1958
1776 I.	Lisburne (8th), John David Malet Vaughan, b. 1918, s. 1965, m.	Viscount Vaughan, b. 1945
1822 I.	* ** Listowel (6th) and 4th UK Baron Hare, 1869, Francis Michael Hare, b. 1964, s. 1997, m.	Hon. Timothy P. H., b. 1966
1905	** Liverpool (5th), Edward Peter Bertram Savile Foljambe, b. 1944, . s. 1969, m	Viscount Hawkesbury, b. 1972
1945	° Lloyd George of Dwyfor (3rd), Owen Lloyd George, b. 1924, s. 1968, m.	Viscount Gwynedd, b. 1951
1785 I.*	Longford (8th) and 2nd UK Baron Pakenham, 1945, Thomas Frank Dermot Pakenham, b. 1933, s. 2001, m.	Hon. Edward M. P., b. 1970
1807	Lonsdale (7th), James Hugh William Lowther, b. 1922, s. 1953, m.	Viscount Lowther, b. 1949
1633 S.	Loudoun (14th), Michael Edward Abney-Hastings, b. 1942, s. 2002, m.	Lord Mauchline, b. 1974
1838	Lovelace (5th) and 12th Brit. Baron King, 1725, Peter Axel William Locke King, b. 1951, s. 1964, m.	None
1795 I.*	Lucan (7th) and 3rd UK Baron Bingham, 1934, Richard John Bingham, b. 1934, s. 1964, m.	Lord Bingham, b. 1967
1880	Lytton (5th) and 18th Engl. Baron, Wentworth, 1529, John Peter Michael Scawen Lytton, b. 1950, s. 1985, m.	Viscount Knebworth, b. 1989
1721	Macclesfield (9th), Richard Timothy George Mansfield Parker, b. 1943, s. 1992, m.	Hon. J. David G. P., b. 1945
1800	Malmesbury (7th), James Carleton Harris, b. 1946, s. 2000, m.	Viscount FitzHarris, b. 1970
1776 & 1792	Mansfield and Mansfield (8th) and 14th Scott. Visct. Stormont, 1621, William David Mungo James Murray, b. 1930, s. 1971, m.	Viscount Stormont, b. 1956
1565 S.*	Mar (14th) and Kellie (16th) (S. 1616) and Baron Erskine of Alloa Tower (life peerage, 2000), James Thorne Erskine, b. 1949, s. 1994, m.	Hon. Alexander D. E., b. 1952
1785 I.	Mayo (10th), Terence Patrick Bourke, b. 1929, s. 1962	Lord Naas, b. 1953
1627 I.*	Meath (15th) and 6th UK Baron, Chaworth, 1831, John Anthony Brabazon, b. 1941, s. 1998, m.	Lord Ardee, b. 1941
1766	Mexborough (8th), John Christopher George Savile, b. 1931, s. 1980, m.	Viscount Pollington, b. 1959
1813	Minto (6th), Gilbert Edward George Lariston Elliot-Murray-Kynynmound, OBE, b. 1928, s. 1975, m.	Viscount Melgund, b. 1953
1562 S.*	Moray (20th) and 12th Brit. Baron Stuart of Castle Stuart, 1796, Douglas John Moray Stuart, b. 1928, s. 1974, m.	Lord Doune, b. 1966
1815	Morley (6th), John St Aubyn Parker, KCVO, b. 1923, s. 1962, m.	Viscount Boringdon, b. 1956

Created	Title, order of succession, name, etc.	Heir
1458	Morton (22nd), John Charles Sholto Douglas, b. 1927, s. 1976, m.	Lord Aberdour, b. 1952
1789	Mount Edgcumbe (8th), Robert Charles Edgcumbe, b. 1939, s. 1982	Piers V. E., b. 1946
1805	° Nelson (9th), Peter John Horatio Nelson, b. 1941, s. 1981, m.	Viscount Merton, b. 1971
1660 S.	Newburgh (12th), Don Filippo Giambattista Camillo Francesco Aldo Maria Rospigliosi, b. 1942, s. 1986, m.	Princess Donna Benedetta F. M. R., b. 1974
1827 I.	Norbury (7th), Richard James Graham-Toler, b. 1967, s. 2000	None
1806 I.*	Normanton (6th) and 9th Brit. Baron Mendip, 1794 and 4th UK Baron, Somerton, 1873, Shaun James Christian Welbore Ellis Agar, b. 1945, s. 1967, m.	Viscount Somerton, b. 1982
1647 S.	** Northesk (14th), David John MacRae Carnegie, b. 1954, s. 1994, m.	Patrick C. C., b. 1940
1801	** Onslow (7th), Michael William Coplestone Dillon Onslow, b. 1938, s. 1971, m.	Viscount Cranley, b. 1967
1696 S.	Orkney (9th), (Oliver) Peter St John, b. 1938, s. 1998, m.	Viscount Kirkwall, b. 1969
1328	Ormonde and Ossory. The marquessate of Ormonde became extinct in 1997 on the death of the 8th Marquess. Viscount Mountgarret is the senior known heir to the Earldoms of Ormonde and Ossory. (see page 52)	Viscount Mountgarret
1925	Oxford and Asquith (2nd), Julian Edward George Asquith, KCMG, b. 1916, s. 1928, w.	Viscount Asquith, OBE, b. 1952
1929	° ** Peel (3rd) and 4th UK Viscount Peel, 1895, William James Robert Peel, b. 1947, s. 1969, m.	Viscount Clanfield, b. 1976
1551	Pembroke (17th) and Montgomery (14th) (1605), Henry George Charles Alexander Herbert, b. 1939, s. 1969	Lord Herbert, b. 1978
1605	Perth (18th), John Eric Drummond, PC, b. 1935, s. 2002, m.	Viscount Strathallan, b. 1965
1905	Plymouth (3rd) and 15th Eng. Baron, Windsor, 1529, Other Robert Ivor Windsor-Clive, b. 1923, s. 1943, m.	Viscount Windsor, b. 1951
1785	Portarlington (7th), George Lionel Yuill Seymour Dawson-Damer, b. 1938, s. 1959, m.	Viscount Carlow, b. 1965
1689	Portland (12th), Count Timothy Charles Robert Noel Bentinck, b. 1953, s. 1997, m.	Viscount Woodstock, b. 1984
1743	Portsmouth (10th), Quentin Gerard Carew Wallop, b. 1954, s. 1984, m.	Viscount Lymington, b. 1981
1804	Powis (8th) and 9th Irish Baron, Clive, 1762, John George Herbert, b. 1952, s. 1993, m.	Viscount Clive, b. 1979
1765	Radnor (8th), Jacob Pleydell-Bouverie, b. 1927, s. 1968, m.	Viscount Folkestone, b. 1955
1831 I.*	Ranfurly (7th) and 8th UK Baron, Ranfurly, 1826, Gerald Françoys Needham Knox, b. 1929, s. 1988, m.	Viscount Northland, b. 1957
1771	Roden (10th), Robert John Jocelyn, b. 1938, s. 1993, m.	Viscount Jocelyn, b. 1989
1801	Romney (7th), Michael Henry Marsham, b. 1910, s. 1975, w.	Julian C. M., b. 1948
1703 S.*	Rosebery (7th) and 3rd UK Earl Midlothian, 1911, Neil Archibald Primrose, b. 1929, s. 1974, m.	Lord Dalmeny, b. 1967
1806 I.	Rosse (7th), William Brendan Parsons, b. 1936, s. 1979, m.	Lord Oxmantown, b. 1969
1801	** Rosslyn (7th), Peter St Clair-Erskine, b. 1958, s. 1977, m.	Lord Loughborough, b. 1986
1457 S.	Rothes (21st), Ian Lionel Malcolm Leslie, b. 1932, s. 1975, m.	Lord Leslie, b. 1958
1861	° ** Russell (5th), Conrad Sebastian Robert Russell, FBA, b. 1937, s. 1987, m.	Viscount Amberley, b. 1968
1915	° St Aldwyn (3rd), Michael Henry Hicks Beach, b. 1950, s. 1992, m.	Hon. David S. H. B., b. 1955
1815	St Germans (10th), Peregrine Nicholas Eliot, b. 1941, s. 1988	Lord Eliot, b. 1966
1660	** Sandwich (11th), John Edward Hollister Montagu, b. 1943, s. 1995, m.	Viscount Hinchingbrooke, b. 1969
1690	Scarbrough (12th) and 13th Irish Visct. Lumley, 1628, Richard Aldred Lumley, b. 1932, s. 1969, m.	Viscount Lumley, b. 1973
1701 S.	Seafield (13th), Ian Derek Francis Ogilvie-Grant, b. 1939, s. 1969, m.	Viscount Reidhaven, b. 1963
1882	** Selborne (4th), John Roundell Palmer, KBE, FRS, b. 1940, s. 1971, m.	Viscount Wolmer, b. 1971
1646 S.	Selkirk. Disclaimed for life 1994. (see Lord Selkirk of Douglas, page 67)	Hon. John A. D.-H., b. 1978
1672	Shaftesbury (10th), Anthony Ashley-Cooper, b. 1938, s. 1961, m.	Lord Ashley, b. 1977
1756 I.*	Shannon (9th) and 8th Brit. Baron Carleton, 1786, Richard Bentinck Boyle, b. 1924, s. 1963	Viscount Boyle, b. 1960
1442	** Shrewsbury and Waterford (22nd) and 7th Eng. Earl Talbot, 1784, Charles Henry John Benedict Crofton Chetwynd Chetwynd-Talbot, b. 1952, s. 1980, m., Premier Earl of England and Ireland	Viscount Ingestre, b. 1978
1961	Snowdon (1st) and Baron Armstrong-Jones (life peerage, 1999), Antony Charles Robert Armstrong-Jones, GCVO, b. 1930, m., Constable of Caernarfon Castle	Viscount Linley, b. 1961
1765	° Spencer (9th), Charles Edward Maurice Spencer, b. 1964, s. 1992, m.	Viscount Althorp, b. 1994
1703 S.*	Stair (14th) and 7th UK Baron, Oxenfoord, 1841, John David James Dalrymple, b. 1961, s. 1996	Hon. David H. D., b. 1963
1984	Stockton (2nd), Alexander Daniel Alan Macmillan, MEP, b. 1943, s. 1986, m.	Viscount Macmillan of Ovenden, b. 1974

Created	Title, order of succession, name, etc.	Heir
1821	Stradbroke (6th), Robert Keith Rous, b. 1937, s. 1983, m.	Viscount Dunwich, b. 1961
1847	Strafford (8th), Thomas Edmund Byng, b. 1936, s. 1984, m.	Viscount Enfield, b. 1964
1606 S.*	Strathmore and Kinghorne (18th) and 16th Scott. Earl, Strathmore, 1677 and 18th Scott. Earl, Kinghorne, 1606 and 5th UK Earl, Strathmore and Kinghorne, 1937, Michael Fergus Bowes Lyon, b. 1957, s. 1987, m.	Lord Glamis, b. 1986
1603	Suffolk (21st) and Berkshire (14th) (1626), Michael John James George Robert Howard, b. 1935, s. 1941, m.	Viscount Andover, b. 1974
1955	Swinton (2nd), David Yarburgh Cunliffe-Lister, b. 1937, s. 1972, m.	Hon. Nicholas J. C.-L., b. 1939
1714	Tankerville (10th), Peter Grey Bennet, b. 1956, s. 1980	Revd the Hon. George A. G. B., b. 1925
1822	° Temple of Stowe (8th), (Walter) Grenville Algernon Temple-Gore-Langton, b. 1924, s. 1988, m.	Lord Langton, b. 1955
1815	Verulam (7th) and 11th Irish Visct. Grimston, 1719 and 16th Scott. Baron Forrester of Corstorphine, 1633, John Duncan Grimston, b. 1951, s. 1973, m.	Viscount Grimston, b. 1978
1729	° Waldegrave (13th), James Sherbrooke Waldegrave, b. 1940, s. 1995, m.	Viscount Chewton, b. 1986
1759	Warwick (9th) and Brooke (9th) (Brit. 1746), Guy David Greville, b. 1957, s. 1996, m.	Lord Brooke, b. 1982
1633 S.*	Wemyss (12th) and March (8th) and 5th UK Baron Wemyss, 1821, Francis David Charteris, KT, b. 1912, s. 1937, m.	Lord Neidpath, b. 1948
1621 I.	Westmeath (13th), William Anthony Nugent, b. 1928, s. 1971, m.	Hon. Sean C. W. N., b. 1965
1624	Westmorland (16th), Anthony David Francis Henry Fane, b. 1951, s. 1993, m.	Hon. Harry St C. F., b. 1953
1876	Wharncliffe (5th), Richard Alan Montagu Stuart Wortley, b. 1953, s. 1987, m.	Viscount Carlton, b. 1980
1801	Wilton (8th) and 6th Baron Ebury (1857), Francis Egerton Grosvenor, b. 1934, s. 1999, m.	Viscount Grey de Wilton, b. 1959
1628	Winchilsea (17th) and Nottingham (12th) (1681), Daniel James Hatfield Finch Hatton, b. 1967, s. 1999, m.	Viscount Maidstone, b. 1998
1766	° Winterton (8th), (Donald) David Turnour, b. 1943, s. 1991, m.	Robert C. T., b. 1950
1956	Woolton (3rd), Simon Frederick Marquis, b. 1958, s. 1969, m.	None
1837	Yarborough (8th), Charles John Pelham, b. 1963, s. 1991, m.	Lord Worsley, b. 1990

COUNTESSES IN THEIR OWN RIGHT

Style, The Right Hon. the Countess (of) _
Husband, Untitled
Children's style, As for children of an Earl
For forms of address, see page 40

Created	Title, order of succession, name, etc.	Heir
1643 S.	Dysart (11th in line), Rosamund Agnes Greaves, b. 1914, s. 1975	Lady Katherine Grant of Rothiemurchus, b. 1918
c.1115 S. **	Mar (31st in line), Margaret of Mar, b. 1940, s. 1975, m., Premier Earldom of Scotland	Mistress of Mar, b. 1963
1947	° Mountbatten of Burma (2nd in line), Patricia Edwina Victoria Knatchbull, CBE, b. 1924, s. 1979, m.	Lord Romsey, b. 1947
c.1235 S.	Sutherland (24th in line), Elizabeth Millicent Sutherland, b. 1921, s. 1963, m.	Lord Strathnaver, b. 1947

VISCOUNTS

Coronet, Sixteen silver balls
Style, The Right Hon. the Viscount _
Wife's style, The Right Hon. the Viscountess _
Children's style, 'The Hon.' before forename and family name
In Scotland, the heir apparent to a viscount may be styled 'The Master of _ (title of peer)'
For forms of address, see page 40

Created	Title, order of succession, name, etc.	Heir
1945	*Addison (4th),* William Matthew Wand Addison, *b.* 1945, *s.* 1992, *m.*	Hon. Paul W. A., *b.* 1973
1946	*Alanbrooke (3rd),* Alan Victor Harold Brooke, *b.* 1932, *s.* 1972,	None
1919	** *Allenby (3rd),* Lt.-Col. Michael Jaffray Hynman Allenby, *b.* 1931, *s.* 1984, *m.*	Hon. Henry J. H. A., *b.* 1968
1911	*Allendale (4th),* Wentworth Peter Ismay Beaumont, *b.* 1948, *s.* 2002, *m.*	Hon. Wentworth A. I. B., *b.* 1979
1642 S.	*Arbuthnott (16th),* John Campbell Arbuthnott, KT, CBE, DSC, FRSE, *b.* 1924, *s.* 1966, *m.*	Master of Arbuthnott, *b.* 1950
1751 I.	*Ashbrook (11th),* Michael Llowarch Warburton Flower, *b.* 1935, *s.* 1995, *m.*	Hon. Rowland F. W. F., *b.* 1975
1917	** *Astor (4th),* William Waldorf Astor, *b.* 1951, *s.* 1966, *m.*	Hon. William W. A., *b.* 1979
1781 I.	*Bangor (8th),* William Maxwell David Ward, *b.* 1948, *s.* 1993, *m.*	Hon. E. Nicholas W., *b.* 1953
1925	*Bearsted (5th),* Nicholas Alan Samuel, *b.* 1950, *s.* 1996, *m.*	Hon. Harry R. S., *b.* 1988
1963	*Blakenham (2nd),* Michael John Hare, *b.* 1938, *s.* 1982, *m.*	Hon. Caspar J. H., *b.* 1972
1935	** *Bledisloe (3rd),* Christopher Hiley Ludlow Bathurst, QC, *b.* 1934, *s.* 1979	Hon. Rupert E. L. B., *b.* 1964
1712	*Bolingbroke (7th) and St John (8th) (1716),* Kenneth Oliver Musgrave St John, *b.* 1927, *s.* 1974	Hon. Henry F. St J., *b.* 1957
1960	*Boyd of Merton (2nd),* Simon Donald Rupert Neville Lennox-Boyd, *b.* 1939, *s.* 1983, *m.*	Hon. Benjamin A. L.-B., *b.* 1964
1717 I.*	*Boyne (11th) and 5th UK Baron Brancepeth,* 1866, Gustavus Michael Stucley Hamilton-Russell, *b.* 1965, *s.* 1995, *m.*	Hon. Gustavus A. E. H.-R., *b.* 1999
1929	*Brentford (4th),* Crispin William Joynson-Hicks, *b.* 1933, *s.* 1983, *m.*	Hon. Paul W. J.-H., *b.* 1971
1929	** *Bridgeman (3rd),* Robin John Orlando Bridgeman, *b.* 1930, *s.* 1982, *m.*	Hon. Luke R. O. B., *b.* 1971
1868	*Bridport (4th) and 7th Duke, Bronte in Sicily, 1799 and 6th Irish Baron Bridport,* 1794, Alexander Nelson Hood, *b.* 1948, *s.* 1969, *m.*	Hon. Peregrine A. N. H., *b.* 1974
1952	** *Brookeborough (3rd),* Alan Henry Brooke, *b.* 1952, *s.* 1987, *m.*	Hon. Christopher A. B., *b.* 1954
1933	*Buckmaster (3rd),* Martin Stanley Buckmaster, OBE, *b.* 1921, *s.* 1974	Hon. Colin J. B., *b.* 1923
1939	*Caldecote (3rd),* Piers James Hampden Inskip, *b.* 1947, *s.* 1999, *m.*	Hon. Thomas J. H. I., *b.* 1985
1941	*Camrose (4th),* Adrian Michael Berry, *b.* 1937, *s.* 2001, *m.*	Hon. Jonathan W. B., *b.* 1970
1954	*Chandos (3rd) and Baron Lyttelton of Aldershot (life peerage, 2000),* Thomas Orlando Lyttelton, *b.* 1953, *s.* 1980, *m.*	Hon. Oliver A. L., *b.* 1986
1665 I.*	*Charlemont (15th) and 19th Irish Baron Caulfeild of Charlemont,* 1620, John Dodd Caulfeild, *b.* 1966, *s.* 2001, *m.*	Hon. Shane A. C., *b.* 1966
1921	*Chelmsford (4th) and UK Baron Chelmsford,* 1858, Frederic Corin Piers Thesiger, *b.* 1962, *s.* 1999	To Barony only, Sir Wilfred P. T., KBE, *b.* 1910
1717 I.	*Chetwynd (10th),* Adam Richard John Casson Chetwynd, *b.* 1935, *s.* 1965, *m.*	Hon. Adam D. C., *b.* 1969
1911	*Chilston (4th),* Alastair George Akers-Douglas, *b.* 1946, *s.* 1982, *m.*	Hon. Oliver I. A.-D., *b.* 1973
1902	*Churchill (3rd) and 5th UK Baron Churchill,* 1815, Victor George Spencer, *b.* 1934, *s.* 1973	To Barony only, Richard H. R. S., *b.* 1926
1718	*Cobham (11th) and 8th Irish Baron Westcote,* 1776, John William Leonard Lyttelton, *b.* 1943, *s.* 1977, *m.*	Hon. Christopher C. L., *b.* 1947
1902	** *Colville of Culross (4th) and 13th Scott. Baron Colville of Culcross,* 1604, John Mark Alexander Colville, QC, *b.* 1933, *s.* 1945, *m.*	Master of Colville, *b.* 1959
1826	*Combermere (6th),* Thomas Robert Wellington Stapleton-Cotton, *b.* 1969, *s.* 2000	Hon. David P. D. S.-C., *b.* 1932
1917	*Cowdray (4th) and 4th UK Baron Cowdray,* 1910, Michael Orlando Weetman Pearson, *b.* 1944, *s.* 1995, *m.*	Hon. Peregrine J. D. P., *b.* 1994
1927	** *Craigavon (3rd),* Janric Fraser Craig, *b.* 1944, *s.* 1974	None
1886	*Cross (3rd),* Assheton Henry Cross, *b.* 1920, *s.* 1932	None
1943	*Daventry (4th),* James Edward FitzRoy Newdegate, *b.* 1960, *s.* 2000, *m.*	Hon. Humphrey J. F. N., *b.* 1995
1937	*Davidson (2nd),* John Andrew Davidson, *b.* 1928, *s.* 1970, *m.*	Hon. Malcolm W. M. D., *b.* 1934

Created	Title, order of succession, name, etc.	Heir
1956	De L'Isle (2nd) and 7th UK Baron de L'Isle and Dudley, 1835, Philip John Algernon Sidney, MBE, b. 1945, s. 1991, m.	Hon. Philip W. E. S., b. 1985
1776 I.*	De Vesci (7th) and 8th Irish Baron Knapton, 1750, Thomas Eustace Vesey, b. 1955, s. 1983, m.	Hon. Oliver I. V., b. 1991
1917	Devonport (3rd), Terence Kearley, b. 1944, s. 1973	Chester D. H. K., b. 1932
1964	Dilhorne (2nd), John Mervyn Manningham-Buller, b. 1932, s. 1980, m.	Hon. James E. M.-B., b. 1956
1622 I.	Dillon (22nd), Henry Benedict Charles Dillon, b. 1973, s. 1982	Hon. Richard A. L. D., b. 1948
1785 I.	Doneraile (10th), Richard Allen St Leger, b. 1946, s. 1983, m.	Hon. Nathaniel W. R. St J. St L., b. 1971
1680 I.*	Downe (12th) and 5th UK Baron Dawnay, 1897, Richard Henry Dawnay, b. 1967, s. 2002	Thomas P. D., b. 1978
1959	Dunrossil (3rd), Andrew William Reginald Morrison, b. 1953, s. 2000, m.	Hon. Callum A. B. M., b. 1994
1964	Eccles (2nd), John Dawson Eccles, CBE, b. 1931, s. 1999, m.	Hon. William D. E., b. 1960
1897	Esher (4th), Lionel Gordon Baliol Brett, CBE, b. 1913, s. 1963, m.	Hon. Christopher L. B. B., b. 1936
1816	Exmouth (10th), Paul Edward Pellew, b. 1940, s. 1970, m.	Hon. Edward F. P., b. 1978
1620 S.	** Falkland (15th), Lucius Edward William Plantagenet Cary, b. 1935, s. 1984, m., Premier Scottish Viscount on the Roll	Master of Falkland, b. 1963
1720	Falmouth (9th) and 26th Eng. Baron Le Despencer, 1264, George Hugh Boscawen, b. 1919, s. 1962, m.	Hon. Evelyn A. H. B., b. 1955
1720 I.*	Gage (8th) and 7th Brit. Baron Gage, 1790, (Henry) Nicolas Gage, b. 1934, s. 1993, m.	Hon. Henry W. G., b. 1975
1727 I.	Galway (12th), George Rupert Monckton-Arundell, b. 1922, s. 1980, m.	Hon. J. Philip M., b. 1952
1478 I.*	Gormanston (17th) and 5th UK Baron Gormanston, 1868, Jenico Nicholas Dudley Preston, b. 1939, s. 1940, w., Premier Viscount of Ireland	Hon. Jenico F. T. P., b. 1974
1816 I.	Gort (9th), Foley Robert Standish Prendergast Vereker, b. 1951, s. 1995, m.	Hon. Robert F. P. V., b. 1993
1900	** Goschen (4th), Giles John Harry Goschen, b. 1965, s. 1977, m.	Hon. Alexander J. E. G., b. 2001
1849	Gough (5th), Shane Hugh Maryon Gough, b. 1941, s. 1951	None
1929	Hailsham, Douglas Martin Hogg, PC, QC, MP, b. 1945, s. 2001, m.	Hon. Quintin J. N. M. H., b. 1973
1891	Hambleden (4th), William Herbert Smith, b. 1930, s. 1948, m.	Hon. William H. B. S., b. 1955
1884	Hampden (6th), Anthony David Brand, b. 1937, s. 1975, m.	Hon. Francis A. B., b. 1970
1936	Hanworth (3rd), David Stephen Geoffrey Pollock, b. 1946, s. 1996, m.	Hon. Richard C. S. P., b. 1951
1791 I.	Harberton (10th), Thomas de Vautort Pomeroy, b. 1910, s. 1980, w.	Henry R. P., b. 1958
1846	Hardinge (6th), Charles Henry Nicholas Hardinge, b. 1956, s. 1984, m.	Hon. Andrew H. H., b. 1960
1791 I.	Hawarden (9th), (Robert) Connan Wyndham Leslie Maude, b. 1961, s. 1991, m.	Hon. Varian J. C. E. M., b. 1997
1960	Head (2nd), Richard Antony Head, b. 1937, s. 1983, m.	Hon. Henry J. H., b. 1980
1550	Hereford (18th), Robert Milo Leicester Devereux, b. 1932, s. 1952, Premier Viscount of England	Hon. Charles R. de B. D., b. 1975
1842	Hill (9th), Peter David Raymond Charles Clegg-Hill, b. 1945, s. 2003	Paul A. R. C.-H., b. 1979
1796	Hood (8th) and 7th Irish Baron, Hood, 1782, Henry Lyttleton Alexander Hood, b. 1958, s. 1999, m.	Hon. Archibald L. S. H., b. 1993
1956	Ingleby (2nd), Martin Raymond Peake, b. 1926, s. 1966, w.	None
1945	Kemsley (3rd), Richard Gomer Berry, b. 1951, s. 1999, m.	Hon. Luke G. B., b. 1998
1911	Knollys (3rd), David Francis Dudley Knollys, b. 1931, s. 1966, m.	Hon. Patrick N. M. K., b. 1962
1895	Knutsford (6th), Michael Holland-Hibbert, b. 1926, s. 1986, m.	Hon. Henry T. H.-H., b. 1959
1954	Leathers (3rd), Christopher Graeme Leathers, b. 1941, s. 1996, m.	Hon. James F. L., b. 1969
1781 I.	Lifford (9th), (Edward) James Wingfield Hewitt, b. 1949, s. 1987, m.	Hon. James T. W. H., b. 1979
1921	Long (4th), Richard Gerard Long, CBE, b. 1929, s. 1967, m.	Hon. James R. L., b. 1960
1957	Mackintosh of Halifax (3rd), (John) Clive Mackintosh, b. 1958, s. 1980, m.	Hon. Thomas H. G. M., b. 1985
1955	Malvern (3rd), Ashley Kevin Godfrey Huggins, b. 1949, s. 1978	Hon. M. James H., b. 1928
1945	Marchwood (3rd), David George Staveley Penny, b. 1936, s. 1979, w.	Hon. Peter G. W. P., b. 1965
1942	Margesson (2nd), Francis Vere Hampden Margesson, b. 1922, s. 1965, m.	Capt. Hon. Richard F. D. M., b. 1960
1660 I.*	Massereene (14th) and Ferrard (7th) (1797) and 7th UK Baron, Oriel, 1821, John David Clotworthy Whyte-Melville Foster Skeffington, b. 1940, s. 1992, m.	Hon. Charles J. C. W.-M. F. S., b. 1973
1802	Melville (9th), Robert David Ross Dundas, b. 1937, s. 1971, m.	Hon. Robert H. K. D., b. 1984
1916	Mersey (4th) and 13th Scott. Lord Nairne, 1681 s. 1995, Richard Maurice Clive Bigham, b. 1934, s. 1979, m.	Master of Nairne, b. 1966
1717 I.*	Midleton (12th) and 9th Brit. Baron Brodrick of Peper Harow, 1796, Alan Henry Brodrick, b. 1949, s. 1988, m.	Hon. Ashley R. B., b. 1980
1962	Mills (3rd), Christopher Philip Roger Mills, b. 1956, s. 1988, m.	None

Created	Title, order of succession, name, etc.	Heir
1716 I.	Molesworth (12th), Robert Bysse Kelham Molesworth, b. 1959, s. 1997	Hon. William J. C. M., b. 1960
1801 I.*	Monck (7th) and 4th UK Baron, Monck, 1866, Charles Stanley Monck, b. 1953, s. 1982. Does not use title	Hon. George S. M., b. 1957
1957	Monckton of Brenchley (2nd), Maj.-Gen. Gilbert Walter Riversdale Monckton, CB, OBE, MC, b. 1915, s. 1965, m.	Hon. Christopher W. M., b. 1952
1946	Montgomery of Alamein (2nd), David Bernard Montgomery, CBE, b. 1928, s. 1976, m.	Hon. Henry D. M., b. 1954
1550 I.*	Mountgarret (17th) and 4th UK Baron Mountgarret, 1911, Richard Henry Piers Butler, b. 1936, s. 1966, m.	Hon. Piers J. R. B., b. 1961
1952	Norwich (2nd), John Julius Cooper, CVO, b. 1929, s. 1954, m.	Hon. Jason C. D. B. C., b. 1959
1651 S. **	Oxfuird (14th), Ian Arthur Alexander Makgill, b. 1969, s. 2003, m.	Hon Robert E. G. M., b. 1969
1873	Portman (10th), Christopher Edward Berkeley Portman, b. 1958, s. 1999, m.	Hon. Luke O. B. P., b. 1984
1743 I.*	Powerscourt (10th) and 4th UK Baron Powerscourt, 1885, Mervyn Niall Wingfield, b. 1935, s. 1973, m.	Hon. Mervyn A. W., b. 1963
1900	Ridley (4th), Matthew White Ridley, KG, GCVO, TD, b. 1925, s. 1964, m.	Hon. Matthew W. R., b. 1958
1960	Rochdale (2nd), St John Durival Kemp, b. 1938, s. 1993, m.	Hon. Jonathan H. D. K., b. 1961
1919	Rothermere (4th), (Harold) Jonathan Esmond Vere Harmsworth, b. 1967, s. 1998, m.	Hon. Vere R. J. H. H., b. 1994
1937	Runciman of Doxford (3rd) and 4th UK Baron, Runciman, 1933, Walter Garrison Runciman (Garry), CBE, FBA, b. 1934, s. 1989, m.	Hon. David W. R., b. 1967
1918	St Davids (3rd) and 20th Eng. Baron Strange of Knokin, 1299 and 8th Eng. Baron, Hungerford, 1426 and Baron De Moleyns, 1445, Colwyn Jestyn John Philipps, b. 1939, s. 1991, m.	Hon. Rhodri C. P., b. 1966
1801	St Vincent (7th), Ronald George James Jervis, b. 1905, s. 1940, m.	Hon. Edward R. J. J., b. 1951
1937	Samuel (3rd), David Herbert Samuel, OBE, Ph.D., b. 1922, s. 1978, m.	Hon. Dan J. S., b. 1925
1911	Scarsdale (4th) and 8th Brit. Baron Scarsdale, 1761, Peter Ghislain Nathaniel Curzon, b. 1949, s. 2000, m.	Hon. David J. N. C., b. 1958
1905 M.	Selby (6th), Christopher Rolf Thomas Gully, b. 1993, s. 2001	Hon. (James) Edward H. G. G., b. 1945
1805	Sidmouth (7th), John Tonge Anthony Pellew Addington, b. 1914, s. 1976, m.	Hon. Jeremy F. A., b. 1947
1940 **	Simon (3rd), Jan David Simon, b. 1940, s. 1993, m.	None
1960 **	Slim (2nd), John Douglas Slim, OBE, b. 1927, s. 1970, m.	Hon. Mark W. R. S., b. 1960
1954	Soulbury (2nd), James Herwald Ramsbotham, b. 1915, s. 1971, w.	Hon. Sir Peter E. R., GCMG, GCVO, b. 1919
1776 I.	Southwell (7th), Pyers Anthony Joseph Southwell, b. 1930, s. 1960, m.	Hon. Richard A. P. S., b. 1956
1942	Stansgate, Rt. Hon. Anthony Neil Wedgwood Benn, b. 1925, s. 1960, w. Disclaimed for life 1963.	Stephen M. W. B., b. 1951
1959	Stuart of Findhorn (3rd), James Dominic Stuart, b. 1948, s. 1999, m.	Hon. Andrew M. S., b. 1957
1957 **	Tenby (3rd), William Lloyd George, b. 1927, s. 1983, m.	Hon. Timothy H. G. L. G., b. 1962
1952	Thurso (3rd), John Archibald Sinclair, b. 1953, s. 1995, m.	Hon. James A. R. s., b. 1984
1721	Torrington (11th), Timothy Howard St George Byng, b. 1943, s. 1961, m.	John L. B., MC, b. 1919
1936	Trenchard (3rd), Hugh Trenchard, b. 1951, s. 1987, m.	Hon. Alexander T. T., b. 1978
1921	Ullswater (2nd), Nicholas James Christopher Lowther, PC, LVO, b. 1942, s. 1949, m.	Hon. Benjamin J. L., b. 1975
1621 I.	Valentia (15th), Richard John Dighton Annesley, b. 1929, s. 1983, m.	Hon. Francis W. D. A., b. 1959
1952 **	Waverley (3rd), John Desmond Forbes Anderson, b. 1949, s. 1990, m.	Hon. Forbes A. R. A., b. 1996
1938	Weir (3rd), William Kenneth James Weir, b. 1933, s. 1975, m.	Hon. James W. H. W., b. 1965
1918	Wimborne (4th) and 5th UK Baron Wimborne, 1880, Ivor Mervyn Vigors Guest, b. 1968, s. 1993	Hon. Julien J. G., b. 1945
1923	Younger of Leckie (5th) James Edward George Younger, MCIM, MBA b. 1955, s. 2003, m.	Hon. Alexander W. G. Y., b. 1993

BARONS/LORDS

Coronet, Six silver balls
Style, The Right Hon. the Lord _ . In the Peerage of Scotland there is no rank of Baron; the equivalent rank is Lord of
Parliament (*see* page 41) and Scottish peers should always be styled 'Lord', never 'Baron'
Wife's style, The Right Hon. the Lady _
Children's style, 'The Hon.' before forename and family name
In Scotland, the heir apparent to a Lord may be styled 'The Master of _ (title of peer)'
For forms of address, *see* page 40

Created	Title, order of succession, name, etc.	Heir
1911	*Aberconway (4th),* (Henry) Charles McLaren, *b.* 1948, *s.* 2003, *m.*	Hon. Charles S. M., *b.* 1984
1873	** *Aberdare (4th),* Morys George Lyndhurst Bruce, KBE, PC, *b.* 1919, *s.* 1957, *m.*	Hon. Alastair J. L. *b.*, *b.* 1947
1835	*Abinger (9th),* James Harry Scarlett, *b.* 1959, *s.* 2002, *m.*	Hon. Peter R. S., *b.* 1961
1869	*Acton (4th) and Baron Acton of Bridgnorth (life peerage, 2000),* Richard Gerald Lyon-Dalberg-Acton, *b.* 1941, *s.* 1989, *m.*	Hon. John C. F. H. L.-D.-A., *b.* 1966
1887	** *Addington (6th),* Dominic Bryce Hubbard, *b.* 1963, *s.* 1982,	Hon. Michael W. L. H., *b.* 1965
1896	*Aldenham (6th) and Hunsdon of Hunsdon (4th)* (1923), Vicary Tyser Gibbs, *b.* 1948, *s.* 1986, *m.*	Hon. Humphrey W. F. G., *b.* 1989
1962	*Aldington (2nd),* Charles Harold Stuart Low, *b.* 1948, *s.* 2001, *m.*	Hon Philip T. A. L., *b.* 1990
1945	*Altrincham (3rd),* Anthony Ulick David Dundas Grigg, *b.* 1934, *s.* 2000, *m.*	Hon. (Edward) Sebastian G., *b.* 1965
1929	*Alvingham (2nd),* Maj.-Gen. Robert Guy Eardley Yerburgh, CBE, *b.* 1926, *s.* 1955, *m.*	Capt. Hon. Robert R. G. Y., *b.* 1956
1892	*Amherst of Hackney (4th),* William Hugh Amherst Cecil, *b.* 1940, *s.* 1980, *m.*	Hon. H. William A. C., *b.* 1968
1881	** *Ampthill (4th),* Geoffrey Denis Erskine Russell, CBE, PC, *b.* 1921, *s.* 1973	Hon. David W. E. R., *b.* 1947
1947	*Amwell (3rd),* Keith Norman Montague, *b.* 1943, *s.* 1990, *m.*	Hon. Ian K. M., *b.* 1973
1863	*Annaly (6th),* Luke Richard White, *b.* 1954, *s.* 1990, *m.*	Hon. Luke H. W., *b.* 1990
1885	*Ashbourne (4th),* Edward Barry Greynville Gibson, *b.* 1933, *s.* 1983, *m.*	Hon. Edward C. d'O. G., *b.* 1967
1835	*Ashburton (7th),* John Francis Harcourt Baring, KG, KCVO, *b.* 1928, *s.* 1991, *m.*	Hon. Mark F. R. B., *b.* 1958
1892	*Ashcombe (4th),* Henry Edward Cubitt, *b.* 1924, *s.* 1962, *m.*	Mark E. C., *b.* 1964
1911	*Ashton of Hyde (3rd),* Thomas John Ashton, TD, *b.* 1926, *s.* 1983, *m.*	Hon. Thomas H. A., *b.* 1958
1800 I.	*Ashtown (7th),* Nigel Clive Crosby Trench, KCMG, *b.* 1916, *s.* 1990, *m.*	Hon. Roderick N. G. T., *b.* 1944
1956	** *Astor of Hever (3rd),* John Jacob Astor, *b.* 1946, *s.* 1984, *m.*	Hon. Charles G. J. A., *b.* 1990
1789 I. *	*Auckland (10th) and 10th Brit. Baron Auckland,* 1793, Robert Ian Burnard Eden, *b.* 1962, *s.* 1997, *m.*	Hon. Ronald J. E., *b.* 1931
1313	*Audley.* Barony in abeyance between three co-heiresses since 1997	
1900	** *Avebury (4th),* Eric Reginald Lubbock, *b.* 1928, *s.* 1971, *m.*	Hon. Lyulph A. J. L., *b.* 1954
1718 I.	*Aylmer (13th),* Michael Anthony Aylmer, *b.* 1923, *s.* 1982, *m.*	Hon. A. Julian A., *b.* 1951
1929	*Baden-Powell (3rd),* Robert Crause Baden-Powell, *b.* 1936, *s.* 1962, *m.*	Hon. David M. B.-P., *b.* 1940
1780	*Bagot (10th),* (Charles Hugh) Shaun Bagot, *b.* 1944, *s.* 2001, *m.*	Richard C. V. B., *b.* 1941
1953	*Baillieu (3rd),* James William Latham Baillieu, *b.* 1950, *s.* 1973, *m.*	Hon. Robert L. B., *b.* 1979
1607 S.	*Balfour of Burleigh (8th),* Robert Bruce, FRSE, *b.* 1927, *s.* 1967, *m.*	Hon. Victoria B., *b.* 1973
1945	*Balfour of Inchrye (2nd),* Ian Balfour, *b.* 1924, *s.* 1988, *m.*	None
1924	*Banbury of Southam (3rd),* Charles William Banbury, *b.* 1953, *s.* 1981, *m.*	None
1698	*Barnard (11th),* Harry John Neville Vane, TD, *b.* 1923, *s.* 1964	Hon. Henry F. C. V., *b.* 1959
1887	*Basing (5th),* Neil Lutley Sclater-Booth, *b.* 1939, *s.* 1983, *m.*	Hon. Stuart W. S.-B., *b.* 1969
1917	*Beaverbrook (3rd),* Maxwell William Humphrey Aitken, *b.* 1951, *s.* 1985, *m.*	Hon. Maxwell F. A., *b.* 1977
1647 S.	*Belhaven and Stenton (13th),* Robert Anthony Carmichael Hamilton, *b.* 1927, *s.* 1961, *m.*	Master of Belhaven, *b.* 1953
1848 I.	*Bellew (7th),* James Bryan Bellew, *b.* 1920, *s.* 1981, *w.*	Hon. Bryan E. B., *b.* 1943
1856	*Belper (5th),* Richard Henry Strutt, *b.* 1941, *s.* 1999, *m.*	Hon. Michael H. S., *b.* 1969
1938	*Belstead (2nd) and Baron Ganzoni (life peerage, 1999),* John Julian Ganzoni, PC, *b.* 1932, *s.* 1958	None
1421	*Berkeley (18th) and Baron Gueterbock (life peerage, 2000),* Anthony Fitzhardinge Gueterbock, OBE, *b.* 1939, *s.* 1992, *m.*	Hon. Thomas F. G., *b.* 1969
1922	*Bethell (4th),* Nicholas William Bethell, MEP, *b.* 1938, *s.* 1967, *m.*	Hon. James N. B., *b.* 1967
1938	*Bicester (3rd),* Angus Edward Vivian Smith, *b.* 1932, *s.* 1968	Hugh C. V. S., *b.* 1934

Created	*Title, order of succession, name, etc.*	*Heir*
1903	*Biddulph (5th)*, (Anthony) Nicholas Colin Maitland Biddulph, *b.* 1959, *s.* 1988, *m.*	Hon. Robert J. M. B., *b.* 1994
1938	*Birdwood (3rd)*, Mark William Ogilvie Birdwood, *b.* 1938, *s.* 1962, *m.*	None
1958	*Birkett (2nd)*, Michael Birkett, *b.* 1929, *s.* 1962, *w.*	Hon. Thomas B., *b.* 1982
1907	*Blyth (4th)*, Anthony Audley Rupert Blyth, *b.* 1931, *s.* 1977, *m.*	Hon. James A. I. B., *b.* 1970
1797	*Bolton (8th)*, Harry Algar Nigel Orde-Powlett, *b.* 1954, *s.* 2001, *m.*	Hon. Thomas O.-P., *b.* 1979
1452 S.	*Borthwick (24th)*, John Hugh Borthwick, *b.* 1940, *s.* 1997, *m.*	Hon. James H. A. B. of Glengelt, *b.* 1940
1922	*Borwick (4th)*, James Hugh Myles Borwick, MC, *b.* 1917, *s.* 1961, *m.*	Hon. Robin S. B., *b.* 1927
1761	*Boston (10th)*, Timothy George Frank Boteler Irby, *b.* 1939, *s.* 1978, *m.*	Hon. George W. E. B. I., *b.* 1971
1942	** *Brabazon of Tara (3rd)*, Ivon Anthony Moore-Brabazon, *b.* 1946, *s.* 1974, *m.*	Hon. Benjamin R. M.-B., *b.* 1983
1880	*Brabourne (7th)*, John Ulick Knatchbull, CBE, *b.* 1924, *s.* 1943, *m.*	Lord Romsey, *b.* 1947
1925	*Bradbury (3rd)*, John Bradbury, *b.* 1940, *s.* 1994, *m.*	Hon. John B., *b.* 1973
1962	*Brain (2nd)*, Christopher Langdon Brain, *b.* 1926, *s.* 1966, *m.*	Hon. Michael C. B., *b.* 1928
1938	*Brassey of Apethorpe (3rd)*, David Henry Brassey, OBE, *b.* 1932, *s.* 1967, *m.*	Hon. Edward B., *b.* 1964
1788	*Braybrooke (10th)*, Robin Henry Charles Neville, *b.* 1932, *s.* 1990, *m.*	George N., *b.* 1943
1957	** *Bridges (2nd)*, Thomas Edward Bridges, GCMG, *b.* 1927, *s.* 1969, *m.*	Hon. Mark T. B., *b.* 1954
1945	*Broadbridge (4th)*, Martin Hugh Broadbridge, *b.* 1929, *s.* 2000, *m.*	Hon. Richard J. M. B., *b.* 1959
1933	*Brocket (3rd)*, Charles Ronald George Nall-Cain, *b.* 1952, *s.* 1967, *m.*	Hon. Alexander C. C. N.-C., *b.* 1984
1860	** *Brougham and Vaux (5th)*, Michael John Brougham, CBE, *b.* 1938, *s.* 1967	Hon. Charles W. B., *b.* 1971
1945	*Broughshane (3rd)*, (William) Kensington Davison, DSO, DFC, *b.* 1914, *s.* 1995	None
1776	*Brownlow (7th)*, Edward John Peregrine Cust, *b.* 1936, *s.* 1978, *m.*	Hon. Peregrine E. Q. C., *b.* 1974
1942	*Bruntisfield (2nd)*, John Robert Warrender, OBE, MC, TD, *b.* 1921, *s.* 1993, *m.*	Hon. Michael J. V. W., *b.* 1949
1950	*Burden (3rd)*, Andrew Philip Burden, *b.* 1959, *s.* 1995	Hon. Fraser W. E. B., *b.* 1964
1529	*Burgh (8th)*, (Alexander) Gregory Disney Leith, *b.* 1958, *s.* 2001, *m.*	Hon. Alexander J. S. L., *b.* 1986
1903	** *Burnham (6th)*, Hugh John Frederick Lawson, *b.* 1931, *s.* 1993, *m.*	Hon. Harry F. A. L., *b.* 1968
1897	*Burton (3rd)*, Michael Evan Victor Baillie, *b.* 1924, *s.* 1962, *m.*	Hon. Evan M. R. B., *b.* 1949
1643	*Byron (13th)*, Robert James Byron, *b.* 1950, *s.* 1989, *m.*	Hon. Charles R. G. B., *b.* 1990
1937	*Cadman (3rd)*, John Anthony Cadman, *b.* 1938, *s.* 1966, *m.*	Hon. Nicholas A. J. C., *b.* 1977
1945	*Calverley (3rd)*, Charles Rodney Muff, *b.* 1946, *s.* 1971, *m.*	Hon. Jonathan E. M., *b.* 1975
1383	*Camoys (7th)*, (Ralph) Thomas Campion George Sherman Stonor, GCVO, PC, *b.* 1940, *s.* 1976, *m.*	Hon. R. William R. T. S., *b.* 1974
1715 I.	*Carbery (11th)*, Peter Ralfe Harrington Evans-Freke, *b.* 1920, *s.* 1970, *m.*	Hon. Michael P. E.-F., *b.* 1942
1834 I.*	*Carew (7th) and 7th UK Baron, Carew,* 1838, Patrick Thomas Conolly-Carew, *b.* 1938, *s.* 1994, *m.*	Hon. William P. C.-C., *b.* 1973
1916	*Carnock (4th)*, David Henry Arthur Nicolson, *b.* 1920, *s.* 1982,	Nigel N., MBE, *b.* 1917
1796 I.*	*Carrington (6th) and 6th Brit. Baron Carrington,* 1797 *and Baron Carington of Upton (life peerage, 1999)*, Peter Alexander Rupert Carington, KG, GCMG, CH, MC, PC, *b.* 1919, *s.* 1938, *m.*	Hon. Rupert F. J. C., *b.* 1948
1812	*Castlemaine (8th)*, Roland Thomas John Handcock, MBE, *b.* 1943, *s.* 1973, *m.*	Hon. Ronan M. E. H., *b.* 1989
1936	*Catto (3rd)*, Innes Gordon Catto, *b.* 1950, *s.* 2001, *m.*	Hon. Alexander G. C., *b.* 1952
1918	*Cawley (4th)*, John Francis Cawley, *b.* 1946, *s.* 2001, *m.*	Hon. William R. H. C., *b.* 1981
1937	*Chatfield (2nd)*, Ernle David Lewis Chatfield, *b.* 1917, *s.* 1967, *m.*	None
1858	*Chesham (6th)*, Nicholas Charles Cavendish, *b.* 1941, *s.* 1989, *m.*	Hon. Charles G. C. C., *b.* 1974
1945	*Chetwode (2nd)*, Philip Chetwode, *b.* 1937, *s.* 1950, *m.*	Hon. Roger C., *b.* 1968
1945	*Chorley (2nd)*, Roger Richard Edward Chorley, *b.* 1930, *s.* 1978, *m.*	Hon. Nicholas R. D. C., *b.* 1966
1858	*Churston (5th)*, John Francis Yarde-Buller, *b.* 1934, *s.* 1991, *m.*	Hon. Benjamin F. A. Y.-B., *b.* 1974
1946	*Citrine (3rd)*, Ronald Eric Citrine, *b.* 1919, *s.* 1997, *m.* Does not use title	None
1800	*Clanmorris (8th)*, Simon John Ward Bingham, *b.* 1937, *s.* 1988, *m.*	Robert D. de B. B., *b.* 1942
1672	*Clifford of Chudleigh (14th)*, Thomas Hugh Clifford, *b.* 1948, *s.* 1988, *m.*	Hon. Alexander T. H. C., *b.* 1985
1299	*Clinton (22nd)*, Gerard Nevile Mark Fane Trefusis, *b.* 1934, *s.* 1965, *m.*	Hon. Charles P. R. F. T., *b.* 1962
1955	*Clitheroe (2nd)*, Ralph John Assheton, *b.* 1929, *s.* 1984, *m.*	Hon. Ralph C. A., *b.* 1962
1919	*Clwyd (3rd)*, (John) Anthony Roberts, *b.* 1935, *s.* 1987, *m.*	Hon. J. Murray R., *b.* 1971
1948	*Clydesmuir (3rd)*, David Ronald Colville, *b.* 1949, *s.* 1996, *m.*	Hon. Richard C., *b.* 1980
1960	** *Cobbold (2nd)*, David Antony Fromanteel Lytton Cobbold, *b.* 1937, *s.* 1987, *m.*	Hon. Henry F. L. C., *b.* 1962

Created	Title, order of succession, name, etc.	Heir
1919	Cochrane of Cults (4th), (Ralph Henry) Vere Cochrane, b. 1926, s. 1990, m.	Hon. Thomas H. V. C., b. 1957
1954	Coleraine (2nd), (James) Martin (Bonar) Law, b. 1931, s. 1980, m.	Hon. James P. B. L., b. 1975
1873	Coleridge (5th), William Duke Coleridge, b. 1937, s. 1984, m.	Hon. James D. C., b. 1967
1946	Colgrain (3rd), David Colin Campbell, b. 1920, s. 1973, m.	Hon. Alastair C. L. C., b. 1951
1917	** Colwyn (3rd), (Ian) Anthony Hamilton-Smith, CBE, b. 1942, s. 1966, m.	Hon. Craig P. H.-S., b. 1968
1956	Colyton (2nd), Alisdair John Munro Hopkinson, b. 1958, s. 1996, m.	Hon. James P. M. H., b. 1983
1841	Congleton (8th), Christopher Patrick Parnell, b. 1930, s. 1967, m.	Hon. John P. C. P., b. 1959
1927	Cornwallis (3rd), Fiennes Neil Wykeham Cornwallis, OBE, b. 1921, s. 1982, m.	Hon. F. W. Jeremy C., b. 1946
1874	Cottesloe (5th), Cdr. John Tapling Fremantle, b. 1927, s. 1994, m.	Hon. Thomas F. H. F., b. 1966
1929	Craigmyle (4th), Thomas Columba Shaw, b. 1960, s. 1998, m.	Hon. Alexander F. S., b. 1988
1899	Cranworth (3rd), Philip Bertram Gurdon, b. 1940, s. 1964, w.	Hon. Sacha W. R. G., b. 1970
1959	** Crathorne (2nd), Charles James Dugdale, b. 1939, s. 1977, m.	Hon. Thomas A. J. D., b. 1977
1892	Crawshaw (5th), David Gerald Brooks, b. 1934, s. 1997, m.	Hon. John P. B., b. 1938
1940	Croft (3rd), Bernard William Henry Page Croft, b. 1949, s. 1997, m.	None
1797 I.	Crofton (7th), Guy Patrick Gilbert Crofton, b. 1951, s. 1989, m.	Hon. E. Harry P. C., b. 1988
1375	Cromwell (7th), Godfrey John Bewicke-Copley, b. 1960, s. 1982, m.	Hon. David G. B-C., b. 1997
1947	Crook (3rd), Robert Douglas Edwin Crook, b. 1955, s. 2001, m.	Hon. Matthew R. C., b. 1990
1920	Cullen of Ashbourne (3rd), Edmund Willoughby Marsham Cokayne, b. 1916, s. 2000, w.	(Hon.) John O'B. M. C., b. 1920
1914	Cunliffe (3rd), Roger Cunliffe, b. 1932, s. 1963, m.	Hon. Henry C., b. 1962
1927	Daresbury (4th), Peter Gilbert Greenall, b. 1953, s. 1996, m.	Hon. Thomas E. G., b. 1984
1924	Darling (2nd), Robert Charles Henry Darling, b. 1919, s. 1936, m.	Hon. R. Julian H. D., b. 1944
1946	Darwen (3rd), Roger Michael Davies, b. 1938, s. 1988, m.	Hon. Paul D., b. 1962
1932	Davies (3rd), David Davies, b. 1940, s. 1944, m.	Hon. David D. D., b. 1975
1812 I.	Decies (7th), Marcus Hugh Tristram de la Poer Beresford, b. 1948, s. 1992, m.	Hon. Robert M. D. de la P. B., b. 1988
1299	de Clifford (27th), John Edward Southwell Russell, b. 1928, s. 1982, m.	Hon. William S. R., b. 1930
1851	De Freyne (7th), Francis Arthur John French, b. 1927, s. 1935, m.	Hon. Fulke C. A. J. F., b. 1957
1821	Delamere (5th), Hugh George Cholmondeley, b. 1934, s. 1979, m.	Hon. Thomas P. G. C., b. 1968
1838	de Mauley (7th), Rupert Charles Ponsonby, b. 1957, s. 2002, m.	Ashley, G. P., b. 1959
1937	** Denham (2nd), Bertram Stanley Mitford Bowyer, KBE, PC, b. 1927, s. 1948, m.	Hon. Richard G. G. B., b. 1959
1834	Denman (5th), Charles Spencer Denman, CBE, MC, TD, b. 1916, s. 1971, w.	Hon. Richard T. S. D., b. 1946
1885	Deramore (6th), Richard Arthur de Yarburgh-Bateson, b. 1911, s. 1964, m.	None
1887	De Ramsey (4th), John Ailwyn Fellowes, b. 1942, s. 1993, m.	Hon. Freddie J. F., b. 1978
1264	de Ros (28th), Peter Trevor Maxwell, b. 1958, s. 1983, m., Premier Baron of England	Hon. Finbar J. M., b. 1988
1881	Derwent (5th), Robin Evelyn Leo Vanden-Bempde-Johnstone, LVO, b. 1930, s. 1986, m.	Hon. Francis P. H. V.-B.-J., b. 1965
1831	de Saumarez (7th), Eric Douglas Saumarez, b. 1956, s. 1991, m.	Hon. Victor T. S., b. 1956
1910	de Villiers (4th), Alexander Charles de Villiers, b. 1940, s. 2001, m.	None
1930	Dickinson (2nd), Richard Clavering Hyett Dickinson, b. 1926, s. 1943, m.	Hon. Martin H. D., b. 1961
1620 I.*	Digby (12th) and 5th Brit. Baron Digby, 1765, Edward Henry Kenelm Digby, KCVO, b. 1924, s. 1964, m.	Hon. Henry N. K. D., b. 1954
1615	Dormer (17th), Geoffrey Henry Dormer, b. 1920, s. 1995, m.	Hon. William R. D., b. 1960
1943	Dowding (3rd), Piers Hugh Tremenheere Dowding, b. 1948, s. 1992	Hon. Mark D. J. D., b. 1949
1439	Dudley (15th), Jim Anthony Hill Wallace, b. 1930, s. 2002, m.	Hon. Jeremy W. G. W., b. 1964
1800 I.	Dufferin and Clandeboye, The 10th Baron died in 1991. Heir had not established his claim to the title at the time of going to press	Sir John Blackwood, Bt., b. 1944
1929	Dulverton (3rd), (Gilbert) Michael Hamilton Wills, b. 1944, s. 1992	Hon. Robert A. H. W., b. 1983
1800 I.	Dunalley (7th), Henry Francis Cornelius Prittie, b. 1948, s. 1992, m.	Hon. Joel H. P., b. 1981
1324 I.	Dunboyne (28th), Patrick Theobald Tower Butler, VRD, b. 1917, s. 1945, m.	Hon. John F. B., b. 1951
1892	Dunleath (6th), Brian Henry Mulholland, b. 1950, s. 1997, m.	Hon. Andrew H. M., b. 1981
1439 I.	Dunsany (20th), Edward John Carlos Plunkett, b. 1939, s. 1999, m.	Hon. Randal P., b. 1983
1780	Dynevor (9th), Richard Charles Uryan Rhys, b. 1935, s. 1962	Hon. Hugo G. U. R., b. 1966
1963	Egremont (2nd) and 7th UK Baron Leconfield, 1859, John Max Henry Scawen Wyndham, b. 1948, s. 1972, m.	Hon. George R. V. W., b. 1983
1643	Elibank (14th), Alan D'Ardis Erskine-Murray, b. 1923, s. 1973, w.	Master of Elibank, b. 1964
1802	Ellenborough (8th), Richard Edward Cecil Law, b. 1926, s. 1945, m.	Maj. Hon. Rupert E. H. L., b. 1955

Created	Title, order of succession, name, etc.	Heir
1509 S.*	Elphinstone (19th) and 5th UK Baron Elphinstone, 1885, Alexander Mountstuart Elphinstone, b. 1980, s. 1994	Hon. Angus J. E., b. 1982
1934 **	Elton (2nd), Rodney Elton, TD, b. 1930, s. 1973, m.	Hon. Edward P. E., b. 1966
1627 S.	Fairfax of Cameron (14th), Nicholas John Albert Fairfax, b. 1956, s. 1964, m.	Hon. Edward N. T. F., b. 1984
1961	Fairhaven (3rd), Ailwyn Henry George Broughton, b. 1936, s. 1973, m.	Maj. Hon. James H. A. B., b. 1963
1916	Faringdon (3rd), Charles Michael Henderson, b. 1937, s. 1977, m.	Hon. James H. H., b. 1961
1756	Farnham (13th), Simon Kenlis Maxwell, b. 1933, s. 2001, m.	Hon. Robin S. M., b. 1965
1856	Fermoy (6th), Patrick Maurice Burke Roche, b. 1967, s. 1984, m.	Hon. E. Hugh B. R., b. 1972
1826	Feversham (6th), Charles Antony Peter Duncombe, b. 1945, s. 1963, m.	Hon. Jasper O. S. D., b. 1968
1798 I.	ffrench (8th), Robuck John Peter Charles Mario ffrench, b. 1956, s. 1986, m.	Hon. John C. M. J. F. ff., b. 1928
1909	Fisher (3rd), John Vavasseur Fisher, DSC, b. 1921, s. 1955, m.	Hon. Patrick V. F., b. 1953
1295	Fitzwalter (21st), (Fitzwalter) Brook Plumptre, b. 1914, m.	Hon. Julian B. P., b. 1952
1776	Foley (8th), Adrian Gerald Foley, b. 1923, s. 1927, w.	Hon. Thomas H. F., b. 1961
1445	Forbes (22nd), Nigel Ivan Forbes, KBE, b. 1918, s. 1953, m., Premier Lord of Scotland	Master of Forbes, b. 1946
1821	Forester (8th), (George Cecil) Brooke Weld-Forester, b. 1938, s. 1977, m.	Hon. C. R. George W.-F., b. 1975
1922	Forres (4th), Alastair Stephen Grant Williamson, b. 1946, s. 1978, m.	Hon. George A. M. W., b. 1972
1917	Forteviot (4th), John James Evelyn Dewar, b. 1938, s. 1993, w.	Hon. Alexander J. E. D., b. 1971
1951 **	Freyberg (3rd), Valerian Bernard Freyberg, b. 1970, s. 1993	None
1917	Gainford (3rd), Joseph Edward Pease, b. 1921, s. 1971, m.	Hon. George P., b. 1926
1818	Garvagh (5th), (Alexander Leopold Ivor) George Canning, b. 1920, s. 1956, m.	Hon. Spencer G. S. de R. C., b. 1953
1942 **	Geddes (3rd), Euan Michael Ross Geddes, b. 1937, s. 1975, m.	Hon. James G. N. G., b. 1969
1876	Gerard (5th), Anthony Robert Hugo Gerard, b. 1949, s. 1992, m.	Hon. Rupert B. C. G., b. 1981
1824	Gifford (6th), Anthony Maurice Gifford, QC, b. 1940, s. 1961, m.	Hon. Thomas A. G., b. 1967
1917	Gisborough (3rd), Thomas Richard John Long Chaloner, b. 1927, s. 1951, m.	Hon. T. Peregrine L. C., b. 1961
1960	Gladwyn (2nd), Miles Alvery Gladwyn Jebb, b. 1930, s. 1996,	None
1899	Glanusk (5th), Christopher Russell Bailey, b. 1942, s. 1997, m.	Hon. Charles H. B., b. 1976
1918 **	Glenarthur (4th), Simon Mark Arthur, b. 1944, s. 1976, m.	Hon. Edward A. A., b. 1973
1911	Glenconner (3rd), Colin Christopher Paget Tennant, b. 1926, s. 1983, m.	Cody C. E. T., b. 1994
1964	Glendevon (2nd), Julian John Somerset Hope, b. 1950, s. 1996,	Hon. Jonathan C. H., b. 1952
1922	Glendyne (3rd), Robert Nivison, b. 1926, s. 1967, m.	Hon. John N., b. 1960
1939 **	Glentoran (3rd), (Thomas) Robin (Valerian) Dixon, CBE, b. 1935, s. 1995, m.	Hon. Daniel G. D., b. 1959
1909	Gorell (4th), Timothy John Radcliffe Barnes, b. 1927, s. 1963, m.	Hon. Ronald A. H. B., b. 1931
1953	Grantchester (3rd), Christopher John Suenson-Taylor, b. 1951, s. 1995, m.	Hon. Jesse D. S.-T., b. 1977
1782	Grantley (8th), Richard William Brinsley Norton, b. 1956, s. 1995	Hon. Francis J. H. N., b. 1960
1794 I.	Graves (10th), Timothy Evelyn Graves, b. 1960, s. 2002	None
1445 s.	Gray (22nd), Andrew Godfrey Diarmid Stuart Campbell-Gray, b. 1964, s. 2003, m.	Master of Grey, b. 1996
1950	Greenhill (3rd), Malcolm Greenhill, b. 1924, s. 1989	None
1927 **	Greenway (4th), Ambrose Charles Drexel Greenway, b. 1941, s. 1975, m.	Hon. Nigel. P. G., b. 1944
1902	Grenfell (3rd) and Baron Grenfell of Kilvey (life peerage, 2000), Julian Pascoe Francis St Leger Grenfell, b. 1935, s. 1976, m.	Francis P. J. G., b. 1938
1944	Gretton (4th), John Lysander Gretton, b. 1975, s. 1989	None
1397	Grey of Codnor (6th), Richard Henry Cornwall-Legh, b. 1936, s. 1996, m.	Hon. Richard S. C. C.-L., b. 1976
1955	Gridley (3rd), Richard David Arnold Gridley, b. 1956, s. 1996, m.	Hon. Carl R. G., b. 1981
1964	Grimston of Westbury (3rd), Robert John Sylvester Grimston, b. 1951, s. 2003, m.	Hon. Gerald C. W. G., b. 1953
1886	Grimthorpe (5th), Edward John Beckett, b. 1954, s. 2003, m.	Hon Harry M. B., b. 1993
1945	Hacking (3rd), Douglas David Hacking, b. 1938, s. 1971, m.	Hon. Douglas F. H., b. 1968
1950	Haden-Guest (5th), Christopher Haden-Guest, b. 1948, s. 1996, m.	Hon. Nicholas H.-G., b. 1951
1886	Hamilton of Dalzell (4th), James Leslie Hamilton, b. 1938, s. 1990, m.	Hon. Gavin G. H., b. 1968
1874	Hampton (7th), John Humphrey Arnott Pakington, b. 1964, s. 2003, m.	None
1939	Hankey (3rd), Donald Robin Alers Hankey, b. 1938, s. 1996, m.	Hon. Alexander M. A. H., b. 1947
1958	Harding of Petherton (2nd), John Charles Harding, b. 1928, s. 1989, m.	Hon. William A. J. H., b. 1969
1910	Hardinge of Penshurst (4th), Julian Alexander Hardinge, b. 1945, s. 1997	Hon. Hugh F. H., b. 1948
1876	Harlech (6th), Francis David Ormsby-Gore, b. 1954, s. 1985, m.	Hon. Jasset D. C. O.-G., b. 1986
1939	Harmsworth (3rd), Thomas Harold Raymond Harmsworth, b. 1939, s. 1990, m.	Hon. Dominic M. E. H., b. 1973

Created	Title, order of succession, name, etc.	Heir
1815	*Harris (8th)*, Anthony Harris, *b.* 1942, *s.* 1996, *m.*	Anthony J. T. H., *b.* 1915
1954	*Harvey of Tasburgh (2nd)*, Peter Charles Oliver Harvey, *b.* 1921, *s.* 1968, *w.*	Charles J. G. H., *b.* 1951
1295	*Hastings (22nd)*, Edward Delaval Henry Astley, *b.* 1912, *s.* 1956, *m.*	Hon. Delaval T. H. A., *b.* 1960
1835	*Hatherton (8th)*, Edward Charles Littleton, *b.* 1950, *s.* 1985, *m.*	Hon. Thomas E. L., *b.* 1977
1776	*Hawke (11th)*, Edward George Hawke, TD, *b.* 1950, *s.* 1992, *m.*	Hon. William M T. H., *b.* 1995
1927	*Hayter (4th)*, George William Michael Chubb, *b.* 1943, *s.* 2003, *m.*	Hon. Thomas F. F. C., *b.* 1986
1945	*Hazlerigg (3rd)*, Arthur Grey Hazlerigg, *b.* 1951, *s.* 2002, *m.*	Hon. Arthur W. G. H., *b.* 1987
1943	*Hemingford (3rd)*, (Dennis) Nicholas Herbert, *b.* 1934, *s.* 1982, *m.*	Hon. Christopher D. C. H., *b.* 1973
1906	*Hemphill (5th)*, Peter Patrick Fitzroy Martyn Martyn-Hemphill, *b.* 1928, *s.* 1957, *m.*	Hon. Charles A. M. M.-H., *b.* 1954
1799 I.	* ** *Henley (8th) and 6th UK Baron Northington*, 1885, Oliver Michael Robert Eden, *b.* 1953, *s.* 1977, *m.*	Hon. John W. O. E., *b.* 1988
1800 I.*	*Henniker (8th) and 4th UK Baron Hertsmere*,1866, John Patrick Edward Chandos Henniker-Major, KCMG, CVO, MC, *b.* 1916, *s.* 1980, *m.*	Hon. Mark I. P. C. H.-M., *b.* 1947
1461	*Herbert (19th)*, David John Seyfried, *b.* 1952, *s.* 2002, *m.*	Hon. Oliver R. S. H., *b.* 1976
1886	*Herschell (3rd)*, Rognvald Richard Farrer Herschell, *b.* 1923, *s.* 1929, *m.*	None
1935	*Hesketh (3rd)*, Thomas Alexander Fermor-Hesketh, KBE, PC, *b.* 1950, *s.* 1955, *m.*	Hon. Frederick H. F.-H., *b.* 1988
1828	*Heytesbury (6th)*, Francis William Holmes à Court, *b.* 1931, *s.* 1971, *m.*	Hon. James W. H. à. C., *b.* 1967
1886	*Hindlip (6th)*, Charles Henry Allsopp, *b.* 1940, *s.* 1993, *m.*	Hon. Henry W A., *b.* 1973
1950	*Hives (3rd)*, Matthew Peter Hives, *b.* 1971, *s.* 1997	Hon. Michael B. H., *b.* 1926
1912	*Hollenden (4th)*, Ian Hampden Hope-Morley, *b.* 1946, *s.* 1999, *m.*	Hon. Edward H.-M., *b.* 1981
1897	*HolmPatrick (4th)*, Hans James David Hamilton, *b.* 1955, *s.* 1991, *m.*	Hon. Ion H. J. H., *b.* 1956
1797 I.	*Hotham (8th)*, Henry Durand Hotham, *b.* 1940, *s.* 1967, *m.*	Hon. William B. H., *b.* 1972
1881	*Hothfield (6th)*, Anthony Charles Sackville Tufton, *b.* 1939, *s.* 1991, *m.*	Hon. William S. T., *b.* 1977
1597	*Howard de Walden (10th)*, Barony in abeyance since 1999 between the four daughters of 9th Baron	
1930	*Howard of Penrith (3rd)*, Philip Esme Howard, *b.* 1945, *s.* 1999, *m.*	Hon. Thomas Philip H., *b.* 1974
1960	*Howick of Glendale (2nd)*, Charles Evelyn Baring, *b.* 1937, *s.* 1973, *m.*	Hon. David E. C. B., *b.* 1975
1796 I.	*Huntingfield (7th)*, Joshua Charles Vanneck, *b.* 1954, *s.* 1994, *m.*	Hon. Gerard C. A. V., *b.* 1985
1866	** *Hylton (5th)*, Raymond Hervey Jolliffe, *b.* 1932, *s.* 1967, *m.*	Hon. William H. M. J., *b.* 1967
1933	*Iliffe (3rd)*, Robert Peter Richard Iliffe, *b.* 1944, *s.* 1996, *m.*	Hon. Edward R. I., *b.* 1968
1543 I.	*Inchiquin (18th)*, Conor Myles John O'Brien, *b.* 1943, *s.* 1982, *m.*	Conor J. A. O'B., *b.* 1952
1962	*Inchyra (2nd)*, Robert Charles Reneke Hoyer Millar, *b.* 1935, *s.* 1989, *m.*	Hon. C. James C. H. M., *b.* 1962
1964	** *Inglewood (2nd)*, (William) Richard Fletcher-Vane, MEP, *b.* 1951, *s.* 1989, *m.*	Hon. Henry W. F. F.-V., *b.* 1990
1919	*Inverforth (4th)*, Andrew Peter Weir, *b.* 1966, *s.* 1982	Hon. John V. W., *b.* 1935
1941	*Ironside (2nd)*, Edmund Oslac Ironside, *b.* 1924, *s.* 1959, *m.*	Hon. Charles E. G. I., *b.* 1956
1952	*Jeffreys (3rd)*, Christopher Henry Mark Jeffreys, *b.* 1957, *s.* 1986, *m.*	Hon. Arthur M. H. J., *b.* 1989
1906	*Joicey (5th)*, James Michael Joicey, *b.* 1953, *s.* 1993, *m.*	Hon. William J. J., *b.* 1990
1937	*Kenilworth (4th)*, (John) Randle Siddeley, *b.* 1954, *s.* 1981, *m.*	Hon. William R. J. S., *b.* 1992
1935	*Kennet (2nd)*, Wayland Hilton Young, *b.* 1923, *s.* 1960, *m.*	Hon. W. A. Thoby Y., *b.* 1957
1776 I.*	*Kensington (8th) and 5th UK Baron Kensington*, 1886, Hugh Ivor Edwardes, *b.* 1933, *s.* 1981, *m.*	Hon. W. Owen A. E., *b.* 1964
1951	*Kenswood (2nd)*, John Michael Howard Whitfield, *b.* 1930, *s.* 1963, *m.*	Hon. Michael C. W., *b.* 1955
1788	*Kenyon (6th)*, Lloyd Tyrell-Kenyon, *b.* 1947, *s.* 1993, *m.*	Hon. Lloyd N. T.-K., *b.* 1972
1947	*Kershaw (4th)*, Edward John Kershaw, *b.* 1936, *s.* 1962, *m.*	Hon. John C. E. K., *b.* 1971
1943	*Keyes (2nd)*, Roger George Bowlby Keyes, *b.* 1919, *s.* 1945, *w.*	Hon. Charles W. P. K., *b.* 1951
1909	*Kilbracken (3rd)*, John Raymond Godley, DSC, *b.* 1920, *s.* 1950	Hon. Christopher J. G., *b.* 1945
1900	*Killanin (4th)*, (George) Redmond Fitzpatrick Morris, *b.* 1947, *s.* 1999, *m.*	Hon. Luke M. G. K *b.* 1975
1943	*Killearn (3rd)*, Victor Miles George Aldous Lampson, *b.* 1941, *s.* 1996, *m.*	Hon. Miles H. M. L., *b.* 1977
1789 I.	*Kilmaine (7th)*, John David Henry Browne, *b.* 1948, *s.* 1978, *m.*	Hon. John F. S. B., *b.* 1983
1831	*Kilmarnock (7th)*, Alastair Ivor Gilbert Boyd, *b.* 1927, *s.* 1975, *m.*	Hon. Robin J. B., *b.* 1941
1941	*Kindersley (3rd)*, Robert Hugh Molesworth Kindersley, *b.* 1929, *s.* 1976, *m.*	Hon. Rupert J. M. K., *b.* 1955
1223 I.	*Kingsale (35th)*, John de Courcy, *b.* 1941, *s.* 1969, *Premier Baron of Ireland*	Nevinson M. de C., *b.* 1958
1902	*Kinross (5th)*, Christopher Patrick Balfour, *b.* 1949, *s.* 1985, *m.*	Hon. Alan I. B., *b.* 1978
1951	*Kirkwood (3rd)*, David Harvie Kirkwood, Ph.D., *b.* 1931, *s.* 1970, *m.*	Hon. James S. K., *b.* 1937

Created	Title, order of succession, name, etc.	Heir
1800 I.	*Langford (9th)*, Col. Geoffrey Alexander Rowley-Conwy, OBE, *b.* 1912, *s.* 1953, *m.*	Hon. Owain G. R.-C., *b.* 1958
1942	*Latham (2nd)*, Dominic Charles Latham, *b.* 1954, *s.* 1970	Anthony M. L., *b.* 1954
1431	*Latymer (8th)*, Hugo Nevill Money-Coutts, *b.* 1926, *s.* 1987, *m.*	Hon. Crispin J. A. N. M.-C., *b.* 1955
1869	*Lawrence (5th)*, David John Downer Lawrence, *b.* 1937, *s.* 1968	None
1947	*Layton (3rd)*, Geoffrey Michael Layton, *b.* 1947, *s.* 1989, *m.*	Hon. David L., *b.* 1914
1839	*Leigh (5th)*, John Piers Leigh, *b.* 1935, *s.* 1979, *m.*	Hon. Christopher D. P. L., *b.* 1960
1962	*Leighton of St Mellons (3rd)*, Robert William Henry Leighton Seager, *b.* 1955, *s.* 1998	Hon. Simon J. L. S., *b.* 1957
1797	*Lilford (7th)*, George Vernon Powys, *b.* 1931, *s.* 1949, *m.*	Hon. Mark V. P., *b.* 1975
1945	*Lindsay of Birker (3rd)*, James Francis Lindsay, *b.* 1945, *s.* 1994, *m.*	Alexander S. L., *b.* 1940
1758 I.	*Lisle (8th)*, Patrick James Lysaght, *b.* 1931, *s.* 1998	Hon. John N. G. L., *b.* 1960
1850	*Londesborough (9th)*, Richard John Denison, *b.* 1959, *s.* 1968, *m.*	Hon. James F. D., *b.* 1990
1541 I.	*Louth (16th)*, Otway Michael James Oliver Plunkett, *b.* 1929, *s.* 1950, *m.*	Hon. Jonathan O. P., *b.* 1952
1458 S.*	*Lovat (16th) and 5th UK Baron*, Lovat, 1837, Simon Fraser, *b.* 1977, *s.* 1995	Hon. Jack F., *b.* 1984
1946	*Lucas of Chilworth (3rd)*, Simon William Lucas, *b.* 1957, *s.* 2001, *m.*	Hon. John R. M. L., *b.* 1995
1663	** *Lucas (11th) and Dingwall (14th) (s. 1609)*, Ralph Matthew Palmer, *b.* 1951, *s.* 1991	Hon. Lewis E. P., *b.* 1987
1929	** *Luke (3rd)*, Arthur Charles St John Lawson-Johnston, *b.* 1933, *s.* 1996, *m.*	Hon. Ian J. St J. L.-J., *b.* 1963
1914	** *Lyell (3rd)*, Charles Lyell, *b.* 1939, *s.* 1943	None
1859	*Lyveden (7th)*, Jack Leslie Vernon, *b.* 1938, *s.* 1999, *m.*	Hon. Colin R. V., *b.* 1967
1959	*MacAndrew (3rd)*, Christopher Anthony Colin MacAndrew, *b.* 1945, *s.* 1989, *m.*	Hon. Oliver C. J. M., *b.* 1983
1776 I.	*Macdonald (8th)*, Godfrey James Macdonald of Macdonald, *b.* 1947, *s.* 1970, *m.*	Hon. Godfrey E. H. T. M., *b.* 1982
1937	*McGowan (4th)*, Harry John Charles McGowan, *b.* 1971, *s.* 2003, *m.*	Hon. Dominic J. W. McG., *b.* 1951
1922	*Maclay (3rd)*, Joseph Paton Maclay, *b.* 1942, *s.* 1969, *m.*	Hon. Joseph P. M., *b.* 1977
1955	*McNair (3rd)*, Duncan James McNair, *b.* 1947, *s.* 1989, *m.*	Hon. William S. A. M., *b.* 1958
1951	*Macpherson of Drumochter (2nd)*, (James) Gordon Macpherson, *b.* 1924, *s.* 1965, *m.*	Hon. James A. M., *b.* 1979
1937	** *Mancroft (3rd)*, Benjamin Lloyd Stormont Mancroft, *b.* 1957, *s.* 1987, *m.*	Hon. Arthur L. S. M., *b.* 1995
1807	*Manners (5th)*, John Robert Cecil Manners, *b.* 1923, *s.* 1972, *w.*	Hon. John H. R. M., *b.* 1956
1922	*Manton (4th)*, Miles Ronald Marcus Watson, *b.* 1958, *s.* 2003, *m.*	Hon. Thomas N. C. D. W., *b.* 1985
1908	*Marchamley (4th)*, William Francis Whiteley, *b.* 1968, *s.* 1994	None
1964	*Margadale (3rd)*, Alastair John Morrison, *b.* 1958, *s.* 2003, *m.*	Hon. Declan J. M., *b.* 1993
1961	*Marks of Broughton (3rd)*, Simon Richard Marks, *b.* 1950, *s.* 1998, *m.*	Hon. Michael M., *b.* 1989
1964	*Martonmere (2nd)*, John Stephen Robinson, *b.* 1963, *s.* 1989	David A. R., *b.* 1965
1776 I.	*Massy (9th)*, Hugh Hamon John Somerset Massy, *b.* 1921, *s.* 1958, *m.*	Hon. David H. S. M., *b.* 1947
1935	*May (3rd)*, Michael St John May, *b.* 1931, *s.* 1950, *m.*	Hon. Jasper B. St J. M., *b.* 1965
1928	*Melchett (4th)*, Peter Robert Henry Mond, *b.* 1948, *s.* 1973	None
1925	*Merrivale (3rd)*, Jack Henry Edmond Duke, *b.* 1917, *s.* 1951, *w.*	Hon. Derek J. P. D., *b.* 1948
1911	*Merthyr*, Trevor Oswin Lewis, Bt., CBE, *b.* 1935, *s.* 1977, *m.* Disclaimed for life 1977.	David T. L., *b.* 1977
1919	*Meston (3rd)*, James Meston, *b.* 1950, *s.* 1984, *m.*	Hon. Thomas J. D. M., *b.* 1977
1838	** *Methuen (7th)*, Robert Alexander Holt Methuen, *b.* 1931, *s.* 1994, *m.*	James P. A. M.-C., *b.* 1952
1711	*Middleton (12th)*, (Digby) Michael Godfrey John Willoughby, MC, *b.* 1921, *s.* 1970, *m.*	Hon. Michael C. J. W., *b.* 1948
1939	*Milford (4th)*, Guy Wogan Philipps, *b.* 1961, *s.* 1999, *m.*	Hon. Archie S. P., *b.* 1997
1933	*Milne (2nd)*, George Douglass Milne, TD, *b.* 1909, *s.* 1948, *m.*	Hon. George A. M., *b.* 1941
1951	** *Milner of Leeds (3rd)*, Richard James Milner, *b.* 1959, *s.* 2003, *m.*	None
1947	*Milverton (2nd)*, Revd Fraser Arthur Richard Richards, *b.* 1930, *s.* 1978, *m.*	Hon. Michael H. R., *b.* 1936
1873	*Moncreiff (6th)*, Rhoderick Harry Wellwood Moncreiff, *b.* 1954, *s.* 2002, *m.*	Hon. Harry J. W. M., *b.* 1986
1884	*Monk Bretton (3rd)*, John Charles Dodson, *b.* 1924, *s.* 1933, *m.*	Hon. Christopher M. D., *b.* 1958
1885	*Monkswell (5th)*, Gerard Collier, *b.* 1947, *s.* 1984, *m.*	Hon. James A. C., *b.* 1977
1728	** *Monson (11th)*, John Monson, *b.* 1932, *s.* 1958, *m.*	Hon. Nicholas J. M., *b.* 1955
1885	** *Montagu of Beaulieu (3rd)*, Edward John Barrington Douglas-Scott-Montagu, *b.* 1926, *s.* 1929, *m.*	Hon. Ralph D.-S.-M., *b.* 1961
1839	*Monteagle of Brandon (6th)*, Gerald Spring Rice, *b.* 1926, *s.* 1946, *m.*	Hon. Charles J. S. R., *b.* 1953

Created	Title, order of succession, name, etc.	Heir
1943	** *Moran (2nd)*, (Richard) John (McMoran) Wilson, KCMG, *b.* 1924, s. 1977, *m.*	Hon. James M. W., *b.* 1952
1918	*Morris (3rd)*, Michael David Morris, *b.* 1937, *s.* 1975, *m.*	Hon. Thomas A. S. M., *b.* 1982
1950	*Morris of Kenwood (2nd)*, Philip Geoffrey Morris, *b.* 1928, *s.* 1954, *m.*	Hon. Jonathan D. M., *b.* 1968
1831	*Mostyn (6th)*, Llewellyn Roger Lloyd-Mostyn, MC, *b.* 1948, *s.* 2000, *m.*	Hon. Gregory P. R. L.-M., *b.* 1984
1933	*Mottistone (4th)*, David Peter Seely, CBE, *b.* 1920, *s.* 1966, *m.*	Hon. Peter J. P. S., *b.* 1949
1945	*Mountevans (3rd)*, Edward Patrick Broke Evans, *b.* 1943, *s.* 1974, *m.*	Hon. Jeffrey de C. R. E., *b.* 1948
1283	** *Mowbray (26th), Segrave (27th) and Stourton (23rd)* (1448), Charles Edward Stourton, CBE, *b.* 1923, *s.* 1965, *m.*	Hon. Edward W. S. S., *b.* 1953
1932	*Moyne (3rd)*, Jonathan Bryan Guinness, *b.* 1930, *s.* 1992, *m.*	Hon. Jasper J. R. G., *b.* 1954
1929	** *Moynihan (4th)*, Colin Berkeley Moynihan, *b.* 1955, *s.* 1997, *m.*	Hon. Nicholas E. B. M., *b.* 1994
1781 I.	*Muskerry (9th)*, Robert Fitzmaurice Deane, *b.* 1948, *s.* 1988, *m.*	Hon. Jonathan F. D., *b.* 1986
1627 S.*	*Napier (14th) and Ettrick (5th) (UK 1872)*, Francis Nigel Napier, KCVO, *b.* 1930, *s.* 1954, *m.*	Master of Napier, *b.* 1962
1868	*Napier of Magdala (6th)*, Robert Alan Napier, *b.* 1940, *s.* 1987, *m.*	Hon. James R. N., *b.* 1966
1940	*Nathan (2nd)*, Roger Carol Michael Nathan, *b.* 1922, *s.* 1963, *m.*	Hon. Rupert H. *b.* N., *b.* 1957
1960	*Nelson of Stafford (3rd)*, Henry Roy George Nelson, *b.* 1943, *s.* 1995, *m.*	Hon. Alistair W. H. N., *b.* 1973
1959	*Netherthorpe (3rd)*, James Frederick Turner, *b.* 1964, *s.* 1982, *m.*	Hon. Andrew J. E. T., *b.* 1993
1946	*Newall (2nd)*, Francis Storer Eaton Newall, *b.* 1930, *s.* 1963, *m.*	Hon. Richard H. E. N., *b.* 1961
1776 I.	*Newborough (8th)*, Robert Vaughan Wynn, *b.* 1949, *s.* 1998, *m.*	Hon. Charles H. R. W., *b.* 1923
1892	*Newton (5th)*, Richard Thomas Legh, *b.* 1950, *s.* 1992, *m.*	Hon. Piers R. L., *b.* 1979
1930	*Noel-Buxton (3rd)*, Martin Connal Noel-Buxton, *b.* 1940, *s.* 1980, *m.*	Hon. Charles C. N.-B., *b.* 1975
1957	*Norrie (2nd)*, (George) Willoughby Moke Norrie, *b.* 1936, *s.* 1977, *m.*	Hon. Mark W. J. N., *b.* 1972
1884	** *Northbourne (5th)*, Christopher George Walter James, *b.* 1926, *s.* 1982, *m.*	Hon. Charles W. H. J., *b.* 1960
1866	** *Northbrook (6th)*, Francis Thomas Baring, *b.* 1954, *s.* 1990, *m.*	To the Baronetcy, Peter B., *b.* 1939
1878	*Norton (8th)*, James Nigel Arden Adderley, *b.* 1947, *s.* 1993, *m.*	Hon. Edward J. A. A., *b.* 1982
1906	*Nunburnholme (6th)*, Stephen Charles Wilson, *b.* 1973, *s.* 2000	Hon. David M. W., *b.* 1983
1950	*Ogmore (2nd)*, Gwilym Rees Rees-Williams, *b.* 1931, *s.* 1976, *m.*	Hon. Morgan R.-W., *b.* 1937
1870	*O'Hagan (4th)*, Charles Towneley Strachey, *b.* 1945, *s.* 1961	Hon. Richard T. S., *b.* 1950
1868	*O'Neill (4th)*, Raymond Arthur Clanaboy O'Neill, TD, *b.* 1933, *s.* 1944, *m.*	Hon. Shane S. C. O'N., *b.* 1965
1836 I.*	*Oranmore and Browne (5th) and 3rd UK Baron, Mereworth (1926)*, Dominick Geoffrey Thomas Browne, *b.* 1929, *s.* 2002,	Hon. Martin M. D. B., *b.* 1931
1933	** *Palmer (4th)*, Adrian Bailie Nottage Palmer, *b.* 1951, *s.* 1990, *m.*	Hon. Hugo B. R. P., *b.* 1980
1914	*Parmoor (4th)*, (Frederick Alfred) Milo Cripps, *b.* 1929, *s.* 1977	Michael L. S. C., *b.* 1942
1937	*Pender (3rd)*, John Willoughby Denison-Pender, *b.* 1933, *s.* 1965, *m.*	Hon. Henry J. R. D.-P., *b.* 1968
1866	*Penrhyn (6th)*, Malcolm Frank Douglas-Pennant, DSO, MBE, *b.* 1908, *s.* 1967, *w.*	Simon D.-P., *b.* 1938
1603	*Petre (18th)*, John Patrick Lionel Petre, *b.* 1942, *s.* 1989, *m.*	Hon. Dominic W. P., *b.* 1966
1918	*Phillimore (5th)*, Francis Stephen Phillimore, *b.* 1944, *s.* 1994, *m.*	Hon. Tristan A. S. P., *b.* 1977
1945	*Piercy (3rd)*, James William Piercy, *b.* 1946, *s.* 1981	Hon. Mark E. P. P., *b.* 1953
1827	*Plunket (8th)*, Robin Rathmore Plunket, *b.* 1925, *s.* 1975, *m.*	Hon. Shaun A. F. S. P., *b.* 1931
1831	*Poltimore (7th)*, Mark Coplestone Bampfylde, *b.* 1957, *s.* 1978, *m.*	Hon. Henry A. W. B., *b.* 1985
1690 S.	*Polwarth (10th)*, Henry Alexander Hepburne-Scott, TD, *b.* 1916, *s.* 1944, *m.*	Master of Polwarth, *b.* 1947
1930	*Ponsonby of Shulbrede (4th) and Baron Ponsonby of Roehampton (life peerage, 2000)*, Frederick Matthew Thomas Ponsonby, *b.* 1958, *s.* 1990	None
1958	*Poole (2nd)*, David Charles Poole, *b.* 1945, *s.* 1993, *m.*	Hon. Oliver J. P., *b.* 1972
1852	*Raglan (5th)*, FitzRoy John Somerset, *b.* 1927, *s.* 1964	Hon. Geoffrey S., *b.* 1932
1932	*Rankeillour (4th)*, Peter St Thomas More Henry Hope, *b.* 1935, *s.* 1967	Michael R. H., *b.* 1940
1953	*Rathcavan (3rd)*, Hugh Detmar Torrens O'Neill, *b.* 1939, *s.* 1994, *m.*	Hon. François H. N. O'N., *b.* 1984
1916	*Rathcreedan (3rd)*, Christopher John Norton, *b.* 1949, *s.* 1990, *m.*	Hon. Adam G. N., *b.* 1952
1868	*Rathdonnell (5th)*, Thomas Benjamin McClintock-Bunbury, *b.* 1938, *s.* 1959, *m.*	Hon. William L. M.-B., *b.* 1966
1911	*Ravensdale (3rd)*, Nicholas Mosley, MC, *b.* 1923, *s.* 1966, *m.*	Hon. Shaun N. M., *b.* 1949
1821	*Ravensworth (8th)*, Arthur Waller Liddell, *b.* 1924, *s.* 1950, *m.*	Hon. Thomas A. H. L., *b.* 1954
1821	*Rayleigh (6th)*, John Gerald Strutt, *b.* 1960, *s.* 1988, *m.*	Hon. John F. S., *b.* 1993
1937	** *Rea (3rd)*, John Nicolas Rea, MD, *b.* 1928, *s.* 1981, *m.*	Hon. Matthew J. R., *b.* 1956
1628 S.	** *Reay (14th)*, Hugh William Mackay, *b.* 1937, *s.* 1963, *m.*	Master of Reay, *b.* 1965
1902	*Redesdale (6th) and Baron Mitford (life peerage 2000)*, Rupert Bertram Mitford, *b.* 1967, *s.* 1991, *m.*	Hon. Bertram D. M., *b.* 2000
1940	*Reith*, Christopher John Reith, *b.* 1928, *s.* 1971, *m.* Disclaimed for life 1972.	Hon. James H. J. R., *b.* 1971
1928	*Remnant (3rd)*, James Wogan Remnant, CVO, *b.* 1930, *s.* 1967, *m.*	Hon. Philip J. R., *b.* 1954

Created	Title, order of succession, name, etc.	Heir
1806	*Rendlesham (9th)*, Charles William Brooke Thellusson, b. 1954, s. 1999, m.	Hon. Peter R. T., b. 1920
1933	*Rennell (3rd)*, (John Adrian) Tremayne Rodd, b. 1935, s. 1978, m.	Hon. James R. D. T. R., b. 1978
1964	*Renwick (2nd)*, Harry Andrew Renwick, b. 1935, s. 1973, m.	Hon. Robert J. R., b. 1966
1885	*Revelstoke (6th)*, James Cecil Baring, b. 1938, s. 2003, m.	Hon. Alexander R. B., b. 1970
1905	*Ritchie of Dundee (5th)*, (Harold) Malcolm Ritchie, b. 1919, s. 1978, m.	Hon. C. Rupert R. R., b. 1958
1935	*Riverdale (3rd)*, Anthony Robert Balfour, b. 1960, s. 1998	Hon. David R. B., b. 1938
1961	*Robertson of Oakridge (2nd)*, William Ronald Robertson, b. 1930, s. 1974, m.	Hon. William B. E. R., b. 1975
1938	*Roborough (3rd)*, Henry Massey Lopes, b. 1940, s. 1992, m.	Hon. Massey J. H. L., b. 1969
1931	*Rochester (2nd)*, Foster Charles Lowry Lamb, b. 1916, s. 1955, w.	Hon. David C. L., b. 1944
1934	*Rockley (3rd)*, James Hugh Cecil, b. 1934, s. 1976, m.	Hon. Anthony R. C., b. 1961
1782	*Rodney (10th)*, George Brydges Rodney, b. 1953, s. 1992, m.	Hon. John G. B. R., b. 1999
1651 S.*	*Rollo (14th) and 5th UK Baron Dunning*, 1869, David Eric Howard Rollo, b. 1943, s. 1997, m.	Master of Rollo, b. 1972
1959	*Rootes (3rd)*, Nicholas Geoffrey Rootes, b. 1951, s. 1992, m.	William B. R., b. 1944
1796 I.*	*Rossmore (7th) and 6th UK Baron, Rossmore*, 1838, William Warner Westenra, b. 1931, s. 1958, m.	Hon. Benedict W. W., b. 1983
1939 **	*Rotherwick (3rd)*, (Herbert) Robin Cayzer, b. 1954, s. 1996, m.	Hon. H. Robin C., b. 1989
1885	*Rothschild (4th)*, (Nathaniel Charles) Jacob Rothschild, OM, GBE, b. 1936, s. 1990, m.	Hon. Nathaniel P. V. J. R., b. 1971
1911	*Rowallan (4th)*, John Polson Cameron Corbett, b. 1947, s. 1993	Hon. Jason W. P. C. C., b. 1972
1947	*Rugby (3rd)*, Robert Charles Maffey, b. 1951, s. 1990, m.	Hon. Timothy J. H. M., b. 1975
1919	*Russell of Liverpool (3rd)*, Simon Gordon Jared Russell, b. 1952, s. 1981, m.	Hon. Edward C. S. R., b. 1985
1876	*Sackville (6th)*, Lionel Bertrand Sackville-West, b. 1913, s. 1965, m.	Robert B. S-W., b. 1958
1964	*St Helens (2nd)*, Richard Francis Hughes-Young, b. 1945, s. 1980, m.	Hon. Henry T. H.-Y., b. 1986
1559 **	*St John of Bletso (21st)*, Anthony Tudor St John, b. 1957, s. 1978, m.	Hon. Oliver B. St J., b. 1995
1887	*St Levan (4th)*, John Francis Arthur St Aubyn, DSC, b. 1919, s. 1978, w.	Hon. O. Piers St. A., b. 1920
1885	*St Oswald (6th)*, Charles Rowland Andrew Winn, b. 1959, s. 1999, m.	Hon. Rowland C. S. H. W., b. 1986
1960	*Sanderson of Ayot*, Alan Lindsay Sanderson, b. 1931, s. 1971, m. Disclaimed for life 1971.	Hon. Michael S., b. 1959
1945	*Sandford (2nd)*, Revd John Cyril Edmondson, DSC, b. 1920, s. 1959, m.	Hon. James J. M. E., b. 1949
1871	*Sandhurst (6th)*, Guy Rees John Mansfield, b. 1949, s. 2002, m.	Hon. Edward J. M., b. 1982
1802	*Sandys (7th)*, Richard Michael Oliver Hill, b. 1931, s. 1961, m.	The Marquess of Downshire
1888	*Savile (3rd)*, George Halifax Lumley-Savile, b. 1919, s. 1931	John A. T. L-S., b. 1947
1447	*Saye and Sele (21st)*, Nathaniel Thomas Allen Fiennes, b. 1920, s. 1968, m.	Hon. Martin G. F., b. 1961
1826	*Seaford (6th)*, Colin Humphrey Felton Ellis, b. 1946, s. 1999, m.	Hon. Benjamin F. T. E., b. 1976
1932 **	*Selsdon (3rd)*, Malcolm McEacharn Mitchell-Thomson, b. 1937, s. 1963, m.	Hon. Callum M. M. M.-T., b. 1969
1489 s.	*Sempill (21st)*, James William Stuart Whitemore Sempill, b. 1949, s. 1995, m.	Master of Semphill, b. 1979
1916	*Shaughnessy (4th)*, Michael James Shaughnessy, b. 1946, s. 2003	Charles, G. P. S., b. 1955
1946	*Shepherd (3rd)*, Graham George Shepherd, b. 1949, s. 2001, m.	Hon. Patrick M. S.
1964	*Sherfield (2nd)*, Christopher James Makins, b. 1942, s. 1996, m.	Hon. Dwight W. M., b. 1951
1902	*Shuttleworth (5th)*, Charles Geoffrey Nicholas Kay-Shuttleworth, b. 1948, s. 1975, m.	Hon. Thomas E. K.-S., b. 1976
1950	*Silkin (3rd)*, Christopher Lewis Silkin, b. 1947, s. 2001	Rory L. S., b. 1954
1963	*Silsoe (2nd)*, David Malcolm Trustram Eve, QC, b. 1930, s. 1976, m.	Hon. Simon R. T. E., b. 1966
1947	*Simon of Wythenshawe (2nd)*, Roger Simon, b. 1913, s. 1960, m. Does not use title	Hon. Matthew S., b. 1955
1449 S.	*Sinclair (17th)*, Charles Murray Kennedy St Clair, CVO, b. 1914, s. 1957, m.	Master of Sinclair, b. 1968
1957	*Sinclair of Cleeve (3rd)*, John Lawrence Robert Sinclair, b. 1953, s. 1985	None
1919	*Sinha (6th)*, Arup Kumar Sinha, b. 1966, s. 1999	Hon. Dilip K. S., b. 1967
1828 **	*Skelmersdale (7th)*, Roger Bootle-Wilbraham, b. 1945, s. 1973, m.	Hon. Andrew B.-W., b. 1977
1916	*Somerleyton (3rd)*, Savile William Francis Crossley, GCVO, b. 1928, s. 1959, m.	Hon. Hugh F. S. C., b. 1971
1784	*Somers (9th)*, Philip Sebastian Somers Cocks, b. 1948, s. 1995	Alan B. C., b. 1930
1959	*Spens (4th)*, Patrick Nathaniel George Spens, b. 1968, s. 2001, m.	Hon. Peter L. S., b. 2000
1780	*Southampton (6th)*, Charles James FitzRoy, b. 1928, s. 1989, m.	Hon. Edward C. F., b. 1955
1640	*Stafford (15th)*, Francis Melfort William Fitzherbert, b. 1954, s. 1986, m.	Hon. Benjamin J. B. F., b. 1983
1938	*Stamp (4th)*, Trevor Charles Bosworth Stamp, MD, FRCP, b. 1935, s. 1987, m.	Hon. Nicholas C. T. S., b. 1978

Created	Title, order of succession, name, etc.	Heir
1839	Stanley of Alderley (8th) and Sheffield (8th) (I. 1738) and 7th UK Baron, Eddisbury, 1848, Thomas Henry Oliver Stanley, b. 1927, s. 1971, m.	Hon. Richard O. S., b. 1956
1318	** Strabolgi (11th), David Montague de Burgh Kenworthy, b. 1914, s. 1953, m.	Andrew D. W. K., b. 1967
1954	Strang (2nd), Colin Strang, b. 1922, s. 1978, m.	None
1955	Strathalmond (3rd), William Roberton Fraser, b. 1947, s. 1976, m.	Hon. William G. F., b. 1976
1936	Strathcarron (2nd), David William Anthony Blyth Macpherson, b. 1924, s. 1937, m.	Hon. Ian D. P. M., b. 1949
1955	** Strathclyde (2nd), Thomas Galloway Dunlop du Roy de Blicquy Galbraith, PC, b. 1960, s. 1985, m.	Hon. Charles W. du R. de B. G., b. 1962
1900	Strathcona and Mount Royal (4th), Donald Euan Palmer Howard, b. 1923, s. 1959, m.	Hon. D. Alexander S. H., b. 1961
1836	Stratheden (6th) and Campbell (6th) (1841), Donald Campbell, b. 1934, s. 1987, m.	Hon. David A. C., b. 1963
1884	Strathspey (6th), James Patrick Trevor Grant of Grant, b. 1943, s. 1992 m.	Hon. Michael P. F. G., b. 1953
1838	Sudeley (7th), Merlin Charles Sainthill Hanbury-Tracy, b. 1939, s. 1941	D. Andrew J. H.-T., b. 1928
1786	Suffield (11th), Anthony Philip Harbord-Hamond, MC, b. 1922, s. 1951, w.	Hon. Charles A. A. H.-H., b. 1953
1893	Swansea (4th), John Hussey Hamilton Vivian, b. 1925, s. 1934, m.	Hon. Richard A. H. V., b. 1957
1907	Swaythling (5th), Charles Edgar Samuel Montagu, b. 1954, s. 1998, m.	Hon. Anthony T. S. M., b. 1931
1919	** Swinfen (3rd), Roger Mynors Swinfen Eady, b. 1938, s. 1977, m.	Hon. Charles R. P. S. E., b. 1971
1935	Sysonby (3rd), John Frederick Ponsonby, b. 1945, s. 1956	None
1831 I.	Talbot of Malahide (10th), Reginald John Richard Arundell, b. 1931, s. 1987, m.	Hon. Richard J. T. A., b. 1957
1946	Tedder (3rd), Robin John Tedder, b. 1955, s. 1994, m.,	Hon. Benjamin J. T., b. 1985
1884	Tennyson (5th), Cdr. Mark Aubrey Tennyson, DSC, b. 1920, s. 1991, m.	David H. A. T., b. 1960
1918	Terrington (6th), Christopher Richard James Woodhouse, MB, FRCS, b. 1946, s. 2001, m.	Hon. Jack H. L. W., b. 1978
1940	Teviot (2nd), Charles John Kerr, b. 1934, s. 1968, m.	Hon. Charles R. K., b. 1971
1616	Teynham (20th), John Christopher Ingham Roper-Curzon, b. 1928, s. 1972, m.	Hon. David J. H. I. R.-C., b. 1965
1964	Thomson of Fleet (2nd), Kenneth Roy Thomson, b. 1923, s. 1976, m.	Hon. David K. R. T., b. 1957
1792	Thurlow (8th), Francis Edward Hovell-Thurlow-Cumming-Bruce, KCMG, b. 1912, s. 1971, w.	Hon. Roualeyn R. H.-T.-C.-B., b. 1952
1876	Tollemache (5th), Timothy John Edward Tollemache, b. 1939, s. 1975, m.	Hon. Edward J. H. T., b. 1976
1564 S.	Torphichen (15th), James Andrew Douglas Sandilands, b. 1946, s. 1975, m.	Robert, P. S., b. 1950
1947	** Trefgarne (2nd), David Garro Trefgarne, PC, b. 1941, s. 1960, m.	Hon. George G. T., b. 1970
1921	Trevethin (4th) and Oaksey (2nd) (1947), John Geoffrey Tristram Lawrence, OBE, b. 1929, s. 1971, m.	Hon. Patrick J. T. L., b. 1960
1880	Trevor (5th), Marke Charles Hill-Trevor, b. 1970, s. 1997, m.	Hon. Iain R. H.-T., b. 1971
1461 I.	Trimlestown (21st), Raymond Charles Barnewall, b. 1930, s. 1997	None
1940	Tryon (3rd), Anthony George Merrik Tryon, b. 1940, s. 1976	Hon. Charles G. B. T., b. 1976
1935	Tweedsmuir (3rd), William de l'Aigle Buchan, b. 1916, s. 1996, m.	Hon. John W. H. de l'A. B., b. 1950
1523	Vaux of Harrowden (11th), Anthony William Gilbey, b. 1940, s. 2002, m.	Hon. Richard H. G. G., b. 1965
1800 I.	Ventry (8th), Andrew Wesley Daubeny de Moleyns, b. 1943, s. 1987, m.	Hon. Francis W. D. de M., b. 1965
1762	Vernon (11th), Anthony William Vernon-Harcourt, b. 1939, s. 2000, m.	Hon. Simon A. V.-H., b. 1969
1922	Vestey (3rd), Samuel George Armstrong Vestey, b. 1941, s. 1954, m.	Hon. William G. V., b. 1983
1841	** Vivian (6th), Nicholas Crespigny Laurence Vivian, b. 1935, s. 1991, m.	Hon. Charles H. C. V., b. 1966
1934	Wakehurst (3rd), (John) Christopher Loder, b. 1925, s. 1970, m.	Hon. Timothy W. L., b. 1958
1723	** Walpole (10th) and 8th Brit. Baron Walpole of Wolterton, 1756, Robert Horatio Walpole, b. 1938, s. 1989, m.	Hon. Jonathan R. H. W., b. 1967
1780	Walsingham (9th), John de Grey, MC, b. 1925, s. 1965, m.	Hon. Robert de. G., b. 1969
1936	Wardington (2nd), Christopher Henry Beaumont Pease, b. 1924, s. 1950, m.	Hon. William S. P., b. 1925
1792 I.	Waterpark (7th), Frederick Caryll Philip Cavendish, b. 1926, s. 1948, m.	Hon. Roderick A. C., b. 1959
1942	Wedgwood (4th), Piers Anthony Weymouth Wedgwood, b. 1954, s. 1970, m.	John W., b. 1919
1861	Westbury (6th), Richard Nicholas Bethell, MBE, b. 1950, s. 2001, m.	Hon. Alexander B., b. 1986
1944	Westwood (3rd), (William) Gavin Westwood, b. 1944, s. 1991, m.	Hon. W. Fergus W., b. 1972
1544/5	Wharton (12th), Myles Christopher David Robertson, b. 1964, s. 2000, m.	Hon. Christopher J. R., b. 1969
1935	Wigram (2nd), (George) Neville (Clive) Wigram, MC, b. 1915, s. 1960, w.	Maj. Hon. Andrew F. C. W., b. 1949
1491	** Willoughby de Broke (21st), Leopold David Verney, b. 1938, s. 1986, m.	Hon. Rupert G. V., b. 1966

Created	Title, order of succession, name, etc.	Heir
1946	Wilson (2nd), Patrick Maitland Wilson, b. 1915, s. 1964, w.	None
1937	Windlesham (3rd) and Baron Hennesy (life peerage, 1999), David James George Hennessy, CVO, PC, b. 1932, s. 1962, w.	Hon. James R. H., b. 1968
1951	Wise (2nd), John Clayton Wise, b. 1923, s. 1968, m.	Hon. Christopher J. C. W., b. 1949
1869	Wolverton (7th), Christopher Richard Glyn, b. 1938, s. 1988,	Hon. Andrew J. G., b. 1943
1928	Wraxall (3rd), Eustace Hubert Beilby Gibbs, KCVO, CMG, b. 1929, s. 2001, m.	Hon. Anthony H. G., b. 1958
1915	Wrenbury (3rd), Revd John Burton Buckley, b. 1927, s. 1940, m.	Hon. William E. B., b. 1966
1838	Wrottesley (6th), Clifton Hugh Lancelot de Verdon Wrottesley, b. 1968, s. 1977, m.	Hon. Stephen J. W., b. 1955
1829	Wynford (9th), John Philip Robert Best, b. 1950, s. 2002, m.	Hon. Harry R. F. B., b. 1987
1308	Zouche (18th), James Assheton Frankland, b. 1943, s. 1965, m.	Hon. William T. A. F., b. 1984

BARONESSES/LADIES IN THEIR OWN RIGHT

Style, The Right Hon. the Lady _ , or The Right Hon. the Baroness _ , according to her preference. Either style may be used, except in the case of Scottish titles (indicated by S.), which are not baronies (see page 41) and whose holders are always addressed as Lady
Husband, Untitled
Children's style, As for children of a Baron
For forms of address, see page 40

Created	Title, order of succession, name, etc.	Heir
1664	Arlington, Jennifer Jane Forwood, b. 1939, s. 1999, w., title called out of abeyance 1999	Hon. Patrick J. D. F., b. 1967
1455	Berners (16th), Pamela Vivien Kirkham, b. 1929, s. 1995, m.	Hon. Rupert W. T. K., b. 1953
1529	Braye (8th), Mary Penelope Aubrey-Fletcher, b. 1941, s. 1985, m.	Two co-heiresses
1321	Dacre (27th), Rachel Leila Douglas-Home, b. 1929, s. 1970, w.	Hon. James T. A. D.-H., b. 1952
1332	** Darcy de Knayth (18th), Davina Marcia Ingrams, DBE, b. 1938, s. 1943, w.	Hon. Caspar D. I., b. 1962
1490 S.	Herries of Terregles (14th), Anne Elizabeth Fitzalan-Howard, b. 1938, s. 1975, w.	Lady Mary Mumford , b. 1940
1602 S.	Kinloss (12th), Beatrice Mary Grenville Freeman-Grenville, b. 1922, s. 1944, m.	Master of Kinloss, b. 1953
1445 S.	** Saltoun (20th), Flora Marjory Fraser, b. 1930, s. 1979, w.	Hon. Katharine I. M. I. F., b. 1957
1628	** Strange (16th), (Jean) Cherry Drummond of Megginch, b. 1928, s. 1986, m.	Hon. Adam H. D. of M., b. 1953
1313	Willoughby de Eresby (27th), (Nancy) Jane Marie Heathcote-Drummond-Willoughby, b. 1934, s. 1983	Two co-heiresses

LIFE PEERS

NEW LIFE PEERAGES *1 September 2002 to 31 August 2003:*
Admiral Sir Michael Boyce, GCB, OBE; The Rt. Revd. George Leonard Carey, PC; The Rt. Hon. William Douglas Cullen, *Lord Justice-General of Scotland and Lord President of the Court of Session;* Sir Robert Walker, PC; Sir Richard Thomas James Wilson, GCB

CREATED UNDER THE APPELLATE JURISDICTION ACT 1876 (AS AMENDED)

BARONS
Created
1986 *Ackner,* Desmond James Conrad Ackner, PC, *b.* 1920, *m.*
1980 *Bridge of Harwich,* Nigel Cyprian Bridge, PC, *b.* 1917, *m.*
1982 *Brightman,* John Anson, Brightman PC, *b.* 1911, *m.*
1991 *Browne-Wilkinson,* Nicolas Christopher Henry Browne-Wilkinson, PC, *b.* 1930, *m.*
1996 *Clyde,* James John Clyde, PC, *b.* 1932, *m.*
1986 *Goff of Chieveley,* Robert Lionel Archibald Goff, PC, *b.* 1926, *m.*
1985 *Griffiths,* (William) Hugh Griffiths, MC, PC, *b.* 1923, *m.*
1998 *Hobhouse of Woodborough,* John Stewart Hobhouse, PC, *b.* 1932, *Lord of Appeal in Ordinary*
1995 *Hoffmann,* Leonard Hubert Hoffmann, PC, *b.* 1934, *m. Lord of Appeal in Ordinary*
1997 *Hutton,* (James) Brian (Edward) Hutton, PC, *b.* 1931, *m. Lord of Appeal in Ordinary*
1988 *Jauncey of Tullichettle,* Charles Eliot Jauncey, PC, *b.* 1925, *m.*
1979 *Lane,* Geoffrey Dawson Lane, AFC, PC, *b.* 1918, *m.*
1993 *Lloyd of Berwick,* Anthony John Leslie Lloyd, PC, *b.* 1929, *m.*
1998 *Millett,* Peter Julian Millett, PC, *b.* 1932, *m. Lord of Appeal in Ordinary*
1992 *Mustill,* Michael John Mustill, PC, *b.* 1931, *m.*
1994 *Nicholls of Birkenhead,* Donald James Nicholls, PC, *b.* 1933, *m. Second Senior Lord of Appeal in Ordinary*
1994 *Nolan,* Michael Patrick Nolan, PC, *b.* 1928, *m.*
1986 *Oliver of Aylmerton,* Peter Raymond Oliver, PC, *b.* 1921, *m.*
1999 *Phillips of Worth Matravers,* Nicholas Addison Phillips, *b.* 1938, *m. Master of the Rolls*
1997 *Saville of Newdigate,* Mark Oliver Saville, PC, *b.* 1936, *m. Lord of Appeal in Ordinary*
1977 *Scarman,* Leslie George Scarman, OBE, PC, *b.* 1911, *m.*
1992 *Slynn of Hadley,* Gordon Slynn, PC, *b.* 1930, *m.*
1995 *Steyn,* Johan van Zyl Steyn, PC, *b.* 1932, *m. Lord of Appeal in Ordinary*
1982 *Templeman,* Sydney William Templeman, MBE, PC, *b.* 1920, *m.*
1992 *Woolf,* Harry Kenneth Woolf, PC, *b.* 1933, *m. Lord Chief Justice of England and Wales*

CREATED UNDER THE LIFE PEERAGES ACT 1958

* Hereditary peer who has been granted a life peerage. For further details, please refer to the Hereditary Peers section, pages 41–62. For example, life peer *Balniel* can be found under his hereditary title *Earl of Crawford and Balcarres.*

BARONS
Created
2000 **Acton of Bridgnorth,* Lord Acton, *b.* 1941, *m.* (*see* Hereditary Peers)
2001 *Adebowale,* Victor Olufemi Adebowale, CBE, *b.* 1962
1998 *Ahmed,* Nazir Ahmed, *b.* 1957, *m.*
1996 *Alderdice,* John Thomas Alderdice, *b.* 1955, *m.*
1988 *Alexander of Weedon,* Robert Scott Alexander, QC, *b.* 1936, *m.*
1976 *Allen of Abbeydale,* Philip Allen, GCB, *b.* 1912, *w.*
1998 *Alli,* Waheed Alli, *b.* 1964
1997 *Alton of Liverpool,* David Patrick Paul Alton, *b.* 1951, *m.*
1992 *Archer of Sandwell,* Peter Kingsley Archer, PC, QC, *b.* 1926, *m.*
1992 *Archer of Weston-super-Mare,* Jeffrey Howard Archer, *b.* 1940, *m.*
1988 *Armstrong of Ilminster,* Robert Temple Armstrong, GCB, CVO, *b.* 1927, *m.*
1999 **Armstrong-Jones,* Earl of Snowdon, GCVO, *b.* 1930, *m.* (*see* Hereditary Peers)
2000 *Ashcroft,* Michael Anthony Ashcroft, KCMG
2000 *Ashdown of Norton-sub-Hamdon,* Jeremy John Durham (Paddy) Ashdown, KBE, PC, *b.* 1941, *m.*
1992 *Ashley of Stoke,* Jack Ashley, CH, PC, *b.* 1922, *w.*
1993 *Attenborough,* Richard Samuel Attenborough, CBE, *b.* 1923, *m.*
1998 *Bach,* William Stephen Goulden Bach, *b.* 1946, *m.*
1997 *Bagri,* Raj Kumar Bagri, CBE, *b.* 1930, *m.*
1997 *Baker of Dorking,* Kenneth Wilfred Baker, CH, PC, *b.* 1934, *m.*
1974 **Balniel,* The Earl of Crawford and Balcarres, *b.* 1927, *m.* (*see* Hereditary Peers)
1974 *Barber,* Anthony Perrinott Lysberg Barber, TD, PC, *b.* 1920, *m.*
1992 *Barber of Tewkesbury,* Derek Coates Barber, *b.* 1918, *m.*
1983 *Barnett,* Joel Barnett, PC, *b.* 1923, *m.*
1997 *Bassam of Brighton,* (John) Steven Bassam, *b.* 1953
1967 *Beaumont of Whitley,* Revd Timothy Wentworth Beaumont, *b.* 1928, *m.*
1998 *Bell,* Timothy John Leigh Bell, *b.* 1941, *m.*
2000 *Bernstein of Craigweil,* Alexander Bernstein, *b.* 1936, *m.*
2001 *Best,* Richard Stuart Best, OBE, *b.* 1945, *m.*
2001 *Bhatia,* Amirali Alibhai Bhatia, OBE, *b.* 1932, *m.*
1997 *Biffen,* (William) John Biffen, PC, *b.* 1930, *m.*
1995 *Bingham of Cornhill,* Thomas Henry Bingham, PC, *b.* 1933, *m. Senior Lord of Appeal in Ordinary*
2000 *Birt,* John Francis Hodgess Birt, *b.* 1944, *m.*
2001 *Black of Crossharbour,* Conrad Moffat Black, OC, PC, *b.* 1944, *m.*
1997 *Blackwell,* Norman Roy Blackwell, *b.* 1952, *m.*
1971 *Blake,* Robert Norman William Blake, FBA, *b.* 1916, *w.*
1994 *Blaker,* Peter Allan Renshaw Blaker, KCMG, PC, *b.* 1922, *m.*

1978   *Blease,* William John Blease, *b.* 1914, *m.*
1995   *Blyth of Rowington,* James Blyth, *b.* 1940, *m.*
1996   *Borrie,* Gordon Johnson Borrie, QC, *b.* 1931, *m.*
1976   *Boston of Faversham,* Terence George Boston, QC, *b.* 1930, *m.*
1996   *Bowness,* Peter Spencer Bowness, CBE, *b.* 1943, *m.*
2003   *Boyce,* Michael Boyce, GCB, OBE, *b.* 1943
1999   *Bradshaw,* William Peter Bradshaw, *b.* 1936, *m.*
1998   *Bragg,* Melvyn Bragg, *b.* 1939, *m.*
1987   *Bramall,* Edwin Noel Westby Bramall, KG, GCB, OBE, MC, *b.* 1923, *m.*
2000   *Brennan,* Daniel Joseph Brennan, QC, *b.* 1942, *m.*
1999   *Brett,* William Henry Brett, *b.* 1942, *m.*
1976   *Briggs,* Asa Briggs, FBA, *b.* 1921, *m.*
2000   *Brittan of Spennithorne,* Leon Brittan, PC, QC, *b.* 1939, *m.*
1997   *Brooke of Alverthorpe,* Clive Brooke, *b.* 1942, *m.*
2001   *Brooke of Sutton Mandeville,* Peter Leonard Brooke, CH, PC, *b.* 1934, *m.*
1998   *Brookman,* David Keith Brookman, *b.* 1937, *m.*
1979   *Brooks of Tremorfa,* John Edward Brooks, *b.* 1927, *m.*
2001   *Browne of Madingley,* Edmund John Phillip Browne, *b.* 1948
1974   *Bruce of Donington,* Donald William Trevor Bruce, *b.* 1912, *m.*
1976   *Bullock,* Alan Louis Charles Bullock, FBA, *b.* 1914, *m.*
1997   *Burlison,* Thomas Henry Burlison, *b.* 1936, *m.*
1998   *Burns,* Terence Burns, GCB, *b.* 1944, *m.*
1998   *Butler of Brockwell,* (Frederick Edward) Robin Butler, KG, GCB, CVO, *b.* 1938, *m.*
1978   *Buxton of Alsa,* Aubrey Leland Oakes Buxton, KCVO, MC, *b.* 1918, *m.*
1987   *Callaghan of Cardiff,* (Leonard) James Callaghan, KG, PC, *b.* 1912, *m.*
1984   *Cameron of Lochbroom,* Kenneth John Cameron, PC, *b.* 1931, *m.*
1981   *Campbell of Alloway,* Alan Robertson Campbell, QC, *b.* 1917, *m.*
1974   *Campbell of Croy,* Gordon Thomas Calthrop Campbell, MC, PC, *b.* 1921, *m.*
2001   *Campbell-Savours,* Dale Norman Campbell-Savours, *b.* 1943, *m.*
2002   *Carey of Clifton,* Rt. Revd George Leonard Carey, PC, *b.* 1935, *m.*
1999   **Carington of Upton,* Lord Carrington, GCMG, *b.* 1919, *m.* (*see* Hereditary Peers)
1999   *Carlile of Berriew,* Alexander Charles Carlile, QC, *b.* 1948, *m.*
1987   *Carlisle of Bucklow,* Mark Carlisle, QC, PC, *b.* 1929, *m.*
1975   *Carr of Hadley,* (Leonard) Robert Carr, PC, *b.* 1916, *m.*
1987   *Carter,* Denis Victor Carter, PC, *b.* 1932, *m.*
1990   *Cavendish of Furness,* (Richard) Hugh Cavendish, *b.* 1941, *m.*
1996   *Chadlington,* Peter Selwyn Gummer, *b.* 1942, *m.*
1964   *Chalfont,* (Alun) Arthur Gwynne Jones, OBE, MC, PC, *b.* 1919, *m.*
2001   *Chan,* Michael Chew Koon Chan, MBE, *b.* 1940, *m.*
1985   *Chapple,* Francis (Frank) Joseph Chapple, *b.* 1921, *w.*
1987   *Chilver,* (Amos) Henry Chilver, FRS, FREng, *b.* 1926, *m.*
1977   *Chitnis,* Pratap Chidamber Chitnis, *b.* 1936, *m.*
1998   *Christopher,* Anthony Martin Grosvenor Christopher, CBE, *b.* 1925, *m.*
1992   *Clark of Kempston,* William Gibson Haig Clark, PC, *b.* 1917, *m.*

2001   *Clark of Windermere,* David George Clark, PC, Ph.D., *b.* 1939, *m.*
1998   *Clarke of Hampstead,* Anthony James Clarke, CBE, *b.* 1932, *m.*
1998   *Clement-Jones,* Timothy Francis Clement-Jones, CBE, *b.* 1949, *m.*
1990   *Clinton-Davis,* Stanley Clinton Clinton-Davis, PC, *b.* 1928, *m.*
1978   *Cockfield,* (Francis) Arthur Cockfield, PC, *b.* 1916, *w.*
2000   *Coe,* Sebastian Newbold Coe, OBE, *b.* 1956, *m.*
2001   *Condon,* Paul Leslie Condon, QPM, *m.*
1981   *Constantine of Stanmore,* Theodore Constantine, CBE, AE, *b.* 1910, *w.*
1992   *Cooke of Islandreagh,* Victor Alexander Cooke, OBE, *b.* 1920, *m.*
1996   *Cooke of Thorndon,* Robin Brunskill Cooke, KBE, PC, Ph.D., *b.* 1926, *m.*
1997   *Cope of Berkeley,* John Ambrose Cope, PC, *b.* 1937, *m.*
2001   *Corbett of Castle Vale,* Robin Corbett, *b.* 1933, *m.*
1991   *Craig of Radley,* David Brownrigg Craig, GCB, OBE, *b.* 1929, *m.*
1987   *Crickhowell,* (Roger) Nicholas Edwards, PC, *b.* 1934, *m.*
1978   *Croham,* Douglas Albert Vivian Allen, GCB, *b.* 1917, *w.*
2003   *Cullen,* William Douglas Cullen, PC, *b.* 1935, *m. Lord Justice General of Scotland and Lord President of the Court of Session*
1995   *Cuckney,* John Graham Cuckney, *b.* 1925, *m.*
1996   *Currie of Marylebone,* David Anthony Currie, *b.* 1946, *m.*
1993   *Dahrendorf,* Ralf Dahrendorf, KBE, Ph.D., D.Phil., FBA, *b.* 1929, *m.*
1997   *Davies of Coity,* (David) Garfield Davies, CBE, *b.* 1935, *m.*
1997   *Davies of Oldham,* Bryan Davies, *b.* 1939, *m.*
1993   *Dean of Harptree,* (Arthur) Paul Dean, PC, *b.* 1924, *m.*
1998   *Dearing,* Ronald Ernest Dearing, *b.* 1930, *m.*
1986   *Deedes,* William Francis Deedes, KBE, MC, PC, *b.* 1913, *m.*
1991   *Desai,* Prof. Meghnad Jagdishchandra Desai, Ph.D., *b.* 1940, *m.*
1997   *Dholakia,* Navnit Dholakia, OBE, *b.* 1937, *m.*
1970   *Diamond,* John Diamond, PC, *b.* 1907, *m.*
1997   *Dixon,* Donald Dixon, PC, *b.* 1929, *m.*
1993   *Dixon-Smith,* Robert William Dixon-Smith, *b.* 1934, *m.*
1988   *Donaldson of Lymington,* John Francis Donaldson, PC, *b.* 1920, *m.*
1985   *Donoughue,* Bernard Donoughue, D.Phil., *b.* 1934
1987   *Dormand of Easington,* John Donkin Dormand, *b.* 1919, *m.*
1994   *Dubs,* Alfred Dubs, *b.* 1932, *m.*
1995   *Eames,* Robert Henry Alexander Eames, Ph.D., *b.* 1937, *m.*
1992   *Eatwell,* John Leonard Eatwell, Ph.D., *b.* 1945, *m.*
1983   *Eden of Winton,* John Benedict Eden, PC, *b.* 1925, *m.*
1999   *Elder,* Thomas Murray Elder, *b.* 1950
1992   *Elis-Thomas,* Dafydd Elis Elis-Thomas, *b.* 1946, *m.*
1985   *Elliott of Morpeth,* Robert William Elliott, *b.* 1920, *m.*
1981   *Elystan-Morgan,* Dafydd Elystan Elystan-Morgan, *b.* 1932, *m.*
2000   **Erskine of Alloa Tower,* Earl of Mar and Kellie, *b.* 1949, *m.* (*see* Hereditary Peers)
1997   *Evans of Parkside,* John Evans, *b.* 1930, *m.*

2000   *Evans of Temple Guiting*, Matthew Evans, CBE, b. 1941, m.

1998   *Evans of Watford*, David Charles Evans, b. 1942, m.

1992   *Ewing of Kirkford*, Harry Ewing, b. 1931, m.

1983   *Ezra*, Derek Ezra, MBE, b. 1919, m.

1997   *Falconer of Thoroton*, Charles Leslie Falconer, QC, b. 1951, m.

1999   *Faulkner of Worcester*, Richard Oliver Faulkner, b. 1946, m.

2001   *Fearn*, Ronald Cyril Fearn, OBE, b. 1931, m.

1996   *Feldman*, Basil Feldman, b. 1926, m.

1999   *Fellowes*, Robert Fellowes, GCB, GCVO, PC, b. 1941, m.

1999   *Filkin*, David Geoffrey Nigel Filkin, CBE, b. 1944

1983   *Fitt*, Gerard Fitt, b. 1926, w.

1979   *Flowers*, Brian Hilton Flowers, FRS, b. 1924, m.

1999   *Forsyth of Drumlean*, Michael Bruce Forsyth, b. 1954, m.

1982   *Forte*, Charles Forte, b. 1908, m.

1999   *Foster of Thames Bank*, Norman Robert Foster, OM, b. 1935, m.

2001   *Fowler*, (Peter) Norman Fowler, PC, b. 1938, m.

1989   *Fraser of Carmyllie*, Peter Lovat Fraser, PC, QC, b. 1945, m.

1997   *Freeman*, Roger Norman Freeman, PC, b. 1942, m.

2000   *Fyfe of Fairfield*, George Lennox Fyfe, b. 1941, m.

1982   *Gallacher*, John Gallacher, b. 1920, m.

1999   *Ganzoni*, Lord Belstead, PC, b. 1932, (see Hereditary Peers)

1997   *Garel-Jones*, (William Armand) Thomas Tristan Garel-Jones, PC, b. 1941, m.

1999   *Gascoyne-Cecil*, The Marquess of Salisbury, PC, b. 1946, m. (see Hereditary Peers)

1999   *Gavron*, Robert Gavron, CBE, b. 1930, m.

1992   *Geraint*, Geraint Wyn Howells, b. 1925, m.

1975   *Gibson*, (Richard) Patrick (Tallentyre) Gibson, b. 1916, m.

1997   *Gilbert*, John William Gilbert, PC, Ph.D., b. 1927, m.

1992   *Gilmour of Craigmillar*, Ian Hedworth John Little Gilmour, PC, b. 1926, m.

1977   *Glenamara*, Edward Watson Short, CH, PC, b. 1912, m.

1999   *Goldsmith*, Peter Henry Goldsmith, QC, b. 1950, m.

1997   *Goodhart*, William Howard Goodhart, QC, b. 1933, m.

1997   *Gordon of Strathblane*, James Stuart Gordon, CBE, b. 1936, m.

1999   *Grabiner*, Anthony Stephen Grabiner, QC, b. 1945, m.

1983   *Graham of Edmonton*, (Thomas) Edward Graham, b. 1925, m.

1983   *Gray of Contin*, James (Hamish) Hector Northey Gray, PC, b. 1927, m.

2000   *Greaves*, Anthony Robert Greaves, b. 1942, m.

1974   *Greene of Harrow Weald*, Sidney Francis Greene, CBE, b. 1910, m.

1975   *Gregson*, John Gregson, b. 1924

2000   *Grenfell of Kilvey*, Lord Grenfell, b. 1935, m. (see Hereditary Peers)

1991   *Griffiths of Fforestfach*, Brian Griffiths, b. 1941, m.

2001   *Grocott*, Bruce Joseph Grocott, PC, b. 1940, m.

2000   *Gueterbock*, Lord Berkley, OBE, b. 1939, m. (see Hereditary Peers)

2001   *Guthrie of Craigiebank*, Charles Ronald Llewelyn Guthrie, GCB, LVO, OBE, b. 1938, m.

1995   *Habgood*, Rt. Revd John Stapylton Habgood, PC, Ph.D., b. 1927, m.

2001   *Hannay of Chiswick*, David Hugh Alexander Hannay, GCMG, CH, b. 1935, m.

1998   *Hanningfield*, Paul Edward Winston White, b. 1940

1983   *Hanson*, James Edward Hanson, b. 1922, m.

1997   *Hardie*, Andrew Rutherford Hardie, QC, PC, b. 1946, m.

1997   *Hardy of Wath*, Peter Hardy, b. 1931, m.

1998   *Harris of Haringey*, (Jonathan) Toby Harris, b. 1953, m.

1979   *Harris of High Cross*, Ralph Harris, b. 1924, m.

1996   *Harris of Peckham*, Philip Charles Harris, b. 1942, m.

1999   *Harrison*, Lyndon Henry Arthur Harrison, b. 1947, m.

1993   *Haskel*, Simon Haskel, b. 1934, m.

1998   *Haskins*, Christopher Robin Haskins, b. 1937, m.

1997   *Hattersley*, Roy Sidney George Hattersley, PC, b. 1932, m.

1992   *Hayhoe*, Bernard John (Barney) Hayhoe, PC, b. 1925, m.

1992   *Healey*, Denis Winston Healey, CH, MBE, PC, b. 1917, m.

1999   *Hennessey*, Lord Windlesham, CVO, b. 1932, m. (see Hereditary Peers)

2001   *Heseltine*, Michael Ray Dibdin Heseltine, CH, PC, b. 1933, m.

1997   *Higgins*, Terence Langley Higgins, KBE, PC, b. 1928, m.

1979   *Hill-Norton*, Peter John Hill-Norton, GCB, b. 1915, m.

2000   *Hodgson of Astley Abbotts*, Robin Granville Hodgson, CBE, b. 1942, m.

1997   *Hogg of Cumbernauld*, Norman Hogg, b. 1938, m.

1991   *Hollick*, Clive Richard Hollick, b. 1945, m.

1990   *Holme of Cheltenham*, Richard Gordon Holme, CBE, b. 1936, m.

1979   *Hooson*, (Hugh) Emlyn Hooson, QC, b. 1925, m.

1996   *Hope of Craighead*, (James Arthur) David Hope, PC, b. 1938, m. Lord of Appeal in Ordinary

1992   *Howe of Aberavon*, (Richard Edward) Geoffrey Howe, CH, PC, QC, b. 1926, m.

1997   *Howell of Guildford*, David Arthur Russell Howell, PC, b. 1936, m.

1978   *Howie of Troon*, William Howie, b. 1924, m.

1997   *Hoyle*, (Eric) Douglas Harvey Hoyle, b. 1930, w.

1997   *Hughes of Woodside*, Robert Hughes, b. 1932, m.

2000   *Hunt of Chesterton*, Julian Charles Roland Hunt, CBE, b. 1941, m.

1997   *Hunt of Kings Heath*, Philip Alexander Hunt, OBE, b. 1949, m.

1980   *Hunt of Tanworth*, John Joseph Benedict Hunt, GCB, b. 1919, m.

1997   *Hunt of Wirral*, David James Fletcher Hunt, MBE, PC, b. 1942, m.

1997   *Hurd of Westwell*, Douglas Richard Hurd, CH, CBE, PC, b. 1930, m.

1996   *Hussey of North Bradley*, Marmaduke James Hussey, b. 1923, m.

1978   *Hutchinson of Lullington*, Jeremy Nicolas Hutchinson, QC, b. 1915, m.

1999   *Imbert*, Peter Michael Imbert, QPM, b. 1933, m.

1997   *Inge*, Peter Anthony Inge, KG, GCB, b. 1935, m.

1987   *Irvine of Lairg*, Alexander Andrew Mackay Irvine, PC, QC, b. 1940, m.

1997   *Islwyn*, Royston John (Roy) Hughes, b. 1925, m.

1997   *Jacobs*, (David) Anthony Jacobs, b. 1931, m.

1997   *Janner of Braunstone*, Greville Ewan Janner, QC,
b. 1928, w.

1999   **Jellicoe of Southampton*, Earl Jellicoe, KBE,
b. 1918, w. (see Hereditary Peers)

1987   *Jenkin of Roding*, (Charles) Patrick (Fleeming)
Jenkin, PC, b. 1926, m.

1981   *Jenkins of Putney*, Hugh Gater Jenkins,
b. 1908, w.

2000   *Joffe*, Joel Goodman Joffe, CBE, b. 1932, m.

2001   *Jones*, (Stephen) Barry Jones, b. 1937, m.

1997   *Jopling*, (Thomas) Michael Jopling, PC,
b. 1930, m.

2000   *Jordan*, William Brian Jordan, CBE, b. 1936, m.

1991   *Judd*, Frank Ashcroft Judd, b. 1935, m.

1980   *Keith of Castleacre*, Kenneth Alexander Keith,
b. 1916, w.

1997   *Kelvedon*, (Henry) Paul Guinness Channon, PC,
b. 1935, m.

2001   *Kilclooney*, John David Taylor, PC, b. 1937, m.

1996   *Kilpatrick of Kincraig*, Robert Kilpatrick, CBE,
b. 1926, m.

1985   *Kimball*, Marcus Richard Kimball, b. 1928, m.

2001   *King of Bridgwater*, Thomas Jeremy King, CH,
PC, b. 1933, m.

1983   *King of Wartnaby*, John Leonard King,
b. 1918, m.

1999   *King of West Bromwich*, Tarsem King, b. 1937

1993   *Kingsdown*, Robert (Robin) Leigh-Pemberton,
KG, PC, b. 1927, m.

1994   *Kingsland*, Christopher James Prout, TD, PC,
QC, b. 1942

1999   *Kirkham*, Graham Kirkham, b. 1944, m.

1975   *Kirkhill*, John Farquharson Smith, b. 1930, m.

1987   *Knights*, Philip Douglas Knights, CBE, QPM,
b. 1920, m.

1991   *Laing of Dunphail*, Hector Laing, b. 1923, m.

1999   *Laird*, John Dunn Laird, b. 1944, m.

1998   *Laming*, (William) Herbert Laming, CBE,
b. 1936, m.

1998   *Lamont of Lerwick*, Norman Stewart Hughson
Lamont, PC, b. 1942, m.

1990   *Lane of Horsell*, Peter Stewart Lane, b. 1925, w.

1997   *Lang of Monkton*, Ian Bruce Lang, PC,
b. 1940, m.

1992   *Lawson of Blaby*, Nigel Lawson, PC,
b. 1932, m.

2000   *Layard*, Peter Richard Grenville Layard,
b. 1934, m.

1999   *Lea of Crondall*, David Edward Lea, OBE,
b. 1937

1993   *Lester of Herne Hill*, Anthony Paul Lester, QC,
b. 1936, m.

1997   *Levene of Portsoken*, Peter Keith Levene, KBE,
b. 1941, m.

1997   *Levy*, Michael Abraham Levy, b. 1944, m.

1989   *Lewis of Newnham*, Jack Lewis, FRS, b. 1928, m.

1999   *Lipsey*, David Lawrence Lipsey, b. 1948, m.

2001   *Livsey of Talgarth*, Richard Arthur Lloyd Livsey,
CBE, b. 1935, m.

1997   *Lloyd-Webber*, Andrew Lloyd Webber,
b. 1948, m.

1997   *Lofthouse of Pontefract*, Geoffrey Lofthouse,
b. 1925, w.

2000   *Luce*, Richard Napier Luce, GCVO, PC,
b. 1936, m.

2000   **Lyttleton of Aldershot*, The Viscount Chandos,
b. 1953, m. (see Hereditary Peers)

1984   *McAlpine of West Green*, (Robert) Alistair
McAlpine, b. 1942, m.

1988   *Macaulay of Bragar*, Donald Macaulay, QC,
b. 1933, m.

1975   *McCarthy*, William Edward John McCarthy,
D.Phil., b. 1925, m.

1976   *McCluskey*, John Herbert McCluskey,
b. 1929, m.

1989   *McColl of Dulwich*, Ian McColl, CBE, FRCS,
FRCSE, b. 1933, m.

1998   *Macdonald of Tradeston*, Angus John
Macdonald, CBE, b. 1940, m.

1991   *Macfarlane of Bearsden*, Norman Somerville
Macfarlane, KT, FRSE, b. 1926, m.

2002   *MacGregor of Pulham Market*, John Roddick
Russell MacGregor, CBE, PC, b. 1937, m.

1982   *McIntosh of Haringey*, Andrew Robert
McIntosh, b. 1933, m.

1979   *Mackay of Clashfern*, James Peter Hymers
Mackay, KT, PC, FRSE, b. 1927, m.

1995   *Mackay of Drumadoon*, Donald Sage Mackay,
PC, b. 1946, m.

1999   *Mackenzie of Culkein*, Hector Uisdean
MacKenzie, b. 1940

1998   *Mackenzie of Framwellgate*, Brian Mackenzie,
OBE, b. 1943, m.

1974   *Mackie of Benshie*, George Yull Mackie, CBE,
DSO, DFC, b. 1919, m.

1996   *MacLaurin of Knebworth*, Ian Charter
MacLaurin, b. 1937, m.

2001   *Maclennon of Rogart*, Robert Adam Ross
Maclennan, PC, b. 1936, m.

1995   *McNally*, Tom McNally, b. 1943, m.

2001   *Maginnis of Drumglass*, Kenneth Wiggins
Maginnis, b. 1938, m.

1991   *Marlesford*, Mark Shuldham Schreiber,
b. 1931, m.

1981   *Marsh*, Richard William Marsh, PC, b. 1928, m.

1998   *Marshall of Knightsbridge*, Colin Marsh
Marshall, b. 1933, m.

1987   *Mason of Barnsley*, Roy Mason, PC, b. 1924, m.

2001   *May of Oxford*, Robert McCredie May, OM,
b. 1936, m.

1997   *Mayhew of Twysden*, Patrick Barnabas Burke
Mayhew, QC, PC, b. 1929, m.

1992   *Merlyn-Rees*, Merlyn Merlyn-Rees, PC,
b. 1920, m.

1978   *Mishcon*, Victor Mishcon, QC, b. 1915, m.

2000   *Mitchell*, Parry Andrew Mitchell, b. 1943

2000   **Mitford*, Lord Redesdale, b. 1967, m.
(see Hereditary Peers)

1997   *Molyneaux of Killead*, James Henry Molyneaux,
KBE, PC, b. 1920

1997   *Monro of Langholm*, Hector Seymour Peter
Monro, AE, PC, b. 1922, m.

1992   *Moore of Lower Marsh*, John Edward Michael
Moore, PC, b. 1937, m.

1986   *Moore of Wolvercote*, Philip Brian Cecil Moore,
GCB, GCVO, CMG, PC, b. 1921, m.

2000   *Morgan*, Kenneth Owen Morgan, b. 1934, m.

2001   *Morris of Aberavon*, John Morris, KG, QC,
b. 1931, m.

1997   *Morris of Manchester*, Alfred Morris, PC,
b. 1928, m.

2001   *Moser*, Claus Adolf Moser, KCB, CBE,
b. 1922, m.

1985   *Murray of Epping Forest*, Lionel Murray, OBE,
PC, b. 1922, m.

1979   *Murton of Lindisfarne*, (Henry) Oscar Murton,
OBE, TD, PC, b. 1914, m.

1997   *Naseby*, Michael Wolfgang Laurence Morris, PC,
b. 1936, m.

1997   *Neill of Bladen*, (Francis) Patrick Neill, QC,
b. 1926, m.

1997   *Newby*, Richard Mark Newby, OBE, b. 1953, m.

1997   *Newton of Braintree*, Antony Harold Newton,
OBE, PC, b. 1937, m.

1994   *Nickson*, David Wigley Nickson, KBE, FRSE,
b. 1929, m.

1975	*Northfield,* (William) Donald Chapman, *b.* 1923
1998	*Norton of Louth,* Philip Norton, *b.* 1951
2000	*Oakeshott of Seagrove Bay,* Matthew Alan Oakeshott, *b.* 1947, *m.*
1997	*Orme,* Stanley Orme, PC, *b.* 1923, *m.*
2001	*Ouseley,* Herman George Ouseley, *b.* 1945, *m.*
1992	*Owen,* David Anthony Llewellyn Owen, CH, PC, *b.* 1938, *m.*
1999	*Oxburgh,* Ernest Ronald Oxburgh, KBE, FRS, Ph.D., *b.* 1934, *m.*
1991	*Palumbo,* Peter Garth Palumbo, *b.* 1935, *m.*
2000	*Parekh,* Bhikhu Chhotalal Parekh, *b.* 1935, *m.*
1992	*Parkinson,* Cecil Edward Parkinson, PC, *b.* 1931, *m.*
1975	*Parry,* Gordon Samuel David Parry, *b.* 1925, *m.*
1999	*Patel,* Narendra Babubhai Patel, *b.* 1938
2000	*Patel of Blackburn,* Adam Hafejee Patel, *b.* 1940
1997	*Patten,* John Haggitt Charles Patten, PC, *b.* 1945, *m.*
1996	*Paul,* Swraj Paul, *b.* 1931, *m.*
1990	*Pearson of Rannoch,* Malcolm Everard MacLaren Pearson, *b.* 1942, *m.*
2001	*Pendry,* Thomas Pendry, *b.* 1934, *m.*
1987	*Peston,* Maurice Harry Peston, *b.* 1931, *m.*
1983	*Peyton of Yeovil,* John Wynne William Peyton, PC, *b.* 1919, *m.*
1998	*Phillips of Sudbury,* Andrew Wyndham Phillips, OBE, *b.* 1939, *m.*
1996	*Pilkington of Oxenford,* Revd Canon Peter Pilkington, *b.* 1933, *w.*
1992	*Plant of Highfield,* Prof. Raymond Plant, Ph.D., *b.* 1945, *m.*
1987	*Plumb,* (Charles) Henry Plumb, *b.* 1925, *m.*
1981	*Plummer of St Marylebone,* (Arthur) Desmond (Herne) Plummer, TD, *b.* 1914, *m.*
2000	**Ponsonby of Roehampton,* Lord Ponsonby of Shulbrede, *b.* 1958 (*see* Hereditary Peers)
2000	*Powell of Bayswater,* Charles David Powell, KCMG, *b.* 1941
1987	*Prior,* James Michael Leathes Prior, PC, *b.* 1927, *m.*
1982	*Prys-Davies,* Gwilym Prys Prys-Davies, *b.* 1923, *m.*
1997	*Puttnam,* David Terence Puttnam, CBE, *b.* 1941, *m.*
1987	*Pym,* Francis Leslie Pym, MC, PC, *b.* 1922, *m.*
1982	*Quinton,* Anthony Meredith Quinton, FBA, *b.* 1925, *m.*
1994	*Quirk,* Prof. (Charles) Randolph Quirk, CBE, FBA, *b.* 1920, *m.*
2001	*Radice,* Giles Heneage Radice, PC, *b.* 1936
1997	*Randall of St Budeaux,* Stuart Jeffrey Randall, *b.* 1938
1978	*Rawlinson of Ewell,* Peter Anthony Grayson Rawlinson, PC, QC, *b.* 1919, *m.*
1976	*Rayne,* Max Rayne, *b.* 1918, *m.*
1997	*Razzall,* (Edward) Timothy Razzall, CBE, *b.* 1943, *m.*
1987	*Rees,* Peter Wynford Innes Rees, PC, QC, *b.* 1926, *m.*
1988	*Rees-Mogg,* William Rees-Mogg, *b.* 1928, *m.*
1991	*Renfrew of Kaimsthorn,* (Andrew) Colin Renfrew, FBA, *b.* 1937, *m.*
1999	*Rennard,* Christopher John Rennard, MBE, *b.* 1960
1979	*Renton,* David Lockhart-Mure Renton, KBE, TD, PC, QC, *b.* 1908, *w.*
1997	*Renton of Mount Harry,* (Ronald) Timothy Renton, PC, *b.* 1932, *m.*
1997	*Renwick of Clifton,* Robin William Renwick, KCMG, *b.* 1937, *m.*
1990	*Richard,* Ivor Seward Richard, PC, QC, *b.* 1932, *m.*
1979	*Richardson,* John Samuel Richardson, LVO, MD, FRCP, *b.* 1910, *w.*
1983	*Richardson of Duntisbourne,* Gordon William Humphreys Richardson, KG, MBE, TD, PC, *b.* 1915, *m.*
1992	*Rix,* Brian Norman Roger Rix, CBE, *b.* 1924, *m.*
1997	*Roberts of Conwy,* (Ieuan) Wyn (Pritchard) Roberts, PC, *b.* 1930, *m.*
1999	*Robertson of Port Ellen,* George Islay MacNeill Robertson, PC, *b.* 1946, *m.*
1992	*Rodger of Earlsferry,* Alan Ferguson Rodger, PC, QC, FBA, *b.* 1944, *Lord of Appeal in Ordinary*
1992	*Rodgers of Quarry Bank,* William Thomas Rodgers, PC, *b.* 1928, *m.*
1999	*Rogan,* Dennis Robert David Rogan, *b.* 1942, *m.*
1996	*Rogers of Riverside,* Richard George Rogers, RA, RIBA, *b.* 1933, *m.*
1977	*Roll of Ipsden,* Eric Roll, KCMG, CB, *b.* 1907, *w.*
2001	*Rooker,* Jeffrey William Rooker, PC, *b.* 1941, *m.*
2000	*Roper,* John Francis Hodgess Roper, *b.* 1935, *m.*
1997	*Russell-Johnston,* (David) Russell Russell-Johnston, *b.* 1932, *m.*
1997	*Ryder of Wensum,* Richard Andrew Ryder, OBE, PC, *b.* 1949, *m.*
1996	*Saatchi,* Maurice Saatchi, *b.* 1946, *m.*
1989	*Sainsbury of Preston Candover,* John Davan Sainsbury, KG, *b.* 1927, *m.*
1997	*Sainsbury of Turville,* David John Sainsbury, *b.* 1940, *m.*
1987	*St John of Fawsley,* Norman Antony Francis St John-Stevas, PC, *b.* 1929
1997	*Sandberg,* Michael Graham Ruddock Sandberg, CBE, *b.* 1927, *m.*
1985	*Sanderson of Bowden,* Charles Russell Sanderson, *b.* 1933, *m.*
1998	*Sawyer,* Lawrence (Tom) Sawyer, *b.* 1943
1979	*Scanlon,* Hugh Parr Scanlon, *b.* 1913, *m.*
2000	*Scott of Foscote,* Richard Rashleigh Folliott Scott, PC, *b.* 1934, *m. Lord of Appeal in Ordinary*
1997	*Selkirk of Douglas,* James Alexander Douglas-Hamilton, MSP, PC, QC, *b.* 1942, *m.*
1996	*Sewel,* John Buttifant Sewel, CBE, *b.* 1946
1999	*Sharman,* Colin Morven Sharman, OBE, *b.* 1943, *m.*
1994	*Shaw of Northstead,* Michael Norman Shaw, *b.* 1920, *m.*
2001	*Sheldon,* Robert Edward Sheldon, PC, *b.* 1923, *m.*
1994	*Sheppard of Didgemere,* Allan John George Sheppard, KCVO, *b.* 1932, *m.*
1998	*Sheppard of Liverpool,* David Stuart Sheppard, *b.* 1929, *m.*
2000	*Shutt of Greetland,* David Trevor Shutt, OBE, *b.* 1942
1971	*Simon of Glaisdale,* Jocelyn Edward Salis Simon, PC, *b.* 1911, *m.*
1997	*Simon of Highbury,* David Alec Gwyn Simon, CBE, *b.* 1939, *m.*
1997	*Simpson of Dunkeld,* George Simpson, *b.* 1942, *m.*
1991	*Skidelsky,* Robert Jacob Alexander Skidelsky, D.Phil., *b.* 1939, *m.*
1997	*Smith of Clifton,* Trevor Arthur Smith, *b.* 1937, *m.*
1999	*Smith of Leigh,* Peter Richard Charles Smith, *b.* 1945, *m.*
1990	*Soulsby of Swaffham Prior,* Ernest Jackson Lawson Soulsby, Ph.D., *b.* 1926, *m.*

1983	*Stallard,* Albert William Stallard, *b.* 1921, *m.*
1997	*Steel of Aikwood,* David Martin Scott Steel, PC, KBE, MSP, *b.* 1938, *m.*
1991	*Sterling of Plaistow,* Jeffrey Maurice Sterling, GCVO, CBE, *b.* 1934, *m.*
1987	*Stevens of Ludgate,* David Robert Stevens, *b.* 1936, *m.*
1999	*Stevenson of Coddenham,* Henry Dennistoun Stevenson, CBE, *b.* 1945, *m.*
1992	*Stewartby,* (Bernard Harold) Ian (Halley) Stewart, RD, PC, FBA, FRSE, *b.* 1935, *m.*
1983	*Stoddart of Swindon,* David Leonard Stoddart, *b.* 1926, *m.*
1969	*Stokes,* Donald Gresham Stokes, TD, FEng., *b.* 1914, *w.*
1997	*Stone of Blackheath,* Andrew Zelig Stone, *b.* 1942, *m.*
2001	*Sutherland of Houndwood,* Stewart Ross Sutherland, KT, *b.* 1941, *m.*
1971	*Tanlaw,* Simon Brooke Mackay, *b.* 1934, *m.*
1996	*Taverne,* Dick Taverne, QC, *b.* 1928, *m.*
1978	*Taylor of Blackburn,* Thomas Taylor, CBE, *b.* 1929, *m.*
1996	*Taylor of Warwick,* John David Beckett Taylor, *b.* 1952, *m.*
1992	*Tebbit,* Norman Beresford Tebbit, CH, PC, *b.* 1931, *m.*
2001	*Temple-Morris,* Peter Temple-Morris, *b.* 1938, *m.*
1996	*Thomas of Gresford,* Donald Martin Thomas, OBE, QC, *b.* 1937, *m.*
1987	*Thomas of Gwydir,* Peter John Mitchell Thomas, PC, QC, *b.* 1920, *w.*
1997	*Thomas of Macclesfield,* Terence James Thomas, CBE, *b.* 1937, *m.*
1981	*Thomas of Swynnerton,* Hugh Swynnerton Thomas, *b.* 1931, *m.*
1977	*Thomson of Monifieth,* George Morgan Thomson, KT, PC, *b.* 1921, *m.*
1990	*Tombs,* Francis Leonard Tombs, FEng., *b.* 1924, *m.*
1998	*Tomlinson,* John Edward Tomlinson, MEP, *b.* 1939
1994	*Tope,* Graham Norman Tope, CBE, *b.* 1943, *m.*
1981	*Tordoff,* Geoffrey Johnson Tordoff, *b.* 1928, *m.*
1999	*Trotman,* Alexander Trotman, *b.* 1933
1993	*Tugendhat,* Christopher Samuel Tugendhat, *b.* 1937, *m.*
2000	*Turnberg,* Leslie Arnold Turnberg, Kt, MD, *b.* 1934, *m.*
1990	*Varley,* Eric Graham Varley, PC, *b.* 1932, *m.*
1996	*Vincent of Coleshill,* Richard Frederick Vincent, GBE, KCB, DSO, *b.* 1931, *m.*
1985	*Vinson,* Nigel Vinson, LVO, *b.* 1931, *m.*
1990	*Waddington,* David Charles Waddington, GCVO, PC, QC, *b.* 1929, *m.*
1990	*Wade of Chorlton,* (William) Oulton Wade, *b.* 1932, *m.*
1992	*Wakeham,* John Wakeham, PC, *b.* 1932, *m.*
1999	*Waldegrave of North Hill,* William Arthur Waldegrave, PC, *b.* 1946, *m.*
1997	*Walker of Doncaster,* Harold Walker, PC, *b.* 1927, *m.*
2003	*Walker of Gestingthorpe,* Robert Walker, PC, *b.* 1938, *m. Lord of Appeal in Ordinary*
1992	*Walker of Worcester,* Peter Edward Walker, MBE, PC, *b.* 1932, *m.*
1974	*Wallace of Coslany,* George Douglas Wallace, *b.* 1906, *m.*
1995	*Wallace of Saltaire,* William John Lawrence Wallace, Ph.D., *b.* 1941, *m.*
1989	*Walton of Detchant,* John Nicholas Walton, TD, FRCP, *b.* 1922, *m.*
1998	*Warner,* Norman Reginald Warner, *b.* 1940, *m.*

1997	*Watson of Invergowrie,* Michael Goodall Watson, MSP, *b.* 1949, *m.*
1999	*Watson of Richmond,* Alan John Watson, CBE, *b.* 1941, *m.*
1992	*Weatherill,* (Bruce) Bernard Weatherill, PC, *b.* 1920, *m.*
1977	*Wedderburn of Charlton,* (Kenneth) William Wedderburn, FBA, QC, *b.* 1927, *m.*
1976	*Weidenfeld,* (Arthur) George Weidenfeld, *b.* 1919, *m.*
1978	*Whaddon,* (John) Derek Page, *b.* 1927, *m.*
1996	*Whitty,* John Lawrence (Larry) Whitty, *b.* 1943, *m.*
1974	*Wigoder,* Basil Thomas Wigoder, QC, *b.* 1921, *m.*
1985	*Williams of Elvel,* Charles Cuthbert Powell Williams, CBE, *b.* 1933, *m.*
1999	*Williamson of Horton,* David (Francis) Williamson, GCMG, CB, *b.* 1934, *m.*
2002	*Wilson of Dinton,* Richard Thomas James Wilson, GCB, *b.* 1942, *m.*
1992	*Wilson of Tillyorn,* David Clive Wilson, KT, GCMG, Ph.D, *b.* 1935, *m.*
1995	*Winston,* Robert Maurice Lipson Winston, FRCOG, *b.* 1940, *m.*
1985	*Wolfson,* Leonard Gordon Wolfson, *b.* 1927, *m.*
1991	*Wolfson of Sunningdale,* David Wolfson, *b.* 1935, *m.*
1999	*Woolmer of Leeds,* Kenneth John Woolmer, *b.* 1940, *m.*
1994	*Wright of Richmond,* Patrick Richard Henry Wright, GCMG, *b.* 1931, *m.*
1984	*Young of Graffham,* David Ivor Young, PC, *b.* 1932, *m.*

BARONESSES
Created

1997	*Amos,* Valerie Ann Amos, *b.* 1954
2000	*Andrews,* Elizabeth Kay Andrews, OBE, *b.* 1943, *m.*
1996	*Anelay of St Johns,* Joyce Anne Anelay, DBE, *b.* 1947, *m.*
1999	*Ashton of Upholland,* Catherine Margaret Ashton, *b.* 1956, *m.*
1999	*Barker,* Elizabeth Jean Barker, *b.* 1961
2000	*Billingham,* Angela Theodora Billingham, D.Phil., *b.* 1921, *w.*
1987	*Blackstone,* Tessa Ann Vosper Blackstone, Ph.D., *b.* 1942
1987	*Blatch,* Emily May Blatch, CBE, PC, *b.* 1937, *m.*
1999	*Blood,* May Blood, MBE, *b.* 1938
2001	*Boothroyd,* Betty Boothroyd, PC, *b.* 1929
1990	*Brigstocke,* Heather Renwick Brigstocke, *b.* 1929, *m.*
1998	*Buscombe,* Peta Jane Buscombe, *b.* 1954, *m.*
1996	*Byford,* Hazel Byford, DBE, *b.* 1941, *m.*
1982	*Carnegy of Lour,* Elizabeth Patricia Carnegy of Lour, *b.* 1925
1992	*Chalker of Wallasey,* Lynda Chalker, PC, *b.* 1942, *m.*
2000	*Cohen of Pimlico,* Janet Cohen, *b.* 1940, *m.*
1982	*Cox,* Caroline Anne Cox, *b.* 1937, *m.*
1998	*Crawley,* Christine Mary Crawley, MEP, *b.* 1950, *m.*
1990	*Cumberlege,* Julia Frances Cumberlege, CBE, *b.* 1943, *m.*
1978	*David,* Nora Ratcliff David, *b.* 1913, *w.*
1993	*Dean of Thornton-le-Fylde,* Brenda Dean, PC, *b.* 1943, *m.*
1974	*Delacourt-Smith of Alteryn,* Margaret Rosalind Delacourt-Smith, *b.* 1916, *m.*
1990	*Dunn,* Lydia Selina Dunn, DBE, *b.* 1940, *m.*

1990	*Eccles of Moulton,* Diana Catherine Eccles, *b.* 1933, *m.*
1972	*Elles,* Diana Louie Elles, *b.* 1921, *m.*
1997	*Emerton,* Audrey Caroline Emerton, DBE, *b.* 1935
1974	*Falkender,* Marcia Matilda Falkender, CBE, *b.* 1932
1994	*Farrington of Ribbleton,* Josephine Farrington, *b.* 1940, *m.*
2001	*Finlay of Llandaff,* Ilora Gillian Finlay, *b.* 1949, *m.*
1974	*Fisher of Rednal,* Doris Mary Gertrude Fisher, *b.* 1919, *w.*
1990	*Flather,* Shreela Flather, *m.*
1997	*Fookes,* Janet Evelyn Fookes, DBE, *b.* 1936
1999	*Gale,* Anita Gale, *b.* 1940
1981	*Gardner of Parkes,* (Rachel) Trixie (Anne) Gardner, *b.* 1927, *m.*
2000	*Gibson of Market Rasen,* Anne Gibson, OBE, *b.* 1940, *m.*
2001	*Golding,* Llinos Golding, *b.* 1933, *m.*
1998	*Goudie,* Mary Teresa Goudie, *b.* 1946, *m.*
1993	*Gould of Potternewton,* Joyce Brenda Gould, *b.* 1932, *m.*
2001	*Greenfield,* Susan Adele Greenfield, CBE, *b.* 1950, *m.*
2000	*Greengross,* Sally Ralea Greengross, OBE, *b.* 1935, *m.*
1991	*Hamwee,* Sally Rachel Hamwee, *b.* 1947
1999	*Hanham,* Joan Brownlow Hanham, CBE, *b.* 1939, *m.*
1999	*Harris of Richmond,* Angela Felicity Harris, *b.* 1944
1996	*Hayman,* Helene Valerie Hayman, PC, *b.* 1949, *m.*
1991	*Hilton of Eggardon,* Jennifer Hilton, QPM, *b.* 1936
1995	*Hogg,* Sarah Elizabeth Mary Hogg, *b.* 1946, *m.*
1990	*Hollis of Heigham,* Patricia Lesley Hollis, D.Phil., *b.* 1941, *m.*
1985	*Hooper,* Gloria Dorothy Hooper, CMG, *b.* 1939
2001	*Howarth of Breckland,* Valerie Georgina Howarth, OBE, *b.* 1940
2001	*Howe of Idlicote,* Elspeth Rosamond Morton Howe, CBE, *b.* 1932, *m.*
1999	*Howells of St Davids,* Rosalind Patricia-Anne Howells, *b.* 1931, *m.*
1991	*James of Holland Park,* Phyllis Dorothy White (P. D. James), OBE, *b.* 1920, *w.*
1992	*Jay of Paddington,* Margaret Ann Jay, PC, *b.* 1939, *m.*
1979	*Jeger,* Lena May Jeger, *b.* 1915, *w.*
1997	*Kennedy of the Shaws,* Helena Ann Kennedy, QC, *b.* 1950, *m.*
1997	*Knight of Collingtree,* (Joan Christabel) Jill Knight, DBE, *b.* 1927, *w.*
1997	*Linklater of Butterstone,* Veronica Linklater, *b.* 1943, *m.*
1996	*Lloyd of Highbury,* Prof. June Kathleen Lloyd, DBE, FRCP, FRCPE, FRCGP, *b.* 1928
1978	*Lockwood,* Betty Lockwood, *b.* 1924, *w.*
1997	*Ludford,* Sarah Ann Ludford, MEP, *b.* 1951
1979	*McFarlane of Llandaff,* Jean Kennedy McFarlane, *b.* 1926
1999	*McIntosh of Hudnall,* Genista Mary McIntosh, *b.* 1946
1997	*Maddock,* Diana Margaret Maddock, *b.* 1945, *m.*
1991	*Mallalieu,* Ann Mallalieu, QC, *b.* 1945, *m.*
1970	*Masham of Ilton,* Susan Lilian Primrose Cunliffe-Lister, *b.* 1935, *m.*
1999	*Massey of Darwen,* Doreen Elizabeth Massey, *b.* 1938, *m.*
2001	*Michie of Gallanach,* Janet Ray Michie, *b.* 1934, *m.*
1998	*Miller of Chilthorne Domer,* Susan Elizabeth Miller, *b.* 1954
1993	*Miller of Hendon,* Doreen Miller, MBE, *b.* 1933, *m.*
2001	*Morgan of Huyton,* Sally Morgan, *b.* 1959, *m.*
1997	*Nicholson of Winterbourne,* Emma Harriet Nicholson, MEP, *b.* 1941, *m.*
1982	*Nicol,* Olive Mary Wendy Nicol, *b.* 1923, *m.*
2000	*Noakes,* Shiela Valerie Masters, DBE, *b.* 1949, *m.*
2000	*Northover,* Lindsay Patricia Granshaw, *b.* 1954
1991	*O'Cathain,* Detta O'Cathain, OBE, *b.* 1938, *m.*
1999	*O'Neill of Bengarve,* Onora Sylvia O'Neill, CBE, Ph.D., *b.* 1941
1989	*Oppenheim-Barnes,* Sally Oppenheim-Barnes, PC, *b.* 1930, *m.*
1990	*Park of Monmouth,* Daphne Margaret Sybil Désirée Park, CMG, OBE, *b.* 1921
1991	*Perry of Southwark,* Pauline Perry, *b.* 1931, *m.*
1974	*Pike,* (Irene) Mervyn (Parnicott) Pike, DBE, *b.* 1918
1997	*Pitkeathley,* Jill Elizabeth Pitkeathley, OBE, *b.* 1940
1981	*Platt of Writtle,* Beryl Catherine Platt, CBE, FEng., *b.* 1923, *m.*
1999	*Prashar,* Usha Kumari Prashar, CBE, *b.* 1948, *m.*
1996	*Ramsay of Cartvale,* Margaret Mildred (Meta) Ramsay, *b.* 1936
1994	*Rawlings,* Patricia Elizabeth Rawlings, *b.* 1939
1997	*Rendell of Babergh,* Ruth Barbara Rendell, CBE, *b.* 1930, *m.*
1998	*Richardson of Calow,* Kathleen Margaret Richardson, OBE, *b.* 1938, *m.*
1997	*Scotland of Asthal,* Patricia Janet Scotland, QC, *b.* 1955, *m.*
2000	*Scott of Needham Market,* Rosalind Carol Scott, *b.* 1957
1991	*Seccombe,* Joan Anna Dalziel Seccombe, DBE, *b.* 1930, *m.*
1998	*Sharp of Guildford,* Margaret Lucy Sharp, *b.* 1938, *m.*
1973	*Sharples,* Pamela Sharples, *b.* 1923, *m.*
1995	*Smith of Gilmorehill,* Elizabeth Margaret Smith, *b.* 1940, *w.*
1999	*Stern,* Vivien Helen Stern, CBE, *b.* 1941
1996	*Symons of Vernham Dean,* Elizabeth Conway Symons, *b.* 1951
1992	*Thatcher,* Margaret Hilda Thatcher, KG, OM, PC, FRS, *b.* 1925, *w.*
1994	*Thomas of Walliswood,* Susan Petronella Thomas, OBE, *b.* 1935, *m.*
1998	*Thornton,* (Dorothea) Glenys Thornton, *b.* 1952, *m.*
1980	*Trumpington,* Jean Alys Barker, PC, *b.* 1922, *w.*
1985	*Turner of Camden,* Muriel Winifred Turner, *b.* 1927, *m.*
1998	*Uddin,* Manzila Pola Uddin, *b.* 1959, *m.*
2000	*Walmsley,* Joan Margaret Walmsley, *b.* 1943
1985	*Warnock,* Helen Mary Warnock, DBE, *b.* 1924, *w.*
1999	*Warwick of Undercliffe,* Diana Mary Warwick, *b.* 1945, *m.*
1999	*Whitaker,* Janet Alison Whitaker, *b.* 1936
1996	*Wilcox,* Judith Ann Wilcox, *b.* 1940, *w.*
1999	*Wilkins,* Rosalie Catherine Wilkins, *b.* 1946
1993	*Williams of Crosby,* Shirley Vivien Teresa Brittain Williams, PC, *b.* 1930, *m.*
1997	*Young of Old Scone,* Barbara Scott Young, *b.* 1948

LORDS SPIRITUAL

The Lords Spiritual are the Archbishops of Canterbury and York and 24 diocesan bishops of the Church of England. The Bishops of London, Durham and Winchester always have seats in the House of Lords; the other 21 seats are filled by the remaining diocesan bishops in order of seniority. The Bishop of Sodor and Man and the Bishop of Gibraltar are not eligible to sit in the House of Lords.

ARCHBISHOPS

Style, The Most Revd and Right Hon. the Lord Archbishop of _
Addressed as Archbishop, *or* Your Grace

Introduced to House of Lords

2003   *Canterbury* (104th), Rowan Douglas Williams, PC, D.Phil, *b.* 1950, *m., cons.* 1992, *elected* 2002
1990   *York* (96th), David Michael Hope, KCVO, PC, D.Phil, LLD, *b.* 1940, *cons.* 1985, *elected* 1985, *trans.* 1995

BISHOPS

Style, The Right Revd the Lord Bishop of _
Addressed as My Lord
elected date of confirmation as diocesan bishop

Introduced to House of Lords (as at 31 August 2003)

1996   *London* (132nd), Richard John Carew Chartres, *b.* 1947, *m., cons.* 1992, *elected* 1995
1994   *Durham* (71st), Nicholas Thomas Wright, D.Phil, *b.* 1948, *m., cons.* 2003, *elected* 2003
1996   *Winchester* (96th), Michael Charles Scott-Joynt, *b.* 1943, *m., cons.* 1987, *elected* 1995
1993   *Oxford* (41st), Richard Douglas Harries, *b.* 1936, *m., cons.* 1987, *elected* 1987
1997   *Southwark* (9th), Thomas Frederick Butler, *b.* 1940, *m., cons.* 1985, *elected* 1991, *trans* 1998
1997   *Manchester* (11th), Nigel Simeon McCulloch, *b.* 1942, *m., cons.* 1986, *elected* 2002, *trans* 2002
1998   *Salisbury* (77th), David Staffurth Stancliffe, *b.* 1942, *m., cons.* 1993, *elected* 1993
1998   *Gloucester* (39th), David Edward Bentley, *b.* 1935, *m., cons.* 1986, *elected* 1993
1999   *Rochester* (106th), Michael James Nazir-Ali, Ph.D., *b.* 1949, *m., cons.* 1984, *elected* 1994
1999   *Portsmouth* (8th), Kenneth William Stevenson, *b.* 1949, *m., cons.* 1995, *elected* 1995
1999   *Derby* (6th), Jonathan Sansbury Bailey, *b.* 1940, *m., cons.* 1992, *elected* 1995

1999   *St Albans* (9th), Christopher William Herbert, *b.* 1944, *m., cons.* 1995, *elected* 1995
2001   *Peterborough* (37th), Ian Cundy, *b.* 1945, *m., cons.* 1992, *elected* 1996
2001   *Chester* (40th), Peter Robert Forster, Ph.D., *b.* 1950, *cons.* 1996, *elected* 1996
2002   *St Edmundsbury and Ipswich* (9th), (John Hubert) Richard Lewis, *b.* 1943, *m., cons.* 1992, *elected* 1997
2002   *Truro* (14th), William Ind, *b.* 1942, *m., cons.* 1987, *elected* 1997
2002   *Worcester* (112th), Peter Stephen Maurice Selby, *b.* 1941, *cons.* 1984, *elected* 1997
2003   *Newcastle* (11th), (John) Martin Wharton, *b.* 1944, *m., cons.* 1992, *elected* 1997
2003   *Sheffield* (6th), John Nicholls, *b.* 1943, *m., cons.* 1990, *elected* 1997
2003   *Coventry* (8th), Colin J. Bennetts, *b.* 1940, *m., cons.* 1994, *elected* 1998
2003   *Liverpool* (7th), James Jones, *b.* 1948, *m., cons.* 1994, *elected* 1998
2003   *Leicester* (6th), Timothy John Stevens, *b.* 1946, *m., cons.* 1999, *elected* 1999
Awaiting introduction   *Southwell* (10th), George Henry Cassidy, *b.* 1942, *m., cons.* 1999, *elected* 1999
Awaiting introduction   *Norwich* (71st), Graham R. James, *b.* 1951, *m., cons.* 1993, *elected* 1999

BISHOPS AWAITING SEATS, in order of seniority *(as at 31 August 2003)*
Exeter (70th), Michael L. Langrish, *b.* 1946, *m., cons.* 1993, *elected* 2000
Ripon and Leeds (12th), John R. Packer, *b.* 1946, *m., cons.* 1996, *elected* 2000
Ely (68th) Dr. Anthony Russell, *b.* 1943, *m., cons.* 1988, *elected* 2000
Carlisle (65th) Graham Dow, *b.* 1942, *m., cons.* 1985, *elected* 2000
Chichester (102nd) John Hind, *b.* 1945, *cons.* 1991, *elected* 2000
Lincoln (71st) Dr John Saxbee, *b.* 1946, *cons.* 1994, *elected* 2001
Bath & Wells (77th) Peter Price, *b.* 1944, *m., cons.* 1997, *elected* 2002
Birmingham (8th) Dr John Tucker Mugabi Sentamu, Ph.D, *b.* 1949, *m., cons.* 1996, *elected* 2002
Bradford (9th) David James, *b.* 1945, *cons.* 1998, *elected* 2002
Bristol (55th) Michael A. Hill, *b.* 1949, *m., cons.* 1998, *elected* 2003
Wakefield (12th) Stephen G. Platten, *b.* 1947, *m., cons.* 2003, *elected* 2003
Lichfield (98th) Jonathan Gledhill, *b.* 1949, *m., cons.* 1996, *elected* 2003
Chelmsford (9th) John Warren Gladwin, *b.*1942, *m., cons.* 1994, *elected* 2003
Blackburn (8th) Nicholas Reade, *b.* 1946, *m. elected* 2003
Guildford (9th) vacant
Hereford (104th) vacant

COURTESY TITLES

From this list it will be seen that, for example, the Marquess of Blandford is heir to the Dukedom of Marlborough, and Viscount Amberley to the Earldom of Russell. Titles of second heirs are also given, and the courtesy title of the father of a second heir is indicated by * e.g. Earl of Burlington, eldest son of *Marquess of Hartington

For forms of address, *see* page 40

MARQUESSES
*Blandford – *Marlborough, D.*
Bowmont and Cessford – *Roxburghe, D.*
Douglas and Clydesdale – *Hamilton, D.*
*Douro – *Wellington, D.*
Graham – *Montrose, D.*
Hamilton – *Abercorn, D.*
*Hartington – *Devonshire, D.*
Kildare – *Leinster, D.*
Stafford – *Sutherland, D.*
Tullibardine – *Atholl, D.*
*Worcester – *Beaufort, D.*

EARLS
Aboyne – *Huntly, M.*
Ancram – *Lothian, M.*
Arundel and Surrey – *Norfolk, D.*
*Bective – *Headfort, M.*
*Belfast – *Donegall, M.*
Brecknock – *Camden, M.*
Burford – *St Albans, D.*
Burlington – *Hartington, M.*
*Cardigan – *Ailesbury, M.*
Compton – *Northampton, M.*
*Dalkeith – *Buccleuch, D.*
*Euston – *Grafton, D.*
Glamorgan – *Worcester, M.*
Grosvenor – *Westminster, D.*
Haddo – *Aberdeen and Temair, M.*
Hillsborough – *Downshire, M.*
Hopetoun – *Linlithgow, M.*
March and Kinrara – *Richmond, D.*
Medina – *Milford Haven, M.*
*Mount Charles – *Conyngham, M.*
Mornington – *Douro, M.*
Mulgrave – *Normanby, M.*
Percy – *Northumberland, D.*
Ronaldshay – *Zetland, M.*
*St Andrews – *Kent, D.*
Shelburne – *Lansdowne, M.*
*Southesk – *Fife, D.*
Sunderland – *Blandford, M.*
*Tyrone – *Waterford, M.*
Ulster – *Gloucester, D.*
*Uxbridge – *Anglesey, M.*
Wiltshire – *Winchester, M.*
Yarmouth – *Hertford, M.*

VISCOUNTS
Alexander – *Caledon, E.*
Althorp – *Spencer, E.*
Amberley – *Russell, E.*
Andover – *Suffolk and Berkshire, E.*
Anson – *Lichfield, E.*
Asquith – *Oxford and Asquith, E.*
Boringdon – *Morley, E.*
Borodale – *Beatty, E.*
Boyle – *Shannon, E.*
Brocas – *Jellicoe, E.*
Campden – *Gainsborough, E.*
Carlow – *Portarlington, E.*
Carlton – *Wharncliffe, E.*
Castlereagh – *Londonderry, M.*
Chelsea – *Cadogan, E.*
Chewton – *Waldegrave, E.*
Chichester – *Belfast, E.*
Clanfield – *Peel, E.*
Clive – *Powis, E.*
Coke – *Leicester, E.*
Corry – *Belmore, E.*
Corvedale – *Baldwin of Bewdley, E.*
Cranborne – *Salisbury, M.*
Cranley – *Onslow, E.*
Crichton – *Erne, E.*
Curzon – *Howe, E.*
Dangan – *Cowley, E.*
Dawick – *Haig, E.*
Drumlanrig – *Queensberry, M.*
Duncannon – *Bessborough, E.*
Dungarvan – *Cork and Orrery, E.*
Dunluce – *Antrim, E.*
Dunwich – *Stradbroke, E.*
Dupplin – *Kinnoull, E.*
Ednam – *Dudley, E.*
Emlyn – *Cawdor, E*
Encombe – *Eldon, E.*
Enfield – *Strafford, E.*
Erleigh – *Reading, M.*
Errington – *Cromer, E.*
FitzHarris – *Malmesbury, E.*
Folkestone – *Radnor, E.*
Forbes – *Granard, E.*
Garmoyle – *Cairns, E.*
Garnock – *Lindsay, E.*
Glenapp – *Inchcape, E.*
Glentworth – *Limerick, E.*
Grey de Wilton – *Wilton, E.*
Grimstone – *Verulam, E.*
Gwynedd – *Lloyd George of Dwyfor, E.*
Hawkesbury – *Liverpool, E.*
Hinchingbrooke – *Sandwich, E.*
Ikerrin – *Carrick, E.*
Ingestre – *Shrewsbury, E.*
Ipswich – *Euston, E.*
Jocelyn – *Roden, E.*
Kelburn – *Glasgow, E.*
Kilwarlin – *Hillsborough, E.*
Kingsborough – *Kingston, E.*
Kirkwall – *Orkney, E.*
Knebworth – *Lytton, E.*
Lascelles – *Harewood, E.*
Linley – *Snowdon, E.*
Loftus – *Ely, M.*
Lowther – *Lonsdale, E.*
Lumley – *Scarbrough, E.*
Lymington – *Portsmouth, E.*
Macmillan of Ovenden – *Stockton, E.*
Maidstone – *Winchilsea, E*
Maitland – *Lauderdale, E.*
Malden – *Essex, E.*
Mandeville – *Manchester, D.*
Melgund – *Minto, E.*
Merton – *Nelson, E.*
Moore – *Drogheda, E.*
Newport – *Bradford, E.*
Northland – *Ranfurly, E*
Newry and Mourne – *Kilmorey, E.*
Petersham – *Harrington, E.*
Pollington – *Mexborough, E*
Raynham – *Townshend, M.*
Reidhaven – *Seafield, E.*
Ruthven of Canberra – *Gowrie, E.*
St Cyres – *Iddesleigh, E.*
Sandon – *Harrowby, E.*
Savernake – *Cardigan, E.*
Slane – *Mount Charles, E.*
Somerton – *Normanton, E.*
Stopford – *Courtown, E.*
Stormont – *Mansfield, E.*
Strathallan – *Perth, E.*
Stuart – *Castle Stewart, E.*
Suirdale – *Donoughmore, E.*
Tamworth – *Ferrers, E.*
Tarbat – *Cromartie, E.*
Vaughan – *Lisburne, E.*
Weymouth – *Bath, M.*
Windsor – *Plymouth, E.*
Wolmer – *Selborne, E.*
Woodstock – *Portland, E.*

BARONS (LORDS)
Aberdour – *Morton, E.*
Apsley – *Bathurst, E.*
Ardee – *Meath, E.*
Ashley – *Shaftesbury, E.*
Balgonie – *Leven and Melville, E.*
Balniel – *Crawford and Balcarres, E.*
Berriedale – *Caithness, E.*
Bingham – *Lucan, E.*
Binning – *Haddington, E.*
Brooke – *Warwick, E.*
Bruce – *Elgin, E.*
Buckhurst – *De La Warr, E*
Burghley – *Exeter, M.*
Cardross – *Buchan, E.*
Carnegie – *Southesk, E.*
Clifton – *Darnley, E.*
Cochrane – *Dundonald, E.*
Courtenay – *Devon, E.*
Dalmeny – *Rosebery, E.*
Doune – *Moray, E.*
Downpatrick – *St Andrews, E.*
Dunglass – *Home, E.*
Eliot – *St Germans, E.*
Eskdail – *Dalkeith, E.*
Formartine – *Haddo, E.*
Gillford – *Clanwilliam, E.*
Glamis – *Strathmore, E.*
Greenock – *Cathcart, E.*
Guernsey – *Aylesford, E.*
Hay – *Erroll, E.*
Herbert – *Pembroke, E.*
Howard of Effingham – *Effingham, E.*
Hyde – *Clarendon, E.*
Inverurie – *Kintore, E.*
Irwin – *Halifax, E.*
Johnstone – *Annandale and Hartfell, E.*
Kenlis – *Bective, E.*
Langton – *Temple of Stowe, E.*
La Poer – *Tyrone, E.*
Leslie – *Rothes, E.*
Leveson – *Granville, E*
Loughborough – *Rosslyn, E.*
Mauchline – *Loudoun, C.*
Medway – *Cranbrook, E.*
Montgomerie – *Eglinton and Winton, E.*
Moreton – *Ducie, E.*

Mount Stuart – *Bute, M*
Naas – *Mayo, E.*
Neidpath – *Wemyss and March, E.*
Norreys – *Lindsey and Abingdon, E.*

North – *Guilford, E.*
Ogilvy – *Airlie, E.*
Oxmantown – *Rosse, E.*
Paget de Beaudesert – *Uxbridge, E.*
Porchester – *Carnarvon, E.*

Ramsay – *Dalhousie, E.*
Romsey – *Mountbatten of Burma, C*
Scrymgeour – *Dundee, E.*
Seymour – *Somerset, D.*
Stanley – *Derby, E.*

Strathnaver – *Sutherland, C.*
Wodehouse – *Kimberley, E.*
Worsley – *Yarborough, E.*

PEERS' SURNAMES WHICH DIFFER FROM THEIR TITLES

The following symbols indicate the rank of the peer holding each title:

C. Countess
D. Duke
E. Earl
M. Marquess
V. Viscount
* Life Peer

Where no designation is given, the title is that of an hereditary Baron or Baroness

Abney-Hastings – *Loudoun, C.*
Acheson – *Gosford, E.*
Adderley – *Norton*
Addington – *Sidmouth, V.*
Adebowale – *A. of Thornes*
Agar – *Normanton, E.*
Aitken – *Beaverbrook*
Akers-Douglas – *Chilston, V.*
Alexander – *A. of Tunis, E.*
Alexander – *A. of Weedon*
Alexander – *Caledon, E.*
Allen – *A. of Abbeydale*
Allen – *Croham*
Allsopp – *Hindlip*
Alton – *A. of Liverpool*
Anderson – *Waverley, V.*
Anelay – *A. of St Johns*
Annesley – *Valentia, V.*
Anson – *Lichfield, E.*
Archer – *A. of Sandwell*
Archer – *A. of Weston-super-Mare*
Armstrong – *A. of Ilminster*
Armstrong-Jones – *Snowdon, E.*
Arthur – *Glenarthur*
Arundell – *Talbot of Malahide*
Ashdown – *A. of Norton-sub-Hamdon*
Ashley – *A. of Stoke*
Ashley-Cooper – *Shaftesbury, E.*
Ashton – *A. of Hyde*
Ashton – *A. of Upholland*
Asquith – *Oxford and Asquith, E.*
Assheton – *Clitheroe*

Astley – *Hastings*
Astor – *A. of Hever*
Aubrey-Fletcher – *Braye*
Bailey – *Glanusk*
Baillie – *Burton*
Baillie Hamilton – *Haddington, E.*
Baker – *B. of Dorking*
Baldwin – *B. of Bewdley, E.*
Balfour – *B. of Inchrye*
Balfour – *Kinross*
Balfour – *Riverdale*
Bampfylde – *Poltimore*
Banbury – *B. of Southam*
Barber – *B. of Tewkesbury*
Baring – *Ashburton*
Baring – *Cromer, E.*
Baring – *Howick of Glendale*
Baring – *Northbrook*
Baring – *Revelstoke*
Barker – *Trumpington*
Barnes – *Gorell*
Barnewall – *Trimlestown*
Bassam – *B. of Brighton*
Bathurst – *Bledisloe, V.*
Beauclerk – *St Albans, D.*
Beaumont – *Allendale, V.*
Beaumont – *B. of Whitley*
Beckett – *Grimthorpe*
Benn – *Stansgate, V.*
Bennet – *Tankerville, E.*
Bentinck – *Portland, E.*
Beresford – *Decies*
Beresford – *Waterford, M.*
Bernstein – *B. of Craigweil*
Berry – *Camrose, V.*
Berry – *Kemsley, V.*
Bertie – *Lindsey, E.*
Best – *Wynford*
Bethell – *Westbury*
Bewicke-Copley – *Cromwell*
Bigham – *Mersey, V.*
Bingham – *B. of Cornhill*
Bingham – *Clanmorris*
Bingham – *Lucan, E.*
Black – *B. of Crossharbour*
Bligh – *Darnley, E.*
Blyth – *B. of Rowington*
Bootle-Wilbraham – *Skelmersdale*
Boscawen – *Falmouth, V.*
Boston – *B. of Faversham*
Bourke – *Mayo, E.*

Bowes Lyon – *Strathmore, E.*
Bowyer – *Denham*
Boyd – *Kilmarnock*
Boyle – *Cork and Orrery, E.*
Boyle – *Glasgow, E.*
Boyle – *Shannon, E.*
Brabazon – *Meath, E.*
Brand – *Hampden, V.*
Brassey – *B. of Apethorpe*
Brett – *Esher, V.*
Bridge – *B. of Harwich*
Bridgeman – *Bradford, E.*
Brittan – *B. of Spennithorne*
Brodrick – *Midleton, V.*
Brooke – *Alanbrooke, V.*
Brooke – *B. of Alverthorpe*
Brooke – *Brookeborough, V.*
Brooke – *B. of Sutton Mandeville*
Brooks – *B. of Tremorfa*
Brooks – *Crawshaw*
Brougham – *Brougham and Vaux*
Broughton – *Fairhaven*
Browne – *Kilmaine*
Browne – *B. of Madingley*
Browne – *Oranmore and Browne*
Browne – *Sligo, M.*
Bruce – *Aberdare*
Bruce – *Balfour of Burleigh*
Bruce – *B. of Donington*
Bruce – *Elgin and Kincardine, E.*
Brudenell-Bruce – *Ailesbury, M.*
Buchan – *Tweedsmuir*
Buckley – *Wrenbury*
Butler – *B. of Brockwell*
Butler – *Carrick, E.*
Butler – *Dunboyne*
Butler – *Mountgarret, V.*
Buxton – *B. of Alsa*
Byng – *Strafford, E.*
Byng – *Torrington, V.*
Callaghan – *C. of Cardiff*
Cambell-Savours – *C.-S. of Allerdale*
Cameron – *C. of Lochbroom*
Campbell – *Argyll, D.*
Campbell – *C. of Alloway*
Campbell – *C. of Croy*
Campbell – *Cawdor, E.*
Campbell – *Colgrain*

Campbell – *Stratheden and Campbell*
Campbell-Gray – *Gray*
Canning – *Garvagh*
Capell – *Essex, E.*
Carey – *C. of Clifton*
Carington – *Carrington*
Carlisle – *C. of Berriew*
Carlisle – *C. of Bucklow*
Carnegie – *Fife, D.*
Carnegie – *Northesk, E.*
Carr – *C. of Hadley*
Cary – *Falkland, V.*
Caulfeild – *Charlemont, V.*
Cavendish – *C. of Furness*
Cavendish – *Chesham*
Cavendish – *Devonshire, D.*
Cavendish – *Waterpark*
Cayzer – *Rotherwick*
Cecil – *Amherst of Hackney*
Cecil – *Exeter, M.*
Cecil – *Rockley*
Chalker – *C. of Wallasey*
Chaloner – *Gisborough*
Channon – *Kelvedon*
Chapman – *Northfield*
Charteris – *Wemyss and March, E.*
Chetwynd-Talbot – *Shrewsbury, E.*
Chichester – *Donegall, M.*
Child Villiers – *Jersey, E.*
Cholmondeley – *Delamere*
Chubb – *Hayter*
Clark – *C. of Kempston*
Clarke – *C. of Hampstead*
Clegg-Hill – *Hill, V.*
Clifford – *C. of Chudleigh*
Cochrane – *C. of Cults*
Cochrane – *Dundonald, E.*
Cocks – *Somers*
Cohen – *C. of Pimlico*
Cokayne – *Cullen of Ashbourne*
Coke – *Leicester, E.*
Cole – *Enniskillen, E.*
Collier – *Monkswell*
Colville – *Clydesmuir*
Colville – *C. of Culross, V.*
Compton – *Northampton, M.*
Condon – *C. of Langdon Green*
Conolly-Carew – *Carew*

Constantine – *C. of Stanmore**

Cooke – *C. of Islandreagh**

Cooke – *C. of Thorndon**

Cooper – *Norwich, V.*

Cope – *C. of Berkeley**

Corbett – *C. of Castle Vale**.

Corbett – *Rowallan*

Cornwall-Leigh – *Grey of Condor*

Courtenay – *Devon, E.*

Craig – *C. of Radley**

Craig – *Craigavon, V.*

Crichton – *Erne, E.*

Crichton-Stuart – *Bute, M.*

Cripps – *Parmoor*

Crossley – *Somerleyton*

Cubitt – *Ashcombe*

Cunliffe-Lister – *Masham of Ilton**

Cunliffe-Lister – *Swinton, E.*

Currie – *C. of Marylebone**

Curzon – *Howe, E.*

Curzon – *Scarsdale, V.*

Cust – *Brownlow*

Dalrymple – *Stair, E.*

Daubeny de Moleyns – *Ventry*

Davies – *D. of Coity**

Davies – *Darwen*

Davies – *D. of Oldham**

Davison – *Broughshane*

Dawnay – *Downe, V.*

Dawson-Damer – *Portarlington, E.*

Dean – *D. of Harptree**

Dean – *D. of Thornton-le-Fylde**

Deane – *Muskerry*

de Courcy – *Kingsale*

de Grey – *Walsingham*

Delacourt-Smith – *Delacourt Smith of Alteryn**

Denison – *Londesborough*

Denison-Pender – *Pender*

Devereux – *Hereford, V.*

Dewar – *Forteviot*

De Yarburgh-Bateson – *Deramore*

Dixon – *Glentoran*

Dodson – *Monk Bretton*

Donaldson – *D. of Lymington**

Dormand – *D. of Easington**

Douglas – *Morton, E.*

Douglas – *Queensberry, M.*

Douglas-Hamilton – *Hamilton, D.*

Douglas-Hamilton – *Selkirk, E.*

Douglas-Hamilton – *Selkirk of Douglas**

Douglas-Home – *Dacre*

Douglas-Home – *Home, E.*

Douglas-Pennant – *Penrhyn*

Douglas-Scott-Montagu – *Montagu of Beaulieu*

Drummond – *Perth, E.*

Drummond of Megginch – *Strange*

Dugdale – *Crathorne*

Duke – *Merrivale*

Duncombe – *Feversham*

Dundas – *Melville, V.*

Dundas – *Zetland, M.*

Eady – *Swinfen*

Eccles – *E. of Moulton**

Eden – *Auckland*

Eden – *E. of Winton**

Eden – *Henley*

Edgcumbe – *Mount Edgcumbe, E.*

Edmondson – *Sandford*

Edwardes – *Kensington*

Edwards – *Crickhowell**

Egerton – *Sutherland, D.*

Eliot – *St Germans, E.*

Elliott – *E. of Morpeth**

Elliot-Murray-Kynynmound – *Minto, E.*

Ellis – *Seaford*

Erskine – *Buchan, E.*

Erskine – *Mar and Kellie, E.*

Erskine-Murray – *Elibank*

Evans – *E. of Parkside**

Evans – *E. of Temple Guiting**

Evans – *E. of Watford**

Evans – *Mountevans*

Evans-Freke – *Carbery*

Eve – *Silsoe*

Ewing – *E. of Kirkford**

Fairfax – *F. of Cameron*

Falconer – *F. of Thoroton**

Fane – *Westmorland, E.*

Farrington – *F. of Ribbleton**

Faulkner – *F. of Worcester**

Fearn – *F. of Southport**

Feilding – *Denbigh, E.*

Felton – *Seaford*

Fellowes – *De Ramsey*

Fermor-Hesketh – *Hesketh*

Fiennes – *Saye and Sele*

Fiennes-Clinton – *Lincoln, E.*

Finch Hatton – *Winchilsea, E.*

Finch-Knightley – *Aylesford, E.*

Finlay – *F. of Llandaff**

Fisher – *F. of Rednal**

Fitzalan-Howard – *Herries of Terregles*

Fitzalan-Howard – *Norfolk, D.*

FitzGerald – *Leinster, D.*

Fitzherbert – *Stafford*

FitzRoy – *Grafton, D.*

FitzRoy – *Southampton*

FitzRoy Newdegate – *Daventry, V.*

Fletcher-Vane – *Inglewood*

Flower – *Ashbrook, V.*

Foljambe – *Liverpool, E.*

Forbes – *Granard, E.*

Forsyth – *F. of Drumlean**.

Forwood – *Arlington*

Foster – *F. of Thames Bank**

Fowler – *F. of Sutton Caulfield**

Fox-Strangways – *Ilchester, E.*

Frankland – *Zouche*

Fraser – *F. of Carmyllie**

Fraser – *F. of Kilmorack**

Fraser – *Lovat*

Fraser – *Saltoun*

Fraser – *Strathalmond*

Freeman-Grenville – *Kinloss*

Fremantle – *Cottesloe*

French – *De Freyne*

Fyfe – *F. of Fairfield**

Galbraith – *Strathclyde*

Ganzoni – *Belstead*

Gardner – *G. of Parkes**

Gascoyne-Cecil – *M. of Salisbury**

Gathorne-Hardy – *Cranbrook, E.*

Gibbs – *Aldenham*

Gibbs – *Wraxall*

Gibson – *Ashbourne*

Gibson – *G. of Market Rasen**

Giffard – *Halsbury, E.*

Gilbey – *Vaux of Harrowden*

Gilmour – *G. of Craigmillar**

Glyn – *Wolverton*

Godley – *Kilbracken*

Goff – *G. of Chieveley**

Golding – *G. of Newcastle-under-Lyme**

Gordon – *Aberdeen, M.*

Gordon – *G. of Strathblane**

Gordon – *Huntly, M.*

Gordon Lennox – *Richmond, D.*

Gore – *Arran, E.*

Gould – *G. of Potternewton**

Graham – *G. of Edmonton**

Graham – *Montrose, D.*

Graham-Toler – *Norbury, E.*

Granshaw – *Northover**

Grant of Grant – *Strathspey*

Granville – *G. of Eye**

Gray – *G. of Contin**

Greaves – *Dysart, C.*

Greenall – *Daresbury*

Greene – *G. of Harrow Weald**

Greville – *Warwick, E.*

Griffiths – *G. of Fforestfach**

Grigg – *Altrincham*

Grimston – *G. of Westbury*

Grimston-Verulam, E.

Grosvenor – *Westminster, D.*

Grosvenor – *Wilton and Ebury, E.*

Guest – *Wimborne, V.*

Gueterbock – *Berkeley*

Guinness – *Iveagh, E.*

Guinness – *Moyne*

Gully – *Selby, V.*

Gummer – *Chadlington**

Gurdon – *Cranworth*

Guthrie – *G. of Craigiebank**

Gwynne Jones – *Chalfont**

Hamilton – *Abercorn, D.*

Hamilton – *Belhaven and Stenton*

Hamilton – *Dudley*

Hamilton – *H. of Dalzell*

Hamilton – *Holm Patrick*

Hamilton-Russell – *Boyne, V.*

Hamilton-Smith – *Colwyn*

Hanbury-Tracy – *Sudeley*

Handcock – *Castlemaine*

Hannay – *H. of Chiswick**

Harbord-Hamond – *Suffield*

Harding – *H. of Petherton*

Hardinge – *H. of Penshurst*

Hardy – *H. of Wath**

Hare – *Blakenham, V.*

Hare – *Listowel, E.*

Harmsworth – *Rothermere, V.*

Harris – *H. of Haringey**

Harris – *H. of High Cross**

Harris – *H. of Peckham**

Harris – *H. of Richmond**

Harris – *Malmesbury, E.*

Harvey – *H. of Tasburgh*

Hastings Bass – *Huntingdon, E.*

Hay – *Erroll, E.*

Hay – *Kinnoull, E.*

Hay – *Tweeddale, M.*

Heathcote-Drummond-Willoughby – *Willoughby de Eresby*

Hely-Hutchinson – *Donoughmore, E.*

Henderson – *Faringdon*

Hennessy – *Windlesham*

Henniker-Major – *Henniker*

Hepburne-Scott – *Polwarth*

Herbert – *Carnarvon, E.*

Herbert – *Hemingford*

Herbert – *Pembroke, E.*

Herbert – *Powis, E.*

Hervey – *Bristol, M.*

Heseltine – *H. of Thenford**

Montagu – *Sandwich, E.*
Montagu – *Swaythling*
Montagu Douglas Scott – *Buccleuch, D.*
Montagu Stuart Wortley – *Wharncliffe, E.*
Montague – *Amwell*
Montgomerie – *Eglinton, E.*
Montgomery – *M. of Alamein, V.*
Moore – *Drogheda, E.*
Moore – *M. of Lower Marsh*
Moore – *M. of Wolvercote*
Moore-Brabazon – *Brabazon of Tara*
Moreton – *Ducie, E*
Morgan – *M. of Huyton*.
Morris – *Killanin*
Morris – *M. of Aberavon*
Morris – *M. of Manchester*
Morris – *Naseby*
Morris – *M. of Kenwood*
Morrison – *Dunrossil, V.*
Morrison — *Margadale*
Moser – *M. of Regents Park*
Mosley – *Ravensdale*
Mountbatten – *Milford Haven, M.*
Muff – *Calverley*
Mulholland – *Dunleath*
Murray – *Atholl, D.*
Murray – *Dunmore, E.*
Murray – *Mansfield and Mansfield, E.*
Murray – *M. of Epping Forest*
Murton – *M. of Lindisfarne*
Nall-Cain – *Brocket*
Napier – *Napier and Ettrick*
Napier – *N. of Magdala*
Needham – *Kilmorey, E.*
Neill – *N. of Bladen*
Nelson – *N. of Stafford*
Nevill – *Abergavenny, M.*
Neville – *Braybrooke*
Newton – *N. of Braintree*
Nicholls – *N. of Birkenhead*
Nicolson – *Carnock*
Nicholson – *N. of Winterbourne*
Nivison – *Glendyne*
Noel – *Gainsborough, E.*
North – *Guilford, E.*
Northcote – *Iddesleigh, E.*
Norton – *Grantley*
Norton – *N. of Louth*
Norton – *Rathcreedan*
Nugent – *Westmeath, E.*
Oakeshott – *O. of Seagrove Bay*
O'Brien – *Inchiquin*
Ogilvie-Grant – *Seafield, E.*
Ogilvy – *Airlie, E.*
Oliver – *O. of Aylmerton*

O'Neill – *O'N of Bengarve*
O'Neill – *Rathcavan*
Orde-Powlett – *Bolton*
Ormsby-Gore – *Harlech*
Ouseley – *O. of Peckham Rye*
Page – *Whaddon*
Paget – *Anglesey, M.*
Pakenham – *Longford, E.*
Pakington – *Hampton*
Palmer – *Lucas and Dingwall*
Palmer – *Selborne, E.*
Park – *P. of Monmouth*
Parker – *Macclesfield, E.*
Parker – *Morley, E.*
Parnell – *Congleton*
Parsons – *Rosse, E.*
Patel – *P. of Blackburn*
Paulet – *Winchester, M.*
Peake – *Ingleby, V.*
Pearson – *Cowdray, V.*
Pearson – *P. of Rannoch*
Pease – *Gainford*
Pease – *Wardington*
Pelham – *Chichester, E.*
Pelham – *Yarborough, E.*
Pellew – *Exmouth, V*
Pendry – *P. of Stalybridge*.
Penny – *Marchwood, V.*
Pepys – *Cottenham, E.*
Perceval – *Egmont, E.*
Percy – *Northumberland, D.*
Perry – *P. of Southwark*
Pery – *Limerick, E.*
Peyton – *P. of Yeovil*
Philipps – *Milford*
Philipps – *St Davids, V.*
Phillips – *P. of Sudbury*
Phillips – *P. of Worth Matravers*
Phipps – *Normanby, M.*
Pilkington – *P. of Oxenford*
Plant – *P. of Highfield*
Platt – *P. of Writtle*
Pleydell-Bouverie – *Radnor, E.*
Plummer – *P. of St Marylebone*
Plumptre – *Fitzwalter*
Plunkett – *Dunsany*
Plunkett – *Louth*
Pollock – *Hanworth, V.*
Pomeroy – *Harberton, V.*
Ponsonby – *Bessborough, E.*
Ponsonby – *de Mauley*
Ponsonby – *P. of Shulbrede*
Ponsonby – *Sysonby*
Powell – *P. of Bayswater*
Powys – *Lilford*
Pratt – *Camden, M.*
Preston – *Gormanston, V.*
Primrose – *Rosebery, E.*
Prittie – *Dunalley*
Prout – *Kingsland*
Ramsay – *Dalhousie, E.*
Ramsay – *R. of Cartvale*

Ramsbotham – *Soulbury, V.*
Randall – *R. of St. Budeaux*
Rawlinson – *R. of Ewell*
Rees-Williams – *Ogmore*
Rendell – *R. of Babergh*
Renfrew – *R. of Kaimsthorn*
Renton – *R. of Mount Harry*
Renwick – *R. of Clifton*
Rhys – *Dynevor*
Richards – *Milverton*
Richardson – *R. of Calow*
Richardson – *R. of Duntisbourne*
Ritchie – *R. of Dundee*
Roberts – *Clwyd*
Roberts – *R. of Conway*
Robertson – *R. of Oakridge*
Robertson – *R. of Port Ellen*
Robertson – *Wharton*
Robinson – *Martonmere*
Roche – *Fermoy*
Rodd – *Rennell*
Rodger – *R. of Earlsferry*
Rodgers – *R. of Quarry Bank*
Rogers – *R. of Riverside*
Roll – *R. of Ipsden*
Roper-Curzon – *Teynham*
Rospigliosi – *Newburgh, E.*
Rous – *Stradbroke, E.*
Rowley-Conwy – *Langford*
Runciman – *R. of Doxford, V.*
Russell – *Ampthill*
Russell – *Bedford, D.*
Russell – *de Clifford*
Russell – *R. of Liverpool*
Ryder – *Harrowby, E.*
Ryder – *R. of Wensum*
Sackville – *De La Warr, E.*
Sackville-West – *Sackville*
Sainsbury – *S. of Preston Candover*
Sainsbury – *S. of Turville*
St Aubyn – *St Levan*
St Clair – *Sinclair*
St Clair-Erskine – *Rosslyn, E.*
St John – *Bolingbroke and St John, V.*
St John – *St John of Blesto*
St John-Stevas – *St John of Fawsley*
St Leger – *Doneraile, V.*
Samuel – *Bearsted, V.*
Sanderson – *S. of Ayot*
Sanderson – *S. of Bowden*
Sandilands – *Torphichen*
Saumarez – *De Saumarez*
Savile – *Mexborough, E.*
Saville – *S. of Newdigate*
Scarlett – *Abinger*
Schreiber – *Marlesford*
Sclater-Booth – *Basing*

Scotland – *S. of Asthal*
Scott – *Eldon, E*
Scott – *S. of Foscotte*
Scott – *S. of Needham Market*.
Scrymgeour – *Dundee, E.*
Seager – *Leighton of St Mellons*
Seely – *Mottistone*
Seyfried – *Herbert*
Seymour – *Hertford, M.*
Seymour – *Somerset, D.*
Sharp – *S. of Guildford*
Shaw – *Craigmyle*
Shaw – *S. of Northstead*
Sheldon – *S. of Ashdon-under-Lyne*
Sheppard – *S. of Didgemere*
Sheppard – *S. of Liverpool*
Shirley – *Ferrers, E.*
Short – *Glenamara*
Shutt – *S. of Greetland*
Siddeley – *Kenilworth*
Sidney – *De L'Isle, V.*
Simon – *S. of Glaisdale*
Simon – *S. of Highbury*
Simon – *S. of Wythenshawe*
Simpson – *S. of Dunkeld*
Sinclair – *Caithness, E.*
Sinclair – *S. of Cleeve*
Sinclair – *Thurso, V.*
Skeffington – *Massereene, V.*
Slynn – *S. of Hadley*
Smith – *Bicester*
Smith – *Hambleden, V.*
Smith – *Kirkhill*
Smith – *S. of Clifton*
Smith – *S. of Gilmorehill*
Smith – *S. of Leigh*
Somerset – *Beaufort, D.*
Somerset – *Raglan*
Soulsby – *S. of Swaffham Prior*
Spencer – *Churchill, V.*
Spencer-Churchill – *Marlborough, D.*
Spring Rice – *Monteagle of Brandon*
Stanhope – *Harrington, E.*
Stanley – *Derby, E.*
Stanley – *Stanley of Alderley and Sheffield*
Stapleton-Cotton – *Combermere, V.*
Steel – *S. of Aikwood*
Sterling – *S. of Plaistow*
Stevens – *S. of Ludgate*
Stevenson – *S. of Coddenham*
Stewart – *Galloway, E.*
Stewart – *Stewartby*
Stoddart – *S. of Swindon*
Stone – *S. of Blackheath*
Stonor – *Camoys*
Stopford – *Courtown, E.*
Stourton – *Mowbray*
Strachey – *O'Hagan*

ORDERS OF CHIVALRY

THE MOST NOBLE ORDER OF THE GARTER (1348)

KG
Ribbon, Blue
Motto, Honi soit qui mal y pense
(Shame on him who thinks evil of it)

The number of Knights Companions is limited to 24

SOVEREIGN OF THE ORDER
The Queen

LADY OF THE ORDER
HRH The Princess Royal, 1994
HRH Princess Alexandra, The Hon. Lady Ogilvy, 2003

ROYAL KNIGHTS
HRH The Prince Philip, Duke of Edinburgh, 1947
HRH The Prince of Wales, 1958
HRH The Duke of Kent, 1985
HRH The Duke of Gloucester, 1997

EXTRA KNIGHTS COMPANIONS AND LADIES
HRH Princess Juliana of the Netherlands, 1958
Grand Duke Jean of Luxembourg, 1972
HM The Queen of Denmark, 1979
HM The King of Sweden, 1983
HM The King of Spain, 1988
HM The Queen of the Netherlands, 1989
HIM The Emperor of Japan, 1998
HM The King of Norway, 2001

KNIGHTS AND LADY COMPANIONS
The Duke of Grafton, 1976
The Lord Richardson of Duntisbourne, 1983
The Lord Carrington, 1985
The Lord Callaghan of Cardiff, 1987
The Duke of Wellington, 1990
Field Marshal the Lord Bramall, 1990
Sir Edward Heath, 1992
The Viscount Ridley, 1992
The Lord Sainsbury of Preston Candover, 1992
The Lord Ashburton, 1994
The Lord Kingsdown, 1994
Sir Ninian Stephen, 1994

The Baroness Thatcher, 1995
Sir Edmund Hillary, 1995
The Duke of Devonshire, 1996
Sir Timothy Colman, 1996
The Duke of Abercorn, 1999
Sir William Gladstone, 1999
Field Marshal The Lord Inge, 2001
Sir Anthony Acland, 2001
The Duke of Westminster, 2003
The Lord Butler of Brockwell, 2003
The Lord Morris of Aberavon, 2003
Prelate, The Bishop of Winchester

Chancellor, The Lord Carrington, KG, GCMG, CH, MC
Register, The Dean of Windsor
Garter King of Arms, P. Gwynn-Jones, CVO
Gentleman Usher of the Black Rod, Lt.-Gen. Sir Michael Willcocks, KCB
Secretary, D. H. B. Chesshyre, LVO

THE MOST ANCIENT AND MOST NOBLE ORDER OF THE THISTLE (REVIVED 1687)

KT
Ribbon, Green
Motto, Nemo me impune lacessit
(No one provokes me with impunity)

The number of Members is limited to 16

SOVEREIGN OF THE ORDER
The Queen

LADY OF THE THISTLE
HRH The Princess Royal, 2000

ROYAL KNIGHTS
HRH The Prince Philip, Duke of Edinburgh, 1952
HRH The Prince of Wales, Duke of Rothesay, 1977

KNIGHTS AND LADIES
The Earl of Wemyss and March, 1966
Sir Donald Cameron of Lochiel, 1973
The Duke of Buccleuch and Queensberry, 1978
The Earl of Elgin and Kincardine, 1981

The Lord Thomson of Monifieth, 1981
The Earl of Airlie, 1985
Sir Iain Tennant, 1986
The Viscount of Arbuthnott, 1996
The Earl of Crawford and Balcarres, 1996
Lady Marion Fraser, 1996
The Lord Macfarlane of Bearsden, 1996
The Lord Mackay of Clashfern, 1997
The Lord Wilson of Tillyorn, 2000
The Lord Sutherland of Houndwood, 2002
Sir Eric Anderson, 2002

Chancellor, The Duke of Buccleuch and Queensberry, KT, VRD
Dean, The Very Revd G. I. Macmillan, CVO
Secretary and Lord Lyon King of Arms, R. O. Blair, LVO, WS
Usher of the Green Rod, Rear-Adm. C. H. Layman, CB, DSO, LVO

THE MOST HONOURABLE ORDER OF THE BATH (1725)

GCB *Military*   GCB *Civil*

GCB Knight (or Dame) Grand Cross
KCB Knight Commander
DCB Dame Commander
CB Companion

Ribbon, Crimson
Motto, Tria juncta in uno
(Three joined in one)

Remodelled 1815, and enlarged many times since. The Order is divided into civil and military divisions. Women became eligible for the Order from 1 January 1971

THE SOVEREIGN

GREAT MASTER AND FIRST OR PRINCIPAL KNIGHT GRAND CROSS
HRH The Prince of Wales, KG, KT, GCB, OM

Dean of the Order, The Dean of Westminster

Bath King of Arms, Gen. Sir Brian
Kenny, GCB, CBE
Registrar and Secretary, Air Vice-
Marshal Sir Richard Peirse, KCVO,
CB
Genealogist, P. Gwynn-Jones, CVO
Gentleman Usher of the Scarlet Rod,
Rear-Adm. I. R. Henderson, CB,
CBE
Deputy Secretary, The Secretary of
the Central Chancery of the
Orders of Knighthood
Chancery, Central Chancery of the
Orders of Knighthood, St James's
Palace, London SW1A 1BH

THE ORDER OF MERIT (1902)

OM *Military*   OM *Civil*

OM
Ribbon, Blue and crimson

This Order is designed as a special
distinction for eminent men and
women without conferring a
knighthood upon them. The Order
is limited in numbers to 24, with the
addition of foreign honorary
members.

THE SOVEREIGN
HRH The Prince Philip, Duke of
Edinburgh, 1968
Revd Prof. Owen Chadwick, KBE,
1983
Sir Andrew Huxley, 1983
Dr Frederick Sanger, 1986
Dame Cicely Saunders, 1989
The Baroness Thatcher, 1990
Dame Joan Sutherland, 1991
Prof. Francis Crick, 1991
Sir Michael Atiyah, 1992
Lucian Freud, 1993
Sir Aaron Klug, 1995
The Lord Foster of Thames Bank,
1997
Sir Denis Rooke, 1997
Sir James Black, 2000
Sir Anthony Caro, 2000
Prof. Sir Roger Penrose, 2000
Sir Tom Stoppard, 2000
HRH The Prince of Wales, 2002
The Lord May of Oxford, 2002
The Lord Rothschild, 2002

Honorary Member, Nelson Mandela,
1995

Secretary and Registrar, The Lord
Fellowes, GCB, GCVO, PC, QSO
Chancery, Central Chancery of the
Orders of Knighthood, St James's
Palace, London SW1A 1BH

THE MOST DISTINGUISHED ORDER OF ST MICHAEL AND ST GEORGE (1818)

GCMG
GCMG   Knight (or Dame) Grand
Cross
KCMG   Knight Commander
DCMG   Dame Commander
CMG   Companion

Ribbon, Saxon blue, with scarlet
centre
Motto, Auspicium melioris aevi
(Token of a better age)

THE SOVEREIGN

GRAND MASTER
HRH The Duke of Kent, KG, GCMG,
GCVO, ADC

Prelate, The Rt. Revd Simon
Barrington-Ward, KCMG
Chancellor, Sir Antony Acland, KG,
GCMG, GCVO
Secretary, The Permanent Under-
Secretary of State at the Foreign
and Commonwealth Office and
Head of the Diplomatic Service
Registrar, Lord Wilson of Tillyorn,
KT, GCMG
King of Arms, Sir Ewen Fergusson,
GCMG, GCVO
Gentleman Usher of the Blue Rod, Sir
Anthony Figgis, KCVO, CMG
Dean, The Dean of St Paul's
Deputy Secretary, The Secretary of
the Central Chancery of the
Orders of Knighthood
Chancery, Central Chancery of the
Orders of Knighthood, St James's
Palace, London SW1A 1BH

THE MOST EMINENT ORDER OF THE INDIAN EMPIRE (1878)

GCIE   Knight Grand Commander
KCIE   Knight Commander
CIE   Companion

Ribbon, Imperial purple
Motto, Imperatricis auspiciis *(Under
the auspices of the Empress)*

THE SOVEREIGN

Registrar, The Secretary of the
Central Chancery of the Orders of
Knighthood
No conferments have been made
since 1947

THE IMPERIAL ORDER OF THE CROWN OF INDIA (1877) FOR LADIES

CI
Badge, the royal cipher in jewels
within an oval, surmounted by an
heraldic crown and attached to a
bow of light blue watered ribbon,
edged white

The honour does not confer any
rank or title upon the recipient
No conferments have been made
since 1947

HM The Queen, 1947
HRH Princess Alice, Duchess of
Gloucester, 1937

THE ROYAL VICTORIAN ORDER (1896)

GCVO   KCVO

GCVO   Knight or Dame Grand
Cross
KCVO   Knight Commander
DCVO   Dame Commander
CVO   Commander
LVO   Lieutenant
MVO   Member

Ribbon, Blue, with red and white
edges
Motto, Victoria

THE SOVEREIGN

Chancellor, The Lord Chamberlain
Secretary, The Keeper of the Privy
Purse
Registrar, The Secretary of the
Central Chancery of the Orders of
Knighthood
Chaplain, The Chaplain of the
Queen's Chapel of the Savoy
Hon. Genealogist, D. H. B.
Chesshyre, LVO

THE MOST EXCELLENT ORDER OF THE BRITISH EMPIRE (1917)

GBE   KBE

The Order was divided into military
and civil divisions in December
1918
GBE   Knight or Dame Grand
Cross
KBE   Knight Commander

DBE	Dame Commander
CBE	Commander
OBE	Officer
MBE	Member

Ribbon, Rose pink edged with pearl grey with vertical pearl stripe in centre (military division); without vertical pearl stripe (civil division)
Motto, For God and the Empire

THE SOVEREIGN

GRAND MASTER
HRH The Prince Philip, Duke of Edinburgh, KG, KT, OM, GBE, PC

Prelate, The Bishop of London
King of Arms, Air Chief Marshal Sir Patrick Hine, GCB, GBE
Registrar, The Secretary of the Central Chancery of the Orders of Knighthood
Secretary, The Secretary of the Cabinet and Head of the Home Civil Service
Dean, The Dean of St Paul's
Gentleman Usher of the Purple Rod, Sir Alexander Michael Graham, GBE, DCL
Chancery, Central Chancery of the Orders of Knighthood, St James's Palace, London SW1A 1BH

ORDER OF THE COMPANIONS OF HONOUR (1917)

CH

Ribbon, Carmine, with gold edges

This Order consists of one class only and carries with it no title. The number of awards is limited to 65 (excluding honorary members)

Anthony, Rt. Hon. John, 1981
Ashley of Stoke, The Lord, 1975
Attenborough, Sir David, 1995
Baker, Dame Janet, 1993
Baker of Dorking, The Lord, 1992
Birtwistle, Sir Harrison, 2000
Brenner, Sydney, 1986
Brook, Peter, 1998
Brooke of Sutton Mandeville, The Lord, 1992
Carrington, The Lord, 1983
Christie, Sir George, 2001
Davis, Sir Colin, 2001
De Chastelain, Gen. John, 1999
Doll, Prof. Sir Richard, 1995
Fraser, Rt. Hon. Malcolm, 1977
Freud, Lucian, 1983

Glenamara, The Lord, 1976
Hamilton, Richard, 1999
Hannay of Chiswick, The Lord, 2003
Hawking, Prof. Stephen, 1989
Healey, The Lord, 1979
Heseltine, The Lord, 1997
Hobsbawm, Prof. Eric, 1998
Hockney, David, 1997
Hodgkin, Sir Howard, 2002
Howard, Sir Michael, 2002
Howe of Aberavon, The Lord, 1996
Hurd of Westwell, The Lord, 1995
Jones, James, 1977
King of Bridgewater, The Lord, 1992
Lange, Rt. Hon. David, 1989
Lessing, Doris, 1999
Lovelock, James, 2002
McKenzie, Prof. Dan Peter, 2003
MacKerras, Sir Charles, 2003
Mahon, Sir Denis, 2002
Major, Rt. Hon. John, 1998
Owen, The Lord, 1994
Patten, Rt. Hon. Christopher, 1997
Pinter, Harold, 2002
Riley, Bridget, 1998
Sanger, Frederick, 1981
Scofield, Paul, 2000
Sisson, Charles, 1993
Smith, Sir John, 1993
Somare, Rt. Hon. Sir Michael, 1978
Talboys, Rt. Hon. Sir Brian, 1981
Tebbit, The Lord, 1987
Varah, Revd Dr. Chad, 1999

Honorary Members, Lee Kuan Yew, 1970; Prof. Anartya Sen, 2000; Bernard Haitink, 2002
Secretary and Registrar, The Secretary of the Central Chancery of the Orders of Knighthood

THE DISTINGUISHED SERVICE ORDER (1886)

DSO

Ribbon, Red, with blue edges

Bestowed in recognition of especial services in action of commissioned officers in the Navy, Army and Royal Air Force and (since 1942) Mercantile Marine. The members are Companions only. A Bar may be awarded for any additional act of service

THE IMPERIAL SERVICE ORDER (1902)

ISO

Ribbon, Crimson, with blue centre

Appointment as Companion of this Order is open to members of the Civil Services whose eligibility is determined by the grade they hold. The Order consists of The Sovereign and Companions to a number not exceeding 1,900, of whom 1,300 may belong to the Home Civil Services and 600 to Overseas Civil Services. The then Prime Minister announced in March 1993 that he would make no further recommendations for appointments to the Order.

Secretary, The Secretary of the Cabinet and Head of the Home Civil Service
Registrar, The Secretary of the Central Chancery of the Orders of Knighthood, St James's Palace, London SW1A 1BH

THE ROYAL VICTORIAN CHAIN (1902)

It confers no precedence on its holders

HM THE QUEEN

HRH Princess Juliana of the Netherlands, 1950
HM The King of Thailand, 1960
HM King Zahir Shah of Afghanistan, 1971
HM The Queen of Denmark, 1974
HM The King of Sweden, 1975
HM The Queen of the Netherlands, 1982
Gen. Antonio Eanes, 1985
HM The King of Spain, 1986
HM The King of Saudi Arabia, 1987
HE Richard von Weizsäcker, 1992
HM The King of Norway, 1994
The Earl of Airlie, 1997
The Rt. Revd and Rt. Hon. Lord Carey of Clifton, 2002

BARONETAGE AND KNIGHTAGE

BARONETS

Style, 'Sir' before forename and surname, followed by 'Bt'.
Wife's style, 'Lady' followed by surname
For forms of address, see page 40

There are five different creations of baronetcies: Baronets of England (creations dating from 1611); Baronets of Ireland (creations dating from 1619); Baronets of Scotland or Nova Scotia (creations dating from 1625); Baronets of Great Britain (creations after the Act of Union 1707 which combined the kingdoms of England and Scotland); and Baronets of the United Kingdom (creations after the union of Great Britain and Ireland in 1801).

Badge of Baronets of the
United Kingdom

Badge of Baronets
of Nova Scotia

Badge of Ulster

The patent of creation limits the destination of a baronetcy, usually to male descendants of the first baronet, although special remainders allow the baronetcy to pass, if the male issue of sons fail, to the male issue of daughters of the first baronet. In the case of baronetcies of Scotland or Nova Scotia, a special remainder of 'heirs male and of tailzie' allows the baronetcy to descend to heirs general, including women. There are four existing Scottish baronets with such a remainder.

The Official Roll of the Baronetage is kept at the Department for Constitutional Affairs by the Registrar of the Baronetage. Anyone who considers that he is entitled to be entered on the Roll may petition the Crown through the Lord Chancellor. Every person succeeding to a baronetcy must exhibit proofs of succession to the Lord Chancellor. A person whose name is not entered on the Official Roll will not be addressed or mentioned by the title of baronet in any official document, nor will he be accorded precedence as a baronet.

BARONETCIES EXTINCT SINCE THE LAST EDITION
Abercromby (cr. 1636); Bowman (cr. 1884);
Leese (cr. 1908); Meysey-Thompson (cr. 1874)

Registrar of the Baronetage, Andrew McDonald
Assistant Registrar, S. Johnson
Office, Department for Constitutional Affairs,
Constitutional Policy Division, 1st Floor Southside,
105 Victoria Street, London SW1E 6QT Tel: 020 7210 1511

KNIGHTS

Style, 'Sir' before forename and surname, followed by
appropriate post-nominal initials if a Knight Grand
Cross, Knight Grand Commander or Knight
Commander

Wife's style, 'Lady' followed by surname
For forms of address, *see* page 40

The prefix 'Sir' is not used by knights who are clerics of the Church of England, who do not receive the accolade. Their wives are entitled to precedence as the wife of a knight but not to the style of 'Lady'.

ORDERS OF KNIGHTHOOD
Knight Grand Cross, Knight Grand Commander, and Knight Commander are the higher classes of the Orders of Chivalry (*see* page 77). Honorary knighthoods of these Orders may be conferred on men who are citizens of countries of which The Queen is not head of state. As a rule, the prefix 'Sir' is not used by honorary knights.

KNIGHTS BACHELOR

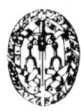

The Knights Bachelor do not constitute a Royal Order, but comprise the surviving representation of the ancient State Orders of Knighthood. The Register of Knights Bachelor, instituted by James I in the 17th century, lapsed, and in 1908 a voluntary association under the title of The Society of Knights (now The Imperial Society of Knights Bachelor by Royal Command) was formed with the primary objects of continuing the various registers dating from 1257 and obtaining the uniform registration of every created Knight Bachelor. In 1926 a design for a badge to be worn by Knights Bachelor was approved and adopted; in 1974 a neck badge and miniature were added.

Knight Principal, Sir Richard Gaskell
Prelate, Rt. Revd and Rt. Hon. The Bishop of London
Registrar, Sir Robert Balchin, DL
Hon. Treasurer, Sir Paul Judge
Clerk to the Council, R. L. Jenkins, LVO, TD
Office, 21 Old Buildings, Lincoln's Inn, London WC2A 3UJ

LIST OF BARONETS AND KNIGHTS

Revised to 31 August 2003
Peers are not included in this list
† Not registered on the Official Roll of the Baronetage at the time of going to press
( ) The date of creation of the baronetcy is given in parenthesis
I Baronet of Ireland
NS Baronet of Nova Scotia
S Baronet of Scotland

If a baronet or knight has a double-barrelled or hyphenated surname, he is listed under the first element of the name
A full entry in italic type indicates that the recipient of a knighthood died during the year in which the honour was conferred. The name is included for purposes of record

Abbott, Sir Albert Francis, Kt., CBE

Abbott, Adm. Sir Peter Charles, GBE, KCB

Abdy, Sir Valentine Robert Duff, Bt. (1850)

Acheson, Prof. Sir (Ernest) Donald, KBE

Ackers, Sir James George, Kt.

Ackers-Jones, Sir David, KBE, CMG

Ackroyd, Sir Timothy Robert Whyte, Bt. (1956)

Acland, Sir Antony Arthur, KG, GCMG, GCVO

Acland, Lt.-Col. Sir (Christopher) Guy (Dyke), Bt., MVO (1890)

Acland, Sir John Dyke, Bt. (1644)

Acland, Maj.-Gen. Sir John Hugh Bevil, KCB, CBE

Adam, Sir Christopher Eric Forbes, Bt. (1917)

Adam, Sir Kenneth Hugo, Kt., OBE

Adams, Sir William James, KCMG

Adsetts, Sir William Norman, Kt., OBE

Adye, Sir John Anthony, KCMG

Agnew, Sir Crispin Hamlyn, Bt. (S. 1629)

Agnew, Sir John Keith, Bt. (1895)

Agnew, Sir Rudolph Ion Joseph, Kt.

Agnew-Somerville, Sir Quentin Charles Somerville, Bt. (1957)

Aiken, Air Chief Marshal Sir John Alexander Carlisle, KCB

Aikens, Hon. Sir Richard John Pearson, Kt.

†Ainsworth, Sir Anthony Thomas Hugh, Bt. (1916)

Aird, Capt. Sir Alastair Sturgis, GCVO

Aird, Sir (George) John, Bt. (1901)

Airy, Maj.-Gen. Sir Christopher John, KCVO, CBE

Aitchison, Sir Charles Walter de Lancey, Bt. (1938)

Akehurst, Gen. Sir John Bryan, KCB, CBE

Alberti, Prof. Sir Kurt George Matthew Mayer, Kt.

Albu, Sir George, Bt. (1912)

Alcock, Air Chief Marshal Sir (Robert James) Michael, GCB, KBE

Aldous, Rt. Hon. Sir William, Kt.

Alexander, Sir Charles Gundry, Bt. (1945)

Alexander, Sir Douglas, Bt. (1921)

Allen, Prof. Sir Geoffrey, Kt., Ph.D., FRS

Allen, Sir John Derek, Kt., CBE

Allen, Hon. Sir Peter Austin Philip Jermyn, Kt.

Allen, Sir Thomas Boaz, Kt., CBE

Allen, Hon. Sir William Clifford, KCMG, MP

Allen, Sir William Guilford, Kt.

Alleyne, Sir George Allanmoore Ogarren, Kt.

Alleyne, Revd John Olpherts Campbell, Bt. (1769)

Alliance, Sir David, Kt., CBE

Allinson, Sir (Walter) Leonard, KCVO, CMG

Alliott, Hon. Sir John Downes, Kt.

Allison, Air Chief Marshal Sir John Shakespeare, KCB, CBE

Althaus, Sir Nigel Frederick, Kt.

Alun-Jones, Sir (John) Derek, Kt.

Ambo, Rt. Revd George, KBE

Amet, Hon. Sir Arnold Karibone, Kt.

Amory, Sir Ian Heathcoat, Bt. (1874)

Anderson, Sir John Anthony, KBE

Anderson, Maj.-Gen. Sir John Evelyn, KBE

Anderson, Sir John Muir, Kt., CMG

Anderson, Sir Leith Reinsford Steven, Kt., CBE

Anderson, Vice-Adm. Sir Neil Dudley, KBE, CB

Anderson, Sir (William) Eric Kinloch, KT

Anderson, Prof. Sir (William) Ferguson, Kt., OBE

Anderton, Sir (Cyril) James, Kt., CBE, QPM

Andrew, Sir Robert John, KCB

Andrews, Sir Derek Henry, KCB, CBE

Andrews, Hon. Sir Dormer George, Kt.

Angus, Sir Michael Richardson, Kt.

Annesley, Sir Hugh Norman, Kt., QPM

Anson, Vice-Adm. Sir Edward Rosebery, KCB

Anson, Sir John, KCB

Anson, Rear-Adm. Sir Peter, Bt., CB (1831)

Anstruther, Sir Ian Fife Campbell, Bt., (S. 1694)

Anstruther-Gough-Calthorpe, Sir Euan Hamilton, Bt. (1929)

Antico, Sir Tristan Venus, Kt.

Antrobus, Sir Edward Philip, Bt. (1815)

Appleyard, Sir Leonard Vincent, KCMG

Appleyard, Sir Raymond Kenelm, KBE

Arbib, Sir Martyn, Kt.

Arbuthnot, Sir Keith Robert Charles, Bt. (1823)

Arbuthnot, Sir William Reierson, Bt. (1964)

Arbuthnott, Prof. Sir John Peebles, Kt., Ph.D., FRSE

Archdale, Capt. Sir Edward Folmer, Bt., DSC, RN (1928)

Arculus, Sir Ronald, KCMG, KCVO

Armitage, Air Chief Marshal Sir Michael John, KCB, CBE

Armour, Prof. Sir James, Kt., CBE

Armstrong, Sir Christopher John Edmund Stuart, Bt., MBE (1841)

Armstrong, Sir Patrick John, Kt., CBE

Armytage, Sir John Martin, Bt. (1738)

Arnold, Rt. Hon. Sir John Lewis, Kt.

Arnold, Sir Malcolm Henry, Kt., CBE

Arnold, Sir Thomas Richard, Kt.

Arnott, Sir Alexander John Maxwell, Bt. (1896)

Arrindell, Sir Clement Athelston, GCMG, GCVO, QC

Arthur, Lt.-Gen. Sir (John) Norman Stewart, KCB

Arthur, Sir Stephen John, Bt. (1841)

Ash, Prof. Sir Eric Albert, Kt., CBE, FRS, FREng.

Ashburnham, Sir James Fleetwood, Bt. (1661)

Ashley, Sir Bernard Albert, Kt.

Ashmore, Admiral of the Fleet Sir Edward Beckwith, GCB, DSC

†Aske, Sir Robert John Bingham, Bt. (1922)

Askew, Sir Bryan, Kt.

Asscher, Prof. Sir (Adolf) William, Kt., MD, FRCP

Astill, Hon. Sir Michael John, Kt.

Astley-Cooper, Sir Alexander Paston, Bt. (1821)

Aston, Sir Harold George, Kt., CBE

Astwood, Hon. Sir James Rufus, KBE

Atcherley, Sir Harold Winter, Kt.

Atiyah, Sir Michael Francis, Kt., OM, Ph.D., FRS

Atkins, Rt. Hon. Sir Robert James, Kt.

Atkinson, Prof. Sir Anthony Barnes, Kt.

Atkinson, Air Marshal Sir David William, KBE

Atkinson, Sir Frederick John, KCB

Atkinson, Sir John Alexander, KCB, DFC

Atkinson, Sir Robert, Kt., DSC, FREng.

Atopare, Sir Sailas, GCMG

Attenborough, Sir David Frederick, Kt., CH, CVO, CBE, FRS

Aubrey-Fletcher, Sir Henry Egerton, Bt. (1782)

Audland, Sir Christopher John, KCMG

Audley, Sir George Bernard, Kt.

Augier, Prof. Sir Fitz-Roy Richard, Kt.

Auld, Rt. Hon. Sir Robin Ernest, Kt.

Austin, Sir Anthony Leonard, Bt. (1894)

Austin, Vice-Adm. Sir Peter Murray, KCB

Austin, Air Marshal Sir Roger Mark, KCB, AFC

Austen-Smith, Air Marshal Sir Roy David, KBE, CB, CVO, DFC

Avei, Sir Moi, KBE

Axford, Sir William Ian, Kt.

Ayckbourn, Sir Alan, Kt., CBE

Aykroyd, Sir James Alexander Frederic, Bt. (1929)

Aykroyd, Sir William Miles, Bt., MC (1920)

Aylmer, Sir Richard John, Bt. (I. 1622)

Bacha, Sir Bhinod, Kt., CMG

Backhouse, Sir Jonathan Roger, Bt. (1901)

Bacon, Sir Nicholas Hickman Ponsonby, Bt. Premier Baronet of England (1611 and 1627)

Bacon, Sir Sidney Charles, Kt., CB, FREng.

Baddeley, Sir John Wolsey Beresford, Bt. (1922)

Baddiley, Prof. Sir James, Kt., Ph.D., D.Sc., FRS, FRSE

Badge, Sir Peter Gilmour Noto, Kt.

Baer, Sir Jack Mervyn Frank, Kt.

Bagge, Sir (John) Jeremy Picton, Bt. (1867)

Bagnall, *Air Chief Marshal* Sir Anthony, GBE, KCB

Bailey, Sir Alan Marshall, KCB

Bailey, Sir Brian Harry, Kt., OBE

Bailey, Sir Derrick Thomas Louis, Bt., DFC (1919)

Bailey, Sir John Bilsland, KCB

Bailey, Sir Richard John, Kt., CBE

Bailey, Sir Stanley Ernest, Kt., CBE, QPM

Bailhache, Sir Philip Martin, Kt.

Baillie, Sir Gawaine George Hope, Bt. (1823)

Bain, *Prof.* Sir George Sayers, Kt.

Baird, Sir Charles William Stuart, Bt. (1809)

†Baird, Sir James Andrew Gardiner, Bt. (S. 1695)

Baird, *Lt.-Gen.* Sir James Parlane, KBE, MD

Baird, *Air Marshal* Sir John Alexander, KBE

Baird, *Vice-Adm.* Sir Thomas Henry Eustace, KCB

Bairsto, *Air Marshal* Sir Peter Edward, KBE, CB

Baker, Sir Bryan William, Kt.

Baker, *Prof.* Sir John Hamilton, Kt., QC

Baker, *Rt. Hon.* Sir (Thomas) Scott (Gillespie), Kt.

Balchin, Sir Robert George Alexander, Kt.

Balderstone, Sir James Schofield, Kt.

Baldwin, *Prof.* Sir Jack Edward, Kt., FRS

Baldwin, Sir Peter Robert, KCB

Ball, *Air Marshal* Sir Alfred Henry Wynne, KCB, DSO, DFC

Ball, Sir Christopher John Elinger, Kt.

Ball, Sir Richard Bentley, Bt. (1911)

Ball, *Prof.* Sir Robert James, Kt., Ph.D.

Ballantyne, *Dr* Sir Frederick Nathaniel, GCMG

Bamford, Sir Anthony Paul, Kt.

Band, *Adm.* Sir Jonathon, KCB

Banham, Sir John Michael Middlecott, Kt.

Bannerman, Sir David Gordon, Bt., OBE (S. 1682)

Bannister, Sir Roger Gilbert, Kt., CBE, DM, FRCP

Barber, Sir (Thomas) David, Bt. (1960)

Barbour, *Very Revd* Robert Alexander Stewart, KCVO, MC

Barclay, Sir Colville Herbert Sanford, Bt. (S. 1668)

Barclay, Sir David Rowat, Kt.

Barclay, Sir Frederick Hugh, Kt.

Barclay, Sir Peter Maurice, Kt., CBE

Barder, Sir Brian Leon, KCMG

Baring, Sir John Francis, Bt. (1911)

Barker, Sir Colin, Kt.

Barker, *Hon.* Sir (Richard) Ian, Kt.

Barlow, Sir Christopher Hilaro, Bt. (1803)

Barlow, Sir Frank, Kt., CBE

Barlow, Sir (George) William, Kt., FREng.

Barlow, Sir John Kemp, Bt. (1907)

Barlow, Sir Thomas Erasmus, Bt., DSC (1902)

Barnard, Sir Joseph Brian, Kt.

Barnes, *The Most Revd.* Brian James, KBE

Barnes, Sir (James) David (Francis), Kt., CBE

Barnes, Sir Kenneth, KCB

Barnewall, Sir Reginald Robert, Bt. (I. 1623)

Baron, Sir Thomas, Kt., CBE

Barraclough, *Air Chief Marshal* Sir John, KCB, CBE, DFC, AFC

Barran, Sir John Napoleon Ruthven, Bt. (1895)

Barratt, Sir Lawrence Arthur, Kt.

Barratt, Sir Richard Stanley, Kt., CBE, QPM

Barratt-Boyes, Sir Brian Gerald, KBE

Barrett, Sir Stephen Jeremy, KCMG

Barrett-Lennard, *Revd* Hugh Dacre, Bt. (1801)

Barrington, Sir Benjamin, Bt. (1831)

Barrington, Sir Nicholas John, KCMG, CVO

Barrington-Ward, *Rt. Rev.* Simon, KCMG

Barron, Sir Donald James, Kt.

Barrow, *Capt.* Sir Richard John Uniacke, Bt. (1835)

Barry, Sir (Lawrence) Edward (Anthony Tress), Bt. (1899)

Barter, Sir Peter Leslie Charles, Kt., OBE

†Bartlett, Sir Andrew Alan, Bt. (1913)

Barttelot, *Col.* Sir Brian Walter de Stopham, Bt., OBE (1875)

Batchelor, Sir Ivor Ralph Campbell, Kt., CBE

Bate, Sir David Lindsay, KBE

Bates, Sir Alan Arthur, Kt., CBE

Bates, Sir Geoffrey Voltelin, Bt., MC (1880)

Bates, Sir Malcolm Rowland, Kt.

Bates, Sir Richard Dawson Hoult, Bt. (1937)

Bateson, *Prof.* Sir Patrick, Kt.

Batho, Sir Peter Ghislain, Bt. (1928)

Bathurst, *Admiral of the Fleet* Sir (David) Benjamin, GCB

Bathurst, Sir Maurice Edward, Kt., CMG, CBE, QC

Batten, Sir John Charles, KCVO

Battersby, *Prof.* Sir Alan Rushton, Kt., FRS

Battishill, Sir Anthony Michael William, GCB

Batty, Sir William Bradshaw, Kt., TD

Baxendell, Sir Peter Brian, Kt., CBE, FREng.

Bayliss, Sir Richard Ian Samuel, KCVO, MD, FRCP

Bayne, Sir Nicholas Peter, KCMG

Baynes, Sir John Christopher Malcolm, Bt. (1801)

Bazley, Sir Thomas John Sebastian, Bt. (1869)

Beach, *Gen.* Sir (William Gerald) Hugh, GBE, KCB, MC

Beache, *Hon.* Sir Vincent Ian, KCMG

Beale, *Lt.-Gen.* Sir Peter John, KBE, FRCP

Beament, Sir James William Longman, Kt., Sc.D., FRS

Beamish, Sir Adrian John, KCMG

Beaumont, *Capt.* the Hon. Sir (Edward) Nicholas (Canning), KCVO

Beaumont, Sir George (Howland Francis), Bt. (1661)

Beaumont, Sir Richard Ashton, KCMG, OBE

Beaumont-Dark, Sir Anthony Michael, Kt

Beatson, *Hon.* Sir Jack, Kt.

Beavis, *Air Chief Marshal* Sir Michael Gordon, KCB, CBE, AFC

Beck, Sir Edgar Philip, Kt.

Beckett, Sir Richard Gervase, Bt., QC (1921)

Beckett, Sir Terence Norman, KBE, FREng.

Beckwith, Sir John Lionel, Kt., CBE

Bedser, Sir Alec Victor, Kt., CBE

Beecham, Sir Jeremy Hugh, Kt.

Beecham, Sir John Stratford Roland, Bt. (1914)

Beetham, *Marshal of the Royal Air Force* Sir Michael James, GCB, CBE, DFC, AFC

Beevor, Sir Thomas Agnew, Bt. (1784)

Beldam, *Rt. Hon.* Sir (Alexander) Roy (Asplan), Kt.

Belich, Sir James, Kt.

Bell, Sir Brian Ernest, KBE

Bell, Sir John Lowthian, Bt. (1885)

Bell, *Prof.* Sir Peter Robert Frank, Kt.

Bell, *Hon.* Sir Rodger, Kt.

Bellamy, *Hon.* Sir Christopher William, Kt.

Bellingham, Sir Anthony Edward Norman, Bt. (1796)

Bender, Sir Brian Geoffrey, KCB

Bengough, *Col.* Sir Piers, KCVO, OBE

Benn, Sir (James) Jonathan, Bt. (1914)

Bennett, *Air Vice-Marshal* Sir Erik Peter, KBE, CB

Bennett, *Hon.* Sir Hugh Peter Derwyn, Kt.

Bennett, *Gen.* Sir Phillip Harvey, KBE, DSO

Bennett, Sir Richard Rodney, Kt., CBE

Bennett, Sir Ronald Wilfrid Murdoch, Bt. (1929)

Benson, Sir Christopher John, Kt.

Benyon, Sir William Richard, Kt.

Beresford, Sir (Alexander) Paul, Kt., MP

Beresford-Peirse, Sir Henry Grant de la Poer, Bt. (1814)

Berger, *Vice-Adm.* Sir Peter Egerton Capel, KCB, LVO, DSC

Berghuser, *Hon.* Sir Eric, Kt., MBE
Beringer, *Prof.* Sir John Evelyn, Kt., CBE
Berman, Sir Franklin Delow, KCMG
Bernard, Sir Dallas Edmund, Bt. (1954)
Bernstein, Sir Howard, Kt.
Berney, Sir Julian Reedham Stuart, Bt. (1620)
Berridge, *Prof.* Sir Michael John, Kt., FRS
Berrill, Sir Kenneth Ernest, GBE, KCB
Berriman, Sir David, Kt.
Berry, *Prof.* Sir Colin Leonard, Kt., FRCPath.
Berry, *Prof.* Sir Michael Victor, Kt., FRS
Berthon, *Vice-Adm.* Sir Stephen Ferrier, KCB
Berthoud, Sir Martin Seymour, KCVO, CMG
Best, Sir Richard Radford, KCVO, CBE
Best-Shaw, Sir John Michael Robert, Bt. (1665)
Bethune, *Hon.* Sir (Walter) Angus, Kt.
Bett, Sir Michael, Kt., CBE
Bevan, Sir Martyn Evan Evans, Bt. (1958)
Bevan, Sir Nicolas, Kt., CB
Bevan, Sir Timothy Hugh, Kt.
Beverley, *Lt.-Gen.* Sir Henry York La Roche, KCB, OBE, RM
Bhattacharyya, *Prof.* Sir Sushantha Kumar, Kt.
Bibby, Sir Michael James, Bt. (1959)
Bichard, Sir Michael George, KCB
Bickersteth, *Rt. Revd* John Monier, KCVO
Biddulph, Sir Ian D'Olier, Bt. (1664)
Bide, Sir Austin Ernest, Kt.
Bidwell, Sir Hugh Charles Philip, GBE
Biggam, Sir Robin Adair, Kt.
Biggs, Sir Norman Paris, Kt.
Bilas, Sir Angmai Simon, Kt., OBE
Billière, *Gen.* Sir Peter Edgar de la Cour de la, KCB, KBE, DSO, MC
Bingham, *Hon.* Sir Eardley Max, Kt.
Birch, Sir John Allan, KCVO, CMG
Birch, Sir Roger, Kt., CBE, QPM
Bird, Sir Richard Geoffrey Chapman, Bt. (1922)
Birkin, Sir John Christian William, Bt. (1905)
Birkin, Sir (John) Derek, Kt., TD
Birkmyre, Sir James, Bt. (1921)
Birrell, Sir James Drake, Kt.
Birtwistle, Sir Harrison, Kt. CH
Bischoff, Sir Winfried Franz Wilhelm, Kt.
Bishop, Sir Frederick Arthur, Kt., CB, CVO
Bishop, Sir Michael David, Kt., CBE
Bisson, *Rt. Hon.* Sir Gordon Ellis, Kt.
Bjelke-Petersen, Sir Johannes, KCMG
Black, Sir James Whyte, Kt., OM, FRCP, FRS
Black, *Adm.* Sir (John) Jeremy, GBE, KCB, DSO

Black, Sir Robert David, Bt. (1922)
Blackburne, *Hon.* Sir William Anthony, Kt.
Blacker, *Gen.* Sir (Anthony Stephen) Jeremy, KCB, CBE
Blackett, Sir Hugh Francis, Bt. (1673)
Blackham, *Vice-Adm.* Sir Jeremy Joe, KCB
Blacklock, *Surgeon Capt. Prof.* Sir Norman James, KCVO, OBE
Blackman, Sir Frank Milton, KCVO, OBE
Blackwood, Sir John Francis, Bt. (1814) Blair, *Lt.-Gen.* Sir Chandos, KCVO, OBE, MC
Blair, Sir Edward Thomas Hunter, Bt. (1786)
Blair, Sir Ian Warwick, Kt., QPM
Blake, Sir Alfred Lapthorn, KCVO, MC
Blake, Sir Francis Michael, Bt. (1907)
Blake, Sir Peter Thomas, Kt, CBE
Blake, Sir (Thomas) Richard (Valentine), Bt. (I. 1622)
Blaker, Sir John, Bt. (1919)
Blakiston, Sir Ferguson Arthur James, Bt. (1763)
Blanch, Sir Malcolm, KCVO
Bland, Sir (Francis) Christopher (Buchan), Kt.
Bland, *Lt.-Col.* Sir Simon Claud Michael, KCVO
Blank, Sir Maurice Victor, Kt.
Blatherwick, Sir David Elliott Spiby, KCMG, OBE
Blelloch, Sir John Nial Henderson, KCB
Blennerhassett, Sir (Marmaduke) Adrian Francis William, Bt. (1809)
Blewitt, *Maj.* Sir Shane Gabriel Basil, GCVO
Blofeld, *Hon.* Sir John Christopher Calthorpe, Kt.
Blois, Sir Charles Nicholas Gervase, Bt. (1686)
Blom-Cooper, Sir Louis Jacques, Kt., QC
Blomefield, Sir Thomas Charles Peregrine, Bt. (1807)
Bloomfield, Sir Kenneth Percy, KCB
Blount, Sir Walter Edward Alpin, Bt., DSC (1642)
Blundell, Sir Thomas Leon, Kt., FRS
Blunden, Sir George, Kt.
Blunden, Sir Philip Overington, Bt. (I. 1766)
Blunt, Sir David Richard Reginald Harvey, Bt. (1720)
Blyth, Sir Charles (Chay), Kt., CBE, BEM
Boardman, *Prof.* Sir John, Kt., FSA, FBA
Bodey, *Hon.* Sir David Roderick Lessiter, Kt.
Bodmer, Sir Walter Fred, Kt., Ph.D., FRS
Body, Sir Richard Bernard Frank Stewart, Kt., MP
Bogan, Sir Nagora, KBE
Boileau, Sir Guy (Francis), Bt. (1838)

Boles, Sir Jeremy John Fortescue, Bt. (1922)
Boles, Sir John Dennis, Kt., MBE
Bolland, Sir Edwin, KCMG
Bollers, *Hon.* Sir Harold Brodie Smith, Kt.
Bolt, *Air Marshal* Sir Richard Bruce, KBE, CB, DFC, AFC
Bolton, Sir Frederic Bernard, Kt., MC
Bona, Sir Kina, KBE
Bonallack, Sir Michael Francis, Kt., OBE
Bond, Sir John Reginald Hartnell, Kt.
Bond, Sir Kenneth Raymond Boyden, Kt.
Bond, *Prof.* Sir Michael Richard, Kt., FRCPsych., FRCPGlas., FRCSE
Bondi, *Prof.* Sir Hermann, KCB, FRS
Bone, Sir Roger Bridgland, KCMG
Bonfield, Sir Peter Leahy, Kt., CBE, FREng.
Bonham, *Maj.* Sir Antony Lionel Thomas, Bt. (1852)
Bonington, Sir Christian John Storey, Kt., CBE
Bonsall, Sir Arthur Wilfred, KCMG, CBE
Bonsor, Sir Nicholas Cosmo, Bt. (1925)
Boolell, Sir Satcam, Kt.
Boord, Sir Nicolas John Charles, Bt. (1896)
Boorman, *Lt.-Gen.* Sir Derek, KCB
Booth, Sir Christopher Charles, Kt., MD, FRCP
Booth, *Prof.* Sir Clive, Kt.
Booth, Sir Douglas Allen, Bt. (1916)
Booth, Sir Gordon, KCMG, CVO
Boothby, Sir Brooke Charles, Bt. (1660)
Bore, Sir Albert, Kt.
Boreel, Sir Stephan Gerard, Bt. (1645)
Boreham, *Hon.* Sir Leslie Kenneth Edward, Kt.
†Borthwick, Sir Anthony Thomas, Bt. (1908)
Borysiewicz, *Prof.* Sir Leszek Krzysztof, Kt.
Bossom, *Hon.* Sir Clive, Bt. (1953)
Boswell, *Lt.-Gen.* Sir Alexander Crawford Simpson, KCB, CBE
Bosworth, Sir Neville Bruce Alfred, Kt., CBE
Bottoms, *Prof.* Sir Anthony Edward, Kt.
Bottomley, Sir James Reginald Alfred, KCMG
Boughey, Sir John George Fletcher, Bt. (1798)
Boulton, Sir Clifford John, GCB
Boulton, Sir William Whytehead, Bt., CBE, TD (1944)
Bourn, Sir John Bryant, KCB
Bowater, Sir Euan David Vansittart, Bt. (1939)
Bowater, Sir (John) Vansittart, Bt. (1914)
Bowden, Sir Andrew, Kt., MBE

Bowden, Sir Nicholas Richard, Bt. (1915)

Bowen, Sir Geoffrey Fraser, Kt.

Bowen, Sir Mark Edward Mortimer, Bt. (1921)

Bowett, *Prof.* Sir Derek William, Kt., CBE, QC, FBA

†Bowlby, Sir Richard Peregrine Longstaff, Bt. (1923)

Bowman, Sir Jeffery Haverstock, Kt.

Bowman-Shaw, Sir (George) Neville, Kt.

Bowness, Sir Alan, Kt., CBE

Bowyer-Smyth, Sir Thomas Weyland, Bt. (1661)

Boyce, Sir Graham Hugh, KCMG

Boyce, Sir Robert Charles Leslie, Bt. (1952)

Boyd, Sir Alexander Walter, Bt. (1916)

Boyd, Sir John Dixon Iklé, KCMG

Boyd, *Prof.* Sir Robert Lewis Fullarton, Kt., CBE, D.Sc., FRS

Boyd-Carpenter, Sir (Marsom) Henry, KCVO

Boyd-Carpenter, *Lt.-Gen.* Hon. Sir Thomas Patrick John, KBE

Boyle, Sir Stephen Gurney, Bt. (1904)

Boynton, Sir John Keyworth, Kt., MC

Boys, *Rt. Hon.* Sir Michael Hardie, GCMG

Boyson, *Rt. Hon.* Sir Rhodes, Kt.

Brabham, Sir John Arthur, Kt., OBE

Bracewell-Smith, Sir Charles, Bt. (1947)

Bradbeer, Sir John Derek Richardson, Kt., OBE, TD

Bradford, Sir Edward Alexander Slade, Bt. (1902)

Bradshaw, Sir Kenneth Anthony, KCB

Braithwaite, Sir (Joseph) Franklin Madders, Kt.

Braithwaite, *Rt. Hon.* Sir Nicholas Alexander, Kt., OBE

Braithwaite, Sir Rodric Quentin, GCMG

Bramley, *Prof.* Sir Paul Anthony, Kt.

Branson, Sir Richard Charles Nicholas, Kt.

Bratza, *Hon.* Sir Nicolas Dušan, Kt.

Brennan, *Hon.* Sir (Francis) Gerard, KBE

Brett, Sir Charles Edward Bainbridge, Kt., CBE

Brickwood, Sir Basil Greame, Bt. (1927)

Bridges, *Hon.* Sir Phillip Rodney, Kt., CMG

Brierley, Sir Ronald Alfred, Kt.

Bright, Sir Graham Frank James, Kt.

Bright, Sir Keith, Kt.

Brigstocke, *Adm.* Sir John Richard, KCB

Brinckman, Sir Theodore George Roderick, Bt. (1831)

†Brisco, Sir Campbell Howard, Bt. (1782)

Briscoe, Sir Brian Anthony, Kt.

Briscoe, Sir John Geoffrey James, Bt. (1910)

Brittan, Sir Samuel, Kt.

Britton, Sir Edward Louis, Kt., CBE

†Broadbent, Sir Andrew George, Bt. (1893)

Broadbent, Sir Richard John, KCB

Brocklebank, Sir Aubrey Thomas, Bt. (1885)

Brodie, Sir Benjamin David Ross, Bt. (1834)

Brodie-Hall, Sir Laurence Charles, Kt., AO, CMG

Broers, *Prof.* Sir Alec Nigel, Kt., Ph.D., FRS

Bromhead, Sir John Desmond Gonville, Bt. (1806)

Bromley, Sir Michael Roger, KBE

Bromley, Sir Rupert Charles, Bt. (1757)

Brook, *Prof.* Sir Richard John, Kt. OBE

†Brooke, Sir Alistair Weston, Bt. (1919)

Brooke, Sir Francis George Windham, Bt. (1903)

Brooke, *Rt. Hon.* Sir Henry, Kt.

Brooke, Sir (Richard) David Christopher, Bt. (1662)

Brooks, Sir Timothy Gerald Martin, KCVO

Brooksbank, Sir (Edward) Nicholas, Bt. (1919)

Broomfield, Sir Nigel Hugh Robert Allen, KCMG

†Broughton, Sir David Delves, Bt. (1661)

Broun, Sir William Windsor, Bt. (S. 1686)

Brown, Sir (Austen) Patrick, KCB

Brown, *Adm.* Sir Brian Thomas, KCB, CBE

Brown, Sir (Cyril) Maxwell Palmer, KCB, CMG

Brown, Sir David, Kt.

Brown, *Vice-Adm.* Sir David Worthington, KCB

Brown, Sir Douglas Denison, Kt.

Brown, *Hon.* Sir Douglas Dunlop, Kt.

Brown, Sir George Francis Richmond, Bt. (1863)

Brown, Sir George Noel, Kt.

Brown, Sir Mervyn, KCMG, OBE

Brown, Sir Peter Randolph, Kt.

Brown, *Rt. Hon.* Sir Simon Denis, Kt.

Brown, *Rt. Hon.* Sir Stephen, GBE

Brown, Sir Stephen David Reid, KCVO

Brown, Sir Thomas, Kt.

Browne, Sir Nicholas Walker, KBE, CMG

Brownrigg, Sir Nicholas (Gawen), Bt. (1816)

Browse, *Prof.* Sir Norman Leslie, Kt., MD, FRCS

Bruce, Sir (Francis) Michael Ian, Bt. (S. 1628)

Bruce, Sir Hervey James Hugh, Bt. (1804)

Bruce-Gardner, Sir Robert Henry, Bt. (1945)

Bruce-Lockhart, Sir Alexander John (Sandy), Kt., OBE

Buckworth-Herne-Soame, Sir Charles John, Bt. (1697)

Brunner, Sir John Henry Kilian, Bt. (1895)

Brunton, Sir (Edward Francis) Lauder, Bt. (1908)

Brunton, Sir Gordon Charles, Kt.

Bryan, Sir Arthur, Kt.

Bryan, Sir Paul Elmore Oliver, Kt., DSO, MC

Bryce, *Hon.* Sir (William) Gordon, Kt., CBE

Bryson, *Adm.* Sir Lindsay Sutherland, KCB, FREng.

Buchan-Hepburn, Sir John Alastair Trant Kidd, Bt. (1815)

Buchanan, Sir Andrew George, Bt. (1878)

Buchanan, *Vice-Adm.* Sir Peter William, KBE

Buchanan, Sir (Ranald) Dennis, Kt., MBE

Buchanan, Sir Robert Wilson (Robin), Kt.

Buchanan-Jardine, *Maj.* Sir (Andrew) Rupert (John), Bt., MC (1885)

Buck, Sir (Philip) Antony (Fyson), Kt., QC

Buckland, Sir Ross, Kt.

Buckley, Sir Michael Sidney, Kt.

Buckley, *Lt.-Cdr.* Sir (Peter) Richard, KCVO

Buckley, *Hon.* Sir Roger John, Kt.

Budd, Sir Alan Peter, Kt.

Budd, Sir Colin Richard, KCMG

Bull, Sir George Jeffrey, Kt.

Bull, Sir Simeon George, Bt. (1922)

Bullard, Sir Julian Leonard, GCMG

Bultin, Sir Bato, Kt., MBE

Bunbury, Sir Michael William, Bt. (1681)

Bunch, Sir Austin Wyeth, Kt., CBE

Bunyard, Sir Robert Sidney, Kt., CBE, QPM

Burbidge, Sir Herbert Dudley, Bt. (1916)

Burden, Sir Anthony Thomas, Kt., QPM

Burdett, Sir Savile Aylmer, Bt. (1665)

Burgen, Sir Arnold Stanley Vincent, Kt., FRS

Burgess, *Gen.* Sir Edward Arthur, KCB, OBE

Burgess, Sir (Joseph) Stuart, Kt., CBE, Ph.D., FRSC

Burgh, Sir John Charles, KCMG, CB

Burke, Sir James Stanley Gilbert, Bt. (I. 1797)

Burke, Sir (Thomas) Kerry, Kt.

Burley, Sir Victor George, Kt., CBE

Burnet, Sir James William Alexander (Sir Alastair Burnet), Kt.

Burnett, *Air Chief Marshal* Sir Brian Kenyon, GCB, DFC, AFC Burnett, Sir Charles David, Bt., (1913)

Burnett, Sir John Harrison, Kt.

Burnett, Sir Walter John, Kt.

Burney, Sir Nigel Dennistoun, Bt.
(1921)
Burns, Sir (Robert) Andrew, KCMG
Burnton, *Hon.* Sir Stanley Jeffrey, Kt.
Burrell, Sir John Raymond, Bt.
(1774)
Burston, Sir Samuel Gerald Wood,
Kt., OBE
Burt, Sir Peter Alexander, Kt.
Burt, *Hon.* Sir Francis Theodore
Page, KCMG
Burton, Sir Carlisle Archibald, Kt.,
OBE
Burton, Sir George Vernon Kennedy,
Kt., CBE
Burton, *Lt.-Gen.* Sir Edmund
Fortescue Gerard, KBE
Burton, Sir Graham Stuart, KCMG
Burton, *Hon.* Sir Michael John, Kt.
Burton, Sir Michael St Edmund,
KCVO, CMG
Bush, *Adm.* Sir John Fitzroy
Duyland, GCB, DSC
Butler, *Rt. Hon.* Sir Adam Courtauld,
Kt.
Butler, *Hon.* Sir Arlington Griffith,
KCMG
Butler, Sir Michael Dacres, GCMG
Butler, Sir (Reginald) Michael
(Thomas), Bt. (1922)
Butler, Sir Percy James, Kt., CBE, DL
Butler, *Hon.* Sir Richard Clive, Kt.
Butler, Sir Richard Pierce, Bt. (1628)
Butter, *Maj.* Sir David Henry, KCVO,
MC
Butterfield, *Hon.* Sir Alexander Neil
Logie, Kt.
Buxton, Sir Jocelyn Charles Roden,
Bt. (1840)
Buxton, *Rt. Hon.* Sir Richard Joseph,
Kt.
Buzzard, Sir Anthony Farquhar, Bt.
(1929)
Byatt, Sir Hugh Campbell, KCVO,
CMG
Byatt, Sir Ian Charles Rayner, Kt.
Byford, Sir Lawrence, Kt., CBE, QPM
Byron, Sir Charles Michael Dennis,
Kt.
†Cable-Alexander, Sir Patrick
Desmond William, Bt. (1809)
Cadbury, Sir (George) Adrian
(Hayhurst), Kt.
Cadbury, Sir (Nicholas) Dominic, Kt.
Cadogan, *Prof.* Sir John Ivan George,
Kt., CBE, FRS, FRSE
Cahn, Sir Albert Jonas, Bt. (1934)
Cain, Sir Henry Edney Conrad, Kt.
Caine, Sir Michael (Maurice
Micklewhite), Kt., CBE
Caines, Sir John, KCB
Calcutt, Sir David Charles, Kt., QC
Calderwood, Sir Robert, Kt.
Caldwell, Sir Edward George, KCB
Callan, Sir Ivan Roy, KCVO, CMG
Callaway, *Prof.* Sir Frank Adams, Kt.,
CMG, OBE
Calman, *Prof.* Sir Kenneth Charles,
KCB, MD, FRCP, FRCS, FRSE
Calne, *Prof.* Sir Roy Yorke, Kt., FRS
Calvert-Smith, Sir David, Kt., QC

Cameron of Lochiel, Sir Donald
Hamish, KT, CVO, TD
Cameron, Sir Ewen James Hanning,
Kt.
Cameron, Sir Hugh Roy Graham,
Kt., QPM
Campbell, Sir Alan Hugh, GCMG
Campbell, *Prof.* Sir Colin Murray,
Kt.
Campbell, *Prof.* Sir Donald, Kt.,
CBE, FRCS, FRCPGlas.
Campbell, Sir Ian Tofts, Kt., CBE,
VRD
Campbell, Sir Ilay Mark, Bt. (1808)
Campbell, Sir James Alexander
Moffat Bain, Bt. (S. 1668)
Campbell, Sir Lachlan Philip
Kemeys, Bt. (1815)
Campbell, Sir Niall Alexander
Hamilton, Bt. (1831)
Campbell, Sir Robin Auchinbreck,
Bt. (S. 1628)
Campbell, *Hon.* Sir Walter Benjamin,
Kt.
Campbell, *Rt. Hon.* Sir William
Anthony, Kt.
Campbell-Orde, Sir John Alexander,
Bt. (1790)
†Carden, Sir Christopher Robert, Bt.
(1887)
Carden, Sir John Craven, Bt.
(I. 1787)
Carew, Sir Rivers Verain, Bt. (1661)
Carey, Sir de Vic Graham, Kt.
Carey, Sir Peter Willoughby, GCB
Carleton-Smith, *Maj.-Gen.* Sir
Michael Edward, Kt., CBE
Carlisle, Sir James Beethoven, GCMG
Carlisle, Sir John Michael, Kt.
Carlisle, Sir Kenneth Melville, Kt.
Carnegie, *Lt.-Gen.* Sir Robin
Macdonald, KCB, OBE
Carnegie, Sir Roderick Howard, Kt.
Carnwath, *Rt. Hon.* Sir Robert John
Anderson, Kt., CVO
Caro, Sir Anthony Alfred, Kt., OM,
CBE
Carr, Sir (Albert) Raymond
(Maillard), Kt.
Carr-Ellison, *Col.* Sir Ralph Harry,
KCVO, TD
Carrick, *Hon.* Sir John Leslie, KCMG
Carrick, Sir Roger John, KCMG, LVO
Carruthers, Sir Ian James, Kt., OBE
Carsberg, *Prof.* Sir Bryan Victor, Kt.
Carswell, *Rt. Hon.* Sir Robert
Douglas, Kt.
Carter, *Prof.* Sir David Craig, Kt.,
FRCSE, FRCSGlas., FRCPE
Carter, Sir John, Kt., QC
Carter, Sir John Alexander, Kt.
Carter, Sir John Gordon Thomas, Kt.
Carter, Sir Philip David, Kt., CBE
Carter, Sir Richard Henry Alwyn,
Kt.
Cartland, Sir George Barrington, Kt.,
CMG
Cartledge, Sir Bryan George, KCMG
Cary, Sir Roger Hugh, Bt. (1955)
Casey, *Rt. Hon.* Sir Maurice Eugene,
Kt.

Cash, Sir Gerald Christopher,
GCMG, GCVO, OBE
Cass, Sir Geoffrey Arthur, Kt.
Cassel, Sir Timothy Felix Harold, Bt.
(1920)
Cassels, Sir John Seton, Kt., CB
Cassels, *Adm.* Sir Simon Alastair
Cassillis, KCB, CBE
Cassidi, *Adm.* Sir (Arthur) Desmond,
GCB
Castell, Sir William Martin, Kt.
Cater, Sir Jack, KBE
Catford, Sir (John) Robin, KCVO,
CBE
Catherwood, Sir (Henry) Frederick
(Ross), Kt.
Catling, Sir Richard Charles, Kt.,
CMG, OBE
Catto, *Prof.* Sir Graeme Robertson
Dawson, Kt.
Cave, Sir John Charles, Bt. (1896)
Cave-Browne-Cave, Sir Robert, Bt.
(1641)
Cayley, Sir Digby William David, Bt.
(1661)
Cayzer, Sir James Arthur, Bt. (1904)
Cazalet, *Hon.* Sir Edward Stephen,
Kt.
Cazalet, Sir Peter Grenville, Kt.
Cecil, *Rear-Adm.* Sir (Oswald) Nigel
Amherst, KBE, CB
Chadwick, *Revd Prof.* Henry, KBE
Chadwick, *Rt. Hon.* Sir John Murray,
Kt., ED
Chadwick, Sir Joshua Kenneth
Burton, Bt. (1935)
Chadwick, *Revd Prof.* (William)
Owen, OM, KBE, FBA
Chadwyck-Healey, Sir Charles
Edward, Bt. (1919)
Chalmers, Sir Iain Geoffrey, Kt.
Chalmers, Sir Neil Robert, Kt.
Chalstrey, Sir (Leonard) John, Kt.,
MD, FRCS
Chan, *Rt. Hon.* Sir Julius, GCMG,
KBE
Chance, Sir (George) Jeremy ffolliott,
Bt. (1900)
Chandler, Sir Colin Michael, Kt.
Chandler, Sir Geoffrey, Kt., CBE
Chantler, *Prof.* Sir Cyril, Kt., MD,
FRCP
Chaplin, Sir Malcolm Hilbery, Kt.,
CBE
Chapman, Sir David Robert
Macgowan, Bt. (1958)
Chapman, Sir George Alan, Kt.
Chapman, Sir Sidney Brookes, Kt.,
MP
Chapple, *Field Marshal* Sir John
Lyon, GCB, CBE
Charles, *Hon.* Sir Arthur William
Hessin, Kt
Charles, Sir George Frederick
Lawrence, KCMG, CBE
Charlton, Sir Robert (Bobby), Kt.,
CBE
Charnley, Sir (William) John, Kt., CB,
FREng.
Chataway, *Rt. Hon.* Sir Christopher,
Kt.

Chatfield, Sir John Freeman, Kt., CBE

Chaytor, Sir George Reginald, Bt. (1831)

Checketts, *Sqn. Ldr.* Sir David John, KCVO

Checkland, Sir Michael, Kt.

Cheshire, *Air Chief Marshal* Sir John Anthony, KBE, CB

Chessells, Sir Arthur David (Tim), Kt.

Chesterton, Sir Oliver Sidney, Kt., MC

Chetwood, Sir Clifford Jack, Kt.

Chetwynd, Sir Arthur Ralph Talbot, Bt. (1795)

Cheung, Sir Oswald Victor, Kt., CBE

Cheyne, Sir Joseph Lister Watson, Bt., OBE (1908)

Chichester, Sir (Edward) John, Bt. (1641)

Chichester-Clark, Sir Robin, Kt.

Chilcot, Sir John Anthony, GCB

Child, Sir (Coles John) Jeremy, Bt. (1919)

Chilton, *Brig.* Sir Frederick Oliver, Kt., CBE, DSO

Chilwell, *Hon.* Sir Muir Fitzherbert, Kt.

Chinn, Sir Trevor Edwin, Kt., CVO

Chipperfield, Sir Geoffrey Howes, KCB

Chisholm, Sir John Alexander Raymond, Kt., FREng.

Chitty, Sir Thomas Willes, Bt. (1924)

Cholmeley, Sir Hugh John Frederick Sebastian, Bt. (1806)

Chow, Sir Chung Kong, Kt.

Chow, Sir Henry Francis, Kt., OBE

Christie, Sir George William Langham, Kt., CH

Christie, Sir William, Kt., MBE

Christopher, Sir Duncan Robin Carmichael, KBE, CMG

Chung, Sir Sze-yuen, GBE, FREng.

Clark, Sir Francis Drake, Bt. (1886)

Clark, Sir Jonathan George, Bt. (1917)

Clark, Sir Robert Anthony, Kt., DSC

Clark, Sir Terence Joseph, KBE, CMG, CVO

Clark, Sir Thomas Edwin, Kt.

Clarke, *Rt. Hon.* Sir Anthony Peter, Kt.

Clarke, Sir Arthur Charles, Kt., CBE

Clarke, Sir (Charles Mansfield) Tobias, Bt. (1831)

Clarke, Sir Ellis Emmanuel Innocent, GCMG

Clarke, Sir Jonathan Dennis, Kt.

Clarke, *Maj.* Sir Peter Cecil, KCVO

Clarke, Sir Robert Cyril, Kt.

Clarke, Sir Rupert William John, Bt., MBE (1882)

Clarke, Sir Stanley William, Kt., CBE

Clay, Sir Richard Henry, Bt. (1841)

Clayton, Sir David Robert, Bt. (1732)

Cleaver, Sir Anthony Brian, Kt.

Cleminson, Sir James Arnold Stacey, KBE, MC

Clerk, Sir Robert Maxwell, Bt., OBE (1679)

Clerke, Sir John Edward Longueville, Bt. (1660)

Clifford, Sir Roger Joseph, Bt. (1887)

Clifford, Sir Timothy Peter Plint, Kt.

Clothier, Sir Cecil Montacute, KCB, QC

Clucas, Sir Kenneth Henry, KCB

Clutterbuck, *Vice-Adm.* Sir David Granville, KBE, CB

Coates, Sir Anthony Robert Milnes, Bt. (1911)

Coates, Sir David Frederick Charlton, Bt. (1921)

Coats, Sir Alastair Francis Stuart, Bt. (1905)

Coats, Sir William David, Kt.

Cobham, Sir Michael John, Kt., CBE

Cochrane, Sir (Henry) Marc (Sursock), Bt. (1903)

Cockburn, Sir John Elliot, Bt. (S. 1671)

Cockburn-Campbell, Sir Alexander Thomas, Bt. (1821)

Cockshaw, Sir Alan, Kt., FREng.

Codrington, Sir Simon Francis Bethell, Bt. (1876)

Codrington, Sir William Alexander, Bt. (1721)

Coghill, Sir Patrick Kendal Farley, Bt. (1778)

Coghlin, *Hon.* Sir Patrick, Kt.

Cohen, Sir Edward, Kt.

Cohen, Sir Ivor Harold, Kt., CBE, TD

Cohen, *Prof.* Sir Philip, Kt., Ph.D, FRS

Cohen, Sir Ronald, Kt.

Coldstream, Sir George Phillips, KCB, KCVO, QC

Cole, Sir (Robert) William, Kt.

Coleridge, *Hon.* Sir Paul James Duke, Kt.

Coles, Sir (Arthur) John, GCMG

Colfox, Sir (William) John, Bt. (1939)

Collett, Sir Christopher, GBE

Collett, Sir Ian Seymour, Bt. (1934)

Collins, *Hon.* Sir Andrew David, Kt.

Collins, Sir Bryan Thomas Alfred, Kt., OBE, QFSM

Collins, Sir John Alexander, Kt

Collins, Sir Kenneth Darlingston, Kt..

Collins, *Hon.* Sir Lawrence Antony, Kt.

Collyear, Sir John Gowen, Kt.

Colman, *Hon.* Sir Anthony David, Kt.

Colman, Sir Michael Jeremiah, Bt. (1907)

Colman, Sir Timothy, KG

Colquhoun of Luss, Sir Ivar Iain, Bt. (1786)

Colt, Sir Edward William Dutton, Bt. (1694)

Colthurst, Sir Richard La Touche, Bt. (1744)

Coltman, Sir (Arthur) Leycester Scott, KBE, CMG

Colvin, Sir Howard Montagu, Kt., CVO, CBE, FBA

Colyer-Fergusson, Sir James Herbert Hamilton, Bt. (1866)

Compton, *Rt. Hon.* Sir John George Melvin, KCMG

Conant, Sir John Ernest Michael, Bt. (1954)

Connell, *Hon.* Sir Michael Bryan, Kt.

Connery, Sir Sean, Kt.

Connor, Sir William Joseph, Kt.

Conran, Sir Terence Orby, Kt.

Cons, *Hon.* Sir Derek, Kt.

Constantinou, Sir Georkios, Kt., OBE

Cook, *Prof.* Sir Alan Hugh, Kt.

Cook, Sir Christopher Wymondham Rayner Herbert, Bt. (1886)

Cooke, *Col.* Sir David William Perceval, Bt. (1661)

Cooke, Sir Howard Felix Hanlan, GCMG, GCVO

Cooke, *Hon.* Sir Jeremy Lionel, Kt.

Cooke, *Prof.* Sir Ronald Urwick, Kt.

Cooksey, Sir David James Scott, Kt.

Cooper, *Gen.* Sir George Leslie Conroy, GCB, MC

Cooper, Sir Henry, Kt.

Cooper, Sir Richard Powell, Bt. (1905)

Cooper, Sir Robert George, Kt., CBE

Cooper, *Maj.-Gen.* Sir Simon Christie, GCVO

Cooper, Sir William Daniel Charles, Bt. (1863)

Coote, Sir Christopher John, Bt., *Premier Baronet of Ireland* (I. 1621)

Copas, *Most Revd* Virgil, KBE, DD

Copisarow, Sir Alcon Charles, Kt.

Corbett, *Maj.-Gen.* Sir Robert John Swan, KCVO, CB

Corby, Sir (Frederick) Brian, Kt.

Cordy-Simpson, *Lt.-Gen.* Sir Roderick Alexander, KBE, CB

Corfield, *Rt. Hon.* Sir Frederick Vernon, Kt.

Corfield, Sir Kenneth George, Kt., FREng.

Corley, Sir Kenneth Sholl Ferrand, Kt.

Cormack, Sir Patrick Thomas, Kt., MP

Corness, Sir Colin Ross, Kt.

Cornforth, Sir John Warcup, Kt., CBE, D.Phil., FRS

Corry, Sir James Michael, Bt. (1885)

Cortazzi, Sir (Henry Arthur) Hugh, GCMG

Cory, Sir (Clinton Charles) Donald, Bt. (1919)

Cory-Wright, Sir Richard Michael, Bt. (1903)

Cossons, Sir Neil, Kt., OBE

†Cotter, Sir Patrick Laurence Delaval Bt. (I. 1763)

Cotterell, Sir John Henry Geers, Bt. (1805)

Cotton, *Hon.* Sir Robert Carrington, KCMG

Cotton, Sir William Frederick, Kt., CBE

Cottrell, Sir Alan Howard, Kt., Ph.D, FRS, FREng.

†Cotts, Sir Richard Crichton Mitchell, Bt. (1921)
Couper, Sir James George, Bt. (1841)
Court, *Hon.* Sir Charles Walter Michael, KCMG, OBE
Courtenay, Sir Thomas Daniel, Kt.
Cousins, *Air Chief Marshal* Sir David, KCB, AFC
Couzens, Sir Kenneth Edward, KCB
Coville, *Air Marshal* Sir Christopher Charles Cotton, KCB
Cowan, *Gen.* Sir Samuel, KCB, CBE
Coward, *Vice-Adm.* Sir John Francis, KCB, DSO
Cowen, *Rt. Hon. Prof.* Sir Zelman, GCMG, GCVO
Cowie, Sir Thomas (Tom), Kt., OBE
Cowperthwaite, Sir John James, KBE, CMG
Cox, Sir Alan George, Kt., CBE
Cox, *Prof.* Sir David Roxbee, Kt., FRS
Cox, Sir Geoffrey Sandford, Kt., CBE
Cox, *Vice-Adm.* Sir John Michael Holland, KCB
Cradock, *Rt. Hon.* Sir Percy, GCMG
Craig, Sir (Albert) James (Macqueen), GCMG
Craig-Cooper, Sir (Frederick Howard) Michael, Kt., CBE, TD
Crane, *Hon.* Sir Peter Francis, Kt.
Craufurd, Sir Robert James, Bt. (1781)
Craven, Sir John Anthony, Kt.
Crawford, *Prof.* Sir Frederick William, Kt., FREng.
Crawley-Boevey, Sir Thomas Michael Blake, Bt. (1784)
Crew, Sir (Michael) Edward, Kt., QPM
Cresswell, *Hon.* Sir Peter John, Kt.
Crichton-Brown, Sir Robert, KCMG, CBE, TD
Crick, *Prof.* Sir Bernard, Kt.
Crill, Sir Peter Leslie, KBE
Crisp, Sir Edmund Nigel Ramsay, KCB
Crisp, Sir (John) Peter, Bt. (1913)
Critchett, Sir Ian (George Lorraine), Bt. (1908)
Crockett, Sir Andrew Duncan, Kt.
Croft, Sir Owen Glendower, Bt. (1671)
Croft, Sir Thomas Stephen Hutton, Bt. (1818)
†Crofton, Sir Hugh Denis, Bt. (1801)
Crofton, *Prof.* Sir John Wenman, Kt.
†Crofton, Sir Julian Malby, Bt. (1838)
Crompton, Sir Dan, Kt., CBE, QPM
Crossland, *Prof.* Sir Bernard, Kt., CBE, FREng.
Crossley, Sir Julian Charles, Bt. (1909)
Crowe, Sir Brian Lee, KCMG
Cruthers, Sir James Winter, Kt.
Cubbon, Sir Brian Crossland, GCB
Cubitt, Sir Hugh Guy, Kt., CBE
Cullen, Sir (Edward) John, Kt., FREng.

Culme-Seymour, Sir Michael Patrick, Bt. (1809)
Culpin, Sir Robert Paul, Kt.
Cummins, Sir Michael John Austin, Kt.
Cunliffe, Sir David Ellis, Bt. (1759)
Cunliffe-Owen, Sir Hugo Dudley, Bt. (1920)
Cunningham, *Lt.-Gen.* Sir Hugh Patrick, KBE
Cunynghame, Sir Andrew David Francis, Bt. (S. 1702)
†Currie, Sir Donald Scott, Bt. (1847)
Curry, Sir Donald Thomas Younger, Kt., CBE
Curtis, Sir Barry John, Kt.
Curtis, *Hon.* Sir Richard Herbert, Kt.
Curtis, Sir William Peter, Bt. (1802)
Curtiss, *Air Marshal* Sir John Bagot, KCB, KBE
Curwen, Sir Christopher Keith, KCMG
Cuschieri, *Prof.* Sir Alfred, Kt.
Cutler, Sir Charles Benjamin, KBE, ED
Dacie, *Prof.* Sir John Vivian, Kt., MD, FRS
Dain, Sir David John Michael, KCVO
Dales, Sir Richard Nigel, KCVO
Dalrymple-Hay, Sir James Brian, Bt. (1798)
Dalrymple-White, *Wg Cdr.* Sir Henry Arthur, Bt., DFC (1926)
Dalton, Sir Alan Nugent Goring, Kt., CBE
Dalton, *Vice-Adm.* Sir Geoffrey Thomas James Oliver, KCB
Daly, *Lt.-Gen.* Sir Thomas Joseph, KBE, CB, DSO
Dalyell, Sir Tam (Thomas), Bt., MP (NS 1685)
Daniel, Sir John Sagar, Kt., D.Sc.
Darby, Sir Peter Howard, Kt., CBE, QFSM
Darell, Sir Jeffrey Lionel, Bt., MC (1795)
Darling, Sir Clifford, GCVO
Dasgupta, *Prof.* Sir Partha Sarathi, Kt.
†Dashwood, Sir Edward John Francis, Bt., *Premier Baronet of Great Britain* (1707)
Dashwood, Sir Richard James, Bt. (1684)
Daunt, Sir Timothy Lewis Achilles, KCMG
Davenport-Handley, Sir David John, Kt., OBE
David, Sir Jean Marc, Kt., CBE, QC
David, *His Hon.* Sir Robin (Robert) Daniel George, Kt.,
Davidson, Sir Robert James, Kt., FREng.
Davies, Sir Alan Seymour, Kt.
Davies, *Hon.* Sir (Alfred William) Michael, Kt.
Davies, Sir (Charles) Noel, Kt.
Davies, *Prof.* Sir David Evan Naughton, Kt., CBE, FRS, FREng.
Davies, *Hon.* Sir (David Herbert) Mervyn, Kt., MC, TD
Davies, Sir David John, Kt.

Davies, Sir Frank John, Kt., CBE
Davies, *Prof.* Sir Graeme John, Kt., FREng.
Davies, Sir John Howard, Kt.
Davies, Sir John Michael, KCB
Davies, *Vice-Adm.* Sir Lancelot Richard Bell, KBE
Davies, Sir Peter Maxwell, Kt., CBE
Davies, Sir Rhys Everson, Kt., QC
Davis, Sir Andrew Frank, Kt., CBE
Davis, Sir Colin Rex, Kt., CH, CBE
Davis, Sir (Ernest) Howard, Kt., CMG, OBE
Davis, Sir John Gilbert, Bt. (1946)
Davis, *Hon.* Sir Nigel Anthony Lambert, Kt.
Davis, Sir Peter John, Kt.
Davis, *Hon.* Sir Thomas Robert Alexander Harries, KBE
Davis-Goff, Sir Robert (William), Bt. (1905)
Davison, *Rt. Hon.* Sir Ronald Keith, GBE, CMG
Davson, Sir Christopher Michael Edward, Bt. (1927)
Dawanincura, Sir John Norbert, Kt., OBE
Dawbarn, Sir Simon Yelverton, KCVO, CMG
Dawson, *Hon.* Sir Daryl Michael, KBE, CB
Dawson, Sir Hugh Michael Trevor, Bt. (1920)
Dawtry, Sir Alan (Graham), Kt., CBE, TD
Day, Sir Derek Malcolm, KCMG
Day, *Air Chief Marshal* Sir John Romney, KCB, OBE, ADC
Day, Sir (Judson) Graham, Kt.
Day, Sir Michael John, Kt., OBE
Day, Sir Simon James, Kt.
Deakin, Sir (Frederick) William (Dampier), Kt., DSO
Deane, *Hon.* Sir William Patrick, KBE
Dear, Sir Geoffrey James, Kt., QPM
Dearlove, Sir Richard Billing, KCMG, OBE
de Bellaigue, Sir Geoffrey, GCVO
†Debenham, Sir Thomas Adam Bt. (1931)
de Deney, Sir Geoffrey Ivor, KCVO
de Hoghton, Sir (Richard) Bernard (Cuthbert), Bt. (1611)
De la Bère, Sir Cameron, Bt. (1953)
de la Rue, Sir Andrew George Ilay, Bt. (1898)
Dellow, Sir John Albert, Kt., CBE
Delves, *Lt.-Gen.* Sir Cedric Norman George, KBE
de Montmorency, Sir Arnold Geoffroy, Bt. (I. 1631)
Denholm, Sir John Ferguson (Ian), Kt., CBE
Denison-Smith, *Lt.-Gen.* Sir Anthony Arthur, KBE
Denman, Sir (George) Roy, KCB, CMG
Denny, Sir Anthony Coningham de Waltham, Bt. (I. 1782)
Denny, Sir Charles Alistair Maurice, Bt. (1913)

Denton, *Prof.* Sir Eric James, Kt.,
CBE, FRS
Derbyshire, Sir Andrew George, Kt.
Derham, Sir Peter John, Kt.
de Trafford, Sir Dermot Humphrey,
Bt. (1841)
Deverell, *Gen.* Sir John Freegard,
KCB, OBE
Devesi, Sir Baddeley, GCMG, GCVO
De Ville, Sir Harold Godfrey Oscar,
Kt., CBE
Devitt, Sir James Hugh Thomas, Bt.
(1916)
de Waal, Sir (Constant Henrik)
Henry, KCB, QC
Dewey, Sir Anthony Hugh, Bt.
(1917)
Dewhurst, *Prof.* Sir (Christopher)
John, Kt.
De Witt, Sir Ronald Wayne, Kt.
Dhenin, *Air Marshal* Sir Geoffrey
Howard, KBE, AFC, GM, MD
Dhrangadhra, HH the Maharaja Raj
Saheb of, KCIE
Dibela, *Hon.* Sir Kingsford, GCMG
Dick-Lauder, Sir Piers Robert, Bt.
(S. 1690)
Dickinson, Sir Harold Herbert, Kt.
Dickinson, Sir Samuel Benson, Kt.
Dilke, Sir Charles John Wentworth,
Bt. (1862)
Dillwyn-Venables-Llewelyn, Sir John
Michael, Bt. (1890)
Dixon, Sir Jeremy, Kt.
Dixon, Sir Jonathan Mark, Bt.
(1919)
Djanogly, Sir Harry Ari Simon, Kt.,
CBE
Dobbs, *Capt.* Sir Richard Arthur
Frederick, KCVO
Dobson, *Vice-Adm.* Sir David Stuart,
KBE
Dodds, Sir Ralph Jordan, Bt. (1964)
Dodds-Parker, Sir (Arthur) Douglas,
Kt.
Dodson, Sir Derek Sherborne
Lindsell, KCMG, MC
Doll, *Prof.* Sir (William) Richard
(Shaboe), Kt., CH, OBE, FRS, DM,
MD, D.Sc.
Dollery, Sir Colin Terence, Kt.
Don-Wauchope, Sir Roger
(Hamilton), Bt. (S. 1667)
Donald, Sir Alan Ewen, KCMG
Donald, *Air Marshal* Sir John
George, KBE
Donaldson, *Prof.* Sir Liam Joseph,
Kt.
Donne, *Hon.* Sir Gaven John, KBE
Donne, Sir John Christopher, Kt.
Donnelly, Sir Joseph Brian, KBE,
CMG
Dookun, Sir Dewoonarain, Kt.
Dorey, Sir Graham Martyn, Kt.
Dorman, Sir Philip Henry Keppel,
Bt. (1923)
Doughty, Sir Graham Martin, Kt.
Doughty, Sir William Roland, Kt.
Douglas, *Hon.* Sir Roger Owen, Kt.
Dover, *Prof.* Sir Kenneth James, Kt.,
D.Litt., FBA, FRSE

Dowell, Sir Anthony James, Kt., CBE
Dowling, Sir Robert, Kt.
Down, Sir Alastair Frederick, Kt.,
OBE, MC, TD
Downes, Sir Edward Thomas, Kt.,
CBE
Downey, Sir Gordon Stanley, KCB
Downs, Sir Diarmuid, Kt., CBE,
FREng.
Downward, *Maj.-Gen.* Sir Peter
Aldcroft, KCVO, CB, DSO, DFC
Downward, Sir William Atkinson,
Kt.
Dowson, Sir Philip Manning, Kt.,
CBE, PRA
Doyle, Sir Reginald Derek Henry,
Kt., CBE
†D'Oyly, Sir Hadley Gregory Bt.
(1663)
Drake, *Hon.* Sir (Frederick) Maurice,
Kt., DFC
Drewry, *Lt.-Gen.* Sir Christopher
Francis, KCB, CBE
Drinkwater, Sir John Muir, Kt., QC
Driver, Sir Eric William, Kt.
Drummond, Sir John Richard Gray,
Kt., CBE
Drury, Sir (Victor William) Michael,
Kt., OBE
Dryden, Sir John Stephen Gyles, Bt.
(1733 and 1795)
du Cann, *Rt. Hon.* Sir Edward Dillon
Lott, KBE
†Duckworth, Sir Edward Richard
Dyce, Bt. (1909)
du Cros, Sir Claude Philip Arthur
Mallet, Bt. (1916)
Dudley-Williams, Sir Alastair
Edgcumbe James, Bt. (1964)
Duff-Gordon, Sir Andrew Cosmo
Lewis, Bt. (1813)
Duffell, *Lt.-Gen.* Sir Peter Royson,
KCB, CBE, MC
Duffy, Sir (Albert) (Edward) Patrick,
Kt., Ph.D.
Dugdale, Sir William Stratford, Bt.,
MC (1936)
Dummett, *Prof.* Sir Michael Anthony
Eardley, Kt., FBA
Dunbar, Sir Archibald Ranulph, Bt.
(S. 1700)
Dunbar, Sir Robert Drummond
Cospatrick, Bt. (S. 1698)
Dunbar, Sir James Michael, Bt. (S.
1694)
Dunbar of Hempriggs, Sir Richard
Francis, Bt. (S. 1706)
Dunbar-Nasmith, *Prof.* Sir James
Duncan, Kt., CBE
Duncan, Sir James Blair, Kt.
Dunlop, Sir Thomas, Bt. (1916)
Dunn, *Air Marshal* Sir Eric Clive,
KBE, CB, BEM
Dunn, *Air Marshal* Sir Patrick
Hunter, KBE, CB, DFC
Dunn, *Rt. Hon.* Sir Robin Horace
Walford, Kt., MC
Dunne, Sir Thomas Raymond,
KCVO
Dunning, Sir Simon William Patrick,
Bt. (1930)

Dunnington-Jefferson, Sir Mervyn
Stewart, Bt. (1958)
Dunstan, *Lt.-Gen.* Sir Donald
Beaumont, KBE, CB
Dunt, *Vice-Adm.* Sir John Hugh, KCB
Duntze, Sir Daniel Evans Bt. (1774)
Dupre, Sir Tumun, Kt., MBE
Dupree, Sir Peter, Bt. (1921)
Durand, Sir Edward Alan
Christopher David Percy, Bt.
(1892)
Durant, Sir (Robert) Anthony
(Bevis), Kt.
Durham, Sir Kenneth, Kt.
Durie, Sir David Robert Campbell,
KCMG
Durkin, *Air Marshal* Sir Herbert,
KBE, CB
Durrant, Sir William Alexander
Estridge, Bt. (1784)
Duthie, *Prof.* Sir Herbert Livingston,
Kt.
Duthie, Sir Robert Grieve (Robin),
Kt., CBE
Dwyer, Sir Joseph Anthony, Kt.
Dyke, Sir David William Hart, Bt.
(1677)
Dyson, *Rt. Hon.* Sir John Anthony,
Kt.
Eady, *Hon.* Sir David, Kt.
Eardley-Wilmot, Sir Michael John
Assheton, Bt. (1821)
Earle, Sir (Hardman) George
(Algernon), Bt. (1869)
Easton, Sir Robert William Simpson,
Kt., CBE
Eaton, *Adm.* Sir Kenneth John, GBE,
KCB
Eberle, *Adm.* Sir James Henry Fuller,
GCB
Ebrahim, Sir (Mahomed)
Currimbhoy, Bt. (1910)
Echlin, Sir Norman David Fenton,
Bt. (I. 1721)
Eckersley, Sir Donald Payze, Kt.,
OBE
Edge, *Capt.* Sir (Philip) Malcolm,
KCVO
†Edge, Sir William, Bt. (1937)
Edmonstone, Sir Archibald Bruce
Charles, Bt. (1774)
Edwardes, Sir Michael Owen, Kt.
Edwards, Sir Christopher John
Churchill, Bt. (1866)
Edwards, Sir Llewellyn Roy, Kt.
Edwards, *Prof.* Sir Samuel Frederick,
Kt., FRS
†Edwards-Moss, Sir David John, Bt.
(1868)
Egan, Sir John Leopold, Kt.
Egerton, Sir Stephen Loftus, KCMG
Eichelbaum, *Rt. Hon.* Sir Thomas,
GBE
Elias, *Hon.* Sir Patrick, Kt.
Eliott of Stobs, Sir Charles Joseph
Alexander, Bt. (S. 1666)
Ellerton, Sir Geoffrey James, Kt.,
CMG, MBE
Elliot, Sir Gerald Henry, Kt.

Elliott, Sir Clive Christopher Hugh, Bt. (1917)
Elliott, Sir David Murray, KCMG, CB
Elliott, *Prof.* Sir John Huxtable, Kt., FBA
Elliott, Sir Randal Forbes, KBE
Elliott, *Prof.* Sir Roger James, Kt., FRS
Ellis, Sir Ronald, Kt., FREng.
Elphinstone, Sir John, Bt. (S. 1701)
Elphinstone, Sir John Howard Main, Bt. (1816)
Elsmore, Sir Lloyd, Kt., OBE
Elton, Sir Arnold, Kt., CBE
Elton, Sir Charles Abraham Grierson, Bt. (1717)
Elwes, Sir Jeremy Vernon, Kt., CBE
Elwood, Sir Brian George Conway, Kt., CBE
Elworthy, Sir Peter Herbert, Kt.
Elworthy, *Air Cdre. Hon.* Sir Timothy Charles, KCVO, CBE
Emery, *Rt. Hon.* Sir Peter Frank Hannibal, Kt., MP
Empey, Sir Reginald Norman Morgan, Kt., OBE
Engle, Sir George Lawrence Jose, KCB, QC
English, Sir Terence Alexander Hawthorne, KBE, FRCS
Epstein, *Prof.* Sir (Michael) Anthony, Kt., CBE, FRS
Errington, *Col.* Sir Geoffrey Frederick, Bt., OBE (1963)
Errington, Sir Lancelot, KCB
Erskine, Sir (Thomas) David, Bt. (1821)
Erskine-Hill, Sir Alexander Rodger, Bt. (1945)
Esmonde, Sir Thomas Francis Grattan, Bt. (I. 1629)
Espie, Sir Frank Fletcher, Kt., OBE
Esplen, Sir John Graham, Bt. (1921)
Essenhigh, *Adm.* Sir Nigel Richard, GCB
Etherton, *Hon.* Sir Terence Michael Elkan Barnet, Kt.
Evans, Sir Anthony Adney, Bt. (1920)
Evans, *Rt. Hon.* Sir Anthony Howell Meurig, Kt., RD
Evans, *Prof.* Sir Christopher Thomas, Kt., OBE
Evans, *Air Chief Marshal* Sir David George, GCB, CBE
Evans, *Hon.* Sir David Roderick, Kt.
Evans, *Hon.* Sir Haydn Tudor, Kt.
Evans, *Prof.* Sir John Grimley, Kt., FRCP
Evans, Sir John Stanley, Kt., QPM
Evans, Sir Richard Harry, Kt., CBE
Evans, Sir Richard Mark, KCMG, KCVO
Evans, Sir Robert, Kt., CBE, FREng.
Evans, Sir (William) Vincent (John), GCMG, MBE, QC
Evans-Lombe, *Hon.* Sir Edward Christopher, Kt.
†Evans-Tipping, Sir David Gwynne, Bt. (1913)
Eveleigh, *Rt. Hon.* Sir Edward Walter, Kt., ERD

Everard, Sir Robin Charles, Bt. (1911)
Every, Sir Henry John Michael, Bt. (1641)
Ewans, Sir Martin Kenneth, KCMG
†Ewart, Sir William Michael, Bt. (1887)
Ewbank, *Hon.* Sir Anthony Bruce, Kt.
Ewin, Sir (David) Ernest Thomas Floyd, Kt., LVO, OBE
Eyre, Sir Reginald Edwin, Kt.
Eyre, Sir Richard Charles Hastings, Kt., CBE
Faber, Sir Richard Stanley, KCVO, CMG
Fagge, Sir John William Frederick, Bt. (1660)
Fairbairn, Sir (James) Brooke, Bt. (1869)
Fairhall, *Hon.* Sir Allen, KBE
Fairlie-Cuninghame, Sir Robert Henry, Bt. (S. 1630)
Fairweather, Sir Patrick Stanislaus, KCMG
Falconer, *Hon.* Sir Douglas William, Kt., MBE
†Falkiner, Sir Benjamin Simon Patrick, Bt. (I. 1778)
Fall, Sir Brian James Proetel, GCVO, KCMG
Falle, Sir Samuel, KCMG, KCVO, DSC
Fang, *Prof.* Sir Harry, Kt., CBE
Fareed, Sir Djamil Sheik, Kt.
Farmer, Sir Thomas, Kt., CBE
Farquhar, Sir Michael Fitzroy Henry, Bt. (1796)
Farquharson, *Rt. Hon.* Sir Donald Henry, Kt.
Farquharson, Sir James Robbie, KBE
Farrar-Hockley, *Gen.* Sir Anthony Heritage, GBE, KCB, DSO, MC
Farrell, Sir Terence, Kt., CBE
Farrer, Sir (Charles) Matthew, GCVO
Farrington, Sir Henry Francis Colden, Bt. (1818)
Fat, Sir (Maxime) Edouard (Lim Man) Lim, Kt.
Faulkner, Sir (James) Dennis (Compton), Kt., CBE, VRD
Fawkes, Sir Randol Francis, Kt.
Fay, Sir (Humphrey) Michael Gerard, Kt.
Fayrer, Sir John Lang Macpherson, Bt. (1896)
Fearn, Sir (Patrick) Robin, KCMG
Feilden, Sir Bernard Melchior, Kt., CBE
Feilden, Sir Henry Wemyss, Bt., (1846)
Fell, Sir David, KCB
Fender, Sir Brian Edward Frederick, Kt., CMG, Ph.D.
Fenn, Sir Nicholas Maxted, GCMG
Fennell, *Hon.* Sir (John) Desmond Augustine, Kt., OBE
Fennessy, Sir Edward, Kt., CBE
Fergus, Sir Howard Archibald, KBE
Ferguson, Sir Alexander Chapman, Kt., CBE
†Ferguson-Davie, Sir Michael, Bt. (1847)

Fergusson of Kilkerran, Sir Charles, Bt. (S. 1703)
Fergusson, Sir Ewan Alastair John, GCMG, GCVO
Feroze, Sir Rustam Moolan, Kt., FRCS
Fersht, *Prof.* Sir Alan Roy, Kt., FRS
Ferris, *Hon.* Sir Francis Mursell, Kt., TD
ffolkes, Sir Robert Francis Alexander, Bt., OBE (1774)
Field, Sir Malcolm David, Kt.
Field, *Hon* Sir Richard Alan, Kt.
Fielding, Sir Colin Cunningham, Kt., CB
Fielding, Sir Leslie, KCMG
Fieldsend, *Hon.* Sir John Charles Rowell, KBE
Fiennes, Sir Ranulph Twisleton-Wykeham, Bt., OBE (1916)
Figg, Sir Leonard Clifford William, KCMG
Figgis, Sir Anthony St John Howard, KCVO, CMG
Figures, Sir Colin Frederick, KCMG, OBE
Finlay, Sir David Ronald James Bell, Bt. (1964)
Finney, Sir Thomas, Kt., OBE
Fisher, Sir George Read, Kt., CMG
Fisher, *Hon.* Sir Henry Arthur Pears, Kt.
Fison, Sir (Richard) Guy, Bt., DSC (1905)
Fitzalan-Howard, *Maj.-Gen.* Lord Michael, GCVO, CB, CBE, MC
†Fitzgerald, *Revd* Daniel Patrick, Bt. (1903)
FitzGerald, Sir Adrian James Andrew, Bt. (1880)
FitzHerbert, Sir Richard Ranulph, Bt. (1784)
Fitzpatrick, *Air Marshal* Sir John Bernard, KBE, CB
Flanagan, Sir Ronald, GBE
Fletcher, Sir James Muir Cameron, Kt.
Floissac, *Hon.* Sir Vincent Frederick, Kt., CMG, OBE
Floyd, Sir Giles Henry Charles, Bt. (1816)
Foley, *Lt.-Gen.* Sir John Paul, KCB, OBE, MC
Foley, Sir (Thomas John) Noel, Kt., CBE
Follett, *Prof.* Sir Brian Keith, Kt., FRS
Foot, Sir Geoffrey James, Kt.
Foots, Sir James William, Kt.
Forbes, *Maj.* Sir Hamish Stewart, Bt., MBE, MC (1823)
Forbes, *Adm.* Sir Ian Andrew, KCB, CBE
Forbes of Craigievar, Sir John Alexander Cumnock, Bt. (S. 1630)
Forbes, *Vice-Adm.* Sir John Morrison, KCB
Forbes, *Hon.* Sir Thayne John, Kt.
Forbes-Leith, Sir George Ian David, Bt. (1923)
Ford, Sir Andrew Russell, Bt. (1929)
Ford, Sir David Robert, KBE, LVO

Ford, *Maj.* Sir Edward William Spencer, GCVO, KCB, ERD

Ford, *Air Marshal* Sir Geoffrey Harold, KBE, CB, FREng.

Ford, *Prof.* Sir Hugh, Kt., FRS, FREng.

Ford, Sir John Archibald, KCMG, MC

Ford, *Gen.* Sir Robert Cyril, GCB, CBE

Foreman, Sir Philip Frank, Kt., CBE, FREng.

Forestier-Walker, Sir Michael Leolin, Bt. (1835)

Forman, Sir John Denis, Kt., OBE

Forrest, *Prof.* Sir (Andrew) Patrick (McEwen), Kt.

Forrest, *Rear-Adm.* Sir Ronald Stephen, KCVO

Forte, Hon. Sir Rocco John Vincent, Kt.

Forwood, Sir Peter Noel, Bt. (1895)

Foster, Sir Andrew William, Kt.

Foster, *Prof.* Sir Christopher David, Kt.

Foster, Sir John Gregory, Bt. (1930)

Foster, Sir Robert Sidney, GCMG, KCVO

Foulkes, Sir Arther Alexander, KCMG

Foulkes, Sir Nigel Gordon, Kt.

Fountain, *Hon.* Sir Cyril Stanley Smith, Kt.

Fowden, Sir Leslie, Kt., FRS

Fowke, Sir David Frederick Gustavus, Bt. (1814)

Fowler, Sir (Edward) Michael Coulson, Kt.

Fox, *Rt. Hon.* Sir Michael John, Kt.

Fox, Sir Paul Leonard, Kt., CBE

Foxley-Norris, *Air Chief Marshal* Sir Christopher Neil, GCB, DSO, OBE

France, Sir Christopher Walter, GCB

Francis, Sir Horace William Alexander, Kt., CBE, FREng.

Frank, Sir Douglas George Horace, Kt., QC

Frank, Sir Robert Andrew, Bt. (1920)

Franklin, Sir Michael David Milroy, KCB, CMG

Franks, Sir Arthur Temple, KCMG

Fraser, Sir Alasdair MacLeod, Kt.

Fraser, Sir Charles Annand, KCVO

Fraser, *Gen.* Sir David William, GCB, OBE

Fraser, Sir Iain Michael Duncan, Bt. (1943)

Fraser, Sir (James) Campbell, Kt.

Fraser, Sir James Murdo, KBE

Fraser, Sir William Kerr, GCB

Frayling, *Prof.* Sir Christopher John, Kt.

Frederick, Sir Christopher St John, Bt. (1723)

Freedman, *Prof.* Sir Lawrence David, KCMG, CBE

Freeland, Sir John Redvers, KCMG

Freeman, Sir James Robin, Bt. (1945)

Freer, *Air Chief Marshal* Sir Robert William George, GBE, KCB

French, *Air Marshal* Sir Joseph Charles, KCB, CBE

Frere, *Vice-Adm.* Sir Richard Tobias, KCB

Fretwell, Sir (Major) John (Emsley), GCMG

Freud, Sir Clement Raphael, Kt.

Friend *Prof.* Sir Richard Henry, Kt.

Froggatt, Sir Leslie Trevor, Kt.

Froggatt, Sir Peter, Kt.

Frossard, Sir Charles Keith, KBE

Frost, Sir David Paradine, Kt., OBE

Frost, Sir Terence Ernest Manitou, Kt., RA

Fry, Sir Peter Derek, Kt.

Fulford, *Hon.* Sir Adrian Bruce, Kt.

Fuller, Sir James Henry Fleetwood, Bt. (1910)

Fuller, *Hon.* Sir John Bryan Munro, Kt.

Furness, Sir Stephen Roberts, Bt. (1913)

Gadsden, Sir Peter Drury Haggerston, GBE, FREng.

Gage, *Hon.* Sir William Marcus, Kt.

Gains, Sir John Christopher, Kt.

Gainsford, Sir Ian Derek, Kt., DDS

Gaius, *Rt. Revd* Saimon, KBE

Galsworthy, Sir Anthony Charles, KCMG

Galway, Sir James, Kt., OBE

Gam, *Rt. Revd* Sir Getake, KBE

Gamble, Sir David Hugh Norman, Bt. (1897)

Gambon, Sir Michael John, Kt., CBE

Garden, *Air Marshal* Sir Timothy, KCB

Gardiner, Sir John Eliot, Kt., CBE

Gardner, Sir Roy Alan, Kt.

Garland, *Hon.* Sir Patrick Neville, Kt.

Garland, *Hon.* Sir Ransley Victor, KBE

Garlick, Sir John, KCB

Garner, Sir Anthony Stuart, Kt.

Garnett, *Adm.* Sir Ian David Graham, KCB

Garnier, *Rear-Adm.* Sir John, KCVO, CBE

Garrard, Sir David Eardley, Kt.

Garrett, Sir Anthony Peter, Kt., CBE

Garrick, Sir Ronald, Kt., CBE, FREng.

Garrioch, Sir (William) Henry, Kt.

Garrod, *Lt.-Gen.* Sir (John) Martin Carruthers, KCB, OBE

Garthwaite, Sir (William) Mark (Charles), Bt. (1919)

Gaskell, Sir Richard Kennedy Harvey, Kt.

Geno, Sir Makena Viora, KBE

Gent, Sir Christopher Charles, Kt.

George, Sir Arthur Thomas, Kt.

George, *Prof.* Sir Charles Frederick, MD, FRCP

George, *Rt. Hon.* Sir Edward Alan John, GBE

George, Sir Richard William, Kt., CVO

Gerken, *Vice-Adm.* Sir Robert William Frank, KCB, CBE

Gethin, Sir Richard Joseph St Lawrence, Bt. (I. 1665)

Ghurburrun, Sir Rabindrah, Kt.

Gibb, Sir Francis Ross (Frank), Kt., CBE, FREng.

Gibbings, Sir Peter Walter, Kt.

Gibbons, Sir (John) David, KBE

Gibbons, Sir William Edward Doran, Bt. (1752)

Gibbs, *Rt. Hon.* Sir Harry Talbot, GCMG, KBE

Gibbs, *Hon.* Sir Richard John Hedley, Kt.

Gibbs, Sir Roger Geoffrey, Kt.

Gibbs, *Field Marshal* Sir Roland Christopher, GCB, CBE, DSO, MC

†Gibson, *Revd* Christopher Herbert, Bt. (1931)

Gibson, Sir Ian, Kt., CBE

Gibson, *Rt. Hon.* Sir Peter Leslie, Kt.

Gibson, *Rt. Hon.* Sir Ralph Brian, Kt.

Gibson-Craig-Carmichael, Sir David Peter William, Bt. (S. 1702 and 1831)

Giddings, *Air Marshal* Sir (Kenneth Charles) Michael, KCB, OBE, DFC, AFC

Giffard, Sir (Charles) Sydney (Rycroft), KCMG

Gilbart-Denham, *Lt.-Col.* Sir Seymour Vivian, KCVO

Gilbert, *Air Chief Marshal* Sir Joseph Alfred, KCB, CBE

Gilbert, Sir Martin John, Kt., CBE

†Gilbey, Sir Walter Gavin, Bt. (1893)

Gill, Sir Anthony Keith, Kt.

Gill, Sir Arthur Benjamin Norman, Kt., CBE

Gillam, Sir Patrick John, Kt.

Gillen, *Hon.* Sir John de Winter, Kt.

Gillett, Sir Robin Danvers Penrose, Bt., GBE, RD (1959)

Gilmour, *Col.* Sir Allan Macdonald, KCVO, OBE, MC

Gilmour, Sir John Edward, Bt., DSO, TD (1897)

Gina, Sir Lloyd Maepeza, KBE

Gingell, *Air Chief Marshal* Sir John, GBE, KCB, KCVO

Girolami, Sir Paul, Kt.

Girvan, *Hon.* Sir (Frederick) Paul, Kt.

Gladstone, Sir (Erskine) William, Bt., KG (1846)

Glen, Sir Alexander Richard, KBE, DSC

Glenn, Sir (Joseph Robert) Archibald, Kt., OBE

Glidewell, *Rt. Hon.* Sir Iain Derek Laing, Kt.

Glover, Sir Victor Joseph Patrick, Kt.

Glyn, Sir Richard Lindsay, Bt. (1759 and 1800)

Goavea, Sir Sinaka Vakai, KBE

Gobbo, Sir James Augustine, Kt., AC

Godber, Sir George Edward, GCB, DM

Goldberg, *Prof.* Sir Abraham, Kt., MD, D.Sc., FRCP

Goldberg, *Prof.* Sir David Paul Brandes, Kt.

Goldman, Sir Samuel, KCB

Goldring, *Hon.* Sir John Bernard, Kt.

Gomersall, Sir Stephen John, KCMG

Gonsalves-Sabola, *Hon.* Sir Joaquim Claudino, Kt
†Gooch, Sir Miles Peter, Bt. (1866)
Gooch, Sir Timothy Robert, Bt., MBE (1746)
Goodall, Sir (Arthur) David Saunders, GCMG
Goodall, *Air Marshal* Sir Roderick Harvey, KBE, CB, AFC
Goode, *Prof.* Sir Royston Miles, Kt., CBE, QC
Goodenough, Sir Anthony Michael, KCMG
Goodenough, Sir William McLernon, Bt. (1943)
Goodhart, Sir Philip Carter, Kt.
Goodhart, Sir Robert Anthony Gordon, Bt. (1911)
Goodhew, Sir Victor Henry, Kt.
Goodison, Sir Alan Clowes, KCMG
Goodison, Sir Nicholas Proctor, Kt.
Goodlad, *Rt. Hon.* Sir Alastair Robertson, KCMG
Goodman, Sir Patrick Ledger, Kt., CBE
Goodson, Sir Mark Weston Lassam, Bt. (1922)
Goodwin, Sir Matthew Dean, Kt., CBE
†Goold, Sir George William, Bt. (1801)
Gordon, Sir Charles Addison Somerville Snowden, KCB
Gordon, Sir Gerald Henry, Kt., CBE, QC
Gordon, Sir Keith Lyndell, Kt., CMG
Gordon, Sir Robert James, Bt. (S. 1706)
Gordon, Sir Sidney Samuel, Kt., CBE
Gordon-Cumming, Sir William Gordon, Bt. (1804)
Gordon Lennox, Lord Nicholas Charles, KCMG, KCVO
†Gore, Sir Nigel Hugh St George, Bt. (I. 1622)
Gore-Booth, Hon. Sir David Alwyn, KCMG, KCVO
Gore-Booth, Sir Josslyn Henry Robert, Bt. (I. 1760)
Gorham, Sir Richard Masters, Kt., CBE, DFC
Goring, Sir William Burton Nigel, Bt. (1627)
Gorman, Sir John Reginald, Kt., CVO, CBE, MC
Gorst, Sir John Michael, Kt.
Goschen, Sir (Edward) Alexander Bt. (1916)
Gosling, Sir (Frederick) Donald, Kt.
Goswell, Sir Brian Lawrence, Kt.
Gough, Sir Charles Brandon, Kt.
Goulden, Sir (Peter) John, GCMG
Goulding, Sir Marrack Irvine, KCMG
Goulding, Sir (William) Lingard Walter, Bt. (1904)
Gourlay, *Gen.* Sir (Basil) Ian (Spencer), KCB, OBE, MC, RM
Gourlay, Sir Simon Alexander, Kt.
Govan, Sir Lawrence Herbert, Kt.
Gow, *Gen.* Sir (James) Michael, GCB

Gowans, Sir James Learmonth, Kt., CBE, FRCP, FRS
†Graaff, Sir David de Villiers, Bt. (1911)
Grabham, Sir Anthony Henry, Kt.
Graham, Sir Alexander Michael, GBE
Graham, Sir James Bellingham, Bt. (1662)
Graham, Sir James Fergus Surtees, Bt. (1783)
Graham, Sir James Thompson, Kt., CMG
Graham, Sir John Alexander Noble, Bt., GCMG (1906)
Graham, Sir John Alistair, Kt.
Graham, Sir John Moodie, Bt. (1964)
Graham, Sir Norman William, Kt., CB
Graham, Sir Peter, KCB, QC
Graham, Sir Peter Alfred, Kt., OBE
Graham, *Lt.-Gen.* Sir Peter Walter, KCB, CBE
†Graham, Sir Ralph Stuart, Bt. (1629)
Graham-Moon, Sir Peter Wilfred Giles, Bt. (1855)
Graham-Smith, *Prof.* Sir Francis, Kt.
Grandy, *Marshal of the Royal Air Force* Sir John, GCB, GCVO, KBE, DSO
Grant, Sir Archibald, Bt. (S. 1705)
Grant, Sir Clifford, Kt.
Grant, Sir (John) Anthony, Kt.
Grant, Sir Patrick Alexander Benedict, Bt. (S. 1688)
Grant, *Lt.-Gen.* Sir Scott Carnegie, KCB
Grant-Suttie, Sir James Edward, Bt. (S. 1702)
Granville-Chapman, *Lt.-Gen.* Sir Timothy John, KCB, CBE
Gratton-Bellew, Sir Henry Charles, Bt. (1838)
Gray, *Hon.* Sir Charles Anthony St John, Kt.
Gray, *Prof.* Sir Denis John Pereira, Kt., OBE, FRCGP
Gray, Sir John Archibald Browne, Kt., Sc.D., FRS
Gray, Sir John Walton David, KBE, CMG
Gray, *Lt.-Gen.* Sir Michael Stuart, KCB, OBE
Gray, Sir Robert McDowall (Robin), Kt.
Gray, Sir William Hume, Bt. (1917)
Graydon, *Air Chief Marshal* Sir Michael James, GCB, CBE
Grayson, Sir Jeremy Brian Vincent Harrington, Bt. (1922)
Green, Sir Allan David, KCB, QC
Green, Sir Andrew Fleming, KCMG
Green, *Hon.* Sir Guy Stephen Montague, KBE
Green, Sir Kenneth, Kt.
Green, Sir Owen Whitley, Kt.
†Green, Sir Simon Lycett, Bt., TD (1886)
Green-Price, Sir Robert John, Bt. (1874)

Greenaway, Sir John Michael Burdick, Bt. (1933)
Greenbury, Sir Richard, Kt.
Greener, Sir Anthony Armitage, Kt.
Greengross, Sir Alan David, Kt.
Greening, *Rear-Adm.* Sir Paul Woollven, GCVO
Greenstock, Sir Jeremy Quentin, GCMG
Greenwell, Sir Edward Bernard, Bt. (1906)
Gregson, Sir Peter Lewis, GCB
Greig, Sir (Henry Louis) Carron, KCVO, CBE
Grenside, Sir John Peter, Kt., CBE
Grey, Sir Anthony Dysart, Bt. (1814)
Grey-Egerton, Sir (Philip) John (Caledon), Bt. (1617)
Grierson, Sir Michael John Bewes, Bt. (S. 1685)
Grierson, Sir Ronald Hugh, Kt.
Griffin, *Maj.* Sir (Arthur) John (Stewart), KCVO
Griffin, Sir (Charles) David, Kt., CBE
Griffiths, Sir Eldon Wylie, Kt.
Grigson, *Hon.* Sir Geoffrey Douglas, Kt.
Grimshaw, Sir Nicholas Thomas, Kt., CBE
Grimwade, Sir Andrew Sheppard, Kt., CBE
Grindrod, *Most Revd* John Basil Rowland, KBE
Grinstead, Sir Stanley Gordon, Kt.
Grose, *Vice-Adm.* Sir Alan, KBE
Gross, *Hon.* Sir Peter Henry, Kt.
Grossart, Sir Angus McFarlane McLeod, Kt., CBE
Grotrian, Sir Philip Christian Brent, Bt. (1934)
Grove, Sir Charles Gerald, Bt. (1874)
Grove, Sir Edmund Frank, KCVO
Grugeon, Sir John Drury, Kt.
Guinness, Sir Howard Christian Sheldon, Kt., VRD
Guinness, Sir John Ralph Sidney, Kt., CB
Guinness, Sir Kenelm Ernest Lee, Bt. (1867)
Guise, Sir John Grant, Bt. (1783)
Gull, Sir Rupert William Cameron, Bt. (1872)
Gumbs, Sir Emile Rudolph, Kt.
Gun-Munro, Sir Sydney Douglas, GCMG, MBE
Gunn, Sir Robert Norman, Kt.
†Gunning, Sir Charles Theodore, Bt. (1778)
Gunston, Sir John Wellesley, Bt. (1938)
Gurdon, *Prof.* Sir John Bertrand, Kt., D.Phil., FRS
Guthrie, Sir Malcolm Connop, Bt.(1936)
Guy, *Gen.* Sir Roland Kelvin, GCB, CBE, DSO
Haddacks, *Vice-Adm.* Sir Paul Kenneth, KCB
Hadfield, Sir Ronald, Kt., QPM
Hadlee, Sir Richard John, Kt., MBE

Hagart-Alexander, Sir Claud, Bt. (1886)

Hague, *Prof.* Sir Douglas Chalmers, Kt., CBE

Halberg, Sir Murray Gordon, Kt., MBE

Hall, Sir Basil Brodribb, KCB, MC, TD

Hall, *Prof.* Sir David Michael Baldock, Kt.

Hall, Sir Douglas Basil, Bt., KCMG (S. 1687)

Hall, Sir Ernest, Kt., OBE

Hall, Sir Graham Joseph, Kt.

Hall, Sir Iain Robert, Kt.

Hall, Sir (Frederick) John (Frank), Bt. (1923)

Hall, Sir John, Kt.

Hall, Sir John Bernard, Bt. (1919)

Hall, Sir Peter Edward, KBE, CMG

Hall, *Prof.* Sir Peter Geoffrey, Kt., FBA

Hall, Sir Peter Reginald Frederick, Kt., CBE

Hall, Sir Robert de Zouche, KCMG

Halliday, *Vice-Adm.* Sir Roy William, KBE, DSC

Halpern, Sir Ralph Mark, Kt.

Halsey, *Revd* John Walter Brooke, Bt. (1920)

Halstead, Sir Ronald, Kt., CBE

Hambling, Sir (Herbert) Hugh, Bt. (1924)

Hamer, *Hon.* Sir Rupert James, KCMG, ED

Hamilton, Sir Andrew Caradoc, Bt. (S. 1646)

Hamilton, *Rt. Hon.* Sir Archibald Gavin, Kt., MP

Hamilton, Sir Edward Sydney, Bt. (1776 and 1819)

Hamilton, Sir James Arnot, KCB, MBE, FREng.

Hamilton-Dalrymple, *Maj.* Sir Hew Fleetwood, Bt., GCVO, (S. 1697)

Hamilton-Spencer-Smith, Sir John, Bt. (1804)

Hammick, Sir Stephen George, Bt. (1834)

Hammond, Sir Anthony Hilgrove, KCB, QC

Hampel, Sir Ronald Claus, Kt.

Hampshire, Sir Stuart Newton, Kt., FBA

Hampson, Sir Stuart, Kt.

Hampton, Sir (Leslie) Geoffrey, Kt.

Hanbury-Tenison, Sir Richard, KCVO

Hancock, Sir David John Stowell, KCB

Hand, *Most Revd* Geoffrey David, KBE

Hanham, Sir Michael William, Bt., DFC (1667)

Hanley, *Rt. Hon.* Sir Jeremy James, KCMG

Hanmer, Sir John Wyndham Edward, Bt. (1774)

Hann, Sir James, Kt., CBE

Hannam, Sir John Gordon, Kt.

Hanson, Sir (Charles) Rupert (Patrick), Bt. (1918)

Hanson, Sir John Gilbert, KCMG, CBE

Harcourt-Smith, *Air Chief Marshal* Sir David, GBE, KCB, DFC

Hardie, Sir Douglas Fleming, Kt., CBE

Harding, Sir George William, KCMG, CVO

Harding, *Marshal of the Royal Air Force* Sir Peter Robin, GCB

Harding, Sir Roy Pollard, Kt., CBE

Hardy, Sir David William, Kt.

Hardy, Sir James Gilbert, Kt., OBE

Hardy, Sir Richard Charles Chandos, Bt. (1876)

Hare, Sir David, Kt., FRSL

Hare, Sir Nicholas Patrick, Bt. (1818)

Harford, Sir (John) Timothy, Bt. (1934)

Hargroves, *Brig.* Sir Robert Louis, Kt., CBE

Harington, *Gen.* Sir Charles Henry Pepys, GCB, CBE, DSO, MC

Harington, Sir Nicholas John, Bt. (1611)

Harland, *Air Marshal* Sir Reginald Edward Wynyard, KBE, CB

Harley, *Gen.* Sir Alexander George Hamilton, KBE, CB

Harman, *Gen.* Sir Jack Wentworth, GCB, OBE, MC

Harman, *Hon.* Sir Jeremiah LeRoy, Kt.

Harman, Sir John Andrew, Kt.

Harmsworth, Sir Hildebrand Harold, Bt. (1922)

Harper, Sir Ewan William, Kt. CBE

Harris, *Prof.* Sir Henry, Kt., FRCP, FRCPath., FRS

Harris, Sir Jack Wolfred Ashford, Bt. (1932)

Harris, *Air Marshal* Sir John Hulme, KCB, CBE

Harris, *Prof.* Sir Martin Best, Kt., CBE

Harris, Sir Thomas George, KBE, CMG,

Harris, Sir William Gordon, KBE, CB, FREng.

Harrison, Sir David, Kt., CBE, FREng.

Harrison, Sir Ernest Thomas, Kt., OBE

Harrison, *Surgeon Vice-Adm.* Sir John Albert Bews, KBE

Harrison, *Hon.* Sir (John) Richard, Kt., ED

Harrison, *Hon.* Sir Michael Guy Vicat, Kt.

Harrison, Sir Michael James Harwood, Bt. (1961)

Harrison, Sir (Robert) Colin, Bt. (1922)

Harrison, Sir Terence, Kt., FREng

Harrop, Sir Peter John, KCB

Hart, Sir Graham Allan, KCB

Hart, *Hon.* Sir Michael Christopher Campbell, Kt.

Hartwell, Sir (Francis) Anthony Charles Peter, Bt. (1805)

Harvey, Sir Charles Richard Musgrave, Bt. (1933)

Harvey-Jones, Sir John Henry, Kt., MBE

Harvie, Sir John Smith, Kt., CBE

Harvie-Watt, Sir James, Bt. (1945)

Haselhurst, *Rt. Hon.* Sir Alan Gordon Barraclough, Kt., MP

Haskard, Sir Cosmo Dugal Patrick Thomas, KCMG, MBE

Haslam, *Rear-Adm.* Sir David William, KBE, CB

Hassett, *Gen.* Sir Francis George, KBE, CB, DSO, LVO

Hastings, Sir Max Macdonald, Kt.

Hastings, Sir Stephen Lewis Edmonstone, Kt., MC

Hatter, Sir Maurice, Kt.

Havelock-Allan, Sir (Anthony) Mark David, Bt. (1858)

Hawkins, Sir Richard Caesar, Bt. (1778)

Hawley, Sir Donald Frederick, KCMG, MBE

†Hawley, Sir Henry Nicholas, Bt. (1795)

Haworth, Sir Philip, Bt. (1911)

Hawthorne, *Prof.* Sir William Rede, Kt., CBE, Sc.D., FRS, FREng.

Hay, Sir David Osborne, Kt., CBE, DSO

Hay, Sir David Russell, Kt., CBE, FRCP, MD

Hay, Sir Hamish Grenfell, Kt.

Hay, Sir John Erroll Audley, Bt. (S. 1663)

†Hay, Sir Ronald Frederick Hamilton, Bt. (S. 1703)

Hayes, Sir Brian, Kt., CBE, QPM

Hayes, Sir Brian David, GCB

Hayman-Joyce, *Lt.-Gen.* Sir Robert John, KCB, CBE

Hayward, Sir Anthony William Byrd, Kt.

Hayward, Sir Jack Arnold, Kt., OBE

Haywood, Sir Harold, KCVO, OBE

Head, Sir Francis David Somerville, Bt. (1838)

Heap, Sir Peter William, KCMG

Heap, *Prof.* Sir Robert Brian, Kt., CBE, FRS

Hearne, Sir Graham James, Kt., CBE

Heath, *Rt. Hon.* Sir Edward Richard George, KG, MBE

Heath, Sir Mark Evelyn, KCVO, CMG

Heathcote, *Brig.* Sir Gilbert Simon, Bt., CBE (1733)

Heathcote, Sir Michael Perryman, Bt. (1733)

Heatley, Sir Peter, Kt., CBE

Hedley, *Hon.* Sir Mark, Kt.

Heiser, Sir Terence Michael, GCB

Henao, Revd Ravu, Kt., OBE

Henderson, Sir Denys Hartley, Kt.

Henderson, Sir (John) Nicholas, GCMG, KCVO

Henley, Sir Douglas Owen, KCB

Hennessy, Sir James Patrick Ivan, KBE, CMG

†Henniker, Sir Adrian Chandos, Bt. (1813)

Henniker-Heaton, Sir Yvo Robert, Bt. (1912)

Henriques, *Hon.* Sir Richard Henry Quixano, Kt.

Henry, *Rt. Hon.* Sir Denis Robert Maurice, Kt.
Henry, *Hon.* Sir Geoffrey Arama, KBE
†Henry, Sir Patrick Denis, Bt. (1923)
Henry, *Hon.* Sir Trevor Ernest, Kt.
Herbecq, Sir John Edward, KCB
Herbert, *Adm.* Sir Peter Geoffrey Marshall, KCB, OBE
Herbert, Sir Walter William, Kt.
Hermon, Sir John Charles, Kt., OBE, QPM
Heron, Sir Conrad Frederick, KCB, OBE
Heron, Sir Michael Gilbert, Kt.
Heron-Maxwell, Sir Nigel Mellor, Bt. (S. 1683)
Hervey, Sir Roger Blaise Ramsay, KCVO, CMG
Hervey-Bathurst, Sir Frederick John Charles Gordon, Bt. (1818)
Heseltine, *Rt. Hon.* Sir William Frederick Payne, GCB, GCVO
Hetherington, Sir Thomas Chalmers, KCB, CBE, TD, QC
Hewetson, Sir Christopher Raynor, Kt., TD
Hewett, Sir Richard Mark John, Bt. (1813)
Hewitt, Sir (Cyrus) Lenox (Simson), Kt., OBE
Hewitt, Sir Nicholas Charles Joseph, Bt. (1921)
Heygate, Sir Richard John Gage, Bt. (1831)
Heywood, Sir Peter, Bt. (1838)
Hezlet, *Vice-Adm.* Sir Arthur Richard, KBE, CB, DSO, DSC
Hibbert, Sir Jack, KCB
Hickey, Sir Justin, Kt.
Hickman, Sir (Richard) Glenn, Bt. (1903)
Hicks, Sir Robert, Kt.
Hidden, *Hon.* Sir Anthony Brian, Kt.
Hielscher, Sir Leo Arthur, Kt.
Higgins, *Hon.* Sir Malachy Joseph, Kt.
Higginson, Sir Gordon Robert, Kt., Ph.D., FREng.
Hill, Sir Arthur Alfred, Kt., CBE
Hill, Sir Brian John, Kt.
Hill, Sir James Frederick, Bt. (1917)
Hill, Sir John McGregor, Kt., Ph.D., FREng.
Hill, Sir John Maxwell, Kt., CBE, DFC
†Hill, Sir John Rowley, Bt. (I. 1779)
Hill, *Vice-Adm.* Sir Robert Charles Finch, KBE, FREng.
Hill-Norton, *Vice-Adm. Hon.* Sir Nicholas John, KCB
Hill-Wood, Sir Samuel Thomas, Bt. (1921)
Hillary, Sir Edmund, KG, KBE
Hillhouse, Sir (Robert) Russell, KCB
Hills, Sir Graham John, Kt.
Hine, *Air Chief Marshal* Sir Patrick Bardon, GCB, GBE
Hirsch, *Prof.* Sir Peter Bernhard, Kt., Ph.D., FRS
Hirst, *Rt. Hon.* Sir David Cozens-Hardy, Kt.

Hirst, Sir Michael William, Kt.
Hoare, *Prof.* Sir Charles Anthony Richard, Kt., FRS
Hoare, Sir Peter Richard David, Bt. (1786)
Hoare, Sir Timothy Edward Charles, Bt., OBE (I. 1784)
Hobart, Sir John Vere, Bt. (1914)
Hobbs, *Maj.-Gen.* Sir Michael Frederick, KCVO, CBE
Hobday, Sir Gordon Ivan, Kt.
Hobhouse, Sir Charles John Spinney, Bt. (1812)
Hockaday, Sir Arthur Patrick, KCB, CMG
†Hodge, Sir Andrew Rowland, Bt. (1921)
Hodge, Sir James William, KCVO, CMG
Hodge, Sir Julian Stephen Alfred, Kt.
Hodges, *Air Chief Marshal* Sir Lewis MacDonald, KCB, CBE, DSO, DFC
Hodgkin, Sir (Gordon) Howard (Eliot), Kt., CH, CBE
Hodgkinson, Sir Michael Stewart, Kt.
Hodgkinson, *Air Chief Marshal* Sir (William) Derek, KCB, CBE, DFC, AFC
Hodgson, Sir Maurice Arthur Eric, Kt., FREng.
Hodson, Sir Michael Robin Adderley, Bt. (I. 1789)
Hoffenberg, *Prof.* Sir Raymond, KBE
Hogg, Sir Christopher Anthony, Kt.
†Hogg, Sir Piers Michael James, Bt. (1846)
Holcroft, Sir Peter George Culcheth, Bt. (1921)
Holderness, Sir Martin William, Bt. (1920)
Holden, Sir Edward, Bt. (1893)
Holden, Sir John David, Bt. (1919)
Holden-Brown, Sir Derrick, Kt.
Holder, Sir John Henry, Bt. (1898)
Holdgate, Sir Martin Wyatt, Kt., CB, Ph.D.
Holdsworth, Sir (George) Trevor, Kt., CVO
Holland, *Hon.* Sir Alan Douglas, Kt.
Holland, *Hon.* Sir Christopher John, Kt.
Holland, Sir Clifton Vaughan, Kt.
Holland, Sir Geoffrey, KCB
Holland, Sir John Anthony, Kt.
Holland, Sir Kenneth Lawrence, Kt., CBE, QFSM
Holland, Sir Philip Welsby, Kt.
Holliday, *Prof.* Sir Frederick George Thomas, Kt., CBE, FRSE
Hollings, *Hon.* Sir (Alfred) Kenneth, Kt., MC
Hollis, *Hon.* Sir Anthony Barnard, Kt.
Hollom, Sir Jasper Quintus, KBE
Holloway, *Hon.* Sir Barry Blyth, KBE
Holm, Sir Carl Henry, Kt., OBE
Holm, Sir Ian (Ian Holm Cuthbert), Kt., CBE

Holman, *Hon.* Sir (Edward) James, Kt.

Holmes, *Prof.* Sir Frank Wakefield, Kt.
Holmes, Sir John Eaton, KBE, CMG, CVO
Holmes-Sellors, Sir Patrick John, KCVO
Holroyd, *Air Marshal* Sir Frank Martyn, KBE, CB
Holt, *Prof.* Sir James Clarke, Kt.
Holt, Sir Michael, Kt., CBE
Home, Sir William Dundas, Bt. (S. 1671)
Honeycombe, *Prof.* Sir Robert William Kerr, Kt., FRS, FREng.
Honywood, Sir Filmer Courtenay William, Bt. (1660)
Hood, Sir Harold Joseph, Bt., TD (1922)
Hookway, Sir Harry Thurston, Kt.
Hooper, *Hon.* Sir Anthony, Kt.
Hope, Sir Colin Frederick Newton, Kt.
Hope, *Rt. Revd and Rt. Hon.* David Michael, KCVO
Hope, Sir John Carl Alexander, Bt. (S. 1628)
Hope-Dunbar, Sir David, Bt. (S. 1664)
Hopkin, Sir (William Aylsham) Bryan, Kt., CBE
Hopkins, Sir Anthony Philip, Kt., CBE
Hopkins, Sir Michael John, Kt., CBE, RA, RIBA
Hopwood, *Prof.* Sir David Alan, Kt., FRS
Hordern, *Rt. Hon.* Sir Peter Maudslay, Kt.
Horlick, *Vice-Adm.* Sir Edwin John, KBE, FREng.
Horlick, Sir James Cunliffe William, Bt. (1914)
Horlock, *Prof.* Sir John Harold, Kt., FRS, FREng.
Horn, *Prof.* Sir Gabriel, Kt., FRS
Hornby, Sir Derek Peter, Kt.
Hornby, Sir Simon Michael, Kt.
Horne, Sir Alan Gray Antony, Bt. (1929)
Horne, *Dr* Sir Alistair Allan, Kt. CBE
Horsbrugh-Porter, Sir John Simon, Bt. (1902)
Horsfall, Sir John Musgrave, Bt., MC, TD (1909)
†Hort, Sir Andrew Edwin Fenton, Bt. (1767)
Horton, Sir Robert Baynes, Kt.
Hosker, Sir Gerald Albery, KCB, QC
Hoskyns, Sir Benedict Leigh, Bt. (1676)
Hoskyns, Sir John Austin Hungerford Leigh, Kt.
Hotung, Sir Joseph Edward, Kt.
Houghton, Sir John Theodore, Kt., CBE, FRS
Houldsworth, Sir Richard Thomas Reginald, Bt. (1887)
Hounsfield, Sir Godfrey Newbold, Kt., CBE
Hourston, Sir Gordon Minto, Kt.
House, *Lt.-Gen.* Sir David George, GCB, KCVO, CBE, MC

Houssemayne du Boulay, Sir Roger William, KCVO, CMG

Houstoun-Boswall, Sir (Thomas) Alford, Bt. (1836)

Howard, Sir David Howarth Seymour, Bt. (1955)

Howard, *Prof.* Sir Michael Eliot, Kt., CH, CBE, MC

Howard-Dobson, *Gen.* Sir Patrick John, GCB

Howard-Lawson, Sir John Philip, Bt. (1841)

Howell, Sir Ralph Frederic, Kt.

Howells, Sir Eric Waldo Benjamin, Kt., CBE

Howes, Sir Christopher Kingston, KCVO, CB

Howlett, *Gen.* Sir Geoffrey Hugh Whitby, KBE, MC

Huggins, *Hon.* Sir Alan Armstrong, Kt.

Hugh-Jones, Sir Wynn Normington, Kt., LVO

Hugh-Smith, Sir Andrew Colin, Kt.

Hughes, *Hon.* Sir Anthony Philip Gilson, Kt.

Hughes, Hon. Sir Davis, Kt.

Hughes, Sir Jack William, Kt.

†Hughes, Sir Thomas Collingwood, Bt. (1773)

Hughes, Sir Trevor Poulton, KCB

Hughes-Morgan, *His Hon. Maj.-Gen.* Sir David John, Bt., CB, CBE (1925)

Hull, *Prof.* Sir David, Kt.

Hulse, Sir Edward Jeremy Westrow, Bt. (1739)

Hum, Sir Christopher Owen, KCMG

Hume, Sir Alan Blyth, Kt., CB

Hunt, Sir John Leonard, Kt.

Hunt, *Adm.* Sir Nicholas John Streynsham, GCB, LVO

Hunt, *Hon.* Sir Patrick James, Kt.

Hunt, Sir Rex Masterman, Kt., CMG

Hunt, Sir Robert Frederick, Kt., CBE, FREng.

Hunt-Davis, *Brig.* Sir Miles Garth, KCVO

Hunter, Sir Alistair John, KCMG

Hunter, Sir Ian Bruce Hope, Kt., MBE

Hunter, *Prof.* Sir Laurence Colvin, Kt., CBE, FRSE

Huntington-Whiteley, Sir Hugo Baldwin, Bt. (1918)

Hurn, Sir (Francis) Roger, Kt.

Hurrell, Sir Anthony Gerald, KCVO, CMG

Hurst, Sir Geoffrey Charles, Kt., MBE

Husbands, Sir Clifford Straugh, GCMG

Hutchinson, *Hon.* Sir Ross, Kt., DFC

Hutchison, Sir James Colville, Bt. (1956)

Hutchison, *Rt. Hon.* Sir Michael, Kt.

Hutchison, Sir Robert, Bt. (1939)

Huxley, *Prof.* Sir Andrew Fielding, Kt., OM, FRS

Huxtable, *Gen.* Sir Charles Richard, KCB, CBE

Ibbs, Sir (John) Robin, KBE

Imbert-Terry, Sir Michael Edward Stanley, Bt. (1917)

Imray, Sir Colin Henry, KBE, CMG

Ingham, Sir Bernard, Kt.

Ingilby, Sir Thomas Colvin William, Bt. (1866)

Inglefield-Watson, Sir John Forbes, Bt. (1895)

Inglis, Sir Brian Scott, Kt.

Inglis of Glencorse, Sir Roderick John, Bt. (S. 1703)

Ingram, Sir James Herbert Charles, Bt. (1893)

Ingram, Sir John Henderson, Kt., CBE

Inkin, Sir Geoffrey David, Kt., OBE

†Innes, Sir David Charles Kenneth Gordon, Bt. (NS 1686)

Innes of Edingight, Sir Malcolm Rognvald, KCVO

Innes, Sir Peter Alexander Berowald, Bt. (S. 1628)

Irvine, Sir Donald Hamilton, Kt., CBE, MD, FRCGP

Irving, *Prof.* Sir Miles Horsfall, Kt., MD, FRCS, FRCSE

Irwin, *Lt.-Gen.* Sir Alistair Stuart Hastings, KCB, CBE

Isaacs, Sir Jeremy Israel, Kt.

Isham, Sir Ian Vere Gyles, Bt. (1627)

Jack, *Hon.* Sir Alieu Sulayman, Kt.

Jack, Sir David, Kt., CBE, FRS, FRSE

Jack, Sir David Emmanuel, GCMG, MBE

Jack, *Hon.* Sir Raymond Evan, Kt.

Jackling, Sir Roger Tustin, KCB. CBE

Jackson, Sir Barry Trevor, Kt.

Jackson, Sir Kenneth Joseph, Kt.

Jackson, *Gen.* Sir Michael David, KCB, CBE

Jackson, Sir Michael Roland, Bt. (1902)

Jackson, Sir Nicholas Fane St George, Bt. (1913)

Jackson, Sir Keith Arnold, Bt. (1815)

Jackson, *Hon.* Sir Rupert Matthew, Kt.

Jackson, Sir William Thomas, Bt. (1869)

Jacob, *Hon.* Sir Robert Raphael Hayim (Robin), Kt.

Jacobi, Sir Derek George, Kt., CBE

Jacobi, *Dr* Sir James Edward, Kt., OBE

Jacobs, Sir Cecil Albert, Kt., CBE

Jacobs, *Hon.* Sir Kenneth Sydney, KBE

Jacomb, Sir Martin Wakefield, Kt.

Jaffray, Sir William Otho, Bt. (1892)

Jagger, Sir Michael Philip, Kt.

James, Sir Cynlais Morgan, KCMG

James, Sir Jeffrey Russell, KBE

James, Sir John Nigel Courtenay, KCVO, CBE

James, Sir Stanislaus Anthony, GCMG, OBE

Jamieson, *Air Marshal* Sir David Ewan, KBE, CB

Jansen, Sir Ross Malcolm, KBE

Janvrin, *Rt. Hon.* Sir Robin Berry, KCB, KCVO

Jardine of Applegirth, Sir Alexander Maule, Bt. (S. 1672)

Jardine, Sir Andrew Colin Douglas, Bt. (1916)

Jarman, *Prof.* Sir Brian, Kt., OBE

Jarratt, Sir Alexander Anthony, Kt., CB

Jarvis, Sir Gordon Ronald, Kt.

Jawara, *Hon.* Sir Dawda Kairaba, Kt.

Jay, Sir Antony Rupert, Kt., CVO

Jay, Sir Michael Hastings, KCMG

Jeewoolall, Sir Ramesh, Kt.

Jefferson, Sir George Rowland, Kt., CBE, FREng.

Jeffreys, *Prof.* Sir Alec John, Kt., FRS

Jeffries, *Hon.* Sir John Francis, Kt.

Jehangir, Sir Cowasji, Bt. (1908)

Jejeebhoy, Sir Jamsetjee, Bt. (1857)

Jenkins, Sir Brian Garton, GBE

Jenkins, Sir Elgar Spencer, Kt., OBE

Jenkins, Sir James Christopher, KCB, QC

Jenkins, Sir Michael Nicholas Howard, Kt., OBE

Jenkins, Sir Michael Romilly Heald, KCMG

Jenkinson, Sir John Banks, Bt. (1661)

Jenks, Sir Maurice Arthur Brian, Bt. (1932)

Jenner, *Air Marshal* Sir Timothy LVO, KCB

Jennings, Sir John Southwood, Kt., CBE, FRSE

Jennings, Sir Peter Neville Wake, Kt., CVO

Jennings, *Prof.* Sir Robert Yewdall, Kt., QC

†Jephcott, Sir Neil Welbourn, Bt. (1962)

Jessel, Sir Charles John, Bt. (1883)

Jewkes, Sir Gordon Wesley, KCMG

Job, Sir Peter James Denton, Kt.

John, Sir David Glyndwr, KCMG

John, Sir Elton Hercules (Reginald Kenneth Dwight), Kt., CBE

Johns, *Air Chief Marshal* Sir Richard Edward, GCB, CBE, LVO

†Johnson, Sir Colpoys Guy, Bt. (1755)

Johnson, *Gen.* Sir Garry Dene, KCB, OBE, MC

Johnson, Sir John Rodney, KCMG

†Johnson, Sir Patrick Eliot, Bt. (1818)

Johnson, *Hon.* Sir Robert Lionel, Kt.

Johnson, Sir Vassel Godfrey, Kt., CBE

Johnson-Ferguson, Sir Ian Edward, Bt. (1906)

Johnston, Sir John Baines, GCMG, KCVO

Johnston, *Lt.-Col.* Sir John Frederick Dame, GCVO, MC

Johnston, *Lt.-Gen.* Sir Maurice Robert, KCB, OBE

Johnston, Sir Thomas Alexander, Bt. (S. 1626)

Johnstone, Sir Geoffrey Adams Dinwiddie, KCMG

Johnstone, Sir (George) Richard Douglas, Bt. (S. 1700)

Johnstone, Sir (John) Raymond, Kt.,
CBE
Jolliffe, Sir Anthony Stuart, GBE
Jolly, Sir Aurthur Richard, KCMG
Jonas, Sir John Peter Jens, Kt., CBE
Jones, Gen. Sir (Charles) Edward
Webb, KCB, CBE
Jones, Air Marshal Sir Edward
Gordon, KCB, CBE, DSO, DFC
Jones, Sir Harry George, Kt., CBE
Jones, Sir John Francis, Kt.
Jones, Sir Keith Stephen, Kt.
Jones, Hon. Sir Kenneth George
Illtyd, Kt.
Jones, Sir Lyndon, Kt.
Jones, Sir (Owen) Trevor, Kt.
Jones, Sir Richard Anthony Lloyd,
KCB
Jones, Sir Robert Edward, Kt.
Jones, Sir Simon Warley Frederick
Benton, Bt. (1919)
†Joseph, Hon. Sir James Samuel, Bt.
(1943)
Jowitt, Hon. Sir Edwin Frank, Kt.
Judge, Rt. Hon. Sir Igor, Kt.
Judge, Sir Paul Rupert, Kt.
Jugnauth, Rt. Hon. Sir Anerood,
KCMG
Jungius, Vice-Adm. Sir James George,
KBE
Jupp, Hon. Sir Kenneth Graham, Kt.,
MC
Kaberry, Hon. Sir Christopher
Donald, Bt. (1960)
Kakaraya, Sir Pato, KBE
Kalms, Sir (Harold) Stanley, Kt.
Kalo, Sir Kwamala, Kt., MBE
Kan Yuet-Keung, Sir, GBE
Kapi, Hon. Sir Mari, Kt., CBE
Kaputin, Sir John Rumet, KBE, CMG
Kausimae, Sir David Nanau, KBE
Kavali, Sir Thomas, Kt., OBE
Kawharu, Prof. Sir Ian Hugh, Kt.
Kay, Prof. Sir Andrew Watt, Kt.
Kay, Rt. Hon. Sir John William, Kt.
Kay, Hon. Sir Maurice Ralph, Kt.
Kaye, Sir Paul Henry Gordon, Bt.
(1923)
Keane, Sir Richard Michael, Bt.
(1801)
Kearney, Hon. Sir William John
Francis, Kt., CBE
Keeble, Sir (Herbert Ben) Curtis,
GCMG
Keegan, Sir John Desmond Patrick,
Kt., OBE
Keene, Rt. Hon. Sir David Wolfe, Kt.
Keith, Hon. Sir Brian Richard, Kt.
Keith, Prof. Sir James, KBE
†Kellett, Sir Stanley Charles, Bt.
(1801)
Kelly, Sir Christopher William, KCB
Kelly, Sir David Robert Corbett, Kt.,
CBE
Kelly, Rt. Hon. Sir (John William)
Basil, Kt.
Kemakeza, Sir Allan, Kt.
Kemball, Air Marshal Sir (Richard)
John, KCB, CBE
Kemp, Sir (Edward) Peter, KCB
Kemp-Welch, Sir John, Kt.
Kenilorea, Rt. Hon. Sir Peter, KBE

Kennaway, Sir John Lawrence, Bt.
(1791)
Kennedy, Sir Francis, KCMG, CBE
Kennedy, Hon. Sir Ian Alexander, Kt.
Kennedy, Prof. Sir Ian McColl, Kt.
Kennedy, Sir Ludovic Henry
Coverley, Kt.
†Kennedy, Sir Michael Edward, Bt.,
(1836)
Kennedy, Rt. Hon. Sir Paul Joseph
Morrow, Kt.
Kennedy, Air Chief Marshal Sir
Thomas Lawrie, GCB, AFC
Kennedy-Good, Sir John, KBE
Kenny, Sir Anthony John Patrick,
Kt., D.Phil., D.Litt., FBA
Kenny, Gen. Sir Brian Leslie Graham,
GCB, CBE
Kentridge, Sir Sydney Woolf, KCMG,
QC
Kenyon, Sir George Henry, Kt.
Kermode, Sir (John) Frank, Kt., FBA
Kermode, Sir Ronald Graham Quale,
KBE
Kerr, Hon. Sir Brian Francis, Kt.
Kerr, Adm. Sir John Beverley, GCB
Kerr, Sir John (Olav), GCMG
Kerry, Sir Michael James, KCB, QC
Kershaw, Prof. Sir Ian, Kt.
Kershaw, Sir (John) Anthony, Kt.,
MC
Keswick, Sir John Chippendale
Lindley, Kt.
Kidd, Sir Robert Hill, KBE, CB
Kikau, Ratu Sir Jone Latianara, KBE
Killen, Hon. Sir Denis James, KCMG
Killick, Sir John Edward, GCMG
Kimber, Sir Charles Dixon, Bt.
(1904)
King, Prof. Sir David Anthony, Kt.,
FRS
King, Sir John Christopher, Bt.
(1888)
King, Vice-Adm. Sir Norman Ross
Dutton, KBE
King, Sir Wayne Alexander, Bt.
(1815)
Kingman, Prof. Sir John Frank
Charles, Kt., FRS
Kingsland, Sir Richard, Kt., CBE,
DFC
Kingsley, Sir Ben, Kt.
Kinloch, Sir David, Bt. (S. 1686)
Kinloch, Sir David Oliphant, Bt.
(1873)
Kipalan, Sir Albert, Kt.
Kirkpatrick, Sir Ivone Elliott, Bt.
(S. 1685)
Kirkwood, Hon. Sir Andrew
Tristram Hammett, Kt.
Kirkwood, Sir Archibald Johnstone,
Kt., MP
Kitcatt, Sir Peter Julian, Kt., CB
Kitson, Gen. Sir Frank Edward, GBE,
KCB, MC
Kitson, Sir Timothy Peter Geoffrey,
Kt.
Kleinwort, Sir Richard Drake, Bt.
(1909)
Klug, Sir Aaron, Kt., OM
Kneller, Sir Alister Arthur, Kt.

Knight, Sir Harold Murray, KBE,
DSC
Knight, Air Chief Marshal Sir
Michael William Patrick, KCB,
AFC
†Knill, Sir Thomas John Pugin
Bartholomew, Bt. (1893)
Knowles, Sir Charles Francis, Bt.
(1765)
Knowles, Sir Durward Randolph,
Kt., OBE
Knowles, Sir Richard Marchant, Kt.
Knox, Sir Bryce Muir, KCVO, MC,
TD
Knox, Sir David Laidlaw, Kt.
Knox, Hon. Sir John Leonard, Kt.
Knox, Hon. Sir William Edward, Kt.
Knox-Johnston, Sir William Robert
Patrick (Sir Robin), Kt., CBE, RD
Koraea, Sir Thomas, Kt.
Kornberg, Prof. Sir Hans Leo, Kt.,
D.Sc., Sc.D., Ph.D., FRS
Korowi, Sir Wiwa, GCMG
Krebs, Prof. Sir John Richard, Kt.,
D.Phil., FRS
Kroto, Prof. Sir Harold Walter, Kt.,
FRS
Kulukundis, Sir Elias George (Eddie),
Kt., OBE
Kurongku, Most Revd Peter, KBE
Lachmann, Prof. Sir Peter Julius, Kt.
Lacon, Sir Edmund Vere, Bt. (1818)
Lacy, Sir Patrick Brian Finucane, Bt.
(1921)
Lacy, Sir John Trend, Kt., CBE
Laddie, Hon. Sir Hugh Ian Lang, Kt.
Laidlaw, Sir Christopher Charles
Fraser, Kt.
Laing, Sir (John) Martin (Kirby), Kt.,
CBE
Laing, Sir (John) Maurice, Kt.
Laing, Sir (William) Kirby, Kt.,
FREng.
Laird, Sir Gavin Harry, Kt., CBE
Lake, Sir (Atwell) Graham, Bt.
(1711)
Laker, Sir Frederick Alfred, Kt.
Lakin, Sir Michael, Bt. (1909)
Laking, Sir George Robert, KCMG
Lamb, Sir Albert Thomas, KBE, CMG,
DFC
Lambert, Sir Anthony Edward,
KCMG
Lambert, Sir John Henry, KCVO,
CMG
†Lambert, Sir Peter John Biddulph,
Bt. (1711)
Lampl, Sir Frank William, Kt.
Lampl, Sir Peter, Kt., OBE
Lamport, Sir Stephen Mark Jeffrey,
KCVO
Landale, Sir David William Neil,
KCVO
Landau, Sir Dennis Marcus, Kt.
Lander, Sir Stephen James, KCB
Lane, Prof. Sir David Philip, Kt.,
FRS, FRSE
†Langham, Sir John Stephen, Bt.
(1660)
Langlands, Sir Robert Alan, Kt.
Langley, Hon. Sir Gordon Julian
Hugh, Kt.

Langley, *Maj.-Gen.* Sir Henry Desmond Allen, KCVO, MBE

Langrishe, Sir James Hercules, Bt. (I. 1777)

Lankester, Sir Timothy Patrick, KCB

Lapli, Sir John Ini, GCMG

Lapun, *Hon.* Sir Paul, Kt.

Larcom, Sir (Charles) Christopher Royde, Bt. (1868)

Large, Sir Andrew McLeod Brooks, Kt.

Large, Sir Peter, Kt., CBE

Latham, *Rt. Hon.* Sir David Nicholas Ramsey, Kt.

Latham, Sir Michael Anthony, Kt.

Latham, Sir Richard Thomas Paul, Bt. (1919)

Latimer, Sir (Courtenay) Robert, Kt., CBE

Latimer, Sir Graham Stanley, KBE

Latour-Adrien, *Hon.* Sir Maurice, Kt.

Laughton, Sir Anthony Seymour, Kt.

Laurence, Sir Peter Harold, KCMG, MC

Laurie, Sir Robert Bayley Emilius, Bt. (1834)

Lauterpacht, Sir Elihu, Kt., CBE, QC

Lauti, *Rt. Hon.* Sir Toaripi, GCMG

Lavan, *Hon.* Sir John Martin, Kt.

Law, *Adm.* Sir Horace Rochfort, GCB, OBE, DSC

Lawes, Sir (John) Michael Bennet, Bt. (1882)

Lawler, Sir Peter James, Kt., OBE

†Lawrence, Sir Clive Wyndham, Bt. (1906)

Lawrence, Sir Henry Peter, Bt. (1858)

Lawrence, Sir Ivan John, Kt., QC

Lawrence, Sir John Patrick Grosvenor, Kt., CBE

Lawrence, Sir William Fettiplace, Bt. (1867)

Lawrence-Jones, Sir Christopher, Bt. (1831)

Laws, *Rt. Hon.* Sir John Grant McKenzie, Kt.

Lawson, Sir Christopher Donald, Kt.

Lawson, Sir Charles John Patrick, Bt. (1900)

Lawson, *Gen.* Sir Richard George, KCB, DSO, OBE

Lawson-Tancred, Sir Henry, Bt. (1662)

Layard, *Adm.* Sir Michael Henry Gordon, KCB, CBE

Lea, *Vice-Adm.* Sir John Stuart Crosbie, KBE

Lea, Sir Thomas William, Bt. (1892)

Leach, *Admiral of the Fleet* Sir Henry Conyers, GCB

Leahy, Sir Daniel Joseph, Kt.

Leahy, Sir John Henry Gladstone, KCMG

Leahy, Sir Terence Patrick, Kt.

Learmont, *Gen.* Sir John Hartley, KCB, CBE

Leask, *Lt.-Gen.* Sir Henry Lowther Ewart Clark, KCB, DSO, OBE

Leather, Sir Edwin Hartley Cameron, KCMG, KCVO

Leaver, Sir Christopher, GBE

Le Bailly, *Vice-Adm.* Sir Louis Edward Stewart Holland, KBE, CB

Le Cheminant, *Air Chief Marshal* Sir Peter de Lacey, GBE, KCB, DFC

†Lechmere, Sir Reginald Anthony Hungerford, Bt. (1818)

Ledger, Sir Philip Stevens, Kt., CBE, FRSE

Lee, Sir Arthur James, KBE, MC

Lee, *Air Chief Marshal* Sir David John Pryer, GBE, CB

Lee, *Brig.* Sir Leonard Henry, Kt., CBE

Lee, Sir Quo-wei, Kt., CBE

Leeds, Sir Christopher Anthony, Bt. (1812)

Lees, Sir David Bryan, Kt.

Lees, Sir Thomas Edward, Bt. (1897)

Lees, Sir Thomas Harcourt Ivor, Bt. (1804)

Lees, Sir (William) Antony Clare, Bt. (1937)

Le Fanu, *Maj.* Sir (George) Victor (Sheridan), KCVO

le Fleming, Sir David Kelland, Bt. (1705)

Legard, Sir Charles Thomas, Bt. (1660)

Legg, Sir Thomas Stuart, KCB, QC

Leggatt, *Rt. Hon.* Sir Andrew Peter, Kt.

Leggatt, Sir Hugh Frank John, Kt.

Leigh, Sir Geoffrey Norman, Kt.

Leigh, Sir Richard Henry, Bt. (1918)

Leighton, Sir Michael John Bryan, Bt. (1693)

Leitch, Sir George, KCB, OBE

Leith-Buchanan, Sir Charles Alexander James, Bt. (1775)

Le Marchant, Sir Francis Arthur, Bt. (1841)

Lemon, Sir (Richard) Dawnay, Kt., CBE

Leng, *Gen.* Sir Peter John Hall, KCB, MBE, MC

Lennox-Boyd, The *Hon.* Sir Mark Alexander, Kt.

Leon, Sir John Ronald, Bt. (1911)

Leonard, *Rt. Revd Monsignor* and *Rt. Hon.* Graham Douglas, KCVO

Lepping, Sir George Geria Dennis, GCMG, MBE

Le Quesne, Sir (Charles) Martin, KCMG

Le Quesne, Sir (John) Godfray, Kt., QC

Lee-Steere, Sir Ernest Henry, KBE

Leslie, Sir Colin Alan Bettridge, Kt.

Leslie, Sir John Norman Ide, Bt. (1876)

Leslie, Sir Peter Evelyn, Kt.

Lester, Sir James Theodore, Kt.

Lethbridge, Sir Thomas Periam Hector Noel, Bt. (1804)

Lever, Sir Jeremy Frederick, KCMG, QC

Lever, Sir Paul, KCMG

Lever, Sir (Tresham) Christopher Arthur Lindsay, Bt. (1911)

Leveson, *Hon.* Sir Brian Henry, Kt.

Levey, Sir Michael Vincent, Kt., LVO

Levine, Sir Montague Bernard, Kt.

Levinge, Sir Richard George Robin, Bt. (I. 1704)

Lewando, Sir Jan Alfred, Kt., CBE

Lewinton, Sir Christopher, Kt.

Lewis, Sir David Courtenay Mansel, KCVO

Lewis, Sir Terence Murray, Kt., OBE, GM, QPM

Lewison, *Hon.* Sir Kim Martin Jordan, Kt.

†Lewthwaite, Sir David Rainald, Bt. (1927)

Ley, Sir Ian Francis, Bt. (1905)

Li, Sir Ka-Shing, KBE

Lickiss, Sir Michael Gillam, Kt.

Liddington, Sir Bruce, Kt.

Liggins, *Prof.* Sir Graham Collingwood, Kt., CBE, FRS

Lightman, *Hon.* Sir Gavin Anthony, Kt.

Lighton, Sir Thomas Hamilton, Bt. (I. 1791)

Likierman, *Prof.* Sir John Andrew, Kt.

Lilleyman, *Prof.* Sir John Stuart, Kt.

Limon, Sir Donald William, KCB

Linacre, Sir (John) Gordon (Seymour), Kt., CBE, AFC, DFM

Lindop, Sir Norman, Kt.

Lindsay, Sir James Harvey Kincaid Stewart, Kt.

Lindsay, *Hon.* Sir John Edmund Frederic, Kt.

Lindsay, Sir Ronald Alexander, Bt., (1962)

†Lindsay-Hogg, Sir Michael Edward, Bt. (1905)

Lipton, Sir Stuart Anthony, Kt.

Lipworth, Sir (Maurice) Sydney, Kt.

Lister-Kaye, Sir John Phillip Lister, Bt. (1812)

Liston-Foulis, Sir Ian Primrose, Bt. (S. 1634)

Lithgow, Sir William James, Bt. (1925)

Little, *Most Revd* Thomas Francis, KBE

Littler, Sir (James) Geoffrey, KCB

Livesay, *Adm.* Sir Michael Howard, KCB

Llewellyn, Sir David St Vincent, Bt. (1922)

Llewellyn-Smith, *Prof.* Sir Christopher Hubert, Kt.

Lloyd, *Prof.* Sir Geoffrey Ernest Richard, Kt., FBA

Lloyd, Sir Ian Stewart, Kt.

Lloyd, Sir Nicholas Markley, Kt.

Lloyd, *Rt. Hon.* Sir Peter Robert Cable, Kt., MP

Lloyd, Sir Richard Ernest Butler, Bt. (1960)

Lloyd, *Hon.* Sir Timothy Andrew Wigram, Kt.

Lloyd-Hughes, Sir Trevor Denby, Kt.

Lloyd-Jones, Sir (Peter) Hugh (Jefferd), Kt

Loane, *Most Revd* Marcus Lawrence, KBE

Lobo, Sir Rogerio Hyndman, Kt., CBE

†Loder, Sir Edmund Jeune, Bt. (1887)

Logan, Sir David Brian Carleton, KCMG

Logan, Sir Donald Arthur, KCMG

Logan, Sir Raymond Douglas, Kt.

Lokoloko, Sir Tore, GCMG, GCVO, OBE

Longmore, *Rt. Hon.* Sir Andrew Centlivres, Kt.

Loram, *Vice-Adm.* Sir David Anning, KCB, CVO

Lord, Sir Michael Nicholson, Kt.

Lorimer, Sir (Thomas) Desmond, Kt.

Los, *Hon.* Sir Kubulan, Kt., CBE

Loughran, Sir Gerald Finbar, KCB

Lovell, Sir (Alfred Charles) Bernard, Kt., OBE, FRS

Lovelock, Sir Douglas Arthur, KCB

Loveridge, Sir John Warren, Kt.

Lovill, Sir John Roger, Kt., CBE

Lowe, *Air Chief Marshal* Sir Douglas Charles, GCB, DFC, AFC

Lowe, Sir Frank Budge, Kt.

Lowe, Sir Thomas William Gordon, Bt. (1918)

Lowson, Sir Ian Patrick, Bt. (1951)

Lowther, *Col.* Sir Charles Douglas, Bt. (1824)

Lowther, Sir John Luke, KCVO, CBE

Loyd, Sir Francis Alfred, KCMG, OBE

Loyd, Sir Julian St John, KCVO

Lu, Sir Tseng Chi, Kt.

Lucas, *Prof.* Sir Colin Renshaw, Kt.

Lucas, Sir Thomas Edward, Bt. (1887)

Lucas-Tooth, Sir (Hugh) John, Bt. (1920)

Lucy, Sir Edmund John William Hugh Cameron-Ramsay-Fairfax, Bt. (1836)

Luddington, Sir Donald Collin Cumyn, KBE, CMG, CVO

Lumsden, Sir David James, Kt.

Lush, *Hon.* Sir George Hermann, Kt.

Lushington, Sir John Richard Castleman, Bt. (1791)

Luttrell, *Col.* Sir Geoffrey Walter Fownes, KCVO, MC

Lyell, *Rt. Hon.* Sir Nicholas Walter, Kt. MP

Lygo, *Adm.* Sir Raymond Derek, KCB

Lyle, Sir Gavin Archibald, Bt. (1929)

Lynch-Blosse, *Capt.* Sir Richard Hely, Bt. (1622)

Lynch-Robinson, Sir Dominick Christopher, Bt. (1920)

Lyne, Sir Roderic Michael John, KBE, CMG

Lyons, Sir Edward Houghton, Kt.

Lyons, Sir James Reginald, Kt.

Lyons, Sir John, Kt.

Lyons, Sir Michael Thomas, Kt.

McAlpine, Sir William Hepburn, Bt. (1918)

Macara, Sir Alexander Wiseman, Kt., FRCP, FRCGP

†Macara, Sir Hugh Kenneth, Bt. (1911)

McAvoy, Sir (Francis) Joseph, Kt., CBE

McCaffrey, Sir Thomas Daniel, Kt.

McCallum, Sir Donald Murdo, Kt., CBE, FREng.

McCamley, Sir Graham Edward, KBE

McCartney, Sir (James) Paul, Kt., MBE

Macartney, Sir John Barrington, Bt. (I. 1799)

McClellan, *Col.* Sir Herbert Gerard Thomas, Kt., CBE, TD

McClintock, Sir Eric Paul, Kt.

McColl, Sir Colin Hugh Verel, KCMG

McCollum, *Rt. Hon.* Sir William, Kt.

McCombe, *Hon.* Sir Richard George Bramwell, Kt.

McConnell, Sir Robert Shean, Bt. (1900)

McCorkell, *Col.* Sir Michael William, KCVO, OBE, TD

MacCormac, Sir Richard Cornelius, Kt., CBE

MacCormick, *Prof.* Sir Donald Neil, Kt., MEP, QC

†McCowan, Sir David William, Bt. (1934)

McCullough, *Hon.* Sir (Iain) Charles (Robert), Kt.

MacDermott, *Rt. Hon.* Sir John Clarke, Kt.

McDermott, Sir (Lawrence) Emmet, KBE

Macdonald of Sleat, Sir Ian Godfrey Bosville, Bt. (S. 1625)

Macdonald, Sir Kenneth Carmichael, KCB

McDonald, Sir Trevor, Kt., OBE

MacDougall, Sir (George) Donald (Alastair), Kt., CBE, FBA

McDowell, Sir Eric Wallace, Kt., CBE

Mace, *Lt.-Gen.* Sir John Airth, KBE, CB

McEwen, Sir John Roderick Hugh, Bt. (1953)

McFarland, Sir John Talbot, Bt. (1914)

MacFarlane, *Prof.* Sir Alistair George James, Kt., CBE, FRS

Macfarlane, Sir (David) Neil, Kt.

Macfarlane, Sir George Gray, Kt., CB, FREng.

McFarlane, Sir Ian, Kt.

McGeoch, *Vice-Adm.* Sir Ian Lachlan Mackay, KCB, DSO, DSC

McGrath, Sir Brian Henry, GCVO

Macgregor, Sir Edwin Robert, Bt. (1828)

McGregor, Sir Ian Alexander, Kt., CBE

McGregor, Sir James David, Kt., OBE

†MacGregor of MacGregor, Sir Malcolm Gregor Charles, Bt. (1795)

McGrigor, *Capt.* Sir Charles Edward, Bt. (1831)

McIntosh, Sir Neil William David, Kt., CBE

McIntosh, Sir Ronald Robert Duncan, KCB

McIntyre, Sir Donald Conroy, Kt., CBE

McIntyre, Sir Meredith Alister, Kt.

Mackay, *Hon.* Sir Colin Crichton, Kt.

MacKay, *Prof.* Sir Donald Iain, Kt.

MacKay, Sir Francis Henry, Kt.

McKay, Sir John Andrew, Kt., CBE

McKay, Sir William Robert, KCB

Mackay-Dick, *Maj.-Gen.* Sir Iain Charles, KCVO, MBE

Mackechnie, Sir Alistair John, Kt.

McKee, *Maj.* Sir (William) Cecil, Kt., ERD

McKellen, Sir Ian Murray, Kt., CBE

Mackenzie, Sir (James William) Guy, Bt. (1890)

Mackenzie, *Gen.* Sir Jeremy John George, GCB, GCVO

†Mackenzie, Sir Peter Douglas, Bt. (S. 1673)

†Mackenzie, Sir Roderick McQuhae, Bt. (S. 1703)

McKenzie, Sir Roy Allan, KBE

Mackerras, Sir (Alan) Charles (MacLaurin), Kt., CH, CBE

Mackeson, Sir Rupert Henry, Bt. (1954)

McKillop, Sir Thomas Fulton Wilson, Kt.

McKinnon, Sir James, Kt.

McKinnon, *Hon.* Sir Stuart Neil, Kt.

Mackintosh, Sir Cameron Anthony, Kt.

Mackworth, Sir Digby (John), Bt. (1776)

McLaren, Sir Robin John Taylor, KCMG

McLaughlin, *Hon.* Mr Justice, Sir Richard, Kt.

Maclean of Dunconnell, Sir Charles Edward, Bt. (1957)

Maclean, Sir Donald Og Grant, Kt.

Maclean, Sir Lachlan Hector Charles, Bt. (NS 1631)

Maclean, Sir Murdo, Kt.

McLeod, Sir Charles Henry, Bt. (1925)

MacLeod, Sir (John) Maxwell Norman, Bt. (1924)

Macleod, Sir (Nathaniel William) Hamish, KBE

McLintock, Sir (Charles) Alan, Kt.

McLintock, Sir Michael William, Bt. (1934)

Maclure, Sir John Robert Spencer, Bt. (1898)

McMahon, Sir Brian Patrick, Bt. (1817)

McMahon, Sir Christopher William, Kt.

McMaster, Sir Brian John, Kt., CBE

Macmillan, Sir (Alexander McGregor) Graham, Kt.

MacMillan, *Lt.-Gen.* Sir John Richard Alexander, KCB, CBE

McMullin, *Rt. Hon.* Sir Duncan Wallace, Kt.

McMurtry, Sir David, Kt., CBE

Macnaghten, Sir Patrick Alexander, Bt. (1836)

McNair-Wilson, Sir Patrick Michael Ernest David, Kt.

McNamara, *Air Chief Marshal* Sir Neville Patrick, KBE

Macnaughton, *Prof.* Sir Malcolm Campbell, Kt.

McNee, Sir David Blackstock, Kt., QPM

McNulty, Sir (Robert William) Roy, Kt., CBE

MacPhail, Sir Bruce Dugald, Kt.

Macpherson, Sir Ronald Thomas Steward (Tommy), CBE, MC, TD

Macpherson of Cluny, *Hon.* Sir William Alan, Kt., TD

McQuarrie, Sir Albert, Kt.

MacRae, Sir (Alastair) Christopher (Donald Summerhayes), KCMG

Macready, Sir Nevil John Wilfrid, Bt. (1923)

MacSween, *Prof.* Sir Roderick Norman McIver, Kt.

Mactaggart, Sir John Auld, Bt. (1938)

Macwhinnie, Sir Gordon Menzies, Kt., CBE

McWilliam, Sir Michael Douglas, KCMG

McWilliams, Sir Francis, GBE

Madden, Sir David Christopher Andrew, KCMG

Madden, Sir Peter John, Bt. (1919)

Maddox, Sir John Royden, Kt.

Madel, Sir (William) David, Kt., MP

Magnus, Sir Laurence Henry Philip, Bt. (1917)

Mahon, Sir (John) Denis, Kt., CH, CBE

Mahon, Sir William Walter, Bt. (1819)

Maiden, Sir Colin James, Kt., D.Phil.

Main, Sir Peter Tester, Kt., ERD

Maingard de la Ville ès Offrans, Sir Louis Pierre René, Kt., CBE

Maini, *Prof.* Sir Ravinder Nath, Kt.

Maino, Sir Charles, KBE

†Maitland, Sir Charles Alexander, Bt. (1818)

Maitland, Sir Donald James Dundas, GCMG, OBE

Malbon, *Vice-Adm.* Sir Fabian Michael, KBE

Malcolm, Sir James William Thomas Alexander, Bt. (S. 1665)

Malet, Sir Harry Douglas St Lo, Bt. (1791)

Mallaby, Sir Christopher Leslie George, GCMG, GCVO

Mallet, Sir William George, GCMG, CBE

Mallick, *Prof.* Sir Netar Prakash, Kt.

Mallinson, Sir William James, Bt. (1935)

Malpas, Sir Robert, Kt., CBE

Mamo, Sir Anthony Joseph, Kt., OBE

Mance, *Rt. Hon.* Sir Jonathan Hugh, Kt.

Mancham, Sir James Richard Marie, KBE

Manchester, Sir William Maxwell, KBE

Mander, Sir Charles Marcus, Bt. (1911)

Manduell, Sir John, Kt., CBE

Mann, *Rt. Revd* Michael Ashley, KCVO

Mann, Sir Rupert Edward, Bt. (1905)

Manning, Sir David Geoffrey, KCMG

Mansel, Sir Philip, Bt. (1622)

Mansfield, *Vice-Adm.* Sir (Edward) Gerard (Napier), KBE, CVO

Mansfield, *Prof.* Sir Peter, Kt.

Mantell, *Rt. Hon.* Sir Charles Barrie Knight, Kt.

Manton, Sir Edwin Alfred Grenville, Kt.

Manuella, Sir Tulaga, GCMG, MBE

Manzie, Sir (Andrew) Gordon, KCB

Mara, *Rt. Hon. Ratu* Sir Kamisese Kapaiwai Tuimacilai, GCMG, KBE

Margetson, Sir John William Denys, KCMG

Mark, Sir Robert, GBE

Markham, Sir Charles John, Bt. (1911)

Marling, Sir Charles William Somerset, Bt. (1882)

Marmot, Prof. Sir Michael Gideon, Kt.

Marr, Sir Leslie Lynn, Bt. (1919)

Marriner, Sir Neville, Kt., CBE

†Marsden, Sir Simon Neville Llewelyn, Bt. (1924)

Marsh, *Prof.* Sir John Stanley, Kt., CBE

Marshall, Sir Arthur Gregory George, Kt., OBE

Marshall, Sir Denis Alfred, Kt.

Marshall, *Prof.* Sir (Oshley) Roy, Kt., CBE

Marshall, Sir Peter Harold Reginald, KCMG

Marshall, Sir (Robert) Michael, Kt.

Martin, Sir Clive Haydon, Kt., OBE

Martin, Sir George Henry, Kt., CBE

Martin, *Vice-Adm.* Sir John Edward Ludgate, KCB, DSC

Martin, *Prof.* Sir Laurence Woodward, Kt.

Martin, Sir (Robert) Bruce, Kt., QC

Marychurch, Sir Peter Harvey, KCMG

Masefield, Sir Charles Beech Gordon, Kt.

Masefield, Sir Peter Gordon, Kt.

Mason, *Hon.* Sir Anthony Frank, KBE

Mason, Sir (Basil) John, Kt., CB, D.Sc., FRS

Mason, *Prof.* Sir David Kean, Kt., CBE

Mason, Sir Frederick Cecil, KCVO, CMG

Mason, Sir Gordon Charles, Kt., OBE

Mason, Sir John Charles Moir, KCMG

Mason, Sir John Peter, Kt., CBE

Mason, Sir Peter James, KBE

Mason, *Prof.* Sir Ronald, KCB, FRS

Massy-Greene, Sir (John) Brian, Kt.

Matane, Sir Paulias Nguna, Kt., CMG, OBE

Mather, Sir (David) Carol (Macdonell), Kt., MC

Mathers, Sir Robert William, Kt.

Matheson of Matheson, Sir Fergus John, Bt. (1882)

Mathewson, Sir George Ross, Kt., CBE, Ph.D., FRSE

Matthews, Sir Peter Alec, Kt.

Matthews, Sir Terence Hedley, Kt., OBE

Maud, The Hon. Sir Humphrey John Hamilton, KCMG

Maughan, Sir Deryck, Kt.

Mawer, Sir Philip John Courtney, Kt.

Mawhinney, *Rt. Hon.* Sir Brian Stanley, Kt., MP

Maxwell, Sir Michael Eustace George, Bt. (S. 1681)

Maxwell-Hyslop, Sir Robert John (Robin), Kt.

Maxwell-Scott, Sir Dominic James, Bt. (1642)

May, *Rt. Hon.* Sir Anthony Tristram Kenneth, Kt.

Mayhew-Sanders, Sir John Reynolds, Kt.

Maynard, *Hon.* Sir Clement Travelyan, Kt.

Mayne, *Very Revd* Michael Clement Otway, KCVO

Meadow, *Prof.* Sir (Samuel) Roy, Kt., FRCP, FRCPE

Medlycott, Sir Mervyn Tregonwell, Bt. (1808)

Megarry, *Rt. Hon.* Sir Robert Edgar, Kt., FBA

Meldrum, Sir Graham, Kt., CBE, QFSM

Melhuish, Sir Michael Ramsay, KBE, CMG

Mellon, Sir James, KCMG

Melmoth, Sir Graham John, Kt.

Menter, Sir James Woodham, Kt., Ph.D., Sc.D., FRS

Merifield, Sir Anthony James, KCVO, CB

Meyer, Sir Anthony John Charles, Bt. (1910)

Meyer, Sir Christopher John Rome, KCMG

Meyjes, Sir Richard Anthony, Kt.

Meyrick, Sir David John Charlton, Bt. (1880)

Miakwe, *Hon.* Sir Akepa, KBE

Michael, Sir Duncan, Kt.

Michael, Sir Peter Colin, Kt., CBE

Middleton, Sir John Maxwell, Kt.

Middleton, Sir Peter Edward, GCB

Miers, Sir (Henry) David Alastair Capel, KBE, CMG

Milbank, Sir Anthony Frederick, Bt. (1882)

Milborne-Swinnerton-Pilkington, Sir Thomas Henry, Bt. (S. 1635)

Milburn, Sir Anthony Rupert, Bt. (1905)

Miles, Sir Peter Tremayne, KCVO

Miles, Sir William Napier Maurice, Bt. (1859)

Millais, Sir Geoffrey Richard Everett, Bt. (1885)

Millar, Sir Oliver Nicholas, GCVO, FBA

Millard, Sir Guy Elwin, KCMG, CVO

Miller, Sir Albert Joel, KCMG, MVO, MBE, QPM, CPM

Miller, Sir Donald John, Kt., FRSE, FREng.

Miller, Sir Harry Holmes, Bt. (1705)

Miller, Sir Hilary Duppa (Hal), Kt.

Miller, *Lt.-Col.* Sir John Mansel, GCVO, DSO, MC

Miller, Sir Jonathan Wolfe, Kt., CBE

Miller, Sir Peter North, Kt.

Miller, Sir Robin Robert William, Kt.

Miller, Sir Ronald Andrew Baird, Kt., CBE

Miller of Glenlee, Sir Stephen William Macdonald, Bt. (1788)

Mills, *Vice-Adm.* Sir Charles Piercy, KCB, CBE, DSC

Mills, Sir Ian, Kt.

Mills, Sir Frank, KCVO, CMG

Mills, Sir John Lewis Ernest Watts, Kt., CBE

Mills, Sir Peter Frederick Leighton, Bt. (1921)

Milman, Sir David Patrick, Bt. (1800)

Milne, Sir John Drummond, Kt.

Milne-Watson, Sir Andrew Michael, Bt. (1937)

Milner, Sir Timothy William Lycett, Bt. (1717)

Milton-Thompson, *Surgeon Vice-Adm.* Sir Godfrey James, KBE

Mirrlees, *Prof.* Sir James Alexander, Kt., FBA

Mitchell, Sir David Bower, Kt.

Mitchell, Sir Derek Jack, KCB, CVO

Mitchell, *Rt. Hon.* Sir James FitzAllen, KCMG

Mitchell, *Very Revd* Patrick Reynolds, KCVO

Mitchell, *Hon.* Sir Stephen George, Kt.

Mitting, *Hon.* Sir John Edward, Kt.

Moate, Sir Roger Denis, Kt.

Mobbs, Sir (Gerald) Nigel, Kt.

Moberly, Sir John Campbell, KBE, CMG

Moberly, Sir Patrick Hamilton, KCMG

Moffat, Sir Brian Scott, Kt., OBE

Moffat, *Lt.-Gen.* Sir (William) Cameron, KBE

Mogg, Sir John Frederick, KCMG

Moir, Sir Christopher Ernest, Bt. (1916)

† Molesworth-St Aubyn, Sir William, Bt. (1689)

†Molony, Sir Thomas Desmond, Bt. (1925)

Monck, Sir Nicholas Jeremy, KCB

Money-Coutts, Sir David Burdett, KCVO

Montagu, Sir Nicholas Lionel John, KCB

Montagu-Pollock, Sir Giles Hampden, Bt. (1872)

Montague-Browne, Sir Anthony Arthur Duncan, KCMG, CBE, DFC

Montgomery, Sir (Basil Henry) David, Bt. (1801)

Montgomery, Sir (William) Fergus, Kt.

Montgomery-Cuninghame, Sir John Christopher Foggo, Bt. (NS 1672)

Moody-Stuart, Sir Mark, KCMG

Moollan, Sir Abdool Hamid Adam, Kt.

Moollan, *Hon.* Sir Cassam (Ismael), Kt.

†Moon, Sir Roger, Bt. (1887)

Moore, *Most Revd* Desmond Charles, KBE

Moore, Sir Francis Thomas, Kt.

Moore, *Maj.-Gen.* Sir (John) Jeremy, KCB, OBE, MC

Moore, Sir John Michael, KCVO, CB, DSC

Moore, *Vice Adm.* Sir Michael Antony Claës, KBE, LVO

Moore, *Prof.* Sir Norman Winfrid, Bt. (1919)

Moore, Sir Patrick Alfred Caldwell, Kt., CBE

Moore, Sir Patrick William Eisdell, Kt., OBE

Moore, Sir Roger George, KBE

Moore, Sir William Roger Clotworthy, Bt., TD (1932)

Moore-Bick, *Hon.* Sir Martin James, Kt.

Moores, Sir Peter, Kt., CBE

Morauta, Sir Mekere, Kt.

Mordaunt, Sir Richard Nigel Charles, Bt. (1611)

Moreton, Sir John Oscar, KCMG, KCVO, MC

Morgan, *Vice-Adm.* Sir Charles Christopher, KBE

Morgan, Sir Graham, Kt.

Morgan, Sir John Albert Leigh, KCMG

Morgan-Giles, *Rear-Adm.* Sir Morgan Charles, Kt., DSO, OBE, GM

Morison, *Hon.* Sir Thomas Richard Atkin, Kt.

Morland, *Hon.* Sir Michael, Kt.

Morland, Sir Robert Kenelm, Kt.

Morpeth, Sir Douglas Spottiswoode, Kt., TD

†Morris, Sir Allan Lindsay, Bt. (1806)

Morris, *Air Marshal* Sir Arnold Alec, KBE, CB

Morris, Sir Derek James, Kt.

Morris, Sir (James) Richard (Samuel), Kt., CBE

Morris, Sir Keith Elliot Hedley, KBE, CMG

Morris, *Prof.* Sir Peter John, Kt.

Morris, Sir Trefor Alfred, Kt., CBE, QPM

Morris, Sir William, Kt.

Morris, *Very Revd* William James, KCVO

Morrison, Sir (Alexander) Fraser, Kt., CBE

Morrison, *Hon.* Sir Charles Andrew, Kt.

Morrison, Sir Howard Leslie, Kt., OBE

Morrison, Sir Kenneth Duncan, Kt., CBE

Morrison-Bell, Sir William Hollin Dayrell, Bt. (1905)

Morrison-Low, Sir James Richard, Bt. (1908)

Morritt, *Rt. Hon.* Sir (Robert) Andrew, Kt., CVO

Morrow, Sir Ian Thomas, Kt.

Morse, Sir Christopher Jeremy, KCMG

Mortimer, Sir John Clifford, Kt., CBE, QC

Morton, *Adm.* Sir Anthony Storrs, GBE, KCB

Morton, Sir (Robert) Alastair (Newton), Kt.

Moseley, Sir George Walker, KCB

Moses, *Hon.* Sir Alan George, Kt.

Moss, Sir David Joseph, KCVO, CMG

Moss, Sir Stirling Craufurd, Kt., OBE

Mostyn, Sir (Joseph) David Frederick, KCB, OBE

†Mostyn, Sir William Basil John, Bt. (1670)

Mott, Sir John Harmer, Bt. (1930)

Mottram, Sir Richard Clive, KCB

†Mount, Sir (William Robert) Ferdinand, Bt. (1921)

Mountain, Sir Denis Mortimer, Bt. (1922)

Mountfield, Sir Robin, KCB

Mowbray, Sir John, Kt.

Mowbray, Sir John Robert, Bt. (1880)

Muir, Sir Laurence Macdonald, Kt.

†Muir, Sir Richard James Kay, Bt. (1892)

Muir-Mackenzie, Sir Alexander Alwyne Henry Charles Brinton, Bt. (1805)

Mulcahy, Sir Geoffrey John, Kt.

Mullens, *Lt.-Gen.* Sir Anthony Richard Guy, KCB, OBE

Mummery, *Rt. Hon.* Sir John Frank, Kt.

Munby, *Hon.* Sir James Lawrence, Kt.

Munn, Sir James, Kt., OBE

Munro, Sir Alan Gordon, KCMG

†Munro, Sir Kenneth Arnold William, Bt. (S. 1634)

†Munro, Sir Keith Gordon, Bt. (1825)

Muria, *Hon.* Sir Gilbert John Baptist, Kt.

Murphy, Sir Leslie Frederick, Kt.

Murray, *Rt. Hon.* Sir Donald Bruce, Kt.

Murray, Sir James, KCMG

Murray, *Prof.* Sir Kenneth, Kt.

Murray, Sir Nigel Andrew Digby, Bt. (S. 1628)

Murray, Sir Patrick Ian Keith, Bt. (S. 1673)

†Murray, Sir Rowland William, Bt. (S. 1630)

Mursell, Sir Peter, Kt., MBE

Musgrave, Sir Christopher John Shane, Bt. (1782)

Musgrave, Sir Christopher Patrick Charles, Bt. (1611)

Musson, *Gen.* Sir Geoffrey Randolph Dixon, GCB, CBE, DSO

Myers, Sir Philip Alan, Kt., OBE, QPM

Myers, *Prof.* Sir Rupert Horace, KBE

Mynors, Sir Richard Baskerville, Bt. (1964)

Naipaul, Sir Vidiadhar Surajprasad, Kt.

Nairn, Sir Michael, Bt. (1904)

Nairne, *Rt. Hon.* Sir Patrick Dalmahoy, GCB, MC

Naish, Sir (Charles) David, Kt.

Nall, Sir Edward William Joseph Bt. (1954)

Namaliu, *Rt. Hon.* Sir Rabbie Langanai, KCMG

†Napier, Sir Charles Joseph, Bt. (1867)

Napier, Sir John Archibald Lennox, Bt. (S. 1627)

Napier, Sir Oliver John, Kt.

Naylor-Leyland, Sir Philip Vyvyan, Bt. (1895)

Neal, Sir Eric James, Kt., CVO

Neal, Sir Leonard Francis, Kt., CBE

Neale, Sir Gerrard Anthony, Kt.

Neave, Sir Paul Arundell, Bt. (1795)

Neill, *Rt. Hon.* Sir Brian Thomas, Kt.

Neill, Sir (James) Hugh, KCVO, CBE, TD

†Nelson, Sir Jamie Charles Vernon Hope, Bt. (1912)

Nelson, *Hon.* Sir Robert Franklyn, Kt.

Neuberger, *Hon.* Sir David Edmond, Kt.

Neubert, Sir Michael John, Kt.

Neville, Sir Roger Albert Gartside, Kt.

New, *Maj.-Gen.* Sir Laurence Anthony Wallis, Kt., CB, CBE

Newall, Sir Paul Henry, Kt., TD

Newby, *Prof.* Sir Howard Joseph, Kt., CBE

Newington, Sir Michael John, KCMG

Newman, Sir Francis Hugh Cecil, Bt. (1912)

Newman, Sir Geoffrey Robert, Bt. (1836)

Newman, *Hon.* Sir George Michael, Kt.

Newman, Sir Kenneth Leslie, GBE, QPM

Newman, *Vice-Adm.* Sir Roy Thomas, KCB

Newsam, Sir Peter Anthony, Kt.

†Newson-Smith, Sir Peter Frank Graham, Bt. (1944)

Newton, Sir (Charles) Wilfred, Kt., CBE

Newton, Sir (Harry) Michael (Rex), Bt. (1900)

Newton, Sir Kenneth Garnar, Bt., OBE, TD (1924)

Ngata, Sir Henare Kohere, KBE

Nichol, Sir Duncan Kirkbride, Kt., CBE

Nicholas, Sir David, Kt., CBE

Nicholas, Sir John William, KCVO, CMG

Nicholls, *Air Marshal* Sir John Moreton, KCB, CBE, DFC, AFC

Nicholls, Sir Nigel Hamilton, KCVO, CBE

Nichols, Sir Richard Everard, Kt.

Nicholson, Sir Bryan Hubert, Kt.

†Nicholson, Sir Charles Christian, Bt. (1912)

Nicholson, *Rt. Hon.* Sir Michael, Kt.

Nicholson, Sir Paul Douglas, Kt.

Nicholson, Sir Robin Buchanan, Kt., Ph.D., FRS, FREng.

Nicoll, Sir William, KCMG

Nightingale, Sir Charles Manners Gamaliel, Bt. (1628)

Nixon, Sir Simon Michael Christopher, Bt. (1906)

Nixon, Sir Edwin Ronald, Kt., CBE

Noble, Sir David Brunel, Bt. (1902)

Noble, Sir Iain Andrew, Bt., OBE (1923)

Nombri, Sir Joseph Karl, Kt., ISO, BEM

Noon, Sir Gulam Kaderbhoy, Kt., MBE

Norman, Sir Arthur Gordon, KBE, DFC

Norman, Sir Mark Annesley, Bt. (1915)

Norman, Sir Robert Henry, Kt., OBE

Norman, Sir Ronald, Kt., OBE

Norrington, Sir Roger Arthur Carver, Kt., CBE

Norris, Sir Eric George, KCMG

Norriss, *Air Marshal* Sir Peter Coulson, KBE, CB, AFC

North, Sir Peter Machin, Kt., CBE, QC, DCL, FBA

North, Sir Thomas Lindsay, Kt.

North, Sir (William) Jonathan (Frederick), Bt. (1920)

Norton-Griffiths, Sir John, Bt. (1922)

Nossal, Sir Gustav Joseph Victor, Kt., CBE

Nott, *Rt. Hon.* Sir John William Frederic, KCB

Nourse, *Rt. Hon.* Sir Martin Charles, Kt.

Nugent, Sir John Edwin Lavallin, Bt. (I. 1795)

Nugent, Sir Robin George Colborne, Bt. (1806)

†Nugent, Sir (Walter) Richard Middleton, Bt. (1831)

Nunn, Sir Trevor Robert, Kt., CBE

Nunneley, Sir Charles Kenneth Roylance, Kt.

Nursaw, Sir James, KCB, QC

Nurse, Sir Paul Maxime, Kt.

Nuttall, Sir Nicholas Keith Lillington, Bt. (1922)

Nutting, Sir John Grenfell, Bt., QC (1903)

Oakeley, Sir John Digby Atholl, Bt. (1790)

Oakes, Sir Christopher, Bt. (1939)

Oakshott, *Hon.* Sir Anthony Hendrie, Bt. (1959)

Oates, Sir Thomas, Kt., CMG, OBE

O'Brien, Sir Frederick William Fitzgerald, Kt.

O'Brien, Sir Richard, Kt., DSO, MC

O'Brien, Sir Timothy John, Bt. (1849)

O'Brien, *Adm.* Sir William Donough, KCB, DSC

O'Connell, Sir Maurice James Donagh MacCarthy, Bt. (1869)

O'Dea, Sir Patrick Jerad, KCVO

Odell, Sir Stanley John, Kt.

Odgers, Sir Graeme David William, Kt.

O'Donnell, Sir Christopher John, Kt.

O'Dowd, Sir David Joseph, Kt., CBE, QPM

Ogden, Sir Robert, Kt., CBE

Ogilvy, *Rt. Hon.* Sir Angus James Bruce, KCVO

Ogilvy, Sir Francis Gilbert Arthur, Bt. (S. 1626)

Ogilvy-Wedderburn, Sir Andrew John Alexander, Bt. (1803)

Ognall, *Hon.* Sir Harry Henry, Kt.

Ohlson, Sir Brian Eric Christopher, Bt. (1920)

Oldham, *Dr* Sir John, Kt., OBE

Oliver, Sir James Michael Yorrick, Kt.

O'Loghlen, Sir Colman Michael, Bt. (1838)

Olver, Sir Stephen John Linley, KBE, CMG

Omand, Sir David Bruce, KCB

O'Nions, *Prof.* Sir Robert Keith, Kt., FRS, Ph.D.

Ondaatje, Sir Christopher, Kt., CBE

Onslow, Sir John Roger Wilmot, Bt. (1797)

Oppenheimer, Sir Michael Bernard Grenville, Bt. (1921)

O'Regan, *Dr* Sir Stephen Gerard (Tipene), Kt.

O'Reilly, Sir Anthony John Francis, Kt.

Orr, Sir David Alexander, Kt., MC

Orr, Sir John, Kt., OBE

Orr-Ewing, Sir (Alistair) Simon, Bt. (1963)

Orr-Ewing, Sir Archibald Donald, Bt. (1886)

Osborn, Sir John Holbrook, Kt.

Osborn, Sir Richard Henry Danvers, Bt. (1662)

Osborne, Sir Peter George, Bt. (I. 1629)

Osmond, Sir Douglas, Kt., CBE

Osmotherly, Sir Edward Benjamin Crofton, Kt., CB

O'Sullevan, Sir Peter John, Kt., CBE

Oswald, *Admiral of the Fleet* Sir (John) Julian Robertson, GCB

Oswald, Sir (William Richard) Michael, KCVO

Otton, Sir Geoffrey John, KCB

Otton, *Rt. Hon.* Sir Philip Howard, Kt.

Oulton, Sir Antony Derek Maxwell, GCB, QC

Ouseley, *Hon.* Sir Brian Walter, Kt.

Outram, Sir Alan James, Bt. (1858)

Owen, Sir Geoffrey, Kt.
Owen, *Hon.* Sir John Arthur Dalziel, Kt.
Owen, *Hon.* Sir Robert Michael, Kt.
Pakenham, *Hon.* Sir Michael Aiden, KBE, CMG
Packer, Sir Richard John, KCB
Page, Sir (Arthur) John, Kt.
Page, Sir Frederick William, Kt., CBE, FREng.
Page, Sir John Joseph Joffre, Kt., OBE
Paget, Sir Julian Tolver, Bt., CVO (1871)
Paget, Sir Richard Herbert, Bt. (1886)
Pain, *Lt.-Gen.* Sir (Horace) Rollo (Squarey), KCB, MC
Paine, Sir Christopher Hammon, Kt., FRCP, FRCR
Palin, *Air Chief Marshal* Sir Roger Hewlett, KCB, OBE
Palliser, *Rt. Hon.* Sir (Arthur) Michael, GCMG
Palmar, Sir Derek James, Kt.
Palmer, Sir (Charles) Mark, Bt. (1886)
Palmer, Sir Geoffrey Christopher John, Bt. (1660)
Palmer, *Rt. Hon.* Sir Geoffrey Winston Russell, KCMG
Palmer, Sir John Edward Somerset, Bt. (1791)
Palmer, *Maj.-Gen.* Sir (Joseph) Michael, KCVO
Palmer, Sir Reginald Oswald, GCMG, MBE
Pantlin, Sir Dick Hurst, Kt., CBE
Paolozzi, Sir Eduardo Luigi, Kt., CBE, RA
Parbo, Sir Arvi Hillar, Kt.
Park, *Hon.* Sir Andrew Edward Wilson, Kt.
Parker, Sir Alan William, Kt., CBE
Parker, Sir Eric Wilson, Kt.
Parker, *Rt. Hon.* Sir Jonathan Frederic, Kt.
Parker, *Maj.* Sir Michael John, KCVO, CBE
Parker, Sir Richard (William) Hyde, Bt. (1681)
Parker, *Rt. Hon.* Sir Roger Jocelyn, Kt.
Parker, Sir (Thomas) John, Kt.
Parker, *Vice-Adm.* Sir (Wilfred) John, KBE, CB, DSC
Parker, Sir William Peter Brian, Bt. (1844)
Parkes, Sir Edward Walter, Kt., FREng.
Parry, Sir Emyr Jones, KCMG
Parry-Evans, *Air Chief Marshal* Sir David, GCB, CBE
Parsons, Sir John Christopher, KCVO
Parsons, Sir (John) Michael, Kt.
Parsons, Sir Richard Edmund (Clement Fownes), KCMG
Partridge, Sir Michael John Anthony, KCB

Pascoe, *Gen.* Sir Robert Alan, KCB, MBE

Pasley, Sir John Malcolm Sabine, Bt. (1794)
Paston-Bedingfeld, *Capt.* Sir Edmund George Felix, Bt. (1661)
Paterson, Sir Dennis Craig, Kt.
Patnick, Sir (Cyril) Irvine, Kt., OBE
Patten, *Hon.* Mr Justice, Sir Nicholas John, Kt.
Pattie, *Rt. Hon.* Sir Geoffrey Edwin, Kt.
Pattinson, Sir (William) Derek, Kt.
Pattison, *Prof.* Sir John Ridley, Kt., DM, FRCPath.
Pattullo, Sir (David) Bruce, Kt., CBE
Paul, Sir John Warburton, GCMG, OBE, MC
Pauncefort-Duncombe, Sir Philip Digby, Bt. (1859)
Payne, Sir Norman John, Kt., CBE, FREng.
Payne-Gallwey, Sir Philip Frankland, Bt. (1812)
Peach, Sir Leonard Harry, Kt.
Peacock, *Prof.* Sir Alan Turner, Kt., DSC
Pearce, Sir Austin William, Kt., CBE, Ph.D., FREng.
Pearce, Sir (Daniel Norton) Idris, Kt., CBE, TD
Pearse, Sir Brian Gerald, Kt.
Pearson, Sir Francis Nicholas Fraser, Bt. (1964)
Pearson, *Gen.* Sir Thomas Cecil Hook, KCB, CBE, DSO
Peart, *Prof.* Sir William Stanley, Kt., MD, FRS
Pease, Sir (Alfred) Vincent, Bt. (1882)
Pease, Sir Richard Thorn, Bt. (1920)
Peat, Sir Gerrard Charles, KCVO
Peat, Sir Michael Charles Gerrard, KCVO
Peck, Sir Edward Heywood, GCMG
Peckham, *Prof.* Sir Michael John, Kt., FRCP, FRCPGlas., FRCR, FRCPath.
Peek, *Vice-Adm.* Sir Richard Innes, KBE, CB, DSC
Peek, Sir William Grenville, Bt. (1874)
Peel, Sir John Harold, KCVO
Peel, Sir (William) John, Kt.
Peirse, *Air Vice-Marshal* Sir Richard Charles Fairfax, KCVO, CB
Pelgen, Sir Harry Friedrich, Kt., MBE
Peliza, Sir Robert John, KBE, ED
Pelly, Sir Richard John, Bt. (1840)
Pemberton, Sir Francis Wingate William, Kt., CBE
Penrose, *Prof.* Sir Roger, Kt., OM, FRS
Penry-Davey, *Hon.* Sir David Herbert, Kt.
Pereira, Sir (Herbert) Charles, Kt., D.Sc., FRS
Perowne, *Vice-Adm.* Sir James Francis, KBE
Perring, Sir John Raymond, Bt. (1963)
Perris, Sir David (Arthur), Kt., MBE
Perry, Sir David Howard, KCB
Perry, Sir (David) Norman, Kt., MBE

Perry, Sir Michael Sydney, GBE
Pervez, Sir Mohammed Anwar, Kt., OBE
Pestell, Sir John Richard, KCVO
Peters, *Prof.* Sir David Keith, Kt., FRCP
Petersen, Sir Jeffrey Charles, KCMG
Peterson, Sir Christopher Matthew, Kt., CBE, TD
†Petit, Sir Jehangir, Bt. (1890)
Peto, Sir Henry George Morton, Bt. (1855)
Peto, Sir Michael Henry Basil, Bt. (1927)
Peto, *Prof.* Sir Richard, Kt., FRS
Petrie, Sir Peter Charles, Bt., CMG (1918)
Pettigrew, Sir Russell Hilton, Kt.
Pettit, Sir Daniel Eric Arthur, Kt.
Pettitt, Sir Dennis, Kt.
Philips, *Prof.* Sir Cyril Henry, Kt.
Philipson-Stow, Sir Christopher, Bt., DFC (1907)
Phillips, Sir Fred Albert, Kt., CVO
Phillips, Sir (Gerald) Hayden, GCB
Phillips, Sir Henry Ellis Isidore, Kt., CMG, MBE
Phillips, Sir Horace, KCMG
Phillips, Sir John David, Kt., QPM
Phillips, Sir Peter John, Kt., OBE
Phillips, Sir Robin Francis, Bt. (1912)
Pickard, Sir (John) Michael, Kt.
Pickthorn, Sir James Francis Mann, Bt. (1959)
Pidgeon, Sir John Allan Stewart, Kt.
†Piers, Sir James Desmond, Bt. (I. 1661)
Piggott-Brown, Sir William Brian, Bt. (1903)
Pigot, Sir George Hugh, Bt. (1764)
Pigott, *Lt.-Gen.* Sir Anthony David, KCB, CBE
Pigott, Sir Berkeley Henry Sebastian, Bt. (1808)
Pike, *Lt.-Gen.* Sir Hew William Royston, KCB, DSO, MBE
Pike, Sir Michael Edmund, KCVO, CMG
Pike, Sir Philip Ernest Housden, Kt., QC
Pilditch, Sir Richard Edward, Bt. (1929)
Pile, Sir Frederick Devereux, Bt., MC (1900)
Pill, *Rt. Hon.* Sir Malcolm Thomas, Kt.
Pilling, Sir Joseph Grant, KCB
Pinker, Sir George Douglas, KCVO
Pinsent, Sir Christopher Roy, Bt. (1938)
Pippard, *Prof.* Sir (Alfred) Brian, Kt., FRS
Pitakaka, Sir Moses Puibangara, GCMG
Pitcher, Sir Desmond Henry, Kt.
Pitchers, *Hon.* Sir Christopher (John), Kt.
Pitchford, *Hon.* Sir Christopher John, Kt.
Pitman, Sir Brian Ivor, Kt.
Pitoi, Sir Sere, Kt., CBE

Pitt, Sir Harry Raymond, Kt., Ph.D., FRS
Pitts, Sir Cyril Alfred, Kt.
Plastow, Sir David Arnold Stuart, Kt.
Platt, Sir Harold Grant, Kt.
Platt, Sir Martin Philip, Bt. (1959)
Pledger, *Air Chief Marshal* Sir Malcolm David, KCB, OBE, AFC
Plumbly, Sir Derek John, KCMG
Pogo, Most *Revd.* Ellison Leslie, KBE
Pohai, Sir Timothy, Kt., MBE
Pole, Sir (John) Richard (Walter Reginald) Carew, Bt. (1628)
Pole, Sir Peter Van Notten, Bt. (1791)
Polkinghorne, *Revd Canon* John Charlton, KBE, FRS
Pollard, Sir Charles, Kt.
†Pollen, Sir Richard John Hungerford, Bt. (1795)
Pollock, Sir George Frederick, Bt. (1866)
Pollock, *Admiral of the Fleet* Sir Michael Patrick, GCB, LVO, DSC
Ponsonby, Sir Ashley Charles Gibbs, Bt., KCVO, MC (1956)
Poole, *Hon.* Sir David Anthony, Kt.
Poore, Sir Herbert Edward, Bt. (1795)
Pope, Sir Joseph Albert, Kt., D.Sc., Ph.D.
Pople, *Prof.* Sir John Anthony, KBE, FRS
Popplewell, *Hon.* Sir Oliver Bury, Kt.
†Porritt, Sir Jonathon Espie, Bt. (1963)
Portal, Sir Jonathan Francis, Bt. (1901)
Porter, Sir Leslie, Kt.
Porter, Sir Robert Wilson, Kt., PC (NI)
Posnett, Sir Richard Neil, KBE, CMG
Potter, *Rt. Hon.* Sir Mark Howard, Kt.
Potter, *Maj.-Gen.* Sir (Wilfrid) John, KBE, CB
Potts, *Hon.* Sir Francis Humphrey, Kt.
Pound, Sir John David, Bt. (1905)
Pountain, Sir Eric John, Kt.
Povey, Sir Keith, Kt., QPM
Powell, Sir Nicholas Folliott Douglas, Bt. (1897)
Powell, Sir Richard Royle, GCB, KBE, CMG
Power, Sir Alastair John Cecil, Bt. (1924)
Power, *Hon.* Sir Noel Plunkett, Kt.
Prance, *Prof.* Sir Ghillean Tolmie, Kt., FRS
Prendergast, Sir (Walter) Kieran, KCVO, CMG
Prentice, *Hon.* Sir William Thomas, Kt., MBE
Prescott, Sir Mark, Bt. (1938)
†Preston, Sir Philip Charles Henry Hulton, Bt. (1815)
Prevost, Sir Christopher Gerald, Bt. (1805)
Price, Sir David Ernest Campbell, Kt.

Price, Sir Francis Caradoc Rose, Bt. (1815)
Price, Sir Frank Leslie, Kt.
Price, Sir Norman Charles, KCB
Prickett, *Air Chief Marshal* Sir Thomas Other, KCB, DSO, DFC
Prideaux, Sir Humphrey Povah Treverbian, Kt., OBE
†Primrose, Sir John Ure, Bt. (1903)
Prince-Smith, Sir (William) Richard, Bt. (1911)
Pringle, *Air Marshal* Sir Charles Norman Seton, KBE, FREng.
Pringle, *Hon.* Sir John Kenneth, Kt.
Pringle, *Lt.-Gen.* Sir Steuart (Robert), Bt., KCB, RM (S. 1683)
Pritchard, Sir Neil, KCMG
Prichard-Jones, Sir John, Bt. (1910)
†Proby, Sir William Henry, Bt. (1952)
Proctor-Beauchamp, Sir Christopher Radstock, Bt. (1745)
Prosser, Sir Ian Maurice Gray, Kt.
Pryke, Sir Christopher Dudley, Bt. (1926)
Puapua, *Rt. Hon.* Sir Tomasi, GCMG, KBE
Pugh, Sir Idwal Vaughan, KCB
Pumfrey, *Hon.* Sir Nicholas Richard, Kt.
Pumphrey, Sir (John) Laurence, KCMG
Purchas, *Rt. Hon.* Sir Francis Brooks, Kt.
Purves, Sir William, Kt., CBE, DSO
Purvis, *Vice-Adm.* Sir Neville, KCB
Quan, Sir Henry (Francis), KBE
Quicke, Sir John Godolphin, Kt., CBE
Quigley, Sir (William) George (Henry), Kt., CB, Ph.D.
Quilliam, *Hon.* Sir (James) Peter, Kt.
Quilter, Sir Anthony Raymond Leopold Cuthbert, Bt. (1897)
Quinlan, Sir Michael Edward, GCB
Quinton, Sir James Grand, Kt.
Radcliffe, Sir Sebastian Everard, Bt. (1813)
Radda, *Prof.* Sir George Karoly, Kt., CBE, FRS
Rae, *Hon.* Sir Wallace Alexander Ramsay, Kt.
Raeburn, Sir Michael Edward Norman, Bt. (1923)
Raikes, *Vice-Adm.* Sir Iwan Geoffrey, KCB, CBE, DSC
Raison, *Rt. Hon.* Sir Timothy Hugh Francis, Kt.
Ralli, Sir Godfrey Victor, Bt., TD (1912)
Ramdanee, Sir Mookteswar Baboolall Kailash, Kt.
Ramphal, Sir Shridath Surendranath, GCMG
Ramphul, Sir Baalkhristna, Kt.
Ramphul, Sir Indurduth, Kt.
Ramsay, Sir Alexander William Burnett, Bt. (1806)
Ramsay, Sir Allan John (Hepple), KBE, CMG
Ramsbotham, *Gen.* Sir David John, GCB, CBE

Ramsbotham, *Hon.* Sir Peter Edward, GCMG, GCVO
Ramsden, Sir John Charles Josslyn, Bt. (1689)
Randle, *Prof.* Sir Philip John, Kt.
Rankin, Sir Ian Niall, Bt. (1898)
Rasch, Sir Simon Anthony Carne, Bt. (1903)
Rashleigh, Sir Richard Harry, Bt. (1831)
Ratford, Sir David John Edward, KCMG, CVO
Rattee, *Hon.* Sir Donald Keith, Kt.
Rattle, Sir Simon Dennis, Kt., CBE
Rawlins, *Surgeon Vice-Adm.* Sir John Stuart Pepys, KBE
Rawlins, *Prof.* Sir Michael David, Kt., FRCP, FRCPED.
Rawlinson, Sir Anthony Henry John, Bt. (1891)
Read, *Air Marshal* Sir Charles Frederick, KBE, CB, DFC, AFC
Read, Sir John Emms, Kt.
†Reade, Sir Kenneth Ray, Bt. (1661)
Reardon-Smith, Sir (William) Antony (John), Bt. (1920)
Reay, *Lt.-Gen.* Sir (Hubert) Alan John, KBE
Redgrave, *Maj.-Gen.* Sir Roy Michael Frederick, KBE, MC
Redgrave, Sir Steven Geoffrey, Kt., CBE
Redmayne, Sir Nicholas, Bt. (1964)
Redwood, Sir Peter Boverton, Bt. (1911)
Reece, Sir Charles Hugh, Kt.
Rees, Sir David Allan, Kt., Ph.D., D.Sc., FRS
Rees, *Prof.* Sir Martin John, Kt., FRS
Reeve, Sir Anthony, KCMG, KCVO
Reeves, *Most Revd* Paul Alfred, GCMG, GCVO
Reffell, *Adm.* Sir Derek Roy, KCB
Refshauge, *Maj.-Gen.* Sir William Dudley, Kt., CBE
Reid, Sir Alexander James, Bt. (1897)
Reid, Sir (Harold) Martin (Smith), KBE, CMG
Reid, Sir Hugh, Bt. (1922)
Reid, Sir Norman Robert, Kt.
Reid, Sir Robert Paul, Kt.
Reid, Sir William Kennedy, KCB
Reiher, Sir Frederick Bernard Carl, KBE, CMG
Reilly, *Lt.-Gen.* Sir Jeremy Calcott, KCB, DSO
Renals, Sir Stanley, Bt. (1895)
Renouf, Sir Clement William Bailey, Kt.
Renshaw, Sir John David Bine, Bt. (1903)
Renwick, Sir Richard Eustace, Bt. (1921)
Reporter, Sir Shapoor Ardeshirji, KBE
Reynolds, Sir David James, Bt. (1923)
Reynolds, Sir Peter William John, Kt., CBE
Rhodes, Sir John Christopher Douglas, Bt. (1919)

Rhodes, Sir Peregrine Alexander, KCMG
Rice, *Maj.-Gen.* Sir Desmond Hind Garrett, KCVO, CBE
Rice, Sir Timothy Miles Bindon, Kt.
Richard, Sir Cliff, Kt., OBE
Richards, Sir Brian Mansel, Kt., CBE, Ph.D.
Richards, Sir Francis Neville, KCMG, CVO
Richards, *Lt.-Gen.* Sir John Charles Chisholm, KCB, KCVO, RM
Richards, Sir Rex Edward, Kt., D.Sc., FRS
Richards, *Hon.* Sir Stephen Price, Kt.
Richardson, Sir Anthony Lewis, Bt. (1924)
Richardson, *Rt. Hon.* Sir Ivor Lloyd Morgan, Kt.
Richardson, Sir (John) Eric, Kt., CBE
Richardson, *Lt.-Gen.* Sir Robert Francis, KCB, CVO, CBE
Richardson, Sir Thomas Legh, KCMG
Richardson-Bunbury, Sir (Richard David) Michael, Bt. (I. 1787)
Richmond, *Prof.* Sir Mark Henry, Kt., FRS
Ricketts, Sir Robert Cornwallis Gerald St Leger, Bt. (1828)
Riddell, Sir John Charles Buchanan, Bt., CVO (S. 1628)
Ridley, Sir Adam (Nicholas), Kt.
Ridley, Sir Michael Kershaw, KCVO
Ridsdale, Sir Julian Errington, Kt., CBE
Rifkind, *Rt. Hon.* Sir Malcolm Leslie, KCMG
Rigby, Sir Anthony John, Bt. (1929)
Rigby, Sir Peter, Kt.
Rimer, *Hon.* Sir Colin Percy Farquharson, Kt.
Ripley, Sir Hugh, Bt. (1880)
Risk, Sir Thomas Neilson, Kt.
Ritako, Sir Thomas Baha, Kt., MBE
Rivett-Carnac, *Revd Canon* (Thomas) Nicholas, Bt. (1836)
Rix, *Rt. Hon.* Sir Bernard Anthony, Kt.
Rix, Sir John, Kt., MBE, FREng.
Robati, Sir Pupuke, KBE
Robb, Sir John Weddell, Kt.
Roberts, *Hon.* Sir Denys Tudor Emil, KBE,
Roberts, Sir Derek Harry, Kt., CBE, FRS, FREng.
Roberts, *Prof.* Sir Edward Adam, KCMG
Roberts, Sir (Edward Fergus) Sidney, Kt., CBE
Roberts, *Prof.* Sir Gareth Gwyn, Kt., FRS
Roberts, Sir Gilbert Howland Rookehurst, Bt. (1809)
Roberts, Sir Hugh Ashley, KCVO
Roberts, Sir Ivor Anthony, KCMG
Roberts, Sir Samuel, Bt. (1919)
Roberts, Sir William James Denby, Bt. (1909)
Robertson, Sir Lewis, Kt., CBE, FRSE
Robins, Sir Ralph Harry, Kt., FREng.

Robinson, Sir Albert Edward Phineas, Kt.
†Robinson, Sir Christopher Philipse, Bt. (1854)
Robinson, Sir Ian, Kt.
Robinson, Sir John James Michael Laud, Bt. (1660)
Robinson, *Dr* Sir Kenneth, Kt.
Robinson, Sir Wilfred Henry Frederick, Bt. (1908)
Robson, *Prof.* Sir James Gordon, Kt., CBE
Robson, Sir John Adam, KCMG
Robson, Sir Stephen Arthur, Kt., CB
Robson, Sir Robert William, Kt., CBE
Roch, *Rt. Hon.* Sir John Ormond, Kt.
Roche, Sir David O'Grady, Bt. (1838)
Roche, Sir Henry John, Kt.
Rodgers, Sir (Andrew) Piers (Wingate Aikin-Sneath), Bt. (1964)
Rodley, *Prof.* Sir Nigel, KBE
Rodrigues, Sir Alberto Maria, Kt., CBE, ED
Rogers, Sir Frank Jarvis, Kt.
Rogers, *Air Chief Marshal* Sir John Robson, KCB, CBE
Rooke, Sir Denis Eric, Kt., OM, CBE, FRS, FREng.
Ropner, Sir John Bruce Woollacott, Bt. (1952)
Ropner, Sir Robert Douglas, Bt. (1904)
Rose, *Rt. Hon.* Sir Christopher Dudley Roger, Kt.
Rose, Sir Clive Martin, GCMG
Rose, Sir David Lancaster, Bt. (1874)
Rose, *Gen.* Sir (Hugh) Michael, KCB, CBE, DSO, QGM
Rose, Sir John Edward Victor, Kt.
Rose, Sir Julian Day, Bt. (1872 and 1909)
Ross, *Maj.* Sir Andrew Charles Paterson, Bt. (1960)
Ross, *Lt.-Gen.* Sir Robert Jeremy, KCB, OBE
Ross, *Lt.-Col.* Sir Walter Hugh Malcolm, KCVO, OBE
Rossi, Sir Hugh Alexis Louis, Kt.
Rotblat, *Prof.* Sir Joseph, KCMG, CBE, FRS
Roth, *Prof.* Sir Martin, Kt., MD, FRCP
Rothschild, Sir Evelyn Robert Adrian de, Kt.
Rougier, *Hon.* Sir Richard George, Kt.
Rowe, *Rear-Adm.* Sir Patrick Barton, KCVO, CBE
Rowe-Beddoe, Sir David Sydney, Kt.
Rowe-Ham, Sir David Kenneth, GBE
Rowland, Sir (John) David, Kt.
Rowlands, *Air Marshal* Sir John Samuel, GC, KBE
Rowley, Sir Charles Robert, Bt. (1836) (1786)
Rowling, Sir John Reginald, Kt.
Rowlinson, *Prof.* Sir John Shipley, Kt., FRS

Roxburgh, *Vice-Adm.* Sir John Charles Young, KCB, CBE, DSO, DSC
Royce, *Hon.* Sir Roger John, Kt.
Royden, Sir Christopher John, Bt. (1905)
Rudd, Sir (Anthony) Nigel (Russell), Kt.
Rudge, Sir Alan Walter, Kt., CBE, FRS
Rugge-Price, Sir James Keith Peter, Bt. (1804)
Ruggles-Brise, Sir John Archibald, Bt., CB, OBE, TD (1935)
Rumbold, Sir Henry John Sebastian, Bt. (1779)
Runchorelal, Sir (Udayan) Chinubhai Madhowlal, Bt. (1913)
Rusby, *Vice-Adm.* Sir Cameron, KCB, LVO
†Russell, Sir (Arthur) Mervyn, Bt. (1812)
Russell, Sir Charles Dominic, Bt. (1916)
Russell, Sir George, Kt., CBE
Russell, Sir Muir, KCB
Russell, *Prof.* Sir Peter Edward Lionel, Kt., D.Litt., FBA
Russell, Sir (Robert) Mark, KCMG
Rutter, *Prof.* Sir Michael Llewellyn, Kt., CBE, MD, FRS
Ryan, Sir Derek Gerald, Bt. (1919)
Rycroft, Sir Richard John, Bt. (1784)
Ryrie, Sir William Sinclair, KCB
Sachs, *Hon.* Sir Michael Alexander Geddes, Kt.
Sainsbury, *Rt. Hon.* Sir Timothy Alan Davan, Kt.
St Clair-Ford, Sir James Anson, Bt. (1793)
†St George, Sir John Avenel Bligh, Bt. (I. 1766)
St John-Mildmay, Sir Walter John Hugh, Bt. (1772)
St Johnston, Sir Kerry, Kt.
Sainty, Sir John Christopher, KCB
Salisbury, Sir Robert William, Kt.
Salt, Sir Patrick MacDonnell, Bt. (1869)
Salt, Sir (Thomas) Michael John, Bt. (1899)
Salusbury-Trelawny, Sir John Barry, Bt. (1628)
Sampson, Sir Colin, Kt., CBE, QPM
Samuel, Sir John Michael Glen, Bt. (1898)
Samuelson, Sir (Bernard) Michael (Francis), Bt. (1884)
Samuelson, Sir Sydney Wylie, Kt., CBE
Sanders, Sir Robert Tait, KBE, CMG
Sanders, Sir Ronald Michael, KCMG
Sanderson, Sir Frank Linton, Bt. (1920)
Sarei, Sir Alexis Holyweek, Kt., CBE
Satchwell, Sir Kevin Joseph, Kt.
Savage, Sir Ernest Walter, Kt.
Savile, Sir James Wilson Vincent, Kt., OBE
Saxby, *Prof.* Sir Robin Keith, Kt.
Say, *Rt. Revd* Richard David, KCVO
Scheele, Sir Nicholas Vernon, KCMG

Schiemann, *Rt. Hon.* Sir Konrad Hermann Theodor, Kt.
Scholar, Sir Michael Charles, KCB
Scholey, Sir David Gerald, Kt., CBE
Scholey, Sir Robert, Kt., CBE, FREng.
Scholtens, Sir James Henry, KCVO
Schreier, Sir Bernard, Kt.
Schubert, Sir Sydney, Kt.
Scipio, Sir Hudson Rupert, Kt.
Scoon, Sir Paul, GCMG, GCVO, OBE
Scott, Sir Anthony Percy, Bt. (1913)
Scott, Sir David Aubrey, GCMG
Scott, Sir James Jervoise, Bt. (1962)
Scott, Sir Kenneth Bertram Adam, KCVO, CMG
Scott, Sir Michael, KCVO, CMG
Scott, *Rt. Hon.* Sir Nicholas Paul, KBE
Scott, Sir Oliver Christopher Anderson, Bt. (1909)
Scott, *Prof.* Sir Philip John, KBE
Scott, Sir Ridley, Kt.
Scott, Sir Robert David Hillyer, Kt.
Scott, Sir Walter John, Bt. (1907)
Scott, *Rear-Adm.* Sir (William) David (Stewart), KBE, CB
Scott-Barrett, *Lt.-Gen.* Sir David William, KBE, MC
Seale, Sir Clarence David, Kt.
Seale, Sir John Henry, Bt. (1838)
Seaman, Sir Keith Douglas, KCVO, OBE
Sebastian, Sir Cuthbert Montraville, GCMG, OBE
† Sebright, Sir Peter Giles Vivian, Bt. (1626)
Seccombe, Sir (William) Vernon Stephen, Kt.
Seconde, Sir Reginald Louis, KCMG, CVO
Sedley, *Rt. Hon.* Sir Stephen John, Kt.
Seely, Sir Nigel Edward, Bt. (1896)
Seeto, Sir Ling James, Kt., MBE
Seeyave, Sir Rene Sow Choung, Kt., CBE
Seligman, Sir Peter Wendel, Kt., CBE
Semple, Sir John Laughlin, KCB
Sergeant, Sir Patrick, Kt.
Series, Sir (Joseph Michel) Emile, Kt., CBE
Serota, Sir Nicholas Andrew, Kt.
Serpell, Sir David Radford, KCB, CMG, OBE
† Seton, Sir Charles Wallace, Bt. (S. 1683)
Seton, Sir Iain Bruce, Bt. (S. 1663)
Severne, *Air Vice-Marshal* Sir John de Milt, KCVO, OBE, AFC
Shackleton, *Prof.* Sir Nicholas John, Kt., Ph.D., FRS
Shaffer, Sir Peter Levin, Kt., CBE
Shakerley, Sir Geoffrey Adam, Bt. (1838)
Shakespeare, Sir Thomas William, Bt. (1942)
Sharp, Sir Adrian, Bt. (1922)
Sharp, Sir Kenneth Johnston, Kt., TD
Sharp, Sir Leslie, Kt., QPM
Sharp, Sir Sheridan Christopher Robin, Bt. (1920)
Sharples, Sir James, Kt., QPM

Shattock, Sir Gordon, Kt.
Shaw, Sir Brian Piers, Kt.
Shaw, Sir (Charles) Barry, Kt., CB, QC
Shaw, Sir Charles De Vere, Bt. (1821)
Shaw, *Prof.* Sir John Calman, Kt., CBE
Shaw, Sir Neil McGowan, Kt.
Shaw, Sir Roy, Kt.
Shaw, Sir Run Run, Kt., CBE
Shaw-Stewart, Sir Houston Mark, Bt., MC, TD (S. 1667)
Shebbeare, Sir Thomas Andrew, KCVO
Sheehy, Sir Patrick, Kt.
Sheen, *Hon.* Sir Barry Cross, Kt.
Sheffield, Sir Reginald Adrian Berkeley, Bt. (1755)
Shehadie, Sir Nicholas Michael, Kt., OBE
Sheil, *Hon.* Sir John, Kt.
Sheinwald, Sir Nigel Elton, KCMG
Sheldon, *Hon.* Sir (John) Gervase (Kensington), Kt.
Shelley, Sir John Richard, Bt. (1611)
Shepherd, Sir Colin Ryley, Kt.
Shepherd, Sir John Alan, KCVO, CMG
Shepperd, Sir Alfred Joseph, Kt.
Sher, Sir Antony, KBE
Sherston-Baker, Sir Robert George Humphrey, Bt. (1796)
Sherman, Sir Alfred, Kt.
Shields, *Prof.* Sir Robert, Kt., MD
Shiffner, Sir Henry David, Bt. (1818)
Silber, *Hon.* Sir Stephen Robert, Kt.
Shinwell, Sir (Maurice) Adrian, Kt.
Shock, Sir Maurice, Kt.
Short, Sir Apenera Pera, KBE
Shortridge, Sir Jon Deacon, KCB
Shuckburgh, Sir Rupert Charles Gerald, Bt. (1660)
Siaguru, Sir Anthony Michael, KBE
Sieff, *Hon.* Sir David, Kt.
Silber, *Rt. Hon.* Sir Stephen Robert, Kt.
Simeon, Sir John Edmund Barrington, Bt. (1815)
Simmons, *Air Marshal* Sir Michael George, KCB, AFC
Simmons, Sir Stanley Clifford, Kt., FRCS, FRCOG
Simms, Sir Neville Ian, Kt., FREng.
Simon, *Hon.* Sir Peregrine Charles Hugh, Kt.
Simonet, Sir Louis Marcel Pierre, Kt., CBE
Simpson, *Hon.* Sir Alfred Henry, Kt.
Simpson, Sir William James, Kt.
Sims, Sir Roger Edward, Kt.
Sinclair, Sir Clive Marles, Kt.
Sinclair, Sir George Evelyn, Kt., CMG, OBE
Sinclair, Sir Ian McTaggart, KCMG, QC
Sinclair, Sir Patrick Robert Richard, Bt. (S. 1704)
Sinclair, Sir Robert John, Kt.
Sinclair-Lockhart, Sir Simon John Edward Francis, Bt. (S. 1636)

Sinden, Sir Donald Alfred, Kt., CBE
Singer, *Prof.* Sir Hans Wolfgang, Kt.
Singer, *Hon.* Sir Jan Peter, Kt.
Sione, Sir Tomu Malaefone, GCMG, OBE
Sitwell, Sir (Sacheverell) Reresby, Bt. (1808)
Skeet, Sir Trevor Herbert Harry, Kt.
Skeggs, Sir Clifford George, Kt.
Skehel, Sir John James, Kt., FRS
Skingsley, *Air Chief Marshal* Sir Anthony Gerald, GBE, KCB
Skinner, Sir (Thomas) Keith (Hewitt), Bt. (1912)
Skipwith, Sir Patrick Alexander d'Estoteville, Bt. (1622)
Slack, Sir William Willatt, KCVO, FRCS
Slade, Sir Benjamin Julian Alfred, Bt. (1831)
Slade, *Rt. Hon.* Sir Christopher John, Kt.
Slaney, *Prof.* Sir Geoffrey, KBE
Slater, *Adm.* Sir John (Jock) Cunningham Kirkwood, GCB, LVO
Sleight, Sir Richard, Bt. (1920)
Sloan, Sir Andrew Kirkpatrick, Kt., QPM
Sloman, Sir Albert Edward, Kt., CBE
Smart, *Prof.* Sir George Algernon, Kt., MD, FRCP
Smart, Sir Jack, Kt., CBE
Smedley, *Hon.* Sir (Frank) Brian, Kt.
Smedley, Sir Harold, KCMG, MBE
Smiley, *Lt.-Col.* Sir John Philip, Bt. (1903)
Smith, Sir Alan, Kt., CBE, DFC
Smith, *Hon.* Sir Andrew Charles, Kt.
Smith, Sir Andrew Thomas, Bt. (1897)
Smith, Sir Christopher Sydney Winwood, Bt. (1809)
Smith, *Prof.* Sir Colin Stansfield, Kt., CBE
Smith, Sir Cyril, Kt., MBE
Smith, *Prof.* Sir David Cecil, Kt., FRS
Smith, Sir David Iser, KCVO
Smith, Sir Dudley (Gordon), Kt.
Smith, *Prof.* Sir Eric Brian, Kt., Ph.D.
Smith, Sir Geoffrey Johnson, Kt., MP
Smith, Sir John Alfred, Kt., QPM
Smith, Sir John Lindsay Eric, Kt., CH, CBE
Smith, Sir Joseph William Grenville, Kt.
Smith, Sir Leslie Edward George, Kt.
Smith, Sir Michael John Llewellyn, KCVO, CMG
Smith, Sir (Norman) Brian, Kt., CBE, Ph.D.
Smith, Sir Paul Brierley, Kt., CBE
Smith, *Hon.* Sir Peter (Winston), Kt.
Smith, Sir Robert Courtney, Kt., CBE
Smith, Sir Robert Haldane, Kt
Smith, Sir Robert Hill, Bt., MP (1945)
Smith, *Prof.* Sir Roland, Kt.
Smith, *Gen.* Sir Rupert Anthony, KCB, DSO, OBE, QGM
Smith-Dodsworth, Sir John Christopher, Bt. (1784)

Smith-Gordon, Sir (Lionel) Eldred (Peter), Bt. (1838)

Smith-Marriott, Sir Hugh Cavendish, Bt. (1774)

Smithers, Sir Peter Henry Berry Otway, Kt., VRD, D.Phil.

Smyth, Sir Timothy John, Bt. (1955)

Soakimori, Sir Frederick Pa-Nukuanca, KBE, CPM

Sobers, Sir Garfield St Auburn, Kt.

Solomon, Sir Harry, Kt.

Somare, *Rt. Hon.* Sir Michael Thomas, GCMG, CH

Somerville, *Brig.* Sir John Nicholas, Kt., CBE

Sorrell, Sir Martin Stuart, Kt.

Soulsby, Sir Peter Alfred, Kt.

Soutar, *Air Marshal* Sir Charles John Williamson, KBE

South, Sir Arthur, Kt.

Southby, Sir John Richard Bilbe, Bt. (1937)

Southern, *Prof.* Sir Edwin Mellor, Kt.

Southgate, Sir Colin Grieve, Kt.

Southgate, Sir William David, Kt.

Southward, Sir Leonard Bingley, Kt., OBE

Southward, *Dr* Sir Nigel Ralph, KCVO

Southwood, *Prof.* Sir (Thomas) Richard (Edmund), Kt., FRS

Souyave, *Hon.* Sir (Louis) Georges, Kt.

Sowrey, *Air Marshal* Sir Frederick Beresford, KCB, CBE, AFC

Sparkes, Sir Robert Lyndley, Kt.

Sparrow, Sir John, Kt.

Spearman, Sir Alexander Young Richard Mainwaring, Bt. (1840)

Spedding, *Prof.* Sir Colin Raymond William, Kt., CBE

Speed, Sir (Herbert) Keith, Kt., RD

Speelman, Sir Cornelis Jacob, Bt. (1686)

Speight, *Hon.* Sir Graham Davies, Kt.

Spencer, Sir Derek Harold, Kt., QC

Spencer, *Vice-Adm.* Sir Peter, KCB

Spencer-Nairn, Sir Robert Arnold, Bt. (1933)

Spicer, Sir James Wilton, Kt.

Spicer, Sir Nicholas Adrian Albert, Bt., MB (1906)

Spicer, Sir (William) Michael Hardy, Kt., MP

Spiers, Sir Donald Maurice, Kt., CB, TD

Spooner, Sir James Douglas, Kt.

Spratt, *Col.* Sir Greville Douglas, GBE, TD

Spring, Sir Dryden Thomas, Kt.

Squire, *Air Chief Marshal* Sir Peter Ted, GCB, DFC, AFC, ADC

Stabb, *Hon.* Sir William Walter, Kt.

Stainton, Sir (John) Ross, Kt., CBE

Stamer, Sir (Lovelace) Anthony, Bt. (1809)

Standard, Sir Kenneth Livingstone, Kt., MD

Stanier, Sir Beville Douglas, Bt. (1917)

Stanier, *Field Marshal* Sir John Wilfred, GCB, MBE

Stanley, *Rt. Hon.* Sir John Paul, Kt., MP

Staples, Sir Richard Molesworth, Bt. (I. 1628)

Stark, Sir Andrew Alexander Steel, KCMG, CVO

Starkey, Sir John Philip, Bt. (1935)

Staughton, *Rt. Hon.* Sir Christopher Stephen Thomas Jonathan Thayer, Kt.

Staveley, Sir John Malfroy, KBE, MC

Stear, *Air Chief Marshal* Sir Michael James Douglas, KCB, CBE

Steel, Sir David Edward Charles, Kt., DSO, MC, TD

Steel, *Hon.* Sir David William, Kt.

Stephen, *Rt. Hon.* Sir Ninian Martin, KG, GCMG, GCVO, KBE

Stephens, Sir (Edwin) Barrie, Kt.

Stephenson, Sir Henry Upton, Bt. (1936)

Sternberg, Sir Sigmund, Kt.

Stevens, Sir Jocelyn Edward Greville, Kt., CVO

Stevens, Sir John, Kt.

Stevens, Sir Laurence Houghton, Kt., CBE

Stevenson, Sir Simpson, Kt.

Stewart, Sir Alan, KBE

Stewart, Sir Alan d'Arcy, Bt. (I. 1623)

Stewart, Sir Brian John, Kt., CBE

Stewart, Sir David James Henderson, Bt. (1957)

Stewart, Sir David John Christopher, Bt. (1803)

Stewart, Sir Edward Jackson, Kt.

Stewart, Sir James Douglas, Kt.

Stewart, Sir James Moray, KCB

Stewart, Sir (John) Simon (Watson), Bt. (1920)

Stewart, Sir John Young, Kt., OBE

Stewart, *Lt.-Col.* Sir Robert Christie, KCVO, CBE, TD

Stewart, Sir Robertson Huntly, Kt., CBE

Stewart, Sir Robin Alastair, Bt. (1960)

Stewart, *Prof.* Sir William Duncan Paterson, Kt., FRS, FRSE

Stewart-Clark, Sir John, Bt., MEP (1918)

Stewart-Richardson, Sir Simon Alaisdair, Bt. (S. 1630)

Stewart-Wilson, *Lt.-Col.* Sir Blair Aubyn, KCVO

Stibbon, *Gen.* Sir John James, KCB, OBE

Stirling, Sir Alexander John Dickson, KBE, CMG

Stirling, Sir Angus Duncan Aeneas, Kt.

Stirling-Hamilton, Sir Malcolm William Bruce, Bt. (S. 1673)

Stirrup, *Air Chief Marshal* Sir Graham Eric, KCB, AFC

Stockdale, Sir Arthur Noel, Kt.

Stockdale, Sir Thomas Minshull, Bt. (1960)

Stoddart, *Wg Cdr.* Sir Kenneth Maxwell, KCVO, AE

Stoker, *Prof.* Sir Michael George Parke, Kt., CBE, FRCP, FRS, FRSE

Stones, Sir William Frederick, Kt., OBE

Stonhouse, *Revd* Michael Philip, Bt. (1628 and 1670)

Stonor, *Air Marshal* Sir Thomas Henry, KCB

Stoppard, Sir Thomas, Kt., OM, CBE

Storey, *Hon.* Sir Richard, Bt., CBE (1960)

Stothard, Sir Peter Michael, Kt.

Stott, Sir Adrian George Ellingham, Bt. (1920)

Stoute, Sir Michael Ronald, Kt.

Stowe, Sir Kenneth Ronald, GCB, CVO

Stracey, Sir John Simon, Bt. (1818)

Strachan, Sir Curtis Victor, Kt., CVO

Strachey, Sir Charles, Bt. (1801)

Strang Steel, Sir (Fiennes) Michael, Bt. (1938)

Strawson, *Prof.* Sir Peter Frederick, Kt., FBA

Street, *Hon.* Sir Laurence Whistler, KCMG

Streeton, Sir Terence George, KBE, CMG

Strickland-Constable, Sir Frederic, Bt. (1641)

Stringer, Sir Donald Edgar, Kt., CBE

Stringer, Sir Howard, Kt.

Strong, Sir Roy Colin, Kt., Ph.D., FSA

Stronge, Sir James Anselan Maxwell, Bt. (1803)

Stroud, *Prof.* Sir (Charles) Eric, Kt., FRCP

Strutt, Sir Nigel Edward, Kt., TD

Stuart, Sir James Keith, Kt.

Stuart, Sir Kenneth Lamonte, Kt.

†Stuart, Sir Phillip Luttrell, Bt. (1660)

†Stuart-Forbes, Sir William Daniel, Bt. (S. 1626)

Stuart-Menteth, Sir James Wallace, Bt. (1838)

Stuart-Paul, *Air Marshal* Sir Ronald Ian, KBE

Stuart-Smith, *Rt. Hon.* Sir Murray, Kt.

Stuart-White, *Hon.* Sir Christopher Stuart, Kt.

Stubbs, Sir William Hamilton, Kt., Ph.D.

Stucley, *Lt.* Sir Hugh George Coplestone Bampfylde, Bt. (1859)

Studd, Sir Edward Fairfax, Bt. (1929)

Studholme, Sir Henry William, Bt. (1956)

†Style, Sir William Frederick, Bt. (1627)

Sugar, Sir Alan Michael, Kt.

Sullivan, *Hon.* Sir Jeremy Mirth, Kt.

Sullivan, Sir Richard Arthur, Bt. (1804)

Sulston, Sir John Edward, Kt.

Sumner, *Hon.* Sir Christopher John, Kt.

Sutherland, Sir John Brewer, Bt. (1921)
Sutherland, Sir William George MacKenzie, Kt.
Sutton, Sir Frederick Walter, Kt., OBE
Sutton, *Air Marshal* Sir John Matthias Dobson, KCB
Sutton, Sir Richard Lexington, Bt. (1772)
Swaffield, Sir James Chesebrough, Kt., CBE, RD
Swaine, Sir John Joseph, Kt., CBE
Swan, Sir Conrad Marshall John Fisher, KCVO, Ph.D.
Swan, Sir John William David, KBE
Swann, Sir Michael Christopher, Bt., TD (1906)
Swartz, *Hon.* Sir Reginald William Colin, KBE, ED
Sweeney, Sir George, Kt.
Sweeting, *Prof.* Sir Martin Nicholas, Kt., OBE, FRS
Sweetnam, Sir (David) Rodney, KCVO, CBE, FRCS
Swinburn, *Lt.-Gen.* Sir Richard Hull, KCB
Swinnerton-Dyer, *Prof.* Sir (Henry) Peter (Francis), Bt., KBE, FRS (1678)
Swinton, *Maj.-Gen.* Sir John, KCVO, OBE
Swire, Sir Adrian Christopher, Kt.
Swire, Sir John Anthony, Kt., CBE
Sykes, Sir David Michael, Bt. (1921)
Sykes, Sir Francis John Badcock, Bt. (1781)
Sykes, Sir Hugh Ridley, Kt.
Sykes, *Prof.* Sir (Malcolm) Keith, Kt.
Sykes, Sir Richard, Kt.
Sykes, Sir Tatton Christopher Mark, Bt. (1783)
Symington, *Prof.* Sir Thomas, Kt., MD, FRSE
Symons, *Vice-Adm.* Sir Patrick Jeremy, KBE
Synge, Sir Robert Carson, Bt. (1801)
Synnott, Sir Hilary Nicholas Hugh, KCMG
Tait, *Adm.* Sir (Allan) Gordon, KCB, DSC
Talbot, *Hon.* Sir Hilary Gwynne, Kt.
Talboys, *Rt. Hon.* Sir Brian Edward, CH, KCB
Tangaroa, *Hon.* Sir Tangoroa, Kt., MBE
Tapps-Gervis-Meyrick, Sir George Christopher Cadafael, Bt. (1791)
Tapsell, Sir Peter Hannay Bailey, Kt., MP
Tate, Sir (Henry) Saxon, Bt. (1898)
Tavaiqia, *Ratu* Sir Josaia, KBE
Tavare, Sir John, Kt., CBE
Tavener, *Prof.* Sir John Kenneth, Kt.
Taylor, *Lt.-Gen.* Sir Allan Macnab, KBE, MC
Taylor, Sir (Arthur) Godfrey, Kt.
Taylor, Sir Cyril Julian Hebden, Kt.
Taylor, Sir Edward Macmillan (Teddy), Kt., MP
Taylor, *Rt. Revd* John Bernard, KCVO

Taylor, Sir Nicholas Richard Stuart, Bt. (1917)
Taylor, *Prof.* Sir William, Kt., CBE
Taylor, Sir William George, Kt.
Teagle, *Vice-Adm.* Sir Somerford Francis, KBE
Tebbit, Sir Donald Claude, GCMG
Tebbit, Sir Kevin Reginald, KCB, CMG
Telford, Sir Robert, Kt., CBE, FREng.
Temple, *Prof.* Sir John Graham, Kt.
Temple, *Maj.* Sir Richard Anthony Purbeck, Bt., MC (1876)
Templeton, Sir John Marks, Kt.
Tennant, Sir Anthony John, Kt.
Tennant, *Capt.* Sir Iain Mark, KT
Tennyson-D'Eyncourt, Sir Mark Gervais, Bt. (1930)
Terry, *Air Marshal* Sir Colin George, KBE, CB
Terry, *Air Chief Marshal* Sir Peter David George, GCB, AFC
†Thatcher, Sir Mark, Bt. (1990)
†Thomas, Sir David John Godfrey, Bt. (1694)
Thomas, Sir Derek Morison David, KCMG
Thomas, Sir Jeremy Cashel, KCMG
Thomas, Sir (John) Alan, Kt.
Thomas, *Prof.* Sir John Meurig, Kt., FRS
Thomas, Sir Keith Vivian, Kt.
Thomas, Sir Quentin Jeremy, Kt., CB
Thomas, Sir Robert Evan, Kt.
Thomas, *Hon.* Sir Roger John Laugharne, Kt.
Thomas, *Hon.* Sir Swinton Barclay, Kt.
Thomas, Sir William James Cooper, Bt., TD (1919)
Thomas, Sir (William) Michael (Marsh), Bt. (1918)
Thompson, Sir Christopher Peile, Bt. (1890)
Thompson, Sir Clive Malcolm, Kt.
Thompson, Sir David Albert, KCMG
Thompson, Sir Donald, Kt.
Thompson, Sir Gilbert Williamson, Kt., OBE
Thompson, *Prof.* Sir Michael Warwick, Kt., D.Sc
Thompson, Sir Nicholas Annesley, Bt. (1963)
Thompson, Sir Nigel Cooper, KCMG, CBE
Thompson, Sir Paul Anthony, Bt. (1963)
Thompson, Sir Peter Anthony, Kt.
Thompson, *Dr* Sir Richard Paul Hepworth, KCVO
Thompson, Sir Thomas d'Eyncourt John, Bt. (1806)
Thomson, Sir (Frederick Douglas) David, Bt. (1929)
Thomson, Sir John Adam, GCMG
Thomson, Sir John (Ian) Sutherland, KBE, CMG
Thomson, Sir Mark Wilfrid Home, Bt. (1925)
Thomson, Sir Thomas James, Kt., CBE, FRCP
Thorn, Sir John Samuel, Kt., OBE

Thorne, Sir Neil Gordon, Kt., OBE, TD
Thorne, Sir Peter Francis, KCVO, CBE
Thornton, Sir (George) Malcolm, Kt.
Thornton, Sir Peter Eustace, KCB
Thornton, Sir Richard Eustace, KCVO, OBE
†Thorold, Sir (Anthony) Oliver, Bt. (1642)
Thorpe, *Rt. Hon.* Sir Mathew Alexander, Kt.
Thouron, Sir John Rupert Hunt, KBE
Thwaites, Sir Bryan, Kt., Ph.D.
Tickell, Sir Crispin Charles Cervantes, GCMG, KCVO
Tikaram, Sir Moti, KBE
Tilt, Sir Robin Richard, Kt.
Timmins, *Col.* Sir John Bradford, KCVO, OBE, TD
Tims, Sir Michael David, KCVO
Tindle, Sir Ray Stanley, Kt., CBE
Tippet, *Vice-Adm.* Sir Anthony Sanders, KCB
Tirvengadum, Sir Harry Krishnan, Kt.
Tod, *Vice-Adm.* Sir Jonathan James Richard, KCB, CBE
Todd, *Prof.* Sir David, Kt., CBE
Todd, Sir Ian Pelham, KBE, FRCS
Tollemache, Sir Lyonel Humphry John, Bt. (1793)
Tololo, Sir Alkan, KBE
Tomkins, Sir Edward Emile, GCMG, CVO
Tomkys, Sir (William) Roger, KCMG
Tomlinson, *Prof.* Sir Bernard Evans, Kt., CBE
Tomlinson, *Hon.* Sir Stephen Miles, Kt.
Tooley, Sir John, Kt.
ToRobert, Sir Henry Thomas, KBE
Torry, Sir Peter James, KCMG
Tory, Sir Geofroy William, KCMG
Touche, Sir Anthony George, Bt. (1920)
Touche, Sir Rodney Gordon, Bt. (1962)
Toulson, *Hon.* Sir Roger Grenfell, Kt.
Tovey, Sir Brian John Maynard, KCMG
ToVue, Sir Ronald, Kt., OBE
Towneley, Sir Simon Peter Edmund Cosmo William, KCVO
Townsend, Sir Cyril David, Kt.
Traill, Sir Alan Towers, GBE
Trant, *Gen.* Sir Richard Brooking, KCB
Treacher, *Adm.* Sir John Devereux, KCB
Treacy, *Hon.* Sir Colman Maurice, Kt.
Treitel, *Prof.* Sir Guenter Heinz, Kt., FBA, QC
Trench, Sir Peter Edward, Kt., CBE, TD
Trescowthick, Sir Donald Henry, KBE
†Trevelyan, Sir Edward (Norman), Bt. (1662)

Trevelyan, Sir Geoffrey Washington, Bt. (1874)
Trezise, Sir Kenneth Bruce, Kt., OBE
Trippier, Sir David Austin, Kt., RD
Tritton, Sir Anthony John Ernest, Bt. (1905)
Trollope, Sir Anthony Simon, Bt. (1642)
Trotman-Dickenson, Sir Aubrey Fiennes, Kt.
Trotter, Sir Neville Guthrie, Kt.
Trotter, Sir Ronald Ramsay, Kt.
Troubridge, Sir Thomas Richard, Bt. (1799)
Troup, *Vice-Adm.* Sir (John) Anthony (Rose), KCB, DSC
Truscott, Sir George James Irving, Bt. (1909)
Tsang, Sir Donald Yam-keun, KBE
Tuck, Sir Bruce Adolph Reginald, Bt. (1910)
Tucker, *Hon.* Sir Richard Howard, Kt.
Tuckey, *Rt. Hon.* Sir Simon Lane, Kt.
Tugendhat, *Hon.* Sir Michael George, Kt.
Tuita, Sir Mariano Kelesimalefo, KBE
Tuite, Sir Christopher Hugh, Bt., Ph.D. (1622)
Tuivaga, Sir Timoci Uluiburotu, Kt.
Tully, Sir William Mark, KBE
Tumim, *His Hon.* Sir Stephen, Kt.
Tupper, Sir Charles Hibbert, Bt. (1888)
Turbott, Sir Ian Graham, Kt., CMG, CVO
Turing, Sir John Dermot, Bt. (S. 1638)
Turnbull, Sir Andrew, KCB, CVO
Turner, Sir Colin William Carstairs, Kt., CBE, DFC
Turner, *Hon.* Sir Michael John, Kt.
Turnquest, Sir Orville Alton, GCMG, QC
Tusa, Sir John, Kt.
Tuti, *Revd* Dudley, KBE
Tweedie, *Prof.* Sir David Philip, Kt.
Tyree, Sir (Alfred) William, Kt., OBE
Tyrwhitt, Sir Reginald Thomas Newman, Bt. (1919)
Unsworth, *Hon.* Sir Edgar Ignatius Godfrey, Kt., CMG
Unwin, Sir (James) Brian, KCB
Ure, Sir John Burns, KCMG, LVO
Urquhart, Sir Brian Edward, KCMG, MBE
Urwick, Sir Alan Bedford, KCVO, CMG
Usher, Sir Andrew John, Bt. (1899)
Usher, Sir Leonard Gray, KBE
Ustinov, Sir Peter Alexander, Kt., CBE
Utting, Sir William Benjamin, Kt., CB
Vai, Sir Mea, Kt., CBE, ISO
Vallance, Sir Iain David Thomas, Kt.
Vallat, Sir Francis Aimé, GBE, KCMG, QC
Vallings, *Vice-Adm.* Sir George Montague Francis, KCB
Vanderfelt, Sir Robin Victor, KBE

Vane, Sir John Robert, Kt., D.Phil., D.Sc., FRS
Vardy, Sir Peter, Kt.Vasquez, Sir Alfred Joseph, Kt., CBE, QC
Vassar-Smith, Sir John Rathbone, Bt. (1917)
Vavasour, Sir Eric Michael Joseph Marmaduke, Bt. (1828)
Veale, Sir Alan John Ralph, Kt., FREng.
Venner, Sir Kenneth Dwight Vincent, KBE
Vereker, Sir John Michael Medlicott, KCB
†Verney, Sir John Sebastian, Bt. (1946)
Verney, *Hon.* Sir Lawrence John, Kt., TD
†Verney, Sir Edmund Ralph, Bt. (1818)
Vernon, Sir Nigel John Douglas, Bt. (1914)
Vernon, Sir (William) Michael, Kt.
Vestey, Sir (John) Derek, Bt. (1921)
Vickers, *Lt.-Gen.* Sir Richard Maurice Hilton, KCB, CVO, OBE
Vincent, Sir William Percy Maxwell, Bt. (1936)
Vineall, Sir Anthony John Patrick, Kt.
Vinelott, *Hon.* Sir John Evelyn, Kt.
Vines, Sir William Joshua, Kt., CMG
von Schramek, Sir Eric Emil, Kt.
†Vyvyan, Sir Ralph Ferrers Alexander, Bt. (1645)
Waddell, Sir James Henderson, Kt., CB
Wade, *Prof.* Sir Henry William Rawson, Kt., QC, FBA
Wade-Gery, Sir Robert Lucian, KCMG, KCVO
Waine, *Rt. Revd* John, KCVO
Waite, *Rt. Hon.* Sir John Douglas, Kt.
Wake, Sir Hereward, Bt., MC (1621)
Wakefield, Sir (Edward) Humphry (Tyrell), Bt. (1962)
Wakefield, Sir Norman Edward, Kt.
Wakefield, Sir Peter George Arthur, KBE, CMG
Wakeford, *Air Marshal* Sir Richard Gordon, KCB, OBE, LVO, AFC
Wakeley, Sir John Cecil Nicholson, Bt., FRCS (1952)
†Wakeman, Sir Edward Offley Bertram, Bt. (1828)
Wales, Sir Robert Andrew, Kt.
Waley-Cohen, Sir Stephen Harry, Bt. (1961)
Walford, Sir Christopher Rupert, Kt.
Walker, Sir Alfred Cecil, Kt.
Walker, *Gen.* Sir Antony Kenneth Frederick, Kt.
Walker, Sir Baldwin Patrick, Bt. (1856)
Walker, Sir David Alan, Kt.
Walker, Sir Harold Berners, KCMG
Walker, *Maj.* Sir Hugh Ronald, Bt. (1906)
Walker, Sir James Graham, Kt., MBE
Walker, Sir John Ernest, Kt., D.Phil., FRS

Walker, *Air Marshal* Sir John Robert, KCB, CBE, AFC
Walker, *Gen.* Sir Michael John Dawson, GCB, CMG, CBE, ADC
Walker, Sir Miles Rawstron, Kt., CBE
Walker, Sir Patrick Jeremy, KCB
Walker, Sir Rodney Myerscough, Kt.
Walker, *Hon.* Sir Timothy Edward, Kt.
Walker, Sir Victor Stewart Heron, Bt. (1868)
Walker-Okeover, *Capt.* Sir Peter Ralph Leopold, Bt. (1886)
Walker-Smith, Sir John Jonah, Bt. (1960)
Wall, Sir John Anthony, Kt., CBE
Wall, Sir (John) Stephen, KCMG, LVO
Wall, *Hon.* Sir Nicholas Peter Rathbone, Kt.
Wall, Sir Robert William, Kt., OBE
Wallace, *Lt.-Gen.* Sir Christopher Brooke Quentin, KBE
Wallace, Sir Ian James, Kt., CBE
Waller, *Rt. Hon.* Sir (George) Mark, Kt.
Waller, Sir Robert William, Bt. (I. 1780)
Wallis, Sir Peter Gordon, KCVO
Wallis, Sir Timothy William, Kt.
Walmsley, *Vice-Adm.* Sir Robert, KCB
†Walsham, Sir Timothy John, Bt. (1831)
Walters, *Prof.* Sir Alan Arthur, Kt.
Walters, Sir Dennis Murray, Kt., MBE
Walters, Sir Frederick Donald, Kt.
Walters, Sir Peter Ingram, Kt.
Walters, Sir Roger Talbot, KBE, FRIBA
Wamiri, Sir Akapite, KBE
Wan, Sir Wamp, Kt., MBE
Ward, *Rt. Hon.* Sir Alan Hylton, Kt.
Ward, Sir John Devereux, Kt., CBE
Ward, *Prof.* Sir John MacQueen, Kt., CBE
Ward, Sir Joseph James Laffey, Bt. (1911)
Ward, Sir Timothy James, Kt.
Wardale, Sir Geoffrey Charles, KCB
Wardlaw, Sir Henry (John), Bt. (S. 1631)
Waring, Sir (Alfred) Holburt, Bt. (1935)
Warmington, Sir David Marshall, Bt. (1908)
Warner, Sir (Edward Courtenay) Henry, Bt. (1910)
Warner, *Prof.* Sir Frederick Edward, Kt., FRS, FREng.
Warner, Sir Gerald Chierici, KCMG
Warner, *Hon.* Sir Jean-Pierre Frank Eugene, Kt.
Warren, Sir (Frederick) Miles, KBE
Warren, Sir Kenneth Robin, Kt.
†Warren, Sir Michael Blackley, Bt. (1784)
Wass, Sir Douglas William Gretton, GCB
Waterhouse, *Hon.* Sir Ronald Gough, GBE
Waterlow, Sir Christopher Rupert, Bt. (1873)

Waterlow, Sir (James) Gerard, Bt. (1930)

Waters, *Gen.* Sir (Charles) John, GCB, CBE

Waters, Sir (Thomas) Neil (Morris), Kt.

Wates, Sir Christopher Stephen, Kt.

Watkins, *Rt. Hon.* Sir Tasker, VC, GBE

Watson, Sir Bruce Dunstan, Kt.

Watson, *Prof.* Sir David John, Kt., Ph.D.

Watson, Sir (James) Andrew, Bt. (1866)

Watson, *Vice-Adm.* Sir Philip Alexander, KBE, LVO

Watson, Sir Ronald Matthew, Kt., CBE

Watt, *Surgeon Vice-Adm.* Sir James, KBE, FRCS

Watts, Sir John Augustus Fitzroy, KCMG, CBE

Watts, Sir Arthur Desmond, KCMG

Watts, *Lt.-Gen.* Sir John Peter Barry Condliffe, KBE, CB, MC

Watts, Sir Philip Beverley, KCMG

Weatherall, *Prof.* Sir David John, Kt., FRS

Weatherall, *Vice-Adm.* Sir James Lamb, KCVO, KBE

Weatherstone, Sir Dennis, KBE

Weatherup, *Hon.* Sir Ronald Eccles, Kt.

Webb, *Prof.* Sir Adrian Leonard, Kt.

Webb, Sir Thomas Langley, Kt.

Webb-Carter, *Gen.* Sir Evelyn John, KCVO, OBE

Webster, *Very Revd* Alan Brunskill, KCVO

Webster, *Vice-Adm.* Sir John Morrison, KCB

Webster, *Hon.* Sir Peter Edlin, Kt.

Wedgwood, Sir (Hugo) Martin, Bt. (1942)

Weekes, Sir Everton DeCourcey, KCMG, OBE

Weinberg, Sir Mark Aubrey, Kt.

Weir, Sir Michael Scott, KCMG

Weir, Sir Roderick Bignell, Kt.

Welby, Sir (Richard) Bruno Gregory, Bt. (1801)

Welch, Sir John Reader, Bt. (1957)

Weldon, Sir Anthony William, Bt. (I. 1723)

Weller, Sir Arthur Burton, Kt., CBE

Wellings, Sir Jack Alfred, Kt., CBE

†Wells, Sir Christopher Charles, Bt. (1944)

Wells, Sir John Julius, Kt.

Wells, Sir William Henry Weston, Kt., FRICS

West, *Adm.* Sir Alan William John, KCB, DSC

West-Russell, *Hon.* Sir David Sturrock, Kt.

Westbrook, Sir Neil Gowanloch, Kt., CBE

Westmacott, Sir Peter John, KCMG

Weston, Sir Michael Charles Swift, KCMG, CVO

Weston, Sir (Philip) John, KCMG

Whalen, Sir Geoffrey Henry, Kt., CBE

Wheeler, Sir Harry Anthony, Kt., OBE

Wheeler, *Air Chief Marshal* Sir (Henry) Neil (George), GCB, CBE, DSO, DFC, AFC

Wheeler, *Rt. Hon.* Sir John Daniel, Kt.

Wheeler, Sir John Hieron, Bt. (1920)

Wheeler, *Gen.* Sir Roger Neil, GCB, CBE

Wheeler-Booth, Sir Michael Addison John, KCB

Wheler, Sir Edward Woodford, Bt. (1660)

Whishaw, Sir Charles Percival Law, Kt.

Whitaker, Sir John James Ingham (Jack), Bt. (1936)

White, *Prof.* Sir Christopher John, Kt., CVO

White, Sir Christopher Robert Meadows, Bt. (1937)

White, Sir David Harry, Kt.

White, *Hon.* Sir Frank John, Kt.

White, Sir George Stanley James, Bt. (1904)

White, *Adm.* Sir Hugo Moresby, GCB, CBE

White, *Hon.* Sir John Charles, Kt., MBE

White, Sir John Woolmer, Bt. (1922)

White, Sir Lynton Stuart, Kt., MBE, TD

White, Sir Nicholas Peter Archibald, Bt. (1802)

White, *Adm.* Sir Peter, GBE

Whitehead, Sir John Stainton, GCMG, CVO

Whitehead, Sir Rowland John Rathbone, Bt. (1889)

Whiteley, *Gen.* Sir Peter John Frederick, GCB, OBE, RM

Whitfield, Sir William, Kt., CBE

Whitmore, Sir Clive Anthony, GCB, CVO

Whitmore, Sir John Henry Douglas, Bt. (1954)

Whitney, Sir Raymond William, Kt., OBE, MP

Whitson, Sir Keith Roderick, Kt.

Wickerson, Sir John Michael, Kt.

Wicks, Sir Nigel Leonard, GCB, CVO, CBE

†Wigan, Sir Michael Iain, Bt. (1898)

Wiggin, Sir Alfred William (Jerry), Kt., TD

†Wiggin, Sir Charles Rupert John, Bt. (1892)

Wigram, *Maj.* Sir Edward Robert Woolmore, Bt. (1805)

Wilbraham, Sir Richard Baker, Bt. (1776)

Wiles, *Prof.* Sir Andrew John, KBE

Wilford, Sir (Kenneth) Michael, GCMG

Wilkes, *Prof.* Sir Maurice Vincent, Kt.

Wilkes, *Gen.* Sir Michael John, KCB, CBE

Wilkinson, Sir (David) Graham (Brook) Bt. (1941)

Wilkinson, *Prof.* Sir Denys Haigh, Kt., FRS

Wilkinson, Sir Philip William, Kt.

Willcocks, Sir David Valentine, Kt., CBE, MC

Willcocks, *Lt.-Gen.* Sir Michael Alan, KCB

Williams, Sir Alwyn, Kt., Ph.D., FRS, FRSE

Williams, Sir Arthur Dennis Pitt, Kt.

Williams, Sir (Arthur) Gareth Ludovic Emrys Rhys, Bt. (1918)

Williams, *Prof.* Sir Bruce Rodda, KBE

Williams, Sir Charles Othniel, Kt.

Williams, Sir Daniel Charles, GCMG, QC

Williams, *Adm.* Sir David, GCB

Williams, *Prof.* Sir David Glyndwr Tudor, Kt.

Williams, Sir David Innes, Kt.

Williams, Sir David Reeve, Kt., CBE

Williams, *Hon.* Sir Denys Ambrose, KCMG

Williams, Sir Donald Mark, Bt. (1866)

Williams, *Prof.* Sir (Edward) Dillwyn, Kt., FRCP

Williams, Sir Francis Owen Garbett, Kt., CBE

Williams, *Prof.* Sir Glanmor, Kt., CBE, FBA

Williams, Sir (John) Kyffin, Kt., OBE, DL, RA

Williams, Sir (Lawrence) Hugh, Bt. (1798)

Williams, Sir Leonard, KBE, CB

Williams, Sir Osmond, Bt., MC (1909)

Williams, Sir Peter Michael, Kt.

Williams, Sir (Robert) Philip Nathaniel, Bt. (1915)

Williams, Sir Robin Philip, Bt. (1953)

Williams, Sir (William) Maxwell (Harries), Kt.

Williams-Bulkeley, Sir Richard Thomas, Bt. (1661)

Williams-Wynn, Sir David Watkin, Bt. (1688)

Williamson, *Marshal of the Royal Air Force* Sir Keith Alec, GCB, AFC

Williamson, Sir Robert Brian, Kt., CBE

Willink, Sir Charles William, Bt. (1957)

Willis, *Vice-Adm.* Sir (Guido) James, KBE

Willis, *Air Chief Marshal* Sir John Frederick, GBE, KCB

Willison, *Lt.-Gen.* Sir David John, KCB, OBE, MC

Wills, Sir David James Vernon, Bt. (1923)

Wills, Sir David Seton, Bt. (1904)

Wilmot, Sir David, Kt., QPM

Wilmot, Sir Henry Robert, Bt. (1759)

Wilsey, *Gen.* Sir John Finlay Willasey, GCB, CBE

Wilshaw, Sir Michael, Kt.

Wilson, *Prof.* Sir Alan Geoffrey, Kt.

Wilson, *Lt.-Gen.* Sir (Alexander) James, KBE, MC

Wilson, Sir Anthony, Kt.

Wilson, *Vice-Adm.* Sir Barry Nigel, KCB

Wilson, *Prof.* Sir Colin Alexander St John, Kt., RA, FRIBA

Wilson, Sir David, Bt. (1920)

Wilson, Sir David Mackenzie, Kt.

Wilson, Sir Geoffrey Masterman, KCB, CMG

Wilson, Sir James William Douglas, Bt. (1906)

Wilson, *Brig.* Sir Mathew John Anthony, Bt., OBE, MC (1874)

Wilson, *Hon.* Sir Nicholas Allan Roy, Kt.

Wilson, Sir Robert Peter, KCMG

Wilson, *Air Chief Marshal* Sir (Ronald) Andrew (Fellowes), KCB, AFC

Wilson, *Hon.* Sir Ronald Darling, KBE, CMG

Wilton, Sir (Arthur) John, KCMG, KCVO, MC

Wingate, *Capt.* Sir Miles Buckley, KCVO

Winkley, Sir David Ross, Kt.

†Winnington, Sir Anthony Edward, Bt. (1755)

Winskill, *Air Cdre* Sir Archibald Little, KCVO, CBE, DFC

Winterton, Sir Nicholas Raymond, Kt.

Winton, Sir Nicholas George, Kt., MBE

Wisdom, Sir Norman, Kt., OBE

Wiseman, Sir John William, Bt. (1628)

Wolfendale, *Prof.* Sir Arnold Whittaker, Kt., FRS

Wolfson, Sir Brian Gordon, Kt.

Wolseley, Sir Charles Garnet Richard Mark, Bt. (1628)

†Wolseley, Sir James Douglas, Bt. (I. 1745)

Wolstenholme, Sir Gordon Ethelbert Ward, Kt., OBE

†Wombell, Sir George Philip Frederick, Bt. (1778)

Womersley, Sir Peter John Walter, Bt. (1945)

Woo, Sir Leo Joseph, Kt.

Woo, Sir Po-Shing, Kt.

Wood, Sir Alan Marshall Muir, Kt., FRS, FREng.

Wood, Sir Andrew Marley, GCMG

Wood, Sir Anthony John Page, Bt. (1837)

Wood, Sir Ian Clark, Kt., CBE

Wood, *Hon.* Sir John Kember, Kt., MC

Wood, Sir Martin Francis, Kt., OBE

Wood, Sir Russell Dillon, KCVO, VRD

Wood, Sir William Alan, KCVO, CB

Woodard, *Rear Adm.* Sir Robert Nathaniel, KCVO

Woodcock, Sir John, Kt., CBE, QPM

Woodhead, *Vice-Adm.* Sir (Anthony) Peter, KCB

Woodhouse, *Rt. Hon.* Sir (Arthur) Owen, KBE, DSC

Wooding, Sir Norman Samuel, Kt., CBE

Woodroffe, *Most Revd* George Cuthbert Manning, KBE

Woods, Sir Robert Kynnersley, Kt., CBE

Woodward, *Hon.* Sir (Albert) Edward, Kt., OBE

Woodward, *Adm.* Sir John Forster, GBE, KCB

Worsley, *Gen.* Sir Richard Edward, GCB, OBE

Worsley, Sir (William) Marcus (John), Bt. (1838)

Worsthorne, Sir Peregrine Gerard, Kt.

Wratten, *Air Chief Marshal* Sir William John, GBE, CB, AFC

Wraxall, Sir Charles Frederick Lascelles, Bt. (1813)

Wrey, Sir George Richard Bourchier, Bt. (1628)

Wrigglesworth, Sir Ian William, Kt.

Wright, Sir Allan Frederick, KBE

Wright, Sir David John, GCMG, LVO

Wright, Sir Denis Arthur Hepworth, GCMG

Wright, Sir Edward Maitland, Kt., D.Phil., LLD, D.Sc., FRSE

Wright, *Hon.* Sir (John) Michael, Kt.

Wright, Sir (John) Oliver, GCMG, GCVO, DSC

Wright, Sir Paul Hervé Giraud, KCMG, OBE

Wright, Sir Peter Robert, Kt., CBE

Wrightson, Sir Charles Mark Garmondsway, Bt. (1900)

Wrigley, *Prof.* Sir Edward Anthony (Sir Tony), Kt., Ph.D., PBA

Wrixon-Becher, Sir John William Michael, Bt. (1831)

Wu, Sir Gordon Ying Sheung, KCMG

Wyldbore-Smith, *Maj.-Gen.* Sir (Francis) Brian, Kt., CB, DSO, OBE

Yacoub, *Prof.* Sir Magdi Habib, Kt., FRCS

Yaki, Sir Roy, KBE

Yang, *Hon.* Sir Ti Liang, Kt.

Yapp, Sir Stanley Graham, Kt.

Yardley, Sir David Charles Miller, Kt., LLD

Yarrow, Sir Eric Grant, Bt., MBE (1916)

Yellowlees, Sir Henry, KCB

Yocklunn, Sir John (Soong Chung), KCVO

Yoo Foo, Sir (François) Henri, Kt.

Young, Sir Anthony Ian, Kt.

Young, Sir Brian Walter Mark, Kt.

Young, Sir Colville Norbert, GCMG, MBE

Young, Sir Dennis Charles, KCMG

Young, *Rt. Hon.* Sir George Samuel Knatchbull, Bt., MP (1813)

Young, *Hon.* Sir Harold William, KCMG

Young, Sir Jimmy Leslie Ronald, Kt., CBE

Young, Sir John Kenyon Roe, Bt. (1821)

Young, *Hon.* Sir John McIntosh, KCMG

Young, Sir John Robertson, GCMG

Young, Sir Leslie Clarence, Kt., CBE

Young, Sir Nicholas Charles, Kt.

Young, Sir Richard Dilworth, Kt.

Young, Sir Robin Urquhart, KCB

Young, Sir Roger William, Kt.

Young, Sir Stephen Stewart Templeton, Bt. (1945)

Young, Sir William Neil, Bt. (1769)

†Younger, Sir Julian William Richard, Bt. (1911)

Yuwi, Sir Matiabe, KBE

Zeeman, *Prof.* Sir (Erik) Christopher, Kt., FRS

Zissman, Sir Bernard Philip, Kt.

Zochonis, Sir John Basil, Kt.

Zoleveke, Sir Gideon Pitabose, KBE

Zunz, Sir Gerhard Jacob (Jack), Kt., FREng.

Zurenuoc, Sir Zibang, KBE

THE ORDER OF ST JOHN

THE MOST VENERABLE ORDER OF THE
HOSPITAL OF ST JOHN OF JERUSALEM (1888)

GCStJ	Bailiff/Dame Grand Cross
KStJ	Knight of Justice/Grace
DStJ	Dame of Justice/Grace
ChStJ	Chaplain
CStJ	Commander
OstJ	Officer
SBStJ	Serving Brother
SSStJ	Serving Sister
EsqStJ	Esquire

Mottoes, Pro Fide *and* Pro Utilitate Hominum
The Order of St John, founded in the early 12th century in Jerusalem, was a religious order with a particular duty to care for the sick. In Britain the Order was dissolved by Henry VIII in 1540 but the British branch was revived in the early 19th century. The branch was not accepted by the Grand Magistracy of the Order in Rome but its search for a role in the tradition of the Hospitallers led to the founding of the St John Ambulance Association in 1877 and later the St John Ambulance Brigade; in 1882 the St John Ophthalmic Hospital was founded in Jerusalem. A royal charter was granted in 1888 establishing the British Order of St John as a British Order of Chivalry with the Sovereign as its head. Since October 1999, a separate Priory of England and the Islands has governed the Order in England, the Channel Islands and the Isle of Man, with a Commandery in Northern Ireland.

The whole Order world-wide is now governed by a Grand Council including the representatives of all 8 Priories (England, Scotland, Wales, South Africa, New Zealand, Canada, Australia and the United States). There are also branches in about 30 other countries, mostly in the Commonwealth. Apart from the St John Ambulance Foundation, the Order is also responsible for the Jerusalem Eye Hospital.

Admission to the Order is conferred in recognition of service, usually in St John Ambulance or the Eye Hospital. Membership does not confer any rank, style, title or precedence on a -recipient.

SOVEREIGN HEAD OF THE ORDER
HM The Queen

GRAND PRIOR
HRH The Duke of Gloucester, KG, GCVO

Lord Prior, Eric Barry
Prelate, The Rt. Revd John Waine
Deputy Lord Prior: Prof. Anthony Mellows, OBE, TD
Sub Prior, Mr John Strachan Headquarters, Priory House, 25 St John's Lane, London EC1M 4PP

DAMES

DAMES GRAND CROSS AND DAMES COMMANDERS

Style, 'Dame' before forename and surname, followed by appropriate post-nominal initials. Where such an award is made to a lady already in enjoyment of a higher title, the appropriate initials follow her name
Husband, Untitled
For forms of address, *see* page 40

Dame Grand Cross and Dame Commander are the higher classes for women of the Order of the Bath, the Order of St Michael and St George, the Royal Victorian Order, and the Order of the British Empire. Dames Grand Cross rank after the wives of Baronets and before the wives of Knights Grand Cross. Dames Commanders rank after the wives of Knights Grand Cross and before the wives of Knights Commanders.

Honorary Dames Commanders may be conferred on women who are citizens of countries of which The Queen is not head of state.

LIST OF DAMES

Revised to 31 August 2003

Women peers in their own right and life peers are not included in this list. Female members of the royal family are not included in this list; details of the orders they hold can be found within the Royal Family section.

If a dame has a double barrelled or hyphenated surname, she is listed under the first element of the name.

A full entry in italic type indicates that the recipient of an honour died during the year in which the honour was conferred. The name is included for the purposes of record.

Abaijah, Dame Josephine, DBE
Abel Smith, Lady, DCVO
Abergavenny, The Marchioness of, DCVO
Airlie, The Countess of, DCVO
Albemarle, The Countess of, DBE
Allen, *Prof.* Dame Ingrid Victoria, DBE
Anderson, *Brig. Hon.* Dame Mary Mackenzie (Mrs Pihl), DBE
Andrews, Dame Julie, DBE
Anglesey, The Marchioness of, DBE
Anson, Lady (Elizabeth Audrey), DBE
Anstee, Dame Margaret Joan, DCMG
Arden, *Rt. Hon.* Dame Mary Howarth (Mrs Mance), DBE
Atkins, Dame Eileen, DBE
Bainbridge, Dame Beryl, DBE
Baker, Dame Janet Abbott (Mrs Shelley), CH, DBE
Ballin, Dame Reubina Ann, DBE
Barrow, Dame Jocelyn Anita (Mrs Downer), DBE
Barstow, Dame Josephine Clare (Mrs Anderson), DBE
Bassey, Dame Shirley, DBE
Beaurepaire, Dame Beryl Edith, DBE
Beer, *Prof.* Dame Gillian Patricia Kempster, DBE, FBA
Bergquist, *Prof.* Dame Patricia Rose, DBE
Bewley, Dame Beulah Rosemary, DBE
Black, Hon. Dame Jill Margaret, DBE
Blackadder, Dame Elizabeth Violet, DBE
Blaize, Dame Venetia Ursula, DBE

Blaxland, Dame Helen Frances, DBE
Booth, *Hon.* Dame Margaret Myfanwy Wood, DBE
Bowtell, Dame Ann Elizabeth, DCB
Boyd, Dame Vivienne Myra, DBE
Barbour, Dame Margaret (Mrs Ash), DBE
Bracewell, *Hon.* Dame Joyanne Winifred (Mrs Copeland), DBE
Brain, Dame Margaret Anne (Mrs Wheeler), DBE
Brazill, Dame Josephine (Sister Mary Philippa), DBE
Bridges, Dame Mary Patricia, DBE
Browne, Lady Moyra Blanche Madeleine, DBE
Browne-Evans, Dame Lois Marie, DBE
Bryans, Dame Anne Margaret, DBE
Buckland, Dame Yvonne Helen Elaine, DBE
Butler-Sloss, *Rt. Hon.* Dame (Ann) Elizabeth (Oldfield), DBE
Buttfield, Dame Nancy Eileen, DBE
Byatt, Dame Antonia Susan, DBE, FRSL
Bynoe, Dame Hilda Louisa, DBE
Caldicott, Dame Fiona, DBE, FRCP, FRCPsych.
Campbell-Preston, Dame Frances Olivia, DCVO
Cartwright, Dame Silvia Rose, DBE
Charles, Dame (Mary) Eugenia, DBE
Clark, *Prof.* Dame Jill MacLeod, DBE
Clark, *Prof.* Dame (Margaret) June, DBE, Ph.D.
Clay, Dame Marie Mildred, DBE
Clayton, Dame Barbara Evelyn (Mrs Klyne), DBE
Collarbone, Dame Patricia, DBE
Corsar, *The Hon.* Dame Mary Drummond, DBE
Coward, Dame Pamela Sarah, DBE
Cox, Dame Laura Mary (The Hon. Mrs Justice), DBE
Davies, Dame Wendy Patricia, DBE
Davis, Dame Karlene Cecile, DBE
Daws, Dame Joyce Margaretta, DBE
Deech, Dame Ruth Lynn, DBE
Dell, Dame Miriam Patricia, DBE
Dench, Dame Judith Olivia (Mrs Williams), DBE
Descartes, Dame Marie Selipha Sesenne, DBE, BEM
Devonshire, The Duchess of, DCVO
Digby, Lady, DBE
Donaldson, Dame (Dorothy) Mary (Lady Donaldson of Lymington), GBE
Duffield, Dame Vivien Louise, DBE
Dugdale, Kathryn, Lady, DCVO
Dumont, Dame Ivy Leona, DCMG
Dyche, Dame Rachael Mary, DBE
Elcoat, Dame Catherine Elizabeth, DBE
Ellison, Dame Jill, DBE
Else, Dame Jean, DBE
Engel, Dame Pauline Frances (Sister Pauline Engel), DBE
Esteve-Coll, Dame Elizabeth Anne Loosemore, DBE
Evans, Dame Anne Elizabeth Jane, DBE
Evans, Dame Madeline Glynne Dervel, DBE, CMG
Evison, Dame Helen June Patricia, DBE
Fenner, Dame Peggy Edith, DBE
Fielding, Dame Pauline, DBE
Fitton, Dame Doris Alice (Mrs Mason), DBE
Fort, Dame Maeve Geraldine, DCMG, DCVO
Fraser, Dame Dorothy Rita, DBE
Friend, Dame Phyllis Muriel, DBE
Fritchie, Dame Irene Tordoff (Dame Rennie Fritchie), DBE
Frost, Dame Phyllis Irene, DBE
Fry, Dame Margaret Louise, DBE

Gallagher, Dame Monica Josephine, DBE
Gardiner, Dame Helen Louisa, DBE, MVO
Giles, *Air Comdt.* Dame Pauline (Mrs Parsons), DBE, RRC
Glen-Haig, Dame Mary Alison, DBE
Goodall, *Dr* Dame (Valerie) Jane, DBE
Goodman, Dame Barbara, DBE
Gordon, Dame Minita Elmira, GCMG, GCVO
Gow, Dame Jane Elizabeth (Mrs Whiteley), DBE
Grafton, The Duchess of, GCVO
Grant, Dame Mavis, DBE
Green, Dame Mary Georgina, DBE
Green, Dame Pauline, DBE
Grey, Dame Beryl Elizabeth (Mrs Svenson), DBE
Grimthorpe, The Lady, DCVO
Guilfoyle, Dame Margaret Georgina Constance, DBE
Guthardt, *Revd Dr* Dame Phyllis Myra, DBE
Hale, *Rt. Hon.* Dame Brenda Marjorie (Mrs Farrand), DBE
Hallett, *Hon.* Dame Heather Carol, DBE
Harper, Dame Elizabeth Margaret Way, DBE
Hedley-Miller, Dame Mary Elizabeth, DCVO, CB
Heilbron, *Hon.* Dame Rose, DBE
Herbison, Dame Jean Marjory, DBE, CMG
Hercus, *Hon.* Dame (Margaret) Ann, DCMG
Higgins, *Prof.* Dame Julia Stretton, DBE, FRS
Higgins, *Prof.* Dame Rosalyn, DBE, QC
Hill, *Air Cdre* Dame Felicity Barbara, DBE
Hine, Dame Deirdre Joan, DBE, FRCP
Hogg, *Hon.* Dame Mary Claire (Mrs Koops), DBE
Hollows, Dame Sharon, DBE
Hurley, *Prof.* Dame Rosalinde (Mrs Gortvai), DBE
Hussey, Lady Susan Katharine (Lady Hussey of North Bradley), DCVO
Imison, Dame Tamsyn, DBE
Isaacs, Dame Albertha Madeline, DBE
James, Dame Naomi Christine (Mrs Haythorne), DBE
Jenkins, Dame (Mary) Jennifer (Lady Jenkins of Hillhead), DBE
Johnson, *Prof.* Dame Louise Napier, DBE, FRS
Jones, Dame Gwyneth (Mrs Haberfeld-Jones), DBE
Keegan, Dame Geraldine Mary Marcella, DBE
Kekedo, Dame Rosalina Violet, DBE
Kelleher, Dame Joan, DBE
Kellett-Bowman, Dame (Mary) Elaine, DBE
Kelly, Dame Lorna May Boreland, DBE
Kershaw, Dame Janet Elizabeth Murray (Dame Betty), DBE
Kettlewell, *Comdt.* Dame Marion Mildred, DBE
King, Dame Thea, DBE
Kirby, Dame Georgina Kamiria, DBE
Kramer, *Prof.* Dame Leonie Judith, DBE
Laine, Dame Cleo (Clementine) Dinah (Mrs Dankworth), DBE
Lamb, Dame Dawn Ruth, DBE
Legge-Schwarzkopf, Dame Elisabeth Friederike Marie Olga, DBE
Lewis, Dame Edna Leofrida (Lady Lewis), DBE
Lott, Dame Felicity Ann Emwhyla (Mrs Woolf), DBE
Louisy, Dame (Calliopa) Pearlette, GCMG
Lympany, Dame Moura, DBE
Lynn, Dame Vera (Mrs Lewis), DBE
Mackinnon, Dame (Una) Patricia, DBE
McKechnie, Dame Sheila Marshall, DBE
McLaren, Dame Anne Laura, DBE, FRCOG, FRS
Macmillan of Ovenden, Katharine, Viscountess, DBE
Mayhew, Dame Judith, DBE
Major, Dame Malvina Lorraine (Mrs Fleming), DBE
Major, Dame Norma Christina Elizabeth, DBE

Markova, Dame Alicia, DBE
Maxwell-Scott, Dame Jean Mary Monica, DCVO
Metcalf, Dame Helen, DBE
Metge, *Dr* Dame (Alice) Joan, DBE
Middleton, Dame Elaine Madoline, DCMG, MBE
Mills, Dame Barbara Jean Lyon, DBE, QC
Mirren, Dame Helen, DBE
Moores, Dame Yvonne, DBE
Morrison, *Hon.* Dame Mary Anne, DCVO
Muirhead, Dame Lorna Elizabeth Fox, DBE
Muldoon, Thea Dale, Lady, DBE, QSO
Mumford, Lady Mary Katharine, DCVO
Munro, Dame Alison, DBE
Murdoch, Dame Elisabeth Joy, DBE
Murray, Dame (Alice) Rosemary, DBE, D.Phil.
Neville, Dame Elizabeth, DBE, QPM
Neville-Jones, Dame (Lilian) Pauline, DCMG
Ogilvie, Dame Bridget Margaret, DBE, Ph.D., D.Sc.
Oliver, Dame Gillian Frances, DBE
Ollerenshaw, Dame Kathleen Mary, DBE, D.Phil.
Oxenbury, Dame Shirley Anne, DBE
Park, Dame Merle Florence (Mrs Bloch), DBE
Paterson, Dame Betty Fraser Ross, DBE
Penhaligon, Dame Annette (Mrs Egerton), DBE
Peters, Dame Mary Elizabeth, DBE
Polak, *Prof.* Dame Julia Margaret, DBE
Poole, Dame Avril Anne Barker, DBE
Porter, Dame Shirley (Lady Porter), DBE
Powell, Dame Sally Ann Vickers, DBE
Prendergast, Dame Simone Ruth, DBE
Prentice, Dame Winifred Eva, DBE
Price, Dame Margaret Berenice, DBE
Purves, Dame Daphne Helen, DBE
Pyke, Lady, DBE
Quinn, Dame Sheila Margaret Imelda, DBE
Rafferty, *Hon.* Dame Anne Judith, DBE
Rawson, *Prof.* Dame Jessica Mary, DBE,
Rees, *Prof.* Dame Lesley Howard, DBE
Reeves, Dame Helen May, DBE
Richardson, Dame Mary, DBE
Riddelsdell, Dame Mildred, DCB, CBE
Ridley, Dame Rosalina Violet, DBE
Ridley, Dame (Mildred) Betty, DBE
Ridsdale, Dame Victoire Evelyn Patricia (Lady Ridsdale), DBE
Rigg, Dame Diana, DBE
Rimington, Dame Stella, DCB
Ritterman, Dame Janet, DBE
Robins, Dame Ruth Laura, DBE
Robottom, Dame Marlene, DBE
Roddick, Dame Anita Lucia, DBE
Roe, Dame Raigh Edith, DBE
Rothschild, *Hon.* Dame Miriam Louisa, DBE, FRS
Rue, Dame (Elsie) Rosemary, DBE
Rumbold, *Rt. Hon.* Dame Angela Claire Rosemary, DBE
Runciman of Doxford, The Viscountess, DBE
Salas, Dame Margaret Laurence, DBE
Salmond, *Prof.* Dame Mary Anne, DBE
Saunders, Dame Cicely Mary Strode, OM, DBE, FRCP
Sawyer, *Hon.* Dame Joan Augusta, DBE
Scardino, Dame Marjorie, DBE
Scott, Dame Catherine Margaret (Mrs Denton), DBE
Seward, Dame Margaret Helen Elizabeth, DBE
Shenfield, Dame Barbara Estelle, DBE
Shirley, Dame Stephanie, DBE
Shovelton, Dame Helena, DBE
Sibley, Dame Antoinette (Mrs Corbett), DBE
Smieton, Dame Mary Guillan, DBE
Smith, Dame Dela, DBE

Smith, *Rt. Hon.* Dame Janet Hilary (Mrs Mathieson), DBE
Smith, Dame Margaret Natalie (Maggie) (Mrs Cross),
    DBE
Smith, Dame Margot, DBE
Soames, Mary, Lady, DBE
Southgate, *Prof.* Dame Lesley Jill, DBE
Spark, Dame Muriel Sarah, DBE
Spencer, Dame Rosemary Jane, DCMG
Steel, *Hon.* Dame (Anne) Heather (Mrs Beattie), DBE
Strachan, Dame Valerie Patricia Marie, DCB
Strathern, *Prof.* Dame Anne Marilyn, DBE
Sutherland, Dame Joan (Mrs Bonynge), OM, DBE
Sutherland, Dame Veronica Evelyn, DBE, CMG
Symmonds, Dame Olga Patricia, DBE
Taylor, Dame Elizabeth, DBE
Taylor, Dame Meg, DBE
Te Atairangikaahu, Te Arikinui, Dame, DBE
Te Kanawa, Dame Kiri Janette, DBE
Thomas, Dame Maureen Elizabeth (Lady Thomas), DBE
Thorneycroft, Carla, Lady, DBE
Tinson, Dame Sue, DBE
Tizard, Dame Catherine Anne, GCMG, GCVO, DBE
Tokiel, Dame Rosa, DBE
Trotter, Dame Janet Olive, DBE
Turner-Warwick, Dame Margaret Elizabeth Harvey, DBE,
    FRCP, FRCPEd.
Uprichard, Dame Mary Elizabeth, DBE
Varley, Dame Joan Fleetwood, DBE
Wagner, Dame Gillian Mary Millicent (Lady Wagner),
    DBE
Wall, (Alice) Anne, (Mrs Michael Wall), DCVO
Wallis, Dame Sheila Ann, DBE
Warburton, Dame Anne Marion, DCVO, CMG
Waterhouse, Dame Rachel Elizabeth, DBE, Ph.D.
Webb, *Prof.* Dame Patricia, DBE
Weir, Dame Gillian Constance (Mrs Phelps), DBE
Weller, Dame Rita, DBE
Weston, Dame Margaret Kate, DBE
Wilson-Barnett, *Prof.* Dame Jenifer, DBE
Winstone, Dame Dorothy Gertrude, DBE, CMG
Wong Yick-ming, Dame Rosanna, DBE

DECORATIONS AND MEDALS

PRINCIPAL DECORATIONS AND MEDALS
In order of wear

VICTORIA CROSS (VC), 1856 (see below)
GEORGE CROSS (GC), 1940 (see below)

BRITISH ORDERS OF KNIGHTHOOD
Baronet's Badge
Knight Bachelor's Badge

Indian Order of Merit (Military)

DECORATIONS
Conspicuous Gallantry Cross (CGC), 1995
Royal Red Cross Class I (RRC), 1883
Distinguished Service Cross (DSC), 1914. For all ranks for actions at sea
Military Cross (MC), December 1914. For all ranks for actions on land
Distinguished Flying Cross (DFC), 1918. For all ranks for acts of gallantry when flying in active operations against the enemy
Air Force Cross (AFC), 1918. For all ranks for acts of courage when flying, although not in active operations against the enemy
Royal Red Cross Class II (ARRC)
Order of British India
Kaisar-i-Hind Medal
Order of St John

MEDALS FOR GALLANTRY AND DISTINGUISHED CONDUCT
Union of South Africa Queen's Medal for Bravery, in Gold
Distinguished Conduct Medal (DCM), 1854
Conspicuous Gallantry Medal (CGM), 1874
Conspicuous Gallantry Medal (Flying)
George Medal (GM), 1940
Queen's Police Medal for Gallantry
Queen's Fire Service Medal for Gallantry
Royal West African Frontier Force Distinguished Conduct Medal
King's African Rifles Distinguished Conduct Medal
Indian Distinguished Service Medal
Union of South Africa Queen's Medal for Bravery, in Silver
Distinguished Service Medal (DSM), 1914
Military Medal (MM), 1916
Distinguished Flying Medal (DFM), 1918
Air Force Medal (AFM)
Constabulary Medal (Ireland)
Medal for Saving Life at Sea (Sea Gallantry Medal)
Indian Order of Merit (Civil)
Indian Police Medal for Gallantry
Ceylon Police Medal for Gallantry
Sierra Leone Police Medal for Gallantry
Sierra Leone Fire Brigades Medal for Gallantry
Colonial Police Medal for Gallantry (CPM)
Queen's Gallantry Medal (QGM), 1974
Royal Victorian Medal (RVM), Gold, Silver and Bronze
British Empire Medal (BEM)
Canada Medal
Queen's Police (QPM) *Medal for Distinguished Service*
Queen's Fire Service Medal (QFSM) for Distinguished Service

Queen's Volunteer Reserves Medal
Queen's Medal for Chiefs

CAMPAIGN MEDALS AND STARS, including authorised United Nations, European Community/Union and North Atlantic Treaty Organisation medals (in order of date of campaign for which awarded)

POLAR MEDALS (in order of date)

Imperial Service Medal

POLICE MEDALS FOR VALUABLE SERVICE
Indian Police Medal for Meritorious Service
Ceylon Police Medal for Merit
Sierra Leone Police Medal for Meritorious Service
Sierra Leone Fire Brigades Medal for Meritorious Service
Colonial Police Medal for Meritorious Service

Badge of Honour

JUBILEE, CORONATION AND DURBAR MEDALS
King George V, King George VI, Queen Elizabeth II and Long and Faithful Service Medals

EFFICIENCY AND LONG SERVICE DECORATIONS AND MEDALS
Medal for Meritorious Service
Accumulated Campaign Service Medal
The Medal for Long Service and Good Conduct (Military)
Naval Long Service and Good Conduct Medal
Medal for Meritorious Service (Royal Navy 1918–28)
Indian Long Service and Good Conduct Medal
Indian Meritorious Service Medal
Royal Marines Meritorious Service Medal (1849–1947)
Royal Air Force Meritorious Service Medal (1918–1928)
Royal Air Force Long Service and Good Conduct Medal
Medal for Long Service and Good Conduct (Ulster Defence Regiment)
Indian Long Service and Good Conduct Medal
Royal West African Frontier Force Long Service and Good Conduct Medal
Royal Sierra Leone Military Forces Long Service and Good Conduct Medal
King's African Rifles and Long Service and Good Conduct Medal
Indian Meritorious Service Medal
Police Long Service and Good Conduct Medal
Fire Brigade Long Service and Good Conduct Medal
African Police Medal for Meritorious Service
Royal Canadian Mounted Police Long Service Medal
Ceylon Police Long Service Medal
Ceylon Fire Services Long Service Medal
Sierra Leone Police Long Service Medal
Colonial Police Long Service Medal
Sierra Leone Fire Brigades Long Service Medal
Mauritius Police Long Service and Good Conduct Medal
Mauritius Police Long Service and Good Conduct Medal
Mauritius Fire Services Long Service and Good Conduct Medal
Mauritius Prisons Service Long Service and Good Conduct Medal
Colonial Fire Brigades Long Service Medal
Colonial Prison Service Medal

Hong Kong Disciplined Services Medal
Army Emergency Reserve Decoration (ERD)
Volunteer Officers' Decoration (VD)
Volunteer Long Service Medal
Volunteer Officers' Decoration for India and the Colonies
Volunteer Long Service Medal for India and the Colonies
Colonial Auxiliary Forces Officers' Decoration
Colonial Auxiliary Forces Long Service Medal
Medal for Good Shooting (Naval)
Militia Long Service Medal
Imperial Yeomanry Long Service Medal
Territorial Decoration (TD), 1908
Ceylon Armed Services Long Service Medal
Efficiency Decoration (ED)
Territorial Efficiency Medal
Efficiency Medal
Special Reserve Long Service and Good Conduct Medal
Decoration for Officers of the Royal Navy Reserve (RD), 1910
Decoration for Officers of the Royal Naval Volunteer Reserve (VRD)
Royal Naval Reserve Long Service and Good Conduct Medal
Royal Naval Volunteer Reserve Long Service and Good Conduct Medal
Royal Naval Auxiliary Sick Berth Reserve Long Service and Good Conduct Medal
Royal Fleet Reserve Long Service and Good Conduct Medal
Royal Naval Wireless Auxiliary Reserve Long Service and Good Conduct Medal
Royal Naval Auxiliary Service Medal
Air Efficiency Award (AE), 1942
Volunteer Reserves Service Medal
Ulster Defence Regiment Medal
Northern Ireland Home Service Medal
Queen's Medal (for Champion Shots of the RN and RM)
Queen's Medal (for Champion Shots of the New Zealand Naval Forces)
Queen's Medal (for Champion Shots in the Military Forces)
Queen's Medal (for Champion Shots of the Air Forces)
Cadet Forces Medal, 1950
Coastguard Auxiliary Service Long Service Medal
Special Constabulary Long Service Medal
Canadian Forces Decoration
Royal Observer Corps Medal
Civil Defence Long Service Medal
Ambulance Service (Emergency Duties) Long Service and Good Conduct Medal
Royal Fleet Auxiliary Service Medal Rhodesia Medal
Royal Ulster Constabulary Service Medal
Northern Ireland Prison Service Medal
Union of South Africa Commemoration Medal
Indian Independence Medal
Pakistan Medal
Ceylon Armed Services Inauguration Medal
Ceylon Police Independence Medal (1948)
Sierra Leone Independence Medal
Jamaica Independence Medal
Uganda Independence Medal
Malawi Independence Medal
Fiji Independence Medal
Papua New Guinea Independence Medal
Solomon Islands Independence Medal
Service Medal of the Order of St John
Badge of the Order of the League of Mercy
Voluntary Medical Service Medal, 1932
Women's Voluntary Service Medal
South African Medal for War Services
Colonial Special Constabulary Medal

HONORARY MEMBERSHIP OF COMMONWEALTH ORDERS

OTHER COMMONWEALTH MEMBERS' ORDERS, DECORATIONS AND MEDALS

FOREIGN ORDERS

FOREIGN DECORATIONS

FOREIGN MEDALS

THE VICTORIA CROSS (1856)
FOR CONSPICUOUS BRAVERY

VC

Ribbon, Crimson, for all Services (until 1918 it was blue for the Royal Navy)

Instituted on 29 January 1856, the Victoria Cross was awarded retrospectively to 1854, the first being held by Lt. C. D. Lucas, RN, for bravery in the Baltic Sea on 21 June 1854 (gazetted 24 February 1857). The first 62 Crosses were presented by Queen Victoria in Hyde Park, London, on 26 June 1857.

The Victoria Cross is worn before all other decorations, on the left breast, and consists of a cross-pattée of bronze, one and a half inches in diameter, with the Royal Crown surmounted by a lion in the centre, and beneath there is the inscription For Valour. Holders of the VC receive a tax-free annuity of £1,300, irrespective of need or other conditions. In 1911, the right to receive the Cross was extended to Indian soldiers, and in 1920 to matrons, sisters and nurses, and the staff of the Nursing Services and other services pertaining to hospitals and nursing, and to civilians of either sex regularly or temporarily under the orders, direction or supervision of the naval, military, or air forces of the Crown.

SURVIVING RECIPIENTS OF THE VICTORIA CROSS
as at August 2003

Annand, Capt. R. W. (Durham Light Infantry)
    1940 World War
Bhan Bhagta Gurung, Havildar (2nd Gurkha Rifles)
    1945 World War
Cruickshank, Flt. Lt. J. A. (RAFVR)
    1944 World War
Fraser, Lt.-Cdr. I. E., DSC (RNR)
    1945 World War
Kenna, Pte. E. (Australian Military Forces, 2/4th (NSW))
    1945 World War
Lachhiman Gurung, Havildar (8th Gurkha Rifles)
    1945 World War
Norton, Capt. G. R., MM (South African Forces, Kaffrarian Rifles)
    1944 World War
Payne, WO K., DSC (USA) (Australian Army Training Team)
    1969 Vietnam

Rambahadur Limbu, *Capt.,* MVO (10th Princess Mary's Gurkha Rifles)
1965 *Sarawak*
Smith, *Sgt.* E. A., CD (Seaforth Highlanders of Canada)
1944 *World War*
Speakman-Pitts, *Sgt.* W. (Black Watch, attached KOSB)
1951 *Korea*
Tulbahadur Pun, *Lt.* (6th Gurkha Rifles)
1944 *World War*
Umrao Singh, *Sub Major* (Royal Indian Artillery)
1944 *World War*
Watkins, *Maj. Rt. Hon.* Sir Tasker, GBE (Welch Regiment)
1944 *World War*
Wilson, *Lt.-Col.* E. C. T. (East Surrey Regiment)
1940 *World War*

THE GEORGE CROSS (1940)
FOR GALLANTRY

GC

Ribbon, Dark blue, threaded through a bar adorned with laurel leaves
Instituted 24 September 1940 (with amendments, 3 November 1942)

The George Cross is worn before all other decorations (except the VC) on the left breast (when worn by a woman it may be worn on the left shoulder from a ribbon of the same width and colour fashioned into a bow). It consists of a plain silver cross with four equal limbs, the cross having in the centre a circular medallion bearing a design showing St George and the Dragon. The inscription *For Gallantry* appears round the medallion and in the angle of each limb of the cross is the Royal cypher 'G VI' forming a circle concentric with the medallion. The reverse is plain and bears the name of the recipient and the date of the award. The cross is suspended by a ring from a bar adorned with laurel leaves on dark blue ribbon one and a half inches wide.

The cross is intended primarily for civilians; awards to the fighting services are confined to actions for which purely military honours are not normally granted. It is awarded only for acts of the greatest heroism or of the most conspicuous courage in circumstances of extreme danger. From 1 April 1965, holders of the Cross have received a tax-free annuity, which is now £1,300. The cross has twice been awarded collectively rather than to an individual: to Malta (1942) and the Royal Ulster Constabulary (1999).

The royal warrant which ordained that the grant of the Empire Gallantry Medal should cease authorised holders of that medal to return it to the Central Chancery of the Orders of Knighthood and to receive in exchange the George Cross. A similar provision applied to posthumous awards of the Empire Gallantry Medal made after the outbreak of war in 1939. In October 1971 all surviving holders of the Albert Medal and the Edward Medal exchanged those decorations for the George Cross.

SURVIVING RECIPIENTS OF THE GEORGE CROSS
as at August 2003

If the recipient originally received the Empire Gallantry Medal (EGM), the Albert Medal (AM) or the Edward Medal (EM), this is indicated by the initials in parenthesis.

Archer, *Col.* B. S. T., GC, OBE, ERD, 1941
Bamford, J., GC, 1952
Beaton, J., GC, CVO, 1974
Bridge, *Lt.-Cdr.* J., GC, GM and BAR, 1944
Butson, *Lt.-Col.* A. R. C., GC, CD, MD (AM), 1948
Bywater, R. A. S., GC, GM, 1944
Errington, H., GC, 1941
Farrow, K., GC (AM), 1948
Flintoff, H. H., GC (EM), 1944
Gledhill, A. J., GC, 1967
Gregson, J. S., GC (AM), 1943
Johnson, *WO1 (SSM)* B., GC, 1990
Kinne, D. G., GC, 1954
Lowe, A. R., GC (AM), 1949
Lynch, J., GC, BEM (AM), 1948
Naughton, F., GC (EGM), 1937
Pratt, M. K., GC, 1978
Purves, Mrs M., GC (AM), 1949
Raweng, Awang anak, GC, 1951
Riley, G., GC (AM), 1944
Rowlands, *Air Marshal* Sir John, GC, KBE, 1943
Stevens, H. W., GC, 1958
Styles, *Lt.-Col.* S. G., GC, 1972
Walker, C., GC, 1972
Walker, C. H., GC (AM), 1942
Walton, E. W. K., GC (AM), DSO, 1948
Wilcox, C., GC (EM), 1949
Wiltshire, S. N., GC (EGM), 1930
Wooding, E. A., GC (AM), 1945

CHIEFS OF CLANS AND NAMES IN SCOTLAND

Only chiefs of whole Names or Clans are included, except certain special instances (marked *) who, though not chiefs of a whole name, were or are for some reason (e.g. the Macdonald forfeiture) independent. Under decision (*Campbell-Gray*, 1950) that a bearer of a 'double or triple-barrelled' surname cannot be held chief of a part of such, several others cannot be included in the list at present.

THE ROYAL HOUSE: HM THE QUEEN

AGNEW: Sir Crispin Agnew of Lochnaw, Bt., QC, 6 Palmerston Road, Edinburgh EH9 1TN
ANSTRUTHER: Sir Ian Fife Campbell Anstruther, Bt., The Estate Office, Barlavington, Petworth, W. Sussex GU28 0LG
ARBUTHNOTT: The Viscount of Arbuthnott, KT, CBE, DSC, Arbuthnott House, Laurencekirk, Kincardineshire AB30 1PA
BARCLAY: Peter C. Barclay of Towie Barclay and of that Ilk, 69 Oakwood Court, London W14 8JF
BORTHWICK: The Lord Borthwick, Crookston, Heriot, Midlothian EH38 5YS
BOYD: The Lord Kilmarnock, MBE, 194 Regent's Park Road, London NW1 8XP
BOYLE: The Earl of Glasgow, Kelburn, Fairlie, Ayrshire KA29 0BE
BRODIE: Alastair Brodie of Brodie, Brodie Castle, Forres, Morayshire IV36 0TE
BRUCE: The Earl of Elgin and Kincardine, KT, Broomhall, Dunfermline, Fife KY11 3DU
BUCHAN: David S. Buchan of Auchmacoy, Auchmacoy House, Ellon, Aberdeenshire
BURNETT: J. C. A. Burnett of Leys, Crathes Castle, Banchory, Kincardineshire
CAMERON: Sir Donald Cameron of Lochiel, KT, CVO, TD, Achnacarry, Spean Bridge, Inverness-shire
CAMPBELL: The Duke of Argyll, Inveraray, Argyll PA32 8XF
CARMICHAEL: Richard J. Carmichael of Carmichael, Carmichael, Thankerton, Biggar, Lanarkshire
CARNEGIE: The Duke of Fife, Elsick House, Stonehaven, Kincardineshire AB3 2NT
CATHCART: The Earl Cathcart, 18 Smith Terrace, London SW3 4DL
CHARTERIS: The Earl of Wemyss and March, KT, Gosford House, Longniddry, East Lothian EH32 0PX
CLAN CHATTAN: K. Mackintosh of Clan Chattan, Fairburn, Felixburg, Zimbabwe
CHISHOLM: Hamish Chisholm of Chisholm (The Chisholm), Elmpine, Beck Row, Bury St Edmunds, Suffolk IP28 8BT
COCHRANE: The Earl of Dundonald, Lochnell Castle, Ledaig, Argyllshire
COLQUHOUN: Sir Ivar Colquhoun of Luss, Bt., Camstraddan, Luss, Dunbartonshire G83 8NX
CRANSTOUN: David A. S. Cranstoun of that Ilk, Corehouse, Lanark
CRICHTON: vacant
CUMMING: Sir Alastair Cumming of Altyre, Bt., Altyre, Forres, Moray
DARROCH: Capt. Duncan Darroch of Gourock, The Red House, Branksome Park Road, Camberley, Surrey
DAVIDSON: Alister G. Davidson of Davidston, 21 Winscombe Street, Auckland, New Zealand
DEWAR: Michael Dewar of that Ilk and Vogrie, Rectory Farm House, Wincanton, Somerset BA9 8ET
DRUMMOND: The Earl of Perth, Stobhall, Perth PH2 6DR
DUNBAR: Sir James Dunbar of Mochrum, Bt., 211 Gardenville Drive, Yorktown, Va 23693, USA

DUNDAS: David D. Dundas of Dundas, 3 Crane Close, Tokai 7945, Cape Town, South Africa
DURIE: Andrew Durie of Durie, CBE, Finnich Malise, Croftamie, Stirlingshire G63 0HA
ELIOTT: Mrs Margaret Eliott of Redheugh, Redheugh, Newcastleton, Roxburghshire
ERSKINE: The Earl of Mar and Kellie, Erskine House, Kirk Wynd, Alloa, Clackmannan FK10 4JF
FARQUHARSON: Capt. A. Farquharson of Invercauld, MC, Invercauld, Braemar, Aberdeenshire AB35 5TT
FERGUSSON: Sir Charles Fergusson of Kilkerran, Bt., Kilkerran, Maybole, Ayrshire
FORBES: The Lord Forbes, KBE, Balforbes, Alford, Aberdeenshire AB33 8DR
FORSYTH: Alistair Forsyth of that Ilk, Ethie Castle, by Arbroath, Angus DD11 5SP
FRASER: The Lady Saltoun, Inverey House, Braemar, Aberdeenshire AB35 5YB
*FRASER (OF LOVAT): The Lord Lovat, Beaufort Lodge, Beauly, Inverness-shire IV4 7AZ
GAYRE: R. Gayre of Gayre and Nigg, Minard Castle, Minard, Inverary, Argyll PA32 8YB
GORDON: The Marquess of Huntly, Aboyne Castle, Aberdeenshire AB34 5JP
GRAHAM: The Duke of Montrose, Buchanan Auld House, Drymen, Stirlingshire
GRANT: The Lord Strathspey, The School House, Lochbuie, Mull, Argyllshire PA62 6AA
GRIERSON: Sir Michael Grierson of Lag, Bt., 40C Palace Road, London SW2 3NJ
GUTHRIE: Alexander Guthrie of Guthrie, 22 William Street, Shenton Park, Perth, Western Australia
HAIG: The Earl Haig, OBE, Bemersyde, Melrose, Roxburghshire TD6 9DP
HALDANE: Martin Haldane of Gleneagles, Gleneagles, Auchterarder, Perthshire
HANNAY: David Hannay of Kirkdale and of that Ilk, Cardoness House, Gatehouse-of-Fleet, Kirkcudbrightshire
HAY: The Earl of Erroll, Woodbury Hall, Sandy, Beds
HENDERSON: John Henderson of Fordell, 7 Owen Street, Toowoomba, Queensland, Australia
HUNTER: Pauline Hunter of Hunterston, Plover's Ridge, Lon Crecrist, Trearddur Bay, Anglesey LL65 2AZ
IRVINE OF DRUM: David C. Irvine of Drum, Holly Leaf Cottage, Banchory, Aberdeenshire AB31 4BR
JARDINE: Sir Alexander Jardine of Applegirth, Bt., Ash House, Thwaites, Millom, Cumbria LA18 5HY
JOHNSTONE: The Earl of Annandale and Hartfell, Raehills, Lockerbie, Dumfriesshire
KEITH: The Earl of Kintore, The Stables, Keith Hall, Inverurie, Aberdeenshire AB51 0LD
KENNEDY: The Marquess of Ailsa, Cassillis House, Maybole, Ayrshire
KERR: The Marquess of Lothian, KCVO, Ferniehurst Castle, Jedburgh, Roxburghshire TN8 6NX
KINCAID: Arabella Kincaid of Kincaid, Stoneyeld, Downton, Ludlow, Shropshire
LAMONT: Peter N. Lamont of that Ilk, 40 Breakfast Road, Marayong, New South Wales, Australia
LEASK: Madam Leask of Leask, 1 Vincent Road, Sheringham, Norfolk
LENNOX: Edward J. H. Lennox of that Ilk, Tods Top Farm, Downton on the Rock, Ludlow, Shropshire
LESLIE: The Earl of Rothes, Tanglewood, West Tytherley, Salisbury, Wilts SP5 1LX
LINDSAY: The Earl of Crawford and Balcarres, KT, GCVO, PC, Balcarres, Colinsburgh, Fife
LOCKHART: Angus H. Lockhart of the Lee, Newholme, Dunsyre, Lanark

LUMSDEN: Gillem Lumsden of that Ilk and Blanerne, Stapely Howe, Hoe Benham, Newbury, Berks

MACALESTER: William St J. S. McAlester of Loup and Kennox, 27 Durnham Road, Christchurch, Dorset BH23 7ND

MACARTHUR: James MacArthur of that Ilk, 14 Hillpark Wood, Edinburgh

MCBAIN: J. H. McBain of McBain, 7025 North Finger Rock Place, Tucson, Arizona, USA

MACDONALD: The Lord Macdonald *(The Macdonald of Macdonald),* Kinloch Lodge, Sleat, Isle of Skye

*MACDONALD OF CLANRANALD: Ranald A. Macdonald of Clanranald, Mornish House, Killin, Perthshire FK21 8TX

*MACDONALD OF SLEAT (CLAN HUSTEAIN): Sir Ian Macdonald of Sleat, Bt., Thorpe Hall, Rudston, Driffield, N. Humberside YO25 0JE

*MACDONELL OF GLENGARRY: Ranald MacDonell of Glengarry, Elonbank, Castle Street, Fortrose, Ross-shire IV10 8TH

MACDOUGALL: vacant

MACDOWALL: Fergus D. H. Macdowall of Garthland, 16 Rowe Road, Ottawa, Ontario K29 2ZS

MACGREGOR: Sir Malcolm MacGregor of MacGregor, Bt., Bannatyne, Newtyle, Blairgowrie, Perthshire PH12 8TR

MACINTYRE: James W. MacIntyre of Glenoe, 15301 Pine Orchard Drive, Apartment 3H, Silver Spring, Maryland, USA

MACKAY: The Lord Reay, 98 Oakley Street, London SW3

MACKENZIE: The Earl of Cromartie, Castle Leod, Strathpeffer, Ross-shire IV14 9AA

MACKINNON: Madam Anne Mackinnon of Mackinnon, 3 Anson Way, Bridgewater, Somerset TA6 3TB

MACKINTOSH: John Mackintosh of Mackintosh *(The Mackintosh of Mackintosh),* Moy Hall, Inverness IV13 7YQ

MACLAREN: Donald MacLaren of MacLaren and Achleskine, Achleskine, Kirkton, Balquhidder, Lochearnhead

MACLEAN: The Hon. Sir Lachlan Maclean of Duart, Bt., CVO, Arngask House, Glenfarg, Perthshire PH2 9QA

MACLENNAN: Ruaraidh MacLennan of MacLennan, Oldmill, Dores, Inverness-shire IV2 6R

MACLEOD: John MacLeod of MacLeod, Dunvegan Castle, Isle of Skye

MACMILLAN: George MacMillan of MacMillan, Finlaystone, Langbank, Renfrewshire

MACNAB: J. C. Macnab of Macnab *(The Macnab),* Leuchars Castle Farmhouse, Leuchars, Fife KY16 0EY

MACNAGHTEN: Sir Patrick Macnaghten of Macnaghten and Dundarave, Bt., Dundarave, Bushmills, Co. Antrim

MACNEACAIL: Iain Macneacail of Macneacail and Scorrybreac, 12 Fox Street, Ballina, NSW, Australia

MACNEIL OF BARRA: Ian R. Macneil of Barra *(The Macneil of Barra),* 95/6 Grange Loan, Edinburgh

MACPHERSON: The Hon. Sir William Macpherson of Cluny, TD, Newton Castle, Blairgowrie, Perthshire

MACTAVISH: E. S. Dugald MacTavish of Dunardry, 3049 Vine Lane, Sebring, Florida 33870, USA

MACTHOMAS: Andrew P. C. MacThomas of Finegand, c/o Roslin Cottage, Pitmedden, Aberdeenshire AB41 7NY

MAITLAND: The Earl of Lauderdale, 12 St Vincent Street, Edinburgh

MAKGILL: The Viscount of Oxfuird, Kemback, Stoke, Nr Andover, Hampshire SP11 ONP

MALCOLM (MACCALLUM): Robin N. L. Malcolm of Poltalloch, Duntrune Castle, Lochgilphead, Argyll

MAR: The Countess of Mar, St Michael's Farm, Great Witley, Worcs WR6 6JB

MARJORIBANKS: Andrew Marjoribanks of that Ilk, 10 Newark Street, Greenock

MATHESON: Maj. Sir Fergus Matheson of Matheson, Bt., Old Rectory, Hedenham, Bungay, Suffolk NR35 2LD

MENZIES: David R. Menzies of Menzies, 42 Panorama Drive, Preston Beach, Western Australia 6215

MOFFAT: Madam Moffat of that Ilk, St Jasual, Bullocks Farm Lane, Wheeler End Common, High Wycombe

MONCREIFFE: The Hon. Peregrine Moncreiffe of Moncreiffe, Easter Moncreiffe, Bridge of Earn, Perthshire

MONTGOMERIE: The Earl of Eglinton and Winton, Balhomie, Cargill, Perth PH2 6DS

MORRISON: Dr Iain M. Morrison of Ruchdi, Magnolia Cottage, The Street, Walberton, Sussex

MUNRO: Hector W. Munro of Foulis, Foulis Castle, Evanton, Ross-shire IV16 9UX

MURRAY: The Duke of Atholl, Blair Castle, Blair Atholl, Perthshire

NESBITT (OR NISBET): Mark Nesbitt of that Ilk, 114 Cambridge Road, Teddington, Middlesex TW11 8DJ

NICOLSON: The Lord Carnock, 90 Whitehall Court, London SW1A 2EL

OGILVY: The Earl of Airlie, KT, GCVO, PC, Cortachy Castle, Kirriemuir, Angus

OLIPHANT: Richard Oliphant of that Ilk, 1B Kylerhea, Breaknish, Isle of Skye IV42 8NH

RAMSAY: The Earl of Dalhousie, Brechin Castle, Brechin, Angus DD7 6SH

RATTRAY: James S. Rattray of Rattray, Craighall, Rattray, Perthshire

RIDDELL: Sir John Riddell of Riddell, CB, CVO, Hepple, Morpeth, Northumberland

ROBERTSON: Alexander G. H. Robertson of Struan *(Struan-Robertson),* The Breach Farm, Goudhurst Road, Cranbrook, Kent

ROLLO: The Lord Rollo, Pitcairns, Dunning, Perthshire

ROSE: Miss Elizabeth Rose of Kilravock, Kilravock Castle, Croy, Inverness

ROSS: David C. Ross of that Ilk and Balnagown, Shandwick, Perth Road, Stanley, Perthshire

RUTHVEN: The Earl of Gowrie, PC, 34 King Street, Covent Garden, London WC2

SCOTT: The Duke of Buccleuch and Queensberry, KT, VRD, Bowhill, Selkirk

SCRYMGEOUR: The Earl of Dundee, Birkhill, Cupar, Fife

SEMPILL: The Lord Sempill, 3 Vanburgh Place, Edinburgh, EH6 8AE

SHAW: John Shaw of Tordarroch, East Craig an Ron, 22 Academy Mead, Fortrose IV10 8TW

SINCLAIR: The Earl of Caithness, 137 Claxton Grove, London W6 8HB

SKENE: Danus Skene of Skene, Orwell House, Manse Road, Milnathort, Fife KY13 9YQ

STIRLING: Fraser J. Stirling of Cader, 44A Oakley Street, London SW3 5HA

STRANGE: Maj. Timothy Strange of Balcaskie, Little Holme, Porton Road, Amesbury, Wilts

SUTHERLAND: The Countess of Sutherland, House of Tongue, Brora, Sutherland

SWINTON: John Swinton of that Ilk, 123 Superior Avenue SW, Calgary, Alberta, Canada

TROTTER: Alexander Trotter of Mortonhall, Charterhall, Duns, Berwickshire

URQUHART: Kenneth T. Urquhart of Urquhart, 507 Jefferson Park Avenue, Jefferson, New Orleans, USA

WALLACE: Ian F. Wallace of that Ilk, 5 Lennox Street, Edinburgh EH4 1QB

WEDDERBURN OF THAT ILK: The Master of Dundee, Birkhill, Cupar, Fife

WEMYSS: David Wemyss of that Ilk, Invermay, Forteviot, Perthshire

THE PRIVY COUNCIL

The Sovereign in Council, or Privy Council, was the chief source of executive power until the system of Cabinet government developed in the 18th century. Now the Privy Council's main functions are to advise the Sovereign and to exercise its own statutory responsibilities independent of the Sovereign in Council.

Membership of the Privy Council is automatic upon appointment to certain government and judicial positions in the United Kingdom, e.g. Cabinet ministers must be Privy Counsellors and are sworn in on first assuming office. Membership is also accorded by The Queen to eminent people in the UK and independent countries of the Commonwealth of which Her Majesty is Queen, on the recommendation of the British Prime Minister. Membership of the Council is retained for life, except for very occasional removals.

The administrative functions of the Privy Council are carried out by the Privy Council Office under the direction of the President of the Council, who is always a member of the Cabinet.

President of the Council, vacant. *See* Stop Press
Clerk of the Council, A. Galloway

MEMBERS *as at August 2003*

HRH The Duke of Edinburgh, 1951
HRH The Prince of Wales, 1977

Aberdare, Lord, 1974
Ackner, Lord, 1980
Airlie, Earl of, 1984
Aldous, Sir William, 1995
Alebua, Ezekiel, 1988
Alison, Michael, 1981
Ampthill, Lord, 1995
Ancram, Michael, 1996
Anderson, Donald, 2000
Anthony, Douglas, 1971
Arbuthnot, James, 1998
Archer of Sandwell, Lord, 1977
Arden, Dame Mary, 2000
Armstrong, Hilary, 1999
Arnold, Sir John, 1979
Arthur, Hon. Owen, 1995
Ashdown of Norton-sub-Hamdon, Lord, 1989
Ashley of Stoke, Lord, 1979
Atkins, Sir Robert, 1995
Auld, Sir Robin, 1995
Baker, Sir Thomas, 2002
Baker of Dorking, Lord, 1984
Barber, Lord, 1963
Barnett, Lord, 1975
Barron, Kevin, 2001

Battle, John, 2002
Beckett, Margaret, 1993
Beith, Alan, 1992
Beldam, Sir Roy, 1989
Belstead, Lord, 1983
Benn, Anthony, 1964
Biffen, Lord, 1979
Bingham of Cornhill, Lord, 1986
Birch, William, 1992
Bisson, Sir Gordon, 1987
Blackstone, Baroness, 2001
Blair, Tony, 1994
Blaker, Lord, 1983
Blanchard, Peter, 1998
Blatch, Baroness, 1993
Blunkett, David, 1997
Boateng, Paul, 1999
Bolger, James, 1991
Booth, Albert, 1976
Boothroyd, Baroness, 1992
Boscawen, *Hon.* Robert, 1992
Bottomley, Virginia, 1992
Boyd, Colin, 2000
Boyson, Sir Rhodes, 1987
Bradley, Keith, 2001
Brathwaite, Sir Nicholas, 1991
Bridge of Harwich, Lord, 1975
Brightman, Lord, 1979
Brittan of Spennithorne, Lord, 1981
Brook, Sir Henry, 1996
Brooke of Sutton Mandeville, Lord, 1988
Brown, Gordon, 1996
Brown, Nicholas, 1997
Brown, Sir Simon, 1992
Brown, Sir Stephen, 1983
Browne-Wilkinson, Lord, 1983
Butler, Sir Adam, 1984
Butler-Sloss, Dame Elizabeth, 1988
Buxton, Sir Richard, 1997
Byers, Stephen, 1998
Caborn, Richard, 1999
Caithness, Earl of, 1990
Callaghan of Cardiff, Lord, 1964
Cameron of Lochbroom, Lord, 1984
Camoys, Lord, 1997
Campbell of Croy, Lord, 1970
Campbell, Walter Menzies, 1999
Campbell, Sir William, 1999
Canterbury, The Archbishop of, 2002
Carey of Clifton, Lord, 1991
Carlisle of Bucklow, Lord, 1979
Carnwath, Sir Robert, 2002
Carr of Hadley, Lord, 1963
Carrington, Lord, 1959
Carswell, Sir Robert, 1993
Carter, Lord, 1997
Casey, Sir Maurice, 1986
Chadwick, Sir John, 1997
Chalfont, Lord, 1964
Chalker of Wallasey, Baroness, 1987
Chan, Sir Julius, 1981
Chataway, Sir Christopher, 1970
Clark of Windermere, Lord, 1997
Clark, Helen, 1990
Clark of Kempston, Lord, 1990

Clarke, Sir Anthony, 1998
Clarke, Charles, 2001
Clarke, Kenneth, 1984
Clarke, Thomas, 1997
Clinton-Davis, Lord, 1998
Clyde, Lord, 1996
Cockfield, Lord, 1982
Colman, Fraser, 1986
Compton, Sir John, 1983
Concannon, John, 1978
Cook, Robin, 1996
Cooke of Thorndon, Lord, 1977
Cope of Berkeley, Lord, 1988
Corfield, Sir Frederick, 1970
Cosgrove, Lady, 2003
Coulsfield, Lord, 2000
Cowen, Sir Zelman, 1981
Cradock, Sir Percy, 1993
Crawford and Balcarres, Earl of, 1972
Creech, *Hon.* Wyatt, 1999
Crickhowell, Lord, 1979
Croom-Johnson, Sir David, 1984
Cullen, *Rt. Hon.* Lord, 1997
Cunningham, Jack, 1993
Curry, David, 1996
Darling, Alistair, 1997
Davies, Denzil, 1978
Davies, Ronald, 1997
Davis, David, 1997
Davis, Terence, 1999
Davison, Sir Ronald, 1978
Dean of Harptree, Lord, 1991
Dean of Thornton-le-Fylde, Baroness, 1998
Deedes, Lord, 1962
Denham, John, 2000
Denham, Lord, 1981
Devonshire, Duke of, 1964
Diamond, Lord, 1965
Dixon, Lord, 1996
Dobson, Frank, 1997
Donaldson of Lymington, Lord, 1979
Dorrell, Stephen, 1994
du Cann, Sir Edward, 1964
Duncan Smith, Iain, 2001
Dunn, Sir Robin, 1980
Dyson, Sir John, 2001
East, Paul, 1998
Eden of Winton, Lord, 1972
Eggar, Timothy, 1995
Eichelaum, Sir Thomas, 1989
Elias, *Hon.* Dame, Sian, 1999
Emery, Sir Peter, 1993
Esquivel, Manuel, 1986
Evans, Sir Anthony, 1992
Eveleigh, Sir Edward, 1977
Farquharson, Sir Donald, 1989
Fellowes, Lord, 1990
Ferrers, Earl, 1982
Field, Frank, 1997
Floissac, Sir Vincent, 1992
Foot, Michael, 1974
Forsyth of Drumlean, The Lord, 1995
Forth, Eric, 1997
Foster, Derek, 1993

Foulkes, George, 2002
Fowler, Lord, 1979
Fox, Sir Michael, 1981
Fraser, Malcolm, 1976
Fraser of Carmyllie, Lord, 1989
Freeman, John, 1966
Freeman, Lord, 1993
Freeson, Reginald, 1976
Garel-Jones, Lord, 1992
Gault, Thomas, 1992
George, Bruce, 2000
George, Sir Edward, 1999
Georges, Telford, 1986
Gibbs, Sir Harry, 1972
Gibson, Sir Peter, 1993
Gibson, Sir Ralph, 1985
Gilbert, Lord, 1978
Gill, Lord, 2002
Gilmour of Craigmillar, Lord, 1973
Glenamara, Lord, 1964
Glidewell, Sir Iain, 1985
Goff of Chieveley, Lord, 1982
Goldsmith, Lord, 2002
Goodlad, Sir Alastair, 1992
Gowrie, Earl of, 1984
Graham, Sir Douglas, 1998
Graham of Edmonton, Lord, 1998
Gray of Contin, Lord, 1982
Griffiths, Lord, 1980
Grocott, Lord, 2002
Gummer, John, 1985
Habgood, Rt. Revd Lord, 1983
Hague, William, 1995
Hain, Peter, 2001
Hale, Dame Brenda, 1999
Hamilton, Sir Archie, 1991
Hamilton, Lord, 2002
Hanley, Sir Jeremy, 1994
Hardie, Lord, 1997
Hardie Boys, Sir Michael, 1989
Harman, Harriet, 1997
Harrison, Walter, 1977
Haselhurst, Sir Alan, 1999
Hattersley, Lord, 1975
Hayhoe, Lord, 1985
Hayman, Baroness, 2000
Healey, Lord, 1964
Heath, Sir Edward, 1955
Heathcoat-Amory, David, 1996
Henry, Sir Denis, 1993
Henry, John, 1996
Heseltine, Lord, 1979
Heseltine, Sir William, 1986
Hesketh, Lord, 1991
Hewitt, Patricia, 2001
Higgins, Lord, 1979
Hirst, Sir David, 1992
Hobhouse of Woodborough, Lord, 1993
Hoffmann, Lord, 1992
Hogg, *Hon.* Douglas, 1992
Hollis of Heigham, Baroness, 1999
Holme of Cheltenham, Lord, 2000
Hoon, Geoffrey, 1999
Hope of Craighead, Lord, 1989
Hordern, Sir Peter, 1993
Howard, Michael, 1990
Howarth, Alan, 2000
Howe of Aberavon, Lord, 1972
Howell of Guildford, Lord, 1979
Hunt, Jonathan, 1989

Hunt of Wirral, Lord, 1990
Hurd of Westwell, Lord, 1982
Hutchison, Sir Michael, 1995
Hutton, Lord, 1988
Hutton, John, 2001
Ingraham, Hubert, 1993
Ingram, Adam, 1999
Irvine of Lairg, Lord, 1997
Jack, Michael, 1997
Janvrin, Sir Robin, 1998
Jauncey of Tullichettle, Lord, 1988
Jay of Paddington, Baroness, 1998
Jellicoe, Earl, 1963
Jenkin of Roding, Lord, 1973
Johnson, Alan, 2003
Johnson Smith, Sir Geoffrey, 1996
Jones, Lord, 1999
Jopling, Lord, 1979
Jowell, Tessa, 1998
Judge, Sir Igor, 1996
Jugnauth, Sir Anerood, 1987
Kaufman, Gerald, 1978
Kay, Sir John, 2000
Keene, Sir David, 2000
Keith, Sir Kenneth, 1998
Kelly, Sir Basil, 1984
Kelvedon, Lord, 1980
Kenilorea, Sir Peter, 1979
Kennedy, Charles, 1999
Kennedy, Jane, 2003
Kennedy, Sir Paul, 1992
King of Bridgwater, Lord, 1979
Kingsdown, Lord, 1987
Kingsland, Lord, 1994
Kinnock, Neil, 1983
Kirkwood, Lord, 2000
Knight, Gregory, 1995
Lamont of Lerwick, Lord, 1986
Lane, Lord, 1975
Lang of Monkton, Lord, 1990
Lange, David, 1984
Latasi, Kamuta, 1996
Latham, Sir David, 2000
Lauti, Sir Toaripi, 1979
Laws, Sir John, 1999
Lawson of Blaby, Lord, 1981
Lawton, Sir Frederick, 1972
Leggatt, Sir Andrew, 1990
Leonard, Rt. Revd Graham, 1981
Letwin, Oliver, 2002
Liddell, Mrs Helen, 1998
Lilley, Peter, 1990
Lloyd of Berwick, Lord, 1984
Lloyd, Sir Peter, 1994
London, The Bishop of, 1995
Longmore, Sir Andrew, 2001
Louisy, Allan, 1981
Luce, Lord, 1986
Lyell, Sir Nicholas, 1990
Mabon, Dickson, 1977
McCartney, Ian, 1999
McCollum, Sir Liam, 1997
McConnell, Jack, 2001
MacDermott, Sir John, 1987
Macdonald of Tradeston, Lord, 1999
Macfadyen, Lord, 2002
MacGregor of Pulham Market, Lord, 1985
MacIntyre, Duncan, 1980
Mackay, Andrew, 1998

McIntosh of Haringey, Lord, 2002
McKay, Ian, 1992
Mackay of Clashfern, Lord, 1979
Mackay of Drumadoon, Lord, 1996
McKinnon, Donald, 1992
Maclean, David, 1995
Maclean, Lord, 2001
McLeish, Henry, 2000
Maclennan of Rogart, Lord, 1997
McMullin, Sir Duncan, 1980
Major, John, 1987
Mance, Sir Jonathan, 1999
Mandelson, Peter, 1998
Mantell, Sir Charles, 1997
Mara, Ratu Sir Kamisese, 1973
Marnoch, Lord, 2001
Marsh, Lord, 1966
Martin, Michael, 2000
Mason of Barnsley, Lord, 1968
Maude, *Hon.* Francis, 1992
Mawhinney, Sir Brian, 1994
May, Sir Anthony, 1998
May, Theresa, 2003
Mayhew of Twysden, Lord, 1986
Meacher, Michael, 1997
Megarry, Sir Robert, 1978
Mellor, David, 1990
Merlyn-Rees, Lord, 1974
Michael, Alun, 1998
Milburn, Alan, 1998
Millan, Bruce, 1975
Millett, Lord, 1994
Milligan, Lord, 2000
Mitchell, Sir James, 1985
Molyneaux of Killead, Lord, 1983
Monro of Langholm, Lord, 1995
Moore, Michael, 1990
Moore of Lower Marsh, Lord, 1986
Moore of Wolvercote, Lord, 1977
Morgan, Rhodri, 2000
Morris, Charles, 1978
Morris, Estelle, 1999
Morris of Aberavon, Lord, 1970
Morris of Manchester, Lord, 1979
Morritt, Sir Robert, 1994
Mowlam, Marjorie, 1997
Moyle, Roland, 1978
Mummery, Sir John, 1996
Murphy, Paul, 1998
Murray, *Hon.* Lord, 1974
Murray, Sir Donald, 1989
Murray of Epping Forest, Lord, 1976
Murton of Lindisfarne, Lord, 1976
Mustill, Lord, 1985
Nairne, Sir Patrick, 1982
Namaliu, Sir Rabbie, 1989
Naseby, Lord, 1994
Needham, Sir Richard, 1994
Neill, Sir Brian, 1985
Newton of Braintree, Lord, 1988
Nicholls of Birkenhead, Lord, 1995
Nicholson, Sir Michael, 1995
Nolan, Lord, 1991
Nott, Sir John, 1979
Nourse, Sir Martin, 1985
Oakes, Gordon, 1979
O'Connor, Sir Patrick, 1980
O'Donnell, Turlough, 1979
O'Flynn, Francis, 1987
Ogilvy, Sir Angus, 1997

Oliver of Aylmerton, Lord, 1980
Oppenheim-Barnes, Baroness, 1979
Orme, Lord, 1974
Osbourne, Lord, 2001
Otton, Sir Philip, 1995
Owen, Lord, 1976
Paeniu, Bikenibeu, 1991
Palliser, Sir Michael, 1983
Palmer, Sir Geoffrey, 1986
Parker, Sir Jonathan, 2000
Parker, Sir Roger, 1983
Parkinson, Lord, 1981
Patten, Christopher, 1989
Patten, Lord, 1990
Patterson, Percival, 1993
Pattie, Sir Geoffrey, 1987
Pendry, Lord, 2000
Penrose, Lord, 2000
Peters, Winston, 1998
Peyton of Yeovil, Lord, 1970
Phillips of Worth Matravers, Lord, 1995
Pill, Sir Malcolm, 1995
Pindling, Sir Lynden, 1976
Portillo, Michael, 1992
Potter, Sir Mark, 1996
Prescott, John, 1994
Price, George, 1982
Primarolo, Dawn, 2002
Prior, Lord, 1970
Prosser, Lord, 2000
Puapua, Sir Tomasi, 1982
Pym, Lord, 1970
Quin, Ms Joyce, 1998
Radice, Lord, 1999
Raison, Sir Timothy, 1982
Ramsden, James, 1963
Rawlinson of Ewell, Lord, 1964
Raynsford, Nick, 2001
Redwood, John, 1993
Rees, Lord, 1983
Reid, John, 1998
Renton, Lord, 1962
Renton of Mount Harry, Lord, 1989
Richard, Lord, 1993
Richardson, Sir Ivor, 1978
Richardson of Duntisbourne, Lord, 1976
Rifkind, Sir Malcolm, 1986
Rix, Sir Bernard, 2000
Roberts of Conwy, Lord, 1991

Robertson of Port Ellen, Lord, 1997
Roch, Sir John, 1993
Rodger of Earlsferry, Lord, 1992
Rodgers of Quarry Bank, Lord, 1975
Rooker, Lord, 1999
Rose, Sir Christopher, 1992
Ross, *Hon.* Lord, 1985
Rumbold, Dame Angela, 1991
Ryder of Wensum, Lord, 1990
Sainsbury, Sir Timothy, 1992
St John of Fawsley, Lord, 1979
Salisbury, Marquess of, 1994
Sandiford, Erskine, 1989
Saville of Newdigate, Lord, 1994
Scarman, Lord, 1973
Schiemann, Sir Konrad, 1995
Scott, Sir Nicholas, 1989
Scott of Foscote, Lord, 1991
Scotland of Asthal, Baroness, 2001
Seaga, Edward, 1981
Sedley, Sir Stephen, 1999
Selkirk of Douglas, Lord, 1996
Shearer, Hugh, 1969
Sheldon, Lord, 1977
Shephard, Gillian, 1992
Shipley, Jennifer, 1998
Short, Clare, 1997
Simmonds, Kennedy, 1984
Simon of Glaisdale, Lord, 1961
Sinclair, Ian, 1977
Slade, Sir Christopher, 1982
Slynn of Hadley, Lord, 1992
Smith, Andrew, 1997
Smith, Christopher, 1997
Smith, Dame Janet, 2002
Smith, Jacqueline, 2003
Somare, Sir Michael, 1977
Spellar, John, 2001
Stanley, Sir John, 1984
Staughton, Sir Christopher, 1988
Steel of Aikwood, Lord, 1977
Stephen, Sir Ninian, 1979
Stewartby, Lord, 1989
Steyn, Lord, 1992
Strang, Gavin, 1997
Strathclyde, Lord, 1995
Straw, Jack, 1997
Stuart-Smith, Sir Murray, 1988
Sutherland, Lord, 2000
Symons of Vernham Dean, Baroness, 2001

Talboys, Sir Brian, 1977
Taylor, Ann, 1997
Tebbit, Lord, 1981
Templeman, Lord, 1978
Thatcher, Baroness, 1970
Thomas, Edmund, 1996
Thomas of Gwydir, Lord, 1964
Thomas, Sir Swinton, 1994
Thomson of Monifieth, Lord, 1966
Thorpe, Jeremy, 1967
Thorpe, Sir Matthew, 1995
Tipping, Andrew, 1998
Tizard, Robert, 1986
Trefgarne, Lord, 1989
Trimble, David, 1997
Trumpington, Baroness, 1992
Tuckey, Sir Simon, 1998
Ullswater, Viscount, 1994
Upton, Simon, 1999
Varley, Lord, 1974
Waddington, Lord, 1987
Waite, Sir John, 1993
Wakeham, Lord, 1983
Waldegrave of North Hill, Lord, 1990
Walker of Doncaster, Lord, 1979
Walker of Gestingthorpe, Lord, 1997
Walker of Worcester, Lord, 1970
Wallace, James, 2000
Waller, Sir Mark, 1996
Ward, Sir Alan, 1995
Watkins, Sir Tasker, 1980
Weatherill, Lord, 1980
Wheeler, Sir John, 1993
Widdecombe, Ann, 1997
Wigley, Dafydd, 1997
Williams, Alan, 1977
Williams of Crosby, Baroness, 1974
Wilson, Brian, 2003
Windlesham, Lord, 1973
Winti, Paias, 1987
Withers, Reginald, 1977
Woodhouse, Sir Owen, 1974
Woolf, Lord, 1986
Wylie, *Hon.* Lord, 1970
York, The Archbishop of, 1991
Young, Sir George, 1993
Young of Graffham, Lord, 1984
Zacca, Edward, 1992

THE PRIVY COUNCIL OF NORTHERN IRELAND

The Privy Council of Northern Ireland had responsibilities in Northern Ireland similar to those of the Privy Council in Great Britain until the Northern Ireland Act 1974 instituted direct rule and a UK Cabinet minister became responsible for the functions previously exercised by the Northern Ireland government.

Membership of the Privy Council of Northern Ireland is retained for life. Since the Northern Ireland Constitution Act 1973 no further appointments have been made. The postnominal initials PC (NI) are used to differentiate its members from those of the Privy Council.

MEMBERS *as at August 2003*

Bailie, Robin, 1971
Bleakley, David, 1971
Craig, William, 1963

Dobson, John, 1969
Kelly, Sir Basil, 1969
Kirk, Herbert, 1962
Long, William, 1966
McIvor, Basil, 1971
Porter, Sir Robert, 1969
Taylor, John, MP, 1970
West, Henry, 1960

PARLIAMENT

The United Kingdom constitution is not contained in any single document but has evolved over time, formed partly by statute, partly by common law and partly by convention. A constitutional monarchy, the United Kingdom is governed by Ministers of the Crown in the name of the Sovereign, who is head both of the state and of the government.

The organs of government are the legislature (Parliament), the executive and the judiciary. The executive consists of HM Government (Cabinet and other Ministers), government departments, local authorities (*see* Local Government and Government Departments and Public Offices). The judiciary (*see* Law Courts and Offices section) pronounces on the law, both written and unwritten, interprets statutes and is responsible for the enforcement of the law; the judiciary is independent of both the legislature and the executive.

THE MONARCHY

The Sovereign personifies the state and is, in law, an integral part of the legislature, head of the executive, head of the judiciary, commander-in-chief of all armed forces of the Crown and 'Supreme Governor' of the Church of England. The seat of the monarchy is in the United Kingdom. In the Channel Islands and the Isle of Man, which are Crown dependencies, the Sovereign is represented by a Lieutenant-Governor. In the member states of the Commonwealth of which the Sovereign is head of state, her representative is a Governor-General; in UK dependencies the Sovereign is usually represented by a Governor, who is responsible to the British Government.

Although in practice the powers of the monarchy are now very limited, restricted mainly to the advisory and ceremonial, there are important acts of government which require the participation of the Sovereign. These include summoning, proroguing and dissolving Parliament, giving royal assent to bills passed by Parliament, appointing important office-holders, e.g. government ministers, judges, bishops and governors, conferring peerages, knighthoods and other honours, and granting pardon to a person wrongly convicted of a crime. The Sovereign appoints the Prime Minister; by convention this office is held by the leader of the political party which enjoys, or can secure, a majority of votes in the House of Commons. In international affairs the Sovereign as head of state has the power to declare war and make peace, to recognise foreign states and governments, to conclude treaties and to annex or cede territory. However, as the Sovereign entrusts executive power to Ministers of the Crown and acts on the advice of her Ministers, which she cannot ignore, royal prerogative powers are in practice exercised by Ministers, who are responsible to Parliament.

Ministerial responsibility does not diminish the Sovereign's importance to the smooth working of government. She holds meetings of the Privy Council (*see* below), gives audiences to her Ministers and other officials at home and overseas, receives accounts of Cabinet decisions, reads dispatches and signs state papers;

she must be informed and consulted on every aspect of national life; and she must show complete impartiality.

COUNSELLORS OF STATE

In the event of the Sovereign's absence abroad, it is necessary to appoint Counsellors of State under letters patent to carry out the chief functions of the Monarch, including the holding of Privy Councils and giving royal assent to acts passed by Parliament. The normal procedure is to appoint as Counsellors three or four members of the royal family among those remaining in the UK.

In the event of the Sovereign on accession being under the age of 18 years, or at any time unavailable or incapacitated by infirmity of mind or body for the performance of the royal functions, provision is made for a regency.

THE PRIVY COUNCIL

The Sovereign in Council, or Privy Council, was the chief source of executive power until the system of Cabinet government developed. Its main function is to advise the Sovereign to approve Orders in Council and to advise on the issue of royal proclamations. The Council's own statutory responsibilities (independent of the powers of the Sovereign in Council) include powers of supervision over the registering bodies for the medical and allied professions. A full Council is summoned only on the death of the Sovereign or when the Sovereign announces his or her intention to marry. (For a full list of Counsellors, *see* The Privy Council section.)

There are a number of advisory Privy Council committees, whose meetings the Sovereign does not attend. Some are prerogative committees, such as those dealing with legislative matters submitted by the legislatures of the Channel Islands and the Isle of Man or with applications for charters of incorporation; and some are provided for by statute, e.g. those for the universities of Oxford and Cambridge and the Scottish universities.

The Judicial Committee of the Privy Council is the court of final appeal from courts of the UK dependencies, courts of independent Commonwealth countries which have retained the right of appeal and courts of the Channel Islands and the Isle of Man.

It also has certain jurisdiction within the United Kingdom, the most important of which is that it is the court of final appeal for 'devolution issues,' i.e. issues as to the legal competences and functions of the legislative and executive authorities established in Scotland, Wales and Northern Ireland by the devolution legislation of 1998.

The Committee is composed of Privy Counsellors who hold, or have held, high judicial office, although usually only three or five hear each case.

Administrative work is carried out by the Privy Council Office under the direction of the President of the Council, a Cabinet Minister.

PARLIAMENT

Parliament is the supreme law-making authority and can legislate for the UK as a whole or for any parts of it separately (the Channel Islands and the Isle of Man are Crown dependencies and not part of the UK). The main functions of Parliament are to pass laws, to provide (by voting taxation) the means of carrying on the work of government and to scrutinise government policy and administration, particularly proposals for expenditure. International treaties and agreements are by custom presented to Parliament before ratification.

Parliament emerged during the late 13th and early 14th centuries. The officers of the King's household and the King's judges were the nucleus of early Parliaments, joined by such ecclesiastical and lay magnates as the King might summon to form a prototype 'House of Lords', and occasionally by the knights of the shires, burgesses and proctors of the lower clergy. By the end of Edward III's reign a 'House of Commons' was beginning to appear; the first known Speaker was elected in 1377.

Parliamentary procedure is based on custom and precedent, partly formulated in the Standing Orders of both Houses of Parliament, and each House has the right to control its own internal proceedings and to commit for contempt. The system of debate in the two Houses is similar; when a motion has been moved, the Speaker proposes the question as the subject of a debate. Members speak from wherever they have been sitting. Questions are decided by a vote on a simple majority. Draft legislation is introduced, in either House, as a bill. Bills can be introduced by a Government Minister or a private Member, but in practice the majority of bills which become law are introduced by the Government. To become law, a bill must be passed by each House (for parliamentary stages, see Bill, page 127) and then sent to the Sovereign for the royal assent, after which it becomes an Act of Parliament.

Proceedings of both Houses are public, except on extremely rare occasions. The minutes (called *Votes and Proceedings in the Commons*, and *Minutes of Proceedings in the Lords*) and the speeches (*The Official Report of Parliamentary Debates*, Hansard) are published daily. Proceedings are also recorded for transmission on radio and television and stored in the Parliamentary Recording Unit before transfer to the National Sound Archive. Television cameras have been allowed into the House of Lords since 1985 and into the House of Commons since 1989; committee meetings may also be televised.

By the Parliament Act of 1911, the maximum duration of a Parliament is five years (if not previously dissolved), the term being reckoned from the date given on the writs for the new Parliament. The maximum life has been prolonged by legislation in such rare circumstances as the two world wars (31 January 1911 to 25 November 1918; 26 November 1935 to 15 June 1945). Dissolution and writs for a general election are ordered by the Sovereign on the advice of the Prime Minister. The life of a Parliament is divided into sessions, usually of one year in length, beginning and ending most often in October or November.

DEVOLUTION

The Scottish Parliament has legislative power over all devolved matters, i.e. matters not reserved to Westminster or otherwise outside its powers. The National Assembly for Wales has power to make secondary legislation in the areas where executive functions have been transferred to it. The Northern Ireland Assembly has legislative authority in the fields previously administered by the Northern Ireland departments. The Assembly was suspended in October 2002 and dissolved in April 2003. For further information, see Regional Government section.

THE HOUSE OF LORDS

London SW1A 0PW
Tel: 020-7219 3000
Information Office: 020-7219 3107
Email: hlinfo@parliament.uk
Web: www.parliament.uk

The House of Lords is the second chamber, or 'Upper House' of the UK's bi-cameral parliament. Until the beginning of the twentieth century, the House of Lords had considerable power, being able to veto any bill submitted to it by the House of Commons. Today the main functions of the House of Lords are to revise legislation, to act as a check on the Government, to provide a forum of independent expertise and to act as a final court of appeal.

The House of Lords has a number of Select Committees. Some relate to the internal affairs of the House – such as its management and administration – while others carry out important investigative work on matters of public interest. There are four main areas of work – Europe, Science, the Economy and the Constitution. House of Lords investigative committees look at broader issues and do not mirror Government Departments as do Select Committees in the Commons.

The House of Lords has judicial powers as the ultimate Court of Appeal for courts in Great Britain and Northern Ireland, except for criminal cases in Scotland. These powers are exercised by the Lords of Appeal in Ordinary (the Law Lords) (see Law Courts and Officers section). On 12 June 2003 the Government announced reforms affecting the role of Lord Chancellor as a judge and Speaker of the House of Lords and establishing a separate Supreme Court (see Government Departments section).

Members of the House of Lords comprise life peers created under the Life Peerages Act 1958, 92 hereditary peers under the House of Lords Act 1999 and Lords of Appeal in Ordinary, i.e. Law Lords, under the Appellate Jurisdiction Act 1876. The Archbishops of Canterbury and York, the Bishops of London, Durham and Winchester, and the 21 senior diocesan bishops of the Church of England are also members.

The House of Lords Act provides for 90 elected hereditary peers to remain in the House of Lords until longer-term reform of the House has been carried out. (42 Conservative, 28 Cross-bench, three Liberal Democrat, two Labour.) Elections for each of the party groups and crossbenches were held in October and November 1999. Fifteen office holders were elected by the Whole House. Two Hereditary Peers, the Earl Marshal and the Lord Great Chamberlain are also members.

Peers are disqualified from sitting in the House if they are:
– aliens, i.e. any peer who is not a British citizen, a Commonwealth citizen (under the British Nationality Act 1981) or a citizen of the Republic of Ireland
– under the age of 21

- undischarged bankrupts or, in Scotland, those whose estate is sequestered
- convicted of treason

Bishops retire at the age of 70 and cease to be members of the house at that time.

Peers who do not wish to attend sittings of the House of Lords may apply for Leave of Absence for the duration of a Parliament.

Members of the House of Lords are unpaid but are entitled to allowances for attendance at sittings of the House. The daily maxima are £122.00 for overnight subsistence, £61.00 for day subsistence and incidental travel, and £51.00 for secretarial costs (as at June 2003).

COMPOSITION *as at 1 July 2003*
Archbishops and Bishops, 24
Life peers under the Appellate Jurisdiction Act 1876, 27
Life peers under the Life Peerages Act 1958, 544 (109 women)
Peers under the House of Lords Act 1999, 92 (4 women)
Total 687

STATE OF PARTIES *as at 1 July 2003**
Conservative, 211
Labour, 187
Liberal Democrats, 65
Cross-bench, 180
Archbishops and Bishops, 24
Other, 7
Total: 674
*Excluding 13 peers on leave of absence from the House

OFFICERS

The House is presided over by the Lord Chancellor, who is *ex officio* Speaker of the House. (On 12 June 2003 the the Government announced proposals to end the role of the Lord Chancellor as a judge and Speaker of the House of Lords, *see* description of Lord Chancellor's role below and Government Departments section).

A panel of deputy Speakers is appointed by Royal Commission. The first deputy Speaker is the Chairman of Committees, appointed at the beginning of each session, who is a salaried officer of the House. He takes the chair when the whole House is in Committee and in some select committees. He is assisted by a panel of deputy chairmen, headed by the salaried Principal Deputy Chairman of Committees, who is also chairman of the European Communities Committee of the House.

The Clerk of the Parliaments is the Accounting Officer and the chief permanent official responsible for the administration of the House. The Gentleman Usher of the Black Rod is responsible for security and other services and also has royal duties as secretary to the Lord Great Chamberlain.

Secretary of State for Constitutional Affairs and Lord Chancellor (£96,960), The Rt. Hon. Lord Falconer of Thoroton, QC
Private Secretary, Mrs S. Albon
Chairman of Committees (£75,706), The Lord Brabazon of Tara
Principal Deputy Chairman of Committees (£70,826), The Lord Grenfell

HOUSE OF LORDS MANAGEMENT BOARD
Staff are placed in the following pay bands according to their level of responsibility and taking account of other factors such as experience and marketability.

Judicial Group 4	£147,198
Senior Band 3	£89,085–£126,816
Senior Band 2	£72,316–£116,964
Senior Band 1A	£60,788–£98,099
Senior Band 1	£54,203–£87,408

Clerk of the Parliaments (Judicial Group 4), P. D. G. Hayter, LVO
Clerk Assistant, (Senior Band 3), M. G. Pownall
Reading Clerk and Clerk of the Journals (Senior Band 2), D. R. Beamish
Clerk of the Committees and Clerk of the Overseas Office (Senior Band 2), Dr R. H. Walters
Principal Finance Officer (Senior Band 1A), E. C. Ollard
Head of Human Resources (Senior Band 1A), Dr F. P. Tudor

DEPARTMENT OF THE GENTLEMAN USHER OF THE BLACK ROD
Gentleman Usher of the Black Rod and Serjeant-at-Arms (Senior Band 2), Lt.-Gen. Sir Michael Willcocks
Yeoman Usher of the Black Rod and Deputy Serjeant-at-Arms, Brig. H. D. C. Duncan, MBE

SELECT COMMITTEES
The main House of Lords select committees, as at October 2003, are as follows:
European Union – Chair, The Lord Grenfell;
  Clerk, S. Burton
European Union – Sub-committees:
  A *(Economic and Financial Affairs, Trade and External Relations) – Chair*, The Lord Radice; *Clerk*, J. Brooke
  B *(Energy, Industry and Transport) – Chair*, The Lord Woolmer of Leeds; *Clerk*, P. Wogan
  C *(Common Foreign and Security Policy) – Chair*, The Lord Jopling; *Clerk*, A. Nelson
  D *(Environment, Agriculture, Public Health and Consumer Protection) – Chair*, The Earl of Selborne; *Clerk*, N. Besly
  E *(Law and Institutions) – Chair*, The Lord Scott of Foscote; *Clerk*, S. Todd
  F *(Social Affairs, Education and Home Affairs) – Chair*, The Baroness Harris of Richmond; *Clerk*, T. Rawsthorne
Constitution Committee – Chair, The Lord Norton of Louth; *Clerk*, I. Mackley
Delegated Powers and Regulatory Reform – Chair, The Lord Dahrendorf; *Clerk*, C. Salmon
Economic Affairs – Chair, The Lord Peston; *Clerk*, S. Michell
Science and Technology – Chair, The Lord Oxburgh, FRCOG; *Clerk*, Dr C. S. Johnson
  I – *Chair*, The Lord Mitchell; *Clerk*, R. Neal
  II – *Chair*, The Lord Oxburgh; *Clerk*, Dr C. S. Johnson
Human Rights Joint Committee – Chair, Jean Corston, MP; *Lords Clerk*, I. Mackley
House of Lords Reform Joint Committee – Chair, Dr Jack Cunningham, MP; *Lords Clerk*, D. Beamish

THE HOUSE OF COMMONS
London SW1A 0AA
Tel: 020-7219 3000
Information Office: Tel: 020-7219 4272
Forthcoming business: Tel: 020-7219 5532
Email: hcinfo@parliament.uk
Web: www.parliament.uk

The members of the House of Commons are elected by universal adult suffrage. For electoral purposes, the United Kingdom is divided into constituencies, each of which returns one member to the House of Commons, the member being the candidate who obtains the largest number of votes cast in the constituency. To ensure equitable representation, the four Boundary Commissions keep constituency boundaries under review and recommend any redistribution of seats which may seem necessary because of population movements, etc. The number of seats was raised to 640 in 1945, reduced to 625 in 1948, and subsequently rose to 630 in 1955, 635 in 1970, 650 in 1983, 651 in 1992 and 659 in 1997. Of the present 659 seats, there are 529 for England, 40 for Wales, 72 for Scotland and 18 for Northern Ireland. The number of Scottish MPs at Westminster is likely to be cut by approximately 12 by 2007.

An electoral reform commission headed by Lord Jenkins of Hillhead proposed in October 1998 that the 'first-past-the-post' system of electing members of the House of Commons should be replaced by an alternative vote top-up system, under which 80–85 per cent of MPs would be elected by an alternative vote method and the remaining 15–20 per cent by approximately an open-list system of proportional representation.

ELECTIONS

Elections are by secret ballot, each elector casting one vote; voting is not compulsory. For entitlement to vote in parliamentary elections, *see* Legal Notes section. When a seat becomes vacant between general elections, a by-election is held.

British subjects and citizens of the Irish Republic can stand for election as Members of Parliament (MPs) provided they are 21 or over and not subject to disqualification. Those disqualified from sitting in the House include:
– undischarged bankrupts
– people sentenced to more than one year's imprisonment
– members of the House of Lords (but hereditary peers not sitting in the Lords are eligible)
– holders of certain offices listed in the House of Commons Disqualification Act 1975, e.g. members of the judiciary, Civil Service, regular armed forces, police forces, some local government officers and some members of public corporations and government commissions.

A candidate does not require any party backing but his or her nomination for election must be supported by the signatures of ten people registered in the constituency. A candidate must also deposit with the returning officer £500, which is forfeit if the candidate does not receive more than 5 per cent of the votes cast. All election expenses at a general election, except the candidate's personal expenses, are subject to a statutory limit of £5,483, plus 4.6 pence for each elector in a borough constituency or 6.2 pence for each elector in a county constituency. These figures are due to be updated before the next General Election.

See pages 133–177 for an alphabetical list of MPs, results of the last general election and results of by-elections since the general election.

STATE OF PARTIES *as at 24 September 2003*
Conservative, 163 (14 women)
Labour, 409 (94 women)

Liberal Democrats, 54 (6 women)
Plaid Cymru, 4
Scottish Nationalist, 5 (1 woman)
Sinn Fein (have not taken their seats), 4 (1 woman)
Social Democratic Labour, 3
Democratic Unionist Party, 5 (1 woman)
Ulster Unionist, 3 (1 woman)
Independent Unionist, 3
Independent (Dr Richard Taylor-Wyre Forest), 1
Independent Conservative (Mr Andrew Hunter), 1
The Speaker and three Deputy Speakers, 4
Total, 658 (118 women)

BUSINESS

The week's business of the House is outlined each Thursday by the Leader of the House, after consultation between the Chief Government Whip and the Chief Opposition Whip. A quarter to a third of the time will be taken up by the Government's legislative programme and the rest by other business. As a rule, bills likely to raise political controversy are introduced in the Commons before going on to the Lords, and the Commons claims exclusive control in respect of national taxation and expenditure. Bills such as the Finance Bill, which imposes taxation, and the Consolidated Fund Bills, which authorise expenditure, must begin in the Commons. A bill of which the financial provisions are subsidiary may begin in the Lords; and the Commons may waive its rights in regard to Lords' amendments affecting finance.

The Commons has a public register of MPs' financial and certain other interests; this is published annually as a House of Commons paper. Members must also disclose any relevant financial interest or benefit in a matter before the House when taking part in a debate, in certain other proceedings of the House, or in consultations with other MPs, with Ministers or with civil servants.

MEMBERS' PAY AND ALLOWANCES

Since 1911 members of the House of Commons have received salary payments; facilities for free travel were introduced in 1924. Annual salary rates since 1911 are as follows:

1911	£400	1985 Jan	£16,904
1931	360	1986 Jan	17,702
1934	380	1987 Jan	18,500
1935	400	1988 Jan	22,548
1937	600	1989 Jan	24,107
1946	1,000	1990 Jan	26,701
1954	1,250	1991 Jan	28,970
1957	1,750	1992 Jan	30,854
1964	3,250	1994 Jan	31,687
1972 Jan	4,500	1995 Jan	33,189
1975 June	5,750	1996 Jan	34,085
1976 June	6,062	1996 July	43,000
1977 July	6,270	1997 April	43,860
1978 June	6,897	1998 April	45,066
1979 June	9,450	1999 April	47,008
1980 June	11,750	2000 April	48,371
1981 June	13,950	2001 April	49,822
1982 June	14,510	2002 April	55,118
1983 June	15,308	2003 April	56,358
1984 Jan	16,106		

In 1969 MPs were granted an allowance for secretarial and research expenses, revised in July 2001. From April 2003 Members receive an Incidental Expenses Provision

(£18,799) and a staffing allowance (between £64,273 and £74,985).

Since 1972 MPs have been able to claim reimbursement for the additional cost of staying overnight away from their main residence while on parliamentary business; this is known as the Additional Costs Allowance and from April 2003 is £20,333 a year.

Members of staff who are paid out of the allowances can benefit from a sum not exceeding 10 per cent of their gross salary which is paid into a pension scheme of their choice. This sum comes from a central budget.

MEMBERS' PENSIONS

Pension arrangements for MPs were first introduced in 1964. The arrangements currently provide a pension of one-fiftieth of salary for each year of pensionable service with a maximum of two-thirds of salary at age 65. Pension is payable normally at age 65, for men and women, or on later retirement. Pensions may be paid earlier, e.g. on retirement due to ill health or at age 60 after 20 years' service. The widow/widower of a former MP receives a pension of five-eighths of the late MP's pension. Pensions are index-linked. Members currently contribute six per cent of salary to the pension fund; there is an Exchequer contribution, currently slightly more than the amount contributed by MPs.

The House of Commons Members' Fund provides for annual or lump sum grants to ex-MPs, their widows or widowers, and children whose incomes are below certain limits or who are experiencing severe hardship. Members contribute £24 a year and the Exchequer £215,000 a year to the fund.

OFFICERS AND OFFICIALS

The House of Commons is presided over by the Speaker, who has considerable powers to maintain order in the House. A deputy Speaker, called the Chairman of Ways and Means, and two Deputy Chairmen may preside over sittings of the House of Commons; they are elected by the House, and, like the Speaker, neither speak nor vote other than in their official capacity.

The staff of the House are employed by a Commission chaired by the Speaker. The heads of the six House of Commons departments are permanent officers of the House, not MPs. The Clerk of the House is the principal adviser to the Speaker on the privileges and procedures of the House, the conduct of the business of the House, and committees. The Serjeant-at-Arms is responsible for security, ceremonial, and for accommodation in the Commons part of the Palace of Westminster.

Speaker (£127,791), The Rt. Hon. Michael J. Martin, MP (Glasgow Springburn)
Chairman of Ways and Means (£93,413), Sir Alan Haselhurst, MP (Saffron Walden)
First Deputy Chairman of Ways and Means (£88,925), Sylvia Heal, MP (Halesowen and Rowley Regis)
Second Deputy Chairman of Ways and Means (£88,925), Sir Michael Lord, MP (Suffolk Central and Ipswich North)

OFFICES OF THE SPEAKER AND CHAIRMAN OF WAYS AND MEANS

Speaker's Secretary (£60,788–£98,099), Sir Nicolas Bevan, CB
Chaplain to the Speaker, Revd Canon R. Wright
Secretary to the Chairman of Ways and Means (£34,979–£50,770), M. Hennessy

DEPARTMENT OF THE CLERK OF THE HOUSE

Clerk of the House of Commons (£143,258), R. B. Sands
Clerk Assistant (£89,085–£126,816), D. G. Millar
Clerk of Committees (£89,085–£126,816), G. Cubie
Clerk of Legislation (£89,085–£126,816), Dr M. R. Jack
Principal Clerks (£72,316–£116,964)
  Table Office, Ms H. E. Irwin
  Journals, W. A. Proctor
Principal Clerks (£60,788–£98,099)
  Overseas Office, J. Boyce Sharpe
  Bills, F. A. Cranmer
  Select Committees, R. W. G. Wilson; D. L. Natzler; D. W. N. Doig
  Delegated Legislation, L. C. Laurence Smyth
Deputy Principal Clerks (£52,403–£87,408), Ms A. Barry; Dr C. R. M. Ward; A. Sandall; A. R. Kennon; S. J. Patrick; D. J. Gerhold; C. J. Poyser; D. F. Harrison; S. J. Priestley; A. H. Doherty; P. A. Evans; R. I. S. Phillips; Dr R. G. James; D. R. Lloyd; B. M. Hutton; J. S. Benger, D.Phil.; Ms E. C. Samson; N. P. Walker; Mrs E. J. Flood; C. G. Lee; C. D. Stanton; Miss L. M. Gardner; F. J. Reid; C. A. Shaw; P. G. Moon; T. W. P. Healey; G. R. Devine; Mrs S. A. R. Davies; Mrs J. N. St J. Mulley; M. Hennessy; P. Aylett
Senior Clerks (£34,979–£50,770), M. Clark; J. D. Whatley; K. C. Fox; J. D. W. Rhys; Mrs E. S. Hunt; Miss S. McGlashen; Mrs C. Oxborough; T. Goldsmith; H. A. Yardley; Ms K. Emms; N. P. Wright; M. Hillyard; J. H. Davies; M. P. Atkins; Ms J. S. Fox; S. Mark; T. Jarvis; G. K. Clarke; G. F. J. Farrar; J. Patterson; C. Porro; S. T. Fiander (acting); D. H. Griffiths (acting); Ms R. Melling, CBE (acting); D. Lees; A. Kidner; T. Byrne
Examiners of Petitions for Private Bills, F. A. Cranmer; Dr F. P. Tudor
Registrar of Members' Interests (£53,534–£87,598), Ms A. Barry
Taxing Officer, F. A. Cranmer

VOTE OFFICE

Deliverer of the Vote (£52,403–£87,408), J. F. Collins
Deputy Deliverers of the Vote (£34,979–£50,770), O. B. T. Sweeney *(Parliamentary)*; F. W. Hallett *(Production)*; R. Brook *(Development)*

LEGAL SERVICES OFFICE

Speaker's Counsel and Head of Legal Services Office (£72,316–£116,964), J. E. G. Vaux
Counsel for European Legislation (£60,788–£98,099), M. Carpenter
Counsel for Legislation, A. D. Preston
Assistant Counsel (£52,403–£87,408), A. Akbar; P. Brooksbank

DEPARTMENT OF THE SERJEANT-AT-ARMS

Serjeant-at-Arms (£72,316–£116,964), M. J. A. Cummins
Deputy Serjeant-at-Arms (£60,788–£98,099), R. M. Morton
Assistant Serjeants-at-Arms (£44,456–£61,557), P. A. J. Wright; J. M. Robertson; M. Harvey

DEPARTMENT OF THE LIBRARY

Librarian (£72,316–£116,964), Miss P. J. Baines
Directors (£52,403–£87,408), K. G. Cuninghame; R. Clements; Miss E. M. McInnes; B. Twigger
Heads of Sections (£44,456–£61,557), Dr C. Pond; Mrs C. Andrews; Mrs J. Lourie; C. Barclay; Mrs C. Gillie; Ms P. J. Strickland; R. Cracknell; S. A. Wise; Dr P. Richards

Senior Library Clerks (£34,979–£50,770), Ms F. Poole;
T. Edmonds; Dr D. Gore; Mrs H. Holden;
Mrs P. Carling; Miss V. Miller; Ms J. Roll;
Ms W. Wilson; Dr P. Bowers; A. Seely; Mrs J. Hough;
G. Danby; Mrs L. Conway; C. Blair; C. Sear; K. Parry;
Dr A. Sleator; Mrs B. Brevitt; Mrs D. Clark; T. Youngs;
Dr S. McGinness; S. Kennedy; T. Jarrett;
Ms R. Winstone; Ms S. Broadbridge;
Mrs G. Garton Grimwood; Mrs S. L. Meagher

DEPARTMENT OF FINANCE AND ADMINISTRATION
Director of Finance and Administration
(£72,316–£116,964), A. J. Walker
Director of Operations (£60,788–£98,099),
A. A. Cameron
Director of Personnel Policy (£52,403–£87,408)
Ms S. Craig
Director of Finance Policy (£52,403–£87,408), C. Ridley
Director of Internal Review Services (£44,456–£61,557),
R. Russell

DEPARTMENT OF THE OFFICIAL REPORT
Editor, W. G. Garland (£60,788–£98,099)
Deputy Editors (£52,403–£87,408), V. A. Widgery;
Miss L. Sutherland; Ms C. Fogarty

REFRESHMENT DEPARTMENT
Director of Catering Services (£68,788–£98,099),
Mrs S. Harrison
Catering Operations Manager (Outbuildings)
(£34,979–£50,770), Ms D. Herd
Food and Beverage Operations Manager, R. Gibbs
Executive Chef (£34,979–£50,770), D. Dorricott
Finance and Administration Manager (£34,797–£50,770),
Mrs J. Rissen
Retail Manager (£34,979–£57,770), Mrs M. DeSouza

SELECT COMMITTEES
The more significant committees, as at July 2003, are:

DEPARTMENTAL COMMITTEES
Accommodation and Works – Chair, Derek Conway, MP;
Clerk, Tom Goldsmith
Administration – Chair, Mrs M. Roe;
Clerk, Tom Goldsmith
Culture, Media and Sport – Chair, Rt. Hon. Gerald
Kaufman, MP; *Clerks*, Fergus Reid; Olivia Davidson
Defence – Chair, Rt. Hon. Bruce George, MP;
Clerks, Steven Mark; Mark Hutton
Education and Skills – Chair, Barry Sheerman, MP,
Clerks, David Lloyd; Annabel Jones
Environment, Food and Rural Affairs – Chair,
Rt. Hon. David Curry, MP; *Clerks*, Miss Kate Emms;
Gavin Devine
Foreign Affairs – Chair, Rt. Hon. Donald Anderson, MP;
Clerks, Steve Priestley; Geoffrey Farrar
Health – Chair, David Hinchliffe, MP; *Clerks*,
Dr John Benger; Jenny McCullough
Home Affairs – Chair, Chris Mullin; MP; *Clerks*,
Dr Robin James; Ms Sarah Ioannou
International Development – Chair, Tony Baldry, MP;
Clerks, Alistair Doherty; Sarah Hartwell
Northern Ireland – Chair, Michael Mates, MP; *Clerk*,
Elizabeth Hunt
*Office of the Deputy Prime Minister: Housing, Planning,
Local Government and the Regions* – Chair,
Andrew Bennett, MP; *Clerk*, Dr David Harrison

Scottish Affairs – Chair, Mrs I. Adams; *Clerk*,
John Whatley
Trade and Industry – Chair, Martin O'Neill, MP; *Clerks*,
Mrs Elizabeth Flood; David Lees
Transport – Chair, Hon. Gwyneth Dunwoody, MP; *Clerks*,
Martyn Atkins; Eve Samson
Treasury – Chair, Rt. Hon. John McFall, MP; *Clerks*,
Crispin Poyser; Alex Kidner
Urban Affairs sub committee: – Chair, Clive Betts, MP;
Clerks, David Harrison; Libby Preston
Welsh Affairs – Chair, Martyn Jones, MP; *Clerk*,
James Davies
Work and Pensions – Chair, Archy Kirkwood, MP; *Clerks*,
Phillip Moon; Mick Hillyard

NON-DEPARTMENTAL COMMITTEES
Draft Corruption Bill (Joint Committee) – Chair,
Lord Slynn of Hadley; *Clerks*, Andrew Kennon;
Mary Robinson
Environmental Audit – Chair, John Horam, MP; *Clerk*,
Jessica Mulley
European Scrutiny – Chair, Jimmy Hood, MP; *Clerk*,
Dorian Gerhold; Jane Fox
Finance and Services – Chair, Stuart Bell; *Clerk*,
Robert Rogers
House of Lords Reform (Joint Committee) – *Clerks*,
Malcolm Jack; David Beamish
Human Rights (Joint Committee) – Chair, Jean Corston;
Clerks, Paul Evans; Thomas Elias
Intelligence and Security (Cabinet Office) – Chair,
Rt. Hon. Ann Taylor; *Clerks*, Alistair Corbett;
Mr Sterling
Modernisation of the House of Commons – Chair,
Rt. Hon. Peter Hain, MP; *Clerks*, George Cubie;
Tom Healey
Procedure – Chair, Nicholas Winterton, MP; *Clerks*,
Simon Patrick; Charlotte Littleboy
Public Accounts – Chair, Edward Leigh, MP; *Clerk*,
Nick Wright
Public Administration – Chair, Tony Wright, MP; *Clerk*,
Phillip Aylett
Regulatory Reform – Chair, Peter Pike, MP; *Clerk*,
Huw Yardley
Science and Technology – Chair, Dr Ian Gibson; *Clerks*,
Chris Shaw; Nerys Wellfoot
Selection – Chair, John McWilliam, MP; *Clerk*, Mark Egan
Statutory Instruments (Joint Committee) – Chair,
David Tredinnick, MP; *Clerks*, Huw Yardley;
Ms Chloe Mawson

PARLIAMENTARY INFORMATION

The following is a short glossary of aspects of the work
of Parliament. Unless otherwise stated, references are to
House of Commons procedures.

BILL – Proposed legislation is termed a bill. The stages
of a public bill (for private bills, *see* page 128) in the
House of Commons are as follows:
First Reading: This stage merely constitutes an order to
have the bill printed.
Second Reading: Debate on the principles of the bill.
Committee Stage: The detailed examination of a bill,
clause by clause. In most cases this takes place in a
standing committee, or the whole House may act as a
committee. A special standing committee may take
evidence before embarking on detailed scrutiny of the
bill. Very rarely, a bill may be examined by a select
committee.

Report Stage: Detailed review of a bill as amended in committee.

Third Reading: Final debate on a bill. Public bills go through the same stages in the House of Lords, except that in almost all cases the committee stage is taken in committee of the whole House.

A bill may start in either House, and has to pass through both Houses to become law. Both Houses have to agree the same text of a bill, so that the amendments made by the second House are then considered in the originating House, and if not agreed, sent back or themselves amended, until agreement is reached.

CHILTERN HUNDREDS – A nominal office of profit under the Crown, the acceptance of which requires an MP to vacate his/her seat. The Manor of Northstead is similar. These are the only means by which an MP may resign.

CONSOLIDATED FUND BILL – A bill to authorise issue of money to maintain Government services. The bill is dealt with without debate.

EARLY DAY MOTION – A motion put on the notice paper by an MP without in general the real prospect of its being debated. Such motions are expressions of back-bench opinion.

FATHER OF THE HOUSE – The Member whose continuous service in the House of Commons is the longest. The present Father of the House is the Rt. Hon. Tam Dalyell.

HOURS OF MEETING – The House of Commons normally meets on Tuesdays, Wednesdays and Thursdays at 11.30 a.m., Mondays at 2.30 p.m. and some Fridays at 9.30 a.m. There are ten Fridays without sittings in each session. (*See* also Westminster Hall Sittings, below). The House of Lords normally meets at 2.30 p.m. Monday to Wednesday and at 3 p.m. on Thursday. In the latter part of the session, the House of Lords sometimes sits on Fridays at 11 a.m.

LEADER OF THE OPPOSITION – In 1937 the office of Leader of the Opposition was recognised and a salary was assigned to the post. Since April 2003 this has been £121,840 (including parliamentary salary of £56,358). The present leader of the Opposition is Iain Duncan Smith.

THE LORD CHANCELLOR – The Lord High Chancellor of Great Britain is *(ex officio)* the Speaker of the House of Lords. Unlike the Speaker of the House of Commons, he is a member of the Government, takes part in debates and votes in divisions. He has none of the powers to maintain order that the Speaker in the Commons has, these powers being exercised in the Lords by the House as a whole. The Lord Chancellor sits in the Lords on one of the Woolsacks, couches covered with red cloth and stuffed with wool. If he wishes to address the House in any way except formally as Speaker, he leaves the Woolsack.

On 12 June 2003 the Prime Minister announced the creation of the Department for Constitutional Affairs, which will incorporate most of the responsibilities of the Lord Chancellor's department. The post of Lord Chancellor and the Department of the Lord Chancellor will eventually be abolished. Other changes announced include the replacement of the law lords by a Supreme Court as the final court of appeal, and the creation of a new Judicial Appointments Commission.

The current Lord Chancellor is Lord Falconer of Thoroton who will continue in the post until his powers are transferred to his new post of Secretary of State for Constitutional Affairs. Lord Falconer currently operates as a conventional Cabinet Minister and head of department, and is located together with his permanent secretary and departmental officials in the offices of the Lord Chancellor's department.

For further information on the new Department for Constitutional Affairs *see* Government section.

NORTHERN IRELAND GRAND COMMITTEE – The Northern Ireland Grand Committee consists of all MPs representing constituencies in Northern Ireland, together with not more than 25 other MPs nominated by the Committee of Selection. The business of the committee includes questions, short debates, ministerial statements, bills, legislative proposals and other matters relating exclusively to Northern Ireland, and delegated legislation.

The Northern Ireland Affairs Committee is one of the departmental select committees, empowered to examine the expenditure, administration and policy of the Northern Ireland Office and the administration and expenditure of the Crown Solicitor's Office.

OPPOSITION DAY – A day on which the topic for debate is chosen by the Opposition. There are 20 such days in a normal session. On 17 days, subjects are chosen by the Leader of the Opposition; on the remaining three days by the leader of the next largest opposition party.

PARLIAMENT ACTS 1911 AND 1949 – Under these Acts, bills may become law without the consent of the Lords, though the House of Lords has the power to delay a public bill for 13 months from its first second reading in the House of Commons.

PRIME MINISTER'S QUESTIONS – The Prime Minister answers questions from 12.00 to 12.30 p.m. on Wednesdays.

PRIVATE BILL – A bill promoted by a body or an individual to give powers additional to, or in conflict with, the general law, and to which a special procedure applies to enable people affected to object.

PRIVATE MEMBER'S BILL – A public bill promoted by a Member who is not a member of the Government.

PRIVATE NOTICE QUESTION – A question adjudged of urgent importance on submission to the Speaker (in the Lords, the Leader of the House), answered at the end of oral questions, usually at 3.30 p.m.

PRIVILEGE – The following are covered by the privilege of Parliament:
(i) freedom from interference in going to, attending at, and going from, Parliament
(ii) freedom of speech in parliamentary proceedings
(iii) the printing and publishing of anything relating to the proceedings of the two Houses is subject to privilege
(iv) each House is the guardian of its dignity and may punish any insult to the House as a whole

QUESTION TIME – Oral questions are answered by Ministers in the Commons from 2.30 to 3.30 p.m. Monday to Wednesday and 11.30 a.m. to 12.30 p.m. on Thursdays. Questions are also taken at the start of the Lords sittings, with a daily limit of four oral questions.

ROYAL ASSENT – The royal assent is signified by letters patent to such bills and measures as have passed both Houses of Parliament (or bills which have been passed under the Parliament Acts 1911 and 1949). The Sovereign has not given royal assent in person since 1854. On occasion, for instance in the prorogation of Parliament, royal assent may be pronounced to the two Houses by Lords Commissioners. More usually royal assent is notified to each House sitting separately in accordance with the Royal Assent Act 1967. The old

French formulae for royal assent are then endorsed on the acts by the Clerk of the Parliaments.

The power to withhold assent resides with the Sovereign but has not been exercised in the UK since 1707.

SELECT COMMITTEES – Consisting usually of ten to fifteen members of all parties, select committees are a means used by both Houses in order to investigate certain matters.

Most select committees in the House of Commons are tied to departments: each committee investigates subjects within a government department's remit. There are other select committees dealing with public accounts (i.e. the spending by the Government of money voted by Parliament) and European legislation, and also domestic committees dealing, for example, with privilege and procedure. Major select committees usually take evidence in public; their evidence and reports are published by The Stationery Office. House of Commons select committees are reconstituted after a general election. For main committees, *see* page127.

The principal select committee in the House of Lords is that on the European Communities, which has, at present, six sub-committees dealing with all areas of Community policy. The House of Lords also has a select committee on science and technology, which appoints sub-committees to deal with specific subjects, and a select committee on delegated powers and deregulation. For committees, *see* page 124. In addition, *ad hoc* select committees have been set up from time to time to investigate specific subjects. There are also some joint committees of the two Houses, e.g. the committees on statutory instruments and on parliamentary privilege.

THE SPEAKER – The Speaker of the House of Commons is the spokesman and chairman of the Chamber. He or she is elected by the House at the beginning of each Parliament or when the previous Speaker retires or dies. The Speaker neither speaks in debates nor votes in divisions except when the voting is equal.

VACANT SEATS – When a vacancy occurs in the House of Commons during a session of Parliament, the writ for the by-election is moved by a Whip of the party to which the member whose seat has been vacated belonged. If the House is in recess, the Speaker can issue a warrant for a writ, should two members certify to him that a seat is vacant.

WELSH AFFAIRS COMMITTEE – The Welsh Affairs Committee, one of the departmental select committees, was empowered to examine the expenditure, administration and policy of the Welsh Office. Following devolution, the role of the select committee has been questioned. If it continues, it will be concerned with the role and responsibilities of the relevant Secretary of State and on occasion the policy of the UK departments as it affects Wales.

WESTMINSTER HALL SITTINGS – Following a report by the Modernisation of the House of Commons Select Committee, the Commons decided in May 1999 to set up a second debating forum. It is known as 'Westminster Hall' and sittings are in the Grand Committee Room on Tuesdays from 10 a.m. to 1 p.m., Wednesdays from 9.30 a.m. to 2 p.m. and Thursdays from 2.30 p.m. for up to three hours. Sittings will be open to the public at the times indicated.

WHIPS – In order to secure the attendance of Members of a particular party in Parliament, particularly on the occasion of an important vote, Whips (originally known as 'Whippers-in') are appointed. The written appeal or circular letter issued by them is also known as a 'whip', its urgency being denoted by the number of times it is underlined. Failure to respond to a three-line whip is tantamount in the Commons to secession (at any rate temporarily) from the party. Whips are provided with office accommodation in both Houses, and Government and some Opposition Whips receive salaries from public funds.

PARLIAMENTARY EDUCATION UNIT – Norman Shaw Building (North), London SW1A 2TT
Tel: 020-7219 2105
Email: edunit@parliament.uk
Web: www.explore.parliament.uk

GOVERNMENT OFFICE

The Government is the body of Ministers responsible for the administration of national affairs, determining policy and introducing into Parliament any legislation necessary to give effect to government policy. The majority of Ministers are members of the House of Commons but members of the House of Lords or of neither House may also hold ministerial responsibility. The Lord Chancellor is always a member of the House of Lords. The Prime Minister is, by current convention, always a member of the House of Commons.

THE PRIME MINISTER

The office of Prime Minister, which had been in existence for nearly 200 years, was officially recognised in 1905 and its holder was granted a place in the table of precedence. The Prime Minister, by tradition also First Lord of the Treasury and Minister for the Civil Service, is appointed by the Sovereign and is usually the leader of the party which enjoys, or can secure, a majority in the House of Commons. Other Ministers are appointed by the Sovereign on the recommendation of the Prime Minister, who also allocates functions amongst Ministers and has the power to obtain their resignation or dismissal individually.

The Prime Minister informs the Sovereign of state and political matters, advises on the dissolution of Parliament, and makes recommendations for important Crown appointments, the award of honours, etc.

As the chairman of Cabinet meetings and leader of a political party, the Prime Minister is responsible for translating party policy into government activity. As leader of the Government, the Prime Minister is responsible to Parliament and to the electorate for the policies and their implementation.

The Prime Minister also represents the nation in international affairs, e.g. summit conferences.

THE CABINET

The Cabinet developed during the 18th century as an inner committee of the Privy Council, which was the chief source of executive power until that time. The Cabinet is composed of about 20 Ministers chosen by the Prime Minister, usually the heads of government departments (generally known as Secretaries of State unless they have a special title, e.g. Chancellor of the Exchequer), the leaders of the two Houses of Parliament, and the holders of various traditional offices.

The Cabinet's functions are the final determination of policy, control of government and co-ordination of government departments. The exercise of its functions is dependent upon enjoying majority support in the House of Commons. Cabinet meetings are held in private, taking place once or twice a week during parliamentary sittings and less often during a recess. Proceedings are confidential, the members being bound by their oath as Privy Counsellors not to disclose information about the proceedings.

The convention of collective responsibility means that the Cabinet acts unanimously even when Cabinet Ministers do not all agree on a subject. The policies of departmental Ministers must be consistent with the policies of the Government as a whole, and once the Government's policy has been decided, each Minister is expected to support it or resign.

The convention of ministerial responsibility holds a Minister, as the political head of his or her department, accountable to Parliament for the department's work. Departmental Ministers usually decide all matters within their responsibility, although on matters of political importance they normally consult their colleagues collectively. A decision by a departmental Minister is binding on the Government as a whole.

POLITICAL PARTIES

Before the reign of William and Mary the principal officers of state were chosen by and were responsible to the Sovereign alone and not to Parliament or the nation at large. Such officers acted sometimes in concert with one another but more often independently, and the fall of one did not, of necessity, involve that of others, although all were liable to be dismissed at any moment.

In 1693 the Earl of Sunderland recommended to William III the advisability of selecting a ministry from the political party which enjoyed a majority in the House of Commons and the first united ministry was drawn in 1696 from the Whigs, to which party the King owed his throne. This group became known as the Junto and was regarded with suspicion as a novelty in the political life of the nation, being a small section meeting in secret apart from the main body of Ministers. It may be regarded as the forerunner of the Cabinet and in the course of time it led to the establishment of the principle of joint responsibility of Ministers, so that internal disagreement caused a change of personnel or resignation of the whole body of Ministers.

The accession of George I, who was unfamiliar with the English language, led to a disinclination on the part of the Sovereign to preside at meetings of his Ministers and caused the appearance of a Prime Minister, a position first acquired by Robert Walpole in 1721 and retained by him without interruption for 20 years and 326 days.

DEVELOPMENT OF PARTIES
In 1828 the Whigs became known as Liberals, a name originally given to it by its opponents to imply laxity of principles, but gradually accepted by the party to indicate its claim to be pioneers and champions of political reform and progressive legislation. In 1861 a Liberal Registration Association was founded and Liberal Associations became widespread. In 1877 a National Liberal Federation was formed, with headquarters in London. The Liberal Party was in power for long periods during the second half of the 19th-century and for several years during the first quarter of the 20th-century, but after a split in the party the numbers elected were small from 1931. In 1988, a majority of the Liberals agreed on a merger with the Social Democratic Party under the title Social and Liberal Democrats; since 1989

they have been known as the Liberal Democrats. A minority continue separately as the Liberal Party.

Soon after the change from Whig to Liberal the Tory Party became known as Conservative, a name believed to have been invented by John Wilson Croker in 1830 and to have been generally adopted about the time of the passing of the Reform Act of 1832 to indicate that the preservation of national institutions was the leading principle of the party. After the Home Rule crisis of 1886 the dissentient Liberals entered into a compact with the Conservatives, under which the latter undertook not to contest their seats, but a separate Liberal Unionist organisation was maintained until 1912, when it was united with the Conservatives.

Labour candidates for Parliament made their first appearance at the general election of 1892, when there were 27 standing as Labour or Liberal-Labour. In 1900 the Labour Representation Committee was set up in order to establish a distinct Labour group in Parliament, with its own whips, its own policy, and a readiness to co-operate with any party which might be engaged in promoting legislation in the direct interest of labour. In 1906 the LRC became known as the Labour Party.

The Council for Social Democracy was announced by four former Labour Cabinet Ministers in January 1981 and in March 1981 the Social Democratic Party was launched. Later that year the SDP and the Liberal Party formed an electoral alliance. In 1988 a majority of SDP agreed on a merger with the Liberal Party but a minority continued as a separate party under the SDP title. In 1990 it was decided to wind up the party organisation and its three sitting MPs were known as independent social democrats. None were returned at the 1992 general election.

Plaid Cymru was founded in 1926 to provide an independent political voice for Wales and to campaign for self-government in Wales.

The Scottish National Party was founded in 1934 to campaign for independence for Scotland.

The Social Democratic and Labour Party was founded in 1970, emerging from the civil rights movement of the 1960s, with the aim of promoting reform, reconciliation and partnership across the sectarian divide in Northern Ireland and of opposing violence from any quarter.

The Democratic Unionist Party was founded in 1971 to resist moves by the Ulster Unionist Party which were considered a threat to the Union. Its aim is to maintain Northern Ireland as an integral part of the UK.

The Ulster Unionist Council first met formally in 1905. Its objectives are to maintain Northern Ireland as an integral part of the UK and to promote the aims of the Ulster Unionist Party.

GOVERNMENT AND OPPOSITION
The government of the day is formed by the party which wins the largest number of seats in the House of Commons at a general election, or which has the support of a majority of members in the House of Commons. By tradition, the leader of the majority party is asked by the Sovereign to form a government, while the largest minority party becomes the official Opposition with its own leader and a 'Shadow Cabinet.' Leaders of the Government and Opposition sit on the front benches of the Commons with their supporters (the back-benchers) sitting behind them.

FINANCIAL SUPPORT

Financial support for Opposition parties in the House of Commons was introduced in 1975 and is commonly known as Short Money, after Edward Short, the Leader of the House at that time, who introduced the scheme. Short money allocation for 2003–4 is:

Conservative	£3,566,927.49
Liberal Democrats	1,210,901.83
Plaid Cymru	72,067.46
SNP	116,605.78
SDLP	56,824.20
Democratic Unionists	82,500.73
Ulster Unionists	98,807.51

A specific allocation for the Leader of the Opposition's office was introduced in April 1999 and has been set at £548,101.65 for the years 2003–4.

Financial support for Opposition parties in the House of Lords was introduced in 1996 and is commonly known as Cranborne Money.

The parties included here are those with MPs sitting in the House of Commons in the present Parliament.

CONSERVATIVE PARTY

Conservative Central Office, 32 Smith Square,
London SW1P 3HH
Tel: 020-7222 9000 Fax: 020-7222 1135
Email: ccoffice@conservatives.com
Web: www.conservatives.com

SHADOW CABINET *as at 22 July 2003*
Leader of the Opposition, Rt. Hon. Iain Duncan Smith, MP
Deputy Leader and Shadow Secretary of State for Foreign and Commonwealth Affairs, Rt. Hon. Michael Ancram, QC, MP
Agriculture (Minister), John Hayes, MP
*Attorney General and Constitutional Affairs in the House of Commons, Bill Cash, MP
Chancellor of the Exchequer, Rt. Hon. Michael Howard, QC, MP
Party Chairman, Rt. Hon. Theresa May, MP
Chief Secretary to the Treasury, Howard Flight, MP
Secretary of State for Culture, Media and Sport, John Whittingdale, OBE, MP
Secretary of State for Defence, Hon. Bernard Jenkin, MP
Secretary of State for Education and Skills, Damian Green, MP
Secretary of State for Environment, Food and Rural Affairs, David Lidington, MP
Secretary of State for Health, Dr Liam Fox, MP
Secretary of State for Home Department, Rt. Hon. Oliver Letwin, MP
Secretary of State for International Development and Minister for Women, Mrs Caroline Spelman, MP
Leader of the House of Commons, Rt. Hon. Eric Forth, MP
Leader of the House of Lords, Rt. Hon. Lord Strathclyde
Lord Chancellor's Department, Rt. Hon. Lord Kingsland, QC, MP
Secretary of State for Local Government and the Regions, Eric Pickles, MP
Secretary of State for Northern Ireland, Quentin Davies, MP
Office of the Deputy Prime Minister, Rt. Hon. David Davis, MP
Secretary of State for Scotland, Mrs Jacqui Lait, MP
Secretary of State for Trade and Industry, Tim Yeo, MP
Secretary of State for Transport, Tim Collins, CBE, MP

Secretary of State for Wales, Nigel Evans, MP
Secretary of State for Work and Pensions, David Willetts, MP
Whip (House of Commons), Rt. Hon. David Maclean, MP
Whip (House of Lords), Rt. Hon. The Lord Cope of Berkeley
*not a member of the shadow cabinet but attends at the invitation of the Leader

SCOTTISH CONSERVATIVE AND UNIONIST PARTY

83 Princes Street, Edinburgh EH2 2ER
Tel: 0131-247 6890 Fax: 0131-247 6891
Email: central.office@scottishtories.org.uk
Web: www.scottishtories.org.uk

Chairman, David Mitchell, CBE
Deputy Chairman, Mrs M. Goodman
Hon. Treasurer, Mrs J. Slater
Campaigns and Operations, Mark Neeham

LABOUR PARTY

16 Old Queen Street, London SW1H 9HP
Tel: 0870-590 0200 Fax: 020-7802 1234
Email: info@new.labour.org.uk
Web: www.labour.org.uk

Parliamentary Party Leader, Rt. Hon. Tony Blair, MP
Deputy Party Leader, Rt. Hon. John Prescott, MP
Leader in the Lords, vacant. *See* Stop Press
Chair, Rt. Hon. Ian McCartney, MP
General Secretary, D. Triesman
General Secretary, Scottish Labour Party, L. Quinn

LIBERAL DEMOCRATS

4 Cowley Street, London SW1P 3NB
Tel: 020-7222 7999 Fax: 020-7799 2170
Email: libdems@cix.co.uk
Web: www.libdems.org.uk

President, Lord Dholakia
Hon. Treasurer, Reg Clark
Chief Executive, Hugh Rickard
Parliamentary Party Leader, Rt. Hon. Charles Kennedy, MP
Shadow Leader in the House of Commons, Paul Tyler, MP
Leader in the Lords, Baroness Williams of Grosby

LIBERAL DEMOCRAT SPOKESMEN *as at August 2003*
Deputy Leader, Rt. Hon. Menzies Campbell, MP
Culture, Media and Sport, Constitution, Nick Harvey, MP
Defence, Paul Keetch, MP
Education and Skills, Phil Willis, MP
Environment, Norman Baker, MP
Food and Rural Affairs, Andrew George, MP
Foreign and Commonwealth Affairs, Rt. Hon. Menzies Campbell, MP
Health, Dr Evan Harris, MP
Home Affairs, Simon Hughes, MP
International Development, Dr Jenny Tonge, MP
Office of the Deputy Prime Minister, Edward Davey, MP
Scotland, John Thurso, MP
Trade and Industry, Dr Vincent Cable, MP
Transport, Don Foster, MP
Treasury, Matthew Taylor, MP
Wales and Northern Ireland, Lembit Opik, MP
Work and Pensions, Prof. Steve Webb, MP
Chair of the Parliamentary Party, Mark Oaten, MP

LIBERAL DEMOCRAT WHIPS
House of Lords, The Lord Roper of Thorney Island
House of Commons, Andrew Stunell, MP *(Chief Whip)*

SCOTTISH LIBERAL DEMOCRATS
4 Clifton Terrace, Edinburgh EH12 5DR
Tel: 0131-337 2314 Fax: 0131-337 3566
Email: administration@scotlibdems.org.uk
Web: www.scotlibdems.org.uk

Party President, Malcolm Bruce, MP
Party Leader, Jim Wallace, MSP
Convener, Tavish Scott
Vice-Convener, Neil Wallace; Karen Freel; Robert Brown
Treasurer, Douglas Herbison
Chief of Staff, Dr Derek Barrie

WELSH LIBERAL DEMOCRATS
Bay View House, 102 Bute Street, Cardiff CF10 5AD
Tel: 029-2031 3400 Fax: 029-2031 3401
Email: ldwales@cix.co.uk
Web: www.welshlibdems.org.uk

Party President, Rob Humphreys
Party Leader, Lembit Opik, MP
Chairman, Rob Humphreys
Treasurer, Phill Lloyd
Secretary, vacant
Administrative Officer, Helen Ceri Jones
Chief Executive, Chris Lines

PLAID CYMRU – THE PARTY OF WALES
18 Park Grove, Cardiff CF10 3BN
Tel: 029-2064 6000 Fax: 029-2064 6001
Email: post@plaidcymru.org
Web: www.plaidcymru.org

Party President, Dafydd Iwan
Chairman, John Dixon
Hon. Treasurer, Jeff Canning
Chief Executive/General Secretary, Dafydd Trystan

SCOTTISH NATIONAL PARTY
107 McDonald Road, Edinburgh EH7 4NW
Tel: 0131-525 8900 Fax: 0131-525 8901
Email: snp.hq@snp.org Web: www.snp.org

Parliamentary Party Leader, John Swinney, MSP
Chief Whip, Bruce Crawford, MSP
National Convener, John Swinney, MSP
Senior Vice-Convener, Roseanna Cunningham, MSP
National Treasurer, Jim Mather, MSP
National Secretary, Stewart Hosie
Chief Executive, Peter Murrell

NORTHERN IRELAND DEMOCRATIC UNIONIST PARTY
91 Dundela Avenue, Belfast BT4 3BU
Tel: 028-9047 1155 Fax: 028-9047 1797
Email: info@dup.org.uk Web: www.dup.org.uk

Parliamentary Party Leader, Ian Paisley, MP, MEP, MLA
Deputy Leader, Peter Robinson, MP, MLA
Chairman, Maurice Morrow, MLA
Chief Executive, Allan Ewart
Hon. Treasurer, Gregory Campbell, MP, MLA
Party Secretary, Nigel Dodds, MP, MLA

SINN FEIN
51/55 Falls Road, Belfast BT12 4PD
Tel: 02890-223000 Fax: 02890-223001
Web: www.sinnfein.ie

Party President, Gerry Adams, MP, MLA
Vice-President, Pat Doherty, MP, MLA
Chief Negotiator, Martin McGuinness, MP, MLA

SOCIAL DEMOCRATIC AND LABOUR PARTY
121 Ormeau Road, Belfast BT7 1SH
Tel: 028-9024 7700 Fax: 028-9023 6699
Email: sdlp@indigo.ie
Web: www.sdlp.ie

Parliamentary Party Leader, Mark Durkan, MLA
Deputy Leader, Ms Brid Rodgers, MLA
Chief Whip, Eddie McGrady, MP
Chairperson, Alex Attwood, MLA
Hon. Treasurer, Geraldine Cosgrove
General Secretary, Geraldine Cosgrove

ULSTER UNIONIST PARTY
429 Holywood Road, Belfast BT4 2LN
Tel: 028-9076 5500 Fax: 028-9076 9419
Email: uup@uup.org Web: www.uup.org
Party Leader, Rt. Hon. David Trimble, MP
Chief Whip, Ald. Roy Beggs, MP

ULSTER UNIONIST COUNCIL
President, Revd Martin Smyth, MP
Leader, Rt. Hon. David Trimble, MP
Chairman of the Executive Committee, James Cooper
Hon. Treasurer, Jack Allen, OBE
Vice-Chairman, Donn McConnell, OBE
Vice-Presidents, Jeffrey Donaldson, MP; Sir Reg Empey,
    OBE; Lord Maginnis of Drumglass; Jim Nicholson, MEP
Hon. Secretaries, Lord Rogan of Lower Iveagh;
    Arlene Foster; Cllr Jim Rodgers; Dermot Nesbitt
Assistant Honorary Treasurer, May Steele, MBE

MEMBERS OF PARLIAMENT

*Abbott, Ms Diane (*b.* 1953) *Lab., Hackney North and Stoke Newington,* Maj. 13,651

*Adams, Gerard (Gerry) (*b.* 1948) *SF, Belfast West,* Maj. 19,342

*Adams, Mrs K. Irene (*b.* 1948) *Lab., Paisley North,* Maj. 9,321

*Ainger, Nicholas R. (*b.* 1949) *Lab., Carmarthen West and Pembrokeshire South,* Maj. 4,538

*Ainsworth, Peter M. (*b.* 1956) *C., Surrey East,* Maj. 13,203

*Ainsworth, Robert W. (*b.* 1952) *Lab., Coventry North East,* Maj. 15,751

*Alexander, Douglas G. (*b.* 1967) *Lab., Paisley South,* Maj. 11,910

Allan, Richard B. (*b.* 1966) *LD, Sheffield Hallam,* Maj. 9,347

*Allen, Graham W. (*b.* 1953) *Lab., Nottingham North,* Maj. 12,240

*Amess, David A. A. (*b.* 1952) *C., Southend West,* Maj. 7,941

*Ancram, Rt. Hon. Michael A. F. J. K. (Earl of Ancram) (*b.* 1945) *C., Devizes,* Maj. 11,896

*Anderson, Rt. Hon. Donald (*b.* 1939) *Lab., Swansea East,* Maj. 16,148

*Anderson, Mrs Janet (*b.* 1949) *Lab., Rossendale and Darwen,* Maj. 5,223

*Arbuthnot, Rt. Hon. James N. (*b.* 1952) *C., Hampshire North East,* Maj. 13,257

*Armstrong, Rt. Hon. Hilary J. (*b.* 1945) *Lab., Durham North West,* Maj. 16,333

Atherton, Ms Candy K. (*b.* 1955) *Lab., Falmouth and Camborne,* Maj. 4,527

Atkins, Ms Charlotte (*b.* 1950) *Lab., Staffordshire Moorlands* Maj. 5,838

*Atkinson, David A. (*b.* 1940) *C., Bournemouth East,* Maj. 3,434

*Atkinson, Peter L. (*b.* 1943) *C., Hexham,* Maj. 2,529

*Austin, John E. (*b.* 1944) *Lab., Erith and Thamesmead,* Maj. 11,167

Bacon, Richard (*b.* 1962) *C., Norfolk South,* Maj. 6,893

*Bailey, Adrian (*b.* 1945) *Lab. Co-op., West Bromwich West,* Maj. 11,355

Baird, Vera (*b.* 1950) *Lab., Redcar,* Maj. 13,443

*Baker, Norman (*b.* 1957) *LD, Lewes,* Maj. 9,710

*Baldry, Anthony B. (*b.* 1950) *C., Banbury,* Maj. 5,219

*Banks, Anthony L. (*b.* 1943) *Lab., West Ham,* Maj. 15,645

Barker, Gregory (*b.* 1966) *C., Bexhill and Battle,* Maj. 10,503

*Barnes, Harold (*b.* 1936) *Lab., Derbyshire North East,* Maj. 12,258

Baron, John (*b.* 1959) *C., Billericay,* Maj. 5,013

Barrett, John (*b.* 1954) *LD, Edinburgh West,* Maj. 7,589

*Barron, Rt. Hon. Kevin J. (*b.* 1946) *Lab., Rother Valley,* Maj. 14,882

*Battle, John D. (*b.* 1951) *Lab., Leeds West,* Maj. 14,935

*Bayley, Hugh (*b.* 1952) *Lab., City of York,* Maj. 13,779

Beard, Nigel C., (*b.* 1936) *Lab., Bexleyheath and Crayford,* Maj. 1,472

*Beckett, Rt. Hon. Margaret (*b.* 1943) *Lab., Derby South,* Maj. 13,855

*Begg, Ms Anne (*b.* 1955) *Lab., Aberdeen South,* Maj. 4,388

*Beggs, Roy (*b.* 1936) *UUP Antrim East,* Maj. 128

*Beith, Rt. Hon. Alan J. (*b.* 1943) *LD, Berwick upon Tweed,* Maj. 8,458

*Bell, Stuart (*b.* 1938) *Lab., Middlesbrough,* Maj. 16,330

Bellingham, Henry (*b.* 1955) *Lab., Norfolk North West,* Maj. 3,485

*Benn, Hilary J. (*b.* 1953) *Lab., Leeds Central,* Maj. 14,381

*Bennett, Andrew F. (*b.* 1939) *Lab., Denton and Reddish,* Maj. 15,330

*Benton, Joseph E. (*b.* 1933) *Lab., Bootle,* Maj. 19,043

Bercow, John S. (*b.* 1963) *C., Buckingham,* Maj. 13,325

*Beresford, Sir Paul (*b.* 1946) *C., Mole Valley,* Maj. 10,153

*Berry, Roger D.Phil. (*b.* 1948) *Lab., Kingswood,* Maj. 13,962

*Best, Harold (*b.* 1939) *Lab., Leeds North West,* Maj. 5,236

*Betts, Clive J. C., (*b.* 1950) *Lab., Sheffield Attercliffe,* Maj. 18,844

Blackman, Ms Elizabeth M. (*b.* 1949) *Lab., Erewash,* Maj. 6,932

*Blair, Rt. Hon. Tony C. L. (*b.* 1953) *Lab., Sedgefield,* Maj. 17,713

Blears, Hazel A. (*b.* 1956) *Lab., Salford,* Maj. 11,012

Blizzard, Robert J. (*b.* 1950) *Lab., Waveney,* Maj. 8,553

*Blunkett, Rt. Hon. David (*b.* 1947) *Lab., Sheffield Brightside,* Maj. 17,049

*Blunt, Crispin J. R. (*b.* 1960) *C., Reigate,* Maj. 8,025

*Boateng, Rt. Hon. Paul Y. (*b.* 1951) *Lab., Brent South,* Maj. 17,380

Borrow, David S. (*b.* 1952) *Lab., Ribble South,* Maj. 3,792

*Boswell, Timothy E. (*b.* 1942) *C., Daventry,* Maj. 9,649

*Bottomley, Peter J. (*b.* 1944) *C., Worthing West,* Maj. 9,037

*Bottomley, Rt. Hon. Virginia H. B. M. (*b.* 1948) *C., Surrey South West,* Maj. 861

*Bradley, Rt. Hon. K. (*b.* 1950) *Lab., Manchester Withington,* Maj. 11,524

Bradley, Peter C. S. (*b.* 1953) *Lab., The Wrekin,* Maj. 3,587

Bradshaw, Benjamin P. J. (*b.* 1960) *Lab., Exeter,* Maj. 11,759

*Brady, Graham (*b.* 1967) *C., Altrincham and Sale West,* Maj. 2,941

Brake, Thomas A. (*b.* 1962) *LD, Carshalton and Wallington,* Maj. 4,547

*Brazier, Julian W. H. TD (*b.* 1953) *C., Canterbury,* Maj. 2,069

Breed, Colin E. (*b.* 1947) *LD, Cornwall South East,* Maj. 5,375

Brennan Kevin (*b.* 1959) *Lab., Cardiff West,* Maj. 11,321

Brooke, Annette (*b.* 1947) *LD, Dorset Mid and Poole North,* Maj. 384

*Brown, Rt. Hon. J. Gordon Ph.D. (*b.* 1951) *Lab., Dunfermline East,* Maj. 15,063

*Brown, Rt. Hon. Nicholas H. (*b.* 1950) *Lab., Newcastle upon Tyne East and Wallsend,* Maj. 14,223

Brown, Russell L. (*b.* 1951) *Lab., Dumfries,* Maj. 8,834

Browne, Desmond (*b.* 1952) *Lab., Kilmarnock and Loudoun,* Maj. 10,334

*Browning, Mrs Angela F. (*b.* 1946) *C., Tiverton and Honiton,* Maj. 6,284

*Bruce, Malcolm G. (*b.* 1944) *LD, Gordon,* Maj. 7,879

Bryant, Chris (*b.* 1962) *Lab., Rhondda,* Maj. 16,047

Buck, Ms Karen P. (*b.* 1958) *Lab., Regent's Park and Kensington North,* Maj. 10,266

*Burden, Richard H. (*b.* 1954) *Lab., Birmingham Northfield,* Maj. 7,798

Burgon, Colin (b. 1948) Lab., Elmet, Maj. 4,171
Burnett, John P. A. (b. 1945) LD, Devon West and Torridge, Maj. 1,194
*Burnham, Andy (b. 1970) Lab., Leigh, Maj. 16,362
*Burns, Simon H. M. (b. 1952) C., Chelmsford West, Maj. 6,261
Burnside, David (b. 1952) UUP Antrim South, Maj. 1,011
Burstow, Paul K. (b. 1962) LD, Sutton and Cheam, Maj. 4,304
Burt, Alastair (b. 1955) C., Bedfordshire North East, Maj. 8,577
*Butterfill, John V. (b. 1941) C., Bournemouth West, Maj. 4,718
*Byers, Rt. Hon. Stephen J. (b. 1953) Lab., Tyneside North, Maj. 20,668
Cable, Dr J. Vincent (b. 1943) LD, Twickenham, Maj. 7,655
*Caborn, Rt. Hon. Richard G. (b. 1943) Lab., Sheffield Central, Maj. 12,544
Cairns, David (b. 1966) Lab., Greenock and Inverclyde, Maj. 9,890
Calton, Patsy (b. 1948) LD, Cheadle, Maj. 33
Cameron, David (b. 1966) C., Witney, Maj. 7,973
Campbell, Alan (b. 1957) Lab., Tynemouth, Maj. 8,678
*Campbell Mrs Anne (b. 1940) Lab., Cambridge, Maj. 8,579
Campbell, Gregory (b. 1953) DUP Londonderry East, Maj. 1,901
*Campbell, Ronald (b. 1943) Lab., Blyth Valley, Maj. 12,188
*Campbell, Rt. Hon. W. Menzies CBE, QC (b. 1941) LD, Fife North East, Maj. 9,736
*Caplin, Ivor K. (b. 1958) Lab., Hove, Maj. 3,171
Carmichael, Alistair (b. 1965) LD, Orkney and Shetland, Maj. 3,475
Casale, Roger M. (b. 1960) Lab., Wimbledon, Maj. 3,744
*Cash, William N. P. (b. 1940) C., Stone, Maj. 6,036
Caton, Martin P. (b. 1951) Lab., Gower, Maj. 7,395
*Cawsey, Ian A. (b. 1960) Lab., Brigg and Goole, Maj. 3,961
Challen, Colin (b. 1953) Lab., Morley and Rothwell, Maj. 12,090
*Chapman, J. K. (Ben) (b. 1940) Lab., Wirral South, Maj. 5,049
*Chapman, Sir Sydney (b. 1935) C., Chipping Barnet, Maj. 2,701
*Chaytor, David M. (b. 1949) Lab., Bury North, Maj. 6,532
*Chidgey, David W. G. (b. 1942) LD, Eastleigh, Maj. 3,058
*Chope, Christopher R. OBE (b. 1947) C., Christchurch, Maj. 13,544
*Clapham, Michael (b. 1943) Lab., Barnsley West and Penistone, Maj. 12,352
*Clappison, W. James (b. 1956) C., Hertsmere, Maj. 4,902
Clark, Ms Helen R. (b. 1954) Lab., Peterborough, Maj. 384
Clark, Dr Lynda M. QC (b. 1949) Lab., Edinburgh Pentlands, Maj. 1,742
Clark, Paul G. (b. 1957) Lab., Gillingham, Maj. 2,272
Clarke, Anthony R. (b. 1963) Lab., Northampton South, Maj. 885
*Clarke, Rt. Hon. Charles R. (b. 1950) Lab., Norwich South, Maj. 8,816
*Clarke, Rt. Hon. Kenneth H. QC (b. 1940) C., Rushcliffe, Maj. 7,357
*Clarke, Rt. Hon. Thomas CBE (b. 1941) Lab., Coatbridge and Chryston, Maj. 15,314

*Clelland, David G. (b. 1943) Lab., Tyne Bridge, Maj. 14,889
*Clifton-Brown, Geoffrey R. (b. 1953) C., Cotswold, Maj. 11,983
*Clwyd, Anne (b. 1937) Lab., Cynon Valley, Maj. 12,998
*Coaker, Vernon R. (b. 1953) Lab., Gedling, Maj. 5,598
*Coffey, Ms M. Ann (b. 1946) Lab., Stockport, Maj. 11,569
*Cohen, Harry M. (b. 1949) Lab., Leyton and Wanstead, Maj. 12,904
Coleman, Iain (b. 1958) Lab., Hammersmith and Fulham, Maj. 2,015
Collins, Timothy W. G. CBE (b. 1964) C., Westmorland and Lonsdale, Maj. 3,147
Colman, Anthony (b. 1943) Lab., Putney, Maj. 2,771
*Connarty, Michael (b. 1947) Lab., Falkirk East, Maj. 10,712
Conway, Derek (b. 1953) C., Old Bexley and Sidcup, Maj. 3,345
*Cook, Frank (b. 1935) Lab., Stockton North, Maj. 14,647
*Cook, Rt. Hon. R. F. (Robin) (b. 1946) Lab., Livingston, Maj. 10,616
Cooper, Ms Yvette (b. 1969) Lab., Pontefract and Castleford, Maj. 16,378
*Corbyn, Jeremy B. (b. 1949) Lab., Islington North, Maj. 12,958
*Cormack, Sir Patrick FSA (b. 1939) C., Staffordshire South, Maj. 6,881
*Corston, Ms Jean A. (b. 1942) Lab., Bristol East, Maj. 13,392
Cotter, Brian J. (b. 1938) LD, Weston-super-Mare, Maj. 338
*Cousins, James M. (b. 1944) Lab., Newcastle upon Tyne Central, Maj. 11,605
*Cox, Thomas M. (b. 1930) Lab., Tooting, Maj. 10,400
*Cran, James D. (b. 1944) C., Beverley and Holderness, Maj. 781
Cranston, Ross F. QC (b. 1948) Lab., Dudley North, Maj. 6,800
*Crausby, David A. (b. 1946) Lab., Bolton North East, Maj. 8,422
Cruddas, Jon (b. 1965) Lab., Dagenham, Maj. 8,693
Cryer, Mrs C., Ann (b. 1939) Lab., Keighley, Maj. 4,005
Cryer, John R. (b. 1964) Lab., Hornchurch, Maj. 1,482
*Cummings, John S. (b. 1943) Lab., Easington, Maj. 21,949
*Cunningham, Rt. Hon. Dr. J. A. (Jack) Ph.D. (b. 1939) Lab., Copeland, Maj. 4,964
*Cunningham, James D. (b. 1941) Lab., Coventry South, Maj. 8,279
Cunningham, Tony (b. 1952) Lab., Workington, Maj. 10,850
*Curry, Rt. Hon. David M. (b. 1944) C., Skipton and Ripon, Maj. 12,930
Curtis-Thomas, Ms Claire (b. 1958) Lab., Crosby, Maj. 8,353
*Dalyell, Tam (b. 1932) Lab., Linlithgow, Maj. 9,129
*Darling, Rt. Hon. Alistair M. (b. 1953) Lab., Edinburgh Central, Maj. 8,142
Davey, Edward J. (b. 1965) LD, Kingston and Surbiton, Maj. 15,676
Davey, Ms Valerie (b. 1940) Lab., Bristol West, Maj. 4,426
David, Wayne (b. 1957) Lab., Caerphilly, Maj. 14,425
*Davidson, Ian G. (b. 1950) Lab. Co-op., Glasgow Pollok, Maj. 11,268
*Davies, Rt. Hon. D. J. Denzil (b. 1938) Lab., Llanelli, Maj. 6,403

Davies, Geraint R. (*b.* 1960) *Lab., Croydon Central,* Maj. 3,984

*Davies, J. Quentin (*b.* 1944) *C., Grantham and Stamford,* Maj. 4,518

*Davis, Rt. Hon. David M. (*b.* 1948) *C., Haltemprice and Howden,* Maj. 1,903

*Davis, Rt. Hon. Terence A. G. (*b.* 1938) *Lab., Birmingham Hodge Hill,* Maj. 11,618

Dawson, T. Hilton (*b.* 1953) *Lab., Lancaster and Wyre,* Maj. 481

Dean, Ms Janet E. A. (*b.* 1949) *Lab., Burton,* Maj. 4,849

*Denham, Rt. Hon. John Y. (*b.* 1953) *Lab., Southampton Itchen,* Maj. 11,223

*Dhanda, Parmjit (*b.* 1971) *Lab., Gloucester,* Maj. 3,880

*Dismore, Andrew H. (*b.* 1954) *Lab., Hendon,* Maj. 7,417

Djanogly, Jonathan (*b.* 1965) *C., Huntingdon,* Maj. 12,792

Dobbin, James (*b.* 1941) *Lab. Co-op., Heywood and Middleton,* Maj. 11,670

*Dobson, Rt. Hon. Frank G. (*b.* 1940) *Lab., Holborn and St Pancras,* Maj. 11,175

Dodds, Nigel MLA (*b.* 1958) *DUP, Belfast North,* Maj. 6,387

Doherty, Pat (*b.* 1945) *SF, Tyrone West,* Maj. 5,040

Donaldson, Jeffrey M. (*b.* 1962) *UUP, Lagan Valley,* Maj. 18,342

*Donohoe, Brian H. (*b.* 1948) *Lab., Cunninghame South,* Maj. 11,230

Doran, Frank (*b.* 1949) *Lab., Aberdeen Central,* Maj. 6,646

*Dorrell, Rt. Hon. Stephen J. (*b.* 1952) *C., Charnwood,* Maj. 7,739

Doughty, Sue (*b.* 1955) *LD, Guildford,* Maj. 538

*Dowd, James P. (*b.* 1951) *Lab., Lewisham West,* Maj. 11,920

Drew, David E. (*b.* 1952) *Lab. Co-op., Stroud,* Maj. 5,039

Drown, Ms Julia K. (*b.* 1962) *Lab., Swindon South,* Maj. 7,341

*Duncan, Alan J. C., (*b.* 1957) *C., Rutland and Melton,* Maj. 8,612

Duncan, Peter (*b.* 1965) *C., Galloway and Upper Nithsdale,* Maj. 74

*Duncan Smith, G. Iain (*b.* 1954) *C., Chingford and Woodford Green,* Maj. 5,487

*Dunwoody, Hon. Mrs Gwyneth P. (*b.* 1930) *Lab., Crewe and Nantwich,* Maj. 9,906

*Eagle, Ms Angela (*b.* 1961) *Lab., Wallasey,* Maj. 12,276

Eagle, Ms Maria (*b.* 1961) *Lab., Liverpool Garston,* Maj. 12,494

Edwards, Huw W. E. (*b.* 1953) *Lab., Monmouth,* Maj. 384

Efford, Clive S. (*b.* 1958) *Lab., Eltham,* Maj. 6,996

*Ellman, Ms Louise J. (*b.* 1945) *Lab. Co-op., Liverpool Riverside,* Maj. 13,950

*Ennis, Jeffrey (*b.* 1952) *Lab., Barnsley East and Mexborough,* Maj. 16,789

*Etherington, William (*b.* 1941) *Lab., Sunderland North,* Maj. 13,354

*Evans, Nigel M. (*b.* 1957) *C., Ribble Valley,* Maj. 11,238

Ewing, Annabelle (*b.* 1960) *SNP, Perth,* Maj. 48

*Fabricant, Michael L. D. (*b.* 1950) *C., Lichfield,* Maj. 4,426

*Fallon, Michael C., (*b.* 1952) *C., Sevenoaks,* Maj. 10,154

Farrelly, Paul (*b.* 1962) *Lab., Newcastle under Lyme,* Maj. 9,986

*Field, Rt. Hon. Frank (*b.* 1942) *Lab., Birkenhead,* Maj. 15,591

*Field, Mark (*b.* 1934) *C., Cities of London and Westminster,* Maj. 4,499

*Fisher, Mark (*b.* 1944) *Lab., Stoke-on-Trent Central,* Maj. 11,845

*Fitzpatrick, James (*b.* 1952) *Lab., Poplar and Canning Town,* Maj. 14,104

*Fitzsimons, Ms Lorna (*b.* 1967) *Lab., Rochdale,* Maj. 5,655

*Flight, Howard E. (*b.* 1948) *C., Arundel and South Downs,* Maj. 13,704

*Flint, Ms Caroline L. (*b.* 1961) *Lab., Don Valley,* Maj. 9,520

Flook, Adrian (*b.* 1963) *C., Taunton,* Maj. 235

*Flynn, Paul P. (*b.* 1935) *Lab., Newport West,* Maj. 9,304

Follett, Ms D. Barbara (*b.* 1942) *Lab., Stevenage,* Maj. 8,566

*Forth, Rt. Hon. Eric (*b.* 1944) *C., Bromley and Chislehurst,* Maj. 9,037

*Foster, Rt. Hon. Derek (*b.* 1937) *Lab., Bishop Auckland,* Maj. 13,926

*Foster, Donald M. E. (*b.* 1947) *LD, Bath,* Maj. 9,894

Foster, Michael (*b.* 1963) *Lab., Worcester,* Maj. 5,766

*Foster, Michael J. (*b.* 1946) *Lab., Hastings and Rye,* Maj. 4,308

*Foulkes, George (*b.* 1942) *Lab. Co-op., Carrick, Cumnock and Doon Valley,* Maj. 14,856

*Fox, Dr Liam (*b.* 1961) *C., Woodspring,* Maj. 8,798

Francis, David Hywel (*b.* 1946) *Lab., Aberavon,* Maj. 16,108

Francois, Mark Ph.D. (*b.* 1965) *C., Rayleigh,* Maj. 8,290

*Gale, Roger J. (*b.* 1943) *C., Thanet North,* Maj. 6,650

*Galloway, George (*b.* 1954) *Lab., Glasgow Kelvin,* Maj. 7,260

*Gapes, Michael J. (*b.* 1952) *Lab. Co-op., Ilford South,* Maj. 13,997

Gardiner, Barry S. (*b.* 1957) *Lab., Brent North,* Maj. 10,205

*Garnier, Edward H. QC (*b.* 1952) *C., Harborough,* Maj. 5,252

George, Andrew H. (*b.* 1958) *LD, St Ives,* Maj. 10,053

*George, Rt. Hon. Bruce T. (*b.* 1942) *Lab., Walsall South,* Maj. 9,931

*Gerrard, Neil F. (*b.* 1942) *Lab., Walthamstow,* Maj. 15,181

*Gibb, Nicholas J. (*b.* 1960) *C., Bognor Regis and Littlehampton,* Maj. 5,643

*Gibson, Dr Ian (*b.* 1938) *Lab., Norwich North,* Maj. 5,863

*Gidley, Sandra (*b.* 1957) *LD, Romsey,* Maj. 2,370

Gildernew, Michelle (*b.* 1970) *SF, Fermanagh and South Tyrone,* Maj. 53

*Gillan, Mrs Cheryl E. K. (*b.* 1952) *C., Chesham and Amersham,* Maj. 11,882

Gilroy Mrs Linda, (*b.* 1949) *Lab. Co-op., Plymouth Sutton,* Maj. 7,517

*Godsiff, Roger D. (*b.* 1946) *Lab., Birmingham Sparkbrook and Small Heath,* Maj. 16,246

Goggins, Paul G. (*b.* 1953) *Lab., Wythenshawe and Sale East,* Maj. 12,608

Goodman, Paul (*b.* 1960) *C., Wycombe,* Maj. 3,168

Gray, James W. (*b.* 1954) *C., Wiltshire North,* Maj. 3,878

Grayling, Chris (*b.* 1962) *C., Epsom and Ewell,* Maj. 10,080

Green, Damian H. (*b.* 1956) *C., Ashford,* Maj. 7,359

Green, Matthew (*b.* 1970) *LD, Ludlow,* Maj. 1,630

*Greenway, John R. (*b.* 1946) *C., Ryedale,* Maj. 4,875

*Grieve, Dominic C. R. (*b.* 1956) *C., Beaconsfield,* Maj. 11,065

*Griffiths, Ms Jane P. (*b.* 1954) *Lab., Reading East,* Maj. 5,588

*Griffiths, Nigel (*b.* 1955) *Lab., Edinburgh South,*
Maj. 5,499

*Griffiths, Winston J. (*b.* 1943) *Lab., Bridgend,*
Maj. 10,045

Grogan, John T. (*b.* 1961) *Lab., Selby,* Maj. 2,138

*Gummer, Rt. Hon. John S. (*b.* 1939) *C., Suffolk Coastal,*
Maj. 4,326

*Hague, Rt. Hon. William J. (*b.* 1961) *C., Richmond,*
Maj. 16,319

*Hain, Rt. Hon. Peter G. (*b.* 1950) *Lab., Neath,*
Maj. 14,816

*Hall, Michael T. (*b.* 1952) *Lab., Weaver Vale,* Maj. 9,637

Hall, Patrick (*b.* 1951) *Lab., Bedford,* Maj. 6,157

Hamilton, David (*b.* 1950) *Lab., Midlothian,* Maj. 9,014

*Hamilton, Fabian (*b.* 1955) *Lab., Leeds North East,*
Maj. 7,089

Hammond, Philip (*b.* 1955) *C., Runnymede and Weybridge,* Maj. 8,360

*Hancock, Michael T. CBE (*b.* 1946) *LD, Portsmouth South,* Maj. 6,094

*Hanson, David G. (*b.* 1957) *Lab., Delyn,* Maj. 8,065

*Harman, Rt. Hon. Harriet QC (*b.* 1950) *Lab., Camberwell and Peckham,* Maj. 14,123

*Harris, Dr Evan (*b.* 1965) *LD, Oxford West and Abingdon,* Maj. 9,185

Harris, Tom (*b.* 1964) *Lab., Glasgow Cathcart,*
Maj. 10,816

Harvard, Dai (*b.* 1949) *Lab., Merthyr Tydfil and Rhymney,* Maj. 14,923

*Harvey, Nicholas B. (*b.* 1961) *LD, Devon North,*
Maj. 2,984

*Haselhurst, Rt. Hon. Sir Alan (*b.* 1937) *C., Saffron Walden,* Maj. 12,004

Hawkins, Nick (*b.* 1957) *C., Surrey Heath,* Maj. 10,819

Hayes, John H. (*b.* 1958) *C., South Holland and the Deepings,* Maj. 11,099

*Heal, Mrs Sylvia L (*b.* 1942) *Lab., Halesowen and Rowley Regis,* Maj. 7,359

*Heald, Oliver (*b.* 1954) *C., Hertfordshire North East,*
Maj. 3,444

Healey, John (*b.* 1960) *Lab., Wentworth,* Maj. 16,449

Heath, David W. CBE (*b.* 1954) *LD, Somerton and Frome,*
Maj. 668

*Heathcoat-Amory, Rt. Hon. David P. (*b.* 1949) *C., Wells,*
Maj. 2,796

*Henderson, Douglas J. (*b.* 1949) *Lab., Newcastle upon Tyne North,* Maj. 14,450

Henderson, Ivan J. (*b.* 1958) *Lab., Harwich,* Maj. 2,596

*Hendrick, Mark (*b.* 1958) *Lab. Co-op., Preston,*
Maj. 12,268

Hendry, Charles (*b.* 1959) *C., Wealden,* Maj. 13,772

Hepburn, Stephen (*b.* 1959) *Lab., Jarrow,* Maj. 17,595

*Heppell, John (*b.* 1948) *Lab., Nottingham East,*
Maj. 10,320

Hermon, Lady Sylvia (*b.* 1956) *UUP, Down North,*
Maj. 7,324

Hesford, Stephen (*b.* 1957) *Lab., Wirral West,* Maj. 4,035

Hewitt, Rt. Hon. Patricia H. (*b.* 1948) *Lab., Leicester West,* Maj. 9,639

Heyes, David (*b.* 1946) *Lab., Ashton under Lyne,*
Maj. 15,518

*Hill, T. Keith (*b.* 1943) *Lab., Streatham,* Maj. 14,270

*Hinchliffe, David M. (*b.* 1948) *Lab., Wakefield,*
Maj. 7,954

Hoban, Mark (*b.* 1964) *C., Fareham,* Maj. 7,009

*Hodge, Mrs Margaret E. MBE (*b.* 1944) *Lab., Barking,*
Maj. 9,534

*Hoey, Ms Catharine (Kate) L. (*b.* 1946) *Lab., Vauxhall,*
Maj. 13,018

*Hogg, Rt. Hon. Douglas M. QC (*b.* 1945) *C., Sleaford and North Hykeham,* Maj. 8,622

Holmes, Paul (*b.* 1957) *LD, Chesterfield,* Maj. 2,586

*Hood, James (*b.* 1948) *Lab., Clydesdale,* Maj. 7,794

*Hoon, Rt. Hon. Geoffrey W. (*b.* 1953) *Lab., Ashfield,*
Maj. 13,268

Hope, Philip I. (*b.* 1955) *Lab. Co-op., Corby,* Maj. 5,700

Hopkins, Kelvin P. (*b.* 1941) *Lab., Luton North,*
Maj. 9,977

*Horam, John R. (*b.* 1939) *C., Orpington,* Maj. 269

*Howard, Rt. Hon. Michael QC (*b.* 1941) *C., Folkestone and Hythe,* Maj. 5,907

*Howarth, Rt. Hon. Alan CBE (*b.* 1967) *Lab.,* Maj. 9,874

*Howarth, George E. (*b.* 1949) *Lab., Knowsley North and Sefton East,* Maj. 18,927

Howarth, J. Gerald D. (*b.* 1947) *C., Aldershot,* Maj. 6,564

*Howells, Dr Kim S. Ph.D. (*b.* 1946) *Lab., Pontypridd,*
Maj. 17,684

Hoyle, Lindsay H. (*b.* 1957) *Lab., Chorley,* Maj. 8,444

*Hughes, Ms Beverley J. (*b.* 1950) *Lab., Stretford and Urmston,* Maj. 13,239

*Hughes, Kevin M. (*b.* 1952) *Lab., Doncaster North,*
Maj. 15,187

*Hughes, Simon H. W. (*b.* 1951) *LD, Southwark North and Bermondsey,* Maj. 9,632

Humble, Mrs Jovanka (Joan) (*b.* 1951) *Lab., Blackpool North and Fleetwood,* Maj. 5,721

*Hume, John MEP (*b.* 1937) *SDLP, Foyle,* Maj. 11,550

*Hunter, Andrew R. F. (*b.* 1943) *C., Basingstoke,* Maj. 880

Hurst, Alan A. (*b.* 1945) *Lab., Braintree,* Maj. 358

*Hutton, Rt. Hon. John (*b.* 1955) *Lab., Barrow and Furness,* Maj. 9,889

Iddon, Brian (*b.* 1940) *Lab., Bolton South East,*
Maj. 12,871

*Illsley, Eric E. (*b.* 1955) *Lab., Barnsley Central,*
Maj. 15,130

*Ingram, Rt. Hon. Adam P. (*b.* 1947) *Lab., East Kilbride,*
Maj. 12,755

*Irranca-Davies, Huw (*b.* 1963) *Lab., Ogmore,* Maj. 5,721

*Jack, Rt. Hon. J. Michael (*b.* 1946) *C., Fylde,* Maj. 9,610

*Jackson, Ms Glenda M. CBE (*b.* 1936) *Lab., Hampstead and Highgate,* Maj. 7,876

*Jackson, Mrs Helen M. (*b.* 1939) *Lab., Sheffield Hillsborough,* Maj. 14,569

*Jackson, Robert V. (*b.* 1946) *C., Wantage,* Maj. 5,600

*Jamieson, David C., (*b.* 1947) *Lab., Plymouth Devonport,*
Maj. 13,033

*Jenkin, Hon. Bernard C., (*b.* 1959) *C., Essex North,*
Maj. 7,186

*Jenkins, Brian D. (*b.* 1942) *Lab., Tamworth,* Maj. 4,598

*Johnson, Alan A. (*b.* 1950) *Lab., Hull West and Hessle,*
Maj. 10,951

Johnson, Boris (*b.* 1964) *C., Henley,* Maj. 8,458

Johnson, Ms Melanie J. (*b.* 1955) *Lab., Welwyn Hatfield,*
Maj. 1,196

Jones, Ms Helen M. Ph.D. (*b.* 1954) *Lab., Warrington North,* Maj. 15,156

*Jones, Jonathan O. (*b.* 1954) *Lab. Co-op., Cardiff Central,*
Maj. 659

Jones, Kevan (*b.* 1964) *Lab., Durham North,* Maj. 18,683

*Jones, Ms Lynne M. Ph.D. (*b.* 1951) *Lab., Birmingham Selly Oak,* Maj. 10,339

*Jones, Martyn D. (*b.* 1947) *Lab., Clwyd South,*
Maj. 8,898

*Jones, Nigel D. (*b.* 1948) *LD, Cheltenham,* Maj. 5,255

*Jowell, Rt. Hon. Tessa J. H. D. (b. 1947) Lab., Dulwich and West Norwood, Maj. 12,310

*Joyce, Eric (b. 1960) Lab., Falkirk West, Maj. 8,532

*Kaufman, Rt. Hon. Gerald B. (b. 1930) Lab., Manchester Gorton, Maj. 11,304

Keeble, Ms Sally C., (b. 1951) Lab., Northampton North, Maj. 7,893

*Keen, D. Alan (b. 1937) Lab. Co-op. Feltham and Heston, Maj. 12,657

Keen, Mrs Ann L. (b. 1948) Lab. Co-op., Brentford and Isleworth, Maj. 10,318

*Keetch, Paul S. (b. 1961) LD, Hereford, Maj. 968

*Kelly, Ms Ruth M. (b. 1968) Lab., Bolton West, Maj. 5,518

*Kemp, Fraser (b. 1958) Lab., Houghton and Washington East, Maj. 19,818

*Kennedy, Rt. Hon. Charles P. (b. 1959) LD, Ross, Skye and Inverness West, Maj. 12,952

*Kennedy, Mrs Jane E. (b. 1958) Lab., Liverpool Wavertree, Maj. 12,319

*Key, S. Robert (b. 1945) C., Salisbury, Maj. 8,703

*Khabra, Piara S. (b. 1922) Lab., Ealing Southall, Maj. 13,683

*Kidney, David N. (b. 1955) Lab., Stafford, Maj. 5,032

*Kilfoyle, Peter (b. 1946) Lab., Liverpool Walton, Maj. 17,996

King, Andrew (b. 1948) Lab., Rugby and Kenilworth, Maj. 2,877

*King, Ms Oona T. (b. 1967) Lab., Bethnal Green and Bow, Maj. 10,057

*Kirkbride, Miss Julie (b. 1960) C., Bromsgrove, Maj. 8,138

*Kirkwood, Archibald J. (b. 1946) LD, Roxburgh and Berwickshire, Maj. 7,511

*Knight, Rt. Hon. Greg (b. 1949) C., Yorkshire East, Maj. 4,682

Knight, Jim (b. 1965) Lab., Dorset South, Maj. 153

*Kumar, Dr Ashok (b. 1956) Lab., Middlesbrough South and Cleveland East, Maj. 9,351

*Ladyman, Dr Stephen J. (b. 1952) Lab., Thanet South, Maj. 1,792

Laing, Mrs Eleanor F. (b. 1958) C., Epping Forest, Maj. 8,426

*Lait, Ms Jacqueline A. H. (b. 1947) C., Beckenham, Maj. 4,959

Lamb, Norman (b. 1957) LD, Norfolk North, Maj. 483

*Lammy, David (b. 1972) Lab., Tottenham, Maj. 16,916

*Lansley, Andrew D. CBE (b. 1956) C., Cambridgeshire South, Maj. 8,403

*Lawrence, Mrs Jacqueline R. (b. 1948) Lab., Preseli Pembrokeshire, Maj. 2,946

Laws, David (b. 1965) LD, Yeovil, Maj. 3,928

*Laxton, Robert (b. 1944) Lab., Derby North, Maj. 6,982

Lazarowicz, Mark (b. 1953) Lab., Edinburgh North and Leith, Maj. 8,817

*Leigh, Edward J. E. (b. 1950) C., Gainsborough, Maj. 8,071

*Lepper, David (b. 1945) Lab. Co-op., Brighton Pavilion, Maj. 9,643

Leslie, Christopher M. (b. 1972) Lab., Shipley, Maj. 1,428

Letwin, Oliver (b. 1956) C., Dorset West, Maj. 1,414

*Levitt, Tom (b. 1954) Lab., High Peak, Maj. 4,489

*Lewis, Ivan (b. 1967) Lab., Bury South, Maj. 12,772

*Lewis, Dr Julian M. (b. 1951) C., New Forest East, Maj. 3,829

*Lewis, Terence (b. 1935) Lab., Worsley, Maj. 11,787

*Liddell, Rt. Hon. Helen (b. 1950) Lab., Airdrie and Shotts, Maj. 12,340

Liddell-Grainger, Ian (b. 1959) C., Bridgwater, Maj. 4,987

*Lidington, David R. Ph.D. (b. 1956) C., Aylesbury, Maj. 10,009

*Lilley, Rt. Hon. Peter B. (b. 1943) C., Hitchin and Harpenden, Maj. 6,663

Linton, J. Martin (b. 1944) Lab., Battersea, Maj. 5,053

*Lloyd, Anthony J. (b. 1950) Lab., Manchester Central, Maj. 13,742

*Llwyd, Elfyn (b. 1951) PC, Meirionnydd nant Conwy, Maj. 5,684

*Lord, Sir Michael N. (b. 1938) C., Suffolk Central and Ipswich North, Maj. 3,469

*Loughton, Timothy P. (b. 1962) C., Worthing East and Shoreham, Maj. 6,139

*Love, Andrew (b. 1949) Lab. Co-op., Edmonton, Maj. 9,772

Lucas, Ian (b. 1960) Lab., Wrexham, Maj. 9,188

*Luff, Peter J. (b. 1955) C., Worcestershire Mid, Maj. 10,627

Luke, Ian (b. 1951) Lab., Dundee East, Maj. 4,475

Lyons, John (b. 1950) Lab., Strathkelvin and Bearsden, Maj. 11,717

*McAvoy, Thomas M. (b. 1943) Lab. Co-op Glasgow Rutherglen, Maj. 12,625

*McCabe, Stephen J. (b. 1955) Lab., Birmingham Hall Green, Maj. 6,648

*McCafferty Ms Christine (b. 1945) Lab., Calder Valley, Maj. 3,094

*McCartney, Rt. Hon. Ian (b. 1951) Lab., Makerfield, Maj. 17,750

*McDonagh, Ms Siobhain A. (b. 1960) Lab., Mitcham and Morden, Maj. 13,785

*MacDonald, Calum A. Ph.D. (b. 1956) Lab., Western Isles, Maj. 1,074

McDonnell, John M. (b. 1951) Lab., Hayes and Harlington, Maj. 13,466

*MacDougall, John (b. 1947) Lab., Fife Central, Maj. 10,075

*McFall, John (b. 1944) Lab. Co-op., Dumbarton, Maj. 9,575

*McGrady, Edward K. (b. 1935) SDLP, Down South, Maj. 13,858

McGuinness, Martin (b. 1950) SF, Ulster Mid, Maj. 9,953

McGuire, Anne (b. 1949) Lab., Stirling, Maj. 6,274

*McIntosh, Miss Anne C. B. (b. 1954) C., Vale of York, Maj. 12,517

McIsaac, Ms Shona (b. 1960) Lab., Cleethorpes, Maj. 5,620

*Mackay, Rt. Hon. Andrew J. (b. 1949) C., Bracknell, Maj. 6,713

McKechin, Ann (b. 1961) Lab., Glasgow Maryhill, Maj. 9,888

McKenna, Ms Rosemary CBE (b. 1941) Lab., Cumbernauld and Kilsyth, Maj. 7,520

*Mackinlay, Andrew S. (b. 1949) Lab., Thurrock, Maj. 9,997

*Maclean, Rt. Hon. David J. (b. 1953) C., Penrith and the Border, Maj. 14,677

*McLoughlin, Patrick A. (b. 1957) C., Derbyshire West, Maj. 7,370

*McNamara, J. Kevin (b. 1934) Lab., Hull North, Maj. 10,721

*McNulty, Anthony J. (b. 1958) Lab., Harrow East, Maj. 11,124

*MacShane, Denis Ph.D. (b. 1948) Lab., Rotherham, Maj. 13,077

Mactaggart, Ms Fiona M. (b. 1953) Lab., Slough, Maj. 12,508

*McWalter, Tony (b. 1945) Lab. Co-op., Hemel Hempstead, Maj. 3,742

*McWilliam, John D. (b. 1941) Lab., Blaydon, Maj. 7,809

Mahmood, Khalid (b. 1961) Lab., Birmingham Perry Barr, Maj. 8,753

*Mahon, Mrs Alice (b. 1937) Lab., Halifax, Maj. 6,129

Malins, Humfrey J. CBE (b. 1945) C., Woking, Maj. 6,759

*Mallaber Ms C., Judith (b. 1951) Lab., Amber Valley, Maj. 7,227

*Mallon, Seamus (b. 1936) SDLP, Newry and Armagh, Maj. 3,575

*Mandelson, Rt. Hon. Peter B. (b. 1953) Lab., Hartlepool, Maj. 14,571

Mann, John (b. 1960) Lab., Bassetlaw, Maj. 9,748

*Maples, John C., (b. 1943) C., Stratford-upon-Avon, Maj. 11,802

Marris, Robert (b. 1955) Lab., Wolverhampton South West, Maj. 3,487

*Marsden, Gordon (b. 1953) Lab., Blackpool South, Maj. 8,262

*Marsden, Paul W. B. (b. 1968) Lab., Shrewsbury and Atcham, Maj. 3,579

*Marshall, David Ph.D. (b. 1941) Lab., Glasgow Shettleston, Maj. 9,818

*Marshall, James Ph.D. (b. 1941) Lab., Leicester South, Maj. 13,243

*Marshall-Andrews, Robert G. QC (b. 1944) Lab., Medway, Maj. 3,780

*Martin, Rt. Hon. Michael J. (b. 1945) The Speaker Glasgow Springburn, Maj. 11,378

*Martlew, Eric A. (b. 1949) Lab., Carlisle, Maj. 5,702

*Mates, Michael J. (b. 1934) C., Hampshire East, Maj. 8,890

*Maude, Rt. Hon. Francis A. A. (b. 1953) C., Horsham, Maj. 13,666

*Mawhinney, Rt. Hon. Sir Brian Ph.D. (b. 1940) C., Cambridgeshire North West, Maj. 8,101

*May, Mrs Theresa M. (b. 1956) C., Maidenhead, Maj. 3,284

*Meacher, Rt. Hon. Michael H. (b. 1939) Lab., Oldham West and Royton, Maj. 13,365

*Meale, J. Alan (b. 1949) Lab., Mansfield, Maj. 11,038

Mercer, Patrick OBE (b. 1956) C., Newark, Maj. 4,073

*Merron, Ms Gillian J. (b. 1959) Lab., Lincoln, Maj. 8,420

*Michael, Rt. Hon. Alun E. (b. 1943) Lab. Co-op., Cardiff South and Penarth, Maj. 12,287

*Milburn, Rt. Hon. Alan (b. 1958) Lab., Darlington, Maj. 9,529

Miliband, David (b. 1966) Lab., South Shields, Maj. 14,090

*Miller, Andrew P. (b. 1949) Lab., Ellesmere Port and Neston, Maj. 10,861

Mitchell, Andrew (b. 1956) C., Sutton Coldfield, Maj. 10,104

*Mitchell, Austin V. D.Phil. (b. 1934) Lab., Great Grimsby, Maj. 11,484

*Moffatt, Mrs Laura J. (b. 1954) Lab., Crawley, Maj. 6,770

*Mole, Chris (b. 1958) Lab., Ipswich, Maj. 4,087

*Moonie, Dr Lewis (b. 1947) Lab. Co-op., Kirkcaldy, Maj. 8,963

*Moore, Michael (b. 1965) LD, Tweeddale, Ettrick and Lauderdale, Maj. 5,157

*Moran, Ms Margaret (b. 1955) Lab., Luton South, Maj. 10,133

Morgan, Ms Julie (b. 1944) Lab., Cardiff North, Maj. 6,165

*Morley, Elliot A. (b. 1952) Lab., Scunthorpe, Maj. 10,372

*Morris, Rt. Hon. Estelle (b. 1952) Lab., Birmingham Yardley, Maj. 2,578

*Moss, Malcolm D. (b. 1943) C., Cambridgeshire North East, Maj. 6,373

Mountford, Ms Kali C., J. (b. 1954) Lab., Colne Valley, Maj. 4,639

*Mudie, George E. (b. 1945) Lab., Leeds East, Maj. 12,643

*Mullin, Christopher J. (b. 1947) Lab., Sunderland South, Maj. 13,667

Munn, Meg (b. 1959) Lab. Co-op., Sheffield Heeley, Maj. 11,704

Murphy, Denis (b. 1948) Lab., Wansbeck, Maj. 13,101

Murphy, Jim (b. 1967) Lab., Eastwood, Maj. 9,141

*Murphy, Rt. Hon Paul P. (b. 1948) Lab., Torfaen, Maj. 16,280

Murrison, Andrew (b. 1961) C., Westbury, Maj. 5,294

Naysmith, J. Douglas (b. 1941) Lab. Co-op., Bristol North West, Maj. 11,087

Norman, Archibald J. (b. 1954) C., Tunbridge Wells, Maj. 9,730

Norris, Dan (b. 1960) Lab., Wansdyke, Maj. 5,113

*Oaten, Mark (b. 1964) LD, Winchester, Maj. 9,634

*O'Brien, Michael (b. 1954) Lab., Warwickshire North, Maj. 9,639

*O'Brien, Stephen (b. 1957) C., Eddisbury, Maj. 4,568

*O'Brien, William (b. 1929) Lab., Normanton, Maj. 9,937

*O'Hara, Edward (b. 1937) Lab., Knowsley South, Maj. 21,316

*Olner, William J. (b. 1942) Lab., Nuneaton, Maj. 7,535

*O'Neill, Martin J. (b. 1945) Lab., Ochil, Maj. 5,349

Opik, Lembit (b. 1965) LD, Montgomeryshire, Maj. 6,234

*Organ, Ms Diana M. (b. 1952) Lab., Forest of Dean, Maj. 2,049

Osborne, George (b. 1971) C., Tatton, Maj. 8,611

Osborne, Mrs Sandra C., (b. 1956) Lab., Ayr, Maj. 2,545

*Ottaway, Richard G. J. (b. 1945) C., Croydon South, Maj. 8,697

*Owen, Albert (b. 1960) Lab., Ynys Môn, Maj. 800

*Page, Richard L. (b. 1941) C., Hertfordshire South West, Maj. 8,181

*Paice, James E. T. (b. 1949) C., Cambridgeshire South East, Maj. 8,990

*Paisley, Revd Ian R. K. MEP (b. 1926) DUP, Antrim North, Maj. 14,224

Palmer, Nicholas D. (b. 1950) Lab., Broxtowe, Maj. 5,873

*Paterson, Owen W. (b. 1956) C., Shropshire North, Maj. 6,241

*Pearson, Ian P. Ph.D. (b. 1959) Lab., Dudley South, Maj. 6,817

*Perham, Ms Linda (b. 1947) Lab., Ilford North, Maj. 2,115

Picking, Anne (b. 1958) Lab., East Lothian, Maj. 10,830

*Pickles, Eric J. (b. 1952) C., Brentwood and Ongar, Maj. 2,821

*Pickthall, Colin (b. 1944) Lab., Lancashire West, Maj. 9,643

*Pike, Peter L. (b. 1937) Lab., Burnley, Maj. 10,498

*Plaskitt, James A. (b. 1954) Lab., Warwick and Leamington, Maj. 5,953

Pollard, Kerry P. (b. 1944) Lab., St Albans, Maj. 4,466

*Pond, Christopher R. (b. 1952) Lab., Gravesham, Maj. 4,862

*Pope, Gregory J. (b. 1960) Lab., Hyndburn, Maj. 8,219

*Portillo, Rt. Hon. Michael (b. 1953) C., Kensington and Chelsea, Maj. 8,771
Pound, Stephen P. (b. 1948) Lab., Ealing North, Maj. 11,837
*Prentice, Ms Bridget T. (b. 1952) Lab., Lewisham East, Maj. 8,959
*Prentice, Gordon (b. 1951) Lab., Pendle, Maj. 4,275
*Prescott, Rt. Hon. John L. (b. 1938) Lab., Hull East, Maj. 15,325
Price, Adam (b. 1968) PC, Carmarthen East and Dinefwr, Maj. 2,590
*Primarolo, Ms Dawn (b. 1954) Lab., Bristol South, Maj. 14,181
*Prisk, Mark (b. 1962) C., Hertford and Stortford, Maj. 5,603
*Prosser, Gwynfor M. (b. 1943) Lab., Dover, Maj. 5,199
Pugh John, (b. 1949) LD, Southport, Maj. 3,007
*Purchase, Kenneth (b. 1939) Lab. Co-op., Wolverhampton North East, Maj. 9,965
Purnell, James (b. 1970) Lab., Stalybridge and Hyde, Maj. 8,859
*Quin, Rt. Hon. Joyce G. (b. 1944) Lab., Gateshead East and Washington West, Maj. 17,904
*Quinn, Lawrence W. (b. 1956) Lab., Scarborough and Whitby, Maj. 3,585
*Rammell, William E. (b. 1959) Lab., Harlow, Maj. 5,228
*Randall, A. John (b. 1955) C., Uxbridge, Maj. 2,098
Rapson, Sydney N. J. (b. 1942) Lab., Portsmouth North, Maj. 5,134
*Raynsford, Rt. Hon. W. R. N. (Nick) (b. 1945) Lab., Greenwich and Woolwich, Maj. 13,433
*Redwood, Rt. Hon. John A. D.Phil. (b. 1951) C., Wokingham, Maj. 5,994
Reed, Andrew J. (b. 1964) Lab., Loughborough, Maj. 6,378
Reid, Alan (b. 1954) LD, Argyll and Bute, Maj. 1,653
*Reid, Rt. Hon. John Ph.D. (b. 1947) Lab., Hamilton North and Bellshill, Maj. 13,561
*Rendel, David D. (b. 1949) LD, Newbury, Maj. 2,415
*Robathan, Andrew R. G. (b. 1951) C., Blaby, Maj. 6,209
Robertson, Angus (b. 1969) SNP, Moray, Maj. 1,744
Robertson, Hugh (b. 1962) C., Faversham and Mid Kent, Maj. 4,183
*Robertson, John (b. 1952) Lab., Glasgow Anniesland, Maj. 11,054
Robertson, Laurence A. (b. 1958) C., Tewkesbury, Maj. 8,663
*Robinson, Geoffrey (b. 1938) Lab., Coventry North West, Maj. 10,874
Robinson, Iris MLA (b. 1949) DUP, Strangford, Maj. 1,110
*Robinson, Peter D. (b. 1948) DUP, Belfast East, Maj. 7,117
*Roche, Mrs Barbara M. R. (b. 1954) Lab., Hornsey and Wood Green, Maj. 10,614
*Roe, Mrs Marion A. (b. 1936) C., Broxbourne, Maj. 8,993
*Rooney, Terence H. (b. 1950) Lab., Bradford North, Maj. 8,969
Rosindell, Andrew (b. 1966) C., Romford, Maj. 5,977
*Ross, Ernest (b. 1942) Lab., Dundee West, Maj. 6,800
*Roy, Frank (b. 1958) Lab., Motherwell and Wishaw, Maj. 10,956
*Ruane, Christopher S. (b. 1958) Lab., Vale of Clwyd, Maj. 5,761
*Ruddock, Mrs Joan M. (b. 1943) Lab., Lewisham Deptford, Maj. 15,293

Ruffley, David L. (b. 1962) C., Bury St Edmunds, Maj. 2,503
Russell, Ms Christine M. (b. 1945) Lab., City of Chester, Maj. 6,894
*Russell, Robert E. (b. 1946) LD, Colchester, Maj. 5,553
*Ryan, Ms Joan M. (b. 1955) Lab., Enfield North, Maj. 2,291
*Salmond, Alexander E. A. (b. 1954) SNP, Banff and Buchan, Maj. 10,503
Salter, Martin J. (b. 1954) Lab., Reading West, Maj. 8,849
*Sanders, Adrian M. (b. 1959) LD, Torbay, Maj. 6,708
*Sarwar, Mohammad (b. 1952) Lab., Glasgow Govan, Maj. 6,400
*Savidge, Malcolm K. (b. 1946) Lab., Aberdeen North, Maj. 4,449
*Sawford, Philip A. (b. 1950) Lab., Kettering, Maj. 665
*Sayeed, Jonathan (b. 1948) C., Bedfordshire Mid, Maj. 8,066
*Sedgemore, Brian C., J. (b. 1937) Lab., Hackney South and Shoreditch, Maj. 15,049
Selous, Andrew (b. 1962) C., Bedfordshire South West, Maj. 776
*Shaw, Jonathan R. (b. 1966) Lab., Chatham and Aylesford, Maj. 4,340
*Sheerman, Barry J. (b. 1940) Lab. Co-op., Huddersfield, Maj. 10,046
*Shephard, Rt. Hon. Gillian P. (b. 1940) C., Norfolk South West, Maj. 9,366
*Shepherd, Richard C., S. (b. 1942) C., Aldridge-Brownhills, Maj. 3,768
Sheridan, Jim (b. 1952) Lab., Renfrewshire West, Maj. 8,575
*Shipley, Ms Debra A. (b. 1957) Lab., Stourbridge, Maj. 3,812
*Short, Rt. Hon. Clare (b. 1946) Lab., Birmingham Ladywood, Maj. 18,143
Simmonds, Mark (b. 1964) C., Boston and Skegness, Maj. 515
Simon, Sion (b. 1969) Lab., Birmingham Erdington, Maj. 9,962
*Simpson, Alan J. (b. 1948) Lab., Nottingham South, Maj. 9,989
*Simpson, Keith (b. 1949) C., Norfolk Mid, Maj. 4,562
Singh, Marsha (b. 1954) Lab., Bradford West, Maj. 4,165
*Skinner, Dennis E. (b. 1932) Lab., Bolsover, Maj. 18,777
*Smith, Rt. Hon. Andrew D. (b. 1951) Lab., Oxford East, Maj. 10,344
*Smith, Ms Angela E. (b. 1959) Lab. Co-op., Basildon, Maj. 7,738
*Smith, Rt. Hon. Christopher R. Ph.D. (b. 1951) Lab., Islington South and Finsbury, Maj. 7,280
*Smith, Ms Geraldine (b. 1961) Lab., Morecambe and Lunesdale, Maj. 5,092
*Smith, Ms Jacqui (b. 1962) Lab., Redditch, Maj. 2,484
*Smith, John W. P. (b. 1951) Lab., Vale of Glamorgan, Maj. 4,700
*Smith, Llewellyn T. (b. 1944) Lab., Blaenau Gwent, Maj. 19,313
*Smith, Sir Robert Bt. (b. 1958) LD, Aberdeenshire West and Kincardine, Maj. 4,821
*Smyth, Revd W. Martin (b. 1931) UUP, Belfast South, Maj. 5,399
*Soames, Hon. A. Nicholas W. (b. 1948) C., Sussex Mid, Maj. 6,898
*Soley, Clive S. (b. 1939) Lab., Ealing Acton and Shepherd's Bush, Maj. 10,789
Southworth, Ms Helen M. (b. 1956) Lab., Warrington South, Maj. 7,387

*Spellar, Rt. Hon. John F. (*b.* 1947) *Lab., Warley,*
Maj. 11,850

Spelman, Mrs Caroline A. (*b.* 1958) *C., Meriden,*
Maj. 3,784

*Spicer, Sir Michael (*b.* 1943) *C., Worcestershire West,*
Maj. 5,374

Spink, Dr Robert (*b.* 1948) *C., Castle Point,* Maj. 985

*Spring, Richard J. G. (*b.* 1946) *C., Suffolk West,*
Maj. 4,295

*Squire, Ms Rachel A. (*b.* 1954) *Lab., Dunfermline West,*
Maj. 10,980

*Stanley, Rt. Hon. Sir John (*b.* 1942) *C., Tonbridge and
Malling,* Maj. 8,250

Starkey, Dr Phyllis M. (*b.* 1947) *Lab., Milton Keynes South
West,* Maj. 6,978

*Steen, Anthony (*b.* 1939) *C., Totnes,* Maj. 3,597

*Steinberg, Gerald N. (*b.* 1945) *Lab., City of Durham,*
Maj. 13,441

*Stevenson, George W. (*b.* 1938) *Lab., Stoke-on-Trent
South,* Maj. 10,489

*Stewart, David J. (*b.* 1956) *Lab., Inverness East, Nairn
and Lochaber,* Maj. 4,716

*Stewart, Ian (*b.* 1950) *Lab., Eccles,* Maj. 14,528

*Stinchcombe, Paul D. (*b.* 1962) *Lab., Wellingborough,*
Maj. 2,355

*Stoate, Dr Howard G. A. (*b.* 1954) *Lab., Dartford,*
Maj. 3,306

*Strang, Rt. Hon Dr Gavin (*b.* 1943) *Lab., Edinburgh East
and Musselburgh,* Maj. 12,168

*Straw, Rt. Hon. J. W. (Jack) (*b.* 1946) *Lab., Blackburn,*
Maj. 9,249

*Streeter, Gary N. (*b.* 1955) *C., Devon South West,*
Maj. 7,144

*Stringer, Graham E. (*b.* 1950) *Lab., Manchester Blackley,*
Maj. 14,464

*Stuart, Mrs Gisela G. (*b.* 1955) *Lab., Birmingham
Edgbaston,* Maj. 4,698

*Stunell, Andrew (*b.* 1942) *LD, Hazel Grove,* Maj. 8,435

*Sutcliffe, Gerard (*b.* 1953) *Lab., Bradford South,*
Maj. 9,662

Swayne, Desmond A. (*b.* 1956) *C., New Forest West,*
Maj. 13,191

Swire, Hugo (*b.* 1959) *C., Devon East,* Maj. 8,195

*Syms, Robert A. R. (*b.* 1956) *C., Poole,* Maj. 7,166

Tami, Mark (*b.* 1963) *Lab., Alyn and Deeside,* Maj. 9,222

*Tapsell, Sir Peter (*b.* 1930) *C., Louth and Horncastle,*
Maj. 7,554

*Taylor, Rt. Hon. Ann (*b.* 1947) *Lab., Dewsbury,*
,Maj. 7,449

*Taylor, Ms Dari J. (*b.* 1944) *Lab., Stockton South,*
Maj. 9,086

Taylor, David L. (*b.* 1946) *Lab. Co-op., Leicestershire North
West,* Maj. 8,157

*Taylor, Sir Edward (Teddy) (*b.* 1937) *C., Rochford and
Southend East,* Maj. 7,034

*Taylor, Ian C., MBE (*b.* 1945) *C., Esher and Walton,*
Maj. 11,538

*Taylor, John M. (*b.* 1941) *C., Solihull,* Maj. 9,407

*Taylor, Matthew O. J. (*b.* 1963) *LD, Truro and St Austell,*
Maj. 8,065

Taylor, Dr Richard (*b.* 1935) *KHHC, Wyre Forest,*
Maj. 17,630

Thomas, Gareth (*b.* 1954) *Lab., Clwyd West,* Maj. 1,115

*Thomas, Gareth R. (*b.* 1967) *Lab., Harrow West,*
Maj. 6,156

*Thomas, Simon (*b.* 1963) *PC, Ceredigion,* Maj. 3,944

*Thurso, John (*b.* 1953) *LD, Caithness, Sutherland and
Easter Ross,* Maj. 2,744

*Timms, Stephen C., (*b.* 1955) *Lab., East Ham,*
Maj. 21,032

*Tipping, S. P. (Paddy) (*b.* 1949) *Lab., Sherwood,*
Maj. 9,373

Todd, Mark W. (*b.* 1954) *Lab., Derbyshire South,*
Maj. 7,851

Tonge, Dr Jennifer L. (*b.* 1941) *LD, Richmond Park,*
Maj. 4,964

*Touhig, J. Donnelly (Don) (*b.* 1947) *Lab. Co-op., Islwyn,*
Maj. 15,309

*Tredinnick, David A. S. (*b.* 1950) *C., Bosworth,*
Maj. 2,280

*Trend, Hon. Michael St J. CBE (*b.* 1952) *C., Windsor,*
Maj. 8,889

*Trickett, Jon H. (*b.* 1950) *Lab., Hemsworth,* Maj. 15,636

*Trimble, Rt. Hon. W. David (*b.* 1944) *UUP, Upper
Bann,* Maj. 2,058

Truswell, Paul A. (*b.* 1955) *Lab., Pudsey,* Maj. 5,626

Turner, Andrew (*b.* 1953) *C., Isle of Wight,* Maj. 2,826

*Turner, Dennis (*b.* 1942) *Lab. Co-op., Wolverhampton
South East,* Maj. 12,464

Turner, Desmond S. (*b.* 1939) *Lab., Brighton Kemptown,*
Maj. 4,922

*Turner, Neil (*b.* 1945) *Lab., Wigan,* Maj. 13,743

*Twigg, J. Derek (*b.* 1959) *Lab., Halton,* Maj. 17,428

*Twigg, Stephen (*b.* 1966) *Lab., Enfield Southgate,*
Maj. 5,546

*Tyler, Paul A. CBE (*b.* 1941) *LD, Cornwall North,*
Maj. 9,832

*Tynan, Bill (*b.* 1940) *Lab., Hamilton South,* Maj. 10,775

*Tyrie, Andrew G. (*b.* 1957) *C., Chichester,* Maj. 11,355

*Vaz, N. Keith A. S. (*b.* 1956) *Lab., Leicester East,*
Maj. 13,422

*Viggers, Peter J. (*b.* 1938) *C., Gosport,* Maj. 2,621

*Vis, R. J. (Rudi) (*b.* 1941) *Lab., Finchley and Golders
Green,* Maj. 3,716

*Walley, Ms Joan L. (*b.* 1949) *Lab., Stoke-on-Trent North,*
Maj. 11,784

*Walter, Robert J. (*b.* 1948) *C., Dorset North,* Maj. 3,797

*Ward, Ms Claire M. (*b.* 1972) *Lab., Watford,* Maj. 5,555

*Wareing, Robert N. (*b.* 1930) *Lab., Liverpool West Derby,*
Maj. 15,853

*Waterson, Nigel C., (*b.* 1950) *C., Eastbourne,* Maj. 2,154

Watkinson, Angela (*b.* 1941) *C., Upminster,* Maj. 1,241

*Watson, Tom (*b.* 1967) *Lab., West Bromwich East,*
Maj. 9,763

Watts, David L. (*b.* 1951) *Lab., St Helens North,*
Maj. 15,901

Webb, Prof. Steven J. (*b.* 1965) *LD, Northavon,*
Maj. 9,877

Weir, Michael (*b.* 1957) *SNP, Angus,* Maj. 3,611

White, Brian A. R. (*b.* 1957) *Lab., Milton Keynes North
East,* Maj. 1,829

*Whitehead, Alan P. V. (*b.* 1950) *Lab., Southampton Test,*
Maj. 11,207

*Whittingdale, John F. L. OBE (*b.* 1959) *C., Maldon and
Chelmsford East,* Maj. 8,462

*Wicks Malcolm H. (*b.* 1947) *Lab., Croydon North,*
Maj. 16,858

*Widdecombe, Rt. Hon. Ann N. (*b.* 1947) *C., Maidstone
and the Weald,* Maj. 10,318

Wiggin, Bill (*b.* 1966) *C., Leominster,* Maj. 10,367

*Wilkinson, John A. D. (*b.* 1940) *C., Ruislip-Northwood,*
Maj. 7,537

*Willetts, David L. (*b.* 1956) *C., Havant,* Maj. 4,207

*Williams, Rt. Hon. Alan J. (*b.* 1930) *Lab., Swansea West,*
Maj. 9,550

*Williams, Betty (*b.* 1944) *Lab., Conwy,* Maj. 6,219

Williams, Hywel (b. 1953) PC, Caernarfon, Maj. 3,511
Williams Roger (b. 1948) LD, Brecon and Radnorshire, Maj. 751
*Willis, G. Philip (b. 1941) LD, Harrogate and Knaresborough, Maj. 8,845
Wills, Michael D. (b. 1952) Lab., Swindon North, Maj. 8,105
*Wilshire, David (b. 1943) C., Spelthorne, Maj. 3,262
*Wilson, Brian D. H. (b. 1948) Lab., Cunninghame North, Maj. 8,398
*Winnick, David J. (b. 1933) Lab., Walsall North, Maj. 9,391
*Winterton, Mrs J. Ann (b. 1941) C., Congleton, Maj. 7,134
*Winterton, Nicholas R. (b. 1938) C., Macclesfield, Maj. 7,200
Winterton, Ms Rosalie (b. 1958) Lab., Doncaster Central, Maj. 11,999
Wishart, Peter (b. 1962) SNP, Tayside North, Maj. 3,283
*Wood, Michael R. (b. 1946) Lab., Batley and Spen, Maj. 5,064
Woodward, Shaun (b. 1958) Lab., St Helens South, Maj. 8,985
*Woolas, Philip J. (b. 1959) Lab., Oldham East and Saddleworth, Maj. 2,726
*Worthington, Anthony (b. 1941) Lab., Clydebank and Milngavie, Maj. 10,724
*Wray, James (b. 1938) Lab., Glasgow Baillieston, Maj. 9,839
Wright, Anthony D. (b. 1954) Lab., Great Yarmouth, Maj. 4,564
*Wright, Anthony W. D.Phil. (b. 1948) Lab., Cannock Chase, Maj. 10,704
Wright, David (b. 1967) Lab., Telford, Maj. 8,383
*Wyatt, Derek M. (b. 1949) Lab., Sittingbourne and Sheppey, Maj. 3,509
*Yeo, Timothy S. K. (b. 1945) C., Suffolk South, Maj. 5,081
*Young, Rt. Hon. Sir George Bt. (b. 1941) C., Hampshire North West, Maj. 12,009
Younger-Ross, Richard (b. 1953) LD, Teignbridge, Maj. 3,011

*Sitting MPs
For by-elections since 2001 see page 177.

GENERAL ELECTION STATISTICS

PARLIAMENTS SINCE 1970

Assembled	Dissolved	yr	m.	d.
29 June 1970	8 February 1974	3	7	10
6 March 1974	20 September 1974	0	6	14
22 October 1974	7 April 1979	4	5	16
9 May 1979	13 May 1983	4	0	4
15 June 1983	18 May 1987	3	11	3
17 June 1987	16 March 1992	4	8	28
27 April 1992	8 April 1997	4	11	12
7 May 1997	14 May 2001	4	0	7
13 June 2001				

GENERAL ELECTION TURNOUT

	2001	1997
England	59.4	71.4
Wales	61.6	73.5
Scotland	58.2	71.3
Northern Ireland	68.0	67.1

VOTES CAST 1997 AND 2001

	1997	2001
Conservative	9,600,940	8,357,622
Labour	13,517,911	10,724,895
Liberal Democrats	5,243,440	4,812,833
Scottish Nationalist	622,260	464,305
Plaid Cymru	161,030	195,892
N. Ireland parties	780,920	635,735
Others	1,361,701	1,177,516
Total	31,287,702	26,368,798

PARLIAMENTARY CONSTITUENCIES AS AT 7 JUNE 2001

The results of voting in each parliamentary division at the general election of 7 June 2001 are given below. The majority in the 1997 general election and any by-election between 1997 and 2001, is given below the 2001 result.

Symbols
* Sitting MP
† Previously MP in another seat

Abbreviations

AL	Asian League
Alliance	Alliance
Anti-Corrupt	Anti-Corruption Forum
BNP	British National Party
Bean	New Millennium Bean
CPA	Christian Peoples Alliance
Ch. D.	Christian Democrat
Choice	People's Choice
Comm.	Communist Party
Community	Independent Community Candidate Empowering Change
C.	Conservative
Country	Countryside Party
Customer	Direct Customer Service Party
Def Welfare	Defend the Welfare State Against Blairism
DUP	Democratic Unionist Party
EIP	English Independence Party
Elvis	Church of the Militant Elvis Party
Ext. Club	Extinction Club
FDP	Fancy Dress Party
Free	Freedom Party
Green	Green Party
Grey	Grey Party
Ind.	Independent

Ind. UU	Independent United Unionist
Ind. Vote	Independent - Vote for Yourself Party
IOW	Isle of Wight Party
JLD P	John Lillburne Democratic Party
JP	Justice Party
KHHC	Kidderminster Hospital and Health Concern
Lab.	Labour
Lab. Co-op.	Labour and Co-operative
LCA	Legalise Cannabis Alliance
LD	Liberal Democrat
LP	Liberated Party
Left All	All Left Alliance
Lib.	Liberal
Loony	Monster Raving Loony Party
Low Excise	Lower Excise Duty Party
Marxist	Marxist Party
Meb. Ker.	Mebyon Kernow
Muslim	Muslim Party
NBP	New Britain Party
NF	National Front
NI Unionist	Northern Ireland Unionist
NI WC	Northern Ireland Women's Coalition
PC	Plaid Cymru
PF	Pathfinders
PJP	People's Justice Party
PUP	Progressive Unionist Party
Pacifist	Pacifist for Peace, Justice, Cooperation, Environment
Pensioner	Pensioner Coalition
Pro Euro C	Pro Euro Conservative Party
ProLife	ProLife Alliance
Prog Dem	Progress Democratic Party Members Decide Policy
Qari	Qari

R & R Loony	Rock & Roll Loony Party
RP	Rate Payer
Ref. UK	Reform UK
Reform	Reform 2000
Res. Motor	Motor Residents and Motorists of Great Britain
SDLP	Social Democratic and Labour Party
SF	Sinn Fein
SNP	Scottish National Party
SSP	Scottish Socialist Party
Scot. Ref.	Scottish Freedom Referendum Party
Scot. U.	Scottish Unionist
Soc.	Socialist Party
Soc. All.	Socialist Alliance
Soc. Alt.	Socialist Alternative Party
Soc. Lab.	Socialist Labour Party
Socialist	Socialist
Speaker	The Speaker
Stuck	Stuckist
Sunrise	Chairman of Sunrise Radio
Tatton	Tatton Group Independent
Third	Third Way
Truth	Truth Party
UK Ind.	UK Independence Party
UKU	United Kingdom Unionist
UUP	Ulster Unionist Party
Unrep.	Unrepresented People's Party
WSA	Welsh Socialist Alliance
Wessex Reg.	Wessex Regionalist
WFLOE	Women for Life on Earth
Women's Co.	Women's Coalition
WP	Workers' Party
WRP	Workers' Revolutionary Party
Wrestling	Jam Wrestling Party

ENGLAND

ALDERSHOT
E. 78,262   T. 45,315 (57.90%)
*Gerald Howarth, C.	19,106
Adrian Collett, LD	12,542
Luke Akehurst, Lab.	11,391
Derek Rumsey, UK Ind.	797
Adam Stacey, Green	630
Arthur Pendragon, Ind.	459
Alan Hope, Loony	390

C. majority 6,564 (14.49%)
1.13% swing LD to C.
(1997: C. maj. 6,621 (12.22%))

ALDRIDGE-BROWNHILLS
E. 62,388   T. 37,810 (60.60%)   C. hold
*Richard Shepherd, C.	18,974
Ian Geary, Lab.	15,206
Mrs Monica Howes, LD	3,251
John Rothery, Soc. All.	379

C. majority 3,768 (9.97%)
2.26% swing Lab. to C.
(1997: C. maj. 2,526 (5.44%))

ALTRINCHAM & SALE WEST
E. 71,820   T. 43,568 (60.66%)   C. hold
*Graham Brady, C.	20,113
Ms Janet Baugh, Lab.	17,172
Christopher Gaskell, LD	6,283

C. majority 2,941 (6.75%)
1.92% swing Lab. to C.
(1997: C. maj. 1,505 (2.91%))

AMBER VALLEY
E. 73,798   T. 44,513 (60.32%)   Lab. hold
*Ms Judy Mallaber, Lab.	23,101
Ms Gillian Shaw, C.	15,874
Ms Kate Smith, LD	5,538

Lab. majority 7,227 (16.24%)
2.49% swing Lab. to C.
(1997: Lab. maj. 11,613 (21.21%))

ARUNDEL & SOUTH DOWNS
E. 70,956   T. 45,889 (64.67%)   C. hold
*Howard Flight, C.	23,969
Derek Deedman, LD	10,265
Charles Taylor, Lab.	9,488
Robert Perrin, UK Ind.	2,167

C. majority 13,704 (29.86%)
1.26% swing LD to C.
(1997: C. maj. 14,035 (27.34%))

ASHFIELD
E. 73,428   T. 39,350 (53.59%)   Lab. hold
*Rt. Hon. G. Hoon, Lab.	22,875
Julian Leigh, C.	9,607
Bill Smith, LD	4,428
Melvin Harby, Ind.	1,471
George Watson, Soc. All.	589
Ms Katrina Howse, Soc. Lab.	380

Lab. majority 13,268 (33.72%)
5.60% swing Lab. to C.
(1997: Lab. maj. 22,728 (44.91%))

ASHFORD
E. 76,699   T. 47,937 (62.50%)   C. hold
*Damien Green, C.	22,739
John Adams, Lab.	15,380
Keith Fitchett, LD	7,236
Richard Boden, Green	1,353
David Waller, UK Ind.	1,229

C. majority 7,359 (15.35%)
2.84% swing Lab. to C.
(1997: C. maj. 5,355 (9.68%))

ASHTON UNDER LYNE
E. 72,820   T. 35,764 (49.11%)   Lab. hold
David Heyes, Lab.	22,340
Tim Charlesworth, C.	6,822
Mrs Kate Fletcher, LD	4,237
Roger Woods, BNP	1,617
Nigel Rolland, Green	748

Lab. majority 15,518 (43.39%)
2.59% swing Lab. to C.
(1997: Lab. maj. 22,965 (48.57%))

AYLESBURY
E. 80,002   T. 49,087 (61.36%)   C. hold
*David Lidington, C.	23,230
Peter Jones, LD	13,221
Keith White, Lab.	11,388
Justin Harper, UK Ind.	1,248

C. majority 10,009 (20.39%)
2.88% swing Lab. to C.
(1997: C. maj. 8,419 (14.63%))

BANBURY
E. 83,392   T. 51,515 (61.77%)   C. hold
*Tony Baldry, C.	23,271
Leslie Sibley, Lab.	18,052
Tony Worgan, LD	8,216
Bev Cotton, Green	1,281
Stephen Harris, UK Ind.	695

C. majority 5,219 (10.13%)
1.02% swing to C.
(1997: C. maj. 4,737 (8.10%))

BARKING
E. 55,229   T. 25,126 (45.49%)   Lab. hold
*Mrs Margaret Hodge, Lab.	15,302
Mike Weatherley, C.	5,768
Anura Keppetipola, LD	2,450
Mark Toleman, BNP	1,606

Lab. majority 9,534 (37.94%)
5.14% swing Lab. to C.
(1997: Lab. maj. 15,896 (48.22%))

BARNSLEY CENTRAL
E. 60,086   T. 27,543 (45.84%)   Lab. hold
*Eric Illsley, Lab.	19,181
Alan Hartley, LD	4,051
Ian McCord, C.	3,608
Henry Rajch, Soc. All.	703

Lab. majority 15,130 (54.93%)
6.26% swing Lab. to LD
(1997: Lab. maj. 24,501 (67.15%))

BARNSLEY EAST & MEXBOROUGH
E. 65,655   T. 32,509 (49.51%)   Lab. hold
*Jeff Ennis, Lab.	21,945
Mrs Sharron Brook, LD	5,156
Matthew Offord, C.	4,024
Terry Robinson, Soc. Lab.	722
George Savage, UK Ind.	662

Lab. majority 16,789 (51.64%)
5.57% swing Lab. to LD
(1997: Lab. maj. 26,763 (61.76%))

BARNSLEY WEST & PENISTONE
E. 65,291   T. 34,564 (52.94%)   Lab. hold
*Michael Clapham, Lab.	20,244
William Rowe, C.	7,892
Miles Crompton, LD	6,428

Lab. majority 12,352 (35.74%)
2.59% swing Lab. to C.
(1997: Lab. maj. 17,267 (40.91%))

BARROW & FURNESS
E. 64,746   T. 39,020 (60.27%)   Lab. hold
*Rt. Hon. J. Hutton, Lab.	21,724
James Airey, C.	11,835
Barry Rabone, LD	4,750
John Smith, UK Ind.	711

Lab. majority 9,889 (25.34%)
2.36% swing Lab. to C.
(1997: Lab. maj. 14,497 (30.06%))

BASILDON
E. 74,121   T. 40,875 (55.15%)   Lab. Co-op hold
*Ms Angela Smith, Lab. Co-op.	21,551
Dominic Schofield, C.	13,813
Ms Jane Smithard, LD	3,691
Frank Mallon, UK Ind.	1,397
Dick Duane, Soc. All.	423

Lab. Co-op majority 7,738 (18.93%)
3.04% swing Lab. Co-op to C.
(1997: Lab. maj. 13,280 (25.02%))

BASINGSTOKE
E. 79,110   T. 47,995 (60.67%)   C. hold
*Andrew Hunter, C.	20,490
Jon Hartley, Lab.	19,610
Steve Sollitt, LD	6,693
Mrs Kim-Elisbeth Graham, UK Ind.	1,202

C. majority 880 (1.83%)
1.18% swing C. to Lab.
(1997: C. maj. 2,397 (4.19%))

BASSETLAW
E. 68,302   T. 38,895 (56.95%)   Lab. hold
John Mann, Lab.	21,506
Mrs Alison Holley, C.	11,758
Neil Taylor, LD	4,942
Kevin Meloy, Soc. Lab.	689

Lab. majority 9,748 (25.06%)
5.68% swing Lab. to C.
(1997: Lab. maj 17,460 (36.43%))

BATH
E. 71,372   T. 46,296 (64.87%)   LD hold
*Don Foster, LD	23,372
Ashley Fox, C.	13,478
Ms Marilyn Hawkings, Lab.	7,269
Mike Boulton, Green	1,469
Andrew Tettenborn, UK Ind.	708

LD majority 9,894 (21.37%)
2.06% swing C. to LD
(1997: C. maj. (17.26%))

BATLEY & SPEN
E. 63,665   T. 38,542 (60.54%)   Lab. hold
*Mike Wood, Lab.	19,224
Mrs Elizabeth Peacock, C.	14,160
Ms Kath Pinnock, LD	3,989
Clive Lord, Green	595
Allen Burton, UK Ind.	574

Lab. majority 5,064 (13.14%)
0.03% swing C. to Lab.
(1997: Lab. maj. 6,141 (13.08%))

BATTERSEA
E. 67,495   T. 36,804 (54.53%)   Lab. hold
*Martin Linton, Lab.	18,498
Mrs Lucy Shersby, C.	13,445
Ms Siobhan Vitelli, LD	4,450
Thomas Barber, Ind.	411

Lab. majority 5,053 (13.73%)
1.21% swing C. to Lab.
(1997: Lab. maj. 5,360 (11.31%))

BEACONSFIELD
E. 68,378   T. 42,044 (61.49%)   C. hold
*Dominic Grieve C.   22,233
Stephen Lathrope, Lab.   9,168
Stephen Lloyd, LD   9,017
Andrew Moffatt, UK Ind.   1,626
C. majority 13,065 (31.07%)
0.95% swing Lab. to C.
(1997: C. maj. 13,987 (27.86%))

BECKENHAM
E. 72,241   T. 45,562 (63.07%)   C. hold
*Mrs Jacqui Lait C.   20,618
Richard Watts, Lab.   15,659
Alex Feakes, LD   7,308
Ms Karen Moran, Green   961
Christopher Pratt, UK Ind.   782
Rif Winfield Lib.   234
C. majority 4,959 (10.88%)
0.89% swing Lab. to C.
(1997 Nov. by-election: C. maj. 1,227
(3.85%); (1997: C. maj. 4,953 (9.11%))

BEDFORD
E. 67,763   T. 40,579 (59.88%)   Lab. hold
*Patrick Hall, Lab.   19,454
Mrs Nicky Attenborough, C.   13,297
Michael Headley, LD   6,425
Dr Richard Rawlins, Ind.   973
Mrs Jennifer Lo Bianco, UK Ind.   430
Lab. majority 6,157 (15.17%)
0.89% swing Lab. to C.
(1997: Lab. maj. 8,300 (16.96%))

BEDFORDSHIRE MID
E. 70,594   T. 46,638 (66.07%)   C. hold
*Jonathan Sayeed, C.   22,109
James Valentine, Lab.   14,043
Graham Mabbutt, LD   9,205
Christopher Laurence, UK Ind.   1,281
C. majority 8,066 (17.29%)
1.89% swing Lab. to C.
(1997: C. maj. 7,090 (13.51%))

BEDFORDSHIRE NORTH EAST
E. 69,451   T. 45,246 (65.15%)   C. hold
Alastair Burt, C.   22,586
Philip Ross, Lab.   14,009
Dan Rogerson, LD   7,409
Ms Ros Hill, UK Ind.   1,242
C. majority 8,577 (18.96%)
3.64% swing Lab. to C.
(1997: C. maj. 5,883 (11.68%))

BEDFORDSHIRE SOUTH WEST
E. 72,126   T. 43,854 (60.80%)   C. hold
Andrew Selous, C.   18,477
Andrew Date, Lab.   17,701
Martin Pantling, LD   6,473
Tom Wise, UK Ind.   1,203
C. majority 776 (1.77%)
0.76% swing Lab. to C.
(1997: C. maj. 132 (0.24%))

BERWICK-UPON-TWEED
E. 56,918   T. 36,308 (63.79%)   LD hold
*Rt. Hon. A. Beith LD   18,651
Glen Sanderson, C.   10,193
Martin Walker, Lab.   6,435
John Pearson, UK Ind.   1,029
LD majority 8,458 (23.30%)
0.94% swing C. to LD
(1997: Lab. maj. 8,042 (19.24%))

BETHNAL GREEN & BOW
E. 79,192   T. 38,470 (48.58%)   Lab. hold
*Ms Oona King, Lab.   19,380
Shahagir Faruk, C.   9,323
Ms Janet Ludlow, LD   5,946
Ms Anna Bragga, Green   1,666
Michael Davidson, BNP   1,267
Dennis Delderfield, NBP   888
Lab. majority 10,057 (26.14%)
0.44% swing C. to Lab.
(1997: Lab. maj. 11,285 (25.26%))

BEVERLEY & HOLDERNESS
E. 75,146   T. 46,375 (61.71%)   C. hold
*James Cran, C.   19,168
Ms Pippa Langford, Lab.   18,387
Stewart Willie, LD   7,356
Stephen Wallis, UK Ind.   1,464
C. majority 781 (1.68%)
0.08% swing Lab. to C.
(1997: C. maj. 811 (1.53%))

BEXHILL & BATTLE
E. 69,010   T. 44,783 (64.89%)   C. hold
Greg Barker, C.   21,555
Stephen Hardy, LD   11,052
Ms Anne Moore-Williams, Lab.   8,702
Nigel Farage, UK Ind.   3,474
C. majority 10,503 (23.45%)
0.40% swing Lab. to C.
(1997: C. maj. 11,100 (22.66%))

BEXLEYHEATH & CRAYFORD
E. 63,580   T. 40,378 (63.51%)   Lab. hold
*Nigel Beard, Lab.   17,593
David Evennett, C.   16,121
Nickolas O'Hare, LD   4,476
Colin Smith, BNP   1,408
John Dunford, UK Ind.   780
Lab. majority 1,472 (3.65%)
1.72% swing Lab. to C.
(1997: Lab. maj. 3,415 (7.08%))

BILLERICAY
E. 78,528   T. 45,598 (58.07%)   C. hold
John Baron, C.   21,608
Ms Amanda Campbell, Lab.   16,595
Frank Bellard, LD   6,323
Nick Yeomans, UK Ind.   1,072
C. majority 5,013 (10.99%)
4.27% swing Lab. to C.
(1997: C. maj. 1,356 (2.45%))

BIRKENHEAD
E. 60,726   T. 28,967 (47.70%)   Lab. hold
*Rt. Hon. F. Field, Lab.   20,418
Brian Stewart, C.   4,827
Roy Wood, LD   3,722
Lab. majority 15,591 (53.82%)
0.86% swing Lab. to C.
(1997: Lab. maj. 21,843 (55.55%))

BIRMINGHAM EDGBASTON
E. 67,405   T. 37,749 (56.00%)   Lab. hold
*Ms Gisela Stuart Lab.   18,517
Nigel Hastilow, C.   13,819
Ms Nicola Davies, LD   4,528
John Gretton, Pro Euro C   454
Sam Brackenbury, Soc. Lab.   431
Lab. majority 4,698 (12.45%)
1.23% swing C. to Lab.
(1997: Lab. maj. 4,842 (9.99%))

BIRMINGHAM ERDINGTON
E. 65,668   T. 30,604 (46.60%)   Lab. hold
Sion Llewelyn Simon, Lab.   17,375
Oliver Lodge, C.   7,413
Ms Sandra Johnson, LD   3,602
Michael Shore, NF   681
Steve Goddard, Soc. All.   669
Mark Nattrass, UK Ind.   521
Ms Judith Sambrook-Marshall,
   Soc. Lab.   343
Lab. majority 9,962 (32.55%)
0.62% swing C. to Lab.
(1997: Lab. maj. 12,657 (31.32%))

BIRMINGHAM HALL GREEN
E. 57,563   T. 33,084 (57.47%)   Lab. hold
*Stephen McCabe, Lab.   18,049
Chris White, C.   11,401
Punjab Singh, LD   2,926
Peter Johnson, UK Ind.   708
Lab. majority 6,648 (20.09%)
0.02% swing Lab. to C.
(1997: Lab. maj. 8,420 (20.14%))

BIRMINGHAM HODGE HILL
E. 55,254   T. 26,465 (47.90%)   Lab. hold
*Rt. Hon. T. Davis, Lab.   16,901
Mrs Debbie Lewis, C.   5,283
Alistair Dow, LD   2,147
Lee Windridge, BNP   889
Parwez Hussain, PJP   561
Dennis Cridge, Soc. Lab.   284
Harvey Vivian, UK Ind.   275
Ayub Khan, Muslim   125
Lab. majority 11,618 (43.90%)
1.16% swing C. to Lab.
(1997: Lab. maj. 14,200 (41.58%))

BIRMINGHAM LADYWOOD
E. 71,113   T. 31,493 (44.29%)   Lab. hold
*Rt. Hon. Ms C. Short, Lab.   21,694
Benjamin Prentice, C.   3,551
Mahmood Chaudhry, LD   2,586
Allah Ditta, PJP   2,112
Surinder Virdee, Soc. Lab.   443
Mahmood Hussain, Muslim   432
James Caffery, ProLife   392
Dr Anneliese Nattrass, UK Ind.   283
Lab. majority 18,143 (57.61%)
1.59% swing Lab. to C.
(1997: Lab. maj. 23,082 (60.78%))

BIRMINGHAM NORTHFIELD
E. 55,922   T. 29,534 (52.81%)   Lab. hold
*Richard Burden, Lab.   16,528
Nils Purser, C.   8,730
Trevor Sword, LD   3,322
Stephen Rogers, UK Ind.   550
Clive Walder, Soc. All.   193
Zane Carpenter, Soc. Lab.   151
Andrew Chaffer, Comm.   60
Lab. majority 7,798 (26.40%)
1.53% swing Lab. to C.
(1997: Lab. maj. 11,443 (29.46%))

BIRMINGHAM PERRY BARR
E. 71,121   T. 37,417 (52.61%)   Lab. hold
Khalid Mahmood, *Lab.*   17,415
David Binns, *C.*   8,662
Jon Hunt, *LD*   8,566
Avtar Singh Jouh, *Soc. Lab.*   1,544
Ms Caroline Johnson, *Soc. All.*   465
Ms Natalya Nattrass, *UK Ind.*   352
Michael Roche, *Marxist*   221
Robert Davidson, *Muslim*   192
Lab. majority 8,753 (23.39%)
8.96% swing Lab. to C.
(1997: Lab. maj. 18,957 (41.32%))

BIRMINGHAM SELLY OAK
E. 71,237   T. 40,100 (56.29%)   Lab. hold
*Dr Lynne Jones, *Lab.*   21,015
Ken Hardeman, *C.*   10,676
David Osborne, *LD*   6,532
Barney Smith, *Green*   1,309
Mrs Beryl Williams, *UK Ind.*   568
Lab. majority 10,339 (25.78%)
1.04% swing Lab. to C.
(1997: Lab. maj. 14,088 (27.87%))

**BIRMINGHAM SPARKBROOK &
SMALL HEATH**
E. 74,358   T. 36,647 (49.28%)   Lab. hold
*Roger Godsiff, *Lab.*   21,087
Qassim Afzal, *LD*   4,841
Shafaq Hussain, *PJP*   4,770
Iftkhar Hussain, *C.*   3,948
Gul Mohammed, *Ind.*   662
Wayne Vincent, *UK Ind.*   634
Abdul Aziz, *Muslim*   401
Salman Mirza, *Soc. All.*   304
Lab. majority 16,246 (44.33%))
5.31% swing Lab. to LD
(1997: Lab. maj. 19,526 (46.76%)

BIRMINGHAM YARDLEY
E. 52,444   T. 30,013 (57.23%)   Lab. hold
*Rt. Hon. Ms E. Morris *Lab.*   14,085
John Hemming, *LD*   11,507
Barrie Roberts, *C.*   3,941
Alan Ware, *UK Ind.*   329
Colin Wren, *Soc. Lab.*   151
Lab. majority 2,578 (8.59%)
2.74% swing Lab. to LD
(1997: Lab. maj. 5,315 (14.07%))

BISHOP AUCKLAND
E. 67,377   T. 38,559 (57.23%)   Lab. hold
*Rt. Hon. D. Foster, *Lab.*   22,680
Mrs Fiona McNish, *C.*   8,754
Chris Foote-Wood, *LD*   6,073
Carl Bennett, *Green*   1,052
Lab. majority 13,926 (36.12%)
4.85% swing Lab. to C.
(1997: Lab. maj. 21,064 (45.82%))

BLABY
E. 73,907   T. 47,642 (64.46%)   C. hold
*Andrew Robathan, *C.*   22,104
David Morgan, *Lab.*   15,895
Geoff Welsh, *LD*   8,286
Edward Scott, *BNP*   1,357
C. majority 6,209 (13.03%)
0.48% swing Lab. to C.
(1997: C. maj. 6,474 (12.08%))

BLACKBURN
E. 72,621   T. 40,484 (55.75%)   Lab. hold
*Rt. Hon. J. Straw, *Lab*   .21,808
John Cotton, *C.*   12,559
Imtiaz Patel, *LD*   3,264
Mrs Dorothy Baxter, *UK Ind.*   1,185
Paul Morris, *Ind.*   577
Terence Cullen, *Soc. Lab.*   559
Frederick Nichol, *Socialist*   532
Lab. majority 9,249 (22.85%)
3.79% swing Lab. to C.
(1997: Lab. maj. 14,451 (30.43%))

**BLACKPOOL NORTH &
FLEETWOOD**
E. 74,456   T. 42,581 (57.19%)   Lab. hold
*Ms Joan Humble, *Lab.*   21,610
Alan Vincent, *C.*   15,889
Steven Bate, *LD*   4,132
Colin Porter, *UK Ind.*   950
Lab. majority 5,721 (13.44%)
1.60% swing Lab. to C.
(1997: Lab. maj. 8,946 (16.64%))

BLACKPOOL SOUTH
E. 74,311   T. 38,792 (52.20%)   Lab. hold
*Gordon Marsden, *Lab.*   21,060
David Morris, *C.*   12,798
Ms Doreen Holt, *LD*   4,115
Mrs Val Cowell, *UK Ind.*   819
Lab. majority 8,262 (21.30%)
0.67% swing Lab. to C.
(1997: Lab. maj. 11,616 (22.63%))

BLAYDON
E. 64,574   T. 37,086 (57.43%)   Lab. hold
*John McWilliam, *Lab.*   20,340
Peter Maughan, *LD*   12,531
Mark Watson, *C.*   4,215
Lab. majority 7,809 (21.06%)
7.55% swing Lab. to LD
(1997: Lab. maj. 16,605 (36.16%))

BLYTH VALLEY
E. 63,274   T. 34,550 (54.60%)   Lab. hold
*Ronnie Campbell, *Lab.*   20,627
Jeff Reid, *LD*   8,439
Wayne Daley, *C.*   5,484
Lab. majority 12,188 (35.28%)
3.24% swing Lab. to LD
(1997: Lab. maj. 17,736 (41.75%))

**BOGNOR REGIS &
LITTLEHAMPTON**
E. 66,903   T. 38,968 (58.25%)   C. hold
*Nick Gibb, *C.*   17,602
George O'Neill, *Lab.*   11,959
Ms Pamela Peskett, *LD*   6,846
George Stride, *UK Ind.*   1,779
Ms Lilias Rider Haggard Cheyne,
  Green   782
C. majority 5,643 (14.48%)
0.64% swing C. to Lab.
(1997: C. maj. 7,321 (15.76%))

BOLSOVER
E. 67,537   T. 38,271 (56.67%)   Lab. hold
*Dennis Skinner, *Lab.*   26,249
Simon Massey, *C.*   7,472
Ms Marie Bradley, *LD*   4,550
Lab. majority 18,777 (49.06%)
4.10% swing Lab. to C.
(1997: Lab. maj. 27,149 (57.26%))

BOLTON NORTH EAST
E. 69,514   T. 38,950 (56.03%)   Lab. hold
*David Crausby, *Lab.*   21,166
Michael Winstanley, *C.*   12,744
Tim Perkins, *LD*   4,004
Kenneth McIvor, *Green*   629
Ms Lynne Lowe, *Soc. Lab.*   407
Lab. majority 8,422 (21.62%)
2.06% swing Lab. to C.
(1997: Lab. maj. 12,669 (25.74%))

BOLTON SOUTH EAST
E. 68,140   T. 34,154 (50.12%)   Lab. hold
*Dr Brian Iddon, *Lab.*   21,129
Haroon Rashid, *C.*   8,258
Frank Harasiwka, *LD*   3,941
Dr William John Kelly, *Soc. Lab.*   826
Lab. majority 12,871 (37.69%)
5.74% swing Lab. to C.
(1997: Lab. maj. 21,311 (49.16%))

BOLTON WEST
E. 66,033   T. 41,214 (62.41%)   Lab. hold
*Ms Ruth Kelly, *Lab.*   19,381
James Stevens, *C.*   13,863
Ms Barbara Ronson, *LD*   7,573
David Toomer, *Soc. All.*   397
Lab. majority 5,518 (13.39%)
0.50% swing Lab. to C.
(1997: Lab. maj. 7,072 (14.39%))

BOOTLE
E. 56,320   T. 27,594 (49.00%)   Lab. hold
*Joe Benton *Lab.*   21,400
Jim Murray, *LD*   2,357
Miss Judith Symes, *C.*   2,194
Dave Flynn, *Soc. Lab.*   971
Peter Glover, *Soc. All.*   672
Lab. majority 19,043 (69.01%)
4.05% swing Lab. to LD
(1997: Lab. maj. 28,421 (74.36%))

BOSTON & SKEGNESS
E. 69,010   T. 40,313 (58.42%)   C. hold
Mark Simmonds, *C.*   17,298
Ms Elaine Bird, *Lab.*   16,783
Duncan Moffatt, *LD*   4,994
Cyril Wakefield, *UK Ind.*   717
Martin Harrison, *Green*   521
C. majority 515 (1.28%)
0.06% swing C. to Lab.
(1997: C. maj. 647 (1.39%))

BOSWORTH
E. 69,992   T. 45,106 (64.44%)   C. hold
*David Tredinnick, *C.*   20,030
Andrew Furlong, *Lab.*   17,750
Jon Ellis, *LD*   7,326
C. majority 2,280 (5.05%)
1.54% swing Lab. to C.
(1997: C. maj. 1,027 (1.97%))

BOURNEMOUTH EAST
E. 60,454   T. 35,799 (59.22%)   C. hold
*David Atkinson, *C.*   15,501
Andrew Garratt, *LD*   12,067
Paul Nicholson, *Lab.*   7,107
George Chamberlaine, *UK Ind.*   1,124
C. majority 3,434 (9.59%)
0.21% swing C. to LD
(1997: C. maj. 4,346 (10.01%))

BOURNEMOUTH WEST
E. 62,038   T. 33,648 (54.24%)   C. hold
*John Butterfill, C.   14,417
David Stokes, Lab.   9,699
Ms Fiona Hornby, LD   8,468
Mrs Cynthia Blake, UK Ind.   1,064
C. majority 4,718 (14.02%)
1.54% swing C. to Lab.
(1997: C. maj. 5,710 (13.90%))

BRACKNELL
E. 81,118   T. 49,225 (60.68%)   C. hold
*Rt. Hon. A. Mackay, C.   22,962
Ms Janet Keene, Lab.   16,249
Ray Earwicker, LD   8,424
Lawrence Boxall, UK Ind.   1,266
Ms Dominica Roberts, (ProLife)   324
C. majority 6,713 (13.64%)
1.97% swing C. to Lab.
(1997: C. maj. 10,387 (17.58%))

BRADFORD NORTH
E. 66,454   T. 35,017 (52.69%)   Lab. hold
*Terry Rooney, Lab.   17,419
Zahid Iqbal, C.   8,450
David Ward, LD   6,924
John Brayshaw, BNP   1,613
Steven Schofield, Green   611
Lab. majority 8,969 (25.61%)
2.44% swing Lab. to C.)

BRADFORD SOUTH
E. 68,450   T. 35,137 (51.33%)   Lab. hold
*Gerry Sutcliffe, Lab.   19,603
Graham Tennyson, C.   9,941
Alexander Wilson-Fletcher, LD   3,717
Peter North, UK Ind.   783
Tony Kelly, Soc. Lab.   571
Ateeq Siddique, Soc. All.   302
George Riseborough, Def Welfare   220
Lab. majority 9,662 (27.50%)
0.61% swing Lab. to C.
(1997: Lab. maj. 12,936 (28.71%))

BRADFORD WEST
E. 71,620   T. 38,370 (53.57%)   Lab. hold
*Marsha Singh, Lab.   18,401
Mohammed Riaz, C.   14,236
John Robinson, Green   2,672
Abdul Rauf Khan, LD   2,437
Imran Hussain, UK Ind.   427
Farhan Khokhar, AL   197
Lab. majority 4,165 (10.85%)
1.17% swing C. to Lab.
(1997: Lab. maj. 3,877 (8.51%))

BRAINTREE
E. 79,157   T. 50,315 (63.56%)   Lab. hold
*Alan Hurst, Lab.   21,123
Brooks Newmark, C.   20,765
Peter Turner, LD   5,664
James Abbott, Green   1,241
Michael Nolan, LCA   774
Charles Cole, UK Ind.   748
Lab. majority 358 (0.71%)
0.95% swing Lab. to C.
(1997: Lab. maj. 1,451 (2.61%))

BRENT EAST
E. 58,095   T. 28,992 (49.90%)   Lab. hold
Paul Daisley, Lab.   18,325
David Gauke, C.   5,278
Ms Nowsheen Bhatti, LD   3,065
Ms Simone Aspis, Green   1,361
Ms Sarah Macken, (ProLife)   392
Ms Iris Cremer, Soc. Lab.   383
Ashwin Tanna, UK Ind.   188
Lab. majority 13,047 (45.00%)
0.01% swing Lab. to C.
(1997: Lab. maj. 15,882 (45.03%))

BRENT NORTH
E. 58,789   T. 33,939 (57.73%)   Lab. hold
*Barry Gardiner, Lab.   20,149
Philip Allott, C.   9,944
Paul Lorber, LD   3,846
Lab. majority 10,205 (30.07%)
9.77% swing C. to Lab.
(1997: Lab. maj. 4,019 (10.53%))

BRENT SOUTH
E. 55,891   T. 28,637 (51.24%)   Lab. hold
*Rt. Hon. P. Boateng, Lab.   20,984
Carupiah Selvarajah, C.   3,604
Havard Hughes, LD   3,098
Mick McDonnell, Soc. All.   491
Thomas Mac Stiofain, (Res. Motor)   460
Lab. majority 17,380 (60.69%)
1.81% swing C. to Lab.
(1997: Lab. maj. 19,691 (57.08%))

BRENTFORD & ISLEWORTH
E. 84,049   T. 44,514 (52.96%)   Lab. hold
*Ms Ann Keen Lab.   23,275
Tim Mack, C.   12,957
Gareth Hartwell, LD   5,994
Nic Ferriday, Green   1,324
Gerald Ingram, UK Ind.   412
Danny Faith, Soc. All.   408
Asa Khaira, Ind.   144
Lab. majority 10,318 (23.18%)
1.26% swing Lab. to C.
(1997: Lab. maj. 14,424 (25.70%))

BRENTWOOD & ONGAR
E. 64,695   T. 43,542 (67.30%)   C. hold
*Eric Pickles, C.   16,558
+Martin Bell, (Ind Bell)   13,737
David Kendall, LD   6,772
Ms Diana Johnson, Lab   .5,505
Ken Gulleford, UK Ind.   611
Peter Pryke, Ind.   239
David Bishop, Elvis   68
Tony Appleton, Ind.   52
C. majority 2,821 (6.48%)
(1997: C. maj. 9,690 (19.10%))

BRIDGWATER
E. 74,079   T. 47,847 (64.59%)   C. hold
Ian Liddell-Grainger, C.   19,354
Ian Thorn, LD   14,367
William Monteith, Lab.   12,803
Ms Vicky Gardner, UK Ind.   1,323
C. majority 4,987 (10.42%)
3.57% swing LD to C.
(1997: C. maj. 1,796 (3.28%))

BRIGG & GOOLE
E. 63,536   T. 41,054 (64.62%)   Lab. hold
*Ian Cawsey, Lab.   20,066
Don Stewart, C.   16,105
David Nolan, LD   3,796
Godfrey Bloom, UK Ind.   688
Michael Kenny, Soc. Lab.   399
Lab. majority 3,961 (9.65%)
2.00% swing Lab. to C.
(1997: Lab. maj. 6,389 (13.65%))

BRIGHTON KEMPTOWN
E. 67,621   T. 39,203 (57.97%)   Lab. hold
*Dr Desmond Turner, Lab.   18,745
Geoffrey Theobald, C.   13,823
Ms Jan Marshall, LD   4,064
Hugh Miller, Green   1,290
Dr James Chamberlain-Webber,
  UK Ind.   543
John McLeod, Soc. Lab.   364
Dave Dobbs, (Free)   227
Ms Elaine Cook, (ProLife)   147
Lab. majority 4,922 (12.56%)
2.45% swing C. to Lab.
(1997: Lab. maj. 3,534 (7.66%))

BRIGHTON PAVILION
E. 69,200   T. 40,723 (58.85%)
  Lab. Co-op hold
*David Lepper, Lab. Co-op.   19,846
David Gold, C.   10,203
Ms Ruth Berry, LD   5,348
Keith Taylor, Green   3,806
Ian Fyvie, Soc. Lab.   573
Bob Dobbs, (Free)   409
Stuart Hutchin, UK Ind.   361
Ms Marie Paragallo, (ProLife)   177
Lab. Co-op majority 9,643 (23.68%)
1.63% swing Lab. Co-op to C.
(1997: Lab. maj. 13,181 (26.93%))

BRISTOL EAST
E. 70,279   T. 40,334 (57.39%)   Lab. hold
*Ms Jean Corston, Lab.   22,180
Jack Lo-Presti, C.   8,788
Brian Niblett, LD   6,915
Geoff Collard, Green   1,110
Roger Marsh, UK Ind.   572
Mike Langley, Soc. Lab.   438
Andy Pryor, Soc. All.   331
Lab. majority 13,392 (33.20%)
0.16% swing Lab. to C.
(1997: Lab. maj. 16,159 (33.52%))

BRISTOL NORTH WEST
E. 76,756   T. 46,692 (60.83%)
  Lab. Co-op hold
*Doug Naysmith, Lab. Co-op.   24,436
Charles Hansard, C.   13,349
Peter Tyzack, LD   7,387
Miss Diane Carr, UK Ind.   1,149
Vince Horrigan, Soc. Lab.   371
Lab. Co-op majority 11,087 (23.74%)
1.57% swing C. to Lab. Co-op
(1997: Lab. maj. 11,382 (20.60%))

BRISTOL SOUTH
E. 72,490   T. 40,970 (56.52%)   Lab. hold
*Ms Dawn Primarolo, *Lab.*   23,299
Richard Eddy, *C.*   9,118
James Main, *LD*   6,078
Glenn Vowles, *Green*   1,233
Brian Drummond, *Soc. All.*   496
Chris Prasad, *UK Ind.*   496
Giles Shorter, *Soc. Lab.*   250
Lab. majority 14,181 (34.61%)
2.08% swing Lab. to C.
(1997: Lab. maj. 19,328 (38.77%))

BRISTOL WEST
E. 84,821   T. 55,665 (65.63%)   Lab. hold
*Ms Valerie Davey, *Lab.*   20,505
Stephen Williams, *LD*   16,079
Mrs Pamela Chesters, *C.*   16,040
John Devaney, *Green*   1,961
Bernard Kennedy, *Soc. Lab.*   590
Simon Muir, *UK Ind.*   490
Lab. majority 4,426 (7.95%)
0.37% swing LD to Lab.
(1997: Lab. maj. 1,493 (2.38%))

BROMLEY & CHISLEHURST
E. 68,763   T. 43,231 (62.87%)   C. hold
*Rt. Hon. E. Forth, *C.*   21,412
Ms Sue Polydorou, *Lab.*   12,375
Geoff Payne, *LD*   8,180
Rob Bryant, *UK Ind.*   1,264
C. majority 9,037 (20.90%)
0.09% swing C. to Lab.
(1997: C. maj. 11,118 (21.08%))

BROMSGROVE
E. 68,115   T. 45,684 (67.07%)   C. hold
*Miss Julie Kirkbride, *C.*   23,640
Peter McDonald, *Lab.*   15,502
Mrs Margaret Rowley, *LD*   5,430
Ian Gregory, *UK Ind.*   1,112
C. majority 8,138 (17.81%)
4.22% swing Lab. to C.
(1997: C. maj. 4,895 (9.38%))

BROXBOURNE
E. 68,982   T. 37,845 (54.86%)   C. hold
*Mrs Marion Roe, *C.*   20,487
David Prendergast, *Lab.*   11,494
Ms Julia Davies, *LD*   4,158
Martin Harvey, *UK Ind.*   858
John Cope, *BNP*   848
C. majority 8,993 (23.76%)
4.80% swing Lab. to C.
(1997: C. maj. 6,653 (14.16%))

BROXTOWE
E. 73,675   T. 49,004 (66.51%)   Lab. hold
*Nick Palmer, *Lab.*   23,836
Mrs Pauline Latham, *C.*   17,963
David Watts, *LD*   7,205
Lab. majority 5,873 (11.98%)
1.20% swing C. to Lab.
(1997: Lab. maj. 5,575 (9.59%))

BUCKINGHAM
E. 65,270   T. 45,272 (69.36%)   C. hold
*John Bercow, *C.*   24,296
Mark Seddon, *Lab.*   10,971
Ms Isobel Wilson, *LD*   9,037
Christopher Silcock, *UK Ind.*   968
C. majority 13,325 (29.43%)
2.18% swing Lab. to C.
(1997: C. maj. 12,386 (25.08%))

BURNLEY
E. 66,393   T. 36,884 (55.55%)   Lab. hold
*Peter Pike, *Lab.*   18,195
Robert Frost, *C.*   7,697
Paul Wright, *LD*   5,975
Steven Smith, *BNP*   4,151
Richard Buttrey, *UK Ind.*   866
Lab. majority 10,498 (28.46%)
4.62% swing Lab. to C.
(1997: Lab. maj. 17,062 (37.71%))

BURTON
E. 75,194   T. 46,457 (61.78%)   Lab. hold
*Ms Janet Dean, *Lab.*   22,783
Mrs Maggie Punyer, *C.*   17,934
David Fletcher, *LD*   4,468
Ian Crompton, *UK Ind.*   984
John Taylor, *(ProLife)*   288
Lab. maority 4,849 (10.44%)
0.59% swing Lab. to C.
(1997: Lab. Maj. 6,330 (11.62%))

BURY NORTH
E. 71,108   T. 44,788 (62.99%)   Lab. hold
*David Chaytor, *Lab.*   22,945
John Walsh, *C.*   16,413
Bryn Hackley, *LD*   5,430
Lab. majority 6,532 (14.58%)
0.15% swing C. to Lab.
(1997: Lab. maj. 7,866 (14.29%))

BURY SOUTH
E. 67,276   T. 39,539 (58.77%)   Lab. hold
*Ivan Lewis, *Lab.*   23,406
Mrs Nicola Le Page, *C.*   10,634
Tim Pickstone, *LD*   5,499
Lab. majority 12,772 (32.30%)
3.80% swing C. to Lab.
(1997: Lab. maj. 12,433 (24.70%))

BURY ST EDMUNDS
E. 76,146   T. 50,257 (66.00%)   C. hold
*David Ruffley, *C.*   21,850
Mark Ereira, *Lab.*   19,347
Richard Williams, *LD*   6,998
John Howlett, *UK Ind.*   831
Mike Brundle, *Ind.*   651
Michael Benwell, *Soc. Lab.*   580
C. majority 2,503 (4.98%)
2.16% swing Lab. to C.
(1997: C. maj. 368 (0.66%))

CALDER VALLEY
E. 75,298   T. 47,425 (62.98%)   Lab. hold
*Mrs Christine McCafferty, *Lab.*   20,244
Mrs Sue Robson-Catling, *C.*   17,150
Michael Taylor, *LD*   7,596
Steve Hutton, *Green*   1,034
John Nunn, *UK Ind.*   729
Philip Lockwood, *LCA*   672
Lab. majority 3,094 (6.52%)
2.27% swing Lab. to C.
(1997: Lab. maj. 6,255 (11.07%))

CAMBERWELL & PECKHAM
E. 53,694   T. 25,104 (46.75%)   Lab. hold
*Rt. Hon. Ms H. Harman, *Lab.*   17,473
Donnachadh McCarthy, *LD*   3,350
Jonathan Morgan, *C.*   2,740
Storm Poorun, *Green*   805
John Mulrenan, *Soc. All.*   478
Robert Adams, *Soc. Lab.*   188
Frank Sweeney, *WRP*   70
Lab. majority 14,123 (56.26%)
0.91% swing Lab. to LD
(1997: Lab. maj. 16,351 (57.43%))

CAMBRIDGE
E. 70,663   T. 42,836 (60.62%)   Lab. hold
*Ms Anne Campbell, *Lab.*   19,316
David Howarth, *LD*   10,737
Graham Stuart, *C.*   9,829
Stephen Lawrence, *Green*   1,413
Howard Senter, *Soc. All.*   716
Len Baynes, *UK Ind.*   532
Ms Clare Underwood, *(ProLife)*   232
Ms Margaret Courtney, *WRP*   61
Lab. majority 8,579 (20.03%)
8.64% swing Lab. to LD
(1997: Lab. maj. 14,137 (27.54%))

CAMBRIDGESHIRE NORTH EAST
E. 79,891   T. 48,051 (60.15%)   C. hold
*Malcolm Moss, *C.*   23,132
Dil Owen, *Lab.*   16,759
Richard Renaut, *LD*   6,733
John Stevens, *UK Ind.*   1,189
Tony Hoey, *(ProLife)*   238
C. majority 6,373 (13.26%)
2.03% swing Lab. to C.
(1997: C. maj. 5,101 (9.20%))

CAMBRIDGESHIRE NORTH WEST
E. 70,569   T. 43,956 (62.29%)   C. hold
*Rt. Hon. Sir B. Mawhinney, *C.*   21,895
Ms Anthea Cox, *Lab.*   13,794
Alastair Taylor, *LD*   6,957
Barry Hudson, *UK Ind.*   881
David Hall, *Ind.*   429
C. majority 8,101 (18.43%)
1.27% swing Lab. to C.
(1997: C. maj. 7,754 (15.88%))

CAMBRIDGESHIRE SOUTH
E. 72,095   T. 48,341 (67.05%)   C. hold
*Andrew Lansley, *C.*   21,387
Ms Amanda Taylor, *LD*   12,984
Dr Joan Herbert, *Lab.*   11,737
Simon Saggers, *Green*   1,182
Mrs Helene Davies, *UK Ind.*   875
Ms Beata Klepacka, *(ProLife)*   176
C. majority 8,403 (17.38%)
0.58% swing Lab. to C.
(1997: C. maj. 8,712 (16.23%))

CAMBRIDGESHIRE SOUTH EAST
E. 81,663   T. 51,886 (63.54%)   C. hold
*James Paice, *C.*   22,927
Ms Sal Brinton, *LD*   13,937
Andrew Inchley, *Lab.*   13,714
Neil Scarr, *UK Ind.*   1,308
C. majority 8,990 (17.33%)
0.27% swing C. to LD
(1997: C. maj. 9,349 (16.46%))

CANNOCK CHASE
E. 73,423   T. 41,064 (55.93%)   Lab. hold
*Dr Tony Wright, *Lab.*   23,049
Gavin Smithers, *C.*   12,345
Stewart Reynolds, *LD*   5,670
Lab. majority 10,704 (26.07%)
0.79% swing Lab. to C.
(1997: Lab. maj. 14,478 (27.65%))

CANTERBURY
E. 74,159   T. 45,132 (60.86%)   C. hold
*Julian Brazier, *C.*   18,711
Ms Emily Thornberry, *Lab.*   16,642
Peter Wales, *LD*   8,056
Ms Hazel Dawe, *Green*   920
Ms Lisa Moore, *UK Ind.*   803
C. majority 2,069 (4.58%)
1.37% swing C. to Lab.
(1997: C. maj. 3,964 (7.33%))

CARLISLE
E. 58,811 T. 34,909 (59.36%) Lab. hold
*Eric Martlew, *Lab.*   17,856
Mike Mitchelson, *C.*   12,154
John Guest, *LD*   4,076
Colin Paisley, *LCA*   554
Paul Wilcox, *Soc. All.*   269
Lab. majority 5,702 (16.33%)
6.04% swing Lab. to C.
(1997: Lab. maj. 12,390 (28.41%))

CARSHALTON & WALLINGTON
E. 67,337 T. 40,612 (60.31%) LD hold
*Tom Brake, *LD*   18,289
Ken Andrew *C.*   13,742
Ms Margaret Cooper, *Lab.*   7,466
Simon Dixon, *Green*   614
Martin Haley, *UK Ind.*   501
LD majority 4,547 (11.20%)
3.26% swing C. to LD
(1997: Lab. maj. 2,267 (4.68%))

CASTLE POINT
E. 68,108 T. 39,763 (58.38%) C. gain
Dr Robert Spink, *C.*   17,738
*Ms Christine Butler, *Lab.*   16,753
Billy Boulton, *LD*   3,116
Ron Hurrell, *UK Ind.*   1,273
Douglas Roberts, *Ind.*   663
Nik Searle, *Truth*   220
C. majority 985 (2.48%)
2.39% swing Lab. to C.
(1997: Lab. maj. 1,116 (2.30%))

CHARNWOOD
E. 74,836 T. 48,265 (64.49%) C. hold
*Rt. Hon. S. Dorrell, *C.*   23,283
Sean Sheahan, *Lab.*   15,544
Ms Susan King, *LD*   7,835
Jamie Bye, *UK Ind.*   1,603
C. majority 7,739 (16.03%)
2.77% swing Lab. to C.
(1997: C. maj. 5,900 (10.50%))

CHATHAM & AYLESFORD
E. 69,759 T. 39,735 (56.96%) Lab. hold
*Jonathan Shaw, *Lab.*   19,180
Sean Hold en, *C.*   14,840
David Lettington, *LD*   4,705
Gregory Knopp, *UK Ind.*   1,010
Lab. majority 4,340 (10.92%)
2.62% swing C. to Lab.
(1997: Lab. maj. 2,790 (5.68%))

CHEADLE
E. 69,002 T. 43,606 (63.20%) LD gain
Ms Patsy Calton, *LD*   18,477
*Stephen Day, *C.*   18,444
Howard Dawber, *Lab.*   6,086
Vincent Cavanagh, *UK Ind.*   599
LD majority, 33 (0.08%)
3.07% swing C. to LD
(1997: C. maj. 3,189 (6.07%))

CHELMSFORD WEST
E. 78,291 T. 48,143 (61.49%) C. hold
*Simon Burns, *C.*   20,446
Adrian Longden, *Lab.*   14,185
Stephen Robinson, *LD*   11,197
Mrs Eleanor Burgess, *Green*   837
Ken Wedon, *UK Ind.*   785
Christopher Philbin, *LCA*   693
C. majority 6,261 (13.01%)
0.62% swing C. to Lab.
(1997: C. maj. 6,691 (11.42%))

CHELTENHAM
E. 67,563 T. 41,835 (61.92%) LD hold
*Nigel Jones, *LD*   19,970
Rob Garnham, *C.*   14,715
Andy Erlam, *Lab.*   5,041
Keith Bessant, *Green*   735
Dancing Ken Hanks, *Loony*   513
Jim Carver *UK Ind.*   482
Anthony Gates, *(ProLife)*   272
Roger Everest, *Ind.*   107
LD majority 5,255 (12.56%)
0.32% swing LD to C.
(1997: Lab. maj. 6,645 (13.21%))

CHESHAM & AMERSHAM
E. 70,021 T. 45,283 (64.67%) C. hold
*Mrs Cheryl Gillan, *C.*   22,867
John Ford, *LD*   10,985
Ken Hulme, *Lab.*   8,497
Ian Harvey, *UK Ind.*   1,367
Nick Wilkins, *Green*   1,114
Ms Gillian Duval, *(ProLife)*   453
C. majority 11,882 (26.24%)
0.16% swing C. to LD
(1997: C. maj. 13,859 (26.55%))

CHESTER, CITY OF
E. 70,382 T. 44,877 (63.76%) Lab. hold
*Ms Christine Russell, *Lab.*   21,760
David Jones, *C.*   14,866
Tony Dawson, *LD*   6,589
Allan Weddell, *UK Ind.*   899
George Rogers, *Ind.*   763
Lab. majority 6,894 (15.36%)
1.70% swing Lab. to C.
(1997: Lab. maj. 10,553 (18.76%))

CHESTERFIELD
E. 73,252 T. 44,441 (60.67%) LD gain
Paul Holmes, *LD*   21,249
Reg Race, *Lab.*   18,663
Simon Hitchcock, *C.*   3,613
Ms Jeannie Robinson, *Soc. All.*   437
Bill Harrison, *Soc. Lab.*   295
Christopher Rawson, *Ind.*   184
LD majority 2,586 (5.82%)
8.53% swing Lab. to LD
(1997: Lab. maj. 5,775 (11.24%))

CHICHESTER
E. 77,703 T. 49,512 (63.72%) C. hold
*Andrew Tyrie, *C.*   23,320
Ms Lynne Ravenscroft, *LD*   11,965
Ms Celia Barlow, *Lab.*   10,627
Douglas Denny, *UK Ind.*   2,308
Gavin Graham, *Green*   1,292
C. majority 11,355 (22.93%)
2.74% swing LD to C.
(1997: C. maj. 9,734 (17.45%))

CHINGFORD & WOODFORD
GREEN
E. 63,252 T. 36,982 (58.47%) C. hold
*Iain Duncan Smith, *C.*   17,834
Ms Jessica Webb, *Lab.*   12,347
John Beanse, *LD*   5,739
Ms Jean Griffin, *BNP*   1,062
C. majority 5,487 (14.84%)
0.99% swing Lab. to C.
(1997: C. maj. 5,714 (12.85%))

CHIPPING BARNET
E. 70,217 T. 42,456 (60.46%) C. hold
*Sir Sydney Chapman, *C.*   19,702
Damien Welfare, *Lab.*   17,001
Sean Hooker, *LD*   5,753
C. majority 2,701 (6.36%)
2.14% swing Lab. to C.
(1997: C. maj. 1,035 (2.09%))

CHORLEY
E. 77,036 T. 47,952 (62.25%) Lab. hold
*Lindsay Hoyle, *Lab.*   25,088
Peter Booth, *C.*   6,644
Stephen Fenn, *LD*   5,372
Graham Frost, *UK Ind.*   848
Lab. majority 8,444 (17.61%)
0.25% swing C. to Lab.
(1997: Lab. maj. 9,870 (17.10%))

CHRISTCHURCH
E. 73,503 T. 49,567 (67.44%) C. hold
*Christopher Chope, *C.*   27,306
Ms Dorothy Webb, *LD*   13,762
Ms Judith Begg, *Lab.*   7,506
Ms Margaret Strange, *UK Ind.*   993
C. majority 13,544 (27.32%)
11.74% swing LD to C.
(1997: C. maj. 2,165 (3.85%))

CITIES OF LONDON &
WESTMINSTER
E. 71,935 T. 33,975 (47.23%) C. hold
Mark Field, *C.*   15,737
Michael Katz, *Lab.*   11,238
Martin Horwood, *LD*   5,218
Hugo Charlton, *Green*   1,318
Colin Merton, *UK Ind.*   464
C. majority 4,499 (13.24%)
0.54% swing Lab. to C.
(1997: C. maj. 4,881 (12.16%))

CLEETHORPES
E. 68,392 T. 42,418 (62.02%) Lab. hold
*Ms Shona McIsaac, *Lab.*   21,032
Stephen Howd, *C.*   15,412
Gordon Smith, *LD*   5,080
Ms Janet Hatton, *UK Ind.*   894
Lab. majority 5,620 (13.25%)
2.47% swing Lab. to C.
(1997: Lab. maj. 9,176 (18.18%))

COLCHESTER
E. 78,955 T. 43,736 (55.39%) LD hold
*Bob Russell, *LD*   18,627
Kevin Bentley, *C.*   13,074
Chris Fegan, *Lab.*   10,925
Roger Lord, *UK Ind.*   631
Leonard Overy-Owen, *Grey*   479
LD majority 5,553 (12.70%)
4.83% swing C. to LD
(1997: Lab. maj. 1,581 (3.04%))

COLNE VALLEY
E. 74,192 T. 46,987 (63.33%) Lab. hold
*Ms Kali Mountford, *Lab.*   18,967
Philip Davies, *C.*   14,328
Gordon Beever, *LD*   11,694
Richard Plunkett, *Green*   1,081
Dr Arthur Quarmby, *UK Ind.*   917
Lab. majority 4,639 (9.87%)
0.65% swing C. to Lab.
(1997: Lab. maj. 4,840 (8.58%))

CONGLETON
E. 71,941   T. 45,083 (62.67%)   C. hold
*Mrs Ann Winterton, C.   20,872
John Flanagan, Lab.   13,738
David Lloyd-Griffiths, LD   9,719
Bill Young, UK Ind.   754
C. majority 7,134 (15.82%)
1.08% swing Lab. to C.
(1997: C. maj. 6,130 (11.48%))

COPELAND
E. 53,526   T. 34,750 (64.92%)   Lab. hold
*Rt. Hon. Dr J. Cunningham, Lab.   17,991
Mike Graham, C.   13,027
Mark Gayler, LD   3,732
Lab. majority 4,964 (14.28%)
7.30% swing Lab. to C.
(1997: Lab. maj. 11,944 (28.89%))

CORBY
E. 72,304   T. 47,222 (65.31%)
                             Lab. Co-op hold
*Phil Hope, Lab. Co-op.   23,283
Andrew Griffith, C.   17,583
Kevin Scudder, LD   4,751
Ian Gillman, UK Ind.   855
Andrew Dickson, Soc. Lab.   750
Lab. Co-op majority 5,700 (12.07%)
4.95% swing Lab. Co-op to C.
(1997: Lab. maj. 11,860 (21.98%))

CORNWALL NORTH
E. 84,662   T. 53,983 (63.76%)   LD hold
*Paul Tyler, LD   28,082
John Weller, C.   18,250
Mike Goodman, Lab.   5,257
Steve Protz, UK Ind.   2,394
LD majority 9,832 (18.21%)
2.79% swing LD to C.
(1997: Lab. maj. 13,933 (23.79%))

CORNWALL SOUTH EAST
E. 79,090   T. 51,753 (65.44%)   LD hold
*Colin Breed, LD   23,756
Ashley Gray, C.   18,381
Bill Stevens, Lab.   6,429
Graham Palmer, UK Ind.   1,978
Dr Ken George, (Meb. Ker.)   1,209
LD majority 5,375 (10.39%)
0.45% swing LD to C.
(1997: Lab. maj. 6,480 (11.28%))

COTSWOLD
E. 68,154   T. 45,981 (67.47%)   C. hold
*Geoffrey Clifton-Brown, C.   23,133
Ms Angela Lawrence, LD   11,150
Richard Wilkins, Lab.   10,383
Mrs Jill Stopps, UK Ind.   1,315
C. majority 11,983 (26.06%)
1.33% swing LD to C.
(1997: C. maj. 11,965 (23.41%))

COVENTRY NORTH EAST
E. 73,998   T. 37,265 (50.36%)   Lab. hold
Bob Ainsworth, Lab.   22,739
Gordon Bell, C.   6,988
Geoffrey Sewards, LD   4,163
Dave Nellist, Soc. All.   2,638
Edward Sheppard, BNP   737
Lab. majority 15,751 (42.27%)
2.34% swing Lab. to C.
(1997: Lab. maj. 22,569 (46.94%))

COVENTRY NORTH WEST
E. 76,652   T. 42,551 (55.51%)   Lab. hold
*Geoffrey Robinson, Lab.   21,892
Andrew Fairburn, C.   11,018
Napier Penlington, LD   5,832
Ms Christine Oddy, Ind.   3,159
Mark Benson, UK Ind.   650
Lab. majority 10,874 (25.56%)
2.50% swing Lab. to C.
(1997: Lab. maj. 16,601 (30.56%))

COVENTRY SOUTH
E. 72,527   T. 40,096 (55.28%)   Lab. hold
*Jim Cunningham, Lab.   20,125
Ms Heather Wheeler, C.   11,846
Vincent McKee, LD   5,672
Rob Windsor, Soc. All.   1,475
Ms Irene Rogers, Ind.   564
Timothy Logan, Soc. Lab.   414
Lab. majority 8,279 (20.65%)
0.61% swing Lab. to C.
(1997: Lab. maj. 10,953 (21.86%))

CRAWLEY
E. 71,626   T. 39,522 (55.18%)   Lab. hold
*Ms Laura Moffatt, Lab.   19,488
Henry Smith, C.   12,718
Ms Linda Seekings, LD   5,009
Brian Galloway, UK Ind.   1,137
Ms Claire Staniford, Loony   388
Arshad Khan, JP   271
Karl Stewart, Soc. Lab.   260
Ms Muriel Hirsch, Soc. All.   251
Lab. majority 6,770 (17.13%)
3.05% swing Lab. to C.
(1997: Lab. maj. 11,707 (23.22%))

CREWE & NANTWICH
E. 69,040   T. 41,547 (60.18%)   Lab. hold
*Mrs Gwyneth Dunwoody, Lab.   22,556
Donald Potter, C.   2,650
David Cannon, LD   5,595
Roger Croston, UK Ind.   746
Lab. majority 9,906 (23.84%)
3.69% swing Lab. to C.
(1997: Lab. maj. 15,798 (31.22%))

CROSBY
E. 57,375   T. 36,866 (64.25%)   Lab. hold
*Ms Claire Curtis-Thomas, Lab.   20,327
Robert Collinson, C.   11,974
Tim Drake, LD   4,084
Mark Holt, Soc. Lab.   481
Lab. majority 8,353 (22.66%)
3.19% swing C. to Lab.
(1997: Lab. maj. 7,182 (16.27%))

CROYDON CENTRAL
E. 77,567   T. 45,860 (59.12%)   Lab. hold
*Geraint Davies, Lab.   21,643
David Congdon, C.   17,659
Paul Booth, LD   5,156
James Feisenberger, UK Ind.   545
Ms Lynda Miller, BNP   449
John Cartwright, Loony   408
Lab. majority 3,984 (8.69%)
0.85% swing C. to Lab.
(1997: Lab. maj. 3,897 (6.99%))

CROYDON NORTH
E. 76,600   T. 41,882 (54.68%)   Lab. hold
*Malcolm Wicks, Lab.   26,610
Simon Allison, C.   9,752
Ms Sandra Lawman, LD   4,375
Alan Smith, UK Ind.   606
Don Madgwick, Soc. All.   539
Lab. majority 16,858 (40.25%)
2.63% swing C. to Lab.
(1997: Lab. maj. 18,398 (35.00%))

CROYDON SOUTH
E. 73,402   T. 45,060 (61.39%)   C. hold
*Richard Ottaway, C.   22,169
Gerry Ryan, Lab.   13,472
Ms Anne Gallop, LD   8,226
Mrs Kathleen Garner, UK Ind.   998
Mark Samuel, Choice   195
C. majority 8,697 (19.30%)
1.35% swing C. to Lab.
(1997: C. maj. 11,930 (22.01%))

DAGENHAM
E. 59,340   T. 27,580 (46.48%)   Lab. hold
Jon Cruddas, Lab.   15,784
Michael White, C.   7,091
Adrian Gee-Turner, LD   2,820
David Hill, BNP   1,378
Berlyne Hamilton, Soc. All.   262
Robert Siggins, Soc. Lab.   245
Lab. majority 8,693 (31.52%)
7.82% swing Lab. to C.
(1997: Lab. maj. 17,054 (47.16%))

DARLINGTON
E. 64,328   T. 40,754 (63.35%)   Lab. hold
*Rt. Hon. A. Milburn, Lab.   22,479
Tony Richmond, C.   12,950
Robert Adamson, LD   4,358
Alan Docherty, Soc. All.   469
Craig Platt, Ind.   269
Ms Amanda Rose, Soc. Lab.   229
Lab. majority 9,529 (23.38%)
4.94% swing Lab. to C.
(1997: Lab. maj. 16,025 (33.27%))

DARTFORD
E. 72,258   T. 44,740 (61.92%)   Lab. hold
*Howard Stoate, Lab.   21,466
Bob Dunn, C.   18,160
Graham Morgan, LD   3,781
Mark Croucher, UK Ind.   989
Keith Davenport, FDP   344
Lab. majority 3,306 (7.39%)
0.47% swing Lab. to C.
(1997: Lab. maj. 4,328 (8.32%))

DAVENTRY
E. 86,537   T. 56,684 (65.50%)   C. hold
*Tim Boswell, C.   27,911
Kevin Quigley, Lab.   18,262
Jamie Calder, LD   9,130
Peter Baden, UK Ind.   1,381
C. majority 9,649 (17.02%)
2.54% swing Lab. to C.
(1997: C. maj. 7,378 (11.95%))

DENTON & REDDISH
E. 69,236   T. 33,593 (48.52%)   Lab. hold
*Andrew Bennett, Lab.   21,913
Paul Newman, C.   6,583
Roger Fletcher, LD   4,152
Alan Cadwallender, UK Ind.   945
Lab. majority 15,330 (45.63%)
0.78% swing C. to Lab.
(1997: Lab. maj. 20,311 (44.08%))

DERBY NORTH
E. 76,489   T. 44,054 (57.60%)   Lab. hold
*Bob Laxton, Lab.   22,415
Barrie Holden, C.   15,433
Robert Charlesworth, LD   6,206
Lab. majority 6,982 (15.85%)
1.53% swing Lab. to C.
(1997: Lab. maj. 10,615 (18.91%))

DERBY SOUTH
E. 77,366   T. 43,075 (55.68%)   Lab. hold
*Rt. Hon. Mrs M. Beckett, Lab.   24,310
Simon Spencer, C.   10,455
Anders Hanson, LD   8,310
Lab. majority 13,855 (32.16%)
0.54% swing C. to Lab.
(1997: Lab. maj. 16,106 (31.08%))

DERBYSHIRE NORTH EAST
E. 71,527   T. 42,124 (58.89%)   Lab. hold
*Harry Barnes, Lab.   23,437
James Hollingsworth, C.   11,179
Mark Higginbottom, LD   7,508
Lab. majority 12,258 (29.10%)
3.08% swing Lab. to C.
(1997: Lab. maj. 18,321 (35.25%))

DERBYSHIRE SOUTH
E. 81,010   T. 51,945 (64.12%)   Lab. hold
*Mark Todd, Lab.   26,338
James Hakewill, C.   18,487
Russell Eagling, LD   5,233
John Blunt, UK Ind.   1,074
Paul Liversuch, Soc. Lab.   564
James Taylor, Ind.   249
Lab. majority 7,851 (15.11%)
4.09% swing Lab. to C.
(1997: Lab. maj. 13,967 (23.29%))

DERBYSHIRE WEST
E. 75,067   T. 50,589 (67.39%)   C. hold
*Patrick McLoughlin, C.   24,280
Stephen Clamp, Lab.   16,910
Jeremy Beckett, LD   7,922
Stuart Bavester, UK Ind.   672
Nick Delves, Loony   472
Robert Goodall, Ind.   333
C. majority 7,370 (14.57%)
2.99% swing Lab. to C.
(1997: C. maj. 4,885 (8.59%))

DEVIZES
E. 83,655   T. 53,249 (63.65%)   C. hold
*Rt. Hon. M. Ancram, C.   25,159
Jim Thorpe, Lab.   13,263
Ms Helen Frances, LD   11,756
Alan Wood, UK Ind.   1,521
Ludovic Kennedy, Ind.   1,078
Ms Vanessa Potter, Loony   472
C. majority 11,896 (22.34%)
1.88% swing Lab. to C.
(1997: C. maj. 9,782 (16.29%))

DEVON EAST
E. 70,278   T. 47,837 (68.07%)   C. hold
Hugo Swire, C.   22,681
Tim Dumper, LD   14,486
Phil Starr, Lab.   7,974
David Wilson, UK Ind.   2,696
C. majority 8,195 (17.13%)
1.44% swing LD to C.
(1997: C. maj. 7,489 (14.25%))

DEVON NORTH
E. 72,100   T. 49,254 (68.31%)   LD hold
*Nick Harvey, LD   21,784
Clive Allen, C.   18,800
Ms Viv Gale, Lab.   4,995
Roger Knapman, UK Ind.   2,484
Tony Bown, Green   1,191
LD majority 2,984 (6.06%)
2.61% swing LD to C.
(1997: Lab. maj. 6,181 (11.27%))

DEVON SOUTH WEST
E. 70,922   T. 46,904 (66.13%)   C. hold
*Gary Streeter, C.   21,970
Christopher Mavin, Lab.   14,826
Phil Hutty, LD   8,616
Roger Bullock, UK Ind.   1,492
C. majority 7,144 (15.23%)
0.58% swing Lab. to C.
(1997: C. maj. 7,433 (14.07%))

DEVON WEST & TORRIDGE
E. 78,976   T. 55,684 (70.51%)   LD hold
*John Burnett, LD   23,474
Geoffrey Cox, C.   22,280
David Brenton, Lab.   5,959
Bob Edwards, UK Ind.   2,674
Martin Quinn, Green   1,297
LD majority 1,194 (2.14%)
0.58% swing LD to C.
(1997: Lab. maj. 1,957 (3.31%))

DEWSBURY
E. 62,344   T. 36,651 (58.79%)   Lab. hold
*Rt. Hon. Mrs A. Taylor, Lab.   18,524
Robert Cole, C.   11,075
Ian Cuthbertson, LD   4,382
Russell Smith, BNP   1,632
Ms Brenda Smithson, Green   560
David Peace, UK Ind.   478
Lab. majority 7,449 (20.32%)
0.50% swing C. to Lab.
(1997: Lab. maj. 8,323 (19.33%))

DON VALLEY
E. 66,244   T. 36,630 (55.30%)   Lab. hold
*Ms Caroline Flint, Lab.   20,009
James Browne, C.   10,489
Phillip Smith, LD   4,089
Tony Wilde, Ind.   800
David Cooper, UK Ind.   777
Nigel Ball, Soc. Lab.   466
Lab. majority 9,520 (25.99%)
3.84% swing Lab. to C.
(1997: Lab. maj. 14,659 (33.66%))

DONCASTER CENTRAL
E. 65,087   T. 33,902 (52.09%)   Lab. hold
*Ms Rosie Winterton, Lab.   20,034
Gary Meggitt, C.   8,035
Michael Southcombe, LD   4,390
David Gordon, UK Ind.   926
Ms Janet Terry, Soc. All.   517
Lab. majority 11,999 (35.39%)
2.85% swing Lab. to C.
(1997: Lab. maj. 17,856 (41.10%))

DONCASTER NORTH
E. 62,124   T. 31,363 (50.48%)   Lab. hold
*Kevin Hughes, Lab.   19,788
Mrs Anita Kapoor, C.   4,601
Colin Ross, LD   3,323
Martin Williams, Ind.   2,926
John Wallis, UK Ind.   725
Lab. majority 15,187 (48.42%)
3.28% swing Lab. to C.
(1997: Lab. maj. 21,937 (54.99%))

DORSET MID & POOLE NORTH
E. 66,675   T. 43,718 (65.57%)   LD gain
Ms Annette Brooke, LD   18,358
*Christopher Fraser, C.   17,974
James Selby-Bennett, Lab.   6,765
Jeff Mager, UK Ind.   621
LD majority 384 (0.88%)
1.11% swing C. to LD
(1997: C. maj. 681 (1.34%))

DORSET NORTH
E. 72,140   T. 47,821 (66.29%)   C. hold
*Robert Walter, C.   22,314
Miss Emily Gasson, LD   18,517
Mark Wareham, Lab.   5,334
Peter Jenkins, UK Ind.   1,019
Joseph Duthie, Low Excise   391
Mrs Cora Bone, Ind.   246
C. majority 3,797 (7.94%)
1.36% swing LD to C.
(1997: C. maj. 2,746 (5.23%))

DORSET SOUTH
E. 69,233   T. 45,345 (65.50%)   Lab gain
Jim Knight, Lab.   19,027
*Ian Cameron Bruce, C.   18,874
Andrew Canning, LD   6,531
Laurence Moss, UK Ind.   913
Lab. majority 153 (0.34%)
0.25% swing C. to Lab.
(1997: C. maj. 77 (0.16%))

DORSET WEST
E. 74,016   T. 49,571 (66.97%)   C. hold
*Oliver Letwin, C.   22,126
Simon Green, LD   20,712
Richard Hyde, Lab.   6,733
C. majority 1,414 (2.85%)
0.29% swing C. to LD
(1997: C. maj. 1,840 (3.44%))

DOVER
E. 69,025   T. 44,960 (65.14%)   Lab. hold
*Gwyn Prosser, Lab.   21,943
Paul Watkins, C.   16,744
Antony Hook, LD   5,131
Lee Speakman, UK Ind.   1,142
Lab. majority 5,199 (11.56%)
5.05% swing Lab. to C.
(1997: Lab. maj. 11,739 (21.66%))

DUDLEY NORTH
E. 68,964   T. 38,564 (55.92%)   Lab. hold
*Ross Cranston, Lab.   20,095
Andrew Griffiths, C.   13,295
Richard Burt, LD   3,352
Simon Darby, BNP   1,822
Lab. majority 6,800 (17.63%)
1.08% swing Lab. to C.
(1997: Lab. maj. 9,457 (19.79%))

DUDLEY SOUTH
E. 65,578   T. 36,344 (55.42%)   Lab. hold
*Ian Pearson, Lab.   18,109
Jason Sugarman, C.   11,292
Ms Lorely Burt, LD   5,421
John Westwood, UK Ind.   859
Ms Angela Thompson Soc. All.   663
Lab. majority 6,817 (18.76%)
4.22% swing Lab. to C.
(1997: Lab. maj. 13,027 (27.19%))

DULWICH & WEST NORWOOD

E. 70,497 T. 38,247 (54.25%) Lab. hold

*Rt. Hon. Ms T. Jowell, *Lab.*	20,999
Nick Vineall, *C.*	8,689
Ms Caroline Pidgeon, *LD*	5,806
Ms Jenny Jones, *Green*	1,914
Brian Kelly, *Soc. All.*	839

Lab. majority 12,310 (32.19%)
2.29% swing Lab. to C.
(1997: Lab. maj. 16,769 (36.76%))

DURHAM NORTH

E. 67,610 T. 38,568 (57.04%) Lab. hold

Kevan Jones, *Lab.*	25,920
Matthew Palmer, *C.*	7,237
Ms Carole Field, *LD*	5,411

Lab. majority 18,683 (48.44%)
3.65% swing Lab. to C.
(1997: Lab. maj. 26,299 (55.75%))

DURHAM NORTH WEST

E. 67,062 T. 39,226 (58.49%) Lab. hold

*Rt. Hon. Ms H. Armstrong, *Lab.*	24,526
William Clouston, *C.*	8,193
Alan Ord, *LD*	5,846
Ms Joan Hartnell, *Soc. Lab.*	661

Lab. majority 16,333 (41.64%)
5.90% swing Lab. to C.
(1997: Lab. maj. 24,754 (53.44%))

DURHAM, CITY OF

E. 69,633 T. 41,486 (59.58%) Lab. hold

*Gerry Steinberg, *Lab.*	23,254
Ms Carol Woods, *LD*	9,813
Nick Cartmell, *C.*	7,167
Mrs Chris Williamson, *UK Ind.*	1,252

Lab. majority 13,441 (32.40%)
7.82% swing Lab. to LD
(1997: Lab. maj. 22,504 (45.80%))

EALING ACTON & SHEPHERD'S BUSH

E. 70,697 T. 37,201 (52.62%) Lab. hold

*Clive Soley, *Lab.*	20,144
Miss Justine Greening, *C.*	9,355
Martin Tod, *LD*	6,171
Nick Grant, *Soc. All.*	529
Andrew Lawrie, *UK Ind.*	476
Carlos Rule, *Soc. All.*	301
Ms Rebecca Ng, *ProLife*	225

Lab. majority 10,789 (29.00%)
1.77% swing Lab. to C.
(1997: Lab. maj. 15,647 (32.55%))

EALING NORTH

E. 77,524 T. 44,957 (57.99%) Lab. hold

*Stephen Pound, *Lab.*	25,022
Charles Walker, *C.*	13,185
Francesco Fruzza, *LD*	5,043
Ms Astra Seibe, *Green*	1,039
Daniel Moss, *UK Ind.*	668

Lab. majority 11,837 (26.33%)
4.94% swing C. to Lab.
(1997: Lab. maj. 9,160 (16.44%))

EALING SOUTHALL

E. 82,373 T. 46,828 (56.85%) Lab. hold

*Piara Khabra, *Lab.*	22,239
Daniel Kawczynski, *C.*	8,556
Avtar Lit, *Sunrise*	5,764
Baldev Sharma, *LD*	4,680
Ms Jane Cook, *Green*	2,119
Salvinder Dhillon, *Community*	1,214
Mushtaq Choudhry, *Ind.*	1,166
Harpal Brar, *Soc,. Lab.*	921
Mohammed Bhutta, *Qari*	169

Lab. majority 13,683 (29.22%)
5.00% swing Lab. to C.
(1997: Lab. maj. 21,423 (39.21%))

EASINGTON

E. 61,532 T. 33,010 (53.65%) Lab. hold

*John Cummings, *Lab.*	25,360
Philip Lovel, *C.*	3,411
Christopher Ord, *LD*	3,408
Dave Robinson, *Soc. Lab.*	831

Lab. majority 21,949 (66.49%)
2.57% swing Lab. to C.
(1997: Lab. maj. 30,012 (71.64%))

EAST HAM

E. 71,255 T. 37,277 (52.31%) Lab. hold

*Stephen Timms, *Lab.*	27,241
Peter Campbell, *C.*	6,209
Ms Bridget Fox, *LD*	2,600
Rod Finlayson, *Soc. Lab.*	783
Ms Johinda Pandhal, *UK Ind.*	444

Lab. majority 21,032 (56.42%)
3.95% swing C. to Lab.
(1997: Lab. maj. 19,358 (48.53%))

EASTBOURNE

E. 73,784 T. 44,770 (60.68%) C. hold

*Nigel Waterson, *C.*	19,738
Chris Berry, *LD*	17,584
Ms Gillian Roles, *Lab.*	5,967
Barry Jones, *UK, Ind.*	907
Ms Theresia Williamson, *Lib.*	574

C. majority 2,154 (4.81%)
0.51% swing LD to C.
(1997: C. maj. 1,994 (3.79%))

EASTLEIGH

E. 74,603 T. 47,573 (63.77%) LD hold

*David Chidgey, *LD*	19,360
Conor Burns, *C.*	16,302
Sam Jaffa, *Lab.*	10,426
Stephen Challis, *UK Ind.*	849
Ms Martha Lyn, *Green*	636

LD majority 3,058 (6.43%)
2.54% swing C. to LD
(1997: LD maj. 754 (1.35%))

ECCLES

E. 68,764 T. 33,182 (48.25%) Lab. hold

*Ian Stewart, *Lab.*	21,395
Peter Caillard, *C.*	6,867
Bob Boyd, *LD*	4,920

Lab. majority 14,528 (43.78%)
2.09% swing Lab. to C.
(1997: Lab. maj. 21,916 (47.96%))

EDDISBURY

E. 69,181 T. 44,387 (64.16%) C. hold

*Stephen O'Brien, *C.*	20,556
Bill Eyres, *Lab.*	15,988
Paul Roberts, *LD*	6,975
David Carson, *UK Ind.*	868

C. majority 4,568 (10.29%)
3.95% swing Lab. to C.
1999 Jul. by-election: C. maj. 1,606
(1997: C. maj. 1,185 (2.39%))

EDMONTON

E. 62,294, T. 34,774 (55.82%) Lab. Co-op hold

*Andy Love, *Lab. Co-op.*	20,481
David Burrowes, *C.*	10,709
Douglas Taylor, *LD*	2,438
Miss Gwyneth Rolph, *UK Ind.*	406
Erol Basarik, *Reform*	344
Howard Medwell, *Soc. All.*	296
Dr Ram Saxena, *Ind.*	100

Lab. Co-op majority 9,772 (28.10%)
0.97% swing Lab. Co-op to C.
(1997: Lab. maj. 13,472 (30.04%))

ELLESMERE PORT & NESTON

E. 68,147 T. 41,528 (60.94%) Lab. hold

*Andrew Miller, *Lab.*	22,964
Gareth Williams, *C.*	12,103
Stuart Kelly, *LD*	4,828
Henry Crocker, *UK Ind.*	824
Geoff Nicholls, *Green*	809

Lab. majority 10,861 (26.15%)
2.18% swing Lab. to C.
(1997: Lab. maj. 16,036 (30.51%))

ELMET

E. 70,041 T. 45,937 (65.59%) Lab. hold

*Colin Burgon, *Lab.*	22,038
Andrew Millard, *C.*	17,867
Ms Madeleine Kirk, *LD*	5,001
Andrew Spence, *UK Ind.*	1,031

Lab. majority 4,171 (9.08%)
3.57% swing Lab. to C.
(1997: Lab. maj. 8,779 (16.22%))

ELTHAM

E. 57,519 T. 33,792 (58.75%) Lab. hold

*Clive Efford, *Lab.*	17,855
Mrs Sharon Massey, *C.*	10,859
Martin Morris, *LD*	4,121
Terry Jones, *UK Ind.*	706
Andrew Graham, *Ind.*	251

Lab. majority 6,996 (20.70%)
1.37% swing Lab. to C.
(1997: Lab. maj. 10,182 (23.45%))

ENFIELD NORTH

E. 67,756 T. 38,143 (56.29%) Lab. hold

*Ms Joan Ryan, *Lab.*	17,888
Nick De Bois, *C.*	15,597
Ms Hilary Leighter, *LD*	3,355
Ramon Johns, *BNP*	605
Brian Hall, *UK Ind.*	247
Michael Akerman, *(ProLife)*	241
Richard Course, *Ind.*	210

Lab. majority 2,291 (6.01%)
4.15% swing Lab. to C.
(1997: Lab. maj. 6,822 (14.31%))

ENFIELD SOUTHGATE

E. 66,418 T. 41,908 (63.10%) Lab. hold

*Stephen Twigg, *Lab.*	21,727
John Flack, *C.*	16,181
Wayne Hoban, *LD*	2,935
Ms Elaine Graham-Leigh, *Green*	662
Roy Freshwater, *UK Ind.*	298
Andrew Malakouna, *Ind.*	105

Lab. majority 5,546 (13.23%)
5.08% swing C. to Lab.
(1997: Lab. maj. 1,433 (3.08%))

EPPING FOREST
E. 72,645   T. 42,414 (58.39%)   C. hold
*Mrs Eleanor Laing, C.   20,833
Christopher Naylor, Lab.   12,407
Michael Heavens, LD   7,884
Andrew Smith, UK Ind.   1,290
C. majority 8,426 (19.87%)
4.98% swing Lab. to C.
(1997: C. maj. 5,252 (9.91%))

EPSOM & EWELL
E. 74,266   T. 46,643 (62.81%)   C. hold
Chris Grayling, C.   22,430
Charles Mansell, Lab.   12,350
John Vincent, LD   10,316
G. Webster-Gardiner, UK Ind.   1,547
C. majority 10,080 (21.61%)
0.17% swing Lab. to C.
(1997: C. maj. 11,525 (21.27%))

EREWASH
E. 78,484   T. 48,596 (61.92%)   Lab. hold
*Ms Liz Blackman, Lab.   23,915
Gregor MacGregor, C.   16,983
Martin Garnett, LD   5,586
Ms Louise Smith, UK Ind.   692
Steven Belshaw, BNP   591
R U Seerius, Loony   428
Peter Waldock, Soc. Lab.   401
Lab. majority 6,932 (14.26%)
0.44% swing Lab. to C.
(1997: Lab. maj. 9,135 (15.14%))

ERITH & THAMESMEAD
E. 66,371   T. 33,351 (50.25%)   Lab. hold
*John Austin, Lab.   19,769
Mark Brooks, C.   8,602
James Kempton, LD   3,800
Hardev Dhillon, Soc. Lab.   1,180
Lab. majority 11,167 (33.48%)
4.21% swing Lab. to C.
(1997: Lab. maj. 17,424 (41.90%))

ESHER & WALTON
E. 73,541   T. 45,531 (61.91%)   C. hold
*Ian Taylor, C.   22,296
Joe McGowan, Lab.   10,758
Mark Marsh, LD   10,241
Bernard Collignon, UK Ind.   2,236
C. majority 11,538 (25.34%)
0.86% swing C. to Lab.
(1997: C. maj. 14,528 (27.07%))

ESSEX NORTH
E. 71,680   T. 44,944 (62.70%)   C. hold
*Bernard Jenkin, C.   21,325
Philip Hawkins, Lab.   14,139
Trevor Ellis LD   7,867
George Curtis, UK Ind.   1,613
C. majority 7,186 (15.99%)
2.65% swing Lab. to C.
(1997: C. maj. 5,476 (10.69%))

EXETER
E. 81,942   T. 52,616 (64.21%)   Lab. hold
*Ben Bradshaw, Lab.   26,194
Mrs Anne Jobson, C.   14,435
Richard Copus, LD   6,512
David Morrish, Lib.   2,596
Paul Edwards, Green   1,240
John Stuart, UK Ind.   1,109
Francis Choules, Soc. All.   530
Lab. majority 11,759 (22.35%)
1.71% swing C. to Lab.
(1997: Lab. maj. 11,705 (18.92%))

FALMOUTH & CAMBORNE
E. 72,833   T. 46,820 (64.28%)   Lab. hold
*Ms Candy Atherton, Lab.   18,532
Nick Serpell, C.   14,005
Julian Brazil, LD   11,453
John Browne, UK Ind.   1,328
Ms Hilda Wasley, Meb. Ker.   853
Paul Holmes, Lib.   649
Lab. majority 4,527 (9.67%)
2.33% swing C. to Lab.
(1997: Lab. maj. 2,688 (5.01%))

FAREHAM
E. 72,678   T. 45,447 (62.53%)   C. hold
Mark Hoban, C.   21,389
James Carr, Lab.   14,380
Hugh Pritchard, LD   8,503
William O'Brien, UK Ind.   1,175
C. majority 7,009 (15.42%)
2.21% swing C. to Lab.
(1997: C. maj. 10,358 (19.85%))

FAVERSHAM & KENT MID
E. 67,995   T. 41,051 (60.37%)   C. hold
Hugh Robertson, C.   18,739
Grahame Birchall, Lab.   14,556
Mike Sole, LD   5,529
Jim Gascoyne, UK Ind.   828
Ms Penny Kemp, Green   799
Norman Davidson, R & R Loony   600
C. majority 4,183 (10.19%)
0.89% swing Lab. to C.
(1997: C. maj. 4,173 (8.41%))

FELTHAM & HESTON
E. 73,229   T. 36,177 (49.40%)
                          Lab. Co-op hold
*Alan Keen, Lab. Co-op.   21,406
Mrs Liz Mammatt, C.   8,749
Andy Darley, LD   4,998
Surinder Cheema, Soc. Lab.   651
Warwick Prachar, Ind.   204
Asa Khaira, Ind.   169
Lab. Co-op majority 12,657 (34.99%)
1.11% swing C. to Lab. Co-op
(1997: Lab. maj. 15,273 (32.76%))

FINCHLEY & GOLDERS GREEN
E. 76,175   T. 43,675 (57.34%)   Lab. hold
*Rudi Vis, Lab.   20,205
John Marshall, C.   16,489
Ms Sarah Teather, LD   5,266
Ms Miranda Dunn, Green   1,385
John de Roeck, UK Ind.   330
Lab. majority 3,716 (8.51%)
1.08% swing C. to Lab.
(1997: Lab. maj. 3,189 (6.34%))

FOLKESTONE & HYTHE
E. 71,503   T. 45,855 (64.13%)   C. hold
*Rt. Hon. M. Howard, C.   20,645
Peter Carroll, LD   14,738
Albert Catterall, Lab.   9,260
John Baker, UK Ind.   1,212
C. majority 5,907 (12.88%)
0.36% swing LD to C.
(1997: C. maj. 6,332 (12.17%))

FOREST OF DEAN
E. 66,240   T. 44,607 (67.34%)   Lab. hold
*Ms Diana Organ, Lab.   19,350
Mark Harper, C.   17,301
David Gayler, LD   5,762
Simon Pickering, Green   1,254
Allen Prout, UK Ind.   661
Gerald Morgan, Ind.   279
Lab. majority 2,049 (4.59%)
4.02% swing Lab. to C.
(1997: Lab. maj. 6,343 (12.64%))

FYLDE
E. 72,207   T. 44,737 (61.96%)   C. hold
*Rt. Hon. M. Jack, C.   23,383
John Stockton, Lab.   13,773
John Begg, LD   6,599
Mrs Lesley Brown, UK Ind.   982
C. majority 9,610 (21.48%)
2.13% swing Lab. to C.
(1997: C. maj. 8,963 (17.22%))

GAINSBOROUGH
E. 65,871   T. 42,319 (64.25%)   C. hold
*Edward Leigh, C.   19,555
Alan Rhodes, Lab.   11,484
Steve Taylor, LD   11,280
C. majority 8,071 (19.07%)
2.39% swing Lab. to C.
(1997: C. maj. 6,826 (14.29%))

GATESHEAD EAST & WASHINGTON
WEST
E. 64,041   T. 33,615 (52.49%)   Lab. hold
*Rt. Hon. Ms J. Quin, Lab.   22,903
Ron Beadle, LD   4,999
Ms Elizabeth Campbell, C.   4,970
Martin Rouse, UK Ind.   743
Lab. majority 17,904 (53.26%)
4.04% swing Lab. to LD
(1997: Lab. maj. 24,950 (57.92%))

GEDLING
E. 68,540   T. 43,816 (63.93%)   Lab. hold
*Vernon Coaker, Lab.   22,383
Jonathan Bullock, C.   16,785
Tony Gillam, LD   4,648
Lab. majority 5,598 (12.78%)
2.74% swing C. to Lab.
(1997: Lab. maj. 3,802 (7.29%))

GILLINGHAM
E. 70,898   T. 42,212 (59.54%)   Lab. hold
*Paul Clark, Lab.   18,782
Tim Butcher, C.   16,510
Jonathan Hunt, LD   5,755
Tony Scholefield, UK Ind.   933
Wynford Vaughan, Soc. All.   232
Lab. majority 2,272 (5.38%)
0.74% swing C. to Lab.
(1997: Lab. maj. 1,980 (3.91%))

GLOUCESTER
E. 81,144   T. 48,223 (59.43%)   Lab. hold
Parmjit Dhanda, Lab.   22,067
Paul James, C.   18,187
Tim Bullamore, LD   6,875
Terry Lines, UK Ind.   822
Stewart Smyth, Soc. All.   272
Lab. majority 3,880 (8.05%)
3.11% swing Lab. to C.
(1997: Lab. maj. 8,259 (14.26%))

GOSPORT
E. 69,626   T. 39,789 (57.15%)   C. hold
*Peter Viggers, C.   17,364
Richard Williams, Lab.   14,743
Roger Roberts, LD   6,011
John Bowles, UK Ind.   1,162
Kevin Chetwynd, Soc. Lab.   509
C. majority 2,621 (6.59%)
3.18% swing C. to Lab.
(1997: C. maj. 6,258 (12.94%))

GRANTHAM & STAMFORD
E. 74,459   T. 46,289 (62.17%)   C. hold
*Quentin Davies, C.   21,329
John Robinson, Lab.   16,811
Ms Jane Carr, LD   6,665
Miss Marilyn Swain, UK Ind.   1,484
C. majority 4,518 (9.76%)
2.34% swing Lab. to C.
(1997: C. maj. 2,692 (5.08%))

GRAVESHAM
E. 69,590   T. 43,639 (62.71%)   Lab. hold
*Chris Pond, Lab.   21,773
Jacques Arnold, C.   16,911
Bruce Parmenter, LD   4,031
William Jenner, UK Ind.   924
Lab. majority 4,862 (11.14%)
0.15% swing C. to Lab.
(1997: Lab. maj. 5,779 (10.85%))

GREAT GRIMSBY
E. 63,157   T. 33,017 (52.28%)   Lab. hold
*Austin Mitchell, Lab.   19,118
James Cousins, C.   7,634
Andrew de Freitas, LD   6,265
Lab. majority 11,484 (34.78%)
1.46% swing Lab. to C.
(1997: Lab. maj. 16,244 (37.70%))

GREAT YARMOUTH
E. 69,131   T. 40,366 (58.39%)   Lab. hold
*Tony Wright, Lab.   20,344
Charles Reynolds, C.   15,780
Maurice Leeke, LD   3,392
Bertie Poole, UK Ind.   850
Lab. majority 4,564 (11.31%)
3.21% swing Lab. to C.
(1997: Lab. maj. 8,668 (17.73%))

GREENWICH & WOOLWICH
E. 62,530   T. 32,536 (52.03%)   Lab. hold
*Rt. Hon. N. Raynsford, Lab.   19,691
Richard Forsdyke, C.   6,258
Russell Pyne, LD   5,082
Stan Gain UK, Ind.   672
Miss Kirstie Paton, Soc. All.   481
Ms Margaret Sharkey, Soc. Lab.   352
Lab. majority 13,433 (41.29%)
1.79% swing Lab. to C.
(1997: Lab. maj. 18,128 (44.87%))

GUILDFORD
E. 76,046   T. 47,842 (62.91%)   LD gain
Ms Sue Doughty, LD   20,358
*Nick St Aubyn, C.   19,820
Ms Joyce Still, Lab.   6,558
Ms Sonya Porter, UK Ind.   736
John Morris, Pacifist   370
LD majority 538 (1.12%)
4.77% swing C. to LD
(1997: C. maj. 4,791 (8.41%))

HACKNEY NORTH & STOKE NEWINGTON
E. 60,444   T. 29,621 (49.01%)   Lab. hold
*Ms Diane Abbott, Lab.   18,081
Mrs Pauline Dye, C.   4,430
Ms Meral Ece, LD   4,170
Chit Yen Chong, Green   2,184
Sukant Chandan, Soc. Lab.   756
Lab. majority 13,651 (46.09%)
0.74% swing Lab. to C.
(1997: Lab. maj. 15,627 (47.57%))

HACKNEY SOUTH & SHOREDITCH
E. 63,990   T. 30,347 (47.42%)   Lab. hold
*Brian Sedgemore, Lab.   19,471
Tony Vickers, LD   4,422
Paul White, C.   4,180
Ms Cecilia Prosper, Soc. All.   1,401
Saim Kokshal, Reform   471
Ivan Beavis, Comm.   259
William Rogers, WRP   143
Lab. majority 15,049 (49.59%)
2.60% swing LD to Lab.
(1997: Lab. maj. 14,980 (44.39%))

HALESOWEN & ROWLEY REGIS
E. 65,683   T. 39,274 (59.79%)   Lab. hold
*Ms Sylvia Heal, Lab.   20,804
Les Jones, C.   13,445
Patrick Harley, LD   4,089
Alan Sheath, UK Ind.   936
Lab. majority 7,359 (18.74%)
1.23% swing Lab. to C.
(1997: Lab. maj. 10,337 (21.20%))

HALIFAX
E. 69,870   T. 40,390 (57.81%)   Lab. hold
*Ms Alice Mahon, Lab.   19,800
James Walsh, C.   13,671
John Durkin, LD   5,878
Mrs Helen Martinek, UK Ind.   1,041
Lab. majority 6,129 (15.17%)
3.50% swing Lab. to C.
(1997: Lab. maj. 11,212 (22.18%))

HALTEMPRICE & HOWDEN
E. 67,055   T. 43,928 (65.51%)   C. hold
*Rt. Hon. D. Davis, C.   18,994
John Neal, LD   17,091
Leslie Howell, Lab.   6,898
Ms Joanne Robinson, UK Ind.   945
C. majority 1,903 (4.33%)
5.41% swing C. to LD
(1997: C. maj. 7,514 (15.16%))

HALTON
E. 63,673   T. 34,470 (54.14%)   Lab. hold
*Derek Twigg, Lab.   23,841
Chris Davenport, C.   6,413
Peter Walker, LD   4,216
Lab. majority 17,428 (50.56%)
1.33% swing Lab. to C.
(1997: Lab. maj. 23,650 (53.22%))

HAMMERSMITH & FULHAM
E. 79,302   T. 44,700 (56.37%)   Lab. hold
*Iain Coleman, Lab.   19,801
Matthew Carrington, C.   17,786
Jon Burden, LD   5,294
Daniel Lopez Dias, Green   1,444
Gerald Roberts, UK Ind.   375
Lab. majority 2,015 (4.51%)
1.30% swing Lab. to C.
(1997: Lab. maj. 3,842 (7.11%))

HAMPSHIRE EAST
E. 78,802   T. 50,289 (63.82%)   C. hold
*Michael Mates, C.   23,950
Robert Booker, LD   15,060
Ms Barbara Burfoot, Lab.   9,866
Stephen Coles, UK Ind.   1,413
C. majority 8,890 (17.68%)
1.13% swing C. to LD
(1997: C. maj. 11,590 (19.93%))

HAMPSHIRE NORTH EAST
E. 71,323   T. 43,947 (61.62%)   C. hold
*Rt. Hon. J. Arbuthnot, C.   23,379
Mike Plummer, LD   10,122
Barry Jones, Lab.   8,744
Graham Mellstrom, UK Ind.   1,702
C. majority 13,257 (30.17%)
1.00% swing LD to C.
(1997: C. maj. 14,398 (28.17%))

HAMPSHIRE NORTH WEST
E. 76,359   T. 48,631 (63.69%)   C. hold
*Rt. Hon. Sir G. Young, C.   24,374
Mick Mumford, Lab.   12,365
Alex Bentley, LD   10,329
Stanley Oram, UK Ind.   1,563
C. majority 12,009 (24.69%)
1.53% swing Lab. to C.
(1997: C. maj. 11,551 (21.13%))

HAMPSTEAD & HIGHGATE
E. 65,309   T. 35,407 (54.21%)   Lab. hold
*Ms Glenda Jackson, Lab.   16,601
Andrew Mennear, C.   8,725
Jonathan Simpson, LD   7,273
Andrew Cornwell, Green   1,654
Ms Helen Cooper, Soc. All.   559
Thomas McDermott, UK Ind.   316
Ms Sister Xnunoftheabove, Ind.   144
Ms Mary Teale, ProLife   92
Amos Klein, Ind.   43
Lab. majority 7,876 (22.24%)
3.96% swing Lab. to C.
(1997: Lab. maj. 13,284 (30.17%))

HARBOROUGH
E. 73,300   T. 46,427 (63.34%)   C. hold
*Edward Garnier, C.   20,748
Ms Jill Hope, LD   15,496
Raj Jethwa, Lab.   9,271
David Knight, UK Ind.   912
C. majority 5,252 (11.31%)
0.49% swing C. to LD
(1997: C. maj. 6,524 (12.30%))

HARLOW
E. 67,074   T. 40,115 (59.81%)   Lab. hold
*Bill Rammell, Lab.   19,169
Robert Halfon, C.   13,941
Ms Lorna Spenceley, LD   5,381
Tony Bennett, UK Ind.   1,223
John Hobbs, Soc. All.   401
Lab. majority 5,228 (13.03%)
4.48% swing Lab. to C.
(1997: Lab. maj. 10,514 (21.99%))

HARROGATE & KNARESBOROUGH
E. 65,185   T. 42,179 (64.71%)   LD hold
*Phil Willis, LD   23,445
Andrew Jones, C.   14,600
Alastair MacDonald, Lab.   3,101
Bill Brown, UK Ind.   761
John Cornforth, ProLife   272
LD majority 8,845 (20.97%)
3.94% swing C. to LD
(1997: LD maj. 6,236 (13.09%))

HARROW EAST
E. 81,575   T. 48,077 (58.94%)   Lab. hold
*Tony McNulty, Lab.   26,590
Peter Wilding, C.   15,466
George Kershaw, LD   6,021
Lab. majority 11,124 (23.14%)
3.02% swing C. to Lab.
(1997: Lab. maj. 9,738 (17.09%))

HARROW WEST
E. 73,505   T. 46,648 (63.46%)   Lab. hold
*Gareth Thomas, Lab.   23,142
Danny Finkelstein, C.   16,986
Christopher Noyce, LD   5,995
Peter Kefford, UK Ind.   525
Lab. majority 6,156 (13.20%)
5.42% swing C. to Lab.
(1997: Lab. maj. 1,240 (2.36%))

HARTLEPOOL
E. 67,652   T. 38,051 (56.25%)   Lab. hold
*Rt. Hon. P. Mandelson, Lab.   22,506
Gus Robinson, C.   7,935
Nigel Boddy, LD   5,717
Arthur Scargill, Soc. Lab.   912
Ian Cameron, Ind.   557
John Booth, Ind.   424
Lab. majority 14,571 (38.29%)
0.54% swing Lab. to C.
(1997: Lab. maj. 17,508 (39.38%))

HARWICH
E. 77,539   T. 48,115 (62.05%)   Lab. hold
*Ivan Henderson, Lab.   21,951
Ian Sproat, C.   19,355
Peter Wilcock, LD   4,099
Tony Finnegan-Butler, UK Ind.   2,463
Clive Lawrance, Ind.   247
Lab. majority 2,596 (5.40%)
1.56% swing C. to Lab.
(1997: Lab. maj. 1,216 (2.28%))

HASTINGS & RYE
E. 70,632   T. 41,218 (58.36%)   Lab. hold
*Michael Foster, Lab.   19,402
Mark Coote, C.   15,094
Graem Peters, LD   4,266
Alan Coomber, UK Ind.   911
Ms Sally Phillips, Green   721
Mrs Gillian Bargery, Ind.   486
John Ord-Clarke, Loony   198
Brett McLean, R & R Loony   140
Lab. majority 4,308 (10.45%)
2.62% swing C. to Lab.
(1997: Lab. maj. 2,560 (5.21%))

HAVANT
E. 70,246   T. 40,437 (57.56%)   C. hold
*David Willetts, C.   17,769
Peter Guthrie, Lab.   13,562
Ms Helena Cole, LD   7,508
Kevin Jacks, Green   793
Tim Cuell, UK Ind.   561
Roy Stanley, Ind.   244
C. majority 4,207 (10.40%)
1.34% swing Lab. to C.
(1997: C. maj. 3,729 (7.72%))

HAYES & HARLINGTON
E. 57,561   T. 32,403 (56.29%)   Lab. hold
*John McDonnell, Lab.   21,279
Robert McLean, C.   7,813
Ms Nahid Boethe, LD   1,958
Gary Burch, BNP   705
Wally Kennedy, Soc. Alt.   648
Lab. majority 13,466 (41.56%)
3.39% swing C. to Lab.
(1997: Lab. maj. 14,291 (34.78%))

HAZEL GROVE
E. 65,107   T. 38,478 (59.10%)   LD hold
*Andrew Stunell, LD   20,020
Ms Nadine Bargery, C.   11,585
Martin Miller, Lab.   6,230
Gerald Price, UK Ind.   643
LD majority 8,435 (21.92%)
1.01% swing LD to C.
(1997: LD maj. 11,814 (23.95%))

HEMEL HEMPSTEAD
E. 72,086   T. 45,833 (63.58%)   Lab. Co-op hold
*Tony McWalter, Lab. Co-op.   21,389
Paul Ivey, C.   17,647
Neil Stuart, LD   5,877
Barry Newton, UK Ind.   920
Lab. Co-op majority 3,742 (8.16%)
0.78% swing C. to Lab. Co-op
(1997: Lab. maj. 3,636 (6.60%))

HEMSWORTH
E. 67,948   T. 35,227 (51.84%)   Lab. hold
*Jon Trickett, Lab.   23,036
Mrs Elizabeth Truss, C.   7,400
Ed Waller, LD   3,990
Paul Turek, Soc. Lab.   801
Lab. majority 15,636 (44.39%)
4.19% swing Lab. to C.
(1997: Lab. maj. 23,992 (52.76%))

HENDON
E. 78,212   T. 40,851 (52.23%)   Lab. hold
*Andrew Dismore, Lab.   21,432
Richard Evans, C.   14,015
Wayne Casey, LD   4,724
Craig Crosbie, UK Ind.   409
Ms Stella Taylor, WRP   164
Michael Stewart, Prog Dem   107
Lab. majority 7,417 (18.16%)
2.93% swing C. to Lab.
(1997: Lab. maj. 6,155 (12.30%))

HENLEY
E. 69,081   T. 44,401 (64.27%)   C. hold
Boris Johnson, C.   20,466
Ms Catherine Bearder, LD   12,008
Ms Janet Mathews, Lab.   9,367
Philip Collings, UK Ind.   1,413
Oliver Tickell, Green   1,147
C. majority 8,458 (19.05%)
1.31% swing C. to LD
(1997: C. maj. 11,167 (21.66%))

HEREFORD
E. 70,305   T. 44,624 (63.47%)   LD hold
*Paul Keetch, LD   18,244
Mrs Virginia Taylor, C.   17,276
David Hallam, Lab.   6,739
Clive Easton, UK Ind.   1,184
David Gillett, Green   1,181
LD majority 968 (2.17%)
5.24% swing LD to C.
(1997: LD maj. 6,648 (12.65%))

HERTFORD & STORTFORD
E. 75,141   T. 47,176 (62.78%)   C. hold
Mark Prisk, C.   21,074
Simon Speller, Lab.   15,471
Ms Mione Gold Spink, LD   9,388
Stuart Rising, UK Ind.   1,243
C. majority 5,603 (11.88%)
0.37% swing C. to Lab.
(1997: C. maj. 6,885 (12.62%))

HERTFORDSHIRE NORTH EAST
E. 68,790   T. 44,645 (64.90%)   C. hold
*Oliver Heald, C.   19,695
Ivan Gibbons, Lab.   16,251
Ms Alison Kingman, LD   7,686
Michael Virgo, UK Ind.   1,013
C. majority 3,444 (7.71%)
0.89% swing Lab. to C.
(1997: C. maj. 3,088 (5.94%))

HERTFORDSHIRE SOUTH WEST
E. 73,367   T. 47,269 (64.43%)   C. hold
*Richard Page, C.   20,933
Graham Dale, Lab.   12,752
Ed Featherstone, LD   12,431
Colin Dale-Mills, UK Ind.   847
Ms Julia Goffin, ProLife   306
C. majority 8,181 (17.31%)
0.39% swing C. to Lab.
(1997: C. maj. 10,021 (18.08%))

HERTSMERE
E. 68,780   T. 41,505 (60.34%)   C. hold
*James Clappison, C.   19,855
Ms Hilary Broderick, Lab.   14,953
Paul Thompson, LD   6,300
James Dry, Soc. Lab.   397
C. majority 4,902 (11.81%)
2.85% swing Lab. to C.
(1997: C. maj. 3,075 (6.11%))

HEXHAM
E. 59,807   T. 42,413 (70.92%)   C. hold
*Peter Atkinson, C.   18,917
Paul Brannen, Lab.   16,388
Philip Latham, LD   6,380
Alan Patterson, UK Ind.   728
C. majority 2,529 (5.96%)
2.74% swing Lab. to C.
(1997: C. maj. 222 (0.49%))

HEYWOOD & MIDDLETON
E. 73,005   T. 38,779 (53.12%)   Lab. Co-op hold
*Jim Dobbin, Lab. Co-op.   22,377
Mrs Marilyn Hopkins, C.   10,707
Ian Greenhalgh, LD   4,329
Philip Burke, Lib.   1,021
Ms Christine West, Ch. D.   345
Lab. Co-op majority 11,670 (30.09%)
2.30% swing Lab. Co-op to C.
(1997: Lab. maj. 17,542 (34.70%))

HIGH PEAK
E. 73,774   T. 48,114 (65.22%)   Lab. hold
*Tom Levitt, Lab.   22,430
Simon Chapman, C.   17,941
Peter Ashenden, LD   7,743
Lab. majority 4,489 (9.33%)
3.03% swing Lab. to C.
(1997: Lab. maj. 8,791 (15.38%))

HITCHIN & HARPENDEN
E. 67,196   T. 44,924 (66.86%)   C. hold
*Rt. Hon. P. Lilley, C.   21,271
Alan Amos, Lab.   14,608
John Murphy, LD   8,076
John Saunders, UK Ind.   606
Peter Rigby, Ind.   363
C. majority 6,663 (14.83%)
1.06% swing Lab. to C.
(1997: C. maj. 6,671 (12.72%))

HOLBORN & ST PANCRAS
E. 62,813   T. 31,129 (49.56%)   Lab. hold
*Rt. Hon. F. Dobson, Lab.   16,770
Nathaniel Green, LD   5,595
Mrs Roseanne Serelli, C.   5,258
Rob Whitley, Green   1,875
Ms Candy Udwin, Soc. All.   971
Joti Brar, Soc. Lab.   359
Magnus Nielsen, UK Ind.   301
Lab. majority 11,175 (35.90%)
8.31% swing Lab. to LD
(1997: Lab. maj. 17,903 (47.11%))

HORNCHURCH
E. 61,008   T. 35,557 (58.28%)   Lab. hold
*John Cryer, Lab.   16,514
Robin Squire, C.   15,032
Ms Sarah Lea, LD   2,928
Lawrence Webb, UK Ind.   893
Mr David Durant, Third   190
Lab. majority 1,482 (4.17%)
4.38% swing Lab. to C.
(1997: Lab. maj. 5,680 (12.93%))

HORNSEY & WOOD GREEN
E. 75,967   T. 44,063 (58.00%)   Lab. hold
*Ms Barbara Roche, Lab.   21,967
Ms Lynne Featherstone, LD   11,353
Jason Hollands, C.   6,921
Ms Jayne Forbes, Green   2,228
Ms Louise Christian, Soc. All.   1,106
Ms Ella Rule, Soc. Lab.   294
Erdil Ataman, Reform   194
Lab. majority 10,614 (24.09%)
13.21% swing Lab. to LD
(1997: Lab. maj. 20,499 (39.82%))

HORSHAM
E. 79,604   T. 50,770 (63.78%)   C. hold
*Rt. Hon. F. Maude, C.   26,134
Hubert Carr, LD   12,468
Ms Janet Sully, Lab.   10,267
Hugo Miller, UK Ind.   1,472
Jim Duggan, Ind.   429
C. majority 13,666 (26.92%)
0.46% swing LD to C.
(1997: C. maj. 14,862 (26.00%))

HOUGHTON & WASHINGTON EAST
E. 67,946   T. 33,641 (49.51%)   Lab. hold
*Fraser Kemp, Lab.   24,628
Tony Devenish, C.   4,810
Richard Ormerod, LD   4,203
Lab. majority 19,818 (58.91%)
2.29% swing Lab. to C.
(1997: Lab. maj. 26,555 (63.49%))

HOVE
E. 70,889   T. 41,988 (59.23%)   Lab. hold
*Ivor Caplin, Lab.   19,253
Mrs Jenny Langston, C.   16,082
Harold de Souza, LD   3,823
Ms Anthea Ballam, Green   1,369
Andy Richards Soc. All.   531
Richard Franklin, UK Ind.   358
Nigel Donovan, Lib.   316
Simon Dobbshead, Free   196
Thomas Major, Ind.   60
Lab. majority 3,171 (7.55%)
0.34% swing Lab. to C.
(1997: Lab. maj. 3,959 (8.23%))

HUDDERSFIELD
E. 64,349   T. 35,383 (54.99%)
                                       Lab. Co-op hold
*Barry Sheerman, Lab. Co-op   18,840
Paul Baverstock, C.   8,794
Neil Bentley, LD   5,300
John Phillips, Green   1,254
Mrs Judith Longman, UK Ind.   613
Graham Hellawell, Soc. All.   374
George Randall, Soc. Lab.   208
Lab. Co-op majority 10,046 (28.39%)
3.59% swing Lab. Co-op to C.
(1997: Lab. maj. 15,848 (35.57%))

HULL EAST
E. 66,473   T. 30,875 (46.45%)   Lab. hold
*Rt. Hon. J. Prescott, Lab.   19,938
Ms Jo Swinson, LD   4,613
Ms Sandip Verma, C.   4,276
Ms Jeanette Jenkinson, UK Ind.   1,218
Ms Linda Muir, Soc. Lab.   830
Lab. majority 15,325 (49.64%)
5.94% swing Lab. to LD
(1997: Lab. maj. 23,318 (57.60%))

HULL NORTH
E. 63,022   T. 28,633 (45.43%)   Lab. hold
*Kevin McNamara, Lab.   16,364
Ms Simone Butterworth, LD   5,643
Paul Charlson, C.   4,902
Ms Tineka Robinson, UK Ind.   655
Roger Smith, Soc. All.   490
Carl Wagner, LCA   478
Christopher Veasey, Ind.   101
Lab. majority 10,721 (37.44%)
6.89% swing Lab. to LD
(1997: Lab. maj. 19,705 (50.79%))

HULL WEST & HESSLE
E. 63,077   T. 28,916 (45.84%)   Lab. hold
*Alan Johnson, Lab.   16,880
John Sharp, C.   5,929
Ms Angela Wastling, LD   4,364
John Cornforth, UK Ind.   878
David Harris, Ind.   512
David Skinner Soc. Lab.   353
Lab. majority 10,951 (37.87%)
1.38% swing Lab. to C.
(1997: Lab. maj. 15,525 (40.48%))

HUNTINGDON
E. 78,604   T. 49,089 (62.45%)   C. hold
Jonathan Djanogly, C.   24,507
Michael Pope, LD   11,715
Takki Sulaiman, Lab.   11,211
Derek Norman, UK Ind.   1,656
C. majority 12,792 (26.06%)
7.26% swing C. to LD
(1997: C. maj. 18,140 (31.84%))

HYNDBURN
E. 66,445   T. 38,243 (57.56%)   Lab. hold
*Greg Pope, Lab.   20,900
Peter Britcliffe, C.   12,681
Bill Greene, LD   3,680
John Tomlin, UK Ind.   982
Lab. majority 8,219 (21.49%)
1.11% swing Lab. to C.
(1997: Lab. maj. 11,448 (23.71%))

ILFORD NORTH
E. 68,893   T. 40,234 (58.40%)   Lab. hold
*Ms Linda Perham, Lab.   18,428
Vivian Bendall, C.   16,313
Gavin Stollar, LD   4,717
Martin Levin, UK Ind.   776
Lab. majority 2,115 (5.26%)
0.67% swing Lab. to C.
(1997: Lab. maj. 3,224 (6.60%))

ILFORD SOUTH
E. 76,025   T. 41,295 (54.32%)
                                       Lab. Co-op hold
*Mike Gapes, Lab. Co-op   24,619
Suresh Kuma, C.   10,622
Ralph Scott, LD   4,647
Harun Khan, UK Ind.   1,407
Lab. Co-op majority 13,997 (33.90%)
2.75% swing C. to Lab. Co-op
(1997: Lab. maj. 14,200 (28.39%))

IPSWICH
E. 68,198   T. 38,873 (57.00%)   Lab. hold
*Jamie Cann, Lab.   19,952
Edward Wild, C.   11,871
Terry Gilbert, LD   5,904
William Vinyard, UK Ind.   624
Peter Leach, Soc. All.   305
Shaun Gratton, Soc. Lab.   217
Lab. majority 8,081 (20.79%)
0.40% swing Lab. to C.
(1997: Lab. maj. 10,439 (21.58%))

ISLE OF WIGHT
E. 106,305   T. 63,482 (59.72%)   C. gain
Andrew Turner, C.   25,223
*Dr Peter Brand, LD   22,397
Ms Deborah Gardiner, Lab.   9,676
David Lott, UK Ind.   2,106
David Holmes, Ind.   1,423
Paul Scivier, Green   1,279
Philip Murray, IOW   1,164
James Spensley, Soc. Lab.   214
C. majority 2,826 (4.45%)
6.61% swing LD to C.
(1997: LD maj. 6,406 (8.76%))

ISLINGTON NORTH
E. 61,970   T. 30,216 (48.76%)   Lab. hold
*Jeremy Corbyn, Lab.   18,699
Ms Laura Willoughby, LD   5,741
Neil Rands, C.   3,249
Chris Ashby, Green   1,876
Steve Cook, Soc. Lab.   512
Emine Hassan, Reform   139
Lab. majority 12,958 (42.88%)
6.38% swing Lab. to LD
(1997: Lab. maj. 19,955 (55.64%))

ISLINGTON SOUTH & FINSBURY
E. 59,515   T. 28,206 (47.39%) Lab. hold
*Rt. Hon. C. Smith, *Lab.*   15,217
Keith Sharp, *LD*   7,937
Mrs Nicky Morgan, *C.*   3,860
Ms Janine Booth, *Soc. All.*   817
Thomas McCarthy, *Ind.*   267
Charles Thomson, *Stuck*   108
Lab. majority 7,280 (25.81%)
7.71% swing Lab. to LD
(1997: Lab. maj. 14,563 (41.24%))

JARROW
E. 63,172   T. 34,479 (54.58%) Lab. hold
*Stephen Hepburn, *Lab.*   22,777
James Selby, *LD*   5,182
Donald Wood, *C.*   5,056
Alan Badger, *UK Ind.*   716
Alan Le Blond, *Ind.*   391
John Bissett, *Soc.*   357
Lab. majority 17,595 (51.03%)
1.37% swing Lab. to LD
(1997: Lab. maj. 21,933 (49.91%))

KEIGHLEY
E. 68,349   T. 43,333 (63.40%) Lab. hold
*Ms Ann Cryer, *Lab.*   20,888
Simon Cooke, *C.*   16,883
Mike Doyle, *LD*   4,722
Michael Cassidy, *UK Ind.*   840
Lab. majority 4,005 (9.24%)
2.30% swing Lab. to C.
(1997: Lab. maj. 7,132 (13.85%))

KENSINGTON & CHELSEA
E. 62,007   T. 28,038 (45.22%)   C. hold
*Rt. Hon. M. Portillo, *C.*   15,270
Simon Stanley, *Lab.*   6,499
Ms Kishwer Falkner, *LD*   4,416
Ms Julia Stephenson, *Green*   1,158
Nicholas Hockney, *UK Ind.*   416
Ms Josephine Quintavalle, *ProLife*   179
Ginger Crab, *Wrestling*   100
C. majority 8,771 (31.28%)
2.81% swing Lab. to C.
(1999 Nov. by-election: C. maj. 6,706
(34.37%); 1997: C. maj. 9,519
(25.66%))

KETTERING
E. 79,697   T. 53,752 (67.45%) Lab. hold
*Philip Sawford, *Lab.*   24,034
Philip Hollobone, *C.*   23,369
Roger Aron, *LD*   5,469
Barry Mahoney, *UK Ind.*   880
Lab. majority 665 (1.24%)
0.45% swing C. to Lab.
(1997: Lab. maj. 189 (0.33%))

KINGSTON & SURBITON
E. 72,687   T. 49,093 (67.54%)   LD hold
*Edward Davey, *LD*   29,542
David Shaw, *C.*   13,866
Phil Woodford, *Lab.*   4,302
Chris Spruce, *Green*   572
Miss Amy Burns, *UK Ind.*   438
John Hayball, *Soc. Lab.*   319
Jeremy Middleton, *Unrep.*   54
LD majority 15,676 (31.93%)
15.92% swing C. to LD
(1997: LD maj. 56 (0.10%))

KINGSWOOD
E. 80,531   T. 52,676 (65.41%) Lab. hold
*Dr Roger Berry, *Lab.*   28,903
Robert Marven, *C.*   14,941
Christopher Greenfield, *LD*   7,747
David Smith, *UK Ind.*   1,085
Lab. majority 13,962 (26.51%)
1.35% swing C. to Lab.
(1997: Lab. maj. 14,253 (23.80%))

KNOWSLEY NORTH & SEFTON EAST
E. 70,781   T. 37,517 (53.00%) Lab. hold
*George Howarth, *Lab.*   25,035
Keith Chapman, *C.*   6,108
Richard Roberts, *LD*   5,173
Ron Waugh, *Soc. Lab.*   574
Thomas Rossiter, *Ind.*   356
David Jones, *Ind.*   271
Lab. majority 18,927 (50.45%)
1.08% swing Lab. to C.
(1997: Lab. maj. 26,147 (52.61%))

KNOWSLEY SOUTH
E. 70,681   T. 36,590 (51.77%) Lab. hold
*Eddie O'Hara, *Lab.*   26,071
David Smithson, *LD*   4,755
Paul Jemetta, *C.*   4,250
Alan Fogg, *Soc. Lab.*   1,068
Ms Mona McNee, *Ind.*   446
Lab. majority 21,316 (58.26%)
5.27% swing Lab. to LD
(1997: Lab. maj. 30,708 (64.53%))

LANCASHIRE WEST
E. 72,858   T. 42,971 (58.98%) Lab. hold
*Colin Pickthall, *Lab.*   23,404
Jeremy Myers, *C.*   13,761
John Thornton, *LD*   4,966
David Hill, *Ind.*   523
David Braid, *Ind.*   317
Lab. majority 9,643 (22.44%)
4.42% swing Lab. to C.
(1997: Lab. maj. 17,119 (31.28%))

LANCASTER & WYRE
E. 78,964   T. 52,350 (66.30%) Lab. hold
*Hilton Dawson, *Lab.*   22,556
Steve Barclay, *C.*   22,075
Ms Liz Scott, *LD*   5,383
Prof John Whitelegg, *Green*   1,595
Dr John Whittaker, *UK Ind.*   741
Lab. majority 481 (0.92%)
0.64% swing Lab. to C.
(1997: Lab. maj. 1,295 (2.20%))

LEEDS CENTRAL
E. 65,497   T. 27,306 (41.69%) Lab. hold
*Hilary Benn, *Lab.*   18,277
Miss Victoria Richmond, *C.*   3,896
Stewart Arnold, *LD*   3,607
David Burgess, *UK Ind.*   775
Steve Johnson, *Soc. All.*   751
Lab. majority 14,381 (52.67%)
1.62% swing Lab. to C.
(1999 Jun. by-election: Lab. maj. 2,293
(17.39%); 1997: Lab. maj. 20,689
(55.90%))

LEEDS EAST
E. 56,400   T. 29,055 (51.52%) Lab. hold
*George Mudie, *Lab.*   18,290
Barry Anderson, *C.*   5,647
Brian Jennings, *LD*   3,923
Raymond Northgreaves, *UK Ind.*   634
Mark King, *Soc. Lab.*   419
Peter Socrates, *Ind.*   142
Lab. majority 12,643 (43.51%)
2.64% swing Lab. to C.
(1997: Lab. maj. 17,466 (48.80%))

LEEDS NORTH EAST
E. 64,123   T. 39,773 (62.03%) Lab. hold
*Fabian Hamilton, *Lab.*   19,540
Owain Rhys, *C.*   12,451
Jonathan Brown, *LD*   6,325
Ms Celia Foote, *Left All*   770
Jeffrey Miles, *UK Ind.*   382
Colin Muir, *Soc. Lab.*   173
Mohammed Zaman, *Ind.*   132
Lab. majority 7,089 (17.82%)
1.27% swing C. to Lab.
(1997: Lab. maj. 6,959 (15.29%))

LEEDS NORTH WEST
E. 72,945   T. 42,451 (58.20%) Lab. hold
*Harold Best *Lab.*   17,794
Adam Pritchard, *C.*   12,558
David Hall-Matthews, *LD*   11,431
Simon Jones, *UK Ind.*   668
Lab. majority 5,236 (12.33%)
2.27% swing C. to Lab.
(1997: Lab. maj. 3,844 (7.79%))

LEEDS WEST
E. 64,218   T. 32,094 (49.98%) Lab. hold
*John Battle, *Lab.*   19,943
Kris Hopkins, *C.*   5,008
Darren Finlay, *LD*   3,350
David Blackburn, *Green*   2,573
William Finley, *UK Ind.*   758
Noel Nowosielski, *Lib.*   462
Lab. majority 14,935 (46.54%)
1.31% swing Lab. to C.
(1997: Lab. maj. 19,771 (49.16%))

LEICESTER EAST
E. 65,527   T. 40,661 (62.05%) Lab. hold
*Keith Vaz, *Lab.*   23,402
John Mugglestone *C.*   9,960
Ms Harpinder Athwal, *LD*   4,989
Dave Roberts, *Soc. Lab.*   837
Clive Potter, *BNP*   772
Shirley Bennett, *Ind.*   701
Lab. majority 13,442 (33.06%)
4.22% swing Lab. to C.
(1997: Lab. maj. 18,422 (41.49%))

LEICESTER SOUTH
E. 72,671   T. 42,142 (57.99%) Lab. hold
*Jim Marshall, *Lab.*   22,958
Richard Hoile, *C.*   9,715
Parmjit Singh Gill, *LD*   7,243
Ms Margaret Layton, *Green*   1,217
Arnold Gardner, *Soc. Lab.*   676
Kirti Ladwa, *UK Ind.*   333
Lab. majority 13,243 (31.42%)
1.43% swing Lab. to C.
(1997: Lab. maj. 16,493 (34.28%))

LEICESTER WEST
E. 65,267   T. 33,219 (50.90%)   Lab. hold
*Rt. Hon. Ms P. Hewitt, *Lab.*   18,014
Chris Shaw, *C.*   8,375
Andrew Vincent, *LD*   5,085
Matthew Gough, *Green*   1,074
Sean Kirkpatrick, *Soc. Lab.*   350
Steve Score, *Soc. All.*   321
Lab. majority 9,639 (29.02%)
1.21% swing Lab. to C.
(1997: Lab. maj. 12,864 (31.44%))

LEICESTERSHIRE NORTH WEST
E. 68,414   T. 45,009 (65.79%)
Lab. Co-op hold
*David Taylor, *Lab. Co-op.*   23,431
Nick Weston, *C.*   15,274
Charlie Fraser-Fleming, *LD*   4,651
William Nattrass, *UK Ind.*   1,021
Robert Nettleton, *Ind.*   632
Lab. Co-op majority 8,157 (18.12%)
3.64% swing Lab. Co-op to C.
(1997: Lab. maj. 13,219 (25.41%))

LEIGH
E. 71,054   T. 35,298 (49.68%)   Lab. hold
Andrew Burnham, *Lab.*   22,783
Andrew Oxley, *C.*   6,421
Ray Atkins, *LD*   4,524
William Kelly, *Soc. Lab.*   820
Chris Best, *UK Ind.*   750
Lab. majority 16,362 (46.35%)
3.50% swing Lab. to C.
(1997: Lab. maj. 24,496 (53.35%))

LEOMINSTER
E. 68,695   T. 46,729 (68.02%)   C. gain
Bill Wiggin, *C.*   22,879
Ms Celia Downie, *LD*   12,512
Stephen Hart, *Lab.*   7,872
Ms Pippa Bennett, *Green*   1,690
Christopher Kingsley, *UK Ind.*   1,590
John Haycock, *Ind.*   186
C. majority 10,367 (22.19%)
2.35% swing LD to C.
(1997: C. maj. 8,835 (17.48%))

LEWES
E. 66,332   T. 45,433 (68.49%)   LD hold
*Norman Baker, *LD*   25,588
Simon Sinnatt, *C.*   15,878
Paul Richards, *Lab.*   3,317
John Harvey, *UK Ind.*   650
LD majority 9,710 (21.37%)
9.36% swing C. to LD
(1997: LD maj. 1,300 (2.65%))

LEWISHAM DEPTFORD
E. 62,869   T. 29,107 (46.30%)   Lab. hold
*Joan Ruddock, *Lab.*   18,915
Ms Cordelia McCartney, *C.*   3,622
Andrew Wiseman, *LD*   3,409
Darren Johnson, *Green*   1,901
Ian Page, *Soc. All.*   1,260
Lab. majority 15,293 (52.54%)
1.78% swing Lab. to C.
(1997: Lab. maj. 18,878 (56.11%))

LEWISHAM EAST
E. 58,302   T. 30,040 (51.52%)   Lab. hold
*Ms Bridget Prentice, *Lab.*   16,116
David McInnes, *C.*   7,157
David Buxton, *LD*   4,937
Barry Roberts, *BNP*   1,005
Ms Jean Kysow, *Soc. All.*   464
Maurice Link, *UK Ind.*   361
Lab. majority 8,959 (29.82%)
1.30% swing Lab. to C.
(1997: Lab. maj. 12,127 (32.42%))

LEWISHAM WEST
E. 60,947   T. 30,815 (50.56%)   Lab. hold
*Jim Dowd, *Lab.*   18,816
Gary Johnson, *C.*   6,896
Richard Thomas, *LD*   4,146
Frederick Pearson, *UK Ind.*   485
Nick Long, *Ind.*   472
Lab. majority 11,920 (38.68%)
0.25% swing C. to Lab.
(1997: Lab. maj. 14,337 (38.19%))

LEYTON & WANSTEAD
E. 61,549   T. 33,718 (54.78%)   Lab. hold
*Harry Cohen, *Lab.*   19,558
Edward Heckels, *C.*   6,654
Alex Wilcock, *LD*   5,389
Ashley Gunstock, *Green*   1,030
Ms Sally Labern, *Soc. All.*   709
M. Skaife D'Ingerthorp, *UK Ind.*   378
Lab. majority 12,904 (38.27%)
0.17% swing Lab. to C.
(1997: Lab. maj. 15,186 (38.62%))

LICHFIELD
E. 63,794   T. 41,680 (65.34%)   C. hold
*Michael Fabricant, *C.*   20,480
Martin Machray, *Lab.*   16,054
Phillip Bennion, *LD*   4,462
John Phazey, *UK Ind.*   684
C. majority 4,426 (10.62%)
5.06% swing Lab. to C.
(1997: C. maj. 238 (0.49%))

LINCOLN
E. 66,299   T. 37,125 (56.00%)   Lab. hold
*Ms Gillian Merron, *Lab.*   20,003
Mrs Christine Talbot, *C.*   11,583
Ms Lisa Gabriel, *LD*   4,703
Roger Doughty, *UK Ind.*   836
Lab. majority 8,420 (22.68%)
0.61% swing Lab. to C.
(1997: Lab. maj. 11,130 (23.91%))

LIVERPOOL GARSTON
E. 65,094   T. 32,651 (50.16%)   Lab. hold
*Ms Maria Eagle, *Lab.*   20,043
Ms Paula Keaveney, *LD*   7,549
Miss Helen Sutton, *C.*   5,059
Lab. majority 12,494 (38.27%)
2.05% swing Lab. to LD
(1997: Lab. maj. 18,417 (42.36%))

LIVERPOOL RIVERSIDE
E. 74,827   T. 25,503 (34.08%)
Lab. Co-op hold
*Ms Louise Ellman, *Lab. Co-op.*   18,201
Richard Marbrow, *LD*   4,251
Miss Judith Edwards, *C.*   2,142
Ms Cathy Wilson, *Soc. All.*   909
Lab. Co-op majority 13,950 (54.70%)
1.23% swing Lab. Co-op to LD
(1997: Lab. maj. 21,799 (57.16%))

LIVERPOOL WALTON
E. 66,237   T. 28,458 (42.96%)   Lab. hold
*Peter Kilfoyle, *Lab.*   22,143
Kiron Reid, *LD*   4,147
Stephen Horgan, *C.*   1,726
Paul Forrest, *UK Ind.*   442
Lab. majority 17,996 (63.24%)
2.00% swing Lab. to LD
(1997: Lab. maj. 27,038 (67.24%))

LIVERPOOL WAVERTREE
E. 72,555   T. 32,138 (44.29%)   Lab. hold
*Ms Jane Kennedy, *Lab.*   20,155
Christopher Newby, *LD*   7,836
Geoffrey Allen, *C.*   3,091
Michael Lane, *Soc. Lab.*   359
Mark O'Brien, *Soc. All.*   349
Neil Miney, *UK Ind.*   348
Lab. majority 12,319 (38.33%)
2.29% swing Lab. to LD
(1997: Lab. maj. 19,701 (42.91%))

LIVERPOOL WEST DERBY
E. 67,921   T. 30,907 (45.50%)   Lab. hold
*Robert Wareing, *Lab.*   20,454
Steve Radford, *Lib.*   4,601
Patrick Moloney, *LD*   3,366
Bill Clare, *C.*   2,486
Lab. majority 15,853 (51.29%)
5.15% swing Lab. to Lib.
(1997: Lab. maj. 25,965 (61.59%))

LOUGHBOROUGH
E. 70,077   T. 44,254 (63.15%)
Lab. Co-op hold
*Andy Reed, *Lab. Co-op.*   22,016
Neil Lyon, *C.*   15,638
Ms Julie Simons, *LD*   5,667
John Bigger, *UK Ind.*   933
Lab. Co-op majority 6,378 (14.41%)
1.75% swing C. to Lab. Co-op
(1997: Lab. maj. 5,712 (10.91%))

LOUTH & HORNCASTLE
E. 71,556   T. 44,460 (62.13%)   C. hold
*Sir Peter Tapsell, *C.*   21,543
David Bolland, *Lab.*   13,989
Ms Fiona Martin, *LD*   8,928
C. majority 7,554 (16.99%)
1.59% swing Lab. to C.
(1997: C. maj. 6,900 (13.81%))

LUDLOW
E. 63,053   T. 43,124 (68.39%)   LD gain
Matthew Green, *LD*   18,620
Martin Taylor-Smith, *C.*   16,990
Nigel Knowles, *Lab.*   5,785
Jim Gaffney, *Green*   871
Phil Gutteridge, *UK Ind.*   858
LD majority 1,630 (3.78%)
8.27% swing C. to LD
(1997: C. maj. 5,909 (12.77%))

LUTON NORTH
E. 65,998   T. 39,126 (59.28%)   Lab. hold
*Kelvin Hopkins, *Lab.*   22,187
Mrs Amanda Sater, *C.*   12,210
Colin Brown, *UK Ind.*   934
Dr Bob Hoyle, *LD*   3,795
Lab. majority 9,977 (25.50%)
2.58% swing C. to Lab.
(1997: Lab. maj. 9,626 (20.34%))

LUTON SOUTH
E. 68,985   T. 39,351 (57.04%)   Lab. hold
*Ms Margaret Moran, *Lab.*   21,719
Gordon Henderson, *C.*   11,586
Rabi Martins, *LD*   4,292
Marc Scheimann, *Green*   798
Charles Lawman, *UK Ind.*   578
Joe Hearne, *Soc. All.*   271
Robert Bolton, *WRP*   107
Lab. majority 10,133 (25.75%)
1.13% swing C. to Lab.
(1997: Lab. maj. 11,319 (23.49%))

MACCLESFIELD
E. 73,123   T. 45,585 (62.34%)   C. hold
*Nicholas Winterton, *C.*   22,284
Stephen Carter, *Lab.*   15,084
Mike Flynn, *LD*   8,217
C. majority 7,200 (15.79%)
0.09% swing C. to Lab.
(1997: C. maj. 8,654 (15.97%))

MAIDENHEAD
E. 68,130   T. 43,318 (63.58%)   C. hold
*Ms Theresa May, *C.*   19,506
Ms Kathryn Newbound, *LD*   16,222
John O'Farrell, *Lab.*   6,577
Dr Denis Cooper, *UK Ind.*   741
Lloyd Clarke, *Loony*   272
C. majority 3,284 (7.58%)
7.98% swing C. to LD
(1997: C. maj. 11,981 (23.54%))

MAIDSTONE & THE WEALD
E. 74,002   T. 45,577 (61.59%)   C. hold
*Rt. Hon. Miss A. Widdecombe, *C.* 22,621
Mark Davis, *Lab.*   12,303
Ms Allison Wainman, *LD*   9,064
John Botting, *UK Ind.*   978
Neil Hunt, *Ind.*   611
C. majority 10,318 (22.64%)
2.36% swing Lab. to C.
(1997: C. maj. 9,603 (17.91%))

MAKERFIELD
E. 68,457   T. 34,856 (50.92%)   Lab. hold
*Rt. Hon. Ian McCartney, *Lab.*   23,879
Mrs Jane Brooks, *C.*   6,129
David Crowther, *LD*   3,990
Malcolm Jones, *Soc. All.*   858
Lab. majority 17,750 (50.92%)
3.61% swing Lab. to C.
(1997: Lab. maj. 26,177 (58.15%))

MALDON & CHELMSFORD EAST
E. 69,201   T. 44,100 (63.73%)   C. hold
*John Whittingdale, *C.*   21,719
Russell Kennedy, *Lab.*   13,257
Ms Jane Jackson, *LD*   7,002
Geoffrey Harris, *UK Ind.*   1,135
Walter Schwarz, *Green*   987
C. majority 8,462 (19.19%)
0.37% swing C. to Lab.
(1997: C. maj. 10,039 (19.92%))

MANCHESTER BLACKLEY
E. 59,111   T. 26,523 (44.87%)   Lab. hold
*Graham Stringer, *Lab.*   18,285
Lance Stanbury, *C.*   3,821
Gary Riding, *LD*   3,015
Kevin Barr, *Soc. Lab.*   485
Ms Karen Reissmann, *Soc. All.*   461
Aziz Bhatti, *Anti-Corrupt*   456
Lab. majority 14,464 (54.53%)
0.13% swing Lab. to C.
(1997: Lab. maj. 19,588 (54.79%))

MANCHESTER CENTRAL
E. 66,268   T. 25,928 (39.13%)   Lab. hold
*Tony Lloyd, *Lab.*   17,812
Philip Hobson, *LD*   4,070
Aaron Powell, *C.*   2,328
Ms Vanessa Hall, *Green*   1,018
Ron Sinclair, *Soc. Lab.*   484
Ms Terrenia Brosnan, *ProLife*   216
Lab. majority 13,742 (53.00%)
2.84% swing Lab. to LD
(1997: Lab. maj. 19,682 (58.69%))

MANCHESTER GORTON
E. 63,834   T. 27,229 (42.66%)   Lab. hold
*Rt. Hon. G. Kaufman, *Lab.*   17,099
Ms Jackie Pearcey, *LD*   5,795
Christopher Causer, *C.*   2,705
Bruce Bingham, *Green*   835
Rashid Bhatti, *UK Ind.*   462
Ms Kirsty Muir, *Soc. Lab.*   333
Lab. majority 11,304 (41.51%)
3.12% swing Lab. to LD
(1997: Lab. maj. 17,342 (47.76%))

MANCHESTER WITHINGTON
E. 67,480   T. 35,050 (51.94%)   Lab. hold
*Rt. Hon. K. Bradley, *Lab.*   19,239
Ms Yasmin Zalzala, *LD*   7,715
Julian Samways, *C.*   5,349
Ms Michelle Valentine, *Green*   1,539
John Clegg, *Soc. All.*   1,208
Lab. majority 11,524 (32.88%)
7.53% swing Lab. to LD
(1997: Lab. maj. 18,581 (42.20%))

MANSFIELD
E. 66,748   T. 36,852 (55.21%)   Lab. hold
*Alan Meale, *Lab.*   21,050
William Wellesley, *C.*   10,012
Tim Hill, *LD*   5,790
Lab. majority 11,038 (29.95%)
6.65% swing Lab. to C.
(1997: Lab. maj. 20,518 (43.26%))

MEDWAY
E. 64,930   T. 38,610 (59.46%)   Lab. hold
*Robert Marshall-Andrews, *Lab.*   18,914
Mark Reckless, *C.*   15,134
Geoffrey Juby, *LD*   3,604
Ms Nikki Sinclaire, *UK Ind.*   958
Lab. majority 3,780 (9.79%)
1.08% swing Lab. to C.
(1997: Lab. maj. 5,354 (11.96%))

MERIDEN
E. 74,439   T. 44,559 (59.86%)   C. hold
*Mrs Caroline Spelman, *C.*   21,246
Ms Christine Shawcroft, *Lab.*   17,462
Nigel Hicks, *LD*   4,941
Richard Adams, *UK Ind.*   910
C. majority 3,784 (8.49%)
3.71% swing Lab. to C.
(1997: C. maj. 582 (1.07%))

MIDDLESBROUGH
E. 67,659   T. 33,717 (49.83%)   Lab. hold
*Stuart Bell, *Lab.*   22,783
Alex Finn, *C.*   6,453
Keith Miller, *LD*   3,512
Geoff Kerr-Morgan, *Soc. All.*   577
Kai Andersen, *Soc. Lab.*   392
Lab. majority 16,330 (48.43%)
2.92% swing Lab. to C.
(1997: Lab. maj. 25,018 (54.28%))

MIDDLESBROUGH SOUTH &
CLEVELAND EAST
E. 71,485   T. 43,991 (61.54%)   Lab. hold
*Dr Ashok Kumar, *Lab.*   24,321
Mrs Barbara Harpham, *C.*   14,970
Ms Linda Parrish, *LD*   4,700
Lab. majority 9,351 (21.26%)
0.73% swing C. to Lab.
(1997: Lab. maj. 10,607 (19.79%))

MILTON KEYNES NORTH EAST
E. 75,526   T. 47,094 (62.35%)   Lab. hold
*Brian White, *Lab.*   19,761
Mrs Marion Rix, *C.*   17,932
David Yeoward, *LD*   8,375
Michael Phillips, *UK Ind.*   1,026
Lab. majority 1,829 (3.88%)
1.71% swing C. to Lab.
(1997: Lab. maj. 240 (0.47%))

MILTON KEYNES SOUTH WEST
E. 76,607   T. 45,384 (59.24%)   Lab. hold
*Dr Phyllis Starkey, *Lab.*   22,484
Iain Stewart, *C.*   15,506
Nazar Mohammad, *LD*   4,828
Alan Francis, *Green*   957
Clive Davies, *UK Ind.*   848
Patrick Denning, *LCA*   500
Dave Bradbury, *Soc. All.*   261
Lab. majority 6,978 (15.38%)
2.45% swing Lab. to C.
(1997: Lab. maj. 10,292 (20.28%))

MITCHAM & MORDEN
E. 65,671   T. 37,961 (57.80%)   Lab. hold
*Ms Siobhain McDonagh, *Lab.*   22,936
Harry Stokes, *C.*   9,151
Nicholas Harris, *LD*   3,820
Tom Walsh, *Green*   926
John Tyndall, *BNP*   642
Adrian Roberts, *UK Ind.*   486
Lab. majority 13,785 (36.31%)
3.83% swing C. to Lab.
(1997: Lab. maj. 13,741 (28.66%))

MOLE VALLEY
E. 67,770   T. 47,072 (69.46%)   C. hold
*Sir Paul Beresford, *C.*   23,790
Ms Celia Savage, *LD*   13,637
Dan Redford, *Lab.*   7,837
Ron Walters, *UK Ind.*   1,333
William Newton, *ProLife*   475
C. majority 10,153 (21.57%)
1.41% swing LD to C.
(1997: C. maj. 10,221 (18.74%))

MORECAMBE & LUNESDALE
E. 68,607   T. 41,655 (60.72%)   Lab. hold
*Ms Geraldine Smith, *Lab.*   20,646
David Nuttall, *C.*   15,554
Chris Cotton, *LD*   3,817
Gregg Beaman, *UK Ind.*   935
Ms Cherith Adams, *Green*   703
Lab. majority 5,092 (12.22%)
0.05% swing C. to Lab.
(1997: Lab. maj. 5,965 (12.12%))

MORLEY & ROTHWELL
E. 71,815 *T.* 38,442 (53.53%) Lab. hold
Colin Challen, *Lab.*   21,919
David Schofield, *C.*   9,829
Stewart Golton, *LD*   5,446
John Bardsley, *UK Ind.*   1,248
Lab. majority 12,090 (31.45%)
0.35% swing Lab. to C.
(1997: Lab. maj. 14,750 (32.14%))

NEW FOREST EAST
E. 66,767 *T.* 42,178 (63.17%) C. hold
*Dr Julian Lewis, *C.*   17,902
Brian Dash, *LD*   14,073
Alan Goodfellow, *Lab.*   9,141
William Howe, *UK Ind.*   1,062
C. majority 3,829 (9.08%)
0.78% swing C. to LD
(1997: C. maj. 5,215 (10.63%))

NEW FOREST WEST
E. 67,806 *T.* 44,087 (65.02%) C. hold
*Desmond Swayne, *C.*   24,575
Mike Bignell, *LD*   11,384
Ms Crada Onuegbu, *Lab.*   6,481
Michael Clark, *UK Ind.*   1,647
C. majority 13,191 (29.92%)
3.57% swing LD to C.
(1997: C. maj. 11,332 (22.78%))

NEWARK
E. 71,089 *T.* 45,147 (63.51%) C. gain
Patrick Mercer, *C.*   20,983
*Ms Fiona Jones, *Lab.*   16,910
David Harding-Price, *LD*   5,970
Donald Haxby, *Ind.*   822
Ian Thomson, *Soc. All.*   462
C. majority 4,073 (9.02%)
7.41% swing Lab. to C.
(1997: Lab. maj. 3,016 (5.80%))

NEWBURY
E. 75,490 *T.* 50,807 (67.30%) LD hold
*David Rendel, *LD*   24,507
Richard Benyon, *C.*   22,092
Steve Billcliffe, *Lab.*   3,523
Ms Delphine Gray-Fisk, *UK Ind.*   685
LD majority 2,415 (4.75%)
5.16% swing LD to C.
(1997: LD maj. 8,517 (15.08%))

NEWCASTLE UPON TYNE
CENTRAL
E. 67,970 *T.* 34,870 (51.30%) Lab. hold
*Jim Cousins, *Lab.*   19,169
Stephen Psallidas, *LD*   7,564
Aidan Ruff, *C.*   7,414
Gordon Potts, *Soc. Lab.*   723
Lab. majority 11,605 (33.28%)
5.44% swing Lab. to LD
(1997: Lab. maj. 16,480 (35.75%))

NEWCASTLE UPON TYNE EAST &
WALLSEND
E. 61,494 *T.* 32,694 (53.17%) Lab. hold
*Rt. Hon. N. Brown, *Lab.*   20,642
David Ord, *LD*   6,419
Tim Troman, *C.*   873
Andrew Gray, *Green*   651
Dr Harash Narang, *Ind.*   563
Ms Blanch Carpenter, *Soc. Lab.*   420
Martin Levy, *Comm.*   126
Lab. majority 14,223 (43.50%)
8.53% swing Lab. to LD
(1997: Lab. maj. 23,811 (57.25%))

NEWCASTLE UPON TYNE NORTH
E. 63,208 *T.* 36,368 (57.54%) Lab. hold
*Doug Henderson, *Lab.*   21,874
Phillip Smith, *C.*   7,424
Graham Soult, *LD*   7,070
Lab. majority 14,450 (39.73%)
1.50% swing Lab. to C.
(1997: Lab. maj. 19,332 (42.74%))

NEWCASTLE-UNDER-LYME
E. 65,739 *T.* 38,674 (58.83%) Lab. hold
Paul Farrelly, *Lab.*   20,650
Mike Flynn, *C.*   10,664
Jerry Roodhouse, *LD*   5,993
Robert Fyson, *Ind.*   773
Paul Godfrey, *UK Ind.*   594
Lab. majority 9,986 (25.82%)
4.60% swing Lab. to C.
(1997: Lab. maj. 17,206 (35.02%))

NORFOLK MID
E. 74,911 *T.* 52,548 (70.15%) C. hold
*Keith Simpson, *C.*   23,519
Daniel Zeichner, *Lab.*   18,957
Ms V. Clifford-Jackson, *LD*   7,621
John Agnew, *UK Ind.*   1,333
Peter Reeve, *Green*   1,118
C. majority 4,562 (8.68%)
3.18% swing Lab. to C.
(1997: C. maj. 1,336 (2.33%))

NORFOLK NORTH
E. 80,061 *T.* 56,220 (70.22%) LD gain
Norman Lamb, *LD*   23,978
*David Prior, *C.*   23,495
Michael Gates, *Lab.*   7,490
Mike Sheridan, *Green*   649
Paul Simison, *UK Ind.*   608
LD majority 483 (0.86%)
1.53% swing C. to LD
(1997: C. maj. 1,293 (2.20%))

NORFOLK NORTH WEST
E. 77,387 *T.* 51,203 (66.16%) C. gain
Henry Bellingham, *C.*   24,846
*Dr George Turner, *Lab.*   21,361
Dr Ian Mack, *LD*   4,292
Ian Durrant, *UK Ind.*   704
C. majority 3,485 (6.81%)
4.57% swing Lab. to C.
(1997: Lab. maj. 1,339 (2.33%))

NORFOLK SOUTH
E. 82,710 *T.* 55,929 (67.62%) C. hold
Richard Bacon, *C.*   23,589
Dr Anne Lee, *LD*   16,696
Mark Wells, *Lab.*   13,719
Ms Stephanie Ross-Wagenknecht,
    Green   1,069
Joseph Neal, *UK Ind.*   856
C. majority 6,893 (12.32%)
0.22% swing LD to C.
(1997: C. maj. 7,378 (11.88%))

NORFOLK SOUTH WEST
E. 83,903 *T.* 52,949 (63.11%) C. hold
*Rt. Hon. Mrs G. Shephard, *C.*   27,633
Ms Anne Hanson, *Lab.*   18,267
Gordon Dean, *LD*   5,681
Ian Smith, *UK Ind.*   1,368
C. majority 9,366 (17.69%)
6.75% swing Lab. to C.
(1997: C. maj. 2,464 (4.19%))

NORMANTON
E. 65,392 *T.* 34,155 (52.23%) Lab. hold
*William O'Brien, *Lab.*   19,152
Graham Smith, *C.*   9,215
Stephen Pearson, *LD*   4,990
Mick Appleyard, *Soc. Lab.*   798
Lab. majority 9,937 (29.09%)
3.93% swing Lab. to C.
(1997: Lab. maj. 15,893 (36.96%))

NORTHAMPTON NORTH
E. 74,124 *T.* 41,494 (55.98%) Lab. hold
*Ms Sally Keeble, *Lab.*   20,507
John Whelan, *C.*   12,614
Richard Church, *LD*   7,363
Dusan Torbica, *UK Ind.*   596
Gordon White, *Soc. All.*   414
Lab. majority 7,893 (19.02%)
0.16% swing Lab. to C.
(1997: Lab. maj. 10,000 (19.34%))

NORTHAMPTON SOUTH
E. 85,271 *T.* 51,029 (59.84%) Lab. hold
*Tony Clarke, *Lab.*   21,882
Shailesh Vara, *C.*   20,997
Andrew Simpson, *LD*   6,355
Derek Clark, *UK Ind.*   1,237
Miss Tina Harvey, *LP*   362
Ms Clare Johnson, *ProLife*   196
Lab. majority 885 (1.73%)
0.22% swing C. to Lab.
(1997: Lab. maj. 744 (1.30%))

NORTHAVON
E. 78,841 *T.* 55,758 (70.72%) LD hold
*Steve Webb, *LD*   29,217
Dr Carrie Ruxton, *C.*   19,340
Robert Hall, *Lab.*   6,450
Mrs Carmen Carver, *UK Ind.*   751
LD majority 9,877 (17.71%)
7.15% swing C. to LD
(1997: LD maj. 2,137 (3.42%))

NORWICH NORTH
E. 74,911 *T.* 45,614 (60.89%) Lab. hold
*Dr Ian Gibson, *Lab.*   21,624
Ms Kay Mason, *C.*   15,761
Ms Moira Toye, *LD*   6,750
Robert Tinch, *Green*   797
Guy Cheyney, *UK Ind.*   471
Michael Betts, *Ind.*   211
Lab. majority 5,863 (12.85%)
2.17% swing Lab. to C.
(1997: Lab. maj. 9,470 (17.20%))

NORWICH SOUTH
E. 65,792 *T.* 42,592 (64.74%) Lab. hold
*Rt. Hon. C. Clarke, *Lab.*   19,367
Andrew French, *C.*   10,551
Andrew Aalders-Dunthorne, *LD*   9,640
Adrian Holmes, *Green*   1,434
Alun Buffrey, *LCA*   620
Edward Manningham, *Soc. All.*   507
Tarquin Mills, *UK Ind.*   473
Lab. majority 8,816 (20.70%)
3.67% swing Lab. to C.
(1997: Lab. maj. 14,239 (28.03%))

NOTTINGHAM EAST
E. 65,339 *T.* 29,731 (45.50%) Lab. hold
*John Heppell, *Lab.*   17,530
Richard Allan, *C.*   7,210
Tim Ball, *LD*   3,874
Pete Radcliff, *Soc. All.*   1,117
Lab. majority 10,320 (34.71%)
2.04% swing Lab. to C.
(1997: Lab. maj. 15,419 (38.80%))

NOTTINGHAM NORTH
E. 64,281 T. 30,042 (46.74%) Lab. hold
*Graham Allen, *Lab.*   19,392
Martin Wright, *C.*   7,152
Rob Lee, *LD*   3,177
Andrew Botham, *Soc. Lab.*   321
Lab. majority 12,240 (40.74%)
2.34% swing Lab. to C.
(1997: Lab. maj. 18,801 (45.42%))

NOTTINGHAM SOUTH
E. 73,049 T. 36,605 (50.11%) Lab. hold
*Alan Simpson, *Lab.*   19,949
Mrs Wendy Manning, *C.*   9,960
Kevin Mulloy, *LD*   6,064
David Bartrop, *UK Ind.*   632
Lab. majority 9,989 (27.29%)
0.13% swing Lab. to C.
(1997: Lab. maj. 13,364 (27.55%))

NUNEATON
E. 72,101 T. 43,312 (60.07%) Lab. hold
*Bill Olner, *Lab.*   22,577
Mark Lancaster, *C.*   15,042
Tony Ferguson, *LD*   4,820
Brian James, *UK Ind.*   873
Lab. majority 7,535 (17.40%)
3.95% swing Lab. to C.
(1997: Lab. maj. 13,540 (25.30%))

OLD BEXLEY & SIDCUP
E. 67,841 T. 42,133 (62.11%) C. hold
Derek Conway, *C.*   19,130
Jim Dickson, *Lab.*   15,785
Ms Belinda Ford, *LD*   5,792
Mrs Janice Cronin, *UK Ind.*   1,426
C. majority 3,345 (7.94%)
0.49% swing Lab. to C.
(1997: C. maj. 3,569 (6.95%))

OLDHAM EAST & SADDLEWORTH
E. 74,511 T. 45,420 (60.96%) Lab. hold
*Phil Woolas, *Lab.*   17,537
Howard Sykes, *LD*   14,811
Craig Heeley, *C*   7,304
Michael Treacy, *BNP*   5,091
Ms Barbara Little, *UK Ind.*   677
Lab. majority 2,726 (6.00%)
0.13% swing Lab. to C.
(1997: Lab. maj. 3,389 (6.26%))

OLDHAM WEST & ROYTON
E. 69,409 T. 39,962 (57.57%) Lab. hold
*Rt. Hon. M. Meacher, *Lab.*   20,441
Duncan Reed, *C.*   7,076
Nick Griffin, *BNP*   6,552
Marc Ramsbottom, *LD*   4,975
David Roney, *Green*   918
Lab. majority 13,365 (33.44%)
0.99% swing Lab. to C.
(1997: Lab. maj. 16,201 (35.42%))

ORPINGTON
E. 74,423 T. 50,912 (68.41%) C. hold
*John Horam, *C.*   22,334
Chris Maines, *LD*   22,065
Chris Purnell, *Lab.*   5,517
John Youles, *UK Ind.*   996
C. majority 269 (0.53%)
2.19% swing C. to LD
(1997: C. maj. 2,952 (4.91%))

OXFORD EAST
E. 74,421 T. 39,848 (53.54%) Lab. hold
*Rt. Hon. A. Smith, *Lab.*   19,681
Steve Goddard, *LD*   9,337
Ms Cheryl Potter, *C.*   7,446
Pritam Singh, *Green*   1,501
John Lister, *Soc. All.*   708
Peter Gardner, *UK Ind.*   570
Fahim Ahmed, *Soc. Lab.*   274
Ms Linda Hodge, *ProLife*   254
Pathmanathan Mylvaganan, *Ind.*   77
Lab. majority 10,344 (25.96%)
8.08% swing Lab. to LD
(1997: Lab. maj. 16,665 (34.81%))

OXFORD WEST & ABINGDON
E. 79,915 T. 51,568 (64.53%) LD hold
*Dr Evan Harris, *LD*   24,670
Ed Matts, *C.*   15,485
Ms Gillian Kirk, *Lab.*   9,114
Mike Woodin, *Green*   1,423
Marcus Watney, *UK Ind.*   451
Ms Sigrid Shreeve, *Ind.*   332
Robert Twigger, *Ext. Club*   93
LD majority 9,185 (17.81%)
3.77% swing C. to LD
(1997: LD maj. 6,285 (10.27%))

PENDLE
E. 62,870 T. 39,732 (63.20%) Lab. hold
*Gordon Prentice, *Lab.*   17,729
Rasjid Skinner, *C.*   13,454
David Whipp, *LD*   5,479
Christian Jackson, *BNP*   1,976
Graham Cannon, *UK Ind.*   1,094
Lab. majority 4,275 (10.76%)
6.13% swing Lab. to C.
(1997: Lab. maj. 10,824 (23.02%))

PENRITH & THE BORDER
E. 67,776 T. 44,249 (65.29%) C. hold
*Rt. Hon. D. Maclean, *C.*   24,302
Kenneth Geyve Walker, *LD*   9,625
Michael Boaden, *Lab.*   8,177
Thomas Lowther, *UK Ind.*   938
Mark Gibson, *LCA*   870
John Moffat, *Ind.*   337
C. majority 14,677 (33.17%)
6.13% swing LD to C.
(1997: C. maj. 10,233 (20.90%))

PETERBOROUGH
E. 64,918 T. 39,812 (61.33%) Lab. hold
*Mrs Helen Brinton, *Lab.*   17,975
Stewart Jackson, *C.*   15,121
Nick Sandford, *LD*   5,761
Julian Fairweather, *UK Ind.*   955
Lab. majority 2,854 (7.17%)
3.98% swing Lab. to C.
(1997: Lab. maj. 7,323 (15.12%))

PLYMOUTH DEVONPORT
E. 73,666 T. 41,719 (56.63%) Lab. hold
*David Jamieson, *Lab.*   24,322
John Glen, *C.*   11,289
Keith Baldry, *LD*   4,513
Michael Parker, *UK Ind.*   958
Tony Staunton, *Soc. All.*   334
Rob Hawkins, *Soc. Lab.*   303
Lab. majority 13,033 (31.24%)
2.73% swing Lab. to C.
(1997: Lab. maj. 19,067 (36.70%))

PLYMOUTH SUTTON
E. 68,438 T. 39,073 (57.09%)
                         Lab. Co-op hold
*Mrs Linda Gilroy, *Lab. Co-op.*   19,827
Oliver Colvile, *C.*   12,310
Alan Connett, *LD*   5,605
Alan Whitton, *UK Ind.*   970
Henry Leary, *Soc. Lab.*   361
Lab. Co-op majority 7,517 (19.24%)
0.29% swing Lab. Co-op to C.
(1997: Lab. maj. 9,440 (19.81%))

PONTEFRACT & CASTLEFORD
E. 63,181 T. 31,391 (49.68%) Lab. hold
*Ms Yvette Cooper, *Lab.*   21,890
Ms Pamela Singleton, *C.*   5,512
Wesley Paxton, *LD*   2,315
John Burdon, *UK Ind.*   739
Trevor Bolderson, *Soc. Lab.*   605
John Gill, *Soc. All.*   330
Lab. majority 16,378 (52.17%)
4.99% swing Lab. to C.
(1997: Lab. maj. 25,725 (62.15%))

POOLE
E. 64,644 T. 39,233 (60.69%) C. hold
*Robert Syms, *C.*   17,710
David Watt, *Lab.*   10,544
Nick Westbrook, *LD*   10,011
John Bass, *UK Ind.*   968
C. majority 7,166 (18.27%)
1.15% swing C. to Lab.
(1997: C. maj. 5,298 (11.32%))

POPLAR & CANNING TOWN
E. 75,173 T. 34,108 (45.37%) Lab. hold
*Jim Fitzpatrick, *Lab.*   20,862
Robert Marr, *C.*   6,758
Ms Alexi Sugden, *LD*   3,795
Paul Borg, *BNP*   1,743
Dr Kambiz Boomla, *Soc. All.*   950
Lab. majority 14,104 (41.35%)
3.41% swing Lab. to C.
(1997: Lab. maj. 18,915 (48.17%))

PORTSMOUTH NORTH
E. 64,256 T. 36,866 (57.37%) Lab. hold
*Syd Rapson, *Lab.*   18,676
Chris Day, *C.*   13,542
Darren Sanders, *LD*   3,795
William McCabe, *UK Ind.*   559
Brian Bundy, *Ind.*   294
Lab. majority 5,134 (13.93%)
2.19% swing C. to Lab.
(1997: Lab. maj. 4,323 (9.55%))

PORTSMOUTH SOUTH
E. 77,095 T. 39,215 (50.87%) LD hold
*Mike Hancock, *LD*   17,490
Philip Warr, *C.*   11,396
Graham Heaney, *Lab.*   9,361
John Molyneux, *Soc. All.*   647
Michael Tarrant, *UK Ind.*   321
LD majority 6,094 (15.54%)
3.58% swing C. to LD
(1997: LD maj. 4,327 (8.37%))

PRESTON

E. 72,077   T. 36,041 (50.00%)
Lab. Co-op hold
*Mark Hendrick, *Lab. Co-op.*   20,540
Graham O'Hare, *C.*   8,272
Bill Chadwick, *LD*   4,746
Bilal Patel, *Ind.*   1,241
Richard Merrick, *Green*   1,019
The Rev David Braid, *Ind.*   223
Lab. Co-op majority 12,268 (34.04%)
2.41% swing Lab. Co-op to C.
(2000 Nov. by-election: Lab. maj. 4,426)
(1997: *Lab. majority* 18,680 (38.86%))

PUDSEY

E. 71,405   T. 45,175 (63.27%) Lab. hold
*Paul Truswell, *Lab.*   21,717
John Procter, *C.*   16,091
Stephen Boddy, *LD*   6,423
David Sewards, *UK Ind.*   944
Lab. majority 5,626 (12.45%)
0.34% swing C. to Lab.
(1997: Lab. maj. 6,207 (11.77%))

PUTNEY

E. 60,643   T. 34,254 (56.48%) Lab. hold
*Tony Colman, *Lab.*   15,911
Michael Simpson, *C.*   13,140
Tony Burrett, *LD*   4,671
Ms Pat Wild, *UK Ind.*   347
Ms Yvonne Windsor, *ProLife*   185
Lab. majority 2,771 (8.09%)
0.66% swing C. to Lab.
(1997: Lab. maj. 2,976 (6.76%))

RAYLEIGH

E. 70,073   T. 42,773 (61.04%)   C. hold
Mark Francois, *C.*   21,434
Paul Clark, *Lab.*   13,144
Geoff Williams, *LD*   6,614
Colin Morgan, *UK Ind.*   1,581
C. majority 8,290 (19.38%)
0.72% swing C. to Lab.
(1997: C. maj. 10,684 (20.83%))

READING EAST

E. 74,637   T. 43,618 (58.44%) Lab. hold
*Ms Jane Griffiths, *Lab.*   19,531
Barry Tanswell, *C.*   13,943
Tom Dobrashian, *LD*   8,078
Ms Miriam Kennett, *Green*   1,053
Miss Amy Thornton, *UK Ind.*   525
Darren Williams, *Soc. All.*   394
Peter Hammerson, *Ind.*   94
Lab. majority 5,588 (12.81%)
2.63% swing C. to Lab.
(1997: Lab. maj. 3,795 (7.55%))

READING WEST

E. 71,688   T. 41,986 (58.57%) Lab. hold
*Martin Salter, *Lab.*   22,300
Stephen Reid, *C.*   13,451
Ms Polly Martin, *LD*   5,387
David Black, *UK Ind.*   848
Lab. majority 8,849 (21.08%)
7.44% swing C. to Lab.
(1997: Lab. maj. 2,997 (6.20%))

REDCAR

E. 66,179   T. 38,198 (57.72%) Lab. hold
Ms Vera Baird, *Lab.*   23,026
Chris Main, *C.*   9,583
Stan Wilson, *LD*   4,817
John Taylor, *Soc. Lab.*   772
Lab. majority 13,443 (35.19%)
4.53% swing Lab. to C.
(1997: Lab. maj. 21,664 (44.25%))

REDDITCH

E. 62,543   T. 37,032 (59.21%) Lab. hold
*Ms Jacqui Smith, *Lab.*   16,899
Mrs Karen Lumley, *C.*   14,415
Michael Ashall, *LD*   3,808
George Flynn, *UK Ind.*   1,259
Richard Armstrong, *Green*   651
Lab. majority 2,484 (6.71%)
3.49% swing Lab. to C.
(1997: Lab. maj. 6,125 (13.69%))

REGENT'S PARK & KENSINGTON NORTH

E. 75,886   T. 37,052 (48.83%) Lab. hold
*Ms Karen Buck, *Lab.*   20,247
Peter Wilson, *C.*   9,981
David Boyle, *LD*   4,669
Dr Paul Miller, *Green*   1,268
China Mieville, *Soc. All.*   459
Alan Crisp, *UK Ind.*   354
Ms Charlotte Regan, *Ind.*   74
Lab. majority 10,266 (27.71%)
1.63% swing Lab. to C.
(1997: Lab. maj. 14,657 (30.96%))

REIGATE

E. 65,023   T. 39,474 (60.71%)   C. hold
*Crispin Blunt, *C.*   18,875
Simon Charleton, *Lab.*   10,850
Ms Jane Kulka, *LD*   8,330
Stephen Smith, *UK Ind.*   1,062
Harold Green, *Ref. UK*   357
C. majority 8,025 (20.33%)
2.13% swing Lab. to C.
(1997: C. maj. 7,741 (16.07%))

RIBBLE SOUTH (SOUTH RIBBLE)

E. 73,794   T. 46,130 (62.51%) Lab. hold
*David Borrow, *Lab.*   21,386
Adrian Owens, *C.*   17,594
Mark Alcock, *LD*   7,150
Lab. majority 3,792 (8.22%)
0.49% swing Lab. to C.
(1997: Lab. maj. 5,084 (9.20%))

RIBBLE VALLEY

E. 74,319   T. 49,171 (66.16%)   C. hold
*Nigel Evans, *C.*   25,308
Mike Carr, *LD*   14,070
Marcus Johnstone, *Lab.*   9,793
C. majority 11,238 (22.85%)
5.63% swing LD to C.
(1997: C. maj. 6,640 (11.60%))

RICHMOND (YORKS)

E. 65,360   T. 44,034 (67.37%)   C. hold
*Rt. Hon. W. Hague, *C.*   25,951
Ms Fay Tinnion, *Lab.*   9,632
Edward Forth, *LD*   7,890
Mrs Melodie Staniforth, *Loony*   561
C. majority 16,319 (37.06%)
8.00% swing Lab. to C.
(1997: C. maj. 10,051 (21.05%))

RICHMOND PARK

E. 72,663   T. 49,151 (67.64%) LD hold
*Dr Jenny Tonge, *LD*   23,444
Tom Harris, *C.*   18,480
Barry Langford, *Lab.*   5,541
James Page, *Green*   1,223
Peter St John Howe, *UK Ind.*   348
Raymond Perrin, *Ind.*   115
LD majority 4,964 (10.10%)
2.45% swing C. to LD
(1997: LD maj. 2,951 (5.19%))

ROCHDALE

E. 69,506   T. 39,412 (56.70%) Lab. hold
*Ms Lorna Fitzsimons, *Lab.*   19,406
Paul Rowen, *LD*   13,751
Ms Elaina Cohen, *C.*   5,274
Nick Harvey, *Green*   728
Mohammed Salim, *Ind.*   253
Lab. majority 5,655 (14.35%)
2.45% swing LD to Lab.
(1997: Lab. maj. 4,545 (9.45%))

ROCHFORD & SOUTHEND EAST

E. 69,991   T. 37,452 (53.51%)   C. hold
*Sir Teddy Taylor, *C.*   20,058
Chris Dandridge, *Lab.*   13,024
Stephen Newton, *LD*   2,780
Adrian Hedges, *Green*   990
Brian Lynch, *Lib.*   600
C. majority 7,034 (18.78%)
4.86% swing Lab. to C.
(1997: C. maj. 4,225 (9.07%))

ROMFORD

E. 59,893   T. 35,701 (59.61%)   C. gain
Andrew Rosindell, *C.*   18,931
*Ms Eileen Gordon, *Lab.*   12,954
Nigel Meyer, *LD*   2,869
Stephen Ward, *UK Ind.*   533
Frank McAllister, *BNP*   414
C. majority 5,977 (16.74%)
9.14% swing Lab. to C.
(1997: Lab. maj. 649 (1.54%))

ROMSEY

E. 70,584   T. 48,459 (68.65%) LD hold
*Mrs Sandra Gidley, *LD*   22,756
Paul Raynes, *C.*   20,386
Stephen Roberts, *Lab.*   3,986
Anthony McCabe, *UK Ind.*   730
Derrick Large, *LCA*   601
LD majority 2,370 (4.89%)
10.73% swing C. to LD
(2000 May by-election: LD maj. 3,311
(8.55%); 1997: C. maj. 8,585 (16.56%))

ROSSENDALE & DARWEN

E. 70,280   T. 41,358 (58.85%) Lab. hold
*Ms Janet Anderson, *Lab.*   20,251
George Lee, *C.*   15,028
Brian Dunning, *LD*   6,079
Lab. majority 5,223 (12.63%)
4.38% swing Lab. to C.
(1997: Lab. maj. 10,949 (21.38%))

ROTHER VALLEY

E. 69,174   T. 36,803 (53.20%) Lab. hold
*Rt. Hon. K. Barron, *Lab.*   22,851
James Duddridge, *C.*   7,969
Ms Win Knight, *LD*   4,603
David Cutts, *UK Ind.*   1,380
Lab. majority 14,882 (40.44%)
5.22% swing Lab. to C.
(1997: Lab. maj. 23,485 (50.88%))

ROTHERHAM

E. 57,931   T. 29,354 (50.67%) Lab. hold
*Denis MacShane, *Lab.*   18,759
Richard Powell, *C.*   5,682
Charles Hall, *LD*   3,117
Peter Griffith, *UK Ind.*   730
Dick Penycate, *Green*   577
Ms Freda Smith, *Soc. All.*   352
Geoffrey Bartholomew, *JLDP*   137
Lab. majority 13,077 (44.55%)
6.24% swing Lab. to C.
(1997: Lab. maj. 21,469 (57.02%))

RUGBY & KENILWORTH
E. 79,764   T. 53,796 (67.44%)   Lab. hold
*Andy King, Lab.   24,221
David Martin, C.   21,344
Ms Gwen Fairweather, LD   7,444
Paul Garratt, UK Ind.   787
Lab. maj 2,877 (5.35%)
2.27% swing C. to Lab.
(1997: Lab. maj. 495 (0.81%))

RUISLIP-NORTHWOOD
E. 60,788   T. 37,141 (61.10%)   C. hold
*John Wilkinson, C.   18,115
Ms Gillian Travis, Lab.   10,578
Mike Cox, LD   7,177
Graham Lee, Green   724
Ian Edward, BNP   547
C. majority 7,537 (20.29%)
1.46% swing Lab. to C.
(1997: C. maj. 7,794 (17.38%))

RUNNYMEDE & WEYBRIDGE
E. 75,569   T. 42,426 (56.14%)   C. hold
*Philip Hammond, C.   20,646
Ms Jane Briginshaw, Lab.   12,286
Chris Bushill, LD   6,924
Christopher Browne, UK Ind.   1,332
Charles Gilman, Green   1,238
C. majority 8,360 (19.70%)
0.27% swing Lab. to C.
(1997: C. maj. 9,875 (19.16%))

RUSHCLIFFE
E. 81,839   T. 54,446 (66.53%)   C. hold
*Rt. Hon. K. Clarke, C.   25,869
Paul Fallon, Lab.   18,512
Jeremy Hargreaves, LD   7,395
Ken Browne, UK Ind.   1,434
Ashley Baxter, Green   1,236
C. majority 7,357 (13.51%)
2.69% swing Lab. to C.
(1997: C. maj. 5,055 (8.14%))

RUTLAND & MELTON
E. 72,448   T. 47,056 (64.95%)   C. hold
*Alan Duncan, C.   22,621
Matthew O'Callaghan, Lab.   14,009
Kim Lee, LD   8,386
Peter Baker, UK Ind.   1,223
Christopher Davies, Green   817
C. majority 8,612 (18.30%)
0.76% swing Lab. to C.
(1997: C. maj. 8,836 (16.78%))

RYEDALE
E. 66,543   T. 43,899 (65.97%)   C. hold
*John Greenway, C.   20,711
Keith Orrell, LD   15,836
David Ellis, Lab.   6,470
Stephen Feaster, UK Ind.   882
C. majority 4,875 (11.11%)
0.37% swing LD to C.
(1997: C. maj. 5,058 (10.37%))

SAFFRON WALDEN
E. 76,724   T. 50,040 (65.22%)   C. hold
*Rt. Hon. Sir A. Haselhurst, C.   24,485
Mrs E. Tealby-Watson, LD   12,481
Ms Tania Rogers, Lab.   11,305
Richard Glover, UK Ind.   1,769
C. majority 12,004 (23.99%)
2.73% swing LD to C.
(1997: C. maj. 10,573 (18.53%))

SALFORD
E. 54,152   T. 22,514 (41.58%)   Lab. hold
*Ms Hazel Blears, Lab.   14,649
Norman Owen, LD   3,637
Chris King, C.   3,446
Peter Grant, Soc. All.   414
Ms Hazel Wallace, Ind.   216
Roy Masterson, Ind.   152
Lab. majority 11,012 (48.91%)
4.89% swing Lab. to LD
(1997: Lab. maj. 17,069 (51.53%))

SALISBURY
E. 80,538   T. 52,603 (65.31%)   C. hold
*Robert Key, C.   24,527
Ms Yvonne Emmerson-Peirce, LD   15,824
Ms Sue Mallory, Lab.   9,199
Malcolm Wood, UK Ind.   1,958
Hamish Soutar, Green   1,095
C. majority 8,703 (16.54%)
2.88% swing C. to LD
(1997: C. maj. 6,276 (10.78%))

SCARBOROUGH & WHITBY
E. 75,213   T. 47,523 (63.18%)   Lab. hold
*Lawrie Quinn, Lab.   22,426
John Sykes, C.   18,841
Tom Pearce, LD   3,977
Jonathan Dixon, Green   1,049
John Jacob, UK Ind.   970
Ms Theresa Murray, ProLife   260
Lab. majority 3,585 (7.54%)
0.94% swing Lab. to C.
(1997: Lab. maj. 5,124 (9.43%))

SCUNTHORPE
E. 59,689   T. 33,625 (56.33%)   Lab. hold
*Elliot Morley, Lab.   20,096
Bernard Theobald, C.   9,724
Bob Tress, LD   3,156
John Cliff, UK Ind.   347
David Patterson, Ind.   302
Lab. majority 10,372 (30.85%)
1.62% swing Lab. to C.
(1997: Lab. maj. 14,173 (34.09%))

SEDGEFIELD
E. 64,925   T. 40,258 (62.01%)   Lab. hold
*Rt. Hon. T. Blair, Lab.   26,110
Douglas Carswell, C.   8,397
Andrew Duffield, LD   3,624
Andrew Spence, UK Ind.   974
Brian Gibson, Soc. Lab.   518
Christopher Driver, R & R Loony   375
Ms Helen John WFLOE   260
Lab. majority 17,713 (44.00%)
4.69% swing Lab. to C.
(1997: Lab. maj. 25,143 (53.37%))

SELBY
E. 77,924   T. 50,272 (64.51%)   Lab. hold
*John Grogan, Lab.   22,652
Michael Mitchell, C.   20,514
Jeremy Wilcock, LD   5,569
Ms Helen Kenwright, Green   902
Bob Lewis, UK Ind.   635
Lab. majority 2,138 (4.25%)
1.28% swing Lab. to C.
(1997: Lab. maj. 3,836 (6.81%))

SEVENOAKS
E. 66,648   T. 42,614 (63.94%)   C. hold
*Michael Fallon, C.   21,052
Ms Caroline Humphreys, Lab.   10,898
Clive Gray, LD   9,214
Mrs Lisa Hawkins, UK Ind.   1,155
Mark Ellis, PF   295
C. majority 10,154 (23.83%)
1.48% swing Lab. to C.
(1997: C. maj. 10,461 (20.86%))

SHEFFIELD ATTERCLIFFE
E. 68,386   T. 35,824 (52.38%)   Lab. hold
*Clive Betts, Lab.   24,287
John Perry, C.   5,443
Ms Gail Smith, LD   5,092
Ms Pauline Arnott, UK Ind.   1,002
Lab. majority 18,844 (52.60%)
1.69% swing C. to Lab.
(1997: Lab. maj. 21,818 (49.23%))

SHEFFIELD BRIGHTSIDE
E. 54,711   T. 25,552 (46.70%)   Lab. hold
*Rt. Hon. D. Blunkett, Lab.   19,650
Matthew Wilson, C.   2,601
Ms Alison Firth, LD   2,238
Brian Wilson, Soc. All.   361
Robert Morris, Soc. Lab.   354
Mark Suter, UK Ind.   348
Lab. majority 17,049 (66.72%)
0.81% swing C. to Lab.
(1997: Lab. maj. 19,954 (58.92%))

SHEFFIELD CENTRAL
E. 62,018   T. 30,069 (48.48%)   Lab. hold
Rt. Hon. R. Caborn, Lab.   18,477
Ali Qadar, LD   5,933
Miss Noelle Brelsford, C.   3,289
Bernard Little, Green   1,008
Nick Riley, Soc. All.   754
David Hadfield, Soc. Lab.   289
Ms Charlotte Schofield, UK Ind.   257
Michael Driver, WRP   62
Lab. majority 12,544 (41.72%)
2.36% swing C. to LD
(1997: Lab. maj. 16,906 (46.43%))

SHEFFIELD HALLAM
E. 60,288   T. 38,246 (63.44%)   LD hold
*Richard Allan, LD   21,203
John Harthman, C.   11,856
Ms Gillian Furniss, Lab.   4,758
Leslie Arnott, UK Ind.   429
LD majority 9,347 (24.44%)
3.12% swing C. to LD
(1997: LD maj. 8,271 (18.19%))

SHEFFIELD HEELEY
E. 62,758   T. 34,139 (54.40%)   Lab. hold
Ms Meg Munn, Lab.   19,452
David Willis, LD   7,748
Ms Carolyn Abbott, C.   4,864
Rob Unwin, Green   774
Brian Fischer, Soc. Lab.   667
David Dunn, UK Ind.   634
Lab. majority 11,704 (34.28%)
2.60% swing Lab. to LD
(1997: Lab. maj. 17,078 (39.48%))

SHEFFIELD HILLSBOROUGH
E. 75,097   T. 42,536 (56.64%) Lab. hold
*Ms Helen Jackson, *Lab.*   24,170
John Commons, *LD*   9,601
Graham King, *C.*   7,801
Peter Webb, *UK Ind.*   964
Lab. majority 14,569 (34.25%)
1.62% swing LD to Lab.
(1997: Lab. maj. 16,451 (31.02%))

SHERWOOD
E. 75,670   T. 45,900 (60.66%) Lab. hold
*Paddy Tipping, *Lab.*   24,900
Brandon Lewis, *C.*   15,527
Peter Harris, *LD*   5,473
Lab. majority 9,373 (20.42%)
4.66% swing Lab. to C.
(1997: Lab. maj. 16,812 (29.74%))

SHIPLEY
E. 69,577   T. 46,020 (66.14%) Lab. hold
*Christopher Leslie, *Lab.*   20,243
David Senior, *C.*   18,815
Ms Helen Wright, *LD*   4,996
Martin Love, *Green*   1,386
Walter Whitacker, *UK Ind.*   580
Lab. majority 1,428 (3.10%)
1.28% swing Lab. to C.
(1997: Lab. maj. 2,996 (5.67%))

SHREWSBURY & ATCHAM
E. 74,964   T. 49,909 (66.58%) Lab. hold
*Paul Marsden, *Lab.*   22,253
Miss Anthea McIntyre, *C.*   18,674
Jonathan Rule, *LD*   6,173
Henry Curteis, *UK Ind.*   1,620
Ms Emma Bullard, *Green*   931
James Gollins, *Ind.*   258
Lab. majority 3,579 (7.17%)
2.08% swing C. to Lab.
(1997: Lab. maj. 1,670 (3.02%))

SHROPSHIRE NORTH
E. 73,716   T. 46,520 (63.11%) C. hold
*Owen Paterson, *C.*   22,631
Michael Ion, *Lab.*   16,390
Ben Jephcott, *LD*   5,945
David Trevanion, *UK Ind.*   1,165
Russell Maxfield, *Ind.*   389
C. majority 6,241 (13.42%)
4.58% swing Lab. to C.
(1997: C. maj. 2,195 (4.26%))

SITTINGBOURNE & SHEPPEY
E. 65,825   T. 37,858 (57.51%) Lab. hold
*Derek Wyatt, *Lab.*   17,340
Adrian Lee, *C.*   13,831
Ms Elvie Lowe, *LD*   5,353
Michael Young, *R & R Loony*   673
Robert Oakley, *UK Ind.*   661
Lab. majority 3,509 (9.27%)
2.54% swing C. to Lab.
(1997: Lab. maj. 1,929 (4.18%))

SKIPTON & RIPON
E. 75,201   T. 49,126 (65.33%) C. hold
*Rt. Hon. D. Curry, *C.*   25,736
Bernard Bateman, *LD*   12,806
Michael Dugher, *Lab.*   8,543
Mrs Nancy Hold sworth, *UK Ind.*   2,041
C. majority 12,930 (26.32%)
2.47% swing LD to C.
(1997: C. maj. 11,620 (21.38%))

SLEAFORD & NORTH HYKEHAM
E. 74,561   T. 48,719 (65.34%) C. hold
*Rt. D. Hogg, *C.*   24,190
Ms Elizabeth Donnelly, *Lab.*   15,568
Robert Arbon, *LD*   7,894
Michael Ward-Barrow, *UK Ind.*   1,067
C. majority 8,622 (17.70%)
4.03% swing Lab. to C.
(1997: C. maj. 5,123 (9.64%))

SLOUGH
E. 72,429   T. 38,998 (53.84%) Lab. hold
*Ms Fiona Mactaggart, *Lab.*   22,718
Mrs Diana Coad, *C.*   10,210
Keith Kerr, *LD*   4,109
Michael Haines, *Ind.*   859
John Lane, *UK Ind.*   738
Choudry Nazir, *Ind.*   364
Lab. majority 12,508 (32.07%)
2.34% swing C. to Lab.
(1997: Lab. maj. 13,071 (27.39%))

SOLIHULL
E. 77,094   T. 48,271 (62.61%) C. hold
*John Taylor, *C.*   21,935
Ms Jo Byron, *LD*   12,528
Brendan O'Brien, *Lab.*   12,373
Andy Moore, *UK Ind.*   1,061
Ms Stephanie Pyne, *ProLife*   374
C. majority 9,407 (19.49%)
0.07% swing LD to C.
(1997: C. maj. 11,397 (19.35%))

SOMERTON & FROME
E. 74,991   T. 52,684 (70.25%) LD hold
*David Heath, *LD*   22,983
Jonathan Marland, *C.*   22,315
Andrew Perkins, *Lab.*   6,113
Peter Bridgwood, *UK Ind.*   919
Ms Jean Pollock, *Lib.*   354
LD majority 668 (1.27%)
0.52% swing C. to LD
(1997: LD maj. 130 (0.23%))

SOUTH HOLLAND & THE DEEPINGS
E. 73,880   T. 46,202 (62.54%) C. hold
*John Hayes, *C.*   25,611
Graham Walker, *Lab.*   14,512
Ms Grace Hill, *LD*   4,761
Malcolm Charlesworth, *UK Ind.*   1,318
C. majority 11,099 (24.02%)
4.04% swing Lab. to C.
(1997: C. maj. 7,991 (15.94%))

SOUTH SHIELDS
E. 61,802   T. 30,448 (49.27%) Lab. hold
David Miliband, *Lab.*   19,230
Miss Joanna Gardner, *C.*   5,140
Marshall Grainger, *LD*   5,127
Alan Hardy, *UK Ind.*   689
Roger Nettleship, *Ind.*   262
Lab. majority 14,090 (46.28%)
5.28% swing Lab. to C.
(1997: Lab. maj. 22,153 (56.84%))

SOUTHAMPTON ITCHEN
E. 76,603   T. 41,373 (54.01%) Lab. hold
*Rt. Hon. J. Denham, *Lab.*   22,553
Mrs Caroline Nokes, *C.*   11,330
Mark Cooper, *LD*   6,195
Kim Rose, *UK Ind.*   829
Gavin Marsh, *Soc. All.*   241
Michael Holmes, *Soc. Lab.*   225
Lab. majority 11,223 (27.13%)
0.37% swing C. to Lab.
(1997: Lab. maj. 14,209 (26.38%))

SOUTHAMPTON TEST
E. 73,893   T. 41,575 (56.26%) Lab. hold
*Alan Whitehead, *Lab.*   21,824
Richard Gueterbock, *C.*   10,617
John Shaw, *LD*   7,522
Garry Rankin-Moore, *UK Ind.*   792
Mark Abel, *Soc. All.*   442
Paramjit Bahia, *Soc. Lab.*   378
Lab. majority 11,207 (26.96%)
0.43% swing C. to Lab.
(1997: Lab. maj. 13,684 (26.10%))

SOUTHEND WEST
E. 64,116   T. 37,375 (58.29%) C. hold
*David Amess, *C.*   17,313
Paul Fisher, *Lab.*   9,372
Richard de Ste Croix, *LD*   9,319
Brian Lee, *UK Ind.*   1,371
C. majority 7,941 (21.25%)
2.64% swing Lab. to C.
(1997: C. maj. 2,615 (5.62%))

SOUTHPORT
E. 70,785   T. 41,153 (58.14%) LD hold
John Pugh, *LD*   18,011
Laurence Jones, *C.*   15,004
Paul Brant, *Lab.*   6,816
David Green, *Lib.*   767
Gerry Kelley, *UK Ind.*   555
LD majority 3,007 (7.31%)
2.44% swing LD to C.
(1997: LD maj. 6,160 (12.18%))

SOUTHWARK NORTH & BERMONDSEY
E. 73,527   T. 36,862 (50.13%) LD hold
*Simon Hughes, *LD*   20,991
Kingsley Abrams, *Lab.*   11,359
Ewan Wallace, *C.*   2,800
Ms Ruth Jenkins, *Green*   752
Ms Lianne Shore, *NF*   612
Rob McWhirter, *UK Ind.*   271
John Davies, *Ind.*   77
LD majority 9,632 (26.13%)
8.91% swing Lab. to LD
(1997: LD maj. 3,387 (8.30%))

SPELTHORNE
E. 68,731   T. 41,794 (60.81%) C. hold
*David Wilshire, *C.*   18,851
Andrew Shaw, *Lab.*   15,589
Martin Rimmer, *LD*   6,156
Richard Squire, *UK Ind.*   1,198
C. majority 3,262 (7.80%)
0.56% swing Lab. to C.
(1997: C. maj. 3,473 (6.69%))

ST ALBANS
E. 66,040   T. 43,761 (66.26%) Lab. hold
*Kerry Pollard, *Lab.*   19,889
Charles Elphicke, *C.*   15,423
Nick Rijke, *LD*   7,847
Christopher Sherwin, *UK Ind.*   602
Lab. majority 4,466 (10.21%)
0.71% swing C. to Lab.
(1997: Lab. maj. 4,459 (8.78%))

ST HELENS NORTH
E. 70,545   T. 37,601 (53.30%) Lab. hold
*Dave Watts, *Lab.*   22,977
Simon Pearce, *C.*   7,076
John Beirne, *LD*   6,609
Stephen Whatham, *Soc. Lab.*   939
Lab. majority 15,901 (42.29%)
2.64% swing Lab. to C.
(1997: Lab. maj. 23,417 (47.57%))

ST HELENS SOUTH
E. 65,122   T. 33,804 (51.91%)   Lab. hold
†Shaun Woodward, *Lab.*   16,799
Brian Spencer, *LD*   7,814
Dr Lee Rotherham, *C.*   4,675
Neil Thompson, *Soc. All.*   2,325
Mike Perry, *Soc. Lab.*   1,504
Bryan Slater, *UK Ind.*   336
Michael Murphy, *Ind.*   271
David Braid, *Ind.*   80
Lab. majority 8,985 (26.58%)
14.33% swing Lab. to LD
(1997: Lab. maj. 23,739 (53.63%))

ST IVES
E. 74,256   T. 49,266 (66.35%)   LD hold
*Andrew George, *LD*   25,413
Miss Joanna Richardson, *C.*   15,360
William Morris, *Lab.*   6,567
Mick Faulkner, *UK Ind.*   1,926
LD majority 10,053 (20.41%)
3.55% swing C. to LD
(1997: LD maj. 7,170 (13.30%))

STAFFORD
E. 67,934   T. 44,366 (65.31%)   Lab. hold
*David Kidney, *Lab.*   21,285
Philip Cochrane, *C.*   16,253
Ms Jeanne Pinkerton, *LD*   4,205
Earl of Bradford, *UK Ind.*   2,315
Michael Hames, *R & R Loony*   308
Lab. majority 5,032 (11.34%)
1.50% swing C. to Lab.
(1997: Lab. maj. 4,314 (8.34%))

STAFFORDSHIRE MOORLANDS
E. 66,760   T. 42,658 (63.90%)   Lab. hold
*Ms Charlotte Atkins, *Lab.*   20,904
Marcus Hayes, *C.*   15,066
John Redfern, *LD*   5,928
Paul Gilbert, *UK Ind.*   760
Lab. majority 5,838 (13.69%)
2.99% swing Lab. to C.
(1997: Lab. maj. 10,049 (19.66%))

STAFFORDSHIRE SOUTH
E. 69,925   T. 42,180 (60.32%)   C. hold
*Sir Patrick Cormack, *C.*   21,295
Paul Kalinauckas, *Lab.*   14,414
Ms Jo Harrison, *LD*   4,891
Mike Lynch, *UK Ind.*   1,580
C. majority 6,881 (16.31%)
0.51% swing Lab. to C.
(1997: C. maj. 7,821 (15.30%))

STALYBRIDGE & HYDE
E. 66,265   T. 32,046 (48.36%)   Lab. hold
James Purnell, *Lab.*   17,781
Andrew Reid, *C.*   8,922
Brendon Jones, *LD*   4,327
Frank Bennett, *UK Ind.*   1,016
Lab. majority 8,859 (27.64%)
3.36% swing Lab. to C.
(1997: Lab. maj. 14,806 (34.36%))

STEVENAGE
E. 69,203   T. 42,453 (61.35%)   Lab. hold
*Ms Barbara Follett, *Lab.*   22,025
Graeme Quar, *C.*   13,459
Harry Davies, *LD*   6,027
Steve Glennon, *Soc. All.*   449
Antal Losonczi, *Ind.*   320
Ms Sarah Bell, *ProLife*   173
Lab. majority 8,566 (20.18%)
1.18% swing Lab. to C.
(1997: Lab. maj. 11,582 (22.54%))

STOCKPORT
E. 66,397   T. 35,383 (53.29%)   Lab. hold
*Ms Ann Coffey, *Lab.*   20,731
John Allen, *C.*   9,162
Mark Hunter, *LD*   5,490
Lab. majority 11,569 (32.70%)
3.91% swing Lab. to C.
(1997: Lab. maj. 18,912 (40.52%))

STOCKTON NORTH
E. 65,192   T. 35,427 (54.34%)   Lab. hold
*Frank Cook, *Lab.*   22,470
Ms Amanda Vigar, *C.*   7,823
Ms Mary Wallace, *LD*   4,208
Bill Wennington, *Green*   926
Lab. majority 14,647 (41.34%)
3.34% swing Lab. to C.
(1997: Lab. maj. 21,357 (48.02%))

STOCKTON SOUTH
E. 71,026   T. 44,209 (62.24%)   Lab. hold
*Ms Dari Taylor, *Lab.*   23,414
Tim Devlin, *C.*   14,328
Mrs Suzanne Fletcher, *LD*   6,012
Lawrie Coombes, *Soc. All.*   455
Lab. majority 9,086 (20.55%)
0.84% swing Lab. to C.
(1997: Lab. maj. 11,585 (22.23%))

STOKE-ON-TRENT CENTRAL
E. 59,750   T. 28,300 (47.36%)   Lab. hold
*Mark Fisher, *Lab.*   17,170
Ms Jill Clark, *C.*   5,325
Gavin Webb, *LD*   4,148
Richard Wise, *Ind.*   1,657
Lab. majority 11,845 (41.86%)
3.83% swing Lab. to C.
(1997: Lab. maj. 19,924 (49.51%))

STOKE-ON-TRENT NORTH
E. 57,998   T. 30,115 (51.92%)   Lab. hold
*Ms Joan Walley, *Lab.*   17,460
Benjamin Browning, *C.*   5,676
Henry Jebb, *LD*   3,580
Lee Wanger, *Ind.*   3,399
Lab. majority 11,784 (39.13%)
2.92% swing Lab. to C.
(1997: Lab. maj. 17,392 (44.98%))

STOKE-ON-TRENT SOUTH
E. 70,032   T. 36,028 (51.45%)   Lab. hold
*George Stevenson, *Lab.*   19,366
Philip Bastiman, *C.*   8,877
Christopher Coleman, *LD*   4,724
Adrian Knapper, *Ind.*   1,703
Steven Batkin, *BNP*   1,358
Lab. majority 10,489 (29.11%)
5.23% swing Lab. to C.
(1997: Lab. maj. 18,303 (39.58%))

STONE
E. 68,847   T. 45,642 (66.29%)   C. hold
*William Cash, *C.*   22,395
John Palfreyman, *Lab.*   16,359
Brendan McKeown, *LD*   6,888
C. majority 6,036 (13.22%)
3.01% swing Lab. to C.
(1997: C. maj. 3,818 (7.20%))

STOURBRIDGE
E. 64,610   T. 39,924 (61.79%)   Lab. hold
*Ms Debra Shipley, *Lab.*   18,823
Stephen Eyre, *C.*   15,011
Chris Bramall, *LD*   4,833
John Knotts, *UK Ind.*   763
Mick Atherton, *Soc. Lab.*   494
Lab. majority 3,812 (9.55%)
0.91% swing Lab. to C.
(1997: Lab. maj. 5,645 (11.36%))

STRATFORD-ON-AVON
E. 85,241   T. 54,914 (64.42%)   C. hold
*John Maples, *C.*   27,606
Dr Susan Juned, *LD*   15,804
Mushtaq Hussain, *Lab.*   9,164
Ronald Mole, *UK Ind.*   1,184
Mick Davies, *Green*   1,156
C. majority 11,802 (21.49%)
0.61% swing C. to LD
(1997: C. maj. 14,106 (22.72%))

STREATHAM
E. 76,021   T. 36,998 (48.67%)   Lab. hold
*Keith Hill, *Lab.*   21,041
Roger O'Brien, *LD*   6,771
Stephen Hocking, *C.*   6,639
Mohammed Sajid, *Green*   1,641
Greg Tucker, *Soc. All.*   906
Lab. majority 14,270 (38.57%)
5.33% swing Lab. to LD
(1997: Lab. maj. 18,423 (41.04%))

STRETFORD & URMSTON
E. 70,924   T. 38,973 (54.95%)   Lab. hold
*Ms Beverley Hughes, *Lab.*   23,804
Jonathan Mackie, *C.*   10,565
John Bridges, *LD*   3,891
Ms Katie Price, *Ind.*   713
Lab. majority 13,239 (33.97%)
2.98% swing C. to Lab.
(1997: Lab. maj. 13,640 (28.01%))

STROUD
E. 78,878   T. 55,175 (69.95%)
                             Lab. Co-op hold
*David Drew, *Lab. Co-op.*   25,685
Neil Carmichael, *C.*   20,646
Ms Janice Beasley, *LD*   6,036
Kevin Cranston, *Green*   1,913
Adrian Blake, *UK Ind.*   895
Lab. Co-op majority 5,039 (9.13%)
2.24% swing C. to Lab. Co-op
(1997: Lab. maj. 2,910 (4.66%))

**SUFFOLK CENTRAL & IPSWICH
NORTH**
E. 74,200   T. 47,104 (63.48%)   C. hold
*Michael Lord, *C.*   20,924
Ms Carole Jones, *Lab.*   17,455
Mrs Ann Elvin, *LD*   7,593
Jonathan Wright, *UK Ind.*   1,132
C. majority 3,469 (7.36%)
0.33% swing Lab. to C.
(1997: C. maj. 3,538 (6.70%))

SUFFOLK COASTAL
E. 75,963   T. 50,407 (66.36%)   C. hold
*Rt. Hon. J. Gummer, *C.*   21,847
Nigel Gardner, *Lab.*   17,521
Tony Schur, *LD*   9,192
Michael Burn, *UK Ind.*   1,847
C. majority 4,326 (8.58%)
1.40% swing Lab. to C.
(1997: C. maj. 3,254 (5.79%))

SUFFOLK SOUTH
E. 68,408   T. 45,293 (66.21%)   C. hold
*Tim Yeo, C.   18,748
Marc Young, Lab.   13,667
Mrs Tessa Munt, LD   11,296
Derek Allen, UK Ind.   1,582
C. majority 5,081 (11.22%)
1.59% swing Lab. to C.
(1997: C. maj. 4,175 (8.03%))

SUFFOLK WEST
E. 71,220   T. 42,445 (59.60%)   C. hold
*Richard Spring, C.   20,201
Michael Jeffreys, Lab.   15,906
Robin Martlew, LD   5,017
Will Burrows, UK Ind.   1,321
C. majority 4,295 (10.12%)
3.16% swing Lab. to C.
(1997: C. maj. 1,867 (3.80%))

SUNDERLAND NORTH
E. 60,846   T. 29,820 (49.01%)   Lab. hold
*Bill Etherington, Lab.   18,685
Michael Harris, C.   5,331
John Lennox, LD   3,599
Neil Herron, Ind.   1,518
David Guynan, BNP   687
Lab. majority 13,354 (44.78%)
3.38% swing Lab. to C.
(1997: Lab. maj. 19,697 (51.55%))

SUNDERLAND SOUTH
E. 64,577   T. 31,187 (48.29%)   Lab. hold
*Chris Mullin, Lab.   19,921
Jim Boyd, C.   6,254
Mark Greenfield, LD   3,675
Joseph Dobbie, BNP   576
Joseph Moore, UK Ind.   470
Ms Rosalyn Warner, Loony   291
Lab. majority 13,667 (43.82%)
2.68% swing Lab. to C.
(1997: Lab. maj. 19,638 (49.18%))

SURREY EAST
E. 75,049   T. 47,049 (62.69%)   C. hold
*Peter Ainsworth, C.   24,706
Jeremy Pursehouse, LD   11,503
Ms Jo Tanner, Lab.   8,994
Anthony Stone, UK Ind.   1,846
C. majority 13,203 (28.06%)
0.23% swing LD to C.
(1997: C. maj. 15,093 (27.61%))

SURREY HEATH
E. 75,858   T. 45,102 (59.46%)   C. hold
*Nicholas Hawkins, C.   22,401
Mark Lelliott, LD   11,582
James Norman, Lab.   9,640
Nigel Hunt, UK Ind.   1,479
C. majority 10,819 (23.99%)
2.89% swing C. to LD
(1997: C. maj. 16,287 (29.76%))

SURREY SOUTH WEST
E. 74,127   T. 49,592 (66.90%)   C. hold
*Rt. Hon. Mrs V. Bottomley, C.   22,462
Simon Cordon, LD   21,601
Martin Whelton, Lab.   4,321
Timothy Clark, Ind.   1,208
C. majority 861 (1.74%)
1.52% swing C. to LD
(1997: C. maj. 2,694 (4.77%))

SUSSEX MID
E. 70,632   T. 45,822 (64.87%)   C. hold
*Nicholas Soames, C.   21,150
Ms Lesley Wilkins, LD   14,252
Paul Mitchell, Lab.   8,693
Petrina Holsworth UK Ind.   1,126
Peter Berry, Loony   601
C. majority 6,898 (15.05%)
1.12% swing LD to C.
(1997: C. maj. 6,854 (12.82%))

SUTTON & CHEAM
E. 63,648   T. 39,723 (62.41%)   LD hold
*Paul Burstow, LD   19,382
Lady Olga Maitland, C.   15,078
Ms Lisa Homan, Lab.   5,263
LD majority 4,304 (10.84%)
3.19% swing C. to LD
(1997: LD maj. 2,097 (4.45%))

SUTTON COLDFIELD
E. 71,856   T. 43,452 (60.47%)   C. hold
Andrew Mitchell, C.   21,909
Robert Pocock, Lab.   11,805
Martin Turner, LD   8,268
Mike Nattrass, UK Ind.   1,186
Ian Robinson, Ind.   284
C. majority 10,104 (23.25%)
2.58% swing C. to Lab.
(1997: C. maj. 14,885 (28.41%))

SWINDON NORTH
E. 69,335   T. 42,328 (61.05%)   Lab. hold
*Michael Wills, Lab.   22,371
Nick Martin, C.   14,266
David Nation, LD   4,891
Brian Lloyd, UK Ind.   800
Lab. majority 8,105 (19.15%)
1.61% swing C. to Lab.
(1997: Lab. maj. 7,688 (15.93%))

SWINDON SOUTH
E. 71,080   T. 43,384 (61.04%)   Lab. hold
*Ms Julia Drown, Lab.   22,260
Simon Coombs, C.   14,919
Geoff Brewer, LD   5,165
Mrs Vicki Sharp, UK Ind.   713
Roly Gillard, R & R Loony   327
Lab. majority 7,341 (16.92%)
2.94% swing C. to Lab.
(1997: Lab. maj. 5,645 (11.04%))

TAMWORTH
E. 69,596   T. 40,250 (57.83%)   Lab. hold
*Brian Jenkins, Lab.   19,722
Ms Luise Gunter, C.   15,124
Ms Jennifer Pinkett, LD   4,721
Paul Sootheran, UK Ind.   683
Lab. majority 4,598 (11.42%)
1.81% swing Lab. to C.
(1997: Lab. maj. 7,496 (15.04%))

TATTON
E. 64,954   T. 41,278 (63.55%)   C. gain
George Osborne, C.   19,860
Steve Conquest, Lab.   11,249
Mike Ash, LD   7,685
Mark Sheppard, UK Ind.   769
Peter Sharratt, Ind.   734
Mrs Viviane Allinson, Tatton   505
John Batchelor, Ind.   322
Jonathan Boyd Hunt, Ind.   154
C. majority 8,611 (20.86%)
(1997: Ind. maj. 11,077 (22.70%))

TAUNTON
E. 81,651   T. 55,225 (67.64%)   C. gain
Adrian Flook, C.   23,033
*Mrs Jackie Ballard, LD   22,798
Andrew Govier, Lab.   8,254
Michael Canton, UK Ind.   1,140
C. majority 235 (0.43%)
2.21% swing LD to C.
(1997: LD maj. 2,443 (4.00%))

TEIGNBRIDGE
E. 85,533   T. 59,310 (69.34%)   LD gain
Richard Younger-Ross, LD   26,343
*Patrick Nicholls, C.   23,332
Christopher Bain, Lab.   7,366
Paul Viscount Exmouth, UK Ind.   2,269
LD majority 3,011 (5.08%)
2.76% swing C. to LD
(1997: C. maj. 281 (0.45%))

TELFORD
E. 59,486   T. 30,875 (51.90%)   Lab. hold
David Wright, Lab.   16,854
Andrew Henderson, C.   8,471
Ms Sally Wiggin, LD   3,983
Ms Nicola Brookes, UK Ind.   1,098
Mike Jeffries, Soc. All.   469
Lab. majority 8,383 (27.15%)
1.63% swing Lab. to C.
(1997: Lab. maj. 11,290 (30.42%))

TEWKESBURY
E. 70,276   T. 45,195 (64.31%)   C. hold
*Laurence Robertson, C.   20,830
Keir Dhillon, Lab.   12,167
Stephen Martin, LD   11,863
Charles Vernall, Ind.   335
C. majority 8,663 (19.17%)
0.19% swing C. to Lab.
(1997: C. maj. 9,234 (17.71%))

THANET NORTH
E. 70,581   T. 41,868 (59.32%)   C. hold
*Roger Gale, C.   21,050
James Stewart Laing, Lab.   14,400
Seth Proctor, LD   4,603
John Moore, UK Ind.   980
David Shortt, Ind.   440
Thomas Holmes, NF   395
C. majority 6,650 (15.88%)
5.12% swing Lab. to C.
(1997: C. maj. 2,766 (5.65%))

THANET SOUTH
E. 61,462   T. 39,431 (64.16%)   Lab. hold
*Dr Stephen Ladyman, Lab.   18,002
Mark Macgregor, C.   16,210
Guy Voizey, LD   3,706
William Baldwin, Ind.   770
Terry Eccott, UK Ind.   501
Bernard Franklin, NF   242
Lab. majority 1,792 (4.54%)
0.92% swing Lab. to C.
(1997: Lab. maj. 2,878 (6.39%))

THURROCK
E. 76,524   T. 37,362 (48.82%)   Lab. hold
*Andrew Mackinlay, Lab.   21,121
Mike Penning, C.   11,124
John Lathan, LD   3,846
Christopher Sheppard, UK Ind.   1,271
Lab. majority 9,997 (26.76%)
4.90% swing Lab. to C.
(1997: Lab. maj. 17,256 (36.55%))

TIVERTON & HONITON

E. 80,646 T. 55,784 (69.17%) C. hold
*Mrs Angela Browning, C. 26,258
Jim Barnard, LD 19,974
Ms Isabel Owen, Lab. 6,647
Alan Langmaid, UK Ind. 1,281
Matthew Burgess, Green 1,030
Mrs Jennifer Roach, Lib. 594
C. majority 6,284 (11.26%)
4.23% swing LD to C.
(1997: C. maj. 1,653 (2.80%))

TONBRIDGE & MALLING

E. 65,939 T. 42,436 (64.36%) C. hold
*Rt. Hon. Sir J. Stanley, C. 20,956
Ms Victoria Hayman, Lab. 12,706
Ms Merilyn Canet, LD 7,605
Ms Lynn Croucher, UK Ind. 1,169
C. majority 8,250 (19.44%)
0.67% swing C. to Lab.
(1997: C. maj. 10,230 (20.78%))

TOOTING

E. 68,447 T. 37,591 (54.92%) Lab. hold
*Tom Cox, Lab. 20,332
Alexander Nicoll, C. 9,932
Simon James, LD 5,583
Matthew Ledbury, Green 1,744
Lab. majority 10,400 (27.67%)
2.45% swing Lab. to C.
(1997: Lab. maj. 15,011 (32.56%))

TORBAY

E. 72,409 T. 47,569 (65.69%) LD hold
*Adrian Sanders, LD 24,015
Christian Sweeting, C. 17,307
John McKay, Lab. 4,484
Graham Booth, UK Ind. 1,512
Ms Pam Neale, Ind. 251
LD majority 6,708 (14.10%)
7.04% swing C. to LD
(1997: LD maj. 12 (0.02%))

TOTNES

E. 72,548 T. 49,246 (67.88%) C. hold
*Anthony Steen, C. 21,914
Ms Rachel Oliver, LD 18,317
Thomas Wildy, Lab. 6,005
Craig Mackinlay, UK Ind. 3,010
C. majority 3,597 (7.30%)
2.84% swing LD to C.
(1997: C. maj. 877 (1.63%))

TOTTENHAM

E. 65,567 T. 31,601 (48.20%) Lab. hold
*David Lammy, Lab. 21,317
Ms Uma Fernandes, C. 4,401
Ms Meher Khan, LD 3,008
Peter Budge, Green 1,443
Weyman Bennett Soc. All. 1,162
Unver Shefki, Reform 270
Lab. majority 16,916 (53.53%)
0.03% swing Lab. to C.
(2000 Jun. by-election: Lab. maj. 5,646
(34.39%); 1997: Lab. Maj. 20,200
(53.58%))

TRURO & ST AUSTELL

E. 79,219 T. 50,295 (63.49%) LD hold
*Matthew Taylor, LD 24,296
Tim Bonner, C. 16,231
David Phillips, Lab. 6,889
James Wonnacott, UK Ind. 1,664
Conan Jenkin, Meb. Ker. 1,137
John Lee, Ind. 78
LD majority 8,065 (16.04%)
3.00% swing LD to C.
(1997: LD maj. 12,501 (22.03%))

TUNBRIDGE WELLS

E. 64,534 T. 40,201 (62.29%) C. hold
*Archie Norman, C. 19,643
Keith Brown, LD 9,913
Ian Carvell, Lab. 9,332
Victor Webb, UK Ind. 1,313
C. majority 9,730 (24.20%)
4.34% swing LD to C.
(1997: C. maj. 7,506 (15.52%))

TWICKENHAM

E. 74,135 T. 49,938 (67.36%) LD hold
*Dr Vincent Cable, LD 24,344
Nick Longworth, C. 16,689
Dean Rogers, Lab. 6,903
Ms Judy Maciejowska, Green 1,423
Ray Hollebone, UK Ind. 579
LD majority 7,655 (15.33%)
3.98% swing C. to
(1997: LD maj. 4,281 (7.36%))

TYNE BRIDGE

E. 58,900 T. 26,032 (44.20%) Lab. hold
*David Clelland, Lab. 18,345
James Cook, C. 3,456
Jonathan Wallace, LD 3,213
James Fitzpatrick, Soc. Lab. 533
Samuel Robson, Soc. All. 485
Lab. majority 14,889 (57.19%)
4.27% swing Lab. to C.
(1997: Lab. maj. 22,906 (65.73%))

TYNEMOUTH

E. 65,184 T. 43,903 (67.35%) Lab. hold
*Alan Campbell, Lab. 23,364
Karl Poulsen, C. 14,686
Ms Penny Reid, LD 5,108
Michael Rollings, UK Ind. 745
Lab. majority 8,678 (19.77%)
1.14% swing Lab. to C.
(1997: Lab. maj. 11,273 (22.04%))

TYNESIDE NORTH

E. 64,914 T. 37,569 (57.88%) Lab. hold
*Rt. Hon. S. Byers, Lab. 26,127
Mark Ruffell, C. 5,459
Simon Reed, LD 4,649
Alan Taylor, UK Ind. 770
Pete Burnett, Soc. All. 324
Ken Capstick, Soc. Lab. 240
Lab. majority 20,668 (55.01%)
2.02% swing Lab. to C.
(1997: Lab. maj. 26,643 (59.05%))

UPMINSTER

E. 56,829 T. 33,851 (59.57%) C. gain
Mrs Angela Watkinson, C. 15,410
*Keith Darvill, Lab. 14,169
Peter Truesdale, LD 3,183
Terry Murray, UK Ind. 1,089
C. majority 1,241 (3.67%)
5.18% swing Lab. to C.
(1997: Lab. maj. 2,770 (6.70%))

UXBRIDGE

E. 58,066 T. 33,418 (57.55%) C. hold
*John Randall, C. 15,751
David Salisbury-Jones, Lab. 13,653
Ms Catherine Royce, LD 3,426
Paul Cannons, UK Ind. 588
C. majority 2,098 (6.28%)
2.26% swing Lab. to C.
(1997 Jul. by-election: C. maj. 3,766
(11.82%); 1997: C. maj. 724 (1.75%))

VALE OF YORK

E. 73,335 T. 48,490 (66.12%) C. hold
*Miss Anne McIntosh, C. 25,033
Christopher Jukes, Lab. 12,516
Greg Stone, LD 9,799
Peter Thornber, UK Ind. 1,142
C. majority 12,517 (25.81%)
3.78% swing Lab. to C.
(1997: C. maj. 9,721 (18.25%))

VAUXHALL

E. 74,474 T. 33,392 (44.84%) Lab. hold
*Ms Kate Hoey, Lab. 19,738
Anthony Bottrall, LD 6,720
Gareth Compton, C. 4,489
Shane Collins, Green 1,485
Ms Theresa Bennett, Soc. All. 853
Martin Boyd, Ind. 107
Lab. majority 13,018 (38.99%)
4.39% swing Lab. to LD
(1997: Lab. maj. 18,660 (47.77%))

WAKEFIELD

E. 75,750 T. 41,254 (54.46%) Lab. hold
*David Hinchcliffe, Lab. 20,592
Mrs Thelma Karran, C. 12,638
Douglas Dale, LD 5,097
Ms Sarah Greenwood, Green 1,075
Ms Janice Cannon, UK Ind. 677
Abdul Aziz, Soc. Lab. 634
Mick Griffiths, Soc. All. 541
Lab. majority 7,954 (19.28%)
4.82% swing Lab. to C.
(1997: Lab. maj. 14,604 (28.93%))

WALLASEY

E. 64,889 T. 37,346 (57.55%) Lab. hold
*Ms Angela Eagle, Lab. 22,718
Mrs Lesley Rennie, C. 10,442
Peter Reisdorf, LD 4,186
Lab. majority 12,276 (32.87%)
3.92% swing Lab. to C.
(1997: Lab. maj. 19,074 (40.72%))

WALSALL NORTH

E. 66,020 T. 32,312 (48.94%) Lab. hold
*David Winnick, Lab. 18,779
Melvin Pitt, C. 9,388
Michael Heap, LD 2,923
Mrs Jenny Mayo, UK Ind. 812
Dave Church, Soc. All. 410
Lab. majority 9,391 (29.06%)
(1997: Lab. maj. 12,588 (29.07%))

WALSALL SOUTH

E. 62,657 T. 34,899 (55.70%) Lab. hold
*Rt. Hon. B. George, Lab. 20,574
Mike Bird, C. 10,643
Bill Tomlinson, LD 2,365
Derek Bennett, UK Ind. 974
Peter Smith, Soc. All. 343
Lab. majority 9,931 (28.46%)
1.15% swing C. to Lab.
(1997: Lab. maj. 11,312 (26.16%))

WALTHAMSTOW
E. 64,403   T. 34,429 (53.46%)   Lab. hold
*Neil Gerrard, Lab.   21,402
Nick Boys Smith, C.   6,221
Peter Dunphy, LD   5,024
Simon Donovan, Soc. Alt.   806
William Phillips, BNP   389
Ms Gerda Mayer, UK Ind.   298
Ms Barbara Duffy, ProLife   289
Lab. majority 15,181 (44.09%)
0.64% swing C. to Lab.
(1997: Lab. maj. 17,149 (42.81%))

WANSBECK
E. 62,989   T. 37,419 (59.41%)   Lab. hold
*Denis Murphy, Lab.   21,617
Alan Thompson, LD   8,516
Mrs Rachael Lake, C.   4,774
Michael Kirkup, Ind.   1,076
Dr Nic Best, Green   954
Gavin Attwell, UK Ind.   482
Lab. majority 13,101 (35.01%)
7.25% swing Lab. to LD
(1997: Lab. maj. 22,367 (49.52%))

WANSDYKE
E. 70,728   T. 49,047 (69.35%)   Lab. hold
*Dan Norris, Lab.   22,706
Chris Watt, C.   17,593
Ms Gail Coleshill, LD   7,135
Francis Hayden, Green   958
Peter Sandell, UK Ind.   655
Lab. majority 5,113 (10.42%)
0.83% swing C. to Lab.
(1997: Lab. maj. 4,799 (8.77%))

WANTAGE
E. 76,129   T. 49,129 (64.53%)   C. hold
*Robert Jackson, C.   19,475
Stephen Beer, Lab.   13,875
Neil Fawcett, LD   13,776
David Brooks-Saxl, Green   1,062
Count Nichola Tolstoy, UK Ind.   941
C. majority 5,600 (11.40%)
0.31% swing Lab. to C.
(1997: C. maj. 6,039 (10.77%))

WARLEY
E. 58,071   T. 31,415 (54.10%)   Lab. hold
*Rt. Hon. J. Spellar, Lab.   19,007
Mark Pritchard, C.   7,157
Ron Cockings, LD   3,315
Harbhajan Dardi, Soc. Lab.   1,936
Lab. majority 11,850 (37.72%)
1.00% swing Lab. to C.
(1997: Lab. maj. 15,451 (39.73%))

WARRINGTON NORTH
E. 72,445   T. 38,910 (53.71%)   Lab. hold
*Ms Helen Jones, Lab.   24,026
James Usher, C.   8,870
Roy Smith, LD   5,232
Jack Kirkham, UK Ind.   782
Lab. majority 15,156 (38.95%)
0.43% swing C. to Lab.
(1997: Lab. maj. 19,527 (38.10%))

WARRINGTON SOUTH
E. 74,283   T. 45,487 (61.23%)   Lab. hold
*Ms Helen Southworth, Lab.   22,409
Ms Caroline Mosley, C.   15,022
Roger Barlow, LD   7,419
Mrs Joan Kelley, UK Ind.   637
Lab. majority 7,387 (16.24%)
1.69% swing C. to Lab.
(1997: Lab. maj. 10,807 (19.62%))

WARWICK & LEAMINGTON
E. 81,405   T. 53,539 (65.77%)   Lab. hold
*James Plaskitt, Lab.   26,108
David Campbell Bannerman, C.   20,155
Ms Linda Forbes, LD   5,964
Ms Clare Kime, Soc. All.   664
Greville Warwick, UK Ind.   648
Lab. majority 5,953 (11.12%)
2.73% swing C. to Lab.
(1997: Lab. maj. 3,398 (5.65%))

WARWICKSHIRE NORTH
E. 73,828   T. 44,409 (60.15%)   Lab. hold
*Mike O'Brien, Lab.   24,023
Geoff Parsons, C.   14,384
William Powell, LD   5,052
John Flynn, UK Ind.   950
Lab. majority 9,639 (21.71%)
2.76% swing Lab. to C.
(1997: Lab. maj. 14,767 (27.23%))

WATFORD
E. 75,724   T. 46,372 (61.24%)   Lab. hold
*Ms Claire Ward, Lab.   20,992
Michael McManus, C.   15,437
Duncan Hames, LD   8,088
Ms Denise Kingsley, Green   900
Edmund Stewart-Mole, UK Ind.   535
Jon Berry, Soc. All.   420
Lab. majority 5,555 (11.98%)
0.75% swing C. to Lab.
(1997: Lab. maj. 5,792 (10.48%))

WAVENEY
E. 76,585   T. 47,167 (61.59%)   Lab. hold
*Bob Blizzard, Lab.   23,914
Lee Scott, C.   15,361
David Young, LD   5,370
Brian Aylett, UK Ind.   1,097
Graham Elliot, Green   983
Rupert Mallin, Soc. All.   442
Lab. majority 8,553 (18.13%)
1.93% swing Lab. to C.
(1997: Lab. maj. 12,453 (21.99%))

WEALDEN
E. 83,066   T. 52,756 (63.51%)   C. hold
Charles Hendry, C.   26,279
Steve Murphy, LD   12,507
Ms Kathy Fordham, Lab.   10,705
Keith Riddle, UK Ind.   1,539
Julian Salmon, Green   1,273
Cyril Thornton, Pensioner   453
C. majority 13,772 (26.11%) 1.03% swing
LD to C.
(1997: C. maj. 14,204 (24.04%))

WEAVER VALE
E. 68,234   T. 39,271 (57.55%)   Lab. hold
*Mike Hall, Lab.   20,611
Carl Cross, C.   10,974
Nigel Griffiths, LD   5,643
Michael Cooksley, Ind.   1,484
Jim Bradshaw, UK Ind.   559
Lab. majority 9,637 (24.54%)
1.65% swing Lab. to C.
(1997: Lab. maj. 13,448 (27.84%))

WELLINGBOROUGH
E. 77,389   T. 51,006 (65.91%)   Lab. hold
*Paul Stinchcombe, Lab.   23,867
Peter Bone, C.   21,512
Peter Gaskell, LD   4,763
Anthony Ellwood, UK Ind.   864
Lab. majority 2,355 (4.62%)
2.14% swing C. to Lab.
(1997: Lab. maj. 187 (0.33%))

WELLS
E. 74,189   T. 51,314 (69.17%)   C. hold
*Rt. Hon. D. Heathcoat-Amory, C.   22,462
Graham Oakes, LD   19,666
Andy Merryfield, Lab.   7,915
Steve Reed, UK Ind.   1,104
Colin Bex, Wessex Reg.   167
C. majority 2,796 (5.45%)
2.25% swing LD to C.
(1997: C. maj. 528 (0.94%))

WELWYN HATFIELD
E. 67,004   T. 42,821 (63.91%)   Lab. hold
*Ms Melanie Johnson, Lab.   18,484
Grant Shapps, C.   17,288
Daniel Cooke, LD   6,021
Malcolm Biggs, UK Ind.   798
Ms Fiona Pinto, ProLife   230
Lab. majority 1,196 (2.79%)
3.89% swing Lab. to C.
(1997: Lab. maj. 5,595 (10.57%))

WENTWORTH
E. 64,033   T. 33,778 (52.75%)   Lab. hold
*John Healey, Lab.   22,798
Mike Roberts, C.   6,349
David Wildgoose, LD   3,652
John Wilkinson, UK Ind.   979
Lab. majority 16,449 (48.70%)
4.32% swing Lab. to C.
(1997: Lab. maj. 23,959 (57.34%))

WEST BROMWICH EAST
E. 61,198   T. 32,664 (53.37%)   Lab. hold
Tom Watson, Lab.   18,250
David MacFarlane, C.   8,487
Ian Garrett, LD   4,507
Steven Grey, UK Ind.   835
Sheera Johal, Soc. Lab.   585
Lab. majority 9,763 (29.89%)
1.43% swing Lab. to C.
(1997: Lab. maj. 13,584 (32.74%))

WEST BROMWICH WEST
E. 66,777   T. 31,840 (47.68%)
                                Lab. Co-op hold
*Adrian Bailey, Lab. Co-op.   19,352
Mrs Karen Bissell, C.   7,997
Mrs Sadie Smith, LD   2,168
John Salvage, BNP   1,428
Kevin Walker, UK Ind.   499
Baghwant Singh, Soc. Lab.   396
Lab. Co-op majority 11,355 (35.66%)
(2000 Nov. by-election: Lab. maj. 3,232
(17.12%); 1997: Speaker maj. 15,423
(42.03%))

WEST HAM
E. 59,828   T. 29,273 (48.93%)   Lab. hold
*Tony Banks, Lab.   20,449
Syed Kamall, C.   4,804
Paul Fox, LD   2,166
Ms Jackie Chandler Oatts, Green   1,197
Gerard Batten, UK Ind.   657
Lab. majority 15,645 (53.45%)
2.24% swing Lab. to C.
(1997: Lab. maj. 19,494 (57.92%))

WESTBURY
E. 75,911 T. 50,628 (66.69%) C. hold
Dr Andrew Murrison, C. 21,299
David Vigar, LD 16,005
Ms Sarah Cardy, Lab. 10,847
Charles Booth-Jones, UK Ind. 1,261
Bob Gledhill, Green 1,216
C. majority 5,294 (10.46%)
0.12% swing C. to LD
(1997: C. maj. 6,068 (10.69%))

WESTMORLAND & LONSDALE
E. 70,637 T. 47,903 (67.82%) C. hold
*Tim Collins, C. 22,486
Tim Farron, LD 19,339
John Bateson, Lab. 5,234
Robert Gibson, UK Ind. 552
Tim Bell, Ind. 292
C. majority 3,147 (6.57%)
1.17% swing C. to LD
(1997: C. maj. 4,521 (8.90%))

WESTON-SUPER-MARE
E. 74,343 T. 46,680 (62.79%) LD hold
*Brian Cotter, LD 18,424
John Penrose, C. 18,086
Derek Kraft Lab. 9,235
Bill Lukins, UK Ind. 650
John Peverelle, Ind. 206
Richard Sibley, Ind. 79
LD majority 338 (0.72%)
0.83% swing LD to C.
(1997: LD maj. 1,274 (2.39%))

WIGAN
E. 64,040 T. 33,591 (52.45%) Lab. hold
*Neil Turner, Lab. 20,739
Mark Page, C. 6,996
Trevor Beswick, LD 4,970
Dave Lowe, Soc. All. 886
Lab. majority 13,743 (40.91%)
5.38% swing Lab. to C.
(1999 Sept. by-election: Lab. maj 6,729)
(1997: Lab. maj. 22,643 (51.67%))

WILTSHIRE NORTH
E. 79,524 T. 52,948 (66.58%) C. hold
*James Gray, C. 24,090
Hugh Pym, LD 20,212
Ms Jo Garton, Lab. 7,556
Neil Dowdney, UK Ind. 1,090
C. majority 3,878 (7.32%)
0.67% swing LD to C.
(1997: C. maj. 3,475 (5.99%))

WIMBLEDON
E. 63,930 T. 41,109 (64.30%) Lab. hold
*Roger Casale, Lab. 18,806
Stephen Hammond, C. 15,062
Martin Pierce, LD 5,341
Rajeev Thacker, Green 1,007
Roger Glencross, CPA 479
Ms Mariana Bell, UK Ind. 414
Lab. majority 3,744 (9.11%)
1.47% swing C. to Lab.
(1997: Lab. maj. 2,980 (6.17%))

WINCHESTER
E. 81,852 T. 59,158 (72.27%) LD hold
*Mark Oaten, LD 32,282
Andrew Hayes, C. 22,648
Stephen Wyeth, Lab. 3,498
Ms Joan Martin, UK Ind. 664
Ms Henrietta Rouse, Wessex Reg. 66
LD majority 9,634 (16.29%)
8.14% swing C. to LD
(1997 Nov. by-election: LD maj 21,556 (39.64%))
(1997: LD maj. 2 (0.00%))

WINDSOR
E. 69,136 T. 42,110 (60.91%) C. hold
*Michael Trend, C. 19,900
Nick Pinfield, LD 11,011
Mark Muller, Lab. 10,137
John Fagan, UK Ind. 1,062
C. majority 8,889 (21.11%)
0.79% swing LD to C.
(1997: C. maj. 9,917 (19.53%))

WIRRAL SOUTH
E. 60,653 T. 39,818 (65.65%) Lab. hold
*Ben Chapman, Lab. 18,890
Anthony Millard, C. 13,841
Phillip Gilchrist, LD 7,087
Lab. majority 5,049 (12.68%)
0.94% swing Lab. to C.
(1997: Lab. maj. 7,004 (14.56%))

WIRRAL WEST
E. 62,294 T. 40,475 (64.97%) Lab. hold
*Stephen Hesford, Lab. 19,105
Chris Lynch, C. 15,070
Simon Holbrook, LD 6,300
Lab. majority 4,035 (9.97%)
2.06% swing Lab. to C.
(1997: Lab. maj. 2,738 (5.84%))

WITNEY
E. 74,624 T. 49,203 (65.93%) C. gain
David Cameron, C. 22,153
Michael Bartlet, Lab. 14,180
Gareth Epps, LD 10,000
Mark Stevenson, Green 1,100
Barry Beadle, Ind. 1,003
Kenneth Dukes, UK Ind. 767
C. majority 7,973 (16.20%)
1.87% swing Lab. to C.
(1997: C. maj. 7,028 (12.46%))

WOKING
E. 71,163 T. 42,910 (60.30%) C. hold
*Humfrey Malins, C. 9,747
Alan Hilliar, LD 12,988
Sabir Hussain, Lab. 8,714
Michael Harvey, UK Ind. 1,461
C. majority 6,759 (15.75%)
2.30% swing LD to C.
(1997: C. maj. 5,678 (11.15%))

WOKINGHAM
E. 68,430 T. 43,848 (64.08%) C. hold
*Rt. Hon. J. Redwood, C. 20,216
Dr Royce Longton, LD 14,222
Matthew Syed, Lab. 7,633
Franklin Carstairs, UK Ind. 897
Peter "Top Cat" Owen Loony 880
C. majority 5,994 (13.67%)
2.51% swing C. to LD
(1997: C. maj. 9,365 (18.69%))

WOLVERHAMPTON NORTH EAST
E. 60,486 T. 31,494 (52.07%)
Lab. Co-op hold
*Ken Purchase, Lab. Co-op. 18,984
Ms Maria Miller, C. 9,019
Steven Bourne, LD 2,494
Thomas McCartney, UK Ind. 997
Lab. Co-op majority 9,965 (31.64%)
0.14% swing C. to Lab. Co-op
(1997: Lab. maj. 12,987 (31.37%))

WOLVERHAMPTON SOUTH EAST
E. 53,931 T. 27,297 (50.61%)
Lab. Co-op hold
*Dennis Turner, Lab. Co-op. 18,409
Adrian Pepper, C. 5,945
Peter Wild, LD 2,389
James Barry, NF 554
Lab. Co-op majority 12,464 (45.66%)
1.04% swing C. to Lab. Co-op
(1997: Lab. maj. 15,182 (43.58%))

WOLVERHAMPTON SOUTH WEST
E. 67,171 T. 40,897 (60.88%) Lab. hold
Robert Marris, Lab. 19,735
David Chambers, C. 16,248
Mike Dixon, LD 3,425
Ms Wendy Walker, Green 805
Doug Hope, UK Ind. 684
Lab. majority 3,487 (8.53%)
0.97% swing Lab. to C.
(1997: Lab. maj. 5,118 (10.46%))

WOODSPRING
E. 71,023 T. 48,758 (68.65%) C. hold
*Dr Liam Fox, C. 21,297
Chanel Stevens, Lab. 12,499
Colin Eldridge, LD 11,816
David Shopland, Ind. 1,412
Dr Richard Lawson, Green 1,282
Fraser Crean, UK Ind. 452
C. majority 8,798 (18.04%)
2.86% swing C. to Lab.
(1997: C. maj. 7,734 (14.08%))

WORCESTER
E. 71,255 T. 44,210 (62.04%) Lab. hold
*Michael Foster, Lab. 21,478
Richard Adams, C. 15,712
Paul Chandler, LD 5,578
Richard Chamings, UK Ind. 1,442
Lab. majority 5,766 (13.04%)
0.67% swing Lab. to C.
(1997: Lab. maj. 7,425 (14.38%))

WORCESTERSHIRE MID
E. 71,985 T. 44,897 (62.37%) C. hold
*Peter Luff, C. 22,937
David Bannister, Lab. 12,310
R. Woodthorpe-Browne, LD 8,420
Tony Eaves, UK Ind. 1,230
C. majority 10,627 (23.67%)
2.57% swing Lab. to C.
(1997: C. maj. 9,412 (18.52%))

WORCESTERSHIRE WEST
E. 66,769 T. 44,807 (67.11%) C. hold
*Sir Michael Spicer, C. 20,597
Mike Hadley, LD 15,223
Waquar Azmi, Lab. 6,275
Ian Morris, UK Ind. 1,574
Malcolm Victory, Green 1,138
C. majority 5,374 (11.99%)
2.10% swing LD to C.
(1997: C. maj. 3,846 (7.80%))

WORKINGTON
E. 65,965   T. 41,822 (63.40%) Lab. hold
Tony Cunningham, *Lab.*   23,209
Tim Stoddart, *C.*   12,359
Ian Francis, *LD*   5,214
John Peacock, *LCA*   1,040
Lab. majority 10,850 (25.94%)
6.93% swing Lab. to C.
(1997: Lab. maj. 19,656 (39.81%))

WORSLEY
E. 69,300   T. 35,363 (51.03%) Lab. hold
*Terry Lewis, *Lab.*   20,193
Tobias Ellwood, *C.*   8,406
Robert Bleakley, *LD*   6,188
Ms Dorothy Entwistle, *Soc. Lab.*   576
Lab. majority 11,787 (33.33%)
2.30% swing Lab. to C.
(1997: Lab. maj. 17,741 (37.93%))

WORTHING EAST & SHOREHAM
E. 71,890   T. 43,068 (59.91%) C. hold
*Tim Loughton, *C.*   18,608
Daniel Yates, *Lab.*   12,469
Paul Elgood, *LD*   9,876
Jim McCulloch, *UK Ind.*   1,195
Christopher Baldwin, *LCA*   920
C. majority 6,139 (14.25%)
1.14% swing C. to Lab.
(1997: C. maj. 5,098 (9.89%))

WORTHING WEST
E. 72,419   T. 43,209 (59.67%) C. hold
*Peter Bottomley, *C.*   20,508
James Walsh, *LD*   11,471
Alan Butcher, *Lab.*   9,270
Tim Cross, *UK Ind.*   1,960
C. majority 9,037 (20.91%)
2.96% swing LD to C.
(1997: C. maj. 7,713 (15.00%))

WREKIN, THE
E. 65,837   T. 41,490 (63.02%) Lab. hold
*Peter Bradley, *Lab.*   19,532
Jacob Rees-Mogg, *C.*   15,945
Ian Jenkins, *LD*   4,738
Denis Brookes, *UK Ind.*   1,275
Lab. majority 3,587 (8.65%)
0.98% swing C. to Lab.
(1997: Lab. maj. 3,025 (6.69%))

WYCOMBE
E. 74,647   T. 44,974 (60.25%) C. hold
Paul Goodman, *C.*   19,064
Chaudhry Shafique, *Lab.*   15,896
Ms Dee Tomlin, *LD*   7,658
Christopher Cooke, *UK Ind.*   1,059
John Laker, *Green*   1,057
David Fitton, *Ind.*   240
C. majority 3,168 (7.04%)
1.26% swing Lab. to C.
(1997: C. maj. 2,370 (4.53%))

WYRE FOREST
E. 72,152   T. 49,062 (68.00%) KHHC
                                            gain
Dr Richard Taylor, *KHHC*   28,487
*David Lock, *Lab.*   10,857
Mark Simpson, *C.*   9,350
James Millington, *UK Ind.*   368
KHHC majority 17,630 (35.93%)
(1997: Lab. maj. 6,946 (12.62%))

WYTHENSHAWE & SALE EAST
E. 72,127   T. 35,055 (48.60%) Lab. hold
*Paul Goggins, *Lab.*   21,032
Mrs Susan Fildes, *C.*   8,424
Ms Vanessa Tucker, *LD*   4,320
Lance Crookes, *Green*   869
Fred Shaw, *Soc. Lab.*   410
Lab. majority 12,608 (35.97%)
1.49% swing C. to Lab.
(1997: Lab. maj. 15,019 (32.99%))

YEOVIL
E. 75,977   T. 48,132 (63.35%) LD hold
David Laws, *LD*   21,266
Marco Forgione, *C.*   17,338
Joe Conway, *Lab.*   7,077
Neil Boxall, *UK Ind.*   1,131
Alex Begg, *Green*   786
Tony Prior, *Lib.*   534
LD majority 3,928 (8.16%)
6.47% swing LD to C.
(1997: LD maj. 11,403 (21.10%))

YORK, CITY OF
E. 80,431   T. 47,980 (59.65%) Lab. hold
*Hugh Bayley, *Lab.*   25,072
Michael McIntyre, *C.*   11,293
Andrew Waller, *LD*   8,519
Bill Shaw, *Green*   1,465
Frank Ormston, *Soc. All.*   674
Richard Bate, *UK Ind.*   576
Graham Cambridge, *Loony*   381
Lab. majority 13,779 (28.72%)
3.23% swing Lab. to C.
(1997: Lab. maj. 20,523 (35.17%))

YORKSHIRE EAST
E. 72,342   T. 43,314 (59.87%) C. hold
Rt. Hon. G. Knight, *C.*   19,861
Ms Tracey Simpson-Laing, *Lab.*   15,179
Ms Mary-Rose Hardy, *LD*   6,300
Trevor Pearson, *UK Ind.*   1,661
Paul Dessoy, *Ind.*   313
C. majority 4,682 (10.81%)
1.99% swing Lab. to C.
(1997: C. maj. 3,337 (6.82%))

WALES

ABERAVON
E. 49,660   T. 30,190 (60.79%) Lab. hold
Hywel Francis, *Lab.*   19,063
Ms Lisa Turnbull, *PC*   2,955
Chris Davies, *LD*   2,933
Ali Miraj, *C.*   2,296
Andrew Tutton, *RP*   1,960
Captain Beany, *Bean*   727
Mr Martin Chapman, *Soc. All.*   256
Lab. majority 16,108 (53.36%)
6.08% swing Lab. to PC
(1997: Lab. maj. 21,571 (59.98%))

ALYN & DEESIDE
E. 60,478   T. 35,421 (58.57%) Lab. hold
Mark Tami, *Lab.*   18,525
Mark Isherwood, *C.*   9,303
Derek Burnham, *LD*   4,585
Richard Coombs, *PC*   1,182
Klaus Armstrong-Braun, *Green*   881
William Crawford, *UK Ind.*   481
Max Cooksey, *Ind.*   253
Glyn Davies, *Comm.*   211
Lab. majority 9,222 (26.04%)
6.53% swing Lab. to C.
(1997: Lab. maj. 16,403 (39.10%))

BLAENAU GWENT
E. 53,353   T. 31,725 (59.46%) Lab. hold
*Llew Smith, *Lab.*   22,855
Adam Rykala, *PC*   3,542
Edward Townsend, *LD*   2,945
Huw Williams, *C.*   2,383
Lab. majority 19,313 (60.88%)
6.68% swing Lab. to PC
(1997: Lab. maj. 28,035 (70.74%))

BRECON & RADNORSHIRE
E. 52,247   T. 37,516 (71.81%) LD hold
Roger Williams, *LD*   13,824
Dr Felix Aubel, *C.*   13,073
Huw Irranca-Davis, *Lab.*   8,024
Brynach Parri, *PC*   1,301
Ian Mitchell, *Ind.*   762
Mrs Elizabeth Phillips, *UK Ind.*   452
Robert Nicholson, *Ind.*   80
LD majority 751 (2.00%)
4.94% swing LD to C.
(1997: LD maj. 5,097 (11.89%))

BRIDGEND
E. 61,496   T. 37,004 (60.17%) Lab. hold
*Win Griffiths, *Lab.*   19,422
Ms Tania Brisby, *C.*   9,377
Ms Jean Barraclough, *LD*   5,330
Ms Monica Mahoney, *PC*   2,652
Ms Sara Jeremy, *ProLife*   223
Lab. majority 10,045 (27.15%)
4.05% swing Lab. to C.
(1997: Lab. maj. 15,248 (35.24%))

CAERNARFON
E. 47,354   T. 29,053 (61.35%) PC hold
Hywel Williams, *PC*   12,894
Martin Eaglestone, *Lab.*   9,383
Ms Bronwen Naish, *C.*   4,403
Melab Owain, *LD*   1,823
Ifor Lloyd, *UK Ind.*   550
PC majority 3,511 (12.08%)
4.75% swing PC to Lab
(1997: PC maj. 7,449 (21.59%))

CAERPHILLY
E. 67,593   T. 38,831 (57.45%) Lab. hold
Wayne David, *Lab.*   22,597
Lindsay Whittle, *PC*   8,172
David Simmonds, *C.*   4,413
Rob Roffe, *LD*   3,649
Lab. majority 14,425 (37.15%)
10.49% swing Lab. to PC
(1997: Lab. maj. 25,839 (57.08%))

CARDIFF CENTRAL
E. 59,785   T. 34,842 (58.28%)
Lab. Co-op. hold
*Jon Owen Jones, *Lab. Co-op.*   13,451
Ms Jenny Willott, *LD*   12,792
Gregory Walker, *C.*   5,537
Richard Grigg, *PC*   1,680
Stephen Bartley, *Green*   661
Julian Goss, *Soc. All.*   283
Frank Hughes, *UK Ind.*   221
Ms Madeleine Jeremy, *ProLife*   217
Lab. Co-op. majority 659 (1.89%)
8.43% swing Lab. Co-op. to LD
(1997: Lab. maj. 7,923 (18.75%))

CARDIFF NORTH
E. 62,634   T. 43,240 (69.04%)   Lab. hold
*Ms Julie Morgan, *Lab.*   19,845
Alastair Watson, *C.*   13,680
John Dixon, *LD*   6,631
Sion Jobbins, *PC*   2,471
Don Hulston, *UK Ind.*   613
Lab. majority 6,165 (14.26%)
1.25% swing Lab. to C.
(1997: Lab. maj. 8,126 (16.76%))

CARDIFF SOUTH & PENARTH
E. 62,125   T. 35,751 (57.55%)
Lab. Co-op. hold
*Rt. Hon. A. Michael, *Lab. Co-op.*   20,094
Ms Maureen Kelly Owen, *C.*   7,807
Dr Rodney Berman, *LD*   4,572
Ms Lila Haines, *PC*   1,983
Justin Callan, *UK Ind.*   501
Dave Bartlett, *Soc. All.*   427
Ms Anne Savoury, *ProLife*   367
Lab. Co-op. majority 12,287 (34.37%)
0.81% swing C. to Lab. Co-op.
(1997: Lab. maj. 13,881 (32.74%))

CARDIFF WEST
E. 58,348   T. 34,083 (58.41%)   Lab. hold
Kevin Brennan, *Lab.*   18,594
Andrew Davies, *C.*   7,273
Ms Jacqui Gasson, *LD*   4,458
Delme Bowen, *PC*   3,296
Ms Joyce Jenking, *UK Ind.*   462
Lab. majority 11,321 (33.22%)
2.79% swing Lab. to C.
(1997: Lab. maj. 15,628 (38.80%))

CARMARTHEN EAST & DINEFWR
E. 54,035   T. 38,053 (70.42%)   PC gain
Adam Price, *PC*   16,130
*Alan Williams, *Lab.*   13,540
David N Thomas, *C.*   4,912
Doiran Evans, *LD*   2,815
Mike Squires, *UK Ind.*   656
PC majority 2,590 (6.81%)
7.54% swing Lab. to PC
(1997: Lab. maj. 3,450 (8.27%))

CARMARTHEN WEST &
PEMBROKESHIRE SOUTH
E. 56,518   T. 36,916 (65.32%)   Lab. hold
*Nick Ainger, *Lab.*   15,349
Robert Wilson, *C.*   10,811
Llyr Hughes Griffiths, *PC*   6,893
William Jeremy, *LD*   3,248
Ian Phillips, *UK Ind.*   537
Nick Turner, *Customer*   78
Lab. majority 4,538 (12.29%)
5.14% swing Lab. to C.
(1997: Lab. maj. 9,621 (22.57%))

CEREDIGION
E. 56,118   T. 34,606 (61.67%)   PC hold
*Simon Thomas, *PC*   13,241
Mark Williams, *LD*   9,297
Paul Davies, *C.*   6,730
David Grace, *Lab.*   5,338
PC majority 3,944 (11.40%)
6.89% swing PC to LD
(2000 Feb. by-election: PC maj. 4,948
(19.74%); 1997: PC maj. 6,961 (17.33%))

CLWYD SOUTH
E. 53,680   T. 33,496 (62.40%)   Lab. hold
*Martyn Jones, *Lab.*   17,217
Tom Biggins, *C.*   8,319
Dyfed Edwards, *PC*   3,982
David Griffiths, *LD*   3,426
Mrs Edwina Theunissen, *UK Ind.*   552
Lab. majority 8,898 (26.56%)
4.25% swing Lab. to C.
(1997: Lab. maj. 13,810 (35.07%))

CLWYD WEST
E. 53,960   T. 34,600 (64.12%)   Lab. hold
*Gareth Thomas, *Lab.*   13,426
Jimmy James, *C.*   2,311
Elfed Williams, *PC*   4,453
Ms Bobbie Feeley, *LD*   3,934
Matthew Guest, *UK Ind.*   476
Lab. majority 1,115 (3.22%)
0.68% swing Lab. to C.
(1997: Lab. maj. 1,848 (4.59%))

CONWY
E. 54,751   T. 34,366 (62.77%)   Lab. hold
*Mrs Betty Williams, *Lab.*   14,366
David Logan, *C.*   8,147
Ms Vicky Macdonald, *LD*   5,800
Ms Ann Owen, *PC*   5,665
Alan Barham, *UK Ind.*   388
Lab. majority 6,219 (18.10%)
3.66% swing C. to Lab
(1997: Lab. maj. 1,596 (3.84%))

CYNON VALLEY
E. 48,591   T. 26,958 (55.48%)   Lab. hold
*Ms Ann Clwyd, *Lab.*   17,685
Steven Cornelius, *PC*   4,687
Ian Parry, *LD*   2,541
Julian Waters, *C.*   2,045
Lab. majority 12,998 (48.22%)
5.44% swing Lab. to PC
(1997: Lab. maj. 19,755 (59.10%))

DELYN
E. 54,732   T. 34,636 (63.28%)   Lab. hold
*David Hanson, *Lab.*   17,825
Paul Brierley, *C.*   9,220
Tudor Jones, *LD*   5,329
Paul Rowlinson, *PC*   2,262
Lab. majority 8,605 (24.84%)
2.29% swing Lab. to C.
(1997: Lab. maj. 11,693 (29.42%))

GOWER
E. 58,943   T. 37,353 (63.37%)   Lab. hold
*Martin Caton, *Lab.*   17,676
John Bushell, *C.*   10,281
Ms Sheila Waye, *LD*   4,507
Ms Sian Caiach, *PC*   3,865
Ms Tina Shrewsbury, *Green*   607
Darran Hickery, (Soc. Lab.)   417
Lab. majority 7,395 (19.80%)
5.11% swing Lab. to C.
(1997: Lab. maj. 13,007 (30.02%))

ISLWYN
E. 51,230   T. 31,691 (61.86%)
Lab. Co-op. hold
*Don Touhig, *Lab. Co-op.*   19,505
Kevin Etheridge, *LD*   4,196
Leigh Thomas, *PC*   3,767
Philip Howells, *C.*   2,543
Paul Taylor, *Ind.*   1,263
Ms Mary Millington, *Soc. Lab.*   417
Lab. Co-op. majority 15,309 (48.31%)
8.71% swing Lab. Co-op. to LD
(1997: Lab. maj. 23,931 (65.73%))

LLANELLI
E. 58,148   T. 36,198 (62.25%)   Lab. hold
*Rt. Hon. D. Davies, *Lab.*   17,586
Dyfan Jones, *PC*   11,183
Simon Hayes, *C.*   3,442
Ken Rees, *LD*   3,065
Ms Jan Cliff, *Green*   515
John Willock, Soc. Lab.   407
Lab. majority 6,403 (17.69%)
10.62% swing Lab. to PC
(1997: Lab. maj. 16,039 (38.92%))

MEIRIONNYDD NANT CONWY
E. 33,175   T. 21,068 (63.51%)   PC hold
*Elfyn Llwyd, *PC*   10,459
Ms Denise Idris Jones, *Lab.*   4,775
Ms Lisa Francis, *C.*   3,962
Dafydd Raw-Rees, *LD*   1,872
PC majority 5,684 (26.98%)
0.36% swing PC to Lab.
(1997: PC maj. 6,805 (27.69%))

MERTHYR TYDFIL & RHYMNEY
E. 55,368   T. 31,684 (57.22%)   Lab. hold
Dai Havard, *Lab.*   19,574
Robert Hughes, *PC*   4,651
Keith Rogers, *LD*   2,385
Richard Cuming, *C.*   2,272
Jeff Edwards, *Ind.*   1,936
Ken Evans, *Soc. Lab.*   692
Anthony Lewis, *ProLife*   174
Lab. majority 14,923 (47.10%)
11.80% swing Lab. to PC
(1997: Lab. maj. 27,086 (69.20%))

MONMOUTH
E. 62,202   T. 44,462 (71.48%)   Lab. hold
*Huw Edwards, *Lab.*   19,021
Roger Evans, *C.*   18,637
Neil Parker, *LD*   5,080
Marc Hubbard, *PC*   1,068
David Rowlands, *UK Ind.*   656
Lab. majority 384 (0.86%)
3.83% swing Lab. to C.
(1997: Lab. maj. 4,178 (8.52%))

MONTGOMERYSHIRE
E. 44,243   T. 28,983 (65.51%)   LD hold
*Lembit Opik, *LD*   14,319
David Jones, *C.*   8,085
Paul Davies, *Lab.*   3,443
David Senior, *PC*   1,969
David William Rowlands, *UK Ind.*   786
Miss Ruth Davies, *ProLife*   210
Reg Taylor, *Ind.*   171
LD majority 6,234 (21.51%)
0.88% swing C. to LD
(1997: LD maj. 6,303 (19.74%))

NEATH
E. 56,107   *T.* 35,020 (62.42%) Lab. hold
*Rt. Hon. P. Hain, *Lab.*   21,253
Alun Llywelyn, *PC*   6,437
David Davies, *LD*   3,335
David Devine, *C.*   3,310
Huw Pudner, *Soc. All.*   483
Gerardo Brienza, *ProLife*   202
Lab. majority 14,816 (42.31%)
11.56% swing Lab. to PC
(1997: Lab. maj. 26,741 (64.84%))

NEWPORT EAST
E. 56,118   *T.* 31,282 (55.74%) Lab. hold
*Rt. Hon. A. Howarth, *Lab.*   17,120
Ian Oakley, *C.*   7,246
Alistair Cameron, *LD*   4,394
Madoc Batcup, *PC*   1,519
Ms Liz Screen, *Soc. Lab.*   420
Neal Reynolds, *UK Ind.*   410
Robert Griffiths, *Comm.*   173
Lab. majority 9,874 (31.56%)
2.36% swing Lab. to C.
(1997: Lab. maj. 13,523 (36.29%))

NEWPORT WEST
E. 59,742   *T.* 35,063 (58.69%) Lab. hold
*Paul Flynn, *Lab.*   18,489
Dr William Morgan, *C.*   9,185
Ms Veronica Watkins, *LD*   4,095
Anthony Salkeld, *PC*   2,510
Hugh Moelwyn-Hughes, *UK Ind.*   506
Terry Cavill, *BNP*   278
Lab. majority 9,304 (26.54%)
4.81% swing Lab. to C.
(1997: Lab. maj. 14,537 (36.16%))

OGMORE
E. 52,185   *T.* 30,353 (58.16%) Lab. hold
*Sir Ray Powell, *Lab.*   18,833
Ms Angela Pulman, *PC*   4,259
Ian Lewis, *LD*   3,878
Richard Hill, *C.*   3,383
Lab. majority 14,574 (48.02%)
9.46% swing Lab. to PC
(1997: Lab. maj. 24,447 (64.22%))

PONTYPRIDD
E. 66,105   *T.* 38,309 (57.95%) Lab. hold
*Dr Kim Howells, *Lab.*   22,963
Bleddyn Hancock, *PC*   5,279
Ms Prudence Dailey, *C.*   5,096
Eric Brooke, *LD*   4,152
Ms Sue Warry, *UK Ind.*   603
Joseph Biddulph, *ProLife*   216
Lab. majority 17,684 (46.16%)
5.61% swing Lab. to PC
(1997: Lab. maj. 23,129 (50.44%))

PRESELI PEMBROKESHIRE
E. 54,283   *T.* 36,777 (67.75%) Lab. hold
*Ms Jackie Lawrence, *Lab.*   15,206
Stephen Crabb, *C.*   12,260
Rhys Sinnet, *PC*   4,658
Alexander Dauncey, *LD*   3,882
Ms Trish Bowen, *Soc. Lab.*   452
Hugh Jones, *UK Ind.*   319
Lab. majority 2,946 (8.01%)
6.29% swing Lab. to C.
(1997: Lab. maj. 8,736 (20.60%))

RHONDDA
E. 56,059   *T.* 34,002 (60.65%) Lab. hold
Chris Bryant, *Lab.*   23,230
Ms Leanne Wood, *PC*   7,183
Peter Hobbins, *C.*   1,557
Gavin Cox, *LD*   1,525
Glyndwr Summers, *Ind.*   507
Lab. majority 16,047 (47.19%)
6.95% swing Lab. to PC
(1997: Lab. maj. 24,931 (61.09%))

SWANSEA EAST
E. 57,273   *T.* 30,072 (52.51%) Lab. hold
*Rt. Hon. D. Anderson, *Lab.*   19,612
John Ball, *PC*   3,464
Robert Speht, *LD*   3,064
Paul Morris, *C.*   3,026
Tony Young, *Green*   463
Tim Jenkins, *UK Ind.*   443
Lab. majority 16,148 (53.70%)
9.15% swing Lab. to PC
(1997: Lab. maj. 25,569 (66.12%))

SWANSEA WEST
E. 57,074   *T.* 32,100 (56.24%) Lab. hold
*Rt. Hon. A. Williams, *Lab.*   15,644
Ms Margaret Harper, *C.*   6,094
Mike Day, *LD*   5,313
Ian Titherington, *PC*   3,404
Richard Lewis, *UK Ind.*   653
Martyn Shrewsbury, *Green*   626
Alec Thraves, *Soc. All.*   366
Lab. majority 9,550 (29.75%)
2.99% swing Lab. to C.
(1997: Lab. maj. 14,459 (35.73%))

TORFAEN
E. 61,110   *T.* 35,242 (57.67%) Lab. hold
*Rt. Hon. P. Murphy, *Lab.*   21,883
Jason Evans, *C.*   5,603
Alan Masters, *LD*   3,936
Stephen Smith, *PC*   2,720
Mrs Brenda Vipass, *UK Ind.*   657
Steve Bell, *Soc. All.*   443
Lab. majority 16,280 (46.19%)
5.27% swing Lab. to C.
(1997: Lab. maj. 24,536 (56.74%))

VALE OF CLWYD
E. 51,247   *T.* 32,346 (63.12%) Lab. hold
*Chris Ruane, *Lab.*   16,179
Brendan Murphy, *C.*   10,418
Graham Rees, *LD*   3,058
John Penri Williams, *PC*   2,300
William Campbell, *UK Ind.*   391
Lab. majority 5,761 (17.81%)
2.54% swing Lab. to C.
(1997: Lab. maj. 8,955 (22.89%))

VALE OF GLAMORGAN
E. 67,071   *T.* 45,184 (67.37%) Lab. hold
*John Smith, *Lab.*   20,524
Lady Susan Inkin, *C.*   15,824
Dewi Smith, *LD*   5,521
Chris Franks, *PC*   2,867
Niall Warry, *UK Ind.*   448
Lab. majority 4,700 (10.40%)
4.57% swing Lab. to C.
(1997: Lab. maj. 10,532 (19.54%))

WREXHAM
E. 50,465   *T.* 30,048 (59.54%) Lab. hold
Ian Lucas, *Lab.*   15,934
Ms Felicity Elphick, *C.*   6,746
Ron Davies, *LD*   5,153
Malcolm Evans, *PC*   1,783
Mrs Jane Brookes, *UK Ind.*   432
Lab. majority 9,188 (30.58%)
0.86% swing Lab. to C.
(1997: Lab. maj. 11,762 (32.30%))

YNYS MON
E. 53,117   *T.* 34,018 (64.04%) Lab. gain
Albert Owen, *Lab.*   11,906
Eilian Williams, *PC*   11,106
Albie Fox, *C.*   7,653
Nick Bennett, *LD*   2,772
Francis Wykes, *UK Ind.*   359
Ms Nona Donald, *Ind.*   222
Lab. majority 800 (2.35%)
4.28% swing PC to Lab
(1997: PC maj. 2,481 (6.21%))

SCOTLAND

ABERDEEN CENTRAL
E. 50,098 T. 26,429 (52.75%) Lab. hold
*Frank Doran, Lab.   12,025
Wayne Gault, SNP   5,379
Ms Eleanor Anderson, LD   4,547
Stewart Whyte, C.   3,761
Andy Cumbers, SSP   717
Lab. majority 6,646 (25.15%)
4.24% swing Lab. to SNP
(1997: Lab. maj. 10,801 (30.32%))

ABERDEEN NORTH
E. 52,746 T. 30,357 (57.55%) Lab. hold
*Malcolm Savidge, Lab.   13,157
Dr Allan Alasdair, SNP   8,708
Jim Donaldson, LD   4,991
Richard Cowling, C.   3,047
Ms Shona Forman, SSP   454
Lab. majority 4,449 (14.66%)
5.70% swing Lab. to SNP
(1997: Lab. maj. 10,010 (26.06%))

ABERDEEN SOUTH
E. 58,907 T. 36,890 (62.62%) Lab. hold
*Ms Anne Begg, Lab.   14,696
Ian Yuill, LD   10,308
Moray Macdonald, C.   7,098
Ian Angus, SNP   4,293
David Watt, SSP   495
Lab. majority 4,388 (11.89%)
2.13% swing LD to Lab.
(1997: Lab. maj. 3,365 (7.64%))

ABERDEENSHIRE WEST & KINCARDINE
E. 61,180 T. 37,914 (61.97%) LD hold
*Sir Robert Smith, LD   16,507
Tom Kerr, C.   11,686
Kevin Hutchens, Lab.   4,669
John Green, SNP   4,634
Alan Manley, SSP   418
LD majority 4,821 (12.72%)
3.28% swing C. to LD
(1997: LD maj. 2,662 (6.16%))

AIRDRIE & SHOTTS
E. 58,349 T. 31,736 (54.39%) Lab. hold
*Rt. Hon. Ms H. Liddell, Lab.   18,478
Ms Alison Lindsay, SNP   6,138
John Love, LD   2,376
Gordon McIntosh, C.   1,960
Ms Mary Dempsey, Scot. U.   1,439
Kenny McGuigan, SSP   1,171
Chris Herriot, Soc. Lab.   174
Lab. majority 12,340 (38.88%)
0.73% swing SNP to Lab.
(1997: Lab. maj. 15,412 (37.42%))

ANGUS
E. 59,004 T. 35,013 (59.34%) SNP hold
Michael Weir, SNP   12,347
Marcus Booth, C.   8,736
Ian McFatridge, Lab.   8,183
Peter Nield, LD   5,015
Bruce Wallace, SSP   732
SNP majority 3,611 (10.31%)
6.67% swing SNP to C.
(1997: SNP maj. 10,189 (23.66%))

ARGYLL & BUTE
E. 49,175 T. 30,957 (62.95%) LD hold
Alan Reid, LD   9,245
Hugh Raven, Lab.   7,592
David Petrie, C.   6,436
Ms Agnes Samuel, SNP   6,433
Des Divers, SSP   1,251
LD majority 1,653 (5.34%)
9.60% swing LD to Lab.
(1997: LD maj. 6,081 (17.03%))

AYR
E. 55,630 T. 38,560 (69.32%) Lab. hold
*Ms Sandra Osborne, Lab.   16,801
Phil Gallie, C.   14,256
Jim Mather, SNP   4,621
Stuart Ritchie, LD   2,089
James Stewart, SSP   692
Joseph Smith, UK Ind.   101
Lab. majority 2,545 (6.60%)
4.01% swing Lab. to C.
(1997: Lab. maj. 6,543 (14.62%))

BANFF & BUCHAN
E. 56,496 T. 30,806 (54.53%) SNP hold
*Alex Salmond, SNP   16,710
Alexander Wallace, C.   6,207
Edward Harris, Lab.   4,363
Douglas Herbison, LD   2,769
Ms Alice Rowan, SSP   447
Eric Davidson, UK Ind.   310
SNP majority 10,503 (34.09%)
1.06% swing C. to SNP
(1997: SNP maj. 12,845 (31.97%))

CAITHNESS, SUTHERLAND & EASTER ROSS
E. 41,225 T. 24,867 (60.32%) LD hold
Viscount John Thurso, LD   9,041
Michael Meighan, Lab.   6,297
John Macadam, SNP   5,273
Robert Rowantree, C.   3,513
Ms Karn Mabon, SSP   544
Gordon Campbell, Ind.   199
LD majority 2,744 (11.03%)
1.64% swing Lab. to LD
(1997: LD maj. 2,259 (7.75%))

CARRICK, CUMNOCK & DOON VALLEY
E. 64,919 T. 40,107 (61.78%)
                               Lab. Co-op hold
*George Foulkes, Lab. Co-op   22,174
Gordon Miller, C.   7,318
Tom Wilson, SNP   6,258
Ms Amy Rogers, LD   2,932
Ms Amanda McFarlane, SSP   1,058
James McDaid, Soc. Lab.   367
Lab. Co-op majority 14,856 (37.04%)
2.90% swing Lab. Co-op to C.
(1997: Lab. maj. 21,062 (42.84%))

CLYDEBANK & MILNGAVIE
E. 52,534 T. 32,491 (61.85%) Lab. hold
*Tony Worthington, Lab.   17,249
Jim Yuill, SNP   6,525
Rod Ackland, LD   3,909
Dr Catherine Pickering, C.   3,514
Ms Dawn Brennan, SSP   1,294
Lab. majority 10,724 (33.01%)
0.54% swing Lab. to SNP
(1997: Lab. maj. 13,320 (34.08%))

CLYDESDALE
E. 64,423 T. 38,222 (59.33%) Lab. hold
*Jimmy Hood, Lab.   17,822
Jim Wright, SNP   10,028
Kevin Newton, C.   5,034
Ms Moira Craig, LD   4,111
Paul Cockshott, SSP   974
Donald MacKay, UK Ind.   253
Lab. majority 7,794 (20.39%)
5.01% swing Lab. to SNP
(1997: Lab. maj. 13,809 (30.41%))

COATBRIDGE & CHRYSTON
E. 52,178 T. 30,311 (58.09%) Lab. hold
*Rt. Hon. T. Clarke, Lab.   19,807
Peter Kearney, SNP   4,493
Alistair Tough, LD   2,293
Patrick Ross-Taylor, C.   2,171
Ms Lynne Sheridan, SSP   1,547
Lab. majority 15,314 (50.52%)
0.39% swing Lab. to SNP
(1997: Lab. maj. 19,295 (51.30%))

CUMBERNAULD & KILSYTH
E. 49,739 T. 29,699 (59.71%) Lab. hold
*Ms Rosemary McKenna, Lab.   16,144
David McGlashan, SNP   8,624
John O'Donnell, LD   1,934
Ms Alison Ross, C.   1,460
Kenny McEwan, SSP   1,287
Thomas Taylor, Scot. Ref.   250
Lab. majority 7,520 (25.32%)
2.78% swing Lab. to SNP
(1997: Lab. maj. 11,128 (30.89%))

CUNNINGHAME NORTH
E. 54,993 T. 33,816 (61.49%) Lab. hold
*Brian Wilson, Lab.   15,571
Campbell Martin, SNP   7,173
Richard Wilkinson, C.   6,666
Ross Chmiel, LD   3,060
Sean Scott, SSP   964
Ms Louise McDaid, Soc. Lab.   382
Lab. majority 8,398 (24.83%)
3.51% swing Lab. to SNP
(1997: Lab. maj. 11,039 (26.84%))

CUNNINGHAME SOUTH
E. 49,982 T. 28,009 (56.04%) Lab. hold
*Brian Donohoe, Lab.   16,424
Bill Kidd, SNP   5,194
Mrs Pam Paterson, C.   2,682
John Boyd, LD   2,094
Ms Rosemary Byrne, SSP   1,233
Bobby Cochrane, Soc. Lab.   382
Lab. majority 11,230 (40.09%)
0.93% swing Lab. to SNP
(1997: Lab. maj. 14,869 (41.95%))

DUMBARTON
E. 56,267 T. 33,994 (60.42%)
                               Lab. Co-op hold
*John McFall, Lab. Co-op   16,151
Iain Robertson, SNP   6,576
Eric Thompson, LD   5,265
Peter Ramsay, C.   4,648
Les Robertson, SSP   1,354
Lab. Co-op majority 9,575 (28.17%)
0.89% swing SNP to Lab. Co-op
(1997: Lab. maj. 10,883 (26.38%))

DUMFRIES
E. 62,931 T. 42,586 (67.67%) Lab. hold
*Russell Brow, *Lab.*   20,830
John Charteris, *C.*   11,996
John Ross Scott, *LD*   4,955
Gerry Fisher, *SNP*   4,103
John Dennis, *SSP*   702
Lab. majority 8,834 (20.74%)
0.64% swing C. to Lab.
(1997: Lab. maj. 9,643 (19.47%))

DUNDEE EAST
E. 56,535 T. 32,358 (57.24%) Lab. hold
Iain Luke, *Lab.*   14,635
Stewart Hosie, *SNP*   10,160
Alan Donnelly, *C.*   3,900
Raymond Lawrie, *LD*   2,784
Harvey Duke, *SSP*   879
Lab. majority 4,475 (13.83%)
5.38% swing Lab. to SNP
(1997: Lab. maj. 9,961 (24.58%))

DUNDEE WEST
E. 53,760 T. 29,242 (54.39%) Lab. hold
*Ernie Ross, *Lab.*   14,787
Gordon Archer, *SNP*   7,987
Ian Hail, *C.*   2,656
Ms Elizabeth Dick, *LD*   2,620
Jim McFarlane, *SSP*   1,192
Lab. majority 6,800 (23.25%)
3.65% swing Lab. to SNP
(1997: Lab. maj. 11,859 (30.56%))

DUNFERMLINE EAST
E. 52,811 T. 30,086 (56.97%) Lab. hold
*Rt. Hon. G. Brown, *Lab.*   19,487
John Mellon, *SNP*   4,424
Stuart Randall, *C.*   2,838
John Mainland, *LD*   2,281
Andy Jackson, *SSP*   770
Tom Dunsmore, *UK Ind.*   286
Lab. majority 15,063 (50.07%)
0.60% swing Lab. to SNP
(1997: Lab. maj. 18,751 (51.26%))

DUNFERMLINE WEST
E. 54,293 T. 30,975 (57.05%) Lab. hold
*Ms Rachel Squire, *Lab.*   16,370
Brian Goodall, *SNP*   5,390
Russell McPhate, *LD*   4,832
James Mackie, *C.*   3,166
Ms Kate Stewart, *SSP*   746
Alastair Harper, *UK Ind.*   471
Lab. majority 10,980 (35.45%)
0.77% swing SNP to Lab.
(1997: Lab. maj. 12,354 (33.91%))

EAST KILBRIDE
E. 66,572 T. 41,690 (62.62%) Lab. hold
*Rt. Hon. A. Ingram, *Lab.*   22,205
Archie Buchanan, *SNP*   9,450
Ewan Hawthorn, *LD*   4,278
Mrs Margaret McCulloch, *C.*   4,238
David Stevenson, *SSP*   1,519
Lab. majority 12,755 (30.59%)
2.52% swing Lab. to SNP
(1997: Lab. maj. 17,384 (35.63%))

EAST LOTHIAN
E. 58,987 T. 36,871 (62.51%) Lab. hold
Mrs Anne Picking, *Lab.*   17,407
Hamish Mair, *C.*   6,577
Ms Judy Hayman, *LD*   6,506
Ms Hilary Brown, *SNP*   5,381
Derrick White, *SSP*   624
Jake Herriot, *Soc. Lab.*   376
Lab. majority 10,830 (29.37%)
1.68% swing Lab. to C.
(1997: Lab. maj. 14,221 (32.74%))

EASTWOOD
E. 68,378 T. 48,368 (70.74%) Lab. hold
*Jim Murphy, *Lab.*   23,036
Raymond Robertson, *C.*   13,895
Allan Steele, *LD*   6,239
Stewart Maxwell, *SNP*   4,137
Peter Murray, *SSP*   814
Dr Manar Tayan, *Ind.*   247
Lab. majority 9,141 (18.90%)
6.35% swing C. to Lab.
(1997: Lab. maj. 3,236 (6.19%))

EDINBURGH CENTRAL
E. 66,089 T. 34,390 (52.04%) Lab. hold
*Rt. Hon. A. Darling, *Lab.*   14,495
Andrew Myles, *LD*   6,353
Alastair Orr, *C.*   5,643
Dr Ian McKee, *SNP*   4,832
Graeme Farmer, *Green*   1,809
Kevin Williamson, *SSP*   1,258
Lab. majority 8,142 (23.68%)
5.15% swing Lab. to LD
(1997: Lab. maj. 11,070 (25.90%))

EDINBURGH EAST &
MUSSELBURGH
E. 59,241 T. 34,454 (58.16%) Lab. hold
*Rt. Hon. Dr G. Strang, *Lab.*   18,124
Rob Munn, *SNP*   5,956
Gary Peacock, *LD*   4,981
Peter Finnie, *C.*   3,906
Derek Durkin, *SSP*   1,487
Lab. majority 12,168 (35.32%)
0.41% swing SNP to Lab.
(1997: Lab. maj. 14,530 (34.50%))

EDINBURGH NORTH & LEITH
E. 62,475 T. 33,234 (53.20%) Lab. hold
Mark Lazarowicz, *Lab.*   15,271
Sebastian Tombs, *LD*   6,454
Ms Kaukab Stewart, *SNP*   5,290
Iain Mitchell, *C.*   4,626
Ms Catriona Grant, *SSP*   1,334
Don Jacobsen, *Soc. Lab.*   259
Lab. majority 8,817 (26.53%)
3.67% swing Lab. to LD
(1997: Lab. maj. 10,978 (26.81%))

EDINBURGH PENTLANDS
E. 59,841 T. 38,932 (65.06%) Lab. hold
*Dr Lynda Clark, *Lab.*   15,797
Sir Malcolm Rifkind, *C.*   14,055
David Walker, *LD*   4,210
Stewart Gibb, *SNP*   4,210
James Mearns, *SSP*   555
William McMurdo, *UK Ind.*   105
Lab. majority 1,742 (4.47%)
3.08% swing Lab. to C.
(1997: Lab. maj. 4,862 (10.63%))

EDINBURGH SOUTH
E. 64,012 T. 37,166 (58.06%) Lab. hold
*Nigel Griffiths, *Lab.*   15,671
Ms Marilyne MacLaren, *LD*   10,172
Geoffrey Buchan, *C.*   6,172
Ms Heather Williams, *SNP*   3,683
Colin Fox, *SSP*   933
Ms Linda Hendry, *LCA*   535
Lab. majority 5,499 (14.80%)
7.19% swing Lab. to LD
(1997: Lab. maj. 11,452 (25.54%))

EDINBURGH WEST
E. 61,895 T. 39,478 (63.78%) LD hold
John Barrett, *LD*   16,719
Ms Elspeth Alexandra, *Lab.*   9,130
Iain Whyte, *C.*   8,894
Alyn Smith, *SNP*   4,047
Bill Scott, *SSP*   688
LD majority 7,589 (19.22%)
2.59% swing LD to Lab.
(1997: LD maj. 7,253 (15.22%))

FALKIRK EAST
E. 57,633 T. 33,702 (58.48%) Lab. hold
*Michael Connarty, *Lab.*   18,536
Ms Isabel Hutton, *SNP*   7,824
Bill Stevenson, *C.*   3,252
Ms Karen Utting, *LD*   2,992
Tony Weir, *SSP*   725
Raymond Stead, *Soc. Lab.*   373
Lab. majority 10,712 (31.78%)
0.20% swing Lab. to SNP
(1997: Lab. maj. 13,385 (32.18%))

FALKIRK WEST
E. 53,583 T. 30,891 (57.65%) Lab. hold
*Eric Joyce, *Lab.*   16,022
David Kerr, *SNP*   7,490
Simon Murray, *C.*   2,321
Hugh O'Donnell, *LD*   2,203
William Buchanan, *Ind.*   1,464
Ms Mhairi McAlpine, *SSP*   707
Hugh Lynch, *Ind.*   490
Ronnie Forbes, *Soc. Lab.*   194
Lab. majority 8,532 (27.62%)
4.15% swing Lab. to SNP
2000 Dec. by-election: Lab. maj. 705
(3.61%)
(1997: Lab. maj. 13,783 (35.92%))

FIFE CENTRAL
E. 59,597 T. 32,512 (54.55%) Lab. hold
John MacDougall, *Lab.*   18,310
David Alexander, *SNP*   8,235
Ms Elizabeth Riches, *LD*   2,775
Jeremy Balfour, *C.*   2,351
Ms Morag Balfour, *SSP*   841
Lab. majority 10,075 (30.99%)
1.33% swing Lab. to SNP
(1997: Lab. maj. 13,713 (33.64%))

FIFE NORTH EAST
E. 61,900 T. 34,692 (56.05%) LD hold
*Rt. Hon. M. Campbell, *LD*   17,926
Mike Scott-Hayward, *C.*   8,190
Ms Claire Brennan, *Lab.*   3,950
Ms Kris Murray-Browne, *SNP*   3,596
Keith White, *SSP*   610
Mrs Leslie Von Goetz, *LCA*   420
LD majority 9,736 (28.06%)
1.66% swing C. to LD
(1997: LD maj. 10,356 (24.75%))

GALLOWAY & UPPER NITHSDALE
E. 52,756   *T.* 35,914 (68.08%)   C. gain
Peter Duncan, *C.*   12,222
Malcolm Fleming, *SNP*   12,148
Thomas Sloan, *Lab.*   7,258
Neil Wallace, *LD*   3,698
Andy Harvey, *SSP*   588
C. majority 74 (0.21%)
6.80% swing SNP to C.
(1997: SNP maj. 5,624 (13.39%))

GLASGOW ANNIESLAND
E. 53,290   *T.* 26,722 (50.14%)   Lab. hold
*John Robertson, *Lab.*   15,102
Grant Thoms, *SNP*   4,048
Christopher McGinty, *LD*   3,244
Stewart Connell, *C.*   2,651
Charlie McCarthy, *SSP*   1,486
Ms Katherine McGavigan, *Soc. Lab.*   191
Lab. majority 11,054 (41.37%)
1.68% swing Lab. to SNP
2000 Nov. by-election: Lab. maj. 6,337
(31.35%)
(1997: Lab. maj. 15,154 (44.73%))

GLASGOW BAILLIESTON
E. 49,268   *T.* 23,261 (47.21%)   Lab. hold
*Jimmy Wray, *Lab.*   14,200
Lachlan McNeill, *SNP*   4,361
David Comrie, *C.*   1,580
Jim McVicar, *SSP*   1,569
Charles Dundas, *LD*   1,551
Lab. majority 9,839 (42.30%)
2.15% swing Lab. to SNP
(1997: Lab. maj. 14,840 (46.59%))

GLASGOW CATHCART
E. 52,094   *T.* 27,386 (52.57%)   Lab. hold
Tom Harris, *Lab.*   14,902
Mrs Josephine Docherty, *SNP*   4,086
Richard Cook, *C.*   3,662
Tom Henery, *LD*   3,006
Ronnie Stevenson, *SSP*   1,730
Lab. majority 10,816 (39.49%)
1.80% swing SNP to Lab.
(1997: Lab. maj. 12,245 (35.90%))

GLASGOW GOVAN
E. 54,068   *T.* 25,284 (46.76%)   Lab. hold
*Mohammad Sarwar, *Lab.*   12,464
Ms Karen Neary, *SNP*   6,064
Bob Stewart, *LD*   2,815
Mark Menzies, *C.*   2,167
Willie McGartland, *SSP*   1,531
John Foster, *Comm.*   174
Badar Mirza, *Ind.*   69
Lab. majority 6,400 (25.31%)
8.14% swing SNP to Lab.
(1997: Lab. maj. 2,914 (9.04%))

GLASGOW KELVIN
E. 61,534   *T.* 26,802 (43.56%)   Lab. hold
*George Galloway, *Lab.*   12,014
Ms Tamsin Mayberry, *LD*   4,754
Frank Rankin, *SNP*   4,513
Miss Davina Rankin, *C.*   2,388
Ms Heather Ritchie, *SSP*   1,847
Tim Shand, *Green*   1,286
Lab. majority 7,260 (27.09%)
4.85% swing Lab. to LD
(1997: Lab. maj. 9,665 (29.60%))

GLASGOW MARYHILL
E. 55,431   *T.* 22,231 (40.11%)   Lab. hold
Ms Ann McKechin, *Lab.*   13,420
Alex Dingwall, *SNP*   3,532
Stuart Callison, *LD*   2,372
Gordon Scott, *SSP*   1,745
Gawain Towler, *C.*   1,162
Lab. majority 9,888 (44.48%)
1.76% swing Lab. to SNP
(1997: Lab. maj. 14,264 (47.99%))

GLASGOW POLLOK
E. 49,201   *T.* 25,277 (51.37%)
                         Lab. Co-op hold
*Ian Davidson, *Lab. Co-op*   15,497
David Ritchie, *SNP*   4,229
Keith Baldssara, *SSP*   2,522
Ms Isabel Nelson, *LD*   1,612
Rory O'Brien, *C.*   1,417
Lab. Co-op majority 11,268 (44.58%)
1.27% swing SNP to Lab. Co-op
(1997: Lab. maj. 13,791 (42.04%))

GLASGOW RUTHERGLEN
E. 51,855   *T.* 29,213 (56.34%)
                         Lab. Co-op hold
*Tommy McAvoy, *Lab. Co-op*   16,760
Ms Anne McLaughlin, *SNP*   4,135
David Jackson, *LD*   3,689
Malcolm Macaskill, *C.*   3,301
Bill Bonnar, *SSP*   1,328
Lab. Co-op majority 12,625 (43.22%)
0.48% swing SNP to Lab. Co-op
(1997: Lab. maj. 15,007 (42.25%))

GLASGOW SHETTLESTON
E. 51,557   *T.* 20,465 (39.69%)   Lab. hold
*David Marshall, *Lab.*   13,235
Jim Byrne, *SNP*   3,417
Ms Rosie Kane, *SSP*   1,396
Lewis Hutton, *LD*   1,105
Campbell Murdoch, *C.*   1,082
Murdo Ritchie, *Soc. Lab.*   230
Lab. majority 9,818 (47.97%)
5.60% swing Lab. to SNP
(1997: Lab. maj. 15,868 (59.18%))

GLASGOW SPRINGBURN
E. 55,192   *T.* 24,104 (43.67%)
                             Speaker hold
*Rt. Hon. M. Martin, *Speaker*   16,053
Sandy Bain, *SNP*   4,675
Ms Carolyn Leckie, *SSP*   1,879
Daniel Houston, *Scot. U.*   1,289
Richard Silvester, *Ind.*   208
Speaker majority 11,378 (47.20%)
(1997: Lab. maj. 17,326 (54.87%))

GORDON
E. 59,996   *T.* 35,001 (58.34%)   LD hold
*Malcolm Bruce, *LD*   15,928
Mrs Nanette Milne, *C.*   8,049
Mrs Rhona Kemp, *SNP*   5,760
Ellis Thorpe, *Lab.*   4,730
John Sangster, *SSP*   534
LD majority 7,879 (22.51%)
2.97% swing C. to LD
(1997: LD maj. 6,997 (16.57%))

GREENOCK & INVERCLYDE
E. 47,884   *T.* 28,419 (59.35%)   Lab. hold
David Cairns, *Lab.*   14,929
Chic Brodie, *LD*   5,039
Andrew Murie, *SNP*   4,248
Alistair Haw, *C.*   3,000
Davey Landels, *SSP*   1,203
Lab. majority 9,890 (34.80%)
3.77% swing Lab. to LD
(1997: Lab. maj. 13,040 (37.59%))

HAMILTON NORTH & BELLSHILL
E. 53,539   *T.* 30,404 (56.79%)   Lab. hold
*Rt. Hon. Dr J. Reid, *Lab.*   18,786
Chris Stephens, *SNP*   5,225
Bill Frain Bell, *C.*   2,649
Keith Legg, *LD*   2,360
Ms Shareen Blackall, *SSP*   1,189
Steve Mayes, *Soc. Lab.*   195
Lab. majority 13,561 (44.60%)
0.16% swing Lab. to SNP
(1997: Lab. maj. 17,067 (44.92%))

HAMILTON SOUTH
E. 46,665   *T.* 26,750 (57.32%)   Lab. hold
*Bill Tynan, *Lab.*   15,965
John Wilson, *SNP*   5,190
John Oswald, *LD*   2,381
Neil Richardson, *C.*   ,876
Ms Gena Mitchell, *SSP*   1,187
Ms Janice Murdoch, *UK Ind.*   151
Lab. majority 10,775 (40.28%)
3.85% swing Lab. to SNP
1999 Sep. by-election:
Lab. maj 556 (2.86%)
(1997: Lab. maj. 15,878 (47.98%))

INVERNESS EAST, NAIRN &
LOCHABER
E. 67,139   *T.* 42,461 (63.24%)   Lab. hold
*David Stewart, *Lab.*   15,605
Angus MacNeil, *SNP*   10,889
Ms Patsy Kenton, *LD*   9,420
Richard Jenkins, *C.*   5,653
Steve Arnott, *SSP*   894
Lab. majority 4,716 (11.11%)
3.10% swing SNP to Lab.
(1997: Lab. maj. 2,339 (4.90%))

KILMARNOCK & LOUDOUN
E. 61,049   *T.* 37,665 (61.70%)   Lab. hold
*Des Browne, *Lab.*   19,926
John Brady, *SNP*   9,592
Donald Reece, *C.*   3,943
John Stewart, *LD*   3,177
Jason Muir, *SSP*   1,027
Lab. majority 10,334 (27.44%)
6.07% swing SNP to Lab.
(1997: Lab. maj. 7,256 (15.30%))

KIRKCALDY
E. 51,559   *T.* 28,157 (54.61%)
                         Lab. Co-op hold
*Dr Lewis Moonie, *Lab. Co-op*   15,227
Ms Shirley-Anne Somerville, *SNP*   6,264
Scott Campbell, *C.*   3,013
Andrew Weston, *LD*   2,849
Dougie Kinnear, *SSP*   804
Lab. Co-op majority 8,963 (31.83%)
0.60% swing SNP to Lab. Co-op
(1997: Lab. maj. 10,710 (30.63%))

LINLITHGOW
E. 54,599 T. 31,655 (57.98%) Lab. hold
*Tam Dalyell, Lab.   17,207
Jim Sibbald, SNP   8,078
Gordon Lindhurst, C.   2,836
Martin Oliver, LD   2,628
Eddie Cornoch, SSP   695
Ms Helen Cronin, R & R Loony   211
Lab. majority 9,129 (28.84%)
0.75% swing SNP to Lab.
(1997: Lab. maj. 10,838 (27.33%))

LIVINGSTON
E. 64,850 T. 36,033 (55.56%) Lab. hold
*Rt. Hon. R. Cook, Lab.   19,108
Graham Sutherland, SNP   8,492
Gordon Mackenzie, LD   3,969
Ian Mowat, C.   2,995
Ms Wendy Milne, SSP   1,110
Robert Kingdon, UK Ind.   359
Lab. majority 10,616 (29.46%)
1.02% swing SNP to Lab.
(1997: Lab. maj. 11,747 (27.43%))

MIDLOTHIAN
E. 48,625 T. 28,724 (59.07%) Lab. hold
David Hamilton, Lab.   15,145
Ian Goldie, SNP   6,131
Ms Jacqueline Bell, LD   3,686
Robin Traquair, C.   2,748
Bob Goupillot, SSP   837
Terence Holden, ProLife   177
Lab. majority 9,014 (31.38%)
1.69% swing SNP to Lab.
(1997: Lab. maj. 9,870 (28.00%))

MORAY
E. 58,008 T. 33,223 (57.27%) SNP hold
Angus Robertson, SNP   10,076
Mrs Catriona Munro, Lab.   8,332
Frank Spencer-Nairn, C.   7,677
Ms Linda Gorn, LD   5,224
Ms Norma Anderson, SSP   821
Bill Jappy, Ind.   802
Nigel Kenyon, UK Ind.   291
SNP majority 1,744 (5.25%)
8.25% swing SNP to Lab.
(1997: SNP maj. 5,566 (14.00%))

MOTHERWELL & WISHAW
E. 52,418 T. 29,673 (56.61%) Lab. hold
*Frank Roy, Lab.   16,681
Jim McGuigan, SNP   5,725
Mark Nolan, C.   3,155
Iain Brown, LD   2,791
Stephen Smellie, SSP   1,260
Ms Claire Watt, Soc. Lab.   61
Lab. majority 10,956 (36.92%)
1.00% swing SNP to Lab.
(1997: Lab. maj. 12,791 (34.93%))

OCHIL
E. 57,554 T. 35,303 (61.34%) Lab. hold
*Martin O'Neill, Lab.   16,004
Keith Brown, SNP   10,655
Alasdair Campbell, C.   4,235
Paul Edie, LD   3,253
Ms Pauline Thompson, SSP   751
Flash Gordon Approaching,
  Loony   405
Lab. majority 5,349 (15.15%)
2.26% swing SNP to Lab.
(1997: Lab. maj. 4,652 (10.63%))

ORKNEY & SHETLAND
E. 31,909 T. 16,733 (52.44%) LD hold
Alistair Carmichael, LD   6,919
Robert Mochrie, Lab.   3,444
John Firth, C.   3,121
John Mowat, SNP   2,473
Peter Andrews, SSP   776
LD majority 3,475 (20.77%)
6.48% swing LD to Lab.
(1997: LD maj. 6,968 (33.72%))

PAISLEY NORTH
E. 47,994 T. 27,153 (56.58%) Lab. hold
*Ms Irene Adams, Lab.   15,058
George Adam, SNP   5,737
Ms Jane Hook, LD   2,709
Craig Stevenson, C.   2,404
Jim Halfpenny, SSP   982
Robert Graham, ProLife   263
Lab. majority 9,321 (34.33%)
1.61% swing Lab. to SNP
(1997: LAB. MAJ. 12,814 (37.54%))

PAISLEY SOUTH
E. 53,351 T. 30,536 (57.24%) Lab. hold
*Douglas Alexander, Lab.   17,830
Brian Lawson, SNP   5,920
Brian O'Malley, C.   3,178
Andrew Cossar, C.   2,301
Ms Frances Curran, SSP   835
Ms Patricia Graham, ProLife   346
Terence O'Donnell, Ind.   126
Lab. majority 11,910 (39.00%)
2.44% swing SNP to Lab.
(1997 Nov. by-election: Lab. maj. 2,731)
(1997: Lab. maj. 12,750 (34.13%))

PERTH
E. 61,497 T. 37,816 (61.49%) SNP hold
Ms Annabelle Ewing, SNP   11,237
Miss Elizabeth Smith, C.   11,189
Ms Marion Dingwall, Lab.   9,638
Ms Vicki Harris, LD   4,853
Frank Byrne, SSP   899
SNP majority 48 (0.13%)
3.46% swing SNP to C.
(1997: SNP maj. 3,141 (7.05%))

RENFREWSHIRE WEST
E. 52,889 T. 33,497 (63.33%) Lab. gain
James Sheridan, Lab.   15,720
Ms Carol Puthucheary, SNP   7,145
David Sharpe, C.   5,522
Ms Clare Hamblen, LD   4,185
Ms Arlene Nunnery, SSP   925
Lab. majority 8,575 (25.60%)
2.77% swing SNP to Lab.
(1997: Lab. maj. 7,979 (20.05%))

ROSS, SKYE & INVERNESS WEST
E. 56,522 T. 34,812 (61.59%) LD hold
*Rt. Hon. C. Kennedy, LD   18,832
Donald Crichton, Lab.   5,880
Ms Jean Urquhart, SNP   4,901
Angus Laing, C.   3,096
Dr Eleanor Scott, Green   699
Stuart Topp, SSP   683
Philip Anderson, UK Ind.   456
James Crawford, Country   265
LD majority 12,952 (37.21%)
13.57% swing Lab. to LD
(1997: LD maj. 4,019 (10.06%))

ROXBURGH & BERWICKSHIRE
E. 47,059 T. 28,797 (61.19%) LD hold
*Archy Kirkwood, LD   14,044
George Turnbull, C.   6,533
Ms C. Maxwell-Stuart, Lab.   4,498
Roderick Campbell, SNP   2,806
Ms Amanda Millar, SSP   463
Peter Neilson, UK Ind.   453
LD majority 7,511 (26.08%)
1.73% swing C. to LD
(1997: LD maj. 7,906 (22.63%))

STIRLING
E. 53,097 T. 35,930 (67.67%) Lab. hold
*Ms Anne McGuire, Lab.   15,175
Geoff Mawdsley, C.   8,901
Ms Fiona Macaulay, SNP   5,877
Clive Freeman, LD   4,208
Dr Clarke Mullen, SSP   1,012
Mark Ruskell, Green   757
Lab. majority 6,274 (17.46%)
1.27% swing C. to Lab.
(1997: Lab. maj. 6,411 (14.93%))

STRATHKELVIN & BEARSDEN
E. 62,729 T. 41,486 (66.14%) Lab. hold
John Lyons, Lab.   19,250
Gordon Macdonald, LD   7,533
Calum Smith, SNP   6,675
Murray Roxburgh, C.   6,635
Willie Telfer, SSP   1,393
Lab. majority 11,717 (28.24%)
7.44% swing Lab. to LD
(1997: Lab. maj. 16,292 (32.77%))

TAYSIDE NORTH
E. 61,645 T. 38,517 (62.48%) SNP hold
Peter Wishart, SNP   15,441
Murdo Fraser, C.   12,158
Thomas Docherty, Lab.   5,715
Ms Julia Robertson, LD   4,363
Ms Rosie Adams, SSP   620
Ms Tina MacDonald, Ind.   220
SNP majority 3,283 (8.52%)
0.30% swing SNP to C.
(1997: SNP maj. 4,160 (9.13%))

TWEEDDALE, ETTRICK &
LAUDERDALE
E. 51,966 T. 33,217 (63.92%) LD hold
*Michael Moore, LD   14,035
Keith Geddes, Lab.   8,878
Andrew Brocklehurst, C   5,118
Richard Thomson, SNP   4,108
Norman Lockhart, SSP   695
John Hein, Lib.   383
LD majority 5,157 (15.53%)
5.86% swing Lab. to LD
(1997: LD maj. 1,489 (3.81%))

WESTERN ISLES
E. 21,807 T. 13,159 (60.34%) Lab. hold
*Calum MacDonald, Lab.   5,924
Alasdair Nicholson, SNP   4,850
Douglas Taylor, C.   1,250
John Horne, LD   849
Ms Joanne Telfer, SSP   286
Lab. majority 1,074 (8.16%)
7.02% swing Lab. to SNP
(1997: Lab. maj. 3,576 (22.20%))

NORTHERN IRELAND

ANTRIM EAST
E. 60,897   T. 36,000 (59.12%) UUP hold
*Roy Beggs, UUP	13,101
Sammy Wilson, DUP	12,973
John Mathews, Alliance	4,483
Danny O'Connor, SDLP	2,641
Robert Mason, Ind.	1,092
Ms Jeanette Graffin, SF	903
Alan Greer, C.	807

UUP majority 128 (0.36%)
9.48% swing UUP to DUP
(1997: UUP maj. 6,389 (18.60%)))

ANTRIM NORTH
E. 74,451   T. 49,217 (66.11%) DUP hold
*Revd Ian Paisley, DUP	24,539
Lexie Scott, UUP	10,315
Sean Farren, SDLP	8,283
John Kelly, SF	4,822
Miss Jayne Dunlop, Alliance	1,258

DUP majority 14,224 (28.90%)
3.01% swing UUP to DUP
(1997: DUP maj. 10,574 (22.89%)))

ANTRIM SOUTH
E. 70,651   T. 44,158 (62.50%) UUP gain
David Burnside, UUP	16,366
*Revd Robert McCrea, DUP	15,355
Sean McKee, SDLP	5,336
Martin Meehan, SF	4,160
David Ford, Alliance	1,969
Norman Boyd, NI Unionist	972

UUP majority 1,011 (2.29%)
10.21% swing UUP to DUP
(2000 Sep. by-election: DUP maj. 822)
(1997: UUP maj. 16,611 (41.33%)))

BELFAST EAST
E. 58,455   T. 36,829 (63.00%) DUP hold
*Peter Robinson, DUP	15,667
Tim Lemon, UUP	8,550
Dr David Alderdice, Alliance	5,832
David Ervine, PUP	3,669
Joe O'Donnell, SF	1,237
Ms Ciara Farren, SDLP	880
Terry Dick, C.	800
Joe Bell, WP	123
Rainbow George Weiss, Ind. Vote	71

DUP majority 7,117 (19.32%)
1.01% swing UUP to DUP
(1997: DUP maj. 6,754 (17.30%))

BELFAST NORTH
E. 60,941   T. 40,932 (67.17%) DUP gain
Nigel Dodds, DUP	16,718
Gerry Kelly, SF	10,331
Alban Maginness, SDLP	8,592
*Cecil Walker, UUP	4,904
Ms Marcella Delaney, WP	253
Rainbow George Weiss, Ind. Vote	134

DUP majority 6,387 (15.60%)
(1997: UUP maj. 13,024 (31.42%))

BELFAST SOUTH
E. 59,436   T. 37,952 (63.85%) UUP hold
*Revd M. Smyth, UUP	17,008
Dr Alasdair McDonnell, SDLP	11,609
Prof Monica McWilliams,	
Women's Co.	2,968
Alex Maskey, SF	2,894
Ms Geraldine Rice, Alliance	2,042
Ms Dawn Purvis, PUP	1,112
Paddy Lynn, WP	204
Rainbow George Weiss, Ind. Vote	115

UUP majority 5,399 (14.23%)
1.29% swing SDLP to UUP
(1997: UUP maj. 4,600 (11.65%))

BELFAST WEST
E. 59,617   T. 40,982 (68.74%)   SF hold
*Gerry Adams, SF	27,096
Alex Attwood, SDLP	7,754
The Revd Eric Smyth, DUP	2,641
Chris McGimpsey, UUP	2,541
John Lowry, WP	736
Mr David Kerr, Third	116
Rainbow George Weiss, Ind. Vote	98

SF majority 19,342 (47.20%)
14.98% swing SDLP to SF
(1997: SF maj. 7,909 (17.24%))

DOWN NORTH
E. 63,212   T. 37,189 (58.83%) UUP gain
Lady Sylvia Hermon, UUP	20,833
*Robert McCartney, UKU	13,509
Ms Marietta Farrell, SDLP	1,275
Julian Robertson, C.	815
Chris Carter, Ind.	444
Eamon McConvey, SF	313

UUP majority 7,324 (19.69%)
11.83% swing UKU to UUP
(1997: UKU maj. 1,449 (3.96%))

DOWN SOUTH
E. 73,519   T. 52,074 (70.83%)
SDLP hold
*Eddie McGrady, SDLP	24,136
Mick Murphy, SF	10,278
Dermot Nesbitt, UUP	9,173
Jim Wells, DUP	7,802
Ms Betty Campbell, Alliance	685

SDLP majority 13,858 (26.61%)
7.97% swing SDLP to SF
(1997: SDLP maj. 9,933 (20.08%))

FERMANAGH & SOUTH TYRONE
E. 66,640   T. 51,974 (77.99%)   SF gain
Ms Michelle Gildernew, SF	17,739
James Cooper, UUP	17,686
Tommy Gallagher, SDLP	9,706
Jim Dixon, Ind. UU	6,843

SF majority 53 (0.10%)
14.22% swing UUP to SF
(1997: UUP maj. 13,688 (28.34%))

FOYLE
E. 70,943   T. 48,879 (68.90%)
SDLP hold
*John Hume, SDLP	24,538
Mitchel McLaughlin, SF	12,988
William Hay, DUP	7,414
Andrew Davidson, UUP	3,360
Colm Cavanagh, Alliance	579

SDLP majority 11,550 (23.63%)
2.47% swing SDLP to SF
(1997: SDLP maj. 13,664 (28.57%))

LAGAN VALLEY
E. 72,671   T. 45,941 (63.22%) UUP hold
*Jeffrey Donaldson, UUP	25,966
Seamus Close, Alliance	7,624
Edwin Poots, DUP	6,164
Ms Patricia Lewsley, SDLP	3,462
Paul Butler, SF	2,725

UUP majority 18,342 (39.93%)
0.86% swing Alliance to UUP
(1997: UUP maj. 16,925 (38.20%))

LONDONDERRY EAST
E. 60,276   T. 39,869 (66.14%) DUP gain
Gregory Campbell, DUP	12,813
*William Ross, UUP	10,912
John Dallat, SDLP	8,298
Francie Brolly, SF	6,221
Mrs Yvonne Boyle, Alliance	1,625

DUP majority 1,901 (4.77%)
7.36% swing UUP to DUP
(1997: UUP maj. 3,794 (9.95%))

NEWRY & ARMAGH
E. 72,466   T. 55,621 (76.75%)
SDLP hold
*Seamus Mallon, SDLP	20,784
Conor Murphy, SF	17,209
Paul Berry, DUP	10,795
Mrs Sylvia McRoberts, UUP	6,833

SDLP majority 3,575 (6.43%)
7.75% swing SDLP to SF
(1997: SDLP maj. 4,889 (9.17%))

STRANGFORD
E. 72,114   T. 43,254 (59.92%) DUP gain
Mrs Iris Robinson, DUP	18,532
*David McNarry, UUP	17,422
Kieran McCarthy, Alliance	2,902
Danny McCarthy, SDLP	2,646
Liam Johnstone, SF	930
Cedric Wilson, NI Unionist	822

DUP majority 1,110 (2.57%)
8.32% swing UUP to DUP
(1997: UUP maj. 5,852 (14.07%))

TYRONE WEST
E. 60,739   T. 48,530 (79.90%)   SF gain
Pat Doherty, SF	19,814
*William Thompson, UUP	14,774
Ms Brid Rodgers, SDLP	13,942

SF majority 5,040 (10.39%)
7.05% swing UUP to SF
(1997: UUP maj. 1,161 (2.51%))

ULSTER MID
E. 61,390   T. 49,936 (81.34%)   SF hold
*Martin McGuinness, SF	25,502
Ian McCrea, DUP	15,549
Ms Eilis Haughey, SDLP	8,376
Francie Donnelly, WP	509

SF majority 9,953 (19.93%)
8.11% swing DUP to SF
(1997: SF maj. 1,883 (3.71%))

UPPER BANN
E. 72,574   T. 51,036 (70.32%) UUP hold
*Rt. Hon. D. Trimble, UUP	17,095
David Simpson, DUP	15,037
Dr Dara O'Hagan, SF	10,770
Ms Dolores Kelly, SDLP	7,607
Tom French, WP	527

UUP majority 2,058 (4.03%)
14.05% swing UUP to DUP
(1997: UUP maj. 9,252 (19.36%))

BY-ELECTIONS SINCE THE 2001 GENERAL ELECTION

BRENT EAST
(18 September 2003)
T. 36.4 %

Sarah Teather, *LD.*	8,158
Robert Evans, *Lab.*	7,040
Uma Fernandes, *C.*	3,368
Noel Lynch, *Green*	638
Brian Butterworth, *Soc. All.*	361
Khidori Fawzi Ibrahim, *Public Services Not War*	219
Winston McKenzie, *Ind.*	197
Kelly McBride, *Ind.*	189
Harold Immanuel, *Ind. Lab.*	188
Brian Hall, *UK Ind.*	140
Iris Cremer, *Soc. Lab.*	111
Neil Walsh, *Ind.*	101
Alan Howling, Lord Hope, *Loony*	59
Aaron Barschack, *No Description*	37
Jiten Bardwaj, *No Description*	35
Rainbow George Weiss, *www.xat.org*	11

LD Majority	1,118

IPSWICH
(22 November 2001)
E.68,244 T. 40.2 %

Chris Mole, *Lab.*	11,881
Paul West, *C.*	7,794
Ms Tessa Munt, *LD*	6,146
Dave Cooper, *CPA*	581
Jonathan Wright, *UK Ind.*	276
Tony Slade, *Green*	255
John Ramirez, *LCA*	236
Peter Leech, *Soc. All.*	152
Nicholas Winskill, *EIP*	84

Lab. Majority	4,087

OGMORE
(14 February 2002)
E.52,209 T.35.2%

Huw Irranca-Davies, *Lab.*	9,548
Bleddyn Hancock, *PC*	3,827
Veronica Watkins, *LD*	1,608
Guto Bebb, *C.*	1,377
Christopher Herriot, *Soc. Lab.*	1,152
Jonathan Spink, *Green*	250
Jeff Hurford, *WSA*	205
Leslie Edwards, *Loony*	187
Captain Beany, *Bean*	122
Revd David Braid, *Ind.*	100

Lab. Majority	5,721

THE GOVERNMENT

THE CABINET AS AT 1 AUGUST 2003

Prime Minister, First Lord of the Treasury and Minister for the Civil Service
The Rt. Hon. Tony Blair, MP, since May 1997
Deputy Prime Minister and First Secretary of State
The Rt. Hon. John Prescott, MP, *Deputy Prime Minister* since May 1997 and *First Secretary of State* since June 2001
Chancellor of the Exchequer
The Rt. Hon. Gordon Brown, MP, since May 1997
Leader of the House of Commons, Lord Privy Seal and Secretary of State for Wales
The Rt. Hon. Peter Hain, MP, since June 2003
Secretary of State for Constitutional Affairs and Lord Chancellor
The Rt. Hon. The Lord Falconer of Thoroton, QC, since June 2003
Secretary of State for Foreign and Commonwealth Affairs
The Rt. Hon. Jack Straw, MP, since June 2001
Secretary of State for the Home Department
The Rt. Hon. David Blunkett, MP, since June 2001
Secretary of State for Environment, Food and Rural Affairs
The Rt. Hon. Margaret Beckett, MP, since June 2001
Secretary of State for International Development
The Rt. Hon. Baroness Amos, MP, since May 2003
Secretary of State for Transport (since May 2002) *and Secretary of State for Scotland* (since June 2003)
The Rt. Hon. Alistair Darling, MP
Secretary of State for Health
The Rt. Hon. John Reid, MP, since June 2003
Secretary of State for Northern Ireland
The Rt. Hon. Paul Murphy, since October 2002
Secretary of State for Defence
The Rt. Hon. Geoff Hoon, MP, since October 1999
Secretary of State for Work and Pensions
The Rt. Hon. Andrew Smith, MP, since May 2002
Leader of the House of Lords and Lord President of the Council vacant[*]
Secretary of State for Trade and Industry
The Rt. Hon. Patricia Hewitt, MP, since June 2001
Secretary of State for Education and Skills
The Rt. Hon. Charles Clarke, MP, since October 2002
Secretary of State for Culture, Media and Sport
The Rt. Hon. Tessa Jowell, MP, since June 2001
Parliamentary Secretary to the Treasury (Chief Whip)
The Rt. Hon. Hilary Armstrong, MP, since June 2001
Minister Without Portfolio and Party Chair
The Rt. Hon. Ian McCartney, MP, since June 2003
Chief Secretary to the Treasury
The Rt. Hon. Paul Boateng, MP, since May 2002

The Minister of State at the Department for Work and Pensions with responsibility for Work, and the Government Chief Whip in the House of Lords attend Cabinet meetings although they are not members of the Cabinet.

[*]The Rt. Hon. Lord Williams of Mostyn died on 20 September 2003. *See* 'Stop Press' for further details.

LAW OFFICERS

Attorney-General
The Rt. Hon. Lord Goldsmith, QC, since June 2001
Lord Advocate
Colin Boyd, QC, since February 2000
Solicitor-General
The Rt. Hon. Harriet Harman, MP, QC, since June 2001
Solicitor-General for Scotland
Mrs Elish Angiolini, QC, since November 2001
Advocate-General for Scotland
Dr Lynda Clark, QC, MP, since May 1999

MINISTERS OF STATE

Cabinet Office
Douglas Alexander, MP *(Chancellor of the Duchy of Lancaster)* Culture, Media and Sport
The Rt. Hon. Richard Caborn, MP *(Sport and Tourism)*
The Rt. Hon. Estelle Morris, MP *(Arts)*
Defence
The Rt. Hon. Adam Ingram, MP *(Armed Forces)*
Office of the Deputy Prime Minister
The Rt. Hon. Keith Hill, MP *(Housing and Planning)*
The Rt. Hon. Nick Raynsford, MP *(Local Government and the Regions)*
The Rt. Hon. Lord Rooker *(Regeneration and Regional Development)*
Education and Skills
David Miliband, MP *(School Standards)*
Margaret Hodge, MBE, MP *(Children)*
Alan Johnson, MP *(Lifelong Learning, Further and Higher Education)*
Environment, Food and Rural Affairs
Elliot Morley, MP *(Environment and Agri-Environment)*
The Rt. Hon. Alun Michael, MP *(Rural Affairs)*
Foreign and Commonwealth Office
Denis MacShane, MP *(Europe)*
The Rt. Hon. The Baroness Symons of Vernham Dean *(Middle East)*
Mike O'Brien, MP *(Trade)*
Health
The Rt. Hon. John Hutton, MP
Rosie Winterton, MP
Home Office
The Rt. Hon. Baroness Scotland of Asthal, QC *(Criminal Justice System and Law Reform)*
Hazel Blears, MP *(Crime Reduction, Policing and Community Safety)*
Beverley Hughes, MP *(Citizenship, Immigration and Counter-Terrorism)*
International Development
Hilary Benn, MP
Northern Ireland Office
Jane Kennedy, MP
The Rt. Hon. John Spellar, MP
Trade and Industry
Stephen Timms, MP *(E-Commerce and Competitiveness)*
Mike O'Brien, MP *(Trade)*
Jacqui Smith, MP *(Deputy Minister for Women)*
Transport
Dr Kim Howells, MP *(Transport)*

Treasury
The Rt. Hon. Dawn Primarolo, MP *(Paymaster-General)*
Ms Ruth Kelly, MP *(Financial Secretary)*
John Healey, MP *(Economic Secretary)*
Work and Pensions
Des Browne, MP *(Work)*
Malcolm Wicks, MP *(Pensions)*

UNDER-SECRETARIES OF STATE

Constitutional Affairs
The Lord Filkin, CBE
David Lammy, MP
Christopher Leslie, MP
Anne McGuire, MP *(Scotland)*
Don Touhig, MP *(Wales)*
Culture, Media and Sport
The Rt. Hon. Lord McIntosh of Haringey *(Media and Heritage)*
Defence
Ivor Caplin, MP *(Veterans)*
The Lord Bach *(Defence Procurement)*
Office of the Deputy Prime Minister
Yvette Cooper, MP
Phil Hope, MP
Education and Skills
The Baroness Ashton of Upholland *(Sure Start, Early Years and Childcare)*
Ivan Lewis, MP
Skills and Vocational Education
Stephen Twigg, MP *(Schools)*
Environment, Food and Rural Affairs
Ben Bradshaw, MP *(Nature Conservation and Fisheries)*
The Lord Whitty of Camberwell *(Food, Farming and Sustainable Energy)*
Foreign and Commonwealth Office
Bill Rammell, MP *(Latin America, Caribbean, OTs, East Asia and Pacific, Russia, Central Asia, and Global Issues)*
Chris Mullin, MP *(Africa, Commonwealth)*
Health
Melanie Johnson, MP *(Public Health)*
Lord Warner of Brockley *(Performance and Quality in the House of Lords)*
Dr Stephen Ladyman, MP *(Community Care)*
Home Office
Paul Goggins, MP *(Correctional Services and Reducing Re-offending)*
Caroline Flint, MP *(Anti-Drugs Co-ordination,Reducing Organised Crime and International and European Issues)*
Fiona Mactaggart, MP *(Race Equality, Community Policy and Civil Renewal)*
International Development
Gareth Thomas, MP
Northern Ireland Office
Ian Pearson, MP
Angela Smith, MP
Trade and Industry
The Lord Sainsbury of Turville, KG *(Science and Innovation)*
Gerry Sutcliffe, MP
Nigel Griffiths, MP *(Small Business)*
Transport
David Jamieson, MP
Tony McNulty, MP
Work and Pensions
The Rt. Hon. The Baroness Hollis of Heigham *(Lords)*
Baroness Ashton of Upholland *(Sure Start)*
Chris Pond, MP *(Work)*
Ms Maria Eagle, MP *(Disabled People)*

GOVERNMENT WHIPS

HOUSE OF LORDS
Captain of the Honourable Corps of the Gentlemen-at-Arms (Chief Whip)
The Lord Grocott
Captain of The Queen's Bodyguard of the Yeoman of the Guard (Deputy Chief Whip)
The Lord Davies of Oldham
Lords-in-Waiting
The Lord Evans of Temple Guiting
The Lord Bassam of Brighton
Baronesses-in-Waiting
The Baroness Farrington of Ribbleton
The Baroness Andrews, OBE
The Baroness Crawley

HOUSE OF COMMONS
Parliamentary Secretary to the Treasury (Chief Whip)
The Rt. Hon. Hilary Armstrong, MP
Treasurer of HM Household (Deputy Chief Whip)
Bob Ainsworth, MP
Comptroller of HM Household
The Rt. Hon. Thomas McAvoy, MP
Vice-Chamberlain of HM Household
Jim Fitzpatrick, MP
Lords Commissioners of HM Treasury
John Heppell, MP; Nick Ainger, MP; Jim Murphy, MP; Joan Ryan, MP; Derek Twigg, MP
Assistant Whips
Fraser Kemp, MP; Charlotte Atkins, MP; Paul Clark, MP; Vernon Coaker, MP; Gillian Merron, MP; Margaret Moran, MP; Bridget Prentice, MP

GOVERNMENT DEPARTMENTS

This section covers central Government departments, executive agencies, regulatory bodies, other statutory independent organisations, and bodies which are government-financed or whose head is appointed by a Government Minister.

THE CIVIL SERVICE

Under the Next Steps programme, launched in 1988, many semi-autonomous executive agencies were established to carry out much of the work of the Civil Service. Executive agencies operate within a framework set by the responsible minister which specifies policies, objectives and available resources. All executive agencies are set annual performance targets by their Minister. Each agency has a chief executive, who is responsible for the day-to-day operations of the agency and who is accountable to the minister for the use of resources and for meeting the agency's targets. The minister accounts to Parliament for the work of the agency. Nearly 80 per cent of civil servants now work in executive agencies. In October 2002 there were about 526,900 permanent civil servants.

The Senior Civil Service was created in 1996 and on 1 April 2001 comprised 3,850 staff from Permanent Secretary to the former Grade 5 level, including all agency chief executives. All Government departments and executive agencies are now responsible for their own pay and grading systems for civil servants outside the Senior Civil Service. In practice the grades of the former Open structure are still in use in some organisations. The Open structure represented the following:

Grade	Title
1	Permanent Secretary
1A	Second Permanent Secretary
2	Deputy Secretary
3	Under-Secretary
4	Chief Scientific Officer B, Professional and Technology Directing A
5	Assistant Secretary, Deputy Chief Scientific Officer, Professional and Technology Directing B
6	Senior Principal, Senior Principal Scientific Officer, Professional and Technology Superintending Grade
7	Principal, Principal Scientific Officer, Principal Professional and Technology Officer

SALARIES 2003–4

MINISTERIAL SALARIES *from 1 April 2003*
Ministers who are Members of the House of Commons receive a parliamentary salary (£56,358) in addition to their ministerial salary.

Prime Minister	£119,056
Cabinet minister (Commons)	£71,433
Cabinet minister (Lords)	£96,960
Minister of State (Commons)	£37,055
Minister of State (Lords)	£75,706
Parliamentary Under-Secretary (Commons)	£28,125
Parliamentary Under-Secretary (Lords)	£65,936

SPECIAL ADVISERS' SALARIES *from 1 April 2002*
Special advisers to Government Ministers are paid out of public funds; their salaries are negotiated individually, but are usually in the range £34,001 to £90,000.

CIVIL SERVICE SALARIES *from 1 April 2003*
Senior Civil Service (SCS)

Permanent Secretary	£118,750–£251,500
Band 3	£89,085–£188,651
Band 2	£72,316–£151,969
Band 1A	£60,788–£120,527
Band 1	£52,403–£110,047

A new Senior Civil Service pay system was introduced from 1 April 2002 with three rather than nine pay bands.

Staff are placed in pay bands according to their level of responsibility and taking account of other factors such as experience and marketability. Movement within and between bands is based on performance.

Other Civil Servants
Following the delegation of responsibility for pay and grading to Government departments and agencies from 1 April 1996, it is no longer possible to show service-wide pay rates for staff outside the Senior Civil Service.

GOVERNMENT DEPARTMENTS

THE CABINET OFFICE
70 Whitehall, London SW1A 2AS
Tel: 020-7270 1234
Web: www.cabinet-office.gov.uk

The Cabinet Office has four main roles: to support the Prime Minister in leading the Government; to support the Government in transacting its business; to lead and support the reform and delivery programme and to co-ordinate security and intelligence. The Department is headed by the Minister for the Cabinet Office (and Chancellor of the Duchy of Lancaster) and has one Minister of State. The Cabinet Office has two Executive Agencies: The Government Car and Despatch Agency (GCDA) and the Central Office of Information (COI) which is a department in its own right.

Prime Minister and Minister for the Civil Service,
  The Rt. Hon. Tony Blair, MP
Parliamentary Private Secretary, Lawrie Quinn, MP
Minister for the Cabinet Office and Chancellor of the Duchy of Lancaster, Douglas Alexander, MP
Principal Private Secretary to the Prime Minister and Head of Policy Directorate (SCS), Jeremy Heywood
Parliamentary Private Secretary, Alan Campbell, MP
Minister of State, Douglas Alexander, MP
Private Secretary, Georgia Hutchinson
Minister without Portfolio and Party Chair, The Rt. Hon. Ian McCartney, MP
Parliamentary Private Secretary, Gareth Thomas, MP
Secretary of the Cabinet and Head of the Home Civil Service, Sir Andrew Turnbull, KCB, CVO
Principal Private Secretary (SCS), Ian Fletcher
Chief Scientific Adviser, Prof. D. King

Security and Intelligence Co-ordinator and Permanent
Secretary, Sir David Omand
Principal Private Secretary (SCS), Sebastian Madden

CEREMONIAL SECRETARIAT
35 Great Smith Street, London SW1P 2BQ
Tel: 020-7276 2728
Honours Nomination Unit: Tel: 020-7276 2774
Ceremonial Officer (SCS), G. Catto

CIVIL CONTINGENCIES SECRETARIAT
10 Great George Street, London SW1P 3AE
Head (SCS), Susan Scholefield, CMG
Deputy Head (SCS), Dr J. Fuller

DEFENCE AND OVERSEAS AFFAIRS SECRETARIAT
Prime Minister's Foreign Policy Adviser and Head of
Secretariat, Sir David Manning, KCMG
Deputy Head (SCS), Desmond Bowen

ECONOMIC AND DOMESTIC SECRETARIAT
Director (SCS), Paul Britton, CB
Deputy Head (SCS), Robin Fellgett

EUROPEAN SECRETARIAT
Prime Minister's European Policy Adviser and Head of
Secretariat, Sir Stephen Wall, KCMG, LVO
Deputy Head (SCS), Katrina Williams, CMG

OFFICE OF THE COMMISSIONER FOR PUBLIC
APPOINTMENTS (OCPA)
3rd Floor, 35 Great Smith Street, London SW1P 3BQ
Tel: 020-7276 2625
The Commissioner for Public Appointments is
responsible for monitoring, regulating and providing
advice to departments on 12,000 ministerial
appointments to public bodies. The Commissioner
publishes a Code of Practice, guidance for departments
and an annual report. The Commissioner has the right to
investigate and will also deal with complaints.
Commissioner for Public Appointments,
Dame Rennie Fritchie, DBE
Senior Policy Adviser, Alistair Howie
Secretary to the Commissioner and Head of the Office (SCS),
J. Barron

OFFICE OF THE CIVIL SERVICE COMMISSIONERS
(OCSC)
3rd Floor, 35 Great Smith Street, London SW1P 3BQ
Tel: 020-7276 2615
The independent Civil Service Commissioners are the
custodians of the rules for selection on merit by fair and
open competition; they publish a Recruitment Code and
audit departments' and agencies' performance against it.
When senior posts at payband two and above are opened
to people from outside the Service the Commissioners
normally chair the recruitment process. The
Commissioners also act as an independent appeals body
under the Civil Service Code.
First Commissioner, Baroness Usha Prashar, CBE
Commissioners (part-time), D. Bell; P. Bounds;
J. Boyle; Ms B. Curtis; Ms S. Forbes, CBE;
Dame Rennie Fritchie, DBE; Prof. E. Gallagher, CBE;
H. Hamill, CB; G. Lemos, CMG; A. MacDonald, CB;
G. Maddrell; Ms G. Peacock, CBE; Dr M. Semple, OBE
Secretary to the Commissioners and Head of the Office (SCS),
Jim Barron

REGULATORY IMPACT UNIT
5th Floor, 22 Whitehall, London SW1A 2WH
Tel: 020-7276 2193
The Regulatory Impact Unit assists Government
Ministers and Departments in finding the right balance
between under-regulating (and so failing to protect the
public) and over-regulating (and so failing to preserve
freedoms, or creating excessive burdens on business). The
Unit also investigates ways of reducing bureaucracy and
red tape in the public and private sectors, and works with
and supports the Better Regulation Task Force.
Director (SCS), Simon Virley
Deputy Directors (SCS), M. Courtney; Ms J. Cruickshank;
Ms S. Grey; Ms K. Hill; Dr P. Rushbrook;
Ms K. Jennings

THE PRIME MINISTER'S DELIVERY UNIT
1 Horse Guards Road, London SW1A 2HQ
Tel: 020-7270 5811
The Prime Minister's Delivery Unit was established in
June 2001 to monitor progress and strengthen the
Government's capacity to deliver its key priorities across
education, health, crime and transport. The Unit reports
to the Prime Minister through the Head of the Civil
Service and the Minister for the Cabinet Office.
Following the Spending Review 2002 the role of the
Delivery Unit now shares responsibility with the
Treasury for the joint Public Service Agreement (PSA)
target to improve public services by working with
departments to help them meet their PSA targets
consistently with fiscal rules. The Unit's work is carried
out by a team of around 40 people drawn from the public
and private sectors. The Unit also draws on the expertise
of a wider group of associates with experience of
successful delivery in the public, private and voluntary
sectors.
Prime Minister's Chief Adviser on Delivery,
Prof. Michael Barber
Deputy Director (SCS), William Jordan *(Accounts, Data*
Analysis and Reporting, Secretariat and Support)
Deputy Director (SCS), Peter Thomas *(Problem Solving and*
Capacity Building)

OFFICE OF THE E-ENVOY
Stockley House, 130 Wilton Road, Victoria, London SW1V 1LQ
Tel: 020-7276 3300
The Office of the E-Envoy is part of the Prime Minister's
Delivery and Reform team based in the Cabinet Office.
The primary focus of the Office of the E-Envoy is to
improve the delivery of public services and achieve long-
term cost savings by joining-up online government
services around the needs of customers. The E-Envoy is
responsible for ensuring that all government services are
available electronically by 2005 with key services
achieving high levels of use.
The Office ensures that the country, its citizens and its
businesses derive maximum benefit from the knowledge
economy. It works to meet the Prime Minister's target for
internet access for all who want it by 2005 and supports
work across Government to develop the UK as a world
leader for electronic business.
E-Envoy, A. Pinder

STRATEGY UNIT
Admiralty Arch, The Mall, London SW1A 2WH
The Strategy Unit (SU) is the result of a merger between
the Performance and Innovation Unit (PIU) and the
Prime Minister's Forward Strategy Unit (PMFSU). The

PIU was created in 1998 to improve the capacity of Government to address strategic, crosscutting issues and promote innovation in the development of policy and in the delivery of the Government's objectives. The PMFSU was created in July 2001 to provide the Prime Minister with long-range policy analysis and thinking. The merged units play the same role, tackling issues on a project basis, and focusing on long term problems that cross public sector institutional boundaries.
Director (SCS), G. Mulgan
Deputy Directors (SCS), J. Rentoul; S. Aldridge; Ms P. Greer; Ms C. Laing

THE PRIME MINISTER'S OFFICE OF PUBLIC SERVICES REFORM
22 Whitehall, London SW1A 2WH
Tel: 020-7276 3600
To strengthen the Government's ability to improve public services, the Prime Minister established the Office of Public Services Reform in 2001, based in the Cabinet Office. The Unit reports directly to the Prime Minister through the Cabinet Secretary. Its role is to advise and work with the Prime Minister and Departments in order to embed the following four principles of reform and deliver customer-focused public services. The principles of reform are: to provide standards within a framework of clear accountability; to give local leaders responsibility and accountability for delivery; to meet the diversity of customer needs, to reduce bureaucracy and to offer greater incentives and rewards for staff; and to provide different ways for users to receive services.
The Unit works on local service projects within health, education, the criminal justice system and local government. It also leads work on understanding customers.
Prime Minister's Adviser on Public Services Reform, Dr Wendy Thomson

CENTRAL SPONSOR FOR INFORMATION ASSURANCE
Stockley House, 130 Wilton Road, London SW1V 1LQ
Tel: 020-7276 3267
The CSIA was established on 1 April 2003. It works with partners in the public and private sectors, as well as its international counterparts, to help safeguard the nation's IT and telecommunications services.
Director, Steve Marsh

CORPORATE DEVELOPMENT GROUP (CDG)
Admiralty Arch, The Mall, London SW1P 3AE
Tel: 020-7276 1566
Director-General (SCS), Ms A. Perkins, CB
Directors (SCS), J. Barker; Ewart Wooldridge; Richard Kornicki; Tim Kemp; Richard Furlong

GOVERNMENT INFORMATION AND COMMUNICATION SERVICE (GICS)
10 Great George St, London SW1P 3AE
Tel: 020-7276 0014
Office of the Head of the Government Information and Communication Service. Responsible for the standards of the service provided by the GICS to Whitehall Departments and their Agencies. Supports the Head of the Civil Service's work. Provides guidance on the strategic development of the GICS, its professional practice, recruitment and promotion. Focuses on cross-departmental communication and management of the central GICS units.

Director-General Government Information and Communication Service (SCS), Mike Granatt, CB
Deputy Head of GICS (Corporate and HR Strategy) (SCS), Ms S. Jenkins
Director of GICS Development Centre (SCS), T. Dunmore
Director of Counter-Terrorist Communication (SCS), Brian Butler
Director of Operations (SCS), Ms L. Salisbury
Head of Government News Network, R. Haslam
Regional Director, East Midlands, P. Smith
   The Belgrave Centre, Talbot Street, Nottingham NG1 5GG
Regional Director, Eastern, Ms M. Basham 2nd Floor, Block A1, Westbrook Centre, Milton Road, Cambridge CB4 1YG
Regional Director, London and South East, Ms V. Burdon
   Hercules Road, London SE1 7DU
Regional Director, North East, C. Child Wellbar House, Gallowgate, Newcastle upon Tyne NE1 4TB
Regional Director, North West, Ms E. Jones
Regional Director, South West, P. Whitbread
   The Pithay, Bristol BS1 2PB
Regional Director, West Midlands, B. Garner
   Five Ways House, Islington Row, Middleway, Edgbaston, Birmingham B15 1SH
   Sunley Tower, Piccadilly Plaza, Manchester M1 4BE
Regional Director, Yorkshire and the Humber, Ms W. Miller
   City House, New Station Street, Leeds LS1 4JG

CORPORATE SERVICES GROUP
9 Whitehall, London SW1A 2DD
Director of Corporate Services and Principal Establishment and Finance Officer, P. Wardle
Deputy Director, Business Development, J. Sweetman
Deputy Director, Financial Management, Ms S. Budden
Deputy Director, Histories and Records, Ms T. Stirling
Deputy Director, Human Resources, Ms C. Francis
Deputy Director, Infrastructure, E. Hepburn
Head, Internal Audit, P. Norris

HER MAJESTY'S STATIONERY OFFICE
St Clements House, 2–16 Colegate, Norwich NR3 1BQ
Tel: 01603-621000
Controller, Carol Tullo

COMMUNICATION GROUP
70 Whitehall, London SW1A 2AS
Tel: 020-7276 1272/0311/0432
Advises on presentation of departmental policy and activity. Handles media and public relations activities other than recruitment publicity and advertising.
Director of Communication, Ms L. Austin
Head of News, J. Bretherton

EXECUTIVE AGENCY
GOVERNMENT CAR AND DESPATCH AGENCY
46 Ponton Road, London SW8 5AX
Tel: 020-7217 3839 Fax: 020-7217 3840
The Agency provides secure transport and mail distribution to Government and the public sector.
Chief Executive, N. Matheson

PRIME MINISTER'S OFFICE
10 Downing Street, London SW1A 2AA
Tel: 020-7270 3000 Fax: 020-7925 0918
Web: www.number-10.gov.uk
Prime Minister, The Rt. Hon Tony Blair, MP
   Principal Private Secretary and Head of Policy Directorate, Jeremy Heywood, CB

Parliamentary Private Secretary, David Hanson, MP
Chief of Staff, Jonathan Powell
Personal Assistant to Prime Minister (Diary), Katie Kay
Director of Political Operations, Pat McFadden
Head of Policy Directorate, Geoff Mulgan
Policy Directorate; Carey Oppenheim; Simon Morys;
  Geoffrey Norris; Arnab Banerji; Sarah Hunter;
  Simon Stevens; Justin Russell; Clare Sumner;
  Alasdair McGowan; Matthew Elson; Patrick Diamond;
  Martin Hurst
Foreign Policy, Matthew Rycroft; David Hallam;
  Liz Lloyd; Roger Liddle
Head of Delivery Unit, Prof. Michael Barber
Head of the Office of Public Services Reform,
  Wendy Thompson
Head of Strategy, Geoff Mulgan
Research and Information Unit, Phil Bassett
Director of Communications and Strategy,
  David Hill
Strategic Communications Unit, Peter Hyman
Direct Communications Unit, Jan Taylor
Prime Minister's Official Spokesmen (PMOS),
  Godric Smith; Tom Kelly
Director of Events and Visits, Fiona Millar
Director of Government Relations, The Baroness Margaret
  Morgan of Huyton
Secretary for Appointments, William Chapman
*Advisor on Education, Public Services and Constitutional
  Reform,* Andrew Adonis
*Advisor on Foreign Policy and Head of the Overseas and
  Defence Secretariat*, Nigel Sheinwald
*Advisor on European Union Affairs and Head of the
  European Secretariat*, Sir Stephen Wall
Parliamentary Clerk, Nicholas Howard

COI COMMUNICATIONS
Hercules Road, London SE1 7DU
Tel: 020-7928 2345 Fax: 020-7928 5037
The Central Office of Information (COI) is a Government
department which offers consultancy, procurement and
project management services to central Government for
publicity. Administrative responsibility for the COI rests
with the Minister for the Cabinet Office.
Chief Executive, A. Bishop
  Senior Personal Secretary, Mrs I. MacMull
Deputy Chief Executive, P. Buchanan

MANAGEMENT BOARD
Members, I. Hamilton; Mrs S. Whetton; G. Beasant;
  A. Wade; Mrs E. Lochhead
Secretary, Mrs I. MacMull

OFFICE OF THE DEPUTY PRIME MINISTER
26 Whitehall, London SW1A 2WH
Tel: 020-7944 4400
Web: www.odpm.gov.uk
The Office of the Deputy Prime Minister was created in
May 2002 taking on responsibility for policy areas from
both the Department for Transport, Local Government
and the Regions and the Cabinet Office. The department
brings together regional and local government (including
the Regional Government Offices), housing, planning
and regeneration, social exclusion and neighbourhood
renewal.
  Regional and local government and the Government's
cross-cutting agenda for neighbourhood renewal and
social inclusion are administered by a single department

under the Deputy Prime Minister, who also has
responsibility for implementing the Regional
Government and Local Government White Papers. The
Deputy Prime Minister will continue to act as the Prime
Minister's deputy across the full range of domestic and
international business, chairing a range of key Cabinet
committees.
Deputy Prime Minister and First Secretary of State, The Rt.
  Hon. John Prescott, MP
  Private Secretary, David Prout
Minister of State, The Rt. Hon. Nick Raynsford, MP
  (Local Government and the Regions)
  Private Secretary, Angela Kerr
Minister of State, The Rt. Hon. Lord Rooker *(Regeneration
  and Regional Development)*
  Private Secretary, Tracy Pennyfather
Minister of State, Keith Hill, MP *(Housing and Planning)*
  Private Secretary, Mark Livesey
Parliamentary Under-Secretary, Phil Hope, MP
  Private Secretary, Karen Abbott
Parliamentary Under-Secretary, Yvette Cooper, MP
  Private Secretary, Sam Wilkinson
Permanent Secretary, Mavis McDonald
  Private Secretary, Andrew Vaughan

DIRECTORATE OF COMMUNICATION
Director of Communication, Derek Plews
Head of Operations, Jane Groom

CORPORATE STRATEGY AND RESOURCES
DIRECTORATE
Director, Peter Unwin
Deputy Director, Mike Bailey

ANALYSIS AND RESEARCH DIRECTORATE
Deputy Director, vacant

FINANCE DIRECTORATE
Deputy Director, Andrew Lean

CORPORATE BUSINESS AND DELIVERY DIVISION
Divisional Manager, Stuart Hoggan

FINANCIAL ACCOUNTING SERVICES DIVISION
Divisional Manager, Alan Beard

INTERNATIONAL AND CENTRAL POLICY DIVISION
Divisional Manager, Shona Dunn

RESOURCE MANAGEMENT CENTRE AND
SECRETARIAT
Branch Head, Fiona Willis

HOUSING, HOMELESSNESS, AND PLANNING GROUP
Director-General (SCS), Genie Turton

HOUSING DIRECTORATE
Director, Neil McDonald

HOMELESSNESS DIRECTORATE
Director, Terrie Alafat
PLANNING DIRECTORATE
Director, Brian Hackland

CHIEF SCIENTIST'S OFFICE
Chief Scientist, David Fisk

LEGAL GROUP
Director-General, David Hogg, CB

LEGAL DIRECTORATE
Director, Sandra Unerman

LOCAL AND REGIONAL GOVERNMENT GROUP
Director-General, Neil Kinghan

FIRE, HEALTH AND SAFETY DIRECTORATE
Director, Clive Norris

LOCAL GOVERNMENT DIRECTORATE OF PRACTICE
Director, John Haward

LOCAL GOVERNMENT FINANCE DIRECTORATE
Director, Bob Linnard
LOCAL GOVERNMENT PERFORMANCE UNIT
Director, Phillip Ward

REGIONAL POLICY AND LOCAL GOVERNANCE
DIRECTORATE
Director, Richard Allan

NEIGHBOURHOOD RENEWAL UNIT
Director-General, Joe Montgomery

NEIGHBOURHOOD RENEWAL OPERATIONS
DIRECTORATE
Director, Alan Riddell

NEIGHBOURHOOD RENEWAL STRATEGY DIRECTORATE
Director, Lindsay Bell

REGIONAL CO-ORDINATION UNIT
River Walk House, Millbank, London SW1P 4RR
Tel: 020-7217 3550
Director-General, Rob Smith
Director, Teresa Vokes

CIVIL RESILIENCE DIRECTORATE
Director, Alun Evans
Regional Directors, Caroline Bowdler *(Government Office
for the East);* Jane Todd *(Government Offices for the East
Midlands);* Liz Meek *(Government Office for London);*
Jonathon Blackie *(Government Office for the North
East);* Keith Barnes *(Government Office for the North
West);* Paul Martin *(Government Office for the South
East);* Jane Henderson *(Government Office for the South
West);* Graham Garbutt *(Government Office for the West
Midlands);* Felicity Everiss *(Government Office for
Yorkshire and the Humber)*

BUSINESS DEVELOPMENT DIVISION
Divisional Managers, Vanessa Scarborough; Sally
Burlington

CHILDREN IN CARE DIVISION
Divisional Manager, Cath Shaw

DEPARTMENTAL TRADE UNION
Chair, Chris Hickey

IMPLEMENTATION DIVISION
Divisional Manager, Jos Joures

SOCIAL EXCLUSION UNIT
Eland House, Bressenden Place, London SW1E 5DU
Tel: 020-7944 3160
Director, Claire Tyler

SUSTAINABLE COMMUNITIES DEVELOPMENT UNIT
Director-General, vacant

SUSTAINABLE COMMUNITIES DIRECTORATE
Director, Andrew Wells

URBAN POLICY DIRECTORATE
Director, David Lunts

RESIDENTIAL PROPERTY TRIBUNAL SERVICE
Senior President, Siobhan McGrath
Head of Corporate Unit, Michael Ross

EXECUTIVE AGENCIES

FIRE SERVICE COLLEGE
Moreton-in-Marsh, Gloucestershire, GL56 0RH
Tel: 01608-650831 Fax: 01608-651788
Web: www.fireservicecollege.ac.uk
The Fire Service College provides unique facilities for
both practical and theoretical fire fighting, fire safety and
accident and emergency training.
Chief Executive, A. R. Currie

ORDNANCE SURVEY
Romsey Road, Southampton SO16 4GU
Tel: 023-8079 2000 Fax: 023-8079 2615
Web: www.ordsvy.gov.uk
The Ordnance Survey department carries out official
surveying and definitive mapping of Great Britain.
Chief Executive, V. Lawrence

PLANNING INSPECTORATE
Temple Quay House, 2 The Square, Temple Quay,
Bristol BS1 6PN
Helpline: 0117-372 6372
Crown Buildings, Cathays Park, Cardiff CF10 3NQ
Tel: 029-2082 3866 Fax: 029-2082 5150
Web: www.planning-inspectorate.gov.uk
The Inspectorate deals with appeals against the decisions
of local authorities on planning applications and appeals
against local authority enforcement notices. It also
provides inspectors to hold inquiries into objections to
local authority planning.
Chief Executive, Katrine Sporle

THE QUEEN ELIZABETH II CONFERENCE CENTRE
Broad Sanctuary, London SW1P 3EE
Tel: 020-7222 5000 Fax: 020-7798 4200
Web: www.qeiicc.co.uk
The Centre provides secure conference facilities for
national and international government and private sector
use.
Chief Executive, John McCarthy

THE RENT SERVICE
5 Welbeck Street, London W1G 9YQ
Tel: 020-7023 6000 Fax: 020-7023 6220
Web: www.therentservice.gov.uk
The Agency combines 77 independent units previously
administered by local authorities.
Chief Executive, Miss C. Copeland

DEPARTMENT FOR CONSTITUTIONAL AFFAIRS (DCA)

Selborne House, 54–60 Victoria Street, London SW1E 6QW
Tel: 020-7210 8500
Web: www.dca.gov.uk

The Department for Constitutional Affairs was created on 12 June 2003, as part of the Government's drive to modernise the constitution. It brings together what had been most of the Lord Chancellor's Department, the UK devolution settlements and, for administrative purposes only, the staff of the Scotland Office and the Wales Office. The new department is charged with building fair, effective and accessible justice services, which contribute towards a safe and secure society and protect the rights of citizens; and to modernise the law and constitution. Among its principal responsibilities are: in partnership with the Home Office and the Crown Prosecution Service to deliver an effective criminal justice system; in partnership with the Home Office to improve the effectiveness of the asylum system; to reform the constitution, in particular establishing a Supreme Court, and a Judicial Appointments Commission; to effectively manage the courts and many tribunals; until the appointment of the Commission, to undertake the appointment and training of the judiciary; to provide legal aid and legal services to help tackle social exclusion; to oversee the legal services market, including regulation and competition; to reform and revise English civil law particularly in the fields of freedom of information, privacy and data sharing, human rights, reform of the House of Lords, the constitutional relationship with the Channel Islands and the Isle of Man, royal, church and hereditary issues, electoral law and policy, referenda and Party funding.

The Department employs over 11,500 civil servants, over 10,000 of whom work in courts and tribunals throughout the country. It includes a number of related bodies: the Law Commission; the Judicial Studies Board; the Official Solicitor and Public Trustee; the Legal Services Ombudsman; the Judge Advocate General's Office; the Magistrates Court Inspectorate; the Commission for Judicial Appointments; the Information Commissioner's Office and the Council on Tribunals. It is the sponsor department for the Legal Services Commission. The Secretary of State for Constitutional Affairs is also responsible for the Land Registry, the Public Record Office, and the Court Service in Northern Ireland. The Scotland and Wales Offices continue to exist under the umbrella of the Department for Constitutional Affairs but report to the Secretaries of State for Scotland and Wales respectively.

Secretary of State for Constitutional Affairs and Lord Chancellor, The Rt. Hon. The Lord Falconer of Thoroton, QC
Principal Private Secretary, Sarah Albon
Special Adviser, Gary Hart
Parliamentary Private Secretaries, Laura Moffat, MP; Geraint Davis, MP
Parliamentary Under-Secretary, David Lammy, MP
Private Secretary, Paul Zimmerman
Parliamentary Under-Secretary, Christopher Leslie, MP
Private Secretary, Grant Morris
Parliamentary Under-Secretary, Lord Filkin, CBE
Private Secretary, David Liddemore
Permanent Secretary, Sir Hayden Phillips, KCB
Private Secretary, Jade Cortes

PERMANENT SECRETARY'S OFFICE
Clerk of the Crown in Chancery, Sir Hayden Phillips, KCB
Deputy Clerk of the Crown in Chancery, vacant
Clerk of the Chamber and Head of the Crown Office, C. I. P. Denyer

COMMUNICATIONS GROUP
Selbourne House, 54/60 Victoria Street, London SW1E 6QW
Tel: 020-7210 2022
Director of Communications, Alan Percival, LVO
Head of External Communications, Mike Wicksteed

CLIENTS AND POLICY GROUP
Tel: 020-7210 2022
Director-General (SCS), Dr J. Spencer
Director, Civil Justice and Legal Services Directorate, D. Nooney
Director, Criminal Justice Directorate, N. Smedley
Director, Constitution, A. McDonald
Director, Public and Private Rights Directorate, A. Finlay
Heads of Divisions, Kay Birch; Keith Budgen; B. Clark; Ms S. Field; Ms S. Johnson; Judith Simpson; E. Adams; John Sills; Edwin Kilby; Belinda Crowe; M. de Pulford; A. Frazer; A. Maultby; Ms M. Shaw; B. Taylor

FINANCE
Selbourne House, 54/60 Victoria Street, London SW1E 6QW
Tel: 020-7210 2801
Director-General, S. Ball
Director of Facilities Management, C. Lyne
Principal Finance Officer, A. Cogbill
Head of Internal Audit, A. Rummins

LEGAL AND JUDICIAL SERVICES
Tel: 020-7210 2810
Directors-General, John Lyon; P. Jenkins
Heads of Divisions, A. Shaw *(Courts Policy);* J. Powell *(Competitions (Courts));* P. Farmer *(Information and Planning);* R. Sams *(Competitions, Tribunals);* D. Staff *(Pay, Pensions and Terms and Conditions);* Ms M. Pigott and Ms J. Killick *(Policy and Correspondence);* P. Fish *(Legal Advice and Litigation);* R. Heaton *(Constitutional Law);* Ms C. Johnston *(Legal Advice and Legislation);* P. G. Harris *(Legal Services Development);* M. Collon *(Drafting Services);* A. Wallace *(International)*

CHIEF EXECUTIVE OPERATIONS
Southside, 105 Victoria Street, London SW1E 6QT
Tel: 020-7210 2177
Chief Executive Operations and Second Permanent Secretary, Ian Magee

CHIEF EXECUTIVE AND DIRECTOR FIELD SERVICES
Southside, 105 Victoria Street, London SW1E 6QT
Tel: 020-7210 1808
Acting Chief Executive, Peter Handcock
Directors, Kevin Pogson; Keith Budgen; Ian Hyams; Kevin Sadler

ECCLESIASTICAL PATRONAGE
10 Downing Street, London SW1S 2AA
Tel: 020-7930 4433

CROWN OFFICE
House of Lords, London SW1A 0PW
Tel: 020-7219 4713

SUPREME COURT GROUP
Strand, London WC2A 2LL
Tel: 020-7947 6000

EXECUTIVE AGENCIES

THE COURT SERVICE
Southside, 105 Victoria Street, London SW1E 6QT
Tel: 020-7210 1646 Fax: 020-7210 2059
Web: www.courtservice.gov.uk
The Court Service provides administrative support to the Supreme Court, the Crown Court, county courts and a number of tribunals in England and Wales.
Chief Executive (acting), P. Handcock
Director of Purchasing and Contract Management (SCS), C. Lyne
Director of Information Services and Communications Technologies (SCS), Ms A. Vernon
Director of Human Resources (acting) (SCS), Ms H. Dudley
Programme Delivery Directors (SCS), D. Barr; J. Lane
Head of Magistrates' Courts Administrative Division (SCS), N. Haighton
Programme Director Magistrates' Courts IT Division and LIBRA Project (SCS), N. Haighton
Director of Tribunals (SCS), S. Smith

HM LAND REGISTRY
32 Lincoln Inn Fields, London WC2A 3PH
Tel: 020-7917 8888

NATIONAL ARCHIVES
Ruskin Avenue, Kew, Surrey TW9 4DU
Tel: 020-8876 3444

PUBLIC GUARDIANSHIP OFFICE
Archway Tower, 2 Junction Road, London N19 5AZ
Tel: 0845-330 2900

DEPARTMENT FOR CULTURE, MEDIA AND SPORT

2–4 Cockspur Street, London SW1Y 5DH
Tel: 020-7211 6200 Fax: 020-7211 6032
Web: www.culture.gov.uk
The Department for Culture, Media and Sport was established in July 1997 and is responsible for Government policy relating to the arts, broadcasting, press freedom and regulation, the film and music industries, museums and galleries, libraries, architecture and the historic environment, sport and recreation, tourism, the National Lottery, gambling, and alcohol and entertainment licensing.
Secretary of State for Culture, Media and Sport, The Rt. Hon. Tessa Jowell, MP
Principal Private Secretary, Hugh Ind
Special Advisers, Nick Bent, Bill Bush
Parliamentary Private Secretary, Gordon Marsden, MP
Minister of State, The Rt. Hon. Estelle Morris, MP *(Arts)*
Private Secretary, David McLaren
Parliamentary Private Secretary, Dr Howard Stoate, MP
Minister of State, The Rt. Hon. Richard Caborn, MP
(Sport and Tourism)
Private Secretary, Graeme Cornell
Parliamentary Private Secretary, Ben Chapman, MP
Parliamentary Under-Secretary, The Rt. Hon. The Lord

McIntosh of Haringey *(Media and Heritage)*
Private Secretary, Gareth Maybury
Permanent Secretary (SCS), Sue Street

STRATEGY AND COMMUNICATIONS DIRECTORATE
Head of Group (SCS), Siobhan Kenny
Head of News (SCS), Paddy Feeny
Head of Education and Social Policy, Phil Clapp
Head of Promotions and Publicity, Graham Newsom
Head of Strategy, Policy, and Delivery, David Roe

CORPORATE SERVICES GROUP
Head of Group (SCS), Nicholas Kroll
Head, Finance and Planning Division (SCS), Keith Smith
Head, Internal Audit, Michael Kirk
Head, Personnel and Central Services Division (SCS), Paul Heron
Head, Public Appointments and Honours, Janet Evans

ARTS AND CULTURE DIRECTORATE
Head of Group (SCS), Alan Davey
Director, Government Art Collection (SCS), Penny Johnson
Head, Arts Division, vacant
Head, Architecture and Historic Environment Division (SCS), Michael Seeney
Head, Cultural Property, Hillary Bauer
Head, Museums and Cultural Property (SCS), Bryony Lodge
Head, Museums and Libraries Sponsorship, Richard Hartman

CREATIVE INDUSTRIES, BROADCASTING AND GAMBLING GROUP
Head of Group (SCS), Andrew Ramsay
Head, Broadcasting Division (SCS), Jon Zeff
Head, Creative Industries Division (SCS), vacant
Head, Gambling and National Lottery Licensing, Elliot Grant
Head, National Lottery Distribution and Communities (SCS), Simon Broadley

TOURISM, LIBRARIES AND COMMUNITIES DIRECTORATE
Head of Group, Brian Leonard
Head, Libraries and Communities (SCS), Mark Ferrero
Head, Tourism Division (SCS), Harry Reeves

SPORT DIRECTORATE
Head of Group (SCS), Alec McGivan
Head, Olympic Games Unit (SCS), David Bawden
Head, Sports Division (SCS), Robert Raine

EXECUTIVE AGENCY

ROYAL PARKS AGENCY
The Old Police House, Hyde Park, London W2 2UH
Tel: 020-7298 2000 Fax: 020-7298 2005
The agency is responsible for maintaining and developing the royal parks.
Chief Executive (G5), William Weston, MVO

DEPARTMENT FOR EDUCATION AND SKILLS

Sanctuary Buildings, Great Smith Street, London SW1P 3BT
Tel: 0870-001 2345 Fax: 020-7925 6000
Email: info@dfes.gsi.gov.uk
Web: www.dfes.gov.uk
Caxton House, Tothill Street, London SW1H 9NA

Tel: 020-7273 3000 Fax: 020-7273 5124
Castle View House, East Lane, Runcorn WA7 2GJ
Tel: 0114-275 3275 Fax: 0114-259 4724
Mowden Hall, Staindrop Road, Darlington DL3 9BG
Tel: 0870-001 2345
Moorfoot, Sheffield S1 4PQ

The Department for Education and Skills aims to help build a competitive economy and inclusive society by creating opportunities for everyone to develop their learning potential and achieve excellence in standards of education and levels of skills. The department's main objectives are to give children an excellent start in education and enable young people and adults to develop and equip themselves with the skills, knowledge and personal qualities needed for life and work.

The Department also sponsors eleven non-departmental public bodies across a variety of professional disciplines and educational services.

Secretary of State for Education and Skills, The Rt. Hon. Charles Clarke, MP
Principal Private Secretary, Chris Wormald
Private Secretaries, Jenny Loosley; Jane Whitfield; Dean Creamer
Special Advisers, Lisa Tremble; Robert Hill
Parliamentary Private Secretary, Gareth Richard Thomas, MP
Minister of State for School Standards, David Miliband, MP
Private Secretary, Nick Carson
Parliamentary Private Secretary, Ian Cawsey, MP
Minister of State for Lifelong Learning, Further and Higher Education, Alan Johnson, MP
Private Secretary, Jo Ware
Parliamentary Private Secretary, Mike Foster, MP
Minister of State for Children, Margaret Hodge, MBE, MP
Private Secretary, Claire Carroll
Parliamentary Private Secretary, vacant
Parliamentary Under-Secretary of State for Schools, Stephen Twigg, MP
Private Secretary, Kathryn McManus
Parliamentary Under-Secretary of State for Sure Start, The Baroness Catherine Ashton of Upholland
Private Secretary, Luke O'Shea
Parliamentary Under-Secretary of State for Young People and Adult Skills, Ivan Lewis, MP
Private Secretary, Jo Bewley
Permanent Secretary, David Normington, CB
Private Secretary, Claudette Sutton
Head of Strategy and Innovation Unit, Anne Jackson
Parliamentary Clerk, John Major
Spokesman in the House of Lords, Baroness Ashton of Upholland

STRATEGY AND COMMUNICATIONS DIRECTORATE (SCD)
Director, M. Stevenson
Heads of Divisions, T. Cook *(Press Office)*; D.-J. Collins *(News)*
Divisional Managers, Ms Y. Diamond *(Corporate Communications)*; J. Ross *(Publicity)*; M. Haroon *(Regional Policy)*

SCHOOLS DIRECTORATE
Director-General, P. Housden
Head of Schools Communication Unit, R. Graham
Divisional Managers, Ms C. Bienkowska *(Strategy and Performance)*

SECONDARY EDUCATION GROUP
Director, P. Wanless
Divisional Managers, Ms S. Todd *(School Diversity)*; N. Flint *(Academies Division)*; B. Shaw *(School Improvement and Excellence)*; J. Coles *(London Challenge Programme)*

STANDARDS AND EFFECTIVENESS UNIT
Director, D. Hopkins
Director of Innovation Unit, M. Gibbons
Leadership and Teacher Development, R. Harrison
Divisional Managers, A. McCully *(Pupil Standards)*; D. Woods *(Transforming Standards Advisers)*; N. Baxter *(School Performance and Accountability)*

RESOURCES, INFRASTRUCTURE AND GOVERNANCE GROUP
Director, S. Crowne
Divisional Managers, Ms C. Macready *(School Admissions, Organisation and Governance)*; A. Wye *(School and LEA Funding)*; Ms S. Brooks *(Schools Capital and Buildings)*; M. Patel *(Schools Building and Design Unit)*

SCHOOL WORKFORCE UNIT
Director, S. Kershaw
Deputy Directors, S. Edwards; S. Hillier; G. Holley
Deputy Director, Local Implementation, R. Blows
Deputy Director, Local Standards Policy, R. Woods

CHILDREN AND FAMILIES GROUP
Director, T. Jeffery
Divisional Managers, Ms S. Scales, I. Whitehouse *(Improving Behaviour and Attendance)*; M. Phipps *(Schools Plus)*; Ms P. Jones *(Pupil Support and Independent Schools)*; Ms A. Gross *(Special Education Needs)*; Ms A. Burns *(Ethnic Minority Achievement Project)*

SURE START UNIT
Director, Ms N. Eisenstadt
Divisional Managers, A. Cranston *(Quality and Standards)*; Ms T. Finkelstein *(Strategy)*; Ms J. Doughty *(Operations)*; N. Tooze *(Infrastructure)*

CHILDREN AND YOUNG PEOPLE'S UNIT
Director, Ms A. Efunshile
Deputy Director, Policy and Strategy, Ms S. Lewis
Assistant Director, Local Partnerships, Ms K. Bundred
Assistant Director, Preventative Strategies and Systems, Ms H. Bennett

PRIMARY EDUCATION AND E-LEARNING GROUP
Director, Ms H. Williams
Divisional Managers, Ms M. Watts *(Curriculum)*; D. Brown; *(ICT in Schools)*; M. Conway *(PE and School Sport and Club Links Project)*

YOUTH DIRECTORATE
Director-General, P. Shaw
Divisional Managers, Ms D. Laurillard *(E-Learning Strategy Unit)*; J. Temple *(Strategy and Funding)*

CONNEXIONS SERVICE NATIONAL UNIT
Chief Executive, Ms A. Weinstock
Divisional Managers, Ms J. Pugh *(Strategy and Communications)*; G. McKenzie *(Operational Policy)*; S. Jackson *(Delivery and Quality)*; Ms J. Haywood *(Activities for Young People and Volunteering)*

QUALIFICATIONS AND YOUNG PEOPLE
Director, R. Hull
Divisional Managers, Ms S. Marshall *(Qualifications for Work);* Ms C. Johnson *(School and College Qualifications);* T. Fellowes *(Young People Learner Support);* A. Davies *(Young People's Policy);* Ms J. Benham *(Examinations System);* Ms C. Hunter *(Youth Co-ordination);* Ms L. Dale *(Review of Post-Qualifications Admissions to HE)*

JOINT INTERNATIONAL UNIT
Director, C. Tucker
Divisional Managers, W. Harris *(European Union);* Ms J. Evans *(European Social Fund);* Ms M. Niven *(International Relations)*

LIFELONG LEARNING DIRECTORATE (LLD)
Director-General, Ms J. Shiner
Divisional Managers, A. Clarke *(Prisoners' Learning and Skills Unit);* J. Temple *(Lifelong Learning Directorate and Youth Directorate)*

ADULT BASIC SKILLS STRATEGY UNIT
Director, Ms S. Pember
Deputy Directors, M. Dawe *(Planning and Delivery);* B. Brooks *(Standards and Achievement)*

ADULT LEARNING GROUP
Director, S. Marston
Divisional Managers, T. Down *(Access to Learning for Adults);* Ms M. Bennett *(Lifelong Learning and Technologies);* S. Perryman *(Skills for Employment);* H. Tollyfield *(Workplace Learning);* Ms S. Orr *(ILA Project);* Ms M. Durie *(Review of Funding of Adult Learning);* Ms J. Mark-Lawson *(ITB Review)*

STUDENT FINANCE GROUP
Director and HE Adviser, N. Sanders, CB
Divisional Managers, P. Swift *(Student Finance Policy);* I. Morrison *(Student Finance Delivery);* Ms N. Graham *(Student Finance Modernisation);* C. Barnham *(Delivery and Strategy Overview);* Ms L. Longstone *(HE Bill Team)*

HIGHER EDUCATION STRATEGY AND IMPLEMENTATION GROUP
Acting Director, M. Hipkins
Divisional Managers, S. Geary *(Foundation Degrees, Employability and Progression Division);* P. Cohen *(Quality and Participation);* Ms R. Green *(Funding and Research);* M. Williams *(Access and Modernisation)*

LEARNING DELIVERY AND STANDARDS GROUP
Director, P. Lauener
Divisional Managers, P. Mucklow *(FE Strategy);* J. Turner *(LSC Unit);* E. Galvin *(Provider Plus);* Ms L. Dale *(Financial and Management Systems Review of the LSC)*

STANDARDS UNIT
Director, Ms J. Williams
Divisional Managers, Ms H. Adcock *(Workforce Development);* D. Taylor *(Teaching and Learning and Success for All Programme Management)*

CORPORATE SERVICES AND DEVELOPMENT DIRECTORATE
Director-General, Ms S. Thomas

Divisional Managers, G. Archer *(Leadership and Personnel);* Ms A.-M. Lawlor *(Change);* M. Daly *(Learning Academy);* C. Moore *(Information Services);* P. Neill *(Commercial Services);* Ms J. Stockwell *(Equality and Diversity Unit);* Ms K. Driver *(e-Delivery)*

LEGAL ADVISER'S OFFICE
Legal Adviser, J. Jones
Divisional Managers, D. Aries *(Lifelong Learning and School Workforce);* F. Clarke *(Effectiveness and Admissions);* P. Kilgarriff *(Governance and Finance);* N. Ash *(Special Needs and Curriculum);* Ms C. Davies *(Equality, Establishment and European Commission);* Ms C. Geist-Divver *(Higher Education and Student Support)*

FINANCE AND ANALYTICAL SERVICES DIRECTORATE (FASD)
Director-General, P. Makeham
Divisional Managers, Ms S. Orr *(Internal Audit);* R. Hinchcliffe *(Programme and Project Management Unit)*

FINANCE
Director, Ms R. Thompson
Divisional Managers, P. Houten *(Finance Strategy);* Ms M. Maddox *(Corporate Planning and Performance);* P. Connor, CBE *(Financial Accounting)*

ANALYTICAL SERVICES
Director, P. Johnson
Divisional Managers, M. Britton *(Qualifications, Pupil Assessment and IT);* J. Elliot *(Central Economics and International);* Ms K. Hancock *(Higher Education);* B. Butcher *(Adults);* T. Moody *(Youth);* Ms A. Brown *(Schools 1);* R. Bartholomew *(Schools 2)*

DEPARTMENT FOR ENVIRONMENT, FOOD AND RURAL AFFAIRS

Nobel House, 17 Smith Square, London SW1P 3JR
Tel: 020-7238 3000 Fax: 020-7238 6591
Web: www.defra.gov.uk

The Department for Environment, Food, and Rural Affairs is responsible for Government policies on agriculture, horticulture and fisheries in England and for policies relating to the food chain. In association with the agriculture departments of the Scottish Executive, the National Assembly for Wales and the Northern Ireland Office, and with the Intervention Board, the department is responsible for negotiations in the EU on the common agricultural and fisheries policies, and for single European market questions relating to its responsibilities. Its remit also includes international agricultural and food trade policy.

The department exercises responsibilities for policies on climate change and international negotiations on sustainable development. It is also responsible for a range of pollution issues relating to waste and recycling, the protection and enhancement of the countryside and the marine environment, flood defence, GM crops, hunting, rural development and other rural issues. It is the licensing authority for veterinary medicines and the registration authority for pesticides. It administers policies relating to the control of animal, plant and fish diseases. It provides scientific, technical and professional services and advice to farmers, growers and ancillary industries, and commissions research to assist in the formulation and assessment of policy and to underpin applied research and development work done by industry. Responsibility for food safety and standards was

transferred to the Food Standards Agency in April 2000.
Secretary of State for Environment, Food and Rural Affairs,
The Rt. Hon. Margaret Beckett, MP
Principal Private Secretary (G7), Gavin Ross
Private Secretaries, Robin Healey; Janice Kerr;
Marianne Jenner
Special Advisers, Sheila Watson; Nicci Collins
Parliamentary Private Secretary, Andy Reed, MP
Minister of State (Environment and Agri-Environment),
Elliot Morley, MP
Private Secretaries, Robert Hitchin; Bradley Bates
Assistant Private Secretaries, Liam McAleese;
Katrina McLeay
Minister of State (Rural Affairs and Urban Quality of Life),
The Rt. Hon. Alun Michael, MP
Private Secretaries, Mike Burbridge; Rory Wallace
Assistant Private Secretaries, Louise Parry; Lewis Mortimer
Parliamentary Private Secretary, Peter Bradley, MP
*Parliamentary Under-Secretary (Nature Conservation and
Fisheries),* Ben Bradshaw, MP
Principal Private Secretary, Kathleen Cameron
Private Secretary, Jodie Tremelling
Assistant Secretary, Richard Wollack
*Parliamentary Under-Secretary (Farming, Food and
Sustainable Energy),* The Lord Whitty of Camberwell
Senior Private Secretary, Charlotte Middleton
Private Secretary, Emily Garner
Assistant Private Secretaries, Fiona Tranter;
Haroona Chughtai
Permanent Secretary (SCS), Brian Bender, CB
Private Secretary, Suzie Daykin
Assistant Private Secretary, Alison Thomas

FOOD, FARMING AND FISHERIES DIRECTORATE
GENERAL
9 Millbank, c/o Nobel House, 17 Smith Square, London
SW1P 3JR Tel: 020-7238 3000
Director-General, Andrew Lebrecht

EU AND INTERNATIONAL POLICY
Director, David Hunter
Heads of Division, David Dawson; Tom Eddy

SUSTAINABLE AGRICULTURE AND LIVESTOCK
PRODUCTS DIRECTORATE
Director, Sonia Phippard
Heads of Division, Nigel Atkinson; Ivor Llewelyn;
Dr Mike Segal; Andrew Slade

FOOD INDUSTRY AND CROPS DIRECTORATE
Director, John Robbs
Heads of Division, Judy Allfrey; Nicholas Denton;
David Jones; Andrew Kuyk; Callton Young;
Heather Hamilton; Dr Stephen Hunter

FISHERIES DIRECTORATE
Fisheries Director, Stephen Wentworth
Heads of Division, Peter Boyling; Richard Cowan;
Barry Edwards; Chris Ryder
Chief Inspector, Sea Fisheries Inspectorate, vacant

ECONOMICS AND STATISTICS DIRECTORATE
East Block, Whitehall Place, London SW1A 2HH
Tel: 020-7270 6000
Director, David Thompson
Heads of Division, Rachel Chandler; Simon Harding;
Peter Helm; Peter Muriel; Stuart Platt; John Watson

LAND USE AND RURAL AFFAIRS DIRECTORATE
GENERAL
Ergon House, c/o Nobel House, 17 Smith Square, London
SW1P 3JR Tel: 020-7238 3000
Director-General, Anna Walker, CB

LAND MANAGEMENT AND RURAL DEVELOPMENT
DIRECTORATE
Director, Jane Brown
Heads of Division, Ray Anderson; Peter Cleasby;
Martin Nesbit; Marcus Nisbet; John Osmond;
Andrew Perrins; Ann Tarran; Alan Taylor

RURAL ECONOMIES AND COMMUNITIES
DIRECTORATE
Director, Paul Elliott
Heads of Division, Christopher Braun; David Coleman;
Graham Cory; Christopher Dunabin; Lindsay Harris

WILDLIFE, COUNTRYSIDE AND FLOOD MANAGEMENT
DIRECTORATE
Director, Sophia Lambert
Heads of Division, Martin Brasher; Martin Capstick;
Susan Carter; Sarah Nason; Noel Cleary

ANIMAL HEALTH AND WELFARE DIRECTORATE
GENERAL
1A Page Street, London SW1P 4PQ
Tel: 020-7904 6000
Chief Veterinary Officer and Director-General,
Jim Scudamore
Deputy Chief Veterinary Officer, Dr Richard Cawthorne
Heads of Division, Nigel Gibbens; Fred Landeg;
Ruth Lysons; David Pritchard; Alick Simmons;
Peter Soul; David Bench

ANIMAL HEALTH AND WELFARE DIRECTORATE
Director, Neil Thornton
Heads of Division, Roy Hathaway; George Noble;
Jill Wordley; Malcolm Hunt

TSE GROUP
Director, Peter Nash
Heads of Division, Mandy Bailey; Catharine Boyle;
Sue Eades; Francis Marlow

ENVIRONMENT PROTECTION DIRECTORATE
GENERAL
Ashdown House, 123 Victoria Street, London SW1E 6DE
Tel: 020-7944 3000
Director-General, Bill Stow, CB

ENVIRONMENT QUALITY AND WASTE DIRECTORATE
Director, Richard Bird
Heads of Division, Sue Ellis; Bob Ryder; Martin Williams;
Lindsay Cornish

CLIMATE, ENERGY AND ENVIRONMENTAL RISK
DIRECTORATE
Director, Henry Derwent
Heads of Division, Colin Church; Jeremy Eppel;
Sarah Hendry; Duncan Prior; Richard Wood

ENVIRONMENTAL PROTECTION STRATEGY
DIRECTORATE
Director, Robert Lowson
Heads of Division, Scott Ghagan; Stephen Claughton;
John Custance; Bob Davies; Sheila
McCabe/Christopher Whaley; Helen Marquard;
Bronwen Jones

WATER AND LAND DIRECTORATE
Director, John Ballard, CB
Heads of Division, Rodney Anderson; Daniel Instone;
John Roberts; Prof. Jeni Colbourne

SOLICITOR AND LEGAL SERVICES DIRECTORATE
GENERAL
Solicitor and Director-General Legal Services, Donald
Macrae
Directors, Stephen Parker; Frances Nash
Heads of Division, Charles Allen; Chris Burke; John
Comber; Ian Corbett; Peter Davis; Brian Dickinson;
Colin Gregory; Nigel Lefton; Alistair McGlone; Mayur
Patel; Jonathan Robinson; Sue Spence; Anne Werbicki
Chief Investigation Officer, Jan Panting

SCIENCE DIRECTORATE
Cromwell House, Dean Stanley Street, London SW1P 3JH
Tel: 020-7238 6000
Chief Scientific Adviser and Head of Directorate,
Prof. Howard Dalton, FRS
Deputy Chief Scientific Adviser, Miles Parker
Heads of Division, Dr Tony Burne; Dr Nick Coulson;
Dr John Sherlock

OPERATIONS AND SERVICE DELIVERY DIRECTORATE
GENERAL
1A Page Street, London SW1P 4PQ Tel: 020-7904 6000
Director-General, Mark Addison

VETERINARY SERVICES
1A Page Street, London SW1P 4PQ Tel: 020-7904 6000
Deputy Chief Veterinary Officer (Services),
Martin Atkinson
Heads of Veterinary Services, John Cross *(West);*
Robert Paul *(North);* Gareth Jones *(East);*
Derick McIntosh *(Scotland)*
Chief Veterinary Officer (Scotland), Charles Milne
Assistant Veterinary Officer (Wales), Tony Edwards
Head of Veterinary Resource Team, Betty Philip
Service Delivery, Richard Drummond
Contingency Planning, Ann Waters

CORPORATE SERVICES DIRECTORATE
East Block, Whitehall Place, London SW1A 2HH
Tel: 020-7270 6000
Director, Richard Allen
Heads of Division, Bronwen Jones; Teresa Newell;
Wendy Cartwright; Tony Nickson; Caroline Smith

COMMUNICATIONS DIRECTORATE
Director of Communications, Lucian Hudson
Head of News, Martyn Smith
Head of Corporate Communications, Kelly Freeman

E-BUSINESS DIRECTORATE
Government Buildings, Epsom Road, Guildford, Surrey
GU1 2LD Tel: 01483-568121
Director, David Rossington
Director of IT, Shaun Soper

Heads of Division, Peter Barber; David Brown; Alan Hill;
David Myers

DELIVERY STRATEGY TEAM
1A Page Street, London SW1P 4PQ Tel: 020-7904 6000
Head, George Trevelyan

POLICY AND CORPORATE STRATEGY
Cromwell House, Dean Bradley Street, London SW1P 3JH
Tel: 020-7238 6000
Director, B. Harding
East of England, Building A, Westbrook Centre, Milton Road,
Cambridge, CB4 1YG Tel: 01223-346700 *Rural Director,*
J. Rabagliati
East Midlands, The Belgrave Centre, Talbot Street,
Nottingham, NG1 5GG *Rural Director,* G. Norbury
North East, Welbar House, Gallowgate, Newcastle-upon-Tyne,
NE1 4TD Tel: 0191-201 3300 *Rural Director,* J. Bainton
North West, Sunley Tower, Piccadilly Plaza, Manchester
M1 4BE Tel: 0161-952 4000 *Regional Director,*
N. Cumberlidge
South-East, Bridge House, 1 Walnut Tree Close, Guildford,
Surrey GU1 4GA Tel: 01483-882255 *Regional Director,*
Ms A. Parker
South-West, 4th and 5th Floors, The Pithay, Bristol BS1 2PB
Tel: 0117-900 1700 *Regional Director,* T. Render
West Midlands, 77 Paradise Circus, Queensway, Birmingham
B1 2DT Tel: 0121-212 5000 *Regional Director,* B. Davies
Yorkshire and the Humberside, PO Box 213, City House, New
Station Street, Leeds LS1 4US. Tel: 0113-280 0600
Regional Director, G. Kingston

RURAL DEVELOPMENT SERVICE
c/o Nobel House, 17 Smith Square, London
SW1P 3JR
Tel: 020-7238 3000
Head of Group, John Adams
Head of Technical Advice, Alan Hooper
Business Process Director, Jeff Robinson

RURAL DEVELOPMENT CENTRES
East, Block B, Government Buildings, Brooklands Avenue,
Cambridge CB2 2DR Tel: 01223-455968 *Regional Manager,*
Martin Edwards; *Regional Director,* Jane Rabagliati
East-Midlands, Block 7, Government Buildings, Chalfont
Drive, Nottingham NG8 3SN Tel: 0115-929 1191
Regional Manager, Sue Buckenham; *Regional Director,*
Graham Norbury
North-East, Government Buildings, Kenton Bar, Newcastle-
upon-Tyne NE5 3EW Tel: 0191-286 3377 *Regional
Manager,* Fiona Gough; *Regional Director,* John Bainton
North-West, Electra Way, Crewe Business Park, Crewe,
Cheshire, CW1 6GJ Tel: 01270-754000 *Regional Manager,*
Tony Percival; *Regional Director,* Neil Cumberlidge
South-East, Block A, Government Buildings, Coley Park,
Reading, Berkshire RG1 6DT Tel: 0118-9581 222 *Regional
Manager,* Nick Beard; *Regional Director,* Alison Parker
South-West, Block 3, Government Buildings, Burghill Road,
Westbury-on-Trym, Bristol BS10 6NJ Tel: 0117-959 1000
Regional Manager, David Sisson; *Regional Director,* Tim
Render
West Midlands, Block C, Government Buildings, Whittington
Road, Worcester WR5 2LQ Tel: 01905-763355 *Regional
Manager,* Carol Deakins; *Regional Director,* Brin Davies
Yorkshire and The Humber, Government Buildings, Otley
Road, Lawnswood Leeds, LS16 5QT Tel: 0113-230 3964
Regional Manager, Mike Silverwood; *Regional Director,*
Gordon Kingston

FINANCE, PLANNING AND RESOURCES DIRECTORATE
East Block, Whitehall Place, London SW1A 2HH
Tel: 020-7270 6000
Finance Director, Andrew Burchell
Deputy Director, Ian Grattidge
Heads of Division, Roger Atkinson; David Fisher; Julie Flint; David Rabey; Richard Wilkinson

POLICY AND CORPORATE STRATEGY UNIT
Cromwell House, Dean Bradley Street, London SW1P 3JH
Tel: 020-7238 6000
Director and Secretary to the Management Board,
   Francesca Okosi

EXECUTIVE AGENCIES

CENTRAL SCIENCE LABORATORY (CSL)
Sand Hutton, York YO41 1LZ
Tel: 01904-462000 Fax: 01904-462111
The Central Science Laboratory (CSL) provides advice, technical and enforcement support, underpinned by appropriate research, to meet both the statutory and policy objectives of DEFRA; it provides research development and advice on a commercial basis to other government departments and to public and private sector organisations both overseas and UK-based.
   CSL's main work areas are: safeguarding food supplies through the identification and control of invertebrate pests, plant pests and diseases; the management of vertebrate wildlife, food and consumer safety with the emphasis on the microbiological and chemical safety, and the quality and nutritional value of food.
   CSL is also concerned with environmental protection through the investigation of the impact of agriculture on the environment, and the promotion of biodiversity in agricultural habitats.
Chief Executive (G3), Prof. M. Roberts
Research Directors (G5), Prof. Tony Hardy *(Agriculture and Environment);* Prof. John Gilbert *(Food)*
Commercial Director, Dr Robert Bolton
Corporate Services Director, Dr Helen Crews
Finance and Procurement Director, Richard Shaw

CENTRE FOR ENVIRONMENT, FISHERIES AND AQUACULTURE SCIENCE
Pakefield Road, Lowestoft, Suffolk NR33 0HT
Tel: 01502-562244 Fax: 01502-513865
The Agency, established in April 1997, provides research and consultancy services in fisheries science and management, aquaculture, fish health and hygiene, environmental impact assessment, and environmental quality assessment.
Chief Executive, Dr P. Greig-Smith

PESTICIDES SAFETY DIRECTORATE
Mallard House, Kings Pool, 3 Peasholme Green, York YO1 7PX
Tel: 01904-640500 Fax: 01904-455733
The Pesticides Safety Directorate is responsible for the evaluation and approval of agricultural pesticides and the development of policies relating to them, in order to protect consumers, users and the environment.
Chief Executive (SCS), Dr H. K. Wilson
Director (Policy) (SCS), Dr S. Popple
Director (Approvals) (SCS), R. Davis
Director (Finance, IT, and Corporate Services),
   Ms K. Dyson

RURAL PAYMENTS AGENCY
Kings House, 33 Kings Road, Reading RG1 3BU
Tel: 0118-958 3626 Fax: 0118-959 7736
The Rural Payments Agency (RPA) is an executive agency of the Department for Environment, Food and Rural Affairs. It is the single paying agency responsible for Common Agricultural Policy (CAP) schemes in England and for certain schemes throughout the UK.
Chief Executive, J. McNeill
Director (Business) S. Vry
Director (CAP), A. Sutton
Director (Finance), A. Kerr
Director (Human Resources), R. Gregg
Director (IS), A. McDermott
Director (Operations), H. MacKinnon

VETERINARY LABORATORIES AGENCY
Woodham Lane, New Haw, Addlestone, Surrey KT15 3NB
Tel: 01932-341111 Fax: 01932-347046
The Veterinary Laboratories Agency safeguards public and animal health through world class veterinary research and surveillance of farmed livestock and wildlife.
Chief Executive, Prof. S. Edwards
Director of Finance, C. Morrey
Director of Research, Prof. J. A. Morris
Director of Surveillance and Laboratory Services,
   R. D. Hancock
Laboratory Secretary, C. Edwards

VETERINARY MEDICINES DIRECTORATE
Woodham Lane, New Haw, Addlestone, Surrey KT15 3LS
Tel: 01932-336911 Fax: 01932-336618
The Veterinary Medicines Directorate is responsible for all aspects of the authorisation and control of veterinary medicines, including post-authorisation surveillance of residues in animals and animal products, and the provision of policy advice to Ministers.
Chief Executive (G4), S. Dean
Director of Corporate Business (G6), C. Bean
Director (Licensing) (G5), D. Mackay
Director (Policy) (G5), J. Fitzgerald

FOREIGN AND COMMONWEALTH OFFICE
King Charles Street, London SW1A 2AH
Tel: 020-7270 1500 Web: www.fco.gov.uk
The Foreign and Commonwealth Office provides, through its staff in the UK and through its diplomatic missions abroad, the means of communication between the British Government and other governments and international governmental organisations on all matters falling within the field of international relations.
   It is responsible for alerting the British Government to the implications of developments overseas; for promoting British interests overseas; for protecting British citizens abroad; for explaining British policies to, and cultivating relationships with, governments overseas; for the discharge of British responsibilities to the overseas territories; for entry clearance UK Visas, with the Home Office and for promoting British business overseas (jointly with the Department of Trade and Industry through British Trade International).
Secretary of State for Foreign and Commonwealth Affairs,
   The Rt. Hon. Jack Straw, MP
Principal Private Secretary, Geoffrey Adams
Special Advisers, Michael Williams; Ed Owen
Parliamentary Private Secretary, Colin Pickthall, MP
Minister of State, Dr Denis MacShane, MP *(Europe)*

Private Secretary, David Dunn
Minister of State, The Rt. Hon. The Baroness Symons of Vernham Dean *(Middle East)*
Private Secretary, Nick Allan
Parliamentary Private Secretary, Charlotte Atkins, MP
Minister of State, Mike O'Brien, MP *(Trade and Foreign Affairs)*
Private Secretary, Peter Elder
Parliamentary Under-Secretary of State, Bill Rammell, MP
Private Secretary, David Whineray
Parliamentary Under-Secretary of State, Chris Mullin, MP
Private Secretary, Tom Fletcher
Permanent Under-Secretary of State and Head of HM Diplomatic Service, Sir Michael Jay, KCMG
Private Secretary, Menna Rawlings
Chief Executive, British Trade International, Sir Stephen Brown, KCVO
Deputy Under-Secretaries, Peter Collecott *(Chief Clerk);* Michael Arthur, CMG *(Economic Director);* Michael Wood, CMG *(Legal Adviser);* Peter Ricketts, CMG *(Political Director);* Stephen Wright, CMG *(Defence Intelligence);* Graham Fry *(Wider World)*

DIRECTORS
Africa, James Bevan
Americas/Overseas Territories, Robert Culshaw, MVO
Asia Pacific, Nigel Cox
Chief Executive FCO Services, Stephen Sage
Consular Services, Paul Sizeland
Finance, Simon Gass, CMG, CVO
Global Issues, Philippa Drew
Information, Dickie Stagg, CMG
International Security, Edward Oakden
Mediterranean, Europe Bilateral, Resources, Dominick Chilcott
Middle East and North Africa, Edward Chaplin, OBE
Personnel, Alan Charlton, CMG
South Asia, Tom Phillips, CMG
Strategy and Innovation, Simon Fraser
Wider Europe, Linda Duffield

SPECIAL REPRESENTATIVES
UK Special Representative for Afghanistan, Tom Phillips, CMG
UK Special Representative for Cyprus, Lord David Hannay, GCMG, CH
UK Special Representative for Georgia, Sir Brian Fall, KCMG
UK Special Representative for Sudan, Alan Goulty, CMG

HEADS OF DEPARTMENTS
Afghanistan Unit, Jan Thompson
Africa Department (Equatorial), Tim Hitchens
Africa Department (Southern), Dr Andrew Pocock
Aviation, Maritime and Energy Department, Andrew Levi
British Trade International, Mike O'Brien, MP *(Chairman)*
China/Hong Kong Department, Denis Keefe
Commonwealth Co-ordination, Asif Ahmad
Consular Assistance Group, Richard Morris
Consular Crisis Group, Ralph Publicover
Consular Service Quality Group, Tim Flear, MVO
Consular Resources Group, David Popplestone
Counter-Proliferation, Tim Dowse
Counter-Terrorism Policy Department, Rob Macaire
Cultural Relations Department, Dr M. Reilly
Diplomatic Service Families Association, E. Salvesen
Diplomatic Service Trade Union Side (DSTUS), S. Watson
Drugs and International Crime Department, Lesley Pallet

Eastern Department, Simon Butt
Eastern Adriatic Department, Karen Pierce, CVO
Economic Policy, Creon Butler
e-Media Unit, Moray Angus
Environment Policy, Valerie Caton
Estate Strategy, Julian Metcalfe
European Union Department (External), Tim Barrow, LVO, MBE
European Union Department (Internal), David Frost
Financial Compliance Unit, David Major
FCO Services, Stephen Sage *(Chief Executive);* James Clark *(Client Services);* Mike Blake *(Facilities Service Delivery);* Patrick Cullen *(ICT Service Delivery);* Dr Vanessa L. Davies *(People and Best Practice Service Delivery);* John Elgie *(Promotions and Events Service Delivery);* Rod Peters *(Supply Chain Service Delivery);* Kerry Simmonds *(Finance);* Elaine Kennedy *(Human Resources)*
Human Resources Directorate *(operational from January 2004 onwards and previously known as the Personnel Directorate),* Alan Charlton, CMG *(Head of HR Directorate);* Andy Heyn *(HR Direct);* Andrew George *(Health and Welfare Policy Team);* Diane Corner and Carole Sweeney *(Legal Policy Team);* David Powell *(Pay and Benefits);* Howard Drake *(Career Development and Senior Management);* Richard Tauwhare *(Training, Learning and Development);* Gerry Reffo *(Performance Assessment and Development);* Simon Pease *(Workforce Planning Team)*
Human Rights Policy, Jon Benjamin
Internal Audit (FCO/DFID), Jon Hews
IT Strategy Unit, Nick Westcott
Latin America Department, Stephen Williams
Legal Advisers, Michael Wood, CMG
Middle East Department, Charles Gray
Near East and North Africa Department, Nicholas Archer
North America Department, vacant
North-East Asia and Pacific Department, Simon Smith
Organisation for Security Co-operation in Europe, Peter January
Overseas Territories Department, Alan Huckle
Parliamentary Relations and Devolution, Matthew Hamlyn
Partnership and Networks Development Unit, Fraser Wheeler
Passports and Documentary Services Group, David Clegg, MVO
Press Office, John Williams *(Press Secretary);* Andrew Patrick *(Head of News Room)*
Procurement Policy, Michael Gower
Protocol Department, Charles de Chassiron, CVO
Public Diplomacy, Paul Madden
Records and Historical, Heather Yasamee
Research Analysis, Simon Buckle
Resource Accounting, Iain Morgan
Resource Budgeting, Tristan Price
Science and Technology, Fiona Clouder Richards
Security Strategy Unit, Peter Millett
Security Policy, Paul Johnston
South Asia, Stephen Smith
South-East Asian Department, Michael Reilly
Sudan, Dr Alistair McPhail
Trade Union Side, Stephen Watson *(TUS Chair);* Pam Chapman *(TUS Secretary)*
United Nations, William Harrison, CVO
UK Visas Joint Entry Clearance Unit (Joint FCO/Home Office Unit), Robin Barnett
Whitehall Liaison Department, Matthew Kidd

BRITISH TRADE INTERNATIONAL

BUSINESS GROUP
Group Director, Peter Tibber

INTERNATIONAL GROUP
Group Director, David Warren

REGIONAL GROUP
Group Director, Ian Jones

STRATEGY AND COMMUNICATIONS GROUP
Group Director, John Reynolds
Invest UK Chief Executive, William Pedder

EXECUTIVE AGENCIES

CORPS OF QUEEN'S MESSENGERS
Support Group, Foreign and Commonwealth Office, London
SW1A 2AH Tel: 020-7270 2779
Superintendent of the Corps of Queen's Messengers,
A. C. Brown
Queen's Messengers, P. Allen; R. Allen; Maj. A. N. D. Bols;
Maj. P. C. H. Dening-Smitherman; Sqn. Ldr. J. S.
Frizzell; Maj. D. A. Griffiths; Sqn Ldr A. Hill; R. Long;
Maj. K. J. Rowbottom; Maj. M. R. Senior; Maj. J. E. A.
Andre; W. Lisle; Maj. J. H. Steele; J. A. Hatfield; Sqn
Ldr P. J. Hearn; S. J. Addy; Lt.-Col. R. I. S. Burgess

WILTON PARK CONFERENCE CENTRE
Wiston House, Steyning, W. Sussex BN44 3DZ
Tel: 01903-815020 Fax: 01903-879647
Wilton Park organises international affairs conferences
and is hired out to Government departments and
commercial users.
Chief Executive, Colin Jennings

DEPARTMENT OF HEALTH
Richmond House, 79 Whitehall, London SW1A 2NL
Tel: 020-7210 3000
Web: www.doh.gov.uk
The Department of Health is responsible for the
provision of the National Health Service in England and
for social care. The department's aims are to support,
protect, promote and improve the nation's health; to
secure the provision of comprehensive, high quality care
for all those who need it, regardless of their ability to pay
or where they live or their age; and to provide responsive
social care and child protection for those who lack the
support they need.
Secretary of State for Health, The Rt. Hon. Dr John Reid, MP
Principal Private Secretary, Dominic Hardy
Private Secretaries, Helena Feinstein; Nicola Hewer
Assistant Secretaries, Susanne Rowe; Rachel Robertson
Special Advisers, Prof. Paul Corrigan; Darren Murphy
Parliamentary Private Secretary, Mike Hall, MP
Minister of State, The Rt. Hon. John Hutton, MP *(NHS and
Delivery)*
Private Secretary, Tony Sampson
Parliamentary Private Secretary, Claire Ward, MP
Minister of State, Rosie Winterton, MP *(Community)*
Private Secretary, Alistair Finney
Parliamentary Private Secretary, Andy Love, MP
Parliamentary Under-Secretary of State, Stephen Ladyman, MP
Private Secretary, Kevin Holton
Parliamentary Under-Secretary of State (Lords), Lord Warner
of Brockley
Acting Private Secretary, Catherine Davies

Parliamentary Under-Secretary of State (Health),
Melanie Johnson, MP
Acting Private Secretary, Emily Stott
Parliamentary Clerk, Neil Townley
Permanent Secretary (SCS), Sir Nigel Crisp
Private Secretaries, Sarah Fisher; Matthew Hamilton
Chief Medical Officer (SCS), Prof. Sir Liam Donaldson,
FRCSED, FRCPED
Private Secretary, Rachel Dickson
Deputy Chief Medical Officer, Prof. Aidan Halligan
Director of National Cancer Services, Prof. Michael
Richards, FRCP

CHIEF NURSING OFFICER'S DIRECTORATE
*Chief Nursing Officer and Director of Nursing–Private
Office London and Leeds,* Ms S. Mullally
Division Head, Ms F. Goldhill; P. Allanson
Assistant Chief Nursing Officer, Ms K. Billingham
Assistant Chief Nursing Officer, D. Moore
Branch Heads, A. Sheehan; R. Thompson; I. Berry;
Mrs S. White; Mrs K. East; Dr S. Hill; A. Sieff;
Ms A. Richardson; D. Mowat
Principal Medical Officer, Dr J. Graham

COMMUNICATIONS DIRECTORATE
Director of Communications, Ms S. Jarvis
Assistant Director of NHS Communications, R. Langford
Deputy Director of Marketing Communications Group,
W. Roberts
Head of Corporate Development, Mrs M. King
Assistant Director (News), J. Hibbs
Deputy Director of Strategic Communications, J. Worne
Assistant Director of Strategy and Planning, S. Pollock
Assistant Director of External Relations, A. Millward

DIRECTORATE OF ACCESS AND CHOICE
Director of Access and Choice, Ms M. Edwards
Head of Capacity, Plurality and Choice, B. Ricketts
Branch Heads; R. Webster; P. Jenkins; M. Svenson;
K. Smith; M. Davies; Ms L. Fleck; Mrs A. Phillips;
R. Cienciala; J. Peers

DIRECTORATE OF CHILDREN, OLDER PEOPLE AND
SOCIAL CARE SERVICES
Chief Inspector, Ms D. Platt, CBE
Deputy Chief Inspector (SSI), Ms A. Nottage
Deputy Director and Head of Social Care Policy,
G. Denham
Director of the Change Agent Team, R. Humphries
National Clinical Director for Children, Prof. A. Aynsley-
Green
National Director for Older People's Services, Prof. I. Philp
Branch Heads, Mrs A. Smith; D. Holmes; Ms K. Tyson;
B. Clark; Ms J. Grauberg; Ms J. Shersby; Mrs C.
Phillips; R. Campbell; A. McNeil; Miss H. Robinson;
C. Muir; Ms C. Brock; J. Stopes-Roe
SSI Directors, G. Mason; J. Fraser; Ms L. Hoare; J. Phillips;
M. Rourke; P. Brearley; J. Cypher; Mrs J. Owen; S. Pitt;
J. Bolton *(Consultant)*

DIRECTORATE OF CORPORATE AFFAIRS
Director of External and Corporate Affairs, H. Taylor
Division Heads, D. Clark; Ms E. Al-Khalifa; A. McKeon;
Ms O. Senior; Dr A. Holt; Ms L. Percival; Dr F. Harvey;
I. Ellul; Miss A. Simkins; Mrs K. Barnard;
Ms C. Moriarty
Branch Heads, Dr J. Smith; Ms J. Howe; Dr P. Clappison;
C. Dobson; Prof. C. Ham; J. Middleton; Ms J. Taylor;

M. Collyer; B. Mussenden; Ms L. Yee; M. Rainsford;
C. Horsey; Mrs L. Wishart; Mrs J. Dainty; A. Angilley;
S. Gallagher; K. Guinness; M. Brownlee; R. Carter;
Ms C. Dowse; Dr G. Lee; Miss S. Fathers; S. Fuchs;
Mrs P. Parr; Ms M. Furr; Mrs S. Lake (Consultant);
D. McNeil; G. Wilmore; Ms M. Field; Mrs J. Hickling;
Ms A. Humphrey; S. Barnsley; T. Baxter;
Mrs H. Shirley-Quirk; Mrs S. Gallagher

FINANCE AND INVESTMENT DIRECTORATE
Director of Finance, R. Douglas
Director of Counter Fraud Services, J. Gee
Branch Heads, J. Tomlinson; P. Kendall; A. MacLellan;
B. Burleigh; P. Coates; Ms L. Eccles; R. Smith;
M. Campbell

MODERNISATION AGENCY
Director of Modernisation Agency, D. Fillingham
Head of National Primary Care Development Team,
Dr J. Oldham
Director of NHS Collaboratives, Ms S. Howard
Director of NHS Leadership Centre, Ms P. Humphris
*Chief Executive of National Institute for Mental Health in
England,* A. Sheehan
Director of New Ways of Working, Ms J. Hargadon
Head of Human Resources, Mrs C. Corrigan
Director National Programme, Health and Social Care,
Ms C. Pond
Head of National Patients Access Team, M. Scott
Consultant, M. Davidge
Branch Heads; Dr S. Lowden; Dr V. Day; Dr K. Harmond,
Dr P. Zollinger-Read *(Consultant);* B. Gowland
(Consultant); Prof. H. Bevan; N. Patten; Dr I. Rutter;
Ms M. Haines; R. Jeffries; J. Mooney; Ms J. Copeland;
Mrs C. Smith; Ms L. Postle; Mrs A. Imison, OBE;
R. Greig; Ms M. Lawless

NHS HUMAN RESOURCES DIRECTORATE
Director of Human Resources, A. Foster
Deputy Directors of Human Resources, M. Staniforth;
D. Amos
*Deputy Director of Human Resources and Head of Learning
and Personnel Development Division,* Prof. M. Pearson
Branch Heads, R. Mundon; P. Loveland; J. Ennis; Ms H.
Fields; Ms S. Goulding; Ms D. Mellor, OBE; B. Dyson;
T. Sands; Dr P. Leech; Mrs G. Redhead; I. Dodge;
M. Sturges; D. Royles

PUBLIC HEALTH AND CLINICAL QUALITY
DIRECTORATE
*Director of Public Health and Clinical Quality Directorate;
Chief Medical Officer,* Sir Liam Donaldson
Deputy Chief Medical Officer (Public Health), vacant
Head of Clinical Quality (Ethics and Genetics), vacant
Head of Public Health Division, Prof. D. Nutbeam
Branch Heads, N. Dean; Ms L. Woodeson; Ms J. Walden;
N. Boyd; Dr D. Harper; Ms C. Hamlyn; Ms I. Sharp;
Dr G. Bickler; Dr V. King; Dr H. Markowe; Mrs P.
Wilson; Dr F. Sim; Prof. Sir I. Kennedy; N. Paterson

RESEARCH ANALYSIS AND INFORMATION
DIRECTORATE
Director of Research Analysis and Information Directorate,
Prof. Sir J. Pattison
Under Secretary and Chief Economic Adviser,
B. McCormick
Head of Information Policy Unit, Dr P. Drury
Director of Statistics, Dr J. Fox

Director of Business and Strategy, Ms K. James
*Director of the Central Office for Research Ethics
Committees,* Prof. T. Stacey
Director-General of NHS IT, R. Granger
Assistant Director of Research and Development,
Dr P. Greenaway
Branch Heads, Ms A. Kauder; N. York; Dr G. Royston;
A. Hare; M. Freeman; Dr P. Westley; Dr J. Stephenson;
M. Taylor; G. Phillpotts; J. Stokoe; R. Willmer; Ms A.
Roberts; R. Staton; A. Sutherland; Ms M. Haines; Dr
D. Franklin; R. Murray; A. Griffiths; Prof. G. Parker;
Dr C. Davies; Ms S. Lonsdale; Dr W. Maton-Howarth

SPECIALIST HEALTH SERVICES DIRECTORATE
*Director of Specialist Health Services and Deputy Chief
Medical Officer,* Prof. Aidan Halligan
Chief Dental Officer, Prof. R. Bedi
Senior Dental Officer, C. Audrey
*Head of Coronary Heart Disease and Stroke Prevention
Policy,* Ms H. Gwynn, CBE
Head of Prison Health, J. Boyington
Head of Specialist Services, D. Hewlett
Branch Heads, Dr M. McGovern; Dr J. Carpenter;
Dr S. Hadjipavlou; Dr M. Piper; Dr C. Howells;
Miss A. Mithani; Dr G. Chapman; Ms A. Stephenson;
S. Waring; G. Larner; R. Bradshaw; S. Reeve

HER MAJESTY'S INSPECTOR OF ANATOMY
Branch Head, Dr J. Metters

SHARED SERVICES
Chief Executive and Programme Director, P. Hewitson

SOLICITOR'S OFFICE, DEPARTMENT FOR WORK AND
PENSIONS
Solicitor, Ms M. Morgan, CB
Director of Legal Services, Mrs G. Kerrigan

ADVISORY COMMITTEES

ADVISORY COMMITTEE ON THE MICROBIOLOGICAL
SAFETY OF FOOD, Room 808C, Aviation House,
125 Kingsway, London, WC2B 6NH Tel: 020-7276 8947
Chairman, Prof. D. Georgala, CBE

COMMITTEE ON THE SAFETY OF MEDICINES,
Market Towers, 1 Nine Elms Lane, London SW8 5NQ
Tel: 020-7273 0000 *Chairman,* Gordon Duff

SPECIAL HEALTH AUTHORITIES

DENTAL VOCATIONAL TRAINING AUTHORITY,
Master's House, Temple Grove, Compton Place Road,
Eastbourne, E. Sussex BN20 8AD Tel: 01323-431189
Chairman, R. Davies *Secretary,* Andrea Goring
FAMILY HEALTH SERVICES APPEAL AUTHORITY (SHA),
30 Victoria Avenue, Harrogate HG1 5PR Tel: 01423-530280
Chief Executive, P. Burns
HEALTH DEVELOPMENT AGENCY, Holborn Gate,
330 High Holborn, London WC1V 7BA Tel: 020-7430 0850
Chair, Ms Y. Buckland; *Chief Executive,* vacant
NATIONAL BLOOD SERVICE, Oak House, Reeds Crescent,
Watford, Herts WD24 4QN Tel: 01923-486800
Chairman, M. Fogden, CB; *Chief Executive,* M. Gorham
NATIONAL INSTITUTE OF CLINICAL EXCELLENCE,
MidCity Place, 71 High Holborn, London WC1V 6NA
Tel: 020-7067 5800 *Chairman,* Prof. Sir Michael
Rawlins; *Chief Executive,* Andrew Dillon

NHS INFORMATION AUTHORITY, Aqueous II, Aston Cross, Rocky Lane, Birmingham B6 5RQ Tel: 0121-333 0333 *Chairman,* Prof. A. Bellingham, CBE; *Chief Executive,* Dr G. Thomas

NHS LITIGATION AUTHORITY, Napier House, 24 High Holborn, London WC1V 6AZ Tel: 020-7430 8700 *Chief Executive,* S. Walker

PRESCRIPTION PRICING AUTHORITY, Bridge House, 152 Pilgrim Street, Newcastle upon Tyne NE1 6SN Tel: 0191-232 5371 *Chairman,* Mrs A. Galbraith *Chief Executive,* N. Scholte

UK TRANSPLANT, Fox Den Road, Stoke Gifford, Bristol BS34 8RR Tel: 0117-975 7575. *Chairman,* Gwyneth Flower; *Chief Executive,* Sue Sutherland

SPECIAL HOSPITALS

ASHWORTH HOSPITAL, Parkbourn, Maghull, Merseyside L31 1HW Tel: 0151-473 0303 *Director of Secure Services/Deputy Chief Executive,* C. Flynn

BROADMOOR HOSPITAL, Crowthorne, Berks RG45 7EG Tel: 01344 773111

RAMPTON HOSPITAL, Retford, Notts DN22 0PD Tel: 01777-248321 *Chief Executive,* J. Taylor

EXECUTIVE AGENCIES

HEALTH PROTECTION AGENCY
The Adelphi, 1–11 John Adams Street, London WC2N 6HP Tel: 020-7339 1300
Chairman, William Stewart, FRS
Chief Executive, Dr Pat Troop

MEDICINES AND HEALTHCARE PRODUCTS REGULATORY AGENCY (MHRA)
Market Towers, 1 Nine Elms Lane, London SW8 5NQ Tel: 020-7273 0000 Fax: 020-7273 0353
The MHRA is responsible for safeguarding public health by ensuring all medicines on the UK market meet appropriate standards of safety, quality and efficacy. This is achieved by a system of licensing, inspection, enforcement and monitoring of medicines after they have been licensed.
Chairman, Prof. Alasdair Breckenridge
Head of Devices Sector, Dr D. Jefferys

NHS ESTATES
1 Trevelyan Square, Boar Lane, Leeds LS1 6AE Tel: 0113-254 7000 Fax: 0113-254 7299
NHS Estates provides advice and guidance in the area of healthcare estate and facilities management to the NHS and the healthcare industry.
Chief Executive, P. Wearmouth

NHS PENSIONS
Hesketh House, 200–220 Broadway, Fleetwood, Lancs FY7 8LG Tel: 01253-774774 Fax: 01253-774860
NHS Pensions administers the NHS occupational pension scheme.
Chief Executive (acting), Mrs P. Corless

NHS PURCHASING AND SUPPLY AGENCY
Premier House, 60 Caversham Road, Reading, Berks RG1 7EB Tel 0118-980 8600
The agency is responsible for ensuring that the NHS makes the most effective use of its resources by getting the best value for money possible when purchasing goods and services.
Chief Executive, D. Eaton

HOME OFFICE

Home Office, 50 Queen Anne's Gate, London SW1H 9AT
Tel: 0870-000 1585 Fax: 020-7273 2065
Web: www.homeoffice.gov.uk

The Home Office deals with those internal affairs in England and Wales which have not been assigned to other Government departments. The Home Secretary is the link between The Queen and the public and exercises certain powers on her behalf, including that of the royal pardon.

The Home Office's objectives are: to build a safe, just and tolerant society and to maintain and enhance public security and protection; to support and mobilise communities so that they are able to shape policy and improvement for their locality, overcome nuisance, anti-social behaviour, maintain and enhance social cohesion and enjoy their homes and public spaces peacefully; to deliver departmental policies and responsibilities fairly, effectively and efficiently; and to make the best use of resources. These objectives reflect the priorities of the Government and the Home Secretary in areas of crime, citizenship and communities, namely: to reduce crime and the fear of crime; to reduce organised and international crime; to combat terrorism and other threats to national security; to ensure the effective delivery of justice; to deliver effective custodial and community sentences; to reduce re-offending and protect the public; to reduce the availability and abuse of dangerous drugs; to regulate entry to and settlement in the UK effectively in the interests of sustainable growth and social inclusion; and to support strong active communities in which people of all races and backgrounds are valued and participate on equal terms.

The Home Office delivers these aims through the prison, probation and immigration services; its agencies and non-departmental public bodies, and by working with partners in private, public and voluntary sectors, individuals and communities.

The Home Secretary is also the link between the UK Government and the governments of the Channel Islands and the Isle of Man.

Secretary of State for the Home Department, The Rt. Hon. David Blunkett, MP
Principal Private Secretary (SCS), Jonathan Sedgwick
Private Secretaries, Gareth Redmond; Kevin O'Connor; Lizzy Gummer; Nicola Thomas; Rebecca Razavi
Special Advisers, Nick Pearce; Katherine Raymond; Matthew Seward; Huw Evans
Minister of State, Hazel Blears, MP *(Crime Reduction, Policing and Community Safety)*
Private Secretary, vacant
Minister of State, Beverley Hughes, MP *(Citizenship, Immigration and Counter-Terrorism)*
Private Secretary, Neil Roberts
Minister of State, The Rt. Hon. Baroness Scotland of Asthal, QC *(Criminal Justice System and Law Reform)*
Private Secretary, Tom Walker
Parliamentary Under-Secretary of State, Caroline Flint, MP *(Anti-Drugs Co-ordination and Organised and International Crime)*
Private Secretary, Peter Grime
Parliamentary Under-Secretary of State, Paul Goggins, MP *(Correctional Services and Reducing Re-Offending)*
Private Secretary, Tony Lord
Parliamentary Under-Secretary of State, Fiona Mactaggart, MP *(Race Equality, Community Policy, and Civil Renewal)*
Private Secretary, Kishor Mistry

Permanent Secretary of State (SCS), John Gieve
Private Secretary, Diana Luchford
Parliamentary Under-Secretary of State, Michael Wills, MP
(Criminal Justice Systems IT and Performance of the Correspondence System)
Private Secretary, Asma Samuel
Parliamentary Clerk, Tony Strutt

COMMUNICATION DIRECTORATE
Director of Communications (SCS), Julia Simpson
Assistant Director and Head of Direct Communications Unit, Geoff Sampher
Customer Communications Manager, Julia Speight
Deputy Director and Head of News (Press Office) (SCS), Terry Norman
Deputy Director of Communications and Head of Marketing and Strategic Communications (SCS), Anne Nash
Head of Internal Communications Unit (SCS), vacant
Head of Information Services Unit (G6), Peter Griffiths

COMMUNITY POLICY DIRECTORATE
Director (SCS), Hilary Jackson
Director, Active Community Unit, Helen Edwards
Deputy Director, Service Delivery (SCS), Amobi Modu
Chief Inspector, Dr Jon Richmond
Superintendent Inspector, James Anderson
Chairman, Commission for Racial Equality, Trevor Phillips

Heads of Units
Animal Procedures and Coroners Unit, Trevor Cobley
Community Cohesion Unit (Acting Head), Susan Hadland;
Entitlement Card Unit, Stephen Harrison
Family Policy Unit, Robin Woodland
Strategic Support Group, Richard Jenkins
Race Equality Unit, Bruce Gill
Regions and Renewals Unit, Betty Moxon

CORPORATE DEVELOPMENT AND SERVICES
DIRECTORATE
Grenadier House, 99–105 Horseferry Road, London SW1P 2DD
Tel: 0870-000 1585
Queen Anne's Gate, London SW1H 9AT
Tel: 0870-000 1585
Director (SCS), Charles Everett
Heads of Units, Mike Fitzpatrick *(Agreement and Service Delivery);* Tony Edwards *(Building and Estate Management);* Andrew Honeyman *(Business Support and Communications);* Robert Scotland *(Commercial and Procurement Unit);* Tony Fitzpatrick *(Home Office Pay and Pensions Service);* Carol Anderson *(Programme Project Management Support Services);* Peter Lowe
Records Management, (Information Management Unit) Richard Thompson
President of HO Sports and Social Association, John Gieve

CRIME REDUCTION AND COMMUNITY SAFETY
GROUP
Director-General (SCS), John Lyon
Directors, Steve Trimmins *(Crime Reduction Centre);* Kevin Bond *(Police Standards);* Stephen Rimmer *(Policing Policy);* Jim Daniell *(Policing and Crime Reduction);* Peter Edwards *(Assistant Director, Crime Reduction Delivery)*
Heads of Units, Paul Pugh *(Police Leadership and Powers Unit);* Jeremy Crump *(Police Personnel Unit);* Andy Ford *(Police Resources Unit);* Dr Anthony Whitehead *(Science Policy Unit);* Martin Parker *(Performance and Strategic Management Unit);* Fenella Taylor

(Management Support Unit); Teresa Burnhams *(Police Performance Delivery Unit);* Charles Goldie *(Criminal Records and Security Industry);* Michael Gillespie *(Public Order and Crime Issues Unit);* Brian Coleman *(Police Scientific and Development Branch);* Clare Checksfield *(Street Crime Action Team);* Ann Ashworth *(Resources Development Unit);* Vic Hogg *(Communities and Law Enforcement Drugs Unit);* Peter Vallance *(Financial Crime Team);* Stephen Webb *(Policing and Organised Crime Unit);* Clive Welsh *(Judicial Co-operation Unit);* Judy Youell *(Strategic Co-ordination and Planning Unit);* Lesley Pallett *(European and International Unit)*

CRIMINAL POLICY GROUP
Director-General (SCS), Moira Wallace, OBE
Director-General, Criminal Justice System IT, Jo Wright
Directors, James Quinault *(Criminal Justice Performance);* Mark Omerod *(Criminal Law and Policy);* Christine Stewart *(Correctional and Rehabilitation Policy);* Althea Efunshile *(Children and Young Peoples Unit)*
Heads of Units, Louise Dominian *(Adult Offenders and Rehabilitation Unit);* Peter Curwen *(Independent Monitoring Board);* Ann-Marie Field *(Local Performance and Delivery Unit);* Clive Manning *(Resources Planning and Communications);* Mark Gladwyn *(Criminal Justice System IT);* Ian Chisholm *(Criminal Procedures and Evidence Unit);* William Arnold *(Criminal Justice System Confidence Unit);* David Reardon *(Criminal Justice System Race Unit);* Elizabeth Moody, Fiona Spencer *(Mental Health Unit);* Simon Hickson *(Juvenile Offenders Unit);* Catherine Lee *(Justice, Victims and Witnesses Unit);* Deborah Grice *(Sentencing and Offenders Unit)*
Chairman, Youth Justice Board, Lord Norman Warner

HUMAN RESOURCES DIRECTORATE
Director (SCS), David Spencer
Personnel Director (SCS), Deborah Louden
Heads of Units, Tony Williams *(Central Personnel Management Unit);* Nigel Benger *(Corporate Support Services Unit);* David McDonough *(Departmental Security Unit);* Eileen Arney *(Human Resources and Development Unit);* Jill Douglas *(Personnel Management and Administration);* vacant *(Assessment and Consultancy Unit)*

IMMIGRATION AND NATIONALITY DIRECTORATE
Advance House, 15 Wellesley Road, Croydon, Surrey CR0 2AG
Tel: 020-8760 3023
Apollo House, 36 Wellesley Road, Croydon, Surrey CR9 3RR
Tel: 0870-000 1585
50 Queen Anne's Gate, London SW1H 9AT
Tel: 020-7273 4000
India Buildings, 3rd Floor, Water Street, Liverpool L2 0QN
Tel: 0151-237 5200
Director-General (SCS), Bill Jeffrey
Deputy Director-General, Operations and Chief Inspectors of Immigration, Dr Chris Mace, CBE; Robin Halward
Deputy Director-General, Policy, Martin Donelly
Directors, Richard Westlake *(Asylum and Appeals Policy Directorate);* Steven Barnett *(Human Resources Directorate);* Stephen Calvard *(Business Information Systems and Technology Directorate);* Chris Hudson *(Integrated Casework Directorate (Croydon));* Jenny Rumble *(International Policy Directorate);* David Stephens *(Finance and Services Directorate);* Freda Chaloner *(National Asylum Support Service);* Alan Underwood *(Integrated Casework Directorate (North));*

Clem Norman *(Immigration Service, Detention)*; Peter Higgins *(Immigration Service, Immigration Control)*; Alex O'Grady *(Organisation, Management and Leadership Development)*

WORK PERMITS UK
Moorfort, Sheffield, S1 4PQ
Director, Alan Underwood
Heads of Units, Mick Seals *(Operations)*; Steve Lamb *(Operations Manager)*; Sylvia Hannah *(Operations Support Manager)*; Roy Saxby *(Managed Migration)*; Neil Hughes *(Charging Development)*; Campbell Gilmore *(Research Projects)*

LEGAL ADVISORS' BRANCH
Senior Legal Advisor (SCS), David Seymour
Deputy Legal Advisor (SCS), David Noble
Assistant Legal Advisors, Richard Clayton; Jim O'Meara; Steve Bramley; Harry Carter; Sally Weston; Rowena Collins-Rice; Caroline Price; Kevan Norris; Steve Braviner Roman

PERFORMANCE AND FINANCE DIRECTORATE
50 Queen Anne's Gate, London SW1H 9AT
Tel: 020-7273 4000
Horseferry House, Dean Ryle Street, London SW1P 2AW
Tel: 020-7273 4000
Director (SCS), William Rye
Heads of Units, Tim Hurdle *(Audit and Assurance Unit)*; Adrian Cory *(Accounting and Finance Unit)*; Betty Sandars *(Special Conference Centre)*; Alison Barnett *(Performance and Finance Support)*; Steven Jenner *(Performance, Delivery and Strategy Team)*; Nichola Roche *(Strategic Policy Team)*; Tony Williams *(Corporate Change Team)*

RESEARCH, DEVELOPMENT AND STATISTICS DIRECTORATE
Director (SCS), Prof. Paul Wiles
Directors, Jon Simmons *(Analysing Crime Programme (SCS))*; Carol Hedderman *(Offending and Crime Justice Group)*
Assistant Directors, David Moxon; Chris Lewis; David Pyle; Carole Willis *(Crime and Policing Group)*; Peter Ward *(Immigration and Community Group)*
Heads of Units, Christine Lehman *(Communication and Development Group)*; Lisa Killham *(Corporate Management Unit)*

CENTRAL POLICE TRAINING AND DEVELOPMENT AUTHORITY (CENTREX)
Chief Executive, Chris Mould
Directors, Andy Humphreys *(Performance and Service Delivery)*; Valerie Vaughan-Dick *(Resources)*

EXECUTIVE AGENCIES

UK PASSPORT SERVICE
Globe House, 89 Ecclestone Square, London SW1V 1PN
Advice line: 0870-521 0410
Chief Executive, Bernard Herdan
Deputy Chief Executive and Director of Operations (G6), K. Sheehan
Director of Systems (G6), J. Davies
Director Finance, Ms A. Cook

CRIMINAL RECORDS BUREAU
Horton House, Exchange Flags, Liverpool L2 3YL
Tel: 0870-909 0811
Chief Executive, Vincent Gaskill
Director of Operation, K. Broadbent

FORENSIC SCIENCE SERVICE
Operational Headquarters, Priory House, Gooch Street North, Birmingham B5 6QQ
Tel: 0121-607 6800
Chief Executive, David Werrett

HM PRISON SERVICE
Cleland House, Page Street, London SW1P 4LN
Director-General, Phil Wheatley

PAROLE BOARD FOR ENGLAND AND WALES
see Prison Service section

PRISONS AND PROBATIONS OMBUDSMAN FOR ENGLAND AND WALES
see Prison Service section

DEPARTMENT FOR INTERNATIONAL DEVELOPMENT

1 Palace Street, London SW1E 5HE
Tel: 020-7023 0000 Fax: 020-7023 0019
Email: enquiry@dfid.gov.uk
Web: www.dfid.gov.uk
Abercrombie House, Eaglesham Road, East Kilbride, Glasgow G75 8EA
Tel: 01355-844000 Fax: 01355-844099

The Department for International Development (DFID) is the UK Government department responsible for promoting sustainable development and reducing poverty.

The central focus of the Government's policy, based on the 1997 and 2000 White Papers on International Development, is a commitment to the internationally agreed Millennium Development Goals, to be achieved by 2015. These seek to eradicate extreme poverty and hunger; achieve universal primary education; promote gender equality and empower women; reduce child mortality; improve maternal health; combat HIV/AIDS, malaria and other diseases; ensure environmental sustainability; and develop a global partnership for development.

DFID's assistance is concentrated in the poorest countries of sub-Saharan Africa and Asia, but also contributes to poverty reduction and sustainable development in middle-income countries, including those in Latin America and Eastern Europe. DFID works in partnership with governments committed to the Millennium Development Goals, and with the private sector and the research community. It also works with multilateral institutions, including the World Bank, United Nations agencies, and the European Commission. DFID has headquarters in London and East Kilbride, offices in many developing countries, and staff based in British embassies and high commissions around the world.

Secretary of State for International Development, The Rt. Hon. Baroness Amos, MP
Principal Private Secretary, Anna Bewes
Special Adviser, Alex Evans
Parliamentary Private Secretary, Tom Levitt, MP
Parliamentary Clerk, Peter Gordon

Minister of State for International Development, Hilary
Benn, MP
Private Secretary, Alison Cochrane
Parliamentary Private Secretary, Dr Ashok Kumar, MP
Parliamentary Under-Secretary of State,
Gareth R. Thomas, MP
Private Secretary, Elizabeth Peri
House of Lords Spokespeople, Baroness Crawley; Baroness
Whitaker *(Liaison Peer)*
Permanent Secretary (SCS), Suma Chakrabarti
Private Secretary, Charlie Whetham
*Director-General, Corporate Performance and Knowledge
Sharing (SCS),* M. Lowcock
Director-General, Policy and International (SCS),
M. Ahmed
Director-General, Regional Programmes (SCS),
Dr N. Brewer, CMG
Non-Executive Directors, N. Shafik *(World Bank);*
W. Griffiths *(Shell)*

AFRICA DIVISION
Director of Division (SCS), G. Stegmann *(SCS)*
Heads of Departments, T. Craddock *(SCS) (Africa Great Lakes
and Horn);* G. Teskey *(Africa Policy);* A. Smith *(SCS)
(Central and Southern Africa and Deputy Director, Africa
Division);* D. Batt *(SCS) (East Africa and Deputy Director,
Africa Division);* B. Thomson *(SCS) (West Africa)*
Heads of Offices, R. Wilson *(SCS) (Malawi);* J. Winter
(SCS) (Ghana); E. Cassidy *(SCS) (Mozambique);*
Ms H. Mealins *(SCS) (Zambia);* M. Wyatt *(SCS)
(Kenya);* Ms C. Sergeant *(SCS) (Tanzania);*
M. Hammond *(SCS) (Uganda);* W. Kingsmill *(SCS)
(Nigeria);* S. Sharpe *(SCS) (Southern Africa);*
Ms G. Wright *(Zimbabwe)*
Heads of Field Offices, J. L. Riley *(Botswana);* Ms I. Thorn
(Lesotho); M. Johnston *(Angola);* Ms G. Yates *(Burundi);*
P. Godfrey *(Dem Rep Congo);* P. Kerby *(Ethiopia);*
Ms R. Malone *(Namibia);* M. James *(Rwanda);* D. Bell
(Somalia); M. Baugh *(Sudan);* Ms K. Wells *(Swaziland)*

ASIA AND PACIFIC DIVISION
Director of Division (SCS), M. Dinham, CBE
Heads of Departments, M. Manuel *(SCS) (Asia Directorate
and Deputy Director, Asia and Pacific Division);*
Ms P. Jenkins *(Director's Cabinet);* H. Taylor *(County
Programmes Unit);* J. Clarke *(SCS) (Asia Policy and
Strategy);* J. Gordon *(Regional Policy Unit);* C. Austin
(Western Asia)
Heads of Offices, P. Ackroyd *(SCS) (Bangladesh);* Ms C.
Seymour-Smith *(SCS) (India);* D. Wood *(SCS) (Nepal);*
D. L. Wood *(Pacific);* M. Mallalieu *(SCS) (South East
Asia);* A. Johnson *(Vietnam);* A. Davis *(SCS) (China);*
Dr R. Hogg *(Afghanistan);* Dr D. Arghiros *(Cambodia);*
vacant *(Indonesia);* Ms P. Thorpe *(Sri Lanka)*
Representatives, R. S. Sharat *(Andhra Pradesh, India);* A.
Chowla *(Madhya Pradesh, India);* Ms S. Pattanayak
(Orissa, India); S. Sengupta *(West Bengal, India)*

EUROPE, MIDDLE EAST AND AMERICAS DIVISION
Director of Division (SCS), Ms C. Miller
Heads of Departments, Ms B. Killen *(SCS) (Europe, Middle
East and Americas Policy);* Ms J. Irvine *(SCS) (Europe
and Central Asia);* R. Teuten *(SCS) (Latin America);* A.
Fernie *(Middle East and North Africa);*
C. Warren *(Overseas Territories)*
Heads of Offices,
S. Bickersteth *(Bolivia);* vacant *(Brazil);* Ms J. Alston
(SCS) (Caribbean); G. Briffa *(Guyana);* V. Heard

(Honduras); Ms E. Carrière *(Jamaica);* Ms G. Taylor
(Nicaragua); M. Lewis *(Peru);* S. Bland *(Russia);*
D. Houston *(Ukraine);*
UK Representative, S. Ray *(SCS) (EBRD)*

POLICY DIVISION
Director of Division (SCS), Ms S. White
Deputy Directors, M. Elliott *(SCS),* Ms S. Moorehead
(SCS), Dr M. Schultz *(SCS)*

OFFICE OF THE CHIEF ADVISERS
Heads of Profession (SCS), A. Wood *(Economics);*
R. Edmunds *(Statistics);* M. Sergeant *(Infrastructure and
Urban Development);* J. Harvey *(Rural Livelihoods);*
J. Warburton *(Environment);* D. Bermingham
(Education)
Chief Advisers (SCS), D. Stanton *(Enterprise Development);*
S. Bass *(Environment);* Dr J. Lob-Levyt *(Human
Development);* Ms S. Unsworth *(Governance);*
Dr A. Norton *(Social Development)*
Deputy Heads of Profession, J. Burton *(Economics);*
S. Tyson *(Health);* M. Everest-Phillips *(Governance);*
Ms P. Holden *(Social Development)*

INTERNATIONAL DIVISION
Director of Division (SCS), P. Grant
Heads of Departments (SCS), M. Mosselmans *(Conflict and
Humanitarian Affairs);* N. Dyer *(European Union);*
Ms M. Cund *(International Financial Institutions);*
Ms D. Melrose *(International Trade);* T. Williams
(United Nations and Commonwealth)
Team Leader, Ms R. Turner *(International Division
Advisory Team)*
UK Permanent Representative, A. Beattie *(SCS) (FAO)*
UK Permanent Delegate, D. L. Stanton *(SCS) (UNESCO)*

CORPORATE PERFORMANCE AND KNOWLEDGE
SHARING DIVISION
Heads of Departments (SCS), Dr C. Kirk *(Evaluation);*
G. McGillivray *(Private Sector Infrastructure/CDC)*

FINANCE AND CORPORATE PERFORMANCE DIVISION
Director of Division, R. Calvert *(SCS)*
Heads of Departments, Ms S. Wardell *(SCS) (Performance
and Effectiveness);* K. Sparkhall *(SCS) (Finance);* M.
Smithson *(Accounts);* M. Noronha *(Internal Audit);* S.
Chard *(SCS) (Procurement)*

HUMAN RESOURCES DIVISION
Director (SCS), D. Fish
Heads of Departments (SCS), J. Anning *(Human Resources
Operations);* I. McKendry *(Human Resources Policy);*
P. Brough *(Overseas Pensions)*

INFORMATION, KNOWLEDGE AND
COMMUNICATIONS DIVISION
Director of Division (SCS), O. Barder
Heads of Departments (SCS), M. Green *(Information and
Civil Society);* D. Gillett *(Information Systems and
Services)*

CDC CAPITAL PARTNERS
One Bessborough Gardens, London SW1V 2JQ
Tel: 020-7828 4488 Fax: 020-7282 6505
CDC Capital Partners provides equity finance to private
sector businesses in emerging markets. It has over 20
offices located across Latin America, Africa, South Asia
and Asia Pacific. CDC is a public limited company with

the Department for International Development as its 100 per cent shareholder.
Chairman, The Lord Cairns, CBE
Deputy Chairman, Ms J. Almond
Chief Executive, P. Fletcher

LORD CHANCELLOR'S DEPARTMENT

Selborne House, 54–60 Victoria Street, London SW1E 6QW
Tel: 020-7210 8500
Web: www.lcd.gov.uk
See Department for Constitutional Affairs

NORTHERN IRELAND OFFICE

11 Millbank, London SW1P 4PN
Tel: 020-7210 3000
Castle Buildings, Stormont, Belfast BT4 3SG
Tel: 01232-520700 Fax: 01232-528195
Web: www.nio.gov.uk

The Northern Ireland Office was established in 1972, when the Northern Ireland (Temporary Provisions) Act transferred the legislative and executive powers of the Northern Ireland Parliament and Government to the UK Parliament and a Secretary of State.

The Northern Ireland Office is responsible primarily for security issues, law and order and prisons, and for matters relating to the political and constitutional future of the province. It also deals with international issues as they affect Northern Ireland.

Under the terms of the 1998 Good Friday Agreement, power was devolved to the Northern Ireland Assembly in 1999. The Assembly took on responsibility for the relevant areas of work previously undertaken by the departments of the Northern Ireland Office covering agriculture and rural development, the environment, regional development, social development, education, higher education, training and employment, enterprise, trade and investment, culture, arts and leisure, health, social services and public safety and finance and personnel. On 14th October 2002 the Northern Ireland Assembly was suspended and Northern Ireland returned to direct rule. For further details, *see* Regional Government section.

Secretary of State for Northern Ireland, The Rt. Hon. Paul Murphy, MP
Parliamentary Private Secretary, Gareth Thomas, MP
Ministers of State, Jane Kennedy, MP, The Rt. Hon. John Spellar, MP
Parliamentary Private Secretary, Shona McIsaac, MP
Parliamentary Under-Secretaries of State, Desmond Browne, MP; Ian Pearson, MP; Angela Smith, MP
Permanent Under-Secretary of State, Sir Joseph Pilling, KCB
Head of the Northern Ireland Civil Service, Gerry Loughran

NORTHERN IRELAND INFORMATION SERVICE
Castle Buildings, Stormont, Belfast BT4 3SG
Tel: 028-9052 0700

EXECUTIVE AGENCIES

COMPENSATION AGENCY, Royston House, Upper Queen Street, Belfast BT1 6FD Tel: 01232-2499444
FORENSIC SCIENCE NORTHERN IRELAND, Seapark, 151 Belfast Road, Carrickfergus, Co. Antrim BT38 8PL Tel: 01232-365744
NORTHERN IRELAND PRISON SERVICE, *see* Prison Service section

SCOTLAND OFFICE

Dover House, Whitehall, London SW1A 2AU
Tel: 020-7270 6754 Fax: 020-7270 6812
Email: scottish.secretary@scotland.gov.uk
Web: www.scottishsecretary.gov.uk

The Scotland Office is the department of the Secretary of State for Scotland, who represents Scottish interests in the Cabinet on matters reserved to the UK Parliament, i.e. constitutional matters, financial and economic matters, defence and international relations, immigration, social security, various matters relating to the single market with the UK (energy, transport, consumer protection) and employment. It also supports the Advocate General, the legal adviser to the UK Government on Scottish law. *See also* Regional Government section and Department for Constitutional Affairs.

Secretary of State for Scotland, The Rt. Hon. Alistair Darling, MP
Private Secretary, Ms J. Colquhoun
Parliamentary Private Secretary, vacant
Parliamentary Under-Secretary of State, Anne McGuire, MP
Private Secretary, Chloe Squire
Parliamentary Private Secretary, vacant
Advocate-General for Scotland, Dr Lynda Clark, QC, MP
Private Secretary, Gary White
Spokesperson in the House of Lords, Lord Evans of Temple Guiting, CBE

DEPARTMENT OF TRADE AND INDUSTRY

1 Victoria Street, London SW1H 0ET
Tel: 020-7215 5000 Fax: 020-7215 0105
Web: www.dti.gov.uk

The Department of Trade and Industry works with businesses, employees and consumers to increase UK productivity and competitiveness. The department's aim is to make the UK a more prosperous country and close the gap with its international competitors by making it easier and more attractive to start and grow new businesses in the UK. The DTI strongly focuses on innovation to help more firms to grow and capture new markets, ensuring fair and open markets at home and overseas to support successful UK businesses and the creation of jobs, and better support for scientific excellence.

Secretary of State for Trade and Industry, Minister for Women and e-Minister, The Rt. Hon. Patricia Hewitt, MP
Principal Private Secretary, Erica Zimmer
Private Secretaries, Angela Pearce; Donald McNeill; Ian Gibbons
Parliamentary Private Secretaries, Andrew Miller, MP; vacant
Minister of State, Stephen Timms, MP *(E-Commerce and Competitiveness)*
Private Secretary, Mike Warnes
Parliamentary Private Secretary, Oona King, MP
Minister of State, Mike O'Brien, MP *(International Trade and Investment)*
Private Secretary, Peter Elder
Parliamentary Private Secretary, Mark Todd, MP
Minister of State, Jacqui Smith, MP *(Industry and the Regions)*
Private Secretary, Giles Smith
Parliamentary Private Secretary, Bob Laxton, MP

Parliamentary Under-Secretary of State, Gerry Sutcliffe, MP
(Competition, Consumers and Markets)
Private Secretary, Sam Myers
Parliamentary Under-Secretary of State, The Lord
Sainsbury of Turville § *(Science and Innovation)*
Private Secretary, Charlotte DuBern
Parliamentary Under-Secretary of State, Nigel Griffiths, MP
(Small Business)
Private Secretary, Louise Robson
Permanent Secretary, Sir Robin Young, KCB
Private Secretary, Tom Ridge
Parliamentary Clerk, Tim Williams
*Chief Scientific Adviser and Head of Office of Science and
Technology,* Prof. Sir David King, KB
Director-General, Research Councils, Dr John Taylor, OBE
Chief Executive British Trade International, Sir Stephen
Brown, KCVO
§ Unpaid

STRATEGY UNIT
Director of Strategy Unit (SCS), Geoff Dart
Chief Economic Adviser (SCS), Vicky Pryce
Director of Communications (SCS), Sheree Dodd

INNOVATION GROUP
Director-General, David Hughes
Director, Facilitating Innovation, John Rhodes
Directors, Jonathan Startup *(Sustainable Development);*
Peter Burke *(Business Planning and Strategy);* vacant
(Technical Innovation and Sustainable Development);
David Reed *(Standards and Technical Regulations)*

BRITISH NATIONAL SPACE CENTRE
Director-General (SCS), Dr Colin Hicks
Deputy Director-General (SCS), David Leadbeater
Director, Space Applications and Programmes, Paula
Freedman

NATIONAL WEIGHTS AND MEASURES LABORATORY
Director and Chief Executive (SCS), Jeffrey Llewellyn
PATENT OFFICE
Chief Executive (SCS), Alison Brimelow

ENERGY GROUP
Director-General, Joan MacNaughton, CB
Heads of Units, Jim Campbell *(Licensing and Consents
Unit);* Derek Davis *(Nuclear and Coal Liabilities Unit);*
Claire Durkin *(Energy Innovation and Business Unit);*
Neil Hirst *(Energy Markets Unit);* Paul McIntyre
(British Energy Team); Rob Wright *(Energy Strategy
Unit)*
Directors, Simon Toole *(Licensing Exploration and
Development);* Nigel Pearce *(Electricity Consents and
Agency Project Management);* Alan Edwards *(Liabilities
Management Unit);* Stephen Spivey *(Nuclear Reform
Bill);* Ian Gregory *(Nuclear Business Relations);* Ann
Taylor *(Coal Health Claims);* Iain Todd *(Energy
Industries Business Unit and Oil and Gas Industry
Development);* Patrick Robinson *(Nuclear Safety and
Security);* Peter Fenwick *(Engineering Inspectorate);* Ian
Downing *(International Nuclear Policy and
Programmes);* Michael Buckland-Smith *(Civil Nuclear
Security);* Liz Baker *(Domestic and European Energy);*
Ann Eggington *(International and Infrastructure);*
Graham White *(Social Issues and Information);* Graham
Turnock *(British Energy);* David Hayes *(Strategic Issues);*
Adrian Gault *(Strategy Development, Research and
Analysis);* John Hobday *(Energy MSU)*

BUSINESS GROUP
Director-General, Mark Gibson
Deputy Director-General, Regions, Katharine Elliott

BUSINESS RELATIONS
Director of Business Relations (SCS), John Alty
Directors (SCS), David Hendon *(Business Relations 2);*
David Saunders *(Business Support);* Mark Higson
(Postal Services); Amanda Brooks *(Change Management
Team);* Sheila Morris *(Business Relations Strategic
Management);* Rosa Wilkinson *(Policy, Business
Relations);* Martin Berry *(Industry Sponsorship Support)*

AEROSPACE AND DEFENCE INDUSTRIES
TECHNOLOGY
Director, (SCS), David Way

AUTOMOTIVE
Director (SCS), Sarah Chambers

BIOSCIENCE
Director (SCS), Monica Darnbrough

CHEMICALS
Director (SCS), Dr David Jennings

CONSTRUCTION INDUSTRIES
Director (SCS), Elizabeth Whatmore

CONSUMER GOODS AND SERVICES
Director (SCS), Jane Swift

JOINT ENVIRONMENTAL MARKETS UNIT
Director (SCS), Duncan Prior

MARINE
Director (SCS), Chris North

MATERIALS AND ENGINEERING
Director (SCS), Simon Edmonds

REGIONS
Directors, Tony Medawar *(RDA Sponsorship and Finance);*
Peter Bunn *(Regional Policy);* John Neve *(Regional
European Funds and Devolution);* Andrew Steele
(Regional Assistance); Barbara Phillips *(Social Enterprise
Unit)*

SMALL BUSINESS SERVICE
Chief Executive (SCS), Martin Wyn-Griffith
Deputy Chief Executive (SCS), Stephen Lyle Smythe
Directors (SCS), Dr Ken Poulter *(Business Services);* Mandy
Mayer *(Strategy and Planning);* Howard Capelin
(Channel Management); Peter Bentley *(Finance Director)*

SERVICES GROUP
Director-General, Dr Catherine Bell

EXPORT CONTROL AND NON PROLIFERATION
Director of Export Control and Non Proliferation (SCS),
Mike O'Shea

FINANCE AND RESOURCE MANAGEMENT
Director of Finance and Resource Management, (SCS),
David Evans

HUMAN RESOURCES AND CHANGE MANAGEMENT
*Director of Human Resources and Change Management
(SCS),* Susan Haird

INFORMATION AND WORKPLACE SERVICES
Director (SCS), Yvonne Gallagher
Directors, Helen Taylor, David Evans *(Internal Audit)*;
Peter Mason *(Finance)*; Curtis Juman *(Resource
Accounting and Budgeting)*; Adam Jackson *(Business
Planning and Performance Management)*; Tim Soane
(Change and Knowledge Management Unit); Rosemary
Heyhoe *(HR Operations)*; Christine Hewitt, Jan Dixon
(HR Strategy and Terms of Employment); Howard Ewing
(People Deployment and Development); Andrew Mathew
(E-Strategy and Major Projects); Liz Maclachlan
(Information Policy and Services); Glyn Williams
(Export Control Organisation)

FAIR MARKETS GROUP
Director-General, Stephen Haddrill

COMPANY LAW AND INVESTIGATIONS
Director of Company Law and Investigations (SCS),
Bernadette Kelly
Directors (SCS), Robert Burns, Keith Masson, Rachel Clark,
Richard Carter *(Company Law)*; John Grewe *(Financial
Reporting Policy)*; Andrew Watchman *(Accountancy
Advisor)*; Anne Willcocks *(Review of Non-Executive
Directors)*; Roger Watson *(Policy and Resources)*; Grahame
Harp *(Investigations and Inspector of Companies)*

CONSUMER AND COMPETITION POLICY
Director of Consumer and Competition Policy (SCS),
Jonathan Rees
Directors (SCS), Pat Sellers *(Mergers)*; David Miner
(Research, Analysis and Evidence Database); Thoss
Shearer *(Economic Regulation and Reform)*; Barbara
Habberjam *(Consumer Advice and Information)*;
Katherine Wright *(Strategy and Delivery)*; Tony Sims
(Europe and International); Adrian Walker-Smith
(Consumer Credit); Fiona Price *(Cross-Market
Intervention)*

EMPLOYMENT RELATIONS
Director of Employment Relations (SCS), Janice Munday
Directors (SCS), Sarah Rhodes *(Dispute Resolution)*; Ros
McCarthy-Ward *(Selected Employment Rights)*; Grant
Fitzner *(Employment Market Analysis and Research)*; Jane
Whewell *(European Strategy and Labour Market
Flexibility)*; Julie Carney *(Participation and Skills)*

LOW PAY COMMISSION
Secretary, Kate Harre

WOMEN AND EQUALITY UNIT
10 Great George Street, London SW1P 3AE
Tel: 020-7273 8880
Director (SCS), Angela Mason
Directors (SCS), Liz Chennells *(Gender Equality and Social
Justice)*; Hilary Samson-Barry *(Productivity and
Diversity)*; Kate Allan *(Equality Co-Ordination)*

EUROPEAN AND WORLD TRADE POLICY
Director, World Trade, Edmund Hosker
Director, Europe, Jo Durning
Directors, Dr Elaine Drage *(EC Trade Policy)*; Hugh Savill
(EU Economic Reform); Tim Abraham *(International
Trade Policy)*; David Andrews *(Market Access)*;
Matthew Cocks *(Future of Europe)*; Peter Dodd
(International Economies); vacant *(State Aid)*

LEGAL SERVICES GROUP
The Solicitor and Director-General, Anthony Inglese
*Director of Legal Resource Management and Business Law
(SCS)*, Carl Warren
*Director of Legal Services A (Business and Consumers)
(SCS)*, Tessa Dunstan
*Director of Legal Services B (Employment Discrimination,
Equality and Intellectual Property) (SCS)*, Alex Brett-
Holt
*Director of Legal Services C (Energy, Communications, EC
and Overseas Trade) (SCS)*, Deborah Collins
Director of Legal Services D (Law Enforcement) (SCS),
Scott Milligan
*Director of Legal Services E (Company Law and British
Energy) (SCS)*, Philip Bovey

BRITISH TRADE INTERNATIONAL
Kingsgate House, 66–74 Victoria Street, London SW1E 6SW
Tel: 020-7215 5000
British Trade International brings together the
Department of Trade and Industry and the Foreign and
Commonwealth Office export and investment operations.
Chair, The Rt. Hon. The Baroness Symons of Vernham
Dean
Vice-Chairmen, Sir David Brown, Sir David John, KCMG
Group Members, R. Turner, OBE; V. Brown; A. Summers;
K. Pathak, OBE; W. Thompson, OBE; D. Jones;
M. Gibson; Sir Peter Mason, KBE; A. Hingston; G. Fry;
S. Hampson; Ms S. Pirie, OBE; Ms J. Stevens; P. Barron,
CBE; Dr J. Bridge
Special Representative for Investment and Trade, HRH The
Duke of York KCVO, GCMG, GCVO

TRADE PARTNERS UK
The Trade Partners UK network provides services to
British exporters and investors at home and overseas.
Chief Executive, Sir David Wright, KCMG, LVO
Deputy Chief Executive and Group Director (SCS), I. Jones
(Regions)
Group Directors (SCS), Q. Quayle *(International)*;
D. Warren *(Business)*; J. Reynolds *(Strategy and
Communications)*

INVEST UK
Chief Executive (SCS), W. Pedder
Directors (SCS), S. O. Leary *(Operations)*; M. Uden
(International)

EXECUTIVE AGENCIES

COMPANIES HOUSE
Crown Way, Cardiff CF143UZ
Tel: 0870-333 3636 Fax: 029-2038 0517
Email: genenquiries@companieshouse.gov.uk
Web: www.companieshouse.gov.uk
London Information Centre, 21 Bloomsbury Street, London
WC1B 3XD Tel: 0870-333 3636 Fax: 029-2038 0517
Edinburgh, 37 Castle Terrace, Edinburgh EH12EB
Tel: 0870-333 3636 Fax: 029-380 517
Birmingham, Central Library, Chamberlain Square,
Birmingham B33 3HQ
Tel: 0870-333 3636 Fax: 029-2038 0517
Leeds, 25 Queen Street, Leeds, LS1 2TW
Tel: 0870-333 3636 Fax: 029-2038 0517
Manchester, 75 Mosley Street, Manchester, M2 2HR
Tel: 0870-333 3636 Fax: 029-2038 0517
Companies House incorporates companies, registers
company documents and provides company information.

Registrar of Companies for England and Wales,
   Claire Clancey
Registrar for Scotland, Jim Henderson

EMPLOYMENT TRIBUNALS SERVICE
19–29 Woburn Place, London WC1H 0LU
Tel: 020-7273 8666 Fax: 020-7273 8670
The Service became an executive agency in 1997 and brought together the administrative support for the employment tribunals and the Employment Appeal Tribunal.
Chief Executive, Roger Heathcote

THE INSOLVENCY SERVICE
PO Box 203, 21 Bloomsbury Street, London WC1B 3QW
Tel: 020-7637 1110 Fax: 020-7636 4709
The Service administers and investigates the affairs of bankrupts and companies in compulsory liquidation; deals with the disqualification of directors in all corporate failures; regulates insolvency practitioners and their professional bodies; provides banking and investment services for bankruptcy and liquidation estates; and advises Ministers on insolvency policy issues.
Inspector-General and Chief Executive, Desmond Flynn
Deputy Inspectors-General, G. Horne; L. T. Cramp

NATIONAL WEIGHTS AND MEASURES LABORATORY (NWML)
Stanton Avenue, Teddington, Middx TW11 0JZ
Tel: 020-8943 7272 Fax: 020-8943 7270
Web: www.nwml.gov.uk
The Laboratory administers weights and measures legislation, carries out type examination, calibration and testing, and runs courses on legal metrology.
Chief Executive, Dr Jeff Llewellyn

PATENT OFFICE
see Intellectual Property section

DEPARTMENT FOR TRANSPORT
Great Minster House, 76 Marsham Street, London SW1P 4DR
Ashdown House, 123 Victoria Street, London SW1E 6DE
Tel: 020-7944 8300 020-7944 4873
Web: www.dft.gov.uk
The Department for Transport was established in May 2002 following the de-merger of the Department of Transport, Local Government and the Regions.
   The department's main responsibilities are aviation, freight, health and safety, integrated and local transport, London Underground, maritime, mobility and inclusion, railways, roads and road safety, shipping and vehicles.
Secretary of State for Transport, The Rt. Hon Alistair
   Darling, MP
Principal Private Secretary, Scott McPherson
Minister of State, The Rt. Hon. Kim Howells, MP
   (Transport)
Private Secretary, Deborah Heenan
Parliamentary Under-Secretary of State, David Jamieson,
   MP *(Transport)*
Private Secretary, Kirstin Blagden
Parliamentary Under-Secretary of State, Tony McNulty
   (Transport)
Private Secretary, Emma Cliffe
Permanent Secretary, David Rowlands
   Private Secretary, Jessica Bowles

BUSINESS DELIVERY SERVICES DIRECTORATE
Director, Hazel Parker-Brown

DRIVER, VEHICLE AND OPERATOR GROUP
Director-General, Stephen Hickey

DRIVER, VEHICLE AND OPERATOR DIRECTORATE
Director, John Plowman

LEGAL SERVICES DIRECTORATE
Director, Christopher Muttukumaru
Divisional Managers, Alan Jones *(Aviation);* Stephen Rock
   (Driving and Road Safety); Hussein Kaya *(Highways);*
   Elizabeth Walsh *(Railways, Operations and
   Construction);* Robert Caune *(Railways, Track and
   Safety);* David Jordan *(Road Vehicles);* Karen Booth
   (Employment and Corporate Services)

RAILWAYS, AVIATION, LOGISTICS, MARITIME AND SECURITY GROUP
Director-General (SCS), vacant
Directors, Roy Griffins *(Aviation Directorate);* Brian
   Wadsworth *(Logistics and Maritime Transport
   Directorate);* Mark Lambirth *(Rail Directorate);* Mike
   Fuhr *(Major Projects Directorate);* Niki Tompkinson
   (Transport Security Directorate); Vivien Bodnar *(People
   and Skills Programme Division)*
Deputy Director, John Grubb *(Transport Security Division)*
Chief Inspectors, Ken Smart *(Air Accidents Investigation
   Branch);* Stephen Meyer *(Marine Accidents Investigation
   Branch)*
Principal Investigator of Rail Accidents, Carolyn Griffiths
   (Rail Accidents Investigation Branch)

ROADS, REGIONAL AND LOCAL TRANSPORT GROUP
Director-General (SCS), Robert Devereux
Directors, Alan Davis *(Integrated and Local Transport
   Directorate);* Dennis Roberts *(Roads and Vehicle
   Directorate);* Bronwyn Hill *(Regional Transport
   Directorate)*

STRATEGY, FINANCE AND DELIVERY GROUP
Director-General, Willy Rickett
Directors, Charles Skinner *(Communication Directorate);*
   David McMillan *(Strategy and Delivery Directorate);*
   Chris Riley *(Transport Analysis and Economics
   Directorate);* Ken Beeton *(Transport Finance
   Directorate);* Ann Frye *(Mobility and Inclusion Unit)*
Chair, Trade Union Side, Chris Hickey

EXECUTIVE AGENCIES

DRIVER AND VEHICLE LICENSING AGENCY
Longview Road, Morriston, Swansea SA6 7JL
Tel: 01792-782341 Fax: 01792-782793
Web: www.dvla.gov.uk
The Agency is responsible for registering and licensing drivers and vehicles, and the collection and enforcement of vehicle exercise duty.
Chief Executive, C. Bennett

DRIVING STANDARDS AGENCY
Stanley House, Talbot Street, Nottingham NG1 5GU
Tel: 0115-901 2500 Fax: 0115-901 2940
Web: www.dsa.gov.uk
The Agency is responsible for carrying out theory and practical driving tests for car drivers, motorcyclists, bus and lorry drivers and for maintaining the registers of

Approved Driving Instructors and Large Goods Vehicle Instructors, as well as supervising Compulsory Basic Training (CBT) for learner motorcyclists. There are five area offices, which manage over 430 practical test centres across Britain.
Chief Executive, G. Austin

HIGHWAYS AGENCY
St Christopher House, Southwark Street, London SE1 0TE
Tel: 020-7921 4574 Fax: 020-7921 4592
Web: www.highways.gov.uk
The Agency is responsible for delivering the Transport Department's road programme and for maintaining the national road network in England.
Acting Chief Executive, Stephen Hickey

MARITIME AND COASTGUARD AGENCY
Spring Place, 105 Commercial Road, Southampton SO15 1EG
Tel: 023-8032 9100 Fax: 023-8032 9298
Web: www.mcga.gov.uk
The agency's aim is to prevent loss of life, continuously improving maritime safety and protecting the marine environment.
Chief Executive, Capt. Stephen Bligh
Chief Coastguard, J. Astbury

VEHICLE CERTIFICATION AGENCY
1 Eastgate Office Centre, Eastgate Road, Bristol BS5 6XX
Tel: 0117-951 5151 Fax: 0117-952 4103
Web: www.vca.gov.uk
The agency is the UK authority responsible for ensuring that vehicles and vehicle parts have been designed and constructed to meet internationally agreed standards of safety and environmental protection.
Chief Executive, D. W. Harvey

VEHICLE AND OPERATOR SERVICES AGENCY (VOSA)
Berkeley House, Croydon Street, Bristol BS5 0DA
Tel: 0117-954 3200 Fax: 0117-954 3212
Web: www.vosa.gov.uk
The Vehicle and Operator Services Agency was formed on 1 April 2003 from the merger of the Vehicle Inspectorate and the Traffic Area Network. The agency is responsible for processing applications for licences to operate heavy goods and public service vehicles and registering bus services; operating and administering testing schemes for all vehicles including statutory annual testing of commercial vehicles, single vehicle approval of imported vehicles and vehicle identity checks; supervision of the MOT scheme; enforcement checks of vehicle safety, drivers' hours and emissions; supporting the independent Traffic Commissioners in carrying out their responsibilities for operator licensing, vocational drivers and bus registration; providing training and advice for commercial operators and MOT testers; investigating vehicle accidents, defects and recalls.
Chief Executive, Maurice R. Newey

HM TREASURY
1 Horse Guards Road, London SW1A 2HQ
Tel: 020-7270 5000
Email: public.enquiries@hm-treasury.gov.uk
Web: www.hm-treasury.gov.uk
The Office of the Lord High Treasurer has been continuously in commission for well over 200 years. The Lord High Commissioners of HM Treasury are the First Lord of the Treasury (who is also the Prime Minister), the Chancellor of the Exchequer and five junior Lords. This Board of Commissioners is assisted at present by the Chief Secretary, the Parliamentary Secretary (who is also the Government Chief Whip in the House of Commons), the Paymaster-General, the Financial Secretary, and the Economic Secretary. The Prime Minister as First Lord is not primarily concerned in the day-to-day aspects of Treasury business; neither are the Parliamentary Secretary and the Junior Lords as Government Whips. Treasury business is managed by the Chancellor of the Exchequer and the other Treasury Ministers, assisted by the Permanent Secretary.
The Chief Secretary is responsible for public expenditure planning and control; public sector pay; value for money in the public services; public service agreements; public/private partnerships and procurement policy; strategic oversight of banking, financial services and insurance; departmental investment strategies; including the Capital Modernisation Fund and Invest to Save Budget; welfare reform; devolution; and resource accounting and budgeting.
The Paymaster-General is responsible for the Inland Revenue and the Valuation Office, with overall responsibility for the Finance Bill. She leads on personal taxation, business taxation, European and international tax issues.
Prime Minister and First Lord of the Treasury,
The Rt. Hon. Tony Blair, MP
Chancellor of the Exchequer,
The Rt. Hon. Gordon Brown, MP
Principal Private Secretary, Mark Bowman
Private Secretaries, Beth Russell; William Price
Parliamentary Private Secretary, Ann Keen, MP
Chief Economic Adviser to the Treasury, Ed Balls
Special Advisers, Ed Miliband; Ian Austin; S. Nye; Spencer Livermore
Council of Economic Advisers, Chris Wales; Paul Gregg; Ms Shriti Vadera; Maeve Sherlock; Stewart Wood
Chief Secretary to the Treasury, The Rt. Hon. Paul Boateng, MP
Private Secretary, Lucy Makinson
Parliamentary Private Secretary, Helen Southworth, MP
Paymaster-General, The Rt. Hon. Dawn Primarolo, MP
Private Secretary, Andy Gordon
Parliamentary Private Secretary, Chris Pond, MP
Financial Secretary to the Treasury, Ruth Kelly, MP
Private Secretary, Rob Gregory
Parliamentary Private Secretary, Tony Wright, MP
Economic Secretary to the Treasury, John Healey, MP
Private Secretary, Sam Woods
Permanent Secretary to the Treasury, Gus O'Donnell, CB
Parliamentary Clerk, David Martin
Parliamentary Secretary to the Treasury and Government Chief Whip, The Rt. Hon. Hilary Armstrong, MP
Private Secretary, Roy Stone
Treasurer of HM Household and Deputy Chief Whip, Bob Ainsworth, MP
Comptroller of HM Household, Thomas McAvoy, MP
Vice-Chamberlain of HM Household, Jim Fitzpatrick, MP
Lord Commissioners of HM Treasury (Whips), John Heppel, MP; Nick Ainger, MP; Jim Murphy, MP; Derek Twigg, MP; Joan Ryan, MP
Assistant Whips, Fraser Kemp, MP; Gillian Merron, MP; Charlotte Atkins, MP; Vernon Coaker, MP; Paul Clark, MP; Margaret Moran, MP; Bridget Prentice, MP

DIRECTORATES
Head of Ministerial Support Team (SCS), M. Bowman
Head of Communications and Strategy Team (SCS),
M. Ellam

MACROECONOMIC POLICY AND INTERNATIONAL
FINANCE
Managing Director, J. Cunliffe
Directors (SCS), S. Brooks; S. Pickford; S. Owen;
M. Dawes
Heads of Teams (SCS), C. M. Kelly; A. Kilpatrick;
D. Ramsden; G. Lloyd; R. Woods; J. de Berker;
A. Holland; I. Walker; H. Thompson; J. Stewart;
J. Ockenden; P. Rankin; B. Warmington; H. Freeman

BUDGET AND PUBLIC FINANCES
Managing Director (SCS), R. Culpin
Directors (SCS), N. Holgate; I. Rogers
Heads of Teams (SCS), P. Betts; I. Taylor; G. Parker;
D. Deaton; D. Richardson; H. John; P. Short; A. Lewis;
P. O'Sullivan; A. Cottrell

PUBLIC SERVICES
Managing Director, N. Macpherson
Directors, L. de Groot; A. Sharples; J. Grice; J. Stephens;
A. Charlesworth
Heads of Teams, R. Dunn; M. Wheatley; A. Ritchie;
A. Graham; L. Atter; P. Johnston; P. Samuel; S. Mullen;
M. Brivah; J. Dodds; J. Hall; J. Taylor; S. Meek

CORPORATE SERVICES AND DEVELOPMENT (CSD)
Managing Director (SCS), H. Douglas
Heads of Teams (SCS), C. Pearson; P. Pelger; S. Norris;
R. Brightwell; B. Cass; S. Sheen

FINANCIAL MANAGEMENT, REPORTING AND AUDIT
Managing Director (SCS), A. Likierman
*Director and Head of Treasury Office of Accounts Team
(SCS),* B. Glicksman
Heads of Teams (SCS), D. Loweth; I. Carruthers; C. Butler;
A. M. Jones; R. Molan; M. Singh; H. Pullinger
FINANCE, REGULATION AND INDUSTRY
Managing Director (SCS), J. Sassoon
Directors (SCS), J. Kingman; W. Owen
Heads of Teams (SCS), S. Beckett; D. Storey; C. Maxwell;
S. Catchpole; D. Lawton; R. Price; G. Spence; P. Mills;
P. Kirkman; L. Makinson; O. Robbins; J. Kohli

EXECUTIVE AGENCIES

NATIONAL SAVINGS AND INVESTMENTS
see Finance section

OFFICE FOR NATIONAL STATISTICS
see Public Bodies section

ROYAL MINT
see Public Bodies section

UNITED KINGDOM DEBT MANAGEMENT OFFICE
Eastcheap Court, 11 Philpot Lane, London, EC3M 8UD
Tel: 020-7862 6500 Fax: 020- 7862 6509
The UK Debt Management Office was launched as an
executive agency of the Treasury in April 1998. The
office has two main functions: it is the Government's debt
manager (issuing gilts, managing the gilt market); and the
Government's cash manager (balancing the Exchequer's
cash flow on a daily basis). On 1 July 2002 the

operations of the Public Loan Works Board (PWLB), and
the Commissioners for the Reduction of the National
Debt (CRND) were integrated with the DMO.
Chief Executive, R. Stheeman

OTHER BODIES
OFFICE OF GOVERNMENT COMMERCE (OGC)
Trevelyan House, 26–30 Great Peter Street, London
SW1P 2BY
Tel: 0845-000 4999
Web: www.ogc.gov.uk

OGC BUYING SOLUTIONS
Royal Liver Building, Pier Head, Liverpool L3 1PE
Tel: 0870-268 2222 Fax: 0151-227 3315
Web: www. ogcbuyingsolutions.gov.uk

DEPARTMENT OF HM PROCURATOR-GENERAL AND
TREASURY SOLICITOR
Queen Anne's Chambers, 28 Broadway, London SW1H 9JS
Tel: 020-7210 3000 Fax: 020-7210 3004
The Treasury Solicitor's Department provides legal
services for many Government departments. Those
without their own lawyers are provided with legal advice,
and both they and other departments are provided with
litigation services. The Treasury Solicitor is also the
Queen's Proctor, and is responsible for collecting Bona
Vacantia on behalf of the Crown. The Department
became an executive agency in 1996.
HM Procurator-General and Treasury Solicitor (SCS), Juliet
Wheldon

LITIGATION DIVISION
(SCS), R. Aitken; Mrs D. Babar; P. Bennett; D. Pearson;
L. John-Charles; A. D. Lawton; B. McKay; P. R.
Messer; D. Palmer; R. Phillips; A. J. Sandal; P. Kent;
H. Giles; S. Cochrane; A. Chapman; P. Whitehurst;
M. Truran

QUEEN'S PROCTOR DIVISION
Queen's Proctor (SCS), Juliet Wheldon
Assistant Queen's Proctor (G6), Ravi Sampanthar

DIRECTORATE OF CORPORATE STRATEGY
Director of Corporate Strategy (SCS), Hilary Jackson
Assistant Director Establishments (G7), Ms H. Donnelly
Assistant Director Finance (G7), C. A. Woolley
Assistant Director Information Systems (G6), M. Gabbidon
Assistant Director Human Resources (G6), Ms M. Esplin
Business Support Manager, E. Blishen

BONA VACANTIA DIVISION
(SCS), Valerie Caln

EUROPEAN DIVISION
(SCS), J. E. Collins; A. Ridout; M. C. P. Thomas

CULTURE, MEDIA AND SPORT DIVISION
(SCS), Ms I. Letwin

CABINET OFFICE AND CENTRAL ADVISORY DIVISION
(SCS), Ms R. Jeffreys, C. House

MINISTRY OF DEFENCE ADVISORY DIVISION
Metropole Building, Northumberland Avenue, London
WC2N 5BL Tel: 020-7218 4691
(SCS), V. Rose; L. Nicoll; H. Morrison; Mrs V. Collett;
M. Hemming

DEPARTMENT FOR EDUCATION AND SKILLS DIVISION
Caxton House, Tothill Street, London SW1H 9NA
Tel: 020-7273 3000
(SCS), F. D. W. Clarke; P. Kilgarriff; D. Macrae; D. Aries;
N. Ash

HM TREASURY ADVISORY DIVISION
1 Horse Guards Road, London SW1A 2HQ
Tel: 020-7270 3000
(SCS), M. A. Blythe; J. R. J. Braggins; J. Jones;
P. Henderson; A. Stewart; S. Cochran

WALES OFFICE
Gwydyr House, Whitehall, London SW1A 2ER
Tel: 020-7270 0549 Fax: 020-7270 0568
Email: wales.office@wales.gov.uk
Web: www.walesoffice.gov.uk
The Wales Office is the department of the Secretary of
State for Wales, who represents Welsh interests in the
Cabinet. *See* also Regional Government section and
Department for Constitutional Affairs.
Secretary of State for Wales, The Rt. Hon. Peter Hain, MP
 Principal Private Secretary, Simon Morris
 Parliamentary Private Secretary, Chris Ruane, MP
Parliamentary Under-Secretary, Don Touhig, MP
 Head of Office, Alison Jackson

DEPARTMENT FOR WORK AND PENSIONS
Richmond House, 79 Whitehall, London SW1A 2NS
Tel: 020-7238 0800 Fax: 020-7238 0763
Email: ministers@dwp.gsi.gov.uk
Web: www.dwp.gov.uk
The Department for Work and Pensions was formed on 8
June 2001 from parts of the former Department of Social
Security and Department for Education and Employment
and the Employment Service. The department helps
unemployed people of working age into work, helps
employers to fill their vacancies and provides financial
support to people unable to help themselves through
back to work programmes. The department also
administers the Child Support system, social security
benefits and the social fund. In addition, the department
has reciprocal social security arrangements with other
countries.
 In April 2002 the Benefits Agency and the
Employment Service was replaced by the Jobcentre Plus
network (responsible for helping people to find jobs and
paying benefits to people of working age), and the
Pension Service which administers the Benefits Agency's
pension-related services.
Secretary of State for Work and Pensions,
 The Rt. Hon. Andrew Smith, MP
 Principal Private Secretary, Susan Park
 Private Secretaries, Liz Wood; Kate Kelly; Charlotte
 Wightwick; Frances Thompson
 Special Advisers, Chris Norton; Tom Clark
 Parliamentary Private Secretary, Ivan Henderson, MP
Minister of State, Des Browne, MP *(Work)*
 Parliamentary Private Secretary, Kali Mountford
 Private Secretary, Caroline Crowther
Minister of State, Malcolm Wicks, MP *(Pensions)*
 Private Secretary, Denise Whitehead
 Assistant Private Secretary, Helen Hutchings
 Parliamentary Private Secretary, David Cairns, MP

Parliamentary Under-Secretary of State (Lords), The Rt.
 Hon. The Baroness Hollis of Heigham, DL *(Children
 and the Family)*
 Private Secretary, Lucy Vause
Parliamentary Under-Secretary of State, Chris Pond, MP
 (Work)
 Private Secretary, Fiona Walshe
Parliamentary Under-Secretary of State, Maria Eagle, MP
 (Disabled People)
 Private Secretary, Emma Davis
Parliamentary Under-Secretary, Baroness Ashton of
 Upholland *(Sure Start)*
Permanent Secretary (SCS), Sir Richard Mottram, KCB
 Private Secretary, Judith Tunstall
 Parliamentary Clerk, Tim Elms

WORKING AGE AND CHILDREN GROUP
Group Director (SCS), Ms U. Brennan
Director, Child Benefit Centre, vacant
Director, Children and Housing, M. Neale
Director, Fraud, Planning and Presentation Strategy,
 R. Clark
Director, National Employment Panel, Ms C. Stratton
Director, Work and Welfare Strategy, M. Richardson

PENSIONS AND DISABILITY GROUP
Managing Director, P. Gray
Director, Disability and Carers, D. Brereton, CB
Director, Disability and Carers Service, J. Sumner
*Director, Joint International Unit (also for Department for
 Education and Skills)* C. Tucker
Director, Pensions Strategy and Client Programme,
 Ms H. Reynolds
Director, Private Pensions, Ms J. Hill
Director, Private Pensions II, Charles Ramsden

CORPORATE AND SHARED SERVICES GROUP FINANCE
Group Director and Principal Finance Officer (SCS),
 J. Codling
Director, Commercial, D. Smith
Director, Corporate Management Information, David Kirk
Director, Financial Services, P. Robinson
Director, Financial Management, M. Davison
Director, Internal Assurance Services, C. Turner

PROGRAMME AND SYSTEMS DELIVERY GROUP
Group Director, R. Westcott
Director, Digital Infrastructure, A. Stott
Director, External Supply, P. Crahan
Director, Joint Programme Management, Ms S. Newton
Director, Planning and Finance, K. Palmer

HUMAN RESOURCES GROUP
Group Director, K. White
Diversity Director, Ms B. Burford
Head of Department, Development, J. Ashe
Head of Department, HR Services, G. Adey
Head of Department, Occupational Psychology,
 Dr M. Dalgliesh
Head of Department, Senior Civil Service, Kim Archer
Head of Department, Training Services, B. Gormley
Head of Department, Workforce Planning, Ms S. Rice

MEDICAL POLICY AND CORPORATE MEDICAL GROUP
Chief Medical Adviser and Medical Director, Dr M. Aylward
Policy Manager, State Incapacity Benefits, Dr P. Sawney
Policy Manager, Disability and Carer Benefits,
 Dr R. Thomas

EU of Medical Advisers in Social Security (UEMASS),
  Dr P. Stidolph
Contractorisation of Medical Services (IMPACT) Project,
  Dr M. Henderson

LAW AND SPECIAL POLICY GROUP
Head of Group, Ms M. Morgan, CB
Director of Legal Services, J. Catlin
Assistant Director, Commercial Branch, R. Powell
Assistant Director, SOL Litigation, Ms A. James
Assistant Director, SOL Prosecutions, Ms S. Edwards

INFORMATION AND ANALYSIS DIRECTORATE
Director, Nick Dyson
Policy Managers, Ajudicational and Constitutional Reform,
  J. Griffiths
Policy Managers, Welfare to Work Strategy,
  Ms B. O'Gorman
Policy Managers, Pension Provision Group, G. Fiegehen

COMMUNICATIONS DIRECTORATE
Director, S. MacDowall
Head of Corporate Communications, K. Young
Head of Marketing, S. O'Neill
Head of Media Relations, Ms S. Dodd

EXECUTIVE AGENCIES

APPEALS SERVICE AGENCY
see Tribunals Section

CHILD SUPPORT AGENCY
Long Benton, Benton Park Road, Newcastle upon Tyne
NE98 1YX
CSA Helpline: 08457-133133
The Agency was set up in April 1993. It is responsible for
the administration of the Child Support Act and for the
assessment, collection and enforcement of maintenance
payments for all new cases.
Chief Executive, D. Smith

JOBCENTRE PLUS
Richmond House, 79 Whitehall, London SW1A 2NS
Tel: 020-7238 0800 Fax: 020-7238-0763
Web: www.jobcentreplus.gov.uk
Jobcentre Plus was formed in April 2002 following the
merger of the Employment Service and some parts of the
Benefits Agency. The agency administers claims for and
payment of social security benefits to help people gain
employment or improve their prospects for work as well
as helping employers to fill their vacancies.
Chief Executive, D. Anderson

THE PENSION SERVICE
Trevelyan House, 30 Great Peter Street, London SW1P 2BY
Public Enquiries: 0113-232 24143
The Pension Service was created in April 2002 to deliver
services to pensioners through a network of twenty-six
pension centres.
Chief Executive, Ms A. Cleveland

VETERANS AGENCY
Norcross, Blackpool, Lancs FY5 3WP
Tel: 0800-169 2277
Email: help@veteransagency.mod.uk
Web: www.veteransagency.mod.uk
The Agency administers the payment of war disablement
and war widows' pensions and provides welfare services
and support to war disablement pensioners, war widows
and their dependants and carers.
Chief Executive, A. Burnham

PUBLIC OFFICES

ADJUDICATOR'S OFFICE
Haymarket House, 28 Haymarket, London SW1Y 4SP
Tel: 020-7930 2292 Fax: 020-7930 2298
Web: www.adjucatorsoffice.gov.uk

The Adjudicator's Office opened in 1993 and investigates complaints about the way the Inland Revenue (including the Valuation Office Agency), Customs and Excise and the Public Guardianship Office have handled a person's affairs.
The Adjudicator, Dame Barbara Mills, DBE, QC
Head of Office, C. Gordon

ADVISORY, CONCILIATION AND ARBITRATION SERVICE
Brandon House, 180 Borough High Street, London SE1 1LW
Tel: 020-7210 3613 Fax: 020-7210 3708
Web: www.acas.org.uk

The Advisory, Conciliation and Arbitration Service (ACAS) was set up under the Employment Protection Act 1975 (the provisions now being found in the Trade Union and Labour Relations (Consolidation) Act 1992).

ACAS is directed by a Council consisting of a full-time chairman and part-time employer, trade union and independent members, all appointed by the Secretary of State for Trade and Industry. The functions of the Service are to promote the improvement of industrial relations in general, to provide facilities for conciliation, mediation and arbitration as means of avoiding and resolving industrial disputes, and to provide advisory and information services on industrial relations matters to employers, employees and their representatives.

ACAS has regional offices in Birmingham, Bristol, Cardiff, Fleet, Glasgow, Leeds, Liverpool, London, Manchester, Newcastle upon Tyne and Nottingham.
Chair, R. Donaghy, OBE
National Conciliator (G6), T. Lippiatt

ANCIENT MONUMENTS BOARD FOR WALES (CADW)
Crown Buildings, Cathays Park, Cardiff CF10 3NQ
Tel: 029-2050 0200 Fax: 029-2082 6375
Email: cadw@wales.gsi.gov.uk
Web: www.cadw.wales.gov.uk

The Ancient Monuments Board for Wales advises the Welsh Assembly Government on its statutory functions in respect of ancient monuments.
Chairman, Prof. R. R. Davies, CBE, FBA, D.Phil
Members, R. G. Keen; Prof. W. Davies, FBA, FSA;
M. J. Garner; Prof. R. A. Griffiths, D.Litt.;
R. Brewer, FSA; Prof. A. Whittle, FBA, D.Phil;
C. Musson, MBE, FSA; Prof. M. Aldhouse-Green, FSA
Secretary, Mrs J. Booker

ARTS COUNCILS

The Arts Council of Great Britain was established as an independent body in 1946 to be the principal channel for the Government's support of the arts. In 1994 the Scottish and Welsh Arts Councils became autonomous and the Arts Council of Great Britain became the Arts Council of England.

The Arts Councils are responsible for the distribution of the proceeds of the National Lottery allocated to the arts.

ARTS COUNCIL ENGLAND
14 Great Peter Street, London SW1P 3NQ
Tel: 0845-300 6200 Fax: 020-7973 6590
Email: enquiries@artscouncil.org.uk
Web: www.artscouncil.org.uk

Arts Council England is the national development agency for the arts in England, distributing public money from Government and the National Lottery. Between 2003 and 2006 Arts Council England will invest £2 billion of public funds in the arts in England. Arts Council Grants for the arts are for individuals, arts organisations, national touring and other people who use the arts in their work.

On 1 April 2002, the Arts Council of England and the nine regional arts boards joined together to form a single development organisation for the arts.

The Government grant for 2003–4 is £335 million.
Chairman, G. Robinson
Members, Sir Norman Adsetts, OBE; T. Bloxham, MBE;
Ms D. Bull, CBE; P. Collard; Ms D. Grubb;
Lady Sue Woodford Hollick; Prof. A. Livingston;
S. Lowe; B. McMaster, CBE; Ms E. Owusu;
W. Sieghart; Prof. S. Timperley; Ms D. Wilson
Chief Executive, P. Hewitt

REGIONAL OFFICES
EAST ENGLAND ARTS, Eden House, 48–49 Bateman
Street, Cambridge CB2 1LR. Tel: 01223-454400.
Chair, Prof. S. Timperley
EAST MIDLANDS ARTS, St Nicholas Court,
25–27 Castle Gate, Nottingham NG1 7AR.
Tel: 0115-989 7520. *Chair,* S. Lowe
LONDON ARTS, 2 Pear Tree Court, London EC1R 0DS.
Tel: 020-7608 6100. *Chair,* Lady Hollick
NORTH EAST, Central Square, Forth Street,
Newcastle upon Tyne NE1 3PJ. Tel: 0191-255 8500.
Chair, P. Collard
NORTH WEST ARTS, Manchester House, 22 Bridge Street,
Manchester M3 3AB. Tel: 0161-834 6644.
Chair, T. Bloxham, MBE
SOUTH EAST ARTS, Sovereign House, Church Street,
Brighton BN1 1RA. Tel: 01273-763000.
Chair, Ms D. Grubb
SOUTH WEST ARTS, Bradninch Place, Gandy Street, Exeter
EX4 3LS. Tel: 01392-218188. *Chair,* Prof. A. Livingston
WEST MIDLANDS ARTS, 82 Granville Street, Birmingham
B1 2LH. Tel: 0121-631 3121. *Chair,* Ms D. Wilson
YORKSHIRE ARTS, 21 Bond Street, Dewsbury, W. Yorks
WF13 1AX. Tel: 01924-455555. *Chair,* Sir Norman
Adsetts

ARTS COUNCIL OF NORTHERN IRELAND

MacNeice House, 77 Malone Road, Belfast BT9 6AQ
Tel: 028-9038 5200 Fax: 028-9066 1715
Email: publicaffairs@artscouncil-ni.org
Web: www.artscouncil-ni.org

The Arts Council of Northern Ireland is the prime distributor of Government funds in support of the arts in Northern Ireland. It is funded by the Department of Culture, Arts and Leisure, and the grant for 2003–4 is around £7.4 million.
Chair, Ms R. Kelly
Vice-Chair, M. Bradley
Members, Mrs E. M. Benson; Mrs K. Bond;
    W Chamberlain; Ms L. Finnegan; Ms J. A. Holmes;
    A. Kennedy; T. Kerr; A. McDowell; B. J. Milligan;
    W H. C. Montgomery; Ms S. M. O'Connor;
    G. O'Heara; P. Spratt
Chief Executive, Ms R. McDonough

ARTS COUNCIL OF WALES

9 Museum Place, Cardiff CF10 3NX
Tel: 029-2037 6500 Fax: 029-2022 1447
Email: info@artswales.org.uk
Web: www.artswales.org.uk

The Arts Council of Wales funds arts organisations in Wales and is funded by the National Assembly for Wales and is the distributor of National Lottery fund to the arts in Wales. The grant for 2002–3 was £20.783 million.
Chairman, Geraint Talfan Davies
Members, D. Davies; Dr H. Walford Davies; E. Fivet;
    S. Garrett; E. ap Gwyn; H. James; D. Jones; P. Ryan,
    OBE; Ms M. A. Elis; Ms J. Roberts; D. W. Walters
Chief Executive, P. Tyndall

SCOTTISH ARTS COUNCIL

12 Manor Place, Edinburgh EH3 7DD
Tel: 0131-226 6051 Fax: 0131-225 9833
Email: help.desk@scottisharts.org.uk
Web: www.scottisharts.org.uk

The Scottish Arts Council is the main arts development agency in Scotland. It is a non-departmental public body, accountable to Scottish Ministers. The Scottish Arts Council investing funds from the Scottish Executive and National Lottery and working with partners to support and develop artistic excellence and creativity throughout Scotland.
Chairman, J. Boyle
Vice-Chair, Ms D. Idiens
Members, Cllr E. Cameron; J. Scott Moncrieff; W. Speirs;
    Ms J. Baker; Ms L. Mitchell; J. Mulgrew
Director, G. Berry

ART GALLERIES AND ASSOCIATED BODIES

NATIONAL GALLERIES OF SCOTLAND

The Mound, Edinburgh EH2 2EL
Tel: 0131-624 6200 Fax: 0131-343 3250

The National Galleries of Scotland comprise the National Gallery of Scotland, the Scottish National Portrait Gallery, the Scottish National Gallery of Modern Art, the Dean Gallery and the Royal Scottish Academy Building. There are also outstations at Paxton House, Berwickshire,

and Duff House, Banffshire. Total Government grant-in-aid for 2003–4 is £12.54 million.

TRUSTEES
Chairman of the Trustees, Mr B. Ivory, CBE
Trustees, Ms V. Atkinson; Ms A. Bonnar; Bailie
    E. Cameron; G. J. N. Gemmell, CBE; M. Ellington;
    Dr I. McKenzie Smith, OBE; Prof. R. Thomson;
    G. Weaver; Dr Ruth Wishart

OFFICERS
Director-General (G4), Sir T. Clifford, FRSE
Keeper of Conservation (G6), M. Gallagher
Head of Press and Information (G7), P. Convery
Head of Education (G7), M. Finn
Registrar (G7), Miss A. Buddle
Buildings (G7), R. Galbraith
Director, National Gallery of Scotland (G6), M. Clarke
Director, Scottish National Portrait Gallery (G6),
    J. Holloway
Curator of Photography, Miss S. F. Stevenson
*Director, Scottish National Gallery of Modern Art and
    Dean Gallery (G6),* R. Calvocoressi

NATIONAL GALLERY

Trafalgar Square, London WC2N 5DN
Tel: 020-7747 2885 Fax: 020-7747 2423
Web: www.nationalgallery.org.uk

The National Gallery, which houses a permanent collection of western painting from the 13th to the 20th century, was founded in 1824, following a parliamentary grant of £60,000 for the purchase and exhibition of the Angerstein collection of pictures. The present site was first occupied in 1838; an extension to the north of the building with a public entrance in Orange Street was opened in 1975, and the Sainsbury wing was opened in 1991. Total Government grant-in-aid for 2002–3 was £20,449 million.

BOARD OF TRUSTEES
Chairman, P. Scott, QC
Trustees, Prof. D. Ades; S. Burke; J. Fenton; M. Getty;
    Prof. J. Higgins; Lady Hopkins; Sir John Kerr;
    Dr D. Landau; J. Lessore; D. A. Moore; J. Snow;
    R. Sondhi; Sir Colin Southgate

OFFICERS
Director, Dr C. Saumarez Smith
Head of Curational Department, Dr S. Foister
Senior Curator, D. Jaffé
Chief Restorer, M. H. Wyld, CBE
Scientific Adviser, Dr A. Roy
Director of Administration, J. MacAuslan
Head of Education, K. Adler
Head of Communications and Media, Clare Gough

NATIONAL PORTRAIT GALLERY

St Martin's Place, London WC2H 0HE
Tel: 020-7306 0055 Fax: 020-7306 0056
Web: www.npg.org.uk

A grant was made in 1856 to form a gallery of the portraits of the most eminent persons in British history. The present building was opened in 1896 and the Ondaatje Wing; including a new Balcony Gallery, Tudor Gallery, IT Gallery, Lecture Theatre and roof-top restaurant opened in May 2000. There are three regional partnerships displaying portraits in appropriate settings: Montacute House, Beningbrough Hall and Bodelwyddan Castle. Total Government grant-in-aid for 2003–4 is £5.7 million.

BOARD OF TRUSTEES
Chairman, Sir David Scholey, CBE
Trustees, The Rt. Hon. Peter Hain, MP; Prof. P. King, CBE, PRA; Ms. F. Fraser; Sir M. Hastings; T. Phillips, CBE, RA; Prof. The Earl Russell, FBA; Mrs A. Shulman; Sir John Weston, KCMG; Baroness Willoughby de Eresby, DL; Prof. D. Cannadine; Prof. L. Jordanova; Dr C. Ondaatje, CBE, OC; Sara Selwood
Director (G3), S. Nairne

ROYAL FINE ART COMMISSION FOR SCOTLAND
Bakehouse Close, 146 Canongate, Edinburgh EH8 8DD
Tel: 0131-556 6699 Fax: 0131-556 6633
Web: www.futurescotland.org

The Commission was established in 1927 and advises Ministers and local authorities on the visual impact and quality of design of construction projects. It is an independent body and gives its opinions impartially.
Chairman, The Rt. Hon. The Lord Cameron of Lochbroom, PC, FRSE
Commissioners, Ms J. Malvenan; R. G. Maund; M. Murray; D. Page; B. Rae; Prof. R. Russell; M. Turnbull; A. Wright; Ms K. Anderson; Mrs M. Hickish; P. Stallan
Secretary, C. Prosser

TATE BRITAIN
Millbank, London SW1P 4RG
Tel: 020-7887 8008 Fax: 020-7887 8007
Web: www.tate.org.uk

Tate Britain displays the national collection of British art. The gallery opened in 1897, the cost of building (£80,000) being defrayed by Sir Henry Tate, who also contributed the nucleus of the present collection. The Turner wing was opened in 1910, and further galleries and a new sculpture hall followed in 1937. In 1979 a further extension was built, and the Clore Gallery, for the Turner collection, was opened in 1987. The Centenary Development was opened in 2001. Tate consists of four galleries: Tate Britain and Tate Modern in London, Tate Liverpool and Tate St Ives.

BOARD OF TRUSTEES
Chairman, D. Verey
Trustees, Prof. D. Ades; Ms H. Alexander; Ms V. Barnsley; Prof. J. Latto; J. Snow; J. Studzinski; Ms G. Wearing; C. Ofili; Ms J. Opie; Sir Howard Davies; P. Myners

OFFICERS
Director, Sir Nicholas Serota
Deputy Director, Alex Beard
Director of Collections, Jan Debbaut
Director, Tate Britain, S. Deuchar
Director, Tate Modern, V. Todoli
Director, Tate Liverpool, C. Gruneberg
Director, Tate St Ives, S. Daniel-McElvoy

TATE MODERN
Bankside, London SE1 9TG
Tel: 020-7887 8008 Booking: 020-7887 8888
Web: www.tate.org.uk

Opened on 11 May 2000, Tate Modern displays the Tate collection of international modern art dating from 1900 to the present day. It includes works by Dalí, Picasso, Matisse and Warhol as well as many contemporary works. It is housed in the former Bankside Power Station in London, redesigned by the Swiss architects Herzog & de Meuron.
Director, V. Todoli

WALLACE COLLECTION
Hertford House, Manchester Square, London W1M 3BN
Tel: 020-7563 9500 Fax: 020-7224 2155
Web: www.wallacecollection.org.

The Wallace Collection was bequeathed to the nation by the widow of Sir Richard Wallace, Bt., in 1897, and Hertford House was subsequently acquired by the Government. Total Government grant-in-aid for 2002–3 was £2.463 million.
Director, Miss R. J. Savill
Head of Finance and Administration (acting), Ms H. Ramsey

ASSEMBLY OMBUDSMAN FOR NORTHERN IRELAND AND NORTHERN IRELAND COMMISSIONER FOR COMPLAINTS
Progressive House, 33 Wellington Place, Belfast BT1 6HN
Tel: 028-9023 3821 Fax: 028-9023 4912
Email: ombudsman@ni-ombudsman.org.uk
Web: www.ni-ombudsman.org.uk

The Ombudsman is appointed under legislation with powers to investigate complaints by people claiming to have sustained injustice in consequence of maladministration arising from action taken by a Northern Ireland Government department, or any other public body within his remit. Staff are presently seconded from the Northern Ireland Civil Service.
Ombudsman, T. Frawley
Deputy Ombudsman, J. MacQuarrie
Directors, C. O'Hare; R. Doherty; H. Mallon; P. Gibson

AUDIT COMMISSIONS

AUDIT COMMISSION FOR LOCAL AUTHORITIES AND THE NATIONAL HEALTH SERVICE IN ENGLAND AND WALES
1 Vincent Square, London SW1P 2PN
Tel: 020-7828 1212 Fax: 020-7976 6187
Web: www.audit-commission.gov.uk

The Audit Commission was set up in 1983 and is responsible for appointing external auditors to local authorities, including the Greater London Authority, and local National Health Service bodies in England and Wales. It is also responsible for promoting the proper stewardship of public finances and value for money in the services provided by local authorities and health bodies.
  The Commission has a chairman, a deputy chairman and up to 18 members who are appointed by the Office

of the Deputy Prime Minister in consultation with the Secretary of State for Wales and the Health Secretaries in England and Wales.

Chair, J. Strachan
Members, Dr. P. Lane; G. Lemos; Cllr N. Skellett; C. Swinson; D. Moss; Sir David Williams; Prof. S. Richards; Dr J. Curson; Sir Graham Hart, KCB; Ms E. Filkin; J. Bowen; R. Hoyle; Ms A. Fresko
Controller of Audit, A. Foster
Commission Secretary, A. Morris
Chief Executive of District Audit Service, A. Meekings

AUDIT SCOTLAND

110 George Street, Edinburgh EH2 4LH
Tel: 0131-477 1234 Fax: 0131-477 4567
Web: www.audit-scotland.gov.uk

Audit Scotland was set up on 1 April 2000 to provide services to the Accounts Commission and the Auditor General for Scotland. Together they help to ensure that the Scottish Executive and public sector bodies in Scotland are held accountable for the proper, efficient and effective use of around £18 billion of public funds.

Audit Scotland's work covers over 200 bodies including local authorities, police and fire boards; NHS boards and trusts; further education colleges; the water authority; departments of the Scottish Executive; executive agencies such as the Prison Service and non-departmental public bodies such as Scottish Enterprise.

Audit Scotland carries out financial and regularity audits to ensure that the public sector bodies adhere to the highest standards of financial management and governance. It also performs audits to ensure that these bodies achieve the best value for money. All of Audit Scotland's work in connection with local authorities, fire and police boards is carried out for the Accounts Commission while its other work is undertaken for the Auditor General.

Auditor General, R. W. Black
Accounts Commission Chairman, A. MacNish
Secretary, W. F. Magee

BANK OF ENGLAND

Threadneedle Street, London EC2R 8AH
Tel: 020-7601 4444 Fax: 020-7601 4771
Email: enquiries@bankofengland.co.uk
Web: www.bankofengland.co.uk

The Bank of England was incorporated in 1694 under royal charter. It is the banker of the Government and it manages the note issue. Since May 1997 it has been operationally independent and its Monetary Policy Committee has had responsibility for setting short-term interest rates to meet the Government's inflation target. As the central reserve bank of the country, the Bank keeps the accounts of British banks, who maintain with it a proportion of their cash resources, and of most overseas central banks. The Bank has three main areas of activity: Monetary Stability, Market Operations and Financial Stability. Its responsibility for banking supervision has been transferred to the Financial Services Authority. (*See* also Financial Services Regulation section).

Governor, M. A. King
Deputy Governors, Sir Andrew Large; Ms R. Lomax
Non-Executive Directors, Sir David Cooksey; Sir Howard Davies; Sir Ian Gibson, CBE; Ms K. A. O'Donovan; G. Hall; Dr D. Julius, CBE; Sir John Bond; Mrs M. Francis; Ms B. Blow; Sir Brian Moffat, OBE;

W. Morris; Mrs L. Powers-Freeling; B. Barber; The Hon. Peter Jay; Dr D. Potter, CBE; Ms H. Rabbatts, CBE
Monetary Policy Committee, The Governor; the Deputy Governors; Prof. S. Nickell; C. Bean; Ms K. Barker; Ms M. Bell; P. Tucker; R. Lambert
Advisers to the Governor, M. Glover; C. Goodhart
Chief Cashier and Deputy Director, Banking and Market Services, Ms M. V. Lowther
Chief Registrar, G. P. Sparkes
Secretary, P. D. Rodgers
The Auditor, Mrs C. Brady

BOARD OF INLAND REVENUE

Somerset House, Strand, London WC2R 1LB
Tel: 020-7438 6622 Fax: 020-7438 7562
Email: library.ir.sh@gtnet.gov.uk
Web: www.inlandrevenue.gov.uk

The Board of Inland Revenue was constituted under the Inland Revenue Board Act 1849. The Board administers and collects direct taxes – income tax, corporation tax, capital gains tax, inheritance tax, stamp duty, and petroleum revenue tax – and advises the Chancellor of the Exchequer on policy questions involving them. The Department's Valuation Office is an executive agency responsible for valuing property for tax purposes. The Contributions Agency of the Department for Work and Pensions which is responsible for the collection of contributions under the National Insurance scheme, became part of the Inland Revenue in April 1999 and is now an executive office called the National Insurance Contributions Office. The Contributions Unit of the Social Security Agency in Northern Ireland also transferred to the Inland Revenue in April 1999.

THE BOARD
Chairman (G1), Sir Nicholas Montagu, KCB
Deputy Chairmen (G2), T. J. Flesher; Ms A. Chant
Head of Revenue Policy, D. Hartnett
Chief Executive, Valuation Office Agency, M. Johns

DIVISIONS
Director, Analysis Research, (G3), Prof. D. Ulph
Director of Business Services (G3), J. Yard
Director, Business Tax (G3), Ms M. Hay
Director, Capital and Savings (G3), M. Williams
Director, Human Resources Division (G3), A. Walker
Director, International (G3), G. Makhlouf
Director, Personal Tax (G3), T. Orhinal
Director, Service Delivery Support (G3), S. Banyard
Director of Special Compliance, C. Hall
Head, Strategy and Planning, S. Norris
Principal of Tax Law Rewrite (G3), R. R. Martin

EXECUTIVE OFFICES
ACCOUNTS OFFICE (CUMBERNAULD), St Mungo's Road, Cumbernauld, Glasgow G70 5TR. *Director,* J. Brown
ACCOUNTS OFFICE (SHIPLEY), Shipley, Bradford, W. Yorks BD98 8AA. *Director,* P. Gronow
CAPITAL TAXES OFFICE (SCOTLAND), Meldrum House, 15 Drumshugh Gardens, Edinburgh, EH3 7UG. *Registrar,* D. Erasmus
CENTRE FOR NON-RESIDENTS, St John's House, Merton Road, Bootle L26 9BB; Fitz Roy House, PO Box 46, Castle Meadow, Nottingham NG2 1BD. *Director,* J. Johnston
ENFORCEMENT AND INSOLVENCY SERVICE, Durrington Bridge House, Barrington Road, Worthing, W. Sussex BN12 4SE. *Director,* R. Steele

FINANCIAL ACCOUNTING OFFICE, South Block, Barrington Road, Worthing, W. Sussex BN12 4XH. *Director,* J. Gant

INLAND REVENUE CAPITAL TAXES, Ferrers House, PO Box 38, Castle Meadow Road, Nottingham NG2 1BB. *Director,* J. Leigh-Pemberton

INTERNAL AUDIT OFFICE, 2nd Floor (North), 22 Kingsway, London WC2B 6NR. *Director,* M. Neate

MARKETING AND COMMUNICATIONS, Ground Floor, New Wing Somerset House, Strand, London WC2R 1LB. *Director of Communications,* I. Schoolar

NATIONAL INSURANCE CONTRIBUTIONS OFFICE, DWP Longbenton, Benton Park Road, Newcastle upon Tyne NE98 1ZZ. *Chief Executive (G3),* A. Fisher

OIL TAXATION OFFICE, Melbourne House, Aldwych, London WC2B 4LL. *Director,* R. Dyall

SAVINGS, PENSIONS AND SHARES, New Wing, Somerset House, London WC2R 1LB. *Director,* Ms C. Rookes

SOLICITOR'S OFFICE, East Wing, Somerset House, London WC2R 1LB. *Solicitor (G2),* P. Ridd

SOLICITOR'S OFFICE (SCOTLAND), Clarendon House, 114–116 George Street, Edinburgh EH2 4LH. *Solicitor,* D. Wishart

SPECIAL COMPLIANCE OFFICE, Angel Court, 199 Borough High Street, London SE1 1HZ. *Director,* C. Hall

STAMP OFFICE, New Wing, Somerset House, London WC2R 1LB. *Director,* C. Lester

IR LEARNING, Lawress Hall, Riseholme Park, Lincoln LN2 2BJ. *Director,* Ms L. Hinnigan

REGIONAL EXECUTIVE OFFICES

INLAND REVENUE CENTRAL ENGLAND, Churchgate, New Road, Peterborough PE1 1TD. *Director,* E. McKeegan

INLAND REVENUE LARGE BUSINESS OFFICE, 1st Floor North, 22 Kingsway, London WC2B 6NR. *Director,* S. Jones

INLAND REVENUE LONDON, New Court, Carey Street, London WC2A 2JE. *Director,* C. R. Massingale

INLAND REVENUE NORTHERN ENGLAND, 1 Munroe Court, White Rose Office Park, Milshaw Park, Leeds. *Director,* R. Cooke

INLAND REVENUE NORTHERN IRELAND, Dorchester House, 52–58 Great Victoria Street, Belfast BT2 7QE. *Director,* Ms. N. Ferguson

INLAND REVENUE SCOTLAND, Clarendon House, 114–116 George Street, Edinburgh EH2 4LH. *Director,* D. Hinstridge

INLAND REVENUE SOUTHERN ENGLAND, 1 Northern Road, Cosham, Portsmouth PO6 3AY. *Director,* T. Sleeman

INLAND REVENUE WALES, 1st Floor, Phase II Building, Ty Glas Avenue, Llanishen, Cardiff CF14 5TS. *Director,* K. Cartwright

VALUATION OFFICE AGENCY

New Court, 48 Carey Street, London WC2A 2JE
Tel: 020-7506 1700 Fax: 020-7506 1998
Web: www.voa.gov.uk
50 Frederick Street, Edinburgh EH2 1NG
Tel: 0131-465 0700 Fax: 0131-465 0799

Chief Executive, M. A. Johns
Chief Valuer, Scotland, A. Ainslie
Chief Valuer, Wales, P. Clement

BOUNDARY COMMISSIONS

The Commissions are constituted under the Parliamentary Constituencies Act 1986. The Speaker of the House of Commons is *ex officio* chairman of all four commissions in the UK. Each of the four commissions is required by law to keep the parliamentary constituencies in their part of the UK under review. The latest Boundary Commission report for England was completed in April 1995 and its proposals took effect at the 1997 general election. The next report must be submitted before April 2006. The latest Scottish report was completed in December 1994, with the European constituencies completed in April 1996.

ENGLAND

1 Drummond Gate, London SW1V 2QQ
Tel: 020-7533 5177 Fax: 020-7533 5176
Deputy Chairman, The Hon. Mr Justice Harrison
Joint Secretaries, R. Farrance; M. Barnett

WALES

1st Floor, Caradog House, 1–6 St Andrews Place, Cardiff CF10 3BE
Tel: 029-2039 5031 Fax: 029-2039 5250
Deputy Chairman, The Hon. Mr Justice Richards
Joint Secretaries, E. H. Lewis; M. Barnett

SCOTLAND

3 Drumsheugh Gardens, Edinburgh EH3 7QJ
Tel: 0131-538 7200 Fax: 0131-538 7240
Deputy Chairman, The Hon. Lady Cosgrove
Secretary, R. Smith

NORTHERN IRELAND

2nd Floor, Forestview, Purdy's Lane, Newtownbreda, Belfast BT8 4AX Tel: 028-9072 6040 Fax: 028-9072 6077
Deputy Chairman, The Hon. Mr Justice Coghlin
Secretary, J. R. Fisher

BRITISH BROADCASTING CORPORATION

Broadcasting House, Portland Place, London W1A 1AA
Tel: 020-7580 4468
BBC Information Line: 0870-010 0222
Web: www.bbc.co.uk
Television Centre, Wood Lane, London W12 7RJ

The BBC was incorporated under royal charter in 1926 as successor to the British Broadcasting Company Ltd. The BBC's current charter came into force on 1 May 1996 and extends to 31 December 2006. The chairman, vice-chairman and other governors are appointed by The Queen-in-Council. The BBC is financed by revenue from receiving licences for the home services and by grant-in-aid from Parliament for the World Service (radio).

BOARD OF GOVERNORS

Chairman, G. Davies
Vice-Chairman, R. Ryder
National Governors, Prof. F. Monds *(N. Ireland)*;
Prof. M. Jones *(Wales)*; Sir Robert Smith *(Scotland)*
Governors, Sir Richard Eyre, CBE; D. Gleeson; Dame Pauline Neville-Jones, DCMG; Baroness Hogg; R. Sondhi; Dame Ruth Deech; Angela Sarkis

BOARD OF MANAGEMENT
EXECUTIVE COMMITTEE
Director-General and Editor-in-Chief, G. Dyke
Directors, Ms J. Bennett *(Television);* Ms J. Abramsky *(Radio);* M. Byford *(BBC World Service);* R. Sambrook *(News);* Ms G. Benson *(Joint Director, Factual and Learning);* A. Yentob *(Drama, Entertainment and Children);* P. Loughrey *(Nations and Regions);* J. Smith *(Finance and Business Affairs);* S. Dando *(Human Resources and Internal);* A. Duncan *(Marketing and Communications);* P. Salmon *(Sport);* Ms C. Thomson *(Public Policy);* Ms C. Fairbairn *(Strategy and Distribution);* A. Highfield *(New Media)*
Chief Executives, R. Gavin *(BBC Worldwide);* R. Flynn, *(BBC Ventures)*

OTHER SENIOR STAFF
Controller, BBC1, L. Heggessey
Controller, BBC2, Ms J. Root
Controller, Radio 1, A. Parfitt
Controller, Radio 2, J. Moir
Controller, Radio 3, R. Wright
Controller, Radio 4, H. Boaden
Controller, Radio 5 Live, B. Shennan
Controller, BBC Scotland, J. McCormick
Controller, BBC Wales, M. Richards
Controller, BBC N. Ireland, A. Carragher
Controller, English Regions, A. Griffee
Secretary, S. Milner

THE BRITISH COUNCIL
10 Spring Gardens, London SW1A 2BN
Tel: 020-7930 8466 Fax: 020-7839 6347
Bridgewater House, 58 Whitworth Street,
Manchester M1 6BB Tel: 0161-957 7000

The British Council was established in 1934, incorporated by Royal Charter in 1940 and granted a supplemental charter in 1993. It is an independent, non-political organisation which promotes Britain abroad. It is the UK's international organisation for educational and cultural relations. The British Council is represented in 216 towns and cities in 109 countries. Total income in 2002–3, including Foreign and Commonwealth Office grants and contracted money, was £455.177 million.
Chairman, The Baroness Kennedy of The Shaws, QC
Deputy Chairman, Sir Tim Lankester, KCB
Director-General, D. Green, CMG

BRITISH FILM INSTITUTE
21 Stephen Street, London W1T 1LN
Tel: 020-7255 1444 Fax: 020-7436 0439
Web: www.bfi.org.uk

The British Film Institute (BFI) offers opportunities for people throughout the UK to experience, learn and discover more about the world of film and moving image culture. The BFI incorporates the BFI National Library, the monthly magazine *Sight and Sound,* the BFI National Film Theatre, the annual London Film Festival and the BFI London IMAX, and provides advice and support for regional cinemas and film festivals across the UK. The BFI also undertakes the preservation of, and promotes access to films, television programmes, computer games, museum collections, stills, posters and designs, and other special collections.
Chairman, Anthony Minghella, CBE
Director, Amanda Nevill

BRITISH PHARMACOPOEIA COMMISSION
Market Towers, 1 Nine Elms Lane, London SW8 5NQ
Tel: 020-7273 0561 Fax: 020-7273 0566

The British Pharmacopoeia Commission sets standards for medicinal products used in human and veterinary medicines and is responsible for publication of the British Pharmacopoeia (a publicly available statement of the standard that a product must meet throughout its shelf-life), the British Pharmacopoeia (Veterinary) and the selection of British Approved Names. It has 15 members who are appointed by the Secretary of State for Health, the Minister for Environment, Food and Rural Affairs, the Scottish Ministers, the National Assembly for Wales, and the relevant Northern Ireland departments.
Chairman, Prof. D. Calam, OBE, D.Phil.
Vice-Chairman, Prof. J. A. Goldsmith
Secretary and Scientific Director, Dr M. G. Lee

BRITISH WATERWAYS
Willow Grange, Church Road, Watford, Herts WD17 4QA
Tel: 01923-201120 Fax: 01923-201400
Email: enquiries.hq@britishwaterways.co.uk
Web: www.britishwaterways.co.uk

British Waterways conserves and manages over 2,000 miles of canals and rivers in England, Scotland and Wales. It is responsible to the Secretary of State for Environment, Food and Rural Affairs. Its responsibilities include maintaining the waterways and structures on and around them; looking after wildlife and the waterway environment; and ensuring that canals and rivers are safe and enjoyable places to visit.
Chairman (part-time), Dr G. Greener
Vice-Chairman, Sir P. Soulsby
Members (part-time), D. Langslow; I. Darling; Ms H. Gordon; C. Christie; Ms S. Achmatowicz; G. Fleming; Ms J. Lewis-Jones; Ms A. Malik; T. Tricker
Chief Executive, R. Evans

BRITISH STANDARDS INSTITUTION, BSI GROUP
389 Chiswick High Road, London W4 4AL
Tel: 020-8996 9000 Fax: 020-8996 7344

British Standards – a part of the BSI Group – is the recognised authority in the UK for the preparation and publication of national standards, both for products and the service sector. About 90 per cent of its standards work is now internationally linked. British Standards are issued for voluntary adoption, though in some cases compliance with a British Standard is required by legislation. Industrial and consumer products and services certified as complying with the relevant British Standard and operating an assessed quality management system are eligible to carry BSI's certification trade mark, known as the 'Kitemark'.
Chairman, Sir David John, KCMG

THE BROADS AUTHORITY
Thomas Harvey House, 18 Colegate, Norwich NR3 1BQ
Tel: 01603-610734 Fax: 01603-765710
Web: www.broads-authority.gov.uk

The Broads Authority is a special statutory authority set up under the Norfolk and Suffolk Broads Act 1988. The functions of the Authority are to conserve and enhance

the natural beauty of the Broads; to provide integrated management of the land and water space of the area; to promote the enjoyment of the Broads by the public; and to protect the interests of navigation. The Authority comprises 35 members, appointed by the local authorities in the area covered, environmental conservation bodies, the Environment Agency, and the Great Yarmouth Port Authority.
Chairman, Prof. K. Turner
Chief Executive, Dr J. Packman

CENTRAL ARBITRATION COMMITTEE
Third Floor, Discovery House, 28–42 Banner Street, London EC1Y 8QE
Tel: 020-7251 9747 Fax: 020-7251 3114
Web: www.cac.gov.uk
Email: enquiries@cac.gov.uk

The Central Arbitration Committee is a permanent independent body which determines claims for statutory recognition and de-recognition of trade unions under the Employment Relations Act 1999, it also adjudicates on disclosure of information cases, issues relating to the European Works Council Directive and arbitrates on trade disputes.
Chairman, Sir Michael Burton
Secretary and Chief Executive, G. Charles

CERTIFICATION OFFICE FOR TRADE UNIONS AND EMPLOYERS' ASSOCIATIONS
180 Borough High Street, London SE1 1LW
Tel: 020-7210 3734/5 Fax: 020-7210 3612

The Certification Office is an independent statutory authority. The Certification Officer is appointed by the Secretary of State for Trade and Industry and is responsible for receiving and scrutinising annual returns from trade unions and employers' associations; for determining complaints concerning trade union elections, certain ballots and certain breaches of trade union rules; for ensuring observance of statutory requirements governing mergers between trade unions and employers' associations; for overseeing the political funds and finances of trade unions and employers' associations; and for certifying the independence of trade unions.
Certification Officer, David Cockburn
Assistant Certification Officer, G. Walker

SCOTLAND
58 Frederick Street, Edinburgh EH2 1NB
Tel: 0131-226 3224 Fax: 0131-200 1300
Assistant Certification Officer for Scotland, J. L. J. Craig

CHARITY COMMISSION
Harmsworth House, 13–15 Bouverie Street, London EC4Y 8DP Tel: 0870-333 0123 Fax: 020-7674 2310
2nd Floor, 20 King's Parade, Queen's Dock, Liverpool L3 4DQ
Tel: 0870-333 0123 Fax: 0151-703 1555
Woodfield House, Tangier, Taunton, Somerset TA1 4BL
Tel: 0870-333 0123 Fax: 01823-345003
Web: www.charitycommission.gov.uk

The Charity Commission for England and Wales is the Government Department whose aim is to give the public confidence in the integrity of charities. It also carries out the functions of the registration, monitoring and support of charities and the investigation of alleged wrong-doing.

The Commission maintains a computerised register of some 187,000 charities. It is accountable to the courts and for its efficiency to the Home Secretary. There are five Commissioners appointed by the Home Office for a fixed term and the Commission has Offices in London, Liverpool and Taunton.
Chief Commissioner (G3), J. Stoker
Acting Legal Commissioner (G3), K. M. Dibble
Commissioners (part-time) (G4), D. Taylor; D. Unwin; Ms G. Peacock
Director of Operations (G4), S. Gillespie
Head of Human Resources, Ms S. Bailey
Heads of Legal Sections (G5), G. S. Goodchild; K. M. Dibble; J. Kilby
Head of Policy Division (G5), Ms R. Chapman
Information Systems Controller (G5), K. Chown

The offices responsible for charities in Scotland and Northern Ireland are:
SCOTLAND – Scottish Charities Office, Crown Office, 25 Chambers Street, Edinburgh EH1 1LA.
Tel: 0131-226 2626
NORTHERN IRELAND – Department for Social Development, Charities Branch, 5th Floor, Churchill House, Victoria Square, Belfast BT1 4SD

CHURCH COMMISSIONERS
1 Millbank, London SW1P 3JZ
Tel: 020-7898 1000 Fax: 020-7898 1131
Email: commissioners.enquiry@c-of-e.org
Web: www.churchcommissioners.org

The Church Commissioners were established in 1948 by the amalgamation of Queen Anne's Bounty (established 1704) and the Ecclesiastical Commissioners (established 1836). They are responsible for the management of the majority of the Church of England's assets, the income from which is predominantly used to help pay for the stipend and pension of the clergy. The Commissioners own 125,000 acres of agricultural land, a number of residential estates in central London and commercial property across Great Britain. They also carry out administrative duties in connection with pastoral reorganisation and redundant churches.

The Commissioners are: the Archbishops of Canterbury and of York; four bishops, three clergy and four lay persons elected by the respective houses of the General Synod; two deans or provosts elected by all the deans and provosts; three persons nominated by The Queen; three persons nominated by the Archbishops of Canterbury and York; three persons nominated by the Archbishops after consultation with others including the lord mayors of London and York and the vice-chancellors of the universities of Oxford and Cambridge; the First Lord of the Treasury; the Lord President of the Council; the Home Secretary; the Lord Chancellor; the Secretary of State for Culture, Media and Sport; and the Speaker of the House of Commons.

INCOME AND EXPENDITURE
for year ended 31 December 2002

	£ million
Net income	113.2
Investments	64.7
Property	42.8
Interest from loans, etc.	11.3
Total expenditure	165.6
Parish ministry support	25.5

Bishop and cathedral clergy stipends	7.5
Bishops' housing	3.4
Grants to cathedrals	2.5
Financial provision for resigning clergy	0.8
Clergy pensions and CHARM subsidy	97.7
Transitional support for pension contributions	8.1
Church buildings	1.6
Bishops' working cost	9.8
Commissioners' administration of national church functions	5.1
Administration costs of other church bodies	1.7

CHURCH ESTATES COMMISSIONERS
First, A. Whittam Smith
Second, S. Bell, MP
Third, The Viscountess Brentford

OFFICERS
Secretary, A. C. Brown
Deputy Secretary (Finance and Investment), C. W. Daws
Official Solicitor, S. Jones

ASSISTANT SECRETARIES
The Accountant, M. Adams
Chief Surveyor and Deputy Secretary, vacant
Computer Manager, J. W. Ferguson
Investments Manager, M. Chaloner
Pastoral, Houses and Redundant Churches, M. D. Elengorn

CIVIL AVIATION AUTHORITY
CAA House, 45–59 Kingsway, London WC2B 6TE
Tel: 020-7379 7311
Web: www.caa.co.uk

The CAA is responsible for the economic regulation of UK airlines and for the safety regulation of UK civil aviation by the certification of airlines and aircraft and by licensing aerodromes, flight crew and aircraft engineers.

The CAA advises the Government on aviation issues, represents consumer interests, conducts economic and scientific research, produces statistical data, and provides specialist services and other training and consultancy services to clients world-wide. It also regulates UK airspace and runs the ATOL flight and air holiday protection scheme.

Chairman, Sir Roy McNulty
Secretary and Legal Adviser, R. J. Britton

THE COAL AUTHORITY
200 Lichfield Lane, Mansfield, Notts NG18 4RG
Tel: 01623-427162 Fax: 01623-622072
Email: thecoalauthority@coal.gov.uk
Web: www.coal.gov.uk

The Coal Authority was established under the Coal Industry Act 1994 to manage certain functions previously undertaken by British Coal, including ownership of unworked coal. It is responsible for licensing coal mining operations and for providing information on coal reserves and past and future coal mining. It settles subsidence claims not falling on coal mining operators. It deals with the management and disposal of property, and with surface hazards such as abandoned coal mine shafts.

Chairman, J. Harris
Chief Executive, Dr I. Roxburgh

COLLEGE OF ARMS (OR HERALDS' COLLEGE)
Queen Victoria Street, London EC4V 4BT
Tel: 020-7248 2762 Fax: 020-7248 6448
Email: enquiries@college-of-arms.gov.uk
Web: www.college-of-arms.gov.uk

The Sovereign's Officers of Arms (Kings, Heralds and Pursuivants of Arms) were first incorporated by Richard III. The powers vested by the Crown in the Earl Marshal (the Duke of Norfolk) with regard to state ceremonial are largely exercised through the College. The College is also the official repository of the arms and pedigrees of English, Welsh, Northern Irish and Commonwealth (except Canadian) families and their descendants, and its records include official copies of the records of Ulster King of Arms, the originals of which remain in Dublin. The 13 officers of the College specialise in genealogical and heraldic work for their respective clients.

Arms have been and still are granted by letters patent from the Kings of Arms. A right to arms can only be established by the registration in the official records of the College of Arms of a pedigree showing direct male line descent from an ancestor already appearing therein as being entitled to arms, or by making application through the College of Arms for a grant of arms. Grants are made to corporations as well as to individuals.

Earl Marshal, The Duke of Norfolk

KINGS OF ARMS
Garter, P. L. Gwynn-Jones, CVO, FSA
Clarenceux, D. H. B. Chesshyre, LVO, FSA
Norroy and Ulster, T. Woodcock, LVO, FSA

HERALDS
Richmond (and Earl Marshal's Secretary), P. L. Dickinson
York, H. E. Paston-Bedingfeld
Chester (and Registrar), T. H. S. Duke
Lancaster, R. J. B. Noel
Windsor, W. G. Hunt, TD

PURSUIVANTS
Rouge Croix, D. V. White
Rouge Dragon, C. E. A. Cheesman

COMMISSION FOR ARCHITECTURE AND THE BUILT ENVIRONMENT
The Tower Building, 11 York Road, London SE1 7NX
Tel: 020-7960 2400 Fax: 020-7960 2444
Email: enquiries@cabe.org.uk
Web: www.cabe.org.uk

The Commission for Architecture and the Built Environment (CABE) is responsible for promoting the importance of high quality architecture and urban design and encouraging the understanding of architecture through educational and regional initiatives. CABE offers free advice to local authorities, public sector clients and others embarking on building projects of any size or purpose.

Chairman, Sir Stuart Lipton
Chief Executive, J. Rouse

COMMISSION FOR INTEGRATED TRANSPORT

Romney House, 5th Floor, 43 Marsham Street,
London SW1P 3HW
Tel: 020-7944 4101 Fax: 020-7944 2919
Email: cfit@dft.gsi.gov.uk
Web: www.cfit.gov.uk

The Commission for Integrated Transport was proposed in the 1998 Transport White Paper and was set up in June 1999. Its role is to provide independent expert advice to the Government in order to achieve a transport system that supports sustainable development. Members of the Commission are appointed by the Secretary of State for Transport.

Chairman (£30,000), Prof. D. Begg
Vice-Chairman (£24,000), Sir Trevor Chinn
Members (£5,431 each), L. Christensen, CBE; S. Francis;
    S. Joseph; D. Leeder; Ms L. Matson; W. Morris;
    H. Holland; N. Scales; M. Parker; Baroness Scott;
    M. Hodgkinson
Ex-Officio Members, Sir Roy McNulty, *(Chairman, Civil
    Aviation Authority)*; T. Matthews *(Chief Executive,
    Highways Agency)*; R. Bowker *(Chairman, British
    Railways Board and Head, Strategic Rail Authority)*;
    Ms J. Wilmot *(Chair, Disabled Persons Transport
    Advisory Committee)*
Secretary (G6), A. Braithwaite

COMMISSION FOR RACIAL EQUALITY

St Dunstan's House, 201–211 Borough High Street,
London SE1 1GZ
Tel: 020-7939 0000 Fax: 020-7939 0001
Email: info@cre.gov.uk Web: www.cre.gov.uk

The Commission for Racial Equality was set up under the 1976 Race Relations Act. It receives an annual grant from the Home Office but works independently of Government. The CRE is run by commissioners appointed by the Home Secretary, and has support from all the main political parties.

The CRE has three main duties: to work towards the elimination of racial discrimination and to promote equality of opportunity; to encourage good relations between people from different racial backgrounds; and to monitor the way the Race Relations Act is working and recommend ways in which it can be improved.

The CRE is the only Government-appointed body with statutory power to enforce the Race Relations Act. It also has a reference library which is open to the public (by appointment only).

Chairman, Trevor Phillips
Chief Executive, Danny Silverstone
Customer Services Manager, Carmen Franco

COMMITTEE ON STANDARDS IN PUBLIC LIFE

35 Great Smith Street, London SW1P 3BQ
Tel: 020-7276 2595 Fax: 020-7276 2585
Web: www.public-standards.gov.uk

The Committee on Standards in Public Life was set up in October 1994. It is a standing body whose chairman and members are appointed by the Prime Minister; three members are nominated by the leaders of the three main political parties. The committee's remit is to examine concerns about standards of conduct of all holders of public office, including arrangements relating to financial and commercial activities, and to make recommendations as to any changes in present arrangements which might be required to ensure the highest standards of propriety in public life. It is also charged with reviewing issues in relation to the funding of political parties. The committee does not investigate individual allegations of misconduct.

Chair, Sir Nigel Wicks, GCB, CVO, CBE
Members, Sir Anthony Cleaver; The Lord Goodhart, QC;
    F. Heaton; The Rt. Hon. Lord MacGregor of Pulham
    Market, OBE; R. Donaghy, OBE; Rabbi Julia
    Neuberger; The Rt. Hon. Chris Smith, MP
Secretary (SCS), Robert Behrens

COMMONWEALTH INSTITUTE

Kensington High Street, London W8 6NQ
Tel: 020-7603 4535 Fax: 020-7602 7374
Email: information@commonwealth.org.uk
Web: www.commonwealth.org.uk

The Commonwealth Institute is an educational trust. Its members are the 54 member states of the Commonwealth who elect a Board of Trustees responsible to them. The Trustees have entered a joint venture with Cambridge University to create a Centre for Commonwealth Education.

Chairman, Ms J. Hanratty, OBE
Vice-Chairman, The Rt. Hon. Lord Fellowes, GCB, GCVO
Company Secretary, Ms J. Curry

COMMONWEALTH WAR GRAVES COMMISSION

2 Marlow Road, Maidenhead, Berks SL6 7DX
Tel: 01628-634221 Fax: 01628-771208
Email: general.enq@cwgc.org
Web: www.cwgc.org

The Commonwealth War Graves Commission (formerly Imperial War Graves Commission) was founded by royal charter in 1917. It is responsible for the commemoration of 1,694,783 members of the forces of the Commonwealth who fell in the two world wars. More than one million graves are maintained in 23,292 burial grounds throughout the world. Over three-quarters of a million men and women who have no known grave or who were cremated are commemorated by name on memorials built by the Commission.

The funds of the Commission are derived from the six participating governments, i.e. the UK, Canada, Australia, New Zealand, South Africa and India.

President, HRH The Duke of Kent, KG, GCMG, GCVO,
    ADC
Chairman, The Secretary of State for Defence in the UK
Vice-Chairman, Gen. Sir John Wilsey, GCB, CBE
Members, The High Commissioners in London for
    Australia, Canada, South Africa, New Zealand and
    India; J. Wilkinson, MP; Sir John Gray, KBE, CMG;
    Dame Susan Tinson, DBE; Sir John Keegan, OBE;
    Adm. Sir Peter Abbott, GBE, KCB; Alan Meale, MP;
    Ian Henderson, CBE, FRICS
Director-General and Secretary to the Commission,
    R. E. Kellaway
Deputy Director-General, R. J. Dalley, CBE
Legal Adviser and Solicitor, G. C. Reddie
Directors, D. R. Parker *(Information and Secretariat)*;
    B. Davidson, MBE *(Works)*; R. D. Wilson
    (Administration); D. C. Parker *(Horticulture)*;
    Ms C. Cecil *(Personnel)*

IMPERIAL WAR GRAVES ENDOWMENT FUND

Trustees, A. C. Barker *(Chairman);* C. G. Clarke;
Gen. Sir John Wilsey, GCB, CBE
Secretary to the Trustees, R. D. Wilson

COMMUNITIES SCOTLAND

Thistle House, 91 Haymarket Terrace, Edinburgh EH12 5HE
Tel: 0131-313 0044 Fax: 0131-313 2680
Web: www.communitiesscotland.gov.uk

Communities Scotland is a Scottish Executive agency,
reporting directly to Ministers. The agency's overall
aim is to improve the quality of life for people in
Scotland by working with others to create sustainable,
healthy and attractive communities. They do this by
regenerating neighbourhoods, empowering communities
and improving the effectiveness of investment.
Chief Executive, Bob Millar

COMMUNITY FUND

St Vincent House, 16 Suffolk Street, London SW1Y 4NL
Tel: 020-7747 5300 Fax: 020-7747 5297
Web: www.community-fund.org.uk

The Fund was set up under the National Lottery Act
1993 to distribute funds from the Lottery to support
charitable, benevolent and philanthropic organisations.
The chair and members are appointed by the Secretary of
State for Culture, Media and Sport. The Fund's aim is to
meet the needs of those at greatest disadvantage in
society and also to improve the quality of life in the
community.

It has UK-wide, county and regional priorities for its
general grants programmes and runs two specialist
programmes for research and international grants.
Chair, Lady Brittan, CBE
Deputy Chairman, Dame Valerie Strachan, DCB
Members, E. Appelbee; S. Burkeman; J. Carroll;
P Cavanagh; D. Graham; K. Hampton;
Prof. J. Kearney; L. MacLeod; S. Malley; R. Martineau;
J. Strachan; E. Watkins; B. Whitaker, CBE; C. Tongue
Chief Executive, R. Buxton

COMPETITION COMMISSION

New Court, 48 Carey Street, London WC2A 2JT
Tel: 020-7271 0100 Fax: 020-7271 0367
Email: info@competition-commission.gsi.gov.uk
Web: www.competition-commission.org.uk

The Commission was established in 1948 as the
Monopolies and Restrictive Practices Commission (later
the Monopolies and Mergers Commission); it became the
Competition Commission in April 1999 under the
Competition Act 1998. Its role is to investigate and
report on matters which are referred to it by the Secretary
of State for Trade and Industry or the Director-General of
Fair Trading or, in the case of regulated utilities, by the
appropriate regulator. It has no power to initiate its own
investigations.

The Appeal Tribunals of the Competition Commission
hears appeals against decisions by the Director-General
of Fair Trading and the utility regulators in respect of the
prohibitions on anti-competitive agreements and abuse of
a dominant position.

The Commission has a full-time chairman and three
deputy chairmen. There are 52 members to carry out
investigations. All are appointed by the Secretary of State
for Trade and Industry for single 8-year terms.

Chairman, Dr D. Morris
Deputy Chairmen, Prof. P. Geroski; Mrs D. Kingsmill,
CBE; P. J. Freeman
President, Appeal Tribunals, His Hon. Sir Christopher
Bellamy, QC
Members, S. Ahmed; Prof. J. Baillie; R. D. D. Bertram;
Mrs S. E. Brown; Miss L. I. Christmas; C. Clarke;
Dr J. Collings; Dr D. Coyle; C. Darke; L. Elks;
N. Garthwaite; W. Gibson; C. Goodall; Prof. C.
Graham; Prof. A. Gregory; Mrs D. Guy; A. Hadfield;
G. H. Hadley; Prof. A. Hamlin; Prof. J. Haskel; P. F.
Hazell; C. E. Henderson, CB; G. L. Holbrook, MBE;
R. Holroyd; Mrs M. J. Hopkirk; Prof. P. F. Klemperer;
Prof. B. Lyons; Dame Barbara Mills, DBE, QC;
Prof. N. C. L. Macdonald; Prof. P. Moizer; Dr E. M.
Monck; Prof. D. Parker; E. Pollard; R. A. Rawlinson;
J. B. K. Rickford, CBE; E. J. Seddon; Dame Helena
Shovelton; DBE; C. R. Smallwood; J. D. S. Stark;
P. Stoddart; Prof. D. J. Trelford; R. Turgoose; Prof. C.
Waddams; S. D. Walzer, M. R. Webster; Prof. S. R. M.
Wilks; C. Wilson; A. M. Young
Secretary, R. Foster

COMPETITION SERVICE

New Court, 48 Carey Street, London WC2A 3BZ
Tel: 020-7271 0395 Fax: 020-7271 0281
Email: info@catribunal.org.uk
Web: www.catribunal.org.uk

The Enterprise Act 2002 created the Competition
Service, a non-departmental public body whose purpose
is to fund and provide support services to the
Competition Appeal Tribunal. Support services include
everything necessary to facilitate the carrying out by the
Competition Appeal Tribunal of its statutory functions
such as administration, accommodation and office
equipment.
Director, Operations, Peter Lambert, OBE

COUNCIL ON TRIBUNALS

81 Chancery Lane, London WC2A 1BQ
Tel: 020-7855 5200 Fax: 020-7855 5201
Email: enquiries@cot.gsi.gov.uk
Web: www.council-on-tribunals.gov.uk

The Council on Tribunals is an independent body that
operates under the Tribunals and Inquiries Act 1992. It
consists of 15 members appointed by the Lord
Chancellor and the Scottish Ministers; one member is
appointed to represent the interests of people in Wales.
The Scottish Committee of the Council generally
considers Scottish tribunals and matters relating only to
Scotland. The Parliamentary Commissioner for
administration is an *ex officio* member of the Council and
the Scottish Committee.

The Council advises on and keeps under review the
constitution and working of the tribunals listed in the
Tribunals and Inquiries Act, and considers and reports on
administrative procedures relating to statutory inquiries.
Some 80 tribunals are currently under the Council's
supervision. It is consulted by and advises Government
departments on a wide range of subjects relating to
adjudicative procedures.
Chairman, The Rt. Hon. The Lord Newton of
Braintree, CBE
Members, Ann Abraham The Parliamentary
Commissioner for Administration *(ex officio);*
R. J. Elliot *(Chairman of the Scottish Committee);*

Mrs C. Berkeley; Mrs S. R. Howdle; Prof.
G. Richardson; P. Waring; S. D. Mannion, QPM;
A. W. Russell, CB; Mrs R. Hepplewhite; Ms P. Letts;
Mrs E. C. Cameron; B. Wilcox; B. Quoroll
Secretary, Mrs P. J. Fairbairn

SCOTTISH COMMITTEE OF THE COUNCIL ON TRIBUNALS
44 Palmerston Place, Edinburgh EH12 5BJ
Tel: 0131-220 1236 Fax: 0131-225 4271
Email: sccot@gtnet.gov.uk
Chairman, R. J. Elliot
Members, The Parliamentary Commissioner for
Administration *(ex officio)*; Mrs B. Bruce; D. Graham;
Mrs. M. Wood; Mrs E. Cameron; Mr S. Mannion;
Mrs A Watson
Secretary, Mrs E. M. MacRae

COUNTRYSIDE AGENCY
John Dower House, Crescent Place, Cheltenham,
Glos GL50 3RA
Tel: 01242-521381 Fax: 01242-584270
Web: www.countryside.gov.uk

The Countryside Agency was set up in April 1999 by
the merger of the Countryside Commission with parts of
the Rural Development Commission. It is a Government
agency which promotes the conservation and
enhancement of the countryside in England and
undertakes activities aimed at stimulating job creation
and the provision of essential services in the countryside.
The Agency is funded by an annual grant from the
Department for Environment, Food and Rural Affairs and
board members are appointed by the Secretary of State.
Chairman, Sir E. Cameron
Deputy Chair, Ms P. Warhurst
Members, Ms K. Ashbrook; Ms J. Bradbury;
Rt. Revd Bishop of Norwich; Sir Martin Doughty;
Dr V. Edwards; P. Fane; A. Hams, OBE; Prof. P. Lowe;
Ms F. Rowe; J. Varley; Norman Glass; Dr Tayo
Adebowale
Chief Executive, R. G. Wakeford
Directors, Miss M. A. Clark, OBE; Tim Lunel; S. Sleet

COUNTRYSIDE COUNCIL FOR WALES/CYNGOR CEFN GWLAD CYMRU
Maes y Ffynnon, Penrhosgarnedd, Bangor,
Gwynedd LL57 2DW
Tel: 01248-385500 Fax: 01248-355782

The Countryside Council for Wales is the Government's
statutory adviser on sustaining natural beauty, wildlife
and the opportunity for outdoor enjoyment in Wales and
its inshore waters. It is funded by the National Assembly
for Wales and accountable to the First Secretary, who
appoints its members.
Chairman, J. Lloyd Jones, OBE
Chief Executive, R. Thomas
Senior Director and Chief Scientist, Dr M. E. Smith
Director, Countryside Policy, Dr J. Taylor
Director, Conservation, Dr D. Parker
Director, Corporate Services, L. Warmington

COURT OF THE LORD LYON
HM New Register House, Edinburgh EH1 3YT
Tel: 0131-556 7255 Fax: 0131-557 2148

The Court of the Lord Lyon is the Scottish Court of

Chivalry (including the genealogical jurisdiction of the
Ri-Sennachie of Scotland's Celtic Kings). The Lord Lyon
King of Arms has jurisdiction, subject to appeal to the
Court of Session and the House of Lords, in questions of
heraldry and the right to bear arms. The Court also
administers the Scottish Public Register of All Arms and
Bearings and the Public Register of All Genealogies.
Pedigrees are established by decrees of Lyon Court and
by letters patent. As Royal Commissioner in Armory, the
Lord Lyon grants patents of arms (which constitute the
grantee and heirs noble in the Noblesse of Scotland) to
virtuous and well-deserving Scotsmen and to petitioners
(personal or corporate) in The Queen's overseas realms of
Scottish connection, and issues birthbrieves.
Lord Lyon King of Arms, R. O. Blair, LVO, WS

HERALDS
Albany, J. A. Spens, MVO, RD, WS
Rothesay, Sir Crispin Agnew of Lochnaw, Bt., QC
Ross, C. J. Burnett, FSA Scot.

PURSUIVANTS
Unicorn, Alastair Campbell of Airds
Carrick, Mrs C. G. W. Roads, MVO
Bute, W. D. H. Sellar
Orkney Herald Extraordinary, Sir Malcolm Innes of
Edingight, KCVO, WS
Linlithgow Pursuivant Extraordinary, J. C. G. George
Lyon Clerk and Keeper of Records, Mrs C. G. W. Roads,
MVO, FSA Scot.
Procurator-Fiscal, George Way of Plean, SSC
Herald Painter, Mrs J. Phillips
Macer, H. M. Love

COVENT GARDEN MARKET AUTHORITY
Covent House, New Covent Garden Market, London SW8
5NX Tel: 020-7720 2211 Fax: 020-7622 5307
Email: info@cgma.gov.uk
Web: www.cgma.gov.uk

The Covent Garden Market Authority is constituted
under the Covent Garden Market Acts 1961 to 1977, the
members being appointed by the Minister of
Environment, Food and Rural Affairs. The Authority
owns and operates the 56-acre New Covent Garden
Markets (fruit, vegetables, flowers) which have been
trading since 1974.
Chairman (part-time), L. Mills, CBE
General Manager, Dr P. M. Liggins
Secretary, C. Farey

CRIMINAL CASES REVIEW COMMISSION
Alpha Tower, Suffolk Street, Queensway, Birmingham B1 1TT
Tel: 0121-633 1800 Fax: 0121-633 1823/1804

The Criminal Cases Review Commission is an
independent body set up under the Criminal Appeal Act
1995. It is a non-departmental public body reporting to
Parliament via the Home Secretary. It is responsible for
investigating suspected miscarriages of justice in England,
Wales and Northern Ireland, and deciding whether or
not to refer cases back to an appeal court. Membership of
the Commission is by royal appointment; the senior
executive staff are appointed by the Commission.
Chairman, Prof. Graham Zellick
Members, B. Capon; L. Elks; A. Foster; I. Nicholl; D. Kyle;

Prof. L. Leigh; J. MacKeith; K. Singh; B. Skitt; D. Jessel; M. Allen; M. Emerton; J. Weeden
Chief Executive, Ms J. Courtney
Director of Finance and Personnel, D. Robson
Legal Advisers, J. Wagstaff; Ms F. Barrie
Police Adviser, R. Barrington

CRIMINAL INJURIES COMPENSATION APPEALS PANEL (CICAP)

11th Floor, Cardinal Tower, 12 Farringdon Road, London EC1M 3HS
Tel: 020-7549 4600 Fax: 020-7436 6804
Email: info@cicap.gov.uk Web: www.cicap.gov.uk
Chairman, R. Goodier
Chief Executive and Secretary to the Panel, R. Burke

CRIMINAL INJURIES COMPENSATION AUTHORITY (CICA)

Morley House, 26–30 Holborn Viaduct, London EC1A 2JQ
Tel: 020-7842 6800 Fax: 020-7436 0804
Web: www.cica.gov.uk
Tay House, 300 Bath Street, Glasgow G2 4JR
Tel: 0141-331 2726 Fax: 0141-331 2287

All applications for compensation for personal injury arising from crimes of violence in England, Scotland and Wales are dealt with at the above locations. (Separate arrangements apply in Northern Ireland.) Applications received up to 31 March 1996 are assessed on the basis of common law damages under the 1990 compensation scheme. Applications received later than 1 April 1996 are assessed under a tariff-based scheme, made under the Criminal Injuries Compensation Act 1995, by the Criminal Injuries Compensation Authority (CICA). There is a separate avenue of appeal to the Criminal Injuries Compensation Appeals Panel (CICAP).
Chief Executive, Howard Webber
Deputy Chief Executive, Edward McKeown
Head of Legal Services, Anne Johnstone

CROFTERS COMMISSION

4–6 Castle Wynd, Inverness IV2 3EQ
Tel: 01463-663450 Fax: 01463-711820
Email: info@crofterscommission.org.uk
Web: www.crofterscommission.org.uk

The Crofters Commission, established in 1955 under the Crofters (Scotland) Act is a government funded organisation whose overall objective is the promotion of thriving and sustainable crofting communities. It works with communities to develop, reorganise and regulate crofting, and advises Scottish Ministers on crofting matters. The Commission administers the Crofting Counties Agricultural Grants Scheme, the Croft Entrant Scheme, the Livestock Improvement Schemes and the Crofting Community Development Scheme. It also provides a free enquiry service.
Chairman, David Green
Chief Executive, Shane Rankin

CROWN ESTATE

16 Carlton House Terrace, London SW1Y 5AH
Tel: 020-7210 4377 Fax: 020-7930 8187
Web: www.crownestate.co.uk

The Crown Estate includes substantial blocks of urban property, primarily in London, almost 120,000 hectares of agricultural land, almost half the foreshore, and the sea bed out to the twelve mile territorial limit throughout the United Kingdom. The Crown Estate is part of the hereditary possessions of the Sovereign 'in right of the Crown', managed under the provisions of the Crown Estate Act 1961 by the Crown Estate Commissioners who have a duty to maintain and enhance the capital value of estate and the income obtained from it. In the year ended 31 March 2003, the gross revenue totalled £230 million and £170.8 million was paid to the Exchequer as surplus revenue.
Chairman (part-time), Ian Grant, CBE
Chief Executive, Roger Bright
Commissioners (part-time), Honor Chapman, CBE; Sir Donald Curry, KB, CBE; Hugh Duberly, CBE; Martin Moore; Dinah Nichols, CB; Ronald Spinney, FRICS
Director of Urban Estates, Tony Bickmore

HEADS OF DEPARTMENTS
Central London Estate, Elspeth Miller
Communications, Irene Belcher
Corporate Planning and Human Resources, Martin Gravestock
Finance and Information Systems, John Lelliott
Internal Audit, John Ford
Legal Adviser and Head of Legal Services, David Harris
Marine Estates, Frank Parrish
Regent Street Strategy and Development, David Shaw
Regent Street Estate Management, Alan Meakin
Regional Estates, Mal Dillon
Residential Estate, Giles Clarke
Rural Estates, Chris Bourchier
Special Projects, Liam Colgan
Valuation, Roland Spence

EDINBURGH OFFICE
6 Bell's Brae, Edinburgh EH4 3BJ
Tel: 0131-260 6070 Fax: 0131-260 6090
Edinburgh Office Manager, Ian Pritchard

WINDSOR ESTATE
The Crown Estate Office, The Great Park, Windsor, Berks SL4 2HT
Tel: 01753-860222 Fax: 01753-859617
Deputy Ranger, P. Everett

HM CUSTOMS AND EXCISE

New King's Beam House, 5th Floor East, 22 Upper Ground, London SE1 9PJ
Tel: 020-7620 1313
National Advice Service: 0845-010 900
Web: www.hmce.gov.uk

Commissioners of Customs were first appointed in 1671 and housed by the King in London. The Excise Department was formerly under the Inland Revenue Department and was amalgamated with the Customs Department in 1909.

HM Customs and Excise is responsible for collecting and administering customs and excise duties and VAT, and advises the Chancellor of the Exchequer on any matters connected with them. The Department is also responsible for preventing and detecting the evasion of revenue laws and for enforcing a range of prohibitions and restrictions on the importation of certain classes of goods. In addition, the Department undertakes certain agency work on behalf of other departments, including the compilation of UK overseas trade statistics from customs import and export documents.

THE BOARD
Chairman (G1), R. Broadbent
Private Secretary, Mrs K. Spendiff

COMMISSIONERS
Director-General Business Services and Taxes (G2),
 M. J. Eland
Director-General Law Enforcement (G2), T. Byrne
Director Logistics and Finance (G3), M. Hanson
Director Intelligence (G3), M. N. Norgrove
Non Executive Directors, Ms R. Pickavance; D. Spencer;
 B. Quirk; T. Hall; Sir Stephen Lander
Solicitor (G2), D. Pickup
Director Regional Business Services and Taxes, R. McAfee
Director Large Business Group, Information and E-Services,
 D. Garlick

DEER COMMISSION FOR SCOTLAND
Knowsley, 82 Fairfield Road, Inverness IV3 5LH
Tel: 01463-231751 Fax: 01463-712931
Email: enquiries@deercom.com
Web: www.dcs.gov.uk

The Deer Commission for Scotland has the general functions of furthering the conservation and control of deer in Scotland. It has the statutory duty, with powers, to prevent damage to agriculture, forestry and the habitat by deer. It is funded by the Scottish Executive.
Chairman (part-time), A. Raven
Director, N. Reiter
Technical Director, D. Balharry

DESIGN COUNCIL
34 Bow Street, London WC2E 7DL
Tel: 020-7420 5200 Fax: 020-7420 5300

The Design Council is a campaigning and lobbying organisation which works with partners in business, education and Government to promote the effective use of good design. It is a registered charity with a Royal Charter and is funded by grant-in-aid from the Department of Trade and Industry.
Chairman, C. Frayling
Chief Executive, D. Kester

DISABILITY RIGHTS COMMISSION (DRC)
DRC, Stratford upon Avon CV37 9BR
DRC Helpline: 0845-762 2633
Web: www.drc-gb.org

The Commission is an executive non-departmental public body established in April 2000. Its role is to advise Government on issues of discrimination against disabled people and the operation of the Disability Discrimination Act 1995. It promotes good practice to employers and service providers and provides advice, information and sometimes legal support to disabled people.
Chair, B. Massie, CBE
Chief Executive, B. Niven
Commissioners, S. Alam; M. Burton; Ms J. Campbell, MBE;
 Ms S. Daniels; M. Devenney; R. Exell, OBE;
 Dr K. Fitzpatrick; C. Holmes, MBE; Mrs E. Noad;
 Ms E. Rank-Petruzziello

THE DUCHY OF CORNWALL
10 Buckingham Gate, London SW1E 6LA
Tel: 020-7834 7346 Fax: 020-7931 9541
Web: www.princeofwales.gov.uk

The Duchy of Cornwall was created by Edward III in 1337 for the support of his eldest son Edward, later known as the Black Prince. It is the oldest of the English duchies. The duchy is acquired by inheritance by the sovereign's eldest son either at birth or on the accession of his parent to the throne, whichever is the later. The primary purpose of the estate remains to provide an income for the Prince of Wales. The estate is mainly agricultural and based in the south-west of England. A recent purchase has increased the landholding to approximately 150,000 acres in 26 counties. The duchy also has some residential property, a number of shops and offices, and a Stock Exchange portfolio. Prince Charles is the 24th Duke of Cornwall.

THE PRINCE'S COUNCIL
Chairman, HRH The Prince of Wales, KG, KT, GCB, OM
Lord Warden of the Stannaries, The Earl Peel
Receiver-General, The Rt. Hon. J. H. Leigh-Pemberton
Attorney-General to the Prince of Wales, N. Underhill, QC
Secretary and Keeper of the Records, W. R. A. Ross
Other members, R. Broadhurst; Mrs. J. Coode;
 W. N. Hood, CBE; Sir Christopher Howes, CB;
 S. Lamport; J. E. Pugsley; The Duke of Westminster

THE DUCHY OF LANCASTER
Lancaster Place, Strand, London WC2E 7ED
Tel: 020-7836 8277 Fax: 020-7836 3098

The estates and jurisdiction known as the Duchy of Lancaster have belonged to the reigning monarch since 1399 when John of Gaunt's son came to the throne as Henry IV. As the Lancaster Inheritance it goes back as far as 1265 when Henry III granted his youngest son Edmund lands and possessions following the Baron's war. In 1267 Henry gave Edmund the County, Honor and Castle of Lancaster and created him the first Earl of Lancaster. In 1351 Edward III created Lancaster a County Palatine.

The Chancellor of the Duchy of Lancaster is responsible for the administration of the Duchy, the appointment of justices of the peace in Lancashire, Greater Manchester and Merseyside and ecclesiastical patronage in the Duchy gift.
Chancellor of the Duchy of Lancaster (and Minister for the Cabinet Office), The Rt. Hon. The Lord Macdonald of Tradeston, CBE
Chairman of the Duchy Council, Sir Michael Bunbury, Bt.
Attorney-General, M. T. F. Briggs, QC
Receiver-General, A. Reid
Clerk of the Council and Chief Executive, P. R. Clarke

ECGD (EXPORT CREDITS GUARANTEE DEPARTMENT)

PO Box 2200, Exchange Tower, Harbour Exchange Square, London E14 9GS
Tel: 020-7512 7000 Fax: 020-7512 7649
Web: www.ecgd.gov.uk

ECGD, the Export Credits Guarantee Department is the UK's export credit agency. A separate government department reporting to the Secretary of State for Trade and Industry, it has more than 80 years' experience of working closely with exporters, project sponsors, banks and buyers to help UK exporters of capital equipment and project-related goods and services. ECGD does this by providing: help in arranging finance packages for buyers of UK goods by guaranteeing bank loans; insurance against non-payment to UK exporters; and, overseas investment insurance – a facility that gives UK investors up to 15 years' insurance against political risks such as war, expropriation and restrictions on remittances.

EXECUTIVE COMMITTEE

Chief Executive and Accounting Officer, H. V. B. Brown
Group Directors, V. P. Lunn-Rockliffe *(Portfolio Asset Management)*; J. R. Weiss *(Business)*; T. M. Jaffray *(Risk Management Group)*; J. Ormerod *(Strategy and Communications Division)*; I. Dickson *(Finance Division)*; S. R. Dodgson *(Central Services Division)*; D. N. Ridley *(General Counsel)*

NON-EXECUTIVE DIRECTORS

D. Harrison; J. Wright; T. Davies

DIRECTORS

Directors, Business Divisions, G. G. Welsh; R. Gotts; M. D. Pentecost
Director, Capital and Pricing Division, J. Croall
Director Country Risk and Economics Division, P. J. Radford
Director, Operational Research and Portfolio Risk Analysis Division, Ms R. A. Kaufman
Director, International Debt and Development Division, E. J. Walsby
Director, Recovery Division, R. F. Lethbridge
Director, Guarantee Management Division, A. C. Faulkner
Director, Portfolio Management Division, Y. Tamir
Director, Information Services Division, Ms L. Woods
Director, Internal Audit and Assurance, G. Cassell

EXPORT GUARANTEES ADVISORY COUNCIL

Chairman, E. P. Airey
Other Members, J. Armitt; Sir S. Brown; J. Elkington; Prof. J. Kydd; D. MacLachlan; Prof. K. Phylaktis; A. Shepherd; Dr R. Thamotheram; M. Roberts

ENGLISH HERITAGE (HISTORIC BUILDINGS AND MONUMENTS COMMISSION FOR ENGLAND)

23 Savile Row, London W1S 2ET
Tel: 020-7973 3000 Fax: 020-7973 3001
Web: www.english-heritage.org.uk

English Heritage was established under the National Heritage Act 1983. On 1 April 1999 it merged with the Royal Commission on the Historical Monuments of England to become the new lead body for England's historic environment. Its duties are to carry out and sponsor archaeological, architectural and scientific surveys and research designed to increase the understanding of England's past and its changing condition; to offer expert advice and skills and give grants to secure the preservation of listed buildings, cathedrals, churches, archaeological sites, ancient monuments and historic houses of England; to encourage the imaginative re-use of historic buildings to aid regeneration of the centres of cities, towns and villages; to manage the historic monuments and historic buildings in England; and to curate and make publicly accessible the National Monuments Record, whose records of over one million historic sites and buildings, and collections of more that 12 million photographs, maps, drawings and reports constitute the central database and archive to England's historic environment.

Chairman, Sir Neil Cossons
Deputy Chairman, A. Fane
Commissioners, M. Cairns; Prof. D. Cannadine; Mrs G. Drummond; P. Gough, CBE; J. Grenville; L. Grossman; M. Jolly, The Earl of Leicester; R. Morris, FSA; L. Sparks; Miss S. Underwood
Chief Executive, Dr S. Thurley

NATIONAL MONUMENTS RECORD, National Monuments Record Centre, Kemble Drive, Swindon SN2 2GZ.
Tel: 01793-414600 Fax: 01793-414606
LONDON SEARCH ROOM, 55 Blandford Street, London SW1H 3AF. Tel: 020-7208 8200 Fax: 020-7224 5333

ENGLISH NATURE

Northminster House, Peterborough PE11UA
Tel: 01733-455000 Fax: 01733-568834
Web: www.english-nature.org.uk

English Nature was established in 1991 and is responsible for advising the Secretary of State for the Environment, Food and Rural Affairs on nature conservation in England. It promotes, directly and through others, the conservation of England's wildlife and natural features. It selects, establishes and manages National Nature Reserves and identifies and notifies Sites of Special Scientific Interest. It provides advice and information about nature conservation, and supports and conducts research relevant to these functions. Through the Joint Nature Conservation Committee, it works with its sister organisations in Scotland and Wales on UK and international nature conservation issues.

Chairman, M. Doughty
Chief Executive, Dr A. Brown
Directors, Dr K. L. Duff; Miss C. E. M. Wood; Ms S. Collins; A. Clements

ENVIRONMENT AGENCY

Rio House, Waterside Drive, Aztec West, Almondsbury, Bristol BS32 4UD
Tel: 01454-624400 Fax: 01454-624409
Email: enquiries@environment-agency.gov.uk
Web: www.environment-agency.gov.uk

The Environment Agency was established in 1996 under the Environment Act 1995 and is a non-departmental public body sponsored by the Department of the Environment, Food and Rural Affairs and the National Assembly for Wales. The Agency is responsible for pollution prevention and control in England and Wales, and for the management and use of water resources, including flood defences, fisheries and navigation. It has head offices in London and Bristol and eight regional offices.

THE BOARD

Chairman, Sir John Harman
Members, C. Beardwood; T. Cantle; A. Dare, CBE;
Prof. R. Macrory; Prof. J. McGlade; G. Manning, OBE;
Prof. P. Matthews; Ms S. Parkin; Prof. D. Ritchie;
G. Wardell; Prof. L. Warren

THE EXECUTIVE

Chief Executive, B. Young
Director of Finance, N. Reader
Director of Personnel, G. Duncan
Director of Environmental Protection, Dr P. Leinster
Director of Water Management, D. King
Director of Operations, A. Robertson
Director of Corporate Affairs, H. McCallum
Director of Legal Services, R. Navarro

EQUAL OPPORTUNITIES COMMISSION

Arndale House, Arndale Centre, Manchester M4 3EQ
Tel: 0845-601 5901 Fax: 0161-838 8303
Email: info@eoc.org.uk
Web: www.eoc.org.uk

MEDIA ENQUIRIES, 36 Broadway, London SW1H 0BH.
Tel: 020-7222 0004
OTHER OFFICES, St Stephens House, 279 Bath Street,
Glasgow G2 4JL Tel: 0845-601 5901
Windsor House, Windsor Lane, Cardiff CF10 3GE
Tel: 029-2034 3552

The Equal Opportunities Commission was established
under the Sex Discrimination Act in 1975. It was set up
as an independent statutory body with the following
powers: to work towards the elimination of
discrimination on the grounds of sex or marriage; to
promote equality of opportunity for women and men; to
keep under review the Sex Discrimination Act and the
Equal Pay Act; and to provide legal advice and assistance
to individuals who have been discriminated against.
Chair, Ms J. Mellor
Deputy Chair, Ms J. Watson
Commissioners, Ms T. Akpeki; Ms S. Ashtiany;
Ms K. Carberry; Ms F. Cannon; Ms J. Drake;
Ms S. Pierce; Ms S. Sharma; D. Smith;
Ms T. Woodcraft; Ms D. Mattinson; Ms R. Arshad;
N. Rhys Wooding
Chief Executive, C. Slocock

EQUALITY COMMISSION FOR NORTHERN IRELAND

Equality House, 7–9 Shaftesbury Square, Belfast, BT2 7DP
Tel: 028-9050 0600 Fax: 028-9033 1544
Email: information@equalityni.org
Web: www.equalityni.org

The Equality Commission was set up in 1999 and is
responsible for promoting equality, eliminating
discrimination on the grounds of race, disability, gender,
religion and political opinion and for overseeing the
statutory duty on public authorities to promote equality
of opportunity.
Chief Commissioner, Mrs J. Harbison
Chief Executive, Ms E. Collins

FILM COUNCIL

10 Little Portland Street, London W1W 7JG
Tel: 020-7861 7861 Fax: 020-7861 7862
Email: info@filmcouncil.org.uk

The Council was created in April 2000 by the
Department for Culture, Media and Sport to develop a
coherent strategy for the development and leadership of
film culture and the film industry. It is responsible for the
majority of the Department for Culture, Media and Sport
funding for film as well as lottery and grant-in-aid (with
the exception of the National Film and Television
School).
Chairman, A. Parker
Deputy Chairman, S. Till
Chief Executive, J. Woodward

FOOD STANDARDS AGENCY (UK)

Aviation House, 125 Kingsway, London WC2B 6NH
Tel: 020-7276 8000 Fax: 020-7276 8004
Web: www.food.gov.uk

The Food Standards Agency (FSA) was established in
April 2000 to protect public health from risks arising in
connection with the consumption of food, and otherwise
to protect the interests of consumers in relation to food.
The Agency has the general function of developing
policy in these areas and provides information and advice
to the Government, other public bodies and consumers. It
also sets standards for and monitors food law
enforcement by local authorities. The Agency is a UK-
wide non-ministerial Government body which is led by a
board, which has been appointed to act in the public
interest. It has executive offices in Scotland, Wales and
Northern Ireland. It is advised by advisory committees on
food safety matters of special interest to each of these
areas.
Chairman, Prof. Sir John Krebs, MD
Acting Deputy Chair, Ms Ann Hemingway
Chief Executive, Dr Jon Bell

EXECUTIVE AGENCY
MEAT HYGIENE SERVICE
Kings Pool, Peasholme Green, York YO1 7PR
Tel: 01904-455500 Fax: 01904-455502

The Meat Hygiene Service was launched on 1 April
1995, and became an Executive Agency of the Food
Standards Agency from 1 April 2000. It protects public
health and animal welfare at slaughter through veterinary
supervision and meat inspection in licensed fresh meat
premises.
Chief Executive (G4), C. J. Lawson

FOOD STANDARDS AGENCY SCOTLAND

St Magnus House, 25 Guild Street, Aberdeen, AB11 6NJ
Tel: 01224-285100 Fax: 01224-285167
Email: scotland@foodstandards.gsi.gov.uk
Web: www.food.gov.uk

FOOD STANDARDS AGENCY WALES

1st Floor, Southgate House, Wood Street, Cardiff CF10 1EW
Tel: 029-2067 8999 Fax: 029-2067 8919
Email: wales@foodstandards.gsi.gov.uk
Web: www.food.gov.uk
Advisory Committee for Wales Chair, Ms A. Hemingway

FOOD STANDARDS AGENCY NORTHERN IRELAND

10B and 10C Clarendon Road, Belfast, BT1 3BG
Tel: 028-9041 7700 Fax: 028-9041 7726
Email: infofsani@foodstandards.gsi.gov.uk
Web: www.food.gov.uk
Advisory Committee for Northern Ireland
Chairman, M. Walker

FOREIGN COMPENSATION COMMISSION

Room SG/III, Old Admiralty Building, Whitehall,
London SW1A 2PA
Tel: 020-7008 1321 Fax: 020-7008 0160

The Commission was set up by the Foreign
Compensation Act 1950 primarily to distribute, under
Orders in Council, funds received from other
governments in accordance with agreements to pay
compensation for expropriated British property and other
losses sustained by British nationals.
Chairman, vacant
Secretary, A. N. Grant

FORESTRY COMMISSION

Silvan House, 231 Corstorphine Road, Edinburgh EH12 7AT
Tel: 0845-367 3787 Fax: 0131-334 3047
Email: enquiries@forestry.gsi.gov.uk
Web: www.forestry.gov.uk

The Forestry Commission is the Government department
responsible for forestry policy in Great Britain. It reports
directly to forestry Ministers (i.e. the Minister of
Environment, Food and Rural Affairs, the Scottish
Ministers and the National Assembly for Wales), to whom
it is responsible for advice on forestry policy and for the
implementation of that policy.

The Commission's principal objectives are to protect
Britain's forests and woodlands; expand Britain's forest
area; enhance the economic value of the forest resources;
conserve and improve the biodiversity, landscape and
cultural heritage of forests and woodlands; develop
opportunities for woodland recreation; and increase
public understanding of and community participation in
forestry. Forest Enterprise, an executive agency of the
Forestry Commission, ceased to exist on 1 April 2003.
Three new bodies, one each for England, Scotland and
Wales have been created in its place.
Chairman (part-time), The Rt. Hon. Lord Clark of
Windermere
Director-General and Deputy Chairman (G2), D. J. Bills,
CBE

FORESTRY COMMISSION ENGLAND, Great Eastern
House, Tenison Road, Cambridge CB1 2BU
Tel: 01223-314546
FORESTRY COMMISSION SCOTLAND, 231 Corstorphine
Road, Edinburgh EH12 7AT Tel: 0131-334 0303
FORESTRY COMMISSION WALES, Victoria Terrace,
Aberystwyth, Ceredigion SY23 2DQ Tel: 01970-625866
FOREST RESEARCH, Alice Holt Lodge, Wrecclesham,
Farnham, Surrey GU10 4LU. Tel: 01420-222555
NORTHERN RESEARCH STATION, Roslin, Midlothian
EH25 9SY Tel: 0131-445 2176

GAMING BOARD FOR GREAT BRITAIN

Berkshire House, 168-173 High Holborn,
London WC1V 7AA
Tel: 020-7306 6200 Fax: 020-7306 6266
Email: enqs@gbgb.org.uk
Web: www.gbgb.org.uk

The Board was established in 1968 and is responsible to
the Secretary of State for Culture, Media and Sport. It is
the regulatory body for casinos, bingo clubs, gaming
machines and all local authority lotteries in Great Britain.
Its functions are to ensure that those involved in
organising gaming and lotteries are fit and proper to do
so and to keep gaming free from criminal infiltration; to
ensure that gaming and lotteries are run fairly and in
accordance with the law; and to advise the Secretary of
State on developments in gaming and lotteries.
Chairman (part-time) (£40,000-£45,000), P. Dean, CBE
Secretary, T. Kavanagh

GOVERNMENT ACTUARY'S DEPARTMENT

15/17 Furnival Street, London EC4A 1AB
Tel: 020-7211 2601 Fax: 020-7211 2640/2650
Email: enquiries@gad.gov.uk
Web: www.gad.gov.uk

The Government Actuary provides a consulting service to
Government departments, the public sector, and overseas
governments. The actuaries advise on social security
schemes and superannuation arrangements in the public
sector at home and abroad, on population and other
statistical studies, and on supervision of insurance
companies and pension funds.
Government Actuary, C. D. Daykin, CB
Directing Actuaries, D. G. Ballantine; A. G. Young
Chief Actuaries, E. I. Battersby; I. A. Boonin;
A. I. Johnston; D. Lewis; G. T. Russell

GOVERNMENT HOSPITALITY

Lancaster House, Stable Yard, St James's, London SW1A 1BB
Tel: 020-7008 8196 Fax: 020-7008 8526

The Government Hospitality Fund was instituted in 1908
for the purpose of organising official hospitality on a
regular basis with a view to the promotion of
international goodwill.
Government Hospitality is now incorporated as part of
the Foreign and Commonwealth Office's Conference and
Visitors Group.
Minister, B. Rammell
Manager of Government Hospitality, R. Alexander

GOVERNMENT OFFICES FOR THE REGIONS

The Government Offices for the Regions manage
expenditure programmes amounting to over £7 billion
per year for various Government departments. The
programmes cover areas such as; sustainable development,
neighbourhood renewal, social inclusion, regeneration,
competitiveness and rural affairs.
Government Offices handle land use planning, housing
and countryside work, road schemes decisions, local
transport priorities, transport interaction with land uses

planning and statutory casework. Government Offices have a sponsorship role for the eight Regional Development Agencies and the London Development Agency and are also involved in training and education and business support issues.

REGIONAL CO-ORDINATION UNIT
Riverwalk House, 157–161 Millbank, London SW1P 4RR
Tel: 020-7217 3029 Fax: 020-7217 3471

Director General, Rob Smith
Director (G3), A. Campbell
Directors, Ian Jones *(Corporate Communications)*; Nick Dexter *(Strategy)*; Teresa Vokes *(Business Development)*; Richard Bruce *(Regional Resilience)*

EAST MIDLANDS
Secretariat: The Belgrave Centre, Stanley Place, Talbot Street, Nottingham NG1 5GG
Tel: 0115-971 2757 Fax: 0115-971 2412
Email: enquiries.goem@go-regions.gsi.gov.uk
Web: www.go-em.gov.uk

Regional Director (G3), Jane Todd
Directors (G5), Robert Smith *(Corporate Affairs)*; Stephen Brooks *(Crime Reduction Directorate)*; Roger Poole *(Derbyshire and Leicestershire Directorate)*; Lindsey Davies *(Health and Social Care)*; Graham Norbury *(Lincolnshire and Rutland Directorate)*; Mike Jackson *(Northamptonshire and Nottingham Directorate)*

EAST OF ENGLAND
Secretariat: Building A, Westbrook Centre, Milton Road, Cambridge CB4 1YG
Tel: 01223-346708 Fax: 01223-346705

Regional Director (G3), Caroline Bowdler
Directors (G5), Hilary Cooper *(Corporate Strategies and Services)*; Martin Oldman *(Business and Europe)*; John Dowie *(Planning and Transport)*; Jane Rabagliati *(Sustainable Development and Rural Affairs)*; John Street *(Learning and Local Government)*; Keith Harding *(Community Safety and Regeneration)*

LONDON
Secretariat: Riverwalk House, 157–161 Millbank, London SW1P 4RR
Tel: 020-7217 3029 Fax: 020-7217 3471

Regional Director (G3), Liz Meek
Directors (G5), Richard Wragg *(Central and South Division)*; Anne Griffiths *(Corporate and Change Management)*; Ellie Roy *(Crime Reduction)*; Jonathan Tillson *(GLA, Business and Europe)*; Marion Kerr *(Central Unit)*; Zyg Kowalczyk *(London Resilience Team)*; Liz Walton *(North and West Division)*; Andrew Melville *(Planning Division)*; vacant *(Thames Gateway)*

NORTH-EAST
Secretariat: Wellbar House, Gallow Gate, Newcastle upon Tyne NE1 4TD
Tel: 0191-202 3811 Fax: 0191-202 3830
Email: general.enquiries.gone@go-regions.gsi.gov.uk

Regional Director (G3), Jonathan Blackie
Directors (G5), Diana Pearce *(Environment Group)*; Denise Caudle *(Communities and Learning Directorate)*;

David Slater *(Competitiveness and Europe Directorate)*; Alan Brown *(Crime Reduction Directorate)*; Jim Darlington *(Planning, Environment and Transport Directorate)*; Bill Kirkup *(Public Health Directorate)*; John Bainton *(Rural Directorate)*; John Heywood *(Strategy and Resources Directorate)*

NORTH-WEST
Secretariat: 12th Floor, Sunley Tower, Piccadilly Plaza, Manchester M1 4BE
Tel: 0161-952 4010 Fax: 0161-952 4019

Regional Director (G3), Keith Barnes
Directors, (G5), Peter Styche *(Communities Group)*; Dr David Higham *(Competitiveness and Infrastructure Group)*; Nigel Burke *(Connexions, Education and Social Inclusion Team)*; David Smith *(Crime Reduction Group)*; Neil Cumberlidge *(Environment and Rural Affairs Group)*; John Flamson *(Europe Directorate – North West)*; John Ashton *(Health Group)*; Brian Holmes *(Neighbourhood Renewal Activity)*; vacant *(Planning Directorate)*

SOUTH-EAST
Secretariat: 2nd Floor, Bridge House, 1 Walnut Tree Close, Guildford, Surrey GU1 4GA
Tel: 01483-882470 Fax: 01483-882269

Regional Director (G3), Paul Martin
Directors (G5), Hugh Marriage *(Crime Reduction)*; Alison Parker *(Europe and DEFRA Issues – Surrey/Sussex)*; Peter Craggs *(Finance and Corporate Management)*; Colin Byrne *(Planning and Innovation – Hants/Isle of Wight)*; Mike Gill *(Public Health)*; Mark Bilsborough *(Regeneration, Housing and Environment – Kent)*; vacant *(Skills, Enterprise and DTI Issues – Berks/Bucks/Oxon)*; vacant *(Transport)*

SOUTH-WEST
Secretariat: 2 Rivergate, Temple Quay, Bristol BS1 6ED
Tel: 0117-900 1701 Fax: 0117-900 1901
Web: www.gosw.gov.uk

Regional Director (G3), Jane Henderson
Directors (G5), Phil McVey *(Children, Young People and Skills)*; Malcolm Davey *(Corporate Services Division)*; Paul Rowlandson *(Crime Reduction)*; Tim Render *(Food, Farming and Rural Development)*; Celia Carrington *(Local Government and Neighbourhood Renewal Division)*; Gabriel Scally *(Public Health)*; Tony Medwar *(Regional Policies and Enterprise)*; Richard Bayly *(Transport and Europe)*

WEST MIDLANDS
Secretariat: 6th Floor, 77 Paradise Circus, Queensway, Birmingham B1 2DT
Tel: 0121-212 5226 Fax: 0121-212 5224
Email: enquiries.gowm@go-regions.gsi.gov.uk

Regional Director (G3), Graham Garbutt
Directors (G5), Jack Markiewicz *(Corporate Services Division)*; Margaret Geary *(Crime Reduction, Social Inclusion and National Division)*; Phillipa Holland *(Northern Division)*; Rod Griffiths *(Public Health Division)*; Chris Marsh *(Regional Policy and Europe)*; James Bradley *(Special Projects)*; Chris Beesley *(South Eastern Division)*; Brin Davies *(Western Division)*

YORKSHIRE AND THE HUMBER

Secretariat: PO Box 213, City House, New Station Street, Leeds LS1 4US
Tel: 0113-283 6681 Fax: 0113-283 5210
Email: enquiries.goyh@go-regions.gsi.gov.uk

Regional Director (G3), Felicity Everiss
Directors (G5), Margaret Jackson *(Competitiveness and Sustainability Group);* Nick Best *(Corporate Services Group);* Greg Dyche *(Crime Reduction Group);* Alison Biddulph *(European Funds);* Carol Cooper-Smith *(Local Authority and Neighbourhood Renewal Group);* Sylvia Yates *(Objective 1 Programme Directorate);* Isobel Mills *(People and Communities Group);* Paul Johnstone *(Public Health);* Mark Robson *(Regional International Trade Directorate);* John Jarvis *(Regional Affairs);* Gordon Kingston *(Rural Affairs Group);* Neville Myers *(Small Business Service)*

HEALTH AND SAFETY COMMISSION

Rose Court, 2 Southwark Bridge, London SE1 9HS
Tel: 020-7717 6000 Fax: 020-7717 6644
Email: hseinformationservices@natbrit.com
Web: www.hse.gov.uk

The Health and Safety Commission was created under the Health and Safety at Work etc. Act 1974, with duties to reform health and safety law, to propose new regulations, and generally to promote the protection of people at work and the public from hazards arising from industrial and commercial activity, including major industrial accidents and the transportation of hazardous materials.

Its members are nominated by organisations representing employers, employees, local authorities and others.
Chairman, B. Callaghan
Members, J. Donovan; Ms J. Edmond-Smith; G. Brumwell; Ms M. Burns; A. Chowdry; O. Tudor; J. Longworth; J. Hackitt
Secretary, M. Dempsey

HEALTH AND SAFETY EXECUTIVE

Rose Court, 2 Southwark Bridge, London SE1 9HS
Tel: 020-7717 6000 Fax: 020-7717 6717

The Health and Safety Executive is the Health and Safety Commission's major instrument. Through its inspectorates it enforces health and safety law in the majority of industrial premises. The Executive advises the Commission in its major task of laying down safety standards through regulations and practical guidance for many industrial processes. The Executive is also the licensing authority for nuclear installations and the reporting officer on the severity of nuclear incidents in Britain, and it is responsible for the Channel Tunnel Safety Authority.
Director-General, T. Walker
Deputy Director-General, Operations, J. McCracken
Deputy Director-General, Policy, K. Timms
Director, Corporate Science and Analytical Service Directorate and Chief Scientist, Dr P. Davies
Director, Field Operations Directorate, Dr A. Ellis
Director, Hazardous Installations Directorate, C. Willby
Director, Health Directorate, S. Caldwell
Director and HM Chief Inspector of the Nuclear Installations Inspectorate, L. Williams
Director of Rail Safety, A. Osborne
Director, Resource and Planning Directorate, V. Dews
Director, Safety Policy, N. Starling

HEALTH PROTECTION AGENCY

Central Office: Level 11, The Adelphi, 10–11 John Adam Street, London WC2N 6HT
Tel: 020-7339 1300 Fax: 020-7339 1301
Email: firstname.surname@ hpa.org.uk
Web: www.hpa.org.uk

The Health Protection Agency (HPA) was set up on 1 April 2003 to provide an integrated approach to protecting public health and reducing the impact of infections, chemicals, poisons and radiation hazards on human health. It brings together the functions and expertise from the Public Health Laboratory Service, including the Communicable Disease Surveillance Centre, the Centre for Applied Microbiology and Research, the National Focus for Chemical Incidents, the Regional Service Provider Units that support the management of chemical incidents, the National Poisons Information Service, and the NHS public health staff responsible for control of infectious disease, emergency planning and other protection support.
Chairman, Sir William Stewart
Chief Executive, Dr Pat Troop

BUSINESS
Porton Down, Salisbury, Wilts SP4 0JG
Director, Prof. Roger Gilmour

CHEMICAL HAZARDS AND POISONS
University of Wales Institute, Western Avenue, Cardiff CF5 2YB
Director, Prof. Stephen Palmer

COMMUNICABLE DISEASE SURVEILLANCE CENTRE
61 Colindale Avenue, NW9 5EQ
Director, Dr A. Nicoll

EMERGENCY RESPONSE
Porton Down, Salisbury, Wilts SP4 0JG
Director, Dr Nigel Lightfoot

LOCAL AND REGIONAL SERVICES
Level 11, The Adelphi, 1–11 John Adam Street, London WC2N 6HT
Director, Dr Mary O'Mahony

SPECIALIST AND REFERENCE MICROBIOLOGY
61 Colindale Avenue, London NW9 5HT
Director, Prof. Pete Borriello

HIGHLANDS AND ISLANDS ENTERPRISE

Cowan House, Inverness Retail and Business Park, Inverness, Scotland IV2 7GF
Tel: 01463-234171 Fax: 01463-244469
Email: hie.general@hient.co.uk
Web: www.hie.co.uk

Highlands and Islands Enterprise (HIE) was set up under the Enterprise and New Towns (Scotland) Act 1991. Its role is to design, direct and deliver enterprise development, training, environmental and social projects and services. HIE is made up of a strategic core body and ten Local Enterprise Companies (LECs) to which many of its individual functions are delegated.
Chairman, Dr J. Hunter
Chief Executive, I. J. R. S Cumming

HISTORIC BUILDINGS COUNCIL FOR WALES
Cathays Park, Cardiff CF10 3NQ
Tel: 029-2050 0200 Fax: 029-2082 6375

The Council's function is to advise the National Assembly for Wales on the historic buildings through Cadw: Welsh Historic Monuments, which is an executive agency of the Assembly.
Chairman, T. Lloyd, FSA
Members, Prof. P. Morgan; Mrs S. Furse; Dr S. Unwin; Dr E. Wiliam; Miss E. Evans; Dr R. Wools
Secretary, Mrs J. Booker

HISTORIC ENVIRONMENT ADVISORY COUNCIL FOR SCOTLAND
Longmore House, Salisbury Place, Edinburgh EH9 1SH
Tel: 0131-668 8810 Fax: 0131-668 8788

The Historic Environment Advisory Council for Scotland is the advisory body to provide to Scottish Ministers advice on issues affecting the historic environment and how the functions of the Scottish Ministers exercisable in relation to the historic environment may be exercised effectively for the benefit of the historic environment. In this context the historic environment means any or all structures and places in Scotland of historical, archaeological or architectural interest or importance.
Chair, Mrs Elizabeth Burns, OBE
Secretary, Dr Malcolm Bangor-Jones

HISTORIC ROYAL PALACES
Hampton Court Palace, Surrey KT8 9AU
Tel: 0870-751 5172 Fax: 020-8781 9754
Web: www.hrp.org.uk

Historic Royal Palaces is a non-departmental public body with charitable status. The Secretary of State for Culture, Media and Sport is still accountable to Parliament for the care, conservation and presentation of the palaces, which are owned by the Sovereign in right of the Crown. The chairman of the trustees is appointed by The Queen on the advice of the Secretary of State.

Historic Royal Palaces is responsible for the Tower of London, Hampton Court Palace, Kensington Palace State Apartments and the Royal Ceremonial Dress Collection, Kew Palace with Queen Charlotte's Cottage, and the Banqueting House, Whitehall.

TRUSTEES
Chairman, Sir Nigel Mobbs
Appointed by The Queen, A. Reid; Sir Hugh Roberts, KCVO, FSA; Field Marshal The Lord Inge, KG, GCB
Appointed by the Secretary of State, Ms A. Heylin, OBE; S. Jones, LVO; Mrs G. Woolfe, MBE; Dr B. Cherry, FSA
Ex officio, Sir Roger Wheeler, GCB, CBE *(Constable of the Tower of London)*

OFFICERS
Chief Executive, M. Day
Director of Conservation, J. Barnes
Director of Finance, Ms A. McLeish
Director of Human Resources, G. Josephs
Director, Palaces Group, R. Giddins
Marketing Director, D. Homan
Resident Governor, HM Tower of London, Maj.-Gen. G. Field, CB, OBE
Retail Director, Ms A. Boyes

HOME-GROWN CEREALS AUTHORITY
Caledonia House, 223 Pentonville Road, London N1 9HY
Tel: 020-7520 3926 Fax: 020-7520 3954

Set up under the Cereals Marketing Act 1965, the HGCA Board consists of seven members representing UK cereal growers, seven representing dealers in, or processors of, grain and two independent members. HGCA's functions are to improve the production and marketing of UK-grown cereals and oilseeds through a research and development programme, to provide a market information service and to promote UK cereals in export markets.
Chairman, A. Pike
Chief Executive, P. V. Biscoe

HONOURS SCRUTINY COMMITTEE
35 Great Smith Street, London SW1P 3BQ
Tel: 020-7276 2770 Fax: 020-7276 2766

The Honours Scrutiny Committee is a committee of Privy Counsellors. The Prime Minister submits certain particulars to the Committee about persons proposed to be recommended for honour at any level other than a peerage for their political services, or for an honour at the level of Knight or Dame for non-political services. The Committee, after such enquiry as it thinks fit, reports to the Prime Minister whether, so far as it believes, the political candidates are fit and proper persons to be recommended and for any non-political candidate, who may have made a political donation, whether this was a factor in the recommendation for an honour.
Chairman, The Lord Thomson of Monifieth, KT, PC
Members, The Baroness Dean of Thornton-le-Fylde, PC; The Lord Hurd of Westwell, CH, CBE
Secretary, Mrs P. G. W. Catto

HORSERACE TOTALISATOR BOARD
Tote House, 74 Upper Richmond Road, London SW15 2SU
Tel: 020-8874 6411 Fax: 020-8874 6107
Web: www.tote.co.uk

The Horserace Totalisator Board (the Tote) was established by the Betting, Gaming and Lotteries Act 1963. Its function is to operate totalisators on approved racecourses in Great Britain, and it also provides on and off-course cash and credit offices. Under the Horserace Totalisator and Betting Levy Board Act 1972, it is further empowered to offer bets at starting price (or other bets at fixed odds) on any sporting event, and under the Horserace Totalisator Board Act 1997 to take bets on any event, except the National Lottery. The chairman and members of the Board are appointed by the Secretary of State, Department of Culture, Media and Sport.

The Government announced in March 2001 that the Tote would eventually be sold to a racing trust, subject to the necessary legislation going through Parliament.
Chairman, P. I. Jones
Chief Executive, W. J. Heaton

HOUSING CORPORATION

Maple House, 149 Tottenham Court Road, London W1T 7BN
Tel: 020-7393 2000 Fax: 020-7393 2111
Email: enquiries@housingcorp.gsx.gov.uk
Web: www.housingcorp.gov.uk

Established by Parliament in 1964, the Housing Corporation regulates and funds registered social landlords, non-profit making bodies run by voluntary committees. There are over 2,000 registered social landlords, most of which are housing associations, who provide homes for more than 1.5 million people. Under the Housing Act 1996, the Corporation's regulatory role was widened to embrace new types of landlords, in particular local housing companies. The Corporation is funded by the Office of the Deputy Prime Minister.
Chairman, The Rt. Hon. The Baroness Dean of Thornton-le-Fylde
Deputy Chairman, E. Armitage, OBE
Chief Executive, Dr N. Perry

HUMAN FERTILISATION AND EMBRYOLOGY AUTHORITY

Paxton House, 30 Artillery Lane, London E1 7LS
Tel: 020-7377 5077 Fax: 020-7377 1871
Email: admin@hfea.gov.uk
Web: www.hfea.gov.uk

The Human Fertilisation and Embryology Authority (HFEA) was established under the Human Fertilisation and Embryology Act 1990. Its function is to license the following activities: the creation or use of embryos outside the body in the provision of infertility treatment services; the use of donated gametes in infertility treatment; the storage of gametes or embryos; and research on human embryos. It maintains a confidential database of all such treatments and of egg and sperm donors, and provides information to patients, clinics and the public. The HFEA also keeps under review information about embryos and, when requested to do so, gives advice to the Secretary of State for Health.
Chairman, S. Leather
Deputy Chairman, Prof. T. Baldwin
Members, Prof. D. Barlow; Prof. C. Barratt;
  Prof. P. Braude; I. Brecker; Ms C. Brown;
  Prof. I. Cameron; Prof. A. Grubb; Prof. N. Haites;
  Dr M. Jamieson; S. Jenkins; W. Merricks; Ms S. Nathan;
  The Right Rev. Dr M. J. Nazir-Ali; Ms S. Nebhrajani
Director of Sub-Committees, Mrs J. Denton

HUMAN GENETICS COMMISSION

Area 652C, Skipton House, 80 London Road,
London SE1 6LH Tel: 020-7972 1518 Fax: 020-7972 1717
Email: hgc@doh.gov.uk
Web: www.hgc.gov.uk

The Human Genetics Commission was established in 1999, subsuming three previous advisory committees. Its remit is to give Ministers strategic advice on how developments in human genetics will impact on people and health care, focusing in particular on the special and ethical implications.
Chairman, Baroness H. Kennedy of the Shaws, QC
Vice-Chair, Prof. A. McCall Smith
Members, Dr W. Albert, Prof. E. Anionwu; Dr S. Bain;
  Prof. J. Burn; Dr H. Harris; Prof. J. Harris;
  Ms S. Leather; Ms H. Newiss; Prof. M. Richards;
  Dr S. Singleton; Mr G. Watts; Mr P. Webb;

Prof. V. van Heyningen; Dr Patrick Morrison;
Dr R. Skinner; Emeritius Prof. Brenda Almond;
Mrs C. Patch; P. Sayers
Head of Secretariat, M. Bale

INDEPENDENT HOUSING OMBUDSMAN

Norman House, 105–109 Strand, London WC2R 0AA
Tel: 020-7836 3630 Fax: 020-7836 3900
Email: ombudsman@ihos.org.uk
Web: www.ihos.org.uk

The Independent Housing Ombudsman (IHO) was established in 1997 under the Housing Act 1996. The Ombudsman deals with complaints against registered social landlords (not including local authorities) and some private landlords. IHO is also managing the pilot Tenancy Deposit Scheme aimed at protecting the deposits of private tenants and resolving any disputes over their return quickly, cheaply and fairly.
Ombudsman, M. Biles
Chair of Board, G. Lewis
Company Secretary, Wilma Jarvie

INDEPENDENT INTERNATIONAL COMMISSION ON DECOMMISSIONING

Dublin Castle, Block M, Ship Street, Dublin 2
Tel: 00 353 1-478 0111 Fax: 00 353 1-478 0600
Rosepark House, Upper Newtownards Road, Belfast BT4 3NX
Tel: 028-9048 8600 Fax: 028-9048 8601

The Commission was established by agreement between the British and Irish Governments in August 1997. Its objective is to facilitate the decommissioning of illegally-held firearms and explosives in accordance with the relevant legislation in both jurisdictions. Its members are appointed jointly by the two Governments; staff are appointed by the Commission. All are drawn from countries other than the UK and the Republic of Ireland.
Commissioners, Gen. J. de Chastelain *(Chairman, Canada)*;
  A. D. Sens *(USA)*
Staff Director, A. Suonio *(Finland)*
Admin/Finances, K. Juntunen; R. Schoen; J. Mladinich

INDEPENDENT REVIEW SERVICE FOR THE SOCIAL FUND

4th Floor, Centre City Podium, 5 Hill Street,
Birmingham B5 4UB
Tel: 0121-606 2100 Fax: 0121-606 2180
Email: sfc@irs-review.org.uk
Web: www.irs-review.org.uk

The Social Fund Commissioner is appointed by the Secretary of State for Work and Pensions. The Commissioner appoints Social Fund Inspectors, who provide an independent review of decisions made by Social Fund Officers in the Department of Work and Pensions.
Social Fund Commissioner, Sir Richard Tilt

INDUSTRIAL INJURIES ADVISORY COUNCIL

6th Floor, The Adelphi, 1–11 John Adam Street, London WC2N 6HT
Tel: 020-7962 8066 Fax: 020-7712 2255
Email: iiac@dial.pipex.com Web: www.iiac.org.uk

The Industrial Injuries Advisory Council is a statutory body under the Social Security Administration Act 1992. It considers and advises the Secretary of State for Work and Pensions on regulations and other questions relating to industrial injuries benefits or their administration.
Chairman, Prof. A. J. Newman Taylor, OBE, FRCP
Administrative Secretary, N. Davidson

INFORMATION COMMISSIONER'S OFFICE

Wycliffe House, Water Lane, Wilmslow, Cheshire SK9 5AF
Tel: 01625-545745 Fax: 01625-524510
Email: data@dataprotection.gov.uk
Web: www.dataprotection.gov.uk

The Data Protection Act 1998 sets rules for processing personal information and applies to some paper records as well as those held on computers.

The Data Protection Act works in two ways; it says that those who record and use personal information (data controllers) must be open about how the information is used and must follow the eight principles of 'good information handling.' It also gives data subjects (individuals who are the subject of personal data) certain rights.

The Commissioner has a number of specific duties under the Act. He is given discretion in the manner in which he fulfils those duties and much of his work, and that of his staff, involves informal advice and consultation with data controllers, data subjects and the various bodies that represent them.

It is the Commissioner's duty to compile and maintain the register of data controllers, and provide facilities for members of the public to examine the register; promote observance of the data protection principles; and disseminate information to the public about the Act and his functions under the Act. The Commissioner also has the power to produce codes of practice.

The Commissioner reports annually to parliament on the performance of his functions under the Act and has obligations to assess breaches of the Act.
Commissioner, Richard Thomas

JOINT NATURE CONSERVATION COMMITTEE

Monkstone House, City Road, Peterborough PE1 1JY
Tel: 01733-562626 Fax: 01733-555948

The Committee was established under the Environmental Protection Act 1990. It advises the Government and others on UK and international nature conservation issues and disseminates knowledge on these subjects. It establishes common standards for the monitoring of nature conservation and research, and provides guidance to English Nature, Scottish Natural Heritage, the Countryside Council for Wales and the Department of the Environment for Northern Ireland.
Chairman, Mrs K. Bryan
Managing Director, D. Steer
Director, Dr M. A. Vincent

LAND REGISTRIES

HM LAND REGISTRY

32 Lincoln's Inn Fields, London WC2A 3PH
Tel: 020-7919 8888 Fax: 020-7955 0110
Email: enquiries.pic@landreg.gov.uk
Web: www.landreg.gov.uk

The registration of title to land was first introduced in England and Wales by the Land Registry Act 1862; HM Land Registry operates today under the Land Registration Acts 1925 to 1997. The object of registering title to land is to create and maintain a register of landowners whose title is guaranteed by the state and so to simplify the transfer, mortgage and other dealings with real property. Registration on sale is now compulsory throughout England and Wales. The register has been open to inspection by the public since 1990.

HM Land Registry is an executive agency and Trading Fund administered under the Lord Chancellor by the Chief Land Registrar.

HEADQUARTERS OFFICE

Chief Land Registrar and Chief Executive, P. Collis
Director for Business Development and Deputy Chief Executive, E. G. Beardsall, CBE
Director of Education and Training, Mrs L. Chamberlain
Director of Facilities, A. Elston
Director of Finance, Ms H. Jackson
Director of Geographic Information, R. Ashwin
Director of Information Systems, I. Johnson
Director of Legal Services, J. V. Timothy
Director of Marketing and Communication, Mrs D. Reynolds
Director of Operations, A. Howarth
Director of Personnel, Mrs L. Daniels
Director of Service Development, P. Norman
Director of Strategy, A. Pemberton

INFORMATION SYSTEMS DIRECTORATE

Burrington Way, Plymouth PL5 3LP
Tel: 01752-635600
Head of IT Services/Strategy Division, P. A. Maycock/ C. Bitton
Head of IT Development Division, J. Formby
Head of IT Directorate Services, K. Deards

LAND CHARGES CREDITS DEPARTMENT

Plumer House, Tailyour Road, Crownhill, Plymouth PL6 5HY
Tel: 01752-636666
Superintendent, Ms M. Telfer

DISTRICT LAND REGISTRIES

BIRKENHEAD (OLD MARKET) – Old Market House, Hamilton Street, Birkenhead CH41 5FL.
Tel: 0151-473 1110. *District Land Registrar,* P. J. Brough
BIRKENHEAD (ROSEBRAE) – Rosebrae Court, Woodside Ferry Approach, Birkenhead CH41 6DU.
Tel: 0151-472 6666. *District Land Registrar,* M. J. Garwood
COVENTRY – Leigh Court, Torrington Avenue, Tile Hill, Coventry CV4 9XZ. Tel: 024-7686 0860. *District Land Registrar,* Mrs D. M. Weaver
CROYDON – Sunley House, Bedford Park, Croydon CR9 3LE. Tel: 020-8781 9103. *District Land Registrar,* F. M. Twambley
DURHAM (BOLDON HOUSE) – Boldon House, Wheatlands Way, Pity Me, Durham DH1 5GJ. Tel: 0191-301 2345.
District Land Registrar, R. B. Fearnley

DURHAM (SOUTHFIELD HOUSE) – Southfield House, Southfield Way, Durham DH1 5TR. Tel: 0191-301 3500. *District Land Registrar,* P. J. Timothy

GLOUCESTER – Twyver House, Bruton Way, Gloucester GL1 1DQ. Tel: 01452-511111. *District Land Registrar,* Mrs J. Jenkins

HARROW – Lyon House, Lyon Road, Harrow, Middx HA1 2EU. Tel: 020-8235 1181. *District Land Registrar,* C. Tate

KINGSTON UPON HULL – Earle House, Colonial Street, Hull HU2 8JN. Tel: 01482-223244. *District Land Registrar,* S. R. Coveney

LANCASHIRE – Wrea Brook Court, Lytham Road, Warton, Preston, PR4 1TE. Tel: 01772-836 700 *District Land Registrar,* Mrs L. Wallwork

LEICESTER – Westbridge Place, Leicester LE3 5DR. Tel: 0116-265 4000. *District Land Registrar,* Mrs J. A. Goodfellow

LYTHAM – Birkenhead House, East Beach, Lytham St Annes, Lancs FY8 5AB. Tel: 01253-849849. *District Land Registrar,* J. Griffiths

NOTTINGHAM (EAST) – Robins Wood Road, Nottingham NG8 3RQ. Tel: 0115-906 5353. *District Land Registrar,* Ms A. M. Goss

NOTTINGHAM (WEST) – Chalfont Drive, Nottingham NG8 3RN. Tel: 0115-935 1166. *District Land Registrar,* P. A. Brown

PETERBOROUGH – Touthill Close, City Road, Peterborough PE1 1XN. Tel: 01733-288288. *District Land Registrar,* C. W. Martin

PLYMOUTH – Plumer House, Tailyour Road, Crownhill, Plymouth PL6 5HY. Tel: 01752-636000. *District Land Registrar,* A. J. Pain

PORTSMOUTH – St Andrew's Court, St Michael's Road, Portsmouth PO1 2JH. Tel: 023-9276 8888. *District Land Registrar,* S. R. Sehrawat

STEVENAGE – Brickdale House, Swingate, Stevenage, Herts SG1 1XG. Tel: 01438-788889. *District Land Registrar,* M. Croker

SWANSEA – Tŷ Bryn Glas, High Street, Swansea SA1 1PW. Tel: 01792-458877. *District Land Registrar,* G. A. Hughes

TELFORD – Parkside Court, Hall Park Way, Telford TF3 4LR. Tel: 01952-290355. *District Land Registrar,* A. M. Lewis

TUNBRIDGE WELLS – Forest Court, Forest Road, Tunbridge Wells, Kent TN2 5AQ. Tel: 01892-510015. *District Land Registrar,* G. R. Tooke

WALES – Tŷ Cwm Tawe, Phoenix Way, Llansamlet, Swansea SA7 9FQ. Tel: 01792-355000. *District Land Registrar,* T. M. Lewis

WEYMOUTH – Melcombe Court, 1 Cumberland Drive, Weymouth, Dorset DT4 9TT. Tel: 01305-363636. *District Land Registrar,* J. Pownall

YORK – James House, James Street, York YO10 3YZ. Tel: 01904-450000. *District Land Registrar,* Mrs R. F. Lovel

REGISTERS OF SCOTLAND
Meadowbank House, 153 London Road,
Edinburgh EH8 7AU
Tel: 0131-659 6111 Fax: 0131-479 3688
Customer Service Centre: 0845-607 0161
Email: customer.services@ros.gov.uk
Web: www.ros.gov.uk

Registers of Scotland is the executive agency responsible for framing and maintaining records relating to property and other legal documents in Scotland. The agency holds 15 registers: two property registers (General Register of Sasines and Land Register of Scotland) and 13 chancery and judicial registers (Register of Deeds in the Books of Council and Session; Register of Protests; Register of Judgements; Register of Service of Heirs; Register of the Great Seal; Register of the Quarter Seal; Register of the Prince's Seal; Register of Crown Grants; Register of Sheriffs' Commissions; Register of the Cachet Seal; Register of Inhibitions and Adjudications; Register of Entails; and Register of Hornings).

Chief Executive and Keeper of the Registers of Scotland, A. W. Ramage
Deputy Keeper, A. G. Rennie
Managing Director, F. Manson

LAW COMMISSION
Conquest House, 37–38 John Street, London WC1N 2BQ
Tel: 020-7453 1220 Fax: 020-7453 1297
Web: www.lawcom.gov.uk

The Law Commission was set up in 1965, under the Law Commissions Act 1965, to make proposals to the Government for the examination of the law in England and Wales and for its revision where it is unsuited for modern requirements, obscure, or otherwise unsatisfactory. It recommends to the Lord Chancellor programmes for the examination of different branches of the law and suggests whether the examination should be carried out by the Commission itself or by some other body. The Commission is also responsible for the preparation of Consolidation and Statute Law (Repeals) Bills.

Chairman, The Hon. Mr Justice Toulson
Commissioners, Judge A. Wilkie, QC; Prof. H. Beale, QC; Prof. M. Partington, CBE; S. Bridge
Secretary, M. W. Sayers

LAW OFFICERS' DEPARTMENTS
Legal Secretariat to the Law Officers, Attorney-General's Chambers, 9 Buckingham Gate, London SW1E 6JP
Tel: 020-7271 2400 Fax: 020-7271 2430
Email: lslo@gtnet.gov.uk
Web: www.lslo.gov.uk
Attorney-General's Chambers, Royal Courts of Justice, Belfast BT1 3JY
Tel: 028-9054 6082 Fax: 028-9054 6049

The Law Officers of the Crown for England and Wales are the Attorney-General and the Solicitor-General. The Attorney-General, assisted by the Solicitor-General, is the chief legal adviser to the Government and is also ultimately responsible for all Crown litigation. He has overall responsibility for the work of the Law Officers' Departments (the Treasury Solicitor's Department, the Crown Prosecution Service, the Serious Fraud Office and the Legal Secretariat to the Law Officers). He has a specific statutory duty to superintend the discharge of their duties by the Director of Public Prosecutions (who heads the Crown Prosecution Service) and the Director of the Serious Fraud Office. The Director of Public Prosecutions for Northern Ireland is also responsible to the Attorney-General for the performance of his functions. The Attorney-General has additional responsibilities in relation to aspects of the civil and criminal law.

Attorney-General (*£99,200), The Rt. Hon. The Lord Goldsmith, QC
Private Secretary, C. Bartlett
Parliamentary Private Secretary, M. Foster, MP

Solicitor-General, The Rt. Hon. Harriet Harman, QC, MP
Legal Secretary (G2), D. Brummell
Deputy Legal Secretary (G3), S. Parkinson

*In addition to a parliamentary salary of £56,358

LEARNING AND SKILLS COUNCIL
Cheylesmore House, Quinton Road, Coventry, West Midlands, CV1 2WT
Tel: 0845-019 4170 Fax: 024-7649 3600
Email: info@lsc.gov.uk Web: www.lsc.gov.uk

The Learning and Skills Council (LSC) was established in April 2001 to replace the Further Education Funding and the Training and Enterprise Councils. It is a non-departmental public body responsible for the planning and funding of post-16 education and training. Its annual budget for 2003–4 is £8 billion. Its remit is to ensure that high quality post-16 provision is available to meet the needs of employers, individuals and communities. The LSC operates through a national office based in Coventry and 47 local departments, which work to promote the equality of opportunity in the workplace, aiming to ensure that the needs of the most disadvantaged in the labour market are met. These local departments in most cases have coterminous boundaries with Small business service franchises.
Chairman, B. Sanderson
Chief Executive, J. Harwood

LEGAL SERVICES COMMISSION
85 Gray's Inn Road, London WC1X 8TX
Tel: 020-7759 0000
Web: www.legalservices.gov.uk

The Legal Services Commission is an executive non-departmental public body created under the Access to Justice Act 1999 to replace the Legal Aid Board. It is responsible for the development and administration of two schemes in England and Wales: the Community Legal Service, which from 1 April 2000 replaced the old civil scheme of legal aid, bringing together networks of funders (eg. Local Authorities) and suppliers into partnership to provide the widest possible access to information and advice; the Criminal Defence Service, which from 2 April 2001 replaced the old system of criminal legal aid and provides criminal services to people accused of crimes.
Chief Executive, Clare Dodgson
Chairman, P. Ely, OBE
Members, A. Edwards; Ms J. Herzog; Ms S. Hewitt; Ms Y. Mosquito; J. Shearer; Ms M. Richards

LIBRARIES

THE BRITISH LIBRARY
96 Euston Road, London NW1 2DB
Tel: 020-7412 7000
Email: visitor-services@bl.uk Web: www.bl.uk

The British Library was established in 1973. It is the UK's national library and occupies a key position in the library and information network. The Library aims to serve scholarship, research, industry, commerce and all other major users of information. Its services are based on collections which include over 16 million volumes, 1 million discs, and 55,000 hours of tape recordings. The Library is now based at two sites: London (St Pancras and

Colindale) and Boston Spa, W. Yorks. Government-grant-in-aid to the British Library in 2003–4 is £88.9 million. The Library's sponsoring department is the Department for Culture, Media and Sport.
Access to the reading rooms at St Pancras is limited to holders of a British Library Reader's Pass; information about eligibility is available from the Reader Admissions Office. The exhibition galleries and public areas are open to all, free of charge.
Opening hours of services vary and specific information should be checked by telephone.

BRITISH LIBRARY BOARD
Chairman, Lord Eatwell
Chief Executive and Deputy Chairman, Mrs L. Brindley
Part-time Members, H. Boyd-Carpenter, CVO;
   Dr C. G. R. Leach; Prof. Dame Jessica Rawson, DBE, D.Litt, FBA; J. Ritblat, FRICS; Prof. L. Colley; S. Olswang; Prof. R. Burgess; S. Forbes, CBE; D. Lewis

BRITISH LIBRARY, BOSTON SPA
Boston Spa, Wetherby, W. Yorks LS23 7BQ
Tel: 01937-546000

BRITISH LIBRARY, ST PANCRAS
96 Euston Road, London NW1 2DB
Tel: 020-7412 7000

PRESS AND PUBLIC RELATIONS Tel: 020-7412 7111
VISITOR SERVICES Tel: 020-7412 7332
EDUCATION SERVICE Tel: 020-7412 7797

SCHOLARSHIP AND COLLECTIONS
Reader Services, Tel: 020-7412 7676
Asia, Pacific and Africa Collections, Tel: 020-7412 7873
British Collections, Tel: 020-7412 7676
Western Manuscripts, Tel: 020-7412 7513
Map Library, Tel: 020-7412 7702
Music Library, Tel: 020-7412 7772
Philatelic Collections, Tel: 020-7412 7635
British Library Sound Archive, Tel: 020-7412 7440
British Library Newspapers, Colindale Avenue, London NW9 5HE. Tel: 020-7412 7353
European and American Collections, Tel: 020-7412 7676

OPERATIONS AND SERVICES
Reader Admissions, Tel: 020-7412 7677

SCIENCE, TECHNOLOGY AND INNOVATION
Science and Technology, Tel: 020-7412 7494/7289
Patents, Tel: 020-7412 7919/7920
Business, Tel: 020-7412 7454
Social Policy Information Service, Tel: 020-7412 7536

NATIONAL PRESERVATION OFFICE Tel: 020-7412 7612

NATIONAL LIBRARY OF SCOTLAND
George IV Bridge, Edinburgh EH1 1EW
Tel: 0131-226 4531 Fax: 0131-622 4803
Email: enquiries@nls.uk Web: www.nls.uk

The Library, which was founded as the Advocates' Library in 1682, became the National Library of Scotland in 1925. It is funded by the Scottish Executive. It contains about seven million books and pamphlets, 20,000 current periodicals, 350 newspaper titles and 120,000 manuscripts. It has an unrivalled Scottish collection.

The Reading Room is for reference and research which cannot conveniently be pursued elsewhere. Admission is by ticket issued to an approved applicant.
Chairman of the Trustees, Prof. Michael Anderson, OBE, FBA, FRSE
Librarian and Secretary to the Trustees (G4), M. Wade
Secretary of the Library (G6), M. C. Graham
Director of General Collections, C. Newton
Director of Special Collections, M. C. T. Simpson
Director of Public Services, A. M. Marchbank

NATIONAL LIBRARY OF WALES/LLYFRGELL GENEDLAETHOL CYMRU
Aberystwyth SY23 3BU
Tel: 01970-632800 Fax: 01970-615709
Web: www.llgc.org.uk

The National Library of Wales was founded by royal charter in 1907, and is funded by the National Assembly for Wales. It contains about four million printed books, 40,000 manuscripts, four million deeds and documents, numerous maps, prints and drawings, and a sound and moving image collection. It specialises in manuscripts and books relating to Wales and the Celtic peoples. It is the repository for pre-1858 Welsh probate records, manorial records and tithe documents, and certain legal records. Admission is by reader's ticket to the Reading Rooms but there is free entry to the exhibition programme.
President, Dr R. Brinley Jones
Librarian (G4), A. M. W. Green
Heads of Departments (G6), M. W. Mainwaring
   (Corporate Services); G. Jenkins *(Collection Services);*
   Dr W. R. M. Griffiths *(Public Services)*

LIGHTHOUSE AUTHORITIES

CORPORATION OF TRINITY HOUSE
Trinity House, Tower Hill, London EC3N 4DH
Tel: 020-7481 6900 Fax: 020-7480 7662
Web: www.trinityhouse.co.uk

Trinity House, the first general lighthouse and pilotage authority in the kingdom, was granted its first charter by Henry VIII in 1514. The Corporation is the general lighthouse authority for England, Wales and the Channel Islands and maintains 72 lighthouses, 13 major floating aids to navigation (e.g. light vessels) and more than 420 buoys. The Corporation also has certain statutory jurisdiction over aids to navigation maintained by local harbour authorities and is responsible for dealing with wrecks dangerous to navigation, except those occurring within port limits or wrecks of HM ships.
   The Trinity House Lighthouse Service is maintained out of the General Lighthouse Fund which is provided from light dues levied on ships calling at ports of the UK and the Republic of Ireland. The Corporation is also a deep-sea pilotage authority and a charitable organisation.
   The affairs of the Corporation are controlled by a board of Elder Brethren and the Secretary. A separate board, which comprises Elder Brethren, senior staff and outside representatives, currently controls the Lighthouse Service. The Elder Brethren also act as nautical assessors in marine cases in the Admiralty Division of the High Court of Justice.

ELDER BRETHREN
Master, HRH The Prince Philip, Duke of Edinburgh, KG, KT, PC

Deputy Master and Executive Chairman, Rear-Adm. J. M. de Halpert, CBE
Wardens, Capt. C. M. C. Stewart *(Rental);* Cdr. M. J. Rivett-Carnac, RN *(Nether)*
Elder Brethren, HRH The Prince of Wales, KG, KT, OM; HRH The Duke of York, GCVO, ADC; Capt. Sir David Tibbits, DSC, RN; Sir Brian Shaw; Capt. J. E. Bury; Capt. J. A. N. Bezant, DSC, RD; Capt. D. J. Cloke; Capt. Sir Miles Wingate, KCVO; The Rt. Hon. Sir Edward Heath, KG, MBE; Capt. P. F. Mason, CBE; Capt. T. Woodfield, OBE; The Rt. Hon. The Lord Simon of Glaisdale; Capt. D. T. Smith, OBE, RN; Cdr. Sir Robin Gillett, Bt., GBE, RD; Capt. Sir Malcolm Edge, KCVO; The Rt. Hon. The Lord Cuckney of Millbank; Capt. D. J. Orr; The Rt. Hon. The Lord Carrington, KG, GCMG, CH, MC; The Rt. Hon. The Lord Mackay of Clashfern; Sir Adrian Swire, AE; The Rt. Hon. The Lord Sterling of Plaistow, CBE; Adm. Sir Jock Slater, GCB, LVO; Capt. J. R. Burton-Hall, RD; Capt. I. Gibb; Cdre. P. J. Melson, CBE, RN; Capt. D. C. Glass; D. F. Potter; Capt. P. Richards, RD; S. P. Sherrard; The Lord Brown of Madingley; The Rt. Hon. The Lord Robertson of Port Ellen; Rear-Adm. Sir Patrick Rowe, KCVO, CBE

OFFICERS
Secretary, P. Galloway
Director of Finance, J. S. Wedge
Director of Engineering, D. Golden
Director of Administration, D. I. Brewer
Legal and Insurance Manager, J. D. Price
Navigation Manager, Mrs K. Hossain
Head of Marketing and Management Services,
   S. J. W. Dunning
Senior Inspector of Shipping, J. R. Dunnett
Media and Communication Officer, H. L. Cooper
Head of Human Resources, P. F. Morgan

NORTHERN LIGHTHOUSE BOARD
84 George Street, Edinburgh EH2 3DA
Tel: 0131-473 3100 Fax: 0131-220 2093
Email: enquiries@nlb.org.uk Web: www.nlb.org.uk

The Lighthouse Board is the general lighthouse authority for Scotland and the Isle of Man. The board owes its origin to an Act of Parliament passed in 1786. At present the Commissioners operate under the Merchant Shipping Act 1995 and are 19 in number.
   The Commissioners control 83 major automatic lighthouses, 118 minor lights and many lighted and unlighted buoys. They have a fleet of two motor vessels.

COMMISSIONERS
The Lord Advocate; the Solicitor-General for Scotland; the Lord Provosts of Edinburgh, Glasgow and Aberdeen; the Provost of Inverness; the Convener of Argyll and Bute Council; the Sheriffs-Principal of North Strathclyde, Tayside, Central and Fife, Grampian, Highlands and Islands, South Strathclyde, Dumfries and Galloway, Lothians and Borders and Glasgow and Strathkelvin; Capt. D. M. Cowell; Adm. Sir Michael Livesay, KCB; P. MacKay, CB; Capt. K. MacLeod; Dr A. Cubie, CBE

OFFICERS
Chief Executive, Capt. J. B. Taylor, RN
Director of Finance, D. Gorman
Director of Engineering, M. Waddell
Director of Operations and Navigational Requirements,
   G. Platten

LOCAL COMMISSIONERS

COMMISSION FOR LOCAL ADMINISTRATION IN ENGLAND

Millbank Tower, Millbank, London SW1P 4QP
Tel: 020-7217 4620 Fax: 020-7217 4621
Enquiry line: 0845-602 1983

Local Commissioners (local government ombudsmen) are responsible for investigating complaints from members of the public against local authorities (but not town and parish councils); English Partnerships (planning matters only); Housing Action Trusts; education appeal panels; police authorities and certain other authorities. The Commissioners are appointed by the Crown on the recommendation of the Deputy Prime Minister.

Certain types of action are excluded from investigation, including personnel matters and commercial transactions unless they relate to the purchase or sale of land. Complaints can be sent direct to the Local Government Ombudsman or through a councillor, although the Local Government Ombudsman will not consider a complaint unless the council has had an opportunity to investigate and reply to a complainant.

A free leaflet *Complaint about the council? How to complain to the Local Government Ombudsman* is available from the Commission's offices.

Chairman and Chief Executive of the Commission and Local Commissioner (£143,258), T. Redmond
Vice-Chairman and Local Commissioner (£108,408), Mrs P. A. Thomas
Local Commissioner (£107,408), J. R. White
Member (ex officio), The Parliamentary Commissioner for Administration, Ann Abraham
Deputy Chief Executive and Secretary (£66,797), N. J. Karney

COMMISSION FOR LOCAL ADMINISTRATION IN WALES

Derwen House, Court Road, Bridgend CF31 1BN
Tel: 01656-661325 Fax: 01656-673279
Email: enquiries@ombudsman-wales.org
Web: www.ombudsman-wales.org

The Local Commissioner for Wales has similar powers to the Local Commissioners in England, but since the end of 2001 he has also had additional powers (similar to the Standards Board for England) to investigate allegations made against local authority members of misconduct. The Commissioner is appointed by the Crown on the recommendation of the Secretary of State for Wales. A free leaflet *Your Local Government Ombudsman in Wales* is available from the Commissioner's office.

Local Commissioner, E. R. Moseley (due to retire in autumn 2003)
Secretary, D. Bowen
Member (ex officio), The Parliamentary Commissioner for Administration

LORD GREAT CHAMBERLAIN'S OFFICE

House of Lords, London SW1A 0PW
Tel: 020-7219 3100 Fax: 020-7219 2500

The Lord Great Chamberlain is a Great Officer of State, the office being hereditary since the grant of Henry I to the family of De Vere, Earls of Oxford. It is now a joint hereditary office rotating on the death of the Sovereign between the Cholmondeley, Carington and the Ancaster families. The Lord Great Chamberlain is responsible for the royal apartments in the Palace of Westminster, i.e. The Sovereign's Robing Room, the Royal Gallery, the administration of the Chapel of St Mary Undercroft and, in conjunction with the Lord Chancellor and the Speaker, Westminster Hall. The Lord Great Chamberlain has the right to perform specific services at a Coronation, he carries out ceremonial duties in the Palace of Westminster when the Sovereign visits the Palace and has particular responsibility for the internal administrative arrangements within the House of Lords for State Openings of Parliament.

Lord Great Chamberlain, The Marquess of Cholmondeley
Secretary to the Lord Great Chamberlain,
  Lt.-Gen. Sir Michael Willcocks, KCB
Clerks to the Lord Great Chamberlain, Ms J. Perodeau;
  Ms Rebecca Russel Ponte

LORD PRIVY SEAL'S OFFICE

Cabinet Office, 70 Whitehall, London SW1A 2AT
Tel: 020-7270 3000
Web: www. cabinetoffice.gov.uk

The Lord Privy Seal is a member of the Cabinet and Leader of the House of Lords. He has no departmental portfolio, but is a member of a number of Cabinet committees. He is responsible to the Prime Minister for the organisation of Government business in the House and has a responsibility to the House itself to advise it on procedural matters and other difficulties which arise. He is the Lords' spokesperson on Northern Ireland issues.

Lord Privy Seal, Leader of the House of Lords,
  The Rt. Hon. The Lord Williams of Mostyn, QC
Principal Private Secretary, Christopher Jacobs
Private Secretary (House of Lords), Andrew Makower

MENTAL HEALTH ACT COMMISSION

Maid Marian House, 56 Hounds Gate, Nottingham NG1 6BG
Tel: 0115-943 7100 Fax: 0115-943 7101
Web: www.mhac.trent.nhs.uk

The Mental Health Act Commission was established in 1983. Its functions are to keep under review the operation of the Mental Health Act 1983; to visit and meet patients detained under the Act; to investigate complaints falling within the Commission's remit; to operate the consent to treatment safeguards in the Mental Health Act; to publish a biennial report on its activities; to monitor the implementation of the Code of Practice; and to advise Ministers. Commissioners are appointed by the Secretary of State for Health.

Chairman, Prof. K. Patel
Vice-Chairman, Ms D. Jenkins
Chief Executive, C. Heginbotham

MILLENNIUM COMMISSION

Portland House, Stag Place, London SW1E 5EZ
Tel: 020-7880 2007 Fax: 020-7880 2000
Email: info@millennium.gov.uk

The Millennium Commission was established in February 1994 and is accountable to the Department for Culture, Media and Sport. It is an independent body which distributes money from National Lottery proceeds to projects to mark the millennium.

Chair, The Rt. Hon. Tessa Jowell, MP
Members, Dr H. Couper; The Earl of Dalkeith;
Ms F. Benjamin; The Rt. Hon. M. Heseltine, MP;
Ms J. Donovan, CBE; M. D' Ancona; Lord Gletoran;
The Rt. Hon. R. Caborn, MP
Director, M. O'Connor

MUSEUMS

THE BRITISH MUSEUM

Great Russell Street, London WC1B 3DG
Tel: 020-7323 8000 Fax: 020-7323 8616
Email: information@thebritishmuseum.ac.uk
Web: www.thebritishmuseum.ac.uk

The British Museum houses the national collection of antiquities, ethnography, coins and paper money, medals, prints and drawings. The British Museum may be said to date from 1753, when Parliament approved the holding of a public lottery to raise funds for the purchase of the collections of Sir Hans Sloane and the Harleian manuscripts, and for their proper housing and maintenance. The building (Montagu House) was opened in 1759. The present buildings were erected between 1823 and the present day, and the original collection has increased to its present dimensions by gifts and purchases. Total government grant-in-aid for 2003–4 is £37 million.

BOARD OF TRUSTEES
Appointed by the Sovereign, HRH The Duke of Gloucester, KG, GCVO
Appointed by the Prime Minister, C. Allen-Jones;
Hasan Askari; Nicholas Barber; Prof. Barry Cunliffe;
The Rt. Hon. Countess of Dalkeith; Sir Michael
Hopkins; Sir Joseph Hotung; Prof. Martin Kemp;
David Lindsell; Christopher McCall; Tom Phillips;
Anna Ritchie; Eric Salama; Prof. Jean Thomas;
Sir Keith Thomas; Richard Lambert
Appointed by the Trustees of the British Museum, Sir John
Boyd *(Chair)*; The Hon. Phillip Lader; Lord Powell
of Bayswater, KCMG; J. Tusa *(Deputy Chair)*;
Lord Browne of Madingley *(Deputy Chair)*

OFFICERS
Director, Neil MacGregor
Deputy Director, Dawn Austwick
Deputy Director, Andrew Burnett
Director of Marketing and Public Affairs, vacant
Director of Operations, Chris Rofe
Director of Resources, D. Austwick, OBE
Head of Building and Estates, K. T. Stannard
Acting Head of Communications, Joanna Mackle
Head of Education, J. F. Reeve
Head of Finance, Chris Herring
Head of Membership Development, Ms M. Fenn
Secretary, T. Doubleday
Visitor Operations Manager, Kerry Foster

KEEPERS
Keeper of Ancient Near East Antiquities, Dr John Curtis
Keeper of Coins and Medals, Andrew Burnett
Keeper of Department of Asia, Robert Knox
Keeper of Ethnography, John Mack
Keeper of Egyptian Antiquities, Vivian Davies
Keeper of Greek and Roman Antiquities, Dr Dyfri Williams
Keeper of Prehistory and Europe, Leslie Webster
Keeper, Presentation, Ian Jenkins

Keeper of Prints and Drawings, Antony Griffiths
Conservation, Documentation and Science, Sheridan Bowman

IMPERIAL WAR MUSEUM

Lambeth Road, London SE1 6HZ
Tel: 020-7416 5320 Fax: 020-7416 5374

The Museum, founded in 1917, illustrates and records all aspects of the two world wars and other military operations involving Britain and the Commonwealth since 1914. It was opened in its present home, formerly Bethlem Hospital, in 1936. The Museum is a multibranch organisation which also includes: the Cabinet War Rooms in Whitehall, HMS Belfast in the Pool of London, Imperial War Museum Duxford in Cambridgeshire and Imperial War Museum North in Trafford.

The total grant-in-aid (including grants for special projects) for 2003–4 is £16.541 million.

OFFICERS
Chairman of Trustees, Adm. Sir Jock Slater, GCB, LVO
Director-General, R. W. K. Crawford, CBE
Secretary and Director of Finance, J. Card
Acting Director of Collections, Miss S. Collier
Director, Cabinet War Rooms, P. Reed
Director of Corporate Services, A. Stoneman
Director of Development, Ms V. Cornwall
Director of HMS Belfast, B. King
Director, Imperial War Museum, Duxford, E. Inman, OBE
Director, Imperial War Museum, North, J. Forrester
Director of Public Services, Miss A. Godwin

MUSEUM OF LONDON

London Wall, London EC2Y 5HN
Tel: 0870-444 3852 Fax: 0870-444 3853
Email: info@museumoflondon.org.uk
Web: www.museumoflondon.org.uk

The Museum of London illustrates the history of London from prehistoric times to the present day. It opened in 1976 and is based on the amalgamation of the former Guildhall Museum and London Museum. The Museum is controlled by a Board of Governors, appointed (nine each) by the Government and the Corporation of London. The Museum is currently funded by a grant of £6.293 million from the Department for Culture, Media and Sport and a grant of £4.519 million from the Corporation of London for 2002–3.
Chairman of Board of Governors, R. Hambro
Director, Prof. J. Lohman

NATIONAL ARMY MUSEUM

Royal Hospital Road, London SW3 4HT
Tel: 020-7730 0717 Fax: 020-7823 6573
Email: info@national-army-museum.ac.uk
Web: www.national-army-museum.ac.uk

The National Army Museum covers the history of five centuries of the British Army. It was established by royal charter in 1960.
Assistant Directors, D. K. Smurthwaite; Dr A. J. Guy;
P. B. Boyden

NATURAL HISTORY MUSEUM
Cromwell Road, London SW7 5BD
Tel: 020-7942 5000

The Natural History Museum originates from the natural history departments of the British Museum, which grew extensively during the 19th century; in 1860 the natural history collection was moved from Bloomsbury to a new location. Part of the site of the 1862 International Exhibition in South Kensington was acquired for the new museum, and the Museum opened to the public in 1881. In 1963 the Natural History Museum became completely independent with its own board of trustees. The Walter Rothschild Zoological Museum, Tring, bequeathed by the second Lord Rothschild, has formed part of the Museum since 1938. The Geological Museum merged with the Natural History Museum in 1985. Total Government grant-in-aid for 2003–4 is £39.6 million.

BOARD OF TRUSTEES
Appointed by the Prime Minister, Prof. Sir Keith O'Nions, FRS *(Chairman);* Dame Anne McLaren, DBE, FRS, FRCOG; Sir Richard Sykes, FRS; Miss J. Mayhew, DBE; Prof. M. Hassell, CBE, FRS; O. Stocken; Prof. J. McGlade; Prof. Dianne Edward, CBE, FRS
Appointed by the Secretary of State for Culture, Media and Sport, Prof. C. Leaver, CBE, FRS
Appointed by the Trustees of the Natural History Museum, The Lord Palumbo; Prof. Sir K. O'Nions, FRS; Prof. Linda Partridge, FRS, FRSE

SENIOR STAFF
Director, Dr N. R. Chalmers
Director of Communications and Development, Ms S. Ament
Director of Estates, K. Rellis
Director of Finance, N. Greenwood
Director of Human Resources, D. Hill
Director of Science, R. Lane
Director, Tring Zoological Museum, Mrs T. Wild
Head of Audit and Review, D. Thorpe
Head of Library and Information Services, G. Higley
Head of Visitor and Operational Services, D. Candlin
Keeper of Mineralogy, Prof. A. Fleet
Keeper of Botany, Dr R. Bateman
Keeper of Entomology, Dr R. Vane-Wright
Keeper of Palaeontology, Dr N. MacLeod
Keeper of Zoology, Prof. P. Rainbow

NATIONAL MARITIME MUSEUM
Greenwich, London SE10 9NF
Tel: 020-8858 4422 Fax: 020-8312 6632

Established by Act of Parliament in 1934, the National Maritime Museum illustrates the maritime history of Great Britain in the widest sense, underlining the importance of the sea and its influence on the nation's power, wealth, culture, technology and institutions. The Museum is in three groups of buildings in Greenwich Park, the main building, the Queen's House (built by Inigo Jones, 1616–35) and the Royal Observatory (including Wren's Flamsteed House). In May 1999, a £20 million Heritage Lottery supported project opened 16 new galleries in a glazed courtyard in the Museum's west wing. Total Government grant-in-aid for 2002–3 was £13.681 million.
Director, R. Clare

NATIONAL MUSEUMS LIVERPOOL
PO Box 33, 127 Dale Street, Liverpool L69 3LA
Tel: 0151-207 0001 Fax: 0151-478 4790

The Board of Trustees of the National Museums Liverpool (formerly National Museums and Galleries on Merseyside) is responsible for the Liverpool Museum, the Merseyside Maritime Museum (incorporating HM Customs and Excise National Museum), the Museum of Liverpool Life, the Lady Lever Art Gallery, the Walker, Sudley House and the Conservation Centre. Total Government grant-in-aid is currently £13 million per year.
Chairman of the Board of Trustees, D. McDonnell
Director, Dr David Fleming
Keeper of Art Galleries, J. Treuherz
Keeper of Conservation, A. Durham
Keeper, Liverpool Museum, J. Millard
Keeper, Merseyside Maritime Museum and Museum of Liverpool Life, M. Stammers

NATIONAL MUSEUMS AND GALLERIES OF WALES/AMGUEDDFEYDD AC ORIELAU CENEDLAETHOL CYMRU
Cathays Park, Cardiff CF10 3NP
Tel: 029-2039 7951 Fax: 029-2037 3219
Email: post@nmgw.ac.uk Web: www.nmgw.ac.uk

The National Museums and Galleries of Wales comprise the National Museum and Gallery Cardiff, the Museum of Welsh Life, St Fagans, Big Pit National Museum of Wales, Blaenafon, the Roman Legionary Museum Caerleon, Turner House Gallery Penarth, the Welsh Slate Museum Llanberis, the Segontium Roman Museum Caernarfon and the Museum of the Welsh Woollen Industry Dre-fach, Felindre. Total funding from the Welsh Assembly Government for 2003–4 is £20.536 million.
President, Paul E. Loveluck, CBE
Vice-President, Dr Susan J. Davies
Treasurer, Gwyn Howells, ACIB

OFFICERS
Director-General, Michael Houlihan
Directors, Dr E. Wiliam *(Collections and Education and Deputy Director);* J. Williams-Davies *(Museum of Welsh Life);* M. Tooby *(National Museum and Gallery);* R. Gwyn *(Strategic Communications);* M. Richards *(Resource Planning);* J. Sheppard *(Finance and IT)*
Keeper of Archaeology, R. Brewer
Keeper of Art, O. Fairclough
Keeper of Bio-diversity and Systematic Biology, Dr P. G. Oliver
Keeper of Geology, Dr M. G. Bassett
Keeper, Welsh Slate Museum and Segontium Roman Museum, Dr D. Roberts
Manager, Big Pit National Museum of Wales, P. Walker
Manager, National Woollen Museum, S. Moss
Manager, Roman Legionary Museum, B. Lewis

NATIONAL MUSEUMS OF SCOTLAND
Chambers Street, Edinburgh EH1 1JF
Tel: 0131-225 7534 Fax: 0131-220 4819
Email: feedback@nms.ac.uk Web: www.nms.ac.uk

The National Museums of Scotland comprise the Royal Museum of Scotland, the National War Museum of Scotland, the Museum of Scottish Country Life, the

Museum of Flight, Shambellie House Museum of Costume and the Museum of Scotland. Total funding from the Scottish Executive for 2002–3 was £17.3 million.

BOARD OF TRUSTEES
Chairman, The Lord Wilson of Tillyorn, KT, GCMG, Ph.D., FRSE
Members, G. S. Johnston, OBE, TD, KCSG, DL, CA; Ms C. Macaulay; Sir Neil McIntosh, CBE, DL; Mrs N. Mahal, DCG; Prof. A. Manning, OBE, Dphil., FRSE, FIbiol.; Prof. J. Murray, CEng; I. Ritchie, CBE, FReng, FRSE; A. J. C. Smith, FCIA; J. A. G. Fiddes, OBE; Prof. M. Lynch, Ph.D., FRSE, FSA (Scot); Miss A. MacLean

OFFICERS
Director, Dr G. Rintoul, Ph.D.
Director of Collections, Jane Carmichael
Director of Facilities Management and Projects, S. Elson, FSA (Scot)
Director of Finance and Resources, A. Patience
Director of Marketing and Development, C. McCallum
Director of Public Programmes, Mary Bryden, FRSA
Head of Corporate Policy and Performance, Sheila McClure
Managing Director, P. Williamson

RESOURCE: THE COUNCIL FOR MUSEUMS, ARCHIVES AND LIBRARIES
16 Queen Anne's Gate, London SW1H 9AA
Tel: 020-7273 1444 Fax: 020-7273 1404
Web: www.resource.gov.uk

Resource: The Council for Museums, Archives and Libraries provides strategic guidance, advice and advocacy across the whole of Government on museum, archive and library matters. It is a non-departmental public body sponsored by the Department for Culture, Media and Sport. Resource came into being in April 2000, replacing the Museums and Galleries Commission (MGC) and the Library and Information Commission (LIC), and now includes archives within its portfolio.
Chairman, Mark Wood
Chief Executive (acting), C. Batt, OBE
Board Members, L. Grossman; V. Gray; A. Chowdhury; Dr M. Crozier; M. Jones; N. MacGregor; J. Ryder; M. Stevenson; A. Watkin; D. Barrie; Ms L. Brindley; B. MacNaught; B. McKee

ROYAL AIR FORCE MUSEUM
Grahame Park Way, London NW9 5LL
Tel: 020-8205 2266 Fax: 020-8200 1751

Situated on the former airfield at RAF Hendon, the Museum illustrates the development of aviation from before the Wright brothers to the present-day RAF. Total Government grant-in-aid for 2002–3, including funding for the outstation at Cosford, is £6.057 million.
Director-General, Dr M. A. Fopp
Directors, H. Hall; A. Wright; S. Garman; K. Ifould
Senior Keeper, P. Elliott

THE SCIENCE MUSEUM
Exhibition Road, London SW7 2DD
Tel: 0870 870 4868 Fax: 020-7942 4447

The Science Museum, part of the National Museum of Science and Industry, houses the national collections of science, technology, industry and medicine. The Museum began as the science collection of the South Kensington Museum and first opened in 1857. In 1883 it acquired the collections of the Patent Museum and in 1909 the science collections were transferred to the new Science Museum, leaving the art collections with the Victoria and Albert Museum. The Wellcome Wing was opened in July 2000.

Some of the Museum's commercial aircraft, agricultural machinery, and road and rail transport collections are at Wroughton, Wilts. The National Museum of Science and Industry also incorporates the National Railway Museum, York and the National Museum of Photography, Film and Television, Bradford.

Total Government grant-in-aid for 2003–4 is £31.248 million.

BOARD OF TRUSTEES
Chairman, The Rt. Hon. Lord Waldegrave of North Hill
Members, Prof. Sir Ron U. Cooke, DSC; Prof. A. Dowling, CBE, FReng; G. Dyke; Dr A. Grocock; Dr D. Gurr; R. Haythornthwaite; The Lord Puttnam, CBE; D. E. Rayner, CBE; Prof. Sir Martin Rees; S. Singh, MBE; M. G. Smith; Prof. R. A. Smith, Ph.D., FReng; Sir William Wells

OFFICERS
Director, Dr. L. Sharp
Head of Commercial Development, M. Sullivan
Interim Head of Change Management, A. Mather
Head of Design, T. Molloy
Head of Estates, J. Bevin
Head of Finance, Ms A. Caine
Head of IT, M. Burns
Head of National Museum of Photography, Film and Television, Ms A. Nevill
Head of National Railway Museum, A. Scott
Head of Physical Sciences and Engineering Group (acting), Dr A. Q. Morton
Head of Science Museum, J. Tucker

VICTORIA AND ALBERT MUSEUM
Cromwell Road, London SW7 2RL
Tel: 020-7942 2000 Web: www.vam.ac.uk

The Victoria and Albert Museum is the national museum of fine and applied art and design. It descends directly from the Museum of Manufactures, which opened in Marlborough House in 1852 after the Great Exhibition of 1851. The Museum was moved in 1857 to become part of the South Kensington Museum. It was renamed the Victoria and Albert Museum in 1899. It also houses the National Art Library and Print Room.

The Museum administers three branch museums: the Museum of Childhood at Bethnal Green, the Theatre Museum in Covent Garden, and the Wellington Museum at Apsley House. The museum in Bethnal Green was opened in 1872 and the building is the most important surviving example of the type of glass and iron construction used by Paxton for the Great Exhibition. Total Government grant-in-aid for 2003–4 is £34.839 million.

BOARD OF TRUSTEES
Chairman, Paula Ridley
Deputy Chairman, vacant
Members, Prof. M. Buck; Viscountess Cobham; R. Dickins; Prof. Sir Christopher Frayling, Ph.D.;

Sir Terence Heiser, GCB; Mrs J. Gordon Clark;
R. Mather; P. Rogers; P. Ruddock; Dame Marjorie
Scardino, DBE; Prof. Sir Christopher White, CVO, FBA
Secretary to the Board of Trustees, J. F. Rider

OFFICERS
Director, M. Jones
Director of Apsley House, the Wellington Museum,
Ms A. Robinson
Director of Collections and Keeper of Asian Department,
Dr D. Swallow
Director of Collections Services, N. Umney
Director of Development, J. McCaffrey
Director of Finance and Resources, I. Blatchford
Director of Learning and Interpretation, D. Anderson, OBE
Director of the Museum of Childhood, Ms D. Lees
Director of Personnel, Mrs G. Henchley
Director of Projects and Estate, Mrs G. F. Miles
Director of Public Affairs, D. Whitmore
Director of the Theatre Museum, G. Marsh
Managing Director of V&A Enterprises Ltd, M. Cass
Head of Conservation, Ms S. Smith
Head of Exhibitions, Mrs L. Lloyd Jones
Head of Photography and Picture Library, J. Stevenson
Head of Records and Collections Services, A. Seal
Head of Regional Liaison and Purchase Grant Fund,
Miss J. Davies
Head of Research Department, Ms C. Sargentson
Keeper of Furniture, Textiles and Fashion Department, C. Wilk
*Keeper of Sculpture, Metalwork, Ceramics and Glass
Department,* Dr P. E. D. Williamson
Keeper of Word and Image Department, Ms S. B. Lambert

NATIONAL AUDIT OFFICE
157–197 Buckingham Palace Road, London SW1W 9SP
Tel: 020-7798 7000 Fax: 020-7798 7070
3–4 Park Place, Cardiff CF10 3DP
Tel: 029-2067 8500 Fax: 029-2067 8501
Email: enquiries@nao.gsi.gov.uk
Web: www.nao.gov.uk

The National Audit Office came into existence under the National Audit Act 1983 to replace and continue the work of the former Exchequer and Audit Department. The Act reinforced the Office's total financial and operational independence from the Government and brought its head, the Comptroller and Auditor-General, into a closer relationship with Parliament as an officer of the House of Commons.
The National Audit Office provides independent information, advice and assurance to Parliament and the public about all aspects of the financial operations of Government departments and many other bodies receiving public funds. It does this by examining and certifying the accounts of these organisations and by regularly publishing reports to Parliament on the results of its value for money investigations of the economy, efficiency and effectiveness with which public resources have been used. The National Audit Office is also the auditor by agreement of the accounts of certain international and other organisations. In addition, the Office authorises the issue of public funds to Government departments.
Comptroller and Auditor-General, Sir John Bourn, KCB
Private Secretary, N. Sayers
Deputy Comptroller and Auditor-General, T. Burr

Assistant Auditors-General, J. Colman; Miss C. Mawhood;
M. Sinclair; Ms W. Kenway-Smith; M. Whitehouse;
J. Rickleton

NATIONAL CONSUMER COUNCIL
20 Grosvenor Gardens, London SW1W 0DH
Tel: 020-7730 3469 Fax: 020-7730 0191
Email: info@ncc.org.uk Web: www.ncc.org.uk

The National Consumer Council (NCC) was set up by the Government in 1975 to give an independent voice to consumers in the UK. Its role is to advocate the consumer interest to decision-makers in national and local government, industry and regulatory bodies, business and the professions. It does this through a combination of research and campaigning. NCC is a non-profit making company limited by guarantee and is largely funded by grant-in-aid from the Department of Trade and Industry. The Council is not a consumer advice or complaints body.
Chair, Mrs D. Hutton, CBE
Chief Executive, Ed Mayo

NESTA – NATIONAL ENDOWMENT FOR SCIENCE, TECHNOLOGY AND THE ARTS
Fishmongers' Chambers, 110 Upper Thames Street,
London EC4R 3TW
Tel: 020-7645 9500 Fax: 020-7645 9501
Web: www.nesta.org.uk

The National Endowment for Science, Technology and the Arts (NESTA) was established under the National Lottery Act 1998 with a £200 million endowment from the proceeds of the National Lottery. It runs four funding programmes: *Invention and Innovation* takes original ideas with commercial or social potential and helps them get to market; *Fellowship* supports exceptionally talented and innovative people, and enables them to pursue a tailor-made programme of personal creative development; *Learning* researches and pioneers initiatives, which will drive education and encourage public engagement with science, technology and the arts; and the *Graduate Pioneer Programme* supports recent graduates from the creative industries.
Chairman, The Lord Puttnam of Queensgate, CBE
Chief Executive, J. Newton

NATIONAL HERITAGE MEMORIAL FUND
7 Holbein Place, London SW1W 8NR
Tel: 020-7591 6000 Fax: 020-7591 6001
Web: www.hlf.org.uk

The National Heritage Memorial Fund was set up under the National Heritage Act 1980 in memory of people who have given their lives for the United Kingdom. The Fund provides grants (and sometimes loans) to organisations based in the United Kingdom, mainly so they can buy items of outstanding interest and of importance to the national heritage. These must either be at risk or have a memorial character. The Fund is administered by 14 trustees who are appointed by the Prime Minister.
The National Lottery Act 1993 designated the Fund as distributor of the heritage share of proceeds from the National Lottery. As a result, the Fund now operates two funds: the Heritage Memorial Fund and the Heritage

Lottery Fund. The Heritage Memorial Fund receives an annual grant from the Department for Culture, Media and Sport.
Chair, L. Forgan
Trustees, Prof. C. Baines; N. Dodd; Sir Angus Grossart, CBE; G. Waterfield; Ms P. Wilson; Ms S. Palmer; Earl of Dalkeith; Prof. T. Pritchard; J. Wright, CBE; Dr M. Phillips; Dr D. Langslow; Madhu Anjali; Catherine Graham-Harrison
Director, Ms C. Souter

NATIONAL LOTTERY COMMISSION

101 Wigmore Street, London W1U 1QU
Tel: 020-7016 3400 Fax: 020-7016 3401
Web: www.natlotcomm.gov.uk

The National Lottery Commission replaced the Office of the National Lottery (OFLOT) in April 1999 under the National Lottery Act 1998. The Commission is responsible for the granting, varying and enforcing of licences to run the National Lottery. Its duties are to ensure that the National Lottery is run with all due propriety, that the interests of players are protected, and, subject to these two objectives, that returns to the 'good causes' are maximised.

Gaming and lotteries in the UK are officially regulated and may only be run by licensed operators or in licensed premises.

The Department of Culture, Media and Sport is responsible for gaming and lottery policy and laws. The National Lottery is the most heavily regulated part of the gaming market. Empowered by the National Lottery Act 1993, the Department of Culture, Media and Sport directs the National Lottery Commission, who in turn regulate Camelot, the lottery operator. Camelot, a private company wholly owned by five shareholders, were granted the second seven-year licence to run the Lottery, which began on 27 January 2002. The main National Lottery draw was relaunched as Lotto in spring 2002. Total sales of Lottery products in 2002–3 were almost £4,600 million; this represented a fall of 5.4 per cent compared to the previous year. Lotto sales dropped by 12.1 per cent, making up just under 74 per cent of total sales revenue. A total of £3,387 million was spent on Lotto tickets alone during 2002–3, and £2,238 million was paid out in prizes.
Chairman, Brian Pomeroy
Commissioners, Ms H. Spicer; T. Hornsby; Ms M. Black; Ms J. Valentine
Chief Executive, M. Harris
Director of Compliance, Ms M. Phillips
Director of Licensing, K. Jones
Director of Performance and Communications, Ms C. Forrester
Director of Resources, Ms C. McCullough

NATIONAL PHYSICAL LABORATORY

Queens Road, Teddington, Middx TW11 0LW
Tel: 020-8977 3222 Fax: 020-8943 6458

The Laboratory is the UK's national standards laboratory. It develops, maintains and disseminates national measurement standards for physical quantities such as mass, length, time, temperature, voltage, force and pressure. It also conducts underpinning research on engineering materials and information technology and disseminates good measurement practice. It is Government-owned but contractor-operated.
Managing Director, Dr B. McGuiness
Director of Marketing and Strategic Planning,
D. C. Richardson

NATIONAL RADIOLOGICAL PROTECTION BOARD

Chilton, Didcot, Oxon OX11 0RQ
Tel: 01235-831600 Fax: 01235-833891
Email: nrpb@nrpb.org
Web: www.nrpb.org

The National Radiological Protection Board is an independent statutory body created by the Radiological Protection Act 1970. It is the national point of authoritative reference on radiological protection for both ionising and non-ionising radiations, and has issued recommendations on limiting human exposure to electromagnetic fields and radiation from a range of sources, including X-rays, the Sun, base stations and mobile phones. Its sponsoring department is the Department of Health.
Chairman, Sir William Stewart, FRS, FRSE
Director, Prof. R. Cox

NATIONAL SAVINGS AND INVESTMENTS

375 Kensington High Street, London W14 8SD
Tel: 020-7348 9200 Fax: 020-7048 9698
Web: www.nsandi.com

National Savings and Investments was established as a Government department in 1969. It became an executive agency of the Treasury in 1996 and is responsible for the design, marketing and administration of savings and investment products for personal savers and investors. In April 1999 Siemens Business Services took over all the back office functions at National Savings and Investments.
Chief Executive, A. Cook
Finance Director, T. Bayley
Commercial Director, G. Cattanach
Partnerships and Operations Director, S. Owen

For details of schemes, *see* National Savings section

NEW OPPORTUNITIES FUND

1 Plough Place, London EC4A 1DE
Tel: 020-7211 1800 Fax: 020-7211 1750
Email: enquiries@nof.org.uk
Web: www.nof.org.uk

The New Opportunities Fund provides lottery funding for health, education and environment projects in order to help create lasting improvements to the quality of life, particularly in disadvantaged communities.

The Fund works with national, regional and local partners from the public, private and voluntary sectors to fund initiatives, with particular focus on the needs of those who are most disadvantaged in society.
Chair of the Board, The Baroness Pitkeathley
Members of the Board, Ms J. Barrow *(Member for England)*; Prof. E. Bolton, CB; Prof. A. Patmore, CBE; D. Mackie; D. Campbell, CBE *(Member for Scotland)*; Prof. S. Griffiths, OBE; Prof. B. Gadd, CBE *(Member for Northern Ireland)*; T. Davies *(Member for Wales)*; D. Carrington; Ms P. Hudson; Ms B. Stephens; G. Thompson, MBE
Chief Executive, S. Dunmore

NORTHERN IRELAND AUDIT OFFICE
106 University Street, Belfast BT7 1EU
Tel: 028-9025 1000 Fax: 028-9025 1106
Email: auditoffice@nics.gov.uk
Web: www.niauditoffice.gov.uk

The primary aim of the Northern Ireland Audit Office is to provide independent assurance, information and advice to the Northern Ireland Assembly on the proper accounting for Northern Ireland departmental and certain other public expenditure, revenue, assets and liabilities; on regularity and propriety; and on the economy, efficiency and effectiveness of the use of resources.
Comptroller and Auditor-General for Northern Ireland,
J. M. Dowdall

NORTHERN IRELAND AUTHORITY FOR ENERGY REGULATION
Brookmount Buildings, 42 Fountain Street, Belfast BT1 5EE
Tel: 028-9031 1575 Fax: 028-9031 1740
Email: ofreg@nics.gov.uk
Web: www.ofreg.nics.gov.uk

The Northern Ireland Authority for Energy Regulation operating as The Office for the Regulation of Electricity & Gas (Ofreg) is the regulatory body for the electricity and gas supply industries in Northern Ireland.
Chairman, Douglas McIldoon

NORTHERN IRELAND HUMAN RIGHTS COMMISSION
Temple Court, 39–41 North Street, Belfast BT1 1NA
Tel: 028-9024 3987 Fax: 028-9024 7844
Email: info@nihrc.org
Web: www.nihrc.org

The Northern Ireland Human Rights Commission was set up in March 1999. Its main functions are to keep under review the law and practice relating to human rights in Northern Ireland, to advise the Government and to promote an awareness of human rights in Northern Ireland. It can also take cases to court. The Commission currently consists of one full-time commissioner and ten part-time commissioners, all appointed by the Secretary of State for Northern Ireland.
Chief Commissioner (£66,000), Prof. B. Dickson
Commissioners (£10,000), Mrs M. A. Dinsmore, QC;
T. Donnelly, MBE; Lady Christine Eames;
Revd H. Good, OBE; Prof. T. Hadden; Ms P. Kelly;
Dr C. McGimpsey; K. McLaughlin; F. McGuinness;
P. Yu

OCCUPATIONAL PENSIONS REGULATORY AUTHORITY
Invicta House, Trafalgar Place, Brighton BN1 4DW
Tel: 01273-627600 Fax: 01273-627688
Email: helpdesk@opra.gov.uk
Web: www.opra.gov.uk

The Occupational Pensions Regulatory Authority (Opra) was set up under the Pensions Act 1995 and became fully operational on 6 April 1997. It is the UK regulator of pension arrangements offered by employers. It maintains a register of stakeholder pensions and regulates payments into stakeholder and personal pensions.
Chairman, H. Maunsell, OBE
Chief Executive, T. Hobman

OFFICE FOR NATIONAL STATISTICS
1 Drummond Gate, London SW1V 2QQ
Tel: 0845-601 3034
Email: info@statistics.gov.uk
Web: www.statistics.gov.uk

The Office for National Statistics was created in 1996 by the merger of the Central Statistical Office and the Office of Population Censuses and Surveys. It is both a Government department and an executive agency of the Treasury and is responsible for preparing, interpreting and publishing key economic statistics for the government and society of the UK. ONS also administers the marriage laws and local registration of births, marriages and deaths in England and Wales; provision of population estimates and projections and statistics on health and other demographic matters in England and Wales; population censuses in England and Wales; surveys for Government departments and public bodies; and promoting these functions within the UK, the European Union and internationally to provide a statistical service to meet European Union and international requirements.

The National Statistics initiative was launched in June 2000. Headed by the National Statistician, with an independent Statistics Commission, providing assurance to Parliament about the integrity of official statistics and statistical practice. The National Statistics brand encompasses the output of the ONS, plus many of the key public interest statistics produced by other Government departments.
National Statistician and Registrar General for England and Wales, Len Cook
Executive Directors, Karen Dunnell *(Surveys and Administrative Sources);* Colin Mowl *(Macroeconomics and Labour Market);* Mike Pepper *(Sources Transformation);* John Pullinger *(Economic and Social Reporting);* Peter Walton *(Organisational Development and Resources);* vacant *(Methodology)*
Deputy Registrar General, Isobel Macdonald-Davies
Corporate Directors, Mike Hughes *(National Statistics and Planning);* Dayantna Joshua *(Information Management);* Peter Murphy *(Finance and Procurement);* Helena Rafalowska *(Communications);* Susan Young *(Human Resources)*
National Statistician's Private Office: Jackie Orme (PS); Timothy Stamp (APS); Brigid Keenan (PA)
Parliamentary Clerks, Robert Smith; Alex Elton-Wall

OFFICE FOR STANDARDS IN EDUCATION (OFSTED)
Alexandra House, 33 Kingsway, London WC2B 6SE
Tel: 020-7421 6800
Early Years Helpline: 0845-601 4771 Fax: 020-7421 6707
Email: geninfo@ofsted.gov.uk
Web: www.ofsted.gov.uk

OFSTED is a non-ministerial Government department established under the Education (Schools Act) 1992. Since April 2001 OFSTED has been responsible for inspecting all educational provision for 16–19 year olds to establish and monitor an independent inspection system for maintained schools in England. Its inspection role also includes the inspection of local education authorities, teacher training institutions and youth work. In September 2001, OFSTED took over the regulation of childcare providers, from 150 local authorities.
HM Chief Inspector, D. Bell
Directorate of Inspection, D. Taylor

Director of Corporate Services, R. Knight
Director of Early Years, M. Smith
Director of Finance, P. Jolly
Director of Strategy and Resources, R. Green

OFFICE OF COMMUNICATIONS (OFCOM)

Riverside House, 2A Southwark Bridge Road, London SE1 9HA
Tel: 020-7981 3000 Fax: 020-7981 3333
Email: wwwenq@ofcom.org.uk
Web: www.ofcom.org.uk

The Office of Communications (Ofcom) was established in 2003 under the Office of Communications Act 2002 to regulate the communications sector in the UK. The Office of Communications merges the functions of five regulatory bodies: the Independent Television Commission (ITC), The Broadcasting Standards Commission (BSC), the Office of Telecommunications (Oftel), the Radio Authority (RAu) and the Radiocommunications Agency (RA). The Office of Communications aims to further the interests of consumers in relevant markets, secure the optimal use of the radio spectrum, ensure the availability throughout the UK of television and radio services and to protect the public from any offensive or potentially harmful effects of broadcast media, as well as safeguarding people from being unfairly treated in television and radio programmes. Members of the Board are appointed by the Secretaries of State for Trade and Industry and for Culture, Media and Sport. Ofcom is scheduled to become fully operational by the end of 2003.
Chief Executive, S. Carter
Chairman, D. Currie
Deputy Chairman, R. Hooper
Members, Ms M. Banerjee; D. Edmonds; I.Hargreaves; Ms K. Meek; Ms S. Nathan; E. Richards
Director of Communications, M. Peacock

OFCOM replaces the following bodies:

BROADCASTING STANDARDS COMMISSION
7 The Sanctuary, London SW1P 3JS
Tel: 020-7808 1000 Fax: 020-7233 0397
Email: bsc@bsc.org.uk
INDEPENDENT TELEVISION COMMISSION
33 Foley Street, London W1W 7TL
Tel: 020-7255 3000 Fax: 020-7306 7800
Email: public.affairs@itc.org.uk
OFTEL
50 Ludgate Hill, London EC4M 7JJ
Tel: 020-7634 8700 Fax: 020-7634 8845
Email: infocent@oftel.gov.uk
RADIO AUTHORITY
Holbrook House, 14 Great Queen Street, Holborn, London WC2B 5DG
Tel: 020-7430 2724 Fax: 020-7405 7062
Email: p&l@radioauthority.org.uk
RADIOCOMMUNICATIONS AGENCY
Wyndham House, 189 Marsh Wall, London E14 9SX
Tel: 020-7211 0211 Fax: 020-7211 0507
Email: library@ra.gsi.gov.uk

OFFICE OF FAIR TRADING

Fleetbank House, 2–6 Salisbury Square, London EC4Y 8JX
Tel: 020-7211 8000 Fax: 020-7211 8800
Email: enquiries@oft.gov.uk
Web: www.oft.gov.uk

The Office of Fair Trading is a non-ministerial Government department headed by a corporate board. It pursues its primary goal of making markets work better for consumers through enforcement of competition and consumer legislation, market studies and communication.

The Consumer Regulation Enforcement Division pursues the Office's consumer protection duties through the Enterprise Act 2002 (which replaced part III of the Fair Trading Act and the Stop Now Orders Regulations in June 2003), the Consumer Credit Act 1974, the Estate Agents Act 1979, the Control of Misleading Advertisements Regulations 1988, the Consumer Protection (Distance Selling) Regulations 2000 and the Unfair Contract Terms in Consumer Contracts Regulations 1999.

The Competition Enforcement Division is responsible for enforcing the Competition Act 1998, as amended by the Enterprise Act 2002, and for reviewing mergers under the UK and EC merger control regimes. It also has responsibility for competition matters arising under other legislation, including the Financial Services Act 1986 and the Broadcasting Act 1990.

The Markets and Policy Initiatives Division conduct market studies, which are made public, helping the Office assess what action, if any, needs to be taken to make markets work better. It negotiates and reviews undertakings following Competition Commission reports. The Division also identifies and assesses the impact of government regulations on competition and co-ordinates the Office's overall relationships with government departments and other bodies involved with consumer and competition issues.

Communications Division's work entails empowering consumers through campaigns, advice and education. It also informs businesses of their rights and duties under competition and consumer laws giving an opportunity for law-abiding businesses to complain about anti-competitive behaviours of others.

The Office of Fair Trading is a UK competent authority in relation to the application of the European Community competition rules and also liaises with the European Commission on consumer protection initiatives.
Chairman, John Vickers
Executive Director, Penny Boys
Non-Executive Directors, Allan Asher, Lord Blackwell, Christine Farnish, Richard Whish, Rosalind Wright

CONSUMER REGULATION ENFORCEMENT DIVISION
Divisional Director (G3), Christine Wade
Branch Directors (G5), Steven Wood, Ray Hall

COMPETITION ENFORCEMENT DIVISION
Divisional Director (G3), Vincent Smith
Branch Directors (G5), Neil Feinson, Chris Mayock, Simon Priddis, Beckett McGrath, Justin Coombs, Alan Williams, Christiane Kent

LEGAL DIVISION
Divisional Director (G3), Miss Pat Edwards
Branch Directors (G5), Frances Barr, Simon Brindley, Louis Christofides, Jessica Farry, Paul Gurowich

MARKETS AND POLICIES INITIATIVES DIVISION
Divisional Director (G3), Jonathan May
Branch Directors (G5), Amelia Fletcher, Daniel Gordon, Chris Rawlins, Graham Winton

COMMUNICATIONS DIVISION
Director of Communications (G5), Mike Ricketts

RESOURCES AND SERVICES
Director of Resources and Services (G5), David Fisher

OFFICE OF GAS AND ELECTRICITY MARKETS (OFGEM)
9 Millbank, London SW1P 3GE
Tel: 020-7901 7000 Fax: 020-7901 7066
Scotland: Regents Court, 70 West Regent Street, Glasgow G2 2QZ
Tel: 0141-331 2678 Fax: 0141-331 2777
Web: www.ofgem.gov.uk

The Office of Gas and Electricity Markets (Ofgem) regulates the gas and electricity industries in England, Scotland and Wales. It was formed in 1999 through the merger of the Office of Gas Supply and the Office of Electricity Regulation.

Ofgem's overriding aim is to promote and protect the interests of gas and electricity customers by promoting competition and regulating monopolies. Ofgem is governed by an authority and its powers are provided for under the Gas Act 1986, the Electricity Act 1989 and the Utilities Act 2000.
Chief Executive, A. Buchanan
Managing Directors, J. Neilson *(Customers and Supply);* Dr B. Moselle *(Competition and Trading Arrangements);* D. Gray *(Regulation and Financial Affairs)*
Chief Operating Officer, R. Field

OFFICE OF MANPOWER ECONOMICS
Oxford House, 8th Floor, 76 Oxford Street, London W1D 1BS
Tel: 020-7467 7244 Fax: 020-7467 7248
Web: www.ome.uk.com

The Office of Manpower Economics was set up in 1971. It is an independent non-statutory organisation which is responsible for servicing independent review bodies which advise on the pay of various public service groups, the Pharmacists Review Panel and the Police Negotiating and Advisory Boards. The Office is also responsible for servicing ad hoc bodies of inquiry and for undertaking research into pay and associated matters as requested by the Government.
OME Director, Dr R. A. Wright
Director, Health Secretariats and OME Deputy Director, vacant
Director, Armed Forces' Secretariat, Mrs C. Haworth
Director, Senior Salaries and Police Negotiating and Advisory Boards Secretariat, S. Palmer
Director, School Teachers' Secretariat, Mrs E. M. Melling
Director, Prison Service Secretariat, M. C. Cahill
Press Liaison Officer, C. P. Jordan

OFFICE OF THE LEGAL SERVICES OMBUDSMAN
3rd Floor, Sunlight House, Quay Street, Manchester M3 3JZ
Tel: 0845-601 0794 Fax: 0161-832 5446
Email: lso@olso.gsi.gov.uk
Web: www.olso.org

The Legal Services Ombudsman is appointed by the Lord Chancellor under the Courts and Legal Services Act 1990 to oversee the handling of complaints against solicitors, barristers, licensed conveyancers, legal executives and patent agents by their professional bodies. A complainant must first complain to the relevant professional body before raising the matter with the Ombudsman. The Ombudsman is independent of the legal profession and her services are free of charge.
Legal Services Ombudsman, Ms Zahida Manzoor, CBE
Operations Director, S. D. Entwistle

OFFICE OF THE LEGAL SERVICES OMBUDSMAN (SCOTTISH)
17 Waterloo Place, Edinburgh, EH1 3DL
Tel: 0131-556 9123 Fax: 0131-556 9292
Email: ombudsman@slso.org.uk
Web: www.slso.org.uk

The Ombudsman investigates complaints about the way in which Scottish professional bodies have handled a complaint against a practitioner.

The Ombudsman also examines complaints about the unwillingness of a professional body to investigate a complaint against a practitioner.
Scottish Legal Services Ombudsman, Mrs L. Costelloe Baker

OFFICE OF THE LORD ADVOCATE
Crown Office, 25 Chambers Street, Edinburgh EH1 1LA
Tel: 0131-226 2626 Fax: 0131-226 6920

The Law Officers for Scotland are the Lord Advocate and the Solicitor-General for Scotland.
Lord Advocate, The Rt. Hon. Colin Boyd, QC
Solicitor-General for Scotland, Ms E. Angiolini, QC
Private Secretary to the Lord Advocate, Ms K. Davidson
Private Secretary to the Solicitor General, R. Kent

OFFICE OF THE PENSIONS OMBUDSMAN
6th Floor, 11 Belgrave Road, London SW1V 1RB
Tel: 020-7834 9144 Fax: 020-7821 0065
Email: enquiries@pensions-ombudsman.org.uk
Web: www.pensions-ombudsman.org.uk

The Pensions Ombudsman is appointed under the Pension Schemes Act 1993 as amended by the Pensions Act 1995. He independently investigates and decides complaints and disputes concerning pension schemes.
Pensions Ombudsman, D. Laverick

OFFICE OF THE RAIL REGULATOR
1 Waterhouse Square, 138–142 Holborn, London EC1N 2TQ
Tel: 020-7282 2000 Fax: 020-7282 2047
Web: www.rail-reg.gov.uk

The Office of the Rail Regulator was set up under the Railways Act 1993. It is headed by the Rail Regulator, who is independent of ministerial control. The Regulator's principal function is to regulate Network Rail's stewardship of the national network and to provide the economic regulation of the monopoly and dominant elements of the rail industry. The Regulator also licenses operators of railway assets, approves agreements for access by those operators to track, stations and light maintenance depots, and enforces domestic competition law. The International Rail Regulator is a statutory office separate from that of the Rail Regulator. The International Rail Regulator licenses the operation of certain international rail services in the European Economic Area, and access to railway infrastructure in Great Britain for the purpose of the operation of such services. The Office of The International Rail Regulator is co-located with the Office of the Rail Regulator, who fulfils both functions.

Rail Regulator, T. Winsor
Director of Corporate Affairs, K. Webb
Director of Rail Market, Access and Performance,
  S. Gooding
Chief Economist and Director of Infrastructure and Economic Regulation, T. Martin
Chief Legal Adviser and Director of Legal Services,
  Ms G. Richmond

OFFICE OF WATER SERVICES

Centre City Tower, 7 Hill Street, Birmingham B5 4UA
Tel: 0121-625 1300 Fax: 0121-625 1400
Email: enquiries@ofwat.gsi.gov.uk
Web: www.ofwat.gov.uk

The Office of Water Services (Ofwat) was set up under the Water Act 1989 and is a non-ministerial Government department headed by the Director-General of Water Services. It is the independent economic regulator of the water and sewerage companies in England and Wales. Ofwat's main duties are to ensure that the companies can finance and carry out the functions specified in the Water Industry Act 1991 and to protect the interests of water customers. There are ten WaterVoice committees which are concerned solely with the interests of water customers. Representation of customer interests at national and European level is the responsibility of the WaterVoice Council.

Director-General of Water Services, P. Fletcher
Chairman, WaterVoice Council, M. Terry

ORDNANCE SURVEY

Romsey Road, Maybush, Southampton SO16 4GU
Tel: 023-8030 5030 Fax: 023-8079 2615
Email: customerservices@ordsvy.gov.uk

Ordnance Survey is the national mapping agency for Great Britain. It is a Government department and executive agency operating as a Trading Fund and reporting to the Office of the Deputy Prime Minister.

Director-General and Chief Executive, Ms V. Lawrence

PARADES COMMISSION

12th Floor, Windsor House, 6–12 Bedford Street,
Belfast BT2 7EL
Tel: 028-9054 8900 Fax: 028-9032 2988
Email: info@paradescommission.com
Web: www.paradescommission.org

The Parades Commission was set up under the Public Processions (Northern Ireland) Act 1998. Its function is to encourage and facilitate local accommodation on contentious parades; where this is not possible, the Commission is empowered to make legal determinations

about such parades, which may include imposing conditions on aspects of the notified parade.

The chairman and members are appointed by the Secretary of State for Northern Ireland; the membership must, as far as is practicable, be representative of the community in Northern Ireland.

Chairman, A. J. Holland
Members, J. Cousins; Revd R. Magee; W. Martin;
  P. Osborne; Sir John Pringle; P. Quinn
Secretary (G5), A. Elliott

PARLIAMENTARY AND HEALTH SERVICE OMBUDSMAN

Millbank Tower, Millbank, London SW1P 4QP
Tel: 0845-015 4033 Fax: 020-7217 4000
Email: opca.enquiries@ombudsman.gsi.gov.uk
Web: www.ombudsman.org.uk
Health Service Ombudsman
Tel: 0845-015 4033 Fax: 020-7217 4000
Email: ohsc.enquiries@ombudsman.gsi.gov.uk

The Parliamentary Ombudsman (also known as the Parliamentary Commissioner for Administration) is independent of Government and is an officer of Parliament. She is responsible for investigating complaints referred to her by MPs from members of the public who claim to have sustained injustice in consequence of maladministration by or on behalf of Government departments and certain non-departmental public bodies. In March 1999 an additional 158 public bodies were brought within the jurisdiction of the Parliamentary Ombudsman. Certain types of action by Government departments or bodies are excluded from investigation. The Parliamentary Ombudsman is also responsible for investigating complaints, referred by MPs, alleging that access to official information has been wrongly refused under the Code of Practice on Access to Government Information 1994.

The Health Service Ombudsman (also known as the Health Service Commissioner) for England and for Wales is responsible for investigating complaints against National Health Service authorities and trusts that are not dealt with by those authorities to the satisfaction of the complainant. Complaints can be referred direct by the member of the public who claims to have sustained injustice or hardship in consequence of the failure in a service provided by a relevant body, failure of that body to provide a service or in consequence of any other action by that body. The Ombudsman's jurisdiction now covers complaints about family doctors, dentists, pharmacists and opticians, and complaints about actions resulting from clinical judgement.

The Health Service Ombudsman is also responsible for investigating complaints that information has been wrongly refused under the Code of Practice on Openness in the National Health Service 1995. The two offices are presently held by the Parliamentary Ombudsman.

Parliamentary Ombudsman and Health Service Ombudsman (G1), Ms A. Abraham
Deputy Parliamentary Commissioner (G3), A. Watson
Directors, Parliamentary Commissioner (G5),
  Ms C. Corrigan; N. Jordan
Directors, Health Service Commissioners (G5), D. R. G. Pinchin; L. Charlton
Finance and Establishment Officer (G5), J. Stevens

PARLIAMENTARY COMMISSIONER FOR STANDARDS

House of Commons, London SW1A 0AA
Tel: 020-7219 0320 Fax: 020-7219 0490

Following recommendations of the Committee on Standards in Public Life, the House of Commons agreed to the appointment of an independent Parliamentary Commissioner for Standards with effect from November 1995. The Commissioner has responsibility for maintaining and monitoring the operation of the Register of Members' Interests; advising Members of Parliament and the Select Committee on Standards and Privileges; interpreting the rules on disclosure and advocacy, and on other questions of propriety. The Commissioner also receives and investigates complaints about the conduct of MPs.
Parliamentary Commissioner for Standards, Sir Philip Mawer

PARLIAMENTARY COUNSEL

36 Whitehall, London SW1A 2AY
Tel: 020-7210 6611 Fax: 020-7210 6632
Web: www.parliamentary-counsel.gov.uk

Parliamentary Counsel draft all Government bills (i.e. primary legislation) except those relating exclusively to Scotland. They also advise on all aspects of parliamentary procedure in connection with such bills and draft Government amendments to them as well as any motions (including financial resolutions) necessary to secure their introduction into, and passage through, Parliament.
First Parliamentary Counsel, E. G. Bowman, CB
Counsel (SCS), Sir E. G. Caldwell; D. W. Saunders, CB;
G. B. Sellers, CB; E. R. Sutherland, CB; P. F. A. Knowles, CB; S. C. Laws, CB; R. S. Parker, CB; Miss C. E. Johnston, CB; P. J. Davies, CB; J. M. Sellers; A. J. Hogarth; Mrs H. J. Caldwell; D. I. Greenberg; Mrs E. A. F. Gardiner; D. J. Cook

PAROLE BOARD FOR ENGLAND AND WALES

Abell House, John Islip Street, London SW1P 4LH
Tel: 020-7217 5314 Fax: 020-7217 5793
Email: info@paroleboard.gov.uk
Web: www.paroleboard.gov.uk

The duty of the Parole Board is to advise the Home Secretary with respect to matters referred to it by him which are connected with the early release or recall of prisoners. Its functions include giving directions concerning the release on licence of prisoners serving discretionary life sentences and of certain prisoners serving long-term determinate sentences.
Chairman, D. Hatch, CBE
Vice-Chairman, The Hon. Mr Justice Gage
Chief Executive, C. Glenn

PAROLE BOARD FOR SCOTLAND

Saughton House, Broomhouse Drive, Edinburgh EH11 3XD
Tel: 0131-244 8347 Fax: 0131-244 6974

The Board directs and advises the Scottish Minister on the release of prisoners on licence, and related matters.
Chairman, Dr J. J. McManus
Vice-Chairman, Mrs M. Casserly
Secretary, L. Brown

PATENT OFFICE

Concept House, Cardiff Road, Newport NP10 8QQ
Tel: 0845-950 0505 Fax: 01633-813600
Email: enquiries@patent.gov.uk
Web: www.patent.gov.uk

The Patent Office is an executive agency of the Department of Trade and Industry. The duties of the Patent Office are to administer the Patent Acts, the Registered Designs Act and the Trade Marks Act, and to deal with questions relating to the Copyright, Designs and Patents Act 1988. The Search and Advisory Service carries out commercial searches through patent information.
Comptroller-General and Chief Executive, Ms A. Brimelow (until end 2003)
Director, Copyright, A. Murphy
Director, Finance, K. Woodrow
Director, Intellectual Property Policy Directorate, G. Jenkins
Director, Patents, R. J. Marchant
Director, Trade Marks and Designs, P. Lawrence
Secretary and Director, IT and Corporate Services, Ms C. Fullerton

PENSIONS COMPENSATION BOARD

11 Belgrave Road, London SW1V 1RB
Tel: 020-7828 9794 Fax: 020-7931 7239

The Pensions Compensation Board was established under the Pensions Act 1995 and is funded by a levy paid by all eligible occupational pension schemes. Its function is to compensate occupational pension schemes for losses due to dishonesty where the employer is insolvent.
Chairman, Sir Bryan Carsberg
Secretary, M. Lydon

POLICE COMPLAINTS AUTHORITY

10 Great George Street, London SW1P 3AE
Tel: 020-7273 6450 Fax: 020-7273 6401
Email: info@pca.gov.uk
Web: www.pca.gov.uk

The Police Complaints Authority was established under the Police and Criminal Evidence Act 1984 to provide an independent system for dealing with complaints by members of the public against police officers in England and Wales. It is funded by the Home Office. The authority has powers to supervise the investigation of certain categories of serious complaints and examines all completed investigations to decide whether officers should face misconduct proceedings. It does not deal with police operational matters; these are usually dealt with by the Chief Constable of the relevant force. The authority will be replaced from April 2004 by the Independent Police Complaints Commission.
Chairman, Sir Alistair Graham
Deputy Chair, I. Bynoe
2nd Deputy Chair, Ms W. Towers
Members, Mrs A. Boustred; D. Gear; Miss M. Mian; D. Petch; S. Swindell; D. Hughes; D. Glass; L. Pilkington; A. Macdougall; S. Hawkins; M. Williams; E. Rassaby; N. Williams; A. Barker; J. Rodgers

POLICE OMBUDSMAN FOR NORTHERN IRELAND
New Cathedral Buildings, St Anne's Square, Belfast BT1 1PG
Tel: 028-9082 8600 Fax: 028-9082 8659
Email: info@policeombudsman.org
Web: www.policeombudsman.org

Founded in November 2000 under the Police (Northern Ireland) Act 1998, the function of the Police Ombudsman for Northern Ireland is to investigate complaints against the police in an impartial, efficient, effective and (as far as is possible) transparent way, to win the confidence of the public and the police. It must report on trends in complaints and react to incidents involving the police, where it is in the public interest, even if no individual complaint has been made.
Ombudsman, N. O'Loan

PORT OF LONDON AUTHORITY
Bakers' Hall, 7 Harp Lane, London EC3R 6LB
Tel: 020-7743 7900 Fax: 020-7743 7999
Web: www.portoflondon.co.uk

The Port of London Authority (PLA) is the port authority for the 93 miles of the tidal River Thames from the Estuary to Teddington. It provides navigational and pilotage services for ships using the Port of London, including the maintenance of shipping channels. The PLA is also actively engaged in the promotion of the Port of London. The Port of London is one of the UK's main three ports, handling over 50 million tonnes of cargo each year. The port comprises over 80 independently owned terminals and port facilities, which handle a very wide range of cargoes.
The PLA is a public trust constituted under the Port of London Act 1908 and subsequent legislation.
Chairman, S. P. Sherrard
Chief Executive, S. C. Cuthbert
Secretary, D. Cartlidge

POSTAL SERVICES COMMISSION
Hercules House, Hercules Road, London SE1 7DB
Tel: 020-7593 2100 Web: www.postcomm.gov.uk
The Postal Services Commission (Postcomm) is an independent regulator set up by the Postal Services Act 2000 to ensure that postal operators, including Royal Mail, meet the needs of their customers throughout the UK. Postcomm monitors the network of post offices in the UK and makes annual reports to the DTI.
Chairman, Graham Corbett

PRISONS AND PROBATION OMBUDSMAN FOR ENGLAND AND WALES
Ashley House, 2 Monck Street, London SW1P 2BQ
Tel: 020-7035 2876 Fax: 020-7035 2860
Email: mail@ppo.gsi.gov.uk
Web: www.ppo.gov.uk

The Ombudsman is appointed by the Home Secretary. He provides a free and independent adjudication service for prisoners and those under probation supervision who have been unable to resolve their grievances with the Prison and Probation Services.
Prisons Ombudsman, S. Shaw

For Scotland, *see* Scottish Prisons Complaints Commission

PRIVY COUNCIL OFFICE
2 Carlton Gardens, London SW1Y 5AA
Tel: 020-7210 1033 Fax: 020-7210 1071

The Office is responsible for the arrangements leading to the making of all royal proclamations and Orders in Council; for certain formalities connected with ministerial changes; for considering applications for the granting (or amendment) of royal charters; for scrutiny and approval of by-laws and statutes of chartered bodies; and for the appointment of high sheriffs and many Crown and Privy Council appointments to governing bodies.
President of the Council (and Leader of the House of Commons), The Rt. Hon. Peter Hain, MP
Principal Private Secretary, G. Jones *(Policy and Legislation)*
Private Secretaries, S. Hillcoat; vacant *(Parliamentary Affairs)*; J. Newman *(Policy)*
Parliamentary Secretary, Ben Bradshaw, MP
Private Secretary, Ms F. Slee
Clerk of the Council, A. Galloway
Deputy Clerk of the Council, G. Donald
Senior Clerk, Ms M. McCullagh
Registrar of the Judicial Committee, J. Watherston

PUBLIC GUARDIANSHIP OFFICE
Archway Tower, 2 Junction Road, London N19 5SZ
Tel: 020-7664 7000 Fax: 020-7664 7705
Email: custserv@guardianship.gov.uk
Web: www.guardianship.gov.uk

The Public Guardianship Office (PGO) is the administrative arm of the Court of Protection.
Established on the 1 April 2001, it has taken over the mental health functions previously undertaken by the Public Trust Office (PTO), which also provides services that promote the financial and social well being of people with mental incapacity.
Chief Executive (Accountant-General), D. Lye
Director of Business Strategy and Innovation, G. Dalton
Director of Client Services, D. Thompson
Director of Communications, L. Joy
Acting Director of Finance, S. Taylor
Director of Human Resource, H. Daley
Director of Information Management, H. Street

RAIL SAFETY AND STANDARDS BOARD
Evergreen House, 160 Euston Road, London NW1 2DX
Tel: 020-7904 7518 Fax: 020-7557 9072
Email: enquiries@rssb.co.uk
Web: www.railwaysafety.org.uk

The Rail Safety and Standards Board was established on 1 April 2003 to help focus the rail industry on the continuous improvement in the safety performance of Britain's railways through facilitating the reduction in risk to passengers and railway workers. Its objectives include: the development of a long-term industry safety strategy; the effective representation of the UK rail industry in the development of EU legislation and standards that impact on the safe interworking of trains and infrastructure; and the facilitation of a research and development programme, education and awareness of safety issues. The Rail Safety and Standards Board is a not-for-profit organisation.

RECORD OFFICES

ADVISORY COUNCIL ON NATIONAL RECORDS AND ARCHIVES

Secretariat: Public Record Office, Kew, Surrey TW9 4DU
Tel: 020-8392 5381 Fax: 020-8392 5286

Following the bringing together of the Public Record Office and the Historical Manuscripts Commission to form the National Archives, the Advisory Council advises on all matters relating to the preservation, use of, and access to historical manuscripts, records and archives of all kinds. The Advisory Council on National Records and Archives encompasses the statutory Advisory Council on Public Records, and will advise on public records issues as before.
Chairman, The Rt. Hon. Lord Phillips
Secretary, T. R. Padfield

CORPORATION OF LONDON RECORDS OFFICE

PO Box 270, Guildhall, London EC2P 2EJ
Tel: 020-7332 1251 Fax: 020-7710 8682
Email: clro@corpoflondon.gov.uk
Web: www.cityoflondon.gov.uk/archives/clro

The Corporation of London Records Office contains the municipal archives of the City of London which are regarded as the most complete collection of ancient municipal records in existence. The collection includes charters of William the Conqueror, Henry II, and later kings and queens to 1957; ancient custumals: Liber Horn, Dunthorne, Custumarum, Ordinacionum, Memorandorum and Albus, Liber de Antiquis Legibus, and collections of statutes; continuous series of judicial rolls and books from 1252 and Council minutes from 1275; records of the Old Bailey and Guildhall sessions from 1603; financial records from the 16th century; the records of London Bridge from the 12th century; and numerous subsidiary series and miscellanea of historical interest.
Keeper of the City Records, The Town Clerk
Head Archivist, D. Jenkins, Ph.D.
City Archives Manager, J. M. Bankes

HOUSE OF LORDS RECORD OFFICE (THE PARLIAMENTARY ARCHIVES)

House of Lords, London SW1A 0PW
Tel: 020-7219 3074 Fax: 020-7219 2570
Email: hlro@parliament.uk Web: www.parliament.uk

Since 1497, the records of Parliament have been kept within the Palace of Westminster. They are in the custody of the Clerk of the Parliaments. In 1946 the Record Office was established to supervise their preservation and their availability to the public.
Some three million documents are preserved, including Acts of Parliament from 1497, journals of the House of Lords from 1510, minutes and committee proceedings from 1610, and papers laid before Parliament from 1531. Amongst the records are the Petition of Right, the Death Warrant of Charles I, the Declaration of Breda, and the Bill of Rights. The House of Lords Record Office also has charge of the journals of the House of Commons (from 1547), and other surviving records of the Commons (from 1572), including documents relating to private bill legislation from 1818. Among other documents are the records of the Lord Great

Chamberlain, the political papers of certain members of the two Houses, and documents relating to Parliament acquired on behalf of the nation. The Record Office makes the records available through a public search room and answers enquiries concerning the archives and history of Parliament.
Clerk of the Records, S. K. Ellison
Assistant Clerks of the Records, D. L. Prior; Dr C. Shenton; Ms F. P. Grey *(Freedom of Information Officer)*

NATIONAL ARCHIVES

Kew, Richmond, Surrey TW9 4DU
Tel: 020-8876 3444 Fax: 020-8878 8905
Web: www.nationalarchives.gov.uk

The National Archives, a government department and an executive agency reporting to the Lord Chancellor, was formed in April 2003 by bringing together the Public Record Office (founded in 1838) and the Historical Manuscripts Commission (founded in 1869).
The National Archives for England, Wales and the United Kingdom acts as the custodian of the nation's collective memory as revealed in the records of government. It also collects and disseminates information about archives relating to British history wherever they are held.
Its aims are: to assist and promote the study of the past through the public records and other archives in order to inform the present and the future; to act as chief source of authoritative advice and guidance on records management, archive policy and related information policy matters within government; to provide impartial advice to custodians of records and papers throughout the public and private sectors on records and archives management.
The National Archives administers the UK's public records system under the Public Records Acts of 1958 and 1967. The records it holds span 1,000 years – from the Domesday Book to the latest government papers to be released – and fill more than 100 miles of shelving. The records held by the National Archives are available to the public, without charge, in the reading rooms.
The National Archives also provides free expert advice to owners, custodians and users of archives throughout the UK. They include central and local government, universities, business and industry, many other individuals and institutions, and a range of public and private grant-awarding bodies.
Chief Executive, Mrs S. Tyacke, CB
Director of Public Services, Dr E. Hallam-Smith
Director of Government and Archival Services, Dr D. Thomas
Director of Corporate Services, Mrs W. Jones
Secretary, Historical Manuscripts Commission, Dr C. Kitching

NATIONAL ARCHIVES OF SCOTLAND

HM General Register House, Edinburgh EH1 3YY
Tel: 0131-535 1314 Fax: 0131-535 1360
Email: enquiries@nas.gov.uk Web: www.nas.gov.uk

The history of the national archives of Scotland can be traced back to the 13th century. The National Archives of Scotland (formerly the Scottish Record Office) is an executive agency of the Scottish Executive and keeps the administrative records of pre-Union Scotland, the registers of central and local courts of law, the public registers of property rights and legal documents, and

many collections of local and church records and private archives. Certain groups of records, mainly the modern records of Government departments in Scotland, the Scottish railway records, the plans collection and private archives of an industrial or commercial nature, are preserved in the branch repository at West Register House in Charlotte Square. The National Register of Archives for Scotland is based in the West Register House.
Keeper of the Records of Scotland, G. P. MacKenzie
Deputy Keepers, Dr P. D. Anderson; D. Brownlee

PUBLIC RECORD OFFICE OF NORTHERN IRELAND
66 Balmoral Avenue, Belfast BT9 6NY
Tel: 028-9025 1318 Fax: 028-9025 5999

The Public Record Office of Northern Ireland is responsible for identifying and preserving Northern Ireland's archival heritage and making it available to the public. It is an executive agency of the Department of Culture, Arts and Leisure.
Chief Executive, Dr G. Slater

REGISTRAR OF PUBLIC LENDING RIGHT
Richard House, Sorbonne Close, Stockton on Tees TS17 6DA
Tel: 01642-604699 Fax: 01642-615641
Email: registrar@plr.uk.com
Web: www.plr.uk.com

Under the Public Lending Right system, in operation since 1983, payment is made from public funds to authors whose books are lent out from public libraries. Payment is made once a year and the amount each author receives is proportionate to the number of times (established from a sample) that each registered book has been lent out during the previous year. The Registrar of PLR, who is appointed by the Secretary of State for Culture, Media and Sport, compiles the register of authors and books. Authors resident in all EC countries are eligible to apply. (The term 'author' covers writers, illustrators, translators, and some editors/compilers.)
   A payment of 4.21 pence was made in 2002–3 for each estimated loan of a registered book, up to a top limit of £6,000 for the books of any one registered author; the money for loans above this level is used to augment the remaining PLR payments. In 2003, the sum of £6.2 million was made available for distribution to 35,078 registered authors and assignees as the annual payment of PLR.
Registrar, Dr J. G. Parker
Chairman of Advisory Committee, C. Francis

SCOTTISH RECORDS ADVISORY COUNCIL
HM General Register House, Edinburgh EH1 3YY
Tel: 0131-535 1403 Fax: 0131-535 1360
Web: www.nas.gov.uk

The Council was established under the Public Records (Scotland) Act 1937. Its members are appointed by the First Minister and it may submit proposals or make representations to the First Minister, the Lord Justice General or the Lord President of the Court of Session on questions relating to the public records of Scotland.
Chairman, Prof. H. MacQueen
Secretary, Dr A. Rosie

REVIEW BODIES

The secretariat for these bodies is provided by the Office of Manpower Economics (*see* above)

ARMED FORCES PAY
The Review Body on Armed Forces Pay was appointed in 1971. It advises the Prime Minister and Government on the pay and allowances of members of naval, military and air forces of the Crown.
Chairman, The Baroness Dean of Thornton-le-Fylde, PC
Members, N. Sherlock; Vice-Adm. Sir Peter Woodhead; Dr A. Wright; J. Davies; Prof. D. Greenaway; Prof. The Lord Patel of Dunkeld; M. Ward

DOCTORS AND DENTISTS
The Review Body on Doctors' and Dentists' Remuneration was set up in 1971. It advises the Prime Minister and Government on the remuneration of doctors and dentists taking any part in the National Health Service.
Chairman, M. Blair, QC
Members, Prof. F. Burchill; Prof. A. Dow; H. Donaldson; Ms D. Page; Dr G. Jones; R. Malone

NURSING STAFF, MIDWIVES, HEALTH VISITORS AND PROFESSIONS ALLIED TO MEDICINE
The Review Body for nursing staff, midwives, health visitors and professions allied to medicine was set up in 1983. It advises the Prime Minister and Government on the remuneration of nursing staff, midwives and health visitors employed in the National Health Service; and also of physiotherapists, radiographers, occupational therapists, orthoptists, chiropodists, dieticians and related grades employed in the National Health Service.
Chairman, Prof. Sir C. Booth
Members, J. Bartlett; W. MacPherson; C. Monks, OBE; Prof. P. Weetman; D. Evans; Sir Patrick Symons, KBE

POLICE ADVISORY BOARD FOR ENGLAND AND WALES
The Police Advisory Board for England and Wales provides advice to the Secretary of State on general questions affecting the police in England and Wales and considers draft regulations which the Secretary of State proposes to make with respect to matters other than hours of duty, leave, pay and allowances or the issue, use and return of police clothing, personal equipment and other effects.
Independent Chair, Prof. Jon Clark
Independent Deputy Chair, Mark Baker
Secretary, Michael Penny

POLICE NEGOTIATING BOARD
The Police Negotiating Board (PNB) was established by Act of Parliament in 1980 to negotiate pay, allowances, hours of duty, leave and pensions of United Kingdom police officers and to make recommendations on these matters to the Home Secretary, Secretary of State for Northern Ireland, and Scottish Ministers.
Independent Chair, Prof. Jon Clark
Independent Deputy Chair, Mark Baker
Secretary, Michael Penny

PRISON SERVICE

The Prison Service Pay Review Body (PSPRB) was set up in 2001. It makes independent recommendations on the pay of prison governors, prison officers and related grades for the Prison Service in England and Wales and for the Northern Ireland Prison Service.

Chairman, Sir Toby Frere, KCB

Members, D. Bourn; B. Brewer; A. Gallico; P. Heard; F. Horisk; Prof. A. Smith; P. Tett; J. Abrams

SCHOOL TEACHERS

The School Teachers' Review Body (STRB) was set up under the School Teachers' Pay and Conditions Act 1991. It is required to examine and report on such matters relating to the statutory conditions of employment of school teachers in England and Wales as may be referred to it by the Secretary of State for Education and Skills.

Chairman, W. Cockburn, CBE, TD

Members, R. Gardner; Dr B. Roberts; J. Singh; R. East; M. Goodridge; J. Stephens

SENIOR SALARIES

The Senior Salaries Review Body (formerly the Top Salaries Review Body) was set up in 1971 to advise the Prime Minister on the remuneration of the judiciary, senior civil servants and senior officers of the armed forces. In 1993 its remit was extended to cover the pay, pensions and allowances of MPs, Ministers and others whose pay is determined by a Ministerial and Other Salaries Order and the allowances of peers. It also advises on the pay of officers and members of the devolved Parliament and Assemblies.

Chairman, J. Baker, CBE

Members, D. Clayman; Prof. S. Dawson; The Baroness Dean of Thornton-le-Fylde, PC; Sir Terry Heiser, GCB; Prof. Sir David Williams, QC; George Staple, CB, QC; J. Rubin; M. Sim Lei; J. McKenna

ROYAL BOTANIC GARDEN EDINBURGH

20A Inverleith Row, Edinburgh EH3 5LR
Tel: 0131-552 7171 Fax: 0131-248 2901
Email: info@rbge.org.uk
Web: www.rbge.org.uk

The Royal Botanic Garden Edinburgh (RBGE) originated as the Physic Garden, established in 1670 beside the Palace of Holyroodhouse. The Garden moved to its present 28-hectare site at Inverleith, Edinburgh, in 1821. There are also three Regional Gardens: Benmore Botanic Garden, near Dunoon, Argyll; Logan Botanic Garden, near Stranraer, Wigtownshire; and Dawyck Botanic Garden, near Stobo, Peeblesshire. Since 1986 RBGE has been administered by a board of trustees established under the National Heritage (Scotland) Act 1985. It receives an annual grant from the Environment and Rural Affairs Department of the Scottish Executive.

RBGE is an international centre for scientific research on plant diversity and for horticulture education and conservation. It has an extensive library, a herbarium with over two million preserved plant specimens, and over 16,500 species in the living collections. Entrance to the garden in Edinburgh is free; there is an admission charge to Regional Gardens.

Chairman of the Board of Trustees, Dr P. Nicholson
Regius Keeper, Prof. S. Blackmore, FRSE

ROYAL BOTANIC GARDENS KEW

Richmond, Surrey TW9 3AB
Tel: 020-8332 5000 Fax: 020-8332 5197
Wakehurst Place, Ardingly, nr Haywards Heath,
W. Sussex RH17 6TN
Tel: 01444-89000 Fax: 01444-894069

The Royal Botanic Gardens (RBG) Kew were originally laid out as a private garden for Kew House for George III's mother, Princess Augusta, in 1759. They were much enlarged in the 19th century, notably by the inclusion of the grounds of the former Richmond Lodge. In 1965 the garden at Wakehurst Place was acquired; it is owned by the National Trust and managed by RBG Kew. Under the National Heritage Act 1983 a board of trustees was set up to administer the gardens, which in 1984 became an independent body supported by grant-in-aid from the Department of Environment, Food and Rural Affairs.

The functions of RBG Kew are to carry out research into plant sciences, to disseminate knowledge about plants and to provide the public with the opportunity to gain knowledge and enjoyment from the gardens' collections. There are extensive national reference collections of living and preserved plants and a comprehensive library and archive. The main emphasis is on plant conservation and bio-diversity.

BOARD OF TRUSTEES

Chairman, The Viscount Blakenham

Members, Baroness Hayman; A. Cahn, CMG; Ms T. Burman; D. Norman; Miss M. Black; Sir Jeffery Bowman; S. de Grey, CBE; R. Lapthorne, CBE; I. Oag; Prof. C. Payne; Ms M. Regan

Director, Prof. P. Crane, FRS

ROYAL COMMISSION FOR THE EXHIBITION OF 1851

Sherfield Building, Imperial College, London SW7 2AZ
Tel: 020-7594 8790 Fax: 020-7594 8794
Email: royalcom1851@imperial.ac.uk
Web: www.royalcommission1851.org.uk

The Royal Commission was incorporated by supplemental charter as a permanent commission after winding up the affairs of the Great Exhibition of 1851. Its object is to promote scientific and artistic education by means of funds derived from its Kensington estate, purchased with the surplus left over from the Great Exhibition. Annual charitable expenditure on educational grants is about £1 million.

President, HRH The Prince Philip, Duke of Edinburgh, KG, KT, PC

Chairman, Board of Management, Sir Alan Rudge, CBE, FRS, FREng

Secretary to Commissioners, M. C. Shirley

ROYAL COMMISSION ON ENVIRONMENTAL POLLUTION

3rd Floor, The Sanctuary, Westminster, London SW1P 3JS
Tel: 020-7799 8970 Email:enquiries@rcep.org.uk
Web: www.rcep.org.uk

The Commission was set up in 1970 to advise on national and international matters concerning the pollution of the environment.

Chairman, Prof. Sir Tom Blundell, FRS

Members, Dr I. Graham-Bryce; CBE; Prof. R. Clift, OBE, FREng; J. Flemming, CBE; Sir Brian Follett, FRS;

Prof. B. Hoskins, CBE, FRS; Dr S. Owens, OBE; Prof. J. Plant, CBE; Prof. P. Ekins; Prof. S. Holgate; J. Speirs; Prof. J. Sprent
Secretary, Dr P. Hinchcliffe

ROYAL COMMISSION ON THE ANCIENT AND HISTORICAL MONUMENTS OF SCOTLAND
John Sinclair House, 16 Bernard Terrace, Edinburgh EH8 9NX
Tel: 0131-662 1456 Fax: 0131-662 1477
Web: www.rcahms.gov.uk

The Royal Commission was established in 1908 and is appointed to provide for the survey and recording of ancient and historical monuments connected with the culture, civilisation and conditions of life of the people in Scotland from the earliest times. It is funded by the Scottish Executive. The Commission compiles and maintains the National Monuments Record of Scotland as the national record of the archaeological and historical environment.
Chairman, Mrs K. Dalyell
Commissioners, Dr B. E. Crawford, FSA; Miss A. C. Riches, OBE, FSA; J. W. T. Simpson; Dr M. A. Mackay; Dr J. Murray; Dr A. Macdonald; Prof. C. D. Morris, FSA, FRSE; Dr S. Nenadic; G. Masterton, CEng
Secretary, R. J. Mercer, FSA, FRSE

ROYAL COMMISSION ON THE ANCIENT AND HISTORICAL MONUMENTS OF WALES
Crown Building, Plas Crug, Aberystwyth SY23 1NJ
Tel: 01970-621200 Fax: 01970-627701
Email: admin@rcahmw.org.uk
Web: www.rcahmw.org.uk

The Royal Commission was established in 1908 and is currently empowered by a Royal Warrant of 2001 to survey, record, publish and maintain a database of ancient and historical and maritime sites and structures, and landscapes in Wales. The Commission is funded by the National Assembly for Wales and is also responsible for the National Monuments Record of Wales, which is open daily for public reference, for the supply of archaeological information to the Ordnance Survey, for the co-ordination of archaeological aerial photography in Wales, and for sponsorship of the regional Sites and Monuments Records.
Chairman, Prof. R. A. Griffiths, D.Litt.
Commissioners, Prof. A. D. Carr, FSA; D. W. Crossley, FSA; N. Harries; J. W. Lloyd, CB; J. Newman, FSA; Prof. P. Sims-Williams, FBA; Dr L. O. W. Smith; Dr E. Williams, FSA
Secretary, P. R. White, FSA

ROYAL MAIL GROUP PLC
148 Old Street, London EC1V 9HQ
Tel: 020-7250 2888
Web: www.royalmailgroup.com

Crown services for the carriage of Government dispatches were set up in about 1516. The conveyance of public correspondence began in 1635 and the mail service was made a parliamentary responsibility with the setting up of a Post Office in 1657. Telegraphs came under Post Office control in 1870 and the Post Office Telephone Service began in 1880. The National Girobank service of the Post Office began in 1968. The Post Office ceased to be a Government department in 1969 when responsibility for the running of the postal, telecommunications, giro and remittance services was transferred to a public authority called The Post Office. The 1981 British Telecommunications Act separated the functions of the Post Office, making it solely responsible for postal services and Girobank. Girobank was privatised in 1990. The Postal Services Act 2000 turned The Post Office into a wholly owned public limited company establishing a regulatory regime under the Postal Service Commission. The Post Office Group changed its name to Consignia plc on 26 March 2001 when its new corporate structure took effect. On 4 November the name was changed to Royal Mail plc.

The chairman, chief executive and members of the Board are appointed by the Secretary of State for Trade and Industry but responsibility for the running of Royal Mail as a whole rests with the Board in its corporate capacity.

BOARD
Chairman, A. Leighton
Chief Executive, A. Crozier
Members, M. Cassoni *(Group Finance Director);* J. Cope *(Group Managing Director Mail Services)*
Non Executive Directors, M. Templeman; Ms R. Thorne; J. Lloyd
Secretary, J. Evans

ROYAL MINT
Llantrisant, Pontyclun CF72 8YT
Tel: 01443-222111 Fax: 01443-623148
Email: information.office@royalmint.gov.uk
Web: www.royalmint.com

The prime responsibility of the Royal Mint is the provision of United Kingdom coinage, but it actively competes in world markets for a share of the available circulating coin business and about half of the coins and blanks it produces annually are exported. The Mint also manufactures special proof and uncirculated quality coins in gold, silver and other metals; military and civil decorations and medals; commemorative and prize medals; and royal and official seals.

The Royal Mint became an executive agency of the Treasury in 1990. The Government announced in July 1999 that the Royal Mint would be given greater commercial freedom to expand its business into new areas and develop partnerships with the private sector.
Master of the Mint, The Chancellor of the Exchequer *(ex officio)*
Chief Executive, G. Sheehan

ROYAL NATIONAL THEATRE
South Bank, London SE1 9PX
Tel: 020-7452 3333 Fax: 020-7452 3344
Web: www.nationaltheatre.org.uk

Chairman, Sir Christopher Hogg
Members, Ms J. Bakewell, CBE; Ms S. MacGregor, OBE; B. Okri; The Rt. Hon. Chris Smith, MP; E. Walker-Arnott; Prof. L. Young; A. Ptaszynski; Ms R. Lomax; N. Wright; J. Hill; Ms N. Horlick; Ms C. Merrick; Ms C. Newling; G. Morris
Company Secretary, Mrs M. McGregor
Director, Nicholas Hytner
Executive Director, Nick Starr

RURAL PAYMENTS AGENCY (RPA)
Kings House, Kings Road, Reading, Berkshire RG1 3BU
Tel: 0118-958 3626 Fax: 0118-959 7736
Email: enquiries@rpa.gsi.gov.uk
Web: www.rpa.gov.uk

The Rural Payments Agency (RPA) is as an executive agency of the Department for Environment, Food and Rural Affairs. It is the single paying agency responsible for Common Agricultural Policy (CAP) schemes in England and for certain schemes throughout the UK.
Chief Executive (G3), J. McNeill
Directors (G5), H. MacKinnon *(Operations);* A. Kerr, *(Finance);* R. Gregg *(Human Resources);* A. MacDermott *(Information Systems);* S. Vry *(Business Development);* I. Pearson *(Operations Development);* A. Sutton *(CAP Schemes);* Ms G. Robinson *(Head of Internal Audit);* B. Stedman *(Head of Inspectorate);* Ms S. Milum *(Group Manager Counter Fraud and Compliance Unit)*

SCOTTISH CRIMINAL CASES REVIEW COMMISSION
5th Floor, Portland House, 17 Renfield Street, Glasgow G2 5AH Tel: 0141-270 7030 Fax: 0141-270 7040/23
Email: info@sccrc.org.uk
Web: www.sccrc.org.uk

The Commission is a non-departmental public body which started operating on 1 April 1999. It took over from the Secretary of State for Scotland powers to consider alleged miscarriages of justice in Scotland and refer cases meeting the relevant criteria to the High Court for determination. Members are appointed by Her Majesty The Queen on the recommendation of the First Minister; senior executive staff are appointed by the Commission.
Chairperson, The Very Revd G. Forbes
Members, Prof. P. Duff; Sir Gerald Gordon, CBE, QC; W. Taylor, QC; R. Anderson, QC; D. Belfall; J. Mackay, QPM
Chief Executive, Gerard Sinclair

SCOTTISH ENTERPRISE
5 Atlantic Quay, 150 Broomielaw, Glasgow G2 8LU
Tel: 0141-248 2700 Fax: 0141-221 3217
Email: network.helpline@scotent.co.uk
Web: www.scottishenterprise.com

Scottish Enterprise was established in 1991 and its purpose is to create jobs and prosperity for the people of Scotland. It is funded largely by the Scottish Executive and is responsible to the Scottish Ministers. Working in partnership with the private and public sectors, Scottish Enterprise aims to further the development of Scotland's economy, to enhance the skills of the Scottish workforce and to promote Scotland's international competitiveness. Scottish Enterprise is concerned with attracting firms to Scotland and, through Scottish Trade International, it helps Scottish companies to compete in world export markets. Scottish Enterprise has a network of 12 Local Enterprise Companies that deliver economic development services at local level.
Chairman, Sir Ian Robinson, CBE
Chief Executive, Dr R. Crawford

SCOTTISH ENVIRONMENT PROTECTION AGENCY
Erskine Court, The Castle Business Park, Stirling FK9 4TR
Tel: 01786-457700 Hotline: 0800 80 70 60
Fax: 01786-446885 Web: www.sepa.org.uk

The Scottish Environment Protection Agency (SEPA) is the public body responsible for environmental protection in Scotland. It regulates potential pollution to land, air and water, the storage, transport and disposal of controlled waste and the safe keeping and disposal of radioactive materials. It does this within a complex legislative framework of Acts of Parliament, EC Directives and Regulations, granting licenses to operations of industrial processes and waste disposal.
SEPA also operates Floodline, 0845-988 1188, a public service providing information on possible risk of flooding 24 hours a day, 365 days a year.
Chairman, K. Collins
Chief Executive, C. Gemmell
Director of Finance and Corporate Support, J. Ford
Acting Director of Strategic Planning, C. MacDonald
Director of Operations, W. Halcrow
Director of Public Affairs and Corporate Communications, J. Beveridge

SCOTTISH LAW COMMISSION
140 Causewayside, Edinburgh EH9 1PR
Tel: 0131-668 2131 Fax: 0131-662 4900
Email: info@scotlawcom.gov.uk
Web: www. scotlawcom.gov.uk

The Commission keeps the law in Scotland under review and makes proposals for its development and reform. It is responsible to the Scottish Ministers through the Scottish Executive Justice Department.
Chairman (part-time), The Hon. Lord Eassie
Commissioners, Prof. G. Maher; Prof. K. G. C. Reid; Prof. J. M. Thomson
Secretary, Miss J. McLeod

SCOTTISH LEGAL AID BOARD
44 Drumsheugh Gardens, Edinburgh EH3 7SW
Tel: 0131-226 7061 Fax: 0131-220 4878
Email: general@slab.org.uk
Web: www.slab.org.uk

The Scottish Legal Aid Board was set up under the Legal Aid (Scotland) Act 1986 to manage legal aid in Scotland. Board members are appointed by Scottish Ministers.
Chairman, Mrs J. Couper
Members, W. Gallagher; Sheriff A. Jessop; N. Kuenssberg; G. McKinstry; D. J. C. Nicol; Prof. J. P. Percy, CBE; Mrs Y. Osman; Mrs M. Scanlan; M. C. Thomson, QC; P. Gray, QC; Mrs E. More
Chief Executive, L. Montgomery

SCOTTISH NATURAL HERITAGE
12 Hope Terrace, Edinburgh EH9 2AS
Tel: 0131-447 4784 Fax: 0131-446 2277
Email: enquiries@snh.gov.uk
Web: www.snh.org.uk

Scottish Natural Heritage was established in 1992 under the Natural Heritage (Scotland) Act 1991. It provides advice on nature conservation to all those whose activities affect wildlife, landforms and features of geological interest in Scotland, and seeks to develop and improve facilities for the enjoyment and understanding of the Scottish countryside. It is funded by the Scottish Executive.

Chairman, Dr J. Markland, CBE
Chief Executive, I. Jardine
Chief Scientific Adviser, C. Galbraith
Directors of Operations, J. Thomson *(West)*; A. Bachell *(East)*; J. Watson *(North)*
Director of Corporate Services, I. Edgeler

SCOTTISH PRISONS COMPLAINTS COMMISSION

Government Buildings, Broomhouse Drive,
Edinburgh EH11 3XD
Tel: 0131-244 8423 Fax: 0131-244 8430

The Commission was established in 1994. It is an independent body to which prisoners in Scottish prisons can make application in relation to any matter where they have failed to obtain satisfaction from the Scottish Prison Service's internal grievance procedures. Clinical judgements made by medical officers, matters which are the subject of legal proceedings and matters relating to sentence, conviction and parole decision-making are excluded from the Commission's jurisdiction. The Commissioner is appointed by the First Minister.
Commissioner, V. Barrett

SCOTTISH PUBLIC SERVICES OMBUDSMAN

23 Walker Street, Edinburgh, EH3 7HX
Tel: 0870-011 5378 Fax: 0870-011 5379
Email: enquiries@scottishombudsman.org.uk
Web: www.scottishombudsman.org.uk

The Scottish Public Services Ombudsman was established in 2002. The Ombudsman investigates complaints about Scottish government departments, councils, housing associations, the national health service and other public bodies. The public bodies which the Scottish Public Services Ombudsman may consider investigating are taken from a list of such bodies outlined in the Scottish Public Services Ombudsman Act 2002. Complaints considered by the Ombudsman can range from complaints about poor service, failure to provide a service, administrative failure and complaints about the NHS including hospital staff, GPs, dentists and other health professionals.
Scottish Public Services Ombudsman, Prof. A. Brown

SEAFISH INDUSTRY AUTHORITY

18 Logie Mill, Logie Green Road, Edinburgh EH7 4HG
Tel: 0131-558 3331 Fax: 0131-558 1442
Email: seafish@seafish.co.uk
Web: www.seafish.org.uk

Established under the Fisheries Act 1981, Seafish works with the seafood industry to satisfy consumers, raise standards, improve efficiency and secure a sustainable future. It is responsible to the four UK fisheries departments.
Chairman, A. Dewar-Durie
Chief Executive, J. Rutherford

THE SECURITY AND INTELLIGENCE SERVICES

Under the Intelligence Services Act 1994, the Intelligence and Security Committee of Parliamentarians was established to oversee the work of GCHQ, MI5 and MI6; in 1999 an Investigator was appointed to the committee in order to reinforce the authority of its findings and establish public confidence in the oversight system. The Act also established the Intelligence Services Tribunal, which hears complaints made against GCHQ and MI6. The Security Service Tribunal and Commissioner (see below) investigate complaints about MI5.

GOVERNMENT COMMUNICATIONS HEADQUARTERS (GCHQ)

Priors Road, Cheltenham, Glos GL52 5AJ
Tel: 01242-221491 Fax: 01242-574349

GCHQ produces signals intelligence in support of national security and the UK's economic wellbeing, and in the prevention or detection of serious crime. Additionally, GCHQ Communications-Electronics Security Group (CESG) provides advice and assistance to Government departments, the armed forces and other national infrastructure bodies on the security of their communications and information systems. GCHQ was placed on a statutory footing by the Intelligence Services Act 1994 and is headed by a director who is directly accountable to the Foreign Secretary. Staff began moving into a new building in Cheltenham in September 2003 and the move is scheduled to be completed by the end of 2004.
Director, D. E. Pepper

INTELLIGENCE SERVICES COMMISSIONER

c/o PO Box 33220, London SW1H 9ZQ
Tel: 020-7273 4514

The Commissioner is appointed by the Prime Minister. He keeps under review the issue of warrants by the Secretaries of State as detailed under the Regulation of Investigatory Powers Act (RIPA) 2000. The Commissioner is also required to submit an annual report on the discharge of his functions to the Prime Minister.
Commissioner, The Rt. Hon. Lord Justice Simon Brown
Private Secretary, D. Payne

INTERCEPTION OF COMMUNICATIONS COMMISSIONER

c/o PO Box 33220, London SW1H 9ZQ
Tel: 020-7273 4514

The Interception of Communications Commissioner is appointed by the Prime Minister for a period of three years. The Commissioner's job is to keep under review the issue of interception warrants and the adequacy of the arrangements for ensuring the product of interception is properly handled. He does this by reviewing the warrant applications that the intercepting agencies have made to the Secretary of State, in order to make sure that the Secretary of State was right to sign the warrants. He also visits the Security Service and other agencies to examine his selection of interception warrants with the officers responsible for the relevant investigations. At the end of each reporting year, the Commissioner submits a report to the Prime Minister which is subsequently laid before Parliament and published.
Commissioner, Sir Swinton Thomas
Private Secretary, D. Payne

INVESTIGATORY POWERS TRIBUNAL
PO Box 33220, London SW1H 9ZQ
Tel: 020-7273 4514

The Investigatory Powers Tribunal replaces the Interception of Communications Tribunal, the Intelligence Services Tribunal, the Security Services Tribunal and the complaints function of the Commissioner appointed under the Police Act 1997.

The Regulation of Investigatory Powers Act 2000 provides for a Tribunal made up of senior members of the legal profession, independent of the Government and appointed by The Queen, to consider all complaints against the intelligence services and those against public authorities in respect of powers covered by RIPA; and to consider proceedings brought under section 7 of the Human Rights Act 1998 against the intelligence services and law enforcement agencies in respect of these powers.
President, The Rt. Hon. Lord Justice John Mummery
Vice-President, Mr Justice Michael Burton
Members, W. Carmichael; Sir David Calcutt, QC;
   Sir Richard Gaskell; Sheriff Principal J. McInnes, QC;
   Sir John Pringle, QC; P. Scott, QC; R. Seabrook, QC
Secretary, Mr D. Payne

NCIS NATIONAL CRIMINAL INTELLIGENCE SERVICE
PO Box 8000, London SE11 5EN
Tel: 020-7238 8000 Web: www.ncis.gov.uk

The National Criminal Intelligence Service (NCIS) provides intelligence about serious and organised crime to law enforcement, government and other relevant national and international agencies.
Director-General, P. Hampson, QPM, CBE
Deputy Director-General, D. Bolt
Director, International Division, R. Wainwright
Director, UK Division, K. Bristow
Director, Resources Division, N. Beard
Director, Finance, Ms M. Ashworth
Director, Special Projects, N. Bailey

SERVICE AUTHORITY
PO Box 2600, London SW1V 2WG
Tel: 020-7238 2600

The Service Authority for NCIS is responsible for ensuring its effective operation. It operates with the Service Authority for the National Crime Squad. There are 26 members of the authorities, of whom the chairman and nine others serve as 'core members' on both authorities.
Chairman, D. Lock
Clerk, T. Simmons
Treasurer, P. Derrick

THE SECRET INTELLIGENCE SERVICE (MI6)
PO Box 1300, London SE1 1BD

The Secret Intelligence Service produces secret intelligence in support of the Government's security, defence, foreign and economic policies. It was placed on a statutory footing by the Intelligence Services Act 1994 and is headed by a chief, known as 'C', who is directly accountable to the Foreign Secretary.
Chief, Sir R. B. Dearlove, OBE, KCMG

THE SECURITY SERVICE (MI5)
PO Box 3255, London SW1P 1AE
Tel: 020-7930 9000

The Security Service is responsible for security intelligence work against covertly organised threats to the UK. These include terrorism, espionage and the proliferation of weapons of mass destruction, and supporting the police and other law enforcement agencies against serious crime. The service also provides security advice to a range of organisations to help reduce vulnerability to threats from individuals, groups or countries hostile to UK interests.
Director-General, Ms E. Manningham-Buller

SENTENCE REVIEW COMMISSIONERS
5th Floor, Windsor House, 12–16 Bedford Street,
Belfast BT2 7SR
Tel: 028-9054 9412 Fax: 028-9054 9427
Email: sentrev@belfast.org.uk
Web: www.sentencereview.org.uk

The Sentence Review Commissioners are appointed by the Secretary of State for Northern Ireland to consider applications from prisoners serving sentences in Northern Ireland for declarations that they are entitled to early release in accordance with the provisions of the Northern Ireland (Sentences) Act 1998. The commissioners have been appointed until 31 July 2005 and are served by staff seconded from the Northern Ireland Office.
Joint Chairmen, Sir John Belloch, KCB; B. Currin
Commissioners, Dr S. Casale; Dr P. Curran; I. Dunbar, CB;
   Mrs M. Gilpin; Dr A. Grounds; D. McFerran;
   Ms C. McGrory; Dr D. Morrow

SERIOUS FRAUD OFFICE
Elm House, 10–16 Elm Street, London WC1X 0BJ
Tel: 020-7239 7272 Fax: 020-7837 1689
Email: public.enquiries@sfo.gsi.gov.uk

The Serious Fraud Office works under the superintendence of the Attorney-General. Its remit is to investigate and prosecute serious and complex fraud. (Other fraud cases are handled by the fraud divisions of the Crown Prosecution Service.) The scope of its powers covers England, Wales and Northern Ireland. The staff includes lawyers, accountants and other support staff investigating teams work closely with the police.
Director, Robert Wardle

SMALL BUSINESS COUNCIL
Kingsgate House, 66–74 Victoria Street, London SW1E 6SW
Tel: 020-7215 8519
Email: sbcsecretariat@sbs.gsi.gov.uk
Web: www.sbs.gov.uk/sbc

The Small Business Council was set up in March 2000. It is a non-departmental public body reporting to the Secretary for Trade and Industry on the needs of small businesses. It produces an annual report.
Chairman, W. Sargent
Members, Ms S. Anderson, CBE; J. Braithwaite. CBE;
   G. Burton; Ms E. Caleb; Dr M. Carter; P. Donaldson;
   Ms S. Gemmell; Ms L. Gradwell; Ms T. Graham, OBE;
   P. Harrod; Ms C. Hughes; S. Johnson; Ms M. Rigby;
   I. Rees; Prof. D. Storey; Mrs S. Brownson, OBE;
   J. Karia; G. Osborne; R. Reed; M. Robinson;
   S. Topman; Prof. M. Ram; Mrs L. Shafer

SMALL BUSINESS SERVICE
Kingsgate House, 66–74 Victoria Street, London SW1E 6SW
Tel: 0114- 259 7788 Fax: 0114-259 7330
Web: www.sbs.gov.uk

The Small Business Service was set up in March 2000. It is an advisory Non-Departmental Public Body reporting to the Secretary for Trade and Industry on the needs of small businesses. It produces an annual report. There are 45 local Business Link franchises throughout England largely coterminous in their boundaries with the new Learning and Skills Council.
Chairman, W. Sargent
Members, Ms S. Anderson, CBE; J. Braithwaite, CBE; G. Burton; Ms E. Caleb; Dr M. Carter; P. Donaldson; Ms S. Gemmell; Ms L. Gradwell; Ms T. Graham, OBE; P. Harrod; Ms C. Hughes; S. Johnson; Ms M. Rigby; I. Rees; Prof. D. Storey; Mrs S. Brownson, OBE; J. Karia; G. Osborne; R. Reed; M. Robinson; S. Topman; Prof. M. Ram; Mrs L. Shafer
Chief Executive, Martin Wyn Griffith

STATISTICS COMMISSION
10 Great George Street, London SW1P 3AE
Tel: 020-7273 8008
Email: statscom@statscom.org.uk
Web: www.statscom.org.uk

The Statistics Commission has been set up to advise on the quality, quality assurance and priority-setting for National Statistics, and on the procedures designed to deliver statistical integrity, to help ensure National Statistics are trustworthy and responsive to public needs. It is independent of both Ministers and the producers of National Statistics. It operates in a transparent way with the minutes of its meetings, correspondence and evidence it receives, and advice it gives, all normally publicly available for scrutiny.
Chairman, Prof. D. Rhind, CBE, FRS, FBA
Members, Miss C. Bowe; Sir Kenneth Calman, KCB; Ms P. Hodgson; Mrs J. Trewsdale; D. Wanless; M. Weale

STRATEGIC RAIL AUTHORITY
55 Victoria Street, London SW1H 0EU
Tel: 020-7654 6000 Fax: 020-7654 6010
Web: www.sra.gov.uk

The Strategic Rail Authority (SRA) formally came into being on 1 February 2001 following the introduction of the Transport Act 2000. On 14 January 2002 it published its Strategic Plan, setting out the strategic priorities for Britain's railways over the next ten years.

As well as providing overall strategic direction for Britain's railways, the SRA has responsibility for consumer protection, the development of rail freight and administering freight grants, and for steering forward investment projects aimed at opening up bottlenecks and expanding network capacity. It is directly responsible for letting and managing passenger rail franchises.

The SRA manages all public sector expenditure in the rail industry and operates under directions and guidance issued by the Secretary of State for Transport. In Scotland it is also subject to directions and guidance from the Scottish Minister for Transport, and to directions and

guidance from the Mayor of London in respect of services operating within the capital.
Chairman and Chief Executive, R. Bowker
Non-executive members, L. D. Adams, OBE; D. A. Begg; W. Gallagher; D. Grayson, CBE; P. H. Kent, CBE; J. Mayhew; D. A. Quarmby, CBE; M. Banerjee, CBE; J. Lewis-Jones; D. Norgrove
Secretary, P. Trewin

TOURISM BODIES

Visit Britain, Visit Scotland Tourist Board, the Wales Tourist Board and the Northern Ireland Tourist Board are responsible for developing and marketing the tourist industry in their respective countries.

VISIT BRITAIN, Thames Tower, Black's Road, London W6 9EL. Tel: 020-8846 9000 Fax: 020-8563-0302 Web: www.visitbritain.com *Chief Executive,* T. Wright
VISIT SCOTLAND, 23 Ravelston Terrace, Edinburgh EH4 3TP. Tel: 0131-332 2433;
Thistle House, Beechwood Park North, Inverness IV2 3ED Tel: 01463-716996 Web: www.visitscotland.com *Chairman,* P. Lederer; *Chief Executive,* P. Riddle
WALES TOURIST BOARD, Brunel House, 2 Fitzalan Road, Cardiff CF24 QUY. Tel: 029-2049 9909
Fax: 029-2048 5031 Email: info@tourism.wales.gov.uk Web: www.visitwales.com *Chief Executive,* J. Jones
NORTHERN IRELAND TOURIST BOARD, St Anne's Court, 59 North Street, Belfast BT1 1NB. Tel: 028-9023 1221 Fax: 028-9024 0960 Email: info@nitb.com Web: www.discovernorthernireland.com *Chief Executive,* A. Clarke

TRANSPORT FOR LONDON
Windsor House, 42–50 Victoria Street, London SW1H 0TL
Web: www.tfl.gov.uk/tfl/

Transport for London (TfL) is responsible for the capital's transport system. Its role is to implement the Mayor of London's Transport Strategy and manage the transport services across London for which the Mayor has responsibility.
Chairman, Ken Livingstone
Vice-Chairman, Dave Wetzel
Commissioner of Transport for London, Bob Kiley

UK FILM COUNCIL INTERNATIONAL
10 Little Portland Street, London W1W 7JG
Tel: 020-7861 7860 Fax: 020-7861 7864
Email: internationalinfo@ukfilmcouncil.org.uk
Web: www.bfc.co.uk

The UK Film Council (formerly the British Film Commission) was originally established in 1991. Its remit is to attract inward investment by promoting the UK as an international production centre to the film and television industries and encouraging the use of British locations, services, facilities and personnel. Working with the UK Screen Agencies, the BFC also provides overseas producers with a bespoke information service and offers practical help and advice to those filming in the UK.
British Film Commissioner, S. Norris
Director, Ms C. Wise

UNITED KINGDOM SPORTS COUNCIL (UK SPORT)

40 Bernard Street, London WC1N 1ST
Tel: 020-7211 5100 Fax: 020-7211 5246
Web: www.uksport.gov.uk

The UK Sports Council (UK Sport) was established by Royal Charter in January 1997. Its role is to lead the UK to sporting excellence by supporting winning athletes, world class events, ethically fair and drug-free sport. UK Sport's aim is for the UK to be in the world's top five sporting nations by 2012, measured by athletic performances at world championships, Olympic and Paralympic games.
Chairman, Sir Rodney Walker
Chief Executive, R. Callicott

UNRELATED LIVE TRANSPLANT REGULATORY AUTHORITY

c/o Department of Health, Room 339, Wellington House,
133–155 Waterloo Road, London SE1 8UG
Tel: 020-7972 4812 Fax: 020-7972 4852
Email: dhmail@doh.gsi.gov.uk/ultra
Web: www.doh.gov.uk/ultra

The Unrelated Live Transplant Regulatory Authority (ULTRA) is a statutory body established in 1990. In every case where the transplant of an organ within the definition of the Human Organ Transplants Act 1989 is proposed between a living donor and a recipient who are not genetically related, the proposal must be referred to ULTRA. Applications must be made by registered medical practitioners.
The Authority comprises a chairman and ten members appointed by the Secretary of State for Health. The secretariat is provided by Department of Health officials.
Chairman, Prof. Sir Roddy MacSween
Members, Prof. J. A. Bradley; Ms D. Bowman; Dr J. F. Douglas; Dr S. Fuggle; Dr R. Gokal; A. J. Hooker; Ms A. Keogh; Prof. A. Rees; Mrs S. Roff; Mrs S. J. Sullivan
Administrative Secretary, E. Scarlett
Medical Secretary, Dr P. Doyle

UK ATOMIC ENERGY AUTHORITY

Harwell, Didcot, Oxon OX11 0RA
Tel: 01235-820220 Fax: 01235-436401
Web: www.ukaea.org.uk

The UKAEA was established by the Atomic Energy Authority Act 1954 and took over responsibility for the research and development of the civil nuclear power programme. The Authority's commercial arm, AEA Technology PLC, was privatised in 1996. UKAEA is now responsible for the safe management and decommissioning of its radioactive plant and for maximising the income from the buildings and land on its sites. UKAEA also undertakes special nuclear tasks for the Government, including the UK's contribution to the international fusion programme.
Chairman, D. Tunnicliffe, CBE
Chief Executive, Dr J. McKeown

WALES YOUTH AGENCY

Leslie Court, Lon-y-Llyn, Caerphilly CF83 1BQ
Tel: 029-2085 5700 Fax: 029-2085 5701
Email: wya@wya.org.uk
Web: www.wya.org.uk

The Wales Youth Agency is an independent organisation funded by the National Assembly for Wales to support the youth service in Wales. Its functions include the encouragement and development of the partnership between statutory and voluntary agencies relating to young people; the promotion of staff development and training; and the extension of marketing and information services in the relevant fields. The board of directors does not receive a salary.
Chairman of the Board of Directors, G. Davies, CBE
Chief Executive, B. Williams

WELSH ADMINISTRATION OMBUDSMAN

5th Floor, Capital Tower, Greyfriars Road, Cardiff CF10 3AG
Tel: 0845-601 0987 Fax: 029-2022 6909
Email: wao.enquiries@ombudsman.gsi.gov.uk
Web: www.ombudsman.org.uk

The Welsh Administration Ombudsman was appointed in July 1999 to investigate complaints by members of the public who have suffered an injustice through maladministration by the National Assembly for Wales and certain public bodies involved in devolved Welsh affairs.
Welsh Administration Ombudsman, Ann Abraham

WELSH DEVELOPMENT AGENCY

Plas Glyndwr, Kingsway, Cardiff CF10 3AH
Tel: 01443-845500 Fax: 01443-845589
Web: www.wda.co.uk

The Agency was established under the Welsh Development Agency Act 1975. Its remit is to help further the regeneration of the economy and improve the environment in Wales. Under the Government of Wales Act 1998, the Land Authority for Wales and the Development Board for Rural Wales merged with the Welsh Development Agency. The Agency is sponsored by the National Assembly for Wales.
The Agency's priorities are to create new businesses and to encourage existing small firms to grow. Its main activities include promoting Wales as a location for inward investment, helping to boost the growth, profitability and competitiveness of indigenous Welsh companies, providing investment capital for industry, encouraging investment by the private sector in property development, grant-aiding land reclamation, and stimulating quality urban and rural development.
Chairman, R. Jones, OBE
Chief Executive, G. Hawker, CBE

WOMEN'S NATIONAL COMMISSION

Room 56/4, Cabinet Office, 35 Great Smith Street,
London SW1P 3BQ
Tel: 020-7276 2555 Fax: 020-7276 2563
Email: wnc@cabinet-office.x.gsi.gov.uk
Web: www.thewnc.org.uk

The Women's National Commission is an independent advisory committee to the Government. Its remit is to ensure that the informed opinions of women are given their due weight in the deliberations of the Government and in public debate on matters of public interest including those of special interest to women. The Commission's sponsoring department is the Cabinet Office.
Chair, Margaret Prosser
Director, Ms J. Veitch

REGIONAL GOVERNMENT

LONDON

GREATER LONDON AUTHORITY (GLA)
City Hall, The Queen's Walk, London SE1 2AA
Tel: 020-7983 4000
Press Office: 020-7983 4071/4072/4090/4067/4228
Email: mayor@london.gov.uk Web: www.london.gov.uk

On 7 May 1998 London voted in favour of the formation of the Greater London Authority. The first elections to the GLA were on Thursday, 4 May 2000 and the new Authority took over its responsibilities on 3 July 2000. On 15 July 2002 the GLA moved to one of London's most spectacular buildings, built on a brown field site on the south bank of the river Thames, adjacent to Tower Bridge.

The structure and objectives of the GLA stem from its eight main areas of responsibility. These are transport, planning, economic development and regeneration, the environment, police, fire and emergency planning, culture and health. The bodies that co-ordinate these functions and report to the GLA are: Transport for London (TfL), the London Development Agency (LDA), the Metropolitan Police Authority (MPA) and the London Fire and Emergency Planning Authority (LFEPA). The GLA also absorbed a number of other London bodies, such as the London Planning Advisory Committee, the London Ecology Unit and the London Research Centre.

The GLA consists of a directly elected Mayor, the Mayor of London, and a separately elected assembly, the London Assembly. The Mayor has the key role of decision making with the Assembly performing the tasks of regulating and scrutinising these decisions. In addition, the GLA has around 600 permanent staff to support the activities of the Mayor and the Assembly, which are overseen by a Head of Paid Service. The Mayor may appoint two political advisors but he may not appoint the Chief Executive, the Monitoring Officer or the Chief Finance Officer. These must be appointed by the Assembly.

The Mayor is also responsible for appointing an advisory Cabinet. The Cabinet functions as part of the Mayor's objective of eliminating barriers to effective decision making and enabling the GLA to speak with one voice on behalf of London. The function of the Mayor's Cabinet is to provide the Mayor with the most sound advice on policy and strategy. Meetings of the Cabinet are designed to be a powerful forum for discussing the issues affecting Londoners. The Cabinet is not intended to fit the Whitehall Cabinet model in that GLA members will not be bound by the convention of collective responsibility, the absence of which does not mean that the Mayor will devolve or federalise his powers. All decisions are made by the Mayor acting on the honest advice of his Cabinet. Cabinet members can be broadly categorised into (a) those with specific policy brief (e.g. in the areas of planning, policing or fire and civil defence) and (b) those who have been chosen to give advice and/or reflect political breadth.

The role of the Mayor can be broken down into a number of key areas: to represent and promote London at home and abroad and speak up for Londoners; to devise strategies and plans to tackle London-wide issues, such as transport, economic development and regeneration, air quality, noise, waste, bio-diversity, planning and culture; to set budgets for Transport for London, the London Development Agency, the Metropolitan Police Authority and the London Fire and Emergency Planning Authority;

to control new transport and economic development bodies and appoint their members; to make appointments to the new police and fire authorities; and to publish regular reports on the state of the environment in London. The role of the Assembly can be broken down into a number of key areas:

* to provide a check and balance on the Mayor
* to scrutinise the Mayor
* to have the power to amend the Mayor's budget by a majority of two-thirds
* to investigate issues of London-wide significance and make proposals to the Mayor
* to provide the Deputy Mayor and the members serving on the police, fire and emergency planning authorities with advice

ELECTIONS AND THE VOTING SYSTEMS
The Assembly will be elected every four years at the same time as the Mayor and consists of 25 members. There is one member from each of the 14 GLA constituencies topped up with 11 London members who are representatives of political parties or individuals standing as independent candidates. The next election will be in May 2004.

The GLA constituencies are: Barnet and Camden; Bexley and Bromley; Brent and Harrow; City and East, covering Barking and Dagenham, the City of London, Newham and Tower Hamlets; Croydon and Sutton; Ealing and Hillingdon; Enfield and Haringey; Greenwich and Lewisham; Havering and Redbridge; North East, covering Hackney, Islington and Waltham Forest; Lambeth and Southwark; West Central, covering Hammersmith and Fulham, Kensington and Chelsea and Westminster; South West, covering Hounslow, Kingston upon Thames and Richmond upon Thames; Merton and Wandsworth.

Two distinct voting systems were used to appoint the existing Mayor and the Assembly. The Mayor was elected using the Supplementary Vote System (SV). With the SVS electors have two votes; one to give the first choice for Mayor and one to give the second choice. Electors cannot vote twice for the same candidate. If one candidate gets more than half of all the first choice votes, he or she becomes Mayor. If no candidate gets more than half the first choice votes, the two candidates with the most first choice votes remain in the election and all the other candidates drop out. The second choice votes on the ballot papers of the candidates who drop out are then counted. Where these second choice votes are for the two remaining candidates they are added to the first choice votes these candidates already have. The candidate with the most first and second choice votes combined would become the Mayor of London.

The Assembly was appointed using the Additional Member System (AM). Under AMS, electors have two votes. The first vote is for a constituency candidate. The second vote is for a party list or individual candidate contesting the London-wide Assembly seats. The 14 constituency members were elected under the first-past-the-post system, the same system used in general and local elections. Electors vote for one candidate and the candidate with the most votes wins. The Additional (London) Members were drawn from party lists or were independent candidates who stood as London Members.

The Greater London Returning Officer (GLRO) was the independent official responsible for running the first election in London. The GLRO had overall responsibility for running a free, fair and efficient election. He was

supported in this by Returning Officers in each of the 14 London Constituencies.
GLRO, Robert V. Hughes, CBE

FUNCTIONS AND STRUCTURE
Every aspect of the Assembly and its activities must be open to the view of the public and therefore accountable. Assembly meetings are open to the public and the reports it produces are available to the public. Other measures such as a twice yearly 'people's question time' also take place. The meetings where the Assembly questions the Mayor are also open to the public.

TRANSPORT FOR LONDON (TfL)
TfL is run by a board of 8–15 members appointed by the Mayor. Its role is:
* to manage the buses, Croydon Tramlink and the Docklands Light Railway (DLR)
* to manage the underground once Public Private partnership contracts are in place
* to manage an important network of roads to be known as the GLA Road Network
* to regulate taxis and minicabs
* to run the London River Services and promote the river for passenger and freight movement
* to help to co-ordinate the Dial-a-Ride and Taxicard schemes for door-to-door services for transport users with mobility problems
* to take responsibility for traffic lights
London Borough Councils maintain the role of highway and traffic authorities for 95 per cent of London's roads. A £5 congestion charge for motorists driving into central London between the hours of 7am and 6.30pm, Mondays to Fridays (excluding public holidays) was introduced on 17 February 2003.
Transport Commissioner for London, Robert Kiley

LONDON DEVELOPMENT AGENCY (LDA)
The LDA promotes economic development and regeneration. It is one of the nine regional development agencies set up around the country to perform this task. The key aspects of the LDA's role are:
* to promote business efficiency, investment and competitiveness
* to promote employment
* to enhance the skills of local people
* to create sustainable development
The London Boroughs retain powers to promote economic development in their local areas.

THE ENVIRONMENT
The Mayor is required to formulate strategies to tackle London's environmental issues including the quality of water, air and land; the use of energy and London's contribution to climate change targets; ground water levels and traffic emissions; and municipal waste management.

METROPOLITAN POLICE AUTHORITY (MPA)
This body, which oversees the policing of London consists of 12 members of the assembly, including the deputy Mayor, 4 magistrates and 7 independents. One of the independents was appointed by the Home Secretary. The role of the MPA is:
* to maintain an efficient and effective police force
* to publish an annual policing plan
* to set police targets and monitor performance
* to be part of the appointment, discipline and removal of senior officers
* to be responsible for the performance budget
The boundaries of the metropolitan police districts have been changed to be in line with the 32 London boroughs. Areas beyond the GLA remit have been incorporated into the Surrey, Hertfordshire and Essex police areas. The City of London has its own police force.

LONDON FIRE AND EMERGENCY PLANNING AUTHORITY (LFEPA)
On 3 July 2000 the existing London Fire and Civil Defence Authority became the London Fire and Emergency Planning Authority. It consists of 17 members, 9 drawn from the assembly and 8 from the London Boroughs. The role of LFEPA is:
* to set the strategy for the provision of fire services
* to ensure that the fire brigade can meet all the normal requirements efficiently
* to ensure that effective arrangements are made for the fire brigade to receive emergency calls and deal with them promptly
* to ensure that information useful to the development of the fire brigades is gathered
* to assist the boroughs with their emergency planning, training and exercises

SALARIES AS AT JULY 2003
Mayor	£110,430
Deputy Mayor	£68,661
Assembly Member	£46,984

MAYOR'S ADVISORY CABINET
Deputy Mayor, Jenny Jones
Chair, Cultural Strategy, Jennette Arnold
Chair, London Development Agency, Honor Chapman, CBE
Chair, London Fire and Emergency Planning Authority, Val Shawcross
Chair of the Metropolitan Police Authority, Toby Harris
City and Business, Judith Mayhew
Community Partnerships, Richard Stone
Disability Rights, Caroline Gooding
Environment, Victor Anderson
Health, Sue Atkinson
Homelessness, Glenda Jackson, MP
Human Rights and Equalities, Graham Tope
Lesbian and Gay Issues, vacant
Liberal Democrats, Lynne Featherstone
Older People, Graeme Matthews
Race Relations, Lee Jasper
Regeneration, Kumar Murshid
Spatial Development and Strategic Planning, Nicky Gavron
Trade Unions, Rod Robertson
Urban Strategy, Richard Rogers
Women and Equality, Diane Abbott, MP

GREATER LONDON ASSEMBLY MEMBERS *as at 21 August 2003*

The Mayor, Ken Livingstone, *(Ind.)*
Anderson, Victor *(Green), London List*
Arnold, Jennette *(Lab.), London List*
Arbour, Anthony *(C.), South West,* maj. 7,059
Barnes, Richard *(C.), Ealing and Hillingdon,* maj. 6,812
Biggs, John *(Lab.), City and East,* maj. 26,121
Bray, Angie *(C.), West Central,* maj. 18,279
Coleman, Brian *(C.), Barnet and Camden,* maj. 551
Duvall, Len *(Lab.), Greenwich and Lewisham,* maj. 17,985
Evans, Jeremy Roger *(C.), Havering and Redbridge,* maj. 8,269
Featherstone, Lynne *(LD), London List*
Gavron, Nicky *(Lab.), Enfield and Haringey,* maj. 3,302
Hamwee, Baroness Sally *(LD), London List*
Harris, Lord Toby *(Lab.), Brent and Harrow,* maj. 4,380
Heath, Samantha *(Lab.), London List*
Hillier, Meg *(Lab.), North East,* maj. 17,603
Howlett, Elizabeth *(C.), Merton and Wandsworth,* maj. 12,870
Johnson, Darren *(Green), London List*

*Johnson, Diana *(Lab.), London List*
Jones, Jennifer *(Green), London List*
†Lynch, Noel *(Green), London List*
Neill, Bob *(C.), Bexley and Bromley,* maj. 34,559
Ollerenshaw, Eric *(C.), London List*
Pelling, Andrew John *(C.), Croydon and Sutton,*
   maj. 17,087
Shawcross, Valerie *(Lab.), Lambeth and Southwark,*
   maj. 15,493
Tope, Graham *(LD), London List*
‡Tuffrey, Mike *(LD), London List*

* Replaced Trevor Phillips *(Lab) London List*
† Replaced Victor Anderson *(Green) London List*
‡ Replaced Louse Bloom *(LD) London List*

OVERALL RESULTS IN MAYORAL
ELECTION *as at May 2000*

First Pref	Party	Votes	%
Ken Livingstone	Ind.	667,877	39.0
Steven Norris	C.	464,434	27.1
Frank Dobson	Lab.	223,884	13.1
Susan Kramer	LD	203,452	11.9
Ram Gidoomal	CPA	42,060	2.4
Darren Johnson	Green	38,121	2.2
Michael Newland	BNP	33,569	2.0
Damian Hockney	UK Ind.	16,234	1.0
Geoffrey Ben-Nathan	PMSS	9,956	0.6
Ashwin Kumar Tanna	Ind.	9,015	0.5
Geoffrey Clements	Natural Law Party	5,470	0.3

Second Pref	Party	Votes	%
Susan Kramer	LD	404,815	28.5
Frank Dobson	Lab.	228,095	16.0
Darren Johnson	Green	192,764	13.6
Steven Norris	C.	188,041	13.2
Ken Livingstone	Ind.	178,809	12.6
Ram Gidoomal	CPA	56,489	4.0
Michael Newland	BNP	45,337	3.2
Damian Hockney	UK Ind.	43,672	3.1
Ashwin Kumar Tanna	Ind.	41,766	2.9
Geoffrey Ben-Nathan	PMSS	23,021	1.6
Geoffrey Clements	Natural Law Party	18,185	1.3

WALES

THE NATIONAL ASSEMBLY FOR WALES
Cathays Park, Cardiff CF1 3NQ
Tel: 029-2082 5111
National Assembly Information Line: 029-2089 8200
Email: webmaster@wales.gov.uk Web: www.wales.gov.uk

In July 1997 the Government announced plans to
establish a National Assembly for Wales. In a referendum
on 18 September 1997 about 50 per cent of the
electorate voted, of whom 50.3 per cent voted in favour
of the Assembly. Elections are to be held every four years.
The First elections were held on 6 May 1999 when
approximately 46 per cent of the electorate voted. On 1
May 2003 the second Welsh Assembly elections took
place.
   The Assembly has 60 members (including the
Presiding Officer), comprising 40 constituency members
and 20 additional regional members from party lists. It
can introduce only secondary legislation and has no
power to raise or lower income tax.
   The National Assembly for Wales has responsibility in
Wales for ministerial functions relating to health and
personal social services; education, except for terms and
conditions of service and student awards; training; the
Welsh language, arts and culture; the implementation of

the Citizen's Charter in Wales; local government;
housing; water and sewerage; environmental protection;
sport; agriculture and fisheries; forestry; land use,
including town and country planning and countryside
and nature conservation; new towns; non-departmental
public bodies and appointments in Wales; ancient
monuments and historic buildings and the Welsh Arts
Council; roads; tourism; financial assistance to industry;
the Strategic Development Scheme in Wales and the
Programme for the Valleys; and the operation of the
European Regional Development Fund in Wales and
other European Union matters.

SALARIES FROM 1 APRIL 2003:

†First Minister	£71,434
†Minister/Presiding Officer	£37,056
Assembly Members	£42,434*

* Reduced by two-thirds if the member is already an MP or an
MEP
† First Minister, Ministers and Presiding Officer also receive the
Assembly Member salary

THE WELSH ASSEMBLY GOVERNMENT
First Minister of the Assembly, Rhodri Morgan, AM
   Principal Private Secretary, L. Conway
   Special Advisers, Paul Griffiths; Mark Drakeford;
   Dr Rachel Jones; Leslie Punter; Nick Bennett
Minister for Business, Karen Sinclair, AM
Minister for Economic Development and Transport,
   Andrew Davies, AM
Minister for Education and Lifelong Learning,
   Jane Davidson, AM
Minister for Environment, Planning and Countryside,
   Carwyn Jones, AM
Minister for Finance, Local Government and Public Services,
   Sue Essex, AM
Minister for Health and Social Services, Jane Hutt, AM
Minister for Social Justice and Regeneration,
   Edwina Hart, AM
Deputy Minister for Communities, Huw Lewis
Deputy Minister for Older People, John Griffiths
Deputy Minister for Transport, Brian Gibbons
Minister for Culture, Welsh Language and Sport,
   Alan Pugh, AM
Permanent Secretary (G1), Sir John Shortridge

EXECUTIVE BOARD
Senior Director, Social Policy and Local Government Affairs,
   George Craig
Senior Director, Economic Affairs, Transport, Planning and
   Environment, Derek Jones
Counsel General, Winston Roddick, QC
Clerk to the Assembly, Paul Silk
Chief Medical Officer and Head of Health Protection and
   Improvement Directorate, Dr Ruth Hall
Director, Agriculture and Rural Affairs, Huw Brodie
Director, Business Information and Management,
   Bryan Mitchell
Director, Economic Development, David Pritchard
Director, Finance, David Richards
Director, Local Government, Housing and Culture,
   Adam Peat
Director, NHS Directorate, Ann Lloyd
Director, Personnel and Accommodation Services,
   Peter Gregory
Director, Research and Development, Barbara Wilson
Director, Social Policy, Helen Thomas
Director, Training and Education, Richard Davies
Director, Transport, Planning and Environment,
   Martin Evans
Director, Welsh European Funding Office, John Clarke

DEPARTMENTS AND OFFICES
Agriculture and Rural Affairs Department
Communications Directorate
Economic Development Department
Finance Group
Health Protection and Improvement Directorate
Local Government Group
NHS Directorate
Office of the Counsel General
Office of the Presiding Officer
Social Services and Communities Group
Strategic Policy Unit
Training and Education Department
Transport, Planning and Environment Group

EXECUTIVE AGENCIES
CADW: Welsh Historic Momuments
Planning Inspectorate
Welsh European Funding Office

MEMBERS OF THE WELSH ASSEMBLY
as at May 2003

Andrews, Leighton, *Lab., Rhondda,* maj. 7,954
Barrett, Ms Lorraine Jayne, *Lab., Cardiff South and Penarth,* maj. 4,114
Bates, Michael, *LD, Montgomeryshire,* maj. 12,297
Black, Peter, *LD, South Wales West region*
Bourne, Prof. Nicholas, *C., Mid and West Wales region*
Burnham, Mrs Eleanor, *LD, North Wales region*
Butler, Mrs Rosemary Janet Mair, *Lab., Newport West,* maj. 3,752
Cairns, Alun, *C., South Wales West region*
Chapman, Ms Christine, *Lab., Cynon Valley,* maj. 7,117
Cuthbert, Jeffrey, *Lab., Caerphilly,* maj. 4,974
Davidson, Ms Jane Elizabeth, *Lab., Pontypridd,* maj. 6,920
Davies, Andrew David, *Lab., Swansea West,* maj. 2,562
Davies, David Thomas Charles, *C., Monmouth,* maj. 8,510
Davies, Edward, *C., Mid and West Wales region*
Davies, Ms Jocelyn, *PC, South Wales East region*
Davies, Ms Janet, *PC, South Wales West region*
Dunwoody-Kneafsey, Moyra Tamsin, *Lab., Preseli Pembrokeshire,* maj. 1,326
Elis-Thomas, Lord Dafydd, *PC, Meirionnydd Nant Conwy,* maj. 8,742
Essex, Ms Susan Linda, *Lab., Cardiff North,* maj. 540
Francis, Elizabeth Ann (Lisa), *C., Mid and West Wales region*
German, Michael, *LD, South Wales East region*
Gibbons, Brian, *Lab., Aberavon,* maj. 7,813
Graham, William, *C., South Wales East region*
Gregory, Ms Janice, *Lab., Ogmore,* maj. 6,504
Griffiths, Albert John, *Lab., Newport East,* maj. 3,464
Gwyther, Ms Christine Margery, *Lab., Carmarthen West and South Pembrokeshire,* maj. 515
Hart, Ms Edwina, *Lab., Gower,* maj. 5,688
Hutt, Ms Jane, *Lab., Vale of Glamorgan,* maj. 2,653
Idris Jones, Ms Denise, *Lab., Conwy,* maj. 72
Isherwood, Mark, *C., North Wales region*
James, Ms Irene, *Lab., Islwyn,* maj. 7,320
Jones, Alun, *PC, Caernarfon,* maj. 5,905
Jones, Carwyn Howell, *Lab., Bridgend,* maj. 2,421
Jones, Ms Elin, *PC, Ceredigion,* maj. 4,618
Jones, Ms Helen, *PC, Mid and West Wales region*
Jones, Ms Laura Anne, *C., South Wales East region*
Jones, Ms Margaret Ann (Ann), *Lab., Vale of Clwyd,* maj. 3,341
Law, Peter, *Lab., Blaenau Gwent,* maj. 11,736
Lewis, Huw, *Lab., Merthyr Tydfil and Rhymney,* maj. 8,160
Lloyd, Dr David, *PC, South Wales West region*

Lloyd, Mrs Val, *Lab., Swansea East,* maj. 3,997
Marek, Dr John, *John Marek Ind., Wrexham,* maj. 973
Melding, David, *C., South Wales Central region*
Mewies, Mrs Sandra Elaine, *Lab., Delyn,* maj.1,624
Morgan, Hywel Rhodri, *Lab., Cardiff West,* maj. 6,837
Morgan, Jonathan, *C., South Wales Central region*
Neagle, Mrs Lynne, *Lab., Torfaen,* maj. 6,964
Pugh, Alun John, *Lab., Clwyd West,* maj. 436
Randerson, Ms Jennifer Elizabeth, *LD, Cardiff Central,* maj. 7,156
Ryder, Mrs Janet, *PC, North Wales region*
Sergeant, Carl, *Lab., Alyn and Deeside,* maj. 3,503
Sinclair, Ms Karen, *Lab., Clwyd South,* maj. 2,891
Thomas, Ms Catherine, *Lab., Llanelli,* maj. 21
Thomas, Ms Gwenda, *Lab., Neath,* maj. 4,946
Thomas, Owen, *PC, South Wales Central region*
Thomas, Rhodri, *PC, Carmarthen East and Dinefwr,* maj. 4,614
Williams, Byrnle, *C., North Wales region*
Williams, Ms Kirsty, *LD, Brecon and Radnorshire,* maj. 5,308
Wood, Ms Leanne, *PC, South Wales Central region*
Wyn Jones, Ieuan, *PC, Ynys Mon,* maj. 2,255

STATE OF THE PARTIES *as at May 2003*

	Constituency AM	Regional AM AMs	Total
Labour	30	0	30
Plaid Cymru	5†	7	12†
Conservative	1	10	11
Liberal Democrats	3	3	6
Others	1	0	1
The Presiding Officer (The Lord Elis-Thomas)	1	0	1

† Excludes the Presiding Officer, who has no party allegiance while in post

WELSH ASSEMBLY *as at May 2003*

CONSTITUENCIES

ABERAVON (S. WALES WEST)
E. 50,208, T. 37.6%
Brian Gibbons, *Lab.*	11,137
Geraint Owen, *PC*	3,324
Ms Claire Waller, *LD*	1,840
Myr Boult, *C.*	1,732
Robert Williams, *Soc. Alt.*	608
Gwenno Saunders, *Ind. Wales*	114
Lab. majority 7,813	

ALYN AND DEESIDE (WALES N.)
E. 60,518, T. 25.1%
Carl Sergeant, *Lab.*	7,036
Matthew Wright, *C.*	3,533
Paul Brighton, *LD*	2,509
Richard Coombs, *PC*	1,160
William Crawford, *UK Ind.*	826
Lab. majority 3,503	

BLAENAU GWENT (S. WALES EAST)
E. 52,927, T. 37.8%
Peter Law, *Lab.*	13,884
Stephen Bard, *LD*	2,148
Rhys Ab Elis, *PC*	1,889
Barrie O'Keefe, *C.*	1,131
Roger Thomas, *UK Ind.*	719
Lab. majority 11,736	

BRECON AND RADNORSHIRE (WALES MID AND W.)
E. 53,739, T. 50.0%

Ms Kirsty Williams *LD*	13,325
Nicholas Bourne, *C.*	8,017
David Rees, *Lab.*	3,130
Brynach Parri, *PC*	1,329
Ms Elizabeth Phillips, *UK Ind.*	1,042
LD majority 5,308	

BRIDGEND (S. WALES WEST)
E. 62,540, T. 35.4%

Carwyn Howell Jones, *Lab.*	9,487
Alun Hugh Cairns, *C.*	7,066
Ms Cheryl Anne Green, *LD*	2,980
Keith Parry, *PC*	1,939
Timothy Charles Jenkins, *UK Ind.*	677
Lab. majority 2,421	

CAERNARFON (WALES N.)
E. 47,173, T. 45.0%

Alun Ffred Jones, *PC*	11,675
Martin Robert Eaglestone, *Lab.*	5,770
Goronwy Owen Edwards, *C.*	2,402
Stephen William Churchman, *LD*	1,392
PC majority 5,905	

CAERPHILLY (S. WALES EAST)
E. 68,152, T. 37.3%

Jeffrey Cuthbert, *Lab.*	11,893
Lindsay Whittle, *PC*	6,919
Ms Laura Jones, *C.*	2,570
Rob Roffe, *LD*	1,281
Ms Ann Blackman, *Ind.*	1,204
Revd Avril Dafydd-Lewis, *Ind.*	930
Ms Brenda Vipass, *UK Ind.*	590
Lab. majority 4,974	

CARDIFF CENTRAL (S. WALES CENTRAL)
E. 62,470, T. 33.7%

Ms Jennifer Elizabeth Randerson, *LD*	11,256
Geoff Miles Mungham, *Lab.*	4,100
Craig Stuart Piper, *C.*	2,378
Owen John Thomas, *PC*	1,795
Raja Gul Raiz, *Soc. All.*	541
Captain Beany, *Bean*	289
Ms Madeleine Elise Jeremy, *ProLife*	239
LD majority 7,156	

CARDIFF NORTH (S. WALES CENTRAL)
E. 64,528, T. 43.9%

Ms Susan Linda Essex, *Lab.*	10,413
Jonathan Morgan, *C.*	9,873
John Leslie Dixon, *LD*	3,474
Hewel William Wyn Jones, *PC*	2,679
Donald Edwin Hulston, *UK Ind.*	1,295
Lab. majority 540	

CARDIFF SOUTH AND PENARTH (S. WALES CENTRAL)
E. 65,505, T. 31.0%

Ms Lorraine Jayne Barrett, *Lab.*	8,978
Ms Dianne Elizabeth Rees, *C.*	4,864
Rodney Simon Berman, *LD*	3,154
Richard Rhys Grigg, *PC*	2,538
David Charles Bartlett, *Soc. Alt.*	585
Lab. majority 4,114	

CARDIFF WEST (S. WALES CENTRAL)
E. 60,523, T. 35.4%

Hywel Rhodri Morgan, *Lab.*	10,420
Ms Heather Douglas, *C.*	3,583
Ms Jacqueline-Anne Gasson, *LD*	2,914
Ms Eluned Mary Bush, *PC*	2,859
Frank Roger Wynne Hughes, *UK Ind.*	929
Lab. majority 6,837	

CARMARTHEN EAST AND DINEFWR
(WALES MID AND W.)
E. 54,110, T. 49.5%

Rhodri Thomas, *PC*	12,969
Anthony Cooper, *Lab.*	8,355
Harri Lloyd-Davies, *C.*	3,576
Steffan John, *LD*	1,866
PC majority 4,614	

CARMARTHEN WEST AND SOUTH PEMBROKESHIRE
(WALES MID AND W.)
E. 56,403, T. 43.0%

Ms Christine Margery Gwyther, *Lab.*	8,384
Llyr Hughes Griffiths, *PC*	7,869
David Nicholas Thomas, *C.*	4,917
Ms Mary Kathleen Megarry, *LD*	2,222
Arthur Ronald Williams, *Ind.*	580
Lab. majority 515	

CEREDIGION (WALES MID AND W.)
E. 52,940, T. 50.0%

Ms Elin Jones, *PC*	11,883
John Davies, *LD*	7,265
Ms Rhianon Passmore, *Lab.*	3,308
Owen Williams *C.*	2,923
Ian Sheldon, *UK Ind.*	940
PC majority 4,618	

CLWYD SOUTH (WALES N.)
E. 53,452, T. 35.1%

Ms Karen Sinclair, *Lab.*	6,814
Dyfed Edwards, *PC*	3,923
Albert Fox, *C.*	3,548
Marc Jones, *John Marek Ind.*	2,210
Derek Burnham, *LD*	1,666
Ms Edwina Theunissen, *UK Ind.*	501
Lab. majority 2,891	

CLWYD WEST (WALES N.)
E. 54,463, T. 40.6%

Alun John Pugh, *Lab.*	7,693
Brynle Williams, *C.*	7,257
Ms Janet Ryder, *PC*	4,715
Ms Eleanor Burnham, *LD*	1,743
Peter Murray, *UK Ind.*	715
Lab. majority 436	

CONWY (WALES N.)
E. 54,443, T. 38.7%

Ms Denise Idris Jones, *Lab.*	6,467
Gareth Jones, *PC*	6,395
Guto ap Owain Bebb, *C.*	5,152
Graham Rees, *LD*	2,914
Lab. majority 72	

CYNON VALLEY (S. WALES CENTRAL)
E. 44,473, T. 37.5%

Ms Christine Chapman, *Lab.*	10,841
David Alun Walters, *PC*	3,724
Robert Owen Humphreys, *LD*	1,120
Daniel Clive Byron Thomas, *C.*	984
Lab. majority 7,117	

DELYN (WALES N.)
E. 54,426, T. 31.4%
Ms Sandra Elaine Mewies, *Lab.*	6,520
Mark Isherwood, *C.*	4,896
David Lloyd, *LD*	2,880
Paul Rowlinson, *PC*	2,588
Lab. majority 1,624

GOWER (S. WALES WEST)
E. 60,523, T. 39.9%
Ms Edwina Hart, *Lab.*	10,334
Stephen James, *C.*	4,646
Ms Sian Caiach, *PC*	3,502
Nicholas Tregoning, *LD*	2,775
Richard Lewis, *UK Ind.*	2,444
Lab. majority 5,688

ISLWYN (S. WALES EAST)
E. 51,170, T. 40.3%
Ms Irene James, *Lab.*	11,246
Brian Hancock, *C.*	3,926
Paul Taylor, *Tinker against the Assembly*	2,201
Ms Terri-Anne Matthews, *C.*	1,848
Huw Price, *LD*	1,268
Lab. majority 7,320

LLANELLI (WALES MID AND W.)
E. 57,428, T. 40.9%
Ms Catherine Thomas, *Lab.*	9,916
Ms Helen Mary Jones, *PC*	9,895
Gareth Jones, *C.*	1,712
Kenneth Rees, *LD*	1,644
Lab. majority 21

MEIRIONYDD NANT CONWY (WALES MID AND W.)
E. 33,742, T. 45.5%
Lord Dafydd Elis-Thomas, *PC*	8,717
Edwin Woodward, *Lab.*	2,891
Lisa Francis, *C.*	2,485
Kenneth Harris, *LD*	1,100
PC majority 5,826

MERTHYR TYDFIL AND RHYMNEY (S. WALES EAST)
E. 55,768, T. 33.5%
Huw Lewis, *Lab.*	11,148
Alun Cox, *PC*	2,988
John Prosser, *C.*	1,539
Neil Greer, *Ind.*	1,423
John Ault, *LD*	1,324
Lab. majority 8,160

MONMOUTH (S. WALES EAST)
E. 62,451, T. 44.9%
David Thomas Charles Davies, *C.*	15,989
Ms Sian Catherine James, *Lab.*	7,479
Ms Alison Leyland Willott, *LD*	2,973
Stephen Vaughan Thomas, *PC*	1,355
C. majority 8,510

MONTGOMERYSHIRE (WALES MID AND W.)
E. 45,598, T. 43.0%
Michael Bates, *LD*	7,869
Edward Davies, *C.*	5,572
Ms Rina Clarke, *Lab.*	2,039
David Senior, *PC*	1,918
David Rowlands, *UK Ind.*	1,107
Robert Mills, *Ind.*	985
LD majority 2,297

NEATH (S. WALES WEST)
E. 56,759, T. 39.4%
| Ms Gwenda Thomas, *Lab.* | 11,332 |

Alun Llewelyn, *PC*	6,386
Ms Helen Jones, *LD*	2,048
Chris Smart, *C.*	2,011
Huw Pudner, *WSA*	410
Lab. majority 4,946

NEWPORT EAST (S. WALES EAST)
E. 56,563, T. 30.4%
Albert John Griffiths, *Lab.*	7,621
Matthew Robert Hatton Evans, *C.*	4,157
Charles Edward Townsend, *LD*	2,768
Mohammad Asghar, *PC*	1,555
Neal John Reynolds, *UK Ind.*	987
Lab. majority 3,464

NEWPORT WEST (S. WALES EAST)
E. 61,238, T. 35.3%
Ms Rosemary Janet Mair Butler, *Lab.*	10,053
William Graham, *C.*	6,301
Phylip Andrew David Hobson, *LD*	2,094
Anthony Michael Salkeld, *PC*	1,678
Hugh Moelwyn Hughes, *UK Ind.*	1,102
Richard Morse, *WSA*	198
Lab. majority 3,752

OGMORE (S. WALES WEST)
E. 49,565, T. 34.3%
Ms Janice Gregory, *Lab.*	9,874
Ms Janet Marion Davies, *PC*	3,370
Ms Jacqueline Radford, *LD*	1,567
Richard John Hill, *C.*	1,532
Christopher Herriott, *Soc. Lab.*	410
Lab. majority 6,504

PONTYPRIDD (S. WALES CENTRAL)
E. 63,204, T. 38.8%
Ms Jane Elizabeth Davidson, *Lab.*	12,206
Delme Ifor Bowen, *PC*	5,286
Michael John Powell, *LD*	3,443
Ms Jayne Louise Cowan, *C.*	2,438
Peter Manuel Gracia, *UK Ind.*	1,025
Lab. majority 6,920

PRESELI PEMBROKESHIRE (WALES MID AND W.)
E. 55,195, T. 41.7%
Moyra Tamsin Dunwoody-Kneafsey, *Lab.*	8,067
Paul Windsor Davies, *C.*	6,741
Sion Tomos Jobbins, *PC*	5,227
Michael Ian Warden, *LD*	2,799
Lab. majority 1,326

RHONDDA (S. WALES CENTRAL)
E. 50,463, T. 46.0%
Leighton Andrews, *Lab.*	14,170
Geraint Davies, *PC*	6,216
Jeff Gregory, *Ind.*	909
Ms Veronica Watkins, *LD*	680
Dr K. T. Rajan, *UK Ind.*	524
Paul Williams, *C.*	504
Lab. majority 7,954

SWANSEA EAST (S. WALES WEST)
E. 57,252, T. 30.7%
Ms Val Lloyd, *Lab.*	8,221
Peter Black, *LD*	4,224
Dr Dewi Evans, PC	2,223
David Alan Robinson, *UK Ind.*	1,474
Peter Morris, *C.*	1,135
Alan Thomson, *WSA*	133
Lab. majority 3,997

SWANSEA WEST (S. WALES WEST)
E. 58,749, T. 33.3%

Andrew David Davies, *Lab.*	7,023
Dr David Rees Lloyd, *PC*	4,461
Arthur Michael Day, *LD*	3,510
Dorian Rowbottom, *C.*	3,106
David Charles Evans, *UK Ind.*	1,040
David Leigh Richards, *WSA*	272

Lab. majority 2,562

TORFAEN (S. WALES EAST)
E. 61,264, T. 32.1%

Ms Lynne Neagle, *Lab.*	10,152
Nicholas Ramsay, *C.*	3,188
Michael German, *LD*	2,746
Aneurin Preece, *PC*	2,092
David Rowlands, *UK Ind.*	1,377

Lab. majority 6,964

VALE OF CLWYD (WALES N.)
E. 49,319, T. 36.5%

Ms Margaret Ann Jones, *Lab.*	8,256
Darren Millar, *C.*	5,487
Malcom Evans, *PC*	2,516
Ms Robina Feeley, *LD*	1,630

Lab. majority 2,769

VALE OF GLAMORGAN (S. WALES CENTRAL)
E. 68,947, T. 40.7%

Ms Jane Hutt, *Lab.*	12,267
David Melding, *C.*	9,614
Christopher Franks, *PC*	3,921
Ms Nilmini de Silva, *LD*	2,049

Lab. majority 2,653

WREXHAM (WALES N.)
E. 50,508, T. 34.5%

Dr John Marek, *John Marek Ind.*	6,539
Ms Susan Lesley Griffiths, *Lab.*	5,566
Ms Janet Finch-Saunders, *C.*	2,228
Tom Rippeth, *LD*	1,701
Peter Ryder, *PC*	1,329

John Marek Ind. majority 973

YNYS MON (WALES N.)
E. 49,998, T. 51.0%

Ieuan Wyn Jones, *PC*	9,452
Peter Rogers, *C.*	7,197
William Jones, *Lab.*	6,024
Nicholas Bennett, *LD*	2,089
Francis Charles Wykes, *UK Ind.*	481

PC majority 2,255

REGIONS

MID AND WEST WALES
E. 409,155 T. 184,198

PC	51,874 (28.2%)
Lab.	46,451 (25.2%)
C.	35,566 (19.3%)
LD	30,177 (16.4%)
Green	7,794 (4.2%)
UK Ind.	5,945 (3.2%)
Mid and West Wales Pensioners	3,968 (2.2%)
Ind. Wales	1,324 (0.7%)
Vote 2 Stop The War	716 (0.4%)
ProLife	383 (0.2%)

PC majority 5,423
(May 1999 PC Majority 30,712)
Additional Members: Prof. N. Bourne, *C.*, G. Davies, *C.*,
  L. Francis, *C.*, H. Jones, *PC*

NORTH WALES
E. 474,300, T. 175,028

Lab.	55,250 (31.6%)
PC.	41,640 (23.8%)
C.	38,543 (22.0%)
LD	17,503 (10.0%)
John Marek Ind.	11,008 (6.3%)
UK Ind.	4,500 (2.6%)
Green	4,200 (2.4%)
Ind. Wales	1,552 (0.9%)
Comm.	522 (0.3%)
ProLife	310 (0.2%)

Lab. majority 13,610
(May 1999 Lab. Majority 4,155)
Additional Members: E. Burnham, *LD*, M. Isherwood, *C.*,
  J. Ryder, *PC*, B. Williams, *C.*

SOUTH WALES CENTRAL
E. 480,113, T. 181,047

Lab.	74,369 (41.1%)
C.	33,404 (18.5%)
PC	27,956 (15.4%)
LD	24,926 (13.8%)
UK Ind.	6,920 (3.8%)
Green	6,047 (3.3%)
Soc. Lab.	3,217 (1.8%)
Bean	1,027 (0.6%)
Ind. Wales	1,018 (0.6%)
Vote 2 Stop The War	1,013 (0.6%)
Comm.	577 (0.3%)
ProLife	573 (0.3%)

Lab. majority 40,965
(May 1999 Lab. Majority 21,484)
Additional Members: D. Melding, *C.*, J. Morgan, *C.*,
  O. Thomas, *PC*, L. Wood, *PC*

SOUTH WALES EAST
E. 469,533, T. 169,731

Lab.	76,522 (45.1%)
C.	34,231 (20.2%)
PC	21,384 (12.6%)
LD	17,661 (10.4%)
UK Ind.	5,949 (3.5%)
Green	5,291 (3.1%)
Soc. Lab.	3,695 (2.2%)
BNP	3,210 (1.9%)
Ind Wales	1,226 (0.7%)
ProLife	562 (0.3%)

Lab. majority 42,291
(May 1999 Lab. Majority 34,814)
Additional Members: J. Davies, *PC*, M. German, *LD*,
  W. Graham, *C.*, L. A. Jones, *C.*

SOUTH WALES WEST
E. 395,596, T. 23,541

Lab.	58,066 (41.6%)
PD	24,799 (17.8%)
C.	20,981 (15.0%)
LD	17,746 (12.7%)
Green	6,696 (4.8%)
UK Ind.	6,113 (4.4%)
Soc. Lab.	3,446 (2.5%)
Ind. Wales	1,346 (1.0%)
ProLife	355 (0.3%)

Lab. majority 33,267
(May 1999 Lab. Majority 19,868)
Additional Members: P. Black, *LD*, A. Cairns, *C.*,
  J. Davies, *PC*, D. Lloyd, *PC*

NORTHERN IRELAND

NORTHERN IRELAND ASSEMBLY

Parliament Buildings, Stormont, Belfast BT4 3XX
Tel: 028-9052 1333 Fax: 028-9052 1961
Web: www.ni-assembly.gov.uk

The Assembly was suspended from midnight on 14 October 2002 and was dissolved on 28 April 2003. The Secretary of State assumed responsibility for the direction of the Northern Ireland departments. The following is an overview of the organisation and structure of the Assembly, which applied when it was operational, and will apply should it be reinstated. Talks to discuss the future of the Assembly have been scheduled to take place in October 2003.

The Assembly has 108 members elected by single transferable vote (six from each of the 18 Westminster constituencies). The first elections took place on 25 June 1998 and members met for the first time on 1 July. Safeguards ensure that key decisions have cross-community support. The executive powers of the Assembly are discharged by an Executive Committee comprising a First Minister and Deputy First Minister (jointly elected by the Assembly on a cross-community basis) and up to ten ministers with departmental responsibilities. Ministerial posts are allocated on the basis of the number of seats each party holds.

The Assembly met in shadow form, pending the establishment of an Executive and the transfer of powers from Parliament. Following devolution it has executive and legislative authority over those areas formerly the responsibility of the Northern Ireland government departments.

Power was initially due to be transferred to the new Executive on 10 March 1999, but disagreements emerged over whether Sinn Fein should be allowed to enter the Executive before IRA weapons had been decommissioned. Further deadlines of 2 April and 30 June were also missed. On 15 July the Assembly met to nominate ministers, with the transfer of power to follow on 18 July. However, as the decommissioning issue had still not been resolved, Unionists failed to nominate ministers (the UUP boycotting the meeting itself) and the process collapsed. On 20 July the two prime ministers announced a review of the implementation of the Agreement to be facilitated by Senator George Mitchell. The scope of the review was tightly drawn, focusing only on the practical implementation of the three principles set out above, effectively decommissioning the Executive. The timing of the review dove-tailed with the inevitably sensitive publication of the Patten Commission's report on policing.

Following a series of meetings involving the parties in London, Mitchell's interim report of 15 November stated that he was increasingly more confident that the parties could find a way through the impasse.

On 18 November, following statements from the UUP, Sinn Fein and the IRA, Senator Mitchell concluded the review indicating that he now believed there was a basis for devolution to occur, for the institutions to be established and for decommissioning to take place as soon as possible. He concluded that devolution should take effect, the Executive Committee should meet and paramilitary organisations should appoint their authorised representatives to the IICD in that order and all in the same day. On 20 November the Secretary of State announced support for the Mitchell proposals and stated that the Assembly should meet on 29 November for the purpose of running d'Hondt procedure for appointing shadow ministers and devolution should take effect after the necessary Parliamentary procedures had been completed on 2 December 1999.

Powers were devolved to Assembly and other institutions established on 2 December on a basis agreed by the parties during the Mitchell review. The Mitchell review created the expectation that the establishment of the institutions and the appointment of authorised representatives produced conditions in which Sinn Fein could influence bringing about the start of decommissioning. But it was a matter of political reality that if decommissioning did not occur by the end of January it would be very difficult for David Trimble to continue as leader of the Ulster Unionist Party beyond this. In late November the Council of the UUP had endorsed the Mitchell outcome but, reflecting the political reality, also recommended that progress on the timing and modalities of decommissioning be reviewed at the end of January 2000 through reports presented to the two governments by the IICD.

Devolution and the institutions were able to flourish on the basis of sufficient cross community support. Unfortunately that support began to ebb when the anticipated progress on decommissioning failed to materialise at the end of January. The two Governments took receipt of General de Chastelain's 31 January report but held back publication in order to explore any hope of credible progress on decommissioning. Both governments tried further efforts to gain clarity on the decommissioning issue.

The Secretary of State announced the suspension legislation on 3 February and warned publicly that it would come into effect on Friday 11 February. On the morning of 11 February, there was some sign that a new IRA proposal was emerging. The Irish Government presented a new position from its leadership. There were still only words and no timescale, but it did include clearer and less equivocal words than before. Unfortunately this was not enough to avert the collapse of the institutions.

Suspension meant that the Assembly could not meet or conduct any business. Parliament Buildings remained open for use by Assembly Members for the purpose of carrying out constituency work and they continued to be paid salaries and allowances – set at the lower pre-devolution shadow rate to reflect the suspension of Assembly business.

Following a period of intensive discussions with pro-Agreement parties during 4 and 5 May at Hillsborough, the Prime Minister and Taoiseach issued a joint statement committing both Government's proposals. On May 6, the IRA responded with a significant and forthcoming statement in which they recognised that:

– the implementation of what the Governments had agreed would provide a new context in which Republicans could pursue their political objectives peacefully.

– in that new context the IRA leadership would initiate a process that would completely and verifiably put arms beyond use.

– the IRA would renew contact with the Decommissioning Commission.

– agreed, as a confidence building measure, to open a number of arms dumps to independent inspectors reporting to the Decommissioning Commission on a regular basis to verify that arms remain secure.

The pro-Agreement parties welcomed these developments. The UUP leader, David Trimble said that the IRA statement "appeared to break new ground". The Prime Minister and the Taoiseach announced on 8 May that they were asking the former Finnish President Martti Ahtisaari and Cyril Ramaphosa, the ANC negotiator, to become the independent inspectors. On 9 May, the Chief Constable of the RUC recognised that the IRA statement marked a significant reduction in the overall threat and announced a number of measures, spread across Northern Ireland, designed as a return to more normal policing.

The Government published the Police Bill on 16 May and gave assurances to Unionists that the legal description of the new police service would incorporate the RUC, while the operational and working name would change to Police Service of Northern Ireland. The Government also took an enabling power to resolve the flying of flags over Government buildings if the devolved Executive could not.

A week later than originally envisaged the Ulster Unionist Council endorsed the Government's proposals on 27 May and devolved government was restored to Northern Ireland with effect from midnight on 29 May 2000.

Following considerable political unrest, David Trimble resigned as Northern Ireland First Minister on 1 July 2001, followed on 18 October by other UUP Ministers. His resignation was an ultimatum to encourage the IRA to start decommissioning their weapons. The administrative elements of his post passed to Sir Reg Empey.

To allow time to resolve this situation the Secretary of State for Northern Ireland ordered 24-hour suspensions of the Assembly on 10 August and 22 September 2001. On 5 November 2001 this period was concluded when David Trimble was elected as First Minister and Mark Durkan was elected as Deputy First Minister to replace Seamus Mallon who had retired.

NORTHERN IRELAND EXECUTIVE
Castle Buildings, Stormont Belfast BT4 3SG
Tel: 028-9052 0700 Fax 028-9052 8195
Web: www.northernireland.gov.uk

During suspension the following departments fall under the control of the Secretary of State for Northern Ireland and his Northern Ireland Office Ministerial team.

Secretary of State for Northern Ireland, The Rt. Hon. Paul Murphy, MP
Minister of State, Jane Kennedy *(Security and Policing, Education, and Employment and Learning)*
Minister of State, John Spellar *(Social Development, and Regional Development)*
Parliamentary Under-Secretary, Ian Pearson *(Europe, Agriculture and Rural Development, Finance and Personnel, and Enterprise, Trade and Investment)*
Parliamentary Under-Secretary, Angela Smith *(Health, Social Services and Public Safety, and Culture, Arts and Leisure)*

OFFICE OF THE FIRST MINISTER AND DEPUTY MINISTER
Stormont Castle, Stormont Estate, Belfast BT4 3TT
Tel: 028-9052 8400 Web: www.ofmdfmni.gov.uk

DEPARTMENT OF AGRICULTURE AND RURAL DEVELOPMENT
Dundonald House, Upper Newtownards Road, Belfast BT4 3SB
Tel: 028-9052 4999 Fax: 028-9052 5003
Web: www.dardni.gov.uk

EXECUTIVE AGENCIES
RIVERS AGENCY, 4 Hospital Road, Belfast BT8 8JP
Tel: 028-9025 3355
FOREST SERVICE, Dundonald House, Belfast BT4 3SB
Tel: 028-9052 4822

DEPARTMENT OF CULTURE, ARTS AND LEISURE
3rd Floor, Interpoint, 20–24 York Street, Belfast BT15 1AQ
Tel: 028-9025 8825 Fax: 028-9025 8906
Web: www.dcalni.gov.uk

EXECUTIVE AGENCIES
THE PUBLIC RECORD OFFICE OF NORTHERN IRELAND,
66 Balmoral Avenue, Belfast BT9 6NY Tel: 028-9025 1318
Fax: 028-9025 5999
THE ORDNANCE SURVEY OF NORTHERN IRELAND,
Colby House, Stranmillis Court, Belfast BT9 5BJ
Tel: 028-9025 5755 Fax: 028-9025 5700

DEPARTMENT OF EDUCATION
Rathgael House, 43 Balloo Road, Bangor, Co. Down BT19 7PR
Tel: 028-9127 9279 Fax: 028-9127 9100
Web: www.deni.gov.uk

DEPARTMENT FOR EMPLOYMENT AND LEARNING
39/49 Adelaide House, Adelaide Street, Belfast BT2 8FD
Tel: 028-9025 7793 Fax: 028-9025 7795
Web: www.delni.gov.uk

DEPARTMENT OF ENTERPRISE, TRADE AND INVESTMENT
Netherleigh, Massey Avenue, Belfast BT4 2JP
Tel: 028-9052 9900 Fax: 028-9052 9550

DEPARTMENT OF THE ENVIRONMENT FOR NORTHERN IRELAND
Clarence Court, 10–18 Adelaide Street, Belfast BT2 8GB
Tel: 028-90540 540 Web: www.doeni.gov.uk

EXECUTIVE AGENCIES
Driver and Licensing Agency (Northern Ireland)
Driver and Vehicle Testing Agency (Northern Ireland)
Environment and Heritage Service
Planning Service

DEPARTMENT OF FINANCE AND PERSONNEL
Rathgael House, Balloo Road, Bangor BT19 7NA
Tel: 028-9127 9279 Web: www.dfpni.gov.uk

EXECUTIVE AGENCIES
BUSINESS DEVELOPMENT SERVICE, Craigantlet Buildings,
Stoney Road, Belfast BT4 3SX Tel: 028-9052 0444
LAND REGISTERS OF NORTHERN IRELAND,
Lincoln Building, 27–45 Great Victoria Street, Belfast BT2 7SL
Tel: 028-9025 1515
NORTHERN IRELAND STATISTICS AND RESEARCH
AGENCY*, McAuley House, 2–14 Castle Street, Belfast
BT1 1SA Tel: 028-9034 8100
RATE COLLECTION AGENCY, Oxford House, 49–55
Chichester Street, Belfast BT1 4HH Tel: 028-9025 2252
VALUATION AND LANDS AGENCY, Queen's Court, 56-66
Upper Queen Street, Belfast BT1 6FD Tel: 028-9025 0700
* Incorporates the General Register Office (Northern Ireland),
Oxford House, 49–55 Chichester Street, Belfast BT1 4HH
Tel: 028-9025 2000

DEPARTMENT OF HEALTH SOCIAL SERVICES
AND PUBLIC SAFETY NORTHERN IRELAND
Castle Buildings, Stormont, Belfast BT4 3SJ
Tel: 028-9052 0000 Fax: 028-9052 0573
Web: www.dhsspsni.gov.uk

EXECUTIVE AGENCIES
Northern Ireland Health and Social Services Estates
Agency

DEPARTMENT FOR REGIONAL DEVELOPMENT
Clarence Court, 10–18 Adelaide Street, Belfast BT2 8GB
Tel: 028-9054 0540 Fax: 028-9054 0064
Web: www.drdni.gov.uk

DEPARTMENT FOR SOCIAL DEVELOPMENT
Churchill House, Victoria Square, Belfast BT1 4SD
Tel: 028-9056 9100 Web: www.dsdni.gov.uk

NORTHERN IRELAND ASSEMBLY
MEMBERS *as at 28 April 2003*

Adams, Gerry, *(SF), West Belfast*
Adamson, Dr Ian, *(UUP), East Belfast*
*Agnew, Fraser, *(UUAP), North Belfast*
Alderdice, Lord, *(Speaker), East Belfast*
††Armitage, Ms Pauline, *(Ind. Unionist), East Londonderry*
Armstrong, Billy, *(UUP), Mid Ulster*
Attwood, Alex, *(SDLP), West Belfast*
Beggs, Roy, *(UUP), East Antrim*
Bell, Billy, *(UUP), Lagan Valley*
Bell, Eileen, *(All.), North Down*
Berry, Paul, *(DUP), Newry and Armagh*
Birnie, Dr Esmond, *(UUP), South Belfast*
†Boyd, Norman, *(NIUP), South Antrim*
Bradley, P. J., *(SDLP), South Down*
Byrne, Joe, *(SDLP), West Tyrone*
Campbell, Gregory, *(DUP), East Londonderry*
Carrick, Mervyn, *(DUP), Upper Bann*
Carson, Ms Joan, *(UUP), Fermanagh and South Tyrone*
Close, Seamus, *(All.), Lagan Valley*
Clyde, Wilson, *(DUP), South Antrim*
Cobain, Fred, *(UUP), North Belfast*
Coulter, Revd Robert, *(UUP), North Antrim*
**Courtney, Anne, *(Ind.), Foyle*
Coyle, Michael, *(SDLP), East Derry*
Dallat, John, *(SDLP), East Londonderry*
Davis, Ivan, *(UUP), Lagan Valley*
De Brun, Ms Bairbre, *(SF), West Belfast*
Dodds, Nigel, *(DUP), North Belfast*
Doherty, Pat, *(SF), West Tyrone*
*Douglas, Boyd, *(UUAP), East Londonderry*
Durkan, Mark, *(SDLP), Foyle*
Empey, Sir Reg, *(UUP), East Belfast*
Ervine, David, *(PUP), East Belfast*
Farren, Dr Sean, *(SDLP), North Antrim*
Fee, John, *(SDLP), Newry and Armagh*
Ford, David, *(All.), South Antrim*
Foster, Sam, *(UUP), Fermanagh and South Tyrone*
Gallagher, Tommy, *(SDLP), Fermanagh and South Tyrone*
Gibson, Oliver, *(DUP), West Tyrone*
Gildernew, Michelle, *(SF), Fermanagh and South Tyrone*
‡Gorman, Sir John, *(UUP), North Down*
Hanna, Carmel. *(SDLP), South Belfast*
***Hamilton, Tom, *(UUP), Strangford*
Haughey, Denis, *(SDLP), Mid Ulster*
Hay, William, *(DUP), Foyle*
Hendron, Dr Joe, *(SDLP), West Belfast*
Hilditch, David, *(DUP), East Antrim*
Hussey, Derek, *(UUP), West Tyrone*
Hutchinson, Billy, *(PUP), North Belfast*
§Hutchinson, Roger, *(Ind. Unionist), East Antrim*

Kane, Gardiner, *(Ind. Unionist), North Antrim*
Kelly, Gerry, *(SF), North Belfast*
Kelly, John, *(SF), Mid Ulster*
Kennedy, Danny, *(UUP), Newry and Armagh*
Leslie, James, *(UUP), North Antrim*
Lewsley, Patricia, *(SDLP), Lagan Valley*
Maginness, Alban, *(SDLP), North Belfast*
Mallon, Séamus, *(SDLP), Newry and Armagh*
Maskey, Alex, *(SF), West Belfast*
McCarthy, Kieran, *(All.), Strangford*
McCartney, Robert, *(UKUP), North Down*
McClarty, David, *(UUP), East Londonderry*
McCrea, Revd William, *(DUP), Mid Ulster*
‡McClelland, Donovan, *(SDLP), South Antrim*
McDonnell, Dr Alasdair, *(SDLP), South Belfast*
McElduff, Barry, *(SF), West Tyrone*
McFarland, Alan, *(UUP), North Down*
McGimpsey, Michael, *(UUP), South Belfast*
McGrady, Eddie, *(SDLP), South Down*
McGuinness, Martin, *(SF), Mid Ulster*
McHugh, Gerry, *(SF), Fermanagh and South Tyrone*
McLaughlin, Mitchell, *(SF), Foyle*
McMenamin, Eugene, *(SDLP), West Tyrone*
McNamee, Pat, *(SF), Newry and Armagh*
McWilliams, Prof. Monica, *(NIWC), South Belfast*
Molloy, Francie, *(SF), Mid Ulster*
Murphy, Connor, *(SF), Newry and Armagh*
Murphy, Mick, *(SF), South Down*
‡Morrice, Ms Jane, *(NIWC), North Down*
Morrow, Maurice, *(DUP), Fermanagh and South Tyrone*
Neeson, Sean, *(All.), East Antrim*
Nelis, Ms Mary, *(SF), Foyle*
Nesbitt, Dermot, *(UUP), South Down*
O'Connor, Danny, *(SDLP), East Antrim*
O'Hagan, Dara, *(SF), Upper Bann*
O'Neill, Eamonn, *(SDLP), South Down*
Paisley, Revd Dr Ian, *(DUP), North Antrim*
Paisley, Ian Jnr., *(DUP), North Antrim*
Poots, Edwin, *(DUP), Lagan Valley*
Ramsey, Sue, *(SF), West Belfast*
Robinson, Iris, *(DUP), Strangford*
Robinson, Ken, *(UUP), East Anrtim*
Robinson, Mark, *(DUP), South Belfast*
Robinson, Peter, *(DUP), East Belfast*
†Roche, Patrick, *(NIUP), Lagan Valley*
Rodgers, Ms Brid, *(SDLP), Upper Bann*
Savage, George, *(UUP), Upper Bann*
Shannon, Jim, *(DUP), Strangford*
Shipley-Dalton, Duncan, *(UUP), South Antrim*
Taylor, The Rt. Hon. John, *(UUP), Strangford*
Tierney, John, *(SDLP), Foyle*
Trimble, The Rt. Hon. David, *(UUP), Upper Bann*
Watson, Denis, *(UUAP), Upper Bann*
§§Weir, Peter, *(DUP), North Down*
Wells, Jim, *(DUP), South Down*
†Wilson, Cedric, *(NIUP), Strangford*
Wilson, Jim, *(UUP) South Antrim*
Wilson, Sammy, *(DUP), East Belfast*

* Elected as independent candidates, formed the United
Unionist Assembly Party (UUAP) with effect from 21
September 1998
† Elected as UK Unionist Candidates, formed Northern Ireland
Unionist Party (NIUP) with effect from 15 January 1999
‡ Elected as Deputy Speakers of the Northern Ireland
Assembly 31 January 2000
§ Roger Hutchinson was expelled from the Northern Ireland
Unionist Party (NIUP) with effect from 2 December 1999
** John Hume, MP, MEP, resigned from the Northern Ireland
Assembly with effect from 1 December 2000. He was replaced
by Anne Courtney
*** Tom Benson died on 24 December 2000. He was replaced
by Tom Hamilton

†† Pauline Armitage was suspended from the UUP with effect from 9 November 2001 and became an Independent Unionist with effect from 30 April 2002

§§ Peter Weir ceased to be a member of the UUP with effect from 9 November 2001 and became a member of the DUP with effect from 30 April 2002

POLITICAL COMPOSITION

UUP	Ulster Unionist Party	26
SDLP	Social Democratic and Labour Party	23
DUP	Democratic Unionist Party	22
SF	Sinn Féin	18
All	Alliance	5
NIUP	Northern Ireland Unionist Party	3
UUAP	United Unionist Assembly Party	3
NIWC	Northern Ireland Women's Coalition	2
PUP	Progressive Unionist Party	2
UKUP	UK Unionist Party	1
Ind. Unionist	Independent Unionist	2
Ind.	Independent	1

THE NORTHERN IRELAND ASSEMBLY *as at July 2000*

CONSTITUENCIES
* Indicates those who were elected

ANTRIM EAST
E. 59,313; *T.* 60.87%
Number of Valid Votes: 35,610
Quota: 5,088
*Roy Beggs, *UUP*
Stewart Dickson, *All.*
*Sean Neeson *All.*
Terence Dick, *C.*
*David Hilditch, *DUP*
Jack McKee, *DUP*
James McKissock, *NLP*
Robert Mason, *Pro-Agree*
William Greer, *PUP*
*Danny O'Connor, *SDLP*
Chrissy McAuley, *SF*
Tommy Kirkham, *UDP*
*Roger Hutchinson, *UKU*
James Brown, *Unionist*
*Ken Robinson, *UUP*
May Steele, *UUP*

ANTRIM NORTH
E. 73,163; *T.* 67.92%
Number of Valid Votes: 49,697
Quota: 7,100
Jayne Dunlop, *All.*
*Gardiner Kane, *DUP*
*Revd Dr Ian Paisley, *DUP*
*Ian Paisley, *DUP*
Oliver McMullan, *Ind. Nat.*
Richard Rodgers, *PUP*
*Sean Farren, *SDLP*
Malachy McCamphill, *SDLP*
Joe Chaill, *SF*
James McCarry, *SF*
Maurice McAllister, *UDP*
William Wright, *United*
Patricia Campbell, *UUP*
*Revd Robert Coulter, *UUP*
*James Leslie, *UUP*

ANTRIM SOUTH
E. 69,297; *T.* 63.48%
Number of Valid Votes: 43,991
Quota: 6,285

*David Ford, *All.*
*Wilson Clyde, *DUP*
Stuart Deigan, *DUP*
M. Oliver Frawely, *Lab.*
Joan Cosgrove, *NI Women*
George Stidolph, *NLP*
Ken Wilkinson, *PUP*
Tommy Burns, *SDLP*
*Donovan McClelland, *SDLP*
Martin Meehan, *SF*
*Norman Boyd, *UKU*
John Hunter, *UUP*
*Duncan Shipley-Dalton, *UUP*
*Jim Wilson, *UUP*

BELFAST EAST
E. 60,432; *T.* 65.51%
Number of Valid Votes: 39,593
Quota: 5,657
*The Lord Alderdice of Knock, *All.*
Richard Good, *All.*
Lesley Donaldson, *C.*
John Norris, *DUP*
*Peter Robinson, *DUP*
*Sammy Wilson, *DUP*
John Lawrence, *Energy*
David Bleakley, *Lab.*
Pearl Sager, *NI Women*
David Collins, *NLP*
*David Ervine, *PUP*
Dawn Purvis, *PUP*
Peter Jones, *SDLP*
Joe Donnell, *SF*
Robert Girvan, *UDP*
Denny Vitty, *UKU*
*Ian Adamson, *UUP*
*Reg Empey, *UUP*
Jim Rodgers, *UUP*
Joe Bell, *WP*

BELFAST NORTH
E. 62,435; *T.* 65.86%
Number of Valid Votes: 41,125
Quota: 5,876
Glyn Roberts, *All.*
*Nigel Dodds, *DUP*
Eric Smyth, *DUP*
Peter Emerson, *Green*
Delores Quinn, *Ind. NCC*
Sam McAughtry, *Lab.*
Kevin Blair, *NLP*
*Billy Hutchinson, *PUP*
*Alban Maginness, *SDLP*
Martin, Morgan, *SDLP*
*Gerry Kelly, *SF*
Martina McIlkenny, *SF*
John White, *UDP*
Stephen Cooper, *UKU*
*Fraser Agnew, *UU*
David Browne, *UUP*
*Fred Cobain, *UUP*
Steven Doran, *WP*

BELFAST SOUTH
E. 61,001; *T.* 66.75%
Number of Valid Votes: 40,724
Quota: 5,818
Steve McBride, *All.*
Roger Lomas, *C.*
Myreve Chambers, *DUP*
*Mark Robinson, *DUP*
Boyd Black, *Lab.*

Niall Cusack, *Lab.*
*Monica McWilliams, *NI Women*
James Anderson, *NLP*
Ernie Purvis, *PUP*
*Carmel Hanna, *SDLP*
*Alasdair McDonnell, *SDLP*
Sean Hayes, *SF*
David Adams, *UDP*
Grant Dillon, *UKU*
William Dixon, *Unionist*
*Esmond Birnie, *UUP*
Jim Clark, *UUP*
*Michael McGimpsey, *UUP*
Paddy Lynn, *WP*

BELFAST WEST
E. 60,542; *T.* 69.03%
Number of Valid Votes: 41,794
Quota: 5,971
Dan McGuiness, *All.*
Margaret Ferris, *DUP*
Michael Kennedy, *NLP*
Hugh Smyth, *PUP*
*Alex Attwood, *SDLP*
*Dr Joe Hendron, *SDLP*
*Gerry Adams, *SF*
*Bairbre De Brun, *SF*
Michael Ferguson, *SF*
*Alex Maskey, *SF*
*Sue Ramsey, *SF*
Mary Cahillane, *Soc.*
Thomas Dalzell-Sheridan, *UKU*
Chris McGimpsey, *UUP*
John Lowry, *WP*

DOWN NORTH
E. 62,785; *T.* 59.42%
Number of Valid Votes: 37,313
Quota: 5,331
*Eileen Bell, *All.*
Gavin Walker, *All.*
Leonard Fee, *C.*
Alan Graham, *DUP*
St. Clair McAlister, *DUP*
Brian Wilson, *Ind.*
Vanessa Baird-Gunning, *Lab.*
*Jane Morrice, *NI Women*
Andrea Gribben, *NLP*
Stewart Currie, *PUP*
Mariette Farrell, *SDLP*
Tom Lindsey, *UDP*
Christopher Carter, *UIV*
*Robert McCartney, *UKUP*
Elizabeth Roche, *UKU*
Ann Chambers, *Ind. Unionist*
*John Gorman, *UUP*
*Alan McFarland, *UUP*
*Peter Weir, *UUP*

DOWN SOUTH
E. 70,864; *T.* 72.46%
Number of Valid Votes: 51,353
Quota: 7,337
Anne-Marie Cunningham, *All.*
*Jim Wells, *DUP*
Patrick O'Connor, *Ind. Lab.*
Malachi Curran, *Lab.*
Anne Carr, *NI Women*
Thoma Mullins, *NLP*
*Patrick Bradley, *SDLP*
Hugh Carr, *SDLP*
*Eddie McGrady, *SDLP*

*Eamon O'Neill, *SDLP*
*Mick Murphy, *SF*
Garret O'Fachtna, *SF*
Frederick Wharton, *UKU*
George Graham, *Unionist*
Norman Hanna, *UUP*
*Dermot Nesbitt, *UUP*
Desmond O'Hagan, *WP*

FERMANAGH AND SOUTH TYRONE
E. 65,241; *T.* 78.23%
Number of Valid Votes: 51,043
Quota: 7,292
Stephen Farry, *All.*
Bert Johnston, *DUP*
*Maurice Morrow, *DUP*
Marie Crawley, *NI Women*
Simeon Gillan, *NLP*
*Tommy Gallagher, *SDLP*
Olive Mullen, *SDLP*
*Michelle Gildernew, *SF*
*Gerry McHugh, *SF*
Pat Treanor, *SF*
Jim Dixon, *UKU*
*Joan Carson, *UUP*
*Sam Foster, *UUP*
Bertie Kerr, *UUP*

FOYLE
E. 68,723; *T.* 71%
Number of Valid Votes: 48,794
Quota: 6,971
Colm Cavanagh, *All.*
*William Hay, *DUP*
Peter MacKenzie, *Green*
Ken Adams, *Lab.*
Donn Brennan, *NLP*
Brian Gurney, *PUP*
Anne Courtney, *SDLP*
*Mark Durkan, *SDLP*
*John Hume, *SDLP*
*John Tierney, *SDLP*
Lynn Fleming, *SF*
*Mitchell McLaughlin, *SF*
*Mary Nelis, *SF*
Georoid O'Heara, *SF*
Jack Allen, *SF*

LAGAN VALLEY
E. 71,525; *T.* 65.02%
Number of Valid Votes: 46,510
Quota: 6,645
*Seamus Close, *All.*
William Bleakes, *C.*
Cecil Calvert, *DUP*
*Edwin Poots, *DUP*
Annie Campbell, *NI Women*
John Cairns, *NLP*
*Patricia Lewsley, *SDLP*
Paul Butler, *SF*
Gary McMichael, *UDP*
*Patrick Roche, *UKU*
*Billy Bell, *UUP*
David Campbell, *UUP*
*Ivan Davis, *UUP*
Ken Hull, *UUP*
Frances McCarty, *WP*

LONDONDERRY EAST
E. 59,216; T. 66.81%
Number of Valid Votes: 39,564
Quota: 5,653
Barbara Dempsey, *All.*
*Gregory Campbell, *DUP*
George Robinson, *DUP*
Maura McCann, *NLP*
David Gilmour, *PUP*
*John Dallat, *SDLP*
*Arthur Doherty, *SDLP*
John McAlhenny, *SF*
Malachy O'Kane, *SF*
David Nicholl, *UDP*
*Boyd Douglas, *UI*
*Pauline Armitage, *UUP*
*David McClarty, *UUP*
Robert McPherson, *UUP*

NEWRY AND ARMAGH
E. 71,450; T. 75.76%
Number of Valid Votes: 54,136
Quota: 7,734
Pete Whitcroft, *All.*
*Paul Berry, *DUP*
Mary Allen, *Ind.*
Kate Fearon, *NI Women*
David Evans, *NLP*
*John Fee, *SDLP*
Frank Feeley, *SDLP*
*Seamus Mallon, *SDLP*
Davy Hyland, *SF*
*Pat McNamee, *SF*
*Conor Murphy, *SF*
William Fraser, *UI*
*Danny Kennedy, *UUP*
Jim Speers, *UUP*

STRANGFORD
E. 70,746; T. 60.67%
Number of Valid Votes: 42,922
Quota: 6,132
*Kieran McCarthy, *All.*
Peter Osborne, *All.*
Thomas Beattie, *C.*
Tommy Jeffers, *DUP*
*Iris Robinson, *DUP*
*Jim Shannon, *DUP*
Andrew Frew, *Green*
Agnes Orr, *Ind. CC*
John Beattie, *Ind. UU*
Jonathan Stewart, *Lab..*
Sarah Mullins, *NLP*
Ricky Johnston, *PUP*
Brian Hanvey, *SDLP*
Paddy McGreevy, *SF*
Blakely McNally, *UDP*
*Cedric Wilson, *UKU*
Wibert Magill, *Unionist*
*Thomas Benson, *UUP*
Ton Hamilton, *UUP*
David McNarry, *UUP*
*John Taylor, *UUP*

TYRONE WEST
E. 58,976; T. 77.91%
Number of Valid Votes: 45,951
Quota: 6,565
Ann Gormely, *All.*
Laurence O'Kane, *CECC*
*Oliver Gibson, *DUP*
Paddy McGown, *Ind. Comm*
Robert Johnstone, *NLP*

*Joe Byrne, *SDLP*
Pat McDonnell, *SDLP*
*Eugene McMenamin, *SDLP*
Seamus Devine, *SF*
*Pat Doherty, *SF*
*Barry McElduff, *SF*
Johnny McLaughlin, *Soc.*
*Derek Hussey, *UUP*
Alasdair Patterson, *UUP*
Tommy Owens, *WP*

ULSTER MID
E. 59,850; T. 83.20%
Number of Valid Votes: 49,798
Quota: 7,115
Yvonne Boyle, *All.*
*Revd William McCrea, *DUP*
Paul MCLean, *DUP*
Mary Daly, *NLP*
*Denis Haughey, *SDLP*
Patsy McGlone, *SDLP*
*John Kelly, *SF*
*Martin McGuinness, *SF*
*Francie Molloy, *SF*
Harry Hutchinson, *Soc.*
*Billy Armstrong, *UUP*
John Junkin, *UUP*
Francie Donnelly, *WP*

UPPER BANN
E. 70,697; T. 71.28%
Number of Valid Votes: 50,399
Quota: 7,200
Frank McQuaid, *All.*
Ruth Allen, *DUP*
*Mervyn Carrick, *DUP*
Brian Silcock, *Ind.*
Alan Evans, *Lab..*
Jack Lyons, *NLP*
Mel Bryne, *SDLP*
*Brid Rodgers, *SDLP*
Francie Murray, *SF*
*Dara O'Hagan, *SF*
Kenny McClinton, *UI*
David Vance, *UKU*
Sam Gardiner, *UUP*
Mark Neale, *UUP*
*George Savage, *UUP*
*David Trimble, *UUP*
*Denis Watson, *UUP*
Tom French, *WP*

SCOTLAND

THE SCOTTISH PARLIAMENT
Edinburgh EH99 1SP
Tel: 0131-348 5000
Email: sp.info@scottish.parliament.uk
Web: www.scottish.parliament.uk

In July 1997 the Government announced plans to establish a Scottish Parliament. In a referendum on 11 September 1997 about 62 per cent of the electorate voted, of whom 74.3 per cent voted in favour of the Parliament and 63.5 in favour of its having tax-raising powers. Elections are to be held every four years. The first elections were held on 6 May 1999 when about 59 per cent of the electorate voted. The first session was held on 12 May 1999 and the Scottish Parliament was officially opened on 1 July 1999 at the Edinburgh Assembly Hall; a new building to house the Parliament is under construction in Edinburgh. On 1 May 2003 the second elections to the Scottish Parliament took place.

The Scottish Parliament has 129 members (including the Presiding Officer), comprising 73 constituency members and 56 additional regional members from party lists. It can introduce primary legislation and has the power to raise or lower the basic rate of income tax by up to three pence in the pound.

The Scottish Parliament is responsible for: education, health, law, environment, economic development, local government, housing, police, fire services, planning, financial assistance to industry, tourism, some transport, heritage and the arts, agriculture, forestry and food standards.

SALARIES FROM 1 APRIL 2003:

First Minister	£71,433*
Ministers	£37,056*
Lord Advocate	£48,418*
Solicitor-General for Scotland	£35,006*
Junior Ministers	£23,210*
MSPs	£49,315†
Presiding Officer	£37,056*
Deputy Presiding Officers	£23,210*

* In addition to the MSP salary of £49,315
† Reduced by two-thirds if the member is already an MP or an MEP

THE SCOTTISH EXECUTIVE

St Andrew's House, Regent Road, Edinburgh EH1 3DG
Tel: 0131-556 8400 Email: ceu@scotland.gov.uk
Web: www.scotland.gov.uk

The Scottish Executive is the devolved government for Scotland. It is responsible for most of the issues of day-to-day concern to the people of Scotland, including health, education, justice, rural affairs and transport and manages an annual budget of around £20 billion.

The Executive was established in 1999, following the first elections to the Scottish Parliament. It is a coalition between the Scottish Lab.our Party and the Scottish Liberal Democrat Party.

The Executive is led by a First Minister who is nominated by the Parliament and in turn appoints the other Scottish Ministers.

Scottish Executive civil servants are accountable to Scottish Ministers, who are themselves accountable to the Scottish Parliament.

First Minister, The Rt. Hon. Jack McConnell, MSP *(Lab.)*
Deputy First Minister and Minister for Enterprise and
   Lifelong Learning, Jim Wallace, QC, MSP *(LD)*
Minister for Communities, Margaret Curran, MSP *(Lab.)*
Minister for Education and Young People, Peter Peacock,
   MSP *(Lab.)*
Minister for Environment and Rural Development, Ross
   Finnie, MSP *(LD)*
Minister for Finance and Public Services, Andy Kerr, MSP
   (Lab.)
Minister for Health and Community Care, Malcolm
   Chisholm, MSP *(Lab.)*
Minister for Justice, Cathy Jamieson, MSP *(Lab.)*
Minister for Parliamentary Business, Patricia Ferguson,
   MSP *(Lab.)*
Minister for Tourism, Culture and Sport, Frank McAveety,
   MSP *(Lab.)*
Minister for Transport, Nicol Stephen, MSP *(LD)*
Lord Advocate, Colin Boyd, QC *(Lab.)*

JUNIOR MINISTERS (NOT MEMBERS OF THE SCOTTISH EXECUTIVE)
Deputy Minister for Communities, Mary Mulligan, MSP
   (Lab.)
Deputy Minister for Education and Young People, Euan
   Robson, MSP *(LD)*
Deputy Minister for Enterprise, and Lifelong Learning,
   Lewis Macdonald, MSP *(Lab.)*
Deputy Minister for Environment and Rural Development,
   Allan Wilson, MSP *(Lab.)*
Deputy Minister for Finance and Parliamentary Business,
   Tavish Scott, MSP *(LD)*
Deputy Minister for Health and Community Care, Tom
   McCabe, MSP *(Lab.)*
Deputy Minister for Justice, Hugh Henry, MSP *(Lab.)*
Solicitor-General for Scotland, Elish Angiolini, QC

SCOTTISH EXECUTIVE CORPORATE SERVICES
Saughton House, Broomhouse Drive, Edinburgh EH11 3XD
Tel: 0131-556 8400
Principal Establishment Officer, A. Robson

FINANCE AND CENTRAL SERVICES DEPARTMENT (FCSD)
St Andrew's House, Regent Road, Edinburgh EH1 3DG
Tel: 0131-244 5598 Fax: 0131-248 5536
Acting Head of Department, Dr A. Goudie

SCOTTISH EXECUTIVE RURAL AFFAIRS DEPARTMENT
Pentland House, 47 Robb's Loan, Edinburgh EH14 1TY
Tel: 0131-556 8400 Fax: 0131-244 6116
Head of Department (SCS), J. S. Graham

EXECUTIVE AGENCIES
Fisheries Research Services
Scottish Agricultural Science Agency
Scottish Fisheries Protection Agency

SCOTTISH EXECUTIVE DEVELOPMENT DEPARTMENT
Victoria Quay, Edinburgh EH6 6QQ Tel: 0131-244 0763
Head of Department (SCS), Mrs Nicola Munro

SCOTTISH EXECUTIVE EDUCATION DEPARTMENT
Victoria Quay, Edinburgh EH6 6QQ Tel: 08457-741741
Head of Department, M. Ewart

EXECUTIVE AGENCIES
Historic Scotland
Scottish Public Pensiolns Agency

SCOTTISH EXECUTIVE ENTERPRISE, TRANSPORT AND LIFELONG LEARNING DEPARTMENT
St Andrew's House, Edinburgh EH1 3DG
Tel: 0131-244 2440
Head of Department, E. W. Frizzell, CB

EXECUTIVE AGENCY
Student Awards Agency for Scotland

SCOTTISH EXECUTIVE HEALTH DEPARTMENT
St Andrew's House, Edinburgh EH1 3DG
Tel: 0131-244 2440
Chief Executive, T. Jones

SCOTTISH EXECUTIVE JUSTICE DEPARTMENT
St Andrew's House, Regent Road, Edinburgh EH1 3DG
Tel: 0131-244 2122 Fax: 0131-244 2121
Head of Department, J. D. Gallagher

EXECUTIVE AGENCIES
National Archives of Scotland
Registers of Scotland
Scottish Prison Service
General Register for Scotland
Mental Welfare Commission for Scotland

MEMBERS OF THE SCOTTISH PARLIAMENT *as at May 2003*

*Adam, Brian, *SNP, Glasgow, Aberdeen North*, Maj. 457
*Aitken, Bill, *C., Glasgow region*
*Alexander, Wendy, *Lab.., Paisley North*, Maj. 4,310
*Baillie, Jackie, *Lab.., Dumbarton*, Maj. 6,612
Baird, Shiona, *Green, North East Scotland region*
Baker, Richard, *Lab.., North East Scotland region*
Ballance, Chris, *Green, South of Scotland region*
Ballard, Mark, *Green, Lothians region*
*Barrie, Scott, *Lab.., Dunfermline West*, Maj. 4,080
*Boyack, Sarah, *Lab.., Edinburgh Central*, Maj. 2,666
*Brankin, Rhona, *Lab.. Co-op, Midlothian*, Maj. 5,542
Brocklebank, Ted, *C., Mid Scotland region*
*Brown, Robert E., *LD, Glasgow region*
*Butler, Bill, *Lab.., Glasgow Anniesland*, Maj. 6,253
Byrne, Rosemary, *SSP, South of Scotland region*
*Canavan, Dennis, *Ind., Falkirk West*, Maj. 10,000
*Chisholm, Malcolm, *Lab.., Edinburgh North and Leith*, Maj. 5,414
*Craigie, Cathie, *Lab.., Cumbernauld and Kilsyth*, Maj. 520
*Crawford, Bruce, *SNP, Mid Scotland region*
*Cunningham, Roseanna, *SNP, Perth*, Maj. 727
Curran, Frances, *SSP, West of Scotland region*
*Curran, Margaret, *Lab.., Glasgow Baillieston*, Maj. 6,178
*Davidson, David, *C., North East Scotland region*
*Deacon, Susan, *Lab.., Edinburgh East and Musselburgh*, Maj. 6,158
*Douglas-Hamilton, James, *C., Lothians region*
*Eadie, Helen, *Lab.. Co-op, Dunfermline East*, Maj. 7,290
*Ewing, Fergus, *SNP, Inverness East, Nairn and Lochaber*, Maj. 1,046
*Ewing, Margaret, *SNP, Moray*, Maj. 5,312
*Fabiani, Linda, *SNP, Central Scotland region*
*Ferguson, Patricia, *Lab.., Glasgow Maryhill*, Maj. 5,368
*Fergusson, Alex, *C., Galloway and Upper Nithsdale*, Maj. 99
*Finnie, Ross, *LD, West of Scotland region*
Fox, Colin, *SSP, Lothians region*
*Fraser, Murdo, *C., Mid Scotland region*
*Gallie, Phil, *C., South of Scotland region*
Gibson, Rob, *SNP, Highland region*
*Gillon, Karen, *Lab.., Clydesdale*, Maj. 6,671
Glen, Marlyn, *Lab.., North East Scotland region*
*Godman, Patricia, *Lab.., Renfrewshire West*, Maj. 2,492
*Goldie, Annabel, *C., West of Scotland region*
*Gorrie, Donald, *LD, Central Scotland region*
*Grahame, Christine, *SNP, South of Scotland region*
*Harper, Robin, *Green, Lothians region*
Harvie, Patrick, *Green, Glasgow region*
*Henry, Hugh, *Lab.., Paisley South*, Maj. 2,453
*Home Robertson, John, *Lab.., East Lothian*, Maj. 8,175
*Hughes, Janis, *Lab.., Glasgow Rutherglen*, Maj. 6,303
*Hyslop, Fiona, *SNP, Lothians region*
*Ingram, Adam, *SNP, South of Scotland region*
*Jackson, Gordon, *Lab.., Glasgow Govan*, Maj. 1,235
*Jackson, Sylvia, *Lab.., Stirling*, Maj. 2,880
*Jamieson, Cathy, *Lab.. Co-op, Carrick, Cumnock and Doon Valley*, Maj. 7,454
*Jamieson, Margaret, *Lab.. Co-op, Kilmarnock and Loudoun*, Maj. 1,210
*Johnstone, Alex, *C., North East Scotland region*
Kane, Rosie, *SSP, Glasgow region*
*Kerr, Andy, *Lab.., East Kilbride*, Maj. 5,281

*Lamont, Johann, *Lab.. Co-op, Glasgow Pollok*, Maj. 3,341
Leckie, Carolyn, *SSP, Central Scotland region*
*Livingstone, Marilyn, *Lab.., Kirkcaldy*, Maj. 4,824
*Lochhead, Richard, *SNP, North East Scotland region*
*Lyon, George, *LD, Argyll and Bute*, Maj. 4,196
*MacAskill, Kenny, *SNP, Lothians region*
*MacDonald, Lewis, *Lab.., Aberdeen Central*, Maj. 1,242
*MacDonald, Margo, *Ind., Lothians region*
*MacIntosh, Kenneth, *Lab.., Eastwood*, Maj. 3,702
*Maclean, Kate, *Lab.., Dundee West*, Maj. 1,066
*MacMillan, Maureen, *Lab.., Highland region*
Martin, Campbell, *SNP, West of Scotland region*
*Martin, Paul, *Lab.., Glasgow Springburn*, Maj. 8,007
*Marwick, Tricia, *SNP, Mid Scotland region*
Mather, Jim, *SNP, Highland region*
*Matheson, Michael, *SNP, Central Scotland region*
Maxwell, Stewart, *SNP, West of Scotland*
May, Christine, *Lab.. Co-op, Fife Central*, Maj. 2,762
*McAveety, Frank, *Lab.., Glasgow Shettleston*, Maj. 6,347
*McCabe, Tom, *Lab.., Hamilton South*, Maj. 4,824
*McConnell, Jack, *Lab.., Motherwell and Wishaw*, Maj. 9,259
McFee, Bruce, *SNP, West of Scotland region*
*McGrigor, Jamie, *C., Highland region*
*McLetchie, David, *C., Edinburgh Pentlands*, Maj. 2,111
*McMahon, Michael, *Lab.., Hamilton North and Bellshill*, Maj. 7,905
*McNeil, Duncan, *Lab.., Greenock and Inverclyde*, Maj. 3,009
*McNeill, Pauline, *Lab.., Glasgow Kelvin*, Maj. 3,289
*McNulty, Des, *Lab.., Clydebank and Milngavie*, Maj. 4,534
Milne, Nanette, *C., North East Scotland region*
Mitchell, Margaret, *C., Central Scotland region*
*Monteith, Brian, *C., Mid Scotland*
*Morgan, Alasdair, *SNP, South of Scotland*
*Morrison, Alasdair, *Lab.., Western Isles*, Maj. 720
*Muldoon, Bristow, *Lab.., Livingston*, Maj. 3,670
*Mulligan, Mary, *Lab.., Linlithgow*, Maj. 1,970
*Mundell, David, *C., South of Scotland region*
Munro, John F., *LD, Ross, Skye and Inverness West*, Maj. 6,848
*Murray, Elaine, *Lab.., Dumfries*, Maj. 1,096
*Neil, Alex, *SNP, Central Scotland region*
*Oldfather, Irene, *Lab.., Cunninghame South*, Maj. 6,076
*Peacock, Peter, *Lab.., Highland region*
*Peattie, Cathy, *Lab.., Falkirk East*, Maj. 6,659
Pringle, Mike, *LD, Edinburgh South*, Maj. 158
Purvis, Jeremy, *LD, Tweeddale, Ettrick and Lauderdale*, Maj. 538
*Radcliffe, Nora, *LD, Gordon*, Maj. 4,071
*Raffan, Keith, *LD, Mid Scotland region*
*Reid, George, *SNP, Ochil*, Maj. 296
*Robison, Shona, *SNP, Dundee East*, Maj. 90
*Robson, Euan, *LD, Roxburgh and Berwickshire*, Maj. 2,490
*Rumbles, Mike, *LD, Aberdeenshire West Kincardine*, Maj. 5,399
Ruskell, Mark, *Green, Mid Scotland region*
*Scanlon, Mary, *C., Highland region*
Scott, Eleanor, *Green, Highland*
*Scott, John, *C., Ayr*, Maj. 1,890
*Scott, Tavish, *LD, Shetland*, Maj. 2,260
*Sheridan, Tommy, *SSP, Glasgow region*
*Smith, Elaine, *Lab.., Coatbridge and Chryston*, Maj. 8,571
*Smith, Iain, *LD, Fife North East*, Maj. 5,055
*Smith, Margaret, *LD, Edinburgh West*, Maj. 5,914
*Stephen, Nicol, *LD, Aberdeen South*, Maj. 8,016
*Stevenson, Stewart, *SNP, Banff and Buchan*, Maj. 8,364
*Stone, Jamie, *LD, Caithness, Sutherland and Easter Ross*, Maj. 2,092
*Sturgeon, Nicola, *SNP, Glasgow region*
Swinburne, John, *SSCUP, Central Scotland region*

*Swinney, John, *SNP, North Tayside,* Maj. 4,503
*Tosh, Murray, *C., West of Scotland region*
Turner, Dr Jean, *Ind., Strathkelvin and Bearsden,* Maj. 38
*Wallace, Jim, *LD, Orkney,* Maj. 1,755
*Watson, Mike (Lord Watson of Invergowrie), *Lab..,
Glasgow Cathcart,* Maj. 5,112
*Welsh, Andrew, *SNP, Angus,* Maj. 6,687
*White, Sandra, *SNP, Glasgow region*
*Whitefield, Karen, *Lab.., Airdrie and Shotts,* Maj. 8,977
*Wilson, Allan, *Lab.., Cunninghame North,* Maj. 3,387
*Sitting MP

STATE OF THE PARTIES *as at May 2003*†

MSPs	Constituency MSPs	Regional	Total
Scottish Lab.our Party	46	4	50
Scottish National Party	9	18	27
Scottish Conservative and Unionist Party	3	15	18
Scottish Liberal Democrats	13	4†	17†
Scottish Green Party	0	7	7
Scottish Socialist Party	0	6	6
Scottish Senior Citizens Unity Party	0	1	1
Independent†	2	1	3
Total	73	56	129

† Independents are: Dennis Canavan, Margo MacDonald and Dr Jean Turner

The Presiding Officer, The Rt. Hon. George Reid, MSP
Deputy Presiding Officers, Trish Godman, MSP *(Lab..);*
Murray Tosh, MSP *(C.)*

SCOTTISH PARLIAMENT *as at May 2003*

CONSTITUENCIES

ABERDEEN CENTRAL
(Scotland North East Region)
E. 49,477 T. 20,964 (42.37%)

Lewis Macdonald *(Lab..)*	6,835
Richard Lochhead *(SNP)*	5,593
Eleanor Anderson *(LD)*	4,744
Alan Butler*(C.)*	2,616
Andy Cumbers, *(SSP)*	1,176

Lab.. Maj. 1,242 (5.92%)
2.13% swing Lab.. to SNP

ABERDEEN NORTH
(Scotland North East Region)
E. 52,898 T. 25,027 (47.31%)

Brian Adam *(SNP)*	8,381
Elaine Thomson *(Lab..)*	7,924
John Reynolds *(LD)*	5,767
Jim Gifford *(C.)*	2,311
Katrine Trolle *(SSP)*	644

SNP Maj. 457 (1.83%)
1.63% swing Lab.. to SNP

ABERDEEN SOUTH
(Scotland North East Region)
E. 58,204 T. 30,124 (51.76%)

Nicol Stephen *(LD)*	13,821
Richard Baker *(Lab..)*	5,805
Ian Duncan *(C.)*	5,230
Maureen Watt *(SNP)*	4,315
Keith Farnsworth *(SSP)*	953

LD Maj. 8,016 (26.61%)
10.77% swing Lab.. to LD

ABERDEENSHIRE WEST AND KINCARDINE
(Scotland North East Region)
E. 62,542 T. 31,636 (50.58%)

Mike Rumbles *(LD)*	14,553
David Davidson *(C.)*	9,154
Ian Angus *(SNP)*	4,489
Kevin Hutchens *(Lab..)*	2,727
Alan Manley *(SSP)*	713

LD Maj. 5,399 (17.07%)
5.33% swing C. to LD

AIRDRIE AND SHOTTS
(Scotland Central Region)
E. 56,680 T. 25,086 (44.26%)

Karen Whitefield *(Lab..)*	14,209
Gil Paterson *(SNP)*	5,232
Alan Melville *(C.)*	2,203
Fraser Coats *(SSP)*	2,096
Kevin Lang *(LD)*	1,346

Lab.. Maj. 8,977 (35.78%)
4.37% swing SNP to Lab..

ANGUS
(Scotland North East Region)
E.60,608 T. 29,789 (49.15%)

Andrew Welsh *(SNP)*	13,251
Alex Johnstone *(C.)*	6,564
John Denning *(Lab..)*	4,871
Dick Speirs *(LD)*	3,802
Bruce Wallace *(SSP)*	1,301

SNP Maj. 6,687 (22.45%)
1.66% swing SNP to C.

ARGYLL AND BUTE
(Highlands and Islands Region)
E. 48,330 T. 27,948 (57.83%)

George Lyon *(LD)*	9,817
David Petrie *(C.)*	5,621
Jim Mather *(SNP)*	5,485
Hugh Raven *(Lab..)*	5,107
Des Divers *(SSP)*	1,667
David Walker *(SPA)*	251

LD Maj. 4,196 (15.01%)
1.68% swing LD to C.

AYR
(Scotland South Region)
E. 55,523 T. 31,591 (56.90%)

John Scott *(C.)*	12,865
Rita Miller *(Lab..)*	10,975
James Dornan *(SNP)*	4,334
Stuart Ritchie *(LD)*	1,769
James Stewart *(SSP)*	1,648

C. Maj. 1,890 (5.98%)
3.02% swing Lab.. to C.

BANFF AND BUCHAN
(Scotland North East Region)
E. 55,358 T. 26,149 (47.24%)

Stewart Stevenson *(SNP)*	13,827
Stewart Whyte *(C.)*	5,463
Ian Brotchie *(Lab..)*	2,885
Debra Storr *(LD)*	2,227
Alan Buchan *(SPA)*	907
Alice Rowan *(SSP)*	840

SNP Maj. 8,364 (31.99%)
1.80% swing SNP to C.

CAITHNESS, SUTHERLAND AND EASTER ROSS
(Highlands and Islands Region)
E. 40,462 T. 21,127 (52.21%)

Jamie Stone *(LD)*	7,742
Deirdre Steven *(Lab..)*	5,650
Rob Gibson *(SNP)*	3,692
Alan McLeod *(C.)*	2,262
Gordon Campbell *(Ind.)*	953
Frank Ward *(SSP)*	828

LD Maj. 2,092 (9.90%)
3.48% swing LD to Lab..

CARRICK, CUMNOCK AND DOON VALLEY
(Scotland South Region)
E. 65,102 T. 34,366 (52.79%)

Cathy Jamieson *(Lab.. Co-op)*	16,484
Phil Gallie *(C.)*	9,030
Adam Ingram *(SNP)*	5,822
Murray Steele *(SSP)*	1,715
Caron Howden *(LD)*	1,315

Lab.. Co-op Maj. 7,454 (21.69%)
3.20% swing Lab.. Co-op to C.

CLYDEBANK AND MILNGAVIE
(Scotland West Region)
E. 51,327 T. 26,514 (51.66%)

Des McNulty *(Lab..)*	10,585
Jim Yuill *(SNP)*	6,051
Rod Ackland *(LD)*	3,224
Mary Leishman *(C.)*	2,885
Dawn Brennan *(SSP)*	1,902
Danny McCafferty *(Ind.)*	1,867

Lab.. Maj. 4,534 (17.10%)
1.49% swing SNP to Lab..

CLYDESDALE
(Scotland South Region)
E. 63,675 T. 32,442 (50.95%)

Karen Gillon *(Lab..)*	14,800
John Brady *(SNP)*	8,129
Alastair Campbell *(C.)*	5,174
Fraser Grieve *(LD)*	2,338
Owen Meharry *(SSP)*	1,422
David Morrison *(SPA)*	579

Lab.. Maj. 6,671 (20.56%)
5.30% swing SNP to Lab..

COATBRIDGE AND CHRYSTON
(Scotland Central Region)
E. 51,521 T. 23,862 (46.32%)

Elaine Smith *(Lab..)*	13,422
James Gribben *(SNP)*	4,851
Donald Reece *(C.)*	2,041
Gordon Martin *(SSP)*	1,911
Doreen Nisbet *(LD)*	1,637

Lab.. Maj. 8,571 (35.92%)
0.73% swing SNP to Lab..

CUMBERNAULD AND KILSYTH
(Scotland Central Region)
E. 48,667 T. 24,404 (50.14%)

Cathie Craigie *(Lab..)*	10,146
Andrew Wilson *(SNP)*	9,626
Kenny McEwan *(SSP)*	1,823
Hugh O'Donnell *(LD)*	1,264
Margaret McCulloch *(C.)*	978
Christopher Donohue *(Ind.)*	567

Lab.. Maj. 520 (2.13%)
5.89% swing Lab.. to SNP

CUNNINGHAME NORTH
(Scotland West Region)
E. 55,319 T. 28,631 (51.76%)

Allan Wilson *(Lab..)*	11,142
Campbell Martin *(SNP)*	7,755
Peter Ramsay *(C.)*	5,542
John Boyd *(LD)*	2,333
Sean Scott *(SSP)*	1,859

Lab.. Maj. 3,387 (11.83%)
1.25% swing Lab. to SNP

CUNNINGHAME SOUTH
(Scotland South Region)
E. 49,877 T. 22,772 (45.66%)

Irene Oldfather *(Lab..)*	11,165
Michael Russell *(SNP)*	5,089
Rosemary Byrne *(SSP)*	2,677
Andrew Brocklehurst *(C.)*	2,336
Iain Dale *(LD)*	1,505

Lab.. Maj. 6,076 (26.68%)
1.78% swing SNP to Lab..

DUMBARTON
(Scotland West Region)
E. 55,575 T. 28,823 (51.86%)

Jackie Baillie *(Lab..)*	12,154
Iain Docherty *(SNP)*	5,542
Eric Thompson *(LD)*	4,455
Murray Tosh *(C.)*	4,178
Les Robertson *(SSP)*	2,494

Lab.. Maj. 6,612 (22.94%)
4.61% swing SNP to Lab..

DUMFRIES
(Scotland South Region)
E. 61,517 T. 32,110 (52.20%)

Elaine Murray *(Lab..)*	12,834
David Mundell *(C.)*	11,738
Andrew Wood *(SNP)*	3,931
Clare Hamblen *(LD)*	2,394
John Dennis *(SSP)*	1,213

Lab.. Maj. 1,096 (3.41%)
3.05% swing Lab.. to C.

DUNDEE EAST
(Scotland North East Region)
E. 53,876 T. 26,348 (48.90%)

Shona Robison *(SNP)*	10,428
John McAllion *(Lab..)*	10,338
Edward Prince *(C.)*	3,133
Clive Sneddon *(LD)*	1,584
James Gourlay *(Ind.)*	865

SNP Maj. 90 (0.34%)
4.68% swing Lab.. to SNP

DUNDEE WEST
(Scotland North East Region)
E. 51,387 T. 25,003 (48.66%)

Kate McLean *(Lab..)*	8,234
Irene McGugan *(SNP)*	7,168
Ian Borthwick *(Ind.)*	4,715
Shona Ferrier *(LD)*	1,878
Jim McFarland *(SSP)*	1,501
Victoria Roberts *(C.)*	1,376
Morag MacLachlan *(SPA)*	131

Lab.. Maj. 1,066 (4.26%)
1.92% swing SNP to Lab..

DUNFERMLINE EAST
(Scotland Mid and Fife Region)
E. 51,220 *T.* 23,154 (45.20%)

Helen Eadie *(Lab.. Co-op)*	11,552
Janet Law *(SNP)*	4,262
Stuart Randall *(C.)*	2,485
Brian Stewart *(Local Hospital)*	1,890
Linda Graham *(SSP)*	1,537
Rodger Spillane *(LD)*	1,428

Lab.. Co-op Maj. 7,290 (31.48%)
1.08% swing SNP to Lab.. Co-op

DUNFERMLINE WEST
(Scotland Mid and Fife Region)
E. 53,915 *T.* 25,240 (46.81%)

Scott Barrie *(Lab..)*	8,664
David Wishart *(Local Hospital)*	4,584
Brian Goodall *(SNP)*	4,392
Jim Tolson *(LD)*	3,636
Jim Mackie *(C.)*	1,868
Andy Jackson *(SSP)*	923
Alastair Harper *(Ind.)*	714
Damien Quigg *(Ind. Q)*	459

Lab.. Maj. 4,080 (16.16%)

EAST KILBRIDE
(Scotland Central Region)
E. 65,472 *T.* 34,087 (52.06%)

Andy Kerr *(Lab..)*	13,825
Linda Fabiani *(SNP)*	8,544
Grace Campbell *(C.)*	3,785
Carolyn Leckie *(SSP)*	2,736
Colin McCartney *(Ind.)*	2,597
Alex Mackie *(LD)*	2,181
John Houston *(Ind. Houston)*	419

Lab.. Maj. 5,281 (15.49%)
0.08% swing Lab.. to SNP

EAST LOTHIAN
(Scotland South Region)
E. 59,227 *T.* 31,204 (52.69%)

John Home Robertson *(Lab..)*	13,683
Judy Hayman *(LD)*	5,508
Stewart Thomson *(C.)*	5,459
Tom Roberts *(SNP)*	5,174
Hugh Kerr *(SSP)*	1,380

Lab.. Maj. 8,175 (26.20%)
6.95% swing Lab.. to LD

EASTWOOD
(Scotland West Region)
E. 67,051 *T.* 38,889 (58.00%)

Ken Macintosh *(Lab..)*	13,946
Jackson Carlaw *(C.)*	10,244
Allan Steele *(LD)*	5,056
Stewart Maxwell *(SNP)*	4,736
Margaret Hinds *(Local Health)*	3,163
Steve Oram *(SSP)*	1,504
Martyn Greene *(SPA)*	240

Lab.. Maj. 3,702 (9.52%)
2.42% swing C. to Lab..

EDINBURGH CENTRAL
(Lothians Region)
E. 60,824 *T.* 28,014 (46.06%)

Sarah Boyack *(Lab..)*	9,066
Andy Myles *(LD)*	6,400
Kevin Pringle *(SNP)*	4,965
Peter Finnie *(C.)*	4,802
Catriona Grant *(SSP)*	2,552
James O'Neill *(SPA)*	229

Lab.. Maj. 2,666 (9.52%)
5.98% swing Lab.. to LD

EDINBURGH EAST AND MUSSELBURGH
(Lothians Region)
E. 57,704 *T.* 29,044 (50.33%)

Susan Deacon *(Lab..)*	12,655
Kenny MacAskill *(SNP)*	6,497
John Smart *(C.)*	3,863
Gary Peacock *(LD)*	3,582
Derek Durkin *(SSP)*	2,447

Lab.. Maj. 6,158 (21.20%)
1.53% swing SNP to Lab..

EDINBURGH NORTH AND LEITH
(Lothians Region)
E. 60,501 *T.* 28,734 (47.49%)

Malcolm Chisholm *(Lab..)*	10,979
Anne Dana *(SNP)*	5,565
Ian Mowat *(C.)*	4,821
Sebastian Tombs *(LD)*	4,785
Bill Scott *(SSP)*	2,584

Lab.. Maj. 5,414 (18.84%)
1.13% swing Lab.. to SNP

EDINBURGH PENTLANDS
(Lothians Region)
E. 58,534 *T.* 33,382 (57.03%)

David McLetchie *(C.)*	12,420
Iain Gray *(Lab..)*	10,309
Ian McKee *(SNP)*	5,620
Simon Clark *(LD)*	3,943
Frank O'Donnell *(SSP)*	1,090

C. Maj. 2,111 (6.32%)
6.80% swing Lab.. to C.

EDINBURGH SOUTH
(Lothians Region)
E. 60,366 *T.* 31,196 (51.68%)

Mike Pringle *(LD)*	10,005
Angus Mackay *(Lab..)*	9,847
Gordon Buchan *(C.)*	5,180
Alex Orr *(SNP)*	4,396
Shirley Gibb *(SSP)*	1,768

LD Maj. 158 (0.51%)
7.61% swing Lab.. to LD

EDINBURGH WEST
(Lothians Region)
E. 60,136 *T.* 33,301 (55.38%)

Margaret Smith *(LD)*	14,434
James Douglas-Hamilton *(C.)*	8,520
Carol Fox *(Lab..)*	5,046
Alyn Smith *(SNP)*	4,133
Pat Smith *(SSP)*	993
Bruce Skivington *(SPA)*	175

LD Maj. 5,914 (17.76%)
3.37% swing C. to LD

FALKIRK EAST
(Scotland Central Region)
E. 56,175 *T.* 27,559 (49.06%)

Cathy Peattie *(Lab..)*	14,235
Keith Brown *(SNP)*	7,576
Thomas Calvert *(C.)*	2,720
Karen Utting *(LD)*	1,651
Mhairi McAlpine *(SSP)*	1,377

Lab.. Maj. 6,659 (24.16%)
6.20% swing SNP to Lab..

FALKIRK WEST
(Scotland Central Region)
E. 52,122 *T.* 26,400 (50.65%)

Dennis Canavan *(Falkirk W)*	14,703
Michael Matheson *(SNP)*	4,703
Lee Whitehill *(Lab.)*	4,589
Iain Mitchell *(C.)*	1,657
Jacqueline Kelly *(LD)*	748

Falkirk W Maj. 10,000 (37.88%)
0.34% swing SNP to Falkirk W

FIFE CENTRAL
(Scotland Mid and Fife Region)
E. 57,633 *T.* 25,597 (44.41%)

Christine May *(Lab.. Co-op)*	10,591
Tricia Marwick *(SNP)*	7,829
Andrew Rodger *(Ind.)*	2,258
James North *(C.)*	1,803
Elizabeth Riches *(LD)*	1,725
Morag Balfour *(SSP)*	1,391

Lab.. Co-op Maj. 2,762 (10.79%)
7.81% swing Lab.. Co-op to SNP

FIFE NORTH EAST
(Scotland Mid and Fife Region)
E. 58,695 *T.* 29,282 (49.89%)

Iain Smith *(LD)*	13,479
Ted Brocklebank *(C.)*	8,424
Capre Ross-Williams *(SNP)*	3,660
Gregor Poynton *(Lab..)*	2,353
Carlo Morelli *(SSP)*	1,366

LD Maj. 5,055 (17.26%)
1.59% swing C. to LD

GALLOWAY AND UPPER NITHSDALE
(Scotland South Region)
E. 51,651 *T.* 29,635 (57.38%)

Alex Fergusson *(C.)*	11,332
Alasdair Morgan *(SNP)*	11,233
Norma Hart *(Lab..)*	4,299
Neil Wallace *(LD)*	1,847
Joy Cherkaoui *(SSP)*	709
Graham Brockhouse *(SPA)*	215

C. Maj. 99 (0.33%)
4.70% swing SNP to C.

GLASGOW ANNIESLAND
(Glasgow Region)
E. 50,795 *T.* 22,165 (43.64%)

Bill Butler *(Lab.. Co-op)*	10,141
Bill Kidd *(SNP)*	3,888
Bill Aitken *(C.)*	3,186
Charlie McCarthy *(SSP)*	2,620
Iain Brown *(LD)*	2,330

Lab.. Co-op Maj. 6,253 (28.21%)
5.19% swing Lab.. Co-op to SNP

GLASGOW BAILLIESTON
(Glasgow Region)
E. 46,346 *T.* 18,270 (39.42%)

Margaret Curran *(Lab..)*	9,657
Lachlan McNeill *(SNP)*	3,479
Jim McVicar *(SSP)*	2,461
Janette McAlpine *(C.)*	1,472
David Jackson *(LD)*	1,201

Lab.. Maj. 6,178 (33.81%)
10.43% swing SNP to Lab..

GLASGOW CATHCART
(Glasgow Region)
E. 49,017 *T.* 22,307 (45.51%)

Mike Watson *(Lab..)*	8,742
David Ritchie *(SNP)*	3,630
Richard Cook *(C.)*	2,888
Malcolm Wilson *(SSP)*	2,819
Pat Lally *(Local Health)*	2,419
Tom Henery *(LD)*	1,741
Robert Wilson *(Parent Ex)*	68

Lab.. Maj. 5,112 (22.92%)
1.50% swing SNP to Lab..

GLASGOW GOVAN
(Glasgow Region)
E. 48,635 *T.* 21,136 (43.46%)

Gordon Jackson *(Lab..)*	7,834
Nicola Sturgeon *(SNP)*	6,599
Jimmy Scott *(SSP)*	2,369
Faisal Butt *(C.)*	1,878
Paul Graham *(LD)*	1,807
Razaq Dean *(Ind.)*	226
John Foster *(CPPDS)*	215
Asif Nasir *(SPA)*	208

Lab.. Maj. 1,235 (5.84%)
0.41% swing Lab.. to SNP

GLASGOW KELVIN
(Glasgow Region)
E. 56,038 *T.* 22,080 (39.40%)

Pauline McNeill *(Lab.)*	7,880
Sandra White *(SNP)*	4,591
Douglas Herbison *(LD)*	3,334
Andy Harvey *(SSP)*	3,159
Gawain Towler *(C.)*	1,816
Alistair McConnachie *(Ind. Green)*	1,300

Lab.. Maj. 3,289 (14.90%)
0.32% swing Lab.. to SNP

GLASGOW MARYHILL
(Glasgow Region)
E. 49,119 *T.* 18,243 (37.14%)

Patricia Ferguson *(Lab..)*	8,997
Bill Wilson *(SNP)*	3,629
Donnie Nicolson *(SSP)*	2,945
Arthur Sanderson *(LD)*	1,785
Robert Erskine *(C.)*	887

Lab.. Maj. 5,368 (29.42%)
5.31% swing SNP to Lab..

GLASGOW POLLOK
(Glasgow Region)
E. 47,134 *T.* 21,538 (45.70%)

Johann Lamont *(Lab.. Co-op)*	9,357
Tommy Sheridan *(SSP)*	6,016
Kenneth Gibson *(SNP)*	4,118
Ashraf Anjum *(C.)*	1,012
Isabel Nelson *(LD)*	962
Robert Ray *(Parent Ex)*	73

Lab.. Co-op Maj. 3,341 (15.51%)
3.35% swing Lab.. Co-op to SSP

GLASGOW RUTHERGLEN
(Glasgow Region)
E. 49,512 *T.* 23,554 (47.57%)

Janis Hughes *(Lab.)*	10,794
Robert Brown *(LD)*	4,491
Anne McLaughlin *(SNP)*	3,511
Gavin Brown *(C.)*	2,499
Bill Bonnar *(SSP)*	2,259

Lab.. Maj. 6,303 (26.76%)
0.21% swing LD to Lab..

GLASGOW SHETTLESTON
(Glasgow Region)
E. 46,730 *T.* 16,547 (35.41%)

Francis McAveety *(Lab.. Co-op)*	9,365
Jim Byrne *(SNP)*	3,018
Rosie Kane *(SSP)*	2,403
Dorothy Luckhurst *(C.)*	982
Lewis Hutton *(LD)*	779

Lab.. Co-op Maj. 6,347 (38.36%)
5.87% swing SNP to Lab.. Co-op

GLASGOW SPRINGBURN
(Glasgow Region)
E. 49,551 *T.* 18,573 (37.48%)

Paul Martin *(Lab..)*	10,963
Frank Rankin *(SNP)*	2,956
Margaret Bean *(SSP)*	2,653
Alan Rodger *(C.)*	1,233
Charles Dundas *(LD)*	768

Lab.. Maj. 8,007 (43.11%)
5.36% swing SNP to Lab..

GORDON
(Scotland North East Region)
E. 60,686 *T.* 28,798 (47.45%)

Nora Radcliffe *(LD)*	10,963
Nanette Milne *(C.)*	6,892
Alasdair Allan *(SNP)*	6,501
Ellis Thorpe *(Lab..)*	2,973
John Sangster *(SSP)*	780
Steven Mathers *(Ind.)*	689

LD Maj. 4,071 (14.14%)
1.48% swing LD to C.

GREENOCK AND INVERCLYDE
(Scotland West Region)
E. 46,045 *T.* 23,781 (51.65%)

Duncan McNeil *(Lab..)*	9,674
Ross Finnie *(LD)*	6,665
Tom Chalmers *(SNP)*	3,532
Tricia McCafferty *(SSP)*	2,338
Charles Dunlop *(C.)*	1,572

Lab.. Maj. 3,009 (12.65%)
1.20% swing Lab.. to LD

HAMILTON NORTH AND BELLSHILL
(Scotland Central Region)
E. 51,965 *T.* 24,195 (46.56%)

Michael McMahon *(Lab..)*	12,812
Alex Neil *(SNP)*	4,907
Charles Ferguson *(C.)*	2,625
Shareen Blackhall *(SSP)*	1,932
Siobhan Mathers *(LD)*	1,477
Gordon McIntosh *(SPA)*	442

Lab.. Maj. 7,905 (32.67%)
7.36% swing SNP to Lab..

HAMILTON SOUTH
(Scotland Central Region)
E. 45,749 *T.* 20,518 (44.85%)

Tom McCabe *(Lab..)*	9,546
John Wilson *(SNP)*	4,722
Margaret Mitchell *(C.)*	2,601
Willie O'Neil *(SSP)*	1,893
John Oswald *(LD)*	1,756

Lab.. Maj. 4,824 (23.51%)
2.09% swing Lab.. to SNP

INVERNESS EAST, NAIRN AND LOCHABER
(Highlands and Islands Region)
E. 66,694 *T.* 34,795 (52.17%)

Fergus Ewing *(SNP)*	10,764
Rhoda Grant *(Lab..)*	9,718
Mary Scanlon *(C.)*	6,205
Patsy Kenton *(LD)*	5,622
Steve Arnott *(SSP)*	1,661
Thomas Lamont *(Ind.)*	825

SNP Maj. 1,046 (3.01%)
0.98% swing Lab.. to SNP

KILMARNOCK AND LOUDOUN
(Scotland Central Region)
E. 61,055 *T.* 31,520 (51.63%)

Margaret Jamieson *(Lab..)*	12,633
Danny Coffey *(SNP)*	11,423
Robin Traquair *(C.)*	3,295
Ian Gibson *(LD)*	1,571
Colin Rutherford *(SSP)*	1,421
May Anderson *(Ind. Anderson)*	404
Matthew Donnelly *(Ind.)*	402
Lyndsay McIntosh *(SPA)*	371

Lab.. Maj. 1,210 (3.84%)
1.59% swing Lab.. to SNP

KIRKCALDY
(Scotland Mid and Fife Region)
E. 49,653 *T.* 21,939 (44.18%)

Marilyn Livingstone *(Lab.. Co-op)*	10,235
Colin Welsh *(SNP)*	5,411
Alex Cole-Hamilton *(LD)*	2,417
Mike Scott-Hayward *(C.)*	2,332
Rudi Vogels *(SSP)*	1,544

Lab.. Co-op Maj. 4,824 (21.99%)
3.10% swing SNP to Lab.. Co-op

LINLITHGOW
(Lothians Region)
E. 54,113 *T.* 27,645 (51.09%)

Mary Mulligan *(Lab..)*	11,548
Fiona Hyslop *(SNP)*	9,578
Gordon Lindhurst *(C.)*	3,059
Martin Oliver *(LD)*	2,093
Steve Nimmo *(SSP)*	1,367

Lab.. Maj. 1,970 (7.13%)
0.77% swing Lab.. to SNP

LIVINGSTON
(Lothians Region)
E. 65,421 *T.* 30,557 (46.71%)

Bristow Muldoon *(Lab..)*	13,327
Peter Johnston *(SNP)*	9,657
Lindsay Paterson *(C.)*	2,848
Paul McGreal *(LD)*	2,714
Robert Richard *(SSP)*	1,640
Stephen Milburn *(SPA)*	371

Lab.. Maj. 3,670 (12.01%)
0.67% swing SNP to Lab..

MIDLOTHIAN
(Lothians Region)
E. 48,319 *T.* 23,556 (48.75%)

Rhona Brankin *(Lab.. Co-op)*	11,139
Graham Sutherland *(SNP)*	5,597
Jacqui Bell *(LD)*	2,700
Rosemary MacArthur *(C.)*	2,557
Bob Goupillot *(SSP)*	1,563

Lab.. Co-op Maj. 5,542 (23.53%)
2.48% swing SNP to Lab.. Co-op

MORAY
(Highlands and Islands Region)
E. 58,242 T. 26,981 (46.33%)

Margaret Ewing (SNP)	11,384
Tim Wood (C.)	6,072
Peter Peacock (Lab..)	5,157
Linda Gorn (LD)	3,283
Norma Anderson (SSP)	1,085

SNP Maj. 5,312 (19.69%)
3.24% swing C. to SNP

MOTHERWELL AND WISHAW
(Scotland Central Region)
E. 51,785 T. 25,388 (49.03%)

Jack McConnell (Lab..)	13,739
Lloyd Quinan (SNP)	4,480
Mark Nolan (C.)	2,542
John Milligan (SSP)	1,961
John Swinburne (SSCUP)	1,597
Keith Legg (LD)	1,069

Lab.. Maj. 9,259 (36.47%)
9.92% swing SNP to Lab..

OCHIL
(Scotland Mid and Fife Region)
E. 55,596 T. 30,416 (54.71%)

George Reid (SNP)	11,659
Richard Simpson (Lab..)	11,363
Malcolm Parkin (C.)	2,946
Catherine Whittingham (LD)	2,536
Felicity Garvie (SSP)	1,102
Flash Gordon Approaching (Loony)	432
William Whyte (ND)	378

SNP Maj. 296 (0.97%)
2.25% swing Lab.. to SNP

ORKNEY
(Highlands and Islands Region)
E. 15,487 T. 8,004 (51.68%)

Jim Wallace (LD)	3,659
Christopher Zawadski (C.)	1,904
John Mowat (SNP)	1,056
John Aberdein (SSP)	914
Richard Meade (Lab..)	471

LD Maj. 1,755 (21.93%)
14.93% swing LD to C.

PAISLEY NORTH
(Scotland West Region)
E. 44,999 T. 22,206 (49.35%)

Wendy Alexander (Lab..)	10,631
George Adam (SNP)	6,321
Allison Cook (C.)	1,871
Brian O'Malley (LD)	1,705
Sean Hurl (SSP)	1,678

Lab.. Maj. 4,310 (19.41%)
1.39% swing SNP to Lab..

PAISLEY SOUTH
(Scotland West Region)
E. 49,818 T. 24,984 (50.15%)

Hugh Henry (Lab..)	10,190
Bill Martin (SNP)	7,737
Eileen McCartin (LD)	3,517
Mark Jones (C.)	1,775
Frances Curran (SSP)	1,765

Lab.. Maj. 2,453 (9.82%)
2.42% swing Lab.. to SNP

PERTH
(Scotland and Mid Fife Region)
E. 61,957 T. 31,614 (51.03%)

Roseanna Cunningham (SNP)	10,717
Alexander Stewart (C.)	9,990
Robert Ball (Lab..)	5,629
Gordon Campbell (LD)	3,530
Philip Stott (SSP)	982
Thomas Burns (Ind.)	509
Ken Buchanan (SPA)	257

SNP Maj. 727 (2.30%)
1.56% swing SNP to C.

RENFREWSHIRE WEST
(Scotland West Region)
E. 50,963 T. 28,302 (55.53%)

Patricia Godman (Lab..)	9,671
Bruce McFee (SNP)	7,179
Annabel Goldie (C.)	6,867
Alison King (LD)	2,902
Gerry MaCartney (SSP)	1,683

Lab.. Maj. 2,492 (8.81%)
0.15% swing SNP to Lab..

ROSS, SKYE AND INVERNESS WEST
(Highlands and Islands Region)
E. 55,777 T. 28,971 (51.94%)

John Farquhar Munro (LD)	12,495
David Thompson (SNP)	5,647
Maureen MacMillan (Lab..)	5,464
Jamie McGrigor (C.)	3,772
Anne McLeod (SSP)	1,593

LD Maj. 6,848 (23.64%)
6.66% swing SNP to LD

ROXBURGH AND BERWICKSHIRE
(Scotland South Region)
E. 45,625 T. 22,511 (49.34%)

Euan Robson (LD)	9,280
Sandy Scott (C.)	6,790
Roderick Campbell (SNP)	2,816
Sam Held (Lab..)	2,802
Graeme McIver (SSP)	823

LD Maj. 2,490 (11.06%)
0.90% swing LD to C.

SHETLAND
(Highlands and Islands Region)
E. 16,677 T. 8,645 (51.84%)

Tavish Scott (LD)	3,989
Willie Ross (SNP)	1,729
John Firth (C.)	1,281
Peter Hamilton (Lab..)	880
Peter Andrews (SSP)	766

LD Maj. 2,260 (26.14%)
7.00% swing LD to SNP

STIRLING
(Scotland and Mid Fife Region)
E. 52,087 T. 29,647 (56.92%)

Sylvia Jackson (Lab..)	10,661
Brian Monteith (C.)	7,781
Bruce Crawford (SNP)	5,645
Kenyon Wright (LD)	3,432
Margaret Stewart (SSP)	1,486
Keith Harding (SPA)	642

Lab.. Maj. 2,880 (9.71%)
1.25% swing Lab.. to C.

STRATHKELVIN AND BEARSDEN
(Scotland West Region)
E. 61,905 *T.* 35,736 (57.73%)
Jean Turner *(Ind.)*	10,988
Brian Fitzpatrick *(Lab..)*	10,950
Jo Swinson *(LD)*	4,950
Fiona McLeod *(SNP)*	4,846
Rory O'Brien *(C.)*	4,002

Ind. Maj. 38 (0.11%)

TAYSIDE NORTH
(Scotland Mid and Fife Region)
E. 62,697 *T.* 33,343 (53.18%)
John Swinney *(SNP)*	14,969
Murdo Fraser *(C.)*	10,466
Gordon MacRae *(Lab..)*	3,527
Bob Forrest *(LD)*	3,206
Rosie Adams *(SSP)*	941
George Ashe *(SPA)*	234

SNP Maj. 4,503 (13.51%)
1.24% swing C. to SNP

TWEEDDALE, ETTRICK AND LAUDERDALE
(Scotland South Region)
E. 50,912 *T.* 26,700 (52.44%)
Jeremy Purvis *(LD)*	7,197
Christine Grahame *(SNP)*	6,659
Catherine Maxwell Stuart *(Lab..)*	5,757
Derek Brownlee *(C.)*	5,686
Norman Lockhart *(SSP)*	1,055
Alex Black *(SPA)*	346

LD Maj. 538 (2.01%)
5.63% swing LD to SNP

WESTERN ISLES
(Highlands and Islands Region)
E. 21,205 *T.* 12,387 (58.42%)
Alasdair Morrison *(Lab..)*	5,825
Alasdair Nicholson *(SNP)*	5,105
Frank Warren *(C.)*	612
Conor Snowden *(LD)*	498
Joanne Telfer *(SSP)*	347

Lab..Maj. 720 (5.81%)
4.59% swing Lab.. to SNP

REGIONS

GLASGOW
E. 492,877 *T.* 39.42%
Lab..	77,040	(39.65%)
SNP	34,894	(17.96%)
SSP	31,116	(16.02%)
C.	15,299	(7.87%)
LD	14,839	(7.64%)
Green	14,570	(7.50%)
SSCUP	4,750	(2.44%)
Soc. Lab..	3,091	(1.59%)
ProLife	2,477	(1.27%)
SUP	2,349	(1.21%)
BNP	2,344	(1.21%)
SPA	612	(0.32%)
UK Ind.	552	(0.28%)
CPPDS	345	(0.18%)
Lab..majority	42,146	(21.69%)

1.64% swing SNP to Lab..

ADDITIONAL MEMBERS
Bill Aitken	*(C.)*
Robert Brown	*(LD)*
Ms Sandra White	*(SNP)*
Ms Nicola Sturgeon	*(SNP)*
Patrick Harvie	*(Green)*
Tommy Sheridan	*(SSP)*
Ms Rosie Kane	*(SSP)*

HIGHLANDS AND ISLANDS
E. 322,874 *T.* 52.22%
SNP	39,497	(23.43%)
Lab..	37,605	(22.30%)
LD	31,655	(18.78%)
C.	26,989	(16.01%)
Green	13,935	(8.27%)
SSP	9,000	(5.34%)
UK Ind.	1,947	(1.15%)
SASSDR	1,822	(1.08%)
CPFRI	1,768	(1.05%)
Soc. Lab..	1,617	(0.96%)
PRSP	1,438	(0.85%)
SPA	793	(0.47%)
Ind.	353	(0.21%)
Rural	177	(0.10%)
SNP majority	1,892	(1.12%)

0.57% swing SNP to Lab..

ADDITIONAL MEMBERS
Jamie McGrigor	*(C.)*
Mrs Mary Scanlon	*(C.)*
Peter Peacock	*(Lab..)*
Ms Maureen MacMillan	*(Lab..)*
Jim Mather	*(SNP)*
Rob Gibson	*(SNP)*
Ms Eleanor Scott	*(Green)*

LOTHIANS
E. 525,918 *T.* 50.52%
Lab..	65,102	(24.50%)
SNP	43,142	(16.24%)
C.	40,173	(15.12%)
Green	31,908	(12.01%)
LD	29,237	(11.01%)
Ind.	27,144	(10.22%)
SSP	14,448	(5.44%)
PP	5,609	(2.11%)
Lib	2,573	(0.97%)
Soc. Lab..	2,181	(0.82%)
UK Ind.	1,057	(0.40%)
Witchery	964	(0.36%)
SPA	879	(0.33%)
ProLife	608	(0.23%)
Ind. C.	383	(0.14%)
Ind. A.	184	(0.07%)
Ind. Gatensbury	78	(0.03%)
Lab.. majority	21,960	(8.27%)

1.89% swing SNP to Lab..

ADDITIONAL MEMBERS
Lord James Douglas-Hamilton	*(C.)*
Kenny MacAskill	*(SNP)*
Ms Fiona Hyslop	*(SNP)*
Robin Harper	*(Green)*
Mark Ballard	*(Green)*
Ms Margo MacDonald	*(Ind.)*
Colin Fox	*(SSP)*

SCOTLAND CENTRAL
E. 541,191 T. 48.61%

Lab..	106,318	(40.41%)
SNP	59,274	(22.53%)
C.	24,121	(9.17%)
SSP	19,016	(7.23%)
SSCUP	17,146	(6.52%)
LD	15,494	(5.89%)
Green	12,248	(4.66%)
Soc. Lab..	3,855	(1.47%)
SUP	2,147	(0.82%)
Ind.	1,265	(0.48%)
SPA	1,192	(0.45%)
UK Ind.	1,009	(0.38%)
Lab.. majority	47,044	(17.88%)

3.19% swing SNP to Lab..

ADDITIONAL MEMBERS
Mrs Margaret Mitchell	(C.)
Donald Gorrie	(LD)
Alex Neil	(SNP)
Michael Matheson	(SNP)
Ms Linda Fabiani	(SNP)
John Swinburne	(SSCUP)
Ms Carolyn Leckie	(SSP)

SCOTLAND MID AND FIFE
E. 503,453 T. 49.68%

Lab..	63,239	(25.29%)
SNP	57,631	(23.04%)
C.	43,941	(17.57%)
LD	30,112	(12.04%)
Green	17,147	(6.86%)
SSP	11,401	(4.56%)
PP	8,380	(3.35%)
FHC	5,064	(2.02%)
SLH	4,662	(1.86%)
UK Ind.	2,355	(0.94%)
Soc. Lab..	2,273	(0.91%)
SPA	1,191	(0.48%)
Christian	1,064	(0.43%)
Ind. Gray	996	(0.40%)
Ind.	637	(0.25%)
Lab.. majority	5,608	(2.24%)

1.22% swing Lab.. to SNP

ADDITIONAL MEMBERS
Murdo Fraser	(C.)
Brian Monteith	(C.)
Ted Brocklebank	(C.)
Keith Raffan	(LD)
Bruce Crawford	(SNP)
Ms Tricia Marwick	(SNP)
Mark Ruskell	(Green)

SCOTLAND NORTH EAST
E. 505,036 T. 48.25%

SNP	66,463	(27.28%)
Lab..	49,189	(20.19%)
LD	45,831	(18.81%)
C.	42,318	(17.37%)
Green	12,724	(5.22%)
SSP	10,226	(4.20%)
PP	5,584	(2.29%)
Fishing	5,566	(2.28%)
Soc. Lab..	2,431	(1.00%)
UK Ind.	1,498	(0.61%)
SPA	941	(0.39%)
Ind.	902	(0.37%)
SNP majority	17,274	(7.09%)

0.10% swing Lab.. to SNP

ADDITIONAL MEMBERS
David Davidson	(C.)
Alex Johnstone	(C.)
Mrs Nanette Milne	(C.)
Ms Marlyn Glen	(Lab..)
Richard Baker	(Lab..)
Richard Lochhead	(SNP)
Ms Shiona Baird	(Green)

SCOTLAND SOUTH
E. 503,109 T. 52.33%

Lab..	78,955	(29.99%)
C.	63,827	(24.24%)
SNP	48,371	(18.37%)
LD	27,026	(10.26%)
Green	15,062	(5.72%)
SSP	14,228	(5.40%)
PP	9,082	(3.45%)
Soc. Lab..	3,054	(1.16%)
UK Ind.	1,889	(0.72%)
SPA	1,436	(0.55%)
Rural	355	(0.13%)
Lab.. majority	15,128	(5.75%)

1.83% swing Lab.. to C.

ADDITIONAL MEMBERS
Phil Gallie	(C.)
David Mundell	(C.)
Ms Christine Grahame	(SNP)
Alasdair Morgan	(SNP)
Adam Ingram	(SNP)
Chris Ballance	(Green)
Ms Rosemary Byrne	(SSP)

SCOTLAND WEST
E. 483,002 T. 61.53%

Lab..	83,931	(28.24%)
LD	71,580	(24.09%)
SNP	50,387	(16.96%)
C.	40,261	(13.55%)
SSP	18,591	(6.26%)
Green	14,544	(4.89%)
SSCUP	7,100	(2.39%)
ProLife	3,674	(1.24%)
Soc. Lab..	3,155	(1.06%)
UK Ind.	1,662	(0.56%)
SUP	1,617	(0.54%)
SPA	674	(0.23%)
Lab.. majority	12,351	(4.16%)

11.70% swing Lab.. to LD

ADDITIONAL MEMBERS
Miss Annabel Goldie	(C.)
Murray Tosh	(C.)
Ross Finnie	(LD)
Campbell Martin	(SNP)
Bruce McFee	(SNP)
Stewart Maxwell	(SNP)
Ms Frances Curran	(SSP)

LOCAL GOVERNMENT

Major changes in local government were introduced in England and Wales in 1974 and in Scotland in 1975 by the Local Government Act 1972 and the Local Government (Scotland) Act 1973. Further significant alterations were made in England by the Local Government Acts of 1985, 1992 and 2000.

The structure in England was based on two tiers of local authorities (county councils and district councils) in the non-metropolitan areas; and a single tier of metropolitan councils in the six metropolitan areas of England and London borough councils in London.

Following reviews of the structure of local government in England by the Local Government Commission, 46 unitary (all-purpose) authorities were created between April 1995 and April 1998 to cover certain areas in the non-metropolitan counties. The remaining county areas continue to have two tiers of local authorities. The county and district councils in the Isle of Wight were replaced by a single unitary authority on 1 April 1995; the former counties of Avon, Cleveland, Humberside and Berkshire have been replaced by unitary authorities; and Hereford and Worcester was replaced by a new county council for Worcestershire (with district councils) and a unitary authority for Herefordshire.

The Local Government (Wales) Act 1994 and the Local Government etc. (Scotland) Act 1994 abolished the two-tier structure in Wales and Scotland with effect from 1 April 1996, replacing it with a single tier of unitary authorities.

Local authorities are empowered or required by various Acts of Parliament to carry out functions in their areas. The legislation concerned comprises public general Acts and 'local' Acts which local authorities have promoted as private bills.

ELECTIONS

Local elections are normally held on the first Thursday in May. Generally, all British subjects, citizens of the Republic of Ireland, Commonwealth and other European Union citizens who are 18 years or over and resident on the qualifying date in the area for which the election is being held, are entitled to vote at local government elections. A register of electors is prepared and published annually by local electoral registration officers.

A returning officer has the overall responsibility for an election. Voting takes place at polling stations, arranged by the local authority and under the supervision of a presiding officer specially appointed for the purpose. Candidates, who are subject to various statutory qualifications and disqualifications designed to ensure that they are suitable persons to hold office, must be nominated by electors for the electoral area concerned.

In England, the Boundary Committee for England is responsible for carrying out periodic reviews of electoral arrangements and making recommendations to the Electoral Commission. The Boundary Committee for England has commenced a major review of local government structure in the north-east, north-west and Yorkshire and the Humber, following the Deputy Prime Minister's announcement on 16 June 2003 that referendums would be held in 2004 for three elected regional assemblies in these areas.

In Wales and Scotland these matters are the responsibility of the Local Government Boundary Commission for Wales and the Boundary Commission for Scotland respectively. The Local Government Act 2000 provided for the Secretary of State to change the frequency and phasing of elections.

THE BOUNDARY COMMITTEE FOR ENGLAND, Trevelyan House, Great Peter Street, London SW1P 2HW. Tel: 020-7271 0500 Web: www.boundarycommittee.org.uk
LOCAL GOVERNMENT BOUNDARY COMMISSION FOR WALES, Caradog House, 1–6 St Andrew's Place, Cardiff CF10 3BE. Tel: 029-2039 5031 Web: www.lgbc-wales.gov.uk
THE BOUNDARY COMMISSION FOR SCOTLAND, 3 Drumsheugh Gardens, Edinburgh EH3 7QJ. Tel: 0131-538 7200 Web: www.bcomm-scotland.gov.uk

INTERNAL ORGANISATION

The council as a whole is the final decision-making body within any authority. Councils are free to a great extent to make their own internal organisational arrangements. The Local Government Act, given Royal assent on 28 July 2000, allows councils to adopt one of three broad categories of a new constitution which include a separate executive. These three categories are:
– A directly elected mayor with a cabinet selected by that mayor.
– A cabinet, either elected by the council or appointed by its leader.
– A directly elected mayor and council manager.

Normally, questions of policy are settled by the full council, while the administration of the various services is the responsibility of committees of councillors. Day-to-day decisions are delegated to the council's officers, who act within the policies laid down by the councillors.

FINANCE

Local government in England, Wales and Scotland is financed from four sources: the council tax, non-domestic rates, government grants, and income from fees and charges for services.

COUNCIL TAX

Under the Local Government Finance Act 1992, from 1 April 1993 the council tax replaced the community charge (which had been introduced in April 1989 in Scotland and April 1990 in England and Wales in place of domestic rates).

The council tax is a local tax levied by each local council. Liability for the council tax bill usually falls on the owner-occupier or tenant of a dwelling which is their sole or main residence. Council tax bills may be reduced because of the personal circumstances of people resident in a property, and there are discounts in the case of dwellings occupied by fewer than two adults.

In England, each county council, each district council and each police authority sets its own council tax rate. The district councils collect the combined council tax, and the county councils and police authorities claim their share from the district councils' collection funds. In Wales, each unitary authority and each police authority sets its own council tax rate. The unitary authorities collect the combined council tax and the police authorities claim their share from the funds. In Scotland, each local authority sets its own rate of council tax.

The tax relates to the value of the dwelling. Each dwelling is placed in one of eight valuation bands, ranging from A to H, based on the property's estimated market value as at 1 April 1991.

The valuation bands and ranges of values in England, Wales and Scotland are:

England

A	Up to £40,000	E	£88,001–£120,000
B	£40,001–£52,000	F	£120,001–£160,000
C	£52,001–£68,000	G	£160,001–£320,000
D	£68,001–£88,000	H	Over £320,000

Wales

A	Up to £30,000	E	£66,001–£90,000
B	£30,001–£39,000	F	£90,001–£120,000
C	£39,001–£51,000	G	£120,001–£240,000
D	£51,001–£66,000	H	Over £240,000

Scotland

A	Up to £27,000	E	£58,001–£80,000
B	£27,001–£35,000	F	£80,001–£106,000
C	£35,001–£45,000	G	£106,001–£212,000
D	£45,001–£58,000	H	Over £212,000

The council tax within a local area varies between the different bands according to proportions laid down by law. The charge attributable to each band as a proportion of the Band D charge set by the council is approximately:

A	67%	E	122%
B	78%	F	144%
C	89%	F	167%
D	100%	G	200%

The Band D rate is given in the tables on the following pages. There may be variations from the given figure within each district council area because of different parish or community precepts being levied.

NON-DOMESTIC RATES

Non-domestic (business) rates are collected by billing authorities; these are the district councils in those areas of England with two tiers of local government and unitary authorities in other parts of England, in Wales and in Scotland. In respect of England and Wales, the Local Government Finance Act 1988 provides for liability for rates to be assessed on the basis of a poundage (multiplier) tax on the rateable value of property (hereditaments). Separate multipliers are set by the Office of the Deputy Prime Minister in England, the National Assembly for Wales and the Scottish Executive, and rates are collected by the billing authority for the area where a property is located. Rate income collected by billing authorities is paid into a national non-domestic rating (NNDR) pool and redistributed to individual authorities on the basis of the adult population figure as prescribed by the Office of the Deputy Prime Minister, the National Assembly for Wales or the Scottish Executive. The rates pools are maintained separately in England, Wales and Scotland. Actual payment of rates in certain cases is subject to transitional arrangements, to phase in the larger increases and reductions in rates resulting from the effects of the 2000 revaluation.

Rates are levied in Scotland in accordance with the Local Government (Scotland) Act 1975. For 1995–6, the Secretary of State for Scotland prescribed a single non-domestic rates poundage to apply throughout the country at the same level as the uniform business rate (UBR) in England. Rate income is pooled and redistributed to local authorities on a per capita basis. For the year 1995–6 payment of rates was subject to transitional arrangements to phase in the effect of the 1995 revaluation.

Rateable values for the 2000 rating lists came into force on 1 April 2000. They are derived from the rental value of property as at 1 April 1998 and determined on certain statutory assumptions by the Valuation Office Agency in England and Wales, and by Regional Assessors in Scotland. New property which is added to the list, and significant changes to existing property, necessitate amendments to the rateable value on the same basis. Rating lists (valuation rolls in Scotland) remain in force until the next general revaluation. Such revaluations take place every five years, the next being in 2005.

Certain types of property are exempt from rates, e.g. agricultural land and buildings, certain businesses and places of public religious worship. Charities and other non-profit-making organisations may receive full or partial relief. Empty property is liable to pay rates at 50 per cent, except for certain specified classes which are exempt entirely.

GOVERNMENT GRANTS

In addition to specific grants in support of revenue expenditure on particular services, central government pays revenue support grant to local authorities. This grant is paid to each local authority so that if each authority spends at the level of its standard spending assessment, all authorities in the same class can set broadly the same council tax.

COMPLAINTS

Local Government Ombudsmen are responsible for investigating complaints from members of the public who claim to have suffered as a consequence of maladministration in local government or in certain local bodies.

The Northern Ireland Commissioner for Complaints fulfils a similar function in Northern Ireland, investigating complaints about local authorities and certain public bodies.

Complaints are made to the relevant local authority in the first instance and complainants may approach the Ombudsmen or Commissioners if not satisfied. Complaints may also be made directly to the Ombudsmen or Commissioners.

The Local Government Act 2000 established a Standards Board and Adjudication Panel in England. The Standards Board investigates any allegations that councillors have breached the council's Code of Conduct and if there is evidence of wrongdoing the Adjudication Panel will consider the report of investigations and if it is upheld, impose a penalty. In Wales the Commission for Local Administration in Wales undertakes the role of the Standards Board.

THE QUEEN'S REPRESENTATIVES

The Lord-Lieutenant of a county is the permanent local representative of the Crown in that county. The appointment of Lord-Lieutenants is now regulated by the Lieutenancies Act 1997. They are appointed by the Sovereign on the recommendation of the Prime Minister. The retirement age is 75. The office of Lord-Lieutenant dates from 1551, and its holder was originally responsible for the maintenance of order and for local defence in the county. The duties of the post include attending on royalty during official visits to the county, performing certain duties in connection with armed forces of the Crown (and in particular the reserve forces), and making presentations of honours and awards on behalf of the Crown. In England, Wales and Northern Ireland, the Lord-Lieutenant usually also holds the office of *Custos Rotulorum*. As such, he or she acts as head of the county's commission of the peace (which recommends the appointment of magistrates).

The office of Sheriff (from the Old English shire-reeve) of a county was created in the tenth century. The Sheriff was the special nominee of the Sovereign, and the office reached the peak of its influence under the Norman kings. The Provisions of Oxford (1258) laid down a yearly tenure of office. Since the mid-16th century the office has been purely civil, with military duties taken over by the Lord-Lieutenant of the county. The Sheriff (commonly known as 'High Sheriff') attends on royalty during official visits to the county, acts as the returning officer during parliamentary elections in county constituencies, attends the opening ceremony when a High Court judge goes on circuit, executes High Court writs, and appoints under-sheriffs to act as deputies. The appointments and duties of the High Sheriffs in England and Wales are laid down by the Sheriffs Act 1887.

The serving High Sheriff submits a list of names of possible future sheriffs to a tribunal which chooses three names to put to the Sovereign. The tribunal nominates the High Sheriff annually on 12 November and the Sovereign picks the name of the Sheriff to succeed in the following year. The term of office runs from 25 March to the following 24 March (the civil and legal year before 1752). No person may be chosen twice in three years if there is any other suitable person in the county.

CIVIC DIGNITIES

District councils in England may petition for a royal charter granting borough or 'city' status to the district. Local councils in Wales may petition for a royal charter granting county borough or 'city' status to the council.

In England and Wales the chairman of a borough or county borough council may be called a mayor, and the chairman of a city council may be called a Lord Mayor if Lord Mayoralty has been conferred on that city. Parish councils in England and community councils in Wales may call themselves 'town councils', in which case their chairman is the town mayor.

In Scotland the chairman of a local council may be known as a convenor; a provost is the equivalent of a mayor. The chairmen of the councils for the cities of Aberdeen, Dundee, Edinburgh and Glasgow are Lord Provosts.

ENGLAND

There are currently 34 non-metropolitan counties; all are divided into non-metropolitan districts. In addition, there are 45 unitary authorities (13 created in April 1996, 13 in April 1997 and 19 in April 1998). At present there are 238 non-metropolitan districts. The populations of most of the new unitary authorities are in the range of 100,000 to 300,000. The non-metropolitan districts have populations broadly in the range of 60,000 to 100,000; some, however, have larger populations, because of the need to avoid dividing large towns, and some in mainly rural areas have smaller populations.

The main conurbations outside Greater London – Tyne and Wear, West Midlands, Merseyside, Greater Manchester, West Yorkshire and South Yorkshire – are divided into 36 metropolitan districts, most of which have a population of over 200,000.

There are also about 10,000 parishes, in 219 of the non-metropolitan and 18 of the metropolitan districts.

ELECTIONS

For districts, non-metropolitan counties and for about 8,000 parishes, there are elected councils, consisting of directly elected councillors. The councillors elect annually one of their number as chairman.

Generally, councillors serve four years and there are no elections of district and parish councillors in county election years. In metropolitan districts, one-third of the councillors for each ward are elected each year except in the year when county elections take place elsewhere. Non-metropolitan districts can choose whether to have elections by thirds or whole council elections. In the former case, one-third of the council, as nearly as may be, is elected in each year of metropolitan district elections. If whole council elections are chosen, these are held in the year midway between county elections.

FUNCTIONS

In non-metropolitan areas, functions are divided between the districts and counties, those requiring the larger area or population are generally the responsibility of the county. The metropolitan district councils, with the larger population in their areas, already had wider functions than non-metropolitan councils, and following abolition of the metropolitan county councils were also given most of their functions. A few functions continue to be exercised over the larger area by joint bodies, made up of councillors from each district.

The allocation of functions is as follows:

County councils: education; strategic planning; traffic, transport and highways; fire service; consumer protection; refuse disposal; smallholdings; social services; libraries

Non-metropolitan district councils: local planning; housing; highways (maintenance of certain urban roads and off-street car parks); building regulations; environmental health; refuse collection; cemeteries and crematoria

Unitary councils: their functions are all those listed above, except that the fire service is exercised by a joint body

Concurrently by county and district councils: recreation (parks, playing fields, swimming pools); museums; encouragement of the arts, tourism and industry

The Police and Magistrates Court Act 1994 set up police authorities in England and Wales separate from the local authorities.

PARISH COUNCILS

Parishes with 200 or more electors must generally have parish councils, which means that over three-quarters of the parishes have councils. A parish council comprises at least five members, the number being fixed by the district council. Elections are held every four years, at the time of the election of the district councillor for the ward including the parish. All parishes have parish meetings, comprising the electors of the parish. Where there is no council, the meeting must be held at least twice a year.

Parish council functions include: allotments; encouragement of arts and crafts; community halls; recreational facilities (e.g. open spaces, swimming pools), cemeteries and crematoria; and many minor functions. They must also be given an opportunity to comment on planning applications. They may, like county and district councils, spend limited sums for the general benefit of the parish. They levy a precept on the district councils for their funds.

The Local Government and Rating Act 1997 gave additional powers to parish councils to spend money on community transport initiatives and crime prevention equipment.

FINANCE

Aggregate external finance for 2003–4 has been determined at £51,551 million. Of this, special grants were estimated at £11,677 million; £24,215 million was in respect of Revenue Support Grant and £15,600 million was support from the national non-domestic rate pool.

In England, the average council tax per dwelling for 2003–4 is £908, an increase from £804 in 2002–3. The average council tax is £939 in shire areas, £969 in London and £780 in metropolitan areas. In England, the average council tax bill for a band D dwelling (occupied by two adults) for 2003–4 is £1,102, an average increase of 12.9 per cent from 2002–3. The average band D council tax is £1,114 in shire areas, £1,058 in London and £1,098 in metropolitan areas. The assumed council tax yield for 2003–4 is £18,094 million.

The provisional amount estimated to be raised from national non-domestic rates from central and local lists is £16,186 million. The amount of national non-domestic rates to be redistributed to authorities from the pool in 2003–4 is £15,600 million. The national non-domestic rate multiplier, or poundage, for 2003–4 is 44.4p.

Under the Local Government and Housing Act 1989, local authorities have four main ways of paying for capital expenditure: borrowing and other forms of extended credit; capital grants from central government towards some types of capital expenditure; 'usable' capital receipts from the sale of land, houses and other assets; and revenue.

The amount of capital expenditure which a local authority can finance by borrowing (or other forms of credit) is effectively limited by the credit approvals issued to it by central government. Most credit approvals can be used for any kind of local authority capital expenditure; these are known as basic credit approvals. Others (supplementary credit approvals) can be used only for the kind of expenditure specified in the approval, and so are often given to fund particular projects or services.

Local authorities can use all capital receipts from the sale of property or assets for capital spending, except in the case of sales of council houses. Generally, the 'usable' part of a local authority's capital receipts consists of 25 per cent of receipts from the sale of council houses and 50 per cent of other housing assets such as shops or vacant land. The balance has to be set aside as provision for repaying debt and meeting other credit liabilities.

EXPENDITURE

Local authority budgeted net revenue expenditure for 2003–2004 is:

Service	£m
Central services (including administration & emergency planning)	2,973
Education	30,186
Social Services	14,083
Police	9,140
Highways and Transport	3,738
Fire	1,852
Planning	1,428
Courts services	391
Mandatory rent allowances	6,028
Mandatory rent rebates	371
Non-housing revenue account housing	1,318
Cultural services (including sport & recreation)	2,680
Environment	3,457
Other services	604
Net current expenditure	78,250
Capital financing	2,317
Capital expenditure charged to revenue account	661

Council tax benefit	2,418
Discretionary non-domestic rate relief	25
Flood defence payments to the Environment Agency	257
Less interest receipts	(657)
Less specific grants outside AEF	(10,799)
Gross revenue expenditure	72,473
Less specific grants inside AEF	(9,187)
Net Revenue expenditure	63,286

AEF = aggregate external finance

LONDON

The Greater London Council was abolished in 1986. London is divided into 32 borough councils, which have a status similar to the metropolitan district councils in the rest of England, and the Corporation of the City of London.

In March 1998 the Government announced proposals for a Greater London Authority (GLA) covering the area of the 32 London boroughs and the City of London, which would comprise a directly elected mayor and a 25-member assembly. A referendum was held in London on 7 May 1998; the turnout was approximately 34 per cent, of whom 72 per cent voted in favour of the GLA. The independent candidate for London Mayor, Ken Livingstone, was elected on 4 May 2000 and the Authority assumed its responsibilities on 3 July 2000. The GLA is responsible for transport, economic development, strategic planning, culture, health, the environment, the police and fire and emergency planning. The separately elected assembly scrutinise the mayor's activities and approve plans and budgets. There are 14 Constituency Assembly members, each representing a separate area of London (each constituency is made up of two or three complete London boroughs). Eleven additional members, making up the total Assembly complement of 25 members, are elected on a London-wide basis, either as independents or from party political lists on the basis of proportional representation. Parties or independent candidates must secure at least five per cent of the vote to be entitled to additional seats.

LONDON BOROUGH COUNCILS

The London boroughs have whole council elections every four years, in the year immediately following the county council election year. The most recent elections took place on 2 May 2002.

The borough councils have responsibility for the following functions: building regulations; cemeteries and crematoria; consumer protection; education; youth employment; environmental health; electoral registration; food; drugs; housing; leisure services; libraries; local planning; local roads; museums; parking; recreation (parks, playing fields, swimming pools); refuse collection and street cleansing; social services; town planning; and traffic management.

THE CORPORATION OF LONDON

The Corporation of London is the local authority for the City of London. Its legal definition is 'The Mayor and Commonalty and Citizens of the City of London'. It is governed by the Court of Common Council, which consists of the Lord Mayor, 24 other aldermen, and 130 common councilmen. The Lord Mayor and two sheriffs are nominated annually by the City guilds (the livery companies) and elected by the Court of Aldermen. Aldermen and councilmen are elected from the 25 wards into which the City is divided; councilmen must stand for re-election annually. The Council is a legislative assembly, and there are no political parties.

The Corporation has the same functions as the London borough councils. In addition, it runs the City of London Police; is the health authority for the Port of London; has health control of animal imports throughout Greater London, including at Heathrow airport; owns and manages public open spaces throughout Greater London; runs the Central Criminal Court; and runs Billingsgate, Smithfield and Spitalfields markets.

THE CITY GUILDS (LIVERY COMPANIES)

The livery companies of the City of London grew out of early medieval religious fraternities and began to emerge as trade and craft guilds, retaining their religious aspect, in the 12th century. From the early 14th century, only members of the trade and craft guilds could call themselves citizens of the City of London. The guilds began to be called livery companies, because of the distinctive livery worn by the most prosperous guild members on ceremonial occasions, in the late 15th century.

By the early 19th century the power of the companies within their trades had begun to wane, but those wearing the livery of a company continued to play an important role in the government of the City of London. Liverymen still have the right to nominate the Lord Mayor and sheriffs, and most members of the Court of Common Council are liverymen.

WALES

The Local Government (Wales) Act 1994 abolished the two-tier structure of eight county and 37 district councils which had existed since 1974, and replaced it, from 1 April 1996, with 22 unitary authorities. The new authorities were elected in May 1995. Each unitary authority has inherited all the functions of the previous county and district councils, except fire services (which are provided by three combined fire authorities, composed of representatives of the unitary authorities) and National Parks (which are the responsibility of three independent National Park authorities).

The Police and Magistrates Courts Act 1994 set up four police authorities with effect from 1 April 1995: Dyfed-Powys, Gwent, North Wales, and South Wales.

COMMUNITY COUNCILS

In Wales community councils are the equivalent of parishes in England. Unlike England, where many areas are not in any parish, communities have been established for the whole of Wales, approximately 865 communities in all. Community meetings may be convened as and when desired.

Community councils exist in 735 communities and further councils may be established at the request of a community meeting. Community councils have broadly the same range of powers as English parish councils. Community councillors are elected for a term of four years.

FINANCE

Non-hypothecated funding for 2003–4 is £3,245 million. This comprises revenue support grant of £2,533 million, support from the national non-domestic rate pool of £660 million, Deprivation Grant of £20 million, Performance Incentive Grant of £30 million and additional Police Grant of £2 million. The non-domestic rating multiplier or poundage for Wales for 2003–4 is 44.0p. The average Band D council tax levied in Wales for 2003–4 is £837,

comprising unitary authorities £702, police authorities £116 and community councils £20.

EXPENDITURE

Local authority budgeted net revenue expenditure for 2003–4 is:

Service	£m
Education	1,892.8
Personal social services	938.5
Police	503.5
Fire	115.7
Other law, order and protective services	28.9
Roads and Transport	247.7
Council tax benefit and administration	19.3
Non-housing revenue account housing, including housing benefit	332.9
Libraries, culture, heritage, sport and recreation	148.5
Local environmental services	284.5
National Parks	14.4
Debt financing costs	260.6
Total other services	354.0
Planning, economic and community development and tourism	92.0
Local tax collection	16.4
Central administrative expenditure	187.1
Other revenue expenditure	58.5
Gross Revenue Expenditure	5,141.2
Less specific government grants	(846.8)
Net revenue expenditure	4,294.4

SCOTLAND

The Local Government etc. (Scotland) Act 1994 abolished the two-tier structure of nine regional and 53 district councils which had existed since 1975 and replaced it, from 1 April 1996, with 29 unitary authorities on the mainland; the three islands councils remained. The new authorities were elected in April 1995. Each unitary authority has inherited all the functions of the regional and district councils, except water and sewerage and reporters panels.

In July 1999 the Scottish Parliament assumed responsibility for legislation on local government. The Government had established a Commission on Local Government and the Scottish Parliament (the McIntosh Commission) to make recommendations on the relationship between local authorities and the new Parliament and on increasing local authorities' accountability. The Commission published its reports in July 1999.

Following this report, the Scottish Executive established the 'Renewing Local Democracy' working group to consider ways in which to make council membership more attractive and councils more representative of their communities. The group would also advise on appropriate membership levels for each council, looking at modernising management practices and local concerns. They also investigated which method of election would be most appropriate, taking account of the following criteria; proportionality and the councillor-ward link, fair provision for independents, allowance for geographical diversity and a close fit between council wards and natural communities, and advise on an appropriate system of remuneration for councillors, taking account of available resources.

The Scottish Executive also set up the Leadership Advisory Panel in August 1999 following the recommendations of the McIntosh Report. The panel worked closely with Scottish local authorities helping them to conduct a self-review of their political management structures and to implement its recommendations.

The Local Government in Scotland Bill was introduced to the Scottish Parliament in May 2002. This Bill centres on three integrated core elements:
– A power for local authorities to promote and improve well-being of their area and/or persons in it
– Statutory underpinning for community planning through the introduction of a duty on local authorities and key partners, including police, health boards and enterprise agencies
– A duty to secure best value

The overall aim of the bill is to provide a framework for more responsive public services, giving councils more flexibility and responsibility to act in the best interests of their communities.

ELECTIONS

The unitary authorities consist of directly elected councillors. The Scottish Local Government (Elections) Act 2002 moved elections from a three-year to a four-year cycle; the last elections took place in May 2003. The 2003 register showed 3,905,553 electors in Scotland.

FUNCTIONS

The functions of the councils and islands councils are: education; social work; strategic planning; the provision of infrastructure such as roads; consumer protection; flood prevention; coast protection; valuation and rating; the police and fire services; civil defence; electoral registration; public transport; registration of births, deaths and marriages; housing; leisure and recreation; development and building control; environmental health; licensing; allotments; public conveniences; and the administration of district courts.

COMMUNITY COUNCILS

Scottish community councils differ from those in England and Wales. Their purpose as defined in statute is to ascertain and express the views of the communities they represent, and to take in the interests of their communities such action as appears to be expedient or practicable. Over 1,100 community councils have been established under schemes drawn up by local authorities in Scotland.

Since April 1996 community councils have had an enhanced role, becoming statutory consultees on local planning issues and on the decentralisation schemes which the new councils have to draw up for delivery of services.

FINANCE

Budgeted aggregate external finance for 2003–4 is £7,128 million, comprising; £4,896 million revenue support grant, non-domestic rate income of £1,590 million and specific grants of £642 million. The non-domestic rate multiplier or poundage for 2003-4 is 47.8p. In 2003–4 a single owned property with a rateable value of £5,000 is eligible for 20 per cent small business rate relief. The average Band D council tax for 2003–4 is £1,009.

EXPENDITURE

The 2003–4 net expenditure budget estimates for local authorities in Scotland were:

Service	£m
Education	3,595.9
Cultural and related services	484.6
Social Work Services	1,769.3
Police	909.3
Roads and transport	467.3
Environmental services	423.2
Fire	230.4
Total planning and development services	137.5
Total	8,017.4

NORTHERN IRELAND

For the purpose of local government Northern Ireland has a system of 26 single-tier district councils.

ELECTIONS

Council members are elected for periods of four years at a time on the principle of proportional representation.

FUNCTIONS

The district councils have three main roles. These are:

Executive: responsibility for a wide range of local services including building regulations; community services; consumer protection; cultural facilities; environmental health; miscellaneous licensing and registration provisions, including dog control; litter prevention; recreational and social facilities; refuse collection and disposal; street cleansing; and tourist development

Representative: nominating representatives to sit as members of the various statutory bodies responsible for the administration of regional services such as drainage, education, fire, health and personal social services, housing, and libraries

Consultative: acting as the medium through which the views of local people are expressed on the operation in their area of other regional services, notably conservation (including water supply and sewerage services), planning and roads, provided by those departments of central government which have an obligation, statutory or otherwise, to consult the district councils about proposals affecting their areas

FINANCE

Local government in Northern Ireland is funded by a system of rates. The ratepayer receives a combined tax bill consisting of the Regional Rate and the District Rate, which is set by each district council. The Regional and District Rates are both collected by the Rate Collection Agency. The product of the District Rates is paid over to each council whilst the product of the Regional Rate supports expenditure by the departments of the Executive and Assembly. Rate bills are calculated by multiplying the property's Net Annual Value (NAV) by the Regional and District Rate poundages respectively. A general revaluation of non domestic properties became effective from 1 April 2003, based on 2001 rental values, however the values of domestic properties continue to be based on 1976 rental values.

For 2003–4 the overall average domestic poundage is 273.30p and the overall average non-domestic rate poundage is 42.06p.

POLITICAL COMPOSITION OF LOCAL COUNCILS

AS AT MAY 2003

Abbreviations

All.	Alliance
BNP	British National Party
C	Conservative
CU	Conservative and Unionist
DUP	Democratic Unionist
Green	Green
IF	Island First
Ind.	Independent
Ind. All.	Independent Alliance
Ind. UU	Independent Unionist
IKHHC	Independent Kidderminster Hospital and Health Concern
Lab.	Labour
LD	Liberal Democrat
Lib.	Liberal
NP	Non-Political/Non-Party
PC	Plaid Cymru
R	Residents Associations/Ratepayers
SD	Social Democrat
SDLP	Social Democratic and Labour Party
SF	Sinn Fein
SNP	Scottish National Party
Soc.	Socialist
Soc. Dem.	Social Democratic
SSP	Scottish Socialist Party
UUP	Ulster Unionist Party

ENGLAND

COUNTY COUNCILS

Bedfordshire	C. 26; Lab. 13; LD 9; Ind. 1
Buckinghamshire	C. 40; LD 9; Lab. 5
Cambridgeshire	C. 34; LD 16; Lab. 9
Cheshire	C. 28; Lab. 17; LD 5; Ind. 1
Cornwall	LD 36; Ind. 25; C. 9; Lab. 9
Cumbria	Lab. 40; C. 33; LD 10
Derbyshire	Lab. 43; C. 13; Ind. 1; LD 7
Devon	LD 21; C. 23; Lab. 5; Ind. 3; Lib. 2
Dorset	C. 23; LD 14; Lab. 4; Ind. 1
Durham	Lab. 53; LD 4; C. 2; Ind. 2
East Sussex	C. 24; LD 13; Lab. 7
Essex	C. 49; Lab. 18; LD 10; Ind. 2
Gloucestershire	C. 27; Lab. 19; LD 16; Ind. 1
Hampshire	C. 46; LD 20; Lab. 8
Hertfordshire	C. 40; Lab. 26; LD 10
Kent	C. 52; Lab. 22; LD 10
Lancashire	Lab. 44; C. 27; LD 5; Other 2
Leicestershire	C. 28; Lab. 15; LD 10; Ind. 1
Lincolnshire	C. 49; Lab. 21; LD 4; Ind. 3
Norfolk	C. 47; Lab. 26; LD 11
North Yorkshire	C. 42; LD 17; Lab. 12; Ind. 3
Northamptonshire	Lab. 39; C. 33; LD 1
Northumberland	Lab. 38; C. 17; LD 9; Ind. 3
Nottinghamshire	Lab. 39; C. 21; LD 3
Oxfordshire	C. 26; Lab. 24; LD 19; Green 1
Shropshire	C. 18; LD 9; Lab. 11; Ind. 6
Somerset	LD 29; C. 24; Lab. 5
Staffordshire	Lab. 36; C. 22; LD 4

Suffolk	Lab. 35; C. 32; LD 12; Ind. 1
Surrey	C. 51; LD 13; Lab. 6; R. 4; Ind. 2
Warwickshire	Lab. 28; C. 20; LD 13; Ind. 1
West Sussex	C. 42; LD 18; Lab. 11
Wiltshire	C. 28; LD 13; Lab. 3; Ind. 3
Worcestershire	C. 26; Lab. 14; LD 8; Ind. 9

DISTRICT COUNCILS

Adur	C. 29; Lab. 8; Ind. 2
Allerdale	Lab. 27; C. 15; LD 5; Ind. 9
Alnwick	LD 10; Ind. 10; Lab. 2; C. 3; Other 4
Amber Valley	C. 25; Lab. 20
Arun	C. 36; LD 11; Lab. 8; Ind. 1
Ashfield	Lab. 16; Ind. 14; C. 1; Green 2
Ashford	C. 25; Lab. 4; LD 5; Ind. 9
Aylesbury Vale	C. 30; LD 25; Ind. 4
Babergh	Ind. 8; LD 18; C. 11; Lab. 6
Barrow-in-Furness	Lab. 21; C. 14; Ind. 3
Basildon	C. 23; Lab. 14; LD 3; Ind. 2
Basingstoke and Deane	C. 26; LD 15; Lab. 15; Ind. 3; Other 1
Bassetlaw	Lab. 25; C. 19; LD 2; Ind. 2
Bedford	C. 18; Lab. 13; LD 12; Ind. 7; Other 4
Berwick-upon-Tweed	LD 9; C. 12; Lab. 2; Ind. 4; Other 2
Blaby	C. 25; Lab. 4; LD 9; Ind. 1
Blyth Valley	Lab. 35; LD 9; Ind. 3; C. 3
Bolsover	Lab. 31; Ind. 6;
Boston	C. 12; Lab. 11; Ind. 5; LD 4
Braintree	Lab. 20; C. 27; Other 7; LD 4; Green 2
Breckland	C. 42; Lab. 8; Ind. 4
Brentwood	LD 18; C. 16; Lab. 3
Bridgnorth	Ind. 8; C. 10; Lab. 2; LD 8; Other 6
Broadland	C. 27; LD 12; Ind. 7; Lab. 3
Bromsgrove	C. 26; Lab. 8; Ind. 1; R. 4
Broxbourne	C. 34; Lab. 2; Ind. 1; BNP 1
Broxtowe	Lab. 15; C. 14; LD 13; Ind. 2
Burnley	Lab. 24; LD 7; C. 3; Ind. 3; BNP 8
Cambridge	LD 26; Lab. 14; C. 2
Cannock Chase	Lab. 20; C. 9; LD 12
Canterbury	C. 24; LD 19; Lab. 7
Caradon	LD 15; Ind. 22; Lab. 1; C. 4
Carlisle	C. 23; Lab. 22; LD 5; Ind. 2
Carrick	LD 29; C. 12; Lab. 1; Ind. 5
Castle Morpeth	Ind. 6; Lab. 10; LD 6; C. 9; Green 1
Castle Point	C. 39; Lab. 2;
Charnwood	Lab. 22; C. 24; LD 6
Chelmsford	LD 20; C. 35; Lab. 2
Cheltenham	LD 21; C. 13; Ind. 4; Lab. 2
Cherwell	C. 34; Lab. 12; LD 4
Chester	Lab. 20; LD 21; C. 18; Ind. 1
Chester-le-Street	Lab. 29; Ind. 4; C. 1
Chesterfield	Lab. 12; LD 36;
Chichester	C. 26; LD 21; Ind. 1
Chiltern	C. 27; LD 12; Other 1

Chorley	Lab. 22; C. 18; LD 4; Ind. 3	Kerrier	Ind. 21; LD 10; Lab. 5; C. 4;
Christchurch	C. 14; LD 8; Ind. 2		Other 4
Colchester	LD 25; C. 24; Lab. 5; Ind. 6	Kettering	Lab. 13; C. 30; Ind. 2
Congleton	C. 27; LD 12; Ind. 5; Lab. 2;	King's Lynn and	
	Other 2	West Norfolk	Lab. 14; C. 35; LD 7; Ind. 6
Copeland	Lab. 31; C. 16; Ind. 3; LD 1	Lancaster	Other 15; Lab. 20; C. 10; LD 8;
Corby	Lab. 16; C. 9; LD 2		Green 7
Cotswolds	C. 24; Ind. 9; LD 8; Other 3	Lewes	LD 28; C. 11; Ind. 2
Craven	C. 11; LD 9; Ind. 10	Lichfield	C. 35; Lab. 16; LD 5
Crawley	Lab. 22; C. 8; LD 2	Lincoln City	Lab. 27; C. 6;
Crewe and Nantwich	Lab. 22; C. 21; Ind. 2; LD 5;	Macclesfield	C. 36; LD 14; Lab. 6; Ind. 1;
	Other 6		Other 3
Dacorum	C. 27; Lab. 21; LD 4	Maidstone	LD 21; C. 21; Lab. 10; Ind. 3
Dartford	Lab. 17; C. 18; Other 6;	Maldon	C. 21; Ind. 4; Lab. 2; Other 4
	Vacant 3	Malvern Hills	LD /Green 19; C. 13; Ind. 5;
Daventry	C. 33; Lab. 4; Vacant 1		Green 1
Derbyshire Dales	C. 24; LD 9; Lab. 5; Ind. 1	Mansfield	Lab. 15; C. 2; LD 4; Ind. 25
Derwentside	Lab. 38; Ind. 16; LD 1	Melton	C. 19; Lab. 4; Ind. 5
Dover	C. 22; Lab. 20; LD 3	Mendip	C. 31; LD 11; Ind. 4
Durham	Lab. 17; LD 30; Ind. 3	Mid Bedfordshire	C. 37; LD 11; Ind. 4; NP 1
Easington	Lab. 44; Ind. 5; LD 2	Mid Devon	Ind. 20; LD 8; C. 11; Lab. 1;
East Cambridgeshire	LD 18; Ind. 6; C. 15		Other 2
East Devon	C. 35; LD 18; Ind. 6	Mid Suffolk	C. 21; LD 11; Lab. 2; Ind. 5;
East Dorset	C. 24; LD 11; Ind. 1		Green 1
East Hampshire	C. 26; LD 18;	Mid Sussex	C. 28; LD 24; Lab. 2
East Hertfordshire	C. 41; LD 7; Ind. 2	Mole Valley	C. 18; LD 16; Lab. 1; Ind. 6
East Lindsey	Ind. 26; Lab. 12; C. 15; LD 6;	New Forest	C. 32; LD 27; Ind. 1
	Green 1	Newark and Sherwood	Lab. 13; C. 23; LD 4; Ind. 6
East Northamptonshire	C. 33; Lab. 3;	Newcastle-under-Lyme	Lab. 29; LD 18; C. 12; Other 1
East Staffordshire	Lab. 16; C. 22; LD 1	North Cornwall	Ind. 18; LD 13; C. 3; Other 2
Eastbourne	LD 14; C. 13;	North Devon	LD 22; Ind. 9; C. 10; Other 2
Eastleigh	LD 30; C. 10; Lab. 4	North Dorset	C. 16; LD 11; Ind. 6
Eden	Ind. 28; LD 4; C. 6	North East Derbyshire	Lab. 36; C. 8; LD 5; Ind. 3;
Ellesmere Port and			Other 1
Neston	Lab. 31; C. 10; LD 2	North Hertfordshire	C. 27; Lab. 16; LD 6
Elmbridge	R. 31; C. 20; LD 8; Lab. 1	North Kesteven	C. 18; LD 5; Lab. 4; Ind. 13
Epping Forest	C. 24; LD 15; Lab. 8; R. 6;	North Norfolk	C. 14; LD 28; Ind. 6
	Ind. 5	North Shropshire	Ind. 20; C. 15; Lab. 4; LD 1
Epsom and Ewell	Ind. 27; LD 6; Lab. 3; C. 2	North Warwickshire	Lab. 16; C. 15; LD 4
Erewash	Lab. 19; C. 26; Ind. 2; LD 4	North West	
Exeter	Lab. 20; LD 10; C. 6; Lib. 4	Leicestershire	Lab. 21; C. 12; LD 3; Ind. 2
Fareham	C. 17; LD 13; Ind. 1	North Wiltshire	LD 26; C. 25; Lab. 1; Ind. 1
Fenland	C. 36; Lab. 3; Ind. 1	Northampton	Lab. 11; LD 17; C. 19
Forest Heath	C. 21; Ind. 6;	Norwich	LD 30; Lab. 14; C. 1; Green 3
Forest of Dean	Lab. 16; Ind. 11; LD 4; C. 17	Nuneaton and	
Fylde	Ind. 22; C. 27; Lib. 2	Bedworth	Lab. 26; C. 8
Gedling	C. 21; Lab. 21; LD 7; Ind. 1	Oadby and Wigston	LD 17; C. 9
Gloucester	C. 14; Lab. 11; LD 11	Oswestry	Ind. 9; LD 6; Lab. 1;
Gosport	LD 12; Lab. 12; C. 10		C. 12; Other 1
Gravesham	Lab. 23; C. 21	Oxford	Lab. 29; LD 15; Ind. 4
Great Yarmouth	C. 26; Lab. 22	Pendle	Lab. 15; LD 23; C. 11
Guildford	LD 19; C. 26; Lab. 2; Ind. 1	Penwith	C. 10; LD 11; Ind. 11; Lab. 2
Hambleton	C. 36; LD 3; Lab. 1; Ind. 4	Preston	Lab. 25; C. 18; LD 11; Ind. 3
Harborough	C. 16; LD 18; Lab. 1; Ind. 2	Purbeck	C. 13; LD 8; Ind. 3
Harlow	C. 12; LD 12; Lab. 9	Redditch	Lab. 10; C. 14; LD 5
Harrogate	LD 24; C. 27; Ind. 1; Other 2	Reigate and Banstead	C. 33; Lab. 4; LD 7; Ind. 1; R. 6
Hart	C. 21; LD 10; Ind. 4	Restormel	LD 22; Ind. 13; C. 9; Other 1
Hastings	Lab. 21; C. 10; LD 1	Ribble Valley	C. 22; LD 15; Ind. 2; Lab. 1
Havant	C. 23; Lab. 8; LD 7	Richmondshire	Ind. 9; LD 8; C. 11; Other 6
Hertsmere	C. 25; Lab. 8; LD 6	Rochford	C. 30; Lab. 3; LD 4; Ind. 2
High Peak	Lab. 18; C. 12; LD 7; Ind. 6	Rossendale	Lab. 18; C. 17; LD 1
Hinckley and Bosworth	LD 8; C. 20; Lab. 6	Rother	C. 25; LD 8; Lab. 3; Ind. 2
Horsham	C. 22; LD 20; Ind. 2	Rugby	C. 18; Lab. 16; LD 10; Ind. 4
Huntingdonshire	C. 36; LD 14; Ind. 3	Runnymede	C. 32; Ind. 6; Lab. 4
Hyndburn	Lab. 17; C. 18;	Rushcliffe	C. 34; LD 10; Lab. 4; Ind. 1;
Ipswich	Lab. 31; C. 12; LD 5		Green 1
Kennet	C. 27; Ind. 8; Lab. 1; LD 3;	Rushmoor	C. 25; LD 10; Lab. 6; Ind. 1
	Other 4	Ryedale	C. 13; Ind. 7; LD 8; Lib. 2

Salisbury	C. 31; LD 9; Lab. 11; Ind. 4
Scarborough	C. 27; Lab. 8; LD 2; Ind. 13
Sedgefield	Lab. 35; Ind. 7; LD 7; C. 1
Sedgemoor	C. 35; Lab. 14; LD 1
Selby	Lab. 14; C. 23; Ind. 3; LD 1
Sevenoaks	C. 32; LD 8; Lab. 9; Ind. 3; Vacant 2
Shepway	C. 16; LD 29; Lab. 1
Shrewsbury and Atcham	C. 22; Lab. 9; LD 6; Ind. 3
South Bedfordshire	C. 31; LD 13; Lab. 6
South Bucks	C. 33; Ind. 6; LD 1
South Cambridgeshire	C. 23; LD 16; Ind. 12; Lab. 4
South Derbyshire	Lab. 21; C. 15
South Hams	C. 28; LD 7; Ind. 2; Lab. 3
South Holland	C. 26; Ind. 8; Other 3; Lab. 1
South Kesteven	C. 31; Ind. 12; Lab. 10; LD 5
South Lakeland	LD 23; C. 18; Lab. 9; Ind. 2
South Norfolk	LD 28; C. 18
South Northamptonshire	C. 30; Lab. 4; Ind. 6; LD 1; Other 1
South Oxfordshire	C. 27; LD 9; Lab. 4; Ind. 4; Other 4
South Ribble	Lab. 17; C. 19; LD 15; Other 4
South Shropshire	Ind. 9; LD 14; C. 10; Other 3
South Somerset	LD 36; C. 17; Ind. 7
South Staffordshire	C. 35; Lab. 8; LD 1; Ind. 3; Other 2
Spelthorne	C. 35; LD 4;
St Albans	C. 21; LD 23; Lab. 13; Ind. 1
St Edmundsbury	C. 28; Lab. 12; Ind. 3; LD 2
Stafford	C. 40; Lab. 14; LD 5
Staffordshire Moorlands	C. 22; Lab. 7; Ind. 4; LD 11; Other 12
Stevenage	Lab. 33; C. 3; LD 3
Stratford-on-Avon	C. 27; LD 22; Ind. 3; Lab. 1
Stroud	C. 27; Lab. 11; LD 6; Green 4; Ind. 3
Suffolk Coastal	C. 43; LD 10; Lab. 2
Surrey Heath	C. 22; LD 13; Lab. 3; Ind. 2
Swale	C. 25; LD 11; Lab. 11
Tamworth	Lab. 18; C. 11; Ind. 1
Tandridge	C. 28; LD 10; Lab. 3; Ind. 1
Taunton Deane	LD 15; C. 31; Ind. 3; Lab. 5
Teesdale	Ind. 12; Lab. 9; C. 3; Other 6
Teignbridge	Ind. 16; C. 14; LD 16
Tendring	Lab. 11; C. 25; Ind. 7; LD 13; Other 4
Test Valley	C. 30; LD 16; Ind. 2
Tewkesbury	C. 18; Ind. 5; Lab. 3; LD 9; Other 3
Thanet	C. 31; Lab. 23; LD 1; Ind. 1
Three Rivers	LD 27; C. 14; Lab. 7
Tonbridge and Malling	C. 33; LD 13; Lab. 7
Torridge	Ind. 27; LD 7; Green 1; C. 1
Tunbridge Wells	C. 33; LD 12; Lab. 3
Tynedale	C. 27; Lab. 9; LD 11; Ind. 5
Uttlesford	LD 31; C. 10; Ind. 3
Vale of White Horse	LD 29; C. 22;
Vale Royal	Lab. 21; C. 22; LD 12; Ind. 2
Wansbeck	Lab. 36; LD 9;
Warwick	Lab. 14; LD 16; C. 10; Ind. 6
Watford	Lab. 8; LD 20; C. 7; Green 1
Waveney	Lab. 20; C. 21; LD 3; Ind. 4
Waverley	C. 27; LD 30;
Wealden	C. 34; LD 15; Ind. 6
Wear Valley	Lab. 25; LD 9; Ind. 6
Wellingborough	Lab. 9; C. 27;
Welwyn & Hatfield	C. 27; Lab. 20; Vacant 1

West Devon	Ind. 10; C. 12; LD 8; Other 1
West Dorset	C. 25; LD 12; Ind. 11
West Lancashire	C. 28; Lab. 26;
West Lindsey	LD 13; C. 17; Ind. 6; Lab. 1
West Oxfordshire	C. 29; LD 12; Ind. 6; Lab. 2
West Somerset	C. 19; Ind. 8; Lab. 2; LD 2
West Wiltshire	LD 19; C. 19; Ind. 4; Lab. 2
Weymouth and Portland	Lab. 13; LD 11; C. 6; Ind. 5
Winchester	LD 29; C. 19; Ind. 4; Lab. 5
Woking	C. 17; LD 12; Lab. 6; Ind. 1
Worcester	C. 19; Lab. 10; Ind. 5; LD 2
Worthing	LD 18; C. 18;
Wychavon	C. 31; LD 12; Lab. 2
Wycombe	C. 46; Lab. 9; LD 2; Ind. 3
Wyre	C. 33; Lab. 21; LD 1
Wyre Forest	Ind. 20; C. 9; Lab. 4; LD 2; Lib. 7

LONDON BOROUGHS

Barking and Dagenham	Lab. 41; R. 4; LD 3; C. 3
Barnet	C. 33; Lab. 24; LD 6
Bexley	Lab. 32; C. 30; LD 1
Brent	Lab. 35; C. 19; LD 9
Bromley	C. 41; LD 13; Lab. 6
Camden	Lab. 35; C. 11; LD 8
Croydon	Lab. 37; C. 32; LD 1
Ealing	Lab. 48; C. 17; LD 4
Enfield	C. 39; Lab. 24;
Greenwich	Lab. 38; C. 9; LD 4
Hackney	Lab. 45; C. 9; LD 3
Hammersmith and Fulham	Lab. 29; C. 17;
Haringey	Lab. 42; LD 15;
Harrow	Lab. 30; C. 28; LD 3; Ind. 2
Havering	C. 26; R. 17; Lab. 10
Hillingdon	C. 31; Lab. 27; LD 7
Hounslow	Lab. 37; C. 14; LD 5; Ind. 4
Islington	LD 36; Lab. 10; Ind. 2
Kensington and Chelsea	C. 42; Lab. 12;
Kingston upon Thames	LD 30; C. 15; Lab. 3
Lambeth	Lab. 28; LD 28; C. 7
Lewisham	Lab. 43; LD 6; C. 2; Other 2; Green 1
Merton	Lab. 32; C. 24; R. 4
Newham	Lab. 59; Ind. 1;
Redbridge	C. 33; Lab. 21; LD 9
Richmond upon Thames	C. 39; LD 15;
Southwark	LD 29; Lab. 28; C. 6
Sutton	LD 43; C. 8; Lab. 3
Tower Hamlets	Lab. 35; LD 16;
Waltham Forest	Lab. 28; C. 18; LD 14
Wandsworth	C. 50; Lab. 10
Westminster	C. 48; Lab. 12

METROPOLITAN BOROUGHS

Barnsley	Lab. 47; Ind. 9; C. 5; LD 4; Other 1
Birmingham	Lab. 57; C. 35; LD 23; Ind. 2
Bolton	Lab. 27; C. 19; LD 14
Bradford	C. 36; Lab. 36; LD 14; Green 3; Ind. 1
Bury	Lab. 28 C. 16; LD 4
Calderdale	C. 25; LD 16; Lab. 10; Ind. 1; BNP 2
Coventry	Lab. 24; C. 23; Other 5; LD 2
Doncaster	Lab. 45; LD 8; C. 7; Other 3
Dudley	Lab. 30; C. 31; LD 10; BNP 1
Gateshead	Lab. 46; LD 19; Lib. 1

Kirklees	LD 30; Lab. 21; C. 16; Green 3; BNP. 1
Knowsley	Lab. 55; LD 11;
Leeds	Lab. 52; LD 20; C. 22; Green 3; Ind. 2
Liverpool	LD 63; Lab. 31; Other 2; Lib. 3
Manchester	Lab. 71; LD 27; Ind. 1
Newcastle-upon-Tyne	Lab. 54; LD 24;
North Tyneside	Lab. 31; C. 21; LD 8
Oldham	LD 24; Lab. 33; C. 2; Ind. 1
Rochdale	Lab. 30; LD 22; C. 8
Rotherham	Lab. 59; C. 4; Ind. 3
Salford	Lab. 51; LD 5; C. 3; Other 1
Sandwell	Lab. 55; C. 9; LD 6; BNP 1
Sefton	Lab. 24; LD 20; C. 19; Other 3
Sheffield	Lab. 49; LD 37; C. 1
Solihull	C. 28; Lab. 13; LD 10
South Tyneside	Lab. 49; LD 5; Ind. 2; C. 1; Other 3
St Helens	Lab. 33; LD 15; C. 6
Stockport	LD 34; Lab. 17; C. 9; Ind. 3
Sunderland	Lab. 63; C. 9; LD 1; Ind. 1; Lib. 1
Tameside	Lab. 47; C. 6; Other 2; LD 2
Trafford	Lab. 31; C. 29; LD 3
Wakefield	Lab. 49; C. 7; LD 3; Ind. 2; Other 2
Walsall	Lab. 27; C. 26; LD 7
Wigan	Lab. 60; Other 5; LD 4; C. 3
Wirral	Lab. 26; C. 23; LD 16; Ind. 1
Wolverhampton	Lab. 34; C. 21; Ind. 5

UNITARY COUNCILS

Bath and North East Somerset	LD 29; Lab. 6; C. 26; Ind. 4
Blackburn with Darwen	Lab. 37; C. 16; LD 8; BNP 1
Blackpool	Lab. 25; C. 13; LD 4
Bournemouth	C. 27; LD 18; Lab. 6; Ind. 6
Bracknell Forest	C. 35; Lab. 6; LD 1
Brighton and Hove	Lab. 24; C. 20; LD 3; Ind. 1; Green 6
Bristol	Lab. 31; LD 28; C. 11
Darlington	Lab. 35; C. 16; LD 2
Derby	Lab. 25; LD 13; C. 12; Ind. 1
East Riding of Yorkshire	C. 28; LD 20; Lab. 8; Ind. 6; SDP 2
Halton	Lab. 47; LD 7; C. 2
Hartlepool	Lab. 22; LD 11; C. 7; Ind. 7
Herefordshire	C. 21; LD 16; Ind. 17; Lab. 4
Isle of Wight	IF 28; C. 13; Lab. 3; Other 4
Kingston-upon-Hull	LD 22; Lab. 27; Ind. 8; C. 2
Leicester	Lab. 20; LD 25; C. 9
Luton	Lab. 23; LD 20; C. 4; Ind. 1
Medway	C. 30; Lab. 17; LD 6; Ind. 2
Middlesbrough	Lab. 32; C. 7; LD 5; Ind. 4
Milton Keynes	LD 27; Lab. 16; C. 7; Ind. 1
North East Lincolnshire	Lab. 7; C. 16; LD 15; Ind. 4
North Lincolnshire	Lab. 21; C. 22;
North Somerset	C. 24; Lab. 10; LD 23; Ind. 3; Green 1
Nottingham	Lab. 36; C. 8; LD 11
Peterborough	C. 30; Lab. 17; LD 4; Lib. 3; Other 3
Plymouth	C. 36; Lab. 18; LD 3
Poole	LD 16; C. 26
Portsmouth	C. 15; Lab. 11; LD 16
Reading	Lab. 35; LD 6; C. 4

Redcar and Cleveland	Lab. 23; C. 13; LD 15; Ind. 8
Rutland	C. 15; Ind. 6; LD 5
Slough	Lab. 26; C. 6; Ind. 1; LD 2; Other 6
South Gloucestershire	LD 33; Lab. 16; C. 21
Southampton	Lab. 19; LD 18; C. 11
Southend-on-Sea	C. 32; Lab. 10; LD 8; Ind. 1
Stockton-on-Tees	Lab. 28; C. 13; LD 6; Ind. 8
Stoke-on-Trent	Lab. 27; Ind. 18; LD 7; C. 5; Other 3
Swindon	Lab. 22; C. 29; LD 8
Telford and Wrekin	Lab. 29; C. 13; Ind. 6; LD 6
Thurrock	Lab. 37; C. 9; Ind. 2; LD 1
Torbay	LD 27; C. 9;
Warrington	Lab. 41; LD 15; C. 4
West Berkshire	LD 26; C. 26
Windsor and Maidenhead	C. 15; LD 34; Other 7; Lab. 1
Wokingham	C. 33; LD 20; Lab. 1
York	Lab. 15; LD 29; Green 2; Ind. 1

WALES

Blaenau Gwent	Lab. 33; LD 3; R. 3; Ind. 2; Ind. Lab. 1
Bridgend	Lab. 40; LD 6; PC 2; C. 1; Ind. 5
Caerphilly	PC 38; Lab. 28; LD 1; Ind. 6
Cardiff	Lab. 49; LD 17; C. 6; PC 1; Ind. 2
Carmarthenshire	Ind. 30; Lab. 29; PC 14; LD 1
Ceredigion	Ind. 22; PC 12; LD 8; Lab. 1; Other 1
Conwy	Lab. 20; Ind. 13; LD 13; PC 8; C. 5
Denbighshire	Ind. 22; Lab. 14; PC 8; C. 2; LD 1
Flintshire	Lab. 43; Other 19; LD 7; C. 1
Gwynedd	PC 43; Ind. 22; Lab. 12; LD 6
Merthyr Tydfil	Lab. 16; Ind. 13; PC 4
Monmouthshire	C. 18; Lab. 19; Ind. 3; LD 2
Neath Port Talbot	Lab. 40; PC 10; Other 14
Newport	Lab. 37; C. 5; PC 1; LD 1 Other 2
Pembrokeshire	Ind. 40; Lab. 13; LD 5; PC 2
Powys	Ind. 58; LD 8; Lab. 6; C. 1
Rhondda Cynon Taff	PC 38; Lab. 26; Ind. 5; LD 6
Swansea	Lab. 46; LD 10; Ind. 9; C. 5; PC 2
Torfaen	Lab. 38; Ind. 3; LD 2; C. 1
Vale of Glamorgan	C. 21; Lab. 18; PC 6; LD 1
Wrexham	Lab. 24; Other 14; LD s10; C. 4
Ynys Mon (Isle of Anglesey)	Ind. 15; PC 3; Other 22

SCOTLAND

Aberdeen	Lab. 14; LD 20; C. 3; SNP 6
Aberdeenshire	LD 28; SNP 18; Ind. 11; C. 11
Angus	SNP 17; Ind. 6; LD 3; C. 2; Lab. 1
Argyll and Bute	Ind. 22; LD 8; SNP 3; C. 3
Clackmannanshire	SNP 6; Lab. 10; C. 1; Ind. 1
Dumfries and Galloway	Lab. 14; Ind. 12; C. 11; LD 5; SNP 5
Dundee	Lab. 10; SNP 11; C. 5; LD 2; Ind. 1
East Ayrshire	Lab. 23; SNP 8; C. 1
East Dunbartonshire	Lab. 9; LD 12; C. 3
East Lothian	Lab. 17; C. 4; SNP 1; LD s1
East Renfrewshire	Lab. 8; C. 7; LD 3; Ind. 2
Edinburgh	Lab. 30; LD 15; C. 13
Eilean Siar (Western Isles)	Ind. 22; Lab. 5; SNP 3
Falkirk	Lab. 14; SNP 9; Ind. 7; C. 2
Fife	Lab. 36; LD 23; SNP 11; C. 2; Other 6
Glasgow	Lab. 71; SNP 3; C. 1; SSP1; LD 3
Highland	Ind. 57; Lab. 8; LD 9; SNP 6
Inverclyde	Lab. 6; LD 13; Other 1
Midlothian	Lab. 15; LD 2; Ind. 1
Moray	Ind. 16; Lab. 5; SNP 3; LD 1; C. 1
North Ayrshire	Scottish Lab. 21; C. 4; SNP 3; Ind. 2
North Lanarkshire	Lab. 54; SNP 11; Ind. 5
Orkney Islands	Ind. 21;
Perth and Kinross	C. 10; SNP 15; Lab. 5; LD 9; Ind. 2
Renfrewshire	Lab. 21; SNP 15; LD 3; C. 1
Scottish Borders	Ind. 15; LD 8; SNP 1; C. 10
Shetland Islands	Ind. 17; Scottish LD 5;
South Ayrshire	Lab. 15; C. 15;
South Lanarkshire	Lab. 51; SNP 9; C. 2; LD 2; Other 3
Stirling	Lab. 12; C. 10;
West Dunbartonshire	Lab. 17; SNP 3; SSP 1; Ind. 1
West Lothian	Lab. 18; SNP 12; C. 1; Ind. 1

NORTHERN IRELAND

Antrim	UUP 8; DUP 5; SDLP 4; SF 2
Ards	UUP 8; DUP 9; All. 4; Ind. 2
Armagh City	UUP 7; SDLP 6; SF5; DUP 4
Ballymena	DUP 11; UUP 7; SDLP 4; Ind. 2
Ballymoney	DUP 8; UUP 5; SDLP 2; SF 1
Banbridge	UU7; DUP 5; SDLP 3; All.1; Ind. 1
Belfast	SF 14; UUP 11; DUP 10; SDLP 9; Other 7
Carrickfergus	DUP 6; All. 5; UUP 4; Ind. 2
Castlereagh	DUP 10; UUP 5; All. 4; SDLP 2; Ind. 2
Coleraine	UUP 10; DUP 7; SDLP 4; Ind. 1
Cookstown	SF 6; SDLP 4; UUP 3; DUP 2; Ind. 1
Craigavon	UUP 7; SDLP 7; DUP 6; SF 4; Ind. UU 2
Derry City	SDLP 13; SF 10; DUP 4; UUP 2; Ind. 1
Down	SDLP 9; UUP 6; SF 4; DUP 2; Ind. 2
Dungannon and South Tyrone	SF 8; UUP 6; SDLP 4; DUP 3; Ind. 1
Fermanagh	SF 9; UUP 7; SDLP 4; DUP 2; Ind. 1
Larne	UUP 4; DUP 5; All. 2; SDLP 2; Ind. 2
Limavady	SDLP 4; SF4; UUP 3; DUP 2; Other 2
Lisburn	UUP 12; DUP 6; SF 4; SDLP 3; Other 5
Magherafelt	SF 7; DUP 3; SDLP 3; UUP 2; Ind. 1
Moyle	SDLP 5; Ind. 3; UUP 3; DUP 2; SF 2
Newry and Mourne	SDLP 10; SF 13; UUP 4; Ind. 2; DUP 1
Newtownabbey	UUP 9; DUP 7; Other 6; SDLP 2; SF 1
North Down	UUP 8; A5; DUP 5; Ind. 7
Omagh	SF 8; SDLP 6; UUP 3; DUP 2; Ind. 2
Strabane	SF 7; SDLP 4; DUP 3; UUP 2;

ENGLAND

The Kingdom of England lies between 55° 46' and 49° 57' 30'' N. latitude (from a few miles north of the mouth of the Tweed to the Lizard), and between 1° 46' E. and 5° 43' W. (from Lowestoft to Land's End). England is bounded on the north by the Cheviot Hills; on the south by the English Channel; on the east by the Straits of Dover (Pas de Calais) and the North Sea; and on the west by the Atlantic Ocean, Wales and the Irish Sea. It has a total area of 50,351 sq. miles (130,410 sq. km): land 50,058 sq. miles (129,652 sq. km); inland water 293 sq. miles (758 sq. km).

POPULATION

The population at the 2001 census was 49,138,831. The average density of the population in 2001 was 3.8 persons per hectare.

FLAG

The flag of England is the cross of St George, a red cross on a white field (cross gules in a field argent). The cross of St George, the patron saint of England, has been used since the 13th century.

RELIEF

There is a marked division between the upland and lowland areas of England. In the extreme north the Cheviot Hills (highest point, The Cheviot, 2,674 ft) form a natural boundary with Scotland. Running south from the Cheviots, though divided from them by the Tyne Gap, is the Pennine range (highest point, Cross Fell, 2,930 ft), the main orological feature of the country. The Pennines culminate in the Peak District of Derbyshire (Kinder Scout, 2,088 ft). West of the Pennines are the Cumbrian mountains, which include Scafell Pike (3,210 ft), the highest peak in England, and to the east are the Yorkshire Moors, their highest point being Urra Moor (1,490 ft).

In the west, the foothills of the Welsh mountains extend into the bordering English counties of Shropshire (the Wrekin, 1,334 ft; Long Mynd, 1,694 ft) and Hereford and Worcester (the Malvern Hills – Worcestershire Beacon, 1,394 ft). Extensive areas of highland and moorland are also to be found in the south-western peninsula formed by Somerset, Devon and Cornwall: principally Exmoor (Dunkery Beacon, 1,704 ft), Dartmoor (High Willhays, 2,038 ft) and Bodmin Moor (Brown Willy, 1,377 ft). Ranges of low, undulating hills run across the south of the country, including the Cotswolds in the Midlands and south-west, the Chilterns to the north of London, and the North (Kent) and South (Sussex) Downs of the south-east coastal areas.

The lowlands of England lie in the Vale of York, East Anglia and the area around the Wash. The lowest-lying are the Cambridgeshire Fens in the valleys of the Great Ouse and the River Nene, which are below sea-level in places. Since the 17th century extensive drainage has brought much of the Fens under cultivation. The North Sea coast between the Thames and the Humber, low-lying and formed of sand and shingle for the most part, is subject to erosion and defences against further incursion have been built along many stretches.

HYDROGRAPHY

The Severn is the longest river in Great Britain, rising in the north-eastern slopes of Plynlimon (Wales) and entering England in Shropshire with a total length of 220 miles (354 km) from its source to its outflow into the Bristol Channel, where it receives on the east the Bristol Avon, and on the west the Wye, its other tributaries being the Vyrnwy, Tern, Stour, Teme and Upper (or Warwickshire) Avon. The Severn is tidal below Gloucester, and a high bore or tidal wave sometimes reverses the flow as high as Tewkesbury (13½ miles above Gloucester). The scenery of the greater part of the river is very picturesque and beautiful, and the Severn is a noted salmon river, some of its tributaries being famous for trout. Navigation is assisted by the Gloucester and Berkeley Ship Canal (16¼ miles), which admits vessels of 350 tons to Gloucester. The Severn Tunnel was begun in 1873 and completed in 1886 at a cost of £2 million and after many difficulties caused by flooding. It is 4 miles 628 yards in length (of which 2¼ miles are under the river). The Severn road bridge between Haysgate, Gwent, and Almondsbury, Glos, with a centre span of 3,240 ft, was opened in 1966.

The longest river wholly in England is the Thames, with a total length of 215 miles (346 km) from its source in the Cotswold hills to the Nore, and is navigable by ocean-going ships to London Bridge. The Thames is tidal to Teddington (69 miles from its mouth) and forms county boundaries almost throughout its course; on its banks are situated London, Windsor Castle, Eton College and Oxford University.

Of the remaining English rivers, those flowing into the North Sea are the Tyne, Wear, Tees, Ouse and Trent from the Pennine Range, the Great Ouse (160 miles), which rises in Northamptonshire, and the Orwell and Stour from the hills of East Anglia. Flowing into the English Channel are the Sussex Ouse from the Weald, the Itchen from the Hampshire Hills, and the Axe, Teign, Dart, Tamar and Exe from the Devonian hills. Flowing into the Irish Sea are the Mersey, Ribble and Eden from the western slopes of the Pennines and the Derwent from the Cumbrian mountains.

The English Lakes, noteworthy for their picturesque scenery and poetic associations, lie in Cumbria, the largest being Windermere (10 miles long), Ullswater and Derwent Water.

ISLANDS

The Isle of Wight is separated from Hampshire by the Solent. The capital, Newport, stands at the head of the estuary of the Medina, Cowes (at the mouth) being the chief port. Other centres are Ryde, Sandown, Shanklin, Ventnor, Freshwater, Yarmouth, Totland Bay, Seaview and Bembridge.

Lundy (the name means Puffin Island), 11 miles north-west of Hartland Point, Devon, is about three miles long and about half a mile wide on average, with a total area of about 1,116 acres, and a population of about 18. It became the property of the National Trust in 1969 and is now principally a bird sanctuary.

The Isles of Scilly consist of about 140 islands and skerries (total area, 6 sq. miles/10 sq. km) situated 28 miles south-west of Land's End in Cornwall. Only five are inhabited: St Mary's, St Agnes, Bryher, Tresco and St Martin's. The population at the 2001 census was 2,153. The entire group has been designated a Conservation Area, a Heritage Coast, and an Area of Outstanding Natural Beauty, and has been given National Nature Reserve status by the Nature Conservancy Council because of its unique flora and fauna. Tourism and the winter/spring flower trade for the home market form the basis of the economy of the Isles. The island group is a recognised rural development area.

EARLY HISTORY

Archaeological evidence suggests that England has been inhabited since at least the Palaeolithic period, though the extent of the various Palaeolithic cultures was dependent upon the degree of glaciation. The succeeding Neolithic and Bronze Age cultures have left abundant remains throughout the country, the best-known of these being the henges and stone circles of Stonehenge (ten miles north of Salisbury, Wilts) and Avebury (Wilts), both of which are believed to have been of religious significance. In the latter part of the Bronze Age the Goidels, a people of Celtic race, and in the Iron Age other Celtic races of Brythons and Belgae, invaded the country and brought with them Celtic civilisation and dialects; place names in England bear witness to the spread of the invasion over the whole kingdom.

THE ROMAN CONQUEST

The Roman conquest of Gaul (57–50 bc) brought Britain into close contact with Roman civilisation, but although Julius Caesar raided the south of Britain in 55 BC and 54 BC, conquest was not undertaken until nearly 100 years later. In AD 43 the Emperor Claudius dispatched Aulus Plautius, with a well-equipped force of 40,000, and himself followed with reinforcements in the same year. Success was delayed by the resistance of Caratacus (Caractacus), the British leader from AD 48–51, who was finally captured and sent to Rome, and by a great revolt in AD 61 led by Boudicca (Boadicea), Queen of the Iceni; but the south of Britain was secured by AD 70, and Wales and the area north to the Tyne by about AD 80.

In AD 122, the Emperor Hadrian visited Britain and built a continuous rampart, since known as Hadrian's Wall, from Wallsend to Bowness (Tyne to Solway). The work was entrusted by the Emperor Hadrian to Aulus Platorius Nepos, legate of Britain from AD 122 to 126, and it was intended to form the northern frontier of the Roman Empire.

The Romans administered Britain as a province under a Governor, with a well-defined system of local government, each Roman municipality ruling itself and its surrounding territory, while London was the centre of the road system and the seat of the financial officials of the Province of Britain. Colchester, Lincoln, York, Gloucester and St Albans stand on the sites of five Roman municipalities, and Wroxeter, Caerleon, Chester, Lincoln and York were at various times the sites of legionary fortresses. Well-preserved Roman towns have been uncovered at or near Silchester (*Calleva Atrebatum*), ten miles south of Reading, Wroxeter (*Viroconium Cornoviorum*), near Shrewsbury, and St Albans (*Verulamium*) in Hertfordshire.

Four main groups of roads radiated from London, and a fifth (the Fosse) ran obliquely from Lincoln through Leicester, Cirencester and Bath to Exeter. Of the four groups radiating from London, one ran south-east to Canterbury and the coast of Kent, a second to Silchester and thence to parts of western Britain and south Wales, a third (later known as Watling Street) ran through Verulamium to Chester, with various branches, and the fourth reached Colchester, Lincoln, York and the eastern counties.

In the fourth century Britain was subject to raids along the east coast by Saxon pirates, which led to the establishment of a system of coastal defences from the Wash to Southampton Water, with forts at Brancaster, Burgh Castle (Yarmouth), Walton (Felixstowe), Bradwell, Reculver, Richborough, Dover, Lympne, Pevensey and Porchester (Portsmouth). The Irish (Scoti) and Picts in the north were also becoming more aggressive; from about AD 350 incursions became more frequent and more formidable. As the Roman Empire came under attack increasingly towards the end of the fourth century, many troops were removed from Britain for service in other parts of the empire. The island was eventually cut off from Rome by the Teutonic conquest of Gaul, and with the withdrawal of the last Roman garrison early in the fifth century, the Romano-British were left to themselves.

SAXON SETTLEMENT

According to legend, the British King Vortigern called in the Saxons to defend him against the Picts, the Saxon chieftains being Hengist and Horsa, who landed at Ebbsfleet, Kent, and established themselves in the Isle of Thanet; but the events during the one-and-a-half centuries between the final break with Rome and the re-establishment of Christianity are unclear. However, it would appear that in the course of this period the raids turned into large-scale settlement by invaders traditionally known as Angles (England north of the Wash and East Anglia), Saxons (Essex and southern England) and Jutes (Kent and the Weald), which pushed the Romano-British into the mountainous areas of the north and west. Celtic culture outside Wales and Cornwall survives only in topographical names. Various kingdoms established at this time attempted to claim overlordship of the whole country, hegemony finally being achieved by Wessex (capital, Winchester) in the ninth century. This century also saw the beginning of raids by the Vikings (Danes), which were resisted by Alfred the Great (871–899), who fixed a limit to the advance of Danish settlement by the Treaty of Wedmore (878), giving them the area north and east of Watling Street, on condition that they adopt Christianity.

In the tenth century the kings of Wessex recovered the whole of England from the Danes, but subsequent rulers were unable to resist a second wave of invaders. England paid tribute (*Danegeld*) for many years, and was invaded in 1013 by the Danes and ruled by Danish kings from 1016 until 1042, when Edward the Confessor was recalled from exile in Normandy. On Edward's death in 1066 Harold Godwinson (brother-in-law of Edward and son of Earl Godwin of Wessex) was chosen King of England. After defeating (at Stamford Bridge, Yorkshire, 25 September) an invading army under Harald Hadraada, King of Norway (aided by the outlawed Earl Tostig of Northumbria, Harold's brother), Harold was himself defeated at the Battle of Hastings on 14 October 1066, and the Norman conquest secured the throne of England for Duke William of Normandy, a cousin of Edward the Confessor.

CHRISTIANITY

Christianity reached the Roman province of Britain from Gaul in the third century (or possibly earlier); Alban, traditionally Britain's first martyr, was put to death as a

Christian during the persecution of Diocletian (22 June 303), at his native town Verulamium; and the Bishops of Londinium, Eboracum (York), and Lindum (Lincoln) attended the Council of Arles in 314. However, the Anglo-Saxon invasions submerged the Christian religion in England until the sixth century when conversion was undertaken in the north from 563 by Celtic missionaries from Ireland led by St Columba, and in the south by a mission sent from Rome in 597 which was led by St Augustine, who became the first archbishop of Canterbury. England appears to have been converted again by the end of the seventh century and followed, after the Council of Whitby in 663, the practices of the Roman Church, which brought the kingdom into the mainstream of European thought and culture.

PRINCIPAL CITIES

There are 50 cities in England and space constraints prevent us from including profiles of them all. The profiles below represent just a selection of England's principal cities – other cities (with date city status conferred) are: Bradford (pre-1900), Brighton and Hove (2000), Chichester (pre-1900), Ely (pre-1900), Gloucester (pre-1900), Hereford (pre-1900), Lichfield (pre-1900), London (pre-1900), Peterborough (pre-1900), Plymouth (1928), Portsmouth (1926), Preston (2002), Ripon (pre-1900), Salford (1926), Southampton (1964), Sunderland (1992), Truro (pre-1900), Wakefield (pre-1900), Wells (pre-1900), Westminster (pre-1900), Wolverhampton (2000) and Worcester (pre-1900).

Certain cities have also been granted a Lord Mayoralty – this grant confers no additional powers or functions and is purely honorific. Cities with Lord Mayors are: Birmingham, Bradford, Bristol, Canterbury, Chester, Coventry, Exeter, Kingston-Upon-Hull, Leeds, Leicester, Liverpool, London, Manchester, Newcastle-upon-Tyne, Norwich, Nottingham, Oxford, Plymouth, Portsmouth, Sheffield and Stoke-on-Trent.

BATH
Bath stands on the River Avon between the Cotswold Hills to the North and the Mendips to the south. In the early eighteenth century, Bath became England's premier spa town where the rich and celebrated members of fashionable society gathered to 'take the waters' and enjoy the town's theatres and assembly rooms. During this period the architect John Wood laid the foundations for a new Georgian city to be built using the honey-coloured stone that Bath is famous for today.

Today Bath is a thriving tourist destination and remains a leading cultural, religious and historical centre with many art galleries and historic sites including; the Pump Room (1790), The Royal Crescent (1767), the Circus (1754), the eighteenth century Assembly Rooms, housing the Museum of Costume, Pulteney Bridge (1771), the Guildhall and the Abbey, now over 500 years old, which is built on the site of the Saxon monastery.

BIRMINGHAM
Birmingham is Britain's second largest city with a population of nearly one million. The generally accepted derivation of 'Birmingham' is the *ham* (dwelling-place) of the *ing* (family) of *Beorma,* presumed to have been Saxon. During the Industrial Revolution the town grew into a major manufacturing centre and in 1889 was granted city status.

Recent developments include the Millennium Point,

incorporating the science museum, Thinktank and Brindleyplace. The Eastside of the city is currently undergoing reconstruction.

The principal buildings are the Town Hall (1834–50); the Council House (1879); Victoria Law Courts (1891); Birmingham University (1906–9); the 13th-century Church of St Martin-in-the-Bull-Ring (rebuilt 1873); Our Lady, Help of Christians Church; the Cathedral (formerly St Philip's Church) (1711); the Roman Catholic Cathedral of St Chad (1839–41); the assay office (1773) and the National Exhibition Centre (1976). There is also the Birmingham Museum and Art Gallery including the Waterhall Gallery which opened in 2001.

BRISTOL
Bristol was a Royal Borough before the Norman Conquest. The earliest form of the name is *Bricgstow.* In 1373 Edward III granted Bristol county status.

The chief buildings include the 12th-century Cathedral (with later additions), with Norman chapter house and gateway, the 14th-century Church of St Mary Redcliffe, Wesley's Chapel, Broadmead, the Merchant Venturers' Almshouses, the Council House (1956), Guildhall, Exchange (erected from the designs of John Wood in 1743), Cabot Tower, the University and Clifton College. The Roman Catholic Cathedral at Clifton was opened in 1973.

The Clifton Suspension Bridge, with a span of 702 feet over the Avon, was projected by Brunel in 1836 but was not completed until 1864. Brunel's SS *Great Britain,* the first ocean-going propeller-driven ship, is now being restored in the City Docks from where she was launched in 1843. The docks themselves have been extensively restored and redeveloped and are becoming a focus for the arts and recreation.

CAMBRIDGE
Cambridge, a settlement far older than its ancient University, lies on the River Cam or Granta. The city is a county town and regional headquarters. Its industries include high technology research and development, and biotechnology. Among its open spaces are Jesus Green, Sheep's Green, Coe Fen, Parker's Piece, Christ's Pieces, the University Botanic Garden, and the Backs, or lawns and gardens through which the Cam winds behind the principal line of college buildings. Historical sites east of the Cam include; King's Parade, Great St Mary's Church, Gibbs' Senate House and King's College Chapel.

University and college buildings provide the outstanding features of Cambridge architecture but several churches (especially St Benet's, the oldest building in the city, and St Sepulchre's, the Round Church) are also notable. The Guildhall (1937) stands on a site of which at least part has held municipal buildings since 1224.

CANTERBURY
Canterbury, the Metropolitan City of the Anglican Communion, dates back to prehistoric times. It was the Roman *Durovernum Cantiacorum* and the Saxon *Cant-wara-byrig* (stronghold of the men of Kent). Here in 597 St Augustine began the conversion of the English to Christianity, when Ethelbert, King of Kent, was baptised.

Of the Benedictine St Augustine's Abbey, burial place of the Jutish Kings of Kent, only ruins remain. St Martin's Church, on the eastern outskirts of the city, is stated by Bede to have been the place of worship of Queen Bertha, the Christian wife of King Ethelbert, before the advent of St Augustine.

In 1170 the rivalry of Church and State culminated in the murder in Canterbury Cathedral, by Henry II's knights, of Archbishop Thomas Becket. His shrine became a great centre of pilgrimage, as described in Chaucer's *Canterbury Tales*. After the Reformation pilgrimages ceased, but the prosperity of the city was strengthened by an influx of Huguenot refugees, who introduced weaving. The poet and playwright Christopher Marlowe was born and reared in Canterbury, and there are also literary associations with Defoe, Dickens, Joseph Conrad and Somerset Maugham.

The Cathedral, with architecture ranging from the 11th to the 15th centuries, is world famous. Modern pilgrims are attracted particularly to the Martyrdom, the Black Prince's Tomb, the Warriors' Chapel and the many examples of medieval stained glass.

The medieval city walls are built on Roman foundations and the 14th-century West Gate is one of the finest buildings of its kind in the country.

The 1,000-seat Marlowe Theatre is a centre for the Canterbury Arts Festival each autumn.

CARLISLE

Carlisle is situated at the confluence of the River Eden and River Caldew, 309 miles north-west of London and about ten miles from the Scottish border. It was granted a charter in 1158.

The city stands at the western end of Hadrian's Wall and dates from the original Roman settlement of *Luguvalium*. Granted to Scotland in the tenth century, Carlisle is not included in the Domesday Book. William Rufus reclaimed the area in 1092 and the castle and city walls were built to guard Carlisle and the western border; the citadel is a Tudor addition to protect the south of the city. Border disputes were common until the problem of the Debateable Lands was settled in 1552. During the Civil War the city remained Royalist; in 1745 Carlisle was besieged for the last time by the Young Pretender (Bonnie Prince Charlie).

The Cathedral, originally a 12th-century Augustinian priory, was enlarged in the 13th and 14th centuries after the diocese was created in 1133. To the south is a restored Tithe Barn and nearby the 18th-century church of St Cuthbert, the third to stand on a site dating from the seventh century.

Carlisle is the major shopping, commercial and agricultural centre for the area, and industries include the manufacture of metal goods, biscuits and textiles. However, the largest employer is the services sector, notably in central and local government, retailing and transport. The city has an important communications position at the centre of a network of major roads, as a stage on the main west coast rail services, and with its own airport at Crosby-on-Eden.

CHESTER

Chester is situated on the River Dee, and was granted borough and city status in 1974. Its recorded history dates from the first century when the Romans founded the fortress of *Deva*. The city's name is derived from the Latin *castra* (a camp or encampment). During the Middle Ages, Chester was the principal port of north-west England but declined with the silting of the Dee estuary and competition from Liverpool. The city was also an important military centre, notably during Edward I's Welsh campaigns and the Elizabethan Irish campaigns. During the Civil War, Chester supported the King and was besieged from 1643 to 1646. Chester's first charter

was granted *c.* 1175 and the city was incorporated in 1506. The office of Sheriff is the earliest created in the country (*c.* 1120s), and in 1992 the Mayor was granted the title of Lord Mayor. He/she also enjoys the title 'Admiral of the Dee'.

The city's architectural features include the city walls (an almost complete two-mile circuit), the unique 13th-century Rows (covered galleries above the street-level shops), the Victorian Gothic Town Hall (1869), the Castle (rebuilt 1788 and 1822) and numerous half-timbered buildings. The Cathedral was a Benedictine abbey until the Dissolution. Remaining monastic buildings include the chapter house, refectory and cloisters and there is a modern free-standing bell tower. The Norman church of St John the Baptist was a cathedral church in the early Middle Ages.

COVENTRY

Coventry is an important industrial centre, producing vehicles, machine tools, agricultural machinery, man-made fibres, aerospace components and telecommunications equipment. New investment has come from financial services, power transmission, professional services, leisure and education.

The city owes its beginning to Leofric, Earl of Mercia, and his wife Godiva who, in 1043, founded a Benedictine monastery. The guildhall of St Mary dates from the 14th century, three of the city's churches date from the 14th and 15th centuries, and 16th-century almshouses may still be seen. Coventry's first cathedral was destroyed at the Reformation, its second in the 1940 blitz (the walls and spire remain) and the new cathedral designed by Sir Basil Spence, consecrated in 1962, now draws numerous visitors.

Coventry is the home of the University of Warwick, Coventry University, the Westwood Business Park, the Cable and Wireless College, the Museum of British Road Transport and the Skydome Arena.

DERBY

Derby stands on the banks of the River Derwent, and its name dates back to 880 when the Danes settled in the locality and changed the original Saxon name of *Northworthy* to *Deoraby*.

Derby has a wide range of industries including aero engines, cars, pipework, specialised mechanical engineering equipment, textiles, chemicals, plastics and the Royal Crown Derby porcelain. The city is an established centre of railway excellence with rail research, engineering, safety testing, infrastructure and train-operating companies.

Buildings of interest include St Peter's Church and the Old Abbey Building (14th century), the Cathedral (1525), St Mary's Roman Catholic Church (1839) and the Industrial Museum, formerly the Old Silk Mill (1721). The traditional city centre is complemented by the Eagle Centre and 'out-of-centre' retail developments. In addition to the Derby Playhouse and the mutli-purpose venue Assembly Rooms, Pride Park Stadium is the home of Derby County Football Club, opened by the Queen in 1997.

The first charter granting a Mayor and Aldermen was that of Charles I in 1637. Previous charters date back to 1154. It was granted city status in 1977.

DURHAM

The city of Durham is a district in the county of Durham and a major tourist attraction because of its prominent Norman Cathedral and Castle set high on a wooded peninsula overlooking the River Wear. The Cathedral was founded as a shrine for the body of St Cuthbert in 995. The present building dates from 1093 and among its many treasures is the tomb of the Venerable Bede (673–735). Durham's Prince Bishops had unique powers up to 1836, being lay rulers as well as religious leaders. As a palatinate, Durham could have its own army, nobility, coinage and courts. The Castle was the main seat of the Prince Bishops for nearly 800 years; it is now used as a college by the University. The University, founded on the initiative of Bishop William Van Mildert, is England's third oldest.

Among other buildings of interest is the Guildhall in the Market Place which dates originally from the 14th century. Work has been carried out to conserve this area as part of the city's contribution to the Council of Europe's Urban Renaissance Campaign. Annual events include Durham's Regatta in June (claimed to be the oldest rowing event in Britain) and the Annual Gala (formerly Durham Miners' Gala) in July.

The economy has undergone a significant change with the replacement of mining as the dominant industry by 'white collar' employment. Although still a predominantly rural area, the industrial and commercial sector is growing and a wide range of manufacturing and service industries are based on industrial estates in and around the city. A research and development centre, linked to the University, also plays an important role in the local economy.

EXETER

Exeter lies on the River Exe ten miles from the sea and was granted a charter by Henry II. The Romans founded *Isca Dumnoniorum* in the first century AD as a legionary fortress, and in the third century a stone wall (much of which remains) was built, providing protection against Saxon, and then Danish invasions. After the Conquest, the city led a resistance to William in the west until reduced by siege. The Normans built the ringwork castle of Rougemont, the gatehouse and towers remain, although the rest was pulled down in 1784. The first bridge across the Exe was built in the early 13th century. The city's main port was situated downstream at Topsham until the construction in the 1560s of the first true canal in England The redevelopment of the canal in 1700 brought seaborne trade directly into the city. Exeter was the Royalist headquarters in the west during the Civil War.

The diocese of Exeter was established by Edward the Confessor in 1050, although a minster existed near the Cathedral site from the late seventh century. A new cathedral was built in the 12th century but the present building, incorporating the Norman Towers, was begun c.1275 and completed about a century later. The Guildhall dates from the 12th century and there are many other medieval buildings in the city, as well as architecture in the Georgian and Regency styles, and the Custom House (1680). Damage suffered by bombing in 1942 led to the redevelopment of the city centre.

Exeter's prosperity from medieval times was based on trade in wool, commemorated by Tuckers Hall. The wool trade flourished until the late 18th century when export trade was hit by the French wars. Subsequently Exeter has developed as an administrative and commercial centre, notably in the distributive trades, light manufacturing industries and tourism.

KINGSTON UPON HULL

Hull (officially Kingston upon Hull) lies at the junction of the River Hull with the Humber, 22 miles from the North Sea, at the 2001 census it had a population of 243,589. It is one of the major seaports of the United Kingdom. The port provides a wide range of cargo services, including ro-ro and container traffic, and handles an estimated million passengers annually on daily sailings to Rotterdam and Zeebrugge. There is a variety of manufacturing and service industries.

The city, restored after heavy air raid damage during the Second World War, has good educational facilities with both the University of Hull and the University of Lincoln being within its boundaries. Hull has been granted Urban Regeneration Company Status, current projects include Hull's £45.5 million Millennium Project and the world's only Submarium. Future developments include the Kingston Communications Stadium with a seating capacity for 25,000 and the £25 million BBC regional centre.

Tourism is a major growth industry and the old town area has been renovated and includes Museums, a marina and shopping complex. Just west of the city is the Humber Bridge, until recently the world's longest single-span suspension bridge.

Kingston upon Hull was so named by Edward I. City status was accorded in 1897 and the office of Mayor raised to the dignity of Lord Mayor in 1914.

LANCASTER

Lancaster was originally a Roman fort and in Anglo-Saxon times a church was built within the ruins of the fort.

In the late 17th century, Lancaster began to trade with the West Indies and the new American colonies. This trade meant the 18th century was an age of great prosperity for the city and there are many splendid buildings dating from this period, including the complete port facility of St George's Quay, with the Custom House and numerous warehouses.

In the Victorian age, Lancaster began to specialise in textiles and two major manufacturing firms, Storeys and Williamsons, dominated the industry, the latter having a world reputation for the production of linoleum.

Lancaster was originally a market town and a borough, gaining its first charter in 1193. In 1937 Lancaster was awarded city status on King George VI's Coronation Day. Today, Lancaster has mainly technology and service industries and is an important centre for education.

LEEDS

Leeds, situated in the lower Aire Valley, is a junction for road, rail, canal and air services and an important manufacturing and commercial centre.

The principal buildings are the Civic Hall (1933), the Town Hall (1858), the Municipal Buildings and Art Gallery (1884) with the Henry Moore Gallery (1982), the Corn Exchange (1863) and the University. The Parish Church (St Peter's) was rebuilt in 1841; the 17th-century St John's Church has a fine interior with a famous English Renaissance screen; the last remaining 18th-century church in the city is Holy Trinity in Boar Lane (1727). Kirkstall Abbey (about three miles from the centre of the city), founded by Henry de Lacy in 1152, is one of the most complete examples of Cistercian houses now remaining. Temple Newsam, birthplace of Lord Darnley, was acquired by the Council in 1922. The present house was largely rebuilt by Sir Arthur Ingram in about 1620. Adel Church, about five miles from the centre of the city, is a fine Norman structure. The new Royal Armouries Museum houses the collection of antique arms and armour formerly held at the Tower of London.

Leeds was first incorporated by Charles I in 1626. The earliest forms of the name are *Loidis* or *Ledes,* the origins of which are obscure.

LEICESTER

Leicester is situated geographically in the centre of England. The city was an important Roman settlement and also one of the five Danish boroughs of Danelaw. In 1485 Richard III was buried in Leicester following his death at the nearby Battle of Bosworth. In 1589 Queen Elizabeth I granted a charter to the city and the ancient title was confirmed by letters patent in 1919.

The textile industry, responsible for Leicester's early expansion, has declined in recent years, although the city still maintains a strong manufacturing base. Cotton mills and factories are now undergoing extensive regeneration and are being converted into offices, apartments, bars and restaurants. The principal buildings include the two universities, the University of Leicester and De Montfort University, as well as the Town Hall, the 13th century Guildhall, De Montfort Hall, Leicester Cathedral, the Jewry Wall (the UK's highest standing Roman wall), St Nicholas Church and St Mary de Castro church. The motte and Great Hall of Leicester can be seen from the castle gardens, situated next to the ancient River Soar.

LINCOLN

Situated 40 miles inland on the River Witham, Lincoln derives its name from a contraction of *Lindum Colonia,* the settlement founded in AD 48 by the Romans to command the crossing of Ermine Street and Fosse Way. Sections of the third-century Roman city wall can be seen, including an extant gateway (Newport Arch), and excavations have discovered traces of a sewerage system unique in Britain. The Romans also drained the surrounding fenland and created a canal system, laying the foundations of Lincoln's agricultural prosperity and also the city's importance in the medieval wool trade as a port and Staple town.

As one of the Five Boroughs of Danelaw, Lincoln was an important trading centre in the ninth and tenth centuries and medieval prosperity from the wool trade lasted until the 14th century. This wealth enabled local merchants to build parish churches, of which three survive, and there are also remains of a 12th century Jewish community (Jew's House and Court, Aaron's House). However, the removal of the Staple to Boston in 1369 heralded a decline, from which the city only recovered fully in the 19th century, when improved fen drainage made Lincoln agriculturally important. Improved canal and rail links led to industrial development, mainly in the manufacture of machinery, components and engineering products.

The castle was built shortly after the Conquest and is unusual in having two mounds; on one motte stands a Keep (Lucy's Tower) added in the 12th century. It currently houses one of the four surviving copies of the Magna Carta. The Cathedral was begun *c.* 1073 when the first Norman bishop moved the see of Lindsey to Lincoln, but was mostly destroyed by fire and earthquake in the 12th century. Rebuilding was begun by St Hugh

and completed over a century later. Other notable architectural features are the 12th-century High Bridge, the oldest in Britain still to carry buildings, and the Guildhall situated above the 15th–16th-century Stonebow gateway.

LIVERPOOL

Liverpool, on the north bank of the River Mersey, three miles from the Irish Sea, is the United Kingdom's foremost port for Atlantic trade. Tunnels link Liverpool with Birkenhead and Wallasey.

There are 2,100 acres of dockland on both sides of the river and the Gladstone and Royal Seaforth Docks can accommodate tanker-sized vessels. Liverpool Free Port was opened in 1984.

Liverpool was created a free borough in 1207 and a city in 1880. From the early 18th century it expanded rapidly with the growth of industrialisation and the Atlantic trade. Surviving buildings from this period include the Bluecoat Chambers (1717, formerly the Bluecoat School), the Town Hall (1754, rebuilt to the original design 1795), and buildings in Rodney Street, Canning Street and the suburbs. Notable from the 19th and 20th centuries are the Anglican Cathedral, built from the designs of Sir Giles Gilbert Scott (the foundation stone was laid in 1904, and the building was completed only in 1980); the Catholic Metropolitan Cathedral (designed by Sir Frederick Gibberd, consecrated 1967) and St George's Hall (1842), regarded as one of the finest modern examples of classical architecture. The refurbished Albert Dock (designed by Jesse Hartley) contains the Merseyside Maritime Museum and Tate Gallery, Liverpool.

In 1852 an Act was obtained for establishing a public library, museum and art gallery; as a result Liverpool had one of the first public libraries in the country. The Brown, Picton and Hornby libraries now form one of the country's major libraries. The Victoria Building of Liverpool University, the Royal Liver, Cunard and Mersey Docks & Harbour Company buildings at the Pier Head, the Municipal Buildings and the Philharmonic Hall are other examples of the city's fine architecture.

MANCHESTER

Manchester (the *Mamucium* of the Romans, who occupied it in AD 79) is a commercial and industrial centre with a population engaged in the engineering, chemical, clothing, food processing and textile industries and in education. Banking, insurance and a growing leisure industry are among the prime commercial activities. The city is connected with the sea by the Manchester Ship Canal, opened in 1894, 35.5 miles long, and accommodating ships up to 15,000 tons. In 2001 Manchester Airport handled just over 19 million terminal, transit, scheduled and charter passengers.

The principal buildings are the Town Hall, erected in 1877 from the designs of Alfred Waterhouse, with a large extension of 1938; the Royal Exchange (1869, enlarged 1921); the Central Library (1934); Heaton Hall; the 17th-century Chetham Library; the Rylands Library (1900), which includes the Althorp collection; the University precinct; the 15th-century Cathedral (formerly the parish church) and G-MEX exhibition centre. Recent developments include the Manchester Arena, the largest indoor arena in Europe, and the Bridgewater Hall. Manchester is the home of the Hallé Orchestra, the Royal Northern College of Music, the Royal Exchange Theatre and seven public art galleries. Metrolink, the light rail system, opened in 1992.

To accommodate The Commonwealth Games held in Manchester in 2002 new sports facilities were built including a stadium, swimming pool complex and the National Cycling Centre.

The town received its first charter of incorporation in 1838 and was created a city in 1853.

NEWCASTLE UPON TYNE

Newcastle upon Tyne, on the north bank of the River Tyne, is eight miles from the North Sea. A cathedral and university city, it is the administrative, commercial and cultural centre for north-east England and the principal port. It is an important manufacturing centre with a wide variety of industries.

The principal buildings include the Castle Keep (12th century), Black Gate (13th century), Blackfriars (13th century), West Walls (13th century), St Nicholas's Cathedral (15th century, fine lantern tower), St Andrew's Church (12th–14th century), St John's (14th–15th century), All Saints (1786 by Stephenson), St Mary's Roman Catholic Cathedral (1844), Trinity House (17th century), Sandhill (16th-century houses), Guildhall (Georgian), Grey Street (1834–9), Central Station (1846–50), Laing Art Gallery (1904), University of Newcastle Physics Building (1962) and Medical Building (1985), Civic Centre (1963), Central Library (1969) and Eldon Square Shopping Development (1976). Open spaces include the Town Moor (927 acres) and Jesmond Dene. Ten bridges span the Tyne at Newcastle.

The city's name is derived from the 'new castle' (1080) erected as a defence against the Scots. In 1400 it was made a county, and in 1882 a city.

NORWICH

Norwich grew from an early Anglo-Saxon settlement near the confluence of the Rivers Yare and Wensum, and now serves as provincial capital for the predominantly agricultural region of East Anglia. The name is thought to relate to the most northerly of a group of Anglo-Saxon villages or *wics*. The city's first known charter was granted in 1158 by Henry II.

Norwich serves its surrounding area as a market town and commercial centre, banking and insurance being prominent among the city's businesses. From the 14th century until the Industrial Revolution, Norwich was the regional centre of the woollen industry, but now the biggest single industry is financial services and principal trades are engineering, printing, shoemaking, double glazing, the production of chemicals and clothing, food processing and technology. Norwich is accessible to seagoing vessels by means of the River Yare, entered at Great Yarmouth, 20 miles to the east.

Among many historic buildings are the Cathedral (completed in the 12th century and surmounted by a 15th-century spire 315 feet in height); the keep of the Norman castle (now a museum and art gallery); the 15th-century flint-walled Guildhall; some thirty medieval parish churches; St Andrew's and Blackfriars' Halls; the Tudor houses preserved in Elm Hill and the Georgian Assembly House. The University of East Anglia is on the city's western boundary.

NOTTINGHAM

Nottingham stands on the River Trent. *Snotingaham* or *Notingeham*, literally the homestead of the people of Snot, is the Anglo-Saxon name for the Celtic settlement of *Tigguocobauc*, or the house of caves. In 878, Nottingham became one of the Five Boroughs of Danelaw. William the Conqueror ordered the construction of Nottingham Castle, while the town itself developed rapidly under Norman rule. Its laws and rights were later formally recognised by Henry II's charter in 1155. The Castle became a favoured residence of King John. In 1642 King Charles I raised his personal standard at Nottingham Castle at the start of the Civil War.

Nottingham is home to Notts County FC (the world's oldest football league side), Nottingham Forest FC, Nottingham Racecourse, Trent Bridge cricket ground and the National Watersports Centre. The principal industries include textiles, pharmaceuticals, food manufacturing, engineering and telecommunications. There are two universities within the city boundaries.

Architecturally, Nottingham has a wealth of notable buildings, particularly those designed in the Victorian era by T. C. Hine and Watson Fothergill. The City Council owns the Castle, of Norman origin but restored in 1878, Wollaton Hall (1580–8), Newstead Abbey (home of Lord Byron), the Guildhall (1888) and Council House (1929). St Mary's, St Peter's and St Nicholas's Churches are of interest, as is the Roman Catholic Cathedral (Pugin, 1842–4). Nottingham was granted city status in 1897.

OXFORD

Oxford is a university city, an important industrial centre, and a market town. Industry played a minor part in Oxford until the motor industry was established in 1912.

Oxford is known for its architecture, its oldest specimens being the reputedly Saxon tower of St Michael's church, the remains of the Norman castle and city walls, and the Norman church at Iffley. It also has many Gothic buildings, such as the Divinity Schools, the Old Library at Merton College, William of Wykeham's New College, Magdalen College and Christ Church and many other college buildings. Later centuries are represented by the Laudian quadrangle at St John's College, the Renaissance Sheldonian Theatre by Wren, Trinity College Chapel, and All Saints Church; Hawksmoor's mock-Gothic at All Souls College, and the 18th-century Queen's College. In addition to individual buildings, High Street and Radcliffe Square both form interesting architectural compositions. Most of the Colleges have gardens, those of Magdalen, New College, St John's and Worcester being the largest.

ST ALBANS

The origins of St Albans, situated on the River Ver, stem from the Roman town of *Verulamium*. Named after the first Christian martyr in Britain, who was executed here, St Albans has developed around the Norman Abbey and Cathedral Church (consecrated 1115), built partly of materials from the old Roman city. The museums house Iron Age and Roman artefacts and the Roman Theatre, unique in Britain, has a stage as opposed to an amphitheatre. Archaeological excavations in the city centre have revealed evidence of pre-Roman, Saxon and medieval occupation.

The town's significance grew to the extent that it was a signatory and venue for the drafting of the Magna Carta. It was also the scene of riots during the Peasants' Revolt, the French King John was imprisoned there after the Battle of Poitiers, and heavy fighting took place there during the Wars of the Roses.

Previously controlled by the Abbot, the town achieved a charter in 1553 and city status in 1877. The street market, first established in 1553, is still an important feature of the city, as are many hotels and inns, surviving from the days when St Albans was an important coach stop. Tourist attractions include historic churches and houses, and a 15th-century clock tower.

The city now contains a wide range of firms, with special emphasis on information and legal services. In addition, it is the home of the Royal National Rose Society, and of Rothamsted Park, the agricultural research centre.

SALISBURY

The history of Salisbury centres around the Cathedral and Cathedral Close. The city evolved from an Iron Age camp a mile to the north of its current position which was strengthened by the Romans and called *Serviodunum*. The Normans built a castle and cathedral on the site and renamed it Sarum. In AD 1220, Bishop Richard Poore and the architect Elias de Derham decided to build a new Gothic style cathedral. The cathedral was completed 38 years later and a community known as New Sarum, now called Salisbury, grew around it. Originally the cathedral had a squat tower. The 404 ft spire that makes the cathedral the tallest medieval structure in the world was added *c*. 1315. A walled Close with houses for the clergy was built around the cathedral, the Medieval Hall still stands today, alongside buildings dating from the 13th to the 20th century; including some designed by Sir Christopher Wren.

A prosperous wool and cloth trade allowed Salisbury to flourish until the 17th century. When the wool trade declined new crafts were established including cutlery, leather and basket work, saddlery, lacemaking, joinery and malting. By 1750 it had become an important road junction and coaching centre and in the Victorian era the railways created a new age of expansion and prosperity. Today Salisbury is a thriving tourist centre.

SHEFFIELD

Sheffield is situated at the junction of the Sheaf, Porter, Rivelin and Loxley valleys with the River Don. Though its cutlery, silverware and plate have long been famous, Sheffield has other and now more important industries: special and alloy steels, engineering, tool-making, medical equipment and media-related industries (in its new Cultural Industries Quarter). Sheffield has two universities and is an important research centre.

The parish church of St Peter and St Paul, founded in the 12th century, became the Cathedral Church of the Diocese of Sheffield in 1914. The Roman Catholic Cathedral Church of St Marie (founded 1847) was created Cathedral for the new diocese of Hallam in 1980. Parts of the present building date from *c*.1435. The principal buildings are the Town Hall (1897), the Cutlers' Hall (1832), City Hall (1932), Graves Art Gallery (1934), Mappin Art Gallery, the Crucible Theatre and the restored 19th-century Lyceum theatre, which dates from 1897 and was reopened in 1990. Three major sports venues were opened in 1990 to 1991. These are Sheffield Arena, Don Valley Stadium and Pond's Forge. The Millennium Galleries opened in 2001. Sheffield was created a city in 1893.

STOKE-ON-TRENT

Stoke-on-Trent, standing on the River Trent and familiarly known as The Potteries, is the main centre of employment for the population of north Staffordshire. The city is the largest clayware producer in the world (china, earthenware, sanitary goods, refractories, bricks and tiles) and also has a wide range of other manufacturing industry, including steel, chemicals, engineering and tyres. Extensive reconstruction has been carried out in recent years.

The city was formed by the federation of the separate municipal authorities of Tunstall, Burslem, Hanley, Stoke, Fenton, and Longton in 1910 and received its city status in 1925.

WINCHESTER

Winchester, the ancient capital of England, is situated on the River Itchen. The city is rich in architecture of all types but the Cathedral takes pride of place. The cathedral was built in 1079–93 and exhibits examples of Norman, Early English and Perpendicular styles. The author Jane Austen is buried in the Cathedral. Winchester College, founded in 1382, is one of the most famous public schools, the original building (1393) remaining largely unaltered. St Cross Hospital, another great medieval foundation, lies one mile south of the city. The almshouses were founded in 1136 by Bishop Henry de Blois, and Cardinal Henry Beaufort added a new almshouse of 'Noble Poverty' in 1446. The chapel and dwellings are of great architectural interest, and visitors may still receive the 'Wayfarer's Dole' of bread and ale.

Excavations have done much to clarify the origins and development of Winchester. Part of the forum and several of the streets from the Roman town have been discovered. Excavations in the Cathedral Close have uncovered the entire site of the Anglo-Saxon cathedral (known as the Old Minster) and parts of the New Minster which was built by Alfred's son Edward the Elder and is the burial place of the Alfredian dynasty. The original burial place of St Swithun, before his remains were translated to a site in the present cathedral, was also uncovered.

Excavations in other parts of the city have thrown much light on Norman Winchester, notably on the site of the Royal Castle (adjacent to which the new Law Courts have been built) and in the grounds of Wolvesey Castle, where the great house built by Bishops Giffard and Henry de Blois in the 12th century has been uncovered. The Great Hall, built by Henry III between 1222 and 1236 survives and houses the Arthurian Round Table.

YORK

The city of York is an archiepiscopal seat. Its recorded history dates from AD 71, when the Roman Ninth Legion established a base under Petilius Cerealis later becoming the fortress of *Eburacum*. In Anglo-Saxon times the city was the royal and ecclesiastical centre of Northumbria, and after capture by a Viking army in AD 866 it became the capital of the Viking kingdom of Jorvik. By the 14th century the city had become a great mercantile centre, mainly because of its control of the wool trade, and was used as the chief base against the Scots. Under the Tudors its fortunes declined, though Henry VIII made it the headquarters of the Council of the North. Excavations on many sites, including Coppergate, have greatly expanded knowledge of Roman, Viking and medieval urban life.

With its development as a railway centre in the 19th century the commercial life of York expanded. The principal industries are the manufacture of chocolate, scientific instruments and sugar.

The city is rich in examples of architecture of all periods. The earliest church was built in ad 627 and, in the 12th to 15th centuries, the present Minster was built in a succession of styles. Other examples within the city are the medieval city walls and gateways, churches and guildhalls. Domestic architecture includes the Georgian mansions of The Mount, Micklegate and Bootham.

ENGLISH COUNTIES AND SHIRES

LORDS-LIEUTENANT AND HIGH SHERIFFS

County/Shire	Lord-Lieutenant	High Sheriff, 2003–4
Bedfordshire	S. C. Whitbread	Andrew Rayment
Berkshire	P. L. Wroughton	Malcolm Kimmins, CVO
Bristol	J. Tidmarsh, MBE	Helen Thornhill
Buckinghamshire	Sir Nigel Mobbs	Hon. Richard Godber
Cambridgeshire	Archibald Hugh Duberly	David Riddington
Cheshire	W. A. Bromley-Davenport	Diana McConnell, CBE
Cornwall	Lady Mary Holborow	Christopher Perkins
Cumbria	J. A. Cropper	Antony Leeming
Derbyshire	J. K. Bather	John Rudd
Devon	E. Dancer, CBE	Philip Tuckett
Dorset	Capt. M. Fulford-Dobson, RN	Eleanor Weld
Durham	Sir Paul Nicholson	Peter Cook
East Riding of Yorkshire	R. Marriott, TD	Hugh Bethell
East Sussex	P. Stewart-Roberts	Alastair Ainslie
Essex	The Lord Petre	Mark Thomasin-Foster, CBE
Gloucestershire	H. W. G. Elwes	Deborah Hutton
Greater London	The Lord Imbert, QPM	Michael Ingall
Greater Manchester	Col. J. B. Timmins, OBE, TD	Susan Hodgkiss
Hampshire	Mrs F. M. Fagan	Hon. Frances Hoare
Herefordshire	Sir Thomas Dunne, KCVO	Georgina Britten-Long
Hertfordshire	S. A. Bowes Lyon	Lady Lyell
Isle of Wight	C. D. J. Bland	Judith Hammer
Kent	A. Willett, CBE	Anthony Monteuuis
Lancashire	The Lord Shuttleworth	Bryan Gray
Leicestershire	Lady Jennifer Gretton	Mrs Julien Margaret Birchall
Lincolnshire	Mrs B. K. Cracroft-Eley	Paul Pumfrey, OBE
Merseyside	A. W. Waterworth	Robert Atlay
Norfolk	Sir Timothy Colman, KG	Sir John Bagge, Bt.
North Yorkshire	The Lord Crathorne	Air Cdre. Simon Bostock
Northumberland	Sir John Riddel, CVO	Jennifer Gibson
Nottinghamshire	Sir Andrew Buchanan, Bt.	William Parente
Oxfordshire	H. L. J. Brunner	Anthony Spink
Rutland	Dr Laurence Howard	Mary Lloyd
Shropshire	A. E. H. Heber-Percy	Mrs Julian Veronica Morgan
Somerset	Lady Gass	Brian Tanner, CBE
South Yorkshire	The Earl of Scarbrough	David Moody
Staffordshire	J. A. Hawley, TD	Sir Stanley Clarke, CBE
Suffolk	The Lord Tollemache	John Thurlow
Surrey	Mrs S. J. F. Goad	Andrew Wates
Tyne and Wear	N. Sherlock	James Wright
Warwickshire	M. Dunne	Roger Wiglesworth
West Midlands	R. R. Taylor, OBE	Michael Evans
West Sussex	H. Wyatt	Mark Scrase-Dickins, CMG
West Yorkshire	J. Lyles, CBE	John Jackson, CBE
Wiltshire	Lt.-Gen. Sir Maurice Johnston, KCB, OBE	David Newbigging, OBE
Worcestershire	M. Brinton	Georgina Britten-Long

COUNTY COUNCILS: CONTACT DETAILS, AREA

Council	Administrative Headquarters	Telephone	Area (Hectares)
Bedfordshire	County Hall, Bedford	01234-363222	119,220
Buckinghamshire	County Hall, Aylesbury	01296-395000	156,509
Cambridgeshire	Shire Hall, Cambridge	01223-717111	340,914
Cheshire	County Hall, Chester	01244-602424	208,344
Cornwall	County Hall, Truro	01872-322000	354,810
Cumbria	The Courts, Carlisle	01228-606060	676,780
Derbyshire	County Hall, Matlock	01629-580000	255,071
Devon	County Hall, Exeter	01392-382000	671,096
Dorset	County Hall, Dorchester	01305-251000	254,181
Durham	County Hall, Durham	0191-383 3000	223,181
East Sussex	Pelham House, Lewes	01273-481000	179,530
Essex	County Hall, Chelmsford	01245-492211	345,619
Gloucestershire	Shire Hall, Gloucester	01452-425000	279,875
Hampshire	The Castle, Winchester	01962-841841	367,860
Hertfordshire	County Hall, Hertford	01992-555555	163,416
Kent	County Hall, Maidstone	01622-671411	373,063
Lancashire	County Hall, Preston	01772-254868	289,780
Leicestershire	County Hall, Leicester	0116-232 3232	208,300
Lincolnshire	County Offices, Lincoln	01522-552222	591,470
Norfolk	County Hall, Norwich	01603-222222	537,234
Northamptonshire	County Hall, Northampton	01604-236236	235,966
Northumberland	County Hall, Morpeth	01670-533000	502,594
North Yorkshire	County Hall, Northallerton	01609-780780	803,741
Nottinghamshire	County Hall, Nottingham	0115-982 3823	208,519
Oxfordshire	County Hall, Oxford	01865-792422	260,595
Shropshire	The Shirehall, Shrewsbury	01743-251000	318,761
Somerset	County Hall, Taunton	01823-355455	345,233
Staffordshire	County Buildings, Stafford	01785-223121	262,355
Suffolk	County Hall, Ipswich	01473-583000	380,207
Surrey	County Hall, Kingston Upon Thames	020-8541 8800	167,011
Warwickshire	Shire Hall, Warwick	01926-410410	197,854
West Sussex	County Hall, Chichester	01243-777100	198,936
Wiltshire	County Hall, Trowbridge	01225-713000	325,548
Worcestershire	County Hall, Worcester	01905-763763	173,529

COUNTY COUNCILS: POPULATION, BAND D COUNCIL TAX, CHIEF EXECUTIVES

Council	Population	Band D Charge[*]	Chief Executive
Bedfordshire	382,100	£947	Dick Wilkinson
Buckinghamshire	475,084	£851	Chris Williams
Cambridgeshire	694,000	£797	Ian Stewart
Cheshire	672,700	£901	C. Taylor
Cornwall	499,114	£782	Peter Stethridge
Cumbria	487,792	£890	Louis Victory
Derbyshire	734,900	£914	Nick Hodgson
Devon	1,059,000	£909	Philip Jenkinson
Dorset	391,517	£916	David Jenkins
Durham	489,700	£903	Kingsley Smith
East Sussex	498,800	£930	Cheryl Miller
Essex	1,316,300	£896	K. Ashurst
Gloucestershire	564,841	£844	Joyce Redfearn
Hampshire	1,260,000	£845	Peter Robertson
Hertfordshire	1,011,000	£850	C. Watson
Kent	1,353,000	£853	Michael Pitt
Lancashire	1,429,400	£938	Chris Trinick
Leicestershire	610,300	£848	J. Sinnott
Lincolnshire	612,000	£810	David Bowles
Norfolk	797,900	£879	Tim Byles
North Yorkshire	570,100	£817	Jeremy Walker
Northamptonshire	629,676	£794	Peter Gould
Northumberland	307,000	£975	Mark Henderson
Nottinghamshire	748,800	£994	Roger Latham
Oxfordshire	632,000	£870	Richard Shaw
Shropshire	283,300	£868	C. Downs
Somerset	498,700	£858	Alan Jones
Staffordshire	810,697	£817	N. Pursey
Suffolk	671,100	£890	M. More
Surrey	1,059,500	£851	Paul Coen
Warwickshire	506,200	£865	Ian Caulfield
West Sussex	750,000	£859	Paul Rigg
Wiltshire	432,973	£845	Keith Robinson
Worcestershire	542,107	£822	Rob Sykes

[*] Average Band D council tax for the authority excluding parish precepts

DISTRICT COUNCILS

District Council	Telephone	Population	Band D Charge*	Chief Executive
Adur	01273-263000	59,627	£1,172	Ian Lowrie
Allerdale	01900-326333	93,000	£1,158	P. Leonard
Alnwick	01665-510505	31,400	£1,201	Bill Batey
Amber Valley	01773-570222	116,560	£1,174	Peter Carney
Arun	01903-737500	140,759	£1,121	Ian Sumnall
Ashfield	01623-450000	109,800	£1,248	Alan Mellor
Ashford	01233-637311	102,661	£1,060	David Hill
Aylesbury Vale	01296-585858	165,749	£1,095	Richard Carr
Babergh	01473-822801	82,310	£1,158	Patricia Rockall
Barrow-in-Furness	01229-894900	71,980	£1,194	Tom Campbell
Basildon	01268-533333	165,668	£1,189	John Robb
Basingstoke and Deane	01256-844844	152,800	£1,042	Gordon Hoadcroft
Bassetlaw	01909-533533	107,831	£1,246	James Molloy
Bedford	01234-267422	147,911	£1,170	Shaun Field
Berwick-upon-Tweed	01289-330044	27,000	£1,200	Jane Pannell
Blaby	0116-275 0555	85,000	£1,109	P. Dolan
Blyth Valley	01670-542322	80,000	£1,183	Geoff Paul
Bolsover	01246-240000	71,800	£1,212	John Fotherby
Boston	01205-314200	54,248	£1,055	Nicola Bulbeck
Braintree	01376-552525	132,468	£1,135	Annie Ralph
Breckland	01362-695333	121,418	£1,090	Rob Garnett
Brentwood	01277-261111	71,502	£1,135	R. McLintock
Bridgnorth	01746-713100	52,200	£1,130	T. Elliott
Broadland	01603-431133	118,800	£1,129	Colin Bland
Bromsgrove	01527-873232	87,837	£1,095	R. Lewis
Broxbourne	01992-785555	83,000	£1,034	Mike Walker
Broxtowe	0115-917 7777	109,700	£1,247	M. Brown
Burnley	01282-425011	89,200	£1,128	Gillian Taylor
CAMBRIDGE CITY	01223-457000	120,650	£1,037	R. Hammond
Cannock Chase	01543-462621	92,127	£1,108	Stephen Brown
CANTERBURY CITY	01227-862000	143,218	£1,083	Colin Carmichael
Caradon	01579-341000	79,649	£1,058	B. Davies
CARLISLE CITY	01228-817000	102,317	£1,185	Peter Stybelski
Carrick	01872-224400	85,300	£1,055	John Winskill
Castle Morpeth	01670-535000	50,000	£1,234	Ken Dunbar
Castle Point	01268-882200	84,800	£1,174	B. Rollinson
Charnwood	01509-263151	158,300	£1,090	G. Henshall
Chelmsford	01245-606606	155,000	£1,136	Martin Easteal
Cheltenham	01242-262626	106,226	£1,138	C. Laird
Cherwell	01295-252535	137,500	£1,139	G. Handley
CHESTER CITY	01244-324324	118,000	£1,138	P. Durham
Chester-le-Street	0191-387 1919	55,000	£1,138	M. Waterson
Chesterfield	01246-345345	98,845	£1,142	D. Shaw
Chichester	01243-785166	106,450	£1,097	J. Marsland
Chiltern	01494-729000	91,717	£1,115	A. Goodrum
Chorley	01257-515151	100,239	£1,180	J. Davies
Christchurch	01202-495000	44,908	£1,157	Mike Turvey
Colchester	01206-282222	159,600	£1,135	Andrea Hill
Congleton	01270-763231	90,758	£1,143	P. Cooper
Copeland	01946-852585	69,200	£1,176	J. Stanforth
Corby	01536-464000	52,000	£1,063	Nigel Rudd
Cotswolds	01285-623000	81,402	£1,141	R. Austin
Craven	01756-700600	52,300	£1,127	Gill Dixon
Crawley	01293-438000	99,730	£1,111	Michael Coughlin
Crewe and Nantwich	01270-537777	114,900	£1,124	Alan Wenham
Dacorum	01442-228000	132,240	£1,077	P. Walker
Dartford	01322-343434	85,911	£1,088	G. Harris
Daventry	01327-871100	72,050	£1,053	S. Atkinson
Derbyshire Dales	01629-761100	69,469	£1,196	D. Wheatcroft
Derwentside	01207-218000	87,455	£1,221	M. Lark
Dover	01304-821199	104,566	£1,091	Nadeem Aziz
DURHAM CITY	0191-386 6111	91,200	£1,157	C. Shearsmith

District Council	Telephone	Population	Band D Charge*	Chief Executive
Easington	0191-527 0501	93,981	£1,272	Paul Wilding
East Cambridgeshire	01353-665555	68,900	£1,053	Sean Gallagher
East Devon	01395-516551	127,400	£1,120	M. Williams
East Dorset	01202-886201	85,000	£1,194	A. Breakwell
East Hampshire	01730-266551	111,750	£1,097	P. Burton
East Hertfordshire	01279-655261	128,919	£1,104	Rachel Stopard
East Lindsey	01507-601111	130,500	£1,026	Paul Haigh
East Northamptonshire	01832-742000	78,511	£1,064	Stephen Baker
East Staffordshire	01283-508000	103,000	£1,111	F. Saunders
Eastbourne	01323-410000	92,000	£1,209	Martin Ray
Eastleigh	02380-688000	115,271	£1,100	Chris Tapp
Eden	01768-864671	49,880	£1,165	Ian Bruce
Ellesmere Port and Neston	0151-356 6789	81,671	£1,138	S. Ewbank
Elmbridge	01372-474474	133,000	£1,150	Michael Lockwood
Epping Forest	01992-564000	120,896	£1,152	J. Burgess
Epsom and Ewell	01372-732000	67,059	£1,108	David Smith
Erewash	0115-907 2244	108,000	£1,158	Tony Harris
EXETER CITY	01392-277888	111,076	£1,105	Philip Bostock
Fareham	01329-236100	108,000	£1,062	A. Davies
Fenland	01354-654321	82,500	£1,106	Tim Pilsbury
Forest Heath	01638-719000	55,000	£1,155	D. Burnip
Forest of Dean	01594-810000	78,498	£1,164	Meg Holborow
Fylde	01253-721222	75,000	£1,154	Ken Lee
Gedling	0115-901 3901	110,200	£1,223	Petar Kanuritch
GLOUCESTER CITY	01452-522232	109,300	£1,128	Paul Smith
Gosport	02392-584242	78,678	£1,098	M. Crocker
Gravesham	01474-564422	92,000	£1,073	Rosemary Leadley
Great Yarmouth	01493-856100	89,900	£1,117	Richard Packham
Guildford	01483-505050	129,200	£1,125	D. Willams
Hambleton	01609-779977	84,111	£1,055	P. Simpson
Harborough	01858-821100	75,200	£1,111	Michael Wilson
Harlow	01279-446611	83,000	£1,198	Doug Patterson
Harrogate	01423-500600	149,800	£1,145	P. Walsh
Hart	01252-622122	87,415	£1,105	Jules Samuels
Hastings	01424-781066	84,500	£1,216	Roy Mawford
Havant	02392-474174	120,500	£1,085	Gwen Andrews
Hertsmere	020-8207 2277	94,947	£1,087	Ron Higgins
High Peak	0845-129 7777	89,300	£1,179	Peter Sloman
Hinckley and Bosworth	01455-238141	100,141	£1,061	J. Corry
Horsham	01403-215100	125,700	£1,094	M. Pearson
Huntingdonshire	01480-388388	158,900	£1,041	David Monks
Hyndburn	01254-388111	78,390	£1,200	David Welfare
Ipswich	01473-432000	114,000	£1,256	J. Hehir
Kennet	01380-724911	74,833	£1,098	Mark Boden
Kerrier	01209-614000	90,990	£1,065	B. Manning Cox
Kettering	01536-410333	82,000	£1,069	D. Cook
King's Lynn and West Norfolk	01553-616200	135,600	£1,129	Geoff Chilton
LANCASTER CITY	01524-582000	138,077	£1,167	M. Cullinan
Lewes	01273-471600	85,900	£1,217	John Crawford
Lichfield	01543-308000	93,835	£1,077	N. Dawes
LINCOLN CITY	01522-881188	82,750	£1,085	Andrew Taylor
Macclesfield	01625-500500	150,144	£1,126	D. Parr
Maidstone	01622-602000	139,000	£1,131	David Petford
Maldon	01621-854477	57,300	£1,141	S. Packham
Malvern Hills	01684-892700	72,196	£1,101	Chris Bocock
Mansfield	01623-463463	98,500	£1,265	R. Goad
Melton	01664-502502	47,488	£1,099	J. Burbidge
Mendip	01749-343399	100,427	£1,125	Graham Jeffs
Mid Bedfordshire	01525-402051	121,300	£1,181	Jaki Salisbury
Mid Devon	01884-255255	68,984	£1,174	P. Edwards
Mid Suffolk	01449-720711	87,000	£1,151	A. Good
Mid Sussex	01444-458166	127,400	£1,112	W. Hatton
Mole Valley	01306-885001	80,300	£1,109	H. Kerswell
New Forest	02380-285000	172,319	£1,111	David Yates
Newark and Sherwood	01636-650000	106,273	£1,294	R. Dix

District Council	Telephone	Population	Band D Charge*	Chief Executive
Newcastle-under-Lyme	01782-717717	123,000	£1,088	F. Harley
North Cornwall	01208-893333	81,000	£1,068	David Brown
North Devon	01271-327711	87,518	£1,164	J. Sunderland
North Dorset	01258-454111	61,360	£1,151	Liz Goodall
North East Derbyshire	01246-231111	99,400	£1,218	C. Gilby
North Hertfordshire	01462-474000	117,000	£1,111	Stuart Philp
North Kesteven	01529-414155	94,400	£1,064	Ruth Marlow
North Norfolk	01263-513811	98,510	£1,131	Philip Burton
North Shropshire	01939-232771	54,581	£1,155	R. Hughes
North Warwickshire	01827-715341	60,747	£1,189	J. Hutchinson
North West Leicestershire	01530-454545	84,788	£1,128	M. Diaper
North Wiltshire	01249-706111	125,370	£1,126	R. Marshall
Northampton	01604-837837	196,300	£1,091	R. Morris
NORWICH CITY	01603-622233	121,700	£1,179	Anne Seex
Nuneaton and Bedworth	02476-376376	118,000	£1,157	Christine Kerr
Oadby and Wigston	0116-288 8961	55,800	£1,112	R. Hyde
Oswestry	01691-671111	37,318	£1,190	Paul Shevlin
OXFORD CITY	01865-249811	134,122	£1,184	Marion Headicar
Pendle	01282-661661	85,111	£1,226	S. Barnes
Penwith	01736-362341	63,000	£1,030	J. McKenna
Preston	01772-906000	135,000	£1,234	J. Carr
Purbeck	01929-556561	44,440	£1,191	P. Croft
Redditch	01527-64252	76,747	£1,112	Christopher Smith
Reigate and Banstead	01737-276000	119,000	£1,140	Nigel Clifford
Restormel	01726-223300	95,800	£1,028	P. Crowson
Ribble Valley	01200-425111	54,244	£1,149	D. Morris
Richmondshire	01748-829100	49,300	£1,145	Harry Tabiner
Rochford	01702-546366	63,050	£1,157	P. Warren
Rossendale	01706-217777	65,000	£1,234	O. Williams
Rother	01424-787878	85,458	£1,178	Derek Stevens
Rugby	01788-533533	88,900	£1,139	Diane Colley
Runnymede	01932-838383	78,048	£1,072	T. Williams
Rushcliffe	0115-981 9911	105,900	£1,226	K. Beaumont
Rushmoor	01252-398398	86,000	£1,090	Andrew Lloyd
Ryedale	01653-600666	48,000	£1,142	H. Mosley
Salisbury	01722-336272	111,476	£1,083	R. Sheard
Scarborough	01723-232323	108,000	£1,141	J. Trebble
Sedgefield	01388-816166	89,000	£1,294	N. Vaulks
Sedgemoor	01278-435435	104,000	£1,093	Kerry Rickards
Selby	01757-705101	72,800	£1,136	M. Connor
Sevenoaks	01732-227000	109,305	£1,125	Robin Hales
Shepway	01303-850388	99,265	£1,121	R. Thompson
Shrewsbury and Atcham	01743-281000	98,032	£1,123	Robin Hooper
South Bedfordshire	01582-472222	111,100	£1,237	J. Ruddick
South Bucks	01753-533333	61,945	£1,089	Chris Furness
South Cambridgeshire	01223-443000	132,000	£1,020	John Ballantyne
South Derbyshire	01283-221000	76,000	£1,155	Frank McArdle
South Hams	01803-861234	81,846	£1,139	R. Bagley
South Holland	01775-761161	76,522	£1,054	Terry Huggins
South Kesteven	01476-406080	120,000	£1,033	Chris Farmer
South Lakeland	01539-733333	103,000	£1,174	P. Cunliffe
South Norfolk	01508-533633	104,334	£1,143	Geoffrey Rivers
South Northamptonshire	01327-322322	79,490	£1,083	Rob Tinlin
South Oxfordshire	01491-823000	128,188	£1,137	David Buckle
South Ribble	01772-421491	103,900	£1,186	Jean Hunter
South Shropshire	01584-813000	40,000	£1,185	G. Biggs
South Somerset	01935-462462	155,770	£1,127	Elaine Peters
South Staffordshire	01902-696000	105,600	£1,058	Les Barnfield
Spelthorne	01784-451499	89,190	£1,105	Karen Satterford
ST ALBANS CITY	01727-866100	130,000	£1,117	Peter Learner
St Edmundsbury	01284-763233	98,000	£1,158	D. Cadman
Stafford	01785-619000	127,000	£1,079	David Rawlings
Staffordshire Moorlands	01538-483483	94,390	£1,095	Simon Baker
Stevenage	01438-242242	79,177	£1,100	I. Paske
Stratford-on-Avon	01789-267575	111,536	£1,119	Paul Lankester

District Council	Telephone	Population	Band D Charge*	Chief Executive
Stroud	01453-766321	108,000	£1,183	David Hagg
Suffolk Coastal	01394-383789	115,200	£1,141	Tom Griffin
Surrey Heath	01276-707100	85,900	£1,139	Barry Catchpole
Swale	01795-424341	123,100	£1,073	J. Edwards
Tamworth	01827-709709	80,000	£1,051	David Weatherley
Tandridge	01883-722000	80,000	£1,141	Philip Thomas
Taunton Deane	01823-356356	100,800	£1,088	S. Fletcher
Teesdale	01833-690000	24,992	£1,159	Charles Anderson
Teignbridge	01626-361101	120,976	£1,156	Howard Davis
Tendring	01255-425501	138,555	£1,118	John Hawkins
Test Valley	01264-368000	114,810	£1,052	Roger Tetstall
Tewkesbury	01684-295010	77,939	£1,089	Teri Turner
Thanet	01843-577000	127,685	£1,107	R. Samuel
Three Rivers	01923-776611	85,000	£1,117	A. Robertson
Tonbridge and Malling	01732-844522	108,600	£1,101	David Hughes
Torridge	01237-476700	56,000	£1,133	Trevor Smale
Tunbridge Wells	01892-526121	103,000	£1,074	R. Stone
Tynedale	01434-652200	58,900	£1,213	Richard Robson
Uttlesford	01799-510510	70,300	£1,139	E. Forbes
Vale of White Horse	01235-520202	112,900	£1,097	Terry Stock
Vale Royal	01606-862862	122,300	£1,139	Anne Bingham-Holmes
Wansbeck	01670-532200	61,138	£1,193	R. Stephenson
Warwick	01926-450000	123,800	£1,102	J. Barrett
Watford	01923-226400	81,520	£1,174	Alistair Robertson
Waveney	01502-562111	110,000	£1,122	Mairi McLean
Waverley	01483-523333	115,800	£1,143	C. Pointer
Wealden	01892-653311	142,700	£1,214	Charles Lant
Wear Valley	01388-765555	61,339	£1,167	Iain Phillips
Wellingborough	01933-229777	70,000	£1,037	T. McArdle
Welwyn & Hatfield	01707-357000	97,546	£1,131	Michel Saminaden
West Devon	01822-813600	48,659	£1,177	D. Incoll
West Dorset	01305-251010	90,300	£1,183	R. Rennison
West Lancashire	01695-577177	108,378	£1,190	William Taylor
West Lindsey	01427-676676	78,000	£1,082	Robert Nelsey
West Oxfordshire	01993-861000	99,000	£1,077	G. Bonner
West Somerset	01984-632291	35,075	£1,113	Tim Howes
West Wiltshire	01225-776655	112,000	£1,118	Jeffrey Ligo
Weymouth and Portland	01305-838000	63,000	£1,240	Tom Grainger
WINCHESTER CITY	01962-840222	107,274	£1,083	S. Eden
Woking	01483-755855	89,840	£1,147	Paul Russell
WORCESTER CITY	01905-723471	95,363	£1,075	D. Wareing
Worthing	01903-239999	100,000	£1,112	S. Grady
Wychavon	01386-565000	112,949	£1,063	S. Pritchard
Wycombe	01494-461000	163,000	£1,093	Richard Cummins
Wyre	01253-891000	105,765	£1,159	R. Wightman
Wyre Forest	01562-820505	96,981	£1,111	W. Delin

* Average Band D council tax rounded to the nearest £, without discounts and inclusive of precepts.
Councils in CAPITAL LETTERS have City Status.

METROPOLITAN BOROUGH COUNCILS

Metropolitan Councils	Telephone	Population	Band D Charge*	Chief Executive
Barnsley	01226-770770	218,000	£1,045	Phil Coppard
BIRMINGHAM CITY	0121-303 9944	977,000	£1,079	Lin Homer
Bolton	01204-333333	267,400	£1,118	B. Knight
BRADFORD CITY	01274-432001	467,665	£1,016	Ian Stewart
Bury	0161-253-5000	181,000	£1,084	M. Kelly
Calderdale	01422-357257	192,400	£1,131	Paul Sheehan
COVENTRY CITY	02476-833333	301,000	£1,172	Stella Manzie
Doncaster	01302-734444	289,897	£1,040	D. Marlow
Dudley	01384-818181	305,155	£1,008	Andrew Sparke
Gateshead	0191-433 3000	200,000	£1,238	L. Elton
Kirklees	01484-221000	392,000	£1,089	A. Elson
Knowsley	0151-489 6000	153,094	£1,114	Steve Gallagher
LEEDS CITY	0113-247 4554	726,757	£985	P. Rogerson
LIVERPOOL CITY	0151-233 3000	439,476	£1,181	David Henshaw
MANCHESTER CITY	0161-234 5000	439,549	£1,106	Howard Bernstein
NEWCASTLE UPON TYNE CITY	0191-232 8520	283,000	£1,241	Ian Stratford
North Tyneside	0191-200 6565	192,000	£1,171	John Marsden
Oldham	0161-911 3000	218,680	£1,219	Mike Chambers
Rochdale	01706-647474	208,950	£1,100	Roger Ellis
Rotherham	01709-382121	253,706	£1,085	G. Fitzgerald
SALFORD CITY	0161-794 4711	220,000	£1,237	John Willis
Sandwell	0121-569 2200	282,900	£1,095	Nigel Summers
Sefton	0151-922 4040	287,700	£1,130	Graham Haywood
SHEFFIELD CITY	0114-272 6444	530,300	£1,155	Bob Kerslake
Solihull	0121-704 6000	205,600	£1,008	Katherine Kerswell
South Tyneside	0191-427 1717	152,710	£1,128	Irene Lucas
St Helens	01744-456000	178,854	£1,142	Carole Hudson
Stockport	0161-480 4949	291,500	£1,150	John Schultz
SUNDERLAND CITY	0191-553 1000	280,800	£1,049	Colin Sinclair
Tameside	0161-342 8355	213,043	£1,089	Michael Greenwood
Trafford	0161-912 1212	225,000	£922	Carole Hassan
WAKEFIELD CITY	01924-306090	319,600	£1,006	John Foster
Walsall	01922-650000	261,599	£1,190	Anne Shepperd
Wigan	01942-244991	310,000	£1,098	Frank Costello
Wirral	0151-638 7070	312,289	£1,151	Stephen Maddox
WOLVERHAMPTON CITY	01902-556556	240,500	£1,132	D. Anderson

* Average Band D council tax rounded to the nearest £, without discounts and inclusive of precepts.
Councils in CAPITAL LETTERS have City Status.

UNITARY COUNCILS

Councils	Telephone	Population	Band D Charge*	Chief Executive
Bath and North East Somerset	01225-477000	165,000	£1,075	John Everitt
Blackburn with Darwen	01254-585585	137,600	£1,160	Philip Watson
Blackpool	01253-477477	153,600	£1,078	S. Weaver
Bournemouth	01202-451451	163,000	£1,109	D. Newell
Bracknell Forest	01344-424642	110,000	£963	Timothy Wheadon
BRIGHTON AND HOVE CITY	01273-290000	248,000	£1,073	D. Panter
BRISTOL CITY	0117-922 2000	380,800	£1,171	Carew Reynell
Darlington	01325-380651	97,838	£1,002	Barry Keel
DERBY CITY	01332-293111	236,429	£1,016	Ray Cowlishaw
East Riding of Yorkshire	01482-887700	314,113	£1,109	D. Stephenson
Halton	0151-424 2061	118,200	£1,010	M. Cuff
Hartlepool	01429-266522	91,200	£1,210	Paul Walker
Herefordshire	01432-260000	167,000	£1,071	Neil Pringle
Isle of Wight	01983-821000	132,938	£1,134	M. Fisher
KINGSTON UPON HULL CITY	01482-609100	243,379	£1,036	Jim Brooks
LEICESTER CITY	0116-254 9922	296,000	£1,042	R. Green
Luton	01582-546000	184,356	£990	Darra Singh
Medway	01634-306000	249,502	£919	Judith Armitt
Middlesbrough	01642-245432	142,300	£1,086	Brian Dinsdale
Milton Keynes	01908-691691	212,810	£1,023	J. Best
North East Lincolnshire	01472-313131	156,000	£1,174	Jim Leivers
North Lincolnshire	01724-296296	162,000	£1,157	Michael Garnett
North Somerset	01934-888888	188,564	£1,076	G. Turner
NOTTINGHAM CITY	0115-915 5555	267,000	£1,144	Gordon Mitchell
PETERBOROUGH CITY	01733-747474	156,500	£1,047	Gillian Beasley
PLYMOUTH CITY	01752-668000	255,000	£1,046	Sohail Faruqi
Poole	01202-633633	140,940	£1,072	John McBride
PORTSMOUTH CITY	02392-822251	186,700	£996	N. Gurney
Reading	0118-939 0900	143,200	£1,156	Trish Haines
Redcar and Cleveland	01642-444000	139,200	£1,132	Colin Moore
Rutland	01572-722577	34,600	£1,236	K. Franklin
Slough	01753-552288	108,208	£988	Cheryl Coppell
South Gloucestershire	01454-868686	245,640	£1,105	Mike Robinson
SOUTHAMPTON CITY	02380-223855	210,388	£1,085	Brad Roynon
Southend-on-Sea	01702-215000	164,400	£944	J. Krawiec
Stockton-on-Tees	01642-393939	178,000	£1,089	George Garlick
STOKE-ON-TRENT CITY	01782-234567	253,200	£1,029	Ita O'Donovan
Swindon	01793-463000	182,600	£1,048	Simon Birch
Telford and Wrekin	01952-202100	158,285	£1,047	Michael Frater
Thurrock	01375-390000	134,806	£1,010	Eric Nath
Torbay	01803-201201	123,000	£1,061	R. Painter
Warrington	01925-444400	191,200	£995	Bernice Law
West Berkshire	01635-42400	144,445	£1,134	Jim Graham
Windsor and Maidenhead	01628-798888	136,400	£971	David Lunn
Wokingham	0118-974 6000	146,252	£1,138	Doug Patterson
YORK CITY	01904-613161	181,326	£988	David Atkinson

* Average Band D council tax rounded to the nearest £, without discounts and inclusive of precepts.
Councils in CAPITAL LETTERS have City Status.

1 Stockton-on-Tees
2 Middlesbrough
3 Blackpool
4 Blackburn
   with Darwen
5 Bolton
6 Bury
7 Rochdale
8 Salford
9 Oldham
10 Liverpool
11 Knowsley
12 St Helens
13 Halton
14 Warrington
15 Trafford
16 Manchester
17 Tameside
18 Stockport
19 Nottingham
20 Telford and
   Wrekin
21 Wolverhampton

22 Walsall
23 Sandwell
24 Dudley
25 Birmingham
26 Solihull
27 Coventry
28 Peterborough
29 South Glos
30 Bristol
31 Bath and
   NE Somerset
32 Windsor and
   Maidenhead
33 Slough
34 Reading
35 Wokingham
36 Bracknell Forest
37 Thurrock
38 Southend
39 Medway
40 Plymouth
41 Torbay

LONDON

1 Hillingdon
2 Harrow
3 Barnet
4 Enfield
5 Waltham Forest
6 Redbridge
7 Barking and Dagenham
8 Havering
9 Ealing
10 Brent
11 Camden
12 Haringey
13 Islington
14 Hackney
15 Newham
16 Hounslow
17 Hammersmith and Fulham

18 Kensington and Chelsea
19 City of Westminster
20 City of London
21 Tower Hamlets
22 Richmond upon Thames
23 Wandsworth
24 Lambeth
25 Southwark
26 Lewisham
27 Greenwich
28 Bexley
29 Kingston upon Thames
30 Merton
31 Sutton
32 Croydon
33 Bromley

LONDON

THE CORPORATION OF LONDON

The City of London is the historic centre at the heart of London known as 'the square mile' around which the vast metropolis has grown over the centuries. The City's residential population at Census day 2001 was 7,186. The civic government is carried on by the Corporation of London through the Court of Common Council.

The City is an international financial centre, generating over £20 billion a year for the British economy. It includes the head offices of the principal banks, insurance companies and mercantile houses, in addition to buildings ranging from the historic Roman Wall and the 15th-century Guildhall, to the massive splendour of St Paul's Cathedral and the architectural beauty of Wren's spires.

The City of London was described by Tacitus in AD 62 as 'a busy emporium for trade and traders'. Under the Romans it became an important administration centre and hub of the road system. Little is known of London in Saxon times, when it formed part of the kingdom of the East Saxons. In 886 Alfred recovered London from the Danes and reconstituted it a burgh under his son-in-law. In 1066 the citizens submitted to William the Conqueror who in 1067 granted them a charter, which is still preserved, establishing them in the rights and privileges they had hitherto enjoyed.

THE MAYORALTY

The Mayoralty was probably established about 1189, the first Mayor being Henry Fitz Ailwyn who filled the office for 23 years and was succeeded by Fitz Alan (1212–14). A new charter was granted by King John in 1215, directing the Mayor to be chosen annually, which has been done ever since, though in early times the same individual often held the office more than once. A familiar instance is that of 'Whittington, thrice Lord Mayor of London' (in reality four times, 1397, 1398, 1406, 1419); and many modern cases have occurred. The earliest instance of the phrase 'Lord Mayor' in English is in 1414. It was used more generally in the latter part of the 15th century and became invariable from 1535 onwards. At Michaelmas the liverymen in Common Hall choose two Aldermen who have served the office of Sheriff for presentation to the Court of Aldermen, and one is chosen to be Lord Mayor for the following mayoral year.

LORD MAYOR'S DAY

The Lord Mayor of London was previously elected on the feast of St Simon and St Jude (28 October), and from the time of Edward I, at least, was presented to the King or to the Barons of the Exchequer on the following day, unless that day was a Sunday. The day of election was altered to 16 October in 1346, and after some further changes was fixed for Michaelmas Day in 1546, but the ceremonies of admittance and swearing-in of the Lord Mayor continued to take place on 28 and 29 October respectively until 1751. In 1752, at the reform of the calendar, the Lord Mayor was continued in office until 8 November, the 'New Style' equivalent of 28 October.

The Lord Mayor is now presented to the Lord Chief Justice at the Royal Courts of Justice on the second Saturday in November to make the final declaration of office, having been sworn in at Guildhall on the preceding day. The procession to the Royal Courts of Justice is popularly known as the Lord Mayor's Show.

REPRESENTATIVES

Aldermen are mentioned in the 11th century and their office is of Saxon origin. They were elected annually between 1377 and 1394, when an Act of Parliament of Richard II directed them to be chosen for life.

The Common Council, elected annually on the first Friday in December, was, at an early date, substituted for a popular assembly called the *Folkmote*. At first only two representatives were sent from each ward, but the number has since been greatly increased. The City of London (Ward Elections) Act gained Royal Assent in November 2002 and allowed for new voting arrangements. These include the introduction of periodic re-elections for the 25 Aldermen, a reduction in the number of Councilmen and a comprehensive review of the 25 electoral ward boundaries.

OFFICERS

Sheriffs were Saxon officers; their predecessors were the *wic-reeves* and *portreeves* of London and Middlesex. At first they were officers of the Crown, and were named by the Barons of the Exchequer; but Henry I (in 1132) gave the citizens permission to choose their own Sheriffs, and the annual election of Sheriffs became fully operative under King John's charter of 1199. The citizens lost this privilege, as far as the election of the Sheriff of Middlesex was concerned, by the Local Government Act 1888; but the liverymen continue to choose two Sheriffs of the City of London, who are appointed on Midsummer Day and take office at Michaelmas.

The office of Chamberlain is an ancient one, the first contemporary record of which is 1237. The Town Clerk (or Common Clerk) is mentioned in 1274.

ACTIVITIES

The work of the Corporation is assigned to a number of committees which present reports to the Court of Common Council. These Committees are: Barbican Centre; Barbican Residential; Board of Govenors of the City of London Freeman's School, the City of London School, London School for Girls, the Guildhall School of Music and Drama and the Museum of London; Bridge House Trust; City Lands and Bridge House Estates; Managers of West Ham Park; Community Services; Education; Epping Forest and Open Spaces; Establishment; Finance; Gresham (city side); Guildhall Yard East Building; Hampstead Heath Management; Libraries; Guildhall Art Galleries and Archives; Livery; Markets; Planning and Transportation; Police; Policy and Resources; Port Health and Environmental Services; Queen's Park and Highgate Wood Management and Standards Committees.

The City's estate, in the possession of which the Corporation of London differs from other municipalities, is managed by the City Lands and Bridge House Estates Committee, the chairmanship of which carries with it the title of Chief Commoner.

The Honourable the Irish Society, which manages the Corporation's estates in Ulster, consists of a Governor and five other Aldermen, the Recorder, and 19 Common Councilmen, of whom one is elected Deputy Governor.

THE LORD MAYOR 2003–4
The Rt. Hon. the Lord Mayor, Alderman *Rt. Hon.* Robert Finch; *Private Secretary,* P. Tribe

THE SHERIFFS 2003–4
Nicholas Anstee *(Alderman Aldersgate);* Geoffrey Bond

OFFICERS, ETC.
Town Clerk, Chris Duffield
Chamberlain, P. Derrick
Chief Commoner (2003), J. Nash, OBE
Clerk, The Honourable the Irish Society, S. Waley,
   75 Watling Street, London EC4M 9BJ Tel: 020-7489 7777

THE ALDERMEN
with office held and date of appointment to that office

Name and Ward	CC	Ald.	Shff	Lord Mayor
Sir Alan Towers-Traill,				
GBE, *Langbourn*	1970	1975	1982	1984
Sir David Rowe-Ham,				
GBE, *Bridge and Bridge Wt.*	–	1976	1984	1986
Sir Alexander Graham,				
GBE, *Queenhithe*	1978	1979	1986	1990
Sir Brian Jenkins,				
GBE, *Cordwainer*	–	1980	1987	1991
Sir Paul Newall, TD,				
Walbrook	1980	1981	1989	1993
Sir Richard Nichols,				
Candlewick	1983	1984	1994	1997
Lord Levene of Portsoken,				
KBE, *Portsoken*	1983	1984	1995	1998
Sir Clive Martin, OBE,				
Aldgate	–	1985	1996	1999
Sir David Howard, Bt	1972	1986	1997	2000
Sir Michael Oliver,				
Bishopsgate Out	1980	1987	1997	2001
Gavyn Arther, *Cripplegate*	1988	1991	1998	2002

All the above have passed the Civic Chair

Robert Finch, *Coleman Street*	–	1992	1999
Michael Savory, *Bread Street*	1980	1996	2001
Richard Agutter,			
Castle Baynard	–	1995	2000
David Brewer, *Bassishaw*	1992	1996	2002
Nicholas Anstee, *Aldersgate*	1987	1996	
John Hughesdon, *Billingsgate*	1991	1997	
Anthony Bull, *Cheap*	1968	1984	
Simon Walsh, *Farringdon Wt.*	1989	2000	
John Stuttard, *Lime Street*	–	2001	
Dr Andrew Parmley, *Vintry*	1992	2001	
David Lewis, *Broad Street*	–	2001	
Robert Hall, *Farringdon Wn*	1995	2002	

Mrs Alison Gowman,
   Dowgate   1991   2002
Richard Walduck, OBE,
   Tower   –   2003

THE COMMON COUNCIL
Deputy: Each Common Councilman so described serves as deputy to the Alderman of her/his ward.

Abrahams, G. (2000)	*Farringdon Wt*
Absalom, J. D. (1994)	*Farringdon Wt.*
Altman, L. P., CBE (1996)	*Cripplegate Wn.*
Angell, E. H. (1991)	*Cripplegate Wt.*
Archibald, *Deputy* W. W. (1986)	*Cornhill*
Ayers, K. E. (1996)	*Bassishaw*
Balls, H. D. (1970)	*Castle Baynard*
Barker, *Deputy* J. A. (1981)	*Cripplegate Wn.*
Barter, S. (1999)	*Langbourn*
Beale, *Deputy* M. J. (1979)	*Lime Street*
Bear, M. D. (2003)	*Portsoken*
Bird, J. L., OBE (1977)	*Bridge*
Boleat, M. J. (2002)	*Cordwainer*
Bradshaw, D. J. (1991)	*Cripplegate Wn.*
Branson, N. A. C. (2002)	*Langbourn*
Brewster, J. W., OBE (1994)	*Bassishaw*
Brooks, W. I. B. (1988)	*Billingsgate*
Byllam-Barnes, J. C. F. B. (1997)	*Cheap*
Caspi, D. R. (1994)	*Bridge*
Cassidy, *Deputy* M. J. (1989)	*Coleman Street*
Catt, B. F. (1982)	*Farringdon Wn.*
Chadwick, R. A. H. (1994)	*Tower*
Charkham, J. P., CBE (1996)	*Farringdon Wt.*
Cohen, Mrs C. M., OBE (1986)	*Lime Street*
Cotgrove, D. (1991)	*Lime Street*
Currie, *Deputy* Miss S. E. M. (1985)	*Cripplegate Wt.*
Daily-Hunt, R. B. (1989)	*Cripplegate Wt.*
Davis, C. B. (1991)	*Bread Street*
Dove, W. H., MBE (1993)	*Bishopsgate*
Duckworth, S. (2000)	*Bishopsgate*
Dudley, The Revd Dr M. R. (2002)	*Aldersgate*
Dunitz, *Deputy* A. A. (1984)	*Portsoken*
Eskenzi, *Deputy* A. N., CBE (1970)	*Farringdon Wn.*
Eve, R. A. (1980)	*Cheap*
Everett, K. M. (1984)	*Candlewick*
Falk, F. A., TD (1997)	*Broad Street*
Farr, M. C. (1998)	*Walbrook*
Farrow, *Deputy* M. W. W. (1996)	*Farringdon Wt.*
Farthing, R. B. C. (1981)	*Aldgate*
FitzGerald, *Deputy* R. C. A. (1981)	*Bread Street*
Forbes, G. B. (1993)	*Bishopsgate*
Fraser, S. J. (1993)	*Coleman Street*
Fraser, *Deputy* W. B. (1981)	*Vintry*
Galloway, *Deputy* A. D. (1981)	*Broad Street*
Gillon, G. M. F. (1995)	*Cordwainer*
Ginsburg, S. (1990)	*Bishopsgate*
Graves, A. C. (1985)	*Bishopsgate*
Halliday, *Deputy* Mrs P. (1992)	*Walbrook*
Hardwick, Dr P. B. (1987)	*Aldgate*
Harris, B. N. (1996)	*Broad Street*
Harris-Jones, Dr R. D. L. (2001)	*Farringdon Wt.*
Hart, *Deputy* M. G. (1970)	*Bridge*
Haynes, J. E. H. (1986)	*Cornhill*
Henderson-Begg, M. (1977)	*Coleman Street*
Hoffman, T. (2002)	*Vintry*
Holland, *Deputy* J., CBE (1972)	*Aldgate*
Holliday, Mrs E. H. L. (1987)	*Vintry*
Hook, J. W. (2000)	*Walbrook*
Jackson, L. St J. T. (1978)	*Bread Street*

Kellett, Mrs M. W. F. (1986)	*Tower*
Kemp, D. L. (1984)	*Coleman Street*
King, A. (1999)	*Queenhithe*
Knowles, *Deputy* S. K. (1984)	*Candlewick*
Lawrence, G. A. (2003)	*Farringdon Wt.*
Leck, P. (1998)	*Aldersgate*
Lee, The Revd Dr B. J. (2001)	*Portsoken*
Littlechild, Mrs V. (1998)	*Cripplegate Wt.*
Lord, C. E. (2000)	*Coleman Street*
Luder, I. D. (1998)	*Farringdon Wt.*
McGuinness, C. (1997)	*Castle Baynard*
McNeil, I. D. (1977)	*Lime Street*
Malins, J. H., QC (1981)	*Farringdon Wt.*
Martinelli, *Deputy* P. J. (1994)	*Bassishaw*
Mayhew, *Deputy* Dame Judith (1986)	*Queenhithe*
Mayhew, J. P. (1996)	*Aldersgate*
Mead, Mrs W. (1997)	*Farringdon Wt.*
Mitchell, *Deputy* C. R. (1971)	*Castle Baynard*
Mobsby, *Deputy* D. J. L. (1985)	*Billingsgate*
Montgomery, B. (1999)	*Dowgate*
Mooney, J. P. (1998)	*Queenhithe*
Moss, A. D. (1989)	*Tower*
Moys, Mrs S. (2000)	*Aldgate*
Nash, *Deputy* Mrs J. C. (1983)	*Aldersgate*
Newman, Mrs P. B. (1989)	*Aldersgate*
Owen, Mrs J. (1975)	*Langbourn*
Owen-Ward, J. R. (1983)	*Bridge*
Page, M. (2002)	*Farringdon Wn.*
Pembroke,	
Deputy Mrs A. M. F. (1978)	*Cheap*
Pollard, J. H. G. (2002)	*Dowgate*
Price, E. E. (1996)	*Farringdon Wt.*
Pulman, *Deputy* G. A. G. (1983)	*Tower*
Punter, C. (1993)	*Cripplegate Wn.*
Quilter, S. D. (1998)	*Cripplegate Wt.*
Regan, R. D. (1998)	*Farringdon Wn.*
Robinson, Mrs D. C. (1989)	*Bishopsgate*
Roney, *Deputy* E. P. T., CBE (1974)	*Bishopsgate*
Sargant, K. A. (1991)	*Cornhill*
Scott, J. (1999)	*Broad Street*
Scriven, R. G., CBE (1984)	*Candlewick*
Shalit, *Deputy* D. M. (1972)	*Farringdon Wn.*
Sherlock, *Deputy* M. R. C. (1992)	*Dowgate*
Snyder, *Deputy* M. J. (1986)	*Cordwainer*
Spanner, J. H., TD (2001)	*Farringdon Wt.*
Stevenson, F. P. (1994)	*Cripplegate Wn.*
Taylor, J. A. F., TD (1991)	*Bread Street*
Thorp, C. R. (1996)	*Billingsgate*
Thorp, D. (2000)	*Farringdon Wt.*
Trotter, J. (1993)	*Billingsgate*
Willoughby, *Deputy* P. J. (1985)	*Bishopsgate*
Wooten, D. H (2002)	*Farringdon Wn.*

THE CITY GUILDS (LIVERY COMPANIES)

The constitution of the livery companies has been unchanged for centuries. There are three ranks of membership: freemen, liverymen and assistants. A person can become a freeman by patrimony (through a parent having been a freeman); by servitude (through having served an apprenticeship to a freeman); or by redemption (by purchase).

Election to the livery is the prerogative of the company, who can elect any of its freemen as liverymen. Assistants are usually elected from the livery and form a Court of Assistants which is the governing body of the company. The Master (in some companies called the

Prime Warden) is elected annually from the assistants.

The register for 2003–4 listed 24,249 liverymen of the guilds entitled to vote at elections at Common Hall.

The order of precedence, omitting extinct companies, is given in parenthesis after the name of each company in the list below. In certain companies the election of Master or Prime Warden for the year does not take place until the autumn. In such cases the Master or Prime Warden for 2002–3 is given.

THE TWELVE GREAT COMPANIES
In order of civic precedence

MERCERS *(1)*. *Hall*, Mercers' Hall, Ironmonger Lane, London EC2V 8HE. *Livery*, 233. *Clerk*, C. H. Parker. *Master*, Sir John Blofeld

GROCERS *(2)*. *Hall*, Grocers' Hall, Princes Street, London EC2R 8AD. *Livery*, 323. *Clerk*, Brig. P. P. Rawlins, MBE. *Master*, G-H Mounsey-Heysham

DRAPERS *(3)*. *Hall*, Drapers' Hall, Throgmorton Avenue, London EC2N 2DQ. *Livery*, 269. *Clerk*, Rear-Admiral A. B. Ross, CB, CBE. *Master*, Peter Bottomley, MP

FISHMONGERS *(4)*. *Hall*, Fishmongers' Hall, London Bridge, London EC4R 9EL. *Livery*, 356. *Clerk*, K. S. Waters. *Prime Warden*, A. N. G. Duckworth-Chad, OBE

GOLDSMITHS *(5)*. *Hall*, Goldsmiths' Hall, Foster Lane, London EC2V 6BN. *Livery*, 275. *Clerk*, R. D. Buchanan-Dunlop CBE. *Prime Warden*, D. A. E. R. Peake

MERCHANT TAYLORS *(6/7)*. 30 Threadneedle Street, London EC2R 8JB. *Livery*, 325. *Clerk*, D. A. Peck. *Master*, John Penton, MBE

SKINNERS *(6/7)*. *Hall*, Skinners' Hall, 8 Dowgate Hill, London EC4R 2SP. *Livery*, 395. *Clerk*, Maj.-Gen. Brian Plummer, CBE. *Master*, C. A. Stuart-Clark

HABERDASHERS *(8)*. *Hall*, 18 West Smithfield, London EC1A 9HQ. *Livery*, 293. *Clerk*, Capt. R. J. Fisher, RN. *Master*, The Hon. L. B. Hacking

SALTERS *(9)*. *Hall*, Salters Hall, 4 Fore Street, London EC2Y 5DE. *Livery*, 168. *Clerk*, Col. M. P. Barneby. *Master*, Dr. P. Doyle, CBE

IRONMONGERS *(10)*. *Hall*, Ironmongers' Hall, Shaftesbury Place Barbican, London EC2Y 8AA. *Livery*, 131. *Clerk*, J. A. Oliver. *Master*, M. J. Crickmay

VINTNERS *(11)*. *Hall*, Vintners' Hall, Upper Thames Street, London EC4V 3BG. *Livery*, 301. *Clerk*, Brig. M. Smythe, OBE. *Master*, M. H. R. Hasslacher

CLOTHWORKERS *(12)*. *Hall*, Clothworkers' Hall, Dunster Court, Mincing Lane, London EC3R 7AH. *Livery*, 215. *Clerk*, A. C. Blessley. *Master*, Paul Wates

OTHER CITY GUILDS
In alphabetical order

ACTUARIES *(91)*. *Hall*, 81 Worrin Road, Shenfield, Brentwood, Essex CM15 8JN. *Livery*, 198. *Clerk*, Mrs J. V. Evans. *Master*, H. R. Wynne-Griffith

AIR PILOTS AND AIR NAVIGATORS, GUILD OF *(81)*. *Hall*, Cobham House, 9 Warwick Court, Gray's Inn, London WC1R 5DJ. *Livery*, 500. *Grand Master*, HRH The Duke of York, CVO, ADC. *Clerk*, Paul Tacon. *Master*, M. J. Willett

APOTHECARIES, SOCIETY OF *(58)*. *Hall*, Apothecaries' Hall, 14 Black Friars Lane, London EC4V 6EJ. *Livery*, 1,758. *Clerk*, Lt.-Col. R. J. Stringer. *Master*, Mrs E. Taylor

ARBITRATORS *(93)*. 13 Hall Gardens, Colney Heath, St. Albans, Herts AL4 0QF. *Livery*, 150. *Clerk*, Mrs G. Duffy. *Master*, Michael Wilkey

ARMOURERS AND BRASIERS *(22)*. *Hall*, Armourers' Hall, 81 Coleman Street, London EC2R 5BJ. *Livery*, 120. *Clerk*, Cdr. T. J. K. Sloane, OBE, RN. *Master*, R. N. Lay, CBE, FRICS

BAKERS *(19)*. *Hall*, Bakers' Hall, Harp Lane, London EC3R 6DP. *Livery*, 370. *Clerk*, J. W. Tompkins. *Master*, F. J. Bergin

BARBERS *(17)*. *Hall*, Barber-Surgeons' Hall, Monkwell Square, Wood Street, London EC2Y 5BL. *Livery*, 200. *Clerk*, Col. P. J. Durrant, MBE. *Master*, Sir Barry Jackson

BASKETMAKERS *(52)*. 48 Seymour Walk, London SW10 9NF. *Livery*, 308. *Clerk*, Maj. G. J. Flint-Shipman, TD. *Prime Warden*, J. R. F. F. Sorrell

BLACKSMITHS *(40)*. 48 Upwood Road, London SE12 8AN. *Livery*, 229. *Clerk*, C. Jeal. *Prime Warden*, Rodney Bole

BOWYERS *(38)*. 5 Archer House, Vicarage Crescent, London SW11 3LF. *Livery*, 96. *Clerk*, Richard Wilkinson. *Master*, C. N. G. Arding

BREWERS *(14)*. *Hall*, Brewers' Hall, Aldermanbury Square, London EC2V 7HR. *Livery*, 170. *Clerk*, Brig. D. J. Ross, CBE. *Master*, H. W. Whitbread

BRODERERS *(48)*. Ember House. 35–37 Creek Road, East Molesey, Surrey KT8 9BE. *Livery*, 173. *Clerk*, P. J. C. Crouch. *Master*, Maj.-Gen. P. G. Brooking, CB, CMG, MBE

BUILDERS MERCHANTS *(88)*. 4 College Hill, London EC4R 2RB. *Livery*, 200. *Clerk*, Miss S. M. Robinson, TD. *Master*, S. J. Somerville

BUTCHERS *(24)*. *Hall*, Butchers' Hall, 87 Bartholomew Close, London EC1A 7EB. *Livery*, 594. *Clerk*, A. J. C. Morrow, CVO. *Master*, William Parker

CARMEN *(77)*. 8 Little Trinity Lane, London EC4V 2AN. *Livery*, 469. *Clerk*, Cdr. R. M. H. Bawtree OBE, RN. *Master*, J. R Henley

CARPENTERS *(26)*. *Hall*, Carpenters' Hall, 1 Throgmorton Avenue, London EC2N 2JJ. *Livery*, 150. *Clerk*, Maj.-Gen. P. T. Stevenson, OBE. *Master*, P. A. Luton

CHARTERED ACCOUNTANTS *(86)*. The Rustlings, Valley Close, Studham, Dunstable LU6 2QN. *Livery*, 342. *Clerk*, C. Bygrave. *Master*, W. I. D. Plaistowe, OBE

CHARTERED ARCHITECTS *(98)*. 82A Muswell Hill Road, London N10 3JR. *Livery*, 168. *Clerk*, D. Cole-Adams. *Master*, Alan Downing

CHARTERED SECRETARIES AND ADMINISTRATORS *(87)*. Saddlers' House, 40 Gutter Lane, London EC2V 6BR. *Livery*, 217. *Clerk*, Col. M. J. Dudding, OBE, TD, FCIS. *Master*, D. W. R. Wright, MBE, LLD, FCIS

CHARTERED SURVEYORS *(85)*. 75 Meadway Drive, Horsell, Woking, Surrey GU21 4TF. *Livery*, 350. *Clerk*, Mrs A. L. Jackson. *Master*, E. T. Hartill

CLOCKMAKERS *(61)*. Room 66–67, Albert Buildings, 49 Queen Victoria Street, London EC4N 4SE. *Livery*, 230. *Clerk*, Gp Capt. P. H. Gibson, MBE. *Master*, C. J. Hurrion

COACHMAKERS AND COACH-HARNESS MAKERS *(72)*. 8 Chandlers Court, Burwell, Cambridge CB5 0AZ. *Livery*, 385. *Clerk*, Gp Capt. G. Bunn, CBE. *Master*, Gp Capt. M. Wills, CVO, OBE

CONSTRUCTORS *(99)*. Forge Farmhouse, Glassenbury, Cranbrook, Kent TN17 2QE. *Livery*, 130. *Clerk*, Tim Nicholson. *Master*, C. D. R. Hattersley

COOKS *(35)*. Registry Chambers, The Old Deanery, Deans Court, London EC4V 5AA. *Livery*, 75. *Clerk*, M. C. Thatcher. *Master*, His Hon. R. E. Hammerton

COOPERS *(36)*. *Hall*, Coopers' Hall, 13 Devonshire Square, London EC2M 4TH. *Livery*, 260. *Clerk*, A. G. R. Carroll. *Master*, David Barker

CORDWAINERS *(27)*. 8 Warwick Court, Gray's Inn, London WC1R 5DJ. *Livery*, 164. *Clerk*, Lt.-Col. J. R. Blundell, RM. *Master*, J. B. Barrett

CURRIERS *(29)*. Hedgerley, 10 The Leaze, Ashton Keynes, Wiltshire SN6 6PE. *Livery*, 96. *Clerk*, D. M. Moss. *Master*, G. W. Simmonds

Cutlers *(18)*. *Hall*, Cutlers' Hall, Warwick Lane, London EC4M 7BR. *Livery*, 100. *Clerk*, J. P. Allen. *Master*, N. W. Bragge

DISTILLERS *(69)*. 71 Lincoln's Inn Fields, London WC2A 3JF. *Livery*, 270. *Clerk*, C. V. Hughes. *Master*, R. W. Hobson

DYERS *(13)*. *Hall*, Dyers' Hall, 10 Dowgate Hill, London EC4R 2ST. *Livery*, 127. *Clerk*, J. R. Chambers, FCA. *Prime Warden*, E. A. M. Lee

ENGINEERS *(94)*. Wax Chandlers' Hall, Gresham Street, London EC2V 7AD. *Livery*, 291. *Clerk*, Air Vice-Marshal G. Skinner RAF. *Master*, Sir David Davies, CBE, FRS, FREng

ENVIRONMENTAL CLEANERS *(97)*. 6 Grange Meadows, Elmswell, Bury St Edmunds, Suffolk IP30 9GE. *Livery*, 256. *Clerk*, M. A. Bizley. *Master*, John R. Broadley

FAN MAKERS *(76)*. Skinners' Hall, 8 Dowgate Hill, London EC4R 2SP. *Livery*, 210. *Clerk*, K. J. Patterson. *Master*, P. V. Lush

FARMERS *(80)*. Chislehurst Business Centre, 1 Bromley Lane, Chislehurst, Kent BR7 6LH. *Livery*, 300. *Clerk*, Miss M. L. Winter. *Master*, N. J. Fiske

FARMERS *(80)*. *Hall*, 3 Cloth Street, London EC1. *Livery*, 300. *Clerk*, Miss M. L. Winter. *Master*, N. J. Fiske

FARRIERS *(55)*. 19 Queen Street, Chipperfield, Kings Langley, Herts WD4 9BT. *Livery*, 345. *Clerk*, Mrs C. C. Clifford. *Master*, R. F. Wallis, FCA

FELTMAKERS *(63)*. The Old Post House, Upton Grey, Basingstoke, Hampshire RG25 2RL. *Livery*, 170. *Clerk*, Maj. J. T. H. Coombs. *Master*, M. D. A. Bentata

FLETCHERS *(39)*. *Hall*, The Farmers and Fletchers Hall, 3 Cloth Street, London EC1A 7LD. *Livery*, 136. *Clerk*, M. Johnson. *Master*, D. L. Dumbrell

FOUNDERS *(33)*. *Hall*, Founders' Hall, Number One, Cloth Fair, London EC1A 7JQ. *Livery*, 175. *Clerk*, A. J. Gillett. *Master*, Jeremy P. Lansdell

FRAMEWORK KNITTERS *(64)*. 86 Park Drive, Upminster, Essex RM14 3AS. *Livery*, 275. *Clerk*, A. J. Clark. *Master*, Mrs S. Richards

FRUITERERS *(45)*. Chapelstones, 84 High Street, Codford, St. Mary, Warminster BA12 0ND. *Livery*, 280. *Clerk*, Lt.-Col. L. G. French. *Master*, P. A. H. Halliday

FUELLERS *(95)*. 26 Merrick Square, London SE1 4JB. *Livery*, 86. *Clerk*, Sir W. Anthony J. Reardon Smith, Bt. *Master*, Douglas Barrow

FURNITURE MAKERS *(83)* Painters' Hall, 9 Little Trinity Lane, London EC4V 2AD. *Livery*, 297. *Clerk*, Mrs J. A. Wright. *Master*, C. A. Rust

GARDENERS *(66)*. 25 Luke Street, London EC2A 4AR. *Livery*, 269. *Clerk*, Col. N. G. S. Gray. *Master*, Mrs J. Owen

GIRDLERS *(23)*. *Hall*, Girdlers' Hall, Basinghall Avenue, London EC2V 5DD. *Livery*, 80. *Clerk*, Lt.-Col. R. Sullivan. *Master*, E. P. G. Sherrard

GLASS-SELLERS *(71)*. 43 Aragon Avenue, Thames Ditton, Surrey KT7 0PY. *Livery*, 230. *Hon. Clerk*, B. J. Rawles. *Master*, Prof. J. R. Whiteman, Ph.D., FIMA, FRSA

GLAZIERS AND PAINTERS OF GLASS *(53)*. *Hall*, Glaziers' Hall, 9 Montague Close, London SE1 9DD. *Livery*, 244. *Clerk*, Col. D. W. Eking. *Master*, B. N. Harris

GLOVERS *(62)*. 73 Clapham Manor Street, London SW4 6DS. *Livery*, 260. *Clerk*, Mrs M. Hood. *Master*, William Loach

GOLD AND SILVER WYRE DRAWERS *(74)*. 'Twizzletwig', The Ballands, South Fetcham, Leatherhead Surrey KT22 9EP. *Livery*, 310. *Clerk*, T. J. Waller. *Master*, Michael C. Roberts

GUNMAKERS *(73)*. The Proof House, 48–50 Commercial Road, London E1 1LP. *Livery*, 238. *Clerk*, J. M. Riches. *Master*, R. Wilkin

HORNERS *(54)*. c/o Clergy House, Hide Place, London SW1P 2NG. *Livery*, 235. *Clerk*, A. R. Layard. *Master*, L. Walters

INFORMATION TECHNOLOGISTS *(100)*. Hall, Information Technologists' Hall, 39A Bartholomew Close, London EC1A 7JN. *Livery*, 255. *Clerk*, Mrs G. Davies. *Master*, Campbell McGarvie

INNHOLDERS *(32)*. Hall, Innholders' Hall, 30 College Street, London EC4R 2RH. *Livery*, 141. *Clerk*, D. E. Bulger. *Master*, J. R. Edwardes Jones

INSURERS *(92)*. The Hall, 20 Aldermanbury, London EC2V 7HY. *Livery*, 374. *Clerk*, L. J. Walters. *Master*, M. K. Bewes

JOINERS AND CEILERS *(41)*. 75 Meadway Drive, Horsell, Woking, Surrey GU21 4TF. *Livery*, 124. *Clerk*, Mrs A. L. Jackson. *Master*, Harry Evans

LAUNDERERS *(89)*. Hall, Launderers Hall, 9 Montague Close, London Bridge, London SE1 9DD. *Livery*, 250. *Clerk*, Mrs J. Polek. *Master*, Margaret Sheppard

LEATHERSELLERS *(15)*. Hall, Leathersellers' Hall, 15 St. Helen's Place, London EC3A 6DQ. *Livery*, 150. *Clerk*, Capt. J. G. F. Cooke, OBE, RN. *Master*, Michael Biscoe

LIGHTMONGERS *(96)*. Crown Wharf, 11a Coldharbour, Blackwall Reach, London E14 9NS. *Livery*, 194. *Clerk*, D. B. Wheatley. *Master*, Ian Crosby

LORINERS *(57)*. 8 Portland Square, London E1W 2QR. *Livery*, 358. *Clerk*, G. B. Forbes. *Master*, Martin Hall-Smith

MAKERS OF PLAYING CARDS *(75)*. 42 Warnford Court, Throgmorton Street, London EC2N 2AT. *Livery*, 141. *Clerk*, P. M. Kennerley. *Master*, R. G. W. Somerville

MARKETORS *(90)*. 13 Hall Gardens, Colney Heath, St Albans, Herts AL4 0QF. *Livery*, 240. *Clerk*, Mrs G. Duffy. *Master*, R. D. Collischon

MASONS *(30)*. 22 Cannon Hill, Southgate, London N14 6LG. *Livery*, 120. *Clerk*, P. F. Clark. *Master*, G. N. Tait

MASTER MARINERS, HONOURABLE COMPANY OF *(78)*. Hall, HQS Wellington, Temple Stairs, Victoria Embankment, London WC2R 2PN. *Livery*, 202. *Admiral*, HRH The Prince Philip, Duke of Edinburgh, KG, KT, OM, GBE, PC. *Clerk*, Cdr. I. S. Gregory, RN. *Master*, Capt. S. T. Culshaw

MUSICIANS *(50)*. 6th Floor, 2 London Wall Building, London EC2M 5PP. *Livery*, 374. *Clerk*, Col. T. P. B. Hoggarth. *Master*, N. Tully

NEEDLEMAKERS *(65)*. 5 Staple Inn, London WC1V 7QH. *Livery*, 230. *Clerk*, M. G. Cook. *Master*, Graham Born

PAINTER-STAINERS *(28)*. Hall, Painters' Hall, 9 Little Trinity Lane, London EC4V 2AD. *Livery*, 320. *Clerk*, Col. W. J. Chesshyre. *Master*, B. P. Botting

PATTENMAKERS *(70)*. 3 The High Street, Sutton Valence, Kent ME17 3AG. *Livery*, 200. *Clerk*, Lt. Col. R. W. Murfin, TD. *Master*, Dame Heather Steel, DBE

PAVIORS *(56)*. 3 Ridgemount Gardens, Enfield, Middx EN2 8QL. *Livery*, 234. *Clerk*, J. L. White. *Master*, R. L. Wilson, CBE

PEWTERERS *(16)*. Hall, Pewterers' Hall, Oat Lane, London EC2V 7DE. *Livery*, 125. *Clerk*, Lt. Col. T. M. Reeve-Tucker, OBE. *Master*, R. G. Wildash

PLAISTERERS *(46)*. Hall, Plaisterers' Hall, 1, London Wall, London EC2Y 5JU. *Livery*, 210. *Clerk*, Mrs. H. Machtus. *Master*, M. J. A. Lepper

PLUMBERS *(31)*. Room 28, 49 Queen Victoria Street, London EC4N 4SA. *Livery*, 332. *Clerk*, Lt.-Col. R. J. A. Paterson-Fox. *Master*, P. Lerwill

POULTERS *(34)*. The Old Butchers, Station Road, Groombridge, Kent TN3 9QX. *Livery*, 178. *Clerk*, Mrs G. W. Butcher. *Master*, J. Keevil

SADDLERS *(25)*. Hall, Saddlers' Hall, 40 Gutter Lane, London EC2V 6BR. *Livery*, 73. *Clerk*, Gp Capt. W. S. Brereton Martin, CBE. *Master*, Timothy Satchell

SCIENTIFIC INSTRUMENT MAKERS *(84)*. 9 Montague Close, London SE1 9DD. *Livery*, 240. *Clerk*, N. J. Watson. *Master*, Dr N. K. Reay

SCRIVENERS *(44)*. HQS Wellington, Temple Stairs, Victoria Embankment, London WC2R 2PN. *Livery*, 183. *Clerk*, A. Hill. *Master*, E. H. C. Cole

SHIPWRIGHTS *(59)*. Ironmongers Hall, Barbican, London EC2Y 8AA. *Livery*, 400. *Permanent Master*, HRH The Prince Philip, Duke of Edinburgh, KG, KT, OM, GBE, PC. *Clerk*, Rear Adm. Derek Anthony, MBE. *Prime Warden*, A. H. Farley

SOLICITORS *(79)*. 4 College Hill, London EC2R 2RB. *Livery*, 200. *Clerk*, N. Cameron. *Master*, J. E. Hume

SPECTACLE MAKERS *(60)*. Apothecaries' Hall, Black Friars Lane, London EC4V 6EL. *Livery*, 353. *Clerk*, Lt.-Col. J. A. B. Salmon OBE, LLB. *Master*, G. W. D. McLaren

STATIONERS AND NEWSPAPER MAKERS *(47)*. Hall, Stationers' Hall, Ave Maria Lane, London EC4M 7DD. *Livery*, 416. *Clerk*, Brig. D. G. Sharp, AFC. *Master*, C. J. P. Straker

TALLOW CHANDLERS *(21)*. Hall, Tallow Chandlers' Hall, 4 Dowgate Hill, London EC4R 2SH. *Livery*, 180. *Clerk*, Brig. R. W. Wilde, CBE. *Master*, Brig. W. K. L. Prasser, CBE, MC

TIN PLATE WORKERS (ALIAS WIRE WORKERS) *(67)*. Bartholomew House, 66 Westbury Road, New Malden, Surrey KT3 5AS. *Livery*, 200. *Clerk*, Michael Henderson-Begg. *Master*, Peter J. Rigby

TOBACCO PIPE MAKERS AND TOBACCO BLENDERS *(82)*. Hackhurst Farm, Lower Dicke,r Hailsham, E. Sussex BN27 4BP. *Livery*, 156. *Clerk*, N. J. Hallings-Pott. *Master*, F. M. Bramwell

TURNERS *(51)*. 182 Temple Chambers, Temple Avenue, London EC4Y 0HP. *Livery*, 165. *Clerk*, E. A. Windsor Clive. *Master*, A. H. Mayer

TYLERS AND BRICKLAYERS *(37)*. 30 Shelley Avenue, Tiptree CO5 0SF. *Livery*, 155. *Clerk*, Barry Blunson. *Master*, John Wilson-Wright

UPHOLDERS *(49)*. Hall in the Wood, 46 Quail Gardens, Selsdon Vale, Croydon CR2 8TF. *Livery*, 205. *Clerk*, J. P. Cody. *Master*, M. S. Gilham

WATER CONSERVATORS *(102)* 22 Broadfields, Headstone Lane, Hatch End, Middlesex HA2 6NH. *Livery*, 185. *Clerk*, R. A. Riley. *Master*, Dr Kevin P. Bond

WAX CHANDLERS *(20)*. Hall, Wax Chandlers' Hall, Gresham Street, London EC2V 7AD. *Livery*, 127. *Clerk*, R. J. Percival. *Master*, J. R. Williams

WEAVERS *(42)*. Saddlers' House, Gutter Lane, London EC2V 6BR. *Livery*, 125. *Clerk*, Mr. J. Snowdon. *Upper Bailiff*, P. M. Afia

WHEELWRIGHTS *(68)*. Ember House, 35–37 Creek Road, East Molesey, Surrey KT8 9BE. *Livery*, 210. *Clerk*, P. J. C. Crouch. *Master*, G. W. S. Davie

WOOLMEN *(43)*. Hollands, Hedsor Road, Bourne End, Bucks SL8 5EE. *Livery*, 137. *Clerk*, F. Allen. *Master*, Col. J. R. Nickell-Lean

WORLD TRADERS *(101)*. 36 Ladbroke Grove, London W11 2PA. *Livery*, 162. *Clerk*, N. R. Pullman. *Master*, E. F. Tracey

FIREFIGHTERS *(103)*. The Insurance Hall, 20 Aldermanbury, London EC2V 7GF. *Livery*, 60. *Clerk*, Mrs M. Holland Prior. *Master*, C. Livett

PARISH CLERKS *(No Livery)*. Acreholt, 33 Medstead Road, Beech, Alton, Hampshire GU34 4AD No. *Livery*, 95. *Clerk*, Lt.-Col. B. J. N. Coombes. *Master*, D. J. L. Mobsby

TAX ADVISERS *(No Livery)*. 504 Bryer Court, Barbican, London EC2Y 8DE, *Freemen*, 130. *Clerk*, C. E. Lord. *Master*, A. V. B. Broke

WATERMEN AND LIGHTERMEN *(No Livery)*. Hall, Watermen's Hall, 16 St. Mary-at-Hill, London EC3R 8EF. *Craft Owning Freemen*, 366. *Clerk*, C. Middlemiss. *Master*, Robert E. Lupton

LONDON BOROUGH COUNCILS

Council	Administrative Headquarters	Telephone	Population	Band D charge*	Chief Executive
Barking and Dagenham	Dagenham, RM10 7BN	020-8592 4500	154,786	£1,048	Graham Farrant
Barnet	Hendon, NW4 4BG	020-8359 2000	315,300	£1,135	Leo Boland
Bexley	Bexleyheath, DA6 7LB	020-8303 7777	220,458	£1,102	Nick Johnson *(acting)*
Brent	Wembley, HA9 9HD	020-8937 1234	263,463	£1,075	Gareth Daniel
Bromley	Bromley, BR1 3UH	020-8464 3333	300,071	£973	David Bartlett
Camden	Judd Street, WC1H 9JE	020-7278 4444	198,400	£1,158	Moira Gibb
CORPORATION OF LONDON	Guildhall, EC2P 2EJ	020-7606 3030	6,700	£742	Chris Duffield
Croydon	Park Lane, Croydon, CR9 3JS	020-8686 4433	337,540	£1,086	David Wechsler
Ealing	New Broadway, W5 2BY	020-8825 6000	311,000	£1,114	Gillian Guy
Enfield	Silver Street, EN1 3XA	020-8366 6565	261,000	£1,123	Rob Leak
Greenwich	Wellington Street, SE18 6PW	020-8854 8888	215,300	£1,088	Mary Nay
Hackney	Mare Street, E8 1EA	020-8356 5000	194,000	£1,158	Max Caller
Hammersmith and Fulham	King Street, W6 9JU	020-8748 3020	157,470	£1,073	Geoff Alltimes
Haringey	High Road, N22 8LE	020-8489 0000	213,000	£1,174	David Warwick
Harrow	Harrow, HA1 2UJ	020-8863 5611	206,814	£1,226	Joyce Markham
Havering	Romford, RM1 3BD	01708-434343	224,250	£1,216	S. Evans
Hillingdon	Uxbridge, UB8 1UW	01895-250111	243,006	£1,154	Dorian Leatham
Hounslow	Lampton Road, Hounslow TW3 4DN	020-8583 2000	240,397	£1,180	Mark Gilks
Islington	Upper Street, N1 2UD	020-7527 2000	174,500	£1,049	Helen Bailey
Kensington and Chelsea	Hornton Street, W8 7NX	020-7937 5464	190,300	£905	Derek Myers
Kingston upon Thames	Kingston upon Thames, KT1 1EU	020-8546 2121	144,313	£1,222	Bruce McDonald
Lambeth	Brixton, SW2 1RW	020-7926 1000	267,500	£995	Faith Boardman
Lewisham	Catford Road, SE6 4RU	020-8314 6000	247,000	£1,082	Barry Quirk
Merton	London Road, Morden SM4 5DX	020-8543 2222	179,000	£1,144	Roger Paine
Newham	Barking Road, East Ham, E6 2RP	020-8430 2000	230,000	£1,005	Dave Burbage
Redbridge	Ilford, IG1 1DD	020-8554 5000	238,635	£1,078	Roger Hampson
Richmond upon Thames	Twickenham, TW1 3AA	020-8891 1411	182,766	£1,268	Gillian Norton
Southwark	Peckam Road, SE5 8UB	020-7525 5000	245,000	£1,034	Robert Coomber
Sutton	St. Nicholas Way, Sutton, SM1 1EA	020-8770 5000	179,768	£1,099	Joanna Simons
Tower Hamlets	Clove Crescent, E14 2BG	020-7364 5000	181,251	£957	Christine Gilbert
Waltham Forest	Forest Road, E17 4JF	020-8496 4201	218,341	£1,171	Simon White
Wandsworth	Wandsworth High Street, SW18 2PU	020-8871 6000	266,600	£584	Gerald Jones
WESTMINSTER	Victoria Street, SW1E 6QP	020-7641 6000	181,700	£570	Peter Rogers

*Average Band D council tax rounded to the nearest £, without discounts and inclusive of precepts. Councils in CAPITAL LETTERS have City Status.

WALES

The Principality of Wales (Cymru) occupies the extreme west of the central southern portion of the island of Great Britain, with a total area of 8,015 sq. miles (20,758 sq. km): land 7,965 sq. miles (20,628 sq. km); inland water 50 sq. miles (130 sq. km). It is bounded on the north by the Irish Sea, on the south by the Bristol Channel, on the east by the English counties of Cheshire, Shropshire, Herefordshire and Gloucestershire, and on the west by St George's Channel.

Across the Menai Straits is the island of Anglesey (Ynys Môn) (276 sq. miles), communication with which is facilitated by the Menai Suspension Bridge (1,000 ft long) built by Telford in 1826, and by the tubular railway bridge (1,100 ft long) built by Stephenson in 1850. Holyhead harbour, on Holy Isle (north-west of Anglesey), provides accommodation for ferry services to Dublin (70 miles).

POPULATION
The population at the 2001 census was 2,903,085 (males 1,403,782; females 1,499,303). The average density of population in 2001 was 1.4 persons per hectare.

RELIEF
Wales is a country of extensive tracts of high plateau and shorter stretches of mountain ranges deeply dissected by river valleys. Lower-lying ground is largely confined to the coastal belt and the lower parts of the valleys. The highest mountains are those of Snowdonia in the north-west (Snowdon, 3,559 ft), Berwyn (Aran Fawddwy, 2,971 ft), Cader Idris (Pen y Gadair, 2,928 ft), Dyfed (Plynlimon, 2,467 ft), and the Black Mountain, Brecon Beacons and Black Forest ranges in the south-east (Carmarthen Van, 2,630 ft, Pen y Fan, 2,906 ft, Waun Fâch, 2,660 ft).

HYDROGRAPHY
The principal river rising in Wales is the Severn, which flows from the slopes of Plynlimon to the English border. The Wye (130 miles) also rises in the slopes of Plynlimon. The Usk (56 miles) flows into the Bristol Channel, through Gwent. The Dee (70 miles) rises in Bala Lake and flows through the Vale of Llangollen, where an aqueduct (built by Telford in 1805) carries the Pontcysyllte branch of the Shropshire Union Canal across the valley. The estuary of the Dee is the navigable portion, 14 miles in length and about five miles in breadth, and the tide rushes in with dangerous speed over the 'Sands of Dee'. The Towy (68 miles), Teifi (50 miles), Taff (40 miles), Dovey (30 miles), Taf (25 miles) and Conway (24 miles), the last named broad and navigable, are wholly Welsh rivers.

The largest natural lake is Bala (Llyn Tegid) in Gwynedd, nearly four miles long and about one mile wide. Lake Vyrnwy is an artificial reservoir, about the size of Bala, and forms the water supply of Liverpool; Birmingham is supplied from reservoirs in the Elan and Claerwen valleys.

WELSH LANGUAGE
According to the 2001 census results, the lowest estimate of percentage of persons aged three years and over able to speak Welsh was:

Blaenau Gwent	9.1	Newport	9.6
Bridgend	10.6	Pembrokeshire	21.5
Caerphilly	10.9	Powys	20.8
Cardiff	10.9	Rhondda Cynon Taf	12.3
Carmarthenshire	50.1	Swansea	13.2
Ceredigion	51.8	Torfaen	10.7
Conwy	29.2	Vale of Glamorgan	11.1
Denbighshire	26.1	Wrexham	14.4
Flintshire	14.1	Ynys Mon (Isle of	
Gwynedd	68.7	Anglesey)	59.8
Merthyr Tydfil	10.0		
Monmouthshire	9.0		
Neath Port Talbot	17.8	Wales	20.5

FLAG
The flag of Wales, the Red Dragon (Y Ddraig Goch), is a red dragon on a field divided white over green (per fess argent and vert a dragon passant gules). The flag was augmented in 1953 by a royal badge on a shield encircled with a riband bearing the words *Ddraig Goch Ddyry Cychwyn* and imperially crowned, but this augmented flag is rarely used.

EARLY HISTORY

The earliest inhabitants of whom there is any record appear to have been subdued or exterminated by the Goidels (a people of Celtic race) in the Bronze Age. A further invasion of Celtic Brythons and Belgae followed in the ensuing Iron Age. The Roman conquest of southern Britain and Wales was for some time successfully opposed by Caratacus (Caractacus or Caradog), chieftain of the Catuvellauni and son of Cunobelinus (Cymbeline). South-east Wales was subjugated and the legionary fortress at Caerleon-on-Usk established by about AD 75–77; the conquest of Wales was completed by Agricola about AD 78. Communications were opened up by the construction of military roads from Chester to Caerleon-on-Usk and Caerwent, and from Chester to Conwy (and thence to Carmarthen and Neath). Christianity was introduced during the Roman occupation, in the fourth century.

ANGLO-SAXON ATTACKS
The Anglo-Saxon invaders of southern Britain drove the Celts into the mountain stronghold of Wales, and into Strathclyde (Cumberland and south-west Scotland) and Cornwall, giving them the name of *Waelisc* (Welsh), meaning 'foreign'. The West Saxons' victory of Deorham (AD 577) isolated Wales from Cornwall and the battle of Chester (AD 613) cut off communication with Strathclyde and northern Britain. In the eighth century the boundaries of the Welsh were further restricted by the annexations of Offa, King of Mercia, and counter-attacks were largely prevented by the construction of an artificial boundary from the Dee to the Wye (Offa's Dyke).

In the ninth century Rhodri Mawr (844–878) united the country and successfully resisted further incursions of the Saxons by land and raids of Norse and Danish pirates by sea, but at his death his three provinces of Gwynedd (north), Powys (mid) and Deheubarth (south) were divided among his three sons, Anarawd, Mervyn and Cadell. Cadell's son Hywel Dda ruled a large part of Wales and codified its laws but the provinces were not united again until the rule of Llewelyn ap Seisyllt (husband of the heiress of Gwynedd) from 1018 to 1023.

THE NORMAN CONQUEST
After the Norman conquest of England, William I created palatine counties along the Welsh frontier, and the Norman barons began to make encroachments into Welsh territory. The Welsh princes recovered many of their losses during the civil wars of Stephen's reign and in the early 13th century Owen Gruffydd, prince of Gwynedd, was the dominant figure in Wales. Under Llywelyn ap Iorwerth (1194–1240) the Welsh united in powerful resistance to English incursions and Llywelyn's privileges and *de facto* independence were recognised in the Magna Carta. His grandson, Llywelyn ap Gruffydd, was the last native prince; he was killed in 1282 during hostilities between the Welsh and English, allowing Edward I of England to establish his authority over the country. On 7 February 1301, Edward of Caernarvon, son of Edward I, was created Prince of Wales, a title subsequently borne by the eldest son of the sovereign.

Strong Welsh national feeling continued, expressed in the early 15th century in the rising led by Owain Glyndŵr, but the situation was altered by the accession to the English throne in 1485 of Henry VII of the Welsh House of Tudor. Wales was politically assimilated to England under the Act of Union of 1535, which extended English laws to the Principality and gave it parliamentary representation for the first time.

EISTEDDFOD
The Welsh are a distinct nation, with a language and literature of their own, and the national bardic festival (Eisteddfod), instituted by Prince Rhys ap Griffith in 1176, is still held annually. These *Eisteddfodau* (sessions) form part of the *Gorsedd* (assembly) and are believed to date from the time of Prydian, a ruling prince in an age many centuries before the Christian era.

PRINCIPAL CITIES

CARDIFF
Cardiff, at the mouth of the Rivers Taff, Rhymney and Ely, is the capital city of Wales and at the 2001 census had a population of 305,353. It was granted city status in 1905. The city has changed dramatically in recent years following the regeneration of Cardiff Bay and construction of a barrage, which has created a permanent freshwater lake and waterfront for the city. As the capital city of Wales, Cardiff is home to the National Assembly for Wales and is a major administrative, retail, business and cultural centre.

The civic centre, is home to many fine buildings including, the City Hall, Castell Coch, Cardiff Castle, Llandaff Cathedral, National Museum of Wales, University Buildings, Law Courts and Temple of Peace and Health and the Millennium Stadium which opened in 1999.

SWANSEA
Swansea *(Abertawe)* is a city and a seaport and at the 2001 census had a population of 223,293. The Gower peninsula was brought within the city boundary under local government reform in 1974.

The principal buildings are the Norman Castle (rebuilt *c*.1330), the Royal Institution of South Wales, founded in 1835 (including Library), the University of Wales Swansea at Singleton, and the Guildhall, containing Frank Brangwyn's British Empire panels. The Dylan Thomas Centre, formerly the old Guildhall, was restored in 1995. More recent buildings include the County Hall, the new Maritime Quarter Marina and leisure centre.

Swansea was chartered by the Earl of Warwick, *c*.1158–84, and further charters were granted by King John, Henry III, Edward II, Edward III and James II, Cromwell (two) and the Marcher Lord William de Breos. It was formally invested with city status in 1969 by HRH The Prince of Wales.

Including the above, there are five places with city status in Wales. The other three (with date city status conferred) are; Bangor (pre-1900), St David's (1994) and Newport which was awarded city status as part of the Golden Jubilee city status competition in 2002.

Cardiff and Swansea have also been granted Lord Mayoralities.

LOCAL COUNCILS

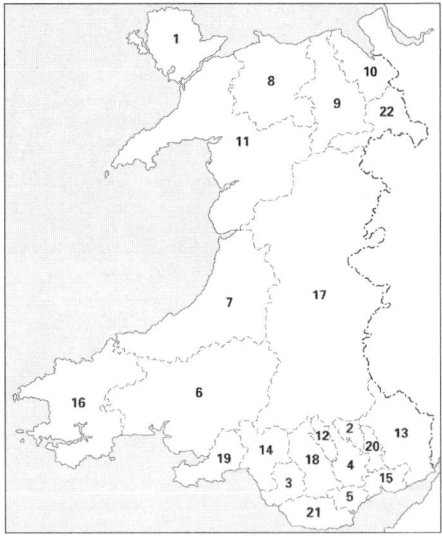

Key	County	Key	County
1	Anglesey	12	Merthyr Tydfil
2	Blaenau Gwent	13	Monmouthshire
3	Bridgend	14	Neath Port Talbot
4	Caerphilly	15	Newport
5	Cardiff	16	Pembrokeshire
6	Carmarthenshire	17	Powys
7	Ceredigion	18	Rhondda, Cynon, Taff
8	Conwy	19	Swansea
9	Denbighshire	20	Torfaen
10	Flintshire	21	Vale of Glamorgan
11	Gwynedd	22	Wrexham

LORDS-LIEUTENANT AND HIGH SHERIFFS

County/Shire	Lord-Lieutenant	High Sheriff, 2003–4
Clwyd	T. Jones, CBE	Nicholas Bankes
Dyfed	The Rt. Hon. Baron Morris of Aberavon, QC	Evan Evans
Gwent	S. Boyle	David Milner
Gwynedd	Prof. E. Sunderland, OBE	Robin Price
Mid Glamorgan	Kate Thomas	John Kendall
Powys	The Hon. Mrs E. S. Legge-Bourke, LVO	Penelope Bourdillon
S. Glamorgan	Capt. N. Lloyd-Edwards	Josephine Homfray
W. Glamorgan	R. C. Hastie, CBE	Jane Clayton

LOCAL COUNCILS

Council	Administrative Headquarters	Telephone	Population	Band D charge*	Chief Executive
Blaenau Gwent	Ebbw Vale	01495-350555	73,000	£975	R. Morrison
Bridgend	Bridgend	01656-643643	129,000	£910	Keri Lewis
Caerphilly	Hengoed	01443-815588	170,000	£825	Malgwyn Davies
CARDIFF CITY	Cardiff	029-2087 2000	327,500	£841	Byron Davies
Carmarthenshire	Carmarthen	01267-234567	168,900	£867	Mark James
Ceredigion	Aberaeron	01545-570881	75,384	£847	Owen Watkin
Conwy	Conwy	01492-574000	109,800	£730	C. Barker
Denbighshire	Ruthin	01824-706000	91,006	£945	Ian Miller
Flintshire	Mold	01352-752121	148,594	£820	Philip McGreevy
Gwynedd	Caernarfon	01286-672255	118,000	£837	Geraint Jones
Merthyr Tydfil	Merthyr Tydfil	01685-725000	55,981	£1,003	Alistair Neill
Monmouthshire	Cwmbran	01633-644644	85,000	£841	Elizabeth Raikes
Neath Port Talbot	Port Talbot	01639-763333	137,954	£1,030	Ken Sawyers
NEWPORT	Newport	01633-244491	138,500	£671	Chris Freegard
Pembrokeshire	Haverfordwest	01437-764551	114,700	£674	Bryn Parry-Jones
Powys	Llandrindod Wells	01597-826000	123,000	£787	Jacky Tonge
Rhondda Cynon Taff	Tonypandy	01443-424000	340,000	£903	Kim Ryley
SWANSEA, CITY	Swansea	01792-636000	231,180	£832	Tim Thorogood
Torfaen	Pontypool	01495-762200	90,500	£824	Peter Durkin
Vale of Glamorgan	Barry	01446-700111	119,281	£783	John Maitland-Evans
Wrexham	Wrexham	01978-292000	125,000	£850	I. Garner
Ynys Mon (Isle of Anglesey)	Ynys, Mon	01248-750057	65,400	£798	Geraint Edwards

* Average Band D council tax rounded to the nearest £, without discounts and inclusive of precepts.
Councils in CAPITAL LETTERS have City Status.

SCOTLAND

The Kingdom of Scotland occupies the northern portion of the main island of Great Britain and includes the Inner and Outer Hebrides, Orkney, Shetland, and many other islands. It lies between 60° 51′ 30″ and 54° 38′ N. latitude and between 1° 45′ 32″ and 6° 14′ W. longitude, with England to the south, the Atlantic Ocean on the north and west, and the North Sea on the east.

The greatest length of the mainland (Cape Wrath to the Mull of Galloway) is 274 miles, and the greatest breadth (Buchan Ness to Applecross) is 154 miles. The customary measurement of the island of Great Britain is from the site of John o' Groats house, near Duncansby Head, Caithness, to Land's End, Cornwall, a total distance of 603 miles in a straight line and approximately 900 miles by road.

The total area of Scotland is 30,420 sq. miles (78,789 sq. km); land 29,767 sq. miles (77,097 sq. km), inland water 653 sq. miles (1,692 sq. km).

POPULATION
The population at the 2001 census was 5,062,011 (males 2,432,494; females 2,629,517). The average density of the population in 2001 was 0.65 persons per hectare.

RELIEF
There are three natural orographic divisions of Scotland. The southern uplands have their highest points in Merrick (2,766 ft), Rhinns of Kells (2,669 ft), and Cairnsmuir of Carsphairn (2,614 ft), in the west; and the Tweedsmuir Hills in the east (Hartfell 2,651 ft, Dollar Law 2,682 ft, Broad Law 2,756 ft).

The central lowlands, formed by the valleys of the Clyde, Forth and Tay, divide the southern uplands from the northern Highlands, which extend almost from the extreme north of the mainland to the central lowlands, and are divided into a northern and a southern system by the Great Glen.

The Grampian Mountains, which entirely cover the southern Highland area, include in the west Ben Nevis (4,406 ft), the highest point in the British Isles, and in the east the Cairngorm Mountains (Cairn Gorm 4,084 ft, Braeriach 4,248 ft, Ben Macdui 4,296 ft). The north-western Highland area contains the mountains of Wester and Easter Ross (Carn Eige 3,880 ft, Sgurr na Lapaich 3,775 ft).

Created, like the central lowlands, by a major geological fault, the Great Glen (60 miles long) runs between Inverness and Fort William, and contains Loch Ness, Loch Oich and Loch Lochy. These are linked to each other and to the north-east and south-west coasts of Scotland by the Caledonian Canal, providing a navigable passage between the Moray Firth and the Inner Hebrides.

HYDROGRAPHY
The western coast is fragmented by peninsulas and islands, and indented by fjords (sea-lochs), the longest of which is Loch Fyne (42 miles long) in Argyll. Although the east coast tends to be less fractured and lower, there are several great drowned inlets (firths), e.g. Firth of Forth, Firth of Tay, Moray Firth, as well as the Firth of Clyde in the west.

The lochs are the principal hydrographic feature. The largest in Scotland and in Britain is Loch Lomond (27 sq. miles), in the Grampian valleys; the longest and deepest is Loch Ness (24 miles long and 800 feet deep), in the Great Glen; and Loch Shin (20 miles long) and Loch Maree in the Highlands.

The longest river is the Tay (117 miles), noted for its salmon. It flows into the North Sea, with Dundee on the estuary, which is spanned by the Tay Bridge (10,289 ft) opened in 1887 and the Tay Road Bridge (7,365 ft) opened in 1966. Other noted salmon rivers are the Dee (90 miles) which flows into the North Sea at Aberdeen, and the Spey (110 miles), the swiftest flowing river in the British Isles, which flows into Moray Firth. The Tweed, which gave its name to the woollen cloth produced along its banks, marks in the lower stretches of its 96-mile course the border between Scotland and England.

The most important river commercially is the Clyde (106 miles), formed by the junction of the Daer and Portrait water, which flows through the city of Glasgow to the Firth of Clyde. During its course it passes over the picturesque Falls of Clyde, Bonnington Linn (30 ft), Corra Linn (84 ft), Dundaff Linn (10 ft) and Stonebyres Linn (80 ft), above and below Lanark. The Forth (66 miles), upon which stands Edinburgh, the capital, is spanned by the Forth Railway Bridge (1890), which is 5,330 feet long, and the Forth Road Bridge (1964), which has a total length of 6,156 ft (over water) and a single span of 3,000 ft.

The highest waterfall in Scotland, and the British Isles, is Eas a'Chùal Aluinn with a total height of 658 ft (200 m), which falls from Glas Bheinn in Sutherland. The Falls of Glomach, on a head-stream of the Elchaig in Wester Ross, have a drop of 370 ft.

GAELIC LANGUAGE
According to the 2001 census, 1.2 per cent of the population of Scotland, mainly in Western Isles, were able to speak the Scottish form of Gaelic.

LOWLAND SCOTTISH LANGUAGE
Several regional Lowland Scottish dialects, known variously as Scots, Scotch, Lallans or Doric, are widely spoken. The General Register Office (Scotland) estimated in 1996 that 1.5 million people, or 30 per cent of the population, are Scots speakers. A question on Scots was not included in the 2001 census.

FLAG
The flag of Scotland is known as the Saltire. It is a white diagonal cross on a blue field (saltire argent in a field azure) and represents St Andrew, the patron saint of Scotland.

THE SCOTTISH ISLANDS

ORKNEY
The Orkney Islands (total area 375.5 sq. miles) lie about six miles north of the mainland, separated from it by the Pentland Firth. Of the 90 islands and islets (holms and skerries) in the group, about one-third are inhabited.

The total population at the 2001 census was 19,245; the 2001 populations of the islands shown here include those of smaller islands forming part of the same council district.

Mainland, 15,339	Rousay, 267
Burray, 357	Sanday, 478
Eday, 121	Shapinsay, 300
Flotta, 81	South Ronaldsay, 854
Hoy, 392	Stronsay, 358
North Ronaldsay, 70	Westray, 563
Papa Westray, 65	

The islands are rich in prehistoric and Scandinavian remains, the most notable being the Stone Age village of Skara Brae, the burial chamber of Maeshowe, the many brochs (towers) and the 12th-century St Magnus Cathedral. Scapa Flow, between the Mainland and Hoy, was the war station of the British Grand Fleet from 1914 to 1919 and the scene of the scuttling of the surrendered German High Seas Fleet (21 June 1919).

Most of the islands are low-lying and fertile, and farming (principally beef cattle) is the main industry. Flotta, to the south of Scapa Flow, is the site of the oil terminal for the Piper, Claymore and Tartan fields in the North Sea.

The capital is Kirkwall (population 6,206) on Mainland.

SHETLAND

The Shetland Islands have a total area of 551 sq. miles and a population at the 2001 census of 21,988. They lie about 50 miles north of the Orkneys, with Fair Isle about half-way between the two groups. Out Stack, off Muckle Flugga, one mile north of Unst, is the most northerly part of the British Isles (60° 51′ 30″ N. lat.).

There are over 100 islands, of which 16 are inhabited. Populations at the 2001 census were:

Mainland, 17,575	Muckle Roe, 104
Bressay, 384	Trondra, 133
East Burra, 66	Unst, 720
Fair Isle, 69	West Burra, 784
Fetlar, 86	Whalsay, 1,034
Housay, 76	Yell, 957

Shetland's many archaeological sites include Jarlshof, Mousa and Clickhimin, and its long connection with Scandinavia has resulted in a strong Norse influence on its place-names and dialect.

Industries include fishing, knitwear and farming. In addition to the fishing fleet there are fish processing factories, while the traditional handknitting of Fair Isle and Unst is supplemented now with machine-knitted garments. Farming is mainly crofting, with sheep being raised on the moorland and hills of the islands. Latterly the islands have become a centre of the North Sea oil industry, with pipelines from the Brent and Ninian fields running to the terminal at Sullom Voe, the largest of its kind in Europe. Lerwick is the main centre for supply services for offshore oil exploration and development.

The capital is Lerwick (population 6,830) on Mainland.

THE HEBRIDES

Until the late 13th century the Hebrides included other Scottish islands in the Firth of Clyde, the peninsula of Kintyre (Argyll), the Isle of Man, and the (Irish) Isle of Rathlin. The origin of the name is stated to be the Greek *Eboudai*, latinised as *Hebudes* by Pliny, and corrupted to its present form. The Norwegian name *Sudreyjar* (Southern Islands) was latinised as *Sodorenses*, a name that survives in the Anglican bishopric of Sodor and Man.

There are over 500 islands and islets, of which about 100 are inhabited, though mountainous terrain and extensive peat bogs mean that only a fraction of the total area is under cultivation. Stone, Bronze and Iron Age settlement has left many remains, including those at Callanish on Lewis, and Norse colonisation influenced language, customs and place-names. Occupations include farming (mostly crofting and stock-raising), fishing and the manufacture of tweeds and other woollens. Tourism is also an important factor in the economy.

The Inner Hebrides lie off the west coast of Scotland and relatively close to the mainland. The largest and best-known is Skye (area 643 sq. miles; pop. 9,251; chief town, Portree), which contains the Cuillin Hills (Sgurr Alasdair 3,257 ft), the Red Hills (Beinn na Caillich 2,403 ft), Bla Bheinn (3,046 ft) and The Storr (2,358 ft). Other islands in the Highland council area include Raasay (pop. 194), Rum, Eigg (pop. 131) and Muck.

Further south the Inner Hebridean islands include Arran (pop. 5,058) containing Goat Fell (2,868 ft); Coll and Tiree (pop. 934); Colonsay and Oronsay (pop. 113); Easdale (pop. 58); Gigha (pop. 110); Islay (area 235 sq. miles; pop. 3,457); Jura (area 160 sq. miles; pop. 188) with a range of hills culminating in the Paps of Jura (Beinn-an-Oir, 2,576 ft, and Beinn Chaolais, 2,477 ft); Lismore (pop. 146); Luing (pop. 220); and Mull (area 367 sq. miles; pop. 2,696; chief town Tobermory) containing Ben More (3,171 ft).

The Outer Hebrides, separated from the mainland by the Minch, now form the Eilean Siar Western Isles Islands Council area (area 1,119 sq. miles; population at the 2001 census 26,502). The main islands are Lewis with Harris (area 770 sq. miles, pop. 19,918), whose chief town, Stornoway, is the administrative headquarters; North Uist (pop. 1,320); South Uist (pop. 1,818); Benbecula (pop. 1,249) and Barra (pop. 1,078). Other inhabited islands include Bernera (233), Berneray (136), Eriskay (133), Grimsay (201), Scalpay (322) and Vatersay (94).

EARLY HISTORY

There is evidence of human settlement in Scotland dating from the third millennium BC, the earliest settlers being Middle Stone Age hunters and fishermen. Early in the second millennium BC, New Stone Age farmers began to cultivate crops and rear livestock; their settlements were on the west coast and in the north, and included Skara Brae and Maeshowe (Orkney). Settlement by the Early Bronze Age 'Beaker folk', so-called from the shape of their drinking vessels, in eastern Scotland dates from about 1800 BC. Further settlement is believed to have occurred from 700 BC onwards, as tribes were displaced from further south by new incursions from the Continent and the Roman invasions from AD 43.

Julius Agricola, the Roman governor of Britain AD 77–84, extended the Roman conquests in Britain by advancing into Caledonia, culminating with a victory at Mons Graupius, probably in AD 84; he was recalled to Rome shortly afterwards and his forward policy was not pursued. Hadrian's Wall, mostly completed by AD 30, marked the northern frontier of the Roman empire except for the period between about AD 144 and 190 when the frontier moved north to the Forth-Clyde isthmus and a turf wall, the Antonine Wall, was manned.

After the Roman withdrawal from Britain, there were centuries of warfare between the Picts, Scots, Britons, Angles and Vikings. The Picts, believed to be a non-Indo-European race, occupied the area north of the Forth. The Scots, a Gaelic-speaking people of northern Ireland, colonised the area of Argyll and Bute (the kingdom of Dalriada) in the fifth century AD and then expanded eastwards and northwards. The Britons, speaking a Brythonic Celtic language, colonised Scotland from the south from the first century BC; they lost control of south-eastern Scotland (incorporated into the kingdom of Northumbria) to the Angles in the early seventh century but retained Strathclyde (south-western Scotland and Cumbria). Viking raids from the late eighth century were followed by Norse settlement in the western and northern isles, Argyll, Caithness and Sutherland from the mid-ninth century onwards.

UNIFICATION

The union of the areas which now comprise Scotland began in AD 843 when Kenneth mac Alpin, king of the Scots from c.834, became also king of the Picts, joining the two lands to form the kingdom of Alba (comprising Scotland north of a line between the Forth and Clyde rivers). Lothian, the eastern part of the area between the Forth and the Tweed, seems to have been leased to Kenneth II of Alba (reigned 971–995) by Edgar of England c.973/4, and Scottish possession was confirmed by Malcolm II's victory over a Northumbrian army at Carham c.1016. At about this time Malcolm II (reigned 1005–34) placed his grandson Duncan on the throne of the British kingdom of Strathclyde, bringing under Scots rule virtually all of what is now Scotland.

The Norse possessions were incorporated into the kingdom of Scotland from the 12th century onwards. An uprising in the mid-12th century drove the Norse from most of mainland Argyll. The Hebrides were ceded to Scotland by the Treaty of Perth in 1266 after a Norwegian expedition in 1263 failed to maintain Norse authority over the islands. Orkney and Shetland fell to Scotland in 1468–9 as a pledge for the unpaid dowry of Margaret of Denmark, wife of James III, though Danish claims of suzerainty were relinquished only with the marriage of Anne of Denmark to James VI in 1590.

From the 11th century, there were frequent wars between Scotland and England over territory and the extent of England's political influence. The failure of the Scottish royal line with the death of Margaret of Norway in 1290 led to disputes over the throne which were resolved by the adjudication of Edward I of England. He awarded the throne to John Balliol in 1292 but Balliol's refusal to be a puppet king led to war. Balliol surrendered to Edward I in 1296 and Edward attempted to rule Scotland himself. Resistance to Scotland's loss of independence was led by William Wallace, who defeated the English at Stirling Bridge (1297), and Robert Bruce, crowned in 1306, who held most of Scotland by 1311 and routed Edward II's army at Bannockburn (1314). England recognised the independence of Scotland in the Treaty of Northampton in 1328. Subsequent clashes include the disastrous battle of Flodden (1513) in which James IV and many of his nobles fell.

THE UNION

In 1603 James VI of Scotland succeeded Elizabeth I on the throne of England (his mother, Mary Queen of Scots,

was the great-granddaughter of Henry VII), his successors reigning as sovereigns of Great Britain. Political union of the two countries did not occur until 1707.

THE JACOBITE REVOLTS

After the abdication (by flight) in 1688 of James VII and II, the crown devolved upon William III (grandson of Charles I) and Mary II (elder daughter of James VII and II). In 1689 Graham of Claverhouse roused the Highlands on behalf of James VII and II, but died after a military success at Killiecrankie.

After the death of Anne (younger daughter of James VII and II), the throne devolved upon George I (great-grandson of James VI and I). In 1715, armed risings on behalf of James Stuart (the Old Pretender, son of James VII and II) led to the indecisive battle of Sheriffmuir, and the Jacobite movement died down until 1745, when Charles Stuart (the Young Pretender) defeated the Royalist troops at Prestonpans and advanced to Derby (1746). From Derby, the adherents of 'James VIII and III' (the title claimed for his father by Charles Stuart) fell back on the defensive and were finally crushed at Culloden (16 April 1746).

PRINCIPAL CITIES

ABERDEEN

Aberdeen, 130 miles north-east of Edinburgh, received its charter as a Royal Burgh in 1124. Scotland's third largest city, Aberdeen lies between two rivers, the Dee and the Don facing the North Sea, the city has a strong maritime history and today is a main centre for offshore oil exploration and production. It is also an ancient university town and distinguished research centre. Other industries include engineering, food processing, textiles, paper manufacturing and chemicals.

Places of interest include King's College, St Machar's Cathedral, Brig o' Balgownie, Duthie Park and Winter Gardens, Hazlehead Park, the Kirk of St Nicholas, Mercat Cross, Marischal College and Marischal Museum, Provost Skene's House, Art Gallery, Gordon Highlanders Museum, Satrosphere Hands-On Discovery Centre, and Aberdeen Maritime Museum.

DUNDEE

The Royal Burgh of Dundee is situated on the north bank of the Tay estuary. The city's port and dock installations are important to the offshore oil industry and the airport also provides servicing facilities. Principal industries include textiles, biotechnology and digital media, lasers, printing, tyre manufacture, food processing, engineering, and tourism.

The unique City Churches – three churches under one roof, together with the 15th-century St Mary's Tower – are the most prominent architectural feature. Dundee has two historic ships: the Dundee-built RRS *Discovery* which took Capt. Scott to the Antarctic lies alongside Discovery Quay, and the frigate *Unicorn*, the only British-built wooden warship still afloat, is moored in Victoria Dock. Places of interest include Mills Public Observatory, the Tay road and rail bridges, Dundee Contemporary Arts Centre, McManus Galleries, Claypotts Castle, Broughty Castle, Verdant Works (Textile Heritage Centre) and the Sensation science centre.

EDINBURGH

Edinburgh is the capital of and seat of government in Scotland. The city is built on a group of hills and contains in Princes Street one of the most beautiful thoroughfares in the world.

The principal buildings are the Castle, which now houses the Stone of Scone and also includes St Margaret's Chapel, the oldest building in Edinburgh, and near it, the Scottish National War Memorial; the Palace of Holyroodhouse; Parliament House, the present seat of the judicature; three universities (Edinburgh, Heriot-Watt, Napier); St Giles' Cathedral; St Mary's (Scottish Episcopal) Cathedral (Sir George Gilbert Scott); the General Register House (Robert Adam); the National and the Signet Libraries; the National Gallery of Scotland; the Royal Scottish Academy; the Scottish National Portrait Gallery; and the Edinburgh International Conference Centre. A new Scottish Parliament building is currently under construction at Holyrood.

GLASGOW

Glasgow, a Royal Burgh, is Scotland's largest city and its principal commercial and industrial centre. The city occupies the north and south banks of the Clyde, formerly one of the chief commercial estuaries in the world. The main industries include engineering, electronics, finance, chemicals and printing. The city is also a key tourist and conference destination.

The chief buildings are the 13th-century Gothic Cathedral, the University (Sir George Gilbert Scott), the City Chambers, the Royal Concert Hall, St Mungo Museum of Religious Life and Art, Pollok House, the School of Art (Mackintosh), Kelvingrove Art Galleries, the Gallery of Modern Art, the Burrell Collection museum and the Mitchell Library. The city is home to the Scottish National Orchestra, Scottish Opera, Scottish Ballet and BBC Scotland and Scottish Television.

INVERNESS

Inverness was granted city status in 2000. The city's name is derived from the Gaelic for 'the mouth of the Ness', referring to the river on which it lies. Inverness is recorded as being at the junction of the old trade routes since 565AD. Today the city is the main administrative centre for the north of Scotland and is the capital of the Highlands. Tourism is one of the city's main industries.

Among the city's most notable buildings is Abertarff House, built in 1593 and the oldest secular building remaining in Inverness. Balnain House, built as a town house in 1726 is a fine example of early Georgian architecture. Once a hospital for Hanoverian soldiers after the battle of Culloden and as billets for the Royal Engineers when completing the 1st Ordnance Survey, today Balnain House is the National Trust for Scotland's regional HQ. The Old High Church, on St Michael's Mount, is the original Parish Church of Inverness and is built on the sight of the earliest Christian church in the city. Parts of the church date back to the 14th century.

Stirling was granted city status in 2002.

Aberdeen, Dundee, Edinburgh and Glasgow have also been granted Lord Mayoralty/Lord Provostship.

LORDS-LIEUTENANT

Title	Name	Title	Name
Aberdeenshire	A. D. M. Farquharson, OBE	Nairn	E. J. Brodie
Angus	Mrs G. L. Osborne	Orkney	G. R. Marwick
Argyll and Bute	K. A. Mackinnon	Perth and Kinross	Sir David Montgomery, Bt.
Ayrshire and Arran	Maj. R. Y. Henderson, TD	Renfrewshire	C. H. Parker, OBE
Banffshire	Mrs Clare Russell	Ross and Cromarty	Capt. R. W. K. Stirling of
Berwickshire	Maj. A. R. Trotter		Fairburn, TD
Caithness	Maj. G. T. Dunnett, TD	Roxburgh, Ettrick and	Dr June Paterson-Brown, CBE
Clackmannan	Mrs S. C. Cruickshank	Lauderdale	
Dumfries	Capt. R. C. Cunningham-	Shetland	J. H. Scott
	Jardine	Stirling and Falkirk	Lt.-Col. J. Stirling of Garden,
Dunbartonshire	Brig. D. D. G. Hardie, TD		CBE, TD
East Lothian	W. Garth Morrison, CBE	Sutherland	Maj.-Gen. D. Houston, CBE
Eilean Siar/Western Isles	A. Matheson, OBE	The Stewartry of	Lt.-Gen. Sir Norman Arthur,
Fife	Mrs C. M. Dean	Kirkcudbright	KCB
Inverness	Donald Angus Cameron of	Tweeddale	Capt. D. Younger
	Lochiel, KT, CVO	West Lothian	Mrs I. G. Brydie, MBE
Kincardineshire	J. D. B. Smart	Wigtown	Maj. E. S. Orr-Ewing
Lanarkshire	G. K. Cox, MBE		
Midlothian	Patrick Robert Prenter, CBE	The Lord Provosts of the four city districts of Aberdeen,	
Moray	Air Vice-Marshal G. A.	Dundee, Edinburgh and Glasgow are Lord-Lieutenants for	
	Chesworth, CB, OBE, DFC	those districts *ex officio*.	

LOCAL COUNCILS

Council	Administrative Headquarters	Telephone	Population	Band D charge*	Chief Executive
ABERDEEN	Aberdeen	01224-522000	211,250	£1,020	Douglas Paterson
Aberdeenshire	Aberdeen	01467-620981	226,940	£966	Alan Campbell
Angus	Forfar	01307-461460	112,000	£933	Sandy Watson
Argyll and Bute	Lochgilphead	01546-602127	89,000	£1,034	James McLellan
Clackmannanshire	Alloa	01259-452000	48,460	£995	Keir Bloomer
Dumfries and Galloway	Dumfries	01387-260000	147,780	£931	Philip Jones
DUNDEE	Dundee	01382-434000	145,663	£1,089	Alex Stephen
East Ayrshire	Kilmarnock	01563-576000	124,000	£1,014	David Montgomery
East Dunbartonshire	Kirkintilloch	0141-578 8000	108,243	£966	Vicki Nash
East Lothian	Haddington	01620-827827	90,180	£993	John Lindsay
East Renfrewshire	Giffnock	0141-577 3000	89,790	£955	Peter Daniels
EDINBURGH	Edinburgh	0131-200 2000	444,020	£1,041	Tom Aitchison
Eilean Siar (Western Isles)	Stornoway	01851-703773	27,940	£867	Bill Howat
Falkirk	Falkirk	01324-506070	145,270	£906	Mary Pitcaithly
Fife	Glenrothes	01592-414141	349,200	£981	Douglas Sinclair
GLASGOW	Glasgow	0141-287 2000	609,370	£1,163	George Black
Highland	Inverness	01463-702000	208,600	£989	Arthur McCourt
Inverclyde	Greenock	01475-717171	84,600	£1,089	Robert Cleary
Midlothian	Dalkeith	0131-270 7500	82,200	£1,072	Trevor Muir
Moray	Elgin	01343-543451	87,350	£907	Alastair Keddie
North Ayrshire	Irvine	01294-324100	140,000	£977	Bernard Devine
North Lanarkshire	Motherwell	01698-302222	321,100	£972	Gavin Whitefield
Orkney	Kirkwall	01856 873 535	19,245	£900	Alistair Buchan
Perth and Kinross	Perth	01738-475000	134,949	£983	Bernadette Malone
Renfrewshire	Paisley	0141-842 5000	172,867	£988	Tom Scholes
Scottish Borders	Melrose	01835-824000	106,300	£935	David Hume
Shetland	Lerwick	01595-693535	21,929	£873	Morgan Goodlad
South Ayrshire	Ayr	01292-612000	113,920	£964	George Thorley
South Lanarkshire	Hamilton	01698-454444	307,000	£971	Michael Docherty
STIRLING	Stirling	0845-277 700	84,700	£1,062	Keith Yates
West Dunbartonshire	Dumbarton	01389-737000	93,378	£1,070	Tim Huntingford
West Lothian	Livingston	01506-777000	159,030	£984	Alex Linkston

* Average Band D council tax without discounts and inclusive of precepts.
Councils in CAPITAL LETTERS have City Status.

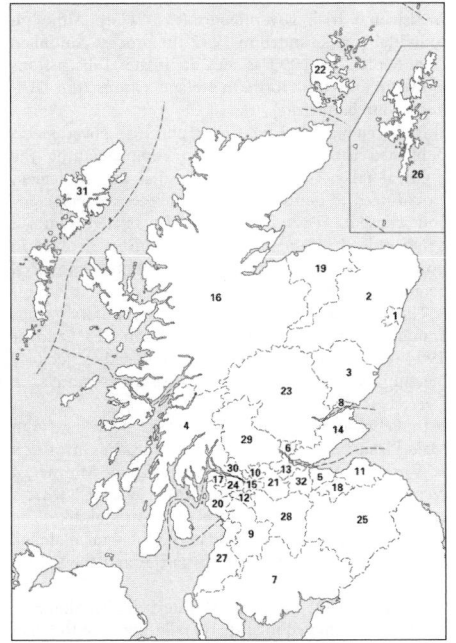

Key	County	Key	County
1	Aberdeen City	17	Inverclyde
2	Aberdeenshire	18	Midlothian
3	Angus	19	Moray
4	Argyll and Bute	20	North Ayrshire
5	City of Edinburgh	21	North Lanarkshire
6	Clackmannanshire	22	Orkney
7	Dumfries and Galloway	23	Perth and Kinross
		24	Renfrewshire
8	Dundee City	25	Scottish Borders
9	East Ayrshire	26	Shetland
10	East Dunbartonshire	27	South Ayrshire
11	East Lothian	28	South Lanarkshire
12	East Renfrewshire	29	Stirling
13	Falkirk	30	West Dunbartonshire
14	Fife	31	Western Isles (Eilean Siar)
15	Glasgow City		
16	Highland	32	West Lothian

NORTHERN IRELAND

Northern Ireland has a total area of 5,467 sq. miles (14,144 sq. km): land, 5,225 sq. miles (13,532 sq. km); inland water and tideways, 249 sq. miles (628 sq. km).

The population of Northern Ireland at the 2001 census was 1,685,267 (males, 821,449; females, 863,818).

In 2001 the number of persons in the various religious denominations (expressed as percentages of the total population) were: Catholic, 40.26; Presbyterian, 20.69; Church of Ireland, 15.30; Methodist Church in Ireland, 3.51; other Christian (including Christian related) 6.07; other religions and philosophies, 0.3; no religion or religion not stated, 13.88.

FLAG

The official national flag of Northern Ireland is now the Union Flag. The flag formerly in use (a white, six-pointed star in the centre of a red cross on a white field, enclosing a red hand and surmounted by a crown) has not been used since the imposition of direct rule.

PRINCIPAL CITIES

BELFAST

Belfast, the administrative centre of Northern Ireland, is situated at the mouth of the River Lagan at its entrance to Belfast Lough. The city grew, owing to its easy access by sea to Scottish coal and iron, to be a great industrial centre.

The principal buildings are of a relatively recent date and include the Parliament Buildings at Stormont, the City Hall, Waterfront Hall, the Law Courts, the Public Library and the Museum and Art Gallery.

Belfast received its first charter of incorporation in 1613 and was created a city in 1888; the title of Lord Mayor was conferred in 1892.

LONDONDERRY

Londonderry (originally Derry) is situated on the River Foyle, and has important associations with the City of London. The Irish Society was created by the City of London in 1610, and under its royal charter of 1613 it fortified the city and was for a long time closely associated with its administration. Because of this connection the city was incorporated in 1613 under the new name of Londonderry.

The city is famous for the great siege of 1688–9, when for 105 days the town held out against the forces of James II until relieved by sea. The city walls are still intact and form a circuit of almost a mile around the old city.

Interesting buildings are the Protestant Cathedral of St Columb's (1633) and the Guildhall, reconstructed in 1912 and containing a number of beautiful stained glass windows, many of which were presented by the livery companies of London.

Three other places in Northern Ireland have been granted city status: Armagh (1994), Newry (2002) and Lisburn (2002).

CONSTITUTIONAL DEVELOPMENTS

Northern Ireland is subject to the same fundamental constitutional provisions which apply to the rest of the United Kingdom. It had its own parliament and government from 1921 to 1972, but after increasing civil unrest the Northern Ireland (Temporary Provisions) Act 1972 transferred the legislative and executive powers of the Northern Ireland parliament and government to the UK Parliament and a Secretary of State. The Northern Ireland Constitution Act 1973 provided for devolution in Northern Ireland through an assembly and executive, but a power-sharing executive formed by the Northern Ireland political parties in January 1974 collapsed in May 1974. Since then Northern Ireland has been governed by direct rule under the provisions of the Northern Ireland Act 1974. This allows Parliament to approve all laws for Northern Ireland and places the Northern Ireland department under the direction and control of the Secretary of State for Northern Ireland.

Attempts were made by successive governments to find a means of restoring a widely acceptable form of devolved government to Northern Ireland. In 1985 the governments of the United Kingdom and the Republic of Ireland signed the Anglo-Irish Agreement, establishing an intergovernmental conference in which the Irish government may put forward views and proposals on certain aspects of Northern Ireland affairs.

Discussions between the British and Irish governments and the main Northern Ireland parties began in 1991. It was agreed that any political settlement would need to address relationships within Northern Ireland, within the island of Ireland (north/south) and between British and Irish governments (east/west). Although round table talks ended in 1992 the process continued from September 1993 as separate bilateral discussions with three of the Northern Ireland parties (the DUP declined to participate).

In December 1993 the British and Irish governments published the Joint Declaration complementing the political talks, and making clear that any settlement would need to be founded on principles of democracy and consent. The declaration also stated that all democratically mandated parties could be involved in political talks as long as they permanently renounced paramilitary violence.

The provisional IRA and loyalist paramilitary groups announced cease-fires on 31 August and 13 October 1994 respectively. The Government initiated exploratory meetings with Sinn Fein and loyalist representatives in December 1994.

In February 1995 the then Prime Minister (John Major) launched *A Framework for Accountable Government in Northern Ireland* and, with the Irish Prime Minister, *A New Framework for Agreement*. These outlined what a comprehensive political settlement might look like. The ideas were intended to facilitate multilateral dialogue involving the Northern Ireland parties and the British government.

In autumn 1995 the Prime Minister said that Sinn Fein would not be invited to all-party talks until the IRA had decommissioned its arms; the IRA ruled out any decommissioning of weapons in advance of a political settlement. An international body chaired by a former US senator, George Mitchell, reported in January 1996 that no weapons would be decommissioned before the start of all-party talks and that a compromise agreement was necessary under which weapons would be decommissioned during negotiations. The Prime Minister accepted the report and proposed the election of representatives to conduct all-party talks. On 9 February 1996 the IRA called off its cease-fire.

PEACE TALKS

Following elections on 30 May 1996, all-party talks opened at Stormont Castle on 10 June 1996 which included nine of the ten parties returned at the election; Sinn Fein representatives were turned away because the IRA had failed to reinstate its cease-fire. On 29 July 1996 the all-party talks were suspended after disagreements over the issue of decommissioning arms. An opening agenda for the talks was agreed in October 1996.

On 25 June 1997 the newly-elected Labour Government said that substantive negotiations should begin in September 1997 with a view to reaching conclusions by May 1998. The British and Irish governments issued a joint paper outlining their proposals for resolving the decommissioning issue. The Government also indicated that if the IRA were to call a cease-fire, it would assess whether it was genuine over a period of six weeks, and if satisfied that it was so, would then invite Sinn Fein to the talks. An IRA cease-fire was declared on 20 July 1997.

When the UK Government announced in August 1997 that Sinn Fein would be present when the substantive talks opened on 15 September, the Unionist and loyalist parties, unhappy at the terms on which Sinn Fein had been admitted, boycotted the opening session. The Ulster Unionist Party, the Progressive Unionist Party and the Ulster Democratic Party re-entered the negotiations on 17 September. Full-scale peace talks began on 7 October. The parties had agreed to concentrate on constitutional issues, with the issue of decommissioning terrorist weapons to be handled by a new independent commission.

On 12 January 1998 the British and Irish governments issued a joint document, *Propositions on Heads of Agreement,* proposing the establishment of various new cross-border bodies; further proposals were presented on 27 January. A draft peace settlement was issued by the talks' chairman, Sen. George Mitchell, on 6 April 1998 but was rejected by the Unionists the following day. On 10 April agreement was reached between the British and Irish governments and the eight Northern Ireland political parties still involved in the talks (the Good Friday Agreement). The agreement provided for an elected New Northern Ireland Assembly; a North/South Ministerial Council, and a British-Irish Council comprising representatives of the British, Irish, Channel Islands and Isle of Man governments and members of the new assemblies for Scotland, Wales and Northern Ireland. Further points included the abandonment of the Republic of Ireland's constitutional claim to Northern Ireland; the decommissioning of weapons; the release of paramilitary prisoners; and changes in policing.

Referendums on the agreement were held in Northern Ireland and the Republic of Ireland on 22 May 1998. In Northern Ireland the turnout was 81 per cent, of which 71.12 per cent voted in favour of the agreement. In the Republic of Ireland, the turnout was about 55 per cent, of which 94.4 per cent voted in favour of both the agreement and the necessary constitutional change. In the UK, the Northern Ireland Act 1998, enshrining the provisions of the Agreement, received Royal Assent in November 1998.

For details of the Northern Ireland Assembly and further political developments in Northern Ireland, *see* the Regional Government section.

OTHER BODIES

Consultations between the First Minister and Deputy First Minister, the British and Irish Governments and the political parties concluded in early 1999 with an agreement to establish six areas for cross-border bodies and a further six areas for co-operation. Treaties between the British and Irish governments establishing the bodies and parallel domestic legislation to underpin them are now in place.

The Good Friday Agreement also provided for a British-Irish Intergovernmental Conference to promote bilateral co-operation at all levels on matters of mutual interest, with a particular focus on non-devolved Northern Ireland matters, and supported by a joint standing Secretariat.

The British-Irish Council operates on the basis of consensus and may reach agreements on common policies in areas of mutual interest. Since its formation in 1999, the Council has met four times at summit level. The last meeting was in Scotland in November 2002.

FINANCE

Northern Ireland's expenditure is funded by the Northern Ireland Consolidated Fund (NICF). Up to date of devolution on 2 December 1999, the NICF was largely financed by Northern Ireland's attributed share of UK taxation and supplemented by a grant-in-aid. From devolution, these separate elements have been subsumed into a single Block Grant. The 2002 Spending Review set the Northern Ireland Departmental Expenditure Limit for 2003–4 at £6,813 million.

LORDS-LIEUTENANT

County	Area* (sq. miles)	Lord-Lieutenant
Antrim	1,093	The Lord O'Neill, TD
Armagh	484	The Earl of Caledon
Belfast City	25	Lady Carswell, OBE
Down	945	Maj. W. J. Hall
Fermanagh	647	The Earl of Erne
Londonderry	798	D. F. Desmond, CBE
Londonderry City	3.4	J. Eaton, TD
Tyrone	1,211	The Duke of Abercorn

DISTRICT COUNCILS

Councils	Telephone	Population	Chief Executive
Antrim, Co. Down	028-9446 3113	50,800	Samuel Magee
Ards, Co. Down	028-9182 4000	71,400	David Fallows
ARMAGH CITY, Co. Armagh	028-3752 9600	55,000	Victor Brownlees
Ballymena, Co. Antrim	028-2566 0300	58,801	M. Rankin
Ballymoney, Co. Antrim	028-2766 0200	26,000	John Dempsey
Banbridge, Co. Down	028-4066 0600	40,000	Robert Gilmore
BELFAST CITY, Co. Antrim and Co. Down	028-9032 0202	277,391	Peter McNaney
Carrickfergus, Co. Antrim	028-9335 1604	38,000	Alan Cardwell
Castlereagh, Co. Down	028-9049 4500	67,000	Adrian Donaldson
Coleraine, Co. Londonderry	028-7034 7034	56,315	Wavell Moore
Cookstown, Co. Tyrone	028-8676 2205	32,500	Michael McGuckin
Craigavon, Co. Armagh	028-3831 2400	79,700	Trevor Reaney
DERRY CITY, Co. Londonderry	028-7136 5151	105,000	A. McGurk
Down, Co. Down	028-4461 0800	61,000	John McGrillen
Dungannon, Co. Tyrone	028-8772 0300	47,000	William Beattie
Fermanagh, Co. Fermanagh	028-6632 5050	57,500	Rodney Connor
Larne, Co. Antrim	028-2827 2313	31,000	Colm McGarry
Limavady, Co. Londonderry	028-7772 2226	32,000	John Stevenson
LISBURN CITY, Co. Antrim	028-9250 9250	108,694	Norman Davidson
Magherafelt, Co. Londonderry	028-7939 7979	40,000	John McLaughlin
Moyle, Co. Antrim	028-2076 2225	15,933	R. Lewis
NEWRY and Mourne, Co. Down and Co. Armagh	028-3031 3031	87,000	Thomas McCall
Newtownabbey, Co. Antrim	028-9034 0000	80,900	Norman Dunn
North Down, Co. Down	028-9127 0371	76,323	Trevor Polley
Omagh, Co. Tyrone	028 8224 5321	48,000	Andrew Kilburn
Strabane, Co. Tyrone	028-7138 2204	37,600	Philip Faithfull

Councils in CAPITAL LETTERS have City Status.

THE ISLE OF MAN
Ellan Vannin

The Isle of Man is an island situated in the Irish Sea, in latitude 54° 3'–54° 25' N. and longitude 4° 18'–4° 47' W., nearly equidistant from England, Scotland and Ireland. Although the early inhabitants were of Celtic origin, the Isle of Man was part of the Norwegian Kingdom of the Hebrides until 1266, when this was ceded to Scotland. Subsequently granted to the Stanleys (Earls of Derby) in the 15th century and later to the Dukes of Atholl, it was brought under the administration of the Crown in 1765. The island forms the bishopric of Sodor and Man.

The total land area is 221 sq. miles (572 sq. km). The report on the 2001 census showed a resident population of 76,315 (males, 37,372; females, 38,943). The main language in use is English. There are no remaining native speakers of Manx Gaelic but 1,527 people are able to speak the language.

CAPITAL ΨDouglas; population (2001), 25,347.

ΨCastletown (3,100) is the ancient capital; the other towns are ΨPeel (3,785) and ΨRamsey (7,322)

FLAG – A red flag charged with three conjoined armoured legs in white and gold

TYNWALD DAY – 5 July

GOVERNMENT
The Isle of Man is a self-governing Crown dependency, having its own parliamentary, legal and administrative system. The British Government is responsible for international relations and defence. Under the UK Act of Accession, Protocol 3, the island's relationship with the European Union is limited to trade alone and does not extend to financial aid. The Lieutenant-Governor is The Queen's personal representative on the island.

The legislature, Tynwald, is the oldest parliament in the world in continuous existence. It has two branches: the Legislative Council and the House of Keys. The Council consists of the President of Tynwald, the Bishop of Sodor and Man, the Attorney-General (who does not have a vote) and eight members elected by the House of Keys. The House of Keys has 24 members, elected by universal adult suffrage. The branches sit separately to consider legislation and sit together, as Tynwald Court, for most other parliamentary purposes.

The presiding officer of Tynwald Court is the President of Tynwald, elected by the members, who also presides over sittings of the Legislative Council. The presiding officer of the House of Keys is Mr Speaker, who is elected by members of the House.

The principal members of the Manx Government are the Chief Minister and nine departmental ministers, who comprise the Council of Ministers.

Lieutenant-Governor, HE Air-Marshal I. MacFadyen, CB, OBE

ADC to the Lieutenant-Governor, C. J. Tummon

President of Tynwald, The Hon. N. Q. Cringle

Speaker, House of Keys, The Hon. J. A. Brown, SHK

The First Deemster and Clerk of the Rolls,
John Michael Kerruish

Clerk of Tynwald, Secretary to the House of Keys and Counsel to the Speaker, Mr Malachy Cornwell-Kelly

Clerk of the Legislative Council and Deputy Clerk of Tynwald, Mrs M. Cullen

Attorney-General, W. J. H. Corlett, QC

Chief Minister, The Hon. R. K. Corkill, MHK

Chief Secretary, Mrs M. Williams

ECONOMY
Most of the income generated in the island is earned in the services sector with financial and professional services accounting for just over half of the national income. Tourism and manufacturing are also major generators of income whilst the island's other traditional industries of agriculture and fishing now play a smaller role in the economy.

Under the terms of Protocol 3, the island has tariff-free access to EU markets for its goods.

The island's unemployment rate is approximately 0.6 per cent and price inflation is around 3.6 per cent per annum.

FINANCE
The budget for 2003–4 provides for net revenue expenditure of £418 million. The principal sources of government revenue are taxes on income and expenditure. Income tax is payable at a rate of 10 per cent on the first £10,000 of taxable income for single resident individuals and 18 per cent on the balance, after personal allowances of £8,000. These bands are doubled for married couples. The rate of income tax is 10 per cent on the first £100 million of taxable income of resident trading companies, rising to 15 per cent on the balance. By agreement with the British Government, the island keeps most of its rates of indirect taxation (VAT and duties) the same as those in the United Kingdom. However, VAT on tourist accommodation, property, repairs and renovations is charged at 5 per cent. A reciprocal agreement on national insurance benefits and pensions exists between the governments of the Isle of Man and the United Kingdom. Taxes are also charged on property (rates), but these are comparatively low.

The major government expenditure items are health, social security and education, which account for 58 per cent of the government budget. The island makes an annual contribution to the United Kingdom for defence and other external services.

The island has a special relationship with the European Union and neither contributes money to nor receives funds from the EU budget.

THE ISLES OF SCILLY

The Isles of Scilly are a cluster of small islands, set 28 miles off the coast of Cornwall in the Atlantic Ocean. There are five inhabited islands; St Mary's, Tresco, St Martin's. Bryher and St. Agnes. The islands are administered by the Council of the Isles of Scilly; a 21 member body, of which 13 are elected by St Mary's residents and 2 by each of the remaining islands.

Administrative Headquarters, Town Hall, St Mary's, Isles of Scilly, TR2 0LW Tel: 01720-422537

Chairman to the Council, Dudley Mumford

THE CHANNEL ISLANDS

The Channel Islands, situated off the north-west coast of France (at distances from ten to 30 miles), are the only portions of the Dukedom of Normandy still belonging to the Crown, to which they have been attached since the Norman Conquest of 1066. They were the only British territory to come under German occupation during the Second World War, following invasion on 30 June to 1 July 1940. The islands were relieved by British forces on 9 May 1945, and 9 May (Liberation Day) is now observed as a bank and public holiday.

The islands consist of Jersey (28,717 acres/11,630 ha), Guernsey (15,654 acres/6,340 ha), and the dependencies of Guernsey: Alderney (1,962 acres/795 ha), Brechou (74/30), Great Sark (1,035/419), Little Sark (239/97), Herm (320/130), Jethou (44/18) and Lihou (38/15) – a total of 48,083 acres/19,474 ha, or 75 sq. miles/194 sq. km. The 2001 census showed the population of Jersey as 87,186; Guernsey, 59,807 and Alderney, 2,294. Sark did not complete the same census but a recent informal census gave their population figure as 591. The official languages are English and French but French is being supplanted by English, which is the language in daily use. In country districts of Jersey and Guernsey and throughout Sark a Norman-French patois is also in use, though to a declining extent.

GOVERNMENT
The islands are Crown dependencies with their own legislative assemblies (the States in Jersey, Guernsey and Alderney, and the Court of Chief Pleas in Sark), and systems of local administration and of law, and their own courts. Acts passed by the States require the sanction of The Queen-in-Council. The British Government is responsible for defence and international relations. The Channel Islands have trading rights alone within the European Union; these rights do not include financial aid.

In both Bailiwicks the Lieutenant-Governor and Commander-in-Chief, who is appointed by the Crown, is the personal representative of The Queen and the channel of communication between the Crown (via the Privy Council) and the island's government.

The government of each Bailiwick is conducted by committees appointed by the States, although in 2001 the States of Jersey decided to move to a ministerial system of government combined with a system of scrutiny, this decision is expected to be implemented within the next two years. Justice is administered by the Royal Courts of Jersey and Guernsey, each consisting of the Bailiff and 12 elected Jurats. The Bailiffs of Jersey and Guernsey, appointed by the Crown, are President of the States and of the Royal Courts of their respective islands.

Each Bailiwick constitutes a deanery under the jurisdiction of the Bishop of Winchester.

ECONOMY
A mild climate and good soil have led to the development of intensive systems of agriculture and horticulture, which form a significant part of the economy. Equally important are invisible earnings, principally from tourism and banking and finance, the low rate of income tax (20p in the £ in Jersey and Guernsey; no tax of any kind in Sark) and the absence of super-tax and death duties, making the islands an important offshore financial centre.

Principal exports are agricultural produce and flowers; imports are chiefly machinery, manufactured goods, food, fuel and chemicals. Trade with the UK is regarded as internal.

British currency is legal tender in the Channel Islands but each Bailiwick issues its own coins and notes (see Finance section). They also issue their own postage stamps; UK stamps are not valid.

JERSEY

Lieutenant-Governor and Commander-in-Chief of Jersey, Chief Marshall Sir John Cheshire, KBE, CB, *apptd* 2001
Secretary and ADC, Lt.-Col. A. J. C. Woodrow, OBE, MC
Bailiff of Jersey, Sir Philip Bailhache, Kt.
Deputy Bailiff, M. C. St J. Birt
Attorney-General, W. J. Bailhache, QC
Receiver-General, P. Lewin
Solicitor-General, Miss S. C. Nicolle, QC
Greffier of the States, M. N. de la Haye
States Treasurer, Mr I. Black

FINANCE

Year to 31 Dec.	2001	2002
Revenue income	£541,759,000	£572,179,000
Revenue expenditure	£470,063,000	£500,654,000
Capital expenditure	£80,700,000	£89,303,000
Public debt	0	0

CHIEF TOWN – ΨSt Helier, on the south coast of Jersey
FLAG – A white field charged with a red saltire cross, and the arms of Jersey in the upper centre

GUERNSEY AND DEPENDENCIES

Lieutenant-Governor and Commander-in-Chief of the Bailiwick of Guernsey and its Dependencies, HE Lieutenant-General Sir John Foley, KCB, OBE, MC, *apptd* 2000
Secretary and ADC, Colonel R. H. Graham, MBE
Bailiff of Guernsey, Sir de Vic Graham Carey
Deputy Bailiff, G. R. Rowland, QC
HM Procureur and Receiver-General, J. N. van Leuven, QC
HM Comptroller, H. E. Roberts, QC
States Supervisor, M. J. Brown

FINANCE

Year to 31 Dec.	2001	2002
Revenue	£280,165,000	£288,320,000
Expenditure	£222,901,000	£239,727,000

CHIEF TOWNS – ΨSt Peter Port, on the east coast of Guernsey; St Anne on Alderney
FLAG – White, bearing a red cross of St George, with a gold cross overall in the centre

ALDERNEY
President of the States, Sir Norman Browse
Clerk of the States, D. V. Jenkins
Clerk of the Court, Mrs S. Kelly

SARK
Seigneur of Sark, J. M. Beaumont, OBE
The Seneschal, Lt.-Col. R. J. Guille, MBE
The Greffier, J. P. Hamon

OTHER DEPENDENCIES
Herm and Lihou are owned by the States of Guernsey; Herm is leased. Jethou is leased by the Crown to the States of Guernsey and is sub-let by the States. Brecqhou is within the legislative and judicial territory of Sark.

EUROPEAN PARLIAMENT

European Parliament elections take place at five-yearly intervals; the first direct elections to the Parliament were held in 1979. In mainland Britain MEPs were elected in all constituencies on a first-past-the-post basis until the elections of June 1999; in Northern Ireland three MEPs have been elected by the single transferable vote system of proportional representation since 1979. From 1979 to 1994 the number of seats held by the UK in the European Parliament was 81. At the June 1994 election the number of seats increased to 87 (England 71, Wales 5, Scotland 8, Northern Ireland 3).

At the European Parliament elections held on 10 June 1999, all British MEPs were elected under a 'closed-list' regional system of proportional representation, with England being divided into nine regions and Scotland and Wales each constituting a region. Parties submitted a list of candidates for each region in their own order of preference. Voters voted for a party or an independent candidate, and the first seat in each region was allocated to the party or candidate with the highest number of votes. The rest of the seats in each region were then allocated broadly in proportion to each party's share of the vote. Each region returned the following number of members: East Midlands, 6; Eastern, 8; London, 10; North East, 4; North West, 10; South East, 11; South West, 7; West Midlands, 8; Yorkshire and the Humber, 7; Wales, 5; Scotland, 8.

If a vacancy occurs due to the resignation or death of an MEP, the vacancy is filled by the next available person on that party's list. If an independent MEP resigns or dies, a by-election is held. Where an MEP leaves the party on whose list he/she was elected, there is no requirement to resign and he/she can remain in office until the next election.

British subjects and citizens of the Irish Republic are eligible for election to the European Parliament provided they are 21 or over and not subject to disqualification. Since 1994, nationals of member states of the European Union have had the right to vote in elections to the European Parliament in the UK as long as they are entered on the electoral register.

MEPs currently receive a salary from the parliaments or governments of their respective member states, set at the level of the national parliamentary salary and subject to national taxation. British MEPs receive a salary of £56,358. MPs who are also MEPs do not receive both salaries in full. Instead they receive the full MPs' salary plus a 'duality rate' equal to one third of the MEP's salary. Thus their total salary is £75,144 (comprising £56,358 plus £18,786).

A proposal that all MEPs should be paid the same rate of salary out of the EU budget, and subject to the EC tax rate, was under negotiation between the European Parliament and the Council of Ministers at the time of going to press.

The next elections of the European Parliament will take place in June 2004.

UK MEMBERS AS AT 20 MAY 2003

* Denotes membership of the last European Parliament
† Replacements since the last election
‡ Previously a member of the UK Independence Party
**Previously a member of the Conservative Party
††Previously a member of the Labour Party

†Adam, Gordon J. (b. 1934), C., North East
Atkins, Rt. Hon. Sir Robert (b. 1946), C., North West
Attwooll, Ms Elspeth M. A. (b. 1943), LD, Scotland
*††Balfe, Richard A. (b. 1944), C., London
Beazley, Christopher J. P. (b. 1952), C., Eastern
Bethell, The Lord (b. 1938), C., London
†Booth, Graham (b. 1940), UK Ind., South West
*Bowe, David R. (b. 1955), Lab., Yorkshire and the Humber
Bowis, John C., OBE (b. 1945), C., London
Bradbourn, Philip, OBE (b. 1951), C., West Midlands
Bushill-Matthews, Philip (b. 1943), C., West Midlands
Callanan, Martin (b. 1961), C., North East
Cashman, Michael (b. 1950), Lab., West Midlands
*Chichester, Giles B. (b. 1946), C., South West
Clegg, Nicholas W. P. (b. 1967), LD, East Midlands
*Corbett, Richard (b. 1955), Lab., Yorkshire and the Humber
*Corrie, John A. (b. 1935), C., West Midlands
Davies, Christopher G. (b. 1954), LD, North West
Deva, Niranjan J. A. (Nirj), FRSA (b. 1948), C., South East
Dover, Den (b. 1938), C., North West
Duff, Andrew N. (b. 1950), LD, Eastern
*Elles, James E. M. (b. 1949), C., South East
Evans, Ms Jillian R. (b. 1959), PC, Wales
Evans, Jonathan P., FRSA (b. 1950), C., Wales
*Evans, Robert J. E. (b. 1956), Lab., London
Farage, Nigel P. (b. 1964), UK Ind., South East
*Ford, J. Glyn (b. 1950), Lab., South West
Foster, Mrs Jacqui (b. 1947), C., North West
Gill, Ms Neena (b. 1956), Lab., West Midlands
Goodwill, Robert (b. 1956), C., Yorkshire and the Humber
Hannan, Daniel J. (b. 1971), C., South East
Harbour, Malcolm (b. 1947), C., West Midlands
Heaton-Harris, Christopher (b. 1967), C., East Midlands
Helmer, Roger (b. 1944), C., East Midlands
†Honeyball, Mary Mrs (b. 1952), Lab., London
*Howitt, Richard (b. 1961), Lab., Eastern
*Hudghton, Ian (b. 1951), SNP, Scotland
*Hughes, Stephen (b. 1952), Lab., North East
Huhne, Christopher M. P., OBE (b. 1954), LD, South East
*Hume, John, MP (b. 1937), SDLP, Northern Ireland
Inglewood, The Lord (b. 1951), C., North West
*Jackson, Mrs Caroline F., D.Phil. (b. 1946), C., South West
Khanbhai, Bashir (b. 1945), C., Eastern
*Kinnock, Mrs Glenys (b. 1944), Lab., Wales
Kirkhope, Timothy J. R. (b. 1945), C., Yorkshire and the Humber
Lambert, Ms Jean D. (b. 1950), Green, London
Lucas, Dr Caroline. (b. 1960), Green, South East
Ludford, The Baroness (b. 1951), LD, London
Lynne, Ms Elizabeth (b. 1948), LD, West Midlands
*McAvan, Ms Linda (b. 1962), Lab., Yorkshire and the Humber
*McCarthy, Ms Arlene (b. 1960), Lab., North West
MacCormick, Prof. D. Neil, FBA (b. 1941), SNP, Scotland
*McMillan-Scott, Edward H. C. (b. 1949), C., Yorkshire and the Humber

*McNally, Mrs Eryl M. (b. 1942), Lab., Eastern
*Martin, David W. (b. 1954), Lab., Scotland
*Miller, William (b. 1954), Lab., Scotland
Moraes, Claude (b. 1965), Lab., London
*Morgan, Ms Eluned (b. 1967), Lab., Wales
*Murphy, Dr Simon F. (b. 1962), Lab., West Midlands
**Newton Dunn, William F. (Bill) (b. 1941), LD, East Midlands
Nicholson of Winterbourne, The Baroness (b. 1941), LD, South East
*Nicholson, James (b. 1945), UUP, Northern Ireland
O'Toole, Ms Barbara M. (b. 1960), Lab., North East
*Paisley, Revd Ian R. K., MP (b. 1926), DUP, Northern Ireland
Parish, Neil (b. 1956), C., South West
*Perry, Roy J. (b. 1943), C., South East
*Provan, James L. C. (b. 1936), C., South East
Purvis, John R., CBE (b. 1938), C., Scotland
*Read, Ms I. M. (b. 1939), Lab., East Midlands

*Simpson, Brian (b. 1953), Lab., North West
*Skinner, Peter W. (b. 1959), Lab., South East
Stevenson, Struan (b. 1948), C., Scotland
Stihler, Catherine D. (elected Catherine Taylor) (b. 1973), Lab., Scotland
Stockton, The Earl of (b. 1943), C., South West
*Sturdy, Robert W. (b. 1944), C., Eastern
Sumberg, David (b. 1941), C., North West
Tannock, Dr Charles (b. 1957), C., London
Titford, Jeffrey (b. 1933), UK Ind., Eastern
*Titley, Gary (b. 1950), Lab., North West
Van Orden, Geoffrey (b. 1945), C., Eastern
Villiers, Ms Theresa (b. 1968), C., London
Wallis, Ms Diana (b. 1954), LD, Yorkshire and the Humber
*Watson, Graham R. (b. 1956), LD, South West
*Watts, Mark F. (b. 1964), Lab., South East
*Whitehead, Philip (b. 1937), Lab., East Midlands
Wyn, Eurig (b. 1944), PC, Wales
*Wynn, Terence (b. 1946), Lab., North West

UK REGIONS AS AT 10 JUNE 1999

Abbreviations

ACPFCA Anti-Corruption Pro Family Christian Alliance
AHRPE   Architect Human Rights Peace in Europe
Anti VAT Independent Anti Value Added Tax
EFP   English Freedom Party
Ind. Profit Independent Making a Profit in Europe
Ind. Stable Independent Open Democracy for Stability
Lower Tax Account for Lower Scottish Taxes
MEP Ind. MEP Independent Labour
Soc. All. Socialist Alliance
SSP   Scottish Socialist Party
WW   Weekly Worker
For other abbreviations, see UK General Election Results

EASTERN
(Bedfordshire, Cambridgeshire, Essex, Hertfordshire, Luton, Norfolk, Peterborough, Southend-on-Sea, Suffolk, Thurrock)

E. 4,067,524	T. 24.45%
C.	425,091 (42.75%)
Lab.	250,132 (25.15%)
LD	118,822 (11.95%)
UK Ind.	88,452 (8.89%)
Green	61,334 (6.17%)
Lib.	16,861 (1.70%)
Pro Euro C.	16,340 (1.64%)
BNP	9,353 (0.94%)
Soc. Lab.	6,143 (0.62%)
NLP	1,907 (0.19%)
C. majority	174,959
(June 1994, Lab. maj. 90,087)	

MEMBERS ELECTED
*R. Sturdy, C.
C. Beazley, C.
B. Khanbhai, C.
G. Van Orden, C.
*Ms E. McNally, Lab.
*R. Howitt, Lab. A. Duff, LD
J. Titford, UK Ind.

EAST MIDLANDS
(Derby, Derbyshire, Leicester, Leicestershire, Northamptonshire, Nottingham, Nottinghamshire, Rutland)

E. 3,199,711	T. 22.61%
C.	285,662 (39.47%)
Lab.	206,756 (28.57%)
LD	92,398 (12.77%)
UK Ind.	54,800 (7.57%)
Green	38,954 (5.38%)
Alt. Lab.	17,409 (2.41%)
Pro Euro C.	11,359 (1.57%)
BNP	9,342 (1.29%)
Soc. Lab.	5,528 (0.76%)
NLP	1,525 (0.21%)
C. majority	78,906
(June 1994, Lab. maj. 229,680)	

MEMBERS ELECTED
R. Helmer, C.
**W. Newton Dunn, LD
C. Heaton-Harris, C.
*Ms M. Read, Lab.
*P. Whitehead, Lab.
N. Clegg, LD

LONDON

E. 4,972,495	T. 22.95%
Lab.	399,466 (35.00%)
C.	372,989 (32.68%)
LD	133,058 (11.66%)
Green	87,545 (7.67%)
UK Ind.	61,741 (5.41%)
Soc. Lab.	19,632 (1.72%)
BNP	17,960 (1.57%)
Lib.	16,951 (1.49%)
Pro Euro C.	16,383 (1.44%)
AHRPE	4,851 (0.43%)
Anti VAT	2,596 (0.23%)
Hum.	2,586 (0.23%)
Hemp	2,358 (0.21%)
NLP	2,263 (0.20%)
WW	846 (0.07%)
Lab. majority	26,477
(June 1994, Lab. maj. 346,850)	

MEMBERS ELECTED
Miss T. Villiers, C.
Dr C. Tannock, C.
The Lord Bethell, C.
J. Bowis, C.
*Ms P. Green, Lab.
C. Moraes, Lab.
*R. Evans, Lab.
**††R. Balfe, Lab.
Ms S. Ludford, LD
Ms J. Lambert, Green

NORTH EAST
(Co. Durham, Darlington, Hartlepool, Middlesbrough, Northumberland, Redcar and Cleveland, Stockton-on-Tees, Tyne and Wear)

E. 1,969,966	T. 19.58%
Lab.	162,573 (42.15%)
C.	105,573 (27.37%)
LD	52,070 (13.50%)
UK Ind.	34,063 (8.83%)
Green	18,184 (4.71%)
Soc. Lab.	4,511 (1.17%)
BNP	3,505 (0.91%)
Pro Euro C.	2,926 (0.76%)
SPGB	1,510 (0.39%)
NLP	826 (0.21%)
Lab. majority	57,000
(June 1994, Lab. maj. 330,689)	

MEMBERS ELECTED
M. Callanan, C.
*A. Donnelly, Lab.
*S. Hughes, Lab.
Ms M. O'Toole, Lab.

NORTHERN IRELAND

Northern Ireland forms a three-member seat with a single transferable vote system

E. 1,190,160	T.57.77%
First Count	
*Revd I. Paisley,	
DUP	192,762 (28.40%)
*J. Hume, SDLP	190,731 (28.10%)
*J. Nicholson,	
UUP	119,507 (17.61%)
M. McLaughlin,	
SF	117,643 (17.33%)
D. Ervine, PUP	22,494 (3.31%)
R. McCartney,	
UKU	20,283 (2.99%)
S. Neeson, All.	14,391 (2.12%)
J. Anderson,	
NLP	998 (0.15%)

MEMBERS ELECTED
*Revd I. Paisley, DUP
*J. Hume, SDLP
*J. Nicholson, UUP (elected on third count)

NORTH WEST

(Blackburn-with-Darwen, Blackpool, Cheshire, Cumbria, Greater Manchester, Halton, Lancashire, Merseyside, Warrington)

E. 5,240,321	T. 19.4%
C.	360,027 (35.39%)
Lab.	350,511 (34.46%)
LD	119,376 (11.74%)
UK Ind.	66,779 (6.57%)
Green	56,828 (5.59%)
Lib.	22,640 (2.23%)
BNP	13,587 (1.34%)
Soc. Lab.	11,338 (1.11%)
Pro Euro C.	9,816 (0.97%)
ACPFCA	2,251 (0.22%)
NLP	2,114 (0.21%)
Ind. Hum.	1,049 (0.10%)
WW	878 (0.09%)
C. majority	9,516
(June 1994, Lab. maj. 444,569)	

MEMBERS ELECTED
The Lord Inglewood, C.
Sir Robert Atkins, C.
D. Sumberg, C.
D. Dover, C.
Mrs J. Foster, C.
*Ms A. McCarthy, Lab.
*G. Titley, Lab.
*T. Wynn, Lab.
*B. Simpson, Lab.
C. Davies, LD

SCOTLAND

E. 3,999,623	T. 24.7%
Lab.	283,490 (28.68%)
SNP	268,528 (27.17%)
C.	195,296 (19.76%)
LD	96,971 (9.81%)
Green	57,142 (5.78%)
SSP	39,720 (4.02%)
Pro Euro C.	17,781 (1.80%)
UK Ind.	12,549 (1.27%)
Soc. Lab.	9,385 (0.95%)
BNP	3,729 (0.38%)
NLP	2,087 (0.21%)
Lower Tax	1,632 (0.17%)
Lab. majority	14,962
(June 1994, Lab. maj. 148,718)	

MEMBERS ELECTED
S. Stevenson, C.
J. Purvis, C.
*D. Martin, Lab.
*W. Miller, Lab.
Ms C. Taylor, Lab.
Ms E. Attwooll, LD
*I. Hudghton, SNP
Prof. N. MacCormick, SNP

SOUTH EAST

(Bracknell Forest, Brighton and Hove, Buckinghamshire, East Sussex, Hampshire, Isle of Wight, Kent, Medway, Milton Keynes, Oxfordshire, Portsmouth, Reading, Slough, Southampton, Surrey, West Berkshire, West Sussex, Windsor and Maidenhead, Wokingham)

E. 6,023,991	T. 24.73%
C.	661,931 (44.42%)
Lab.	292,146 (19.61%)
LD	228,136 (15.31%)
UK Ind.	144,514 (9.70%)
Green	110,571 (7.42%)
Pro Euro C.	27,305 (1.83%)
BNP	12,161 (0.81%)
Soc. Lab.	7,281 (0.49%)
NLP	2,767 (0.19%)
Ind. Stable	1,857 (0.12%)
Ind. Profit	1,400 (0.09%)
C. majority	369,785
(June 1994, C. maj. 230,122)	

MEMBERS ELECTED
*J. Provan, C.
*R. Perry, C.
D. Hannan, C.
*J. Elles, C.
N. Deva, C.
*P. Skinner, Lab.
*M. Watts, Lab.
The Baroness Nicholson of Winterbourne, LD
C. Huhne, LD
Dr Caroline Lucas, Green
N. Farage, UK Ind.

SOUTH WEST

(Bath and North East Somerset, Bournemouth, Bristol, Cornwall, Devon, Dorset, Gloucestershire, North Somerset, South Gloucestershire, Swindon, Torbay, Wiltshire)

E. 3,775,332	T. 27.61%
C.	434,645 (41.70%)
Lab.	188,362 (18.07%)
LD	171,498 (16.45%)
UK Ind.	111,012 (10.65%)
Green	86,630 (8.31%)
Lib.	21,645 (2.08%)
Pro Euro C.	11,134 (1.07%)
BNP	9,752 (0.94%)
Soc. Lab.	5,741 (0.55%)
NLP	1,968 (0.19%)
C. majority	246,283
(June 1994, LD maj. 3,796)	

MEMBERS ELECTED
*Dr Caroline Jackson, C.
*G. Chichester, C.
The Earl of Stockton, C.
N. Parish, C.
*G. Ford, Lab.
*G. Watson, LD
M. Holmes, UK Ind.

WALES

E. 2,229,826	T. 28.99%
Lab.	199,690 (31.88%)
PC	185,235 (29.57%)
C.	142,631 (22.77%)
LD	51,283 (8.19%)
UK Ind.	19,702 (3.15%)
Green	16,146 (2.58%)
Pro Euro C.	5,834 (0.93%)
Soc. Lab.	4,283 (0.68%)
NLP	1,621 (0.26%)
Lab. majority	14,455
(June 1994, Lab. maj. 368,271)	

MEMBERS ELECTED
J. Evans, C.
*Ms G. Kinnock, Lab.
*Ms E. Morgan, Lab.
Ms J. Evans, PC
E. Wyn, PC

WEST MIDLANDS
(Herefordshire, Shropshire,
Staffordshire, Stoke-on-Trent,
Telford and Wrekin, Warwickshire,
West Midlands Metropolitan area,
Worcestershire)

E. 4,034,992	T. 21.03%
C.	321,719 (37.91%)
Lab.	237,671 (28.00%)
LD	95,769 (11.28%)
UK Ind.	49,621 (5.85%)
Green	49,440 (5.83%)
MEP Ind.	36,849 (4.34%)
Lib.	14,954 (1.76%)
BNP	14,344 (1.69%)
Pro Euro C.	11,144 (1.31%)
Soc. All.	7,203 (0.85%)
Soc. Lab.	5,257 (0.62%)
EFP	3,066 (0.36%)
NLP	1,647 (0.19%)
C. majority	84,048

(June 1994, Lab. maj. 268,888)

MEMBERS ELECTED
*J. Corrie, C.
P. Bushill-Matthews, C.
M. Harbour, C.
P. Bradbourn, C.
*S. Murphy, Lab.
M. Cashman, Lab.
Ms N. Gill, Lab.
Ms E. Lynne, LD

YORKSHIRE AND THE HUMBER
(East Riding of Yorkshire, Kingston
upon Hull, North East Lincolnshire,
North Lincolnshire, North Yorkshire,
South Yorkshire, West Yorkshire,
York)

E. 3,795,388	T. 19.60%
C.	272,653 (36.64%)
Lab.	233,024 (31.32%)
LD	107,168 (14.40%)
UK Ind.	52,824 (7.10%)
Green	42,604 (5.73%)
Alt. Lab.	9,554 (1.28%)
BNP	8,911 (1.20%)
Pro Euro C.	8,075 (1.09%)
Soc. Lab.	7,650 (1.03%)
NLP	1,604 (0.22%)
C. majority	39,629

(June 1994, Lab. maj. 344,310)

MEMBERS ELECTED
*E. McMillan-Scott, C.
T. Kirkhope, C.
R. Goodwill, C.
*Ms L. McAvan, Lab.
*D. Bowe, Lab.
*R. Corbett, Lab.
Ms D. Wallis, LD

For further information about the
European   Parliament,   visit
www.europarl.org.uk.
   The county and unitary areas
listed   after   each   European
Parliamentary constituency name are
a guide to the areas covered by each
constituency.
   For information about which areas
of the country are covered by a
particular region, please contact the
Home Office.

LAW COURTS AND OFFICES

THE JUDICIAL COMMITTEE OF THE PRIVY COUNCIL

The Judicial Committee of the Privy Council is the final court of appeal for the United Kingdom overseas territories and Crown dependencies and those independent Commonwealth countries which have retained this avenue of appeal (Antigua and Barbuda, The Bahamas, Barbados, Belize, Brunei, Dominica, Grenada, Jamaica, Kiribati, Mauritius, New Zealand, St Christopher and Nevis, St Lucia, St Vincent and the Grenadines, Trinidad and Tobago, and Tuvalu). The Committee also hears appeals against pastoral schemes under the Pastoral Measure 1983.

Under the devolution legislation enacted in 1998, the Judicial Committee of the Privy Council is the final arbiter in disputes as to the legal competence of things done or proposed by the devolved legislative and Executive authorities in Scotland, Wales and Northern Ireland.

In 2002 the Judicial Committee dealt with a total of 89 appeals and 46 petitions for special leave to appeal.

The members of the Judicial Committee include past and present Lord Chancellors and Lords of Appeal in Ordinary, and other Privy Counsellors who hold or have held high judicial office in the United Kingdom and in certain designated courts of Commonwealth countries from which appeals lie to the Judicial Committee.

JUDICIAL COMMITTEE OF THE PRIVY COUNCIL,
Downing Street, London SW1A 2AJ.
Tel: 020-7276 0483/5.
Registrar of the Privy Council, J. A. C. Watherston
Chief Clerk, F. G. Hart

THE JUDICATURE OF ENGLAND AND WALES

The legal system of England and Wales is separate from those of Scotland and Northern Ireland and differs from them in law, judicial procedure and court structure, although there is a common distinction between civil law (disputes between individuals) and criminal law (acts harmful to the community).

The supreme judicial authority for England and Wales is the House of Lords, which is the ultimate Court of Appeal from all courts in Great Britain and Northern Ireland (except criminal courts in Scotland) for all cases except those concerning the interpretation and application of European Community law, including preliminary rulings requested by British courts and tribunals, which are decided by the European Court of Justice (*see* European Union section). Under the Human Rights Act 1998, which came into force on 2 October 2000, the European Convention on Human Rights is incorporated into British law; unresolved cases are still referred to the European Court of Human Rights. As a Court of Appeal the House of Lords consists of the Lord Chancellor and the Lords of Appeal in Ordinary (law lords).

SUPREME COURT OF JUDICATURE
The Supreme Court of Judicature comprises the Court of Appeal, the High Court of Justice and the Crown Court. The High Court of Justice is the superior civil court and

is divided into three divisions. The Chancery Division is concerned mainly with equity, bankruptcy and contentious probate business. The Queen's Bench Division deals with commercial and maritime law, serious personal injury and medical negligence cases, cases involving a breach of contract and professional negligence actions. The Family Division deals with matters relating to family law. Sittings are held at the Royal Courts of Justice in London or at 126 District Registries outside the capital. High Court judges sit alone to hear cases at first instance. The Restrictive Practices Court, set up under the Restrictive Trade Practices Act 1956, and the Technology and Construction Court which deals with cases that require expert evidence on technical and other issues concerning mainly the construction industry, defective products, property valuations, and landlord and tenant disputes, are also currently part of the High Court, although the Restrictive Practices Court is due to be abolished following the establishment of the Competition Commission. Appeals from the High Court are heard in the Court of Appeal (Civil Division), presided over by the Master of the Rolls, and may go on to the House of Lords.

In December 1999 the Lord Chancellor began a wide-ranging, independent review of the criminal courts in England and Wales. Lord Justice Auld lead the review into how the criminal courts work at every level. The report *Review of the Criminal Courts of England and Wales* was published in October 2001 and assesses what should be done to modernise and improve the criminal justice system so that its aims can be achieved more effectively.

CRIMINAL CASES
In criminal matters the decision to prosecute in the majority of cases rests with the Crown Prosecution Service, the independent prosecuting body in England and Wales. The Service is headed by the Director of Public Prosecutions, who works under the superintendence of the Attorney-General. Certain categories of offence continue to require the Attorney-General's consent for prosecution.

The Crown Court sits in about 90 centres, divided into six circuits, and is presided over by High Court judges, full-time circuit judges, and part-time recorders, sitting with a jury in all trials which are contested. Since 12 April 2000, the distinction between assistant recorders and recorders has changed. Consequently, there are now only full recorders. The post of Assistant Recorder remains on the statute book but appointments are no longer made. There were 1,325 full recorders at 1 June 2002. The Crown Court deals with trials of the more serious criminal offences, the sentencing of offenders committed for sentence by magistrates' courts (when the magistrates consider their own power of sentence inadequate), and appeals from magistrates' courts. Magistrates usually sit with a circuit judge or recorder to deal with appeals and committals for sentence. Appeals from the Crown Court, either against sentence or conviction, are made to the Court of Appeal (Criminal Division), presided over by the Lord Chief Justice. A further appeal from the Court of Appeal to the House of Lords can be brought if a point of law of general public importance is considered to be involved.

Minor criminal offences (summary offences) are dealt

with in magistrates' courts, which usually consist of three unpaid lay magistrates (justices of the peace) sitting without a jury, who are advised on points of law and procedure by a legally-qualified clerk to the justices. There were 24,520 justices of the peace at 1 April 2002. In busier courts a full-time, salaried and legally-qualified stipendiary magistrate presides alone. Cases involving people under 18 are heard in youth courts, specially constituted magistrates' courts. Preliminary proceedings in a serious case to decide whether there is evidence to justify committal for trial in the Crown Court are also dealt with in the magistrates' courts. Appeals from magistrates' courts against sentence or conviction are made to the Crown Court. Appeals upon a point of law are made to the High Court, and may go on to the House of Lords.

CIVIL CASES

Most minor civil cases are dealt with by the county courts, of which there are around 222 (details may be found in the local telephone directory). Cases are heard by circuit judges, courts or district judges (magistrates' courts). There were 411 district judges and 107 District Judges (magistrates' courts) at 1 September 2003. For cases involving small claims there are special simplified procedures. Where there are financial limits on county court jurisdiction, claims which exceed those limits may be tried in the county courts with the consent of the parties, subject to the Court's agreement, or in certain circumstances on transfer from the High Court. Outside London, bankruptcy proceedings can be heard in designated county courts. Magistrates' courts can deal with certain classes of civil case and committees of magistrates license public houses, clubs and betting shops. For the implementation of the Children Act 1989, a new structure of hearing centres was set up in 1991 for family proceedings cases, involving magistrates' courts (family proceedings courts), divorce county courts, family hearing centres and care centres. Appeals in family matters heard in the family proceedings courts go to the Family Division of the High Court; affiliation appeals and appeals from decisions of the licensing committees of magistrates go to the Crown Court. Appeals from county courts may be heard in the High Court of Appeal (civil division) and may go on to the House of Lords.

CORONERS' COURTS

Coroners' courts investigate violent and unnatural deaths or sudden deaths where the cause is unknown. Cases may be brought before a local coroner (a senior lawyer or doctor) by doctors, the police, various public authorities or members of the public. Where a death is sudden and the cause is unknown, the coroner may order a post-mortem examination to determine the cause of death rather than hold an inquest in court.

Judicial appointments are made by The Queen; the most senior appointments are made on the advice of the Prime Minister and other appointments on the advice of the Lord Chancellor.

Under the provisions of the Criminal Appeal Act 1995, a Commission was set up to direct and supervise investigations into possible miscarriages of justice and to refer cases to the courts on the grounds of conviction and sentence; these functions were formerly the responsibility of the Home Secretary.

THE HOUSE OF LORDS

AS FINAL COURT OF APPEAL

The Lord High Chancellor and Secretary of State for Constitutional Affairs (£202,736), The Rt. Hon. The Lord Falconer of Thoroton, *born* 1951, *apptd* 2003

LORDS OF APPEAL IN ORDINARY *as at 14 July 2003* (each £175,055)
Style, The Rt. Hon. Lord—

Rt. Hon. Lord Bingham of Cornhill, *born* 1933, *apptd* 2000
Rt. Hon. Lord Nicholls of Birkenhead, *born* 1933, *apptd* 1994
Rt. Hon. Lord Steyn, *born* 1932, *apptd* 1995
Rt. Hon. Lord Hoffmann, *born* 1934, *apptd* 1995
Rt. Hon. Lord Hope of Craighead, *born* 1938, *apptd* 1996
Rt. Hon. Lord Hutton, *born* 1931, *apptd* 1997
Rt. Hon. Lord Saville of Newdigate, *born* 1936, *apptd* 1997
Rt. Hon. Lord Hobhouse of Woodborough, *born* 1932, *apptd* 1998
Rt. Hon. Lord Millett, *born* 1932, *apptd* 1998
Rt. Hon. Lord Scott Foscote, *born* 1934, *apptd* 2000
Rt. Hon. Lord Rodger of Earlsferry, *born* 1944, *apptd* 2001
Rt. Hon. Lord Walker of Gestingthorpe, *born* 1938, *apptd* 2002

JUDICIAL OFFICE OF THE HOUSE OF LORDS, House of Lords, London SW1A 0PW. Tel: 020-7219 3111
Registrar, The Clerk of the Parliaments

SUPREME COURT OF JUDICATURE

COURT OF APPEAL
The Master of the Rolls (£181,176), The Rt. Hon. Lord Phillips of Worth Matravers, *born* 1938, *apptd* 2000
Secretary, Mrs L. Grace
Clerk, Ms J. Jones

LORDS JUSTICES OF APPEAL *as at 14 July 2003* (each £166,394)
Style, The Rt. Hon. Lord/Lady Justice [surname]
Rt. Hon. Sir Paul Kennedy, *born* 1935, *apptd* 1992
Rt. Hon. Sir Simon Brown, *born* 1937, *apptd* 1992
Rt. Hon. Sir Christopher Rose, *born* 1937, *apptd* 1992
Rt. Hon. Sir Peter Gibson, *born* 1934, *apptd* 1993
Rt. Hon. Sir Robin Auld, *born* 1937, *apptd* 1995
Rt. Hon. Sir Malcolm Pill, *born* 1938, *apptd* 1995
Rt. Hon. Sir William Aldous, *born* 1936, *apptd* 1995
Rt. Hon. Sir Alan Ward, *born* 1938, *apptd* 1995
Rt. Hon. Sir Konrad Schiemann, *born* 1937, *apptd* 1995
Rt. Hon. Sir Mathew Thorpe, *born* 1938, *apptd* 1995
Rt. Hon. Sir Mark Potter, *born* 1937, *apptd* 1996
Rt. Hon. Sir Henry Brooke, *born* 1936, *apptd* 1996
Rt. Hon. Sir Igor Judge, *born* 1941, *apptd* 1996
Rt. Hon. Sir George Waller, *born* 1940, *apptd* 1996
Rt. Hon. Sir John Mummery, *born* 1938, *apptd* 1996
Rt. Hon. Sir Charles Mantell, *born* 1937, *apptd* 1997
Rt. Hon. Sir John Chadwick, ED, *born* 1941, *apptd* 1997
Rt. Hon. Sir Richard Buxton, *born* 1938, *apptd* 1997
Rt. Hon. Sir Anthony May, *born* 1940, *apptd* 1997
Rt. Hon. Sir Simon Tuckey, *born* 1941, *apptd* 1998
Rt. Hon. Sir Anthony Clarke, *born* 1943, *apptd* 1998
Rt. Hon. Sir John Laws, *born* 1945, *apptd* 1999

Rt. Hon. Sir Stephen Sedley, *born* 1939, *apptd* 1999

Rt. Hon. Sir Jonathan Mance, *born* 1943, *apptd* 1999

Rt. Hon. Dame Brenda Hale, DBE, *born* 1945, *apptd* 1999

Rt. Hon. Sir David Latham, *born* 1942, *apptd* 2000

Rt. Hon. Sir John William Kay, *born* 1943, *apptd* 2000

Rt. Hon. Sir Bernard Anthony Rix, *born* 1943, *apptd* 2000

Rt. Hon. Sir Jonathan Parker, *born* 1937, *apptd* 2000

Rt. Hon. Dame Mary Howarth Arden, DBE, *born* 1947, *apptd* 2000

Rt. Hon. Sir David Wolfe Keene, *born* 1941, *apptd* 2000

Rt. Hon. Sir John Anthony Dyson, *born* 1943, *apptd* 2001

Rt. Hon. Sir Andrew Centlivres Longmore, *born* 1944, *apptd* 2001

Rt. Hon. Sir Robert John Carnwath, CVO, *born* 1945, *apptd* 2002

Rt. Hon. Sir Thomas Baker, *born* 1937, *apptd* 2002

Rt. Hon. Dame Janet Hilary Smith, DBE, *born* 1940, *apptd* 2002

Rt. Hon. Sir Roger Laugharne Thomas, *born* 1947, *apptd* 2003

Ex officio Judges, The Lord High Chancellor; the Lord Chief Justice of England; the Master of the Rolls; the President of the Family Division; and the Vice-Chancellor

COURT OF APPEAL (CIVIL DIVISION)
Vice-President, The Rt. Hon. Lord Justice Simon Brown

COURT OF APPEAL (CRIMINAL DIVISION)
Vice-President, The Rt. Hon. Lord Justice Rose
Judges, The Lord Chief Justice of England; the Master of the Rolls; Lords Justices of Appeal; and Judges of the High Court of Justice

COURTS-MARTIAL APPEAL COURT
Judges, The Lord Chief Justice of England; the Master of the Rolls; Lords Justices of Appeal; and Judges of the High Court of Justice

HIGH COURT OF JUSTICE

CHANCERY DIVISION
President, The Lord High Chancellor
The Vice-Chancellor (£175,055), The Rt. Hon. Sir Andrew Moritt, CVO, *born,* 1938 *apptd* 2000
Clerk, W. Northfield, BEM

JUDGES (each £147,198)
Style, The Hon. Mr/Mrs Justice [surname]

Hon. Sir John Lindsay, *born* 1935, *apptd* 1992

Hon. Sir Edward Evans-Lombe, *born* 1937, *apptd* 1993

Hon. Sir Robin Jacob, *born* 1941, *apptd* 1993

Hon. Sir William Blackburne, *born* 1944, *apptd* 1993

Hon. Sir Gavin Lightman, *born* 1939, *apptd* 1994

Hon. Sir Colin Rimer, *born* 1944, *apptd* 1994

Hon. Sir Hugh Laddie, *born* 1946, *apptd* 1995

Hon. Sir Timothy Lloyd, *born* 1946, *apptd* 1996

Hon. Sir David Neuberger, *born* 1948, *apptd* 1996

Hon. Sir Andrew Park, *born* 1939, *apptd* 1997

Hon. Sir Nicholas Pumfrey, *born* 1951, *apptd* 1997

Hon. Sir Michael Hart, *born* 1948, *apptd* 1998

Hon. Sir Lawrence Collins, *born* 1941, *apptd* 2000

Hon. Sir Nicholas John Patten, *born* 1950, *apptd* 2000

Hon. Sir Terence Michael Barnet Etherton, *born* 1951, *apptd* 2001

Hon. Sir Peter Winston Smith, *born* 1952, *appt* 2002

Hon. Sir Kim Lewison, *born* 1952, *apptd* 2003

HIGH COURT OF JUSTICE IN BANKRUPTCY
Judges, The Vice-Chancellor and judges of the Chancery Division of the High Court

COMPANIES COURT
Judges, The Vice-Chancellor and judges of the Chancery Division of the High Court

PATENT COURT (APPELLATE SECTION)
Judge, The Hon. Mr Justice Jacob

QUEEN'S BENCH DIVISION
The Lord Chief Justice of England and Wales (£200,236)
The Rt. Hon. the Lord Woolf, *born* 1933, *apptd* 2000
Private Secretary, E. Adams
Clerk, J. Bond
Vice-President, The Rt. Hon. Lord Justice May, *born* 1940, *apptd* 2002

JUDGES *as at 14 July 2003* (each £147,198)
Style, The Hon. Mr/Mrs Justice [surname]

Hon. Sir Stuart McKinnon, *born* 1938, *apptd* 1988

Hon. Sir Douglas Dunlop Brown, *born* 1931, *apptd* 1996

Hon. Sir Michael Morland, *born* 1929, *apptd* 1989

Hon. Sir Roger Buckley, *born* 1939, *apptd* 1989

Hon. Sir Peter Cresswell, *born* 1944, *apptd* 1991

Hon. Sir Christopher Holland, *born* 1937, *apptd* 1992

Hon. Sir Richard Curtis, *born* 1933, *apptd* 1992

Hon. Sir Anthony Colman, *born* 1938, *apptd* 1992

Hon. Sir Thayne Forbes, *born* 1938, *apptd* 1993

Hon. Sir Michael Sachs, *born* 1932, *apptd* 1993

Hon. Sir Stephen Mitchell, *born* 1941, *apptd* 1993

Hon. Sir Rodger Bell, *born* 1939, *apptd* 1993

Hon. Sir Michael Harrison, *born* 1939, *apptd* 1993

Hon. Sir William Gage, *born* 1938, *apptd* 1993

Hon. Sir Thomas Morison, *born* 1939, *apptd* 1993

Hon. Sir Andrew Collins, *born* 1942, *apptd* 1994

Hon. Sir Maurice Kay, *born* 1942, *apptd* 1995

Hon. Sir Anthony Hooper, *born* 1937, *apptd* 1995

Hon. Sir Alexander Butterfield, *born* 1942, *apptd* 1995

Hon. Sir George Newman, *born* 1941, *apptd* 1995

Hon. Sir David Poole, *born* 1938, *apptd* 1995

Hon. Sir Martin Moore-Bick, *born* 1946, *apptd* 1995

Hon. Sir Gordon Langley, *born* 1943, *apptd* 1995

Hon. Sir Robert Nelson, *born* 1942, *apptd* 1996

Hon. Sir Roger Toulson, *born* 1946, *apptd* 1996

Hon. Sir Michael Astill, *born* 1938, *apptd* 1996

Hon. Sir Alan Moses, *born* 1945, *apptd* 1996

Hon. Sir David Eady, *born* 1943, *apptd* 1997

Hon. Sir Jeremy Sullivan, *born* 1945, *apptd* 1997

Hon. Sir David Penry-Davey, *born* 1942, *apptd* 1997

Hon. Sir Stephen Richards, *born* 1950, *apptd* 1997

Hon. Sir David Steel, *born* 1943, *apptd* 1998

Hon. Sir Charles Gray, *born* 1942, *apptd* 1998

Hon. Sir Nicolas Bratza, *born* 1945, *apptd* 1998

Hon. Sir Michael Burton, *born* 1946, *apptd* 1998

Hon. Sir Rupert Jackson, *born* 1948, *apptd* 1999

Hon. Dame Heather Hallett, DBE, *born* 1949, *apptd* 1999

Hon. Sir Patrick Elias, *born* 1947, *apptd* 1999

Hon. Sir Richard Aikens, *born* 1948, *apptd* 1999

Hon. Sir Stephen Silber, *born* 1944, *apptd* 1999
Hon. Sir John Goldring, *born* 1944, *apptd* 1999
Hon. Sir Peter Crane, *born* 1940, *apptd* 2000
Hon. Dame Anne Rafferty, DBE, *born* 1950, *apptd* 2000
Hon. Sir Geoffrey Grigson, *born* 1944, *apptd* 2000
Hon. Sir Richard Gibbs, *born* 1941, *apptd* 2000
Hon. Sir Richard Henriques, *born* 1943, *apptd* 2000
Hon. Sir Stephen Tomlinson, *born* 1952, *apptd* 2000
Hon. Sir Andrew Smith, *born* 1947, *apptd* 2000
Hon. Sir Stanley Burnton, *born* 1942, *apptd* 2000
Hon. Sir Patrick Hunt, *born* 1943, *apptd* 2000
Hon. Sir Christopher Pitchford, *born* 1947, *apptd* 2000
Hon. Sir Brian Leveson, *born* 1949, *apptd* 2000
Hon. Sir Duncan Ouseley, *born* 1950, *apptd* 2000
Hon. Sir Raymond Jack, *born* 1942, *apptd* 2001
Hon. Sir Richard McCombe, *born* 1952, *apptd* 2001
Hon. Sir Robert Owen, *born* 1944, *apptd* 2001
Hon. Sir Colin Mackay, *born* 1943, *apptd* 2001
Hon. Sir John Mitting, *born* 1947, *apptd* 2001
Hon. Sir David Evans, *born* 1946, *apptd* 2001
Hon. Sir Nigel Davis, *born* 1951, *apptd* 2001
Hon. Sir Peter Gross, *born* 1952, *apptd* 2001
Hon. Sir Brian Keith, *born* 1944, *apptd* 2001
Hon. Sir Jeremy Cooke, *born* 1949, *apptd* 2001
Hon. Sir Richard Field, *born* 1947, *apptd* 2002
Hon. Sir Christopher Pitchers, *born* 1942, *apptd* 2002
Hon. Sir Adrian Fulford, *born* 1953, *apptd* 2002
Hon. Sir Colman Treacy, *born* 1949, *apptd* 2002
Hon. Sir Peregrine Simon, *born* 1950, *apptd* 2002
Hon. Sir Roger Royce, *born* 1944, *apptd* 2002
Hon. Dame Laura Cox, DBE, *born* 1951, *apptd* 2002
Hon. Sir Jack Beatson, *born* 1948, *apptd* 2003
Hon. Sir Michael Tugendhat, *born* 1944, *apptd* 2003

FAMILY DIVISION
President (£175,055), The Rt. Hon. Dame Elizabeth
  Butler-Sloss, DBE, *born* 1933, *apptd* 1999
Secretary, Mrs S. Leung
Clerk, Mrs S. Bell

JUDGES *as at 14 July 2003* (each £147,198)
Style, The Hon. Mr/Mrs Justice [surname]

Hon. Sir Robert Johnson, *born* 1933, *apptd* 1989
Hon. Dame Joyanne Bracewell, DBE, *born* 1934, *apptd*
  1990
Hon. Sir Peter Singer, *born* 1944, *apptd* 1993
Hon. Sir Nicholas Wilson, *born* 1945, *apptd* 1993
Hon. Sir Nicholas Wall, *born* 1945, *apptd* 1993
Hon. Sir Andrew Kirkwood, *born* 1944, *apptd* 1993
Hon. Sir Hugh Bennett, *born* 1943, *apptd* 1995
Hon. Sir Edward Holman, *born* 1947, *apptd* 1995
Hon. Dame Mary Hogg, DBE, *born* 1947, *apptd* 1995
Hon. Sir Christopher Sumner, *born* 1939, *apptd* 1996
Hon. Sir Anthony Hughes, *born* 1948, *apptd* 1997
Hon. Sir Arthur Charles, *born* 1948, *apptd* 1998
Hon. Sir David Bodey, *born* 1947, *apptd* 1999
Hon. Dame Jill Black, DBE, *born* 1954, *apptd* 1999
Hon. Sir James Munby, *born* 1948, *apptd* 2000
Hon. Sir Paul Coleridge, *born* 1949, *apptd* 2000
Hon. Sir Mark Hedley, *born* 1946, *apptd* 2002

TECHNOLOGY AND CONSTRUCTION COURT
St Dunstan's House, 133–137 Fetter Lane, London
  EC4A 1HD. Tel: 020-7947 6022

JUDGES (each £119,160)
The Hon. Mr Justice Forbes (*Presiding Judge*)
His Hon. Judge Havery, QC
His Hon. Judge Lloyd, QC
His Hon. Judge Thornton, QC
His Hon. Judge Wilcox
His Hon. Judge Toulmin, CMG, QC
His Hon. Judge Seymour, QC

Court Manager, Ms L. Fletcher

LORD CHANCELLOR'S DEPARTMENT
see Government Departments and Public Offices section

SUPREME COURT DEPARTMENTS AND OFFICES
Royal Courts of Justice, London WC2A 2LL
Tel: 020-7947 6000

DIRECTOR'S OFFICE
Director, Mark Camley
Group Manager and Deputy Director, J. Selch
Group Manager, Family Proceedings and Probate Service,
  R. P. Knight
Finance and Performance Officer, K. Richardson

ADMIRALTY AND COMMERCIAL REGISTRY AND
MARSHAL'S OFFICE
Registrar, P. Miller
Admiralty Marshal and Court Manager, K. Houghton

BANKRUPTCY AND COMPANIES COURT
Chief Registrar, vacant
Bankruptcy Registrars, S. Baister; G. W. Jaques;
  J. A. Simmonds; P. J. S. Rawson; C. Derrett
Court Manager, Jane O'Connor

CENTRAL OFFICE OF THE SUPREME COURT
Senior Master of the Supreme Court (QBD) and Queen's
  Remembrancer, R. L. Turner
Masters of the Supreme Court (QBD), M. Tennant;
  P. Miller; I. H. Foster; G. H. Rose; P. G. A. Eyre;
  H. J. Leslie; J. G. G. Ungley; S. Whittaker; B. Yoxall;
  B. J. F. Fontaine
Court Manager, M. A. Brown

CHANCERY CHAMBERS
Chief Master of the Supreme Court, J. I. Winegarten
Masters of the Supreme Court, J. A. Moncaster; R. A.
  Bowman; N. W. Bragge; T. J. Bowles; Price
Court Manager, G. Robinson
Conveyancing Counsel of the Supreme Court, W. D. Ainger;
  H. M. Harrod; A. C. Taussig

COURT OF APPEAL CIVIL DIVISION
Head of the Civil Appeals Office, David Gladwell
Court Manager, Mrs S. Morson

COURT OF APPEAL CRIMINAL DIVISION
Registrar, R. A. Venne
Deputy Registrar, Mrs L. G. Knapman
Chief Clerk, M. Bishop

CROWN OFFICE OF THE SUPREME COURT
Master of the Crown Office, and Queen's Coroner and
  Attorney, R. A. Venne
Head of Crown Office, Mrs L. G. Knapman
Group Manager, M. Bishop

EXAMINERS OF THE COURT
Empowered to take examination of witnesses in all Divisions of the High Court.
Examiners, A. G. Dyer; A. W. Hughes; Mrs G. M. Kenne; R. M. Planterose; M. W. M. Chism

SUPREME COURT COSTS OFFICE
Senior Cost Judge, P. T. Hurst
Masters of the Supreme Court, T. H. Seager-Berry; C. C. Wright; P. R. Rogers; J. E. O'Hare; C. D. N. Campbell; J. Simons
Court Manager, Geoff Waterhouse

COURT OF PROTECTION
Archway Towers, 11th Floor, 2 Junction Road, London N19 5SZ
Tel: 020-7664 7317
Master, D. A. Lush

ELECTION PETITIONS OFFICE
Room E113, Royal Courts of Justice, Strand, London WC2A 2LL. Tel: 020-7947 6131

The office accepts petitions and deals with all matters relating to the questioning of parliamentary, European Parliament and local government elections, and with applications for relief under the Representation of the People legislation.
Prescribed Officer, R. L. Turner
Chief Clerk, Mrs A. J. Burns

OFFICE OF THE LORD CHANCELLOR'S VISITORS
Archway Towers, 11th Floor, 2 Junction Road, London N19 5SZ. Tel 020-7664 7317

Legal Visitor, A. R. Tyrrell
Medical Visitors, S. E. Mahapatra; A. Bailey; T. Heads; E. Campbell; J. A. O. Russell; J. Waite

OFFICIAL RECEIVERS' DEPARTMENT
21 Bloomsbury Street, London WC1B 3QW
Tel: 020-7637 1110

Inspector General, D. Flynn
Deputies, L. Gramp; G. Horna

OFFICIAL SOLICITOR'S DEPARTMENT
81 Chancery Lane, London WC2B 6HD
Tel: 020-7911 7127

Official Solicitor to the Supreme Court, L. C. Oates
Deputy Official Solicitor, E. Solomons
Chief Clerk, Edward Bloomfield

PRINCIPAL REGISTRY (FAMILY DIVISION)
First Avenue House, 42–49 High Holborn, London WC1V 6NP.
Tel: 020-7947 6000

Senior District Judge, G. B. N. A. Angel
District Judges,
  A. R. S. Bassett-Cross; M. C. Berry; H. Black; Miss S. M. Bowman; Miss H. C. Bradley; G. C. Brasse; Miss P. Cushing; K. E. Green; R. Harper; Maple; C. Million; Mrs K. T. Moorhouse; Redgrave; Miss L. D. Roberts; Robinson; M. J. Segal; K. J. White; P. Waller
Family and Probate Service Group Manager, R. P. Knight
District Probate Registrars,
Birmingham and Stoke-on-Trent, Miss P. Walbeoff
Brighton and Maidstone, P. Ellwood

Bristol, Exeter and Bodmin, R. H. P. Joyce
Cardiff, Bangor and Carmarthen, P. Curran *(deputy)*
Ipswich, Norwich and Peterborough, Miss H. Whitby
Leeds, Lincoln and Sheffield, A. P. Dawson
Liverpool, Lancaster and Chester, C. Fox
Manchester and Nottingham, P. Burch
Newcastle, Carlisle, York and Middlesborough, P. Sanderson
Oxford, Gloucester and Leicester, R. R. Da Costa
Winchester, A. K. Biggs

JUDGE ADVOCATES
THE JUDGE ADVOCATE OF THE FLEET
c/o Chichester Combined Court, Southgate, Chichester PO19 1SX. Tel: 01243-520741

Judge Advocate of the Fleet (£102,999), His Hon. Judge Sessions

OFFICE OF THE JUDGE ADVOCATE-GENERAL OF THE FORCES
(Joint Service for the Army and the Royal Air Force)
81 Chancery Lane, London WC2A IBQ Tel: 020-7218 8089

Judge Advocate-General (£107,408), vacant
Vice-Judge Advocate-General (£103,353), E. G. Moelwyn-Hughes
Judge Advocates *(£90,176), M. A. Hunter; J. P. Camp; C. R. Burn; R. C. C. Seymour; I. H. Pearson; R. G. Chapple; J. F. T. Bayliss; M. R. Elsom
Style for Judge Advocates, Judge Advocate [surname]
*salary includes £4,000 inner London weighting

HIGH COURT AND CROWN COURT CENTRES
First-tier centres deal with both civil and criminal cases and are served by High Court and circuit judges. Second-tier centres deal with criminal cases only and are served by High Court and circuit judges. Third-tier centres deal with criminal cases only and are served only by circuit judges.

MIDLAND CIRCUIT
First-tier – Birmingham, Lincoln, Nottingham, Stafford, Warwick
Second-tier – Leicester, Northampton, Shrewsbury, Worcester, Wolverhampton
Third-tier – Coventry, Derby, Hereford, Stoke-on-Trent
Circuit Administrator (Acting), Mrs D. Ponsonby, The Priory Courts, 6th Floor, 33 Bull Street, Birmingham B4 6DW.
Tel: 0121-681 3201
Group Managers: Mrs J. Grosvenor *(acting), West Midlands;* R. Perry *(acting), Warwickshire Group;* D. Bennett, *Staffordshire/West Mercia Group;* A. Phillips; *East Midlands Group*

NORTH-EASTERN CIRCUIT
First-tier – Leeds, Newcastle upon Tyne, Sheffield, Teesside
Second-tier – Bradford, York
Third-tier – Doncaster, Durham, Kingston-upon-Hull, Great Grimsby
Circuit Administrator, S. Proudlock, 18th Floor, West Riding House, Albion Street, Leeds LS1 5AA. Tel: 0113-251 1200
Group Managers: Linda Mayhew *(acting), North and West Yorkshire Group;* David Keane, *Tyne Tees Group;* Sarah Greenhough *(acting), Humberside and South Yorkshire Group*

NORTHERN CIRCUIT
First-tier – Carlisle, Liverpool, Manchester (Crown Square), Preston
Third-tier – Barrow-in-Furness, Bolton, Burnley, Lancaster; Manchester (Minshull Street)
Circuit Administrator, C. A. Mayer, 15 Quay Street, Manchester M60 9FD. Tel: 0161-833 1005
Group Managers: Miss G. Hague, Greater Manchester Group; R. Knott, Merseyside Group; S. McNally, Lancashire and Cumbria Group

SOUTH-EASTERN CIRCUIT
First-tier – Chelmsford, Lewes, Norwich
Second-tier – Ipswich, London (Central Criminal Court), Luton, Maidstone, Reading, St Albans
Third-tier – Aylesbury, Basildon, Bury St Edmunds, Cambridge, Canterbury, Chichester, Croydon, Guildford, King's Lynn, London (Blackfriars, Harrow, Inner London Sessions House, Isleworth, Kingston, Middlesex Guildhall, Snaresbrook, Southwark, Wood Green, Woolwich), Southend
Circuit Administrator, D. Ryan, CBE, New Cavendish House, 18 Maltravers Street, London WC2R 3EU.
Tel: 020-7947 7232
Group Managers: D. Weston (London Crown); L. Lennon (London County); J. Cave (Kent and Sussex); M. Littlewood (East Anglia, Bedfordshire and Hertfordshire); S. Townley (Thames Valley, Surrey and Oxford)

The High Court in Greater London sits at the Royal Courts of Justice.

WALES AND CHESTER CIRCUIT
First-tier – Caernarfon, Cardiff, Chester, Mold, Swansea
Second-tier – Carmarthen, Merthyr Tydfil, Newport, Welshpool
Third-tier – Dolgellau, Haverfordwest, Knutsford, Warrington
Circuit Administrator, N. Chipnall, Churchill House, Churchill Way, Cardiff CF10 4HH.
Tel: 029-2041 5500
Group Managers: G. Pickett, South Wales Group; G. Kenney, North Wales and Cheshire Group; Mrs D. Thomas, Swansea Group

WESTERN CIRCUIT
First-tier – Bristol, Exeter, Truro, Winchester
Second-tier – Dorchester, Gloucester, Plymouth, Weymouth
Third-tier – Barnstaple, Bournemouth, Newport (IOW), Portsmouth, Salisbury, Southampton, Swindon, Taunton
Circuit Administrator, R. White, Bridge House, Sion Place, Clifton, Bristol BS8 4BN. Tel: 0117-974 3763
Group Managers: N. Jeffery, East Group; D. Gentry, West Group

CIRCUIT JUDGES

*Senior Circuit Judges, each £119,160
Circuit Judges at the Central Criminal Court, London (Old Bailey Judges), each £119,160
Circuit Judges, each £110,362
Style, His/Her Hon. Judge [surname]
Senior Presiding Judge, The Rt. Hon. Lord Justice Judge

MIDLAND CIRCUIT
Presiding Judges, The Hon. Mr Justice Goldring; The Hon. Mr Justice Gibbs

I. D. G. Alexander, QC; Miss C. Alton; D. Bennett; R. Benson; R. Bray; D. Brunning; J. Burgess; Miss J. Butler, QC; J. Cavell; *F. Chapman; M. Coates; R. Cole; N. B. Coles, QC; I. Collis; T. Corrie; P. De Mille (shared with South-Eastern Circuit); Miss P. Deeley; C. H. Durman; M. R. Eades; P. Eccles, QC; T. Faber; Miss E. Fisher; J. Fletcher; A. Geddes; R. Griffith-Jones; V. Hall; A. Hamilton; D. Hamilton; S. Hammond; Miss A. W. Hampton; C. Harris, QC; M. Heath; E. Hindley, QC; C. Hodson; H. Hughes; R. Inglis; R. Jenkins; F. Kirkham; A. MacDuff, QC; P. McCahill, QC; D. McCarthy; A. McCreath; D. McEvoy, QC; M. McKenna; J. Machin; L. Marshall; W. D. Matthews; H. R. Mayor, QC; C. Metcalf; A. Mitchell; N. Mitchell; P. Morrell; I. Morris; M. Mott; A. H. Norris, QC; R. O'Rorke; S. Oliver-Jones, QC; R. Onions; R. Orme; J. Orrell; D. Perrett, QC; *R. Pollard; D. Pugsley; J. Pyke; J. Rubery; R. Rundell; J. Shand; D. Stanley; M. Stokes, QC; G. Styler; A. Taylor; J. Teare; S. Tonking; S. Waine; J. Wait; *R. Wakerley, QC (Recorder of Birmingham); J. Warner; C. Wide, QC; W. Wood, QC

NORTH-EASTERN CIRCUIT
Presiding Judges, The Hon. Mr Justice Henriques; The Hon. Mr Justice Andrew Smith

NORTH AND WEST YORKSHIRE GROUP
R. Adams; R. Bartfield; G. N. Barr Young; J. E. Barry; C. O. J. Behrens; P. Benson; B. Bush; P. J. Charlesworth; G. Cliffe; P. J. Cockroft; J. Dobkin; A. C. Finnerty; M. S. Garner; R. A. Grant; S. P. Grenfell; S. J. Gullick; T. S. A. Hawkesworth, QC; P. M. L. Hoffman; P. Hunt; R. Ibbotson; N. H. Jones, QC; G. H. Kamil; T. D. Kent-Jones, TD; P. Langan, QC; K. M. P. Macgill; A. G. McCallum; R. M. Scott; J. Spencer, QC; S. M. Spencer, QC; J. S. H. Stewart, QC; R. C. Taylor; T. Walsh; J. S. Wolstenholme

TYNE TEES GROUP
P. J. B. Armstrong; B. Bolton; P. H. Bowers; A. N. J. Briggs; D. M. A. Bryant; M. C. Carr; M. L. Cartledge; E. J. Faulks; P. J. Fox, QC; T. Hewitt; D. Hodson; A. T. Lancaster; P. R. Lowden; J. T. Milford; J. P. Moir; M. G. C. Moorhouse; L. Spittle; M. Taylor; C. T. Walton; J. De G. Walford; G. Whitburn, QC; D. R. Wood

HUMBERSIDE AND SOUTH YORKSHIRE GROUP
T. W. Barber; D. R. Bentley, QC; J. W. Bullimore; A. C. Carr; M. T. Cracknell; J. Davies; J. Dowse; A. R. Goldsack, QC; P. Heppel, QC; L. Hull; P. Jones; K. R. Keen, QC; S. W. Lawler, QC; M. K. Mettyear; R. J. Moore; M. J. A. Murphy, QC; J. H. Reddihough; P. E. Robertshaw; J. Shipley; L. Sutcliffe; J. A. Swanson

NORTHERN CIRCUIT
Presiding Judges, The Hon. Mr Justice McCombe; The Hon. Mr Justice Leveson

M. P. Allweis; J. M. Appleby; J. F. Appleton; E. K. Armitage, QC; R. K. Atherton; Miss P. H. Badley; S. W. Baker; R. C. W. Bennett; A. N. H. Blake; C. Bloom, QC; D. Boulton; L. F. M. Brown; R. Brown; J. K. Burke, QC; M. D. Byrne; I. B. Campbell; B. I. Caulfield; D. Clark; *D. C. Clarke, QC (Recorder of Liverpool); G. M. Clifton;

C. J. Cornwall; I. W. Crompton; Miss J. M. P. Daley; B. R. Duckworth; S. B. Duncan; Miss D. B. Eaglestone; T. K. Earnshaw; G. A. Ensor; P. S. Fish; Miss B. A. Forrester; J. R. B. Geake; D. S. Gee; W. George; J. A. D. Gilliland, QC; N. B. D. Gilmour, QC; H. B. Globe, QC; C. L. Goldstone, QC; I. M. Hamilton; J. A. Hammond; D. Harris, QC; T. B. Hegarty, QC; M. J. Henshell; F. R. B. Holloway; R. C. Holman; A. D. Hope; N. J. G. Howarth; G. W. Humphries; C. James; M. Kershaw, QC *(Commercial Circuit Judge)*; E. M. Knopf; Miss L. J. Kushner, QC; P. M. Lakin; B. L. Lever; B. Lewis; J. Lewis; A. C. Lowcock; A. P. Lyon; D. Lynch; D. I. Mackay; J. B. Macmillan; *D. G. Maddison *(Recorder of Manchester)*; B. C. Maddocks; C. J. Mahon; W. P. Morris; T. J. Mort; L. A. Newton; *C. P. L. Openshaw, QC; F. D. Owen; J. A. Phillips; J. C. Phipps; P. R. Raynor, QC; J. H. Roberts; Miss M. Roddy; Miss G. D. Ruaux; M. W. Rudland; A. A. Rumbelow, QC; H. Singer; E. Slinger; A. Smith; P. Smith; Miss E. M. Steel; M. T. Steiger, QC; S. Stewart, QC; D. R. Swift; P. Sycamore; C. B. Tetlow; I. J. C. Trigger; Miss B. J. Watson; K. Wilkinson; B. Woodward

SOUTH-EASTERN CIRCUIT
Presiding Judges, The Hon. Mr Justice Aikens; The Hon. Mrs Justice Rafferty; The Hon. Mr Justice Bell

M. F. Addison; P. C. Ader; J. Altman; Mrs S. C. Andrew; A. R. L. Ansell; M. G. Anthony; S. A. Anwyl, QC; Charles Atkins; E. H. Bailey; F. Baker, QC; C. G. Ball, QC; A. F. Balston; G. S. Barham; B. J. Barker, QC; W. E. Barnett, QC; R. A. Barratt, QC; K. Bassingthwaighte; *G. A. Bathurst-Norman; P. J. L. Beaumont, QC (Common Serjeant); R. V. M. E. Behar; Mrs C. V. Bevington; N. C. van der Bijl; I. G. Bing; M. G. Binning; W. J. Birtles; J. E. Bishop; B. M. B. Black; H. O. Blacksell, QC; J. G. Boal, QC; A. V. Bradbury; G. B. Breen; R. G. Brown; J. M. Bull, QC; J. P. Burke; L. S. Burn, QC; The Hon. C. W. Byers; J. Q. Campbell; M. J. Carroll; M. T. Catterson; B. E. F. Catlin; P. C. Clegg; Miss S. Coates; N. J. Coleman; S. H. Colgan; *P. H. Collins, CBE; S. S. Coltart; C. D. Compston; T. A. C. Coningsby, QC; J. G. Connor; R. D. Connor; R. A. Cooke; P. E. Copley; T. G. E. Corrie; Dr E. A. Cotran; P. R. Cowell; R. C. Cox; M. L. S. Cripps; C. A. Critchlow; J. F. Crocker; D. L. Croft, QC; D. M. Cryan; P. Curl; Mrs P. M. T. Dangor; A. M. Darroch; M. Dean, QC; P. G. Dedman; J. E. Devaux; P. Dodgson; P. H. Downes; W. H. Dunn, QC; C. M. Edwards; D. R. Ellis; R. C. Elly; C. Elwen; Fabyan Evans; Miss D. Faber; J. D. Farnworth; P. Fingret; P. E. J. Focke, QC; G. C. F. Forrester; Ms D. A. Freedman; M. Fysh, QC; L. Gerber; C. A. H. Gibson; Miss A. F. Goddard, QC; D. N. Goodin; C. G. M. Gordon; J. B. Gosschalk; A. A. Goymer; C. Gratwicke; B. S. Green, QC; A. E. Greenwood; P. Grobel, TD, VRD; G. H. Gypps; J. Hall; D. A. B. R. Hallgarten, QC; Miss G. Hallon; J. Hamilton; Miss S. Hamilton, QC; C. R. H. Hardy; C. Harris, QC; M. F. Harris; W. G. Hawkesworth; R. G. Hawkins, QC; J. M. Haworth; R. J. Haworth; R. M. Hayward; P. Hayward-Smith, QC; D. E. A. Higgins; A. N. Hitching; H. E. G. Hodge, OBE; K. M. J. Hollis; J. F. Holt; K. A. D. Hornby; M. Hucker; J. C. A. Hughes, QC; J. G. Hull; QC; M. J. Hyam *(Recorder of London)*; D. A. Inman; A. B. Issard-Davies; D. G. A. Jackson; Dr P. J. E. Jackson; T. J. C. Joseph; I. G. F. Karsten, QC; S. S. Katkhuda; C. J. B. Kemp; M. Kennedy, QC; W. A. Kennedy; G. M. P. F. Khayat, QC; A. W. P. King; T. R. King; B. J. Knight, QC; P. E. Knowles; Stephen Kramer; Capt. J. B. R. Langdon, RN; P. H. Latham; T. Lawrence; D. M. Levy, QC; C. C. D.

Lindsay, QC; S. H. Lloyd; F. R. Lockhart; N. G. E. Loraine-Smith; J. A. M. Lowen; Mrs C. M. Ludlow; Capt. S. Lyons; A. G. McDowall; R. J. McGregor-Johnson; G. Jones Nicholas; B. M. McIntyre; R. G. McKinnon; W. N. McKinnon; N. A. McKittrick; J. McMullen, QC; K. C. Macrae; T. Maher; F. J. M. Marr-Johnson; D. N. N. Martineau; D. Matheson, QC; V. Mayer; N. A. Medawar, QC; G. Meeran; D. J. Mellor; G. D. Mercer; P. N. De Mille; Miss A. E. Mitchell; C. R. Mitchell; D. C. Mitchell; F. I. Mitchell; H. M. Morgan; A. P. Morris; D. Morton Jack; C. J. Moss, QC; R. T. Moss; Miss M. J. S. Mowat; G. S. Murdoch, QC; T. M. E. Nash; M. H. D. Neligan; A. I. Niblett; Mrs M. F. Norrie-Walker; Brig. A. P. Norris, OBE; P. W. O'Brien; M. A. Oppenheimer; D. C. J. Paget, QC; A. Patience, QC; Mrs N. Pearce; Prof. D. S. Pearl; Miss V. A. Pearlman; B. P. Pearson; N. A. J. Philpot; T. D. Pillay; A. B. Pitts; D. C. Pitman; J. R. Platt; J. R. Playford, QC; Miss I. M. Plumstead; T. G. Pontius; S. Pratt; R. J. C. V. Prendergast; J. Price; D. W. Radford; D. J. Rennie; J. R. Reid, QC; M. P. Reynolds; M. S. Rich, QC; D. J. Richardson; N. P. Riddell; G. Rivlin, QC; S. D. Robbins; J. M. Roberts; J. Roberts, QC; W. M. Rose; J. Rylance; T. R. G. Ryland; J. E. A. Samuels, QC; R. B. Sanders; A. R. G. Scott-Gall; J. S. Sennitt; D. Serota, QC; J. L. Sessions; D. R. A. Sich; A. G. Simmons; K. T. Simpson; P. R. Simpson; S. P. Sleeman; C. M. Smith, QC; S. A. R. Smith; Miss Z. P. Smith; E. Southwell; S. B. Spence; S. M. Stephens, QC; P. R. Statman; Mrs L. J. Stern, QC; N. A. Stewart; D. M. A. Stokes, QC; G. Stone, QC; T. M. F. Stow, QC; J. B. C. Tanzer, QC; A. M. Tapping; C. Thomas; P. J. Thompson; A. G. Y. Thorpe; C. H. Tilling; C. J. M. Tyrer; J. E. van der Werff; T. L. Viljoen; J. P. Wadsworth, QC; Miss A. P. Wakefield; R. Wakefield; R. Walker; S. P. Waller; A. R. Webb; C. S. Welchman; A. F. Wilkie, QC; S. R. Wilkinson; Miss J. A. Williams; R. J. Winstanley; R. L. J. Wood; S. E. Woollam; D. Worsley; M. P. Yelton; M. K. Zeidman, QC K. H. Zucker, QC

WALES AND CHESTER CIRCUIT
Presiding Judges, The Hon. Mr Justice Roderick Evans; The Hon. Mr Justice Pitchford

K. Barnett; M. R. Burr; J. R. Case; N. M. Chambers, QC; S. Clarke; J. Curran; D. L. Daniel; D. Davies; R. L. Denyer, QC; J. B. S. Diehl, QC; R. Dutton; E. Edwards; G. O. Edwards, QC; M. Farmer, QC; M. Furness; W. Gaskell; D. Halbert; D. Hale; J. D. Durham Hall, QC; G. R. Hickinbottom; R. P. Hughes; T. M. Hughes, QC; G. Jones; H. Jones; G. Kilfoil; C. Llewellyn-Jones, QC; C. Masterman; The Lord Elystan Morgan of Aberteifi; D. W. Morgan; D. G. Morris; D. C. Morton; H. Moseley, QC; I. C. Parry; G. A. L. Price, QC; P. Price, QC; E. M. Rees; D. W. Richards; P. Richards; J. M. T. Rogers, QC; *J. G. Williams, QC; N. F. Woodward

WESTERN CIRCUIT
Presiding Judges, The Hon. Mrs Justice Hallett; The Hon. Mr Justice David Steel

P. R. Barclay; J. F. Beashel; R. Bond; J. G. Boggis, QC; G. Boney, QC; J. Bonvin; *M. J. L. Brodrick; J. M. Burford, QC; *R. D. Bursell, QC; G. W. A. Cottle; M. G. Cotterill; *T. Crowther, QC; K. C. Cutler; P. Darlow; S. Darwall Smith; Susan P. Darwall Smith; Mrs L. Davies; J. Foley; F. Gilbert, QC; D. L. Griffiths; J. D. Griggs; C. M. A. Hagen; A. M. Havelock-Allan, QC; P. J. Hooton; M. K. Harington; R. Rooke Hetherington; I. Hughes, QC; G. Hume Jones; J. R. Jarvis; C. Leigh, QC; T. Longbotham; T.

Mackean; I. S. McKintosh; J. G. McNaught; The Lord Meston, QC; T. J. Milligan; J. O. Neligan; S. K. O'Malley; S. K. Overend; R. Price; R. C. Pryor, QC; M. W. Roach; R. Rucker; J. Rudd; A. Rutherford; D. H. Selwood; R. M. Shawcross; D. Smith, QC; G. Tabor, QC; W. E. M. Taylor; D. K. Ticehurst, QC; D. I. H. Tyzack, QC; N. Vincent; R. C. B. Wade; J. H. Weeks, QC; J. S. Wiggs

DISTRICT JUDGES
District Judges (each £88,546)

MIDLAND CIRCUIT
S. W. Arnold; M. Asokan; P. Atkinson; C. Beale; A. Brown; A. Butler; M. Cardinal; D. Cernik; R. Chapman; A. Cleary; J. Cochrane; R. Cole; D. J. Cooke; T. Cotterill; T. Davies; E. Dickinson; D. D. Douce; P. Dowling; L. Eaton; M. Ellery; A. Elliott; S. Gailey; F. Goddard; R. Hearne; R. L. Hudson; J. Ilsley; J. Jack; A. Jenkins; A. Jones; P. Kesterton; K. Lacy; I. Lettall; D. Lipman; P. McHale; P. Mackenzie; A. Marston; A. Maw; R. Merriman; D. Millard; A. Mithani; R. J. Morton; D. O'Regan; B. Oliver; D. Owen; M. Parry; P. Rank; F. Reeson; T. Ridgway; S. Rogers; P. Sanghera; R. Savage; L. H. Schroeder; V. Sehdev; V. Stamenkovich; R. Stevens, OBE, A. F. Suckling; R. J. Toombs; W. A. Vincent; P. Wartnaby; P. Waterworth; R. Whitehurst

NORTH-EASTERN CIRCUIT
S. T. Alderson; H. Anderson; C. A. Arkless; I. D. Atherton; A. M. Babbington; H. J. Bailey; C. W. Bellamy; I. P. Besford; C. M. Birkby; J. Bower; J. A. Buchan; P. E. Bullock; I. L. Buxton; P. Cuthbertson; G. J. Edwards; I. S. Fairwood; J. Flanagan; P. R. Giles; M. M. Glentworth; N. W. Goudie; S. J. Greenwood; M. F. Handley; R. V. M. Hall; J. E. Harrison; P. G. Hawksworth; H. F. Heath; N. G. Hickinbottom; R. N. Hill; T. W. Hill; J. R. A. Howard; R. A. Jordan; D. Kirkham; A. M. Large; D. E. Lascelles; P. E. Lawton; G. Y. Lingard; R. Loomba; G. Lord; J. E. Mainwaring-Taylor; G. M. Marley; P. C. Mort; D. A. Oldham; J. F. W. Peters; A. P. Powell; M. F. Rhodes; D. M. Robertson; J. S. Robinson; S. Rodgers; D. Scott-Phillips; I. F. Slim; S. E. Spencer; B. D. Stapely; D. M. Stocken; J. A. Taylor; P. W. J. Traynor; D. J. R. Weston; P. J. E. Wildsmith; J. S. Wilson; H. P. Wood; M. J. Young

NORTHERN CIRCUIT
G. R. Ashton; R. R. P. Ackroyd; I. Bennett; P. H. Berkson; Ms A. J. C. Brazier; R Bryce; M. E. Buckley; Ms V. Buckley; A. P. Carr; D. B. Chapman; J. L. Clark; J. R. Clegg; J. F. Coffey; P. St J. Dignan; E. Donnelly; J. F. Duerden; C. R. Fairclough; G. J. Fitzgerald; D. R. Fletcher; R. M. Forrester; C. R. Fox; C. E. Freeman; B. N. Gaunt; J. M. Geedes; M. Gosnell; M. J. Gregory; D. Griffiths; A. J. J. Harrison; N. Harrison; L. Henthorn; J. D. Heyworth; J. Horan; M. A. Hovington; G. A. Humphreys-Roberts; S. C. Jackson; J. A. James; E. Johnson; A. Jones; E. R. Jones; G. A. Needham; G. Nuttall; N. A. Law; R. A. McCullagh; B. V. McGrath; Ms M. A. Mornington; L. C. Osborne; J. K. Park; M. I. Peake; I. J. Pickup; J. J. B. Rawlins; A. M. Saffman; D. J. Shannon; Ms J. Shaw; M. J. Simpson; R. Smedley; G. D. Smith; W. H. Stansfield; L. S. Stephens Ms P. S. Stockton; L. G. Sykes; C M Swindley; R. Talbot; B. W. Travers; M. W. Turner; M. J. Wilby; P. T. Wilby; S. Wright

SOUTH-EASTERN CIRCUIT
J. L. Allen; P. R. Ayers; J. D. Banks; P. W. Bazley-White; J. L. Beattie; R. H. L. Blomfield; A. J. Blundson, M. Birchall; G.

Brett; G. H. Burgess; L. M. Burgess; D. W. Caddick; A. R. Campbell; P. R. Carr; C. B. Chandler; J. H.G. Chrispin; E. Cohen; L. Cohen; J. I. Collier; B. R. J. Cole; A. J. Coni; C. N. Darbyshire; C. Dabezies; R. A. Davis; S. A. F. Davies; J. R. Davidson; I. M. Diamond; R. D. Dudley; C. M. Edwards; I. Evans; D. Eynon; M. Fawcett; G. B. Field; S. H. D. Fink; N. G. Freeborough; J. M. Fortgang; V. W. Gatter; P. Gamba; S. M. Gerlis; M. C. Gilchrist; P. S. Gill; J. Gittens; P. M. L. Glover; S. G. Gold; G. A. Green; N. J. Gregory; E. J. Habershon; D. F. Hallett; C. Hamilton; S. Hasan; M. J. Haselgrove; D. N. Hayes; R. M. Henry; S. Henson; P. F. Hewetson-Brown; M. Hickman; R. S. Hicks; R. M. Jacey; N. E. Jackson; G. S. Jackson; W. Jackson; T. H. N. Jenkins; S. V. Jones; J. I. Karet; J. L. C. Kirby; H. E. Kemp; D. C. Lamdin; M. Langley; I. H. Lay; Lee; C. J. Letham; H. A. J. Letts; S. E. Levinson; B. G. Lightman; McHale; McKinnon; N. Madge; H. L. Manners; M. J. Marin; R. Matthews; J. S. Merrick; L. D. Millard; A. J. Mills; E. C. Millward; R. J. Mitchell; S. R. Mitchell; C. B. Molle; S. I. Morley; A. Morris; P. Mostyn; D. Mullis; R. M. Naqvi; M. J. Parker; M. J. Payne; G. L. Pearl; P. Pearl; P. H. Pelly; P. R. Pescod; S. Plaskow; Polden; K. A. Price; A. L. Raeside; M. A. Read; J. M. Rhodes; J. T. Robinson; P. Rogers; M. Royall; B. I. Rutland; Scott-Gam; Sessions; F. W. Shanks; I. Sheratte; G. Silverman; H. Silverman; M. N. Skerratt; E. J. Silverwood-Cope; M. M. Short; R. Southcombe; R. G. Sparrow; E. Stary; G. M. Stephenson; D. Steel; P. A. Sturdy; J. E. Taylor; J. R. K. Taylor;R. P. Taylor; A. K. Taylor; E. R. W. Temple; R. C. Tetlow; A. D. Thomas; I. G. Tilbury; M. Trent; M. Walker; A. S. Wharton; A. N. Wicks; G. K. Wilding; F. J. Wilkinson; E. Willers; S. L. Williams; J. E. Wright; A. J. Worthington; M. Zimmels

WALES AND CHESTER CIRCUIT
D. J. Asplin; V. S. Batcup; C. F. Beattie; G. H. F. Carson; J. L. Davies; C. R. Dawson; Mrs H. Dawson; J. M. Doel; P. M. Evans; Miss R. Evans; I. G. Ewing; Mrs J. E. Garland-Thomas; W. H. Godwin; S. G. Harrison; R. L. Hendicott; R. A. Hoffman; D. L. Hughes; D. P. Jenkins; T. A. John; T. J. Lewis; P. H. Llewellyn, OBE; C. W. Newman; R. North; Mrs C. E. O'Leary; C. G. Perry; D. Wyn Rees; V. Reeves; J. E. Regan; S. Rogers; R. Singh, CBE; A. A. Wallace; A. J. P. Weaver; O. W. Williams

WESTERN CIRCUIT
C. M. Ackner; C. E. H. Ackroyd; R. D. I. Adam; J D. Ainsworth; R. C. Bird; D. Carney; B. R. Carron; G. F. Cawood; M. T. Cooper; P. W. Corrigan; J. P. Crosse; M. Dancey; M. P. H. Daniel; A. M. R. Dowell; Ms J. Exton; D. J. Field; J. Freeman; J .W. Frenkel; C. Fuller; R. A. F. Griggs; A. M. Harvey; J. Hurley; J. R. Ing; R. D. S. James; P. D. Jolly; B. G. Meredith; P. Mildred; P. Mitchell; A. D. Moon; N. J. Murphy; R. F. D. Naylor; M. Rutherford; A. L. Simons; P. N. Singleton; B. J. A. Smith; J. Sparrow; Mrs G. Stuart Brown; M. H. Tennant; A. B. Thomas; J. L. Thomas; C. J. Tromans; J. Turner; A. J. Wainwright; A. Walker; I. E. Weintroub; D. R. White; R. A. Wilson

DISTRICT JUDGES (MAGISTRATES' COURTS)
The Provisional and Metropolitan Division has been changed; all former Provincial and Metropolitan Stipendiary Magistrates can serve nationally within any district and are now called District Judges (Magistrates, Courts).

District Judges (each £92,546) salary includes £4,000 inner London weighting

M. A. Abelson; Mrs J. H. Alderson; R. W. Anderson; Mrs A. Arnold; A. Berg; J. S. Bennett; J. A. Browne; P. H. R. Browning; N. R. Cadbury; A. L. Calloway; J. J. Charles; D. J. Chinery; R. F. S. Clancy; T. M. Chatelier; T. G. Cowling; C. R. Darnton; S. N. Day; Mrs S. E. Driver; P. K. Dodd, OBE; T. M. English; P. R. Farmer; J. Finestein; P. J. Firth; D. R. Fletcher; J. G. Foster; M. J. Friel; I. Gillespie; K. A. Gray; R. House; M. L. R. Harris; N. P. Heley; R. Holland; J. A. Jellema; R. D. Kitson; Ms B. A. Knight; I. S. Lomax; C. M. McColl; D. V. Manning-Davies; D. M. Meredith; B. Morgan; Ms L. Morgan; M. C. Morris; P. T. Nuttall; J. B. Prowse; P. B. Richardson; G. G. Richards; M. A. Rosenberg; F. J. Rutherford; Mrs F. M. Shelvey; T. R. W. R. Stone; P. C. Tain; D. R. G. Tapp; D. L. Thomas; W. D. Thomas; M. J. Walker; P. Ward; P. H. Wassell; G. R. Watkins; Miss P. J. Watkins; C. S. Wiles; J. I. Woollard; R. J. Zara

METROPOLITAN DISTRICTS
Bow Street, T. H. Workman *(Senior District Judge)*; C. L. Pratt; H. N. Evans
Brent Magistrates Court, Mrs K. J. Marshall
Camberwell Green, Miss S. V. Green
Croydon Magistrates Court, A. P. Carr
East Central Division, Miss D. Quick; I. M. Baker; P. A. M. Clark; J. V. Perkins; R. A. McPhee
Greenwich, D. A. Cooper M. Kelly; H. C. F. Riddle; P. S. Wallis
Feltham Magistrates, S. N. Day
Hendon Magistrates Court, C. S. Wiles
Horseferry Road, C. P. M. Davidson; A. R. Davies; A. T. Evans; Mrs K. R. K. Keating; Miss C. S. R. Tubbs
North East London, G. E. Cawdron
South-Western, K. I. Grant; Miss D. Wickham; P. M. M. Gillibrand
Stratford Magistrates Court, H. Gott; Miss S. Sims
Thames, Mrs J. Comyns; S. E. Dawson; Miss A. M. Rose; M. J. Read; Miss F. J. McIvor
Tower Bridge, G. F. S. Black; S. Somjee; T. Stone
West London Magistrates' Court, J. Coleman; S. N. Cooper; D. K. Lachhar; J. R. D. Philips; D. Simpson; Miss S. F. Williams

GREATER LONDON MAGISTRATES' COURTS AUTHORITY 185 Marylebone Road, London, NW1 5QL Tel: 0845 601 3600
Justices' Chief Executive and Clerk to the Committee (Acting), Michael Heap
Training Manager, Mrs R. Marsh
Director of Human Resources, Miss S. Campbell
Director of Finance, T. Summers
Director of Legal Operations, M. Eldridge

CROWN PROSECUTION SERVICE
50 Ludgate Hill, London EC4M 7EX
Tel: 020-7796 8000 Email: enquiries@cps.gov.uk
Web: www.cps.gov.uk
The Crown Prosecution Service (CPS) is responsible for the independent review and conduct of criminal proceedings instituted by police forces in England and Wales, with the exception of cases conducted by the Serious Fraud Office and certain minor offences.
The Service is headed by the Director of Public Prosecutions (DPP), who works under the superintendence of the Attorney General, and a Chief Executive. The Service comprises a headquarters and 42 Areas, each Area corresponding to a police area in England

and Wales. Each Area is headed by a Chief Crown Prosecutor, supported by an Area Business Manager.

Director of Public Prosecutions (SCS), Sir David Calvert-Smith, QC
Chief Executive (SCS), R. Foster
Directors (SCS), C. Newell *(Casework);* G. Patten *(Policy);* J. Graham *(Finance);* Ms C. Hamon *(Business Information Systems);* Ms A. O'Connor *(Human Resources)*
Head of Communications (SCS), Mrs S. Cunningham
Head of Management Audit Services (SCS), R. Capstick

CPS AREAS
ENGLAND
CPS AVON AND SOMERSET 2nd Floor, Froomsgate House, Rupert Street, Bristol BS1 2QJ Tel: 0117-930 2800.
Chief Crown Prosecutor (SCS), D. Archer
CPS BEDFORDSHIRE Sceptre House, 7–9 Castle Street, Luton LU1 3AJ Tel: 01582-816600.
Chief Crown Prosecutor (SCS), R. Newcombe
CPS CAMBRIDGESHIRE Justinian House, Spitfire Close, Ermine Business Park, Huntingdon, Cambs PE29 6XY. Tel: 01480-825200.
Chief Crown Prosecutor (SCS), R. Crowley
CPS CHESHIRE 2nd Floor, Windsor House, Pepper Street, Chester CH1 1TD Tel: 01244-408600.
Chief Crown Prosecutor (SCS), B. Hughes
CPS CLEVELAND 5 Linthorpe Road, Middlesbrough, Cleveland TS1 1TX Tel: 01642-204500.
Chief Crown Prosecutor (SCS), D. Magson
CPS CUMBRIA 1st Floor, Stocklund House, Castle Street, Carlisle CA3 8SY Tel: 01228-882900.
Chief Crown Prosecutor (SCS), D. Farmer
CPS DERBYSHIRE 7th Floor, St Peter's House, Gower Street, Derby DE1 1SB Tel: 01332-614000.
Chief Crown Prosecutor (SCS), D. Adams
CPS DEVON AND CORNWALL Hawkins House, Pynes Hill, Rydon Lane, Exeter EX2 5SS Tel: 01392-288000.
Chief Crown Prosecutor (SCS), A. Cresswell
CPS DORSET 1st Floor, Oxford House, Oxford Road, Bournemouth BH8 8HA Tel: 01202-498700.
Chief Crown Prosecutor (SCS), J. Revell
CPS DURHAM Elvet House, Hallgarth Street, Durham DH1 3AT Tel: 0191-383 5800.
Chief Crown Prosecutor (SCS), J. Corrighan
CPS ESSEX County House, 100 New London Road, Chelmsford CM2 0RG Tel: 01245-455800.
Chief Crown Prosecutor (SCS), J. Bell
CPS GLOUCESTERSHIRE 2 Kimbrose Way, Gloucester GL1 2DB Tel: 01452-872400.
Chief Crown Prosecutor (SCS), W. Cole
CPS GREATER MANCHESTER PO Box 237, 8th Floor, Sunlight House, Quay Street, Manchester M60 3PS Tel: 0161-827 4700.
Chief Crown Prosecutor (SCS), T. Taylor
CPS HAMPSHIRE AND ISLE OF WIGHT 3rd Floor, Black Horse House, 8–10 Leigh Road, Eastleigh, Hants SO50 9FH Tel: 02380-673800.
Chief Crown Prosecutor (SCS), R. Daw
CPS HERTFORDSHIRE Queen's House, 58 Victoria Street, St Albans, Herts AL1 3HZ Tel: 01727-798700.
Chief Crown Prosecutor (SCS), C. Ingham
CPS HUMBERSIDE 2nd Floor, King William House, Market Place, Lowgate, Kingston-upon-Hull HU1 1RS Tel: 01482-621000.
Chief Crown Prosecutor (SCS), B. Marshall

CPS KENT Priory Gate, 29 Union Street, Maidstone, Kent
ME14 1PT Tel: 01622-356300.
Chief Crown Prosecutor (SCS), Ms E. Howe
CPS LANCASHIRE 3rd Floor, Unicentre, Lord's Walk, Preston
PR1 1DH Tel: 01772-208100.
Chief Crown Prosecutor (SCS), D. Dickenson
CPS LEICESTERSHIRE Princes Court, 34 York Road, Leicester
LE1 5TU Tel: 0116-204 6700.
Chief Crown Prosecutor (SCS), M. Howard
CPS LINCOLNSHIRE Crosstrend House, 10A Newport,
Lincoln LN1 3DF Tel: 01522-585900.
Chief Crown Prosecutor (SCS), Ms A. Kerr
CPS LONDON 2nd Floor, The Flagship, 142 Holborn, London
EC1N 2NQ Tel: 020-7796 8000.
Chief Crown Prosecutor (SCS), Ms D. Sharpling
CPS MERSEYSIDE 7th Floor (South), Royal Liver Building, Pier
Head, Liverpool L3 1HN Tel: 0151-239 6400.
Chief Crown Prosecutor (SCS), J. Holt
CPS NORFOLK Haldin House, Old Bank of England Court,
Queen Street, Norwich NR2 4SX Tel: 01603-693000.
Chief Crown Prosecutor (SCS), P. Tidey
CPS NORTH YORKSHIRE 6th Floor, Ryedale Building,
60 Piccadilly, York YO1 1NS Tel: 01904-731700.
Chief Crown Prosecutor (SCS), R. Turnbull
CPS NORTHAMPTONSHIRE Beaumont House, Cliftonville,
Northampton NN1 5BE Tel: 01604-823600.
Chief Crown Prosecutor (SCS), C. Chapman
CPS NORTHUMBRIA 1st Floor, Benton House,
136 Sandyford Road, Newcastle upon Tyne NE2 1QE
Tel: 0191-260 4200.
Chief Crown Prosecutor (SCS), Ms N. Reasbeck
CPS NOTTINGHAMSHIRE 2 King Edward Court, King
Edward Street, Nottingham NG1 1EL Tel: 0115-852 3300.
Chief Crown Prosecutor (SCS), Ms K. Carty
CPS SOUTH YORKSHIRE Greenfield House, 32 Scotland
Street, Sheffield S3 7DQ Tel: 0114-229 8600.
Chief Crown Prosecutor (SCS), Mrs J. Walker
CPS STAFFORDSHIRE 11A Princes Street, Stafford
ST16 2EU Tel: 01785-272200.
Chief Crown Prosecutor (SCS), H. Ireland
CPS SUFFOLK Saxon House, 1 Cromwell Square, Ipswich
IP1 1TS Tel: 01473-282100.
Chief Crown Prosecutor (SCS), C. Yule
CPS SURREY One Onslow Street, Guildford, Surrey
GU1 4YA Tel: 01483-468200.
Chief Crown Prosecutor (SCS), Ms S. Hebblethwaite
CPS SUSSEX City Gates, 185 Dyke Road, Brighton
BN3 1TL Tel: 01273-765600.
Chief Crown Prosecutor (SCS), Mrs A. Saunders
CPS THAMES VALLEY The Courtyard, Lombard Street,
Abingdon, Oxon OX14 5SE Tel: 01235-551900.
Chief Crown Prosecutor (SCS), S. Clements
CPS WARWICKSHIRE Rossmore House, 10 Newbold Terrace,
Leamington Spa, Warks CV32 4EA Tel: 01926-455000.
Chief Crown Prosecutor (SCS), M. Lynn
CPS WEST MERCIA Artillery House, Heritage Way, Droitwich,
Worcester WR9 8YB Tel: 01905-825000.
Chief Crown Prosecutor (SCS), J. England
CPS WEST MIDLANDS 14th Floor, Colmore Gate, 2 Colmore
Row, Birmingham B3 2QA Tel: 0121-262 1300.
Chief Crown Prosecutor (SCS), D. Blundell
CPS WEST YORKSHIRE Oxford House, Oxford Row, Leeds
LS1 3BE Tel: 0113-290 2700.
Chief Crown Prosecutor (SCS), N. Franklin
CPS WILTSHIRE 2nd Floor, Fox Talbot House, Bellinger Close,
Malmesbury Road, Chippenham, Wilts SN15 1BN
Tel: 01249-766100.
Chief Crown Prosecutor (SCS), N. Hawkins

WALES
CPS DYFED POWYS Heol Penlanffos, Tanerdy, Carmarthen,
Dyfed SA31 2EZ Tel: 01267-242100.
Chief Crown Prosecutor (SCS), S. Rowlands
CPS GWENT 6th Floor, Chartist Tower, Upper Dock Street,
Newport, Gwent NP20 1DW Tel: 01633-261100.
Chief Crown Prosecutor (SCS), C. Woolley
CPS NORTH WALES Bromfield House, Ellice Way, Wrexham
LL13 7YW Tel: 01978 346000.
Chief Crown Prosecutor (SCS), P. Whittaker
CPS SOUTH WALES 20th Floor, Capital House, Greyfriars
Road, Cardiff CF1 3PL Tel: 029-2080 3900.
Chief Crown Prosecutor (SCS), H. Heycock

THE SCOTTISH JUDICATURE

Scotland has a legal system separate from and differing
greatly from the English legal system in enacted law,
judicial procedure and the structure of courts.

In Scotland the system of public prosecution is headed
by the Lord Advocate and is independent of the police,
who have no say in the decision to prosecute. The Lord
Advocate, discharging his functions through the Crown
Office in Edinburgh, is responsible for prosecutions in
the High Court, sheriff courts and district courts.
Prosecutions in the High Court are prepared by the
Crown Office and conducted in court by one of the law
officers, by an advocate-depute, or by a solicitor
advocate. In the inferior courts the decision to prosecute
is made and prosecution is preferred by procurators fiscal,
who are lawyers and full-time civil servants subject to the
directions of the Crown Office. A permanent legally-
qualified civil servant known as the Crown Agent is
responsible for the running of the Crown Office and the
organisation of the Procurator Fiscal Service, of which he
is the head.

Scotland is divided into six sheriffdoms, each with a
full-time sheriff principal. The sheriffdoms are further
divided into sheriff court districts, each of which has a
legally-qualified resident sheriff or sheriffs, who are
judges of the court.

In criminal cases sheriffs principal and sheriffs have
the same powers; sitting with a jury of 15 members, they
may try more serious cases on indictment, or, sitting
alone, may try lesser cases under summary procedure.
Minor summary offences are dealt with in district courts
which are administered by the district and the islands
local government authorities and presided over by lay
justices of the peace (of whom there are about 4,000)
and, in Glasgow only, by district judges (magistrates'
courts). Juvenile offenders (children under 16) may be
brought before an informal children's hearing comprising
three local lay people. The superior criminal court is the
High Court of Justiciary which is both a trial and an
appeal court. Cases on indictment are tried by a High
Court judge, sitting with a jury of 15, in Edinburgh and
on circuit in other towns. Appeals from the lower courts
against conviction or sentence are heard also by the High
Court, which sits as an appeal court only in Edinburgh.
There is no further appeal to the House of Lords in
criminal cases.

In civil cases the jurisdiction of the sheriff court
extends to most kinds of action. Appeal against decisions
of the sheriff may be made to the sheriff principal and
thence to the Court of Session, or direct to the Court of
Session, which sits only in Edinburgh. The Court of
Session is divided into the Inner and the Outer House.
The Outer House is a court of first instance in which

cases are heard by judges sitting singly, sometimes with a jury of 12. The Inner House, itself subdivided into two divisions of equal status, is mainly an appeal court. Appeals may be made to the Inner House from the Outer House as well as from the sheriff court. An appeal may be made from the Inner House to the House of Lords.

The judges of the Court of Session are the same as those of the High Court of Justiciary, the Lord President of the Court of Session also holding the office of Lord Justice General in the High Court. Senators of the College of Justice are Lords Commissioners of Justiciary as well as judges of the Court of Session. On appointment, a Senator takes a judicial title, which is retained for life. Although styled The Hon./Rt. Hon. Lord, the Senator is not a peer.

The office of coroner does not exist in Scotland. The local procurator fiscal inquires privately into sudden or suspicious deaths and may report findings to the Crown Agent. In some cases a fatal accident inquiry may be held before the sheriff.

COURT OF SESSION AND HIGH COURT OF JUSTICIARY

The Lord President and Lord Justice General (£181,176)
The Rt. Hon. the Lord Cullen of Whitekirk, *born* 1935, *apptd* 2001
Private Secretary, A. Maxwell

INNER HOUSE
Lords of Session (each £166,394)

FIRST DIVISION
The Lord President
Rt. Hon. Lord Marnoch (Michael Bruce), *born* 1938, *apptd* 1990
Rt. Hon. Lord Penrose, (George Penrose), *born* 1938, *apptd* 1990
Rt. Hon. Lord Hamilton (Arthur Hamilton), *born* 1942, *apptd* 1995
Rt. Hon. Lady Cosgrove (Hazel Aronson), *born* 1946, *apptd* 1996

SECOND DIVISION
Lord Justice Clerk (£175,055), The Rt. Hon. Lord Gill (Brian Gill), *born* 1942, *apptd* 2001
Rt. Hon. Lord Kirkwood (Ian Kirkwood), *born* 1932, *apptd* 1987
Rt. Hon. Lord MacLean (Ranald MacLean), *born* 1938, *apptd* 1990
Rt. Hon. Lord Osborne (Kenneth Osborne), *born* 1937, *apptd* 1990
Rt. Hon. Lord MacFadyen (Donald MacFadyen), *born* 1945, *apptd* 1995

OUTER HOUSE
Lords of Session (each £147,198)
Hon. Lord Abernethy (Alistair Cameron), *born* 1938, *apptd* 1992
Hon. Lord Johnston (Alan Johnston), *born* 1942, *apptd* 1994
Hon. Lord Dawson (Thomas Dawson), *born* 1948, *apptd* 1995
Hon. Lord Nimmo Smith (William Nimmo Smith), *born* 1942, *apptd* 1996
Hon. Lord Philip (Alexander Philip), *born* 1942, *apptd* 1996
Hon. Lord Kingarth (Derek Emslie), *born* 1949, *apptd* 1997

Hon. Lord Bonomy (Iain Bonomy), *born* 1946, *apptd* 1997
Hon. Lord Eassie (Ronald Mackay), *born* 1945, *apptd* 1997
Hon. Lord Reed (Robert Reed), *born* 1956, *apptd* 1998
Hon. Lord Wheatley (John Wheatley), *born* 1941, *apptd* 2000
Hon. Lady Paton (Ann Paton), *born* 1952, *apptd* 2000
Hon. Lord Carloway (Colin Sutherland), *born* 1954, *apptd* 2000
Hon. Lord Clarke (Matthew Clarke), *born* 1947, *apptd* 2000
Rt. Hon. The Lord Hardie (Andrew Hardie), *born* 1946, *apptd* 2000
Rt. Hon. The Lord Mackay of Drumadoon (Donald Mackay), *born* 1946, *apptd* 2000
Hon. Lord McEwan (Robin McEwan), *born* 1943, *apptd* 2000
Hon. Lord Menzies (Duncan Menzies), *born* 1953, *apptd* 2001
Hon. Lord Drummond Young (James Drummond Young), *born* 1950, *apptd* 2001
Hon. Lord Emslie (Nigel Emslie), *born* 1947, *apptd* 2001
Hon. Lady Smith (Anne Smith), *born* 1955, *apptd* 2001
Hon. Lord Brodie (Philip Brodie), *born* 1950, *apptd* 2002
Hon. Lord Bracadale (Alastair Campbell), *born* 1949, *apptd* 2003

COURT OF SESSION AND HIGH COURT OF JUSTICIARY
Parliament House, Parliament Square, Edinburgh EH1 1HQ
Tel 0131-225 2595

Principal Clerk of Session and Justiciary (£41,620-£57,701), J. L. Anderson
Deputy Principal Clerk of Justiciary (£32,249-£46,766), N. Dowie
Deputy Principal Clerk of Session and Principal Extractor (£32,249-£46,766), D. Shand
Deputy in Charge of Offices of Court, (£23,972-£30,565) Mrs P. McFarlane
Deputy Principal Clerk (Keeper of the Rolls) (£32,249-£46,766), D. Shand
Deputy Clerks of Session and Justiciary (£23,972-£30,565), N. J. Dowie; I. F. Smith; T. Higgins; T. B. Cruickshank; Q. A. Oliver; F. Shannly; A. S. Moffat; G. G. Ellis; W. Dunn; A. Finlayson; C. Armstrong; J. McLean; M. Weir; R. M. Sinclair; B. Watson; D. W. Cullen; I. D. Martin; N. McGinley; J. Lynn; E. Dickson; K. Carter; Mrs G. Combe; R. T. MacPherson; P. A. Johnston; D. Bruton; A. Whyte; D. MacLeod; A. McKay; C. MacGrane; L. Maclachlan; A. Thompson

SCOTTISH EXECUTIVE JUSTICE DEPARTMENT
Hayweight House, 23 Lauriston Street, Edinburgh EH3 9DQ
Tel: 0131-229 9200

The Judicial Appointments and Finance Division is responsible for the provision of sufficient Judges and Sheriffs to meet the needs of the business of the supreme and Sheriffs Court in Scotland. It is also responsible for providing the Secretariat for the independent Judicial Appointments Board for Scotland as well as providing resources for the efficient administration of a number of specialist courts and tribunals.

Head of Judicial Appointments and Finance Division (SCS),
D. Stewart

SCOTTISH COURT SERVICE
Hayweight House, 23 Lauriston Street, Edinburgh EH3 9DQ
Tel: 0131-229 9200

The Scottish Court Service is an executive agency within the Scottish Executive Justice Department. It is responsible to the Scottish Ministers for the provision of staff, court houses and associated services for the Supreme and Sheriff Courts.
Chief Executive, J. Ewing

SHERIFF COURT OF CHANCERY
27 Chambers Street, Edinburgh EH1 1LB
Tel: 0131-225 2525

The Court deals with service of heirs and completion of title in relation to heritable property.
Sheriff of Chancery, I. D. Macphail, QC

HM COMMISSARY OFFICE
27 Chambers Street, Edinburgh EH1 1LB
Tel: 0131-225 2525

The Office is responsible for issuing confirmation, a legal document entitling a person to execute a deceased person's will, and other related matters.
Commissary Clerk, David Shand

SCOTTISH LAND COURT
1 Grosvenor Crescent, Edinburgh EH12 5ER
Tel: 0131-225 3595

The court deals with disputes relating to agricultural and crofting land in Scotland.
Chairman (£111,210), The Hon. Lord McGhie (James McGhie), QC
Members, D. J. Houston; D. M. Macdonald; J. Kinloch (part-time)
Principal Clerk, K. H. R. Graham, WS

SHERIFFDOMS
SALARIES

Sheriff Principal	£119,160
Sheriff	£110,362
Area Director	£32,293–£63,490
Sheriff Clerk	£12,719–£43,873
*Floating Sheriff	

GLASGOW AND STRATHKELVIN

Sheriff Principal, E. F. Bowen, QC
Area Director West, I. Scott

SHERIFFS AND SHERIFF CLERKS
Glasgow, B. Kearney; B. A. Lockhart; Mrs A. L. A. Duncan; A. C. Henry; J. K. Mitchell; A. G. Johnston; Miss S. A. O. Raeburn, QC; D. Convery; I. A. S. Peebles, QC; C. W. McFarlane, QC; H. Matthews, QC; J. A. Baird; Mrs P. M. M. Bowman; Miss R. E. A. Rae, QC; A. W. Noble; J. D. Friel; Mrs D. M. MacNeill, QC; J. A. Taylor; C. A. L. Scott; S. Cathcart; *Ms L. M. Ruxton; I. H. L. Miller; Mrs F. L. Reith, QC; W. J. Totten; *M. G. O'Grady, QC; A. C. Normand; W. H. Holligan
Sheriff Clerk, C. Binning

GRAMPIAN, HIGHLANDS AND ISLANDS

Sheriff Principal, Sir Stephen S. T. Young, Bt., QC
Area Director North, J. Robertson

SHERIFFS AND SHERIFF CLERKS
Aberdeen and Stonehaven, A. S. Jessop; Mrs A. M. Cowan; C. J. Harris, QC; G. K. Buchanan; D. J. Cusine; *P. P. Davies; *K. M. Stewart; *Sheriff Clerks,* Mrs E. Laing *(Aberdeen);* A. Hempseed *(Stonehaven)*
Elgin, I. A. Cameron; *Sheriff Clerk,* M. McBey
Fort William, W. D. Small *(also Oban); Sheriff Clerk Depute,* S. McKenna
Inverness, Lochmaddy, Portree, Stornoway, Dingwall, Tain, Wick and Dornoch, D. Booker-Milburn; A. Pollock; D. O. Sutherland; A. L. MacFadyen; *Sheriff Clerks,* A. Bayliss *(Inverness);* M. McBey *(Dingwall); Sheriff Clerks Depute,* Miss M. Campbell *(Lochmaddy and Portree);* Miss A. B. Armstrong *(Stornoway);* L. MacLachlan *(Tain);* Mrs J. McEwan *(Wick);* K. Kerr *(Dornoch)*
Kirkwall and Lerwick, C. S. Mackenzie; *Sheriff Clerks Depute,* A. Moore *(Kirkwall);* M. Flanagan *(Lerwick)*
Peterhead and Banff, K. A. McLernan; *M. Garden, *Sheriff Clerk, (Peterhead); Sheriff Clerk Depute,* Mrs F. L. MacPherson *(Banff)*

LOTHIAN AND BORDERS

Sheriff Principal, I. D. Macphail, QC
Area Director East, M. Bonar

SHERIFFS AND SHERIFF CLERKS
Edinburgh, R. G. Craik, QC *(also Peebles);* R. J. D. Scott *(also Peebles);* Miss I. A. Poole; A. M. Bell; J. M. S. Horsburgh, QC; G. W. S. Presslie *(also Haddington);* J. A. Farrell; A. Lothian; C. N. Stoddart; M. McPartlin; J. D. Allan; K. M. MacIver; N. M. P. Morrison, QC; Miss M. M. Stephen; Mrs M. L. E. Jarvie, QC; *Mrs K. E. C. Mackie; *N. J. MacKinnon; *D. W. M. McIntyre; *J. C. C. McSherry; *Sheriff Clerk,* J. Ross
Linlithgow, G. R. Fleming; P. Gillam; *W. D. Muirhead; M. G. R. Edington; *Sheriff Clerk,* R. D. Sinclair
Haddington, G. W. S. Presslie *(also Edinburgh); Sheriff Clerk,* J. O'Donnell
Jedburgh and Duns, T. A. K. Drummond, QC; *Sheriff Clerk,* I. W. Williamson
Peebles, R. G. Craik, QC *(also Edinburgh);* R. J. D. Scott *(also Edinburgh); Sheriff Clerk Depute,* M. L. Kubeczka
Selkirk, T. A. K. Drummond, QC; *Sheriff Clerk Depute,* L. McFarlane

NORTH STRATHCLYDE

Sheriff Principal, B. A. Kerr, QC
Area Director West, I. Scott

SHERIFFS AND SHERIFF CLERKS
Campbeltown, *W. Dunlop *(also Paisley); Sheriff Clerk Depute,* Miss E. Napier Dumbarton, J. T. Fitzsimons; T. Scott; S. W. H. Fraser; *Sheriff Clerk,* S. Bain
Dunoon, Mrs C. M. A. F. Gimblett; *Sheriff Clerk Depute,* J. McGraw
Greenock, J. Herald *(also Rothesay);* V. J. Canavan; *Mrs R. Swanney; *Sheriff Clerk,* J. Tannahill
Kilmarnock, T. M. Croan; C. G. McKay; Mrs I. S. McDonald *(also Paisley); Sheriff Clerk,* G. Waddell
Oban, W. D. Small *(also Fort William); Sheriff Clerk Depute,* D. Irwin

Paisley, J. Spy; N. Douglas; D. J. Pender; *W. Dunlop *(also Campbeltown),* G. C. Kavanagh; Ms S. M. Sinclair; *C. W. Pettigrew; *Ms S. A. Waldron; *A. M. Cubie; *Sheriff Clerk,* Miss S. Hindes
Rothesay, J. Herald *(also Greenock); Sheriff Clerk Depute,* Mrs C. K. McCormick

SOUTH STRATHCLYDE, DUMFRIES AND GALLOWAY

Sheriff Principal, J. C. McInnes, QC
Area Director West, I. Scott

SHERIFFS AND SHERIFF CLERKS
Airdrie, R. H. Dickson; J. C. Morris, QC; A. D. Vannet; Mrs M. M. Galbraith *(also Lanark), Sheriff Clerk,* D. Forrester
Ayr, N. Gow, QC; C. B. Miller; J. McGowan; *Sheriff Clerk,* Miss C. D. Cockburn
Dumfries, K. G. Barr; K. A. Ross; *Sheriff Clerk,* P. McGonigle
Hamilton, D. C. Russell; W. E. Gibson; J. H. Stewart; Miss J. Powrie; H. S. Neilson; S. C. Pender; T. Welsh, QC; D. M. Bicket; Mrs M. Smart; *H. K. Small; *J. Montgomery; *Ms C. A. Kelly; *W. S. S. Ireland; *Sheriff Clerk,* P. Feeney
Lanark, Ms N. C. Stewart; A. D. Vannett *(also Airdrie); Sheriff Clerk,* Mrs M. McLean
Stranraer and Kirkcudbright, J. R. Smith; *Sheriff Clerks,* W. McIntosh *(Stranraer);* B. Lindsay *(Kirkcudbright)*

TAYSIDE, CENTRAL AND FIFE

Sheriff Principal, R. A. Dunlop, QC
Area Director East, M. Bonar

SHERIFFS AND SHERIFF CLERKS
Alloa, W. M. Reid; *Sheriff Clerk,* R. G. McKeand
Arbroath and Forfar, K. A. Veal; C. N. R. Stein; *Sheriff Clerks,* M. Herbertson *(Arbroath);* S. Munro *(Forfar)*
Cupar, G. J. Evans; *Sheriff Clerk,* A. Nicol
Dundee, R. A. Davidson; A. L. Stewart, QC; J. P. Scott; *I. D. Dunbar; F. R. Crowe; *L. Wood; *Sheriff Clerk,* D. Nicoll
Dunfermline, I. C. Simpson; Mrs I. G. McColl; *R. J. Macleod; *D. M. Mackie; *Sheriff Clerk,* W. McCulloch
Falkirk, A. V. Sheehan; A. J. Murphy; *C. Caldwell; *Sheriff Clerk,* R. McMillan
Kirkcaldy, F. J. Keane; G. W. M. Liddle; B. G. Donald; *Sheriff Clerk,* W. Jones
Perth, M. J. Fletcher; J. K, Tierney; L. D. R. Foulis; *D. C. W. Pyle; *Sheriff Clerk,* J. Murphy
Stirling, The Hon. R. E. G. Younger; A. W. Robertson

STIPENDIARY MAGISTRATES

GLASGOW
R. Hamilton, *apptd* 1984; J. B. C. Nisbet, *apptd* 1984; R. B. Christie, *apptd* 1985; Mrs J. A. M. MacLean, *apptd* 1990

CROWN OFFICE AND PROCURATOR FISCAL SERVICE

CROWN OFFICE
25 Chambers Street, Edinburgh EH1 1LA Tel: 0131-226 2626; Web: www.crownoffice.gov.uk

Crown Agent (£96,700), N. McFadyen
Deputy Crown Agent (£76,369), W. A. Gilchrist

PROCURATORS FISCAL
SALARIES

Area Fiscals	£51,250–£184,500
District Procurator Fiscal, upper level	£51,250–£117,875
District Procurator Fiscal, lower level	£42,750–£52,300

GRAMPIAN AREA
Area Procurator Fiscal, J. Watt *(Aberdeen)*
Procurators Fiscal, Miss C. Frame; A. J. M. Colley; A. B. Hutchinson; E. K. Barbour; S. Ralph

HIGHLAND AND ISLANDS AREA
Area Procurator Fiscal, G. Napier *(Inverness)*
Procurators Fiscal, R. W. Urquhart; Ms A. Wyllie; Ms S. Foard; J. F. Bamber; D. S. Teale; G. Aitken; A. Laing; A. MacDonald; D. MacKenzie

LANARKSHIRE AREA
Area Procurator Fiscal, J. Brisbane *(Hamilton)*
Procurators Fiscal, D. Spiers; Mrs A. C. Donaldson; S. Houston

CENTRAL AREA
Area Procurator Fiscal, Mrs G. M. Watt *(Stirling)*
Procurators Fiscal, R. McQuaid; M. Bell

TAYSIDE AREA
Area Procurator Fiscal, B. Heywood *(Dundee)*
Procurators Fiscal, A. J. Wheelan; J. I. Craigen; D. Griffiths; B. Bott

FIFE AREA
Area Procurator Fiscal, C. Ritchie *(Kirkcaldy)*
Procurators Fiscal, E. B. Russell; Miss H. Clark; J. Robertson

LOTHIAN AND BORDERS AREA
Area Procurator Fiscal, D. Brown *(Edinburgh)*
Procurators Fiscal, A. R. G. Fraser; A. J. P. Reith; A. J. R. Fraser; R. Stott; W. Gallacher; M. Ward

AYRSHIRE AREA
Area Procurator Fiscal, Mrs J. E. Cameron *(Kilmarnock)*
Procurators Fiscal, I. L. Murray; S. Waldron

ARGYLL AREA
Area Procurator Fiscal, J. Miller *(Paisley)*
Procurators Fiscal, F. Redman; C. C. Donnelly; D. L. Webster; W. S. Carnegie; B. R. Maguire; G. F. Williams

DUMFRIES AND GALLOWAY
Area Procurator Fiscal, D. Howdle *(Dumfries)*
Procurators Fiscal, J. Service; N. Patrick

GLASGOW AREA
Area Procurator Fiscal, L. A. Higson *(Glasgow)*

NORTHERN IRELAND JUDICATURE

In Northern Ireland the legal system and the structure of courts closely resemble those of England and Wales; there are, however, often differences in enacted law.

The Supreme Court of Judicature of Northern Ireland comprises the Court of Appeal, the High Court of Justice and the Crown Court. The practice and procedure of these courts is similar to that in England. The superior civil court is the High Court of Justice, from which an appeal lies to the Northern Ireland Court of Appeal; the House of Lords is the final civil appeal court.

The Crown Court, served by High Court and county court judges, deals with criminal trials on indictment. Cases are heard before a judge and, except those involving offences specified under emergency legislation, a jury. Appeals from the Crown Court against conviction or sentence are heard by the Northern Ireland Court of Appeal; the House of Lords is the final court of appeal.

The decision to prosecute in cases tried on indictment and in summary cases of a serious nature rests in Northern Ireland with the Director of Public Prosecutions, who is responsible to the Attorney-General. Minor summary offences are prosecuted by the police.

Minor criminal offences are dealt with in magistrates' courts by a legally qualified resident magistrate and, where an offender is under 17, by juvenile courts each consisting of a resident magistrate and two lay members specially qualified to deal with juveniles (at least one of whom must be a woman). On 19 August 2002 there were 878 justices of the peace in Northern Ireland. Appeals from magistrates' courts are heard by the county court, or by the Court of Appeal on a point of law or an issue as to jurisdiction.

Magistrates' courts in Northern Ireland can deal with certain classes of civil case but most minor civil cases are dealt with in county courts. Judgments of all civil courts are enforceable through a centralised procedure administered by the Enforcement of Judgments Office.

SUPREME COURT OF JUDICATURE

The Royal Courts of Justice, Belfast BT1 3JF
Tel 028-9023 5111

Lord Chief Justice of Northern Ireland (£181,176), The Rt. Hon. Sir Robert Carswell, *born* 1934, *apptd* 1997
Principal Secretary, S. T. A. Rogers

LORDS JUSTICES OF APPEAL (each £166,394)
Style, The Rt. Hon. Lord Justice [surname]

Rt. Hon. Sir Michael Nicholson, *born* 1933, *apptd* 1995
Rt. Hon. Sir William McCollum, *born* 1933, *apptd* 1997
Rt. Hon. Sir Anthony Campbell, *born* 1936, *apptd* 1998

PUISNE JUDGES (each £137,377)
Style, The Hon. Mr Justice [surname]

Hon. Sir John Sheil, *born* 1938, *apptd* 1989
Hon. Sir Brian Kerr, *born* 1948, *apptd* 1993
Hon. Sir Malachy Higgins, *born* 1944, *apptd* 1993
Hon. Sir Paul Girvan, *born* 1948, *apptd* 1995
Hon. Sir Patrick Coghlin, *born* 1945, *apptd* 1997
Hon. Sir John Gillen, *born* 1947, *apptd* 1998

Hon. Sir Richard McLaughlin, *born* 1947, *apptd* 1999
Hon. Sir Ronald Weatherup, *born* 1947, *apptd* June 2001

MASTERS OF THE SUPREME COURT (each £82,639)
Master, Queen's Bench and Appeals and Clerk of the Crown, J. W. Wilson, QC
Master, High Court, C. J. McCorry
Master, Office of Care and Protection, F. B. Hall
Master, Chancery Office, R. A. Ellison
Master, Bankruptcy and Companies Office, C. W. G. Redpath
Master, Probate and Matrimonial Office, Miss M. McReynolds
Master, Taxing Office, J. C. Napier

OFFICIAL SOLICITOR
Official Solicitor to the Supreme Court of Northern Ireland, Miss B. M. Donnelly

COUNTY COURTS

JUDGES (each £102,999)

Style, His/Her Hon. Judge [surname]

Judge Brady, QC; Judge Burgess, Judge Curran, QC; Judge Finnegan; Judge Foote, QC; Judge Gibson, QC; Judge Lockie; Judge Markey, QC; Judge McFarland; Judge McKay, QC; Judge Martin *(Chief Social Security and Child Support Commissioner);* Her Hon. Judge Kennedy; Judge Smyth, QC; His Hon. Judge Marriman, QC

RECORDERS
Belfast (£125,248), Judge Hart, QC
Londonderry, Her Hon. Judge Philpott, QC

MAGISTRATES' COURTS

RESIDENT MAGISTRATES (each £82,639)

There are 19 resident magistrates in Northern Ireland.

CROWN SOLICITOR'S OFFICE PO Box 410, Royal Courts of Justice, Belfast BT1 3JY Tel: 028-9054 2555
Crown Solicitor, O. G. Paulin

DEPARTMENT OF THE DIRECTOR OF PUBLIC PROSECUTIONS 93 Chichester Street, Belfast BT1 3TR
Tel: 028-9054 2444

Director of Public Prosecutions, Sir Alasdair Fraser, CB, QC
Deputy Director of Public Prosecutions, W. R. Junkin

NORTHERN IRELAND COURT SERVICE
Windsor House, Bedford Street, Belfast BT2 7LT
Tel: 028-9032 8594
Director (G3), D. A. Lavery

TRIBUNALS

AGRICULTURAL LAND TRIBUNALS
c/o DEFRA, Ergon House, Horseferry Road, London SW1P 2AL
Tel: 020-7238 5677 Fax: 020-7238 6553

Agricultural Land Tribunals settle disputes and other issues between agricultural landlords and tenants, and drainage disputes between neighbours.

There are seven tribunals covering England and one covering Wales. For each tribunal the Lord Chancellor appoints a chairman and one or more deputies (barristers or solicitors of at least seven years standing). The Lord Chancellor also appoints lay members to three statutory panels: the 'landowners' panel, the 'farmers' panel and the 'drainage' panel.

Each tribunal is an independent statutory body with jurisdiction only within its own area. A separate tribunal is constituted for each case, and consists of a chairman (who may be the chairman or one of the deputy chairmen) and two lay members nominated by the chairman.
Chairmen (England), W. D. M. Wood; P. A. de la Piquerie; N. Thomas; G. L. Newsom; His Hon. Judge Robert Taylor; J. H. Weatherill; His Hon. Judge Machin, QC
Deputy Chairmen, Ms A. M. Seifert; T. D. Bowles; J. E. Mitting; P. Bleasdale; W. M. Kingston; M. E. Heywood; Mrs S. Evans; His Hon. Judge W. H. R. Crawford; M. O. Rodger; P. Morgan, QC; A. R. Gore; J. G. Orme, TD
Chairman (Wales), W. J. Owen
Deputy Chairman (Wales), B. L. Y. Richards

THE APPEALS SERVICE
4th Floor, 19–30 Alfred Place, Whittington House, London WC1E 7LW Tel: 020-7712 2600
Web: www.appeals-service.gov.uk

The Appeals Service arranges and hears appeals on decisions on social security, child support, housing benefit, council tax benefit, vaccine damage, tax credits and compensation recovery.

Judicial authority for the Service rests with the president, while administrative responsibility is exercised by the Appeals Service Agency, which is an executive agency of the Department for Work and Pensions.
President, His Hon. Judge Michael Harris
Chief Executive, Appeals Service Agency, Christina Townsend

COMMONS COMMISSIONERS
Room Zone 1/05b, Temple Quay House, 2 The Square, Temple Quay, Bristol BS1 6EB
Tel: 0117-372 8973 Fax: 0117-372 8969

The Commons Commissioners are responsible for deciding disputes arising under the Commons Registration Act 1965. They also enquire into the ownership of unclaimed common land and village greens. Commissioners are appointed by the Lord Chancellor.
Chief Commons Commissioner (part-time), E. F. Cousins
Clerk, N. Wilson

COMPETITION APPEAL TRIBUNAL
New Court, 48 Carey Street, London WC2A 3BZ
Tel: 020-7271 0395 Fax: 020-7271 0281
Email: info@catribunal.org.uk
Web: www.catribunal.org.uk

The Competition Appeal Tribunal (CAT) is a specialist tribunal created by the Enterprise Act 2002 to hear certain cases in the sphere of UK competition law and merger control. The CAT hears appeals against decisions of the Office of Fair Trading and the regulators of the privatised utilities under the Competition Act 1998; it hears applications for judicial review of decisions of the Secretary of State, the Office of Fair Trading or the Competition Commission under provisions of the Enterprise Act 2002; and it also has jurisdiction under the Competition Act 1998 to award damages for established breaches of EC or UK competition law. It is further envisaged that the CAT will hear appeals against decisions of OFCOM. The CAT is headed by the President and has a panel of 20 members with backgrounds in law, economics, business, accountancy and regulation.
President, Sir Christopher Bellamy
Members, Prof. A. Bain, OBE; M. Blair, QC; P. Clayton; B. Colgate; M. Davey; P. Grant-Hutchison; Prof. P. Grinyer; Ms S. Hewitt; Ms A. Kelly; Hon. A. Lewis; G. Mathers; Prof. J. Pickering; R. Prosser, OBE; Dr A. Pryor, CB; Ms P. Quigley, WS; A. Scott, TD; Ms V. Smith-Hillman; Prof. P. Stoneman; D. Summers; Prof. G. Zellick
Registrar, Charles Dhanowa

COPYRIGHT TRIBUNAL
Harmsworth House, 13–15 Bouverie Street, London EC4Y 8DP
Tel: 020-7596 6510 Minicom: 0845-922 2250
Fax: 020-7596 6526
Email: copyright.tribunal@patent.gov.uk
Web: www.patent.gov.uk/copy/tribunal/index.htm

The Copyright Tribunal resolves disputes over copyright licences, principally where there is collective licensing.

The chairman and two deputy chairmen are appointed by the Lord Chancellor. Up to eight ordinary members are appointed by the Secretary of State for Trade and Industry.
Chairman, C. P. Tootal
Secretary, Miss J. E. M. Durdin

THE EMPLOYMENT TRIBUNALS (ENGLAND AND WALES)
7th Floor, 19–29 Woburn Place, London WC1H 0LU
Tel: 020-7273 8666 Fax: 020-7273 8670
Web: www.employmenttribunals.gov.uk

Employment Tribunals for England and Wales sit in 12 regions. The tribunals deal with matters of employment law, redundancy, dismissal, contract disputes, sexual, racial and disability discrimination and related areas of dispute which may arise in the workplace. A public register of applications is held at Southgate Street, Bury St Edmunds, Suffolk IP33 2AQ. The tribunals are funded by the Department of Trade and Industry; administrative support is provided by the Employment Tribunals Service.

Chairmen, who may be full-time or part-time, are legally qualified. They are appointed by the Lord Chancellor. Tribunal members are appointed by the Secretary of State for Trade and Industry.
President, G. Meeran

CENTRAL OFFICE OF THE EMPLOYMENT TRIBUNALS (SCOTLAND)
Eagle Building, 215 Bothwell Street, Glasgow G2 7TS
Tel: 0141-204 0730 Fax: 0141-204 0732

Tribunals in Scotland have the same remit as those in England and Wales. Chairmen are appointed by the Lord President of the Court of Session and lay members by the Secretary of State for Trade and Industry.
President, C. M. Milne
Regional Chairman, S. F. R. Patrick

EMPLOYMENT APPEAL TRIBUNAL
Central Office: Audit House, 58 Victoria Embankment, London EC4Y 0DS Tel: 020-7273 1041 Fax: 020-7273 1045
Divisional Office: 52 Melville Street, Edinburgh EH3 7HS
Tel: 0131-225 3963 Fax: 0131-220 6694
Web: www.employmentappeals.gov.uk

The Employment Appeal Tribunal hears appeals on a question of law arising from any decision of an employment tribunal. A tribunal consists of a judge and two lay members, one from each side of industry. They are appointed by The Queen on the recommendation of the Lord Chancellor and the Secretary of State for Trade and Industry. Administrative support is provided by the Employment Tribunals Service.
President, The Hon. Mr Justice Burton
Scottish Chairman, The Hon. Lord Johnson
Registrar, P. Donleavy
Deputy Registrar, Ms J. Johnson
Deputy Registrar at Divisional Office, J. Sadler

GENERAL COMMISSIONERS OF INCOME TAX
Lord Chancellor's Department, Selborne House, 54–60 Victoria Street, London SW1E 6QW
Tel: 020-7210 8990 Fax: 020-7210 0660

General Commissioners of Income Tax operate under the Taxes Management Act 1970. They are unpaid judicial officers who sit in some 425 Divisions throughout the United Kingdom to hear appeals against decisions by the Inland Revenue on a variety of taxation matters. The Commissioners' jurisdiction was extended in 1999 to hear National Insurance appeals. The Lord Chancellor appoints General Commissioners (except in Scotland, where they are appointed by the Scottish Executive). There are approximately 2,600 General Commissioners appointed throughout the United Kingdom. In each Division, Commissioners appoint a Clerk, who is normally legally qualified, who makes the administrative arrangements for appeal hearings and advises the Commissioners on points of law and procedure. The Lord Chancellor's Department pays the Clerks' remuneration.

Appeals from the General Commissioners are by way of case stated, on a point of law, to the High Court (the Court of Session in Scotland or the Court of Appeal in Northern Ireland).

In 2002, approximately 34,500 cases were listed before the General Commissioners.

IMMIGRATION APPELLATE AUTHORITY
Taylor House, 88 Rosebery Avenue, London EC1R 4QU
Tel: 020-7862 4200 Web: www.iaa.org.uk

The Immigration Appellate Authorities' powers are now derived from the Immigration and Asylum Act 1999. Immigration Adjudicators hear appeals from immigration decisions concerning the need for, and the refusal of, leave to enter or remain in the UK, refusals to grant asylum, decisions to make deportation orders and directions to remove persons subject to immigration control from the UK.

The Immigration Appeal Tribunal provides a second appellate level for those dissatisfied with an Adjudicator's decision. Leave to appeal needs to be obtained. From the Tribunal there is an appeal to the Court of Appeal on a point of law only.

An adjudicator sits alone. The Tribunal sits in divisions of three, normally a legally qualified member and two lay members.

IMMIGRATION APPEAL TRIBUNAL
Field House, 15 Breams Buildings, Chancery Lane, London EC4A 1DZ Tel: 020-7073 4026

President, The Hon. Mr Justice Collins
Deputy President, C. M. G. Ockelton
Vice-Presidents, J. Barnes; K. Eshun; J. R. A. Fox; M. W. Rapinet; G. Warr; Dr H. H. W. Storey; J. G. Freeman; D. K. Allen; K. Drabu; P. Moulden; A. Mackey; J. H. E. Latter; S. L. Batiste; J. A. J. C. Gleeson
Vice-Presidents, J. Gleeson; D. J. Parkes

IMMIGRATION APPEAL ADJUDICATORS
Chief Adjudicator, His Hon. Judge H. Hodge, OBE
Deputy Chief Adjudicator, E. Arfon-Jones

IMMIGRATION SERVICES TRIBUNAL
48–49 Chancery Lane, London WC2A 1JR
Tel: 020-7947 7200 Fax: 020-7947 7798

The Immigration Services Tribunal is an independent judicial body set up to provide a forum in which appeals against decisions of the Immigration Services Commissioner and complaints made by the Immigration Services Commissioner can be heard and determined. The cases exclusively concern people providing advice and representation services in connection with immigration matters.

The Tribunal forms part of the Court Service. It is the responsibility of the Lord Chancellor. There is a president, who is the judicial head; other judicial members, who must be legally qualified; lay members who must have substantial experience in immigration services or in the law and procedure relating to immigration; and a secretary who is responsible for administration. The tribunal can sit anywhere in the UK.
President, Hon. Judge Seddon Cripps
Judicial Members, D. Bean, QC; G. Marriott; Judge Burgess; B. Kennedy, QC; D. W. Hunter, QC
Members, P. Barnett; O. Conway; M. Hoare; S. Maguire; A. Montgomery; I. Newton; M. Quayum; S. Rowland; P. Fisher
Immigration Services Tribunal Staff, D. Duncan

INDUSTRIAL TRIBUNALS AND THE FAIR EMPLOYMENT TRIBUNAL (NORTHERN IRELAND)

Long Bridge House, 20–24 Waring Street, Belfast BT1 2EB
Tel: 028-9032 7666 Fax: 028-9023 0184

The industrial tribunal system in Northern Ireland was set up in 1965 and has a similar remit to the employment tribunals in the rest of the UK. There is also a Fair Employment Tribunal, which hears and determines individual cases of alleged religious or political discrimination in employment. Employers can appeal to the Fair Employment Tribunal if they consider the directions of the Equality Commission to be unreasonable, inappropriate or unnecessary, and the Equality Commission can make application to the Tribunal for the enforcement of undertakings or directions with which an employer has not complied.

The president, vice-president and part-time chairmen of the Fair Employment Tribunal are appointed by the Lord Chancellor. The full-time chairman and the part-time chairmen of the industrial tribunals and the panel members to both the industrial tribunals and the Fair Employment Tribunal are appointed by the Department of Higher and Further Education Training and Employment.

President of the Industrial Tribunals and the Fair Employment Tribunal, J. Maguire, CBE
Vice-President of the Industrial Tribunals and the Fair Employment Tribunal, Mrs M. P. Price
Secretary, Miss A. Loney

INFORMATION TRIBUNAL

c/o The Lord Chancellor's Department, Selborne House, 54–60 Victoria Street, London SW1E 6QN
Tel: 020-7210 2668 Fax: 020-7210 1415

The Information Tribunal determines appeals against notices issued by the Information Commissioner. The chairman and deputy chairman are appointed by the Lord Chancellor and must be legally qualified. Lay members are appointed by the Lord Chancellor to represent the interests of data users or data subjects. A tribunal consists of a chairman sitting with equal numbers of the lay members. There is a separate panel of the tribunal which hears national security appeals; the president of this panel is the Rt. Hon. Sir Anthony Evans, RD.

Chairman, David Marks
Secretary, Charlotte Mercer
Information Commissioner, R. Thomas

LANDS TRIBUNAL

48–49 Chancery Lane, London WC2A 1JR
Tel: 020-7947 7200 Fax: 020-7947 7215

The Lands Tribunal is an independent judicial body which determines questions relating to the valuation of land, rating appeals from valuation tribunals; appeals from leasehold valuation tribunals, the discharge or modification of restrictive covenants, and compulsory purchase compensation. The tribunal may also arbitrate under references by consent. The president and members are appointed by the Lord Chancellor.

President, G. R. Bartlett, QC
Members, P. H. Clarke, FRICS; N. J. Rose, FRICS; P. R. Francis, FRICS
Member (part-time), His Hon. Judge Rich, QC
Registrar, D. Scannell

LANDS TRIBUNAL FOR SCOTLAND

1 Grosvenor Crescent, Edinburgh EH12 5ER
Tel: 0131-225 7996 Fax: 0131-226 4812
Web: www.lands-tribunal-scotland.org.uk

The Lands Tribunal for Scotland has the same remit as the tribunal for England and Wales but also covers questions relating to tenants' rights to buy their homes under the Housing (Scotland) Act 1987. The president is appointed by the Lord President of the Court of Session.

President, The Hon. Lord McGhie, QC
Members, A. R. MacLeary, FRICS
Member (part-time), J. N. Wright, QC
Clerk, N. M. Tainsh

MENTAL HEALTH REVIEW TRIBUNALS

Secretariat: Health Service Directorate, Room LG02 Wellington House, 133–155 Waterloo Road, London SE1 8UG
Tel: 020-7972 4577 Fax: 020-7972 4884

The Mental Health Review Tribunals are independent judicial bodies which review the cases of patients compulsorily detained under the provisions of the Mental Health Act 1983. They have the power to discharge the patient, to recommend leave of absence, delayed discharge, transfer to another hospital or that a guardianship order be made, to reclassify both restricted and unrestricted patients, and to recommend consideration of a supervision application. There are four tribunals in England, each headed by a regional chairman who is appointed by the Lord Chancellor on a part-time basis. Each tribunal is made up of at least three members, and must include a lawyer, who acts as president, a medical member and a lay member.

There are five regional offices:
LIVERPOOL, 3rd Floor, Cressington House, 249 St Mary's Road, Garston, Liverpool L19 0NF.
Tel: 0151-728 5400
LONDON (NORTH), Spur 3, Block 1, Government Buildings, Honeypot Lane, Stanmore, Middx HA7 1AY.
Tel: 020-7972 3754
LONDON (SOUTH), LG01, 133–155 Wellington House, Waterloo Road, London SE1 8UG. Tel: 020-7972 4287
NOTTINGHAM, Spur A, Block 5, Government Buildings, Chalfont Drive, Western Boulevard, Nottingham NG8 3RZ. Tel: 0115-942 8308
WALES, 4th Floor, Crown Buildings, Cathays Park, Cardiff CF1 3NQ. Tel: 029-2082 5328

NATIONAL HEALTH SERVICE TRIBUNAL (SCOTLAND)

40 Craiglockhart Road, North, Edinburgh EH14 1BT
Tel/Fax: 0131-443 2575

The tribunal considers representations that the continued inclusion of a doctor, dentist, optometrist or pharmacist on a health board's list would be prejudicial to the efficiency of the service concerned. The tribunal sits when required and is composed of a chairman, one lay member, and one practitioner member drawn from a representative professional panel. The chairman is appointed by the Lord President of the Court of Session, and the lay member and the members of the professional panel are appointed by the First Minister.

Chairman, M. G. Thomson, QC
Lay member, J. D. M. Robertson, CBE
Clerk to the Tribunal, W. Bryden

PENSIONS APPEAL TRIBUNAL
Central Office (England and Wales), 48–49 Chancery Lane, London WC2A 1JF Tel: 020-7947 7034 Fax: 020-7947 7492
Web: www.pensionsappealtribunal.gov.uk

The Pensions Appeal Tribunals are responsible for hearing appeals from ex-servicemen or women and widows who have had their claims for a war pension rejected by the Secretary of State for Work and Pensions. The Entitlement Appeal Tribunals hear appeals in cases where the Secretary of State has refused to grant a war pension. The Assessment Appeal Tribunals hear appeals against the Secretary of State's assessment of the degree of disablement caused by an accepted condition. The tribunal members are appointed by the Lord Chancellor.
President, Dr H. M. G. Concannon
Tribunal Manager, Miss L. Nay

PENSIONS APPEAL TRIBUNALS FOR SCOTLAND
20 Walker Street, Edinburgh EH3 7HS Tel: 0131-220 1404
President, C. N. McEachran, QC

OFFICE OF THE SOCIAL SECURITY AND CHILD SUPPORT COMMISSIONERS
5th Floor, Newspaper House, 8–16 Great New Street, London EC4A 3BN Tel: 020-7353 5145 Fax: 020-7936 2171
23 Melville Street, Edinburgh EH3 7PW
Tel: 0131-225 2201

The Social Security Commissioners are the final statutory authority to decide appeals relating to entitlement to social security benefits. The Child Support Commissioners are the final statutory authority to decide appeals relating to child support. Appeals may be made in relation to both matters only on a point of law. The Commissioners' jurisdiction covers England, Wales and Scotland. There are 18 commissioners; they are all qualified lawyers.
Chief Social Security Commissioner and Chief Child Support Commissioner, His Hon. Judge Michael Harris
Secretary, Ms L. Armes (London); S. Niven (Edinburgh)

OFFICE OF THE SOCIAL SECURITY COMMISSIONERS AND CHILD SUPPORT COMMISSIONERS FOR NORTHERN IRELAND
1st Floor, Headline Building, 10–14 Victoria Street, Belfast BT1 3GG Tel: 028-9033 2344 Fax: 028-9031 3510
Email: socialsecuritycommissioners@courtsni.gov.uk
Web: www.courtsni.gov.uk

The role of Northern Ireland Social Security Commissioners and Child Support Commissioners is similar to that of the Commissioners in Great Britain. There are two commissioners for Northern Ireland.
Chief Commissioner, His Hon. Judge Martin, QC
Commissioner, Mrs M. F. Brown
Registrar of Appeals, W. R. Brown

THE SOLICITORS' DISCIPLINARY TRIBUNAL
3rd Floor, Gate House, 1 Farringdon Street, London EC4M 7NS
Tel: 020-7329 4808 Fax: 020-7329 4833
Email: enquiries@solicitorsdt.com
Web: www.solicitorstribunal.org.uk

The Solicitors' Disciplinary Tribunal is an independent statutory body whose members are appointed by the Master of the Rolls. The tribunal considers applications made to it alleging either professional misconduct and/or a breach of the statutory rules by which solicitors are bound against an individually named solicitor, former solicitor, registered foreign lawyer, or solicitor's clerk. The president and solicitor members do not receive remuneration.
President, A. Isaacs
Clerk to the Tribunal, Mrs S. C. Elson

THE SCOTTISH SOLICITORS' DISCIPLINE TRIBUNAL
22 Rutland Square, Edinburgh EH1 2BB
Tel: 0131-229 5860 Fax: 0131-229 0255

The Scottish Solicitors' Discipline Tribunal is an independent statutory body with a panel of 18 members, ten of whom are solicitors; members are appointed by the Lord President of the Court of Session. Its principal function is to consider complaints of misconduct against solicitors in Scotland.
Chairman, G. F. Ritchie
Clerk, J. V. Lea, WS

SPECIAL COMMISSIONERS
15–19 Bedford Avenue, London WC1B 3AS
Tel: 020-7612 9700 Fax: 020-7436 4150/4151

The Special Commissioners are an independent body appointed by the Lord Chancellor to hear complex appeals against decisions of the Board of Inland Revenue and its officials.
Presiding Special Commissioner, His Hon. Stephen Oliver, QC
Clerk, R. P. Lester

SPECIAL IMMIGRATION APPEALS COMMISSION
Taylor House, 88 Rosebery Avenue, London EC1R 4QU
Tel: 020-7862 4200

The Commission was set up under the Special Immigration Appeals Commission Act 1997. Its main function is to consider appeals against orders for deportations in cases which involve, in the main, considerations of national security. Members are appointed by the Lord Chancellor.
Chairman, The Hon. Mr Justice Collins

TRAFFIC COMMISSIONERS
c/o Scottish Traffic Area, Argyle House, 3 Lady Lawson Street, Edinburgh EH3 9SE Tel: 0131-200 4955 Fax: 0131-529 8501

The Traffic Commissioners are responsible for licensing operators of heavy goods and public service vehicles. There are seven Commissioners in the eight traffic areas covering Britain. Each Traffic Commissioner constitutes a tribunal for the purposes of the Tribunals and Inquiries Act 1992.
Senior Traffic Commissioner, P. Brown

TRANSPORT TRIBUNAL
48–49 Chancery Lane, London WC2A 1JR Tel: 020-7947 7200
Fax: 020-7947 7798 Email: transport@courtservice.gsi.gov.uk
Web: www.transporttribunal.gov.uk

The Transport Tribunal hears appeals against decisions made by Traffic Commissioners at public inquiries. The tribunal consists of a legally qualified president, two legal

members who may sit as chairmen, and five lay members. The president and legal members are appointed by the Lord Chancellor and the lay members by the Secretary of State for Transport.
President (part-time), H. B. H. Carlisle, QC
Legal member (part-time), His Hon. Judge Brodrick; J. Beech; F. Burton
Lay members, D. Yeomans; P. Steel; L. Milliken; G. Inch; S. James; J. Robinson
Secretary, G. Evans

VALUATION TRIBUNALS

Valuation Tribunal Management Board, 2nd Floor, Walton House, 11 Parade, Leamington Spa, Warks CV32 4DG
Tel: 01926-423825 Fax: 01926-423 207
Web: www.valuation-tribunals.gov.uk

The Valuation Tribunals hear appeals concerning the council tax, non-domestic rating and land drainage rates in England and Wales. There are 56 tribunals in England and four in Wales; those in England are funded by the Office of the Deputy Prime Minister and those in Wales by the National Assembly for Wales. A separate tribunal is constituted for each hearing, and normally consists of a chairman and two other members. Members are appointed by a representative of the local authorities and the Valuation Tribunal president and serve on a voluntary basis. The Valuation Tribunal Management Board considers all matters affecting valuation tribunals in England, and the Council of Wales Valuation Tribunals performs the same function in Wales.
Chairman, Valuation Tribunal Management Board, P. Wood, OBE
Valuation Tribunals National Officer, B. P. Massen, MBE
President, Council of Wales Valuation Tribunals, J. H. Owens

VAT AND DUTIES TRIBUNALS

15–19 Bedford Avenue, London WC1B 3AS
Tel: 020-7612 9700 Fax: 020-7436 4150/4151

VAT and Duties Tribunals are administered by the Lord Chancellor in England and Wales, and by the First Minister in Scotland. They are independent and decide disputes between taxpayers and Customs and Excise. In England and Wales, the president and chairmen are appointed by the Lord Chancellor and members by the Treasury. Chairmen in Scotland are appointed by the Lord President of the Court of Session.
President, His Hon. Stephen Oliver, QC
Vice-President, England and Wales, J. D. Demack
Vice-President, Scotland, T. G. Coutts, QC
Vice-President, Northern Ireland, His Hon. J. McKee, QC
Registrar, R. P. Lester

TRIBUNAL CENTRES

EDINBURGH, 44 Palmerston Place, Edinburgh EH12 5BJ. Tel: 0131-226 3551
LONDON (including Belfast), 15–19 Bedford Avenue, London WC1B 3AS. Tel: 020-7612 9700
MANCHESTER, 9th Floor, Westpoint, 501 Chester Road, Manchester M16 5HU. Tel: 0161-868 6600

THE POLICE SERVICE

There are 52 police forces in the United Kingdom. Most forces' area is coterminous with one or more local authority areas. Policing in London is carried out by the Metropolitan Police and the City of London Police; in Northern Ireland by the Police Service of Northern Ireland; and by the Isle of Man, States of Jersey and Guernsey forces in their respective islands and bailiwicks. National services include the National Crime Squad and the National Criminal Intelligence Service (NCIS).

The police authorities of English and Welsh forces comprise local councillors, magistrates and independent members. In Scotland, there are six joint police boards made up of local councillors; the other two police authorities are councils. In London the Metropolitan Police Authority oversees police operations. A committee of the Corporation of London including councillors and magistrates oversees the City of London Police. In Northern Ireland the Secretary of State appoints the policing board.

Police authorities in England, Scotland and Wales are financed by central and local government grants and a precept on the council tax. The Northern Ireland Policing Board is wholly funded by central government. The police authorities, subject to the approval of the Home Secretary (in England and Wales), the Secretary of State for Northern Ireland and to regulations, are responsible for appointing the Chief Constable. In England and Wales they are responsible for publishing annual policing plans and annual reports, setting local objectives and a budget, and levying the precept. The police authorities in Scotland are responsible for setting a budget, providing the resources necessary to police the area adequately, appointing officers of the rank of Assistant Chief Constable and above, and determining the number of officers and civilian staff in the force. The Northern Ireland Policing Board exercises these functions in Northern Ireland.

The Home Secretary, the Secretary of State for Northern Ireland and the Scottish Executive are responsible for the organisation, administration and operation of the police service. They make regulations covering matters such as police ranks, discipline, hours of duty and pay and allowances. All police forces are subject to inspection by HM Inspectors of Constabulary, who report to the Home Secretary, Scottish Executive or Secretary of State for Northern Ireland.

COMPLAINTS

The investigation and resolution of a serious complaint against a police officer in England and Wales is subject to the scrutiny of the Police Complaints Authority. An officer who is dismissed, required to resign or reduced in rank, whether as a result of a complaint or not, may appeal to a police appeals tribunal established by the relevant police authority. In Scotland, Chief Constables are obliged to investigate a complaint against one of their officers; if there is a suggestion of criminal activity, the complaint is investigated by an independent public prosecutor. In Northern Ireland complaints are investigated by the Police Ombudsman.

BASIC RATES OF PAY *since 1 April 2003*

Chief Constable of Police Services of Northern Ireland	
No fixed term	£120,057–£129,042
Fixed term appointment	£126,234–£135,669
Chief Constables of Greater Manchester, Strathclyde and West Midlands	
No fixed term	£106,134–£119,775
Fixed term appointment	£111,309–£125,622
Chief Constable	
No fixed term	£80,835–£115,590
Fixed term appointment	£84,879–£121,230
Deputy Chief Constable	
No fixed term	80% of their Chief Constable's pay or £77,427, whichever is higher
Fixed term appointment	80% of their Chief Constable's pay or £81,298, whichever is higher
Assistant Chief Constable	
No fixed term	£67,449–£77,427
Fixed term appointment	£70,824–£81,297
Chief Superintendent*	£58,242–£61,617
Superintendent*	£49,077–£57,249
Chief Inspector†	£41,562–£44,052
Inspector†	£37,551–£42,387
Sergeant	£29,307–£32,940
Constable	£18,666–£29,307

*The rank of Chief Superintendent was re-introduced on 1 January 2002 and so pay arrangements take effect from that date. Superintendents who were not given the rank of Chief Superintendent on its re-introduction receive full protection of their existing Superintendent range 2 salary (£57,249–£60,924).
†Includes London salary range, applicable only to officers in the Metropolitan and City of London polices forces.

Metropolitan Police

Commissioner	£163,299–£175,512
Deputy Commissioner	£132,657–£142,575
Assistant Commissioner	£112,767–£126,234
Deputy Assistant Commissioner*	80% of the basic salary of the assistant commissioner
Commander	
No fixed term	£67,449–£77,427
Fixed term appointment	£70,824–£81,297

*This rank was formally introduced on 1 January 2002, pay arrangements take effect from that date

City of London Police

Commissioner	
No fixed term	£92,448–£107,397
Fixed term appointment	£97,071–£112,767
Assistant Commissioner	
No fixed term	80% of the basic salary of the commissioner or £77,427, whichever is higher
Fixed term appointment	80% of the basic salary of the commissioner or £81,297, whichever is higher

THE SPECIAL CONSTABULARY

Each police force has its own special constabulary, made up of volunteers who work in their spare time. Special Constables have full police powers.

NATIONAL CRIME SQUAD

Headquarters: PO Box 2500, London SW1V 2WF.
Tel: 020-7238 2500
The National Crime Squad was established on 1 April 1998, replacing the six regional crime squads in England and Wales. It investigates national and international organised and serious crime. It also supports police forces investigating serious crime. The Squad is accountable to the National Crime Squad Service Authority.
Director General: W. Hughes, QPM

NCS AND NCIS SERVICE AUTHORITIES

Headquarters: PO Box 2600, London SW1V 2WG.
Tel: 020-7238 2600
The Service Authorities are responsible for ensuring the effective operation of the National Crime Squad and National Criminal Intelligence Service. Each Authority has eleven members, of whom eight sit on both Authorities as core members. The Service Authorities are non-departmental public bodies.
Chairman: D. Lock, *Clerk,* A. Mulholland

NATIONAL MISSING PERSONS BUREAU

Headquarters: New Scotland Yard, Broadway, London SW1H 0BG. Tel: 0207-230 4029
The Police National Missing Persons Bureau (PNMPB) acts as a central clearing house of information, receiving reports about vulnerable missing persons that are still outstanding after 14 days and details of unidentified persons or remains within 48 hours of being found from all forces in England and Wales. Reports are also received from Scottish police forces, the Police Services of Northern Ireland and foreign police forces via Interpol. The Bureau also manages the Missing Kids website, www.ukmissingkids.com
Director: G. Pugh

POLICE INFORMATION TECHNOLOGY ORGANISATION

Headquarters: New Kings Beam House, 22 Upper Ground, London SE1 9QY. Tel: 020-8358 5618
The Police Information Technology Organisation (PITO) is a non-departmental public body funded by grant-in-aid from central Government and by charges from the services provided. It provides information technology, communications systems and services to the police and other criminal justice organisations in the UK and also has a role in the purchasing of goods and services for the police.
Chairman: Lt.-Gen. Sir Edmund Burton, KBE
Chief Executive: P. Webb

FORENSIC SCIENCE SERVICE

Headquarters: Priory House, Gooch Street North, Birmingham B5 6QQ. Tel: 0121-607 6800
The Forensic Science Service (FSS) is an executive agency of the Home Office providing forensic science services to the police forces in England and Wales. It employs over 2,500 people, including over 1,600 trained scientists and has seven laboratories throughout the country.
Chief Executive: D. Werrett, Ph.D.

POLICE FORCES AND AUTHORITIES

Strength: strength of force as known at February 2003

ENGLAND

AVON AND SOMERSET CONSTABULARY, PO Box 37, Portishead, Bristol, BS20 8QJ Tel: 01275-818181
Fax: 01275-816890 *Strength,* 3,185
Chief Constable, S. Pilkington, QPM
BEDFORDSHIRE POLICE, Police Headquarters, Woburn Road, Kempston, Bedford, MK43 9AX Tel: 01234-841212
Fax: 01234-842006 *Strength,* 1,145
Chief Constable, P. Hancock
CAMBRIDGESHIRE CONSTABULARY, Hinchingbrooke Park, Huntingdon, PE29 6NP Tel: 01480-456111
Fax: 01480-422447 *Strength,* 1,373
Chief Constable, T. Lloyd, QPM
CHESHIRE CONSTABULARY, Castle Esplanade, Chester, CH1 2PP Tel: 01244-350000 Fax: 01244-612269
Strength, 2,146 *Chief Constable,* P. Fahy
CLEVELAND POLICE, PO Box 70, Ladgate Lane, Middlesbrough, TS8 9EH Tel: 01642-326326
Fax: 01642-301200 *Strength,* 1,560
Chief Constable, B. Shaw, QPM
CUMBRIA CONSTABULARY, Carleton Hall, Penrith, Cumbria, CA10 2AU Tel: 01768-891999 Fax: 01768-217099
Strength, 1,136 *Chief Constable,* M. Baxter
DERBYSHIRE CONSTABULARY, Butterley Hall, Ripley, Derbyshire, DE5 3RS Tel: 01773-570100 Fax: 01773-572225
Strength, 2,024 *Chief Constable,* D. F. Coleman
DEVON AND CORNWALL CONSTABULARY, Middlemoor, Exeter, EX2 7HQ Tel: 08705-777444 *Strength,* 3,200
Chief Constable, Maria Wallis, QPM
DORSET POLICE HEADQUARTERS, Winfrith, Dorchester, Dorset, DT2 8DZ Tel: 01929-462727 Fax: 01202-223987
Strength, 1,402 *Chief Constable,* Mrs J. Stichbury, QPM
DURHAM CONSTABULARY, Aykley Heads, Durham, DH1 5T, Tel: 0191-386 4929 Fax: 0191-375 2160
Strength, 1,657 *Chief Constable,* P. T. Garvin
ESSEX POLICE, PO Box 2, Springfield, Chelmsford, Essex, CM2 6DA Tel: 01245-491491 Fax: 01245-452259 *Strength,* 3,060 *Chief Constable* D. F. Stevens, QPM
GLOUCESTERSHIRE CONSTABULARY, Holland House, Lansdown Road, Cheltenham, Glos GL51 6QH,
Tel: 0845-0901234 Fax: 01242-221362 *Strength,* 1,174
Chief Constable, T. Brain, Ph.D.
GREATER MANCHESTER POLICE, PO Box 22 (S West PDO), Chester House, Boyer Street, Manchester, M16 0RE Tel: 0161-872 5050 Fax: 0161-856 2666 *Strength,* 7,111
Chief Constable, Michael J. Todd, QPM, M.Phil.
HAMPSHIRE CONSTABULARY, West Hill, Winchester, Hants, SO22 5DB Tel: 0845-045 4545 Fax: 01962-871204
Strength, 3,500 *Chief Constable,* P. R. Kernaghan, QPM
HERTFORDSHIRE CONSTABULARY, Stanborough Road, Welwyn Garden City, Herts, AL8 6XF Tel: 01707-354200
Fax: 01707-354409, *Strength,* 1,851
Chief Constable, P. Acres, QPM
HUMBERSIDE POLICE, Priory Road Police Station, Priory Road, Hull, HU1 5SF Tel: 01482-326111
Fax: 01482-220337 *Strength,* 2,102,
Chief Constable, D. Westwood, QPM, Ph.D.
KENT CONSTABULARY, Sutton Road, Maidstone, Kent, ME15 9BZ Tel: 01622-690690 Fax: 01622-654109
Strength, 3,439 *Chief Constable,* Sir David Phillips, QPM
LANCASHIRE CONSTABULARY, PO Box 77, Hutton, Nr. Preston, Lancs, PR4 5SB Tel: 01772-614444
Fax: 01772-618843 *Strength,* 3,451
Chief Constable, Paul R. Stephenson, QPM
LEICESTERSHIRE CONSTABULARY, St John's, Enderby, Leicester, LE19 2BX Tel: 0116-222 2222 Fax: 0116-248 2227
Strength, 2,061 *Chief Constable,* Matthew Baggott

LINCOLNSHIRE POLICE, PO Box 999, Lincoln, LN5 7PH
Tel: 01522-532222 *Strength,* 1,266
Chief Constable, R. J. N. Childs, QPM
MERSEYSIDE POLICE, PO Box 59, Liverpool, L69 1JD
Tel: 0151-709 6010 Fax: 0151-777 8999 *Strength,* 4,257
Chief Constable, N. Bettison, QPM
NORFOLK CONSTABULARY, Operations and
Communications Centre, Falconers Chase, Wymondham,
Norfolk, NR18 0WW Tel: 01953-424242 Fax: 01953-424299
Strength, 1,440 *Chief Constable,* A. Hayman
NORTHAMPTONSHIRE POLICE, Wootton Hall,
Northampton, NN4 0JQ Tel: 01604-700700
Fax: 01604-703028 *Strength,* 1,224
Chief Executive, C. Fox, QPM
NORTHUMBRIA POLICE, Ponteland, Newcastle upon Tyne,
NE20 0BL Tel: 01661-872555 Fax: 01661-869788
Strength, 4,031 *Chief Constable,* J. C. Strachan, QPM
NORTH YORKSHIRE POLICE, Newby Wiske Hall,
Northallerton, N. Yorks, DL7 9HA Tel: 01609-783131
Fax: 01609-789213 *Strength,* 1,427
Chief Constable, Ms. D. M. Canning
NOTTINGHAMSHIRE POLICE, Sherwood Lodge, Arnold,
Nottingham, NG5 8PP Tel: 0115-967 0999
Fax: 0115-967 0900 *Strength,* 2,400
Chief Constable, S. M. Green, QPM
SOUTH YORKSHIRE POLICE, Snig Hill, Sheffield, S3 8LY
Tel: 0114-220 2020 Fax: 0114-252 3243 *Strength,* 3,223
Chief Constable, M. Hedges, QPM
STAFFORDSHIRE POLICE, Cannock Road, Stafford,
ST17 0QG Tel: 01785-257717 Fax: 01785-232563 *Strength,*
2,218 *Chief Constable,* John W. Giffard, CBE, QPM
SUFFOLK CONSTABULARY HEADQUARTERS,
Martlesham Heath, Ipswich, IP5 3QS Tel: 01473-613500
Fax: 01473-613737 *Strength,* 1,264
Chief Constable, A. McWhirter
SURREY POLICE, Mount Browne, Sandy Lane, Guildford,
Surrey, GU3 1HG Tel: 01483-571212 Fax: 01483-300279
Strength, 1,995 *Chief Constable,* Denis O'Connor, CBE,
QPM
SUSSEX POLICE, Malling House, Lewes, Sussex, BN7 2DZ
Tel: 0845-607 0999 Fax: 01273-404274 *Strength,* 3,038
Chief Constable, Ken Jones, QPM
THAMES VALLEY POLICE, Kidlington, Oxon, OX5 2NX,
Tel: 01865-846000 Fax: 01865-846160 *Strength,* 3,821
Chief Constable, Peter Neyroud
WARWICKSHIRE POLICE, Leek Wootton, Warwick, CV35
7QB Tel: 01926-415000 *Strength,* 1,008
Chief Constable, John Burbeck, QPM, FIMgt
WEST MERCIA CONSTABULARY, Hindlip Hall, Hindlip, PO
Box 55, Worcester, WR3 8SP Tel: 01905-723000
Fax: 01905-454226 *Strength,* 2,401
Chief Constable, P. Hampson, QPM
WEST MIDLANDS POLICE, PO Box 52, Lloyd House,
Colmore Circus, Queensway, Birmingham, B4 6NQ
Tel: 0845-113 5000 *Strength,* 7,573
Chief Constable, Paul Scott-Lee, QPM
WEST YORKSHIRE POLICE, PO Box 9, Wakefield, W. Yorks,
WF1 3QP Tel: 01924-375222 *Strength,* 4,927
Chief Constable, C. R. Cramphorn
WILTSHIRE CONSTABULARY, London Road, Devizes, Wilts,
SN10 2DN Tel: 01380-722341 Fax: 01380-734135
Strength, 1,193 *Chief Constable,* Dame Elizabeth
Neville, DBE, QPM, Ph.D.

WALES

DYFED-POWYS POLICE, PO Box 99, Llangunnor,
Carmarthen, Carmarthenshire, SA31 2PF
Tel: 01267-222020 Fax: 01267-234262 *Strength,* 1,164
Chief Constable, T. Grange, QPM
GWENT POLICE, Croesyceiliog, Cwmbran, Torfaen, NP44 2XJ
Tel: 01633-838111 Fax: 01633-865211 *Strength,* 1,261
Chief Constable, K. Turner, OSTJ, QPM

NORTH WALES POLICE, Colwyn Bay, Conwy, LL29 8AW
Tel: 01492-517171 Fax: 01492-511232 *Strength,* 1,528
Chief Constable, R. Brunstrom
SOUTH WALES POLICE, Cowbridge Road, Bridgend,
CF31 3SU Tel: 01656-655555 Fax: 01656-869399 *Strength,*
3,157 *Chief Constable,* Sir Anthony Burden, OSTJ, QPM

SCOTLAND

CENTRAL SCOTLAND POLICE, Police Headquarters,
Randolphfield, Stirling, FK8 2HD Tel: 01786-456000
Fax: 01786-451177 *Strength,* 730 *Chief Constable,*
Andrew Cameron, QPM
DUMFRIES AND GALLOWAY CONSTABULARY, Police
Headquarters, Cornwall Mount, Dumfries, DG1 1PZ
Tel: 01387-252112 Fax: 01387-262059 *Strength,* 462
Chief Constable, D. J. R. Strang, QPM
FIFE CONSTABULARY, Detroit Road, Glenrothes, Fife, KY6
2RJ Tel: 01592-418888 Fax: 01592-418444 *Strength,* 930
Chief Constable, Peter M. Wilson, QPM
GRAMPIAN POLICE, Queen Street, Aberdeen, AB10 1ZA
Tel: 01224-386000 Fax: 01224-643366 *Strength,* 1,271
Chief Constable, Andrew G. Brown, QPM
LOTHIAN AND BORDERS POLICE, Fettes Avenue,
Edinburgh, EH4 1RB Tel: 0131-311 3131
Fax: 0131-311 3038 *Strength,* 2,602
Chief Constable, Paddy Tomkins, RCDS
NORTHERN CONSTABULARY, Old Perth Road, Inverness,
IV2 3SY Tel: 01463-715555 Fax: 01463-230800
Strength, 664 *Chief Constable,* Ian J. Latimer
STRATHCLYDE POLICE, Police Headquarters,
173 Pitt Street, Glasgow, G2 4JS Tel: 0141-532 2000
Fax: 0141-532 2475 *Strength,* 7,188
Chief Constable, William Rae, QPM
TAYSIDE POLICE, PO Box 59, West Bell Street, Dundee, DD1
9JU Tel: 01382-223200 Fax: 01382-200449 *Strength,* 1,170
Chief Constable, John Vine, QPM

NORTHERN IRELAND

POLICE SERVICE OF NORTHERN IRELAND, Brooklyn,
Knock Road, Belfast, BT5 6LE Tel: 028-9065 0222
Fax: 028-9070 0029 *Strength,* 9,851
Chief Constable, H. S. T. Orde

ISLANDS

GUERNSEY POLICE, Police Headquarters, Hospital Lane, St Peter
Port, Guernsey, GY1 2QN Tel: 01481-725111
Fax: 01481-256432 *Strength,* 177
Chief Officer, M. H. Wyeth
STATES OF JERSEY POLICE, PO Box 789, St Helier, Jersey,
JE2 3ZA Tel: 01534-612612 Fax: 01534-612613
Strength, 241 *Chief Officer,* Graham Power, QPM
ISLE OF MAN CONSTABULARY, Police Headquarters,
Glencrutchery Road, Douglas, Isle of Man, IM2 4RG
Tel: 01624-631212 Fax: 01624-628113 *Strength,* 239
Chief Constable, M. Culverhouse

Source: Police and Constabulary Almanac 2003

METROPOLITAN POLICE SERVICE

NEW SCOTLAND YARD, 8–10 Broadway, London SW1H 0BG
Tel 020-7230 1212 *Strength,* (February 2003), 40,145

Commissioner: Sir John Stevens, QPM, LLB, M.Phil.
Deputy Commissioner: Ian Blair, QPM, MA (Oxon)
Chief of Staff, Deputy Assistant Commissioner:
    C. A. Howlett, QPM

TERRITORIAL POLICING
Assistant Commissioner: T. Godwin, OBE
Deputy Assistant Commissioners: S. House; A Trotter, QPM

SPECIALIST OPERATIONS
Assistant Commissioner: D. Veness, CBE, QPM
Deputy Assistant Commissioners: S. Becks; P. J. Clarke, CVO

SPECIALIST CRIME
Assistant Commissioner: T. Ghaffur, QPM
Deputy Assistant Commissioners: W. I. Griffiths; M. Fuller

HUMAN RESOURCES
Assistant Commissioner: B. Hogan-Howe, MBA
Director, M. Tiplady

CITY OF LONDON POLICE
37 Wood Street, London EC2P 2NQ, Tel: 020-7601 2222
Strength, (February 2003), 735

Though small, the City of London has one of the most important financial centres in the world and the force has particular expertise in areas such as fraud investigation as well as the areas required of any police force. The force has a wholly elected police authority, the police committee of the Corporation of London, which appoints the Commissioner.
Commissioner: J. Hart, QPM, Ph.D.
Assistant Commissioner: M. Bowron
Commander: F. Armstrong

BRITISH TRANSPORT POLICE
15 Tavistock Place, London WC1H 9SJ, Tel: 020-7388 7541
Strength, (February 2003), 2,132

British Transport Police is the national police force for the railways in England, Wales and Scotland, including the London Underground system, Docklands Light Railway, Midland Metro Tram system and Croydon Tramlink. The Chief Constable reports to the British Transport Police Committee. The members of the Committee are appointed by the Strategic Rail Authority and include representatives of Network Rail and London Underground Ltd as well as independent members. Officers are paid the same as other police forces.
Chief Constable: I. Johnston, CBE, QPM
Deputy Chief Constable: J. A. Lake

MINISTRY OF DEFENCE POLICE
MDP Wethersfield, Braintree, Essex CM7 4AZ
Tel: 01371-854000 *Strength,* (March 2003), 3,291

The Ministry of Defence Police is a civilian police force with specific responsibility for meeting the requirements of the MOD and associated customers, including visiting forces and the Royal Mint. Other specialist services include marine policing, dogs, firearms and Police Search Teams. The Force also has its own Criminal Investigation Department with specialist officers working in the field of fraud investigation and can also offer crime prevention advice. MDP officers are also serving as a part of the British contingent of police officers supporting the United Nations policing operations.
Chief Constable: D. L. Clarke, QPM
Deputy Chief Constable: D. A. Ray, QPM, MA, LLM
Head of Secretariat: P. A. Crowther

ROYAL PARKS CONSTABULARY
Police Station, Hyde Park, London W2 2UH,
Tel: 020-7298 2000 *Strength,* (February 2003), 156

The Royal Parks Constabulary is maintained by the Royal Parks Agency, an executive agency of the Department for Culture, Media and Sport, and is responsible for the policing of eight royal parks in and around London. These comprise an area in excess of 5,000 acres. Officers of the force are appointed under the Parks Regulations Act 1872 as amended and are paid around 87 per cent of the Metropolitan Police rate.
Chief Officer: Supt. D. Pollock
Deputy Chief Officer: Acting Chief Inspector K. Quinn

UNITED KINGDOM ATOMIC ENERGY AUTHORITY CONSTABULARY
Building E6, Culham Science Centre, Abingdon,
Oxon OX14 3DB, Tel: 01235-463760
Strength, (March 2003), 559

The Constabulary is responsible for policing the United Kingdom Atomic Energy Authority, URENCO (Uranium Enrichment Services Worldwide) and British Nuclear Fuels plc establishments and for escorting nuclear material between establishments within the UK and worldwide. The Chief Constable is responsible, through the United Kingdom Atomic Energy Authority Police Authority, to the President of the Board of Trade.
Chief Constable: W. F. Pryke
Deputy Chief Constable: P. P. Crossan

STAFF ASSOCIATIONS

Police officers are not permitted to join a trade union or to take strike action. All ranks have their own staff associations.

ASSOCIATION OF CHIEF POLICE OFFICERS OF
ENGLAND, WALES AND NORTHERN IRELAND,
7th Floor, 25 Victoria Street, London SW1H 0EX.
Tel: 020-7227 3434.

THE POLICE SUPERINTENDENTS' ASSOCIATION OF
ENGLAND AND WALES, 67A Reading Road, Pangbourne,
Reading RG8 7JD. Tel: 0118-984 4005.
National Secretary: Chief Supt. D. Palmer

THE POLICE FEDERATION OF ENGLAND AND WALES,
15–17 Langley Road, Surbiton, Surrey KT6 6LP.
Tel: 020-8335 1000. *General Secretary:* C. E. Elliott

ASSOCIATION OF CHIEF POLICE OFFICERS IN
SCOTLAND, Police Headquarters, 173 Pitt Street, Glasgow
G2 4JS. Tel: 0141-532 2052. *Hon. Secretary:* W. Rae, QPM

THE ASSOCIATION OF SCOTTISH POLICE
SUPERINTENDENTS, Secretariat, 173 Pitt Street, Glasgow
G2 4JS. Tel: 0141-221 5796.
President: Chief Supt. A. Shanks

THE SCOTTISH POLICE FEDERATION, 5 Woodside Place,
Glasgow G3 7QF. Tel: 0141-332 5234.
General Secretary: D. J. Keil, QPM

THE SUPERINTENDENTS' ASSOCIATION OF
NORTHERN IRELAND, 77–79 Garnerville Road, Belfast
BT4 2NX. Tel: 028-909 22160.
Hon. Secretary: Supt. H. R. Phillips, MCIPD

THE POLICE FEDERATION FOR NORTHERN IRELAND,
77–79 Garnerville Road, Belfast BT4 2NX.
Tel: 028-9076 4200. *Secretary:* R. Wilson

THE PRISON SERVICE

The prison services in the United Kingdom are the responsibility of the Home Secretary, the Scottish Executive Justice Department and the Secretary of State for Northern Ireland. The chief director generals (Chief Executive in Scotland), officers of the Prison Service, the Scottish Prison Service and the Northern Ireland Prison Service are responsible for the day-to-day running of the system.

There are 137 prison establishments in England and Wales, 20 in Scotland and three in Northern Ireland. Convicted prisoners are classified according to their assessed security risk and are housed in establishments appropriate to that level of security. There are no open prisons in Northern Ireland. Female prisoners are housed in women's establishments or in separate wings of mixed prisons. Remand prisoners are, where possible, housed separately from convicted prisoners. Offenders under the age of 21 are usually detained in a young offender institution, which may be a separate establishment or part of a prison.

Nine prisons are now run by the private sector, and in England and Wales all escort services have been contracted out to private companies. Two prisons are being built and financed under the Private Finance Initiative and will also be run by private contractors. In Scotland, one prison (Kilmarnock) was built and financed by the private sector and is being operated by private contractors.

There are independent prison inspectorates in England and Wales and Scotland which report annually on conditions and the treatment of prisoners. HM Chief Inspector of Prisons for England and Wales also performs an inspectorate role for prisons in Northern Ireland. Every prison establishment also has an independent board of visitors or visiting committee made up of local volunteers.

Any prisoner whose complaint is not satisfied by the internal complaints procedures may complain to the Prisons Ombudsman for England and Wales or the Scottish Prisons Complaints Commission. There is no Prisons Ombudsman for Northern Ireland, but complaints by prisoners regarding maladministration may be made to the Parliamentary Commissioner for Administration.

From May 2003, the nine private sector prisons in England and Wales became the direct responsibility of the Commissioner for Correctional Services, a new post in the Home Office with overall responsibility for HM Prison Service, HM Probation Service and the Youth Justice Board. The Commissioner also has responsibility for correctional services policy, the prisons and probation inspectorates, the Prisons Ombudsman and the Board of Visitors. Martin Narey became Commissioner in March 2003. At the same time, Phil Wheatley took over as Director General of the Prison Service with responsibility for running the public prisons in England and Wales.

AVERAGE PRISON POPULATION MARCH 2003 (UK)

	Remand	Sentenced	Other
ENGLAND AND WALES			
Male	11,863	55,613	1,008
Female	1,045	3,378	47
Total	12,908	58,991	1,055
SCOTLAND			
Male	—	—	—
Female	—	—	—
Total	1,018	5,168	—
N. IRELAND			
Male	363	767	1,130
Female	8	18	26
Total	371	785	1,156
UK TOTAL	14,297	64,944	2,211

The projected prison population for 2007 in England and Wales is 78,100 if custody rates and sentence lengths remain at 2001 levels.

Sources: Home Office – Research Development Statistics; Scottish Prison Service *– Annual Report and Accounts;* Northern Ireland Prison Service – Annual Report 2002–3

SENTENCED PRISON POPULATION BY SEX AND OFFENCE (ENGLAND AND WALES)
as at 31 March 2003

	Male	Female
Violence against the person	12,370	546
Sexual offences	5,495	21
Burglary	8,730	217
Robbery	7,773	405
Theft, handling	4,161	469
Fraud and forgery	923	111
Drugs offences	8,745	1,288
Other offences	6,476	279
Offence not known	874	34
In default of payment of a fine	33	4
*Total	55,580	3,374

*figures do not include civil (non-criminal) prisoners
Source: Home Office *– Research Development Statistics*

SENTENCED POPULATION BY LENGTH OF SENTENCE *as at 31 March 2003* (ENGLAND AND WALES)

	Adults	Young Offenders
Less than 12 months	5,991	1,898
12 months to less than 4 years	16,923	4,838
4 years to less than 10 years	22,304	1,822
Life	5,058	157
*Total	50,276	8,715

*Figures include fine defaulters and non-criminals
Source: Home Office *– Research Development Statistics*

AVERAGE DAILY SENTENCED POPULATION BY
LENGTH OF SENTENCE 2002–3 (SCOTLAND)

	Adults	Young Offenders
Less than 4 years	2,120	433
4 years or over (including life)	2,506	169
Total	4,626	602

Source: Scottish Prison Service – *Annual Report and Accounts 2002–3*

PRISON SUICIDES APRIL 2002 – MARCH 2003
(ENGLAND AND WALES)

Males	92
Females	13
Total	105
Rate per 1,000 prisoners in custody	1.47

Source: Safer Custody Group – Annual Report 2002–3

OPERATING COSTS OF PRISON SERVICE IN
ENGLAND AND WALES 2002–3

	£
Staff costs	1,213,596,000
Other administrative costs	1,261,219,000
Operating income	(235,804,000)
Net operating costs for the year	2,405,237,000
Charge on capital employed	292,702,000
Net operating costs	2,405,237,000
Average cost per prisoner place	
(reflecting establishment costs only)	38,753

Source: HM Prison Service – *Annual Report and Accounts 2002–3*

OPERATING COSTS OF SCOTTISH PRISON
SERVICE 2002–3

	£
Total income	2,990,000
Total expenditure	209,214,000
Staff costs	121,912,000
Running costs	63,939,000
Other current expenditure	23,363,000
Operating cost	(206,224,000)
Cost of capital charges	(23,264,000)
Interest payable and similar charges	(7,000)
Interest receivable	68,000
Net cost of operations after interest	229,427,000
Lockerbie Trial Costs	0
Cost for financial year	(229,427,000)
Average annual cost per prisoner per place	28,110

Source: Scottish Prison Service – *Annual Report and Accounts 2002–3*

OPERATING COSTS OF NORTHERN IRELAND
PRISON SERVICE 2002–3

	£
Income	(267,000)
Staff Costs	75,069,000
Depreciation and other charges	7,102,000
Other Operating Costs	21,505,000
Total Expenditure	103,676,000
Net cost of Operations	103,409,000

Source: Northern Ireland Prison Service – *Annual Report and Accounts 2002–3*

THE PRISON SERVICES

HM PRISON SERVICE
Cleland House, Page Street, London SW1P 4LN
Tel: 0870-000 1397 Web: www.hmprisonservice.gov.uk

SALARIES *from January 2003*

Senior Manager A	£45,600–£65,840
Senior Manager B	£43,990–£62,833
Senior Manager C	£39,160–£56,574
Senior Manager D	£34,870–£51,806
Manager E	£24,680–£38,989
Manager F	£20,390–£33,029
Manager G	£19,320–£27,069

THE PRISON SERVICE MANAGEMENT BOARD
Director-General (SCS), P. Wheatley
Deputy Director-General (SCS), Director of High Security Prisons (SCS), P. Atherton
Director of Operations (SCS), M. Spurr
Director of Personnel (SCS), G. Hadley
Director of Finance (SCS), A. Beasley
Director of Corporate Affairs (SCS), D. Howard
Director of Resettlement (SCS), P. Wrench
Head of the Prison Health Policy Unit (SCS), J. Boyington
Board Secretary and Head of Secretariat (SMD), K. Everett
Race Equality Advisor, Ms J. Clements
Legal Adviser, S. Bramley

AREA MANAGERS (SCS)
Eastern, D. McAllister; *East Midlands (North),* S. Wagstaffe; *East Midlands (South),* B. Perry; *London,* B. Duff; *North East,* M. Egan; *North West,* I. Lockwood; *South East (Thames Valley and Hampshire),* Mrs S. Payne; *South East (Kent Surrey and Sussex),* A. Smith; *South West,* J. Petherick; *Wales,* J. May; *West Midlands,* B. Payling; *Yorkshire and Humberside,* P. Earnshaw
Head of Women's Estate, N. Clifford
Operational Manager for Women's Estate, H. Banks
Operational Manager for Juvenile Estate, D. Waplington
Operational Manager for High Security Prisons, P. Atherton

PRISON ESTABLISHMENTS – ENGLAND AND
WALES
CNA Average number of in use certified normal accommodation places without overcrowding 2002–3.

Prisoners as at 25 July 2003, 73,927
Adult Prisoners as at 25 July 2003, 62,700
Young Offenders as at 25 July 2003, 11,227

ACKLINGTON, Morpeth, Northumberland NE65 9XF. *CNA,* 786. *Governor,* P. Atkinson
ALBANY, Newport, Isle of Wight PO30 5RS. *CNA,* 446. *Governor,* C. Allison
ALTCOURSE (private prison), Higher Lane, Fazakerley, Liverpool L9 7LH. *CNA,* 614. *Director,* W. MacGowan
††ASHFIELD (private prison), Shortwood Road, Pucklechurch, Bristol BS16 9QT. CNA, 407. *Director,* Ms V. O'Dea
ASHWELL, Oakham, Leics LE15 7LF. *CNA,* 499. *Governor,* D. Walmsley
*ASKHAM GRANGE, Askham Richard, York YO26 5RF. *CNA,* 141. *Governor,* Ms D. Elaine
‡AYLESBURY, Bierton Road, Aylesbury, Bucks HP20 1EH. *CNA,* 418. *Governor,* D. Kennedy

†BEDFORD, St Loyes Street, Bedford MK40 1HG. *CNA*, 332. *Governor*, A. Cross

†BELMARSH, Western Way, Thamesmead, London SE28 0EB. *CNA*, 792. *Governor*, G. Hughes

†BIRMINGHAM, Winson Green Road, Birmingham B18 4AS. *CNA*, 706. *Governor*, M. Shann

†BLAKENHURST, Hewell Lane, Redditch, Worcs B97 6QS. *CNA*, 647. *Governor*, F. Parker

BLANTYRE HOUSE, Goudhurst, Cranbrook, Kent TN17 2NH. *CNA*, 122. *Governor*, C. Bartlett

BLUNDESTON, Lowestoft, Suffolk NR32 5BG. *CNA*, 393. *Governor*, Ms T. Clark

†‡BRINSFORD, New Road, Featherstone, Wolverhampton WV10 7PY. *CNA*, 477. *Governor*, T. Watson

†BRISTOL, Cambridge Road, Bristol BS7 8PS. *CNA*, 443. *Governor*, K. Lockyer

†BRIXTON, PO Box 369, Jebb Avenue, London SW2 5XF. *CNA*, 638. *Governor*, J. Podmore

*†‡BROCKHILL, Redditch, Worcester B97 6RD. *CNA*, 164. *Governor*, B. Treen

*†‡BUCKLEY HALL (private prison), Buckley Farm Lane, Rochdale, Lancs OL12 9DP. *CNA*, 350. *Governor*, S. Morrison

†BULLINGDON, PO Box 50, Bicester, Oxon OX25 1WD. *CNA*, 767. *Governor*, S. Saunders

*‡BULLWOOD HALL, High Road, Hockley, Essex SS5 4TE. *CNA*, 180. *Governor*, T. Hassall

CAMP HILL, Newport, Isle of Wight PO30 5PB. *CNA*, 481. *Governor*, B. Bennett

CANTERBURY, 46 Longport, Canterbury CT1 1PJ. *CNA*, 198. *Governor*, H. Rinaldi

†CARDIFF, Knox Road, Cardiff CF24 1UG. *CNA*, 518. *Governor*, P. Tidball

‡CASTINGTON, Morpeth, Northumberland NE65 9XG. *CNA*, 410. *Governor*, M. Bell

CHANNINGS WOOD, Denbury, Newton Abbott, Devon TQ12 6DW. *CNA*, 594. *Governor*, N. Evans

†‡CHELMSFORD, 200 Springfield Road, Chelmsford, Essex CM2 6LQ. *CNA*, 442. *Governor*, S. Rodford

COLDINGLEY, Bisley, Woking, Surrey GU24 9EX. *CNA*, 375. *Governor*, J. Dixon

*COOKHAM WOOD, Rochester, Kent ME1 3LU. *CNA*, 120. *Governor*, S. West

DARTMOOR, Princetown, Yelverton, Devon PL20 6RR. *CNA*, 692. *Governor*, C. Sturt

‡DEERBOLT, Bowes Road, Barnard Castle, Co. Durham DL12 9BG. *CNA*, 477. *Governor*, A. Tallentire

†‡DONCASTER (private prison), Off North Bridge, Marshgate, Doncaster DN5 8UX. *CNA*, 771. *Director*, A. Bramley

†DORCHESTER, North Square, Dorchester DT1 1JD. *CNA*, 156. *Governor*, S. Holland

DOVEGATE (private prison), Uttoxeter, ST14 8XR. *CNA*, 800. *Director*, K. Rogers

§DOVER, The Citadel, Western Heights, Dover CT17 9DR. *CNA*, 316. *Governor*, V. Whitecross

*DOWNVIEW, Sutton Lane, Sutton, Surrey SM2 5PD. *CNA*, 326. *Governor*, D. Lancaster

*DRAKE HALL, Eccleshall, Staffs ST21 6LQ. *CNA*, 312. *Governor*, J. Huntington

*†DURHAM, Old Elvet, Durham DH1 3HU. *CNA*, 632. *Governor*, M. Newell

*EAST SUTTON PARK, Sutton Valence, Maidstone, Kent ME17 3DF. *CNA*, 94. *Governor*, Revd R. Carter

*†‡EASTWOOD PARK, Falfield, Wotton-under-Edge, Glos GL12 8DB. *CNA*, 299. *Governor*, T. Beeston

†‡ELMLEY, Church Road, Eastchurch, Sheerness, Kent ME12 4DZ. *CNA*, 763. *Governor*, B. Pollett

ERLESTOKE, Devizes, Wilts SN10 5TU. *CNA*, 348. *Governor*, K. Brown

EVERTHORPE, Brough, E. Yorks HU15 1RB. *CNA*, 438. *Governor*, A. Rice

†EXETER, New North Road, Exeter EX4 4EX. *CNA*, 317. *Governor*, I. Mulholland

FEATHERSTONE, New Road, Wolverhampton WV10 7PU. *CNA*, 599. *Governor*, M. Pascoe

†‡FELTHAM, Bedfont Road, Feltham, Middx TW13 4ND. *CNA*, 823. *Governor*, N. Pascoe

FORD, Arundel, W. Sussex BN18 0BX. *CNA*, 538. *Governor*, K. Kan

FOREST BANK (private prison), Agecroft Road, Pendlebury, Manchester M27 8UE. *CNA*, 800. *Governor*, I. Woods

*FOSTON HALL, Foston, Derbys DE65 5DN. *CNA*, 225. *Governor*, P. Scriven

FRANKLAND, Brasside, Durham DH1 5YD. *CNA*, 652. *Governor*, P. Copple

FULL SUTTON, Full Sutton, York YO41 1PS. *CNA*, 596. *Governor*, B. Mullen

GARTH, Ulnes Walton Lane, Leyland, Preston PR5 3NE. *CNA*, 633. *Governor*, B. McColm

GARTREE, Gallow Field Road, Market Harborough, Leics LE16 7RP. *CNA*, 375. *Governor*, R. Daly

†‡GLEN PARVA, Tigers Road, Wigston, Leicester LE18 4TN. *CNA*, 664. *Governor*, B. Edwards

†GLOUCESTER, Barrack Square, Gloucester GL1 2JN. *CNA*, 230. *Governor*, D. Chalmers

GRENDON, Grendon Underwood, Aylesbury, Bucks HP18 0TL. *CNA*, 523. *Governor*, P. Bennett

‡GUYS MARSH, Shaftesbury, Dorset SP7 0AH. *CNA*, 496. *Governor*, Mrs D. Calvert

§HASLAR, Dolphin Way, Gosport, Hampshire, PO12 2AW. *CNA*, 160. *Governor*, M. Jones

‡HATFIELD, Thorne Road, Hatfield, Doncaster DN7 6EL. *CNA*, 180. *Governor*, T. Watson

HAVERIGG, Millom, Cumbria LA18 4NA. *CNA*, 554. *Governor*, S. McCullagh

HEWELL GRANGE, Redditch, Worcs B97 6QQ. *CNA*, 184. *Governor*, N. Croft

†‡HIGH DOWN, Sutton Lane, Sutton, Surrey SM2 5PJ. *CNA*, 649. *Governor*, T. Butt

*†‡HIGHPOINT (NORTH AND SOUTH), Stradishall, Newmarket, Suffolk CB8 9YG. *CNA*, 800. *Governor*, S. Pryor

†‡HINDLEY, Gibson Street, Bickershaw, Wigan, Lancs WN2 5TH. *CNA*, 538. *Governor*, J. Blake

‡HOLLESLEY BAY COLONY, Woodbridge, Suffolk IP12 3JW. *CNA*, 329. *Governor*, M. Wood

*†‡HOLLOWAY, Parkhurst Road, London N7 0NU. *CNA*, 508. *Governor*, E. Willetts

HOLME HOUSE, Holme House Road, Stockton-on-Tees TS18 2QU. *CNA*, 857. *Governor*, M. Lees

†HULL, Hedon Road, Hull HU9 5LS. *CNA*, 610. *Governor*, M. Read

‡HUNTERCOMBE, Huntercombe Place, Nuffield, Henley-on-Thames RG9 5SB. *CNA*, 360. *Governor*, E. Jones

KINGSTON, 122 Milton Road, Portsmouth PO3 6AS. *CNA*, 193. *Governor*, J. Robinson

KIRKHAM, Freckleton Road, Preston PR4 2RN. *CNA*, 561. *Governor*, D. Thomas

KIRKLEVINGTON GRANGE, Yarm, Cleveland TS15 9PA. *CNA*, 183. *Governor*, A. Richer

LANCASTER, The Castle, Lancaster LA1 1YL. *CNA*, 196. *Governor*, S. Ellis

‡LANCASTER FARMS, Far Moor Lane, Stone Row Head, off Quernmore Road, Lancaster LA1 3QZ. *CNA*, 496.
Governor, T. Williams
LATCHMERE HOUSE, Church Road, Ham Common, Richmond, Surrey TW10 5HH. *CNA*, 195.
Governor, T. Hinchliffe
†LEEDS, Armley, Leeds LS12 2TJ. *CNA*, 806.
Governor, S. Tasker
LEICESTER, Welford Road, Leicester LE2 7AJ. *CNA*, 199.
Governor, R. Kellett
†‡LEWES, Brighton Road, Lewes, E. Sussex BN7 1EA. *CNA*, 485. *Governor*, P. Carroll
LEYHILL, Wotton-under-Edge, Glos GL12 8BT. *CNA*, 469.
Governor, R. Booty
†LINCOLN, Greetwell Road, Lincoln LN2 4BD. *CNA*, 453.
Governor, J. Tilly
§LINDHOLME, Bawtry Road, Hatfield Woodhouse, Doncaster DN7 6EE. *CNA*, 753. *Governor*, M. Ward
LITTLEHEY, Perry, Huntingdon, Cambs PE28 0SR.
CNA, 624. *Governor*, J. Morgan
†LIVERPOOL, 68 Hornby Road, Liverpool L9 3DF.
CNA, 1,202. *Governor*, J. Smith
LONG LARTIN, South Littleton, Evesham, Worcs WR11 8TZ.
CNA, 598. *Governor*, F. Masserick
LOWDHAM GRANGE (private prison), Lowdham, Notts NG14 7DA. *CNA*, 504. *Director*, P. Wright
*†‡LOW NEWTON, Brasside, Durham DH1 5AD. *CNA*, 248.
Governor, D. Thompson
MAIDSTONE, 36 County Road, Maidstone ME14 1UZ.
CNA, 548. *Governor*, J. Galbally
MANCHESTER, Southall Street, Manchester M60 9AH.
CNA, 953. *Governor*, C. Sheffield
‡MOORLAND OPEN, Thorne Road, Hatfield, Doncaster DN7 6EL. *CNA*, 260. *Governor*, B. McCourt
‡MOORLAND CLOSED, Bawtry Road, Hatfield Woodhouse, Doncaster DN7 6BW. *CNA*, 740.
Governor, B. McCourt
*MORTON HALL, Swinderby, Lincoln LN6 9PT. *CNA*, 265.
Governor, L. Saunders
THE MOUNT, Molyneaux Avenue, Bovingdon, Hemel Hempstead HP3 0NZ. *CNA*, 704. *Governor*,
P. Wailen
*†‡NEW HALL, Dial Wood, Flockton, Wakefield WF4 4AX.
CNA, 327. *Governor*, S. Snell
‡NORTHALLERTON, 15A East Road, Northallerton, N. Yorks DL6 1NW. *CNA*, 153. *Governor*, B. Shaw
NORTH SEA CAMP, Freiston, Boston, Lincs PE22 0QX.
CNA, 294. *Governor*, K. Beaumont
†NORWICH, Mousehold, Norwich NR1 4LU. *CNA*, 536.
Governor, J. Knight
†NOTTINGHAM, Perry Road, Sherwood, Nottingham NG5 3AG. *CNA*, 388. *Governor*, K. Lloyd
‡ONLEY, Willoughby, Rugby, Warks CV23 8AP. *CNA*, 640.
Governor, S. McAllister
†PARC (private prison), Heol Hopcyn John, Bridgend CF35 6AR. *CNA*, 828. *Director*, J. Mullen
†PARKHURST, Newport, Isle of Wight PO30 5NX.
CNA, 478. *Governor*, S. Metcalf
†PENTONVILLE, Caledonian Road, London N7 8TT.
CNA, 897. *Governor*, G. Davies
‡PORTLAND, Easton, Portland, Dorset DT51DL. *CNA*, 505.
Governor, S. Twinn
†PRESTON, 2 Ribbleton Lane, Preston PR1 5AB. *CNA*, 423.
Governor, A. Brown
RANBY, Ranby, Retford, Notts DN22 8EU. *CNA*, 680.
Governor, P. Wragg
†‡READING, Forbury Road, Reading RG1 3HY. *CNA*, 195.
Governor, N. Leader

*RISLEY, Risley, Warrington WA3 6BP. *CNA*, 896. *OC*, 835.
Governor, P. Norbury
†‡ROCHESTER, 1 Fort Road, Rochester, Kent ME1 3QS.
CNA, 374. *Governor*, C. Kershaw
RYE HILL (private prison), Onley, Rugby CV23 8AM.
CNA, 600. *Director*, S. Mitson
*SEND, Ripley Road, Send, Woking, Surrey GU237LJ.
CNA, 220. *Governor*, B. Ritchie
SHEPTON MALLET, Cornhill, Shepton Mallet, Somerset BA4 5LU. *CNA*, 170. *Governor*, B. McAlley
†SHREWSBURY, The Dana, Shrewsbury SY1 2HR.
CNA, 184. *Governor*, M. Bolton
SPRING HILL, Grendon Underwood, Aylesbury, Bucks, HP18 0TH. *CNA*, 256. *Governor*, T. Newell
STAFFORD, 54 Gaol Road, Stafford ST16 3AW. *CNA*, 638.
Governor, P. L. Taylor
STANDFORD HILL, Church Road, Eastchurch, Isle of Sheppey, Kent ME12 4AA. *CNA*, 437.
Governor, T. Robson
STOCKEN, Stocken Hall Road, Stretton, nr Oakham, Leics LE15 7RD. *CNA*, 556. *Governor*, D. Taylor
‡STOKE HEATH, Stoke Heath, Market Drayton, Shropshire TF9 2JL. *CNA*, 572. *Governor*, C. James
*†‡STYAL, Wilmslow, Cheshire SK9 4HR. *CNA*, 416.
Governor, Ms M. Moulden
SUDBURY, Ashbourne, Derbys DE6 5HW. *CNA*, 511.
Governor, C. Davidson
SWALESIDE, Brabazon Road, Eastchurch, Isle of Sheppey, Kent ME12 4AX. *CNA*, 747.
Governor, M. Conway
†SWANSEA, 200 Oystermouth Road, Swansea SA1 3SR.
CNA, 219. *Governor*, P. Taylor
‡SWINFEN HALL, Lichfield, Staffs WS14 9QS. *CNA*, 311.
Governor, P. Knapton
‡THORN CROSS, Arley Road, Appleton Thorn, Warrington WA4 4RL. *CNA*, 316. *Governor*, S. Lawrence
‡USK, 47 Maryport Street, Usk, Gwent NP5 1XP. *CNA*, 257.
Governor, P. Morgan
THE VERNE, Portland, Dorset DT5 1EQ. *CNA*, 552.
Governor, M. Cook
WAKEFIELD, 5 Love Lane, Wakefield WF2 9AG. *CNA*, 754.
Governor, J. Slater
†WANDSWORTH, Heathfield Road, London SW18 3HS.
CNA, 1,134. *Governor*, J. Heavans
‡WARREN HILL, Hollesley, Woodbridge, Suffolk IP12 3JW.
CNA, 214. *Governor*, S. Robinson
WAYLAND, Griston, Thetford, Norfolk IP25 6RL. *CNA*, 620.
Governor, J. Shanley
WEALSTUN, Wetherby, W. Yorks LS23 7AZ. *CNA*, 640.
Governor, S. Tilley
WEARE, Portland Dock, Castletown, Portland, Dorset DT5 1PZ. *CNA*, 400.
Governor, Ms S. F. McCormick
WELLINGBOROUGH, Millers Park, Doddington Road, Wellingborough, Northants NN8 2NH. *CNA*, 516.
Governor, J. Lewis
‡WERRINGTON, Werrington, Stoke-on-Trent ST9 0DX.
CNA, 134. *Governor*, F. Flynn
‡WETHERBY, York Road, Wetherby, W. Yorks LS22 5ED.
CNA, 360. *Governor*, I. Blakeman
WHATTON, 14 Cromwell Road, Nottingham NG13 9FQ.
CNA, 294. *Governor*, V. Hart
WHITEMOOR, Longhill Road, March, Cambs PE15 0PR.
CNA, 500. *Governor*, M. Lomas
*WINCHESTER, Romsey Road, Winchester SO22 5DF.
CNA, 437. *Governor*, J. Gomersall
WOLDS (private prison), Everthorpe, Brough, E. Yorks HU15 2JZ. *CNA*, 348. *Director*, D. McDonnell

†‡§WOODHILL, Tattenhoe Street, Milton Keynes MK4 4DA. *CNA, 677. Governor,* P. Haley

WORMWOOD SCRUBS, PO Box 757, Du Cane Road, London W12 0AE. *CNA, 1,176. Governor,* K. Munns

WYMOTT, Ulnes Walton Lane, Leyland, Preston PR5 3LW. *CNA, 809. Governor,* A. Scott

SCOTTISH PRISON SERVICE
Calton House, 5 Redheughs Rigg, Edinburgh EH12 9HW
Tel: 0131-556 8400; Web: www.sps.gov.uk

SALARIES 2002–3
The following pay bands have applied since 1 October 2002. Senior managers in the Scottish Prison Service, including governors and deputy governors of prisons, are paid across three pay bands:

Band I	£48,000–£58,000
Band H	£38,100–£48,100
Band G	£30,000–£40,000

Chief Executive of Scottish Prison Service, A. Cameron
Director, Human Resources, B. Allison
Director, Finance and Information Systems, W. Pretswell
Director, Strategy and Business Performance, K. Thomson
Deputy Director, Rehabilitation and Care, A. Spencer
Deputy Director, Estates and Buildings, D. Williams
Operations Director, South and West, M. Duffy
Operations Director, North and East, P. Withers
Head of Training, Scottish Prison Service College, W. Rattray
Head of Communications, T. Fox

PRISON ESTABLISHMENTS
Prisoners Average number of prisoners as at May 2003
*ABERDEEN, Craiginches, 4 Grampian Place, Aberdeen AB11 8FN. *Prisoners, 201. Governor,* A. Mooney
BARLINNIE, Barlinnie, Glasgow G33 2QX. *Prisoners, 1,059. Governor,* W. McKinlay
CASTLE HUNTLY, Castle Huntly, Longforgan, nr Dundee DD2 5HL. *Prisoners, 134. Governor,* I. Whitehead
*‡CORNTON VALE, Cornton Road, Stirling FK9 5NU. *Prisoners, 229. Governor,* S. Brookes
*‡DUMFRIES, Terregles Street, Dumfries DG2 9AX. *Prisoners, 132. Governor,* C. McGeever
EDINBURGH, 33 Stenhouse Road, Edinburgh EH11 3LN. *Prisoners, 689. Governor,* D. Croft
‡GLENOCHIL, King O'Muir Road, Tullibody, Clackmannanshire FK10 3AD. *Prisoners, 590. Governor,* K. Donegan
GREENOCK, Gateside, Greenock PA16 9AH. *Prisoners, 312. Governor,* S. Swan
*INVERNESS, Porterfield, Duffy Drive, Inverness IV2 3HH. *Prisoners, 130. Governor,* A. MacDonald
KILMARNOCK (private prison), Bowhouse, Mauchline Road, Kilmarnock KA1 5JH. *Prisoners, 533. Governor,* N. Cameron
LOW MOSS, Low Moss, Bishopbriggs, Glasgow G64 2QB. *Prisoners, 335. Governor,* E. Fairbairn
NORANSIDE, Noranside, Fern, by Forfar, Angus DD8 3QY. *Prisoners, 101. Governor,* I. Whitehead
PERTH, 3 Edinburgh Road, Perth PH2 8AT. *Prisoners, 461. Governor,* W. Millar
PETERHEAD, Salthouse Head, Peterhead, Aberdeenshire AB42 2YY. *Prisoners, 290. Governor,* I. Gunn
‡POLMONT, Brightons, Falkirk, Stirlingshire FK2 0AB. *Prisoners, 425. Governor,* D. Gunn

SHOTTS, Shotts ML7 4LE. *Prisoners, 514. Governor,* A. Park

NORTHERN IRELAND PRISON SERVICE
Dundonald House, Upper Newtownards Road, Belfast BT4 3SU.
Tel: 028-9052 2922 Fax: 028-9052 5100
Email: info@niprisonservice.gov.uk
Web: www.niprisonservice.gov.uk

SALARIES 2002–3
Governor 1	£60,010–£62,143
Governor 2	£54,312–£55,684
Governor 3	£46,763–£49,155
Governor 4	£39,276–£41,281
Governor 5	£33,986–£36,993

A Northern Ireland allowance is also payable

PRISON ESTABLISHMENTS
Prisoners/Young Offenders: average number of prisoners/young offenders as at June 2003

‡HYDEBANK WOOD YOC, Hospital Road, Belfast BT8 8NA. *Young Offenders, 191*
*§MAGHABERRY, Old Road, Ballinderry Upper, Lisburn, Co. Antrim BT28 2PT. *Prisoners, 659*
MAGILLIGAN, Point Road, Limavady, Co. Londonderry BT49 0LR. *Prisoners, 314*

* Women's establishment or establishment with units for women
† Remand Centre or establishment with units for remand prisoners
‡ Young Offender Institution or establishment with units for young offenders
§ Immigration Holding Centre

DEFENCE

The armed forces of the United Kingdom comprise the Royal Navy, the Army and the Royal Air Force. The Queen is Commander-in-Chief of all the armed forces. The Ministry of Defence, headed by the Secretary of State, provides the support structure for the armed forces. Within the Ministry of Defence, the Defence Council has overall responsibility for running the armed forces. Beneath the Ministers lies the top management of the Ministry of Defence, headed jointly by the Permanent Secretary and the Chief of Defence Staff. The Permanent Secretary is the Government's principal civilian adviser on defence and has the primary responsibility for policy, finance, management and administration. He is also personally accountable to Parliament for the expenditure of all public money voted for defence purposes. The Chief of the Defence Staff is the professional head of the Armed Forces in the UK and the principal military adviser to the Secretary of State and the Government.

The Defence Management Board (DMB) is the executive board of the Defence Council. Chaired by the Permanent Secretary, it acts as the main executive board of the Ministry of Defence, providing senior level leadership and strategic management of defence.

The Central Staff, headed by the Vice-Chief of the Defence Staff and the Second Permanent Under-Secretary of State is the policy core of the Department. The Defence Procurement Agency is responsible for purchasing equipment. The Defence Logistics Organisation (DLO) was created to bring together the logistics support organisations in the Royal Navy, Army and Royal Air Force and centre staff in one organisation.

A permanent Joint Headquarters for the conduct of joint operations was set up at Northwood in 1996. The Joint Headquarters connects the policy and strategic functions of the MoD Head Office with the conduct of operations and is intended to strengthen the policy/executive division. A Joint Rapid Deployment Force was established in August 1996 and a Joint Rapid Reaction Force was set up in April 1999.

Britain pursues its defence and security policies through its membership of NATO (to which most of its armed forces are committed), the Western European Union, the European Union, the Organisation for Security and Co-operation in Europe and the UN (see International Organisations section).

ARMED FORCES STRENGTHS *as at 1 April 2003*

All Services	206,920
Men	189,010
Women	17,920
Royal Naval Services	41,550
Army	112,130
Royal Air Force	53,240

Source: Ministry of Defence

SERVICE PERSONNEL *as at 1 April 2003*

	Royal Navy	Army	RAF	All Services
1975 strength	76,200	167,100	95,000	338,300
1990 strength	63,210	152,810	89,680	305,710
1999 strength	43,700	109,720	55,210	208,640
2001 strength	42,420	109,530	53,700	205,650
2002 strength	41,630	110,050	53,000	204,690
2003 strength	41,550	112,130	53,240	206,920

Figures are for UK Regular Forces (including both trained and untrained personnel), and exclude Gurkhas, full-time Reserve Service personnel, the Home Service battalions of the Royal Irish Regiment, mobilised reservists and Naval Activated Reservists

Source: Ministry of Defence

CIVILIAN PERSONNEL

1975 level	316,700
1990 level	172,300
1999 level	115,600
2000 level	115,100
2001 level	111,700
2002 level	103,400
2003 level	88,710

Does not include casual personnel
Source: UK Defence Statistics 2002

DEPLOYMENT OF UK PERSONNEL

SERVICE PERSONNEL IN UK AS AT 1 JULY 2003*

	England	Wales	Scotland	N. Ireland	Unknown
All Services	139,000	2,110	13,870	5,160	8,580
Officers	23,380	300	1,850	580	1,270
Other Ranks	115,630	1,800	12,020	4,580	7,310
Army‡	69,950	920	3,040	4,620	4,710
Officers	9,770	110	550	490	380
Other Ranks	60,180	810	2,490	4,130	4,330
Navy†‡	31,950	20	4,890	150	660
Officers	6,310	10	570	10	160
Other Ranks	25,640	10	4,320	140	500
RAF‡	37,110	1,160	5,950	380	3,210
Officers	7,290	180	730	80	740
Other Ranks	29,810	980	5,220	310	2,470

* Figures are for UK Regular Forces, both Trained and Untrained, located in the UK. They exclude Gurkhas, full-time Reserve Service personnel, the Home Service battalions of the Royal Irish Regiment and mobilised reservists.
† Naval Service personnel on sea service in home waters are included against the local authority containing the home port of their ship.
‡ The titles Naval Service, Army and Royal Air Force include Nursing services.
Source: Ministry of Defence

SERVICE PERSONNEL OVERSEAS *as at 1 October 2002*

	Breakdown	Total
All Services		41,980
Officers	5,740	
Other Ranks	36,240	
Army		33,070
Officers	3,840	
Ranks	29,230	
Royal Navy		3,840
Officers	760	
Ranks	3,080	
RAF		5,080
Officers	1,140	
Ranks	3,940	

Source: Ministry of Defence

NUCLEAR FORCES

Britain's nuclear forces comprise four ballistic missile submarines carrying Trident missiles and equipped with nuclear warheads. All nuclear free-fall bombs have been taken out of service.

ARMS CONTROL

The 1990 Conventional Armed Forces in Europe (CFE) Treaty, which commits all NATO and former Warsaw Pact members to limiting their holdings of five major classes of conventional weapons, has been adapted to reflect the changed geo-strategic environment and negotiations continue for its implementation. The Open Skies Treaty, which the UK signed in 1992 and which entered into force in 2002, allows for the overflight of party states by other party states using unarmed observation aircraft.

In 1968 the UK signed and ratified the Nuclear Non-Proliferation Treaty, which came into force in 1970 and was indefinitely and unconditionally extended in 1995. In 1996 the UK signed the Comprehensive Nuclear Test Ban Treaty and ratified it in 1998. The UK is a party to the 1972 Biological and Toxin Weapons Convention, which provides for a world-wide ban on biological weapons, and the 1993 Chemical Weapons Convention, which came into force in 1997 and provides for a verifiable world-wide ban on chemical weapons.

DEFENCE BUDGET (DEPARTMENTAL EXPENDITURE LIMIT PLANS)

Projection	£ billion
2003–4	30.8
2004–5	31.5
2006–6	32.3

Source: The Budget 2003

MINISTRY OF DEFENCE

Old War Office, Whitehall, London SW1A 2EU
Tel 020-7218 9000
Public Enquiry Office: Tel 020-7218 6645
Web: www.mod.uk

Officers promoted in an acting capacity to a more senior rank are listed under the more senior rank. Promotion to five-star rank is no longer usual in peacetime.

GRADE EQUIVALENTS

Grade 1 equivalents: (5*) Admiral of the Fleet, (5*) Field Marshal, (5*) Marshal of the RAF, (4*) Admiral, (4*) General, (4*) Air Chief Marshal.
Grade 2 equivalents: (3*) Vice Admiral, (3*) Lieutenant-General, (3*) Air Marshal

Secretary of State for Defence, The Rt. Hon. Geoffrey Hoon, MP
Private Secretary (SCS), P. Watkins
Special Advisers, R. Taylor; M. Dogher
Parliamentary Private Secretary, Liz Blackman, MP
Minister of State for the Armed Forces, The Rt. Hon. Adam Ingram, MP
Parliamentary Private Secretary, Alan Campbell, MP
Team PPS, Syd Rapson, MP
Private Secretary (SCS), G. Dean
Parliamentary Under-Secretary of State for Defence and Minister for Defence Procurement, Lord Bach
Private Secretary (SCS), B. Palmer
Parliamentary Under-Secretary of State for Defence and Minister for Veterans, Ivor Caplin, MP
Private Secretary (SCS), A. Cruttwell
Permanent Under-Secretary of State (SCS), Sir Kevin Tebbit, KCB, CMG
Second Permanent Under-Secretary, Ian Andrews, CBE, TD
Chief of Defence Staff, Gen. Sir Michael Walker, GCB, CMG, CBE, ADC

THE DEFENCE COUNCIL

The Defence Council is the Senior Committee of the Ministry of Defence, which was established by Royal Prerogative under the Letters Patent in April 1964. The Letters Patent confer on the Defence Council the command over all of the Armed Forces and charge the Council with such matters relating to the administration of the Armed Forces as the Secretary of State for Defence should direct them to execute. It is chaired by the Secretary of State for Defence and consists of: the Minister of State for the Armed Forces, the Parliamentary Under-Secretary of State for Defence and Minister for Defence Procurement, the Parliamentary Under-Secretary of State for Defence and Minister for Veterans; the Permanent Under-Secretary of State, the Chief of the Defence Staff; the Chief of the Naval Staff and First Sea Lord, the Chief of the General Staff, the Chief of the Air Staff; the Vice-Chief of the Defence Staff, the Second Permanent Under-Secretary of State, the Chief Scientific Advisor, the Chief of Defence Procurement and the Chief of Defence Logistics.

CHIEFS OF STAFF

CHIEF OF THE NAVAL STAFF

First Sea Lord and Chief of the Naval Staff (4),*
   Adm. Sir Alan West, KCB, DSC
Asst Chief of the Naval Staff (2),*
   Rear-Adm. A. J. Johns, CBE

CHIEF OF THE GENERAL STAFF

Chief of the General Staff (4),*
   Gen. Sir Mike Jackson, KCB, CBE, DSO, ADC
Asst Chief of the General Staff (2),*
   Maj.-Gen. F. R. Dannatt, CBE, MC
Director-General, Development and Doctrine (2),*
   Maj.-Gen. J. B. A. Bailey, MBE

CHIEF OF THE AIR STAFF

Chief of the Air Staff (4),*
   Air Chief Marshal Sir Jock Stirrup, KCB, AFC, ADC
Asst Chief of the Air Staff (2),*
   Air Vice-Marshal P. O. Sturley, CB, MBE
British-American Community Relations Co-ordinator (2),*
   Air Marshal Sir John Kemball, KCB, CBE, RAF (retd)
Head of Air Historical Branch (RAF) and Publications

Clearance Branch (Air) (SCS), Sebastian Cox
Chairman Joint Air Navigation Services Council,
  Sir M. Field
Director, Airspace Policy (2*),
  Air Vice-Marshal J. R. D. Arscott

CENTRAL STAFFS
Vice-Chief of the Defence Staff,
  Air Chief Marshal Sir Anthony Bagnall, GBE, KCB,
  OBE
Second Permanent Under-Secretary of State (SCS),
  I. Andrews, CBE, TD
Deputy CDS (Equipment Capability) (3*),
  Lt.-Gen. R. H. G. Fulton
Capability Manager (Information Superiority) (SCS),
  Air Vice-Marshal S. G. G. Dalton
Capability Manager (Strategic Deployment) (2*),
  Rear-Adm. C. R. Style
Director of Science (Concepts and Technology) (SCS),
  Dr J. Jones
Capability Manager (Manoeuvre) (2*),
  Maj.-Gen. A. C. Figgures, CBE
Director of Science (Manoeuvre) (SCS), Dr D. J. Ferbrache
Capability Manager (Strike) (2*),
  Air Vice-Marshal N. J. Day, CBE
Asst CDS (Resources and Plans),
  Rear-Adm. R. I. A. McLean, OBE
Director-General (Service Personnel Policy),
  Elizabeth McLoughlin
Defence Housing Executive (SCS), John Wilson
*Director of Finance and Secretariat (Defence Housing
  Executive) (SCS)*, R. Mansell
Surgeon-General (3*),
  Surgeon Vice-Adm. I. L. Jenkins, CVO, QHS, FRCS
Deputy Chief of Defence Staff (Health)
  Lt.-Gen. K. O'Donoghue
Director-General (Resources and Plans) (SCS),
  Tom McKane
Director of Defence Resources and Plans (SCS), G. Lester
Director of Capability Resources and Scrutiny (SCS),
  David Williams
Director of Performance and Analysis (SCS), Ian Woodman
Director-General Equipment (SCS), Stephen French
Director of Equipment Secretariat (SCS), David Kirk
Director-General (Financial Management) (SCS), B. Mann
Director of Finance Policy (SCS), Bill Davis
Corporate Financial Controller (SCS), J. Thornton
Senior Economic Adviser (SCS), N. V. Davies
Director-General Central Budget, Carl Mantell
Chief Executive, Defence Bills Agency (SCS), N. Swanney
Director-General of Corporate Communication (SCS),
  A. J. D. Pawson
Director of News (SCS), Pam Teare
Director of Corporate Communications Services (SCS),
  C. Williams
*Secretary to the Defence Press and Broadcasting Advisory
  Committee (2*)*, Rear-Adm. N. J. Wilkinson, (retd)
Director of Resettlement, Cdre. A. Picton
Deputy CDS (Commitments) (3*), Lt.-Gen. R. A. Fry
Asst. Chief of the Defence Staff (Operations) (2*),
  Air Vice-Marshal C. R. Loader
Director-General Operational Policy (SCS), I. Lee
Head of Balkans Secretariat (SCS), John Tesh
Head of Overseas Secretariat (SCS), J. Jarvis
Head of Gulf Veterans Illness Unit (SCS), Daniel
  Applegate

Policy Director (SCS), Simon Webb
Asst. Chief of the Defence Staff (Policy) (2*),
  Air Vice-Marshal D. A. Hobart
Director of Policy Planning (SCS), Gavin Barlow
Personnel Director, Richard Hatfield
Director-General Management and Organisation (SCS),
  Nick Evans
Director of Management and Consultancy Services (SCS),
  David Reynolds
Director of Change Programme (SCS), Gary Lewitt
*Director of Organisation and Management Development
  (SCS)*, A. Tourle
Directors of Business Delivery (SCS), M. Preston;
  Alison Stevenson
Director-General Civilian Policy (SCS), John Pitt-Brooke
Chief Constable/Chief Executive, MOD Police,
  D. Lloyd Clarke
*Director of Claims and Legal (Finance and Secretariat)
  (SCS)*, Mrs J. Alexander
Chief Executive, Defence Estates (SCS),
  Vice-Adm. P. A. Dunt
Commandant Joint Services Command and Staff College (2*),
  Maj.-Gen. J. C. McColl, CBE

DEFENCE INTELLIGENCE STAFF
Old War Office Building, Whitehall, London SW1A 2EU
Tel 020-7218 6645 Fax 020-7218 1562
Chief of Defence Intelligence (3*), Lt.-Gen. A. P. Ridgway
Deputy Chief of Defence Intelligence (SCS), Martin Howard
Director Intelligence Programmes and Resources (SCS),
  P. I. Bailey
*Head of Defence Intelligence Secretariat and
  Communications Information Systems (SCS)*,
  C. A. Younger
Director, Intelligence Regional Issues (1*), Brig. J. G. Rose
Director, Intelligence Global Issues (SCS),
  J. M. Cunningham
Director, Intelligence Scientific and Technical (SCS),
  P. W. Roper
Director-General, Intelligence Collection (2*),
  Maj.-Gen. M. Laurie, CBE

DEFENCE SCIENTIFIC STAFF
Chief Scientific Adviser (SCS) (Grade 1A),
  Prof. Sir Keith O'Nions, FRS
Science and Technology Director, Graham Jordan
Director, Science and Technology Policy, P. Hollinshead
Director of Finance and Secretariat (SCS), R. Mansell
Director-General (Scrutiny and Analysis) (SCS),
  N. J. Bennett
Director-General (Research and Technology) (SCS),
  Dr A. Markin
Director of Strategic Technologies (SCS), P. W. Taylor

COMMANDER-IN-CHIEF FLEET
C.-in-C. Fleet, Adm. Sir Jonathon Band, KCB
Deputy C.-in-C. Fleet, Vice-Adm. M. Stanhope, OBE
Chief of Staff (Support), Rear-Adm. T. C. Chittenden
Chief of Staff (Warfare), Rear-Adm. T. P. McClement, OBE
Command Secretary, Jonathon Day
Commander Operations, Rear-Adm. N. S. R. Kilgour
Flag Officer Sea Training, Rear-Adm. J. C. Rapp
Commander UK Maritime Force, Rear-Adm. D. G. Snelson
Commander UK Amphibious Force, Maj.-Gen. A. A. Milton

SECOND SEA LORD/COMMANDER-IN-CHIEF NAVAL HOME COMMAND

Second Sea Lord and C.-in-C. Naval Home Command,
Vice-Adm. J. M. Burnell-Nugent, CBE, ADC
Director-General, Naval Personnel (Strategy and Plans) and Chief of Staff to Second Sea Lord and C.-in-C. Naval Home Command, Rear-Adm. R. F. Cheadle
Asst Under-Secretary of State (Naval Personnel) (SCS),
P. W. D. Hatt
Flag Officer Training and Recruiting (2),*
Rear-Adm. P. R. Davies, CBE
Naval Secretary and Chief Executive, Naval Manning Agency (2),* Rear-Adm. M. W. C. Kerr
Surgeon General (Naval) (2),*
Surgeon Rear-Adm. I. L. Jenkins, CVO, QHS, FRCS
Director-General, Naval Chaplaincy Services,
The Ven. B. K. Hammett, QHC

ADJUTANT-GENERAL'S DEPARTMENT

Adjutant-General, Lt.-Gen. A. Irwin, KCB, CBE
Deputy Adjutant-General and Director-General Service Conditions, Maj.-Gen. W. R. Rollo, CBE
Chief of Staff, Brig. T. N. Tyler
Director of Manning (Army) (1),* Brig. K. H. Cima
Head, Command Secretariat (SCS), Miss E. G. Cassidy
Director-General, Army Training and Recruiting and Chief Executive, Army Training and Recruiting Agency,
Maj.-Gen. A. D. Leakey, CBE
Chaplain-General, Ven J. Blackburn, QHC
Director-General, Army Medical Services,
Maj.-Gen. L. P. Lillywhite, QHP, MBE
Director, Army Legal Services,
Maj.-Gen. D. M. Howell, OBE
Military Secretary and Chief Executive, Army Personnel Centre, Maj-Gen. F. R. Viggers, MBE
Commandant, Royal Military Academy, Sandhurst,
Maj.-Gen. A. S. Ritchie, CBE
Commandant, Royal Military College of Science,
Maj.-Gen. J. C. B. Sutherell

COMMANDER-IN-CHIEF LAND COMMAND

C.-in-C., Land Command,
Lt.-Gen. Sir Timothy Granville-Chapman, KCB, CBE
Deputy C.-in-C., Land Command, and Inspector-General, Territorial Army, Maj.-Gen. J. F. Deverell
Chief of Staff, HQ Land Command,
Maj.-Gen. A. R. D. Shirreff, CBE
Commander Regional Forces, Lt.-Gen. J. P. Kiszely, MC

HQ STRIKE COMMAND

Air Officer Commanding-in-Chief,
Air Chief Marshal Brian Burridge, CBE, ADC
Deputy Commander-in-Chief Strike Command,
Air Vice-Marshal G. L. Torpy
Chief of Air Staff, Air Chief-Marshal Sir Jock Stirrup,
KCB, AFC, ADC
Deputy Chief of Staff Operations,
Air Vice-Marshal A. V. M. Cliffe
Air Officer Logistics and Communications Information Systems, Air Vice-Marshal P. J. Scott
Air Officer Administration and Air Officer Commanding Directly Administered Units,
Air Vice-Marshal R. McConnell
Command Secretary (SCS), Ian McEwen
Air Officer Commanding, No. 1 Group,
Air Vice-Marshal Christopher Moran

Air Officer Commanding, No. 2 Group,
Air Vice-Marshal N. D. A. Maddox, CBE
Air Officer Commanding, No. 3 Group,
Air-Vice Marshal A. D. White

HQ PERSONNEL AND TRAINING COMMAND

Air Member for Personnel and Commander-in-Chief Personnel and Training Command, Air Marshal
Sir Joe French, KCB, CBE
Chief of Staff, Air Vice-Marshal J. A. Collier, CBE
Chief Executive, Training Group Defence Agency,
Air Vice-Marshal A. Miller
Air Officer Administration and Air Officer Commanding Directly Administered Units, Air Vice-Marshal R. C. Moore
Director Plans and Reserves, Air Cdre. D. N. Case
Commandant, RAF College, Cranwell,
Air Cdre Barter, CBE
Air Secretary and Chief Executive, RAF Personnel Management Agency, Air Vice-Marshal I. M. Stewart, AFC
Director-General, Medical Services (RAF),
Air Vice-Marshal W. J. Pike
Director, Legal Services (RAF),
Air Vice-Marshal R. A. Charles
Chaplain-in-Chief (RAF), Ven. R. D. Hesketh

DEFENCE PROCUREMENT AGENCY (DPA)

215 MOD Abbey Wood, Bristol BS34 8JH
Tel 0117-913 0249 Fax 0117-913 0902
Chief of Defence Procurement and Chief Executive, DPA,
Vice-Adm. Sir Peter Spencer, KCB

EXECUTIVE AGENCIES

DEFENCE LOGISTICS ORGANISATION (DLO)
DLO Headquarters, Spur 4, E Block, Ensleigh, Bath BA1 5AB
Chief of Defence Logistics,
Air Chief Marshal Sir Malcolm Pledger, KCB, OBE, AFC

DLO'S BUSINESS UNITS

ARMY BASE REPAIR ORGANISATION (ABRO)
Building 203, Monxton Road, Andover, Hampshire SP11 8HT
Tel: 01264-383295
BRITISH FORCES POST OFFICE (BFPO),
Inglis Barracks, Mill Hill, London NW7 1PX
Tel: 020-8818 6310
CORPORATE TECHNICAL SERVICES (CTS), DLO,
Monxton Road, Andover SP11 8HT
Tel: 01264-382515
DEFENCE CATERING GROUP,
Room 102, Fosseway, Ensleigh, Bath BA1 5AB
Tel: 01225-447943
DEFENCE COMMUNCATION SERVICES AGENCY (DCSA),
Basil Hill Site, Park Lane, Corsham, Wilts SN13 9NR
Tel: 01225-814785
DEFENCE FUELS GROUP, West Moors, Wimborne, Dorset
BH21 6QS Tel: 01202-654351
DEFENCE STORAGE AND DISTRIBUTION AGENCY,
Ploughley Road, Lower Arncott, Bicester, Oxon OX25 2LD
Tel: 01869-256840
DEFENCE SUPPLY CHAIN
Monxton Road, Andover, Hampshire SP11 8HT
Tel: 01264-383846

DEFENCE TRANSPORT AND MOVEMENTS AGENCY, (DTMA), Building 211, DLO Andover, Monxton, Road, Andover, Hampshire SP11 8HT Tel: 01480-452451

EQUIPMENT SUPPORT (AIR), DLO, Room J103, Cranswick House, RAF Wyton, Huntingdon, Cambs PE28 2EA

Tel: 01480-452451

EQUIPMENT SUPPORT (LAND), Building 300, DLO, Monxton Road, Andover, Hampshire SP11 8HT Tel: 01264-383512

PAYD PROJECT, Building 209, DLO Andover, Monxton Road, Andover, Hants SP11 8HT Tel: 01264-348051

WARSHIP SUPPORT AGENCY, Corporate Communications Group, Birch 1c, Abbey Wood, Bristol, BS34 8JH

OTHER EXECUTIVE AGENCIES

ARMED FORCES PERSONNEL ADMINISTRATION AGENCY (AFPAA), Building 182, RAF Innsworth, Gloucester GL3 1HW Tel: 01452-712612

ARMY PERSONNEL CENTRE, Kentigern House, 65 Brown Street, Glasgow G2 8EX Tel: 0141-224 2023

ARMY TRAINING AND RECRUITING AGENCY, Trenchard Lines, Upavon, Pewsey, Wilts SN9 6BE

Tel: 01980-615220

DEFENCE ANALYTICAL SERVICES AGENCY (DASA), 1st Floor, St Georges Court, 2–12 Bloomsbury Way, London WC1A 2SH Tel: 020-7305 2192

DEFENCE AVIATION REPAIR AGENCY, (DARA) Head Office, Building 145, St Athan, Barry, Vale of Glamorgan CF62 4WA

Tel: 01446-798834

DEFENCE AVIATION SAFETY CENTRE (DASC), PO Box 333, RAF Bentley Priory, Stanmore, Middlesex HA7 3YN

DEFENCE BILLS AGENCY (DBA), Room 410, Mersey House, Drury Lane, Liverpool L2 7PX

Tel: 0151-242 2234

DEFENCE DENTAL AGENCY (DDA), RAF Halton, Aylesbury, Bucks HP22 5PG

Tel: 01296-623535

DEFENCE ESTATES, Kingston Road, Sutton Coldfield, W. Midlands B75 7RL Tel: 0121-311 2140

DEFENCE GEOGRAPHIC AND IMAGERY INTELLIGENCE AGENCY, Watson Building, Elmwood Avenue, Feltham TW13 7AH Tel: 020-8818 2133

DEFENCE HOUSING EXECUTIVE, 6th Floor, Ibex House, 42–47 Minories, London EC3N 1DY

Tel: 020-7423 4816

DEFENCE INTELLIGENCE AND SECURITY CENTRE (DISC), Chicksands, Shefford, Beds SG17 5PR

Tel: 01462-752228

DEFENCE MEDICAL EDUCATION AND TRAINING AGENCY (DMETA), MacKenzie Block, Fort Blockhouse, Gosport, Hants PO12 2AB Tel: 023-9276 5141

DEFENCE PROCUREMENT AGENCY (DPA), Maple 2219, MOD Abbey Wood, Bristol BS34 8JH Tel: 0117-913 0000

DEFENCE SCIENCE AND TECHNOLOGY LABORATORY (DSTL), Porton Down, Salisbury, Wiltshire SP4 0JQ

Tel: 01980-613121

DEFENCE VETTING AGENCY, Building 107, Imphal Barracks, Fulford Road, York YO10 4AS Tel: 01904-665820

DISPOSAL SERVICES AGENCY, 6 Hercules Road, London SE1 7DJ Tel: 020-7305 3072

THE DUKE OF YORK'S ROYAL MILITARY SCHOOL (DYRMS), Dover, Kent CT15 5EQ Tel: 01304-245024

MEDICAL SUPPLIES AGENCY, Drummond Barracks, Ludgershall, Andover, Hants SP11 9RU Tel: 01980-608622

MET OFFICE, Fitzroy Road, Exeter, EX1 3PB

Tel: 01344-856608

MINISTRY OF DEFENCE POLICE, Wethersfield, Braintree, Essex CM7 4AZ Tel: 01371-854000

NAVAL MANNING AGENCY, Victory Building, HM Naval Base, Portsmouth PO1 3LS Tel: 023-9272 7401.

NAVAL RECRUITING AND TRAINING AGENCY (NRTA), Victory Building, HM Naval Base, Portsmouth PO1 3LS

Tel: 023-9272 7641

PAY AND PERSONNEL AGENCY, PO Box 99, Bath BA1 1YT

Tel: 01225-828126

QUEEN VICTORIA SCHOOL, Dunblane, Perthshire FK15 0JY

Tel: 01786-822288

QINETIQ, Ively Road, Farnborough, Hampshire GU14 0LX

Tel: 01252-392000

RAF PERSONNEL MANAGEMENT AGENCY, RAF Innsworth, Gloucester GL3 1EZ Tel: 01452-712612

RAF TRAINING GROUP DEFENCE AGENCY, RAF Innsworth, Gloucester GL3 1EZ Tel: 01452-712612, ext. 5302

SERVICE CHILDREN'S EDUCATION, HQ UKSCE, Building 5, Wegberg Military Complex, BFPO 40.

Tel: 00-49 2161-908 2295

UK NATIONAL CODIFICATION BUREAU, Room 2.4.23, Kentigern House, 65 Brown Street, Glasgow G2 8EX

Tel: 0141-224 2066

UNITED KINGDOM HYDROGRAPHIC OFFICE, Admiralty Way, Taunton, Somerset TA1 2DN

Tel: 01823-337900

VETERANS AGENCY, Tomlinson House, Norcross, Thornton Cleveleys, FY5 3WP Freephone: 0800-169 2277

THE ROYAL NAVY

LORD HIGH ADMIRAL OF THE UNITED KINGDOM
HM The Queen

ADMIRALS OF THE FLEET
HRH The Prince Philip, Duke of Edinburgh, KG, KT, OM, GBE, AC, QSO, PC, *apptd* 1953
The Lord Hill-Norton, GCB, *apptd* 1971
Sir Michael Pollock, GCB, LVO, DSC, *apptd* 1974
Sir Edward Ashmore, GCB, DSC, *apptd* 1977
Sir Henry Leach, GCB, *apptd* 1982
Sir Julian Oswald, GCB, *apptd* 1993
Sir Benjamin Bathurst, GCB, *apptd* 1995

ADMIRALS
Walker, Sir Michael, GCB, CMG, CBE, ADC *(Chief of Defence Staff)*
West, Sir Alan, KCB, DSC *(First Sea Lord and Chief of Naval Staff)*
Forbes, Sir Ian, KCB, CBE *(Deputy Supreme Allied Commander Transformation)*
Band, Sir Jonathon, KCB *(C.-in-C. Fleet, C.-in-C. East Atlantic, and Commander Allied Naval Forces North)*
Garnett, Sir Ian, KCB *(Chief of Staff Supreme Headquarters Allied Powers Europe)*

VICE-ADMIRALS
Haddacks, Sir Paul, KCB *(Director of International Military Staff, NATO)*
Burnell-Nugent, James Michael, CBE, ADC *(Second Sea Lord and C.-in-C. Naval Home Command)*
Dunt, Peter Arthur, CB *(Chief Executive Defence Estate Agency)*
Stanhope, Mark, OBE *(Deputy C.-in-C. Fleet)*
HRH The Prince of Wales, KG, KT, OM, GCB and Great Master of the Order of the Bath, AK, QSO, PC, ADC(P)

REAR-ADMIRALS

HRH The Princess Royal, KG, KT, GCVO *(Chief Commandant for Women in the Royal Navy)*

Davies, Peter Roland, CBE *(Flag Officer Training and Recruiting and Chief Executive, Naval Recruiting and Training Agency)*

Stevens, Robert Patrick, CB *(Chief of Staff to Commander Allied Naval Forces, Southern Europe)*

Kerr, Mark William Graham *(Naval Secretary and Chief Executive, Naval Manning Agency)*

Wood, Michael George, CBE *(Director-General Defence Logistics (Operations))*

Ward, Rees Graham John, CB *(Chief Executive, Defence Communications Services Agency)*

Snelson, David George, *(Commander UK Maritime Forces)*

Guild, Nigel Charles Forbes, CB *(Executive Director 4, Defence Procurement Agency, Controller of the Navy)*

Dymock, Anthony Knox, CB *(Head of British Defence Staff, Washington)*

Reeve, Jonathon, CB *(Deputy Chief Executive, Warship Support Agency and Navy Member for Logistics)*

Harris, Nicholas Henry Linton, MBE *(Flag Officer Scotland, N. England and N. Ireland, and Naval Base Commander Clyde)*

Lockwood, Roger Graham *(Senior Naval Member of the Directing Staff Royal College of Defence Studies)*

McLean, Rory Alistair Ian, OBE *(Asst Chief of the Defence Staff (Resources and Planning))*

McClement, Timothy Pentreath, OBE *(Chief of Staff (Warfare) to C.-in-C. Fleet, Rear-Adm. Surface Ships)*

Lidbetter Scott, *(Air Officer Commanding No.3 Group and Flag Officer Maritime Aviation)*

Kilgour, Niall Stuart Roderick *(Commander (Operations) to C.-in-C. Fleet and Rear-Adm. Submarines)*

Rapp, James Campsie *(Flag Officer Sea Training)*

Style, Charles Rodney, CBE *(Capability Manager (Strategic Deployment), DCDS (ES))*

Edleston, Hugh Anthony Harold Greswell *(Military Adviser to the High Representative in Bosnia and Hercegovina)*

Goodall, Simon Richard James, CBE *(Director-General Training and Education)*

Kidner, Peter Jonathon *(Chief Executive Defence Medical Education and Training Agency)*

Bossier, Robin Paul *(Deputy Commander Strike Force South)*

Cheadle, Richard Frank *(Chief of Staff to Second Sea Lord and C.-in-C. Naval Home Command)*

Johns, Adrian James, CBE *(Assistant Chief of Naval Staff)*

HM Fleet *as at 1 August 2003*

SUBMARINES

Vanguard Class	Vanguard, Vengeance, Victorious, Vigilant
Swiftsure Class	Sceptre, Sovereign, Spartan, Splendid, Superb
Trafalgar Class	Talent, Tireless, Torbay, Trafalgar, Trenchant, Triumph, Turbulent
AIRCRAFT CARRIERS	Ark Royal, Illustrious, Invincible
AMPHIBIOUS ASSAULT SHIP	Ocean, Albion
DESTROYERS	
Type 42 Batch 1	Cardiff, Glasgow, Newcastle
Type 42 Batch 2	Exeter, Liverpool, Nottingham, Southampton

Type 42 Batch 3	Edinburgh, Gloucester, Manchester, York
FRIGATES	
Type 23	Argyll, Iron Duke, Lancaster, Marlborough, Monmouth, Montrose, Norfolk
Type 22	Campbeltown, Chatham, Cornwall, Cumberland
OFFSHORE PATROL	
Castle Class	Dumbarton Castle, Leeds Castle
Island Class	Anglesey, Guernsey, Lindisfarne
MINEHUNTERS	
Hunt Class	Atherstone, Brecon, Brocklesby, Cattistock, Chiddingfold, Cottesmore, Dulverton, Hurworth, Ledbury, Middleton, Quorn
Sandown Class	Bangor, Bridport, Grimsby, Inverness, Pembroke, Penzance, Sandown, Walney, Westminster, Northumberland, Richmond, Somerset, Grafton, Sutherland, Kent, Portland, St Albans
PATROL CRAFT	
Archer Class P2000 Fast Training Boats	Archer, Biter, Blazer, Charger, Dasher, Example, Exploit, Explorer, Express, Puncher, Pursuer, Raider, Smiter, Tracker, Ranger, Trumpeter
SURVEY VESSELS	
Antarctic Patrol Ship	Endurance
Ocean Survey Vessels	Scott
Coastal Survey Vessels	Roebuck, Gleaner
Multi-Role Survey Vessels	HMS Echo, Ramsey, Blyth, Shoreham

OTHER PARTS OF THE NAVAL SERVICE

ROYAL MARINES

The Royal Marines were formed in 1664 and are part of the Naval Service. Their primary purpose is to conduct amphibious and land warfare. The principal operational units are 3 Commando Brigade Royal Marines, an amphibious all-arms brigade trained to operate in arduous environments, which is a core element of the UK's Joint Rapid Reaction Force; Fleet Protection Group Royal Marines, which is responsible for the security of nuclear weapon facilities; and Special Boat Service, the maritime special forces. The Royal Marines also provide detachments for warships and land-based naval parties as required. The headquarters of the Royal Marines is at Portsmouth and principal bases are at Plymouth, Arbroath, Poole, Taunton and Chivenor. The Corps of Royal Marines is about 6,500 strong.

Capability Manager (Information Superiority),
  S. G. G. Dalton

Commandant-General, Royal Marines,
  Maj-Gen. A. A. Milton, OBE

Chief of Staff, NATO Joint Headquarters North,
  Maj.-Gen. D. Wilson, CBE

Director-General, Joint Doctrine and Concepts Centre,
  I. W. McNicoll, CBE

ROYAL MARINES RESERVE (RMR)
The Royal Marines Reserve is a commando-trained volunteer force with the principal role, when mobilised, of supporting the Royal Marines. The current strength of the RMR is about 1,000.
Director, RMR, J. P. C. Hea

ROYAL FLEET AUXILIARY SERVICE (RFA)
The Royal Fleet Auxiliary Service is a civilian-manned flotilla of 19 ships. Its primary role is to supply the Royal Navy at sea with fuel, ammunition, food and stores, enabling it to maintain operations away from its home ports. It also provides secure logistic support and amphibious operations for the Army and Royal Marines, and forward ship maintenance and repair and sea-borne aviation training facilities for the Royal Navy.

FLEET AIR ARM
The Fleet Air Arm (FAA) provides the Royal Navy with a multi-role aviation combat capability able to operate autonomously at short notice world-wide in all environments, over the sea and land. The FAA has some 6200 people, which comprises 11.5 per cent of the total Royal Naval strength. It operates some 200 combat aircraft and more than 50 support/training aircraft.

ROYAL NAVAL RESERVE (RNR)
The Royal Naval Reserve is an integral part of the Naval Service. It comprises up to 3,850 men and women nation-wide who volunteer to train in their spare time to enable the Royal Navy to meet its operational commitments, at sea and ashore, in crisis or war.

The standard annual training commitment is 24 days, including 12 days' continuous operational training.
Director Naval Reserves, Capt. C. G. Massie-Taylor, OBE, RN

QUEEN ALEXANDRA'S ROYAL NAVAL NURSING SERVICE
The first nursing sisters were appointed to naval hospitals in 1884 and the Queen Alexandra's Royal Naval Nursing Service (QARNNS) gained its current title in 1902. Nursing ratings were introduced in 1960 and men were integrated into the Service in 1982.
Patron, HRH Princess Alexandra, the Hon. Lady Ogilvy, GCVO
Matron-in-Chief and Director of Naval Nursing Services, Capt. M. Bowen

THE ARMY

THE QUEEN

FIELD MARSHALS
HRH The Prince Philip, Duke of Edinburgh, KG, KT, OM, GBE, AC, QSO, PC, *apptd* 1953
HRH The Duke of Kent, KG, GCMG, GCVO, ADC, *apptd* 1993
Sir Roland Gibbs, GCB, CBE, DSO, MC, *apptd* 1979
The Lord Bramall, KG, GCB, OBE, MC, *apptd* 1982
The Lord Vincent of Coleshill GBE, KCB, DSO, *apptd* 1991
Sir John Stanier, GCB, MBE, *apptd* 1985
Sir John Chapple, GCB, CBE, *apptd* 1992
The Lord Inge, KG, GCB (Col. Green Howards, Col. Cmdt. APTC), *apptd* 1994

GENERALS
Walker, Sir Michael, GCB, CMG, CBE, ADC Gen *(Chief of the Defence Staff)*
Deverell, Sir John, KCB, OBE, Col. Cmdt. LI, Col. Cmdt. SASC *(C.-in-C. Allied Forces Northern Europe)*
Granville-Chapman, Sir Timothy, KCB, CBE, ADC, Gen *(C-in-C. Land Command)*
Jackson, Sir Mike, KCB, CBE, DSO, ADC, Col. Cmdt. Parachute Regiment, Col. Cmdt. AG Corps, Hon. Col. The Rifle Volunteers *(Chief of the General Staff)*

LIEUTENANT-GENERALS
Irwin, Sir Alistair, KCB, CBE, *(Adjutant-General)*
Delves, C. N. G., CBE, DSO *(Commander Field Army Land Command)*
O'Donoghue, K., CBE *(Deputy Chief of the Defence Staff (Health))*
Reith, J. G., CB, CBE *(Chief of Joint Operations Permanent Joint Headquarters)*
Kiszely J. P., MC *(Commander Regional Forces Land Command)*
Palmer, A. M. D., CBE *(Deputy Chief of the Defence Staff (Personnel))*
Trousdell, P. C. C., CB *(General Officer Commanding Northern Ireland)*
Ridgway, A. P., CBE *(Chief of Defence Intelligence)*
Dannatt, F. R., CBE, MC *(Commander Allied Rapid Reaction Corps)*
HRH The Prince of Wales, KG, KT, GCB and Great Master of the Order of the Bath, OM, QSO, PC, ADC(P)

MAJOR-GENERALS
Searby, R. V., CB *(Senior British Loan Service Officer, Oman)*
Elliott, C. H., CBE, *(Defence Services Secretary)*
Raper, A. J., CBE *(Director-General Strategy and Logistic Development/Quartermaster General)*
Watt, C. R., CBE *(GOC London District and Major General Commanding the Household Division)*
Grant Peterkin, A. P., OBE *(Military Secretary and Chief Executive, Army Personnel Centre)*
Viggers, F. R., MBE *(Deputy Commanding General Joint Task Force 7)*
Moore-Bick, J. D., CBE, *(GOC United Kingdom Support Command Germany)*
Gordon, R. D. S., CBE *(Force Commander UN Mission to Ethiopia and Eritrea)*
Judd, D. L., CB *(GOC 4th Division)*
Brims, R. V., CBE *(Deputy Chief Joint Operations (Operations) Permanent Joint Headquarters)*
Gilchrist, P. *(Executive Director 2, Defence Procurement Agency/Master General of the Ordnance)*
Cross, T., CBE *(Deputy International, Office of Reconstruction and Humanitarian Assistance)*
Figgures, A. C., CBE *(Capability Manager (Manoeuvre))*
Laurie, M. I., CBE, *(Director-General Intelligence Collection)*
McColl, J. C., CBE, DSO *(Commandant Joint Services Command and Staff College)*
Gamon, J. A., CBE, QHDS *(Chief Executive of the Defence Dental Agency)*
Richards, D. J., CBE, DSO *(Assistant Chief to the General Staff)*
Shaw, J. M., MBE *(GOC Theatre Troops Land Command)*
Monro, S. H. R. H., CBE *(Deputy Commander NATO Rapid Deployable Corps (Italy))*
Baxter, R., CBE *(Commandant Royal Military College of Science)*

Ritchie, A.S., CBE *(Commandant Royal Military Academy, Sandhurst)*
Bailey, J. B. A., MBE *(Director-General Development and Doctrine)*
Cima, K. H. *(Senior Army Member, Royal College of Defence Studies)*
Williams, P. G., OBE *(Head of Nato Military Liaison Mission Moscow)*
Short, J. H. T., OBE *(Chief of Staff Joint Headquarters (North))*
Lamb, G. C. M., OBE *(GOC 3rd (UK) Division)*
Rollo, W. R., CBE *(Deputy Adjutant General and Director-General, Service Conditions (Army))*
Leakey, A. D., CBE *(Director-General Army Training and Recruiting)*
Wood, M. D., CBE *(Director-General Defence Supply Chain)*
Huntley, M. *(Director-General Equipment Support (Land))*
Wall, P. A., CBE *(GOC 1st (UK) Armoured Division)*
Parker, N. R., CBE *(GOC 2nd Division)*
Cottam, N. J., OBE *(GOC 5th Division)*
Shirreff, A. R. D., CBE *(Chief of Staff Land Command)*
Duncan, A. D. A., DSO, OBE *(Director-General Training Support (Land))*
Cumming, A. A. J. R., CBE *(Kosovo Protection Corps Co-ordinator)*
Houghton, J. N. R., CBE *(Chief of Staff Allied Rapid Reaction Corps)*
Pearson, P. T. C., CBE (*Deputy Commander Operations SFOR)*
Howell, D. M., OBE *(Director Army Legal Services)*
Lillywhite, L. P., MBE, QHS *(Director-General Army Medical Services)*
Blackburn, Ven J., QHC *(Chaplain General)*

CONSTITUTION OF THE ARMY

The regular forces include the following arms, branches and corps. They are listed in accordance with the order of precedence within the British Army. All enquiries with regard to records of serving personnel (Regular and Territorial Army) should be directed to: Relations with the Public, Army Personnel Office, Kentigern House, 65 Brown Street, Glasgow G2 8EX. Tel: 0141-224 2023/3303.

THE ARMS
HOUSEHOLD CAVALRY – The Household Cavalry Regiment (The Life Guards and The Blues and Royals)
ROYAL ARMOURED CORPS – Cavalry Regiments: 1st The Queen's Dragoon Guards; The Royal Scots Dragoon Guards (Carabiniers and Greys); The Royal Dragoon Guards; The Queen's Royal Hussars (The Queen's Own and Royal Irish); 9th/12th Royal Lancers (Prince of Wales's); The King's Royal Hussars; The Light Dragoons; The Queen's Royal Lancers; Royal Tank Regiment, comprising two regular regiments
ARTILLERY – Royal Regiment of Artillery
ENGINEERS – Corps of Royal Engineers
SIGNALS – Royal Corps of Signals

THE INFANTRY
The Foot Guards and regiments of Infantry of the Line are grouped in divisions as follows:

GUARDS DIVISION – Grenadier, Coldstream, Scots, Irish and Welsh Guards. *Divisional Office,* HQ Infantry, Warminster Training Centre, Warminster, Wilts. *Training Centre,* Infantry Training Centre, Vimy Barracks, Catterick, N. Yorks
SCOTTISH DIVISION – The Royal Scots (The Royal Regiment); The Royal Highland Fusiliers (Princess Margaret's Own Glasgow and Ayrshire Regiment); The King's Own Scottish Borderers; The Black Watch (Royal Highland Regiment); The Highlanders (Seaforth, Gordons and Camerons); The Argyll and Sutherland Highlanders (Princess Louise's). *Divisional Office,* HQ Infantry, Warminster Training Centre, Warminster, Wilts. *Training Centre,* Infantry Training Centre, Vimy Barracks, Catterick, N. Yorks
QUEEN'S DIVISION – The Princess of Wales's Royal Regiment (Queen's and Royal Hampshire's); The Royal Regiment of Fusiliers; The Royal Anglian Regiment. *Divisional Office,* HQ Infantry, Warminster Training Centre, Warminster, Wilts. *Training Centre,* Infantry Training Centre, Vimy Barracks, Catterick, N. Yorks
KING'S DIVISION – The King's Own Royal Border Regiment; The King's Regiment; The Prince of Wales's Own Regiment of Yorkshire; The Green Howards (Alexandra, Princess of Wales's Own Yorkshire Regiment); The Queen's Lancashire Regiment; The Duke of Wellington's Regiment (West Riding). *Divisional Office,* HQ Infantry, Warminster Training Centre, Warminster, Wilts. Training Centre, Infantry Training Centre, Vimy Barracks, Catterick, N. Yorks
PRINCE OF WALES'S DIVISION – The Devonshire and Dorset Regiment; The Cheshire Regiment; The Royal Welch Fusiliers; The Royal Regiment of Wales (24th/41st Foot); The Royal Gloucestershire, Berkshire and Wiltshire Regiment; The Worcestershire and Sherwood Foresters Regiment (29th/45th Foot); The Staffordshire Regiment (The Prince of Wales's). Divisional Office, HQ Infantry, Warminster Training Centre, Warminster, Wilts. Training Centre, Infantry Training Centre, Vimy Barracks, Catterick, N. Yorks
LIGHT DIVISION – The Light Infantry; The Royal Green Jackets. *Divisional Office,* HQ Infantry, Warminster Training Centre, Warminster, Wilts. *Training Centre,* Infantry Training Centre, Vimy Barracks, Catterick, N. Yorks
THE ROYAL IRISH REGIMENT (one general service and three home service battalions) (27th (Inniskilling), 83rd, 87th and the Ulster Defence Regiment). *Regimental HQ and Training Centre,* St Patrick's Barracks, BFPO 808
BRIGADE OF GURKHAS – The Royal Gurkha Rifles; The Queen's Gurkha Engineers; Queen's Gurkha Signals; The Queen's Own Gurkha Logistic Regiment. *Regimental HQ,* Airfield Camp, Netheravon, Wilts. *Gurkha Company,* Infantry Training Centre, Vimy Barracks, Catterick, N. Yorks
THE PARACHUTE REGIMENT (three regular battalions) – Regimental HQ, Flagstaff House, Colchester, Essex. Training Centre, Infantry Training Centre, Vimy Barracks, Catterick, N. Yorks
SPECIAL AIR SERVICE REGIMENT – Stirling Lines, Hereford
ARMY AIR CORPS – *Regimental HQ and Training Centre,* Middle Wallop, Stockbridge, Hants

SERVICES

Royal Army Chaplains' Department – *Regimental HQ,* HQ AG, Upavon, Pewsey, Wilts. *Training Centre,* Armed Forces Chaplaincy Centre, Amport House, Amport, Andover, Hants

The Royal Logistic Corps – *Regimental HQ,* Blackdown Barracks, Deepcut, Camberley, Surrey. *Training Centre,* Princess Royal Barracks, Deepcut, Camberley, Surrey

Royal Army Medical Corps – *Regimental HQ,* former Army Staff College, Slim Road, Camberley, Surrey and *Training Centre,* Defence Medical Services Keogh Barracks, Ash Vale, Aldershot, Hants

Corps of Royal Electrical and Mechanical Engineers – *Regimental HQ* and *Training Centre,* Hazebrouck Barracks, Isaac Newton Road, Arborfield, Reading, Berks

Adjutant-General's Corps – Staff and Personnel Support Branch (SPS), Provost Branch (Royal Military Police and Military Provost Staff Corps (RMP and MPS), Educational and Training Services Branch (ETS), Army Legal Services Branch (ALS), Regimental HQ, Worthy Down, Winchester, Hants. *Training Centres,* SPS and ETS Worthy Down, Winchester, Hants; RMP and MPS, Roussillon Barracks, Chichester, West Sussex.

Royal Army Veterinary Corps – *Regimental HQ,* former Army Staff College, Slim Road, Camberley, Surrey, *Training Centre,* Defence Animal Centre, Melton Mowbray, Leics.

Royal Army Dental Corps – *Regimental HQ,* former Army Staff College, Slim Road, Camberley, Surrey, *Training Centre,* Evelyn Woods Road, Aldershot, Hants

Intelligence Corps – *Directorate HQ* and *Training Centre,* Chicksands, Shefford, Beds

Army Physical Training Corps – *Regimental HQ,* Trenchard Lines, Upavon, Pewsey, Wilts, *Training Centre,* Army School of Physical Training, Fox Lines, Queen's Avenue, Aldershot, Hants

Queen Alexandra's Royal Army Nursing Corps – *Regimental HQ,* former Army Staff College, Slim Road, Camberley, *Training Centres,* Army Nursing Training is carried out at Universities of Birmingham and Portsmouth

Corps of Army Music – *Directorate HQ* and *Training Centre,* Army School of Music, Kneller Hall, Kneller Road, Twickenham, Middx

ARMY EQUIPMENT

HOLDINGS *as at August 2002*

Tanks	386
Armoured combat vehicles	2,978
Artillery pieces	302
Landing craft	8
Helicopters	296

THE TERRITORIAL ARMY (TA)

The Territorial Army provides formed units and individuals as an essential part of the Army's order of battle for operations across all military tasks in order to ensure that the Army is capable of mounting and sustaining operations at nominated states of readiness. It also provides a basis for regeneration, while at the same time maintaining links with the local community and society at large. From 1 December 2002 its established strength has been 41,893.

Inspector-General, Lt.-Gen. J. P. Kiszely, MC

QUEEN ALEXANDRA'S ROYAL ARMY NURSING CORPS

The Queen Alexandra's Royal Army Nursing Corps (QARANC) was founded in 1902 as Queen Alexandra's Imperial Military Nursing Service (QAIMNS) and gained its present title in 1949. The QARANC has trained nurses for the register since 1950 and also trains and employs Health Care Assistants to Level 3 NVQ.

Director of Army Nursing Services (DANS) and Matron in Chief Army, Col. K. George

THE ROYAL AIR FORCE

THE QUEEN

MARSHALS OF THE ROYAL AIR FORCE

HRH The Prince Philip, Duke of Edinburgh, KG, KT, OM, GBE, AC, QSO, PC, *apptd* 1953

Sir John Grandy, GCB, GCVO, KBE, DSO, *apptd* 1971

Sir Michael Beetham, GCB, CBE, DFC, AFC, *apptd* 1982

Sir Keith Williamson, GCB, AFC, *apptd* 1985

The Lord Craig of Radley, GCB, OBE, *apptd* 1988

AIR CHIEF MARSHALS

HRH Princess Alice, Duchess of Gloucester, GCB, CI, GCVO, GBE

Stirrup, Sir Jock, KCB, AFC, ADC *(Chief of the Air Staff)*

Bagnall, Sir Anthony, KCB, GBE *(Vice Chief of Defence Staff)*

Burridge, Brian, CBE *(C.-in-C. RAF Strike Command)*

Pledger, Sir Malcolm, KCB, OBE, AFC *(Chief of Defence Logistics)*

AIR MARSHALS

Goodall, Sir Roderick, KBE, CB, AFC *(Chief of Staff, Component Command Air North)*

French, Sir Joe, CBE, KCB *(Air Member for Personnel and C.-in-C. Personnel and Training Command)*

Torpy, Glenn *(Deputy C.-in-C. RAF Strike Command)*

Wright, R. A., AFC *(UK Military Representative to NATO and the EU)*

HRH The Prince of Wales, KG, KT, GCB and Great Master of the Order of the Bath, OM, QSO, PC, ADC(P)

AIR VICE-MARSHALS

Thompson, J. H., CB *(Director-General, Saudi Arabia Armed Forces Project)*

Stewart, I. M., CB, AFC *(Air Secretary and Chief Executive, RAF Personnel Management Agency)*

Sturley, P. O., CB, MBE *(Assistant Chief of the Air Staff)*

Rimmer, T. W., CB, OBE *(Commander British Forces Cyprus)*

Couzens, D. C. *(Senior Directing Staff (Air), Royal College of Defence Studies)*

Scott, P. J., CB *(Air Officer Commanding Logistics and Communications Information Systems)*

Vallance, A. G. B., CB, OBE *(Executive Assistant Chief of Staff Command Structure Implementation, SHAPE)*

Thornton, B. M. *(Director-General Equipment Support (Air))*

Walker, P. B., CBE *(Assistant Chief of Staff Policy and Requirements, SHAPE)*

Hobart, D. A. *(Assistant Chief of the Defence Staff (Policy))*

Day, N. J., CBE *(Capability Manager (Strike) MOD)*

Willis, G. E. *(Director Projects)*

Miller, G. A., CBE *(Air Officer Commanding Training Group)*

Robinson, P. A., OBE *(Deputy Chief of Joint Operations (Operational Support), PJHQ)*

Jones, G., CBE, MBE *(Assistant Chief of Staff (Resources), Regional Headquarters, Allied Forces Southern Europe)*

McNicoll, I. W., CBE *(Director-General Joint Doctrine and Concepts Centre)*

Smith, A. J., OBE *(Director-General Operations, Defence Logistics Organisation)*

Maddox, N. D. A., CBE *(Air Officer Commanding No 2 Group)*

White, A. D., *(Air Officer Commanding No 3 Group)*

Loader, C. R., *(Assistant Chief of Defence Staff (Operations))*

Luker, P. D., OBE, AFC *(Commander Joint Helicopter Command)*

Collier, J. A., CBE *(Chief of Staff, Headquarters Personnel and Training Command)*

Pocock, D. J., *(Head of Personnel Change Programme, MOD)*

Dalton, S. G. G., *(Capability Manager (Information Superiority), MOD)*

Moore, R. C., MBE *(Air Officer Administration, RAF Personnel and Training Command)*

Cliffe, J. A., *(Deputy Chief of Staff (Operations), RAF Strike Command)*

Williams, D. N., OBE *(Executive Director 3, Defence Procurement Agency)*

Peach, S. W., CBE *(Director-General Intelligence Collection, MOD)*

Charles, R. A., *(Director Legal Services, RAF)*

Pike, W. J., QHP *(Director-General, Medical Services (RAF))*

R. D. Hesketh, The Ven. *(Chaplain-in-Chief to the Royal Air Force) (Holds rank relative to Air Vice-Marshal)*

CONSTITUTION OF THE ROYAL AIR FORCE

The RAF consists of two commands, Strike Command and Personnel and Training Command.

Strike Command is responsible for all the RAF's front line forces. Restructured on 1 April 2000, the Command consists of three groups each organised around specific operational duties. No 1 Group comprises the tactical fast jet forces responsible for attack, offensive support and air defence operations. No 2 Group provides the overarching enabling forces – Air Transport and Air Refuelling – and it includes the RAF Regiment and air combat support units. No 3 Group is the Air Battle management group and it includes Airborne Early Warning, Maritime Patrol, and Search and Rescue aircraft.

Personnel and Training Command (PTC), created on 1 April 1994, is responsible for all aspects of recruiting, training, career management, welfare, conditions of service, and resettlement of RAF regular and reserve forces. Two Agencies form an integral part of PTC. The RAF Training Group Defence Agency deals with the recruitment and selection of all RAF personnel and delivery of RAF non-operational flying and ground training, whilst the RAF Personnel Management Agency (RAF PMA), is responsible for the management of the careers of uniformed personnel serving in the Regular and Reserve Air Forces, and posts and deploys personnel to meet the Services military tasks in times of war, crisis and peace.

RAF EQUIPMENT *as at 1 April 2003*[*]
AIRCRAFT

Tornado	203
Harrier	60
Jaguar	46
Canberra	5
Nimrod	23
VC10	18
Tristar	8
Hercules	44
C17 Globemaster	4
BAe 125	5
BAe 146	2
Sentry E-3D	6
Hawk	99
Dominie	9
Islander	1
Jetstream	11
Tucano	67

HELICOPTERS

Chinook	34
Puma	33
Sea King	21
Gazelle	1
Merlin	22
Squirrel	31
Griffin	14

BATTLE OF BRITAIN MEMORIAL FLIGHT

Lancaster	1
Hurricane	2
Spitfire	5
Dakota	1
Chipmunk	2

[*] All figures shown relate to the Required Operating Fleet. The actual number of aircraft will, in many cases, vary from the figure given due to reasons such as operational commitments and engineering programmes.

ROYAL AUXILIARY AIR FORCE (RAuxAF)

The Auxiliary Air Force was formed in 1924 to train an elite corps of civilians to serve their country in flying Squadrons in their spare time. In 1947 the Force was awarded the prefix 'Royal' in recognition of its distinguished war service and The Sovereign's Colour for the Royal Auxiliary Air Force was presented in 1989.

Air Commodore-in-Chief, HM The Queen

Honorary Inspector-General Royal Auxiliary Air Force,
AVM. B. H. Newton, CB, CVO, OBE

Inspector Royal Auxiliary Air Force,
Gp. Capt. R. G. Kemp, QVRM, AE, ADC

PRINCESS MARY'S ROYAL AIR FORCE NURSING SERVICE

The Princess Mary's Royal Air Force Nursing Service (PMRAFNS) was formed on 1st June 1918 as the Royal Air Force Nursing Service. In June 1923, His Majesty King George V gave his Royal Assent for the Royal Air Force Nursing Service to be known as the Princess Mary's Royal Air Force Nursing Service. Men were integrated into the PMRAFNS in 1980 and now serve as officers and other ranks.

Patron and Air Chief Commandant,
HRH Princess Alexandra, the Hon. Lady Ogilvy, GCVO

Director of Nursing Services and Matron-in-Chief,
Gp Capt. R. A. Reid, OBE, ARRC, QHNS

SERVICE SALARIES

The following rates of pay apply from 1 April 2003.

The pay rates shown are for Army personnel. The rates apply also to personnel of equivalent rank and pay band in the other services (*see* below for table of relative ranks).

Rank	Daily	Annual
Second Lieutenant	£55.12	£20,173.92
Lieutenant		
On appointment	£66.25	£24,247.50
After 1 year in rank	£68.00	£24,888.00
After 2 years in rank	£69.74	£25,524.84
After 3 years in rank	£71.48	£26,161.68
After 4 years in rank	£73.22	£26,798.52
Captain		
On appointment	£84.89	£31,069.74
After 1 year in rank	£87.17	£31,904.22
After 2 years in rank	£89.47	£32,746.02
After 3 years in rank	£91.78	£33,591.48
After 4 years in rank	£94.07	£34,429.62
After 5 years in rank	£96.37	£35,271.42
After 6 years in rank	£98.66	£36,109.56
After 7 years in rank	£99.82	£36,534.12
After 8 years in rank	£100.96	£36,951.36
Major		
On appointment	£106.94	£39,140.04
After 1 year in rank	£109.58	£40,106.28
After 2 years in rank	£112.21	£41,068.86
After 3 years in rank	£114.86	£42,038.76
After 4 years in rank	£117.50	£43,005.00
After 5 years in rank	£120.15	£43,974.90
After 6 years in rank	£122.79	£44,941.14
After 7 years in rank	£125.43	£45,907.38
After 8 years in rank	£128.07	£46,873.62

Rank	Daily	Annual
Lieutenant-Colonel		
On appointment	£150.09	£54,932.94
After 1 year in rank	£152.08	£55,661.28
After 2 years in rank	£154.06	£56,385.96
After 3 years in rank	£156.02	£57,103.32
After 4 years in rank	£158.00	£57,828.00
After 5 years in rank	£159.97	£58,549.02
After 6 years in rank	£161.95	£59,273.70
After 7 years in rank	£163.92	£59,994.72
After 8 years in rank	£165.91	£60,723.06
Colonel		
On appointment	£173.81	£63,614.46
After 1 year in rank	£176.10	£64,452.60
After 2 years in rank	£178.39	£65,290.74
After 3 years in rank	£180.67	£66,125.22
After 4 years in rank	£182.96	£66,963.36
After 5 years in rank	£185.24	£67,797.84
After 6 years in rank	£187.52	£68,632.32
After 7 years in rank	£189.82	£69,474.12
After 8 years in rank	£192.11	£70,312.26
Brigadier		
On appointment	£208.48	£76,303.68
After 1 year in rank	£210.70	£77,116.20
After 2 years in rank	£212.92	£77,928.72
After 3 years in rank	£215.14	£78,741.24
After 4 years in rank	£217.37	£79,557.42

PERFORMANCE MANAGEMENT AND PAY SYSTEM FOR SENIOR MILITARY OFFICERS

Revised pay rates effective from 1 April 2003 for all military officers of 2* rank and above (excluding medical and dental officers). Officers enter relevant scale at scale points, provided they have served a minimum of 6 months in rank and, subject to satisfactory performance, become eligible for an incremental award on 1 April of each year.

MAJOR-GENERAL (2*)

Scale 1	£232.72	£85,174
Scale 2	£237.37	£86,877
Scale 3	£242.02	£88,580
Scale 4	£246.68	£90,284
Scale 5	£251.33	£91,986
Scale 6	£255.98	£93,690
Scale 7	£260.63	£95,392

LIEUTENANT-GENERAL (3*)

Scale 1	£271.70	£99,443
Scale 2	£278.49	£101,927
Scale 3	£285.28	£104,412
Scale 4	£292.06	£106,895
Scale 5	£298.85	£109,379
Scale 6	£305.64	£111,863
Scale 7	n/a	n/a

GENERAL (4*)

Scale 1	£334.57	£122,453
Scale 2	£343.25	£125,628
Scale 3	£351.92	£128,804
Scale 4	£360.60	£131,980
Scale 5	£369.28	£135,156
Scale 6	£377.96	£138,332
Scale 7	n/a	n/a

Field Marshal – appointments to this rank will not usually be made in peace time. The salary for holders of the rank is equivalent to the salary of a 5-Star General, a salary created only in times of war. In peace time, the equivalent rank to Field Marshal is the Chief of the Defence Staff. From 1 April 2003, the annual salary for the Chief of the Defence Staff is £182,005.

SALARIES OF OFFICERS COMMISSIONED FROM THE SENIOR RANKS *as at 1 April 2003*

Rank	Daily	Annual
Level 15	£113.48	£41,533.68
Level 14	£112.73	£41,259.18
Level 13	£111.96	£40,977.36
Level 12	£110.44	£40,421.04
Level 11	£108.94	£39,872.04
Level 10	£107.42	£39,315.72
Level 9	£105.90	£38,759.40
Level 8	£104.39	£38,206.74
Level 7*	£102.50	£37,515.00
Level 6	£101.33	£37,086.78
Level 5	£100.16	£36,658.56
Level 4**	£97.81	£35,798.46
Level 3	£96.65	£35,373.90
Level 2	£95.47	£34,942.02
Level 1***	£93.13	£34,085.58

*Minimum entry point for SUY, SCCs and LEs with over 15 years' service
**Minimum entry point for SUY, SCCs and LEs with between 12–15 years' service
***Minimum entry point for SUY, SCCs and LEs with under 12 years' service

SOLDIERS' SALARIES

The pay structure below officer level is divided into pay bands. Jobs at each rank are allocated to bands according to their score in the job evaluation system. Length of service is from age 18.

Scale A: committed to serve for less than 6 years, or those with less than 9 years' service who are serving on Open Engagement

Scale B: committed to serve for 6 years but less than 9 years

Scale C: committed to serve for 9 years or more, or those with more than 9 years' service who are serving on Open Engagement

Rates of pay effective from 1 April 2003 are:

	Lower Band		Higher Band	
	Daily	Annual	Daily	Annual
Private				
Level 1	£35.74	£13,080.84	£35.74	£13,080.84
Level 2	£37.84	£13,849.44	£41.07	£15,031.62
Level 3	£39.93	£14,614.38	£45.34	£16,594.44
Level 4	£43.44	£15,899.04	£48.75	£17,842.50
Lance Corporal (levels 5–7 also applicable to Privates)				
Level 5	£45.77	£16,751.82	£53.91	£19,731.06
Level 6	£47.68	£17,450.88	£56.53	£20,689.98
Level 7	£49.73	£18,201.18	£59.12	£21,637.92
Level 8	£52.01	£19,035.66	£61.78	£22,611.48
Level 9	£53.89	£19,723.74	£64.80	£23,716.80

	Lower Band		Higher Band	
	Daily	Annual	Daily	Annual
Corporal				
Level 1	£59.12	£21,637.92	£61.78	£22,611.48
Level 2	£61.78	£22,611.48	£64.80	£23,716.80
Level 3	£64.80	£23,716.80	£67.97	£24,877.02
Level 4	£65.30	£23,899.80	£69.55	£25,455.30
Level 5	£65.81	£24,086.46	£71.24	£26,073.84
Level 6	£66.32	£24,273.12	£72.71	£26,611.86
Level 7	£66.82	£24,456.12	£74.30	£27,193.80

	Lower Band		Higher Band	
	Daily	Annual	Daily	Annual
Sergeant				
Level 1	£67.21	£24,598.86	£73.35	£26,846.10
Level 2	£68.96	£25,239.36	£75.24	£27,537.84
Level 3	£70.69	£25,872.54	£77.15	£28,236.90
Level 4	£71.41	£26,136.06	£78.12	£28,591.92
Level 5	£73.27	£26,816.82	£79.64	£29,148.24
Level 6	£75.80	£27,742.80	£81.17	£29,708.22
Level 7	£76.37	£27,951.42	£82.68	£30,260.88

	Lower Band		Higher Band	
	Daily	Annual	Daily	Annual
Staff Sergeant				
Level 1	£74.40	£27,230.40	£82.74	£30,282.84
Level 2	£75.37	£27,585.42	£84.75	£31,018.50
Level 3	£77.81	£28,478.46	£86.76	£31,754.16
Level 4	£79.63	£29,144.58	£88.77	£32,489.82
Warrant Officer II				
(levels 5–7 also applicable to staff Sergeants)				
Level 5	£80.72	£29,543.52	£90.80	£33,232.80
Level 6	£84.37	£30,879.42	£92.80	£33,964.80
Level 7	£85.66	£31,351.56	£94.14	£34,455.24
Level 8	£86.76	£31,754.16	£95.49	£34,949.34
Level 9	£88.73	£32,475.18	£96.84	£35,443.44

	Lower Band		Higher Band	
	Daily	Annual	Daily	Annual
Warrant Officer I				
Level 1	£86.42	£31,629.72	£94.22	£34,484.52
Level 2	£88.10	£32,244.60	£96.08	£35,165.28
Level 3	£89.88	£32,896.08	£97.73	£35,769.18
Level 4	£91.66	£33,547.56	£99.52	£36,424.32
Level 5	£93.45	£34,202.70	£101.30	£37,075.80
Level 6	£96.08	£35,165.28	£103.10	£37,734.60
Level 7	£98.78	£36,153.48	£104.68	£38,312.88

RELATIVE RANK – ARMED FORCES

Royal Navy	Army	Royal Air Force
1 Admiral of the Fleet	1 Field Marshal	1 Marshal of the RAF
2 Admiral (Adm.)	2 General (Gen.)	2 Air Chief Marshal
3 Vice-Admiral (Vice-Adm.)	3 Lieutenant-General (Lt.-Gen.)	3 Air Marshal
4 Rear-Admiral (Rear-Adm.)	4 Major-General (Maj.-Gen.)	4 Air Vice-Marshal
5 Commodore (Cdre)	5 Brigadier (Brig.)	5 Air Commodore (Air Cdre)
6 Captain (Capt.)	6 Colonel (Col.)	6 Group Captain (Gp Capt.)
7 Commander (Cdr.)	7 Lieutenant-Colonel (Lt.-Col.)	7 Wing Commander (Wg Cdr.)
8 Lieutenant-Commander (Lt.-Cdr.)	8 Major (Maj.)	8 Squadron Leader (Sqn Ldr)
9 Lieutenant (Lt.)	9 Captain (Capt.)	9 Flight Lieutenant (Flt. Lt.)
10 Sub-Lieutenant (Sub-Lt.)	10 Lieutenant (Lt.)	10 Flying Officer (FO)
11 Acting Sub-Lieutenant (Acting Sub-Lt.)	11 Second Lieutenant (2nd Lt.)	11 Pilot Officer (PO)

SERVICE RETIRED PAY *on compulsory retirement*

Those who leave the services having served at least five years, but not long enough to qualify for the appropriate immediate pension, now qualify for a preserved pension and terminal grant, both of which are payable at age 60. The tax-free resettlement grants shown below are payable on release to those who qualify for a preserved pension and who have completed nine years service from age 21 (officers) or 12 years from age 18 (other ranks)

The annual rates for army personnel are given. The rates apply also to personnel of equivalent rank in the other services, including the nursing services.

OFFICERS
Applicable to officers who give full pay service on the active list on or after 31 March 2003. Pensionable earnings for senior officers (*) is defined as the total amount of basic pay received during the year ending on the day prior to retirement, or the amount of basic pay received during any 12 month period within 3 years prior to retirement, whichever is the higher. Figures for Senior Officers are percentage rates of pensionable earnings on final salary arrangements on or after 31 March 2002.

No. of years reckonable service over age 21	Capt. and below	Major	Lt.-Col.	Colonel	Brigadier	Major-General*	Lieutenant-General*	General*
16	£10,291	£12,256	£16,070	£18,608	£22,210	–	–	–
17	£10,766	£12,838	£16,813	£19,469	£23,076	–	–	–
18	£11,240	£13,421	£17,557	£20,329	£23,941	–	–	–
19	£11,714	£14,003	£18,300	£21,190	£24,807	–	–	–
20	£12,188	£14,585	£19,043	£22,051	£25,673	–	–	–
21	£12,663	£15,167	£19,787	£22,912	£26,539	–	–	–
22	£13,137	£15,749	£20,530	£23,772	£27,405	–	–	–
23	£13,611	£16,331	£21,274	£24,633	£28,271	–	–	–
24	£14,086	£16,913	£22,017	£25,494	£29,137	38.5%	–	–
25	£14,560	£17,495	£22,760	£26,355	£30,003	39.7%	–	–
26	£15,034	£18,077	£23,504	£27,215	£30,868	40.8%	–	–
27	£15,508	£18,659	£24,247	£28,076	£31,734	42.0%	42.0%	–
28	£15,983	£19,241	£24,990	£28,937	£32,600	43.1%	43.1%	–
29	£16,457	£19,823	£25,734	£29,798	£33,466	44.3%	44.3%	–
30	£16,931	£20,405	£26,477	£30,658	£34,332	45.4%	45.4%	45.4%
31	£17,406	£20,987	£27,221	£31,519	£35,198	46.6%	46.6%	46.6%
32	£17,880	£21,570	£27,964	£32,380	£36,064	47.7%	47.7%	47.7%
33	£18,354	£22,152	£28,707	£33,241	£36,930	48.9%	48.9%	48.9%
34	£18,828	£22,734	£29,451	£34,101	£37,795	50.0%	50.0%	50.0%

WARRANT OFFICERS, NCOS AND PRIVATES

Applicable to soldiers who give full pay service on or after 31 March 2003.

No. of years reckonable service	Below Corporal	Corporal	Sergeant	Staff Sergeant	Warrant Officer Level II	Warrant Officer Level I
22	£6,071	£7,856	£8,612	£9,810	£10,321	£11,137
23	£6,283	£8,130	£8,913	£10,152	£10,681	£11,526
24	£6,494	£8,404	£9,214	£10,495	£11,041	£11,915
25	£6,706	£8,678	£9,514	£10,837	£11,402	£12,303
26	£6,918	£8,952	£9,815	£11,180	£11,762	£12,692
27	£7,130	£9,227	£10,115	£11,522	£12,122	£13,081
28	£7,342	£9,501	£10,416	£11,865	£12,482	£13,470
29	£7,554	£9,775	£10,717	£12,207	£12,843	£13,858
30	£7,766	£10,049	£11,017	£12,549	£13,203	£14,247
31	£7,978	£10,323	£11,318	£12,892	£13,563	£14,636
32	£8,190	£10,598	£11,618	£13,234	£13,923	£15,024
33	£8,402	£10,872	£11,919	£13,577	£14,284	£15,413
34	£8,613	£11,146	£12,220	£13,919	£14,644	£15,802
35	£8,825	£11,420	£12,520	£14,262	£15,004	£16,191
36	£9,037	£11,694	£12,821	£14,604	£15,364	£16,579
37	£9,249	£11,969	£13,122	£14,946	£15,725	£16,968

RESETTLEMENT GRANTS

Terminal grants are in each case three times the rate of retired pay or pension. There are special rates of retired pay for certain other ranks not shown above. Lower rates are payable in cases of voluntary retirement.

A gratuity of £3,380 is payable for officers with short service commissions for each year completed. Resettlement grants are: officers £11,631; non-commissioned ranks £7,857.

EDUCATION

Responsibility for education in England lies with the Secretary of State for Education and Skills; in Wales, with the Minister for Education and Lifelong Learning; in Scotland, with Scottish Ministers; and in Northern Ireland with the Education Minister and the Minister for Employment and Learning.

The main concerns of the education departments are the formulation of national policies for education and the maintenance of consistency in educational standards. They are responsible for the broad allocation of resources for education, for the rate and distribution of educational buildings and for the supply, training and superannuation of teachers. In England, the Teacher Training Agency is responsible for recruitment into the profession.

EXPENDITURE

In the UK in 2001–2, total managed expenditure on education was:

	2001–2 outturn £m	2002–3 estimated outturn £m
Under fives	2,844	3,106
Schools	29,055	30,982
Further education	7,266	7,965
Higher education	5,969	6,277
Student support	1,502	1,861
Miscellaneous services, research and administration	2,718	3,381
TOTAL	49,354	53,572

Total managed expenditure on education in real terms from 1993–4 to 2002–3 was:

	£bn		£bn
1993–4	40.5	1998–9	41.9
1994–5	41.9	1999–2000	42.9
1995–6	41.7	2000–1	45.3
1996–7	41.4	2001–2	49.4
1997–8	41.3	2002–3 (estimated)	52.0

Most of this expenditure, except that for higher and further education in England, Wales and Scotland (which is met by the respective funding agencies), is incurred by local authorities, which make their own expenditure decisions according to their local situations and needs. Expenditure on education by central government and local authorities in the UK was:

	2001–2 outturn £m	2002–3 estimated outturn £m
Central government	15,497	17,395
Local authorities	30,799	32,715

Planned central government expenditure on education is:

	£m
2003–4	18,849
2004–5	20,339
2005–6	21,743

The following table shows total managed expenditure on education as a percentage of GDP:

	%
2000–1 outturn	4.6
2001–2 outturn	4.9
2002–3 estimated outturn	5.1

The bulk of direct expenditure by the DfES, the National Assembly for Wales and the Scottish Executive is directed towards supporting higher education in universities and colleges through the Higher Education Funding Councils (HEFCs). Funding for further education and, in England and Wales, sixth form colleges, is channelled through the funding councils for that sector and, in Wales, through the National Council-ELWA. In addition, the DfES currently funds student support in England and Wales (although Wales will be taking over responsibility for student support in Wales at a future date, still to be agreed), the City Technology Colleges, the City College for the Technology of the Arts, and pays grants under the specialist schools programme.

In Wales the National Assembly also funds curriculum development, educational services and research, and supports bilingual education. In Scotland the main elements of central government expenditure, in addition to those outlined above, are grant-aided special schools, student awards and bursaries (through the Student Awards Agency for Scotland), teachers, curriculum development, special educational needs and community education. In Northern Ireland the Department of Education also administers the teachers' superannuation scheme, pays teachers' salaries and funds grant-maintained integrated and voluntary grammar schools. The Department for Employment and Learning directly funds higher education, student awards and further education.

LOCAL EDUCATION ADMINISTRATION

In England and Wales the education service is administered by local education authorities (LEAs), which have day-to-day responsibility for providing most state primary and secondary education in their areas. They share with the appropriate funding bodies the duty to provide adult education to meet local needs.

The LEAs own and maintain most schools and some colleges, build new ones and provide equipment. LEAs are financed largely from the council tax and aggregate external finance from the Office of the Deputy Prime Minister in England and the National Assembly for Wales.

LEA-maintained schools usually manage their own budgets. The LEA allocates funds to the school, largely on the basis of pupil numbers, and the school governing body is responsible for overseeing spending and for most aspects of staffing, including appointments and dismissals. LEAs also have intervention powers to add additional governors, take back a school's delegated budget or replace the governing body of a school with an interim executive when a school is placed in special measures, is judged to have serious weaknesses or is causing concern and has not complied with a formal warning from the LEA.

The duty of providing education locally in Scotland rests with the education authorities. They are responsible for the construction of buildings, the employment of teachers and other staff, and the provision of equipment and materials. Devolved School Management is in place for all primary, secondary and special schools. Education authorities are required to establish school boards consisting of parents and teachers as well as co-opted members, responsible, among other things, for the appointment of staff.

The Standards in Scotland Schools etc. Act 2000 set out a School Improvement Framework which gives strategic direction to school education through five National Priorities in Education. These define the outcomes that education authorities and their schools have to deliver for young people. The national priorities cover: attainment and achievement; framework for learning; inclusion and equality; values and citizenship; and learning for life.

Education is administered locally in Northern Ireland by five education and library boards, which fund controlled and maintained schools and whose costs are met in full by the Northern Ireland Executive. All grant-aided schools include elected parents and teachers on their boards of governors. Provision has been made for schools wishing to provide integrated education to have grant-maintained integrated status, funded directly by the Department of Education. All schools and colleges of further education have full responsibility for their own budgets, including staffing costs.

THE INSPECTORATE

ENGLAND
The Office for Standards in Education (Ofsted) is a non-ministerial government department in England headed by HM Chief Inspector of Schools (HMCI). Ofsted's remit is to help improve the quality and standards of childcare through regular independent inspection and regulation. It must also provide advice to the Secretary of State based on inspection evidence. Ofsted must report on all maintained schools in England, local education authorities (supported by the Audit Commission), initial teacher training courses, the private, voluntary and independent nursery sector (including childminders and day-care establishments), independent schools, (including independent special schools), youth services, service children's education, and all education and training for ages 16–19 in sixth form and further education colleges. Ofsted also reports on the impact of government initiatives such as the national numeracy and literacy strategies.

A new inspection framework, Framework 2003 – Inspecting Schools, came into effect in September 2003. Schools are inspected at least once every six years.

There are 252 HMIs, 1,020 childcare inspectors and 24 area divisional managers on Ofsted's permanent staff.

WALES
Estyn: Arolygiaeth Ei Mawrhydi dros Addysg a Hyfforddiant yng Nghymru (Her Majesty's Inspectorate for Education and Training in Wales) is responsible for inspecting early years' provision in the non-maintained sector, primary schools, secondary schools, special schools (including independent special schools), pupil referral units, independent schools, further education,

voluntary youth agencies, local education authorities, teacher education and training, work-based training, Careers Wales companies, the education, guidance and training elements of the New Deal and adult education. Its remit also includes providing advice to the National Assembly for Wales on a wide range of education and training matters. There are 56 HMIs, 112 registered inspectors, 447 team members and 35 lay inspectors in Wales.

SCOTLAND
HM Inspectorate of Education (HMIE) is an executive agency of the Scottish Executive. HM Inspectors (HMI) inspect or review and report on education in primary, secondary and special schools, further education institutions (under contract to the Scottish Further Education Funding Council), initial teacher education, community learning, care and welfare of pupils, the education functions of local authorities and in other contexts as necessary. They work in collaboration with the Care Commission in integrated inspection of pre-school education centres and residential schools. HMIs work in teams alongside lay members and associate assessors, who are practising teachers seconded for the inspection. The inspection of higher education is the responsibility of inspectors appointed to the Higher Education Funding Council for Scotland. There are one senior chief inspector, five chief inspectors, ten assistant chief inspectors and 70 inspectors in Scotland.

NORTHERN IRELAND
Inspection is carried out in Northern Ireland by the Education and Training Inspectorate, which provides services for the Department of Education, the Department for Employment and Learning and the Department of Culture, Arts and Leisure. Schools are inspected currently once every five to seven years. In further education and training, extended inspections are carried out once every eight years and focused inspections at least every four years. In addition, the Inspectorate provides advice to ministers and departments to assist in the formulation of policies in education and training. The Inspectorate comprises one chief inspector, four assistant chief inspectors, 10 managing inspectors and 47 inspectors.

SCHOOLS AND PUPILS

Full-time education is compulsory in Great Britain for all children between five and 16 years and between four and 16 years in Northern Ireland. About 93 per cent of children receive free education from public funds and the rest attend fee-paying schools or are educated at home. Provision is being increased for pre-school children and many pupils remain at school after the minimum leaving age. No fees are charged in any publicly maintained school in England, Wales and Scotland. In Northern Ireland, fees may be charged in voluntary schools and are paid by pupils in preparatory departments of grammar schools, but pupils admitted to the secondary departments of grammar schools, unless they come from outside Northern Ireland, do not pay fees.

PUPIL NUMBERS
In the maintained sector in the UK in 2002 there were:

Primary pupils	5,245,000
Secondary pupils	3,949,000

ENGLAND AND WALES

There are two main types of school in England and Wales: schools maintained by the state, which charge no fees; and independent schools, which charge fees. Schools maintained by the state, with the exception in England of Academies and City Technology Colleges, are maintained by local education authorities (LEAs).

Schools maintained by the state are classified as community, voluntary or foundation schools. Community schools are owned by LEAs and wholly funded by them. They are non-denominational and provide primary and secondary education. Schools in the voluntary category provide primary and secondary education and many have a particular religious ethos. Although the buildings are in many cases provided by the voluntary body, the LEA financially maintains them. There are two subdivisions in the voluntary category: voluntary controlled, and voluntary aided. In the case of voluntary controlled schools, the LEA bears all the costs. In voluntary aided schools, although the managers or governors are responsible for repairs, improvements and alterations to the building, central government may reimburse up to 90 per cent of approved capital expenditure, while the LEA pays for internal maintenance and other running costs. Foundation schools provide primary and secondary education. They can have a religious character, although most do not. They are funded by the LEA, although the land and buildings will be owned by a foundation or by the governors.

The number of schools by category in 2001 was:

	England	Wales
Maintained schools: total	22,862	1,851
Community, including community special	14,465	1,565
Voluntary aided	4,283	162
Voluntary controlled	2,740	112
Foundation, including foundation special	893	12
CTCs and CCTAs*	15	–
Academies	9	–
Independent schools	2,181	56

* In England only

LEAs are required to provide the schools that they maintain with a delegated budget to cover their running costs, including staffing costs. LEAs can retain funding of various centrally provided services, including transport and some special educational needs. The LEA acts as admission authority for most community and some voluntary schools.

Governing bodies – All publicly maintained schools have a governing body, usually made up of a number of parent and local community representatives, governors appointed by the LEA if the school is LEA-maintained, the head teacher (unless he or she chooses otherwise), and serving teachers and other staff. Schools can appoint up to two sponsor governors; sponsor governors are persons who give substantial assistance to the school, financially or in kind, or who provide services to the school. Governing bodies are responsible for the overall policies of schools and their academic aims and objectives.

City Technology Colleges (CTCs) and City Colleges for the Technology of the Arts (CCTAs) are found in England only, and are state-aided but independent of LEAs. Their aim is to widen the choice of secondary education in disadvantaged urban areas and to teach a broad curriculum with an emphasis on science, technology, business understanding and arts technologies. Capital costs are shared by government and business sponsors, and running costs are covered by a per capita grant from the DfES in line with comparable costs in an LEA-maintained school.

The Specialist Schools Programme is open to all state secondary schools in England that wish to specialise in teaching one of ten specialist areas: arts, business and enterprise, engineering, humanities, languages, mathematics and computing, music, science, sports, and technology. Schools can also combine two specialisms. The schools must raise £50,000 in unconditional sponsorship (schools with fewer than 500 pupils on the roll are required to raise a smaller sum), prepare four-year development plans with measurable targets in the specialist subject area, and make provision for sharing resources and good practice with other schools and the wider community. In return, in addition to the normal funding arrangements, the schools receive business sponsorship (up to four sponsor governors may sit on governing bodies) and a capital grant of up to £100,000 from central government, together with extra annual funding of up to £126,000 a year, (although capping relief for schools with over 1,200 is in place for four financial years initially) to assist the delivery of an enhanced curriculum. In August 2003 there were 1,454 designated specialist schools.

Academies – Academies are schools open to all abilities. They are usually in disadvantaged areas and are established by sponsors from business or faith or voluntary groups. Sponsors and the DfES provide capital costs, and running costs are met in full by the DfES. Academies either replace seriously failing schools with poor examination results or are established to meet a demand for places. The first three academies opened in September 2002 and a further nine opened in September 2003.

Excellence in Cities (EiC) is a programme of support designed to raise school standards and pupil expectations in disadvantaged urban communities. Excellence Clusters bring the core strands of the EiC programme to smaller pockets of deprivation elsewhere.

Federations are groups of two or more schools with a formal agreement to work together to raise standards.

The Beacon Schools programme was set up to help raise standards across primary and secondary education by sharing and spreading locally and nationally the good practice identified in successful schools. The programme is currently being phased out and the last contracts will end by August 2004. A new programme at secondary level, the *Leading Edge Partnership Programme* builds on the success of the beacon schools programme and supports innovative approaches to addressing critical learning challenges; 103 partnerships were announced in summer 2003. In addition, a *Leading Practice* programme is currently being developed to recognise and spread best practice.

Independent/State School Partnerships were launched in 1998 and forge links between independent and state schools to enhance the opportunities on offer to pupils. From September 2003, a £1.6 million government package will fund 47 new partnership projects.

Education Action Zones were established from 1997 to develop local partnerships between schools, parents, the community, businesses and local authorities to find solutions to educational underachievement. They were set up as statutory bodies with a maximum five-year lifespan.

SCOTLAND

Education authority schools (known as public schools) are financed by local government, partly through revenue support grants from central government, and partly from local taxation. Devolved management from the local authority to the school is in place for more than 88 per cent of all school-level expenditure. A small number of grant-aided schools, mainly in the special sector, are conducted by boards of managers and receive grants direct from the Scottish Executive Education Department.

Independent schools charge fees and receive no direct grant, but are subject to inspection and registration.

The number of schools by category in September 2001 was:

Publicly funded schools	2,855
Independent schools	155
TOTAL	3,010

NORTHERN IRELAND

Controlled schools are managed by the education and library boards (ELBs) through boards of governors consisting of representatives of transferors (mainly the Protestant churches), parents, teachers and the ELB. Within the controlled sector there is a small number of controlled integrated schools. Voluntary maintained schools are managed by boards of governors consisting of members nominated by trustees (mainly Roman Catholic) with representatives of teachers, parents and the ELB. Voluntary schools receive grants towards capital costs and running costs in whole or in part. A majority are entitled to capital grants at 100 per cent. Voluntary non-maintained schools are mainly voluntary grammar schools managed by boards of governors consisting of representatives of parents, teachers and, in most cases, the Department of Education and the ELB, as well as those appointed as provided in each school's scheme of management.

Integrated schools exist to educate Protestant and Roman Catholic children together. Latest figures show that there are currently 46 integrated schools, comprising 17 integrated second level colleges and 29 integrated primary schools. There are also 13 integrated nursery schools.

The number of schools by type in 2001–2 was:

Nursery*	96
Primary	920
Secondary: total	235
grammar	71
other	164
Non-maintained mainstream	25
Special (maintained)	48
TOTAL	1,324

* Excludes voluntary and private pre-school education centres

THE STATE SYSTEM

PRE-SCHOOL EDUCATION

Pre-school education is for children from two to five years. It is not compulsory, although a free place is available for each four-year-old who requires it and provision for three-year-olds in the public sector is being increased. In England by April 2004 there will be a free place for each three-year-old whose parents want one. In Wales, a free part-time place in a maintained or non-maintained setting is available for each child from the term following their third birthday. The Early Years

Advisory Panel is responsible for making recommendations to the Minister on the strategy for expanding early years' provision in Wales. In Scotland, pre-school education places are available for all three- and four-year-olds whose parents want one. Northern Ireland has a compulsory school-starting age of four, and since March 2003 one year of pre-school education has been available for each child whose parents want it.

Pre-school education takes place variously in nursery schools (3,216 in the public sector in 2001), nursery classes in primary schools, or pre-school education centres.

The proportion of all three- and four-year-olds in the UK enrolled in pre-school education as at January 2001, by sector, was:

	Public sector	Private and voluntary Sector	All providers
	%	%	%
UK	63	28	92
England	63	32	95
Wales	80	–	80
Scotland	59	21	80
Northern Ireland	53	8	61

'Sure Start' is a UK-wide initiative that brings together early education, childcare, health and family support to ensure the wellbeing of families in disadvantaged areas. Children are covered from conception to 14 (including those with special educational needs) and to 16 for those with disabilities. Sure Start aims to increase the availability of childcare for all children; improve health, education and emotional development for young people; and support parents in their role and in developing their employment aspirations.

PRIMARY EDUCATION

Primary education begins at five years in Great Britain and four years in Northern Ireland. In England, Wales and Northern Ireland the transfer to secondary school is generally made at 11 years. In Scotland, the primary school course lasts for seven years and pupils transfer to secondary courses at about the age of 12.

Primary schools consist mainly of infant schools for children aged five to seven, junior schools for those aged seven to 11, and combined junior and infant schools for both age groups. First schools in some parts of England cater for ages five to ten as the first stage of a three-tier system of first, middle and secondary schools.

Primary schools (UK) 2001–2	
No. of primary schools	22,800
No. of pupils (including nurseries)	5,245,500
No. of pupils (excluding nurseries)	4,423,700

Pupil-teacher ratios in public sector mainstream primary schools were:

	2000–1	2001–2
UK	22.3	22.0
England	22.9	22.5
Wales	21.5	21.0
Scotland	19.0	18.9
Northern Ireland	20.1	19.8

The average size of classes 'as taught' was 26.0 in 2001–2, compared with 26.4 in 2000–1. (Figures refer to 'all classes' rather than 'one-teacher classes' only.)

MIDDLE SCHOOLS

Middle schools take children from first schools, mostly in England, cover varying age ranges between eight and 14 and usually lead on to comprehensive upper schools.

SECONDARY EDUCATION

Secondary schools are for children aged 11 to 16 and for those who choose to stay on to 18. At 16, many students prefer to move on to tertiary or sixth form colleges. Most secondary schools in England, Wales and Scotland are co-educational. The largest secondary schools have over 1,500 pupils, but only 6.2 per cent of schools take over 1,000 pupils.

Secondary schools 2001–2

	England	Wales	Scotland	N. Ireland
No. of pupils (000s)	3,264.1	212.0	317.7	155.5
Average class size	22.0	21.2	n/a	n/a
Pupil-teacher ratio	16.9	16.4	12.9	14.4

In England and Wales the main types of maintained secondary schools are: comprehensive schools, whose admission arrangements are without reference to ability or aptitude; deemed middle schools, for children aged between eight and 14 years who then move on to senior comprehensive schools at 12, 13 or 14; and secondary grammar schools, with selective intake, providing an academic course from 11 to 16–18 years.

In Scotland all pupils in education authority secondary schools attend schools with a comprehensive intake. Most of these schools provide a full range of courses appropriate to all levels of ability from first to sixth year.

In most areas of Northern Ireland there is a selective system of secondary education with pupils transferring either to grammar schools (35 per cent of pupils in 2001) or secondary schools (65 per cent of pupils in 2001) at 10–11 years of age. Grammar schools provide an academic type of secondary education with A-levels at the end of the seventh year, while secondary non-grammar schools follow a curriculum suited to a wider range of aptitudes and abilities.

SPECIAL EDUCATION

Wherever possible, taking parents' wishes into account, children with special educational needs (SEN) are educated in ordinary schools, which are required to publish their policy for pupils with such needs. Local education authorities in England and Wales and education and library boards in Northern Ireland are required to identify and secure provision for the needs of children with learning difficulties, to involve the parents in any decision.

In Scotland, school placing is a matter of agreement between education authorities and parents. Parents have the right to say which school they want their child to attend, and a right of appeal where their wishes are not being met.

Maintained special schools are run by education authorities which pay all the costs of maintenance, but under the terms of local management, those able and wishing to manage their own budgets may choose to do so. Non-maintained special schools are run by voluntary bodies; they may receive some grant from central government for capital expenditure and for equipment but their current expenditure is met primarily from the fees charged to education authorities for pupils placed in the schools. Some independent schools provide education wholly or mainly for children with special educational needs. The number of pupils in maintained schools identified as having special educational needs in 2001–2 was:

	No.	%
UK	292,400	2.9
England	249,000	3.0
Wales	16,900	3.3
Scotland	17,100	2.0
Northern Ireland	9,400	2.7

ALTERNATIVE PROVISION

There is no legal obligation on parents in the UK to educate their children at school provided that the local education authority is satisfied that the child is receiving full-time education suited to its age, abilities and aptitudes. The education authority need not be informed that a child is being educated at home unless the child is already registered at a state school. In that case the parents must arrange for the child's name to be removed from the school's register (by writing to the head teacher) before education at home can begin. Failure to do so leaves the parents liable to prosecution for condoning non-attendance. Estimates suggest that home education in 2000 involved 25,000 families or 150,000 children.

INDEPENDENT SCHOOLS

Independent schools charge fees and are owned and managed under special trusts, with profits being used for the benefit of the schools concerned. There are 2,400 independent schools in Britain, educating over 620,000 pupils, or 7 per cent of the total school-age population.

The number of pupils at independent schools in 2002 was:

UK	620,000
England	571,000
Wales	9,500
Scotland	32,300
Northern Ireland	7,400

The annual survey carried out by the Independent Schools Council (ISC) shows that 1.03 per cent more pupils were being educated in independent schools in 2003 than in 2002.

The Independent Schools Council, formed in 1974, acts on behalf of the seven independent schools' associations which constitute it. These associations are: Headmasters' and Headmistresses' Conference, the Girls Schools Association, the Independent Schools Association, the Society of Headmasters and Headmistresses of Independent Schools, the Incorporated Association of Preparatory Schools, the Association of Governing Bodies of Independent Schools Independent Schools Bursars Association.

There are 1,277 schools in membership of the ISC, educating 80 per cent of all children educated outside the state sector. Most of the schools outside ISC membership are likely to be privately owned.

The ISC has overall responsibility for the Independent Schools Inspectorate (ISI), which works under a framework agreed with the DfES and Ofsted. A school must pass an ISI accreditation inspection to qualify for membership of an association within ISC. Schools are evaluated on their educational standards (including attainment, learning and behaviour), quality of teaching, assessment and recording, curriculum, staffing, premises and resources, links with parents and the community, pupils' personal development and pastoral care, management, efficiency, aims and ethos. ISC schools are subject to inspection every six years.

In 2002 over half of the 11-year-olds who took national curriculum key stage 2 tests at preparatory schools achieved the level expected of 14-year-olds. At GCSE, 53.1 per cent of all exams taken by independent school candidates achieve either an A* or A grade (compared to the national average of 16.4 per cent) and at A-level, about 66 per cent of entries were awarded an A or B grade (national average, 42.6 per cent).

In 2002, over 113,000 pupils at ISC schools received help with their fees in the form of bursaries and scholarships from the schools. In 2002, ISC member schools spent £490 million (an average of £973 per pupil) on new and improved buildings and equipment.

THE CURRICULUM

ENGLAND

The national curriculum was introduced in primary and secondary schools between autumn 1989 and autumn 1996, for the period of compulsory schooling from five to 16. It is mandatory in all maintained schools. Following a review in 1999, a revised curriculum was introduced in schools from September 2000.

The statutory subjects are:

Core subjects	Foundation subjects
English	Design and Technology
Mathematics	Information and
Science	Communication Technology
	History
	Geography
	Art and Design
	Music
	Physical Education

At key stage three (11- to 14-year-olds) a modern foreign language is introduced. At key stage four (14- to 16-year-olds) pupils are required to continue to study the core subjects, plus physical education, design and technology, a modern foreign language, and information and communication technology. Citizenship is a compulsory subject for secondary pupils. Other foundation subjects are optional and other subjects, such as drama, dance and classical languages, are taught when the resources of individual schools permit. Religious education must be taught across all key stages.

Statutory assessment takes place on entry to primary school and national tests and tasks in English and mathematics at key stage one (five- to seven-year-olds), with the addition of science at key stages two (seven- to 11-year-olds) and three (11- to 14-year-olds), are in place. Teachers make their own assessments of their pupils' progress to set alongside the test results. At key stage four, the GCSE and vocational equivalents are the main form of assessment.

The DfES publishes tables showing pupils' performance in A-level, AS-level, GCSE, GNVQ and Vocational A-level examinations school by school. LEAs are required to publish similar information in November each year showing the results of national curriculum tests and teacher assessments for seven, 11- and 14-year-olds.

In September 2002, the percentages of pupils reaching or exceeding the expected level of performance at each key stage were:

	Key stage 1 level 2 or above	Key stage 2 level 4 or above	Key stage 3 level 5 or above
English	–	75	67
Reading	84	80	–
Writing	86	60	–
Spelling	78	–	–
Maths	90	73	67
Science	–	86	67

The Qualifications and Curriculum Authority (QCA) is an independent government agency funded by the DfES. It is responsible for ensuring that the curriculum and qualifications available to young people and adults are of high quality, coherent and flexible and its remit ranges from the under-fives to higher level vocational qualifications.

WALES

The national curriculum was introduced simultaneously in Wales and, although it is broadly similar, has separate and distinctive characteristics which are reflected, where appropriate, in the programmes of study. Following a review of the curriculum in Wales, changes were introduced from September 2000.

Welsh is compulsory for pupils at all key stages, either as a first or as a second language. According to the January 2002 schools' census and the 2002 national curriculum assessment results, 20 per cent of primary school pupils are taught in classes where Welsh is used as a medium of teaching to some degree.

In November 2002, additional funding of £9.5 million was announced for Welsh language education; £7 million will be used to support bilingual nursery education in 2004–6. The percentage of children speaking Welsh fluently in primary school has increased from 13.2 per cent in 1988 to 16.8 per cent in 2002.

Schools perform tests and tasks in all the national curriculum subjects except at key stage 1, where teacher assessment is the sole means of assessing attainment. Approximately 38,000 pupils in each of the key stages 2 and 3 take the tests each year.

In 2002, the percentage of pupils reaching or exceeding the expected level of performance at each key stage (teacher assessment results in parenthesis) were:

	Key stage 1 7-year-olds level 2 or above	Key stage 2 11-year-olds level 4 or above	Key stage 3 14-year-olds level 5 or above
English	(83.0)	76.0 (79.0)	64.0 (62.0)
Welsh (first language)	(87.0)	74.0 (75.0)	72.0 (71.0)
Mathematics	(88.0)	75.0 (73.0)	66.0 (62.0)
Science	(88.0)	83.0 (86.0)	66.0 (67.0)

Awdurdod Cymwysterau, Cwricwlwm ac Asesu Cymru (ACCAC)/the Qualifications, Curriculum and Assessment Authority for Wales advises government on the matters within its remit. ACCAC is funded by the National Assembly for Wales.

SCOTLAND

The content and management of the curriculum in Scotland are not prescribed by statute but are the responsibility of education authorities and individual head teachers. Advice and guidance are provided by the Scottish Executive Education Department and Learning and Teaching Scotland, which also has a developmental role. Those bodies have produced guidelines on the structure and balance of the curriculum as well as for each of five broad curriculum areas for the five to 14 age group. There are also guidelines on assessment across the whole curriculum, on reporting to parents, and on the use of national tests for reading, writing and mathematics at six levels. Testing is carried out by the school when the teacher judges that a pupil has completed a level; most pupils are expected to move from one level to the next at roughly 18-month to two-year intervals.

Guidance on the curriculum for 14- to 16-year-olds recommends study within each of eight modes: language and communication; mathematical studies; science; technology; social studies; creative activities; physical education; and religious and moral education. There is also a recommended percentage of time to be devoted to each area over the two years. Provision is made for teaching in Gaelic in Gaelic-speaking areas.

For 16- to 18-year-olds, National Qualifications, a unified framework of courses and awards which brings together both academic and vocational courses, was introduced in 1999. The Scottish Qualifications Authority awards the certificates.

NORTHERN IRELAND

The statutory Northern Ireland curriculum is made up of religious education and five broad areas of study at primary level and six at secondary level. Provided the requirements of the statutory curriculum are met, it is for each school to decide what additional subjects should be made available for pupils.

Pupils at key stages 1 and 2 study religious education, English, mathematics, science, history and geography (known as the environment and society area of study), art and design, music and PE (the creative and expressive area of study), Irish (in Irish-speaking schools only) and four educational cross-curricular themes (education for mutual understanding, cultural heritage, health education and information technology). At key stage 3, pupils also study technology and design, plus a foreign language (pupils in Irish-speaking schools can study a foreign language or continue studying Irish) and two extra cross-curricular themes (economic awareness and careers education). At key stage 4, pupils can drop technology and design, art and design, music and can choose one subject from history, geography, business studies, home economics, economics, political studies or social and environmental studies.

The Northern Ireland Council for the Curriculum, Examinations and Assessment (CCEA) is currently reviewing the curriculum and it is envisaged that a revised curriculum will be phased in from September 2004 over the rest of the decade.

The assessment of pupils is broadly in line with practice in England and Wales and takes place at the ages of eight, 11 and 14. The GCSE is used to assess 16-year-olds.

The CCEA monitors and advises the Department of Education and teachers on all matters relating to the curriculum, assessment arrangements and examinations in grant-aided schools. It conducts GCSE, A- and AS-level examinations, pupil assessment at key stages one, two and three and administers the transfer procedure tests.

PUBLIC EXAMINATIONS AND QUALIFICATIONS

ENGLAND, WALES AND NORTHERN IRELAND

In 1988 a single system of examinations, the General Certificate of Secondary Education (GCSE), which is usually taken after five years of secondary education was introduced. The GCSE is the main method of assessing the performance of pupils at age 16 in all national curriculum subjects required to be assessed at the end of compulsory schooling. The structure of the examination reflects national curriculum requirements where these apply. GCSE short-course qualifications are available in some subjects. As a rule the syllabus comprises half the content of a full GCSE course.

The GCSE differs from its predecessors in that there are syllabuses based on national criteria covering course objectives, content and assessment methods; differentiated assessment (i.e. different papers or questions for different ranges of ability) and grade-related criteria (i.e. grades awarded on absolute rather than relative performance). The GCSE certificates are awarded on an eight-point scale, A* to G. All GCSE syllabuses, assessments and grading procedures are monitored by the Qualifications and Curriculum Authority to ensure that they conform to the national criteria.

In 2002, 51.5 per cent of 15 to 16-year-olds gained at least five results at grade C or better at GCSE or General National Vocational Qualification (GNVQ) equivalent.

Students are increasingly encouraged to continue their education post-16. For those who do so, in addition to the vocational qualifications outlined below, there are General Certificate of Education (GCE) and Vocational Certificate of Education (VCE) Advanced (A-level) examinations. A-level courses usually last two years and have traditionally provided the foundation for entry to higher education. Following extensive consultations in 1996 and 1997 which indicated the need to broaden the post-16 curriculum, new A-level qualifications were introduced in September 2000. The new Advanced Subsidiary (AS) level examinations represents the first half of a full A-level, and is assessed accordingly. The new A-level qualification consists of six units (three AS units and three A2 units). Students who go on to complete the full A-level will be assessed on their attainment in all six units, which may be taken either in stages or at the end of the course. A-levels and AS-levels are marked on a six-point scale from A to E.

There is also the opportunity for A-level candidates to take additional papers known as Advanced Extension Awards (which replaced Special papers). The awards were designed to stretch the most able A-level students.

Many maintained schools offer BTEC Firsts and an increasing number offer BTEC Nationals. National Vocational Qualifications (NVQs) in the form of General NVQs (GNVQs) are also available to students in schools. The Advanced Vocational Certificate of Education (AVCE) exists in three, six and 12-unit forms.

The City & Guilds Diploma of Vocational Education is intended for a wide ability range. Within guidelines and to meet specified criteria, schools and colleges design their own courses. These stress activity-based learning, core skills (which include application of number, communication and information technology), and work experience. The diploma is of value to those who want to find out what aptitudes they may have and to prepare themselves for work but who may not yet be committed to a particular occupation. It can be taken alongside

GCSEs and can provide a context for the introduction of GNVQ units into the key stage four curriculum.

The various examining boards in England have combined into three unitary awarding bodies (UABs), which offer both academic and vocational qualifications: GNVQs, GCSEs, AS- and A-levels. The bodies are the Assessment and Qualifications Alliance (AQA), Edexcel (shortly to become London Qualifications), and Oxford, Cambridge and RSA Examinations (OCR). The Joint Council for General Qualifications (JCGQ) comprises the three English UABs, the Welsh Joint Education Committee and the Northern Ireland Council for the Curriculum, Examinations and Assessment.

SCOTLAND

Scotland has its own system of public examinations. In 1999 a new system of National Qualifications was introduced and has been implemented for all pupils in the fifth and sixth year of secondary education (post-16).

Five levels of study are offered: Access, Intermediate 1, Intermediate 2, Higher and Advanced Higher. The new Higher National course and Advanced Higher National course are direct replacements for the old SCE Higher grade and the Certificate of Sixth Year Studies respectively. National Qualifications are included on the Scottish Credit and Qualifications Framework (see below), with Access equating to levels 1 to 3, Intermediate 1 to level 4, Intermediate 2 to level 5, Higher to level 6 and Advanced Higher to level 7.

National Courses consist of blocks of study called National Units. A unit usually consists of around 40 hours of study and there are three units in a course. Unit awards demonstrate that a learner has achieved competence in a particular area of study.

National Course awards are graded by external assessment, which consists of an examination, coursework or performance, or a combination of two or more of these. National Course awards also require candidates to pass all unit assessments of the course. A typical National Course external assessment requires candidates to demonstrate long-term retention of knowledge, high levels of problem solving, integration of knowledge across a whole course and an ability to apply knowledge and skills in novel situations. The range of subjects has been expanded to include vocational qualifications.

The new National Qualifications system has been introduced in a few schools for pupils in their fourth year of secondary education, but the majority of this lower age group still take the traditional Standard Grade examinations at the end of a two-year course.

Awards at Standard Grade are set at three levels: Credit (leading to awards at grade 1 or 2); General (leading to awards at grade 3 or 4); and Foundation (leading to awards at grade 5 or 6). Grade 7 is awarded to those who, although they have completed the course, have not attained any of these levels. Normally pupils will take examinations covering two pairs of grades, either grades 1–4 or grades 3–6. Most candidates take seven or eight Standard Grade examinations. The three levels of Standard Grade equate to levels 3 to 5 of the SCQF.

THE INTERNATIONAL BACCALAUREATE DIPLOMA

The International Baccalaureate Diploma is an internationally recognised two-year pre-university course and examination designed to facilitate the mobility of students and to promote international understanding. There are 51 schools and colleges in the UK which offer the diploma.

TEACHERS

ENGLAND AND WALES

All teachers working in maintained primary, special and secondary schools, non-maintained special schools and pupil referral units are required to register with the General Teaching Council (GTCE) in England and the General Teaching Council for Wales (GTCW) in Wales.

New entrants to the teaching profession in state primary and secondary schools are required to be graduates and to have Qualified Teacher Status (QTS). QTS is achieved by successfully completing a course of initial teacher training (ITT), traditionally either a Bachelor of Education (BEd) degree or the Postgraduate Certificate of Education (PGCE) at an accredited institution. New entrants are statutorily required to serve a one-year induction period during which they will have a structured programme of support.

In recent years various employment-based routes to QTS have been developed. The Graduate Teacher Programme is designed for mature, well-qualified people who can quickly take on teaching responsibilities and who need to earn a living while they train. Applicants must be over 24, unless they have already qualified as teachers overseas. Trainees undergo up to a year of school-based training. The schools involved receive up to £13,000 to cover the trainee's salary in addition to a grant of up to £4,000 to cover training costs. 'Training only' grants are also available to schools which themselves fund trainees' salaries. The Registered Teacher Programme is designed to attract into the teaching profession entrants over 24 years of age without a degree or formal teaching qualification but with at least two years of higher education; entrants are paid a salary and complete a degree while undergoing training for up to two years.

Teachers in further education are not required to have QTS, though roughly half have a teaching qualification and most have industrial, commercial or professional experience. A qualification for aspiring head teachers, the National Professional Qualification for Headship, has been introduced. The National College for School Leadership administers this qualification and others and acts as a focus for development and support. In Wales, the NPQH and other headship programmes are administered by the Welsh Assembly Government.

The Department for Education and Skills and the Welsh Assembly Government have introduced various schemes in an attempt to address the shortage of teachers in England and Wales. Eligible graduates training for the PGCE receive an annual training salary of £6,000 paid in instalments during their course. Teachers who successfully gain QTS in a priority subject on a PGCE course and who then go on to teach that subject may receive a further £4,000 as a lump sum after completing their first year of work and will, moreover, be assisted to pay off their student loans over a period of up to 10 years if certain conditions are met; the priority subjects are: English, Welsh (in Wales), design and technology, information technology, mathematics, modern foreign languages and science.

Providers of initial teacher training in England may receive funds from the TTA to help promote courses in certain subjects and to offer financial support to students undertaking them. The subjects are: design and technology, geography, information technology, mathematics, modern languages, music, religious education and science. In Wales, placement grants supported by the Higher Education Funding Council for

Wales (HEFCW) provide £1,000 per funded student on undergraduate priority courses – the same subjects that attract the £4,000 training grant – and £600 to students on other undergraduate courses.

The TTA administers a returners' programme for qualified teachers who wish to refresh their skills before returning to the profession.

The TTA funds all types of teacher training in England, whether run by universities, colleges or schools, and some educational research. In Wales funding is undertaken by the HEFCW. On an integrated England and Wales basis the TTA also acts as a central source of information and advice about entry to teaching. The General Teaching Council, an independent professional council, advises the Secretary of State and the TTA. The separate General Teaching Council for Wales operates on a similar basis.

The Specialist Teacher Assistant (STA) scheme provides trained support to qualified teachers in the teaching of reading, writing and arithmetic to young pupils.

In January 2003 the DfES, Welsh Assembly Government, employers and teaching unions signed a national agreement, 'Raising Standards and Tackling Workload', setting out a three-year programme of reforms to provide more classroom support for teachers.

SCOTLAND

The General Teaching Council (GTC) for Scotland advises central government on matters relating to teacher supply and the professional suitability of all teacher training courses. The GTC is also the body responsible for disciplinary procedures in cases of professional misconduct. All teachers in maintained schools must be registered with the GTC, initially for a two-year probationary period which can be extended if necessary. Only graduates are accepted as entrants to the profession; primary school teachers undertake either a four-year vocational degree course or a one-year postgraduate course, while teachers of academic subjects in secondary schools undertake the latter. There is also a combined degree sometimes known as a concurrent degree.

The Scottish Qualification for Headship has been introduced for aspiring head teachers. The colleges of education provide both in-service and pre-service training for teachers which is subject to inspection by HM Inspectorate of Education. The colleges are funded by the Scottish Higher Education Funding Council, which also sets intake levels for teacher education courses.

NORTHERN IRELAND

All new entrants to teaching in grant-aided schools are graduates and hold an approved teaching qualification. Initial teacher training, provided by the two universities and two colleges of education, is integrated with induction and early in-service training, the latter over a period of three years. The colleges are concerned with teacher education mainly for the primary school sector. They also provide BEd courses for intending secondary school teachers of religious education, commercial studies and craft, design and technology. With these exceptions, the professional training of teachers for secondary schools is provided in the education departments of the universities. A review of primary and secondary teacher training has taken place as a result of which all student teachers spend more time in the classroom.

The General Teaching Council for Northern Ireland advises government on professional issues, maintains a register of professional teachers and acts as a disciplinary body.

SERVING TEACHERS 2000–1 *(full-time)* (thousands):

	E&W	Scotland	NI*	Total UK
Maintained nursery and primary schools	181.8	21.6	8.6	211.9
Maintained secondary schools	193.2	22.6	9.7	225.6
Non-maintained mainstream schools	49.7	2.5	0.1	52.3
All special schools	13.7	2.1	0.8	16.6
TOTAL	438.4	48.8	19.1	506.3

*Provisional

SALARIES

Qualified teachers in England, Wales and Northern Ireland, other than the leadership group (which includes head teachers, deputy head teachers and advanced skills teachers) are paid on an 11-point scale, six points on the main pay scale and five on the upper scale. Entry points and placement depend on relevant experience. There are additional cash allowances for management responsibilities, special needs work and recruitment and retention factors as calculated by the relevant body, i.e. the governing body or the LEA. The 'advanced skills teacher' grade was introduced to enhance prospects in the classroom for the most able teachers; this grade does not apply in Northern Ireland. Experienced teachers are assessed against national standards to move onto the upper pay scale, after which they receive performance-related pay increases. There is a statutory superannuation scheme. Teachers working in the inner London area are paid on a separate pay scale while those working in the outer and fringe London areas receive additional allowances.

Salary scales for teachers in England, Wales and Northern Ireland are:

Head teacher	£35,544–£88,155+
Principal (Northern Ireland)	£83,904
Deputy head/Vice-principal (Northern Ireland)	from £31,416
Advanced skills teacher	£29,757–£47,469
Teacher	£18,105–£33,150
Inner London	
Head teacher	£41,487–£94,098+
Deputy head teacher	from £37,359
Advanced skills teacher	£35,700–£53,412
Teacher	£21,522–£39,093

Teachers in Scotland are paid on a seven-point scale. The entry point depends on type of qualification and additional allowances are payable under a range of circumstances. Salary scales for teachers in Scotland from 1 August 2003 are:

Head teacher/Depute head teacher	£35,565–£67,449
Principal teacher	£32,388–£37,782
Chartered teacher	£26,601–£35,199
Main grade	£18,000–£28,707

POST-16 EDUCATION

In the United Kingdom in 1999–2000, 72 per cent of 16-year-olds and 57 per cent of 17-year-olds were in post-compulsory education, either at school or in full-time further education. There were almost 5.0 million further education students in the UK during the academic year 2000–1, of which over 75 per cent were part-time. The number of students by country of study in 2000–1 was:

	Full-time	Part-time
UK	1,086,000	3,903,400
England	979,300	3,346,100
Wales	44,600	186,200
Scotland*	41,300	313,800
Northern Ireland†	20,700	57,300

* Enrolments, not head count
† Provisional

In 2001–2, there were 483 further education colleges in the UK. In 2000–1, there were 56,000 full-time lecturers in further education institutions.

ENGLAND AND WALES

Further education and sixth form colleges are funded directly by central government through the Learning and Skills Council in England, which operates through 47 local offices, and the National Council for Education and Training in Wales.

Further education colleges are controlled by autonomous further education corporations, which include substantial representation from industry and commerce, and which own their own assets and employ their own staff. Their funding is determined in part by the number of students enrolled and their level of achievement.

Much further education tends to be broadly vocational in purpose and employers are often involved in designing courses. It ranges from lower-level technical and commercial courses and government-sponsored training, through courses for those aiming at higher-level posts in industry, commerce and administration, to professional courses. Facilities exist for GCE A- and AS-levels, GCSEs, GNVQs and a full range of vocational qualifications. These courses can form the foundation for progress to higher education qualifications. Many students attend part-time, either through day or block release from employment, or in the evenings. Adult learners usually form the largest proportion of students in further education colleges, often studying part-time in the evening or at weekends.

The main courses and examinations in the vocational field, all of which link in with the National Vocational Qualification (NVQ) framework, are offered by the following bodies, but there are also many others.

Edexcel resulted from the merger of the Business and Technology Education Council (BTEC) and London Examinations. It provides programmes of study across a wide range of subject areas. Qualifications offered include GNVQs, NVQs, GCSEs, AS- and A-levels, National and Higher National diplomas and certificates, and other BTEC qualifications.

City & Guilds specialise in developing qualifications and assessments for work-related and leisure qualifications. They offer nationally and internationally recognised certificates in over 500 vocational qualifications. The progressive structure of awards spans seven levels, from foundation to the highest level of professional competence.

Oxford, Cambridge and RSA Examinations cover the full range of academic and vocational qualifications. The latter include accounting, business administration, customer service, management, language schemes, information technology and teaching qualifications. A wide range of NVQs and GNVQs are offered and a policy operates of credit accumulation, so that candidates can take a single unit or complete qualifications.

WORK-BASED LEARNING

Modern Apprenticeships are a way for young people aged 16–24 to get hands-on experience and on-the-job training while gaining respected qualifications. The Learning and Skills Council provides financial assistance to employers towards the cost of the training and assessment. Apprenticeships normally last between one and three years and there are two levels: Foundation (FMA) and Advanced (AMA) at NVQ levels 2 and 3 respectively. Both of these lead to:
- National Vocational Qualifications
- Key Skills qualifications – transferable work-related skills like IT and communication, problem solving, application of number, improving learning and performance and teamwork
- Technical certificates – vocationally related qualifications that provide the basic knowledge of the NVQ

In England and Wales in 2001–2 there were 65,800 new starts on AMA schemes and 119,800 new starts on FMA schemes. The overall number of participants in AMAs in March 2002 was 125,400.

SCOTLAND

The Scottish Further Education Funding Council funds further education colleges and the Scottish Qualifications Authority (SQA) is the statutory awarding body for qualifications in the national education and training system in Scotland. It is both the main awarding body for qualifications for work including Scottish Vocational Qualifications (SVQs) and is also their accrediting body. The SQA is by statute required clearly to separate its awarding and accrediting functions.

There are three main qualification 'families' in Scottish further education: National Qualifications; Higher National Qualifications (HNC and HND); and SVQs. In addition to Standard Grade qualifications, National Qualifications are available at five levels: Access, Intermediate 1, Intermediate 2, Higher and Advanced Higher. Another feature of the qualifications system is the Scottish Group Award (SGA). SGAs are built up unit by unit and allow opportunity for credit transfer from other qualifications (such as Standard Grade or SVQ), providing a further option for learners, especially adult learners.

SVQs are competence-based qualifications suitable for work-place delivery but they can also be taken in further education colleges and other centres where work-place conditions can be simulated.

The Scottish Credit and Qualifications Framework (SCQF) includes qualifications across academic and vocational sectors in a single credit-based framework. It comprises 12 levels, covering all mainstream qualifications from Access level in National Qualifications to postgraduate qualifications, and including SVQs.

In the academic year 2001–2 there were 514,877 student enrolments on vocational and non-vocational courses in further education colleges.

NORTHERN IRELAND

All further education colleges are independent corporate bodies like their counterparts in the rest of the UK. Responsibility for the sector lies with the Department for Employment and Learning, which funds the colleges directly. The colleges own their own property, are responsible for their own services and employ their own staff.

The governing bodies of the colleges must include at least 50 per cent membership who are engaged or employed in business, industry, or any profession.

Northern Ireland has 16 institutions of further education, and in 2001–2 there were 21,422 full-time and 58,445 part-time enrolments on vocational further education courses.

STUDENT SUPPORT

The means-tested Education Maintenance Allowance (EMA) for eligible 16- to 19-year-old students continuing their education beyond school-leaving age is being piloted in certain areas in England and Scotland where there are problems of poverty and low tertiary enrolment rates. It is a weekly allowance worth up to £40 (£30 in Scotland), which is payable subject to conditions laid out under a learning agreement. EMAs will be introduced on a national basis from September 2004.

Also available to students in that age group are means-tested discretionary payments from LEAs and free or subsidised travel to and from school or college. Adults may apply for funds which also cover financial help with childcare, allocated by central government through the funding bodies. The discretionary access fund also exists, administered by the institutions.

In England, the Adult Learning Grant is currently being piloted. It offers an allowance of up to £30 per week to young adults on low incomes studying full time for a first full level 2 qualification (five GCSEs or equivalent) or for young adults studying full time for a first level 3 qualification (two A-levels or equivalent).

Eligible Welsh-domiciled students aged over 18 on further education courses, whether full-time or part-time (subject to a minimum contact requirement), receive a means-tested non-repayable Assembly Learning Grant. The grant is administered by local education authorities. Discretionary Financial Contingency Funds are also available to all students suffering hardship and are administered by the institutions themselves.

Eligible Scottish-domiciled further education students can apply to their college for discretionary support in the form of bursaries. These can include allowances for maintenance, travel, study, two homes, dependants and special educational needs. College students receiving EMAs may also be eligible for the non-maintenance elements. In addition, colleges administer discretionary funds in the form of hardship, childcare and young students' retention funds.

In February 2003, it was announced that EMAs will be rolled out across Scotland in the academic year 2004–5 and administered by the Scottish Further Education Funding Council (SFEFC) for those on further education courses and by local authorities for those at school.

Full-time students over 19 years of age and resident in Northern Ireland, on certain vocational courses, may benefit from discretionary non-repayable Access Bursaries. The bursaries are administered by the education and library boards. Discretionary Access Funds exist, administered by the institutions themselves, for which any students suffering hardship are eligible to apply. Support for further education students in Northern Ireland includes free tuition to all full-time students up to age 18 and to all full-time students over 18 undertaking a vocational course at level 3 or below. In addition, financial help is provided by colleges through a discretionary support fund for both full-time and part-time students whose access to and participation in further education is inhibited by financial considerations.

VOCATIONAL QUALIFICATIONS

National Vocational Qualifications (NVQs) are work-related competence-based qualifications. They are designed to reflect the skills and knowledge needed to do a job effectively, and represent national standards recognised by employers. General National Vocational Qualifications (GNVQs) provide a vocational alternative to academic qualifications in colleges and schools for 16–19 year olds. Each GNVQ is related to a broad area of work and is a unit-based qualification assessed through a combination of continuous assessment and short test papers. They are available in 14 vocational areas at two levels: Foundation and Intermediate. In June 2002, over 66,000 young people took the Intermediate GNVQ and over 14,000 took the Foundation GNVQ.

The Vocational Certificate of Education (VCE), sometimes known as the Vocational A-level, replaced Advanced GNVQs. It is available in different forms: the three-unit VCE Advanced Subsidiary (equivalent to one GCE AS-level), the six-unit VCE Advanced Level (equivalent to one GCE A-level), and the 12-unit VCE Double Award (equivalent to two GCE A-levels). In 2002, 12,411 took VCEs at Advanced Level, and 42,291 took the Double Award.

'New Deal' is a government programme administered by the Department for Work and Pensions. It aims to help unemployed people to get off benefits and into employment, and to improve the skills base of the workforce. The programme is mandatory for young jobseekers aged 18–24 and for those aged 25 and over who are claiming Jobseeker's Allowance.

HIGHER EDUCATION

The term higher education is used to describe education above A-level, Higher and Advanced Higher Grade and their equivalent, which is provided in universities, colleges of higher education and in some further education colleges.

The Further and Higher Education Act 1992 and parallel legislation in Scotland removed the distinction between higher education provided by the universities and that provided in England and Wales by the former polytechnics and colleges of higher education and in Scotland by the former central institutions and others. It allowed all polytechnics, and other higher education institutions which satisfy the necessary criteria, to award their own taught course and research degrees and to adopt the title of university. All the polytechnics, art colleges and some colleges of higher education have since done so. The change of name does not affect the legal constitution of the institutions. Funding is by the Higher Education Funding Councils for England, Wales and Scotland and directly by the Department for Employment and Learning in Northern Ireland.

A White Paper, *The Future of Higher Education,* published in January 2003, sets out the Government's plans for reform and investment in universities and higher education colleges, and includes proposals for changes in the student finance system.

STUDENT NUMBERS IN THE UK

The number of first-year UK-domiciled students in higher education in 2001–2 was:

	Total	Full-time	Part-time
Total postgraduate	168,760	–	–
Research for higher degree	15,710	10,175	5,535
Taught course for higher degree	64,510	27,385	37,125
Other postgraduate	88,540	34,220	54,320
Total undergraduate	649,680	–	–
First degree	338,280	302,420	35,860
Other undergraduate	311,400	55,260	256,140
TOTAL	818,445	–	–

In 2001–2, the higher education qualifications obtained by both UK- and overseas-domiciled students were:

	Full-time	Part-time
First degrees	244,120	30,320
Other undergraduate	40,310	51,485
Higher degrees	61,605	28,765
Other postgraduate	34,880	30,015
TOTAL	380,915	140,580

Advice to government on matters relating to the universities is provided by the Higher Education Funding Councils for England, Wales and Scotland, and by the Higher Education Council in Northern Ireland. The former receive a block grant from central government which they allocate to the universities and colleges. In Northern Ireland the grant is allocated directly to institutions by the Department for Employment and Learning.

There are now 89 universities in the UK whereas only 48 existed prior to the Further and Higher Education Acts 1992. Of the 89, 72 are in England (including the University of London, which has a federal structure), two in Wales (one a federal institution comprising six constituent institutions and two university colleges), 13 in Scotland (14 including the Open University Scotland) and two in Northern Ireland. There are also 64 colleges of higher education, some of which are multidisciplinary while others specialise, for example, in teacher training. Some award their own degrees and qualifications, while others are validated by a university or a national body.

The pre-1992 universities each have their own system of internal government but broad similarities exist. Most are run by two main bodies: the senate, which deals primarily with academic issues and consists of members elected from within the university; and the council, which is the supreme body and is responsible for all appointments and promotions, and bidding for and allocation of financial resources. At least half the members of the council are drawn from outside the university. Joint committees of senate and council are common.

Those universities which were formerly polytechnics or other higher education institutions and the colleges of higher education are run by higher education corporations, which are controlled by boards of governors.

The non-residential Open University provides courses nationally leading to degrees, diplomas and certificates. Teaching is through a combination of specially produced textbooks, television programmes, audio- and videotapes, correspondence, tutorials, short residential courses and computer software. No qualifications are needed for entry. The Open University offers a modular programme of undergraduate courses by credit accumulation and post-experience and postgraduate courses, including a programme of higher degrees which comprises BPhil, MPhil and PhD through research, and MA, MBA and MSc through taught courses. The Open University in England, Wales and Northern Ireland is funded by the Higher Education Funding Council for England (HEFCE) and in Scotland by the Scottish Higher Education Funding Council (SHEFC). The Open University received £158.3 million in grants from the various funding bodies in 2001–2. In 2002, 143,753 undergraduates were registered.

The University for Industry (UfI) promotes learning ranging from basic skills to specialised technological and management skills. It aims to help individuals to improve their chances of employment, improve their career prospects and boost business competitiveness. It works as a public-private partnership in England, Wales and Northern Ireland. UfI's services are delivered through learndirect, which provides access to courses, over 80 per cent of which are online. There are over 2000 learndirect centres.

SCOTLAND

The Scottish Higher Education Funding Council (SHEFC) funds 20 institutions of higher education, including 14 universities. The universities are broadly managed as described above and the remaining colleges are managed by independent governing bodies which include representatives of industrial, commercial, professional and educational interests. Most of the courses outside the universities have a vocational orientation and a substantial number are sandwich courses.

NORTHERN IRELAND

In Northern Ireland higher education is provided in the 16 colleges of further education, the two universities and the two university colleges. These institutions offer a range of courses, including first and postgraduate degrees, PGCEs, undergraduate diplomas and certificates, and professional qualifications.

ACADEMIC STAFF

Each university and college appoints its own academic staff on its own conditions. However, there is a common salary structure and, except for Oxford and Cambridge, a common career structure in the pre-1992 universities and a common salary structure for the post-1992 universities. The Universities and Colleges Employers Association (UCEA) is the employers' association for subscribing universities and other higher education institutions in the UK. It provides a framework within which representatives of institutions can discuss salaries, conditions of service, employee relations and all matters connected with the employment of staff and employees. The services of the UCEA include collective bargaining and an annual salary survey.

Teaching staff in higher education require no formal teaching qualification, but the Institute of Teaching and

Learning in Higher Education, funded by the funding councils, has been established to set up an accreditation scheme for higher education teachers and to encourage innovation in teaching and learning. Teacher trainers are required to spend a certain amount of time in schools to ensure that they have sufficient recent practical experience.

The number of full-time academic staff in all UK institutions in 2001–2 was:

	Total	Male	Female
UK	119,900	78,675	41,225
England	96,850	63,330	33,520
Wales	5,770	3,885	1,885
Scotland	14,330	9,520	4,810
Northern Ireland	2,955	1,945	1,005

Salary scales for staff in the pre-1992 universities differ from those in the former polytechnics and colleges; it is planned eventually to amalgamate them. The salary scales for pre-1992 non-clinical academic staff throughout the UK from 1 August 2003 are:

Grade	Spinal points	Salary
Professor		from £42,246
Senior lecturer	20–27	£36,464–£44,549
Lecturer B	12–22	£27,174–£38,923
Lecturer A	8–11	£22,954–£26,327

Salary scales for pre-1992 academic related staff from 1 August 2003 are:

Grade	Spinal points	Salary
Grade 6		from £42,246
Grade 5	20–27	£36,464–£44,549
Grade 4	16–21	£31,715–£37,975
Grade 3	14–18	£29,478–£34,838
Grade 2	7–15	£21,852–£30,640
Grade 1	4–9	£18,893–£24,097

Salary scales for post-1992 academic staff from 1 August 2003 are:

Grade	Spinal points	Salary
Principal lecturer	0–9	£33,230–£41,784
Senior lecturer	(b)–8	£26,592–£35,367
Lecturer	9–15	£22,954–£28,621
Researcher B	1–11	£18,230–£27,534
Researcher A	1–6	£12,512–£17,088

Salary scales in Scotland from 1 August 2003 are:

Grade	Spinal points	Salary
Senior lecturer	8–17	£31,715–£43,317
Lecturer	1–13	£24,097–£38,923

FINANCE

The total income of institutions of higher education in the UK in 2001–2 was:

	£m	%
Funding Council grants	5,692.1	39.3
Tuition fees, education grants and contracts	3,338.2	23.0
Research grants and contracts	2,433.4	16.8
Other income	2,769.1	19.1
Endowment and investment income	258.1	1.8
TOTAL	14,490.9	100

COURSES

In the UK all universities and some colleges award their own degrees and other qualifications and may act as awarding and validating bodies for neighbouring colleges which are not yet accredited. The power to award degrees is regulated by law and it is an offence to purport to award a UK degree unless authorised to do so. The Quality Assurance Agency for Higher Education, funded by subscriptions from universities and higher education colleges/institutions and through contracts with the main higher education funding bodies, advises government on applications for degree-awarding powers.

The Quality Assurance Agency for Higher Education is governed by a board representing a range of interests. Of its 14 members, four are appointed by the representative bodies of the heads of higher education institutions, four are appointed by the funding bodies in higher education and six are independent directors with experience of industry, commerce or finance or the practice of a profession.

Facilities exist for full-time and part-time study, day release, sandwich or block release. Credit accumulation and transfer (CATS) is a system of study which allows a student to achieve a final qualification by accumulating credits for courses of study successfully achieved, or even professional experience, over a period.

Higher education courses comprise: first degree and postgraduate (including research); Diploma in Higher Education (DipHE); Higher National Diploma (HND) and Higher National Certificate (HNC); and preparation for professional examinations.

The Diploma of Higher Education (DipHE) is commonly a two-year diploma usually intended to serve as a stepping stone to a degree course or other further study. The DipHE is awarded by the institution itself if it is accredited; by an accredited institution of its choice if not. The BTEC Higher National Certificate (HNC) is awarded after two years part-time study. The BTEC Higher National Diploma (HND) is awarded after two years full-time, or three years sandwich-course or part-time study.

The foundation degree, launched in 2001, is a vocational higher education qualification which forms either a self-contained qualification or a basis for further study leading to an honours degree or further professional qualifications.

Undergraduate courses lead to the title of Bachelor, Bachelor of Arts (BA) and Bachelor of Science (BSc) being the most common, except in certain Scottish universities where master is sometimes used for a first degree in arts subjects. For a higher degree the titles are Master of Arts (MA), Master of Science (MSc) and the research degrees of Master of Philosophy (MPhil) and

Doctor of Philosophy (PhD or, at a few universities, DPhil).

Most undergraduate courses at universities and colleges of higher education run for three years, but some take four years or longer. Postgraduate studies vary in length.

Post-experience short courses form a large part of higher education provision, reflecting the need to update professional and technical training. Most of these courses fund themselves.

ADMISSIONS

The target proportion of 18- to 30-year-olds entering full-time higher education by 2010 is set in England at 50 per cent. Institutions suffer financial penalties if the number of students laid down for them by the funding councils is exceeded, but the individual university or college decides which students to accept. The formal entry requirements to most degree courses are two or more A-levels at grade E or above (or equivalent), and to HND courses one A-level (or equivalent). In practice, most offers of places require qualifications in excess of this, higher requirements usually reflecting the popularity of a course or institution. These requirements do not, however, exclude applications from students with a variety of non-GCSE qualifications or unquantified experience and skills.

For admission to a degree, DipHE or HND, potential students apply through a central clearing house, the Universities and Colleges Admission Service (UCAS). Applicants are supplied with an application form and the UCAS Handbook, available from schools, colleges and careers offices or direct from UCAS, and may apply to a maximum of six institutions/courses. The only exception among universities is the Open University, which conducts its own admissions.

Applications for undergraduate teacher training courses are made through UCAS. Details of initial teacher training courses in Scotland can be obtained from colleges of education and those universities offering such courses, and from Universities Scotland.

For admission as a postgraduate student, universities and colleges normally require a good first degree in a subject related to the proposed course of study or research. Most applications are made to individual institutions, except for teaching and social work.

FEES

Entrants to undergraduate courses domiciled in England, Wales and Northern Ireland pay, directly to the institution, an annual contribution to their fees (up to £1,125 in 2003–4) depending on their own level of income or that of their spouse or parents. Those whose parents' residual income is less than £20,970 pay nothing and those whose parents have a residual income of £31,231 or more pay the full £1,125. The fee contribution represents about 20 per cent of the average cost of a higher education course in the UK and the balance is paid by the education authority or, in Northern Ireland, by the education and libraries board. Students from EU member countries pay fees at home student rates and, if studying at institutions in England, Wales and Northern Ireland, are liable to make an annual contribution to fees assessed against family income. Among the classes of students exempt from payment are: Scottish-domiciled and EU students at Scottish institutions; students from England, Wales and Northern

Ireland in the fourth year of a four-year degree course at a Scottish institution; existing students with mandatory awards (see below), for whom the grant-awarding body pays; students on certain courses of initial teacher training; medical students in the fifth year of their course; health professionals on National Health Service bursaries; and full-time or part-time students on benefit or low incomes.

For students on an access course, fees start from about £200; financial help with this is available. For part-time or flexible learning tuition fees vary, and tuition is free for those on a low income or for those who receive certain benefits.

STUDENT SUPPORT

LOANS

Since September 1998, the means-tested loan has been the main form of support for most undergraduate students in the UK on full-time or sandwich undergraduate courses of higher education. Students apply through LEAs in England and Wales, education and library boards in Northern Ireland and the Students Awards Agency in Scotland.

Of the maximum loan, 75 per cent is available to all eligible students regardless of income; the remaining 25 per cent is means tested by the LEA. The loan rates for 2003–4 are:

Living in college/lodgings in London area	£4,930
Living in college/lodgings elsewhere	£4,000
Living in parental home	£3,165

Extra income assessed loans are available to students whose courses last more than 30 term-time weeks or who need to study abroad in certain high-cost countries. Loans of up to £500 are available to part-time students on low incomes or with dependent children.

Loans are available to students on designated courses, certain residency conditions also apply. In 2001–2, 809,300 loans were taken up, to the value of £2,485.2 million.

Repayment of the loans begins in the April following the end of the course. Those who pay tax through PAYE have repayments deducted from their salaries once they earn more than £10,000 a year. The self-employed make repayments through their tax returns. Repayments are calculated at 9 per cent of income over the £10,000 threshold. If income falls below £10,000, repayments cease until income rises above £10,000.

NON-REPAYABLE GRANTS AND ALLOWANCES

Eligible students, such as single parents, others with dependants or those leaving care, are entitled to apply for various additional means-tested supplementary grants for help in meeting certain living and other costs, for childcare and for each child at school. Disabled students are eligible for non means-tested Disabled Students' Allowances.

Eligible Welsh-domiciled undergraduates from low-income families, whether on full-time or part-time courses, receive a means-tested non-repayable Assembly Learning Grant of up to £1,500 per year. The grant is administered by local education authorities.

Eligible Scottish-domiciled students from low income families at institutions in Scotland may apply for a Young

Students' Bursary. The maximum available in 2003–4 is £2,100.

Full-time students on a low income who are resident in Northern Ireland may benefit from discretionary non-repayable Access Bursaries of up to £2,000. The award of a bursary carries a reduction in student loan entitlement. The bursaries are administered by the education and library boards.

LEARNER SUPPORT AND ACCESS FUNDS

Funds, variously known as hardship or access funds (Financial Contingency Funds in Wales and Support Funds in Northern Ireland) are allocated by central government to the appropriate funding councils in England and Wales and to the Student Awards Agency in Scotland, and are administered by further and higher education institutions. In Northern Ireland they are allocated by central government directly to the institution. Their purpose is to provide help for individual students facing financial difficulties. All students, whether full- or part-time, undergraduate or postgraduate, may apply. Universities and colleges set their own criteria and manage their own procedures within the national framework. The amount payable depends on individual circumstances and on the amount the institution has available. Some colleges offer non-repayable bursaries from hardship funds, i.e. a payment for each year of the course, to students who might be prevented from completing their studies due to financial problems. Individual colleges and universities may also offer emergency funds.

POSTGRADUATE AWARDS

Grants for postgraduate study are discretionary and competition for them is fierce. They comprise maintenance grants for students undertaking doctoral research or taught masters degrees, are not means-tested and are dependent on the class of first degree (especially for research degrees); and flat-rate maintenance grants, which replace the former 30-week bursaries for new entrants from the academic year 2000–1. There are additional allowances for disabled students, those with dependants and for fieldwork expenses. Postgraduate students, with the exception of students in England, Wales and Northern Ireland on loan-bearing diploma courses such as teacher training, are not eligible to apply for student loans.

Awards are funded by the British Academy, the Higher Education Funding Councils for England and Wales, the Scottish Higher Education Funding Council and the Department for Employment and Learning for Northern Ireland, among others.

ADULT AND CONTINUING EDUCATION

In the UK, the duty of securing adult and continuing education leading to academic or vocational qualifications is statutory. The Learning and Skills Council in England, the National Council for Education and Training in Wales and the Further Education Funding Council in Scotland are responsible for and fund those courses which take place in their sector and lead to academic and vocational qualifications, prepare students to undertake further or higher education courses, or confer basic skills; the Higher Education Funding Councils fund advanced courses of continuing education. The LEAs have the power, although not the duty, to provide those courses which do not fall within the remit of the funding bodies. Funding in Northern Ireland is through the education and library boards and other non-statutory providers.

The involvement of universities in adult education and continuing education has diversified considerably. Birkbeck College in the University of London caters solely for part-time students. The post-1992 universities and the colleges of higher education, because of their range of courses and flexible patterns of student attendance, provide opportunities in the field of adult and continuing education. The Forum for the Advancement of Continuing Education promotes collaboration between institutions of higher education active in this area. The Open University, in partnership with the BBC, provides distance teaching leading to first degrees, and also offers post-experience and higher degree courses.

Of the voluntary bodies, the biggest is the Workers' Educational Association (WEA), which operates throughout the UK and provides over 10,000 courses, reaching more than 110,000 adults. The WEA is a charity supported by funding from the Learning and Skills Council in England and by the Scottish Executive and local authorities in Scotland.

NIACE, the National Institute of Adult Continuing Education, has a broad remit to promote lifelong learning opportunities for adults. NIACE works to develop increased participation in education and training in England and Wales, particularly for those currently under-represented. It does this through research and project work, conferences, publications and the provision of an information service to educational providers. NIACE Dysgu Cymru, the Welsh committee, receives financial support from the National Assembly for Wales, support in kind from local authorities, and advises government, voluntary bodies and education providers on adult continuing education and training matters in Wales. In Scotland, advice on adult and community education, and promotion thereof, is provided by Community Learning Scotland; in April 2002 Community Learning Scotland ceased to be a non-departmental public body and some of its functions transferred to the Communities Scotland agency. In Northern Ireland, those functions are undertaken by the Department for Employment and Learning.

The Universities' Association for Continuing Education (UACE) represents and promotes the interests of continuing education and lifelong learning providers within higher education.

EDUCATION DIRECTORY

LOCAL EDUCATION AUTHORITIES

ENGLAND

COUNTY COUNCILS

BEDFORDSHIRE, Bedfordshire Local Education Authority, County Hall, Cauldwell Street, Bedford MK42 9AP. Tel: 01234-363222 Web: www.bedfordshire.gov.uk *Director,* David Doran

BUCKINGHAMSHIRE, Buckinghamshire Local Education Authority, County Hall, Walton Street, Aylesbury HP20 1UA. Tel: 01296-382603 Web: www.buckscc.gov.uk *Chief Education Officer,* P. J. Mooney

CAMBRIDGESHIRE, School Organisation and Planning, Box ELH 1505, Shire Hall, Castle Hill, Cambridge CB3 0AP. Tel: 01223-718550 Web: www.cambridgeshire.gov.uk *Director,* A. Baxter

CHESHIRE, Cheshire Local Education Authority, County Hall, Chester, CH1 1SQ. Tel: 01244-602424 Web: www.cheshire.gov.uk *Director of Education and Community,* D. Cracknell

CORNWALL, Education, Arts and Libraries, County Hall, Truro TR1 3AY. Tel: 01872-322000 Web: www.cornwall.gov.uk *Director,* G. Aver

CUMBRIA, Education Department, Cumbria County Council, 5 Portland Square, Carlisle, CA1 1PU. Tel: 01228-606877 Web: www.cumbria.gov.uk/education *Director of Education,* J. Nellist

DERBYSHIRE, Derbyshire Local Education Authority, County Hall, Matlock, DE4 3AG. Tel: 01629-585814 Web: www.derbyshire.gov.uk *Chief Education Officer,* R. V. Taylor

DEVON, Education, Arts and Libraries, County Hall, Topsham Road, Exeter EX2 4QG. Tel: 01392-382059 Web: www.devon.gov.uk *Director,* A. G. Smith

DORSET, Dorset Local Education Authority, County Hall, Colliton Park, Dorchester DT1 1XJ. Tel: 01305-224110 Web: www.dorsetcc.gov.uk *Director,* D. Goddard

DURHAM, Durham Local Education Authority, County Hall, Durham DH1 5UJ. Tel: 0191-383 3319 Web: www.durham.gov.uk *Director,* K. Mitchell

EAST SUSSEX, Education Department, PO Box 4, County Hall, St Anne's Crescent, Lewes BN7 1SG. Tel: 01273-481000 Web: www.eastsussexcc.gov.uk *Director of Education,* Ms D. Stokoe

ESSEX, Learning and Social Care, PO Box 47, Chelmsford CM2 6WN. Tel: 01245-492211 Web: www.essexcc.gov.uk *Deputy Chief Executive,* Liz Railton

GLOUCESTERSHIRE, Gloucestershire Local Education Authority, Shire Hall, Westgate Street, Gloucester GL1 2TG. Tel: 01452-425300 Web: www.gloscc.gov.uk *Director of Education,* Jo Davidson

HAMPSHIRE, Hampshire Local Education Authority, County Office, Education Department, The Castle Winchester SO23 8UG. Tel: 01962-846452 Web: www.hants.gov.uk/education *County Education Officer,* A. J. Seber

HERTFORDSHIRE, Children, Schools and Families, County Hall, Pegs Lane, Hertford SG13 8DE. Tel: 01992-555555 Web: www.hertsdirect.org *Director,* R. Shostak

ISLE OF WIGHT, Education and Community Development, County Hall, High Street, Newport PO30 1UD. Tel: 01983-823400 Web: www.iwight.com *Director,* D. Pettitt

KENT, Education and Libraries, Sessions House, County Hall, Maidstone ME14 1XQ. Tel: 01622-671411 Web: www.kent.gov.uk *Strategic Director,* Graham Badman

LANCASHIRE, Education and Cultural Services, PO Box 61, County Hall, Preston PR1 8RJ. Tel: 01772-254868 Web: www.lancashire.gov.uk *Director,* S. Mulvany

LEICESTERSHIRE, Leicestershire Local Education Authority, County Hall, Glenfield, Leicester LE3 8RF. Tel: 0116-265 6300 Web: www.leics.gov.uk *Director,* Mrs J. A. M. Strong

LINCOLNSHIRE, Education and Cultural Services, County Offices, Newland, Lincoln LN1 1YQ. Tel: 01522-552222 Web: www.lincolnshire.gov.uk *Director,* Dr C. Berry

NORFOLK, Norfolk Local Education Authority, County Hall, Martineau Lane, Norwich NR1 2DL. Tel: 01603-222146 Web: www.norfolk.gov.uk *Director,* Dr B. C. Slater

NORTH YORKSHIRE, North Yorkshire Local Education Authority, County Hall, Northallerton, N. Yorks DL7 8AE. Tel: 01609-780780 Web: www.northyorks.gov.uk *Director,* Cynthia Welbourn

NORTHAMPTONSHIRE, Education Services, Northamptonshire County Council, PO Box 216, John Dryden House, 8–10 The Lakes, Northampton NN4 7DD. Tel: 01604-236252 Web: www.northamptonshire.gov.uk *Corporate Director,* Mrs B. Bignold

NORTHUMBERLAND, Education Department, County Hall, Morpeth NE61 2EF. Tel: 01670-533601 *Director,* Dr L. Davis

NOTTINGHAMSHIRE, Nottinghamshire Local Education Authority, County Hall, West Bridgford, Nottingham NG2 7QP. Tel: 0115-982 3823 Web: www.nottinghamshire.gov.uk *Director,* P. Tulley

OXFORDSHIRE, Oxfordshire Local Education Authority, Education Department, Macclesfield House, New Road, Oxford OX1 1NA. Tel: 01865-815449 Web: www.oxfordshire.gov.uk *Director of Education and Culture,* Keith Bartley

SHROPSHIRE, Education Directorate, The Shirehall, Abbey Foregate, Shrewsbury SY2 6ND. Tel: 01743-254307 Web: www.shropshireonline.gov.uk *Corporate Director,* Mrs E. Nicholson

SOMERSET, Somerset Local Education Authority, County Hall, Taunton TA1 4DY. Tel: 01823-355455 Web: www.somerset.gov.uk *Corporate Director – Lifelong Learning,* M. Jennings

STAFFORDSHIRE, Education Service, Staffordshire County Council, Tipping Street, Stafford ST16 2DH. Tel: 01785-223121 Web: www.staffordshire.gov.uk *Director,* Mrs J. C. Hawkins

SUFFOLK, Suffolk Local Education Authority, Suffolk County Council, St Andrew House, County Hall, Ipswich IP4 1LJ. Tel: 01473-584631 Web: www.suffolkcc.gov.uk *Director,* D. J. Peachey

SURREY, Surrey Local Education Authority, County Hall, Penrhyn Road, Kingston upon Thames KT1 2DJ. Tel: 0845-600 9009 Web: www.surreycc.gov.uk *Director,* Dr P. Gray

WARWICKSHIRE, Warwickshire Local Education Authority, 22 Northgate Street, Warwick CV34 4SP. Tel: 01926-410410 Web: www.warwickshire.gov.uk
County Education Officer, E. Wood
WEST SUSSEX, Education and the Arts, County Hall, Chichester PO19 1RF. Tel: 01243-777750 Web: www.westsussex.gov.uk *Director,* R. Back
WILTSHIRE, Children, Education and Libraries Department, County Hall, Bythesea Road, Trowbridge BA14 8JB. Tel: 01225-713000 Web: www.wiltshire.gov.uk
Chief Education Officer, R. W. Wolfson
WORCESTERSHIRE, Educational Services, Educational Services Directorate, PO Box 73, Worcester WR5 2YA. Tel: 01905-766859 Web: www.worcestershire.gov.uk
Director, J. Kramer

UNITARY AND METROPOLITAN BOROUGH COUNCILS

BARNSLEY, Barnsley Local Education Authority, Berneslai Close, Barnsley S70 2HS. Tel: 01226-773500
Executive Director, Education, Ms J. Potter
BATH AND NORTH EAST SOMERSET, Bath and North East Somerset Local Education Authority, PO Box 25, Riverside, Temple Street, Keynsham, Bristol BS31 1DN. Tel: 01225-477000 Web: www.bathnes.gov.uk
Education Director, M. Young
BIRMINGHAM, Education Offices, Margaret Street, Birmingham B3 3BU. Tel: 0121 303 2550 Web: www.bgfl.org
Chief Education Officer, Tony Howell
BLACKBURN WITH DARWEN, Education and Lifelong Learning, Town Hall, Blackburn BB1 7DY. Tel: 01254-477477 Web: www.blackburn.gov.uk *Director,* Peter Morgan
BLACKPOOL, Education, Leisure and Cultural Services, Progress House, Clifton Road, Blackpool FY4 4US. Tel: 01253-476555
Strategic Director Community, Dr D. Sanders
BOLTON, Education and Culture, Paderborn House, Civic Centre, Bolton BL1 1JW. Tel: 01204-333333
Director, Mrs M. Blenkinsop
BOURNEMOUTH, Education Directorate, Dorset House, 20–22 Christchurch Road, Bournemouth BH1 3NL. Tel: 01202-456220/456219 *Director,* P. Deshpande
BRACKNELL FOREST, Bracknell Forest Local Education Authority, Seymour House, 38 Broadway, Bracknell, Berks RG12 1AU. Tel: 01344-424642 Web: www.bracknell-forest.gov.uk
Director of Education, T. Eccleston
BRADFORD, Education Bradford, Future House, Bolling Road, Bradford BD4 7EB. Tel: 01274-385500 Web: www.educationbradford.com
Managing Director, Mark Pattison
BRIGHTON AND HOVE, Children, Families and Schools, PO Box 2503, Kings House, Grand Avenue, Hove BN3 2SU. Tel: 01273-290000 Web: www.brighton-hove.gov.uk
Strategic Director, David Hawker
BRISTOL, Education and Lifelong Learning, The Council House, College Green, Bristol BS99 7EB. Tel: 0117-903 7961 Web: www.bristol-lea.org.uk
Director of Education and Lifelong Learning, John Gaskin
BURY, Bury Local Education Authority, Athenaeum House, Market Street, Bury BL9 0BN. Tel: 0161-253 5652
Chief Education Officer, H. Williams
CALDERDALE, Schools and Children's Services, Northgate House, Northgate, Halifax HX1 1UN. Tel: 01422-357257 Web: www.calderdale.gov.uk
Group Director, Ms C. White

COVENTRY, Lifelong Learning, Council Offices, Earl Street, Coventry CV1 5RS. Tel: 024-7683 1511 Web: www.coventry.gov.uk
Strategic Director, Roger Edwardson
DARLINGTON, Darlington Local Education Authority, Darlington Borough Council, Town Hall, Darlington DL1 5QT. Tel: 01325-380651 Web: www.darlington.gov.uk
Director, G. Pennington
DERBY, Derby City Education Service, Middleton House, 27 St Mary's Gate, Derby DE1 3NN. Tel: 01332-716924 Web: www.derby.gov.uk *Director,* A. Flack
DONCASTER, Doncaster Local Education Authority, Directorate of Education and Culture, PO Box 266, The Council House, College Road, Doncaster DN1 3AD. Tel: 01302-737103 *Executive Director,* M. S. Eales
DUDLEY, Education and Lifelong Learning, Westox House, 1 Trinity Road, Dudley DY1 1JQ. Tel: 01384-814225 Web: www.dudley.gov.uk *Director,* John Freeman
EAST RIDING OF YORKSHIRE, Lifelong Learning, East Riding of Yorkshire Council, County Hall, Beverley HU17 9BA. Tel: 01482-392020 Web: www.eastriding.gov.uk
Director of Lifelong Learning, Jon Mager
GATESHEAD, Learning and Culture Service, Civic Centre, Regent Street, Gateshead NE8 1HH. Tel: 0191-433 3000 Web: www.gateshead.gov.uk *Director,* Brian H. Edwards
HALTON, Education and Social Inclusion, Halton Borough Council, Grosvenor House, Halton Lea, Runcorn WA7 2WD. Tel: 0151-424 2061 *Director,* G. Talbot
HARTLEPOOL, Hartlepool Local Education Authority, Civic Centre, Victoria Road, Hartlepool TS24 8AY. Tel: 01429-266522 Web: www.hartlepool.gov.uk
Director, J. J. Fitt
HEREFORDSHIRE, Herefordshire Local Education Authority, Education and Conference Centre, PO Box 185, Hereford HR4 9ZR. Tel: 01432-260000 Web: www.education.herefordshire.gov.uk
Director, Dr E. Oram
KINGSTON UPON HULL, Learning Services, Essex House, Manor Street, Kingston upon Hull HU1 1YD. Tel: 01482-613161 *Corporate Director,* Helen McMullen
KIRKLEES, Kirklees Education Service, Oldgate House, 2 Oldgate, Huddersfield HD1 6QW. Tel: 01484-225242 Web: www.kirkleesmc.gov.uk
Director of Lifelong Learning, G. Tonkin
KNOWSLEY, Education and Lifelong Learning, Education Offices, Huyton Hey Road, Huyton, Knowsley L36 5YH. Tel: 0151-443 3220 Web: www.knowsley.gov.uk
Director, S. Munby
LEEDS, Education Leeds, Merrion House, 110 Merrion Centre, Leeds LS2 8DT. Tel: 0113-247 5590 Web: www.educationleeds.co.uk
Chief Executive, Chris Edwards
LEICESTER, Leicester Local Education Authority, Marlborough House, 38 Welford Road, Leicester LE2 7AA. Tel: 0116-252 7807
Corporate Director of Education and Lifelong Learning, S. Andrews
LIVERPOOL, Liverpool Local Education Authority, 4th Floor, Lewis Buildings, 4 Renshaw Street, Liverpool L1 4AD. Tel: 0151-233 3000 Web: www.liverpool.gov.uk
Executive Director, Colin Hilton
LUTON, Lifelong Learning, Unity House, 111 Stuart Street, Luton LU1 5NP. Tel: 01582-548001 Web: www.luton.gov.uk
Corporate Director, T. Dessent
MANCHESTER, Manchester Local Education Authority, Overseas House, Quay Street, Manchester M3 3BB. Tel: 0161-234 5000 *Chief Education Officer,* M. Waters

MEDWAY, Medway Local Education Authority, Civic Centre, Strood, Rochester, Kent ME2 4AY. Tel: 01634-306000 Web: www.medway.gov.uk *Director of Education,* R. Collinson

MIDDLESBROUGH, Middlesbrough Local Education Authority, PO Box 69, Vancouver House, Gurney Street, Middlesbrough TS1 1EL. Tel: 01642-729601 *Corporate Director,* Terry Redmayne

MILTON KEYNES, Milton Keynes Learning and Development Directorate, Civic Offices, Saxon Court, 505 Avebury Boulevard, Milton Keynes MK9 3HS. Tel: 01908-253325 Web: www.mkweb.co.uk *Head of Education and Chief Education Officer,* J. McElligott

NEWCASTLE UPON TYNE, Education and Libraries, Civic Centre, Newcastle upon Tyne NE1 8PU. Tel: 0191-232 8520 Web: www.newcastle.gov.uk *Director,* P. Turner

NORTH EAST LINCOLNSHIRE, Learning and Child Care, 7 Eleanor Street, Grimsby DN32 9DU. Tel: 01472-323021 Web: www.nelincs.gov.uk *Director,* Geoff Hill

NORTH LINCOLNSHIRE, Education and Personal Development, PO Box 35, Hewson House, Station Road, Brigg DN20 8XJ. Tel: 01724-297240 Web: www.northlincs.gov.uk *Director,* Dr Trevor Thomas

NORTH SOMERSET, North Somerset Local Education Authority, PO Box 51, Town Hall, Weston-super-Mare BS23 1ZZ. Tel: 01934-888888 Web: www.n-somerset.gov.uk *Director,* Colin Diamond

NORTH TYNESIDE, North Tyneside Local Education Authority, Town Hall, High Street East, Wallsend, Tyne & Wear NE28 7RR. Tel: 0191-200 6565 Web: www.northtyneside.gov.uk *Education Director,* Anne Marie Carrie

NOTTINGHAM CITY, Nottingham City Local Education Authority, Sandfield Centre, Sandfield Road, Lenton, Nottingham NG7 1QH. Tel: 0115-915 0706 Web: www.nottinghamschools.co.uk *Director,* Heather Tomlinson

OLDHAM, Education and Cultural Services, PO Box 40, Civic Centre, West Street, Oldham OL1 1XJ. Tel: 0161-911 4260 Web: www.oldham.gov.uk *Executive Director,* Ms Chris Berry

PETERBOROUGH, Peterborough Local Education Authority, Bayard Place, Broadway, Peterborough PE1 1FB. Tel: 01733-748444 Web: www.peterborough.gov.uk *Director,* R. Clayton

PLYMOUTH, Department for Lifelong Learning, City of Plymouth, Plymouth PL1 2AA. Tel: 01752-307400 Web: www.pgfl.plymouth.gov.uk *Director,* Bronwen Lacey

POOLE, Poole Local Education Authority, Civic Centre, Poole, Dorset BH15 2RU. Tel: 01202-633202 Web: www.boroughofpoole.com *Policy Director – Education,* John Nash

PORTSMOUTH, Portsmouth Local Education Authority, Civic Offices, Guildhall Square, Portsmouth PO1 2AL. Tel: 023-9284 1209 Web: www.portsmouthcc.gov.uk *Director of Education and Lifelong Learning,* Linda Fisher

READING, Education and Community Services, Civic Centre, PO Box 2623, Reading RG1 7WA. Tel: 0118-939 0900 Web: www.reading.gov.uk *Director,* Andrew Daykin

REDCAR AND CLEVELAND, Redcar and Cleveland Local Education Authority, Council Offices, Kirkleatham Street, Redcar TS10 1YA. Tel: 01642-444342 Web: www.redcar-cleveland.gov.uk *Director,* Jenny Lewis

ROCHDALE, Rochdale Local Education Authority, PO Box 70, Municipal Offices, Smith Street Rochdale OL16 1YD. Tel: 01706-647474 *Director of Education,* T. Piggott

ROTHERHAM, Education, Culture and Leisure Services, Education Office, Norfolk House, Walker Place, Rotherham S65 1AS. Tel: 01709-382121 Web: www.rotherham.gov.uk *Executive Director,* Ms D. Billups

RUTLAND, Education, Youth and Culture, Catmose, Oakham, Rutland LE15 6HP. Tel: 01572-722577 Web: www.rutnet.co.uk *Director,* Ms C. Chambers

SALFORD, Education and Leisure Directorate, Minerva House, Pendlebury Road, Swinton, Manchester. Tel: 0161-778 0123 Web: www.salford.gov.uk *Director,* Mrs J. Baker

SANDWELL, Education and Lifelong Learning, PO Box 41, Shaftesbury House, 402 High Street, West Bromwich, West Midlands B70 9LT. Tel: 0121-569 2000 Web: www.lea.sandwell.gov.uk *Executive Director,* E. Griffiths

SEFTON, Children, Schools and Families Service, Town Hall, Oriel Road, Bootle, Merseyside L20 7AE. Tel: 0151-922 4040 Web: www.sefton.gov.uk/education *Strategic Director,* Bryn Marsh

SHEFFIELD, Sheffield Local Education Authority, Education Directorate, Town Hall, Pinstone Street, Sheffield S1 2HH. Tel: 0114-273 5722 Web: www.sheffield.gov.uk *Executive Director,* Jonathan Crossley-Holland

SLOUGH, Slough Local Education Authority, Town Hall, Bath Road, Slough SL1 3UQ. Tel: 01753-875730 *Director of Learning and Cultural Services,* Christopher Spencer

SOLIHULL, Education and Children's Services, PO Box 20, Council House, Solihull B91 3QU. Tel: 0121-704 6656 Web: www.solihull.gov.uk *Director of Education and Children's Services,* K. Crompton

SOUTH GLOUCESTERSHIRE, South Gloucestershire Education Service, Bowling Hill, Chipping Sodbury, Glos BS37 6JX. Tel: 01454-868686 Web: www.southglos.gov.uk *Director of Education,* Ms T. Gillespie

SOUTH TYNESIDE, Lifelong Learning and Leisure, Town Hall and Civic Offices, Westoe Road, South Shields NE33 2RL. Tel: 0191-427 1717 *Director,* Barbara Hughes

SOUTHAMPTON, Lifelong Learning and Leisure, Southampton City Council, 5th Floor, Frobisher House, Nelson Gate, Southampton SO15 1BZ. Tel: 023-8083 2771 Web: www.southampton.gov.uk *Executive Director,* I. Sandbrook

SOUTHEND-ON-SEA, Education and Lifelong Learning, Civic Centre, Victoria Avenue, Southend-on-Sea SS2 6ER. Tel: 01702-215890 *Director,* Lorraine O'Reilly

ST HELENS, Education and Leisure Services, Rivington Centre, Rivington Road, St Helens WA10 4ND. Tel: 01744-455328 Web: www.sthelens.gov.uk *Director,* Mrs S. Richardson

STOCKPORT, Education Division, Town Hall, Stockport SK1 3XE. Tel: 0161-474 3808 *Director for Education,* Ed Blundell

STOCKTON-ON-TEES, Education, Leisure and Cultural Services, Municipal Buildings, PO Box 228, Church Road, Stockton-on-Tees TS18 1XE. Tel: 01642-393441 Web: www.stockton.gov.uk *Director,* S. T. Bradford

STOKE-ON-TRENT, Stoke-on-Trent Local Education Authority, Floor 2, Civic Centre, Glebe Street, Stoke-on-Trent ST4 1HH. Tel: 01782-232014 Web: www.stoke.gov.uk/education *Director,* N. Rigby

SUNDERLAND, Education Directorate, PO Box 101, Civic Centre, Sunderland SR2 7DN. Tel: 0191-553 1000 Web: www.sunderland.gov.uk
Director of Education and Community Services, Barbara Comiskey
SWINDON, Education and Community, Sanford House, Sanford Street, Swindon SN1 1QH. Tel: 01793-463069 Web: www.swindon.gov.uk
Director of Education, Hilary Pitts
TAMESIDE, Education and Cultural Services, Council Offices, Wellington Road, Ashton under Lyne, Lancs OL6 6DL. Tel: 0161-342 2201 Web: www.tameside.gov.uk
Strategic Director, P. Lawday
TELFORD AND WREKIN, Education and Culture, PO Box 440, Civic Offices, Telford, Shropshire TF3 4WF. Tel: 01952-202402 Web: www.telford.gov.uk
Corporate Director, Mrs C. Davies
THURROCK, Thurrock Local Education Authority, PO Box 118, Grays, Essex RM17 6GF. Tel: 01375-652652 Web: www.thurrock.gov.uk/education
Corporate Director – Education, Steve Beynon
TORBAY, Education Services Directorate, Oldway Mansion, Paignton, Devon TQ3 2TE. Tel: 01803-208208
Strategic Director of Education, Frank Weeple
TRAFFORD, Lifelong Learning, PO Box 40, Trafford Town Hall, Talbot Road, Stretford, Trafford, Greater Manchester M32 0EL. Tel: 0161-912 1212
Executive Director, Chris Pratt
WAKEFIELD, Wakefield Local Education Authority, County Hall, Bond Street, Wakefield WF1 2QL. Tel: 01924-306090 Web: www.wakefield.gov.uk
Chief Education Officer, J. McLeod
WALSALL, Education and Community Services, Civic Centre, Darwall Street, Walsall WS1 1TP. Tel: 01922-652301 Web: www.walsall.gov.uk *Director,* Elaine Simpson
WARRINGTON, Education and Lifelong Learning Department, Warrington Borough Council, New Town House, Buttermarket Street, Warrington, Cheshire WA1 2NJ. Tel: 01925-442971 *Director,* M. L. Roxburgh
WEST BERKSHIRE, Children and Young People, Avonbank House, West Street, Newbury, Berks RG14 1BZ. Tel: 01635-519722 Web: www.westberks.gov.uk
Corporate Director, Ian Pearson
WIGAN, Wigan Local Education Authority, Gateway House, Standishgate, Wigan, Lancs WN1 1AE. Tel: 01942-828891 Web: www.wiganmbc.gov.uk *Director,* R. J. Clark
WINDSOR AND MAIDENHEAD, Windsor and Maidenhead Local Education Authority, Town Hall, St Ives Road, Maidenhead, Berks SL6 1RF. Tel: 01628-796367 Web: www.rbwm.gov.uk *Director,* M. D. Peckham
WIRRAL, Education Cultural Services Department, Hamilton Building, Conway Street, Birkenhead, Wirral CH41 4FD. Tel: 0151-666 2121 *Director,* Howard Cooper
WOKINGHAM, Education and Cultural Services, Wokingham District Council, Shute End, Wokingham, Berks RG40 1WN. Tel: 0118-974 6100 Web: www.wokingham.gov.uk
Director, A. Roberts
WOLVERHAMPTON, Department for Lifelong Learning, Wolverhampton City Council, St Peter's Square, Wolverhampton WV1 1RR. Tel: 01902-554100 Web: www.wolverhampton.gov.uk
Co-ordinating Director, Roy Lockwood
YORK, Education and Leisure, Mill House, North Street, York YO1 6JD. Tel: 01904-613161 Web: www.york.gov.uk
Director, Patrick Scott

LONDON
*Inner London borough
BARKING AND DAGENHAM, Education, Arts and Libraries, Town Hall, Barking, Essex IG11 7LU. Tel: 020-8227 3181/3662 Web: www.bardaglea.org.uk
Director, R. Luxton
BARNET, Barnet Local Education Authority, The Old Town Hall, Friern Barnet Lane, London N11 3DL. Tel: 020-8359 2000 Web: www.barnet.gov.uk
Director of Education, Jill Stansfield
BEXLEY, Bexley Local Education Authority, Hill View, Hill View Drive, Welling, Kent DA16 3RY. Tel: 020-8303 7777 Web: www.bexley.gov.uk
Chief Education Officer, P. McGee
BRENT, Education, Arts and Libraries, Chesterfield House, 9 Park Lane, Wembley, Middx HA9 7RW. Tel: 020-8937 3190 Web: www.brent.gov.uk *Director,* John Christie
BROMLEY, Bromley Local Education Authority, Civic Centre, Stockwell Close, Bromley BR1 3UH. Tel: 020-8313 4066 Web: www.bromley.gov.uk *Director,* Ken Davis
*CAMDEN, Camden Local Education Authority, Crowndale Centre, 218–220 Eversholt Street, London NW1 1BD. Tel: 020-7974 1505 *Director,* R. Litchfield
*CITY OF LONDON, Economic Development and Education Office, Education Service, Corporation of London, PO Box 270, Guildhall, London EC2P 2EJ. Tel: 020-7332 1750
City Education Officer, D. Smith
*CITY OF WESTMINSTER, City of Westminster Local Education Authority, City Hall, 64 Victoria Street, London SW1E 6QP. Tel: 020-7641 1947 Web: www.westminster.gov.uk
Director of Education, Mrs Phyl Crawford
CROYDON, Croydon Local Education Authority, Taberner House, Park Lane, Croydon CR9 1TP. Tel: 020-8760 5452 Web: www.croydon.gov.uk *Director,* D. Sands
EALING, London Borough of Ealing Education Department, Perceval House, 14–16 Uxbridge Road, London W5 2HL. Tel: 020-8825 5599 Web: www.ealing.gov.uk
Director, Caroline Whalley
ENFIELD, Enfield Local Education Authority, PO Box 56, Civic Centre, Silver Street, Enfield, Middx EN1 3XQ. Tel: 020-8379 3201 *Director,* Ms E. Graham
*GREENWICH, Greenwich Local Education Authority, Riverside House, Woolwich High Street, London SE18 6DF. Tel: 020-8921 8238 Web: www.greenwich.gov.uk
Director, P. Burnett
*HACKNEY, The Learning Trust, Hackney Technology and Learning Centre, 1 Reading Lane, London E8 1GQ. Tel: 020-8356 8436 Web: www.learningtrust.co.uk
Director, Alan Wood
*HAMMERSMITH, Hammersmith and Fulham Local Education Authority, Town Hall, King Street, London W6 9JU. Tel: 020-8748 3020 Web: www.lbhf.gov.uk
Director, Sandy Adamson
HARINGEY, Haringey Local Education Authority, 48 Station Road, Wood Green, London N22 7TY. Tel: 020-8489 0000 Web: www.haringey.gov.uk *Director,* P. Roberts
HARROW, People First, PO Box 22, Civic Centre, Station Road, Harrow HA1 2UW. Tel: 020-8863 5611 Web: www.harrow.gov.uk
Director of Learning and Community Development, Javed Khan
HAVERING, Education, The Broxhill Centre, Broxhill Road, Harold Hill, Romford RM4 1XN. Tel: 01708-432488
Acting Executive Director, David MacLean
HILLINGDON, Education, Youth and Leisure Services, Civic Centre, High Street, Uxbridge UB8 1UW. Tel: 01895-250528
Corporate Director, P. O'Hear

HOUNSLOW, Hounslow Local Education Authority, Civic Centre, Lampton Road, Hounslow, Middx TW3 4DN. Tel: 020-8583 2000 Web: www.hounslow.gov.uk *Director,* Robert Garnett

*ISLINGTON, Islington Education Department, Laycock Street, Islington, London N1 1TH. Tel: 020-7527 5666 Web: www.islington.gov.uk *Director of Regeneration and Education,* Mohammed Mehmet

*KENSINGTON AND CHELSEA, Education, Libraries and Arts, The Royal Borough of Kensington and Chelsea, Town Hall, Hornton Street, London W8 7NX. Tel: 020-7361 3303 Web: www.rbkc.gov.uk *Executive Director,* Jacky Griffin

KINGSTON UPON THAMES, Education and Leisure Services, Guildhall 2, Kingston upon Thames KT1 1EU. Tel: 020-8546 2121 Web: www.kingston.gov.uk *Director,* P. Leeson

*LAMBETH, Lambeth Education, International House, Canterbury Crescent, London SW9 7QE. Tel: 020-7926 1000 Web: www.lambeth.gov.uk *Director,* Phyllis Dunipace

*LEWISHAM, Education and Culture, 3rd Floor, Laurence House, 1 Catford Road, London SE6 4RU. Tel: 020-8314 8527 Web: www.lewisham.gov.uk *Executive Director,* Ms F. Sulke

MERTON, Education, Leisure and Libraries, Civic Centre, London Road, Morden, Surrey SM4 5DX. Tel: 020-8545 3251 Web: www.merton.gov.uk *Director of Education, Leisure and Libraries,* Mrs Sue Evans

NEWHAM, Broadway House, 322 High Street, Stratford, London E15 1AJ. Tel: 020-8430 2000 *Director of Education and Community Learning,* Ms P. Maddison

REDBRIDGE, Education and Lifelong Learning, Lynton House, 255–259 High Road, Ilford, Essex IG1 1NN. Tel: 020-8478 3020 Web: www.redbridge.gov.uk *Director,* E. Grant

RICHMOND UPON THAMES, Education, Arts and Leisure, London Borough of Richmond upon Thames, 1st Floor, Regal House, London Road, Twickenham TW1 3QB. Tel: 020-8891 7500 Web: www.richmond.gov.uk *Director of Education and Leisure Services,* Anji Phillips

*SOUTHWARK, Southwark Education, John Smith House, 144–152 Walworth Road, London SE17 1JL. Tel: 020-7525 5050/5001 Web: www.southwark.lgfl.net *Director of Education and Culture,* Dr Roger Smith

SUTTON, Learning for Life, The Grove, Carshalton, Surrey SM5 3AL. Tel: 020-8770 5000 Web: www.sutton.gov.uk *Strategic Director,* Dr I. Birnbaum

*TOWER HAMLETS, Tower Hamlets Local Education Authority, Town Hall, Mulberry Place, 5 Clove Crescent, London E14 2BG. Tel: 020-7364 5000 Web: www.towerhamlets-pdc.org.uk *Corporate Director – Education,* Stephen Grix

WALTHAM FOREST, EduAction (Waltham Forest), Education Centre, 97 Queens Road, Walthamstow, London E17 8QS. Tel: 020-8496 5900 *Director,* Graham Moss

*WANDSWORTH, Wandsworth Local Education Authority, Town Hall, Wandsworth High Street, London SW18 2PU. Tel: 020-8871 8013 Web: www.wandsworth.gov.uk *Director,* P. Robinson

WALES

ANGLESEY, Education and Leisure Department, Ffordd Glanhwfa, Llangefni, Anglesey LL77 7EY. Tel: 01248-752921 Web: www.ynysmon.gov.uk *Director,* R. P. Jones

BLAENAU GWENT, Education Department, Festival House, Victoria Business Park, Ebbw Vale, Blaenau, Gwent NP23 6ER. Tel: 01495-355337 *Director of Lifelong Learning and Strategic Partnerships,* J. Pearce

BRIDGEND, Education, Leisure and Community Services, Bridgend County Borough Council, Sunnyside, Bridgend CF31 4AR. Tel: 01656-642600 Web: www.bridgend.gov.uk *Director,* D. Matthews

CAERPHILLY, Caerphilly Local Education Authority, Council Offices, Caerphilly Road, Ystrad Mynach, Hengoed CF82 7EP. Tel: 01443-815588 *Director,* David Hopkins

CARDIFF, Schools Service, County Hall, Atlantic Wharf, Cardiff CF10 4UW. Tel: 029-2087 2700 Web: www.cardiff.gov.uk *Head of Service,* H. Knight

CARMARTHENSHIRE, Lifelong Learning and Leisure, Pibwrlwyd, Carmarthen SA31 2NH. Tel: 01267-224501 Web: www.carmathenshire.gov.uk *Director,* Alun G. Davies

CEREDIGION, Education and Community Services, Swyddfa'r Sir, Marine Terrace, Aberystwyth SY23 2DE. Tel: 01970-633600 *Director,* R. J. Williams

CONWY, Conwy Local Education Authority, Government Buildings, Dinerth Road, Colwyn Bay LL28 4UL. Tel: 01492-575031/032 Web: www.conwy.gov.uk *Director,* R. E. Williams

DENBIGHSHIRE, Directorate of Lifelong Learning, Denbighshire County Council, Caledfryn, Smithfield Road, Denbigh, Denbighshire LL16 3RJ. Tel: 01824-706777 Web: www.denbighshire.gov.uk *Director,* S. Bowen

FLINTSHIRE, Education and Children's Services and Recreation, County Hall, Mold CH7 6ND. Tel: 01352-704010 Web: www.flintshire.gov.uk *Director,* John R. Clutton

GWYNEDD, Education, Culture and Leisure, Cyngor Gwynedd, Council Offices, Caernarfon LL55 1SH. Tel: 01286-672255 Web: www.gwynedd.gov.uk *Director,* D. Whittall

MERTHYR TYDFIL, Merthyr Tydfil Council Education Department, Ty Keir Hardie, Riverside Court, Avenue De Clichy, Merthyr Tydfil CF47 8XD. Tel: 01685-724600 Web: www.mnet2000.org.uk *Corporate Chief Officer,* W. V. Morgan

MONMOUTHSHIRE, Lifelong Learning and Leisure, Monmouthshire County Council, Floor 5, County Hall, Cwmbran NP44 2XH. Tel: 01633-644487 Web: www.monmouthshire.gov.uk *Director,* P. Cooke

NEATH PORT TALBOT, Neath Port Talbot Local Education Authority, Civic Centre, Port Talbot SA13 1PJ. Tel: 01639-763298 Web: www.neath-porttalbot.gov.uk *Director,* K. Napieralla

NEWPORT, Newport Local Education Authority, Civic Centre, Newport NP20 4UR. Tel: 01633-232257 Web: www.newport.gov.uk *Chief Education Officer,* D. Griffiths

PEMBROKESHIRE, Education and Community Services, County Hall, Haverfordwest SA61 1TP. Tel: 01437-764551 Web: www.pembrokeshire.gov.uk *Director,* G. Davies

POWYS, Children, Families and Lifelong learning, County Hall, Llandrindod Wells LD1 5LG. Tel: 01597-826422 Web: www.education.powys.gov.uk *Group Director,* M. Barker

RHONDDA, CYNON Taff Education and Children's Services, Ty Trevithick, Abercynon, Mountain Ash CF45 4UQ. Tel: 01443-744000 *Group Director,* D. Jones

SWANSEA, Swansea Local Education Authority, County Hall, Oystermouth Road, Swansea SA1 3SN. Tel: 01792-636351 Web: www.swansea.gov.uk/learningforlife *Director,* R. Parry

TORFAEN, Education Department, County Hall, Croesyceiliog, Cwmbran, Torfaen NP44 2WN. Tel: 01633-648610 Web: www.torfaen.gov.uk *Director,* M. de Val

VALE OF GLAMORGAN, Learning and Development Directorate, The Vale of Glamorgan Council, Civic Offices, Holton Road, Barry CF63 4RU. Tel: 01446-709138 Web: www.valeofglamorgan.gov.uk *Director,* B. Jeffreys

WREXHAM, Education and Leisure Services, Wrexham County Borough Council, Ty Henblas, Queen's Square, Wrexham LL13 8AZ. Tel: 01978-297421 Web: www.wrexham.gov.uk *Director,* Terry Garner

SCOTLAND

ABERDEEN CITY, Learning and Leisure, Summerhill Education Centre, Stronsay Drive, Aberdeen AB15 6JA. Tel: 01224-522000 Web: www.aberdeen-education.org.uk *Corporate Director,* J. Stodger

ABERDEENSHIRE, Aberdeenshire Local Education Authority, Woodhill House, Westburn Road, Aberdeen AB16 5GJ. Tel: 01224-664630 Web: www.aberdeenshire.gov.uk *Director,* H. Vernal

ANGUS, Angus Council Education Authority, County Buildings, Market Street, Forfar DD8 3WE. Tel: 01307-461460 Web: www.angus.gov.uk *Director of Education,* Jim Anderson

ARGYLL AND BUTE, Argyll and Bute Council, Education, Argyll House, Alexandra Parade, Dunoon, Argyll PA23 8AJ. Tel: 01369-704000 Web: www.argyll-bute.gov.uk *Director of Education,* Archibald Morton

CLACKMANNANSHIRE, Services to People, Lime Tree House, Castle Street, Alloa FK10 1EX. Tel: 01259-452374 Web: www.clacksweb.org.uk *Director,* Dave Jones

DUMFRIES AND GALLOWAY, Dumfries and Galloway Local Education Authority, Education Department, 30 Edinburgh Road, Dumfries DG1 1NW. Tel: 01387-260427 *Director of Education and Community Services,* F. Sanderson

DUNDEE CITY, Dundee City Council Education Department, Floor 8, Tayside House, Crichton Street, Dundee DD1 3RJ. Tel: 01382-433111 Web: www.dundeecity.gov.uk *Director of Education,* Mrs A. Wilson

EAST AYRSHIRE, East Ayrshire Local Education Authority, Council Headquarters, London Road, Kilmarnock KA3 7BU. Tel: 01563-576017 Web: www.east-ayrshire.gov.uk *Director,* J. Mulgrew

EAST DUNBARTONSHIRE, East Dunbartonshire Local Education Authority, Boclair House, 100 Milngavie Road, Bearsden, Glasgow G61 2TQ. Tel: 0141-578 8000 Web: www.eastdunbarton.gov.uk *Strategic Director – Community,* Ms S. Bruce

EAST LOTHIAN, Education and Community Services, East Lothian Council, John Muir House, Haddington EH41 3HA. Tel: 01620-827562 Web: www.eastlothian.gov.uk *Director of Education and Community Services,* A. Blackie

EAST RENFREWSHIRE, Education Department, Council Offices, Eastwood Park, Rouken Glen Road, Giffnock G46 6UG. Tel: 0141-577 3479 Web: www.eastrenfrewshire.gov.uk *Director,* John Wilson

EDINBURGH, CITY OF, City of Edinburgh Local Education Authority, Wellington Court, 10 Waterloo Place, Edinburgh EH1 3EG. Tel: 0131-469 3000 *Director,* Education, R. Jobson

EILEAN SIAR/WESTERN ISLES, Eilean Siar/Western Isles, Council Offices, Sandwick Road, Stornoway, Isle of Lewis HS1 2BW. Tel: 01851-703773 *Director of Education,* Murdo Macleod

FALKIRK, Falkirk Local Education Authority, McLaren House, Marchmont Avenue, Polmont, Falkirk FK2 0NZ. Tel: 01324-506600 Web: www.falkirk.gov.uk *Director,* Dr G. Young

FIFE, Education Service, Fife House, North Street, Glenrothes KY7 5PN. Tel: 01592-413667 Web: www.fife.gov.uk *Head of Education,* Roger Stewart

GLASGOW CITY, Glasgow City Council Education Offices, Nye Bevan House, 20 India Street, Glasgow G2 4PF. Tel: 0141-287 6998 Web: www.glasgow.gov.uk *Director,* Ronnie O'Connor

HIGHLAND, Education, Culture and Sport, Council Buildings, Glenurquhart Road, Inverness IV3 5NX. Tel: 01463-702802 Web: www.highland.gov.uk *Director,* B. Robertson

INVERCLYDE, Inverclyde Education Services, 105 Dalrymple Street, Greenock PA15 1HT. Tel: 01475-712824 *Director,* B. McLeary

MIDLOTHIAN, Midlothian Council Education Authority, Fairfield House, 8 Lothian Road, Dalkeith EH22 3ZG. Tel: 0131-270 7500 Web: www.midlothian.gov.uk *Director,* D. MacKay

MORAY, Educational Services, Council Offices, High Street, Elgin IV30 1BX. Tel: 01343-563001 Web: www.moray.gov.uk *Director,* Donald Duncan

NORTH AYRSHIRE, Educational Services, Cunninghame House, Irvine KA12 8EE. Tel: 01294-324400 Web: www.north-ayrshire.gov.uk *Corporate Director,* J. Travers

NORTH LANARKSHIRE, North Lanarkshire Local Education Authority, Municipal Buildings, Kildonan Street, Coatbridge ML5 3BT. Tel: 01236-812222 Web: www.northlan.gov.uk *Director,* Michael O'Neill

ORKNEY ISLANDS, Education and Recreation, Council Offices, School Place, Kirkwall, Orkney KW15 1NY. Tel: 01856-873535 Web: www.orkney.gov.uk *Director,* Leslie Manson

PERTH AND KINROSS, Education and Children's Services, Pullar House, 35 Kinnoull Street, Perth PH1 5GD. Tel: 01738-476200 *Acting Director,* George Waddell

RENFREWSHIRE, Renfrewshire Council Education and Leisure Services, Council Headquarters, South Building, Cotton Street, Paisley PA1 1LE. Tel: 0141-842 5601 Web: www.renfrewshire.gov.uk *Director of Education of Leisure,* Ms S. Rae

SCOTTISH BORDERS, Scottish Borders Local Education Authority, Scottish Borders Council, Council Headquarters, Newtown St Boswells, Melrose, Roxburghshire TD6 0SA. Tel: 01835-824000 Web: www.scottishborders.gov.uk *Director,* G. Roger

SHETLAND ISLANDS, Community Services Department, Shetland Islands Council, Hayfield House, Hayfield Lane, Lerwick, Shetland ZE1 0QD. Tel: 01595-744000 Web: www.shetland.gov.uk *Head of Education,* Alex Jamieson

SOUTH AYRSHIRE, Education, Culture and Lifelong Learning, County Buildings, Wellington Square, Ayr KA7 1DR. Tel: 01292-612201 Web: www.south-ayrshire.gov.uk *Director,* Mike McCabe

SOUTH LANARKSHIRE, South Lanarkshire Local Education Authority, Council Headquarters, Almada Street, Hamilton ML3 0AE. Tel: 01698-454545 Web: www.southlanarkshire.gov.uk *Executive Director,* Ms M. Allan

STIRLING, Children's Services, Stirling Council, Viewforth, Stirling FK8 2ET. Tel: 01786-442678 Web: www.stirling.gov.uk *Director,* Gordon Jeyes

WEST DUNBARTONSHIRE, Education and Cultural Services, Council Offices, Garshake Road, Dumbarton G82 3PU. Tel: 01389-737301 *Director,* I. McMurdo

WEST LOTHIAN, West Lothian Council Education Services, Lindsay House, South Bridge Street, Bathgate EH48 1TS. Tel: 01506-776000
Director of Education and Cultural Services, Ms K. Reid

NORTHERN IRELAND

BELFAST, Belfast Education and Library Board, 40 Academy Street, Belfast BT1 2NQ. Tel: 028-9056 4000
Web: www.belb.org.uk *Chief Executive,* David Cargo

NORTH, North Eastern Education and Library Board, County Hall, 182 Galgorm Road, Ballymena, Co. Antrim BT42 1HN. Tel: 028-2565 3333 Web: www.neelb.org.uk
Chief Executive, G. Topping

SOUTH EASTERN, South Eastern Education and Library Board, Headquarters Offices, Grahamsbridge Road, Dundonald, Belfast BT16 2HS. Tel: 028-9056 6200
Web: www.seelb.org.uk *Chief Executive,* J. B. Fitzsimons

SOUTHERN, Southern Education and Library Board, 3 Charlemont Place, The Mall, Armagh BT61 9AX. Tel: 028-3751 2200 Web: www.selb.org
Chief Executive, Mrs H. McClenaghan

WESTERN, Western Education and Library Board, 1 Hospital Road, Omagh, Co. Tyrone BT79 0AW. Tel: 028-8241 1411 Web: www.welbni.org *Chief Executive,* P. J. Martin

ISLANDS

GUERNSEY, Guernsey Local Education Authority, The Grange, St Peter Port, Guernsey GY1 1RQ. Tel: 01481-710821
Director, D. T. Neale

ISLE OF MAN, Isle of Man Department of Education, St. George's Court, Upper Church Street, Douglas, Isle of Man IM1 2SG. Tel: 01624-685820 Web: www.gov.im
Director, John Cain

ISLES OF SCILLY, Isles of Scilly Local Education Authority, Town Hall, St Mary's, Isles of Scilly TR21 0LW. Tel: 01720-422537
Secretary for Education, P. S. Hygate

JERSEY, States Jersey Education Sport and Culture Committee, PO Box 142, Jersey JE4 8QJ. Tel: 01534-509500 Web: www.esc.gov.je
Director of Education, Sport and Culture, T. W. McKeon

ADVISORY BODIES

SCHOOLS

BRITISH EDUCATIONAL COMMUNICATIONS AND TECHNOLOGY AGENCY, Milburn Hill Road, Science Park, Coventry CV4 7JJ. Tel: 024-7641 6994
Web: www.becta.org.uk *Chief Executive,* O. Lynch

EDUCATION OTHERWISE, PO Box 7420, London N9 9SG. Helpline: 0870-730 0074
Web: www.education-otherwise.org

INTERNATIONAL BACCALAUREATE ORGANISATION, Peterson House, Malthouse Avenue, Cardiff Gate, Cardiff CF23 8GL. Tel: 029-2054 7777 Web: www.ibo.org
Academic Director, Prof. J. Thompson

LEARNING AND SKILLS COUNCIL, Cheylesmore House, Quinton Road, Coventry CV1 2WT. Tel: 0845-019 4170
Web: www.lsc.gov.uk *Chief Executive,* John Harwood

SPECIAL EDUCATIONAL NEEDS AND DISABILITY TRIBUNAL, 7th Floor, Windsor House, 50 Victoria Street, London SW1H 0NW. Tel: 01325-392555
Web: www.sentribunal.gov.uk *President,* Trevor Aldridge

INDEPENDENT SCHOOLS

ASSOCIATION OF GOVERNING BODIES OF INDEPENDENT SCHOOLS, Field House, Newton Tony, Salisbury, Wilts SP4 0HF. Tel: Web: www.agbis.org.uk
Secretary, Shane Ruther-Jerome

INDEPENDENT SCHOOLS COUNCIL, Grosvenor Gardens House, 35–37 Grosvenor Gardens, London SW1W 0BS. Tel: 020-7798 1500 Web: www.isis.org.uk
General Secretary, Dr A. B. Cooke

INDEPENDENT SCHOOLS EXAMINATIONS BOARD, Jordan House, Christchurch Road, New Milton, Hants BH25 6QJ. Tel: 01425-621111 Web: www.iseb.co.uk
General Secretary, Mrs J. Williams

FURTHER EDUCATION

LEARNING AND SKILLS DEVELOPMENT AGENCY, Regent Arcade House, 19–25 Argyll Street, London W1F 7LS. Tel: 020-7297 9000 Web: www.lsda.org.uk
Chief Executive, Chris Hughes

ACER (ASSOCIATION OF COLLEGES IN THE EASTERN REGION), Suite 1, Lancaster House, Meadow Lane, St Ives, Huntingdon, Cambs PE27 4LG. Tel: 01480-468198
Web: www.acer.ac.uk *Chief Executive,* Veronica Windmill

AOSEC (ASSOCIATION OF SOUTH EAST COLLEGES), Building 33, The University of Reading, London Road, Reading RG1 5AQ. Tel: 0118-378 6319
Web: www.aosec.org.uk *Chief Executive,* B. Knowles

CENTRA (EDUCATION AND TRAINING SERVICES) LTD, Duxbury Park, Duxbury Hall Road, Chorley, Lancs PR7 4AT. Tel: 01257-241428 Web: www.centra.org.uk
Chief Executive, P. Wren

EMFEC (EAST MIDLAND FURTHER EDUCATION COUNCIL), Robins Wood House, Robins Wood Road, Aspley, Nottingham NG8 3NH. Tel: 0115-854 1616
Web: www.emfec.co.uk *Chief Executive,* Ms J. Gardiner

NCFE, Citygate, St James Boulevard, Newcastle upon Tyne NE1 4JE. Tel: 0191-239 8000 Web: www.ncfe.org.uk
Chief Executive, Isabel Sutcliffe

SOUTH WEST ASSOCIATION FOR EDUCATION AND TRAINING, Bishops Hull House, Bishops Hull, Taunton, Somerset TA1 5EP. Tel: 01823-335491
Web: www.swafet.org.uk *Chief Executive,* Liz McGrath

WELSH JOINT EDUCATION COMMITTEE, 245 Western Avenue, Cardiff CF5 2YX. Tel: 029-2026 5000 Web: www.wjec.co.uk *Chief Executive,* Wyn G. Roberts

HIGHER EDUCATION

ASSOCIATION OF COMMONWEALTH UNIVERSITIES, John Foster House, 36 Gordon Square, London WC1H 0PF. Tel: 020-7380 6700 Web: www.acu.ac.uk
Secretary-General, Prof. M. G. Gibbons

NORTHERN IRELAND HIGHER EDUCATION COUNCIL, 4th Floor, Room 407, Adelaide House, 39–49 Adelaide Street, Belfast, BT2 8FD. Tel: 02890-257400
Web: *Chairman,* Tony Hopkins, CBE

QUALITY ASSURANCE AGENCY FOR HIGHER EDUCATION, Southgate House, Southgate Street, Gloucester GL1 1UB. Tel: 01452-557000
Web: www.qaa.ac.uk *Chief Executive,* P. R. Williams

UNIVERSITIES SCOTLAND, 53 Hanover Street, Edinburgh EH2 2PJ. Tel: 0131-226 1111
Web: www.universities-scotland.ac.uk
Director, D. Caldwell

UNIVERSITIES UK, Woburn House, 20 Tavistock Square, London WC1H 9HQ. Tel: 020-7419 4111
Web: www.universitiesuk.ac.uk
President, Baroness Diana Warwick

CURRICULUM COUNCILS

ACCAC, Castle Buildings, Womanby Street, Cardiff CF10 1SX.
Tel: 029-2037 5400 Web: www.accac.org.uk
Chief Executive, J. V. Williams
COUNCIL FOR THE CURRICULUM, EXAMINATIONS
AND ASSESSMENT, 29 Clarendon Road, Clarendon Dock,
Belfast BT1 3BG. Tel: 028-9026 1200
Web: www.ccea.org.uk
Chief Executive, G. Boyd
LEARNING AND TEACHING SCOTLAND, Gardyne Road,
Dundee DD5 1NY Tel: 01382-443600; 74 Victoria Crescent
Road, Glasgow G12 9JN. Tel: 0141-337 5000
Web: www.ltscotland.com *Chief Executive,* M. Baughan
QUALIFICATIONS AND CURRICULUM AUTHORITY,
83 Piccadilly, London W1Y 8QA. Tel: 020-7509 5555
Web: www.qca.org.uk *Chairman,* Dr Ken Boston

EXAMINING BODIES

ASSESSMENT AND QUALIFICATIONS ALLIANCE (AQA),
Devas Street, Manchester M15 6EX.
Tel: 0161-953 11800 Web: www.aqa.org.uk
Director-General, Dr Mike Cresswell
EDEXCEL, Stewart House, 32 Russell Square, London
WC1B 5DN. Tel: 0870-240 9800
Web: www.edexcel.org.uk *Chief Executive,* John Kerr
OCR (OXFORD CAMBRIDGE AND RSA
EXAMINATIONS), Head Office, 1 Regent Street,
Cambridge CB2 1GG Tel: 01223-552552
Web: www.ocr.org.uk *Chief Executive,* Dr R. McLone

SCOTLAND
SCOTTISH QUALIFICATIONS AUTHORITY, Hanover
House, 24 Douglas Street, Glasgow G2 7NQ.
Tel: 0141-242 2214 Web: www.sqa.org.uk
Chief Executive, David Fraser

WALES
WELSH JOINT EDUCATION COMMITTEE, 245 Western
Avenue, Cardiff CF5 2YX. Tel: 029-2026 5000
Web: www.wjec.co.uk *Chief Executive,* Wyn G. Roberts

NORTHERN IRELAND
NORTHERN IRELAND COUNCIL FOR THE
CURRICULUM, EXAMINATIONS AND ASSESSMENT,
29 Clarendon Road, Belfast, County Antrim BT1 3BG.
Tel: 028-9026 1200 Web: www.ccea.org.uk
Chief Executive, G. Boyd

GSCE
See above: AQA, EDEXCEL, NORTHERN IRELAND
COUNCIL FOR THE CURRICULUM, EXAMINATIONS
AND ASSESSMENT, WELSH JOINT EDUCATION
COMMITTEE

A-LEVEL
See above: AQA, EDEXCEL, NORTHERN IRELAND
COUNCIL FOR THE CURRICULUM, EXAMINATIONS
AND ASSESSMENT, OCR, WELSH JOINT EDUCATION
COMMITTEE

FURTHER EDUCATION
CITY & GUILDS, 1 Giltspur Street, London EC1A 9DD.
Tel: 020-7294 2468 Web: www.city-and-guilds.co.uk
Director-General, C. Humphries, CBE
EDEXCEL, OCR, *see above*

FUNDING COUNCILS

FURTHER EDUCATION
LEARNING AND SKILLS COUNCIL, Cheylesmore House,
Quinton Road, Coventry CV1 2WT Tel: 0845-019 4170
Web: www.lsc.gov.uk *Chief Executive,* J. Harwood
NATIONAL COUNCIL – ELWA, Linden Court, The Orchards,
Ilex Close, Cardiff CF14 5DZ Tel: 029-2076 1861
Web: www.elwa.org.uk *Chief Executive,* S. Martin
SCOTTISH FUNDING COUNCILS FOR FURTHER AND
HIGHER EDUCATION, Donaldson House, 97 Haymarket
Terrace, Edinburgh EH12 5HD Tel: 0131-313 6500
Web: www.sfc.ac.uk *Chief Executive,* Roger McClure

HIGHER EDUCATION
HIGHER EDUCATION FUNDING COUNCIL FOR
ENGLAND, Northavon House, Coldharbour Lane, Bristol
BS16 1QD Tel: 0117-931 7317 Web: www.hefce.ac.uk
Chief Executive, Sir Howard Newby
HIGHER EDUCATION COUNCIL – ELWA, Linden Court,
The Orchards, Ilex Close, Cardiff CF14 5DZ
Tel: 029-2076 1861 Web: www.elwa.org.uk
Chief Executive, S. Martin
SCOTTISH FUNDING COUNCILS FOR FURTHER AND
HIGHER EDUCATION, Donaldson House, 97 Haymarket
Terrace, Edinburgh EH12 5HD Tel: 0131-313 6500
Web: www.shefc.ac.uk *Chief Executive,* Roger McClure
STUDENT AWARDS AGENCY FOR SCOTLAND, Gyleview
House, 3 Redheughs Rigg, Edinburgh EH12 9HH
Tel: 0131-476 8212 Web: www.saas.gov.uk
Chief Executive, D. Stephen
STUDENT LOANS COMPANY LTD, 100 Bothwell Street,
Glasgow G2 7JD Tel: 0141-306 2000
Web: www.slc.co.uk *Chief Executive,* C. Ward
TEACHER TRAINING AGENCY, Portland House, Stag Place,
London SW1E 5TT Tel: 020-7925 3700
Web: www.teach-tta.gov.uk *Chief Executive,* R. Tabberer

ADMISSIONS AND COURSE INFORMATION

CAREERS RESEARCH AND ADVISORY CENTRE, Sheraton
House, Castle Park, Cambridge CB3 0AX Tel: 01223-460277
Web: www.crac.org.uk
GRADUATE TEACHER TRAINING REGISTRY, Rosehill,
New Barn Lane, Cheltenham, Glos GL52 3LZ
Tel: 0820-1122205 Web: www.gttr.ac.uk
GTTR Unit Manager, Mrs J. Pearce
SOCIAL WORK ADMISSIONS SYSTEM, Rosehill,
New Barn Lane, Cheltenham, Glos GL52 3LZ
Tel: 01242-544600 *SWAS Unit Manager,* Mrs J. Pearce
UNIVERSITIES AND COLLEGES ADMISSIONS SERVICE,
Rosehill, New Barn Lane, Cheltenham, Glos GL52 3LZ
Tel: 01242-222444 Web: www.ucas.com
Chief Executive, M. A. Higgins
UNIVERSITIES SCOTLAND, 53 Hanover Street,
Edinburgh EH2 2PJ Tel: 0131-226 1111
Web: www.universities-scotland.ac.uk
Director, D. Caldwell

UNIVERSITIES

UNIVERSITY OF ABERDEEN (1495)
King's College, Aberdeen, AB24 3FX
Tel: 01224-272000
Web: www.abdn.ac.uk
Full-time students (2002–3), 10,450
Academic Registrar, Dr T. Webb
Chancellor, The Lord Wilson of Tillyorn, GCMG
Rector, Miss C. Dickson Wright
Secretary, S. Cannon
Vice-Chancellor and Principal, Prof. Duncan C. Rice

UNIVERSITY OF ABERTAY DUNDEE (1994)
Bell Street, Dundee, DD1 1HG
Tel: 01382-308000
Web: www.abertay.ac.uk
Full-time students (2002–3), 3,814
Chancellor, The Rt. Hon. Earl of Airlie, KT, GCVO, PC
Registrar, Philip Henry
University Secretary and Director of Operations,
  Ms Caroline Lamb
Vice-Chancellor, Prof. Bernard King

ANGLIA POLYTECHNIC UNIVERSITY (1992)
Rivermead Campus, Bishop Hall Lane, Chelmsford CM1 1SQ
Tel: 01245-493131
Web: www.anglia.ac.uk
Full-time students (2002–3), 18,853
Chancellor, Lord Ashcroft, KCMG
Secretary and Clerk, S. G. Bennett
Vice-Chancellor, Michael Malone-Lee, CB

ASTON UNIVERSITY (1895)
Aston Triangle, Birmingham B4 7ET
Tel: 0121-359 3611
Web: www.aston.ac.uk
Full-time students (2002–3), 6,600
Chancellor, Sir Adrian Cadbury (1979)
Registrar and Secretary, David Packham
Vice-Chancellor, Prof. Mike Wright

UNIVERSITY OF BATH (1966)
Claverton Down, Bath BA2 7AY
Tel: 01225-388388
Web: www.bath.ac.uk
Full-time students (2002–3), 7,191
Chancellor, The Lord Tugendhat (1998)
Registrar, Jonathan Bursey
Vice-Chancellor, Prof. Glynis Breakwell

UNIVERSITY OF BIRMINGHAM (1900)
Edgbaston, Birmingham, BH15 2TT
Tel: 0121-414 3344
Web: www.bham.ac.uk
Full-time students (2002–3), 26,500
Chancellor, Sir Dominic Cadbury (2002)
Registrar and Secretary, David Allen
Vice-Chancellor, Prof. Michael Sterling, DEng, FREng

BOURNEMOUTH UNIVERSITY (1992)
Fern Barrow, Poole, Dorset BH12 5BB
Tel: 01202-524111
Web: www.bournemouth.ac.uk
Full-time students (2002–3), 9,741
Chancellor, Lord John Taylor of Warwick (1992)
Registrar, Noel Richardson
Vice-Chancellor, Prof. Gillian Slater

UNIVERSITY OF BRADFORD (1966)
Richmond Building, Richmond Road, Bradford BD7 1DP
Tel: 01274-232323
Web: www.brad.ac.uk
Full-time students (2002–3), 8,356
Chancellor, The Baroness Lockwood of Dewsbury (1997)
Registrar and Secretary, N. J. Andrew
Vice-Chancellor, Prof. Chris Taylor

UNIVERSITY OF BRIGHTON (1992)
Mithras House, Lewes Road, Brighton, BN2 4AT
Tel: 01273-600900
Web: www.bton.ac.uk
Full-time students (2002–3), 15,000
Chairman of the Board, Sir Michael Checkland
Director, Prof. Sir David Watson
Registrar and Secretary, Ms C. E. Moon

UNIVERSITY OF BRISTOL (1876)
Senate House, Tyndall Avenue, Bristol, BS8 1TH
Tel: 0117-928 9000
Web: www.bristol.ac.uk
Full-time students (2002–3), 13,828
Chancellor, Sir Jeremy Morse, KMCG, D.Litt, LLD (1989)
Registrar, D. Pretty, FRCOG
Secretary, Dr K. McKenzie
Vice-Chancellor, Prof. Eric Thomas

BRUNEL UNIVERSITY (1966)
Uxbridge, Middx UB8 3PH
Tel: 01895-274000
Web: www.brunel.ac.uk
Full-time students (2002–3), 12,000
Academic and Principal Registrar, J. B. Alexander
Chancellor, The Rt. Hon Lord Wakeham, PC, JP, DL (1998)
Vice-Chancellor and Principal, Prof. Steven Schwartz

UNIVERSITY OF BUCKINGHAM (1983)
Buckingham, MK18 1EG
Tel: 01280-814080
Web: www.buckingham.ac.uk
Full-time students (2002–3), 720
Chancellor, Sir Martin Jacomb (1998)
Secretary, Prof. John Clarke
Vice-Chancellor, Dr Terence Kealey

UNIVERSITY OF CAMBRIDGE (1209)
The Old Schools, Trinity Lane, Cambridge CB2 1TN
Tel: 01223-337733
Web: www.cam.ac.uk

UNIVERSITY OFFICERS
Chancellor, HRH The Prince Philip, Duke of Edinburgh,
  KG, KT, OM, GBE, PC (1977)
Commissary, The Lord Mackay of Clashfern, KT, PC,
  FRSE (2002)
Deputy High Steward, The Lord Richardson of
  Duntisbourne, MBE, TD, PC (1983)
Academic Secretary, G. P. Allen (Wolfson)
Director of the Fitzwilliam Museum, D. D. Robinson
  (Magdalene) (1995)
High Steward, Dame Bridget Ogilvie (Girton) (2001)
Librarian, P. K. Fox (Selwyn) (1994)
Orator, A. J. Bowen (Jesus) (1993)
Registrary, T. J. Mead, Ph.D. (Wolfson) (1997)
Secretary-General of the Faculties, D. A. Livesey, Ph.D.
  (Emmanuel) (1992)
Treasurer, Mrs J. Womack (Trinity Hall) (1993)

Vice-Chancellor, Prof. Alison Richard, Ph.D. (Newnham) (2003)

COLLEGES AND HALLS *with dates of foundation*
CHRIST'S (1505) *Master,* Prof. Malcolm Bowie, D.Phil., FBA (2002)
CHURCHILL (1960) *Master,* Sir John Boyd, KCMG (1996)
CLARE (1326) *Master,* Professor A. J. Badger, Ph.D. (2003)
CLARE HALL (1966) *President,* Prof. Ekhart Salje, Ph.D., FRS (2001)
CORPUS CHRISTI (1352) *Master,* Prof. H. Ahmed, FREng (2000)
DARWIN (1964) *Master,* Prof. W. A. Brown
DOWNING (1800) *Master,* Prof. B. J. Everitt, Ph.D. (2003)
EMMANUEL (1584) *Master,* Lord Wilson of Dinton, GCB (2002)
FITZWILLIAM (1966) *Master,* Prof. B. F. G. Johnson, Ph.D, FRS (1999)
GIRTON (1869) *Mistress,* Prof. Dame Marylin Strathern, Ph.D., FBA (1998)
GONVILLE AND CAIUS (1348) *Master,* N. McKendrick (1996)
HOMERTON (1824) *Principal,* Dr K. B. Pretty
HUGHES HALL (1985) (for post-graduate students) *President,* Prof. P. Richards, MD, Ph.D. (1998)
JESUS (1496) *Master,* Prof. R. Mair, Ph.D., FREng (2001)
KING'S (1441) *Provost,* Prof. P. P. G. Bateson
*LUCY CAVENDISH COLLEGE (1965) (for women research students and mature and affiliated undergraduates) *President,* Dame Veronica Sutherland, CMG (2001)
MAGDALENE (1542) *Master,* D. D. Robinson (2002)
*NEW HALL (1954) *President,* Mrs A. Longsdale (1996)
*NEWNHAM (1871) *Principal,* Baroness O'Neill of Bengarve, CBE (1992)
PEMBROKE (1347) *Master,* Sir Roger Tomkys
PETERHOUSE (1284) *Master,* Lord Wilson of Tillyorn, KT, GCMG, Ph.D., FRSE (2002)
QUEENS' (1448) *President,* The Lord Eatwell (1997)
ROBINSON (1977) *Warden,* A. D. Yates (2001)
ST CATHARINE'S (1473) *Master,* Prof. D. S. Ingram (2000)
ST EDMUND'S (1896) *Master,* Prof. Sir Brian Heap, FRS (1996)
ST JOHN'S (1511) *Master,* Prof. P. Goddard, FRS (1994)
SELWYN (1882) *Master,* Prof. R. J. Bowring, Litt.D (2000)
SIDNEY SUSSEX (1596) *Master,* Prof. S. J. N. Dawson (1999)
TRINITY (1546) *Master,* Prof. A. K. Sen, Ph.D. (1998)
TRINITY HALL (1350) *Master,* Prof. P. F. Clarke, Lit.D., FBA (2000)
WOLFSON (1965) *President,* G. Johnson, Ph.D. (1994),

*College for women only

UNIVERSITY OF CENTRAL ENGLAND IN BIRMINGHAM (1992)
Perry Barr, Birmingham, B42 2SU
Tel: 0121-331 5000
Web: www.uce.ac.uk
Full-time students (2002–3), 12,500
Chancellor, Cllr Mahmood Hussein
Registrar and Secretary, Maxine Penlington
Vice-Chancellor, Dr P. C. Knight, CBE

UNIVERSITY OF CENTRAL LANCASHIRE (1992)
Preston, PR1 2HE
Tel: 01772-201201
Web: www.uclan.ac.uk
Full-time students (2002–3), 29,000
Academic Registrar, Lesley Munro
Chancellor, Sir Richard Evans, CBE, DL (2002)
Vice-Chancellor, Dr Malcolm McVicar

CITY UNIVERSITY (1996)
Northampton Square, London EC1V 0HB
Tel: 020-7040 5060
Web: www.city.ac.uk
Full-time students (2002–3), 10,000
Academic Registrar, Ms F. Owen
Chancellor, The Rt. Hon. The Lord Mayor of London
Secretary, I. Creagh
Vice-Chancellor, Prof. D. W. Rhind, Ph.D., DSc

COVENTRY UNIVERSITY (1992)
Priory Street, Coventry CV1 5FB
Tel: 024-76 887688
Web: www.coventry.ac.uk
Full-time students (2002–3), 20,000
Academic Registrar, Kate Quantrell
Chancellor, The Lord Plumb, DL (1995)
Secretary, Dr John Gledhill
Vice-Chancellor, Dr Michael Goldstein, CBE

CRANFIELD UNIVERSITY (1969)
Cranfield, Beds MK43 0AL
Tel: 01234-750111
Web: www.cranfield.ac.uk
Full-time students (2002–3), 2,740
Academic Registrar and Secretary, David Buck
Chancellor, The Lord Vincent of Coleshill, GBE, KCB, DSO
Vice-Chancellor, Prof. Frank Hartley, DSc (1998)

DE MONTFORT UNIVERSITY (1992)
The Gateway, Leicester LE1 9BH
Tel: 0116-255 1551
Web: www.dmu.ac.uk
Full-time students (2002–3), 16,700
Academic Registrar, Eugene Critchlow
Chancellor, Baroness Prashar of Runnymede, CBE (1998)
Chief Executive and Vice-Chancellor, Prof. Philip Tasker
Secretary, Ms Linda Jones

UNIVERSITY OF DERBY (1992)
Kedleston Road, Derby DE22 1GB
Tel: 01332-590500
Web: www.derby.ac.uk
Full-time students (2002–3), 25,000
Chancellor, Sir Christopher Ball
Registrar, June Hughes
Secretary, Dr Paul Bridges
Vice-Chancellor, Prof. Roger Waterhouse

UNIVERSITY OF DUNDEE (1967)
Dundee DD1 4HN
Tel: 01382-344000
Web: www.dundee.ac.uk
Full-time students (2002–3), 12,000
Academic Secretary, Dr David Duncan
Chancellor, Sir James Black, FRCP, FRS (1992)
Rector, Fred MacAulay, 1998–2001
Vice-Chancellor, Sir Alan Langlands

UNIVERSITY OF DURHAM (1832)
The University Office, Durham DH1 3HP
Tel: 0191-334 2000
Web: www.dur.ac.uk
Full-time students (2002–3), 11,597
Chancellor, Sir Peter Ustinov, CBE, FRSL, FRSA, FRSL
Registrar and Secretary, J. V. Hogan, Ph.D.
Vice-Chancellor, Prof. Sir Kenneth Calman, KCB, MD, Ph.D.

COLLEGES
COLLINGWOOD, *Principal,* Jane H. M. Taylor, D.PHIL. (2001)
GEORGE STEPHENSON, *Principal,* Prof. A. C. Darnell (2001)
GREY, *Acting Master,* A. E. Cleaver (2002)
HATFIELD, *Acting Master,* Angel B. Scott (2002)
JOHN SNOW, *Principal,* Prof. H. M. Evans, PH.D. (2002)
ST AIDAN'S, *Principal,* J. S. Ashworth (1998)
ST CHAD'S, *Principal,* Revd J. P. M. Cassidy, PH.D. (1997)
ST CUTHBERT'S SOCIETY, *Acting Principal,* B. Robertson (2003)
ST HILD AND ST BEDE, *Principal,* J. A. Pearson, PH.D. (2000)
ST JOHN'S, *Principal,* Rt. Revd Prof. S. W. Sykes (1999)
ST MARY'S, *Principal,* Miss J. L Hobbs (1999)
TREVELYAN, *Principal,* N. Martin, PH.D. (2000)
UNIVERSITY, *Master,* Prof. M. E. Tucker, PH.D. (2000)
USHAW, *President,* Revd J. O'Keefe (1996)
USTINOV COLLEGE (Graduate Society), *Principal,* Susan J. Scott (2003)
VAN MILDERT, *Principal,* G. Patterson (2000)

UNIVERSITY OF EAST ANGLIA (1963)
Norwich NR4 7TJ
Tel: 01603-456161
Web: www.uea.ac.uk
Full-time students (2002–3), 13,000
Chancellor, Sir Geoffrey Allen, FRS, FREng. (1994)
Registrar and Secretary, Brian Summers
Vice-Chancellor, Prof. David Eastwood

UNIVERSITY OF EAST LONDON (1898)
Longbridge Road, Dagenham, Essex RM8 2AS
Tel: 020-8223 3000
Web: www.uel.ac.uk
Full-time students (2002–3), 14,500
Chancellor, The Lord Rix, CBE, DL (1997)
Registrar and Secretary, Alan Ingle
Vice-Chancellor, Prof. Michael Thorne

UNIVERSITY OF EDINBURGH (1583)
Old College, South Bridge, Edinburgh EH8 9YL
Tel: 0131-650 1000
Web: www.ed.ac.uk
Full-time students (2002–3), 20,483
Chancellor, HRH The Prince Philip, Duke of Edinburgh, KG, KT, OM, GBE, PC, FRS (1952)
Principal and Vice-Chancellor, Prof. Tim O'Shea, FBA, FRSE
Rector, Tam Dalyell, MP
Secretary, Melvyn Cornish

UNIVERSITY OF ESSEX (1964)
Wivenhoe Park, Colchester CO4 3SQ
Tel: 01206-873333
Web: www.essex.ac.uk
Full-time students (2002–3), 6,686
Chancellor, Lord Phillips of Sudbury

Registrar and Secretary, Dr Tony Rich
Vice-Chancellor, Prof. Ivor Crewe

UNIVERSITY OF EXETER (1955)
Northcote House, The Queen's Drive, Exeter EX4 4QJ
Tel: 01392-661000
Web: www.exeter.ac.uk
Full-time students (2002–3), 9,622
Chancellor, The Lord Alexander of Weedon, QC (1998)
Registrar and Secretary, I. H. C. Powell
Vice-Chancellor, Prof. Steven Smith

UNIVERSITY OF GLAMORGAN (1992)
Pontypridd CF37 1DL
Tel: 01443-480480 Freephone: 0800-716925
Web: www.glam.ac.uk
Full-time students (2002–3), 10,090
Academic Registrar, John O'Shea
Chancellor, The Rt. Hon. the Lord Morris of Aberavon, QC (1994)
Vice-Chancellor, Prof. Sir Adrian Webb

UNIVERSITY OF GLASGOW (1451)
Gilbert Scott Building, University Avenue, Glasgow G12 8QQ
Tel: 0141-339 8855
Web: www.gla.ac.uk
Full-time students (2002–3), 19,180
Chancellor, Sir William Kerr Fraser, GCB, LLD, FRSE
Rector, Greg Hemphill
Secretary, Dugald Mackie, FRSA
Vice-Chancellor, Sir Muir Russell, KCB, FRSE

GLASGOW CALEDONIAN UNIVERSITY (1993)
City Campus, 70 Cowcaddens Road, Glasgow G4 0BA
Tel: 0141-331 3000
Web: www.caledonian.ac.uk
Full-time students (2002–3), 14,000
Principal and Vice-Chancellor, I. A. Johnston, Ph.D., CB, FIPO, FRSA
Pro Vice Chancellor, Prof. G. Dickson, (2003)
Secretary to University Court, B. M. Murphy

UNIVERSITY OF GLOUCESTERSHIRE (2001)
The Park, Cheltenham, Glos GL50 2QF
Tel: 01242-532700
Web: www.glos.ac.uk
Full-time students, (2002–3), 6,063
Academic Registrar, Peter Griffiths
Chancellor, Lord Carey of Clifton
Vice-Chancellor, Dame Janet Trotter

UNIVERSITY OF GREENWICH (1992)
Old Royal Naval College, Park Row, London SE10 9LS
Tel: 020-8331 8000
Web: www.gre.ac.uk
Full-time students (2002–3), 11,745
Academic Registrar, Christine Rose
Chancellor, The Rt. Hon. Lord Holme of Cheltenham, CBE
Vice-Chancellor, Prof. Rick Trainor

HERIOT-WATT UNIVERSITY (1966)
Edinburgh EH14 4AS
Tel: 0131-449 5111
Web: www.hw.ac.uk
Full-time students (2002–3), 6,100
Chancellor, The Lord Mackay of Clashfern KT, PC (1979)
Secretary, P. L. Wilson
Vice-Chancellor, Prof. John Archer, FREng.

UNIVERSITY OF HERTFORDSHIRE (1992)
College Lane, Hatfield, Herts, AL10 9AB
Tel: 01707-284000
Web: www.herts.ac.uk
Full-time students (2002–3), 16,656
Chancellor, The Lord MacLaurin of Knebworth, (1996)
Registrar and Secretary, Philip Waters
Vice-Chancellor, Prof. R. J. T. Wilson

UNIVERSITY OF HUDDERSFIELD (1992)
Queensgate, Huddersfield HD1 3DH
Tel: 01484-422288
Web: www.hud.ac.uk
Full-time students (2002–3), 17,347
Chancellor, Sir Ernest Hall, OBE (1996)
Secretary, Tony Mears
Vice-Chancellor, Prof. John Tarrant

UNIVERSITY OF HULL (1927)
Cottingham Road, Hull HU6 7RX
Tel: 01482-346311
Web: www.hull.ac.uk
Full-time students (2002–3), 17,000
Chancellor, The Lord Armstrong of Ilminster, GCB, CVO (1994)
Quality Director and Registrar and Secretary, Frances Owen
Vice-Chancellor, Prof. David Drewry

KEELE UNIVERSITY (1962)
Keele, Staffs ST5 5BG
Tel: 01782-621111
Web: www.keele.ac.uk
Full-time students (2002–3), 5,636
Chancellor, Prof. Sir David Weatherall, MB, FRCP (1986)
Registrar and Secretary, S. J. Morris
Vice-Chancellor, Prof. Janet Finch CBE

UNIVERSITY OF KENT AT CANTERBURY (1965)
Canterbury, Kent CT2 7NZ
Tel: 01227-764000
Web: www.kent.ac.uk
Full-time students (2002–3), 9,300
Chancellor, Sir Crispin Tickell, GCMG, KCVO
Registrar and Secretary, Nick McHard
Vice-Chancellor, Prof. David Melville

KINGSTON UNIVERSITY (1992)
River House, 53–57 High Street, Kingston upon Thames, Surrey KT1 1LQ
Tel: 020-8547 2000
Web: www.kingston.ac.uk
Full-time students (2002–3), 12,000
Chancellor, Sir Peter Hall
Secretary, Raficq Abdula, MBE
Vice-Chancellor, Prof. Peter Scott

UNIVERSITY OF LANCASTER (1964)
Bailrigg, Lancaster LA1 4YW
Tel: 01524-65201
Web: www.lancs.ac.uk
Full-time students (2002–3), 9,385.5
Chancellor, HRH Princess Alexandra, the Hon. Lady Ogilvy, GCVO (1964)
Secretary, Fiona Aiken
Vice-Chancellor, Prof. Paul Wellings

THE UNIVERSITY OF LEEDS (1904)
Leeds LS2 9JT
Tel: 0113-343 1751
Web: www.leeds.ac.uk
Full-time students (2002–3), 27,841
Chancellor, Lord Bragg of Wigton
Secretary, J. Roger Gair
Vice-Chancellor, Prof. Sir Alan Wilson

LEEDS METROPOLITAN UNIVERSITY (1992)
City Campus, Leeds LS1 3HE
Tel: 0113-283 2600
Web: www.lmu.ac.uk
Full-time students (2002–3), 15,505
Chancellor, Leslie Silver, OBE (1989)
Secretary, Steve Denton
Vice-Chancellor, Prof. Simon Lee

UNIVERSITY OF LEICESTER (1957)
University Road, Leicester LE1 7RH
Tel: 0116-252 2522
Web: www.le.ac.uk
Full-time students (2002–3), 9,000
Chancellor, Sir Michael Atiyah, OM, FRS, Ph.D., D.Sc. (1995)
Registrar and Secretary, K. J. Julian
Vice-Chancellor, Prof. R. Burgess, Ph.D.

UNIVERSITY OF LINCOLN (1992)
Brayford, Pool, Lincoln LN6 7TS
Tel: 01522-882000
Web: www.ulh.ac.uk
Full-time students (2002–3), 8,000
Chancellor, Dame Elizabeth Esteve-Coll
Registrar, Edmund Fitzpatrick
Vice-Chancellor, Prof. David Chiddick

UNIVERSITY OF LIVERPOOL (1903)
Senate House, Abercromby Square, Liverpool L69 3BX
Tel: 0151-794 2000
Web: www.liv.ac.uk
Full-time students (2002–3), 16,381
Chancellor, Rt. Hon. Lord Owen, CH (1996)
Registrar and Secretary, M. D. Carr
Vice-Chancellor, Prof. J. D. Bone, FRSA

LIVERPOOL JOHN MOORES UNIVERSITY (1992)
Egerton Court, 2 Rodaney Street, Liverpool L3 5UX
Tel: 0151-231 2121
Web: www.livjm.ac.uk
Full-time students (2002–3), 15,000
Chancellor, Ms C. Booth, QC
Registrar and Secretary, Ms A. Wild
Vice-Chancellor, Prof. M. Brown

UNIVERSITY OF LONDON (1836)
Senate House, Malet Street, London WC1E 7HU
Tel: 020-7862 8000
Web: www.lon.ac.uk
Academic Registrar, Mrs G. F. Roberts
Chairman of the Council, The Rt. Hon. The Lord Brooke of Sutton Mandeville, CH, PC
Chancellor, HRH The Princess Royal, KG, GCVO, FRS (1981)
Director of Administration, J. R. Davidson
Vice-Chancellor, Prof. Sir Graeme Davies (2003)
Visitor, HM the Queen in Council

COLLEGES

BIRKBECK, Malet Street, London WC1E 7HX. *Master,* Prof.
D. Latchman (2003)

COURTAULD INSTITUTE OF ART, Somerset House, Strand,
London WC2R 0RN. *Director,* Prof. J. Cuno (2003)

GOLDSMITHS COLLEGE, Lewisham Way, New Cross,
London SE14 6NW. *Warden,* Prof. B. Pimlott, FBA (1998)

HEYTHROP COLLEGE, Kensington Square, London
W8 5HQ. *Principal,* Revd Dr J. McDade, SJ, BD (1999)

IMPERIAL COLLEGE OF SCIENCE, TECHNOLOGY AND
MEDICINE (incl. Imperial College Schools of Medicine at
Charing Cross, Hammersmith and St Mary's hospitals and at
the National Heart and Lung Institute), South Kensington,
London SW7 2AZ. *Rector,* Sir Richard Sykes, FRS (2001)

INSTITUTE OF EDUCATION, 20 Bedford Way, London
WC1H 0AL. *Director,* Prof. G. Whitty (2000)

KING'S COLLEGE LONDON (incl. Guy's, King's and St.
Thomas' Schools of Medicine, Dentistry and Biomedical
Sciences), Strand, London WC2R 2LS. *Principal,* Prof. A.
Lucas, Ph.D. (1993)

LONDON BUSINESS SCHOOL, Sussex Place, Regent's Place,
London NW1 4SA. *Dean,* Prof. L. D'Andrea Tyson (2002)

LONDON SCHOOL OF ECONOMICS AND POLITICAL
SCIENCE, Houghton Street, London WC2A 2AE. *Director,*
Prof. A. Giddens (1997)

LONDON SCHOOL OF HYGIENE AND TROPICAL
MEDICINE, Keppel Street, London WC1E 7HT. *Dean,* Prof.
A. Haines (2001)

QUEEN MARY, Mile End Road, London E1 4NS. *Principal,*
Prof. A. Smith, FRS, Ph.D. (1998)

ROYAL HOLLOWAY (incorporating St Bartholomew's and the
Royal London School of Medicine and Dentistry), Egham Hill,
Egham, Surrey TW20 0EX. *Principal,* Prof. S. Hill (2002)

ROYAL VETERINARY COLLEGE, Royal College Street,
London NW1 0TU. *Principal and Dean,* Prof. L. E.
Lanyon, CBE (1989)

ST GEORGE'S HOSPITAL MEDICAL SCHOOL, Cranmer
Terrace, London SW17 0RE.
Principal, Prof. R. Boyd (1996)

SCHOOL OF ORIENTAL AND AFRICAN STUDIES,
Thornhaugh Street, Russell Square, London WC1N 1AX.
Dean, Prof. C. Bundy (2001)

SCHOOL OF PHARMACY, 29–39 Brunswick Square, London
WC1N 1AX.
Dean, Prof. A. T. Florence, CBE, Ph.D. (1989)

ROYAL ACADEMY OF MUSIC, Marylebone Road, London
NW1 5HT.
Principal, Prof. Curtis Price, Ph.D., FKC (1995)

UNIVERSITY COLLEGE LONDON, Gower Street, London
WC1N 6BT. *Provost and President,* Prof. Sir Derek
Roberts (2002)

INSTITUTES AND ASSOCIATE INSTITUTIONS

BRITISH INSTITUTE IN PARIS, 9–11 rue de Constantine,
75340 Paris, Cedex 07, France. *London Office:* Senate
House, Malet Street, London WC1E 7HU.
Director, Prof. C. L. Campos, OBE, Ph.D. (1978)

INSTITUTE OF CANCER RESEARCH, Royal Cancer
Hospital, Chester Beatty Laboratories, 17A Onslow Gardens,
London SW7 3AL. *Chief Executive,* Prof. P. Rigby (1999)

UNIVERSITY MARINE BIOLOGICAL STATION, Isle of
Cumbrae, Scotland KA28 0EG

SCHOOL OF ADVANCED STUDY,
Institute of Advanced Legal Studies, Charles Clore House,
17 Russell Square, London WC1B 5DR.
Director, Prof. B. A. K. Rider (1995)

INSTITUTE OF CLASSICAL STUDIES, Senate House,
Malet Street, London WC1E 7HU.
Director, Prof. G. B. Waywell, FSA (1996)

INSTITUTE OF COMMONWEALTH STUDIES,
27–28 Russell Square, London WC1B 5DS.
Director, Prof. T. Shaw (2001)

INSTITUTE OF ENGLISH STUDIES, Senate House, Malet
Street, London WC1E 7HU.
Director, Prof. W. Gould (2000)

INSTITUTE OF GERMANIC STUDIES, 29 Russell Square,
London WC1B 5DP.
Director, Prof. R. Görner, Ph.D. (1999)

INSTITUTE OF HISTORICAL RESEARCH, Senate House,
Malet Street, London WC1E 7HU.
Director, Prof. D. Cannadine (1998)

INSTITUTE OF LATIN AMERICAN STUDIES,
31 Tavistock Square, London WC1H 9HA.
Director, Prof. J. Dunkerley (1998)

INSTITUTE OF ROMANCE STUDIES, Senate House, Malet
Street, London WC1E 7HU. *Director,* Prof. J. Still (2002)

INSTITUTE OF UNITED STATES STUDIES, Senate House,
Malet Street, London WC1E 7HU.
Director, Prof. G. L. McDowell, Ph.D. (2002)

WARBURG INSTITUTE, Woburn Square, London
WC1H 0AB. *Director,* Prof. C. Hope

EXTERNAL PROGRAMME, Senate House, Malet Street,
London WC1E 7HU. *Director,* J. McConnell (1992)

PHILOSOPHY PROGRAMME, Senate House, Malet Street,
London WC1E 7HU. *Director,* Prof. T. Crane

LONDON METROPOLITAN UNIVERSITY (2002)

London City Campus, 31 Jewry Street, London EC3N 2EY
Tel: 020-7320 1000
Web: www.londonmet.ac.uk
Full-time students (2002–3), 19,000
Academic Registrar, Jill Grinstead
Chief Executive, Brian Roper
Secretary, John MacParland
Vice-Chancellor, Prof. Roderick Floud

LOUGHBOROUGH UNIVERSITY (1966)

Ashby Road, Loughborough, Leics LE11 3TU
Tel: 01509-263171
Web: www.lboro.ac.uk
Full-time students (2002–3), 13,500
Chancellor, Sir John Jennings, CBE (1989)
Registrar and Secretary, John Town
Vice-Chancellor, Prof. David Wallace, CBE, FRS, FREng

UNIVERSITY OF LUTON (1993)

Park Square, Luton LU1 3JU
Tel: 01582-734111
Web: www.luton.ac.uk
Full-time students (2002–3), 11,000
Chancellor, Sir Robin Biggam (2001)
Vice-Chancellor, Dr Dai John

UNIVERSITY OF MANCHESTER (1185)
Oxford Road, Manchester M13 9PL
Tel: 0161-275 2000
Web: www.man.ac.uk
Full-time students (2002–3), 21,784
Chancellor, Anna Ford, LLD (1994)
Registrar and Secretary, Eddie Newcomb, OBE, FRSA
Vice-Chancellor, Prof. Sir Martin Harris, CBE, DL, Ph.D.

UNIVERSITY OF MANCHESTER INSTITUTE OF
SCIENCE AND TECHNOLOGY (UMIST) (1824)
PO Box 88, Manchester M60 1QD
Tel: 0161-236 3311
Web: www.umist.ac.uk
Full-time students (2002–3), 7,000
Chancellor, Sir Terry Leahy (1995)
Registrar and Secretary, Jon Baldwin
Vice-Chancellor, Prof. John Garside

MANCHESTER METROPOLITAN UNIVERSITY
(1992)
All Saints, Manchester M15 6BH
Tel: 0161-247 2000
Web: www.mmu.ac.uk
Full-time students (2002–3), 26,000
Chancellor, Dame Janet Smith
Registrar, Janusz Karczewski-Slowikowski
Secretary, Stephen Heaton
Vice-Chancellor, Mrs Alexandra Burslem

MIDDLESEX UNIVERSITY (1992)
White Hart Lane, London N17 8HR
Tel: 020-8411 5000
Web: www.mdx.ac.uk
Full-time students (2002–3), 22,500
Chancellor, The Rt. Hon. Lord Sheppard of Didgemere
Registrar, Colin Davis
Vice-Chancellor, Prof. Michael Driscoll, FRSA

NAPIER UNIVERSITY (1992)
Craighouse Campus, Craighouse Road, Edinburgh EH10 5LG
Tel: 0131-444 2266
Web: www.napier.ac.uk
Full-time students (2002–3), 12,000 (1993)
Principal and Vice-Chancellor, Joan Stringer
Secretary, Dr Gerry Webber

UNIVERSITY OF NEWCASTLE UPON TYNE
(1963)
6 Kensington Terrace, Newcastle upon Tyne NE1 7RU
Tel: 0191-222 6000
Web: www.ncl.ac.uk
Full-time students (2002–3), 14,656
Chancellor, Rt. Hon. Christopher Patten, CH (1999)
Registrar, Dr. J Hogan
Vice-Chancellor, Prof. C. R. W. Edwards

NORTHUMBRIA UNIVERSITY AT NEWCASTLE
(1992)
Ellison Building, Ellison Place, Newcastle upon Tyne NE1 8ST
Tel: 0191-232 6002
Web: www.northumbria.ac.uk
Full-time students (2002–3), 18,404
Chancellor, Lord Glenamara, CH, PC (1984)
Registrar, Cheryl Penna
Secretary, Richard Bott
Vice-Chancellor, Prof. Kel Fidler

UNIVERSITY OF NOTTINGHAM (1948)
University Park, Nottingham NG7 2RD
Tel: 0115-951 5151
Web: www.nottingham.ac.uk
Full-time students (2002–3), 24,500
Chancellor, Prof. F. Yang, Litt.D. (1993)
Registrar, K. H. Jones
Vice-Chancellor, Prof. Sir Colin Campbell, DL, LLB, FRSA, LLD

NOTTINGHAM TRENT UNIVERSITY (1992)
Burton Street, Nottingham NG1 4BU
Tel: 0115-941 8418
Web: www.ntu.ac.uk
Full-time students (2002–3), 16,385
Chairman of the Board of Governors, John Peace
Registrar, David Samson
Secretary, Stephen Smith
Vice-Chancellor, Prof. Ray Cowell, Ph.D.

OPEN UNIVERSITY (1969)
Walton Hall, Milton Keynes MK7 6AA
Tel: 01908-274066
Web: www.open.ac.uk
Students (2002–3), 79,000
Chancellor, Baroness Betty Boothroyd of Sandwell, MP
Head of Student Recruitment and Retention, Ms Helen Niven
Secretary, Fraser Woodburn
Vice-Chancellor, Prof. Brenda Gourley

UNIVERSITY OF OXFORD (*c.* 12th century)
University Offices, Wellington Square, Oxford OX1 2JD
Tel: 01865-270000
Web: www.ox.ac.uk
Students in residence 2002–3, 16,411
Assessor, Dr T. C. Buchanan (Kellogg), elected 2003
Bodley's Librarian, R. P. Carr (Balliol), appointed 1997
Chancellor, The Rt. Hon. Chris Patten, CH, elected 2003
Director of the Ashmolean Museum, Dr C. Brown (Worcester), elected 1998
High Steward, The Rt. Hon. Lord Bingham of Cornhill (Balliol), elected 2002
Keeper of Archives, S. Bailey, elected 2000
Proctors, Prof. D. A. Hills (Lincoln), Dr I. W. Archer (Keble), elected 2003
Public Orator, Prof. J. Griffin (Balliol), elected 1997
Registrar of the University, D. R. Holmes (St John's), elected 1998
Secretary of the Chest, J. R. Clements (Merton), elected 1995
Secretary of the Faculties and Academic Registrar, A. P Weale (Worcester), elected 1984
Surveyor to the University, Ms J. Wood
Vice-Chancellor, Sir Colin Lucas (Balliol), elected 1997

COLLEGES AND HALLS *with dates of foundation*
ALL SOULS (1438) *Warden,* Prof. J. Davis, FBA, Ph.D. (1995)
BALLIOL (1263) *Master,* A. Graham (1998)
BLACKFRIARS (1221) *Regent,* Revd F. G. Kerr (1998)
BRASENOSE (1509) *Principal,* Prof. R. Cashmore, FRS (2003)
CAMPION HALL (1896) *Master,* Revd Dr G. J. Hughes (1998)
CHRIST CHURCH (1546) *Dean,* Very Revd J. H. Drury (1991)
CORPUS CHRISTI (1517) *President,* Sir Timothy Lankester, KCB (2001)

EXETER (1314) *Rector,* Prof. M. Butler (1993)
GREEN (1979) *Warden,* Sir John Hanson, KCMG, CBE (1997)
GREYFRIARS (1910) *Warden,* Revd Dr T. G. Weinandy (1996)
HARRIS MANCHESTER (1786) *Principal,* Revd R. Waller, Ph.D. (1988)
HERTFORD (1974) *Principal,* Sir Walter Bodmer, FRS, FRCPath. (1996)
JESUS (1571) *Principal,* Sir Peter North, CBE, FBA (1984)
KEBLE (1868) *Warden,* Prof. A. Cameron, CBE, Ph.D., FBA, FSA (1994)
KELLOGG (1990) *President,* Dr G. P Thomas (1990)
LADY MARGARET HALL (1878) *Principal,* Dr Frances Lannon, FRHist. (2002)
LINACRE (1962) *Principal,* Prof. P. A. Slack, FBA (1996)
LINCOLN (1427) *Rector,* Prof. P. Langford (2000)
MAGDALEN (1458) *President,* A. D. Smith, CBE (1998)
MANSFIELD (1886) *Principal,* Dr D. Walford, FRCPath., FRCP, FFPHM (1996)
MERTON (1264) *Warden,* Prof. Dame J. Rawlson, CBE, FBA (1994)
NEW COLLEGE (1379) *Warden,* Prof. A. J. Ryan, FBA (1996)
NUFFIELD (1958) *Warden,* Sir Tony Atkinson, FBA (1994)
ORIEL (1326) *Provost,* Dr. E. W. Nicholson
PEMBROKE (1624) *Master,* Giles Henderson, CBE (2001)
QUEEN'S (1340) *Provost,* Sir Alan Budd (1999)
REGENT'S PARK (1820) *Principal,* Revd Dr P. S. Fiddes (1989)
ST ANNE'S (1952) (Society of Oxford Home-Students), *Principal,* Dame Ruth Deech (1991)
ST ANTONY'S (1953) *Warden,* Sir Marrack Goulding, KCMG (1997)
ST BENET'S HALL (1897) *Master,* Revd H. Wansbrough, OSB (1991)
ST CATHERINE'S (1963) *Master,* Prof. Roger Ainsworth (2003)
ST CROSS (1965) *Master,* Prof. Andrew Goudie (2003)
ST EDMUND HALL (c.1278) *Principal,* Prof. D. M. P. Mingos, FRS, FRSC (1999)
*ST HILDA'S (1893) *Principal,* Lady Judith English (2001)
ST HUGH'S (1886) *Principal,* A, Dilnot, CBE (2002)
ST JOHN'S (1555) *President,* Sir Michael Scholar, KCB (2001)
ST PETER'S (1929) *Master,* Prof. Bernard Silverman, FRS (2003)
SOMERVILLE (1879) *Principal,* Dame Fiona Caldicott, DBE, FRCP, FRCPsych. (1996)
TEMPLETON (1965) *President,* Sir David Rowland (1998)
TRINITY (1554) *President,* The Hon. Michael J. Beloff, FRSA (1996)
UNIVERSITY (1249) *Master,* Lord Butler of Brockwell, GCB, CVO (1998)
WADHAM (1610) *Warden,* J. Fleming (2003)
WOLFSON (1966) *President,* Prof. Sir Gareth Roberts, FRS, Ph.D. (2000)
WORCESTER (1714) *Provost,* R. G. Smethurst (1991)
WYCLIFFE HALL (1877) *Principal,* Revd Dr A. E. McGrath (1995)

*College for women only

OXFORD BROOKES UNIVERSITY (1992)
Gipsy Lane, Oxford OX3 0BP
Tel: 01865-484848
Web: www.brookes.ac.uk
Full-time students (2002–3), 15,570
Chancellor, Jon Snow
Vice-Chancellor, Prof. Graham Upton

UNIVERSITY OF PAISLEY (1992)
Paisley PA1 2BE
Tel: 0141-848 3000
Web: www.paisley.ac.uk
Full-time students (2002–3), 10,300
Chancellor, Sir Robert Smith
Registrar and Secretary, David Rigg
Secretary, J. Fraser
Vice-Chancellor and Principal, Prof. John Macklin

UNIVERSITY OF PLYMOUTH (1992)
Drake Circus, Plymouth PL4 8AA
Tel: 01752-600600
Web: www.plymouth.ac.uk
Full-time students (2002–3), 17,000
Academic Registrar and University Secretary, Miss J. Hopkinson
Vice-Chancellor, Prof. J. Levinsky

UNIVERSITY OF PORTSMOUTH (1992)
University House, Winston Churchill Avenue, Portsmouth PO1 2UP
Tel: 023-9284 8484
Web: www.port.ac.uk
Full-time students (2002–3), 15,500
Academic Registrar, Andy Rees
Chancellor, Lord Palumbo of Walbrook
Vice-Chancellor, Prof. John Craven

QUEEN'S UNIVERSITY OF BELFAST (1908)
Belfast BT7 1NN
Tel: 028-9024 5133
Web: www.qub.ac.uk
Full-time students (2002–3), 16,000
Chancellor, Senator George Mitchell
Registrar, James O'Kane
Vice-Chancellor, Prof. Sir George Bain

UNIVERSITY OF READING (1926)
Whiteknights, PO Box 217, Reading RG6 6AH
Tel: 0118-987 5123
Web: www.reading.ac.uk
Full-time students (2002–3), 10,585
Chancellor, Lord Carrington, KG, GCMG, CH, MC, PC (1992)
Registrar, D. C. R. Frampton
Vice-Chancellor, Prof. Gordon Marshall, (2003)

ROBERT GORDON UNIVERSITY (1992)
Schoolhill, Aberdeen AB10 1FR
Tel: 01224-262000
Web: www.rgu.ac.uk
Full-time students (2002–3), 8,230
Chancellor, Sir Bob Reid (1993)
Registrar, Ms Hilary Douglas
Secretary, Dr Adrian Graves, D.Phil.
Vice-Chancellor and Principal, Prof. William Stevely, D.Phil.

ROYAL COLLEGE OF ART (1837)
Kensington Gore, London SW7 2EU
Tel: 020-7590 4444
Web: www.rca.ac.uk
Students (2002–3), 816
Provost, Lord Snowdon, GCVO (1995)
Registrar, Alan Selby
Vice-Provost, Prof. Sir Christopher Frayling

ROYAL COLLEGE OF MUSIC
Prince Consort Road, London SW7 2BS
Tel: 020-7589 3643
Web: www.rcm.ac.uk
Full-time students (2002–3), 500
Dean and Deputy Director, Dr J. Cox
Director, Dame Janet Ritterman, DBE
Registrar and Secretary, K. A. Porter

UNIVERSITY OF ST ANDREWS (1411)
College Gate, St Andrews, Fife KY16 9AJ
Tel: 01334-476161
Web: www.st-and.ac.uk
Full-time students (2002–3), 6,401
Chancellor, Sir Kenneth Dover, LL D, D.Litt., FRSE, FBA
   (1981)
Secretary and Registrar, David Corner
Vice-Chancellor, Brian Lang, Ph.D

UNIVERSITY OF SALFORD (1896)
Salford, Greater Manchester M5 4WT
Tel: 0161-295 5000
Web: www.salford.ac.uk
Full-time students (2002–3), 15,000
Chancellor, Sir Walter Bodmer, Ph.D., FRS
Registrar, Dr M. D. Winton, Ph.D.
Vice-Chancellor, Prof. M. Harloe

UNIVERSITY OF SHEFFIELD (1905)
Western Bank, Sheffield S10 2TN
Tel: 0114-222 2000
Web: www.shef.ac.uk
Full-time students (2002–3), 20,889
Chancellor, Sir Peter Middleton
Registrar and Secretary, Dr D. E. Fletcher
Vice-Chancellor, Prof. R. F. Boucher

SHEFFIELD HALLAM UNIVERSITY (1992)
City Campus, Howard Street, Sheffield S1 1WB
Tel: 0114-225 5555
Web: www.shu.ac.uk
Full-time students (2002–3), 21,880
Chancellor, Lord Prof. Robert Winston (1992)
Registrar, Jane Tory
Secretary, Tom Colsten
Vice-Chancellor, Prof. Diana Green

UNIVERSITY OF SOUTHAMPTON (1952)
Highfield, Southampton SO17 1BJ
Tel: 023-8059 5000
Web: www.soton.ac.uk
Full-time students (2002–3), 16,851
Chancellor, The Rt. Hon Earl of Selbourne (1996)
Registrar and Secretary, John Lauwerys
Vice-Chancellor, Prof. Bill Wakeham

SOUTH BANK UNIVERSITY (1992)
103 Borough Road, London SE1 0AA
Tel: 020-7928 8989
Web: www.sbu.ac.uk
Full-time students (2002–3), 13,500
Chancellor, Sir Trevor McDonald, OBE
Secretary, Ms K. Stephenson
Vice-Chancellor, Prof. D. Hopkin

STAFFORDSHIRE UNIVERSITY (1992)
College Road, Stoke-on-Trent ST4 2DE
Tel: 01782-294000
Web: www.staffs.ac.uk
Full-time students (2002–3), 18,500
Chancellor, vacant
Dean of Students, Francesca Francis
Secretary, Ken Sproston
Vice-Chancellor, Prof. Christine King

UNIVERSITY OF STIRLING (1967)
Stirling FK9 4LA
Tel: 01786-473171
Web: www.stir.ac.uk
Full-time students (2002–3), 6,800
Academic Registrar, Douglas Wood
Acting Principal and Vice-Chancellor, Prof. C. Hallett,
   Ph.D., FRSE
Chancellor, Dame Diana Rigg
University Secretary, Kevin Clarke

UNIVERSITY OF STRATHCLYDE (1796)
McCance Building, John Anderson Campus, Glasgow G1 1XQ
Tel: 0141-552 4400
Web: www.strath.ac.uk
Full-time students (2002–3), 15,000
Academic Registrar, Dr S. M. Mellows
Chairman of Court, A. S. Hunter
Chancellor, Rt. Hon. Lord Hope of Craighead, PC (1998)
Secretary, Dr Peter West
Vice-Chancellor, Prof. Andrew Hamnett

UNIVERSITY OF SUNDERLAND (1992)
Langham Tower, Ryhope Road, Sunderland SR2 7EE
Tel: 0191-515 2000
Web: www.sunderland.ac.uk
Full-time students (2002–3), 8,500
Chancellor, The Lord Puttnam of Queensgate, CBE
   (1998)
Rector, Revd Alison Marshall
Secretary, J. D. Pacey
Vice-Chancellor, Prof. P. Fidler, MBE

UNIVERSITY OF SURREY (1966)
Guildford, Surrey GU2 7XH
Tel: 01483-300800
Web: www.surrey.ac.uk
Full-time students (2002–3), 9,500
Chancellor, HRH The Duke of Kent, KG, GCMG, GCVO
   (1977)
Registrar, Peter Beardsley, FRSA
University Secretary and Clerk to the Council,
   James Strawson
Vice-Chancellor, Prof. P. J. Dowling CBE, FRS, FREng.,
   FRS

UNIVERSITY OF SURREY ROEHAMPTON
Roehampton Lane, London SW15 5PU
Tel: 020-8392 3000/3232
Web: www.roehampton.ac.uk
Full-time students (2002–3), 8000
Chancellor, HRH The Duke of Kent, KG, GCMG, GCVO
Vice Chancellor, Dr Bernadette Porter

UNIVERSITY OF SUSSEX (1961)
Sussex House, Falmer, Brighton BN1 9RH
Tel: 01273-606755
Web: www.sussex.ac.uk
Full-time students (2002–3), 10,000
Chancellor, Lord Richard Attenborough, CBE (1998)
Registrar and Secretary, Neil Gershon
Vice-Chancellor, Prof. Alisdair Smith

UNIVERSITY OF TEESSIDE (1992)
Middlesbrough, Tees Valley TS1 3BA
Tel: 01642-218121
Web: www.tees.ac.uk
Chancellor, Lord Leon Brittan of Spennithorn (1993)
Registrar, Kathryn Turnbull
University Secretary, J. M. McClintock
Vice-Chancellor, Prof. D. Fraser

THAMES VALLEY UNIVERSITY (1992)
St Mary's Road, Ealing, London W5 5RF
Tel: 020-8579 5000
Web: www.tvu.ac.uk
Full-time students (2002–3), 13,500
Chancellor, Sir William Stubbs
Secretary, A. M. Dalton
Vice-Chancellor, Prof. Geoff Crispin

UNIVERSITY OF ULSTER (1984)
Cromore Road, Coleraine Co., Londonderry BT52 1SA
Tel: 08700 400 700
Web: www.ulster.ac.uk
Full-time students (2002–3), 23,000
Chancellor, Sir Richard Nichols (1993)
Director of Planning and Governance Services, Irene Aston
Secretary, J. Hunter
Vice-Chancellor, Prof. P. G. McKenna

UNIVERSITY OF WALES
King Edward VII Avenue, Cathays Park, Cardiff CF10 3NS
Tel: 029-2038 2656
Web: www.wales.ac.uk (1893)
Chancellor, HRH The Prince of Wales, KG, KT, GCB, OM, PC (1976)
Secretary-General, Lynne E. Williams, Ph.D.
Senior Vice-Chancellor, Prof. D. Llwyd Morgan, D.Phil., D.Litt.

MEMBER INSTITUTES
UNIVERSITY OF WALES, ABERYSTWYTH, Old College, King Street, Aberystwyth SY23 2AX. Tel: 01970-623111. *Vice-Chancellor,* Prof. D. Llwyd Morgan, D.Phil., D.Litt.
UNIVERSITY OF WALES, BANGOR, Bangor, Gwynedd LL57 2DG. Tel: 01248-351151. *Vice-Chancellor,* Prof. H. R. Evans, Ph.D., FREng (1995)
UNIVERSITY OF WALES, CARDIFF, PO Box 920, Cardiff CF10 3XP. Tel: 01222-874000.
Vice-Chancellor, Dr D. Grant, CBE, FEng. (2001)

UNIVERSITY OF WALES COLLEGE, NEWPORT, Caerleon Campus, PO Box 179, Newport NP6 1YG.
Tel: 01633-430088. *Principal,* Prof. J. R. Lusty, Ph.D., FRSC (2002)
UNIVERSITY OF WALES, COLLEGE OF MEDICINE, Heath Park, Cardiff CF14 4XN. Tel: 01222-747747.
Vice-Chancellor, Prof. S. Tomlinson, MD, FRCP (2001)
UNIVERSITY OF WALES INSTITUTE, CARDIFF, Llandaff Centre, Western Avenue, Cardiff CF5 2SG.
Tel: 01222-506070 *Principal,* A. J. Chapman, Ph.D. (1998)
UNIVERSITY OF WALES, LAMPETER, Lampeter SA48 7ED. Tel: 01570-422351 *Vice-Chancellor,*
Prof. K. G. Robbins, D.Litt., D.Phil., FRSED (1992)
UNIVERSITY OF WALES, SWANSEA, Singleton Park, Swansea SA2 8PP. Tel: 01792-205678. *Vice-Chancellor,* Prof. R. Williams, Ph.D., FRS (1994)

UNIVERSITY OF WARWICK (1965)
Coventry CV4 7AL
Tel: 024-7652 3523
Web: www.warwick.ac.uk
Full-time students (2002–3), 18,000
Chancellor, Sir Nicholas Scheele (1989)
Registrar, Dr J. W. Nicholls
Vice-Chancellor, Prof. V. D. Vandelinde, FRS

UNIVERSITY OF WESTMINSTER (1992)
309 Regent Street, London W1B 2UW
Tel: 020-7911 5000
Web: www.wmin.ac.uk
Full-time students (2002–3), 12,282
Academic Registrar, Evelyne Rugg
Chairman to the Court of Governors, Sir Alan Thomas (1996)
Vice-Chancellor and Rector, Dr Geoffrey Copland

UNIVERSITY OF THE WEST OF ENGLAND (1992)
Frenchay Campus, Coldharbour Lane, Bristol BS16 1QY
Tel: 0117-965 6261
Web: www.uwe.ac.uk
Full-time students (2002–3), 18,000
Academic Secretary, Carole Webb
Chancellor, The Rt. Hon. Dame Elizabeth Butler-Sloss, DBE (1993)
Vice-Chancellor, A. C. Morris, CBE

UNIVERSITY OF WOLVERHAMPTON (1992)
Wulfruna Street, Wolverhampton WV1 1SB
Tel: 01902-321000
Web: www.wlv.ac.uk
Full-time students (2002–3), 14,223
Chancellor, Lord Paul of Marylebone
Registrar, Jane Nelson
Secretary, Tony Lee
Vice-Chancellor, Prof. John Brooks, Ph.D., DSc

UNIVERSITY OF YORK (1963)
Heslington, York YO10 5DD
Tel: 01904-430000
Web: www.york.ac.uk
Full-time students (2002–3), 8,000
Chancellor, Dame Janet Baker, CH, DBE (1991)
Registrar and Secretary, D. J. Foster
Vice-Chancellor, Prof. B. Cantor, Ph.D., FREng, FIM, (2002)

PROFESSIONAL EDUCATION
Excluding postgraduate study

The organisations listed below are those which, by providing specialist training or conducting examinations, control entry into a profession, or are responsible for maintaining a register of those with professional qualifications in their sector.

EU RECOGNITION
It is possible for those with professional qualifications obtained in the UK to have these recognised in other European Union countries. A booklet, *Europe Open for Professions,* and further information can be obtained from:
DEPARTMENT FOR EDUCATION AND SKILLS, Room E3B, Moorfoot, Sheffield S1 4PQ. Tel: 0114-259 4151
Email: carol.rowlands@dfes.gsi.gov.uk
Web: www.dfes.gov.uk/europeopen
Contact, Carol Rowlands

ACCOUNTANCY
The main bodies granting membership on examination after a period of practical work are:
ASSOCIATION OF CHARTERED CERTIFIED ACCOUNTANTS (ACCA), 29 Lincoln's Inn Fields, London WC2A 3EE. Tel: 020-7396 7000
Web: www.accaglobal.com *Chief Executive,* Anthea Rose
CIMA (THE CHARTERED INSTITUTE OF MANAGEMENT ACCOUNTANTS), 26 Chapter Street, London SW1P 4NP.
Tel: 020-7663 5441 Web: www.cimaglobal.com
Chief Executive, Charles Tilley
INSTITUTE OF CHARTERED ACCOUNTANTS IN ENGLAND AND WALES, Chartered Accountants' Hall, PO Box 433, Moorgate Place, London EC2P 2BJ.
Tel: 020-7920 8100 Web: www.icaew.co.uk
Secretary General, Peter Owen
INSTITUTE OF CHARTERED ACCOUNTANTS OF SCOTLAND, CA House, 21 Haymarket Yards, Edinburgh EH12 5BH. Tel: 0131-347 0100 Web: www.icas.org.uk
Chief Executive, David Brew

ACTUARIAL SCIENCE
The UK actuarial profession is controlled by the Institute of Actuaries in London and the Faculty of Actuaries in Edinburgh. The Faculty and the Institute together set examinations, continuing professional development, professional codes and disciplinary standards. UK qualified actuaries may be Fellows of either organisation. Practising certificates are issued on certain actuaries for their statutory role in the financial management of life offices and most pension schemes.
FACULTY OF ACTUARIES IN SCOTLAND,
Maclaurin House, 18 Dublin Street, Edinburgh EH1 3PP.
Tel: 0131-240 1300 Web: www.actuaries.org.uk
Secretary, Richard Machonachie
INSTITUTE OF ACTUARIES, Staple Inn Hall, High Holborn, London WC1V 7QJ. Tel: 020-7632 2100
Education Executive, Careers and Library,
Napier House, 4 Worcester Street, Oxford OX1 2AW.
Tel: 01865-268200
Web: www.actuaries.org.uk
Secretary General, Caroline Instance

ARCHITECTURE
The Education Committee of the Royal Institute of British Architects sets standards and guides the whole system of architectural education throughout the UK. The Architects Registration Board is the independent regulator for the architects' profession in the UK. It was established to simultaneously protect the interest of consumers and to safeguard the reputation of architects. RIBA recognises courses at 36 schools of architecture in the UK for exemption from their own examinations as well as courses at 51 overseas schools.
ARCHITECTURAL ASSOCIATION (INC.),
34–36 Bedford Square, London WC1B 3ES.
Tel: 020-7887 4000
Web: www.aaschool.ac.uk
Chief Executive, Mohsen Mostafavi
ARCHITECTS REGISTRATION BOARD, 8 Weymouth Street, London W1W 5BU. Tel: 020-7580 5861
Web: www.arb.org.uk
Chief Executive and Registrar, Robin Vaughan
ROYAL INSTITUTE OF BRITISH ARCHITECTS,
66 Portland Place, London W1N 4AD. Tel: 020-7580 5533
Web: www.architecture.com

BANKING
Professional organisations granting qualifications after examination are:
INSTITUTE OF FINANCIAL SERVICES, IFS House,
4/9 Burgate Lane, Canterbury CT1 2XJ. Tel: 01227-818609
Web: www.ifslearning.com
Chief Executive Officer, G. Shreeve
CHARTERED INSTITUTE OF BANKERS IN SCOTLAND, Drumsheugh House, 38b Drumsheugh Gardens, Edinburgh EH3 7SW. Tel: 0131-473 7777
Web: www.ciobs.org.uk
Chief Executive, Prof. Charles Munn, FCIBS

BUILDING AND CONSTRUCTION
Examinations are conducted by:
RICS (ROYAL INSTITUTION OF CHARTERED SURVEYORS), 12 Great George Street, Parliament Square, London SW1P 3AD. Tel: 020-7222 7000
Web: www.rics.org.uk *Chief Executive,* J. Armstrong
CHARTERED INSTITUTE OF BUILDING, Englemere, Kings Ride, Ascot, Berks SL5 7TB. Tel: 01344-630700
Web: www.ciob.org.uk *Chief Executive,* Chris Blythe
INSTITUTE OF CLERKS OF WORKS OF GREAT BRITAIN, 1st and 2nd Floors, The Old House, The Lawns, 33 Thorpe Road, Peterborough W5 3TJ. Tel: 01733-564033

BUSINESS, MANAGEMENT AND ADMINISTRATION
Professional bodies conducting training and/or examinations include:
ASSOCIATION OF MBAS, 25 Hosier Lane, London EC1A 9LQ. Tel: 020-7246 2686
Web: www.mba.org.uk *Director-General,* M. A. Jones
CAM FOUNDATION, Moor Hall, Cookham, Maidenhead, Berks SL6 9QH. Tel: 01628-427180
Web: www.camfoundation.com
CHARTERED INSTITUTE OF HOUSING, Octavia House, Westwood Business Park, Westwood Way, Coventry CV4 8JP. Tel: 024-7685 1700 Web: www.cih.org
Chief Executive, D. Butler
CHARTERED INSTITUTE OF PERSONNEL AND DEVELOPMENT, CIPD House, Camp Road, London SW19 4UX. Tel: 020-8971 9000 Web: www.cipd.co.uk
Director-General, G. Armstrong

CHARTERED INSTITUTE OF PURCHASING AND SUPPLY, Easton House, Easton on the Hill, Stamford, Lincs PE9 3NZ. Tel: 01780-756777 Web: www.cips.org *Chief Executive,* Ken James

CHARTERED MANAGEMENT INSTITUTE, Management House, Cottingham Road, Corby, Northants NN17 1TT. Tel: 01536-204222 Web: www.managers.org.uk *Director-General,* Mary Chapman

HENLEY MANAGEMENT COLLEGE, Greenlands, Henley on Thames, Oxon RG9 3AU. Tel: 01491-571454 Web: www.henleymc.ac.uk

INSTITUTE OF ADMINISTRATIVE MANAGEMENT, 16 Park Crescent, London W1B 1BA. Tel: 020-7612 7099 Web: www.instam.org *Chief Executive,* David Woodgate

INSTITUTE OF CHARTERED SECRETARIES AND ADMINISTRATORS AND ADMINISTRATORS, 16 Park Crescent, London W1B 1AH. Tel: 020-7580 4741 Web: www.icsa.org.uk *Chief Executive,* John Ainsworth

INSTITUTE OF CHARTERED SHIPBROKERS, 3 St Helen's Place, London, EC3A 6EJ. Tel: 020-7628 5559 Web: www.ics.org.uk *Director-General,* Alan Phillips

INSTITUTE OF EXPORT, Export House, Minerva Business Park, Lynch Wood, Peterborough PE2 6FT. Tel: 01733-404400 Web: www.export.org.uk *Chief Executive,* Hugh Allen

INSTITUTE OF HEALTHCARE MANAGEMENT, PO Box 33239, London SW1W 0WN. Tel: 020-7881 9235 Web: www.ihm.org.uk *Chief Executive,* S. Marples

INSTITUTE OF QUALITY ASSURANCE, 12 Grosvenor Crescent, London SW1X 7EE. Tel: 020-7245 6722 Web: www.iqa.org

CHIROPRACTIC

The General Chiropractic Council (GCC) is the statutory regulatory body for chiropractors and its role and remit is defined in the Chiropractors Act 1994. It is illegal for anyone in the UK to use the title 'chiropractor' unless registered with the GCC.

BRITISH CHIROPRACTIC ASSOCIATION, Blagrave House, Blagrave Street, Reading, Berks RG1 1QB, Tel: 0118-950 5950 Web: www.chiropractic-uk.co.uk

COLLEGE OF CHIROPRACTORS, PO Box 2739, 106 London Street, Reading RG1 4BF. Tel: 0118-950 2070

GENERAL CHIROPRACTIC COUNCIL, 344–354 Gray's Inn Road, London WC1X 8BP. Tel: 020-7713 5155 Web: www.gcc-uk.org

SCOTTISH CHIROPRACTIC ASSOCIATION, Laigh Hatton Farm, Old Greenock Road, Bishopton, Renfrewshire PA7 5PB. Tel: 01505-863151 Web: www.sca-chiropractic.org

UNITED CHIROPRACTIC ASSOCIATION, Chichester House, 145A London Road, Kingston upon Thames, Surrey KT2 6SR. Tel: 020-8939 4599

DANCE

The Council for Dance Education and Training (CDET) accredits courses at the following: ArtsEdLondon, Arts Educational Tring Park; Central School of Ballet; Bird College of Performing Arts; Elmhurst–The School for Dance and Performing Arts; The Hammond School; The Italia Conti Academy of Theatre Arts Ltd; Laban; Laine Theatre Arts Ltd; London Contemporary Dance School; London Studio Centre; Midlands Academy of Dance and Drama; Merseyside Dance and Drama Centre; Northern Ballet School; Performers College; Stella Mann College; Studios La Pointe; Royal Academy of Dancing; The Urdang Academy.

The accreditation of a course in a school does not necessarily imply that other courses of a different type or duration in the same school are also accredited.

CDET has approved the teacher registration systems of the following: British Ballet Organisation; British Theatre Dance Association; Cecchetti Society; Imperial Society of Teachers of Dancing; Royal Academy of Dancing.

COUNCIL FOR DANCE EDUCATION AND TRAINING, Toynbee Hall, 28 Commercial Street, London E1 6LS. Tel: 020-7247 4030 Web: www.cdet.org.uk

IMPERIAL SOCIETY OF TEACHERS OF DANCING, Imperial House, 22–26 Paul Street, London EC2A 4QE. Tel: 020-7377 1577 Web: www.istd.org *Chief Executive,* Michael J. Browne

INTERNATIONAL DANCE TEACHERS' ASSOCIATION, International House, 76 Bennett Road, Brighton BN2 5JL. Tel: 01273-685652 Web: www.idta.co.uk

ROYAL ACADEMY OF DANCE, 36 Battersea Square, London SW11 3RA. Tel: 020-7326 8000 Web: www.rad.org.uk *Chief Executive,* L. Rittner

ROYAL BALLET SCHOOL, 46 Floral Street, London WC2E 9DA. Tel: 020-7836 8899 Web: www.royalballetschool.co.uk *Director,* Ms G. Stock, AM

DEFENCE

ROYAL COLLEGE OF DEFENCE STUDIES, Seaford House, 37 Belgrave Square, London SW1X 8NS. Tel: 020-7915 4800 Web: www.da.mod.uk/rcds *Commandant,* Lt.-Gen. (Retd) Sir Christopher Wallace, KBE

JOINT SERVICES COMMAND AND STAFF COLLEGE, Faringdon Road, Watchfield, Swindon, Wilts SN6 8TS. Tel: 01793-788000 Web: www.jscsc.org.uk *Commandant,* Maj.-Gen. J. C. McColl, CBE

ROYAL NAVAL COLLEGE

BRITANNIA ROYAL NAVAL COLLEGE, Dartmouth, Devon TQ6 0HJ. Tel: 01803-677108 *Commodore,* Cdre C. A. Johnstone-Burt, OBE, ADC

MILITARY COLLEGES

DIRECTORATE OF EDUCATIONAL AND TRAINING SERVICES (ARMY), Trenchard Lines, Upavon, Pewsey, Wilts SN9 6BE. Tel: 01980-618719/618701 Web: www.agc-ets.co.uk *Director,* Brig. M. St. J. Filler

ROYAL MILITARY ACADEMY SANDHURST, Camberley, Surrey GU15 4PQ. Tel: 01276-63344 Web: www.sandhurst.mod.uk *Commandant,* Maj.-Gen. A. S. Ritchie, CBE

ROYAL MILITARY COLLEGE OF SCIENCE, Cranfield University, RMCS Shrivenham, Swindon SN6 8LA. Tel: 01793-782551 Web: www.rmcs.cranfield.ac.uk

ROYAL AIR FORCE COLLEGES

The Royal Airforce College Cranwell provides initial training for all officer and non-commissioned aircrew entrants to the RAF. It also provides postgraduate training through the Joint Elementary Flying School, Number 3 Flying Training School and the Department of Specialist Ground Training. Headquarters Central Flying School, the headquarters for the RAF University Air Squadrons and Headquarters Air Cadets are also located at Cranwell.

ROYAL AIR FORCE COLLEGE, Cranwell, Sleaford, Lincs, NG34 8HB. Tel: 01400-261201 Web: www.cranwell.raf.mod.uk

TRAINING DEVELOPMENT WING, RAF Halton, Aylesbury, Bucks HP22 5PG. Tel: 01296-623535 ext. 6363

DENTISTRY

In order to practise in the UK, a dentist must be registered with the General Dental Council. To be registered a person must be qualified in one of the following ways: hold the degree or diploma in dental surgery of a university in the UK or hold the licentiate in dental surgery awarded by one of the Royal Surgical Colleges in the UK; have completed the Council's International Qualifying Examination (IQE); be a European Community or European Economic Area national holding an appropriate European diploma; hold a registered overseas diploma or be an EEA national holding a primary dental qualification from outside the EEA but has acquired a right to practise in the EEA. The holder of a dental degree or diploma other than those referred to above may be eligible for temporary registration to enable him or her to practise dentistry in the United Kingdom for a limited period and in specified posts without the need to take further examinations. The Dentists Register and Rolls of Dental Auxiliaries are maintained by:

GENERAL DENTAL COUNCIL, 37 Wimpole Street, London W1G 8DQ. Tel: 020-7887 3800 Web: www.gdc-uk.org

DIETETICS

The professional association is the British Dietetic Association. Full membership is open to dieticians holding a recognised qualification, who must also be registered with the Health Professions Council (*see* Professions Supplementary to Medicine).

THE BRITISH DIETETIC ASSOCIATION, 5th Floor, Charles House, 148–149 Great Charles Street, Queensway, Birmingham B3 3HT. Tel: 0121-200 8080 Web: www.bda.uk.com

DRAMA

The national validating body for courses providing training in drama for the professional theatre is the National Council for Drama Training (NCDT). NCDT accredits courses at 21 drama schools in England, Scotland and Wales. It also sponsors annual seminars on graduate showcases, television training and skills needs in the small sector. There are two useful guides for students entering drama school: *A Practical Guide to Vocational Training in Dance and Drama* and *An Applicant's Guide to Auditioning and Interviewing at Dance and Drama*. These publications and numerous information sheets and useful links are available on the NCDT's website (*see* below).

NATIONAL COUNCIL FOR DRAMA TRAINING, 5 Tavistock Place, London WC1H 9SS. Tel: 020-7387 3650 Web: www.ncdt.co.uk

ENGINEERING

Engineering Council (UK) sets the standards for the accreditation for academic courses in universities and colleges and the practical training in industry. The Council also runs the National Register of Chartered Engineers, Incorporated Engineers and Engineering Technicians.

The principal qualifying bodies are:

BRITISH COMPUTER SOCIETY, 1 Sanford Street, Swindon SN1 1HJ. Tel: 01793-417417 Web: www.bcs.org *Chief Executive,* David Clarke

CHARTERED INSTITUTE OF BUILDING SERVICES ENGINEERS, 222 Balham High Road, London SW12 9BS. Tel: 020-8675 5211 Web: www.cibse.org *Chief Executive,* Julian Amey

ENGINEERING COUNCIL (UK), 10 Maltravers Street, London WC2 R3E. Tel: 020-7240 7891 Web: www.engc.org.uk *Chairman,* Sir Colin Terry

ENGINEERING AND TECHNOLOGY BOARD, 10 Maltravers Street, London WC2R 3ER. Tel: 020-7240 7333 Web: www.etechb.co.uk

INSTITUTE OF MARINE ENGINEERING, SCIENCE AND TECHNOLOGY, 80 Coleman Street, London EC2R 5BJ. Tel: 020-7382 2600 Web: www.imarest.org *Director-General,* K. F. Read

INSTITUTE OF MATERIALS, MINERALS AND MINING, 1 Carlton House Terrace, London SW1Y 5DB. Tel: 020-7451 7300 Web: www.iom3.org *Chief Executive,* Dr B. Rickinson

INSTITUTE OF MEASUREMENT AND CONTROL, 87 Gower Street, London WC1E 6AF. Tel: 020-7387 4949 Web: www.instmc.org.uk *Secretary,* M. J. Yates

INSTITUTE OF PHYSICS, 76 Portland Place, London W1B 1NT. Tel: 020-7470 4800 Web: www.iop.org *Chief Executive,* Julia King

INSTITUTION OF CHEMICAL ENGINEERS, Davis Building, 165–189 Railway Terrace, Rugby, Warks CV21 3HQ. Tel: 01788-578214 Web: www.icheme.org *Chief Executive,* Dr Trevor Evans

INSTITUTION OF CIVIL ENGINEERS, 1 Great George Street, London, SW1P 3AA. Tel: 020-7222 7722 Web: www.ice.org.uk *Acting Chief Executive,* Amar Bhogal

INSTITUTION OF ELECTRICAL ENGINEERS, Savoy Place, London WC2R 0BL. Tel: 020-7240 1871 Web: www.iee.org.uk *Chief Executive,* Dr Alf Roberts

INSTITUTION OF GAS ENGINEERS AND MANAGERS, 12 York Gate, London NW1 4QG. Tel: 020-7487 0650 Web: www.igaseng.com *Chief Executive Officer,* G. Davies

INSTITUTION OF MECHANICAL ENGINEERS, 1 Birdcage Walk, London SW1H 9JJ. Tel: 020-7222 7899 Web: www.imeche.org.uk *Director-General,* Sir Michael Moore, KBE, LVO

INSTITUTION OF STRUCTURAL ENGINEERS, 11 Upper Belgrave Street, London SW1X 8BH. Tel: 020-7235 4535 Web: www.istructe.org.uk *Chief Executive and Secretary,* Dr K. J. Eaton Scottish Branch, 15 Beresford Place, East Trinity Road, Edinburgh EH5 3SL. Tel: 0131-552 8852 Web: www.istructe.org.uk *Chief Executive and Secretary,* Dr K. J. Eaton

ROYAL AERONAUTICAL SOCIETY, 4 Hamilton Place, London W1J 7BQ. Tel: 020-7670 4300 Web: www.raes.org.uk *Director,* K. Mans

ROYAL INSTITUTION OF NAVAL ARCHITECTS, 10 Upper Belgrave Street, London SW1X 8BQ. Tel: 020-7235 4622 Web: www.rina.org.uk *Chief Executive,* T. Blakeley

FILM AND TELEVISION

Postgraduate training for those intending to make a career in film, television and new media production is provided by the National Film and Television School, which offers MA courses in animation direction, documentary direction, fiction direction, producing, screenwriting, production design, editing, cinematography, sound post-production and composing for film and television. The school also runs a Diploma course in sound recording and the Advanced Programme/Project Development Lab for post-MA students. Short courses enabling professionals to update or expand their skills, are run by the National Short Course Training Programme. There is also the

Finishing School, a new industry-accredited, Digital Post-Production training workshop and creative laboratory.
NATIONAL FILM AND TELEVISION SCHOOL,
Beaconsfield Studios, Station Road, Beaconsfield, Bucks
HP9 1LJ. Tel: 01494-731425 Web: www.nftsfilm-tv.ac.uk
Chief Executive, Stephen Bayly

FOOD AND NUTRITION SCIENCE
See DIETETICS

FORESTRY AND TIMBER STUDIES
Professional organisations include:
COMMONWEALTH FORESTRY ASSOCIATION,
PO Box 142, Bicester, Oxon OX26 6ZJ. Tel: 01865-271037
Chairman, Dr J. S. Maini
INSTITUTE OF CHARTERED FORESTERS,
7A St Colme Street, Edinburgh EH3 6AA.
Tel: 0131-225 2705 Web: www.charteredforesters.org
Executive Director, Mrs M. W. Dick, FRSA, OBE
ROYAL FORESTRY SOCIETY OF ENGLAND, WALES AND
NORTHERN IRELAND, 102 High Street, Tring, Herts
HP23 4AF. Tel: 01442-822028 Web: www.rfs.org.uk
Director, Dr J. E. Jackson
ROYAL SCOTTISH FORESTRY SOCIETY, Hagg-on-Esk,
Canonbie, Dumfriesshire DG14 0BE. Tel: 01387-371518
Web: www.rsfs.org *President*, P. J. Fothergill

FUEL AND ENERGY SCIENCE
The principal professional body is:
INSTITUTE OF PETROLEUM, 61 New Cavendish Street,
London W1G 7AR. Tel: 020-7467 7100
Web: www.petroleum.co.uk
Director-General, Mrs L. Kingham

HOTELKEEPING, CATERING AND INSTITUTIONAL MANAGEMENT
See also DIETETICS
The qualifying professional body in these areas is:
HOTEL AND CATERING INTERNATIONAL
MANAGEMENT ASSOCIATION, Trinity Court, 34 West
Street, Sutton, Surrey SM1 1SH. Tel: 020-8661 4900
Web: www.hcima.org.uk
Chief Executive, Philippe Rossiter

INSURANCE
Organisations conducting examinations and awarding
diplomas are:
ASSOCIATION OF AVERAGE ADJUSTERS, The Baltic
Exchange, St Mary Axe, London EC3A 8BH.
Tel: 020-7623 5501 Web: www.average-adjusters.com
Chairman, Tim Madge
CHARTERED INSTITUTE OF LOSS ADJUSTERS,
Peninsular House, 36 Monument Street, London EC3R 8LJ.
Tel: 020-7337 9960 Web: www.cila.co.uk
Executive Director, Graham Cave
CHARTERED INSURANCE INSTITUTE,
20 Aldermanbury, London EC2V 7HY. Tel: 020-8989 8464
Web: www.cii.co.uk *Director-General*, Dr Sandy Scott

JOURNALISM
Courses for trainee newspaper journalists are available at
30 centres. One-year full-time courses are available for
selected students, three-year degree programmes and
18-week courses for graduates. Particulars of all these
courses are available from the National Council for the
Training of Journalists. Short courses for mid-career
development are available, as are various distance
learning courses.

For periodical journalists, there are twelve centres
running courses approved by the Periodicals Training
Council (PTC). The PTC also provides career information
for people wishing to join the industry.
NATIONAL COUNCIL FOR THE TRAINING OF
JOURNALISTS, Latton Bush Centre, Southern Way, Harlow,
Essex CM18 7BL. Tel: 01279-430009 Web: www.nctj.com
PERIODICALS TRAINING COUNCIL, Queens House,
55–56 Lincoln Inn Field, London WC2A 3LJ.
Tel: 020-7404 4168 Web: www.ppa.co.uk/ptc

LAW
THE BAR
Admission to the Bar of England and Wales is controlled
by the Bar Council, called by the Inns of Court.
Admission to the Bar of Northern Ireland by the
Honorable Society of the Inn of Court of Northern
Ireland and admission as an Advocate of the Scottish Bar
is controlled by the Faculty of Advocates. The governing
body of the barristers' branch of the legal profession in
England and Wales is the General Council of the Bar (the
Bar Council). The governing body in Northern Ireland is
the Honorable Society of the Inn of Court of Northern
Ireland, and the Faculty of Advocates is the governing
body of the Scottish Bar. The education and examination
of students training for the Bar of England and Wales is
regulated by the General Council of the Bar. Those who
intend to practise at the Bar of England and Wales must
pass the Bar's vocational course. The Inns of Court
School of Law (now part of the Institute of Law at City
University) provides professional legal training for
barristers and solicitors. The School is the largest
provider of the Bar Vocational Course (BVC) and runs a
Legal Practice Course (LPC). Applications are handled by
the Bar Council's Centralised Applications Clearing
House (CACH).
BVCONLINE, The General Council of the Bar, 2–3 Curistor
Street, London EC4A 1NE. Tel: 020-7440 4000
Web: www.bvconline.co.uk *Chief Executive*, N. Morison
FACULTY OF ADVOCATES, Advocates Library, Parliament
House, Edinburgh EH1 1RF. Tel: 0131-226 5071
Web: www.advocates.org.uk *Dean*, G. N. H. Emslie, QC
GENERAL COUNCIL OF THE BAR, 3 Bedford Row, London
WC1R 4DB. Tel: 020-7242 0082
Web: www.barcouncil.org.uk
INSTITUTE OF LAW, City University, Northampton Square,
London EC1V 0HB. Web: www.city.ac.uk/law
HONORABLE SOCIETY OF THE INN OF COURT OF
NORTHERN IRELAND, The Under-treasurer's Office, Royal
Courts of Justice, Belfast BT1 3JF. Tel: 028-9072 4699
INNS OF COURT SCHOOL OF LAW, 4 Gray's Inn Place,
Gray's Inn, London WC1R 5DX. Tel: 020-7404 5787
Web: www.city.ac.uk/icsl

The Inns of Court
GRAY'S INN, 8 South Square, London, WC1R 5ET,
Tel: 020-7458 7800 Web: www.graysinn.org.uk
Treasurer, The Rt. Hon. Sir Paul Kennedy, QC
INNER TEMPLE, London EC4Y 7HL. Tel: 020-7797 8250
Web: www.innertemple.org.uk
Treasurer, Richard Southwell, QC
HONOURABLE SOCIETY OF LINCOLN'S INN, Treasury
Office, Lincoln's Inn, London WC2A 3TL.
Tel: 020-7405 1393 Web: www.lincolnsinn.org.uk
Under-Treasurer, Col. D. Hills, MBE
MIDDLE TEMPLE, Middle Temple Lane, London EC4Y 9AT.
Tel: 020-7427 4800 Web: www.middletemple.org.uk
Treasurer, Rt. Hon. Lord Justice Rose, QC

SOLICITORS

The College of Law is the largest provider of vocational legal education and training for students wishing to become solicitors and barristers in England and Wales. It also offers training after qualification and a wide range of distance-learning courses. There are a number of other institutions offering the necessary courses, namely the Legal Practice Course and the Common Professional Examination (conversion course for non-law graduates). The Law Society of England and Wales, the Law Society of Scotland and the Law Society of Northern Ireland control the education and examination of trainee solicitors and the admission of solicitors.

COLLEGE OF LAW, Braboeuf Manor, Portsmouth Road, St Catherine's, Guildford, Surrey GU3 1HA.
Tel: 01483-460200 Web: www.lawcol.org.uk

LAW SOCIETY OF ENGLAND AND WALES,
113 Chancery Lane, London WC2A 1PL.
Tel: 020-7242 1222 Web: www.lawsociety.org.uk

LAW SOCIETY OF SCOTLAND, 26 Drumsheugh Gardens, Edinburgh EH3 7YR. Tel: 0131-226 7411
Web: www.lawscot.org.uk

LAW SOCIETY OF NORTHERN IRELAND, Law Society House, 98 Victoria Street, Belfast BT1 3JZ.
Tel: 028-9023 1614 Web: www.lawsoc-ni.org
Chief Executive and Secretary, J. W. Bailie

LIBRARIANSHIP AND INFORMATION SCIENCE/MANAGEMENT

The Chartered Institute of Library and Information Professionals accredits degree and postgraduate courses in library and information science which are offered by 17 universities in the UK. A full list of accredited degree and postgraduate courses is available from its Membership, Careers and Qualifications Department and on its website (*see* below).

CHARTERED INSTITUTE OF LIBRARY AND INFORMATION PROFESSIONALS, 7 Ridgmount Street, London WC1E 7AE. Tel: 020-7255 0500
Text phone 020-7255 0505 Web: www.cilip.org.uk

MEDICINE

All doctors must be registered with the General Medical Council (GMC), which is responsible for protecting the public by setting standards for professional practice, overseeing medical education, keeping a register of qualified doctors and taking action where a doctor's fitness to practise is in doubt. A doctor not registered with the GMC is not a "legally qualified" medical practitioner for the purposes of the Medical Act 1983. In order to be eligible for registration, doctors must obtain a primary medical qualification recognised by the GMC and have satisfactorily completed a year of general clinical training. Special arrangements apply to doctors qualified outside the UK. Once registered, doctors undertake general professional and basic specialist training as senior house officers. Further specialist training is provided by the royal colleges, faculties and societies listed below.

The United Examining Board holds qualifying examinations for candidates who have trained overseas. These candidates must also have spent a period at a UK medical school.

FACULTY OF PHARMACEUTICAL MEDICINE,
1 St Andrew's Place, Regents Park, London NW1 4LB.
Tel: 020-7224 0343 Web: www.fpm.org.uk
Faculty Administrator, Mrs Kathryn Swanston

GENERAL MEDICAL COUNCIL, 178 Great Portland Street, London W1N 6JE. Tel: 020-7580 7642
Web: www.gmc-uk.org

JOINT COMMITTEE ON POSTGRADUATE TRAINING FOR GENERAL PRACTICE, 14 Princes Gate, London SW7 1PU. Tel: 020-7581 3232
Web: www.jcptgp.org.uk *Chairman,* Dr John Toby, CBE

ROYAL COLLEGE OF GENERAL PRACTITIONERS,
14 Princes Gate, London SW7 1PU. Tel: 020-7581 3232
Web: www.rcgp.org.uk *Hon. Secretary,* Dr M. Baker

SCOTTISH COUNCIL FOR POSTGRADUATE MEDICAL AND DENTAL EDUCATION, 2nd Floor, Hanover Buildings, 66 Rose Street, Edinburgh EH2 2NN. Tel: 0131-225 4365

UNITED EXAMINING BOARD, Apothecaries Hall, Black Friars Lane, London EC4V 6EJ. Tel: 020-7236 1180
Chairman, Prof J. S. P. Lumley

COLLEGES/SOCIETIES HOLDING POSTGRADUATE MEMBERSHIP AND DIPLOMA

FACULTY OF ACCIDENT AND EMERGENCY MEDICINE, 35–43 Lincoln's Inn Fields, London WC2A 3PE.
Tel: 020-7405 7071 Web: www.faem.org.uk
President, I. W. R. Anderson

FACULTY OF PUBLIC HEALTH MEDICINE,
4 St Andrews Place, London NW1 4LB. Tel: 020-7935 0243
Web: www.fphm.org.uk *Faculty Secretary,* P. Scourfield

ROYAL COLLEGE OF ANAESTHETISTS,
48–49 Russell Square, London WC1B 4JY.
Tel: 020-7813 1900 Web: www.rcoa.ac.uk
The College Secretary, Kevin Story

ROYAL COLLEGE OF OBSTETRICIANS AND GYNAECOLOGISTS 27 Sussex Place, Regent's Park, London, NW1 4RG. Tel: 020-7772 6200
Web: www.rcog.org.uk
College Secretary, P. A. Barnett

ROYAL COLLEGE OF PAEDIATRICS AND CHILD HEALTH, 50 Hallam Street, London W1W 6DE.
Tel: 020-7307 5600 Web: www.rcpch.ac.uk
College Secretary, Len Tyler

ROYAL COLLEGE OF PATHOLOGISTS, 2 Carlton House Terrace, London SW1Y 5AF. Tel: 020-7451 6700
Web: www.rcpath.org.uk *Chief Executive,* D. Ross

ROYAL COLLEGE OF PHYSICIANS, 11 St Andrews Place, Regent's Park, London NW1 4LE. Tel: 020-7935 1174
Web: www.rcplondon.ac.uk
President, Prof. Sir George Alberti

ROYAL COLLEGE OF PHYSICIANS AND SURGEONS OF GLASGOW, 232–242 St Vincent Street, Glasgow G2 5RJ. Tel: 0141-221 6072 Web: www.rcpsglasg.ac.uk
President, Prof. A. R. Lorimer

ROYAL COLLEGE OF PHYSICIANS OF EDINBURGH,
9 Queen Street, Edinburgh EH2 1JQ. Tel: 0131-225 7324
Web: www.rcpe.ac.uk
President, Dr N. D. C. Finlayson, OBE

ROYAL COLLEGE OF PSYCHIATRISTS, 17 Belgrave Square, London SW1X 8PG. Tel: 020-7235 2351
Web: www.rcpsych.ac.uk *President,* Dr Mike Shooter

ROYAL COLLEGE OF RADIOLOGISTS, 38 Portland Place, London W1B 1JQ. Tel: 020-7636 4432 Web: www.rcr.ac.uk
President, Dr Dan Ash

ROYAL COLLEGE OF SURGEONS OF EDINBURGH,
Nicolson Street, Edinburgh EH8 9DW. Tel: 0131-527 1600
Web: www.rcsed.ac.uk *Chief Executive,* J. R. C. Foster

ROYAL COLLEGE OF SURGEONS OF ENGLAND,
35–43 Lincoln's Inn Fields, London WC2A 3PE.
Tel: 020-7405 3474 Web: www.rcseng.ac.uk
Chief Executive, Craig Duncan

SOCIETY OF APOTHECARIES OF LONDON,
14 Black Friars Lane, London EC4V 6EJ. Tel: 020-7236 1189
Web: www.apothecaries.org *The Clerk*, R. J. Stringer

PROFESSIONS SUPPLEMENTARY TO MEDICINE
The standard of professional education in art, drama and music therapies, biomedical sciences, chiropody, dietetics, occupational therapy, orthoptics, prosthetics and orthotics, physiotherapy and radiography is regulated by the Health Professions Council. It also ensures that the registration of professionals is linked to continual professional development.
HEALTH PROFESSIONS COUNCIL, Park House,
184 Kennington Park Road, London SE11 4BU.
Tel: 020-7582 0866 Web: www.hpc-uk.org

ART, DRAMA AND MUSIC THERAPIES
A postgraduate qualification in the relevant therapy is required. Details of accredited training programmes in the UK can be obtained from the following organisations:
ASSOCIATION OF PROFESSIONAL MUSIC THERAPISTS,
26 Hamlyn Road, Glastonbury, Somerset BA6 8HT.
Tel: 01458-834919 Web: www.apmt.org.uk
Administrator, Mrs D. Asbridge
BRITISH ASSOCIATION OF ART THERAPISTS, Mary Ward House, 5 Tavistock Place, London WC1H 9SN.
Tel: 020-7383 3774 Web: www.baat.org
BRITISH ASSOCIATION OF DRAMA THERAPISTS,
41 Broomhouse Lane, London SW6 3DP.
Tel: 020-7731 0160 Web: www.badth.demon.co.uk

BIOMEDICAL SCIENCES
Qualifications from higher education establishments and training in medical laboratories are required for membership of the Institute of Biomedical Science.
INSTITUTE OF BIOMEDICAL SCIENCE, 12 Coldbath Square, London EC1R 5HL. Tel: 020-7713 0214
Web: www.ibms.org

CHIROPODY
Professional recognition is granted by the Society of Chiropodists and Podiatrists to students who are awarded BSc degrees in Podiatry or Podiatric Medicine after attending a course of full-time training for three or four years at one of the 13 recognised schools in the UK (ten in England and Wales, two in Scotland and one in Northern Ireland). Qualifications granted and degrees recognised by the Society are approved for the purpose of State Registration, which is a condition of employment within the National Health Service.
SOCIETY OF CHIROPODISTS AND PODIATRISTS,
1 Fellmongers Path, Tower Bridge Road, London SE1 3LY.
Tel: 020-7234 8620 Web: www.feetforlife.org
Chief Executive, Ms Hilary De Lyon

COMPLEMENTARY MEDICINE
Professional courses are validated by:
INSTITUTE FOR COMPLEMENTARY MEDICINE,
PO Box 194, London SE16 7QZ. Tel: 020-7237 5165
Web: www.icmedicine.co.uk

OCCUPATIONAL THERAPY
The professional qualification and eligibility for state registration may be obtained upon successful completion of a validated course in any of the institutions approved by the College of Occupational Therapists. The courses are normally degree-level courses based in higher education institutions. For full information visit the website below.

COLLEGE OF OCCUPATIONAL THERAPISTS,
106–114 Borough High Street, London SE1 1LB.
Tel: 020-7357 6480 Web: www.cot.co.uk
FACULTY OF OCCUPATIONAL MEDICINE, 6 St Andrew's Place, London NW1 4LB. Tel: 020-7317 5890
Web: www.facoccmed.ac.uk *President*, Dr W. J. Gunnyeon

ORTHOPTICS
Orthoptists undertake the diagnosis and treatment of all types of squint and other anomalies of binocular vision, working in close collaboration with ophthalmologists. The training and maintenance of professional standards are the responsibility of the Health Professions Council (*see* Professions Supplementary to Medicine). The professional body is the British Orthoptic Society. Training is at degree level.
THE BRITISH ORTHOPTIC SOCIETY, Tavistock House North, Tavistock Square, London WC1H 9HX.
Tel: 020-7387 7992 Web: www.orthoptics.org.uk
Hon. Chairman, June Carpenter

PHYSIOTHERAPY
Full-time three- or four-year degree courses are available at 30 higher education institutions in the UK. Information about courses leading to eligibility for Membership of the Chartered Society of Physiotherapy and to State Registration is available from the Chartered Society of Physiotherapy.
CHARTERED SOCIETY OF PHYSIOTHERAPY,
14 Bedford Row, London WC1R 4ED. Tel: 020-7306 6666
Web: www.csp.org.uk

PROSTHETICS AND ORTHOTICS
Prosthetists provide artificial limbs, while orthotists provide devices to support or control a part of the body. It is necessary to obtain an honours degree to become a prosthetist/orthotist. Training is centred at two UK universities, University of Salford and University of Strathclyde.
BRITISH ASSOCIATION OF PROSTHETISTS AND ORTHOTISTS, Sir James Clark Building, Abbey Mill Business Centre, Paisley PA1 1TJ. Tel: 0141-561 7217
Web: www.bapo.com

RADIOGRAPHY AND RADIOTHERAPY
In order to practise both diagnostic and therapeutic radiography in the UK, it is necessary to have successfully completed a course of education and training recognised by the Privy Council. Such courses are offered by universities throughout the UK and lead to the award of a degree in radiography. Further information is available from the The Society and College of Radiographers.
SOCIETY AND COLLEGE OF RADIOGRAPHERS,
207 Providence Square, Mill Street, London SE1 2EW.
Tel: 020-7740 7200 Web: www.sor.org

MERCHANT NAVY TRAINING SCHOOLS
OFFICERS
WARSASH MARITIME CENTRE, Southampton Institute, Newtown Road, Warsash, Southampton SO31 9ZL.
Tel: 01489-576161 Web: www.solent.ac.uk/wmc/
Head, John Milligan
SEAFARERS
NATIONAL SEA TRAINING CENTRE, North West Kent College, Dering Way, Gravesend, Kent DA12 2JJ.
Tel: 01322-629600 Web: www.nwkcollege.ac.uk
Director of Faculty – *NSTC,* I. R. Goodwin

MUSIC

ASSOCIATED BOARD OF THE ROYAL SCHOOLS OF MUSIC, The Board conducts graded music examinations in over 86 countries and provides other services to music education through its professional development department and publishing company.
ASSOCIATED BOARD OF THE ROYAL SCHOOLS OF MUSIC, 24 Portland Place, London W1B 1LU. Tel: 020-7636 5400 Web: www.abrsm.org;
Chief Executive, R. Morris
GUILDHALL SCHOOL OF MUSIC & DRAMA, Silk Street, Barbican, London EC2Y 8DT. Tel: 020-7628 2571 Web: www.gsmd.ac.uk
Principal, Baroness McIntosh of Hudnall
LONDON COLLEGE OF MUSIC AND MEDIA, Thames Valley University, St Mary's Road, London W5 5RF. Tel: 020-8231 2304 Web: elgar.tvu.ac.uk
ROYAL ACADEMY OF MUSIC, Marylebone Road, London NW1 5HT. Tel: 020-7873 7373 Web: www.ram.ac.uk
Principal, Prof. Curtis Price
ROYAL COLLEGE OF ORGANISTS, 7 St Andrew Street, London EC4A 3LQ. Tel: 020-7936 3606 Web: www.rco.org.uk *The Registrar,* Gordon St. J. Clarke
ROYAL NORTHERN COLLEGE OF MUSIC, 124 Oxford Road, Manchester M13 9RD. Tel: 0161-907 5200 Web: www.rncm.ac.uk *Principal,* Prof. E. Gregson
ROYAL SCOTTISH ACADEMY OF MUSIC AND DRAMA, 100 Renfrew Street, Glasgow G2 3DB. Tel: 0141-332 4101 Web: www.rsamd.ac.uk *Principal,* John Wallace, OBE
TRINITY COLLEGE OF MUSIC, King Charles Court, Old Royal Naval College, London SE10 9JF. Tel: 020-8305 4444 Web: www.tcm.ac.uk *Principal,* G. Henderson

NURSING

All nurses must be registered with the Nursing and Midwifery Council (NMC). Courses leading to registration as a nurse or midwife are at least three years in length. There are also some programmes which are combined with degrees. Students study in colleges of nursing or in institutions of higher education. Courses offer a combination of theoretical and practical experience in a variety of settings. Different courses lead to different types of registration, including Registered Nurse (RN), Registered Mental Nurse (RMN), Registered Learning Disabilities Nurse (RLDN), Registered Sick Children's Nurse (RSCN), Registered Midwife (RM) and Registered Health Visitor (RHV). The NMC is responsible for validating courses in nursing and midwifery.
The Royal College of Nursing is the largest professional union representing nurses and provides higher education through its Institute.
UK CENTRAL COUNCIL FOR NURSING, MIDWIFERY AND HEALTH VISITING, 23 Portland Place, London W1N 4JT. Tel: 020-7637 7181 Web: www.nmc-uk.org

OPHTHALMIC AND DISPENSING OPTICS
Professional bodies are:
THE ASSOCIATION OF BRITISH DISPENSING OPTICIANS, Godmersham Park Mansion, Godmersham, Kent CT4 7DT. Tel: 01227-738829 Web: www.abdo.org.uk
General Secretary, Sir Anthony Garrett, CBE
THE COLLEGE OF OPTOMETRISTS, 42 Craven Street, London WC2N 5NG. Tel: 020-7839 6000 Web: www.college-optometrists.org
Chief Executive, P. D. Leigh

OSTEOPATHY

Osteopathy is the first of the professions previously outside conventional medical services to achieve statutory recognition under a new body the General Osteopathic Council. Since May 2000 all practising osteopaths have had to be registered with the General Osteopathic Council and the title 'osteopath' is protected by law. To gain entry to the register all newly qualified osteopaths have to be in possession of a recognised qualification from a course of training accredited by the General Osteopathic Council. The General Osteopathic Council is responsible for regulating, developing, and promoting the profession.
GENERAL OSTEOPATHIC COUNCIL, Osteopathy House, 176 Tower Bridge Road, London SE1 3LU. Tel: 020-7357 6655 Web: www.osteopathy.org.uk
Chief Executive & Registrar, Miss M. J. Craggs

PHARMACY
The Royal Pharmaceutical Society of Great Britain is the regulatory and professional body for pharmacists in all aspects of practice. It has a statutory duty to maintain the registers of pharmacists and pharmacy premises. To be eligible to register students must have a degree in pharmacy followed by one year pre-registration training at a premises recognised by the Society and must pass a registration examination.
ROYAL PHARMACEUTICAL SOCIETY OF GREAT BRITAIN, 1 Lambeth High Street, London SE1 7JN. Tel: 020-7735 9141 Web: www.rpsgb.org.uk
Secretary and Registrar, Ms A. M Lewis

PHOTOGRAPHY
The professional body is:
BRITISH INSTITUTE OF PROFESSIONAL PHOTOGRAPHY, Fox Talbot House, Amwell End, Ware, Herts SG12 9HN. Tel: 01920-464011 Web: www.bipp.com *Chief Executive,* Alex Mair

PRINTING
Details of training courses in printing can be obtained from the Institute of Printing and the British Printing Industries Federation. In addition to these examining and organising bodies, examinations are held by various independent regional examining boards in further education.
INSTITUTE OF PRINTING, The Mews, Hill House, Clanricarde Road, Tunbridge Wells, Kent TN1 1PJ. Tel: 01892-538118 Web: www.instituteofprinting.org
BRITISH PRINTING INDUSTRIES FEDERATION, Farringdon Point, 29–35 Farringdon Rd, London EC1M 3JF. Tel: 020-7915 8300 Web: www.bpif.org.uk
Chief Executive, Michael Johnson

SCIENCE
Professional qualifications are awarded by:
THE ROYAL SOCIETY OF CHEMISTRY, Burlington House, Piccadilly, London W1J 0BA. Tel: 020-7437 8656. Web: www.rsc.org
Secretary-General and Chief Executive, Dr D. Giachardi
INSTITUTE OF BIOLOGY, 20–22 Queensberry Place, London SW7 2DZ. Tel: 020-7581 8333 Web: www.iob.org *Chief Executive,* Prof. Alan Malcolm

SPEECH AND LANGUAGE THERAPY

The Royal College of Speech and Language Therapists accredits education and training courses leading to qualification as a speech and language therapist.

ROYAL COLLEGE OF SPEECH AND LANGUAGE
  THERAPISTS, 2 White Hart Yard, London SE1 1NX.
  Tel: 020-7378 1200 Web: www.rcslt.org
  Chief Executive, Kamini Gadhok

SURVEYING

The qualifying professional bodies include:

ASSOCIATION OF BUILDING ENGINEERS, Lutyens House,
  Billing Brook Road, Weston Favell, Northampton NN3 8NW.
  Tel: 01604-404121 Web: www.abe.org.uk
  Chief Executive, David Gibson
INSTITUTE OF REVENUES, RATING AND VALUATION,
  41 Doughty Street, London, WC1N 2LF. Tel: 020-7831 3505
  Web: www.irrv.org.uk *Director,* David Magor
ROYAL INSTITUTION OF CHARTERED SURVEYORS,
  12 Great George Street, Parliament Square, London
  SW1P 3AD. Tel: 020-7222 7000
  Web: www.rics.org *Chief Executive,* J. H. A. J. Armstrong

TEACHING

To work as a qualified teacher in a school in England and Wales, Qualified Teacher Status (QTS) must be acquired by completing a programme of Initial Teacher Training. Teaching is an all-graduate profession. Those without a first degree may take a Bachelor of Education (BEd) or a Bachelor of Arts/Science (BA/BSc) with QTS, full-time for three or four years, depending on the programme followed. These degrees combine subject and professional studies with teaching practice.

For those who already have a first degree, the most common route is through a one-year Postgraduate Certificate of Education (PGCE). This may be taken full-time or part-time, or as a distance-learning programme. Postgraduates may also gain QTS through training in a school (School-Centred Initial Teacher Training). Graduates aged 24 or above can apply to train through the Graduate Teacher Programme which offers a salary while employed in a school as a trainee teacher, usually for one year.

Further information about how to become a teacher in England and Wales is available on the Teacher Training Agency's website (*see* below) or in *The Initial Teacher Training Handbook* (£9.99 plus p&p) available from UCAS on +44 (0)1242 544610. Further personal advice is available from the Teaching Information Line, 0845-600 0991. In Wales the Higher Education Funding Council – ELWA funds initial teacher training and accredits providers of initial teacher training in Wales. They also produce Performance Information on Initial Teacher Training Providers in Wales. Details of courses in Scotland can be obtained from universities and the Graduate Teacher Training Registry (GTTR). Details of courses in Northern Ireland can be obtained from the Department of Education for Northern Ireland.

TEACHER TRAINING AGENCY, Portland House, Stag Place,
  London SW1E 5TT. Tel: 020-7925 3700
  Web: www.canteach.gov.uk

TEXTILES

TEXTILE INSTITUTE, 1st Floor, St James's Buildings, Oxford
  Street, Manchester M1 6FQ. Tel: 0161-237 1188
  Web: www.texi.org
  Membership Director, Steven Kirkwood

THEOLOGICAL COLLEGES

There is no overall body which accredits theological colleges unless they have contacts with other academic Institutions. Theological colleges, as opposed to colleges which offer courses in theology, usually have denominational contacts and offer theology as a part of training for the ministry in that particular denomination. *See* Religion in the UK section for contact details of denominations in the UK.

VETERINARY MEDICINE

The regulatory body for veterinary medicine is the Royal College of Veterinary Surgeons, which keeps the register of those entitled to practise veterinary medicine. Holders of recognised degrees from any of the six UK university veterinary schools or from certain EU or overseas universities are entitled to be registered, and holders of certain other degrees may take a statutory membership examination.

The British Veterinary Association is the professional body representing veterinary surgeons. The British Veterinary Nursing Association is the professional body representing veterinary nurses.

ROYAL COLLEGE OF VETERINARY SURGEONS, Belgravia
  House, 62–64 Horseferry Road, London SW1P 2AF.
  Tel: 020-7222 2001 Web: www.rcvs.org.uk
BRITISH VETERINARY NURSING ASSOCIATION,
  Level 15, Terminus House, Terminus Street, Harlow, Essex
  CM20 1XA. Tel: 01279-450567 Web: www.bvna.org.uk

INDEPENDENT SCHOOLS

The following pages list those independent schools (in the UK) whose Head is a member of the Headmasters' and Headmistresses' Conference, the Society of Headmasters and Headmistresses of Independent Schools or the Girls' Schools Association. The list includes name of school, location, date founded, number of pupils, termly fees (day and board) and the name of head (with date of appointment). This section has been compiled with the assistance of Klaus Boehm and Jenny Lees-Spalding, editors of *Guide to Independent Schools 2004*.

School	Date Founded	No of pupils	Termly fees Day	Board	Head (with date of appointment)
ENGLAND					
The Abbey School, Berkshire	1887	990	£2,600	–	Barbara E. Stanley (2002)
Abbotsholme School, Staffordshire	1889	252	£4,095	£5,995	Stephen Fairclough (2003)
Abingdon School, Oxfordshire	1256	796	£3,135	£5,720	Mark Turner (2002)
Ackworth School, West Yorkshire	1779	542	£2,859	£4,981	Martin Dickinson (1995)
Adcote School for Girls, Shropshire	1907	95	£3,025	£5,365	Robin Case (2002)
Aldenham School, Hertfordshire	1597	447	£4,260	£6,144	Richard Harman (2000)
Alderley Edge School for Girls, Cheshire	1876	610	£2,044	–	Mrs Kathy Mills (1999)
The Alice Ottley School, Worcester	1883	640	£2,606	–	Mrs Morag Chapman (1999)
Alleyn's School, London	1619	932	£3,160	–	Colin Diggory (2002)
Ampleforth College, York	1802	535	£3,475	£6,515	Revd Gabriel Everitt, OSB (2004)
Ardingly College, West Sussex	1858	707	£4,695	£6,265	John Franklin (1998)
Arnold School, Lancashire	1896	1,169	£2,065	–	Barry M. Hughes (2003)
The Arts Educational School, Hertfordshire	1945	267	£5,425	£6,740	Stefan Anderson (2002)
Ashford School, Kent	1898	488	£3,300	£5,718	Mrs Paula Holloway (2000)
Ashville College, North Yorkshire	1877	840	£2,630	£4,985	A. Fleck (2003)
The Atherley School, Hampshire	1926	450	£2,220	–	Mrs Maureen Bradley (1999)
Austin Friars St Monica's, Cumbria	1951	446	£2,488	–	Nicholas J. B. O'Sullivan (2000)
Bablake School, Coventry	1344	1,000	£2,097	–	Dr S. Nuttall (1991)
Badminton School, Bristol	1858	399	£3,695	£6,580	Mrs Jan Scarrow (1997)
Bancroft's School, Essex	1737	1,184	£3,063	–	Dr Peter Scott (1996)
Barnard Castle School, Durham	1883	677	£2,690	£4,545	M. D. Featherstone (1997)
Batley Grammar School, West Yorkshire	1612	407	£2,218	–	Brian Battye (1998)
Battle Abbey School, East Sussex	1912	271	£3,263	£5,242	Roger Clark (1998)
Bearwood College, Berkshire	1827	356	£3,885	£6,025	S. G. Aiano (1998)
Bedales School, Hampshire	1893	414	£5,453	£7,133	Keith Budge (2001)
Bedford School, Bedford	1552	1,100	£3,858	£6,067	Dr I. Philip Evans, OBE (1990)
Bedford High School, Bedford	1882	898	£2,666	£5,232	Mrs Gina Piotrowska (2000)
Bedford Modern School, Bedford	1566	1,100	£2,481	–	Stephen Smith (1996)
Bedgebury School, Kent	1860	366	£3,650	£5,875	Mrs Hilary Moriarty (2000)
Beechwood School, Kent	1915	350	£3,305	£5,350	Nicholas Beesley (1999)
The Belvedere School GDST, Liverpool	1880	560	£2,159	–	Mrs Gillian Richards (1997)
Benenden School, Kent	1923	470	–	£7,150	Mrs Claire Oulton (2000)
Berkhamsted Collegiate School, Hertfordshire	1541	1,470	£3,642	£5,793	Dr Priscilla Chadwick (1996)
Bethany School, Kent	1866	340	£3,378	£5,255	Nicholas Dorey (1997)
Birkdale School, Sheffield	1915	800	£2,399	–	Robert J. Court (1994)
Birkenhead School, Wirral	1860	808	£2,196	–	Stuart Haggett (1988)
Birkenhead High School GDST, Merseyside	1901	830	£2,159	–	Mrs Carole Evans (1997)
Bishop's Stortford College, Hertfordshire	1868	399	£3,661	£5,079	John G. Trotman (1997)
Blackheath High School GDST, London	1880	590	£2,695	–	Mrs Elizabeth Laws (2000)
Bloxham School, Oxfordshire	1860	385	£5,258	£6,795	Mark Allbrook (2002)
Blundell's School, Devon	1604	553	£3,885	£6,090	Jonathan Leigh (1991)
Bolton School Boys' Division, Lancashire	1524	1,106	£2,243	–	Mervyn Brooker (2003)
Bolton School Girls' Division, Lancashire	1877	1,204	£2,243	–	Miss E. J. Panton (1993)
Bootham School, York	1823	420	£3,480	£5,325	Ian Small (1988)
Box Hill School, Surrey	1959	350	£3,250	£5,400	Dr Rodney Atwood (1987)
Bradfield College, Berkshire	1850	600	£5,440	£6,800	Peter Smith (1986)
Bradford Girls' Grammar School, West Yorkshire	1875	809	£2,459	–	Mrs L. J. Warrington (1987)
Bradford Grammar School, West Yorkshire	1548	1,063	£2,400	–	Stephen Davidson (1996)

School	Date Founded	No of pupils	Termly fees Day	Board	Head (with date of appointment)
Brentwood School, Essex	1557	1,115	£3,316	£5,745	John Kelsall (1993)
Brighton College, East Sussex	1845	692	£4,195	£6,503	Dr Anthony Seldon (1997)
Bristol Cathedral School, Bristol	1542	440	£2,375	–	K. J. Riley (1993)
Bristol Grammar School, Bristol	1532	1,249	£2,330	–	David Mascord (1999)
Bromley High School GDST, Kent	1883	912	£2,695	–	Mrs Lorna Duggleby (2001)
Bromsgrove School, Worcestershire	1548	1,102	£3,260	£5,650	T. M. Taylor (1986)
Bruton School for Girls, Somerset	1900	500	£2,850	£4,860	Mrs Barbara Bates (1999)
Bryanston School, Blandford, Dorset	1928	640	£5,512	£6,890	Tom Wheare (1983)
Burgess Hill School for Girls, West Sussex	1906	720	£2,995	£5,235	Mrs Susan Gorham (2001)
Bury Grammar School, Lancashire	1726	826	£2,020	–	Keith Richards (1990)
Bury Grammar School (Girls), Lancashire	1884	1,033	£2,020	–	Mrs R. S. Georghiou (2003)
Canford School, Dorset	1923	592	£5,064	£6,751	John D. Lever (1992)
Casterton School, Cumbria	1823	340	£2,994	£5,004	A. F. Thomas (1990)
Caterham School, Surrey	1811	974	£3,320	£6,192	Rob Davey (1995)
Central Newcastle High School GDST, Newcastle upon Tyne	1895	1,001	£2,159		Mrs Lindsey Jane Griffin (2000)
Channing School, London	1885	527	£3,095	–	Mrs Elizabeth Radice (1999)
Charterhouse, Surrey	1611	697	£5,712	£6,910	Revd John Witheridge (1996)
Cheadle Hulme School, Cheshire	1855	1,425	£2,264	–	Paul Dixon (2001)
Cheltenham College, Gloucestershire	1841	562	£5,046	£6,708	P. A. Chamberlain (1997)
The Cheltenham Ladies' College, Gloucestershire	1853	860	£4,070	£6,116	Mrs Vicky Tuck (1996)
Chetham's School of Music, Manchester	1653	285	£5,650	£7,300	Mrs Claire Moreland (1999)
Chigwell School, Essex	1629	730	£3,050	£4,636	David Gibbs (1995)
Christ's Hospital, West Sussex	1552	837	Means tested	Means tested	Dr Peter Southern (1996)
Churcher's College, Hampshire	1722	782	£2,675	–	G. W. Buttle (1988)
City of London School, London	1442	895	£3,339	–	David Levin (1999)
City of London Freemen's School, Surrey	1854	840	£3,369	£5,362	D. C. Haywood (1987)
City of London School for Girls, London	1894	679	£3,204	–	Dr Yvonne Burne (1995)
Claremont Fan Court School, Surrey	1922	600	£3,190	£5,292	Mrs Patricia Farrar (1984)
Clayesmore School, Dorset	1896	294	£4,376	£6,093	Martin Cooke (2000)
Clifton College, Bristol	1862	650	£3,866	£5,643	Stephen Spurr (2000)
Clifton High School, Bristol	1877	767	£2,490	–	Mrs M. C. Culligan (1998)
Cobham Hall School, Kent	1962	205	£4,220	£6,140	Helen Davy (2003)
Colfe's School, London	1652	1,041	£3,036	–	Andrew Chicken (2001)
Colston's Collegiate School, Bristol	1710	929	£2,157	£4,495	D. G. Crawford (1995)
Colston's Girls' School, Bristol	1891	443	£2,149	–	Mrs Lesley Jones (2003)
Combe Bank School, Kent	1924	450	£3,410	–	Mrs Rosemary Martin (2000)
Concord College, Shropshire	1949	280	£2,044	£5,778	Antony Morris (1975)
Cranleigh School, Surrey	1865	590	£5,290	£6,665	Guy Waller (1997)
Croham Hurst School, Surrey	1899	558	£2,750	–	Miss Sue Budgen (1994)
Croydon High School for Girls GDST, Surrey	1874	902	£2,695	–	Miss Lorna M. Ogilvie (1998)
Culford School, Suffolk	1881	680	£3,884	£5,967	John Richardson (1992)
The Dame Alice Harpur School, Bedford	1882	974	£2,589	–	Mrs Jill Berry (2000)
Dauntsey's School, Wiltshire	1542	699	£3,580	£5,990	S. B. Roberts (1997)
Dean Close School, Gloucestershire	1886	456	£4,640	£6,585	Revd Timothy M. Hastie-Smith (1998)
Denstone College, Staffordshire	1868	437	£3,006	£4,620	David Derbyshire (1997)
Derby High School, Derby	1892	600	£2,270	–	Dr George H. Goddard (1983)
Dover College, Kent	1871	354	£2,995	£5,720	Howard Blackett (1997)
Downe House, Berkshire	1907	537	£4,890	£6,750	Mrs Emma McKendrick (1997)
Downside School, Bath	1606	335	£3,062	£5,867	Dom Leo Maidlow Davis (2003)
Duke of York Royal Military School, Kent	1803	500	–	£650	John Cummings (1999)
Dulwich College, London	1619	1,450	£3,410	£6,755	Graham G. Able (1997)
Dunottar School, Surrey	1926	425	£2,820	–	Mrs Jeanne Hobson (2001)
Durham School, Durham	1414	360	£3,612	£5,518	N. G. Kern (1997)
Durham High School for Girls, Durham	1884	575	£2,345	–	Mrs Ann J Templeman (1998)
Eastbourne College, East Sussex	1867	552	£4,140	£6,345	Charles M. P. Bush (1993)
Edgbaston High School for Girls, Birmingham	1876	930	£2,215	–	Miss Elizabeth Mullinger (1998)
Elizabeth College, Channel Islands	1563	740	£1,630	–	Dr N. D. Argent (2001)
Ellesmere College, Shropshire	1884	472	£3,700	£5,720	B. J. Wignall (1996)
Elmhurst in Association with Birmingham Royal Ballet, Surrey	c.1910	186	£3,859	£4,948	John McNamara (1995)

School	Date Founded	No of pupils	Termly fees Day	Board	Head (with date of appointment)
Eltham College, London	1842	779	£3,175	£6,547	Paul Henderson (2000)
Emanuel School, London	1594	721	£3,195	–	Mrs Anne-Marie Sutcliffe (1998)
Embley Park School, Hampshire	1946	450	£3,040	£4,975	David Chapman (1987)
Epsom College, Surrey	1855	698	£4,709	£6,674	Stephen Borthwick (2000)
Eton College, Berkshire	1440	1,287	–	£6,987	Anthony R. M. Little (2002)
Exeter School, Devon	1633	860	£2,315	–	Robert Griffin (2003)
Farlington School, West Sussex	1896	472	£3,140	£4,995	Mrs Trina Mawer (1992)
Farnborough Hill, Hampshire	1889	484	£2,525	–	Miss Jacqueline Thomas (1997)
Farringtons & Stratford House, Kent	1911	500	£2,810	£5,160	Mrs Catherine James (1999)
Felsted School, Essex	1564	432	£4,648	£6,300	Stephen Roberts (1993)
Forest School, London	1834	1,170	£3,171	£4,970	A. G. Boggis (1992)
Framlingham College, Suffolk	1864	419	£3,545	£5,515	Mrs Gwendolen Randall (1994)
Francis Holland School, London, NW1	1878	395	£3,250	–	Mrs Gillian Low (1998)
Francis Holland School, London, SW1	1878	480	£3,400	–	Miss Stephanie Pattenden (1997)
Frensham Heights School, Surrey	1925	470	£4,100	£6,100	Peter M. de Voil (1993)
Friends' School, Essex	1702	348	£3,160	£5,266	Andy Waters (2001)
Fulneck School, West Yorkshire	1753	411	£2,495	£4,595	Mrs Honorée Gordon (1996)
Giggleswick School, North Yorkshire	1512	492	£4,200	£6,260	Geoffrey Boult (2001)
The Godolphin School, Wiltshire	1726	410	£3,800	£6,000	Miss Jill Horsburgh (1996)
Godolphin & Latymer School, London	1905	700	£3,490	–	Miss Margaret Rudland (1986)
The Grange School, Cheshire	1933	1,125	£1,910	–	Jennifer Stephen (1997)
Greenacre School for Girls, Surrey	1933	430	£2,720	–	Mrs Pat Wood (1990)
Gresham's School, Norfolk	1555	517	£4,850	£6,255	A. R. Clark (2002)
Guildford High School, Surrey	1888	910	£2,925	–	Mrs Fiona Boulton (2002)
The Haberdashers' Aske's Boys' School, Hertfordshire	1690	1,300	£3,200	–	Peter Hamilton (2002)
Haberdashers' Aske's School for Girls, Hertfordshire	1690	1,135	£2,625	–	Mrs Penelope Penney (1991)
Haileybury, Hertford	1862	710	£4,993	£6,650	Stuart Westley (1996)
Hampton School, Middlesex	1556	1,065	£3,085	–	Barry Martin (1997)
Harrogate Ladies' College, North Yorkshire	1893	380	£3,170	£5,300	Dr Margaret J Hustler (1996)
Harrow School, Middlesex	1572	785	–	£6,995	Barnaby Lenon (1999)
Headington School, Oxford	1915	903	£2,895	£5,495	Mrs Anne Coutts (2003)
Heathfield School, Berkshire	1899	220	–	£6,700	Mrs Frances King (2003)
Heathfield School GDST, Middlesex	1900	617	£2,695	–	Miss Christine Juett (1997)
Hereford Cathedral School, Hereford	1384	900	£2,510	–	Dr Howard Tomlinson (1987)
Hethersett Old Hall School, Norwich	1928	273	£2,615	£5,170	Mrs Janet Mark (2000)
Highgate School, North Road, London	1565	1,100	£3,810	–	Richard Kennedy (1989)
The Hulme Grammar School for Boys, Lancashire	1611	720	£1,999	–	Ken Jones (2000)
Hurstpierpoint College, West Sussex	1849	373	£4,630	£5,980	Stephen Meek (1995)
Hymers College, Hull	1893	968	£2,030	–	John Morris (1990)
Ipswich School, Suffolk	1390	710	£2,728	£4,746	Ian Galbraith (1992)
Ipswich High School GDST, Suffolk	1878	700	£2,159	–	Miss Valerie MacCuish (1993)
James Allen's Girls' School, London	1741	770	£3,117	–	Mrs Marion Gibbs (1994)
The John Lyon School, Middlesex	1876	550	£3,150	–	Dr Christopher Ray (2001)
Kelly College, Devon	1877	360	£4,000	£6,200	Mark Steed (2001)
Kent College, Kent	1885	658	£3,600	£6,150	G. G. Carminati (2002)
Kent College, Kent	1886	595	£3,700	£5,970	Mrs Anne E. Upton (2002)
King Edward VII & Queen Mary School, Lancashire	1908	875	£1,995	–	Robert Karling (2003)
King Edward's School, Somerset	1552	970	£2,622	–	Miss Caroline Thompson (2002)
King Edward's School, Birmingham	1552	875	£2,370	–	Roger Dancey (1998)
King Edward VI High School for Girls, Birmingham	1883	550	£2,330	–	Miss Sarah Evans (1996)
King Edward VI School, Hampshire	1553	930	£2,662	–	Julian Thould (2002)
King Edward's School, Surrey	1553	484	£3,860	£5,500	Kerr Fulton-Peebles (2000)
King Henry VIII School, Coventry	1545	1,117	£2,097	–	G. Fisher (2000)
King's School, Somerset	1519	337	£4,345	£5,875	R. I. Smyth (1992)
The King's School, Kent	597	777	£5,050	£6,960	Keith Wilkinson (1996)
The King's School, Chester	1541	703	£2,373	–	Timothy J. Turvey (2000)
The King's School, Cambridgeshire	970	920	£4,130	£5,980	Richard Youdale (1991)
The King's School, Gloucester	1541	515	£3,424	–	Peter Lacey (1992)

School	Date Founded	No of pupils	Termly fees Day	Board	Head (with date of appointment)
The King's School in Macclesfield, Cheshire	1502	1,400	£2,200	–	S. Coyne (2000)
King's School, Kent	1541	745	£3,900	£6,700	Dr I. R. Walker (1986)
King's College, Somerset	1522	430	£4,010	£6,040	Christopher Ramsey (2002)
King's High School for Girls, Warwick	1879	565	£2,391	–	Elizabeth Surber (2001)
The King's School, Worcester	1541	1,299	£2,768	–	T. H. Keyes (1998)
King's College School, London	1829	750	£3,910	–	Tony Evans (1997)
The Kingsley School, Warwickshire	1884	622	£2,385	–	Mrs Christine A. Mannion Watson (1997)
Kingston Grammar School, Surrey	1561	620	£3,140	–	C. D. Baxter (1991)
Kingswood School, Bath	1748	618	£2,721	£5,763	Gary M. Best (1987)
Kirkham Grammar School, Lancashire	1549	970	£2,065	£3,800	Douglas Walker (2002)
La Sagesse School, Newcastle upon Tyne	1912	300	£2,295	–	Miss Linda Clark (1994)
The Lady Eleanor Holles School, Middlesex	1711	872	£3,056	–	Miss Elizabeth Candy (1981)
Lancing College, West Sussex	1848	416	£4,555	£6,550	P. M. Tinniswood (1998)
Langley School, Norwich	1910	370	£2,625	£5,250	J. G. Malcolm (1997)
Latymer Upper School, London	1624	970	£3,550	–	Peter Winter (2002)
Lavant House Rosemead, West Sussex	1919	140	£2,995	£4,745	Mrs M. Scott (2001)
Leeds Grammar School, Leeds	1552	1,380	£2,583	–	Dr Mark Bailey (1999)
Leeds Girls' High School, Leeds	1876	993	£2,455	–	Ms Sue Fishburn (1997)
Leicester Grammar School, Leicester	1981	700	£2,335	–	Christopher King (2001)
Leicester High School for Girls, Leicester	1906	435	£2,170	–	Mrs J. Burns (2003)
Leighton Park School, Berkshire	1890	425	£4,312	£6,244	John Dunston (1996)
The Leys School, Cambridge	1875	525	£4,000	£6,250	Revd Dr John C. A. Barrett (1990)
Licensed Victuallers' School, Berkshire	1803	800	£2,945	£5,195	Ian Mullins (1996)
Lincoln Minster School, Lincoln	1996	687	£2,510	£4,750	Clive Rickart (1999)
Liverpool College, Liverpool	1840	1,950	£2,355	–	Brian Christian (2002)
Longridge Towers School, Northumberland	1983	311	£2,200	£4,525	Dr Michael Barron (1983)
Lord Wandsworth College, Hampshire	1920	504	£4,270	£5,730	Ian Power (1997)
Loughborough Grammar School, Leicestershire	1495	1,010	£2,466	£4,350	Paul Fisher (1998)
Loughborough High School, Leicestershire	1849	584	£2,244	–	Miss Bridget O'Connor (2002)
Magdalen College School, Oxford	1480	615	£2,882	–	A. D. Halls (1998)
Malvern College, Worcestershire	1865	523	£4,615	£6,960	Hugh Carson (1997)
Malvern Girls' College, Worcestershire	1893	400	£4,350	£6,700	Mrs Philippa M. C. Leggate (1997)
The Manchester Grammar School, Manchester	1515	1,440	£2,147	–	Dr G. M. Stephen (1994)
Manchester High School for Girls, Manchester	1874	920	£2,095	–	Mrs Christine Lee-Jones (1998)
Marlborough College, Wiltshire	1843	860	£5,175	£6,900	Edward Gould (1993)
Marymount International School, Surrey	1955	230	£4,067	£6,900	Sister Rosaleen Sheridan (1990)
The Maynard School, Devon	1658	470	£2,424	–	Dr Daphne West (2000)
Merchant Taylors' School, Liverpool	1620	894	£2,025	–	Simon Dawkins (1986)
Merchant Taylors' School, Middlesex	1561	765	£3,542	–	Jon Gabitass (1991)
Merchant Taylors' School for Girls, Liverpool	1888	920	£2,025	–	Mrs J. I. Mills (1994)
Mill Hill School, London	1807	600	£3,975	£6,239	William R. Winfield (1996)
Millfield School, Somerset	1935	1,253	£4,550	£6,885	Peter M. Johnson (1998)
Milton Abbey School, Dorset	1954	225	£4,950	£6,600	W. J. Hughes-D'Aeth (1995)
Moira House School, East Sussex	1875	400	£3,455	£5,885	Mrs Ann Harris (1997)
Monkton Combe School, Avon	1868	348	£4,310	£6,260	Michael Cuthbertson (1990)
Moreton Hall, Shropshire	1913	300	£4,630	£6,330	J. Forster (1992)
The Mount School, York	1785	431	£3,300	£5,220	Mrs Diana Gant (2001)
Mount St Mary's College, Derbyshire	1842	321	£2,675	£4,825	Philip MacDonald (1998)
New Hall School, Essex	1642	700	£3,660	£5,750	Mrs K. A. Jeffrey (2002)
Newcastle upon Tyne Church High School, Newcastle upon Tyne	1885	617	£2,233	–	Mrs Lesley Smith (1996)
Newcastle-under-Lyme School, Staffordshire	1602	1,080	£1,996	–	Robert Dillow (2002)
North London Collegiate School, Middlesex	1850	1,009	£3,028	–	Mrs Bernice McCabe (1997)
Northampton High School, Northampton	1878	831	£2,345	–	Mrs L. A. Mayne (1988)
Northamptonshire Grammar School, Northampton	1989	380	£2,640	–	Simon Larter (1996)
Northwood College, Middlesex	1878	777	£2,795	–	Mrs Ruth Mercer (2002)
Norwich School, Norwich	1547	794	£2,460	–	J. B. Hawkins (2002)

School	Date Founded	No of pupils	Termly fees Day	Board	Head (with date of appointment)
Norwich High School for Girls GDST, Norwich	1875	887	£2,159	–	Mrs Valerie Bidwell (1985)
Notre Dame Senior School, Surrey	1937	375	£2,800	–	Mrs Margaret McSwiggan (1999)
Notting Hill and Ealing High School GDST, London	1873	830	£2,695	–	Mrs Susan Whitfield (1991)
Nottingham High School, Nottingham	1513	820	£2,564	–	Christopher Parker, CBE (1995)
Nottingham High School for Girls GDST, Nottingham	1875	1,117	£2,159	–	Mrs Angela Rees (1996)
Oakham School, Rutland	1584	1,044	£3,480	£5,800	Dr Joseph A. F. Spence (2002)
Old Palace School of John Whitgift, Surrey	1889	850	£2,283	–	Mrs Joy Hancock (2000)
The Oratory School, Berkshire	1859	400	£4,695	£6,510	Clive Dytor, MC (2001)
Oswestry School, Shropshire	1407	453	£3,120	£5,245	Paul Stockdale (2001)
Oundle School, Peterborough	1556	1,050	£3,049	£6,141	Dr Ralph Townsend (1999)
Our Lady's Convent Senior School, Oxfordshire	1860	390	£2,380	–	Mrs Glynne Butt (1996)
Oxford High School GDST, Oxford	1875	913	£2,159	–	Miss Felicity Lusk (1997)
Pangbourne College, Berkshire	1917	362	£4,372	£6,233	Dr Kenneth Greig (2000)
Parsons Mead School, Surrey	1897	316	£2,880	–	Mrs Patricia Taylor (2000)
The Perse School, Cambridge	1615	630	£3,048	–	Nigel Richardson (1994)
The Perse School for Girls, Cambridge	1881	715	£2,832	–	Miss Tricia Kelleher (2001)
Peterborough High School, Peterborough	1895	350	£2,599	£4,735	Mrs Sarah Dixon (1999)
Pipers Corner School, Buckinghamshire	1930	450	£3,020	£5,020	Mrs Valerie Stattersfield (1996)
Pocklington School, York	1514	610	£2,740	£4,686	Nicholas Clements (2000)
Polam Hall School, Durham	1854	480	£2,385	£4,895	Mrs Susanne Davison (*Acting* 2003)
The Portsmouth Grammar School, Hampshire	1732	884	£2,724	–	Dr Timothy Hands (1997)
Portsmouth High School GDST, Hampshire	1882	616	£2,159	–	Miss P. Hulse (1999)
The Princess Helena College, Hertfordshire	1820	168	£3,790	£5,545	Anne-Marie Hodgkiss (1998)
Prior Park College, North Somerset	1830	535	£3,158	£5,695	Giles Mercer (1996)
Prior's Field School, Surrey	1902	305	£3,303	£4,939	Mrs Jenny Dwyer (1999)
Priory School, Birmingham	1933	320	£2,195	–	Mrs Elaine Brook (2001)
The Purcell School, Hertfordshire	1962	167	£6,127	£7,837	John Tolputt (1999)
Putney High School GDST, London	1893	800	£2,695	–	Dr Denise V. Lodge (2002)
Queen Anne's School, Reading	1894	336	£4,135	£6,120	Mrs Deborah Forbes (1993)
Queen Elizabeth's Grammar School, Lancashire	1509	830	£2,320	–	Dr David Hempsall (1995)
Queen Elizabeth Grammar School, West Yorkshire	1591	950	£2,360	–	Michael Gibbons (2001)
Queen Elizabeth's Hospital, Bristol	1590	560	£2,284	£4,209	Stephen Holliday (2000)
Queen Margaret's School, York	1901	369	£3,197	£5,046	Dr Geoffrey A. H. Chapman (1992)
The Queen's School, Chester	1878	621	£2,300	–	Mrs C. M. Buckley (2001)
Queen's College London, London	1848	380	£3,600	–	Miss M. M. Connell (1999)
Queen's College, Somerset	1843	672	£3,363	£5,070	Christopher J. Alcock (2001)
Queenswood, Hertfordshire	1894	418	£4,765	£6,400	Clarissa Farr (1996)
Radley College, Oxfordshire	1847	620	–	£6,855	Angus McPhail (2000)
Ratcliffe College, Leicester	1847	600	£3,180	£4,789	Peter Farrar (1999)
Read School, North Yorkshire	1667	280	£2,025	£4,380	Richard Hadfield (1996)
Reading Blue Coat School, Berkshire	1646	617	£2,940	–	S. J. W. McArthur (1997)
The Red Maids' School, Bristol	1634	420	£2,095	–	Mrs Isobel Tobias (2001)
Redland High School for Girls, Bristol	1882	668	£2,340	–	Dr Ruth A. Weeks (2002)
Reed's School, Surrey	1813	460	£4,389	£5,806	D. W. Jarrett (1997)
Reigate Grammar School, Surrey	1675	860	£2,856	–	David Thomas (2001)
Rendcomb College, Gloucestershire	1920	350	£4,265	£5,380	Gerry Holden (1999)
Repton School, Derby	1557	540	£4,720	£6,360	R. A. Holroyd (2003)
Rishworth School, West Yorkshire	1724	560	£2,495	£4,895	Richard Baker (1999)
RNIB New College Worcester, Worcester	–	115	£7,972	£11,486	Nick Ratcliffe (2000)
Roedean School, East Sussex	1885	412	£3,900	£6,975	Mrs Carolyn Shaw (2003)
Rossall School, Lancashire	1844	415	£2,600	£6,545	Tim Wilbur (2001)
The Royal Ballet School, London	1929	205	£5,545	£7,639	Gailene Stock (1999)
The Royal Grammar School, Surrey	1509	850	£3,047	–	Timothy Young (1992)
Royal Grammar School, Newcastle upon Tyne	1510	1,127	£2,135	–	James F. X. Miller (1994)

School	Date Founded	No of pupils	Termly fees Day	Board	Head (with date of appointment)
Royal Grammar School, Worcester	1291	1,003	£2,424		– W. A. Jones (1993)
The Royal High School GDST, Bath	1864	900	£2,159	£4,235	James Graham-Brown (2000)
Royal Hospital School, Suffolk	1712	680	£3,073	£4,834	Nicholas Ward (1995)
The Royal Masonic School, Hertfordshire	1788	772	£2,661	£4,373	Mrs Diana Rose (2002)
Royal Russell School, Surrey	1853	810	£3,080	£6,120	Dr John Jennings (1996)
The Royal School Haslemere, Surrey	1840	356	£3,407	£5,382	Mrs Lynne Taylor-Gooby (1999)
Rugby School, Warwickshire	1567	790	£4,260	£6,870	Patrick Derham (2001)
Ryde School, Isle of Wight	1921	720	£2,230	£4,550	Dr Nick J. England (1997)
Rye St Antony School, Oxford	1930	400	£2,750	£4,675	Miss Alison Jones (1990)
St Albans School, Hertfordshire	1100	730	£3,155		– Andrew Grant (1993)
St Albans High School for Girls, Hertfordshire	1889	855	£2,670		– Mrs Carol Y. Daly (1994)
St Antony's Leweston School, Dorset	1891	252	£3,750	£5,647	Henry J. MacDonald (1999)
St Bede's School, East Sussex	1978	685	£3,670	£5,970	Stephen Cole (2001)
St Bees School, Cumbria	1583	305	£3,710	£6,088	Philip J. Capes (2000)
St Benedict's School, London	1902	551	£2,870		– Christopher J. Cleugh (2002)
St Catherine's School, Surrey	1885	711	£3,080	£5,065	Mrs A. Phillips (2000)
St Christopher School, Hertfordshire	1915	609	£3,320	£5,835	Colin Reid (1981)
St David's School, Middlesex	1716	437	£2,800	£5,133	Ms P. A. Bristow (1999)
St Dominic's Priory School, Staffordshire	1934	360	£2,029		– Mrs Jacqueline Hildreth (1994)
St Dunstan's College, London	c1446	946	£3,229		– Ian Davies (1998)
St Dunstan's Abbey, Devon	1867	330	£2,370	£4,786	Mrs T. Smith (2001)
St Edmund's School, Kent	1749	562	£4,135	£6,405	A. Nicholas Ridley (1994)
St Edward's School, Gloucestershire	1987	450	£2,880		– Dr Andrew J. Nash (2001)
St Edward's School, Oxford	1863	640	£5,323	£6,800	David Christie (1988)
St Elphin's School, Derbyshire	1844	210	£2,995	£4,985	Dr Deborah Mouat (2003)
St Felix & St George's School, Suffolk	1897	340	£3,500	£5,500	Mrs Wendy Holland (2002)
St George's School, Berkshire	c1900	301	£3,900	£6,230	Mrs Joanna Grant-Peterkin (1999)
St George's College, Surrey	1869	850	£3,325		– Joseph A. Peake (1994)
The School of St Helen & St Katharine, Oxfordshire	1903	602	£2,537		– Mrs Cynthia Hall (1993)
St Helen's School, Middlesex	1899	965	£2,855	£5,325	Mrs Mary Morris (2000)
St James's School, Worcestershire	1896	140	£3,904	£6,343	Rosalind Hayes (2003)
St John's School, Surrey	1851	454	£4,280	£6,070	Christopher Tongue (1992)
St Joseph's College, Suffolk	1937	592	£2,651	£4,604	Mrs S. Grant (2001)
St Lawrence College, Kent	1879	515	£3,970	£6,400	Mark Slater (1996)
St Leonards-Mayfield School, East Sussex	1863	380	£3,790	£5,820	Mrs Julia Dalton (2000)
St Mary's School Ascot, Berkshire	1885	350	£4,395	£6,420	Mrs Mary Breen (1999)
St Mary's School, Wiltshire	1873	290	£4,500	£6,660	Mrs Helen Wright (2003)
St Mary's School, Cambridge	1898	471	£2,710	£5,820	Mrs Jayne Triffitt (2001)
St Mary's College, Merseyside	1919	965	£1,993		– Jean Marsh (2003)
St Mary's School, Buckinghamshire	1872	300	£2,915		– Mrs Fanny Balcombe (1995)
St Mary's School, Dorset	1945	340	£3,750	£5,660	Mrs Margaret McSwiggan (2003)
St Mary's School, Oxfordshire	1872	200	£4,327	£6,490	Mrs Susan Sowden (1994)
St Paul's School, London	1509	829	£4,287	£6,377	R. S. Baldock (1992)
St Paul's Girls' School, London	1509	680	£3,530		– Miss Elizabeth Diggory (1998)
St Peter's School, York	627	500	£3,297	£5,536	Andrew Trotman (1995)
St Swithun's School, Hampshire	1884	462	£3,555	£5,870	Dr Helen L. Harvey (1995)
St Teresa's School, Surrey	1928	348	£3,160	£5,470	Mrs Mary Prescott (1997)
Scarborough College, North Yorkshire	1898	510	£2,478	£3,650	T. L. Kirkup (1996)
Seaford College, West Sussex	1884	404	£3,750	£5,700	Toby J. Mullins (1997)
Sedbergh School, Cumbria	1525	440	£4,675	£6,266	Christopher Hirst (1995)
Sevenoaks School, Kent	1432	972	£3,943	£6,353	Mrs Catherine Ricks (2002)
Sheffield High School GDST, Sheffield	1878	967	£2,159		– Mrs Valerie Dunsford (2004)
Sherborne School, Dorset	1550	550	£5,345	£6,945	S. F. Eliot (2000)
Sherborne School for Girls, Dorset	1899	360	£4,995	£6,820	Mrs Geraldine Kerton-Johnson (1999)
Shiplake College, Oxfordshire	1959	300	£4,035	£5,985	N. V. Bevan (1988)
Shrewsbury School, Shropshire	1552	700	£4,715	£6,710	Jeremy Goulding (2001)
Shrewsbury High School GDST, Shropshire	1885	647	£2,159		– Mrs Marilyn Cass (2000)
Sibford School, Oxfordshire	1842	367	£2,633	£5,313	Susan Freestone (1997)
Sir William Perkins's School, Surrey	1725	560	£2,612		– Miss Susan Ross (1994)

School	Date Founded	No of pupils	Termly fees Day	Head (with date of appointment) Board
Solihull School, Solihull	1560	978	£2,400	– John Claughton (2001)
South Hampstead High School GDST, London	1876	934	£2,695	– Mrs V. L. Ainley (2001)
Stamford School, Lincolnshire	1532	652	£2,600	£4,976 Dr Peter Mason (1997)
Stamford High School, Lincolnshire	1877	653	£2,600	£4,976 Dr Peter Mason (1997)
Stanbridge Earls School, Hampshire	1952	199	£4,762	£6,424 Nicholas Hall (2001)
Stockport Grammar School, Cheshire	1487	1,410	£2,124	– I. Mellor (1996)
Stonar, Wiltshire	1895	450	£2,750	£4,950 Mrs Clare Osborne (2002)
Stonyhurst College, Lancashire	1593	397	£3,665	£6,326 Adrian Aylward (1996)
Stover School, Devon	1932	510	£2,295	£4,995 Philip Bujak (1995)
Stowe School, Buckingham	1923	588	£5,140	£6,850 Dr Anthony Wallersteiner (2003)
Streatham Hill & Clapham High School GDST, London	1887	830	£2,695	– Mrs Susan Mitchell (2002)
Sunderland High School, Sunderland	1884	600	£2,085	– Dr Angela Slater (1998)
Surbiton High School, Surrey	1884	1,211	£2,790	– Dr Jennifer Longhurst (2001)
Sutton High School GDST, Surrey	1884	763	£2,695	– Stephen Callaghan (2003)
Sutton Valence School, Kent	1576	440	£3,960	£6,270 Joe Davies (2001)
Sydenham High School for Girls GDST, London	1887	690	£2,695	– Mrs Kathryn Pullen (2002)
Talbot Heath, Dorset	1886	652	£2,580	£4,320 Mrs Christine Dipple (1991)
Teesside High School, Stockton-on-Tees	1970	470	£2,270	– Mrs Hilary French (2000)
Tettenhall College, West Midlands	1863	488	£2,618	£4,369 Dr P. C. Bodkin (1994)
Tonbridge School, Kent	1553	720	£4,915	£6,956 J. M. Hammond (1990)
Tormead School, Surrey	1905	730	£2,765	– Mrs Susan Marks (2001)
Trinity School of John Whitgift, Surrey	1596	880	£2,996	– Christopher Tarrant (1999)
Truro School, Cornwall	1880	814	£2,526	£4,927 Paul K. Smith (2001)
Truro High School, Cornwall	1880	430	£2,435	£4,570 Michael McDowell (2000)
Tudor Hall School, Oxfordshire	1850	270	£3,650	£5,664 Miss Wendy Griffiths (2004)
University College School, London	1830	1,040	£3,805	– Kenneth Durham (1996)
Uppingham School, Rutland	1584	721	£4,690	£6,700 Dr Stephan Winkley (1991)
Victoria College, Channel Islands	1852	900	£1,084	– Robert Cook (2000)
Wakefield Girls' High School, West Yorkshire	1878	670	£2,360	– Mrs Patricia Langham (1987)
Walthamstow Hall, Kent	1838	460	£3,595	– Mrs Jill Milner (2002)
Warminster School, Wiltshire	1707	570	£2,900	£5,050 David Dowdles (1998)
Warwick School, Warwick	c.914	1,086	£2,594	£5,536 Edward Halse (2002)
Welbeck College, Nottinghamshire	1953	220	–	£5,502 Tony Halliwell (1999)
Wellingborough School, Northamptonshire	1595	832	£2,871	– Ralph Ullmann (1993)
Wellington College, Berkshire	1853	775	£5,480	£6,850 A. Hugh Munro (2000)
Wellington School, Somerset	1837	850	£2,475	£4,610 A. J. Rogers (1990)
Wells Cathedral School, Somerset	c.1150	745	£3,435	£5,765 Elizabeth Cairncross (2000)
Wentworth College, Dorset	1871	235	£2,950	£4,750 Miss Sandra D. Coe (1990)
West Buckland School, Devon	1858	728	£2,710	£4,760 John Vick (1997)
Westfield School, Newcastle upon Tyne	1959	370	£2,295	– Mrs Marion Farndale (1992)
Westholme School, Lancashire	1923	1,106	£1,875	– Mrs Lillian Croston (1988)
Westminster School, London	1560	700	£5,173	£6,886 Tristram Jones-Parry (1998)
Westonbirt School, Gloucestershire	1928	230	£4,220	£6,055 Mrs Mary Henderson (1999)
Whitgift School, Surrey	1596	1,150	£3,325	– Dr Christopher Barnett (1991)
William Hulme's Grammar School, Manchester	1887	639	£2,259	– Stephen R. Patriarca (2000)
Wimbledon High School GDST, London	1880	900	£2,695	– Mrs Pamela Wilkes (2001)
Winchester College, Hampshire	1382	700	£6,812	£7,170 Tommy Cookson (2003)
Windermere St Anne's School, Cumbria	1863	394	£2,743	£4,964 Miss W. A. Ellis (2000)
Withington Girls' School, Manchester	1890	640	£2,100	– Mrs Janet Pickering (2000)
Woldingham School, Surrey	1842	530	£3,785	£6,330 Miss Diana Vernon (2000)
Wolverhampton Grammar School, Wolverhampton	1512	732	£2,610	– Dr Bernard Trafford (1990)
Woodbridge School, Suffolk	1577	920	£3,080	£5,338 Stephen H. Cole (1994)
Woodhouse Grove School, West Yorkshire	1812	670	£2,660	£4,680 David Humphreys (1996)
Worksop College, Nottinghamshire	1890	395	£3,775	£5,515 Roy A. Collard (1994)
Worth School, West Sussex	1933	440	£4,240	£5,758 Peter Armstrong (2002)
Wrekin College, Shropshire	1880	420	£3,530	£5,840 Stephen Drew (1998)
Wychwood School, Oxford	1897	150	£2,620	£4,150 Mrs S. M. P. Wingfield Digby (1997)
Wycliffe College, Gloucestershire	1882	783	£4,250	£6,290 Dr Tony Collins (1998)

School	Date Founded	No of pupils	Termly fees Day	Head (with date of appointment) Board
Wycombe Abbey School, Buckinghamshire	1896	536	£5,025	£6,700 Mrs Pauline Davies (1998)
Yarm School, Cleveland	1978	900	£2,541	– David M. Dunn (1999)
The Yehudi Menuhin School, Surrey	1963	59	£9,056	£9,297 Nicolas Chisholm (1988)

WALES

School	Date Founded	No of pupils	Termly fees Day	Head (with date of appointment) Board
Christ College, Brecon,	1541	320	£4,046	£5,215 D. P. Jones (1996)
Haberdashers' Monmouth School for Girls, Monmouth	1892	698	£2,773	£4,794 Dr Brenda Despontin (1997)
Howell's School, Denbighshire,	1540	340	£2,980	£4,430 Mrs Louise Robinson (2001)
Howell's School GDST, Cardiff	1860	728	£2,159	– Mrs Jane Fitz (1991)
Llandovery College, Carmarthenshire	1847	260	£3,223	£4,866 Peter Hogan (2000)
Monmouth School, Monmouth	1614	668	£2,820	£4,701 Tim Haynes (1995)
Rougemont School, Gwent	1920	726	£2,240	– Dr Jonathan Tribbick (2002)
Rydal Penrhos School, North Wales	1885	394	£3,279	£5,495 Michael S. James (1998)

SCOTLAND

School	Date Founded	No of pupils	Termly fees Day	Head (with date of appointment) Board
Craigholme School, Glasgow	1894	551	£2,235	– Mrs Gillian Burt (1990)
High School of Dundee, Dundee	1239	1,100	£2,330	– A. Michael Duncan (1997)
The Edinburgh Academy, Edinburgh	1824	777	£2,568	£5,284 John Light (1995)
Fernhill School, Glasgow	1972	165	£1,840	– Mrs Louisa M. McLay (1992)
Fettes College, Edinburgh	1870	592	£4,429	£6,443 Michael Spens (1998)
George Heriot's School, Edinburgh	1628	1,547	£2,260	– Alistair Hector (1998)
George Watson's College, Edinburgh	1741	2,250	£2,368	£4,898 Gareth H. Edwards (2001)
The Glasgow Academy, Glasgow	1846	1,110	£2,340	– David Comins (1994)
The High School of Glasgow, Glasgow	1124	1,046	£2,369	– Robin Easton (1983)
Glenalmond College, Perthshire	1841	405	£4,335	£6,380 Gordon Woods (2003)
Hutchesons' Grammar School, Glasgow	1641	2,086	£2,145	– John Knowles (1999)
Kelvinside Academy, Glasgow	1878	640	£2,460	– John Broadfoot (1998)
Kilgraston School, Perthshire	1920	236	£3,385	£5,730 Mrs Juliet L. Austin (1993)
Lomond School, Argyll & Bute	1845	535	£2,375	£5,080 Angus Macdonald (1986)
Loretto School, Midlothian	1827	405	£4,243	£6,359 Michael Mavor (2001)
The Mary Erskine School, Edinburgh	1694	699	£2,463	£4,676 David Gray (2000)
Merchiston Castle School, Edinburgh	1833	413	£4,470	£6,295 Andrew Hunter (1998)
Morrison's Academy, Perthshire	1860	530	£2,305	£5,585 Ian Bendall (2001)
Robert Gordon's College, Aberdeen	1732	1,450	£2,300	– Brian Lockhart (1996)
St Columba's School, Renfrewshire	1897	700	£2,237	– David G. Girdwood (2002)
St George's School for Girls, Edinburgh	1888	1,000	£2,595	£5,105 Dr Judith McClure (1994)
St Margaret's School for Girls, Aberdeen	1846	396	£2,294	– Mrs Lyn McKay (2001)
St Margaret's School, Edinburgh	1855	580	£2,120	£4,430 Mrs Eileen Davis (2001)
Stewart's Melville College, Edinburgh	1832	710	£2,342	£4,760 David Gray (2000)
Strathallan School, Perth	1913	448	£4,227	£6,254 Bruce K. Thompson (2000)

NORTHERN IRELAND

School	Date Founded	No of pupils	Termly fees Day	Head (with date of appointment) Board
Belfast Royal Academy, Belfast	1785	1,582	£80	– W. S. F. Young (2000)
Campbell College, Belfast	1894	690	£533	£2,605 Dr Ivan Pollock (1987)
Coleraine Academical Institution, Londonderry	1860	730	£25	– Robert S. Forsythe (1984)
The Methodist College, Belfast	1868	2,370	£80–£1,416	£3,400 Dr Wilfred Mulryne (1988)
The Royal Belfast Academical Institution, Belfast	1810	1,050	£210	– Michael Ridley (1990)
The Royal School, Co Tyrone	1614	660	£40	£1,527 P. D. Hewitt (1984)

NATIONAL ACADEMIES OF SCHOLARSHIP

THE BRITISH ACADEMY (1902)

10 Carlton House Terrace, London SW1Y 5AH
Tel: 020-7969 5200 Fax: 020-7969 5300
Web: www.britac.ac.uk

The British Academy is an independent, self-governing learned society for the promotion of the humanities and social sciences. It supports advanced academic research and is a channel for the Government's support of research in those disciplines.

The Fellows are scholars who have attained distinction in one of the branches of study that the Academy exists to promote. Candidates must be nominated by existing Fellows. There are 729 Fellows, 13 Honorary Fellows and 312 Corresponding Fellows overseas.

President, The Viscount Runciman, PBA
Treasurer, Prof. R. J. P. Kain, FBA
Foreign Secretary, Prof. C. N. J. Mann, FBA
Publications Secretary, Dr D. J. McKitterick, FBA
Secretary, P. W. H. Brown, CBE

ROYAL ACADEMY OF ARTS (1768)

Burlington House, Piccadilly, London W1J 0BD
Tel: 020-7300 8000 Fax: 020-7300 8001
Web: www.royalacademy.org.uk

The Royal Academy of Arts is an independent, self-governing society devoted to the encouragement and promotion of the fine arts.

Membership of the Academy is limited to 80 Royal Academicians, all being painters, engravers, sculptors or architects. Candidates are nominated and elected by the existing Academicians. There is also a limited class of honorary membership and there were 20 honorary members as at June 2003.

President, Prof. P. King, CBE, PRA
Treasurer, Prof. P. Huxley, RA
Keeper, Prof. B. Neiland, RA
Secretary, Miss L. Fitt

THE ROYAL ACADEMY OF ENGINEERING (1976)

29 Great Peter Street, London SW1P 3LW Tel: 020-7222 2688
Fax: 020-7233 0054 Web: www.raeng.org.uk

The Royal Academy of Engineering was established as the Fellowship of Engineering in 1976. It was granted a royal charter in 1983 and its present title in 1992. It is an independent, self-governing body whose object is the pursuit, encouragement and maintenance of excellence in the whole field of engineering, in order to promote the advancement of the science, art and practice of engineering for the benefit of the public.

Election to the Fellowship is by invitation only from nominations supported by the body of Fellows. Fellows are chosen from engineers of all disciplines. At June 2003 there were 1,294 Fellows, of these 1,186 were full Fellows, 23 Honorary Fellows and 85 Foreign Members. The Duke of Edinburgh is the Senior Fellow and the Duke of Kent is a Royal Fellow.

President, Sir Alec Broers, FRS, FREng
Senior Vice-President, Sir Duncan Michael, FREng
Vice-Presidents, G. A. Campbell, FREng; Prof. P. J. Dowling, CBE, FREng, FRS; Dr S. E. Ion, OBE, FREng; P. C. Ruffles, CBE, FRS, FREng; Prof. R. W. E. Shannon, FREng; Sir Peter Williams, CBE, FRS, FREng
Hon. Treasurer, J. W. Herbert, FREng
Hon. Secretaries, Prof. R. W. E. Shannon, FREng *(International Activities);* Prof. G. F. Hewitt, FREng, FRS *(Education and Training)*
Chief Executive, J. Burch

THE ROYAL SCOTTISH ACADEMY (1838)

The Mound, Edinburgh EH2 2EL Tel: 0131-225 6671
Web: www.royalscottishacademy.org

The Scottish Academy was founded in 1826 to arrange exhibitions of contemporary paintings and to establish a society of fine art in Scotland. The Academy was granted a royal charter in 1838.

Members are elected from the disciplines of painting, sculpture, architecture and printmaking. Elections are from nominations put forward by the existing membership. At mid-2002 there were three Senior Academicians, six Senior Associates, 36 Academicians, 39 Associates, 4 non-resident Associates and 28 Honorary Members.

President, I. McKenzie Smith, OBE, PRSA
Secretary, W. Scott, RSA
Treasurer, I. Metzstein, RSA
Administrative Secretary, B. Laidlaw, ACIS

ROYAL SOCIETY (1660)

6–9 Carlton House Terrace, London SW1Y 5AG
Tel: 020-7839 5561 Fax: 020-7930 2170
Web: www.royalsoc.ac.uk

The Royal Society is an independent academy promoting the natural and applied sciences. Founded in 1660, the Society has three roles, as the UK academy of science, as a learned Society and as a funding agency. It is an independent, self-governing body under a royal charter, promoting and advancing all fields of physical and biological sciences, of mathematics and engineering, medical and agricultural sciences and their application.

Fellows are elected for their contributions to science, both in fundamental research resulting in greater understanding, and also in leading and directing scientific and technological progress in industry and research establishments. A maximum of 42 new Fellows, who must be citizens or residents of the British Commonwealth countries or Ireland, may be elected annually.

Up to six Foreign Members, who are selected from those not eligible to become Fellows because of citizenship or residency, are elected annually for their contributions to science.

One Honorary Fellow may be elected each year from those not eligible for election as Fellows or Foreign members. There are approximately 1,300 Fellows and Foreign Members covering all scientific disciplines.

President, Lord May of Oxford, Kt., AC
Treasurer, Prof. D. Wallace, CBE, FRS
Biological Secretary, Prof. P. Bateson, FRS
Physical Secretary, Prof. J. Enderby, CBE, FRS
Foreign Secretary, Prof. Dame J. Higgins, DBE, FRS
Executive Secretary, S. Cox, CVO

THE ROYAL SOCIETY OF EDINBURGH (1783)

22–26 George Street, Edinburgh EH2 2PQ Tel: 0131-240 5000
Fax: 0131-240 5024 Web: www.royalsoced.org.uk

The Royal Society of Edinburgh (RSE) is Scotland's
National Academy. A wholly independent, non party-
political body with charitable status, the RSE provides a
forum for broadly-based interdisciplinary activity in
Scotland. This includes organising conferences and
lectures both for the specialist and for the general public;
providing independent, expert advice to key decision
making bodies, including Government and Parliament;
strengthening links between academia and industry and
boosting wealth generation at home. The Society's
Research Awards programme annually awards nearly half
a million pounds to exceptionally talented young
academics and potential entrepreneurs in Scotland.

Fellows are elected by ballot after being nominated by
at least four existing Fellows.

At June 2003 there were 1,244 Ordinary Fellows, 69
Honorary Fellows and 16 Corresponding Fellows.

President, Lord Sutherland of Houndwood, Kt., FBA,
FRSE

Vice-Presidents, Sir David Carter, FRSE; Prof. A. C.
Walker, FRSE; Prof. Gavin McCrone, CB, FRSE

Treasurer, Prof. Sir Laurence Hunter, CBE, FRSE

General Secretary, Prof. A. Miller, CBE, FRSE

THE RESEARCH COUNCILS

The Government funds basic and applied civil science research, mostly through the seven research councils, which are supported by the Department of Trade and Industry. The councils support research and training in universities and other higher education establishments. They also receive income for research commissioned by Government departments and the private sector. A total of £356 million of resource is being added to the science budget over three years from 2002 to increase basic research. Of this, £252 million, (including £12 million of capital) will be directed to cross-councils research programmes in genomics, e-science and basic technology. The remaining £104 million of resource is added to the science budget, mainly to provide an uplift to existing council programmes. In July 2000, the Chancellor announced a further £1 billion of investment in science infrastructure over the years 2002–4, comprising £755 million from Government and £225 million from the Wellcome Trust.

The Government science budget for 2002–3 included the following allocations:

	2002–3 £m	2003–4 £m
BBSRC	232.603	250.151
ESRC	82.763	91.533
EPSRC	461.540	489.911
MRC	371.930	387.151
NERC	205.414	216.750
PPARC	220.383	232.208
*CCLRC	8.113	9.952
Pensions	28.450	29.740
Royal Society	28.745	29.245
Royal Academy of Engineering	4.770	5.270
DIAMOND	20.000	20.000
OST Administrative Costs	11.192	11.192
OST initiatives	3.100	3.350
Foresight Challenge	3.000	5.000
Joint Research Equipment Initiative	10.000	10.000
University Challenge	5.000	–
Higher Education Innovation Fund	20.000	40.000
Joint Infrastructure Fund	–	–
Science Enterprise Challenge	5.000	10.000
Science Research Investment Fund	125.000	250.000
Cambridge/MIT	14.000	14.000
Exchange Rate and Contingency Reserve	15.464	16.014
Exploitation of Discoveries at PSREs	–	–
Capital not yet allocated	34.000	34.000

* partially funded by the European Union

BIOTECHNOLOGY AND BIOLOGICAL SCIENCES RESEARCH COUNCIL (BBSRC)
Polaris House, North Star Avenue, Swindon SN21UH
Tel: 01793-413200

The BBSRC promotes and supports research and postgraduate training relating to the understanding and exploitation of biological systems; advances knowledge and technology; provides trained scientists to meet the needs of biotechnological-related industries; and provides advice, disseminates knowledge, and promotes public understanding of biotechnology and the biological sciences.
Chairman, Dr P. Ringrose
Chief Executive, Prof. J. Goodfellow, CBE

INSTITUTES
BABRAHAM INSTITUTE, Babraham Hall, Babraham, Cambridge CB2 4AT. Tel: 01223-496000.
Director, Dr R.G. Dyer

INSTITUTE FOR ANIMAL HEALTH, Compton Laboratory, Compton, Newbury, Berks RG20 7NN.
Tel: 01635-578411. *Director,* Prof. P. P. Pastoret

BBSRC/MRC NEUROPATHOGENESIS UNIT, Ogston Building, West Mains Road, Edinburgh EH9 3JF.
Tel: 0131-667 5204.

PIRBRIGHT LABORATORY, Ash Road, Pirbright, Woking, Surrey GU24 0NF. Tel: 01483-232441.
Director, Dr A. I. Donaldson

ROTHAMSTED RESEARCH, Rothamsted, Harpenden, Herts AL5 2JQ. Tel: 01582-763133. *Director,* Prof. I. R. Crute

BROOM'S BARN, Higham, Bury St Edmunds, Suffolk IP28 6NP. Tel: 01284-812200. *Director,* Dr J. D. Pidgeon

INSTITUTE OF FOOD RESEARCH, Norwich Research Park, Colney Lane, Norwich NR4 7UA.
Tel: 01603-255000. *Director,* Prof. A. Robertson

INSTITUTE OF GRASSLAND AND ENVIRONMENTAL RESEARCH, Aberystwyth Research Centre, Plas Gogerddan, Aberystwyth SY23 3EB. Tel: 01970-823000.
Director, Prof. C. Pollock, OBE

NORTH WYKE RESEARCH STATION, Okehampton, Devon EX20 2SB. Tel: 01837-883500. *Head,* Prof. S. Jarvis

JOHN INNES CENTRE, Norwich Research Park, Colney, Norwich NR4 7UH. Tel: 01603-452571.
Director, Prof. C. Lamb

ROSLIN INSTITUTE, Roslin, Midlothian EH25 9PS.
Tel: 0131-527 4200. *Director,* Prof. John Clarke

SILSOE RESEARCH INSTITUTE, Wrest Park, Silsoe, Bedford MK45 4HS. Tel: 01525-860000.
Director, Prof. B. Day

SCOTTISH AGRICULTURAL AND BIOLOGICAL RESEARCH INSTITUTES

BIOMATHEMATICS AND STATISTICS SCOTLAND (BIOSS) (administered by SCRI), University of Edinburgh, James Clerk Maxwell Building, The King's Buildings, Mayfield Road, Edinburgh EH9 3JZ. Tel: 0131-650 4901.
Director, R. A. Kempton
HANNAH RESEARCH INSTITUTE, Mauchline Road, Ayr KA6 5HL. Tel: 01292-674000.
Director, Prof. M. Peaker, FRS

420   Research Councils

MACAULAY LAND USE RESEARCH INSTITUTE,
Craigiebuckler, Aberdeen AB15 8QH. Tel: 01224-498200.
Director, Prof. E. M. Gill
MOREDUN RESEARCH INSTITUTE, Pentlands Science
Park, Bush Loan, Penicuik, Midlothian EH26 0PZ.
Tel: 0131-445 5111. *Director,* Prof. Q. A. McKellar
ROWETT RESEARCH INSTITUTE, Greenburn Road,
Bucksburn, Aberdeen AB21 9SB. Tel: 01224-712751.
Director, Prof. P. J. Morgan
SCOTTISH CROP RESEARCH INSTITUTE (SCRI),
Invergowrie, Dundee DD2 5DA. Tel: 01382-562731.
Director, Prof. J. Hillman, FRSE

COUNCIL FOR THE CENTRAL LABORATORY OF THE RESEARCH COUNCILS (CCLRC)

Rutherford Appleton Laboratory, Chilton, Didcot, Oxon
OX11 0QX Tel: 01235-445553 Fax: 01235-446665
Web: www.cclrc.ac.uk

The CCLRC is a non-departmental body of the Office of
Science and Technology, which is part of the Department
of Trade and Industry. It is the national portal and centre
for key, large-scale research facilities in support of science
and engineering research. In particular, the CCLRC has
strategic and operational roles in respect of neutron
scattering, synchrotron radiation and high power laser
facilities. These will enable UK researchers to carry out
world-leading science. As well as providing strategic
advice, the CCLRC also provides facilities for scientists to
research a broad spectrum of applications, from the
molecular structure of drugs enabling them to be targeted
to maximise efficiency and minimise side effects, to the
discovery of planets in distant galaxies.

The CCLRC operates the Rutherford Appleton
Laboratory in Oxfordshire, the Daresbury Laboratory in
Cheshire and the Chilbolton Observatory in Hampshire.
Chairman, Prof. Sir Graeme Davies
Chief Executive, Prof. J. Wood

CHILBOLTON OBSERVATORY, Stockbridge, Hampshire
SO20 6BJ. Tel: 01264 860391
DARESBURY LABORATORY, Daresbury, Warrington,
Cheshire WA4 4AD. Tel: 01925-603000
RUTHERFORD APPLETON LABORATORY, Chilton, Didcot,
Oxon OX11 0QX. Tel: 01235-821900

ECONOMIC AND SOCIAL RESEARCH COUNCIL (ESRC)

Polaris House, North Star Avenue, Swindon SN2 1UJ
Tel: 01793-413000

The purpose of the ESRC is to promote and support
research and postgraduate training in the social sciences;
to advance knowledge and provide trained social
scientists; to provide advice on, and disseminate
knowledge and promote public understanding of the
social sciences.
Chairman, F. Cairncross, CBE
Chief Executive, I. Diamond

RESEARCH CENTRES
CENTRE FOR THE ANALYSIS OF SOCIAL EXCLUSION,
London School of Economics, Houghton Street, London
WC2A 2AE. Tel: 020-7955 7419.
Director, Prof. J. Hills
CENTRE FOR BUSINESS RESEARCH, Department of
Applied Economics, University of Cambridge, Sidgwick

Avenue, Cambridge CB3 9DE. Tel: 01223-335248.
Director, Prof. A. Hughes
CENTRE FOR ECONOMIC LEARNING AND SOCIAL
EVOLUTION, Department of Economics, University College
London, Gower Street, London WC1E 6BT.
Tel: 020-7387 7050.
Research Director (Acting), Prof. T. Börgers
CENTRE FOR ECONOMIC PERFORMANCE, London
School of Economics, Houghton Street, London WC2A 2AE.
Tel: 020-7955 7048.
Directors, Prof. R. Layard; Prof. R. Freeman
CENTRE FOR MICROECONOMIC ANALYSIS OF PUBLIC
POLICY (CMAPP), Institute for Fiscal Studies, 7 Ridgmount
Street, London WC1E 7AE. Tel: 020-7636 3784.
Director, Prof. R. Blundell
CENTRE FOR ORGANISATION AND INNOVATION,
Institute of Work Psychology, University of Sheffield,
Sheffield S10 2TN. Tel: 0114-222 3287. *Director,* Prof. T.
Wall
CENTRE FOR RESEARCH IN DEVELOPMENT,
INSTRUCTION AND TRAINING, Department of
Psychology, University of Nottingham, Nottingham NG7 2RD.
Tel: 0115-951 5312. *Director,* Prof. D. Wood
CENTRE FOR RESEARCH INTO ELECTIONS AND
SOCIAL TRENDS, Social and Community Planning
Research, 35 Northampton Square, London EC1V 0AX.
Tel: 020-7250 1866. *Director,* Prof. R. Jowell
CENTRE ON MICRO-SOCIAL CHANGE, University of
Essex, Wivenhoe Park, Colchester, Essex CO4 3SQ.
Tel: 01206-872957. *Director,* Prof. J. Ermisch
CENTRE FOR RESEARCH ON INNOVATION AND
COMPETITION, Faculty of Economic and Social Studies,
University of Manchester M13 9PL. Tel: 0161-275 2000.
Directors, Prof. S. Metcalfe; Prof. R. Coombs
CENTRE FOR SKILLS, KNOWLEDGE AND
ORGANISATIONAL PERFORMANCE (SKOPE) University
of Oxford, Department of Economics, Manor Road, Oxford,
OX1 3UP. Tel: 01865-271087.
Director, K. Mayhews
CENTRE FOR SOCIAL AND ECONOMIC RESEARCH ON
THE GLOBAL ENVIRONMENT, School of Environmental
Sciences, University of East Anglia, Norwich NR4 7TJ.
Tel: 01603-593176.
Director, Prof. R. K. Turner
CENTRE FOR THE STUDY OF GLOBALISATION AND
REGIONALISATION, Department of Political Science,
University of Warwick, Coventry CV4 7AL.
Tel: 024-7652 3916. *Directors,* Prof. R. Higgott; J. Whalley
COMPLEX PRODUCT SYSTEMS INNOVATION CENTRE,
SPRU, Mantell Building, University of Sussex, Brighton
BN1 9RF. Tel: 01273-686758.
Director, Prof. M. Hobday
FINANCIAL MARKETS CENTRE, London School of
Economics, Houghton Street, London WC2A 2AE.
Tel: 020-7955 7002. *Director,* Prof. D. Webb
TRANSPORT STUDIES UNIT, Centre for Transport Studies,
University College London, Gower Street, London WC1E
6BT. Tel: 020-7380 7009.
Director, Prof. P. Goodwin

RESOURCE CENTRES
CENTRE FOR APPLIED SOCIAL SURVEYS, SOCIAL AND
COMMUNITY PLANNING RESEARCH, 35 Northampton
Square, London EC1V 0AX.
Tel: 020-7250 1866.
Director, R. Thomas

CENTRE FOR ECONOMIC POLICY RESEARCH,
90–98 Goswell Road, London EC1V 7DB.
Tel: 020-7878 2900. *Director,* Prof. R. Portes
ESRC DATA ARCHIVE, University of Essex, Wivenhoe Park,
Colchester, Essex CO4 3SQ. Tel: 01206-872001.
Director, K. Schurer
ESRC UK CENTRE FOR EVIDENCE BASED POLICY,
Queen Mary and Westfield College, Department of Politics,
Mile End Road, London E1 4NS.
Director, Prof. K. Young
INTERNATIONAL BIBLIOGRAPHY OF THE SOCIAL
SCIENCES, British Library of Political and Economic Science,
London School of Economics, Houghton Street,
London WC2A 2AE. Tel: 020-7955 7000.
Director, Ms J. Sykes
INTERNATIONAL BIBLIOGRAPHY OF THE SOCIAL
SCIENCES: ON-LINE RESOURCE CENTRE, LSE, 10
Portugal Street, London WC2A 2HD. Tel: 020-7955 7455.
Director, Ms. L. Brindley
QUALITATIVE DATA ARCHIVAL RESOURCE CENTRE,
Department of Sociology, University of Essex, Colchester,
Essex CO4 3SQ. Tel: 01206-873058.
Director, Prof. P. Thompson
RESOURCE CENTRE FOR ACCESS TO DATA IN EUROPE,
Department of Geography, University of Durham, Durham
DH1 3HP. Tel: 0191-374 7350.
Director, Prof. R. Hudson

ENGINEERING AND PHYSICAL SCIENCES RESEARCH COUNCIL (EPSRC)

Polaris House, North Star Avenue, Swindon SN2 1ET
Tel: 01793-444000

The EPSRC is the largest of the UK Research Councils and funds research and postgraduate training in engineering, the physical sciences and basic technology in universities and other organisations throughout the UK. It also provides advice, disseminates knowledge and promotes public understanding in these areas.
Chairman, Prof. Dame Julia Higgins, FRS, FREng
Chief Executive, Prof. J. O'Reilly, FREng, CEng

MEDICAL RESEARCH COUNCIL (MRC)

20 Park Crescent, London W1B 1AL Tel: 020-7636 5422
Fax: 020-7436 2663 Web: www.mrc.ac.uk

The purpose of the MRC is to promote medical and related biological research. The council employs its own research staff and funds research by other institutions and individuals, complementing the research resources of the universities and hospitals.
Chairman, Sir Anthony Cleaver
Chief Executive, Prof. G. K. Radda, CBE, D.Phil., FRS
Chairman, Neurosciences and Mental Health Board, Prof. N. J. Rothwell
Chairman, Molecular and Cellular Medicine Board, Prof. I. C. MacLennan
Chairman, Physiological Medicine and Infections Board, Prof. J. Saville
Chairman, Health Services and Public Health Research Board, Prof. R. Fitzpatrick

LABORATORY OF MOLECULAR BIOLOGY,
Hills Road, Cambridge CB2 2QH. Tel: 01223-248011.
Director, Dr R. Henderson, FRS

RESEARCH UNITS

MRC ANATOMICAL NEUROPHARMACOLOGY UNIT,
Tel: 01865-271865 Web: mrcanu.pharm.ox.ac.uk
MRC BIOCHEMICAL AND CLINICAL MAGNETIC
RESONANCE UNIT, Tel: 01865-221111
Web: www.bioch.ox.ac.uk/mrs
MRC BIOMEDICAL NMR CENTRE,
Tel: 020-8816 2427; Web: www.mmrcentre.mrc.ac.uk
MRC BIOSTATISTICS UNIT, Tel: 01223-330397
Web: www.mrc-bsu.cam.ac.uk
MRC CANCER CELL UNIT, Tel: 01223-763240
Web: www.hutchison-mrc.cam.ac.uk
MRC CELL BIOLOGY UNIT, Tel: 020-7679 7806
Web: www.ucl.ac.uk/lmcb
MRC CENTRE CAMBRIDGE, Tel: 01223-248011
MRC CENTRE LONDON, Tel: 020-7670 4691
MRC CENTRE OXFORD, Tel: 01865-811179
MRC/UCL CENTRE DEVELOPMENT FOR MEDICAL
MOLECULAR VIROLOGY, Tel: 020-7679 9119
Web: www.ucl.ac.uk/windeyer-institute/institute/mrc.htm
MRC/UNIVERSITY OF NEWCASTLE CENTRE
DEVELOPMENT IN CLINICAL BRAIN AGEING,
Tel: 0191-256 3206
Web: www.ncl.ac.uk/iah/wolfson.htm
MRC CENTRE FOR DEVELOPMENTAL
NEUROBIOLOGY, Tel: 020-7848 6521
Web: www.kcl.ac.uk/depsta/biomedical/mrcdevbiol
MRC/UNIVERSITY OF EDINBURGH CENTRE FOR
INFLAMMATION RESEARCH, Tel: 0131-651 3094
Web: www.med.ed.ac.uk/idg/inflamrs.htm
MRC CENTRE FOR PROTEIN ENGINEERING,
Tel: 01223-402100 Web: www.mrc-cpe.cam.ac.uk
MRC/UNIVERSITY OF BRISTOL CENTRE FOR
SYNAPTIC PLASTICITY, Tel: 0117-928 7402;
Web: www.bris.ac.uk/depts/synaptic
MRC CLINICAL SCIENCES CENTRE,
Tel: 020-8383 8250 Web: www.csc.mrc.ac.uk
MRC CLINICAL TRIALS UNIT, Tel: 020-7670 4700;
Web: www.ctu.mrc.ac.uk
MRC COGNITION AND BRAIN SCIENCES UNIT,
Tel: 01223-355294 Web: www.mrc-cbu.cam.ac.uk
MRC DUNN HUMAN NUTRITION UNIT,
Tel: 01223-252700 Web: www.mrc-dunn.cam.ac.uk
MRC ENVIRONMENTAL EPIDEMIOLOGY UNIT,
Tel: 023-8077 7624 Web: www.mrc.soton.ac.uk
MRC FUNCTIONAL GENETICS UNIT,
Tel: 01865-272169 Web: www.mrcfgu.ox.ac.uk
MRC GENESERVICE, Tel: 01223-496750
Web: www.hgmp.mrc.ac.uk/geneservice
MRC/UNIVERSITY OF SUSSEX GENOME DAMAGE AND
STABILITY CENTRE, Tel: 01273-678 123
Web: www.biols.susx.ac.uk/gdsc
MRC HEALTH SERVICES RESEARCH COLLABORATION,
Tel: 0117-928 7343 Web: www.hsrc.ac.uk
MRC HUMAN GENETICS UNIT, Tel: 0131-332 2471;
Web: www.hgu.mrc.ac.uk
MRC HUMAN IMMUNOLOGY UNIT,
Tel: 01865-222336
Web: www.imm.ox.ac.uk/pages/research/human-
immunology.htm
MRC HUMAN REPRODUCTIVE SCIENCES UNIT,
Tel: 0131-242 6200 Web: www.hrsu.mrc.ac.uk
MRC IMMUNOCHEMISTRY UNIT, Tel: 01865-275354;
Web: www.bioch.ox.ac.uk/immunoch

MRC INSTITUTE FOR ENVIRONMENT AND HEALTH, Tel: 0116-223 1600 Web: www.le.ac.uk/ieh

MRC INSTITUTE OF HEARING RESEARCH, Tel: 0115-922 3431 Web: www.ihr.mrc.ac.uk

MRC LABORATORIES FAJARA, The Gambia. Tel: +220 495442 to 495446 Web: www.extra.mrc.ac.uk/gambia

MRC LABORATORY OF MOLECULAR BIOLOGY, Tel: 01223-248011 Web: www.mrc-lmb.cam.ac.uk

MRC/UCL LABORATORY FOR MOLECULAR CELL BIOLOGY, Tel: 020-7679 7806 Web: www.ucl.ac.uk/lmcb

MRC MAMMALIAN GENETICS UNIT, Tel: 01235-841000 Web: www.har.mrc.ac.uk

MRC MOLECULAR HAEMOTOLOGY UNIT, Tel: 01865-222443 Web: www.imm.ox.ac.uk/groups/mrc_molhaem

MRC UK MOUSE GENOME CENTRE, Tel: 01235-841000 Web: www.mgc.har.mrc.ac.uk

MRC NATIONAL INSTITUTE FOR MEDICAL RESEARCH, Tel: 020-8959 3666 Web: www.nimr.mrc.ac.uk

MRC PRION UNIT, Tel: 020-7837 4888 Web: www.prion.ucl.ac.uk

MRC PROTEIN PHOSPHORYLATION UNIT, Tel: 01382-344241 Web: www.dundee.ac.uk/lifesciences/mrcppu

MRC RADIATION AND GENOME STABILITY UNIT, Tel: 01235-841000 Web: www.ragsu.har.mrc.ac.uk

MRC RESOURCE CENTRE FOR HUMAN NUTRITION RESEARCH, Tel: 01223-426356 Web: www.mrc-hnr.cam.ac.uk

MRC ROSALIND FRANKLIN CENTRE FOR GENOMICS RESEARCH, Tel: 01223-494500 Web: www.hgmp.mrc.ac.uk

MRC SOCIAL AND PUBLIC HEALTH SCIENCES UNIT, Tel: 0141-357 3949 Web: www.msoc-mrc.gla.ac.uk

MRC SOCIAL, GENETIC AND DEVELOPMENTAL PSYCHIATRY CENTRE, Tel: 020-7848 0873 Web: www.iop.kcl.ac.uk/iop/departments/sgdpsy/index.shtml

MRC TOXICOLOGY UNIT, Tel: 0116-252 5544 Web: www.le.ac.uk/mrctox

MRC VIROLOGY UNIT, Tel: 0141-330 4017 Web: www.vir.gla.ac.uk

NATURAL ENVIRONMENT RESEARCH COUNCIL (NERC)

Polaris House, North Star Avenue, Swindon SN2 1EU
Tel: 01793-411500 Fax: 01793-411501 Web: www.nerc.ac.uk

The UK's Natural Environment Research Council (NERC) funds and carries out impartial scientific research in the sciences of the environment. Its work covers the full range of atmospheric, earth, terrestrial and aquatic sciences, from the depth of the oceans to the upper atmosphere. Its mission is to gather and apply knowledge, create understanding and predict the behaviour of the natural environment and its resources.
Chairman, R. Margetts, CBE, FREng
Chief Executive, Prof. J. Lawton, CBE, FRS

RESEARCH CENTRES

BRITISH ANTARCTIC SURVEY, High Cross, Madingley Road, Cambridge, CB3 0ET. Tel: 01223-221400. *Director,* Prof. C. Rapley

BRITISH GEOLOGICAL SURVEY, Kingsley Dunham Centre, Keyworth, Nottingham, NG12 5GG. Tel: 0115-936 3100. *Executive Director,* Dr D. Falvey

CENTRE FOR ECOLOGY AND HYDROLOGY (CEH), Corporate Planning Office, Polaris House, North Star Avenue, Swindon, SN2 1EU. Tel: 01793-442524. *Director,* Prof. P. Nuttall, OBE

PROUDMAN OCEANOGRAPHIC LABORATORY, Bidston Observatory, Bidston, Prenton, Birkenhead, CH43 7RA. Tel: 0151-653 8633. *Director,* Dr E. Hill

COLLABORATIVE CENTRES

CENTRE OF OBSERVATION OF AIR-SEA INTERACTIONS AND FLUXES, Plymouth Marine Laboratory, Prospect Place, Plymouth, PL1 3DH. *Director,* Prof. J. Aiken

CENTRE FOR OBSERVATION AND MODELLING OF EARTHQUAKES AND TECTONICS, COMET Centre of Excellence, Department of Earth Sciences, University of Oxford, Parks Road, Oxford OX1 3PR. Tel: 01865-272000. *Head of Department,* Prof. J. Woodhouse

CENTRE FOR POLAR OBSERVATION AND MODELLING, Department of Space and Climate Physics, Pearson Building, University College London, Gower Street, London WC1E 6BT. Tel: 020-7679 3031. *Director,* Dr B. Parson

CENTRE FOR POPULATION BIOLOGY, Imperial College, Silwood Park, Ascot, SL5 7PY. Tel: 0200-7594 2474. *Director,* Prof. J. Godfray

CLIMATE AND LAND SURFACE SYSTEMS INTERACTION CENTRE, University of Wales Swansea, Singleton Park, Swansea, SA2 8PP. Tel: 01792-295647. *Director,* Prof. M. Barnsley

DATA ASSIMILATION RESEARCH CENTRE, DEPARTMENT OF METEOROLOGY, University of Reading, Reading RG6 6BB. Tel: 0118-931 6981. *Director,* Prof. R. O'Neill

ENVIRONMENTAL SYSTEMS SCIENCE CENTRE, UNIVERSITY OF READING, PO Box 238, Reading, RG6 6AL. Tel: 0118- 931 8741. *Director,* Prof. R. Gurney

NATIONAL INSTITUTE FOR ENVIRONMENTAL E-SCIENCE, Centre for Mathematical Science, Wilberforce Road, Cambridge, CB3 0WA. Tel: 01223-764289. *Director,* Dr M. Dove

NERC CENTRES FOR ATMOSPHERIC SCIENCE, University of Reading, Earley Gate, PO Box 243, Reading RG6 6BB. Tel: 0118-931 6979. *Director,* Prof. A. Thorpe

NCAS ATMOSPHERIC CHEMISTRY MODELLING SUPPORT UNIT, Dept of Chemistry, University of Cambridge, Lensfield Road, Cambridge, CB2 1EW. Tel: 01223-336473. *Director,* Prof. J. Pyle

NCAS BRITISH ATMOSPHERIC DATA CENTRE, RUTHERFORD APPLETON LABORATORY, CHILTON, Didcot, OX11 0QX. Tel: 01235-446432. *Director,* Dr B. Lawrence

NERC CENTRE FOR GLOBAL ATMOSPHERIC MODELLING, Department of Meteorology, University of Reading, PO Box 243, Earley Gate, Reading, RG6 6BB. Tel: 0118-931 8315. *Director,* Prof. J. Slingo

NCAS DISTRIBUTED INSTITUTE FOR ATMOSPHERIC COMPOSITION, School of Chemistry, University of Leeds, Leeds, LS2 9JT. Tel: 0113-343 6450. *Director,* Prof. M. Pilling

NCAS FACILITY FOR AIRBORNE ATMOSPHERIC MEASUREMENTS, Physics Dept, UMIST, PO Box 88, Manchester, M60 1QD. Tel: 0161-200 3936. *Director,* Prof. P. Jonas

NCAS UNIVERSITIES FACILITY FOR ATMOSPHERIC MEASUREMENTS, School of Environment, University of Leeds, Leeds, LS2 9JT. Tel: 0113-343 1632.
Director, Dr A. Blyth
NCAS UNIVERSITIES WEATHER RESEARCH NETWORK, Dept of Meteorology, University of Reading, PO Box 243, Earley Gate, Reading, RG6 6BB. Tel: 0118-931 6311.
Director, Prof. P. Mason
NERC CENTRE FOR TERRESTRIAL CARBON DYNAMICS, University of Sheffield, Hicks Building, Hounsfield Road, Sheffield S3 7RH. Tel: 0114-222 3803
PLYMOUTH MARINE LABORATORY, Prospect Place, West Hoe, Plymouth, PL1 3DH. Tel: 01752-633100.
Director, Prof. N. Owens
SCOTTISH ASSOCIATION FOR MARINE SCIENCE, Dunstaffnage Marine Laboratory, by Dunbeg, Oban, Argyll, PA37 IQA. Tel: 01631-559000.
Director, Prof. G. Shimmield
SEA MAMMAL RESEARCH UNIT, Gatty Marine Laboratory, University of St Andrews, Fife, KY16 8LB. Tel: 01334-462630, *Director,* Prof. I. Boyd
SOUTHAMPTON OCEANOGRAPHY CENTRE, University of Southampton, European Way, Southampton, SO14 3ZH. Tel: 023-8059 6666. *Director,* Prof. H. Roe
TYNDALL CENTRE, School of Environmental Sciences, University of East Anglia, Norwich, Norfolk NR4 7TJ. Tel: 01603-593900. *Director,* Dr M. Hulme

PARTICLE PHYSICS AND ASTRONOMY RESEARCH COUNCIL (PPARC)

Polaris House, North Star Avenue, Swindon SN2 1SZ
Tel: 01793-442000 Fax: 01793-442002
Email: pr.pus@pparc.ac.uk

The Particle Physics and Astronomy Research Centre (PPARC) is the UK's strategic science investment agency. It funds research, education and public understanding in four broad areas of science – particle physics, astronomy, cosmology and space sciences.

PPARC is government funded and provides research grants and studentships to scientists in British universities, gives researchers access to world-class facilities and funds the UK membership of international bodies such as the European Laboratory for Particle Physics (CERN), the European Space Agency (ESA) and The European Southern Observatory (ESO). It also contributes money to the UK telescopes overseas on La Palma, Hawaii, Australia and in Chile, the UK Astronomy Technology Centre at the Royal Observatory, Edinburgh and the MERLIN/VLBI National Facility.
Chairman, P. Warry
Chief Executive, Prof. I. Halliday, FRSE, FInstP

ISAAC NEWTON GROUP OF TELESCOPES, Apartado de Coreos 321, Santa Cruz de la Palma, Tenerife 38780, Canary Islands. Tel: 00 3422-411048.
Director, R. Rutten
JOINT ASTRONOMY CENTRE, 660 N A'ohoku Place, University Park, Hilo, Hawaii 96720. Tel: Hawaii 961 3756.
Head, Prof. G. Davies
UK ASTRONOMY TECHNOLOGY CENTRE, Blackford Hill, Edinburgh EH9 3HJ. Tel: 0131-668 8100.
Director, Dr A. Russell

RESEARCH AND TECHNOLOGY ORGANISATIONS

The following industrial and technological research bodies are members of the Applied Industrial Research Trading Organisations (AIRTO). Members' activities span a wide range of disciplines from life sciences to engineering. Their work includes basic research, development and design of innovative products or processes, instrumentation testing and certification, and technology and management consultancy. AIRTO publishes a directory to help clients identify the organisations that might be able to assist them. AIRTO, PO Box 85, Leatherhead, Surrey KT22 7RY. Tel: 01372- 374153. *President,* Dr B. Blunden, OBE
ADVANCED MANUFACTURING TECHNOLOGY RESEARCH INSTITUTE, Hulley Road, Macclesfield, Cheshire SK10 2NE. Tel: 01625-425421.
Managing Director, P. Sholl
AIRCRAFT RESEARCH ASSOCIATION LTD, Manton Lane, Bedford MK41 7PF. Tel: 01234-350681.
Chief Executive, B. Timmins
BLC (THE LEATHER TECHNOLOGY CENTRE), Leather Trade House, Kings Park Road, Moulton Park, Northants NN3 6JD. Tel: 01604-679999.
Chief Executive, M. Parsons
BRE (BUILDING RESEARCH ESTABLISHMENT), Garston, Watford, Hertfordshire, WD2 7JR. Tel: 01923-664000.
Chief Executive, Dr M. Wyatt
BREWING RESEARCH INTERNATIONAL (*Alcoholic beverages*), Lyttel Hall, Coopers Hill Road, Nutfield, Surrey RH1 4HY. Tel: 01737-822272.
Director-General, Dr M. Kierstan
BRITISH MARITIME TECHNOLOGY LTD, Orlando House, 1 Waldegrave Road, Teddington, Middx TW11 8LZ. Tel: 01923-664000. *Chief Executive,* R. Swann.
BRITISH TEXTILE TECHNOLOGY GROUP, Wira House, West Park Ring Road, Leeds LS16 6QL. Tel: 0113-259 1999; Shirley House, Wilmslow Road, Didsbury, Manchester M20 2RB. Tel: 0161-445 8141.
Chief Executive, A. King
BUILDING SERVICES RESEARCH AND INFORMATION ASSOCIATION, Old Bracknell Lane West, Bracknell, Berks RG12 7AH. Tel: 01344-426511.
Chief Executive, A. Eastwell
CAMPDEN AND CHORLEYWOOD FOOD RESEARCH ASSOCIATION, Chipping Campden, Glos GL55 6LD. Tel: 01386-842000.
Director-General, Prof. C. Dennis
CENTRAL LABORATORY OF THE RESEARCH COUNCILS, Chilton, Didcot, Oxfordshire, OX11 OQX. Tel: 01235-821900. *Chief Executive,* Prof. J. Wood
CERAM RESEARCH (BRITISH CERAMIC RESEARCH LTD), Queen's Road, Penkhull, Stoke-on-Trent ST4 7LQ. Tel: 01782-764444. *Chief Executive,* Dr N. E. Sanderson
CIRIA (CONSTRUCTION INDUSTRY RESEARCH AND INFORMATION ASSOCIATION), 6 Storey's Gate, London SW1P 3A. Tel: 020-7222 8891.
Director-General, Dr T. Broyd
CRL *(Specialist products, technology licences, research and development),* Dawley Road, Hayes, Middx UB3 1HH. Tel: 020-8848 9779. *Managing Director,* Dr B. Holcroft
FIRA INTERNATIONAL LTD (FURNITURE INDUSTRY RESEARCH ASSOCIATION), Maxwell Road, Stevenage, Herts SG1 2EW. Tel: 01438-313433.
Managing Director, H. Davies

HR WALLINGFORD GROUP LTD *(Hydroinformatics and engineering)*, Howbery Park, Wallingford, Oxon OX10 8BA. Tel: 01491-835381. *Chief Executive,* Dr S. W. Huntington

ITRI LIMITED, *(Tin and chemicals)*, Kingston Lane, Uxbridge, Middlesex UB8 3PJ. Tel: 01895-272406. *Chief Executive,* D. Bishop

LGC, Queens Road, Teddington, Middx TW11 0LY. Tel: 020-8943 7300. *Chief Executive and Government Chemist,* Dr R. Worswick

LEATHERHEAD FOOD INTERNATIONAL, Randalls Road, Leatherhead, Surrey KT22 7RY. Tel: 01372-376761. *Director,* J. Bevington

MATERIALS ENGINEERING RESEARCH LABORATORY LTD, Tamworth Road, Hertford SG13 7DG. Tel: 01992-500120. *Managing Director,* Dr. R. H. Martin

MOTOR INDUSTRY RESEARCH ASSOCIATION, Watling Street, Nuneaton, Warks CV10 0TU. Tel: 024-7635 5000. *Managing Director,* J. R. Wood

MOTOR INSURANCE REPAIR RESEARCH CENTRE, Colthorp Lane, Thatcham, Berks, RG19 4NP. Tel: 01635-868855. *Chief Executive,* P. Roberts

THE NATIONAL COMPUTING CENTRE LTD, Oxford House, Oxford Road, Manchester M1 7ED. Tel: 0161-228 6333. *Chief Executive,* M. Gough

NATIONAL PHYSICAL LABORATORY, Queens Road, Teddington, Middx TW11 0LW. Tel: 020-8977 3222. *Chief Executive,* Dr B. McGuiness

NCIMB LIMITED *(Microbiological supply and bacterial culture collection)*, 23 St Machar Drive, Aberdeen, AB24 3RY. Tel: 01224-273332. *Chief Executive,* Dr A. Syms

PAINT RESEARCH ASSOCIATION, 8 Waldegrave Road, Teddington, Middx TW11 8LD. Tel: 020-8977 4427. *Acting Managing Director, Company Secretary and Finance Director,* J. Marshall

PERA GROUP *(Multi-disciplinary research, design, development and consultancy)*, Middle Aston House, Middle Aston, Oxon OX6 3PT. Tel: 01869-347755. *Chief Executive,* Dr P. Davies, CBE

QINETIQ, *(Science Consultancy)*, Cody Building, Ively Road, Farnborough, Hants GU14 0LX. Tel: 01252-394555. *Chief Executive,* Sir John Chisholm, FEng

RAPRA TECHNOLOGY LTD *(Rubber and plastics)*, Shawbury, Shrewsbury SY4 4NR. Tel: 01939-250383; North East Centre, 18 Belasis Court, Belasis Technology Park, Billingham TS23 4AZ. Tel: 01642-370406. *Managing Director,* A. Ward

SATRA TECHNOLOGY CENTRE *(Footwear, apparel, safety products and furniture)*, Satra House, Rockingham Road, Kettering, Northants NN16 9JH. Tel: 01536-410000. *Chief Executive,* Dr R.E. Whittaker

SCOTCH WHISKY RESEARCH INSTITUTE, The Robertson Trust Building, Research Park North, Riccarton, Edinburgh, EH14 4AP. Tel: 0131 449-8900. *Director,* Dr G. M. Steele

SIRA LTD *(Measurement, instrumentation, control and optical systems technology)*, South Hill, Chislehurst, Kent BR7 5EH. Tel: 020-8467 2636. *Managing Director,* Prof. R. A. Brook

SMITH INSTITUTE *(Mathematics and computing)*, PO Box 183, Guildford, Surrey GU2 5GG. Tel: 01483-579108. *Chairman of the Council,* Dr B. Smith, CBE

SPORTS TURF RESEARCH INSTITUTE, St Ives Estate, Bingley, W. Yorks BD16 1AU. Tel: 01274-565131. *Chief Executive,* Dr G. McKillop

STEEL CONSTRUCTION INSTITUTE, Silwood Park, Ascot, Berks SL5 7QN. Tel: 01344-623345. *Director,* Dr G. Owens

TNO BIBRA INTERNATIONAL LTD, Woodmansterne Road, Carshalton, Surrey SM5 4DS. Tel: 020-8652 1000, *Director,* Dr G. van der Veek

TRADA TECHNOLOGY LTD *(Timber and wood-based products)*, Chiltern House, Stocking Lane, Hughenden Valley, High Wycombe, Bucks HP14 4ND. Tel: 01494-563091. *Managing Director,* A. Abbott

TWI ABINGTON HALL, Abington, Cambridge DCB 6AL. Tel: 01223-891162. *Chief Executive,* A.B.M. Braithwaite, OBE

SOCIAL WELFARE

NATIONAL HEALTH SERVICE

The National Health Service (NHS) came into being on 5 July 1948 under the National Health Service Act 1946, covering England and Wales, and under separate legislation for Scotland and Northern Ireland. The NHS is now administered by the Secretary of State for Health (in England), the National Assembly for Wales, the Scottish Executive and the Secretary of State for Northern Ireland.

The function of the NHS is to provide a comprehensive health service designed to secure improvement in the physical and mental health of the people and to prevent, diagnose and treat illness. It was founded on the principle that treatment should be provided according to clinical need rather than ability to pay, and should be free at the point of delivery. However, the possibility for charges to be made in specific cases is provided for in legislation and examples of charges that have been introduced by statute are those for prescriptions and for some dental and ophthalmic treatment. Those visiting the UK, but who are not normally resident, are subject to certain charges.

The NHS covers a comprehensive range of hospital, specialist, family practitioner (medical, dental, ophthalmic and pharmaceutical), artificial limb and appliance, ambulance, and community health services. Everyone normally resident in the UK is entitled to use any of these services.

STRUCTURE

The structure of the NHS remained relatively stable for the first 30 years of its existence. In 1974, a three-tier management structure comprising Regional Health Authorities, Area Health Authorities and District Management Teams was introduced in England, and the NHS became responsible for community health services. In 1979 Area Health Authorities were abolished and District Management Teams were replaced by District Health Authorities.

The National Health Service and Community Care Act 1990 provided for more streamlined Regional Health Authorities and District Health Authorities, and for the establishment of Family Health Services Authorities (FHSAs) and NHS Trusts. The concept of the 'internal market' was introduced into health care, whereby care was provided through NHS contracts where health authorities or boards and GP fundholders (the purchasers) were responsible for buying health care from hospitals, non-fundholding GPs, community services and ambulance services (the providers).

NHS Trusts operate as self-governing health care providers independent of health authority control and responsible to the Secretary of State. Until 1999 they derived their income principally from contracts to provide services to health authorities and fund-holding GPs. In Northern Ireland, 19 health and social services trusts are responsible for providing health and social services in an organisational model unique to Northern Ireland.

The Act also paved the way for the Community Care

reforms, which were introduced in April 1993 and changed the way care is administered for elderly people, the mentally ill, the physically handicapped and people with learning disabilities.

ENGLAND

The eight Regional Health Authorities in England were abolished in April 1996 and replaced by eight regional offices which, together with the headquarters in Leeds, formed the NHS Executive. In April 2002, as an interim arrangement, the eight regional offices were replaced by four Directorates of Health and Social Care (DsHSC). In February 2003, the abolition of DsHSCs was announced.

In April 1996 the District Health Authorities and Family Health Service Authorities were merged to form 100 unified Health Authorities (HAs) in England. In April 2002, 28 new health authorities were formed from the existing HAs. In October 2002, as part of the new arrangements set out in the NHS Reform and Health Care Professions Act 2002, these new health authorities were renamed Strategic Health Authorities (SHAs) and charged with creating a strategic framework for managing the performance of Primary Care Trusts and building the capacity of health services locally.

The first 17 Primary Care Trusts (PCTs) became operational in England on 1 April 2000. At 1 April 2003 a total of 303 PCTs covered all areas of England. PCTs were created to give primary care professionals greater control over how resources are best used to benefit patients. PCTs are responsible for tackling health inequalities, developing primary and community health services and commissioning secondary care services. They are free-standing statutory bodies undertaking many of the functions previously exercised by former Health Authorities, such as securing the provision of services and integrating health and social care.

Each PCT is overseen by a lay board, comprising a Chairman and non-executive directors who are appointed by the NHS Appointments Commission and who are members of the local community to be served by the PCT. The Board's role is to provide strategic oversight and verification to the work of the Executive, which is made up of health professionals. The Executive committee guides the board on priorities, services policies and investment plans.

The 28 SHAs are: Avon, Gloucestershire and Wiltshire; Bedfordshire and Hertfordshire; Birmingham and the Black Country; Cheshire and Merseyside; County Durham and Tees Valley; Coventry, Warwickshire, Herefordshire and Worcestershire; Cumbria and Lancashire; Dorset and Somerset; Essex; Greater Manchester; Hampshire and Isle of Wight; Kent and Medway; Leicestershire, Northamptonshire and Rutland; Norfolk, Suffolk and Cambridgeshire; North and East Yorkshire and Northern Lincolnshire; North Central London; North East London; North West London; Northumberland, Tyne and Wear; Shropshire and Staffordshire; South East London; South West London; South West Peninsula; South Yorkshire; Surrey and Sussex; Thames Valley; Trent; and West Yorkshire.

Contact details for all the SHAs, PCTs and other NHS organisations in England can be found in the *Local*

Services Search section on the NHS website: www.nhs.uk or by calling the Public Enquiry Office on 020-7210 4850.

WALES
In Wales there were five HAs which replaced the former 17 HAs and FHSAs in April 1996. The HAs set up 22 Local Health Groups (LHGs), coterminous with local authority areas (*see* Local Government Section), which began work in April 1999. Originally they advised HAs, but in March 2003 the five HAs were abolished and the LHGs took up a role similar to PCTs; assuming responsibility for commissioning services and devising strategies for improving health. They also integrate the delivery of primary and community care. A governing body including GPs and other health professional, social services and community representatives administers each group.

Contact details for the LHGs and other NHS organisations in Wales are available in the *NHS Wales Directory* section on the Welsh NHS website: www.wales.nhs.uk

SCOTLAND
In Scotland there are 15 Health Boards with similar responsibilities to those of the SHAs. The Health Act 1999 replaced the internal market with Local Health Care Co-operatives. As at June 2003, there were over 70 Local Health Care co-operatives, made up of groups of general practitioner services, responsible for fundholding and primary care in their areas.

Health Boards
ARGYLL AND CLYDE, Ross House, Hawkhead Road, Paisley PA2 7BN Tel: 0141-842 7200
  Chief Executive, N. Campbell
AYRSHIRE AND ARRAN, Boswell House, 10 Arthur Street, Ayr KA7 1QJ Tel: 01292-611040
  Chief Executive, Wai Yin Hatton
BORDERS, Newstead, Melrose, Roxburghshire TD6 9BD Tel: 01896-825500 *Chief Executive,* J. Glennie
DUMFRIES AND GALLOWAY, Grierson House, The Crichton Royal, Bankend Road, Dumfries DG1 4ZG Tel: 01387-272700 *Chief Executive,* M. Wright
FIFE, Springfield House, Cupar KY15 5UP Tel: 01334-656200 *Chief Executive,* G. Brechin
FORTH VALLEY, 33 Spittal Street, Stirling FK8 1DX Tel: 01786-463031 *Chief Executive,* Fiona Mackenzie
GRAMPIAN, Summerfield House, 2 Eday Road, Aberdeen AB15 6RE Tel: 01224-663456.
  Chief Executive, Alec Cumming
GREATER GLASGOW, Dalian House, 350 St Vincent Street, Glasgow G3 8YZ Tel: 0141-201 4444
  Chairman, Prof. Sir John Arbuthnott
HIGHLAND, Assynt House, Beechwood Park, Inverness IV2 3HG Tel: 01463-717123
  General Manager, Dr Robin Gibbins
LANARKSHIRE, 14 Beckford Street, Hamilton, Lanarkshire ML3 0TA Tel: 01698-281313
  Chief Executive, D. Pigott
LOTHIAN, Deaconess House, 148 Pleasance, Edinburgh EH8 9RS Tel: 0131-536 9000
  Chief Executive, Prof. J. Barbour, OBE
ORKNEY, Garden House, New Scapa Road, Kirkwall, Orkney KW15 1BQ Tel: 01856-885400
  Chief Executive, Mrs J. Wellden
SHETLAND, Brevik House, South Road, Lerwick ZE1 0TG Tel: 01595-696767 *Chief Executive,* Miss S. Laurenson
TAYSIDE, Kings Cross, Clepington Road, Dundee DD3 8EA Tel: 01382-818479 *Chief Executive,* Prof. T. Wells

WESTERN ISLES, 37 South Beach Street, Stornoway, Isle of Lewis HS1 2BB Tel: 01851-702997
  Chief Executive, M. MacLennan

Health Promotion Authority
HEALTH SCOTLAND, Woodburn House, Canaan Lane, Edinburgh EH10 4SG Tel: 0131-536 5500
  Chief Executive, Graham Robertson

NORTHERN IRELAND
In Northern Ireland there are four Health and Social Services Boards responsible for commissioning services to meet the needs of their respective populations. They are also responsible for assessing the needs of that population, establishing objectives and developing policies and priorities to meet these objectives:

EASTERN, Champion House, 12–22 Linenhall Street, Belfast BT2 8BS Tel: 028-9032 1313
  Chief Executive, Dr Paula Kilbane, FRCP
NORTHERN, County Hall, 182 Galgorm Road, Ballymena BT42 1QB Tel: 028-2565 3333
  Chief Executive, S. MacDonnell
SOUTHERN, Tower Hill, Armagh BT61 7DR Tel: 028-3741 0041 *Chief Executive,* C. Donaghy
WESTERN, 15 Gransha Park, Clooney Road, Londonderry BT47 6FN Tel: 028-7186 0086
  Chief Executive, S. Lindsay

Health Promotion Authority
HEALTH PROMOTION AGENCY FOR NORTHERN IRELAND, 18 Ormeau Avenue, Belfast BT2 8HS
Tel: 028-9031 1611 *Chief Executive,* Dr B. Gaffney

COMMUNITY HEALTH COUNCILS
There are Community Health Councils (CHCs) throughout the UK; their role is to represent the interests of the public to NHS Trusts, PCTs and SHAs and their equivalents in Wales and Scotland. The Government announced in the NHS Plan, published in July 2000, that CHCs would be abolished and replaced by a wholly new system, in order to increase public consultation and patient involvement in the NHS. As a result the 184 CHCs in England will no longer exist from 1 December 2003.

THE NHS PLAN
In July 2000 the government launched The NHS Plan, a ten year strategy to modernise the health service. In April 2002, the Secretary of State published the document *Delivering the NHS Plan: Next Steps on Investment, Next Steps on Reform,* which included: plans for major expansions in NHS capacity (buildings, beds and staff) with the aim of reducing waiting times for treatment; creating 'foundation' hospitals which will have greater independence from central government; financial penalties for local authorities whose delays lead to delayed patient discharge; and the creation of a new health inspectorate, *Commission for Healthcare Audit and Inspection (CHAI).* The document states expectations of net increases above the September 2001 staff census of at least 15,000 consultants and GPs, 35,000 nurses, midwives and health visitors and 30,000 therapists and scientists by 2008.

FINANCE

The NHS is still funded mainly through general taxation, although in recent years more reliance has been placed on the NHS element of National Insurance contributions, patient charges and other sources of income.

In the April 2002 Budget, the Chancellor announced a five-year spending plan for the NHS. Over the years 2003–4 to 2007–8, these plans mean that expenditure on the NHS in the UK will increase on average by 7.2 per cent a year over and above inflation, 7.4 per cent a year for England. The spending plans are set out in the table below:

£ million	UK	% real terms increase*	England	% real terms increase*
2003–4	74,800	7.0	61,300	7.1
2004–5	82,200	7.1	67,400	7.2
2005–6	90,500	7.4	74,400	7.6
2006–7	99,400	7.2	81,800	7.3
2007–8	109,400	7.4	90,200	7.5

* calculated using GDP deflator at 27 June 2003
Source: Department of Health

NATIONAL HEALTH SERVICE EXPENDITURE 2001–2 OUTTURN (England)

	£ million
Hospitals, community health, family health (discretionary) and related services and NHS Trusts	43,464
Family health services (non-discretionary)	4,839
Central and other services*	975
Total	49,279

* includes: environmental health, health promotion, support to the voluntary sector and expenditure on the administration of the Department of Health
Source: Department of Health

GOVERNMENT EXPENDITURE ON WELFARE SERVICES 2000–1

	£ million
Central government	49
Local authorities running expenses	12,048
Capital expenditure	128
Total	12,226

Source: The Stationery Office – Annual Abstract of Statistics 2003 (Crown copyright)

EMPLOYEES AND SALARIES

EMPLOYEES
NHS HOSPITAL AND COMMUNITY HEALTH SERVICE STAFF (Great Britain) 2001

Medical and dental staff	76,000
Nursing, midwifery and health visitors	440,000
Other non-medical staff	171,000
General medical practitioners	37,000
General dental practitioners	22,000

Source: National Statistics – Social Trends 2003 (Crown copyright)

SALARIES
General Practitioners (GPs), dentists, optometrists and pharmacists are self-employed, and are employed by the NHS under contract. On 20 June 2003 GPs accepted a new practice-based contract which rewards practices for delivering quality and a wider range of services. Dentists receive payment for items of treatment for individual adult patients and, in addition, a continuing care payment for those registered with them. Optometrists receive approved fees for each sight test they carry out. Pharmacists receive professional fees from the NHS and

are refunded the cost of prescriptions supplied. Doctors in training receive additional supplements reflecting the intensity and out-of-hours elements of their duties, these can range from 20–100 per cent of the basic salary.

SALARIES at 1 April 2003 for Hospital Medical and Dental Staff and Nurses (these figures do not include merit awards, discretionary points or banding supplements):

Consultant	£54,340–£70,715
Specialist Registrar	£26,760–£39,000
Registrar	£26,760–£32,460
Senior House Officer	£23,940–£33,570
House Officer	£19,185–£21,655
Nursing Grades H–I (Modern Matron)	£25,815–£33,820
Nursing Grades G–I (Senior Ward Sister)*	£23,110–£33,820
Nursing Grade F (Ward Sister)*	£19,585–£25,360
Nursing Grade E (Senior Staff Nurse)	£17,660–£21,325
Nursing Grade D (Staff Nurse)	£16,525–£18,240
Nursing Grade C (Enrolled Nurse and some Nursing auxiliary staff)	£13,465–£16,525
Nursing Grades A–B	£10,050–£12,615

* Includes discretionary points

HEALTH SERVICES

PRIMARY AND COMMUNITY HEALTH CARE
Primary and community health care services comprise the family health services (i.e. the general medical, personal medical, pharmaceutical, dental, and ophthalmic services) and community services (including preventive activities such as vaccination, immunisation and fluoridation). Nursing services including practice nurses, community nurses and health visitors and ante- and post-natal care.

PRIMARY MEDICAL SERVICES
In England, Primary Medical Services are the responsibility of Primary Care Trusts (PCTs) who contract with GPs to provide the service to the NHS. They do so in one of two ways: by providing general medical services (GMS) under national rules or by successfully applying to become a personal medical service (PMS) pilot, with a contract that is largely locally determined. As at 1 April 2003, 39 per cent of GPs were in PMS.

In Wales, responsibility for primary medical services rests with Local Health Groups (LHGs) and in Scotland with Local Health Care Co-operatives (see Structure section).

Any vocationally trained doctor may provide general or personal medical services. The average number of patients on a doctor's list in the UK as at September 2002 was 1,838. GPs may also have private fee-paying patients, but not if that patient is already an NHS patient on that doctor's patient list.

A person who is ordinarily resident in the UK is eligible to register with a GP (or PMS provider) for free primary care treatment. Should a patient have difficulty in registering with a doctor, he or she should contact the local PCT for help. When a person is away from home he/she can still access primary care treatment from a GP if they ask to be treated as a temporary resident. In an emergency any doctor in the service will give treatment and advice.

GPs are responsible for the care of their patients 24 hours a day, 7 days a week, but can fulfil the terms of their contract by delegating or transferring responsibility for out-of-hours (OOH) care to an accredited provider. Under the new GMS contract, practices will be able to opt out of responsibility for patient care during the OOH period. When they do so, it will become a Primary Care Trust (PCT) responsibility. PCTs will be able to provide the OOH cover themselves or commission the service from an OOH provider.

Increasingly, some secondary care services, such as minor operations and consultations can be provided in a primary care setting. The number of such practitioners is growing and the new GMS contract provides a platform for further expansion.

In addition, drop-in services are being developed. A total of 42 NHS Walk-in Centres are operational across the country, with a further centre planned to open in October 2003. They are nurse-led and provide treatment for minor ailments and injuries, health information and self-help advice with extended opening hours (normally every day of the year from 7am-10pm Monday to Friday, and 9am-10pm Saturday and Sunday).

HEALTH COSTS

Some people are exempt or entitled to help with health costs such as prescription charges, ophthalmic and dental costs, and in some cases help towards travel costs to and from hospital. The Social Market Foundation (SMF) Commission is currently reviewing the prescription charge system and released its first report, *A fairer prescription for NHS charges*, in June 2003.

The following list is being reviewed and is only intended as a general guide to those who are entitled to help or are exempt:
– children under 16 and young people in full time education who are under 19
– people aged 60 or over
– pregnant women and women who have had a baby in the last 12 months
– people receiving Income Support and/or Jobseeker's Allowance
– people receiving Tax Credits
– people with a specified medical condition
– people with impaired hearing
– patients of a genito-urinary medicine clinic
– people who need help to go out or live in residential care or a nursing home
– people supported by Local Authority after leaving care
– NHS in-patients
– NHS out-patients for all medication given at the hospital
– patients of the Community Dental Service
– people registered blind or partially sighted
– people who need complex lenses
– war pensioners

People in other circumstances may also be eligible for help; Booklet HC11, available from main post offices, local social security offices and online: www.doh.gov.uk/nhscharges gives further details.

PHARMACEUTICAL SERVICE

Patients may obtain medicines and appliances under the NHS from any pharmacy whose owner has entered into arrangements with the PCT to provide this service; the number of these pharmacies in England and Wales as at March 2002 was 10,463. There are also some suppliers who only provide special appliances. In rural areas, where access to a pharmacy may be difficult, patients may be able to obtain medicines, etc., from a dispensing doctor.

Except for contraceptives (for which there is no charge), a charge of £6.30 is payable for each item supplied unless the patient is exempt and the declaration on the back of the prescription form is completed. Prepayment certificates (£32.90 valid for four months, £90.40 valid for a year) may be purchased by those patients not entitled to exemption who require frequent prescriptions.

DENTAL SERVICE

Dentists, like doctors, may take part in the NHS and also have private patients. Over 18,000 dentists in England provide NHS general dental services. They are responsible to the PCTs in whose areas they provide services. Patients may go to any dentist who is taking part in the NHS and is willing to accept them. Patients are required to pay 80 per cent of the cost of NHS dental treatment. Since 1 April 2003 the maximum charge allowed for an NHS course of treatment has been £372. There is no charge for arrest of bleeding or repairs to dentures; home visits by the dentist or re-opening a surgery in an emergency are charged for as treatment given in the normal way.

GENERAL DENTAL SERVICE 2002–3 (ENGLAND)

Number of dentists	18,369
Number of patients registered	
Adults	16,800,000
Children	6,700,000
Number of courses of treatment	
Adults	26,300,000
Expenditure (£ million)	
Gross expenditure	1,700
Paid by patients	500
Paid out of public funds	1,200
Source: Department of Health	

GENERAL OPHTHALMIC SERVICES

General Ophthalmic Services are administered by PCTs. Testing of sight may be carried out by any ophthalmic medical practitioner or ophthalmic optician (optometrist). The optician must give the prescription to the patient, who can take this to any supplier of glasses to have them dispensed. Only registered opticians can supply glasses to children and to people registered as blind or partially sighted. At the end of March 2002 there were 7,856 practising Optometrists in Great Britain. Approximately 17 million sight tests were carried out in 2001–2.

The NHS sight test costs £16.72. Free eyesight tests and help towards the cost is available to people in certain circumstances. Help is also available for the purchase of glasses. (*see* Health Costs section or booklet HC11)

COMMUNITY CHILD HEALTH SERVICES

Pre-school services at GP surgeries or child health clinics provide regular monitoring of children's physical, mental and emotional health and development, and advice to parents on their children's health and welfare.

The School Health Service provides for the medical and dental examination of schoolchildren, and advises the local education authority, the school, the parents and the pupil of any health factors which may require special consideration during the pupil's school life. GPs are increasingly undertaking child health monitoring in order to improve the preventive health care of children.

All Primary Care Trusts (PCTs) are working with Local Authorities under accredited local health and education partnerships to recruit more schools into the Healthy Schools Programme which was established in 1999 as a joint initiative between the Department of Health and the Department for Education and Skills.

HEALTH ACTION ZONES
Health Action Zones were set up by the government in areas of deprivation and poor health to tackle health inequalities and modernise services. The 26 zones had populations ranging from 180,000 to 1.4 million in certain areas.

Responsibility for further development of initiatives within Health Action Zones (HAZ) now rests with PCTs. PCTs within HAZs have had their budgets adjusted accordingly and have responsibility for spending HAZ money within their area in a way that will address health inequalities.

HOSPITALS AND OTHER SERVICES
Hospital, medical, dental, nursing, ophthalmic and ambulance services are provided by the NHS to meet all reasonable requirements. Facilities for the care of expectant and nursing mothers and young children, and other services required for the diagnosis and treatment of illness, are also provided. Rehabilitation services (occupational therapy, physiotherapy and speech therapy) may also be provided, and surgical and medical appliances are supplied where appropriate. Specialists and consultants who work in NHS hospitals can also engage in private practice, including the treatment of their private patients in NHS hospitals.

FOUNDATION TRUSTS
The *Health and Social Care (Community Health and Standards) Bill,* published in March 2003, included proposals for the creation of NHS Foundation Trusts. Trusts will provide and develop services for NHS patients, within the NHS and subject to NHS systems of inspection, but they will be controlled and run locally rather than nationally.

Foundation Trusts will be free to borrow money for investment from the public and private sectors and to retain operating surpluses to invest in new services. They will be able to recruit and employ their own staff and offer extra rewards for improvements in productivity. They will operate under the terms of authorisation issued by an Independent Regulator and be inspected by the Commission for Healthcare Audit and Inspection (CHAI).

Hospitals attaining a three-star rating in the annual performance tables will be able to apply for foundation trust status. Suitability to become a NHS Foundation Trust will also depend on an evaluation of financial performance as well as management, vision and leadership potential. Subject to legislation the first NHS Foundation Trusts will become fully operational from April 2004.

PRIVATE FINANCE INITIATIVE
The Private Finance Initiative (PFI) was launched in 1992, and involves the private sector in designing, building, financing and operating new hospitals, which are then leased to the NHS. The NHS Plan committed the NHS to entering into a new public private partnership, Partnerships for Health, a joint venture between the Department of Health and Partnerships UK plc (PUK) established in September 2001. Both parties committed an initial £5 million of equity funding to the company whose role is to support the development of NHS Local Improvement Finance Trusts (LIFT) by implementing a standard approach to procurement as well as providing some equity. LIFTs will be set up as limited companies with the local NHS, Partnerships for Health and the private sector as shareholders. £195 million has been earmarked by the Department of Health as enabling funding for LIFTs. LIFT will build and refurbish primary care premises, which it will own and then rent to GPs on a lease basis (as well as other parties such as chemists, opticians, dentists etc).

CHARGES
NHS trusts can provide accommodation in single rooms or small wards, if not required for patients who need privacy for medical reasons. The patient is still an NHS patient, but there may be a charge for these additional facilities. NHS trusts can charge for certain patient services that are considered to be additional treatments over and above the normal service provision. There is no blanket policy to cover this and each case should be considered in the light of the patient's clinical need. However, if an item or service is considered to be an integral part of a patient's treatment by their clinician, then a charge should not be made.

In some NHS hospitals, accommodation and services are available for the treatment of private patients where it does not interfere with care for NHS patients. Income generated by treating private patients is then put back into the local NHS services. Private patients undertake to pay the full costs of medical treatment, accommodation, medication and other related services. Charges for private patients are set locally.

AMBULANCE SERVICE
The NHS provides emergency ambulance services free of charge via the 999 emergency telephone service. Air ambulances, provided through local charities and partially funded by the NHS, are used throughout the UK. They assist with cases where access may be difficult or heavy traffic could hinder road progress. Non-emergency ambulance services are provided free of charge to patients who are deemed to require them on medical grounds.

In 2002–3 in England approximately 5 million emergency calls were made to the ambulance service, an increase of 7 per cent on the previous year. There were about 3.2 million emergency patient journeys. By 1 April 2001 all services had introduced call prioritisation. The prioritisation procedures require all emergency calls to be classified as either immediately life threatening (category A) or other emergency (category B/C). Services are expected to reach 75 per cent of Category A (life threatening) calls within eight minutes and 95 per cent of category B/C calls within 19 minutes in rural areas and 14 minutes in urban areas. In 2002–3, 74.6 per cent of life threatening calls resulted in emergency response arriving at the scene of the incident within 8 minutes (70.7 per cent in 2001–2). Eighteen services met or exceeded the 75 per cent target. For category B/C calls, 14 services responded to 95 per cent or more calls within 14 or 19 minutes.

NHS DIRECT
NHS Direct is a telephone service staffed by nurses which gives patients advice on how to look after themselves as well as directing them to the appropriate part of the NHS for treatment if necessary. Tel: 0845-4647.

BLOOD SERVICES
There are four national bodies which co-ordinate the blood donor programme in the UK. Donors give blood at local centres on a voluntary basis.

NATIONAL BLOOD SERVICE, Oak House, Reeds Crescent, Watford, Herts WD24 4QN Tel: 01923-486800
Chief Executive, M. Gorham
SCOTTISH NATIONAL BLOOD TRANSFUSION SERVICE, 21 Ellens Glen Road, Edinburgh EH17 7QT
Tel: 0131-536 5700
National Director, A. Macmillan Douglas
WELSH BLOOD SERVICE, Ely Valley Road, Talbot Green, Pontyclun CF72 9WB Tel: 01443-622000
Acting Director, Dr D. Evans
NORTHERN IRELAND BLOOD TRANSFUSION SERVICE, Belfast City Hospital Complex, Lisburn Road, Belfast BT9 7TS
Tel: 028-9032 1414 *Chief Executive,* Dr W. McClelland

HOSPICES

Hospice or palliative care may be available for patients with life-threatening illnesses. It may be provided at the patient's home or in a voluntary or NHS hospice or in hospital, and is intended to ensure the best possible quality of life for the patient during their illness, and to provide help and support to both the patient and the patient's family. The National Council for Hospices and Specialist Palliative Care Services co-ordinates NHS and voluntary services in England, Wales and Northern Ireland; the Scottish Partnership Agency for Palliative and Cancer Care performs the same function in Scotland.
NATIONAL COUNCIL FOR HOSPICE AND SPECIALIST PALLIATIVE CARE SERVICES, 1st Floor, 34–44 Britannia Street, London WC1X 9JG Tel: 020-7520 8299
Chief Executive, Ms E. S. Richardson
SCOTTISH PARTNERSHIP FOR PALLIATIVE CARE, 1A Cambridge Street, Edinburgh EH1 2DY
Tel: 0131-229 0538 *Director,* Mrs P. Wallace

NUMBER OF BEDS AND PATIENT ACTIVITY 2001

	England	Wales
In-patients:		
Average daily available beds	186,000*	14,400
Average daily occupation of beds	156,000*	11,700
Persons waiting for admission at 31 March	1,035,000	65,600
Day-case admissions	3,620,000*	130,000
Ordinary admissions	8,645,000*	509,400
Out-patient attendances:		
New patients	12,714,000	697,100
Total attendances	44,008,000	761,900
Accident and emergency:		
New cases	12,853,000	877,700
Total attendances	14,044,000	1,009,800
Ward attendances	1,089,000	–

* 2000 figures

SCOTLAND

In-patients:	
Average available staffed beds	32,100
Average occupied beds	25,800
Out-patient attendances:	
New patients	2,744,000
Total attendances	6,382,000

Source: The Stationery Office – *Annual Abstract of Statistics 2003* (Crown copyright)

WAITING LISTS

At the end of March 2003 the total number of patients waiting to be admitted to NHS hospitals in England was 992,045, a decrease of 4.1 per cent on the previous year. The number of patients who had been waiting more than one year was 73, a decrease of 99 per cent on the

previous year, when the total was 21,900. Under the charter *Your Guide to the NHS,* patients are guaranteed admission within 18 months of being placed on a waiting list. Only 11 patients had been waiting longer than 15 months at the end of March 2003 and no patients had been waiting over 18 months.

NHS CHARTERS

The original Patient's Charter was published in 1991 and came into force in 1992; an expanded version was published in 1995. The Charter set out the rights of patients in relation to the standards of service they should expect to receive at all times and standards of service that the NHS aimed to provide.

The Patient's Charter was replaced nationally in 2001 with *Your Guide to the NHS,* which is part of the wider programme of change for patients set out in the NHS Plan. The 'Guide' provides information on how to get treatment and gives information on and sets targets for waiting times for outpatients appointments and access to GP appointments, it also gives specific details on when these targets and other improvements will be achieved. The guide also contains statements on the minimum standards which patients can expect and developments that the NHS will make. The guide makes clear what patients have a right to expect from the NHS and what is expected from patients. A full version of the guide is available online: www.nhs.uk/nhsguide

COMPLAINTS

The charter *Your Guide to the NHS* includes the right to complain about NHS services and sets out how to do this and what the patient can expect if they make a complaint. Patients can expect all complaints to be investigated and a full written reply to be provided by a relevant chief executive or complaints manager within four weeks of receiving the complaint. There are three levels to the NHS complaints procedure: the first level involves resolution of a complaint locally, following a direct approach to the relevant service provider; the second level involves an independent review procedure if the complaint is not resolved locally. As a final resort, patients may approach the Health Service Commissioner or Ombudsman (in Northern Ireland, the Commissioner for Complaints) if they are dissatisfied with the response of the NHS to a complaint.

RECIPROCAL ARRANGEMENTS

Citizens of countries in the European Economic Area (EEA – *see* European Union section) who are resident in the UK are entitled to receive emergency health care either free of charge or for a reduced charge when they are temporarily visiting other member states of the EEA. Form E111, available at post offices, should be obtained before travelling. There are also bilateral agreements with several other countries, including Australia and New Zealand, for the provision of urgent medical treatment either free of charge or for a reduced charge.

EEA nationals visiting the UK and visitors from other countries with which the UK has bilateral healthcare agreements, are entitled to receive emergency healthcare on the NHS on the same terms as it is available to UK residents.

PERSONAL SOCIAL SERVICES

The Secretary of State for Health is responsible, under the Local Authority Social Services Act 1970, for the provision of social services for elderly people, disabled people, families and children, and those with mental disorders. Personal Social Services are administered by local authorities according to policies and standards set by central government. Each authority has a Director of Social Services and a Social Services Committee responsible for the social services functions placed upon them. Local authorities provide, enable and commission care after assessing the needs of their population. The private and voluntary sectors also play an important role in the delivery of social services, and an estimated six million people in Great Britain provide substantial regular care for a member of their family.

Under the Care Standards Act 2000, the National Care Standards Commission (NCSC) was set up to regulate social, private and voluntary care services throughout England. From 1 April 2002 NCSC took responsibility for the registration and inspection of services replacing the system of inspection by local authority and Health Authority inspection units. Care homes, children's homes, domiciliary care agencies, residential family centres, voluntary adoption agencies, independent fostering agencies, private and voluntary hospitals and clinics, exclusively private doctors and nurses agencies all have to register with the NCSC. The Commission is also responsible for inspecting Local Authority fostering and adoption services and the welfare aspects of boarding schools.

In April 2002 the Secretary of State for Health announced plans to establish two new independent inspectorates to strengthen the accountability of those responsible for commissioning the delivery of health and social services. There will be a legal obligation for the two commissions to co-operate fully with one another. Legislation to establish the new commissions; The Commission for Social Care Inspection (CSCI) and the Commission for Healthcare Audit and Inspection (CHAI) was introduced into Parliament in March 2003. The CHAI and CSCI are not expected to be legally fully operational before April 2004.

FINANCE

The Personal Social Services programme is financed partly by central government, with decisions on expenditure allocations being made at local authority level.

STAFF

PERSONAL SOCIAL SERVICES STAFF 2001 (GREAT BRITAIN)

Full-time equivalents

Home help service	40,200
Field social workers	35,200
Residential care staff	53,800
Day care establishments staff	29,500
All other staff (including management and administration and ancillary staff)	53,300
Total staff	212,000

Source: National Statistics – *Annual Abstract of Statistics 2003* (Crown copyright)

ELDERLY PEOPLE

Services for elderly people are designed to enable them to remain living in their own homes for as long as possible. Local authority services include advice, domestic help, meals in the home, alterations to the home to aid mobility, emergency alarm systems, day and/or night attendants, laundry services and the provision of day centres and recreational facilities. Charges may be made for these services. Respite care may also be provided in order to allow carers temporary relief from their responsibilities.

Local authorities and the private sector also provide 'sheltered housing' for elderly people, sometimes with resident wardens.

If an elderly person is admitted to a residential home, charges are made according to a means test; if the person cannot afford to pay, the costs are met by the local authority.

DISABLED PEOPLE

Services for disabled people are designed to enable them to remain living in their own homes wherever possible. Local authority services include advice, adaptations to the home, meals in the home, help with personal care, occupational therapy, educational facilities and recreational facilities. Respite care may also be provided in order to allow carers temporary relief from their responsibilities.

Special housing may be available for disabled people who can live independently, and residential accommodation for those who cannot.

FAMILIES AND CHILDREN

Local authorities are required to provide services aimed at safeguarding the welfare of children in need and, wherever possible, allowing them to be brought up by their families. Services include advice, counselling, help in the home and the provision of family centres. Many authorities also provide short-term refuge accommodation for women and children.

DAY CARE

In allocating day-care places to children, local authorities give priority to children with special needs, whether in terms of their health, learning abilities or social needs. They also provide a registration and inspection service in relation to childminders, play groups and private day nurseries in the local authority area. In 2001 in England, Wales and Northern Ireland there were 301,000 registered day nurseries of which 19,000 were provided by local authorities, 334,000 registered child-minders of which 3,000 were provided by local authorities, and 354,000 registered play groups of which of which 7,000 were provided by local authorities.

Out of school clubs have been introduced in recent years and in 2001 there were 165,000 such places in England, Wales and Northern Ireland.

CHILD PROTECTION

Children considered to be at risk of physical injury, neglect or sexual abuse are placed on the local authority's child protection register. Local authority social services staff, school nurses, health visitors and other agencies work together to prevent and detect cases of abuse. In England at 31 March 2002 there were 25,700 children on child protection registers, a four per cent decrease from March 2001. Of the children registered during 2001–2 39 per cent were at risk of neglect, 19 per cent of physical injury, 10 per cent of sexual abuse and 17 per cent of emotional abuse. In Scotland, at 31 March 2002, there were 2,018 children on local child protection registers and in Wales there were 1,965 children registered.

LOCAL AUTHORITY CARE

Local authorities are required to provide accommodation for children who have no parent or guardian or whose parents or guardians are unable or unwilling to care for them. A family proceedings court may also issue a care order in cases where a child is being neglected or abused, or is not attending school; the court must be satisfied that this would positively contribute to the well-being of the child.

The welfare of children in local authority care must be properly safeguarded. Children may be placed with foster families, who receive payments to cover the expenses of caring for the child or children, or in residential care.

Children's homes may be run by the local authority or by the private or voluntary sectors; all homes are subject to inspection procedures. In England at 31 March 2001, 58,900 children were in the care of local authorities. Of these, 38,400 were in foster placements.

ADOPTION

Local authorities are required to provide an adoption service, either directly or via approved voluntary societies. In the UK, in 2001, 6,589 children (under 18 years old) were entered onto the Adopted Children Register; 5,982 in England and Wales, 468 in Scotland and 139 in Northern Ireland.

PEOPLE WITH LEARNING DISABILITIES

Services for people with learning disabilities are designed to enable them to remain living in the community wherever possible. Local authority services include short-term care, support in the home, the provision of day care centres, and help with other activities outside the home. Residential care is provided for the severely or profoundly disabled.

MENTALLY ILL PEOPLE

Under the Care Programme Approach, mentally ill people should be assessed by specialist services and receive a care plan, and a key worker should be appointed for each patient. Regular reviews of the patient's progress should be conducted. Local authorities provide help and advice to mentally ill people and their families, and places in day centres and social centres. Social workers can apply for a mentally disturbed person to be compulsorily detained in hospital. Where appropriate, mentally ill people are provided with accommodation in special hospitals, local authority accommodation, or homes run by private or voluntary organisations. Patients who have been discharged from hospitals may be placed on a supervision register. A Mental Health National Service Framework was published in September 1999 setting national standards on how to prevent and treat mental illness.

PLACES AVAILABLE IN RESIDENTIAL CARE HOMES, BY SECTOR (*as at March 2001*)

	Public Sector	Independent Sector
Older People	39,200	197,600
People with physical, sensory or learning difficulties	7,500	52,900
People with mental health problems*	3,900	36,200
Other people	200	3,700
Total places	50,900	290,300

* Includes residential beds for older mentally infirm people

Source: National Statistics – *Social Trends 2003* (Crown copyright)

NATIONAL INSURANCE AND RELATED CASH BENEFITS

The state insurance and assistance schemes, comprising schemes of national insurance and industrial injuries insurance, national assistance, and non-contributory old age pensions, came into force from 5 July 1948. The Ministry of Social Security Act 1966 replaced national assistance and non-contributory old age pensions with a scheme of non-contributory benefits. These and subsequent measures relating to social security provision in Great Britain were consolidated by the Social Security Act 1975, the Social Security (Consequential Provisions) Act 1975, and the Industrial Injuries and Diseases (Old Cases) Act 1975. Corresponding measures were passed for Northern Ireland. The Social Security Pensions Act 1975 introduced a new state pensions scheme in 1978, and the graduated pension scheme 1961 to 1975 has been wound up, existing rights being preserved. Under the Pensions Act 1995 the age of retirement is to be 65 for both men and women, this being phased in between 2010 and 6 April 2020. The Pensioners' Payments and Social Security Act 1979 provided for a Christmas bonus for pensioners in 1979 and in succeeding years. The Child Benefit Act 1975 replaced family allowances (introduced 1946) with child benefit and one-parent benefit. Some of this legislation has been superseded by the provisions of the Social Security Acts 1969 to 1992. The Government is reforming the social security system. The Welfare Reform and Pensions Act became law on 11 November 1999. Changes in benefits came into effect from April 2001.

NATIONAL INSURANCE SCHEME

The National Insurance (NI) scheme operates under the Social Security Contributions and Benefits Act 1992 and the Social Security Administration Act 1992, and orders and regulations made thereunder. The scheme is financed by contributions payable by earners, employers and others (*see* below) and by a Treasury grant. Money collected under the scheme is used to finance the National Insurance Fund (from which contributory benefits are paid) and to contribute to the cost of the National Health Service.

NATIONAL INSURANCE FUND

Estimated receipts and payments of the National Insurance Fund for 2003–4:

Receipts	£'000s
Net National Insurance contributions	60,443,000
Compensation from Consolidated Fund for Statutory Sick Pay and Statutory Maternity Pay recoveries	1,162,000
Income from investments	1,367,000
State scheme premiums	137,000
Other receipts	64,000
Total receipts	63,173,000

Payments	£'000s
Benefits	53,698,000
Benefits increase due to proposed changes	1,279,000
Personal and stakeholder pensions contracted-out rebates	3,914,000
Age-related rebates for contracted-out money purchase schemes	136,000

Transfers to Northern Ireland	260,000
Administration	978,000
Redundancy fund payments (net)	234,000
Other payments	20,000
Total receipts	60,520,000

Balances	£'000s
Opening balance	26,693,000
Excess of receipts over payments	2,653,000
Balance at end of year	29,345,000

CONTRIBUTIONS

There are six classes of NI contributions:

Class 1	paid by employees and their employers
Class 1A	paid by employers who provide employees with certain benefits in kind for private use, such as company cars
Class 1B	paid by employers who enter into a Pay As You Earn (PAYE) Settlement Agreement with the Inland Revenue
Class 2	paid by self-employed people
Class 3	voluntary contributions paid to protect entitlement to the State Pension and who do not pay enough NI contributions in another class
Class 4	paid by the self-employed on their taxable profits over a set limit. These are normally paid by self-employed people in addition to Class 2 contributions. Class 4 contributions do not count towards benefits.

The lower and upper earnings limits and the percentage rates referred to below apply from April 2003 to April 2004 unless otherwise stated.

CLASS 1

Class 1 contributions are paid where a person:
- is an employed earner (employee), office holder (e.g. company director) or employed under a contract of service in Great Britain or Northern Ireland
- is 16 or over and under state pension age
- earns at or above the Earnings Threshold of £89.00 per week (including overtime pay, bonus, commission, etc., without deduction of superannuation contributions)

Class 1 contributions are made up of primary and secondary contributions. Primary contributions are those paid by the employee and these are deducted from earnings by the employer. Since 6 April 2001 the employee's and employer's earnings thresholds have been the same and are referred to as the earnings threshold. Primary contributions are not paid on earnings below the earnings threshold of £89.00. Contributions are payable at the rate of eleven per cent on earnings between the earnings threshold and the upper earnings limit of £585.00 per week (9.4 per cent for contracted-out employment). Above the upper earnings limit one per cent is payable.

Some married women or widows pay a reduced rate of 4.85 per cent on earnings between the earnings threshold and upper earnings limits and one per cent above this. It is no longer possible to elect to pay the reduced rate but those who had reduced liability before 12 May 1977 may retain it so long as certain conditions are met. *See* leaflet CA09 (widows) or leaflet CA13 (married women).

Secondary contributions are paid by employers of employed earners at the rate of 12.8 per cent on all earnings above the earnings threshold of £89.00 per week. There is no upper earnings limit for employers' contributions. Employers operating contracted-out salary related schemes pay reduced contributions of 9.3 per cent; those with contracted-out money-purchase schemes pay 11.8 per cent. The contracted-out rate applies only to that portion of earnings between the earnings threshold and the upper earnings limits. Employers' contributions below and above those respective limits are assessed at the appropriate not contracted-out rate.

CLASS 2

Class 2 contributions are paid where a person is self-employed and is 16 or over and under state pension age. Contributions are paid at a flat rate of £2.00 per week regardless of the amount earned. However, those with earnings of less than £4,095 a year can apply for Small Earnings Exception, e.g. exemption from liability to pay Class 2 contributions. Those granted exemption from Class 2 contributions may pay Class 2 or Class 3 contributions voluntarily. Self-employed earners (whether or not they pay Class 2 contributions) may also be liable to pay Class 4 contributions based on profits. There are special rules for those who are concurrently employed and self-employed.

Married women and widows can no longer choose not to pay Class 2 contributions but those who elected not to pay Class 2 contributions before 12 May 1977 may retain the right so long as certain conditions are met.

Class 2 contributions are collected by the National Insurance Contributions Office (NICO), an executive agency of the Inland Revenue, by direct debit or quarterly bills. *See* leaflets CWL2 and CA02.

CLASS 3

Class 3 contributions are voluntary flat-rate contributions of £6.95 per week payable by persons over the age of 16 who would otherwise be unable to qualify for retirement pension and certain other benefits because they have an insufficient record of Class 1 or Class 2 contributions. This may include those who are not working, those not liable for Class 1 or Class 2 contributions or those excepted from Class 2 contributions. Married women and widows who on or before 11 May 1977 elected not to pay Class 1 (full rate) or Class 2 contributions cannot pay Class 3 contributions while they retain this right.

Class 3 contributions are collected by the NICO by quarterly bills or direct debit. *See* leaflet CA08.

CLASS 4

Self-employed people whose profits and gains are over £4,615 a year pay Class 4 contributions in addition to Class 2 contributions. This applies to self-employed earners over 16 and under the state pension age. Class 4 contributions are calculated at eight per cent of annual profits or gains between £4,615 and £30,940 and one per cent above. Class 4 contributions are assessed and collected by the Inland Revenue together with Schedule D tax. It is possible, in some circumstances, to apply for exceptions from liability to pay Class 4 contributions or to have the amount of contribution reduced (where Class 1 contributions are payable on earnings assessed for Class 4 contributions). *See* leaflet CWL2.

PENSIONS

The Social Security Pensions Act (1975) came into force in 1978. It aimed to:
- reduce reliance on means-tested benefit in old age, widowhood and chronic ill-health
- ensure that occupational pension schemes which are contracted out of the state scheme fulfil the conditions of a good scheme
- ensure that pensions are adequately protected against inflation
- ensure that men and women are treated equally in state and occupational schemes

Legislation and regulations introduced since 1978 go further towards fulfilling these aims and more changes came into effect in April 1997. One of the changes is to equalise the state pension age for men (currently 65 years) and women (currently 60 years) from 6 April 2020. The change will be phased in over the ten years leading up to 6 April 2020. As a result the state pension age is as follows:
- the pension age for men remains at 65
- the pension age for women born on or before 5 October 1950 remains at 60
- the pension age for women born on or between 6 October 1950 and 5 October 1951 is 61
- the pension age for women born on or between 6 October 1951 and 5 October 1952 is 62
- the pension age for women born on or between 6 October 1952 and 5 October 1953 is 63
- the pension age for women born on or between 6 October 1953 and 5 October 1954 is 64
- the pension age for women born on 6 October 1954 or later is 65

STATE PENSION SCHEME

The state pension scheme consists of the basic State Pension and the State Second Pension, also known as the Additional Pension, which reformed the State Earnings-Related Pension Scheme (SERPS) from 6 April 2002.

The amount of basic State Pension paid is dependent on the number of 'qualifying years' a person has in their 'working life'. A 'qualifying year' is a tax year in which a person pays Class 1 National Insurance contributions (NI) at the standard rate or class 2 or 3 NI contributions for the whole year (see National Insurance section). Those in receipt of Carer's Allowance, Disabled Person's Tax Credit, Jobseeker's Allowance, Incapacity Benefit, Severe Disablement Allowance or approved training have contributions credited to them for each week they receive benefit or fulfil certain other conditions. For those reaching pensionable age on or after 6 April 1999, a Class 3 credit of earnings will be awarded for each week from 6 April 1995 that Family Credit or, subsequently, Working Families' Tax Credit, has been received. 'Working life' is counted from the start of the tax year in which a person reaches 16 to the end of the tax year before the one in which they reach pensionable age: for men this is normally 49 years and for women this varies between 44 and 49 years depending on birth date (see above). To get the full rate (100 per cent) basic pension a person must have qualifying years for about 90 per cent of their working life. To get the minimum basic pension (25 per cent) a person will need ten or eleven qualifying years. Married women who are not entitled to a pension on their own contributions may get a pension on their husband's contributions. It is possible for people who are unable to work because they care for children or a sick or disabled person at home to reduce the number of qualifying years required. This is called home responsibilities protection (HRP) and can be given for any tax year since April 1978; the number of years for which HRP is given is deducted from the number of qualifying years needed. From April 2002, HRP may also qualify the recipient for Additional Pension through the State Second Pension.

The amount of Additional Pension or SERPS paid depends on the amount of earnings a person has, or is treated as having, between the lower and upper earnings limits for each complete tax year between 6 April 1978 (when the scheme started) and the tax year before they reach state pension age. The right to Additional Pension does not depend on the person's right to basic State Pension. The amount of Additional Pension paid also depends on when a person reaches state pension age; changes phased in from 6 April 1999 mean that pensions are calculated differently from that date. Men or women widowed before 6 October 2002 inherit all their late spouse's additional pension. From 6 October 2002, the maximum percentage of SERPS that a person can inherit from a late spouse will depend on their late spouse's date of birth:

Maximum %		
SERPS entitlement for surviving spouse	*d.o.b (men)*	*d.o.b (women)*
100%	5/10/37 or earlier	5/10/42 or earlier
90%	6/10/37 to 5/10/39	6/10/42 to 5/10/44
80%	6/10/39 to 5/10/41	6/10/44 to 5/10/46
70%	6/10/41 – 5/10/43	6/10/46 to 5/10/48
60%	6/10/43 – 5/10/45	6/10/48 to 5/7/50
50%	6/10/45 or later	6/7/50 or later

The maximum Additional Pension (Second State Pension) a person can inherit from a late spouse is 50 per cent.

There are four categories of State Pension provided under the Social Security Contributions and Benefits Act 1992:
- Category A, a contributory pension made up of a Basic Pension dependent on the number of qualifying years in your working life and an Additional Pension dependent on earnings since April 1978.
- Category B, a contributory pension made up of basic and additional elements, payable to married women, widows and widowers based on their spouse's qualifying years and earnings. From 6 April 2010 both men and women will be able to get a Basic Pension based on their spouse's National Insurance contributions, if this is better than the pension based on their own contribution record.
- Category C, this pension is now obsolete.
- Category D, a non-contributory pension for those aged 80 and over.

Graduated retirement benefit is also available to those who paid graduated NI contributions into the scheme when it existed between April 1961 and April 1975.

The Pension Service provides a state pension forecasting service, for more information telephone: 0845-300 0168.

From 1978 to 2002, Additional Pension was called the State Earnings-Related Pension Scheme (SERPS). SERPS covered all earnings by employees from 6 April 1978 to 5 April 1997 on which standard rate class 1 National Insurance had been paid and earnings between 6 April 1997 and 5 April 2002 if the standard rate class 1 contributions had been contracted-in.

In 2002 The Welfare Reform and Pensions Act 1999 replaced SERPS with an Additional Pension – the State Second Pension, targeted towards low and moderate earners and certain carers and people with long-term illness or disability. If earnings are above the annual National Insurance Lower Earnings Limit (£4,004 for 2003–4) but below the new low earnings threshold (£11,200 a year for 2003–4), the State Second Pension regards this as earnings of £11,200 and it is treated equivalently. Carers and people with long term illness and disability will be considered as at the low earnings threshold for each complete tax year even if they do not work at all, or earn less than the annual Lower Earnings Limit.

CONTRACTED-OUT PENSION SCHEMES
Personal Pension Schemes
Since July 1988, an employee has been able to start a personal pension which, if it meets certain conditions, can be used in place of Additional Pension. These pensions are known as Appropriate Personal Pensions (APPs). That part of an APP derived from the protected rights (rights comprising mainly the NI contribution rebate and its investment return) is intended to provide benefits broadly equivalent to those given up in the Additional Pension. At retirement, a contracted-out deduction will be made from Additional Pension built up from 6 April 1987 to 5 April 1997. The reduction may be more or less than that part of the pension derived from the protected right. From 6 April 1997 and 5 April 2002, members of an APP scheme will not have built up any entitlement to Additional Pension during the period of their membership. From 6 April 2002, employees contracted-out into a personal pension and earning between the lower earnings limit and the low earnings threshold (£4,004 and £11,200 in 2003–4) will be treated as having earnings of £11,200, meaning that in addition to their APP, they will build up entitlement to Additional Pension as well.

Stakeholder Pension Schemes
Stakeholder pensions became available in April 2001. They are intended to be low charge, flexible and portable pensions for people that may not otherwise be able to save for their retirement. It is possible to invest up to £3,600 (including tax relief) annually in a stakeholder pension scheme without evidence of earnings. The minimum contribution cannot be set higher than £20 and providers are prohibited from levying a management charge of more than 1 per cent of the value of the individual fund annually. The charge is taken directly from the fund. People who are already members of occupational pension schemes may also contribute to a stakeholder pension scheme and it is possible to contribute to a scheme on someone else's behalf, for example that of a non-working partner.

As with a personal pension, if it meets certain conditions, it can be used to contract out of the State Second Pension (formerly the State Earnings Related Pension Scheme (SERPS)).

When someone contracts out of the State scheme with either an APP or a Stakeholder Pension, both the employee and their employers pay NI contributions at the full not contracted out rate. At the end of the tax year to which those NI contributions relate, the Inland Revenue pays an age-related rebate (increases with age) and tax relief on the employee's share of the rebate direct to the scheme for investment on behalf of the employee.

OCCUPATIONAL PENSION SCHEMES
Contracted-Out Salary-Related (COSR) Scheme
– this scheme provides a pension related to earnings
– any notional additional pension built up from 6 April 1978 to 5 April 1997 will be reduced by the amount of Guaranteed Minimum Pension (GMP) built up during that period (the contracted-out deduction)
– from 6 April 1997 these schemes no longer provide a GMP. Instead, as a condition for contracting out they have to satisfy a reference scheme test to ensure that the benefits provided are at least as good as a prescribed standard
– when someone contracts out of the Additional Pension through a COSR scheme, both the scheme member and the employer pay a reduced rate of NI contributions (known as the rebate) to compensate for the State benefit given up

Contracted-Out Money Purchase (COMP) Scheme
– this scheme provides a pension based on the value of the fund at retirement i.e. the money paid in, along with the investment return.
– that part of the COMP fund derived from protected rights is intended to provide benefits broadly equivalent to those given up in the Additional Pension
– a contracted-out deduction, which may be more or less than that part of the pension derived from the protected rights will be made from any additional pension built up from 6 April 1988 to 5 April 1997. Between 6 April 1997 and 5 April 2002 members of a COMP scheme will not have built up any entitlement to Additional Pension during the period of their membership
– as with a COSR scheme, when someone contracts out of the Additional Pension through a COMP scheme, both the scheme member and the employer pay a reduced rate of NI contributions to compensate for the State benefit given up. In addition, at the end of the tax year to which the contributions relate, the Inland Revenue pay an additional age-related rebate direct to the scheme for investment on behalf of the employer

Contracted-Out Mixed Benefit (COMB) Scheme
A mixed benefit scheme has two active sections, one salary related and the other money purchase. Scheme rules set out which section individual employees may join and the circumstances (if any), in which members may move between sections. Each section must satisfy the respective contracting-out conditions for COSR and COMP schemes.

From April 2002, members of contracted-out occupational schemes earning above £4004 (in 2003–4) may build up entitlement to Additional Pension through the State Second Pension as well as that built up in their occupational pension.

The Pensions Advisory Service (OPAS) gives free help and advice to people who have problems with occupational or personal pensions. There are two bodies for pension complaints. The financial Ombudsman Service deals with complaints which predominantly concern the sale and or marketing of occupational, stakeholder and personal pensions. The Pensions Ombudsman deals with complaints which predominantly concern the management (after sale or marketing) of occupational, stakeholder and personal pensions. The Occupational Pensions Regulatory Authority (OPRA) was set up by parliament to help make sure occupational pension schemes are safe and well run, it can impose penalties where there are breaches of the law.

BENEFITS

Leaflets relating to the various benefits and contribution conditions for different benefits are available from local social security offices; leaflet GL23 *Social Security Benefit Rates* is a general guide to benefit rates and contributions. The benefits payable under the Social Security Acts are:

CONTRIBUTORY BENEFITS
Jobseeker's Allowance (contribution-based)
Incapacity Benefit
Maternity Allowance
Widow's Benefit and Bereavement Benefit
State Pensions, categories A and B

NON-CONTRIBUTORY BENEFITS
Jobseeker's Allowance (income-based)
Maternity Allowance
Child Benefit
Guardian's Allowance
Carer's Allowance
Severe Disablement Allowance
Attendance Allowance
Disability Living Allowance
State Pensions, categories C and D
Income Support
Pension Credit
Housing Benefit
Council Tax Benefit
Social Fund

BENEFITS FOR INDUSTRIAL INJURIES AND
DISABLEMENT

EMPLOYER PAYMENTS
Statutory Adoption Pay
Statutory Maternity Pay
Statutory Paternity Pay
Statutory Sick Pay

TAX CREDITS

From April 2003 Working Families' Tax Credit, Disabled Person's Tax Credit and the Children's Tax Credit were replaced with Working Tax Credit and Child Tax Credit. Tax Credits are administered by the Inland Revenue and are awarded for up to 12 months, although they can be adjusted during the year to reflect changes of income or circumstances.

WORKING TAX CREDIT

Working Tax Credit is made up of a basic payment with additional payments for couples, lone parents, people working over 30 hours a week, disabled workers and people aged 50 or over returning to work after a period of benefits. The tax credit will be paid with wages to people who are employed and direct to the self-employed. It is available to:
- People with dependant children and/or a disability, working at least 16 hours a week
- People aged 25 or over and working at least 30 hours a week

The aim of the tax credit system is to provide a guaranteed income from full-time work for those aged 25 or over without children or a disability, of £183 a week for couples, and £154 a week for single people.

WORKING TAX CREDIT 2003–4

Annual Income/status*	Tax Credit per annum
£5,000	
single	–
couple	–
single adult with a disability	£3,565
£8,000	
single	£1,065
couple	£2,565
single adult with a disability	£3,105
£10,000	
single	£320
couple	£1,820
single adult with a disability	£2,360
£15,000	
single	–
couple	–
single adult with a disability	£515

* Those with incomes of £5,000 a year are assumed to work part-time (working between 16 and 30 hours a week). families with an income of £8,000 a year or more, at least one adult is assumed to be working 30 or more hours a week.

CHILD TAX CREDIT

Child Tax Credit combines all income-related support for children and is paid direct to the main carer. The credit is made up of a main 'family' payment with additional payments for each extra child in the household, for children with a disability and an extra payment for children who are severely disabled. Child Tax Credit is available to households where:
- there is at least one dependant child under 16 years old.
- there is at least one dependant young person under 19 years old and in full-time non-advanced education or registered with the Careers or Connexions Service (does not include Scotland or Northern Ireland)

CHILD CARE

In families where a lone parent or both partners in a couple work for at least 16 hours a week, or where one partner works and the other is disabled, the family is entitled to child care payments. This payment can contribute up to £94.50 a week to the cost of child care for one child and up to £140 a week for two children. Families can only claim if they use an approved child care provider.

CHILD TAX CREDIT 2003–4
(£ per year)

Annual Income	One Child		Two Children	
	No Childcare	Maximum Childcare	No Childcare	Maximum Childcare
0	1,990	1,990	3,435	3,435
5,000	5,015	9,955	6,460	13,780
8,000	4,555	9,495	6,000	13,320
10,000	3,810	8,750	5,255	12,575
15,000	1,965	6,905	3,410	10,730
20,000	545	5,055	1,560	8,880
25,000	545	3,205	545	7,030
30,000	545	1,355	545	5,180
35,000	545	545	545	3,330
40,000	545	545	545	1,480
45,000	545	545	545	545
50,000	545	545	545	545
60,000	–	–	–	–

CONTRIBUTORY BENEFITS

Entitlement to contributory benefits depends on contribution conditions being satisfied either by the claimant or by some other person (depending on the kind of benefit). The class or classes of contribution which for this purpose are relevant to each benefit are:

Jobseeker's Allowance (contribution-based)	Class 1
Incapacity Benefit	Class 1 or 2
Maternity Allowance	Class 1 or 2
Widow's Benefits	Class 1, 2 or 3
State Pensions, categories A and B	Class 1, 2 or 3

The system of contribution conditions relates to yearly levels of earnings on which contributions have been paid.

JOBSEEKER'S ALLOWANCE

Jobseeker's allowance (JSA) replaced unemployment benefit and income support for unemployed people under pension age from 7 October 1996. There are two routes of entitlement. Contribution-based JSA is paid as a personal rate (i.e. additional benefit for dependants is not paid) to those who have made sufficient NI contributions in two particular tax years. Savings and partner's earnings are not taken into account and payment can be made for up to six months. Rates of JSA correspond to income support rates.

Claims for this benefit are made through Jobcentre Plus offices and Jobcentres. A person wishing to claim JSA must be unemployed, capable of work and available for any work which they can reasonably be expected to do, usually for at least 40 hours per week. They must agree and sign a 'jobseeker's agreement', which will set out each claimant's plans to find work, and must actively seek work. If they refuse work or training their benefit may be suspended for between one and 26 weeks.

A person will be disqualified from JSA for up to 26 weeks if they have left a job voluntarily or through misconduct, if they refuse to take up an offer of employment or if they fail to attend a training scheme or employment programme. In these circumstances, it may be possible to receive hardship payments, particularly where the claimant or their family is vulnerable, e.g. if sick or pregnant, or for those with children or caring responsibilities. See leaflet JSAL5.

INCAPACITY BENEFIT

Incapacity benefit is available to those who are incapable of work but cannot get statutory sick pay from their employer. It is not payable to those over State Pension age. However, people who are already in receipt of short-term incapacity benefit when they reach State Pension age may continue to receive this benefit for up to 52 weeks. Eligibility for incapacity benefit is restricted to people who have paid National Insurance contributions for one of the previous three years, although some exceptions do apply. The amount of incapacity benefit payable may be reduced where a claimant receives more than a specified amount of occupational or personal pension. Severely disabled people aged between 16 and 19 should receive incapacity benefit without meeting the national insurance contribution conditions. There are three rates of incapacity benefit:

– short-term lower rate for the first 28 weeks of sickness
– short-term higher rate from weeks 29 to 52
– long-term rate from week 53 onwards

The terminally ill and those entitled to the highest rate care component of disability living allowance are paid the long-term rate after 28 weeks. Incapacity benefit is taxable after 28 weeks.

Two rates of age addition are paid with long-term benefit based on the claimant's age when incapacity started. The higher rate is payable where incapacity for work commenced before the age of 35; and the lower rate where incapacity commenced before the age of 45. Increases for dependants are also payable with short and long-term incapacity benefit.

There are two medical tests of incapacity: the 'own occupation' test and the 'personal capability' assessment. Those who worked before becoming incapable of working will be assessed, for the first 28 weeks of incapacity, on their ability to do their own job. After 28 weeks (or from the start of incapacity for those who were not working) claimants are assessed on their ability to carry out a range of work-related activities. See leaflets IB1 and IB214. From October 2001 all new benefit claimants in the 51 Jobcentre Plus areas receive a service combining jobs and benefits advice and support. The government plans to extend this as Jobcentre Plus is rolled out nationally. New Incapacity Benefit claimants will be invited back for work-focused interviews at intervals of not longer than three years. The interviews are not medical tests, but if the claimant is due for a medical test around the same time, their local office will aim to schedule both together. People who are severely disabled and those who are terminally ill will not be asked to attend these interviews.

BEREAVEMENT BENEFITS

Bereavement benefits replaced widow's benefit on 9 April 2001. Those claiming widow's benefit before this date will continue to receive them under the old scheme for as long as they qualify. The new system provides bereavement benefits for widows and widowers providing that their deceased spouse paid National Insurance contributions. The new system offers benefits in three forms:

Bereavement Payment – may be received by a man or woman who is under the state pension age at the time of their spouse's death, or whose husband or wife was not entitled to a Category A retirement pension when he or she died. It is a single tax-free lump sum of £2,000 payable immediately on becoming a widow or widower.

Widowed Parent's Allowance – a taxable benefit payable to the surviving partner if he or she is entitled or treated as entitled to child benefit, or to a widow if she is expecting her husband's baby

Bereavement Allowance – a taxable weekly benefit paid for 52 weeks after the spouse's death. A widow or widower may receive this pension if aged 45 or over at the time of his or her spouse's death or if his or her Widowed Parent's Allowance ends before 52 weeks. If aged 55 or over he or she will receive the full Bereavement Allowance

It is not possible to receive Widowed Parent's Allowance and Bereavement Allowance at the same time. Bereavement benefits and widow's benefit, in any form, ceases upon remarriage or is suspended during a period of cohabitation as man and wife without being legally married. See leaflet GL14, D49 (D49S for deaths that occur in Scotland).

STATE PENSION: CATEGORIES A AND B

Category A pension is payable for life to men and women who reach State Pension age and who satisfy the contributions conditions. Category B pension is payable for life to married women, widows and widowers and is based on their wife or husband's contributions. It is payable to a married women only when the wife and husband have claimed their State Pension and they have both reached State Pension age (from April 2010, a married man will be able to qualify for a Category B pension from his wife's contributions). A Category B pension is also payable on widowhood after the State Pension age regardless of whether the wife or husband had qualified for their State Pension. There are special rules for those who are widowed before reaching State Pension age.

A person may defer claiming their pension for five years after State Pension age. In doing so they may earn increments which will increase the weekly amount paid when they claim their State Pension. If a married man defers his Category A pension, his wife cannot claim a Category B pension on his contributions but she may earn increments on her State Pension during this time. A woman can defer her Category B pension, and earn increments, even if her husband is claiming his Category A pension.

The basic state pension is £75.45 per week plus any additional (earnings-related) pension the person may be entitled to. An increase of £46.35 is paid for an adult dependant, providing the dependant's earnings do not exceed the rate of Jobseeker's Allowance for a single person (*see* below). Before April 2003 it was also possible to get an increase of Category A and B pensions for a child or children. From April 2003 provision for children is made through Child Tax Credits. An age addition of 25p per week is payable if a retirement pensioner is aged 80 or over.

Since 1989 pensioners have been allowed to have unlimited earnings without affecting their State Pension. Income support can be paid where a person's income is below a set level and pensioners may also be entitled to housing and council tax benefits.

GRADUATED RETIREMENT BENEFIT

Graduated NI contributions were first payable from 1961 and were calculated as a percentage of earnings between certain bands. They were discontinued in 1975. Any graduated pension which an employed person over 18 and under 70 (65 for a woman) had earned by paying graduated contributions will be paid when the contributor claims State Pension or at 70 (65 for a woman), in addition to any State Pension for which he or she qualifies. A husband or wife can only get a graduated pension in return for his/her own graduated contributions, but not for his/her spouse's.

Graduated retirement benefit is at a weekly rate for each 'unit' of graduated contributions paid by the employee (half a unit or more counts as a whole unit); the rate varies from person to person. A unit of graduated pension can be calculated by adding together all graduated contributions and dividing by 7.5 (men) or 9.0 (women). If a person defers making a claim beyond 65 (60 for a woman), entitlement may be increased by one seventh of a penny per £1 of its weekly rate for each complete week of deferred retirement, as long as the retirement is deferred for a minimum of seven weeks.

In April 2002 the Pension Service, part of the Department for Work and Pensions was set up and is due to be expanded over the next two years. This organisation aims to provide an improved service for pensioners, through its network of pension centres and local services.

WEEKLY RATES OF BENEFIT *from April 2003*

Jobseeker's Allowance (JSA) (contribution-based)

Person under 18	£32.90
Person aged 18–24	£43.25
Person aged 25 to state pension age	£54.65

From October 2003 people between 60 and State Pension age can choose to claim Pension Credits instead of JSA.

Short-term Incapacity Benefit

Person under pension age – lower rate	£54.50
*Person under pension age – higher rate	£64.35
Increase for adult dependant	£33.65
*Person over pension age	£69.20
Person over pension age – higher rate	£72.15
Increase for adult dependant	£41.50

Long-term Incapacity Benefit

Person under pension age	£72.15
Increase for adult dependant	£43.15
Age addition – lower rate	£7.60
Age addition – higher rate	£15.15

Widow's Benefits (from 8 April 2003)

*Widowed mother's allowance	£77.45
*Widow's pension, full entitlement (aged 55 and over at time of spouse's death)	£77.45

*Amount of widow's pension by age of widow at spouse's death (for deaths occurring before 11 April 1988 refer to the age-points in brackets):

aged 54 (49)	£72.03
aged 53 (48)	£66.61
aged 52 (47)	£61.19
aged 51 (46)	£55.76
aged 50 (45)	£50.34
aged 49 (44)	£44.92
aged 48 (43)	£39.50
aged 47 (42)	£34.08
aged 46 (41)	£28.66
aged 45 (40)	£23.24

Bereavement Benefit (from 8 April 2003)

Bereavement payment (lump sum)	£2,000.00
*Widowed parents allowance	£77.45
*Bereavement allowance, full entitlement (aged 55 and over at time of spouse's death)	£77.45

*Amount of bereavement allowance by age of widow/widower at spouse's death:

aged 54	£72.03
aged 53	£66.61
aged 52	£61.19
aged 51	£55.76
aged 50	£50.34
aged 49	£44.92
aged 48	£39.50
aged 47	£34.08
aged 46	£28.66
aged 45	£23.24

State Pension: categories A and B

Single person	£77.45
Increase for adult dependant	£46.35

*These benefits attract an increase for each dependant child (in addition to child benefit) of £9.85 for the first or only child and £11.35 for each subsequent child

NON-CONTRIBUTORY BENEFITS
These benefits are paid from general taxation and are not dependent on NI contributions. Unless otherwise stated, a benefit is tax-free and is not means tested.

JOBSEEKER'S ALLOWANCE (INCOME-BASED)
Those who do not qualify for contribution-based Jobseeker's Allowance (JSA(c)), those who have exhausted their entitlement to contribution-based JSA or those for whom contribution-based JSA provides insufficient income may qualify for income-based JSA. Rates of JSA correspond to income support rates. The amount paid depends on age, number of dependants, amount of income and savings. Income-based JSA comprises of three parts:
- a personal allowance for the jobseeker and his/her partner and an allowance for each child or young person for whom they are responsible (*see* below)
- premiums for people with special needs
- premiums for housing costs.

The rules of entitlement are the same as for contribution-based JSA.

If one person in a couple was born after 28 October 1957 and neither person in the couple has responsibility for a child or children, then the couple will have to make a joint claim for JSA if they wish to receive income-based JSA.

From April 2003 claimants may choose to claim Child Tax Credit instead of an increase of JSA for children.

MATERNITY ALLOWANCE
Maternity Allowance (MA) covers women who are self-employed or otherwise do not qualify for Statutory Maternity Pay (SMP). In order to qualify for payment, a woman must have been employed and/or self-employed for at least 26 weeks in the 66 week period up to and including the week before the baby is due (test period). She must also have average weekly earning of at least £30 (Maternity Allowance Threshold) in any 13 weeks of the test period. Women who are self-employed will be deemed to have earnings at or above the Maternity Allowance Threshold. A woman can choose to start receiving MA from the 11th week before the week in which the baby is due up to the day following the day of birth. This will depend on when the woman stops work to have her baby or if the baby is born before she stops work. However, where the woman is absent from work for pregnancy related illness on or after the Sunday of the 4th week before the baby is due to be born, MA will start the day following the first day of absence from work for a pregnancy related illness. MA is paid up to 26 weeks and is only paid while the woman is not working.

CHILD BENEFIT
Child Benefit is payable for virtually all children aged under 16, and for those aged 16 to 18 who are studying full-time up to and including A-level or equivalent standard. It is also payable for a short period if the child has left school recently and is registered for work or work-based training for young people at a careers office or with the Connexions Service.

Child Benefit (Lone Parent), a higher rate of benefit for the eldest child of lone parents, was abolished for new lone parents from 6 July 1988. For lone parents who have continuously satisfied the entitlement conditions since before that date it may be payable in certain specified circumstances. *See* leaflets CH1 and CH11.

GUARDIAN'S ALLOWANCE
Where the parents of a child are dead, the person who has the child in his/her family may claim a Guardian's Allowance in addition to Child Benefit. In specified circumstances the allowance is payable on the death of only one parent. *See* leaflet NI14.

CARER'S ALLOWANCE
Carer's Allowance (CA) is a benefit payable to people who spend at least 35 hours per week caring for a severely disabled person. To qualify for CA a person must be caring for someone in receipt of one of the following benefits:
- the middle or highest rate of disability living allowance care component
- either rate of attendance allowance
- constant attendance allowance, paid at not less than the normal maximum rate, under the industrial injuries or war pension schemes

See leaflets SD1 and SD4.

SEVERE DISABLEMENT ALLOWANCE
From April 2001 Severe Disablement Allowance (SDA) has not been available to new claimants. Those claiming SDA before that date will continue to receive it for as long as they qualify. *See* leaflet NI252.

ATTENDANCE ALLOWANCE
This is payable to disabled people who claim after the age of 65 and who need a lot of care or supervision because of physical or mental disability for a period of at least six months. Attendance Allowance has two rates: the lower rate is for day or night care, and the higher rate is for day and night care. People not expected to live for more than six months because of an illness can receive the highest rate of Attendance Allowance straight away. *See* leaflets DS702 and SD1.

DISABILITY LIVING ALLOWANCE
This is payable to disabled people who claim before the age of 65 who have personal care and/or mobility needs because of an illness or disability for a period of at least three months and are likely to have those needs for a further six months or more. The allowance has two components: the care component, which has three rates, and the mobility component, which has two rates. The rates depend on the care and mobility needs of the claimant. People not expected to live for more then six months because of an illness will automatically receive the highest rate of the care component. *See* leaflets DS704 and SD1.

RETIREMENT PENSION: CATEGORY D
Category D pension is provided for people aged 80 and over if they are not entitled to another category of pension or are entitled to less than the Category D rate.

WEEKLY RATES OF BENEFIT *from April 2003*
Jobseeker's Allowance (income-based)

Person under 18, living with family	£32.90
Person under 18, living away from home	£43.25
Person aged 18–24	£43.25
Person aged 25 to state pension age	£54.65
Couple with one or both under 18	£32.90–£85.75
	(depending on circumstances)
Couple aged 18 to state pension age	£85.75
Dependant children and young persons	
premium up to 16	£38.50
16–19 years	£38.50

| Family premium | £15.75 |
| Family premium (lone parent) | £15.90 |

Maternity Allowance

| Standard rate | £100 or 90% of the women's average weekly earnings if this is less than £100 |
| Increase for adult dependant | £33.65 |

Child Benefit

Eldest child	£15.75
Eldest child of certain lone parents	£17.55
Each subsequent child	£10.55

Guardian's allowance

| Eldest child | £9.85 |
| Each subsequent child | £11.35 |

| *Carer's Allowance | £43.15 |
| Increase for dependant adult | £25.80 |

Severe Disablement Allowance

| †Basic rate | £43.60 |

Age related addition:

Under 40	£15.15
40–49	£9.70
50–59	£4.85

Additions may be payable for dependant adults

Attendance allowance

| Higher rate | £57.20 |
| Lower rate | £38.30 |

Disability living allowance

Care component

Higher rate	£57.20
Middle rate	£38.30
Lowest rate	£15.15

Mobility component

| Higher rate | £39.95 |
| Lower rate | £15.15 |

State Pension: category D

| Single person | £46.35 |
| Increase for wife/other adult dependant | £27.70 |

*These benefits attract an increase for each dependant child (in addition to child benefit) of £9.85 for the first or only child and £11.35 for each subsequent child
†The age addition applies to the age when incapacity began

INCOME SUPPORT

Income support is a benefit for those aged 16 and over whose income is below a certain level. It can be paid to people who are not expected to sign on as unemployed (income support for unemployed people was replaced by jobseeker's allowance in October 1996) and who are:
– incapable of work due to sickness or disability
– bringing up children alone
– looking after a person who has a disability
– registered blind
Pension Credit replaced Income Support for people aged 60 or over on 6 October 2003.

Some people who are not in these categories may also be able to claim income support.

Income support is also payable to people who work for less than 16 hours a week on average (or 24 hours for a

partner). Some people can claim income support if they work longer hours.

Income support is not payable if the claimant, or claimant and partner, have capital or savings in excess of £8,000. For capital and savings in excess of £3,000, a deduction of £1 is made for every £250 or part of £250 held. Different limits apply to people permanently in residential care and nursing homes: the upper limit is £16,000 and deductions apply for capital in excess of £10,000.

Sums payable depend on fixed allowances laid down by law for people in different circumstances. If both partners are entitled to income support, either may claim it for the couple. People receiving income support may be able to receive housing benefit, help with mortgage or home loan interest and help with health care. They may also be eligible for help with exceptional expenses from the Social Fund. Special rates may apply to some people living in residential care or nursing homes. Leaflet IS20 gives a detailed explanation of income support.

In October 1998 the Government's voluntary New Deal for Lone Parents programme became available throughout the UK. All lone parents receiving income support are assigned a personal adviser at a Jobcentre who will provide guidance and support with a view to enabling the claimant to find work.

INCOME SUPPORT PREMIUMS
Income support premiums are additional weekly payments for those with special needs. People qualifying for more than one premium will normally only receive the highest single premium for which they qualify. However, family premium, disabled child premium, severe disability premium and carer premium are payable in addition to other premiums.

People with children may qualify for:
– the family premium if they have at least one child (a higher rate is paid to lone parents, although from 6 April 1998 it has not been available to new claimants)
– the disabled child premium if they have a child who receives disability living allowance or is registered blind

Carers may qualify for:
– the carer premium if they or their partner are in receipt of carer's allowance

Long-term sick or disabled people may qualify for:
– the disability premium if they or their partner are receiving certain benefits because they are disabled or cannot work; are registered blind; or if the claimant has been incapable of work or receiving statutory sick pay for at least 364 days (196 days if the person is terminally ill), including periods of incapacity separated by eight weeks or less
– the severe disability premium if the person lives alone and receives attendance allowance or the middle or higher rate of disability living allowance care component and no one receives carer's allowance for caring for that person. This premium is also available to couples where both partners meet the above conditions

People aged 60 and over may qualify for:
– the pensioner premium if they or their partner are aged 60 to 74
– the enhanced pensioner premium if they or their partner are aged 75 to 79
– the higher pensioner premium if they or their partner are aged 80 or over. This is also available to people over 60 who receive attendance allowance, disability

living allowance, long-term incapacity benefit or severe disablement allowance, or who are registered blind

WEEKLY RATES OF BENEFIT *from April 2003*
Income support
Single person
under 18	£32.90
under 18 (higher)	£43.25
aged 18–24	£43.25
aged 25 and over	£54.65
aged under 18 and a single parent (lower)	£32.90
aged under 18 and a single parent (higher)	£43.25
aged 18 and over and a single parent	£54.65

Couples*
Both under 18	£65.30
one or both aged 18 or over	£85.75
For each child in a family from birth to day before 19th birthday	£38.50

Premiums
Family premium	£15.75
Family (lone parent) premium	£15.90
Disabled child premium	£41.30
Carer premium	£25.10
Disability premium	
Single	£23.30
Couple	£33.25
Enhanced disability premium	
Single	£11.40
Enhanced disabled child premium	£16.60
Severe disability premium	
Lower rate (single person and some couples)	£42.95
Higher rate (couples)	£85.90
Pensioner premium	
Single	£47.45
Couple	£70.05
Higher pensioner premium	
Single	£47.45
Couple	£70.05
Enhanced pensioner premium	
Single	£47.45
Couple	£70.05
Bereavement premium	£19.45

*Where one or both partners are aged under 18, their personal allowance will depend on their situation

PENSION CREDIT
Pension Credit was introduced on 6 October 2003 and replaces Income Support for those aged 60 and over.

There are two elements to Pension Credit:

The Guarantee Credit
The guarantee credit provides a guaranteed minimum income, with additional elements for people who have:
– relevant housing costs
– severe disabilities
– caring responsibilities

Income from State Pension, private pensions, income from capital, earnings and certain benefits are taken into account when calculating the guarantee credit. For savings and capital in excess of £6,000 a deduction of £1 is made for every £500 or part of £500 held.

People receiving the guarantee credit element of Pension Credit may be able to receive Housing Benefit, Council Tax Benefit and help with health care.

The Savings Credit
Single people aged 65 or over (and couples where one member is 65 or over) may be entitled to a savings credit which will reward pensioners who have modest income or savings. The savings credit is calculated by taking into account any qualifying income above the savings credit threshold. For 2003–4 the threshold is £77.45 for single people and £123.80 for couples. The savings credit gives pensioners a cash addition calculated at 60p for every pound of qualifying income they have between the savings credit threshold and the guarantee credit. After this, the maximum reward will be reduced by 40p for every pound of income above the guarantee level. The maximum savings credit is £14.79 per week (£19.20 a week for couples).

Income that qualifies towards the savings credit includes state pensions, earnings, second pensions and capital above £6,000.

Where only the savings credit is in payment, people need to claim standard housing benefit or council tax benefit. Although local authorities take any savings credit into account in the housing benefit/council tax benefit assessment, the housing benefit/council tax benefit applicable amount for people aged 65 and over is enhanced to ensure that gains in Pension Credit are not depleted.

WEEKLY RATES OF BENEFIT *from October 2003*
Standard minimum guarantee:	
single	£102.10
couple	£155.80
Additional amount for:	
severe disability	£42.90
carers	£25.10
Savings credit threshold	
single	£77.45
couple	£123.80

HOUSING BENEFIT
Housing benefit is designed to help people with rent (including rent for accommodation in guesthouses, lodgings or hostels). It does not cover mortgage payments. The amount of benefit paid depends on:
– the income of the claimant, and partner if there is one, including earned income, unearned income (any other income including some other benefits) and savings
– number of dependants
– certain extra needs of the claimant, partner or any dependants
– number and gross income of people sharing the home who are not dependent on the claimant
– how much rent is paid
Housing benefit is not payable if the claimant, or claimant and partner, have savings of over £16,000. The amount of benefit is affected if savings held exceed £3,000 (£6,000 for pensioners and £10,000 for people living in care homes). Housing benefit is not paid for meals, fuel or certain service charges that may be included in the rent. Deductions are also made for most non-dependants who live in the same accommodation as the claimant (and their partner).

The maximum amount of benefit (which is not necessarily the same as the amount of rent paid) may be paid where the claimant is in receipt of income support or income-based jobseeker's allowance or where the claimant's income is less than the amount allowed for their needs. Any income over that allowed for their needs will mean that their benefit is reduced. *See* leaflets GL16 and RR2.

COUNCIL TAX BENEFIT

Nearly all the rules which apply to housing benefit apply to council tax benefit, which helps people on low incomes to pay council tax bills. The amount payable depends on how much council tax is paid and who lives with the claimant. The benefit may be available to those receiving income support or income-based Jobseeker's Allowance or to those whose income is less than that allowed for their needs. Any income over that allowed for their needs will mean that their council tax benefit is reduced. Deductions are made for non-dependants.

The maximum amount that is payable for those living in properties in council tax bands A to E is 100 per cent of the claimant's council tax liability. This also applies to those living in properties in bands F to H who were in receipt of the benefit at 31 March 1998 if they have remained in the same property. From 1 April 1998 council tax benefit for new claimants living in property bands F to H (or existing claimants moving into these bands) was restricted to the level payable for band E.

If a person shares a home with one or more adults (not their partner) who are on a low income, it may be possible to claim a second adult rebate. Those who are entitled to both council tax benefit and second adult rebate will be awarded whichever is the greater. Second adult rebate may be claimed by those not in receipt of council tax benefit.

THE SOCIAL FUND

REGULATED PAYMENTS

Sure Start Maternity Grant

The Sure Start Maternity Grant (SSMG) is a one-off payment of £500 for parents on low incomes to buy essential items for new babies. To qualify, mothers and expectant mothers must also receive health and welfare advice for themselves and their child from an approved health professional. SSMG can be claimed any time from the 29th week of pregnancy until the child is three months old. Those eligible are mothers or their partners in receipt of Income Support, income-based Jobseeker's Allowance, Child Tax Credit at a rate higher than the family element or Working Tax Credit where a disability or severe disability element is in payment.

Funeral Payments

Payable for the necessary cost of burial or cremation, plus other funeral expenses reasonably incurred up to £700, to people receiving Income Support, income-based Jobseeker's Allowance, Child Tax Credit at a higher rate than the family element, Working Tax Credit where a disability or severe disability element is in payment, Council Tax Benefit or Housing Benefit who have good reason for taking responsibility for the funeral expenses. These payments are recoverable from any estate of the deceased.

Cold Weather Payments

A payment of £8.50 when the average temperature over seven consecutive days is recorded at or forecast to be 0°C or below in the qualifying person's area. Payments are made to people on Income Support or income-based Jobseeker's Allowance and who have a child under five or whose benefit includes a pensioner or disability premium. Payments do not have to be repaid.

Winter Fuel Payments

An annual payment of £200 per household paid to most people aged 60 or over. The majority of eligible people are paid automatically before Christmas, although a few need to claim. Payments do not have to be repaid.

DISCRETIONARY PAYMENTS

Community Care Grants

These are intended to help people on Income Support or income-based Jobseeker's Allowance or receiving payments on account of such benefits (or those likely to receive these benefits on leaving residential or institutional accommodation) to live as independently as possible in the community; ease exceptional pressures on families; care for a prisoner or young offender released on temporary licence; help people set up home as part of a resettlement programme and/or assist with certain travelling expenses. They do not have to be repaid.

Budgeting Loans

These are interest-free loans to people who have been receiving income support or income-based Jobseeker's Allowance, or payments on account of such benefits for at least 26 weeks, for intermittent expenses that may be difficult to budget for.

Crisis Loans

These are interest-free loans to anyone, whether receiving benefit or not, who is without resources in an emergency, where there is no other means of preventing serious damage or serious risk to their health or safety.

SAVINGS

Savings over £500 (£1,000 for people aged 60 or over) are taken into account for Community Care Grants and Budgeting Loans. All savings are taken into account for Crisis Loans. Savings are not taken into account for Sure Start Maternity Grants, Funeral Payments, Cold Weather or Winter Fuel Payments.

INDUSTRIAL INJURIES AND DISABLEMENT BENEFITS

The industrial injuries scheme, administered under the Social Security Contributions and Benefits Act 1992, provides a range of benefits designed to compensate for disablement resulting from an industrial accident (i.e. an accident arising out of and in the course of an employed earner's employment) or from a prescribed disease due to the nature of a person's employment. Those who are self-employed are not covered by this scheme.

INDUSTRIAL INJURIES DISABLEMENT BENEFIT

A person must be at least 14 per cent disabled (except for certain respiratory diseases) in order to qualify for this benefit. The amount paid depends on the degree of disablement:
 – those assessed as 14–19 per cent disabled are paid at the 20 per cent rate
 – those with disablement of over 20 per cent will have the percentage rounded up or down to the nearest ten per cent, e.g. a disablement of 44 per cent will be paid at the 40 per cent rate while a disablement of 45 per cent will be paid at the 50 per cent rate.

Benefit is payable 15 weeks (90 days) after the date of the accident or onset of the disease and may be payable for a limited period or for life. The benefit is payable whether the person works or not and those who are incapable of work are entitled to draw statutory sick pay or incapacity benefit in addition to industrial injuries disablement benefit. It may also be possible to claim the following allowances:

– reduced earnings allowance for those who are unable to return to their regular work or work of the same standard and who had their accident (or whose disease started) before 1 October 1990
– retirement allowance for those who were entitled to reduced earnings allowance who have reached State Pension age
– constant attendance allowance for those with a disablement of 100 per cent who need constant care. There are four rates of allowance depending on how much care the person needs
– exceptionally severe disablement allowance for those who are entitled to constant care attendance allowance at one of the higher rates and who need constant care permanently
See leaflets SD6, SD7 and SD8.

OTHER BENEFITS
People who are disabled because of an accident or disease that was the result of work that they did before 5 July 1948 are not entitled to industrial injuries disablement benefit. They may, however, be entitled to payment under the workmen's compensation scheme or the pneumoconiosis, byssinosis and miscellaneous diseases benefit scheme. See leaflet GL23.

WEEKLY RATES OF BENEFIT *from April 2003*
*Disablement benefit/pension
Degree of disablement:

100 per cent	£116.80
90	£105.12
80	£93.44
70	£81.76
60	£70.08
50	£58.40
40	£46.72
30	£35.04
20	£23.36
†Unemployability supplement	£72.15
Addition for adult dependant	
(subject to earnings rule)	£43.15
Reduced earnings allowance (maximum)	£46.72
Retirement allowance (maximum)	£11.68
Constant attendance allowance	
(normal maximum rate)	£46.80
Exceptionally severe disablement allowance	£46.80

*There is a weekly benefit for those under 18 with no dependants which is set at a lower rate
†This benefit attracts an increase for each dependent child (in addition to child benefit) of £9.85 for the first child and £11.35 for each subsequent child

CLAIMS AND QUESTIONS

Entitlement to benefit and regulated Social Fund payments is determined by a decision maker on behalf of the Secretary of State for the Department of Work and Pensions. A claimant who is dissatisfied with that decision can ask for an explanation. They can dispute the decision by applying to have it revised or, in particular circumstances, superseded. If they are still dissatisfied they can go to the Appeals Service where it will be heard by an independent tribunal. There is a further right of appeal to a Social Security Commissioner against the tribunal's decision but this is on a point of law only and leave to appeal must first be obtained.

Decisions on claims and applications for housing benefit and council tax benefit are made by Local Authority decision makers. The explanation, dispute and appeals process is the same as for other benefits. See leaflets GL24 and NI260DMA.

Decisions on applications to the discretionary Social Fund are made by Social Fund Officers. Applicants can ask for a review within 28 days of the date on the decision letter. The Social Fund Review Officer will review the case and there is a further right of review to an independent Social Fund Inspector.

EMPLOYER PAYMENTS

STATUTORY MATERNITY PAY
Employers pay statutory maternity pay (SMP) to pregnant women who have been employed by them full or part-time for at least 26 weeks into the 15th week before the week the baby is due, and whose earnings on average at least equal the lower earnings limit applied to NI contributions (£77 per week from April 2003). All women who meet these conditions receive payment of 90 per cent of their average earnings for the first six weeks, followed by a maximum of 20 weeks at £100.00 or 90 per cent of the woman's average weekly earnings if this is less than £100. SMP can be paid, at the earliest, 11 weeks before the week in which the baby is due, up to the day following the birth. Women can decide when they wish their maternity leave to start and can work until the baby is born. However, where the woman is absent from work for a pregnancy related illness on or after the Sunday of the 4th week before the baby is due to be born, SMP will start the day following the first day of absence from work for the pregnancy related illness. SMP is not payable for any week in which the woman works. Employers are reimbursed for 92 per cent of the SMP they pay. Small employers with annual gross NI payments of £40,000 or less recover 100 per cent of the SMP paid out plus 4.5 per cent in compensation for the secondary National Insurance Contributions paid on SMP. See Leaflet NI17A and Inland Revenue guide for employers E15.

STATUTORY PATERNITY PAY
Employers pay statutory paternity pay (SPP) to employees who are taking leave when a child is born or placed for adoption. To qualify the employee must:
– have responsibility for the child's upbringing
– be the biological father of the child (or the child's adopter), or the husband/partner of the mother or adopter
– be taking time off work to care for the child and/or support the mother or adopter
– have been employed by the same employer for at least 26 weeks ending with the 15th week before the baby is due (or the week in which the adopter is notified of having been matched with a child)
– continue working for the employer up to the child's birth (or placement for adoption)
– have earnings on average at least equal to the lower earnings limit applied to NI contributions (£77 per week from April 2003)
Employees who meet these conditions receive payment of £100 or 90 per cent of the employee's average weekly earnings if this is less than £100. The employee can choose to be paid for one or two consecutive weeks. The earliest the SPP period can begin is the date of the child's birth or placement for adoption. The SPP period must be completed within eight weeks of that date. SSP is not payable for any week in which the employee works. Employers are reimbursed in the same way as for

Statutory Maternity Pay. *See* Department of Trade and Industry leaflet PL514 and PL515.

STATUTORY ADOPTION PAY
Employers pay statutory adoption pay (SAP) to employees taking adoption leave from their employers. To qualify for SAP the employee must:
- be newly matched with a child by an adoption agency
- have been employed by the same employer for at least 26 weeks ending the week in which they have been notified of being matched with a child
- have earnings at least equal to the lower earnings limit applied to NI contributions (£77 per week from April 2003)

Employees who meet these conditions receive payment of £100 or 90 per cent of their average weekly earnings if this is less than £100 for up to 26 weeks. The SAP period can start from the date of the child's placement. SAP is not payable for any week in which the employee works. Where a couple adopt a child only one of them may receive SAP, the other may be able to receive Statutory Paternity Pay (SPP) if they meet the eligibility criteria. Employers are reimbursed in the same way as for Statutory Maternity Pay. *See* Department of Trade and Industry leaflet PL515

STATUTORY SICK PAY
Employers pay statutory sick pay (SSP) for up to 28 weeks to any employee incapable of work for four or more consecutive days. SSP is payable to employees between the ages of 16 and 65 who have average earnings at or above the point at which earnings become relevant for NI purposes (£77 from April 2003) in a specified period. SSP is paid at £64.35 per week and is subject to PAYE and NI contributions. Employees who cannot obtain SSP may be able to claim Incapacity Benefit. Employers may be able to recover some SSP costs. *See* Inland Revenue Leaflets CA86 Employees and CA30 Employer Manual.

WAR PENSIONS
The Veteran's Agency (originally known as The War Pensions Agency) became an executive agency of the Ministry of Defence in June 2001. The Agency makes awards to war pensions under The Naval, Military and Air Forces, Etc. (Disablement and Death) Service Pensions Order 1983 to members of the armed forces in respect of disablement due to service. There is also a scheme for civilians and civil defence workers in respect of the 1939–45 war, and other schemes for groups such as merchant seamen and Polish armed forces who served under British command, during World War II.

PENSIONS
War disablement pension is awarded for the disabling effects of any injury, wound or disease which is the result of, or has been aggravated by, conditions of service in the armed forces. It can only be paid once the person has left the armed forces. The amount of pension paid depends on the severity of disablement, which is assessed by comparing the health of the claimant with that of a healthy person of the same age and sex. The person's earning capacity or occupation are not taken into account in this assessment. A pension is awarded if the person has a disablement of 20 per cent or more and a lump sum is usually payable to those with a disablement of less than 20 per cent. No award is made for noise-induced sensorineural hearing loss where the assessment of disablement is less than 20 per cent.

War widow/widower's pension is payable where the spouse's death was due to, or hastened by, service in the armed forces or where the spouse was in receipt of a war disablement pension constant attendance allowance (or would have been if not in hospital). A war widow/widower's pension is also payable if the spouse was getting War Disablement Pension at the 80 per cent rate or higher and was receiving unemployability supplement at the time of death. War widows/widowers receive a standard rank-related rate but a lower weekly rate is payable to war widows/widowers of Personnel below the rank of Major who are under the age of 40, without children and capable of maintaining themselves. This is increased to the standard rate at age 40. Allowances are paid for children (in addition to child benefit) and adult dependants. An age allowance is automatically given when the widow/widower reaches 65 and increased at ages 70 and 80.

All war pensions and war widow/widower's pensions are tax-free and pensioners living overseas receive the same amount as those resident in the UK.

SUPPLEMENTARY ALLOWANCES
A number of supplementary allowances may be awarded to a war pensioner which are intended to meet various needs which may result from disablement or death and take account of its particular effect on the pensioner or spouse. The principal supplementary allowances are unemployability supplement, allowance for lowered standard of occupation and constant attendance allowance. Others include exceptionally severe disablement allowance, severe disablement occupational allowance, treatment allowance, mobility supplement, comforts allowance, clothing allowance, age allowance and widow/widower's age allowance. Rent and children's allowances are also available on war widow/widower's pensions.

DEPARTMENT FOR WORK AND PENSIONS BENEFITS
Most benefits are paid in addition to the basic war disablement pension or war widow/widower's pension, but may be affected by supplementary allowances in payment. Any State Pension for which a war widow/widower qualifies on their own NI contribution record can be paid in addition to war widow/widower's pension.

CLAIMS AND QUESTIONS
To claim a war pension it is necessary to contact the nearest war pensioners' welfare service office, the address of which is available from local social security offices, or to write to the Veteran's Agency, Norcross, Blackpool FY5 3WP. Claims can also be made through authorised agents, usually ex-service organisations such as the RBL, BLESMA etc. General advice on any war pensions matter can be obtained by ringing the War Pensions Freeline (UK only) on 0800-169 2277. If living overseas, call (00 44) (125) 386-6043;
Email: help@veteransagency.mod.uk
Web: www.veteransagency.mod.uk

THE WATER INDUSTRY

ENGLAND AND WALES

The water industry supplies around 18,000 million litres of water every day. Around 2.8 million tests are carried out to check drinking water quality every year and 99.86 per cent of samples meet all British/European standards. In England and Wales the Secretary of State for Environment, Food and Rural Affairs and the National Assembly for Wales have overall responsibility for water policy and oversee environmental standards for the water industry.

THE WATER COMPANIES

Until 1989 nine regional water authorities in England and the Welsh Water Authority in Wales were responsible for water supply and the development of water resources, sewerage and sewage disposal, pollution control, freshwater fisheries, flood protection, water recreation and environmental conservation. The Water Act 1989 provided for the creation of a privatised water industry under public regulation. The functions of the regional water authorities were taken over by ten holding companies and the regulatory bodies and have since been consolidated into the Water Industry Act 1991.

Water UK is the industry association that represents all UK water and wastewater service suppliers at national and European level. Water UK provides a framework for the water industry to engage with government, regulators, stakeholder organisations and the public. Water UK is funded directly by its members who are the service suppliers for England, Scotland, Wales and Northern Ireland; every member has a seat on the Water UK Council.

WATER UK, 1 Queen Anne's Gate, London SW1H 9BT
Tel: 020-7344 1844 Web: www.water.org.uk.
Chief Executive: Pamela Taylor

WATER SERVICE COMPANIES

ANGLIAN WATER SERVICES LTD (part of AWG PLC), Anglian House, Ambury Road, Huntingdon, Cambs PE29 3NZ. Tel: 01480-323000
Web: www.anglianwater.co.uk

BOURNEMOUTH & WEST HAMPSHIRE WATER PLC, George Jessel House, Francis Avenue, Bournemouth, Dorset BH11 8NB. Tel: 01202-591111
Web: www.bwhwater.co.uk

BRISTOL WATER PLC, PO Box 218, Bridgwater Road, Bristol BS99 7AU. Tel: 0117-966 5881
Web: www.bristolwater.co.uk

CAMBRIDGE WATER PLC, 41 Rustat Road, Cambridge CB1 3QS. Tel: 01223-403000
Web: www.cambridge-water.co.uk

DEE VALLEY WATER PLC, Packsaddle, Wrexham Road, Rhostyllen, Wrexham LL14 4EH Tel: 01978-846946

DWR CYMRU CYFYNGEDIG (WELSH WATER),
Pentwyn Road, Nelson, Treharris, Mid Glamorgan CF46 6LY.
Tel: 01443-452300 Web: www.dwrcymru.co.uk

ESSEX & SUFFOLK WATER PLC (subsidiary of Northumbrian Water Ltd), Hall Street, Chelmsford, Essex CM2 0HH Tel: 01245-491234 Web: www.eswater.co.uk

FOLKESTONE & DOVER WATER SERVICES LTD, Cherry Garden Lane, Folkestone, Kent CT19 4QB
Tel: 01303-298800

MID KENT WATER PLC, Snodland, Kent ME6 5AH
Tel: 01634-873111 Web: www.midkentwater.co.uk

NORTHUMBRIAN WATER LTD, Abbey Road, Pity Me, Durham DH1 5FJ. Tel: 0191-383 2222 Web: www.nwl.co.uk

PORTSMOUTH WATER PLC, PO Box 8, West Street, Havant, Hampshire PO9 1LG. Tel: 02392-499888
Web: www.portsmouthwater.co.uk

SEVERN TRENT PLC, 2297 Coventry Road, Birmingham B26 3PU. Tel: 0121-722 4000
Web: www.severn-trent.com

SOUTH EAST WATER PLC, 3 Church Road, Haywards Heath, West Sussex RH16 3NY.
Tel: 01444-448200 Web: www.southeastwater.co.uk

SOUTH STAFFORDSHIRE WATER PLC, Green Lane, Walsall, West Midlands WS2 7PD. Tel: 01922-638282
Web: www.south-staffs-water.co.uk

SOUTH WEST WATER LTD, Peninsula House, Rydon Lane, Exeter EX2 7HR. Tel: 01392-446688
Web: www.swwater.co.uk

SOUTHERN WATER, Southern House, Yeoman Road, Worthing, W. Sussex BN13 3NX. Tel: 01903-264444
Web: www.southernwater.co.uk

SUTTON AND EAST SURREY WATER PLC, London Road, Redhill, Surrey RH1 1LY. Tel 01737-772000
Web: www.waterplc.com

TENDRING HUNDRED WATER SERVICES LTD, Mill Hill, Manningtree, Essex CO11 2AZ. Tel: 01206-399200
Web: www.thws.co.uk

THAMES WATER UTILITIES LTD, 14 Cavendish Place, London W1M 0NU. Tel: 020-7636 8686
Web: www.thames-water.com

THREE VALLEYS WATER PLC, PO Box 48, Bishops Rise, Hatfield, Hertfordshire AL10 9HL. Tel: 01707-268111
Web: www.3valleys.co.uk

UNITED UTILITIES WATER PLC, Dawson House, Liverpool Road, Great Sankey, Warrington WA5 3LW.
Tel: 01925-234000 Web: www.unitedutilities.com

WESSEX WATER SERVICES LTD, Claverton Down, Bath BA2 7WW. Tel: 01225-526000 Web: wessexwater.co.uk

YORKSHIRE WATER SERVICES LTD, Western House, Western Way, Halifax Road, Bradford BD6 2LZ.
Tel: 01274-600111 Web: www.yorkshirewater.com

ISLAND WATER AUTHORITIES
(NOT MEMBERS OF WATER UK)

COUNCIL OF THE ISLES OF SCILLY, Town Hall, St Mary's, Isles of Scilly TR21 0LW Tel: 01720-422902

ISLE OF MAN WATER AUTHORITY, Drill House, Tromode Road, Isle of Man IM2 5PA Tel: 01624-624414

THE JERSEY NEW WATERWORKS COMPANY LTD, Mulcaster House, Westmount Road, St Helier, Jersey JE1 1DG Tel: 01534-509999

THE STATES OF GUERNSEY WATER BOARD, PO Box 30, South Esplanade, St Peter Port, Guernsey GY1 3AS
Tel: 01481-724552

WATER SUPPLY AND CONSUMPTION 2001–2

	Supply		Consumption			
	Supply from Treatment Works (Ml/day)	Total Leakage (Ml/day)	Household (l/head/day) Unmetered	Metered	Non-household (l/prop/day) Unmetered	Metered
WATER AND SEWERAGE COMPANIES						
Anglian	1,159	224	150	119	587	3,130
Dwr Cymru	894	245	151	132	686	2,391
Northumbrian	754	161	148	128	849	4,673
Severn Trent	1,870	340	141	134	600	2,217
South West	445	83	160	123	822	1,698
Southern	598	92	164	151	551	2,730
Thames	2,765	865	161	150	913	3,423
United Utilities	1,933	452	142	136	704	2,683
Wessex	374	79	147	129	2,332	2,458
Yorkshire	1,307	297	149	138	123	2,896
Total	12,099	2,840	–	–	–	–
Average	–	–	150	134	741	2,766
WATER ONLY COMPANIES						
Total	3,226	575	–	–	–	–
Average	–	–	153	136	839	2,853

Source: Office of Water Services

REGULATORY BODIES

The Office of Water Services (Ofwat) was set up under the Water Act 1989 and is the independent economic regulator of the water and sewerage companies in England and Wales. Overall responsibility for water policy and overseeing environmental standards for the water industry lies with the Department for Environment, Food and Rural Affairs and the National Assembly for Wales. Ofwat's main duty is to ensure that the companies can finance and carry out their statutory functions and to protect the interests of water customers. Ofwat is a non-ministerial government department headed by the Director General of Water Services.

Under the Competition Act 1998, from 1 March 2000 the Competition Commission has heard appeals against the regulator's decisions regarding anti-competitive agreements and abuse of a dominant position in the marketplace. The 2003 Water Bill placed a new duty on Ofwat to have regard to sustainable development.

The Environment Agency was set up by the 1995 Environment Act as a non-departmental public body and is sponsored largely by the Department for Environment, Food and Rural Affairs and the National Assembly of Wales. The Environment Agency has statutory duties and powers in relation to water resources, pollution control, flood defence, fisheries, recreation, conservation and navigation in England and Wales. They are also responsible for issuing permits, licences, consents and registrations such as industrial licences to abstract water and fishing licences.

The Drinking Water Inspectorate (DWI) is the drinking water quality regulator for England and Wales, responsible for assessing the quality of the drinking water supplied by the water companies and investigating any incidents affecting drinking water quality, initiating prosecution where necessary. The DWI also provides scientific advice on drinking water policy issues to the Department of the Environment, Food and Rural Affairs and the National Assembly for Wales.

OFWAT, Centre City Tower, 7 Hill Street, Birmingham, B5 4UA
Tel: 0121-625 1300 Email: enquiries@ofwat.gsi.gov.uk
Web: www.ofwat.gov.uk
Director General: Philip Fletcher

METHODS OF CHARGING

In England and Wales, most domestic customers still pay for domestic water supply and sewerage services through charges based on the old rateable value of their property. It is expected that in 2003–4 about 25 per cent of householders will be charged according to consumption, which is recorded by meter. Industrial and most commercial customers are charged according to consumption.

Under the Water Industry Act 1999, water companies can continue basing their charges on the old rateable value of property. Domestic customers can continue paying on an unmeasured basis unless they choose to pay according to consumption. After having a meter installed (which is free of charge), a customer can revert to unmeasured charging within 12 months. Domestic, school and hospital customers cannot be disconnected for non-payment.

In November 1999 Ofwat set new price limits for the period 2000–5. Ofwat will set price limits for 2005–10 in November 2004.

AVERAGE HOUSEHOLD WATER BILLS 2003–4

	Unmetered (£)	Metered (£)
Water	116	96
Sewerage	129	113
Combined	245	209

SCOTLAND

Overall responsibility for national water policy in Scotland rested with the Secretary of State for Scotland until July 1999 when it was devolved to the Scottish Ministers. Until The Local Government (Scotland) Act 1994, water supply and sewerage services were local authority responsibilities. The Central Scotland Water Development Board had the function of developing new sources of water supply for the purpose of providing water in bulk to water authorities whose limits of supply were within the board's area. Under the Act, three new public water authorities, covering the north, east and west of Scotland respectively, took over the provision of water and sewerage services from April 1996. The Central Scotland Water Development Board was then abolished. The new authorities were accountable to the Secretary of State for Scotland, and since July 1999 have been accountable to the Scottish Ministers. The Act also established the Scottish Water and Sewerage Customers Council representing consumer interests. It monitored the performance of the authorities; approved charges schemes; investigated complaints; and advised the Secretary of State. The Water Industry Act 1999, whose Scottish provisions were accepted by the Scottish Executive, abolished the Scottish Water and Sewerage Customers Council and replaced it in November 1999 by a Water Industry Commissioner.

The Water Industry (Scotland) Act 2002 resulted from the Scottish Executive's proposal that a single authority was better placed than three separate authorities to harmonise changes across the Scottish water industry. This lead to Scottish Water replacing the three existing water authorities, East of Scotland Water, North of Scotland Water and West of Scotland Water, from 31 March 2002. Scottish Water is a public sector company, structured and managed like a private company, but remains answerable to the Scottish Parliament. Scottish Water is regulated by the Water Industry Commissioner for Scotland, the Scottish Environment Protection Agency (SEPA), and the Drinking Water Quality Regulator for Scotland. The Water Industry Commissioner is responsible for regulating all aspects of economic and customer service performance, including water and sewerage charges and SEPA is responsible for environmental issues, including controlling pollution and promoting the cleanliness of Scotland's rivers, lochs and coastal waters.

METHODS OF CHARGING

Scottish Water sets charges for domestic and non-domestic water and sewerage provision through charges schemes which are regulated by the Water Industries Commissioner for Scotland. Scottish Water is required to harmonise charges across the country by April 2005.

WATER RESOURCES 2001–2

	Yield (ml/day)
Reservoirs and Lochs	3,077
River Intakes	357
Boreholes	104
Springs	26
Total	3,564

Source: The Scottish Executive Water Services Unit (Crown Copyright)

WATER CONSUMPTION 2001–2*

Total daily demand	2,408.7
Total potable demand	2,399.1
Unmetered	1,876.4
Metered	522.8
Non-potable†	9.6

* 'Non-potable' supplied for industrial purposes. Metered supplies in general relate to commercial and industrial use and unmetered to domestic use

Source: The Scottish Executive Water Services Unit (Crown Copyright)

SCOTTISH WATER, 26 Castle Drive, Carnegie Campus, Dunfermline KY11 8GG
Tel: 01383-848200 Web: www.scottishwater.co.uk
THE WATER INDUSTRY COMMISSIONER FOR SCOTLAND, Ochil House, Springkerse Business Park, Stirling, FK7 7XE. Tel: 01786-430200
Web: www.watercommissioner.co.uk
SCOTTISH ENVIRONMENT PROTECTION AGENCY (SEPA), Erskine Court, Castle Business Park, Stirling FK9 4TR. Tel: 01786-457700 Web: www.sepa.org.uk

NORTHERN IRELAND

In Northern Ireland ministerial responsibility for water services lies with The Minister of the Department for Regional Development. The Water Service, which is an executive agency of the Department for Regional Development, is responsible for policy and co-ordination with regard to supply, distribution and cleanliness of water, and the provision and maintenance of sewerage services.

The Water Service is divided into four regions, the Eastern, Northern, Western and Southern Divisions. The main divisional offices are based in Belfast, Ballymena, Londonderry and Craigavon respectively.

METHODS OF CHARGING

Until last year the Water Service was funded mainly through the regional rate (part of which was appropriated in-aid of the Department) and direct charges principally for metered water. However, the regional rate is no longer appropriated-in-aid and following devolution the Water service is now funded by parliamentary vote and direct charges. The department's policy is to meter all properties that are not exclusively domestic. They are, however, granted an allowance of 200 cubic metres per annum to reflect domestic usage – this is known as the domestic usage allowance. Customers are charged only for water used in excess of the domestic usage allowance together with a standing charge, which is intended to cover the costs of meter provision, maintenance, reading and billing. This allowance is not granted if rates are not paid on the property. Traders operating from de-rated, rate exempt or rate rebated premises are required to pay for the treatment and disposal of trade effluent which they discharge into the public sewer.

NORTHERN IRELAND WATER SERVICE, Northland House, 3 Frederick Street, Belfast, BT1 2NR. Tel: 028-90 244711 Web: www.doeni.gov.uk/water

ENERGY

The main primary sources of energy in Britain are oil, natural gas, coal, nuclear power and water power. The main secondary sources (e.g. sources derived from the primary sources) are electricity, coke and smokeless fuels and petroleum products. The Department for the Environment, Food and Rural Affairs (DEFRA) is responsible for promoting energy efficiency.

INDIGENOUS PRODUCTION OF PRIMARY FUELS
Million tonnes of oil equivalent

	2002
Coal	20.5
Petroleum	127.2
Natural gas	104.1
Primary electricity	20.8
Nuclear	20.3
Natural flow hydro	0.5
Total	272.6

INLAND ENERGY CONSUMPTION BY PRIMARY FUEL
Million tonnes of oil equivalent, seasonally adjusted

	2002
Coal	39.9
Petroleum	77.4
Natural gas	97.9
Primary electricity	21.6
Nuclear	20.3
Natural flow hydro	0.5
Net Imports	0.7
Total	236.8

TRADE IN FUELS AND RELATED MATERIALS 2002

	Quantity*	Value†
IMPORTS		
Coal and other solid fuel	19.8	875
Crude petroleum	44.6	4,985
Petroleum products	22.9	3,208
Natural gas	2.7	271
Electricity	0.8	179
Total	91.0	9,518
Total ‡	–	8,726
EXPORTS		
Coal and other solid fuel	0.7	62
Crude petroleum	86.6	9,739
Petroleum products	32.3	4,164
Natural gas	10.8	862
Electricity	0	94
Total	130.4	14,922
Total ‡	–	14,922

* Million tonnes of oil equivalent
† £ million
‡ Adjusted to exclude estimated costs of insurance, freight, etc.
Source: HM Customs & Excise

OIL

Until the 1960s Britain imported almost all its oil supplies. In 1969 oil was discovered in the Arbroath field of the UK Continental Shelf (UKCS). The first oilfield to be brought into production was the Argyll field in 1975, and since the mid-1970s Britain has been a major producer of crude oil.

Licences for exploration and production are granted to companies by the Department of Trade and Industry; the leading British oil companies are BP and Shell. At the end of 2002, 1,062 Seaward Production Licences and 124 onshore Petroleum Exploration and Development Licences had been awarded, and there were 154 offshore oilfields in production. In 2002 there were 9 oil refineries and three smaller refining units processing crude and process oils. There are estimated to be reserves of 1,300 million tonnes of oil remaining in the UKCS. Royalties are payable on fields approved before April 1982 and petroleum revenue tax is levied on fields approved between 1975 and March 1993.

DRILLING ACTIVITY 2002

Number of wells started	Offshore	Onshore
Exploration and appraisal	44	14
Exploration	16	–
Appraisal	28	–
Development	249	18

VALUE OF UKCS OIL AND GAS PRODUCTION AND INVESTMENT
£ million

	2000	2001
Total income	25,518	24,493
Operating costs	4,359	4,335
Gross trading profits*	20,906	20,079
Percentage contribution to GVA	2.6	2.4
Exploration expenditure	348	411
Other Capital investment	2,748	3,509
Percentage contribution to industrial investment	12	15

*Net of stock appreciation

INDIGENOUS PRODUCTION AND REFINERY RECEIPTS

	2001	2002
Indigenous production (thousand tonnes)	116,678	115,944
Crude oil	108,387	107,430
NGLs*	8,292	8,514
Refinery receipts (thousand tonnes)		
Indigenous	29,403	28,556
Other†	4,331	2,333
Net foreign imports	50,613	54,114

* Natural gas liquids: condensates and petroleum gases derived at onshore treatment plants
† Mainly recycled products

DELIVERIES OF PETROLEUM PRODUCTS FOR INLAND CONSUMPTION BY ENERGY USE
Thousand tonnes

	2001	2002
Industry	6,057	5,748
Transport	48,966	48,718
Domestic	3,196	3,260
Other	2,272	1,562
Total	60,491	59,288

Source: Department of Trade and Industry

COAL

Coal has been mined in Britain for centuries and the availability of coal was crucial to the industrial revolution of the 18th and 19th centuries. Mines were in private ownership until 1947 when they were nationalised and came under the management of the National Coal Board, later the British Coal Corporation. In addition to producing coal at its own deep-mine and opencast sites, of which there were 850 in 1955, British Coal was responsible for licensing private operators.

Under the Coal Industry Act 1994, the Coal Authority was established to take over ownership of coal reserves and to issue licences to private mining companies as part of the privatisation of British Coal. The Coal Authority also deals with the physical legacy of mining, e.g. subsidence damage claims, and is responsible for holding and making available all existing records. The mines were sold as five separate businesses in 1994 and coal production in the UK is now undertaken entirely in the private sector. By mid April 2002 there were 18 large deep mines in operation.

The main UK customer for coal is the electricity supply industry. A review of energy policy was undertaken during 1998 and the Government announced measures in its October 1998 Energy White Paper which included a freeze on new applications to build gas-fired power stations in order to increase opportunities for coal-fired power stations. The moratorium on new gas-fired power stations was lifted in 2000 in the light of two measures to improve the competitiveness of coal fired generation. Firstly the government reached an agreement with the European Commission to make available temporary state aid for the coal industry with such aid to end with the termination of the European Coal and Steel Community Treaty in 2002. Secondly there was the reform of the electricity wholesale market and the replacement of The Pool with the New Electricity Trading Arrangement (NETA) which took effect from 27 March 2001. An Energy White Paper published on 24 February 2003 stated that coal generation still provides around a third of the UK's power output, but recognised that for a low-carbon economy the development of cleaner coal technologies is required. By 2020 coal generation's contribution to the UK's power output is likely to be significantly lower than today.

COAL PRODUCTION AND FOREIGN TRADE
Thousand tonnes

	2001	2002p
Total production	31,930	30,038
Deep-mined	17,347	16,391
Opencast	14,166	13,147
Imports*	35,542	28,686
Exports†	550	535

* Includes an estimate for slurry

† As recorded in the Overseas Trade Statistics of the United Kingdom, although these are based on estimates from extra-EC trade until monthly statistics for intra-EC trade become available from HM Customs and Excise

p provisional

INLAND COAL USE
Thousand tonnes

	2001	2002
Fuel producers		
Collieries	10	9
Electricity generators	50,996	47,528
Heat generation*	709	641
Coke ovens and blast furnaces	7,896	6,433
Other conversion industries†	495	436
Final users		
Industry‡	1,743	986
Domestic	2,538	2,435
Public administration, commerce and agriculture	147	73
Total	64,535	58,539

* Generation of heat for sale under the provision of a contract

† Low temperature carbonisation and patent fuel plants

‡ Includes estimates of imports

Source: Department of Trade and Industry

GAS

From the late 18th-century gas in Britain was produced from coal. In the 1960s town gas began to be produced from oil-based feedstocks using imported oil. In 1965 gas was discovered in the North Sea in the West Sole field, which became the first gasfield in production in 1967, and from the late 1960s natural gas began to replace town gas. Britain is now the world's fourth largest producer of gas and in 1998 only 1.5 per cent of gas available for consumption in the UK was imported. From October 1998 Britain was connected to the continental European gas system via a pipeline from Bacton, Norfolk to Zeebrugge, Belgium. At the end of October 2002 there were 4,100 miles of high pressure gas pipelines and 170,300 miles of local transmission and distribution pipelines owned and operated in the UK by National Grid Transco.

The gas industry in Britain was nationalised in 1949 and operated as the Gas Council. The Gas Council was replaced by the British Gas Corporation in 1972 and the industry became more centralised. The British Gas Corporation was privatised in 1986 as British Gas PLC.

In 1993 the Monopolies and Mergers Commission found that British Gas's integrated business in Great Britain as a gas trader and the owner of the gas transportation system could be expected to operate against the public interest. In February 1997, British Gas demerged its trading arm to become two separate companies BG PLC and Centrica PLC. BG Group, as the company is now known, is an international natural gas company whose principal business is finding and developing gas reserves and building gas markets. Its core operations are located in the UK, South America, Egypt, Trinidad & Tobago, Kazakhstan and India. Centrica runs the trading and services operations under the British Gas brand name in Great Britain. In October 2000 BG demerged its pipeline business, Transco, which became part of Lattice Group, finally merging with the National Grid Group in 2002 to become National Grid Transco.

Competition was gradually introduced into the industrial gas market from 1986. Supply of gas to the domestic market was opened to companies other than British Gas, starting in April 1996 with a pilot project in the West Country and Wales. From spring 1997 competition was progressively introduced throughout the rest of Britain in stages which were completed in May 1998. The majority of gas companies are now part of larger multi-utility companies, often operating internationally.

BG GROUP PLC, 100 Thames Valley Park Drive, Reading RG6 1PT Tel: 0118-935 3222
Chairman, Sir R. V. Giordano
Chief Executive, F. Chapman

CENTRICA PLC, Millstream, Maidenhead Road, Windsor, Berkshire SL4 5GD Tel: 01753-494000
Chief Executive, Sir Roy Gardner

NATIONAL GRID TRANSCO PLC, National Grid House, Kirby Corner Road, Coventry, CV4 8JY
Tel: 024-7642 3000 Web: www.nationalgrid.com

UK NATURAL GAS PRODUCTION
GWh

	2000	2001
Power stations	324,679	311,545
Coal extraction and manufacture		
of solid fuels	6	4
Coke ovens	–	–
Petroleum Refineries	3,641	4,192
Nuclear fuel production	1,272	1,210
Production and distribution of		
other energy	619	451
Total final producers	330,217	317,402

Source: The Stationery Office: *Annual Abstract of Statistics 2003* (Crown copyright)

NATURAL GAS CONSUMPTION
GWh

	2000	2001
Iron and steel industry	21,118	20,972
Other industries	14,387	12,568
Domestic	369,909	379,163
Public administration	44,088	45,455
Agriculture	1,315	1,327
Miscellaneous	63,477	64,724
Total final users	514,294	524,209

Source: The Stationery Office: *Annual Abstract of Statistics 2003* (Crown copyright)

ELECTRICITY

The first power station in Britain generating electricity for public supply began operating in 1882. In the 1930s a national transmission grid was developed and it was reconstructed and extended in the 1950s and 1960s. Power stations were operated by the Central Electricity Generating Board.

Under the Electricity Act 1989, 12 regional electricity companies (RECs), which were responsible for the distribution of electricity from the national grid to consumers, were formed from the former area electricity boards in England and Wales. Four companies were formed from the Central Electricity Generating Board:

three generating companies (National Power PLC, Nuclear Electric PLC and PowerGen PLC) and the National Grid Company PLC, which owned and operated the transmission system. National Power and PowerGen were floated on the stock market in 1991. National Power was demerged in October 2000 to form two separate companies: International Power PLC and Innogy PLC, which manages the bulk of National Power's UK assets. Nuclear Electric was split into two parts in 1996 British Energy (*see* Nuclear Energy) and Magnox Electric, which owns the magnox nuclear reactors, remained in the public sector and was integrated into British Nuclear Fuels (BNFL) in 1998. The National Grid Company was floated on the stock exchange in 1995 and formed a new holding company, National Grid Group. National Grid Group completed a merger with Lattice in 2002 to form National Grid Transco, a public limited company. Generators and suppliers participate in a competitive wholesale trading market known as NETA (New Electricity Trading Arrangements) which began in March 2001, replacing the Electricity Pool. The introduction of competition into the domestic electricity market was completed in May 1999. With the gas market also open, most suppliers now offer their customers both gas and electricity. Overall, there is a trend towards larger multi-utility companies, often operating internationally.

In Scotland, three new companies were formed under the Electricity Act 1989: Scottish Power PLC and Scottish Hydro-Electric PLC, which are responsible for generation, transmission, distribution and supply; and Scottish Nuclear Ltd. Scottish Power and Scottish Hydro-Electric were floated on the stock market in 1991. Scottish Hydro-Electric merged with Southern Electric in 1998 to become Scottish and Southern Energy PLC. Scottish Nuclear was incorporated into British Energy in 1996.

In Northern Ireland, Northern Ireland Electricity PLC was set up in 1993 under a 1991 Order in Council. In 1993 it was floated on the stock exchange and in 1998 it became part of the Viridian Group and is responsible for distribution and supply.

The Electricity Association is the electricity industry's main trade association, providing representational and professional services for the electricity companies. EA Technology provides distribution and utilisation research, development and technology transfer.

ELECTRICITY ASSOCIATION LTD, 30 Millbank, London SW1P 4RD. Tel: 020-7963 5700
Web: www.electricity.org.uk
EA TECHNOLOGY LTD, Capenhurst, Chester CH1 6ES. Tel: 0151-339 4181 Web: www.eatechnology.com
NATIONAL GRID TRANSCO PLC, National Grid House, Kirby Corner Road, Coventry, CV4 8JY
Tel: 024-7642 3000 Web: www.nationalgrid.com

ELECTRICITY GENERATION, SUPPLY AND CONSUMPTION
GWh

	2000	2001
Electricity generated	377,309	385,826
Major power producers: total	341,783	352,985
Conventional thermal, gas turbines		
and oil engines	131,062	139,409
Combined cycle gas turbine		
stations	117,935	117,183

	2000	2001
Nuclear stations	85,063	90,093
Hydro-electric stations:		
Natural flow	4,331	3,216
Pumped storage	2,694	2,356
Renewables other than hydro	698	728
Other generators: total	35,525	32,841
Electricity used on works: total	16,333	17,376
Major generating companies	14,952	15,994
Other generators	1,381	1,382
Electricity supplied (gross): total		
Major power producers: total	326,831	336,991
Conventional thermal, gas turbines		
and oil engines	124,828	132,655
Combined cycle gas turbine		
stations	116,110	115,124
Nuclear stations	78,334	82,985
Hydro-electric stations		
Natural flow	4,316	3,204
Pumped storage	2,603	2,340
renewables other than hydro	640	683
Other generators: total	34,144	31,459
Electricity used in pumping		
Major power producers	3,499	3,210
Electricity supplied (net): total	357,476	365,240
Major power producers	323,332	333,781
Other generators	34,144	31,459
Net Imports	14,174	10,399
Electricity Available	371,650	375,640
Losses in transmission etc	31,241	32,213
Electricity Consumption: total	340,409	343,427
Fuel industries	9,702	8,463
Final users: total	330,707	334,964
Industrial sector	114,915	113,589
Domestic sector	111,842	115,336
Other sectors	103,950	106,039

Source: The Stationery Office – *Annual Abstract of Statistics 2003* (Crown copyright)

REGULATION OF THE GAS AND ELECTRICITY INDUSTRIES

The Office of the Gas and Electricity Markets (Ofgem) regulates the gas and electricity industries in Great Britain. It was formed in 1999 by the merger of the Office of Gas Supply and the Office of Electricity Regulation. Ofgem's overriding aim is to protect and promote the interests of all gas and electricity customers by promoting competition and regulating monopolies. It is governed by an authority and its powers are provided for under the Gas Act 1986, the Electricity Act 1989 and the Utilities Act 2000.

NUCLEAR POWER

Nuclear reactors began to supply electricity to the national grid in 1956. It is generated at six magnox reactors, seven advanced gas-cooled reactors (AGRs) and one pressurised water reactor (PWR), Sizewell 'B' in Suffolk. In 1989 nuclear stations were withdrawn from privatisation. In 1996 Nuclear Electric Ltd and Scottish Nuclear Ltd became operating subsidiaries of British Energy and the magnox stations were transferred to Nuclear Electric which became Magnox Electric, later part of British Nuclear Fuels Ltd (BNFL). In September 2002 the Government stepped in to provide a loan facility to British Energy which was facing insolvency and a major financial restructuring package was announced in November 2002. In March 2003 British Energy received formal approvals for loan standstill agreements from its creditors and the Government agreed to extend the loan facility until September 2004.

The UK Atomic Energy Authority (UKAEA) is responsible for the decommissioning of nuclear reactors and other nuclear facilities used in research and development. UKAEA is a non-departmental public body, funded mainly by the Department of Trade and Industry. UK Nirex, which was set up by the nuclear generating companies with the agreement of the Government, is responsible for the disposal of intermediate and some low-level nuclear waste. The Nuclear Safety Directorate of the Health and Safety Executive is the nuclear industry's regulator.

ELECTRICITY AND GAS SUPPLIERS

With both the gas and electricity markets open, most suppliers now offer their customers both gas and electricity. The majority of gas/electricity companies have become part of larger multi-utility companies, often operating internationally. The following is a selection of some of the suppliers offering gas and electricity. Organisations in italics are subsidiaries of the companies listed directly above.

ATLANTIC ELECTRIC & GAS LTD, Regus House, Malthouse Avenue, Cardiff Gate Business Park, Cardiff CF23 8RU Tel: 0870 013 2080 Fax: 02920 263310 Web: atlanticeg.com

AQUILA NETWORKS, Whittington Hall, Whittington, Worcester WR5 2RB Tel: 08457-353637 Web: www.aquila-networks.co.uk

CENTRICA PLC, Millstream, Maidenhead Road, Windsor, Berkshire SL4 5GD Tel: 01753-494000

BRITISH GAS/SCOTTISH GAS, Tel: 0845-600 5001 Web: www.house.co.uk

INNOGY HOLDINGS, Windmill Hill Business Park, Whitehill Way, Swindon SN5 6PB Tel: 01793-877777 Fax: 01793-892525 Web: www.innogy.com

Npower, Oak House, Bridgewater Road, Warndon, Worcester WR4 9FP Tel: 01793 877 777 Web: www.npower.com

EDF ENERGY, Templar House, 81–87 High Holborn, London WC1V 6NU Tel: 020-7242 9050 Fax: 020-7242 2815 Web: www.edfenergy.com

Seeboard Energy, Forest Gate, Brighton Road, Crawley, RH11 9BH Tel: 01293 565 888 Fax: 01293 657 327 Web: www.seeboard.com

SWEB, Osprey Road, Exeter, EX2 7H7 Tel: 0800-365 000 Fax: 01392-448911 Web: www.sweb.co.uk

POWERGEN, Westwood Way, Westwood Business Park, Coventry CV4 8LG Tel: 024-7642 4000 Fax: 024-7642 5432 Web: www.pgen.com

East Midlands Electricity, Pegasus Business Park, East Midlands Airport, Derby DE74 2TU Tel: 0800-096 3080 Web: www.eme.co.uk

SCOTTISHPOWER PLC, 1 Atlantic Quay, Glasgow G2 8SP Tel: 0141-248 8200 Fax: 0141-248 8300 Web: www.scottishpower.com

SCOTTISH AND SOUTHERN ENERGY, 200 Dunkeld Road,
Perth PH1 3AQ Tel: 01738-456 000 Fax: 01738 456 520
Web: www.scottish-southern.co.uk
Scottish Hydro-Electric, 200 Dunkeld Road,
Perth PH1 3GH Tel: 0845-300 2141
Web: www.hydro.co.uk
Southern Electric, PO Box 6009,
Basingstoke RG21 8ZD Tel: 0845-7444 555
SWALEC, PO Box 6009, Basingstoke RG21 8ZD
Tel: 0800-052 5252 Web: www.swalec.co.uk
VIRGIN HOME, Freepost LON1 4908, Exeter, EX2 7BF
Tel: 0800-028 8269 Web: www.virginhome.co.uk
VIRIDIAN GROUP, Danesfort House, 120 Malone Road,
Belfast, BT9 5HT Tel: 028-9068 9448
Web: www.viridiangroup.co.uk
Northern Ireland Electricity, 120 Malone Road, Belfast BT9
5HT Tel: 028-9066 1100 Fax: 028-9066 3579
Web: www.nie.co.uk

RENEWABLE ENERGY SOURCES 2001

	Percentages
Biofuels and wastes	85.6
Landfill gas	27.0
Sewage gas	5.4
Wood combustion	15.1
Straw combustion	4.8
Waste combustion	21.5
Other biofuels	11.8
Hydro	11.3
Large-scale	10.7
Small-scale	0.6
Wind and wave	2.7
Geothermal and active solar heating	0.4
Total	100

Source: Department of Trade and Industry

RENEWABLE SOURCES

Renewable sources of energy principally include biofuels, hydro, wind and solar. Renewable sources accounted for 3.1 million tonnes of oil equivalent of primary energy use in 2001; of this, about 2.4 million tonnes was used to generate electricity and about 0.7 million tonnes to generate heat.

The Non-Fossil Fuel Obligation (NFFO) Renewables Orders have been the Government's principal mechanism for developing renewable energy sources. NFFO Renewables Orders require the regional electricity companies to buy specified amounts of electricity from specified non-fossil fuel sources.

In January 2000 the government announced a target for renewables to supply 10 per cent of UK electricity by 2010. A new renewables obligation was introduced in England and Wales in April 2002 to give incentives to generators to supply progressively higher levels of renewable energy over time. These measures included:
- The exemption of renewable electricity sources from the Climate Change Levy.
- The creation of a renewables support programme worth £250 million from 2002–5
- The creation of a strategic framework for a major expansion of offshore wind generation
- The formation of a new organisation within the Government (Renewables UK) to help the industry grow and compete internationally

In July 2003 the DTI announced that the world's biggest wind farms will be built in three sites off the English coast (the Thames Estuary, the Wash on the east coast and from Morecambe Bay to north Wales), providing enough power for one in six British homes.

TRANSPORT

CIVIL AVIATION

Since the privatisation of British Airways in 1987, UK airlines have been operated entirely by the private sector. In 2002, total capacity of British airlines amounted to 41 billion tonne-km, of which 31 billion tonne-km was on scheduled services. In 2002 British airlines carried 106.5 million passengers, 72.2 million on scheduled services and 34.3 million on charter flights. Following the 11 September terrorist attacks passenger traffic fell by 6 per cent (to December 2001). In 2002, traffic at the five main London airports grew by three per cent over 2001 and regional airlines saw a growth of four per cent in 2002, largely due to the expansion of no-frills airlines. The number of passengers is estimated to be growing at 5 per cent each year.

Leading British airlines include British Airways, Britannia Airways, BMI British Midland, Air 2000, My Travel, Thomas Cook Airlines, Monarch, Virgin Atlantic, and easyJet.

There are around 140 licensed civil aerodromes in Britain, with Heathrow and Gatwick handling the highest volume of passengers. BAA PLC owns and operates the seven major airports: Heathrow, Gatwick, Stansted, Southampton, Glasgow, Edinburgh and Aberdeen, which between them handle about 70 per cent of air passengers and a high percentage of air cargo traffic in Britain. Other airports are controlled by local authorities or private companies.

The Civil Aviation Authority (CAA), an independent statutory body, is responsible for the regulation of UK airlines. This includes economic and airspace regulation, air safety, consumer protection and environmental research and consultancy. All commercial airline companies must be granted an Air Operator's Certificate, which is issued by the CAA to operators meeting the required safety standards. The CAA issues airport safety licences, which must be obtained by any airport used for public transport and training flights. All British-registered aircraft must be granted an airworthiness certificate, and the CAA issues professional licences to pilots, flight crew, ground engineers and air traffic controllers. The CAA also manages the Air Travel Organiser's License (ATOL), the UK's principal travel protection scheme. The CAA's costs are met entirely from charges on those whom it regulates; there is no direct Government funding of the CAA's work.

The Transport Act, passed by parliament on 29 November 2000, separated the CAA from its subsidiary, National Air Traffic Services (NATS), which plans and provides air traffic control services throughout the United Kingdom, over the eastern part of the North Atlantic and at most of Britain's major airports. In 2003 NATS handled an estimated two million flights carrying over 160 million passengers. In March 2001, the Airline Group, a consortium of seven UK airlines (British Airways, BMI British Midland, Virgin Atlantic, Britannia, Monarch, easyJet and My Travel), was selected by the government as its strategic partner for NATS. The Airline Group plans to invest 1 billion of private capital in NATS over 10 years. In July 2001, under the terms of a Public Private Partnership, 46 per cent of shares in NATS were sold to the Airline Group, 5 per cent to staff and 49 per cent were retained by the government.

AIR PASSENGERS 2002*

ALL UK AIRPORTS: TOTAL	192,259,025
LONDON AREA AIRPORTS: TOTAL	117,138,199
Battersea Heliport	–
Gatwick (BAA)	29,627,420
Heathrow (BAA)	63,362,097
London City	1,602,335
Luton	6,486,770
Southend	5,055
Stansted (BAA)	16,054,522
OTHER UK AIRPORTS: TOTAL	72,677,161
Aberdeen (BAA)	2,550,477
Barra	8,294
Barrow-in-Furness	–
Belfast City	1,896,081
Belfast International	3,576,785
Benbecula (HIAL)†	31,560
Biggin Hill	1,144
Birmingham	8,027,730
Blackpool	70,385
Bournemouth	394,810
Bristol	3,445,945
Cambridge	1,277
Campbeltown (HIAL)†	8,356
Cardiff	1,425,436
Carlisle	62
Coventry	3,942
Dundee	45,400
East Midlands	3,236,592
Edinburgh (BAA)	6,930,649
Exeter	348,403
Glasgow (BAA)	7,803,627
Gloucestershire	195
Hawarden	1,912
Humberside	492,433
Inverness (HIAL)†	386,824
Islay (HIAL)†	20,728
Isle of Man	731,571
Kent International	52
Kirkwall (HIAL)†	106,271
Leeds/Bradford	1,530,019
Lerwick (Tingwall)	2,068
Liverpool	2,835,871
Londonderry	199,146
Lydd	3,088
Manchester	18,809,185
Newcastle upon Tyne	3,426,952
Norwich	423,968
Penzance Heliport	135,891
Plymouth	100,913
Prestwick	1,490,415
St Mary's, Isles of Scilly	148,346
Scatsta	246,187
Sheffield City	13,104
Shoreham	537
Southampton (BAA)	789,325
Stornoway (HIAL)†	94,283
Sumburgh (HIAL)†	133,899
Teesside	671,131
Tiree (HIAL)†	5,297
Tresco, Isles of Scilly (Heliport)	44,558
Unst	–
Wick (HIAL)†	26,037

CHANNEL IS. AIRPORTS: TOTAL	2,443,665
Alderney	72,861
Guernsey	882,814
Jersey	1,487,990

*Total terminal, transit, scheduled and charter passengers.
Passengers carried on air taxi services are excluded
†Highlands and Islands Airports Ltd (HIAL)
Source: Civil Aviation Authority

CAA, CAA House, 45–59 Kingsway, London, WC2B 6TE
Tel: 020-7379 7311 Web: www.caa.co.uk

BAA PLC, 130 Wilton Road, London, SW1V 1LQ
Tel: 020-7932 6654 Web: www.baa.co.uk
Heathrow Airport	0870-000 0123
Gatwick Airport	0870-000 2468
Stansted Airport	0870-000 0303
Glasgow Airport	0141-887 1111
Edinburgh Airport	0131-333 1000
Aberdeen Airport	01224-722331
Southampton Airport	023-8062 0021

BRITISH AIRWAYS, Waterside, PO Box 365,
Harmondsworth, UB7 0GB Web: www.britishairways.com
BRITANNIA AIRWAYS, Britannia House, London Luton
International Airport, Luton, Bedfordshire, LU2 9ND
Tel: 01582-424155 Web: www.britanniaairways.com
BMI BRITISH MIDLAND, Donington Hall, Castle Donington,
Derby, DE74 2SB Tel: 01332-854321 Web: www.flybmi.com
AIR 2000, Commonwealth House, Chicago Avenue,
Manchester Airport, M90 3DP Tel: 0870-757 2757
Web: www.air2000.com
MY TRAVEL, Parkway One, Parkway Business Centre,
300 Princess Road, Manchester, M14 7QU
Tel: 0870-238 7777 Web: www.mytravel.com
THOMAS COOK AIRLINES, Tel: 0870-750 0316
Web: www.thomascook.co.uk
MONARCH, Prospect House, Prospect Way, London Luton
Airport, LU2 9NR Tel: 01582-400000
Web: www.monarch-airlines.com
VIRGIN ATLANTIC, Manor Royal, Crawley, West Sussex
RH10 9NU Tel: 01293-747747
Web: www.virgin-atlantic.com
EASYJET, London Luton Airport, LU2 9LS Tel: 0871-750 0100
Web: www.easyjet.com

RAILWAYS

Britain pioneered railways and a railway network was developed across Britain by private companies in the 19th century. In 1948 the main railway companies were nationalised and were run by a public authority, the British Transport Commission. The Commission was replaced by the British Railways Board in 1963, operating as British Rail. On 1 April 1994, responsibility for managing the track and railway infrastructure passed to a newly-formed company, Railtrack plc. In October 2001 Railtrack was put into administration under the Railways Act 1993 and Ernst and Young was appointed as administrator. In October 2002 Railtrack was taken out of administration and replaced by the not-for-profit company Network Rail. The British Railways Board continued as operator of all train services until 1996–7 when they were sold or franchised to the private sector.

OTHER RAIL SYSTEMS
Plans for a public-private partnership (PPP) for London Underground were pushed through by the government in February 2002 despite opposition from the Mayor of London and a range of transport organisations. Under the PPP, long-term contracts with private companies estimate

to enable around £16 billion to be invested in renewing and upgrading the Underground's infrastructure over 15 years. Responsibility for stations, trains, operations, signalling and safety will remain in the public sector. In 2001–2 there were 953 million passenger journeys on the London Underground, down 2 per cent on the previous year.

Britain has seven other metro systems: in Birmingham, Glasgow, Newcastle, Manchester, Sheffield and the Croydon Tramlink and Docklands Light Railway in London. The latest to open was the Croydon Tramlink in May 2000.

Light rail and metro systems in Great Britain contributed to the growth in public transport, with 141 million passenger journeys in 2001–2, up five per cent on the previous year. The Government's 10-year Transport Plan target is to double light rail use in England by 2010. The Sunderland extension to Tyne and Wear Metro opened in March 2002, the Nottingham Express Transit (NET) opened in November 2003 and construction for the Leeds Supertram began in March 2003.

RAIL REGULATOR
Under the Railways Act 1993 and the Transport Act 2000 the Rail Regulator exercises statutory powers to regulate Network Rail, which owns the national rail network (track, signalling, bridges, tunnels and stations). The network is operated under a network licence, which is issued by the Government but enforced by the Regulator who is independent of the Government. The Regulator also ensures the network provider has the necessary funds to maintain, renew and expand the network, that all train operators are ensured fair access to the network and, under the Competition Act 1998, prevents anti-competitive practices.

Regulations, which took effect on 28 June 1998, established licensing and access arrangements for certain international train services in Great Britain; these are overseen by the International Rail Regulator.

The Strategic Rail Authority (SRA) was created to provide strategic leadership to the rail industry and formally came into being on 1 February 2001 following the passing of the Transport Act 2000. In January 2002 it published its first Strategic Plan, setting out the strategic priorities for Britain's railways over the next ten years. In addition to its co-ordinating role, the SRA is responsible for allocating Government funding to railways, awarding and monitoring the franchises for operating rail services, as well as a number of other statutory functions; particularly relating to customer protection. Many of the current passenger rail franchises are due to expire in 2004. In November 2002 the SRA issued a franchising policy statement specifying that new franchises should set service levels and quality standards and the private sector should be charged with delivering the standards set. The SRA envisages these new franchises will be for lengths of between five and eight years.

SERVICES
For privatisation, domestic passenger services were divided into 25 train-operating units, which were franchised to private sector operators via a competitive tendering process overseen by the Strategic Rail Authority (SRA). The franchise agreements were for between five and 15 years. The Government continues to subsidise loss-making but socially necessary rail services. The SRA is responsible for monitoring the performance of the franchisees, allocating and administering government subsidy payments, proposing closures to the Rail Regulator and designating experimental services.

There are currently 25 train operating companies (TOCs): Anglia; Arriva Trains Merseyside; Arriva Trains Northern; c2c; Central Trains; Chiltern; Connex South Eastern; First Great Eastern; First Great Western; First North Western Trains; Gatwick Express; Great North Eastern Railways; Island Line (Isle of Wight); Midland Mainline; ScotRail; Silverlink; South Central; South West Trains; Thameslink; Thames Trains; Virgin Crosscountry; Virgin West Coast; Wales and Borders; WAGN and Wessex Trains.

In addition, Eurostar and Eurotunnel provide services through the channel tunnel, but are not subject to the franchise process. The Heathrow Express service is a subsidiary of the airports group BAA.

Network Rail publishes a national timetable which contains details of rail services operated over the network, coastal shipping information and connections with Ireland, the Isle of Man, the Isle of Wight, the Channel Islands and some European destinations.

The national rail enquiries service offers information about train times and fares for any part of the country:

NATIONAL RAIL ENQUIRIES Tel: 08457-484950
 Web: www.nationalrail.co.uk
TRANSPORT FOR LONDON Tel: 020-7941 4500
 Web: www.transportforlondon.gov.uk
EUROSTAR Tel: 08705-186186
 Web: www.eurostar.com

Rail Users' Consultative Committees (RUCCs) were set up under the Railways Act 1993 to protect the interests of users of the services and facilities provided on Britain's rail network. The Transport Act 2000 changed their name to the Rail Passenger Committees (RPCs) and transferred sponsorship from the Rail Regulator to the SRA. There are eight RPCs nationwide, six for England and one each for Scotland and Wales. They are statutory bodies and have a legal right to make recommendations for changes. The London Transport Users' Committee represents users of buses, the Underground, Croydon Tramlink and the Docklands Light Railway as well as rail users' interests. In summer 2000 the Greater London Assembly and Mayor established Transport for London with a view to developing a strategy for transport in the capital.

On privatisation, British Rail's bulk freight haulage companies and Rail Express Systems, which carries Royal Mail traffic, were sold to English, Welsh and Scottish Railways (EWS), which also purchased Railfreight Distribution (international freight) in 1997. In 2001–2 94.4 billion-tonne-kilometres of freight was transported by EWS and other freight companies.

NETWORK RAIL, 40 Melton Street, London NW1 2EE
 Tel: 020-7557 8000 Web: www.networkrail.com
ASSOCIATION OF TRAIN OPERATING COMPANIES,
 40 Bernard Street, London WC1N 1BY.
 Tel: 020-7904 3010 Web: www.atoc.org
OFFICE OF THE RAIL REGULATOR (ORR),
 1 Waterhouse Square, 138–142 Holborn, London
 EC1N 2TQ. Tel: 020-7282 2000 Web: www.rail-reg.gov.uk
 Rail Regulator and International Rail Regulator, Tom
 Winsor
STRATEGIC RAIL AUTHORITY, 55 Victoria Street, London,
 SW1H 0EU. Tel: 020-7654 6000 Web: www.sra.gov.uk
 Chairman and Chief Executive, Richard Bowker

NETWORK RAIL
Network Rail is run as a commercial business but has members instead of shareholders. The members have similar rights to those of shareholders in a public company except they do not receive dividends or share

capital and thereby having no financial or economic interest in Network Rail. All of Network Rail's profits are reinvested into maintaining and upgrading the rail infrastructure.

Network Rail owns and maintains 21,000 miles of track, owns and provide access to 2,500 stations and operates and maintains more than 9,000 level crossings and 40,000 bridges and tunnels. In addition to providing the timetables for the passenger and freight operators Network Rail is responsible for all the signalling and electrical control equipment needed to operate the rail network.

RAIL SAFETY
The Railways (Safety Case) Regulations 2000 came into force on 31 December 2000 and transferred responsibility for safety cases from Railtrack to HM Railway Inspectorate, part of the Health and Safety Executive (HSE). The regulations demand that rail operators such as Network Rail, London Underground, the station and train operators must prepare a comprehensive safety case and have it accepted by HSE before being allowed to operate their business. The Office of the Rail Regulator (ORR) will not grant a licence to a railway operator without an accepted safety case or an exemption being in place.

Amendments to railway safety case regulations were announced in March 2003 and came into force on 1 April 2003. The requirement for infrastructure controllers to obtain an independent assessment of safety cases in addition to the Health and Safety Executive's acceptance was removed and the requirement to obtain annual independent health and safety audits of train and station operations was transferred from HSE to individual operators. These changes pave the way for the creation of the Rail Safety and Standards Board (RSSB), the new industry body charged with promoting health and safety.

ACCIDENTS ON RAILWAYS

	2000–1	2001–2
Train accidents: total	1,801	1,705
Persons killed: total	17	5
Passengers	10	0
Railway staff	4	0
Others	3	5
Persons injured: total	235	52
Passengers	178	21
Railway staff	42	23
Others	15	8
Other accidents through movement		
of railway vehicles		
Persons killed	17	21
Persons injured	949	909
Other accidents on railway premises		
Persons killed	5	6
Passengers	3	3
Railway staff	1	1
Others	1	2
Persons injured	4,130	3,906
Trespassers and suicides		
Persons killed	300	275
Persons injured	177	179

Source: Department for Transport

THE CHANNEL TUNNEL
The earliest recorded scheme for a submarine transport connection between Britain and France was in 1802. Tunnelling has begun simultaneously on both sides of the Channel three times: in 1881, in the early 1970s, and on 1 December 1987, when construction workers began to

bore the first of the three tunnels which form the Channel Tunnel. They 'holed through' the first tunnel (the service tunnel) on 1 December 1990 and tunnelling was completed in June 1991. The tunnel was officially inaugurated by The Queen and President Mitterrand of France on 6 May 1994.

The submarine link comprises three tunnels. There are two rail tunnels, each carrying trains in one direction, which measure 24.93 ft (7.6 m) in diameter. Between them lies a smaller service tunnel, measuring 15.75 ft (4.8 m) in diameter. The service tunnel is linked to the rail tunnels by 130 cross-passages for maintenance and safety purposes. The tunnels are 31 miles (50 km) long, 24 miles (38 km) of which is under the sea-bed at an average depth of 132 ft (40 m). The rail terminals are situated at Folkestone and Calais, and the tunnels go underground at Shakespeare Cliff, Dover, and Sangatte, west of Calais.

Eurostar is the high speed passenger train connecting London with Paris in three hours and Brussels in two hours 40 minutes, via the Channel Tunnel. There are up to 14 trains each way per day on the Paris route and eight each way per day on the Brussels route. Some trains stop en route at Ashford (Kent) and Avignon, Calais, Disneyland Paris and Lille in France. Vehicle shuttle services operate between Folkestone and Calais.

RAIL LINKS

The route for the British Channel Tunnel Rail Link will run from Folkestone to a new terminal at St Pancras station, London, with new intermediate stations at Ebbsfleet, Kent, and Stratford, east London; at present services run into a terminal at Waterloo station, London.

Construction of the rail link is being financed by the private sector with a substantial government contribution. A private sector consortium, London and Continental Railways Ltd (LCR), is responsible for the design, construction and ownership of the rail link, and comprises Union Railways and the UK operator of Eurostar. Construction was expected to be completed in 2003, but on 28 January 1998 LCR informed the Government that it was unable to fulfil its obligations. On 3 June 1998 the Government announced a new funding agreement with LCR. The rail link will be constructed in two phases: phase one, from the Channel Tunnel to Fawkham Junction (where an existing connection allows trains to continue to Waterloo), began in October 1998 and was to be completed in 2003; phase two, from Fawkham Junction to St Pancras, will be built between 2001 and 2007. Infrastructure developments in France have been completed and high-speed trains run from Calais to Paris and from Lille to the South of France.

The first phase of the Channel Tunnel high-speed link through Kent was due to open in October 2003 and the second stage through to St Pancras is due to open in 2007.

ROADS

HIGHWAY AUTHORITIES

The powers and responsibilities of highway authorities in England and Wales are set out in the Highways Act 1980; for Scotland there is separate legislation.

Responsibility for trunk road motorways and other trunk roads in Great Britain rests in England with the Secretary of State for Transport, in Scotland with the Scottish Executive, and in Wales with the Welsh Assembly. The costs of construction, improvement and maintenance are paid for by central government in England and by the Welsh Assembly in Wales. The highway authority for non-trunk roads in England, Wales and Scotland is, in general, the local authority in whose area the roads lie. With the establishment of the Greater London Authority in July 2000, Transport for London became the highway authority for roads in London.

In Northern Ireland the Department of Regional Development is the statutory road authority responsible for public roads and their maintenance and construction; the Roads Service executive agency carries out these functions on behalf of the Department.

FINANCE

In England all aspects of trunk road and motorway funding are provided directly by the Government to the Highways Agency which operates, maintains and improves around 6,400 miles of motorways and trunk roads on behalf of the Secretary of State. For the financial year 2003–4 the Highways Agency was allocated £1,760 million of which £705 million was for maintenance, £755 million for major new roads including private finance payments and £300 million on smaller improvements and traffic management measures.

Central Government support for local authority capital expenditure on roads and other transport infrastructure is provided through grant and credit approvals as part of the Local Transport Plan (LTP). Local Authorities bid for resources on the basis of a five-year programme built around delivering integrated transport strategies. As well as covering the structural maintenance of local roads and the construction of major new road schemes, LTP funding also includes smaller-scale safety and traffic management measures with associated improvements for public transport, cyclists and pedestrians.

For the financial year 2002–3 local authorities received a total of £55 million in the form of a Transport Supplementary Grant and an estimated £1,350 million in supplementary credit approvals including annual capital guidelines. The costs of repayment and interest on the borrowing are funded through the Revenue Support Grant Settlement (RSG).

Support for the routine maintenance of local roads is also provided through the RSG system. For 2002–3 the amount identified for local highway maintenance by Central Government was £1,955 million (£1,905 million in 2001–2). However, RSG is a general, unhypothecated grant and local authorities set their own spending priorities.

Total expenditure by central Government in Wales on trunk roads, motorways and transport services including grants to local authorities and credit approval in 2001–2 was £216.6 million. Forecast expenditure for 2003–4 was £260.4 million.

Until 1999 the Scottish Office received a block vote from Parliament and the Secretary of State for Scotland determined how much was spent on roads. Since 1 July 1999 all decisions on transport expenditure have been devolved to the Scottish Executive. The estimated total expenditure on motorways and trunk road in Scotland during 2002–3 was £788 million based on the Annual Expenditure Report of the Scottish Executive, this includes the cost of capital and depreciation charges.

In Northern Ireland estimated expenditure on roads for 2002–3 was £213.2 million and £223.3 million has been allocated for expenditure in 2003–4.

The Transport Act 2000 gave Welsh and English local authorities (outside London) powers to introduce road user charging or workplace parking levy schemes. The Act requires that the net revenue raised is used to improve local transport services and facilities for at least ten years. The aim is to reduce congestion and encourage greater use of alternative modes of transport. Schemes developed by local authorities require Government approval. The Government's Ten Year Plan for Transport assumes that 8 large road user charging and 12 large workplace parking levy schemes will be developed by 2010. Charging schemes in London are allowed under the 1999 Greater London Authority Act. The Central London Congestion Charge Scheme began on 17 February 2003.

TARGETED PROGRAMME OF IMPROVEMENTS (TPI)

The 1998 Roads Review increased the emphasis given to making better use of the existing road network and improving road maintenance. In addition a carefully targeted programme of major trunk road improvements was announced which initially consisted of 37 schemes. The current programme contains 75 schemes, funded conventionally or through public-private partnerships, with a total value of around £3.2 billion. One of the most significant schemes to open in 2002–3 was the Silverstone bypass, part of a major improvement for the A43. A series of 22 studies were announced in March 1999 to look at transport problems across all modes. Road schemes that emerge from these studies will be progressed through the regional planning guidance (RPG) system. This is now the method by which trunk road schemes will enter the TPI. As at the beginning of April 2003 19 studies the government had issued final reports. Based on these studies the government announced a major national road expansion programme on 10 July 2003.

ROAD LENGTHS (in miles) *2002*

	Total roads	Trunk roads (including Motorways)	Motorways*
England†	177,420	6,598	1,804
Wales	21,128	1,068	83
Scotland†	33,121	2,024	229
N. Ireland	15,380	760	83

*There were in addition 26.1 miles of local authority motorways in England
† 2001 lengths

MOTORWAYS

ENGLAND AND WALES

M1	London to Yorkshire
M2	London to Faversham
M3	London to Southampton
M4	London to South Wales
M5	Birmingham to Exeter
M6	Catthorpe to Carlisle
M10	St Albans spur
M11	London to Cambridge
M18	Rotherham to Goole
M20	London to Folkestone
M23	London to Gatwick
M25	London orbital
M26	M20 to M25 spur
M27	Southampton bypass
M32	M4 to Bristol spur
M40	London to Birmingham
M42	South-west of Birmingham to Measham
M45	Dunchurch spur
M48	M4 to South Wales
M49	M4 to M5
M50	Ross spur
M53	Chester to Birkenhead
M54	M6 to Telford
M55	Preston to Blackpool
M56	Manchester to Chester
M57	Liverpool outer ring
M58	Liverpool to Wigan
M60	Manchester ring road
M61	Manchester to Preston
M62	Liverpool to Hull
M65	Calder Valley
M66	Manchester Whitefield to Ramsbottom
M67	Manchester Hyde to Denton
M69	Coventry to Leicester
M180	South Humberside
M271	West of Southampton
M275	M27 to Portsmouth
M606	M62 to Bradford
M621	M1 to M62

SCOTLAND

M8	Edinburgh-Newhouse (Glasgow)
M9	Edinburgh to Dunblane and M9 Spur to A8000
M73	Jn. 4 of M74 to A80 (Mollinsburn)
M74	Glasgow-Gretna
M77	Jn. 22 of M8 to Malletsheugh (Ayr Road)
M80	Jn. 9 of M9 (Stirling) to Jn. 4 of M80/A80 (Haggs) and M80 Stepps Bypass
M90	Forth Bridge Road/Inverkeithing to Perth
M876	Kincardine Bridge to Jn. 5 of M80
M898	Jn. 30 of M8 to Erskine Bridge
A823(M)	Jn. 2 of M90 to A823 (Dunfermline)

NORTHERN IRELAND

M1	Belfast to Dungannon
M2	Belfast to Antrim
M2	Ballymena bypass
M3	Belfast Cross Harbour Bridge
M5	M2 to Greencastle
M12	M1 to Craigavon
M22	Antrim to Randalstown

ROAD USE

ESTIMATED TRAFFIC ON ALL ROADS (GREAT BRITAIN) 2001

Million vehicle kilometres	
All motor vehicles	473,700
Cars and taxis	383,700
Two-wheeled motor vehicles	4,800
Buses and coaches	4,900
Light vans	51,100
Other goods vehicles	29,200
Total goods vehicles	80,300
Pedal cycles	4,000

ROAD GOODS TRANSPORT (GREAT BRITAIN) 2002

Analysis by mode of working and by gross weight of vehicle

Estimated tonne kilometres (thousand million)	149.8
Own account	39.2
Public haulage	110.6

By gross weight of vehicle (billion tonne kilometres)

Estimated tonnes lifted (millions)	1,627
Own account	608
Public haulage	1,019

By gross weight of vehicle (million tonnes)

Not over 25 tonnes	283
Over 25 tonnes	1,343

BUSES

Nearly all bus and coach services in Great Britain are provided by private sector companies. The Transport Act 2000 outlines a 10-year transport plan intended to promote bus use, through agreements between local authorities and bus operators and to improve the standard and efficiency of services. The 10-year plan sets targets for bus patronage and reliability of services. There are a number of ways in which the Government supports bus services:

– Bus Service Operators Grant (BSOG) is paid directly to bus operators according to how much fuel they use and refunds around 80 percent of the duty paid on that fuel

- Local authorities outside London have a duty to secure socially necessary bus services not provided commercially. Services are tendered and let to commercial operators in return for payment from the local authority
- Rural Bus subsidy grant is currently paid to 73 local authorities
- Urban Bus Challenge aims to improve transport in deprived urban areas and awarded £18 million to 34 projects in 2002

Since June 2001 it has been a statutory minimum requirement for all local authorities to provide at least half fares and a free bus pass to pensioners and disabled people in the area. Local authorities recompense operators for the reduced fare revenue.

In London, Transport for London (TfL) has overall responsibility for setting routes, service standards and fares for the bus network. Almost all routes are competitively tendered to commercial operators. The amount of GLA transport grant allocated to London Buses to bridge the gap between farebox income and the cost of providing the service in 2001–2 was around £200 million, this is budgeted to rise to £300 million in 2002–3. London also benefits from a share of the funding schemes listed above.

In Northern Ireland, passenger transport services are provided by Ulsterbus Limited and Citybus Limited, two wholly owned subsidiaries of the Northern Ireland Transport Holding Company. Along with Northern Ireland Railways, Ulsterbus and Citybus operate under the brand name of Translink and are publicly owned. Ulsterbus is responsible for virtually all bus services in Northern Ireland except Belfast city services which are operated by Citybus.

BUSES AND COACHES (GREAT BRITAIN) 2000–1

Vehicle kilometres (millions)	4,145
Passenger journeys (millions)	4,309
Passenger receipts (£ million)	4,420

Source: Department for Transport .

TAXIS

A taxi is a public transport vehicle with fewer than nine passenger seats, which is licensed to 'ply for hire'. This distinguishes taxis from private hire vehicles which must be booked in advance through an operator.

In London, taxis and their drivers are licensed by The Public Carriage Office (PCO) which is part of Transport for London (TfL). At the end of December 2001 there were 59,682 licensed taxis in England, of which 20,500 were in London. In Wales 3,381 taxis were licensed at the end of 2001. In Scotland 9,343 taxis were licensed in 2001.

AVERAGE TAXI FARE FOR A FOUR-MILE JOURNEY BY REGION 2002

Region	Fare in £
London (Transport for London)	9.10
North East	5.64
North West	5.96
Yorkshire & the Humber	5.85
East Midlands	6.09
West Midlands	6.14
East	6.58
South East	6.87
South West	7.14
Wales	6.07

ROAD SAFETY

In March 2000, the Government published a new road safety strategy, *Tomorrow's Roads – Safer for Everyone*, which set new casualty reduction targets for 2010. The new targets include a 40 per cent reduction in the overall number of people killed or seriously injured in road accidents, a 50 per cent reduction in the number of children killed or seriously injured and a 10 per cent reduction in the slight casualty rate, all compared with the average for 1994–8.

There were 302,605 casualties on roads in Great Britain in 2002, 3 per cent less than in 2001. Road traffic levels were 3 per cent higher, but the casualty rate per 100 million vehicle kilometres was six per cent lower. Child casualties fell by nine per cent with 179 child fatalities, 18 per cent less than in 2001. Car user casualties decreased by 3 per cent on the 2001 level to 197,425, although fatalities were only marginally lower. Pedestrian casualties were 38,784 in 2002, 4 per cent less than 2001 and pedal cyclist casualties fell by 11 per cent to 17,107.

ROAD ACCIDENT CASUALTIES 2002

	Fatal	Serious	Slight	All Severities
England	2,980	31,287	234,764	269,031
Wales	147	1,485	12,704	14,336
Scotland	304	3,204	15,730	19,238
Great Britain	3,431	35,976	263,198	302,605

	Killed	Injured
1965	7,952	389,985
1970	7,499	355,869
1975	6,366	318,584
1980	6,010	323,000
1985	5,165	312,359
1990	5,217	335,924
1995	3,621	306,885
1996	3,598	316,704
1997	3,599	323,945
1998	3,421	321,791
1999	3,423	316,887
2000	3,409	316,872
2001	3,450	313,309
2002	3,431	302,605

Source: Department for Transport

DRIVING LICENCES

It is necessary to hold a valid full licence in order to drive unaccompanied on public roads in the UK. Learner drivers must obtain a provisional driving licence before starting to learn to drive and must then pass theory and practical tests to obtain a full driving licence.

There are separate tests for driving motor cycles, cars, passenger-carrying vehicles (PCVs) and large goods vehicles (LGVs). Drivers must hold full car entitlement before they can apply for PCV or LGV entitlements.

The Driver and Vehicle Licensing Agency (DVLA) no longer issues paper licences, however, those currently in circulation will remain valid until they expire or the details on them change. The photocard driving licence was introduced to comply with the second EC directive on driving licences. This requires a photograph of the driver to be included on all UK licences issued from July 2001. In March 2000 the DVLA ceased issuing paper licences. To apply for a first photocard driving licence, individuals are required to complete the forms *Application for a Driving Licence* (D1) and *Application for a Photocard Driving Licence* (D750). Application forms are available from post offices.

The minimum age for driving motor cars, light goods vehicles up to 3.5 tonnes and motor cycles is 17 (moped, 16). Since June 1997, drivers who collect six or more penalty points within two years of qualifying lose their licence and are required to take another test. A leaflet, *What You Need to Know About Driving Licences* (form D100), is available from post offices.

The DVLA is responsible for issuing driving licences, registering and licensing vehicles, and collecting excise duty in Great Britain. In Northern Ireland the Driver and Vehicle Licensing Agency (Northern Ireland) has similar responsibilities.

DRIVING LICENCE FEES *as at 1 April 2003*

First provisional licence	£29.00
Changing a provisional to a full licence after passing a driving test (includes car, motorcycle, medium/large vehicle, minibus/bus)	£12.00
Duplicate (if lost, stolen or defaced)	£17.00
Replacement (change of name and/or address)	Free
Exchange (including adding or removing entitlements/test passes and removing expired endorsements)	£18.00
After revocation under the New Drivers Act	£29.00
Renewal	
Car licence (at age 70 and over)	£6.00
Full licence (medium/large vehicle, minibus/bus)	£29.00
Provisional (medium/large vehicle, minibus/bus)	£29.00
For medical reasons	Free
Exchanging licences from other countries	
Full Northern Ireland car licence	£18.00
Full Northern Ireland for medium/large vehicle, minibus/bus	£29.00
Full EC/EEA or other foreign licence	£29.00
New full licence after disqualification	£35.00
New full licence after disqualification for some drink driving offences	£50.00

DRIVING TESTS

The Driving Standards Agency is responsible for carrying out driving tests and approving driving instructors in Great Britain. In Northern Ireland the Driver and Vehicle Testing Agency (Northern Ireland) is responsible for testing drivers and vehicles.

DRIVING TESTS TAKEN/PERCENTAGE PASSED
April 2002–March 2003

Type of Test	Number Taken	Percentage Passed
Practical Tests		
Car	1,317,608	43.21%
Motorcycle	84,039	64.68%
Large goods vehicle	61,566	49.50%
Passenger carrying vehicle	10,851	44.00%
Theory Tests		
Car	1,275,723	61.62%
Motorcycle	87,548	80.42%
Large goods vehicle	38,392	72.77%
Passenger carrying vehicle	9,043	72.48%

The theory and practical driving tests can be booked by postal application, online at www.dsa.gov.uk or by telephoning 0870-010 1372.

DRIVING TEST FEES (weekday rate/evening and Saturday rate) *since November 2002**

For cars	£39.00/48.00
For motor cycles	£48.00/£57.00
For lorries, buses	£76.00/£94.00
Extended Test for cars (after disqualification)	£78.00/£96.00
Extended Test for motorcycles (after disqualification)	£96.00/£114.00
Motorcycle Compulsory Basic Training (CBT) Certificate	£8.00
Theory Test for all categories	£20.50

* Correct at the time of going to press. Figures were due to be revised November 2003 – *see* DSA website for further information: www.dsa.gov.uk

MOTOR VEHICLES

Vehicles must be licensed by the DVLA or the DVLNI before they can be driven on public roads. They must also be approved as roadworthy by the Vehicle Certification Agency. The Vehicle Inspectorate carries out annual testing and inspection of goods vehicles, buses and coaches.

There were 30,557 thousand vehicles licensed at the DVLA at the end of 2002.

MOTOR VEHICLES LICENSED BY BODY TYPE 2002
Thousands

Cars	25,782
Taxis (black cabs only)	39
Motor cycles	1,070
Three Wheelers	21
Light goods vehicles	2,343
Goods vehicles	625
Buses and coaches	173
Agricultural vehicles	292
Other vehicles	213
Total	30,557

Source: Department for Transport: *Vehicle Licensing Statistics 2002.*

VEHICLE LICENCES

Registration and first licensing of vehicles is through local offices of the Driver and Vehicle Licensing Agency in Swansea. Local facilities for relicensing are available at any post office which deals with vehicle licensing. Applicants will need to take their vehicle registration document; if this is not available the applicant must complete form V62 which is held at post offices. Postal applications can be made to the post offices shown in the V100 booklet, available at any post office. This V100 also provides guidance on registering and licensing vehicles.

Details of the present duties chargeable on motor vehicles are available at post offices and Local Offices. The Vehicle Excise and Registration Act 1994 provides *inter alia* that any vehicle kept on a public road but not used on roads is chargeable to excise duty as if it were in use. All non-commercial vehicles constructed before 1 January 1973 are exempt from vehicle excise duty.

VEHICLE EXCISE DUTY RATES *from 1 May 2003*
REGISTERED BEFORE 1 MARCH 2001

	Twelve Months £	Six Months £		Twelve Months £	Six Months £
Motor Cars			*Tricycles*		
Light vans, cars, taxis, etc.			Not over 150 cc	15.00	–
Under 1549cc	110.00	60.50	All Others	60.00	33.00
Over 1549cc	165.00	90.75	*Buses**		
Motor Cycles (With or without			Seating 9–16 persons	165.00 (165.00)	90.75 (90.75)
sidecar)			Seating 17–35 persons	220.00 (165.00)	121.00 (90.75)
Not over 150 cc	15.00	–	Seating 36–60 persons	330.00 (165.00)	181.50 (90.75)
151-400 cc	30.00	–	Seating over 61 persons	500.00 (165.00)	275.00 (90.75)
401-600 cc	45.00	–	* Figures in parentheses refer to reduced pollution vehicles.		
All other motorcycles	60.00	33.00			

REGISTERED ON OR AFTER 1 MARCH 2001

Band	CO_2 Emissions (g/km)	Diesel Car 12 month rate £	6 month rate £	Petrol Car 12 month rate £	6 month rate £	Alternative Fuel Car 12 month rate £	6 month rate £
AAA	Up to 100	75.00	41.25	65.00	35.75	55.00	30.25
AA	101-120	85.00	46.75	75.00	41.25	65.00	35.75
A	121-150	115.00	63.25	105.00	57.75	95.00	52.25
B	151-165	135.00	74.25	125.00	68.75	115.00	63.25
C	166-185	155.00	85.25	145.00	79.75	135.00	74.25
D	Over 185	165.00	90.75	160.00	88.00	155.00	85.25

MOT TESTING

Cars, motor cycles, motor caravans, light goods and dual-purpose vehicles more than three years old must be covered by a current MoT test certificate. However, some vehicles i.e. minibuses may require a certificate at one year old. All certificates must be renewed annually. The MoT testing scheme is administered by the Vehicle Operator Services Agency (VOSA) on behalf of the Secretary of State for Transport.

A fee is payable to MoT testing stations, which must be authorised to carry out tests. The maximum fees, which are prescribed by regulations, are:

For cars and light vans	£39.25	
For solo motor cycles	£14.65	
For motor cycle combinations	£24.05	
For three-wheeled vehicles	£28.15	
Motor caravans	£39.25	
Dual purpose vehicles	£39.25	
Public service vehicles		
(up to 8 seats)	£39.25	
Ambulances and Taxis	£39.25	
Private passenger vehicles and		
ambulances		
With 9-12 passenger seats	£41.10	£46.20*
13-16 passenger seats	£44.45	£60.20*
Over 16 passenger seats	£60.35	£93.30
For light goods vehicles		
between 3,000 and 3,500 kg	£43.15	

*Including seatbelt installation check

METHOD OF TRAVEL TO WORK, *Great Britain*
(percentage)*

	1997	2002
Car, van, minibus, works van	71	70
Bus, coach, private bus	8	8
Train (incl. Underground and light rail)	6	7
Walk	11	11
Other	5	5
All	100	100

* All figures are rounded
Source: DfT/The Stationery Office – *Transport Statistics Great Britain* (Crown copyright)

SHIPPING AND PORTS

Since earliest times sea trade has played a central role in Britain's economy. By the 17th-century Britain had built up a substantial merchant fleet and by the early 20th century it dominated the world shipping industry. Until the late 1990s the size and tonnage of the UK-registered trading fleet had been steadily declining. In December 1998 the Government published, *British Shipping: Charting a New Course*, which outlined strategies to promote the long-term interests of British shipping. By the end of 2002 the number of ships in the UK fleet had increased by almost a third whilst tonnage more than doubled; and the UK-flagged merchant fleet now constitutes over 1 per cent of the world fleet. Freight is carried by liner and bulk services, almost all scheduled liner services being containerised. About 95 per cent by weight of Britain's overseas trade is carried by sea; this amounts to 75 per cent of its total value. Passengers and vehicles are carried by roll-on, roll-off ferries, hovercraft, hydrofoils and high-speed catamarans. There were about 49 million ferry passengers a year in 2001, of whom 28 million travelled internationally. The leading British operators of passenger services are P&O Ferries and Stena Line (which has a Swedish parent company). Lloyd's of London provides the most comprehensive shipping intelligence service in the world. *Lloyd's Shipping Index*, published daily, lists some 25,000 ocean-going vessels and gives the latest known report of each.

PORTS

There are about 100 commercially significant ports in Great Britain, including such ports as London, Dover, Forth, Tees and Hartlepool, Grimsby and Immingham, Sullom Voe, Milford Haven, Southampton, Felixstowe and Liverpool. Belfast is the principal freight port in Northern Ireland.

Broadly speaking, ports are owned and operated by private companies, local authorities or trusts. The largest operator is Associated British Ports which owns 21 ports. Total traffic through UK ports in 2001 amounted to 566 million tonnes, a decrease of 1 per cent on the previous year's figure of 573 million tonnes.

MARINE SAFETY

From 1 October 2002 all roll-on, roll-off ferries operating to and from the UK are required to meet the new international safety standards on stability established by the Stockholm Agreement.

The Maritime and Coastguard Agency (MCA) was established on 1 April 1998 by the merger of the Coastguard Agency and the Marine Safety Agency. It is an executive agency of the Department for Transport. The Agency's aims are to minimise loss of life amongst seafarers and coastal users, respond to maritime emergencies, develop, promote and enforce high standards of marine safety and to minimise the risk of pollution of the marine environment from shipping activities. HM Coastguard co-ordinates all civil maritime Search and Rescue around the UK and over a large part of the eastern Atlantic. There are about 560 full-time Coastguard Officers and a further 3,100 Auxiliary Coastguards. Each year HM Coastguard responds to around 12,000 incidents of which 6,500 are accidents to which search and rescue resources are deployed.

Locations hazardous to shipping in coastal waters are marked by lighthouses and other lights and buoys. The lighthouse authorities are the Corporation of Trinity House (for England, Wales and the Channel Islands), the Northern Lighthouse Board (for Scotland and the Isle of Man), and the Commissioners of Irish Lights (for Northern Ireland and the Republic of Ireland). Trinity House maintains 72 lighthouses, 13 major floating aids to navigation and more than 429 buoys, the Northern Lighthouse Board maintains 201 lighthouses and 131 buoys; and Irish Lights 80 lighthouses and 146 buoys.

Harbour authorities are responsible for pilotage within their harbour areas; and the Ports Act 1991 provides for the transfer of lights and buoys to harbour authorities where these are used for mainly local navigation.

UK-OWNED TRADING VESSELS

OF 500 GROSS TONS AND OVER *as at end 2001*

Type of vessel	No.	Gross tonnage
Tankers	114	2,579,000
Bulk carriers	38	1,845,000
Specialised carriers	10	100,000
Fully cellular Container	77	2,525,000
Ro-Ro (passenger & cargo)	103	1,355,000
Other general cargo	116	409,000
Passenger	18	636,000
TOTAL	476	9,449,000

Source: Lloyd's Register of Shipping

UK INTERNATIONAL PASSENGER MOVEMENTS BY SEA 2001

Arrivals plus departures[*]

All passenger movements[†]	28,250,000
Irish Republic, European continent and Mediterranean Sea area	27,754,000
Rest of the World	27,000
Pleasure Cruises[†]	470,000

[*]Passengers are included at both departure and arrival if their journeys begin and end at a UK seaport

[†]provisional figures
Source: Department for Transport

RELIGION IN THE UK

The 2001 census included a voluntary question on religion for the first time (although the question had been included in previous censuses in Northern Ireland); 92 per cent of people chose to answer the question. In the UK, 71.6 per cent of people in Britain identified themselves as Christian (42.1 million people). After Christianity, the next most prevalent faith was Islam with 2.7 per cent describing their religion as Muslim (1.6 million people). The next largest religious groups were Hindus (559,000), followed by Sikhs (336,000), Jews (267,000), Buddhists (152,000) and people from Other religions (179,000). Together, these groups accounted for less than 3 per cent of the total UK population. People in Northern Ireland were most likely to say that they identified with a religion (86 per cent) compared with 77 per cent in England and Wales and 67 per cent in Scotland. About 16 per cent of the UK population stated that they had no religion. This category included those who identified themselves as agnostics, atheists, heathens and Jedi Knights.

CENSUS 2001 RESULTS – RELIGIONS IN THE UK
(thousands)

Christian	42,079	71.6%
Buddhist	152	0.3%
Hindu	559	1.0%
Jewish	267	0.5%
Muslim	1,591	2.7%
Sikh	336	0.6%
Other religion	179	0.3%
All religions	45,163	76.8%
No religion	9,104	15.5%
Not stated	4,289	7.3%
All no religion/not stated	13,626	23.2%
Total	58,789	100%

Source: Census 2001

ADHERENTS TO RELIGIONS IN THE UK *(millions)*

	1975	1985	1995	2000
Christian (Trinitarian)	40.2	39.1	38.1	37.5
Non-Trinitarian	0.7	1.0	1.3	1.3
Hindu	0.3	0.4	0.4	0.5
Jew	0.4	0.3	0.3	0.3
Muslim	0.4	0.9	1.2	1.4
Sikh	0.2	0.3	0.6	0.6
Other	0.1	0.3	0.3	0.4
Total	42.3	42.3	42.2	42.0

Source: Christian Research – *UK Christian Handbook Religious Trends No. 3 2002–3*

INTER-CHURCH AND INTER-FAITH CO-OPERATION

The main umbrella body for the Christian churches in the UK is the Churches Together in Britain and Ireland. There are also ecumenical bodies in each of the constituent countries of the UK: Churches Together in England, Action of Churches Together in Scotland, CYTÛN (Churches Together in Wales), and the Irish Council of Churches. The Free Churches' Council comprises most of the Free Churches in England and Wales, and the Evangelical Alliance represents evangelical Christians.

The Inter Faith Network for the United Kingdom promotes co-operation between faiths, and the Council of Christians and Jews works to improve relations between the two religions. Churches Together in Britain and Ireland also has a Commission on Inter-Faith Relations.

ACTION OF CHURCHES TOGETHER IN SCOTLAND, Scottish Churches House, Kirk Street, Dunblane, Perthshire FK15 0AJ Tel: 01786-823588 Fax: 01786-825844 Email: ecumenical@acts-scotland.org Web: www.acts-scotland.org. *General Secretary,* Revd Dr Kevin Franz

CHURCHES TOGETHER IN BRITAIN AND IRELAND, Inter-Church House, 35–41 Lower Marsh, London SE1 7SA Tel: 020-7523 2121 Fax: 020-7928 0010 Email: info@ctbi.org.uk Web: www.ctbi.org.uk *General Secretary,* Dr D. Goodbourn

CHURCHES TOGETHER IN ENGLAND, 27 Tavistock Square, London WC1H 9HH Tel: 020-7529 8141 Fax: 020-7529 8134 Web: www.churches-together.org.uk *General Secretary,* The Revd Bill Snelson

COUNCIL OF CHRISTIANS AND JEWS, Camelford House, 87–89 Albert Embankment, London SE1 7TP Tel: 020-7820 0090 Fax: 020-7820 0504 Email: cjrelations@ccj.org.uk Web: www.ccj.org.uk *Director,* Sr M. Shepherd, NDS

CYTÛN (CHURCHES TOGETHER IN WALES) - Tŷ John Penri, 11 St Helen's Road, Swansea SA1 4AL Tel: 01792-460876. Web: www.cytun.org.uk

EVANGELICAL ALLIANCE, Whitefield House, 186 Kennington Park Road, London SE11 4BT Tel: 020-7207 2100 Fax: 020-7207 2150 Email: london@eauk.org Web: www.eauk.org *General Director,* Revd J. Edwards

INTER FAITH NETWORK FOR THE UNITED KINGDOM, 8A Lower Grosvenor Place, London SW1W 0EN Tel: 020-7931 7766 Fax: 020-7931 7722 Email: ifnet.uk@interfaith.org.uk Web: www.interfaith.org.uk *Director,* Brian Pearce, OBE

IRISH COUNCIL OF CHURCHES, Inter-Church Centre, 48 Elmwood Avenue, Belfast BT9 6AZ Tel: 028-9066 3145 Fax: 028-9066 4160 Email: icpep@email.com Web: www.irishchurches.org *General Secretary,* Dr R. D. Stevens

CHRISTIANITY

Christianity is a monotheistic faith based on the person and teachings of Jesus Christ and all Christian denominations claim his authority. Central to its teaching is the concept of God and his son Jesus Christ, who was crucified and resurrected in order to enable mankind to attain salvation.

The Jewish scriptures predicted the coming of a *Messiah,* an 'anointed one', who would bring salvation. To Christians, Jesus of Nazareth, a Jewish rabbi (teacher), who was born in Palestine, was the promised Messiah. Jesus' birth, teachings, crucifixion and subsequent resurrection are recorded in the *Gospels,* which, together with other scriptures that summarise Christian belief, form the *New Testament.* This, together with the Hebrew scriptures, entitled the *Old Testament* by Christians, makes up the *Bible,* the sacred texts of Christianity.

BELIEFS
Christians believe that sin distanced mankind from God, and that Jesus was the Son of God, sent to redeem mankind from that sin by his death. In addition, many believe that Jesus will return again at some future date, triumph over evil and establish a kingdom on earth, thus inaugurating a new age. The Gospel assures Christians that those who believe in Jesus and obey his teachings will be forgiven their sins and will be resurrected from the dead.

PRACTICES
Christian practices vary widely between different Christian churches, but prayer is universal to all, as is charity, giving for the maintenance of the church buildings, for the work of the church, and to the poor and needy. In addition, certain days of observance, i.e. the *Sabbath, Easter* and *Christmas,* are celebrated by most Christians. The Orthodox, Roman Catholic and Anglican churches celebrate many more days of observance, based on saints and significant events in the life of Jesus. The belief in sacraments, physical signs believed to have been ordained by Jesus Christ to symbolise and convey spiritual gifts, varies greatly between Christian denominations; *Baptism* and the *Eucharist* are practised by most Christians. Baptism, symbolising repentance and faith in Jesus is an act marking entry into the Christian community; the Eucharist, the ritual re-enactment of the Last Supper, Jesus' final meal with his disciples, is also practised by most denominations. Other sacraments, such as anointing the sick, the laying on of hands to symbolise the passing on of the office of priesthood or to heal the sick and speaking in tongues, where it is believed that the person is possessed by the Holy Spirit, the Spirit of God, are less common. In denominations where infant baptism is practised, confirmation is common, where the person repeats the commitments made for him or her at infancy. Matrimony and the ordination of priests are also widely believed to be sacraments. Many Protestants only view baptism and the Eucharist as sacraments; the Quakers and the Salvation Army reject the use of sacraments.

Most Christians believe that God actively guides the Church.

THE EARLY CHURCH
The apostles were Jesus' first converts and are recognised by Christians as the founders of the Christian community. The new faith spread rapidly throughout the eastern provinces of the Roman Empire. Early Christianity was subject to great persecution until 313 AD, when Emperor Constantine's Edict of Toleration confirmed its right to exist and it became established as the religion of the Roman Empire in 381 AD.

The Christian faith was slowly formulated in the first millennium of the Christian era. Between AD 325 and 787 there were seven Oecumenical Councils at which bishops from the entire Christian world assembled to resolve various doctrinal disputes. The estrangement between East and West began after Constantine moved the centre of the Roman Empire from Rome to Constantinople, and it grew after the division of the Roman Empire into eastern and western halves. Linguistic and cultural differences between Greek East and Latin West served to encourage separate ecclesiastical developments which became pronounced in the tenth and early 11th centuries.

Administration of the church was divided between five ancient patriarchates: Rome and all the West, Constantinople (the imperial city – the 'New Rome'),

Jerusalem and all Palestine, Antioch and all the East, and Alexandria and all Africa. Of these, only Rome was in the Latin West and after the schism in 1054, Rome developed a structure of authority centralised on the Papacy, while the Orthodox East maintained the style of localised administration.

Papal authority over the doctrine and jurisdiction of the Church in western Europe was unrivalled after the split with the Eastern Orthodox Church until the Protestant Reformation in the 16th century.

CHRISTIANITY IN BRITAIN
An English Church already existed when Pope Gregory sent Augustine to evangelise the English in AD 596. Conflicts between Church and State during the Middle Ages culminated in the Act of Supremacy in 1534, which repudiated papal supremacy and declared King Henry VIII to be the supreme head of the Church in England. Since 1559 the English monarch has been termed the Supreme Governor of the Church of England.

In 1560 the jurisdiction of the Roman Catholic Church in Scotland was abolished and the first assembly of the Church of Scotland ratified the Confession of Faith, drawn up by a committee including John Knox. In 1592 Parliament passed an Act guaranteeing the liberties of the Church and its presbyterian government. King James VI (James I of England) and later Stuart monarchs attempted to reintroduce episcopacy, but a presbyterian church was finally restored in 1690 and secured by the Act of Settlement (1690) and the Act of Union (1707).

PORVOO DECLARATION
The Porvoo Declaration was drawn up by representatives of the British and Irish Anglican churches and the Nordic and Baltic Lutheran churches and was approved by the General Synod of the Church of England in July 1995. Churches that approve the Declaration regard baptised members of each other's churches as members of their own, and allow free interchange of episcopally ordained ministers within the rules of each church.

NON-CHRISTIAN RELIGIONS

BAHÁ'Í FAITH
Mirza Husayn-'Ali, known as *Bahá'u'lláh* (Glory of God) was born in Iran in 1817 and became a follower of the *Báb,* a religious reformer and prophet who was imprisoned for his beliefs and executed on the grounds of heresy in 1850. *Bahá'u'lláh* was himself imprisoned in 1852, and in 1853 he had a vision that he was the Promised One foretold by the *Báb.* He was exiled after his release from prison and eventually was exiled to Acre, now in Israel, where he continued to compose the Bahá'í sacred scriptures. He died in 1892 and was succeeded by his son, Abdu'l-Bahá, as spiritual leader, under whose guidance the faith spread to Europe and North America. He was followed by Shoghi Effendi, his grandson, who translated many of *Bahá'u'lláh's* works into English. Upon his death in 1957, a democratic system of leadership was brought into operation.

The Bahá'í faith recognises the unity and relativity of religious truth and teaches that there is only one God, whose will has been revealed to mankind by a series of messengers, such as Zoroaster, Abraham, Moses, Buddha, Krishna, Christ, Muhammad, the Báb and Bahá'u'lláh, who were seen as the founders of separate religions, but whose common purpose was to bring God's message to mankind. It teaches that all races and both sexes are equal and deserving of equal opportunities and treatment, that education is a fundamental right and encourages a fair distribution of wealth. In addition, mankind is exhorted to establish a world federal system to promote peace, tolerance and the free movement of people, goods and ideas.

A Feast is held every 19 days, which consists of prayer and readings of Bahá'í scriptures, consultation on community business, and social activities. Music, food and beverages usually accompany the proceedings. There is no clergy; each local community elects a local assembly, which co-ordinates community activities, enrols new members, counsels and assists members in need, and conducts Bahá'í marriages and funerals. A national assembly is elected annually by locally elected delegates, and every five years the national spiritual assemblies meet together to elect the Universal House of Justice, the supreme international governing body of the Bahá'í Faith. World-wide there are over 13,000 local spiritual assemblies; there are around five million members residing in about 235 countries, of which 182 have national organisations.

THE BAHÁ'Í OFFICE OF PUBLIC INFORMATION,
   27 Rutland Gate, London SW7 1PD Tel: 020-7584 2566
   Fax: 020-7584 9402 Email: nsa@bahai.org.uk
   Web: www.bahai.org.uk *Secretary of the National UK Spiritual Assembly*, The Hon. Barnabus Leith

BUDDHISM

Buddhism originated in northern India, in the teachings of Siddharta Gautama, who was born near Kapilavastu about 560 BC and became the *Buddha* (Enlightened One).

Fundamental to Buddhism is the concept of rebirth. Each life carries with it the consequences of the conduct of earlier lives (known as the law of *karma*). This cycle of death and rebirth is broken only when the state of *nirvana* has been reached. Buddhism steers a middle path between belief in personal immortality and belief in death as the final end.

The Four Noble Truths of Buddhism (*dukkha*, suffering; *tanha*, a thirst or desire for continued existence which causes dukkha; *nirvana*, the final liberation from desire and ignorance; and *ariya*, the path to nirvana) are all held to be universal and to sum up the *dhamma* or true nature of life. Necessary qualities to promote spiritual development are *sila* (morality), *samadhi* (meditation) and *panna* (wisdom).

There are two main schools of Buddhism: *Theravada* Buddhism, the earliest extant school, which is more traditional, and *Mahayana* Buddhism, which began to develop about 500 years after the Buddha's death and is more liberal; it teaches that all people may attain Buddhahood. Important schools that have developed within Mahayana Buddhism are *Zen* Buddhism, *Nichiren* Buddhism and Pure Land Buddhism or *Amidism*. There are also distinctive Tibetan forms of Buddhism. Buddhism began to establish itself in the West in the early 20th century.

The scripture of Theravada Buddhism is the *Pali Canon*, which dates from the first century BC. Mahayana Buddhism uses a Sanskrit version of the Pali Canon but also has many other works of scripture.

There is no set time for Buddhist worship, which may take place in a temple or in the home. Worship centres around meditation, acts of devotion centring on the image of the Buddha, and, where possible, offerings to a relic of the Buddha. Buddhist festivals vary according to

local traditions and within Theravada and Mahayana Buddhism. For religious purposes Buddhists use solar and lunar calendars, the New Year being celebrated in April. Other festivals mark events in the life of the Buddha.

There is no supreme governing authority in Buddhism. In the United Kingdom communities representing all schools of Buddhism have developed and operate independently. The Buddhist Society was established in 1924; it runs courses and lectures, and publishes books about Buddhism. It represents no one school of Buddhism.

There are estimated to be at least 300 million Buddhists world-wide, and more than 500 groups and centres, an estimated 25,000 adherents and up to 20 temples or monasteries in the UK.

THE BUDDHIST SOCIETY, 58 Eccleston Square, London
   SW1V 1PH Tel: 020-7834 5858 Fax: 020-7976 5238
   Email: info@thebuddhistsociety.org.uk
   Web: www.thebuddhistsociety.org.uk.
FRIENDS OF THE WESTERN BUDDHIST ORDER,
   London Buddhist Centre, 51 Roman Road, E2 0HU
   Tel: 0845-458 4716 Web: www.lbc.org.uk
THE NETWORK OF BUDDHIST ORGANISATIONS,
   6 Tyne Road, Bishopston, Bristol BS7 8EE Tel: 0117-924 8819
   Email: sally@bristol-chan.co.uk Web: www.nbo.org.uk
OFFICE OF TIBET (The Official UK Agency for HH the
   Dalai Lama), Tibet House, 1 Culworth Street, London
   NW8 7AF Tel: 020-7722 5378
SOKA GAKKAI UK, Taplow Court, Taplow, Maidenhead,
   Berkshire SL6 0ER Tel: 01628-773 163 Web: www.sgi-uk.org

HINDUISM

Hinduism has no historical founder but had become highly developed in India by about 1200 BC. Its adherents originally called themselves Aryans; Muslim invaders first called the Aryans 'Hindus' (derived from 'Sindhu', the name of the river Indus) in the eighth century.

Most Hindus hold that *satya* (truthfulness), *ahimsa* (non-violence), honesty, sincerity and devotion to God are essential for good living. They believe in one supreme spirit *(Brahman)*, and in the transmigration of *atman* (the soul). Most Hindus accept the doctrine of *karma* (consequences of actions), the concept of *samsara* (successive lives) and the possibility of all atmans achieving *moksha* (liberation from samsara) through *jnana* (knowledge), *yoga* (meditation), *karma* (work or action) and *bhakti* (devotion).

Most Hindus offer worship to *murtis* (images of deities) representing different incarnations or aspects of Brahman, and follow their *dharma* (religious and social duty) according to the traditions of their *varna* (social class), *ashrama* (stage in life), *jati* (caste) and *kula* (family).

Hinduism's sacred texts are divided into *shruti* ('that which is heard'), including the *Vedas*; or *smriti* ('that which is remembered'), including the *Ramayana*, the *Mahabharata*, the *Puranas* (ancient myths), and the sacred law books. Most Hindus recognise the authority of the *Vedas*, the oldest holy books, and accept the philosophical teachings of the *Upanishads*, the *Vedanta Sutras* and the *Bhagavad-Gita*.

Brahman is omniscient, omnipotent, limitless and all-pervading, and is usually worshipped in His deity form. Brahma, Vishnu and Shiva are the most important gods worshipped by Hindus; their respective consorts are Saraswati, Lakshmi and Durga or Parvati, also known as Shakti. There are believed to have been ten *avatars* (incarnations) of Vishnu, of whom the most important are

Rama and Krishna. Other popular gods are Ganesha, Hanuman and Subrahmanyam. All gods are seen as aspects of the supreme God, not as competing deities.

Orthodox Hindus revere all gods and goddesses equally, but there are many denominations, including the Hare-Krishna movement (ISKCon), the Arya Samaj, the Swami Narayan Hindu mission and the Satya Sai-Baba movement, in which worship is concentrated on one deity. The *guru* (spiritual teacher) is seen as the source of spiritual guidance.

Hinduism does not have a centrally-trained and ordained priesthood. The pronouncements of the *shankaracharyas* (heads of monasteries) of Shringeri, Puri, Dwarka and Badrinath are heeded by the orthodox but may be ignored by the various sects.

The commonest form of worship is a *puja*, in which offerings of water, flowers, food, fruit, incense and light are made to a deity. Puja may be done either in a home shrine or a *mandir* (temple). Many British Hindus celebrate *samskars* (purification rites) to name a baby, the sacred thread (an initiation ceremony), marriage and cremation.

The largest communities of Hindus in Britain are in Leicester, London, Birmingham and Bradford, and developed as a result of immigration from India, eastern Africa and Sri Lanka.

There are an estimated 800 million Hindus world-wide; there are about 380,000 adherents and over 150 temples in the UK.

ARYA PRATINIDHI SABHA (UK) AND ARYA SAMAJ LONDON, 69A Argyle Road, London W13 0LY
Tel: 020-8991 1732
BHARATIYA VIDYA BHAVAN, Institute of Indian Art and Culture, 4A Castletown Road, London W14 9HE
Tel: 020-7381 4608 *Executive Director,* Dr M. N. Nandakumara
INTERNATIONAL SOCIETY FOR KRISHNA CONSCIOUSNESS (ISKCon), Bhaktivedanta Manor, Dharam Marg, Hilfield Lane, Aldenham, Watford, Herts WD2 8EZ Tel: 01923-857244
Email: bhaktivedanta.manor@pamho.net
Web: www.krishnatemple.com
Temple President, Gauri Das
NATIONAL COUNCIL OF HINDU TEMPLES (UK), Bhakrivedanta Manor, Dharam Marg, Hilfield Lane, Aldenham, Watford WD2 8EZ Tel: 01923-856269/857244
Secretary, Bimal Krishna Das
SWAMINARAYAN HINDU MISSION (SHRI SWAMINARAYAN MANDIR), 105–119 Brentfield Road, London NW10 8LD Tel: 020-8965 2651
Fax: 020-8965 6313 Email: admin@mandir.org
Web: www.swaminarayan-baps.org.uk
Secretary, Arvindkumar Patel
VISHWA HINDU PARISHAD (UK), 48 Wharfedale Gardens, Thornton Heath, Surrey CR7 6LB
Tel: 020-8684 9716 *General Secretary,* K. Ruparelia

ISLAM

Islam (which means 'peace arising from submission to the will of Allah' in Arabic) is a monotheistic religion which was taught in Arabia by the Prophet Muhammad, who was born in Mecca (Al-Makkah) in 570 CE. Islam spread to Egypt, North Africa, Spain and the borders of China in the century following the Prophet's death, and is now the predominant religion in Indonesia, the Near and Middle East, northern and parts of western Africa, Pakistan, Bangladesh, Malaysia and some of the former Soviet republics. There are also large Muslim communities in other countries.

For Muslims (adherents of Islam), there is one God *(Allah),* who holds absolute power. His commands were revealed to mankind through the prophets, who include Abraham, Moses and Jesus, but His message was gradually corrupted until revealed finally and in perfect form to Muhammad through the angel *Jibril* (Gabriel) over a period of 23 years. This last, incorruptible message has been recorded in the *Qur'an* (Koran), which contains 114 divisions called *surahs,* each made up of ayahs, and is held to be the essence of all previous scriptures. The *Ahadith* are the records of the Prophet Muhammad's deeds and sayings (the *Sunnah*) as recounted by his immediate followers. A culture and a system of law and theology gradually developed to form a distinctive Islamic civilisation. Islam makes no distinction between sacred and worldly affairs and provides rules for every aspect of human life. The *Shari'ah* is the sacred law of Islam based upon prescriptions derived from the Qur'an and the *Sunnah* of the Prophet.

The 'five pillars of Islam' are *shahadah* (a declaration of faith in the oneness and supremacy of Allah and the messengership of Muhammad); *salat* (formal prayer, to be performed five times a day facing the *Ka'bah* (sacred house in the holy city of Al-Makkah)); *zakat* (welfare due); *sawm* (fasting during the month of Ramadan); and *hajj* (pilgrimage to Al-Makkah); some Muslims would add *jihad* (striving for the cause of good and resistance to evil).

Two main groups developed among Muslims. *Sunni* Muslims accept the legitimacy of Muhammad's first four *caliphs* (successors as head of the Muslim community) and of the authority of the Muslim community as a whole. About 90 per cent of Muslims are Sunni Muslims.

Shi'ites recognise only Muhammad's son-in-law Ali as his rightful successor and the *Imams* (descendants of Ali, not to be confused with *imams* (prayer leaders or religious teachers)) as the principal legitimate religious authority. The largest group within Shi'ism is *Twelver Shi'ism,* which has been the official school of law and theology in Iran since the 16th century; other subsects include the *Ismailis,* the *Druze* and the *Alawis,* the latter two differing considerably from the main body of Muslims.

The *Ibadhis* of Oman are neither Sunni nor Shi'a, deriving from the strictly observant *Khariji* (Seceeders).

There is no organised priesthood, but learned men such as *ulama, imams* and *ayatollahs* are accorded great respect. The *Sufis* are the mystics of Islam. Mosques are centres for worship and teaching and also for social and welfare activities.

Islam was first known in western Europe in the eighth century AD when 800 years of Muslim rule began in Spain. Later, Islam spread to eastern Europe. More recently, Muslims came to Europe from Africa, the Middle East and Asia in the late 19th century. Both the Sunni and Shi'a traditions are represented in Britain, but the majority of Muslims in Britain adhere to Sunni Islam.

Efforts to establish a representative central organisation recognised by all Muslims in Britain are beginning to yield good results with the emergence of the Muslim Council of Britain. In addition, there are many other Muslim organisations in Britain.

There are about 1,000 million Muslims world-wide, with nearly two million adherents and about 1,200 mosques in Britain.

IMAMS AND MOSQUES COUNCIL, 20–22 Creffield Road, London W5 3RP Tel: 020-8992 6636 *Chairman of the Council and Principal of the Muslim College,* Dr M. A. Z. Badawi

ISLAMIC CULTURAL CENTRE, 146 Park Road, London
NW8 7RG Tel: 020-7724 3363 Fax: 020-7724 0493
Email: islamic200@aol.com
Web: www.islamicculturalcentre.co.uk
Director, Dr A. Al-Dubayan

MUSLIM COUNCIL OF BRITAIN, Suite 5, Boardman House,
64 Broadway, Stratford, London E15 1NT
Tel: 020-8432 0585 Fax: 020-8432 0587
Email: admin@mcb.org.uk Web: www.mcb.org.uk
Secretary-General, Iqbal Sacranie

MUSLIM WORLD LEAGUE, 46 Goodge Street, London
W1P 1FJ Tel: 020-7636 7568
Acting Director, Abdelbasit E Abdelbasit

UNION OF MUSLIM ORGANISATIONS OF THE UK AND
ÉIRE, 109 Campden Hill Road, London W8 7TL
Tel: 020-7229 0538/7221 6608

JAINISM

Jainism traces its history to Vardhamana Jnatiputra, known as *Tirthankara Mahavira* (The Great Hero) whose traditional dates were 599–527 BC. He was the last of a series of 24 *Jinas* (those who overcome all passions and desires) or *Tirthankaras* (those who show a way across the ocean of life) stretching back to remote antiquity. Born to a noble family in north-eastern India, he renounced the world for the life of a wandering ascetic and after 12 years of austerity and meditation he attained enlightenment. He then preached his message until, at the age of 72, he passed away and reached *moksha*, total liberation from the cycle of death and rebirth.

Jains deny the authority of the *Vedas,* the Hindu sacred scriptures. They recognise some of the minor deities of the Hindu pantheon, but the supreme objects of worship are the *Tirthankaras.* The pious Jain does not ask favours from the *Tirthankaras,* but seeks to emulate their example in his or her own life.

Jains believe that the universe is eternal and self-subsisting: there is no omnipotent creator God ruling it and the destiny of the individual is in his or her own hands. *Karma,* the fruit of past actions, determines the place of every living being and rebirth may be in the heavens, on earth as a human, an animal or other lower being, or in the hells. The ultimate goal of existence is *moksha* or *nirvana,* a state of perfect knowledge and tranquility for each individual soul, which can be achieved only by gaining enlightenment.

The path to liberation is defined by the Three Jewels, *samyak darsana* (right thought), *samyak jnana* (right knowledge) and *samyak charitra* (right conduct).

There are about 25,000 Jains in Britain, sizeable communities in North America and East Africa and smaller groups in many other countries.

INSTITUTE OF JAINOLOGY, Unit 18, Silicon Business
Centre, 26/28 Wadsworth Road, Greenford, Middx, UB6 7JZ
Tel: 020-8997 2300

JAIN CENTRE, 32 Oxford Street, Leicester, LE1 5XU
Tel: 0116-254 3091

JUDAISM

Judaism is the oldest monotheistic faith. The primary authority of Judaism is the Hebrew Bible or *Tanakh,* which records how the descendants of Abraham were led by Moses out of their slavery in Egypt to Mount Sinai where God's law *(Torah)* was revealed to them as the chosen people. The *Talmud,* which consists of commentaries on the *Mishnah* (the first text of rabbinical Judaism), is also held to be authoritative, and may be divided into two main categories: the *halakah* (dealing with legal and ritual matters) and the *Aggadah* (dealing with theological and ethical matters not directly concerned with the regulation of conduct). The *Midrash* comprises rabbinic writings containing biblical interpretations in the spirit of the Aggadah. The *halakah* has become a source of division; Orthodox Jews regard Jewish law as derived from God and therefore unalterable; Reform and Liberal Jews seek to interpret it in the light of contemporary considerations; and Conservative Jews aim to maintain most of the traditional rituals but to allow changes in accordance with tradition. Reconstructionist Judaism, a 20th-century movement, regards Judaism as a culture rather than a theological system and accepts all forms of Jewish practice.

The family is the basic unit of Jewish ritual, with the synagogue playing an important role as the centre for public worship and religious study. A synagogue is led by a group of laymen who are elected to office. The Rabbi is primarily a teacher and spiritual guide. The Sabbath is the central religious observance. Most British Jews are descendants of either the *Ashkenazim* of central and eastern Europe or the *Sephardim* of Spain, Portugal and the Middle East.

The Chief Rabbi of the United Hebrew Congregations of the Commonwealth is appointed by a Chief Rabbinate Conference, and is the rabbinical authority of the mainstream Orthodox sector of the Ashkenazi Jewish community, the largest body of which is the United Synagogue. His formal ecclesiastical authority is not recognised by the Reform Synagogues of Great Britain (the largest progressive group), the Union of Liberal and Progressive Synagogues, the Sephardi community, or the Assembly of Masorti Synagogues. He is, however, generally recognised both outside the Jewish community and within it as the public religious representative of the totality of British Jewry. The Chief Rabbi is President of the London *Beth Din.*

Beth Din (Court of Judgement) is a rabbinic court. The *Dayanim* (Assessors) adjudicate in disputes or on matters of Jewish law and tradition; they also oversee dietary law administration.

The Board of Deputies of British Jews, established in 1760, is the representative body of British Jewry. The basis of representation is mainly synagogal, but communal organisations are also represented. It watches over the interests of British Jewry, acts as the central voice of the community and seeks to counter anti-Jewish discrimination and antisemitic activities.

In November 1998 a Consultative Committee was established comprising representatives of the Assembly of Masorti Synagogues, Reform Synagogues of Great Britain, Union of Liberal and Progressive Synagogues and the United Synagogue. The Committee holds discussions to further communal harmony and development.

There are over 12.5 million Jews world-wide; in Great Britain and Ireland there are an estimated 285,000 adherents and about 365 synagogues. Of these, 191 congregations and about 175 rabbis and ministers are under the jurisdiction of the Chief Rabbi; 99 orthodox congregations have a more independent status; and 79 congregations are outside the jurisdiction of the Chief Rabbi.

CHIEF RABBINATE, Adler House, 735 High Road, London
N12 0US Tel: 020-8343 6301 Fax: 020-8343 6301
Email: info@chiefrabbi.org Web: www.chiefrabbi.org.
Chief Rabbi, Prof. Jonathan Sacks
Executive Director, Syma Weinberg

BETH DIN (COURT OF THE CHIEF RABBI), 735 High Road, London N12 0US Tel: 020-8343 6270 Fax: 020-8343 6257 Email: info@bethdin.org.uk.
Registrar, D. Frei; *Dayanim,* Rabbi Chanoch Ehrentreu; Ivan Binstock; Menachem Gelley; Yonason Abraham; I. Berger
BOARD OF DEPUTIES OF BRITISH JEWS, 6 Bloomsbury Square, London WC1A 2LP. Tel: 020-7543 5400 Fax: 020-7543 0010 Email: info@bod.org.uk Web: www.bod.org.uk *President,* Jo Wagerman, OBE; *Director-General,* Neville Nagler
ASSEMBLY OF MASORTI SYNAGOGUES, 1097 Finchley Road, London NW11 0PU Tel: 020-8201 8772 Fax: 020-8201 8917 Email: office@masorti.org.uk Web: www.masorti.org.uk
Executive Director, M. Gluckman
FEDERATION OF SYNAGOGUES, 65 Watford Way, London NW4 3AQ Tel: 020-8202 2263 Fax: 020-8203 0610
Chief Executive, G. D. Coleman
BETH DIN OF THE FEDERATION OF SYNAGOGUES, 65 Watford Way, London NW4 3AQ Tel: 020-8202 2263 *Registrar,* Rabbi S. Unsdorfer; *Dayanim,* Yisroel Lichtenstein; Berel Berkovits; M. D. Elzas
REFORM SYNAGOGUE OF GREAT BRITAIN, The Sternberg Centre for Judaism, 80 East End Road, London N3 2SY Tel: 020-8349 5640 Email: admin@reformjudaism.org.uk Web: www.reformjudaism.org.uk
Chief Executive, Rabbi Tony Bayfield
SPANISH AND PORTUGUESE JEWS' CONGREGATION, 2 Ashworth Road, London W9 1JY Tel: 020-7289 2573 Fax: 020-7289 2709 Email: howardmiller@spsyn.org.uk
Chief Executive, Howard Miller
UNION OF LIBERAL AND PROGRESSIVE SYNAGOGUES, The Montagu Centre, 21 Maple Street, London W1T 4BE Tel: 020-7580 1663 Fax: 020-7436 4184 Email: montagu@ulps.org Web: www.ulps.org.
UNION OF ORTHODOX HEBREW CONGREGATIONS, 140 Stamford Hill, London N16 6QT Tel: 020-8802 6226 *Principal Rabbinical Authority,* Rabbi Ephraim Padwa
UNITED SYNAGOGUE HEAD OFFICE, Adler House, 735 High Road, London N12 0US Tel: 020-8343 8989 Fax: 020-8343 6262 Web: www.unitedsynagogue.org.uk
Chief Executive, Rabbi Saul Zneimer

SIKHISM

The Sikh religion dates from the birth of Guru Nanak in the Punjab in 1469. 'Guru' means teacher but in Sikh tradition has come to represent the divine presence of God giving inner spiritual guidance. Nanak's role as the human vessel of the divine guru was passed on to nine successors, the last of whom (Guru Gobind Singh) died in 1708. The immortal guru is now held to reside in the sacred scripture, *Guru Granth Sahib,* and so to be present in all Sikh gatherings.

Guru Nanak taught that there is one God and that different religions are like different roads leading to the same destination. He condemned religious conflict, ritualism and caste prejudices. The fifth Guru, Guru Arjan Dev, largely compiled the Sikh Holy Book, a collection of hymns *(gurbani)* known as the *Adi Granth.* It includes the writings of the first five Gurus and the ninth Guru, and selected writings of Hindu and Muslim saints whose views are in accord with the Gurus' teachings. Guru Arjan Dev also built the Golden Temple at Amritsar, the centre of Sikhism. The tenth Guru, Guru Gobind Singh, passed on the guruship to the sacred scripture, Guru Granth Sahib. He also founded the *Khalsa,* an order intended to fight against tyranny and injustice. Male initiates to the order added 'Singh' to their given names and women added 'Kaur'. Guru Gobind Singh also made five symbols obligatory: *kaccha* (a special undergarment), *kara* (a steel bangle), *kirpan* (a small sword), *kesh* (long unshorn hair, and consequently the wearing of a turban), and *kangha* (a comb). These practices are still compulsory for those Sikhs who are initiated into the Khalsa (the *Amritdharis*). Those who do not seek initiation are known as *Sehajdharis.*

There are no professional priests in Sikhism; anyone with a reasonable proficiency in the Punjabi language can conduct a service. Worship can be offered individually or communally, and in a private house or a *gurdwara* (temple). Sikhs are forbidden to eat meat prepared by ritual slaughter; they are also asked to abstain from smoking, alcohol and other intoxicants. Such abstention is compulsory for the *Amritdharis.*

There are about 20 million Sikhs world-wide and about 500,000 adherents and 250 gurdwaras in Great Britain. Every gurdwara manages its own affairs and there is no central body in the UK. The Sikh Missionary Society provides an information service.

SIKH MISSIONARY SOCIETY UK, 10 Featherstone Road, Southall, Middx UB2 5AA Tel: 020-8574 1902
Hon. General Secretary, M. S. Chahal
WORLD SIKH FOUNDATION (THE SIKH COURIER INTERNATIONAL), 33 Wargrave Road, South Harrow, Middx HA2 8LL Tel: 020-8864 9228
Secretary, Mrs H. B. Bharara

ZOROASTRIANISM

Zoroastrianism was founded by Zarathushtra (or Zoroaster in its hellenised form) in Persia. Linguistic analysis of the earliest extant Zoroastrian texts suggests that he lived around 1500 BC. Zarathushtra's words are recorded in five poems called the *Gathas,* which, together with other scriptures, forms the *Avesta.*

Zoroastrianism teaches that there is one God, *Ahura Mazda* (the Wise Lord), and that all creation stems ultimately from God; the Gathas teach that human beings have free will, are responsible for their own actions and can choose between good and evil: Choosing *Asha* (truth or righteousness), with the aid of *Vohu Manah* (good mind), leads to happiness for the individual and society, whereas choosing evil leads to unhappiness and conflict. The *Gathas* also encourage hard work, good deeds and charitable acts. Zoroastrians believe that after death, the immortal soul is judged by God, and is then sent to paradise or hell, where it will stay until the end of time. It will be resurrected for the final judgement.

In Zoroastrian places of worship, an urn containing fire is the central feature; the fire symbolises purity, light, and truth and is a visible symbol of the *Fravashi* or *Farohar,* the presence of *Ahura Mazda* in every human being.

Zoroastrians respect nature and much importance is attached to cultivating land and protecting the air, the earth and water. The practice of leaving corpses on mountain tops or towers developed to avoid pollution.

Zoroastrians were persecuted in Iran following the Arab invasion of Persia in the seventh century AD, which also brought Islam and a group migrated to India in the tenth century AD, who are known as Parsis, to avoid harassment and persecution; there are fewer than 150,000 Zoroastrians worldwide, of which 7,000 reside in Britain, mainly in London and the south east.
ZOROASTRIAN TRUST FUNDS OF EUROPE, 88 Compayne Gardens, London NW6 3RU Tel: 020-7328 6018 Email: secretary@ztfe.com Web: www.ztfe.com

THE CHURCHES

There are two established, i.e. state, churches in the United Kingdom: the Church of England and the Church of Scotland. There are no established churches in Wales or Northern Ireland, though the Church in Wales, the Scottish Episcopal Church and the Church of Ireland are members of the Anglican Communion.

THE CHURCH OF ENGLAND

The Church of England is the established (i.e. national) church in England and seeks to serve the nation through its dioceses and parishes. It traces its life back to the first coming of Christianity to England. Its position is defined by the ancient creeds of the Church and by the 39 Articles of Religion (1571), the Book of Common Prayer (1662) and the Ordinal. The Church of England is thus both catholic and reformed. It is the mother church of the Anglican Communion.

THE ANGLICAN COMMUNION
The Anglican Communion consists of 40 independent provincial or national Christian churches throughout the world, many of which are in Commonwealth countries and originated from missionary activity by the Church of England. Every ten years all the bishops in the Communion meet at the Lambeth Conference, convened by the Archbishop of Canterbury. The Conference has no policy-making authority but is an important forum for discussing and forming consensus around issues common concern. The Anglican Consultative Council was set up in 1968 to liaise between the member churches and provinces of the Anglican Communion. It meets every three years. Meetings of the Anglican primates have taken place every two years since 1979.

There are about 80 million Anglicans and 800 archbishops and bishops world-wide.

STRUCTURE
The Church of England is divided into the two provinces of Canterbury and York, each under an archbishop. The two provinces are subdivided into 44 dioceses.

Legislative provision for the Church of England is made by the General Synod, established in 1970. It also discusses and expresses opinion on any other matter of religious or public interest. The General Synod has 580 members in total, divided between three houses: the House of Bishops, the House of Clergy and the House of Laity. It is presided over jointly by the Archbishops of Canterbury and York and normally meets twice a year. The Synod has the power, delegated by Parliament, to frame statute law (known as a Measure) on any matter concerning the Church of England. A Measure must be laid before both Houses of Parliament, who may accept or reject it but cannot amend it. Once accepted the Measure is submitted for royal assent and then has the full force of law. In addition to the General Synod, there are Synods at diocesan level.

The Archbishops' Council was established in January 1999. Its creation was the result of changes to the Church of England's national structure proposed in 1995 and subsequently approved by the Synod and Parliament. The Council's purpose, set out in the National Institutions Measure 1998, is 'to co-ordinate, promote and further the work and mission of the Church of England'. It reports to the General Synod. The Archbishops' Council comprises the Archbishops of Canterbury and York, ex officio, the Prolocutors elected by the Convocations of Canterbury and York, the Chairman and Vice-Chairman of the House of Laity, elected by that House, two bishops, two clergy and two lay persons elected by their respective Houses of the General Synod, and up to six persons appointed jointly by the two Archbishops with the approval of the General Synod.

There are also a number of national Boards, Councils and other bodies working on matters such as social responsibility, mission, Christian unity and education which report to the General Synod through the Archbishops' Council.

GENERAL SYNOD OF THE CHURCH OF ENGLAND, Church House, Great Smith Street, London SW1P 3NZ Tel: 020-7898 1000 *Joint Presidents*, The Archbishops of Canterbury and York
HOUSE OF BISHOPS: *Chairman*, The Archbishop of Canterbury; *Vice-Chairman*, The Archbishop of York
HOUSE OF CLERGY: *Chairmen (alternating)*, Canon Bob Baker; Canon Glyn Webster
HOUSE OF LAITY: *Chairman*, Dr Christina Baxter; *Vice-Chairman*, Brian McHenry
ARCHBISHOPS' COUNCIL, Church House, Great Smith Street, London SW1P 3NZ Tel: 020-7898 1000 *Joint Presidents*, The Archbishops of Canterbury and York *Secretary-General*, William Fittall

THE ORDINATION OF WOMEN
The canon making it possible for women to be ordained to the priesthood was promulgated in the General Synod in February 1994 and the first 32 women priests were ordained on 12 March 1994.

MEMBERSHIP
In 2001, 153,000 people were baptised, the Church of England had an electoral roll membership of 1.4 million, and each week about 1.2 million people attended services. As at December 2002 there were over 16,000 churches and places of worship. At December 2002 there were 370 dignitaries (including bishops, archdeacons and cathedral clergy); 8,712 parochial stipendiary clergy; 399 non parochial stipendiary clergy; 1,159 chaplains etc; 35 lay workers and Church Army evangelists; 8,384 licensed readers and 1,900 readers with permission to officiate and active emeriti; and approximately 4,600 active retired ordained clergy.

FULL-TIME DIOCESAN CLERGY 2002 AND CHURCH ELECTORAL ROLL 2001

	Clergy Male	Female	Membership
Bath and Wells	202	31	43,000
Birmingham	160	26	19,500
Blackburn	217	17	39,400
Bradford	103	12	13,200
Bristol	121	25	20,000
Canterbury	143	18	22,700
Carlisle	133	20	24,800
Chelmsford	347	53	54,500
Chester	230	35	53,400

Chichester	321	10	60,600
Coventry	120	23	18,100
Derby	156	18	22,200
Durham	192	27	27,700
Ely	122	26	21,200
Europe	98	1	9,800
Exeter	243	24	34,100
Gloucester	128	19	27,200
Guildford	153	36	32,700
Hereford	83	22	19,800
Leicester	136	28	17,200
Lichfield	293	51	55,200
Lincoln	166	38	30,900
Liverpool	197	34	33,100
London	464	60	64,600
Manchester	244	42	40,500
Newcastle	128	22	18,600
Norwich	181	21	27,000
Oxford	338	72	62,300
Peterborough	132	22	19,800
Portsmouth	100	12	20,500
Ripon and Leeds	112	29	19,700
Rochester	190	29	33,800
St Albans	216	55	47,200
St Edmundsbury and Ipswich	139	23	26,400
Salisbury	193	33	49,700
Sheffield	157	28	22,000
Sodor and Man	19	0	2,800
Southwark	295	63	48,500
Southwell	137	29	18,900
Truro	114	12	17,900
Wakefield	141	28	24,900
Winchester	221	25	24,200
Worcester	125	28	22,700
York	210	35	40,300
TOTAL	7,920	1,262	1,372,000

STIPENDS 2003–4

Archbishop of Canterbury	£60,820
Archbishop of York	£53,280
Bishop of London	£49,690
Other diocesan bishops	£33,010
Suffragan bishops	£27,090
Assistant Bishops (full-time)	£26,010
Deans and provosts	£27,090
Archdeacons (recommended)	£26,910
Residentiary canons	£22,070
Incumbents and clergy of similar status	£17,940*

*National Stipends Benchmark

CANTERBURY
104th ARCHBISHOP AND PRIMATE OF ALL ENGLAND
Most Revd and Rt. Hon. Rowan Williams *cons.* 1992,
  apptd 2002; Lambeth Palace, London SE1 7JU
  Signs Rowan Cantuar
BISHOPS SUFFRAGAN
Dover, Rt. Revd Stephen Venner, *cons.* 1994, *apptd* 1999;
  Upway, St Martin's Hill, Canterbury, Kent CT1 1PR
Maidstone, Rt. Revd Graham Cray, *cons.* 2001, *apptd*
  2001, Bishop's House, Pett Lane, Charing, Ashford, Kent
  TN27 0DL
Ebbsfleet, Rt. Revd Andrew Burnham, *cons.* 2001, *apptd*
  2001 (provincial episcopal visitor); Bishop's House, Dry
  Sandsford, Oxon OX13 6JP
Richborough, Rt. Revd Keith Newton, *cons.* 2002, *apptd*
  2002 (provincial episcopal visitor); 6 Mellis Gardens,
  Woodford Green, Essex IG8 0BH

DEAN
Very Revd Robert Willis, *apptd* 2001

CANONS RESIDENTIARY
Edward Condry, *apptd* 2003; Richard Marsh, *apptd* 2001

Organist, D. Flood, FRCO, *apptd* 1988

ARCHDEACONS
Canterbury, Ven. Patrick Evans, *apptd* 2002
Maidstone, Ven. Philip Down, *apptd* 2002

Vicar-General of Province and Diocese, Chancellor Sheila
  Cameron, QC
Commissary-General, His Hon. Judge Richard Walker
Joint Registrars of the Province, F. E. Robson, OBE;
  B. J. T. Hanson, CBE
Diocesan Registrar and Legal Adviser, Richard Sturt
Diocesan Secretary, David Kemp, Diocesan House, Lady
  Wootton's Green, Canterbury CT1 1NQ Tel: 01227-459401

YORK
96th ARCHBISHOP AND PRIMATE OF ENGLAND
Most Revd and Rt. Hon. David M. Hope, KCVO, D.Phil.,
  LLD, *cons.* 1985, *trans.* 1995; Bishopthorpe, York
  YO23 2GE. *Signs* David Ebor

BISHOPS SUFFRAGAN
Hull, Rt. Revd Richard M. C. Frith, *cons.* 1998, *apptd*
  1998; Hullen House, Woodfield Lane, Hessle, Hull
  HU13 0ES
Selby, Rt. Revd Martin Wallace, *cons.* 2003, *apptd* 2003;
  c/o Bishopthorpe, York YO23 2GE
Whitby, Rt. Revd Robert S. Ladds, *cons.* 1999, *apptd*
  1999; 60 West Green, Stokesley, Middlesbrough TS9 5BD
Beverley, Rt. Revd Martyn Jarrett, *cons.* 1994, *apptd* 2000
  (provincial episcopal visitor); 3 North Lane, Roundhay,
  Leeds LS8 2QJ

DEAN
vacant

CANONS RESIDENTIARY
Glyn Webster, *apptd* 1999; Edward. R. Norman, Ph.D.,
  DD, *apptd* 1999; Jonathan Draper, *apptd* 2000; Jeremy
  Fletcher, *apptd* 2002

CANONS LAY
Lindsay Mackinlay, *apptd* 2000; Carol Rymer, *apptd*
  2000; Dr Allen Warren, *apptd* 2000; Brig.
  Peter Lyddon (as Chapter Steward), *apptd* 2000;
  Peter Collier, QC, *apptd* 2001

Organist, Philip Moore, FRCO, *apptd* 1983

ARCHDEACONS
Cleveland, Ven. Paul Ferguson, *apptd* 2001
East Riding, Ven. Peter Harrison, *apptd* 1998
York, Ven. Richard Seed, *apptd* 1999

Official Principal and Auditor of the Chancery Court,
  Sir John Owen, QC
Chancellor of the Diocese, His Hon. Judge Coningsby, QC,
  apptd 1977
*Vicar-General of the Province and Official Principal of the
  Consistory Court,* His Hon. Judge Coningsby, QC
Registrar and Legal Secretary, Lionel Lennox
Diocesan Secretary, Colin Sheppard, Diocesan House, Aviator
  Court, Clifton Moor, York YO30 4WJ Tel: 01904-699500

LONDON *(Province of Canterbury)*
132nd BISHOP
Rt. Revd and Rt. Hon Richard J. C. Chartres, *cons.* 1992, *apptd.* 1995; The Old Deanery, Dean's Court, London EC4V 5AA *Signs* Richard Londin

AREA BISHOPS
Edmonton, Rt. Revd Peter W. Wheatley, *cons.* 1999, *apptd* 1999; 27 Thurlow Road, London NW3 5PP
Kensington, Rt. Revd Michael J. Colclough, *cons.* 1996, *apptd* 1996; 19 Campden Hill Square, London W8 7JY
Stepney, Rt. Revd Canon Stephen J. Oliver, *cons. apptd* 2003
Willesden, Rt. Revd Peter Broadbent, *cons.* 2001, *apptd* 2001; 173 Willesden Lane, London NW6 7YN

BISHOP SUFFRAGAN
Fulham, Rt. Revd John C. Broadhurst, *cons.* 1996, *apptd* 1996; 26 Canonbury Park South, London N1 2FN

DEAN OF ST PAUL'S
Very Revd John H. Moses, Ph.D., *apptd* 1996

CANONS RESIDENTIARY
Philip Buckler, *apptd* 1999; Edmund Newall, *apptd* 2001; Peter Chapman, *apptd* 2001; Martin Warner, *apptd* 2003; Lucy Winckett, *apptd* 2003

Registrar and Receiver of St Paul's, Maj.–Gen. John Milne

Organist, John Scott, FRCO, *apptd* 1990

ARCHDEACONS
Charing Cross, Ven. Dr William Jacob, *apptd* 1996
Hackney, Ven. Lyle Dennen, *apptd* 1999
Hampstead, Ven. Michael Lawson, *apptd* 1999
London, Ven. Peter Delaney, *apptd* 1999
Middlesex, Ven. Malcolm Colmer, *apptd* 1996
Northolt, Ven. Christopher Chessun, *apptd* 2001

Chancellor, Nigel Seed, QC, *apptd* 2002
Registrar and Legal Secretary, Paul Morris
Diocesan Secretary, Keith Robinson,
London Diocesan House, 36 Causton Street, London SW1P 4AU. Tel: 020-7932 1226

DURHAM *(Province of York)*
71st BISHOP
Rt. Revd Dr N. Thomas Wright, *cons.* 2003, *apptd* 2003; Auckland Castle, Bishop Auckland DL14 7NR.
Signs Thomas Dunelm

BISHOP SUFFRAGAN
Jarrow, Rt. Revd John Pritchard, *cons.* 2002, *apptd* 2002; Bishop's House, Ivy Lane, Low Fell, Gateshead NE9 6QD

DEAN
Very Revd Michael Sadgrove, *apptd* 2003

CANONS RESIDENTIARY
Prof David Brown, *apptd* 1990; Stephen Conway, *apptd* 2002; Martin Kitchen, *apptd* 1997; David Whittington, *apptd* 1998; David Kennedy, *apptd* 2001
Organist, James Lancelot, FRCO, *apptd* 1985

ARCHDEACONS
Auckland, Ven. Ian Jagger, *apptd* 2001
Durham, Ven. Stephen Conway, *apptd* 2002

Sunderland, Ven. Stuart Bain, *apptd* 2002

Chancellor, Revd Canon Rupert Bursell, QC, *apptd* 1989
Registrar and Legal Secretary, A. N. Fairclough
Diocesan Secretary, Jonathan Cryer, Auckland Castle, Bishop Auckland, Co. Durham DL14 7QJ Tel: 01388-604515

WINCHESTER *(Canterbury)*
96th BISHOP
Rt. Revd Michael C. Scott-Joynt, *cons.* 1987, *trans.* 1995: Wolvesey, Winchester SO23 9ND *Signs* Michael Winton

BISHOPS SUFFRAGAN
Basingstoke, Rt. Revd Trevor Willmott, *cons.* 2002, *apptd* 2002. Bishopswood End, Kingswood Rise, Four Marks, Alton, Hants GU34 5BD
Southampton, vacant Ham House, The Crescent, Romsey SO51 7NG

DEAN
Very Revd Michael Till, *apptd* 1996

Dean of Jersey (A Peculiar), Very Revd John Seaford, *apptd* 1993
Dean of Guernsey (A Peculiar), Very Revd Marc Trickey, *apptd* 1995

CANONS RESIDENTIARY
Keith Anderson, *apptd* 2003; Charles Stewart, *apptd* 1997; Ven. John Guille, *apptd* 1998

Organist, Andrew Lumsden, ARCO, *apptd* 2002

ARCHDEACONS
Bournemouth, Ven. Adrian Harbidge, *apptd* 1998
Winchester, Ven. John Guille, *apptd* 1998

Chancellor, Christopher Clark, *apptd* 1993
Registrar and Legal Secretary, Peter White
Diocesan Secretary, Ray Anderton, Church House, 9 The Close, Winchester, Hants SO23 9LS
Tel: 01962-844644

BATH AND WELLS *(Canterbury)*
77th BISHOP
Rt. Revd Peter Price, *cons.* 1997, *apptd* 2002; The Palace, Wells BA5 2PD *Signs* Peter Bath & Wells

BISHOP SUFFRAGAN
Taunton, Rt. Revd Andrew John Radford, *cons.* 1998, *apptd* 1998; The Bishop's Lodge, Monkton Heights, West Monkton, Taunton, Somerset TA2 8LU

DEAN
vacant

CANONS RESIDENTIARY
Richard Acworth, *apptd* 1993; Russell Bowman-Eadie, *apptd* 2002; Melvyn Matthews, *apptd* 1997; Patrick Woodhouse, *apptd* 2000

Organist, Malcolm Archer, *apptd* 1996

ARCHDEACONS
Bath, Ven. Robert Evens, *apptd* 1996
Taunton, Ven. John Reed, *apptd* 1999
Wells, Ven. Richard Acworth, *apptd* 1993

Chancellor, Timothy Briden, apptd 1993
Registrar and Legal Secretary, Tim Berry
Diocesan Secretary, Nicholas Denison, The Old Deanery,
Wells, Somerset BA5 2UG Tel: 01749-670777

BIRMINGHAM (Canterbury)
8th BISHOP
Rt. Revd Dr John Sentamu, cons. 1996, apptd 2002;
Bishop's Croft, Harborne, Birmingham B17 0BG
Signs John Birmingham

BISHOP SUFFRAGAN
Aston, Rt. Revd John Austin, cons. 1992, apptd 1992;
Strensham House, 8 Strensham Hill, Moseley, Birmingham
B13 8AG

PROVOST
The Very Revd Gordon Mursell, apptd 2000

CANONS RESIDENTIARY
Revd David Lee, apptd 1996; Revd Gary O'Neill,
apptd 1997

Organist, Marcus Huxley, FRCO, apptd 1986

ARCHDEACONS
Aston, Ven. John Barton, apptd 1990
Birmingham, Ven. Hayward Osborne, apptd 2001

Chancellor, vacant
Vice-Chancellor, David Pittaway
Registrar and Legal Secretary, Hugh Carslake
Diocesan Secretary, Jim Drennan, 175 Harborne Park Road,
Harborne, Birmingham B17 0BH Tel: 0121-426 0400

BLACKBURN (York)
8th BISHOP
Rt. Revd Nicholas Reade, apptd 2003, due to be cons.
March 2004; Bishop's House, Ribchester Road, Blackburn
BB1 9EF Signs Nicholas Blackburn

BISHOPS SUFFRAGAN
Burnley, Rt. Revd John Goddard, cons. 2000, apptd 2000;
Dean House, 449 Padiham Road, Burnley BB12 6TE
Lancaster, Rt. Revd Stephen Pedley, cons. 1998,
apptd 1998; The Vicarage, Shireshead, Forton,
Preston PR3 0AE

DEAN
Very Revd Christopher Armstrong, apptd 2001

CANONS RESIDENTIARY
David Galilee, apptd 1995; Andrew Hindley, apptd 1996;
Peter Ballard, apptd 1998; Andrew Clitherow, apptd
2000

Organist, Richard Tanner, apptd 1998

ARCHDEACONS
Blackburn, Ven. John Hawley, apptd 2002
Lancaster, Ven. Colin Williams, apptd 1999

Chancellor, John Bullimore, apptd 1990
Registrar and Legal Secretary, Thomas Hoyle
Diocesan Secretary, Revd Michael Wedgeworth,
Diocesan Office, Cathedral Close, Blackburn BB1 5AA
Tel: 01254-54421

BRADFORD (York)
9th BISHOP
Rt. Revd David James, apptd 2002; Bishopscroft,
Ashwell Road, Heaton, Bradford BD9 4AU.
Signs David Bradford

DEAN
Very Revd Dr Christopher David Hancock, apptd 2002

CANON RESIDENTIARY
Derek Jackson, apptd 2000; David Brierley, apptd 2002

Organist, Andrew Teague, FRCO, apptd 2003

ARCHDEACONS
Bradford, Ven. Guy Wilkinson, apptd 1999
Craven, Ven. Malcolm Grundy, apptd 1994

Chancellor, John de G. Walford, apptd 1999
Registrar and Legal Secretary, Stuart Robinson
Diocesan Secretary, Malcolm Halliday, Kadugli House,
Elmsley Street, Steeton, Keighley BD20 6SE
Tel: 01535-650555

BRISTOL (Canterbury)
55th BISHOP
Rt. Revd Michael Hill, cons. 1998, apptd 2003;
Wethered House, 11 The Avenue, Clifton, Bristol BS8 3HG
Signs Michael Bristol

BISHOP SUFFRAGAN
Swindon, Rt. Revd Michael Doe, cons. 1994, apptd 1994;
Mark House, Field Rise, Old Town, Swindon SN1 4HP

DEAN
Very Revd Robert W. Grimley, apptd 1997

CANONS RESIDENTIARY
Peter Johnson, apptd 1990; Douglas Holt, apptd 1998;
Brendan Clover, apptd 1999

Organist, Mark Lee, apptd 1998

ARCHDEACONS
Bristol, Ven. Tim McClure, apptd 1999
Malmesbury, Ven. Alan Hawker, apptd 1998

Chancellor, Sir David Calcutt, QC, apptd 1971
Registrar and Legal Secretary, Tim Berry
Diocesan Secretary, Lesley Farrall, Diocesan Church House,
23 Great George Street, Bristol, Avon BS1 5QZ
Tel: 0117-906 0100

CARLISLE (York)
66th BISHOP
Rt. Revd Graham Dow, cons. 1985, apptd 2000;
Rose Castle, Dalston, Carlisle CA5 7BZ
Signs Graham Carlisle

BISHOP SUFFRAGAN
Penrith, Rt. Revd James Newcome, cons. 2002, apptd
2002; Holm Croft, Castle Road, Kendal, Cumbria LA9 7AU

DEAN
Very Revd Graeme Knowles, apptd 1998

CANONS RESIDENTIARY
Rex Chapman, *apptd* 1978; David Weston, *apptd* 1994;
   Colin Hill, *apptd* 1996

Organist, Jeremy Suter, FRCO, *apptd* 1991

ARCHDEACONS
Carlisle, Ven. David Thomson, *apptd* 2002
West Cumberland, Ven. Alan Davis, *apptd* 1996
Westmorland and Furness, Ven. George Howe, *apptd* 2000
Chancellor, Geoffrey Tattersall, QC, *apptd* 2003
Registrar and Legal Secretary, Susan Holmes
Diocesan Secretary, Canon Colin Hill, Church House, West
   Walls, Carlisle CA3 8UE Tel: 01228-522573

CHELMSFORD *(Canterbury)*
9th BISHOP
Rt. Revd John Warren Gladwin, *cons.* 1994, *apptd* 2003,
   due to be trans. January 2004; Bishopscourt, Margaretting,
   Ingatestone CM4 0HD *Signs* John Chelmsford

BISHOPS SUFFRAGAN
Barking, Rt. Revd David Hawkins, *apptd* 2002
Bradwell, Rt. Revd Laurence Green, *cons.* 1993,
   apptd 1993; The Vicarage, Orsett Road,
   Horndon-on-the-Hill, Stanford-le-Hope, Essex SS17 8NS
Colchester, Rt. Revd Christopher Morgan, 1 Fitzwalter
   Road, Colchester, Essex CO3 3SS

PROVOST
Very Revd Peter S. M. Judd, *apptd* 1997

CANONS RESIDENTIARY
Andrew Knowles, *apptd* 1998; Walter King, *apptd* 2001

Master of Music, Peter Nardone, *apptd* 2000

ARCHDEACONS
Colchester, Ven. Martin Wallace, *apptd* 1997
Harlow, Ven. Peter Taylor, *apptd* 1996
Southend, Ven. David Lowman, *apptd* 2001
West Ham, Ven. Michael Fox, *apptd* 1996

Chancellor, George Pulman, *apptd* 2001
Registrar and Legal Secretary, Brian Hood
Diocesan Secretary, David Phillips, 53 New Street,
   Chelmsford, Essex CM1 1AT Tel: 01245-294400

CHESTER *(York)*
40th BISHOP
Rt. Revd Peter R. Forster, Ph.D., *cons.* 1996, *apptd* 1996;
   Bishop's House, Chester CH1 2JD *Signs* Peter Cestr

BISHOPS SUFFRAGAN
Birkenhead, Rt. Revd David A. Urquhart, *cons.* 2000,
   apptd 2000; Bishop's Lodge, 67 Bidston Road, Oxton,
   Birkenhead CH43 6TR
Stockport, Rt. Revd Nigel Stock, *cons.* 2000, *apptd* 2000;
   Bishop's Lodge, Back Lane, Dunham Town, Altrincham,
   Cheshire WA14 4SG

DEAN
Very Revd Dr Gordon McPhate

CANONS RESIDENTIARY
Trevor Dennis, *apptd* 1994; Christopher Burkett, *apptd*
   2000; John Roff, *apptd* 2000; Judy Hunt, *apptd* 2002

Organist and Director of Music, David Poulter, FRCO,
   apptd 1997
ARCHDEACONS
Chester, Revd, *apptd* 2002
Macclesfield, Ven. Richard Gillings, *apptd* 1994

Chancellor, David Turner, QC, *apptd* 1998
Registrar and Legal Secretary, Alan McAllester
Diocesan Secretary, Stephen P. A. Marriott, Church House,
   Lower Lane, Aldford, Chester CH3 6HP Tel: 01244-620444

CHICHESTER *(Canterbury)*
102nd BISHOP
Rt. Revd John Hind, *cons.* 1991, *apptd* 2001; The Palace,
   Chichester PO19 1PY *Signs* John Cicestr

BISHOPS SUFFRAGAN
Horsham, Rt. Revd Lindsay G. Urwin, *cons.* 1993, *apptd*
   1993; Bishop's House, 21 Guildford Road, Horsham,
   W. Sussex RH12 1LU
Lewes, Rt. Revd Wallace P. Benn, *cons.* 1997, *apptd* 1997;
   Bishop's Lodge, 16A Prideaux Road, Eastbourne, E. Sussex
   BN21 2NB

DEAN
Revd Nicholas Frayling, *apptd* 2002

CANONS RESIDENTIARY
Peter Atkinson, *apptd* 1997; John Ford, *apptd* 2000;
   Peter Kefford, *apptd* 2001

Organist, Alan Thurlow, FRCO, *apptd* 1980

ARCHDEACONS
Chichester, Ven. Douglas McKittrick, *apptd* 2002
Horsham, Ven. Roger Combes, *apptd* 2003
Lewes and Hastings, vacant

Chancellor, Mark Hill
Registrar and Legal Secretary, Tim Gleeson
Diocesan Secretary, Jonathan Prichard, Diocesan Church
   House, 211 New Church Road, Hove, E. Sussex BN3 4ED
   Tel: 01273-421021

COVENTRY *(Canterbury)*
8th BISHOP
Rt. Revd Colin J. Bennetts; *cons.* 1994, *apptd* 1997;
   The Bishop's House, 23 Davenport Road,
   Coventry CV5 6PW. *Signs* Colin Coventry

BISHOP SUFFRAGAN
Warwick, Rt. Revd Anthony M. Priddis, *cons.* 1996,
   apptd 1996; 139 Kenilworth Road, Coventry CV4 7AP

DEAN
Very Revd John Irvine, *apptd* 2001

CANONS RESIDENTIARY
Andrew White, *apptd* 1998; Stuart Beake, *apptd* 2000;
   Justin Welby, *apptd* 2002; Adrian Daffern, *apptd* 2003

Director of Music, Rupert Jeffcoat, *apptd* 1997

ARCHDEACONS
Coventry, Ven. Mark Bryant, *apptd* 2001
Warwick, Ven. Michael Paget-Wilkes, *apptd* 1990

Chancellor, Sir William Gage, *apptd* 1980

Registrar and Legal Secretary, David Dumbleton
Diocesan Secretary, Isobel Chapman, Church House, Palmerston Road, Coventry CV5 6FJ Tel: 024-7671 0500

DERBY *(Canterbury)*
6th BISHOP
Rt. Revd Jonathan S. Bailey, *cons.*1992, *apptd* 1995; Derby Church House, Full Street, Derby DE1 3DR
Signs Jonathan Derby

BISHOP SUFFRAGAN
Repton, Rt. Revd David C. Hawtin, *cons.* 1999, *apptd* 1999; Repton House, Lea, Matlock, Derbys DE4 5JP

DEAN
Very Revd Michael F. Perham, *apptd* 1998

CANONS RESIDENTIARY
Barrie Gauge, *apptd* 1999; Nicholas Henshall, *apptd* 2002; Andrew Brown, *apptd* 2003
Organist, Peter Gould, *apptd* 1982

ARCHDEACONS
Chesterfield, Ven. David Garnett, *apptd* 1996
Derby, Ven. Ian Gatford, *apptd* 1992

Chancellor, His Hon. Judge John Bullimore, *apptd* 1981
Registrar and Legal Secretary, Mrs Nadine Waldron
Diocesan Secretary, Bob Carey, Derby Church House, Full Street, Derby DE1 3DR Tel: 01332-382233

ELY *(Canterbury)*
68th BISHOP
Rt. Revd Dr Anthony Russell, *cons.* 1988, *apptd* 2000; The Bishop's House, Ely, Cambs CB7 4DW
Signs Anthony Ely

BISHOP SUFFRAGAN
Huntingdon, Rt. Revd Dr John Inge, *cons.* 2003, *apptd* 2003; 14 Lynn Road, Ely, Cambs CB6 1DA

DEAN
Very Revd Dr Michael Chandler, *apptd* 2003

CANONS RESIDENTIARY
Peter Sills, *apptd* 2000

Organist, Paul Trepte, FRCO, *apptd* 1991

ARCHDEACONS
Ely, Ven. Jeffrey Watson, *apptd* 1993
Huntingdon Wisbech, Ven. John Beer, *apptd* 1997

Chancellor, William Gage, QC
Registrar, Peter Beesley
Diocesan Secretary, Dr Matthew Lavis, Bishop Woodford House, Barton Road, Ely, Cambs CB7 4DX Tel: 01353-652701

EXETER *(Canterbury)*
70th BISHOP
Rt. Revd Michael L. Langrish, *cons.* 1993, *apptd* 2000; The Palace, Exeter, EX1 1HY *Signs* Michael Exon

BISHOPS SUFFRAGAN
Crediton, Rt. Revd Richard S. Hawkins, *cons.* 1988, *apptd* 1996; 10 The Close, Exeter EX1 1EZ

Plymouth, Rt. Revd John H. Garton, *cons.* 1996, *apptd* 1996; 31 Riverside Walk, Tamerton Foliot, Plymouth PL5 4AQ

DEAN
Very Revd Keith Jones, *apptd* 1996

CANONS RESIDENTIARY
David Ison, *apptd* 1997; Neil Collings, *apptd* 1999; Carl Turner, *apptd* 2001
Director of Music, Andrew Millington, *apptd* 1999

ARCHDEACONS
Barnstaple, Ven. David Gunn-Johnson, *apptd* 2003
Exeter, Ven. Dr Paul Gardner, *apptd* 2003
Plymouth, Ven. Tony Wilds, *apptd* 2001
Totnes, Ven. Richard Gilpin, *apptd* 1996

Chancellor, Sir David Calcutt, QC, *apptd* 1971
Registrar and Legal Secretary, R. K. Wheeler
Diocesan Secretary, Mark Beedell, Diocesan House, Palace Gate, Exeter, Devon EX1 1HX Tel: 01392-272686

GIBRALTAR IN EUROPE *(Canterbury)*
BISHOP
Rt. Revd Geoffrey Rowell, *cons.* 1994, *apptd* 2001; Bishop's Lodge, Church Road, Worth, Cranley, West Sussex, RH10 7RT

BISHOP SUFFRAGAN
In Europe Rt. Revd David Hamid, *cons.* 2002, *apptd* 2002; 14 Tufton Street, London SW1P 3QZ
Dean, Cathedral Church of the Holy Trinity, Gibraltar, Very Revd Kenneth Robinson
Chancellor, Pro-Cathedral of St Paul, Valletta, Malta, Canon Alan Woods
Chancellor, Pro-Cathedral of the Holy Trinity, Brussels, Belgium, Canon Nigel Walker

ARCHDEACONS
Eastern, Ven. Patrick Curran
North-West Europe, Ven. Geoffrey Allen
France, Ven. Anthony Wells
Gibraltar, Ven. Howell Sasser
Italy, Ven. Gordon Reid
Scandinavia and Germany, Ven. David Ratcliff
Switzerland, Ven. Peter Hawker, OBE

Chancellor, Sir David Calcutt, QC
Registrar and Legal Secretary, John Underwood
Diocesan Secretary, Adrian Mumford, 14 Tufton Street, London SW1P 3QZ Tel: 020-7898 1155

GLOUCESTER *(Canterbury)*
39th BISHOP
Rt. Revd David Bentley, *cons.* 1986, *apptd* 1993; Bishopscourt, Pitt Street, Gloucester GL1 2BQ.
Signs David Gloucester (*due to retire* 31 December 2003)

BISHOP SUFFRAGAN
Tewkesbury, Rt. Revd John S. Went, *cons.* 1995, *apptd* 1995; Green Acre, 166 Hempsted Lane, Hempsted, Gloucester GL2 5LG

DEAN
Very Revd Nicholas Bury, *apptd* 1997

CANONS RESIDENTIARY
Neil Heavisides, *apptd* 1993; David Hoyle, *apptd* 2002; Guy Bridgewater, *apptd* 2002; Celia Thomson, *apptd* 2003

Director of Music, Andrew Nethsingha, *apptd* 2002

ARCHDEACONS
Cheltenham, Ven. Hedley Ringrose, *apptd* 1998
Gloucester, Ven. Geoffrey Sidaway, *apptd* 2000

Chancellor and Vicar-General, June Rodgers, *apptd* 1990
Registrar and Legal Secretary, Chris Peak
Diocesan Secretary, Michael Williams, Church House, College Green, Gloucester GL1 2LY Tel: 01452-410022

GUILDFORD *(Canterbury)*
9th BISHOP
vacant; Willow Grange, Woking Road, Guildford GU4 7QS
Tel: 01483-590500 Fax: 01483-590501

BISHOP SUFFRAGAN
Dorking, Rt. Revd Ian Brackley, *cons.* 1996, *apptd* 1995;
Dayspring, 13 Pilgrims Way, Guildford GU4 8AD

DEAN
The Very Revd Victor Stock, *apptd* 2002

CANONS RESIDENTIARY
Dr Maureen Palmer, *apptd* 1996; Julian Hubbard, *apptd* 1999; Dr Nicholas Thistlethwaite, *apptd* 1999; Jonathan Frost, *apptd* 2002
Organist, Stephen Farr, FRCO, *apptd* 1999

ARCHDEACONS
Dorking, Ven. Mark Wilson, *apptd* 1996
Surrey, Ven. Robert Reiss, *apptd* 1996

Chancellor, The Worshipful Andrew Jordan
Registrar and Legal Secretary, Peter Beesley
Diocesan Secretary, Stephen Marriott

HEREFORD *(Canterbury)*
104th BISHOP
Rt. Revd John Oliver, *cons.* 1990, *apptd* 1990 *(due to retire 30 November 2003);* The Palace, Hereford HR4 9BN

BISHOP SUFFRAGAN
Ludlow, Ven. Michael Wrenford Hooper, *cons.* 2002, *apptd* 2002; Bishop's House, Halford, Craven Arms, Shropshire SY7 9BT

DEAN
Very Revd Michael Tavinor, *apptd* 2002

CANONS RESIDENTIARY
John Tiller, *apptd* 1984; Val Hamer, *apptd* 2002; Andrew Piper, *apptd* 2002

Organist, Geraint Bowen, FRCO, *apptd* 2001

ARCHDEACONS
Hereford, Ven. John Tiller, *apptd* 2002
Ludlow, Michael Wrenford Hooper, *apptd* 2002

Chancellor, Val Hamer
Joint Registrars and Legal Secretaries, Tom Jordan; Peter Beesley

Diocesan Secretary, Sylvia Green, The Palace, Hereford HR4 9BL Tel: 01432-353863

LEICESTER *(Canterbury)*
6th BISHOP
Rt. Revd Timothy J. Stevens, *cons.* 1995, *apptd* 1999; Bishop's Lodge, 10 Springfield Road, Leicester LE2 3BD
Signs Timothy Leicester

DEAN
Very Revd Vivienne F. Faull, *apptd* 2000

CANONS RESIDENTIARY
Michael Wilson, *apptd* 1988; John Craig, *apptd* 2002

Master of Music, Jonathan Gregory, *apptd* 1994

ARCHDEACONS
Leicester, Ven. Richard Atkinson, *apptd* 2002
Loughborough, Ven. Ian Stanes, *apptd* 1992

Chancellor, James Behrens
Registrar and Legal Secretary, Trevor Kirkman
Diocesan Secretary, Andrew Howard; Church House, 3–5 St Martin's East, Leicester LE1 5FX Tel: 0116-248 7400

LICHFIELD *(Canterbury)*
98th BISHOP
Rt. Revd Jonathan Gledhill *cons.* 1996, *apptd* 2003; Bishop's House, The Close, Lichfield WS13 7LG

BISHOPS SUFFRAGAN
Shrewsbury, Rt. Revd Alan Smith, *cons.* 2001, *apptd* 2002; 68 London Road, Shrewsbury SY2 6PG
Stafford, Rt. Revd Christopher J. Hill, *cons.* 1996, *apptd* 1996; Ash Garth, Broughton Crescent, Barlaston, Staffs ST12 9DD
Wolverhampton, Rt. Revd Michael G. Bourke, *cons.* 1993, *apptd* 1993; 61 Richmond Road, Wolverhampton WV3 9JH

DEAN
Very Revd Michael Yorke, *apptd* 1999

CANONS RESIDENTIARY
A. N. Barnard, *apptd* 1977; C. W. Taylor, *apptd* 1995; Ven. Christopher Liley, *apptd* 2001

Organist, Philip Scriven, *apptd* 2002

ARCHDEACONS
Lichfield, Ven. Christopher Liley, *apptd* 2001
Salop, Ven. John Hall, *apptd* 1998
Stoke-on-Trent, Ven. Godfrey Owen Stone *apptd* 2002
Walsall, Ven. Tony Sadler, *apptd* 1997

Chancellor, His Hon. Judge John Shand
Joint Registrars and Legal Secretaries, J. P. Thorneycroft; N. Blackie
Diocesan Secretary, D. R. Taylor, St Mary's House, The Close, Lichfield, Staffs WS13 7LD Tel: 01543-306030

LINCOLN *(Canterbury)*
71st BISHOP
Rt. Revd Dr John Saxbee, *cons.* 1994, *apptd* 2002; Bishop's House, Eastgate, Lincoln LN2 1QQ
Signs John Lincoln

BISHOPS SUFFRAGAN
Grantham, Rt. Revd Alastair L. J. Redfern, *cons.* 1997,
  apptd 1997; Fairacre, 234 Barrowby Road, Grantham, Lincs
  NG31 8NP
Grimsby, Rt. Revd David D. J. Rossdale, *cons.* 2000, *apptd*
  2000; Bishop's House, Church Lane, Irby-upon-Humber,
  Grimsby DN37 7JR

DEAN
Very Revd Alexander Knight, *apptd* 1998

CANONS RESIDENTIARY
Alan Nugent, *apptd* 2003; Gavin Kirk, *apptd* 2003

Organist, Colin Walsh, FRCO, *apptd* 1988

ARCHDEACONS
Lincoln, Ven. Arthur Hawes, *apptd* 1995
Lindsey, Ven. Dr Timothy Ellis, *apptd* 2001
Stow, see Lindsey

Chancellor, Peter N. Collier, QC, *apptd* 1999
Registrar and Legal Secretary, Derek Wellman
Diocesan Secretary, Philip Hamlyn Williams, The Old
  Palace, Lincoln LN2 1PU Tel: 01522-529241

LIVERPOOL *(York)*
7th BISHOP
Rt. Revd James Jones, *cons.* 1994, *apptd* 1998;
  Bishop's Lodge, Woolton Park, Liverpool L25 6DT
  Signs James Liverpool

BISHOP SUFFRAGAN
Warrington, Rt. Revd David Jennings, *cons.* 2000, *apptd*
  2000; 34 Central Avenue, Eccleston Park, Prescot,
  Merseyside L34 2QP

DEAN
Rt. Revd Dean Dr Rupert W. N. Hoare

CANONS RESIDENTIARY
Mark Boyling, *apptd* 1994; Anthony Hawley, *apptd*
  2002

Organist, Prof. Ian Tracey, *apptd* 1980

ARCHDEACONS
Liverpool, Ven Richard Panter, *apptd* 2002
Warrington, Ven. Peter Bradley, *apptd* 2001

Chancellor, Hon. Sir Mark Hedley
Registrar and Legal Secretary, Roger Arden
Diocesan Secretary, Mike Eastwood, Church House, 1
  Hanover Street, Liverpool L1 3DW Tel: 0151-709 9722

MANCHESTER *(York)*
11th BISHOP
Rt. Revd Nigel McCulloch, *cons.* 1986, *apptd* 2002,
  trans. 2002; Bishopscourt, Bury New Road, Manchester M7
  4LE *Signs* Nigel Manchester

BISHOPS SUFFRAGAN
Bolton, Rt. Revd David K. Gillett, *cons.* 1999, *apptd*
  1999; 4 Bishop's Lodge, Bolton Road, Hawkshaw, Bury
  BL8 4JN
Hulme, Rt. Revd Stephen R. Lowe, *cons.* 1999, *apptd.*
  1999; 14 Moorgate Avenue, Withington, Manchester
  M20 1HE

Middleton, Rt. Revd Michael A. O. Lewis, *cons.* 1999,
  apptd 1999; The Hollies, Manchester Road, Rochdale
  OL11 3QY

DEAN
Very Revd Kenneth Riley, *apptd* 1993

CANONS RESIDENTIARY
John Atherton, Ph.D., *apptd* 1984; Paul Denby, *apptd*
  1995

Organist, Christopher Stokes, *apptd* 1992

ARCHDEACONS
Bolton, John Applegate, *apptd* 2002
Manchester, Ven. Alan Wolstencroft, *apptd* 1998
Rochdale, Ven. Andrew Ballard, *apptd* 2000

Chancellor, J. L. L. Holden
Registrar and Legal Secretary, Michael Darlington
Diocesan Secretary, Nigel Spraggins, 1st Floor, Diocesan
  Church House, 90 Deansgate, Manchester M3 2GH
  Tel: 0161-833 9521

NEWCASTLE *(York)*
11th BISHOP
Rt. Revd J. Martin Wharton, *cons.* 1992, *apptd* 1997;
  Bishop's House, 29 Moor Road South, Gosforth,
  Newcastle upon Tyne NE3 1PA *Signs* Martin Newcastle

STIPENDIARY ASSISTANT BISHOP
Rt. Revd Paul Richardson, *cons.* 1987, *apptd* 1999

HON. ASSISTANT BISHOP
Rt. Revd K. E. Gill, *cons.* 1972, *apptd* 1998

DEAN
Very Revd Christopher C. Dalliston, *apptd* 2003

CANONS RESIDENTIARY
Peter Strange, *apptd* 1986; Ven. Peter Elliott, *apptd*
  1993; Geoffrey Miller, *apptd* 1999; David Elkington,
  apptd 2002

Director of Music, Scott Farrell, *apptd* 2002

ARCHDEACONS
Lindisfarne, Ven. Robert Langley, *apptd* 2001
Northumberland, Ven. Peter Elliott, *apptd* 1993

Chancellor, Prof. David McClean, *apptd* 1998
Registrar and Legal Secretary, Jane Lowdon
Diocesan Secretary, Philip Davies, Church House, St John's
  Terrace, North Shields, NE29 6HS Tel: 0191-270 4100

NORWICH *(Canterbury)*
71st BISHOP
Rt. Revd Graham R. James, *cons.* 1993, *apptd* 2000;
  Bishop's House, Norwich NR3 1SB. *Signs* Graham Norvic

BISHOPS SUFFRAGAN
Lynn, vacant
Thetford, Rt. Revd David J. Atkinson, *cons.* 2001, *apptd*
  2001; Rectory Meadow, Bramerton, Norwich NR14 7DW

DEAN
vacant

CANONS RESIDENTIARY
Ven. Clifford Offer, *apptd* 1994; Richard Hanmer,
  apptd 1994; Jeremy Haselock, *apptd* 1998;
  Michael Kitchener, *apptd* 1999

Organist, David Dunnett, *apptd* 1996

ARCHDEACONS
Lynn, Ven. Martin Gray, *apptd* 1999
Norfolk, Ven. David Hayden, *apptd* 2002
Norwich, Ven. Clifford Offer, *apptd* 1994

Chancellor, The Hon. Mr Justice Blofeld, *apptd* 1998
Registrar and Legal Secretary, John Herring
Diocesan Secretary, Revd Richard Bowett, Diocesan House,
  109 Dereham Road, Easton, Norwich, Norfolk NR9 5ES
  Tel: 01603-880853

OXFORD *(Canterbury)*
41st BISHOP
Rt. Revd Richard D. Harries, *cons.* 1987, *apptd* 1987;
  Diocesan Church House, North Hinksey Lane, Oxford
  OX2 0NB *Signs* Richard Oxon

AREA BISHOPS
Buckingham, Rt. Revd Alan Wilson *cons.* 2003, *apptd*
  2003; Sheridan, Grimms Hill, Great Missenden, Bucks
  HP16 9BD
Dorchester, Rt. Revd Colin Fletcher, *cons.* 2000, *apptd*
  2000; Arran House, Sandy Lane, Yarnton, Oxon OX5 1PB
Reading, vacant

DEAN OF CHRIST CHURCH
vacant

CANONS RESIDENTIARY
Oliver O'Donovan, *apptd* 1982; Marilyn Parry, *apptd*
  2001; Nicholas Coulton, *apptd* 2002; Ven. John
  Morrison, *apptd* 1998

Organist, Stephen Darlington, FRCO, *apptd* 1985

ARCHDEACONS
Berkshire, Ven. Norman Russell, *apptd* 1998
Buckingham, Ven. Sheila Watson, *apptd* 2002
Oxford, Ven. John Morrison, *apptd* 1998

Chancellor, Dr Rupert Bursell *apptd* 2001
Registrar and Legal Secretary, Dr F. E. Robson and Revd.
  Canon John Rees
Diocesan Secretary, Rosemary Pearce, Diocesan Church
  House, North Hinksey, Oxford OX2 0NB Tel: 01865-208202

PETERBOROUGH *(Canterbury)*
37th BISHOP
Rt. Revd Ian P. M. Cundy, *cons.* 1992, *apptd* 1996;
  Bishop's Lodging, The Palace, Peterborough PE1 1YA
  Signs Ian Petriburg

BISHOP SUFFRAGAN
Brixworth, Rt. Revd Frank White, *cons.* 2002, *apptd*
  2002; 4 The Avenue, Dallington, Northampton NN1 4RZ

DEAN
Very Revd Michael Bunker, *apptd* 1992

CANONS RESIDENTIARY
David Painter, *apptd* 2000; Bill Croft, *apptd* 2001;
  Stephen Cottrell, *apptd* 2001

Organist, Christopher Gower, FRCO, *apptd* 1977

ARCHDEACONS
Northampton, Ven. Michael Chapman, *apptd* 1991
Oakham, Ven. David Painter, *apptd* 2000

Chancellor, Thomas Coningsby, QC, *apptd* 1989
Registrar and Legal Secretary, Canon Raymond Hemingray
Diocesan Secretary, Richard Pestell, Diocesan Office, The
  Palace, Peterborough, Cambs PE1 1YB Tel: 01733-887000

PORTSMOUTH *(Canterbury)*
8th BISHOP
Rt. Revd Dr Kenneth W. Stevenson, *cons.* 1995, *apptd*
  1995; Bishopsgrove, 26 Osborn Road, Fareham,
  Hants PO16 7DQ *Signs* Kenneth Portsmouth

DEAN
Very Revd D. C. Brindley, *apptd* 2002

CANONS RESIDENTIARY
David Isaac, *apptd* 1990; Gavin Kirk, *apptd* 1998;
  Michael Tristram *apptd.* 2003

Organist, David Price, *apptd* 1996

ARCHDEACONS
Isle of Wight, Ven. Trevor Reader, *apptd* 2003
Portsdown, Ven. Christopher Lowson, *apptd* 1999
The Meon, Ven. Peter Hancock, *apptd* 1999

Chancellor (acting), C. Clark, QC
Registrar and Legal Secretary, Hilary Tyler
Diocesan Secretary, Michael Jordan, Cathedral House,
  St Thomas's Street, Portsmouth, Hants PO1 2HA
  Tel: 023-9282 5731

RIPON AND LEEDS *(York)*
12th BISHOP
Rt. Revd John R. Packer, *cons.* 1996, *apptd* 2000; Bishop
  Mount, Ripon HG4 5DP. *Signs* John Ripon and Leeds

DEAN
Very Revd John Methuen, *apptd* 1995

CANONS RESIDENTIARY
Michael Glanville-Smith, *apptd* 1990; Keith Punshon,
  apptd 1996

Organist, Simon Morley *apptd* 2003

ARCHDEACONS
Leeds, Ven. John Oliver, *apptd* 1992
Richmond, Ven. Kenneth Good, *apptd* 1993

Chancellor, His Hon. Judge Grenfell, *apptd* 1992
Registrars and Legal Secretaries, Christopher Tunnard,
  Nichola Harding
Diocesan Secretary, Philip Arundel, Diocesan Office,
  St Mary's Street, Leeds LS9 7DP Tel: 0113-200 0540

ROCHESTER *(Canterbury)*
106th BISHOP
Rt. Revd Dr Michael Nazir-Ali, *cons.* 1984, *apptd* 1994;
Bishopscourt, Rochester ME1 1TS *Signs* Michael Roffen
BISHOP SUFFRAGAN
Tonbridge, Rt. Revd Dr Brian C. Castle, *cons.* 2002, *apptd*
2002; Bishop's Lodge, 48 St Botolph's Road, Sevenoaks
TN13 3AG

DEAN
vacant

CANONS RESIDENTIARY
Jonathan Meyrick, *apptd* 1998; Canon Ralph Godsall,
apptd 2001
Director of Music, Roger Sayer, FRCO, *apptd* 1995

ARCHDEACONS
Bromley, Ven. Garth Norman, *apptd* 1994
Rochester, Ven. Peter Lock, *apptd* 2000
Tonbridge, Ven. Clive Mansell, *apptd* 2002

Chancellor, His Hon. Judge Michael Goodman, *apptd*
1971
Registrar and Legal Secretary, Michael Thatcher
Diocesan Secretary, Mrs Louise Gilbert, St Nicholas Church,
Boley Hill, Rochester ME1 1SL Tel: 01634-830333

ST ALBANS *(Canterbury)*
9th BISHOP
Rt. Revd Christopher W. Herbert, *cons.* 1995, *apptd*
1995; Abbey Gate House, St Albans AL3 4HD
Signs Christopher St Albans

BISHOPS SUFFRAGAN
Bedford, Rt. Revd Richard N. Inwood, *apptd* 2002
Hertford, Rt. Revd Christopher R. J. Foster, *cons.* 2001,
apptd 2001; Hertford House, Abbey Mill Lane,
St Albans AL3 4HE

DEAN
Very Revd Christopher Lewis, *apptd* 1993

CANONS RESIDENTIARY
Michael Sansom, *apptd* 1988; Iain Lane, *apptd* 2000;
Richard Wheeler, *apptd* 2001; Dennis Stamps, *apptd*
2002; Stephen Lake, *apptd* 2001

Organist, Andrew Lucas, *apptd* 1998

ARCHDEACONS
Bedford, Ven. Malcolm Lesiter, *apptd* 1993
Hertford, Ven. Trevor Jones, *apptd* 1997
St Albans, Ven. Helen Cunliffe, *apptd* 2003

Chancellor, Roger Kaye, *apptd* 2002
Registrar and Legal Secretary, David Cheetham
Diocesan Secretary, Susan Pope, Holywell Lodge,
41 Holywell Hill, St Albans AL1 1HE Tel: 01727-854532

ST EDMUNDSBURY AND IPSWICH
(Canterbury)
9th BISHOP
Rt. Revd J. H. Richard Lewis, *cons.* 1992, *apptd* 1997;
Bishop's House, 4 Park Road, Ipswich IP1 3ST *Signs* Richard
St Edmundsbury and Ipswich

BISHOP SUFFRAGAN
Dunwich, Rt. Revd Clive Young, *cons.* 1999, *apptd* 1999;
28 Westerfield Road, Ipswich IP4 2UJ

DEAN
Very Revd James Atwell, *apptd* 1995

CANONS RESIDENTIARY
Martin Shaw, *apptd* 1989; Andrew Todd, *apptd* 2001;
Peter Barham, *apptd* 2003
Organist, James Thomas, *apptd* 1997

ARCHDEACONS
Ipswich, Ven. Terry Gibson, *apptd* 1987
Sudbury, Ven. John Cox, *apptd* 1995
Suffolk, Ven. Geoffrey Arrand, *apptd* 1994

Chancellor, The Hon. Mr Justice Blofeld, *apptd* 1974
Registrar and Legal Secretary, James Hall
Diocesan Secretary, Nicholas Edgell, Churchgates House,
Cutler Street, Ipswich IP1 1QU Tel: 01473-298500

SALISBURY *(Canterbury)*
77th BISHOP
Rt. Revd David S. Stancliffe, *cons.* 1993, *apptd* 1993;
South Canonry, The Close, Salisbury SP1 2ER
Signs David Sarum

BISHOPS SUFFRAGAN
Ramsbury, Rt. Revd Peter F. Hullah, *cons.* 1999, *apptd*
1999
Sherborne, Rt. Revd Timothy M. Thornton, *cons.* 2001,
apptd 2001

DEAN
vacant

CANONS RESIDENTIARY
Jeremy Davies, *apptd* 1985; D. M. K. Durston, *apptd*
1992; June Osborne, *apptd* 1995

Organist, Simon Lole, *apptd* 1997

ARCHDEACONS
Dorset, Ven. Alistair Magowan, *apptd* 2000
Sherborne, Ven. Paul Wheatley, *apptd* 1991
Wilts, Ven. Barney Hopkinson, *apptd* 1998
Sarum, Ven. Alan Jeans, *apptd* 2003

Chancellor, His Hon. Judge Samuel Wiggs, *apptd* 1997
Registrar and Legal Secretary, Andrew Johnson
Acting Diocesan Secretary, Christopher Love, Church
House, Crane Street, Salisbury SP1 2QB Tel: 01722-411922

SHEFFIELD *(York)*
6th BISHOP
Rt. Revd John (Jack) Nicholls, *cons.* 1990, *apptd* 1997;
Bishopscroft, Snaithing Lane, Sheffield S10 3LG
Signs Jack Sheffield

BISHOP SUFFRAGAN
Doncaster, Rt. Revd Cyril Guy Ashton, *cons.* 2000, *apptd*
2000; Bishop's House, 3 Farrington Court, Wickersley,
Rotherham S66 1JQ

DEAN
Very Revd Peter Bradley, *apptd* 2003

CANONS RESIDENTIARY
Ven. Richard Blackburn, *apptd* 1999; Ven. Paul Shackerley, *apptd* 2002; Ven. Howard Such, *apptd* 2003
Master of Music, Neil Taylor, *apptd* 1997

ARCHDEACONS
Doncaster, Ven. Robert Fitzharris, *apptd* 2001
Sheffield, Ven. Richard Blackburn, *apptd* 1999
Chancellor, Prof. David McClean, *apptd* 1992
Registrar and Legal Secretary, Mrs Miranda Myers
Diocesan Secretary, Tony Beck, FCIS, Diocesan Church House, 95–99 Effingham Street, Rotherham S65 1BL
Tel: 01709-309100

SODOR AND MAN *(York)*
80th BISHOP
vacant; The Bishop's House, Quarterbridge Road, Douglas, Isle of Man IM2 3RF

CANONS
Brian Kelly, *apptd* 1980; Hinton Bird, *apptd* 1993; Duncan Whitworth, *apptd* 1996; Malcolm Convery, *apptd* 1999

ARCHDEACON
Isle of Man, Ven. Brian Partington, OBE, *apptd* 1996

Vicar-General and Chancellor, Clare Faulds
Registrar and Legal Secretary, Christopher Callow
Diocesan Secretary, Christine Roberts, Holly Cottage, Ballaughton Meadows, Douglas, Isle of Man IM2 1JG
Tel: 01624-626994

SOUTHWARK *(Canterbury)*
9th BISHOP
Rt. Revd Dr Tom F. Butler, *cons.* 1985, *apptd* 1998; Bishop's House, 38 Tooting Bec Gardens, London SW16 1QZ
Signs Thomas Southwark

AREA BISHOPS
Croydon, Rt. Revd Nicholas Baines, *cons.* 2003, *apptd* 2003
Kingston upon Thames, Rt. Revd Richard Cheetham, *cons.* 2002, *apptd* 2002
Woolwich, Rt. Revd Dr Colin O. Buchanan, *cons.* 1985, *apptd* 1996; 37 South Road, Forest Hill, London SE23 2UJ

DEAN
Very Revd Colin B. Slee, OBE, *apptd* 1994

CANONS RESIDENTIARY
Jeffrey John, *apptd* 1997; Bruce Saunders, *apptd* 1997; Andrew Nunn, *apptd* 1999; Stephen Roberts, *apptd* 2000

Organist, Peter Wright, FRCO, *apptd* 1989

ARCHDEACONS
Croydon, Ven. Tony Davies, *apptd* 1994
Lambeth, vacant
Lewisham, Ven. Christine Hardman, *apptd* 2001
Reigate, Ven. Daniel Kajumba, *apptd* 2001
Southwark, Ven. Douglas Bartles-Smith, *apptd* 1985
Wandsworth, Ven. David Gerrard, *apptd* 1989
Chancellor, Charles George, QC

Registrar and Legal Secretary, Paul Morris
Diocesan Secretary, Simon Parton, Trinity House, 4 Chapel Court, Borough High Street, London SE1 1HW
Tel: 020-7939 9400

SOUTHWELL *(York)*
10th BISHOP
Rt. Revd George H. Cassidy, *cons.* 1999, *apptd* 1999; Bishop's Manor, Southwell NG25 0JR
Signs George Southwell

BISHOP SUFFRAGAN
Sherwood, Rt. Revd Alan W. Morgan, *cons.* 1989, *apptd* 1989; Dunham House, Westgate, Southwell, Notts NG25 0JL

DEAN
Very Revd David Leaning, *apptd* 1991

CANONS RESIDENTIARY
Richard Davey, *apptd* 1999; Jacqueline Jones, *apptd* 2003

Organist, Paul Hale, *apptd* 1989

ARCHDEACONS
Newark, Ven. Nigel Peyton, *apptd* 1999
Nottingham, Ven. Gordon Ogilvie, *apptd* 1996

Chancellor, John Shand, *apptd* 1981
Registrar and Legal Secretary, Christopher Hodson
Diocesan Secretary, Dunham House, Westgate, Southwell, Notts NG25 0JL Tel: 01636-817204

TRURO *(Canterbury)*
14th BISHOP
Rt. Revd William Ind, *cons.* 1987, *apptd* 1997; Lis Escop, Truro TR3 6QQ. *Signs* William Truro

BISHOP SUFFRAGAN
St Germans, Revd Royden Screech, *cons.* 2000, *apptd* 2000

DEAN
Very Revd Michael A. Moxon, LVO, *apptd* 1998

CANONS RESIDENTIARY
Perran Gay, *apptd* 1994; Peter Walker, *apptd* 2001

Organist, Robert Sharpe, *apptd* 2002

ARCHDEACONS
Cornwall, Ven. Rodney Whiteman, *apptd* 2000
Bodmin, Ven. Clive Cohen, *apptd* 2000

Chancellor, Timothy Briden, *apptd* 1998
Registrar and Legal Secretary, Michael Follett
Diocesan Secretary, Sheri Sturgess, Diocesan House, Kenwyn, Truro TR1 1JQ Tel: 01872-274351

WAKEFIELD *(York)*
12th BISHOP
Rt. Revd Stephen Platten, *cons.* 2003, *apptd* 2003; Bishop's Lodge, Woodthorpe Lane, Wakefield, WF2 6JL
Signs Stephen Wakefield

BISHOP SUFFRAGAN
Pontefract, Rt. Revd Anthony William Robinson, *cons.* 2003, *apptd* 2002; Pontefract House, 181A Manygates Lane, Wakefield WF2 7DR

DEAN
Very Revd George P. Nairn-Briggs, *apptd* 1997

CANONS RESIDENTIARY
Richard Capper, *apptd* 1997; Robert Gage, *apptd* 1997; Ian Gaskell, *apptd* 1998; John Holmes, *apptd* 1998

Organist, Jonathan Bielby, FRCO, *apptd* 1972

ARCHDEACONS
Halifax, Ven. Robert Freeman, *apptd* 2003
Pontefract, Ven. Jonathan Greener, *apptd* 2003
Chancellor, Peter Collier, QC, *apptd* 1992
Registrar and Legal Secretary, Linda Box
Diocesan Secretary, Ashley Ellis, Church House, 1 South Parade, Wakefield WF1 1LP Tel: 01924-371802

WORCESTER *(Canterbury)*
112th BISHOP
Rt. Revd Dr Peter S. M. Selby, *cons.* 1984, *apptd* 1997; The Bishop's House, Hartlebury Castle, Kidderminster DY11 7XX *Signs* Peter Wigorn

SUFFRAGAN BISHOP
Dudley, Rt. Revd Dr David S. Walker, *cons.* 2000, *apptd* 2000; The Bishop's House, Bishop's Walk, Cradley Heath B64 7JF

DEAN
Very Revd Peter J. Marshall, *apptd* 1997

CANONS RESIDENTIARY
Bruce Ruddock, *apptd.* 1999; Ven. Dr Joy Tetley, *apptd* 1999; Alvyn Pettersen, *apptd* 2002

Organist, Adrian Lucas, *apptd* 1996

ARCHDEACONS
Dudley, Ven. Fred Trethewey, *apptd* 2001
Worcester, Ven. Dr Joy Tetley
Chancellor, Charles Mynors, *apptd* 1999
Registrar and Legal Secretary, Michael Huskinson
Diocesan Secretary, Robert Higham, The Old Palace, Deansway, Worcester WR1 2JE Tel: 01905-20537

ROYAL PECULIARS
WESTMINSTER

The Collegiate Church of St Peter

Dean, Very Revd Dr Wesley Carr, *apptd* 1997
Sub Dean and Archdeacon, David Hutt, *apptd* 1995
Canons of Westminster, David Hutt, *apptd* 1995; Michael Middleton, *apptd* 1997; Robert Wright, *apptd* 1998; Dr Tom Wright, *apptd* 1999
Chapter Clerk and Receiver-General, Maj.-Gen. David Burden, CB, CBE, Chapter Office, 20 Dean's Yard, London SW1P 3PA
Organist, James O'Donnell, *apptd* 1999
Registrar, Stuart Holmes, MVO
Legal Secretary, Christopher Vyse, *apptd* 2000

WINDSOR

The Queen's Free Chapel of St George within Her Castle of Windsor

Dean, Rt. Revd David Conner, *apptd* 1998
Canons Residentiary, John White, *apptd* 1982; Laurence Gunner, *apptd* 1996; John Ovenden, *apptd* 1998
Chapter Clerk, Lt.-Col. Nigel Newman, LVO, *apptd* 1990, Chapter Office, The Cloisters, Windsor Castle, Windsor, Berks SL4 1NJ
Organist, vacant

OTHER ANGLICAN CHURCHES

THE CHURCH IN WALES
The Anglican Church was the established church in Wales from the 16th century until 1920, when the estrangement of the majority of Welsh people from Anglicanism resulted in disestablishment. Since then the Church in Wales has been an autonomous province consisting of six sees. The bishops are elected by an electoral college comprising elected lay and clerical members, who also elect one of the diocesan bishops as Archbishop of Wales.

The legislative body of the Church in Wales is the Governing Body, which has 350 members divided between the three orders of bishops, clergy and laity. Its President is the Archbishop of Wales and it meets twice annually. Its decisions are binding upon all members of the Church. The Church's property and finances are the responsibility of the Representative Body. There are about 90,000 members of the Church in Wales, with about 650 stipendiary clergy and 1,071 parishes.

THE GOVERNING BODY OF THE CHURCH IN WALES, 39 Cathedral Road, Cardiff CF1 9XF Tel: 029-2034 8200
Provincial Secretary, J. Shirley
12th ARCHBISHOP OF WALES, The Most Revd Dr Barry C. Morgan (Bishop of Llandaff), *elected* 2003
Signs Barry Cambrensis
BISHOPS
Bangor (79th), Rt. Revd F. J. Saunders Davies, *b.* 1937, *cons.* 2000, *elected* 1999; Tŷ'r Esgob, Bangor, Gwynedd LL57 2SS *Signs* Saunders Bangor. *Stipendiary clergy,* 72
Llandaff (102nd), Most. Revd Dr Barry C. Morgan, *b.* 1947, *cons.* 1993, *trans.* 1999; Llys Esgob, The Cathedral Green, Llandaff, Cardiff CF5 2YE *Signs* Barry Landav. *Stipendiary clergy,* 146
Monmouth (9th), Rt. Revd Dominic Walker, *b.* 1948, *cons.* 1997, *elected* 2003; Bishopstow, Stow Hill, Newport NP20 4EA *Signs,* Dominic Monmouth. *Stipendiary clergy,* 106
St Asaph (74th), Rt. Revd John S. Davies, *b.* 1943, *cons.* 1999, *elected* 1999; Esgobty, St Asaph, Denbighshire LL17 0TW *Signs* John St Asaph. *Stipendiary clergy,* 116
St David's (127th), Rt. Revd Carl N. Cooper, *b.* 1960, *cons.* 2002, *elected* 2002; Llys Esgob, Abergwili, Carmarthen SA31 2JG *Signs* Carl St Davids. *Stipendiary clergy,* 126
Swansea and Brecon (8th), Rt. Revd Anthony E. Pierce, *b.* 1941, *cons.* 1999, *elected* 1999; Ely Tower, Brecon, Powys LD3 9DE. *Signs* Anthony Swansea & Brecon. *Stipendiary clergy,* 85

The stipend for a diocesan bishop of the Church in Wales is £31,073 a year for 2003–4.

THE SCOTTISH EPISCOPAL CHURCH
The Scottish Episcopal Church was founded after the Act of Settlement (1690) established the presbyterian nature of the Church of Scotland. The Scottish Episcopal Church is in full communion with the Church of England

but is autonomous. The governing authority is the General Synod, an elected body of approximately 170 members which meets once a year. The diocesan bishop who convenes and presides at meetings of the General Synod is called the Primus and is elected by his fellow bishops.

There are 45,077 members of the Scottish Episcopal Church, of whom 29,821 are communicants. There are seven bishops, approximately 482 serving clergy, and 313 churches and places of worship.

THE GENERAL SYNOD OF THE SCOTTISH EPISCOPAL CHURCH, 21 Grosvenor Crescent, Edinburgh EH12 5EE Tel: 0131-225 6357 Web: www.scottishepiscopal.com
Secretary-General, J. F. Stuart
PRIMUS OF THE SCOTTISH EPISCOPAL CHURCH, Most Revd A. Bruce Cameron (Bishop of Aberdeen and Orkney), *elected* 2000

BISHOPS
Aberdeen and Orkney, A. Bruce Cameron, *b.* 1941, *cons.* 1992, *elected* 1992. *Clergy,* 54
Argyll and the Isles, vacant, *Clergy* 22
Brechin, Neville Chamberlain, *b.* 1939, *cons.* 1997, *elected* 1997. *Clergy,* 35
Edinburgh, Brian Smith, *b.* 1943, *cons.* 1993, *elected* 2001. *Clergy,* 162
Glasgow and Galloway, Idris Jones, *b.* 1943, *cons.* 1998, *elected* 1998. *Clergy,* 99
Moray, Ross and Caithness, John Crook, *b.* 1940, *cons.* 1999, *elected* 1999. *Clergy,* 31
St Andrews, Dunkeld and Dunblane, Michael H. G. Henley, *b.* 1938, *cons.* 1995, *elected* 1995. *Clergy,* 86

The minimum stipend of a diocesan bishop of the Scottish Episcopal Church for 2003–4 is £26,442 (i.e. 1.5 times the minimum clergy stipend of £17,628)

THE CHURCH OF IRELAND

The Anglican Church was the established church in Ireland from the 16th century but never secured the allegiance of a majority of the Irish and was disestablished in 1871. The Church of Ireland is divided into the provinces of Armagh and Dublin, each under an archbishop. The provinces are subdivided into 12 dioceses.

The legislative body is the General Synod, which has 660 members in total, divided between the House of Bishops and the House of Representatives. The Archbishop of Armagh is elected by the House of Bishops; other episcopal elections are made by an electoral college.

There are about 375,000 members of the Church of Ireland, with two archbishops, ten bishops, about 600 clergy and about 1,100 churches and places of worship.

CENTRAL OFFICE, Church of Ireland House, Church Avenue, Rathmines, Dublin 6 Tel: (00 353) (1) 4978422
Chief Officer and Secretary of the Representative Church Body, D. C. Reardon

PROVINCE OF ARMAGH
ARCHBISHOP OF ARMAGH AND PRIMATE OF ALL IRELAND, Most Revd Robert H. A. Eames, Ph.D., *b.* 1937, *cons.* 1975, *trans.* 1986. *Clergy,* 55

BISHOPS
Clogher, Michael G. Jackson, *b.* 1956, *cons.* 2002, *apptd* 2002. *Clergy,* 32
Connor, Alan E. T. Harper, OBE, *b.* 1944, *cons.* 2002, *apptd* 2002. *Clergy,* 106
Derry and Raphoe, Kenneth R. Good, *b.* 1592, *cons.* 2002, *apptd* 2002. *Clergy,* 51
Down and Dromore, Harold C. Miller, *b.* 1950, *cons.* 1997, *apptd* 1997. *Clergy,* 116
Kilmore, Elphin and Ardagh, Kenneth H. Clarke, *b.* 1949, *cons.* 2001, *apptd* 2001. *Clergy,* 21
Tuam, Killala and Achonry, Richard C. A. Henderson, DPhil, *b.* 1957, *cons.* 1998, *apptd* 1998. *Clergy,* 13

PROVINCE OF DUBLIN
ARCHBISHOP OF DUBLIN, BISHOP OF GLENDALOUGH, AND PRIMATE OF IRELAND, Most Revd John R. W. Neill, *b.* 1945, *apptd* 2002 *Clergy,* 86

BISHOPS
Cashel and Ossory, Peter F. Barrett, *b.* 1956, *cons.* 2003, *apptd* 2003. *Clergy,* 42
Cork, Cloyne and Ross, W. Paul Colton, *b.* 1960, *cons.* 1999, *apptd* 1999. *Clergy,* 30
Limerick and Killaloe, Michael H. G. Mayes, *b.* 1941, *cons.* 1993, *trans.* 2000. *Clergy,* 19
Meath and Kildare, (Most Revd) Richard L. Clarke, Ph.D., *b.* 1949, *cons.* 1996, *apptd* 1996. *Clergy,* 26

OVERSEAS

PRIMATES
PRIMATE AND PRESIDING BISHOP OF AOTEAROA, NEW ZEALAND AND POLYNESIA, Rt. Revd John Paterson (Bishop of Auckland), *cons.* 1995, *apptd* 1998
PRIMATE OF AUSTRALIA, Most Revd Peter Carnley (Archbishop of Perth), *cons.* 1981, *apptd* 2000
PRIMATE OF BRAZIL, Most Revd Orlando Santos de Oliveira (Bishop of Southern Brazil)
ARCHBISHOP OF THE PROVINCE OF BURUNDI, Most Revd Samuel Ndayisenga (Bishop of Buye), *apptd* 1998
ARCHBISHOP AND PRIMATE OF CANADA, Most Revd Michael G. Peers, *cons.* 1977, *elected* 1986
ARCHBISHOP OF THE PROVINCE OF CENTRAL AFRICA, Most Revd Bernard A. Malango (Bishop of Northern Zambia), *elected* 2000
PRIMATE OF THE CENTRAL REGION OF AMERICA, Most Revd Martin de Jesus Barahona (Bishop of El Salvador)
ARCHBISHOP OF THE PROVINCE OF CONGO, Most Revd Dr Dirokpa Balufuga Fidhle (Bishop of Bukavu)
PRIMATE OF THE PROVINCE OF HONG KONG SHENG KUNG HUI, Most Revd Peter Kwong (Bishop of Hong Kong Island), *cons.* 1981, *apptd* 1998
ARCHBISHOP OF THE PROVINCE OF THE INDIAN OCEAN, Most Revd Remi Rabenirina (Bishop of Antananarivo), *cons.* 1984, *apptd* 1995
PRESIDENT-BISHOP OF JERUSALEM AND THE MIDDLE EAST, Most Revd George Handford (Bishop of Cyprus and the Gulf)
ARCHBISHOP OF THE PROVINCE OF KENYA, Most Revd Benjamin M. P. Nzimbi (Bishop of All Saints Cathedral Diocese)
ARCHBISHOP OF THE PROVINCE OF KOREA, Most Revd Paul Hwan Yoon (Bishop of Taejon), *cons.* 1987, *apptd* 2000

ARCHBISHOP OF THE PROVINCE OF MELANESIA, Most Revd Sir Ellison L. Pogo, KBE (Bishop of Central Melanesia), *cons.* 1981, *apptd* 1994

ACTING PRIMATE OF MEXICO, Rt. Revd Martiniano Garcia-Montiel,

ARCHBISHOP OF THE PROVINCE OF MYANMAR, Most Revd Samuel San Si Htay (Bishop of Yangon), *cons.* 2001, *apptd* 2001

ARCHBISHOP OF THE PROVINCE OF NIGERIA, Most Revd Peter Akinola (Bishop of Abuja), *cons.* 1989, *apptd* 2000

PRIMATE OF NIPPON SEI KO KAI, Most Revd James Toru Uno (Bishop of Kita Kanto)

ARCHBISHOP OF PAPUA NEW GUINEA, Most Revd James Ayong (Bishop of Aipo Rongo), *cons.* 1995, *elected* 1996

PRIME BISHOP OF THE PHILIPPINES, Most Revd Ignacio C. Soliba, *cons.* 1991, *apptd* 1997

ARCHBISHOP OF THE PROVINCE OF RWANDA, Most Revd Emmanuel Musaba Kolini (Bishop of Kigali), *cons.* 1980, *apptd* 1997

PRIMATE OF THE PROVINCE OF SOUTH EAST ASIA, Most Revd Datuk Yong Ping Chung (Bishop of Sabah), *cons.* 1990 *apptd* 1999

METROPOLITAN OF THE PROVINCE OF SOUTHERN AFRICA, Most Revd Njongonkulu W. H. Ndungane (Archbishop of Capetown), *cons.* 1991, *trans.* 1996

PRESIDING BISHOP OF THE SOUTHERN CONE OF AMERICA, Most Revd Gregory James Venables (Bishop of Argentina)

ARCHBISHOP OF THE PROVINCE OF THE SUDAN, Most Revd Joseph Marona (Bishop of Juba) *cons.* 1984, *apptd* 2000

ARCHBISHOP OF THE PROVINCE OF TANZANIA, Most Revd Donald L. Mtetemela (Bishop of Ruaha), *cons.* 1982, *apptd* 1998

ARCHBISHOP OF THE PROVINCE OF UGANDA, Most Revd Livingstone Mpalanyi-Nkoyoyo. *cons.* 1980

PRESIDING BISHOP AND PRIMATE OF THE USA, Most Revd Frank T. Griswold III, *cons.* 1985, *apptd* 1997

ARCHBISHOP OF THE PROVINCE OF WEST AFRICA, Most Revd Robert Okine (Bishop of Koforidua), *cons.* 1981, *apptd* 1993

ARCHBISHOP OF THE PROVINCE OF THE WEST INDIES, Most Revd Drexel Gomez (Bishop of Nassau and the Bahamas), *cons.* 1972, *apptd* 1998

OTHER CHURCHES AND EXTRA-PROVINCIAL DIOCESES

ANGLICAN CHURCH OF BERMUDA, Rt. Revd Ewen Ratteray, *apptd* 1996, *extra-provincial to Canterbury*

CHURCH OF CEYLON, *extra-provincial to Canterbury* Bishop of Colombo, Rt. Revd Duleep de Chickera, Bishop of Kurunagala, Rt. Revd Kumara Illangasinghe

EPISCOPAL CHURCH OF CUBA, Rt. Revd Jorge Perera Hurtado, *apptd* 1995

LUSITANIAN CHURCH *(Portuguese Episcopal Church)*, Rt. Revd Fernando Soares, *apptd* 1971, *extra-provincial to Canterbury*

SPANISH REFORMED EPISCOPAL CHURCH, Rt. Revd Carlos Lopez-Lozano, *apptd* 1995, *extra-provincial to Canterbury*

EXTRA-PROVINCIAL TO PROVINCE IX OF THE EPISCOPAL CHURCH IN THE USA:
PUERTO RICO, Rt. Revd David Andres Alvarez-Velazquez, *cons.* 1987

VENEZUELA, Rt. Revd Orlando Guerrero, *cons.* 1995

MODERATORS OF CHURCHES IN FULL COMMUNION WITH THE ANGLICAN COMMUNION

CHURCH OF BANGLADESH, Rt. Revd Michael S. Baroi (Bishop of Dhaka)

CHURCH OF NORTH INDIA, Most Revd Zechariah J. Terom (Bishop of Chotanagpur)

CHURCH OF SOUTH INDIA, Most Revd Dr Kunnumpurathu Joseph Samuel (Bishop of East Kerala), *cons.* 1990, *apptd* 2000

CHURCH OF PAKISTAN, Rt. Revd Samuel Azariah (Bishop of Raiwind)

THE CHURCH OF SCOTLAND

The Church of Scotland is the established (i.e. national) church of Scotland. The Church is Reformed in doctrine, and presbyterian in constitution, i.e. based on a hierarchy of councils of ministers and elders and, since 1990, of members of a diaconate. At local level the Kirk Session consists of the parish minister and ruling elders. At district level the presbyteries, of which there are 47 in Britain, consist of all the ministers in the district, one ruling elder from each congregation, and those members of the diaconate who qualify for membership. The General Assembly is the supreme authority, and is presided over by a Moderator chosen annually by the Assembly. The Sovereign, if not present in person, is represented by a Lord High Commissioner who is appointed each year by the Crown.

The Church of Scotland has about 570,000 members, 1,100 ministers and 1,500 churches. There are about 100 ministers and other personnel working overseas.

Lord High Commissioner (2003), The Rt. Hon. Lord Steel of Aikwood

Moderator of the General Assembly (2003), The Rt. Revd Prof. Iain R. Torrance

Principal Clerk, Very Revd Dr F. A. J. Macdonald

Depute Principal Clerk, Revd. M. A. MacLean

Procurator, P. S. Hodge

Law Agent and Solicitor of the Church, Mrs J. S. Wilson

Parliamentary Agent, I. McCulloch *(London)*

General Treasurer, D. F. Ross

Secretary, Church and Nation Committee, Revd Dr D. Sinclair

CHURCH OFFICE, 121 George Street, Edinburgh EH2 4YN
Tel: 0131-225 5722

PRESBYTERIES AND CLERKS

Edinburgh, Revd W. P. Graham
West Lothian, Revd D. Shaw

Lothian, J. D. McCulloch, DL
Melrose and Peebles, Revd A. J. Morton
Duns, Revd J. S. H. Cutler
Jedburgh, Revd N. R. Combe

Annandale and Eskdale, Revd C. B. Haston
Dumfries and Kirkcudbright, Revd G. M. A. Savage
Wigtown and Stranraer, Revd D. W. Dutton
Ayr, Revd J. Crichton
Irvine and Kilmarnock, Revd C. G. G. Brockie
Ardrossan, Revd D. Broster

Lanark, Revd G. J. Elliott
Greenock and Paisley, vacant
Glasgow, Revd D. W. Lunan

Hamilton, Revd J. H. Wilson
Dumbarton, Revd D. P. Munro

Argyll, vacant

Falkirk, Revd I. W. Black
Stirling, Revd M. MacCormick

Dunfermline, Revd W. E. Farquhar
Kirkcaldy, A. Moore
St Andrews, Revd P. Meager
Dunkeld and Meigle, Revd J. Russell
Perth, Revd D. G. Lawson
Dundee, Revd J. A. Roy
Angus, Revd M. I. G. Rooney

Aberdeen, Revd A. M. Douglas
Kincardine and Deeside, Revd J. W. S. Brown
Gordon, Revd E. Glen
Buchan, Revd M. M. McKay
Moray, Revd G. M. Wood

Abernethy, Revd J. A. I. MacEwan
Inverness, Revd A. S. Younger
Lochaber, Revd D. M. Anderson

Ross, Revd T. M. McWilliam
Sutherland, Revd J. L. Goskirk
Caithness, Mrs M. Gillies, MBE
Lochcarron-Skye, Revd A. I. MacArthur
Uist, Revd M. Smith
Lewis, Revd T. S. Sinclair

Orkney, Revd T. G. Hunt
Shetland, Revd C. H. M.Greig
England, Revd W. A. Cairns

Europe, Revd J. A. Cowie

The minimum stipend of a minister in the Church of Scotland in 2003 was £19,486.

THE ROMAN CATHOLIC CHURCH

The Roman Catholic Church is one world-wide Christian Church acknowledging as its head the Bishop of Rome, known as the Pope (Father). He leads a communion of followers of Christ, who believe they continue his presence in the world as servants of faith, hope and love to all society. The Pope is held to be the successor of St Peter and thus invested with the power which was entrusted to St Peter by Jesus Christ. A direct line of succession is therefore claimed from the earliest Christian communities. With the fall of the Roman Empire the Pope also became an important political leader. His territory is now limited to the 107 acres of the Vatican City State, created to provide some independence to the Pope from Italy and other nations.

The Pope exercises spiritual authority over the Church with the advice and assistance of the Sacred College of Cardinals, the supreme council of the Church. He is also advised by bishops in communion with him, by a group of officers which form the Roman Curia and by his ambassadors, called Apostolic Nuncios, who liaise with the Bishops' Conference in each country.

Those members of the College of Cardinals who are under the age of 80 elect a successor of the Pope following his death. The assembly of the Cardinals called

to the Vatican for the election of a new Pope is known as the Conclave. In complete seclusion the Cardinals vote by a secret ballot; a two-thirds majority is necessary before the vote can be accepted as final. When a Cardinal receives the necessary number of votes, the Dean of the Sacred College formally asks him if he will accept election and the name by which he wishes to be known. On his acceptance of the office of Supreme Pontiff, the Conclave is dissolved and the first Cardinal Deacon announces the election to the assembled crowd in St Peter's Square.

The number of cardinals was fixed at 70 by Pope Sixtus V in 1586, but has been steadily increased since the pontificate of John XXIII and at the end of July 2001 stood at 189, plus two cardinals created 'in pectore' (their names being kept secret by the Pope for fear of persecution; they are thought to be Chinese).

The Pope has full legislative, judicial and adminstrative power over the whole church. He is aided in his administration by the Curia, which is made up of a number of departments. The Secretariat of State is the central office for carrying out the Pope's instructions and is presided over by the Cardinal Secretary of State. It maintains relations with the departments of the Curia, with the episcopate, with the representatives of the Holy See in various countries, governments and private persons. The congregations and pontifical councils are the Pope's ministries and include departments such as the Congregation for the Doctrine of Faith, whose field of competence concern faith and morals; the Congregation for the Clergy and the Congregation for the Evangelisation of Peoples, the Pontifical Council for the Family and the Pontifical Council for the Promotion of Christian Unity.

The Vatican State does not have diplomatic representatives. The Holy See, composed of the Pope and those who help him in his mission for the Church, is recognised by the Conventions of Vienna as an International Moral Body. The representatives of the Holy See are known as Apostolic Nuncios. Where representation is only to the local churches and not to the government of a country, the Papal representative is known as an apostolic delegate. The Roman Catholic Church has an estimated 840 million adherents under the care of of around 2,500 diocesan bishops world-wide.

SOVEREIGN PONTIFF
His Holiness Pope John Paul II (Karol Wojtyła), *born* Wadowice, Poland, 18 May 1920; *ordained priest* 1946; *appointed Archbishop* of Kraków 1964; *created Cardinal* 1967; *assumed pontificate* 16 October 1978

SECRETARIAT OF STATE
Secretary of State, HE Cardinal Angelo Sodano
First Section (General Affairs), Archbishop Leonardo
   Sandri (Titular Archbishop of Cittanova)
Second Section (Relations with other states), Most Revd J. L.
   Tauran (Titular Archbishop of Telepte)

BISHOPS' CONFERENCE
The Roman Catholic Church in England and Wales consists of a total of 22 dioceses and is governed by the Bishops' Conference, membership of which includes the Diocesan Bishops, the Apostolic Exarch of the Ukrainians, the Bishop of the Forces and the Auxiliary Bishops. The Conference is headed by the President *(HE Cardinal Cormac Murphy-O'Connor, Archbishop of Westminster)* and Vice-President *(The Most Revd Patrick*

Kelly, *Archbishop of Liverpool*). There are five departments, each with an episcopal chairman: the Department for Christian Life and Worship (the Bishop of Menevia), the Department for Mission and Unity (the Bishop of Portsmouth), the Department for Catholic Education and Formation (the Archbishop of Birmingham), the Department for Christian Responsibility and Citizenship (the Archbishop of Cardiff), and the Department for International Affairs (the Bishop of Leeds).

The Bishops' Standing Committee, made up of all the Archbishops and the chairman of each of the above departments, has general responsibility for continuity of policy between the plenary sessions of the Conference. It prepares the Conference agenda and implements its decisions. It is serviced by a General Secretariat. There are also agencies and consultative bodies affiliated to the Conference.

The Bishops' Conference of Scotland is the permanently constituted assembly of the Bishops of Scotland. The Conference is headed by the President (The Most Revd Keith P. O'Brien, Archbishop of St. Andrews and Edinburgh). To promote its work, the Conference establishes various agencies which have an advisory function in relation to the Conference. The more important of these agencies are called Commissions and each one has a Bishop President who, with the other members of the Commissions, are appointed by the Conference.

The Irish Episcopal Conference has as its president Archbishop Brady of Armagh. Its membership comprises all the Archbishops and Bishops of Ireland and it appoints various Commissions to assist it in its work. There are three types of Commissions: (a) those made up of lay and clerical members chosen for their skills and experience, and staffed by full-time expert secretariats; (b) Commissions whose members are selected from existing institutions and whose services are supplied on a part-time basis; and (c) Commissions of Bishops only.

The Roman Catholic Church in the UK has an estimated 1,712,010 members, 6,854 priests, and 4,587 churches.

Bishops' Conferences secretariats:

ENGLAND AND WALES, 39 Eccleston Square, London SW1V 1BX Tel: 020-7630 8220 Fax: 020-7901 4821
Email: secretariat@cbcew.org.uk
Web: www.catholic-ew.org.uk
General Secretary, Mgr Andrew Summersgill
SCOTLAND, 64 Aitken Street, Airdrie, Lanarkshire ML6 6LT
General Secretary, Rt. Revd Mgr Henry Docherty
IRELAND, Columba Centre, Maynooth, County Kildare.
Secretary, The Most Revd William Lee (Bishop of Waterford and Lismore); *Executive Secretary*, Revd Aidan O'Boyle

GREAT BRITAIN

APOSTOLIC NUNCIO TO GREAT BRITAIN
The Most Revd Pablo Puente, 54 Parkside, London SW19 5NE Tel: 020-8944 7189

ENGLAND AND WALES
THE MOST REVD ARCHBISHOPS
Westminster, H. E. Cardinal Cormac Murphy-O'Connor, cons. 1977, apptd 2000
Auxiliaries, James J. O'Brien, cons. 1977; George Stack, cons. 2001; Bernard Longley cons. 2003; Alan Hopes

cons. 2003. *Clergy*, 779. *Archbishop's Residence*, Archbishop's House, Ambrosden Avenue, London SW1P 1QJ
Tel: 020-7798 9033
Birmingham, Vincent Nichols, cons. 1992, apptd 2000
Auxiliaries, Philip Pargeter, cons. 1990. *Clergy*, 511.
Diocesan Curia, Cathedral House, St Chad's Queensway, Birmingham B4 6EX Tel: 0121-236 5535
Cardiff, Peter Smith, cons. 1995, apptd 2001. *Clergy*, 126.
Diocesan Curia, Archbishop's House, 41–43 Cathedral Road, Cardiff CF11 9HD. Tel: 029-2022 0411
Liverpool, Patrick Kelly, cons. 1984, apptd 1996
Auxiliary, Vincent Malone, cons. 1989. Clergy, 492.
Diocesan Curia, Archdiocese of Liverpool, Centre for Evangelisation, Croxteth Drive, Sefton Park, Liverpool L17 1AA Tel: 0151-522 1000
Southwark, Michael Bowen, cons. 1970, apptd 1977
Auxiliaries, John Hine, cons. 2001; Howard Tripp, cons. 1980. *Clergy*, 518. *Diocesan Curia*, Archbishop's House, 150 St George's Road, London SE1 6HX Tel: 020-7928 5592

THE RT. REVD BISHOPS
Arundel and Brighton, Kieran Conry, cons. 2001, apptd 2001. *Clergy*, 204. *Diocesan Curia*, Bishop's House, The Upper Drive, Hove, E. Sussex BN3 6NE. Tel: 01273-506387
Brentwood, Thomas McMahon, cons. 1980, apptd 1980.
Clergy, 175. *Bishop's Office*, Cathedral House, Ingrave Road, Brentwood, Essex CM15 8AT Tel: 01277-232266
Clifton, Declan Lang, cons. 2001, apptd 2001. *Clergy*, 251. *Bishop's House*, St Ambrose, North Road, Leigh Woods, Bristol BS8 3PW Tel: 0117-973 3072
East Anglia, Michael Evans, cons. 2003, apptd 2003.
Clergy, 129. *Diocesan Curia*, The White House, 21 Upgate, Poringland, Norwich NR14 7SH Tel: 01508-495358
Hallam, John Rawsthorne, cons. 1981, apptd 1997.
Clergy, 75. *Bishop's House*, 75 Norfolk Road, Sheffield S2 3SZ Tel: 0114-278 7988
Hexham and Newcastle, Michael Ambrose Griffiths, cons. 1992, apptd 1992. *Clergy*, 221. *Diocesan Curia*, Bishop's House, East Denton Hall, 800 West Road, Newcastle upon Tyne NE5 2BJ Tel: 0191-228 0003
Lancaster, Patrick O'Donoghue, cons. 1993, apptd 2001. *Clergy*, 248. *Bishop's Residence*, Bishop's House, Cannon Hill, Lancaster LA1 5NG Tel: 01524-32231
Leeds, David Konstant, cons. 1977, apptd 1985. *Clergy*, 226. *Diocesan Curia*, Hinsley Hall, 62 Headingley Lane, Leeds LS6 2BU Tel: 0113-261 8000
Menevia (Wales), Mark Jabalé, cons. 2001, apptd 2001.
Clergy, 60. *Diocesan Curia*, 27 Convent Street, Greenhill, Swansea SA1 2BX Tel: 01792-644017
Middlesbrough, John Crowley, cons. 1986, apptd 1992.
Clergy, 182. *Diocesan Curia*, 50A The Avenue, Linthorpe, Middlesbrough, Cleveland TS5 6QT Tel: 01642-850505
Northampton, Kevin McDonald, cons. 2001, apptd 2001.
Clergy, 159. *Diocesan Curia*, Bishop's House, Marriott Street, Northampton NN2 6AW Tel: 01604-715635
Nottingham, Malcolm McMahon, cons. 2000, apptd 2000. *Clergy*, 214. *Bishop's House*, 27 Cavendish Road East, The Park, Nottingham NG7 1BB Tel: 0115-947 4786
Plymouth, Christopher Budd, cons. 1986, apptd 1985.
Clergy, 170. *Diocesan Curia*, Bishop's House, 31 Wyndham Street West, Plymouth PL1 5RZ
Tel: 01752-224414
Portsmouth, F. Crispian Hollis, cons. 1987, apptd 1989.
Clergy, 282. *Bishop's Residence*, Bishop's House, Edinburgh Road, Portsmouth, Hants PO1 3HG Tel: 023-9282 0894
Salford, Terence J. Brain, cons. 1991, apptd 1997. *Clergy*, 346. *Bishop's House*, Wardley Hall, Worsley, Manchester M28 2ND Tel: 0161-794 2825

Shrewsbury, Brian Noble, *cons.* 1995, *apptd* 1995. *Clergy,* 190. *Diocesan Curia,* 2 Park Road South, Prenton, Wirral CH43 4UX Tel: 0151-652 9855

Wrexham (Wales), Edwin Regan, *cons.*1994, *apptd* 1994. *Clergy,* 83. *Diocesan Curia,* Bishop's House, Sontley Road, Wrexham LL13 7EW Tel: 01978-262726

SCOTLAND

THE MOST REVD ARCHBISHOPS

St Andrews and Edinburgh, Keith Patrick O'Brien, *cons.* 1985, *apptd* 1985 *Clergy,* 188 *Archbishop's House,* 42 Greenhall Gardens, Edinburgh EH10 4BJ Tel: 0131-447 3337

Glasgow, Mario Joseph Conti, *cons.* 1977, *apptd* 2002 *Clergy,* 252 *Diocesan Curia,* 196 Clyde Street, Glasgow G1 4JY Tel: 0141-226 5898

THE RT. REVD BISHOPS

Aberdeen, vacant. *Clergy,* 46. *Diocesan Curia,* Bishop's House, 3 Queen's Cross, Aberdeen AB15 4XU Tel: 01224-319154

Argyll and the Isles, Ian Murray, *cons.* 1999, *apptd* 1999. *Clergy,* 26. *Diocesan Curia,* Bishop's House, Esplanade, Oban, Argyll PA34 5AB Tel: 01631-567436

Dunkeld, Vincent Logan, *cons.* 1981. *Clergy,* 47. *Diocesan Curia,* 24–28 Lawside Road, Dundee DD3 6XY Tel: 01382-225453

Galloway, Maurice Taylor, *cons.* 1981, *apptd* 1981 *Clergy,* 56. *Diocesan Curia,* 8 Corsehill Road, Ayr KA7 2ST Tel: 01292-266750

Motherwell, Joseph Devine, *cons.* 1977, *apptd* 1983. *Clergy,* 134. *Diocesan Curia,* Coursington Road, Motherwell ML1 1PP Tel: 01698-269114

Paisley, John A. Mone, *cons.* 1984, *apptd* 1988. *Clergy,* 56. *Diocesan Curia,* Diocesan Centre, Cathedral Precincts, Incle Street, Paisley PA1 1HR Tel: 0141-847 6130

BISHOPRIC OF THE FORCES

Thomas Matthew Burns, *cons.* 2002, *apptd* 2002. Administration: Bishopric of the Forces, Middle Hill, Aldershot, Hants GU11 1PP Tel: 01252-349004

IRELAND

There is one hierarchy for the whole of Ireland. Several of the dioceses have territory partly in the Republic of Ireland and partly in Northern Ireland.

APOSTOLIC NUNCIO TO IRELAND

Most Revd Giuseppe Lazzarotto (Titular Archbishop of Numana), 183 Navan Road, Dublin 7 Tel: (00 353) (1) 838 0577 Fax: (00 353) 1 838 0276

THE MOST REVD ARCHBISHOPS

Armagh, Sean Brady, *cons.* 1995, *apptd* 1996 *Auxiliary,* Gerard Clifford, *cons.* 1991. *Clergy,* 183. *Diocesan Curia,* Ara Coeli, Armagh BT61 7QY Tel: 028-3752 2045

Cashel, Dermot Clifford, *cons.* 1986, *apptd* 1988. *Clergy,* 128. *Archbishop's Residence,* Archbishop's House, Thurles, Co. Tipperary. Tel: (00 353) (504) 21512

Dublin, H. E. Cardinal Desmond Connell, *cons.* 1988, *apptd* 1988, *elevated* 2001 *Coadjutor Archbishop,* Diarmuid Martin, *apptd* 2003 *Auxiliaries,* Eamonn Walsh, *cons.* 1990; Fiachra O'Ceallaigh, *cons* 1994; Martin Drennan, *cons.* 1997; Raymond Field, *cons.* 1997. *Clergy,* 994. *Archbishop's Residence,* Archbishop's House, Dublin 9 Tel: (00 353) (1) 836 0723

Tuam, Michael Neary, *cons.* 1992, *apptd* 1995. *Clergy,* 141. *Archbishop's Residence,* Archbishop's House, Tuam, Co. Galway Tel: (00 353) (93) 24166

THE MOST REVD BISHOPS

Achonry, Thomas Flynn, *cons.* 1975, *apptd* 1977. *Clergy,* 62. *Bishop's Residence,* Bishop's House, Ballaghadaderreen, Co. Roscommon Tel: (00 353) (907) 60021

Ardagh and Clonmacnois, Colm O'Reilly, *cons.* 1983, *apptd* 1983. *Clergy,* 68. *Diocesan Office,* Bishop's House, St Michael's, Longford, Co. Longford Tel: (00 353) (43) 46432

Clogher, Joseph Duffy, *cons.* 1979, *apptd* 1979. *Clergy,* 108. *Bishop's Residence,* Bishop's House, Monaghan Tel: (00 353) (47) 81019

Clonfert, John Kirby, *cons.* 1988. *Clergy,* 71. *Bishop's Residence,* St Brendan's, Coorheen, Loughrea, Co. Galway Tel: (00 353) (91) 841560

Cloyne, John Magee, *cons.* 1987, *apptd* 1987. *Clergy,* 155. *Diocesan Centre,* Cobh, Co. Cork Tel: (00 353) (21) 4811430

Cork and Ross, John Buckley, *cons.* 1984, *apptd* 1998. *Clergy,* 153. *Diocesan Office,* Cork and Ross Offices, Redemption Road, Cork Tel: (00 353) (21) 4301717

Derry, Seamus Hegarty, *cons.* 1982, *apptd* 1994. *Clergy,* 138. *Bishop's Residence,* Bishop's House, St Eugene's Cathedral, Derry BT48 9AP Tel: 028-7126 2302 *Auxiliary,* Francis Lagan, *cons.* 1988

Down and Connor, Patrick J. Walsh, *cons.* 1983, *apptd* 1991. *Clergy,* 240. *Bishop's Residence,* Lisbreen, 73 Somerton Road, Belfast, Co. Antrim BT15 4DE Tel: 028-9077 6185 *Auxiliaries,* Anthony Farquhar, *cons.* 1983; Donal McKeown, *cons.* 2001

Dromore, John McAreavey, *cons.* 1999, *apptd* 1999. *Clergy,* 78. *Bishop's Residence,* Bishop's House, Violet Hill, Newry, Co. Down BT35 6PN Tel: 028-3026 2444

Elphin, Christopher Jones, *cons.* 1994, *apptd* 1994. *Clergy,* 70. *Bishop's Residence,* St Mary's, Sligo Tel: (00 353) (71) 9162670

Ferns, Éamonn Walsh, *cons.* 1990, *apptd* 2002. *Clergy,* 138. *Bishop's Office,* Bishop's House, Summerhill, Wexford Tel: (00 353) (53) 22177

Galway and Kilmacduagh, James McLoughlin, *cons.* 1993, *apptd* 1993. *Clergy,* 87. *Diocesan Office,* The Cathedral, Galway Tel: (00 353) (91) 563566

Kerry, William Murphy, *cons.* 1995, *apptd* 1995. *Clergy,* 127. *Bishop's Residence,* Bishop's House, Killarney, Co. Kerry Tel: (00 353) (64) 31168

Kildare and Leighlin, James Moriarty, *apptd* 2002. *Clergy,* 127. *Bishop's Residence,* Bishop's House, Carlow Tel: (00 353) (59) 917 6725

Killala, John Fleming, *cons.* 2002, *apptd* 2002. *Clergy,* 52. *Bishop's Residence,* Bishop's House, Ballina, Co. Mayo Tel: (00 353) (96) 21518

Killaloe, William Walsh, *cons.* 1994. *Clergy,* 149. *Bishop's Residence,* Westbourne, Ennis, Co. Clare Tel: (00 353) (65) 28638

Kilmore, Leo O'Reilly, *cons.* 1997, *apptd* 1998. *Clergy,* 98. *Bishop's Residence,* Bishop's House, Cullies, Co. Cavan Tel: (00 353) (49) 4331496

Limerick, Donal Murray, *cons.* 1982, *apptd* 1996. *Clergy,* 136. *Diocesan Offices,* 66 O'Connell Street, Limerick Tel: (00 353) (61) 315856

Meath, Michael Smith, *cons.* 1984, *apptd* 1990. *Clergy,* 141. *Bishop's Residence,* Bishop's House, Dublin Road, Mullingar, Co. Westmeath Tel: (00 353) (44) 48841

Ossory, Laurence Forristal, *cons.* 1980, *apptd* 1981. *Clergy,* 92. *Bishop's Residence,* Sion House, Kilkenny Tel: (00 353) (56) 62448

Raphoe, Philip Boyce, *cons.* 1995, *apptd* 1995. *Clergy,* 90. *Bishop's Residence,* Ard Adhamhnáin, Letterkenny, Co. Donegal Tel: (00 353) (74) 9121208
Waterford and Lismore, William Lee, *cons.* 1993, *apptd* 1993. *Clergy,* 114. *Bishop's Residence,* John's Hill, Waterford. Tel: (00 353) (51) 874663

PATRIARCHS IN COMMUNION WITH THE ROMAN CATHOLIC CHURCH

Alexandria, HB Cardinal Stephanos II Ghattas (Patriarch for Catholic Copts)
Antioch, HB Ignace Pierre VIII Abdel-Ahad
Jerusalem, HB Michel Sabbah
Babilonia of the Chaldeans, HB Raphael I Bidawid
Cilicia of the Armenians, HB Jean Pierre XVIII Kasparian
Oriental India, Archbishop Raul Nicolau Gonsalves
Lisbon, HE Jose da Cruz Policarpo
Venice, HE Archbishop Angelo Scola

OTHER CHURCHES IN THE UK

AFRICAN AND AFRO-CARIBBEAN CHURCHES

There are more than 160 Christian churches or groups of African or Afro-Caribbean origin in the UK. These include the Apostolic Faith Church, the Cherubim and Seraphim Church, the New Testament Church Assembly, the New Testament Church of God, the Wesleyan Holiness Church and the Aladura Churches.

The Afro-West Indian United Council of Churches and the Council of African and Afro-Caribbean Churches UK (which was initiated as the Council of African and Allied Churches in 1979 to give one voice to the various Christian churches of African origin in the UK) are the media through which the member churches can work jointly to provide services they cannot easily provide individually.

There are about 70,000 adherents of African and Afro-Caribbean churches in the UK, and over 1,000 congregations. The Council of African and Afro-Caribbean Churches UK has about 17,000 members, 250 ministers and 125 congregations.
COUNCIL OF AFRICAN AND AFRO-CARIBBEAN CHURCHES UK, 31 Norton House, Sidney Road, London SW9 0UJ Tel: 020-7274 5589 Fax: 020-7274 4726
Chairman, His Grace The Most Revd Father Olu A. Abiola, OBE

ASSOCIATED PRESBYTERIAN CHURCHES OF SCOTLAND

The Associated Presbyterian Churches came into being in 1989 as a result of a division within the Free Presbyterian Church of Scotland. Following two controversial disciplinary cases, the culmination of deepening differences within the Church, a presbytery was formed calling itself the Associated Presbyterian Churches (APC). The Associated Presbyterian Churches has about 1,000 members, 10 ministers and 20 churches.
Clerk of the Scottish Presbytery, Revd A. N. McPhail, Fernhill, Polvinster Road, Oban PA34 5TN Tel: 01631-567076

THE BAPTIST CHURCH

Baptists trace their origins to John Smyth, who in 1609 in Amsterdam reinstituted the baptism of conscious believers as the basis of the fellowship of a gathered church. Members of Smyth's church established the first Baptist church in England in 1612. They came to be known as 'General' Baptists and their theology was Arminian, whereas a later group of Calvinists who adopted the baptism of believers came to be known as 'Particular' Baptists. The two sections of the Baptists were united into one body, the Baptist Union of Great Britain and Ireland, in 1891. In 1988 the title was changed to the Baptist Union of Great Britain.

Baptists emphasise the complete autonomy of the local church, although individual churches are linked in various kinds of associations. There are international bodies (such as the Baptist World Alliance) and national bodies, but some Baptist churches belong to neither. However, in Great Britain the majority of churches and associations belong to the Baptist Union of Great Britain. There are also Baptist Unions in Wales, Scotland and Ireland which are much smaller than the Baptist Union of Great Britain, and there is some overlap of membership.

There are over 40 million Baptist church members world-wide; in the Baptist Union of Great Britain there are 140,730 members, 1,890 pastors and 2,119 churches. In the Baptist Union of Scotland there are 14,001 members, 159 pastors and 174 churches. In the Baptist Union of Wales (Undeb Bedyddwyr Cymru) there are 17,774 members, 106 pastors and 473 churches. In the Association of Baptist Churches (formerly the Baptist Union of Ireland) there are 7,965 members, 89 pastors and 111 churches.
President of the Baptist Union of Great Britain (2003–4), Revd John Rackley
General Secretary, Revd David Coffey, Baptist House, PO Box 44, 129 Broadway, Didcot, Oxon OX11 8RT Tel: 01235-517700 Email: info@baptist.org.uk Web: www.baptist.org.uk
General Director of the Baptist Union of Scotland, Revd William Slack, 14 Aytoun Road, Glasgow G41 5RT Tel: 0141-423 6169 Fax: 0141-424 1422 Email: admin@scottishbaptist.org.uk
President of the English Assembly of the Baptist Union of Wales (2003–4), F. S. Maull
President of the Welsh Assembly of the Baptist Union of Wales (2003–4), Revd Denzil John
General Secretary of the Baptist Union of Wales, Revd P. D. Richards, 94 Stryd Mansel, Swansea SA1 5TZ Tel: 01792-655468
General Secretary of the Association of Baptist Churches in Ireland, Revd W. Colville, The Baptist Centre, 19 Hillsborough Road, Moira BT67 0HG Tel: 028-9261 9267 Email: abc@thebaptistcentre.org

THE CONGREGATIONAL FEDERATION

The Congregational Federation was founded by members of Congregational churches in England and Wales who did not join the United Reformed Church in 1972. There are also churches in Scotland and France affiliated to the Federation. The Federation exists to encourage congregations of believers to worship in free assembly, but it has no authority over them and emphasises their right to independence and self-government.

The Federation has 10,234 members, 71 recognised ministers and 297 churches in England, Wales and Scotland.

President of the Federation (2002–3), Felicity Cleaves
General Secretary, Revd M. Heaney, The Congregational
Centre, 8 Castle Gate, Nottingham NG1 7AS
Tel: 0115-911 1460

THE FREE CHURCH OF ENGLAND

The Free Church of England is a union of two bodies in
the Anglican tradition, the Free Church of England,
founded in 1844 as a protest against the Oxford
Movement in the established Church, and the Reformed
Episcopal Church, founded in America in 1873 but
which also had congregations in England. As both
Churches sought to maintain the historic faith, tradition
and practice of the Anglican Church since the
Reformation, they decided to unite as one body in
England in 1927. The historic episcopate was conferred
on the English Church in 1876 through the line of the
American bishops, who had pioneered an open table
Communion policy towards members of other
denominations.

The Free Church of England has 1,400 members, 41
ministers and 25 churches in England. It also has three
house churches and three ministers in New Zealand and
one church and one minister in St Petersburg, Russia.
General Secretary, Revd R. E. Talbot, 32 Bonnywood Road,
Hassocks, W. Sussex BN6 8HR Tel: 01273-845092

THE FREE CHURCH OF SCOTLAND

The Free Church of Scotland was formed in 1843 when
over 400 ministers withdrew from the Church of
Scotland as a result of interference in the internal affairs
of the church by the civil authorities. In 1900, all but 26
ministers joined with others to form the United Free
Church (most of which rejoined the Church of Scotland
in 1929). In 1904 the remaining 26 ministers were
recognised by the House of Lords as continuing the Free
Church of Scotland.

The Church maintains strict adherence to the
Westminster Confession of Faith (1648) and accepts the
Bible as the sole rule of faith and conduct. Its General
Assembly meets annually. It also has links with Reformed
Churches overseas. In January 2000, a division occurred
within the church, the larger body retains the name of
the Free Church of Scotland with the smaller body
known as the Free Church of Scotland (Continuing) and
has around 2,000 members. The Free Church of Scotland
has 13,600 members, 76 ministers and 130 churches.
General Treasurer, I. D. Gill, The Mound, Edinburgh EH1 2LS
Tel: 0131-226 5286
Email: offices@freechurchofscotland.org.uk

THE FREE PRESBYTERIAN CHURCH OF SCOTLAND

The Free Presbyterian Church of Scotland was formed in
1893 by two ministers of the Free Church of Scotland
who refused to accept a Declaratory Act passed by the
Free Church General Assembly in 1892. The Free
Presbyterian Church of Scotland is Calvinistic in doctrine
and emphasises observance of the Sabbath. It adheres
strictly to the Westminster Confession of Faith of 1648.

The Church has about 3,000 members in Scotland and
about 4,000 in overseas congregations. It has 19
ministers and 50 churches in the UK.

Moderator, Revd H. M. Cartwright, Napier House,
8 Collinton Road, Edinburgh EH10 5DS
Clerk of Synod, Revd J. MacLeod, 16 Matheson Road,
Stornoway, Isle of Lewis HS1 2LA Tel: 01851-702755

THE HOLY APOSTOLIC CATHOLIC ASSYRIAN CHURCH OF THE EAST

The Holy Apostolic Catholic Assyrian Church of the East
traces its beginnings to the middle of the first century. It
spread from Upper Mesopotamia throughout the
territories of the Persian Empire. The Assyrian church of
the East became theologically separated from the rest of
the Christian community following the Council of
Ephesus in 431. The Church is headed by the Catholicos
Patriarch and is episcopal in government. The liturgical
language is Syriac (Aramaic). The Assyrian Church of the
East and the Roman Catholic Church agreed a common
Christological declaration in 1994 and a process of
dialogue between the Assyrian Church of the East and
the Chaldean Catholic Church, which is in communion
with Rome but shares the Syriac liturgy, was instituted in
1996.

The Church numbers about 400,000 members in the
Middle East, India, Europe, North America and
Australasia. There are around 600 members in the UK.

The Church in Great Britain forms part of the diocese
of Europe under Mar Odisho Oraham.
Representative in Great Britain, Very Revd Younan Y.
Younan, 66 Montague Road, London W7 3PQ
Tel: 020-8579 7259

THE INDEPENDENT METHODIST CHURCHES

The Independent Methodist Churches seceded from the
Wesleyan Methodist Church in 1805 and remained
independent when the Methodist Church in Great Britain
was formed in 1932. They are mainly concentrated in the
industrial areas of the north of England.

The churches are Methodist in doctrine but their
organisation is congregational. All the churches are
members of the Independent Methodist Connexion of
Churches. The controlling body of the Connexion is the
Annual Meeting, to which churches send delegates. The
Connexional President is elected annually. Between
annual meetings the affairs of the Connexion are handled
by departmental committees. Ministers are appointed by
the churches and trained through the Connexion. The
ministry is open to both men and women and is unpaid.

There are 2,552 members, 108 ministers and 96
churches in Great Britain.
Connexional President (2003–5), Geoffrey Lomas
General Secretary, W. C. Gabb, 66 Kirkstone Drive,
Loughborough LE11 3RW Tel: 01942-223526

THE LUTHERAN CHURCH

Lutheranism is based on the teachings of Martin Luther,
the German leader of the Protestant Reformation. The
authority of the scriptures is held to be supreme over
Church tradition. The teachings of Lutheranism are
explained in detail in 16th century confessional writings,
particulary the Augsburg Confession. Lutheranism is one
of the largest Protestant denominations and it is
particularly strong in northern Europe and the USA.
Some Lutheran churches are episcopal, while others have
a synodal form of organisation; unity is based on doctrine

rather than structure. Most Lutheran churches are members of the Lutheran World Federation, based in Geneva.

Lutheran services in Great Britain are held in eighteen languages to serve members of different nationalities. Services usually follow ancient liturgies. English-language congregations are members either of the Lutheran Church in Great Britain, or of the Evangelical Lutheran Church of England. The Lutheran Church in Great Britain and other Lutheran churches in Britain are members of the Lutheran Council of Great Britain, which represents them and co-ordinates their common work.

There are over 70 million Lutherans world-wide; in Great Britain there are about 100,000 members, 50 clergy and 100 congregations.

General Secretary of the Lutheran Council of Great Britain, Revd T. Bruch, 30 Thanet Street, London WC1H 9QH
Tel: 020-7554 2900 Fax 020-7383 3081
Email: enquiries@lutheran.org.uk
Web: www.lutheran.org.uk

THE METHODIST CHURCH

The Methodist movement started in England in 1729 when the Revd John Wesley, an Anglican priest, and his brother Charles met with others in Oxford and resolved to conduct their lives and study by 'rule and method'. In 1739 the Wesleys began evangelistic preaching and the first Methodist chapel was founded in Bristol in the same year. In 1744 the first annual conference was held, at which the Articles of Religion were drawn up. Doctrinal emphases included repentance, faith, the assurance of salvation, social concern and the priesthood of all believers. After John Wesley's death in 1791 the Methodists withdrew from the established Church to form the Methodist Church. Methodists gradually drifted into many groups, but in 1932 the Wesleyan Methodist Church, the United Methodist Church and the Primitive Methodist Church united to form the Methodist Church in Great Britain as it now exists.

The governing body and supreme authority of the Methodist Church is the Conference, but there are also 33 district synods, consisting of all the ministers and selected lay people in each district, and circuit meetings of the ministers and lay people of each circuit.

There are over 60 million Methodists world-wide; in Great Britain in 2001 there are 327,724 members, 3,626 ministers, 9,951 lay preachers and 6,378 churches.

President of the Conference in Great Britain (2003–4), Revd N. G. Richardson
Vice-President of the Conference (2002–3), Mrs J. Jarvis
Secretary of the Conference, Revd David G. Deeks,
Methodist Church, 25 Marylebone Road, London NW1 5JR
Tel: 020-7486 5502 Fax: 020-7467 5226
Email: generalsecretary@methodistchurch.org.uk
Web: www.methodist.org.uk

THE METHODIST CHURCH IN IRELAND
The Methodist Church in Ireland is closely linked to British Methodism but is autonomous. It has a community roll of 55,009, 15,924 members, 201 ministers, 299 lay preachers and 193 churches.
President of the Methodist Church in Ireland (2003–4), Revd W. James Rea, 35 Thomas Street, Portadown, Co. Armagh Tel: 028 3833 3030
Secretary of the Methodist Church in Ireland, Revd E. T. I. Mawhinney, 1 Fountainville Avenue, Belfast BT9 6AN
Tel: 028-9032 4554

THE (EASTERN) ORTHODOX CHURCH

The Eastern (or Byzantine) Orthodox Church is a communion of self-governing Christian churches recognising the honorary primacy of the Oecumenical Patriarch of Constantinople.

The position of Orthodox Christians is that the faith was fully defined during the period of the Oecumenical Councils. In doctrine it is strongly trinitarian, and stresses the mystery and importance of the sacraments. It is episcopal in government. The structure of the Orthodox Christian year differs from that of western Churches.

Orthodox Christians throughout the world are estimated to number about 300 million.

PATRIARCHS OF THE EASTERN ORTHODOX CHURCH
Archbishop of Constantinople, New Rome and Ecumenical Patriarch, Bartholomew, *elected* 1991
Pope and Patriarch of Alexandria and All Africa, Petros VII, *elected* 1997
Patriarch of Antioch and All the East, Ignatius IV, *elected* 1979
Patriarch of the Holy City of Jerusalem and All Palestine, Irenaeos *elected* 2001
Patriarch of Moscow and All Russia, Aleksy II, *elected* 1990
Catholicos-Patriarch of All Georgia, Archbishop of Mtsheta and Tbilisi, Ilia II, *elected* 1977
Archbishop of Pec, Metropolitan of Belgrade and Karlovci, Patriarch of Serbia, Pavle, *elected* 1990
Patriarch of All Romania, Locum Tenens of Caesarea in Cappadocia, Metropolitan of Ungro-Vlachia, Archbishop of Bucharest, Teoctist, *elected* 1986
Patriarch of Bulgaria, Maxim, *elected* 1971

HEADS OF AUTOCEPHALOUS ORTHODOX CHURCHES
Archbishop of New Justiniana and All Cyprus, Chrysostomos, *elected* 1977
Archbishop of Athens and All Greece, Christodoulos, *elected* 1998
Archbishop of Tirana and All Albania, Anastasios, *elected* 1992
Metropolitan of Warsaw and All Poland, Sawa, *elected* 1998
Metropolitan of The Czech Lands and Slovakia, Nicholas, *elected* 2000

EASTERN ORTHODOX CHURCHES IN THE UK
THE PATRIARCHATE OF ANTIOCH
There are ten parishes served by 15 clergy. In Great Britain the Patriarchate is represented by the Revd Fr Samir Gholam, St George's Cathedral, 1A Redhill Street, London NW1 4BG Tel: 020-7383 0403.

THE GREEK ORTHODOX CHURCH (PATRIARCHATE OF CONSTANTINOPLE)
The presence of Greek Orthodox Christians in Britain dates back at least to 1677 when Archbishop Joseph Geogirenes of Samos fled from Turkish persecution and came to London. The present Greek cathedral in Moscow Road, Bayswater, was opened for public worship in 1879 and the Diocese of Thyateira and Great Britain was established in 1922. There are now 125 parishes and other communities (including monasteries) in the UK, served by five bishops, 110 clergy, nine cathedrals and about 93 churches.

In Great Britain the Patriarchate of Constantinople is represented by Archbishop Gregorios of Thyateira and Great Britain, Thyateira House, 5 Craven Hill, London W2 3EN Tel: 020-7723 4787 Fax: 020-7224 9301.

THE RUSSIAN ORTHODOX CHURCH (PATRIARCHATE OF MOSCOW) AND THE RUSSIAN ORTHODOX CHURCH OUTSIDE RUSSIA

The records of Russian Orthodox Church activities in Britain date from the visit to England of Tsar Peter I in the early 18th century. Clergy were sent from Russia to serve the chapel established to minister to the staff of the Imperial Russian Embassy in London.

In Great Britain the Patriarchate of Moscow is represented by Bishop Basil of Sergievo, 94a Banbury Road, Oxford OX2 6JT. He is assisted by one bishop and 30 clergy. There are 30 parishes and smaller communities.

The Russian Orthodox Church Outside Russia is represented by Archbishop Mark of Berlin, Germany and Great Britain, c/o Dean of English-Language Parishes, Very Revd Archimandrite Alexis, The Church of Saint Edward, St Cyprian's Avenue, Brookwood, Surrey GU24 0BL Tel: 01483-487763 Web: www.rocorbritishisles.org. There are eight communities, including two monasteries in England and one in Northern Ireland.

THE SERBIAN ORTHODOX CHURCH (PATRIARCHATE OF SERBIA)

There are 33 parishes and smaller communities in Great Britain served by 11 clergy. The Patriarchate of Serbia is represented by the Episcopal Vicar, the Very Revd Milenko Zebić, 131 Cob Lane, Bournville, Birmingham B30 1QE Tel: 0121-458 5273

OTHER NATIONALITIES

Most of the Ukrainian parishes in Britain have joined the Patriarchate of Constantinople, leaving a small number of Ukrainian parishes in Britain under the care of other patriarchates (not all of which are recognised by the other Orthodox Churches). The Latvian, Polish and some Belarusian parishes are also under the care of the Patriarchate of Constantinople. The Patriarchate of Romania has one parish served by two clergy. The Patriarchate of Bulgaria has one parish served by one priest. The Belarusian Autocephalous Orthodox Church has five parishes served by two priests.

THE ORIENTAL ORTHODOX CHURCHES

The term 'Oriental Orthodox Churches' is now generally used to describe a group of six ancient eastern churches which reject the Christological definition of the Council of Chalcedon (AD 451) and use Christological terms in different ways from the Eastern Orthodox Church. There are about 34 million members of the Oriental Orthodox Churches.

PATRIARCHS OF THE ORIENTAL ORTHODOX CHURCHES

ARMENIAN ORTHODOX CHURCH – *Supreme Patriarch Catholicos of All Armenians (Etchmiadzin)*, Karekin II, *elected* 1999; *Catholicos of Cilicia*, Aram I, *elected* 1995; *Patriarch of Jerusalem*, Torkom II, *elected* 1994; *Patriarch of Constantinople*, Mesrob II, *elected* 1998
COPTIC ORTHODOX CHURCH – *Pope of Alexandria and Patriarch of the See of St Mark*, Shenouda III, *elected* 1971

ERITREAN ORTHODOX CHURCH – *Patriarch of Eritrea*, Jacob II, *elected*
ETHIOPIAN ORTHODOX CHURCH – *Patriarch of Ethiopia*, Paulos, *elected* 1992
MALANKARA ORTHODOX SYRIAN CHURCH – *Catholicos of the East*, Basilios Mar Thoma Mathews II, *elected* 1991
SYRIAN ORTHODOX CHURCH – *Patriarch of Antioch and All the East*, Ignatius Zakka I, *elected* 1980

ORIENTAL ORTHODOX CHURCHES IN THE UK

THE ARMENIAN ORTHODOX CHURCH (PATRIARCHATE OF ETCHMIADZIN)

The Armenian Orthodox Church is the longest established Oriental Orthodox community in Great Britain. It is represented by the Rt. Revd Bishop Nathan Hovhannisian, Armenian Primate of Great Britain, Armenian Vicarage, Iverna Gardens, London W8 6TP Tel: 020-7937 0152 Email: armchurchlondon@aol.com

THE COPTIC ORTHODOX CHURCH

The Coptic Orthodox Church is the largest Oriental Orthodox community in Great Britain. The senior bishop in Great Britain is Metropolitan Seraphim of Glastonbury, The British Orthodox Church, 10 Heathwood Gardens, London SE7 8EP Tel: 020-8854 3090 Email: boc@nildram.co.uk Coptic Orthodox Church Tel: 01438-745232

THE ERITREAN ORTHODOX CHURCH

In Great Britain the Eritrean Orthodox Church is represented by Bishop Markos, 78 Edmund Street, Camberwell, London SE5 7NR

THE MALANKARA ORTHODOX SYRIAN CHURCH

The Malankara Orthodox Syrian Church is part of the Diocese of Europe, UK and Canada under Metropolitan Thomas Mar Makarios. The church in Great Britain can be contacted via Fr Abraham Thomas, Flat 2, 97 Cranfield Road, Brockley, London SE4 1TR Tel: 020-8691 9456.

THE SYRIAN ORTHODOX CHURCH

The Syrian Orthodox Church in Great Britain comes under the Patriarchal Vicar, whose representative is Fr Touma Hazim Dakkama, Antiochian, 5 Canning Road, Croydon CR0 6QA Tel: 020-8654 7531

THE COUNCIL OF ORIENTAL ORTHODOX CHURCHES, The Armenian Vicarage, Iverna Gardens, London W8 6TP Tel: 020-7937 0152
President, Rt. Revd Bishop Nathan Hovhannisian

PENTECOSTAL CHURCHES

Pentecostalism is inspired by the descent of the Holy Spirit upon the apostles at Pentecost. The movement began in Los Angeles, USA, in 1906 and is characterised by baptism with the Holy Spirit, divine healing, speaking in tongues (glossolalia), and a literal interpretation of the scriptures. The Pentecostal movement in Britain dates from 1907. Initially, groups of Pentecostalists were led by laymen and did not organise formally. However, in 1915 the Elim Foursquare Gospel Alliance (more usually called the Elim Pentecostal Church) was founded in Ireland by George Jeffreys and in 1924 about 70 independent assemblies formed a fellowship, the Assemblies of God in

Great Britain and Ireland. The Apostolic Church grew out of the 1904–5 revivals in South Wales and was established in 1916, and the New Testament Church of God was established in England in 1953. In recent years many aspects of Pentecostalism have been adopted by the growing charismatic movement within the Roman Catholic, Protestant and Eastern Orthodox churches.

There are about 105 million Pentecostalists worldwide, with about 200,000 adult adherents in Great Britain and Ireland.

THE APOSTOLIC CHURCH, International Administration Offices, PO Box 389, 24–27 St Helens Road, Swansea SA1 1ZH Tel: 01792-473992

National Leader, Pastor R. W. Jones
Administrator, Pastor A. Saunders

The Apostolic Church has about 110 churches, 5,500 adherents and 91 ministers

THE ASSEMBLIES OF GOD IN GREAT BRITAIN AND IRELAND, PO Box 7634, Nottingham NG11 6ZY Tel: 0115-921 7272 Fax: 0115-921 7273 Email: info@aog.org.uk

General Superintendent, P. C. Weaver
General Administrator, D. H. Gill

The Assemblies of God has 640 churches, about 60,000 adherents (including children) and 896 accredited ministers

THE ELIM PENTECOSTAL CHURCH, PO Box 38, Cheltenham, Glos GL50 3HN Tel: 01242-519904 Email: info@elimhq.com

General Superintendent, Revd J. J. Glass
Administrator, Pastor B. Hunter

The Elim Pentecostal Church has 600 churches, 68,500 adherents and 650 accredited ministers

THE NEW TESTAMENT CHURCH OF GOD, Main House, Overstone Park, Overstone, Northampton NN6 0AD Tel: 01604-643311

National Overseer, Bishop Eric Arthur Brown.

The New Testament Church of God has 118 organised congregations, about 9,750 members, about 10,000 adherents and 282 accredited ministers

PLYMOUTH BRETHREN

The Brethren was founded in Dublin in 1827–28. It rejected denominationalism and clericalism and based itself on the structures and practices of the early Church. Many groups sprang up and that at Plymouth became the best known, which resulted in the designation by others as Plymouth Brethren. Other groups are based in Ireland, USA, Burma and Guyana.

Early worship had a prescribed form but quickly assumed an unstructured, non-liturgical format. There were services devoted to worship, usually involve the breaking of bread, and separate preaching meetings. There was no salaried ministry.

A theological dispute led in 1848 to schism between the Open Brethren and the Closed or Exclusive Brethren, each branch later suffering further divisions.

Open Brethren churches are completely independent, but freely co-operate with each other. Churches are run by appointed elders. Exclusive Brethren churches believe in a universal fellowship between congregations. They do not have elders, but appoint respected members of their congregation to perform certain administrative functions.

The Brethren are established throughout the UK, Ireland, Europe, India, Africa and Australasia. Total membership in the UK is 81,638.

GOSPEL TRACT PUBLICATIONS, 7 Beech Avenue, Dumbreck, Glasgow G41 5BY Tel: 0141-427 4661
CHAPTER TWO, Fountain House, Conduit Mews, London SE18 7AP Tel: 020-8316 5389

THE PRESBYTERIAN CHURCH IN IRELAND

The Presbyterian Church in Ireland is Calvinistic in doctrine and presbyterian in constitution. Presbyterianism was established in Ireland as a result of the Ulster plantation in the early 17th century, when English and Scottish Protestants settled in the north of Ireland.

There are 21 presbyteries and five regional synods under the chief court known as the General Assembly. The General Assembly meets annually and is presided over by a Moderator who is elected for one year. The ongoing work of the Church is undertaken by 18 boards under which there are a number of specialist committees.

There are about 279,000 Presbyterians in Ireland, mainly in the north, in 557 congregations and with 400 ministers.

Moderator (2003–4), Rt. Revd Ivan McKay
Clerk of Assembly and General Secretary, Revd Dr Donald Watts, Church House, Belfast BT1 6DW Tel: 028-9032 2284

THE PRESBYTERIAN CHURCH OF WALES

The Presbyterian Church of Wales or Calvinistic Methodist Church of Wales is Calvinistic in doctrine and presbyterian in constitution. It was formed in 1811 when Welsh Calvinists severed the relationship with the established church by ordaining their own ministers. It secured its own confession of faith in 1823 and a Constitutional Deed in 1826, and since 1864 the General Assembly has met annually, presided over by a Moderator elected for a year. The doctrine and constitutional structure of the Presbyterian Church of Wales was confirmed by Act of Parliament in 1931–2.

The Church has 37,820 members, 94 ministers and 815 churches.

Moderator (2003–4), Revd D. Owen
General Secretary, Revd Ifan Roberts, 53 Richmond Road, Cardiff CF24 3WJ Tel: 029-2049 4913

THE RELIGIOUS SOCIETY OF FRIENDS (QUAKERS)

Quakerism is a movement, not a church, which was founded in the 17th century by George Fox and others in an attempt to revive what they saw as 'primitive Christianity'. The movement was based originally in the Midlands, Yorkshire and north-west England, but there are now Quakers in 36 countries around the world. The colony of Pennsylvania, founded by William Penn, was originally Quaker.

Emphasis is placed on the experience of God in daily life rather than on sacraments or religious occasions. There is no church calendar. Worship is largely silent and there are no appointed ministers; the responsibility for conducting a meeting is shared equally among those present. Social reform and religious tolerance have always been important to Quakers, together with a commitment to non-violence in resolving disputes.

There are 213,800 Quakers world-wide, with over 16,000 in Great Britain and Ireland. There are about 470 meetings in Great Britain.

CENTRAL OFFICES: (GREAT BRITAIN) Friends House,
173 Euston Road, London NW1 2BJ
Tel: 020-7663 1000 Fax: 020-7663 1001
Email: betha@quaker.org.uk
Web: www.quaker.org.uk

THE SALVATION ARMY

The Salvation Army was founded by a Methodist minister, William Booth, in the east end of London in 1865, and has since become established in 108 countries world-wide. In 1878 it adopted a quasi-military command structure intended to inspire and regulate its endeavours and to reflect its view that the Church was engaged in spiritual warfare. Salvationists emphasise evangelism and the provision of social welfare.

There are over 1.5 million members worldwide, 17,201 active officers (full-time ordained ministers) and 15,670 worship centres and outposts world-wide. In Great Britain and Ireland there are 48,600 members, 1,484 active officers and 822 worship centres.

International Leader, Gen. John Gowans
UK Leader, Commissioner Alex Hughes
TERRITORIAL HEADQUARTERS, 101 Newington
   Causeway, London SE1 6BN Tel: 020-7367 4500
   Email: thq@salvationarmy.org.uk

THE SEVENTH-DAY ADVENTIST CHURCH

The Seventh-day Adventist Church was founded in 1863 in the USA and the first church in the UK was established in 1886. Its members look forward to the second coming of Christ and observe the Sabbath (the seventh day) as a day of rest, worship and ministry. The Church bases its faith and practice wholly on the Bible and has developed 27 core beliefs.

The World Church is divided into 13 divisions, each made up of unions of churches. The Seventh-day Adventist Church in the British Isles is known as the British Union Conference of Seventh-day Adventists and is a member of the Trans-European Division. In the British Isles the administrative organisation of the church is arranged in three tiers: the local churches; the regional conferences for south England, north England, Wales, Scotland and Ireland; and the national headquarters.

There are over 12 million members and 49,724 churches in 204 countries. In the UK and Ireland there are 21,864 members and 251 churches.

President of the British Union Conference, C. R. Perry
BRITISH ISLES HEADQUARTERS, Stanborough Park,
   Watford WD25 9JZ Tel: 01923-672251

THE (SWEDENBORGIAN) NEW CHURCH

The New Church is based on the teachings of the 18th century Swedish scientist and theologian Emanuel Swedenborg (1688–1772), who believed that Jesus Christ appeared to him and instructed him to reveal the spiritual meaning of the Bible. He claimed to have visions of the spiritual world, including heaven and hell, and conversations with angels and spirits. He published several theological works, including descriptions of the spiritual world and a Bible commentary.

The Second Coming of Jesus Christ is believed to have already taken place and is still taking place, being not an actual physical reappearance of Christ, but rather His return in spirit. It is also believed that concurrent with our life on earth is life in a parallel spiritual world, of which we are usually unconscious until death.

There are around 30,000 Swedenborgians world-wide, with 1,148 members, 27 Churches and 11 ministers in the UK.

THE GENERAL CONFERENCE OF THE NEW CHURCH,
   Swedenborg House, 20 Bloomsbury Way, London
   WC1A 2TH Tel: 020-7229 9340

UNDEB YR ANNIBYNWYR CYMRAEG

The Union of Welsh Independents

The Union of Welsh Independents was formed in 1872 and is a voluntary association of Welsh Congregational Churches and personal members. It is mainly Welsh-speaking. Congregationalism in Wales dates back to 1639 when the first Welsh Congregational Church was opened in Gwent. Member churches are Calvinistic in doctrine, although a wide range of interpretations are permitted, and congregationalist in organisation. Each church has complete independence in the government and administration of its affairs.

The Union has 32,500 members, 220 ministers and 500 member churches.

President of the Union (2003–4) Revd Meirion Evans
General Secretary, Revd D. Myrddin Hughes,
   Ty John Penry, 11 Heol Sant Helen, Swansea SA1 4AL
   Tel: 01792-652542 Fax: 01792-650647

THE UNITED REFORMED CHURCH

The United Reformed Church was first formed by the union of most of the Congregational churches in England and Wales with the Presbyterian Church of England in 1972. Congregationalism dates from the mid 16th century. It is Calvinistic in doctrine, and its followers form independent self-governing congregations bound under God by covenant, a principle laid down in the writings of Robert Browne (1550–1633). From the late 16th century the movement was driven underground by persecution, but the cause was defended at the Westminster Assembly in 1643 and the Savoy Declaration of 1658 laid down its principles. Congregational churches formed county associations for mutual support and in 1832 these associations merged to form the Congregational Union of England and Wales.

Presbyterianism in England also dates from the mid 16th century, and was Calvinistic and evangelical in its doctrine. It was governed by a hierarchy of courts.

In the 1960s there was close co-operation locally and nationally between Congregational and Presbyterian Churches. This led to union negotiations and a Scheme of Union, supported by Act of Parliament in 1972. In 1981 a further unification took place, with the Reformed Association of Churches of Christ becoming part of the URC. In 2000 a third union took place, with the Congregational Union of Scotland. In its basis the United Reformed Church reflects local church initiative and responsibility with a conciliar pattern of oversight. The General Assembly is the central body, and is made up of equal numbers of ministers and lay members.

The United Reformed Church is divided into 13 Synods, each with a Synod Moderator, and 78 Districts. There are 87,732 members, 628 full-time stipendiary ministers, 83 part-time stipendiary ministers, 173 non-stipendiary ministers, 16 active church related community workers and 1,719 local churches.

General Secretary, Revd Dr David C. Cornick, 86 Tavistock
Place, London WC1H 9RT Tel: 020-7916 2020
Fax: 7916 2021 Email: david.cornick@urc.org.uk

THE WESLEYAN REFORM UNION

The Wesleyan Reform Union was founded by Methodists
who left or were expelled from Wesleyan Methodism in
1849 following a period of internal conflict. Its doctrine
is conservative evangelical and its organisation is
congregational, each church having complete
independence in the government and administration of
its affairs.

The Union has 1,947 members, 17 ministers, 131 lay
preachers and 108 churches.

President (2003–4), Revd P. Henson
General Secretary, Revd A. J. Williams, Wesleyan Reform
Church House, 123 Queen Street, Sheffield S1 2DU
Tel: 0114-272 1938

NON-TRINITARIAN CHURCHES

CHRISTADELPHIANISM

Christadelphians believe that the Bible is the word of
God and that it reveals both God's dealing with mankind
in the past and his plans for the future. These plans centre
on the work of Jesus Christ, who is believed shortly to
return to earth to establish God's kingdom.
Christadelphians have existed since the 1850s, beginning
in the USA through the work of an Englishman, Dr John
Thomas.

THE CHRISTADELPHIAN MAGAZINE AND PUBLISHING
ASSOCIATION, 404 Shaftmoor Lane, Birmingham B28 8SZ
Tel: 0121-777 6324 Fax: 0121-778 5024

THE CHURCH OF CHRIST, SCIENTIST

The Church of Christ, Scientist was founded by Mary
Baker Eddy in the USA in 1879 to 'reinstate primitive
Christianity and its lost element of healing'. Christian
Science teaches the need for spiritual regeneration and
salvation from sin, but is best known for its reliance on
prayer alone in the healing of sickness. Adherents believe
that such healing is a law, or Science, and is in direct line
with that practised by Jesus Christ (revered, not as God,
but as the Son of God) and by the early Christian
Church.

The denomination consists of The First Church of
Christ, Scientist, in Boston, Massachusetts, USA (the
Mother Church) and its branch churches in over 80
countries world-wide. The Bible and Mary Baker Eddy's
book, *Science and Health with Key to the Scriptures,* are
used at services; there are no clergy. Those engaged in
full-time healing are called practitioners, of whom there
are 3,500 world-wide.

No membership figures are available, since Mary Baker
Eddy felt that numbers are no measure of spiritual vitality
and ruled that such statistics should not be published.
There are over 2,000 branch churches world-wide,
including nearly 120 in the UK.

CHRISTIAN SCIENCE COMMITTEE ON PUBLICATION,
9 Elysium Gate, 126 New Kings Road, London SW6 4LZ
Tel: 020-7384 8600 Fax: 020-7371 9204
Email: cs@compub.org
District Manager for Great Britain and Ireland, Tony Lobl

THE CHURCH OF JESUS CHRIST OF LATTER-DAY SAINTS

The Church (often referred to as 'the Mormons') was
founded in New York State, USA, in 1830, and came to
Britain in 1837. The oldest continuous branch in the
world is to be found in Preston, Lancs. Mormons are
Christians who claim to belong to the 'Restored Church'
of Jesus Christ. They believe that true Christianity died
when the last original apostle died, but that it was given
back to the world by God and Christ through Joseph
Smith, the Church's founder and first president. They
accept and use the Bible as scripture, but believe in
continuing revelation from God and use additional
scriptures, including *The Book of Mormon: Another
Testament of Jesus Christ.* The importance of the family is
central to the Church's beliefs and practices. Church
members set aside Monday evenings as Family Home
Evenings when Christian family values are taught.
Polygamy was formally discontinued in 1890.

The Church has no paid ministry; local congregations
are headed by a leader chosen from amongst their
number. The world governing body, based in Utah, USA,
is the three-man First Presidency, assisted by the Quorum
of the Twelve Apostles.

There are more than 11 million members world-wide,
with about 180,000 adherents in Britain in over 350
congregations.

President of the Europe West Area (including Britain), Elder
Harold G. Hillam
BRITISH HEADQUARTERS, Church Offices, 751 Warwick
Road, Solihull, W. Midlands B91 3DQ Tel: 0121-712 1202

JEHOVAH'S WITNESSES

The movement now known as Jehovah's Witnesses grew
from a Bible study group formed by Charles Taze Russell
in 1872 in Pennsylvania, USA. In 1896 it adopted the
name of the Watch Tower Bible and Tract Society, and in
1931 its members became known as Jehovah's Witnesses.
Jehovah's (God's) Witnesses believe in the Bible as the
word of God, and consider it to be inspired and
historically accurate. They take the scriptures literally,
except where there are obvious indications that they are
figurative or symbolic, and reject the doctrine of the
Trinity. Witnesses also believe that the earth will remain
for ever and that all those approved of by Jehovah will
have eternal life on a cleansed and beautified earth; only
144,000 will go to heaven to rule with Christ. They
believe that the second coming of Christ began in 1914
and his thousand-year reign on earth is imminent, and
that Armageddon (a final battle in which evil will be
defeated) will precede Christ's rule of peace. They refuse
to take part in military service, and do not accept blood
transfusions.

The 10-member world governing body is based in
New York, USA. There is no paid ministry, but each
congregation has elders assigned to look after various
duties and every Witness is assigned homes to visit in
their congregation.

There are over 6 million Jehovah's Witnesses world-
wide, with 130,000 Witnesses in the UK organised into
over 1,400 congregations.

BRITISH ISLES HEADQUARTERS, Watch Tower House, The
Ridgeway, London NW7 1RN
Tel: 020-8906 2211 Fax: 020-8371 0051
Email: pr@wtbts.org.uk Web: www.watchtower.org

UNITARIAN AND FREE CHRISTIAN CHURCHES

Unitarianism has its historical roots in the Judaeo-Christian tradition but rejects the deity of Christ and the doctrine of the trinity. It allows the individual to embrace insights from all the world's faiths and philosophies, as there is no fixed creed. It is accepted that beliefs may evolve in the light of personal experience.

Unitarian communities first became established in Poland and Transylvania in the 16th century. The first avowedly Unitarian place of worship in the British Isles opened in London in 1774. The General Assembly of Unitarian and Free Christian Churches came into existence in 1928 as the result of the amalgamation of two earlier organisations.

There are about 6,000 Unitarians in Great Britain and Ireland, and about 150 Unitarian ministers. Nearly 200 self-governing congregations and fellowship groups, including a small number overseas, are members of the General Assembly.

GENERAL ASSEMBLY OF UNITARIAN AND FREE
  CHRISTIAN CHURCHES, Essex Hall, 1–6 Essex Street,
  London WC2R 3HY Tel: 020-7240 2384
  Fax: 020-7240 3089 Email: ga@unitarian.org.uk
  Web: www.unitarian.org.uk
  General Secretary, Jeffrey J. Teagle

COMMUNICATIONS

POSTAL SERVICES

On 26 March 2001 the Post Office became a public limited company and adopted a new name, Consignia plc. On 13 June 2003, it was announced that Consignia's name would be changed to Royal Mail Group plc. Royal Mail Group plc operates Parcelforce, Post Office and Royal Mail, which handles over 80 millions items of mail each day. The Postal Services Commission (Postcomm), an independent regulator accountable to parliament, oversees postal operations in the UK and is tasked with the gradual introduction of competition into postal services.

POSTCOMM, 6 Hercules Road, London SE1 7DB
Tel: 020-7593 2100 Web: www.postcomm.gov.uk
POSTWATCH, 28 Grosvenor Gardens, London SW1W 0TT
Tel: 08456-013265
Postwatch is the consumer organisation responsible for postal services and takes up complaints on behalf of consumers against any licensed provider of postal services.

Below are details of a number of popular postal services along with prices at the time of going to press. For further details please contact the relevant service provider, i.e. Royal Mail or Parcelforce.

INLAND POSTAL SERVICES AND REGULATIONS

INLAND LETTER POST RATES*

Not over	1st class†	2nd class†
60 g	28p	20p
100 g	42p	34p
150 g	60p	46p
200 g	75p	56p
250 g	88p	69p
300 g	£1.01	80p
350 g	£1.15	91p
400 g	£1.37	£1.10
450 g	£1.56	£1.25
500 g	£1.74	£1.42
600 g	£2.10	£1.68
700 g	£2.64	£1.92
750 g	£2.83	£2.04
800 g	£3.06	(not
900 g	£3.36	admissible
1,000 g	£3.67	over 750 g)

Costs for first class items over 1kg are £3.67 and then 89p for each extra 250g or part thereof.
*Postcards travel at the same rates as letter post
† First class letters are normally delivered the following day and second class post within three days

UK PARCEL RATES

Standard Tariff
Not over	
1 kg	£3.32
1.5 kg	£4.27
2 kg	£4.58
4 kg	£6.91
6 kg	£7.54
8 kg	£8.59
10 kg	£9.23
30 kg	£10.76

OVERSEAS POSTAL SERVICES AND REGULATIONS

Royal Mail divides the world into three zones: Europe; Zone 1 (USA, Canada, South America, the Middle East, Africa, parts of Asia and the Indian sub-continent, most of south east Asia and Hong Kong); Zone 2 (the rest of the world, including Asia and Australasia).

OVERSEAS SURFACE MAIL RATES (WORLD ZONES 1 & 2)

Letters
Not over		Not over	
20 g	37p	450 g	£3.25
60 g	61p	500 g	£3.59
100 g	87p	750 g	£5.29
150 g	£1.21	1,000 g	£6.99
200 g	£1.55	1,250 g	£8.69
250 g	£1.89	1,500 g	£10.39
300 g	£2.23	1,750 g	£12.09
350 g	£2.57	2,000 g	£13.79
400 g	£2.91		

AIRMAIL LETTER RATES

Europe: Letters
Not over		Not over	
20 g	38p	280 g	£2.40
40 g	53p	300 g	£2.55
60 g	69p	320 g	£2.70
80 g	85p	340 g	£2.85
100 g	£1.01	360 g	£3.00
120 g	£1.17	380 g	£3.15
140 g	£1.32	400 g	£3.30
160 g	£1.47	420 g	£3.45
180 g	£1.62	440 g	£3.60
200 g	£1.77	460 g	£3.75
220 g	£1.93	480 g	£3.90
240 g	£2.09	500 g	£4.05
260 g	£2.25	1,000 g	£7.80
		*2,000 g	£15.30

* Max. 2 kg

Zones 1 & 2: Letters
Postcards	Not over 10g	Not over 20g	Over 20g
42p	47p	68p	price varies

SPECIAL DELIVERY SERVICES

ROYAL MAIL SPECIAL DELIVERY
A guaranteed next working day delivery service by 12.00 p.m. to most UK destinations for first class letters and packets. Prices start at £3.75. Customers can choose the level of compensation payable in the event that an item is lost or damaged, up to a maximum of £2,500.

SWIFTAIR AND AIRSURE
Express airmail services. The fee for Swiftair is £3.30 plus airmail postage. The fee for Airsure is £4.00 plus airmail postage.

RECORDED MAIL
Provides a record of posting and delivery of letters and ensures a signature on delivery. This service is recommended for items of little or no monetary value. All packets must be handed to the post office and a certificate of posting issued. Charges: 64p plus the standard first or second class postage. The International Signed For service costs £2.85 on top of the airmail postage.

OTHER SERVICES

BUSINESS SERVICES
A range of services are available to help businesses manage their postal needs most effectively. These include: business collection, freepost, business reply services, business packaging for special deliveries and international mailing options.

COMPENSATION (INLAND AND INTERNATIONAL)
Compensation for loss or damage to an item sent varies according to the service used to send the item. For inland post, compensation may be paid where it can be shown that a letter was damaged or lost in the post due to the fault of Royal Mail, its employees or agents. Royal Mail does not accept responsibility for loss or damage arising from faulty packing. For international post, compensation up to £28 may be given for loss or damage occurring in the UK.

PASSPORT APPLICATIONS
Around 2,000 post offices process passport applications. To find out your nearest office, and for further information, *see* contact details below.

TRACK AND TRACE
This service enables customers to track the progress of items sent using selected Royal Mail and Parcelforce Worldwide services. *See* below for contact details.

REDIRECTION
By agent of addressee: mail other than parcels, business reply and freepost items may be reposted free not later than the day after delivery (not counting Sundays and public holidays) if unopened and if original addressee's name is unobscured. Parcels may be redirected free within the same time limits only if the original and substituted address are in the same local parcel delivery area (or the London postal area). Registered packets must be taken to a post office and are re-registered free up to the day after delivery.

By the Post Office: a printed form obtainable from the Post Office must be signed by the person to whom the letters are to be addressed. A fee is payable for each different surname on the application form. Charges: up to 1 calendar month, £6.45 (abroad via airmail, £12.90); up to 3 calendar months, £14.05 (£28.10); up to 6 calendar months, £21.60 (£43.20); up to 12 calendar months, £32.40 (£64.80).

INTERNATIONAL PREPAID PRODUCTS
Prepaid products are a convenient and secure way of packaging items that are to be sent overseas. There are a number of different types of prepaid products to choose from, depending on the weight of the article to be sent, ranging in price up to £6.00.

SMALL PACKETS POST AND PRINTED PAPERS (INTERNATIONAL)
Permits the transmission of goods up to 2 kg to all countries, in the same mails as printed papers. Packets can be sealed and can contain personal correspondence relating to the contents. Registration is allowed as insurance as long as the item is packed in a way complying with any insurance regulations. A customs declaration is required and the packet must be marked with 'small packet' and a return address.

Surface mail: worldwide

Not over		Not over	
100 g	60p	450 g	£2.00
150 g	80p	500 g	£2.20
200 g	1.00p	750 g	£3.20
250 g	£1.20	1,000 g	£4.20
300 g	£1.40	1,500 g	£6.20
350 g	£1.60	2,000 g	£8.20
400 g	£1.80		

CONTACT DETAILS
Royal Mail general enquiries: 08457-740740
Royal Mail business enquiries: 08457-950950
Postcode enquiry line: 08457-111222 or 0906-302 1222
Online shop: 08457-641641
Parcelforce Worldwide: 08708-501150
Post Office enquires: 08457-223344
Track and Trace: 08456-092609
Web: www.royalmail.com

IDD CODES

INTERNATIONAL DIRECT DIALLING (IDD)

International dialling codes are composed of four elements which are dialled in sequence:

(i)	the international code
(ii)	the country code
(iii)	the area code
(iv)	the telephone number

Calls to some countries must be made via the international operator.

*Can vary depending on area and/or carrier

Country	IDD from UK	IDD to UK
Afghanistan	00 93	00 44
Albania	00 355	00 44
Algeria	00 213	00 44
Andorra	00 376	00 44
Angola	00 244	00 44
Anguilla	00 1 264	11 44
Antigua and		
Barbuda	00 1 268	11 44
Argentina	00 54	00 44
Armenia	00 374	810 44
Aruba	00 297	00 44
Ascension Island	00 247	00 44
Australia	00 61	00 11 44
Austria	00 43	00 44
Azerbaijan	00 994	810 44
Azores	00 351	00 44
Bahamas	00 1 242	11 44
Bahrain	00 973	0 44
Bangladesh	00 880	00 44
Barbados	00 1 246	11 44
Belarus	00 375	810 44
Belgium	00 32	00 44
Belize	00 501	00 44
Benin	00 229	00 44
Bermuda	00 1 441	11 44
Bhutan	00 975	00 44
Bolivia	00 591	00 44
Bosnia-Hercegovina		
Muslim-Croat		
Federation	00 387	00 44
Republika Srpska	00 381	00 44
Botswana	00 267	00 44
Brazil	00 55	00 44
British Virgin Islands	00 1 284	11 44
Brunei	00 673	00 44
Bulgaria	00 359	00 44
Burkina Faso	00 226	00 44
Burundi	00 257	90 44
Cambodia	00 855	00 44
Cameroon	00 237	00 44
Canada	00 1	011 44
Canary Islands	00 34	00 44
Cape Verde	00 238	0 44
Cayman Islands	00 1 345	11 44
Central African		
Republic	00 236	19 44
Chad	00 235	15 44
Chile	00 56	00 44
China	00 86	00 44
Hong Kong	00 852	1 44
Macao	00 853	00 44
Colombia	00 57	9 44

Country	IDD from UK	IDD to UK
Comoros	00 269	00 44
Congo, Dem. Rep. of	00 243	00 44
Congo, Republic of	00 242	00 44
Cook Islands	00 682	00 44
Costa Rica	00 506	00 44
Côte d'Ivoire	00 225	00 44
Croatia	00 385	00 44
Cuba	00 53	119 44
Cyprus	00 357	00 44
Czech Republic	00 420	00 44
Denmark	00 45	00 44
Djibouti	00 253	00 44
Dominica	00 1 767	11 44
Dominican Republic	00 1 809	11 44
East Timor	00 670	00 44
Ecuador	00 593	00 44
Egypt	00 20	00 44
El Salvador	00 503	0 44
Equatorial Guinea	00 240	00 44
Eritrea	00 291	00 44
Estonia	00 372	800 44
Ethiopia	00 251	0044
Falkland Islands	00 500	0 44
Færøe Islands	00 298	9 44
Fiji	00 679	5 44
Finland	00 358	00 44*
France	00 33	00 44
French Guiana	00 594	00 44
French Polynesia	00 689	00 44
Gabon	00 241	00 44
The Gambia	00 220	00 44
Georgia	00 995	810 44
Germany	00 49	00 44
Ghana	00 233	00 44
Gibraltar	00 350	00 44
Greece	00 30	00 44
Greenland	00 299	99 44
Grenada	00 1 473	11 44
Guadeloupe	00 590	00 44
Guam	00 1 671	1 44
Guatemala	00 502	00 44
Guinea	00 224	00 44
Guinea-Bissau	00 245	99 44
Guyana	00 592	1 44
Haiti	00 509	00 44
Honduras	00 504	00 44
Hungary	00 36	00 44
Iceland	00 354	00 44
India	00 91	00 44
Indonesia	00 62	001 44*
		008 44*
Iran	00 98	00 44
Iraq	00 964	00 44
Ireland, Republic of	00 353	00 44
Israel	00 972	00 44*
Italy	00 39	00 44
Jamaica	00 1 876	11 44
Japan	00 81	001 44*
		0041 44*
		0061 44*
Jordan	00 962	00 44*
Kazakhstan	00 7	810 44
Kenya	00 254	00 44
Kiribati	00 686	00 44
Korea, North	00 850	00 44
Korea, South	00 82	001 44*
		002 44*
Kuwait	00 965	00 44
Kyrgyzstan	00 996	00 44
Laos	00 856	00 44
Latvia	00 371	00 44

Country	IDD from UK	IDD to UK	Country	IDD from UK	IDD to UK
Lebanon	00 961	00 44	St Helena	00 290	00 44
Lesotho	00 266	00 44	St Lucia	00 1 758	11 44
Liberia	00 231	00 44	St Pierre and		
Libya	00 218	00 44	Miquelon	00 508	00 44
Liechtenstein	00 423	00 44	St Vincent and the		
Lithuania	00 370	810 44	Grenadines	00 1 784	1 44
Luxembourg	00 352	00 44	Samoa	00 685	0 44
Macedonia	00 389	99 44	Samoa, American	00 684	00 44
Madagascar	00 261	00 44	San Marino	00 378	00 44
Madeira	00 351	00 44*	São Tomé and		
Malawi	00 265	00 44	Príncipe	00 239	00 44
Malaysia	00 60	00 44	Saudi Arabia	00 966	00 44
Maldives	00 960	00 44	Senegal	00 221	00 44
Mali	00 223	00 44	Serbia &		
Malta	00 356	00 44	Montenegro	00 381	99 44
Mariana Islands,			Seychelles	00 248	00 44
Northern	00 1 670	11 44	Sierra Leone	00 232	00 44
Marshall Islands	00 692	11 44	Singapore	00 65	1 44
Martinique	00 596	00 44	Slovakia	00 421	00 44
Mauritania	00 222	00 44	Slovenia	00 386	00 44
Mauritius	00 230	00 44	Solomon Islands	00 677	00 44
Mayotte	00 269	10 44	Somalia	00 252	16 44
Mexico	00 52	98 44	South Africa	00 27	09 44
Micronesia, Federated			Spain	00 34	00 44
States of	00 691	11 44	Sri Lanka	00 94	00 44
Moldova	00 373	810 44	Sudan	00 249	00 44
Monaco	00 377	00 44	Suriname	00 597	00 44
Mongolia	00 976	00 44	Swaziland	00 268	00 44
Montenegro	00 381	99 44	Sweden	00 46	00 44
Montserrat	00 1 664	11 44	Switzerland	00 41	00 44
Morocco	00 212	00 44	Syria	00 963	00 44
Mozambique	00 258	00 44	Taiwan	00 886	2 44
Myanmar	00 95	00 44	Tajikistan	00 992	810 44
Namibia	00 264	00 44	Tanzania	00 255	00 44
Nauru	00 674	00 44	Thailand	00 66	1 44
Nepal	00 977	00 44	Tibet	00 86	00 44
Netherlands	00 31	00 44	Togo	00 228	00 44
Netherlands Antilles	00 599	00 44	Tonga	00 676	00 44
New Caledonia	00 687	00 44	Trinidad and		
New Zealand	00 64	00 44	Tobago	00 1 868	11 44
Nicaragua	00 505	00 44	Tristan da Cunha	–	–
Niger	00 227	00 44	Tunisia	00 216	00 44
Nigeria	00 234	9 44	Turkey	00 90	00 44
Niue	00 683	00 44	Turkmenistan	00 993	810 44
Norfolk Island	00 672	101 44	Turks and Caicos		
Norway	00 47	00 44	Islands	00 1 649	00 44
Oman	00 968	00 44	Tuvalu	00 688	00 44
Pakistan	00 92	00 44	Uganda	00 256	00 44
Palau	00 680	11 44	Ukraine	00 380	810 44
Panama	00 507	00 44	United Arab		
Papua New Guinea	00 675	5 44	Emirates	00 971	00 44
Paraguay	00 595	002 44	Uruguay	00 598	00 44
Peru	00 51	00 44	USA	00 1	011 44
Philippines	00 63	00 44	Alaska	00 1 907	011 44
Poland	00 48	00 44	Hawaii	00 1 808	011 44
Portugal	00 351	00 44	Uzbekistan	00 998	810 44
Puerto Rico	00 1 787	11 44	Vanuatu	00 678	00 44
Qatar	00 974	00 44	Vatican City State	00 390 66982	00 44
Réunion	00 262	00 44	Venezuela	00 58	00 44
Romania	00 40	00 44	Vietnam	00 84	00 44
Russia	00 7	810 44	Virgin Islands (US)	00 1 340	11 44
Rwanda	00 250	00 44	Yemen	00 967	00 44
St Christopher and			Zambia	00 260	00 44
Nevis	00 1 869	11 44	Zimbabwe	00 263	00 44

MOBILE COMMUNICATIONS

2003 Current Subscriber Base	O_2	Vodafone	T-Mobile	Orange	Hutchison*
Total	11,640,000	12,166,080	12,400,000	13,312,000	NA
Market Share	23.5%	24.6%	25.0%	26.9%	NA

*Launched March 2003

The UK mobile communications industry is continuing to undergo a period of transformation primarily as the result of introducing new technologies (expanding the traditional mobile operator service offering to customer) which has had major financial implications for all market players. The Government sold the 3G operating licences for considerable profit and Network Operators are trying to recoup both this cost and the costs associated with technology upgrades by developing more ambitious services and encouraging consumer use of more expensive handsets.

INDUSTRY PLAYERS

The mobile communications industry has a number of players: Network Operators who own the infrastructure and provide services; Service Providers and MVNOs who do not own infrastructure but have commercial agreements with the Network Operators; and the Regulator who is responsible for setting the controls of the mobile market, implementing EU-wide legislation and ensuring that industry players do not behave anti-competitively.

NETWORK OPERATORS
Until recently there were four network operators rolling out their mobile networks and actively offering mobile services. A fifth, Hutchison 3G, was launched in March 2003. Network Operators are responsible for setting tariffs, billing, offering services and maintaining the network infrastructure.

UK MOBILE NETWORK OPERATORS

Operator	Ownership	Licence	Launch Date
O_2	Formerly BT Cellnet	Tacs-900	January 1985
	100% O_2	GSM	January 1994
Vodafone	100% Vodafone	Tacs-900	January 1985
		GSM	July 1992
T-Mobile	Formerly One2One 100% - Deutsche Telekom	GSM 1800	September 1993
Orange	100% - France Telecom	GSM 1800	April 1994
Hutchison 3G	65% - Hutchison Whampoa	UMTS	March 2003
	20% - DoCoMo		
	15% - KPN		

ALTERNATIVE SERVICE PROVIDERS
Mobile services are also provided by Service Providers and MVNOs. Service Providers were introduced into the UK as a means to stimulate competition within the market. Service Providers buy airtime wholesale from the Network Operators and sell it on to end users. This agreement means that they can set their own tariff structures and have a direct billing relationship with end users. The incumbent network operators (those who have been operating since the start) O_2 and Vodafone have an obligation under the terms of their licences to offer wholesale minutes of airtime to Service Providers. Orange and T-Mobile, as later entrants to the market, have not been subject to this condition. There are said to be around 50 Service Providers operating in the UK market including One.Tel, Sainsbury's, Sony Cellular Services and Martin Dawes. In order to maintain a viable business operation many of these Service Providers have diversified their product offering away from pure mobile services to other telecom or Internet based services.

The newest players offering mobile services are MVNOs, Mobile Virtual Network Operators. Whereas a number of Network Operators are obliged to open their networks to Service Providers, none of the Network Operators are currently obliged to open their networks to MVNOs. The main difference between Service Providers and MVNOs is the degree of ownership over the equipment used. An MVNO has its own mobile network code, issues its own SIM cards (Subscriber Identity Module card – the 'brain' of a handset), operates its own mobile switching centre and has a pricing structure fully independent from the Network Operator. The most successful MVNO to date is Virgin Mobile, which operates on the back of the T-Mobile network. As the company does not have infrastructure costs, Virgin Mobile has been able to keep costs low and attract a large number of customers in a relatively short space of time. Other emerging MVNOs include Energis and FT Mobile, a joint venture between the Financial Times and the Carphone Warehouse.

TYPES OF MOBILE SERVICE
Network Operators, Service Providers and MVNOs offer two basic types of service: contract and pre-paid. Contracts (generally paid on a monthly basis though fixed to a minimum contract term) mean that the end user pays a fixed subscription fee each month that entitles them to a number of basic services (for example voicemail or SMS) and gives them a certain amount of 'free' airtime/access to services each month. Pre-paid subscribers have access to the same services but pay in advance and simply top up their account when it is running low. The introduction of pre-paid services has allowed industry players to target additional consumer segments, in particular the youth market and customers who do not have an acceptable credit rating for a contract service. Pre-paid has proved to be a very popular option as it allows customers to control their spend. As at 1 January 2003, the split between pre-paid and contract customers in the UK was 68:32.

NETWORK TECHNOLOGY

THE DEVELOPMENT OF MOBILE INFRASTRUCTURE

The first technology introduced in the UK was an analogue technology called TACS which was adopted in 1985. In 1992 Vodafone launched a new digital GSM network, usually referred to as 2G or second generation. BT Cellnet (now O$_2$) and two more entrants launched GSM services in the following two years making the UK one of Europe's most competitive markets.

More recently, GSM networks have been modified to enable them to transfer packet-switch data and this technology is known as GPRS (General Packet Radio Service). GPRS is not a completely new network, rather an upgrade from the existing GSM infrastructure and is also referred to as 2.5G. The main difference between GSM and GPRS technology is the ability to transmit data as well as voice across the network. This is a result of higher bandwidth and with GPRS, as shown in the table above.

The industry is still waiting for the fully-fledged delivery of next generation mobile services, 3G, or UMTS (Universal Mobile Telecommunications System). The main difference with UMTS lies in its capacity to offer even faster data transmission speeds than GPRS, therefore allowing data facilities such as MMS (multi-media services) and access to the internet. Additionally, UMTS has the potential to offer further advantages over GSM/GPRS such as international roaming whereas at present, despite GSM's widespread presence, other mobile technologies used in other parts of the world are incompatible with GSM handsets, for instance in parts of Asia and in America.

As 3G or UMTS technology is an entirely new network, Network Operators must hold a licence to deploy it. The UK was the third European country to licence 3G operators after Finland and Spain but was the first to auction its licences. Auctions are not new to the European communications industry – many of the second and third entrants to Europe's communications markets had to bid for their licences – but what was spectacular about the UK's 3G auction was the size of the bids. While industry observers had speculated that the auction might reach £4 billion, in the event a total of £22 billion was raised from the sale of the spectrum.

UK 3G LICENCE WINNERS AND TOTAL COST

Hutchison 3G UK	Licence A	2x 15MHz paired 5MHz unpaired	€7 billion
Vodafone	Licence B	2x15MHz paired	€9.6 billion
BT Cellnet	Licence C	2x10 MHz paired 5MHz unpaired	€6.5 billion
One2One	Licence D	2x10 MHz paired 5MHz unpaired	€6.4 billion
Orange	Licence E	2x10 MHz paired 5MHz unpaired	€6.6 billion
TOTAL			€36.1 billion

DATA SERVICES

GSM from analogue brought clearer voice quality, while the upgrade from GSM through GPRS to UMTS brings not only improved voice quality but also new services, primarily data-based services as seen in the table below.

DATA SERVICES MIGRATION PATH

Mobile Infrastructure	Data Services available
GSM (2G) Speed: 10kb/sec	• Phone calls • Voice mail • Receipt of simple email messages
GPRS (2.5G) Speed: 64-144kb/sec	• Phone calls/fax • Voice mail • Receipt and transmission of large emails • Web browsing • Navigation/maps
UMTS (3G) Speed: 144kb-2mb/sec	• Phone calls/fax • Global roaming • Receipt and transmission of large emails • High speed web • Navigation/maps • Videoconferencing • TV Streaming • Electronic agenda meeting reminder

The provision of improved and new services is crucially important for the industry as it reaches saturation point (88 per cent of the UK population now owns a mobile handset). In order to maintain revenues, Network Operators now have to refocus from customer acquisition strategies to increasing customer service usage levels/ARPU (average revenue per user), as well as encouraging more frequent handset renewal.

2G & 2.5G DATA SERVICES

To date, the most popular and readily available data service has been SMS (Short Messaging Service). SMS, or 'text messaging', allows consumers to send and receive text messages up to 160 characters long on their mobile phones. Due to its simplicity and popularity, particularly among young users, the number of SMS messages being sent has increased dramatically.

With increased familiarity and accessibility of SMS technology, new services (sending logos, basic pictures and downloading personal ringtones) have also been introduced. These types of services are referred to as EMS, Enhanced Messaging Services. For example, Vodafone has launched its 'Live!' service which offers mobile users access to multimedia services, including the taking, sending and receiving of photos with an integrated camera, Java games, email, ringtones and chat as well as the 'traditional' SMS and mobile phone calls.

TOTAL NUMBER OF SMS SENT IN THE UK (PER MONTH)

Date	December '99	December '00	December '01	December '02
Number of Messages	271 million	756 million	1.3 billion	1.6 billion

WAP, Wireless Application Protocol, is a software language that allows Internet-style data to be downloaded and viewed on a mobile phone. Consumers access content from mobile portals which, like traditional Internet portals, aggregate and display mobile Internet content in an accessible manner. As could be expected, there are a number of independent mobile Internet portals and content sites springing up for UK consumers. However, given the slow data rate of a GSM network and the size of a mobile phone screen, WAP applications have, so far, been uninspiring.

3G DATA SERVICES

The main difference between UMTS and GPRS/GSM from the customer's viewpoint is the extension of data services that will be accessible through one's mobile. All operators have launched 3G style services over their GPRS networks though these services will be further enhanced (for example introduction of video messaging) once the move to the 3G network has taken place (and all technical problems have been resolved). Hutchison 3G has been the first to launch its highly advertised '3' service which offers video calling, content browsing, interactive games and location based services which took place in March 2003.

REGULATION

Regulation of the mobile industry underwent significant change in 2003, with the passing of a Communications Act in the UK and the implementation of new EU Directives covering framework, authorisation, access and interconnection, and universal services. The new EU framework aims to develop a pro-competitive, light-touch regulatory framework.

From the point of view of the mobile industry, the key features of the Communications Act 2003 are:

- *The abolition of licensing requirements* – the removal of licensing requirements means that Ofcom will draw up sets of conditions for providers in the areas of universal service, significant market power, access and privileged supplier obligations
- *The provision for spectrum trading* – when an operator is awarded a mobile licence, the allocated spectrum can only be used by that named company; under the new Act, licences will be able to transfer the entitlement to use the spectrum to another player
- *New enforcement provisions for dealing with anti-competitive behaviour* – Ofcom will be given the power to levy a fine of up to 10 per cent of turnover (or suspend a licence in extreme cases) should a mobile operator breach the conditions of its licence instead of having to refer cases to the Competition Authority.

In the UK, regulation is the responsibility of the Office of Communications (Ofcom) which replaces the Radio Authority, the Radio Communications Agency, Oftel, the Broadcasting Standards Commission and the Independent Television Commission.

CONTACTS

DEPARTMENT OF TRADE AND INDUSTRY (DTI)
1 Victoria Street, London SW1H OET
Tel: 020-7215 5000 or 020-7215 1783 Fax: 020-7215 2909
Web: www.dti.gov.uk

OFCOM
Riverside House, 2A Southwark Bridge Road, London SE1 9HA
Tel: 020-7981 3000 Fax: 020-7981 3333
Web: www.ofcom.org.uk

O_2
260 Bath Road, Slough SL1 4DX
Tel: 01753-565 000 Fax: 01753-565 010
Web: www.O2.co.uk

HUTCHISON 3G UK
43 New Bond Street, London W1Y 9HB
Tel: 020-7499 1886 Fax: 020-7491 7266
Web: www.three.co.uk

ORANGE PLC
50 George Street, London W1U 7DZ
Tel: 020-7984 1600 Fax: 020-7984 1601
Web: www.orange.co.uk

T-MOBILE
Imperial Place, Maxwell Road, Borehamwood WD6 1EA
Tel: 020-8214 2121 Fax: 020-8214 3601
Web: www.t-mobile.co.uk

VODAFONE GROUP
The Courtyard, 2–4 London Road, Newbury RG14 1JX
Tel: 01635-33251 Fax: 01635-45713
Web: www.vodafone.co.uk

INFORMATION TECHNOLOGY

ANCESTRY AND DEVELOPMENT

The ancestors of the modern computer are the Difference Engine and the Analytical Engine devised by mathematician Charles Babbage. Designed in 1820 to automatically compute mathematical tables, Babbage abandoned construction of his mechanical, clockwork-like Difference Engine in the 1840s for personal and financial reasons. In 1834 he began work on his Analytical Engine. Unlike the Difference Engine, the Analytical Engine was designed as a general-purpose tool with a store to hold information.

Babbage's work relied heavily on mechanics and physical machinery. It was not until the twentieth century invention of the electrical vacuum tube, and then the transistor, that computers became a feasible means to solving problems.

FIRST GENERATION

War has been a significant factor in the development of the computer. In 1943, during World War II, the British and Americans developed electro-mechanical computers. Colossus, a British effort, was specifically developed to crack German coding ciphers, whilst an American effort, Harvard Mark I, was developed as a more general-purpose electro-mechanical programmable computer (partly for atom bomb research). Regarded as early first generation computers, these machines primarily comprised wired circuits and vacuum valves. Punched cards and paper tape were largely employed as the input, output and main storage systems. ENIAC (Electronic Numerical Integrator and Computer) was completed in 1946 at the University of Pennsylvania, USA. Capable of carrying out 100,000 calculations a second, it was remarkable for its day despite weighing thirty tons.

SECOND GENERATION

Similar to light bulbs, valves were prone to failure, requiring tedious checks to resolve problems (ENIAC alone contained 18,000 vacuum valves). In 1947, the transistor was invented. Performing the same role as a vacuum valve but less prone to failure, smaller and more efficient, the transistor allowed smaller 'second generation' computers to be developed throughout the 1950s and early 1960s.

THIRD GENERATION

In 1958 Jack St Claire Kilby produced the first integrated circuit 'microchip'. A microchip is comprised of a large number of transistors and other components bonded to a wafer ('chip') of silicon, interconnected by a surface film of conductive material rather than by wires. By reducing distance between components, savings are made in both size and electricity. In 1963 the first 'third generation' computers based on microchip technology appeared.

FOURTH GENERATION

In 1971 Intel produced the first 'microprocessor' heralding a 'fourth generation' of computers. The Intel 4004 (capable of 60,000 instructions per second) grouped much of the processing functions onto a single microchip. Around the same time, Intel invented the RAM (random access memory) chip which grouped significant amounts of memory onto a single chip. Supercomputers and mainframes, utilising scores of microprocessors, had terrific power in the order of 150 million instructions per second. Developments such as multi-layer circuits, and the use of copper instead of gold in microchips, yielded improvements in size and performance through miniaturisation. The size of the transistor was scaled down from thumb size to far smaller than the thickness of a human hair, allowing for greater density and thus exponentially increasing the total power of the computer.

NEXT GENERATION

Most modern computers are still regarded as 'fourth generation' as they use essentially the same technology, albeit highly miniaturised. The future of computer technology is widely thought to be dependent on the physics of light. Already used extensively in the computer industry for high-speed communications, light offers future possibilities for both calculation and storage.

Gordon Moore, co-founder of Intel, observed in 1965 that the number of transistors per square inch had doubled every 12 months since the inception of the integrated circuit. The pace of development has slowed somewhat. The widely recognised definition of the so-called 'Moore's Law' is that data density doubles every 18 months and is likely to do so for the next few decades.

PROGRAMMING LANGUAGES

Numerous programming languages have been adopted with the common purpose of devising a program of instructions for computers to follow to achieve a task. The languages are categorised by generation:

1GL or first-generation language is the machine language that the processor chips execute in raw binary form (strings of zeros and ones).

2GL or second-generation language. Assembly language is a human-understandable language insofar as it uses names as well as numbers. An assembler program takes assembly language and turns it into a machine code program. Very common in early systems where resources (speed, storage) were at a premium, it is typically only used today as an output from 3GL and higher systems.

3GL or third-generation language is a 'high-level' programming language typically more readable and concise than assembly language.

4GL or fourth generation language is designed to be closer to natural language than a 3GL language.

5GL or fifth-generation programming uses graphical development environments to create source language to be compiled with a 3GL or 4GL language compiler. Often a mix of generations is used, with a high level language (4 or 5GL) used to produce interface elements and a lower level language used to provide the processing power.

OPERATING SYSTEMS

An operating system (OS) is a set of utility programs that acts as the liaison between the computer user, the hardware (processor unit, memory) and its peripherals (disks, mouse, display, printer, network, etc.) and the program that the user is running (e.g. a word processor). The first computers had no operating system, and each program had to directly control the hardware on its own, adding greatly to the burden of programming. Early operating systems were hardware and manufacturer-specific with assembly language or machine code as the programming language. Each computer model or series tended to have its own specific operating system. UNIX was one of the first operating systems that could be ported (converted) to a variety of system hardware. This ability was enabled largely through the use of the 'C' programming language.

PERSONAL COMPUTER OPERATING SYSTEMS

Since the 1990s, the personal computer world has been dominated by Microsoft Corporation. Although not a significant manufacturer of computer equipment, the Microsoft Corporation has built on its market share secured in the 1980s with MS-DOS to become the market leading operating system provider. Microsoft's MS Windows personal computer operating systems are installed on more computers than any other commercial operating system.

Microsoft's main personal computer rival is Apple. Established in the 1970s, Apple became highly successful with its Apple I, II and III range of personal computers, and is one of the few personal computer companies from that time that has continued to manufacture both its own hardware and operating system to run upon it. It is now also known for its design innovation from the iMac and iBook.

THE NET

Prior to the Internet (or 'the Net' or 'the Web' as it is known colloquially) computers tended to be connected together by hardware and protocols that were specific to each particular connection. Typically, links were point-to-point (a link had to be directly and physically established between the two computers). In 1969 ARPANET was formed by the US Department of Defence to establish a way for the computer capability of the military to be dispersed so that no one centre was critical to the operation of the network as a whole. This was achieved by interconnecting computers both directly and by way of other intermediary computers; thus if one computer was hit by a nuclear bomb, other pathways of communication could be established. The interconnections, when drawn, appeared as a mesh, or net or web. ARPANET was extended to non-military users such as universities early in the 1970s, with initial international links appearing in 1972.

The introduction of domain names (e.g. www.acblack.com/whitakers) in 1984 offered an easier means of using the Web. Prior to domain names one had to remember IP numbers (e.g.192.168.1.100) for accessing destination computers. However, before 1989 the Internet was still primarily limited to government agencies, the military, academic and research organisations and some big businesses.

In 1989, what most people perceive as 'the Net' was born. It was effectively invented at CERN (the European Particle Physics Laboratory) by Tim Berners-Lee as a way for scientists to share information by placing it in a prescribed format on a server. Initially text only, development of computer capability allowed inclusion of images.

By 1993 a whole new industry of ISPs (Internet Service Providers) had begun, allowing computer users to dial up via a modem and access the Internet and to view the Web through a browser (see glossary). Developments through the late 1990s have allowed music, video, games, text, graphics and telephone calls to travel the Internet. The future is likely to see the majority of telephone calls, and probably video, being transmitted over the Internet for at least part of their journey. Expansion of fibre-optic cable networks to homes and businesses will underpin this. The advent of high-capacity mobile phones will also facilitate and demand expansion of the Internet.

GLOSSARY OF TERMS

The following is a selected list of modern computing terms. It is by no means exhaustive but is intended to cover those that the average computer user might encounter.

3G: Third Generation wireless – a populist term commonly used to describe high bandwidth (2 Mbps) wireless technologies for mobile phones. So called 3G as it follows 1st generation analogue and 2nd generation digital mobile services. Deployed 3G is still in its infancy but when fully deployed 3G technology will offer high speed and capacity transmission of sound, vision and data to and from wireless devices and networks. European operator licences for 3G services were sold in Europe early this century for billions of Euros however few comprehensive networks have been completed and consumer uptake has been slow. Many consider pornography will be a major driving force in 3G uptake.

AIRPORT: Apple, the first single manufacturer to popularise Wi-Fi technology, markets its Wi-Fi technology under this trade mark. See Wi-Fi.

ADSL: Asymmetric Digital Subscriber Line – high speed internet connection, four or more times faster than a modem, but using the same standard cables as regular telephone. Faster at downloading than uploading (hence asymmetric).

ANIMATED GIF: A multi-layered GIF file that allows simple animations to be created by transitions between the layers. Banner advertising on the Internet tends to utilise animated GIFs. See also GIF.

BLOG: A blog (short for weblog) is an online personal journal that is frequently updated and intended to be read by the public. Blogs generally represent the personality of the author and may include philosophy, commentary on Internet and other social issues, and links to favourite websites. Blogs are kept by 'bloggers'.

BLUETOOTH: Standard for short-range (10 metre) wireless connectivity between devices such as laptops, cell phones and printers to interact without cables. Bluetooth can presently operate at speeds of up to 2Mbps (the exact speed varies on the generation of the technology).

BROADBAND INTERNET: Generic term to describe high speed Internet-using technologies such as ISDN, ADSL etc. as opposed to narrowband Internet connections via modem.

BROWSER: Typically referring to a 'web browser' program that allows a computer user to view web page content on their computer, e.g. Microsoft Explorer, Netscape Navigator, AOL, etc.

BURN: To 'burn', 'toast' or 'rip' a file or files to a CD-ROM or similar media means to copy the files to the media from hard disk (or other source). Derived from the fact that CD-ROMs are burnt by a laser during the process of writing to the disk.

C: A 3GL programming language developed in the late 1960s in parallel with the UNIX operating system. Primarily limited to UNIX until the mid-1980s when standards such as POSIX emerged, allowing C to be widely adopted on many operating systems. UNIX used C as its core programming language. There are many derivatives such as C+ (object oriented) or C# (Microsoft's proposed alternative to Java).

CAT-5: An electrical performance and cable quality standard prescribed to support high-speed Ethernet networks. There are higher category and capability specifications denoted by higher numbers but Cat-5 is the most commonly installed today.

CD: Compact Disc – a digital disk format capable of storing 650 megabytes of information per side. A laser head detects pits etched into the substrate of the spinning disk and interprets them as information. Widely used in an audio format for storing recorded music. The computer format CD-ROM is likely to be superceded by the higher capacity DVD in the next few years. CD-RAM/CD-RW and CD-R are modifiable versions that use lasers to alter the disk substrate to make the pits interpreted later as information. See also DVD.

DNS: Domain Name Server – a server that translates domain names into the IP numbers used by programs to directly access computers on the Internet. Each server has an IP number and a name. DNS is analogous to the telephone directory enquiry service, providing a means of looking up and locating a computer connected to the Internet.

DOMAIN: A set of words, numbers and letters separated by dots used to identify an Internet server or group of servers, e.g. www.whitakersalmanack.co.uk, where 'www' denotes a web (http) server, 'whitakers almanack' denotes the organisation name, 'co' denotes that the organisation is a company and 'uk' denotes United Kingdom (there are alternatives for every country but 'us' is typically omitted for the United States).

DVD: Digital Versatile Disc – DVD-ROM is a high capacity (read only) disk format that has the same form factor as CD-ROM but can store several gigabytes of information on each surface and can have four readable surfaces (through laser focusing technology). DVD-RAM is a modifiable version. Various formats are available, the most common being that used to store high-quality digital video, an alternative to the laser disk or videotape. See also CD.

EMAIL: Electronic mail – an email message is a document that is addressed to one or more persons from an individual address. Usually containing a message, it can also include other documents. It has superceded the telex, telegram, postcard and letter for rapidly exchanging information. The advent of the Internet has seen an explosion in the use of email in modern life. Without encryption or digital signature, an Internet email is not secure.

ETHERNET: Utilising simple, standard and relatively cheap cable and connectors, Ethernet has become the standard for local area networks. Ethernet employs a system whereby each computer listens for information addressed to its own unique address. Before transmitting, each computer waits for silence on the line; if multiple computers start transmitting simultaneously, they each detect the 'collision' and wait a random period of time before trying again, thus allowing communications to proceed politely.

EXTRANET: An extranet is a secure and private subset of the Internet, protected by security protocols and typically used for exchanging information and services between a specific group.

FILE SERVER: A computer on a network that stores computer files that users can access from other computers on the network. Popular modern systems include Microsoft Windows, UNIX, Novell NetWare, and MacOS Server.

FIREWALL: Computer or device to protect a network from security risks posed by the Internet. Just as a firewall protects parts of a building from a fire raging on the other side, a network firewall stops risks posed by the Internet from egressing into a private network.

FIREWIRE: Apple Computer's implementation of IEEE 1394. See also IEEE 1394.

FTP: File Transfer Protocol – an Internet protocol whereby an FTP client program can exchange files with a remote server.

GBPS: Giga bits per second – denoting 1,000 million bits transmitted per second.

GIF: Graphics Interchange Format – compressed graphic format suitable for logos and non-photographic images. Invented by Unisys to allow images to be sent electronically in an efficient manner.

GPRS: General Packet Radio Services – a service for continuous wireless communication over the Internet from mobile phones and computers. Presently available in data rates of between 56 and 114K Bps, GPRS tends to be charged by volume of information transferred rather than by time, which allows a more economic continuous connection compared with direct dial over a modem.

HTML: HyperText Mark-up Language – a small programming language used to denote or mark-up how an internet page should be presented to a user from an HTTP server via a web browser. HTTP is an evolving standard that has grown greatly from its first version to accommodate new types of web content and features provided by the different web browsers (e.g. Netscape and Internet Explorer).

HTTP: HyperText Transfer Protocol – an Internet protocol whereby a web server sends web pages, images and files to a web browser. HTTP is an evolving protocol.

IEEE 1394: High-speed serial (400 Mbps) connection standard for hard disks, digital video cameras and other multimedia devices. Popularised as iLink (Sony) and FireWire (Apple).

iLINK: Sony's implementation of IEEE 1394. See also IEEE 1394.

IMAP: Internet Mail Access Protocol – an Internet protocol IMAP allows a user to review, manipulate and store email on a central server from one or more workstations without necessitating message removal from the server.

INTERNET: An abstract concept applied to describe the global network of INTER-connected computer NET-works of computers. See body of article.

INTRANET: Subset of the Internet, using Internet protocols over a local area network, common today for publishing information and services within an organisation.

IRC: Internet Relay Chat – protocol that allows users to 'chat' online with other users using their keyboards. Under IRC a user can log into various chat rooms under their own name or an alias and have a text 'conversation' in real time with other users.

ISDN: Integrated Services Digital Network – widely adopted in the United Kingdom and Europe but not North America, ISDN allows both digital computer data and voice telephony to exist simultaneously on the same cable circuits. Data can be digitally exchanged at 64 Kbps per circuit. Typically used for point-to-point file transfer of large documents when it was first introduced, more recently it has been used for 'dial-up' Internet.

JPEG: Joint Photographic Experts Group – compressed graphic format suitable for compression of photographic images in a manner that simplifies the image, losing definition in the process. As the level of compression increases so too does the image degradation.

KBPS: Kilo bits per second – measure of transmission speed, denoting 1,000 bits transmitted per second.

LINUX: A UNIX-like operating system first developed as a free or low cost system for personal computers. Linux was first developed by Linus Torvalds however large portions of its source code are now in the public domain and there are many distributions (versions) available. It is increasingly popular for business enterprise applications, highly scalable and can be used for anything from running a vehicles engine management system to controlling a supercomputing cluster. *See also* UNIX.

MACOS: Operating system developed by Apple Computer for use on their own Macintosh computers.

MBPS: Mega bits per second – denoting 1 million bits transmitted per second.

MODEM: Modulator/demodulator – a device that modulates digital signals from a computer into analogue signals for transmission over a standard telephone line and demodulates an incoming analogue signal and converts it to a digital signal for the computer.

MP3: Motion Picture Group 1 layer 3 – popular format for compressing audio information for transmission over the Internet for later playback on personal computers, music players and other devices.

MPEG: Motion Picture Encoding Group – popular format standard for compressing video and audio information for transmission over the Internet for later playback on personal computers and on hand-held devices.

MS-DOS: Microsoft Corporation's Disk Operating System – an early OS commercially developed, but not invented, by Microsoft for use on early Intel-based personal computers. *See also* Operating System.

NNTP: Network News Transfer Protocol – an Internet protocol that implements a bulletin board on a global scale. Using a NNTP browser one can subscribe and contribute to one or more news groups covering a large variety of topics.

OPERATING SYSTEM (OS): Computer software developed to provide computer programs with standard facilities to interact with users and with computer hardware (via drivers). *See also* MS-DOS, UNIX, MacOS.

PNG: An improved royalty-free graphics file replacement for GIF.

POP3: Post Office Protocol 3 – an Internet protocol whereby a workstation can collect email from a personal mailbox on an email server and move it to a user's own machine.

PRINT SERVER: A computer or device on a network that manages the sharing of one or more printers between multiple computers over a network. Many modern printers have a print server built in.

ROUTER: Where multiple networks are joined together, a router acts like a fast sorting office, examining the destination address of each information packet and passing or routing it to the appropriate network. Routers can select the most efficient route for packets.

SMTP: Simple Mail Transfer Protocol – an Internet protocol whereby a workstation can send email to a server or whereby two servers can exchange email.

SNMP: Simple Network Management Protocol – widely used protocol for remotely monitoring and managing network device status and function.

SPAM: A term used for unsolicited, generally junk, email. To spam someone is to send them (multiple) junk emails. Junk email is becoming a major internet issue with some estimates suggesting that spam is becoming more prevalent than legitimate email. Most spam contains offers of pornography, get-rich schemes, prescription drugs, low cost finance or discount goods or services. Many legislatures around the globe are taking steps to ban or regulate it.

STUFFIT: Popular Apple Macintosh mechanism to compress to compress information in order to save resources. Stuffit is a proprietary brand name of Aladdin Systems. *See also* Zip.

TAR: Compression – a common mechanism on UNIX and Linux operating systems to compress information in order to save resources.

TCP/IP: Transmission Control Protocol/Internet Protocol – a protocol which is the lifeblood of the Internet, TCP/IP defines how information and requests generated by all other protocols are transmitted over the Internet. Information on the Internet is chopped up into small chunks or packets which are addressed with a destination and origination address. It sometimes happens that a packet gets lost and TCP/IP dictates how such a loss is handled.

UNIX: *See* body of article. Modern versions include Linux, MacOS X, Solaris, FreeBSD.

USB: Universal Serial Bus – standard for connecting serial devices such as scanners, mice, keyboards, modems and printers to computers. With USB, speeds of 10 Mbps and higher are possible.

USB 2: Universal Serial Bus 2 – a revised, higher performance version of USB.

URL: Uniform Resource Locator – address of an Internet file accessible on the Internet, e.g. http://www.whitakersalmanack.co.uk.

VIRUS: A computer program or script written for the express purpose of replicating itself onto as many machines as possible (much like its biological namesake) often with negative side effects to the host computer and computer network. Such effects vary from harmless screen messages to corruption of document integrity, network overload or compromising data security or privacy. Historically transmitted slowly by floppy disk and over networks within offices, the prevalence of email means viruses can spread globally within minutes.

WAP: Wireless Application Protocol – a set of standards to define how portable devices connected via radio waves (such as cell phones) can access Internet services.

WARCHALKING: To 'warchalk' is to mark an open or security-exposed Wi-Fi or other wireless network by writing symbols on or outside the relevant buildings in chalk. The idea of warchalking derives from the early days of computer networks, when curious hackers would engage in wardialling expeditions. These involved telephoning a lot of numbers to see which of them answered with a data, rather than a dial tone. *See* Wi-Fi.

WAR DRIVING: The activity of locating and exploiting security exposed Wi-Fi and other wireless networks to gain access to the network resource or information on or accessible to that network. *See* Wi-Fi.

WI-FI: Industry brand name for the increasingly popular hi frequency wireless local area Ethernet networking technology specification IEEE 802.11. Most prevalent is the 802.11b specification offering speeds of up to 11 Mps.

WLAN: Wireless local area network where information is transferred by radio frequency rather than wires between computers and base stations. As radio waves can pass through objects such as walls, it is becoming increasingly important for WLANs to be secured by encryption against unauthorised access.

XML: Extensible Mark-up Language, similar to HTML but more powerful, XML allows information to be encoded or tagged in a manner that is both human and computer readable. The advent of XML has greatly simplified the exchange of information between many formerly incompatible systems.

ZIP: Compression – a popular mechanism on PCs to compress to compress information in order to save resources. *See also* Stuffit.

THE ENVIRONMENT

Europe's environment has improved in several respects over the last decade. A report published by the European Environment Agency in May 2003, represents the third assessment of Europe's environment and is the first to include the whole of the Russian Federation and the eleven other eastern European, Caucasus and central Asian states. The two previous assessments were published in 1995 and 1998. The report revealed that most progress has come from measures to limit pollution, or as a result of economic recession and restructuring, and that properly developed and implemented environmental policies have led to significant improvements in several areas, such as emissions to air and water. However, it also highlighted that policies to curb waste have made no significant headway; the process of integrating environmental concerns into areas such as transport policy is at an early stage and environmental impacts caused by economic development are typically not taken into account. The report concluded that policies that take full account of environmental concerns, with a balance between regulatory measures to deal with specific problems and economic and other instruments, will be needed for Europe to make the transition to more sustainable development.

Environmental policies are developed at several levels – international conventions and protocols (of which there are over 50), European Directives (of which there are over 300) and national legislation and strategies.

EUROPEAN UNION MEASURES

The European Union (EU) is developing an interlinked set of policies – the sixth Environmental Action Programme, the Cardiff process for the integration of environment into other policies and the EU sustainable development strategy – which form the framework for more detailed strategies.

The Environmental Action Programme began in the 1970s. The Sixth Environmental Action Programme, *Environment 2010: Our Future, Our Choice*, was adopted in January 2001 and sets the programme to 2010. It proposes five priority areas: improving the implementation of existing legislation; integrating environmental concerns into other policies; working more closely with the market; empowering citizens and helping them to change behaviour and taking account of the environment in land-use planning and management decisions. The programme focuses on four topics: climate change, nature and biodiversity, environment and health, and natural resources and waste.

SUSTAINABLE DEVELOPMENT AND LOCAL AGENDA 21

The environmental agenda is increasingly becoming part of a wider move to address sustainability which incorporates social, environmental and economic development. In 2002, the World Summit on Sustainable Development was held in Johannesburg and Governments agreed on a series of commitments in five priority areas – water and sanitation, energy, health,

agriculture and biodiversity. Targets include halving the number of people who lack access to clean water or proper sanitation by 2015 and reducing biodiversity loss by 2010. Following the summit, the United Nations Commission on Sustainable Development has agreed its programme for the next 15 years. It will work in two year cycles, with the first (2004–5) focusing on water, sanitation and human settlements. This will be followed by energy, climate change, atmosphere and industrial development in 2006–7.

As part of the EU's preparation for the World Summit, a sustainable development strategy was adopted in May 2001. It sets out long-term objectives, such as limiting major threats to public health and breaking the link between economic growth and transport growth. The UK published its first national sustainable development strategy in 1994 and its first set of sustainable development indicators in 1996. The latest strategy *A Better Quality of Life* was published in May 1999. A full review of the strategy started in May 2003 with a revised version to be in place by 2005. The review will take a fresh look at how sustainable development can be achieved in the UK.

The current strategy provides a framework for integrating social, environmental and economic policies to meet four objectives: social progress, to protect the environment, prudent use of natural resources and to maintain high and stable levels of economic growth and employment. The strategy contains 19 headline and sub-headline indicators. In February 2003, the government published its third annual progress report which found that ten of the headline indicators showed significant improvement, five had no significant change, three had declined and there was no comparable data for one.

The Scottish Executive launched its statement on sustainable development, together with 24 initial indicators in April 2002 and further indicators published in February 2003.

Local authorities also have a role to play in sustainable development. Under Local Agenda 21, which came out of the UN Conference on Environment and Development in Rio, Brazil in 1992, local authorities have an obligation to draw up sustainable development strategies for their areas. At the World Summit, the UK government committed itself to taking further action towards the implementation of Agenda 21 and achieving the Millennium Development Goals which have grown out of agreements and declarations at UN Conferences.

Many businesses are also working towards sustainable development and some are assessing and reporting their own progress using the Global Reporting Initiative (GRI).

WASTE

Waste policy in the UK follows a number of principles: the waste hierarchy of reduce, reuse, recycle, dispose; the proximity principle of disposing of waste close to its generation and national self sufficiency.

Directives from Europe are playing an increasingly important role in driving UK policy, particularly regarding commercial and industrial waste. For instance, the Landfill Directive, which was adopted in July 1999, sets stringent targets for reducing the amount of waste sent to landfill. The directive should have been implemented by July 2001, but regulations were not laid before the UK parliament for implementation in England and Wales until April 2002. The Scottish Executive laid its measures before parliament in February 2003.

The proposed European integrated products policy aims to internalise the environmental costs of products throughout their life-cycle via market forces, by focusing on eco-design and incentives to ensure increased demand for greener products. Greater responsibility for end-of-life products is already being addressed by the producer responsibility directives for packaging waste, which came into force in the UK in 1997; the end-of-life-vehicle directive, which entered into force in December 2001 and for which the UK is currently consulting on regulations and the directives on waste from electrical and electronic equipment and on the restriction of the use of certain hazardous substances in such equipment which came into effect in February and must be law in member states by August 2004. The UK is currently consulting on legislation.

The UK also has its own targets. In May 2000 a Waste Strategy for England and Wales was published. The strategy aims to tackle the amount of waste produced; increase recycling rates through statutory targets for local authorities; reduce the amount of waste sent to landfill; and develop markets and end-uses for secondary materials. To meet the targets the public and local authorities will have to vastly increase their current recycling rates. In 2001–2, 12.4 per cent of household waste was recycled (including composting), up from 11.2 per cent in 2000–1. In November 2001, the UK government held a waste summit to start the process of looking at forward policies to implement the strategy. This was followed in December 2001 by a study undertaken by the Prime Minister's Strategy Unit into how the UK can tackle its growing waste problem and meet EU Landfill Directive targets. The unit made a number of recommendations in November 2002, to which the government has committed.

Scotland also has a national waste strategy which aims to encourage more effective use of natural resources through greater efficiency, waste minimisation, recycling and increased value recovery from waste. The National Waste Plan for Scotland was published in February 2003.

The Northern Ireland waste strategy, published in 2000, is currently under review. The current strategy is a framework to help achieve the goal of sustainable waste management and meet the targets for the diversion of waste from landfill.

CLIMATE CHANGE AND AIR POLLUTION

The UK's response to climate change is driven by the international Framework Convention on Climate Change. This is a binding agreement that has been signed and ratified by 188 countries. It came into force in the UK in March 1994 and is intended to reduce the risks of global warming by limiting 'greenhouse' gas emissions.

Progress towards the convention's targets are assessed at regular conferences. In 1997 the Kyoto Protocol to the convention was adopted. It covers the six main greenhouse gases – carbon dioxide, methane, nitrous oxide, hydrofluorocarbons (HFCs), perfluorocarbons (PFCs), and sulphur hexafluoride. Under the protocol industrialised countries agreed to legally binding targets for cutting emissions of greenhouse gases by 5.2 per cent below 1990 levels by 2008–12. EU members agreed to an 8 per cent reduction and the UK's target is a 12.5 per cent cut. A report published in May 2003 shows that, by 2000, the UK reduced its greenhouse gas emissions by 12.8 per cent below 1990 levels. Meanwhile, the latest data from the European Environment Agency, also published in May 2003, shows that emissions of greenhouse gases from the EU have increased for a second consecutive year. Emissions were 1 per cent higher in 2001 than 2000, although levels were still 2.3 per cent below 1990 levels.

The protocol set three ways for countries to increase the flexibility and reduce the cost of making emission cuts – the clean development mechanism, emissions trading and joint implementation. At the seventh Conference of the Parties in Marrakech, Morocco in November 2001 the operational details of the Kyoto Protocol were finalised. The eighth Conference of the Parties, in New Delhi, India, in October 2002, considered technical issues and progress was made to ensure the Kyoto Protocol is a success when it comes into force. The protocol will enter into force 90 days after has been ratified by 55 governments, including developed countries representing at least 55 per cent of that group's CO_2 emissions. It had been expected to enter into force in early 2003. Currently 109 countries have ratified the protocol, with developed countries representing 43.9 per cent of emissions. The US has stated that it will not ratify the treaty.

In November 2000, a UK climate change programme was published which sets out how the UK intends to meet its Kyoto target and progress towards its domestic goal of a 20 per cent cut in carbon dioxide emissions by 2010, some of the policies mentioned are already in place. The proposed measures include: a climate change levy which came into effect in April 2002 applied to sales of electricity, coal, natural gas and liquefied petroleum gas to the business and public sectors; agreements with energy intensive sectors to meet targets; integrated pollution prevention and control (see below); cutting transport congestion and pollution; energy efficiency standards of performance requiring electricity and gas suppliers to help domestic consumers save energy; better countryside management; cuts in fertiliser use; new targets for improving energy management of public buildings and emissions trading.

The voluntary greenhouse gas emissions trading scheme started in April 2002 allowing businesses to buy an emission allowance to meet emissions targets or to sell surplus emission allowances. The scheme's first year has been successful with nearly 1,000 companies transferring over seven million tonnes of carbon dioxide.

The European Commission also set up a European Climate Change Programme in 2000 to identify measures to meet the Kyoto target. It plans to introduce a mandatory emissions trading scheme at company level for carbon dioxide in the European Union beginning in 2005. The scheme proposes 'cap and trade', whereby governments will have to impose total carbon dioxide caps on companies, which they would then be able to trade as carbon dioxide allowances within the European Union. Other conventions covering air pollution include the Convention on Long Range Transboundary Air Pollution which was adopted in 1979 and came into force in 1993.

The UK has also developed its own policy on air pollution. The Environmental Protection Act 1990 established two regimes: integrated pollution control (IPC) to regulate emissions to any environmental medium from certain industrial processes and local air pollution control to regulate emissions to air from smaller processes. The European Integrated Pollution Prevention and Control (IPPC) Directive was largely based on the UK's IPC regime. This new regime came into force in the UK in August 2000 (and Scotland in September 2000) after much delay and wrangling over details. Although IPPC is very similar to the UK's IPC it covers many more installations and includes returning sites to a satisfactory state on closure, using energy efficiently and noise and vibration regulation. IPPC has been implemented in the UK through the replacement to the Environmental Protection Act – the Pollution Prevention and Control regulations 2000.

The UK's National Air Quality Strategy was first published in 1997 and revised in 2000. The strategy sets air quality objectives for the main pollutants (benzene 1-3, butadiene, carbon monoxide, lead, nitrogen dioxide, sulphur dioxide, ozone, and particulates) to be met by 2003–8. An addendum was added in February 2003 with tighter objectives for particulates, benzene and carbon monoxide and a new objective for polycyclic aromatic hydrocarbons. Under the strategy, all district and unitary authorities have a duty to review air quality, including likely future air quality, in their areas. This is accompanied by an assessment of whether air quality objectives are being, or are likely to be, met. If authorities find that any part of their area breaches the objectives, an air quality management area must be declared and an action plan drawn up for improvements.

WATER

Water quality targets are set at both EU and UK level for drinking water sources, wastewater discharges, rivers, coastal water and bathing water. The EU's water framework directive, which entered into force in December 2000, has an objective to achieve 'good water status' throughout the EU by 2015. The UK published its Water Bill in February 2003.

The Water Environment and Water Services Bill for Scotland completed its passage through the Scottish parliament in early 2003. It establishes a source-to-sea planning framework for river basin management.

The EC Bathing Water Directive sets standards for bathing waters. This applies to 391 coastal and nine inland bathing waters in the UK. This directive is over 25 years old. The commission presented a proposal for a new directive in October last year which would set a much tighter bathing water quality standard than the existing Directive.

The Environment Agency sets river quality objectives for each stretch of river. Water quality is currently protected through licensing abstraction and regulating discharges. Consents to discharge sewage and industrial effluent are regulated under the Water Resources Act 1991 and the IPPC regime. Discharge consents are based on the river quality objectives and relevant EU directives and specify the concentration and quantity permitted.

The European Urban Waste Water Treatment Directive sets minimum standards for sewage treatment before discharge into coastal waters with the levels of treatment needed depending on the sensitivity of the receiving water. In 1999 the government set more stringent UK targets for all significant coastal discharges to have a minimum of secondary treatment by 2005.

ENERGY

In February 2003, the UK government published a White Paper setting out a long-term strategy for UK Energy policy combining environmental, security of supply, competitiveness and social goals. It builds on the Performance and Innovation Unit's (now the Prime Minister's Strategy Unit) Energy Review, published a year earlier.

SELECTED UK TARGETS

GLOBAL ATMOSPHERE
• Reduce greenhouse gas emissions to 12.5 per cent below 1990 levels by 2010
• Reduce carbon dioxide emissions to 20 per cent below 1990 levels by 2010, and by 60 per cent by 2050

AIR QUALITY
• Reduce sulphur dioxide emissions by 63 per cent based on 1990 levels by 2010
• Reduce emissions of nitrogen oxides by 41 per cent based on 1990 levels by 2010
• Reduce emissions of volatile organic compounds by 40 per cent based on 1990 levels by 2010
• Reduce ammonia emissions by 17 per cent based on 1990 levels by 2010

FRESH WATER AND SEA
• 97 per cent of bathing waters to meet European directive standards consistently by 2005
• Provide secondary treatment for all significant coastal discharges (over 2,000 population equivalent) by 2005
• Reduce the lengths of poor and seriously polluted rivers in Scotland by 351km^2 by 2006.

WASTE
• Reduce industrial and commercial waste going to landfill by 85 per cent of 1998 levels by 2005
• Recover 40 per cent of municipal waste by 2005, 45 per cent by 2010 and 67 per cent by 2015
• Recycle or compost 25 per cent of household waste by 2005, 30 per cent by 2010 and 33 per cent by 2015
• Reduce biodegradable municipal waste sent to landfill to 75 per cent of 1995 levels by 2010, 50 per cent by 2013 and 35 per cent by 2020
• Ensure 65 per cent of UK newspaper feedstock content is waste paper by end of 2003 and 70 per cent by end of 2006
• Proposed re-use and recovery of 85 per cent of the mass of end-of-life vehicles with a minimum of 80 per cent recycling by 2006, 95 per cent and 85 per cent by 2015
• EU target to reduce the amount of waste going to final disposal by 20 per cent by 2010 and 50 per cent by 2050
• Provide segregated kerbside waste collection to over 90 per cent of households in Scotland by 2020
• Stop the growth in municipal waste in Scotland by 2010

LAND
• Ensure 60 per cent of all new housing is built on re-used sites

ENERGY
• Provide 10 per cent of electricity generated from new renewable sources by 2010
• Provide 40 per cent of electricity from renewable sources by 2020 in Scotland

CONSERVATION AND HERITAGE

CONSERVATION OF THE COUNTRYSIDE

NATIONAL PARKS

ENGLAND AND WALES

The ten National Parks of England and Wales were set up under the provisions of the National Parks and Access to the Countryside Act 1949 to conserve and protect scenic landscapes from inappropriate development and to provide access to the land for public enjoyment.

The Countryside Agency (established on 1 April 1999 from the merger of the Countryside Commission and the Rural Development Commission) is the statutory body which has the power to designate National Parks in England, and the Countryside Council for Wales is responsible for National Parks in Wales. Designations in England are confirmed by the Secretary of State for Environment, Food and Rural Affairs and those in Wales by the National Assembly for Wales. The designation of a National Park does not affect the ownership of the land or remove the rights of the local community. The majority of the land in the National Parks is owned by private landowners (74 per cent) or by bodies such as the National Trust (7 per cent) and the Forestry Commission (7 per cent). The National Park Authorities own only 2.3 per cent of the land.

The Environment Act 1995 replaced the existing National Park boards and committees with free-standing National Park Authorities (NPAs). NPAs are the sole local planning authorities for their areas and as such influence land use and development, and deal with planning applications. Their duties include conserving and enhancing the natural beauty, wildlife and cultural heritage of the National Parks; promoting opportunities for public understanding and enjoyment of the National Parks; and fostering the economic and social well-being of the communities within National Parks. The NPAs publish management plans as statements of their policies and appoint their own officers and staff.

Membership of the NPAs differs slightly between England and Wales. In England membership is split between representatives of the constituent local authorities and members appointed by the Secretary of State (of whom one half, minus one, are nominated by the parish councils in the park), with the local authority representatives in a majority of one. The Countryside Agency advises the Secretary of State on appointments not nominated by the parish councils. In Wales two-thirds of NPA members are appointed by the constituent local authorities and one-third by the National Assembly for Wales, advised by the Countryside Council for Wales.

Central government provides 75 per cent of the funding for the parks through the National Park Grant. The remaining 25 per cent is supplied by the local authorities concerned, drawing on monies ring-fenced by central Government for National Park purposes. The National Parks (with date designation confirmed) are:

BRECON BEACONS (1957), Powys (66 per cent)/Carmarthenshire/Rhondda, Cynon and Taff/Merthyr Tydfil/Blaenau Gwent/Monmouthshire, 1,349sq. km/519 sq. miles – The park is centred on the Beacons, Pen y Fan, Corn Du and Cribyn, but also includes the valley of the Usk, the Black Mountains to the east and the Black Mountain to the west. There are information centres at Brecon, Craig-y-nos Country Park, Abergavenny and Llandovery, a study centre at Danywenallt and a day visitor centre near Libanus.
Information Office, Plas y Ffynnon, Cambrian Way, Brecon, Powys LD3 7HP. Tel: 01874-624437
Email: enquiries@breconbeacons.org
National Park Officer, Christopher Gledhill

DARTMOOR (1951 and 1994), Devon, 954 sq. km/368 sq. miles – The park consists of moorland and rocky granite tors, and is rich in prehistoric remains. There are information centres at Haytor, Newbridge, Princetown and Postbridge.
Information Office, Parke, Bovey Tracey, Devon TQ13 9JQ. Tel: 01626-832093 Email: hq@dartmoor-npa.gov.uk
Chief Executive, Nick Atkinson

EXMOOR (1954), Somerset (71 per cent)/Devon, 693 sq. km/268 sq. miles – Exmoor is a moorland plateau inhabited by wild ponies and red deer. There are many ancient remains and burial mounds. There are information centres at Lynmouth, County Gate, Dulverton and Combe Martin.
Information Office, Exmoor House, Dulverton, Somerset TA21 9HL. Tel: 01398-323665
Email: info@exmoor-nationalpark.gov.uk
National Park Officer, Nigel Stone

LAKE DISTRICT (1951), Cumbria, 2,292 sq. km/885 sq. miles – The Lake District includes England's highest mountains (Scafell Pike, Helvellyn and Skiddaw) but it is most famous for its glaciated lakes. There are information centres at Broughton, Keswick, Waterhead, Hawkshead, Seatoller, Bowness, Grasmere, Coniston, Glenridding and Pooley Bridge and a park centre at Brockhole, Windermere.
Information Office, Murley Moss, Oxenholme Road, Kendal, Cumbria, LA9 7RL. Tel: 01539-724555
Email: hq@lake-district.gov.uk
National Park Officer, Paul Tiplady

NORTH YORK MOORS (1952), North Yorkshire (96 per cent)/Redcar and Cleveland, 1,432 sq. km/554 sq. miles – The park consists of woodland and moorland, and includes the Hambleton Hills and the Cleveland Way. There are information centres at Danby, Sutton Bank and at The Old Coastguard Station in Robin Hood's Bay.
Information Office, The Old Vicarage, Bondgate, Helmsley, York YO6 5BP. Tel: 01439-770657
Email: general@northyorkmoors-npa.gov.uk
National Park Officer, Andrew Wilson

NORTHUMBERLAND (1956), Northumberland, 1,049 sq. km/405 sq. miles – The park is an area of hill country stretching from Hadrian's Wall to the Scottish Border. There are information centres at Ingram, Once Brewed and Rothbury.
Information Office, Eastburn, South Park, Hexham, Northumberland HE46 1BS. Tel: 01434-605555
Email: admin@nnpa.org.uk
National Park Officer, Graham Taylor

PEAK DISTRICT (1951), Derbyshire (64 per cent)/Staffordshire/South Yorkshire/Cheshire/West Yorkshire/Greater Manchester, 1,438 sq. km/555 sq.

miles – The Peak District includes the gritstone moors of the 'Dark Peak' and the limestone dales of the 'White Peak'. There are information centres at Bakewell, Edale, Castleton and Upper Derwent.
Information Office, Aldern House, Baslow Road, Bakewell, Derbyshire DE45 1AE. Tel: 01629-816200
Email: aldern@peakdistrict-npa.gov.uk
National Park Officer, Jim Dixon
PEMBROKESHIRE COAST (1952 and 1995), Pembrokeshire, 620 sq. km/240 sq. miles – The park includes cliffs, moorland and a number of islands, including Skomer. There are information centres at St David's and Newport.
Information Office, Winch Lane, Haverfordwest, Pembrokeshire SA61 1PY. Tel: 01437-764636
Email: pcnp@pembrokeshirecoast.org.uk
National Park Officer, Nick Wheeler
SNOWDONIA/ERYRI (1951), Gwynedd/Conwy, 2,142 sq. km/827 sq. miles – Snowdonia is an area of deep valleys and rugged mountains. There are information centres at Aberdyfi, Beddgelert, Betws y Coed, Blaenau Ffestiniog, Conwy, Dolgellau and Harlech.
Information Office, Penrhyndeudraeth, Gwynedd LL48 6LF. Tel: 01766-770274 Email: parc@eryri-npa.gov.uk
Chief Executive, Aneurin Phillips
YORKSHIRE DALES (1954), North Yorkshire (88 per cent)/Cumbria, 1,769 sq. km/683 sq. miles – The Yorkshire Dales are composed primarily of limestone overlaid in places by millstone grit. The three peaks of Ingleborough, Whernside and Pen-y-Ghent are within the park. There are information centres at Grassington, Hawes, Aysgarth Falls, Malham, Reeth and Sedbergh.
Information Office, Yorebridge House, Bainbridge, Leyburn, N. Yorks DL8 3BP. Tel: 01969-650456
Email: info@yorkshiredales.org.uk
Chief Executive, David Butterworth

Two other areas considered to have equivalent status to the National Parks are The Broads and the New Forest. The Broads Authority, a special statutory authority, was established in 1989 to develop, conserve and manage the Norfolk and Suffolk Broads. In 1992 the Government declared its intention of giving the New Forest a status equivalent to that of a national park by declaring it an 'area of national significance'. In 1999 the Countryside Agency began the process of designating the New Forest and The South Downs (within the Sussex Downs and east Hampshire 'Areas of Outstanding Natural Beauty') as National Parks.

THE BROADS (1989), Norfolk, 303 sq. km/117 sq. miles – The Broads are located between Norwich and Great Yarmouth on the flood plains of the five rivers flowing through the area to the sea. The area is one of fens, winding waterways, woodland and marsh. The 40 or so broads are man-made, and are connected to the rivers by dikes, providing over 200 km of navigable waterways. There are information centres at Beccles, Hoveton, North west Tower (Yarmouth), Potterheigham, Ranworth and Toad Hole.
The Broads Authority, Thomas Harvey House, 18 Colegate, Norwich NR3 1BQ. Tel: 01603 610734
Email: broads@broads-authority.gov.uk
Chief Executive, Dr John Packman
THE NEW FOREST Hampshire, 580 sq. km/224 sq. miles – The forest has been protected since 1079 when it was declared a royal hunting forest. The area consists of forest, ancient woodland and heathland.

Much of the Forest is managed by the Forestry Commission, which provides several camp-sites. The main villages are Brockenhurst, Burley and Lyndhurst, which has a visitor centre.
The New Forest Committee, 4 High Street, Lyndhurst, Hants SO43 7BD. Tel: 023-8028 4144.
Chairman, E. Johnson, FRICS
Committee Officer, M. Jago
THE SOUTH DOWNS, West Sussex/Hampshire,1,637 sq. km/632 sq. miles – The South Downs contains a diversity of natural habitats, including flower-studded chalk grassland, ancient woodland, flood meadow, lowland heath and rare chalk heathland.
Sussex Downs Conservation Board, Chantonbury House, Storrington, West Sussex, RH20 4LT. Tel: 01903-741234
Email: info@southdowns-aonb.gov.uk
Chief Officer: Martin Beaton

SCOTLAND

On 9 August 2000 The National Parks (Scotland) Bill received Royal Assent, providing the Parliament with the ability to create National Parks in Scotland. The first two Scottish National Parks; *Loch Lomond and the Trossachs and the Cairngorms*, became operational in 2002 and 2003 respectively. The Act gives Scottish Parks wider powers than in England and Wales, including statutory responsibilities for the economy and rural communities. Membership of the two NPAs in Scotland consists of 20 per cent directly elected members. The remaining 80 per cent are chosen by the Secretary of State, 40 per cent of which are nominated by the constituent Local Authorities. In Scotland, the National Parks are central Government bodies and wholly funded by the Scottish Executive.
CAIRNGORMS (2003), Morayshire, 3,800 sq. km/1,461 sq. miles – The Cairngorms National Park is the largest in the UK. It displays a vast collection of landforms and includes four of Scotland's highest mountains.
Information Office, 14 The Square, Grantown-on-Spey, Morayshire, PH26 3HG. Tel: 01479-873535
Email: mainoffice@cairngorms.prestel.co.uk
Chief Executive, Jane Hope
LOCH LOMOND AND THE TROSSACHS (2002), Argyll and Bute/Stirling/West Dunbartonshire, 1,865 sq. km/720 sq. miles – The park boundaries encompass lochs, rivers, forests, 20 mountains above 3,000 ft. including Ben Moore and a further 20 mountains between 2,500 ft. and 3,000 ft.
Information Office, The Old Station, Balloch Road, Balloch, Alexandria, G83 8SS. Tel: 01389-722600
Email: info@lochlomond-trossachs.org
Chief Executive, Bill Dalrymple

NORTHERN IRELAND

There is power to designate National Parks in Northern Ireland under the Amenity Lands Act 1965 and the Nature Conservation and Amenity Lands Order (Northern Ireland) 1985.

AREAS OF OUTSTANDING NATURAL BEAUTY

ENGLAND AND WALES

Under the National Parks and Access to the Countryside Act 1949, provision was made for the designation of Areas of Outstanding Natural Beauty (AONBs) by the

Countryside Commission. The Countryside Agency is now responsible for AONBs in England and since April 1991 the Countryside Council for Wales has been responsible for the Welsh AONBs. Designations in England are confirmed by the Secretary of State for Environment, Food and Rural Affairs and those in Wales by the National Assembly for Wales. The Countryside and Rights of Way Act 2000 provided for the creation of conservation boards for individual AONBs and placed greater responsibility on local authorities to protect them.

Although less emphasis is placed upon the provision of open-air enjoyment for the public than in the national parks, AONBs are areas which are no less beautiful and require the same degree of protection to conserve and enhance the natural beauty of the countryside. This includes protecting flora and fauna, geological and other landscape features. In AONBs planning and management responsibilities are split between county and district councils and the newly established conservation boards (where they exist). In Wales, unitary authorities have sole responsibility for the planning and management. Several AONBs cross local authority boundaries. Finance for the AONBs is provided by grant-aid.

The 41 Areas of Outstanding Natural Beauty (with date of designation confirmed) are:

ANGLESEY (1967), Anglesey, 221 sq. km/85 sq. miles
ARNSIDE AND SILVERDALE (1972), Cumbria/ Lancashire, 75 sq. km/29 sq. miles
BLACKDOWN HILLS (1991), Devon/Somerset, 370 sq. km/143 sq. miles
CANNOCK CHASE (1958), Staffordshire, 68 sq. km/26 sq. miles
CHICHESTER HARBOUR (1964), Hampshire/West Sussex, 74 sq. km/29 sq. miles
CHILTERNS (1965; extended 1990), Bedfordshire/ Hertfordshire/Buckinghamshire/ Oxfordshire, 833 sq. km/322 sq. miles
CLWYDIAN RANGE (1985), Denbighshire/Flintshire, 157 sq. km/60 sq. miles
CORNWALL (1959; Camel estuary 1983), 958 sq. km/370 sq. miles
COTSWOLDS (1966; extended 1990), Gloucestershire/ Wiltshire/Warwickshire/Worcestershire/Somerset, 2,038 sq. km/787 sq. miles
CRANBORNE CHASE AND WEST WILTSHIRE DOWNS (1983), Dorset/Hampshire/Somerset/Wiltshire, 983 sq. km/379 sq. miles
DEDHAM VALE (1970; extended 1978, 1991), Essex/ Suffolk, 90 sq. km/35 sq. miles
DORSET (1959), 1,129 sq. km/436 sq. miles
EAST DEVON (1963), 268 sq. km/103 sq. miles
EAST HAMPSHIRE (1962), 383 sq. km/148 sq. miles
FOREST OF BOWLAND (1964), Lancashire/North Yorkshire, 802 sq. km/310 sq. miles
GOWER (1956), Swansea, 188 sq. km/73 sq. miles
HIGH WEALD (1983), Kent/Surrey/East Sussex/West Sussex, 1,460 sq. km/564 sq. miles
HOWARDIAN HILLS (1987), North Yorkshire, 204 sq. km/79 sq. miles
ISLE OF WIGHT (1963), 189 sq. km/73 sq. miles
ISLES OF SCILLY (1976), 16 sq. km/6 sq. miles
KENT DOWNS (1968), 878 sq. km/339 sq. miles
LINCOLNSHIRE WOLDS (1973), 558 sq. km/215 sq. miles
LLEYN (1957), Gwynedd, 161 sq. km/62 sq. miles
MALVERN HILLS (1959), Herefordshire/Worcestershire/ Gloucestershire, 105 sq. km/40 sq. miles

MENDIP HILLS (1972; extended 1989), Somerset, 198 sq. km/76 sq. miles
NIDDERDALE (1994), North Yorkshire, 603 sq. km/233 sq. miles
NORFOLK COAST (1968), 451 sq. km/174 sq. miles
NORTH DEVON (1960), 171 sq. km/66 sq. miles
NORTH PENNINES (1988), Cumbria/Durham/ Northumberland, 1,983 sq. km/766 sq. miles
NORTHUMBERLAND COAST (1958), 135 sq. km/52 sq. miles
QUANTOCK HILLS (1957), Somerset, 99 sq. km/38 sq. miles
SHROPSHIRE HILLS (1959), 804 sq. km/310 sq. miles
SOLWAY COAST (1964), Cumbria, 115 sq. km/44 sq. miles
SOUTH DEVON (1960), 337 sq. km/130 sq. miles
SOUTH HAMPSHIRE COAST (1967), 77 sq. km/30 sq. miles
SUFFOLK COAST AND HEATHS (1970), 403 sq. km/ 156 sq. miles
SURREY HILLS (1958), 419 sq. km/162 sq. miles
SUSSEX DOWNS (1966), 983 sq. km/379 sq. miles
TAMAR VALLEY (1995), Cornwall/Devon, 195 sq. km/ 115 sq. miles
NORTH WESSEX DOWNS (1972), Berkshire/ Hampshire/Oxfordshire/Wiltshire, 1,730 sq. km/668 sq. miles
WYE VALLEY (1971), Monmouthshire/Gloucestershire/ Herefordshire, 326 sq. km/126 sq. miles

NORTHERN IRELAND

The Department of the Environment for Northern Ireland, with advice from the Council for Nature Conservation and the Countryside, designates Areas of Outstanding Natural Beauty in Northern Ireland. At present there are nine and these cover a total area of approximately 284,948 hectares (704,103 acres).

ANTRIM COAST AND GLENS, Co. Antrim, 70,600 ha/174,452 acres
CAUSEWAY COAST, Co. Antrim, 4,200 ha/10,378 acres
LAGAN VALLEY, Co. Down, 2,072 ha/5,119 acres
LECALE COAST, Co. Down, 3,108 ha/7,679 acres
MOURNE, Co. Down, 57,012 ha/140,876 acres
NORTH DERRY, Co. Londonderry, 12,950 ha/31,999 acres
RING OF GULLION, Co. Armagh, 15,353 ha/37,938 acres
SPERRIN, Co. Tyrone/Co. Londonderry, 101,006 ha/249,585 acres
STRANGFORD LOUGH, Co. Down, 18,647 ha/46,077 acres

NATIONAL SCENIC AREAS

In Scotland, National Scenic Areas have a broadly equivalent status to AONBs. Scottish Natural Heritage recognises areas of national scenic significance. At the end of June 2003 there were 40, covering a total area of 1,001,800 hectares (2,475,448 acres).

Development within National Scenic Areas is dealt with by local authorities, who are required to consult Scottish Natural Heritage concerning certain categories of development. Disagreements between Scottish Natural Heritage and local authorities are referred to the Scottish Executive. Land management uses can also be modified in the interest of scenic conservation.

ASSYNT-COIGACH, Highland, 90,200 ha/222,884 acres
BEN NEVIS AND GLEN COE, Highland/Argyll and
Bute/Perth and Kinross, 101,600 ha/251,053 acres
CAIRNGORM MOUNTAINS, Highland/Aberdeenshire/
Moray, 67,200 ha/166,051 acres
CUILLIN HILLS, Highland, 21,900 ha/54,115 acres
DEESIDE AND LOCHNAGAR, Aberdeenshire/Angus,
40,000 ha/98,840 acres
DORNOCH FIRTH, Highland, 7,500 ha/18,532 acres
EAST STEWARTRY COAST, Dumfries and Galloway,
4,500 ha/11,119 acres
EILDON AND LEADERFOOT, Scottish Borders, 3,600
ha/8,896 acres
FLEET VALLEY, Dumfries and Galloway, 5,300 ha/
13,096 acres
GLEN AFFRIC, Highland, 19,300 ha/47,690 acres
GLEN STRATHFARRAR, Highland, 3,800 ha/9,390
acres
HOY AND WEST MAINLAND, Orkney Islands, 14,800
ha/36,571 acres
JURA, Argyll and Bute, 21,800 ha/53,868 acres
KINTAIL, Highland, 15,500 ha/38,300 acres
KNAPDALE, Argyll and Bute, 19,800 ha/48,926 acres
KNOYDART, Highland, 39,500 ha/97,604 acres
KYLE OF TONGUE, Highland, 18,500 ha/45,713 acres
KYLES OF BUTE, Argyll and Bute, 4,400 ha/10,872
acres
LOCH NA KEAL, MULL, Argyll and Bute, 12,700 ha/
31,382 acres
LOCH LOMOND, Argyll and Bute/Stirling/West
Dunbartonshire, 27,400 ha/67,705 acres
LOCH RANNOCH AND GLEN LYON, Perth and
Kinross/Stirling, 48,400 ha/119,596 acres
LOCH SHIEL, Highland, 13,400 ha/33,111 acres
LOCH TUMMEL, Perth and Kinross, 9,200 ha/22,733
acres
LYNN OF LORN, Argyll and Bute, 4,800 ha/11,861
acres
MORAR, MOIDART AND ARDNAMURCHAN, Highland,
13,500 ha/33,358 acres
NORTH-WEST SUTHERLAND, Highland, 20,500 ha/
50,655 acres
NITH ESTUARY, Dumfries and Galloway, 9,300 ha/
22,980 acres
NORTH ARRAN, North Ayrshire, 23,800 ha/58,810
acres
RIVER EARN, Perth and Kinross, 3,000 ha/7,413 acres
RIVER TAY, Perth and Kinross, 5,600 ha/13,838 acres
ST KILDA, Western Isles, 900 ha/2,224 acres
SCARBA, LUNGA AND THE GARVELLACHS, Argyll and
Bute, 1,900 ha/4,695 acres
SHETLAND, Shetland Islands, 11,600 ha/28,664 acres
SMALL ISLES, Highland, 15,500 ha/38,300 acres
SOUTH LEWIS, HARRIS AND NORTH UIST, Western
Isles, 109,600 ha/270,822 acres
SOUTH UIST MACHAIR, Western Isles, 6,100 ha/15,073
acres
THE TROSSACHS, Stirling, 4,600 ha/11,367 acres
TROTTERNISH, Highland, 5,000 ha/12,355 acres
UPPER TWEEDDALE, Scottish Borders, 10,500 ha/
25,945 acres
WESTER ROSS, Highland, 145,300 ha/359,036 acres

THE NATIONAL FOREST

The National Forest is being planted across 200 square
miles of Derbyshire, Leicestershire and Staffordshire.
About 30 million trees, of mixed species but mainly
broadleaved, will be planted, and will eventually cover
about one-third of the designated area. The project is
funded by the Department for Environment, Food and
Rural Affairs. It was developed in 1992–5 by the
Countryside Commission and is now run by the National
Forest Company, which was established in April 1995.
Since then almost 5 million trees have been planted on
2,500 hectares of land across 480 sites. Under the
National Forest Tender Scheme, anybody wishing to
undertake a project can submit a competitive bid to the
National Forest Company.

NATIONAL FOREST COMPANY, Enterprise Glade,
Bath Lane, Moira, Swadlincote, Derbyshire DE12 6BD.
Tel: 01283-551211.
Chief Executive, Miss S. Bell, OBE

SITES OF SPECIAL SCIENTIFIC INTEREST

Site of Special Scientific Interest (SSSI) is a legal notification applied to land in England, Scotland or Wales
which English Nature (EN), Scottish Natural Heritage
(SNH) or the Countryside Council for Wales (CCW)
identifies as being of special interest because of its flora,
fauna, geological or physiographical features. In some
cases, SSSIs are managed as nature reserves.

EN, SNH and CCW must notify the designation of a
SSSI to the local planning authority, every owner/
occupier of the land, and the Secretary of State for
Environment, Food and Rural Affairs, the First Minister
in Scotland or the National Assembly for Wales. Forestry
and agricultural departments and a number of other
bodies are also informed of this notification.

Objections to the notification of a SSSI can be made
and ultimately considered at a full meeting of the Council
of EN or CCW. In Scotland an objection will be dealt
with by the appropriate area board or the main board of
SNH, depending on the nature of the objection.
Unresolved objections on scientific grounds must be
referred to the Advisory Committee on SSSI.

The protection of these sites depends on the co-
operation of individual landowners and occupiers.
Owner/occupiers must consult EN, SNH or CCW and,
in England and Wales, gain written consent before they
can undertake certain listed activities on the site. In
Scotland, owner/occupiers can carry out a listed
operation four months after consultation, unless SNH
obtains a Nature Conservation Order from Scottish
Ministers. Funds are available through management
agreements and grants to assist owners and occupiers in
conserving sites' interests. As a last resort a site can be
purchased.

The number and area of SSSIs in Britain as at May
2003 was:

	No.	Hectares	Acres
England	4,112	1,055,390	2,607,868
Scotland	1,450	1,004,700	2,482,580
Wales*	1,019	262,612	648,652

* Some sites in Wales amalgamated 2002–3

NORTHERN IRELAND

In Northern Ireland 196 Areas of Special Scientific
Interest (ASSIs) have been declared by the Department of
the Environment for Northern Ireland. These cover a
total area of 92,127.39 hectares (227,643.66 acres).

NATIONAL NATURE RESERVES

National Nature Reserves are defined in the National Parks and Access to the Countryside Act 1949 as land designated for the study and preservation of flora and fauna, or of geological or physiographical features.

English Nature (EN), Scottish Natural Heritage (SNH) or the Countryside Council for Wales (CCW) can designate as a National Nature Reserve land which is being managed as a nature reserve under an agreement with one of the statutory nature conservation agencies; land held and managed by EN, SNH or CCW; or land held and managed as a nature reserve by another approved body. EN, SNH or CCW can make by-laws to protect reserves from undesirable activities; these are subject to confirmation by the Secretary of State for Environment, Food and Rural Affairs, the National Assembly for Wales or the Scottish Ministers in Scotland.

The number and area of National Nature Reserves in Britain as at May 2003 was:

	No.	Hectares	Acres
England	214	87,697	216,699
Scotland	73	131,131	324,020
Wales	66	24,123	59,584

NORTHERN IRELAND

National Nature Reserves are established and managed by the Department of the Environment for Northern Ireland, with advice from the Council for Nature Conservation and the Countryside. There are 48 National Nature Reserves covering 4,746.3 hectares (11,723 acres).

LOCAL NATURE RESERVES

Local Nature Reserves are defined in the National Parks and Access to the Countryside Act 1949 as land designated for the study and preservation of flora and fauna, or of geological or physiographical features. The Act gives local authorities in England, Scotland and Wales the power to acquire, declare and manage local nature reserves in consultation with English Nature, Scottish Natural Heritage and the Countryside Council for Wales. Conservation trusts can also own and manage non-statutory local nature reserves.

The number and area of designated Local Nature Reserves in Britain as at May 2003 was:

	No.	Hectares	Acres
England	806	26,643	65,835
Scotland	36	9,392	23,207
Wales	53	4,887	12,071

FOREST NATURE RESERVES

In 1999 responsibility for forestry was transferred to Scottish Ministers and the National Assembly for Wales. Westminster retained responsibility for forestry in England and for international issues. In April 2003 Forest Enterprise, an executive agency of the Forestry Commission, ceased to exist as a single agency. Three new bodies for England, Scotland and Wales were created in its place. The Forest Enterprise manages 665,000 hectares in Scotland, 258,500 hectares in England and 130,000 hectares in Wales.

Forest Nature Reserves extend in size from under 50 hectares (124 acres) to over 500 hectares (1,236 acres). The largest include the Black Wood of Rannoch, by Loch Rannoch; Cannop Valley Oakwoods, Forest of Dean; Culbin Forest, near Forres; Glen Affric, near Fort Augustus; Kylerhea, Skye; Pembrey, Carmarthen Bay; Starr Forest, in Galloway Forest Park; and Wyre Forest, near Kidderminster.

NORTHERN IRELAND

There are 34 Forest Nature Reserves in Northern Ireland, covering 1,512 hectares (3,736 acres). They are designated and administered by the Forest Service, an agency of the Department of Agriculture and Rural Development for Northern Ireland. There are also 16 National Nature Reserves on Forest Service-owned property.

MARINE NATURE RESERVES

The Secretary of State for Environment, Food and Rural Affairs, the National Assembly for Wales and the Scottish Executive have the power to designate Marine Nature Reserves. English Nature, Scottish Natural Heritage and the Countryside Council for Wales select and manage these reserves. Marine Nature Reserves may be established in Northern Ireland under a 1985 Order.

Marine Nature Reserves provide protection for marine flora and fauna, and geological and physiographical features on land covered by tidal waters or parts of the sea in or adjacent to the UK. Reserves also provide opportunities for study and research.

The three statutory Marine Nature Reserves are:

LUNDY (1986), Bristol Channel
KOMER (1990), Dyfed
STRANGFORD LOUGH (1995), Northern Ireland

Non-statutory marine reserves have also been set up by conservation groups.

EUROPEAN MARINE SITES

The 1992 EC Habitats Directive and the 1979 Birds Directive allow the UK government to establish Special Areas of Conservation (SACs) or Special Protection Areas (SPAs) for animals and birds on land and at sea. Where the designated area includes sea or seashore it is described as a European marine site. The 1998–2002 UK Marine SACs project formed a demonstration initiative, funded partly by the EU, to establish management schemes for twelve of the marine SACs in the UK.

WORLD HERITAGE SITES

The Convention Concerning the Protection of the World Cultural and Natural Heritage was adopted by UNESCO in 1972 and ratified by the UK in 1984. As at June 2003 the convention had been ratified by 172 states. The convention provides for the identification, protection and conservation of cultural and natural sites of outstanding universal value.

Cultural sites may be:
– monuments
– groups of buildings
– sites of historic, aesthetic, archaeological, scientific, ethnologic or anthropologic value
– historic areas of towns
– 'cultural landscapes', i.e. sites whose characteristics are marked by significant interactions between human populations and their natural environment

Natural sites may be:
– those with remarkable physical, biological or geological formations
– those with outstanding universal value from the point of view of science, conservation or natural beauty
– the habitat of threatened species and plants

Governments which are party to the convention nominate sites in their country for inclusion in the World Cultural and Natural Heritage List. Nominations are considered by the World Heritage Committee, an inter-governmental committee composed of 21 representatives of the parties to the convention. The committee is advised by the International Council on Monuments and Sites (ICOMOS), the International Centre for the Study of the Preservation and Restoration of Cultural Property (ICCROM) and the World Conservation Union (IUCN). ICOMOS evaluates and reports on proposed cultural sites, ICCROM provides expert advice and training on how to conserve the listed sites and IUCN advises on proposed natural sites. The Department for Culture, Media and Sport represents the UK government in matters relating to the convention.

A prerequisite for inclusion in the World Cultural and Natural Heritage List is the existence of an effective legal protection system in the country in which the site is situated (e.g. listing, conservation areas and planning controls in the United Kingdom) and a detailed management plan to ensure the conservation of the site. Inclusion in the list does not confer any greater degree of protection on the site than that offered by the national protection framework.

If a site is considered to be in serious danger of decay or damage the committee may add it to a complementary list, the World Heritage in Danger List. Sites on this list may benefit from particular attention or emergency measures.

Financial support for the conservation of sites on the World Cultural and Natural Heritage List is provided by the World Heritage Fund. This is administered by the World Heritage Committee, which determines the financial and technical aid to be allocated. The fund's income is derived from contributions of the parties to the convention, voluntary contributions from other States, other United Nations and intergovernmental organisations, public or private bodies and individuals, through interest due on the fund and from events organised for the benefit of the fund.

DESIGNATED SITES

As at 3 July 2003 there were 754 sites in 128 countries on the World Cultural and Natural Heritage List. Of these, 22 are in the United Kingdom and three in British overseas territories; 19 are listed for their cultural significance (†) and six for their natural significance (*). The year in which sites were designated appears in parentheses.

UNITED KINGDOM
†Bath – the city (1987)
†Blaenarvon, Wales (2000)
Blenheim Palace and park, Oxfordshire (1987)
†Canterbury Cathedral, St Augustine's Abbey, St Martin's Church, Kent (1988)
†Castle and town walls of King Edward I, north Wales – Beaumaris, Anglesey, Caernarfon Castle, Conwy Castle, Harlech Castle (1986)
†Derwent Valley Mills, Derbyshire (2001)
*Dorset and East Devon Coast (2001)
†Durham Cathedral and Castle (1986)
†Edinburgh Old and New Towns (1995)
*Giant's Causeway and Causeway coast, Co. Antrim (1986)
†Greenwich, London – maritime Greenwich, including the Royal Naval College, Old Royal Observatory, †Queen's House, town centre (1997)
†Hadrian's Wall, northern England (1987)
†Heart of Neolithic Orkney (1999)
†Ironbridge Gorge, Shropshire – the world's first iron bridge and other early industrial sites (1986)
†New Lanark, South Lanarkshire, Scotland (2001)
*St Kilda, Western Isles (1986)
†Royal Botanic Gardens, Kew (2003)
†Saltaire, West Yorkshire (2001)
†Stonehenge, Avebury and related megalithic sites, Wiltshire (1986)
†Studley Royal Park, Fountains Abbey, St Mary's Church, N. Yorkshire (1986)
†Tower of London (1988)
†Westminster Abbey, Palace of Westminster, St Margaret's Church, London (1987)

BRITISH OVERSEAS TERRITORIES
*Henderson Island, Pitcairn Islands, South Pacific Ocean (1988)
*Gough Island wildlife reserve (part of Tristan da Cunha), South Atlantic Ocean (1995)
*St George town and related fortifications, Bermuda (2000)

HISTORIC ENVIRONMENT DIVISION, Department for Culture, Media and Sport, 2–4 Cockspur Street, London SW1Y 5DH. Tel: 020-7211 6000
Email: enquiries@culture.gov.uk
WORLD HERITAGE CENTRE, UNESCO, 7 Place de Fontenoy, 75352 Paris 07 SP, France. Email: wh-info@unesco.org
Web: www.unesco.org
INTERNATIONAL CENTRE FOR THE STUDY OF THE PRESERVATION AND RESTORATION OF CULTURAL PROPERTY (ICCROM), Via di San Michele 13, Rome, Italy. Tel: (00 39) (06) 585 531 Web: www.iccrom.org
INTERNATIONAL COUNCIL ON MONUMENTS AND SITES (ICOMOS), 10 Barley Mow Passage, London W4 4PH. Tel. 020-8994 6477 Email: icomos-uk@iconos.org
Web: www.icomos.org
THE WORLD CONSERVATION UNION (IUCN), Rue Mauverney 28, 1196 Gland, Switzerland. Tel: (00 41) (22) 999 0000 Email: mail@hq.iucn.org Web: www.iucn.org

CONSERVATION OF WILDLIFE AND HABITATS

The UK is party to a number of international conventions.

RAMSAR CONVENTION

The 1971 Ramsar Convention on Wetlands of International Importance especially as Waterfowl Habitat, entered into force in the UK in May 1976. By June 2003, 136 countries were party to the convention.

The aim of the convention is the conservation and wise use of wetlands and their flora and fauna. Governments that are party to the convention must designate wetlands and include wetland conservation considerations in their land-use planning. A total of 1,288 wetland sites, totalling 109 million hectares have been designated for inclusion in the List of Wetlands of International Importance. The UK currently has 169 designated sites covering 859,023 hectares. The member countries meet every three years to assess the progress of the convention and the next meeting is scheduled for November 2005.

The UK has set targets under the Ramsar Strategic Plan, 2003–8. Progress towards these is monitored by the UK Ramsar Committee, known as the Joint Working Party. The UK and the Republic of Ireland have established a formal protocol to ensure common monitoring standards for waterbirds in the two countries.
RAMSAR CONVENTION BUREAU, Rue Mauverney 28, CH-1196 Gland, Switzerland. Tel: (00 41) (22) 999 0170
Web: www.ramsar.org

BIODIVERSITY

There is much synergy between the Ramsar Convention and the 1992 Convention on Biological Diversity. In 1996 the Ramsar Secretariat became a lead partner in implementing activities under the Convention on Biological Diversity with joint work plans. The UK ratified the Convention on Biological Diversity in June 1994. There are currently 187 parties to the convention.

The objectives are the conservation of biological diversity, the sustainable use of its components and the fair and equitable sharing of the benefits arising out of the use of genetic resources. There are thematic work programmes addressing marine and coastal, forest, inland waters, dry land and sub-humid land.

The Conference of the Parties to the Convention on Biological Diversity adopted a supplementary agreement to the Convention known as the *Cartagena Protocol on Biosafety* on 29 January 2000. The protocol seeks to protect biological diversity from potential risks that may be posed by introducing modified living organisms, resulting from modern biotechnology, into the environment. As of June 2003 52 countries (not including the UK) were party to the protocol.

The UK published its own Biodiversity Action Plan in 1994. A report from the UK Biodiversity Steering Group, published in 1995, proposed monitoring a list of 1,252 species to check on biodiversity within the UK.

A report, *Sustaining the Variety of Life: 5 years of the UK Biodiversity Action Plan*, was published in March 2001 and made a number of recommendations including to support actions for conservation of species and habitats at UK, county and local levels. There are now a significant number of local biodiversity action plans across the UK. The England Biodiversity Group with DEFRA and the Biodiversity Policy Unit launched a Biodiversity Strategy for England on 24 October 2002.
BIODIVERSITY POLICY UNIT, Zone 1/10b, Temple Quay House, 2 The Square, Temple Quay, Bristol BS1 6EB.
Tel: 0117-372 8974 Email: biodiversity.defra@gtnet.gov.uk
Web: www.ukbap.org.uk

CITES

The 1973 Convention on International Trade in Endangered Species of Wild Fauna and Flora (CITES) came into force in the UK in July 1975. Currently 162 countries are members. The countries party to the convention ban commercial international trade in an agreed list of endangered species and regulate and monitor trade in others species that might become endangered. The convention covers more than 30,000 species.

The Conference of the Parties to CITES meets every two to three years to review the convention's implementation. The Global Wildlife Division at the Department for Environment, Food and Rural Affairs carries out the government's responsibilities under CITES and the Bonn Convention on the Conservation of Migratory Species of Wild Animals.
CITES SECRETARIAT, International Environment House, Chemin des Anémones, CH-1219 Châtelaine, Geneva, Switzerland. Tel: (00 41) (22) 917 8139/8140.
Email: cities@unep.ch Web: www.cites.org

BONN CONVENTION

The 1979 Convention on Conservation of Migratory Species of Wild Animals came into force in the UK in October 1979. By 1 September 2003, 84 countries were party to the convention.

It requires the protection of listed endangered migratory species and encourages international agreements covering these and other threatened species. International agreements can range from legally binding treaties to less formal memoranda of understanding.

Six agreements have been concluded to date under the convention. They aim to conserve: seals in the Wadden Sea, bat populations in Europe; small cetaceans of the Baltic and North Seas; African-Eurasian migratory waterbirds; cetaceans of the Mediterranean and Black Seas; and albatrosses and petrels. A further seven memorandums of understanding have been agreed for the Siberian Crane, Slender-billed Curlew, marine turtles of the Atlantic coast of Africa, Indian Ocean and South-East Asia, the middle-European population of the Great Bustard, Bukhara Deer and the Aquatic Warbler.
UNEP/CMS SECRETARIAT, Martin-Luther-King-Str. 8, D-53175, Bonn, Germany. Tel: (00 49) (228) 815 2401/2
Email: cms@unep.de Web: www.wcmc.org.uk/cms

BERN CONVENTION

The 1979 Bern Convention on the Conservation of European Wildlife and Natural Habitats came into force in the UK in June 1982. Currently there are 45 Contracting Parties and a number of other states attend meetings as observers.

The aims are to conserve wild flora and fauna and their natural habitats, especially where this requires the co-operation of several countries, and to promote such co-operation. The convention gives particular emphasis to endangered and vulnerable species.

All parties to the convention must promote national conservation policies and take account of the conservation of wild flora and fauna when setting planning and development policies. Reports on contracting parties' conservation policies must be submitted to the Standing Committee every four years.

SECRETARIAT OF THE BERN CONVENTION STANDING COMMITTEE, Council of Europe, 67075 Strasbourg-Cedex, France. Tel: (00 33) (3) 8841 3192 Web: www.nature.coe.int

EUROPEAN WILDLIFE TRADE REGULATION

The Council (EC) Regulation on the Protection of Species of Wild Fauna and Flora by Regulating Trade Therein came into force in the UK on 1 June 1997. It is intended to standardise wildlife trade regulations across Europe and to improve the application of CITES. Approximately 30,000 plant and animal species are protected under the regulation.

UK LEGISLATION

The Wildlife and Countryside Act 1981 gives legal protection to a wide range of wild animals and plants. Subject to parliamentary approval, the Secretary of State for Environment, Food and Rural Affairs may vary the animals and plants given legal protection. The most recent variation of Schedules 5 and 8 came into effect in March and April 1998. During 2003 a public consultation took place under the quinquennial review and revisions will be made to the Schedules in 2004 by secondary legislation.

Under Section 9 of the Act it is an offence to kill, injure, take, possess or sell (whether alive or dead) any wild animal included in Schedule 5 of the Act and to disturb its place of shelter and protection or to destroy that place.

Under Section 13 of the Act it is illegal without a licence to pick, uproot, sell or destroy plants listed in Schedule 8. Since January 2001, under the Countryside and Rights of Way Act 2000, persons found guilty of an offence under part 1 of the Wildlife and Countryside Act 1981 face a maximun penalty of up to £5,000 and/or up to six months custodial sentence per specimen.

The Act lays down a close season for wild birds (other than game birds) from 1 February to 31 August inclusive, each year. Exceptions to these dates are made for:

Capercaillie and (except Scotland) *Woodcock* – 1 February to 30 September

Snipe – 1 February to 11 August

Birds listed on Schedule 2, part 1 (see below) (below high water mark) – 21 February to 31 August

Birds listed on Schedule 2, Part 1, which may be killed or taken outside the close season (except on Sundays and on Christmas Day in Scotland, and on Sundays in prescribed areas of England and Wales) are Capercaille, coot, certain wild duck (gadwall, goldeneye, mallard, pintail, pochard, shoveler, teal, tufted duck, wigeon), certain wild geese (Canada, greylag, pink-footed, white-fronted (in England and Wales only)), moorhen, golden plover and woodcock.

Section 16 of the 1981 Act allows licences to be issued on either an individual or general basis, to allow the killing, taking and sale of certain birds for specified reasons such as public health and safety.

All other British birds are fully protected by law throughout the year.

Animals protected by Schedule 5

Adder (*Vipera berus*)
Allis shad (*Alosa alosa*)
Atlantic Stream Crayfish (*Austropotomobius pallipes*)
Anemone, Ivell's Sea (*Edwardsia ivelli*)
Anemone, Starlet Sea (*Nematosella vectensis*)
Apus, Tadpole shrimp (*Triops cancriformis*)
Bat, Horseshoe (*Rhinolophidae,* all species)
Bat, Typical (*Vespertilionidae,* all species)
Beetle (*Graphoderus zonatus*)
Beetle (*Hypebaeus flavipes*)
Beetle, Lesser Silver Water (*Hydrochara caraboides*)
Beetle, Mire Pill (*Curimopsis nigrita*)
Beetle, Rainbow Leaf (*Chrysolina cerealis*)
Beetle, Stag (*Lucanus cervus*)
Beetle, Violet Click (*Limoniscus violaceus*)
Beetle, Water (*Paracymus aeneus*)
Burbot (*Lota lota*)
Butterfly, Adonis Blue (*Lysandra bellargus*)
Butterfly, Black Hairstreak (*Strymonidia pruni*)
Butterfly, Brown Hairstreak (*Thecla betulae*)
Butterfly, Chalkhill Blue (*Lysandra coridon*)
Butterfly, Chequered Skipper (*Carterocephalus palaemon*)
Butterfly, Duke of Burgundy Fritillary (*Hamearis lucina*)
Butterfly, Glanville Fritillary (*Melitaea cinxia*)
Butterfly, Heath Fritillary (*Mellicta athalia* (or *Melitaea athalia*))
Butterfly, High Brown Fritillary (*Argynnis adippe*)
Butterfly, Large Blue (*Maculinea arion*)
Butterfly, Large Copper (*Lycaena dispar*)
Butterfly, Large Heath (*Coenonympha tullia*)
Butterfly, Large Tortoiseshell (*Nymphalis polychloros*)
Butterfly, Lulworth Skipper (*Thymelicus acteon*)
Butterfly, Marsh Fritillary (*Eurodryas aurinia*)
Butterfly, Mountain Ringlet (*Erebia epiphron*)
Butterfly, Northern Brown Argus (*Aricia artaxerxes*)
Butterfly, Pearl-bordered Fritillary (*Boloria euphrosyne*)
Butterfly, Purple Emperor (*Apatura iris*)
Butterfly, Silver Spotted Skipper (*Hesperia comma*)
Butterfly, Silver-studded Blue (*Plebejus argus*)
Butterfly, Small Blue (*Cupido minimus*)
Butterfly, Swallowtail (*Papilio machaon*)
Butterfly, White Letter Hairstreak (*Stymonida w-album*)
Butterfly, Wood White (*Leptidea sinapis*)
Cat, Wild (*Felis silvestris*)
Cicada, New Forest (*Cicadetta montana*)
Cricket, Field (*Gryllus campestris*)
Cricket, Mole (*Gryllotalpa gryllotalpa*)
Damselfly, Southern (*Coenagrion mercuriale*)
Dolphin (*Cetacea*)
Dormouse (*Muscardinus avellanarius*)
Dragonfly, Norfolk Aeshna (*Aeshna isosceles*)
Frog, Common (*Rana temporaria*)
Goby, Couch's (*Gobius couchii*)
Goby, Giant (*Gobius cobitis*)
Grasshopper, Wart-biter (*Decticus verrucivorus*)
Hatchet Shell, Northern (*Thyasira gouldi*)
Hydroid, Marine (*Clavopsella navis*)
Lagoon Snail (*Paludinella littorina*)
Lagoon Snail, De Folin's (*Caecum armoricum*)
Lagoon Worm, Tentacled (*Alkmaria romijni*)

Lily, Snowdon (*Lloydia serotina*)
Liverwort (*Petallophyllum ralfsi*)
Liverwort, Lindenberg's Leafy (*Adelanthus lindenbergianus*)
Marsh-mallow, Rough (*Althaea hirsuta*)
Marshwort, Creeping (*Apium repens*)
Milk-parsley, Cambridge (*Selinum carvifolia*)
Moss (*Drepanocladius vernicosus*)
Moss, Alpine copper (*Mielichoferia mielichoferi*)
Moss, Baltic bog (*Sphagnum balticum*)
Moss, Blue dew (*Saelania glaucescens*)
Moss, Blunt-leaved bristle (*Orthotrichum obtusifolium*)
Moss, Bright green cave (*Cyclodictyon laetevirens*)
Moss, Cordate beard (*Barbula cordata*)
Moss, Cornish path (*Ditrichum cornubicum*)
Moss, Derbyshire feather (*Thamnobryum angustifolium*)
Moss, Dune thread (*Bryum mamillatum*)
Moss, Flamingo (*Desmatodon cernuus*)
Moss, Glaucous beard (*Barbula glauca*)
Moss, Green shield (*Buxbaumia viridis*)
Moss, Hair silk (*Plagiothecium piliferum*)
Moss, Knothole (*Zygodon forsteri*)
Moss, Large yellow feather (*Scorpidium turgescens*)
Moss, Millimetre (*Micromitrium tenerum*)
Moss, Multifruited river (*Cryphaea lamyana*)
Moss, Nowell's limestone (*Zygodon gracilis*)
Moss, Rigid apple (*Bartramia stricta*)
Moss, Round-leaved feather (*Rhyncostegium rotundifolium*)
Moss, Schleicher's thread (*Bryum schleicheri*)
Moss, Triangular pygmy (*Acaulon triquetrum*)
Moss, Vaucher's feather (*Hypnum vaucheri*)
Mudwort, Welsh (*Limosella australis*)
Naiad, Holly-leaved (*Najas marina*)
Naiad, Slender (*Najas flexilis*)
Orache, Stalked (*Halimione pedunculata*)
Orchid, Early spider (*Ophrys sphegodes*)
Orchid, Fen (*Liparis loeselii*)
Orchid, Ghost (*Epipogium aphyllum*)
Orchid, Lapland marsh (*Dactylorhiza lapponica*)
Orchid, Late spider (*Ophrys fuciflora*)
Orchid, Lizard (*Himantoglossum hircinum*)
Orchid, Military (*Orchis militaris*)
Orchid, Monkey (*Orchis simia*)
Pannaria, Caledonia (*Panneria ignobilis*)
Parmelia, New Forest (*Parmelia minarum*)
Parmentaria, Oil stain (*Parmentaria chilensis*)
Pear, Plymouth (*Pyrus cordata*)
Penny-cress, Perfoliate (*Thlaspi perfoliatum*)
Pennyroyal (*Mentha pulegium*)
Pertusaria, Alpine moss (*Pertusaria bryontha*)
Physcia, Southern grey (*Physcia tribacioides*)
Pigmyweed (*Crassula aquatica*)
Pine, Ground (*Ajuga chamaepitys*)
Pink, Cheddar (*Dianthus gratianopolitanus*)
Pink, Childing (*Petroraghia nanteuilii*)
Plantain, Floating water (*Luronium natans*)
Polypore, Oak (*Buglossoporus pulvinus*)
Pseudocyphellaria, Ragged (*Pseudocyphellaria lacerata*)
Psora, Rusty Alpine (*Psora rubiformis*)
Puffball, Sandy Stilt (*Battarraea phalloides*)
Ragwort, Fen (*Senecio paludosus*)
Ramping-fumitory, Martin's (*Fumaria martinii*)
Rampion, Spiked (*Phyteuma spicatum*)
Restharrow, Small (*Ononis reclinata*)
Rock-cress, Alpine (*Arabis alpina*)
Rock-cress, Bristol (*Arabis stricta*)
Rustwort, Western (*Marsupella profunda*)
Sandwort, Norwegian (*Arenaria norvegica*)

Sandwort, Teesdale (*Minuartia stricta*)
Saxifrage, Drooping (*Saxifraga cernua*)
Saxifrage, Marsh (*Saxifrage hirulus*)
Saxifrage, Tufted (*Saxifraga cespitosa*)
Solenopsora, Serpentine (*Solenopsora liparina*)
Solomon's-seal, Whorled (*Polygonatum verticillatum*)
Sow-thistle, Alpine (*Cicerbita alpina*)
Spearwort, Adder's-tongue (*Ranunculus ophioglossifolius*)
Speedwell, Fingered (*Veronica triphyllos*)
Speedwell, Spiked (*Veronica spicata*)
Spike rush, Dwarf (*Eleocharis parvula*)
Stack Fleawort, South (*Tephroseris integrifolia* (*ssp maritima*))
Star-of-Bethlehem, Early (*Gagea bohemica*)
Starfruit (*Damasonium alisma*)
Stonewort, Bearded (*Chara canescens*)
Stonewort, Foxtail (*Lamprothamnium papulosum*)
Strapwort (*Corrigiola litoralis*)
Sulphur-tresses, Alpine (*Alectoria ochroleuca*)
Threadmoss, Long-leaved (*Bryum neodamense*)
Turpswort (*Geocalyx graveolens*)
Violet, Fen (*Viola persicifolia*)
Viper's-grass (*Scorzonera humilis*)
Water-plantain, Ribbon-leaved (*Alisma gramineum*)
Wood-sedge, Starved (*Carex depauperata*)
Woodsia, Alpine (*Woodsia alpina*)
Woodsia, Oblong (*Woodsia ilvenis*)
Wormwood, Field (*Artemisia campestris*)
Woundwort, Downy (*Stachys germanica*)
Woundwort, Limestone (*Stachys alpina*)
Yellow-rattle, Greater (*Rhinanthus serotinus*)

MOST UNDER THREAT

The animals and birds considered to be most under threat in Great Britain by the Joint Nature Conservation Committee are the high brown fritillary butterfly; violet click beetle; new forest burnet moth; corncrake; aquatic warbler; tree sparrow; wryneck; water vole; red squirrel; allis shad; and twaite shad.

HISTORIC BUILDINGS AND MONUMENTS

Under the Planning (Listed Buildings and Conservation Areas) Act 1990, the Secretary of State for Culture, Media and Sport has a statutory duty to compile lists of buildings or groups of buildings in England which are of special architectural or historic interest. Under the Ancient Monuments and Archaeological Areas Act 1979 as amended by the National Heritage Act 1983, the Secretary of State is also responsible for compiling a schedule of ancient monuments. Decisions are taken on the advice of English Heritage.

Listed buildings are classified into Grade I, Grade II* and Grade II. There are currently about 370,000 individual listed buildings in England, of which about 92 per cent are Grade II listed. Almost all pre-1700 buildings are listed, and most buildings of 1700 to 1840. English Heritage carries out thematic surveys of particular types of buildings with a view to making recommendations for listing, and members of the public may propose a building for consideration. The main purpose of listing is to ensure that care is taken in deciding the future of a building. No changes which affect the architectural or historic character of a listed building can be made without listed building consent (in addition to planning permission where relevant). Applications for listed building consent are normally dealt with by the local planning authority, although English Heritage is always consulted about proposals affecting Grade I and Grade II* properties. It is a criminal offence to demolish a listed building, or alter it in such a way as to affect its character, without consent.

There are currently about 18,300 scheduled monuments in England. English Heritage is carrying out a Monuments Protection Programme assessing archaeological sites with a view to making recommendations for scheduling, and members of the public may propose a monument for consideration. All monuments proposed for scheduling are considered to be of national importance. Where buildings are both scheduled and listed, ancient monuments legislation takes precedence. The main purpose of scheduling a monument is to preserve it for the future and to protect it from damage, destruction or any unnecessary interference. Once a monument has been scheduled, scheduled monument consent is required before any works can be carried out. The scope of the control is more extensive and more detailed than that applied to listed buildings, but certain minor works, as detailed in the Ancient Monuments (Class Consents) Order 1994, may be carried out without consent. It is a criminal offence to carry out unauthorised work to scheduled monuments.

Under the Planning (Listed Buildings and Conservation Areas) Act 1990 and the Ancient Monuments and Archaeological Areas Act 1979, the Secretary of State for Wales is responsible for listing buildings and scheduling monuments in Wales on the advice of CADW, the Historic Buildings Council for Wales and the Royal Commission on the Ancient and Historical Monuments of Wales. The criteria for evaluating buildings are similar to those in England and the same listing system is used. There are approximately 26,400 listed buildings and approximately 3,500 scheduled monuments in Wales.

Under the Planning (Listed Buildings and Conservation Areas) (Scotland) Act 1997 and the Ancient Monuments and Archaeological Areas Act 1979, Scottish Ministers are responsible for listing buildings and scheduling monuments in Scotland on the advice of Historic Scotland, the Historic Buildings Council for Scotland and the Royal Commission on the Ancient and Historical Monuments of Scotland. The criteria for evaluating buildings are similar to those in

England but an A, B, C categorisation is used. There are approximately 46,000 listed buildings and 6,500 scheduled monuments in Scotland.

Under the Planning (Northern Ireland) Order 1991 and the Historic Monuments and Archaeological Objects (Northern Ireland) Order 1995, the Department of the Environment for Northern Ireland Executive is responsible for listing buildings and scheduling monuments in Northern Ireland on the advice of the Historic Buildings Council for Northern Ireland and the Historic Monuments Council for Northern Ireland. The criteria for evaluating buildings are similar to those in England but no statutory grading system is used. There are approximately 8,500 listed buildings and 1,500 scheduled monuments in Northern Ireland.

OPENING TO THE PUBLIC

The following is a selection of the many historic buildings and monuments open to the public. Admission charges and opening hours vary. Many properties are closed in winter (usually November-March) and some are also closed in the mornings. Most properties are closed on Christmas Eve, Christmas Day, Boxing Day and New Year's Day, and many are closed on Good Friday. During the winter season, many English Heritage monuments are closed on Mondays and Tuesdays and monuments in the care of CADW are closed on Sunday mornings. In Northern Ireland many monuments are closed on Mondays except on bank holidays. Information about a specific property should be checked by telephone.

ENGLAND

For more information on any of the English Heritage properties listed below, the official website is:
www.english-heritage.org.uk.
For more information on any of the National Trust properties listed below, the official website is:
www.nationaltrust.org.uk.
EH English Heritage property
NT National Trust property

A LA RONDE (NT), Summer Lane, Exmouth, Devon.
  Tel: 01395-265514. Unique 16-sided house completed c.1796
ALNWICK CASTLE, Northumberland NE66 1NQ.
  Tel: 01665-510777 Web: www.alnwick.com
  Seat of the Dukes of Northumberland since 1309; Italian Renaissance-style interior. New gardens with spectacular water features
ALTHORP, Northants NN7 4HQ. Tel: 0870-167 9000
  Web: www.althorp.com
  Spencer family seat. Diana, Princess of Wales memorabilia
ANGLESEY ABBEY (NT), Cambridge CB5 9EJ.
  Tel: 01223-811200. House built c.1600. Houses many paintings and a unique clock collection. Gardens and Lode Mill
APSLEY HOUSE, London W1 . Tel: 020-7499 5676
  Web: www.apsleyhouse.org.uk
  Built by Robert Adam 1771–8, home of the Dukes of Wellington since 1817 and known as 'No. 1 London'. Collection of fine and decorative arts
ARUNDEL CASTLE, W. Sussex BN18 9AB. Tel: 01903-883136
  Web: www.arundelcastle.org
  Castle dating from the Norman Conquest. Seat of the Dukes of Norfolk

AVEBURY (NT), Wilts. Tel: 01672-539250.
Remains of stone circles constructed 4,000 years ago surrounding the later village of Avebury
BANQUETING HOUSE, Whitehall, London SW1A 2ER. Tel: 0870-751 5178 Web: www.hrp.org.uk
Designed by Inigo Jones; ceiling paintings by Rubens. Site of the execution of Charles I
BASILDON PARK (NT), Reading RG8 9NR. Tel: 0118-984 3040.
Palladian house built in 1776–83 by John Carr
BATTLE ABBEY (EH), E. Sussex. Tel: 01424-773792. Remains of the abbey founded by William the Conqueror on the site of the Battle of Hastings
BEAULIEU, Hants SO42 7ZN. Tel: 01590-612345 Web: www.beaulieu.co.uk
House and gardens, Beaulieu Abbey and exhibition of monastic life, National Motor Museum
BEESTON CASTLE (EH), Cheshire CW6 9TX. Tel: 01829-260464. Thirteenth-century inner ward with gatehouse and towers, and remains of outer ward built by Ranulf sixth Earl of Chester
BELTON HOUSE (NT), Leics NG32 2LS. Tel: 01476-566116.
Fine 17th-century house, formal gardens in landscaped park
BELVOIR CASTLE, Leics NG32 1PD. Tel: 01476-871002 Web: www.belvoircastle.com.
Seat of the Dukes of Rutland; 19th-century Gothic-style castle
BERKELEY CASTLE, Glos GL13 9BQ. Tel: 01453-810332.
Completed 1153; site of the murder of Edward II (1327)
BLENHEIM PALACE, Woodstock, Oxon OX20 1PX. Tel: 01993-811091 Web: www.blenheimpalace.com.
Seat of the Dukes of Marlborough and Winston Churchill's birthplace; designed by Vanbrugh
BLICKLING HALL (NT), Norwich NR11 6NF. Tel: 01263-738030. Jacobean house with state rooms, temple and 18th-century orangery
BODIAM CASTLE (NT), E. Sussex TN32 5UA. Tel: 01580-830436. Well-preserved medieval moated castle, built 1385
BOLSOVER CASTLE (EH), Derbys. Tel: 01246-822844.
Notable 17th-century buildings
BOSCOBEL HOUSE (EH), Shropshire. Tel: 01902-850244.
Timber-framed 17th-century hunting lodge, refuge of fugitive Charles II
BOUGHTON HOUSE, Northants. Tel: 01536-515731 Web: www.boughtonhouse.org.uk
17th-century house with French-style additions. Home of the Dukes of Buccleuch and Queensbury
BOWOOD HOUSE, Wilts SN11 0LZ. Tel: 01249-812102 Web: www.bowood-estate.co.uk
An 18th-century house in Capability Brown park, with lake, temple and arboretum
BROADLANDS, Hants SO51 9ZD. Tel: 01794-505010 Web: www.broadlands.net
Palladian mansion in Capability Brown parkland. Mountbatten exhibition
BRONTË PARSONAGE, Haworth, W. Yorks BD22 8DR. Tel: 01535-642323 Web: www.bronte.org,uk
Home of the Brontë sisters; museum and memorabilia
BUCKFAST ABBEY, Devon TQ11 0EE. Tel: 01364-642500 Web: www.buckfast.org.uk
Benedictine monastery on medieval foundations
BUCKINGHAM PALACE, London SW1A 1AA. Tel: 020-7839 1377 Web: www.royal.gov.uk
Purchased by George III in 1762, and the Sovereign's official London residence since 1837. Eighteen state rooms, including the Throne Room, and Picture Gallery
BUCKLAND ABBEY (NT), Devon PL20 6EY. Tel: 01822-853607. A 13th-century Cistercian monastery. Home of Sir Francis Drake

BURGHLEY HOUSE, Stamford, Lincs. Tel: 01780-752451 Web: www.burghley.co.uk
Late Elizabethan house built by William Cecil, first Lord Burghley.
CALKE ABBEY (NT), Derbys DE73 1LE. Tel: 01332-863822.
Baroque 18th-century mansion
CARISBROOKE CASTLE (EH), Isle of Wight PO30 1XY. Tel: 01983-523112 Web: www.carisbrookecastlemuseum.org.uk
Norman castle; prison of Charles I 1647–8
CARLISLE CASTLE (EH), Cumbria CA3 8UR. Tel: 01228-606000. Medieval castle, prison of Mary Queen of Scots
CARLYLE'S HOUSE (NT), Cheyne Row, London SW3 5HL. Tel: 020-7352 7087. Home of Thomas Carlyle
CASTLE ACRE PRIORY (EH), Norfolk. Tel: 01760-755394.
Remains include 12th-century church and prior's lodgings
CASTLE DROGO (NT), Devon EX6 6PB. Tel: 01647-433306.
Granite castle designed by Lutyens
CASTLE HOWARD, N. Yorks YO60 7DA. Tel: 01653-648444 Web: www.castlehoward.co.uk
Designed by Vanbrugh 1699–1726; mausoleum designed by Hawksmoor
CASTLE RISING (EH), Norfolk. Tel: 01553-631330.
A 12th-century keep in a massive earthwork with gatehouse and bridge
CHARTWELL (NT), Kent TN16 1PS. Tel: 01732-868381
Home of Sir Winston Churchill
CHATSWORTH, Derbys. Tel: 01246-582204 Web: www.chatsworth-house.co.uk
Tudor mansion in magnificent parkland
CHESTERS ROMAN FORT (EH), Northumberland. Tel: 01434-681379. Roman cavalry fort
CHYSAUSTER ANCIENT VILLAGE (EH), Cornwall. Tel: 07831-757934. Romano-Cornish village, 2nd- and 3rd-century AD, on a probably late Iron Age site
CLIFFORD'S TOWER (EH), York. Tel: 01904-646940.
A 13th-century tower built on a mound
CLIVEDEN (NT), Maidenhead SL6 0JA. Tel: 01628-605069.
Former home of the Astors, now an hotel set in garden and woodland
CORBRIDGE ROMAN SITE (EH), Northumberland. Tel: 01434-632349. Excavated central area of a Roman town and successive military bases
CORFE CASTLE (NT), Wareham BH20 5EZ. Tel: 01929-481294.
Ruined former royal castle dating from 11th-century
CROFT CASTLE (NT), Herefordshire HR6 9PW. Tel: 01568-780246. Pre-Conquest border castle with Georgian-Gothic interior
DEAL CASTLE (EH), Kent. Tel: 01304-372762.
Largest of the coastal defence forts built by Henry VIII
DICKENS HOUSE, 48 Doughty Street, London WC1. Tel: 020-7405 2127 Web: www.dickensmuseum.com
House occupied by Dickens 1837–9; manuscripts, furniture and portraits
DR JOHNSON'S HOUSE, 17 Gough Square, London EC4A 3DE. Tel: 020-7353 3745 Web: www.drjh.dircon.co.uk.
Home of Samuel Johnson
DOVE COTTAGE, Grasmere, Cumbria LA22 9SH. Tel: 01539-435544 Web: www.wordsworth.org.uk
Wordsworth's home 1799–1808; museum
DOVER CASTLE (EH), Kent CT16 1HU. Tel: 01304-201628.
Castle with Roman, Saxon and Norman features; wartime operations rooms
DUNSTANBURGH CASTLE (EH), Northumberland. Tel: 01665-576231. A 14th-century castle on a cliff, with a substantial gatehouse-keep
ELTHAM PALACE (EH), Court Yard, Eltham, London SE9 5QE. Tel: 020-8294 2548. Combines a 1930s country house and remains of medieval palace set in moated gardens.
FARLEIGH HUNGERFORD CASTLE (EH), Somerset BA2 7RS. Tel: 01225-754026. Late 14th-century castle with two courts; chapel with tomb of Sir Thomas Hungerford

FARNHAM CASTLE KEEP (EH), Surrey GU9 0AG.
Tel: 01252-713393. Large 12th-century shell-keep

FOUNTAINS ABBEY (NT), nr Ripon, N. Yorks HG4 3DY.
Tel: 01765-608888 Web: www.fountainsabbey.org.uk
Deer park, visitor centre and St Mary's Church. Ruined
Cistercian monastery; 18th-century landscaped gardens
of Studley Royal estate

FRAMLINGHAM CASTLE (EH), Suffolk. Tel: 01728-724189
Web: www.framlingham.com
Castle (c.1200) with high curtain walls enclosing an
almshouse (1639)

FURNESS ABBEY (EH), Cumbria. Tel: 01229-823420. Remains
of church and conventual buildings founded in 1123

GLASTONBURY ABBEY, Somerset BA6 9EL.
Tel: 01458-832267 Web: www.glastonburyabbey.com
Ruins of a 12th-century abbey rebuilt after fire. Site of
an early Christian settlement

GOODRICH CASTLE (EH), Herefordshire.
Tel: 01600-890538. Remains of 13th- and 14th-century
castle with 12th-century keep

GREENWICH, London SE10. Royal Observatory.
Tel: 020-8858 6565 Web: www.rog.nmm.ac.uk
Former Royal Observatory (founded 1675) housing the
time ball and zero meridian of longitude. The Queen's
House. Tel: 020-8858 4422. Designed for Queen Anne,
wife of James I, by Inigo Jones. Painted Hall and Chapel
(Royal Naval College)

GRIMES GRAVES (EH), Norfolk. Tel: 01842-810656. Neolithic
flint mines. One shaft can be descended

GUILDHALL, London EC2P 2EJ. Tel: 020-7332 1460.
Centre of civic government of the City. Built c.1441;
facade built 1788–9

HADDON HALL, Derbys DE45 1LA. Tel: 01629-812855
Web: www.haddonhall.co.uk
Well-preserved 12th-century manor house

HAILES ABBEY (EH), Glos GL54 5PB. Tel: 01242-602398.
Ruins of a 13th-century Cistercian monastery

HAM HOUSE (NT), Richmond, Surrey TW10 7RS.
Tel: 020-8940 1950. Stuart house with fine interiors

HAMPTON COURT PALACE, East Molesey, Surrey KT8 9AU.
Tel: 0870-752 7777 Web: www.hrp.org.uk
A 16th-century palace with additions by Wren. Gardens
with maze; Tudor tennis court (summer only)

HARDWICK HALL (NT), Derbys S44 5QJ. Tel: 01246-850430.
Built 1591–7 for Bess of Hardwick; notable furnishings

HARDY'S COTTAGE (NT), Dorset DT2 8QJ. Tel: 01305-262366.
Birthplace and home of Thomas Hardy

HAREWOOD HOUSE, W. Yorks. Tel: 0113-288 6331
Web: www.harewood.org
An 18th-century house designed by John Carr and
Robert Adam; park by Capability Brown

HATFIELD HOUSE, Herts AL9 5NQ. Tel: 01707-287000
Web: www.hatfield-house.co.uk
Jacobean house built by Robert Cecil; surviving wing of
Royal Palace of Hatfield (1497)

HELMSLEY CASTLE (EH), N. Yorks YO62 5AB. Tel: 01439-
770442. A 12th-century keep and curtain wall with
16th-century buildings. Spectacular earthwork defences

HEVER CASTLE, Kent. Tel: 01732-865224
Web: www.hevercastle.co.uk
A 13th-century double-moated castle, childhood home
of Anne Boleyn

HOLKER HALL, Cumbria. Tel: 01539-558328
Web: www.holker-hall.co.uk
Former home of the Dukes of Devonshire; award-
winning gardens

HOLKHAM HALL, Norfolk NR23 1AB. Tel: 01328-710227
Web: www.holkham.co.uk
Fine Palladian mansion

HOUSESTEADS ROMAN FORT (EH), Northumberland.
Tel: 01434-344363 Web: www.hadrians-wall.org
Excavated infantry fort on Hadrian's Wall with extra-
mural civilian settlement

HUGHENDEN MANOR (NT), High Wycombe HP14 4LA.
Tel: 01494-755565. Home of Disraeli; small formal garden

JANE AUSTEN'S HOUSE, Chawton, Hants GU34 1SD.
Tel: 01420-83262. Jane Austen's home 1809–17

KEDLESTON HALL (NT), Derby DE22 5JH. Tel: 01332-842191.
A classical Palladian mansion built 1759–65; complete
Robert Adam interiors.

KELMSCOTT MANOR, nr Lechlade, Glos GL7 3HJ.
Tel: 01367-252486 Web: www.kelmscottmanor.co.uk
Summer home of William Morris, with products of
Morris and Co.

KENILWORTH CASTLE (EH), Warks. Tel: 01926-852078.
Largest castle ruin in England

KENSINGTON PALACE, London W8 4PX. Tel: 0870-751 5170
Web: www.hrp.org.uk
Built in 1605 and enlarged by Wren; bought by William
and Mary in 1689. Birthplace of Queen Victoria. Royal
Ceremonial Dress Collection

KENWOOD HOUSE (EH), Hampstead Lane, London NW3.
Tel: 020-8348 1286. Adam villa housing the Iveagh bequest
of paintings and furniture. Open-air concerts in summer

KEW, Surrey TW9 3AB. Tel: 020-8332 5655
Web: www.rbgkew.org
Queen Charlotte's Cottage

KINGSTON LACY HOUSE (NT), Dorset BH21 4EA.
Tel: 01202-882402. A 17th-century house with 19th-
century alterations; important art collection

KNEBWORTH HOUSE, Herts SG3 6PY. Tel: 01438-812661
Web: www.knebworthhouse.com
Tudor manor house concealed by 19th-century Gothic
decoration; Lutyens gardens

KNOLE (NT), Kent TN15 0RP. Tel: 01732-450608. House
dating from 1456 set in parkland; fine art treasures

LAMBETH PALACE, London SE1 7JU. Tel: 020-7898 1200
Web: www.archbishopofcanterbury.org
Official residence of the Archbishop of Canterbury. A
19th-century house with parts dating from the 12th-
century

LANERCOST PRIORY (EH), Cumbria CA8 2HQ. Tel: 01697-
73030. The nave of the Augustinian priory church,
c.1166, is still used; remains of other claustral buildings

LANHYDROCK (NT), Cornwall PL30 5AD. Tel: 01208-73320.
House dating from the 17th-century; 45 rooms,
including kitchen and nursery

LEEDS CASTLE, Kent ME17 1PL. Tel: 01622-765400
Web: www.leeds-castle.com
Castle dating from 9th-century, on two islands in lake

LEVENS HALL, Cumbria LA8 0PD. Tel: 01539-560321
Web: www.levenshall.co.uk
Elizabethan house with unique topiary garden (1694).
Steam engine collection

LINCOLN CASTLE, LN1 3AA. Tel: 01522-511068.
Built by William the Conqueror in 1068

LINDISFARNE PRIORY (EH), Northumberland.
Tel: 01289-389200. Bishopric of the Northumbrian
kingdom destroyed by the Danes; re-established in the
11th-century as a Benedictine priory, now ruined

LITTLE MORETON HALL (NT), Cheshire CW12 4SD.
Tel: 01260-272018. Timber-framed moated manor house
with knot garden

LONGLEAT HOUSE, Wilts BA12 7NW. Tel: 01985-844400
Web: www.longleat.co.uk
Elizabethan house in Italian Renaissance style

LULLINGSTONE ROMAN VILLA (EH), Kent.
Tel: 01322-863467. Large villa occupied for much of the
Roman period; fine mosaics

MANSION HOUSE, London EC4N 8BH. Tel: 020-7626 2500
Web: www.cityoflondon.gov.uk
The official residence of the Lord Mayor of London

MARBLE HILL HOUSE (EH), Twickenham, Middx TW1 2NL.
Tel: 020-8892 5115. English Palladian villa with Georgian
paintings and furniture

MICHELHAM PRIORY, E. Sussex. Tel: 01323-844224.
Tudor house built onto an Augustinian priory
MIDDLEHAM CASTLE (EH), N. Yorks DL8 4QR. Tel: 01969-
623899. A 12th-century keep within later fortifications.
Childhood home of Richard III
MONTACUTE HOUSE (NT), Somerset TA15 6XP. Tel: 01935-
823289. Elizabethan house with National Portrait
Gallery. Portraits from the period
MOUNT GRACE PRIORY (EH), N. Yorks DL6 3JG. Tel: 01609-
883494. Carthusian monastery, with remains of monastic
buildings
NETLEY ABBEY (EH), Hants SO31 5GA. Tel: 023-8045 3076.
Remains of Cistercian abbey, used as house in Tudor
period
OLD SARUM (EH), Wilts. Tel: 01722-335398.
Earthworks enclosing remains of the castle and the 11th-
century cathedral
ORFORD CASTLE (EH), Suffolk. Tel: 01394-450472.
Circular keep of c.1170 and remains of coastal defence
castle built by Henry II
OSBORNE HOUSE (EH), Isle of Wight. Tel: 01983-200022.
Queen Victoria's seaside residence
OSTERLEY PARK HOUSE (NT), Isleworth, Middx TW7 4RB.
Tel: 020-8232 5050 Web: www.osterleypark.org.uk
Elizabethan mansion set in parkland
PENDENNIS CASTLE (EH), Cornwall. Tel: 01326-316594.
Well-preserved coastal defence castle
PENSHURST PLACE, Kent TN11 8DG. Tel: 01892-870307
Web: www.penhurstplace.com
House with medieval Baron's Hall and 14th-century
gardens
PETWORTH (NT), W. Sussex GU28 0AE. Tel: 01798-343929.
Late 17th-century house set in deer park
PEVENSEY CASTLE (EH), E. Sussex. Tel: 01323-762604. Walls
of a 4th-century Roman fort; remains of an 11th-century
castle
PEVERIL CASTLE (EH), Derbys S33 8WQ. Tel: 01433-620613.
A 12th-century castle defended on two sides by
precipitous rocks
POLESDEN LACEY (NT), Surrey RH5 6BD. Tel: 01372-458203.
Regency villa remodelled in the Edwardian era. Fine
paintings and furnishings
PORTCHESTER CASTLE (EH), Hants PO3 5LY. Tel: 023-9237
8291. Walls of a late Roman fort enclosing a Norman
keep and an Augustinian priory church
POWDERHAM CASTLE, Devon EX6 8JQ.
Tel: 01626-890243 Web: www.powderham.co.uk
Medieval castle with 18th- and 19th-century alterations.
Historic home of the Earl of Devon
RABY CASTLE, Co. Durham DL2 3AH. Tel: 01833-660202
Web: www.rabycastle.com
A 14th-century castle with walled gardens
RAGLEY HALL, Warks B49 5NJ. Tel: 01789-762090
Web: www.ragleyhall.com
A 17th-century house with gardens, park and lake
RICHBOROUGH ROMAN FORT (EH), Kent. Tel: 01304-
612013. Landing-site of the Claudian invasion in AD 43
RICHMOND CASTLE (EH), N. Yorks. Tel: 01748-822493.
A 12th-century keep with 11th-century curtain wall and
domestic buildings
RIEVAULX ABBEY (EH), N. Yorks YO6 5LB. Tel: 01439-798228.
Remains of a Cistercian abbey founded c.1131
ROCHESTER CASTLE (EH), Kent ME1 1SX.
Tel: 01634-402276. An 11th-century castle partly on the
Roman city wall, with a square keep of c.1130
ROCKINGHAM CASTLE, Northants. Tel: 01536-770240.
Built by William the Conqueror
ROYAL PAVILION, Brighton. Tel: 01273-290900.
Palace of George IV, in Chinese style with Indian
exterior and Regency gardens
RUFFORD OLD HALL (NT), Lancs L40 1SG.
Tel: 01704-821254. A 16th-century hall with unique screen

ST AUGUSTINE'S ABBEY (EH), Kent. Tel: 01227-767345.
Remains of Benedictine monastery, with Norman church,
on site of abbey founded AD 598 by St Augustine
ST MAWES CASTLE (EH), Cornwall TR2 3AA. Tel: 01326-
270526. Coastal defence castle built by Henry VIII
ST MICHAEL'S MOUNT (NT), Cornwall TR17 0EF.
Tel: 01736-710507. A 12th-century castle with later
additions, off the coast at Marazion
SANDRINGHAM, Norfolk PE35 6EN. Tel: 01553-772675
Web: www.sandringhamestate.co.uk
The Queen's private residence; a neo-Jacobean house
built in 1870
SCARBOROUGH CASTLE (EH), N. Yorks. Tel: 01723-372451.
Remains of 12th-century keep and curtain walls
SHERBORNE CASTLE, Dorset. Tel: 01935-813182.
Web: www.sherbournecastle.com
Sixteenth-century castle built by Sir Walter Raleigh
SHUGBOROUGH (NT), Staffs ST17 0XB. Tel: 01889-881388.
House set in 18th-century park with monuments,
temples and pavilions in the Greek Revival style. Seat of
the Earls of Lichfield
SKIPTON CASTLE, N. Yorks BD23 1AX. Tel: 01756-792442
Web: www.skiptoncastle.co.uk
D-shaped castle with six round towers and beautiful
inner courtyard
SMALLHYTHE PLACE (NT), Kent TN30 7NG.
Tel: 01580-762334. Half-timbered 16th-century house;
home of Ellen Terry 1899–1928. Barn Theatre
STANFORD HALL, Leics LE17 6DH. Tel: 01788-860250
Web: www.stanfordhall.co.uk
William and Mary house with Stuart portraits.
Motorcycle museum
STONEHENGE (EH), Wilts. Tel: 01980-624715. Prehistoric
monument consisting of concentric stone circles
surrounded by a ditch and bank
STONOR PARK, Oxon RG9 6HF. Tel: 01491-638587. Medieval
house with Georgian facade. Centre of Roman
Catholicism after the Reformation
STOURHEAD (NT), Wilts BA12 6QD. Tel: 01747-841152.
English Palladian mansion with famous gardens
STRATFIELD SAYE HOUSE, Hants RG7 2BT.
Tel: 01256-882882 Web: www.stratfield-saye.co.uk
House built 1630–40; home of the Dukes of Wellington
since 1817
STRATFORD-UPON-AVON, Warks. Shakespeare's
Birthplace Trust with Shakespeare Centre; Anne
Hathaway's Cottage, home of Shakespeare's wife; Mary
Arden's House, home of Shakespeare's mother; Nash's
House and New Place, where Shakespeare died; and
Hall's Croft, home of Shakespeare's daughter.
Tel: 01789-204016 Web: www.shakespeare.org.uk. Also
Grammar School attended by Shakespeare, Holy Trinity
Church, where Shakespeare is buried, Royal Shakespeare
Theatre (burnt down 1926, rebuilt 1932) and Swan
Theatre (opened 1986)
SUDELEY CASTLE, Glos GL54 5JD. Tel: 01242-602308
Web: www.sudeleycastle.co.uk
Castle built in 1442; restored in the 19th-century
SYON HOUSE, Brentford, Middx TW8 8JF. Tel: 020-8560 0883
Web: www.syonpark.co.uk
Built on the site of a former monastery; Adam interior
TILBURY FORT (EH), Essex RM18 7NR. Tel: 01375-858489.
A 17th-century coastal fort
TINTAGEL CASTLE (EH), Cornwall. Tel: 01840-770328.
A 12th-century cliff-top castle and Dark Age settlement
site
TOWER OF LONDON, London EC3N 4AB. Tel: 0870-756 6060
Web: www.hrp.org.uk.
Royal palace and fortress begun by William the
Conqueror in 1078. Houses the Crown Jewels
TRERICE (NT), Cornwall TR8 4PG. Tel: 01637-875404.
Elizabethan manor house

TYNEMOUTH PRIORY AND CASTLE (EH), Tyne and Wear.
Tel: 0191-257 1090. Remains of a Benedictine priory,
founded c.1090, on Saxon monastic site
UPPARK (NT), W. Sussex GU31 5QR. Tel: 01730-825857.
Late 17th-century house, completely restored after fire.
Fetherstonhaugh art collection
WALMER CASTLE (EH), Kent. Tel: 01304-364288.
One of Henry VIII's coastal defence castles, now the
residence of the Lord Warden of the Cinque Ports
WALTHAM ABBEY (EH), Essex. Tel: 01992-702200.
Ruined abbey including the nave of the abbey church,
'Harold's Bridge' and late 14th-century gatehouse.
Traditionally the burial place of Harold II (1066)
WARKWORTH CASTLE (EH), Northumberland.
Tel: 01665-711423. A 15th-century keep amidst earlier
ruins, with 14th-century hermitage upstream
WARWICK CASTLE, Warks CV34 4QU. Tel: 0870-442 2000
Web: www.warwickcastle.co.uk
Medieval castle with Madame Tussaud's waxworks, in
Capability Brown parkland
WHITBY ABBEY (EH), N. Yorks. Tel: 01947-603568
Remains of Norman church on the site of a monastery
founded in AD 657
WILTON HOUSE, Wilts SP2 0BJ. Tel: 01722-746720
Web: www.wiltonhouse.co.uk
A 17th-century house on the site of a Tudor house and
Saxon abbey
WINDSOR CASTLE, Berks SL4 1NJ. Tel: 020-7321 2233
Web: www.royal.gov.uk
Official residence of The Queen; oldest royal residence
still in regular use. Also St George's Chapel
WOBURN ABBEY, Beds MK17 9WA. Tel: 01525-290666
Web: www.woburnabbey.co.uk
Built on the site of a Cistercian abbey; seat of the Dukes
of Bedford. Important art collection; antiques centre
WROXETER ROMAN CITY (EH), Shropshire.
Tel: 01743-761330. Second-century public baths and part
of the forum of the Roman town of Viroconium

WALES

For more information on any of the National Trust properties
listed below, the official website is: www.nationaltrust.org.uk.
For more information on any of the CADW properties listed
below, the official website is: www.cadw.wales.gov.uk.
(C) Property of CADW: Welsh Historic Monuments
(NT) National Trust property

BEAUMARIS CASTLE (C), Anglesey. Tel: 01248-810361.
Concentrically-planned castle, still almost intact
CAERLEON ROMAN BATHS AND AMPHITHEATRE (C), nr
Newport. Tel: 01633-422518. Rare example of a legionary
bath-house and late 1st-century arena surrounded by
bank for spectators
CAERNARFON CASTLE (C). Tel: 01286-677617.
Important Edwardian castle built, with the town wall,
between 1283 and 1330
CAERPHILLY CASTLE (C) CF83 1JD. Tel: 029-2088 3143.
Concentrically-planned castle (c.1270) notable for its
scale and use of water defences
CARDIFF CASTLE CF10 2RB. Tel: 029-2087 8100.
Castle built on the site of a Roman fort; spectacular
towers and rich interior
CASTELL COCH (C), nr Cardiff CF15 7JS.
Tel: 029-2081 0101. Rebuilt 1875-90 on medieval
foundations
CHEPSTOW CASTLE (C) NP16 5EY. Tel: 01291-624065.
Rectangular keep amid extensive fortifications
CONWY CASTLE (C). Tel: 01492-592358.
Built by Edward I, 1283-7
CRICCIETH CASTLE (C) Gwynedd LL52 0DP.
Tel: 01766-522227. Native Welsh 13th-century castle,
altered by Edward I

DENBIGH CASTLE (C) LL16 3NB. Tel: 01745-813385.
Remains of the castle (begun 1282), including triple-
towered gatehouse
HARLECH CASTLE (C). Tel: 01766-780552.
Well-preserved Edwardian castle, constructed 1283-90,
on an outcrop above the former shoreline
PEMBROKE CASTLE SA71 4LA. Tel: 01646-681510
Web: www.pembrokecastle.co.uk
Castle founded in 1093; Great Tower built 1200;
birthplace of King Henry VII
PENRHYN CASTLE (NT), Bangor LL57 4HN.
Tel: 01248-353084. Neo-Norman castle built in the
19th-century. Industrial railway museum
PORTMEIRION, Gwynedd LL48 6ET. Tel: 01766-770228
Web: www.portmeirion.wales.com
Village in Italianate style
POWIS CASTLE (NT), nr Welshpool SY21 8RF.
Tel: 01938-551944. Medieval castle with interior in variety
of styles; 17th-century gardens and Clive of India museum
RAGLAN CASTLE (C) NP15 2BT. Tel: 01291-690228.
Remains of 15th-century castle with moated hexagonal
keep
ST DAVIDS BISHOP'S PALACE (C), St Davids.
Tel: 01437-720517. Remains of residence of Bishops of St
Davids built 1328-47
TINTERN ABBEY (C), nr Chepstow. Tel: 01291-689251.
Remains of 13th-century church and conventual
buildings of a Cistercian monastery
TRETOWER COURT AND CASTLE (C), nr Crickhowell NP8
2RF. Tel: 01874-730279. Medieval house with remains of
12th-century castle nearby

SCOTLAND

For more information on any of the Historic Scotland properties
listed below, the official website is: www.historic-scotland.gov.uk.
For more information on any of the National Trust For Scotland
properties listed below, the official website is: www.nts.org.uk.
(HS) Historic Scotland property
(NTS) National Trust for Scotland property

ANTONINE WALL, between the Clyde and the Forth.
Built about AD 142, consists of ditch, turf rampart and
road, with forts every two miles
BALMORAL CASTLE, nr Braemar. Tel: 01339-742334
Web: www.balmoralcastle.com. Baronial-style castle built
for Victoria and Albert. The Queen's private residence
BLACKHOUSE, ARNOL (HS), Lewis, Western Isles.
Tel: 01851-710395. Traditional Lewis thatched house
BLAIR CASTLE, Blair Atholl PH18 5TL. Tel: 01796-481207
Web: www.blair-castle.co.uk
Mid 18th-century mansion with 13th-century tower;
seat of the Dukes of Atholl
BONAWE IRON FURNACE (HS), Argyll and Bute PA35 1JQ.
Tel: 01866-822432.Charcoal-fuelled ironworks founded in
1753
BOWHILL, Selkirk TD7 5ET. Tel: 01750-22204.
Seat of the Dukes of Buccleuch and Queensberry; fine
collection of paintings, including portrait miniatures
BROUGH OF BIRSAY (HS), Orkney. Tel: 01856 841815.
Remains of Norse church and village on the tidal island
of Birsay.
CAERLAVEROCK CASTLE (HS), nr Dumfries DG1 4RN.
Tel: 01387-770244. Fine early classical Renaissance building
CALANAIS STANDING STONES (HS), Lewis, Western Isles.
Tel: 01851-621422. Standing stones in a cross-shaped
setting, dating from 3000 BC
CATERTHUNS (BROWN AND WHITE) (HS), nr Brechin.
Two large Iron Age hill forts
CAWDOR CASTLE, Inverness IV12 5RD. Tel: 01667-404615
Web: www.cawdorcastle.com
A 14th-century keep with 15th- and 17th-century
additions

CLAVA CAIRNS (HS), Highlands. Tel: 01667-460232.
Late Neolithic or early Bronze Age cairns
CRATHES CASTLE (NTS), nr Banchory AB31 5QJ.
Tel: 01330-844525. A 16th-century baronial castle in
woodland, fields and gardens
CULZEAN CASTLE (NTS), S. Ayrshire KA19 8LE.
Tel: 01655-884455. An 18th-century Adam castle with
oval staircase and circular saloon
DRYBURGH ABBEY (HS), Scottish Borders. Tel: 01835-822381.
A 12th-century abbey containing tomb of Sir Walter
Scott
DUNVEGAN CASTLE, Skye IV55 8WF. Tel: 01470-521206
Web: www.dunvegancastle.com
A 13th-century castle with later additions; home of the
chiefs of the Clan MacLeod; trips to seal colony
EDINBURGH CASTLE (HS) EH1 2NG. Tel: 0131-225 9846.
Includes the Scottish Crown Jewels, Scottish National
War Memorial, Scottish United Services Museum and
historic apartments
EDZELL CASTLE (HS), nr Brechin. Tel: 01356-648631.
Medieval tower house; unique walled garden
EILEAN DONAN CASTLE, Wester Ross. Tel: 01599-555202.
A 13th-century castle with Jacobite relics
ELGIN CATHEDRAL (HS), Moray. Tel: 01343-547171.
A 13th-century cathedral with fine chapterhouse
FLOORS CASTLE, Kelso. Tel: 01573-223333.
Largest inhabited castle in Scotland; seat of the Dukes of
Roxburghe
FORT GEORGE (HS), Highlands. Tel: 01667-462777.
An 18th-century fort
GLAMIS CASTLE, Angus. Tel: 01307-840393
Web: www.strathmore-estates.co.uk
Seat of the Lyon family (later Earls of Strathmore and
Kinghorne) since 1372
GLASGOW CATHEDRAL (HS). Tel: 0141-552 6891.
Medieval cathedral with elaborately vaulted crypt
GLENELG BROCHS (HS), Highlands. Tel: 01667-470232.
Two broch towers with well-preserved structural features
HOPETOUN HOUSE, nr Edinburgh EH30 9SL.
Tel: 0131-331 2451 Web: www.hopetounhouse.com
House designed by Sir William Bruce, enlarged by
William Adam
HUNTLY CASTLE (HS). Tel: 01466-793191.
Ruin of a 16th- and 17th-century house
INVERARAY CASTLE, Argyll. Tel: 01499-302203. Gothic-style
18th-century castle; seat of the Dukes of Argyll
IONA ABBEY, Inner Hebrides. Tel: 01681-700793.
Monastery founded by St Columba in AD 563
JARLSHOF (HS), Shetland. Tel: 01950-460112. Remains from
Stone Age
JEDBURGH ABBEY (HS), Scottish Borders. Tel: 01835-863925.
Romanesque and early Gothic church founded c.1138
KELSO ABBEY (HS), Scottish Borders. Remains of great abbey
church founded 1128 by David I
LINLITHGOW PALACE (HS) EH49 7AL. Tel: 01506-842896.
Ruin of royal palace in park setting. Birthplace of Mary,
Queen of Scots
MAES HOWE (HS), Orkney. Tel: 01856-761606.
Neolithic tomb
MEIGLE SCULPTURED STONES (HS), Angus.
Tel: 01828-640612. Celtic Christian stones
MELROSE ABBEY (HS), Scottish Borders. Tel: 01896-822562.
Ruin of Cistercian abbey founded c.1136
MOUSA BROCH (HS), Shetland. Tel: 01466-793191
Finest surviving Iron Age broch tower
NEW ABBEY CORN MILL (HS), nr Dumfries.
Tel: 01387-850260. Water-powered mill
PALACE OF HOLYROODHOUSE, Edinburgh.
Tel: 0131-556 5100 Web: www.royal.gov.uk
The Queen's official Scottish residence. Main part of the
palace built 1671–9
RING OF BROGAR (HS), Orkney. Tel: 01865-841815.
Neolithic circle of upright stones with an enclosing ditch

RUTHWELL CROSS (HS), Dumfries and Galloway.
Tel: 01387-870249. Seventh-century Anglian cross
ST ANDREWS CASTLE AND CATHEDRAL (HS), Fife KY16
9AR. Tel: 01334-477196 (castle); 01334-472563 (cathedral).
Ruins of 13th-century castle and remains of the largest
cathedral in Scotland
SCONE PALACE, Perth PH2 6BD. Tel: 01738-552300
Web: www.scone-palace.net
House built 1802–13 on the site of a medieval palace.
Home of the Earls of Mansfield
SKARA BRAE (HS), Orkney. Tel: 01856-841815.
Stone-Age village with adjacent 17th-century house
SMAILHOLM TOWER (HS), Scottish Borders.
Tel: 01573-460365. Well-preserved tower-house
STIRLING CASTLE (HS) FK8 1EJ. Tel: 01786-450000.
Great Hall and gatehouse of James IV, palace of James V,
Chapel Royal remodelled by James VI
TANTALLON CASTLE (HS), E. Lothian EH39 5PN.
Tel: 01620-892727. Fortification with earthwork defences
and a 14th-century curtain wall with towers
THREAVE CASTLE (HS), Dumfries and Galloway.
Tel: 0831-168541. Late 14th-century tower on an island;
reached by boat, long walk to castle
URQUHART CASTLE (HS), Loch Ness IV63 6XJ.
Tel: 01456-450551. Castle remains with well-preserved
tower

NORTHERN IRELAND

For more information on any of the National Trust properties
listed below, the official website is: www.nationaltrust.org.uk. For
the Northern Ireland Environment and Heritage Service, the
official website is: www.ehsni.gov.uk
EHS Property in the care of the Northern Ireland Environment
and Heritage Service
NT National Trust property

CARRICKFERGUS CASTLE (EHS), Co. Antrim.
Tel: 028-9335 1273. Castle begun in 1180 and garrisoned
until 1928
CASTLE COOLE (NT), Enniskillen BT74 6JY. Tel: 028-6632
2690. An 18th-century mansion by James Wyatt in
parkland
CASTLE WARD (NT), Co. Down BT30 7LS. Tel: 028-4488 1204.
An 18th-century house with Classical and Gothic
facades
DEVENISH ISLAND (EHS), Co. Fermanagh.
Tel: 028-6862 1588. Island monastery founded in the 6th
century by St Molaise
DOWNHILL CASTLE (NT), Co. Londonderry.
Tel: 028-7084 8728. Ruins of palatial house in landscaped
estate including Mussenden Temple.
DUNLUCE CASTLE (EHS), Co. Antrim. Tel: 028-9054 3037.
Ruins of 16th-century stronghold of the MacDonnells
FLORENCE COURT (NT), Co. Fermanagh BT92 1DB. Tel: 028-
6634 8249. Mid-18th-century house with rococo
plasterwork
GREY ABBEY (EHS), Co. Down. Tel: 028-9054 3037.
Substantial remains of a Cistercian abbey founded in
1193.
HILLSBOROUGH FORT (EHS), Co. Down.
Tel: 028-9268 9717. Built in 1650
MOUNT STEWART (NT), Co. Down. Tel: 028-4278 8387.
An 18th-century house, childhood home of Lord
Castlereagh
NENDRUM MONASTERY (EHS), Mahee Island, Co. Down.
Tel: 028-9054 3037. Founded in the 5th century by St
Machaoi
TULLY CASTLE (EHS), Co. Fermanagh. Tel: 028-9023 5000.
Fortified house and bawn built in 1613
WHITE ISLAND (EHS), Co. Fermanagh.
Tenth-century monastery and 12th-century church.
Access by ferry

MUSEUMS AND GALLERIES

There are approximately 2,500 museums and galleries in the United Kingdom. Around 1,800 are registered with Resource: The Council for Museums, Archives and Libraries, formerly the Museums and Galleries Commission, which indicates that they have an appropriate constitution, are soundly financed, have adequate collection management standards and public services, and have access to professional curatorial advice. Museums must achieve full or provisional registration status in order to be eligible for grants from Resource and from Area Museums Councils. Many registered museums are run by a local authority.

The national museums and galleries receive direct government grant-in-aid. These are: British Museum; Imperial War Museum; National Army Museum; National Galleries of Scotland; National Gallery; National Maritime Museum; National Museums and Galleries on Merseyside; National Museum of Wales; National Museums of Scotland; National Portrait Gallery; Natural History Museum; RAF Museum; Royal Armouries; Science Museum; Tate Gallery; Ulster Folk and Transport Museum; Ulster Museum; Victoria and Albert Museum; Wallace Collection. An online art museum (www.24hourmuseum.org.uk) has also been awarded national collection status.

Local authority museums are funded by the local authority and may also receive grants from Resource. Independent museums and galleries mainly rely on their own resources but are also eligible for grants from the Museums and Galleries Commission.

Area Museum Councils, which are independent charities, give advice and support to the museums in their area and may offer improvement grants. They also circulate exhibitions and assist with training and marketing. For further information see the Public Bodies section.

OPENING TO THE PUBLIC

The following is a selection of the museums and art galleries in the United Kingdom. Opening hours and admission charges vary. Most museums are closed on Christmas Eve, Christmas Day, Boxing Day and New Year's Day; many are closed on Good Friday, and some are closed on May Day Bank Holiday. Some smaller museums close at lunchtimes. Information about a specific museum or gallery should be checked by telephone. For further information about museums and galleries in the UK, including local authority status and whether a collection is designated pre-eminent, contact the Museums Association on 020-7426 6970.

ENGLAND

BARNARD CASTLE, Co. Durham – *The Bowes Museum*, Westwick Road DR12 8NP. Tel: 01833-690606
  Web: www.bowesmuseum.org.uk
  European art from the late medieval period to the 19th-century; music and costume galleries; English period rooms from Elizabeth I to Victoria; local archaeology

BATH – *American Museum*, Claverton Manor BA2 7BD.
  Tel: 01225-460503 Web: www.americanmuseum.org
  American decorative arts from the 17th- to 19th-century
Museum of Costume, Bennett Street BA1 2QH.
  Tel: 01225-477789 Web: www.museumofcostume.co.uk
  Fashion from the 16th-century to the present day
Roman Baths Museum, Pump Room, Stall Street BA1 1LZ.
  Tel: 01225-477785 Web: www.romanbaths.co.uk
  Museum adjoins the remains of a Roman baths and temple complex
Victoria Art Gallery, Bridge Street BA2 4AT.
  Tel: 01225-477772 Web: www.victoriagal.org.uk
  European Old Masters and British art since the 18th-century
BEAMISH, Co. Durham – Beamish, The North of England Open Air Museum, DH9 0RG Tel: 0191-370 4000
  Web: www.beamish.org.uk
  Recreated northern town c.1900, with rebuilt and furnished local buildings, colliery village, farm, railway station, tramway, Pockerley Manor and horse-yard (set c.1800)
BEAULIEU, Hants – National Motor Museum. SO42 7ZN.
  Tel: 01590-612345 Web: www.beaulieu.co.uk
  Displays of over 250 vehicles dating from 1895 to the present day
BIRMINGHAM – *Aston Hall*, Trinity Road, B6 6JD.
  Tel: 0121-327 0062 Web: www.bmag.org.uk/aston_hall
  Jacobean House containing paintings, furniture and tapestries from the 17th- to 19th-century
Barber Institute of Fine Arts, off Edgbaston Park Road, B15 2TS.
  Tel: 0121-414 7333 Web: www.barber.org.uk
  Fine arts, including Old Masters
Birmingham Nature Centre, Pershore Road, Edgbaston, B5 7RL.
  Tel: 0121-472 7775. Indoor and outdoor enclosures displaying wildlife, especially British and European
City Museum and Art Gallery, Chamberlain Square B3 3DH.
  Tel: 0121-303 2834,
  Web: www.bmag.org.uk/museum_and_art_gallery
  Includes notable collection of Pre-Raphaelites
Museum of the Jewellery Quarter, Vyse Street, Hockley B18 6HA.Tel: 0121-554 3598
  Web: www.bmag.org.uk/jewellery_quarter
  Built around a real jewellery workshop
Soho House, Soho Avenue B18 5LB. Tel: 0121-554 9122
  Web: www.bmag.or.uk/soho_house
  Eighteenth-century home of industrialist Matthew Boulton
BOVINGTON CAMP, Dorset – *Tank Museum* BH20 6JG.
  Tel: 01929-405096 Web: www.tankmuseum.co.uk
  Collection of 300 tanks from the earliest days of tank warfare to the present
BRADFORD – *Cartwright Hall Art Gallery*, Lister Park BD9 4NS. Tel: 01274-751212.
  British 19th- and 20th-century fine art
Industrial Museum and Horses at Work, Moorside Road BD2 3HP. Tel: 01274-435900.
  Engineering, textiles, transport and social history exhibits, including recreated back-to-back cottages, shire horses and horse tram-rides

National Museum of Photography, Film and Television, Bradford BD1 1NQ. Tel: 0870-710200 Web: www.nmpft.org.uk
Photography, film and television interactive exhibits. Features the UK's first IMAX cinema and the only public Cinerama screen in the world

BRIGHTON – *Booth Museum of Natural History*, Dyke Road BN1 5AA. Tel: 01273-292777. Zoology, botany and geology collections; British birds in recreated habitats

Brighton Museum and Art Gallery, Royal Pavilion Gardens, BN1 1EE. Tel: 01273-290900. Includes fine art and design, fashion, non-Western art, Brighton history

BRISTOL – *Arnolfini*, Narrow Quay BS1 4QA
Tel: 0117-929 9191 Web: www.arnolfini.demon.co.uk
Contemporary visual arts, dance, performance, music, talks and workshops

Blaise Castle House Museum, Henbury BS10 7QS.
Tel: 0117-903 9818 Web: www.bristol-city.gov.uk
Agricultural and social history collections in an 18th-century mansion

Bristol Industrial Museum, Princes Wharf BS1 4RN.
Tel: 0117-925 1470 Web: www.bristol-city.gov.uk
Industrial, maritime and transport collections

City Museum and Art Gallery, Queen's Road BS8 1RL
Tel: 0117-922 3571 Web: www.bristol-city.gov.uk
Includes fine and decorative art, oriental art, Egyptology and Bristol ceramics and paintings

CAMBRIDGE – *Duxford Airfield*, Duxford CB2 4QR
Tel: 01223-835000 Web: www.iwm.org.uk
Displays of military and civil aircraft, tanks, guns and naval exhibits

Fitzwilliam Museum, Trumpington Street CB2 1RB.
Tel: 01223-332900 Web: www.fitzmuseum.cam.ac.uk
Antiquities, fine and applied arts, clocks, ceramics, manuscripts, furniture, sculpture, coins and medals, temporary exhibitions

Sedgwick Museum of Earth Sciences, Downing Street, CB2 3EQ. Tel: 01223-333456 Web: www.sedgwickmuseum.org
Extensive geological collection

University Museum of Archaeology and Anthropology, Downing Street CB2 3DZ. Tel: 01223-333516 Archaeology and anthropology from all parts of the world

University Museum of Zoology, Downing Street CB2 3EJ.
Tel: 01223-336650 Web: www.zoo.cam.ac.uk
Extensive zoological collection

Whipple Museum of the History of Science, Free School Lane CB2 3RH. Tel: 01223-330906
Web: www.hps.cam.ac.uk/whipple
Scientific instruments from the 14th-century to the present

CARLISLE – *Tullie House Museum and Art Gallery*, Castle Street CA3 8TP. Tel: 01228-534781
Web: www.tulliehouse.co.uk
Prehistoric archaeology, Hadrian's Wall, Viking and medieval Cumbria, and the social history of Carlisle; also British 19th- and 20th-century art and English porcelain

CHATHAM – *World Naval Base* ME4 4TZ Tel: 01634-823800
Web: www.worldnavalbase.org.uk
Maritime attractions including HMS Cavalier, the UK's last World War II destroyer

Royal Engineers Museum, Brompton Barracks ME4 4UG.
Tel: 01634-406397 Web: www.army.mod.uk/royalengineers
Regimental history, ethnography, decorative art and photography

CHELTENHAM – *Art Gallery and Museum*, Clarence Street GL50 3JT. Tel: 01242-237431
Web: www.cheltenhammuseum.org.uk
Paintings, arts and crafts

CHESTER – *Grosvenor Museum*, Grosvenor Street CH1 2DD.
Tel: 01244-402008
Web: www.chestercc.gov.uk/heritage/museum/home
Roman collections, natural history, art, Chester silver, local history and costume

CHICHESTER – *Weald and Downland Open Air Museum*, Singleton PO18 0EU. Tel: 01243-811363
Web: www.wealddown.co.uk
Rebuilt vernacular buildings from south-east England; includes medieval houses, agricultural and rural craft buildings and a working watermill

COLCHESTER – *Colchester Castle Museum*, Castle Park CO1 1YG. Tel: 01206-282939
Web: www.colchestermuseums.org.uk
Largest Norman keep in Europe standing on foundations of roman Temple of Claudius; tours of the Roman vaults, castle walls and chapel with medieval and prison displays

COVENTRY – *Herbert Art Gallery and Museum*, Jordan Well CV1 5QP. Tel: 024-7683 2381
Web: www.coventrymuseum.org.uk
Local history, archaeology and industry, and fine and decorative art

Museum of British Road Transport, Hales Street CV1 1PN.
Tel: 024-7683 2425 Web: www.mbrt.co.uk
Hundreds of motor vehicles and bicycles

CRICH, nr Matlock, Derbys – *Crich Tramway Museum* BE4 5DP. Tel: 01773-852565 Web: www.tramway.co.uk
Open-air working museum with tram rides

DERBY – *Derby Museum and Art Gallery*, The Strand DE1 1BS.
Tel: 01332-716659 Web: www.derby.gov.uk/museums
Includes paintings by Joseph Wright of Derby and Derby porcelain

Industrial Museum, off Full Street DE1 3AR.
Tel: 01332-255308 Web: www.derby.gov.uk/museums
Rolls-Royce aero engine collection and a railway engineering gallery

Pickford's House Museum, Friar Gate DE1 1DA.
Tel: 01332-255363 Web: www.derby.gov.uk/museums
Georgian Town House by architect Joseph Pickford; reconstructed period rooms and garden

DEVIZES – *Wiltshire Heritage Museum*, Long Street SN10 1NS. Tel: 01380-727369
Web: www.wiltshireheritage.org.uk
Natural and local history, art gallery, archaeological finds from Bronze Age, Iron Age, Roman and Saxon sites

DORCHESTER – *Dorset County Museum*, High West Street, DT1 1XA. Tel: 01305-262735
Web: www.dorsetcountymuseum.com
Includes a collection of Thomas Hardy's manuscripts, books, notebooks and drawings

DOVER – *Dover Museum*, Market Square CT16 1PB.
Tel: 01304-201066 Web: www.dovermuseum.co.uk
Contains Dover Bronze Age Boat Gallery and archaeological finds from the Bronze Age, Roman and Saxon sites.

ELLESMERE PORT – *Boat Museum*, South Pier Road CH65 4FW. Tel: 0151-355 5017 Web: www.boatmuseum.co.uk
Craft and boating history

EXETER – *Royal Albert Memorial Museum and Art Gallery*, Queen Street EX4 3RX. Tel: 01392-665858
Web: www.exeter.gov.uk
Natural history, archaeology, worldwide fine and decorative art including Exeter silver

GATESHEAD – *Shipley Art Gallery*, Prince Consort Road NE8 4JB. Tel: 0191-477 1495.
Contemporary crafts

Baltic Centre for Contemporary Art, South Shore Road, Gateshead, NE8 3BA. Tel: 0191-478 1810
Web: www.balticmill.com
Presents a constantly changing programme of contemporary art exhibitions and events

GAYDON, Warwick – *British Motor Industry Heritage Trust,* Heritage Motor Centre, Banbury Road CV35 0BJ. Tel: 01926-641188: Web; www.heritage.org.uk
History of British motor industry from 1895 to present; classic vehicles; engineering gallery; Corgi and Lucas collections

GLOUCESTER – *National Waterways Museum,* Llanthony Warehouse, Gloucester Docks GL1 2EH. Tel: 01452-318200
Web: www.nwm.org.uk
Two-hundred-year history of Britain's canals and inland waterways

GOSPORT, Hants – *Royal Navy Submarine Museum,* Haslar Jetty Road PO12 2AS. Tel: 023-9252 9217
Web: www.rnsubmus.co.uk
Underwater warfare, including the submarine Alliance; historical and nuclear galleries; and first Royal Navy submarine

GRASMERE, Cumbria – *Dove Cottage and the Wordsworth Museum* LA22 9SH. Web: www.wordsworth.org.uk

HALIFAX – *Eureka! The Museum for Children,* Discovery Road HX1 2NE. Tel: 01422-330069 Web: www.eureka.org.uk
Hands-on museum designed for children up to age 12

HULL – *Ferens Art Gallery,* Queen Victoria Square HU1 3RA. Tel: 01482-613902
Web: www.hullcc.gov.uk/museums/index.htm
European art, especially Dutch 17th-century paintings, British portraits from 17th- to 20th-century, and marine paintings

Hull Maritime Museum, Queen Victoria Square HU1 3DX. Tel: 01482-613902 Web: www.hullcc.gov.uk/museums
Whaling, fishing and navigation exhibits

HUNTINGDON – *Cromwell Museum,* Grammar School Walk PE29 3LF. Tel: 01480-375830
Web: www.edweb.camcnty.gov.uk/cromwell.
Portraits and memorabilia relating to Oliver Cromwell

IPSWICH – *Christchurch Mansion and Wolsey Art Gallery,* Christchurch Park IP4 2BE. Tel: 01473-253246.
Tudor house with paintings by Gainsborough, Constable and other Suffolk artists; furniture and 18th-century ceramics. Art gallery for temporary exhibitions

LEEDS – *City Art Gallery,* The Headrow LS1 3AA. Tel: 0113-247 8248 Web: www.leeds.gov.uk/artgallery
British and European paintings including English watercolours, modern sculpture, Henry Moore gallery, print room

Leeds Industrial Museum at Armley Mills, Canal Road, Armley LS12 2QF. Tel: 0113-263 7861
Web: www. leeds.gov.uk/armleymills
Largest woollen mill in world

Lotherton Hall, Aberford LS25 3EB. Tel: 0113-281 3259
Web: www.leeds.gov.uk/lothertonhall
Costume and oriental collections in furnished Edwardian house; deer park and bird garden

Royal Armouries Museum, Armouries Drive LS10 1LT. Tel: 0113-220-1916 Web: www.armouries.org.uk/leeds
National collection of arms and armour from BC to present; demonstrations of foot combat in museum's five galleries; falconry and mounted combat in the tiltyard

Temple Newsam House LS15 0AE. Tel: 0113-264 7321
Web: www.leeds.gov.uk/templenewsam
Old Masters and 17th- and 18th-century decorative art in furnished Jacobean/Tudor house

LEICESTER – *Jewry Wall Museum,* St Nicholas Circle LE1 4LB. Tel: 0116-225 4971 Web: www.leicestermuseums.ac.uk
Archaeology, Roman Jewry Wall and baths, and mosaics

New Walk Museum and Art Gallery, New Walk LE1 7EA. Tel: 0116-255 4100 Web: www.leicestermuseums.ac.uk
Natural history, geology, ancient Egypt gallery, European art and decorative arts

Snibston Discovery Park, Coalville LE67 3LN. Tel: 01530-278444.
Open-air science and industry museum on site of a coal mine; country park with nature trail

LINCOLN – *Museum of Lincolnshire Life,* Burton Road LN1 3LY. Tel: 01522-528448.
Social history and agricultural collection

Usher Gallery, Lindum Road LN2 1NN. Tel: 01522-527980.
Watches, miniatures, porcelain, silver; collection of Peter de Wint works; Lincolnshire topography and Royal Lincs Regiment memorabilia

LIVERPOOL – *Lady Lever Art Gallery,* Wirral CH62 5EQ. Tel: 0151-478 4136 Web: www.ladyleverartgallery.org.uk
Paintings, furniture and porcelain

Liverpool Museum, William Brown Street L3 8EN. Tel: 0151-478 4399 Web: www.nmgm.org.uk
Includes Egyptian mummies, weapons and classical sculpture; planetarium, aquarium, vivarium and natural history centre

Merseyside Maritime Museum, Albert Dock L3 4AQ. Tel: 0151-478 4499 Web: www.nmgm.org.uk
Floating exhibits, working displays and craft demonstrations; incorporates HM Customs and Excise National Museum

Museum of Liverpool Life, Pier Head, Albert Dock L3 1PZ. Tel: 0151-478 4080 Web: www.nmgm.org.uk
The history of Liverpool

Sudley House, Mossley Hill Road L18 8BX. Tel: 0151-724 3245.
Late 18th- and 19th-century British paintings in former shipowner's home

Tate Gallery Liverpool, Albert Dock L3 4BB. Tel: 0151-702 7400 Web: www.tate.org.uk/liverpool
Twentieth-century painting and sculpture

Walker Art Gallery, William Brown Street L3 8EL. Tel: 0151-478 4199 Web: www.nmgm.org.uk
Paintings from the 14th- to 20th-century

LONDON: GALLERIES – *Barbican Art Gallery,* Barbican Centre EC2Y 8DS. Tel: 020-7638 8891
Web: www.barbican.org.uk
Temporary exhibitions

Courtauld Gallery, Somerset House, Strand, WC2R 0RN. Tel: 020-7848 2526 Web: www.courtauld.ac.uk
The University of London galleries

Dulwich Picture Gallery, Gallery Road, SE21 7AD. Tel: 020-8693 5254 Web: www.dulwichpicturegallery.org.uk
Built by Sir John Soane to house 17th- and 18th-century paintings

Hayward Gallery, Belvedere Road, SE1 8XZ. Tel: 020-7960 5226 Web: www.hayward.org.uk
Temporary exhibitions

National Gallery, Trafalgar Square, WC2N 5DN. Tel: 020-7747 2885 Web: www.nationalgallery.org.uk
Western painting from the 13th- to 20th-century; early Renaissance collection in the Sainsbury wing

National Portrait Gallery, St Martin's Place, WC2H 0HE. Tel: 020-7306 0055 Web: www.npg.org.uk
Portraits of eminent people in British history

Percival David Foundation of Chinese Art, Gordon Square, WX1H 0PD. Tel: 020-7387 3909
Web: www.pdfmuseum.org.uk
Chinese ceramics from 10th- to 18th-century
Photographers Gallery, Great Newport Street, WC2H 7HY. Tel: 020-7831 1772 Web: www.photonet.org.uk
Temporary exhibitions
The Queen's Gallery, Buckingham Palace, SW1A 1AA. Tel: 020-7839 1377 Web: www.royal.org.uk
Art from the Royal Collection
Royal Academy of Arts, Piccadilly, W1V 0DS. Tel: 020-7300 8000 Web: www.royalacademy.org.uk
British art since 1750 and temporary exhibitions; annual Summer Exhibition
Saatchi Gallery, County Hall, South Bank.
Contemporary art including paintings, photographs, sculpture and installations
Serpentine Gallery, Kensington Gardens, W2 3XA. Tel: 020-7298 1515 Web: www.serpentinegallery.org
Temporary exhibitions of British and international contemporary art
Tate Britain, Millbank SW1P 4RG. Tel: 020-7887 8000 Web: www.tate.org.uk
British painting and 20th-century painting and sculpture.
Tate Modern, Bankside, SE1 9TG. Tel: 020-7887 8000 Web: www.tate.org.uk
International modern art from 1900 to the present
Wallace Collection, Manchester Square, W1U 3BN. Tel: 020-7563 9500 Web: www.the-wallace-collection.org.uk
Paintings and drawings, French 18th-century furniture, armour, porcelain, clocks and sculpture
Whitechapel Art Gallery, Whitechapel High Street, E1 7QX. Tel: 020-7522 7888 Web: www.whitechapel.org
Temporary exhibitions of modern art
LONDON: MUSEUMS – *Bank of England Museum,* Threadneedle Street, EC2R 8AH (entrance from Bartholomew Lane). Tel: 020-7601 5545
Web: www.bankofengland.co.uk
History of the Bank since 1694
Bethnal Green Museum of Childhood, Cambridge Heath Road, E2 9PA. Tel: 020-8983 5200
Web: www.museumofchildhood.org.uk
Toys, games and exhibits relating to the social history of childhood
British Museum, Great Russell Street, WC1B 3DG. Tel: 020-7323 8000 Web: www.thebritishmuseum.ac.uk
Antiquities, coins, medals, prints and drawings
Cabinet War Rooms, King Charles Street, SW1A 2AQ. Tel: 020-7930 6961 Web: www.iwm.org.uk/cabinet
Underground rooms used by Churchill and the Government during the Second World War
Commonwealth Experience, Kensington High Street W8 6NQ. Tel: 020-7603 4535 Web: www.commonwealth.org.uk
Exhibitions on Commonwealth nations, visual arts and crafts; Interactive World
Cutty Sark, Greenwich, SE10 9HT. Tel: 020-8858 3445 Web: www.cuttysark.org.uk
Restored and re-rigged tea clipper with exhibits on board.
Design Museum, Shad Thames, SE1. Tel: 020-7378 6055 Web: www.designmuseum.org.uk
The development of design and the mass-production of consumer objects
Estorick Collection, Canonbury Square, N1 2AN Tel: 020-7704 9522 Web: www.estorickcollection.com
Stages the main Estorick Collection of modern Italian art together with temporary loan exhibitions

Firepower! The Royal Artillery Museum, Royal Arsenal, Woolwich, SE18 6ST. Tel: 020-8855 7755
Web: www.firepower.org.uk
The history and development of artillery over the last 700 years including the collections of the Royal Regiment of Artillery
Geffrye Museum, Kingsland Road, E2 8EA. Tel: 020-7739 9893 Web: www.geffrye-museum.org.uk
English urban domestic interiors from 1600 to present day; also paintings, furniture, decorative arts, walled herb garden and period garden rooms
Gilbert Collection, The Strand WC2R 1LA. Tel: 020-7420 9400 Web: www.gilbert-collection.org.uk
The collection comprises some 800 works of art including European silver, gold snuff boxes and Italian mosaics
HMS Belfast, Morgan's Lane, Tooley Street, SE1 2JH. Tel: 020-7940 6300 Web: www.iwm.org.uk/belfast
Life on a World War II warship
Horniman Museum and Gardens, London Road SE23 3PQ. Tel: 020-8699 1872 Web: www.horniman.ac.uk
Museum of ethnography, musical instruments, natural history and aquarium; reference library; sunken, water and flower gardens
Imperial War Museum, Lambeth Road SE1 6HZ. Tel: 020-7416 5320 Web: www.iwm.org.uk
All aspects of the two world wars and other military operations involving Britain and the Commonwealth since 1914
Jewish Museum, Camden Town, Albert Street NW1 7NB. Tel: 020-7284 1997 Web: www.jewishmuseum.org.uk
Jewish life, history and religion
Jewish Museum, Finchley, East End Road N3 2SY. Tel: 020-8349 1143 Web: www.jewishmuseum.org.uk
Jewish life in London and Holocaust education
London's Transport Museum, Covent Garden WC2E 7BB. Tel: 020-7379 6344 Web: www.ltmuseum.co.uk
Vehicles, photographs and graphic art relating to the history of transport in London
MCC Museum, Lord's NW8 8QN. Tel: 020-7616 8595 Web: www.lords.org
Cricket museum. Conducted tours by appointment with Tours Manager.
Museum in Docklands, East India Quay, Hertsmere Road, E14 4AL Tel: 0870-444 3856
Web: www.museumindocklands.org.uk
Explores the story of London's river, port and people over 2,000 years; from Roman times through to the recent regeneration of London's Docklands.
Museum of Garden History, Lambeth Palace Road SE1 7LB. Tel: 020-7401 8865 Web: www.museumgardenhistory.org
Exhibition of aspects of garden history and re-created 17th-century garden
Museum of London, 150 London Wall, EC2Y 5HN Tel: 020-7600 3699 Web: www.museum-london.org.uk
History of London from prehistoric times to present day
National Army Museum, Royal Hospital Road SW3 4HT. Tel: 020-7730 0717 Web: www.national-army-museum.ac.uk
Five-hundred-year history of the British soldier; exhibits include model of the Battle of Waterloo and Army for Today gallery
Natural History Museum, Cromwell Road SW7 5BD. Tel: 020-7942 5000 Web: www.nhm.ac.uk
Natural history collections

National Maritime Museum, Greenwich SE10 9NF.
Tel: 020-8858 4422 Web; www.nmm.ac.uk
Comprises the main building, the Royal Observatory and the Queen's House. Maritime history of Britain; collections include globes, clocks, telescopes and paintings
Petrie Museum of Egyptian Archaeology, University College London, Malet Place WC1E 6BT. Tel: 020-7679 2884
Web: www.petrie.ucl.ac.uk
Egyptian archaeology collection
Royal Air Force Museum, Hendon, NW9 5LL. Tel: 020-8205 2266 Web: www.rafmuseum.org.uk
National museum of aviation with over 70 full-size aircraft; aviation from before the Wright brothers to the present-day RAF; flight simulator
Royal Mews, Buckingham Palace SW1A 1AA.
Tel: 020-7321 2233 Web: www.royal.gov.uk
Carriages, coaches, stables and horses
Science Museum, Exhibition Road, SW7 2DD.
Tel: 0870 870 4771 Web: museum.org.uk
Science, technology, industry and medicine collections
Shakespeare Globe Theatre Tour and Exhibition, Bankside SE1 9DT. Tel: 020-7902 1400 Web: www.shakespeare-globe.org
Recreation of Elizabethan theatre using 16th-century techniques
Sherlock Holmes Museum, Baker Street NW1 6XE.
Tel: 020-7935 8866 Web: www.sherlock-holmes.co.uk
Recreated rooms of the fictional detective
Sir John Soane's Museum, Lincoln's Inn Fields WC2A 3BP.
Tel: 020-7405 2107 Web: www.soane.org
Art and antiques
Theatre Museum, Russell Street WC2E 7PR . Tel: 020-7943 4700 Web: www.theatremuseum.vam.ac.uk
History of the performing arts
Tower Bridge Experience, SE1 2UP. Tel: 020-7403 3761
Web: www.towerbridge.org.uk
History of the bridge and display of Victorian steam machinery; panoramic views from walkways
Victoria and Albert Museum, Cromwell Road SW7 2RL.
Tel: 020-7942 2000 Web: www.vam.ac.uk
Includes National Art Library and Print Room. Fine and applied art and design, including furniture, glass, textiles, dress collections
Wellington Museum, Apsley House, W1J 7NT. Tel: 020-7499 5676 Web: www.apsleyhouse.org.uk
Wimbledon Lawn Tennis Museum, Church Road SW19 5AE.
Tel: 020-8946 6131 Web: www.wimbledon.org/museum
Tennis trophies, fashion and memorabilia; view of Centre Court
MANCHESTER – *Gallery of Costume,* Rusholme M14 5LL
Tel: 0161-224 5217 Web: www.manchestergalleries.org
Exhibits from the 16th- to 20th–century
Imperial War Museum North, Trafford Wharf Road, Trafford Park, Manchester, M17 1TZ. Tel: 0161-877 9240
Web: www.iwm.org.uk/north
Manchester Art Gallery, Mosley Street M2 3JL.
Tel: 0161-235 8888 Web: www.manchestergalleries.org
Manchester Museum, Oxford Road M13 9PL Tel: 0161-275 2634 Web: www.museum.man.ac.uk
Archaeology, archery, botany, Egyptology, entomology, ethnography, geology, natural history, numismatics, oriental and zoology collections
Museum of Science and Industry, Castlefield M3 4FP.
Tel: 0161-832 2244 Web: www.msim.org.uk
On site of world's oldest passenger railway station; galleries relating to space, energy, power, transport, aviation, textiles and social history; interactive science centre

People's History Museum, Pump House, Left Bank M3 3ER. Tel: 0161-839 6061 Web: www.peopleshistorymuseum.org.uk
Political and working life history
Whitworth Art Gallery, Oxford Road M15 6ER.
Tel: 0161-275 7450 Web: www.whitworth.man.ac.uk
Watercolours, drawings, prints, textiles, wallpapers and 20th-century British art
MONKWEARMOUTH – *Monkwearmouth Station Museum,* North Bridge Street SR5 1AP. Tel: 0191-567 7075.
Victorian train station
NEWCASTLE UPON TYNE – *Hancock Museum,* Barras Bridge NE2 4PT. Tel: 0191-222 6765.
Natural history. Egyptology
Laing Art Gallery, New Bridge Street NE1 8AG.
Tel: 0191-232 7734.
British and European art, ceramics, glass, silver, textiles and costume; Art on Tyneside display
Newcastle Discovery Museum, Blandford Square NE1 4JA.
Tel: 0191-232 6789.
Science and industry, local history, fashion and Tyneside's maritime history; Turbinia (first steam-driven vessel) gallery
NEWMARKET – *National Horseracing Museum,* High Street CB8 8JL. Tel: 01638-667333 Web: www.nhrm.co.uk
The Essential Horse Millennium Exhibition, horseracing exhibits and tours of local trainers' yards and studs
NORTHAMPTON – *Central Museum and Art Gallery,* Guildhall Road NN1 1DP. Tel: 01604-238548
Web: www.northampton.gov.uk/museums
Boot and shoe collection
NORTH SHIELDS – *Stephenson Railway Museum,* Middle Engine Lane NE29 8DX. Tel: 0191-200 7145.
Locomotive engines and rolling stock
NOTTINGHAM – *Brewhouse Yard Museum,* Castle Boulevard NG7 1FB. Tel: 0115-915 3600.
Daily life from the 17th- to 20th-century
Castle Museum and Art Gallery NG1 6EL. Tel: 0115-915 3700.
Paintings, ceramics, silver and glass; history of Nottingham
Industrial Museum, Wollaton Park NG8 2AE. Tel: 0115-915 3900. Lacemaking machinery, steam engines and transport exhibits
Museum of Costume and Textiles, Castle Gate NG1 6AF.
Tel: 0115-915 3500. Costume displays from 1790 to the mid-20th century in period rooms
Natural History Museum, Wollaton Park NG8 2AE. Tel: 0115-915 3900. Local natural history and wildlife dioramas
OXFORD – *Ashmolean Museum,* Beaumont Street OX1 2PH.
Tel: 01865-278000 Web: www.ashmol.ox.ac.uk
European and Oriental fine and applied arts, archaeology, Egyptology and numismatics
Museum of Modern Art, Pembroke Street OX1 1BP.
Tel: 01865-722733 Web: www.moma.org.uk
Temporary exhibitions
Museum of the History of Science, Broad Street OX1 3AZ.
Tel: 01865-277280 Web: www.mhs.ox.ac.uk
Displays include early scientific instruments, chemical apparatus, clocks and watches
Oxford University Museum of Natural History, Parks Road OX1 3PW. Tel: 01865-272950 Web: www.oum.ox.ac.uk
Entomology, geology, mineralogy and zoology
Pitt Rivers Museum, South Parks Road OX1 3PP.
Tel: 01865-270927 Web: www.prm.ox.ac.uk
Ethnographic and archaeological artefacts

PLYMOUTH – *City Museum and Art Gallery,* Drake Circus PL4
8AJ. Tel: 01752-304774
Web: www.plymouthmuseum.gov.uk
Local and natural history, ceramics, silver, Old Masters,
temporary exhibitions
The Dome, The Hoe PL1 2NZ. Tel: 01752-600608.
Maritime history museum
PORTSMOUTH – *Charles Dickens Birthplace Museum,* Old
Commercial Road PO1 4QL. Tel: 023-9282 7261
Web: www.charlesdickensbirthplace.co.uk
Dickens memorabilia
D-Day Museum, Clarence Esplanade PO5 3NT.
Tel: 023-9282 7261 Web: www.ddaymuseum.co.uk
Includes the Overlord Embroidery
Flagship Portsmouth, HM Naval Base. Incorporates the *Royal
Naval Museum* (Tel: 023-9272 7562
Web: www.royalnavalmuseum.org), HMS *Victory*
(Tel: 023-9282 2034 Web: www.hms-victory.com), HMS
Warrior (Tel: 023-9229 1379 Web: www.hmswarrior.org), the
Mary Rose (Tel: 023-9275 0521 Web: www.maryrose.org)
and the *Dockyard Museum.* History of the Royal Navy
and of the dockyard and the trades in it
PRESTON – *Harris Museum and Art Gallery*, Market Square
PR1 2PP. Tel: 01772-258248
British art since the 18th-century, ceramics, glass,
costume and local history; also contemporary exhibitions
READING – *Rural History Centre,* University of Reading,
Whiteknights RG6 6AG. Tel: 0118-931 8660
Web: www.rdg.ac.uk
History of farming and the countryside over the last
200 years
ST ALBANS – *Verulamium Museum,* St Michael's AL3 4SW.
Tel: 01727-751810 Web: www.stalbansmuseums.org.uk
Iron Age and Roman Verulamium, including wall
plasters, jewellery, mosaics and room reconstructions
ST IVES, Cornwall – *Tate Gallery St Ives,* Porthmeor Beach
TR26 1TG. Tel: 01736-796226 Web: www.tate.org.uk/stives
Modern art, much by artists associated with St Ives.
Includes the Barbara Hepworth Museum and Sculpture
Garden
SALISBURY – *Salisbury and South Wiltshire Museum,* The
Close SP1 2EN Tel: 01722-332151
Web: www.salisburymuseum.org.uk
Archaeology collection
SHEFFIELD – *City Museum and Mappin Art Gallery,* Weston
Park S10 2TP. Tel: 0114-278 2600
Web: www.sheffieldgalleries.org.uk
Includes applied arts, natural history, Bronze Age
archaeology and ethnography, 19th- and 20th-century
art
Graves Art Gallery, Surrey Street S1 1XZ. Tel: 0114-278 2600.
Twentieth-century British art, Grice Collection of
Chinese ivories
Kelham Island Industrial Museum, off Alma Street.
Tel: 0114-272 2106. Local industrial and social history
Ruskin Gallery and Ruskin Craft Gallery, Arundle Gate S1 2PP.
Tel: 0114-278 2600.
SOUTHAMPTON – *City Art Gallery,* Commercial Road SO14
7LP. Tel: 023-8083 2277
Web: www.southampton.gov.uk/art
Fine art, especially 20th-century British
Maritime Museum, Town Quay SO14 2AR. Tel: 023-8063 5904.
Southampton maritime history
Museum of Archaeology, Town Quay SO14 2NY. Tel: 023-8063
5904. Roman, Saxon and medieval archaeology
Tudor House Museum and Garden, Bugle Street SO14 2AD.
Tel: 023-8063 5904. Restored 16th-century garden;
social history exhibitions

SOUTH SHIELDS – *Arbeia Roman Fort,* Baring Street NE33
2BB. Tel: 0191-456 1369. Excavated ruins
South Shields Museum and Art Gallery, Ocean Road NE33 2JA.
Tel: 0191-456 8740. South Tyneside history, including
reconstructed street
STOKE-ON-TRENT – *Etruria Industrial Museum,* Etruria ST4
7AF. Tel: 01782-233144. Britain's sole surviving steam-
powered potter's mill
Gladstone Pottery Museum, Longton ST3 1PQ.
Tel: 01782-319232. A working Victorian pottery
Potteries Museum and Art Gallery, Hanley ST1 3DE.
Tel: 01782-232323. Pottery, china and porcelain
collections and a Mark XVI Spitfire. Pottery factory
tours are available by arrangement, at the following:
Royal Doulton, Burslem; *Spode,* Stoke; *Wedgwood,*
Barlaston; *W. Moorcroft,* Cobridge; *H & R Johnson Tiles,*
Tunstall; *Staffordshire Enamels,* Longton; *Royale Stratford
China,* Fenton
STYAL, Cheshire – *Quarry Bank Mill* SK9 4LA.
Tel: 01625-527468 Web: www.quarrybankmill.org.uk
Working mill illustrating history of cotton industry;
costumed guides at restored Apprentice House
SUNDERLAND – *Sunderland Museum and Winter Gardens,*
Sunderland SR1 1PP. Tel: 0191-553 2323.
Fine and decorative art, local history and gardens
TELFORD – *Ironbridge Gorge Museums* TF8 7DQ.
Tel: 01952-432166 Web: www.ironbridge.org.uk
Includes first iron bridge; Blists Hill (late Victorian
working town); Museum of Iron; Jackfield Tile
Museum; Coalport China Museum; Tar Tunnel;
Broseley Pipeworks
WAKEFIELD – *Yorkshire Sculpture Park,* West Bretton WF4
4LG. Tel: 01924-830302 Web: www.ysp.co.uk
Open-air sculpture gallery including works by Moore,
Hepworth, Frink and others in 300 acres of parkland
WASHINGTON – *Washington 'F' Pit Museum,* Albany Way
Colliery-related collection
WORCESTER – *City Museum and Art Gallery,* Foregate Street
WR1 1DT. Tel: 01905-25371
Web: www.worcestercitymuseums.org.uk
Includes a military museum, River Severn Gallery and
changing art exhibitions
*Museum of Worcester Porcelain and Royal Worcester Visitor
Centre,* Severn Street WR1 2NE. Tel: 01905-746000
Web: www.royal-worcester.co.uk
WROUGHTON, nr Swindon, Wilts – *Science Museum,*
Wroughton Airfield. Tel: 01793-814466.
Aircraft displays and some of the Science Museum's
transport and agricultural collection
YEOVIL, Somerset – *Fleet Air Arm Museum,* Royal Naval Air
Station, Yeovilton BA22 8HT. Tel: 01935-840565
Web: www.fleetairarm.com
History of naval aviation; historic aircraft, including
Concorde 002
YORK – *Beningbrough Hall,* Beningbrough YO30 1DD.
Tel: 01904-470666. Portraits from the National Portrait
Gallery
Castle Museum, Eye of York YO1 9RY. Tel: 01904-650333
Web: www.york.castle.museum
Reconstructed streets; costume and military collections
City Art Gallery, Exhibition Square YO1 7EW.
Tel: 01904-697979 Web: www.york.art.museum
European and British painting spanning seven
centuries; modern pottery
Jorvik – The Viking City, Coppergate YO1 9WT.
Tel: 01904-543403 Web: www.jorvik-viking-centre.co.uk
Reconstruction of Viking York

National Railway Museum, Leeman Road YO26 4XJ.
Tel: 01904-621261 Web: www.nrm.org.uk
Includes locomotives, rolling stock and carriages
Yorkshire Museum, Museum Gardens YO1 7FR.
Tel: 01904-687687 Web: www.york.yorkshire.museum
Yorkshire life from Roman to medieval times; geology gallery

WALES

BLAENAFON, Torfaen – *Big Pit National Mining Museum* NP4 9XP. Tel: 01495-790311 Web: www.nmgw.ac.uk/bigpit
Colliery with underground tour
BODELWYDDAN, Denbighshire – *Bodelwyddan Castle* LL18 5YA. Tel: 01745-584060
Web: www.bodelwyddan-castle.co.uk
Portraits from the National Portrait Gallery, furniture from the Victoria and Albert Museum and sculptures from the Royal Academy
CAERLEON – *Roman Legionary Museum* NP6 1AE.
Tel: 01633-423134 Web: www.nmgw.ac.uk/rlm
Material from the site of the Roman fortress of Isca and its suburbs
CARDIFF – *National Museum and Gallery Cardiff,* Cathays Park CF10 3NP. Tel: 029-2039 7951
Web: www.nmgw.ac.uk/nmgc
Includes natural sciences, archaeology and Impressionist paintings
Museum of Welsh Life, St Fagans CF5 6XB.
Tel: 029-2057 3500 Web: www.nmgw.ac.uk/mwl
Open-air museum with re-erected buildings, agricultural equipment and costume
DRE-FACH FELINDRE, nr Llandysul – *Museum of the Welsh Woollen Industry* SA44 5UP. Tel: 01559-370929
Web: www.nmgw.ac.uk/mwwi
Exhibitions, a working woollen mill and craft workshops
LLANBERIS, nr Caernarfon – *Welsh Slate Museum* LL55 4TY.
Tel: 01286-870630 Web: www.nmgw.ac.uk/wsm
Former slate quarry with original machinery and plant; slate crafts demonstrations
LLANDRINDOD WELLS – *National Cycle Collection,* Automobile Palace, Temple Street LD1 5DL.
Tel: 01597-825531 Web: www.cyclemuseum.org.uk.
Over 200 bicycles on display, from 1818 to the present day
SWANSEA – *Glynn Vivian Art Gallery and Museum,* Alexandra Road SA1 5DZ. Tel: 01792-655006
Web: www.swansea.gov.uk/glynnvivian
Paintings, ceramics, Swansea pottery and porcelain, clocks, glass and Welsh art
Swansea Museum, Victoria Road SA1 1SN. Tel: 01792-653763
Web: www.swansea.gov.uk/culture
Archaeology, social history, Swansea pottery

SCOTLAND

ABERDEEN – *Aberdeen Art Gallery,* Schoolhill AB10 1FQ.
Tel: 01224-523700 Web: www.aagm.co.uk
Art from the 18th- to 20th-century
Aberdeen Maritime Museum, Shiprow AB11 5BY.
Tel: 01224-337700 Web: www.aagm.co.uk
Maritime history, incl. shipbuilding and North Sea oil
EDINBURGH – *Britannia,* Leith docks EH6 6JJ.
Tel: 0131-555 5566 Web: www.royalyachtbritannia.co.uk
Former royal yacht with royal barge and royal family picture gallery. Tickets must be pre-booked
City Art Centre, Market Street EH1 1DE. Tel: 0131-529 3993
Web: www.cac.org.uk
Late 19th- and 20th-century art and temporary exhibitions
Museum of Childhood, High Street EH1 1TG.
Tel: 0131-529 4142 Web: www.cac.org.uk
Toys, games, clothes and exhibits relating to the social history of childhood
Museum of Edinburgh, Canongate EH8 8DD.
Tel: 0131-529 4143 Web: www.cac.org.uk
Local history, silver, glass and Scottish pottery
Museum of Flight, East Fortune Airfield, East Lothian EH39 5LF.
Tel: 01620-880308. Display of aircraft
Museum of Scotland, Chambers Street EH1 1JF.
Tel: 0131-247 4422 Web: www.nms.ac.uk
Scottish history from prehistoric times to the present
Museum of Scottish Country Life, East Kilbride G76 9HR.
Tel: 0131-247 4377 Web: www.nms.ac.uk
History of rural life and work
National Gallery of Scotland, The Mound EH2 2EL.
Tel: 0131-624 6200 Web: www.nationalgalleries.org
Paintings, drawings and prints from the 16th- to 20th-century, and the national collection of Scottish art
National War Museum of Scotland, Edinburgh Castle EH1 2NG.
Tel: 0131-225 7534 Web: www.nms.ac.uk
History of Scottish military and conflicts
The People's Story, Canongate EH8 8BN. Tel: 0131-529 4057
Web: www.cac.org.uk
Edinburgh life since the 18th-century
Royal Museum of Scotland, Chambers Street EH1 1JF.
Tel: 0131-247 4219 Web: www.nms.ac.uk
Scottish and international collections from prehistoric times to the present
Scottish National Gallery of Modern Art, Belford Road EH4 3DR. Tel: 0131-624 6200 Web: www.nationalgalleries.org
20th-century painting, sculpture and graphic art
Scottish National Portrait Gallery, Queen Street EH2 1JD.
Tel: 0131-624 6200 Web; www.nationalgalleries.org
Portraits of eminent people in Scottish history, and the national collection of photography
The Writers' Museum, Lawnmarket EH1 2PA.
Tel: 0131-529 4901 Web: www.cac.org.uk
Robert Louis Stevenson, Walter Scott and Robert Burns exhibits
FORT WILLIAM – *West Highland Museum,* Cameron Square PH33 6AJ. Tel: 01397-702169
Web: www.fort-william.net/museum
Includes tartan collections and exhibits relating to 1745 uprising

GLASGOW – *Burrell Collection*, Pollokshaws Road G43 1AT.
Tel: 0141-287 2550. Paintings, textiles, furniture,
ceramics, stained glass and silver from classical times to
the 19th-century
Gallery of Modern Art, Queen Street G1 3AZ. Tel: 0141-229
1996. Collection of contemporary Scottish and world art
Glasgow Art Gallery and Museum, Kelvingrove G3 8AG.
Tel: 0141-287 2699. Includes Old Masters, 19th-century
French paintings and armour collection. Closed until
2006 for refurbishment.
Hunterian Art Gallery, Hillhead Street G12 8QQ.
Tel: 0141-330 4221 Web: www.hunterian.gla.ac.uk
Rennie Mackintosh and Whistler collections; Old
Masters, Scottish paintings and modern paintings,
sculpture and prints
McLellan Galleries, Sauchiehall Street G2 3EH.
Tel: 0141-331 1854. Temporary exhibitions
Museum of Transport, Bunhouse Road G3 8DP.
Tel: 0141-287 2720. Includes a reproduction of a 1938
Glasgow street, cars since the 1930s, trams and a
Glasgow subway station
People's Palace Museum, Glasgow Green G40 1AT.
Tel: 0141-554 0223 Web: www.glasgow.gov.uk
History of Glasgow since 1175
St Mungo Museum of Religious Life and Art, Castle Street
G4 0RH. Tel: 0141-553 2557.
Explores universal themes through objects of all the
main world religions

NORTHERN IRELAND

BELFAST – *Ulster Museum*, Botanic Gardens BT9 5AB.
Tel: 028-9038 3000 Web: www.ulstermuseum.org.uk
Irish antiquities, natural and local history, fine and
applied arts
HOLYWOOD, Co. Down – *Ulster Folk and Transport Museum*,
Cultra BT18 0EU. Tel: 028-9042 8428
Web: www.nidex.com/uftm
Open-air museum with original buildings from Ulster
town and rural life c.1900; indoor galleries including
Irish rail and road transport and Titanic exhibitions
LONDONDERRY – *The Tower Museum*, Union Hall Place
BT48 6LU. Tel: 028-7137 2411. Tells the story of Ireland
through the history of Londonderry
OMAGH, Co. Tyrone – *Ulster American Folk Park*, Castletown
BT78 5QY. Tel: 028-8224 3292 Web: www.folkpark.com
Open-air museum telling the story of Ulster's
emigrants to America; restored or recreated dwellings
and workshops; ship and dockside gallery

SIGHTS OF LONDON

For historic buildings and museums and galleries in London, *see* the Historic Buildings and Monuments and Museums and Galleries sections.

ALEXANDRA PALACE, Alexandra Palace Way, Wood Green, N22 7AY. Tel: 020-8365 2121. Web: www.alexandrapalace.com. The Victorian Palace was severely damaged by fire in 1980 but was restored, and reopened in 1988. Alexandra Palace now provides modern facilities for exhibitions, conferences, banquets and leisure activities. There is an ice rink, a boating lake, the Phoenix Bar and a conservation area.

BARBICAN CENTRE, Silk Street, EC2Y 8DS. Tel: 020-7638 4141. Web: www.barbican.org.uk Owned, funded and managed by the Corporation of London, the Barbican Centre opened in 1982 and houses the Barbican Theatre, a studio theatre called The Pit, the Barbican Hall and is home to the London Symphony Orchestra. There are also three cinemas, six conference rooms, two art galleries, a sculpture court, a lending library, trade and banqueting facilities, a conservatory, shops, restaurants, cafes and bars.

BRIDGES. The bridges over the Thames (from east to west) are:

The Queen Elizabeth II Bridge, opened 1991, from Dartford to Thurrock
Tower Bridge, opened 1894
London Bridge, opened after rebuilding by Rennie, 1831; the new London Bridge opened 1973
Alexandra Bridge (railway bridge), built 1863–6
Southwark Bridge (Rennie), built 1814–19; rebuilt 1912–21
Millennium Bridge, opened June 2000; reopened after modification February 2002
Blackfriars Railway Bridge, completed 1864
Blackfriars Bridge, built 1760–9; rebuilt 1860–9; widened 1907–10
Waterloo Bridge (Rennie), opened 1817; rebuilt 1937–42
Hungerford Footbridge, opened 2002
Hungerford Railway Bridge (Brunel), suspension bridge built 1841–5; replaced by present railway and footbridge 1863
Westminster Bridge opened 1750; rebuilt 854–62
Lambeth Bridge, built 1862; rebuilt 1929–32
Vauxhall Bridge, built 1811–16; rebuilt 1895–1906
Grosvenor Bridge (railway bridge), built 1859–60; rebuilt 1963–7
Chelsea Bridge, built 1851–8; replaced by suspension bridge 1934; widened 1937
Albert Bridge, opened 1873; restructured (Bazalgette) 1884; strengthened 1971–3
Battersea Bridge (Holland), opened 1772; rebuilt (Bazalgette) 1890
Battersea Railway Bridge, opened 1863
Wandsworth Bridge, opened 1873; rebuilt 1940
Putney Railway Bridge, opened 1889
Putney Bridge, built 1727–9; rebuilt (Bazalgette) 1882–6; starting point of Oxford and Cambridge Boat Race
Hammersmith Bridge, built 1824–7; rebuilt (Bazalgette) 1883–7; closed 1997–99 for safety work
Barnes Railway Bridge (also pedestrian), built 1846–9; restructured 1893
Chiswick Bridge, opened 1933
Kew Railway Bridge, opened 1869

Kew Bridge, built 1758–9; rebuilt and renamed King Edward VII Bridge 1903
Richmond Lock, lock, weir and footbridge opened 1894
Twickenham Bridge, opened 1933
Richmond Railway Bridge, opened 1848; restructured 1906–8
Richmond Bridge, built 1774–7; widened 1937
Teddington Lock, footbridge opened 1889; marks the end of the tidal reach of the Thames
Kingston Bridge, built 1825–8; widened 1914
Hampton Court Bridge, built 1753; replaced by iron bridge 1865; present bridge built 1933

CEMETERIES. *Abney Park,* Stamford Hill, N16 (35 acres), tomb of General Booth, founder of the Salvation Army, and memorials to many Nonconformist divines. *Brompton,* Old Brompton Road, SW10 (40 acres), graves of Sir Henry Cole, Emmeline Pankhurst, John Wisden. *City of London Cemetery and Crematorium,* Aldersbrook Road, E12 (200 acres). *Golders Green Crematorium,* Hoop Lane, NW11 (12 acres), with Garden of Rest and memorials to many famous men and women. *Hampstead,* Fortune Green Road, NW6 (36 acres), graves of Kate Greenaway, Lord Lister, Marie Lloyd. *Highgate,* Swains Lane, N6 (38 acres), tombs of George Eliot, Faraday and Marx; guided tours only, west side. *Kensal Green,* Harrow Road, W10 (70 acres), tombs of Thackeray, Trollope, Sydney Smith, Wilkie Collins, Tom Hood, George Cruikshank, Leigh Hunt, I. K. Brunel and Charles Kemble. Churchyard of the former *Marylebone Chapel,* Marylebone High Street, W1, Charles Wesley and his son Samuel Wesley buried; chapel demolished in 1949, now Garden of Rest. *Nunhead,* Linden Grove, SE15 (26 acres), closed in 1969, subsequently restored and opened for burials. *St Marylebone Cemetery and Crematorium,* East End Road, N2 (47 acres). *West Norwood Cemetery and Crematorium,* Norwood High Street, SE27 (42 acres), tombs of Sir Henry Bessemer, Mrs Beeton, Sir Henry Tate and Joseph Whitaker (Whitaker's Almanack).

CENOTAPH, Whitehall, London SW1. The word 'cenotaph' means 'empty tomb'. The monument, erected 'To the Glorious Dead', is a memorial to all ranks of the sea, land and air forces who gave their lives in the service of the Empire during the First World War. Designed by Sir Edwin Lutyens and erected as a temporary memorial in 1919, it was replaced by a permanent structure unveiled by George V on Armistice Day 1920. An additional inscription was made after the Second World War to commemorate those who gave their lives in that conflict.

CHARTERHOUSE, Charterhouse Square, EC1M 6AN. Tel: 020-7253 9503. A Carthusian monastery from 1371 to 1537, purchased in 1611 by Thomas Sutton, who endowed it as a residence for aged men 'of gentle birth' and a school for poor scholars (removed to Godalming in 1872).

CHELSEA PHYSIC GARDEN, 66 Royal Hospital Road, SW3 4HS. Tel: 020-7352 5646; Web: www.chelseaphysicgarden.co.uk. A garden of general botanical research and education, maintaining a wide range of rare and unusual plants. The garden was established in 1673 by the Society of Apothecaries.

DOWNING STREET, SW1. Number 10 Downing Street is the official town residence of the Prime Minister, No. 11 to the Chancellor of the Exchequer and No. 12 is the office of the Government Whips. The street was named after Sir George Downing, Bt., soldier and diplomat, who was MP for Morpeth from 1660 to 1684. *Chequers*, a Tudor mansion in the Chilterns near Princes Risborough, was presented by Lord and Lady Lee of Fareham in 1917 to serve, from 1921, as a country residence for the Prime Minister of the day.

GEORGE INN, Borough High Street, SE1. The last galleried inn in London, built in 1677. Now run as an ordinary public house.

GREENWICH, SE10. *The Royal Naval College*, Tel: 020-8269 4791, was until 1873 the Greenwich Hospital. It was built by Charles II, largely from designs by John Webb, and by Queen Mary II and William III, from designs by Wren. It stands on the site of an ancient abbey, a royal house and Greenwich Palace which was constructed by Henry VII. Henry VIII, Mary I and Elizabeth I were born in the royal palace and Edward VI died there. *Greenwich Park* (196.5 acres) was enclosed by Humphrey, Duke of Gloucester, and laid out by Charles II from the designs of Le Nôtre. On a hill in Greenwich Park is the Royal Observatory (founded 1675). Its buildings are now managed by the National Maritime Museum and the earliest building is named Flamsteed House, after John Flamsteed (1646–1719), the first Astronomer Royal. *The Cutty Sark*, the last of the famous tea clippers, has been preserved as a memorial to ships and men of a past era. Sir Francis Chichester's round-the-world yacht, *Gipsy Moth IV*, can also be seen.

HORSE GUARDS, Whitehall, SW1. Archway and offices built about 1753. The mounting of the guard takes place at 11a.m. (10a.m. on Sundays) and the dismounted inspection at 4p.m. Only those with the Queen's permission may drive through the gates and archway into *Horse Guards' Parade*, where the Colour is 'trooped' on The Queen's official birthday.

THE HOUSES OF PARLIAMENT
    The House of Commons, Westminster, London, SW1A 0AA. Tel: 020-7219 4272. Email: hcinfo@parliament.uk
    The House of Lords, Westminster, London, SW1A 0PW. Tel: 020-7219 310. Email: hlinfo@parliament.uk

The royal palace of Westminster, originally built by Edward the Confessor, was the normal meeting place of Parliament from about 1340. St Stephen's Chapel was used from about 1550 for the meetings of the House of Commons, which had previously been held in the Chapter House or Refectory of Westminster Abbey. The House of Lords met in an apartment of the royal palace.

The fire of 1834 destroyed much of the palace and the present Houses of Parliament were erected on the site from the designs of Sir Charles Barry and Augustus Welby Pugin between 1840 and 1867. The chamber of the House of Commons was destroyed by bombing in 1941 and a new Chamber designed by Sir Giles Gilbert Scott was used for the first time in 1950.

Westminster Hall and the Crypt Chapel was the only part of the old palace of Westminster to survive the fire of 1834. It was built by William Rufus (1097–9) and altered by Richard II (1394–9). The hammerbeam roof of carved oak dates from 1396–8. The Hall was the scene of the trial of Charles I.

The Victoria Tower of the House of Lords is about 330 ft high, and when Parliament is sitting the Union flag flies by day from its flagstaff. *The Clock Tower* of the House of Commons is about 320 ft high and contains

'Big Ben', the hour bell said to be named after Sir Benjamin Hall, First Commissioner of Works when the original bell was cast in 1856. This bell, which weighed 16 tons 11 cwt, was found to be cracked in 1857. The present bell (13.5 tons) is a recasting of the original and was first brought into use in 1859. The dials of the clock are 23 ft in diameter, the hands being 9 ft and 14 ft long (including balance piece). A light is displayed from the Clock Tower at night when Parliament is sitting.

During session tours of the Houses of Parliament are only available to UK residents who have made advance arrangements through an MP or peer. Overseas visitors are no longer provided with permits to tour the Houses of Parliament during session, although they can tour during the summer opening and attend debates for both houses in the Strangers' Galleries (*see below*).

During the summer recess tours of the Houses of Parliament can be booked via Firstcall on: 0870-906 3773 or at: www.firstcalltickets.com. They can also be bought on site at the ticket office located at St Stephen's Entrance.

The Strangers' Gallery of the House of Commons is open to the public when the house is sitting. To acquire tickets in advance UK residents should write to their local MP, overseas visitors should apply to their Embassy or High Commission in the UK for a permit. If none of these arrangements have been made, visitors should join the public queue outside St Stephen's Entrance, where there is also a queue for entry to the House of Lords Gallery.

INNS OF COURT. *The Inner* and *Middle Temple*, Fleet Street/Victoria Embankment, EC4, Tel: 020-7797 8250, have occupied since the early 14th-century the site of the buildings of the Order of Knights Templars. *Inner Temple Hall* is open by appointment on application to the Treasury Office. *Middle Temple Hall* (1562–70) is open to the public when not in use. The Inner Temple Garden is normally open to the public on weekdays between 12.30pm and 3pm. *Temple Church*, EC4, Tel: 020-7353 3470, has a nave which forms one of five remaining round churches in England. *Master of the Temple*, Revd R. Griffith-Jones.

Lincoln's Inn, Chancery Lane/Lincoln's Inn Fields, WC2. Tel: 020-7405 1393; Email: mail@lincolnsinn.org.uk. Occupies the site of the palace of a former Bishop of Chichester and of a Black Friars monastery. The hall and library buildings are of 1845, although the library is first mentioned in 1474; the old hall (late 15th-century) and the chapel were rebuilt c. 1619–23. Halls open by appointment, chapel and gardens, Monday–Friday 12–2.30p.m. Chapel services Sunday 11.30a.m. during law terms. *Lincoln's Inn Fields* (7 acres). The square was laid out by Inigo Jones.

Gray's Inn, Holborn/Gray's Inn Road, WC1. Tel: 020-7458 7800. Web: www.graysinn.org.uk. Founded early 14th-century; Hall 1556–8.

No other 'Inns' are active, but there are remains of Staple Inn, a gabled front on Holborn (opposite Gray's Inn Road). *Clement's Inn* (near St Clement Danes Church), *Clifford's Inn*, Fleet Street, and *Thavies Inn*, Holborn Circus, are all rebuilt. *Serjeants' Inn*, Fleet Street, and another (demolished 1910) of the same name in Chancery Lane, were composed of Serjeants-at-Law, the last of whom died in 1922.

LLOYD'S, One Lime Street, EC3M 7HA. Tel: 020-7327 1000. Web: www.lloydsoflondon.com. International insurance market which evolved during the 17th-century from

Lloyd's Coffee House. The present building was opened for business in May 1986, and houses the Lutine Bell. Underwriting is on three floors with a total area of 114,000 sq. ft.

LONDON EYE, The Thames South Bank, SE1 Tel: 0870-5000 600; Web: www.londoneye.com. Opened in February 2000 as London's millennium landmark, this 450ft observation wheel is the capital's fourth largest structure. The wheel provides a 30 minute ride offering spectacular panoramic views of the capital.

LONDON PARKS, ETC.
ROYAL PARKS

Bushy Park (1,099 acres), Middx. Adjoining Hampton Court, contains avenue of horse-chestnuts enclosed in a fourfold avenue of limes planted by William III. 'Chestnut Sunday' (when the trees are in full bloom with their 'candles') is usually about 1 to 15 May.

Green Park (53 acres), W1. Between Piccadilly and St James's Park, with Constitution Hill leading to Hyde Park Corner.

Greenwich Park (183.5 acres), SE10

Hyde Park (350 acres), W1/W2. From Park Lane to Kensington Gardens, containing the Serpentine lake. Fine gateway at Hyde Park Corner, with Apsley House, the Achilles Statue, Rotten Row and the Ladies' Mile. To the north-east is the Marble Arch, originally erected by George IV at the entrance to Buckingham Palace and re-erected in the present position in 1851.

Kensington Gardens (275 acres), W2/W8. From the western boundary of Hyde Park to Kensington Palace, containing the Albert Memorial, Serpentine Gallery and Peter Pan statue.

Kew, Royal Botanic Gardens Richmond, Surrey, TW9 3AB. Tel: 020-8332 5655. Email: info@kew.org

Regent's Park and Primrose Hill (472 acres), NW1. From Marylebone Road to Primrose Hill surrounded by the Outer Circle and divided by the Broad Walk leading to the Zoological Gardens.

Richmond Park (2,500 acres), Middx

St James's Park (93 acres), SW1. From Whitehall to Buckingham Palace. Ornamental lake of 12 acres. The original suspension bridge built in 1857 was replaced in 1957. The Mall leads from the Admiralty Arch to Buckingham Palace, Birdcage Walk from Storey's Gate to Buckingham Palace. Hampton Court Gardens (54 acres), Middx

Hampton Court Green (17 acres), Middx
Hampton Court Park (622 acres), Middx

CORPORATION OF LONDON OPEN SPACES

Ashtead Common (500 acres), Surrey
Burnham Beeches and Fleet Wood (540 acres), Bucks. Purchased by the Corporation for the benefit of the public in 1880, Fleet Wood (65 acres) being presented in 1921.
Coulsdon Common (133 acres), Surrey
Epping Forest (6,000 acres), Essex. Purchased by the Corporation and opened to the public in 1882. The present forest is 12 miles long by 1 to 2 miles wide, about one-tenth of its original area.
Farthing Downs (121 acres), Surrey
Hampstead Heath (789 acres), NW3. Including -Golders Hill (36 acres) and Parliament Hill (271 acres)
Highgate Wood (70 acres), N6/N10
Kenley Common (138 acres), Surrey
Queen's Park (30 acres), NW6
Riddlesdown (90 acres), Surrey

Spring Park (51 acres), Kent
West Ham Park (77 acres), E15
West Wickham Common (25 acres), Kent
Woodredon and Warlies Park Estate (740 acres), Waltham Abbey.
Also smaller open spaces within the City of London, including *Finsbury Circus Gardens*.

LONDON PLANETARIUM, Marylebone Road, NW1 5LR. Tel: 0870-400 3000. Web: www.london-planetarium.com Star show and interactive exhibits.

LONDON ZOO, Regent's Park, NW1. Tel: 020-7722 3333. Web: www.londonzoo.org

MADAME TUSSAUD'S, Marylebone Road, NW1 5LR. Tel: 0870-400 3000. Web: www.madame-tussauds.com Waxwork exhibition.

MARKETS. The London markets are mostly administered by the Corporation of London. *Billingsgate* (fish), Thames Street site dating from 1875, a market site for over 1,000 years, moved to the Isle of Dogs in 1982. *Borough*, SE1 (vegetables, fruit, flowers, etc.), established on present site 1756, privately owned and run. *Covent Garden* (vegetables, fruit, flowers, etc.), established in 1661 under a charter of Charles II, moved in 1973 to Nine Elms. *Leadenhall*, EC3 (meat, poultry, fish, etc.), built 1881, part recently demolished. *London Fruit Exchange*, Brushfield Street, built by Corporation of London 1928–9 as buildings for Spitalfields market; not connected with the market since it moved in 1991. *Petticoat Lane*, Middlesex Street, E1, a market has existed on the site for over 500 years, now a Sunday morning market selling almost anything. *Portobello Road*, W11, originally for herbs and horse-trading from 1870; became famous for antiques after the closure of the Caledonian Market in 1948. *Smithfield, Central Meat, Fish, Fruit, Vegetable and Poultry Markets*, built 1851–66, the site of St Bartholomew's Fair from 12th-to 19th-century, new hall built 1963, market refurbished 1993–4. *Spitalfields*, E1 (vegetables, fruit, etc.), established 1682, modernised 1928, moved to Leyton in 1991. A much smaller market still exists on the original site on Commercial Street, selling arts, crafts, books, clothes and antiques on Sundays.

MARLBOROUGH HOUSE, Pall Mall, SW1A 5HX. Built by Wren for the first Duke of Marlborough and completed in 1711, the house reverted to the Crown in 1835. In 1863 it became the London house of the Prince of Wales and was the London home of Queen Mary until her death in 1953. In 1959 Marlborough House was given by The Queen as the headquarters for the Commonwealth Secretariat and it was opened as such in 1965. The Queen's Chapel, Marlborough Gate was begun in 1623 from the designs of Inigo Jones for the Infanta Maria of Spain, and completed for Queen Henrietta Maria.

LONDON MONUMENT (commonly called The Monument), Monument Street, EC3. Built from designs of Wren, 1671–7, to commemorate the Great Fire of London, which broke out in Pudding Lane on 2 September 1666. The fluted Doric column is 120 ft high; the moulded cylinder above the balcony supporting a flaming vase of gilt bronze is an additional 42 ft; and the column is based on a square plinth 40 ft high (with fine carvings on the west face) making a total height of 202 ft. Splendid views of London from gallery at top of column (311 steps).

MONUMENTS (sculptor's name in parenthesis). *Albert Memorial* (Durham), Kensington Gore; *Royal Air Force* (Blomfield), Victoria Embankment; *Viscount Alanbrooke*,

Whitehall; *Beaconsfield*, Parliament Square; *Beatty* (Macmillan), Trafalgar Square; *Belgian Gratitude* (setting by Blomfield, statue by Rousseau), Victoria Embankment; *Boadicea* (or Boudicca), Queen of the Iceni (Thornycroft), Westminster Bridge; *Brunel* (Marochetti), Victoria Embankment; *Burghers of Calais* (Rodin), Victoria Tower Gardens, Westminster; *Burns* (Steel), Embankment Gardens; *Canada Memorial* (Granche), Green Park; *Carlyle* (Boehm), Chelsea Embankment; *Cavalry* (Jones), Hyde Park; *Edith Cavell* (Frampton), St Martin's Place; *Cenotaph* (Lutyens), Whitehall; *Charles I* (Le Sueur), Trafalgar Square; *Charles II* (Gibbons), South Court, Chelsea Hospital; *Churchill* (Roberts-Jones), Parliament Square; *Cleopatra's Needle*, Thames Embankment, (68.5 ft high, *c.*1500 BC, erected in 1877–8; the sphinxes are Victorian); *Clive* (Tweed), King Charles Street; *Captain Cook* (Brock), The Mall; *Crimean*, Broad Sanctuary; *Oliver Cromwell* (Thornycroft), outside Westminster Hall; *Cunningham* (Belsky), Trafalgar Square; *Gen. Charles de Gaulle,* Carlton Gardens; *Lord Dowding* (Faith Winter), Strand; *Duke of Cambridge* (Jones), Whitehall; *Duke of York* (124 ft), Carlton House Terrace; *Edward VII* (Mackennal), Waterloo Place; *Elizabeth I* (1586, oldest outdoor statue in London; from Ludgate), Fleet Street; *Eros* (Shaftesbury Memorial) (Gilbert), Piccadilly Circus; *Marechal Foch* (Mallisard, copy of one in Cassel, France), Grosvenor Gardens; *Charles James Fox* (Westmacott), Bloomsbury Square; *George III* (Cotes Wyatt), Cockspur Street; *George IV* (Chantrey), riding without stirrups, Trafalgar Square; *George V* (Reid Dick), Old Palace Yard; *George VI* (Macmillan), Carlton Gardens; *Gladstone* (Thornycroft), Strand; *Guards'* (Crimea) (Bell), Waterloo Place; *(Great War)* (Ledward, figures, Bradshaw, cenotaph), Horse Guards' Parade; *Haig* (Hardiman), Whitehall; *Sir Arthur (Bomber) Harris* (Faith Winter), Strand; *Irving* (Brock), north side of National Portrait Gallery; *James II* (Gibbons and/or pupils), Trafalgar Square; *Jellicoe* (Wheeler), Trafalgar Square; *Samuel Johnson* (Fitzgerald), opposite St Clement Danes; *Kitchener* (Tweed), Horse Guards' Parade; *Abraham Lincoln* (Saint-Gaudens, copy of one in Chicago), Parliament Square; *Milton* (Montford), St Giles, Cripplegate; *The Monument* (*see* above); *Mountbatten,* Foreign Office Green; *Nelson* (170 ft 2 in), Trafalgar Square, with Landseer's lions (cast from guns recovered from the wreck of the Royal George); *Florence Nightingale* (Walker), Waterloo Place; *Palmerston* (Woolner), Parliament Square; *Peel* (Noble), Parliament Square; *Pitt* (Chantrey), Hanover Square; *Portal* (Nemon), Embankment Gardens; *Prince Consort* (Bacon), Holborn Circus; *Queen Elizabeth Gate*, Hyde Park Corner; *Raleigh* (Macmillan), Whitehall; *Richard I* (Coeur de Lion) (Marochetti), Old Palace Yard; *Roberts* (Bates), Horse Guards' Parade; *Franklin D. Roosevelt* (Reid Dick), Grosvenor Square; *Royal Artillery* (South Africa) (Colton), The Mall; *(Great War)*, Hyde Park Corner; *Captain Scott* (Lady Scott), Waterloo Place; *Shackleton* (Sarjeant Jagger), Kensington Gore; *Shakespeare* (Fontana, copy of one by Scheemakers in Westminster Abbey), Leicester Square; *Smuts* (Epstein), Parliament Square; *Sullivan* (Goscombe John), Victoria Embankment; *Trenchard* (Macmillan), Victoria Embankment; *Victoria Memorial,* in front of Buckingham Palace; *Raoul Wallenberg* (Phillip Jackson), Great Cumberland Place; *George Washington* (Houdon copy), Trafalgar Square; *Wellington* (Boehm), Hyde Park Corner, (Chantrey) riding without stirrups, outside Royal Exchange; *John Wesley* (Adams Acton), City Road; *William III* (Bacon),

St James's Square; *Wolseley* (Goscombe John), Horse Guards' Parade.

PORT OF LONDON. Port of London Authority, Bakers' Hall, 7 Harp Lane, EC3R 6LB. Tel: 020-7743 7900. Web: www.portoflondon.co.uk The Port of London covers the tidal section of the River Thames from Teddington to the seaward limit (the outer Tongue buoy and the Sunk light vessel), a distance of 150km. The governing body is the Port of London Authority (PLA). Cargo is handled at privately operated riverside terminals between Fulham and Canvey Island, including the enclosed dock at Tilbury, 40km below London Bridge. Passenger vessels and cruise liners can be handled at moorings at Greenwich, Tower Bridge and Tilbury.

ROMAN REMAINS. The city wall of Roman Londinium was largely rebuilt during the medieval period but sections may be seen near the White Tower in the Tower of London; at Tower Hill; at Coopers' Row; at All Hallows, London Wall, its vestry being built on the remains of a semi-circular Roman bastion; at St Alphage, London Wall, showing a succession of building repairs from the Roman until the late medieval period; and at St Giles, Cripplegate. Sections of the great forum and basilica, more than 165m², have been encountered during excavations in the area of Leadenhall, Gracechurch Street and Lombard Street. Traces of Roman activity along the river include a massive riverside wall built in the late Roman period, and a succession of Roman timber quays along Lower and Upper Thames Street. Finds from these sites can be seen at the Museum of London.

Other major buildings are the amphitheatre at Guildhall; remains of bath-buildings in Upper and Lower Thames Street; and the temple of Mithras in Walbrook.

ROYAL ALBERT HALL, Kensington Gore, SW7 2AP. Tel: 020-7589 8212. Web: www.royalalberthall.com. The elliptical hall, one of the largest in the world, was completed in 1871, and since 1941 has been the venue each summer for the Promenade Concerts founded in 1895 by Sir Henry Wood. Other events include pop and classical music concerts, dance, opera, sporting events, conferences and banquets.

ROYAL HOSPITAL, CHELSEA, Royal Hospital Road, SW3 4SR. Tel: 020-7881 5466. Founded by Charles II in 1682, and built by Wren; opened in 1692 for old and disabled soldiers. The extensive grounds include the former Ranelagh Gardens and are the venue for the Chelsea Flower Show each May. *Governor,* Gen. Sir Jeremy Mackenzie, GCB, OBE.

ROYAL OPERA HOUSE, Covent Garden, WC2E 9DD. Tel: Information line and box office 020-7304 4000. Web: www.royalopera.org. Home of The Royal Ballet (1931) and The Royal Opera (1946). The Royal Opera House is the third theatre to be built on the site, opening 1858; the first was opened in 1732.

ST JAMES'S PALACE, Pall Mall, SW1A 1BP. Tel: 020-7930 4832. Web: www.royal.gov.uk. Built by Henry VIII; the Gatehouse and Presence Chamber remain; later alterations were made by Wren and Kent. Representatives of foreign powers are still accredited 'to the Court of St James's'. Clarence House (1825), the official London residence of the Prince of Wales and his sons, stands within the St James's Palace environs.

ST PAUL'S CATHEDRAL, St Paul's Churchyard, EC4M 8AD. Tel: 020-7246 8348.
Email: chapterhouse@stpaulscathedral.org.uk.

Web: www.stpauls.co.uk Built 1675–1710, cost £747,660. The cross on the dome is 365 ft above the ground level, the inner cupola 218 ft above the floor. 'Great Paul' in the south-west tower weighs nearly 17 tons. The organ by Father Smith (enlarged by Willis and rebuilt by Mander) is in a case carved by Grinling Gibbons, who also carved the choir stalls.

SOMERSET HOUSE, Strand and Victoria Embankment, WC2. The river façade (600 ft long) was built in 1776–86 from the designs of Sir William Chambers; the eastern extension, which houses part of King's College, was built by Smirke in 1829. Somerset House was the property of Lord Protector Somerset, at whose attainder in 1552 the palace passed to the Crown, and it was a royal residence until 1692. Somerset House has recently undergone extensive renovation and is home to the Gilbert Collection, Hermitage Rooms and the Courtauld Institute Gallery. Open-air concerts and ice-skating (November–January) are held in the courtyard.

SOUTH BANK, SE1. Tel: 020-7921 0600. Web: www.rfh.org.uk. The arts complex on the south bank of the River Thames which consists of the Royal Festival Hall (opened in 1951 for the Festival of Britain), the adjacent 1,056-seat Queen Elizabeth Hall, the Purcell Room, and the Voice Box.

The National Film Theatre (Opened 1952) Tel: 020-7928 3232. Web: www.bfi.org.uk. Administered by the British Film Institute, has three auditoria showing over 2,000 films a year. The London Film Festival is held here every November. There is also an IMAX cinema with 500 seats.

The Royal National Theatre Tel: 020-7452 3000. Web: www.nationaltheatre.org.uk. Opened in 1976 and stages classical, modern, new and neglected plays in its three auditoria: the Olivier theatre, the Lyttelton theatre and the Cottesloe theatre.

SOUTHWARK CATHEDRAL, Montague Close, SE1 9DA. Tel: 020-7367 6700. Email: cathedral@dswark.org.uk. Web: www.dswark.org. Mainly 13th-century, but the nave is largely rebuilt. The tomb of John Gower (1330–1408) is between the Bunyan and Chaucer memorial windows in the north aisle; Shakespeare's effigy, backed by a view of Southwark and the Globe Theatre, is in the south aisle; the tomb of Bishop Andrewes (died 1626) is near the screen. The lady chapel was the scene of the consistory courts of the reign of Mary (Gardiner and Bonner) and is still used as a consistory court. John Harvard, after whom Harvard University is named, was baptised here in 1607, and the chapel by the north choir aisle is his memorial chapel.

THAMES EMBANKMENTS. *The Victoria Embankment,* on the north side from Westminster to Blackfriars, was constructed by Sir Joseph Bazalgette (1819–91) for the Metropolitan Board of Works, 1864–70; the seats, of which the supports of some are a kneeling camel, laden with spicery, and of others a winged sphinx, were presented by the Grocers' Company and by W. H. Smith, MP, in 1874; the Albert Embankment, on the south side from Westminster Bridge to Vauxhall, 1866–9; the Chelsea Embankment, 1871–4. The total cost exceeded £2,000,000. Bazalgette also inaugurated the London main drainage system, 1858–65. A medallion (*Flumini vincula posuit*) has been placed on a pier of the Victoria Embankment to commemorate the engineer.

THAMES FLOOD BARRIER. Officially opened in May 1984, though first used in February 1983, the barrier consists of ten rising sector gates which span 570 yards from bank to bank of the Thames at Woolwich Reach. When not in use the gates lie horizontally, allowing shipping to navigate the river normally; when the barrier is closed, the gates turn through 90 degrees to stand vertically more than 50 feet above the river bed. The barrier took eight years to complete and can be raised within about 30 minutes.

THAMES TUNNELS. *The Rotherhithe Tunnel,* opened 1908, connects Commercial Road, E14, with Lower Road, Rotherhithe, SE16; it is 1 mile 332 yards long, of which 525 yards are under the river. The first *Blackwall Tunnel* (northbound vehicles only), opened 1897, connects East India Dock Road, Poplar, with Blackwall Lane, East Greenwich. The height restriction on the northbound tunnel is 13ft 4in. A second tunnel (for southbound vehicles only) opened 1967. The lengths of the tunnels measured from East India Dock Road to the Gate House on the south side are 6,215 ft (old tunnel) and 6,152 ft. *Greenwich Tunnel* (pedestrians only), opened 1902, connects the Isle of Dogs, Poplar, with Greenwich; it is 406 yards long. *The Woolwich Tunnel* (pedestrians only), opened 1912, connects North and South Woolwich below the passenger and vehicular ferry from North Woolwich Station, E16, to High Street, Woolwich, SE18; it is 552 yards long.

WALTHAM CROSS, Herts. At Waltham Cross is one of the crosses (partly restored) erected by Edward I to mark a resting place of the corpse of Queen Eleanor on its way to Westminster Abbey. Ten crosses were erected, but only those at Geddington, Northampton and Waltham survive; 'Charing' Cross originally stood near the spot now occupied by the statue of Charles I at Whitehall.

WESTMINSTER ABBEY, Broad Sanctuary, London, SW1P. Tel: 0207-7222 5152. Email: info@westminster-abbey.org Web: www.westminster-abbey.org
Founded as a Benedictine monastery over 1,000 years ago, the Church was rebuilt by Edward the Confessor in 1065 and again by Henry III in the 13th-century. The Abbey is the resting place for monarchs including Edward I, Henry III, Henry V, Henry VII, Elizabeth I, Mary I and Mary Queen of Scots, and has been the setting of coronations since that of William the Conqueror in 1066. In Poets' Corner there are memorials to many literary figures, and many scientists and musicians are also remembered here. The grave of the Unknown Warrior is to be found in the nave.

WESTMINSTER CATHEDRAL, Ashley Place, SW1P 1QW. Tel: 020-7798 9055. Web: www.westminstercathedral.org.uk
Roman Catholic cathedral built 1895–1903 from the designs of J. F. Bentley. The campanile is 283 feet high.

LONDON TOURIST BOARD AND CONVENTION BUREAU, 1 Warwick Row, London, SW1E 5ER. Tel: Tourist information (60p per minute): 09068-663344. Web: www.londontouristboard.com

LONDON THEATRES

ADELPHI THEATRE, Strand, WC2E 7NA.
Tube: Charing Cross. Tel: 020-7344 0055

ALBERY THEATRE, St Martin's Lane, WC2N 4AH.
Tube: Leicester Sq. Tel: 020-7369 1761

ALDWYCH THEATRE, Aldwych, WC2B 4DF.
Tube: Covent Garden. Tel: 020-7416 6003

APOLLO THEATRE, Shaftesbury Avenue, W1V 7HD.
Tube: Piccadilly Circus. Telephone: 020-7494 5070

APOLLO VICTORIA THEATRE, 17 Wilton Rd., SW1V 1LL.
Tube: Victoria Tel: 0870-400 0650

ARTS THEATRE, Great Newport Street, WC1E 7HF.
Tube: Leicester Sq. Tel: 020-7836 3334

BARBICAN THEATRE, Barbican Centre, EC2Y 8BQ.
Tube: Barbican. Tel: 020-7638 8891

CAMBRIDGE THEATRE, Earlham Street, WC2 9HH.
Tube: Covent Garden. Tel: 020-7494 5080

COMEDY THEATRE, Panton Street, SW1Y 4DN.
Tube: Leicester Sq. Tel: 020-7369 1731

CRITERION THEATRE, Piccadilly Circus, W1V 9LB.
Tube: Piccadilly Circus. Tel: 020-7369 1747

DOMINION THEATRE, Tottenham Court Road,
W1P OAG.Tube: Tottenham Court Rd. Tel: 0870-607 7460

DONMAR WAREHOUSE, Earlham Street, WC2H 9LD.
Tube: Covent Garden. Tel: 020-7369 1732

DRURY LANE, Theatre Royal, Catherine St., WC2B 5JF.
Tube: Covent Garden. Tel: 020-7494 5000

DUCHESS THEATRE, Catherine St., WC2B 5LA.
Tube: Covent Garden. Tel: 020-7494 5075

DUKE OF YORK'S THEATRE, St. Martin's Lane, WC2H 4BG.
Tube: Leicester Sq. Tel: 020-7836 5122

FORTUNE THEATRE, Russell St., WC2B 5HH.
Tube: Covent Garden. Tel: 020-7836 2238

GARRICK THEATRE, Charing Cross Rd., WC2H OHH.
Tube: Charing Cross.Tel: 020-7494 5085

GIELGUD THEATRE, Shaftesbury Ave., W1V 8AR.
Tube: Piccadilly Circus. Tel: 020-7494 5065

HAYMARKET THEATRE, Haymarket, SW1Y 4HT.
Tube: Piccadilly Circus. Tel: 020-7930 8800

HER MAJESTY'S THEATRE, Haymarket, SW1Y 4QL.
Tube: Piccadilly Circus. Tel: 020-7494 5400

LONDON PALLADIUM, Argyll Street, W1A 3AB.
Tube: Oxford Circus. Tel: 020-7494 5020

LYCEUM THEATRE, Wellington St., WC2E 7DA.
Tube: Covent Garden. Tel: 0870-243 9000

LYRIC THEATRE, Shaftesbury Ave., W1V 7HA
Tube: Piccadilly Circus. Tel: 020-7494 5045

NEW AMBASSADORS THEATRE, West St., WC2H 9ND.
Tube: Leicester Sq. Tel: 020-7836 6111

NEW LONDON THEATRE, Drury Lane, WC2B 5PW.
Tube: Holborn. Tel: 0207404 4079

OLD VIC THEATRE, Waterloo Road, SE1 8NB.
Tube: Waterloo. Tel: 020-7369 1722

PALACE THEATRE, Shaftesbury Ave., W1V 8AY.
Tube: Leicester Square. Tel: 020-7434 0909

PHOENIX THEATRE, Charing Cross Rd., WC2H OJP.
Tube: Tottenham Court Rd. Tel: 020 7369 1733

PICCADILLY THEATRE, Denman Street, W1V 8DY.
Tube: Piccadilly Circus. Tel: 020-7369 1734

PLAYHOUSE THEATRE, Northumberland Ave., WC2N 5DE.
Tube: Embankment. Tel: 020-7907 7024

PRINCE EDWARD THEATRE, Old Compton Street,
W1V 6HS. Tube: Leicester Sq./Tottenham Court Rd.
Tel: 020-7447 5400

PRINCE OF WALES THEATRE, Coventry Street, W1V 8AS.
Tube: Piccadilly Circus. Tel: 020-7839 5972

QUEENS THEATRE, Shaftesbury Avenue, W1V 8BA.
Tube: Piccadilly Circus. Tel: 020-7494 5041

ROYAL ALBERT HALL, Kensington Gore, SW7 2AP.
Tube: South Kensington. Tel: 020-7589 8212

ROYAL COURT DOWNSTAIRS, Sloane Square, SW1W 8AS.
Tube: Sloane Sq. Tel: 020-7565 5000

ROYAL COURT UPSTAIRS, Sloane Square, SW1W 8AS.
Tube: Sloane Sq. Tel: 020-7565 5000

ROYAL FESTIVAL HALL, South Bank SE1 8XX.
Tube: Waterloo. Tel: 020-7960 4242

SAVOY THEATRE, Strand, WC2R OET. Tube: Charing Cross.
Tel: 020-7836 8888

SHAFTESBURY THEATRE, Shaftesbury Ave., WC2H 8DP.
Tube: Holborn. Tel: 0870-906 3798

ST MARTIN'S THEATRE, West St., WC2H 9NH.
Tube: Leicester Sq. Tel: 020-7836 1443

STRAND THEATRE, Strand, WC2B 5LD.
Tube: Charing Cross. Tel: 020-7930 8800

VAUDEVILLE THEATRE, Strand, WC2R ONH.
Tube: Charing Cross. Tel: 0207-836 9987

THE VENUE (Notre Dame Hall), Leicester Place, W1.
Tube: Leicester Sq. Tel: 0870-899 3335

VICTORIA PALACE THEATRE, Victoria St., SW1E 5EA.
Tube: Victoria. Tel: 020-7834 1317

WHITEHALL THEATRE, Whitehall, SW1 2DY.
Tube: Charing Cross. Tel: 020-7369 1755

WYNDHAM'S THEATRE, Charing Cross Road, WC2H ODA.
Tube: Leicester Sq. Tel: 020-7369 1746/020-7369 1796

YOUNG VIC, The Cut, SE1 8LZ. Tube: Waterloo.
Tel: 020-7928 6363

HALLMARKS

Hallmarks are the symbols stamped on gold, silver or platinum articles to indicate that they have been tested at an official Assay Office and that they conform to one of the legal standards. With certain exceptions, all gold, silver or platinum articles are required by law to be hallmarked before they are offered for sale. Hallmarking was instituted in England in 1300 under a statute of Edward I.

MODERN HALLMARKS

Since 1 January 1999, UK hallmarks have consisted of three compulsory symbols – the sponsor's mark, the fineness (standard) mark and the assay office mark. Traditional marks such as the year date letter, the Britannia for 958 silver, the lion passant for 925 silver (lion rampant in Scotland) and the orb for 950 platinum may be added voluntarily. The distinction between UK and foreign articles has been removed, and more finenesses are now legal, reflecting the more common finenesses elsewhere in Europe.

SPONSOR'S MARK
Instituted in England in 1363, the sponsor's mark was originally a device such as a bird or fleur-de-lis. Now it consists of the initial letters of the name or names of the manufacturer or firm. Where two or more sponsors have the same initials, there is a variation in the surrounding shield or style of letters.

FINENESS (STANDARD) MARK
The fineness (standard) mark indicates that the content of the precious metal in the alloy from which the article is made, is not less than the legal standard. The legal standard is the minimum content of precious metal by weight in parts per thousand, and the standards are:

Gold	999	
	990	
	916.6	(22 carat)
	750	(18 carat)
	585	(14 carat)
	375	(9 carat)
Silver	999	
	958.4	(Britannia)
	925	(sterling)
	800	
Platinum	999	
	950	
	900	
	850	

ASSAY OFFICE MARK
This mark identifies the particular assay office at which the article was tested and marked. The British assay offices are:

LONDON, Goldsmiths' Hall, London EC2V 8AQ.
Tel: 020-7606 8971

BIRMINGHAM, Newhall Street, Birmingham B3 1SB.
Tel: 0121-236 6951 Web: www.theassayoffice.co.uk

SHEFFIELD, 137 Portobello Street, Sheffield S1 4DS.
Tel: 0114-275 5111 Web: www.assayoffice.co.uk

EDINBURGH, 24A Broughton Street, Edinburgh EH1 3RH.
Tel: 0131-556 1144 Web: www.assayofficescotland.com

Assay offices formerly existed in other towns, e.g. Chester, Exeter, Glasgow, Newcastle, Norwich and York, each having its own distinguishing mark.

DATE LETTER
The date letter shows the year in which an article was assayed and hallmarked. Each alphabetical cycle has a distinctive style of lettering or shape of shield. The date letters were different at the various assay offices and the particular office must be established from the assay office mark before reference is made to tables of date letters. Date letter marks became voluntary from 1 January 1999.

The table below shows specimen shields and letters used by the London Assay Office on silver articles in each period from 1498. The same letters are found on gold articles but the surrounding shield may differ. Since 1 January 1975, each office has used the same style of date letter and shield for all articles.

OTHER MARKS

FOREIGN GOODS
Foreign goods imported into the UK are required to be hallmarked before sale, unless they already bear a convention mark (*see* below) or a hallmark struck by an independent assay office in the European Economic Area which is deemed to be equivalent to a UK hallmark.

The following are the assay office marks used for gold until the end of 1998. For silver and platinum the symbols remain the same but the shields differ in shape.

 London

 Birmingham

 Sheffield

 Edinburgh

CONVENTION HALLMARKS

Special marks at authorised assay offices of the signatory countries of the International Convention on Hallmarking (Austria, the Czech Republic, Denmark, Finland, Ireland, the Netherlands, Norway, Portugal, Sweden, Switzerland and the UK) are legally recognised in the United Kingdom as approved hallmarks. These consist of a sponsor's mark, a common control mark, a fineness mark (arabic numerals showing the standard in parts per thousand), and an assay office mark. There is no date letter.

The fineness marks are:

Gold	999	
	990	
	916	(22 carat)
	750	(18 carat)
	585	(14 carat)
	375	(9 carat)
Silver	999	
	925	(sterling)
	800	
Platinum	999	
	950	
	900	
	850	

The common control marks are:

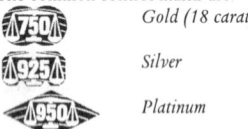

Gold (18 carat)

Silver

Platinum

COMMEMORATIVE MARKS

There are three other marks to commemorate special events: the silver jubilee of King George V and Queen Mary in 1935, the coronation of Queen Elizabeth II in 1953, and her silver jubilee in 1977. During 1999 and 2000 there was a voluntary additional Millennium Mark. A new mark to commemorate the golden jubilee of Queen Elizabeth II was available during 2002.

LONDON (GOLDSMITHS' HALL) DATE

LETTERS FROM 1498

	Black letter, small	1498–9	1517–8
	Lombardic	1518–9	1537–8
	Roman and other capitals	1538–9	1557–8
	Black letter, small	1558–9	1577–8
	Roman letter, capitals	1578–9	1597–8
	Lombardic, external cusps	1598–9	1617–8
	Italic letter, small	1618–9	1637–8
	Court hand	1638–9	1657–8
	Black letter, capitals	1658–9	1677–8
	Black letter, small	1678–9	1696–7
	Court hand	1697	1715–6
	Roman letter, capitals	1716–7	1735–6
	Roman letter, small	1736–7	1738–9
	Roman letter, small	1739–40	1755–6
	Old English, capitals	1756–7	1775–6
	Roman letter, small	1776–7	1795–6
	Roman letter, capitals	1796–7	1815–6
	Roman letter, small	1816–7	1835–6
	Old English, capitals	1836–7	1855–6
	Old English, small	1856–7	1875–6
	Roman letter, capitals [A to M square shield N to Z as shown]	1876–7	1895–6
	Roman letter, small	1896–7	1915–6
	Black letter, small	1916–7	1935–6
	Roman letter, capitals	1936–7	1955–6
	Italic letter, small	1956–7	1974
	Italic letter, capitals	1975	

FINANCE

BRITISH CURRENCY

The unit of currency is the pound sterling (£) of 100 pence.
The decimal system was introduced on 15 February 1971.

COIN

Gold Coins	‡Bi-colour Coins
*One hundred pounds	Two pounds £2
£100	
*Fifty pounds £50	Nickel-Brass Coins
*Twenty-five pounds £25	§Two pounds £2
*Ten pounds £10	One pound £1
Five pounds £5	
Two pounds £2	Cupro-Nickel Coins
Sovereign £1	Crown £5 (since 1990)
Half-Sovereign 50p	50 pence 50p
	Crown 25p (pre-1990)
Silver Coins	20 pence 20p
(*Britannia coins)	10 pence 10p
Two pounds £2	5 pence 5p
One pound £1	
50 pence 50p	Bronze Coins
Twenty pence 20p	2 pence 2p
†Maundy Money	1 penny 1p
Fourpence 4p	
Threepence 3p	¶ Copper-plated Steel Coins
Twopence 2p	2 pence 2p
Penny 1p	1 penny 1p

*Britannia coins: gold bullion coins introduced 1987; silver coins introduced 1997

† Gifts of special money distributed by the Sovereign annually on Maundy Thursday to the number of aged poor men and women corresponding to the Sovereign's own age

‡ Cupro-nickel centre and nickel-brass outer ring

§ Commemorative coins; not intended for general circulation

¶ Since September 1992, although in 1998 the 2p was struck in both copper-plated steel and bronze

GOLD COIN
Gold ceased to circulate during the First World War. Since then controls on buying, selling and holding gold coin have been imposed at various times but subsequently have been revoked. Under the Exchange Control (Gold Coins Exemption) Order 1979, gold coins may now be imported and exported without restriction, except gold coins which are more than 50 years old and valued at a sum in excess of £8,000; these cannot be exported without specific authorisation from the Department of Trade and Industry.

Value Added Taxation on the sale of gold coins was revoked in 2000.

SILVER COIN
Prior to 1920 silver coins were struck from sterling silver, an alloy of which 925 parts in 1,000 were silver. In 1920 the proportion of silver was reduced to 500 parts. From 1 January 1947 all 'silver' coins, except Maundy money, have been struck from cupro-nickel, an alloy of copper 75 parts and nickel 25 parts, except for the 20p, composed of copper 84 parts, nickel 16 parts. Maundy coins continue to be struck from sterling silver.

BRONZE COIN
Bronze, introduced in 1860 to replace copper, is an alloy of copper 97 parts, zinc 2.5 parts and tin 0.5 part. These proportions have been subject to slight variations in the past. Bronze was replaced by copper-plated steel in September 1992 with the exception of 1998 when the 2p was made in both copper plated steel and bronze.

LEGAL TENDER

Gold (dated 1838 onwards, if not below least current weight)	to any amount
£5 (Crown since 1990)	to any amount
£2	to any amount
£1	to any amount
50p	up to £10
25p (Crown pre-1990)	up to £10
20p	up to £10
10p	up to £5
5p	up to £5
2p	up to 20p
1p	up to 20p

The £1 coin was introduced in 1983 to replace the £1 note.

The following coins have ceased to be legal tender:

Farthing	31 December 1960
Halfpenny ($\frac{1}{2}$d)	1 July 1969
Half-crown	1 January 1970
Threepence	31 August 1971
Penny (1d)	31 August 1971
Sixpence	30 June 1980
Halfpenny ($\frac{1}{2}$p)	31 December 1984
old 5 pence	31 December 1990
old 10 pence	30 June 1993
old 50 pence	28 February 1998

Since 1982 the word 'new' in 'new pence' displayed on decimal coins has been dropped.

The Channel Islands and the Isle of Man issue their own coinage, which are legal tender only in the island of issue.

	Metal	Standard weight (g)	Standard diameter (mm)
Penny	Bronze	3.564	20.3
Penny	copper-plated steel	3.564	20.3
2 pence	Bronze	7.128	25.9
2 pence	copper-plated steel	7.128	25.9
5p	cupro-nickel	3.25	18.0
10p	cupro-nickel	6.5	24.5
20p	cupro-nickel	5.0	21.4
25p Crown	cupro-nickel	28.28	38.6
50p	cupro-nickel	8.00	27.3
£1	nickel-brass	9.5	22.5
£2	nickel-brass	15.98	28.4
‡£2	cupro-nickel, nickel-brass	12.00	28.4
£5 Crown	Cupro-nickel	28.28	38.6

The 'remedy' is the amount of variation from standard permitted in weight and fineness of coins when first issued from the Mint.

The Trial of the Pyx is the examination by a jury to ascertain that coins made by the Royal Mint, which have been set aside in the pyx (or box), are of the proper weight, diameter and composition required by law. The trial is held annually, presided over by the Queen's Remembrancer (the Senior Master of the Supreme Court), with a jury of freemen of the Company of Goldsmiths.

BANKNOTES

Bank of England notes are currently issued in denominations of £5, £10, £20 and £50 for the amount of the fiduciary note issue, and are legal tender in England and Wales. No £1 notes have been issued since 1984 and in March 1998 the outstanding notes were written off in accordance with the provision of the Currency Act 1983.

The current E series of notes was introduced from June 1990, replacing the D series (see below). The historical figures portrayed in this series are:

£5	May 2002–	Elizabeth Fry
£5	June 1990–	George Stephenson‡
£10	November 2000–	Charles Darwin*
£20	June 1991–2001	Michael Faraday†
£20	June 1999–	Sir Edward Elgar
£50	April 1994–	Sir John Houblon

†Withrawn from circulation on 28 February 2001.
*The version of the Bank of England £10 banknote issued in April 1992, bearing a portrait of Charles Dickens, ceased to be legal tender from 31 July 2003
‡ Not legal tender after 2 November 2003

NOTE CIRCULATION
Note circulation is highest at the two peak spending periods of the year, around Christmas and during the summer holiday period. The total value of notes in circulation at 3 January 2003 was £35,896 million, compared to £32,574 million at 23 December 2000.

The value of notes in circulation at the end of February 2001 and 2002 was:

	2001	2002
£5	£1,041m	£1,044m
£10	£6,107m	£5,928m
£20	£14,381m	£16,335m
£50	£4,657m	£5,203m
Other notes†	£1,009m	£874m
Total	£27,195m	£29,384m

† Includes higher value notes used internally in the Bank of England, e.g. as cover for the note issues of banks in Scotland and Northern Ireland in excess of their permitted issue

LEGAL TENDER
Banknotes which are no longer legal tender are payable when presented at the head office of the Bank of England in London.

The white notes for £10, £20, £50, £100, £500 and £1,000, which were issued until April 1943, ceased to be legal tender in May 1945, and the white £5 note in March 1946.

The white £5 note issued between October 1945 and September 1956, the £5 notes issued between 1957 and 1963 (bearing a portrait of Britannia) and the first series to bear a portrait of The Queen, issued between 1963 and 1971, ceased to be legal tender in March 1961, June 1967 and September 1973 respectively.

The series of £1 notes issued during the years 1928 to 1960 and the 10 shilling notes issued from 1928 to 1961 (those without the royal portrait) ceased to be legal tender in May and October 1962 respectively. The £1 note first issued in March 1960 (bearing on the back a representation of Britannia) and the £10 note first issued in February 1964 (bearing a lion on the back), both bearing a portrait of The Queen on the front, ceased to be legal tender in June 1979. The £1 note first issued in 1978 ceased to be legal tender on 11 March 1988. The 10 shilling note was replaced by the 50p coin in October 1969, and ceased to be legal tender on 21 November 1970.

The D series of banknotes was introduced from 1970 and ceased to be legal tender from the dates shown below. The predominant identifying feature of each note was the portrayal on the back of a prominent figure from British history:

£1	Feb. 1978–March 1988	Sir Isaac Newton
£5	Nov. 1971–Nov. 1991	The Duke of Wellington
£10	Feb. 1975–May 1994	Florence Nightingale
£20	July 1970–March 1993	William Shakespeare
£50	March 1981–Sept. 1996	Sir Christopher Wren

The £1 coin was introduced on 21 April 1983 to replace the £1 note.

OTHER BANKNOTES
SCOTLAND – Banknotes are issued by three Scottish banks. The Royal Bank of Scotland issues notes for £1, £5, £10, £20 and £100. Bank of Scotland and the Clydesdale Bank issue notes for £5, £10, £20, £50 and £100. Scottish notes are not legal tender in Scotland but they are an authorised currency.

NORTHERN IRELAND – Banknotes are issued by four banks in Northern Ireland. The Bank of Ireland, the Northern Bank and the Ulster Bank issue notes for £5, £10, £20, £50 and £100. The First Trust Bank issues notes for £10, £20, £50 and £100. Northern Ireland notes are not legal tender in Northern Ireland but they circulate widely and enjoy a status comparable to that of Bank of England notes.

CHANNEL ISLANDS – The States of Guernsey issues its own currency notes and coinage. The notes are for £1, £5, £10, £20 and £50, and the coins are for 1p, 2p, 5p, 10p, 20p, 50p, £1, £2 and £5. The States of Jersey issues its own currency notes and coinage. The notes are for £1, £5, £10, £20 and £50, and the coins are for 1p, 2p, 5p, 10p, 20p, 50p, £1 and £2.

THE ISLE OF MAN – The Isle of Man Government issues notes for £1, £5, £10, £20 and £50. Although these notes are only legal tender in the Isle of Man, they are accepted at face value in branches of the clearing banks in the UK. The Isle of Man issues coins for 1p, 2p, 5p, 10p, 20p, 50p, £1, £2 and £5.

Although none of the series of notes specified above is legal tender in the UK, they are generally accepted by the banks irrespective of their place of issue. At one time the banks made a commission charge for handling Scottish and Irish notes but this was abolished some years ago.

BANKING

There are two main types of deposit-taking institutions: banks and building societies, although National Savings and Investments also provides savings products. Banks and building societies are supervised by the Financial Services Authority and National Savings and Investments is accountable to the Treasury. As a result of the conversion of several building societies into banks in the 1990s, the size of the banking sector, which was already substantially greater than the non-bank deposit-taking sector, increased further.

The main institutions within the British banking system are the Bank of England (the central bank), retail banks, investment banks and overseas banks. In its role as the central bank, the Bank of England acts as banker to the Government and as a note-issuing authority; it also oversees the efficient functioning of payment and settlement systems.

Since May 1997, the Bank of England has had operational responsibility for monetary policy. At monthly meetings of its monetary policy committee the Bank sets the interest rate at which it will lend to the money markets.

OFFICIAL INTEREST RATES 2000–2003

13 January 2000	5.75%
10 February 2000	6.00%
8 February 2001	5.75%
5 April 2001	5.50%
10 May 2001	5.25%
2 August 2001	5.00%
18 September 2001	4.75%
4 October 2001	4.50%
8 November 2001	4.00%
6 February 2003	3.75%
10 July 2003	3.50%

RETAIL BANKS

The major retail banks are Abbey National, Alliance and Leicester, Barclays (including Woolwich), HBOS (Halifax and Bank of Scotland), HSBC, Lloyds TSB, National Westminster (which became a wholly owned subsidiary of The Royal Bank of Scotland on 31 January 2003), Northern Rock and The Royal Bank of Scotland.

Retail banks offer a wide variety of financial services to companies and individuals, including current and deposit accounts, loan and overdraft facilities, automated teller (cash dispenser) machines, cheque guarantee cards, credit cards and debit cards. All banks offer varying degrees of telephone and Internet banking facilities and many also offer investment services, such as pensions, insurance and mortgages.

The Financial Ombudsman Service provides independent and impartial arbitration in disputes between a bank and its customer.

Banking hours differ according to the bank and throughout the UK, although most are open 9.00–4.30 Monday to Friday, with the majority also open on Saturday mornings. For customers using internet banking facilities, 24-hour access is available to individual accounts and most telephone banking services operate extended working hours.

PAYMENT CLEARINGS

The Association for Payment Clearing Services (APACS) was set up in 1985 as a non-statutory association of major banks and building societies and is now an umbrella organisation for money transmission and payment clearings in the UK. It manages three clearing companies:
- BACS Ltd (Banker's Automated Clearing Services) is responsible for bulk electronic clearing, processing direct debits, direct credits and standing orders
- the Cheque and Credit Clearing Company Ltd operates bulk clearing systems for inter-bank cheques and paper credit items in Great Britain
- CHAPS Ltd (Clearing House Automated Payment System) provides multi-national same-day clearing for electronic funds transfers in sterling and euro

Membership of APACS is open to any member of a payment scheme which is widely used or significant in the UK. Until September 2002, membership of APACS was linked to membership of the clearing companies or special interest groups. As at June 2003, APACS had 32 members, comprising the major banks, building societies and Royal Mail Group.

ASSOCIATION FOR PAYMENT CLEARING SERVICES (APACS), Mercury House, Triton Court, 14 Finsbury Square, London EC2A 1LQ. Tel: 020-7711 6200 Fax: 020-7256 5527 Web: www.apacs.org.uk.

BACS LTD, De Havilland Road, Edgware, Middx HA8 5QA. Tel: 0870-010 0699

CHEQUE AND CREDIT CLEARING COMPANY LTD, Mercury House, Triton Court, 14 Finsbury Square, London EC2A 1LQ. Tel: 020-7711 6200 Web: www.apacs.org.uk

CHAPS CLEARING COMPANY LTD, Mercury House, Triton Court, 14 Finsbury Square, London EC2A 1LQ. Tel: 020-7711 6277

MAJOR RETAIL BANKS: FINANCIAL RESULTS 2002

Bank Group	Profit/loss before taxation £m	Profit/loss after taxation £m	Total assets £m
Abbey National	(984)	(1,136)	205,721
Alliance and Leicester	468	340	41,249
Barclays (incorporating Woolwich)	3,205	2,250	403,066
HBOS (Halifax/Bank of Scotland)	2,630	1,865	312,275
Lloyds/TSB	2,607	1,843	252,758
HSBC	2,285	1,477	218,378
Northern Rock	3,262	2,297	41,920
The Royal Bank of Scotland Group (incorporating National Westminster)	4,763	3,207	412,000
National Westminster	2,584	1,871	171,887

FINANCIAL SERVICES REGULATION

THE FINANCIAL SERVICES AUTHORITY

The FSA has been the single regulator for financial services in the UK since 1 December 2001, when the Financial Services and Markets Act 2000 (FSMA) came into force. The FSA's aim is to maintain efficient, orderly and clean financial markets and help consumers get a fair deal.

The FSA is required to pursue four statutory objectives:
– maintaining market confidence
– raising public awareness
– protecting consumers
– reducing financial crime

The legislation also requires the FSA to carry out its general functions, whilst having regard to:
– the need to use its resources in the most efficient way
– the responsibilities of regulated firms' own management
– being proportionate in imposing burdens or restrictions on the industry
– facilitating innovation
– the international character of financial services and the competitive position of the United Kingdom
– the need to facilitate, and not have unnecessarily adverse effect, on competition

THE FSA AS AN ORGANISATION

The FSA is a company limited by guarantee, financed by levies on the industry. It receives no funds from the public purse. It is accountable to Treasury Ministers and, through them, to Parliament. Under the new legislation the FSA must report annually on the achievement of its statutory objectives to the Treasury, which is required to lay the report before Parliament.

The FSA's governing body is a board appointed by the Treasury. The Board sets overall FSA policy. Day-to-day operational decisions and management of the staff are the responsibility of the Executive.

The FSA currently has about 2,300 staff. Its total budget for 2003–4 is £215.4 million. The FSA regulates approximately 10,000 institutions. This total includes over 7,500 investment firms, over 660 banks, around 70 building societies, almost 1,000 insurance companies and friendly societies, around 700 credit unions and the Lloyd's insurance market. In addition the FSA regulates about 180,000 approved individuals.

FSA CENTRAL REGISTER/CONSUMER HELPLINE

The FSA maintains a Central Register of all firms that are, or were, authorised to carry on investment business and authorised deposit takers. The entry for each firm gives its name, address and telephone number; a reference number; its authorisation status; and states which organisation regulates it; and whether it can handle client money.

The Consumer Helpline is available to members of the public seeking information about firms listed on the register. In addition, the Helpline explains complaints procedures and provides information on what is and is not regulated by the FSA.

Consumer Helpline: 0845-606 1234 Web: www.fsa.gov.uk

FINANCIAL SERVICES AUTHORITY, 25 the North Colonade, Canary Wharf, London E14 5HS.
Tel: 020-7066 1000. Fax: 020-7066 1099.
Chairman, Callum McCarthy
Chief Executive, John Tiner

COMPENSATION

Under the FSMA the Financial Services Compensation Scheme (FSCS) replaced eight previous compensation schemes. It provides compensation if an authorised firm is unable or likely to be unable to pay claims against it. This is usually when a firm stops trading or is insolvent. The FSCS covers deposits, insurance and investments. The FSCS is independent from the FSA, with separate staff and premises. However, the FSA appoints the board of the FSCS and makes its rules. The FSCS is funded by levies on authorised firms.

THE FINANCIAL SERVICES COMPENSATION SCHEME, 7th Floor, Lloyds Chambers, 1 Portsoken Street, E1 8BN.
Tel: 020-7892 7300. Fax: 020-7892 7301.
Email: enquires@fscs.org.uk Web: www.fscs.org.uk
Chairman, Nigel Hamilton.
Chief Executive, Suzanne McCarthy

DESIGNATED PROFESSIONAL BODIES

Professional firms are exempt from requiring direct regulation by the FSA if they carry out only certain restricted activities that arise out of, or are complementary to the provision of professional services, such as arranging the sale of shares on the instructions of executors or trustees or providing services to small, private companies. These firms are, however, supervised by Designated Professional Bodies (DPBs). There are a number of safeguards to protect consumers dealing with firms that do not require direct regulation. These arrangements include:
– FSA's power to ban a specific firm from taking advantage of the exemption and to restrict the regulated activities permitted to the firms
– rules which require professional firms to ensure that their clients are aware that they are not authorised persons
– a requirement for the DPBs to supervise and regulate the firms and inform the FSA on how the professional firms carry on their regulated activities

The DPBs are:

INSTITUTE OF CHARTERED ACCOUNTANTS IN ENGLAND AND WALES, Chartered Accountants' Hall, PO Box 433, Moorgate Place, London EC2P 2BJ.
Tel: 020-7920 8100 Web: www.icaew.co.uk

INSTITUTE OF CHARTERED ACCOUNTANTS OF SCOTLAND, CA House, 21 Haymarket Yards, Edinburgh EH12 5BH. Tel: 0131-347 0100. Web: www.icas.org.uk

INSTITUTE OF CHARTERED ACCOUNTANTS IN IRELAND, 11 Donegall Square South, Belfast BT1 5JE.
Tel: 028-9032 1600 Web: www.icai.ie

ASSOCIATION OF CHARTERED CERTIFIED ACCOUNTANTS, 29 Lincoln's Inn Fields, London WC2A 3EE.
Tel: 020-7396 7000 Web: www.acca.co.uk

INSTITUTE OF ACTUARIES, Staple Inn Hall, High Holborn,
London WC1V 7QJ. Tel: 020-7632 2100
Web: www.actuaries.org.uk

THE LAW SOCIETY OF ENGLAND AND WALES,
113 Chancery Lane, London WC2A 1PL. Tel: 020-7242 1222
Web: www.lawsoc.org.uk

LAW SOCIETY OF NORTHERN IRELAND, Law Society
House, 98 Victoria Street, Belfast BT1 3JZ.
Tel: 028-9023 1614 Web: www.lawsoc-ni.org

LAW SOCIETY OF SCOTLAND, 26 Drumsheugh Gardens,
Edinburgh EH3 7YR. Tel: 0131-226 7411
Web: www.lawscot.org.uk

RECOGNISED INVESTMENT EXCHANGES

The FSA supervises eight Recognised Investment
Exchanges (RIEs). These are organised markets on which
member firms can trade investments such as equities and
derivatives. Examples are the London Stock Exchange
and the London Metal exchange. As a regulator the FSA
must also focus on the impact of changes brought about
by the continued growth in electronic trading by
exchanges and other organisations. Issues such as how
these changes affect market quality, reliability and access
are important and the FSA works with the exchanges to
ensure that new systems meet regulatory requirements.
There are currently six RIEs which are listed with their
year of recognition:*

INTERNATIONAL PETROLEUM EXCHANGE (IPE) (1988),
International House, 1 St Katharine's Way, London E1W
1UY. Tel: 020-7481 0643. Fax: 020-7481 8485
Web: www.ipe.uk.com

LONDON INTERNATIONAL FINANCIAL FUTURES
EXCHANGE (LIFFE) (1988), Cannon Bridge House,
1 Cousins Lane, London EC4R 3XX. Tel: 020-7623 0444
Web: www.liffe.com

LONDON METAL EXCHANGE (LME) (1988), 56 Leadenhall
Street, London EC3A 2DX. Tel: 020-7264 5555.
Fax: 020-7264 5541 Web: www.lme.co.uk

LONDON STOCK EXCHANGE (LSE) (1988), Old Broad
Street, London EC2N 1HP. Tel: 020-7797 1000.
Web: www.londonstockexchange.com

OM LONDON SECURITIES AND DERIVATIVES
EXCHANGE (1989), 131 Finsbury Pavement, London EC2A
1NT. Tel: 020-7065 8000. Fax: 020-7065 8001
Web: www.omgroup.com

VIRT-X EXCHANGE LTD (2001), 34th Floor, One Canada
Square, London E14 5AA. Tel: 020-7074 4444
Web: virt.x.com
*Jiway Ltd was recognised on 31 October 2000 but
recognition was revoked at Jiway's request on 28 June 2002.
CordealMTS was recognised on 25 May 2000 but recognition
was revoked at CordealMTS' request on 29 November 2002.

RECOGNISED CLEARING HOUSES

The FSA is also responsible for recognising and
supervising Recognised Clearing Houses. These are
bodies which organise the settlement of transactions on
Recognised Investment Exchanges. There are currently
two Recognised Clearing Houses after EuroCCP had its
recognition revoked on 21 January 2003:
CREST CO LTD (1996), 33 Cannon Street, London
EC4M 5SB. Tel: 020-7849 0000. Fax: 020-7849 0130.
Email: info@crestco.co.uk Web: www.crestco.co.uk

LONDON CLEARING HOUSE LTD (LCH) (1988), Aldgate
House, 33 Aldgate High Street, London EC3N 1EA.
Tel: 020-7426 7000. Fax: 020-7426 7001
Web: www.lch.com

OMBUDSMAN SCHEMES

The Financial Ombudsman Service has been set up by the
Financial Services and Markets Act to provide consumers
with a free, independent service for resolving disputes
with financial firms. It brought together eight existing
complaints-handling schemes within the financial sector
including the Banking Ombudsman, the Insurance
Ombudsman, the Investment Ombudsman and the
Personal Investment Authority Ombudsman. It can make
binding awards up to £100,000.
The Financial Ombudsman Service can help with most
financial complaints about:
– Banking services
– Credit cards
– Endowment policies
– Financial and investment advice
– Insurance policies
– Investment and fund management
– Life assurance
– Mortgages
– Personal pension plans
– Saving plans and accounts
– Stocks and shares
– Unit trusts and income bonds

Complainants must first complain to the firm involved.
They do not have to accept the ombudsman's decision
and are free to go to court if they wish.
    The Pensions Ombudsman is appointed and operates
under the Pension Schemes Act 1993 as amended by the
Pensions Act 1995; he is responsible to Parliament. He
investigates and decides complaints and disputes
concerning occupational and personal pension schemes,
primarily alleged maladministration by the persons
responsible for managing pension schemes.

FINANCIAL OMBUDSMAN SERVICE, South Quay Plaza,
183 Marsh Wall, London, E14 9SR
Consumer Helpline: 0845-080 1800 Tel: 020-7964 1000
Fax: 020-7964 1001
Web: www.financial-ombudsman.org.uk
Email: enquiries@financial-ombudsman.org.uk
Chief Ombudsman: W. Merricks
Principal Ombudsmen: Banking and Loans: D. Thomas;
Insurance: T. Boorman; *Investment:* J. Whittles

THE PENSIONS OMBUDSMAN, 6th Floor, 11 Belgrave
Road, London SW1V 1RB. Tel: 020-7834 9144.
Pensions Ombudsman, D. Laverick

THE TAKEOVER PANEL

The Takeover Panel was set up in 1968 in response to concern about practices unfair to shareholders in take-over bids for public and certain private companies. Its principal objective is to ensure equality of treatment, and fair opportunity for all shareholders to consider on its merits an offer that would result in the change of control of a company. It is a non-statutory body that operates the City code on take-overs and mergers.

The chairman, deputy chairmen and three lay members of the panel are appointed by the Bank of England. The remainder are representatives of the banking, insurance, investment, pension fund and accountancy professional bodies and the CBI.

THE PANEL ON TAKEOVERS AND MERGERS, PO Box 226, The Stock Exchange Building, London, EC2P 2JX. Tel: 020-7382 9026. Web: www. takeoverpanel.org.uk
Chairman, Peter Scott, QC

NATIONAL SAVINGS AND INVESTMENTS

National Savings and Investments (formerly National Savings) is one of the largest savings organisations in the UK, and is a government department and executive agency of HM Treasury. Savings and investment products are offered to personal savers and investors and the money is used to manage the national debt more effectively. When people invest in National Savings and Investments they are lending money to the government which pays them interest in return.

INVESTMENT AND ORDINARY ACCOUNTS

Interest is earned at 0.6 per cent per year on each ordinary account for every complete calendar month in which the balance is £500 or more. The minimum deposit is £10; maximum balance £10,000 plus interest credited.

The investment account pays a higher rate of interest depending on the account balance (the current rate can be found at any post office). The minimum deposit is £20; maximum balance £100,000 plus interest credited.

Since April 1999 Individual Savings Accounts (ISAs) have been offered by National Savings and Investments. A cash mini ISA can be opened with £10. Interest is calculated daily on balances of over £1 and is free of tax. The same regulations apply as for ISAs offered by all companies.

PREMIUM BONDS

Premium Bonds are a government security which were first introduced in 1956. Premium Bonds enable savers to enter a regular draw for tax-free prizes, while retaining the right to get their money back. A sum equivalent to interest on each bond is put into a prize fund and distributed by monthly prize draws. (The rate of interest is 2.25 per cent per year from 1 June 2002.) The prizes are drawn by ERNIE (electronic random number indicator equipment) and are free of all UK income tax and capital gains tax.

Bonds are in units of £1, with a minimum purchase of £100; above this, purchases must be in multiples of £10, up to a maximum holding limit of £20,000 per person. The scheme offers a facility to reinvest prize wins automatically. Upon completion of an automatic prize reinvestment mandate, holders receive new bonds which are immediately eligible for future prize draws. Bonds can only be held in the name of an individual and not by organisations.

Bonds become eligible for prizes once they have been held for one clear calendar month following the month of purchase. Each £1 unit can win only one prize per draw, but it will be awarded the highest for which it is drawn. Bonds remain eligible for prizes until they are repaid. When a holder dies, bonds remain eligible for prizes up to and including the twelfth monthly draw after the month in which the holder dies.

Since the first prize draw in 1957, over 100 million prizes totalling £645 billion have been distributed.

INCOME BONDS

National Savings and Investments Income Bonds were introduced in 1982. They are suitable for those who want to receive regular monthly payments of interest while preserving the full cash value of their capital. The bonds are sold in multiples of £500. The minimum holding is £500 and the maximum £1,000,000 (sole or joint holding).

Interest is calculated on a day-to-day basis and paid monthly. Interest is taxable but is paid without deduction of tax at source. The bonds have a guaranteed life of ten years, but may be repaid at par before maturity on giving three months' notice. Repayment is also possible without giving notice but incurs a penalty. If the sole or sole surviving holder dies, however, no fixed period of notice is required and there is no loss of interest for repayment made within the first year.

PENSIONERS GUARANTEED INCOME BONDS

Pensioners Guaranteed Income Bonds were introduced in January 1994 and are designed for people aged 60 and over who wish to receive regular monthly payments with a rate of interest that is fixed for a five-year period whilst preserving the full cash value of their investment. A two-year fixed rate term bond was introduced in May 1999. In October 2000 a new one-year fixed rate term bond was also introduced.

The minimum limit for each purchase is £500. The maximum holding is £1,000,000 (sole or joint holding); within those limits bonds can be bought for any amount in pounds and pence. The rate of interest is fixed and guaranteed for the first one, two or five years, depending on the term invested in. Interest is taxable but is paid without deduction of tax at source.

Holders can apply for repayment (or part repayment of a bond subject to the minimum holding limits) by giving 60 days' notice (if repayment is before the fifth anniversary date). No interest is earned during the notice period. If repayment is requested within two weeks of any fifth anniversary of purchase, there is no formal period of notice. Repayment is possible without giving notice but a penalty is incurred. On the death of a holder or sole surviving investor in a joint holding, repayment will be made without notice. Interest will be paid in full up to the date of repayment.

CHILDREN'S BONUS BONDS

Children's Bonus Bonds were introduced in 1991. The latest issue, Issue 6, was introduced on 21 February 2003. They can be bought for any child under 16 and will go on growing in value until he or she is 21. The bonds are sold in multiples of £25. The minimum holding is £25. The maximum holding in Issue 6 is £1,000 per child. This is in addition to holdings of earlier issues of the bond (excluding interest and bonuses). Bonds for children under 16 must be held by a parent or guardian.

Children's Bonus Bonds (Issue 6) earn 3.35 AER (Annual Equivalent Rate) over five years. AER is based on what the interest return would be if interest was compounded on the initial deposit and paid annually. All returns are totally exempt from UK income tax. No interest is earned on bonds cashed in before the first anniversary of purchase. Bonuses are only payable if the bond is held until the next bonus date. Bonds over five years old continue to earn interest and bonuses until the holder is 21, when they should be cashed in. If bonds are not cashed in on the holder's 21st birthday, they earn no interest after that birthday.

FIXED RATE SAVINGS BOND

Fixed Rate Savings Bonds are lump sum investments that earn guaranteed rates of interest over set periods of time (one year, three years and five years). Interest, from which basic rate tax is deducted at source, can be paid out or reinvested into the bond monthly, annually or at the end of the term. Holders can also choose where the interest is paid.

CAPITAL BONDS

National Savings and Investments Capital Bonds were introduced in 1989. The latest series, Series 10, was introduced on 24 February 2003. Capital Bonds offer capital growth over five years with guaranteed returns at fixed rates. The interest is taxable each year (for those who pay income tax) but is not deducted at source. The minimum purchase is £100. There is a maximum holding limit of £250,000 from Series B onwards.

Capital Bonds will be repaid in full with all interest gained at the end of five years. No interest is earned on bonds repaid in the first year. Reinvestment or extension terms may also be available.

NATIONAL SAVINGS AND INVESTMENTS TREASURER'S ACCOUNT

The Treasurer's Account, introduced in September 1996, offers attractive rates and security to non-profit making organisations such as charities, friendly societies, clubs, etc. The minimum holding is £10,000 and the maximum is £2 million. Interest is paid at the rate of 2.60 per cent a year on holdings of £10,000 to £24,999, 2.80 per cent a year on holdings of £25,000 to £99,999, and 3.80 per cent a year on holdings of £100,000 and above.

NATIONAL SAVINGS AND INVESTMENTS CERTIFICATES

RECENT ISSUES

Interest, index-linked increase, bonus or other sum payable is free of UK income tax (including investment income surcharge) and capital gains tax.

From June 1982, savings certificates of the 7th to 43rd Issues have been extended on general extension rates as they reach the end of their existing extension periods. The percentage interest rate is determined by the Treasury and any change in this general extension rate will be applicable from the first of the month following its announcement. Under the system, a certificate earns interest for each complete period of three months beyond the expiry of the previous extension terms. Within each three-month period, interest is calculated separately for each month at the rate applicable from the beginning of that month. The interest for each month is one-twelfth of the annual rate (i.e. it does not vary with the number of days in the month) and is capitalised annually on the anniversary of the date of purchase. The current rate of interest under the general extension rate is given in leaflets available at post offices. Since October 2001, the holders of other Issues have had the option to reinvest or rollover.

National Savings and Investments can be contacted on 0845-964 500 or by email at customerenquiries@nsandi.com Visit the National Savings and Investments website at www.nsandi.com

THE NATIONAL DEBT

Net central government borrowing each year represents an addition to the National Debt. At the end of March 2002 the National Debt amounted to some £434,544 million of which about £3,697 million was in currencies other than sterling. Of the £430,847 million sterling debt, £278,798 million consisted of gilt-edged stock. Of this, 33 per cent had a maturity of up to five years, 38 per cent a maturity of over five years and up to 15 years, and 29 per cent a maturity of over 15 years or undated. The remaining sterling debt was made up mainly of national savings (£59,963 million), certificates of tax deposits, Treasury bills, and Ways and Means advances (very short-term internal government borrowing).

Sizeable trust funds have been established over the past 50 years for the purpose of reducing the National Debt. The National Fund was established in 1927 with an original gift of £499,878. At 5 April 2001 it was valued at £195,273,150; it is administered by Baring Trust Co. Ltd. The Elsie Mackay Fund was established in 1929 with an original gift of £527,809 to run for 45–50 years. It was wound up in 1979, when it was valued at £4,902,864. The John Buchanan Fund was established in 1932 with gifts totalling £36,702 to run for 50 years. It was wound up in 1982, when it was valued at £204,138.

On 1 July 2002 the National Debt Office (part of the National Investment and Loans Office) was integrated with the UK Debt Management Office. The National Investment and Loans Office ceased to exist from 1 July 2002.

THE LONDON STOCK EXCHANGE

The London Stock Exchange serves the needs of industry and investors by providing facilities for raising capital and a central market-place for securities trading. This market-place covers government stocks (called gilts), UK and overseas company shares (called equities and fixed interest stocks), and other instruments such as covered warrants and Exchange Traded Funds (EFTs).

PRIMARY MARKETS

The Exchange enables companies to raise capital for development and growth through the issue of securities. For a company entering the market for the first time there is a choice of Exchange markets, depending upon the size, history and requirements of the company. The first is the Main Market. A company's securities are admitted to the Official List by the UK Listing Authority (UKLA), a division of the Financial Services Authority, and also admitted to trading by the Exchange.

The Alternative Investment Market (AIM) was established in June 1995. It enables small, young and growing companies to raise capital, widen their investor base and have their shares traded on a regulated market without the expense of a full Exchange listing. Many companies use AIM as a stepping-stone to a full listing.

Once admitted to the AIM, all companies are obliged to keep their shareholders informed of their progress, making announcements of a price-sensitive nature through a Primary Information Provider.

At the end of 2002 there were 1,701 UK companies listed on the London Stock Exchange; their equity capital had a total market value of £1,148 billion. In addition, 419 international companies were listed, with a total equity market value of £1,902 billion. By the end of 2002 AIM had attracted 704 companies, with a total capitalisation of £103 billion.

UK equity turnover in 2002 was £1,815,034 million with an average 149,000 bargains a day. International equity turnover in 2002 totalled £2,780,317 million.

BIG BANG

During 1986 the London Stock Exchange went through the greatest period of change in its 200-year history. In March 1986 it opened its doors for the first time to overseas and corporate membership of the Exchange, allowing banks, insurance companies and overseas securities houses to become members of the Exchange and to buy existing member firms. On 27 October 1986, three major reforms took place, changes which became known as 'Big Bang':

- the abolition of scales of minimum commissions, allowing clients to negotiate freely with their brokers about the charge for their services
- the abolition of the separation of member firms into brokers and jobbers: firms are now broker/dealers, able to act as agents on behalf of clients; to act as principals buying and selling shares for their own account; and to become registered market makers, making continuous buying and selling prices in specific securities

- the introduction of the Stock Exchange Automated Quotations (SEAQ) system

Since the introduction of SEAQ in 1986, dealing in stocks and shares has taken place by telephone in the firms' own dealing rooms, rather than face to face on the floor of the Exchange. The Stock Exchange Electronic Trading Service (SETS), launched in 1997, introduced order-driven trading in which deals are executed electronically on an electronic order book. SETS runs alongside SEAQ and allows remote access to the Exchange. The new systems also provide increased investor protection. All deals taking place via the Exchange systems are recorded on a database which can be used to resolve disputes or to carry out investigations.

Firms Trading on the London Stock Exchange buy and sell shares on behalf of the public, as well as institutions such as pension funds or insurance companies. In return for transacting the deal, the broker will charge a commission, which is usually based upon the value of the transaction. The market makers, or wholesalers, in each security do not charge a commission for their services, but will quote the broker two prices, a price at which they will buy and a price at which they will sell. It is the middle of these two prices which is published in lists of share prices in newspapers.

REGULATION

The Financial Services Authority (FSA) has overall responsibility for regulating the UK's financial industry under the provisions of the Financial Services Act 1986. This Act requires investment businesses to be authorised and regulated by a self-regulating organisation (SRO) and compels business to be conducted through a recognised investment exchange (RIE). The London Stock Exchange is an RIE, regulating three main markets: UK equities, international equities and gilts.

DEMUTUALISATION AND LISTING

On 15 March 2000, the 298 members voted to become shareholders in a demutualised London Stock Exchange, making possible the further commercialisation of the company.

At the end of May 2001 the exchange announced its intention to list on its own main market. The exchange listed on 20 July following an annual general meeting on 19 July 2001. The full listing is intended to enable the Exchange to exploit business opportunities with greater flexibility.

LONDON STOCK EXCHANGE, Old Broad Street, London EC2N 1HP. Tel: 020-7797 1000
Web: www.londonstockexchange.com
Non-Executive Chairman, C. Gibson-Smith
Chief Executive, C. Furse
Executive Directors, M. Wheatley, J. Howell
Non-Executive Directors, G. Allen, CBE;
Baroness Cohen; O. Fanjul; M. Marks;
P. Meinertzhagen; I. Salter; N. Stapleton; R. Webb, QC

INSURANCE

AUTHORISATION AND REGULATION OF INSURANCE COMPANIES

On 1 December 2001 the Financial Services Authority (FSA) assumed its powers under the Financial Services and Markets Act 2000. This saw the FSA take over full responsibility for a wide range of issues including the authorisation of insurance companies operating in the UK; the regulation of investment related insurance products and the preparations for a statutory regulation regime for general insurance products.

FINANCIAL SERVICES AUTHORITY 25 The North Colonnade, London E14 5HS Tel: 020-7676 1000 Fax: 020-7676 1099 Web: www.fsa.gov.uk

AUTHORISATION
As far as authorisation is concerned, the FSA's role is to ensure that firms to which it grants authorisation satisfy the necessary financial criteria, that the senior managers of the company are 'fit and proper persons' and that unauthorised firms are not permitted to trade. This part of the FSA's role was previously undertaken by HM Treasury under the Insurance Companies Act 1982 which was repealed when the Financial Services and Markets Act came fully into force. At the end of 2002 there were around 1,000 insurance companies and friendly societies with authorisation from the FSA to transact one or more classes of insurance business in the UK. However, the single European insurance market, established in 1994, gave insurers authorised in the European Union automatic UK authorisation without further formality. This means a potential market of over 5,000 insurance companies.

REGULATION
At present, only investment-related life insurance contracts are statutorily regulated. This is achieved by the formulation (after consultation) by the FSA of rules and guidance for regulated organisations. The FSA is also responsible for consumer education and the reduction of financial crime, particularly money laundering.

COMPLAINTS

Private policyholders with a complaint against their financial services provider must firstly take the matter to the highest level within the company. Thereafter, if it remains unresolved, they can refer their problem, free of charge, to the Financial Services Ombudsman who examines the facts of a complaint and delivers a decision which is binding on the insurer (but not the policy holder). Small businesses with a turnover of up to £1 million are able to access the scheme. The Financial Ombudsman Service also covers other areas of the financial services industry including banks, building societies and investment firms.

FINANCIAL SERVICES OMBUDSMAN SERVICE South Quay Plaza, 183 Marsh Wall, London E14 9SR. Tel 020-7964 1000 Fax: 020-7964 1002 Web: www.financial-ombudsman.org.uk *Ombudsman:* Walter Merricks

ASSOCIATION OF BRITISH INSURERS

Over 97 per cent of the world-wide business of UK insurance companies is transacted by the 400 members of the Association of British Insurers (ABI). The ABI is a trade association which protects and promotes the interests of life and general insurers. Only insurers authorised in the UK or EU are eligible for membership. Brokers and intermediaries may not join the ABI but there are a number of trade associations representing different sectors of the intermediary market.

ASSOCIATION OF BRITISH INSURERS (ABI) 51 Gresham Street, London EC2V 7HQ Web: www.abi.org.uk *Chairman:* Richard Harvey *Director General:* Mary Francis

GENERAL INSURANCE STANDARDS COUNCIL

The General Insurance Standards Council (GISC) is a non-statutory regulatory organisation for the general insurance industry. It was initially intended that the GISC would regulate the sales, advisory and service standards of insurers, intermediaries and brokers. However, in December 2001 the Treasury announced that the selling of general insurance would be regulated by the FSA. The need for this move was not based on any perceived inadequacy in the GISC but the requirements of the EC Intermediaries Directive that required statutory regulation which the GISC could not achieve. No date has been fixed for the transfer of responsibilities to FSA but this is not expected to be before early 2005.

GENERAL INSURANCE STANDARDS COUNCIL 110 Cannon Street, London EC4N 6EU Web: www.gisc.co.uk

BALANCE OF PAYMENTS

The insurance industry contributes 1.4 per cent to the UK's Gross Domestic Product (GDP). In 2001 insurance companies generated net exports of £3.8 billion.

TAKE-OVERS AND MERGERS

Falling stock markets and poor underwriting results made insurance companies unattractive targets in 2002. The result was a continuation of the quiet period for take-overs and mergers. One life insurance CEO summed up the situation by saying that takeovers and mergers were "just not on the agenda".

GENERAL INSURANCE

The echoes of 11 September 2001 continued to reverberate around the insurance world in 2002. A more accurate estimate of $50 billion was placed on the claims arising from the disaster and in July 2002 it was announced that the UK scheme for offering cover for terrorist damage was being extended to cover 'all risks'. This would have the effect of including cover for damage caused by nuclear attack, impact by aircraft and the use of chemical and biological weapons by terrorists. These were not previously thought necessary for inclusion.

Liability insurance was also topical as a hardening general insurance market made price rises for employers' liability and the availability of any cover difficult for some businesses. This gave rise to an announcement of both a Government review of the legislation that makes employers' liability compulsory and an investigation into the availability of cover by the Office of Fair Trading.

In June 2002, the House of Lords ruled that people who had contracted the lung disease mesothelioma following exposure to several sources and where it could not be established when exposure first took place, were entitled to receive compensation. This overturned a lower court decision which might have allowed insurers to avoid paying claims.

The perennial problem of insurance fraud also continued throughout the year, with a revised estimate of the cost of fraudulent claims being estimated at £1 billion per year despite numerous campaigns, research and warnings.

Work also continued throughout the year in preparation for the statutory regime for the regulation of general insurance. This is expected to come into force in early 2005 and the FSA has begun the consultation and negotiation process over its proposals concerning the conduct of business rules.

Against a background of further rises in weather damage claims (by 34 per cent to £1,251 million) insurers maintained pressure on the government to improve flood defences. Insurers maintain that cover is available to all but a relatively small number of homeowners but in some cases, although cover may be available, it comes at a very high price.

For most other types of general insurance claims the amount paid also continued to rise in 2002. Commercial theft claims rose by 25 per cent over the previous year and commercial fire claims were at their highest level since records began. The exception to the trend was the figure for domestic subsidence claims which fell to £213 million and has steadily fallen since 1997. Inevitably, with claims rising and the market maintaining its tough stance following 11 September 2001, premiums are likely to continue to rise.

LONDON INSURANCE MARKET

The London Insurance Market is a unique wholesale marketplace and a distinct, separate sector of the UK insurance and reinsurance industry. It is the world's leading market for internationally traded insurance and reinsurance, its business comprising mainly overseas non-life large and high-exposure risks. The market is centred on the City of London, which provides the required financial, banking, legal and other support services. Currently there are 71 Lloyd's syndicates, 70 insurance companies and 32 Protection and Indemnity Clubs operating in the market. In 2001 the market had a written gross premium income of around £20,000 million. Around 140 Lloyd's brokers service the market.

The trade association for the international insurers and reinsurers writing primarily non-marine insurance and all classes of reinsurance business in the London Market is the International Underwriting Association (IUA).

INTERNATIONAL UNDERWRITING ASSOCIATION

London Underwriting Centre, 3 Mincing Lane, London EC3R 7DD. Web: www.iua.co.uk

BRITISH INSURANCE COMPANIES

The following insurance company figures refer to members and certain non-members of the ABI.

CLAIMS STATISTICS

	1998 £m	1999 £m	2000 £m	2001 £m	2002 £m
Theft	747	708	740	728	773
Fire	884	866	855	1,049	1,108
Weather	1,002	861	1,298	932	1,251
Domestic Subsidence	437	364	350	265	213
Business Interruption	236	123	202	97	269
Total	3,306	2,922	3,445	3,071	3,614

WORLD-WIDE GENERAL BUSINESS TRADING RESULT

	2000 £m	2001 £m
Net Written Premiums	38,265	39,387
Underwriting profit (loss) for one year account business	(4,182)	(2,889)
Marine, Aviation, Transport	(368)	(136)
Other	(477)	(414)
Total Underwriting Result	(5,028)	(3,439)
Net investment income	5,352	4,733
Overall trading profit	324	1,294
Profit as % of premium income	0.8%	3.3%

LLOYD'S OF LONDON

Lloyd's of London is an international market for almost all types of general insurance. Lloyd's currently has a capacity to accept insurance premiums of over £14,000 million. Much of this business comes from outside Great Britain and makes a valuable contribution to the balance of payments.

A policy is underwritten at Lloyd's by a mixture of private and corporate members, corporate members having been admitted for the first time in 1992. Specialist underwriters accept insurance risks at Lloyd's on behalf of members (referred to as 'Names') grouped in syndicates. There are currently 72 syndicates of varying sizes, each managed by an underwriting agent approved by the Council of Lloyd's.

Individual members are still in the majority at Lloyd's with a total of 2,466 individuals as opposed to 837 corporate members. In 2002 the market capacity of the corporate sector was £11,473 while individuals represented £1,800 million of capacity.

Lloyd's is incorporated by an Act of Parliament (Lloyd's Acts 1971 onwards) and is governed by a Council comprising six working and six external members together with six nominated members whose appointment is confirmed by the Governor of the Bank of England. Market management has always been handled by a Market Board of 18 members, with regulation being supervised by a Regulatory Board of 15 members, but at the end of 2002 Lloyd's Members voted at an Extraordinary General Meeting to accept a proposal from the Chairman's Strategy Group (CSG) to replace the Market and Regulatory Boards with a new Lloyd's Franchise Board.

The Corporation is a non-profit making body chiefly financed by its members' subscriptions. It provides the premises, administrative staff and services enabling

Lloyd's underwriting syndicates to conduct their business. It does not, however, assume corporate liability for the risks accepted by its members. Individual members are responsible to the full extent of their personal means for their underwriting affairs.

At present, Lloyd's syndicates have no direct contact with the public. All business is transacted through insurance brokers accredited by the Corporation of Lloyd's. In addition, non-Lloyd's brokers in the UK, when guaranteed by Lloyd's brokers, are able to deal directly with Lloyd's motor syndicates, a facility which has made the Lloyd's market more accessible to the insuring public.

The FSA has ultimate responsibility for the regulation of the Lloyd's market. However, in situations where Lloyd's internal regulatory and compensation arrangements are more far-reaching, as for example with the Lloyd's Central Fund, which safeguards claim payments to policyholders, the regulatory role is delegated to the Council of Lloyd's.

Lloyd's also provides the most comprehensive shipping intelligence service in the world. The shipping and other information received from Lloyd's agents, shipowners, news agencies and other sources throughout the world is collated and distributed to the media as well as to the maritime and commercial sectors in general. *Lloyd's List* is London's oldest daily newspaper and contains news of general commercial interest as well as shipping information. *Lloyd's Shipping Index*, also published daily, lists some 25,000 ocean-going vessels in alphabetical order and gives the latest known report of each.

DEVELOPMENTS IN 2002

Historically, Lloyd's has always published its accounts on a three-year basis. However, 2002 saw a change to this arrangement with the published figures being on a yearly basis. This makes it considerably easier to compare the Lloyd's results with those of the insurance company market which has always reported on a yearly basis.

Against a background of poor investment returns and losses in the insurance company market, the result for 2002 is all the more remarkable. The market recorded a profit of £834 million which must have been very pleasing to Lloyd's not least because of the doom-laden forecasts from some pundits which greeted the record £3.1 billion loss for 2001. This figure did of course include Lloyd's share of the 11 September claims – the largest share of the gross loss of any insurer. During 2002 the estimate for the cost to Lloyd's of claims arising from this event rose from £1,300 million to £2,000 million.

In common with the general insurance companies Lloyd's is predicting further premium rises but it is not clear how long the current 'hard' market can be maintained.

LLOYD'S OF LONDON One Lime Street, London EC3M 7HA. Tel: 020-7327 1000 Web: www.lloydsoflondon.co.uk
Chairman: Peter Levene
Chief Executive: Nick Prettejohn

LLOYD'S MEMBERSHIP

	2000	2001	2002
Individual	3,296	2,848	2,466
Corporate	853	895	837

TOTAL MARKET CAPACITY

	2000 £m	2001 £m	2002 £m
Individual	2,003	1,800	1,766
Corporate	8,062	9,258	11,473
Total	10,065	11,058	13,239

LLOYD'S GLOBAL ACCOUNTS

	1999 and prior years of account £m	2000 pure year result £m
Gross premiums written (net of brokerage)	9,055	9,524
Outward reinsurance premiums	3,270	3,338
Net premiums	5,785	6,186
Reinsurance to close premiums received from earlier years of account	5,604	—
Amounts retained to meet all known and unknown outstanding liabilities brought forward	680	—
	12,069	6,186
Gross claims paid	9,909	6,335
Reinsurers' share	3,379	1,991
Net claims	6,170	4,344
Reinsurance premiums paid to close the year of account	5,651	2,446
Amounts retained to meet all known and unknown outstanding liabilities carried forward	1,977	1,190
	13,798	7,980
Underwriting result	(1,729)	(1,877)
Profit/(loss) on exchange	(25)	(15)
Syndicate operating expenses	(551)	(575)
Balance on technical account	(2,305)	(2,467)
Investment income	518	484
Investment expenses and charges	(9)	(10)
Investment gains less losses	78	66
Result before personal expenses	(1,718)	(1,927)
Personal expenses	(234)	(276)
Result after personal expenses	(1,952)	(2,203)

NET PREMIUM INCOME BY TERRITORY 2001

	UK £m	Overseas £m
Motor	8,886	4,742
Non-Motor	15,048	7,520
Marine, Aviation and Transport	461	348
Reinsurance	1,249	331
Total General Business	25,644	12,941
Ordinary long-term	92,473	17,069
Industrial long-term	605	—
Total Long-term Business	93,078	17,069

WORLD-WIDE GENERAL BUSINESS UNDERWRITING RESULT

	2000			2001		
	UK	Overseas	Total	UK	Overseas	Total
Motor						
Premiums: £m	7,896	5,400	13,296	8,886	4,742	13,628
Profit (loss): £m	(921)	(699)	1,620	(123)	(307)	(430)
% of premiums	11.7	12.9	12.2	1.4	6.5	3.2
Non-motor						
Premiums: £m	13,517	8,331	21,848	15,048	7,520	22,568
Profit (loss): £m	(886)	(1,304)	(2,190)	(636)	(1,148)	(1,784)
% of premiums	6.6	15.7	10	4.2	15.3	8

LLOYD'S PREMIUM INCOME 2001 BY CATEGORY

	MAT	Home Foreign	Reinsurance	Accident & Health	Motor	Property	Liability	Pecuniary Loss	Total
	£m	£m	£m	£m	£m	£m	£m	£m	£m
Gross Premiums	2,853	4,696	2,896	181	1,435	552	756	185	13,554
Net Premiums	2,252	4,141	1,949	162	1,329	439	600	161	10,033

LIFE AND LONG-TERM INSURANCE AND PENSIONS

'Challenging' was the term used by insurers to describe their business in 2002. Firstly, there were a number of reviews by the regulators into how their business was conducted. One of these looked at the future of polarisation (the way the current legislation insists that intermediaries can only sell the products of either one insurer or the whole market); another examined the need to reform the pension annuities system, while a further investigation was conducted into the problems facing low-cost endowment policyholders who need to buy more insurance if their policy is to pay off their mortgage at the end of the term. Developments on the latter saw a further batch of over 10 million letters being sent to policyholders in May 2002 giving their endowment policy a health check. It's thought that around 25 per cent of these letters warned there was a very real chance of a shortfall.

The middle of the year saw the publication of two major reports into different aspects of savings. Firstly Ron Sandler, former Chief Executive of Lloyd's, produced his report, commissioned by the Treasury. This called for simpler products and light-touch regulation as a way of encouraging everyone to save more. The Sandler Report was followed, in the same week, by the Pickering Report which took up the same theme when it called for simpler and more easily understood pension contracts. Both reports were largely welcomed by the life and pensions industry but it is difficult to see how the proposals in either report can actually have a marked effect on the savings gap (estimated by the ABI to be £29 billion) without the Government offering savers or employers financial incentives to get us all to save more.

It was hoped that the Stakeholder Pension launched in September 2001 would be one element that might help to close the savings gap. However, after a strong start, sales of stakeholder pensions began to falter as the year progressed with sales falling to 50,000 per month by the autumn and only 33,000 per month by the end of the year.

Against a background of these problems and low interest rates, the new business figures proved to be less depressing than might have been expected. The industry recorded a small increase overall of 1 per cent to £11.1 billion (up from £11 billion in 2001).

WORLD-WIDE LONG-TERM PREMIUM INCOME 1997–2001

	1997	1998	1999	2000	2001
UK Life Insurance					
Regular Premium	12,606	12,567	13,085	13,041	12,033
Single Premium	14,022	17,539	23,584	25,931	25,233
Total	26,629	30,106	36,670	38,971	37,266
Personal Pensions					
Regular Premium	6,961	7,375	8,042	8,046	7,637
Single Premium	9,889	9,788	10,874	13,442	17,544
Total	16,849	17,164	18,916	21,488	25,181
Occupational Pensions					
Regular Premium	4,557	4,601	4,604	4,143	3,563
Single Premium	11,215	18,228	26,371	49,798	24,981
Total	15,773	22,829	30,975	53,941	28,544
Other (e.g. Income protection, Annuities)	1,085	1,135	1,008	1,438	1,482
Total UK Premium Income	60,335	71,234	87,569	115,838	92,473
Overseas Premium Income					
Regular Premium	4,966	4,872	5,118	6,575	6,902
Single Premium	9,471	10,113	12,943	13,893	17,069
Total	14,438	14,985	18,061	20,468	23,970
Total World-wide Premium Income	75,825	87,171	106,488	137,060	117,083

PAYMENTS TO POLICYHOLDERS

	2000 £m	2001 £m
Payments to UK policyholders	82,600	88,300
Payments to overseas policyholders	12,900	12,900
Total	95,500	101,200

PRIVATE MEDICAL INSURANCE 1997–2001

	1997	1998	1999	2000	2001
Number of policyholders (000s)					
Corporate	1,954	2,043	2,207	2,325	2,506
Personal	1,263	1,209	1,193	1,145	1,097
Total	3,217	3,251	3,400	3,470	3,603
Number of people covered (000s)					
Corporate	3,979	4,157	4,237	4,517	4,704
Personal	2,144	1,984	1,892	1,949	1,829
Total	6,123	6,141	6,179	6,580	6,534
Gross Earned Premiums, £m					
Corporate	881	966	1,027	1,092	1,253
Personal	996	1,004	1,039	1,146	1,221
Total	1,877	1,970	2,066	2,239	2,473
Gross Claims Incurred, £m	1,503	1,632	1,708	1,788	1,919

INVESTMENTS OF INSURANCE COMPANIES 2001

Investment of funds	Long-term business £m	General business £m
Index-linked British Government securities	21,824	1,419
Non-index-linked British Government securities	93,941	10,774
Other UK public sector debt securities	12,067	469
Overseas government, provincial and municipal securities	36,604	10,404
Debentures, loan shares, preference and guaranteed stocks and shares		
UK	105,914	6,678
Overseas	52,987	9,286
Ordinary stocks and shares		
UK	296,066	11,064
Overseas	124,552	5,278
Unit trusts		
Equities	61,822	1,402
Fixed interest	4,348	255
Loans secured on property	15,566	1,166
Real property and ground rents	56,125	3,233
Other invested assets	91,603	24,884
Total invested assets	973,418	86,312
Net investment income	37,477	4,733

NEW BUSINESS

	New Individual Regular Premiums				New Individual Single Premiums					Group Business	
	Life	Pensions	Collective Investment Schemes	Total Regular	Life	Pensions	Pension Annuities & Income Drawdown	Collective Investment Schemes	Total Single	Regular	Single
1998	1,603	1,611	388	3,602	17,853	5,557	7,563	7,170	38,143	965	3,186
1999	1,683	1,474	570	3,728	23,505	6,999	7,569	8,587	46,660	978	4,723
2000	1,334	1,593	626	3,553	25,109	7,329	7,911	8,718	49,067	940	4,250
2001	1,221	2,417	473	4,112	25,129	8,766	8,545	7,582	50,022	1,139	7,273
2002	1,338	2,243	417	3,998	23,923	11,268	9,543	7,287	52,022	1,073	8,184

MUTUAL SOCIETIES

The term 'mutual societies' covers member-based organisations registered under the Building Societies Acts, the Friendly Societies Acts and the Industrial and Provident Societies Acts, many of which are familiar long-established names.

Until 30 November 2001 the various statutory responsibilities for the supervision and registration of mutual societies rested with the Chief Registrar of Friendly Societies (CR), the Building Societies Commission (BSC) and the Friendly Societies Commission (FSC). The office of CR and the government department of the Registry of Friendly Societies (RFS), from which the BSC and FSC were more recently supported, dated back to 1875. However, the existence in one form or another of an office for the registration of friendly societies and a Registrar dated back to 1829, when its function was initially seen as bringing regulation and social control over a potentially revolutionary popular movement.

In 1997 the Government announced the creation of a single financial regulatory authority for the UK, the Financial Services Authority (FSA). The FSA initially supported the functions of the CR, BSC and FSC under contract. On the full entry into force of the Financial Services and Markets Act 2000 on 1 December 2001, the responsibilities and powers of the BSC, FSC and CR passed to the FSA. Information on the numbers of mutual societies with additions to and removals from the register in the year to 30 November 2002 are given in the following table:

	On register at beginning of year	Added during year	Removed during year	On register at end of year
Friendly Societies Acts				
Friendly societies				
Orders	13	–	–	13
Collecting societies	11	–	–	11
Other centralised societies	217	–	9	208
Total	241	–	9	232
Others				
Branches of orders	612	1	7	606
Benevolent societies	55	–	–	55
Working men's clubs	1,842	–	30	1,812
Specially authorised societies	101	–	3	98
Total	2,610	1	40	2,570
Industrial and Provident Societies Acts				
Housing	2,941	44	70	2,915
Social and Recreation	3,269	47	34	3,282
Agricultural	807	2	50	759
General service	1,021	92	28	1,085
Retail, wholesale and productive	198	12	7	203
Fishing	68	–	–	68
Credit Unions	697	29	39	687
Total	9,001	226	228	8,999
Building Societies Act				
Building Societies	66	–	1	65

FRIENDLY SOCIETIES IN BRITAIN

Four different classes of society are registered under the Friendly Societies Act 1974. These are friendly societies, benevolent societies, working men's clubs and specially authorised societies. Friendly societies are voluntary mutual organisations, where the main purposes are assisting members during sickness, unemployment or retirement, and the provision of life assurance. Many of the older traditional societies complement their business activities by social activity and a general care for individual members in ways normally outside the scope of a purely commercial organisation. There are three main categories of friendly societies: societies with separately registered branches, commonly called orders; centralised societies, which conduct business directly with members (having no separately registered branches); and collecting societies which have traditionally conducted home service assurance. Collecting societies benefit from a number of deregulatory measures included in the Financial Services and Markets Act 2000 involving relaxation for the future administration of existing contracts and by the removal of special requirements, in the industrial assurance legislation, concerning the selling of future contracts. Such business is subject to the general conduct of business rules governing the marketing and selling of investment products.

The Friendly Societies Act 1992 created a new legislative framework for friendly societies, enabling them to provide a wider range of services to their members and allowing them to compete on more equal terms with other financial institutions. At the same time it provided for more flexible prudential supervision to safeguard members of societies.

The Act enabled friendly societies to incorporate and establish subsidiaries to provide various financial and other services to their members and the public. The activities which subsidiaries are able to conduct include those to establish and manage unit trust schemes and personal equity plans; to arrange for the provision of credit, whether as agents or providers; to carry on long-term or general insurance business; to provide insurance intermediary services; to provide fund management services for trustees of pension funds; to administer estates and execute trusts of wills; and to establish and manage sheltered housing, residential homes for the elderly, hospitals and nursing homes.

The Act established a new framework to oversee friendly societies, including a Friendly Societies Commission, now superseded by the FSA, whose principal functions are to regulate the activities of friendly societies, promote their financial stability and protect members' funds. All friendly societies carrying on insurance or non-insurance business require authorisation by the FSA, which has a broad range of prudential powers.

At 31 December 2001 there were 37 'life directive' societies, i.e. those subject to the requirements of EU Life Insurance Directives, and five 'incorporated' societies which were transacting long-term insurance business but not subject to the Directives. These 42 societies accounted for over 95 per cent of the total funds of the movement at 31 December 2001. Of the remaining 194 societies on the register, representing five per cent of the movement, almost 70 per cent were not authorised to accept new business thought they continued to have liabilities to meet.

LIFE DIRECTIVE AND INCORPORATED SOCIETIES

	2000	2001
No. of Societies	43	42
Membership (000s)	5,512	4,936
Contribution income (£000s)	1,219, 663	1,285,166
Investment income (£000s)	255,772	45,130
Benefits paid (£000s)	1,201,628	1,252,807
Management expenses (£000s)	327,864	235,895
Total assets	15,019,152	14,285,338

No new friendly societies may now be registered under the 1974 Act. Benevolent societies are established for any charitable or benevolent purpose, to provide the same type of benefits as would be permissible for a friendly society, but in contrast the benefits must be for persons who are not members instead of, or in addition to, members. Working men's clubs provide social and recreational facilities for members. Specially authorised societies are registered for any purpose authorised by the Treasury as a purpose to which some or all of the provisions of the 1974 Act ought to be extended. Examples are societies for the promotion of science, literature and the fine arts, or to enable members to pursue an interest in sports and games.

INDUSTRIAL AND PROVIDENT SOCIETIES IN BRITAIN

The Industrial and Provident Societies Act 1965 provides for the registration of societies and lays down the broad framework within which they must operate. Internal relations of societies are governed by their registered rules. Registration under the Act confers upon a society corporate status by its registered name with perpetual succession and a common seal, and limited liability. A society qualifies for registration if it is carrying on an industry, business or trade, and it satisfies the FSA either (a) that it is a bona fide co-operative society, or (b) that in view of the fact that its business is being, or is intended to be, conducted for the benefit of the community, there are special reasons why it should be registered under the Act rather than as a company under the Companies Act.

The Credit Unions Act 1979 added a new class of society registrable under the 1965 Act. It also made provision for the supervision of these savings and loan bodies. Unlike other classes, where the role of the FSA remains solely that of a registration authority, for Credit Unions (CUs) it became also the financial supervisor. On 2 July 2002 a new system of regulation by the FSA for all CUs came into effect. The key features of the new regulatory regime for CUs were:

– to meet a basic test of solvency (with additional capital requirements for the larger CUs)
– to maintain a minimum liquidity ratio
– to meet the standard in FSA's rules for approved persons
– to operate an effective complaints scheme with access to the Financial Ombudsman
– to participate in the Financial Services Compensation Scheme providing members with deposit protection for the first time

New legislation for industrial and provident societies, the Industrial and Provident Societies Act 2002, came into force in September 2002. It introduced two measures. The first brought industrial and provident societies into line with building societies on voting thresholds for conversion to company status. A resolution to convert would need to secure a 75 per cent majority on a minimum vote of 50 per cent of the membership to be successful. The second measure enabled the legislation to be amended more easily to bring it into line with company law.

Comparative figures for 2001 show that the housing sector remained the largest in terms of asset holdings at £30,724 million, followed by the general service sector at £25,409 million. Registration statistics for the year to November 2002 show that the clubs sector remained largest in terms of numbers of societies with 3,269 clubs on the register at the beginning of the year, increasing to 3,282 by the end. The total number of societies (excluding credit unions) showed a net increase from 8,304 to 8,312 in the year to 30 November 2002.

Total membership in the credit union sector continued to grow with 366,000 members at the end of 2001 compared to 325,000 a year earlier. However, in 2001 there were only 23 new credit unions registered – the lowest number since 1987 – and 18 credit unions closed. In 2002 the total number of credit unions reduced from 698 to 686 following 30 new registrations and 42 closures, 16 of which were due to mergers.

The principal statistics for all classes of society are given below. In this case, the figures relate to the end of 2001 except for the agriculture sector which are given as at the end of 2000.

	No. of societies	No. of members 000s	Funds of members £000s	Total assets £000s
Retail	133	4,558	1,904,469	3,233,109
Wholesale productive	65	45	858,925	2,573,656
Agricultural	817	1,101	229,784	601,400
Fishing	68	3	7,422	15,814
Clubs	3,205	1,828	358,202	511,302
General service	1,108	605	2,193,797	25,409,438
Housing	2,865	434	9,078,603	30,724,286
Credit unions	698	366	248,674	263,404

BUILDING SOCIETIES IN THE UK

The Building Societies Act 1997, which received royal assent on 21 March 1997, made substantive amendments to, but did not replace, the Building Societies Act 1986. It liberalised the statutory regime for building societies to enable them to compete on more level terms with other financial institutions without having to forego their mutual status.

The Building Societies Act 1986 gave building societies a completely new legal framework for the first time since the initial comprehensive building society legislation in 1874. The 1986 Act set out detailed provisions in relation to:

- the constitution of building societies
- building societies' powers in relation to raising funds, advances, loans, other assets and the provision of services
- the powers of control of the Building Societies Commission (now superseded by the FSA)
- protection of investors, and complaints and disputes
- management of building societies, accounts and audit
- mergers and transfers of business

The 1986 Act was prescriptive in respect of building societies' powers and the way in which they were exercised. However, it gave numerous powers to the Building Societies Commission and/or the Treasury to make statutory instruments which, subject to parliamentary approval, can amend, extend and supplement the provisions of the Act. Since it came into force on 1 January 1987 the Act had been amended and extended considerably, especially in respect of building societies' powers.

The main purposes of the Building Societies Act 1997 are:

- remove the prescriptive powers' regime relating to building societies and to replace it with a permissive regime with appropriately revised balance-sheet 'nature limits', thus increasing the commercial freedom of societies and allowing increased competition and wider choice for customers
- enhance the powers of control of the Building Societies Commission (now superseded by the FSA)
- introduce a package of measures to enhance the accountability of building societies' boards to their members
- make changes to the provisions relating to the transfer of a building society's business to a company

The Act came fully into force on 21 October 1997. Under it a building society may pursue any activities set out in its memorandum, subject only to:

- principal purpose: its purpose or principal purpose must be that of making loans which are secured on residential properties and are funded substantially by its members
- lending limit: at least 75 per cent of its business assets must be loans fully secured on residential property
- funding limit: at least 50 per cent of its funds must be raised in the form of shares held by individual members
- restrictions: subject to certain exceptions, it must not act as a market maker in securities, commodities or currencies; trade in commodities or currencies; enter into transactions involving derivatives, except in relation to hedging; nor create a floating charge over its assets
- prudential: it must comply with the criteria of prudential management

All authorised building societies, after making the necessary changes to their memoranda and rules, are now operating under the more liberal statutory regime set out in the 1997 Act.

OMBUDSMAN SCHEME

Complaints about the actions of building societies may be resolved through societies' own internal complaints procedures. All authorised building societies are, in addition, members of the Building Societies Ombudsman scheme which provides an independent service to consider and determine complaints which are within its remit. The Financial Services and Markets Act 2000 brings together the Building Societies Ombudsman and seven others including the Banking Ombudsman and the Insurance Ombudsman, in a single Financial Ombudsman Service. This new complaints-handling organisation provides consumers with a free, informal and independent service for resolving disputes with most providers of financial products and services.

From 1 April 2000 this new body provided a complaints handling service on behalf of each of the existing schemes. On 1 December 2001 the Financial Ombudsman Service received powers in its own right as the new legislation was brought into force. Complainants may contact the Service at South Quay Plaza, 183 Marsh Wall, London E14 9SR. Tel: 020-8964 1000.

Statistics for building society service activity, liabilities and assets for the five years 1998–2002 are set out in the following tables:

BUILDING SOCIETIES 1998–2002
SERVICE ACTIVITY

			Estate	Staff					Advances During Year	
	Societies		Agency			Shareholders	Depositors	Borrowers	Number	Amount
Year	Authorised	Branches	Offices	Full time	Part time	000s	000s	000s	000s	£m
1998	71	2,502	593	33,155	9,996	21,195	909	3,136	521	24,244
1999	69	2,384	611	32,722	10,379	21,774	722	3,044	519	26,555
2000	67	2,361	607	32,334	10,823	22,237	740	3,107	548	31,514
2001	65	2,126	241	28,200	9,150	20,310	568	2,750	509	31,845
2002	65	2,103	229	28,982	9,257	20,724	511	2,688	558	37,303

LIABILITIES

	Funding							
		Deposits from		Taxation and other	Capital		Life fund	Total liabilities and
Year	Shares	individuals	Wholesale	liabilities	Reserves	Other	liabilities	capital
1998	103,289.0	6,168.0	27,264.5	2,105.0	8,305.6	1,551.4	7,329.9	156,014.2
1999	109,137.6	5,055.4	29,523.8	2,259.8	8,733.0	1,529.9	901.0	157,140.5
2000	119,295.5	5,531.0	38,047.5	2,033.6	9,577.0	1,861.7	1,397.8	177,747.1
2001	119,815.2	4,385.1	33,600.1	1,532.0	9,152.2	1,391.7	1,498.7	171,375.0
2002	132,373.0	4,191.2	33,459.6	1,401.1	9,932.8	1,684.8	1,410.3	184,452.8

ASSETS

	Loans fully secured on land to:							
	Individuals on residential		Other loans and		Office	Other	Life fund	Total
Year	properties	Others	investments	Liquidity	premises	assets	assets	assets
1998	108,789.0	7,495.5	1,212.1	28,343.0	927.3	1,917.4	7,329.9	156,014.2
1999	113,190.2	7,219.3	1,480.7	31,207.9	1,037.7	2,103.7	901.0	157,140.5
2000	125,555.9	8,544.2	1,230.0	37,900.8	1,044.7	2,073.7	1,397.8	177,747.1
2001	119,515.7	8,805.9	1,551.1	37,158.1	1,007.9	1,837.6	1,498.7	171,375.0
2002	129,001.3	9,882.7	1,877.1	39,201.8	1,050.6	2,029.0	1,410.3	184,452.8

AUTHORISED SOCIETIES *at end July 2003*

Name of Building Society[1]	Members[2]	Total Assets[3]
Barnsley, Regent Street, Barnsley S70 2EH	65,000	293,054
Bath, 20 Charles Street, Bath BA1 1HY	22,500	130,372
Beverley, 57 Market Place, Beverley HU17 8AA	13,000	72,436
Britannia, Britannia House, Cheadle Road, Leek ST13 5RG	2,235,271	18,670,600
Buckinghamshire, High Street, Chalfont St Giles HP8 4QB	9,391	112,264
Cambridge, 51 Newmarket Road, Cambridge CB5 8FF	123,980	620,780
Catholic, 7 Strutton Ground, London SW1P 2HY	3,620	35,754
Century, 21 Albany Street, Edinburgh EH1 3QW	3,725	16,409
Chelsea, Thirlestaine Hall, Thirlestaine Road, Cheltenham GL53 7AL	574,000	6,708,400
Chesham, 12 Market Square, Chesham HP5 1ER	21,000	180,273
Cheshire, Castle Street, Macclesfield SK11 6AF	422,000	3,558,862
Chorley and District, Key House, Foxhole Road, Chorley PR7 1NZ	18,702	120,478
City of Derry, 43 Carlisle Road, Londonderry BT48 6JJ	2,235	19,590
Clay Cross, Eyre Street, Clay Cross, Chesterfield S45 9NS	5,216	21,684
Coventry, PO Box 9, High Street, Coventry CV1 5QN	595,000	8,057,900
Cumberland, Cumberland House, Castle Street, Carlisle CA3 8RX	180,000	933,409
Darlington, Sentinel House, Lingfield Way, Darlington DL1 4PR	95,784	503,451
Derbyshire, Duffield Hall, Duffield, Derby DE56 1AG	389,113	3,657,209
Dudley, Dudley House, Stone Street, Dudley DY1 1NP	23,000	152,143
Dunfermline, Caledonia House, Carnegie Avenue, Dunfermline KY11 8PJ	343,000	1,828,327
Earl Shilton, 22 The Hollow, Earl Shilton, Leicester LE9 7NB	13,081	84,003
Ecology, 18 Station Road, Cross Hills, Keighley BD20 7EH	8,196	45,648
Furness, 51–55 Duke Street, Barrow-in-Furness LA14 1RT	110,052	623,082
Hanley Economic, Granville House, Festival Park, Hanley, Stoke-on-Trent ST1 5TB	35,000	257,207
Harpenden, 14 Station Road, Harpenden AL5 4SE	17,200	94,360
Hinckley and Rugby, Upper Bond Street, Hinckley LE10 1DG	98,000	539,570
Holmesdale, 43 Church Street, Reigate RH2 0AE	8,350	127,179
Ipswich, 44 Upper Brook Street, Ipswich IP4 1DP	59,270	325,619
Kent Reliance, Reliance House, Sun Pier, Chatham ME4 4ET	85,000	609,904
Lambeth, 118–120 Westminster Bridge Road, London SE1 7XE	78,875	296,693
Leeds and Holbeck, 105 Albion Street, Leeds LS1 5AS	583,416	4,845,300
Leek United, 50 St Edward Street, Leek ST13 5DH	68,000	564,184
Loughborough, 6 High Street, Loughborough LE11 2QB	22,000	174,764
Manchester, 24 Queen Street, Manchester M2 5AH	22,969	345,810
Mansfield, Regent House, Mansfield NG18 1SS	27,500	174,764
Market Harborough, Welland House, The Square, Market Harborough LE16 7PD	63,876	334,084
Marsden, 6–20 Russell Street, Nelson BB9 7NJ	78,000	311,266
Melton Mowbray, 39 Nottingham Street, Melton Mowbray LE13 1NR	66,000	321,365
Mercantile, Mercantile House, Silverlink Business Park, Wallsend NE28 9NY	44,030	215,802
Monmouthshire, John Frost Square, Newport NP20 1PX	52,225	364,495
National Counties, National Counties House, Church Street, Epsom KT17 4NL	38,206	744,389

Name of Building Society[1]	Members[2]	Total Assets[3]
Nationwide, Nationwide House, Pipers Way, Swindon SN38 1NW	10,000,000	85,417,700
Newbury, 17–20 Bartholomew Street, Newbury RG14 5LY	48,217	406,583
Newcastle, Portland House, New Bridge Street, Newcastle upon Tyne NE1 8AL	407,000	2,586,700
Norwich and Peterborough, Peterborough Business Park, Lynch Wood, Peterborough PE2 6WZ	433,000	2,567,237
Nottingham, 5–13 Upper Parliament Street, Nottingham NG1 2BX	216,212	1,812,380
Penrith, 7 King Street, Penrith CA11 7AR	6,885	68,576
Portman, Portman House, Richmond Hill, Bournemouth BH2 6EP	1,304,236	10,372,600
Principality, PO Box 89, Principality Buildings, Queen Street, Cardiff CF10 1UA	370,000	3,088,385
Progressive, 33–37 Wellington Place, Belfast BT1 6HH	119,360	923,854
Saffron Walden, 1A Market Street, Saffron Walden CB10 1HX	81,935	436,357
Scarborough, Prospect House, PO Box 6, Scarborough YO11 3WZ	152,007	1,282,087
Scottish, 23 Manor Place, Edinburgh EH3 7XE	26,728	183,299
Shepshed, Bull Ring, Shepshed, Loughborough LE12 9QD	10,300	56,405
Skipton, The Bailey, Skipton BD23 1DN	500,000	6,705,843
Stafford Railway, 4 Market Square, Stafford ST16 2JH	12,878	89,504
Staffordshire, Jubilee House, PO Box 66, 84 Salop Street, Wolverhampton WV3 0SA	220,000	1,688,936
Stroud and Swindon, Rowcroft, Stroud GL5 3BG	217,000	1,887,134
Swansea, 11 Cradock Street, Swansea SA1 3EW	5,005	57,755
Teachers, Allenview House, Hanham Road, Wimborne BH21 1AG	20,364	216,292
Tipton and Coseley, 70 Owen Street, Tipton DY4 8HG	31,515	208,399
Universal, Universal House, Kings Manor, Newcastle upon Tyne NE1 6PA	58,000	467,802
Vernon, 19 St Petersgate, Stockport SK1 1HF	37,980	173,900
West Bromwich, 374 High Street, West Bromwich B70 8LR	517,206	4,296,200
Yorkshire, Yorkshire House, Yorkshire Drive, Bradford BD5 8LJ	1,793,548	13,521,314

[1] Building Society are the last words in every society's name
[2] Includes both investing and borrowing members. Some totals are estimated or the latest available
[3] From the latest available balance sheet – mainly as at 31 December 2002

ECONOMIC STATISTICS

THE BUDGET 2003

GOVERNMENT RECEIPTS £ billion

BUDGET 2003

	Outturn 2001–2	Outturn Estimate 2002–3	Projection 2003–4
Inland Revenue			
Income tax (gross of tax credits)	110.2	113.3	122.1
Corporation tax[1]	32.1	29.6	30.8
Tax credits[2]	–2.3	–3.4	–4.5
Petroleum revenue tax	1.3	1.0	1.5
Capital gains tax	3.0	1.7	1.2
Inheritance tax	2.4	2.4	2.4
Stamp duties	7.0	7.6	7.9
Social Security contributions	63.2	64.3	74.5
INLAND REVENUE (NET OF TAX CREDITS)	216.9	216.5	235.8
Customs and excise			
Value added tax	61.0	63.6	66.6
Fuel duties	21.9	22.1	23.0
Tobacco duties	7.8	8.1	8.0
Spirits duties	1.9	2.3	2.4
Wine duties	2.0	1.9	1.9
Beer and cider duties	3.1	3.1	3.1
Betting and gaming duties	1.4	1.3	1.3
Air passenger duty	0.8	0.8	0.8
Insurance premium tax	1.9	2.1	2.2
Landfill tax	0.5	0.5	0.7
Climate change levy	0.6	0.8	0.9
Aggregates levy	0.0	0.2	0.3
Customs duties and levies	2.0	1.9	1.9
CUSTOMS AND EXCISE	104.9	108.8	113.1
Vehicle excise duties	4.2	4.6	4.8
Oil royalties	0.5	0.5	0.0
Business rates[3]	18.0	18.7	18.6
Council tax	15.3	16.6	18.6
Other taxes and royalties[4]	9.9	10.8	11.9
NET TAXES AND SOCIAL SECURITY CONTRIBUTIONS[5]	369.7	376.5	402.9
Accrual adjustments on taxes	0.6	–0.3	3.6
Less own resources contribution to EC budget	–3.6	–2.5	–2.5
Less PC corporation tax payments	–0.1	–0.1	–0.1
Tax credits[6]	0.9	1.1	0.6
Interest and dividends	4.5	4.1	4.0
Other receipts[7]	17.9	18.2	19.8
CURRENT RECEIPTS	389.9	397.1	428.3
North Sea Revenues[8]	5.2	5.0	4.7

[1] National Accounts measure: gross of enhanced and payable tax credits.
[2] Includes enhanced company tax credits
[3] Includes district council rates in Northern Ireland paid by business.
[4] Includes money paid into the National Lottery Distribution Fund.
[5] Includes VAT and 'traditional own resources' contributions to EC budget. Cash basis.
[6] Excludes Children's Tax Credit and other tax credits that score as a tax repayment in the National Accounts
[7] Includes gross operating surplus and rent; net of oil royalties.
[8] Consists of North Sea corporation tax, petroleum revenue tax and royalties.
Source: The Stationery Office – Budget 2003 (Crown Copyright).

GOVERNMENT EXPENDITURE

The Economic and Fiscal Strategy Report in June 1998 introduced changes to the public expenditure control regime. Three-year departmental expenditure limits (DELs) now apply to most government departments. Spending which cannot easily be subject to three-year planning is reviewed annually in the Budget as annually managed expenditure (AME). Current and capital expenditure are treated separately.

DEPARTMENTAL EXPENDITURE LIMITS
RESOURCE AND CAPITAL BUDGETS £ billion

	Outturn 2001–2	Estimate 2002–3	Plans 2003–4
RESOURCE BUDGET			
Education and Skills[1]	17.0	20.6	22.0
Health[1]	52.1	57.4	63.0
of which NHS	50.9	55.1	60.8
Transport	4.4	6.0	7.3
Office of the Deputy Prime Minister	2.7	4.1	4.8
Local Government	36.9	37.4	41.0
Home Office	10.3	11.3	11.7
Lord Chancellor's Departments	3.1	3.3	3.1
Attorney General's Departments	0.4	0.5	0.5
Defence	32.3	41.4[2]	30.8
Foreign and Commonwealth Office	1.4	1.6	1.7
International Development	3.2	3.6	3.6
Trade and Industry	5.4	4.6	4.7
Environment, Food and Rural Affairs	2.7	2.7	2.7
Culture, Media and Sport	1.2	1.3	1.4
Work and Pensions	6.2	7.5	8.0
Scotland[3]	16.0	17.3	18.4
Wales[3]	8.2	9.1	9.8
Northern Ireland Executive[3]	5.7	6.2	6.4
Northern Ireland Office	1.0	1.2	1.1
Chancellor's Departments	4.1	4.6	4.6
Cabinet Office	1.5	1.7	1.8
Invest to Save budget	0.0	0.0	0.0
Capital Modernisation Fund	0.0	0.0	0.0
Reserve	0.0	0.0	0.7
Unallocated special reserve[4]	0.0	2.0	0.0
Allowance for shortfall	0.0	–3.8	0.0
TOTAL RESOURCE BUDGET DEL	215.8	241.6	249.1
CAPITAL BUDGET			
Education and Skills	2.1	2.6	3.3
Health	1.8	2.1	3.0
of which NHS	1.7	2.0	2.9

Transport	2.4	3.0	3.3
Office of the Deputy Prime Minister	1.8	1.5	1.9
Local Government	0.1	0.2	0.3
Home Office	0.6	0.9	1.1
Lord Chancellor's Departments	0.1	0.1	0.1
Attorney General's Departments	0.0	0.0	0.0
Defence	5.8	6.3	6.1
Foreign and Commonwealth Office	0.1	0.1	0.1
International Development	0.0	0.0	0.0
Trade and Industry	0.1	0.4	0.5
Environment, Food and Rural Affairs	0.3	0.4	0.3
Culture, Media and Sport	0.0	0.1	0.1
Work and Pensions	0.1	0.2	0.0
Scotland[3]	1.4	2.0	2.0
Wales[3]	0.5	0.8	0.8
Northern Ireland Executive[3]	0.4	0.6	0.4
Northern Ireland Office	0.0	0.1	0.1
Chancellor's Departments	0.2	0.4	0.3
Cabinet Office	0.2	0.2	0.6
Invest to Save Budget	0.0	0.0	0.0
Capital Modernisation Fund	0.0	0.0	0.0
Reserve	0.0	0.0	0.8
Allowance for shortfall	0.0	−1.2	0.0
TOTAL CAPITAL BUDGET DEL	18.0	20.7	25.1
Depreciation	−9.6	−18.3	−10.4
TOTAL DEPARTMENTAL EXPENDITURE LIMITS	224.1	244.0	263.8

[1] From 2003–4 this includes employer contributions for cost of pension increases.
[2] One-off increase in defence non-cash expenditure in line with agreed asset management policy.
[3] For Scotland, Wales and Northern Ireland, the split between current and capital budgets is decided by the respective executives.
[4] This was the remaining contingency provision for costs of military operations in Iraq after an allocation of a preliminary £1 billion to the Ministry of Defence from the £3 billion total.

Source: The Stationery Office – *Budget 2003* (Crown Copyright).

ANNUALLY MANAGED EXPENDITURE (FORECASTS)

£ billion

	Outturn 2001–2	Estimate 2002–3	Projection 2003–4
Departmental expenditure limits	224.1	244.0	263.8
Social security benefits	101.1	105.5	111.0
Tax credits[1]	8.7	9.8	11.7
Housing revenue account subsidies	4.5	4.3	4.3
Common agricultural policy	3.7	2.6	2.3
Net public service pensions	10.1	3.5	0.2
National Lottery	1.7	1.9	2.2
Non-cash items in AME	23.4	27.9	25.2
Other departmental expenditure	0.2	2.3	2.2
Net payment to EC institutions[2]	0.8	2.3	2.3
Locally financed expenditure	19.8	20.7	23.0
Central government gross debt interest	22.1	20.8	21.8
Public corporations' own-financed capital expenditure	1.5	2.2	2.6
AME margin	0.0	0.0	1.0
Accounting adjustments	−32.2	−26.7	−18.0
Annually managed expenditure	165.5	177.0	191.9

[1] All child allowances in Income Support and Jobseekers' Allowance which, from 2003–4 are part of the Child Tax Credit, have been included in the tax credits line and excluded from the social security benefits line. This is in order to give figures a consistent definition over the forecast period.
[2] Only includes Member States.

Source: The Stationery Office – *Budget 2003* (Crown Copyright).

PUBLIC SECTOR FINANCES

£ billion

PUBLIC SECTOR CAPITAL EXPENDITURE

	Outturn 2001–2	Estimate 2002–3	Projection 2003–4
Capital Budget DEL	18.0	20.7	25.1
Locally-financed expenditure	1.2	1.3	1.5
National Lottery	0.9	0.9	1.2
Public corporations' own-financed capital expenditure	1.5	2.2	2.6
Other capital spending in AME	1.3	0.9	2.9
AME margin	0.0	0.0	0.1
Public sector gross investment[1]	23.0	26.0	33.4
Less depreciation	13.4	13.8	14.4
Public sector net investment	9.6	12.2	18.9
Proceeds from the sale of fixed assets[2]	4.3	4.5	3.8

[1] This and previous lines are all net of sales of fixed assets.
[2] Projections of total receipts from the sale of fixed assets by public sector.

Source: The Stationery Office – *Budget 2003* (Crown Copyright).

BALANCE OF PAYMENTS 2001

£ million

CURRENT ACCOUNT	
Trade in goods	
Exports	191,754
Imports	225,295
Trade in goods balance	−33,541
Services balance	10,472
Investment income	8,982
Transfers balance	−7,144
CURRENT BALANCE	−21,087

Source: The Stationery Office – *Annual Abstract of Statistics 2003* (Crown copyright).

UK TRADE ON A BALANCE OF PAYMENTS BASIS

£ million

	Exports	Imports	Balance
1991	103,939	114,162	−10,223
1992	107,863	120,913	−13,050
1993	122,039	135,295	−13,066
1994	135,143	146,269	−11,126
1995	153,577	165,600	−12,023
1996	167,196	180,918	−13,722
1997	171,923	184,265	−12,342
1998	164,056	185,869	−21,813
1999	166,166	193,538	−27,372
2000	187,936	218,262	−30,326
2001	191,754	225,295	−33,541

Source: The Stationery Office – Annual Abstract of Statistics 2003 (Crown copyright).

VALUE OF UK EXPORTS 2001
BY AREA   £ million

European Union	111,414
Other western Europe	7,167
North America	33,772
Other OECD countries	10,910
Oil exporting countries	6,472
Rest of the world	22,019

Source: The Stationery Office – Annual Abstract of Statistics 2003 (Crown copyright).

VALUE OF UK IMPORTS 2001
BY AREA   £ million

European Union	116,617
Other western Europe	12,477
North America	34,989
Other OECD countries	17,385
Oil exporting countries	3,979
Rest of the World	39,848

Source: The Stationery Office – Annual Abstract of Statistics 2003 (Crown copyright).

EMPLOYMENT

UK EMPLOYMENT BY AGE AND GENDER (2002)
Thousands and percentages in brackets

Age	Male	Female
16–17	321 (41.7)	328 (44.8)
18–24	1,759 (71.2)	1,605 (64.8)
25–34	3,487 (88.1)	2,968 (71.6)
35–49	5,482 (88.2)	4,828 (75.6)
50–64(m)/59(f)	3,544 (69.9)	2,446 (65.1)
65+(m)/60+(f)	293 (7.6)	598 (9.1)
All aged 16 and over	14,886 (66.7)	12,773 (53.1)

Source: The Stationery Office – Annual Abstract of Statistics 2003 (Crown copyright).

DISTRIBUTION OF THE UK WORKFORCE
(AT MID-JUNE 2002)

Employees	25,718,000
Self-employed	3,500,000
HM Forces	204,000
Government-supported trainee	97,000
Claimant unemployed	953,000

Source: The Stationery Office – Annual Abstract of Statistics 2003 (Crown copyright).

UK EMPLOYEE JOBS, BY INDUSTRY (2002)

Service industries	20,375,000
Manufacturing industries	3,668,000
Energy and water supply	177,000
Agriculture, hunting, forestry and fishing	255,000
Mining and quarrying	75,000

Source: The Stationery Office – Annual Abstract of Statistics 2003 (Crown copyright).

AVERAGE GROSS WEEKLY EARNINGS OF FULL-TIME EMPLOYEES ON ADULT RATES (GREAT BRITAIN) 2002

All adults	£464.70
All men	£513.80
Men, manual	£368.20
Men, non-manual	£610.40
All women	£383.40
Women, manual	£251.00
Women, non-manual	£405.20

Source: The Stationery Office – Annual Abstract of Statistics 2003 (Crown copyright).

UNEMPLOYMENT BY AGE AND GENDER 2002
(UK)   Thousands and percentages in brackets

Age	Male	Female
16–17	90 (22.0)	73 (18.3)
18–24	244 (12.2)	148 (8.4)
25–34	195 (5.3)	148 (4.7)
35–49	226 (4.0)	161 (3.2)
50–64(m)/59(f)	144 (3.9)	73 (2.9)
65+(m)/60+(f)	10 (3.3)	12 (1.9)
All aged 16+	909 (5.8)	615 (4.6)

Source: The Stationery Office – Annual Abstract of Statistics 2003 (Crown copyright).

INDUSTRIAL STOPPAGES 2001 (UK) BY DURATION

Not more than 5 days	162,000
6–10 days	15,000
11–20 days	7,000
21–30 days	1,000
31–50 days	4,000
More than 50 days	5,000
Total number of stoppages	194,000

Source: The Stationery Office – Annual Abstract of Statistics 2003 (Crown copyright).

TRADE UNIONS (UK)

Year	No. of unions at end of year	Total membership at end of year
1990	327	9,960,000
1991	306	9,555,000
1992	315	9,171,000
1993	302	8,848,000
1994	281	8,297,000
1995	271	8,111,000
1996	261	7,982,000
1997	257	7,841,000
1998	243	7,894,000
1999	241	7,940,000
2000	230	7,823,000

Source: The Stationery Office – Annual Abstract of Statistics 2003 (Crown copyright)

HOUSEHOLD INCOME AND EXPENDITURE

AVERAGE INCOME OF HOUSEHOLDS BEFORE AND AFTER TAXES AND BENEFITS, 2000–1
(£ per year)

Number of households in the UK population	25,030,000
Original income	23,234
Disposable income	21,242
Post-tax income	16,855

Source: The Stationery Office – *Annual Abstract of Statistics 2003* (Crown copyright).

AVERAGE WEEKLY HOUSEHOLD EXPENDITURE ON COMMODITIES AND SERVICES (2001–2)

	£	As % of total
Housing	66.70	17
Fuel and power	11.70	3
Food	62.20	16
Alcoholic drink	14.60	4
Tobacco	5.60	1
Clothing and footwear	22.40	6
Household goods	33.10	8
Household services	23.70	6
Personal goods and services	14.80	4
Motoring expenditure	58.30	15
Fares and other travel costs	9.50	2
Leisure goods	19.90	5
Leisure services	52.30	13
Miscellaneous	1.90	–
Total	396.80	100

Source: The Stationery Office – *Annual Abstract of Statistics 2002* (Crown copyright).

HOUSEHOLD EXPENDITURE ON SELECTED ITEMS BY FAMILY TYPE 2001–2
(£ per week)

	Couples		Singles	
	Dependent children	No children	Dependent children	No children
Restaurant meals	12.70	14.70	5.00	7.00
Take away meals	5.90	3.70	3.70	2.10
Confectionery	1.00	0.20	1.00	0.10
Ice cream	0.40	0.10	0.20	0.00
Holiday abroad	17.20	21.50	5.90	6.90
National lottery and scratchcards	2.50	2.90	1.10	1.30
Newspapers	1.60	2.00	0.70	1.10
Cinema and theatre	1.70	1.30	0.90	1.10
All household expenditure	552.20	477.80	266.20	257.10

Source: The Stationery Office – *Social Trends 2002* (Crown copyright).

SOURCES OF GROSS HOUSEHOLD INCOME 2001–2

AVERAGE WEEKLY INCOME BY SOURCE (£)

Wages and salaries	377.40
Self-employment	47.70
Investments	19.70
Annuities and pensions (other than social security benefits)	36.10
Social security benefits	63.20
Other sources	6.80
Total	551.00

SOURCES AS A PERCENTAGE OF TOTAL HOUSEHOLD INCOME

Wages and salaries	69
Self-employment	9
Investments	4
Annuities and pensions (other than social security benefits)	7
Social security benefits	11
Other sources	1
Total	100

Source: The Stationery Office – *Annual Abstract of Statistics 2003* (Crown copyright).

AVAILABILITY OF CERTAIN DURABLE GOODS 2001–2
% of households

Car	74
One	44
Two	24
Three or more	6
Central heating, full or partial	92
Washing machine	93
Fridge/freezer or deep freezer	95
Dishwasher	27
Telephone	94
Home computer	49
Internet Access	40
Video recorder	90

Source: The Stationery Office – *Annual Abstract of Statistics 2003* (Crown copyright).

SAVINGS

SAVINGS BY ECONOMIC STATUS AND AMOUNT 2000–1 IN GREAT BRITAIN
(percentages)

	No savings	Less than £1,500	£1,500– £10,000	£10,000– £20,000	£20,000 and above
Self-employed	21	25	28	10	15
Single or couple, both in full-time work	29	30	26	7	7
Couple, one in full-time work, one in part-time work	17	26	32	11	13
Couple, one in full-time work, one not working	25	24	26	10	15
One or more in part-time work	40	24	16	7	14
Head of household or spouse aged 60 or over	27	17	25	10	21
Head of household or spouse unemployed	73	19	5	1	2
Head of household or spouse sick or disabled	70	16	7	2	4
Total Households	34	23	23	8	12

Source: The Stationery Office – *Social Trends 2003* (Crown copyright).

CREDIT AND DEBIT CARD USAGE

PLASTIC CARD HOLDERS IN GREAT BRITAIN BY AGE 2001   *(percentages)*

	16–24	*25–34*	*35–44*	*45–54*	*55–64*	*65 and over*	*All adults 16 and over*
Any credit/charge card	31	61	70	71	68	65	62
Debit card	79	87	87	90	88	84	86
Store/retailer card	19	34	43	42	37	34	35
Cheque guarantee card	36	72	79	82	79	75	71
ATM card*	89	91	87	90	88	84	88
Any plastic card	90	94	92	93	90	84	90

*Cards used in ATM for cash withdrawals and other bank services. Includes single function ATM cards and multi-function debit cards, but excludes credit and charge cards.

Source: The Stationery Office – *Social Trends 2003* (Crown copyright).

AVERAGE DWELLING PRICES

BY REGION AND TYPE OF ACCOMMODATION 2001

	Bungalow	*Detached house*	*Semi-detached house*	*Terraced house*	*Purpose-built flat/maisonette*	*Other**	*All Dwellings*
United Kingdom	113,419	173,295	99,412	87,470	90,356	121,456	112,835
England	121,577	182,487	104,220	92,193	101,867	130,306	119,563
North East	79,281	116,619	60,170	45,945	52,544	68,483	69,813
North West	95,386	139,939	75,486	54,486	69,710	76,864	82,403
Yorkshire & the Humber	87,588	127,888	65,334	52,775	58,499	71,512	76,368
East Midlands	91,274	134,679	68,850	58,028	52,973	74,093	87,280
West Midlands	111,508	162,802	78,857	65,879	69,063	77,526	97,650
East	118,186	202,021	118,771	96,546	78,346	78,349	127,858
London	196,184	331,324	231,228	187,493	138,939	176,471	182,325
South East	169,281	254,138	146,033	117,133	93,559	94,913	156,964
South West	130,157	185,670	107,483	87,641	81,472	88,955	118,639
Wales	87,675	126,644	66,922	53,079	61,009	55,525	79,628
Scotland	89,983	121,705	66,255	58,190	53,585	69,609	73,570
Northern Ireland	82,441	124,012	76,529	57,302	38,838	50,145	79,885

* Includes converted flats

Source: The Stationery Office – *Social Trends 2003* (Crown copyright).

COST OF LIVING AND INFLATION RATES

The first cost of living index to be calculated took July 1914 as 100 and was based on the pattern of expenditure of working-class families in 1914. The cost of living index was superseded in 1947 by the general index of retail prices (RPI), although the older term is still popularly applied to it.

The Harmonised Index of Consumer Prices (HICP) was introduced in 1997 to enable comparisons within the European Union using an agreed methodology. The HICP does not replace the RPI for UK domestic use.

GENERAL INDEX OF RETAIL PRICES

The general index of retail prices measures the changes month by month in the average level of prices of goods and services purchased by households in the United Kingdom. The Office for National Statistics reviews the components of the Retail Price Index once every year to reflect changes in consumer preferences and the establishment of new products. The expenditure of high-income households (top 4 per cent) and of households mainly dependent on state pensions is excluded.

The index is compiled using a selection of around 650 goods and services, and the prices charged for these items are collected at regular intervals in about 150 locations throughout the country. For the index, the price changes are weighted in accordance with the pattern of consumption of the average family.

INFLATION RATE

The twelve-monthly percentage change in the 'all items' index of the RPI is usually referred to as the rate of inflation. The percentage change in prices between any two months/years can be obtained using the following formula:

$$\frac{\text{Later date RPI} - \text{Earlier date RPI}}{\text{Earlier date RPI}} \times 100$$

e.g. to find the rate of inflation for 1988, using the annual averages for 1987 and 1988:

$$\frac{106.9 - 101.0}{101.9} \times 100$$

PURCHASING POWER OF THE POUND

Changes in the internal purchasing power of the pound may be defined as the 'inverse' of changes in the level of prices; when prices go up, the amount which can be purchased with a given sum of money goes down. To find the purchasing power of the pound in one month or year, given that it was 100p in a previous month or year, the calculation would be:

$$100p \times \frac{\text{Earlier month/year RPI}}{\text{Later month/year RPI}}$$

Thus, if the purchasing power of the pound is taken to be 100p in 1975, the comparable purchasing power in 2002 would be:

$$100p \times \frac{34.2}{176.2} = 19.4p$$

For longer term comparisons, it has been the practice to use an index which has been constructed by linking together the RPI for the period 1962 to date; an index derived from the consumers expenditure deflator for the period from 1938 to 1962; and the prewar 'cost of living' index for the period 1914 to 1938. This long-term index enables the internal purchasing power of the pound to be calculated for any year from 1914 onwards. It should be noted that these figures can only be approximate.

	Long-term index of consumer goods and services (Jan. 1987 = 100)	Comparable purchasing power of £1 in 1998	Rate of inflation (annual average)
1914	2.8	58.18	
1915	3.5	46.54	
1920	7.0	23.27	
1925	5.0	32.58	
1930	4.5	36.20	
1935	4.0	40.72	
1938	4.4	37.02	
There are no official figures for 1939–45			
1946	7.4	22.01	
1950	9.0	18.10	
1955	11.2	14.54	
1960	12.6	12.93	
1965	14.8	11.00	
1970	18.5	8.80	
1975	34.2	4.76	
1980	66.8	2.44	18.0
1981	74.8	2.18	11.9
1982	81.2	2.01	8.6
1983	84.9	1.92	4.6
1984	89.2	1.83	5.0
1985	94.6	1.72	6.1
1986	97.8	1.67	3.4
1987	101.9	1.60	4.2
1988	106.9	1.52	4.9
1989	115.2	1.41	7.8
1990	126.1	1.29	9.5
1991	133.5	1.22	5.9
1992	138.5	1.18	3.7
1993	140.7	1.16	1.6
1994	144.1	1.13	2.4
1995	149.1	1.09	3.5
1996	152.7	1.07	2.4
1997	157.5	1.03	3.1
1998	162.9	1.00	3.4
1999	165.4	0.98	1.5
2000	170.3	0.96	3.0
2001	173.3	0.94	1.8
2002	176.2	0.92	1.7

The RPI figures are published around the middle of each month. They are available as a recorded message which can be heard by telephoning 020-7533 5866. Each month an updated Consumer Price Indices bulletin is published by the Office for National Statistics. Information is also available on the National Statistics website.

OFFICE FOR NATIONAL STATISTICS, 1 Drummond Gate, London SW1V 2QQ. Public Enquiries Line: 020-7533 5874
Web: www.statistics.gov.uk

TAXATION

INCOME TAX

Income tax is charged on the taxable income of individuals for a year of assessment commencing on 6 April and ending on the following 5 April. Many changes have been introduced during recent years which affect both the calculation of income chargeable to tax and the rate or rates at which the amount of tax due must be determined. The following information is confined to the year of assessment 2003–4 ending on 5 April 2004 and has only limited application to earlier years.

An individual's liability to satisfy income tax for 2003–4 is determined by establishing the level of taxable income for the year. This income must then be allocated between three different headings, namely: (a) all income excluding that arising from savings and dividends; (b) income from savings; (c) company dividends, including distributions.

Once this allocation has been completed the first calculation must be limited to taxable income excluding that arising from both savings and dividends. This income will be reduced by an individual's personal allowance and any other available allowances. The first £1,960 of taxable income remaining is assessed to income tax at the starting rate of 10 per cent. The next £28,540 is taxable at the basic rate of 22 per cent. Should any excess over £30,500 (£1,960 plus £28,540) remain, this will be taxable at the higher rate of 40 per cent.

The second calculation is limited to income from savings, if any. Liability may arise at the starting rate of 10 per cent, the lower rate of 20 per cent or the higher rate of 40 per cent. There is no liability to income tax at the basic rate of 22 per cent. The appropriate rate which must be used is determined by adding income from savings to other taxable income, excluding dividends. To the extent that the addition does not increase taxable income above £1,960, income from savings is taxed at the starting rate of 10 per cent. Should this level be exceeded but total income does not reach £30,500 any excess remains taxable at the lower rate of 20 per cent. Where the addition of income from savings extends taxable income above £30,500 the excess is taxed at the higher rate of 40 per cent.

Finally, any company dividends are taxed at either the Schedule F ordinary rate of 10 per cent or the Schedule F upper rate of 32.5 per cent. The amount of dividends (with the addition of any tax credit) must be added to taxable income comprising general income together with income from savings. If this addition does not increase total taxable income above £30,500 dividends remain taxable at the ordinary rate of 10 per cent only. However, if or to the extent that the addition discloses dividends exceeding the £30,500 level the excess is taxed at the upper rate of 32.5 per cent.

Trustees administering settled property and personal representatives dealing with the estate of a deceased person are chargeable to income tax at the basic rate of 22 per cent. Where trustees retain discretionary powers or income from settled property is accumulated, liability may be increased to 34 per cent.

Companies residing in the UK are not liable to income tax but suffer corporation tax on income, profits and gains. Income arising overseas will often incur liability to foreign taxation. If that income is also chargeable to UK income tax, excessive liability could arise. The UK has concluded double taxation agreements with the governments of many overseas territories and these ensure that the same slice of income is not doubly taxed.

HUSBAND AND WIFE

A husband and wife are separately taxed, with each entitled to his or her personal allowance. A married man 'living with' his wife can only obtain a married couple's allowance if one party to the marriage was over the age of 64 years before 6 April 2000. In the absence of any claim, this allowance must be used by the husband but where any balance remains the surplus may be transferred to the wife. It is possible for a married woman to claim half the basic married couple's allowance as of right. The entire basic allowance may be claimed by the wife, if her husband so agrees. Each spouse may obtain other allowances and reliefs where the required conditions are satisfied. Income must be accurately allocated between the couple by reference to the individual beneficially entitled to that income. Where income arises from jointly-held assets, this must be apportioned equally between husband and wife. However, in those cases where the beneficial interests in jointly-held assets are not equal, a special declaration can be made to apportion income by reference to the actual interests in that income.

SELF-ASSESSMENT

Self-assessment for income tax purposes affects individuals, trustees and personal representatives. Central to self-assessment is the requirement to deliver a completed tax return. This must normally be submitted by 31 January following the end of the year of assessment (the previous 5 April) to which the return relates. The taxpayer must also calculate the amount of income tax due. If a taxpayer wishes the Inland Revenue to calculate the tax due, the return must be forwarded to the Inland Revenue not later than the previous 30 September.

It is the responsibility of the taxpayer to submit payments of income tax on time. There are three different dates on which payments may fall due:
(a) an interim payment due on 31 January in the year of assessment itself
(b) a second interim payment due on the following 31 July
(c) a balancing payment, or possibly a repayment, on the following 31 January
The two interim payments will be based on tax payable for the previous year of assessment but liability may be reduced where income has fallen or avoided entirely where the amounts are not substantial.

The impact of self-assessment is largely restricted to some nine million persons receiving tax returns. These comprise self-employed individuals, those receiving income from the exploitation of land in the UK, company directors, others with investment income liable to higher rate income tax, trustees and personal representatives. Elderly persons receiving small amounts of untaxed income may be excluded from the need to complete a tax return.

Failure to submit completed tax returns by 31 January or to discharge payments of income tax on time will incur a liability to interest, surcharges and penalties.

INCOME TAXABLE

Throughout a period of many years income tax has been assessed under a range of different Schedules. Each Schedule applies to determine the extent of liability and establishes the amount to be included in taxable income. In some instances the actual income arising in a year of assessment will be charged to income tax for that year. A different basis must be used for business profits taxable under Case I or Case II of Schedule D. This basis requires taxable profits to be those for the business accounting period ending in the year of assessment, with special adjustments for the opening and closing years of a business. Other income assessable under Schedule D will be that which arises in the actual year of assessment.

The use of the various Schedules has gradually been eroded. Schedule B no longer applies following the withdrawal of income tax liability on most commercial woodlands in the UK. Schedule C has also been withdrawn as a result of further changes. The most recent casualty was Schedule E which ceased to apply on 6 April 2003, although this did not affect future liability to income tax on matters previously dealt with under that Schedule.

The contents of the remaining Schedules are outlined below, with a brief reference to the now obsolete Schedule E.

Schedule A

Tax is charged under Schedule A on the annual profits or gains arising from a business carried on for the exploitation of land in the UK. The determination of profits from a Schedule A business adopts principles identical to those used when establishing the profits or gains of a trade, profession or vocation. Rents and other income from the exploitation of land are included in the calculation, and outgoings incurred wholly and exclusively for the purposes of the Schedule A business may be deducted from income.

Schedule A does not extend to profits from farming, market gardening or woodlands, nor does it apply to mineral rents and royalties. Premiums arising on the grant of a lease for a period not exceeding 50 years in duration are treated as rents. However, the amount of the taxable premium may be reduced by 2 per cent for each complete year, after the first 12 months, of the leasing period. Income arising from the provision of certain furnished holiday accommodation attracts a number of tax advantages not otherwise available for most income chargeable under Schedule A. Receipts not exceeding £4,250 annually and accruing to an individual from letting property furnished in his or her own home are usually excluded from liability to income tax.

Schedule D

This Schedule is divided into six Cases:

Cases I and II – profits arising from trades, professions and vocations, including farming and market gardening. Profits must be calculated on an accounting basis which provides 'a true and fair view' of business results. This remains subject to any statutory adjustment which may be required. For example, only sums laid out 'wholly and exclusively' for the purposes of a business may be subtracted from receipts, notwithstanding that those outgoings may reflect a proper accounting charge. Capital expenditure incurred on assets used for business purposes will often produce an entitlement to capital allowances which reduce the profits chargeable. These profits may also be reduced by claims for loss relief and other matters.

Case III – interest on government stocks not taxed at source, interest on National Savings and Investments deposits and discounts. Interest up to £70 on ordinary National Savings and Investments deposits is exempt from income tax. The exemption applies to both husband and wife separately. Interest on National Savings and Investments special investment accounts is not exempt. Interest and other items of savings income incur liability at the starting rate, lower rate or the higher rate depending on the level of the recipient's income.

Cases IV and V – interest from overseas securities, rents, dividends and most other income accruing outside the UK. Assessment is based on the full amount of income arising, whether remitted to the UK or retained overseas, but individuals who are either not domiciled in the UK or who are ordinarily resident overseas may be taxed on a remittance basis. Interest received on most overseas investments is chargeable at the same rates as those which apply to interest from sources within the UK. Overseas dividends are usually taxed at 10 per cent or 32.5 per cent.

Case VI – sundry profits and annual receipts not assessed under any other Case or Schedule. These may include insurance commissions, post-cessation receipts from a discontinued business and numerous other receipts specifically charged under Case VI.

Schedule E

This Schedule ceased to apply after 5 April 2003. Matters previously dealt with under Schedule E have been replaced by the following three headings, none of which involves the use of a Schedule:
(a)   employment income
(b)   pension income
(c)   social security income
This change in approach has not significantly affected the calculation of, and liability to, income tax (see below).

Schedule F

This Schedule is concerned with dividends and distributions received from a UK resident company.

EMPLOYMENT INCOME

Net taxable earnings arising in a year of assessment ending on 5 April are chargeable to income tax as employment income. This charge reflects taxable earnings remaining after subtracting the total of allowable deductions.

Taxable earnings will include all salaries, wages, director's fees and other money sums. In addition, the value of a wide range of benefits must be added. These benefits include the provision of living accommodation on advantageous terms and advantages arising from the use of vouchers.

Further taxable benefits accrue to directors and employees who are not classed as 'lower paid'. These exempt individuals receive earnings of no more than £8,500 calculated by including potentially taxable benefits. Such taxable benefits include the reimbursement of expenses, the availability of motor cars for private motoring, the provision of fuel for private motoring, interest free loans and other benefits provided at the employer's expense. The cost of providing a limited range of childcare facilities and a works bus for the transportation of employees may be ignored. Mileage allowances paid to employees who provide their own motor vehicles or cycles for business travel may also be excluded, unless they exceed stated limits.

All taxable earnings received by an individual who is resident, ordinarily resident and domiciled in the UK are chargeable to income tax. However, limitations may apply where there is some foreign element.

A 'receipts basis' applies for determining the year of assessment to which taxable earnings must be allocated. In general, the date of receipt will comprise the earlier of the date of payment or the date entitlement arises. In the case of company directors it is the earlier of these two dates, with the addition of the following three, which establishes the time of receipt: the date earnings are credited in the company's books; where earnings for a period are determined after the end of that period, the date of determination; where earnings for a period are determined in that period, the last day of that period.

In arriving at the amount of net taxable earnings all expenses incurred wholly, exclusively and necessarily in the performance of the duties, together with the cost of business travel, may be deducted. Fees and subscriptions paid to certain professional bodies and learned societies may also be deducted. In addition, fees paid to managers by entertainers, actors and others in respect of taxable earnings may be deducted, up to a maximum of 17.5 per cent.

Compensation for loss of office and other sums received on the termination of an employment are assessable to income tax. However, the first £30,000 may be excluded with only the balance remaining chargeable, unless the compensatory payment is linked with the retirement of the recipient or the performance of their duties.

A range of other matters loosely linked to an employment may also create employment income. Rules similar to those outlined above apply also to the holder of an office.

PENSION INCOME

Pensions received from various sources, including an occupational pension scheme, personal pension scheme, retirement annuity scheme and from other types of arrangement are treated as pension income chargeable to income tax. Liability is based on the amounts received in a year of assessment. However, where the pension is attributable to certain payments made overseas, only 90 per cent is taxable.

SOCIAL SECURITY INCOME

Many social security benefits are not liable to income tax. However, benefits which are taxable as social security income include the state retirement pension, widow's pension, widowed mother's allowance and jobseeker's allowance. Short-term sick pay and maternity pay payable by an employer are also chargeable to tax. Incapacity benefit remains taxable but no liability arises on most short-term benefit.

PAY AS YOU EARN

The Pay as You Earn (PAYE) system is not an independent form of taxation but is designed to collect income tax by deduction from most taxable earnings. When paying taxable earnings to employees an employer is usually required to deduct income tax and to account for that tax to the Inland Revenue. In many cases this deduction procedure will fully exhaust the individual's liability to income tax, unless there is other income. The date of 'receipt' used to establish the time employment income arises also identifies the date of 'payment' when establishing liability to PAYE.

The PAYE system is used to collect tax on certain payments made 'in kind'. The system is also applied when collecting tax on many pensions, jobseeker's benefits, some incapacity benefits and maternity pay.

INCOME FROM SAVINGS

Many payments of interest made by building societies and banks are received after the deduction of income tax at the lower rate of 20 per cent. However, investors not liable to income tax may arrange to receive interest gross with no tax being deducted on payment.

Interest of this nature represents 'income from savings'; an expression which also extends to interest on government securities, interest on a restricted range of National Savings and Investments products and the income element of purchased life annuities. In addition, 'income from savings' may extend to other income of a similar nature arising outside the United Kingdom. Not all forms of investment income are included in the list, notable exceptions comprising income from letting property and company dividends.

A great deal of interest arising from sources in the United Kingdom will be received after deduction of income tax at the lower rate of 20 per cent. Although this interest is not taxable at the basic rate it remains chargeable at the starting rate of 10 per cent, the lower rate of 20 per cent or the higher rate of 40 per cent. Where such interest, when added to other income, excluding dividends, falls within the starting rate band tax will be due at 10 per cent. As tax will have been suffered by deduction at the lower rate of 20 per cent a repayment of the excess may well be obtained from the Inland Revenue. To the extent that interest from savings when added to other income exceeds £1,960 but does not exceed £30,500, liability arises at the lower rate of 20 per cent. In those situations where, or to the extent that, income from savings when added to other income produces a combined total exceeding £30,500, liability arises at the higher rate of 40 per cent. As income tax will usually have been deducted at source at the rate of 20 per cent, higher rate liability arises at a further 20 per cent (40 per cent less 20 per cent).

DIVIDENDS

Dividends and other distributions paid by a UK resident company have a tax credit attached equal to one-ninth of the sum received in 2003–4. Therefore, a recipient shareholder also residing in the UK who receives a cash dividend of £90 will have a tax credit of £10. The gross dividend or distribution (sum received plus tax credit) is regarded as having suffered income tax, equal to the tax credit, at the rate of 10 per cent. Where the shareholder is not liable, or not fully liable, to income tax it is not possible to claim a repayment of the tax credit. However, for 2003–4 dividends are taxed at the Schedule F ordinary rate of 10 per cent or the Schedule F upper rate of 32.5 per cent. Where the total income of an individual is not unduly substantial the amount of the tax credit, namely 10 per cent, will be offset against the Schedule F ordinary rate of income tax, which is also 10 per cent, leaving no further liability. Should the gross amount of dividends or distributions when added to other taxable income exceed £30,500 the excess is chargeable at the

Schedule F upper rate of 32.5 per cent. The amount of the tax credit will then reduce tax otherwise payable at the upper rate. Although the rates of 10 per cent and 32.5 per cent apply primarily to dividends and distributions from United Kingdom companies, they also extend to income of a similar nature arising outside the UK.

INCOME NOT TAXABLE

Income which is not taxable in 2003–4 includes interest on National Savings and Investments certificates, most scholarship income, bounty payments to members of the armed services and annuities payable to the holders of certain awards. Dividend income arising from qualifying investments in personal equity plans (PEPs) and venture capital trusts is exempt from tax. Although tax credits on dividends from such trusts can no longer be recovered it is possible for PEP managers to obtain repayment of credits during a five-year period ending on 5 April 2004. Payments made to an individual for the adoption of a child, together with income received under maintenance agreements and court orders made following separation or divorce will not be liable to tax. Nor will payments made under many deeds of covenant be recognised for tax purposes, unless the recipient is a charity. Interest arising on a tax exempt special savings account (TESSA) opened with a building society or bank will be exempt from tax if the account is maintained throughout a five-year period.

A popular investment, the individual savings account (ISA), is available to United Kingdom residents aged 18 years and over. The ISA may have three components, namely cash, stocks and shares and life assurance. Interest on the cash component, usually comprising bank or building society deposits, is exempt from income tax. Dividends on most quoted holdings in the stocks and shares component are also immune from liability to income tax, with tax credits being repaid for years up to and including that ending on 5 April 2004. Income and gains accruing to the provider of the life assurance component will be free of all liability to taxation.

A maximum subscription of £7,000 can be made by an individual to an ISA during 2003–4. Of this sum no more than £3,000 can be allocated to the cash component and £1,000 to the life assurance component. Potential investors are provided with the choice of whether to invest in a maxi-ISA or in mini-ISAs. Should a maxi-ISA be selected, the entire £7,000 can be invested in stocks and shares, but the use of a mini-ISA limits such an investment to £3,000 with the balance of £4,000 capable of being used to invest in the cash and life assurance components.

Although new TESSA accounts can no longer be opened, where an existing TESSA matures at the end of a five-year period the capital (but not the income) proceeds can be separately invested in the cash component of an ISA. This is in addition to the normal limits governing investment in an ISA.

FOSTER CARERS

Profits arising to an individual from the provision of foster care are chargeable to income tax. Previously, the calculation of these taxable profits produced a great deal of uncertainty but a new arrangement has been introduced for 2003–4 and future years. When determining the application of this arrangement for a year of assessment, an individual must calculate two factors, namely:

(a) a fixed amount of £10,000 for a given residence in a year. Where the residence is shared by two or more individuals providing foster care the amount of £10,000 must be suitably apportioned. Should the period of review fall short of a full twelve-month period, £10,000 must be suitably reduced.

(b) an amount per week for each foster child, comprising £200 per week for a child aged under 11 years and £250 per week for a child aged 11 or above.

Should the total receipts of an individual from the provision of foster care fall below the aggregate of (a) and (b) no liability to income tax will arise. However, should the receipts exceed the aggregate of (a) and (b) the individual is provided with a choice, namely:

(i) to calculate profits in the normal way on total receipts less actual expenses and capital allowances, or

(ii) to treat as taxable profits the amount by which total receipts from the provision of foster care exceed the aggregate of (a) and (b), without any separate relief for expenses or capital allowances.

ALLOWANCES

Allowances which can be obtained for 2003–4 are shown below.

Personal allowance

Basic personal allowance	£4,615
Those over 64 on 5 April 2004	£6,610
Those over 74 on 5 April 2004	£6,720

The increased allowance for older individuals is available for those who died during the year of assessment but who would otherwise have achieved the appropriate age not later than 5 April 2004. The amount of the increased personal allowance for older taxpayers will be reduced by one-half of total income in excess of £18,300. This reduction in the allowance will continue until it has been reduced to the basic personal allowance of £4,615. The personal allowance is given as a deduction in calculating taxable income and may therefore produce relief at the rate of 10, 22 or 40 per cent, as appropriate.

Married couple's allowance

A married man who was 'living with' his wife at any time in the year ending on 5 April 2004 will be entitled to a married couple's allowance if at least one party to the marriage reached the age of 65 years before 6 April 2000. The allowance, which therefore applies only to those born before 6 April 1935, cannot be obtained where a husband or wife reaches 65 on some future date.

The allowance is £5,565. It may be increased to £5,635 where either party to the marriage was 75 or over on 5 April 2004. Where an individual would otherwise have reached the age of 75 by 5 April 2004 but who died earlier in the year, the increased allowance is given. The amount of the married couple's allowance will be reduced where the income of the husband (excluding the income of the wife) exceeds £18,300. In this situation the amount to be deducted from the allowance will comprise:

(a) one-half of the husband's total income in excess of £18,300, less

(b) the amount of any reduction made when calculating the husband's increased personal allowance.

This reduction in the married couple's allowance cannot reduce that allowance below a basic allowance of £2,150.

If husband and wife were married during 2003–4 the married couple's allowance must be reduced by one-twelfth for each complete month commencing on 6 April 2003 and preceding the date of marriage.

Unlike the personal allowance, the married couple's allowance does not reduce taxable income. Relief is granted by reducing the tax otherwise payable by 10 per cent of the allowance. For example, where the basic allowance of £2,150 is available, the amount of tax payable may be reduced by £215. Should the amount of the reduction exceed tax otherwise payable, no tax will be due, nor will any repayment arise.

In the absence of any further action, the married couple's allowance will be given to the husband. If he is unable to utilise all or any part of that allowance due to an absence of income, the husband may transfer the unused portion to his wife. The decision whether or not to transfer remains at the discretion of the husband. However, a wife may file an election to obtain one-half of the basic married couple's allowance of £2,150 as of right, leaving the husband with the balance of that allowance. Alternatively, the couple may jointly elect that the entire basic allowance should be allocated to the wife only. Should either spouse be unable to utilise his or her share of the total married couple's allowance the unused part may be transferred to the other spouse.

Blind person's allowance
An allowance of £1,510 is available to an individual if at any time during the year ending on 5 April 2004, he or she was registered as blind. If the individual is 'living with' a wife or husband, any unused part of the blind person's allowance can be transferred to the other spouse. The allowance reduces taxable income and may therefore give rise to relief at the taxpayer's highest rate of income tax suffered.

CHILDREN'S TAX CREDIT
A children's tax credit was available for two years only in 2001–2 and 2002–3. The credit could be claimed by an individual who had one or more qualifying children resident with him or her during all or part of the tax year. The credit for 2002–3 was £5,290 and given at the rate of 10 per cent as a deduction from income tax otherwise payable. However, where the income of the claimant incurred liability to income tax at the higher rate of 40 per cent, the credit of £5,290 was reduced by two-thirds of the income chargeable at the higher rate. Special rules applied to identify the person with the higher rate of income in the case of husband and wife or a man and woman 'living together'.

An addition to the children's tax credit was available for 2002–3 only. To obtain this addition it had to be shown that a baby was born during the year of assessment and resided with the claimant. The amount of the additional 'baby rate' credit was £5,200 which was added to the normal children's tax credit of £5,290 to produce an aggregate of £10,490. This aggregate remained subject to the restrictions shown above where the claimant, or some other person, had sufficient income to produce liability at the higher rate of 40 per cent.

The children's tax credit has been discontinued and does not apply for 2003–4 and future years. It has been replaced by the child tax credit which combines all income-related support for children under a single system.

MAINTENANCE PAYMENTS
Relief for maintenance payments made in 2003–4 to a separated spouse or a divorced former spouse is limited to £2,150 or the amount of the payment, whichever is smaller. A further requirement before relief can be obtained is that at least one of the parties to the transaction had reached his/her 65th birthday before 6 April 2000. No relief is available to younger parties. Relief is given at the rate of 10 per cent and subtracted from the amount of tax otherwise due by the payer. The maintenance payment is exempt from liability to income tax in the hands of the recipient.

INTEREST
In some instances, interest paid by a business proprietor may be included when calculating profits chargeable to income tax under Case I or Case II of Schedule D. In addition, relief for interest paid on a loan applied to acquire or develop land and buildings for letting may be obtained by including the outlay in the calculation of income chargeable under Schedule A. However, many private individuals cannot obtain relief in this manner and must satisfy stringent requirements before relief will be forthcoming. In general terms it is a requirement that before interest can qualify for relief it must be paid for a qualifying purpose. Relief will not be available to the extent that interest exceeds a reasonable commercial rate and no relief is forthcoming for interest on an overdraft.

Interest paid in 2003–4 which can be treated as laid out for a qualifying purpose will include the following payments:
(a) Interest on a loan used to acquire an interest in a close company or in a partnership, or to advance money to such a person or body
(b) Interest on a loan to a member of a partnership to acquire machinery or plant for use in the partnership business
(c) Interest on a loan to an employed person to acquire machinery or plant for the purposes of his or her employment
(d) Interest on a loan made for the purpose of contributing capital to an industrial co-operative
(e) Interest on a loan applied for investment in an employee-controlled company
(f) Interest on a loan to personal representatives to provide funds for the payment of inheritance tax
(g) Interest on a loan made to elderly persons for the purchase of an annuity where the loan is secured on land. If the loan exceeds £30,000, relief is limited to interest on this amount. This relief is restricted to income tax at the basic rate of 22 per cent. Whilst the relief remains for some borrowers, it cannot be obtained for interest only new loans taken out after 8 March 1999.

Relief under headings (a) to (f) is given by deducting interest from taxable income. This enables the taxpayer to obtain relief at his or her top rate of tax suffered.

CHARITABLE DONATIONS
A number of charitable donations and qualify for tax relief and may involve donations of money or transferable assets. A popular arrangement is the Gift Aid scheme which requires the making of a money payment to a recognised charity. Providing that the donor receives little or no benefit in return, and certain formalities are complied with, the donation is then treated as a net sum paid after deducting income tax at the basic rate of 22 per cent. On the assumption that the donor suffers a

sufficient amount of income tax at that rate, no additional income tax will be payable. However, if the donor suffers liability at the higher rate of 40 per cent, he/she may obtain relief for the outlay at the difference between the basic rate of 22 per cent and the higher rate of 40 per cent – 18 per cent – on the grossed up amount of the donation.

OTHER OUTGOINGS

Many employees pay contributions to an approved occupational pension scheme. The amount of their contributions may be deducted when calculating net taxable earnings treated as employment income. Relief should also be available for any additional voluntary contributions paid. Self-employed individuals and those receiving earnings not covered by an occupational pension scheme may contribute under personal pension scheme arrangements or under stakeholder schemes. Individuals may also pay premiums under retirement annuity schemes if the arrangements were concluded before 1 July 1988. Contributions paid under all headings and which do not exceed upper limits may obtain income tax relief by deduction from taxable income.

Subject to a maximum of £150,000 in 2003–4, the cost of subscribing for shares in an unquoted trading company or companies may qualify for relief under the Enterprise Investment Scheme. Many requirements must be satisfied before this relief can be obtained, but a husband and wife may each take advantage of the £150,000 maximum. Relief is given by reducing tax payable at the rate of 20 per cent of the share subscription cost. Further relief on an outlay, up to a maximum of £100,000 and also given at the rate of 20 per cent, is available for a subscription of shares in a venture capital trust company.

TAX CREDITS

A new child tax credit and a working tax credit became payable to individuals on and after 6 April 2003. Although the title of both credits incorporates the word 'tax', neither affects the amount of income tax payable or repayable. Both take the form of social security benefits.

CAPITAL GAINS TAX

An individual is potentially chargeable to capital gains tax on chargeable gains that accrue from disposals made by him/her during a year of assessment. The following information is largely confined to the year of assessment 2003–4, ending on 5 April 2004.

Liability extends to individuals who are either resident or ordinarily resident for the year but special rules apply where a person permanently leaves the UK or comes to this territory for the purpose of acquiring residence. Non-residents are not usually liable to capital gains tax unless they carry on a business in the UK through a branch or agency. However, individuals who left the UK after 16 March 1998 and who have been resident or ordinarily resident in at least four of the seven years preceding departure may remain liable to capital gains tax unless they reside overseas throughout a period of five complete tax years. Exceptions from this may apply where there is a disposal of assets acquired in the period of absence.

Trustees residing in the UK, together with personal representatives are chargeable to capital gains tax at the flat rate of 34 per cent but chargeable gains accruing to companies are assessable to corporation tax.

In earlier years, capital gains tax was chargeable on the net chargeable gains accruing to a person in a year of assessment after subtracting the annual exemption for that year. Net chargeable gains represented capital gains less capital losses arising from disposals carried out during the year. Unused losses brought forward from an earlier year could be offset against current net chargeable gains, but in the case of individuals were not to reduce the net gains below the annual exemption limit. It was possible to utilise trading losses against chargeable gains where those losses had not been offset against income.

TAPER RELIEF

However, the calculation of net gains chargeable to capital gains tax is now governed by the availability of taper relief. The purpose of this relief, which replaced the former indexation allowance, is to require that only a percentage of gains become chargeable to capital gains tax. Taper relief draws a distinction between business assets and non-business assets. The expression 'business asset' broadly identifies an asset used for business purposes in addition to some holdings of shares in both trading and non-trading companies. Where the nature of an asset has changed during the period of ownership from a business asset to a non-business asset, or vice versa, the asset must be effectively broken down into two parts. This may be particularly relevant where the period overlaps 5 April 2000, 5 April 2002 or 5 April 2003 when, on each occasion, some previously non-business assets were re-classified as business assets.

The percentage which must be used to calculate taper relief is governed by the number of complete years of ownership falling after 5 April 1998. Initially an additional 'bonus year' could be added for most assets acquired before 17 March 1998. This 'bonus year' continues to apply to non-business assets but has been withdrawn where the disposal of a business asset takes place after 5 April 2000.

The maximum percentage attributable to business assets was initially achieved after an ownership period extending throughout ten years but this period was reduced to one of four years only where the disposal occurred after 5 April 2000 and before 6 April 2002. Finally, where the disposal of business assets takes place on and after 6 April 2002 the ownership period has been further reduced. Once that period exceeds one year only 50 per cent of the gain will be chargeable, falling to 25 per cent where two whole years are exceeded. No corresponding changes have been made to the ownership period of non-business assets, which has remained unchanged since the introduction of taper relief on 6 April 1998. The percentages of gains chargeable for disposals taking place on and after 6 April 2003 are shown in the following table:

No. of whole years of ownership	Percentage of gain chargeable	
	Business assets	Non-business assets
	%	%
1	50.0	100
2	25.0	100
3	–	95
4	–	90
5	–	85
6	–	80
7	–	75

No. of whole years of ownership	Percentage of gain chargeable	
	Business assets	Non-business assets
	%	%
8	–	70
9	–	65
10	–	60

If only chargeable gains arise from disposals carried out in 2003–4 the taper relief, if any, must be calculated by reference to each disposal. The aggregate sum of taper relief will then be subtracted from the total chargeable gains to produce the net gains for the year. Where disposals made in 2003–4 give rise to both gains and losses, the losses must be subtracted from the gains and taper relief calculated on the net sum remaining. It is necessary to allocate the losses between the gains where there are two or more disposals. Losses brought forward from an earlier year must also be subtracted when calculating the net gains qualifying for taper relief. However, the losses brought forward are not to reduce the net gains below the annual exemption limit of £7,900 which applies for 2003–4.

ANNUAL EXEMPTION

The initial slice of net gains arising in a tax year is exempt from liability to capital gains tax. This slice, comprising the annual exemption, is £7,900 for 2003–4. Should any part of the exemption remain unused, this cannot be carried forward to a future year.

RATES OF TAX

The net gains remaining, if any, calculated after subtracting the annual exemption, incur liability to capital gains tax for 2003–4. Although income tax rates are used for this purpose, liability arises only at the starting rate of 10 per cent, the lower rate of 20 per cent, the higher rate of 40 per cent, or a combination of the three rates. Unlike some income tax commitments, there is no liability at the basic rate of 22 per cent.

The first step is to calculate the amount of taxable income chargeable to income tax. This will include income from savings, company dividends and all other forms of taxable income. The second step is to add the amount of net chargeable gains to the taxable income chargeable to income tax. To the extent that this does not increase the aggregate total above £1,960, capital gains tax will be charged at the rate of 10 per cent. If the aggregate total exceeds £1,960 but does not exceed £30,500 any balance needed to reach £1,960 is chargeable at 10 per cent and the excess at 20 per cent. If, or to the extent that, any part of the chargeable gains exceed the limit of £30,500 the excess is chargeable at 40 per cent. Although some income tax rates are used, capital gains tax remains an entirely separate tax. Capital gains tax for 2003–4 falls due for payment in full on 31 January 2005. If payment is delayed, interest or surcharges may be imposed.

HUSBAND AND WIFE

Independent taxation requires that a husband and wife 'living together' are separately assessed to capital gains tax. Each spouse must independently calculate his or her gains and losses, with each entitled to the benefit of taper relief, if any, and the annual exemption of £7,900 for 2003–2004. No liability to capital gains tax arises from the transfer of assets between husband and wife 'living together'.

DISPOSAL OF ASSETS

Before chargeable gains potentially liable to capital gains tax can arise, a disposal or deemed disposal of an asset must take place. This occurs not only where assets are sold or exchanged but applies on the making of a gift. There is also a disposal of assets where any capital sum is derived from assets, e.g. where compensation is received for loss or damage to an asset. The date on which a disposal must be treated as having taken place will determine the year of assessment into which the chargeable gain or allowable loss falls. In those cases where a disposal is made under an unconditional contract, the time of disposal will be that when the contract was entered into and not the subsequent date of conveyance or transfer. A disposal under a conditional contract or option is treated as taking place when the contract becomes unconditional or the option is exercised. Disposals by way of gift are undertaken when the gift becomes effective.

VALUATION OF ASSETS

The amount received as consideration for the disposal of an asset will be the sum from which very limited outgoings must be deducted for the purpose of establishing the gain or loss. In cases where the consideration does not accurately reflect the value of the asset, a different basis must be used. This applies, in particular, where an asset is transferred by way of gift or otherwise than by a bargain made at arm's length. Such transactions are deemed to take place for a consideration representing market value, which will determine both the disposal proceeds accruing to the transferor and the cost of acquisition accruing to the transferee.

Market value represents the price which an asset might reasonably be expected to fetch on a sale in the open market. In the case of unquoted shares or securities, it is to be assumed that the hypothetical purchaser in the open market would have available all the information which a prudent prospective purchaser of shares or securities might reasonably require if that person were proposing to purchase them from a willing vendor by private treaty and at arm's length. The market value of unquoted shares or securities will often be established following negotiations with the Shares Valuation Division of the Inland Revenue. The valuation of land and interests in land in the UK will be dealt with by the District Valuer. Special rules apply to determine the market value of shares quoted on the Stock Exchange.

DEDUCTION FOR OUTGOINGS

Once the actual or notional disposal proceeds have been determined, it only remains to subtract eligible outgoings for the purpose of computing the gain or loss. There is the general rule that any outgoings deducted, or which are available to be deducted, when calculating income tax liability must be ignored. Subject to this, deductions will usually be limited to:

(a) the cost of acquiring the asset, together with incidental costs wholly and exclusively incurred in connection with the acquisition

(b) expenditure incurred wholly and exclusively on the asset in enhancing its value, being expenditure reflected in the state or nature of the asset at the time of the disposal, and any other expenditure wholly and exclusively incurred in establishing, preserving or defending title to, or a right over, the asset

(c) the incidental costs of making the disposal

Where the disposal concerns a leasehold interest having less than 50 years to run, any expenditure falling under (a) and (b) must be written off throughout the duration of the lease using a 'curved line' approach.

INDEXATION ALLOWANCE

For many years an indexation allowance could be inserted when calculating a gain on the disposal of an asset. The allowance was based on percentage increases in the retail prices index between the month of March 1982, or the month in which expenditure was incurred if later, and the month of disposal.

Taper relief has largely replaced the indexation allowance for disposals made after 5 April 1998. However, where an asset was acquired before this date, the indexation allowance will be calculated to the month of April 1998 and frozen. The frozen allowance then enters into the calculation of chargeable gain, if any, when the asset is disposed of at some later date. The adjustment for the indexation allowance must be made before calculating taper relief on the net sum remaining.

EXEMPTIONS

There is a general exemption from liability to capital gains tax where the net gains of an individual for 2003–4 do not exceed £7,900. This general exemption applies separately to a husband and wife whether or not the parties are 'living together'. The disposal of many assets will not give rise to chargeable gains or allowable losses and these assets include:

(a) private motor cars
(b) government securities
(c) loan stock and other securities (but not shares)
(d) options and contracts relating to securities within (b) and (c)
(e) National Savings and Investments Certificates, Premium Bonds, Defence Bonds and National Development Bonds
(f) currency of any description acquired for personal expenditure outside the UK
(g) decorations awarded for valour
(h) betting wins and pools, lottery or games prizes
(i) compensation or damages for any wrong or injury suffered by an individual in his or her person, profession or vocation
(j) life assurance and deferred annuity contracts where the person making the disposal is the original beneficial owner
(k) dwelling-houses and land enjoyed with the residence which is an individual's only or main residence
(l) tangible movable property, the consideration for the disposal of which does not exceed £6,000
(m) certain tangible movable property which is a wasting asset having a life not exceeding 50 years
(n) assets transferred to charities and other bodies
(o) works of art, historic buildings and similar assets
(p) assets used to provide maintenance funds for historic buildings
(q) assets transferred to trustees for the benefit of employees
(r) assets held in a Personal Equity Plan or Individual Savings Account

DWELLING-HOUSES

Exemption from capital gains tax will usually be available for any gain which accrues to an individual from the disposal of, or of an interest in, a dwelling-house or part of a dwelling-house which has been his or her only or main residence. The exemption extends to land which has been occupied and enjoyed with the residence as its garden or grounds. Some restriction may be necessary where the land exceeds half a hectare.

The gain will not be chargeable to capital gains tax if the dwelling-house, or part, has been the individual's only or main residence throughout the period of ownership, or throughout the entire period except for all or any part of the final three years. A proportionate part of the gain will be exempt in other cases if the dwelling-house has been the individual's only or main residence for part only of the period of ownership. In the case of property acquired before 31 March 1982, the period of ownership is treated as commencing on this date. Where part of the dwelling-house has been used exclusively for business purposes, that part of the gain attributable to business use will not be exempt. In those cases where part of a qualifying dwelling-house has been used to provide rented residential accommodation, this non-personal use may frequently be ignored when calculating exemption from capital gains tax, unless relatively substantial sums are involved. Dwellings occupied by dependent relatives, separated spouses or divorced former spouses, may also qualify for the exemption, but only where occupation commenced before 6 April 1988.

ROLL-OVER RELIEF

Persons carrying on business will often undertake the disposal of an asset and use the proceeds to finance the acquisition of a replacement asset. Where this situation arises, a claim for roll-over relief may be available. The broad effect of such a claim is that all or part of the gain arising on the disposal of the old asset may be disregarded. The gain or part is then subtracted from the cost of acquiring the replacement asset. As this cost is reduced, any gain arising from the future disposal of the replacement asset will be correspondingly increased, unless a further roll-over situation then develops. It remains a requirement that both the old and the replacement asset must be used for the purpose of the taxpayer's business or for the purpose of business carried out by a company in which the taxpayer retains an interest. Relief will only be available if the acquisition of the replacement asset takes place within a period commencing twelve months before, and ending three years after, the disposal of the old asset, although the Inland Revenue retains a discretion to extend this period where the circumstances were such that it was impossible for the taxpayer to acquire the replacement asset before the expiration of the normal time limit. Whilst many business assets qualify for roll-over relief there are exceptions.

Roll-over relief may also be available where a gain arises on the disposal of land or buildings to an authority capable of exercising compulsory purchase powers. Similar relief may be forthcoming where shares in a company are transferred to trustees administering an employees' share incentive plan for the benefit of persons employed by that company or group of companies of which the company is a member.

DEFERRAL RELIEF

A form of roll-over relief, known as 'deferral relief' enables gains arising on the disposal of an asset to be matched, in whole or in part, with a subscription for shares in a restricted range of unquoted companies, including certain companies whose shares are dealt in on the Alternative Investment Market. Where matching can be achieved any part of the gain arising on disposal, not exceeding the cost of the qualifying share subscription, may become the subject of a claim. Unlike the usual form of roll-over relief, this claim for deferral relief does not eliminate or reduce the chargeable gain. It has the effect of deferring that gain until the time of some future event, which will usually be identified by the disposal of the newly acquired shares or the loss of UK residential status by the shareholder. A similar form of deferral relief is available for gains arising on other disposals which are matched with a qualifying share investment in a venture capital trust company. To the extent of the gain arising, which must not exceed the amount of the investment qualifying for income tax relief, that gain is deferred until the time of a future event, which will normally comprise the disposal of shares in the venture capital trust or the loss of UK residential status.

HOLD-OVER RELIEF – GIFTS

The gift of an asset is treated as a disposal made for a consideration equal to market value, with a corresponding acquisition by the transferee at an identical value. In the case of gifts made by individuals and a limited range of trustees to a transferee resident in the UK, a form of hold-over relief may be available. Relief, which must be claimed, is limited to the transfer of certain assets, including the following:

(a)   assets used for the purposes of a trade or similar activity carried on by the transferor or his/her personal company

(b)   shares or securities of a trading company which is not listed on a stock exchange

(c)   shares or securities of a trading company which is listed but which is the transferor's personal company

(d)   many interests in agricultural property qualifying for agricultural property relief for inheritance tax purposes

(e)   assets involved in transactions which are lifetime transfers for inheritance tax purposes, other than potentially exempt transfers

The transfer of shares or securities to a company is now precluded from obtaining relief. The effect of a valid claim for hold-over relief is similar to that following a claim for roll-over relief on the disposal of business assets, but adjustments may be necessary where some consideration is given for the transfer, the asset has not been used for business purposes throughout the period of ownership, or not all assets of a company are used for business purposes.

RETIREMENT RELIEF

Retirement relief was previously available to an individual who disposed by way of sale or gift of the whole or part of a business. The main condition for obtaining this relief was that throughout a period of at least one year the business had been owned either by the individual or by a trading company in which the individual retained a sufficient shareholding interest. The relief also extended to cases where an individual disposed by way of sale or gift of shares or securities of a company. To obtain this extension it had to be demonstrated that the company was a trading company, the individual retained a sufficient shareholding interest, and the individual was engaged as a full-time working officer or employee.

An individual who had attained the age of 50 years at the time of disposal could qualify for retirement relief which sheltered gains from liability to capital gains tax.

No retirement relief was forthcoming if the disposal occurred before the individual's fiftieth birthday, unless that individual was compelled to retire early on the grounds of ill health.

In recent years the amount of retirement relief has gradually reduced until it entirely ceased to be available for disposals taking place after 5 April 2003. As a result, retirement relief cannot affect liability to capital gains tax for 2003–4.

DEATH

No capital gains tax is chargeable on the value of assets retained at the time of death. However, the personal representatives administering the deceased's estate are deemed to acquire those assets for a consideration representing market value on death. This ensures that any increase in value occurring before the date of death will not be chargeable to capital gains tax. If a legatee or other person acquires an asset under a will or intestacy no chargeable gain will accrue to the personal representatives, and the person taking the asset will also be treated as having acquired it at the time of death for its then market value.

INHERITANCE TAX

Liability to inheritance tax may arise on a limited range of lifetime gifts and other dispositions and also on the value of assets retained, or deemed to be retained, at the time of death. An individual's domicile at the time of any gift or on death is an important matter. Domicile will generally be determined by applying normal rules, although special considerations may be necessary where an individual was previously domiciled in the UK but subsequently acquired a domicile of choice overseas. In addition, individuals who have been resident in the UK for at least 17 of the previous 20 years at the time of an event are treated as domiciled in the UK for this purpose. Where a person was domiciled, or treated as domiciled, in the UK at the time of a disposition or on death the location of assets is immaterial and full liability to inheritance tax arises. Individuals domiciled outside the UK are, however, chargeable to inheritance tax only on transactions affecting assets located in the UK. The assets of husband and wife are not merged for inheritance tax purposes. Each spouse is treated as a separate individual entitled to receive the benefit of his or her exemptions, reliefs and rates of tax. Where husband and wife retain similar assets, e.g. shares in the same family company, special 'related property' provisions may require the merger of those assets for valuation purposes only.

LIFETIME GIFTS AND DISPOSITIONS

Gifts and dispositions made during lifetime fall under four broad headings, namely:

(a)   dispositions which are not transfers of value
(b)   exempt transfers
(c)   potentially exempt transfers
(d)   chargeable transfers

Dispositions which are not transfers of value
Several lifetime transactions are not treated as transfers of value and may be entirely disregarded for inheritance tax purposes. These include transactions not intended to confer gratuitous benefit, the provision of family maintenance, the waiver of the right to receive remuneration or dividends, and the grant of agricultural tenancies for full consideration.

Exempt transfers

The main exempt transfers are:

Transfers between spouses – Transfers between husband and wife are usually exempt. However, if the transferor is, but the transferee spouse is not, domiciled in the UK, transfers will be exempt only to the extent that the total does not exceed £55,000. Unlike the requirement used for income tax and capital gains tax purposes, it is immaterial whether husband and wife are living together.

Annual exemption – The first £3,000 of gifts and other dispositions made in a year ending on 5 April is exempt. If the exemption is not used, or not wholly used, in any year the balance may be carried forward to the following year only. The annual exemption will only be available for a potentially exempt transfer if that transfer becomes chargeable by reason of the donor's subsequent death.

Small gifts – Outright gifts of £250 or less to any person in one year ending on 5 April are exempt.

Normal expenditure – A transfer made during lifetime and comprising normal expenditure is exempt. To obtain this exemption it must be shown that:

(a) the transfer was made as part of the normal expenditure of the transferor;

(b) taking one year with another, the transfer was made out of income; and

(c) after allowing for all transfers of value forming part of normal expenditure the transferor was left with sufficient income to maintain his or her usual standard of living

Gifts in consideration of marriage – These are exempt if they satisfy certain requirements. The amount allowed will be governed by the relationship between the donor and a party to the marriage. The allowable amounts comprise:

(a) gifts by a parent, £5,000

(b) gifts by a grandparent, £2,500

(c) gifts by a party to the marriage, £2,500

(d) gifts by other persons, £1,000

Gifts to charities – These are exempt from liability.

Gifts to political parties – Gifts which satisfy certain requirements are generally exempt.

Gifts for national purposes – Gifts made to certain bodies are exempt from liability. These bodies include, among others, the National Gallery, the British Museum, the National Trust, the National Art Collections Fund, the National Heritage Memorial Fund, the Historic Buildings and Monuments Commission for England (English Heritage), any local authority, and any university or university college in the UK.

A number of other gifts made for the public benefit are also exempt.

Potentially exempt transfers

Lifetime gifts and dispositions which are neither to be ignored nor comprise exempt transfers incur possible liability to inheritance tax. However, relief is available for a range of potentially exempt transfers. These comprise gifts made by an individual to:

(a) a second individual

(b) trustees administering an accumulation and maintenance trust

(c) trustees administering a disabled person's trust

The accumulation and maintenance trust mentioned in (b) must provide that on reaching a specified age, not exceeding 25 years, a beneficiary will become absolutely entitled to trust assets or obtain an interest in possession in the income from those assets. Additions to the above list affect settled property administered by trustees where an individual, or individuals, retain an interest in possession. The transfer of assets to, the removal of assets from, or the rearrangement of interests in such property comprise potentially exempt transfers if the person transferring an interest and the person benefiting from the transfer are both individuals.

No immediate liability to inheritance tax will arise on the making of a potentially exempt transfer. Should the donor survive for a period of seven years, immunity from liability will be confirmed. However, the donor's death within the seven-year inter vivos period produces liability if the amounts involved are sufficiently substantial (see below).

Chargeable transfers

Any remaining lifetime gifts or dispositions which are neither to be ignored nor represent exempt transfers or potentially exempt transfers, incur liability to inheritance tax.

GIFTS WITH RESERVATION

A lifetime gift of assets made at any time after 17 March 1986 may incur additional liability to inheritance tax if the donor retains some interest in the subject matter of the gift. This may arise, for example, where a parent transfers a dwelling-house to a son or daughter and continues to occupy the property or to enjoy some benefit from that property. The retention of a benefit may be ignored where it is enjoyed in return for full consideration, perhaps a commercial rent, or where the benefit arises from changed circumstances which could not have been foreseen at the time of the original gift. The gift with reservation provisions will not usually apply to most exempt transfers.

There are three possibilities which may arise where the donor reserves or enjoys some benefit from the subject matter of a previous gift and subsequently dies, namely:

(a) if no benefit is enjoyed within a period of seven years before death there can be no further liability

(b) if the benefit ceased to be enjoyed within a period of seven years before the date of death, the original donor is deemed to have made a potentially exempt transfer representing the value of the asset at the time of cessation

(c) if the benefit is enjoyed at the time of death, the value of the asset must be included when arriving at the value of the deceased's estate on death

It must be emphasised that the existence of a benefit enjoyed at any time within a period of seven years before death will establish liability to tax on gifts with reservation, notwithstanding that the gift may have been made many years earlier, providing it was undertaken after 17 March 1986.

DEATH

Immediately before the time of death an individual is deemed to make a transfer of value. This transfer will comprise the value of assets forming part of the deceased's estate after subtracting most liabilities. Any exempt transfers may, however, be excluded. These include transfers for the benefit of a surviving spouse, a charity and a qualifying political party, together with bequests to approved bodies and for national purposes.

Death may also trigger three additional liabilities:

(a) A potentially exempt transfer made within the period of seven years ending on death loses its potential status and becomes chargeable to inheritance tax

(b) The value of gifts made with reservation may incur liability if any benefit was enjoyed within a period of seven years preceding death
(c) Additional tax may become payable for chargeable lifetime transfers made within seven years before death

VALUATIONS

The valuation of assets establishes the value transferred for lifetime dispositions and also the value of a person's estate at the time of death. The value of property will represent the price which might reasonably be expected from a sale in the open market.

In some cases it may be necessary to incorporate the value of 'related property'. This will include property comprised in the estate of the transferor's spouse and certain property previously transferred to charities. The purpose of the related property valuation rules is not to add the value of the property to the estate of the transferor. Related property must be merged to establish the aggregate value of the respective interests and this value is then apportioned, usually on a *pro rata* basis, to the separate interests.

The value of shares and securities listed on the Stock Exchange will be determined by extracting figures from the daily list of official prices.

Where quoted shares and securities are sold or the quotation is suspended within a period of 12 months following the date of death, a claim may be made to substitute the proceeds or subsequent value for the value on death. This claim will only be beneficial if the gross proceeds realised are lower or the value has fallen below market value at the time of death. A similar claim may be available for interests in land sold within a period of four years following death.

RELIEF FOR SELECTED ASSETS

Special relief is made available for certain assets as follows:

Woodlands

Where woodlands pass on death the value will usually be included in the deceased's estate. However, an election may be made in respect of land in the UK on which trees or underwood is growing to delete the value of those assets. Relief is confined to the value of trees or underwood and does not extend to the land on which they are growing. Liability to inheritance tax will arise if and when the trees or underwood are subsequently sold.

Agricultural property

Relief is available for the agricultural value of agricultural property. Such property must be occupied and used for agricultural purposes and relief is confined to the agricultural value only.

The value transferred, either on a lifetime gift or on death, must be determined. This value may then be reduced by a percentage. For events taking place after 9 March 1992, a 100 per cent deduction will be available if the transferor retained vacant possession or could have obtained that possession within a period of 12 months following the transfer. In other cases, notably including land let to tenants, a lower deduction of 50 per cent is usually available. However, this lower deduction may be increased to 100 per cent if the letting was made after 31 August 1995.

It remains a requirement that the agricultural property was either occupied by the transferor for the purposes of agriculture throughout a two-year period ending on the date of the transfer, or was owned by him or her throughout a period of seven years ending on that date and also occupied for agricultural purposes.

Business property

Where the value transferred is attributable to relevant business property, that value may be reduced by a percentage. The reduction in value applies to:
(a) property consisting of a business or an interest in a business (i.e. a partnership)
(b) securities of an unquoted company which, together with any unquoted shares in the same company provided the transferor with control
(c) other unquoted shares in a company
(d) shares or securities of a quoted company which provided the transferor with control
(e) any land, building, machinery or plant which, immediately before the transfer, was used wholly or mainly for the purposes of a business carried on by a company of which the transferor had control
(f) any land, building, machinery or plant which, immediately before the transfer, was used wholly or mainly for the purposes of a business carried on by a partnership of which the transferor was a partner
(g) any land, building, machinery or plant which, immediately before the transfer, was used wholly or mainly for the purposes of a business carried on by the transferor and was then settled property in which he/she retained an interest in possession

The percentage deduction has changed from time to time but for events occurring after 5 April 1996, a deduction of 100 per cent is available for assets falling within (a), (b) and (c). A deduction of 50 per cent remains for assets within (d) to (g).

It is a general requirement that the property must have been retained for a period of two years before the transfer or death and restrictions may be necessary if the property has not been used wholly for business purposes. The same property cannot obtain both business property relief and the relief available for agricultural property.

CALCULATION OF TAX PAYABLE

The calculation of inheritance tax payable adopts the use of a cumulative total. Each chargeable lifetime transfer is added to the total with a final addition made on death. The top slice added to the total for the current event determines the rate at which inheritance tax must be paid. However, the cumulative total will only include transfers made within a period of seven years before the current event and those undertaken outside this period must be excluded.

Lifetime chargeable transfers

The value transferred by the limited range of lifetime chargeable transfers must be added to the seven-year cumulative total to calculate whether any inheritance tax is due. Should the nil rate band be exceeded, tax will be imposed on the excess at the rate of 20 per cent. However, if the donor dies within a period of seven years from the date of the chargeable lifetime transfer, additional tax may be due. This is calculated by applying tax at the full rate or 40 per cent in substitution for the rate of 20 per cent previously used. The amount of tax is then reduced to a percentage by applying tapering relief. This percentage is governed by the number of years from the date of the lifetime gift to the date of death, as follows:

Period of years before death	
Not more than 3	100%
More than 3 but not more than 4	80%
More than 4 but not more than 5	60%
More than 5 but not more than 6	40%
More than 6 but not more than 7	20%

Should this exercise produce liability greater than that previously paid at the 20 per cent rate on the lifetime transfer, additional tax, representing the difference, must be discharged. Where the calculation shows an amount falling below tax paid on the lifetime transfer, no additional liability can arise nor will the shortfall become repayable.

Tapering relief will, of course, only be available if the calculation discloses a liability to inheritance tax. There can be no liability to the extent that the lifetime transfer falls within the nil rate band.

Potentially exempt transfers

Where a potentially exempt transfer loses immunity from liability due to the donor's death within the seven-year *inter vivos* period, the value transferred by that transfer enters into the cumulative total. Any liability to inheritance tax will be calculated by applying the full rate of 40 per cent, reduced to the percentage governed by tapering relief if the original transfer occurred more than three years before death. Liability can only arise to the extent, if any, that the nil rate band is exceeded.

Death

The final addition to the seven-year cumulative total will comprise the value of an estate on death. Inheritance tax will be calculated by applying the full rate of 40 per cent to the extent the nil rate band is exceeded. No tapering relief can be obtained.

RATES OF TAX

In earlier times there were several rates of inheritance tax which progressively increased as the value transferred grew in size. However, since 1988 there have been only three rates, namely:
(a) a nil rate
(b) a lifetime rate of 20 per cent
(c) a full rate of 40 per cent
The nil rate band usually changes on an annual basis and for events taking place after 5 April 2003 applies to the first £255,000. Any excess over this level is taxable at 20 per cent or 40 per cent as the case may be.

PAYMENT OF TAX

Inheritance tax usually falls due for payment six months after the end of the month in which the chargeable transaction takes place. Where a transfer other than that made on death occurs after 5 April and before the following 1 October, tax falls due on the following 30 April, although there are some exceptions to this. Inheritance tax attributable to the transfer of certain land, controlling shareholding interests, unquoted shares, businesses and interests in businesses, together with agricultural property, may usually be satisfied by instalments spread over ten years. Except in the case of non-agricultural land, where interest is charged on outstanding instalments, no liability to interest arises where tax is paid on the due date. In all cases, delay in the payment of tax may incur a liability to discharge interest.

SETTLED PROPERTY

Complex rules apply to establish inheritance tax liability on settled property. Where a person is beneficially entitled to an interest in possession, that person is effectively deemed to own the property in which the interest subsists. It follows that where the interest comes to an end during the beneficiary's lifetime and some other person becomes entitled to the property or interest, the beneficiary is treated as having made a transfer of value. However, this will usually comprise a potentially exempt transfer. In addition, no liability will arise where the property vests in the absolute ownership of the beneficiary retaining the interest in possession. The death of a person entitled to an interest in possession will require the value of the underlying property to be added to the value of the deceased's estate.

In the case of other settled property where there is no interest in possession (e.g. discretionary trusts), liability to tax will arise on each ten-year anniversary of the trust. There will also be liability if property ceases to be held on discretionary trusts before the first ten-year anniversary date is reached or between anniversaries. The rate of tax suffered will be governed by several considerations, including previous dispositions made by the settlor of the trust, transactions concluded by the trustees, and the period throughout which property has been held in trust.

Accumulation and maintenance settlements which require assets to be distributed, or interests in income to be created, not later than a beneficiary's 25th birthday may be exempt from any liability to inheritance tax.

CORPORATION TAX

Profits, gains and income accruing to companies resident in the UK incur liability to corporation tax. Non-resident companies are immune from this tax unless they carry on a trade in the UK through a permanent establishment, branch or office. Companies residing outside the UK may be liable to income tax at the basic rate on other income arising in the UK, perhaps from letting property. The following comments are confined to companies resident in the UK. Liability to corporation tax is governed by the profits, gains or income for an accounting period. This is usually the period for which financial accounts are made up, and in the case of companies preparing accounts to the same accounting date annually will comprise successive periods of 12 months.

RATE OF TAX

The amount of profits or income for an accounting period must be determined on normal taxation principles. The special rules which apply to individuals where a source of income is acquired or discontinued are ignored and consideration is confined to the actual profits or income for an accounting period.

The rate of corporation tax is fixed for a financial year ending on 31 March. Where the accounting period of a company overlaps this date and there is a change in the rate of corporation tax, profits and income must be apportioned.

The main rate of corporation tax for each of the five financial years ending on the 31 March 2000 to 31 March 2005 inclusive is 30 per cent. This may be reduced to a lower level where profits fall within the small companies' rate or companies' starting rate bands. Although the main rate of tax for the year ending on 21 March 2005 is known, the small companies rate and the starting rate for the same year will not be announced until a later date.

SMALL COMPANIES' RATE

Where the profits of a company do not exceed stated limits, corporation tax becomes payable at the small companies' rate. This may be replaced by a lower starting rate where profits are very small, as discussed later. It is the amount of profits and not the size of the company which governs the application of both the small companies' rate and the starting rate.

For each of the financial years ending on 31 March 2000, 31 March 2001 and 31 March 2002 the small companies' rate remained at 20 per cent. It was then reduced to 19 per cent for the two years ending on 31 March 2003 and 31 March 2004.

The level of profits which a company may derive without losing the benefit of the small companies' rate is £300,000 for each of the five years. However, if profits exceed £300,000 but fall below £1,500,000, marginal small companies' rate relief applies. The effect of marginal relief is that the average rate of corporation tax imposed on all profits steadily increases from the lower small companies' rate of 19 per cent (or previously 20 per cent) to the main rate of 30 per cent, with tax being imposed on profits in the margin at an increased rate. Where a change in the rate of tax is introduced and the accounting period of a company overlaps 31 March, profits must be apportioned to establish the appropriate rate for each part of those profits.

The lower limit of £300,000 and the upper limit of £1,500,000 apply to a period of 12 months and must be proportionately reduced for shorter periods. Some restriction in the small companies' rate and the marginal rate may be necessary if there are two or more associated companies, namely companies under common control.

The small companies' rate is not available for close investment-holding companies.

COMPANIES' STARTING RATE

A companies' starting rate is available for each of the four financial years ending on 31 March 2001, 2002, 2003 and 2004. This rate applies where profits of a twelve-month period do not exceed £10,000, with marginal relief where profits exceed this figure but are not in excess of £50,000. The starting rate was 10 per cent for each of the financial years ending on 31 March 2001 and 31 March 2002 and zero for the two financial years ending on 31 March 2003 and 31 March 2004. The effect of marginal relief is to increase the average rate of tax suffered until it reaches the small companies' rate for the same financial year.

PAYMENT OF TAX

Corporation tax charged on profits for an accounting period usually falls due for payment in a single lump sum nine months after the end of that period. Most companies discharge corporation tax on this basis but other arrangements concern large companies for accounting periods ending on or after 1 July 1999. These companies must discharge their liability by four instalments. The receipt of annual profits amounting to £1,500,000 or more is sufficient to identify a large company. Where a company is a member of a group the profits of the entire group must be merged to establish whether the company is large.

CAPITAL GAINS

Chargeable gains arising to a company are calculated in a manner similar to that used for individuals. However, the withdrawal of the indexation allowance after April 1998, and the introduction of taper relief from the same date, have no application to companies. Nor are companies entitled to the annual exemption of £7,900. However, many gains arising to companies from the disposal of substantial shareholdings after 31 March 2002 are exempt from tax. Companies do not suffer capital gains tax on chargeable gains but incur liability to corporation tax. Tax is due on the full chargeable gain of an accounting period after subtracting relief for losses, if any.

DISTRIBUTIONS

Dividends and other qualifying distributions made by a UK resident company on or after 6 April 1999 are not satisfied after deduction of income tax. Similar outgoings made by a company previously required the payment of advance corporation tax but this obligation no longer applies. The only effect which the payment of a dividend or the making of a distribution now has on a company is that the outlay cannot form an ingredient in the calculation of profits.

INTEREST

On making many payments of interest a company is required to deduct income tax at the lower rate of 20 per cent and account for the tax deducted to the Inland Revenue. The gross amount of interest paid will usually be included in the calculation of profits on which corporation tax becomes payable. The requirement to deduct tax will not usually apply where payments are being made to a second company.

GROUPS OF COMPANIES

Each company within a group is separately charged to corporation tax on profits, gains and income. However, where one group member realises a loss for which special rules apply, other than a capital loss, a claim may be made to offset the deficiency against profits of some other member of the same group.

The transfer of capital assets from one member of a group to a fellow member will usually incur no liability to tax on chargeable gains.

COMPLIANCE

For several years a 'pay and file' system affected all companies. A feature of this system required that tax should be payable nine months following the end of the accounting period involved, with accounts and returns being submitted three months later. This system was replaced following the introduction of self-assessment which extends to all companies for accounting periods ending after 30 June 1999.

Self-assessment requires that the corporation tax return should normally be submitted not later than 12 months following the end of the accounting period to which it relates. In addition, a copy of the financial accounts must be included. Failure to file the return within the appropriate time limit will incur a liability to penalties.

VALUE ADDED TAX

Value added tax (VAT) is charged on the value of the supplies made by a registered trader and extends to both the supply of goods and the supply of services. It is administered by Customs and Excise. Liability to account for VAT arises on the value of goods imported into the UK from sources outside the European Community. In contrast goods imported by a trader from a second trader in a member state of the European Community attract no VAT on importation. Instead there is an acquisition tax whereby a trader who acquires goods must include the acquisition in his normal VAT return and account for the tax due. A UK trader who exports goods to a member state will not be required to account for VAT on the supply, if that trader observes the requirements laid down by regulations.

REGISTRATION

All traders, including professional persons and companies, making taxable supplies of a value exceeding stated limits are required to register for VAT purposes. Taxable supplies represent the supply of goods and services potentially chargeable with VAT. The limits which govern mandatory registration are amended periodically, and from 10 April 2003 an unregistered trader must register:

(a) at any time, if there are reasonable grounds for believing that the value of taxable supplies in the next 30 days will exceed £56,000

(b) at the end of any month if the value of taxable supplies in the 12 months then ending has exceeded £56,000.

Liability to register under (b) may be avoided if it can be shown that the value of supplies in the period of 12 months then beginning will not exceed £54,000. There may, however, be liability to register immediately where a business is taken over from another trader as a 'going concern'. Other limits apply where goods are acquired from within the European Community.

Where the limits governing mandatory registration have been exceeded, the trader must notify Customs and Excise. In the event of failure to provide prompt notification, the person concerned will be required to account for VAT from the proper registration date. A trader whose taxable supplies do not reach the mandatory registration limits may apply for voluntary registration. This step may be thought advisable to recover input tax or to compete with other registered traders.

A registered trader may submit an application for deregistration if the value of taxable supplies subsequently falls. From 10 April 2003, an application for deregistration can be made if the value of taxable supplies for the year beginning on the application date is not expected to exceed £54,000.

INPUT TAX

A registered trader will both suffer tax (input tax) when obtaining goods or services for the purposes of his business and also become liable to account for tax (output tax) on the value of goods and services which he or she supplies. Relief can usually be obtained for input tax suffered, either by setting that tax against output tax due or by repayment. Most items of input tax can be relieved in this manner. Where a registered trader makes both exempt supplies and taxable supplies to his customers or clients, there may be some restriction in the amount of input tax which can be recovered.

OUTPUT TAX

When making a taxable supply of goods or services, a registered trader must account for output tax, if any, on the value of the supply. Usually the price charged by the registered trader will be increased by adding VAT but failure to make the required addition will not remove liability to account for output tax. The liability to account for output tax, and also relief for input tax, may be affected where a trader is using a special second-hand goods scheme.

EXEMPT SUPPLIES

No VAT is chargeable on the supply of goods or services which are treated as exempt supplies. These include the provision of burial and cremation facilities, insurance, finance and education. The granting of a lease to occupy land or the sale of land will usually comprise an exempt supply, but there are numerous exceptions. In particular, the sale of new non-domestic buildings or certain buildings used by charities cannot be treated as exempt supplies. A taxable person may elect to tax rents and other supplies relating to buildings and agricultural land not used for residential or charitable purposes. Exempt supplies do not enter into the calculation of taxable supplies which governs liability to mandatory registration. Such supplies made by a registered trader may, however, limit the amount of input tax which can be relieved. It is for this reason that the election may be useful.

RATES OF TAX

Two main rates of VAT have applied for many years, namely:

(a) a zero, or nil, rate

(b) a standard rate of 17.5 per cent

In addition, a special reduced rate of 5 per cent applies to a limited range of supplies including domestic fuels, installation of energy saving materials in domestic premises and children's car seats. From 1 June 2002 the 5 per cent rate was extended to include a range of residential conversions and renovations.

ZERO-RATING

A large number of supplies are zero-rated. The following list is not exhaustive but indicates the wide range of supplies which may be included under this heading:

(a) the supply of many items of food and drink. This does not include ice creams, chocolates, sweets, potato crisps and alcoholic drinks. Nor does it extend to supplies made in the course of catering or to items supplied for consumption in a restaurant or café. Whilst the supply of cold items, e.g. sandwiches for consumption away from the supplier's premises, is zero-rated, the supply of hot food, e.g. fish and chips, is not

(b) animal feeding stuffs

(c) sewerage and water, unless for industrial purposes

(d) books, brochures, pamphlets, leaflets, newspapers, maps and charts

(e) talking books for the blind and handicapped, and wireless sets for the blind

(f) supplies of services, other than professional services, when constructing a new domestic building or a building to be used by a charity. The supply of materials for such a building is zero-rated, together with the sale or the grant of a long lease. Alterations to some protected buildings are zero-rated

(g) the transportation of persons in a vehicle, ship or aircraft designed to carry not less than 10 persons

(h) supplies of drugs, medicines and other aids for the handicapped

(i) supplies of children's clothing and footwear

(j) supplies of pedal cycle helmets

(k) exports

Although no tax is due on a zero-rated supply, this does comprise a taxable supply which must be included in the calculation governing liability to register.

COLLECTION OF TAX

Registered traders submit VAT returns for accounting periods usually of three months in duration but arrangements can be made to submit returns on a monthly basis. Very large traders must account for tax on a monthly basis but this does not affect the three-monthly return. The return will show both the output tax due for supplies made by the trader in the accounting period and also the input tax for which relief is claimed. If the output tax exceeds input tax the balance must be remitted with the VAT return. Where input tax suffered exceeds the output tax due the registered trader may claim recovery of the excess from Customs and Excise.

This basis for collecting tax explains the structure of VAT. Where supplies are made between registered traders the supplier will account for an amount of tax which will usually be identical to the tax recovered by the person to whom the supply is made. However, where the supply is made to a person who is not a registered trader there can be no recovery of input tax and it is on this person that the final burden of VAT eventually falls.

Where goods are acquired by a UK trader from a supplier within a member state of the European Community, the trader must also account for the tax due on acquisition.

An optional annual accounting scheme is available for registered traders having an annual turnover of taxable supplies not exceeding £600,000. Such traders may render returns annually. Nine interim payments of VAT will be made on account, with a final balancing payment accompanying submission of the return. The number of interim payments may be reduced if turnover is small.

A further flat rate optional scheme came into operation on 25 April 2002 and was initially available to businesses having a tax exclusive annual taxable turnover not exceeding £100,000, a figure increased to £125,000 by including exempt and other non-taxable income. These amounts were increased to £150,000 and £187,500 respectively from 10 April 2003. Businesses able to satisfy these requirements may discharge VAT by calculating a flat rate percentage of their total turnover. The rate used is governed by the trade sector into which the business falls.

BAD DEBTS

Many retailers operate special retail schemes for calculating the amount of VAT due. These schemes are based on the volume of consideration received in an accounting period. Should a customer fail to pay for goods or services supplied, there will be no consideration on which to calculate VAT.

To avoid the problem of bad debts incurred by traders not operating a special retail scheme, an optional system of cash accounting is available. This scheme, confined to traders with annual taxable supplies not exceeding £600,000, enables returns to be made on a cash basis, in substitution for the normal supply basis. Traders using such a scheme will not include bad debts in the calculation of cash receipts.

Where neither the cash accounting arrangements nor a special retail scheme applies, output tax falls due on the value of the supply and liability is not affected by failure to receive consideration. However, where a debt is more than six months old, relief for bad debts will be forthcoming. The calculation of the six-month period commences from the date on which payment for the supply falls due. In those cases where a supplier obtains relief for a bad debt, the person to whom the supply has been made must refund to Customs and Excise any input tax relief which may have been granted.

OTHER SPECIAL SCHEMES

In addition to the schemes for retailers, there are several special schemes applied to calculate the amount of VAT due and which also limit the ability to recover input tax.

FARMERS

Farmers may elect to apply a special flat rate scheme. This scheme is available to farmers who are not registered traders.

STAMP DUTIES

For the majority of people, contact with stamp duty arises when they purchase a property. Stamp duty is payable by the buyer as a way of raising money for the government based on the purchase price of a property, or stocks and shares. For more comprehensive information visit www.inlandrevenue.gov.uk or call the stamp duty enquiry line on 0845-603 0135.

STAMP DUTY REGIME (until 1 December 2003)
CONVEYANCE OR TRANSFER ON SALE[†]
Value not exceeding £60,000, *nil*
Value of £60,001–£250,000, 1 per cent
Value of £250,001–£500,000, 3 per cent
Value exceeding £500,000, 4 per cent
Stamp duty for stocks and shares is levied at a rate of 0.5 per cent.

LEASES (INCLUDING AGREEMENTS FOR LEASES)
A letting agreement for any definite term less than a year of any furnished property where the rent exceeds £5,000 per annum attracts a fixed duty of £5.

Of any lands, tenements etc. in consideration of any rent, according to the following:
Term not exceeding seven years or indefinite (and rent exceeding £5000 p.a.), 1 per cent
Term between 7 and 35 years, 2 per cent
Term between 35 and 100 years, 12 per cent
Term exceeding 100 years, 24 per cent

Where a consideration other than rent is payable, the same rule applies where the consideration does not exceed £60,000 as under conveyance or transfer on sale (except stock or marketable securities), provided that any rent payable does not exceed £600 a year and a certificate of value is included in the conveyance or transfer and the reduced rates of 1 per cent for consideration not exceeding £250,000, 3 per cent for consideration not exceeding £500,000 and 4 per cent for consideration exceeding £500,000 apply.
Where a lease is granted pursuant to a prior written agreement for lease, the agreement itself is liable to duty. Credit for any duty paid on the agreement will be given against the duty payable on the lease and the Commissioners will place a denoting stamp on the lease. Where there is no prior written agreement for lease, the lease must contain a certificate that it has not been made in pursuance of such an agreement.

STAMP DUTY LAND TAX (from 1 December 2003)
In April 2002, the government announced proposals to modernise stamp duty charges on UK land and buildings. It is intended that the revised regime will prevent tax-avoidance in high-value commercial transactions while at the same time reducing the burden on smaller businesses and modernising the administration of tax for individuals. The new regime comes into force in general for land transactions completed on or after 1 December 2003. It also applies where a contract for a land transaction is 'substantially performed' after that date. There are special rules for contracts entered into before 1 December 2003 which are completed or 'substantially performed' after that date, and also for contracts entered into on or before 10 July 2003 (Royal Assent of Finance Act 2003).
From 1 December, Stamp Duty Land Tax will be a tax on transactions involving interests in land in the UK, rather than one triggered by the execution of a document as was previously the case. Tax will become automatically

payable on the due date, which will be 30 days after the 'effective date' of the transaction. The effective date is generally the date that the purchaser acquires the subject matter of the transaction but it can also be the date that a contract for a land transaction is 'substantially performed'.
Under the new system, stamp duty on transactions involving property other than land, shares and interests in partnerships will be abolished, removing many transactions from a tax burden.
The majority of individuals buying or renting residential property will see no immediate changes under the new regime, although there will be some administrative changes, and the ability to notify liability and pay stamp duty electronically should help speed up the house-buying process.
Charges on the grant of new leases are also affected under the new system, bringing them closer into line with the charge on transfers of freehold land and buildings. From 1 December 2003, the charge will follow modern commercial practice in valuing the rent payable over the term of the lease at its discounted net present value (NPV) and there will be a single rate of 1 per cent of the NPV of rental payments where the NPV exceeds the zero rate band threshold of £60,000 (residential property) or £150,000 (non-residential property). Duty on premium is the same as for transfers of property.

ALTERNATIVE PROPERTY FINANCE ARRANGEMENTS
Modernisation of the law allows for fairer treatment of property purchases by individuals financed by certain types of alternative mortgage product, such as an 'Islamic mortgage'. From 1 December 2003, the stamp duty burden on individuals using such products will be on a level footing with purchases financed by conventional mortgage products.

CONVEYANCE OR TRANSFER ON SALE[†]
As above, however, a nil rate of stamp duty also applies to non-residential property values not exceeding £150,000.
Since 30 November 2001 stamp duty exemption has been available for the purchase of property not exceeding £150,000 in certain designated disadvantaged areas of the UK. In April 2003 this exemption was extended to purchases of commercial property not exceeding £150,000.

LATE PAYMENT
Transaction returns must be delivered and payment of the tax must be paid within 30 days of the effective date of the transaction. Penalties and interest are payable if transactions are notified late.

STAMP DUTY RESERVE TAX
This is charged where there is an agreement for the transfer of chargeable securities unless the charge is cancelled by a payment of stamp duty. The tax is payable by or on behalf of the buyer who is required to report the transaction and pay the tax on the seventh day of the month following that in which the agreement is made or becomes unconditional. Penalties and interest are imposed for late payment or reporting.

[†] Readers should note that when assessing how much stamp duty is payable, the entire purchase price must be taken into account. For example, on a property purchased for £300,000, 3 per cent, £9,000 is payable.

Note: The Treasury has the power to change the structure of lease duty prior to 1 December 2003. At the time of going to press, this power had not been exercised.

LEGAL NOTES

IMPORTANT

These notes outline certain aspects of the law as they might affect the average person. They are intended only as a broad guideline and are by no means definitive. The law is constantly changing so expert advice should always be taken. In some cases, sources of further information are given in these notes.

It is always advisable to consult a solicitor without delay; timely advice will set your mind at rest but sitting on your rights can mean that you lose them. Anyone who does not have a solicitor already can contact the following for assistance in finding one: Citizens' Advice Bureau (www.nacab.org.uk), the Community Legal Service (www.legalservices.gov.uk), the Law Society of England and Wales (113 Chancery Lane, London WC2A 1PL. Tel: 020-7242 1222 Web: www.lawsociety.co.uk) or the Law Society of Scotland (26 Drumsheugh Gardens, Edinburgh EH3 7YR. Tel: 0131-226 7411 Web: www.lawscot.org.uk).

The community legal service fund and legal aid and assistance schemes exist to make the help of a lawyer available to those who would not otherwise be able to afford one. Entitlement depends on an individual's means but a solicitor or Citizens' Advice Bureau will be able to advise about entitlement.

ABORTION

Under the provisions of the Abortion Act 1967, a legally-induced abortion must be
– performed by a registered medical practitioner
– carried out in an NHS hospital or other approved premises
– certified by two registered medical practitioners as justified on one or more of the following grounds:
  (a) that the pregnancy has not exceeded its twenty-fourth week and that the continuance of the pregnancy would involve risk, greater than if the pregnancy were terminated, of injury to the physical or mental health of the pregnant woman or any existing children of her family
  (b) that the termination is necessary to prevent grave permanent injury to the physical or mental health of the pregnant woman
  (c) that the continuance of the pregnancy would involve risk to the life of the pregnant woman, greater than if the pregnancy were terminated
  (d) that there is a substantial risk that if the child were born it would suffer from such physical or mental abnormalities as to be seriously handicapped

In determining whether the continuance of a pregnancy would involve such risk of injury to health as is mentioned in grounds (a) or (b), account may be taken of the pregnant woman's actual or reasonably foreseeable environment.

The requirements relating to the opinion of two registered medical practitioners and to the performance of the abortion at an NHS hospital or other approved place cease to apply in circumstances where a registered medical practitioner is of the opinion, formed in good faith, that a termination is immediately necessary to save the life, or to prevent grave permanent injury to the physical or mental health, of the pregnant woman.

Further information and advice can be obtained from:
FAMILY PLANNING ASSOCIATION (UK)
2–12 Pentonville Road, London N1 9FP
Tel: 0845-310 1334

FAMILY PLANNING ASSOCIATION (SCOTLAND)
Unit 10, Firhill Business Centre, 76 Firhill Road,
Glasgow G20 7BA
Tel: 0141-576 5088

ADOPTION OF CHILDREN

The Adoption and Children Act 2002 reforms the framework for domestic and intercountry adoption in England and Wales and, at the time of writing (1 August 2003), is only partially in force.

Anyone over 21 (or 18 if the natural birth parent wants to adopt with a partner who must be over 21) can legally adopt a child. Married couples must adopt 'jointly', unless one partner cannot be found, is incapable of making an application, or if a separation is likely to be permanent. Unmarried couples may not adopt 'jointly' although one partner in that couple may adopt. The only organisations allowed to arrange adoptions are the social services departments of local authorities or voluntary agencies which are registered with the local authorities.

Once an adoption has been arranged, a court order is necessary to make it legal. These are obtained from the High Court (Family Division) or from a magistrates, county or family proceedings court. The child's natural parents (or guardians) must consent to the adoption, unless the court dispenses with the consent, e.g. where the natural parent has neglected the child or is incapable of giving consent. Once adopted, the child has the same status as a child born to the adoptive parents and the natural parents cease to have any rights or responsibilities where the child is concerned. The adopted child will be treated as the natural child of the adoptive parents for the purposes of intestate succession, national insurance, family allowances, etc. The adopted child ceases to have any rights to the estates of his/her natural parents.

It is an offence for a person other than an adoption agency to make arrangements for the adoption of a child or place a child for adoption unless the proposed adopter is a relative or is acting according to a court order. It is also an offence to receive a child who is placed in breach of this rule and it is an offence to make or receive payments for adoption.

REGISTRATION AND CERTIFICATES

All adoptions in England and Wales are registered in the Adopted Children Register kept by the Office of National Statistics, and by the General Register Office for Scotland. Certificates from the registers can be obtained in a similar way to birth certificates.

TRACING NATURAL PARENTS OR CHILDREN WHO HAVE BEEN ADOPTED

An adult adopted person may apply to the Registrar-General for information to enable him/her to obtain a full birth certificate. For those adopted before 12 November 1975 it is obligatory to receive counselling services before this information is given; for those adopted after that date counselling services are optional. There is also an Adoption Contact Register (created after the 1989 Act) in which details of adult adopted people and of their relatives may be recorded. The BAAF can provide addresses of organisations which offer advice, information and counselling to adopted people, adoptive parents and people who have had their children adopted.

Further information can be obtained from:
BRITISH ASSOCIATION FOR ADOPTION AND FOSTERING (BAAF)
Skyline House, 200 Union Street, London SE1 0LX.
Tel: 020-7593 2000 Web: www.baaf.org.uk

SCOTLAND
The relevant legislation is the Adoption (Scotland) Act 1978 (as amended by the Children Act 1995) and the provisions are similar to those described above. In Scotland, petitions for adoption are made to the Sheriff Court or the Court of Session.

Further information can be obtained from:
BRITISH ASSOCIATION FOR ADOPTION AND FOSTERING (BAAF)
BAAF Scottish Centre, 40 Shandwick Place,
Edinburgh EH2 4RT. Tel: 0131-225 9285

SCOTTISH ADOPTION ADVICE SERVICE
16 Sandyford Place, Glasgow G3 7NB
Tel: 0141-248 7530

BIRTHS (REGISTRATION)

The birth of a child must be registered within 42 days of birth at the register office of the district in which the baby was born. In England and Wales it is possible to give the particulars to be registered at any other register office. Responsibility for registering the birth rests with the parents, except in the case of an illegitimate child, when the mother is responsible for registration. Responsibility rests firstly with the parents (in Scotland, if the father of the child is not married to the mother and has not been married to her since the child's conception, the mother alone is responsible for registration) but if they fail, particulars may be given to the registrar by:
– a relative of either parent (in Scotland only)
– the occupier of the house or hospital in which the baby was born
– a person present at the birth
– the person who is responsible for the child
Failure to register the birth within 42 days without reasonable cause may leave the parents liable to a penalty in England and Wales and may lead to a court decree being granted by a sheriff in Scotland.

If the parents were married at the time of the birth, either parent may register the birth and details about both parents will be entered on the register. If the parents were unmarried at the time of the birth, the father's details are entered only if both parents attend or if the parents have made a statutory declaration confirming the identity of the father. Copies of the forms necessary to make such a declaration are available at the register offices. A short birth certificate is issued when the birth is registered. If a birth occurs in England and Wales and has not been registered within 12 months of its occurrence it is possible for the late registration of the birth to be authorised by the Registrar General provided certain requirements can be met.

BIRTH ABROAD
Births of British subjects occurring abroad are registered with consular officers or the High Commission and certificates of birth are subsequently available from the Registrar-General.

SCOTLAND
In Scotland the birth of a child must be registered within 21 days at the register office of either the district in which the baby was born or the district in which the mother was resident at the time of the birth.

If the child is born, either in or out of Scotland, on a ship, aircraft or land vehicle that ends its journey at any place in Scotland, the child, in most cases, will be registered as if born in that place.

CERTIFICATES OF BIRTHS, DEATHS OR MARRIAGES

Certificates of births, deaths or marriages that have taken place in England and Wales since 1837 can be obtained from the Office of National Statistics (General Register Office) or the Family Records Centre. Applications can be made:
– by a personal visit
– by postal application (forms can be downloaded from www.statistics.gov.uk)
Certificates are also available from the Superintendent Registrar for the district in which the event took place or, in the case of marriage certificates, from the minister of the church in which the marriage took place. Any register office can advise about the best way to obtain certificates. The fees for certificates are:

From the Family Records Centre, London by personal application:
Full certificate of birth, death or marriage, £7.00
Full certificate of adoption, £7.00
Short certificate of birth, £7.00
Short certificate of adoption, £5.50

By postal application:
Full certificate of birth, marriage or death, £11.50
Full certificate of birth, marriage or death with ONS index reference supplied, £8.50
Short abbreviated certificate of birth, £11.50
Short abbreviated certificate of adoption, £9.50
Extra copies of the same birth, marriage or death certificate issued at the same time, £7.00
A Priority Service is also available with certificates despatched on the working day following receipt of your application.
Visit www.statistics.gov.uk or call 0870-243 7788 for further information.

Indexes prepared from the registers are available for searching by the public at the Family Records Centre in London or at a Superintendent Registrar's Office; indexes at the latter relate only to births, deaths and marriages which occurred in that registration district. There is no charge for searching the indexes in the Public Search Room at the Family Records Centre but a general search fee is charged for searches at a Superintendent Registrar's Office. A fee is charged for verifying index references against the records.

The Society of Genealogists has many records of baptisms, marriages and deaths prior to 1837.

SCOTLAND

Certificates of births, deaths or marriages that have taken place in Scotland since 1855 can be obtained from the General Register Office for Scotland or from the appropriate local registrar. The General Register Office for Scotland also keeps the Register of Divorces (including decrees of declaration of nullity of marriage), and holds parish registers dating from before 1855.

Fees for certificates are:

Certificates (full or abbreviated) of birth, death, marriage or adoption:
Personal application: £11.00
Postal or telephone ordering: £13.00
Internet ordering: £16.00
A priority service for a response within 24 hours is available for an additional fee of £10.00

General search in the indexes to the statutory registers and parochial registers, per day or part thereof:
Full day search (i.e. 9 a.m. to 4.30 p.m.), £17.00
Afternoon (i.e. 1 p.m. to 4.30 p.m.) search £10.00
Discounted full day (i.e. 9 a.m. to 4.30 p.m.) search with payment being made not less than 14 days in advance, £13.00 (only available for the period December 2003 to January 2004)
One week search, £65.00
Four week search, £220.00
One quarter search, £500.00
One year search, £1,500.00
Online searching is also available.
For more information visit: www.scotlandspeople.gov.uk

Further information can be obtained from:
THE GENERAL REGISTER OFFICE, Office for National Statistics, Smedley Hydro, Trafalgar Road, Southport, Merseyside PR8 2HH. Tel: 0870-243 7788
FAMILY RECORDS CENTRE, 1 Myddelton Street, London EC1R 1UW. Monday, Wednesday, Friday 9.00am to 5.00pm, Tuesday 10.00am to 7.00pm, Thursday 9.00am to 7.00pm, Saturday 9.30am to 5.00pm.
THE GENERAL REGISTER OFFICE FOR SCOTLAND, New Register House, Edinburgh EH1 3YT. Tel: 0131-314 4452 Web: www.gro-scotland.gov.uk
THE SOCIETY OF GENEALOGISTS, 14 Charterhouse Buildings, Goswell Road, London EC1M 7BA Tel: 020-7251 8799

BRITISH CITIZENSHIP

The British Nationality Act 1981 which came into force on 1 January 1983 established three types of citizenship to replace the single form of Citizenship of the UK and Colonies created by the British Nationality Act 1948. The three forms of citizenship are: British Citizenship; British Dependent Territories Citizenship; and British Overseas Citizenship. Three residual categories were created: British Subjects; British Protected Persons; and British Nationals (Overseas).

BRITISH CITIZENSHIP

Almost everyone who was a citizen of the UK and colonies and had a right of abode in the UK prior to the 1981 Act became British citizens when the Act came into force. British citizens have the right to live permanently in the UK and are free to leave and re-enter the UK at any time.

A person born on or after 1 January 1983 in the UK (including, for this purpose, the Channel Islands and the Isle of Man) is entitled to British citizenship if he/she falls into one of the following categories:
– he/she has a parent who is a British citizen
– he/she has a parent who is settled in the UK
– he/she is a newborn infant found abandoned in the UK
– his/her parents subsequently settle in the UK
– he/she lives in the UK for the first ten years of his/her life and is not absent for more than 90 days in each of those years
– he/she is adopted in the UK and one of the adopters is a British Citizen
A person born outside the UK may acquire British citizenship if he/she falls into one of the following categories:
– he/she has a parent who is a British citizen otherwise than by descent, e.g. a parent who was born in the UK
– he/she has a parent who is a British citizen serving the Crown overseas
– the Home Secretary consents to his/her registration while he/she is a minor
– he/she is a British Dependent Territories citizen, a British Overseas citizen, a British subject or a British protected person and has been lawfully resident in the UK for five years
– he/she is a British Dependent Territories citizen who acquired that citizenship from a connection with Gibraltar
– he/she is adopted or naturalised
Where parents are married, the status of either may confer citizenship on their child. If a child is illegitimate, the status of the mother determines the child's citizenship.

Under the 1981 Act, Commonwealth citizens and citizens of the Republic of Ireland were entitled to registration as British citizens before 1 January 1988. In 1985, citizens of the Falkland Islands were granted British citizenship.

Renunciation of British citizenship must be registered with the Home Secretary and will be revoked if no new citizenship or nationality is acquired within six months. If the renunciation was required in order to retain or acquire another citizenship or nationality, the citizenship may be reacquired once. The Secretary of State may deprive a person of a citizenship status if he is satisfied that the person has done anything seriously prejudicial to the vital interests of the United Kingdom, or a British overseas territory, unless making the order would have the effect of rendering a person stateless. A person may also be deprived of a citizenship status which results from his registration or naturalisation if the Secretary of State is satisfied that the registration or naturalisation was obtained by means of fraud, false representation or concealment of a material fact.

BRITISH DEPENDENT TERRITORIES CITIZENSHIP

Under the 1981 Act, this type of citizenship was conferred on citizens of the UK and colonies by birth, naturalisation or registration in British Dependent Territories. British Dependent Territories citizens may be entitled to registration as British citizens on completion of five years' legal residence in the UK.

On 1 July 1997 citizens of Hong Kong who did not qualify to register as British citizens under the British Nationality (Hong Kong) Act 1990 lost their British Dependent Territories citizenship on the handover of sovereignty to China; they may, however, have applied to register as British Nationals (Overseas).

BRITISH OVERSEAS CITIZENSHIP
Under the 1981 Act, this type of citizenship was conferred on any UK and colonies citizens who did not qualify for British citizenship or citizenship of the British Dependent Territories. British Overseas citizenship may be acquired by the wife and minor children of a British Overseas citizen in certain circumstances. British Overseas citizens may be entitled to registration as British citizens on completion of five years' legal residence in the UK.

RESIDUAL CATEGORIES
British subjects, British protected persons and British Nationals (Overseas) may be entitled to registration as British citizens on completion of five years' legal residence in the UK.

Citizens of the Republic of Ireland who were also British subjects before 1 January 1949 can retain that status if they fulfil certain conditions.

EUROPEAN UNION CITIZENSHIP
British citizens (including Gibraltarians who are registered as such) are also EU citizens and are entitled to travel freely to other EU countries to work, study, reside and set up a business. EU citizens have the same rights with respect to the United Kingdom.

NATURALISATION
Naturalisation is granted at the discretion of the Home Secretary. The basic requirements are five years' residence (three years if the applicant is married to a British citizen), good character, adequate knowledge of the English, Welsh or Scottish Gaelic language, and an intention to reside permanently in the UK.

STATUS OF ALIENS
Aliens may not hold public office or vote in Britain and they may not own a British ship or aircraft. Citizens of the Republic of Ireland are not deemed to be aliens. Certain provisions of the Immigration and Asylum Act 1999 make provision about immigration and asylum and about procedures in connection with marriage by superintendent registrar's certificate.

CONSUMER LAW

SALE OF GOODS
A sale of goods contract is the most common type of contract. It is governed by the Sale of Goods Act 1979 (as amended by the Sale and Supply of Goods Act 1994). The Act provides protection for buyers by implying terms into every sale of goods contract. These terms are:
– a condition that the seller will pass good title to the buyer (unless the seller agrees to transfer only such title as he has)
– where the seller sells goods by reference to a description, a condition that the goods will match that description and, where the sale is by sample and description, a condition that the bulk of the goods will correspond with such sample and description
– where goods are sold by a business seller, a condition that the goods will be of satisfactory quality if they meet the standard that a reasonable person would regard as satisfactory taking into account any description of the goods, the price, and all other relevant circumstances, including any public statement on the specific characteristics of the goods made by the seller, producer or his representative particularly in advertising or labelling. The quality of the goods includes their state and condition, relevant aspects being whether they are suitable for their common purpose, their appearance and finish, freedom from minor defects and their safety and durability. This term will not be implied, however, if a buyer has examined the goods and should have noticed the defect or if the seller specifically drew the buyer's attention to the defect
– where goods are sold by a business seller, a condition that the goods are reasonably fit for any purpose made known to the seller by the buyer, unless the buyer does not rely on the seller's judgement, or it is not reasonable for him/her to do so
– where goods are sold by sample, conditions that the bulk of the sample will correspond with the sample in quality, that the buyer will have a reasonable opportunity of comparing the two and that the goods are free from any defect rendering them unsatisfactory which would not be obvious from the sample

Some of the above terms can be excluded from contracts by the seller. The seller's right to do this is, however, restricted by the Unfair Contract Terms Act 1977. The Act offers more protection to a buyer who 'deals as a consumer', that is where the sale is a business sale, the goods are of a type ordinarily bought for private use and the goods are bought by a buyer who is not a business buyer. In a sale by auction or competitive tender, a buyer never deals as consumer. Also, a seller can never exclude the implied term as to title mentioned above.

HIRE-PURCHASE AGREEMENTS
Terms similar to those implied in contracts of sales of goods are implied into contracts of hire-purchase, under the Supply of Goods (Implied Terms) Act 1973. The 1977 Act limits the exclusion of these implied terms as before.

SUPPLY OF GOODS AND SERVICES
Under the Supply of Goods and Services Act 1982, similar terms are also implied in other types of contract under which ownership of goods passes, e.g. a contract for 'work and materials' such as supplying new parts while servicing a car, and contracts for the hire of goods. These types of contracts have additional implied terms:
– that the supplier will use reasonable care and skill
– that the supplier will carry out the service in a reasonable time (unless the time has been agreed)
– that the supplier will make a reasonable charge (unless the charge has already been agreed)
The 1977 Act limits the exclusion of these implied terms in a similar manner as before.

UNFAIR TERMS
The Unfair Terms in Consumer Contracts Regulations 1999 apply to contracts between business sellers (or suppliers of goods and services) and consumers, where the terms have not been individually negotiated, i.e where the terms were drafted in advance so that the consumer was unable to influence those terms. An unfair term is one which operates to the detriment of the consumer. An unfair term does not bind the consumer but the contract will continue to bind the parties if it is capable of existing without the unfair term. The regulations contain a non-exhaustive list of terms which are regarded as unfair. Whether a term is regarded as fair or not will depend on many factors, including the nature

of the goods or services, the surrounding circumstances (such as the bargaining strength of both parties) and the other terms in the contract.

TRADE DESCRIPTIONS

It is a criminal offence under the Trade Descriptions Act 1968 for a business seller to apply a false trade description of goods or to supply or offer to supply any goods to which a false description has been applied. A 'trade description' includes descriptions of quality, size, composition, fitness for purpose and method, and place and date of manufacture of the goods. It is also an offence to give a false indication of the price of goods.

FAIR TRADING

The Fair Trading Act 1973 is designed to protect the consumer. It provides for the appointment of a Director-General of Fair Trading, one of whose duties is to review commercial activities in the UK relating to the supply of goods and services to consumers. An example of a practice which has been prohibited by a reference made under this Act is that of business sellers posing in advertisements as private sellers.

CONSUMER PROTECTION

Under the Consumer Protection Act 1987, producers of goods are liable for any injury or for any damage exceeding £275 caused by a defect in their product (subject to certain defences).

The Consumer Protection (Cancellation of Contracts Concluded Away from Business Premises) Regulations 1987 allow consumers a seven-day period in which to cancel contracts for the supply of goods and services, where the contracts were made during an unsolicited visit to the consumer's home or workplace. This only applies to contracts where the cost exceeds £35.

Consumers are also afforded protection under the Consumer Protection (Distance Selling) Regulations 2000.

CONSUMER CREDIT

In matters relating to the provision of credit (or the supply of goods on hire or hire-purchase), consumers are also protected by the Consumer Credit Act 1974. Under this Act a licence, issued by the Director-General of Fair Trading, is required to conduct a consumer credit or consumer hire business or to deal in credit brokerage, debt adjusting, counselling or collecting. Any 'fit' person may apply to the Director-General of Fair Trading for a licence, which is normally renewable after ten years. A licence is not necessary if such types of business are only transacted occasionally, or if only exempt agreements are involved. The provisions of the Act only apply to 'regulated' agreements, i.e. those that are with individuals or partnerships, those that are not exempt (such as certain local authority and building society loans), and those where the total credit does not exceed £25,000. Provisions include:
- the terms of the regulated agreement can be altered by the creditor provided the agreement gives him/her the right to do so; in such cases the debtor must be given proper notice of this
- in order for a creditor to enforce a regulated agreement, the agreement must comply with certain formalities and must be properly executed. The debtor must also be given specified information by the creditor or his/her broker or agent during the negotiations which take place before the signing of the agreement. The agreement must state certain

information such as the amount of credit, the annual interest rate, the amount and timing of repayments
- if an agreement is signed other than at the creditor's (or credit broker's or negotiator's) place of business and oral representations were made in the debtor's presence during discussions pre-agreement, the debtor has a right to cancel the agreement. Time for cancellation expires five clear days after the debtor receives a second copy of the agreement. The agreement must inform the debtor of his right to cancel and how to cancel
- if the debtor is in arrears (or otherwise in breach of the agreement), the creditor must serve a default notice before taking any action such as repossessing the goods
- if the agreement is a hire-purchase or conditional sale agreement, the creditor cannot repossess the goods without a court order if the debtor has paid one-third of the total price of the goods
- in agreements where the debtor is required to make grossly exorbitant payments or where the agreement grossly contravenes the ordinary principles of fair trading, the debtor may request that the court alter or set aside some of the terms of the agreement. The agreement can also be reopened during enforcement proceedings by the court itself

Where a credit reference agency has been used to check the debtor's financial standing, the creditor must give the agency's name to the debtor, who is entitled to see the agency's file on him. A fee of £1 is payable to the agency.

SCOTLAND

The legislation governing the sale and supply of goods applies to Scotland as follows:
- the Sale of Goods Act 1979 applies with some modifications and it has been amended by the Sale and Supply of Goods Act 1994
- the Supply of Goods (Implied Terms) Act 1973 applies
- the Supply of Goods and Services Act 1982 does not extend to Scotland but some of its provisions were introduced by the Sale and Supply of Goods Act 1994
- only Parts II and III of the Unfair Contract Terms Act 1977 apply
- the Trade Descriptions Act 1968 applies with minor modifications
- the Consumer Credit Act 1974 applies
- the Consumer Protection Act 1987 applies
- the General Product Safety Regulations 1994 apply
- the Unfair Terms in Consumer Contracts Regulations 1999 apply
- the Unfair Terms in Consumer Contracts (Amendment) Regulations 2001 apply
- the Consumer Protection (Distance Selling) Regulations 2000 apply
- the Sale and Supply of Goods to Consumers Regulations 2002 apply

PROCEEDINGS AGAINST THE CROWN

Until 1947, proceedings against the Crown were generally possible only by a procedure known as a petition of right, which put the litigant at a considerable disadvantage. The Crown Proceedings Act 1947 placed the Crown (not the Sovereign in his/her private capacity, but as the embodiment of the State) largely in the same position as a private individual. The Act did not, however, extinguish or limit the Crown's prerogative or statutory powers, and it granted immunity to HM ships and aircraft. It also left certain Crown privileges unaffected. The Act largely abolished the special procedures which previously applied to civil proceedings by and against the Crown. Civil proceedings may be instituted against the appropriate government department or against the Attorney-General.

In Scotland proceedings against the Crown founded on breach of contract could be taken before the 1947 Act and no special procedures applied. The Crown could, however, claim certain special pleas. The 1947 Act applies in part to Scotland and brings the practice of the two countries as closely together as the different legal systems permit. As a result of the Scotland Act 1998 actions against government departments should be raised against the Lord Advocate or the Advocate General. Actions should be raised against the Lord Advocate where the department involved administers a devolved matter. Devolved matters include agriculture, education, housing, local government, health and justice. Actions should be raised against the Advocate General where the department is dealing with a reserved matter. Reserved matters include defence, foreign affairs and social security.

DEATHS

WHEN A DEATH OCCURS
If the death (including stillbirth) was expected, the doctor who attended the deceased during their final illness should be contacted. If the death was sudden and unexpected, the family doctor (if known) and police should be contacted. If the cause of death is quite clear the doctor will provide:
- a medical certificate that shows the cause of death
- a formal notice that states that the doctor has signed the medical certificate and that explains how to get the death registered

If the death was known to be caused by a natural illness but the doctor wishes to know more about the cause of death, he/she may ask the relatives for permission to carry out a post-mortem examination.

In England and Wales a coroner is responsible for investigating deaths occurring in the following circumstances:
- where there is no doctor who can issue a medical certificate of cause of death
- when no doctor has treated the deceased during his or her last illness or when the doctor attending the patient did not see him or her within 14 days before death, or after death; or
- when the death occurred during an operation or before recovery from the effect of an anaesthetic; or
- when the death was sudden and unexplained or attended by suspicious circumstances; or
- when the death might be due to an industrial injury or disease, or to accident, violence, neglect or abortion, or to any kind of poisoning; or
- the death occurred in prison or in police custody

The doctor will write on the formal notice that the death has been referred to the coroner; if the post mortem shows that death was due to natural causes, the coroner may issue a notification which gives the cause of death so that the death can be registered. If the cause of death was violent or unnatural, the coroner is obliged to hold an inquest.

In Scotland the office of coroner does not exist. The local procurator fiscal inquires into sudden or suspicious deaths. A fatal accident inquiry will be held before the sheriff where the death has resulted from an accident during the course of the employment of the person who has died, or where the person who has died was in legal custody, or where the Lord Advocate deems it in the public interest that an inquiry be held.

REGISTERING A DEATH
In England and Wales the death must be registered by the registrar of births and deaths for the district in which it occurred; details can be obtained from the doctor or local council, or at a post office or police station. From April 1997, information concerning a death can be given before any registrar of births and deaths in England and Wales. The registrar will pass the relevant details to the registrar for the district where the death occurred, who will then register the death.

In England and Wales the death must normally be registered within five days; in Scotland it must be registered within eight days. If the death has been referred to the coroner/local procurator fiscal it cannot be registered until the registrar has received authority from the coroner/local procurator fiscal to do so. Failure to register a death involves a penalty in England and Wales and may lead to a court decree being granted by a sheriff in Scotland.

If the death occurred at a house or hospital, the death may be registered by:
- any relative of the deceased
- any person present at the death
- the occupier or any inmate of the house or hospital if he/she knew of the occurrence of the death
- any person making the funeral arrangements
- in Scotland, the deceased's executor or legal representative.

The person registering the death should take the medical certificate of the cause of death with them; it is also useful, though not essential, to take the deceased's birth and marriage certificates, NHS medical card (if possible), pension documents and life assurance details. The registrar will issue a certificate for burial or cremation and a certificate of registration of death; both are free of charge. A death certificate is a certified copy of the entry in the death register; these can be provided on payment of a fee and may be required for the following purposes:
- the will
- bank and building society accounts
- savings bank certificates and premium bonds
- insurance policies
- pension claims

If the death occurred abroad or on a foreign ship or aircraft, the death should be registered according to the local regulations of the relevant country and a death certificate should be obtained. The death can also be registered with the British Consul in that country and a record will be kept at the General Register Office. This avoids the expense of bringing the body back.

After 12 months (3 months in Scotland) of death or the finding of a dead body, no death can be registered without the consent of the Registrar-General.

BURIAL AND CREMATION
In most circumstances in England and Wales a certificate for burial or cremation must be obtained from the registrar before the burial or cremation can take place. If the death has been referred to the coroner, an order for burial or a certificate for cremation must be obtained. In Scotland a body may be buried (but not cremated) before the death is registered.

Funeral costs can normally be repaid out of the deceased's estate and will be given priority over any other claims. If the deceased has left a will it may contain directions concerning the funeral; however, these directions need not be followed by the executor.

The deceased's papers should also indicate whether a grave space had already been arranged. Most town churchyards and many suburban churchyards are no longer open for burial because they are full. Most cemeteries are non-denominational and may be owned by local authorities or private companies; fees vary.

If the body is to be cremated, an application form, two cremation certificates (for which there is a charge) or a certificate for cremation if the death was referred to the coroner, and a certificate signed by the medical referee must be completed in addition to the certificate for burial or cremation (the form is not required if the coroner has issued a certificate for cremation). All the forms are available from the funeral director or crematorium. Most crematoria are run by local authorities; the fees usually include the medical referee's fee and the use of the chapel. Ashes may be scattered, buried in a churchyard or cemetery, or kept.

The registrar must be notified of the date, place and means of disposal of the body within 96 hours (England and Wales) or three days (Scotland).

If the death occurred abroad or on a foreign ship or aircraft, a local burial or cremation may be arranged. If the body is to be brought back to England or Wales, a death certificate from the relevant country or an authorisation for the removal of the body from the country of death from the coroner or relevant authority will be required. To arrange a funeral in England and Wales, an authenticated translation of a foreign death certificate or a death certificate issued in Scotland or Northern Ireland which must show the cause of death, is needed, together with a certificate of no liability to register from the registrar in England and Wales in whose sub-district it is intended to bury or cremate the body. If it is intended to cremate the body, a cremation order will be required from the Home Office or a certificate for cremation.

Further information can be obtained from:
THE GENERAL REGISTER OFFICE, Office for National Statistics, Smedley Hydro, Trafalgar Road, Southport, Merseyside PR8 2HH. Tel: 0870-243 7788
THE GENERAL REGISTER OFFICE FOR SCOTLAND, New Register House, Edinburgh EH1 3YT. Tel: 0131-314 4452

DIVORCE AND RELATED MATTERS

ENGLAND AND WALES

There are two types of matrimonial suit: those seeking the annulment of a marriage, and those seeking a judicial separation or divorce. To obtain an annulment, judicial separation or divorce in England and Wales, one or both of the parties must have their permanent home in England and Wales when the petition is started, or have been living in England and Wales for at least a year on the day the petition is started. All cases are commenced in divorce county courts or in the Divorce Registry in London. If a suit is defended it may be transferred to the High Court.

NULLITY OF MARRIAGE

Various circumstances will render a marriage invalid including if: the marriage has not been consumated; one partner had a venereal disease at the time of the marriage and the other did not know about it; the female partner was pregnant at the time of marriage with another person's child and the male partner did not know of the pregnancy; the parties were within the prohibited degrees of consanguinity, affinity or adoption; the parties were not male and female; either of the parties was already married; either of the parties was under the age of 16; the formalities of the marriage were defective, e.g. the marriage did not take place in an authorised building, and both parties knew of the defect.

SEPARATION

A couple may enter into an agreement to separate by consent but for the agreement to be valid it must be followed by an immediate separation; a solicitor should be contacted.

Judicial separation does not dissolve a marriage and it is not necessary to prove that the marriage has irretrievably broken down. Either party can petition for a judicial separation at any time; the grounds listed below as grounds for divorce are also grounds for judicial separation. To petition for judicial separation the parties do not have to prove that they have been married for 12 months or more. A financial settlement between spouses which accompanies a judicial separation will not bind the court after instigation of divorce proceedings.

DIVORCE

Neither party can petition for divorce until at least one year after the date of the marriage. The sole ground for divorce is the irretrievable breakdown of the marriage; this must be proved on one or more of the following grounds:

– the respondent has committed adultery and the petitioner finds it intolerable to live with him/her; however, the petitioner cannot rely on an act of adultery by the other party if they have lived together for more than six months after the discovery that adultery had been committed
– the respondent has behaved in such a way that the petitioner cannot reasonably be expected to continue living with him/her
– the respondent deserted the petitioner for two years immediately before the petition. Desertion may be defined as a voluntary withdrawal from cohabitation by the respondent without just cause and against the wishes of the petitioner; where one party is guilty of serious misconduct which forces the other party to leave, the party at fault is said to be guilty of constructive desertion
– the respondent and the petitioner have lived separately for two years immediately before the petition and the respondent consents to the decree
– the respondent and the petitioner have lived separately for five years immediately before the petition

A total period of less than six months during which the parties have resumed living together is disregarded in determining whether the prescribed period of separation or desertion has been continuous (but cannot be included as part of the period of separation).

The Matrimonial Causes Act 1973 requires the solicitor for the petitioner in certain cases to certify whether the possibility of a reconciliation has been discussed with the petitioner.

THE DECREE NISI

A decree nisi does not dissolve or annul the marriage but must be obtained before a divorce or annulment can take place.

Where the suit is undefended, the evidence normally takes the form of a sworn written statement made by the petitioner which is considered by a district judge. If the judge is satisfied that the petitioner has proved the contents of the petition, he/she will set a date for the pronouncement of the decree nisi in open court; neither party need attend.

If the judge is not satisfied that the petitioner has proved the contents of the petition, or if the suit is defended, the petition will be heard in open court with the parties giving oral evidence.

THE DECREE ABSOLUTE

The decree nisi is usually made absolute after six weeks and on the application of the petitioner. If the judge thinks it may be necessary to exercise any of his/her powers under the Children Act 1989, he/she can in exceptional circumstances delay the granting of the decree absolute. The decree absolute dissolves or annuls the marriage. Where the couple were married in accordance with Jewish or other religious usages, the court may require them to produce a declaration that they have taken such steps as are required to dissolve the marriage in accordance with those usages before a decree absolute is issued.

CHILDREN

Neither parent is now awarded 'custody' of any children of the marriage in England and Wales. Both parents, if married, have 'parental responsibility'. Either parent can exercise this, independently of the other. However, in the case of unmarried parents, the mother has automatic parental responsibility and the father must apply to the courts for a parental responsibility order. Any dispute between the parents can be resolved by the courts. In all court cases concerning children, whether connected to a matrimonial suit or not, the welfare of the child is the paramount consideration.

MAINTENANCE, ETC.

Either party may be liable to pay maintenance to their former spouse. If there were any children of the marriage, both parents have a legal responsibility to support them financially if they can afford to do so. These so-called ancillary matters, including any property settlements, may be settled before the divorce goes through but currently can go on long after the marriage is dissolved.

The courts are responsible for assessing maintenance for the former spouse, taking into account each party's income and essential outgoings and other aspects of the case. The court also deals with any maintenance for a child that has been treated by the spouses as a 'child of the family', e.g. a stepchild, and any property settlements.

The Child Support Agency (CSA) was set up under the Child Support Act 1991 and is now responsible for assessing the maintenance that absent parents should pay for their natural or adopted children (whether or not a marriage has taken place). The CSA accepts applications only when all the people involved are habitually resident in the UK; the courts will continue to deal with cases where one of the people involved lives abroad. The CSA deals with all new cases, and is gradually taking on cases where the parent with care (or his/her new partner) was already receiving income support, family credit or disability working allowance before 5 April 1993. People with existing court orders or written maintenance agreements made before 5 April 1993 should continue to use the courts. Where it is already collecting child maintenance, the CSA has the power to offer a collection and enforcement service for certain other payments of maintenance.

A formula is used to work out how much child maintenance is payable. The formula ensures that after the payment of child maintenance the absent parent's income, and that of any second family he/she may now have, remains significantly above basic income support rates. Also, no absent parent will normally be assessed to pay more than 30 per cent of his/her net income in current child maintenance, or more than 33 per cent if he/she is also liable for any arrears. Absent parents are normally expected to pay at least a minimum amount of child maintenance.

A scheme has begun to be introduced since the end of 1996 which allows departures from the formula in certain tightly defined circumstances, e.g. the high costs of travel to maintain contact with a child, or to have a property and capital transfer ('clean break' settlement) entered into before April 1993 taken into account; there will also be some additional grounds which may result in liability being increased.

Some cases involving unusual circumstances are treated as special cases and the assessment is modified. Where there is financial need (e.g. because of disability or continuing education), maintenance may be ordered by the court for children even beyond the age of 18.

The level of maintenance is reviewed automatically every two years. Either parent can report a change of circumstances and request a review at any time. An independent complaints examiner for the CSA was appointed in early 1997.

If the absent parent does not pay the child maintenance, the CSA may make an order for payments to be deducted directly from his/her salary or wages; if all other methods fail, the CSA may take court action to enforce the payment. In cases where the parent maintaining a child has a high income an application can be made under the Children Act 1989 for top-up payments. Applications for lump sum and property adjustment orders are also made under this statute.

COURT ORDERS

A spouse can apply for a court order on the grounds that the other spouse:
- has failed to pay reasonable maintenance for the applicant
- has failed to make a proper contribution towards the reasonable maintenance of a 'child of the family'
- has deserted the applicant
- has behaved in such a way that the applicant cannot reasonably be expected to live with the respondent

If the case is proved, the court can order:
- periodical payments for the applicant and/or a 'child of the family'
- a lump sum payment to the applicant and/or a 'child of the family'

In deciding what orders (if any) to make, the court must consider guidelines which are similar to those governing financial orders in divorce cases. There are also special provisions relating to consent orders and separation by agreement. An order may be enforceable even if the parties are living together, but in some cases it will cease to have effect if they continue to do so for six months.

MATRIMONIAL PROPERTY

Married couples can own property in two ways. The first is according to the title deeds (joint ownership) and the second relates to contributions to the property (beneficial interest). Just because a couple jointly own a property does not mean that in the event of divorce that the proceeds of matrimonial property will be distributed evenly. When deciding on what financial orders to make the court will take into consideration the length of marriage, the parties' ages, the parties' needs, the parties' earning capacity and the needs of the children to the marriage.

COHABITING COUPLES

Rights of unmarried couples are not the same as for married couples. By virtue of this it may be worth considering entering into a contract which establishes how money and property should be divided in the event of a relationship breakdown. These contracts are commonly known as 'separation deeds' or 'cohabitation contracts'.

DOMESTIC VIOLENCE

If one spouse has been subjected to violence at the hands of the other, it is now possible to obtain a court order very quickly to restrain further violence and if necessary to have the other spouse excluded from the home. Such orders may also relate to unmarried couples and to a range of other relationships including parents and children.

SCOTLAND

Although there is separate legislation for Scotland covering nullity of marriage, judicial separation, divorce and ancillary matters, the provisions are in most respects the same as those for England and Wales. The following is confined to major points on which the law in Scotland differs.

An action for 'declarator of nullity' can be brought only in the Court of Session. Where a spouse is capable of sexual intercourse but refuses to consummate the marriage, this is not a ground of nullity in Scots law, though it could be a ground for divorce. The fact that a spouse was suffering from venereal disease at the time of marriage and the other spouse did not know this is not a ground of nullity in Scots law, neither is the fact that a wife was pregnant by another man at the time of marriage and her husband did not know this.

An action for judicial separation or divorce may be raised in the Court of Session; it may also be raised in the Sheriff Court if either party was resident in the sheriffdom for 40 days immediately before the date of the action or for 40 days ending not more than 40 days before the date of the action. The fee for starting a divorce petition in the Sheriff Court is £81.

When adultery is cited as proof that the marriage has broken down irretrievably, it is not necessary in Scotland to prove also that it is intolerable for the pursuer to live with the defender. In the case of desertion, irretrievable breakdown is not established if, after the two year desertion period has expired, the parties resume living together at any time after the end of three months from the date when they first resume living together.

Where a divorce action has been raised, it may be sisted or put on hold for a variety of reasons.

If the parties do cohabit during such postponement, no account is taken of the cohabitation if the action later proceeds.

In actions for divorce and separation, the court has the power to award a residence order in respect of any children of the marriage. The welfare of the children is of paramount importance, and the fact that a spouse has caused the breakdown of the marriage does not in itself preclude him/her from being awarded residence.

A simplified procedure for 'do-it-yourself' divorce was introduced in 1983 for certain divorces. If the action is based on two or five years' separation and will not be opposed, and if there are no children under 16 and no financial claims, and there is no sign that the applicant's spouse is unable to manage his or her affairs through mental illness or handicap, the applicant can write directly to the local sheriff court or to the Court of Session for the appropriate forms to enable him or her to proceed. The fee is £62, unless the applicant receives income support, family credit or legal advice and assistance, in which case there is no fee.

An extract decree, which brings the marriage to an end, will be made available 14 days after the divorce has been granted.

Further information can be obtained from:
THE PRINCIPAL REGISTRY, First Avenue House, 42–49 High Holborn, London WC2V 6NP.
THE COURT OF SESSION, Parliament House, Parliament Square, Edinburgh EH1 1RQ. Tel: 0131-225 2595
THE CHILD SUPPORT AGENCY, National Enquiry Line: 08457-133133 Minicom: 08457-138924
Web: www.csa.gov.uk

EMPLOYMENT LAW

PAY AND CONDITIONS

The Employment Rights Act 1996 consolidates the statutory provisions relating to employees' rights. Employers must give each employee employed for more than one month a written statement containing the following information:
- names of employer and employee
- date when employment began
- remuneration and intervals at which it will be paid
- job title or description of job
- hours and place(s) of work
- holiday entitlement and holiday pay
- entitlement to sick leave and sick pay
- details of pension scheme(s)
- length of notice period that employer and employee need to give to terminate employment, or the end date for a fixed-term contract
- details of any collective agreement which affects the terms of employment
- details of disciplinary and grievance procedures
- if the employee is to work outside the UK for more than one month, the period of such work and the currency in which payment is made

This must be given to the employee within two months of the start of their employment. The Working Time Regulation 1998, the National Minimum Wage Act 1998 and the Employment Relations Act 1999 now supplement the 1996 Act.

FLEXIBLE WORKING

The Employment Act 2002 gives employees the right to apply for a flexible working pattern for the purpose of caring for a child and is intended to cover anyone who has responsibility as a parent of an eligible child. If an application under the Act is rejected, it is open to the employee to take the case to the employment tribunal.

SICK PAY

Employees absent from work through illness or injury are entitled to receive Statutory Sick Pay (SSP) from the employer for a maximum period of 28 weeks in any three-year period. This applies to all employees, both men and women, up to the age of 65.

MATERNITY AND PATERNITY PAY

The Employment Act 2002 has changed the legislation relating to paternity, maternity and adoption leave and pay. Fathers are now entitled to two weeks' paid paternity leave following the birth of a child or the placement of a child for adoption. Maternity leave and pay have also been altered: ordinary maternity leave has been increased to 26 weeks and new mothers now have the option to take 26 weeks' additional maternity leave. The payment period for statutory maternity pay and maternity allowance was also extended to 26 weeks. Where an adoptive child is newly placed with an adoptive parent, the parent has a right to 26 weeks paid adoption leave. Where a married couple adopt a child, it is intended that only one spouse will be entitled to take adoption leave, with the other spouse being entitled, subject to certain criteria, to two weeks' paternity leave. The rights to paternity leave and adoption leave are in addition to the right to 13 parental leave weeks (18 weeks for the parents of disabled children) provided for in the regulations made under the Employment Rights Act 1996.

SUNDAY TRADING

The Sunday Trading Act 1994 gave new rights to shop workers. They have the right not to be dismissed, selected for redundancy or to suffer any detriment (such as the denial of overtime, promotion or training) if they refuse to work on Sundays. This does not apply to those who, under their contracts, are employed to work on Sundays.

TERMINATION OF EMPLOYMENT

An employee may be dismissed without notice if guilty of gross misconduct but in other cases a period of notice must be given by the employer. The minimum periods of notice specified in the Employment Rights Act 1996 are:
- at least one week if the employee has been continuously employed for one month or more but for less than two years
- at least two weeks if the employee has been continuously employed for two years or more. A week is added for every complete year of continuous employment up to 12 years
- at least 12 weeks for those who have been continuously employed for 12 years or more
- longer periods apply if these are specified in the contract of employment

If an employee is dismissed with less notice than he/she is entitled to, the employer is generally liable to pay wages for the period of proper notice (or for the period of the contract for those on fixed-term contracts). Generally, no notice needs to be given of the expiry of a fixed-term contract.

REDUNDANCY

An employee dismissed because of redundancy may be entitled to a lump sum. This applies if:
- the employee has at least two years' continuous service
- the employee is actually dismissed by the employer (even in cases of voluntary redundancy)
- dismissal is due to a reduction in the work force

An employee may not be entitled to a redundancy payment if offered a new job by the same employer. The amount of payment depends on the length of service, the salary and the age of the employee. The redundancy payment is guaranteed by the State in cases where the employer becomes insolvent (subject to the conditions above).

UNFAIR DISMISSAL

Complaints about unfair dismissal are dealt with by an employment tribunal. Any employee, with one years' continuous service subject to exceptions, regardless of their hours of work, can make a complaint to the tribunal. At the tribunal the employer must prove that the dismissal was due to one or more of the following reasons:
- the employee's capability for the job
- the employee's conduct
- redundancy
- a legal restriction preventing the continuation of the employee's contract
- some other substantial reason (including breaking the law)

If so, the tribunal must decide whether the employer acted reasonably in dismissing the employee for that reason. If the employee is found to have been unfairly dismissed, the tribunal can order that he/she be reinstated or compensated. Any person believing that they may have been unfairly dismissed should contact their local Citizens' Advice Bureau. A claim must be brought within 3 months of the date of termination.

The maximum award for unfair dismissal is £53,500 which relates to dismissals occurring on or after 1 February 2003.

DISCRIMINATION

Discrimination in employment on the grounds of sex, race, colour, nationality, ethnic or national origins, married status or (subject to wide exceptions) disability is unlawful. Discrimination legislation also covers sexual harassment and gender reassignment. Discrimination on the grounds of age is not unlawful. The following legislation applies to those employed in Great Britain but not to employees in Northern Ireland or (subject to EC exceptions) to those who work mainly abroad:
- The Equal Pay Act 1970 (as amended) entitles men and women to equality in matters related to their contracts of employment. Those doing like work for the same employer are entitled to the same pay and conditions regardless of their sex
- The Sex Discrimination Act 1975 (as amended by the Sex Discrimination Act 1986) makes it unlawful to discriminate on grounds of sex or marital status. This covers all aspects of employment, including advertising for recruits, terms offered, opportunities for promotion and training, and dismissal procedures
- The Race Relations Act 1976 gives individuals the right not to be discriminated against in employment matters on the grounds of race, colour, nationality, or ethnic or national origins. It applies to all aspects of employment
- The Disability Discrimination Act 1995 makes discrimination against a disabled person in all aspects of employment unlawful. Unlike sex and race discrimination, an employer may show that the treatment is justified and that the employer acted reasonably. Employers with fewer than 15 employees are exempt.

The Equal Opportunities Commission, the Commission for Racial Equality and the Disability Rights Commission have the function of eliminating such discriminations in the workplace and can provide further information and assistance.

In Northern Ireland similar provisions exist but are constituted in separate legislation which also provides protection against religious discrimination.

The Employment Relations Act 1999 made a number of important changes to the existing law:
- a right of accompaniment. A worker attending a serious disciplinary or grievance hearing will have a right to be accompanied by a trade union representative or co-worker of their choice
- a new scheme of compulsory trade union recognition following a workplace ballot
- greater protection from dismissal for striking employees

HUMAN RIGHTS

On 2 October 2000 the Human Rights Act 1998 came into force. This Act incorporates the European Convention on Human Rights into the law of the United Kingdom.

The main principles of the Act are as follows:
- all legislation must be interpreted by the courts as compatible with the Convention so far as it is possible to do so
- subordinate legislation (e.g. statutory instruments) which are incompatible with the Convention can be struck down by the courts
- primary legislation (e.g. Acts of Parliament) which is incompatible with the Convention cannot be struck down by a court, but the higher courts can make a declaration of incompatibility which is a signal to Parliament to change the law
- all public authorities (including courts and tribunals) must not act in a way which is incompatible with the Convention;
- individuals whose Convention rights have been infringed by a public authority may bring proceedings against that authority, but the Act is not intended to create new rights as between individuals.

The main human rights protected by the Convention are the right to life (article 2); protection from torture and inhuman or degrading treatment (article 3); protection from slavery or forced labour (article 4); the right to liberty and security of the person (article 5); right to a fair trial (article 6); the right not to be subject to retrospective criminal offences (article 7); right to private and family life (article 8); freedom of thought, conscience and religion (article 9); freedom of expression (article 10); freedom of association and assembly (article 11); right to marry and found a family (article 12); protection from discrimination (article 14); the right to property (article 1 Protocol No.1) and the right to education (article 2 Protocol No.1). Most of the Convention rights are subject to limitations which are 'necessary in a democratic society'.

ILLEGITIMACY AND LEGITIMATION

The Children Act 1989 gives the mother parental responsibility for the child when she is not married to the father. The unmarried father can acquire parental responsibility either by agreement with her (in prescribed form) or by applying to the court. The Adoption and Children Act 2002 (not yet fully in force) also makes provision for a father who is not married to the child's mother to acquire parental responsibility for the child if he becomes registered as the child's father. If an illegitimate child is to be adopted, the father's consent is required only where he has been awarded parental rights by the court.

Every child born to a married woman during marriage is presumed to be legitimate, unless the couple are separated under court order when the child is conceived, in which case the child is presumed not to be the husband's child. It is possible to challenge the presumption of legitimacy or illegitimacy through civil proceedings.

In Scotland, the relevant legislation is the Children (Scotland) Act 1995, which also gives the mother parental responsibility for her child whether or not she is married to the child's father. The father has automatic parental rights only if married to the mother. An unmarried father has no automatic parental rights but can acquire parental responsibility by applying to the court or by acquiring them under a parental responsibilities and parental rights agreement made with the mother. A child's father will only have automatic rights and responsibilities if he was married to the mother at the time of conception or subsequently marries her. The father of any child, regardless of parental rights, has a duty to aliment that child until he/she is 18 (25 if he/she is still in full-time education).

LEGITIMATION
Under the Legitimacy Act 1976, an illegitimate person automatically becomes legitimate when his/her parents marry. This applies even where one of the parents was married to a third person at the time of the birth. In such cases it is necessary to re-register the birth of the child. In Scotland, the relevant legislation is the Legitimation (Scotland) Act 1968, the Adoption (Scotland) Act 1978 and the Law Reform Parent and Child) Scotland Act 1986 which gives illegitimate and legitimate persons equal status.

JURY SERVICE

In England and Wales a person charged with any but the most minor offences is entitled to be tried by jury. No such right exists in Scotland, although more serious offences are heard before a jury. In England and Wales there are 12 members of a jury in a criminal case and eight members in a civil case. In Scotland there are 12 members of a jury in a civil case in the Court of Session (the civil jury being confined to the Court of Session and a restricted number of actions), and 15 in a criminal trial. Jurors are normally asked to serve for ten working days, although jurors selected for longer cases are expected to sit for the duration of the trial.

Every parliamentary or local government elector between the ages of 18 and 70 who has lived in the UK (including, for this purpose, the Channel Islands and the Isle of Man) for any period of at least five years since reaching the age of 13 is qualified to serve on a jury unless he/she is ineligible or disqualified.

ENGLAND AND WALES
Those ineligible for jury service include:
- those who have at any time been judges, magistrates or senior court officials
- those who have within the previous ten years been concerned with the administration of justice
- priests of any religion and vowed members of religious communities
- certain sufferers from mental illness

Those disqualified from jury service include:
- those who have at any time been sentenced by a court in the UK (including, for this purpose, the Channel Islands and the Isle of Man) to a term of imprisonment or custody of five years or more
- those who have within the previous ten years served

any part of a sentence of imprisonment, youth custody or detention, been detained in a young offenders' institution, received a suspended sentence of imprisonment or order for detention, or received a community service order
– those who have within the previous five years been placed on probation
– those who are on bail in criminal proceedings

Those who may be excused as of right from jury service include:
– persons over the age of 65
– members and officers of the Houses of Parliament
– members of the National Assembly for Wales
– representatives to the European Parliament
– full-time serving members of the armed forces
– registered and practising members of the medical, dental, nursing, veterinary and pharmaceutical professions
– those who have served on a jury in the previous two years
The court has the discretion to excuse a juror from service, or defer the date of service, if the service would be a hardship to the juror. If a person serves on a jury knowing himself/herself to be ineligible or disqualified, he/she is liable to be fined up to £5,000 if disqualified and up to £1,000 for all other offences. The defendant can object to any juror if he/she can show cause.

A juror may claim travelling expenses, a subsistence allowance and an allowance for other financial loss (e.g. loss of earnings or benefits, fees paid to carers or child-minders) up to a stated limit.

It is an offence for a juror to disclose what happened in the jury room even after the trial is over. A jury's verdict must normally be unanimous, but if no verdict has been reached after two hours' consideration (or such longer period as the court deems to be reasonable) a majority verdict is acceptable if ten jurors agree to it.

SCOTLAND

Qualification criteria for jury service in Scotland are similar to those in England and Wales, except that the maximum age for a juror is 65, members of the judiciary are ineligible for ten years after ceasing to hold their post, and others concerned with the administration of justice are only eligible for service five years after ceasing to hold office. Certain persons who have the right to be excused include full-time members of the medical, dental, nursing, veterinary and pharmaceutical professions, full-time members of the armed forces, ministers of religion, persons who have served on a jury within the previous 5 years, members of the Scottish Parliament, members of the Scottish Executive and junior Scottish Ministers. If you have been convicted of a serious crime then you are automatically disqualified. Those who are incapable by reason of a mental disorder may also be excused. The maximum fine for a person serving on a jury knowing himself/herself to be ineligible is £1,000. The maximum fine for failing to attend without good cause is also £1,000.

Further information can be obtained from:
THE COURT SERVICE, SOUTHSIDE, 105 Victoria Street, London SW1E 6QT. Tel: 020-7210 2266
THE CLERK OF JUSTICIARY, High Court of Justiciary, Lawnmarket, Edinburgh EH1 1RF. Tel: 0131-240 6900

LANDLORD AND TENANT

RESIDENTIAL LETTINGS
The provisions outlined here apply only where the tenant lives in a separate dwelling from the landlord and where the dwelling is the tenant's only or main home. It does not apply to licensees such as lodgers, guests or service occupiers.

The 1996 Housing Act radically changed certain aspects of the legislation referred to below, in particular the grant of assured and assured shorthold tenancies under the Housing Act 1988.

ASSURED SHORTHOLD TENANCIES
If a tenancy was granted on or after 15 January 1989 and before 28 February 1997, the tenant may have an assured tenancy giving that tenant greater rights. The tenant could, for example, stay in possession of the dwelling for as long as the tenant observed the terms of the tenancy. The landlord cannot obtain possession from such a tenant unless the landlord can establish a specific ground for possession (set out in the Housing Act 1988) and obtains a court order. The rent payable is that agreed with the landlord unless the rent has been fixed by the rent assessment committee of the local authority. The tenant or the landlord may request that the committee set the rent in line with open market rents for that type of property. Any rent increases that are to take place should be written into the agreement but failing that, the landlord must give advance notice of the increase.

Under the Housing Act 1996, most new lettings entered into on or after 28 February 1997 will be assured shorthold tenancies. This means that tenants are given limited rights. The landlord must obtain a court order, however, to obtain possession if the tenant refuses to vacate at the end of the tenancy. If the tenant owes two months rent or more, the landlord can serve notice proceedings and apply to the courts for an order for possession. If the tenancy is an assured shorthold tenancy, the court must grant the order.

REGULATED TENANCIES
Before the Housing Act 1988 came into force (15 January 1989) there were regulated tenancies; some are still in existence and are protected by the Rent Act 1977. Under this Act it is possible for the landlord or the tenant to apply to the local rent officer to have a 'fair' rent registered. The fair rent is then the maximum rent payable.

SECURE TENANCIES
Secure tenancies are generally given to tenants of local authorities, housing associations and certain other bodies. This gives the tenant lifelong tenure unless the terms of the agreement are broken by the tenant. In certain circumstances those with secure tenancies may have the right to buy their property. In practice this right is generally only available to council tenants.

AGRICULTURAL PROPERTY
Tenancies in agricultural properties are governed by the Agricultural Holdings Act 1986 and the Rent (Agricultural) Act 1976, which give similar protections to those described above, e.g. security of tenure, right to compensation for disturbance, etc. The Agricultural Holdings (Scotland) Act 1991 applies similar provisions to Scotland.

EVICTION

Under the Protection from Eviction Act 1977 (as amended by the Housing Act 1988), a landlord must give reasonable notice that he/she is to evict the tenant, and in most cases a possession order, granted in court, is necessary. Notice is generally to be at least four weeks and in prescribed statutory form (notices are available from law stationers). It is illegal for a landlord to evict a person by putting their belongings onto the street, by changing the locks and so on. It is also illegal for a landlord to harass a tenant in any way in order to persuade him/her to give up the tenancy.

LANDLORD RESPONSIBILITIES

Under the Landlord and Tenant Act 1985, where the term of the lease is less than seven years the landlord is responsible for maintaining the structure and exterior of the property and all installations for the supply of water, gas and electricity, for sanitation, and for heating and hot water.

LEASEHOLDERS

Legally leaseholders have bought a long lease rather than a property and in certain limited circumstances the landlord can end the tenancy. Under the Leasehold Reform Act 1967 (as amended by the Housing Acts 1969, 1974 and 1980), leaseholders of houses may have the right to buy the freehold or to take an extended lease for a term of 50 years. This applies to leases where the term of the lease is over 21 years and where the leaseholder has occupied the house as his/her main residence for the last three years, or for a total of three years over the last ten.

The Leasehold Reform, Housing and Urban Development Act came into force in 1993 and allows the leaseholders of flats in certain circumstances to buy the freehold of the building in which they live.

Responsibility for maintenance of the structure, exterior and interior of the building should be set out in the lease. Usually the upkeep of the interior of his/her part of the property is the responsibility of the leaseholder, and responsibility for the structure, exterior and common interior areas is shared between the freeholder and the leaseholder(s).

If leaseholders are in any way dissatisfied with treatment from their landlord or with charges made in respect of lease extensions, they are entitled to have their situation evaluated by the Leasehold Valuation Tribunal.

The Commonhold and Leasehold Reform Act 2002 (not in force at the time of writing (1 August 2003)) makes provision for the freehold estate in land to be registered as commonhold land and for the legal interest in the land to be vested in a 'commonhold association' i.e. a private limited company.

BUSINESS LETTINGS

The Landlord and Tenant Acts 1927 and 1954 (as amended) give security of tenure to the tenants of most business premises. The landlord can only evict the tenant on one of the grounds laid down in the 1954 Act, and in some cases where the landlord repossesses the property the tenant may be entitled to compensation.

SCOTLAND

In Scotland assured and short assured tenancies exist for lettings after 2 January 1989 and are similar to assured tenancies in England and Wales. The relevant legislation is the Housing (Scotland) Act 1988.

Most tenancies created before 2 January 1989 were regulated tenancies and the Rent (Scotland) Act 1984 still applies where these exist. The Act defines, among other things, the circumstances in which a landlord can increase the rent when improvements are made to the property. The provisions of the Rent Act do not apply to tenancies where the landlord is the Crown, a local authority, the development corporation of a new town or a housing corporation.

The Housing (Scotland) Act 1987 and its provisions relate to local authority responsibilities for housing, the right to buy, and local authority secured tenancies. The provisions are broadly similar to England and Wales.

In Scotland, business premises are not controlled by statute to the same extent as in England and Wales, although the Tenancy of Shops (Scotland) Act 1949 gives some security to tenants of shops. Tenants of shops can apply to the sheriff, within 21 days of being served a notice to quit, for a renewal of tenancy if threatened with eviction. This application may be dismissed on various grounds including where the landlord has offered to sell the property to the tenant at an agreed price or, in the absence of agreement as to price, at a price fixed by a single arbiter appointed by the parties or the sheriff. The Act extends to properties where the Crown or government departments are the landlords or the tenants.

Under the Leases Act 1449 the landlord's successors (either purchasers or creditors) are bound by the agreement made with any tenants so long as the following conditions are met:
– the lease, if for more than one year, must be in writing
– there must be a rent
– there must be a term of expiry
– the tenant must have entered into possession
– the subjects of the lease must be land
– the landlord, if owner, must be infeft – i.e. the title deeds are recorded in the Register of Sasines or the Land Register

LEGAL AID

The Access to Justice Act 1999 has transformed what used to be known as the Legal Aid system. The Legal Aid Board has been abolished and replaced from 1 April 2000 with the Legal Services Commission (85 Gray's Inn Road, London, WC1X 8TX. Tel: 020-7759 0000 Web: www.legalservices.gov.uk). The Legal Services Commission is responsible for the development and administration of two legal funding schemes in England and Wales, namely the Criminal Defence Service which replaced the old system of criminal legal aid, and the Community Legal Service fund, which replaced the old civil scheme of legal aid. The Community Legal Service is designed to increase access to legal information and advice by involving a much wider network of funders and providers in giving publicly funded legal services. In Scotland, provision of legal aid is governed by the Legal Aid (Scotland) Act 1986.

CIVIL LEGAL AID

From 1 January 2000, only organisations (solicitors or Citizens' Advice Bureau) with a contract with the Legal Services Commission have been able to give initial help in any civil matter. Moreover, from that date decisions about funding were devolved from the Legal Services Commission to contracted organisations in relation to any level of publicly funded service in family and immigration cases. For other types of case, applications for public funding are made through a solicitor (or other contracted legal services providers) in much the same way as the former Legal Aid. From 1 April 2001 the so-called civil contracting scheme was extended to cover all levels of service for all types of cases.

Under the new civil funding scheme there are broadly seven levels of service available:
- legal help
- help at court (the first two types of service are limited to advice and assistance with preparing a case, but do not include representation)
- approved family help – either general family help or help with mediation (special levels of service for family cases)
- legal representation – either investigative help or full representation (this covers assistance with representation in court)
- support funding – either investigative support or litigation support (this is a new type of assistance which allows the costs of a privately funded case to be topped up from public funds. It is only available for personal injury claims)
- family mediation
- such other services as are specifically authorised by the Lord Chancellor

In general, public funding is not available for the following type of cases:
- personal injury (except for the availability of support funding and clinical negligence claims)
- allegations of negligent damage to property
- conveyancing
- boundary disputes
- the making of wills
- matters of trust law
- defamation proceedings
- partnership disputes and company law
- other matters arising out of the carrying on of a business.

ELIGIBILITY
Eligibility for funding from the Community Legal Service depends broadly on five factors :
- the level of service sought (see above)
- whether the applicant qualifies financially
- the merits of the applicant's case
- a costs-benefits analysis (if the costs are likely to outweigh any benefit that might be gained from the proceedings, funding may be refused)
- whether there is any public interest in the case being litigated (i.e. whether the case has a wider public interest beyond that of the parties involved – for example, a human rights case)

The limits on capital and income above which a person is not entitled to public funding vary with the type of service sought.

CONTRIBUTIONS
Some of those who qualify for Community Legal Service funding will have to contribute towards their legal costs. Contributions must be paid by anyone who has a disposable income or disposable capital exceeding a prescribed amount. The rules relating to applicable contributions are complex and detailed information can be obtained from the Legal Services Commission.

STATUTORY CHARGE
A statutory charge is made if a person receives money or property in a case for which they have received legal aid. This means that the amount paid by the Community Legal Service fund on their behalf is deducted from the amount that the person receives. This does not apply if the court has ordered that the costs be paid by the other party (unless the amount paid by the other party does not cover all of the costs) or if the payments are for maintenance.

CONTINGENCY OR CONDITIONAL FEES
This system was introduced by the Courts and Legal Services Act 1990. It offers legal representation on a "no win, no fee" basis. It provides an alternative form of assistance, especially for those cases which are ineligible for funding by the Community Legal Service. The main area for such work is in the field of personal injuries which claims are now largely exempt from public funding (except for clinical negligence claims).

Not all solicitors offer such a scheme and different solicitors may well have different terms. The effect of the agreement is that solicitors will not make any charges until the case is concluded successfully. If a case is won then the losing party will usually have to pay towards costs, with the winning party contributing around one-third.

SCOTLAND
Civil legal aid is available for cases in the following:
- the House of Lords
- the Court of Session
- the Lands Valuation Appeal Court
- the Scottish Land Court
- sheriff courts
- the Lands Tribunal for Scotland
- the Employment Appeal Tribunals
- the Restrictive Practices Court

Civil legal aid is not available for defamation actions, small claims or simplified divorce procedures.

Eligibility for civil legal aid is assessed in a similar way to that in England and Wales, though the financial limits differ in some respects and are as follows:
- a person is eligible if his yearly disposable income is £9,307 or less and disposable capital is £6,100 or less
- if disposable income is between £2,851 and £9,307, contributions are payable
- if disposable capital exceeds £6,100, contributions are payable and legal aid may be refused if disposable capital is over £10,170
- those receiving income support or income related job seeker's allowance qualify automatically.

CRIMINAL LEGAL AID
The courts will grant criminal legal aid if it is desirable in the interests of justice (e.g. if there are important questions of law to be argued or the case is so serious that if found guilty the person may go to prison) and the person needs help to pay their legal costs.

Criminal legal aid covers the cost of preparing a case and legal representation (including the cost of a barrister) in criminal proceedings. It is also available for appeals against verdicts or sentences in magistrates' courts, the Crown Court or the Court of Appeal. It is not available for bringing a private prosecution in a criminal court.

If granted criminal legal aid, either the person may choose their own solicitor or the court will assign one. Contributions to the legal costs must be paid by anyone who has a disposable income or disposable capital which exceeds a prescribed amount. The rules relating to applicable contributions are complex and detailed information can be obtained from the Legal Services Commission.

DUTY SOLICITORS

The Legal Aid Act 1988 also provides free advice and assistance to anyone questioned by the police (whether under arrest or helping the police with their enquiries). No means test or contributions are required for this.

SCOTLAND

Legal advice and assistance operates in a similar way in Scotland. A person is eligible:
- if disposable income does not exceed £192 a week. If disposable income is between £81 and £192 a week, contributions are payable
- if disposable capital does not exceed £1,330 (if the person has dependant relatives, the savings allowance is higher).

The procedure for application for criminal legal aid depends on the circumstances of each case. In solemn cases (more serious cases, such as murder) heard before a jury, a person is automatically entitled to criminal legal aid until they are given bail or placed in custody. Thereafter, it is for the court to decide whether to grant legal aid. The court will do this if the person accused cannot meet the expenses of the case without undue hardship on him or his dependants. In less serious cases the procedure depends on whether the person is in custody:
- anyone taken into custody has the right to free legal aid from the duty solicitor up to and including the first court appearance
- if the person is not in custody and wishes to plead guilty, they are not entitled to criminal legal aid but may be entitled to legal advice and assistance, including assistance by way of representation
- if the person is not in custody and wishes to plead not guilty, they can apply for criminal legal aid. This must be done within 14 days of the first court appearance at which they made the plea

The criteria used to assess whether or not criminal legal aid should be granted is similar to the criteria for England and Wales. When meeting with your solicitor, take evidence of your financial position such as details of savings, bank statements, pay slips, pension book or benefits book.

Further information can be obtained from:
THE SCOTTISH LEGAL AID BOARD,
44 Drumsheugh Gardens, Edinburgh EH3 7SW
Tel: 0131-226 7061

MARRIAGE

Any two persons may marry provided that:
- they are at least 16 years old on the day of the marriage (in England and Wales persons under the age of 18 must generally obtain the consent of their parents; if consent is refused an appeal may be made to the High Court, the county court or a court of summary jurisdiction)
- they are not related to one another in a way which would prevent their marrying
- they are unmarried (a person who has already been married must produce documentary evidence that the previous marriage has been ended by death, divorce or annulment)
- they are not of the same sex
- they are capable of understanding the nature of a marriage ceremony and of consenting to marriage
- the marriage would be regarded as valid in any foreign country of which either party is a citizen

DEGREES OF RELATIONSHIP

A marriage between persons within the prohibited degrees of consanguinity, affinity or adoption is void.

A man may not marry his mother, daughter, granddaughter, granddaughter, sister, aunt, niece, great-grandmother, great-granddaughter, adoptive mother, former adoptive mother, adopted daughter or former adopted daughter. In some circumstances he may now be allowed to marry his former wife's daughter, former wife's granddaughter, father's former wife or grandfather's former wife.

A woman may not marry her father, son, grandfather, grandson, brother, uncle, nephew, great-grandfather, great-grandson, adoptive father, former adoptive father, adopted son or former adopted son. In some circumstances she may now be allowed to marry her former husband's son, former husband's grandson, mother's former husband or grandmother's former husband.

ENGLAND AND WALES

TYPES OF MARRIAGE CEREMONY

It is possible to marry by either religious or civil ceremony. A religious ceremony can take place at a church or chapel of the Church of England or the Church in Wales, or at any other place of worship which has been formally registered by the Registrar-General.

A civil ceremony can take place at a register office, a registered building or any other premises approved by the local authority.

An application for an approved premises licence must be made by the owners or trustees of the building concerned; it cannot be made by the prospective marriage couple. Approved premises must be regularly open to the public so that the marriage can be witnessed; the venue must be deemed to be a permanent and immovable structure. Open-air ceremonies are prohibited.

Non-Anglican marriages may also be solemnised following the issue of a Registrar-General's licence in unregistered premises where one of the parties is seriously ill, is not expected to recover, and cannot be moved to registered premises. Detained and housebound persons may be married at their place of residence.

MARRIAGE IN THE CHURCH OF ENGLAND OR THE CHURCH IN WALES

Marriage by banns

The marriage must take place in a parish in which one of the parties lives, or in a church in another parish if it is the usual place of worship of either or both of the parties. The banns must be called in the parish in which the marriage is to take place on three Sundays before the day of the ceremony; if either or both of the parties lives in a different parish the banns must also be called there. After three months the banns are no longer valid.

Marriage by common licence

The vicar who is to conduct the marriage will arrange for a common licence to be issued by the diocesan bishop; this dispenses with the necessity for banns. One of the parties must have lived in the parish for 15 days immediately before the issuing of the licence or must usually worship at the church. Affidavits are prepared from the personal instructions of one of the parties and the licence will be given to the applicant in person.

Marriage by special licence

A special licence is granted by the Archbishop of Canterbury in special circumstances for the marriage to take place at any place, with or without previous residence in the parish, or at any time. Application must be made to the Faculty Office of the Archbishop of Canterbury, 1 The Sanctuary, London SW1P 3JT Tel: 020-7222 5381.

Marriage by certificate
The marriage can be conducted on the authority of the superintendent registrar's certificate, provided that the vicar's consent is obtained. One of the parties must live in the parish or must usually worship at the church.

MARRIAGE BY OTHER RELIGIOUS CEREMONY
One of the parties must normally live in the registration district where the marriage is to take place. In addition to giving notice to the superintendent registrar it may also be necessary to book a registrar to be present at the ceremony.

CIVIL MARRIAGE
A marriage may be solemnised at any register office, registered building or approved premises in England and Wales. The superintendent registrar of the district should be contacted, and, if the marriage is to take place at approved premises, the necessary arrangements at the venue must also be made.

NOTICE OF MARRIAGE
Unless it is to take place by banns or under common or special licence in the Church of England or the Church in Wales, a notice of the marriage must be given in person to the superintendent registrar. Notice of marriage may be given in the following ways:
– by certificate. Both parties must have lived in a registration district in England or Wales for at least seven days immediately before giving notice at the local register office. If they live in different registration districts, notice must be given in both districts. The marriage can take place in any register office or other approved premises in England and Wales no sooner than 16 days after notice has been given
– by licence (often known as 'special licence'). One of the parties must have lived in a registration district in England or Wales for at least 15 days before giving notice at the register office; the other party need only be a resident of, or be physically in, England and Wales on the day notice is given. The marriage can take place one clear day (other than a Sunday, Christmas Day or Good Friday) after notice has been given

A notice of marriage is valid for 12 months. It is not therefore possible to give formal notice of a marriage more than three months before it is to take place, but it should be possible to make an advance (provisional) booking 12 months before the ceremony. In this case it is still necessary to give formal notice three months before the marriage. When giving notice of the marriage it is necessary to produce official proof, if relevant, that any previous marriage has ended in divorce or death by producing a decree absolute or death certificate; it is also useful, but not necessary, to take birth certificates or passports as proof of age and identity.

SOLEMNISATION OF THE MARRIAGE
On the day of the wedding there must be at least two other people present who are prepared to act as witnesses and sign the marriage register. A registrar of marriages must be present at a marriage in a register office or at approved premises, but an authorised person may act in

the capacity of registrar in a registered building.

If the marriage takes place at approved premises, the room must be separate from any other activity on the premises at the time of the ceremony, and no food or drink can be sold or consumed in the room during the ceremony or for one hour beforehand.

The marriage must be solemnised between 8 a.m. and 6 p.m., with open doors. At some time during the ceremony the parties must make a declaration that they know of no legal impediment to the marriage and they must also say the contracting words; the declaratory and contracting words may vary according to the form of service. A civil marriage cannot contain any religious aspects, but it may be possible for non-religious music and/or poetry readings to be included. It may also be possible to embellish the marriage vows taken by the couple.

CIVIL FEES
Marriage at a Register Office
By superintendent registrar's certificate, £94.00
This includes a fee of £34.00 for the registrar's attendance on the day of the wedding

Marriage on Approved Premises
By superintendent registrar's certificate, £60.00
An additional fee will also be payable for the superintendent registrar's and registrar's attendance at the marriage. This is set locally by the local authority responsible. A further charge is likely to be made by the owners of the building for the use of the premises. For marriages taking place in a religious building other than the Church of England or Church of Wales, an additional fee of £40.00 is payable for the registrar's attendance at the marriage unless an "Authorised Person" appointed by the trustees of the building have agreed to register the marriage. Additional fees may be charged by the trustees of the building for the wedding and by the person who performs the ceremony.

ECCLESIASTICAL FEES
(Church of England and Church in Wales[*])
Marriage by banns
For publication of banns, £18.00
For certificate of banns issued at time of publication, £9.00
For marriage service, £162.00
Marriage by common licence
Fee for licence, £60.00
Marriage by special licence
Fee for licence, £125.00
[*]Some of these fees may not apply to the Church in Wales

SCOTLAND
REGULAR MARRIAGES
A regular marriage is one which is celebrated by a minister of religion or authorised registrar or other celebrant. Each of the parties must complete a marriage notice form and return it to the district registrar for the area in which they are to be married, irrespective of where they live, at least 15 days before the ceremony is due to take place. The district registrar must then enter the date of receipt and certain details in a marriage book kept for this purpose, and must also enter the names of the parties and the proposed date of marriage in a list which is displayed in a conspicuous place at the registration office until the date of the marriage has passed. All persons wishing to enter into a regular marriage in Scotland must follow the same preliminary

procedure regardless of whether they intend to have a religious or civil ceremony. Before the marriage ceremony takes place any person may submit an objection in writing to the district registrar.

A marriage schedule, which is prepared by the registrar, will be issued to one or both of the parties in person up to seven days before a religious marriage; for a civil marriage the schedule will be available at the ceremony. The schedule must be handed to the celebrant before the ceremony starts; it must be signed immediately after the wedding and the marriage must be registered within three days.

The authority to conduct a religious marriage is deemed to be vested in the authorised celebrant rather than the building in which it takes place; open-air religious ceremonies are therefore permissible in Scotland.

From 10 June 2002 it has been possible, under the Marriage (Scotland) Act 2002, for venues or couples to apply to the local council for a licence to allow a civil ceremony to take place at a venue other than a registration office. To obtain further information, a venue or couple should contact the district registrar in the area they wish to marry. A list of licensed venues is also available on the General Registers of Scotland website at www.gro-scotland.gov.uk.

MARRIAGE BY COHABITATION WITH HABIT AND REPUTE
If two people live together constantly as husband and wife and are generally held to be such by the neighbourhood and among their friends and relations, there may arise a presumption from which marriage can be inferred. Before such a marriage can be registered, however, a decree of declarator of marriage must be obtained from the Court of Session.

CIVIL FEES
The fee for a religious marriage is £93.50, comprising a fee of £20.00 per person for the statutory notice of an intention to marry, a £45 fee for the solemnisation of the marriage in a register office and an £8.50 fee for a copy of the marriage certificate. The cost of marrying in a registration office or under a local authority licence can vary.

Further information can be obtained from:
THE GENERAL REGISTER OFFICE, Office for National Statistics, Smedley Hydro, Trafalgar Road, Southport, Merseyside PR8 2HH. Tel: 0870-243 7788
THE GENERAL REGISTER OFFICE FOR SCOTLAND, New Register House, Edinburgh EH1 3YT. Tel: 0131-225 4452

TOWN AND COUNTRY PLANNING

The planning system is important in helping to protect the environment, as well as assisting individuals in assessing their land rights. There are a number of Acts governing the development of land and buildings in the UK and advice should always be sought from a Citizen's Advice Bureau or local planning authority before undertaking building works on any land or property. If building takes place which requires planning permission without permission being sought in advance, the situation may need to be rectified.

PLANNING PERMISSION
Planning permission is needed if the work involves:
– making a material change in use, such as dividing off part of the house so that it can be used as a separate home or dividing off part of the house for commercial use, e.g. for a workshop
– going against the terms of the original planning permission, e.g. there may be a restriction on fences in front gardens on an open-plan estate
– building, engineering for mining, except for the permissions below
– new or wider access to a main road
– additions or extensions to flats or maisonettes
Planning permission is not needed to carry out internal alterations or work which does not affect the external appearance of the building.

There are certain types of development for which the Secretary of State for the Environment has granted general permissions (permitted development rights). These include:
– house extensions and additions (including conservatories, loft conversions, garages and dormer windows). Up to 10 per cent or up to 50 cubic metres (whichever is the greater) can be added to the original house for terraced houses. Up to 15 per cent or 70 cubic metres (whichever is the greater) to other kinds of houses. The maximum that can be added to any house is 115 cubic metres
– buildings such as garden sheds and greenhouses so long as they are no more than 3 metres high (or 4 metres if the roof is ridged), are no nearer to a highway than the house, and at least half the ground around the house remains uncovered by buildings
– adding a porch with a ground area of less than 3 square metres and that is less than 3 metres in height
– putting up fences, walls and gates of under 1 metre in height if next to a road and under 2 metres elsewhere
– laying patios, paths or driveways for domestic use

OTHER RESTRICTIONS
It may be necessary to obtain other types of permissions before carrying out any development. These permissions are separate from planning permission and apply regardless of whether or not planning permission is needed, e.g.:
– building regulations will probably apply if a new building is to be erected, if an existing one is to be altered or extended, or if the work involves building over a drain or sewer. The building control department of the local authority will advise on this
– any alterations to a listed building or the grounds of a listed building must be approved by the local authority
– local authority approval is necessary if a building (or, in some circumstances, gates, walls, fences or railings) in a conservation area is to be demolished; each local authority keeps a register of all local buildings that are in conservation areas
– many trees are protected by tree preservation orders and must not be pruned or taken down without local authority consent
– bats and other species are protected and English Nature, the Countryside Council for Wales or Scottish Natural Heritage must be notified before any work is carried out that will affect the habitat of protected species, e.g. timber treatment, renovation or extensions of lofts
– any development in areas designated as a National Park, an Area of Outstanding National Beauty, a National Scenic Area or in the Norfolk or Suffolk Broads is subject to greater restrictions. The local planning authority will advise or refer enquirers to the relevant authority

If you think you require planning permission, contact your local authority.

VOTERS' QUALIFICATIONS

Those entitled to vote at parliamentary, European Union (EU) and local government elections are those who are:
- on the electoral roll. Local authorities administer the roll and non-registration can lead to a fine of up to £1,000
- over 18 years old
- Commonwealth (which includes British) citizens or citizens of the Republic of Ireland

British citizens resident abroad are entitled to vote, for 15 years after leaving Britain, as overseas electors in parliamentary and EU elections in the constituency in which they were last resident. Members of the armed forces, Crown servants and employees of the British Council who are overseas and their spouses are entitled to vote regardless of how long they have been abroad.

European Union citizens resident in the UK may vote in EU and local government elections.

The main categories of people who are not entitled to vote are:
- sitting peers in the House of Lords
- patients detained under mental health legislation who have criminal convictions
- those serving prison sentences
- those convicted within the previous five years of corrupt or illegal election practices

Under the Representation of the Peoples Act 2000, several new groups of people are permitted to vote for the first time. These include: people who live on barges; unconvicted or remand prisoners; people in mental health hospitals (other than those with criminal convictions) and homeless people who have made a 'declaration of local connection'.

REGISTERING TO VOTE
Voters must be entered on an electoral register, which runs from 16 February in one year to 15 February in the following year. The registration officer for each constituency is responsible for preparing and publishing the register. A registration form is sent to all households in the autumn of each year and the householder is required to provide details of all occupants who are eligible to vote, including ones who will reach their 18th birthday in the year covered by the register. Those who fail to give the required information or who give false information are liable to be fined. A draft register is usually published at the end of November. Any person whose name has been omitted may ask to be registered and should contact the registration officer. Anyone on the register may object to the inclusion of another person's name, in which case he/she should notify the registration officer, who will investigate that person's eligibility. Supplementary electors lists are published throughout the duration of the register.

VOTING
Voting is not compulsory in the UK. Those who wish to vote must generally vote in person at the allotted polling station. Those who will be away at the time of the election, those who will not be able to attend in person due to physical incapacity or the nature of their occupation, and those who have changed address during the period for which the register is valid, may apply for a postal vote or nominate a proxy to vote for them. Overseas electors who wish to vote must do so by proxy.

Further information can be obtained from the local authority's electoral registration officer in England and Wales or the electoral registration office in Scotland, or the Chief Electoral Officer in Northern Ireland.

WILLS AND INTESTACY

In a will a person leaves instructions as to the disposal of their property after they die. A will is also used to appoint executors (who will administer the estate), give directions as to the disposal of the body, appoint guardians for children and, for larger estates, can operate to reduce the level of inheritance tax. It is best to have a will drawn up by a solicitor but if a solicitor is not employed, the following points must be taken into account:
- if possible the will must not be prepared on behalf of another person by someone who is to benefit from it or who is a close relative of a major beneficiary
- the language used must be clear and unambiguous and it is better to avoid the use of legal terms where the same thing can be expressed in plain language
- it is better to rewrite the whole document if a mistake is made. If necessary, alterations can be made by striking through the words with a pen, and the signature or initials of the testator and the witnesses must be put in the margin opposite the alteration. No alteration of any kind should be made after the will has been executed
- if the person later wishes to change the will or part of it, it is better to write a new will revoking the old. The use of codicils (documents written as supplements or containing modifications to the will) should be left to a solicitor
- the will should be typed or printed, or if handwritten be legible and preferably in ink. Commercial will forms can be obtained from some stationers.

The form of a will varies to suit different cases – a solicitor will be able to advise as to wording, however, 'DIY' will-writing kits can be purchased from good stationery shops and many banks offer a will writing service.

LAPSED LEGATEES
If a person who has been left property in a will dies before the person who made the will, the gift fails and will pass to the person entitled to everything not otherwise disposed of (the residuary estate).

If the person left the residuary estate dies before the person who made the will, their share will generally pass to the closest relative(s) of the person who made the will (as in intestacy) unless the will names a beneficiary such as a charity who will take as a 'long stop' if this gift is unable to take effect for any reason. It is always better to draw up a new will if a beneficiary predeceases the person who made the will.

EXECUTORS
It is usual to appoint two executors, although one is sufficient. No more than four persons can deal with the estate of the person who has died. The name and address of each executor should be given in full (the addresses are not essential but including them adds clarity to the document). Executors should be 18 years of age or over. An executor may be a beneficiary of the will.

WITNESSES
A person who is a beneficiary of a will, or the spouse of a beneficiary at the time the will is signed, must not act as a witness or else he/she will be unable to take his/her gift.

Husband and wife can both act as witnesses provided neither benefits from the will.

It is better that a person does not act as an executor and as a witness, as he/she can take no benefit under a will to which he/she is witness. The identity of the witnesses should be made as explicit as possible.

EXECUTION OF A WILL
The person making the will should sign his/her name at the foot of the document, in the presence of the two witnesses. The witnesses must then sign their names while the person making the will looks on. If this procedure is not adhered to, the will will be considered invalid. There are certain exceptional circumstances where these rules are relaxed, e.g. where the person may be too ill to sign.

CAPACITY TO MAKE A WILL
Anyone aged 18 or over can make a will. However, if there is any suspicion that the person making the will is not, through reasons of infirmity or age, fully in command of his/her faculties, it is advisable to arrange for a medical practitioner to examine the person making the will at the time it is to be executed to verify his/her mental capacity and to record that medical opinion in writing, and to ask the examining practitioner to act as a witness. If a person is not mentally able to make a will, the Court may do this for him/her by virtue of the Mental Health Act 1983.

REVOCATION
A will may be revoked or cancelled in a number of ways:
- a later will revokes an earlier one if it says so; otherwise the earlier will is impliedly revoked by the later one to the extent that it contradicts or repeats the earlier one
- a will is also revoked if the physical document on which it is written is destroyed by the person whose will it is. There must be an intention to revoke the will. It may not be sufficient to obliterate the will with a pen
- a will is revoked when the person marries, unless it is clear from the will that the person intended the will to stand after the marriage
- where a marriage ends in divorce or is annulled or declared void, gifts to the spouse and the appointment of the spouse as executor fail unless the will says that this is not to happen. A former spouse is treated as having predeceased the testator. A separation does not change the effect of a married person's will.

PROBATE AND LETTERS OF ADMINISTRATION
Probate is granted to the executors named in a will and once granted, the executors are obliged to carry out the instructions of the will. Letters of administration are granted where no executor is named in a will or is willing or able to act or where there is no will or no valid will; this gives a person, often the next of kin, similar powers and duties to those of an executor.

Applications for probate or for letters of administration can be made to the Principal Registry of the Family Division, to a district probate registry or to a probate sub-registry. Applicants will need the following documents: the original will (if any); a certificate of death; oath for executors or administrators; particulars of all property and assets left by the deceased; a list of debts and funeral expenses. Certain property, up to the value of £5,000, may be disposed of without a grant of probate or letters of administration.

WHERE TO FIND A PROVED WILL
Since 1858 wills which have been proved, that is wills on which probate or letters of administration have been granted, must have been proved at the Principal Registry of the Family Division or at a district probate registry. The Lord Chancellor has power to direct where the original documents are kept but most are filed where they were proved and may be inspected there and a copy obtained. The Principal Registry also holds copies of all wills proved at district probate registries and these may be inspected at First Avenue House, High Holborn. An index of all grants, both of probate and of letters of administration, is compiled by the Principal Registry and may be seen either at the Principal Registry or at a district probate registry.

It is also possible to discover when a grant of probate or letters of administration is issued by requesting a standing search. In response to a request and for a small fee, a district probate registry will supply the names and addresses of executors or administrators and the registry in which the grant was made, of any grant in the estate of a specified person made in the previous 12 months or following six months. This is useful for applicants who may be beneficiaries to a will but who have lost contact with the deceased and for creditors of the deceased.

SCOTLAND
In Scotland any person over 12 and of sound mind can make a will. The person making the will can only freely dispose of the heritage and what is known as the 'dead's part' of the estate because:
- the spouse has the right to inherit one-third of the moveable estate if there are children or other descendants, and one-half of it if there are not
- children are entitled to one-third of the moveable estate if there is a surviving spouse, and one-half of it if there is not

The remaining portion is the dead's part, and legacies and bequests are payable from this. Debts are payable out of the whole estate before any division.

From August 1995, wills no longer needed to be 'holographed' and it is now only necessary to have one witness. The person making the will still needs to sign each page. It is better that the will is not witnessed by a beneficiary although the attestation would still be sound and the beneficiary would not have to relinquish the gift.

Subsequent marriage does not revoke a will but the birth of a child who is not provided for may do so. A will may be revoked by a subsequent will, either expressly or by implication, but in so far as the two can be read together both have effect. If a subsequent will is revoked, the earlier will is revived.

Wills may be registered in the sheriff court Books of the Sheriffdom in which the deceased lived or in the Books of Council and Session at the Registers of Scotland.

CONFIRMATION
Confirmation (the Scottish equivalent of probate) is obtained in the sheriff court of the sheriffdom in which the deceased was resident at the time of death. Executives are either 'nominate' (named by the deceased in the will) or 'dative' (appointed by the court in cases where no executor is named in a will or in cases of intestacy). Applicants for confirmation must first provide an inventory of the deceased's estate and a schedule of debts, with an affidavit. In estates under £25,000 gross, confirmation can be obtained under a simplified procedure at reduced fees, with no need for a solicitor. The local sheriff clerk's office can provide assistance.

Further information can be obtained from:
PRINCIPAL REGISTRY (FAMILY DIVISION),
First Avenue House, 42–49 High Holborn,
London, WC2V 6NP. Tel: 020 7947 6980.
REGISTERS OF SCOTLAND, Meadowbank House,
153 London Road, Edinburgh, EH8 7AU. Tel: 0131-659 6111

INTESTACY

Intestacy occurs when someone dies without leaving a will or leaves a will which is invalid or which does not take effect for some reason. Intestacy can be partial, for instance, if there is a will which disposes of some but not all of the testator's property. In such cases the person's estate (property, possessions, other assets following the payment of debts) passes to certain members of the family. The relevant legislation is the Administration of Estates Act 1925, as amended by various legislation including the Intestates Estates Act 1952, the Law Reform (Succession) Act 1995, and the Trusts of Land and Appointment of Trustees Act 1996 and Orders made there under. Some of the provisions of this legislation are described below. If a will has been written that disposes of only part of a person's property, these rules apply to the part which is undisposed of.

If the person (intestate) leaves a spouse who survives for 28 days and children (legitimate, illegitimate and adopted children and other descendants), the estate is divided as follows:

– the spouse takes the 'personal chattels' (household articles, including cars, but nothing used for business purposes), £125,000 free of tax (with interest payable at 6 per cent from the time of the death until payment) and a life interest in half of the rest of the estate (which can be capitalised by the spouse if he/she wishes)
– the rest of the estate goes to the children[*]

If the person leaves a spouse who survives for 28 days but no children:

– the spouse takes the personal chattels, £200,000 free of tax (interest payable as before) and full ownership of half of the rest of the estate
– the other half of the rest of the estate goes to the parents (equally, if both alive) or, if none, to the brothers and sisters of the whole blood[*]
– if there are no parents or brothers or sisters of the whole blood or their children, the spouse takes the whole estate

If there is no surviving spouse, the estate is distributed among those who survive the intestate as follows:

– to surviving children[*], but if none to
– parents (equally, if both alive), but if none to
– brothers and sisters of the whole blood[*], but if none to
– brothers and sisters of the half blood[*], but if none to
– grandparents (equally, if more than one), but if none to
– aunts and uncles of the whole blood[*], but if none to
– aunts and uncles of the half blood[*], but if none to
– the Crown, Duchy of Lancaster or the Duke of Cornwall (*bona vacantia*)

[*] To inherit, a member of these groups must survive the intestate and attain 18, or marry under that age. If they die under 18 (unless married under that age), their share goes to others, if any, in the same group. If any member of these groups predeceases the intestate leaving children, their share is divided equally among their children.

In England and Wales the provisions of the Inheritance (Provision for Family and Dependants) Act 1975 may allow other people to claim provision from the deceased's assets. This Act also applies to cases where a will has been made and allows a person to apply to the Court if they feel that the will or rules of intestacy or both do not make adequate provision for them. The Court can order payment from the deceased's assets or the transfer of property from them if the applicant's claim is accepted. The application must be made within six months of the grant of probate or letters of administration and the following people can make an application:

– the spouse
– a former spouse who has not remarried
– a child of the deceased
– someone treated as a child of the deceased's family
– someone maintained by the deceased
– someone who has cohabited for two years before the death in the same household as the deceased and as the husband or wife of the deceased

SCOTLAND

The rules of distribution are contained in the Succession (Scotland) Act 1964.

A surviving spouse is entitled to 'prior rights'. This means that the spouse has the right to inherit:

– the matrimonial home up to a value of £130,000, or one matrimonial home if there is more than one, or, in certain circumstances, the value of the matrimonial home
– the furnishings and contents of that home, up to the value of £22,000
– a cash sum of £35,000 if the deceased left children or other descendants, or £58,000 if not

These figures are increased from time to time by regulations.

Once prior rights have been satisfied jus relicti(ae) and legitim are settled. Legal rights are:

Jus relicti(ae) – the right of a surviving spouse to one-half of the net moveable estate, after satisfaction of prior rights, if there are no surviving children; if there are surviving children, the spouse is entitled to one-third of the net moveable estate

Legitim – the right of surviving children to one-half of the net moveable estate if there is no surviving spouse; if there is a surviving spouse, the children are entitled to one-third of the net moveable estate after the satisfaction of prior rights

Where there are no surviving spouse or children, half of the estate is taken by the parents and half by the brothers and sisters. Failing that, the lines of succession, in general, are:

– to descendants
– if no descendants, then to collaterals (i.e. brothers and sisters) and parents
– surviving spouse
– if no collaterals or parents or spouse, then to ascendants collaterals (i.e. aunts and uncles), and so on in an ascending scale
– if all lines of succession fail, the estate passes to the Crown

Relatives of the whole blood are preferred to relatives of the half blood. The right of representation, i.e. the right of the issue of a person who would have succeeded if he/she had survived the intestate, also applies.

INTELLECTUAL PROPERTY

COPYRIGHT

Copyright protects all original literary, dramatic, musical and artistic works (including photographs, maps and plans), published editions of works, computer programs, sound recordings, films (including video), broadcasts (including satellite broadcasts) and cable programmes (including on-line information services). Under copyright the creators of these works can control the various ways in which their material may be exploited, the rights broadly covering copying, adapting, issuing (including renting and lending) copies to the public, performing in public, and broadcasting the material. In 2002 an Act was passed allowing the transfer of copyright works to formats accessible to visually impaired persons without infringement of copyright.

Copyright protection in the United Kingdom is automatic and there is no registration system. The main legislation is the Copyright, Designs and Patents Act 1988, which has been amended by other Acts and by Statutory Instrument to take account of EC Directives. As a result of an EC Directive effective from January 1996, the term of copyright protection for literary, dramatic, musical and artistic works lasts until 70 years after the death of the author, and for film lasts for 70 years after the death of the last to survive of the director, author of the screenplay, author of the dialogue and composer of music specially created for the film. Sound recordings are protected for 50 years after their publication, and broadcasts and cable programmes for 50 years from the end of the year in which the first broadcast/transmission is made. Published editions remain under copyright protection for 25 years from the end of the year in which the edition was published.

The main international treaties protecting copyright are the Bern Convention for the Protection of Literary and Artistic Works, the Rome Convention for the Protection of Performers, Producers of Phonograms and Broadcasting Organisations, and the Universal Copyright Convention (UCC); the UK is a signatory to these conventions. Copyright material created by UK nationals or residents is protected in each country which is a member of the conventions by the national law of that country. A list of participating countries may be obtained from the Patent Office.

Two treaties which strengthen and update international standards of protection, particularly in relation to new technologies were agreed in December 1996: WIPO (World Intellectual Property Organisation) Copyright Treaty, and the WIPO Performance and Phonograms Treaty. In May 2001 the European Union passed a new Directive, which in 2003 became law in the UK, aimed at harmonising copyright law throughout the EU. In the UK this will require changes to the application of certain aspects of copyright to digital media.

LICENSING

Use of copyright material without seeking permission in each instance may be permitted under "blanket" licences available from copyright licensing agencies. The International Federation of Reproduction Rights Organisations facilitates agreements between its member licensing agencies and on behalf of its members with organisations such as the WIPO, UNESCO, the European Union and the Council of Europe.

PATENTS

A patent is a document issued by the Patent Office relating to an invention and giving the proprietor monopoly rights, effective within the United Kingdom (including the Isle of Man). In return the patentee pays a fee to cover the costs of processing the patent and publicly discloses details of the invention.

To qualify for a patent an invention must be new, must exhibit an inventive step, and must be capable of industrial application. The patent is valid for a maximum of 20 years from the date on which the application was filed, subject to payment of annual fees from the end of the fourth year.

The Patent Office, established in 1852, is responsible for ensuring that all stages of an application comply with the Patents Act 1977, and that the invention meets the criteria for a patent.

The WIPO is responsible for administering many of the international conventions on intellectual property. The Patent Co-operation Treaty allows inventors to file a single application for patent rights in some or all of the contracting states. This application is searched by an International Searching Authority and published by the International Bureau of WIPO. It may also be the subject of an (optional) international preliminary examination. Applicants must then deal directly with the patent offices in the countries where they are seeking patent rights.

The European Patent Convention, linked to the Patent Co-operation Treaty, allows inventors to obtain patent rights in all the contracting states by filing a single European patent application which is processed by the European Patent Office (EPO). Once granted, the patent is subject to national laws in each signatory country. To comply with security requirements, an applicant resident in the UK must file a European patent application with the UK Patent Office unless the Patent Office gives permission for it to be filed directly with the EPO.

TRADE MARKS

Trade marks are a means of identification, whether a word or device or a combination of both, a logo, or the shape of goods or their packaging, which enable traders to make their goods or services readily distinguishable from those supplied by other traders. Registration prevents other traders using the same or similar trade marks for similar products or services for which the mark is registered.

In the UK trade marks are registered at the Trade Marks Registry in the Patent Office. In order to qualify for registration a mark must be capable of distinguishing its proprietor's goods or services from those of other undertakings. It should be non-deceptive and not easily confused with a mark that has already been registered for the same or similar goods or services. The relevant current legislation is the Trade Marks Act 1994.

It is possible to obtain an international trade mark registration, effective in 71 countries, under the Madrid Agreement or the Madrid Protocol, to which the UK is party. British companies can obtain international trade mark registration through a single application to WIPO in those countries party to the protocol.

EC trade mark regulation is now in force and is

administered by the Office for Harmonisation in the Internal Market (Trade Marks and Designs) in Alicante, Spain. The office registers EC trade marks, which are a unitary right valid throughout the European Union. The national registration of trade marks in member states is continuing in parallel with the EC trade mark.

DESIGN PROTECTION

Design protection covers the outward appearance of an article and takes two forms in the UK, registered design and design right, which are not mutually exclusive. Registered design protects the aesthetic appearance of an article, including shape, configuration, pattern or ornament, although artistic works such as sculptures are excluded, being generally protected by copyright. In order to qualify for protection, a design must be new and materially different from earlier UK published designs. The owner of the design must apply to the Designs Registry at the Patent Office. Initial registration lasts for five years and is extendible in five-yearly steps to a maximum of 25 years. The current legislation is the Registered Designs Act 1949 (as amended).

There is no international design registry currently available to UK applicants; in general, separate applications must be made in each country in which protection is sought. However, the EC Directive for the Legal Protection of Designs was adopted in 1998 to harmonise laws on certain aspects of design protection throughout the European Union. Member states had to amend their laws to comply with the Directive by 28 October 2001.

Design right is an automatic right which applies to the shape or configuration of articles and does not require registration. Unlike registered design, two-dimensional designs do not qualify for protection but designs of semiconductor chips (topographies) are protected by design right. Designs must be original and non-commonplace. The term of design right is ten years from first marketing of the design and the right is effective only in the UK. The current legislation is Part 3 of the Copyright, Designs and Patents Act 1988, amended on 9 December 2001 to incorporate the European Designs Directive.

LEGAL DEPOSIT

Publishers are legally obliged to send one copy of every new printed publication distributed in the United Kingdom or Republic of Ireland to each of the legal deposit libraries within one month of publication. This is based on the Copyright Act of 1911 and the Irish Copyright Act 1963, replaced by similar provisions in the Copyright and Related Rights Act 2000. All printed publications come within the scope of legal deposit. A code of practice exists in the UK for the deposit of non-printed publications, including microform and electronic media. Work is currently in progress towards the Legal Deposit Libraries Bill, with the aim of extending legal deposit legislation to include automatically non-print publications.

The aim of legal deposit is to keep a complete national archive of published works as a current reference and information source. The legal deposit libraries are the British Library, the Bodleian Library in Oxford, Cambridge University Library, the National Library of Scotland, the National Library of Wales, and Trinity College Library in Dublin.

INTELLECTUAL PROPERTY ORGANISATIONS

COPYRIGHT LIBRARIES AGENCY, 100 Euston Street, London NW1 2HQ Tel: 020-7388 5061

CHARTERED INSTITUTE OF PATENT AGENTS, 95 Chancery Lane, London WC2A 1DT Tel: 020-7405 9450 Web: www.cipa.org.uk.

DESIGNS REGISTRY, The Patent Offiice, Cardiff Road Newport NP10 8QQ Tel: 0845-950-0505

EUROPEAN PATENT OFFICE, Headquarters, Erhardtstrasse 27, D-8000, Munich 2, Germany Tel: 49-892 3990 Web: www.european-patent-offiice.org

INTERNATIONAL FEDERATION OF REPRODUCTION RIGHTS ORGANISATIONS (IFRRO), rue du Prince Royal 87, B-1050 Brussels, Belgium Tel: 32-551 0899 Web: www.ifrro.org

LEGAL DEPOSIT OFFICE, The British Library, Boston Spa, Wetherby, W. Yorks LS23 7BY Tel: 01937-546267

NEWSPAPER LEGAL DEPOSIT OFFICE, The British Library, Newspaper Library, Colindale Avenue, London NW9 5LF Tel: 020-7412 7378

OFFICE FOR HARMONISATION IN THE INTERNAL MARKET (TRADE MARKS AND DESIGNS), Avenida de Europa 4, E-03080 Alicante, Spain Tel: 34-965 139100

THE PATENT OFFICE, Cardiff Road, Newport NP10 8QQ Tel: 0845-950 0505

SCIENCE REFERENCE LIBRARY, 96 Euston Road, London NW1 2DB Tel: 020-7412 7494

STATIONERS' HALL REGISTRY LTD, The Registrar, Stationers' Hall, Ave Maria Lane, London EC4M 7DD Tel: 020-7248 2934

TRADE MARKS REGISTRY, The Patent Offiice, Cardiff Road Newport NP10 8QQ Tel: 0845-950 0505

WORLD INTELLECTUAL PROPERTY ORGANISATION (WIPO), 34 chemin des Colombettes, CH-1211 Geneva 20, Switzerland. Tel: 41-22 338 9111 Web: www.wipo.int

COPYRIGHT LICENSING/COLLECTING AGENCIES

AUTHORS' LICENSING AND COLLECTING SOCIETY, Marlborough Court, 14–18 Holborn, London EC1N 2LE Tel: 020-7395 0600 Web: www.alcs.co.uk

COPYRIGHT LICENSING AGENCY LTD, 90 Tottenham Court Road, London W1T 0LP Tel: 020-7631 5555 Web: www.cla.co.uk

DESIGN AND ARTISTS COPYRIGHT SOCIETY, Parchment House, 13 Northburgh Street, London EC1V 0JP Tel: 020-7336 8811 Web: www.dacs.co.uk

EDUCATIONAL RECORDING AGENCY LTD, New Premier House, 150 Southampton Row, London WC1B 5AL Tel: 020-7837 3222 Web: www.era.org.uk

INTERNATIONAL FEDERATION OF THE PHONOGRAPHIC INDUSTRIES, 54 Regent Street, London W1B 5RE Tel: 020-7878 7900 Web: www.ifpi.org

MCPS-PRS ALLIANCE,Copyright House, 29–33 Berners Street, London W1T 3AB Tel: 020-7580 5544 Web: www.mcps-prs-alliance.co.uk

NEWSPAPER LICENSING AGENCY, 7–9 Church Road, Wellington Gate, Tunbridge Wells, Kent TN1 1NL Tel: 01892-525274 Web: www.nla.co.uk

PHONOGRAPHIC PERFORMANCE LTD, 1 Upper James Street, London W1F 9DE Tel: 020-7534 1000 Web: www.ppluk.com.

PUBLISHERS LICENSING SOCIETY, 37–41 Gower Street, London WC1E 6HH Tel: 020-7299 7730 Web: www.pls.org.uk

VIDEO PERFORMANCE LTD, 1 Upper James Street, London W1F 9DE Tel: 020-7534 1400

THE MEDIA

CROSS-MEDIA OWNERSHIP

The Communications Act, which received Royal Assent on 17 July 2003, has overhauled the rules surrounding cross-media ownership. Some of them have been simplified and relaxed to encourage dispersion of ownership and new market entry, although last minute amendments were made to the bill's controversial proposal which would have allowed national newspaper groups to buy Channel 5. There continue to be rules preventing the most influential media in any community being controlled by too narrow a range of interests. Within individual markets this means scrapping the restriction on the ownership of more than one national TV or radio service, as set out in the Broadcasting Act 1996.

Cross-media regulation has been reduced to three core rules:

– A rule limiting joint-ownership of national newspapers and ITV: no-one controlling more than 20 per cent of the national newspaper market may hold any licence for ITV or hold a stake in any of its services. A company may not own more than a 20 per cent share in such a service if more than 20 per cent of its stock is in turn owned by a national newspaper proprietor with more than 20 per cent of the market
– No-one owning a regional ITV licence may own more than 20 per cent of the local/regional newspaper market in the same region
– There will also be a scheme to uphold the plurality of ownership that exists in local media. This should ensure that at least 3 local commercial radio operators, and at least 3 local or regional commercial media voices (in TV, radio and newspapers), exist in most local communities.

As a consequence, some new forms of cross-holding have been introduced:

– Joint-ownership of national TV and national radio licences.
– Joint ownership of a regional Channel 3 licence and a local radio licence in the same area (as long as there are two or more other radio stations that reach more than 50 per cent of the adult population in the radio station's area).
– Ownership of more than 20 per cent of the national newspaper market and national and/or local radio licences.

From the end of 2003, the licensing and regulation of much of the UK's communications sector, including radio, television, telecommunications and spectrum management, is the responsibility of a single unified body, the Office of Communications (OFCOM). *See* below for regulators presiding until then.

OFFICE OF COMMUNICATIONS, Riverside House,
2A Southwark Bridge Road, London SE1 9HA
Tel: 020-7981 3000 Fax: 020-7981 3333
Email: wwwenq@ofcom.org.uk
Web: www.ofcom.org.uk

BROADCASTING

The British Broadcasting Corporation is responsible for public service broadcasting in the UK. Its constitution and finances are governed by royal charter and agreement. On 1 May 1996 a new royal charter came into force, establishing the framework for the BBC's activities until 2006.

The Independent Television Commission (ITC) and the Radio Authority, set up under the terms of the Broadcasting Act 1990, are due to be replaced by a single broadcasting regulator, OFCOM, at the end of 2003. Until OFCOM is fully operational the ITC is the regulator and licensing authority for all commercially-funded television services, including cable and satellite services, while the Radio Authority is the regulator and licensing authority for all independent radio services.

COMPLAINTS

The Broadcasting Standards Commission was set up in April 1997 under the Broadcasting Act 1996 and was formed from the merger of the Broadcasting Complaints Commission and the Broadcasting Standards Council. It is to be replaced by OFCOM at the end 2003. Until then the Commission considers and adjudicates upon complaints of unfair treatment or unwarranted infringement of privacy in all broadcast programmes and advertisements on television, radio, cable, satellite and digital services. It also monitors the portrayal of violence and sex, and matters of taste and decency.

BROADCASTING STANDARDS COMMISSION,
7 The Sanctuary, London SW1P 3JS Tel: 020-7808 1000
Chairman, Lord Dubs of Battersea; Deputy Chairman,
Lady Suzanne Warner; Director, Paul Bolt

TELEVISION

All channels are broadcast in colour on 625 lines UHF from a network of transmitting stations. In February 1997 the BBC's transmission network was sold to the Castle Tower Consortium (now Crown Castle International), which runs both its analogue and Digital Terrestrial Television. ITV transmission services are owned and operated by NTL. Transmissions are available to 99.4 per cent of the population.

The total number of television licences in force in the UK at the end of 2003 was around 23 million of which over 99 per cent were for colour televisions. Annual television licence fees from 1 April 2003 are black and white £38.50; colour £116.00.

No overall statistics are available for subscriptions in the UK to satellite television services. Over a quarter of all homes in the UK and Ireland received their television via satellite. A further four million households receive Sky channels via cable.

DIGITAL TELEVISION

Digital broadcasting has dramatically increased the number and reception quality of television channels. It uses digital modulation to improve reception and digital compression to make more effective use of the frequency channels available through PAL, the analogue system currently used. A set-top digital decoder or an integrated digital television set is required to convert the digital signals into analogue sound and picture waves in order to watch the digital channels. A basic package is available for free and services are also offered by cable and satellite companies.

The Broadcasting Act 1996 provided for the licensing of 20 or more digital terrestrial television channels (on six frequency channels or 'multiplexes'). In June 1997 the licences to run the remaining digital multiplexes were awarded by the ITC to British Digital Broadcasting (subsequently called Ondigital and ITV Digital), a consortium led by Carlton Communications and Granada. The first digital services went on air in autumn 1998. Analogue broadcasting will eventually be discontinued, with the frequencies sold to mobile telephone companies.

In June 2002, following the collapse of the ITV Digital terrestrial service, a consortium made up of the BBC, BSkyB and Crown Castle, the transmitter company, was awarded the DTT (Digital Terrestrial Television) licence by the Independent Television Commission. Freeview, the new digital network, was launched on 30 October 2002. By 31 March 2003 digital penetration had reached over 43.9 per cent of UK households.

ESTIMATED AUDIENCE SHARE *for 12 months to 30 June 2003*

	Percentage[*]
ITV companies	24.0
BBC 1	26.3
BBC 2	11.3
Channel 4	9.6
Five	6.4
S4C Wales	0.3
Cable, satellite and digital channels	18.6

Source: Independent Television Commission
[*]Rounded to one decimal point and only channels achieving a share of more than 0.1 per cent are included

BBC TELEVISION
Television Centre, Wood Lane, London W12 7RJ
Tel: 020-8743 8000 Web: www.bbc.co.uk/info

The BBC's experiments in television broadcasting started in 1929 and in 1936 the BBC began the world's first public service of high-definition television from Alexandra Palace. The BBC broadcasts two UK-wide terrestrial television services, BBC One and BBC Two; outside England these services are designated BBC Scotland on One, BBC Scotland on Two, BBC One Northern Ireland, BBC Two Northern Ireland, BBC Wales on One and BBC Wales on Two. The BBC's digital services include BBC One, BBC Two, BBC Three, BBC Four, BBC Knowledge, BBC News 24 and BBC Parliament. The services are funded by the licence fee.

BBC WORLDWIDE LTD
Woodlands, 80 Wood Lane, London W12 0TT
Tel 020-8433 2000 Fax: 020-8749 0538
Web: www.bbcworldwide.com

BBC Worldwide Limited is the commercial arm, and a wholly owned subsidiary, of the British Broadcasting Corporation. The company was formed in 1994 and exists in order to maximise the value of the BBC's programme and publishing assets for the benefit of the licence payer, re-investing profit in public service programming. BBC Worldwide's businesses include international programming distribution, TV channels, magazines, books, videos, spoken word, music, DVDs, licensed product, CD-ROMs, English language teaching, videos for education and training, interactive telephony, co-production, library footage sales, exhibitions, live events, film and media monitoring.

INDEPENDENT TELEVISION
The ITV network comprises 16 independent regional television licensees, whose licences are (until OFCOM is fully operational) awarded by the Independent Television Commission (ITC) for a minimum of ten years. These companies broadcast across 15 regions of the UK (there are 2 licences for London). The ITV Network Centre commissions and schedules programmes and, as with the BBC, 25 per cent of programmes must come from independent producers. There are over 1,500 independent production companies in the UK which generate over £1bn of programming.

Channel 4 and S4C (the fourth channel in Wales) were set up to provide programmes with a distinctive character and which appeal to interests not catered for by ITV and are also funded through advertising. Channel 5 began broadcasting in 1997 and now reaches about 80 per cent of the population.

ITV NETWORK CENTRE/ITV ASSOCIATION
200 Gray's Inn Road, London WC1X 8HF
Tel: 020-7843 8000 Web: www.itv.com

The ITV Network Centre is wholly owned by the ITV companies and undertakes commissioning and scheduling of programmes shown across the ITV network and, as with the BBC, 25 per cent of programmes must come from independent producers. In addition to the terrestrial channel ITV1, in December 1998 ITV launched its digital ITV2, aimed at a younger audience.
Chairman, ITV Council, Donald Emslie

INDEPENDENT TELEVISION NETWORK COMPANIES
ANGLIA TELEVISION LTD (owned by Granada Media Group) *(eastern England)*, Anglia House, Norwich NR1 3JG
Tel: 01603-615151
  Web: www.angliatv.co.uk
BORDER TELEVISION PLC *(the Borders)*, The Television Centre, Carlisle CA1 3NT Tel: 01228-525101
  Web: www.border-tv.com
CARLTON LONDON, 101 St Martin's Lane, London WC2N 4RF Tel: 020-7240 4000
  Web: www.carlton.com
CARLTON CENTRAL INDEPENDENT TELEVISION LTD *(the Midlands)*, Central Court, Gas Street, Birmingham B1 2JT Tel: 0121-643 9898 Web: www.carlton.com
CARLTON WESTCOUNTRY TELEVISION LTD *(south-west England)*, Language Science Park, Plymouth PL7 5BG
Tel: 01752-333333
  Web: www.carlton.com
CHANNEL TELEVISION LTD *(Channel Islands)*, The Television Centre, St Helier, Jersey JE1 3ZD
Tel: 01534-816816 Web: www.channeltv.co.uk

GMTV LTD *(breakfast television)*, The London Television Centre, Upper Ground, London SE1 9TT Tel: 020-7827 7000 Web: www.gmtv.co.uk

GRAMPIAN TELEVISION PLC (owned by Scottish Media) *(northern Scotland)*, Queen's Cross, Aberdeen AB15 2XJ Tel: 01224-846846 Web: www.grampiantv.co.uk

GRANADA TELEVISION LTD (owned by Granada Media) *(north-west England)*, Quay Street, Manchester M60 9EA Tel: 0161-832 7211 Web: www.granadatv.co.uk

HTV GROUP PLC *(Wales and western England)*, HTV Wales, The Television Centre, Culverhouse Cross, Cardiff CF5 6XJ Tel: 029-2059 0590 Web: www.htvwales.com HTV West, The Television Centre, Bath Road, Bristol BS4 3HG Tel: 0117-972 2722 Web: www.htvwest.com

LONDON WEEKEND TELEVISION LTD (owned by Granada Media) *(London (weekends))*, The London Television Centre, Upper Ground, London SE1 9LT Tel: 020-7620 1620 Web: www.lwt.co.uk

MERIDIAN BROADCASTING LTD *(south and south-east England)*, The Television Centre, Southampton SO14 0PZ Tel: 023-8022 2555 Web: www.meridian.tv.co.uk

SCOTTISH TELEVISION PLC (owned by Scottish Media) *(central Scotland)*, 200 Renfield Street, Glasgow G2 3PR Tel: 0141-300 3000 Web: www.scottishtv.co.uk

TYNE TEES TELEVISION LTD (owned by Granada Media) *(north-east England)*, The Television Centre, City Road, Newcastle-upon-Tyne NE1 2AL Tel: 0191-261 0181

ULSTER TELEVISION PLC *(Northern Ireland)*, Havelock House, Ormeau Road, Belfast BT7 1EB Tel: 028-9032 8122 Web: www.u.tv

YORKSHIRE TELEVISION LTD (owned by Granada Media) *(Yorkshire)*, The Television Centre, Kirkstall Road, Leeds LS3 1JS Tel: 0113-243 8283 Web: www.yorkshire-television.tv

OTHER INDEPENDENT TELEVISION COMPANIES

CHANNEL FOUR TELEVISION CORPORATION, 124 Horseferry Road, London SW1P 2TX Tel: 020-7396 4444 Web: www.channel4.com. Provides a service to the UK except Wales. Its remit is to cater for interests under-represented by the ITV network companies. Channel 4 sells its own advertising.

FIVE BROADCASTING LTD, 22 Long Acre, London WC2E 9LY Tel: 020-7550 5555 Web: www.five.tv

INDEPENDENT TELEVISION NEWS LTD, 200 Gray's Inn Road, London WC1X 8XZ Tel: 020-7833 3000 Web: www.itn.co.uk

TELETEXT LTD, Building 10, Chiswick Park, 566 Chiswick High Road London W4 5TS Tel: 0870-731 3000 Web: www.teletext.com. Provides teletext services for the ITV companies and Channel 4

WELSH FOURTH CHANNEL AUTHORITY (Sianel Pedwar Cymru), Parc Ty Glas, Llanishen, Cardiff CF4 5DU Tel: 029-2074 7444. S4C schedules Welsh language and most Channel 4 programmes.

DIRECT BROADCASTING BY SATELLITE TELEVISION

BRITISH SKY BROADCASTING LTD, 6 Centaurs Business Park, Grant Way, Isleworth, Middx TW7 5QD Tel: 020-7705 3000

British Sky Broadcasting is the UK's broadband entertainment company, delivering sports, movies, entertainment, news and interactive services to 16 million viewers in 6.7 million households throughout the UK

and Eire. BSkyB's own channels such as Sky News, Sky One and Sky Sports are available in a further 5.3 million homes receiving cable services in the UK and Ireland.

Sky Digital, launched on 1 October 1998, offers over 300 channels, pay-per-view services and interactive entertainment, including email, on-screen shopping and voting. In 2001 BSkyB introduced the next generation integrated digital satellite set-top box/personal video recorder, Sky+. BSkyB is listed on the London and New York Stock Exchanges. For more information visit www.sky.com

RADIO

UK domestic radio services are broadcast across three wavebands: FM (or VHF), medium wave and long wave (used by BBC Radio 4). In the UK the FM waveband extends in frequency from 87.5 MHz to 108 MHz and the medium wave band extends from 531 kHz to 1602 kHz. Some radios are still calibrated in wavelengths rather than frequency. To convert frequency to wavelength, divide 300,000 by the frequency in kHz.

A number of radio stations are now being broadcast in both analogue and digital as well as a growing number in digital alone.

DIGITAL RADIO

Digital radio allows more services to be broadcast to a higher technical quality and provides the data facility for text and pictures. It improves the robustness of high fidelity radio services, especially compared with current FM and AM radio transmissions. It was developed in a collaborative research project under the pan-European EUREKA initiative and has been adopted as a world standard for new digital radio systems. The frequencies allocated for terrestrial digital radio in the UK are 217.5 to 230 MHz. Plans are underway for developing a framework for frequencies in the 1.5 GHz (or L-Band) range.

The Broadcasting Act 1996 provided for the licensing of digital radio services (on seven frequency channels or 'multiplexes'). The BBC has been allocated a multiplex capable of broadcasting six to eight national stereo services; BBC digital broadcasts began in the London area in September 1995. A national digital multiplex has also been made available to the three independent national radio stations, and local and regional services (BBC and commercial) will use the remaining five multiplexes. The Radio Authority, which is to be replaced by OFCOM at the end of 2003, is responsible for awarding licences for capacity on the non-BBC multiplexes. The first national independent radio digital licence was awarded to Digital One, which began broadcasting in November 1999. The first local multiplex licence was awarded in May 1999 (to CE Digital, for Birmingham) and commenced broadcasting in May 2000.

It is necessary to possess a digital radio set in order to receive digital radio broadcasts. Several types of sets are available including portable radios, hi-fi stacks, car radios and PC cards. The latter bring digital radio to the desktop and associated data to the computer screen. At the time of writing the cost of portables started at £99, car-radios at £200 (plus installation), hi-fi units at about £200, PC cards at £50.

ESTIMATED AUDIENCE SHARE *as at end June 2003*

	Percentage
BBC Radio 1	7.6
BBC Radio 2	16.3
BBC Radio 3	1.1
BBC Radio 4	11.4
BBC Radio 5 Live	4.4
BBC Local/Regional	11.3
BBC World Service	0.7
All BBC	53.0
All Commercial	44.9
Classic FM	4.5
TalkSport	1.6
Total Virgin Radio	1.6
Local commercial	36.5
Other	1.9

Source: RAJAR/RSL

BBC RADIO
Broadcasting House, Portland Place, London W1A 1AA
Tel: 020-7580 4468

BBC Radio broadcasts network services to the UK, Isle of Man and the Channel Islands. There is also a tier of national services in Wales, Scotland and Northern Ireland and 40 local radio stations in England and the Channel Islands. In Wales and Scotland there are also dedicated language services in Welsh and Gaelic respectively. The frequency allocated for digital BBC broadcasts is 225.648 MHZ.

BBC NETWORK RADIO SERVICES
RADIO 1 (Contemporary pop music and entertainment news) – 24 hours a day. *Frequencies:* 97.6–99.8 FM, coverage 99%
RADIO 2 (Popular music, entertainment, comedy and the arts) – 24 hours a day. *Frequencies:* 88–90.2 FM, coverage 99%
RADIO 3 (Classical music, classic drama, documentaries and features) – 24 hours a day. *Frequencies:* 90.2–92.4 FM, coverage 99%
RADIO 4 (News, documentaries, drama, entertainment, and cricket on long wave in season) – 5.55 am–1.00 am daily, with BBC World Service overnight. *Frequencies:* 92.4–94.6 FM and 198 LW, coverage 99%
RADIO 5 LIVE (News and sport) – 24 hours a day. *Frequencies:* 693 and 909 MW
RADIO 6 (Digital only) (Contemporary and classic pop and rock music) – 24 hours a day.
RADIO 7 (Digital only) (Comedy and drama) – 7 am to 1 am.
BRITISH ASIAN RADIO (Digital only) (news, music and sport for British Asians)
1XTRA (Digital only) (new black music) – 24 hours a day.

BBC NATIONAL RADIO SERVICES
RADIO CYMRU (Welsh-language) *Frequencies:* 92.4–94.6 FM, 95.7 FM *(Llanfyllin)*, 96.1 FM *(Llandinam)*, 96.8 FM and 103.5–105 FM, coverage 97%
RADIO FOYLE, *Frequencies:* 792 AM; 93.1 MW
RADIO NAN GAIDHEAL (Gaelic service) *Frequencies:* 103.5–105 FM, 990 MW in Aberdeen, coverage 90%.
RADIO SCOTLAND *Frequencies:* 810 MW plus two local fillers; 92.4–94.7 FM, coverage 99%. Local programmes on FM as above: Highlands; North-East; Borders; South-West (also 585 MW); Orkney; Shetland

RADIO ULSTER *Frequencies:* 1341 MW (873 MW Enniskillen), plus two local fillers; 92.4–95.4 FM, coverage 96%. Local programmes on RADIO FOYLE
RADIO WALES *Frequencies:* 882 MW plus two local fillers; 95.1 FM, 95.9 FM *(Gwent)*, 103.9 FM *(Cardiff)*, 95.4 FM *(Wrexham)*, coverage 97%

BBC LOCAL RADIO STATIONS
There are 40 local stations serving England and the Channel Islands:

BERKSHIRE, PO Box 1044, Reading RG94 8FH.
  Tel: 0645 311444. *Frequencies:* 94.6, 95.4, 104.1, 104.4 FM
BRISTOL, PO Box 194, Bristol BS99 7QT.
  Tel: 0117-974 1111. *Frequencies:* 94.9, 95.5, 104.6, 1548 MW
CAMBRIDGESHIRE, PO Box 96, Hills Road, Cambridge CB2 1LD. Tel: 01223-259696. *Frequencies:* 95.7/96.0 FM, 1026/1449 MW
CLEVELAND, PO Box 95FM, Newport Road, Middlesbrough TS1 5DG. Tel: 01642-225211. *Frequencies:* 95.0/95.8 FM
CORNWALL, Phoenix Wharf, Truro, Cornwall TR1 1UA.
  Tel: 01872-275421. *Frequencies:* 95.2/96.0/103.9 FM, 630/657 MW
CUMBRIA, Annetwell Street, Carlisle CA3 8BB.
  Tel: 01228-592444. *Frequencies:* 95.2/95.6/96.1/104.1 FM, 756/837/1458 MW
DERBY, PO Box 269, Derby DE1 3HL.
  Tel: 01332-361111. *Frequencies:* 94.2/95.3/104.5 FM, 1116 MW
DEVON, PO Box 5, Plymouth PL1 1XT.
  Tel: 01752-260323. *Frequencies:* 3.4/96.0/95.8/94.8 FM, 801, 855, 990, 1458 MW
ESSEX, 198 New London Road, Chelmsford CM2 9XB.
  Tel: 01245-616000. *Frequencies:* 95.3/103.3 FM, 729/765/1530 MW
GLOUCESTERSHIRE, London Road, Gloucester GL1 1SW.
  Tel: 01452-308585 *Frequencies:* 95/95.8/104.7 FM
GMR (GREATER MANCHESTER RADIO), PO Box 951, Oxford Road, Manchester M60 1SD. Tel: 0161-200 2000.
  Frequencies: 95.1/104.6 FM
GUERNSEY, Commerce House, Les Banques, St Peter Port, Guernsey GY1 2HS. Tel: 01481-728977. *Frequencies:* 1116 AM, 93.2 FM
HEREFORD AND WORCESTER, Hylton Road, Worcester WR2 5WW. Tel: 01905-748485.
  Frequencies: 94.7/104.0/104.6 FM, 818/738 MW
HUMBERSIDE, 9 Chapel Street, Hull HU1 3NU.
  Tel: 01482-323232. *Frequencies:* 95.9 FM, 1485 MW
JERSEY, 18 Parade Road, St Helier, Jersey JE2 3PL.
  Tel: 01534-870000. *Frequencies:* 1026 AM, 88.8 FM
KENT, Sun Pier, Chatham, Kent ME4 4EZ.
  Tel: 01634-830505. *Frequencies:* 96.7/97.6/104.2 FM, 774/1602 MW
LANCASHIRE, 26 Darwen Street, Blackburn BB2 2EA.
  Tel: 01254-262411. *Frequencies:* 95.5/103.9/104.5 FM, 855/1557 MW
LEEDS, Broadcasting House, Woodhouse Lane, Leeds LS2 9PN.
  Tel: 0113-244 2131. *Frequencies:* 774 AM, 92.4/95.3/103.9 FM, 774 MW
LEICESTER/ASIAN NETWORK, Epic House, Charles Street, Leicester LE1 3SH. Tel: 0116-251 6688. *Frequency:* 104.9 FM
LINCOLNSHIRE, PO Box 219, Newport, Lincoln LN1 3XY.
  Tel: 01522-511411. *Frequencies:* 94.9 FM, 1368 MW
LONDON, BBC London Live, 35c Marylebone High Street, London W1A 4LG. Tel: 020-7224 2424. *Frequency:* 94.9 FM
MERSEYSIDE, 55 Paradise Street, Liverpool L1 3BP.
  Tel: 0151-708 5500. Frequency: 95.8 FM, 1485 MW

NEWCASTLE, Broadcasting Centre, Barrack Road, Newcastle upon Tyne NE99 1RN. Tel: 0191-232 4141.
Frequencies: 95.4/96.0/103.7/104.4 FM, 206 MW
NORFOLK, Norfolk Tower, Surrey Street, Norwich NR1 3PA. Tel: 01603-617411.
Frequencies: 95.1/104.4 FM, 855/873 MW
NORTHAMPTON, Broadcasting House, Abington Street, Northampton NN1 2BH. Tel: 01604-239100. *Frequencies:* 103.6/104.2 FM, 1107 MW
NOTTINGHAM, York House, Mansfield Road, Nottingham NG1 3JB. Tel: 0115-955 0500.
Frequencies: 95.5/103.8 FM, 1584 MW
OXFORD, BBC Radio Oxford, 269 Banbury Road, Oxford OX2 7DW. Tel: 01865-311444. *Frequency:* 95.2 FM
SHEFFIELD, Ashdell Grove, 60 Westbourne Road, Sheffield S10 2QU. Tel: 0114-268 6185.
Frequencies: 88.6/94.7/104.1 FM
SHROPSHIRE, 2–4 Boscobel Drive, Shrewsbury SY1 3TT. Tel: 01743-248484. *Frequencies:* 95.0/96.0 FM, 1584 MW
SOLENT, Broadcasting House, Havelock Road, Southampton SO14 7PW. Tel: 023-8063 1311. *Frequencies:* 96.1/ FM, 999 MW
SOMERSET SOUND, Broadcasting House, Park Street, Taunton, Somerset TA1 4DA. Tel: 01823-348920. *Frequency:* 1566 AM
SOUTHERN COUNTIES, Broadcasting Centre, Guildford GU2 5AP. Tel: 01483-306306.
Frequencies: 95–95.3/104–104.8 FM
STOKE, Cheapside, Hanley, Stoke-on-Trent ST1 1JJ. Tel: 01782-208080. *Frequencies:* 94.6/104.1 FM, 1503 MW
SUFFOLK, Broadcasting House, St Matthew's Street, Ipswich IP1 3EP. Tel: 01473-250000.
Frequencies: 95.5/103.9/104.6 FM
SWINDON, PO Box 1234, Trowbridge, Swindon & Salisbury. Tel: 01793-513 626. *Frequencies:* 103.6 FM
THREE COUNTIES RADIO, PO Box 3CR, Luton, Beds LU1 5XL. Tel: 01582-637400. *Frequencies:* 95.5/103.8/104.5 FM, 630/1161 MW
WILTSHIRE SOUND, Broadcasting House, Prospect Place, Swindon SN1 3RW. Tel: 01793-513626. *Frequencies:* 103.5/103.6/104.3/104.9 FM, 1332/1368 MW
WM (COVENTRY AND WARWICKSHIRE), Holt Court, 1 Greyfriars Road, Coventry CV1 2WR. Tel: 024-7623 1231.
Frequencies: 94.8/103.7/104.0 FM
WM (WEST MIDLANDS), Pebble Mill Road, Birmingham B5 7SD. Tel: 0121-432 8484. *Frequency:* 95.6 FM.
YORK, 20 Bootham Row, York YO3 7BR. Tel: 01904-641351. *Frequencies:* 95.5/103.7/104.3 FM, 666/1260 MW

BBC WORLD SERVICE
Bush House, Strand, London WC2B 4PH
Tel: 020-7240 3456

The BBC World Service broadcasts over 1,280 hours of programmes a week in 43 languages including English. It has a weekly audience of 150 million globally, of whom 42 million listen to English language services. Many services are also available by satellite and on the Internet. *UK frequencies:* 648 MW in Southern England and on BBC Radio 4 at night.

The World Service is organised into five world regions, each responsible for programmes in English as well as regional languages.

AFRICA AND THE MIDDLE EAST, Arabic, French, Hausa, Kinyarwanda/Kirundi, Portuguese, Somali and Swahili; English programmes including *Network Africa* and *Focus on Africa*

ASIA AND THE PACIFIC, Bengali, Burmese, Cantonese, Hindi, Indonesian, Mandarin, Nepali, Sinhala, Tamil, Thai, Urdu and Vietnamese; English programmes including *East Asia Today*
EUROPE, Albanian, Bulgarian, Croatian, Czech, Greek, Hungarian, Macedonian, Polish, Romanian, Serbian, Slovak and Slovene; English programmes including *The World Today*
FORMER SOVIET UNION AND SOUTH-WEST ASIA, Azeri, Kazakh, Kyrgyz, Pashto, Persian, Russian, Turkish, Ukrainian and Uzbek
THE AMERICAS, Portuguese for Brazil, Spanish; English programmes including *The World* (a global news magazine for American listeners), *Caribbean Report* and *Calling the Falklands*
BBC ENGLISH teaches English world-wide through radio, television and a wide range of published courses
BBC MARKET INTELLIGENCE carries out audience research and sells printed publications and data
BBC MONITORING supplies news and information from the output of overseas radio and television stations and news agency sources
BBC WORLD SERVICE TRAINING runs journalism, management and skills training courses for overseas broadcasters
BBC WORLD SERVICE TRUST is a registered charity established in 1999 by BBC World Service. It promotes development through the innovative use of the media in the developing world. The trust presently works in 23 countries worldwide, tackling health, education and good governance.

INDEPENDENT RADIO
The Radio Authority began advertising new licences for the development of independent radio in January 1991. Since then it has awarded three national licences and 261 new local radio licences (including sixteen regional licences). The Authority has also licensed one "additional service" licence (to use the spare capacity in an existing channel which is not used by the programme service), and around 3,922 short-term restricted service licences (for temporary low-powered radio services). It licenses satellite (78) and cable services, and long-term restricted service licences (108) for stations serving non-commercial establishments such as hospitals and universities. The first (and only) national commercial digital multiplex licence was awarded in October 1998. Since then the Authority has awarded 39 local digital multiplex licences and continues to advertise new local multiplex licences. The Radio Authority is one of the five broadcasting regulators, mentioned above, to be replaced by OFCOM at the end of 2003.

The Commercial Radio Companies Association is the trade body for commercial radio companies in the United Kingdom. It is a voluntary, non profit making body, funded by the subscriptions of its member radio companies, who share the cost of CRCA in proportion to their shares of the industry's broadcasting revenue, and was formed by the first radio companies when Independent Radio began in 1973.

THE RADIO AUTHORITY, Holbrook House, 14 Great Queen Street, London WC2B 5DG. Tel: 020-7430 2724.
Fax: 020 7405 7062 Web: www.radioauthority.org.uk
COMMERCIAL RADIO COMPANIES ASSOCIATION, 77 Shaftesbury Avenue, London W1V 7AD.
Tel: 020-7306 2603 Email: info@crca.co.uk.
Web: www.crca.co.uk. *Chief Executive,* P. Brown

INDEPENDENT NATIONAL RADIO STATIONS

CLASSIC FM, 7 Swallow Place, London W1B 2AG.
Tel: 020-7343 9000. 24 hours a day. *Frequencies:*
99.9/101.9 FM

TALK SPORT, 18 Hatfields, London SE1 8DJ.
Tel: 020-7959 7800. 24 hours a day.
Frequencies: 1053/1089 AM

VIRGIN 1250, 1 Golden Square, London W1F 9DJ.
Tel: 020-7434 1215. 24 hours a day.
Frequencies: 1215/1197/1233/1242/1260 AM

INDEPENDENT REGIONAL RADIO STATIONS

100.7 HEART FM *(west Midlands)*, 1 The Square, 111 Broad
Street, Birmingham B15 1AS. Tel: 0121-626 1007.
Frequency: 100.7 FM

CENTURY 105 *(north-west)*, Century House, Waterfront
Quay, Salford Quays, Manchester M5 2XW.
Tel: 0161-400 0105. *Frequency:* 105.4 FM

CENTURY 106 *(east Midlands)*, City Link, Nottingham NG2
4NG. Tel: 0115-910 6100. *Frequency:* 106.0 FM

CENTURY RADIO *(north-east)*, Century House, PO Box 100,
Gateshead NE8 2YY. Tel: 0191-477 6666.
Frequencies: 100.7/101.8/96.2/96.4 FM

GALAXY 105 *(Yorkshire)*, Joseph's Well, Westgate, Leeds LS3
1AB. Tel: 0113-213 0105. *Frequencies:* 105.1 FM (Leeds);
105.6 FM (Bradford and Sheffield); 105.8 FM (Hull)

GALAXY 105-106 *(north-east)*, Kingfisher Way, Silverlink
Business Park, Tyne and Wear NE28 9NX.
Tel: 0191-206 8000. *Frequencies:* 105.3/105.6/106.4 FM

JAZZ FM 100.4 *(north-west)*, 8 Exchange Quay, Manchester
M5 3EJ. Tel: 0161-877 1004. *Frequency:* 100.4 FM

REAL RADIO (YORKSHIRE), Sterling Court, Capitol Park,
Leeds WF3 1EL. Tel 0113 2381114.
Frequencies: 106-108 FM

VIBE FM *(east)*, Alpha Business Park, 6–12 White House Road,
Ipswich, Suffolk IP3 5LT Tel: 01473-467500. *Frequencies:*
107.7 FM (Peterborough); 105.6 FM (Cambridge); 106.1 FM
(Norwich); 106.4 FM (Ipswich)

VIBE 101, Radio House, 1 Passage Street, Bristol BS2 0JF.
Tel 0117-901 0101 *Frequencies:* 97.2/101 FM

WAVE 105 FM *(Solent)*, 5 Manor Court, Barnes Wallis Road,
Segensworth East, Fareham, Hants PO15 5TH.
Tel: 01489-481050. *Frequencies:* 105.2 FM (Solent); 105.8
FM (Poole)

INDEPENDENT LOCAL RADIO STATIONS
England

2-TEN FM, PO Box 2020, Reading RG31 7FG.
Tel: 0118-945 4400. *Frequencies:* 97.0/102.9/103.4 FM

2BR, Imex Lomeshaye Business Village, Nelson, Lancs BB9 7DR.
Tel: 01282-690000. *Frequency:* 99.8 FM

2CR FM, 5 Southcote Road, Bournemouth BH1 3LR.
Tel: 01202-259259. *Frequency:* 102.3 FM

96 TRENT FM, 29–31 Castle Gate, Nottingham NG1 7AP.
Tel: 0115-952 7000. *Frequencies:* 96.2/96.5 FM

96.3 RADIO AIRE, 51 Burley Road, Leeds LS3 1LR.
Tel: 0113-283 5500. *Frequency:* 96.3 FM

96.4 FM BRMB, Nine Brindley Place, 4 Oozells Square,
Birmingham B1 2DJ. Tel: 0121-245 5000. *Frequency:* 96.4 FM

96.4 THE EAGLE, Dolphin House, North Street, Guildford,
Surrey GU1 4AA. Tel: 01483-300964. *Frequency:* 96.4 FM

96.9 VIKING FM, Commercial Road, Hull HU1 2SG.
Tel: 01482-325141. *Frequency:* 96.9 FM

97.2 STRAY FM, the Hamlet, Hornbeam Park Avenue,
Harrogate HG2 8RE. Tel: 01423-522972. *Frequency:* 97.2 FM

97.4 ROCK FM, PO Box 974, Preston PR1 1XS.
Tel: 01772-556301. *Frequency:* 97.4 FM

97.4 VALE FM, Longmead, Shaftesbury, Dorset SP7 8PL.
Tel: 01747-855711. *Frequency:* 97.4 FM

100.7 HEART FM, 1 The Square, 11 Broad Street, Birmingham
B15 1AS. Tel: 0121-695 0000. *Frequency:* 100.7 FM

102.4 WISH FM, Orrell Lodge, Orrell Road, Orrell, Wigan WN5
8HJ. Tel: 01942-761024. *Frequency:* 102.4 FM

102.7 HEREWARD FM, PO Box 225, Queensgate Centre,
Peterborough PE1 1XJ. Tel: 01733-460460.
Frequency: 102.7 FM

103.2 POWER FM, Radio House, Whittle Avenue,
Segensworth West, Fareham, Hants PO15 5SH.
Tel: 01489-589911. *Frequency:* 103.2 FM

103.4 THE BEACH, PO Box 103.4, Lowestoft, Suffolk NR32
2TL. Tel: 0845-345 1035. *Frequency:* 103.4 FM

106.9 SILK FM, Radio House, Bridge Street, Macclesfield,
Cheshire SK11 6DJ. Tel: 01625-268000.
Frequency: 106.9 FM

107 OAK FM, 7 Waldron Court, Prince William Road,
Loughborough, Leics LE11 5GD. Tel: 01509-211711.
Frequency: 107.0 FM

107.2 WIRE FM, Warrington Business Park, Long Lane,
Warrington WA2 8TX. Tel: 01925-445545.
Frequency: 107.2 FM

107.4 TELFORD FM, PO Box 1074, Telford TF3 3WG.
Tel: 01952-280011. *Frequency:* 107.4 FM

107.5 3TR FM, Riverside Studios, Boreham Mill, Bishopstrow,
Warminster, Wiltshire BA12 9HQ. Tel: 01985-211111.
Frequency: 107.5

107.5 WIN FM, PO Box 1072, The Books, Winchester SO23
8FT. Tel: 01962-841071. *Frequency:* 107.2 FM

107.6 KESTREL FM, 2nd Floor, Paddington House, The Walks
Shopping Centre, Basingstoke, Hants RG21 7LJ.
Tel: 01256-694000. *Frequency:* 107.6 FM

107.7 THE WOLF, 10th Floor, Mander House,
Wolverhampton WV1 3NB. Tel: 01902-571070.
Frequency: 107.7 FM

107.8 ARROW FM, Priory Meadow Centre, Hastings,
E. Sussex TN34 1PJ. Tel: 01424-461177.
Frequency: 107.8 FM

ALPHA 103.2, Radio House, 11 Woodland Road, Darlington
DL3 7BJ. Tel: 01325-255552. *Frequency:* 103.2 FM

ASIAN SOUND RADIO, Globe House, Southall Street,
Manchester M3 1LG. Tel: 0161-288 1000.
Frequencies: 1377/963 AM

B97 CHILTERN FM, 55 Goldington Road, Bedford MK40 3LT.
Tel: 01234-272400. *Frequency:* 96.9 FM

BATH FM, Station House, Ashley Avenue, Lower Weston, Bath
BA1 3DS. Tel: 01225-471571. *Frequency:* 107.9 FM

THE BAY, PO Box 969, St George's Quay, Lancaster LA1 3LD.
Tel: 01524-848747. *Frequencies:* 96.9/102.3/103.2 FM

BCR FM, Royal Clarence House, York Buildings, High Street,
Bridgewater, Somerset TA6 4WE. Tel: 01278-727701.
Frequencies: 107.4 FM

BEACON FM, 267 Tettenhall Road, Wolverhampton
WV6 0DE. Tel: 01902-461300. *Frequencies:* 97.2 FM
(Wolverhampton and Black Country); 103.1 FM (Shrewsbury
and Telford)

THE BEAR FM 102, The Guard House Studios, Banbury Road,
Stratford upon Avon, Warwickshire CV37 7HX.
Tel: 01789-262636. *Frequency:* 102 FM

BRIGHT 106.4, The Market Place Shopping Centre, Burgess
Hill, West Sussex RH15 9NP. Tel: 01444-239822.
Frequency: 106.4 FM

BROADLAND 102, St George's Plain, 47–49 Colegate,
Norwich NR3 1DB. Tel: 01603-630621. *Frequency:* 102.4 FM

CAPITAL GOLD (1152), Nine Brindleyplace, 4 Oozells Square,
Birmingham B1 2DJ. Tel: 0121-245 5000.
Frequency: 1152 AM

CAPITAL GOLD (1170 AND 1557), Radio House, Whittle
Avenue, Segensworth West, Fareham, Hants PO15 5SH.
Tel: 01489-589911. *Frequencies:* 1170/1557 AM

CAPITAL GOLD (1242 AND 603), Radio House, John Wilson Business Park, Whitstable, Kent CT5 3QX. Tel: 01227-772004. *Frequencies:* 603 AM (East Kent); 1242 AM (Maidstone and Medway)

CAPITAL GOLD (1323 AND 945), Radio House, PO Box 2000, Brighton BN41 2SS. Tel: 01273-430111. *Frequencies:* 945/1323 AM

CAPITAL GOLD (1548), 30 Leicester Square, London WC2H 7LA. Tel: 020-7766 6000. *Frequency:* 1548 AM

CENTRE FM, 5–6 Aldergate, Tamworth, Staffs B79 7DJ. Tel: 01827-318000. *Frequencies:* 101.6/102.4 FM

CENTURY (106), City Link, Nottingham NG2 4NG. Tel: 0115-910 6100. *Frequency:* 106 FM

CENTURY RADIO, Century House, PO Box 100, Gateshead NE8 2YY. Tel: 0191-477 6666. *Frequencies:* 96.2/96.4/100.7/101.8 FM

CFM, PO Box 964, Carlisle, Cumbria CA1 3NG. Tel: 01228-818964. *Frequencies:* 96.4 FM (Penrith); 102.5 FM (Carlisle); 102.2 FM (Workington); 103.4 FM (Whitehaven)

CHANNEL 103 FM, 6 Tunnell Street, St Helier, Jersey JE2 4LU. Tel: 01534-888103. *Frequency:* 103.7 FM

CHILTERN FM (96.9), 55 Goldington Road, Bedford, Beds MK40 3LT. Tel: 01234-272400. *Frequency:* 96.9 FM

CHILTERN FM (97.6), Chiltern Road, Dunstable, Beds LU6 1HQ. Tel: 01582-676200. *Frequency:* 97.6 FM

CHOICE FM, 291–299 Borough High Street, London SE1 1JG. Tel: 020-7378 3969. *Frequency:* 96.9 FM

CHOICE (107.1), 291–299 Borough High Street, London SE1 1JG. Tel: 020-8348 1033. *Frequency:* 107.1 FM

CLASSIC GOLD 666/954, Hawthorn House, Exeter Business Park, Exeter EX1 3QS. Tel: 01392-444444. *Frequencies:* 666/954 AM

CLASSIC GOLD 774, Bridge Studios, Eastgate Centre, Gloucester GL1 1SS. Tel: 01452-313200. *Frequency:* 774 AM

CLASSIC GOLD 792/828, Chiltern Road, Dunstable, Beds LU6 1HQ. Tel: 01582-676200. *Frequencies:* 792 AM (Bedford); 828 AM (Luton)

CLASSIC GOLD 828, 5 Southcote Road, Bournemouth, Dorset BH1 3LR. Tel: 01202-259259. *Frequency:* 828 AM

CLASSIC GOLD 936/1161 AM, PO Box 2000, Swindon SN4 7EX. Tel: 01793-842600. *Frequencies:* 936 AM (West Wilts); 1161 AM (Swindon)

CLASSIC GOLD 954/1530, PO Box 262, Worcester WR6 5ZE and 18 Broad Street, Hereford HR4 9AP. Tel: 01905-740600. *Frequencies:* 954 AM (Hereford); 1530 AM (Worcester)

CLASSIC GOLD 1260, One Passage Street, Bristol BS2 0JF. Tel: 0117-984 3200. *Frequency:* 1260 AM

CLASSIC GOLD 1332 AM, PO Box 2020, Queensgate Centre, Peterborough PE1 1LL. Tel: 01733-460460. *Frequency:* 1332 AM

CLASSIC GOLD 1359, Hertford Place, Coventry CV1 3TT. Tel: 024-7686 8200. *Frequency:* 1359 AM

CLASSIC GOLD 1431/1485, The Chase, Calcot, Reading, Berks RG31 7RB. Tel: 0118-945 4400. *Frequencies:* 1431/1485 AM

CLASSIC GOLD 1557, 19–21 St Edmunds Road, Northampton NN1 5DY. Tel: 01604-795600. *Frequency:* 1557 AM

CLASSIC GOLD 1152 AM, Earl's Acre, Plymouth PL3 4HX. Tel: 01752 275600. *Frequency:* 1152 AM

CLASSIC GOLD AMBER (SUFFOLK), Alpha Business Park, 6–12 White House Road, Ipswich IP1 5LT. Tel: 01473-461000. *Frequencies:* 1170 AM (Ipswich); 1251 AM (Bury St Edmunds)

CLASSIC GOLD GEM, 29–31 Castle Gate, Nottingham NG1 7AP. Tel: 0115-952 7000. *Frequencies:* 945/999 AM

CLASSIC GOLD BREEZE, Radio House, Clifftown Road, Southend-on-Sea Essex SS1 1SX. Tel: 01702-333711. *Frequencies:* 1359/1431 AM

CLASSIC GOLD WABC, 267 Tettenhall Road, Wolverhampton WV6 0DE. Tel: 01902-461300. *Frequencies:* 990 AM (Wolverhampton); 1017 AM (Shrewsbury and Telford)

CLUB ASIA, Aisa House, 227–247 Gascoigne Road, Barking, Essex IG11 7LN. Tel: 020 8594 6662. *Frequencies:* 936/972 AM

COMPASS FM, 26 Wellowgate, Grimsby DN32 0RA. Tel: 01472-346666. *Frequency:* 96.4 FM

CONNECT FM, Unit 1, Centre 2000, Kettering, Northants, NN16 8PU. Tel: 01536-412413. *Frequency:* 97.2 FM/107.4 FM

COUNTY SOUND RADIO 1566 MW, Dolphin House, North Street, Guildford GU1 4AA. Tel: 01483-300964. *Frequency:* 1566 MW

DEARNE FM, PO Box 350, Barnsley S71 1YD. Tel: 01226-733325. *Frequency:* to be confirmed

DEE 106.3, 2 Chantry Court, Chester CH1 4QN. Tel: 01244 391000. *Frequency:* 106.3

DELTA FM 97.1, 65 Weyhill, Haslemere, Surrey GU27 1HN. Tel: 01428-651971. *Frequency:* 97.1/101.6/102 FM

DERBY'S RAM FM, 35–36 Irongate, Derby DE1 3GA. Tel: 01332 205599. *Frequency:* 102.8 FM

DREAM 100 FM, Northgate House, St Peter's Street, Colchester, CO1 1HT. Tel: 01206-764466. *Frequency:* 100.2 FM

DREAM 107.7, Cater House, High Street, Chelmsford CM1 1AL. Tel: 01245-259400. *Frequency:* 107.7 FM

DUNE FM, The Power Station, Victoria Way, Southport PR8 1RR. Tel: 01704-502500. *Frequency:* 107.9 FM

ESSEX FM, Radio House, Clifftown Road, Southend-on-Sea, Essex SS1 1SX. Tel: 01702-333711. *Frequencies:* 96.3 FM (Southend); 97.5 FM (Southend Centre); 102.6 FM (Chelmsford)

FM 102 – THE BEAR, The Guard House Studios, Banbury Road, Stratford-upon-Avon, Warks CV37 7HX. Tel: 01789-262636. *Frequency:* 102.0 FM

FM 103 HORIZON, The Broadcast Centre, 14 Vincent Avenue, Crownhill, Milton Keynes MK8 0AB. Tel: 01908-269111. *Frequency:* 103.3 FM

FM 107.6 THE FIRE, Quadrant Studios, 1d Christ Church Road, Bournemouth BH1 2AD. Tel: 01202-318100. *Frequency:* 107.6 FM

FOSSEWAY RADIO, PO Box 107, Hinckley, Leics LE10 1WR. Tel: 01455-614151. *Frequency:* 107.9 FM

FOX FM, Brush House, Pony Road, Oxford OX4 2XR. Tel: 01865-871038. *Frequencies:* 102.6/97.4 FM

FRESH RADIO, Firth Mill, Skipton, North Yorkshire, BD23 2PT. Tel: 01756-799991. *Frequencies:* 936 MW (Hawes); 1413 MW (Skipton)

FUSION 107.3 FM, Astra House, Arklow Road, London SE14 6EB. Tel: 020-8691 9202. *Frequency:* 107.3 FM

GALAXY 102, 1 The Square, 111 Broad Street, Birmingham B15 1AS. Tel: 0121-695 0000. *Frequency:* 102.0 FM

GALAXY 102.2, 1 The Square, 111 Broad Street, Birmingham B15 1AS. Tel: 0121-695 0000. *Frequency:* 102.2 FM

GALAXY 105, Joseph's Well, Westgate, Leeds LS3 1AB. Tel: 0113-213 0105. *Frequencies:* 105.1 FM (Leeds); 105.6 FM (Bradford and Sheffield); 105.8 FM (Hull)

GALAXY 105-106, Kingfisher Way, Silverlink Business Park, Tyne and Wear NE28 9NX. Tel: 0191-206 8000. *Frequencies:* 105.3/105.6/106.4 FM

GEMINI FM, Hawthorn House, Exeter Business Park, Exeter EX1 3QS. Tel: 01392-444444. *Frequencies:* 96.4/97.0/103.0 FM

GWR FM (BRISTOL AND BATH), PO Box 2000, Watershed, Canon's Road, Bristol BS99 7SN. Tel: 0117-984 3200. *Frequencies:* 96.3 FM (Bristol); 103.0 FM (Bath)

GWR FM (SWINDON AND WEST WILTSHIRE), PO Box 2000, Swindon SN4 7EX. Tel: 01793-842600. *Frequencies:* 97.2 FM (Swindon); 102.2 FM (West Wilts); 96.5 FM (Marlborough)

HALLAM FM, Radio House, 900 Herries Road, Sheffield S6 1RH. Tel: 0114-209 1000. *Frequencies:* 97.4 FM (Sheffield); 102.9 FM (Barnsley); 103.4 FM (Doncaster)

HEART 106.2, The Chrysalis Building, Bramley Road, London W10 6SP. Tel: 020-7468 1062. *Frequency:* 106.2 FM

HEART FM, *see* 100.7 Heart FM

HERTBEAT 106.9 FM, The Pump House, Knebworth Park, Hertfordshire SG3 6HQ. *Frequencies:* 106.7/106.9 FM

HOME 107.9, The Old Stableblock, Lockwood Park, Huddersfield HD1 3UR. Tel: 01484-321107. *Frequency:* 107.9 FM

IMAGINE FM, Regent House, Heaton Lane, Stockport SK4 1BX. Tel: 0161-285 4545. *Frequencies:* 96.4 FM (Cheshire); 104.9 FM (Stockport)

INVICTA FM, Radio House, John Wilson Business Park, Whitstable, Kent CT5 3QX. Tel: 01227-772004. *Frequencies:* 103.1 FM (Maidstone and Medway); 102.8 FM (Canterbury); 95.9 FM (Thanet); 97.0 FM (Dover); 96.1 FM (Ashford)

ISLAND FM, 12 Westerbrook, St Sampsons, Guernsey GY2 4QQ. Tel: 01481-242000. *Frequencies:* 93.7 FM (Alderney); 104.7 FM (Guernsey)

ISLE OF WIGHT RADIO, Dodnor Park, Newport, Isle of Wight PO30 5XE. Tel: 01983-822557. *Frequencies:* 102.0/107.0 FM

IVEL FM, 99 Preston Grove, Yeovil BA20 2DB. Tel: 01935-827839. *Frequency:* to be confirmed

JAZZ FM 102.2, 26–27 Castlereagh Street, London W1H 5PL. Tel: 020-7706 4100. *Frequency:* 102.2 FM

JAZZ FM 100.4, 8 Exchange Quay, Manchester M5 3EJ. Tel: 0161-877 1004. *Frequency:* 100.4 FM

JUICE 107.2, PO Box 107, Brighton BN1 1QG. Tel: 01273-386107. *Frequency:* 107.2 FM

JUICE 107.6, 27 Fleet Street, Liverpool L1 4AR. Tel: 0151-707 3107. *Frequency:* 107.6 FM

KCR 106.7, The Studios, Cables Retail Park, Prescot, Knowsley L34 5NQ. Tel: 0151-290 1501. *Frequency:* 106.7 FM

KEY 103, Castle Quay, Castlefield, Manchester M15 4PR. Tel: 0161-288 5000. *Frequency:* 103 FM

KICK FM, The Studios, 42 Bone Lane, Newbury, Berks RG14 5SD. Tel: 01635-841600. *Frequencies:* 105.6/107.4 FM

KISS 100, Mappin House, 4 Winsley Street, London W1W 8HF. Tel: 020-7700 6100. *Frequency:* 100.0 FM

KIX 96, Watch Close, Spon Street, Coventry CV1 3LN. Tel: 024-7652 5656. *Frequency:* 96.2 FM

KM-FM FOR CANTERBURY, 9 St. Georges Place, Canterbury, Kent CT1 1UU. Tel: 01227-789106. *Frequency:* 106 FM

KM-FM FOR FOLKESTONE & DOVER, 93–95 Sandgate Road, Folkstone, Kent CT20 2BQ. Tel: 01303-220303. *Frequencies:* 96.4/106.8 FM

KM-FM MEDWAY, Berkely House, 186 High Street, Rochester ME1 1EY. Tel: 01634-841111. *Frequencies:* 107.9/100.4

KM-FM THANET, Imperial House, 2–14 High Street, Margate, Kent CT9 1DH. Tel: 01843-220222. *Frequency:* 107.2

KM-FM WEST KENT, 1 East Street, Tonbridge, Kent, TN9 1AR. Tel: 01732-369200. *Frequencies:* 96.2/101.6 FM

LAKELAND RADIO, Lakeland Food Park, Plumgarths, Crook Road, Kendal, Cumbria LA8 8QJ. Tel: 01539-737380. *Frequencies:* 100.1/100.8

LANTERN FM, 2b Lauder Lane, Roundswell Business Park, Barnstaple EX31 3TA. Tel: 01271-340340. *Frequency:* 96.2 FM

LBC 97.3 FM, The Chrysalis Building, Bramley, London W10 6SP. Tel: 020-7314 7300. *Frequency:* 97.3 FM

LBC NEWS 1152 AM, The Chrysalis Building, Bramley, London W10 6SP. Tel: 020-7314 7309. *Frequency:* 1152 AM

LEICESTER SOUND, 6 Dominus Way, Meridian Business Park, Leicester LE19 1RP. Tel: 0116-256 1300. *Frequency:* 105.4 FM

LINCS FM, Witham Park, Waterside South, Lincoln LN5 7JN. Tel: 01522-549900. *Frequencies:* 102.2/96.7 FM (Grantham Relay)/97.6 FM (Scunthorpe Relay)

LITE FM, 5 Church Street, Peterborough PE1 1XJ. Tel: 01733-898106. *Frequency:* 106.8 FM

LONDON GREEK RADIO, 437 High Road, London N12 0AF. Tel: 020-8800 8001. *Frequency:* 103.3 FM

LONDON TURKISH RADIO, 185B High Road, Wood Green, London N22 6BA. Tel: 020-8881 0606. *Frequency:* 1584 AM

MAGIC 105.4 FM, Mappin House, 4 Winsley Street, London W1W 8AF. Tel: 020-7955 1054. *Frequency:* 105.4 FM

MAGIC 828, 51 Burley Road, Leeds LS3 1LR. Tel: 0113-283 5500. *Frequency:* 828 AM

MAGIC 999, St Paul's Square, Preston, Lancs, PR1 1YE. Tel: 01772-477700. *Frequency:* 999 AM

MAGIC 1152 AM, Newcastle upon Tyne NE99 1BB. Tel: 0191-420 3040. *Frequency:* 1152 AM

MAGIC 1161 AM, Commercial Road, Hull HU1 2SG. Tel: 01482-325141. *Frequency:* 1161 AM

MAGIC 1170, Radio House, Yales Crescent, Thornaby, Stockton-on-Tees, Cleveland TS17 6AA. Tel: 01642-888222. *Frequency:* 1170 AM

MAGIC 1548, St John's Beacon, 1 Houghton Street, Liverpool L1 1RL. Tel: 0151-472 6800. *Frequency:* 1548 AM

MAGIC AM, Radio House, 900 Herries Road, Sheffield S6 1RH. Tel: 0114-285 2121. *Frequencies:* 990/1305/1548 AM

MAIDSTONE'S CTR, PO Box 500, Maidstone ME16 8XQ. Tel: 01622-726621. *Frequency:* 105.6 to be confirmed

MANCHESTER'S MAGIC (1152), Castle Quay, Castlefield, Manchester M15 4PR. Tel: 0161-288 5000. *Frequency:* 1152 AM

MANSFIELD 103.2, The Media Suite, Brunts Business Centre, Samuel Brunts Way, Mansfield, Notts NG18 2AH. Tel: 01623-646666. *Frequency:* 103.2 FM

MEAN COUNTRY 1035, 43–51 Wembley Hill Road, London HA9 8AU. Tel: 020-8795 1035. *Frequency:* 1035 AM

MERCIA FM, Hertford Place, Coventry CV1 3TT. Tel: 024-7686 8200. *Frequencies:* 97.0/102.9 FM

MERCURY FM, The Stanley Centre, Kelvin Way, Crawley, W. Sussex RH10 2SE. Tel: 01293-519161. *Frequencies:* 97.5/102.7 FM

METRO RADIO, Newcastle upon Tyne NE99 1BB. Tel: 0191-420 0971. *Frequencies:* 97.1 FM (Northumberland, Tyne and Wear, Durham); 103.0 FM (Tyne Valley); 102.6 FM (Alnwick); 103.2 FM (Hexham)

MINSTER FM, PO Box 123, Dunnington, York YO19 5ZX. Tel: 01904-488888. *Frequencies:* 104.7 FM (York); 102.3 FM (Thirsk)

MIX 96, Friars Square Studios, 11 Bourbon Street, Aylesbury, Bucks HP20 2PZ. Tel: 01296-399396. *Frequency:* 96.2 FM

NORTHANTS 96, 19–21 St Edmunds Road, Northampton NN1 5DY. Tel: 01604-795601. *Frequency:* 96.6 FM

NORTH NORFOLK RADIO, Stody Estate Office, Melton Constable, Norfolk NR24 2ER. Tel 01502-565639. *Frequency:* to be confirmed

OCEAN FM, Radio House, Whittle Avenue, Segensworth West, Fareham, Hants PO15 5SH. Tel: 01489-589911. *Frequencies:* 96.7/97.5 FM

ORCHARD FM, Haygrove House, Taunton, Somerset TA3 7BT. Tel: 01823-338448. *Frequencies:* 96.5 FM (Taunton); 97.1 FM (Yeovil); 102.6 FM (Somerset)

PASSION FM 107.9, 270 Woodstock Road, Oxford OX2 7NW. Tel: 01865-351980. *Frequency:* 107.9

PEAK 107 FM, Radio House, Foxwood Road, Chesterfield, Derbys S41 9RF. Tel: 01246-269107. *Frequencies:* 107.4 FM (Chesterfield and NE Derbyshire); 102.0 FM (Matlock and Bakewell)

PIRATE FM 102, Carn Brea Studios, Wilson Way, Redruth, Cornwall TR15 3XX. Tel: 01209-314400. *Frequencies:* 102.2 FM (East Cornwall and West Devon); 102.8 FM (West Cornwall and Isles of Scilly)

FM PLYMOUTH SOUND, Earl's Acre, Plymouth PL3 4HX. Tel: 01752-275600. *Frequencies:* 96.6/97.0 FM

PREMIER CHRISTIAN RADIO, 22 Chapter Street, London SW1P 4NP. Tel: 020-7316 1300.
Frequencies: 1305/1332/1413 AM

THE PULSE, Pennine House, Forster Square, Bradford BD1 5NE. Tel: 01274-203040. *Frequencies:* 97.5 FM (Bradford); 102.5 FM (Huddersfield and Halifax)

Q103 FM, Enterprise House, The Vision Park, Chivers Way, Histon, Cambridge CB4 9WW. Tel: 01223-235255.
Frequencies: 103.0 FM (Cambridge); 97.4 FM (Newmarket)

QUAY WEST RADIO, Harbour Studios, The Esplanade, Watchet, Somerset TA23 0AJ. Tel: 01984-634900.
Frequency: 102.4 FM

RADIO CITY 96.7, St John's Beacon, 1 Houghton Street, Liverpool L1 1RL. *Frequency:* 96.7 FM

RAM FM, *see* Derby's RAM FM

READING 107 FM, Radio House, Madejski Stadium, Reading, Berkshire RG2 0FN. Tel: 0118-986 2555. *Frequency:* 107 FM

REVOLUTION, PO Box 962, Oldham OL1 1FE.
Tel: 0161-628 8787. *Frequency:* 96.2 FM

RIDINGS FM, PO Box 333, Wakefield WF2 7QY.
Tel: 01924-367177. *Frequency:* 106.8 FM

ROCK FM, *see* 97.4 Rock FM

RUGBY FM, Dunsmore Business Centre, Spring Street, Rugby, Warwickshire CV21 3HH. Tel 01788-541100.
Frequency: 107.1 FM

RUTLAND RADIO, Rutland Business Centre, Gaol Street, Oakham, Rutland LE15 6AY. Tel: 01572-757868.
Frequencies: 107.2 FM (Rutland); 97.4 FM (Stamford)

SABRAS RADIO, Radio House, 63 Melton Road, Leicester LE4 6PN. Tel: 0116-261 0666. *Frequency:* 1260 AM

SAGA 105.7 FM, 3rd floor, Crown House, Beaufort Court, 123 Hayley Road, Edgbaston, Birmingham B16 8LD.
Tel: 0121-452 1057. *Frequency:* 105.7 FM

SAGA 106.6 FM, Saga radio House, Alder Court, Riverside Business Park Nottingham NG2 1RX. Tel: 0115-986 1066.
Frequency: 106.6 FM

SEVERN SOUND FM, Bridge Studios, Eastgate Centre, Gloucester GL1 1SS. Tel: 01452-313200.
Frequencies: 103.0/102.4 FM

SGR COLCHESTER, Abbeygate Two, 9 Whitewell Road, Colchester CO2 7DE. Tel: 01206-575859.
Frequency: 96.1 FM

SGR-FM, Radio House, Alpha Business Park, 6-12 White House Road, Ipswich IP1 5LT. Tel: 01473-461000. *Frequencies:* 97.1 FM (Ipswich); 96.4 FM (Bury St Edmunds)

SIGNAL 1, Stoke Road, Stoke-on-Trent ST4 2SR.
Tel: 01782-441300. *Frequencies:* 96.9/102.6 FM

SIGNAL 2, Stoke Road, Stoke-on-Trent ST4 2SR.
Tel: 01782-441300. *Frequency:* 1170 AM

SOUL CITY 107.5, Lambourne House, 7 Western Road, Romford, Essex RM1 3LP. Tel 0870-6071075.
Frequency: 107.5 FM

SOUTH CITY FM, City Studios, Marsh Lane, Southampton, SO14 3ST. Tel: 023-8022 0020. *Frequency:* 107.8 FM

SOUTHERN FM, Radio House, PO Box 2000, Brighton BN41 2SS. Tel: 01273-430111. *Frequencies:* 102.0 FM (Hastings); 102.4 FM (Eastbourne); 96.9 FM (Newhaven); 103.5 FM (Brighton)

SOUTH HAMS RADIO, Unit 19, South Hams Business Park, Churchstow, Knightsbridge, Devon TQ7 3QH.
Tel: 01548-854595. *Frequency:* 100.5 FM (Totnes); 100.8 FM (Dartmouth); 101.2 FM (South Hams); 101.9 FM (Ivybridge)

SOVEREIGN RADIO, 14 St Mary's Walk, Hailsham, E. Sussex BN27 1AF. Tel: 01323-442700. *Frequency:* 107.5 FM

SPECTRUM RADIO, 4 Ingate Place, Battersea, London SW8 3NS. Tel: 020-7627 4433. *Frequency:* 558 AM

SPIRE FM, City Hall Studios, Malthouse Lane, Salisbury, Wilts SP2 7QQ. Tel: 01722-416644. *Frequency:* 102.0 FM

SPIRIT FM, Dukes Court, Bognor Road, Chichester, W. Sussex PO19 8FX. Tel: 01243-773600. *Frequencies:* 96.6/102.3 FM

SPLASH FM, Guildbourne Centre, Worthing, West Sussex BN11 1L2. Tel: 01903-233005. *Frequency:* 107.7 FM

STAR 106.6, The Observatory Shopping Centre, Slough, Berks SL1 1LH. Tel: 01753-551066. *Frequency:* 106.6 FM

STAR 107, Brunel Mall, London Road, Stroud, Gloucestershire, GL5 2BP. Tel: 01453-767369. *Frequency:* 107.2/9

STAR 107.1 & 107.5, 5 Church Mews, Wisbech, Cambridgeshire PE13 1HL. Tel: 01945-467465.
Frequencies: 107.1, 107.5 FM

STAR 107.3, Bristol Evening Post Building, Temple Way, Bristol BS99 7HD. Tel: 0117-910 6600. *Frequency:* 107.3 FM

STAR 107.5, Cheltenham Film Studios, 1st Floor, West Suite, Arle Court, Hatherley Lane, Cheltenham, Gloucester GL51 6PN. Tel: 01242-699555. *Frequency:* 107.5 FM

STAR 107.7 FM, 11 Beaconsfield Road, Weston-Super-Mare BS23 1YE. Tel: 01934-624455. *Frequency:* 107.7 FM

STAR 107.9, Radio House, Sturton Street, Cambridge CB1 2QF. Tel: 01223-722300. *Frequency:* 107.9 FM

SUN FM, PO Box 1034, Sunderland SR5 2YL. Tel: 0191-548 1034. *Frequency:* 103.4 FM

SUNRISE FM, Sunrise House, 30 Chapel Street, Little Germany, Bradford BD1 5DN. Tel: 01274-735043.
Frequency: 103.2 FM

SUNRISE RADIO, Sunrise House, Sunrise Road, Southall, Middx UB2 4AU. Tel: 020-8574 6666. *Frequency:* 1458 AM

SUNSHINE 855, Sunshine House, Waterside, Ludlow, Shropshire SY8 1PE. Tel: 01584-873795.
Frequency: 855 AM

SWAN FM, PO Box 1170, High Wycombe, Bucks HP13 6WQ. Tel: 01494-446611. *Frequency:* 1170 FM

TEN 17, Latton Bush Centre, Southern Way, Harlow, Essex CM18 7BU. Tel: 01279-431017. *Frequency:* 101.7 FM

TFM, Radio House, Yale Crescent, Thornaby, Stockton-on-Tees TS17 6AA. Tel: 01642-888222. *Frequency:* 96.6 FM

THAMES 107.8, The Old Post Office, 110–112 Tolworth, Broadway, Surbiton, Surrey KT6 7JD. Tel: 020-8288 1300.
Frequency: 107.8 FM

TIME FM, 2–6 Basildon Road, Abbey Wood, London SE2 0EW. Tel: 020-8311 3112. *Frequency:* 106.8

TOWER FM, The Mill, Brownlow Way, Bolton BL1 2RA.
Tel: 01204-387000. *Frequency:* 107.4 FM

VIBE FM, Alpha Business Park, 6–12 White House Road, Ipswich, Suffolk IP31 5LT. Tel: 01473-461000.
Frequencies: 105.6 FM (Cambridge); 106.1 FM (Norwich); 106.4 FM (Ipswich); 107.7 FM (Peterborough)

VICTORY 107.4, Media House, Tipner Wharf, Twyford Avenue, Portsmouth PO2 8PE. Tel: 023-9263 9922.
Frequency: 107.4 FM

VIRGIN 105.8, 1 Golden Square, London W1F 9DJ.
Tel: 020-7434 1215. *Frequency:* 105.8 FM

WAVE 96.5, 965 Mowbray Drive, Blackpool FY3 7JR.
Tel: 01253-304965. *Frequency:* 96.5 FM

WAVE 105 FM, 5 Manor Court, Barnes Wallis Road,
Segensworth East, Fareham, Hampshire PO15 5TH.
Tel: 01489-481050. *Frequencies:* 105.2 FM (Solent); 105.8
FM (Poole)

WESSEX FM, Radio House, Trinity Street, Dorchester DT1 1DJ.
Tel: 01305-250333. *Frequencies:* 97.2/96.0 FM

WIRRAL'S BUZZ 97.1, Media House, Claughton Road,
Birkenhead CH41 6EY. Tel: 0151-6501700
Frequency: 97.1 FM

WYVERN FM, 5–6 Barbourne Terrace, Worcester WR1 3JZ.
Tel: 01905-612212. *Frequencies:* 97.6 FM (Hereford); 102.8
FM (Worcester); 96.7 FM (Kidderminster)

XFM, 30 Leicester Square, London WC2H 7LA.
Tel: 020-7766 6600. *Frequency:* 104.9 FM

YORKSHIRE COAST RADIO, PO Box 1024, Bridlington, East
Yorkshire YO15 2YW. Tel: 01262-404400.
Tel: 01723-500962. *Frequencies:* 96.2/103.1 FM

YORKSHIRE COAST RADIO BRIDLINGTON'S BEST, Old
Harbour Master's Office, Harbour Road, Bridlington, E. Yorks
YO15 5NR. Tel: 01262-404400. *Frequency:* 102.4 FM

Wales

96.4 FM THE WAVE, PO Box 964, Victoria Road, Gowerton,
Swansea SA4 3AB. Tel: 01792-511964. *Frequency:* 96.4 FM

102.5 RADIO PEMBROKESHIRE, Unit 14, The Old School
Estate, Station Road, Narbarth, Pembrokeshire SA67 7DU.
Tel: 01834-869384. *Frequency:* 102.5 FM

106.3 BRIDGE FM, 25 Wyndham Street, Bridgend CF31 1EY.
Tel: 01656-647777. *Frequency:* 106.3 FM

CAPITAL GOLD, West Canal Wharf, Cardiff CF10 5XL.
Tel: 029-2023 7878. *Frequencies:* 1359 AM (Cardiff); 1305
AM (Newport)

CHAMPION FM, Llys y Dderwen, Parc Menai, Bangor LL57
4BN. Tel: 01248-671888. *Frequency:* 103.0 FM

CLASSIC GOLD MARCHER 1260 AM, The Studios, Mold
Road, Wrexham LL11 4AF. Tel: 01978-752202.
Frequency: 101.2

COAST FM, 41 Conwy Road, Colwyn Bay LL28 5AB.
Tel: 01492-533733. *Frequency:* 96.3 FM

MFM 103.4, The Studios, Mold Road, Gwersyllt, Nr Wrexham
LL11 4AF. Tel: 01978 752202. *Frequency:* 103.4 FM

RADIO CEREDIGION, Yr Hen Ysgol Gymraeg, Ffordd
Alexandra, Aberystwyth SY23 1LF. Tel: 01970-627999.
Frequencies: 96.6/97.4/103.3/FM

RADIO MALDWYN, The Studios, The Park, Newtown, Powys
SY16 2NZ. Tel: 01686-623555. *Frequency:* 756 AM

REAL RADIO, PO Box 6105, Ty-Nant Court, Cardiff CF15 8YF.
Tel: 029-2023 1863. *Frequencies:* 105/106 FM

RED DRAGON FM, Radio House, West Canal Wharf, Cardiff
CF10 4DJ. Tel: 029-2066 2066. *Frequencies:* 103.2 FM
(Cardiff); 97.4 FM (Newport)

SWANSEA SOUND, PO Box 1170, Victoria Road, Gowerton,
Swansea SA4 3AB. Tel: 01792-511170. *Frequency:* 1170 AM

VALLEYS RADIO, Festival Park, Victoria, Ebbw Vale
NP23 8XW. Tel: 01495-301116. *Frequencies:* 999/1116 AM

Scotland

96.3 QFM, 65 Sussex Street, Glasgow G41 1DX.
Tel: 0141-429 9430. *Frequency:* 96.3 FM

ARGYLL FM, 27–29 Longrow, Campbeltown, Argyll PA28
6ER. Tel: 01586-551800. *Frequencies:* 107.1/107.7/
106.5 FM

BEAT 106, Four Winds Pavilion, Pacific Quay, Glasgow G51
1EB. Tel: 0141-566 6106. *Frequencies:* 105.7/106.1 FM

CASTLE ROCK FM, Pioneer Park Studios, Unit 3,
80 Castlegreen Street, Dumbarton G82 1JB.
Tel: 01389-734422. *Frequency:* 103 FM

CENTRAL FM, 201 High Street, Falkirk FK1 1DU.
Tel: 01324-611164. *Frequency:* 103.1 FM

CLAN FM, Radio House, Rowantree Avenue, Newhouse
Industrial Estate, Newhouse ML1 5RX. Tel: 01689-733107.
Frequency: 107.5/107.9 FM

CLYDE 1 (FM) AND 2 (AM), Clydebank Business Park,
Clydebank, Glasgow G81 2RX. Tel: 0141-565 2200.
Frequencies: 102.5 FM; 103.3 FM (Firth of Clyde); 97.0 FM
(Vale of Leven); 1152 AM

CLYDE 2, Clydebank Business Park, Glasgow G81 2RX.
Tel: 0141 565 2200. *Frequency:* 1152 AM

CULLIN FM, Tigh Lisigarry, Bridge Road, Porttee, Isle of Skye
IV51 9ER. Tel: 01478-612921 *Frequency:* to be confirmed

FORTH ONE, Forth House, Forth Street, Edinburgh EH1 3LE.
Tel: 0131-556 9255. *Frequencies:* 1548 AM,
97.3/97.6/102.2 FM

FORTH 2, Forth House, Forth Street, Edinburgh EH1 3LE.
Tel: 0131-556 9255. *Frequencies:* 1548 AM

HEARTLAND FM, Atholl Curling Rink, Lower Oakfield,
Pitlochry, Perthshire PH16 5HQ. Tel: 01796-474040.
Frequency: 97.5 FM

ISLES FM, PO Box 333, Stornoway, Isle of Lewis HS1 2PU.
Tel: 01851-703333. *Frequency:* 103.0 FM

KINGDOM FM, Haig House, Haig Business Park, Markinch,
Fife KY7 6AQ. Tel: 01592-753753.
Frequencies: 95.2/96.1 FM

LOCHBROOM FM, Radio House, Mill Street, Ullapool, Ross-
shire IV26 2UN. Tel: 01854-613131. *Frequency:* 102.2 FM

MORAY FIRTH RADIO, Scorguie Place, Inverness IV3 8UJ.
Tel: 01463-224433. *Frequencies:* 97.4 FM, 1107 AM; *local
opt-outs:* MFR Speysound 96.6 FM, MFR Keith Community
Radio 102.8 FM; MFR Kinnaird Radio 96.7 FM; MFR
Caithness 102.5 FM

NECR (NORTH-EAST COMMUNITY RADIO), The Shed,
School Road, Kintore, Aberdeenshire AB51 0UX.
Tel: 01467-632909. *Frequencies:* 97.1 FM (Braemar); 102.1
FM (Meldrum and Inverurie); 102.6 FM (Kildrummy); 103.2
FM (Colpy)

NEVIS RADIO, Inverlochy, Fort William, Inverness-shire PH33
6PR. Tel: 01397-700007. *Frequencies:* 96.6 FM (Fort
William); 97.0 FM (Glencoe); 102.3 FM (Skye); 102.4 FM
(Loch Leven)

NORTHSOUND ONE (FM) AND TWO (AM), Abbotswell
Road, West Tullos, Aberdeen AB12 3AJ. Tel: 01224-337000.
Frequencies: 1035 AM, 96.9/97.6/103.0 FM

OBAN FM, 132 George Street, Oban, Argyll PA34 5NT.
Tel: 01631-570057. *Frequency:* 103.3 FM

RADIO BORDERS, Tweedside Park, Galashiels TD1 3TD.
Tel: 01896-759444. *Frequencies:* 96.8/97.5/103.1/103.4 FM

RADIO TAY AM AND TAY FM, 6 North Isla Street, Dundee
DD3 7JQ. Tel: 01382-200800. *Frequencies:* 1161 AM, 102.8
FM (Dundee); 1584 AM, 96.4 FM (Perth)

REAL RADIO SCOTLAND, PO Box 101, Parkway Court,
Glasgow Business Park, Glasgow G69 6GA.
Tel: 0141-781 1011. *Frequencies:* 100-101 FM

RIVER FM, Stadium House, Alderstone Road, Livingston EH54
7DN. *Frequency:* to be confirmed

RNA FM, Arbroath Infirmary, Rosemount Road, Arbroath,
Angus DD11 2AT. Tel: 01241-879660. *Frequency:* 96.6 FM

SIBC, Market Street, Lerwick, Shetland ZE1 0JN.
Tel: 01595-695299. *Frequencies:* 96.2/102.2 FM

SOUTH WEST SOUND, Unit 40, The Loreburne Centre, High
St, Dumfries DG1 2BD. Tel: 01387-250999.
Frequencies: 96.5/97.0/103.0 FM

TWO LOCHS RADIO, Gairloch, Ross-shire IV21 2LR.
Tel: 0870-7414657. *Frequency:* to be confirmed
WAVE 102, 8 South Tay Street, Dundee DD1 1PA.
Tel: 01382-901000. *Frequency:* 102 FM
WAVES RADIO PETERHEAD, Unit 2, Blackhouse Industrial
Estate, Peterhead AB42 1BW. Tel: 01779-491012.
Frequency: 101.2 FM
WEST FM, Radio House, 54a Holmston Road, Ayr KA7 3BE.
Tel: 01292-283662. *Frequency:* 97.5 FM
WEST SOUND AM AND WEST FM, Radio House, 54a
Holmston Road, Ayr KA7 3BE. Tel: 01292-283662.
Frequencies: 1035 AM, 96.7 FM (Ayr); 97.5 FM (Girvan)

Northern Ireland
CITY BEAT 96.7, Lamont Buildings, Stranmillis Embankment,
Belfast BT9 5FN. Tel: 028-9020 5967. *Frequency:* 96.7 FM
COOL FM, PO Box 974, Belfast BT1 1RT. Tel: 028-9181 7181.
Frequency: 97.4 FM
DOWNTOWN RADIO, Newtownards, Co. Down BT23 4ES.
Tel: 028-9181 5555. *Frequencies:* 1026 AM (Belfast); 96.4
FM (Limavady); 96.6 FM (Enniskillen); 97.1 FM (Larne); 102.3
FM (Ballymena); 102.4 FM (Londonderry); 103.1 FM (Newry);
103.4 FM (Newcastle); 102.6 AM (Belfast)
MID 106, 2c Park Avenue, Burn Road, Clookstown BT80 8AH.
Tel: 02886-758696. *Frequency:* 106 FM
Q97.2 FM, 24 Cloyfin Road, Coleraine BT52 2NU.
Tel: 028-7035 9100. *Frequency:* 97.2 FM
Q101.2 FM WEST, 42A Market Street, Omagh, Co. Tyrone
BT78 1EN, 1A Belmore Mews, Enniskillen, Co. Fermanagh.
Tel: 028-8224 5777/ 028-6632 0777. *Frequency:* 101.2
Q102.9 FM, The Riverside Suite, 87 Rossdowney Road,
Waterside, Londonderry BT47 5SU. Tel: 028-7134 4449.
Frequency: 102.9 FM

Channel Islands
104.7 ISLAND FM, 12 Westerbrook, St Sampsons, Guernsey
GY2 4QQ. Tel: 01481-242000. *Frequencies:* 104.7 FM
(Guernsey); 93.7 FM (Alderney)
CHANNEL 103 FM, 6 Tunnell Street, St Helier, Jersey JE2 4LU.
Tel: 01534-888103. *Frequency:* 103.7 FM

DIGITAL MULTIPLEXES

The information contained in this section is correct at the
time of writing (August 2003), however it is advisable to
check with the multiplex operator for full listings.

CAPITAL RADIO DIGITAL, 30 Leicester Square, London
WC2H 7LA Tel: 020-7766 6000

Cardiff & Newport, Programme services: Red Dragon FM,
Capital Gold, Centry, Xfm, BBC Radio Wales, BBC Radio
Cymru. *Frequency:* 11C
Kent, Programme services: Invicta FM, Capital Gold, Kent
Digital Extra, Saga Radio, Xfm, Kiss, Swale Sound, Totally
Radio, BBC Radio Kent. *Frequency:* 11C
South Hampshire, Programme services: Ocean FM, 103.2
Power FM, Capital Gold, Wave 105.2, Saga, Passion for the
Planet, South City FM, BBC Radio Solent. *Frequency:* 11C
Sussex coast, Programme services: Southern FM, Capital
Gold, Juice 107.2, Xfm, Saga, Kiss, Gaydar Radio, Spirit FM,
Totally radio, BBC Southern Counties Radio. *Frequency:* 11B

CE DIGITAL LTD, 30 Leicester Square, London WC2H 7LA
Tel: 020-7766 6000.

Birmingham, Programme services: BRMB; Capital Gold;
Xfm; Magic; Radio XL; Kiss; Sunrise; BBC Radio WM.
Frequency: 11C
London, Programme services: Capital FM; Capital Gold;
Capital Disney; Kiss; Xfm, Magic; News Direct; Sunrise Radio;
LBC; Smash! Hits, Century London. *Frequency:* 12C
Manchester, Programme services: Key 103; Magic; Kiss;
Capital Gold; Xfm; Asian Sound Radio; BBC GMR.
Frequency: 11C

DIGITAL ONE, 7 Swallow Place, London W1B 2AG
Tel: 020-7288 4600 Programme services: Classic FM; Virgin
Radio; TalkSport; Planet Rock; Core; Life; Oneword;
PrimeTimeRadio. *Frequencies:* 11D (England and Wales);
12A (Scotland)

THE DIGITAL RADIO GROUP, 7 Swallow Place; London
W1R 7AA Tel: 020-7911 7300 Programme services: The
Arrow; AbracaDABra; Choice; Liquid; Passion for the Planet;
Gaydar Radio; Mean Country; The Storm; Breeze; SBN
Frequency: 11B

EMAP DIGITAL RADIO LTD, Radio House, 900 Herries Road,
Sheffield S6 1RH Tel: 0114-209 1033

Central Lancashire, Emap Performance, Mappin House,
4 Winsley Street, London W1W 8HF Tel; 020-7436 1515
Programme services: 97.4 Rock FM; Kiss; Magic 999; Classic
Gold; Xfm; 3C; Smash! Hits; BBC Radio Lancashire.
Frequency: 12A
Humberside, Programme services: Viking FM; Magic 1161;
Lincs FM; Classic Gold; Xfm; Smash! Hits; Kiss; BBC Radio
Humberside. *Frequency:* 11B
Leeds, Programme services: 96.3 Aire FM; Classic Gold; Kiss;
Magic 828; Ridings FM; Xfm; Smash! Hits; BBC Radio Leeds.
Frequency: 12D
Liverpool, Programme services: Radio City 96.7; Magic
1548; Kiss; Classic Gold; Xfm; 3C; Smash! Hits; BBC Radio
Merseyside. *Frequency:* 12D
South Yorkshire, Programme services: Hallam FM; Magic;
Kiss; Trax FM; Classic Gold; Xfm; Smash! Hits; BBC Radio
Sheffield. *Frequency:* 11C
Teesside, Programme services: Classic Gold; Kiss; Magic
1170; 96.6 TFM; Xfm; 3C; Smash! Hits; BBC Radio
Cleveland. *Frequency:* 11B
Tyne and Wear, Programme services: Metro FM; Magic
1152; Kiss; 3C; Classic Gold; Xfm; Smash! Hits; BBC Radio
Newcastle. *Frequency:* 11C

MXR, The Chrysalis Building, 13 Bramley Road, London W10
6SP Tel: 020-7470 2213

North East England, Programme services: Heart; The
Arrow; Smooth; Digital News Network; Jazz FM; Galaxy;
Century FM; Urban Choice; Capital Disney. *Frequency:* 12C
North West England, Programme services: Urban Choice;
Heart; The Arrow; Smooth; Digital News Network; Galaxy;
Jazz FM; Century FM; Capital Disney. *Frequency:* 12C
South Wales/Severn Estuary, Programme services: Urban
Choice; Heart; The Arrow; Smooth; Digital News Network;
Galaxy; Jazz FM; Real Radio; Capital Disney. *Frequency:* 12C
West Midlands, Programme services: Heart; The Arrow;
Smooth; Digital News Network; Galaxy; Jazz FM; Saga
Radio; *Frequency:* 12A

Yorkshire, Programme services: Capital Disney, Urban Choice, Heart; Jazz FM, The Arrow, Smooth, Digital New Network, Galaxy, Real Radio. *Frequency:* 12A

NOW DIGITAL LTD, PO Box 2000, Bristol BS99 7SN
Tel: 020-7911 7300 Web: www.now-digital.com

Bournemouth, Programme services: 2CR FM, Classic Gold; Kiss; Wave 105; Saga; Passion for the Planet; The Storm; SBN; BBC Radio Solent. *Frequency:* 11B
Bristol/Bath, Programme services: GWR FM; Classic Gold; The Storm; Xfm; Kiss; Saga; Passion for the Planet; now.data; BBC Radio Bristol. *Frequency:* 11B
Coventry, Programme services: Mercia FM; Classic Gold 1359; Kix 96; The Storm; Sunrise radio; SBN; Kiss; YAAR; BBC Radio Coventry and Warwickshire. *Frequency:* 12B
Exeter & Torbay, Programme services: Gemini FM; Classic Gold; Kiss; The Storm; Passion for the Planet; SBN; BBC Radio Devon. *Frequency:* 11C
Leicester, Programme services: Leicester Sound; Classic Gold GEM; Galaxy; Capital Disney; Sabras Sound; A Plus; Century 106; BBC Radio Leicester. Frequency:11B
Norwich, Programme services: Broadland 102; Classic Gold Amber; Vibe; 106.4 The Beach; The Storm; Passion for the Planet; 3C; SBN; AbracaDABra; Smash! Hits. *Frequency:* 11B
Nottingham, Programme services: 96 Trent FM; Classic Gold GEM; 106 Centry FM; Saga; Galaxy; Capital Disney; The Storm; A Plus; BBC Radio Nottingham. Frequency 12C
Peterborough, Programme services: Hereward FM; Classic Gold; Vibe; 3C; Passion for the Planet; SBN; Smash! Hits; BBC Radio Cambridge. *Frequency:* 12D
Southend and Chelmsford, Programme services: Essex FM; Breeze; The Rhythm; Dance service; Easy Listening Service; Ritz; Flix; BBC Radio Essex. *Frequency:* 12D
Swindon and West Wiltshire, Programme services: Kiss; Capital Disney; The Storm; SBN; GWR FM Bath; GWR FM Wilts; Saga; Swindon FM; BBC Radio Swindon, BBC Radio Witshire.
Wolverhampton, Shrewsbury and Telford, Programme services: Beacon FM; Classic Gold WABC; The Storm; The Rhythm; Xfm; Sunrise radio; BBC Radio WM; BBC Radio Shropshire. *Frequency:* 11B

SCORE DIGITAL, 3 South Ave, Clydebank Business Park, Glasgow G81 2RX Tel: 0141-565 2347
Web: www.scoredigital.co.uk

Ayr, Programme services: West FM, West Sound; 3C; UCA Radio; The Storm; Smash! Hits; BBC Radio Scotland; BBC Radio Gaidheal. *Frequency:* 11B
Dundee & Perth, Programme services: Tay FM; Tay AM; 3C; The Access Channel; The Storm; Smash! Hits; BBC Scotland; BBC Nan Gaidheal. *Frequency:* 11B
Edinburgh, Programme services: Forth One; Forth 2; 3C; Sunrise Radio; Xfm; Saga Radio; BBC Radio Scotland. *Frequency:* 12D
Glasgow, Clyde 1; Clyde 2; 3C; Sunrise radio; 96.3 QFM; Xfm; Kiss; Saga Radio; BBC Radio Scotland. *Frequency:* 11C
Inverness, Programme services: MFR; 3C; MFR 1107; BBC Radio Scotland; BBC Nan Gaidheal. *Frequency:* 11B
Northern Ireland, Programme services: Downtown; Cool FM; City Beat; Q102.9; Classic FM; PrimeTime; 3C; Kiss; BBC Radio Ulster. *Frequency:* 12D

SWITCHDIGITAL LTD, 18 Hatfields, London SE1 8DJ
Tel: 020-7959 7800 Web: www.switchdigital.com

Aberdeen, Programme services: Kiss; Smash! Hits; Waves Radio; NECR; Northsound One; Northsound Two; BBC Radio Scotland; BBC Nan Gaidheal. *Frequency:* 11C
Central Scotland, Programme services: Galaxy Jazz FM; Beat 106; Real Radio; The Arrow; Heart; Smash! Hits; BBC Radio Nan Galdheal. *Frequency:* 11D
Greater London, Programme services: Hits; Galaxy; YAAR; The Groove; Travel Now; Heart 106.2 FM; Jazz FM; Saga Radio, Spectrum Radio 558AM; BBC London Live. *Frequency:* 12A

TWG – EMAP (B & H) LTD, 18 Hatfields, London SE1 8DJ.
Tel: 020-7959 7800

Bradford & Huddersfield, Programme services: The Pulse; Classic Gold; Sunrise Radio; Smash! Hits; Kiss. *Frequency:* 11B
Stoke-on Trent, Programme services: Signal 1; Signal 2; Kiss; Smash! Hits; The Storm; BBC Radio Stoke. *Frequency:* 12D
Swansea, Programme services: The Wave; Swansea Sound; Kiss; Smash! Hits; BBC Radio Cymru; BBC Radio Wales. *Frequency* 12A

THE PRESS

The newspaper and periodical press in the UK is large and diverse, catering for a wide variety of views and interests. There is no state control or censorship of the press, though it is subject to the laws on publication and the Press Complaints Commission was set up by the industry as a means of self-regulation.

The press is not state-subsidised and receives few tax concessions. The income of most newspapers and periodicals is derived largely from sales and from advertising; the press is the largest advertising medium in Britain.

SELF-REGULATION

The Press Complaints Commission was founded by the newspaper and magazine industry in January 1991 to replace the Press Council (established in 1953). It is a voluntary, non-statutory body set up to operate the press's self-regulation system following the Calcutt report in 1990 on privacy and related matters, when the industry feared that failure to regulate itself might lead to statutory regulation of the press. The performance of the Press Complaints Commission was reviewed after 18 months of operation (the *Calcutt Review of Press Self-Regulation,* presented to Parliament in January 1993) to determine whether statutory measures were required. No proposals for replacing the self-regulation system have been made to date. The Commission is funded by the industry through the Press Standards Board of Finance.

COMPLAINTS

The Press Complaints Commission's aims are to consider, adjudicate, conciliate, and resolve complaints of unfair treatment by the press; and to ensure that the press maintains the highest professional standards with respect for generally recognised freedoms, including freedom of expression, the public's right to know, and the right of the press to operate free from improper pressure. The Commission judges newspaper and magazine conduct by a code of practice drafted by editors, agreed by the industry and ratified by the Commission.

Six of the Commission's members are editors of national, regional and local newspapers and magazines, and nine, including the chairman, are drawn from other fields. One member has been appointed Privacy Commissioner with special powers to investigate complaints about invasion of privacy.

PRESS COMPLAINTS COMMISSION, 1 Salisbury Square, London EC4Y 8JB Tel: 020-7353 1248 Fax: 020-7353 8355
Email: complaints@pcc.org.uk
Web: www.pcc.org.uk
Chairman, Sir Christopher Meyer

NEWSPAPERS

Newspapers are mostly financially independent of any political party, though most adopt a political stance in their editorial comments, usually reflecting proprietorial influence. Ownership of the national and regional daily newspapers is concentrated in the hands of large corporations whose interests cover publishing and communications. The rules on cross-media ownership, as amended by the Broadcasting Act 1996, which limited the extent to which newspaper organisations may become involved in broadcasting, have been relaxed by the Communications Act 2003. Newspapers with over 20 per cent share of national circulation may own national and/or local radio licences.

There are about 13 daily and 14 Sunday national papers and several hundred local papers that are published weekly or twice-weekly. Scotland, Wales and Northern Ireland all have at least one daily and one Sunday national paper.

Newspapers are usually published in either broadsheet or tabloid format. The 'quality' daily papers, e.g. those providing detailed coverage of a wide range of public matters, have a broadsheet format. The tabloid papers take a more popular approach and are more illustrated.

CIRCULATION (*net average for July 2003*)
National Daily Newspapers

Daily Express	899,686
Daily Mail	2,338,367
Daily Mirror	1,786,376
Daily Record	486,071
Daily Star	770,950
Daily Telegraph	878,735
Financial Times	139,160
Racing Post	73,243
The Guardian	339,325
The Independent	181,563
The Scotsman	67,572
The Sun	3,306,990
The Times	590,487

National Sunday Newspapers

Independent on Sunday	175,539
News of the World	3,595,120
Sunday Express	897,220
The People	1,001,232
Scotland on Sunday	76,024
Sport First	20,664
Mail on Sunday	2,289,436
Sunday Mail	593,085
Sunday Mirror	1,520,979
Sunday Sport	182,577
Sunday Telegraph	673,365
Sunday Times	1,145,954
The Business	66,882
The Observer	389,869

Source: Audit Bureau of Circulations Ltd, July 2003. For further information please see www.abc.org.uk

NATIONAL DAILY NEWSPAPERS

DAILY EXPRESS
　Ludgate House, 245 Blackfriars Road,
　London SE1 9UX Tel: 020-7928 8000 Fax: 020-7633 0244
　Web: www.express.co.uk *Editor:* Chris Williams
DAILY MAIL
　Northcliffe House, 2 Derry Street, London W8 5TT
　Tel: 020-7938 6000 Fax: 020-7937 3251
　Web: www.dailymail.co.uk *Editor:* Paul Dacre
DAILY MIRROR
　1 Canada Square, Canary Wharf, London E14 5AP
　Tel: 020-7293 3000 Fax: 020-7293 3409
　Web: www.mirror.co.uk *Editor:* Piers Morgan

DAILY RECORD
1 Central Quay, Glasgow G3 8DA
Tel: 0141-309 3000 Fax: 0141-309 3340
Web: www.record-mail.co.uk/rm *Editor:* Bruce Waddell

DAILY SPORT
19 Great Ancoats Street, Manchester M60 4BT
Tel: 0161-236 4466 Fax: 0161-236 4535
Editor-in-Chief: Tony Livesey

DAILY STAR
Ludgate House, 245 Blackfriars Road, London SE1 9UX
Tel: 020-7928 8000 Fax: 020-7922 7960
Web: www.megastar.co.uk *Editor:* Peter Hill

THE DAILY TELEGRAPH
1 Canada Square, Canary Wharf, London E14 5DT
Tel: 020-7538 5000 Fax: 020-7538 6242
Web: www.telegraph.co.uk *Editor:* Charles Moore

FINANCIAL TIMES
1 Southwark Bridge, London SE1 9HL
Tel: 020-7873 3000 Fax: 020-7873 3076
Web: www.ft.com *Editor:* Andrew Gowers

THE GUARDIAN
119 Farringdon Road, London EC1R 3ER
Tel: 020-7278 2332 Fax: 020-7837 2114
164 Deansgate, Manchester M60 2RR
Tel: 0161-832 7200 Fax: 0161-832 5351
Web: www.guardian.co.uk
Editor: Alan Rusbridger

THE HERALD
London Office, 3 Waterhouse Square,
138–142 Holborn, London EC1N 2NY
Tel: 020-7882 1060
Editor: Mark Douglas-Home

THE INDEPENDENT
Independent House, 191 Marsh Wall, London E14 9RS
Tel: 020-7005 2000 Fax: 020-7005 2999
Web: www.independent.co.uk
Editor-in-Chief: Simon Kelner

MORNING STAR
(formerly Daily Worker)
People's Press Printing Society Ltd, William Rust House,
52 Beachy Road, London E3 2NS Tel: 020-8510 0815
Fax: 020-8986 5694 *Editor:* John Haylett

THE SCOTSMAN
Barclay House, 108 Holyrood Road, Edinburgh EH8 8AS
Tel: 0131-620 8620 Fax: 0131-620 8615
Web: www.scotsman.com *Editor:* Iain Martin

THE SUN
News Group Newspapers Ltd, Virginia Street, London
E1 9XP Tel: 020-7782 4000 Fax: 020-7488 3253
Web: www.the-sun.co.uk *Editor:* Rebekah Wade

THE TIMES
1 Pennington Street, London E98 1TT
Tel: 020-7782 5000 Fax: 020-7488 3242
Web: www.thetimes.co.uk *Editor:* Robert Thomson

WEEKLY NEWSPAPERS

THE BUSINESS
292 Vauxhall Bridge Road, London SW1V 1DE
Tel: 020-7961 0000 Fax: 020-7961 0101
Editor-in-Chief: Andrew Neil

DAILY STAR SUNDAY
Express Newspapers, Ludgate House,
245 Blackfriars Road, London SE1 9UX
Tel: 020-7928 8000 Fax: 020-7922 7960
Editor: Hugh Whittow

INDEPENDENT ON SUNDAY
Independent House, 191 Marsh Wall, London E14 9RS
Tel: 020-7005 2000 Fax: 020-7005 2999
Web: www.independent.co.uk
Editor-at-Large: Janet Street-Porter

MAIL ON SUNDAY
Northcliffe House, 2 Derry Street, London W8 5TS
Tel: 020-7938 6000 Fax: 020-7937 3829
Web: www.mailonsunday.co.uk *Editor:* Peter Wright

NEWS OF THE WORLD
1 Virginia Street, London E1 9XR Tel: 020-7782 1000
Fax: 020-7583 9504 Web: www.newsoftheworld.co.uk
Editor: Andy Coulson

THE OBSERVER
119 Farringdon Road, London EC1R 3ER
Tel: 020-7278 2332 Fax: 020-7713 4250
Web: www.observer.co.uk *Editor:* Roger Alton

THE PEOPLE
(formerly Sunday People)
1 Canada Square, Canary Wharf, London E14 5AP
Tel: 020-7293 3000 Fax: 020-7293 3517
Web: www.thepeople.co.uk *Editor:* Mark Thomas

SCOTLAND ON SUNDAY
108 Holyrood Road, Edinburgh EH8 8AS
Tel: 0131-620 8620 Fax: 0131-620 8491
Web: www.scotlandonsunday.com *Editor:* John McLellan

SUNDAY EXPRESS
Ludgate House, 245 Blackfriars Road, London SE1 9UX
Tel: 020-7928 8000 Fax: 020-7620 1653
Web: www.express.co.uk *Editor:* Martin Townsend

SUNDAY HERALD
Scottish Media Publishing Ltd, 200 Renfield Street,
Glasgow G2 3PR Tel: 0141-302 7800 Fax: 0141-302 7815
Web: www.sundayherald.com *Editor:* Andrew Jaspan

SUNDAY LIFE
124 Royal Avenue, Belfast BT1 1EB Tel: 028-9026 4300
Fax: 028-9055 4507 *Editor:* Martin Lindsay

SUNDAY MAIL
1 Central Quay, Glasgow G3 8DA
Tel: 0141-309 3000 Fax: 0141-309 3582
Web: www.record-mail.co.uk/rm *Editor:* Allan Rennie

SUNDAY MIRROR
1 Canada Square, Canary Wharf, London E14 5AP
Tel: 020-7293 3000 Fax: 020-7293 3939
Web: www.mirror.co.uk *Editor:* Mark Thomas

SUNDAY POST
D.C. Thomson & Co. Ltd, 144 Port Dundas Road,
Glasgow G4 0HZ Tel: 0141-332 9933 Fax: 0141-331 1595
Editor: David Pollington

SUNDAY SPORT
19 Great Ancoats Street, Manchester M60 4BT
Tel: 0161-236 4466 Fax: 0161-236 4535
Editor: Paul Carter

SUNDAY TELEGRAPH
1 Canada Square, Canary Wharf, London E14 5DT
Tel: 020-7538 5000 Fax: 020-7513 2504
Editor: Dominic Lawson

THE SUNDAY TIMES
1 Pennington Street, London E98 1ST
Tel: 020-7782 5000 Fax: 020-7782 5658
Web: www.sunday-times.co.uk *Editor:* John Witherow

WALES ON SUNDAY
Thomson House, Havelock Street, Cardiff CF10 1XR
Tel: 029-2058 3583 Fax: 029-2058 3725
Editor: Tim Gordon

REGIONAL DAILY NEWSPAPERS

EAST ANGLIA
CAMBRIDGE EVENING NEWS
Winship Road, Milton, Cambs CB4 6PP
Tel: 01223-434434 Fax: 01223-434415
Editor: Colin Grant
EAST ANGLIAN DAILY TIMES
30 Lower Brook Street, Ipswich, Suffolk IP4 1AN
Tel: 01473-230023 Fax: 01473-324871 *Editor:* Terry Hunt
EASTERN DAILY PRESS
Prospect House, Rouen Road, Norwich NR1 1RE
Tel: 01603-628311 Fax: 01603-612930
Web: www.ecn.co.uk *Editor:* Peter Franzen
EVENING NEWS
Prospect House, Rouen Road, Norwich NR1 1RE
Tel: 01603-628311 Fax: 01603-219060
Editor: David Bourn

EAST MIDLANDS
BURTON MAIL
Burton Daily Mail Ltd, 65–68 High Street,
Burton on Trent DE14 1LE Tel: 01283-512345
Fax: 01283-515351 *Editor:* Paul Hazeldine
CHRONICLE & ECHO, NORTHAMPTON
Northamptonshire Newspapers Ltd, Upper Mounts,
Northampton NN1 3HR Tel: 01604-467000
Fax: 01604-467190 *Editor:* Mark Edwards
DERBY EVENING TELEGRAPH
Northcliffe House, Meadow Road, Derby DE1 2DW
Tel: 01332-291111 Fax: 01322-253027
Web: www.thisisderbyshire.co.uk *Editor:* Mike Norton
THE LEICESTER MERCURY
St George Street, Leicester LE1 9FQ Tel: 0116-251 2512
Fax: 0116-253 0645 *Editor:* Nick Carter
NOTTINGHAM EVENING POST
Castle Wharf House, Nottingham NG1 7EU
Tel: 0115-948 2000 Fax: 0115-964 4049
Web: www.thisisnottingham.co.uk *Editor:* Graham Glen

LONDON
EVENING STANDARD
Northcliffe House, 2 Derry Street, London W8 5EE
Tel: 020-7938 6000
Web: www.thisislondon.com *Editor:* Veronica Wadley

NORTH
EVENING CHRONICLE
Newcastle Chronicle and Journal Ltd, Groat Market,
Newcastle upon Tyne NE1 1ED Tel: 0191-232 7500
Fax: 0191-232 2256 *Editor:* Paul Robertson
EVENING GAZETTE
Gazette Media Company Ltd, Borough Road, Middlesbrough
TS1 3AZ Tel: 01642-245401 Fax: 01642-232014
Editor: Steve Dyson
HARTLEPOOL MAIL
Northeast Press Ltd, New Clarence House, Wesley Square,
Hartlepool TS24 8BX Tel: 01429-274441 Fax: 01429-869024
Editor: Paul Napier
THE JOURNAL
Groat Market, Newcastle upon Tyne NE1 1ED
Tel: 0191-232 7500 Fax: 0191-261 8869
Editor: Gerard Henderson
NORTH-WEST EVENING MAIL
Newspaper House, Abbey Road, Barrow-in-Furness, Cumbria
LA14 5QS Tel: 01229-840150 Fax: 01229-840164/832141
Editor: Steve Brauner

THE NORTHERN ECHO
Priestgate, Darlington, Co. Durham DL1 1NF
Tel: 01325-381313 Fax: 01325-380539
Editor: Peter Barron
THE SUNDAY SUN
Groat Market, Newcastle upon Tyne NE1 1ED
Tel: 0191-201 6251 Fax: 0191-230 0238
Editor: Peter Montellier
SUNDERLAND ECHO
Echo House, Pennywell, Sunderland, Tyne & Wear SR4 9ER
Tel: 0191-501 5800 Fax: 0191-534 5975
Web: www.sunderlandtoday.co.uk *Editor:* Rob Lawson

NORTH WEST
BOLTON EVENING NEWS
Newspaper House, Churchgate, Bolton, Lancs BL1 1DE
Tel: 01204-522345 Fax: 01204-365068
Web: www.thisisbolton.co.uk
DAILY POST
PO Box 48, Old Hall Street, Liverpool L69 3EB
Tel: 0151-227 2000 Fax: 0151-472 2474
Editor: Jane Wolstenholme
THE GAZETTE, BLACKPOOL
Blackpool Gazette & Herald Ltd, Avroe House, Avroe
Crescent, Blackpool Business Park, Squires Gate, Blackpool
FY4 2DP Tel: 01253-400888 Fax: 01253-361870
Web: www.blackpoolgazette.co.uk
Editor: David Helliwell
LANCASHIRE EVENING POST
Oliver's Place, Fulwood, Preston PR2 9ZA
Tel: 01772-254841 Fax: 01772-880173
Editor: Simon Reynolds
LANCASHIRE EVENING TELEGRAPH
Newspaper House, High Street, Blackburn BB1 1HT
Tel: 01254-678678 Web: www.thisislancashire.co.uk
Editor: Kevin Young
LIVERPOOL ECHO
PO Box 48, Old Hall Street, Liverpool L69 3EB
Tel: 0151-227 2000 Fax: 0151-236 4682
Web: www.liverpool.com *Editor:* Mark Dickinson
MANCHESTER EVENING NEWS
164 Deansgate, Manchester M60 2RD
Tel: 0161-832 7200 Fax: 0161-834 3814
Editor: Paul Horrocks
OLDHAM CHRONICLE
PO Box 47, Union Street, Oldham, Lancs OL1 1EQ
Tel: 0161-633 2121 Fax: 0161-627 0905
Web: www.oldham-chronicle.co.uk *Editor:* Jim Williams

SOUTH EAST
EVENING ECHO
Newspaper House, Chester Hall Lane, Basildon, Essex
SS14 3BL Tel: 01268-522792 Fax: 01268-469281
Editor: Martin McNeill
MEDWAY MESSENGER
395 High Street, Chatham, Kent ME4 4PQ
Tel: 01634-830600 Fax: 01634-829484
THE NEWS, PORTSMOUTH
The News Centre, Hilsea, Portsmouth PO2 9SX
Tel: 023-9266 4488 Fax: 023-9267 3363
Web: www.thenews.co.uk *Editor:* Mike Gilson
READING EVENING POST
8 Tessa Road, Reading, Berks RG1 8NS
Tel: 0118-918 3000 Fax: 0118-959 9363
Editor: Andy Murrill

THE SOUTHERN DAILY ECHO
Newspaper House, Test Lane, Redbridge, Southampton
SO16 9JX Tel: 023-8042 4777 Fax: 023-8042 4770
Editor: Ian Murray

SWINDON EVENING ADVERTISER
100 Victoria Road, Old Town, Swindon SN1 3BE
Tel: 01793-528144 Fax: 01793-542434
Web: www.thisiswiltshire.co.uk *Editor:* Simon O'Neill

SOUTH WEST

THE BATH CHRONICLE
Bath Newspapers, Windsor House, Windsor Bridge, Bath
BA2 3AU Tel: 01225-322322 Fax: 01225-322291
Editor: David Gledhill

BRISTOL EVENING POST
Temple Way, Bristol BS99 7HD Tel: 0117-934 3000
Editor: Mike Lowe

THE CITIZEN
Gloucestershire Newspapers Ltd, St John's Lane, Gloucester
GL1 2AY Tel: 01452-424442 Fax: 01452-420664
Editor: Ian Mean

DORSET ECHO
Newscom, Fleet House, Hampshire Road, Weymouth, Dorset
DT4 9XD Tel: 01305-830930 Fax: 01305-830956
Editor: David Murdock

EVENING HERALD
17 Brest Road, Derriford Business Park, Plymouth, Devon PL6
5AA Tel: 01752-765529 Fax: 01752-765527
Web: www.thisisplymouth.co.uk *Editor:* Alan Qualtrough

EXPRESS & ECHO
Express & Echo Publications Ltd, Heron Road, Sowton,
Exeter, Devon EX2 7NF Tel: 01392-442211
Fax: 01392-442294/442287 *Editor:* Steve Hall

GLOUCESTERSHIRE ECHO
Cheltenham Newspaper Co. Ltd, 1 Clarence Parade,
Cheltenham, Glos GL50 3NY Tel: 01242-271900
Fax: 01242-271803 *Editor:* Anita Syvret

SUNDAY INDEPENDENT WEST OF ENGLAND
Southern Newspapers plc, Burrington Way, Plymouth
PL5 3LN Tel: 01752-206600 Fax: 01752-206164
Editor: Nikki Rowlands

WESTERN DAILY PRESS
Bristol Evening Post and Press Ltd, Temple Way, Bristol BS99
7HD Tel: 0117-934 3000 Fax: 0117-934 3574
Web: www.westpress.co.uk *Editor:* Terry Manners

THE WESTERN MORNING NEWS
Brest Road, Derriford, Plymouth PL6 5AA
Tel: 01752-765500 Fax: 01752-765535
Editor: Barrie Williams

WEST MIDLANDS

BIRMINGHAM EVENING MAIL
PO Box 78, Weaman Street, Birmingham B4 6AY
Tel: 0121-236 3366 Fax: 0121-233 0271
Editor: Roger Borrell

THE BIRMINGHAM POST
PO Box 18, 28 Colmore Circus, Birmingham B4 6AX
Tel: 0121-236 3366 Fax: 0121-625 1105
Acting Editor: Roger Borrell

COVENTRY EVENING TELEGRAPH
Corporation Street, Coventry CV1 1FP
Tel: 024-7663 3633 Fax: 024-7655 0869
Editor: Alan Kirby

EXPRESS & STAR
Queen Street, Wolverhampton WV1 1ES
Tel: 01902-313131 Fax: 01902-319721
Web: www.westmidlands.com

THE SENTINEL
Staffordshire Sentinel Newspapers Ltd, Sentinel House,
Etruria, Stoke-on-Trent ST1 5SS Tel: 01782-602525
Fax: 01782-602616 Web: www.thisisstaffordshire.co.uk
Editor: Sean Dooley

SHROPSHIRE STAR
Ketley, Telford TF1 5HU Tel: 01952-242424
Fax: 01952-254605 *Editor:* Sarah Jane Smith

SUNDAY MERCURY
Colmore Circus, Birmingham B4 6AZ Tel: 0121-234 5567
Fax: 0121-233 0271 *Editor:* David Brookes

WORCESTER EVENING NEWS
Berrows House, Hylton Road, Worcester WR2 5JX
Tel: 01905-748200 Fax: 01905-748009
Web: www.thisisworcester *Editor:* Stewart Gilbert

YORKSHIRE/HUMBERSIDE

EVENING COURIER
PO Box 19, King Cross Street, Halifax HX1 2SF
Tel: 01422-260200 Fax: 01422-260341
Web: www.halifaxcourier.co.uk *Editor:* John Furbisher

EVENING PRESS
York and County Press, PO Box 29, 76–86 Walmgate, York
YO1 9YN Tel: 01904-653051 Fax: 01904-612853
Web: www.thisisyork.co.uk

GRIMSBY TELEGRAPH
80 Cleethorpe Road, Grimsby, North East Lincolnshire
DN31 3EH Tel: 01472-360360 Fax: 01472-372257
Web: www.thisisgrimsby.co.uk Editor: Peter Moore

THE HUDDERSFIELD DAILY EXAMINER
Examiner News & Information Services Ltd,
PO Box A26, Queen Street South, Huddersfield HD1 2TD
Tel: 01484-430000 Fax: 01484-437789
Web: www.examiner.co.uk

THE STAR
York Street, Sheffield S1 1PU Tel: 0114-276 7676
Fax: 0114-272 5978 Web: www.sheffweb.co.uk
Editor: Peter Charlton

TELEGRAPH & ARGUS
Hall Ings, Bradford, West Yorkshire BD1 1JR
Tel: 01274-729511 Fax: 01274-723634
Web: www.thisisbradford.co.uk
Editor: Perry Austin-Clarke

YORKSHIRE EVENING POST
PO Box 168, Wellington Street, Leeds LS1 1RF
Tel: 0113-2432701 Fax: 0113-2388535
Editor: N. R. Hodgkinson

YORKSHIRE POST
Wellington Street, Leeds LS1 1RF Tel: 0113-243 2701
Fax: 0113-238 8537 Web: www.yorkshireposttoday.co.uk
Editor: Rachel Campey

SCOTLAND

ABERDEEN EVENING EXPRESS
Aberdeen Journals Ltd, PO Box 43, Lang Stracht, Mastrick,
Aberdeen AB15 6DF Tel: 01224-690222 Fax: 01224-699575
Editor: Donald Martin

THE COURIER AND ADVERTISER
D.C. Thomson & Co. Ltd, 80 Kingsway East, Dundee DD4
8SL Tel: 01382-223131 Fax: 01382-454590
Web: www.thecourier.co.uk

DUNDEE EVENING TELEGRAPH AND POST
D.C. Thomson & Co. Ltd, 80 Kingsway East, Dundee DD4 8SL
Tel: 01382-223131 Fax: 01382-454590
Web: www.eveningtelegraph.co.uk

EDINBURGH EVENING NEWS
108 Holyrood Road, Edinburgh EH8 8AS
Tel: 0131-620 8620 Fax: 0131-620 8696
Editor: Ian Stewart

GLASGOW EVENING TIMES
200 Renfield Street, Glasgow G2 3PR
Tel: 0141-302 7000 Fax: 0141-302 6600
Web: www.eveningtimes.co.uk
Editor: Charles McGhee

INVERNESS COURIER
PO Box 13, 9–11 Bank Lane, Inverness IV1 1QW
Tel: 01463-233059 Fax: 01463-243439
Editor: Jim Love

PAISLEY DAILY EXPRESS
Scottish and Universal Newspapers Ltd,
14 New Street, Paisley, Renfrewshire PA1 1YA
Tel: 0141-887 7911 Fax: 0141-889 7148
Web: www.insidescotland.co.uk
Acting Editor: Anne Dalrymple

THE PRESS AND JOURNAL
Lang Stracht, Aberdeen AB15 6DF Tel: 01224-690222
Web: www.thisisnorthscotland.co.uk
Editor: Derek Tucker

WALES
SOUTH WALES ARGUS
South Wales Argus Ltd, Cardiff Road, Maesglas, Newport,
Gwent NP20 3QN Tel: 01633-777219 Fax: 01633-777202
Editor: Gerry Keighley

SOUTH WALES ECHO
Thomson House, Havelock Street, Cardiff CF10 1XR
Tel: 029-2058 3622/2022 3333 Fax: 029-2058 3624
Editor: Alastair Milburn

THE WESTERN MAIL
Thomson House, Havelock Street, Cardiff CF10 1XR
Tel: 029-2058 3583 Fax: 029-2058 3652
Editor: Alan Edmunds

NORTHERN IRELAND
BELFAST TELEGRAPH
124–144 Royal Avenue, Belfast BT1 1EB Tel: 028-9026 4000
Fax: 028-9033 1332 Web: www.belfasttelegraph.co.uk
Editor: Edmund Curran

IRISH NEWS
113–117 Donegall Street, Belfast BT1 2GE
Tel: 028-9032 2226 Fax: 028-9033 7505
Web: www.irishnews.com *Editor:* Noel Doran

NEWS LETTER
46–56 Boucher Crescent, Boucher Road, Belfast BT12 6QY
Tel: 028-9068 0000 Fax: 028-9066 4412
Web: www.newsletter.co.uk *Editor:* Nigel Wareing

CHANNEL ISLANDS
GUERNSEY PRESS AND STAR
Braye Road, Vale, Guernsey GY1 3BW
Tel: 01481-240240 Fax: 01481-240235
Editor: Richard Digard

JERSEY EVENING POST
PO Box 582, Five Oaks, St Saviour, Jersey JE4 8XQ
Tel: 01534-611611 Fax: 01534-611622
Editor: Chris Bright

PERIODICALS

ACCOUNTANCY
40 Bernard Street, London WC1N 1LD Tel: 020-7833 3291
Web: www.accountancymagazine.com
Editor: Chris Quick

ACCOUNTANCY AGE
VNU Business Publications, VNU House,
32–34 Broadwick Street, London W1A 2HG
Tel: 020-7316 9236 Web: www.accountancyage.com
Editor: Damian Wild

ACCOUNTING & BUSINESS
Association of Chartered Certified Accountants,
10–11 Lincolns Inn Fields, London WC2A 3BP
Tel: 020-7396 5966 Web: www.accaglobal.com
Editor: John Rogers Prosser

ACE TENNIS MAGAZINE
Tennis GB, 9–11 North End Road, London W14 8ST
Tel: 020-7605 8000 *Editor:* Nigel Billen

ACTIVE LIFE
Computer Publishing, 221–223 High Street, Berkhamstead,
Herts HP4 1AD Tel: 01442-289600 *Editor:* Paul Jacques

ACUMEN
6 The Mount, Higher Furzeham, Brixham, South Devon
TQ5 8QY Tel: 01803-851098 *Editor:* Patricia Oxley

AEROPLANE MONTHLY
IPC Magazines Ltd, King's Reach Tower, Stamford Street,
London SE1 9LS Tel: 020-7261 5849
Web: www.aeroplanemonthly.com *Editor:* Michael Oakey

AFRICA CONFIDENTIAL
Blackwell Publishers Ltd,
73 Farringdon Road, London EC1M 3JQ
Tel: 020-7831 3511 Web: www.africa-confidential.com
Editor: Patrick Smith

AFRICAN BUSINESS
IC Publications Ltd, 7 Coldbath Square, London EC1R 4LQ
Tel: 020-7713 7711 *Editor:* Anver Versi

AIR INTERNATIONAL
Key Publishing Ltd, PO Box 100, Stamford, Lincs PE9 1XQ
Tel: 01780-755131 *Editor:* Malcolm English

AIR PICTORIAL INTERNATIONAL
HPC Publishing, Drury Lane, St Leonards-on-Sea, East Sussex
TN38 9BJ Tel: 01424-720477 *Editor:* Barry C. Wheeler

AMATEUR GARDENING
IPC Media Ltd, Westover House, West Quay Road, Poole,
Dorset BH15 1JG Tel: 01202-440840
Editor: Tim Rumball

AMATEUR PHOTOGRAPHER
(incorporating Photo Technique)
IPC Magazines Ltd, King's Reach Tower, Stamford Street,
London SE1 9LS Tel: 020-7261 5100
Editor: Garry Coward-Williams

AMATEUR STAGE
Platform Publications Ltd, Hampden House,
2 Weymouth Street, London W1W 5BT Tel: 020-7636 4343
Web: www.amdram.org.uk/amstagel.htm
Editor: Charles Vance

AMBIT
17 Priory Gardens, London N6 5QY Tel: 020-8340 3566
Web: www.ambitmag.co.uk *Editor:* Martin Bax

AN MAGAZINE
AN: The Artists Information Company,
1st Floor, 7–15 Pink Lane, Newcastle upon Tyne NE1 5DW
Tel: 0191-241 8000 Web: www.a-n.co.uk

ANGLING TIMES
EMAP Active, Bushfield House, Orton Centre, Peterborough
PE2 5UW Tel: 01733-232600 *Editor:* Richard Lee

ANIMALS AND YOU
D.C. Thomson & Co Ltd, Albert Square, Dundee DD1 9QJ
Tel: 01382-223131

ANTIQUES & ART INDEPENDENT
PO Box 1945, Comely Bank, Edinburgh EH4 1AB
Tel: 07000-268478 Web: www.antiquesnews.co.uk
Publisher/Editor: Tony Keniston

ANTIQUES AND COLLECTABLES
Merricks Media Ltd, Charlotte House, 12 Charlotte Street,
Bath BA1 2NE Tel: 01225-786800
Web: www.antiques-collectables.co.uk
Editor: Diana Cambridge

APOLLO
1–2 Castle Lane, London SW1E 6DR Tel: 020-7233 6640
Editor: David Ekserdjian

THE ARCHITECTS' JOURNAL
EMAP Business Communications, 151 Rosebery Avenue,
London EC1R 4GB Tel: 020-7505 6700
Editor: Isabel Allen

ARCHITECTURAL DESIGN
John Wiley & Sons Ltd, 4th Floor, International House, Ealing
Broadway Centre, London W5 5DB Tel: 020-8326 3800
Web: www.wiley.co.uk/ad/ *Editor:* Helen Castle

THE ARCHITECTURAL REVIEW
EMAP Construct, 151 Rosebury Avenue, London EC1R 4GB
Tel: 020-7505 6725 Web: www.arplus.com
Editor: Peter Davey

ARCHITECTURE TODAY
161 Rosebery Avenue, London EC1R 4QX Tel: 020-7837 0143
Editors: Ian Latham, Mark Swenarton

ARENA
EMAP East, Endeavour House,
189 Shaftesbury Avenue, London WC2H 8JG
Tel: 020-7437 9011 *Editor:* Anthony Noguera

ART BUSINESS TODAY
The Fine Art Trade Guild, 16–18 Empress Place, London
SW6 1TT Tel: 020-7381 6616
Web: www.fineart.co.uk/Abtonline/abt.htm
Editor: Mike Sims

ART MONTHLY
4th Floor, 28 Charing Cross Road, London WC2H 0DB
Tel: 020-7240 0389 Web: www.artmonthly.co.uk
Editor: Patricia Bickers

THE ART NEWSPAPER
70 South Lambeth Road, London SW8 1RL
Tel: 020-7735 3331 Web: www.theartnewspaper.com
Editor: Anna Somers Cocks

ART REVIEW
Art Review Ltd, Hereford House, 23–24 Smithfield Street,
London EC1A 9LB Tel: 020-7236 4880
Web: www.art-review.com
Editor: Meredith Etherington-Smith

ARTISTS AND ILLUSTRATORS
The Fitzpatrick Building, 188–194 York Way, London N7 9QR
Tel: 020-7700 8500 *Editor:* James Hobbs

ASIAN TIMES
Ethnic Media Group, Unit 2.01, Technology Centre, 65
Whitechapel Road, London E1 1DU Tel: 020-7650 2000
Editor: Emenike Pio

ASTRONOMY NOW
Pole Star Publications, PO Box 175, Tonbridge, Kent TN10 4ZY
Tel: 01903-266165 *Managing Editor:* Steven Young

ATHLETICS WEEKLY
Descartes Publishing Ltd, 83 Park Road, Peterborough PE1 2TN
Tel: 01733-898440 *Editor:* Jason Henderson

THE AUTHOR
84 Drayton Gardens, London SW10 9SB
Tel: 020-7373 6642 *Editor:* Fanny Blake

AUTO EXPRESS
Dennis Publishing Ltd, 30 Cleveland Street, London W1T 4JD
Tel: 020-7907 6200 Web: www.autoexpress.co.uk
Editor: David Johns

AUTOCAR
Haymarket Publishing Ltd, 60 Waldegrave Road, Teddington,
Middlesex TW11 8LG Tel: 020-8267 5630
Editor: Steve Fowler

BALANCE
Diabetes UK, 10 Parkway, London NW1 7AA
Tel: 020-7424 1000 Web: www.diabetes.org.uk
Editor: Martin Cullen

THE BANKER
Tabernacle Court, 16–28 Tabernacle Street, London EC2 4DD
Tel: 020-7382 8000 *Editor-in-Chief:* Stephen Timewell

BAPTIST TIMES
PO Box 54, 129 Broadway, Didcot, Oxon OX11 8XB
Tel: 01235-517670 *Editor:* Hazel Southam

THE BEANO
D.C. Thomson & Co. Ltd, Albert Square, Dundee DD1 9QJ
Tel: 01382-223131

BELLA
H. Bauer Publishing, Academic House, 24–28 Oval Road,
London NW1 7DT Tel: 020-7241 8000
Editor: Rebecca Fleming

BEST
The National Magazine Company,
33 Broadwick Street, London W1F 0DQ Tel: 020-7439 5000
Editor: Louise Court

THE BIG ISSUE
1–5 Wandsworth Road, London SW8 2LN
Tel: 020-7526 3200
Editor: Matt Ford

BIKE
EMAP Automotive Ltd, Media House, Lynchwood,
Peterborough PE2 6EA Tel: 01733-468000
Editor: Tim Thompson

BIRDING WORLD
Sea Lawn, Coast Road, Cley next the Sea, Holt, Norfolk
NR25 7RZ Tel: 01263-740913
Web: www.birdingworld.co.uk *Editor:* Steve Gantlett

BIRDWATCH
Solo Publishing Ltd, 3rd Floor, Leroy House,
436 Essex Road, London N1 3QP
Tel: 020-7704 9495 Web: www.birdwatch.co.uk
Editor: Dominic Mitchell

BIZARRE
IFG, 9 Dallington Street, London EC1V 0BQ
Tel: 020-7687 7000 Web: www.bizarremag.com
Editor: Ben Raworth

BLISS!
EMAP Elan Ltd, Endeavour House,
189 Shaftesbury Avenue, London WC2H 8JG
Tel: 020-7437 9011 Web: www.blissmag.co.uk
Editor: Helen Johnston

BLUEPRINT
ETP Ltd, Rosebery House, 41 Springfield Road, Chelmsford
CM2 6JJ Tel: 01245-491717 *Editor:* Grant Gibson

BMA NEWS
British Medical Association, BMA House, Tavistock Square,
London WC1H 9JP Tel: 020-7383 6122
Joint Editors: Julia Bell, Caroline Jones

BOARDS
Yachting Press Ltd, 196 Eastern Esplanade, Southend-on-
Sea, Essex SS1 3AB Tel: 01702-582245 Web:
www.boards.co.uk
Editor: Bill Dawes

BOOK AND MAGAZINE COLLECTOR
Diamond Publishing Ltd, 45 St Mary's Road, London W5 5RQ
Tel: 020-8579 1082 *Editor:* Crispin Jackson

THE BOOKSELLER
VNU Entertainment Media Ltd, 5th Floor, Endeavour House,
189 Shaftesbury Avenue, London WC2H 8TJ
Tel: 020-7420 6006 Web: www.thebookseller.com
Editor: Nicholas Clee

THE BRITISH JOURNAL OF PHOTOGRAPHY
Timothy Benn Publishing, 39 Earlham Street, London
WC2H 9LT Tel: 020-7306 7000 Web: www.bjphoto.co.uk
Editor: Jon Tarrant

BRITISH JOURNALISM REVIEW
BJR Publishing Ltd, c/o Sage Publications,
6 Bonhill Street, London EC2A 4PU Tel: 020-7374 0645
Editor: Bill Hagerty

BRITISH MEDICAL JOURNAL
BMA House, Tavistock Square, London WC1H 9JR
Tel: 020-7387 4499 Web: www.bmj.com
Editor: Richard Smith

BROADCAST
EMAP Media, 33–39 Bowling Green Lane, London EC1R 0DA
Tel: 020-7505 8014   *Editor:* Conor Dignam

BUILDING
The Builder Group plc, 7th Floor, Anchorage House,
2 Clove Crescent, London E14 2BE Tel: 020-7560 4000
Editor: Adrian Barrick

BUILDING DESIGN
CMP Information Ltd, Ludgate House,
245 Blackfriars Road, London SE1 9UY Tel: 020-7861 6467
Editor: Robert Booth

BUILT ENVIRONMENT
Alexandrine Press, 1 The Farthings, Marcham, Oxon OX13 6QD
Tel: 01865-391518 *Editor:* Prof. Sir Peter Hall

BURLINGTON MAGAZINE
14–16 Duke's Road, London WC1H 9SZ Tel: 020-7388 1228
Editor: Richard Shone

BUSINESS LIFE
Cedar Communications, Haymarket House, 1 Oxenden
Street, London SW1Y 4EE Tel: 020-7925 2544
Web: www.cedarcom.co.uk *Editor:* Alex Finer

BUSINESS SCOTLAND
Peebles Media Group, Bergius House, Clifton Street, Glasgow
G3 7LA Tel: 0141-567 6000 *Editor:* Graham Lironi

BUSINESS TRAVELLER
Perry Publications Ltd, Nestor House, Playhouse Yard, London
EC4V 5EX Tel: 020-7778 0000 Web: www.btonline.co.uk
Editor: Julia Brookes

CAMPAIGN
Haymarket Business Publications Ltd, 22 Bute Gardens, London
W6 7HN Tel: 020-8267 4656 *Editor:* Caroline Marshall

CANAL & RIVERBOAT
PO Box 618, Norwich NR7 0QT Tel: 01603-708930
Web: www.canalandriverboat.com *Editor:* Chris Cattrall

CAR
EMAP Automotive Ltd, 3rd Floor, Media House, Lynchwood,
Peterborough PE2 6EA Tel: 01733-468000
Editor: Greg Fountain

CAR MECHANICS
Cudham Tithe Barn, Berrys Hill, Cudham, Kent TW16 3AG
Tel: 01959-541444 *Editor:* Phil Weeden

CARAVAN MAGAZINE
IPC Country & Leisure Media Ltd, Focus House, Dingwall
Avenue, Croydon CR9 2TA Tel: 020-8774 0600
Web: www.caravanmagazine.co.uk *Editor:* Steve Rowe

CARIBBEAN TIMES
(incorporating African Times)
Ethnic Media Group, Unit 2.01, Technology Centre,
65 Whitehchapel Road, London E1 1DU Tel: 020-7650 2000
Editor: Ron Shillingford

CAROUSEL THE GUIDE TO CHILDREN'S BOOKS
The Saturn Centre, 54–76 Bissell Street, Birmingham B5 7HX
Tel: 0121-622 7458 Web: www.carouselguide.co.uk
Editor: Jenny Blanch

CATERER & HOTELKEEPER
Reed Business Information Ltd, Quadrant House,
The Quadrant, Sutton, Surrey SM2 5AS Tel: 020-8652 8680
Editor: Forbes Mutch

THE CATHOLIC HERALD
Herald House, Lambs Passage, Bunhill Row, London EC1Y 8TQ
Tel: 020-7588 3101 Web: www.catholicherald.co.uk
Editor: Dr William Oddie

CATHOLIC TIMES
1st Floor, St James's Buildings, Oxford Street, Manchester
M1 6FP Tel: 0161-236 8856 *Editor:* Stefano Hatfield

CHARTERED SECRETARY
16 Park Crescent, London W1B 1AH Tel: 020-7612 7045
Web: www.charteredsecretary.net *Editor:* Will Booth

CHAT
IPC Connect Ltd, King's Reach Tower, Stamford Street, London
SE1 9LS Tel: 020-7261 6565 Web: www.ipcmedia.com

CHILD EDUCATION
Scholastic Ltd, Villiers House, Clarendon Avenue,
Leamington Spa, Warks. CV32 5PR Tel: 01926-887799
Web: www.scholastic.co.uk *Editor:* Jeremy Sugden

THE CHINA QUARTERLY
School of Oriental and African Studies, Thornhaugh Street,
Russell Square, London WC1H 0XG Tel: 020-7898 4063
Editor: Dr Julia Strauss

CHOICE
1st Floor, 2 King Street, Peterborough PE1 1LT
Tel: 01733-555123 *Editor:* Norman Wright

CHRISTIAN HERALD
Christian Media, 96 Dominion Road, Worthing,
West Sussex BN14 8JP Tel: 01903-821082
Web: www.christianherald.org.uk

CHURCH OF ENGLAND NEWSPAPER
20–26 Brunswick Place, London N1 6DZ Tel: 020-7417 5800
Web: www.churchnewspaper.com

CHURCH TIMES
33 Upper Street, London N1 0PN Tel: 020-7359 4570
Web: www.churchtimes.co.uk *Editor:* Paul Handley

CLASSIC & SPORTS CAR
Haymarket Specialist Motoring Publications Ltd, Somerset
House, Somerset Road, Teddington, Middlesex TW11 8RT
Tel: 020-8267 5399 *Editor:* James Elliott

CLASSIC CARS
EMAP Automotive Ltd, Media House, Lynchwood,
Peterborough Business Park, Peterborough PE2 6EA
Tel: 01733-468219 *Editor:* Martyn Moore

CLASSICAL MUSIC
Rhinegold Publishing Ltd, 241 Shaftesbury Avenue, London
WC2H 8TF Tel: 020-7333 1742 Web: www.rhinegold.co.uk
Editor: Keith Clarke

CLASSICS
SPL, Berwick House, 8–10 Knoll Rise, Orpington, Kent
BR6 0PS Tel: 01689-887200 *Editor:* Tim Morgan

CLIMBER
Warners Group Publications plc, West Street, Bourne, Lincs
PE10 9PH Tel: 01778-391117 *Editor:* Bernard Newman

COIN NEWS
Token Publishing Ltd, Orchard House, Duchy Road,
Heathpark, Honiton, Devon EX14 1YD Tel: 01404-46972
Editor: John W. Mussell

COMPANY
National Magazine House, 72 Broadwick Street, London
W1V 2BP Tel: 020-7439 5000 *Editor:* Sam Baker

COMPUTER WEEKLY
Reed Business Information Ltd, Quadrant House,
The Quadrant, Sutton, Surrey SM2 5AS Tel: 020-8652 3122
Web: www.computerweekly.com *Editor:* Karl Schneider

COMPUTING
VNU Business Publications, VNU House,
32–34 Broadwick Street, London W1A 2HG
Tel: 020-7316 9158 Web: www.computingnet.co.uk
Editor: Colin Barker

CONDÉ NAST TRAVELLER
Vogue House, Hanover Square, London W1S 1JU
Tel: 020-7499 9080 Web: www.cntraveller.co.uk
Editor: Sarah Miller

CONTEMPORARY
Suite K101, Tower Bridge Business Complex, 100 Clements
Road, London SE16 4DG Tel: 020-7740 1704
Web: www.contemporary-magazine.com
Editor: Keith Patrick

COSMOPOLITAN
National Magazine House, 72 Broadwick Street, London
W1V 2BP Tel: 020-7439 5000
Editor-in-Chief: Lorraine Candy

COUNTRY HOMES AND INTERIORS
IPC Magazines Ltd, King's Reach Tower, Stamford Street,
London SE1 9LS Tel: 020-7261 6451
Editor: Deborah Barker

COUNTRY LIFE
IPC Media Ltd, King's Reach Tower, Stamford Street, London
SE1 9LS Tel: 020-7261 7058 *Editor:* Clive Aslet

COUNTRY LIVING
National Magazine House, 72 Broadwick Street, London
W1F 9EP Tel: 020-7439 5000 Web: www.countryliving.co.uk
Editor: Susy Smith

COUNTRY WALKING
EMAP Active Ltd, Bretton Court, Bretton, Peterborough
PE3 8DZ Tel: 01733-264666 *Editor:* Jonathon Manning

CRITICAL QUARTERLY
Contributions Ollie Garrett, School of English, Queen's
Building, The Queen's Drive, Exeter EX4 4QH
Web: www.criticalquarterly.co.uk

CYCLE SPORT
IPC Leisure & Media Ltd, 5th Floor, Focus House,
9 Dingwall Avenue, Croydon CR9 2TA
Tel: 020-8774 0889
Managing Editor: Robert Garbutt

DAIRY FARMER
CMP Information Ltd, Sovereign House, Sovereign Way,
Tonbridge, Kent TN9 1RW Tel: 01732-377273
Editor: Peter Hollinshead

DANCING TIMES
The Dancing Times Ltd, 45–47 Clerkenwell Green,
London EC1R 0EB Tel: 020-7250 3006
Web: www.dancing-times.co.uk *Editor:* Mary Clarke

DECANTER
IPC Country & Leisure Media Ltd, 1st Floor, Broadway House,
2–6 Fulham Broadway, London SW6 1AA
Tel: 020-7610 3929 Web: www.decanter.com

DISABILITY NOW
6 Market Road, London N7 9PW Tel: 020-7619 7323
Web: www.disabilitynow.org.uk *Editor:* Mary Wilkinson

DIVER
55 High Street, Teddington, Middlesex TW11 8HA
Tel: 020-8943 4288 Web: divernet@www.divernet.com
Editor: Nigel Eaton

DRAPERS
EMAP Communications, Greater London House, Hampstead
Road, London NW1 7EJ Tel: 020-7391 3300
Web: www.drapersrecord.com
Editor-in-Chief: Eric Musgrave

EARLY MUSIC
Oxford University Press, 70 Baker Street, London W1M 7DN
Tel: 020-7616 5902 Web: www.em.oupjournals.org
Editor: Tess Knighton

THE ECOLOGIST
Unit 18, Chelsea Wharf, 15 Lots Road, London SW10 0QJ
Tel: 020-7351 3578

ECONOMICA
STICERD, London School of Economics, Houghton Street,
London WC2A 2AE Tel: 020-7955 7855
Editors: Prof. F. A. Cowell, Prof. A. Manning,
Prof. T. Ellingsen

THE ECONOMIST
25 St James's Street, London SW1A 1HG
Tel: 020-7830 7000 Web: www.economist.com
Editor: Bill Emmott

ELECTRICAL REVIEW
Cumulus Business Media, Anne Boleyn House, 9–13 Ewell
Road, Cheam, Surrey SM3 8BZ Tel: 020-8652 8736
Managing Editor: Bill Evett

ELLE (UK)
Hachette Filipacchi UK, 16–18 Berners Street, London
W1T 3LN Tel: 020-7150 7000 *Editor:* Sarah Bailey

EMPIRE
Endeavour House, 189 Shaftesbury Avenue, London
WC2H 8JG Tel: 020-7439 9011
Web: www.empireonline.com

THE ENGINEER
Centaur Communications Ltd, St Giles House, 50 Poland
Street, London W1F 7AX Tel: 020-7970 4106
Web: www.e4engineering.com

THE ENGLISH GARDEN
Romsey Publishing Ltd, Jubilee House, 2 Jubilee Place,
London SW3 3TQ Tel: 020-7751 4800 *Editor:* Julia Watson

THE EROTIC REVIEW
4th Floor, Maddox House, 1 Maddox Street, London W1S 2PZ
Tel: 020-7439 8999 Web: www.theeroticreview.co.uk
Editor: Rowan Pelling

ESQUIRE
National Magazine House, 72 Broadwick Street, London
W1F 9EP Tel: 020-7439 5000 *Editor:* Simon Tiffin

ESSENTIALS
IPC Media, King's Reach Tower, Stamford Street, London
SE1 9LS Tel: 020-7261 6970 *Editor:* Karen Livermore

EUROPEAN CHEMICAL NEWS
Reed Business Information, Quadrant House,
The Quadrant, Sutton, Surrey SM2 5AS Tel: 020-8652 8147
Editor: John Baker

THE FACE
EMAP Elan Ltd, Exmouth House, Pine Street, London EC1R
0JL Tel: 020-7689 9999 *Editor:* Neil Stevenson

FAMILY LAW
21 St Thomas Street, Bristol BS1 6JS Tel: 0117-923 0600
Web: www.familylaw.co.uk
Editors: Elizabeth Walsh, Miles McColl

FARMERS WEEKLY
Reed Business Information, Quadrant House,
The Quadrant, Sutton, Surrey SM2 5AS Tel: 020-8652 4911
Web: www.fwi.co.uk *Editor:* Stephen Howe

FHM
EMAP Elan Network, Mappin House, 4 Winsley Street,
London W1W 8HF Tel: 020-7436 1515 Web: www.fhm.com
Editor: David Davies

THE FIELD
IPC Media Ltd, King's Reach Tower, Stamford Street, London
SE1 9LS Tel: 020-7261 5198 Web: www.thefield.co.uk

FILM REVIEW
Visual Imagination Ltd, 9 Blades Court, Deodar Road,
London SW15 2NU Tel: 020-8875 1520 *Editor:* Neil Corry

FINANCIAL ADVISER
FT Finance Ltd, Maple House, 149 Tottenham Court Road,
London W1P 9LL Tel: 020-7896 2525 *Editor:* Hal Austin

FIRE
Queensway House, 2 Queensway, Redhill, Surrey RH1 1QS
Tel: 01737-855431 *Editor:* Andrew Lynch

FISHING NEWS
Telephone House, 69–77 Paul Street, London EC2A 4LQ
Tel: 020-7017 4531 *Editor:* Tim Oliver

FLIGHT INTERNATIONAL
Reed Business Information Ltd, Quadrant House,
The Quadrant, Sutton, Surrey SM2 5AS Tel: 020-8652 3842
Web: www.flightinternational.com
Editor: Murdo Morrison

FORTEAN TIMES
Box 2409, London NW5 4NP Tel: 020-7687 7002
Web: www.forteantimes.com *Editors:* David Sutton

THE FRIEND
New Premier House, 150 Southampton Row, London
WC1B 5BQ Tel: 020-7387 7549 Web: www.thefriend.org
Editor: Harry Albright

THE GARDEN
4th Floor, Churchgate, New Road, Peterborough PE1 1TT
Tel: 01733-775775 *Editor:* Ian Hodgson

GAY TIMES
Ground Floor, Worldwide House, 116–134 Bayham Street,
London NW1 0BA Tel: 020-7482 2576
Editor: Vicky Powell

GEOGRAPHICAL JOURNAL
Royal Geographical Society (with the Institute of British
Geographers), Kensington Gore, London SW7 2AR
Tel: 020-7591 3026 *Editor:* Prof. A. Millinglon

GEOLOGICAL MAGAZINE
Cambridge University Press, The Edinburgh Building,
Shaftesbury Road, Cambridge CB2 2RU
Tel: 01223-312393

GLAMOUR
The Condé Nast Publications Ltd, 6–8 Old Bond Street, London
W15 4PH Tel: 020-7499 9080 Web: www.glamour.com
Editor: Jo Elvin

GOLF MONTHLY
IPC Magazines Ltd, King's Reach Tower, Stamford Street,
London SE1 9LS Tel: 020-7261 7237 *Editor:* Jane Carter

GOOD HOUSEKEEPING
National Magazine House, 72 Broadwick Street, London
W1F 9EP Tel: 020-7439 5000 Web: www.natmags.co.uk
Editor-in-Chief: Lindsay Nicholson

GQ
Condé Nast Publications, Vogue House, Hanover Square,
London W1S 1JU Tel: 020-7499 9080
Web: www.gq/magazine.co.uk *Editor:* Dylan Jones

GRANTA
2–3 Hanover Yard, Noel Road, London N1 8BE
Tel: 020-7704 9776 Web: www.granta.com
Editor: Ian Jack

GREEN FUTURES
Overseas House, 19–23 Ironmonger Row, London EC1V 3QN
Web: www.greenfutures.org.uk *Editor:* Martin Wright

THE GROCER
William Reed Publishing Ltd, Broadfield Park, Crawley, West
Sussex RH11 9RT Tel: 01293-613400
Web: www.foodanddrink.co.uk *Editor:* Julian Hunt

HARPERS & QUEEN
National Magazine House, 72 Broadwick Street, London
W1F 9EP Tel: 020-7439 5000 *Editor:* Lucy Yeomans

HELLO!
Wellington House, 69–71 Upper Ground, London SE1 9PQ
Tel: 020-7667 8700 *Editor:* Ronnie Whelan

HI-FI NEWS
IPC Country & Leisure Media Ltd, Focus House, Dingwall
Avenue, Croydon CR9 2TA Tel: 020-8774 0846
Editor: Steve Harris

HISTORY TODAY
20 Old Compton Street, London W1D 4TW
Tel: 020-7534 8000 *Editor:* Peter Furtado

HORSE & HOUND
IPC Media Ltd, King's Reach Tower, Stamford Street, London
SE1 9LS Tel: 020-7261 6315
Web: www.horseandhound.co.uk

HORSE AND RIDER
Haslemere House, Lower Street, Haslemere, Surrey GU27 2PE
Tel: 01428-651551
Web: www.horseandridermagazine.co.uk
Editor: Alison Bridge

HOSPITAL DOCTOR
Reed Healthcare Publishing, Quadrant House,
The Quadrant, Sutton, Surrey SM2 5AS Tel: 020-8652 8745
Editor: Mike Broad

HOUSE & GARDEN
Vogue House, Hanover Square, London W1S 1JU
Tel: 020-7499 9080 *Editor:* Susan Crewe

HOUSEBUILDER
56–64 Leonard Street, London EC2A 4JX
Tel: 020-7608 5130 Web: www.house-builder.co.uk

I-D MAGAZINE
124 Tabernacle Street, London EC2A 4SA
Tel: 020-7490 9710 *Editor:* Avril Mair

IDEAL HOME
IPC Media Ltd, King's Reach Tower, Stamford Street, London
SE1 9LS Tel: 020-7261 5000

IN BRITAIN
Romsey Publishing Group, Jubilee House,
2 Jubilee Place, London SW3 3TQ Tel: 020-7751 4800
Web: www.inbritain.co.uk *Editor:* Andrea Spain

INDEX ON CENSORSHIP
Lancaster House, 33 Islington High Street, London N1 9LH
Tel: 020-7278 2313 Web: www.indexoncensorship.org
Editor-in-Chief: Ursula Owen

INTERMEDIA
International Institute of Communications,
35 Portland Place, London W1B 1AE Tel: 020-7323 9622
Editor: Martin Sims

INTERNATIONAL AFFAIRS
Royal Institute of International Affairs, Chatham House,
10 St James's Square, London SW1Y 4LE
Tel: 020-7957 5700 Web: www.riia.org

INVESTORS CHRONICLE
Maple House, 149 Tottenham Court Road, London W1T 7LB
Tel: 020-7896 2525 *Editor:* Matthew Vincent

JANE'S DEFENCE WEEKLY
Sentinel House, 163 Brighton Road, Coulsdon, Surrey
CR5 2YH Tel: 020-8700 3700 *Editor:* Clifford Beal

JEWISH CHRONICLE
25 Furnival Street, London EC4A 1JT Tel: 020-7415 1500
Editor: Edward J. Temko

JEWISH TELEGRAPH
Telegraph House, 11 Park Hill, Bury Old Road, Prestwich,
Manchester M25 0HH Tel: 0161-740 9321
Web: www.jewishtelegraph.com *Editor:* Paul Harris

**JOURNAL OF ALTERNATIVE AND COMPLEMENTARY
MEDICINE**
9 Rickett Street, London SW6 1RU Tel: 020-7385 0012
Editor: Graeme Miller

JUSTICE OF THE PEACE
LexisNexis UK, Halsbury House, 35 Chancery Lane, London
WC2A 1EL Tel: 020-7400 2828

KERRANG!
EMAP Performance 2001, PO Box 2930, London W1A 6DZ
Tel: 020-7436 1515 *Editor:* Ashley Bird

LANCET
32 Jamestown Road, London NW1 7BY Tel: 020-7424 4910
Web: www.thelancet.com *Editor:* Dr Richard Horton

LAND & LIBERTY
Suite 427, The London Fruit Exchange, Brushfield Street,
London E1 6EL Tel: 020-7377 8885
Web: www.landandliberty.org.uk *Editor:* Peter Gibb

THE LAWYER
Centaur Communications Group, 50 Poland Street, London
W1V 4AX Tel: 020-7970 4614 Web: www.thelawyer.com
Editor: Catrin Griffiths

LEVIATHAN QUARTERLY
Bears Hay Farm, Brookhay Lane, Fradley, Lichfield WS13 8RG
Tel: 01543-411161 *Editor:* Michael Hulse

THE LINGUIST
The Institute of Linguists, Saxon House, 48 Southwark
Street, London SE1 1UN Tel: 020-7226 2822
Web: www.linguistonline.co.uk *Editor:* Pat Treasure

THE LITERARY REVIEW
44 Lexington Street, London W1F 0LW Tel: 020-7437 9392
Editor: Nancy Sladek

LOADED
IPC Media Ltd, King's Reach Tower, Stamford Street, London
SE1 9LS Tel: 020-7261 5000 Web: www.uploaded.com
Editor: Scott Manson

THE LONDON MAGAZINE: A REVIEW OF LITERATURE
AND THE ARTS
32 Addison Grove, London W4 1ER Tel: 020-8400 5882
Web: www.londonmagazine.ukf.net
Editor: Sebastian Barker

LONDON REVIEW OF BOOKS
28 Little Russell Street, London WC1A 2HN
Tel: 020-7209 1101 *Editor:* Mary-Kay Wilmers

MACUSER
Dennis Publishing Ltd, 30 Cleveland Street, London W1T 4JD
Tel: 020-7907 6000 Web: www.macuser.co.uk

MACWORLD
IDG Communications, 99 Gray's Inn Road, London WC1X 8TY
Tel: 020-7831 9252 Web: www.macworld.co.uk

MAKING MUSIC
VViP Highgate Studios, 53–79 Highgate Road, London
NW5 1TW Tel: 020-7331 1170
Web: www.makingmusic.co.uk

MANAGEMENT TODAY
174 Hammersmith Road, London W6 7JP Tel: 020-8267 4610
Editor: Matthew Gwyther

MARIE CLAIRE
European Magazines Ltd, 2 Hatfields, London SE1 9PG
Tel: 020-7261 5240 *Editor:* Marie O'Riordan

MARKETING WEEK
St Giles House, 50 Poland Street, London W1F 7AX
Tel: 020-7970 4000 Web: www.marketing-week.co.uk
Editor: Stuart Smith

MAXIM
Dennis Publishing Ltd, 30 Cleveland Street, London W1T 4JD
Tel: 020-7907 6410 Web: www.maxim-magazine.co.uk

MEDIA WEEK
Quantum Business Media Ltd, Quantum House, 19
Scarbrook Road, Croydon CR9 1LX Tel: 020-8565 4317
Editor: Tim Burrowes

METHODIST RECORDER
122 Golden Lane, London EC1Y 0TL Tel: 020-7251 8414
Web: www.methodistrecorder.co.uk
Managing Editor: Moira Sleight

MIXMAG
EMAP plc, Mappin House, 4 Winsley Street, London W1N 8HF
Tel: 020-7436 1515 Web: www.mixmag.net
Editor: Viv Crask

MODERN LANGUAGE REVIEW
Modern Humanities Research Association,
c/o Maney Publishing, Hudson Road, Leeds LS9 7DL

MODERN PAINTERS
3rd Floor, 52 Bermondsey Street, London SE1 3UD
Tel: 020-7407 9246 Web: www.modernpainters.co.uk
Editor: Karen Wright

MOJO
EMAP Metro, Mappin House, 4 Winsley Street, London
W1W 8HF Tel: 020-7436 1515 Web: www.mojo4music.com
Editor: Phil Alexander

MUSIC TEACHER
Rhinegold Publishing Ltd, 241 Shaftesbury Avenue, London
WC2H 8TF Tel: 020-7333 1747 *Editor:* Lucien Jenkins

MUSIC WEEK
United Business Media International, 7th Floor, Ludgate House,
245 Blackfriars Road, London SE1 9UR Tel: 020-7579 4143
Editor: Ajax Scott

THE NATIONAL TRUST MAGAZINE
The National Trust, 36 Queen Anne's Gate, London SW1H 9AS
Tel: 020-7222 9251 Web: www.nationaltrust.org.uk
Editor: Gaynor Aaltonen

NATURE
Macmillan Magazines Ltd, The Macmillan Building,
4 Crinan Street, London N1 9XW Tel: 020-7833 4000
Web: www.nature.com *Editor:* Philip Campbell

NAUTICAL MAGAZINE
Brown, Son & Ferguson Ltd, 4–10 Darnley Street, Glasgow
G41 2SD Tel: 0141-429 1234 Web: www.skipper.co.uk

NEW HUMANIST
1 Gower Street, London WC1E 6HD Tel: 020-7436 1151
Web: www.newhumanist.org.uk *Editor:* Frank Jordans

NEW INTERNATIONALIST
55 Rectory Road, Oxford OX4 1BW Tel: 01865-728181
Web: www.newint.org *Editor:* Vanessa Baird

NEW LAW JOURNAL
LexisNexis UK, Halsbury House,
35 Chancery Lane, London WC2A 1EL Tel: 020-7400 2500
Editor: Jane Maynard, *Assistant Editor:* Alex Godfree

NEW MUSICAL EXPRESS
IPC Magazines Ltd, 25th Floor, King's Reach Tower, Stamford
Street, London SE1 9LS Tel: 020-7261 5000
Editor: Conor McNicholas

NEW SCIENTIST
RBI Ltd, 151 Wardour Street, London W1F 8WE
Tel: 020-8652 3500 Web: www.NewScientist.com
Editor: Jeremy Webb

NEW STATESMAN
Victoria Station House, 191 Victoria Street, London SW1E 5NE
Tel: 020-7828 1232 *Editor:* Peter Wilby

NEW THEATRE QUARTERLY
Oldstairs, Kingsdown, Deal, Kent CT14 8ES
Editors: Clive Barker, Simon Trussler

NEW WOMAN
EMAP Elan, Endeavour House, 189 Shaftesbury Avenue,
London WC2H 8JG Tel: 020-7437 9011
Web: www.newwoman.co.uk *Editor:* Sara Cremer

THE NEWSPAPER
Young Media Ltd, PO Box 121, Tonbridge, Kent TN12 5ZR
Tel: 01622-871036 Web: www.thenewspaper.org.uk
Editor: Simon Hobbs

NOW
IPC Media Ltd, King's Reach Tower, Stamford Street, London
SE1 9LS Tel: 020-7261 7366 *Editor:* Jane Ennis

NURSING TIMES
EMAP Healthcare, Greater London House, Hampstead Road,
London NW1 7EJ Tel: 020-7874 0500
Editor: Rachel Downey

OK! MAGAZINE
Northern & Shell plc, Ludgate House, 245 Blackfriars Road,
London SE1 9UX Tel: 020-7928 8000
Editor: Nic McCarthy

THE OLDIE
65 Newman Street, London W1T 3EG Tel: 020-7436 8801
Web: www.theoldie.co.uk *Editor:* Richard Ingrams
OPERA
36 Black Lion Lane, London W6 9BE Tel: 020-8563 8893
Web: www.opera.co.uk *Editor:* John Allison
OPERA NOW
241 Shaftesbury Avenue, London WC2H 8TF
Tel: 020-7333 1740 Web: www.rhinegold.co.uk
Editor: Ashutosh Khandekar
ORGANIC GARDENING
Sandvoe, North Roe, Shetland ZE2 9RY Tel: 01806-533319
Editor: Gaby Bartai Bevan
PC ANSWERS
Future Publishing Ltd, 30 Monmouth Street, Bath BA1 2BW
Tel: 01225-442244 Web: www.pcanswers.co.uk
PCS VIEW
Public and Commercial Services Union, 160 Falcon Road,
London SW11 2LN Tel: 020-7924 2727
Web: www.pcs.org.uk *Editor:* Sharon Breen
PENSIONS WORLD
LexisNexis UK, Tolley House, 2 Addiscombe Road, Croydon
CR9 5AF Tel: 020-8686 9141
Web: www.pensionsworld.co.uk
Editor: Stephanie Hawthorne
PERIOD LIVING & TRADITIONAL HOMES
EMAP East, Mappin House, 4 Winsley Street, London
W1W 8HF Tel: 020-7343 8775 *Editor:* Sharon Parsons
PERSONAL FINANCE
Charterhouse Communications, Arnold House, 36–41
Holywell Lane, London EC2A 3SF Tel: 020-7827 5454
THE PINK PAPER
2nd Floor, Medius House, 63–69 New Oxford Street, London
WC1A 1DN Tel: 020-7845 4300 *Editor:* Tris Reid-Smith
POETRY REVIEW
22 Betterton Street, London WC2H 9BX Tel: 020-7420 9880
Web: www.poetrysociety.org.uk
Editors: Robert Potts, David Herd
POLICE REVIEW
Jane's Information Group, The Quadrangle,
1st Floor, 180 Wardour Street, London W1F 8FY
Tel: 020-7851 9701 *Editor:* Catriona Marchant
THE POLITICAL QUARTERLY
Blackwell Publishers Ltd, 108 Cowley Road, Oxford OX4 1JF
Tel: 01865-791100 Web: www.blackwellpublishers.co.uk
PR WEEK
Haymarket Marketing Publications, 174 Hammersmith Road,
London W6 7JP Tel: 020-8267 4520 *Editor:* Kate Nicholas
THE PRACTITIONER
CMP Information Ltd, City Reach, 5 Greenwich View Place,
Millharbour, London E14 9NN Tel: 020-7861 6478
PRESS GAZETTE
Quantum Business Media Ltd, Quantum House,
19 Scarbrook Road, Croydon CR9 1LX Tel: 020-8565 4200
Editor: Ian Reeves
PRIMA
National Magazine Company, 72 Broadwick Street, London
W1F 9EP Tel: 020-7439 5000 *Editor:* Maire Fahey
PRINTING WORLD
CMP Information, Sovereign House, Sovereign Way,
Tonbridge, Kent TN9 1RW Tel: 01732-377329
Editor: Gareth Ward
PRIVATE EYE
6 Carlisle Street, London W1V 5RG Tel: 020-7437 4017
Web: www.private-eye.co.uk *Editor:* Ian Hislop
PROFESSIONAL PHOTOGRAPHER
Archant Specialist Ltd, The Mill, Bearwalden Business Park,
Wendens Ambo, Saffron Walden, Essex CB11 4GB
Tel: 01799-544246

PROSPECT
Prospect Publishing Ltd, 2 Bloomsbury Place, London
WC1A 2QA Tel: 020-7255 1281
Web: www.prospect-magazine.co.uk
Editor: David Goodhart
PUBLISHING NEWS
39 Store Street, London WC1E 7DS Tel: 020-7692 2900
Web: www.publishingnews.co.uk *Editor:* Jane Ellis
PULSE
CMP Information Ltd, City Reach, 5 Greenwich View Place,
Millharbour, London E14 9NN Tel: 020-7861 6483
Editor: Howard Griffiths
Q MAGAZINE
EMAP Performance, Mappin House, 4 Winsley Street,
London W1W 8HF Tel: 020-7436 1515 Web:
www.q4music.com
Editor: Paul Rees
RA MAGAZINE
Royal Academy of Arts, Burlington House, Piccadilly, London
W1J 0BD Tel: 020-7300 5820
Web: www.royalacademy.org.uk *Editor:* Sarah Greenberg
RADIO TIMES
BBC Worldwide Ltd, 80 Wood Lane, London W12 0TT
Tel: 020-8433 3400 Web: www.radiotimes.com
Editor: Gill Hudson
RAILWAY GAZETTE INTERNATIONAL
Reed Business Information, Quadrant House,
The Quadrant, Sutton, Surrey SM2 5AS
Tel: 020-8652 8608 Web: www.railwaygazette.com
RAILWAY MAGAZINE
IPC Media Ltd, King's Reach Tower, Stamford Street, London
SE1 9LS Tel: 020-7261 5821 *Editor:* Nick Pigott
THE RAMBLER
The Ramblers Association, 2nd Floor,
Camelford House, 87–90 Albert Embankment, London
SE1 7TW Tel: 020-7339 8500 Web: www.ramblers.org.uk
READER'S DIGEST
The Reader's Digest Association Ltd, 11 Westferry Circus,
Canary Wharf, London E14 4HE Tel: 020-7715 8000
Web: www.readersdigest.co.uk
Editor-in-Chief: Katherine Walker
RECORD COLLECTOR
45 St Mary's Road, London W5 5RQ Tel: 020-8579 1082
Web: www.recordcollectormag.com *Editor:* Andy Davis
RED
Hachette Filipacchi UK Ltd, 16–18 Berners Street, London
W1T 3LN Tel: 020-7150 7000 *Editor:* Trish Halpin
RED PEPPER
Socialist Newspaper Publications Ltd, 1B Waterlow Road,
London N19 5NJ Web: www.redpepper.org.uk
Editor: Hilary Wainwright
REPORT
ATL, 7 Northumberland Street, London WC2N 5RD
Tel: 020-7782 1517 Web: www.askatl.org.uk
Editor: Heather Pinnell
RESTAURANT MAGAZINE
3rd Floor, 9 Carnaby Street, London W1F 9PE
Tel: 020-7434 9190 *Editor:* Chris Maillard
RETAIL WEEK
Emap Retail, 33–39 Bowling Green Lane, London EC1R 0DA
Tel: 020-7520 1500 *Editor:* Neill Denny
RUSI JOURNAL
Whitehall, London SW1A 2ET Tel: 020-7930 5854
Web: www.rusi.org *Editor:* Dr Terence McNamee
SAGA MAGAZINE
Saga Publishing Ltd, The Saga Building, Enbrook Park,
Folkestone, Kent CT20 3SE Tel: 01303-771523
Editor: Emma Soames

THE SCHOOL LIBRARIAN
The School Library Association, Unit 2, Lotmead Business
Village, Lotmead Farm, Wanborough, Swindon SN4 0UY
Tel: 01793-791787 Web: www.sla.org.uk
THE SCOTS MAGAZINE
D.C. Thomson & Co. Ltd, 2 Albert Square, Dundee DD1 9QJ
Tel: 01382-223131
SCREEN INTERNATIONAL
EMAP Business Publishing, 33–39 Bowling Green Lane,
London EC1R 0DA Tel: 020-7505 8080
Web: www.screendaily.com
Managing Editor: Leo Barraclough
SEA ANGLER
EMAP Active Ltd, Bushfield House, Orton Centre,
Peterborough PE2 5UW Tel: 01733-237111 *Editor:* Mel Russ
SEA BREEZES
Media House, Tromode, Douglas, Isle of Man IM4 4SB
Tel: 01624-626018 *Editor:* A.C. Douglas
SHE
National Magazine House, 72 Broadwick Street, London
W1F 9EP Tel: 020-7439 5000 *Editor:* Eve Cameron
SHIPS MONTHLY
IPC Country & Leisure (Marine), 222 Branston Road,
Burton-on-Trent, Staffs DE14 3BT Tel: 01283-542721
Editor: Iain Wakefield
SIGHT AND SOUND
British Film Institute, 21 Stephen Street, London W1T 1LN
Tel: 020-7255 1444 *Editor:* Nick James
THE SIGN
G. J. Palmer & Sons Ltd, St Mary's Works, St Mary's Plain,
Norwich, Norfolk NR3 3BH Tel: 01603-615995
SKI AND BOARD
The Ski Club of Great Britain, The White House, 57–63
Church Road, London SW19 5SB Tel: 0845-4580780
Web: www.skiclub.co.uk *Editor:* Arnie Wilson
SLIMMING MAGAZINE
EMAP Esprit, Greater London House, Hampstead Road,
London NW1 7EJ Tel: 020-7347 1854 *Editor:* Rashmi Madan
SMASH HITS
EMAP Performance, Mappin House, 4 Winsley Street, London
W1W 8HF Tel: 020-7436 1515 *Editor:* Lisa Smosarski
SOLICITORS JOURNAL
Wilmington Business Information Ltd, Paulton House, 8
Shepherdess Walk, London N1 7LB Tel: 020-7490 0049
THE SPECTATOR
56 Doughty Street, London WC1N 2LL Tel: 020-7405 1706
Editor: Boris Johnson
THE STAGE
(incorporating Television Today)
Stage House, 47 Bermondsey Street, London SE1 3XT
Tel: 020-7403 1818 Web: www.thestage.co.uk
STAMP MAGAZINE
IPC Media Ltd, Focus Network, 9 Dingwall Avenue, Croydon
CR9 2TA Tel: 020-8774 0772 *Editor:* Steve Fairclough
THE STRAD
Orpheus Publications, SMG, 3 Waterhouse Square, 138–142
Holborn, London EC1N 2NY Tel: 020-7882 1040
Web: www.thestrad.com *Editor:* Naomi Sadler
STUDIO SOUND
Miller Freeman Entertainment Ltd, 8 Montague Close,
London SE1 9UR Tel: 020-7940 8500
SUGAR
Hachette Filipacchi, 64 North Row, London W1K 7LL
Tel: 020-7150 7000 *Editor:* Claire Irvin
SWIMMING MAGAZINE
Swimming Times Ltd, Harold Fern House, Derby Square,
Loughborough LE11 5AL Tel: 01509-618766
Editor: Peter Hassall

THE TABLET
1 King Street Cloisters, Clifton Walk, London W6 0QZ
Tel: 020-8748 8484 Web: www.thetablet.co.uk/
Editor: John Wilkins
TATE
Condé Nast Publications Ltd, Vogue House, Hanover Square,
London W1S 1JU Tel: 020-7499 9080
Editor: Robert Violette
TATLER
Vogue House, Hanover Square, London W1S 1JU
Tel: 020-7499 9080 Web: www.tatler.co.uk
Editor: Geordie Greig
THE TEACHER
National Union of Teachers, Hamilton House, Mabledon
Place, London WC1H 9BD Tel: 020-7380 4708
Editor: Mitch Howard
TEMPO
Cambridge University Press, The Edinburgh Building,
Shaftesbury Road, Cambridge CB2 2RU
Editor: Calum MacDonald
TENNIS WORLD
Umbrella Media, 5 Blythe Mews, Olympia, London W14 0HW
Tel: 020-7605 0000 *Editor:* Charlotte James
THERAPY WEEKLY
EMAP Healthcare Ltd, Greater London House, Hampstead
Road, London NW1 7EJ Tel: 020-7874 0360
Editor: Steve Bagshaw
THIRD WAY
This Caring Business, 1 St Thomas' Road, Hastings, East
Sussex TN34 3LG Tel: 01424-718406
Editor: Vivien Shepherd
THIS ENGLAND
PO Box 52, Cheltenham, Glos GL50 1YQ
Tel: 01242-537900 *Editor:* Roy Faiers
TIME OUT
Time Out Group Ltd, Universal House, 251 Tottenham Court
Road, London W1T 7AB Tel: 020-7813 3000
Web: www.timeout.com *Editor:* Laura Lee Davies
THE TIMES EDUCATIONAL SUPPLEMENT
Admiral House, 66–68 East Smithfield, London E1W 1BX
Tel: 020-7782 3000 Web: www.tes.co.uk
Editor: Bob Doe
TIMES EDUCATIONAL SUPPLEMENT SCOTLAND
Scott House, 10 South St Andrew Street, Edinburgh EH2 2AZ
Tel: 0131-557 1133 *Editor:* Neil Munro
TIMES HIGHER EDUCATION SUPPLEMENT
Admiral House, 66–68 East Smithfield, London E1W 1BX
Tel: 020-7782 3000 *Editor:* John O'Leary
THE TIMES LITERARY SUPPLEMENT
Admiral House, 66–68 East Smithfield, London E1W 1BX
Tel: 020-7782 3000 *Editor:* Peter Stothard
TOTAL FILM
99 Baker Street, London W1U 6FP Tel: 020-7317 2600
Editor: Matt Mueller
TRAVELLER
Wexas Ltd, 45 Brompton Road, London SW3 1DE
Tel: 020-7589 0500 Web: www.traveller.org.uk
Editor: Jonathan Lorie
TRIBUNE
9 Arkwright Road, London NW3 6AN Tel: 020-7433 6410
Editor: Mark Seddon
TVTIMES MAGAZINE
IPC Media Ltd, 10th Floor, King's Reach Tower, Stamford
Street, London SE1 9LS Tel: 020-7261 7000
Editor: Mike Hollingsworth
THE UNIVERSE
1st Floor, St James's Buildings, Oxford Street, Manchester
M1 6FP Tel: 0161-236 8856 *Editor:* Joe Kelly

VANITY FAIR
Vogue House, Hanover Square, London W1S 1JU
Tel: 020-7499 9080 Web: www.vanityfair.co.uk
London Editor: Henry Porter

VETERINARY REVIEW
John C. Alborough Ltd, Lion Lane, Needham Market, Suffolk
IP6 8NT Tel: 01449-723800 *Editor:* David Watson

VIZ COMIC
PO Box 1PT, Newcastle upon Tyne NE99 1PT
Web: www.viz.co.uk

VOGUE
Vogue House, Hanover Square, London W1S 1JU
Tel: 020-7499 9080 Web: www.vogue.co.uk
Editor: Alexandra Shulman

THE WAR CRY
The Salvation Army, 101 Newington Causeway, London
SE1 6BN Tel: 020-7367 4900
Web: www.salvationarmy.org/warcry
Editor: Major Nigel Bovey

THE WEEKLY NEWS
D.C. Thomson & Co. Ltd, Albert Square, Dundee DD1 9QJ
Tel: 01382-223131

WEIGHT WATCHERS MAGAZINE
Bloomsbury House Ltd, 1 Cecil Court, 49–55 London Road,
Enfield, Middlesex EN2 6DN Tel: 020-8342 2222
Editor: Pat Kane

WINE
Quest Magazines Ltd, Wilmington Publishing, 6–8
Underwood Street, London N1 7JQ Tel: 020-7549 2572
Editor: Catharine Lowe

THE WISDEN CRICKETER
The New Boathouse, 136–142 Bramley Road, London
W10 6SR Tel: 020-7565 3080
Editors: Emma John, Stephen Fay

WOMAN
IPC Media, King's Reach Tower, Stamford Street, London
SE1 9LS Tel: 020-7261 5000 *Editor:* Carole Russell

WOMAN'S OWN
IPC Connect Ltd, King's Reach Tower, Stamford Street,
London SE1 9LS Tel: 020-7261 5000
Editor: Elsa McAlonan

WOMAN'S WEEKLY
IPC Media Ltd, King's Reach Tower, Stamford Street, London
SE1 9LS Tel: 0870-4445000 *Editor:* Gilly Sinclair

THE WORLD OF INTERIORS
Condé Nast Publications Ltd, Vogue House, Hanover Square,
London W1S 1JU Tel: 020-7499 9080
Web: www.worldofinteriors.co.uk *Editor:* Rupert Thomas

THE WORLD TODAY
The Royal Institute of International Affairs, Chatham House,
10 St James's Square, London SW1Y 4LE
Tel: 020-7957 5712 Web: www.theworldtoday.org
Editor: Graham Walker

WRITERS' FORUM
(incorporating World Wide Writers)
Writers' International Ltd, PO Box 3229, Bournemouth
BH1 1ZS Web: www.writers-forum.com
Publisher John Jenkins

WRITERS' NEWS
PO Box 168, Wellington Street, Leeds LS1 1RF
Tel: 0113-238 8333 *Editor:* Derek Hudson

YACHTING MONTHLY
IPC Media Ltd, Room 2215, King's Reach Tower, Stamford
Street, London SE1 9LS Tel: 020-7261 6040
Editor: Paul Gelder

ZEST
National Magazine House, 72 Broadwick Street, London
W1F 9EP Tel: 020-7439 5000 *Editor:* Alison Pylkkanen

BOOK PUBLISHERS

There are over 50,000 active publishers in the UK, but many of these are subsidiaries of larger publishing houses. Bibliographic data agency Whitaker Information Services recorded 125,390 titles published in 2002, a 5 per cent increase on the previous year's total. The increase was mostly driven by academic, professional and electronic lists, which accounted for more than half of the new titles added to WIS' database last year. The following list comprises a selection of publishers, their contact details and a letter code indicating the type of books published.

A	Fiction
B	Education
C	Religious
D	Technical and Scientific
E	Legal and Parliamentary
F	Medical
G	Commercial and Professional
H	Naval and Military
I	Dictionaries
J	Reference Books
K	Maps and Atlases
L	Directories and Guides
M	Music and Dance
N	Poetry, Film and Drama
O	Illustrated
P	Art and Architecture
Q	History, Archaeology, Biography
R	Politics, Sociology, Political Economy
S	Philosophy
T	Other Academic
U	Children's Books
V	Sports, Hobbies and Interests
W	Foreign language
X	General Literature, e.g. Travel, Essays, Humour

AA PUBLISHING
Automobile Association, Fanum House, Basingstoke, Hants RG21 4EA. Tel: 0990-448866 Fax: 01256-322575 Web: www.theaa.com **K, L, O**

GEORGE ALLEN & UNWIN PUBLISHERS
77–85 Fulham Palace Road, London W6 8JB. Tel: 020-8741 7070 Fax: 020-8307 4440 Web: www.fireandwater.com **U**

ALLISON & BUSBY
Suite 111, Bon Marché Centre, 241–251 Ferndale Road, London SW9 8BJ. Tel: 020-7738 7888 Fax: 020-7733 4244 Web: www.allisonandbusby.ltd.uk **A, U**

ARROW BOOKS
20 Vauxhall Bridge Road, London SW1V 2SA. Tel: 020-7840 8400 Fax: 020-7233 8791 Web: www.randomhouse.co.uk **A**

ASHGATE PUBLISHING
Gower House, Croft Road, Aldershot, Hants GU11 3HR. Tel: 01252-331551 Fax: 01252-344405. **C, D, E, F, G, H, J, M, P, Q, R, S, T**

AURUM PRESS
25 Bedford Avenue, London WC1B 3AT. Tel: 020-7637 3225 Fax: 020-7580 2469 Web: www.aurumpress.co.uk **H, N, P, Q, V, X**

BANTAM
61–63 Uxbridge Road, London W5 5SA. Tel: 020-8579 2652 Fax: 020-8579 5479. Web: www.booksattransworld.co.uk **A, O, Q, R, V, X**

B.T. BATSFORD
The Chrysalis Building, Bramley Road, London W10 6SP. Tel: 020–7221 2213 Web: www.chrysalis.com **N, P, Q, V**

BERLITZ PUBLISHING CO.
Lincoln House, 296–302 High Holborn, London W1V 7JH. Tel: 020-7611 9640 Fax: 020-7611 9656 **X. W**

A & C BLACK PUBLISHERS
37 Soho Square, London W1D 3QZ. Tel: 020-7758 0200 Fax: 020-7758 0222 Web: www.acblack.com **B, I, J, L, M, N, O, P, Q, U, V**

BLACK SWAN
61–63 Uxbridge Road, London W5 5SA. Tel: 020-8579 2652 Fax: 020-8579 5479 Web: www.booksattransworld.co.uk **A**

BLACKWELL PUBLISHING
9600 Garsington Road, Oxford OX4 2DQ. Tel: 01865-776868 Fax: 01865-71459 Web: www.blackwellpublishing.com **C, D, F, O, Q, R, S, T, W**

BLOODAXE BOOKS
Highgreen Tarset, Northumberland NE48 1RP. Tel: 01434-240500 Fax: 01434-240505 **A, N**

BLOOMSBURY PUBLISHING PLC
38 Soho Square, London W1D 3HB. Tel: 020-7494 2111 Fax: 020-7434 0151 Web: www.bloomsburymagazine.com **A, I, J, U**

BOWKER
Windsor Court, East Grinstead House, East Grinstead, West Sussex RH19 1XA. Tel: 01342-336149 Fax: 01342-336192 Web: www.bowker.co.uk **J, L**

BOXTREE
4 Crinan Street, London N1 9XW. Tel: 020-7843 4640 **M, N, O, V**

MARION BOYARS PUBLISHERS
24 Lacy Road, London SW15 1NL. Tel: 020-8788 9522 Fax: 020-8789 8122 Web: www.marionboyars.co.uk **A, N**

ANDREW BRODIE
37 Soho Square, London W1D 3QZ. Tel: 020-7758 0200 Fax: 020-7758 0222 Web: www.acblack.com **B**

CADOGAN GUIDES
Highlands House, 165 The Broadway, London SW19 1NE.
Tel: 020-8544 8051 Fax: 020-8544 8081
Web: www.cadoganguides.com **L, X**

CAMBRIDGE UNIVERSITY PRESS
The Edinburgh Building, Shaftesbury Road, Cambridge
CB2 2RU.. Tel: 01223-312393 Fax: 01223-315052
Web: www.cambridge.org. **B, C, G, Q, R, S, T**

CANONGATE BOOKS
14 High Street, Edinburgh EH1 1TE. Tel: 0131-557 5111
Fax: 0131-557 5211 Web: www.canongate.net
A, C, M, N, V, X

JONATHAN CAPE
20 Vauxhall Bridge Road, London SW1V 2SA.
Tel: 020-7840 8400 Fax: 020-7233 8791
Web: www.randomhouse.co.uk **A, N, Q**

FRANK CASS & CO.
Crown House, 47 Chase Side, Southgate, London N14 5BP.
Tel: 020-8920 2100 Fax: 020-8447 8548
Web: www.frankcass.com **H, Q, R**

CASSELL, Orion House, 5 Upper St Martin's Lane, London
WC2H 9EA. Tel: 020-7240 3444 Fax: 020-7379 6158

CASSELL ILLUSTRATED
2–4 Heron Quays, London E14 4JP. Tel: 020-7531 8400
Fax: 020-7531 8650 Web: www.octopus-publishing.co.uk
O

CAVENDISH PUBLISHING
The Glass House, Wharton Street, London WC1X 9PX.
Tel: 020-7278 8000 Fax: 020-7278 8080
Web: www.cavendishpublishing.com **E, F, G, J**

CENTURY
20 Vauxhall Bridge Road, London SW1V 2SA.
Tel: 020-7840 8400 Fax: 020-7233 8791
Web: www.randomhouse.co.uk **A, Q, X**

CHAMBERS HARRAP PUBLISHERS
7 Hopetoun Crescent, Edinburgh EH7 4AY.
Tel: 0131-556 5929 Fax: 0131-556 5313I **J, W**

CHATTO & WINDUS
20 Vauxhall Bridge Road, London SW1V 2SA.
Tel: 020-7840 8400 Fax: 020-7233 8791
Web: www.randomhouse.co.uk **A, Q, R**

CONSTABLE & ROBINSON
3 The Lanchester, 162 Fulham Palace Road, London
W6 9ER. Tel: 020-8741 3663 Fax: 020-8748 7562
Web: www.constablerobinson.com **A, H, J, P, Q, U, X**

CORGI
61–63 Uxbridge Road, London W5 5SA. Tel: 020-8579 2652
Fax: 020-8579 5479 Web: www.booksattransworld.co.uk
A, Q, X

DAVID & CHARLES
Brunel House, Newton Abbot, Devon TQ12 4PU.
Tel: 01626-323200 Fax: 01626-323319 **O**

DEBRETT'S PEERAGE LIMITED
Brunel House, 55–57 North Wharf Road, London W2 1LA.
Tel: 020-7915 9633 Fax: 020-7753 4212
Web: www.debretts.co.uk **J**

DORLING KINDERSLEY
80 Strand, London WC2R 0RL. Tel: 020-7010 3000
Fax: 020-7010 6060 Web: www.penguin.co.uk
All categories

DOUBLEDAY
61–63 Uxbridge Road, London W5 5SA. Tel: 020-8579 2652
Fax: 020-8579 5479 Web: www.booksattransworld.co.uk
A, O, Q, R, X

GERALD DUCKWORTH & CO.
61 Frith Street, London W1D 3JL. Tel: 020-7434 4242
Fax: 020-7434 4420 Web: www.ducknet.co.uk **H, Q, T**

EBURY PRESS
20 Vauxhall Bridge Road, London SW1V 2SA.
Tel: 020-7840 8400 Fax: 020-7233 8791
Web: www.randomhouse.co.uk **C, F, J, M, O, Q, V, X**

EDINBURGH UNIVERSITY PRESS
22 George Square, Edinburgh EH8 9LF. Tel: 0131-650 4218
Fax: 0131-662 0053 **R, T**

EGMONT BOOKS
239 Kensington High Street, London W8 6SA.
Tel: 020-7761 3500 Fax: 020-7761 3510, **U**

ELSEVIER SCIENCE
The Boulevard, Langford Lane, Kidlington, Oxford OX5 1GB.
Tel: 01865-843000 Fax: 01865-843010B **D, G, P, T**

ENCYCLOPAEDIA BRITANNICA (UK)
2nd Floor, Unity Wharf, Mill Street, London SE1 2BH.
Tel: 020-7500 7800 Fax: 020-7500 7878
Web: www.britannica.co.uk **J, K, U**

EVANS BROTHERS
2A Portman Mansions, Chiltern Street, London W1V 6NR.
Tel: 020-7487 0920 Fax: 020-7487 0921
Web: www.evansbooks.co.uk **B, J, N, U**

EVERYMAN PUBLISHERS PLC
Gloucester Mansions, 140A Shaftesbury Avenue, London
WC2H 8HD. Tel: 020-7539 7600 Fax: 020-7379 4060
Web: www.everyman.ukcom **A, L, O, X**

EXLEY PUBLICATIONS
16 Chalk Hill, Watford, Herts. WD19 4BG.
Tel: 01923-250505 Fax: 01923-818733/249795 **O, X**

FABER & FABER
3 Queen Square, London WC1N 3AU. Tel: 020-7465 0045
Fax: 020-7465 0034 Web: www.faber.co.uk
A, N, Q, U, X

FOLENS
Apex Business Centre, Boscombe Road, Dunstable LU5 4RL.
Tel: 0870-609 1237 Fax: 0870-609 1236
Web: www.folens.com **B**

G.T. FOULIS & CO.
Sparkford, Yeovil, Somerset BA22 7JJ. Tel: 01963-440635
Fax: 01963-440023 **D, J, Q, V**

FOURTH ESTATE
77–85 Fulham Palace Road, London W6 8JB.
Tel: 020-8741 7070 Fax: 020-8307 4440
Web: www.fireandwater.com **A, Q, A**

SAMUEL FRENCH
52 Fitzroy Street, London W1T 5JR. Tel: 020-7387 9373
Fax: 020-7387 2161
Web: www.samuelfrench-london.co.uk **N**

VICTOR GOLLANCZ
Orion House, 5 Upper St Martin's Lane, London WC2H 9EA
Tel: 020-7240 3444 Fax: 020-7379 6158

GOWER PUBLISHING
Gower House, Croft Road, Aldershot, Hants GU11 3HR.
Tel: 01252-331551 Fax: 01252-344405 **G**

GRANTA PUBLICATIONS
2–3 Hanover Yard, Noel Road, London N1 8BE.
Tel: 020-7704 9776 Fax: 020-7354 0474
Web: www.granta.com **A, Q, R, X**

HAMISH HAMILTON
80 Strand, London WC2R 0RL. Tel: 020-7010 3000
Fax: 020-7010 6060 Web: www.penguin.co.uk **A**

HAMLYN
2–4 Heron Quays, London E14 4JP. Tel: 020-7531 8400
Fax: 020-7531 8650 Web: www.octopus-publishing.co.uk
J, M, O, P, V

HARCOURT PUBLISHERS
Harcourt Place, 32 Jamestown Road, London NW1 7BY.
Tel: 020-7424 4200 Fax: 020-7482 2293
Web: www.harcourt-international.com **F**

HARLEQUIN MILLS & BOON
Eton House, 18–24 Paradise Road, Richmond, Surrey TW9
1SR. Tel: 020-8288 2800 Fax: 020-8288 2899 **A**

HARPERCOLLINS PUBLISHERS
77–85 Fulham Palace Road, London W6 8JB.
Tel: 020-8741 7070 Fax: 020-8307 4440
Web: www.fireandwater.com
A, B, H, I, J, K, L, O, Q, R, U, V, X

HAYNES PUBLISHING
Sparkford, Yeovil, Somerset BA22 7JJ. Tel: 01963-440635
Fax: 01963-440023 **D, I, J, K, L**

HEINEMANN EDUCATIONAL
Halley Court, Jordan Hill, Oxford, OX2 8EJ. Tel: 01865 311366
Fax: 01865 314641 Web: www.harcourteducation.co.uk **B**

WILLIAM HEINEMANN
20 Vauxhall Bridge Road, London SW1V 2SA.
Tel: 020-7840 8400 Fax: 020-7233 8791
Web: www.randomhouse.co.uk **B**

CHRISTOPHER HELM
37 Soho Square, London W1D 3QZ. Tel: 020-7758 0200
Fax: 020-7758 0222 Web: www.acblack.com **V**

HODDER HEADLINE
338 Euston Road, London NW1 3BH. Tel: 020-7873 6000
Fax: 020-7873 6024
A, B, C, D, F, G, H, J, M, O, R, U, V, X

HUTCHINSON
20 Vauxhall Bridge Road, London SW1V 2SA.
Tel: 020-7840 8400 Fax: 020-7233 8791
Web: www.randomhouse.co.uk

JANE'S INFORMATION GROUP
163 Brighton Road, Coulsdon, Surrey CR5 2YH.
Tel: 020-8700 3700 Fax: 020-8763 1005
Web: www.janes.com **H**

JARROLD PUBLISHING
Whitefriars, Norwich NR3 1TR. Tel: 01603-763300
Fax: 01603-662748L **Q**

JORDAN PUBLISHING
21 St Thomas Street, Bristol BS1 6JS. Tel: 0117-923 0600
Fax: 0117-925 0486 Web: www.jordanpublishing.co.uk **E**

KINGFISHER PUBLICATIONS PLC
New Penderel House, 283–288 High Holborn, London WC1V
7HZ. Tel: 020-7903 9999 Fax: 020-7242 4979, **C, D, J, Q, X**

JESSICA KINGSLEY PUBLISHERS
116 Pentonville Road, London N1 9JB. Tel: 020-7833 2307
Fax: 020-7837 2917 Web: www.jkp.com **B, C, D, F, G, R, S, T**

KLUWER ACADEMIC/PLENUM PUBLISHERS
241 Borough High Street, London SE1 1GB.
Tel: 020-7940 7490 Fax: 020-7940 7495
Web: www.wkap.nl. **D, F, S T**

LADYBIRD
80 Strand, London WC2R 0RL. Tel: 020-7010 3000
Fax: 020-7010 6060 Web: www.penguin.co.uk **U**

LETTS EDUCATIONAL
Chiswick Centre, 414 Chiswick High Road, London W4 5TF.
Tel: 020-8996 3333 Fax: 020-8742 8390
Web: www.lettsed.co.uk **B**

LEXISNEXIS UK
Halsbury House, 35 Chancery Lane, London WC2A 1EL.
Tel: 020-7400 2500 Fax: 020-7400 2842
Web: www.butterworths.com **E, G**

LONELY PLANET PUBLICATIONS
72–82 Rosebery Avenue, London EC1R 4RW.
Tel: 020-7428 4800 Fax: 020-7428 4828
Web: www.lonelyplanet.com **K, L, W**

LONGMAN
Edinburgh Gate, Harlow, Essex CM20 2JE.
Tel: 01279-623623 Fax: 01279-431059
Web: www.pearsoned.com **B**

LUTTERWORTH PRESS
PO Box 60, Cambridge CB1 2NT. Tel: 01223-350865
Fax: 01223-366951 Web: www.lutterworth.com
B, C, O, P, Q, T, U, V

MACMILLAN PUBLISHERS
The Macmillan Building, 4 Crinan Street, London N1 9XW.
Tel: 020-7833 4000 Fax: 020-7843 4640
A, B, D, F, J, Q, R, S, T, W

MANCHESTER UNIVERSITY PRESS
Oxford Road, Manchester M13 9NR. Tel: 0161-275 2310
Fax: 0161-274 3346
Web: www.manchesteruniversitypress.co.uk
E, N, P, Q, R, S, T, W

MCGRAW-HILL EDUCATION
McGraw-Hill House, Shoppenhangers Road, Maidenhead,
Berks. SL6 2QL. Tel: 01628-502500
Fax: 01628-770224 Web: www.mcgraw-hill.co.uk
B, D, F, G, J, R

METHUEN PUBLISHING
215 Vauxhall Bridge Road, London SW1V 1EJ.
Tel: 020-7798 1600 Fax: 020-7828 2098 A, N, X

MICHELIN TRAVEL PUBLICATIONS
Hannay House, 39 Clarendon Road, Watford, Herts.
WD17 1JA. Tel: 01923-205240 Fax: 01923-205241
Web: www.viamichelin.com K, X

JOHN MURRAY
338 Euston Road, London NW1 3BH. Tel: 020-7873 6000
B, H, Q, R

NEW HOLLAND PUBLISHERS (UK)
Garfield House, 86 Edgware Road, London W2 2EA.
Tel: 020-7724 7773 Fax: 020-7258 1293
Web: www.newhollandpublishers.com V, X

W.W. NORTON & COMPANY
Castle House, 75–76 Wells Street, London W1T 3QT.
Tel: 020-7323 1579 Fax: 020-7436 4553.
H, M, N, P, Q, R, S, T, W, X

OCTOPUS PUBLISHING GROUP
2–4 Heron Quays, London E14 4JP. Tel: 020-7531 8400
Fax: 020-7531 8650 Web: www.octopus-publishing.co.uk
B, J, K, U, V

OPEN UNIVERSITY PRESS
Celtic Court, 22 Ballmoor, Buckingham MK18 1XW.
Tel: 01280-823388 Fax: 01280-823233
Web: www.openup.co.uk B, F, R, T

ORCHARD BOOKS
96 Leonard Street, London EC2A 4XD. Tel: 020-7739 2929
Fax: 020-7739 2318 Web: www.wattspublishing.co.uk U

THE ORION PUBLISHING GROUP
Orion House, 5 Upper St Martin's Lane, London WC2H 9EA.
Tel: 020-7240 3444 Fax: 020-7379 6158

OSPREY PUBLISHING
Elms Court, Chapel Way, Botley, Oxford OX2 9LP.
Tel: 01865-727022 Fax: 01865-727017
Web: www.ospreypublishing.com H, Q

PETER OWEN
73 Kenway Road, London SW5 0RE.
Tel: 020-7373 5628/370 6093 Fax: 020-7373 6760
Web: www.peterowen.com A

OXFORD UNIVERSITY PRESS
Great Clarendon Street, Oxford OX2 6DP.
Tel: 01865-556767 Fax: 01865-556646
Web: www.oup.com
B, C, D, E, F, G, I, J, K, P, Q, R, S, T, W, X

PEARSON EDUCATION
Edinburgh Gate, Harlow, Essex CM20 2JE
Tel: 01279-623623 Fax: 01279-431059
Web: www.pearsoned.com B, J

PENGUIN GROUP (UK)
80 Strand, London WC2R 0RL. Tel: 020-7010 3000
Fax: 020-7010 6060 Web: www.penguin.co.uk
A, B, I, J, K, L, N, O, Q, T, U, V, X

PHAIDON PRESS
Regent's Wharf, All Saints Street, London N1 9PA.
Tel: 020-7843 1000 Fax: 020-7843 1010 P

PIATKUS BOOKS
5 Windmill Street, London W1T 2JA. Tel: 020-7631 0710
Fax: 020-7436 7137 Web: www.piatkus.co.uk
A, C, F, G, H, M, Q, X

PLUTO PRESS
345 Archway Road, London N6 5AA. Tel: 020-8348 2724
Fax: 020-8348 9133 Web: www.plutobooks.com R T

T & AD POYSER
37 Soho Square, London W1D 3QZ. Tel: 020-7758 0200
Fax: 020-7758 0222 Web: www.acblack.com V

PUFFIN
80 Strand, London WC2R 0RL. Tel: 020-7010 3000,
Fax: 020-7010 6060 Web: www.penguin.co.uk U

QUARTET BOOKS
27 Goodge Street, London W1T 2LD. Tel: 020-7636 3992
Fax: 020-7637 1866 A, M, Q, X

QUARTO PUBLISHING PLC
6 Blundell Street, London N7 9BH. Tel: 020-7700 6700
Fax: 020-7700 4191 Web: www.quarto.com P, V

RAGGED BEARS PUBLISHING
Milborne Wick, Sherborne, Dorset DT9 4PW
Tel: 01963-251018 Fax: 01963-250889
Web: www.raggedbears.co.uk U

RANDOM HOUSE GROUP
20 Vauxhall Bridge Road, London SW1V 2SA.
Tel: 020-7840 8400 Fax: 020-7233 8791
Web: www.randomhouse.co.uk A, B, C, G, Q, R, S, T, X

THE READER'S DIGEST ASSOCIATION
11 Westferry Circus, Canary Wharf, London E14 4HE.
Tel: 020-7715 8000 Fax: 020-7715 8600 A, J, X

REAKTION BOOKS
77–79 Farringdon Road, London EC1M 3JU.
Tel: 020-7404 9930 Fax: 020-7404 9931
Web: www.reaktionbooks.co.uk P

WILLIAM REED DIRECTORIES
Broadfield Park, Crawley, West Sussex RH11 9RT.
Tel: 01293-610400 Fax: 01293-610310
Web: www.william-reed.co.uk

ROUGH GUIDES
80 Strand, London WC2R 0RL. Tel: 020-7010 3000,
Fax: 020-7010 6060 Web: www.roughguides.com X

ROUTLEDGE
11 New Fetter Lane, London EC4P 4EE. Tel: 020-7583 9855
Fax: 020-7842 2298 Web: www.tandf.co.uk
C, G, H, I, J, K, L, M, N, P, Q, R, S, T, W

SCHOFIELD & SIMS
Dogley Mill, Fenay Bridge, Huddersfield HD8 0NQ.
Tel: 01484-607080 Fax: 01484-606815 B

SCHOLASTIC CHILDREN'S BOOKS
Commonwealth House, 1–19 New Oxford Street, London
WC1A 1NU. Tel: 020-7421 9000 Fax: 020-7421 9001 U

SEVERN HOUSE PUBLISHERS
9–15 High Street, Sutton, Surrey SM1 1DF.
Tel: 020-8770 3930 Fax: 020-8770 3850
Web: www.severnhouse.com A

SIMON & SCHUSTER
Africa House, 64–78 Kingsway, London WC2B 6AH
Tel: 020-7316 1900 Fax: 020-7316 0331/2
Web: www.simonsays.co.uk A, J, M, X

SPCK
Holy Trinity Church, Marylebone Road, London NW1 4DU.
Tel: 020-7643 0382 Fax: 020-7643 0391
Web: www.spck.org.uk C

SWEET & MAXWELL
100 Avenue Road, London NW3 3PF. Tel: 020-7393 7000
Fax: 020-7393 7010 Web: www.smlawpub.co.uk E

TATE PUBLISHING
The Lodge, Millbank, London SW1P 4RG
Tel: 020-7887 8869/70 Fax: 020-7887 8878
Web: www.tate.org.uk P

TAYLOR & FRANCIS GROUP PLC
11 New Fetter Lane, London EC4P 4EE. Tel: 020-7583 9855
Fax: 020-7842 2298 Web: www.tandf.co.uk J, Q, R, S

THAMES & HUDSON
181A High Holborn, London WC1V 7QX.
Tel: 020-7845 5000 Fax: 020-7845 5050
Web: www.thamesandhudson.com P

NELSON THORNES
Delta Place, 27 Bath Road, Cheltenham, Glos. GL53 7TH.
Tel: 01242-267100 Fax: 01242-221914
Web: www.nelsonthornes.com B

TIME WARNER BOOKS UK
Brettenham House, Lancaster Place, London WC2E 7EN.
Tel: 020-7911 8000 Fax: 020-7911 8100
A, J, O, Q, R, V, X

TRANSWORLD PUBLISHERS
61–63 Uxbridge Road, London W5 5SA.
Tel: 020-8579 2652 Fax: 020-8579 5479
Web: www.booksattransworld.co.uk
A, D, H, J, Q, U, V, X

TSO (THE STATIONERY OFFICE)
Duke Street, Norwich NR3 1PD. Tel: 0870-6005522
Fax: 0870-6005533 Web: www.tso.co.uk E, G, J, L

USBORNE PUBLISHING
Usborne House, 83–85 Saffron Hill, London EC1N 8RT.
Tel: 020-7430 2800 Fax: 020-7430 1562
Web: www.usborne.com U

V&A PUBLICATIONS
160 Brompton Road, London SW3 1HW. Tel: 020-7942 2966
Fax: 020-7942 2977 Web: www.vandashop.co.uk/books P

VIKING
80 Strand, London WC2R 0RL. Tel: 020-7010 3000
Fax: 020-7010 6060 Web: www.penguin.co.uk O, U

VIRAGO
Brettenham House, Lancaster Place, London WC2E 7EN.
Tel: 020-7911 8000 Fax: 020-7911 8100 A, N

VIRGIN BOOKS
Thames Wharf Studios, Rainville Road, London W6 9HA.
Tel: 020-7386 3300 Fax: 020-7386 3360 M, N, X

WALKER BOOKS
87 Vauxhall Walk, London SE11 5HJ. Tel: 020-7793 0909
Fax: 020-7587 1123 Web: www.walkerbooks.co.uk U

WARD LOCK
Orion House, 5 Upper St Martin's Lane, London WC2H 9EA.
Tel: 020-7240 3444 Fax: 020-7379 6158

WATTS PUBLISHING GROUP, 96 Leonard Street, London
EC2A 4XD. Tel: 020-7739 2929 Fax: 020-7739 2181
Web: www.wattspublishing.co.uk B, U

WEIDENFELD & NICOLSON
Orion House, 5 Upper St Martin's Lane, London WC2H 9EA.
Tel: 020-7240 3444 Fax: 020-7379 6158

WHICH?
2 Marylebone Road, London NW1 4DF. Tel: 020-7770 7000
Fax: 020-7770 7660 E, F, J, L T, X

WILEY EUROPE
The Atrium, Southern Gate, Chichester, West Sussex
PO19 8SQ. Tel: 01243-779777 Fax: 01243-775878
Web: www.wileyeurope.com
B, D, F, G, I, J, P, Q, R, S, T, W

THE WOMEN'S PRESS
Top Floor, 27 Goodge Street, London W1T 2LD.
Tel: 020-7636 3992 Fax: 020-7637 1866
Web: www.the-womens-press.com A, R T, U

YALE UNIVERSITY PRESS LONDON
47 Bedford Square, London WC1B 3DP. Tel: 020-7079 4900
Fax: 020-7079 4901 P, Q, R, S, T

ANNUAL REFERENCE BOOKS

This list comprises a selection of popular reference books and their price. If the address of the editorial office differs from the address to which orders should be sent, the address given is usually the one for orders.

THE AAPPL YEARBOOK OF PHOTOGRAPHY (£30)
10 Hillside, London SW19 4NH. Tel: 020-8971 2094
Fax: 020-8971 2094

A.S.K. HOLLIS – THE DIRECTORY OF UK ASSOCIATIONS (£190)
Harlequin House, 7 High Street, Teddington, Middlesex TW11 8EL. Tel: 020-8977 7711 Fax: 020-8977 1133
Web: www.hollis-pr.com

ADVERTISER'S ANNUAL (£260)
Harlequin House, 7 High Street, Teddington TW11 8EL.
Tel: 020-8977 7711 Fax: 020-8977 1133
Web: www.hollis-pr.co.uk

ALMANACH DE GOTHA (£60)
Boydell & Brewer Ltd, PO Box 9, Woodbridge, Suffolk IP12 3DF. Tel: 01394-411320 Fax: 01394-411477
Web: www.boydell.co.uk

ANNUAL ABSTRACT OF STATISTICS (£39.50)
PO Box 29, Norwich NR3 1GN. Tel: 0870-600 5522
Fax: 0870-600 5533 Web: www.tso.co.uk

THE ANNUAL REGISTER (£155)
28A Hills Road, Cambridge CB2 1LA. Tel: 01223-508050
Fax: 01223-508049

ANTHONY AND BERRYMAN MAGISTRATES' COURT GUIDE (£37.50)
2 Addiscombe Road, Croydon, Surrey CR9 5AF.
Tel: 020-8662 2000 Fax: 020-8662 2012

ANTIQUE SHOPS OF BRITAIN, GUIDE TO THE (£14.95)
Antique Collectors' Club, Sandy Lane, Old Martlesham, Woodbridge, Suffolk IP12 4SD. Tel: 01394-389950
Fax: 01394-389999 Web: www.antique-acc.com

ASLIB DIRECTORY OF INFORMATION SOURCES IN THE UNITED KINGDOM (£350)
Aslib / Europa Publications, 11 New Fetter Lane, London EC4P 4EE. Tel: 020-7842 2110 Fax: 020-7842 2249

ASTRONOMICAL ALMANAC (£35)
PO Box 29, Norwich NR3 1GN. Tel: 0870-600 5522
Fax: 0870-600 5533 Web: www.tso.co.uk

ATHLETICS: ASSOCIATION OF TRACK AND FIELD STATISTICIANS YEAR BOOK (£17.95)
Vine House Distribution Ltd, Waldenbury, North Common, Chailey, E. Sussex BN8 4DR. Tel: 01825-723398
Fax: 01825-724188

BANKERS' ALMANAC, THE (£585)
Windsor Court, East Grinstead House, East Grinstead, W. Sussex RH19 1XA. Tel: 01342-335946
Fax: 01342-335969 Web: www.bankersalmanac.com

BENEDICTINE AND CISTERCIAN MONASTIC YEAR BOOK (£1.50)
Ampleforth Abbey, York YO62 4EN. Tel: 01439-766466
Fax: 01439-766467 Web: www.benedictines.org.uk

BENN'S MEDIA: UNITED KINGDOM (£179)
Riverbank House, Angel Lane, Tonbridge, Kent TN9 1SE.
Tel: 01732-377211 Fax: 01732-377440
Web: www.cmpdata.co.uk

BRITISH AND INTERNATIONAL MUSIC YEAR BOOK (£32.50)
Rhinegold Publishing, 241 Shaftesbury Avenue, London WC2H 8TF. Tel: 020-7333 1721 Fax: 020-7333 1769

BRITISH DESIGN AND ART DIRECTION ANNUAL (£69)
71 Great Russell Street, London WC1B 3BP.
Tel: 020-7430 8850 Fax: 020-7430 8880

BRITISH EXPORTS (£195)
Windsor Court, East Grinstead House, East Grinstead, W. Sussex RH19 1XA. Tel: 01342-335876
Fax: 01342-335998 Web: www.kompass.co.uk

BRITISH PERFORMING ARTS YEAR BOOK (£28.45)
Rhinegold Publishing, 241 Shaftesbury Avenue, London WC1H 8TF. Tel: 020-7333 1721 Fax: 020-7333 1769

BRITISH PLASTICS AND RUBBER DIRECTORY (£18)
MCM Publishing, 37 Nelson Road, Caterham, Surrey CR3 5PP. Tel: 01883-347059 Fax: 01883-341350
Web: www.polymer-age.co.uk

BRITISH THEATRE DIRECTORY (£42.95)
70–76 Bell Street, Marylebone, London NW1 6SP.
Tel: 020-7224 9666 Fax: 020-7224 9688
Web: www.rhpco.co.uk

BROWN'S NAUTICAL ALMANAC DAILY TIDE TABLES (£47)
4–10 Darnley Street, Glasgow G41 2SD. Tel: 0141-429 1234
Fax: 0141-420 1694 Web: www.skipper.co.uk

BUILDING SOCIETIES YEAR BOOK (£60)
Arnold House, 36–41 Holywell Lane, London EC2A 3SF.
Tel: 020-7827 5454 Fax: 020-7827 0567
Web: www.moneypages.com

BUSES YEAR BOOK (£13.99)
Ian Allen Publishing, Riverdene Business Park, Molesey Road, Hersham, Surrey 01932-2666600

BUTTERWORTHS LAW DIRECTORY AND LEGAL SERVICES DIRECTORY (£64.29)
Martindale Hubbell, Holden House, 57 Rathbone Place, London WC2A 1EL. Tel: 020-7868 4890

CHARITY CHOICE UNITED KINGDOM (£69.95)
Paulton House, 8 Shepherdess Walk, London N1 7LB.
Tel: 020-7549 8670

CHEMIST AND DRUGGIST DIRECTORY (£128)
Riverbank House, Angel Lane, Tonbridge, Kent TN9 1SE.
Tel: 01732-377591 Fax: 01732-377440
Web: www.look4industry.co.uk

CHURCH OF ENGLAND YEARBOOK (£28)
Church House Publishing, Church House, Great Smith Street, London SW1P 3NZ. Tel: 020-7898 1578 Fax: 020-7898 1449
Web: www.chpublishing.co.uk

CHURCH OF SCOTLAND YEAR BOOK (£12)
121 George Street, Edinburgh EH2 4YN. Tel: 0131-343 6039
Fax: 0131-220 3113

CITY OF LONDON DIRECTORY AND LIVERY COMPANIES GUIDE (£24.50)
Seatrade House, 42–48 North Station Road, Colchester CO1 1RB. Tel: 01206-545121 Fax: 01206-545190

CIVIL SERVICE YEAR BOOK (£42.50)
PO Box 29, Norwich NR3 1GN. Tel: 0870-600 5522
Fax: 0870-600 5533 Web: www.tso.co.uk

COMMONWEALTH YEAR BOOK (£55)
PO Box 29, Norwich NR3 1GN. Tel: 0870-600 5522
Fax: 0870-600 5533

CONCRETE YEARBOOK (£67)
151 Rosebery Avenue, London EC1R 4GB. Tel: 020-7505 6600 Fax: 020-7505 3813 Web: www.nceplus.co.uk

CURRENT LAW YEAR BOOK (£175)
Cheriton House, North Way, Andover, Hants SP10 5BE.
Tel: 020-7449 1111 Fax: 020-7449 1144

DEBRETT'S PEOPLE OF TODAY (£140)
Brunel House, 55–57 North Wharf Road, London W2 1LA.
Tel: 020-7915 9633 Fax: 020-7753 4212
Web: www.debretts.co.uk

DIMENSIONS (£20)
Charities Aid Foundation, Kings Hill, West Malling, Kent
ME19 4TA. Tel: 01732-520125 Fax: 01732-520001
Web: www.cafonline.org

DIPLOMATIC SERVICE LIST (£27.50)
PO Box 29, Norwich NR3 1GN. Tel: 0870-600 5522
Fax: 0870-600 5533 Web: www.tso.co.uk

DIRECTORY OF DIRECTORS (£295)
Windsor Court, East Grinstead House, East Grinstead,
W. Sussex RH19 1XA. Tel: 01342-332042 Fax: 01342-332072
Web: www.reedinfo.co.uk

DIRECTORY OF LOCAL AUTHORITIES (£42.50)
Cheriton House, North Way, Andover, Hants SP10 5BE

DIRECTORY OF PUBLISHING (£80)
The Tower Building, 11 York Road, London SE1 7NX.
Tel: 020-7922 0880 Fax: 020-7922 0881
Web: www.continuumbooks.com

DIRECTORY TO THE FURNITURE AND FURNISHINGS
INDUSTRY (£120)
Riverbank House, Angel Lane, Tonbridge, Kent TN9 1SE.
Tel: 01732-377591 Fax: 01732-377440
Web: www.cmpdata.co.uk

DOD'S PARLIAMENTARY COMPANION (£150)
1 Douglas Street, London SW1P 4PA. Tel: 020-7643 7630
Fax: 020-7828 7269 Web: www.dodonline.co.uk

EDUCATION AUTHORITIES' DIRECTORY
AND ANNUAL (£78)
Darby House, Bletchingley Road, Merstham, Redhill, Surrey
RH1 3DN. Tel: 01737-642223 Fax: 01737-644283
Web: www.schoolgovernment.co.uk/pages/pub/ead.htm

EDUCATION YEAR BOOK (£98)
128 Long Acre, London WC2E 9AN. Tel: 020-7447 2000

ELECTRONICS AND ELECTRICAL BUYER'S GUIDE (£99)
CMP Information Ltd, Data and Information Services
Division, Riverbank House, Angel Lane, Tonbridge,
Kent TN9 1SE. Tel: 01732-377591 Fax: 01732-377440
Web: www.electronics-electrical.co.uk

ENGINEERING BUYERS GUIDE (£90)
CMP Information Ltd, Data and Information Services
Division, Riverbank House, Angel Lane, Tonbridge,
Kent TN9 1SE. Tel: 01732-377591 Fax: 01732-377440
Web: www.cmpinformation.co.uk

EUROPA DIRECTORY OF INTERNATIONAL
ORGANISATIONS (£175)
11 New Fetter Lane, London EC4P 4EE. Tel: 020-7842 2110
Fax: 020-7842 2249 Web: www.europapublications.co.uk

EUROPA WORLD YEAR BOOK (£570)
11 New Fetter Lane, London EC4P 4EE. Tel: 020-7842 2110
Fax: 020-7842 2249

EUROPEAN GLASS DIRECTORY AND BUYER'S
GUIDE (£156)
2 Queensway, Redhill, Surrey RH1 1QS

EVANDALE'S DIRECTORY OF WORLD
UNDERWRITERS (£280)
Informa Publishing, Sheepen Place, Colchester,
Essex CO3 3LP. Tel: 01206-772223
Web: www.informalaw.com

FILM REVIEW (£19.95)
61A Priory Road, Kew Gardens, Richmond, Surrey TW9 3DH.
Tel: 020-8940 5198 Fax: 020-8940 7679
Web: www.rhbooks.com

FOOD TRADES DIRECTORY OF THE UK
AND EUROPE (£205)
32 Vauxhall Bridge Road, London SW1V 2SS.
Tel: 020-7973 6665 Fax: 020-7973 4798
Web: www.foodtrades.co.uk

FREELANCE PHOTOGRAPHER'S MARKET
HANDBOOK (£14.95)
Focus House, 497 Green Lanes, London N13 4BP.
Tel: 020-8882 3315 Fax: 020-8886 5174
Web: www.thebfp.com

FROZEN AND CHILLED FOODS YEAR BOOK (£120)
PO Box 88, Edenbridge, Kent TN8 6ZW. Tel: 01738-868288
Fax: 01738-865874 Web: www.frozenandchilledfoods.com

GOOD BRITAIN GUIDE (£14.99)
The Book Service Ltd, Colchester Road, Frating Green,
Colchester CO7 7DW. Tel: 01206-256000
Fax: 01206-255715

GOOD FOOD GUIDE (£15.99)
Which?, Dept WLB, Freepost, Hertford SG14 1YB.
Tel: 0800-252 1000

GOOD GARDENS GUIDE (£14.99)
Macmillan Distribution, Houndmills, Basingstoke,
London RG21 6XS. Tel: 01256-302692

GUARDIAN MEDIA GUIDE (£17.99)
119 Farringdon Road, London EC1R 3ER.
Tel: 020-7713 4338 Fax: 020-7713 4368
Web: www.guardian.co.uk

GUIDE TO FIRST EDITION PRICES (£15.99)
Coverley House, Carlton, Leyburn, North Yorkshire DL8 4AY.
Tel: 01969-640399 Fax: 01969-640399
Web: www.tartaruspress.com

GUINNESS WORLD RECORDS (£18)
Macmillan Distribution, Brunel Road, Houndmills,
Basingstoke, Hants RG21 2XS. Tel: 01256-302692

HOLLIS SPONSORSHIP AND DONATIONS
YEARBOOK (£125)
Harlequin House, 7 High Street, Teddington TW11 8EL.
Tel: 020-8977 7711 Fax: 020-8977 1133
Web: www.hollis-pr.com

HOLLIS UK PRESS AND PUBLIC RELATIONS
ANNUAL (£145)
Harlequin House, 7 High Street, Teddington TW11 8EL.
Tel: 020-8977 7711 Fax: 020-8977 1133
Web: www.hollis-pr.com

HOUSING AND PLANNING YEAR BOOK (£120)
128 Long Acre, London WC2E 9AN. Tel: 020-7447 2000

INDEPENDENT SCHOOLS YEAR BOOK (£30)
37 Soho Square, London WID 3QZ. Tel: 020-8894 3066
Fax: 020-8893 3957 Web: www.isyb.co.uk

INSURANCE DIRECTORY (£280)
39 Earlham Street, London WC2H 9LT. Tel: 020-7306 7000
Fax: 020-7306 7141

INTERNATIONAL SHOWCASE: THE MUSIC BUSINESS
GUIDE (£55)
Harlequin House, 7 High Street, Teddington TW11 8EL.
Tel: 020-8977 7711 Fax: 020-8977 1133
Web: www.hollis-pr.com

INTERNATIONAL WHO'S WHO (£275)
11 New Fetter Lane, London EC4P 4EE. Tel: 020-7822 4300
Fax: 020-7822 4329 Web: www.europapublications.co.uk

JANE'S ALL THE WORLD'S AIRCRAFT (£403)
Sentinel House, 163 Brighton Road, Coulsdon,
Surrey CR5 2YH. Tel: 020-8700 3700 Fax: 020-8700 3715
Web: www.janes.com

JANE'S ARMOUR AND ARTILLERY (£395)
Sentinel House, 163 Brighton Road, Coulsdon,
Surrey CR5 2YH. Tel: 020-8700 3807 Fax: 020-8700 3715
Web: www.janes.com

JANE'S FIGHTING SHIPS (£380)
Sentinel House, 163 Brighton Road, Coulsdon, Surrey
CR5 2NH. Tel: 020-8700 3700 Fax: 020-8700 3715
Web: www.janes.com

JANE'S INFANTRY WEAPONS (£366)
Sentinel House, 163 Brighton Road, Coulsdon,
Surrey CR5 2NH. Tel: 020-8700 3700 Fax: 020-8700 3715
Web: www.janes.com

JANE'S WORLD RAILWAYS (£419)
Sentinel House, 163 Brighton Road, Coulsdon,
Surrey CR5 2NH. Tel: 020-8700 3807 Fax: 020-8700 3715
Web: www.janes.com

JEWISH YEAR BOOK (£29.50)
Vallentine Mitchell & Co Ltd, Crown House, 47 Chase Side,
Southgate, London N14 5BP. Tel: 020-8920 2100
Fax: 020-8447 8548 Web: www.vmbooks.com

KEESING'S RECORD OF WORLD EVENTS (£195)
Keesing's Worldwide, 28A Hills Road, Cambridge CB2 1LA.
Tel: 01223-508050 Fax: 01223-508049

KELLY'S INDUSTRIAL DIRECTORY (£299)
Windsor Court, East Grinstead House, East Grinstead,
W. Sussex RH19 1XA. Tel: 01342-335876
Fax: 01342-335998 Web: www.kellysarch.com

**LAW SOCIETY'S DIRECTORY OF SOLICITORS AND
BARRISTERS, THE** (£95)
Marston Book Services, PO Box 312, Abingdon, Oxon
OX14 4YN. Tel: 01235-465656 Fax: 01235-465660

LAXTON'S BUILDING PRICE BOOK (£105)
Linacre House, Jordan Hill, Oxford, Oxon OX2 8DP
Web: www.bh.com

**LIBRARY AND INFORMATION PROFESSIONALS
YEARBOOK, THE CHARTERED
INSTITUTE OF** (£37.50)
Bookpoint Ltd, 130 Milton Park, Abingdon, Oxon OX14 4SB.
Tel: 01235-827794 Fax: 01235-400454

**LLOYD'S LIST OF SHIPOWNERS, MANAGERS &
MANAGING AGENTS** (£220)
Lombard House, 3 Princess Way, Redhill, Surrey RH1 1UP.
Tel: 01737-379700 Fax: 01737-379701

LLOYD'S LIST PORTS OF THE WORLD (£250)
Informa UK Limited, Sheepen Place, Colchester,
Essex CO3 3LP. Tel: 01206-772222

LLOYD'S MARITIME DIRECTORY (£275)
Sheepen Place, Colchester CO3 3LP. Tel: 01206-772222
Fax: 01206-772092 Web: www.informamaritime.com

**LLOYD'S REGISTER OF INTERNATIONAL SHIPOWNING
GROUPS** (£495)
Lombard House, 3 Princess Way, Redhill, Surrey RH1 1UP.
Tel: 01737-379000 Fax: 01737-379001
Web: www.lrfairplay.com

LLOYD'S REGISTER OF SHIPS (£730)
Lombard House, 3 Princess Way, Redhill, Surrey RH1 1UP.
Tel: 01737-379700 Fax: 01737-379701

LYLE OFFICIAL ANTIQUES REVIEW (£12.05)
Penguin Direct, Pearson Customer Operations, Edinburgh
Gate, Harlow, Essex CM20 2JE Fax: 0870-850 5777

MARKETING HANDBOOK (£85)
Harlequin House, 7 High Street, Teddington TW11 8EL.
Tel: 020-8977 7711 Fax: 020-8977 1133
Web: www.hollis-pr.com

MEDAL YEARBOOK (£17.95)
Orchard House, Duchy Road, Heathpark, Honiton,
Devon EX14 1YD. Tel: 01404-46972 Fax: 01404-44788
Web: www.tokenpublishing.com

MILLER'S ANTIQUES PRICE GUIDE (£24.99)
Littlehampton Book Services, Faraday Close, Durrington,
Worthing BN13 3RB. Tel: 01903-828911
Web: www.millers.uk.com

**MILLER'S CLASSIC MOTORCYCLES YEARBOOK AND
PRICE GUIDE** (£14.99)
Littlehampton Book Services, Faraday Close, Durrington,
Worthing BN13 3RB. Tel: 01903-828911
Web: www.millers.uk.com

**MINING ANNUAL REVIEW AND METALS AND
MINERALS ANNUAL REVIEW** (£110)
PO Box 10, Edenbridge, Kent TN8 5NE. Tel: 020-7216 6060
Fax: 020-7216 6050 Web: www.mining-journal.com

**MOTOR INDUSTRY OF GREAT BRITAIN WORLD
AUTOMOTIVE STATISTICS** (£155)
Forbes House, Halkin Street, London SW1X 7DS.
Tel: 020-7235 7000 Fax: 020-7235 7112
Web: www.smmt.co.uk

MUNICIPAL YEAR BOOK (£219)
32 Vauxhall Bridge Road, London SW1V 2SS.
Tel: 020-7973 6402 Fax: 020-7973 5052
Web: www.municipalyearbook.co.uk

**NATURE YEARBOOK OF SCIENCE
AND TECHNOLOGY** (£150)
Macmillan Distribution Ltd, Brunel Road, Houndmills,
Basingstoke, Hampshire RG21 6XS. Tel: 01256-329242
Fax: 01256-328339

**OFFICIAL FORMULA ONE ANNUAL OF
THE SEASON** (£35)
The Turnmill Building, 63 Clerkenwell Road,
London EC1M 5NP

OFFSHORE OIL AND GAS DIRECTORY (£99)
CMP Information Ltd, Data and Information Services
Division, Riverbank House, Angel Lane, Tonbridge,
Kent TN9 1SE. Tel: 01732-377591 Fax: 01732-377454
Web: www.cmpdata.co.uk

PACKAGING INDUSTRY DIRECTORY (£99)
CMP Informations Ltd, Data and Information Services
Division, Riverbank House, Angel Lane, Tonbridge,
Kent TN9 1SE. Tel: 01732-377591 Fax: 01732-377454
Web: www.cmpdata.co.uk

PEARS CYCLOPEDIA (£16.99)
Pearson, Edinburgh Gate, Harlow, Essex CM20 2JE.
Tel: 01279-623928

PRIMARY EDUCATION DIRECTORY (£55)
Darby House, Bletchingley Road, Merstham, Redhill
RH1 3DN. Tel: 01737-642223 Fax: 01737-644283
Web: www.schoolgovernment.co.uk/pages/pub/
ped2002.htm

PRINTING TRADES DIRECTORY (£115)
Riverbank House, Angel Lane, Tonbridge, Kent TN1 1SE.
Tel: 01732-377591 Fax: 01732-377440
Web: www.cmpdata.co.uk

RAILWAY DIRECTORY (£199)
PO Box 935, Finchingfield, Braintree, Essex CM7 4LN.
Tel: 01371-810433 Fax: 01371-811065

REEDS NAUTICAL ALMANAC (£32.95)
The Book Barn, White Chimney Row, Westbourne,
Hampshire PO10 8RS. Tel: 01243-377977
Fax: 01243-379136 Web: www.nauticaldata.com

REGIONAL TRENDS (£39.50)
PO Box 29, Norwich NR3 1GN. Tel: 0870-600 5522
Fax: 0870-600 5533 Web: www.tso.co.uk

RETAIL DIRECTORY OF THE UK (£195)
32 Vauxhall Bridge Road, London SW1V 2SS.
Tel: 020-7973 6400 Fax: 020-7233 5056
Web: www.hemming-group.co.uk

RIBA DIRECTORY OF PRACTICES (£50)
Construction House, 56–64 Leonard Street, London
EC2A 4LT. Tel: 020-7251 0791 Fax: 020-7608 2375
Web: www.ribabookshop.com

ROYAL AND ANCIENT GOLFER'S HANDBOOK (£20)
Pan Macmillan Ltd, 20 New Wharf Road, London N1 9RR.
Tel: 020-7014 6000 Fax: 020-7014 6141
Web: www.panmacmillan.com

ROYAL SOCIETY YEAR BOOK (£25)
6–9 Carlton House Terrace, London SW1Y 5AG.
Tel: 020-7451 2500 Fax: 020-7930 2170
Web: www.royalsoc.ac.uk

SCOTTISH LAW DIRECTORY (£40)
Customer Services, LexisNexis UK, 2 Addiscombe Road,
Croydon CR9 5AF. Tel: 020-8662 2000 Fax: 020-8662 2012
Web: www.lexisnexis.co.uk

SOCIAL SERVICES YEAR BOOK (£130)
128 Long Acre, London WC2E 9AN. Tel: 020-7447 2000

SOCIAL TRENDS (£39.50)
PO Box 29, Norwich NR3 1GN. Tel: 0870-600 5522
Fax: 0870-600 5533 Web: www.tso.co.uk

SPINK STANDARD CATALOGUE OF BRITISH
COINS (£18)
69 Southampton Row, London WC1B 4ET.
Tel: 020-7563 4045 Fax: 020-7563 4068
Web: www.spink-online.com

SPON'S ARCHITECTS' AND BUILDERS'
PRICE BOOK (£120)
Spon Press, New Fetter Lane, London EC4B 4FH.
Tel: 08700-768858 Fax: 020-7842 2300
Web: www.pricebooks.co.uk

SPON'S MECHANICAL AND ELECTRICAL SERVICES
PRICE BOOK (£120)
Spon Press, New Fetter Lane, London EC4B 4FH.
Tel: 08700-768858 Fax: 020-7842 2300
Web: www.pricebooks.co.uk

STATESMAN'S YEARBOOK (£75)
Macmillan Building, Crinan Street, London N1 9XW.
Tel: 020-7843 4665 Fax: 020-7843 4650
Web: www.palgrave.com

STOCK EXCHANGE YEARBOOK (£270)
Caritas Data, Paulton House, 8 Shepherdess Walk,
London N1 7LB. Tel: 020-7566 8210 Fax: 020-7566 8238

STONE'S JUSTICES' MANUAL (£376.05)
Customer Services, LexisNexis UK, 2 Addiscombe Road,
Croydon CR9 5AF. Tel: 020-8662 2000 Fax: 020-8662 2012

UK KOMPASS REGISTER (£495)
East Grinstead, Windsor Court, East Grinstead,
W. Sussex RH19 1XA. Tel: 0800-0185882
Fax: 01342-335998 Web: www.kompass.co.uk

UK: THE OFFICIAL YEARBOOK OF THE UNITED
KINGDOM AND NORTHERN IRELAND (£37.50)
PO Box 29, Norwich NR3 1GN. Tel: 0870-600 5522
Fax: 0870-600 5533 Web: www.tso.co.uk

UNITED KINGDOM MINERALS YEARBOOK (£40)
Economic Minerals and Geochemical Baseline,
British Geological Survey, Keyworth, Notts NG12 5GG.
Tel: 0115-936 3100 Fax: 0115-936 3200
Web: www.mineralsuk.com

VOLUNTARY AGENCIES DIRECTORY (£30)
NCVO Publications, Earlstrees Court, Earlstrees Road,
Corby, Northants NN17 4HH. Tel: 0800-2798798
Fax: 0870-1911220 Web: www.ncvo-vol.org.uk

WHITAKER'S BOOKS IN PRINT (£580)
Woolmead House West, Bear Lane, Farnham, Surrey
GU9 7LG. Tel: 01252-742500 Fax: 01252-742501
Web: www.whitaker.co.uk

WHITAKER'S RED BOOK – THE DIRECTORY OF
PUBLISHERS (£16.50)
Woolmead House West, Bear Lane, Farnham, Surrey
GU9 7LG. Tel: 01252-742500 Fax: 01252-742501
Web: www.whitaker.co.uk

THE WHITEHALL COMPANION (£170)
PO Box 29, Norwich NR3 1GN. Tel: 0870-600 5522
Fax: 0870-600 5533 Web: www.tso.co.uk

WHO'S WHO (£130) 37 Soho Square, London W1D 3QZ.
Tel: 020-7287 5366 Fax: 020-7734 6856
Web: www.acblack.com

WILLING'S PRESS GUIDE (£299)
Chess House, 34 Germain Street, Chesham, Bucks HP5 1ST.
Tel: 0870-736 0010 Fax: 0870-736 0011
Web: www.willingspress.com

WISDEN CRICKETERS' ALMANACK (£35)
13 Old Aylesfield, Froyle Road, Golden Pot, Nr. Alton, Hants
GU34 4BY. Tel: 01420-83415 Web: www.wisden.com

WORLD OF LEARNING (£395) Europa Publications,
11 New Fetter Lane, London EC4P 4EE. Tel: 020-7822 4300
Fax: 020-7842 4329 Web: www.europapublications.co.uk

WORLD PRESS PHOTO YEARBOOK (£12.95)
Thames and Hudson, 181A High Holborn, London
WC1V 7QX. Tel: 020-7845 5000 Fax: 020-7845 5050
Web: www.thamesandhudson.com

WORLD RADIO TV HANDBOOK (£19.95)
WRTH Publications Ltd, PO Box 290, Oxford OX2 7FT.
Tel: 01865-516717 Fax: 01865-516717
Web: www.wrth.com

WORLD SHIPPING DIRECTORY (£265)
Lombard House, 3 Princess Way, Redhill, Surrey RH1 1UP.
Tel: 01737-379700 Fax: 01737-379001
Web: www.lrfairplay.com

WRITERS' AND ARTISTS' YEARBOOK (£13.99)
37 Soho Square, London W1D 3QZ. Tel: 020-7287 5338
Fax: 020-7734 6856 Web: www.acblack.com

YEARBOOK OF ASTRONOMY (£14.99)
20 New Wharf Road, London N1 9RR. Tel: 020-7014 6000
Fax: 020-7014 6001

ZURICH INVESTMENT AND SAVINGS HANDBOOK
(£29.99)
Edinburgh Gate, Harlow, Essex CM20 2JE.
Tel: 01279-623928 Fax: 01279-414130
Web: www.pearsoneduc.com

EMPLOYERS' AND TRADE ASSOCIATIONS

Most national employers' associations are members of the Confederation of British Industry (CBI).

CBI
Centre Point, 103 New Oxford Street, London WC1A 1DU
Tel: 020-7379 7400

The CBI was founded in 1965 and is an independent non-party political body financed by industry and commerce. It exists primarily to ensure that the Government understands the intentions, needs and problems of British business. It is the recognised spokesman for the business viewpoint and is consulted as such by the Government.

The CBI has a direct corporate membership employing over 4 million, and a trade association membership over 6 million of the workforce.

The governing body of the CBI is the 200-strong Council, which meets four times a year in London under the chairmanship of the President. It is assisted by 17 expert standing committees which advise on the main aspects of policy. There are 12 regional councils and offices, covering the administrative regions of England, Wales, Scotland and Northern Ireland. There is also an office in Brussels and one in Washington.

President, Sir John Egan
Director-General, Digby Jones
Secretary, P. Forder
WALES: Ground Floor Unit 3, Columbus Walk,
Brigantine Place, Atlantic Wharf, Cardiff CF10 4WW.
Tel: 029-2045 3710. *Regional Director:* David Rosser
SCOTLAND: 16 Robertson Street, Glasgow G2 8DS.
Tel: 0141-222 2184. *Regional Director:* I. McMillan
NORTHERN IRELAND: Scottish Amicable Building,
11 Donegall Square, Belfast BT1 5SE. Tel: 028-9032 6658.
Regional Director: N. Smyth

ASSOCIATIONS

ADVERTISING ASSOCIATION, Abford House, 15 Wilton
Road, London SW1V 1NJ. Tel: 020-7828 2771
Fax: 020-7931 0376 Web: www.adassoc.org.uk
Director-General: Andrew Brown
ASSOCIATION OF BRITISH INSURERS, 51 Gresham Street,
London EC2V 7HQ. Tel: 020-7600 3333 Fax: 020-7696 8999
Web: www.abi.org.uk *Director-General:* M. Francis
ASSOCIATION OF PRIVATE MARKET OPERATORS,
4 Worrygoose Lane, Rotherham, S. Yorks S60 4AD.
Tel: 01709-700072 Fax: 01709-703648
Web: www.apmomarkets.co.uk
General Secretary: David J. Glasby
BLC LEATHER TECHNOLOGY CENTRE LTD, Leather
Trade House, Kings Park Road, Moulton Park, Northampton
NN3 6JD. Tel: 01604-679999 Fax: 01604-679998
Web: www.blcleathertech.com
Managing Director: Mr M. W. Parsons
BOSS FEDERATION, 645 Ajax Avenue, Slough,
Berks SL1 4BG. Tel: 0845-450 1565 Fax: 0870-770 6789
Web: www.bossfed.co.uk *Chief Executive:* K. Davies
BRITISH APPAREL AND TEXTILE CONFEDERATION,
5 Portland Place, London W1B 1PW. Tel: 020-7636 7788
Fax: 020-7636 7515 Web: www.batc.co.uk
Director-General: J. R. Wilson, OBE

BRITISH BANKERS' ASSOCIATION, Pinners Hall,
105–108 Old Broad Street, London EC2N 1EX.
Tel: 020-7216 8800 Fax: 020-7216 8811
Web: www.bba.org.uk *Chief Executive:* Ian Mullen
BRITISH BEER AND PUB ASSOCIATION, Market Towers,
1 Nine Elms Lane, London SW8 5NQ. Tel: 020-7627 9191
Fax: 020-7627 9123 Web: www.blra.co.uk
Chief Executive Officer: R. Hayward, OBE
BRITISH CLOTHING INDUSTRY ASSOCIATION LTD,
5 Portland Place, London W1B 1PW. Tel: 020-7636 7788
Fax: 020-7636 7515 *Director:* J. R. Wilson, OBE
BRITISH MARINE FEDERATION, Marine House,
Thorpe Lea Road, Egham, Surrey TW20 8BF.
Tel: 01784-223600 Fax: 01784-439678
Chief Executive: John Clarke, CBE, LVO, MBE
BRITISH PLASTICS FEDERATION, 6 Bath Place, Rivington
Street, London EC2A 3JE. Tel: 020-7457 5000
Fax: 020-7457 5045 Web: www.bpf.co.uk
Director-General: P. Davis, OBE
BRITISH PORTS ASSOCIATION, Africa House,
64–78 Kingsway, London WC2B 6AH. Tel: 020-7242 1200
Fax: 020-7430 7474 Web: www.britishports.org.uk
Director: D. Whitehead
BRITISH PRINTING INDUSTRIES FEDERATION,
Farringdon Point, 29–35 Farringdon Road, London EC1M
3JF. Tel: 020-7915 8300 Fax: 020-7405 7784
Web: www.bpif.org.uk *Chief Executive:* Michael Johnson
BRITISH PROPERTY FEDERATION, 7th Floor, 1 Warwick
Row, London SW1E 5ER. Tel: 020-7828 0111
Fax: 020-7834 3442 Web: www.bpf.co.uk
Chief Executive: Mrs L. Peace
BRITISH RETAIL CONSORTIUM, 2nd Floor, 21 Dartmouth
Street, London SW1H 9BP. Tel: 020-7854 8900
Fax: 020-7854 8901 *Director-General:* W. Moyes
BRITISH RUBBER MANUFACTURERS' ASSOCIATION
LTD, 6 Bath Place, Rivington Street, London EC2A 3JE.
Tel: 020-7457 5040 Fax: 020-7972 9008
Web: www.brma.co.uk *Director:* A. J. Dorken
THE CHAMBER OF SHIPPING LTD, Carthusian Court,
12 Carthusian Street, London EC1M 6EZ.
Tel: 020-7417 2800 Fax: 020-7726 2080
Web: www.british-shipping.org
Director-General: Mr M. Brownrigg, KBE
CHEMICAL INDUSTRIES ASSOCIATION LTD,
Kings Buildings, Smith Square, London SW1P 3JJ.
Tel: 020-7963 6702 Fax: 020-7834 4470
Web: www.cia.org.uk
Director-General: Mrs Judith Hackitt
COMMERCIAL RADIO COMPANIES ASSOCIATION
(CRCA), The Radiocentre, 77 Shaftesbury Avenue,
London W1D 5DU. Tel: 020-7306 2603 Fax: 020-7470 0062
Web: www.crca.co.uk *Chief Executive:* P. Brown
CONFEDERATION OF PASSENGER TRANSPORT UK,
Imperial House, 15–19 Kingsway, London WC2B 6UN.
Tel: 020-7240 3131 Fax: 020-7240 6565
Web: www.cpt-uk.org/cpt
Director-General: Brian Nimick, OBE
CONSTRUCTION CONFEDERATION, Construction House,
56–64 Leonard Street, London EC2A 4JX.
Tel: 020-7608 5000 Fax: 020-7608 5001
Web: www.constructionconfederation.co.uk
Chief Executive: S. Ratcliffe

CONSTRUCTION PRODUCTS ASSOCIATION,
26 Store Street, London WC1E 7BT. Tel: 020-7323 3770
Fax: 020-7323 0307 Web: www.constprod.org.uk
Chief Executive: M. G. Ankers, FRSA

DAIRY INDUSTRY ASSOCIATION LTD. (DIAL),
19 Cornwall Terrace, London NW1 4QP. Tel: 020-7486 7244
Fax: 020-7935 3920 Web: www.dia-ltd.org.uk
Director-General: J. Begg

ENGINEERING EMPLOYERS' FEDERATION, Broadway
House, Tothill Street, London SW1H 9NQ.
Tel: 020-7222 7777 Fax: 020-7222 2782
Web: www.eef.org.uk *Director-General:* M. J. Temple

THE FEDERATION OF BAKERS, 6 Catherine Street,
London WC2B 5JW. Tel: 020-7420 7190
Fax: 020-7379 0542 Web: www.bakersfederation.org.uk
Director: J. S. White

FEDERATION OF BRITISH ELECTROTECHNICAL AND
ALLIED MANUFACTURERS' ASSOCIATIONS (BEAMA),
Westminster Tower, 3 Albert Embankment, London SE1 7SL.
Tel: 020-7793 3000 Fax: 020-7793 3003
Web: www.beama.org.uk
Director-General: David Dossett

FEDERATION OF MASTER BUILDERS, Gordon Fisher
House, 14–15 Great James Street, London WC1N 3DP.
Tel: 020-7242 7583 Fax: 020-7404-0296
Web: www.fmb.org.uk *Director-General:* I. Davis

FINANCE AND LEASING ASSOCIATION, 2nd Floor,
Imperial House, 15–19 Kingsway, London WC2B 6UN.
Tel: 020-7836 6511 Fax: 020-7420 9600
Web: www.fla.org.uk *Director-General:* M. A. Hall, MVO

FOOD AND DRINK FEDERATION, 6 Catherine Street,
London WC2B 5JJ. Tel: 020-7836 2460 Fax: 020-7836 0580
Web: www.fdf.org.uk *Director-General:* Sylvia Jay

FREIGHT TRANSPORT ASSOCIATION LTD, Hermes
House, St John's Road, Tunbridge Wells, Kent TN4 9UZ.
Tel: 01892-526171 Fax: 01892-534989
Web: www.fta.co.uk *Chief Executive:* Richard Turner

INSTITUTE OF CHARTERED FORESTERS, 7A St. Colme
Street, Edinburgh EH3 6AA. Tel: 0131-225 2705
Web: www.charteredforesters.org
Executive Director: Ms M. Dick, OBE

KNITTING INDUSTRIES' FEDERATION LTD,
53 Oxford Street, Leicester LE1 5XY. Tel: 0116-254 1608
Fax: 0116-254 2273 Web: www.emnet.co.uk/kif/
Director: Anne Carvell

MANAGEMENT CONSULTANCIES ASSOCIATION,
49 Whitehall, London SW1A 2BX. Tel: 020-7321 3990
Fax: 020-7321 3991 Web: www.mca.org.uk
Executive Director: B. Petter

THE NATIONAL FARMERS' UNION (NFU), Agriculture
House, 164 Shaftesbury Avenue, London WC2H 8HL.
Tel: 020-7331 7200 Fax: 020-7331 7313
Web: www.nfu.org.uk *Director-General:* R. Macdonald

NATIONAL FEDERATION OF RETAIL NEWSAGENTS,
Yeoman House, Sekforde Street, London EC1R 0HF.
Tel: 020-7253 4225 Fax: 020-7250 0927
Web: www.nfrn.org.uk *Chief Executive:* R. Clarke

NATIONAL MARKET TRADERS' FEDERATION, Hampton
House, Hawshaw Lane, Hoyland, Barnsley S74 0HA.
Tel: 01226-749021 Fax: 01226-740329
Web: www.nmtf.co.uk *General Secretary:* D. E. Feeny

NEWSPAPER PUBLISHERS ASSOCIATION LTD,
34 Southwark Bridge Road, London SE1 9EU.
Tel: 020-7207 2200 Fax: 020-7928 2067
Director: S. Oram

NEWSPAPER SOCIETY, Bloomsbury House, 74–77 Great
Russell Street, London WC1B 3DA. Tel: 020-7636 7014
Fax: 020-7631 5119 Web: www.newspapersoc.org.uk
Director: D. Newell

THE PAPER FEDERATION OF GREAT BRITAIN,
Papermakers House, Rivenhall Road, Swindon SN5 7BD.
Tel: 01793-889600 Fax: 01793-878700 Web:
www.paper.org.uk *Director-General:* Dr Martin Oldman

THE PUBLISHERS ASSOCIATION, 29B Montague Street,
London WC1B 5BH. Tel: 020-7691 9191
Fax: 020-7691 9199 Web: www.publishers.org.uk
Chief Executive: A. R. Williams, OBE

THE ROAD HAULAGE ASSOCIATION LTD, Roadway
House, 35 Monument Hill, Weybridge, Surrey KT13 8RN.
Tel: 01932-841515 Fax: 01932-852516 Web: www.rha.net
Chief Executive: R. King

SOCIETY OF BRITISH AEROSPACE COMPANIES LTD,
Duxbury House, 60 Petty France, London SW1H 9EU.
Tel: 020-7227 1000 Fax: 020-7227 1067
Web: www.sbac.co.uk *Director-General:* Dr Sally Howes

SOCIETY OF MOTOR MANUFACTURERS AND
TRADERS LTD, Forbes House, Halkin Street, London SW1X
7DS. Tel: 020-7235 7000 Fax: 020-7235 7112
Web: www.smmt.co.uk
Chief Executive: C. Macgowan

THE SPORT INDUSTRIES FEDERATION, Federation
House, National Agricultural Centre, Stoneleigh Park,
Kenilworth, Warks CV8 2RF. Tel: 08708-709399
Fax: 02476-414990 Web: www.sports-life.com
Operations Director: D. J. Pomfret

THE TIMBER TRADE FEDERATION, Clareville House,
26–27 Oxendon Street, London SW1Y 4EL.
Tel: 020-7839 1891 Fax: 020-7930 0094
Web: www.ttf.co.uk *Director-General:* P. C. Martin

UK OFFSHORE OPERATORS ASSOCIATION LTD, Second
Floor, 232–242 Vauxhall Bridge Road, London SW1V 1AY.
Tel: 020-7802 2400 Fax: 020-7802 2401
Web: www.oilandgas.org.uk
Director-General: J. May

UK PETROLEUM INDUSTRY ASSOCIATION LTD,
9 Kingsway, London WC2B 6XF. Tel: 020-7240 0289
Fax: 020-7379 3102 Web: www.ukpia.com
Director-General: M. Webb

ULSTER FARMERS' UNION, 475 Antrim Road, Belfast
BT15 3DA. Tel: 028-9037 0222 Fax: 028-9037 1231
Web: www.ufuni.org *Director-General:* C. Black

TRADE UNIONS

Nearly 80 per cent of trade union members belong to unions affiliated to the TUC.

The Central Arbitration Committee arbitrates on trade disputes, adjudicates on disclosure of information complaints, determines claims for statutory recognition under the Employment Relations Act 1999 and certain issues relating to the implementation of the European Works Council Directive.

THE CENTRAL ARBITRATION COMMITTEE, 3rd Floor, Discovery House, 28–42 Banner Street, London EC1Y 8QE. Tel: 020-7251 9747 Fax: 020-7251 3114
Web: www.cac.gov.uk
Chairman, Sir Michael Burton
Secretary and Chief Executive, Graeme Charles

TRADES UNION CONGRESS (TUC)
Congress House, 23–28 Great Russell Street, London WC1B 3LS
Tel 020-7636 4030 Fax 020-7636 0632
Web: www.tuc.org.uk

The Trades Union Congress, founded in 1868, is an independent association of trade unions. The TUC promotes the rights and welfare of those in work and helps the unemployed. It helps its member unions promote membership in new areas and industries, and campaigns for rights at work for all employees, including part-time and temporary workers, whether union members or not. TUC representatives sit on many public bodies at national and international level. It makes representations to government, political parties, employers and international bodies such as the European Union.

The governing body of the TUC is the annual Congress. Between Congresses, business is conducted by a General Council, which meets five times a year, and an Executive Committee, which meets monthly. The full-time staff is headed by the General Secretary who is elected by Congress and is a permanent member of the General Council.

There are some 69 affiliated unions with a membership of nearly 6,700,000.
President (2003–4), Roger Lyons
General Secretary, B. Barber, elected 2002

SCOTTISH TRADES UNION CONGRESS
333 Woodlands Road, Glasgow G3 6NG
Tel 0141-337 8100 Fax 0141-337 8101
Email: info@stuc.org.uk

The Congress was formed in 1897 and acts as a national centre for the trade union movement in Scotland. The STUC promotes the rights and welfare of those in work and helps the unemployed. It helps its member unions to promote membership in new areas and industries, and campaigns for rights at work for all employees, including part-time and temporary workers, whether union members or not. It makes representations to government and employers. In July 2002 it consisted of 47 unions with a total membership of 626,816 and 30 directly affiliated Trade Councils.

The Annual Congress in April elects a 39-member General Council on the basis of six industrial sections.
Chairperson, Pauline Frazer
General Secretary, Bill Speirs

AFFILIATED UNIONS *as at July 2003*

ABBEY NATIONAL GROUP UNION (ANGU), 2nd Floor, 16–17 High Street, Tring, Herts HP23 5AH.
Tel: 01442-891122 Web: www.angu.org.uk
General Secretary: Linda Rolph, *Membership:* 9,150
ACCORD, Simmons House, 46 Old Bath Road, Charvil, Reading RG10 9QR. Tel: 0118-934 1808
Web: www.accord-myunion.org
General Secretary: Ged Nichols, *Membership:* 25,000
ALLIANCE AND LEICESTER GROUP UNION OF STAFF (ALGUS), 22 Upper King Street, Leicester LE1 6XE.
Tel: 0116-285 6585 Web: www.algus.org.uk
General Secretary: Clare Clark, *Membership:* 2,800
AMICUS (FORMERLY AEEU), Hayes Court, West Common Road, Bromley, Kent BR2 7AU. Tel: 020-8462 7755
Web: www.aeeu.org.uk *General Secretary:*
Derek Simpson, *Membership:* 1,132,311
AMICUS (FORMERLY MSF), MSF Centre, 33–37 Moreland Street, London EC1V 8HA. Tel: 020-7505 3000
Web: www.msf.org.uk *General Secretary:* Roger Lyons, *Membership:* 1,132,211
ASSOCIATED SOCIETY OF LOCOMOTIVE ENGINEERS AND FIREMEN (ASLEF), 9 Arkwright Road, London NW3 6AB. Tel: 020-7317 8600 Web: www.aslef.org.uk
General Secretary: Mick Rix, *Membership:* 17,789
ASSOCIATION FOR COLLEGE MANAGEMENT (ACM), 10 De Montfort Street, Leicester LE1 7GG.
Tel: 0116-275 5076 Web: ww.acm.uk.com
General Secretary: Peter Pendle, *Membership:* 3,600
ASSOCIATION OF EDUCATIONAL PSYCHOLOGISTS (AEP), 26 The Avenue, Durham DH1 4ED.
Tel: 0191-384 9512 Web: www.aep.org.uk
General Secretary: B. Harrison-Jennings, *Membership:* 2,642
ASSOCIATION OF FIRST DIVISION CIVIL SERVANTS (FDA), 2 Caxton Street, London SW1H 0QH.
Tel: 020-7343 1111 Web: www.fda.org.uk
General Secretary: J. Baume, *Membership:* 11,500
ASSOCIATION OF FLIGHT ATTENDANTS (AFA), United Airlines Cargo Centre, AFA Council 07, Shoreham Road East, Heathrow Airport, Hounslow TW6 3UA. Tel: 020-8276 6723
Web: www.unitedafa.org/councils/7-london.html
President: Kevin Creighan, *Membership:* 750
ASSOCIATION OF MAGISTERIAL OFFICERS (AMO), 1 Fellmongers Path, 176 Tower Bridge Road, London SE1 3LY. Tel: 020-7403 2244 Web: www.amo-online.org.uk
General Secretary: Rosie Eagleson, *Membership:* 6,795
ASSOCIATION OF TEACHERS AND LECTURERS (ATL), 7 Northumberland Street, London WC2N 5RD.
Tel: 020-7930 6441 Web: www.askatl.org.uk
General Secretary: Dr Mary Boustead, *Membership:* 160,000
ASSOCIATION OF UNIVERSITY TEACHERS (AUT), Egmont House, 25–31 Tavistock Place, London WC1H 9UT.
Tel: 020-7670 9700 Web: www.aut.org.uk
General Secretary: Sally Hunt, *Membership:* 46,206
BAKERS, FOOD AND ALLIED WORKERS' UNION (BFAWU), Stanborough House, Great North Road, Stanborough, Welwyn Garden City, Herts AL8 7TA.
Tel: 01707-260150 Web: www.bfawu.org
General Secretary: Joe Marino, *Membership:* 29,800
BRITANNIA STAFF UNION (BSU), Court Lodge, Leonard Street, Leek, Staffordshire ST13 5JP. Tel: 01538-399627
Web: www.britanniasu.org.uk
General Secretary: David O'Dowd, *Membership:* 2,400

BRITISH AIR LINE PILOTS ASSOCIATION (BALPA), 81 New Road, Harlington, Hayes, Middx UB3 5BG. Tel: 020-8476 4000 Web: www.balpa.org *General Secretary:* Jim McAuslan, *Membership:* 8,072

BRITISH ASSOCIATION OF COLLIERY MANAGEMENT – TECHNICAL, ENERGY AND ADMINISTRATIVE MANAGEMENT (BACM-TEAM), 17 South Parade, Doncaster, S. Yorks DN1 2DR. Tel: 01302-815551 Web: www.bacmteam.org.uk *General Secretary:* Pat Carragher, *Membership:* 4,027

BRITISH ORTHOPTIC SOCIETY (BOS), Tavistock House North, Tavistock Square, London WC1H 9HX. Tel: 020-7387 7992 Web: www.orthoptics.org.uk *Hon. Secretary:* Rosie Auld, *Membership:* 1,003

BROADCASTING, ENTERTAINMENT, CINEMATOGRAPH AND THEATRE UNION (BECTU), 373–377 Clapham Road, London SW9 9BT. Tel: 020-7346 0900 Web: www.bectu.org.uk *General Secretary:* Roger Bolton, *Membership:* 24,728

CARD SETTING MACHINE TENTERS' SOCIETY (CSMTS), 48 Scar End Lane, Staincliffe, Dewsbury, W. Yorks WF13 4NY. Tel: 01924-400206 *Secretary:* Anthony John Moorhouse, *Membership:* 88

CERAMIC AND ALLIED TRADES UNION (CATU), Hillcrest House, Garth Street, Hanley, Stoke-on-Trent ST1 2AB. Tel: 0800-731 7680 Web: www.catu.org.uk *General Secretary:* G. Bagnall, *Membership:* 13,500

THE CHARTERED SOCIETY OF PHYSIOTHERAPY (CSP), 14 Bedford Row, London WC1R 4ED. Tel: 020-7306 6666 Web: www.csp.org.uk *Chief Executive:* P. Gray, *Membership:* 38,000

COMMUNICATION WORKERS UNION (CWU), 150 The Broadway, Wimbledon, London SW19 1RX. Tel: 020-8971 7200 Web: www.cwu.org *General Secretary:* B. Hayes, *Membership:* 280,000

COMMUNITY AND DISTRICT NURSING ASSOCIATION (CDNA), Westel House, 32–38 Uxbridge Road, Ealing, London W5 2BS. Tel: 020-8280 5342 Web: www.cdna.tvu.ac.uk *Chair:* Ms A. Duffy, *Membership:* 4,000

COMMUNITY AND YOUTH WORKERS UNION (CYWU), Unit 302, The Argent Centre, 60 Frederick Street, Birmingham B1 3HS. Tel: 0121-244 3344 Web: www.cywu.org.uk *General Secretary:* D. Nicholls, *Membership:* 4,300

CONNECT, THE UNION FOR PROFESSIONALS IN COMMUNICATIONS, 30 St George's Road, London SW19 4BD. Tel: 020-8971 6000 Web: www.connectuk.org *General Secretary:* A. Askew, *Membership:* 19,102

DIAGEO STAFF ASSOCIATION (DSA), Sun Works Cottage, Park Royal Brewery, London NW10 7RR. Tel: 020-8965 7700 *Executive Chairman:* D. Orton, *Membership:* 605

EDUCATIONAL INSTITUTE OF SCOTLAND (EIS), 46 Moray Place, Edinburgh EH3 6BH. Tel: 0131-225 6244 Web: www.eis.org.uk *General Secretary:* Ronald A. Smith, *Membership:* 52,552

ENGINEERING AND FASTENER TRADE UNION (EFTU), 22 Willow Avenue, Edgbaston, Birmingham, West Midlands B17 8HD. Tel: 0121-420 2204 *General Secretary:* Andrew Evans, *Membership:* 110

EQUITY, Guild House, Upper St Martin's Lane, London WC2H 9EG. Tel: 020-7379 6,000 Web: www.equity.org.uk *General Secretary:* Ian McGarry, *Membership:* 35,000

THE FIRE BRIGADES UNION (FBU), Bradley House, 68 Coombe Road, Kingston upon Thames, Surrey KT2 7AE. Tel: 020-8541 1765 Web: www.fbu.org.uk *General Secretary:* A. Gilchrist, *Membership:* 52,000

GENERAL UNION OF LOOM OVERLOOKERS (GULO), 9 Wellington Street, St John's, Blackburn, Lancs BB1 8AF. Tel: 01254-51760 *General Secretary:* Don Rishton, *Membership:* 286

GMB, 22–24 Worple Road, London SW19 4DD. Tel: 020-8947 3131 Web: www.gmb.org.uk *General Secretary:* J. Edmonds, *Membership:* 700,000

GRAPHICAL, PAPER AND MEDIA UNION (GPMU), Keys House, 63–67 Bromham Road, Bedford MK40 2AG. Tel: 01234-351521 Web: www.gpmu.org.uk *General Secretary:* A. D. Dubbins, *Membership:* 200,676

HOSPITAL CONSULTANTS AND SPECIALISTS ASSOCIATION (HCSA), 1 Kingsclere Road, Overton, Basingstoke, Hants RG25 3JA. Tel: 01256-771777 Web: www.hcsa.com *Administrative Director:* G. Poynton, *Membership:* 2,850

INDEPENDENT UNION OF HALIFAX STAFF (IUHS), Simmons House, 46 Old Bath Road, Charvil, Reading, Berks RG10 9QR. Tel: 0118-934 1808 *General Secretary:* G. Nichols, *Membership:* 24,000

ISTC, Swinton House, 324 Gray's Inn Road, London WC1X 8DD. Tel: 020-7239 1200 Web: www.istc-tu.org *General Secretary:* M. J. Leahy, *Membership:* 50,100

MUSICIANS' UNION (MU), 60–62 Clapham Road, London SW9 0JJ. Tel: 020-7582 5566 Web: www.musiciansunion.org.uk *General Secretary:* John Smith, *Membership:* 31,312

NASUWT (NATIONAL ASSOCIATION OF SCHOOLMASTERS/UNION OF WOMEN TEACHERS), Hillscourt Education Centre, Rose Hill, Rednal, Birmingham B45 8RS. Tel: 0121-453 6150 Web: www.teachersunion.org.uk *General Secretary:* Eamonn O'Kane, *Membership:* 200,000

NATIONAL ASSOCIATION OF COLLIERY OVERMEN, DEPUTIES AND SHOTFIRERS (NACODS), 37 Church Street, Barnsley S70 2AR. Tel: 01226-203743 Web: www.nacods.co.uk *General Secretary:* Ian Parker, *Membership:* 800

NATIONAL ASSOCIATION OF CO-OPERATIVE OFFICIALS (NACO), 6A Clarendon Place, Hyde, Cheshire SK14 2QZ. Tel: 0161-351 7900 *General Secretary:* L. W. Ewing, *Membership:* 2,363

NATFHE (THE UNIVERSITY AND COLLEGE LECTURERS' UNION), 27 Britannia Street, London WC1X 9JP. Tel: 020-7837 3636 Web: www.natfhe.org.uk *General Secretary:* P. Mackney, *Membership:* 66,000

NATIONAL ASSOCIATION OF PROBATION OFFICERS (NAPO), 4 Chivalry Road, London SW11 1HT. Tel: 020-7223 4887 Web: www.napo.org.uk *General Secretary:* Ms J. McKnight, *Membership:* 6,526

NATIONAL UNION OF DOMESTIC APPLIANCES AND GENERAL OPERATIVES (NUDAGO), 1st Floor, 7–8 Imperial Buildings, Corporation Street, Rotherham, S. Yorks S60 1PB. Tel: 01709-382820 *General Secretary:* A. McCarthy, *Membership:* 2,500

NATIONAL UNION OF JOURNALISTS (NUJ), Headland House, 308–312 Gray's Inn Road, London WC1X 8DP. Tel: 020-7278 7916 Web: www.nuj.org.uk *General Secretary:* Jeremy Dear, *Membership:* 20,000

NATIONAL UNION OF KNITWEAR, FOOTWEAR AND APPAREL TRADES (KFAT), 55 New Walk, Leicester LE1 7EA. Tel: 0116-255 6703 Web: www.kfat.org.uk *General Secretary:* P. Gates, *Membership:* 12,471

NATIONAL UNION OF LOCK AND METAL WORKERS (NULMW), Bellamy House, Wilkes Street, Willenhall, W. Midlands WV13 2BS. Tel: 01902-366651 *General Secretary:* R. Ward, *Membership:* 4,112

NATIONAL UNION OF MARINE, AVIATION AND SHIPPING TRANSPORT OFFICERS (NUMAST), Oceanair House, 750–760 High Road, London E11 3BB. Tel: 020-8989 6677 Web: www.numast.org *General Secretary:* Brian Orrell, *Membership:* 19,133

NATIONAL UNION OF MINEWORKERS (NUM), Miners' Offices, 2 Huddersfield Road, Barnsley, S. Yorks S70 2LS. Tel: 01226-215555 *National Secretary:* S. Kemp, *Membership:* 5,000

NATIONAL UNION OF RAIL, MARITIME AND TRANSPORT WORKERS (RMT), Unity House, 39 Chalton Street, London NW1 1JD. Tel: 020-7387 4771 Web: www.rmt.org.uk *General Secretary:* Bob Crow, *Membership:* 60,400

NATIONAL UNION OF TEACHERS (NUT), Hamilton House, Mabledon Place, London WC1H 9BD. Tel: 020-7388 6191 Web: www.teachers.org.uk *General Secretary:* D. McAvoy, *Membership:* 247,252

NATIONWIDE GROUP STAFF UNION (NGSU), Middleton Farmhouse, 37 Main Road, Middleton Cheney, Banbury, Oxfordshire OX17 2QT. Tel: 01295-710767 Web: www.ngsu.org.uk *General Secretary:* Tim Poil, *Membership:* 11,520

PRISON OFFICERS' ASSOCIATION (POA), Cronin House, 245 Church Street, London N9 9HW. Tel: 020-8803 0255 *General Secretary:* B. Caton, *Membership:* 30,401

PROFESSIONAL FOOTBALLERS ASSOCIATION (PFA), 20 Oxford Court, Bishopsgate, Manchester M2 3WQ. Tel: 0161-236 0575 Web: www.givemefootball.com *Chief Executive:* G. Taylor, *Membership:* 3,848

PROSPECT, Prospect House, 75–79 York Road, London SE1 7AQ. Tel: 020-7902 6600 Web: www.prospect.org.uk *General Secretary:* P. Noon, *Membership:* 74,261

PUBLIC AND COMMERCIAL SERVICES UNION (PCS), 160 Falcon Road, London SW11 2LN. Tel: 020-7924 2727 Web: www.pcs.org.uk *General Secretary:* Mark Serwotka, *Membership:* 288,000

SHEFFIELD WOOL SHEAR WORKERS' UNION (SWSWU), 17 Galsworthy Road, Sheffield S5 8QX. *Secretary:* B. Whomersley, *Membership:* 15

THE SOCIETY OF CHIROPODISTS AND PODIATRISTS (SCP), 1 Fellmonger's Path, Tower Bridge Road, London SE1 3LY. Tel: 020-7234 8620 Web: www.feetforlife.org *Chief Executive:* Ms H. B. De Lyon, *Membership:* 8,500

THE SOCIETY OF RADIOGRAPHERS (SOR), 207 Providence Square, Mill Street, London SE1 2EW. Tel: 020-7740 7200 Web: www.sor.org *Chief Executive Officer:* Ann Cattell, *Membership:* 15,516

TRANSPORT AND GENERAL WORKERS' UNION (T&G), Transport House, 128 Theobalds Road, London WC1X 8TN. Tel: 020-7611 2500 Web: www.tgwu.org.uk *General Secretary:* W. Morris, *Membership:* 848,809

TRANSPORT SALARIED STAFFS' ASSOCIATION (TSSA), Walkden House, 10 Melton Street, London NW1 2EJ. Tel: 020-7387 2101 Web: www.tssa.org.uk *General Secretary:* R. A. Rosser, *Membership:* 32,500

UBAC (REPRESENTING STAFF IN THE BRADFORD AND BINGLEY GROUP AND ALLTEL MORTGAGE SOLUTIONS), 18D Market Place, Malton, N. Yorks YO17 7LX. Tel: 01653-697634 *General Secretary:* D. Matthews, *Membership:* 2,584

UNDEB CENEDLAETHOL ATHRAWON CYMRU (NATIONAL UNION OF THE TEACHERS OF WALES), Pen Roc, Rhodfa'r Môr, Aberystwyth, Ceredigion SY23 2AZ. Tel: 01970-639950 Web: www.athrawon.com *General Secretary:* E. Williams, *Membership:* 4,099

UNIFI, Sheffield House, 1B Amity Grove, London SW20 0LG. Tel: 020-8946 9151 Web: www.unifi.org.uk *General Secretary:* E. Sweeney, *Membership:* 146,000

UNION OF CONSTRUCTION, ALLIED TRADES AND TECHNICIANS (UCATT), UCATT House, 177 Abbeville Road, London SW4 9RL. Tel: 020-7622 2442 Web: www.ucatt.org.uk *General Secretary:* G. Brumwell, *Membership:* 123,000

UNION OF SHOP, DISTRIBUTIVE AND ALLIED WORKERS (USDAW), Oakley, 188 Wilmslow Road, Fallowfield, Manchester M14 6LJ. Tel: 0161-224 2804 Web: www.usdaw.org.uk *General Secretary:* Sir W. Connor, *Membership:* 319,352

UNION OF TEXTILE WORKERS (UTW), 18 West Street, Leek, Staffs ST13 8AA. Tel: 01538-382068 *General Secretary:* A. Hitchmough, *Membership:* 1,389

UNISON, 1 Mabledon Place, London WC1H 9AJ. Tel: 0845-355 0845 Web: www.unison.org.uk *General Secretary:* D. Prentis, *Membership:* 1,300,500

WRITERS' GUILD OF GREAT BRITAIN (WGGB), 15 Britannia Street, London WC1X 9JN. Tel: 020-7833 0777 Web: www.writersguild.org.uk *General Secretary:* Bernie Corbett, *Membership:* 2,000

YORKSHIRE INDEPENDENT STAFF ASSOCIATION (YISA), c/o Yorkshire Building Society, 3/5 Saturday Market, Beverley HU17 8BB. Tel: 01482-862 058 *Chair:* Yvonne Goode, *Membership:* 1,270

NON-AFFILIATED UNIONS *as at July 2003*

BRITISH DENTAL ASSOCIATION, 64 Wimpole Street, London W1G 8YS. Tel: 020-7935 0875 Fax: 020-7487 5232 Web: www.bda-dentistry.org.uk *Chief Executive:* I. Wylie, *Membership:* 18,000

CHARTERED INSTITUTE OF JOURNALISTS, 2 Dock Offices, Surrey Quays Road, London SE16 2XU. Tel: 020-7252 1187 Fax: 020-7232 2302 Web: www.ioj.co.uk *General Secretary:* C. Underwood, *Membership:* 1,100

NATIONAL ASSOCIATION OF HEAD TEACHERS (NAHT), 1 Heath Square, Boltro Road, Haywards Heath, W. Sussex RH16 1BL. Tel: 01444-472472 Fax: 01444-472473 Web: www.naht.org.uk *General Secretary:* David Hart, OBE, *Membership:* 32,500

NATIONAL SOCIETY FOR EDUCATION IN ART AND DESIGN, The Gatehouse, Corsham Court, Corsham, Wilts SN13 0BZ. Tel: 01249-714825 Fax: 01249-716138 Web: www.nsead.org *General Secretary:* Dr J. M. Steers, *Membership:* 2,226

PRISON GOVERNORS ASSOCIATION, Room 718, Horseferry House, Dean Ryle Street, London SW1P 2AW. Tel: 020-7217 8591 Fax: 020-7217 8923 Web: www.prisongovernors.org.uk *General Secretary:* D. Roddan *Membership:* 1,000

RETAIL BOOK, STATIONERY AND ALLIED TRADES EMPLOYEES' ASSOCIATION, 8-9 Commercial Road, Swindon SN1 5NF. Tel: 01793-615811 Fax: 01793-421319 *President:* D. Pickles, *Membership:* 5,000

ROYAL COLLEGE OF MIDWIVES, 15 Mansfield Street, London W1G 9NH. Tel: 020-7312 3535 Fax: 020-7312 3536 Web: www.rcm.org.uk *General Secretary:* Dame Karlene Davis DBE *Membership:* 37,000

SECONDARY HEADS ASSOCIATION, 130 Regent Road, Leicester LE1 7PG. Tel: 0116-299 1122 Fax: 0116-299 1123 Web: www.sha.org.uk *General Secretary:* Dr J. E. Dunford, OBE *Membership:* 10,300

SOCIETY OF AUTHORS, 84 Drayton Gardens, London SW10 9SB. Tel: 020-7373 6642 Fax: 020-7373 5768 Web: www.societyofauthors.org *General Secretary:* M. Le Fanu, OBE, *Membership:* 7,000

UNITED ROAD TRANSPORT UNION, 76 High Lane, Chorlton-cum-Hardy, Manchester M21 9EF. Tel: 0800-526639 Fax: 0161-861 0976 Web: www.urtu.com *General Secretary:* Robert Monks, *Membership:* 20,000

SPORTS BODIES

SPORTS COUNCILS

CENTRAL COUNCIL OF PHYSICAL RECREATION, Francis House, Francis Street, London SW1P 1DE. Tel: 020-7854 8500 Fax: 020-7854 8501 Web: www.ccpr.org.uk
General Secretary: M. Denton
SPORT ENGLAND, 16 Upper Woburn Place, London WC1H 0QP. Tel: 020-7273 1500 Fax: 020-7383 5740
Web: www.sportengland.org *Chairman:* Patrick Carter
SPORTSCOTLAND, Caledonia House, South Gyle, Edinburgh EH12 9DQ. Tel: 0131-317 7200 Fax: 0131-317 7202
Web: www.sportscotland.org.uk
Chief Executive: I. Robson
SPORTS COUNCIL FOR NORTHERN IRELAND, House of Sport, Upper Malone Road, Belfast BT9 5LA. Tel: 028-9038 1222 Fax: 028-9068 2757 Web: www.sportni.net
Chief Executive: E. McCartan
SPORTS COUNCIL FOR WALES, Sophia Gardens, Cardiff CF11 9SW. Tel: 029-2030 0500 Fax: 029-2030 0600
Web: www.sports-council-wales.co.uk
Chief Executive: Dr H. Jones
UK SPORT, 40 Bernard Street, London WC1N 1ST.
Tel: 020-7211 5100 Fax: 020-7211 5246
Web: www.uksport.gov.uk
Chief Executive: Richard Callicott

ANGLING

NATIONAL FEDERATION OF ANGLERS, Halliday House, Egginton Junction, Derbyshire DE65 6GU.
Tel: 01283-734735 Fax: 01283-734799
Web: www.nfadirect.com
Administration Manager: Mrs J. A. Price

ARCHERY

GRAND NATIONAL ARCHERY SOCIETY, Lilleshall National Sports Centre, Newport, Shropshire TF10 9AT.
Tel: 01952-677888 Fax: 01952-606019 Web: www.gnas.org
Chief Executive: D. Sherratt

ASSOCIATION FOOTBALL

THE FOOTBALL ASSOCIATION, 25 Soho Square, London W1D 4FA. Tel: 020-7745 4545 Fax: 020-7745 4546
Web: www.the-fa.com
Chairman: G. Thompson
FOOTBALL ASSOCIATION OF WALES, Plymouth Chambers, 3 Westgate Street, Cardiff CF10 1DP.
Tel: 029-2037 2325 Fax: 029-2034 3961
Web: www.faw.org.uk *Secretary-General:* D. G. Collins
THE FOOTBALL LEAGUE LTD, 11 Connaught Place, London W2 2ET. Tel: 0870-4420 1888 Fax: 0870-442 1188
Web: www.football-league.co.uk
Chairman: Sir Brian Mawhinney
IRISH FOOTBALL LEAGUE, 96 University Street, Belfast BT7 1HE. Tel: 028-9024 2888 Fax: 028-9033 0773
Web: www.irish-league.co.uk *Secretary:* H. Wallace
SCOTTISH FOOTBALL ASSOCIATION, Hampden Park, Glasgow G42 9AY. Tel: 0141-616 6000 Fax: 0141-616 6001
Web: www.scottishfa.co.uk *Chief Executive:* D. Taylor
SCOTTISH FOOTBALL LEAGUE, The National Stadium, Hampden Park, Glasgow G42 9EB. Tel: 0141-620 4160
Fax: 0141-620 4161 Web: www.scottishfootballleague.com
Secretary: Peter Donald

ATHLETICS

ATHLETICS ASSOCIATION OF WALES, The Manor, Coldra Woods, Newport NP18 1WA. Tel: 01633-416633
Fax: 01633-416699 Web: www.welshathletics.org
Hon. Secretary: Jan Evans
NORTHERN IRELAND ATHLETIC FEDERATION, Athletics House, Old Coach Road, Belfast BT9 5PR.
Tel: 028-9060 2707 Fax: 028-9030 9939
Web: www.niathletics.org
Secretary: J. Allen
SCOTTISH ATHLETICS, Caledonia House, South Gyle, Edinburgh EH12 9DQ. Tel: 0131-539 7320
Web: www.scottishathletics.org.uk
President: Mr Frank Clement
UK ATHLETICS, Athletics House, 10 Harborne Road, Edgbaston, Birmingham B15 3AA. Tel: 0121-456 5098
Fax: 0121-456 8752 Web: www.ukathletics.net
Chief Executive: D. Moorcroft, OBE

BADMINTON

BADMINTON ASSOCIATION OF ENGLAND LTD, National Badminton Centre, Bradwell Road, Loughton Lodge, Milton Keynes MK8 9LA. Tel: 01908-268400
Fax: 01908-268412 Web: www.baofe.co.uk
Chief Executive: S. Baddeley
SCOTTISH BADMINTON UNION, Cockburn Centre, 40 Bogmoor Place, Glasgow G51 4TQ.
Tel: 0141-445 1218 Fax: 0141-425 1218
Web: www.scotbadminton.demon.co.uk
Chief Executive: Miss A. Smillie
WELSH BADMINTON UNION, 4th Floor, Plymouth Chambers, 3 Westgate Street, Cardiff CF10 1DP.
Tel: 029-2022 2082 Fax: 029-2039 4282
Web: www.welshbadminton.net
Director of Badminton: L. Williams

BASEBALL

BASEBALLSOFTBALL UK, Ariel House, 74A Charlotte Street, London W1T 4QJ. Tel: 020-7453 7055 Fax: 020-7453 7007
Web: www.baseballsoftballuk.com
Chief Executive: B. Fromer

BASKETBALL

BASKETBALL SCOTLAND, Caledonia House, South Gyle, Edinburgh EH12 9DQ. Tel: 0131-317 7260
Fax: 0131-317 7489 Web: www.basketball-scotland.com
Chief Executive: Rodger Thompson
ENGLISH BASKETBALL ASSOCIATION, EIS Sheffield Coleridge Road, Sheffield S9 5DA Tel: 0870-7744225
Fax: 0870-7744226 Web: www.englandbasketball.co.uk
Chief Executive: S. Kirkland

BILLIARDS AND SNOOKER

WORLD LADIES BILLIARDS AND SNOOKER ASSOCIATION, PO Box 16, 231 Ramnoth Road, Wisbech, Cambs PE13 2SX. Tel: 01945-588598
WORLD PROFESSIONAL BILLIARDS AND SNOOKER ASSOCIATION, Ground Floor, Albert House, 111–117 Victoria Street, Bristol BS1 6AX.
Tel: 0117-317 8200 Fax: 0117-317 8300
Web: www.worldsnooker.com

BOBSLEIGH

BRITISH BOBSLEIGH ASSOCIATION, Department of Sports Development and Recreation, University of Bath, Claverton Down, Bath BA2 7AY. Tel: 01225-826802 Fax: 01225-826802 Web: www.british-bobsleigh.com
Chairman: R. B. B. Ropner

BRITISH BOB SKELETON ASSOCIATION, Department of Sports Development and Recreation, University of Bath, Claverton Down, Bath BA2 7AY. Tel: 01225-323696 Fax: 01225-323696 Web: www.icetrack.org.uk
Administrator: Sarah Robinson

BOWLS

BRITISH ISLES BOWLS COUNCIL, 23 Leysland Avenue, Countesthorpe, Leics LE8 5XX. Tel: 0116-277 3234 Fax: 0116-277 3234 *Hon. Secretary:* Mr Swatland

ENGLISH BOWLING ASSOCIATION, Lyndhurst Road, Worthing, W. Sussex BN11 2AZ. Tel: 01903-820222 Fax: 01903-820444 Web: www.bowlsengland.com
Chief Executive: A. Allcock, MBE

ENGLISH INDOOR BOWLING ASSOCIATION, David Cornwell House, Bowling Green, Leicester Road, Melton Mowbray, Leics LE13 0FA. Tel: 01664-481900 Fax: 01664-428888 Web: www.eiba.co.uk
Secretary: S. A. Rodufu

ENGLISH WOMEN'S BOWLING ASSOCIATION, EWBA Office, Victoria Park, Archery Road, Leamington Spa, Warks CV31 3PT. Tel: 01926-430686 Fax: 01926-332024
Chief Administrator: Mrs P. A. Biddlecombe

ENGLISH WOMEN'S INDOOR BOWLING ASSOCIATION, 3 Moulton Business Park, Scirocco Close, Northampton NN3 6AP. Tel: 01604-494163 Fax: 01604-494434
Secretary: Mrs T. Thomas

BOXING

THE AMATEUR BOXING ASSOCIATION OF ENGLAND LTD, Crystal Palace National Sports Centre, London SE19 2BB. Tel: 020-8778 0251 Fax: 020-8778 9324
Chairman: J. Smart

BRITISH AMATEUR BOXING ASSOCIATION, 96 High Street, Lochee, Dundee DD2 3AY. Tel: 01382-611412/508261 Fax: 01382-509425
Chief Executive: F. Hendry

BRITISH BOXING BOARD OF CONTROL LTD, The Old Library, Trinity Street, Cardiff CF10 1BH. Tel: 02920-367000 Fax: 02920-367019 Web: www.bbbofc.com
General Secretary: S. J. Block

CANOEING

BRITISH CANOE UNION, John Dudderidge House, Adbolton Lane, West Bridgford, Nottingham NG2 5AS. Tel: 0115-982 1100 Fax: 0115-982 1797 Web: www.bcu.org.uk *Chief Executive:* P. Owen

CHESS

BRITISH CHESS FEDERATION, The Watch Oak, Chain Lane, Battle, E. Sussex TN33 0YD. Tel: 01424-775222 Fax: 01424-775904 Web: www.bcf.ndirect.co.uk
President: Gerry Walsh

CRICKET

ENGLAND AND WALES CRICKET BOARD, Lord's Cricket Ground, London NW8 8QN. Tel: 020-7432 1200 Fax: 020-7289 5619 Web: www.ecb.co.uk
Chief Executive: T. Lamb

MCC, Lord's Cricket Ground, London NW8 8QN. Tel: 020-7616 8500 Fax: 020-7289 9100 Web: www.lords.org
Secretary and Chief Executive: R. D. V. Knight

CROQUET

CROQUET ASSOCIATION, c/o Cheltenham Croquet Club, Old Bath Road, Cheltenham GL53 7DF. Tel: 01242-242318 Fax: 01242-243573 Web: www.croquet.org.uk
Secretary: N. R. Graves

CYCLING

BRITISH CYCLING FEDERATION, National Cycling Centre, Stuart Street, Manchester M11 4DQ. Tel: 0870-871 2000 Fax: 0870-871 2001 Web: www.britishcycling.org.uk
Chief Executive: P. King

CYCLING TIME TRIALS, 77 Arlington Drive, Pennington, Leigh, Lancs WN7 3QP. Tel: 01942-603976 Fax: 01942-262326 Web: www.ctt.org.uk
National Secretary: P. Heaton

DARTS

BRITISH DARTS ORGANISATION, 2 Pages Lane, Muswell Hill, London N10 1PS. Tel: 020-8883 5544 Fax: 020-8883 0109 Web: www.bdodarts.com *Director:* O. A. Croft

EQUESTRIANISM

BRITISH EQUESTRIAN FEDERATION, National Agricultural Centre, Stoneleigh Park, Kenilworth, Warks CV8 2RH. Tel: 024-7669 8871 Fax: 024-7669 6484 Web: www.bef.co.uk *Chief Executive:* A. Finding

BRITISH EVENTING, National Agricultural Centre, Stoneleigh Park, Kenilworth, Warks CV8 2RN. Tel: 024-7669 8856 Fax: 024-7669 7235 Web: www.britisheventing.com
Chief Executive: P. Durrant

ETON FIVES

ETON FIVES ASSOCIATION, 3 Bourchier Close, Sevenoaks, Kent TN13 1PD. Tel: 01732-458775 Web: www.etonfives.co.uk
Secretary: M. R. Fenn

FENCING

BRITISH FENCING ASSOCIATION, 1 Baron's Gate, 33–35 Rothschild Road, London W4 5HT. Tel: 020-8742 3032 Fax: 020-8742 3033 Web: www.britishfencing.com
President: Keith Smith

GLIDING

BRITISH GLIDING ASSOCIATION, Kimberley House, Vaughan Way, Leicester LE1 4SE. Tel: 0116-253 1051 Fax: 0116-251 5939 Web: www.gliding.co.uk
General Secretary: B. Rolfe

GOLF

LADIES' GOLF UNION, The Scores, St Andrews, Fife KY16 9AT. Tel: 01334-475811 Fax: 01334-472818. Web: www.lgu.org *Secretary/CEO:* Andy Salmon

THE ROYAL AND ANCIENT GOLF CLUB OF ST ANDREWS, Golf Place, St Andrews, Fife KY16 9JD. Tel: 01334-460000 Fax: 01334-460001 Web: www.randa.org. *Secretary* P. Dawson

GREYHOUND RACING
NATIONAL GREYHOUND RACING CLUB LTD, Twyman
House, 16 Bonny Street, London NW1 9QD.
Tel: 020-7267 9256 Fax: 020-7482 1023
Web: www.ngrc.org.uk
Chief Executive: F. Melville

GYMNASTICS
BRITISH GYMNASTICS, Ford Hall, Lilleshall National Sports
Centre, Newport, Shropshire, TF10 9NB.
Tel: 0845-1297129 Fax: 0845-1249089
Web: www.british-gymnastics.org
Chief Executive: Alan Sommerville

HOCKEY
ENGLAND HOCKEY, The National Hockey Stadium, The
Stadium, Silbury Boulevard, Milton Keynes MK9 1HA.
Tel: 01908-544644 Fax: 01908-241106
Web: www.hockeyonline.co.uk
Interim Chief Executive: Andrew Hode
SCOTTISH HOCKEY UNION, 589 Lanark Road, Edinburgh
EH14 5DA. Tel: 0131-453 9070 Fax: 0131-453 9079
Web: www.scottish-hockey.org.uk *Chairman:* G. Ralph
WELSH HOCKEY UNION 80 Woodville Road, Cathays,
Cardiff CF24 4ED. Tel: 029-2023 3257 Fax: 029-2023 3258
Web: www.welsh-hockey.co.uk *Chairman:* A. J. Rookes

HORSE-RACING
BRITISH HORSERACING BOARD, 42 Portman Square,
London W1H 0EN. Tel: 020-7396 0011 Fax: 020-7935 3626
Web: www.bhb.co.uk
Chief Executive: G. Nichols
THE JOCKEY CLUB, 42 Portman Square, London W1H 6EN.
Tel: 020-7486 4921 Fax: 020-7935 8703
Web: www.thejockeyclub.co.uk
Senior Steward: J. Richmond-Watson

ICE HOCKEY
ICE HOCKEY UK, 47 Westminster Buildings, Theatre Square,
Nottingham NG1 6LG. Tel: 0115-924 1441
Fax: 0115-924 3443, Web: www.icehockeyuk.co.uk
Chairman: Stuart Robertson

ICE SKATING
NATIONAL ICE SKATING ASSOCIATION OF THE UK
LTD, National Ice Centre, Lower Parliament Street,
Nottingham NG1 1LA. Tel: 0115-853 3100
Fax: 0115-853 3101 Web: www.nisa-org.uk
General Secretary: Keith Horton

JUDO
BRITISH JUDO ASSOCIATION, 7A Rutland Street, Leicester
LE1 1RB. Tel: 0116-255 9669 Fax: 0116-255 9660
Web: www.britishjudo.org.uk
Head of Corporate Affairs: Donald Steel

LACROSSE
ENGLISH LACROSSE ASSOCIATION, 26 Wood Street,
Manchester. Tel: 0161-834 4582 Fax: 0161-834 4582
Web: www.englishlacrosse.co.uk
Co-Presidents: Sue Redfern and David Walkden

LAWN TENNIS
LAWN TENNIS ASSOCIATION, The Queen's Club,
Palliser Road, London W14 9EG. Tel: 020-7381 7000
Fax: 020-7381 3773 *Secretary:* J. C. U. James

MARTIAL ARTS
MARTIAL ARTS DEVELOPMENT COMMISSION, PO Box
416, Wembley, Middlesex HA0 3WD. Tel: 0870-770 0461
Fax: 0870-770 0462 Web: www.madec.org
Administration Manager: Dawn Howe

MOTOR SPORTS
MOTORCYCLE GREAT BRITAIN, AUTO-CYCLE UNION,
ACU House, Wood Street, Rugby, Warks CV21 2YX.
Tel: 01788-566400 Fax: 01788-573585
Web: www.acu.org.uk www.motorcyclinggb.com
General Secretary: P. Miller
BRITISH SUPERBIKES RACE ORGANISATION, MCRCB,
PO Box 6450, Woodford Halse, Daventry NN11 3ZD.
Tel: 01327-264010 Fax: 01327-264034
Manager: D. R. Barnfield
THE MOTOR SPORTS ASSOCIATION, Motor Sports House,
Riverside Park, Colnbrook, Berks SL3 0HG.
Tel: 01753-765000 Fax: 01753-682938
Web: www.msauk.org *Chief Executive:* Colin Hilton
SCOTTISH AUTO CYCLE UNION LTD, 28 West Main
Street, Uphall, W. Lothian EH52 5DW. Tel: 01506-858354
Fax: 01506-855792 Web: www.sacu.co.uk
Office Manager: Eric Jones

MOUNTAINEERING
BRITISH MOUNTAINEERING COUNCIL, 177–179 Burton
Road, West Didsbury, Manchester M20 2BB.
Tel: 0870-010 4878 Fax: 0161-445 4500
Web: www.thebmc.co.uk
Chief Officer (BMC): D. Turnbull

MULTI-SPORT BODIES
BRITISH OLYMPIC ASSOCIATION, 1 Wandsworth Plain,
London SW18 1EH. Tel: 020-8871 2677 Fax: 020-8871 9104
Web: www.olympics.org.uk *Chief Executive:* S. Clegg
BRITISH UNIVERSITIES SPORTS ASSOCIATION, 8 Union
Street, London SE1 1SZ. Tel: 020-7357 8555
Fax: 020-7403 0127 Web: www.busa.org.uk
Chief Executive: G. Gregory-Jones
COMMONWEALTH GAMES FEDERATION,
4th Floor, 26 Upper Brook Street, London W1K 7QE.
Tel: 020-7491 8801 Fax: 020-7409 7803
Web: www.thecgf.com
Chief Executive Officer: Michael Hooper

NETBALL
ALL ENGLAND NETBALL ASSOCIATION LTD, Netball
House, 9 Paynes Park, Hitchin, Herts SG5 1EH.
Tel: 01462-442344 Fax: 01462-442343
Web: www.england-netball.co.uk
Chief Executive: Mrs P. Harrison
NETBALL NORTHERN IRELAND, House of Sport,
Upper Malone Road, Belfast BT9 5LA. Tel: 028-9038 1222
Secretary: Mrs E. Curran
NETBALL SCOTLAND, Suite 1A, 2nd Floor, Central
Chambers, 93 Hope Street, Glasgow G2 4LD.
Tel: 0141-572 0114 Fax: 0141-572 0052
Web: www.netballscotland.freeserve.co.uk
WELSH NETBALL ASSOCIATION, 2nd Floor, 33–35
Cathedral Rd, Cardiff CF11 9HB. Tel: 029-2023 7048
Fax: 029-2022 6430 Web: www.welshnetball.co.uk
Chief Executive Officer: Mrs S. J. Holvey

ORIENTEERING

BRITISH ORIENTEERING FEDERATION, Riversdale, Dale
Road North, Darley Dale, Matlock, Derbys DE4 2HX.
Tel: 01629-734042 Fax: 01629-733769
Web: www.britishorienteering.org.uk
Chief Executive: Robin Field

POLO

THE HURLINGHAM POLO ASSOCIATION, Manor Farm,
Little Coxwell, Faringdon, Oxfordshire SN7 7LW.
Tel: 01367-242828 Fax: 01367-242829
Web: www.hpa-polo.co.uk
Chief Executive: D. J. B. Woodd

RIFLE SHOOTING

NATIONAL RIFLE ASSOCIATION, Bisley Camp, Brookwood,
Woking, Surrey GU24 0PB. Tel: 01483-797777
Fax: 01483-797285 Web: www.nra.org.uk
Secretary General: Mr R. J. Fishwick
NATIONAL SMALL-BORE RIFLE ASSOCIATION, Lord
Roberts House, Bisley Camp, Brookwood, Woking, Surrey
GU24 0NP. Tel: 01483-476969 Fax: 01483-476392
Web: www.nsra.co.uk *Secretary:* Lt.-Col. J. D. Hoare

ROWING

AMATEUR ROWING ASSOCIATION LTD,
The Priory, 6 Lower Mall, London W6 9DJ.
Tel: 020-8237 6700 Fax: 020-8237 6749
Web: www.ara-rowing.org
National Manager: Mrs R. Napp
HENLEY ROYAL REGATTA, Regatta Headquarters, Henley-
on-Thames, Oxon RG9 2LY Tel: 01491-572153
Fax: 01491-575509 Web: www.hrr.co.uk
Secretary: R. S. Goddard

RUGBY FIVES

THE RUGBY FIVES ASSOCIATION, 32 Ashbourne Grove,
East Dulwich, London SE22 8RL. Tel: 0208-693 0488
Web: www.rfa.org.uk. *General Secretary:* Ian Fuller

RUGBY LEAGUE

BRITISH AMATEUR RUGBY LEAGUE ASSOCIATION,
West Yorkshire House, 4 New North Parade, Huddersfield
HD1 5JP. Tel: 01484-544131 Fax: 01484-519985
Web: www.barla.org.uk *Chief Executive:* I. Cooper
THE RUGBY FOOTBALL LEAGUE, Red Hall, Red Hall Lane,
Leeds LS17 8NB. Tel: 0113-232 9111 Fax: 0113-232 3666
Web: www.rfl.uk.com *Chairman:* Richard Lewis

RUGBY UNION

IRISH RUGBY FOOTBALL UNION, 62 Lansdowne Road,
Ballsbridge, Dublin 4. Tel: 00 353-1-647 3800
Fax: 00 353-1-647 3801, Web: www.irishrugby.ie
Chief Executive: P. R. Browne
RUGBY FOOTBALL UNION, Rugby House, Rugby Road,
Twickenham TW1 1DS. Tel: 020-8892 2000
Fax: 020-8892 9816 Web: www.rfu.com
Chief Executive: F. Baron
RUGBY FOOTBALL UNION FOR WOMEN, Rugby House,
Rugby Road, Twickenham, Middlesex TW1 1DS.
Tel: 020-8831 7996 Fax: 020-8892 9816
Web: www.rfu-women.co.uk *Chairman:* Sue Eakers
SCOTTISH RUGBY UNION, Murrayfield, Roseburn Street,
Edinburgh EH12 5PJ. Tel: 0131-346 5000
Fax: 0131-346 5001 Web: www.sru.org.uk
Chief Executive: W. S. Watson

SCOTTISH WOMEN'S RUGBY UNION, Scottish Rugby
Union, Roseburn Terrace, Murrayfield, Edinburgh EH12 5PJ.
Tel: 0131-346 5163 Fax: 0131-346 5001
Web: www.sru.org.uk *Chairwoman:* Sandra Kinnear
WELSH RUGBY UNION LTD, 1st Floor, Golate House,
101 St Mary Street, Cardiff CF10 1GE. Tel: 029-2093 4000
Fax: 029-2093 4054 Web: www.wru.co.uk
Group Chief Executive: D. Moffett

SHOOTING

CLAY PIGEON SHOOTING ASSOCIATION LTD, Edmonton
House, Bisley Camp, Brookwood, Woking, Surrey GU24 0NP.
Tel: 01483-485400 Fax: 01483-485410
Web: www.cpsa.co.uk *Director:* Mr P. J. Boakes

SKIING

SNOWSPORT GB, Hillend, Biggar Road, Midlothian EH10 7EF.
Tel: 0131-445 7676 Fax: 0131-445 4949
Web: www.bssf.co.uk
Operations Director: Mrs F. McNeilly
SKIING AND SNOWBOARDING, Snowsport Scotland,
Hillend, Biggar Road, Midlothian EH10 7EF.
Tel: 0131-445 4151 Fax: 0131-445 4949
Web: www.snowsportscotland.org

SPEEDWAY

SPEEDWAY CONTROL BOARD, ACU Headquarters, Wood
Street, Rugby, Warks CV21 2YX. Tel: 01788-565603
Fax: 01788-552308 *Chairman:* E. Bartlett

SQUASH RACKETS

SCOTTISH SQUASH, Caledonia House, South Gyle,
Edinburgh EH12 9DQ. Tel: 0131-317 7343
Fax: 0131-317 7734 Web: www.scottishsquash.org
Administration Manager: Derek Welch
ENGLAND SQUASH, National Squash Centre, Rowsley Street,
Manchester M11 3FF. Tel: 0161-438 4317
Web: www.englandsquash.com
Chief Executive: Nick Rider
SQUASH WALES, St Mellons Country Club, St Mellons,
Cardiff CF3 2XR. Tel: 01633-682108 Fax: 01633-680998
Web: www.squashwales.co.uk
Administrator: Mrs D. Selley

SWIMMING

AMATEUR SWIMMING ASSOCIATION, Harold Fern House,
Derby Square, Loughborough, Leics LE11 5AL.
Tel: 01509-618700 Fax: 01509-618701
Web: www.britishswimming.org
Chief Executive: D. Sparkes
SCOTTISH SWIMMING, National Swimming Academy,
University of Stirling, Stirling FK9 4LA.
Tel: 01786-466520 Fax: 01786-466521
Web: www.scottishswimming.com
Chief Executive: P. Bush
WELSH AMATEUR SWIMMING ASSOCIATION, Wales
National Pool, Sketty Lane, Swansea SA2 8QG.
Tel: 01792-513636 Web: www.welshasa.co.uk
Head of Administration: Julie Tyler

TABLE TENNIS

ENGLISH TABLE TENNIS ASSOCIATION, Queensbury
House, Havelock Road, Hastings, E. Sussex TN34 1HF.
Tel: 01424-722525 Fax: 01424-422103
Web: www.etta.co.uk *Chief Executive:* R. Yule

VOLLEYBALL

ENGLISH VOLLEYBALL ASSOCIATION, 27 South Road,
West Bridgford, Nottingham NG2 7AG. Tel: 0115-981 6324
Fax: 0115-945 5429 Web: www.volleyballengland.org
Chief Executive Officer: T. Ojasoo
SCOTTISH VOLLEYBALL ASSOCIATION, 48 The Pleasance,
Edinburgh EH8 9TJ. Tel: 0131-556 4633 Fax: 0131-557 4314
Web: www.scottishvolleyball.org *Director:* N. S. Moody

WALKING

RACE WALKING ASSOCIATION, Hufflers, Heard's Lane,
Shenfield, Brentwood, Essex CM15 0SF.
Tel: 01277-220687 Fax: 01277-212380
Web: www.racewalkingassociation.btinternet.co.uk
Hon. General Secretary: P. J. Cassidy

WATER SKIING

BRITISH WATER SKI FEDERATION, British Water Ski,
The Tower, Thorpe Road, Chertsey, Surrey KT16 8PH.
Tel: 01932-570885 Fax: 01932-566719
Web: www.britishwaterski.co.uk
Executive Officer: Ms G. Hill

WEIGHTLIFTING

BRITISH WEIGHTLIFTERS ASSOCIATION (BWLA), 131
Hurst Street, Oxford OX4 1HE. Tel: 01865-200339 Fax:
01865-790096 Web: www.bawla.com *Chief Executive:* S.
Cannon

WRESTLING

BRITISH WRESTLING ASSOCIATION, 12 Westwood Lane,
Brimington, Chesterfield, Derbyshire S43 1PA.
Tel: 01246-236443 Fax: 01246-236443
Web: www.britishwrestling.org *Chairman:* M. Morley

YACHTING

ROYAL YACHTING ASSOCIATION, RYA House, Ensign Way,
Hamble, Southampton, Hampshire SO31 4YA.
Tel: 0845-3450400 Fax: 0845-3450329
Web: www.rya.org.uk *Chief Executive:* R. P. Carr

CLUBS

LONDON CLUBS

ALPINE CLUB (1857), 55 Charlotte Road, London EC2A 3QF.
Tel: 020-7613 0755 Web: www.alpine-club.org.uk
Hon. Secretary: R. M. Scott

AMERICAN WOMEN'S CLUB (1899), 68 Old Brompton
Road, London SW7 3LQ. Tel: 020-7589 8292
Fax: 020-7283 9006 Web: www.awclondon.org
President: J. Kocher (Women Only)

ANGLO-BELGIAN CLUB (1955), 60 Knightsbridge, London
SW1X 7LF. Tel: 020-7235 2121 Fax: 020-7245 9470
Chairman: Sir John Gray, KBE, CMG

ARMY AND NAVY CLUB (1837), 36 Pall Mall, London SW1Y
5JN. Tel: 020-7930 9721 Fax: 020-7930 9720
Web: www.armynavyclub.co.uk
Chief Executive and Secretary: Cdr. J. A. Holt, MBE, RN

ARTS CLUB (1863), 40 Dover Street, London W1S 4NP.
Tel: 020-7499 8581 Fax: 020-7409 0913
Web: www.theartsclub.co.uk *Secretary:* Tony Derrett

THE ATHENAEUM (1824), 107 Pall Mall, London SW1Y 5ER.
Tel: 020-7930 4843 Fax: 020-7839 4114 *Secretary:* J. Ford

AUTHORS' CLUB (1892), 40 Dover Street, London W1S 4NP.
Tel: 020-7499 8581 Fax: 020-7409 0913
Web: www.theartsclub.fsnet.co.uk
Club Secretary: Mrs A. de La Grange

BEEFSTEAK CLUB (1876), 9 Irving Street, London WC2H
7AH. Tel: 020-7930 5722 Fax: 020-7925 2325
Secretary: Sir John Lucas-Tooth Bt. (Men Only)

BROOKS'S (1764), St James's Street, London SW1A 1LN.
Tel: 020-7493 4411 Fax: 020-7499 3736
Secretary: G. Snell (Men Only)

BUCK'S CLUB (1919), 18 Clifford Street, London W1S 3RF.
Tel: 020-7734 2337 Fax: 020-7287 2097
Secretary: Mrs G. Thompson (Men Only)

THE CALEDONIAN CLUB (1891), 9 Halkin Street, London
SW1X 7DR. Tel: 020-7235 5162 Fax: 020-7235 4635
Web: www.caledonian-club.org.uk *Secretary:* P. J. Varney

CANNING CLUB (1910), 4 St James's Square, London SW1Y
4JU. Tel: 020-7827 5757 Fax: 020-7827 5758
Secretary: T. M. Harrington

CARLTON CLUB (1832), 69 St James's Street, London SW1A
1PJ. Tel: 020-7493 1164 Fax: 020-7495 4090
Web: www.carltonclub.co.uk *Secretary:* A. E. Telfer

CAVALRY AND GUARDS CLUB (1893), 127 Piccadilly,
London W1J 7PX. Tel: 020-7499 1261 Fax: 020-7495 5956
Secretary: Cdr. I. R. Wellesley-Harding, RN

CHELSEA ARTS CLUB (1891), 143 Old Church Street,
London SW3 6EB. Tel: 020-7376 3311 Fax: 020-7351 5986
Web: chelseaartsclub.com *Secretary:* D. Winterbottom

CITY LIVERY CLUB (1914), 20 Aldermanbury, London EC2V
7HP. Tel: 020-7814 0200 Fax: 020-7814 0201
Web: www.cityliveryclub.com *Hon. Secretary:* J. Slater

CITY OF LONDON CLUB (1832), 19 Old Broad Street,
London EC2N 1DS. Tel: 020-7588 7991 Fax: 020-7374 2020
Web: www.cityclub.uk.com *Chief Executive:* Glenn Jones
(Men Only)

CITY UNIVERSITY CLUB (1895), 50 Cornhill, London EC3V
3PD. Tel: 020-7626 8571 Fax: 020-7626 8572
Web: www.cityuniversityclub.co.uk
Secretary: Miss R. C. Graham

THE CRUISING ASSOCIATION (1908), London, CA House,
1 Northey Street, Limehouse Basin, London E14 8BT.
Tel: 020-7537 2828 Fax: 020-7537 2266
Web: www.cruising.org.uk
General Secretary: Mrs L. Hammett

EAST INDIA CLUB (1849), 16 St James's Square, London
SW1Y 4LH. Tel: 020-7930 1000 Fax: 020-7321 0217
Secretary: M. Howell (Men Only)

FARMERS CLUB (1842), 3 Whitehall Court, London SW1A
2EL. Tel: 020-7930 3751 Fax: 020-7839 7864
Web: www.thefarmersclub.com
Secretary: Gp Capt. G. P. Carson

FLYFISHERS' CLUB (1884), 69 Brook Street, London W1K
4ER. Tel: 020-7629 5958
Secretary: Cdr. T. H. Boycott, OBE, RN (Men Only)

GARRICK CLUB (1831), 15 Garrick Street, London WC2E
9AY. Tel: 020-7379 6478 Fax: 020-7379 5966
Web: www.garrickclub.co.uk
Secretary: M. J. Harvey (Men Only)

THE GROUCHO CLUB (1985), 45 Dean Street, London W1D
4QB. Tel: 020-7439 4685 Fax: 020-7437 0373
Chief Executive: Joel Cadbury

HURLINGHAM CLUB (1869), Ranelagh Gardens, London
SW6 3PR. Tel: 020-7471 8231 Fax: 020-7736 2055
Secretary: Lucie Salmon

THE KENNEL CLUB (1873), 1–5 Clarges Street, London W1J
8AB. Tel: 0870-606 6750 Fax: 020-7518 1058
Web: www.the-kennel-club.org.uk
Chief Executive: Rosemary Smart

LANSDOWNE CLUB (1934), 9 Fitzmaurice Place, London
W1J 5JD. Tel: 020-7629 7200 Fax: 020-7408 0246
Web: www.lansdowneclub.com
Chief Executive and Secretary: M. Anderson

LONDON ROWING CLUB (1856), Embankment, Putney,
London SW15 1LB. Tel: 020-8788 1400 Fax: 020-8874 9056
Web: www.londonrc.org.uk *Hon. Secretary:* N. A. Smith

MCC (MARYLEBONE CRICKET CLUB) (1787), Lord's
Cricket Ground, London NW8 8QN. Tel: 020-7289 1611
Fax: 020-7289 9100 Web: www.lords.org
Secretary & Chief Executive: R. D. V. Knight

THE NATIONAL CLUB (1845), c/o Carlton Club, 69 St James's
Street, London SW1A 1PJ. Tel: 020-8579 0874
Fax: 020-8363 2269 *Hon. Secretary:* I. A. Sowton (Men Only)

NATIONAL LIBERAL CLUB (1882), Whitehall Place, London
SW1A 2HE. Tel: 020-7930 9871 Fax: 020-7839 4768
Web: www.nlc.org.uk *Secretary:* S. J. Roberts

NAVAL AND MILITARY CLUB (1862), 4 St James's Square,
London SW1Y 4JU. Tel: 020-7827 5757 Fax: 020-7827 5758
Web: www.navalandmilitaryclub.co.uk
Club Secretary: M. G. G. Ebbitt

NAVAL CLUB (1946), 38 Hill Street, London W1J 5NS.
Tel: 020-7493 7672 Fax: 020-7629 7995
Web: www.navalclub.co.uk
Chief Executive: Cdr. J. L. L. Prichard

NEW CAVENDISH CLUB (1920), 44 Great Cumberland
Place, London W1H 7BS. Tel: 020-7723 0391
Fax: 020-7262 8411 *General Manager:* J. P. Dauvergne

ORIENTAL CLUB (1824), Stratford House, Stratford Place,
London W1C 1ES. Tel: 020-7629 5126 Fax: 020-7629 0494
Secretary: S. C. Doble

PORTLAND CLUB (1816), 69 Brook Street, London W1Y 2ER.
Tel: 020-7499 1523 *Secretary:* J. Burns, CBE

PRATT'S CLUB (1841), 14 Park Place, London SW1A 1LP. Tel:
020-7493 0397 Fax: 020-7499 3736 *Secretary:* G. Snell
(Men Only)

THE QUEEN'S CLUB (1886), Palliser Road, London W14
9EQ. Tel: 020-7385 3421 Fax: 020-7386 8295
Web: www.queensclub.co.uk *Secretary:* J. A. S. Edwardes

REFORM CLUB (1836), 104–105 Pall Mall, London SW1Y
5EW. Tel: 020-7930 9374 Fax: 020-7930 1857
Web: www.reformclub.com *Secretary:* R. A. M. Forrest

ROEHAMPTON CLUB (1901), Roehampton Lane, London SW15 5LR. Tel: 020-8480 4200 Fax: 020-8480 4265 Web: www.roehamptonclub.co.uk
Chief Executive: Mark Wilson

ROYAL AIR FORCE CLUB (1918), 128 Piccadilly, London W1J 7PY. Tel: 020-7399 1000 Fax: 020-7355 1516 Web: www.rafclub.org.uk *Secretary:* P. N. Owen

ROYAL AUTOMOBILE CLUB (1897), Pall Mall Clubhouse, 89 Pall Mall, London SW1Y 5HS. Tel: 020-7930 2345 Fax: 020-7976 1086 Web: www.royalautomobileclub.co.uk.
Secretary: A. I. G. Kennedy

ROYAL OCEAN RACING CLUB (1925), 20 St James's Place, London SW1A 1NN. Tel: 020-7493 2248 Fax: 020-7493 5252 Web: www.rorc.org
General Manager: P. C. Wykeham-Martin

ROYAL OVER-SEAS LEAGUE (1910), Over-Seas House, Park Place, St James's Street, London SW1A 1LR. Tel: 020-7408 0214 Fax: 020-7499 6738 Web: www.rosl.org.uk
Director-General: R. F. Newell, LVO

ST STEPHEN'S CLUB (1870), 34 Queen Anne's Gate, London SW1H 9AB. Tel: 020-7222 1382 Fax: 020-7222 8740 Web: www.ststephensclub.co.uk
Chief Executive: James M. Wilson

SAVAGE CLUB (1857), 1 Whitehall Place, London SW1A 2HD. Tel: 020-7930 8118 Fax: 020-7930 5209 Web: www.savageclub.com
Hon. Secretary: The Ven. B. H. Lucas CB (Men Only)

SAVILE CLUB (1868), 69 Brook Street, London W1K 4ER. Tel: 020-7629 5462 Fax: 020-7499 7087 Web: www.savileclub.co.uk *Secretary:* N. Storey (Men Only)

THAMES ROWING CLUB (1860), Putney Embankment, London SW15 1LB. Tel: 020-8788 0798 Fax: 020-8788 0798 Web: www.thamesrc.demon.co.uk
Hon. Secretary: Jess Wright

THE TRAVELLERS CLUB (1819), 106 Pall Mall, London SW1Y 5EP. Tel: 020-7930 8688 Fax: 020-7930 2019 Web: www.csma.org.uk *Secretary:* M. S. Allcock (Men Only)

TURF CLUB (1868), 5 Carlton House Terrace, London SW1Y 5AQ. Tel: 020-7930 8555 Fax: 020-7930 7206 *Secretary:* Lt.-Col. O. R. StJ. Breakwell, MBE

OXFORD AND CAMBRIDGE CLUB (1972), 71 Pall Mall, London SW1Y 5HD. Tel: 020-7930 5151 Fax: 020-7930 9490 Web: www.oxfordandcambridgeclub.co.uk
Secretary: G. R. Buchanan

THE UNIVERSITY WOMEN'S CLUB (1886), 2 Audley Square, London W1K 1DB. Tel: 020-7499 2268 Fax: 020-7499 7046 Web: www.univeristywomensclub.com
Club Secretary: Miss Lynne Paterson (Women Only)

VICTORY SERVICES CLUB (1907), 63-79 Seymour Street, London W2 2HF. Tel: 020-7723 4474 Fax: 020-7402 9496 Web: www.vsc.co.uk
Chief Executive: Brig. R. N. Lennox, CBE

WHITE'S (1693), 37–38 St James's Street, London SW1A 1JG. Tel: 020-7493 6671 Fax: 020-7495 6674 *Secretary:* D. A. Anderson (Men Only)

CLUBS OUTSIDE LONDON AND YACHT CLUBS

THE ATHENAEUM (1797), Church Alley, Liverpool L1 3DD. Tel: 0151-709 7770 Fax: 0151-709 0418 Web: www.athena.force9.co.uk
Honorary Secretary: H. Thompson

BATH AND COUNTY CLUB (1858), Queen's Parade, Bath BA1 2NJ. Tel: 01225-423732 Fax: 01225-423997 Web: www.bathandcountyclub.com
President: Sir Alec Morris, KBE, CB

BEMBRIDGE SAILING CLUB (1886), Embankment Road, Bembridge, Isle of Wight PO35 5NR. Tel: 01983-872237 Fax: 01983-874950 Web: www.bembridgesailingclub.org
Secretary: Lt.-Col. M. J. Samuelson, RM

BRISTOL CHANNEL YACHT CLUB (1875), 744 Mumbles Road, Mumbles, Swansea SA3 4EL. Tel: 01792-366000 Fax: 01792-360000 *Hon. Secretary:* R. L. Morgan

CARDIFF AND COUNTY CLUB (1866), Westgate Street, Cardiff CF10 1DA. Tel: 029-2022 0846 Fax: 029-2037 3393 *Hon. Secretary:* Cdr. J. E. Payn, RD (Men Only)

CASTLE CLUB (1865), 3 The Esplanade, Rochester, Kent ME1 1QE. Tel: 01634-843168 *Hon Secretary:* R. C. Abel (Men Only)

CHICHESTER YACHT CLUB (1967), Chichester Marina, Birdham, Chichester, W. Sussex PO20 7EJ. Tel: 01243-512918 Fax: 01243-512627 Web: www.cyc.co.uk *Secretary:* I. M. Clarke

CLIFTON CLUB (1882), 22 The Mall, Clifton, Bristol BS8 4DS. Tel: 0117-974 5039 Fax: 0117-974 3910 *Secretary:* P. J. Organ (Men Only)

DISTRICT AND UNION CLUB (1849), Northwood, 1 West Park Road, Blackburn BB2 6DE. Tel: 01254-51474 *Hon. Secretary:* R. W. Edge (Men Only)

DURHAM COUNTY CLUB (1890), 52 Old Elvet, Durham DH1 3HJ. Tel: 0191-384 8156 *Secretary:* S. Smith

ESSEX YACHT CLUB (1890), HQS Bembridge, Foreshore, Leigh-on-Sea, Essex SS9 1BD. Tel: 01702-478404 Web: www.sailinginleigh.com *Hon. Secretary:* Mrs K. Hanman

FREWEN CLUB (1869), 98 St Aldate's, Oxford OX1 1BT. Tel: 01865-243816 *Hon. Secretary:* B. R. Boyt (Men Only)

HOVE CLUB (1882), 28 Fourth Avenue, Hove, E. Sussex BN3 2PJ. Tel: 01273-730872 Fax: 01273-732481 *Secretary:* R. L. Silverthorne (Men Only)

KENT AND CANTERBURY CLUB (1873), The Elms, 17 Old Dover Road, Canterbury CT1 3JB. Tel: 01227-462181 Web: www.kcgc.org.uk *Secretary:* K. D. Bassey

THE LEAMINGTON TENNIS COURT CLUB (1846), 50 Bedford Street, Leamington Spa, Warks CV32 5DT. Tel: 01926-424977 Fax: 01926 435724
Chairman: P. F. T. Bromwich (Men Only)

LEANDER CLUB (1818), Henley-on-Thames, Oxon RG9 2LP. Tel: 01491-575782 Fax: 01491-410291 Web: www.leander.co.uk *Hon. Secretary:* I. Codrington

THE LEEDS CLUB (1849), 3 Albion Place, Leeds LS1 6JL. Tel: 0113-242 1591 Fax: 0113-245 0755 Web: www.leedsclub.org.uk
General Manager: Nicholas Fawcett

THE NEW CLUB (1874), 2 Atherstone Lawn, Montpellier Parade, Cheltenham GL50 1UD. Tel: 01242-541121 Fax: 01242-541154 Web: www.newclub.org.uk
Hon. Secretary: I. Dunbar

THE NORFOLK CLUB (1770), 17 Upper King Street, Norwich NR3 1RB. Tel: 01603-626767 Fax: 01603-610652 *Secretary:* G. G. Hardaker

NORTHAMPTON AND COUNTY CLUB (1873), George Row, Northampton NN1 1DF. Tel: 01604-632962 *Secretary:* D. J. Harrop

NORTH BAILEY CLUB (1842), 24 North Bailey, Durham DH1 3EW. Tel: 0191-384 3724 Fax: 0191-384 7060 Web: www.dus.org.uk
Permanent Secretary: Mrs M. C. Cleaver

NORTHERN CONSTITUTIONAL CLUB (1882), 37 Pilgrim Street, Newcastle upon Tyne, Tyne & Wear NE1 6QE. Tel: 0191-232 0884 *Hon. Secretary:* D. Blake

OLD BOYS' AND PARK GREEN CLUB (1771), 7 Churchside, Macclesfield, Cheshire SK10 1HG. Tel: 01625-423292 *Hon. Secretary:* C. J. Q. Brooks (Men Only)

PAIGNTON CLUB (1882), The Esplanade, Paignton, Devon TQ4 6ED. Tel: 01803-559682 Fax: 01803-559043 *Hon. Secretary:* P. Grafton

PARKSTONE YACHT CLUB (1895), Pearce Avenue, Poole, Dorset BH14 8EH. Tel: 01202-738824 Fax: 01202-716394 Web: www.parkstoneyc.co.uk
General Manager: M. Simms
PENARTH YACHT CLUB (1880), The Esplanade, Penarth, Vale of Glamorgan CF64 3AU. Tel: 029-2070 8196 Web: www.penarthyachtclub.com
Hon. Secretary: R. S. McGregor
PHYLLIS COURT CLUB (1906), Marlow Road, Henley-on-Thames, Oxon RG9 2HT. Tel: 01491-570500
Fax: 01491-570528 Web: www.phylliscourt.co.uk
Chief Executive: R. Edwards
POOLE HARBOUR YACHT CLUB (1949), 40 Salterns Way, Lilliput, Poole, Dorset BH14 8JR. Tel: 01202-709971
Fax: 01202-700398 Web: www.salterns.co.uk
Managing Director: J. N. J. Smith
THE POOLE YACHT CLUB (1865), New Harbour Road West, Hamworthy, Poole, Dorset BH15 4AQ. Tel: 01202-672687
Fax: 01202-661174 Web: www.pooleyc.co.uk
General Manager: C. Ewing
ROYAL AIR FORCE YACHT CLUB (1932), Riverside House, Rope Walk, Hamble, Southampton SO31 4HD.
Tel: 023-8045 2208 Fax: 023-8045 8001
Web: www.rafyc.co.uk *Hon. Secretary:* J. Chitson
ROYAL ANGLESEY YACHT CLUB (1802), 6–7 Green Edge, Beaumaris, Anglesey LL58 8BY. Tel: 01248-810295
Fax: 01248-811788 Web: www.royalangleseyyc.org.uk
Hon. Secretary: Jackie Williams
ROYAL CANOE CLUB (1866), The Clubhouse, Trowlock Way, Teddington, Middx TW11 9QZ. Tel: 020-8977 5269
Fax: 020-8977 5269 Web: www.royalcanoeclub.com
Hon. Secretary: Mrs J. S. Evans
ROYAL CHANNEL ISLANDS YACHT CLUB (1862), Le Mont du Boulevard, St Brelade, Jersey JE3 8AD.
Tel: 01534-745783 Fax: 01534-490042
Hon. Secretary: B. Murray
ROYAL CINQUE PORTS YACHT CLUB (1872), 5 Waterloo Crescent, Dover, Kent CT16 1LA. Tel: 01304-206262
Fax: 01304-206262 *The Commodore:* Dr R. Hadley
ROYAL CORINTHIAN YACHT CLUB (1872), The Quay, Burnham-on-Crouch, Essex CM0 8AX. Tel: 01621-782105
Fax: 01621-784965 Web: www.royalcorinthian.co.uk
Hon. Secretary: J. Hill
ROYAL DART YACHT CLUB (1866), Priory Street, Kingswear, Dartmouth, Devon TQ6 0AB. Tel: 01803-752496
Fax: 01803-752496 Web: www.royaldart.co.uk
Hon. Secretary: M. D. Deeley
ROYAL DORSET YACHT CLUB (1875), 11 Custom House Quay, Weymouth, Dorset DT4 8BG. Tel: 01305-786258
Fax: 01305-786258 Web: www.rdyc.freeuk.com
Secretary: Mrs M. Tye
ROYAL FOWEY YACHT CLUB (1881), Whitford Yard, Fowey, Cornwall PL23 1BH. Tel: 01726-833573 Fax: 01726-833573
Web: www.rfyc.fowey.org.uk *Commodore:* G. R. Coombs
ROYAL HARWICH YACHT CLUB (1843), Woolverstone, Ipswich IP9 1AT. Tel: 01473-780319 Fax: 01473-780919
Web: www.rhyc.demon.co.uk *Secretary:* Colin Burrows
ROYAL LYMINGTON YACHT CLUB (1922), Bath Road, Lymington, Hants SO41 3SE. Tel: 01590-672677
Fax: 01590-671642 Web: www.rlymyc.org.uk
Secretary: I. Gawn
ROYAL MERSEY YACHT CLUB (1844), Bedford Road East, Rock Ferry, Birkenhead, Merseyside CH42 1LS.
Tel: 0151-645 3204 Web: www.royalmersey.co.uk
Hon. Secretary: P. A. Bastow
ROYAL NAVAL CLUB AND ROYAL ALBERT YACHT CLUB (1867), 17 Pembroke Road, Portsmouth PO1 2NT.
Tel: 023-9282 5924 Fax: 023-9282 4491
Web: www.mc-rayc.co.uk *Secretary:* Cdr. P. Bolas, RN
ROYAL NORFOLK AND SUFFOLK YACHT CLUB (1859), Royal Plain, Lowestoft, Suffolk NR33 0AQ.

Tel: 01502-566726 Fax: 01502-517981
Commodore: Dr D. J. Turner
ROYAL PLYMOUTH CORINTHIAN YACHT CLUB (1877), Madeira Road, Plymouth PL1 2NY. Tel: 01752-664327
Fax: 01752-256140 Web: www.rpcyc.com
Hon. Secretary: A. L. Cooper
ROYAL SOLENT YACHT CLUB (1878), The Square, Yarmouth, Isle of Wight PO41 0NS. Tel: 01983-760256
Fax: 01983-761172 Web: www.royalsolentyc.org.uk
Secretary: Mrs S. Tribe
ROYAL SOUTHAMPTON YACHT CLUB (1875), 1 Channel Way, Ocean Village, Southampton SO14 3QF.
Tel: 023-8022 3352 Fax: 023-8033 0613
Web: www.rsyc.org.uk *Secretary:* A. M. Paterson
ROYAL SOUTHERN YACHT CLUB (1837), Rope Walk, Hamble, Southampton SO31 4HB. Tel: 023-8045 0300
Fax: 023-8045 0310 Web: www.royal-southern.co.uk
Secretary: G. H. Robinson
ROYAL TEMPLE YACHT CLUB (1857), 6 Westcliff Mansions, Ramsgate, Kent CT11 9HY. Tel: 01843-591766
Fax: 01843-583211 Web: www.rtyc.com
Hon. Secretary: R. Green
ROYAL THAMES YACHT CLUB (1775), London, 60 Knightsbridge, London SW1X 7LF. Tel: 020-7235 2121
Fax: 020-7245 9470 Web: www.royalthames.com
Secretary: Capt. D Goldson, RN
ROYAL TORBAY YACHT CLUB (1863), 12 Beacon Terrace, Torquay, Devon TQ1 2BH. Tel: 01803-292006
Fax: 01803-200297 Web: www.royaltorbay.org.uk
Secretary: R. M. Porteous
ROYAL ULSTER YACHT CLUB (1866), 101 Clifton Road, Bangor, Co. Down BT20 5HY. Tel: 028-9127 0568
Fax: 028-9127 3525 Web: www.royalulsteryachtclub.org
Commodore: HRH The Duke of Gloucester
ROYAL WELSH YACHT CLUB (1847), Porth-Yr-Aur, Caernarfon LL55 1SN. Tel: 01286-672599
Web: www.rwyc.org.uk *Commodore:* E. Hudson Davies
ROYAL WESTERN YACHT CLUB OF ENGLAND (1827), Queen Anne's Battery, Plymouth PL4 0TW.
Tel: 01752-660077 Fax: 01752-224299
Web: www.rwyc.org
General Manager/Club Secretary: Miss L. Clark
ROYAL WINDERMERE YACHT CLUB (1860), Fallbarrow Road, Bowness-on-Windermere, Windermere, Cumbria LA23 3DJ. Tel: 01539-443106
Hon. Secretary: Mrs M. A. Kirk
ROYAL YACHT SQUADRON (1815), The Castle, Cowes, IOW PO31 7QT. Tel: 01983-292191 Fax: 01983-200253
Web: www.rys.org.uk
Secretary: Capt. P. D. Mansfield, RN
ROYAL YORKSHIRE YACHT CLUB (1847), 1 Windsor Crescent, Bridlington, E. Yorks YO15 3HX.
Tel: 01262-672041 Fax: 01262-678319
Web: www.ryyc.org.uk *Secretary:* Anita L. Ingham
STOURBRIDGE OLD EDWARDIAN CLUB (1898), Drury Lane, Stourbridge, W. Midlands DY8 1BL. Tel: 01384-395635
Hon. Secretary: C. M. Bowen-Davies (Men Only)
THAMES ESTUARY YACHT CLUB (1895), 3 The Leas, Westcliff-on-Sea, Essex SS0 7ST. Tel: 01702-345967
Web: homepages.rya-online.net/teyc/
Hon. Secretary: L. S. Skinner
ULSTER REFORM CLUB (1885), 4 Royal Avenue, Belfast BT1 1DA. Tel: 028-9032 3411 Fax: 028-9031 2833
Web: www.ulsterreformclub.com
General Manager: A. W. Graham
UNITED CLUB (1870), Pier Steps, St Peter Port, Guernsey GY1 2LF. Tel: 01481-725722
President: B. J. George (Men Only)
VICTORIA CLUB (1853), Beresford Street, St Helier, Jersey JE2 4WN. Tel: 01534-723381 Fax: 01534-874700
Secretary: C. J. Blackstone

SOCIETIES AND INSTITUTIONS

Although this section is arranged in alphabetical order, organisations are usually listed by the key word in their title. The date following the organisation's name is the year of its foundation.

2CARE (1929), 11 Harwood Road, London, SW6 4QP. Tel: 020-7371 0118 Fax: 020-7371 7519
Chief Executive, Miss E. C. R. O'Sullivan

ABBEYFIELD SOCIETY (1956), Abbeyfield House, 53 Victoria Street, St Albans, Herts, AL1 3UW. Tel: 01727-857536 Fax: 01727-846168
Web: www.abbeyfield.com
Chief Executive B. House

ABOLITION OF VIVISECTION, BRITISH UNION FOR THE (1898), 16A Crane Grove, London, N7 8NN. Tel: 020-7700 4888 Fax: 020-7700 0252
Web: www.buav.org
Chief Executive, Ms M. Thew

ACCOUNTANTS IN ENGLAND AND WALES, INSTITUTE OF CHARTERED (1880), Chartered Accountants' Hall, PO Box 433, Moorgate Place, London, EC2P 2BJ. Tel: 020-7920 8100 Fax: 020-7920 0547
Web: www.icaew.co.uk
Secretary-General, Peter Owen

ACCOUNTANTS, ASSOCIATION OF CHARTERED CERTIFIED (1904), 29 Lincoln's Inn Fields, London, WC2A 3EE. Tel: 020-7396 7000 Fax: 020-7396 7070
Web: www.accaglobal.com
Chief Executive, Mrs A. L. Rose

ACCOUNTANTS, INSTITUTE OF FINANCIAL (1916), Burford House, 44 London Road, Sevenoaks, Kent, TN13 1AS. Tel: 01732-458080 Fax: 01732-455848
Web: www.ifa.org.uk
Chief Executive, J. M. Dean

ACCOUNTING TECHNICIANS, ASSOCIATION OF (1980), 154 Clerkenwell Road, London, EC1R 5AD. Tel: 020-7837 8600 Fax: 020-7837 6970
Web: www.aat.co.uk
Chief Executive, Ms J. Scott Paul

ACE STUDY TOURS (1958), Babraham, Cambridge, CB2 4AP. Tel: 01223-835055 Fax: 01223-837394
Web: www.study-tours.org
General Secretary, Paul Barnes

ACOUSTICS, INSTITUTE OF (1974), 77A St Peter's Street, St Albans, Herts, AL1 3BN. Tel: 01727-848195
Fax: 01727-850553 Web: www.ioa.org.uk
Chief Executive, Roy D. Bratby

ACTION FOR BLIND PEOPLE (1857), 14–16 Verney Road, London, SE16 3DZ. Tel: 020-7635 4800 Fax: 020-7635 4900
Web: www.afbp.org
Chief Executive, S. Remington

ACTION RESEARCH (1952), Vincent House, Horsham, W. Sussex, RH12 2DP. Tel: 01403-210406 Fax: 01403-210541
Web: www.actionresearch.org.uk
Chief Executive, Simon Moore

ACTORS' CHARITABLE TRUST, THE (1896), 255–256 Africa House, 64–78 Kingsway, London, WC2B 6BD. Tel: 020-7242 0111 Fax: 020-7242 0234
Web: www.tactactors.org
General Secretary, R. Ashby

ACTUARIES IN SCOTLAND, FACULTY OF (1856), 18 Dublin Street, Edinburgh, EH1 3PP. Tel: 0131-240 1300 Fax: 0131-240 1313 Web: www.actuaries.org.uk

ACTUARIES, INSTITUTE OF (1848), Staple Inn Hall, High Holborn, London, WC1V 7QJ. Tel: 020-7632 2100 Fax: 020-7632 2111 Web: www.actuaries.org.uk
Secretary-General, Caroline Instance, MIPD

ADAM SMITH INSTITUTE (1977), 23 Great Smith Street, London, SW1P 3BL. Tel: 020-7222 4995 Fax: 020-7222 7544
Web: www.adamsmith.org.uk
Director, Dr E. Butler

ADULT SCHOOL ORGANISATION, NATIONAL (1899), Riverton, 370 Humberstone Road, Leicester, LE5 0SA. Tel: 0116-253 8333 Fax: 0116-251 3626
Web: www.naso.org.uk
General Secretary, Mrs P. C. Dean

ADVERTISING STANDARDS AUTHORITY (1962), 2 Torrington Place, London, WC1E 7HW. Tel: 020-7580 5555 Fax: 020-7631 3051 Web: www.asa.org.uk
Director-General, Christopher Graham

AFRICAN INSTITUTE, INTERNATIONAL (1926), SOAS, Thornhaugh Street, Russell Square, London, WC1H 0XG. Tel: 020-7898 4420 Fax: 020-7898 4419
Web: www.iaionthe.net
Hon. Director, Prof. P. Spencer

AFRICAN MEDICAL AND RESEARCH FOUNDATION, UK (1961), 4 Grosvenor Place, London, SW1X 7HJ. Tel: 020-7201 6070 Fax: 020-7201 6170
Web: www.amref.org
Executive Director, A. Heroys

AGE CONCERN CYMRU, 4th Floor, 1 Cathedral Road, Cardiff, CF11 9SD. Tel: 029-2037 1566 Fax: 029-2039 9562
Director, R. W. Taylor

AGE CONCERN ENGLAND (1940), Astral House, 1268 London Road, London, SW16 4ER. Tel: 020-8765 7200 Helpline: 0800-009966 Fax: 020-8765 7211 Web: www.ageconcern.org.uk
Director-General, G. Lishman, OBE

AGE CONCERN SCOTLAND (1943), 113 Rose Street, Edinburgh, EH2 3DT. Tel: 0131-220 3345 Fax: 0131-220 2779 Web: www.ageconcernscotland.org.uk
Director, Ms M. O'Neill

AGRICULTURAL ENGINEERS ASSOCIATION (1875), Samuelson House, Paxton Road, Orton Centre, Peterborough, PE2 5LT. Tel: 01733-362925 Fax: 01733-370664 Web: www.aea.uk.com
Director-General, J. Vowles

AIDS TRUST, NATIONAL (1987), New City Cloisters, 196 Old Street, London, EC1V 9FR. Tel: 020-7814 6767 Fax: 020-7216 0111 Web: www.nat.org.uk

ALCOHOLICS ANONYMOUS (1947), PO Box 1, Stonebow House, Stonebow, York, YO1 2NJ. Tel: 01904-644026 National Helpline: 0845-769 7555 Fax: 01904-629091 Web: www.alcoholics-anonymous.org.uk
General-Secretary, J. Keeney

ALMSHOUSES, NATIONAL ASSOCIATION OF (1951), Billingbear Lodge, Carter's Hill, Workingham, Berks, RG40 5RU. Tel: 01344-452922 Fax: 01344-862062 Web: www.almshouses.org
Director, Maj.-Gen. A. de C. L. Leask

ALZHEIMER'S SOCIETY (1979), Gordon House, 10 Greencoat Place, London, SW1P 1PH. Tel: 020-7306 0606. Helpline: 0845-300 0336 Fax: 020-7306 0808 Web: www.alzheimers.org.uk
Chief Executive, H. Cayton

AMNESTY INTERNATIONAL UNITED KINGDOM (1961), 99–119 Rosebery Avenue, London, EC1R 4RE. Tel: 020-7814 6200 Fax: 020-7833 1510 Web: www.amnesty.org.uk
Director Ms K. Allen

ANCIENT MONUMENTS SOCIETY (1924), St Ann's Vestry Hall, 2 Church Entry, London, EC4V 5HB. Tel: 020-7236 3934 Fax: 020-7329 3677 Web: www.ancientmonumentssociety.org.uk
Secretary M. J. Saunders, MBE

ANGLO-BELGIAN SOCIETY (1982), 5 Hartley Close, Bickley, Kent, BR1 2TP. Tel: 020-8467 8442 Fax: 020-8467 8442
Hon. Secretary, P. R. Bresnan

ANGLO-BRAZILIAN SOCIETY (1943), 32 Green Street, London, W1K 7AU. Tel: 020-7493 8493 Web: www.anglobraziliansociety.org
Secretary, E. Dell'Aglio

ANGLO-DANISH SOCIETY (1924), Hillgate House, 26 Old Bailey, London, EC4M 7HW. Tel: 01753-883510
Chairman, Mr P. J. Willoughby, FCA

ANIMAL CONCERN, PO Box 5178, Dumbarton, G82 5YJ. Tel: 01389-841639 Web: www.animalconcern.com

ANIMAL HEALTH TRUST (1942), Lanwades Park, Kentford, Newmarket, Suffolk, CB8 7UU. Tel: 08700-502 424 Fax: 08700-502 425 Web: www.aht.org.uk
Executive Chairman, E. A. Chandler

ANTHROPOSOPHICAL SOCIETY IN GREAT BRITAIN (1923), Rudolf Steiner House, 35 Park Road, London, NW1 6XT. Tel: 020-7723 4400 Fax: 020-7724 4364 Web: www.anth.org.uk
General Secretary, N. C. Thomas

ANTI-SLAVERY INTERNATIONAL (1839), Thomas Clarkson House, The Stableyard, Broomgrove Road, London, SW9 9TL. Tel: 020-7501 8920 Fax: 020-7738 4110 Web: www.antislavery.org
Director, M. Cunneen

ANTIQUARIES OF LONDON, SOCIETY OF (1707), Burlington House, Piccadilly, London, W1J 0BE. Fax: 020-7287 6967 Web: www.sal.org.uk
General-Secretary, D. Morgan Evans, FSA

ANTIQUARIES OF SCOTLAND, SOCIETY OF (1780), Royal Museum, Chambers Street, Edinburgh, EH1 1JF. Tel: 0131-247 4115/4133 Fax: 0131-247 4163 Web: www.socantscot.org
Director Mrs F. Ashmore, FSA

ANTIQUE DEALERS' ASSOCIATION, BRITISH (1918), 20 Rutland Gate, London, SW7 1BD. Tel: 020-7589 4128 Fax: 020-7581 9083 Web: www.bada.org
Secretary-General, Mrs E. J. Dean

APOTHECARIES OF LONDON, SOCIETY OF (1617), 14 Black Friars Lane, London, EC4V 6EJ. Tel: 020-7236 1189 Fax: 020-7329 3177 Web: www.apothecaries.org
Clerk, R. J. Stringer

ARCHAEOLOGY, COUNCIL FOR BRITISH (1944), Bowes Morrell House, 111 Walmgate, York, YO1 9WA. Tel: 01904-671417 Fax: 01904-671384 Web: www.britarch.ac.uk
President, Dr F. Pryor

ARCHITECTS BENEVOLENT SOCIETY (1850), 43 Portland Place, London, W1B 1QH. Tel: 020-7580 2823 Fax: 020-7580 7075 Web: www.absnet.org.uk
Secretary, K. Robinson

ARCHITECTURAL HERITAGE FUND (1976), Clareville
House, 26–27 Oxendon Street, London, SW1Y 4EL.
Tel: 020-7925 0199 Fax: 020-7930 0295
Web: www.ahfund.org.uk
Director, J. Thompson

ARCHIVISTS, SOCIETY OF (1947), Prioryfield House,
20 Canon Street, Taunton, Somerset, TA1 1SW.
Tel: 01823-327030 Fax: 01823-271719
Web: www.archives.org.uk
Executive Secretary, P. S. Cleary

ARLIS (ART LIBRARIES SOCIETY UK AND IRELAND)
(1969), 18 College Road, Bromsgrove, Worcs, B60 2NE.
Tel: 01527-579298 Fax: 01527-579298
Web: www.arlis.org.uk
Administrator, Ms S. French

ARMY CADET FORCE ASSOCIATION (1930), Holderness
House, 51–61 Clifton Street, London, EC2A 4DW.
Tel: 020-7426 8377 Fax: 020-7426 8378
Web: www.armycadets.com
General Secretary, Brig. I. D. T. McGill, CBE

ART COLLECTIONS FUND, NATIONAL (1903), Mallais
House, 7 Cromwell Place, London, SW7 2JN.
Tel: 020-7225 4800 Fax: 020-7225 4848
Web: www.art-fund.org
Director, D. Barrie

ARTHRITIS CARE (1949), 18 Stephenson Way, London,
NW1 2HD. Tel: 020-7380 6500 Fax: 020-7380 6505
Web: www.arthritiscare.org.uk
Chief Executive, William Butler

ARTISTS, FEDERATION OF BRITISH (1961), 17 Carlton
House Terrace, London, SW1Y 5BD. Tel: 020-7930 6844
Fax: 020-7839 7830 Web: www.mallgalleries.org.uk
Chairman, J. R. S. Boas

ASIAN AFFAIRS, THE ROYAL SOCIETY FOR (1901),
2 Belgrave Square, London, SW1X 8PJ. Tel: 020-7235 5122
Fax: 020-7259 6771 Web: www.rsaa.org.uk
Chairman, Sir Harold Walker, KCMG

ASIAN FAMILY COUNSELLING SERVICE (1985), Suite 51,
The Lodge, Windmill Place, 2–4 Windmill Lane, Southall,
UB2 4NJ. Tel: 020-8571 3933 Fax: 020-8571 3933.
Director, R. Atma

ASLIB (THE ASSOCIATION FOR INFORMATION
MANAGEMENT) (1924), Temple Chambers, 3–7 Temple
Avenue, London, EC4Y 0HP. Tel: 020-7583 8900
Fax: 020-7583 8401 Web: www.aslib.com
Chief Executive, R. Bowes

ASSOCIATION OF HIGH SHERIFFS OF ENGLAND &
WALES (1971), 14 Glebe Road, Letchworth, Herts, SG6
1DR. Tel: 01462-620356 Fax: 01462-618247
Web: www.shrievalty-association.org.uk
Hon. Secretary, Michael McCartney

ASTHMA CAMPAIGN, NATIONAL (1990),
Providence House, Providence Place, London, N1 0NT.
Tel: 020-7226 2260 Fax: 020-7704 0740
Web: www.asthma.org.uk

ATS AND WRAC ASSOCIATION BENEVOLENT FUND
(1944), AGC Centre, Worthy Down, Winchester, Hants,
SO21 2RG. Tel: 01962-887612 Fax: 01962-887478.
General Secretary, Maj. D. M. McElligott

AUDIT BUREAU OF CIRCULATIONS (1931), Saxon House,
211 High Street, Berkhamsted, Herts, HP4 1AD.
Tel: 01442-870800 Fax: 01442-200700.
Web: www.abc.org.uk
Chief Executive, C. Boyd

AUTHORS, SOCIETY OF, 84 Drayton Gardens, London,
SW10 9SB. Tel: 020-7373 6642 Fax: 020-7373 5768
Web: www.societyofauthors.org
General Secretary, M. Le Fanu, OBE

AUTOMOBILE ASSOCIATION (1905), Fanum House,
Basingstoke, Hants, RG21 4EA. Tel: 0990-500600
Fax: 01256-493389 Web: www.theaa.com
Managing Director, Roger Wood

AYRSHIRE ARCHAEOLOGICAL AND NATURAL
HISTORY SOCIETY (1947), 17 Bellrock Avenue, Prestwick,
KA9 1SQ. Tel: 01292-282109/479077 Web:
www.ayrshirearchaeologicalandnaturalhistorysociety.org.uk
Hon. Secretary, Mrs Sheena Andrew

BALTIC AIR CHARTER ASSOCIATION (1949),
The Baltic Exchange, St Mary Axe, London, EC3A 8BH.
Tel: 020-7623 5501 Fax: 020-7369 1623
Web: www.baca.org.uk
Chairman, Mrs Geraldine Malempre

BALTIC EXCHANGE (1744), St Mary Axe, London,
EC3A 8BH. Tel: 020-7623 5501 Fax: 020-7369 1622
Web: www.balticexchange.com
Chief Executive, J. Buckley

BALTIC EXCHANGE CHARITABLE SOCIETY (1978),
13 Norton Folgate, Bishopsgate, London, E1 6DB,
Tel: 020-7247 6863 Fax: 020-7247 6758
Secretary, D. A. Painter

BAR ASSOCIATION FOR LOCAL GOVERNMENT AND
THE PUBLIC SERVICE (1945), c/o Birmingham City
Council, Ingleby House, 11–14 Cannon Street, Birmingham,
B2 5EN. Tel: 0121-303 9991 Fax: 0121-303 1312
Web: www.balgps.freeserve.co.uk
Chairman, M. F. N. Ahmad

BARNARDO'S (1866), Tanners Lane, Barkingside, Ilford, Essex,
IG6 1QG. Tel: 020-8550 8822 Fax: 020-8551 6870
Web: www.barnardos.org.uk
Chief Executive, R. Singleton

BARONETAGE, STANDING COUNCIL OF THE (1903),
3 Eastcroft Road, West Ewell, Epsom, Surrey, KT19 9TX.
Tel: 020-8393 6620 Fax: 020-8393 8845
Web: www.baronetage.org
Chairman, Sir Geoffrey Errington, Bt., OBE

BEE-KEEPERS' ASSOCIATION, BRITISH (1874), National
Beekeeping Centre, Stoneleigh Park, Kenilworth, Warks,
CV8 2LG. Tel: 0247-669 6679 Fax: 0247-669 0682
Web: www.bbka.demon.co.uk
General Secretary, P. B. Spencer

BERKSHIRE ARCHAEOLOGICAL SOCIETY (1871),
43 Laburnham Road, Maidenhead, Berks, SL6 4DE.
Tel: 01628-631225
Hon. Secretary, L. J. Over

BEVIN BOYS ASSOCIATION (1989), School Cottage,
49A Hogshill Street, Beaminster, Dorset, DT8 3AG.
Tel: 01308-861488 Fax: 01308-861488
Vice President and Public Relations, W. H. Taylor, MBE

BIBLE SOCIETY, BRITISH AND FOREIGN (1804),
Stonehill Green, Westlea, Swindon, SN5 7DG.
Tel: 01793-418100 Fax: 01793-418118
Web: www.biblesociety.org.uk
Chief Executive, James Catford

BIBLIOGRAPHICAL SOCIETY (1892),
c/o Institute of English Studies, Room 304, Senate House,
Malet Street, London, WC1E 7HU. Tel: 020-7862 8675
Fax: 020-7862 8720 Web: www.bibsoc.org.uk
Hon. Secretary, M. L. Ford

BIOLOGY, INSTITUTE OF (1950), 20–22 Queensberry Place,
London, SW7 2DZ. Tel: 020-7581 8333
Fax: 020-7823 9409 Web: www.iob.org
Chief Executive, Prof. A. D. B. Malcolm

BIRMINGHAM AND WARWICKSHIRE
ARCHAEOLOGICAL SOCIETY (1870), c/o Birmingham
and Midland Institute, Margaret Street, Birmingham, B3 3BS.
Web: www.bwas.swinternet.co.uk
Hon. Secretary, Miss S. Middleton

BLIND, NATIONAL LIBRARY FOR THE (1828), Far
Cromwell Road, Bredbury, Stockport, Cheshire, SK6 2SG.
Tel: 0161-355 2000 Fax: 0161-355 2098
Web: www.nlbuk.org
Chief Executive, Helen Brazier

BLOOD SERVICE, NATIONAL, Oak House, Reeds Crescent,
Watford, Herts, WO24 4QN. Tel: 01923-486800
Fax: 01923-486801 Web: www.blood.co.uk
Chief Executive, Martin Gorham

BLUE CROSS (1897), Shilton Road, Burford, Oxon, OX18 4PF.
Tel: 01993-822651 Fax: 01993-823083
Web: www.bluecross.org.uk
Chief Executive, John Rutter

BODLEIAN, FRIENDS OF THE (1925), Bodleian Library,
Oxford, OX1 3BG. Tel: 01865-277022/277234
Fax: 01865-277182/277187
Web: www.bodley.ox.ac.uk/friends
Secretary, G. Groom

BOOK AID INTERNATIONAL (1954), 39–41 Coldharbour
Lane, London, SE5 9NR. Tel: 020-7733 3577
Fax: 020-7978 8006 Web: www.bookaid.org
Director, Mrs S. Harrity, MBE

BOOKSELLERS ASSOCIATION OF THE UK & IRELAND
LTD (1895), Minster House, 272 Vauxhall Bridge Road,
London, SW1V 1BA. Tel: 020-7802 0802
Fax: 020-7802 0803 Web: www.booksellers.org.uk
Chief Executive, T. E. Godfray

BOTANICAL ARTS, THE SOCIETY OF (1985),
1 Knapp Cottages, Wyke, Gillingham, Dorset, SP8 4NQ.
Tel: 01747-825718 Fax: 01747-826835
Web: www.soc-botanical-artists.org
Executive Secretary, P. Henderson

BOTANICAL SOCIETY OF SCOTLAND (1836), c/o Royal
Botanic Garden, Inverleith Row, Edinburgh, EH3 5LR.
Tel: 0131-552 7171 Fax: 0131-248 2901
Hon. General Secretary, Dr P. Cochrane

BOTANICAL SOCIETY OF THE BRITISH ISLES (1836),
c/o Department of Botany, The Natural History Museum,
Cromwell Road, London, SW7 5BD. Tel: 020-7942 5002
Web: www.bsbi.org.uk
Hon. General Secretary, Miss A. Burns

BOYS' BRIGADE (1883), Felden Lodge, Hemel Hempstead,
Herts, HP3 0BL. Tel: 01442-231681 Fax: 01442-235391
Web: www.boys-brigade.org.uk
Acting Chief Executive, Malcolm Hayden

BREWING, INSTITUTE & GUILD OF (1886),
33 Clarges Street, London, W1J 7EE. Tel: 020-7499 8144
Fax: 020-7499 1156 Web: www.igb.org.uk
Chief Executive, B. E. A. Pegnall

BRISTOL AND GLOUCESTERSHIRE ARCHAEOLOGICAL
SOCIETY (1876), 22 Beaumont Road, Gloucester, GL2 0EJ.
Tel: 01452-302610 Web: www.bgas.org.uk
Hon. Secretary, D. J. H. Smith, FSA

BRITAIN-NEPAL SOCIETY (1960), 95B Eaton Place, London,
SW1X 8LZ. Tel: 07765-251345
Hon. Secretary, Stuart Sessions, MBE

BRITISH EXECUTIVE SERVICE OVERSEAS (1972),
164 Vauxhall Bridge Road, London, SW1V 2RB.
Tel: 020-7630 0644 Fax: 020-7630 0624
Web: www.beso.org
Chief Executive, G. Ramsey, CBE

BRITISH INSTITUTE IN EASTERN AFRICA (1959),
10 Carlton House Terrace, London, SW1Y 5AH.
Tel: 020-7969 5201 Fax: 020-7969 5401
Web: www.britac.ac.uk/institutes/eafrica
London Secretary, Mrs J. Moyo

BRITISH INTERPLANETARY SOCIETY (1933), 27–29 South
Lambeth Road, London, SW8 1SZ. Tel: 020-7735 3160
Fax: 020-7820 1504 Web: www.bis-spaceflight.com
Executive Secretary, Suszann Parry

BRITISH ISRAEL WORLD FEDERATION (1919),
8 Blades Court, Deodar Road, London, SW15 2NU.
Tel: 020-8877 9010 Fax: 020-8871 4770
Web: www.britishisrael.co.uk
Hon. Secretary, M. A. Clark

BRITISH MEDICAL ASSOCIATION (1832), BMA House,
Tavistock Square, London, WC1H 9JP. Tel: 020-7387 4499
Fax: 020-7383 6400 Web: www.bma.org.uk
Secretary, J. Strachan

BRITISH REFUGEE COUNCIL (1992), Bondway House,
3–9 Bondway, London, SW8 1SJ. Tel: 020-7582 6922
Fax: 020-7582 3969 Web: www.refugeecouncil.org.uk
Chair, Naaz Coker

BTBS THE BOOK TRADE CHARITY (1837), The Foyle
Centre, The Retreat, Kings Langley, Herts, WD4 8LT.
Tel: 01923-263128, Fax: 01923-270732
Web: www.booktradecharity.demon.co.uk
Chief Executive, David Hicks

BUCKINGHAMSHIRE ARCHAEOLOGICAL SOCIETY
(1847), County Museum, Church Street, Aylesbury, Bucks,
HP20 2QP. Tel: 01296-678114
Hon. Secretary, Mrs M. E. A. Brown

BUDGERIGAR SOCIETY (1925), Spring Gardens,
Northampton, NN1 1DR. Tel: 01604-624549
Fax: 01604-627108 Web: www.budgerigarsociety.com
General Secretary, D. Whittaker

BUILDING ENGINEERS, ASSOCIATION OF (1925), Lutyens
House, Billing Brook Road, Weston Favell, Northampton,
NN3 8NW. Tel: 01604-404121 Fax: 01604-784200
Web: www.abe.org.uk
Chief Executive, D. Gibson

BUILDING SERVICES ENGINEERS, CHARTERED
INSTITUTION OF (1898), Delta House, 222 Balham High
Road, London, SW12 9BS. Tel: 020-8675 5211
Fax: 020-8675 5449 Web: www.cibse.org
Chief Executive, J. Amey

BUILDING SOCIETIES ASSOCIATION (1869),
3 Savile Row, London, W1S 3PB. Tel: 020-7437 0655
Fax: 020-7734 6416 Web: www.bsa.org.uk
Director-General, A. Coles

BUSINESS RECOVERY PROFESSIONALS, ASSOCIATION
OF (1990), Halton House, 20–23 Holborn, London,
EC1N 2JE. Tel: 020-7831 6563 Fax: 020-7405 7047
Web: www.r3.org.uk
Chief Operating Officer, R. M. Stancombe

CAFOD (CATHOLIC FUND FOR OVERSEAS
DEVELOPMENT) (1962), Romero Close, Stockwell Road,
London, SW9 9TY. Tel: 020-7733 7900
Fax: 020-7274 9630 Web: www.cafod.org.uk
Director, C. Bain

CALOUSTE GULBENKIAN FOUNDATION (1956),
98 Portland Place, London, W1B 1ET. Tel: 020-7636 5313
Fax: 020-7908 7580 Web: www.gulbenkian.org.uk
Director, Ms P. Ridley

CAMBRIDGE ANTIQUARIAN SOCIETY (1840),
99 Cambridge Road, Girton, Cambridge, CB3 0PN.
Hon. Secretary, Ms E. Allan

CAMBRIDGE PRESERVATION SOCIETY, (1928),
Wandlebury Ring, Gog Magog Hills, Babraham, Cambridge,
CB2 4AE. Tel: 01223-243830 Fax: 01223-243830
Web: www.cpswandlebury.org
Director, B. Pearce

CAMERON FUND (1970), Tavistock House North, Tavistock
Square, London, WC1H 9HR. Tel: 020-7388 0796
Fax: 020-7554 6334 Web: www.cameronfund.org.uk
Secretary, Mrs L. Dluska-Miziura

CAMPAIGN FOR FREEDOM OF INFORMATION (1984),
Suite 102, 16 Baldwin Gardens, London, EC1N 7RJ.
Tel: 020-7831 7477 Fax: 020-7831 7461
Web: www.cfoi.org.uk
Director, M. Frankel

CAMPAIGN FOR NATIONAL DEMOCRACY, BCM
Natdems, London, WC1N 3XX. Tel: 07071-226074
Web: www.natdems.org.uk
Chairman, Ian Anderson

CAMPAIGN FOR NUCLEAR DISARMAMENT (CND)
(1958), 162 Holloway Road, London, N7 8DQ.
Tel: 020-7700 2393 Fax: 020-7700 2357
Web: www.cnduk.org
Chair, Carol Naughton

CANADA-UNITED KINGDOM CHAMBER OF
COMMERCE (1921), 38 Grosvenor Street, London,
W1K 4DP. Tel: 020-7258 6576 Fax: 020-7258 6594
Web: www.canada-uk.org
Executive Director, K. Stephens

CANCER RESEARCH UK (2002), PO Box 123, London,
WC2A 3PX. Tel: 020-7242 0200 Fax: 020-7654 3210
Web: www.cancerresearchuk.org
Chief Executive, Sir Paul Nurse

CARERS UK (1988), Ruth Pitter House, 20–25 Glasshouse Yard, London, EC1A 4JT. Tel: 020-7490 8818 Fax: 020-7490 8824 Web: www.carersonline.org.uk
Chief Executive, Ms D. Whitworth

CARNEGIE HERO FUND TRUST (1908), Abbey Park House, Dunfermline, Fife, KY12 7PB. Tel: 01383-723638 Fax: 01383-721862
Chief Executive, B. A. Anderson

CARNEGIE UNITED KINGDOM TRUST (1913), Comely Park House, Dunfermline, Fife, KY12 7EJ. Tel: 01383-721445 Fax: 01383-620682 Web: www.carnegieuktrust.org.uk
Chief Executive, C. John Naylor, OBE

CAST METAL ENGINEERS, INSTITUTE OF (1904), National Metalforming Centre, 47 Birmingham Road, West Bromwich, B70 6PY. Tel: 0121-601 6979 Fax: 0121-601 6981 Web: www.icme.org.uk
Secretary, A. M. Turner

CATHEDRALS FABRIC COMMISSION FOR ENGLAND (1991), Church House, Great Smith Street, London, SW1P 3NZ. Tel: 020-7898 1863 Fax: 020-7898 1881
Secretary, Ms Paula Griffiths

CATHOLIC HOUSING AID SOCIETY (1956), 209 Old Marylebone Road, London, NW1 5QT. Tel: 020-7723 7273 Fax: 020-7723 5943 Web: www.chasnational.org.uk
Director, Ms R. Rafferty

CATHOLIC TRUTH SOCIETY (1868), 40–46 Harleyford Road, London, SE11 5AY. Tel: 020-7640 0042 Fax: 020-7640 0046 Web: www.cts-online.org.uk
General Secretary, F. Martin

CATHOLIC UNION OF GREAT BRITAIN (1872), St Maxmilian Kolbe House, 63 Jeddo Road, London, W12 9EE. Tel: 020-8749 1321 Fax: 020-8735 0816 Web: www.catholicunion.org/new
Secretary, P. H. Higgs

CATTLE ASSOCIATION (DAIRY), NATIONAL (1998), Brick House, Risbury, Leominster, Herefordshire, HR6 0NQ. Tel: 01568-760632 Fax: 01568-760523
Executive Secretary, Tim Brigstocke

CATTLE BREEDERS' CLUB, BRITISH (1950), Lake Villa, Bradworthy, Holsworthy, Devon, EX22 7SQ. Tel: 01409-241579 Fax: 01409-241579
Secretary, Mrs L. Lewin

CENTRAL AND CECIL HOUSING TRUST (1926), 2 Priory Road, Kew, Richmond, Surrey, TW9 3DG. Tel: 020-8940 9828 Fax: 020-8332 1044 Web: www.ccht.org.uk
Chief Executive, G. Brighton

CENTREPOINT (1969), Neil House, 7 Whitechapel Road, London, E1 1DU. Tel: 020-7426 5300 Fax: 020-7426 5301 Web: www.centrepoint.org.uk
Chief Executive, Anthony Lawton

CEREDIGION HISTORICAL SOCIETY, Henllys, Lôn Tyllwyd, Llanfarian, Aberystwyth, SY23 4UH. Tel: 01970-625818.
Hon. Secretary, T. G. Davies

CHAMBERS OF COMMERCE, SCOTTISH (1948), 30 George Square, Glasgow, G2 1EQ. Tel: 0141-204 8316 Fax: 0141-221 2336 Web: www.scottishchambers.org.uk
Director, Robert Leitch

CHAMBERS OF COMMERCE, THE BRITISH, 1st Floor, 65 Petty France, St James Park, London, SW1H 9EU. Tel: 020-7654 5800 Fax: 020-7654 5819 Web: www.chamberonline.co.uk
President, Isabella Moore

CHARITIES AID FOUNDATION (1924), Kings Hill, West Malling, Kent, ME19 4TA. Tel: 01732-520000 Fax: 01732-520001 Web: www.cafonline.org
Chief Executive, Stephen Ainger

CHILDBIRTH TRUST, NATIONAL (1956), Alexandra House, Oldham Terrace, Acton, London, W3 6NH.
Tel: 0870-770 3236 Enquiries: Tel: 0870 444 8707 Fax: 0870-770 3237 Web: www.nctpregnancyandbabycare.com and www.nctms.co.uk
Chief Executive, Ms B. Phipps

CHILDREN 1ST (1884), 83 Whitehouse Loan, Edinburgh, EH9 1AT. Tel: 0131-446 2300 Fax: 0131-446 2339 Web: www.children1st.org.uk
Chief Executive, Margaret McKay

CHILDREN'S SOCIETY (1881), Edward Rudolf House, Margery Street, London, WC1X 0JL. Tel: 020-7841 4000 Fax: 020-7841 4500 Web: www.childrenssociety.org.uk
Chief Executive, Bob Reitermeier

CHRISTIAN AID SCOTLAND, 41 George IV Bridge, Edinburgh, EH1 1EL. Tel: 0131-220 1254 Fax: 0131-225 8861 Web: www.christian-aid.org.uk
National Secretary, Revd J. Wylie

CHRISTIAN EDUCATION (1965), 1020 Bristol Road, Selly Oak, Birmingham, B29 6LB. Tel: 0121-472 4242 Fax: 0121-472 7575 Web: www.christianeducation.org.uk
Chief Executive, Peter Fishpool

CHRISTIAN KNOWLEDGE, SOCIETY FOR PROMOTING (SPCK) (1698), Holy Trinity Church, Marylebone Road, London, NW1 4DU.
Tel: 020-7643 0382 Fax: 020-7643 0391 Web: www.spck.org.uk
General Secretary, G. C. King

CHRISTIANS AND JEWS, COUNCIL OF (1942), 5th Floor, Camelford House, 87–89 Albert Embankment, London, SE1 7TP. Tel: 020-7820 0090 Fax: 020-7820 0504 Web: www.ccj.org.uk
Director, Sr M. Shepherd

CHURCH BELL RINGERS, CENTRAL COUNCIL OF (1891), The Cottage, School Hill, Warnham, Horsham, RH12 3QN. Tel: 01403-269743 Web: www.cccbr.org.uk
Secretary, Mr I. H. Oram

CHURCH HISTORY SOCIETY, SCOTTISH (1927), Crown Manse, 39 Southside Road, Inverness, IV2 4XA. Tel: 01463-231140 Fax: 01463-230537
Hon. Secretary, Revd Dr P. H. Donald

CHURCH HOUSE, CORPORATION OF (1888), Church House, Dean's Yard, London, SW1P 3NZ. Tel: 020-7898 1310 Fax: 020-7898 1321
Secretary, C. D. L. Menzies

CHURCH LADS' AND CHURCH GIRLS' BRIGADE (1891), 2 Barnsley Road, Wath upon Dearne, Rotherham, S. Yorks, S63 6PY. Tel: 01709-876535 Fax: 01709-878089 Web: www.clcgb.org.uk
General Secretary, A. J. Reed Screen

CHURCH MISSION SOCIETY, Partnership House, 157 Waterloo Road, London, SE1 8UU. Tel: 020-7928 868 Fax: 020-7401 3215 Web: www.cms-uk.org
General Secretary, Revd Canon T. Dakin

CHURCH MONUMENTS SOCIETY (1979), 34 Bridge Street, Shepshed, Leicestershire, LE12 9AD. Tel: 01509-569035 Web: www.churchmonumentssociety.org
Hon. Secretary, Dr Sophie Oosterwijk

CHURCH UNION (1859), Faith House, 7 Tufton Street, London, SW1P 3QN. Tel: 020-7222 6952 Fax: 020-7976 7180 Web: www.churchunion.care4free.net
House Manager, Mrs J. Miller

CHURCHES, COUNCIL FOR THE CARE OF (1921), Church House, Great Smith Street, London, SW1P 3NZ. Tel: 020-7898 1866 Fax: 020-7898 1881
Secretary, Paula Griffiths

CHURCHES, FRIENDS OF FRIENDLESS (1957), St Ann's Vestry Hall, 2 Church Entry, London, EC4V 5HB. Tel: 020-7236 3934 Fax: 020-7329 3677 Web: www.friendsoffrriendlesschurches.org.uk
Hon. Director, M. Saunders, MBE

CHURCHILL SOCIETY - LONDON (1990), c/o 18 Grove Lane, Ipswich, Suffolk, IP4 1NR. Tel: 01473-413533 Fax: 01473-413533 www.churchill-society-london.orguk/index.htm.
General Secretary, N. H. Rogers

CHURCHILL SOCIETY, INTERNATIONAL (1968), PO Box 1257, Melksham, Wilts, SN12 6GQ. Tel: 01380-828609 Fax: 01380-828609 Web: www.winstonchurchill.org
Chairman, N. B. Knocker, OBE

CITIZENS ADVICE (1939), Myddelton House, 115–123 Pentonville Road, London, N1 9LZ. Tel: 020-7833 2181 Fax: 020-7833 4371 Web: www.citizensadvice.org.uk
Chief Executive, D. Harker

CITY PAROCHIAL FOUNDATION (1891), 6 Middle Street, London, EC1A 7PH. Tel: 020-7606 6145 Fax: 020-7600 1866 Web: www.cityparochial.org.uk
Clerk, B. Mehta, OBE

CLASSICAL ASSOCIATION (1903), Senate House, Malet Street, London, WC1E 7HU. Tel: 020-7862 8706 Fax: 020-7862 8729 Web: www.sas.ac.uk/icls/classass
Secretary, C. L. Roberts

CLEAN AIR AND ENVIRONMENTAL PROTECTION, NATIONAL SOCIETY FOR (1898), 44 Grand Parade, Brighton, BN2 9QA. Tel: 01273-878770 Fax: 01273-606626 Web: www.nsca.org.uk
Secretary-General, R. Mills

CLUBS FOR YOUNG PEOPLE, NATIONAL ASSOCIATION OF (1925), 371 Kennington Lane, London, SE11 5QY. Tel: 020-7793 0787 Fax: 020-7820 9815 Web: www.nacyp.org.uk
National Director, C. Groves

CO-OPERATIVE GROUP (CWS) LTD. (1863), PO Box 53, New Century House, Manchester, M60 4ES. Tel: 0161-834 1212 Fax: 0161-834 4507 Web: www.co-op.co.uk
Chief Executive, M. D. Beaumont

CO-OPERATIVE PARTY, 77 Weston Street, London, SE1 3SD. Tel: 020-7357 0230 Fax: 020-7407 4476 Web: www.co-op-party.org.uk
Secretary, P. Hunt

CO-OPERATIVES UK (1869), Holyoake House, Hanover Street, Manchester, M60 0AS. Tel: 0161-246 2900 Fax: 0161-831 7684 Web: www.co-opunion.co.uk
Chief Executive, Ms P. Green

COMMONWEALTH, ENGLISH-SPEAKING UNION OF THE (1918), Dartmouth House, 37 Charles Street, London, W1J 5ED. Tel: 020-7529 1550 Fax: 020-7495 6108 Web: www.esu.org
Director-General, Mrs V. Mitchell, OBE

COMMUNICATORS IN BUSINESS, BRITISH ASSOCIATION FOR (1949), Suite A, First Floor, The Auriga Building, Davy Avenue, Knowlhill, Milton Keynes, MK5 8ND. Tel: 0870-121 7606 Fax: 0870-121 7601 Web: www.cib.uk.com
Secretary-General, Mrs K. Jones

CONFED (1972), Humanities Building, University of Manchester, Oxford Road, Manchester, M13 9PL. Tel: 0161-236 5766 Fax: 0161-236 6742
Assistant Director, Sarah Caton

CONSERVATION OF HISTORIC AND ARTISTIC WORKS, INTERNATIONAL INSTITUTE FOR (1950), 6 Buckingham Street, London, WC2N 6BA. Tel: 020-7839 5975 Fax: 020-7976 1564 Web: www.iiconservation.org
Secretary-General, J. Ashley-Smith

CONSULTING SCIENTISTS, ASSOCIATION OF (1958), PO Box 4040, Thorpe-le-Soken, Clacton-on-Sea, CO16 0EL. Tel: 01255-862526 Fax: 01255-862526 Web: www.consultingscientists.co.uk
Secretary, Dr D. Simpson

CONSUMERS' ASSOCIATION (1957), 2 Marylebone Road, London, NW1 4DF. Tel: 020-7770 7000 Fax: 020-7770 7600 Web: www.which.net
Director, Ms S. McKechnie, OBE

CORAM FAMILY (1739), 49 Mecklenburgh Square, London, WC1N 2QA. Tel: 020-7520 0300 Fax: 020-7520 0301 Web: www.coram.org.uk
Chief Executive, Dr G. Pugh, OBE

CORONER'S SOCIETY OF ENGLAND AND WALES (1846), 21 Dingle Road, Pedmore, Stourbridge, DY9 0RS.
Hon. Secretary, Vic Round

CORPORATE TREASURERS, ASSOCIATION OF (1979), Ocean House, 10–12 Little Trinity Lane, London, EC4V 2DJ. Tel: 020-7213 9728 Fax: 020-7248 2591 Web: www.treasurers.org
Chief Executive, Richard Raeburn

COUNSEL AND CARE, (1954), Twyman House, 16 Bonny Street, London, NW1 9PG. Tel: 020-7241 8555 Fax: 020-7267 6877 Web: www.counselandcare.org.uk
Chief Executive, M. Green

COUNSELLING AND PSYCHOTHERAPY, BRITISH ASSOCIATION FOR (1977), 1 Regent Place, Rugby, Warks, CV21 2PJ. Tel: 0870-443 5252 Fax: 0870-443 5160 Web: www.bacp.co.uk
Chief Executive, L. Clarke

COUNTRYSIDE ALLIANCE (1998), Old Town Hall, 367 Kennington Road, London, SE11 4PT. Tel: 020-7840 9200 Fax: 020-7793 8484 Web: www.countryside-alliance.org
Chief Executive, R. Burge

COUNTY CHIEF EXECUTIVES, ASSOCIATION OF (1974), Office of the Chief Executive, County Hall, Trowbridge, Wiltshire, BA14 8JF. Tel: 01225-713101 Fax: 01225-713092
Hon. Secretary, K. Robinson

COUNTY TREASURERS, SOCIETY OF, Derbyshire County Council, County Hall, Matlock, Derbyshire, DE4 3AH. Tel: 01629-585068 Fax: 01629-585985 Web: www.sctnet.org.uk
Hon. Secretary, Peter Swaby

CPRE (COUNCIL FOR THE PROTECTION OF RURAL ENGLAND) (1926), 128 Southwark Street, London, SE1 0SW. Tel: 020-7981 2800 Fax: 020-7981 2899 Web: www.cpre.org.uk
Director, Ms K. Parminter

CRAFTS COUNCIL (1971), 44A Pentonville Road, London, N1 9BY. Tel: 020-7278 7700 Fax: 020-7837 6891 Web: www.craftscouncil.org.uk
Director, Dr Louise Taylor

CRISIS UK (1967), 64 Commercial Street, London, E1 6LT. Tel: 0870-011 3335 Fax: 0870-011 3336 Web: www.crisis.org.uk
Chief Executive, S. Ghosh

CRUELTY TO ANIMALS, SCOTTISH SOCIETY FOR THE PREVENTION OF (1839), Braehead Mains, 603 Queensferry Road, Edinburgh, EH4 6EA. Tel: 0131-339 0222 Fax: 0131-339 4777 Web: www.scottishspca.org
Chief Executive, I. R. Gardiner

CRUSE BEREAVEMENT CARE (1959), 126 Sheen Road, Richmond, Surrey, TW9 1UR. Tel: 020-8939 9530. Helpline: 0870-167 1677 Fax: 020-8940 7638 Web: www.crusebereavementcare.org.uk
Chief Executive, Anne Viney

CTC (THE UK'S NATIONAL CYCLISTS' ORGANISATION), 69 Meadrow, Godalming, Surrey, GU7 3HS. Tel: 0870-873 0060 Fax: 0870-873 0064 Web: www.ctc.org.uk
Director, K. Mayne

CYSTIC FIBROSIS TRUST (1964), 11 London Road, Bromley, Kent, BR1 1BY. Tel: 020-8464 7211 Fax: 020-8313 0472 Web: www.cftrust.org.uk
Chief Executive, Mrs R. Barnes

DATA (DESIGN AND TECHNOLOGY ASSOCIATION) (1989), 16 Wellesbourne House, Walton Road, Wellesbourne, Warks, CV35 9JB. Tel: 01789-470007 Fax: 01789-841955 Web: www.data.org.uk
Chief Executive, J. Jupe

DEAF ASSOCIATION, BRITISH (1890), 1–3 Worship Street, London, EC2A 2AB. Tel: 020-7588 3529 Fax: 020-7588 3527 Web: www.bda.org.uk
Chief Executive, J. McWhinney

DEMOS (1993), The Mezzanine, Elizabeth House, 39 York Road, London, SE1 7NQ. Tel: 020-7401 5330 Fax: 020-7401 5331 Web: www.demos.co.uk
Director, T. Bentley

DENTAL ASSOCIATION, BRITISH (1880), 64 Wimpole Street, London, W1G 8YS. Tel: 020-7563 4563 Fax: 020-7487 4563 Web: www.bda-dentistry.org.uk
Chief Executive, Ian Wylie

DENTAL COUNCIL, GENERAL (1956), 37 Wimpole Street, London, W1G 8DQ. Tel: 020-7887 3800 Fax: 020-7224 3294 Web: www.gdc-uk.org
Chief Executive & Registrar, Antony Townsend

DESIGN AND INDUSTRIES ASSOCIATION (1915), Business Design Centre, 52 Upper Street, London, N1 0QH. Tel: 020-7288 6212 Fax: 020-7288 6190 Web: www.dia.org.uk *Chairman,* Paul Williams

DEVON ARCHAEOLOGICAL SOCIETY (1929), RAM Museum, Queen Street, Exeter, EX4 3RX. Tel: 01392-265858
Hon. Secretary, Lorinda Legge

DIANA, PRINCESS OF WALES MEMORIAL FUND (1997), County Hall, Westminster Bridge Road, London, SE1 7PB. Tel: 020-7902 5500 Fax: 020-7902 5511 Web: www.theworkcontinues.org.uk
Chief Executive, Dr A. Purkis, OBE

DIRECTORS, INSTITUTE OF (1903), 116 Pall Mall, London, SW1Y 5ED. Tel: 020-7839 1233 Fax: 020-7930 1949 Web: www.iod.com
Chief Executive, A. Main Wilson

DIRECTORY & DATABASE PUBLISHERS ASSOCIATION (1970), PO Box 23034, London, W6 0RJ. Tel: 020-8846 9707 Fax: 0870-168 0552 Web: www.directory-publisher.co.uk
Secretary, Ms R. Pettit

DISPENSING OPTICIANS, ASSOCIATION OF BRITISH (1925), 199 Gloucester Terrace, London, W2 6LD. Tel: 020-7298 5100 Fax: 020-7298 5111 Web: www.abdo.org.uk
General Secretary, Sir Anthony Garrett, CBE

DITCHLEY FOUNDATION (1958), Ditchley Park, Enstone, Chipping Norton, Oxon, OX7 4ER. Tel: 01608-677346 Fax: 01608-677399 Web: www.ditchley.co.uk
Director, Sir Nigel Broomfield, KCMG

DORSET NATURAL HISTORY AND ARCHAEOLOGICAL SOCIETY (1875), Dorset County Museum, Dorchester, Dorset, DT1 1XA. Tel: 01305-262735 Fax: 01305-257180 Web: www.dorsetcountymuseum.com

DOWN'S SYNDROME ASSOCIATION (1970), 155 Mitcham Road, London, SW17 9PG. Tel: 020-8682 4001 Fax: 020-8682 4012 Web: www.downs-syndrome.org.uk
Director, Ms C. Boys

DOWSERS, BRITISH SOCIETY OF (1933), Sycamore Barn, Hastingleigh, Ashford, Kent, TN25 5HW. Tel: 01233-750253 Fax: 01233-750253 Web: www.britishdowsers.org
General Secretary, M. D. Rust

DRAINAGE AUTHORITIES, ASSOCIATION OF (1937), The Mews, 3 Royal Oak Passage, High Street, Huntingdon, Cambs, PE29 3EA. Tel: 01480-411123 Fax: 01480-431107 Web: www.ada.org.uk
Chief Executive, D. Noble

DRIVING SOCIETY, BRITISH (1957), 27 Dugard Place, Barford, Warwick, CV35 8DX. Tel: 01926-624420 Fax: 01926-624633 Web: www.britishdrivingsociety.co.uk
Secretary, Mrs J. M. Dillon

THE DUKE OF EDINBURGH'S AWARD, Gulliver House, Madeira Walk, Windsor, Berks, SL4 1EU. Tel: 01753-727400 Fax: 01753-810666 Web: www.theaward.org
Director, Vice-Adm M. P. Gretton, CB

DYSLEXIA INSTITUTE (1972), Park House, Wick Road, Egham, Middx, TW20 0HH. Tel: 01784-222300 Fax: 01784-222333 Web: www.dyslexia-inst.org.uk
Chief Executive, Shirley Cramer

EAST HERTFORDSHIRE ARCHAEOLOGICAL SOCIETY (1898), 1 Marsh Lane, Stanstead Abbots, Ware, Herts, SG12 8HH. Tel: 01920-870664
Hon. Secretary, Mrs M. C. Readman

EAST OF ENGLAND AGRICULTURAL SOCIETY (1797), East of England Showground, Peterborough, PE2 6XE Tel: 01733-234451 Fax: 01733-370038 Web: www.eastofengland.org.uk
Chief Executive, Andrew Mercer

ECCLESIOLOGICAL SOCIETY (1839), c/o Society of Antiquaries of London, Burlington House, London, W1V 0HS. Tel: 020-7738 2965 Fax: 020-7924 7958 Web: www.ecclsoc.org
Hon. Secretary, Dr James F. Johnston

ECONOMIC AFFAIRS, INSTITUTE OF (1955), 2 Lord North Street, Westminster, London, SW1P 3LB. Tel: 020-7799 8900 Fax: 020-7799 2137 Web: www.iea.org.uk
Director-General, J. Blundell

EDINBURGH CHAMBER OF COMMERCE (1786), 27 Melville Street, Edinburgh, EH3 7JF. Tel: 0131-477 7000 Fax: 0131-477 7002 Web: www.ecce.org
Chief Executive, W. Furness

EDITORS, SOCIETY OF (1999), University Centre, Granta Place, Cambridge, CB2 1RU. Tel: 01223-304080 Fax: 01223-304090 Web: www.societyofeditors.org
Executive Director, R. Satchwell

EDUCATIONAL RESEARCH IN ENGLAND AND WALES, NATIONAL FOUNDATION FOR (1946), The Mere, Upton Park, Slough, SL1 2DQ. Tel: 01753-574123 Fax: 01753-691632 Web: www.nfer.ac.uk.
Director, Dr S. Hegarty

EGYPT EXPLORATION SOCIETY (1882), 3 Doughty Mews, London, WC1N 2PG. Tel: 020-7242 1880 Fax: 020-7404 6118 Web: www.ees.ac.uk
Secretary-General, Dr P. A. Spencer

ELECTORAL REFORM SOCIETY (1884), 6 Chancel Street, London, SE1 0UU. Tel: 020-7928 1622 Fax: 020-7401 7789 Web: www.electoral-reform.org.uk
Chief Executive, Dr K. G. H. Ritchie

ELGAR FOUNDATION (1935), The Elgar Birthplace Museum, Lower Broadheath, Worcester, WR2 6RH. Tel: 01905-333224 Fax: 01905-333426 Web: www.elgarmuseum.org
Museum Director, Catherine Sloan

ELGAR SOCIETY (1951), c/o 29 Van Diemens Close, Chinnor, Oxon, OX39 4QE. Tel: 01844-354096 Fax: 01844-354459 Web: www.elgar.org
Hon. Secretary, Ms W. Hillary

EMERGENCY PLANNING SOCIETY (1993), Northumberland House, 11 The Pavement, Popes Lane, London, W5 4NG. Tel: 020-8579 7971 Fax: 020-8579 7972 Web: www.emergplansoc.org.uk
Hon. Secretary, M. Slaney

ENABLE (1954), 7 Buchanan Street, Glasgow, G1 3HL. Tel: 0141-226 4541 Fax: 0141-204 4398 Web: www.enable.org.uk
Director, N. Dunning

ENERGY, INSTITUTE OF (1927), 18 Devonshire Street, London, W1G 7AU. Tel: 020-7580 7124 Fax: 020-7580 4420 Web: www.instenergy.org.uk
Chief Executive and Secretary, John Ingham

ENERGYWATCH (2000), 4th Floor, Artillery House, Artillery Row, London, SW1P 1RT. Tel: 020-7799 8340 Fax: 020-7799 8341 Web: www.energywatch.org.uk
Chief Executive, Stephen Reid

ENGINEERING COUNCIL (UK), THE (2002), 10 Maltravers Street, London, WC2R 3ER. Tel: 020-7240 7891 Fax: 020-7379 5586 Web: www.engc.org.uk
Executive Director, A. V. Ramsay

ENGINEERING DESIGNERS, INSTITUTION OF (1945), Courtleigh, Westbury Leigh, Westbury, Wilts, BA13 3TA. Tel: 01373-822801 Fax: 01373-858085 Web: www.ied.org.uk
Secretary, E. Brodhurst

ENGINEERS, INSTITUTION OF BRITISH (1928), Clifford Hill Court, Clifford Chambers, Stratford-upon-Avon, CV37 8AA. Tel: 01789-298739 Fax: 01789-294442 Web: www.britishengineers.com
President, Dr John Fenton

ENGINEERS, SOCIETY OF (1854), Guinea Wiggs, Nayland, Colchester, Essex, CO6 7NF. Tel: 01206-263332 Fax: 01206-262624 Web: www.society-of-engineers.org.uk
Chief Executive, Mrs L. C. A. Wright

ENVIRONMENT COUNCIL, THE (1970), 212 High Holborn, London, WC1V 7BF. Tel: 020-7836 2626 Fax: 020-7242 1180 Web: www.the-environment-council.org.uk
Deputy Chief Executive, S. Lansdell

ENVIRONMENTAL HEALTH, CHARTERED INSTITUTE OF (1883), Chadwick Court, 15 Hatfields, London, SE1 8DJ. Tel: 020-7928 6006 Fax: 020-7827 5866 Web: www.cieh.org.uk
Chief Executive, G. Jukes

EPILEPSY ACTION (1950), New Anstey House, Gate Way Drive, Yeadon, Leeds, LS19 7XY. Tel: 0113-210 8800 Helpline: 0808-800 5050 Fax: 0113-391 0300 Web: www.epilepsy.org.uk
Chief Executive, P. Lee

EPILEPSY, NATIONAL SOCIETY FOR (1892), Chesham Lane, Chalfont St Peter, Bucks, SL9 0RJ. Tel: 01494-601300 Fax: 01494-871927 Web: www.epilepsynse.org.uk
Chief Executive, Graham Faulkner

ESTATE AGENTS, NATIONAL ASSOCIATION OF (1962), Arbon House, 21 Jury Street, Warwick, CV34 4EH. Tel: 01926-496800 Fax: 01926-400953 Web: www.naea.co.uk
President, Julie Westby, FNAEA

ESTATE AGENTS, OMBUDSMAN FOR (1998), Beckett House, 4 Bridge Street, Salisbury, Wilts, SP1 2LX. Tel: 01722-333306 Fax: 01722-332296 Web: www.oea.co.uk
Ombudsman, S. R. Carr-Smith

EVANGELICAL LIBRARY, 78A Chiltern Street, London, W1U 5HB. Tel: 020-7935 6997 Web: www.elib.org.uk
Librarian, S. J. Taylor

EX-SERVICES MENTAL WELFARE SOCIETY (1919), Hollybush House, Hollybush, nr Ayr, KA6 7EA. Tel: 01292-560214 Fax: 01292-560871 Web: www.combatstress.com
Clinical Manager, Mrs F. Robertson

EXPORT, INSTITUTE OF (1935), Minerva Business Park, Lynchwood, Peterborough, PE2 6FT. Tel: 01733-404400 Fax: 01733-404444 Web: www.export.org.uk
Director-General, Maria McCaffery, MBE

FAIR ISLE BIRD OBSERVATORY TRUST (1948), Fair Isle Bird Observatory, Fair Isle, Shetland, ZE2 9JU. Tel: 01595-760258 Fax: 01595-760258 Web: www.fairislebirdobs.co.uk
Administrator, H. Shaw

FAITH AND THOUGHT (1865), 41 Marne Avenue, Welling,
Kent, DA16 2EY. Tel: 020-8303 0465 Fax: 020-8303 0465
Web: www.faithandthought.org.uk
Chairman of Council, T. C. Mitchell

FAMILY HISTORY SOCIETIES, FEDERATION OF (1974),
PO Box 2425, Coventry, CV5 6YX. Tel: 07041-492032
Fax: 07041-492032 Web: www.ffhs.org.uk
Administrator, Maggie Loughran

FAMILY WELFARE ASSOCIATION (1869), 501–505
Kingsland Road, London, E8 4AU. Tel: 020-7254 6251
Fax: 020-7245 5443 Web: www.fwa.org.uk
Chief Executive, Ms H. Dent

FAUNA AND FLORA INTERNATIONAL (1903), Great
Eastern House, Tenison Road, Cambridge, CB1 2TT.
Tel: 01223-571000 Fax: 01223-461481
www.fauna-flora.org *Executive Director,* M. Rose

FIELD ARCHAEOLOGISTS, INSTITUTE OF (1982),
University of Reading, 2 Earley Gate, PO Box 239, Reading,
RG6 6AU. Tel: 0118-378 6446 Fax: 0118-378 6448
Web: www.archaeologists.net *Director,* P. Hinton

FILM CLASSIFICATION, BRITISH BOARD OF (1912),
3 Soho Square, London, W1D 3HD. Tel: 020-7440 1570
Fax: 020-7287 0141 Web: www.bbfc.co.uk
Director, R. Duval

FLAG INSTITUTE, THE, 44 Middleton Road, Acomb, York,
YO24 3AS
President, Robin Ashburner

FLEET AIR ARM OFFICERS' ASSOCIATION (1957), 4 St
James's Square, London, SW1Y 4JU. Tel: 020-7930 7722
Fax: 020-7930 7728 Web: www.fleetairarmoa.org
Administration Director, Cdr J. D. O. Macdonald, RN

FOOD FROM BRITAIN, 4th Floor, Manning House, 22
Carlisle Place, London, SW1P 1JA. Tel: 020-7233 5111
Fax: 020-7233 9515 Web: www.foodfrombritain.com
Chief Executive, D. McNair

FOOD SCIENCE AND TECHNOLOGY, INSTITUTE OF
(1964), 5 Cambridge Court, 210 Shepherd's Bush Road,
London, W6 7NJ. Tel: 020-7603 6316 Fax: 020-7602 9936
Web: www.ifst.org
Chief Executive, Ms H. G. Wild

FOOTBALLERS' ASSOCIATION, PROFESSIONAL (1907),
20 Oxford Court, Bishopsgate, Manchester, M2 3WQ.
Tel: 0161-236 0575 Fax: 0161-228 7229
Web: www.givemefootball.com
Chief Executive, G. Taylor

FOREIGN PRESS ASSOCIATION IN LONDON (1888),
11 Carlton House Terrace, London, SW1Y 5AJ.
Tel: 020-7930 0445 Fax: 020-7925 0469
www.foreign-press.org.uk
General Secretary, B. Jenner

FORENSIC SCIENCES, BRITISH ACADEMY OF,
Anaesthetic Unit, The Royal London Hospital, Whitechapel,
London, E1 1BB. Tel: 020-7377 9201
Fax: 020-7377 7126
Secretary-General, Dr P. J. Flynn

FOUNDATION FOR THE STUDY OF INFANT DEATHS
(1971), 11–19 Artillery Row, London, SW1P 1RT
Tel: 0870-787 0885 Helpline: 0870-787 0554
Fax: 020-7222 8002 Web: www.sids.org.uk/fsid/
Director, Mrs J. Epstein

FPA (FAMILY PLANNING ASSOCIATION) (1930),
2–12 Pentonville Road, London, N1 9FP. Tel: 020-7837 5432
Fax: 020-7837 3042 Web: www.fpa.org.uk
Chief Executive, Ms A. Weyman

FRANCO-BRITISH SOCIETY (1904), Room 623, Linen Hall,
162–168 Regent Street, London, W1R 5TB.
Tel: 020-7734 0815 Fax: 020-7734 0815
Web: www.francobritishsociety.org.uk
Executive Secretary, Mrs K. Brayn

FREEMEN OF ENGLAND AND WALES (1966), Richmond
House, Beech Close, Oversley Green, Alcester, Warwickshire,
B49 6PP Tel: 01789-762 574
Hon. Secretary, R. E. Leek

FREEMEN OF THE CITY OF LONDON, GUILD OF (1908),
4 Dowgate Hill, London, EC4R 2SH.
Tel: 020-8541 1435 Fax: 020-8541 1455
Clerk, Brigadier M. I. Keun

FREEMEN'S GUILD, CITY OF COVENTRY (1946),
47 Brownshill Green Road, Coventry, CV6 2AP.
Tel: 024-7627 4321
Web: www.coventryfreemensguild.co.uk
Hon. Clerk, K. Talbot

FRIENDLY SOCIETIES, ASSOCIATION OF (1995),
10–13 Lovat Lane, London, EC3R 8DT. Tel: 020-7397 9550
Fax: 020-7397 9551 Web: www.afs.org.uk

FRIENDS OF CATHEDRAL MUSIC (1956), Aeron House,
Llangeitho, Tregaron, Ceredigion, SY25 6SU
Web: www.fcm.org.uk
Secretary, M. J. Cooke

FRIENDS OF THE EARTH SCOTLAND (1978),
72 Newhaven Road, Edinburgh, EH6 5QG.
Tel: 0131-554 9977 Fax: 0131-554 8656
Web: www.foe-scotland.org.uk
Director, K. Dunion, OBE

FRIENDS OF THE NATIONAL LIBRARIES (1931), c/o
Department of Manuscripts, The British Library, 96 Euston
Road, London, NW1 2DB. Tel: 020-7412 7559
Chairman, Lord Egremont

FURNITURE HISTORY SOCIETY (1964), 1 Mercedes Cottages, St John's Road, Haywards Heath, W. Sussex, RH16 4EH. Tel: 01444-413845 Fax: 01444-413845
Membership Secretary, Dr B. Austen

GALLIPOLI ASSOCIATION (1969), Earleydene Orchard, Earleydene, Ascot, Berks, SL5 9JY. Tel: 01344-626523
Web: www.gallipoli-association.org
Hon. Secretary, J. C. Watson Smith

GAME CONSERVANCY TRUST, Fordingbridge, Hants, SP6 1EF. Tel: 01425-652381 Fax: 01425-655848
Web: www.gct.org.uk
Chief Executive, Teresa Dent

GARDENERS' ASSOCIATION, THE GOOD (1966), 4 Lisle Place, Wotton-under-Edge, Glos, GL12 7AZ.
Tel: 01453-520322 Web: www.goodgardeners.org.uk
Secretary, Matthew Adams

GARDENS SCHEME CHARITABLE TRUST, NATIONAL (1927), Hatchlands Park, East Clandon, Guildford, Surrey, GU4 7RT. Tel: 01483-211535 Fax: 01483-211537
Web: www.ngs.org.uk
Chief Executive, Beryl Evans

GAS ENGINEERS & MANAGERS, INSTITUTION OF (1863), 12 York Gate, London, NW1 4QG. Tel: 020-7487 0650
Fax: 020-7224 4762 Web: www.igem.org.uk
Chief Executive, G. Davies

GEMMOLOGICAL ASSOCIATION AND GEM TESTING LABORATORY OF GREAT BRITAIN (1931), 27 Greville Street (Saffron Hill entrance), London, EC1N 8TN.
Tel: 020-7404 3334 Fax: 020-7404 8843
Director, Terry Davidson

GENEALOGISTS AND RESEARCHERS IN ARCHIVES, ASSOCIATION OF (1968), 29 Badgers Close, Horsham, W. Sussex, RH12 5RU Web: www.agra.org.uk
Company Secretary, David R. Young

GENEALOGISTS ENTERPRISES LTD, SOCIETY OF (1911 AND 1999), 14 Charterhouse Buildings, Goswell Road, London, EC1M 7BA. Tel: 020-7251 8799
Fax: 020-7250 1800 Web: www.sog.org.uk
Acting Chief Executive, June Perrin

GENEALOGY SOCIETY, SCOTTISH (1953), Library and Family History Centre, 15 Victoria Terrace, Edinburgh, EH1 2JL. Tel: 0131-220 3677 Fax: 0131-220 3677
Web: www.scotsgenealogy.com
Hon. Secretary, Miss J. P. S. Ferguson

GENTLEPEOPLE, GUILD OF AID FOR (1921), 10 St Christopher's Place, London, W1U 1HZ. Tel: 020-7935 0641
Fax: 020-7486 0128
Secretary, Miss N. E. Inkson

GEOLOGICAL SOCIETY OF LONDON (1807), Burlington House, Piccadilly, London, W1J 0BJ. Tel: 020-7434 9944
Fax: 020-7439 8975 Web: www.geolsoc.org.uk
Executive Secretary, E. Nickless

GIFTED CHILDREN, NATIONAL ASSOCIATION FOR (1967), Suite 14, Challenge House, Bletchley, Milton Keynes, MK3 6DP. Tel: 0870-770 3217 Fax: 0870-770 3219
Web: www.nagcbritain.org.uk
Director, K. Bore

GILBERT AND SULLIVAN SOCIETY (1924), 7/20 Hampden Gurney Street, London, W1H 5AX.
Hon. Secretary, Miss V. C. Colin-Russ

GINGERBREAD (1970), 7 Sovereign Close, London, E1W 3HW. Tel: 020-7488 9300. Helpline: 0800-018 4318
Fax: 020-7488 9333 Web: www.gingerbread.org.uk
Chief Executive, Ms A. L. Ball

GIRLGUIDING UK (1910), 17–19 Buckingham Palace Road, London, SW1W 0PT. Tel: 020-7834 6242
Fax: 020-7828 8317 Web: www.girlguiding.org.uk
Chief Guide, Mrs Jenny Leach

GIRLS' BRIGADE ENGLAND AND WALES, PO Box 196, 129 The Broadway, Didcot, OX11 8XN. Tel: 01235-510425
Fax: 01235-510429 Web: www.girlsbrigadeew.org.uk
National Director, Ruth Gilson

GIRLS' VENTURE CORPS AIR CADETS (1964), Phoenix House, 3 Handley Square, Finningley Airport, Doncaster, DH9 3GH. Tel: 01302-775020 Web: www.gvcac.org.uk
Chair, Mrs Y. McCarthy

GLASS TECHNOLOGY, SOCIETY OF (1916), Don Valley House, Savile Street East, Sheffield, S4 7UQ.
Tel: 0114-263 4455 Fax: 0114-263 4411
Web: www.sgt.org
Managing Editor, D. Moore

GLIDING ASSOCIATION, BRITISH (1929), Kimberley House, Vaughan Way, Leicester, LE1 4SE. Tel: 0116-253 1051
Fax: 0116-251 5939 Web: www.gliding.co.uk
Secretary, B. Rolfe

GRAPHOLOGISTS, BRITISH INSTITUTE OF, 24–26 High Street, Hampton Hill, Hampton, Middx, TW12 1PD.
Tel: 01753-891241 Web: www.britishgraphology.org
Chairman, Elaine Quigley

GREEK INSTITUTE (1969), 34 Bush Hill Road, London, N21 2DS. Tel: 020-8360 7968 Fax: 020-8360 7968
Web: www.greekinstitute.co.uk
Director, Dr K. Tofallis

GREENPEACE UK, Canonbury Villas, London, N1 2PN.
Tel: 020-7865 8100 Fax: 020-7865 8200
Web: www.greenpeace.org.uk
Executive Director, Stephen Tindale

GURKHA WELFARE TRUST (1969), 2nd Floor, 1 Old Street, London, EC1V 9XB. Tel: 020-7251 5234 Fax: 020-7251 5248
Web: www.gwt.org.uk
Director, E. D. Powell-Jones

HAEMOPHILIA SOCIETY (1950), Chesterfield House, 385 Euston Road, London, NW1 3AU. Tel: 020-7380 0600 Fax: 020-7387 8220 Web: www.haemophilia.org.uk
Chief Executive, Ms K. Pappenheim

HAIG HOMES (1929), Alban Dobson House, Green Lane, Morden, Surrey, SM4 5NS. Tel: 020-8685 5777
Fax: 020-8685 5778 Web: www.haighomes.org.uk
Major General, P. V. R. Besgrove

HAKLUYT SOCIETY (1846), c/o Map Library, The British Library, 96 Euston Road, London, NW1 2DB.
Tel: 01428-641850 Web: www.hakluyt.com
Hon. Secretary, Prof. W. F. Ryan

HALIFAX ANTIQUARIAN SOCIETY (1900), 66 Drub Lane, Gomersal, Cleckheaton, W. Yorks, BD19 4BU.
Tel: 01274-865418 Web: www.halifaxhistory.org.uk
Hon. Secretary, J. H. Patchett

HARVEIAN SOCIETY OF LONDON (1831),
Lettsom House, 11 Chandos Street, London, W19 9EB.
Tel: 020-7580 1043 Fax: 020-7580 5793
Executive Secretary, Col. R. Kinsella-Bevan

HAWICK ARCHAEOLOGICAL SOCIETY (1856), Orrock House, Stirches Road, Hawick, Roxburghshire, TD9 7HF.
Tel: 01450-375546
Hon. Secretary, I. W. Landles

HEALTH CARE ASSOCIATION, BRITISH (1930), 24A Main Street, Garforth, Leeds, LS25 1AA. Tel: 0113-232 0903
Fax: 0113-232 0904 Web: www.bhca.org.uk
Chief Executive, Mrs C. Bell

HEALTH PROFESSIONS WALES (2002), 2nd Floor, Golate House, 101 St Mary Street, Cardiff, CF10 1DX.
Tel: 029-2026 1400 Fax: 029-2026 1499
Web: www.hpw.org.uk
Chief Executive, Mrs Barbara Bale

HEALTH PROMOTION AND EDUCATION, INSTITUTE OF, Department of Oral Health and Development, University Dental Hospital, Higher Cambridge Street, Manchester, M15 6FH. Tel: 0161-275 6610 Fax: 0161-275 6299
Web: www.ihpe.org.uk
Hon. Secretary, Prof. A. S. Blinkhorn

HEALTHCARE MANAGEMENT, INSTITUTE OF, PO Box 33239, London, SW1W 0WN. Tel: 020-7881 9235
Fax: 020-7881 9236 Web: www.ihm.org.uk
Chief Executive, Maurice Cheng

HEARING CONCERN (BRITISH ASSOCIATION FOR THE HARD OF HEARING) (1947), 7–11 Armstrong Road, London, W3 7JL. Tel: 020-8743 1110
Helpline: 0845-0744600 Fax: 020-8742 9043
Web: www.hearingconcern.org.uk
Director, Fiona Robertson

HEART FOUNDATION, BRITISH (1961), 14 Fitzhardinge Street, London, W1H 6DH. Tel: 020-7935 0185
Fax: 020-7486 5820 Web: www.bhf.org.uk
Director General, Maj.-Gen. L. F. H. Busk, CB

HEDGEHOG PRESERVATION SOCIETY, BRITISH (1982), Hedgehog House, Dhustone, Ludlow, Shropshire, SY8 3LQ.
Tel: 01584-890801 Fax: 01584-891313
Web: www.software-technics.com/bhps
Chief Executive, Fay Vass

HELLENIC STUDIES, SOCIETY FOR THE PROMOTION OF (1879), Senate House, Malet Street, London, WC1E 7HU.
Tel: 020-7862 8730 Fax: 020-7862 8731
Web: www.sas.ac.uk/icls/hellenic/
Executive Secretary, R. W. Shone

HELP THE AGED (1961), 207–221 Pentonville Road, London, N2 9UZ. Tel: 020-7278 1114 Fax: 020-7278 1116
Web: www.helptheaged.org.uk
Director General, C. M. Lake, CBE

HERALDIC AND GENEALOGICAL STUDIES, INSTITUTE OF (1961), 79–82 Northgate, Canterbury, Kent, CT1 1BA.
Tel: 01227-768664 Fax: 01227-765617
Web: www.ihgs.ac.uk
Registrar, J. Palmer

HERALDRY SOCIETY, THE (1947), PO Box 772, Guildford, Surrey, GU3 3ZX. Tel: 01483-237373
Fax: 01483-237375
Web: www.theheraldrysociety.com
Secretary, Mrs M. Miles, MBE, RD

HERPETOLOGICAL SOCIETY, BRITISH, c/o Zoological Society of London, Regent's Park, London, NW1 4RY.
Tel: 020-8452 9578
Secretary, Mrs M. Green

HISTORIC HOUSES ASSOCIATION (1973), 2 Chester Street, London, SW1X 7BB. Tel: 020-7259 5688
Fax: 020-7259 5590 Web: www.hha.org.uk
Director-General, R. C. Wilkin, LVO, MBE

HISTORICAL ASSOCIATION, THE (1906), 59A Kennington Park Road, London, SE11 4JH. Tel: 020-7735 3901
Fax: 020-7582 4989 Web: www.history.org.uk
Chief Executive, Mrs M. Stiles

HOROLOGICAL INSTITUTE, BRITISH (1858), Upton Hall, Upton, Newark, Notts, NG23 5TE. Tel: 01636-813795
Fax: 01636-812258 Web: www.bhi.co.uk
General Manager, Martin Taylor

HORSE SOCIETY, THE BRITISH (1947), Stoneleigh Deer Park, Kenilworth, Warks, CV8 2XZ. Tel: 08701-202244 Fax: 01926-707800 Web: www.bhs.org.uk
Chief Executive, Mrs Kay Driver

HOSPITAL FEDERATION, INTERNATIONAL (1947), 46 Grosvenor Gardens, London, SW1W 0EB. Tel: 020-7881 9222 Fax: 020-7881 9223 Web: www.hospitalmanagement.net and www.ihf.co.uk
Director General, Prof. Per-Gunnar Svensson

HOSPITAL SATURDAY FUND (1873), 24 Upper Ground, London, SE1 9PD. Tel: 020-7928 6662 Fax: 020-7928 0446 Web: www.hsf.eu.com
Chief Executive, K. R. Bradley

HOSTELLING INTERNATIONAL NORTHERN IRELAND, 22–32 Donegall Road, Belfast, BT12 5JN. Tel: 028-9032 4733 Fax: 028-9043 9699 Web: www.hini.org.uk
Hon. Secretary, D. Forsythe

HOWARD LEAGUE FOR PENAL REFORM, THE (1866), 1 Ardleigh Road, London, N1 4HS. Tel: 020-7249 7373 Fax: 020-7249 7789 Web: www.howardleague.org
Director, Ms F. Crook

HUGUENOT SOCIETY OF GREAT BRITAIN AND IRELAND (1885), The Huguenot Library, University College, Gower Street, London, WC1E 6BT. Tel: 020-7679 5199 Web: www.huguenotsociety.org.uk
Hon. Secretary, Mrs M. Bayliss

HUMANE RESEARCH TRUST (1962), Brook House, 29 Bramhall Lane South, Bramhall, Stockport, Cheshire, SK7 2DN. Tel: 0161-439 8041 Fax: 0161-439 3713 Web: www.btinternet.com/~shawweb/hrt/
Chairman, K. Cholerton

HUMANIST ASSOCIATION, BRITISH (1896), 1 Gower Street, London, WC1E 6HD. Tel: 020-7430 0908 Fax: 020-7430 1271 Web: www.humanism.org.uk
Executive Director, Hanne Stinson

HYDROGRAPHIC SOCIETY, THE (1972), PO Box 103, Plymouth, PL4 7YP. Tel: 01752-223512 Fax: 01752-223512 Web: www.hydrographicsociety.org
Hon. Secretary, P. J. H. Warden

HYMN SOCIETY OF GREAT BRITAIN AND IRELAND (1936), 7 Paganel Road, Minehead, Somerset, TA24 5ET. Tel: 01643-703530 Fax: 01643-703530 Web: www.hymnsocgbi.org
Secretary, Revd G. Wrayford

ICAN (THE CHARITY FOR CHILDREN WITH SPEECH AND LANGUAGE DIFFICULTIES) (1888), 4 Dyers Buildings, Holborn, London, EC1N 2QP. Tel: 0845-225 4071 Fax: 0845-225 4072 Web: www.ican.org.uk
Chief Executive, Ms G. Edelman

IMMIGRATION ADVISORY SERVICE (1970), 3rd Floor, County House, 190 Great Dover Street, London, SE1 4YB. Tel: 020-7357 7511 Fax: 020-7403 5875 Web: www.iasuk.org
Director of Operations, Michael Pickett

INDEPENDENT SCHOOLS CAREERS ORGANISATION (1973), 12A Princess Way, Camberley, Surrey, GU15 3SP. Tel: 01276-21188 Fax: 01276-691833 Web: www.isco.org.uk
National Director, J. D. Stuart

INDEPENDENT SCHOOLS COUNCIL (1986), Grosvenor Gardens House, 35–37 Grosvenor Gardens, London, SW1W 0BS. Tel: 020-7798 1590 Fax: 020-7798 1591 Web: www.iscis.uk.net
General Secretary, Dr A. B. Cooke, OBE

INDEPENDENT SCHOOLS' BURSARS ASSOCIATION (1932), Unit 11–12, Manor Farm, Cliddesden, Hampshire, RG25 2JB. Tel: 01256-330369 Fax: 01256-330376 Web: www.theisba.org.uk
General Secretary, M. J. Sant

INDEXERS, SOCIETY OF (1957), Blades Enterprise Centre, John Street, Sheffield, S2 4SU. Tel: 0114-292 2350 Fax: 0114-292 2351 Web: www.indexers.org.uk
Secretary, Mrs Ann Kingdom

INDUSTRY AND PARLIAMENT TRUST (1977), 1 Buckingham Place, London, SW1E 6HR. Tel: 020-7630 3700 Fax: 020-7630 3701 Web: www.ipt.org.uk
Director, F. R. Hyde-Chambers, OBE

INSTITUTE OF FINANCIAL SERVICES, 90 Bishopsgate, London, EC2N 4DQ. Tel: 020-7444 7111 Fax: 020-7444 7115 Web: www.ifslearning.com
Chief Executive, Gavin Shreeve

INSURANCE BROKERS' ASSOCIATION, BRITISH (1978), BIBA House, 14 Bevis Marks, London, EC3A 7NT. Tel: 020-7623 9043 Fax: 020-7626 9676 Web: www.biba.org.uk
Chief Executive, R. M. Williams

INTERCONTINENTAL CHURCH SOCIETY (1823), 1 Athena Drive, Tachbrook Park, Warwick, CV34 6NL. Tel: 01926-430347 Fax: 01926-888092 Web: www.ics-uk.org
Chief Executive, The Revd Canon Ian Watson

INTERNATIONAL FRIENDSHIP LEAGUE (1931), 3 Creswick Road, Acton, London, W3 9HE. Tel: 020-8752 0055 Fax: 020-8752 0066 Web: www.itl-peacehaven.co.uk.
Chairman, M. Hewett

INTERNATIONAL PEN (1921), 9–10 Charterhouse Buildings, Goswell Road, London, EC1M 7AT. Tel: 020-7253 4308 Fax: 020-7253 5711 Web: www.internatpen.org
International Secretary, T. Carlbom

INTERNATIONAL POLICE ASSOCIATION (BRITISH SECTION) (1950), 1 Fox Road, West Bridgford, Nottingham, NG2 6AJ. Tel: 0115-981 3638 Web: www.ipa-uk.org
Executive Officer, Mrs E. Jones

INTERNATIONAL STUDENTS HOUSE (1962), 1 Park Crescent, London, W1B 1SH. Tel: 020-7631 8300 Fax: 020-7631 8315 Web: www.ish.org.uk
Executive Director, Peter Anwyl

INTERSERVE (1852), 325 Kennington Road, London, SE11 4QH. Tel: 020-7735 8227 Fax: 020-7587 5362 Web: www.interserveonline.org.uk
National Director, R. Clark

INVALIDS-AT-HOME (1965), Bamford Cottage, South Hill Avenue, Harrow, Middx, HA1 3PA. Tel: 020-8864 3818
Executive Officer, Mrs Mary Rose

IRAN SOCIETY (1935), 2 Belgrave Square, London, SW1X 8PJ. Tel: 020-7235 5122 Fax: 020-7259 6771 Web: www.iransoc.dircon.co.uk
Hon. Secretary, R. Mackenzie

ISLE OF WIGHT NATURAL HISTORY AND ARCHAEOLOGICAL SOCIETY (1919), Salisbury Gardens, Dudley Road, Ventnor, Isle of Wight, PO38 1EJ. Tel: 01983-855385
Hon. Secretary, Dr M. Jackson

JACQUELINE DU PRÉ MUSIC BUILDING LTD (1995), St Hilda's College, Oxford, OX4 1DY. Tel: 01865-276821 Fax: 01865-286674 Web: www.sthildas.ox.ac.uk/jdp
Manager, Ms M. A. Frappat

JAPAN SOCIETY (1891), Swire House, 59 Buckingham Gate, London, SW1E 6AJ. Tel: 020-7828 6330 Fax: 020-7828 6331 Web: www.japansociety.org.uk
Executive Director, Capt. Robert Guy

JERUSALEM AND THE MIDDLE EAST CHURCH ASSOCIATION, 1 Hart House, The Hart, Farnham, Surrey, GU9 7HJ. Tel: 01252-726994 Fax: 01252-735558 Web: www.jmeca.org.uk
Secretary, Mrs V. Wells

JOHN STUART MILL INSTITUTE (1992), 1 Whitehall Place, London, SW1A 2HE. Tel: 01582-615067 Web: www.jsminstitute.org.uk
Hon. Secretary, J. Wates

JOURNALISTS, CHARTERED INSTITUTE OF (1884), 2 Dock Offices, Surrey Quays Road, London, SE16 2XU. Tel: 020-7252 1187 Fax: 020-7232 2302 Web: www.ioj.co.uk
General Secretary, C. J. Underwood

JUSTICE (1957), 59 Carter Lane, London, EC4V 5AQ. Tel: 020-7329 5100 Fax: 020-7329 5055 Web: www.justice.org.uk
Director, Roger Smith

JUSTICES' CLERKS' SOCIETY, 2nd Floor, Port of Liverpool Building, Pier Head, Liverpool, L3 1BY. Tel: 0151-255 0790 Fax: 0151-236 4458 Web: www.jc-society.co.uk
Chief Executive, Sid Brighton

KENT ARCHAEOLOGICAL SOCIETY (1857), Three Elms, Woodlands Lane, Shorne, Gravesend, Kent, DA12 3HH. Web: www.kentarchaeology.org.uk
Hon. General Secretary, A. I. Moffat

KIPLING SOCIETY, THE (1927), 6 Clifton Road, London, W9 1SS. Tel: 020-7286 0194 Fax: 020-7286 0194 Web: www.kipling.org.uk
Hon. Secretary, Jane Keskar

LANDOWNERS' FEDERATION, SCOTTISH (1906), Stuart House, Eskmills Business Park, Musselburgh, EH21 7PB. Tel: 0131-653 5400 Fax: 0131-653 5401 Web: www.slf.org.uk
Director, Dr M. S. Hankey

LAW REPORTING FOR ENGLAND AND WALES, INCORPORATED COUNCIL OF (1865), Megarry House, 119 Chancery Lane, London, WC2A 1PP. Tel: 020-7242 6471 Fax: 020-7831 5247 Web: www.lawreports.co.uk
Secretary, J. Cobbett

LCIA (LONDON COURT OF INTERNATIONAL ARBITRATION) (1892), The Internartional Dispute Resolution, 8 Breams Buildings, Chancery Lane, London, EC4A 1HP. Tel: 020-7405 8008 Fax: 020-7405 8009 Web: www.icia-arbitration.com
Director General and Registrar, Adrian Winstanley

THE LEAGUE OF THE HELPING HAND (1907), Little Finches, Wheatsheaf Road, Henfield, Sussex, TW10 7AL. Tel: 020-8940 7303 Fax: 020-8940 7303
Secretary, Mrs Moira Parrot

LEGAL EXECUTIVES, INSTITUTE OF (1963), Kempston Manor, Kempston, Bedford, MK42 7AB. Tel: 01234-841000 Fax: 01234-840373 Web: www.ilex.org.uk
Secretary General, Mrs D. Burleigh

LEGAL SCHOLARS, SOCIETY OF (1908), Law Faculty, Southampton University, Southampton, SO17 1BJ. Tel: 023-8059 3416 Fax: 023-8059 3024 Web: www.law.warwick.ac.uk/sls/
Hon. Secretary, Prof. N. J. Wikeley

LEPROSY MISSION (ENGLAND AND WALES) (1874), Goldhay Way, Orton Goldhay, Peterborough, PE2 5GZ. Tel: 01733-370505 Fax: 01733-404880 Web: www.leprosymission.org.uk
National Director, Warren Lancaster

LEUKAEMIA RESEARCH FUND (1960), 43 Great Ormond Street, London, WC1N 3JJ. Tel: 020-7405 0101 Fax: 020-7405 3139 Web: www.lrf.org.uk
Chief Executive, D. L. Osborne

LIBERAL PARTY, THE (1877), 323 Hurcott Road, Kidderminster, DY10 2RQ. Tel: 01562-68361 Fax: 01562-68361 Web: www.liberal.org.uk
Membership Secretary, Paul Harrison

LIBERTY (NATIONAL COUNCIL FOR CIVIL LIBERTIES) (1934), 21 Tabard Street, London, SE1 4LA. Tel: 020-7403 3888 Fax: 020-7407 5354 Web: www.liberty-human-rights.org.uk
Director, John Wadham

LIBRARIES ASSOCIATION, PRIVATE (1956), Ravelston, South View Road, Pinner, Middx, HA5 3YD. Web: www.the-old-school.demon.co.uk/pla.htm
Hon. Secretary, James Brown

LIBRARY AND INFORMATION PROFESSIONALS, THE CHARTERED INSTITUTE OF (2002), 7 Ridgmount Street, London, WC1E 7AE. Tel: 020-7255 0500; Textphone: 020-7255 0505 Fax: 020-7255 0501 Web: www.cilip.org.uk
Chief Executive, Dr R. A. McKee, FRSA, MCLIP

LIBRARY, CITY BUSINESS (1970), Corporation of London, 1 Brewers' Hall Garden, London, EC2V 5BX. Tel: 020-7332 1812 Fax: 020-7332 1847 Web: www.cityoflondon.gov.uk/libraries
Business Librarian, G. P. Humphreys, MCLIP, FRSA

LIBRARY, SCOTTISH NATURAL HISTORY (1970), Foremount House, Kilbarchan, Renfrewshire, PA10 2EZ. Tel: 01505-702419,
Director, Dr J. A. Gibson

LIFE SAVING SOCIETY UK, THE ROYAL (1891), River House, High Street, Broom, Warks, B50 4HN. Tel: 01789-773994, 01789-773995 Web: www.lifesavers.org.uk
Chief Executive, D. Standley

LINGUISTS, INSTITUTE OF (1910), Saxon House, 48 Southwark Street, London, SE1 1UN. Tel: 020-7940 3100 Fax: 020-7940 3101 Web: www.iol.org.uk
Director, H. Pavlovich

LIONS CLUBS INTERNATIONAL (BRITISH ISLES AND IRELAND) (1950), 257 Alcester Road South, Kings Heath, Birmingham, B14 6DT. Tel: 0121-441 4544 Fax: 0121-441 4510
Office Manager, Mrs J. Davis

LLOYD'S OF LONDON, One Lime Street, London, EC3M 7HA. Tel: 020-7327 6930 Fax: 020-7327 6512 Web: www.lloyds.com
Chief Executive Officer, N. E. T. Prettejohn

LOCAL AUTHORITY CHIEF EXECUTIVES AND SENIOR MANAGERS, SOCIETY OF (1972), Hope House, 45 Great Peter Street, London, SW1P 3LT. Tel: 0845-601 0649 Fax: 020-7233 3302 Web: www.solace.org.uk
Director-General, David Clark

LOCAL GOVERNMENT ASSOCIATION (1997), Local Government House, Smith Square, London, SW1P 3HZ. Tel: 020-7664 3131 Fax: 020-7664 3030 Web: www.lga.gov.uk
Chief Executive, Sir Brian Briscoe

LONDON AND MIDDLESEX ARCHAEOLOGICAL SOCIETY (1855), c/o Museum of London, 150 London Wall, London, EC2Y 5HN. Web: www.lamas.org.uk
Hon. Secretary, Karen Fielder

LONDON APPRECIATION SOCIETY (1932), 45 Friars Avenue, Friern Barnet, London, N20 0XG.
Chairman, Anthea H. Gray

LONDON CHAMBER OF COMMERCE AND INDUSTRY (1881), 33 Queen Street, London, EC4R 1AP. Tel: 020-7248 4444 Fax: 020-7489 0391 Web: www.londonchamber.co.uk
Chief Executive, Colin Stanbridge

LONDON CITY MISSION (1835), 175 Tower Bridge Road, London, SE1 2AH. Tel: 020-7407 7585 Fax: 020-7403 6711 Web: www.lcm.org.uk
General Secretary, Revd J. McAllen

LONDON FLOTILLA (1937), 40 Endlesham Road, London, SW12 8JL. Tel: 020-8673 1879 Fax: 020-8673 1879
Deputy Chairman and Hon. Membership Recruitment Secretary, Lt.-Cdr. H. C. R. Upton, RD, RNR

LONDON LIBRARY, THE (1841), 14 St James's Square, London, SW1Y 4LG. Tel: 020-7930 7705 Fax: 020-7766 4766 Web: www.londonlibrary.co.uk
Librarian, Inez T. P. A. Lynn

LONDON MAGISTRATES' CLERKS' ASSOCIATION (1889), c/o Marylebone Magistrates' Court, 181 Marylebone Road, London, NW1 5QJ. Tel: 020-7506 3704 Fax: 020-7724 9163
Hon. Secretary, C. Rees

LONDON PLAYING FIELDS SOCIETY (1890), Fraser House, 29 Albemarle Street, London, W1S 4JB. Tel: 020-7493 3211 Fax: 020-7409 3405 Web: www.lpfs.org.uk
Chief Executive, Dr C. Goodson-Wickes, DL

LONDON SOCIETY, THE (1912), Mortimer Wheeler House, 46 Eagle Wharf Road, London, N1 7ED. Tel: 020-7253 9400 Web: www.lonsoc.org.uk/lonsoc/

LORD'S DAY OBSERVANCE SOCIETY (1831), 3 Epsom Business Park, Kiln Lane, Epsom, Surrey, KT17 1JF. Tel: 01372-728300 Fax: 01372-722400 Web: www.lordsday.co.uk
General Secretary, J. G. Roberts

LOTTERIES COUNCIL, THE (1979), 2 Regan Road, Moira, Ashby-de-la Zouch, DE12 6DS. Tel: 01283-229811 Fax: 01283-229810 Web: www.lotteriescouncil.org.uk
Chairman, Mr A. Austin

LUNG FOUNDATION, BRITISH (1985), 78 Hatton Garden, London, EC1N 8LD. Tel: 020-7831 5831 Fax: 020-7831 5832 Web: www.lunguk.org
Chief Executive, Dame Helena Shovelton

MACA (THE MENTAL AFTER CARE ASSOCIATION) (1859), 1st Floor, Lincoln House, 296–302 High Holborn, London, WC1V 7JH. Tel: 020-7061 3400 Fax: 020-7061 3401
Chief Executive, G. Hitchon

MACMILLAN CANCER RELIEF (1911), 89 Albert Embankment, London, SE1 7UQ. Tel: 020-7840 7840 Fax: 020-7840 7841 Web: www.macmillan.org.uk
Chief Executive, Peter Cardy

MAILING PREFERENCE SERVICE (1983), 3rd Floor, DMA House, 70 Margaret Street, London, W1W 8SS. Tel: 020-7291 3310 Fax: 020-7323 4226
Web: www.mpsonline.org.uk
Director of Compliance Operations, Ms T. Kelly

MANIC DEPRESSION FELLOWSHIP (1983), Castle Works, 21 St George's Road, London, SE1 6ES. Tel: 020-7793 2600 Fax: 020-7793 2639 Web: www.mdf.org.uk
Chief Executive, Michelle Rowett

MANPOWER SOCIETY LTD (1970), Beacon House, 85 East Avenue, Talbotwoods, Bournemouth, Dorset, BH3 7BU. Tel: 01202-768091 Fax: 01202-766133
Web: www.mansoc.demon.co.uk
President, Dr Clive Purkis

MARIE CURIE CANCER CARE (1948), 89 Albert Embankment, London, SE1 7TP. Tel: 020-7599 7777 Fax: 020-7599 7788 Web: www.mariecurie.org.uk
Chief Executive, Thomas Hughes-Hallett

MARINE BIOLOGICAL ASSOCIATION OF THE UK (1884), Citadel Hill, Plymouth, PL1 2PB. Tel: 01752-633207 Fax: 01752-633102 Web: www.mba.ac.uk
Director, Prof. S. J. Hawkins

MARINE ENGINEERING, SCIENCE AND TECHNOLOGY, INSTITUTE OF (1889), 80 Coleman Street, London, EC2R 5BJ. Tel: 020-7382 2600 Fax: 020-7382 2670
Web: www.imarest.org
Director-General, K. F. Read, CBE

MARINE SCIENCE, SCOTTISH ASSOCIATION FOR (1884), Dunstaffnage Marine Laboratory, Oban, Argyll, PA37 1QA. Tel: 01631-559000 Fax: 01631-559001
Web: www.sams.ac.uk
Director, Prof. G. B. Shimmield, FIBiol, FRSE

MARINE SOCIETY, THE (1756), 202 Lambeth Road, London, SE1 7JW. Tel: 020-7261 9535 Fax: 020-7401 2537
Web: www.marine-society.org
Director, Capt. J. J. Howard

MARIO LANZA EDUCATIONAL FOUNDATION (1976), 21 Park Road, Norhan, Middlesex, EN6 4NN
Hon. Secretary, Mrs Sadie A. Lewis

MARRIAGE CARE (1946), Clitherow House, 1 Blythe Mews, Blythe Road, London, W14 0NW. Tel: 020-7371 1341 Fax: 020-7371 4921 Web: www.marriagecare.org.uk
Chief Executive, Terry Prendergast

MASONIC TRUST FOR GIRLS AND BOYS (1982), 31 Great Queen Street, London, WC2B 5AG. Tel: 020-7405 2644 Fax: 020-7831 4094 Web: www.mtgb.org
Secretary, Lt.-Col. J. C. Chambers

MASONS, GRAND LODGE OF MARK MASTER (1856), Mark Masons' Hall, 86 St James's Street, London, SW1A 1PL. Tel: 020-7839 5274 Fax: 020-7930 9750
Grand Secretary, T. J. Lewis

MATERIALS, MINERALS AND MINING, INSTITUTE OF (1868), Danum House, 6A South Parade, Doncaster, S. Yorks, DN1 2DY. Tel: 01302-320486 Fax: 01302-340554 Web: www.iom3.org
Chief Executive, Dr Bernie Rickinson

MATHEMATICAL ASSOCIATION (1871), 259 London Road, Leicester, LE2 3BE. Tel: 0116-221 0013 Fax: 0116-212 2835 Web: www.m-a.org.uk
Office Manager, Ms M. Murray

MATHEMATICS AND ITS APPLICATIONS, INSTITUTE OF (1964), Catherine Richards House, 16 Nelson Street, Southend-on-Sea, Essex, SS1 1EF. Tel: 01702-354020 Fax: 01702-354111 Web: www.ima.org.uk
Executive Director, David Joudan

MEASUREMENT AND CONTROL, INSTITUTE OF (1944), 87 Gower Street, London, WC1E 6AF. Tel: 020-7387 4949 Fax: 020-7388 8431 Web: www.instmc.org.uk
Secretary, M. J. Yates

MECHANICAL ENGINEERS, INSTITUTION OF (1847), 1 Birdcage Walk, London, SW1H 9JJ. Tel: 020-7222 7899 Fax: 020-7222 8553 Web: www.imeche.org.uk
Director-General, Sir Michael Moore, KBE, LVO

MEDIAWATCH-UK (1965), 3 Willow House, Kennington Road, Ashford, Kent, TN24 0NR. Tel: 01233-633936 Fax: 01233-633836 Web: www.mediawatchuk.org
Director, J. C. Beyer

MEDICAL COUNCIL, GENERAL (1858), 178 Great Portland Street, London, W1W 5JE. Tel: 020-7580 7642 Fax: 020-7915 3641 Web: www.gmc-uk.org
President, Sir Graeme Catto

MEDICAL SOCIETY OF LONDON (1773), Lettsom House, 11 Chandos Street, London, W1G 9EB. Tel: 020-7580 1043 Fax: 020-7580 5793
Registrar, Col. R. Kinsella-Bevan

MEDICAL WOMEN'S FEDERATION (1917), Tavistock House North, Tavistock Square, London, WC1H 9HX. Tel: 020-7387 7765 Fax: 020-7388 9216
Web: www.mwfonline.org.uk
President, Dr Pauline Brimblecombe

MENCAP (ROYAL MENCAP SOCIETY) (1946), 123 Golden Lane, London, EC1Y 0RT. Tel: 020-7454 0454
Fax: 020-7608 3254 Web: www.mencap.co.uk
Chief Executive, F. Heddell, CBE

MENSA LTD, BRITISH (1946), St John's House, St Johns Square, Wolverhampton, WV2 4AH. Tel: 01902-772771
Fax: 01902-392500 Web: www.mensa.org.uk
Chief Executive, J. Stevenage

MENTAL HEALTH FOUNDATION, 7th Floor, 83 Victoria Street, London, SW1H 0HW. Tel: 020-7802 0300
Fax: 020-7802 0301 Web: www.mentalhealth.orguk and www.learningdisabilities.org.uk

MENTAL HEALTH, SCOTTISH ASSOCIATION FOR (1923), Cumbrae House, 15 Carlton Court, Glasgow, G5 9JP. Tel: 0141-568 7000 Fax: 0141-568 7001
Web: www.samh.org.uk
Chief Executive, Ms S. M. Barcus

MERCHANT NAVY WELFARE BOARD (1948), 30 Palmerston Road, Southampton, SO14 1LL. Tel: 023-8033 7799
Fax: 023-8063 4444 Web: www.mnb.org.uk
General Secretary, Capt. D. A. Parsons

MIDDLE EAST ASSOCIATION, THE (1961), Bury House, 33 Bury Street, London, SW1Y 6AX. Tel: 020-7839 2137
Fax: 020-7839 6121 Web: www.the-mea.co.uk
Director-General, James Lawday

MIGRAINE ACTION ASSOCIATION (1958), Unit 6, Oakley Hay Lodge Business Park, Great Oakley, Northants, NN18 9AS. Tel: 01536-461338 Fax: 01536-461444
Web: www.migraine.org.uk
Director, Mrs A. Turner

MIND (NATIONAL ASSOCIATION FOR MENTAL HEALTH) (1946), Granta House, 15–19 Broadway, London, E15 4BQ. Tel: 020-8519 2122 Fax: 020-8215.2468
Web: www.mind.org.uk
Chief Executive, Richard Brook

MINERALOGICAL SOCIETY (1876), 41 Queen's Gate, London, SW7 5HR. Tel: 020-7584 7516
Fax: 020-7823 8021 Web: www.minersoc.org
General Secretary, Dr F. Wall

MISSING PERSONS HELPLINE, NATIONAL (1992), Roebuck House, 284–286 Upper Richmond Road West, London, SW14 7JE. Tel: 020-8392 4590 Helpline: 0500-700700 Message Home Helpline: 0800-700740 Fax: 020-8878 7752 Web: www.missingpersons.org and www.messagehome.org.uk
Co-Founders, Mrs M. Asprey, OBE; Mrs J. Newman, OBE

MOTOR INDUSTRY, INSTITUTE OF THE (1920), Fanshaws, Brickendon, Hertford, SG13 8PQ. Tel: 01992-511521
Fax: 01992-511548 Web: www.motor.org.uk
Chief Executive, Sarah Sillars

MULTIPLE SCLEROSIS SOCIETY (1953), MS National Centre, 372 Edgware Road, Staples Corner, London, NW2 6ND. Tel: 020-8438 0700 Fax: 020-8438 0701
Web: www.mssociety.org.uk
Chief Executive, Mike O'Donovan

MUSIC HALL SOCIETY, BRITISH, 82 Fernlea Road, London, SW12 9RW. Tel: 020-8673 2175
Hon. Secretary, Mrs D. Masterton

MUSIC INFORMATION CENTRE, BRITISH (1967), 10 Stratford Place, London, W1C 1BA. Tel: 020-7499 8567
Fax: 020-7499 4795 Web: www.bmic.co.uk
Director, M. Greenall

MUSICIANS BENEVOLENT FUND (1921), 16 Ogle Street, London, W1W 6JA. Tel: 020-7636 4481 Fax: 020-7637 4307
Web: www.mbf.org.uk
Chief Executive, Ms H. Faulkner

NACRO, THE CRIME REDUCTION CHARITY (1966), 169 Clapham Road, London, SW9 0PU. Tel: 020-7582 6500
Fax: 020-7735 4666 Web: www.nacro.org.uk
Chief Executive, P. Cavadino

NATIONAL EXTENSION COLLEGE (1963), Michael Young Centre, Purbeck Road, Cambridge, CB2 2HN.
Tel: 01223-400200 Fax: 01223-400322
Web: www.nec.ac.uk
Chief Executive, Alison West

NATIONAL SOCIETY, THE (1811), Church House, Great Smith Street, London, SW1P 3NZ. Tel: 020-7898 1518
Fax: 020-7898 1493 Web: www.natsoc.org.uk
General Secretary, Canon J. Hall

NATIONAL TRUST FOR SCOTLAND, THE (1931), Wemyss House, 28 Charlotte Square, Edinburgh, EH2 4ET. Tel: 0131-243 9300 Fax: 0131-243 9301
Web: www.nts.org.uk
Chief Executive, Robin Pellew

NATIONAL TRUST, THE (1895), 36 Queen Anne's Gate, London, SW1H 9AS. Tel: 0870-609 5380
Fax: 020-7222 5097 Web: www.nationaltrust.org.uk
Director-General, Fiona Reynolds

NATURALISTS' ASSOCIATION, BRITISH (1905), 1 Bracken Mews, London, E4 7UT Web: www.bna-naturalists.org
Hon. Membership Secretary, Mrs Y. H. Griffiths

NAUTICAL RESEARCH, SOCIETY OF (1910), c/o National Maritime Museum, Greenwich, London, SE10 9NF. Tel: 020-8312 6712 Fax: 020-8312 6722
Web: www.snr.org.uk
Hon. Secretary, Liza Verity

NAVY RECORDS SOCIETY (1893), c/o Department of War Studies, King's College, The Strand, London, WC2R 2LS. Web: www.navyrecordssociety.com
Hon. Secretary, Dr A. D. Lambert

NCH (1869), 85 Highbury Park, London, N5 1UD. Tel: 020-7704 7000 Fax: 020-7226 2537
Web: www.nch.org.uk
Chief Executive, D. Mead

NEW ENGLISH ART CLUB (1886), 17 Carlton House Terrace, London, SW1Y 5BD. Tel: 020-7930 6844 Fax: 020-7839 7830 Web: www.mallgalleries.org.uk
President, Ken Howard

NEWCASTLE UPON TYNE, SOCIETY OF ANTIQUARIES OF (1813), Black Gate, Castle Garth, Newcastle upon Tyne, NE1 1RQ. Tel: 0191-261 5390.
Web: www.newcastle-antiquaries.org.uk
Secretary, N. Hodgson

NEWSPAPER PRESS FUND (1864), Dickens House, 35 Wathen Road, Dorking, Surrey, RH4 1JY. Tel: 01306-887511 Fax: 01306-888212
Director, D. Ilott

NHS CONFEDERATION, THE (1997), 1 Warwick Row, London, SW1E 5ER. Tel: 020-7959 7272 Fax: 020-7959 7273 Web: www.nhsconfed.net
Chief Executive, Dr Gill Morgan

NORFOLK AND NORWICH ARCHAEOLOGICAL SOCIETY (1846), 30 Brettingham Avenue, Norwich, NR4 6XG. Tel: 01603-455913
Secretary, R. Bellinger

NOTARIES SOCIETY, THE (1882), 23 New Street, Woodbridge, Suffolk, IP12 1DN. Tel: 01394-384134 Fax: 01394-382906 Web: www.thenotariessociety.org.uk
Secretary, A. G. Dunford

NSPCC (NATIONAL SOCIETY FOR THE PREVENTION OF CRUELTY TO CHILDREN) (1884), 42 Curtain Road, London, EC2A 3NH. Tel: 020-7825 2500
Fax: 020-7825 2525 Web: www.nspcc.org.uk
Chief Executive, Mary Marsh

NUCLEAR ENERGY SOCIETY, BRITISH, 1–7 Great George Street, London, SW1P 3AA. Tel: 020-7665 2241
Fax: 020-7799 1325 Web: www.bnes.org.uk
Secretary, I. M. Andrews, FRSA

NUFFIELD FOUNDATION, THE (1943), 28 Bedford Square, London, WC1B 3JS. Tel: 020-7631 0566
Fax: 020-7323 4877 Web: www.nuffieldfoundation.org
Director, A. Tomei

NUFFIELD TRUST (1940), 59 New Cavendish Street, London, W1G 7LP. Tel: 020-7631 8450 Fax: 020-7631 8451
Web: www.nuffieldtrust.org.uk
Secretary, J. Wyn Owen, CB

NURSING AND MIDWIFERY COUNCIL (2002), 23 Portland Place, London, W1B 1PZ. Tel: 020-7637 7181
Fax: 020-7436 2924 Web: www.nmc-uk.org
Chief Executive, Sarah Thewlis

NUTRITION FOUNDATION, BRITISH (1967), High Holborn House, 52–54 High Holborn, London, WC1V 6RQ. Tel: 020-7404 6504 Fax: 020-7404 6747
Web: www.nutrition.org.uk
Director-General, Prof. R. S. Pickard, PhD, CBiol

OCCUPATIONAL SAFETY AND HEALTH, INSTITUTION OF (1945), The Grange, Highfield Drive, Wigston, Leics, LE18 1NN. Tel: 0116-257 3100 Fax: 0116-257 3101
Web: www.iosh.co.uk
Chief Executive, R. W. H. Strange

OFFICERS' ASSOCIATION, THE (1920), 48 Pall Mall, London, SW1Y 5JY. Tel: 020-7930 0125 Fax: 020-7930 9053 Web: www.officersassociation.org.uk
General Secretary, Maj.-Gen. A. I. Ramsay, CBE, DSO

OPAS (THE PENSIONS ADVISORY SERVICE) (1983), 11 Belgrave Road, London, SW1V 1RB. Tel: 0845-601 2923 Fax: 020-7233 8016 Web: www.opas.org.uk
Chief Executive, M. McLean, OBE

OPEN SPACES SOCIETY (1865), 25A Bell Street, Henley-on-Thames, Oxon, RG9 2BA. Tel: 01491-573535 Fax: 01491-573051 Web: www.oss.org.uk
General Secretary, Miss K. Ashbrook

OPEN-AIR MISSION, THE (1853), 19 John Street, London, WC1N 2DL. Tel: 020-7405 6135 Fax: 020-7405 6135
Web: www.btinternet.com/~oamission
Secretary, A. N. Banton

OPERATIC AND DRAMATIC ASSOCIATION, NATIONAL (1899), NODA House, 55–60 Lincoln Road, Peterborough, PE1 2RZ. Tel: 0870-770 2480 Fax: 0870-770 2490
Web: www.noda.org.uyk
Chief Executive, M. Pemberton

OPERATIONS ENGINEERS, THE SOCIETY OF (2000), 22 Greencoat Place, London, SW1P 1PR. Tel: 020-7630 1111 Fax: 020-7630 6677 Web: www.soe.org.uk *Chief Executive,* T. Fisher, MBA, IENG

OPTICAL COUNCIL, GENERAL (1959), 41 Harley Street, London, W1G 8DJ. Tel: 020-7580 3898 Fax: 020-7436 3525 Web: www.optical.org *Chief Executive and Registrar,* P. C. Coe

ORDERS AND MEDALS RESEARCH SOCIETY (1942), PO Box 1904, Southam, CV47 2ZX. Tel: 01295-690009 Web: www.omrs.org.uk *General Secretary,* P. M. R. Helmore

OSTEOPATHIC COUNCIL, GENERAL (1993), Osteopathy House, 176 Tower Bridge Road, London, SE1 3LU. Tel: 020-7357 6655 Fax: 020-7357 0011 Web: www.osteopathy.org.uk *Chief Executive & Registrar,* Miss M. J. Craggs

OSTEOPATHIC MEDICINE, LONDON COLLEGE OF, 8–10 Boston Place, London, NW1 6QH. Tel: 020-7262 1128 Fax: 020-7723 7492, *Clinic Manager,* Mrs A. Dalby

OSTEOPOROSIS SOCIETY, NATIONAL (1986), Camerton, Bath, BA2 0PJ. Tel: 01761-471771 Fax: 01761-471104 Web: www.nos.org.uk *Communications Manager,* Trevor Reid

OUTWARD BOUND SCOTLAND (1941), Loch Eil Centre, Achdalieu, Corpach, Fort William, Inverness-shire, PH33 7NN. Tel: 01397-772866 Fax: 01397-773905 Web: www.outwardbound-uk.org *Director,* Sir Michael Hobbs, KCVO, CBE

OVERSEAS DEVELOPMENT INSTITUTE, 111 Westminster Bridge Road, London, SE1 7JD. Tel: 020-7922 0300 Fax: 020-7922 0399 Web: www.odi.org.uk *Director,* S. Maxwell

OVERSEAS SERVICE PENSIONERS' ASSOCIATION (1960), 138 High Street, Tonbridge, Kent, TN9 1AX. Tel: 01732-363836 *Secretary,* D. F. B. Le Breton, CBE

OXFAM GREAT BRITAIN (1942), Oxfam House, 274 Banbury Road, Oxford, OX2 7DZ. Tel: 01865-311311 Web: www.oxfam.org.uk *Director,* B. Stocking, CMG

OXFORD PRESERVATION TRUST (1927), 10 Turn Again Lane, St Ebbes, Oxford, OX1 1QL. Tel: 01865-242918 Fax: 01865-251022 Web: www.oxfordpreservation.org.uk *Secretary,* Mrs D. Dance

OXFORDSHIRE ARCHITECTURAL AND HISTORICAL SOCIETY (1839), 53 Radley Road, Abingdon, Oxon, OX14 3PN. Tel: 01235-525960 Web: www.oahs.org.uk *Hon. Secretary,* Dr A. J. Dodd

PALAEONTOLOGICAL ASSOCIATION (1957), c/o Department of Geological Sciences, The University, South Road, Durham, DH1 3LE. Tel: 0121-414 4173 Fax: 0191-374 2510 Web: www.palass.org *Secretary,* Dr H. A. Armstrong

PARLIAMENTARY AND SCIENTIFIC COMMITTEE (1939), 3 Birdcage Walk, Westminster, London, SW1H 9JJ. Tel: 020-7222 7085 Fax: 020-7222 7189. *Administrative Secretary,* Dr A. Whitehouse

PASTEL SOCIETY (1898), 17 Carlton House Terrace, London, SW1Y 5BD. Tel: 020-7930 6844 Fax: 020-7839 7830 Web: www.mallgalleries.org.uk *Secretary,* Brian Gallagher

PASTORAL PSYCHOLOGY, GUILD OF (1937), PO Box 1107, London, W3 6ZP. Tel: 020-8993 8366 Fax: 020-8993 3148 Web: www.guildofpastoralpsychology.org.uk *Chairman,* Mary Jo Radcliffe

PATENTEES AND INVENTORS, INSTITUTE OF (1919), Suite 505A, Triumph House, 189 Regent Street, London, W1B 4JY. Tel: 020-8541 4197 Fax: 020-8541 4195 Web: www.invent.org.uk *Secretary,* Ms R. Magnus

PATIENTS ASSOCIATION (1963), PO Box 935, Harrow, Middx, HA1 3YJ. Tel: 020-8423 9111 Helpline: 0845-608 4455 Fax: 020-8423 9119 Web: www.patients-association.com *Director,* M. Stone

PEABODY TRUST (1862), 45 Westminster Bridge Road, London, SE1 7JB. Tel: 020-7928 7811 Fax: 020-7261 9187 Web: www.peabody.org.uk *Chief Executive,* Richard McCarthy

PETROLEUM, INSTITUTE OF (1913), 61 New Cavendish Street, London, W1G 7AR. Tel: 020-7467 7100 Fax: 020-7255 1472 Web: www.petroleum.co.uk *Director-General,* Mrs L. Kingham

PHARMACOLOGICAL SOCIETY, BRITISH, (1931), 16 Angel Gate, City Road, London, EC1V 2SG. Tel: 020-7417 0110 Fax: 020-7417 0114 Web: www.bps.ac.uk *Executive Officer,* Ms S. J. Stagg

PHILOLOGICAL SOCIETY (1842), School of Oriental and African Studies, University of London, Thornhaugh Street, London, WC1H 0XG. *Hon. Secretary,* Dr Lutz Marten

PHOTOGRAPHY, BRITISH INSTITUTE OF PROFESSIONAL (1901), Fox Talbot House, Amwell End, Ware, Herts, SG12 9HN. Tel: 01920-464011 Fax: 01920-487056 Web: www.bipp.com
Executive Secretary, A. Mair

PHYSICS AND ENGINEERING IN MEDICINE, INSTITUTE OF, Fairmount House, 230 Tadcaster Road, York, YO24 1ES. Tel: 01904-610821 Fax: 01904-612279 Web: www.ipem.org.uk
General Secretary, R. W. Neilson

PHYSIOLOGICAL SOCIETY, THE (1876), PO Box 11319, London, WC1V 6YB. Tel: 020-7269 5710 Fax: 020-7269 5720 Web: www.physoc.org
Executive Secretary, David Sewell

PIERS SOCIETY, NATIONAL (1979), 4 Tyrell Road, Benfleet, Essex, SS7 5DH. Tel: 01268 757291 Fax: 01268-757291 Web: www.piers.co.uk
Secretary, T. Wardley

PIG ASSOCIATION, BRITISH (1884), Scotsbridge House, Scots Hill, Rickmansworth, Herts, WD3 3BB. Tel: 01923-695295 Fax: 01923-695347 Web: www.britishpigs.org
Chief Executive, M. Bates

PILGRIM TRUST, THE (1930), Cowley House, 9 Little College Street, London, SW1P 3XS. Tel: 020-7222 4723 Fax: 020-7976 0461 Web: www.thepilgrimtrust.org.uk
Director, Miss G. Nayler

PILGRIMS OF GREAT BRITAIN, THE (1902), Allington Castle, Maidstone, Kent, ME16 0NB. Tel: 01622-606404 Fax: 01622-606402
Hon. Secretary, M. P. S. Barton, DL

PLAIN ENGLISH CAMPAIGN (1979), PO Box 3, New Mills, High Peak, SK22 4QP. Tel: 01663-744409 Fax: 01663-747038 Web: www.plainenglish.co.uk
Director, Ms C. Maher

PLAYING FIELDS ASSOCIATION, NATIONAL (1925), Stanley House, St Chads Place, London, WC1X 9HH. Tel: 020-7833 5360 Fax: 020-7833 5365 Web: www.playing-fields.com
Director, Ms E. Davies

PLUNKETT FOUNDATION (1919), 23 Hanborough Business Park, Long Hanborough, Oxford, OX29 8SG. Tel: 01993-883636 Fax: 01993-883576 Web: www.plunkett.co.uk
Director, R. Moreton

POETRY SOCIETY, THE (1909), 22 Betterton Street, London, WC2H 9BX. Tel: 020-7420 9880 Fax: 020-7240 4818 Web: www.poetrysociety.org.uk
Director, Jules Mann

POLIO FELLOWSHIP, BRITISH (1939), Ground Floor, Unit A, Eagle Office Centre, The Runway, South Ruislip, Middx, HA4 6SE. Tel: 0800-018 0586 Fax: 020-8842 0555 Web: www.britishpolio.org
Chief Executive, A. Kemp, CQSW

POLITE SOCIETY AND CAMPAIGN FOR COURTESY, THE (1986), 18 The Avenue, Basford, Newcastle-under-Lyme, Staffs, ST5 0LY. Tel: 01782-61440
Secretary, The Revd Ian Gregory

POSTWATCH (2001), 28–30 Grosvenor Gardens, London, SW1W 0TT. Tel: 08456-013265 Fax: 020-7730 3044 Web: www.postwatch.co.uk
Chairman, Peter Carr

POWYSLAND CLUB (1867), Llgyad y Dyffryn, Llanidloes, Powys, SY18 6JD. Tel: 01686-412277 Web: www.powyslandclub.co.uk
Hon. Secretary, Miss P. M. Davies

PRAYER BOOK SOCIETY, THE (1975), St James Garlickhythe, Garlick Hill, London, EC4V 2AF. Tel: 0118-984 2582 Fax: 0118-984 5220 Web: www.prayerbookuk.com
Chairman, Roger Evans

PRINCE'S TRUST, THE (1976), 18 Park Square East, London, NW1 4LH. Tel: 0800-842842 Fax: 020-7543 1200 Web: www.princes-trust.org.uk
Chief Executive, Sir Tom Shebbeare, CVO

PRINCESS ROYAL TRUST FOR CARERS (1991), 142 Minories, London, EC3N 1LB. Tel: 020-7480 7788 Fax: 020-7481 4729 Web: www.carers.org
Chief Executive, Ms A. Ryan

PRINTERS' CHARITABLE CORPORATION (1827), 7 Cantelupe Mews, Cantelupe Road, East Grinstead, W. Sussex, RH19 3BG. Tel: 01342-318882 Fax: 01342-318887 Web: www.printerscharitablecorporation.co.uk

PRINTING, INSTITUTE OF (1980), The Mews, Hill House, Clanricarde Road, Tunbridge Wells, Kent, TN1 1PJ. Tel: 01892-538118 Fax: 01892-518028 Web: www.institute of printing.org
Secretary-General, D. Freeland

PRISON VISITORS, NATIONAL ASSOCIATION OF (1924), 32 Newnham Avenue, Bedford, ME41 9PT Tel: 01234-359763 Web: www.napu.org.uk
General Secretary, Mrs A. G. McKenna

PROFESSIONAL CLASSES AID COUNCIL (1921), 10 St Christopher's Place, London, W1U 1HZ. Tel: 020-7935 0641 Fax: 020-7486 0128
Secretary, Miss N. E. Inkson

PROTECTION OF ANCIENT BUILDINGS, SOCIETY FOR THE (1877), 37 Spital Square, London, E1 6DY. Tel: 020-7377 1644 Fax: 020-7247 5296
Web: www.spab.org.uk
Secretary, P. Venning, FSA

PROTECTION OF WILD BIRDS, SCOTTISH SOCIETY FOR THE (1927), Foremount House, Kilbarchan, Renfrewshire, PA10 2EZ. Tel: 01505-702419
Secretary, Dr J. A. Gibson

PROTESTANT ALLIANCE (1845), 77 Ampthill Road, Flitwick, Bedford, MK45 1BD. Tel: 01525-712348 Fax: 01525-712348
General Secretary, Dr S. J. Scott-Pearson

PSORIASIS ASSOCIATION (1968), 7 Milton Street, Northampton, NN2 7JG. Tel: 01604-711129
Fax: 01604-792894
Web: www.psoriasis-association.org.uk
Chief Executive, Gladys Edwards

PSYCHICAL RESEARCH, SOCIETY FOR (1882), 49 Marloes Road, London, W8 6LA. Tel: 020-7937 8984
Fax: 020-7937 8984 Web: www.spr.ac.uk
Secretary, P. M. Johnson

PSYCHOLOGICAL SOCIETY, BRITISH (1901), St Andrews House, 48 Princess Road East, Leicester, LE1 7DR.
Tel: 0116-254 9568 Fax: 0116-247 0787
Web: www.bps.org.uk
Chief Executive, B. A. Brooking

PUBLIC POLICY RESEARCH, INSTITUTE FOR (1988), 30–32 Southampton Street, London, WC2E 7RA.
Tel: 020-7470 6100 Fax: 020-7470 6111
Web: www.ippr.org
Director, M. Taylor

PUBLIC POLICY, THE SCHOOL OF (1996), University College London, 29 Tavistock Square, London, WC1H 9QU.
Tel: 020-7679 4999 Fax: 020-7679 4969
Web: www.ucl.ac.uk/spp/
Executive Administrator, Miss S. A. Welham

PURCHASING AND SUPPLY, CHARTERED INSTITUTE OF (1932), Easton House, Easton on the Hill, Stamford, Lincs, PE9 3NZ. Tel: 01780-756777 Fax: 01780-751610
Web: www.cips.org
Chief Executive, K. James

QUALITY ASSURANCE, INSTITUTE OF (1919), 12 Grosvenor Crescent, London, SW1X 7EE.
Tel: 020-7245 6722 Fax: 020-7245 6788
Web: www.iqa.org *Director-General,* F. R. Steer, MBE

QUEEN ELIZABETH'S FOUNDATION FOR DISABLED PEOPLE (1934), Leatherhead Court, Leatherhead, Surrey, KT22 0BN. Tel: 01372-841100 Fax: 01372-844072
Web: www.qefd.org
Chief Executive, Cynthia Robinson

QUEEN VICTORIA CLERGY FUND (1897), Church House, Dean's Yard, London, SW1P 3NZ. Tel: 020-7898 1310
Fax: 020-7898 1321
Secretary, C. D. L. Menzies

QUEEN VICTORIA SCHOOL (1908), Dunblane, Perthshire, FK15 0JY. Tel: 01786-822288 Fax: 0131-310 2955/2926
Web: www.qvs.org.uk
Headmaster, B. Raine

QUEEN'S ENGLISH SOCIETY, THE (1973), 20 Jessica Road, London, SW18 2QN. Tel: 020-8874 2200
Web: www.queens-english-society.com
Hon. Secretary, Miss P. Raper

QUEEN'S NURSING INSTITUTE (1887), 3 Albemarle Way, London, EC1V 4RQ. Tel: 020-7490 4227 Fax: 020-7490 1269
Web: www.qni.org.uk
Director, Mrs J. Hesketh

RAIL PASSENGERS COUNCIL (1949), Whittles House, 14 Pentonville Road, London, N1 9HF. Tel: 020-7713 2700
Fax: 020-7713 2729 Web: www.railpassengers.org.uk

RAILWAY AND CANAL HISTORICAL SOCIETY (1954), 3 West Court, West Street, Oxford, OX2 0NP.
Tel: 01865-240514
Web: www.bodley.ox.ac.uk/external/rchs/index.html
Hon. Secretary, M. Searle

RAILWAY BENEVOLENT INSTITUTION (1858), Electra Way, Crewe Business Park, Crewe, Cheshire, CW1 6HS.
Tel: 01270-251316 Fax: 01270-503966
Director, B. R. Whitnall

RAILWAY CLUB (1899), Room 208, 25 Marylebone Road, London, NW1 5JS.
Hon. Secretary, J. M. Burgess

RAINY DAY TRUST (1843), Brooke House, 4 The Lakes, Bedford Road, Northampton, NN4 7YD. Tel: 01604-622023
Fax: 01604-631252
General Secretary, Mrs D. Webb

RAMBLERS' ASSOCIATION (1935), 2nd Floor, Camelford House, 87–90 Albert Embankment, London, SE1 7TW.
Tel: 020-7339 8500 Fax: 020-7339 8501
Web: www.ramblers.org.uk
Chief Executive, Nick Barrett

RARE BREEDS SURVIVAL TRUST (1973), National Agricultural Centre, Stoneleigh Park, Kenilworth, Warks, CV8 2LG. Tel: 024-7669 6551 Fax: 024-7669 6706
Web: www.rbst.org.uk
Chief Executive, Ms R. Mansbridge

RED CROSS, BRITISH (1870), 9 Grosvenor Crescent, London, SW1X 7EJ. Tel: 020-7235 5454 Fax: 020-7245 6315
Web: www.redcross.org.uk
Chief Executive, Sir Nicholas Young

REGULAR FORCES EMPLOYMENT ASSOCIATION LTD (1885), 49 Pall Mall, London, SW1Y 5JG.
Tel: 020-7321 2011 Web: www.rfea.org.uk
Chief Executive, Air Cdre. Peter G. Johnson, OBE

RELATE (1938), Herbert Gray College, Little Church Street, Rugby, Warks, CV21 3AP. Tel: 01788-753241
Fax: 01788-535007 Web: www.relate.org.uk
Chief Executive, Ms A. Sibson

RESEARCH DEFENCE SOCIETY (1908), 58 Great Marlborough Street, London, W1F 7JY. Tel: 020-7287 2818
Fax: 020-7287 2627 Web: www.rds-online.org.uk
Executive Director, Dr M. Matfield

RETIRED NURSES' NATIONAL HOME (1934), Riverside Avenue, Bournemouth, BH7 7EE. Tel: 01202-396418
Fax: 01202-302530 Web: www.rnnh.co.uk
Chairman, Ms J. Deacon

RETIREMENT PENSIONS ASSOCIATIONS, NATIONAL FEDERATION OF (1940), Thwaites House, Railway Road, Blackburn, BB1 5AX. Tel: 01254-52606 Fax: 01254-52606
General Secretary, R. Stansfield

REVENUES, RATINGS AND VALUATION (1882), 41 Doughty Street, London, WC1N 2LF. Tel: 020-7831 3505
Fax: 020-7831 2048 Web: www.irrv.org.uk
Director, D. Magor, IRRV, OBE

RICHARD III SOCIETY (1924), 4 Oakley Street, London, SW3 5NN. Web: www.richardiii.net
Secretary, Miss E. M. Nokes

RNIB (ROYAL NATIONAL INSTITUTE OF THE BLIND) (1868), 105 Judd Street, London, WC1H 9NE.
Tel: 0845-669999 Fax: 020-7388 2034
Web: www.rnib.org.uk
Director-General, I. Bruce

ROAD SAFETY OFFICERS (1971), Pin Point, 1–2 Rosslyn Crescent, Harrow, HA1 2SB. Tel: 0870-010 4442
Fax: 0870-333 7772 Web: www.irso.org.uk
Chairman, R. Doherty

ROADS AND ROAD TRANSPORT HISTORY ASSOCIATION (1992), Copper Beeches, 134 Wood End Road, Erdington, Birmingham, B24 8BN. Tel: 0121-382 5036
Fax: 0121-686 3603
Chairman, Prof. John Hibbs, OBE, PHD, FCIT

ROMAN STUDIES, SOCIETY FOR THE PROMOTION OF (1910), Senate House, Malet Street, London, WC1E 7HU.
Tel: 020-7862 8727 Fax: 020-7862 8728
Web: www.sas.ac.uk/icls/roman/
Secretary, Dr H. M. Cockle

ROUND TABLES OF GREAT BRITAIN AND IRELAND, NATIONAL ASSOCIATION OF (1927), Marchesi House, 4 Embassy Drive, Edgbaston, Birmingham, B15 1TP.
Tel: 0121-456 4402 Fax: 0121-456 4185
Web: www.roundtable.org.uk
General Secretary, J. Handley

ROYAL AERONAUTICAL SOCIETY (1866), 4 Hamilton Place, London, W1J 7BQ. Tel: 020-7670 4302
Fax: 020-7670 4309
Chief Executive, K. Mans

ROYAL AGRICULTURAL SOCIETIES, COUNCIL FOR AWARDS OF (1970), 'Alsace', 48 High Park Road, Ryde, Isle of Wight, PO33 1BX. Tel: 01983-566770
Fax: 01983-566770
Secretary, Dr J. Wibberley, FRAGS

ROYAL AGRICULTURAL SOCIETY OF THE COMMONWEALTH (1957), 2 Grosvenor Gardens, London, SW1W 0DH. Tel: 020-7259 9678
Fax: 020-7259 9675 Web: www.commagshow.org
Hon. Secretary, C. Runge, FRAGS

ROYAL AIR FORCES ASSOCIATION, 117 Loughborough Road, Leicester, LE4 5ND. Tel: 0116-266 5224
Fax: 0116-266 5012 Web: www.rafa.org.uk
Secretary-General, Gary Martin

ROYAL ARMOURED CORPS WAR MEMORIAL BENEVOLENT FUND, c/o RHQ RTR, Bovington Camp, Wareham, Dorset, BH20 6JA. Tel: 01929-403331
Fax: 01929-403488
Secretary, Maj. A. Henzie, MBE

ROYAL ARTILLERY ASSOCIATION, Artillery House, Front Parade, Royal Artillery Barracks, Woolwich, London, SE18 4BH. Tel: 020-8781 3003 Fax: 020-8854 3617
Web: www.raa.uk.com
General Secretary, Lt.-Col. N. G. W. Lang

ROYAL ASSOCIATION OF BRITISH DAIRY FARMERS, Dairy House, 60 Kenilworth Road, Leamington Spa, Warks, CV32 6JX. Tel: 01926-887477 Fax: 01926-887585
Chief Executive, N. Everington

ROYAL BIRMINGHAM SOCIETY OF ARTISTS (1814), 4 Brook Street, Birmingham, B3 1SA. Tel: 0121-236 4353
Fax: 0121-236 4555 Web: www.rbsa.org.uk
Gallery Director, Marie Considine

ROYAL BRITISH LEGION SCOTLAND (1921), New Haig House, Logie Green Road, Edinburgh, EH7 4HR.
Tel: 0131-557 5819 Web: www.rblscotland.org
General Secretary, Wing Cdre. R. J. Woodroffe, MBE

ROYAL CALEDONIAN SCHOOLS TRUST (1815),
80A High Street, Bushey, Watford, Herts, WD23 3HD.
Tel: 020-8421 8845 Fax: 020-8421 8845
Web: www.royalcaledonianschools.org.uk
Chief Executive, J. Horsfield

ROYAL CAMBRIAN ACADEMY OF ARTS (1882),
Crown Lane, Conwy, LL32 8AN. Tel: 01492-593413
Fax: 01492-593413 Web: www.rcaconwy.co.uk
President, Sir Kyffin Williams

ROYAL CELTIC SOCIETY (1820), 23 Rutland Street,
Edinburgh, EH1 2RN. Tel: 0131-228 6449
Fax: 0131-229 6987
Secretary, J. G. Camerson, WS

ROYAL CHORAL SOCIETY (1872), Studio 9, 92 Lots Road,
London, SW10 0QD. Tel: 020-7376 3718 Fax: 020-7376 3719
Web: www.royalchoralsociety.co.uk
Administrator, Helen Body

ROYAL COLLEGE OF GENERAL PRACTITIONERS (1952),
14 Princes Gate, London, SW7 1PU.
Tel: 020-7581 3232 Fax: 020-7225 3047
Web: www.rcgp.org.uk
Chairman of Council, David Haslam

ROYAL COLLEGE OF NURSING (1916), 20 Cavendish
Square, London, W1G 0RN. Tel: 020-7409 3333
Fax: 020-7647 3434 Web: www.rcn.org.uk
General Secretary, Dr Beverly Malone

ROYAL COLLEGE OF OBSTETRICIANS AND
GYNAECOLOGISTS (1929), 27 Sussex Place, Regent's Park,
London, NW1 4RG. Tel: 020-7772 6200 Fax: 020-7723 0575
Web: www.rcog.org.uk
College Secretary, P. A. Barnett

ROYAL COLLEGE OF PATHOLOGISTS, 2 Carlton House
Terrace, London, SW1Y 5AF. Tel: 020-7451 6700
Fax: 020-7451 6701 Web: www.rcpath.org
Chief Executive, Daniel Ross

ROYAL COLLEGE OF PSYCHIATRISTS (1841), 17 Belgrave
Square, London, SW1X 8PG. Tel: 020-7235 2351
Fax: 020-7245 1231 Web: www.rcpsych.ac.uk
Chief Executive, Mrs V. Cameron

ROYAL COLLEGE OF RADIOLOGISTS (1975),
38 Portland Place, London, W1N 4JQ. Tel: 020-7636 4432
Fax: 020-7323 3100 Web: www.rcr.ac.uk.
Chief Executive, A. Hall

ROYAL COLLEGE OF SURGEONS OF ENGLAND (1800),
35–43 Lincoln's Inn Fields, London, WC2A 3PE.
Tel: 020-7405 3474 Fax: 020-7869 6005
Web: www.rcseng.ac.uk
Chief Executive, Craig Duncan

ROYAL COLLEGE OF VETERINARY SURGEONS (1844),
Belgravia House, 62–64 Horseferry Road, London,
SW1P 2AF. Tel: 020-7222 2001 Fax: 020-7222 2004
Web: www.rcvs.org.uk
Registrar, Miss J. C. Hern

ROYAL FACULTY OF PROCURATORS IN GLASGOW,
12 Nelson Mandela Place, Glasgow, G2 1BT.
Tel: 0141-331 0533 Fax: 0141-332 4714
Web: www.rfpg.org
General Manager, I. C. Pearson

ROYAL FORESTRY SOCIETY OF ENGLAND, WALES AND
NORTHERN IRELAND (1882), 102 High Street, Tring,
Herts, HP23 4AF. Tel: 01442-822028 Fax: 01442-890395
Web: www.rfs.org.uk
Director, Dr J. E. Jackson

ROYAL GEOGRAPHICAL SOCIETY (WITH THE
INSTITUTE OF BRITISH GEOGRAPHERS) (1830),
1 Kensington Gore, London, SW7 2AR. Tel: 020-7591 3000
Fax: 020-7591 3001 Web: www.rgs.org
Director, Dr R. Gardner, CBE

ROYAL HIGHLAND AND AGRICULTURAL SOCIETY OF
SCOTLAND (1784), Royal Highland Centre, Ingliston,
Edinburgh, EH28 8NF. Tel: 0131-335 6200
Fax: 0131-333 5236 Web: www.rhass.org.uk
Chief Executive, R. Jones

ROYAL HISTORICAL SOCIETY (1868), University College
London, Gower Street, London, WC1E 6BT.
Tel: 020-7387 7532 Fax: 020-7387 7532
Web: www.rhs.ac.uk
Executive Secretary, Mrs J. N. McCarthy

ROYAL HOSPITAL FOR NEURO-DISABILITY (1854),
West Hill, Putney, London, SW15 3SW. Tel: 020-8780 4500
Fax: 020-8780 4501 Web: www.rhn.org.uk
Chief Executive, Peter Franklyn

ROYAL HUMANE SOCIETY (1774), Brettenham House,
Lancaster Place, London, WC2E 7EP. Tel: 020-7836 8155
Fax: 020-7836 8155 Web: www.royalhumane.org
Secretary, Maj.-Gen. C. Tyler, CB

ROYAL INSTITUTE OF BRITISH ARCHITECTS,
66 Portland Place, London, W1B 1AD. Tel: 020-7580 5533
Information: 0906-302 0400 Fax: 020-7255 1541
Web: www.architecture.org
Chief Executive, Richard Hastilow

ROYAL INSTITUTE OF NAVIGATION (1947), 1 Kensington
Gore, London, SW7 2AT. Tel: 020-7591 3130
Fax: 020-7591 3131 Web: www.rin.org.uk
Director, Gp Capt. D. W. Broughton, MBE

ROYAL INSTITUTE OF OIL PAINTERS (1882), 17 Carlton
House Terrace, London, SW1Y 5BD. Tel: 020-7930 6844
Fax: 020-7839 7830 Web: www.mallgalleries.org.uk
Secretary, Brian Roxby

ROYAL INSTITUTE OF PAINTERS IN WATER COLOURS
(1831), 17 Carlton House Terrace, London, SW1Y 5BD.
Tel: 020-7930 6844 Fax: 020-7839 7830
Web: www.mallgalleries.org.uk
Secretary, P. Dawson

ROYAL INSTITUTE OF PHILOSOPHY, THE (1925),
14 Gordon Square, London, WC1H 0AR.
Tel: 020-7387 4130 Fax: 020-7383 4061
Web: www.royalinstitutephilosophy.org
Director, Prof. A. O'Hear

ROYAL INSTITUTION OF CHARTERED SURVEYORS
(1868), 12 Great George Street, Parliament Square, London,
SW1P 3AD. Tel: 020-7222 7000 Fax: 020-7222 9430
Web: www.rics.org
Chief Executive, J. H. A. J. Armstrong

ROYAL INSTITUTION OF GREAT BRITAIN, THE (1799),
21 Albemarle Street, London, W1S 4BS. Tel: 020-7409 2992
Fax: 020-7629 3569 Web: www.ri.ac.uk
Director, Baroness Greenfield, CBE

ROYAL INSTITUTION OF NAVAL ARCHITECTS (1860),
10 Upper Belgrave Street, London, SW1X 8BQ.
Tel: 020-7235 4622 Fax: 020-7259 5912
Web: www.rina.org.uk
Chief Executive, T. Blakeley

ROYAL LITERARY FUND (1790), 3 Johnson's Court, off Fleet
Street, London, EC4A 3EA. Tel: 020-7353 7150
Fax: 020-7353 1350 Web: www.rlf.org.uk
General Secretary, Ms E. M. Gunn

ROYAL LONDON SOCIETY FOR THE BLIND (1838),
Dorton House, Seal, Sevenoaks, Kent, TN15 0ED.
Tel: 01732-592500 Fax: 01732-592506
Web: www.rlsb.org.uk
Chief Executive, Brian J. Cooney

ROYAL NATIONAL COLLEGE FOR THE BLIND (1872),
College Road, Hereford, HR1 1EB. Tel: 01432-265725
Fax: 01432-376628 Web: www.rncb.ac.uk
Principal, Mrs R. Burge

ROYAL NATIONAL LIFEBOAT INSTITUTION (1824), West
Quay Road, Poole, Dorset, BT15 1HZ. Tel: 01202-663000
Fax: 01202-663167 Web: www.rnli.org.uk
Chief Executive, A. Freemantle, MBE

ROYAL NAVAL ASSOCIATION, 82 Chelsea Manor Street,
London, SW3 5QJ. Tel: 020-7352 6764 Fax: 020-7352 7385
Web: www.royal-naval-association.co.uk
General Secretary, Cdre Barry Leighton, CBE

ROYAL NAVAL BENEVOLENT SOCIETY FOR OFFICERS
(1739), 70 Porchester Terrace, London, W2 3TP.
Tel: 020-7402 5231 Fax: 020-7402 5533
Secretary, Cdr. W. K. Ridley, OBE, RN

ROYAL NAVAL BENEVOLENT TRUST (1922), Castaway
House, 311 Twyford Avenue, Portsmouth, PO2 8PE.
Tel: 023-9269 0112/9266 0296 Fax: 023-9266 0852
Web: www.rnbt.org.uk
Chief Executive, Cdr. J. Owens, RN

ROYAL PATRIOTIC FUND CORPORATION (1854),
40 Queen Anne's Gate, London, SW1H 9AP.
Tel: 020-7233 1894 Fax: 020-7233 1799
Secretary, Col. R. J. Sandy

ROYAL PHARMACEUTICAL SOCIETY OF GREAT
BRITAIN (1841), 1 Lambeth High Street, London, SE1 7JN.
Tel: 020-7735 9141 Fax: 020-7735 7629
Web: www.rpsgb.org.uk
Secretary and Registrar, Ms A. M. Lewis, OBE

ROYAL PHILATELIC SOCIETY LONDON (1869),
41 Devonshire Place, London, W1G 6JY. Tel: 020-7486 1044
Fax: 020-7486 0803 Web: www.rpsl.org.uk
Hon. Secretary, K. B. Fitton

ROYAL PHOTOGRAPHIC SOCIETY (1853), The Octagon,
Milsom Street, Bath, BA1 1DN. Tel: 01225-462841
Fax: 01225-448688 Web: www.rps.org
President, John R. Page

ROYAL SCHOOL OF CHURCH MUSIC (1927), Cleveland
Lodge, Westhumble, Dorking, Surrey, RH5 6BW.
Tel: 01306-872800 Fax: 01306-887260
Web: www.rscm.com
Director-General, Prof. J. Harper

ROYAL SCHOOL OF NEEDLEWORK (1872), Apartment 12A,
Hampton Court Palace, Surrey, KT8 9AU.
Tel: 020-8943 1432 Fax: 020-8943 4910
Web: www.royal-needlework.co.uk
Principal, Mrs E. Elvin

ROYAL SCOTTISH AGRICULTURAL BENEVOLENT
INSTITUTION (1897), South Bungalow, Ingliston,
Edinburgh, EH28 8NB. Tel: 0131-333 1023
Fax: 0131-333 1027 Web: www.rsabi.org.uk
Director, John N. Macdonald

ROYAL SOCIETY FOR THE ENCOURAGEMENT OF ARTS,
MANUFACTURES AND COMMERCE (RSA) (1754),
8 John Adam Street, London, WC2N 6EZ. Tel: 020-7930 5115
Fax: 020-7839 5805 Web: www.thersa.org
Director, Penny Egan

ROYAL SOCIETY FOR THE PREVENTION OF
ACCIDENTS (1917), ROSPA House, Edgbaston Park,
353 Bristol Road, Birmingham, B5 7ST. Tel: 0121-248 2000
Fax: 0121-248 2001 Web: www.rospa.com
Chief Executive, Dr J. Hooper

ROYAL SOCIETY FOR THE PREVENTION OF CRUELTY TO ANIMALS (1824), Wilberforce Way, Horsham, W. Sussex, RH13 9RS. Tel: 0870-010 1181 Fax: 0870-753 0048 Web: www.rspca.org.uk
Director-General, Jackie Ballard

ROYAL SOCIETY FOR THE PROMOTION OF HEALTH, THE (1876), 38A St George's Drive, London, SW1V 4BH. Tel: 020-7630 0121 Fax: 020-7976 6847 Web: www.rsph.org
Chief Executive, S. Royston

ROYAL SOCIETY FOR THE PROTECTION OF BIRDS (RSPB) (1889), The Lodge, Sandy, Beds, SG19 2DL. Tel: 01767-680551 Fax: 01767-692365 Web: www.rspb.org.uk
Chief Executive, G. R. Wynne

ROYAL SOCIETY OF BRITISH ARTISTS (1775), 17 Carlton House Terrace, London, SW1Y 5BD. Tel: 020-7930 6844 Fax: 020-7839 7830 Web: www.mallgalleries.org.uk
President, Cav. Romeo di Girolamo

ROYAL SOCIETY OF CHEMISTRY (1841), Burlington House, Piccadilly, London, W1V 0BA. Tel: 020-7437 8656 Fax: 020-7437 8883 Web: www.rsc.org and www.chemsoc.org
Secretary-General and Chief Executive, Dr D. Giachardi

ROYAL SOCIETY OF LITERATURE (1820), Somerset House, Strand, London, WC2R 1LA. Tel: 020-7845 4676 Fax: 020-7845 4679 Web: www.rslit.org
Secretary, Maggie Fergusson

ROYAL SOCIETY OF MARINE ARTISTS (1945), 17 Carlton House Terrace, London, SW1Y 5BD. Tel: 020-7930 6844 Fax: 020-7839 7830 Web: www.mallgalleries.org.uk
Secretary, D. Howell

THE ROYAL SOCIETY OF MEDICINE (1805), 1 Wimpole Street, London, W1G 0AE. Tel: 020-7290 2900 Fax: 020-7290 2992 Web: www.rsm.ac.uk
Executive Director, Dr A. Grocock

ROYAL SOCIETY OF MINIATURE PAINTERS, SCULPTORS AND GRAVERS (1895), 1 Knapp Cottages, Wyke, Gillingham, Dorset, SP8 4NQ. Tel: 01747-825718 Fax: 01747-826835 Web: www.royal-miniature-society.org.uk
Executive Secretary, Mrs P. Henderson

THE ROYAL SOCIETY OF MUSICIANS OF GREAT BRITAIN (1738), 10 Stratford Place, London, W1C 1BA. Tel: 020-7629 6137 Fax: 020-7629 6137
Secretary, Mrs M. Gibb

ROYAL SOCIETY OF PORTRAIT PAINTERS (1891), 17 Carlton House Terrace, London, SW1Y 5BD. Tel: 020-7930 6844 Fax: 020-7839 7830 Web: www.mallgalleries.org.uk
Secretary, D. Cobley

ROYAL SOCIETY OF ST GEORGE (1894), 127 Sandgate Road, Folkestone, Kent, CT20 2BH. Tel: 01303-241795 Fax: 01303-211710 Web: www.royalsocietyofstgeorge.com
Chairman, J. C. Clemence, QPM

ROYAL SOCIETY OF TROPICAL MEDICINE AND HYGIENE (1907), Manson House, 26 Portland Place, London, W1B 1EY. Tel: 020-7580 2127 Fax: 020-7436 1389 Web: www.rstmh.org
Hon. Secretaries, Prof. R. D. Ward and Prof. G. Pasvol

THE ROYAL STAR AND GARTER HOME FOR DISABLED EX-SERVICE MEN AND WOMEN (1916), Richmond Hill, Richmond, Surrey, TW10 6RR. Tel: 020-8940 3314 Fax: 020-8940 1953 Web: www.starandgarter.org
Chief Executive, Lynn McDougall

ROYAL TOWN PLANNING INSTITUTE, 41 Botolph Lane, London, EC3R 8DL. Tel: 020-7929 9494 Fax: 020-7929 9490 Web: www.rtpi.org.uk *Secretary-General,* R. Upton

ROYAL ULSTER AGRICULTURAL SOCIETY, The King's Hall, Balmoral, Belfast, BT9 6GW. Tel: 028-9066 5225 Fax: 028-9066 1264 Web: www.balmoralshow.co.uk
Chief Executive, Michael Guest

ROYAL UNITED KINGDOM BENEFICENT ASSOCIATION (1863), 6 Avonmore Road, London, W14 8RL. Tel: 020-7605 4200 Fax: 020-7605 4201 Web: www.rukba.org.uk
Chief Executive, Jonathan Powell

ROYAL ZOOLOGICAL SOCIETY OF SCOTLAND (1909), Scottish National Zoological Park, Edinburgh Zoo, Edinburgh, EH12 6TS. Tel: 0131-334 9171 Fax: 0131-314 0382 Web: www.edinburghzoo.org.uk
Chief Executive, David Windmill

RURAL SCOTLAND (1926), 3rd Floor, Gladstone's Land, 483 Lawnmarket, Edinburgh, EH1 2NT. Tel: 0131-225 7012/3 Fax: 0131-225 6592 Web: www.aprs.org.uk
Director, Mrs J. Geddes

RURAL WALES, CAMPAIGN FOR THE PROTECTION OF (1928), Ty Gwyn, 31 High Street, Welshpool, Powys, SY21 7YD. Tel: 01938-552525 Fax: 01938-552741 Web: www.cprw.org.uk
Director, M. Williams

SALMON AND TROUT ASSOCIATION (1903), Fishmongers' Hall, London Bridge, London, EC4R 9EL. Tel: 020-7283 5838 Fax: 020-7626 5137 Web: www.salmon-trout.org
Director, P. R. J. Knight

SALTIRE SOCIETY (1936), 9 Fountain Close, 22 High Street, Edinburgh, EH1 1TF. Tel: 0131-556 1836 Fax: 0131-557 1675 Web: www.saltiresociety.org.uk
Administrator, Mrs K. Munro

SALVATION ARMY, THE (1865), 101 Newington Causeway, London, SE1 6BN. Tel: 0845-634 0101 Fax: 020-7367 4728 Web: www.salvationarmy.org.uk
General, John Larsson

SAMARITANS (1953), The Upper Mill, Kingston Road, Ewell, Surrey, KT17 2AF. Tel: 020-8394 8300 Fax: 020-8394 8301 Web: www.samaritans.org
Chief Executive, S. Armson

SANE (1986), 1st Floor, Cityside House, 40 Adler Street, London, E1 1EE. Tel: 020-7375 1002. Helpline: 0845-767 8000 Fax: 020-7375 2162 Web: www.sane.org.uk
Chief Executive, Ms M. Wallace, MBE

SAVE BRITAIN'S HERITAGE (1975), 70 Cowcross Street, London, EC1M 6EJ. Tel: 020-7253 3500 Fax: 020-7253 3400 Web: www.savebritainsheritage.org
Secretary, A. Wilkinson

SAVE THE CHILDREN UK (1919), 17 Grove Lane, London, SE5 8RD. Tel: 020-7703 5400 Fax: 020-7703 2278 Web: www.savethechildren.org.uk
Director, General, M. Aaronson

SCHOOL LIBRARY ASSOCIATION (1937), Unit 2, Lotmead Business Village, Lotmead Farm, Wanborough, nr Swindon, SN4 0UY. Tel: 01793-791787 Fax: 01793-791786 Web: www.sla.org.uk
Chief Executive, Ms K. Lemaire

SCHOOLMASTERS AND SCHOOLMISTRESSES, SOCIETY OF (1798), c/o L. I. Baggott, SGBI Office, Queen Mary House, Manor Park Road, Chislehurst, Kent, BR7 5PY. Tel: 020-8468 7997 Fax: 020-8468 7200
Acting Secretary, L. I. Baggott, FCA

SCHOOLMISTRESSES AND GOVERNESSES BENEVOLENT INSTITUTION (1848), Queen Mary House, Manor Park Road, Chislehurst, Kent, BR7 5PY. Tel: 020-8468 7997 Fax: 020-8468 7200
Director, L. I. Baggott, FCA

SCIENCE, BRITISH ASSOCIATION FOR THE ADVANCEMENT OF (1831), 23 Savile Row, London, W1S 2EZ. Tel: 020-7973 3500 Fax: 020-7973 3063 Web: www.the-ba.net
Chief Executive, Dr R. Jackson

SCOPE (1952), 6 Market Road, London, N7 9PW. Tel: 0808-800 3333 Fax: 01908-321051 Web: www.scope.org.uk/
Chief Executive, T. Manwaring

SCOTTISH NATIONAL WAR MEMORIAL, The Castle, Edinburgh, EH1 2YT. Tel: 0131-226 7393 Fax: 0131-225 8920 Web: www.snwm.org
Secretary to the Trustees, Lt.-Col. I. Shepherd

SEA CADET ASSOCIATION, THE, 202 Lambeth Road, London, SE1 7JF. Tel: 020-7928 8978 Fax: 020-7928 8914 Web: www.sea-cadets.org
Chief Executive, Cdre. R. M. Parker, RN

SECRETARIES AND ADMINISTRATORS, INSTITUTE OF CHARTERED (1891), 16 Park Crescent, London, W1B 1AH. Tel: 020-7580 4741 Fax: 020-7323 1132 Web: www.icsa.org.uk
Chief Executive, M. J. Ainsworth

SECULAR SOCIETY, NATIONAL (1866), 25 Red Lion Square, London, WC1R 4RL. Tel: 020-7404 3126 Fax: 020-7404 3126 Web: www.secularism.org.uk
Executive Director, K. P. Wood

SENSE (THE NATIONAL DEAF, BLIND AND RUBELLA ASSOCIATION), 11–13 Clifton Terrace, London, N4 3SR. Tel: 020-7272 7774 Fax: 020-7272 6012 Web: www.sense.org.uk
Chief Executive, A. Best

SHAFTESBURY HOMES AND ARETHUSA (1843), The Chapel, Royal Victoria Patriotic Building, Trinity Road, London, SW18 3SX. Tel: 020-8875 1555 Fax: 020-8875 1954
Chief Executive, Ms A. Chesney

SHAFTESBURY SOCIETY, THE (1844), 16 Kingston Road, London, SW19 1JZ. Tel: 020-8239 5555 Fax: 020-8239 5580 Web: www.shaftesburysociety.org
Chief Executive, Mrs Mary Bishop

SHELLFISH ASSOCIATION OF GREAT BRITAIN (1903), Fishmongers' Hall, London Bridge, London, EC4R 9EL. Tel: 020-7283 8305 Fax: 020-7929 1389 Web: www.shellfish.org.uk
Director, Dr P. Hunt

SHELTER (NATIONAL CAMPAIGN FOR HOMELESS PEOPLE), 88 Old Street, London, EC1V 9HU. Tel: 020-7505 4699 Shelterline: 0808-800 4444 Fax: 020-8505 2169 Web: www.shelter.org.uk
Director, Adam Sampson

SHERLOCK HOLMES SOCIETY OF LONDON (1934), 13 Crofton Avenue, Orpington, Kent, BR6 8DU. Tel: 01689-811314 Web: www.sherlock-holmes.org.uk
Membership Secretary, R. J. Ellis

SHIPBROKERS, INSTITUTE OF CHARTERED, 3 St Helen's Place, London, EC3A 6EJ. Tel: 020-7628 5559 Fax: 020-7628 5445 Web: www.ics.org.uk
Director-General, D. A. Phillips

SHROPSHIRE ARCHAEOLOGICAL AND HISTORICAL SOCIETY (1877), Westcott Farm, Pontesbury, Shrewsbury, SY5 0SQ. Tel: 01743-790531
Chairman, J. B. Lawson

SIGHT SAVERS INTERNATIONAL (ROYAL COMMONWEALTH SOCIETY FOR THE BLIND) (1950), Grosvenor Hall, Bolnore Road, Haywards Heath, W. Sussex, RH16 4BX. Tel: 01444-446600 Fax: 01444-446688
Web: www.sightsavers.org
Executive Director, R. Porter

SIMPLIFIED SPELLING SOCIETY (1908), 4 Valette Way, Wellesbourne, Warwick, CV35 9TB.
Web: www.spellingsociety.org
Membership Secretary, John Gledhill

SIR OSWALD STOLL FOUNDATION (1917), 446 Fulham Road, London, SW6 1DT. Tel: 020-7385 2110
Fax: 020-7381 7485 Web: www.oswaldstoll.org.uk
Chief Executive, R. C. Brunwin

SOCIAL WORKERS, BRITISH ASSOCIATION OF (1970), 16 Kent Street, Birmingham, B5 6RD. Tel: 0121-622 3911
Fax: 0121-622 4860 Web: www.basw.co.uk
Director, I. Johnston

SOCIETY OF WILDLIFE ARTISTS (1964), 17 Carlton House Terrace, London, SW1Y 5BD. Tel: 020-7930 6844
Fax: 020-7839 7830 Web: www.mallgalleries.org.uk
Secretary, Andrew Stock

SOIL ASSOCIATION (1946), Bristol House, 40–56 Victoria Street, Bristol, BS1 6BY. Tel: 0117-929 0661
Fax: 0117-925 2504 Web: www.soilassociation.org
Director, P. Holden

SOLICITORS IN THE SUPREME COURT OF SCOTLAND, SOCIETY OF (1784), SSC Library, Parliament House, 11 Parliament Square, Edinburgh, EH1 1RF. Tel: 0131-225 6268
Fax: 0131-225 2270 Web: www.ssclibrary.co.uk
Secretary, I. L. S. Balfour

SOMERSET ARCHAEOLOGICAL AND NATURAL HISTORY SOCIETY (1849), Taunton Castle, Taunton, Somerset, TA1 4AA. Tel: 01823-272429 Fax: 01823-272429
Web: www.sanhs.org
Hon. Secretary, Alex Maxwell-Findlater

SOUTH AMERICAN MISSION SOCIETY (1844), Allen Gardiner Cottage, Pembury Road, Tunbridge Wells, Kent, TN2 3QU. Tel: 01892-538647 Fax: 01892-525797
Web: www.samsgb.org
General Secretary, Revd. Canon J. W. Sutton

SOUTH WALES INSTITUTE OF ENGINEERS, THE, 2nd Floor, Empire House, Mount Stuart Square, Cardiff, CF10 5FN. Tel: 029-2048 1726 Fax: 029-2045 1953
Web: www.swie.org.uk
Hon. Secretary, T. H. Rhodes

SPEAKERS CLUBS, ASSOCIATION OF (1971), Beanlands Chase, 20 Rivermead Drive, Garstang, Preston, Lancashire, PR3 1JJ. Tel: 01995-602560 Fax: 01995-602560,
www.the-asc.org.uk
National Secretary, Mrs D. M. Dickinson

SPORT AND THE ARTS, FOUNDATION FOR (1991), PO Box 20, Liverpool, L13 1HB. Tel: 0151-259 5505
Fax: 0151-230 0664
Secretary, G. Endicott, OBE

SPORT HORSE BREEDING OF GREAT BRITAIN (1886), 96 High Street, Edenbridge, Kent, TN8 5AR.
Tel: 01732-866277 Fax: 01732-867464
Web: www.sporthorsegb.co.uk
General Secretary, Mrs K. P. Hall

SPORTS MEDICINE, INSTITUTE OF (1965), Department of Surgery, Royal Free and University College Medical School, 67/73 Riding House Street, London, W1W 7 EJ.
Tel: 020-7813 2832 Fax: 020-7813 2832
Hon. Secretary, Dr W. T. Orton

SPURGEON'S CHILD CARE (1867), 74 Wellingborough Road, Rushden, Northants, NN10 9TY. Tel: 01933-412412
Fax: 01933-412010 Web: www.spurgeonschildcare.org
Chief Executive, D. C. Culwick

SSAFA FORCES HELP (1885), 19 Queen Elizabeth Street, London, SE1 2LP. Tel: 020-7403 8783 Fax: 020-7403 8815
Web: www.ssafa.org.uk
Controller, Maj.-Gen. P. Sheppard, CB, CBE

ST ALBANS AND HERTFORDSHIRE ARCHITECTURAL AND ARCHAEOLOGICAL SOCIETY (1845), 24 Rose Walk, St Albans, Herts, AL4 9AF. Tel: 01727-853204
Hon. Secretary, B. E. Moody

ST DEINIOL'S RESIDENTIAL LIBRARY (1894), Hawarden, Deeside, Flintshire, CH5 3DF. Tel: 01244-532350
Fax: 01244-520643 Web: www.stdeiniolschester.ac.uk.
Warden and Chief Librarian, Revd P. B. Francis

ST DUNSTAN'S (AN INDEPENDENT FUTURE FOR BLIND EX-SERVICE MEN AND WOMEN) (1915), 2–14 Harcourt Street, London, W1H 4HD. Tel: 020-7723 5021
Fax: 020-7262 6199 Web: www.st-dunstans.org.uk
Chief Executive, Robert Leader

ST JOHN AMBULANCE, 27 St John's Lane, London, EC1M 4BU. Tel: 020-7324 4000 Fax: 020-7324 4001
Web: www.sja.org.uk
Chief Executive, Roger Holmes

STEWART SOCIETY, THE (1899), 53 George Street, Edinburgh, EH2 2HT. Tel: 0131-220 4512 Fax: 0131-220 4512
Web: www.stewartsociety.org
Secretary, Mrs C. Larkins, MVO

STOKE-ON-TRENT, MUSEUM ARCHAEOLOGICAL
SOCIETY, CITY OF (1959), The Potteries Museum and Art
Gallery, Hanley, Stoke-on-Trent, ST1 3DW. Tel: 01782-232323
Web: www.stoke.gov.uk/museums/pmag/
archaeology/archsoc.htm
Chairman, E. E. Royle, MBE

STRATEGIC PLANNING SOCIETY, THE (1967),
Lafone House, The Leathermarket, London, SE1 3ER.
Tel: 020-7636 7737 Fax: 020-7323 1692
Web: www.sps.org.uk
General Manager, Annette Quinn

STRUCTURAL ENGINEERS, INSTITUTION OF (1908),
11 Upper Belgrave Street, London, SW1X 8BH.
Tel: 020-7235 4535 Fax: 020-7235 4294
Web: www.istructe.org.uk
Chief Executive, Dr K. J. Eaton

STUDENTS, NATIONAL UNION OF (1922), Nelson
Mandela House, 461 Holloway Road, London, N7 6LJ.
Tel: 020-7272 8900 Fax: 020-7263 5713
Web: www.nusonline.co.uk

SUFFOLK HORSE SOCIETY (1877), The Market Hill,
Woodbridge, Suffolk, IP12 4LU. Tel: 01394-380643
Fax: 01394-610058 Web: www.suffolkhorsesociety.org.uk
Secretary, Mrs A. V. Hillier

SUFFOLK INSTITUTE OF ARCHAEOLOGY AND
HISTORY (1848), Roots, Church Lane, Playford, Ipswich,
IP6 9DS. Web: www.suffolkarch.org.uk
Hon. Secretary, B. J. Seward

SUNDERLAND ANTIQUARIAN SOCIETY (1900),
c/o Simonburn, 7 Crow Lane, Mid Herrington, Sunderland,
SR3 3TE. Tel: 0191-522 0517
President, D. W. Smith

SURVIVAL INTERNATIONAL (1969), 6 Charterhouse
Buildings, London, EC1M 7ET. Tel: 020-7687 8700
Fax: 020-7687 8701 Web: www.survival-international.org
Director, S. Corry

SUSSEX ARCHAEOLOGICAL SOCIETY (1846), Bull House,
92 High Street, Lewes, E. Sussex, BN7 1XH.
Tel: 01273-486260 Fax: 01273-486990
Web: www.sussexpast.co.uk
Chief Executive, J. Manley

SUZY LAMPLUGH TRUST (1986), 14 East Sheen Avenue,
London, SW14 8AS. Tel: 020-8392 1839 Fax: 020-8392 1830
Web: www.suzylamplugh.org
Hon. Trust Director, Diana Lamplugh, OBE

SWEDENBORG SOCIETY (1810), 20/21 Bloomsbury Way,
London, WC1A 2TH. Tel: 020-7405 7986
Fax: 020-7831 5848 Web: www.swedenborg.org.uk
Secretary, Richard Lines

TEACHERS OF MATHEMATICS, ASSOCIATION OF (1952),
7 Shaftesbury Street, Derby, DE23 8YB. Tel: 01332-346599
Fax: 01332-204357 Web: www.atm.org.uk
Hon. Secretary, S. Welford

TEACHERS, COLLEGE OF (1849), Institute of Education, 57
Gordon Square, London, WC1H 0NU. Tel: 020-7947 9536
Fax: 020-7947 9536 Web: www.collegeofteachers.ac.uk.
Chief Executive Officer, R. Page

TELECOMMUNICATIONS USERS' ASSOCIATION (1965),
Woodgate Studios, 2–8 Games Road, Cockfosters, Barnet,
Herts, EN4 9HN. Tel: 020-8449 8844 Fax: 020-8447 4901
Web: www.tua.co.uk
Executive Chairman, W. E. Mieran

TERRENCE HIGGINS TRUST (1982), 52–54 Grays Inn Road,
London, WC1X 8JU. Tel: 020-7831 0330
Fax: 020-7242 0121 Web: www.tht.org.uk

TEXTILE INSTITUTE (1925), 1st Floor, St James's Building,
Oxford Street, Manchester, M1 6FQ. Tel: 0161-237 1188
Fax: 0161-236 1991 Web: www.texi.org
Membership Director, Steven Kirkwood

THEATRES TRUST (1976), 22 Charing Cross Road, London,
WC2H 0QL. Tel: 020-7836 8591 Fax: 020-7836 3302
Web: www.theatrestrust.org.uk
Director, P. Longman

THORESBY SOCIETY (1889), Claremont, 23 Clarendon
Road, Leeds, LS2 9NZ. Tel: 0113-245 7910
Web: www.thoresby.org.uk
Hon. Secretary, Jim Morgan

TIN TECHNOLOGY LTD, Kingston Lane, Uxbridge,
Middx, UB8 3PJ. Tel: 01895-272406 Fax: 01895-251841
Web: www.tintechnology.com
Director, D. Bishop

TOC H (1915), 1 Forest Close, Wendover, Aylesbury, Buck
HP22 6BT. Tel: 01296-623911 Fax: 01296-696137
Web: www.toch.org.uk
Director, Revd G. Smith

TOWNSWOMEN'S GUILDS, CHAMBER OF COMMERCE
HOUSE, 75 Harborne Road, Birmingham, B15 3DA.
Tel: 0121-456 3435 Fax: 0121-452 1890
Web: www.townswomen.org.uk
National Secretary, Mrs D. Calvert

TRADE MARK ATTORNEYS, INSTITUTE OF (1934),
Canterbury House, 2–6 Sydenham Road, Croydon, CR0 9XE.
Tel: 020-8686 2052 Fax: 020-8680 5723
Web: www.itma.org.uk
Secretary, Mrs M. J. Tyler

TRADING STANDARDS INSTITUTE (1881), 3–5 Hadleigh Business Centre, 351 London Road, Hadleigh, Essex, SS7 2BT. Tel: 0870-872 9000 Fax: 0870-872 9025 Web: www.tradingstandards.gov.uk. *Chief Executive,* Ron Gainsford

TRANSLATION AND INTERPRETING, INSTITUTE OF (1986), Fortuna House, South Fifth Street, Milton Keynes, MK9 2EU. Tel: 01908-325250 Fax: 01908-325259 Web: www.iti.org.uk *Chief Executive,* A. Wheatley

TREE COUNCIL, THE, (1974), 51 Catherine Place, London, SW1E 6DY. Tel: 020-7828 9928 Fax: 020-7828 9060 Web: www.treecouncil.org.uk *Director-General,* Pauline Buchanan Black

TREE FOUNDATION, INTERNATIONAL (1924), Sandy Lane, Crawley Down, W. Sussex, RH10 4HS. Tel: 01342-712536 Fax: 01342-718282 Web: www.internationaltreefoundation.org *Chief Executive,* Kay Saxton

TURNER SOCIETY (1975), BCM Box Turner, London,, WC1N 3XX. Web: www.turnersociety.org.uk *Chairman,* Eric Shanes

UK YOUTH (1911), 2nd Floor, Kirby House, 20–24 Kirby Street, London, EC1N 8TS. Tel: 020-7242 4045 Fax: 020-7242 4125 Web: www.ukyouth.org.uk *Chief Executive,* J. Bateman

UNITED GRAND LODGE OF ENGLAND (1717), Freemasons' Hall, Great Queen Street, London, WC2B 5AZ. Tel: 020-7831 9811 Fax: 020-7831 6021 Web: www.grandlodge-england.org *Grand Master,* HRH The Duke of Kent, KG, GCMG, GCVO

UNITED NATIONS ASSOCIATION OF GREAT BRITAIN AND NORTHERN IRELAND (1945), 3 Whitehall Court, London, SW1A 2EL. Tel: 020-7930 2931 Fax: 020-7930 5893 Web: www.una-uk.org *Director,* M. C. Harper

UNITED REFORMED CHURCH HISTORY SOCIETY (1972), Westminster College, Madingley Road, Cambridge, CB3 0AA. Tel: 01223-741300 *Hon. Secretary,* Revd E. J. Brown

UNIVERSITIES UK, Woburn House, 20 Tavistock Square, London, WC1H 9HQ. Tel: 020-7419 4111 Web: www.universitiesuk.ac.uk' *Chief Executive,* Baroness Warwick

USPG (1701), 157 Waterloo Road, London, SE1 8XA. Tel: 020-7928 8681 Fax: 020-7928 2371 Web: www.uspg.org.uk *Secretary,* Rt. Revd M. Rumalshah

VEGAN SOCIETY, THE (1944), Donald Watson House, 7 Battle Road, St Leonards-on-Sea, E. Sussex, TN37 7AA. Tel: 0845-458 8244 Fax: 01424-717064 Web: www.vegansociety.com *Chief Executive,* Rick Savage

VEGETARIAN SOCIETY OF THE UNITED KINGDOM LTD (1847), Parkdale, Dunham Road, Altrincham, Cheshire, WA14 4QG. Tel: 0161-925 2000 Fax: 0161-926 9182 Web: www.vegsoc.org *Chief Executive,* Ms T. Fox

VERNACULAR ARCHITECTURE GROUP, THE (1952), 'Ashley', Willows Green, Chelmsford, Essex, CM3 1QD. Tel: 01245-361408 Web: www.vag.org.uk *Hon. Secretary,* Mrs B. A. Watkin

VETERINARY ASSOCIATION, BRITISH (1883), 7 Mansfield Street, London, W1G 9NQ. Tel: 020-7636 6541 Fax: 020-7436 2970 Web: www.bva.co.uk

VICTIM SUPPORT (NATIONAL ASSOCIATION OF VICTIMS SUPPORT SCHEMES) (1979), National Office, Cranmer House, 39 Brixton Road, London, SW9 6DZ. Tel: 020-7735 9166 Victim Support Line: 0845-3030 900 Fax: 020-7582 5712 Web: www.victimsupport.org *Chief Executive,* Dame Helen Reeves, DBE

VICTIM SUPPORT SCOTLAND (1985), 15–23 Hardwell Close, Edinburgh, EH8 9RX. Tel: 0131-668 4486 Fax: 0131-662 5400 Web: www.victimsupportsco.org *Chief Executive,* D. McKenna

VICTORIA CROSS AND GEORGE CROSS ASSOCIATION (1956), Horse Guards, Whitehall, London, SW1A 2AX. Tel: 020-7930 3506 Fax: 020-7930 4303 *Secretary,* Mrs D. Grahame, MVO

VICTORIAN SOCIETY, THE (1958), 1 Priory Gardens, Bedford Park, London, W4 1TT. Tel: 020-8994 1019 Fax: 020-8747 5899 Web: www.victorian-society.org.uk *Director,* Dr Ian Dungavell

VIKING SOCIETY FOR NORTHERN RESEARCH (1892), Department of Scandinavian Studies, University College, Gower Street, London, WC1E 6BT. Tel: 020-7679 7176 Fax: 020-7679 7750 *Hon. Secretaries,* Prof. M. P. Barnes; Prof. J. Jesh

VISITSCOTLAND (1969), 23 Ravelston Terrace, Edinburgh, EH4 3TP. Tel: 0131-332 2433. Fax: 0131-332 4441 Web: www.visitscotland.com and www.scotexchange.net *Chief Executive,* Philip Riddle

VOLUNTARY ORGANISATIONS, SCOTTISH COUNCIL FOR, Mansfield Traquair Centre, 15 Mansfield Place, Edinburgh, EH3 6BB. Tel: 0131-556 3882 Fax: 0131-556 0279 Web: www.scvo.org.uk *Chief Executive,* M. Sime

VSO (VOLUNTARY SERVICE OVERSEAS) (1958),
317 Putney Bridge Road, London, SW15 2PN.
Tel: 020-8780 7200 Fax: 020-8780 7300
Web: www.vso.org.uk
Chief Executive, M. Goldring

WALES TOURIST BOARD (1969), Brunel House, 2 Fitzalan
Road, Cardiff, CF24 0UY. Tel: 029-2049 9909
Fax: 029-2048 5031 Web: www.visitwales.com
Chief Executive, Jonathan Jones

WASTES MANAGEMENT, CHARTERED INSTITUTION OF
(1898), 9 Saxon Court, St Peter's Gardens, Northampton,
NN1 1SX. Tel: 01604-620426 Fax: 01604-621339
Web: www.iwm.co.uk
Chief Executive, M. J. Philpott

WATER AND ENVIRONMENTAL MANAGEMENT,
CHARTERED INSTITUTION OF (1895), 15 John Street,
London, WC1N 2EB. Tel: 020-7831 3110
Fax: 020-7405 4967 Web: www.ciwem.org.uk
Executive Director, N. Reeves

WELLBEING - HEALTH RESEARCH CHARITY FOR
WOMEN AND BABIES (1965), 27 Sussex Place, Regent's
Park, London, NW1 4SP. Tel: 020-7772 6400
Fax: 020-7724 7725 Web: www.wellbeing.org.uk
Director, Mrs J. Arnell

WELLCOME TRUST, THE (1936), The Wellcome Building,
183 Euston Road, London, NW1 2BE. Tel: 020-7611 8888
Fax: 020-7611 8545 Web: www.wellcome.ac.uk
Director, Dr Mike Dexter

WES WORLD-WIDE EDUCATION SERVICE LTD, Canada
House, 272 Field End Road, Eastcote, Ruislip, Middx,
HA4 9NA. Tel: 020-8582 0317 Fax: 020-8429 4838
Web: www.wesworldwide.com
Director, Mrs T. Mulder-Reynolds

WESLEY HISTORICAL SOCIETY (1893), 34 Spiceland Road,
Northfield, Birmingham, B31 1NJ.
Tel: 0121-475 4914
General Secretary, Dr E. D. Graham

WEST LONDON MISSION (1893), 19 Thayer Street,
London, W1U 2QJ. Tel: 020-7935 6179
Fax: 020-7487 3965
Web: www.wlm.org.uk
Superintendent, Revd Geoff Cornell

WESTMINSTER FOUNDATION FOR DEMOCRACY
(1992), 2nd Floor, 125 Pall Mall, London, SW1Y 5EA.
Tel: 020-7930 0408 Fax: 020-7930 0449
Web: www.wfd.org
Chief Executive, David French

WILDFOWL AND WETLANDS TRUST, THE (1946),
Slimbridge, Glos, GL2 7BT. Tel: 01453-891900
Fax: 01453-890827 Web: www.wwt.org.uk
Managing Director, A. E. Richardson

WILDLIFE TRUST, SCOTTISH (1964), Cramond House,
Cramond Glebe Road, Edinburgh, EH4 6NS
Tel: 0131-312 7765 Fax: 0131-312 8705
Web: www.swt.org.uk
Chief Executive, S. Sankey

WILLIAM MORRIS SOCIETY AND KELMSCOTT
FELLOWSHIP, (1955), Kelmscott House, 26 Upper Mall,
London, W6 9TA. Tel: 020-8741 3735 Fax: 020-8748 5207
Web: www.morrissociety.org
Hon. Secretary, P. Faulkner

WILTSHIRE ARCHAEOLOGICAL AND NATURAL
HISTORY SOCIETY (1853), Wiltshire Heritage Museum,
41 Long Street, Devizes, Wilts, SN10 1NS.
Tel: 01380-727369 Fax: 01380-722150
Web: www.wiltshireheritage.org.uk
Curator, Dr P. H. Robinson

WINE AND SPIRIT ASSOCIATION, THE (1824), Five Kings
House, 1 Queen Street Place, London, EC4R 1XX.
Tel: 020-7248 5377 Fax: 020-7489 0322
Web: www.wsa.org.uk
Director, Q. Rappoport

WINE, INSTITUTE OF MASTERS OF (1955), Five Kings
House, 1 Queen Street Place, London, EC4R 1QS.
Tel: 020-7236 4426 Fax: 020-7213 0499
www.masters-of-wine.org
Executive Director, Jane Carr

WOMEN ARTISTS, THE SOCIETY OF (1855), 1 Knapp
Cottages, Wyke, Gillingham, Dorset, SP8 4NQ.
Tel: 01747-825718 Fax: 1747-826835
www.society-women-artists.org.uk
Executive Secretary, Mrs P. Henderson

WOMEN GRADUATES, BRITISH FEDERATION OF (1907),
4 Mandeville Courtyard, 142 Battersea Park Road, London,
SW11 4NB. Tel: 020-7498 8037 Fax: 020-7498 5213
Web: www.bfwg.org.uk
Secretary, Mrs A. B. Stein

WOMEN OF GREAT BRITAIN, NATIONAL COUNCIL OF,
36 Danbury Street, London, N1 8JU. Tel: 020-7354 2395
Fax: 020-7354 9214 Web: www.ncwgb.org
President, Mrs Hilary Sillars

WOMEN'S ENGINEERING SOCIETY (1919), 22 Old Queen
Street, London, SW1H 9HW. Tel: 020-7233 1974
Web: www.wes.org.uk
Secretary, Mrs C. MacGillivray

WOMEN'S INSTITUTES OF NORTHERN IRELAND,
FEDERATION OF (1932), 209–211 Upper Lisburn Road,
Belfast, BT10 0LL. Tel: 028-9030 1506/9060-1781
Fax: 020-9043 1127
General Secretary, Mrs I. A. Sproule

WOMEN'S INSTITUTES, NATIONAL FEDERATION OF,
104 New Kings Road, London, SW6 4LY. Tel: 020-7371 9300
Fax: 020-7736 3652 Web: www.womens-insitute.co.uk
General Secretary, Mrs J. Osborne

WOMEN'S ROYAL NAVAL SERVICE BENEVOLENT TRUST
(1941), 311 Twyford Avenue, Portsmouth, PO2 8PE. Tel:
023-9265 5301 Fax: 023-9267 9040
General Secretary, Mrs S. Tarabella

WOMEN'S ROYAL VOLUNTARY SERVICE (1938), Milton
Hill House, Milton Hill, Abingdon, Oxfordshire, OX13 6AD.
Tel: 01235-442900 Fax: 01235-861166
Web: www.wrvs.org.uk
Chief Executive, M. Lever

WOMEN'S RURAL INSTITUTES, SCOTTISH (1917),
42 Heriot Row, Edinburgh, EH3 6ES. Tel: 0131-225 1724
Fax: 0131-225 8129 Web: wwww.swri.org.uk
General Secretary, Mrs A. Peacock

THE WOODLAND TRUST (1972), Autumn Park, Dysart
Road, Grantham, Lincs, NG31 6LL. Tel: 01476-581111
Fax: 01476-590808 Web: www.woodland-trust.org.uk
Chief Executive, Mike Townsend

WOOD PRESERVING AND DAMP-PROOFING
ASSOCIATION, BRITISH (1930), 1 Gleneagles House,
Vernon Gate, Derby, DE1 1UP. Tel: 01332-225100
Fax: 01332-225101 Web: www.bwpda.co.uk
Director, Dr C. R. Coggins

WORCESTERSHIRE ARCHAEOLOGICAL SOCIETY (1854),
26 Albert Park Road, Malvern, WR14 1HN.
Tel: 01299-250416 Fax: 01299-251890
Web: www.worcestershire.gov.uk/museum
Hon. Secretary, Dr J. W. Dunleavey

WORLD MISSION, COUNCIL FOR (1977), Ipalo House,
32–34 Great Peter Street, London, SW1P 2DB.
Tel: 020-7222 4214 Fax: 020-7233 1747
Web: www.cwmission.org.uk
General Secretary, Revd Dr D. van der Water

YORKSHIRE AGRICULTURAL SOCIETY (1837), Great
Yorkshire Showground, Harrogate, N. Yorks, HG2 8PW.
Tel: 01423-541000 Fax: 01423-541414
Web: www.yas.co.uk
Chief Executive, Nigel Pulling

YORKSHIRE ARCHAEOLOGICAL SOCIETY (1863),
Claremont, 23 Clarendon Road, Leeds, LS2 9NZ.
Tel: 0113-245 7910 Fax: 0113-244 1979
Web: www.yas.org.uk
Hon. Secretary, Ms J. Heron

YORKSHIRE SOCIETY, THE (1812), 35 Waldorf Heights,
Camberley, Surrey. Tel: 01276-516484
Secretary, G. G. Prince, FCIS, TD

YOUTH HOSTELS ASSOCIATION (ENGLAND & WALES)
(1930), Trevelyan House, Dimple Road, Matlock, DE4 3YH.
Tel: 01629-592600 Fax: 01629-592702
Web: www.yha.org.uk
Chief Executive, R. Clarke

YOUTH HOSTELS ASSOCIATION, SCOTTISH, (1931),
7 Glebe Crescent, Stirling, FK8 2JA. Tel: 01786-891400
Fax: 01786-891333 Web: www.syha.org.uk
Chief Executive, Lorna MacDonald

YOUTHACTION NORTHERN IRELAND (1944), Hampton,
Glenmachan Park, Belfast, BT4 2PJ. Tel: 028-9076 0067
Fax: 028-9076 8799 Web: www.youthaction.org
Director, Ms J. Trimble

YWCA ENGLAND & WALES (1855), Clarendon House,
52 Cornmarket Street, Oxford, OX1 3EJ. Tel: 01865-304200
Fax: 01865-204805 Web: www.ywca-gb.org.uk
Chief Executive, Ms G. Tishler

ZOOLOGICAL SOCIETY OF LONDON (1826), Regent's
Park, London, NW1 4RY. Tel: 020-7722 3333
Fax: 020-7586 5743 Web: www.zsl.org
Director-General, Dr Michael Dixon

ZOOLOGICAL SOCIETY, NORTH OF ENGLAND (1934),
Chester Zoo, Upton by Chester, Chester, CH2 1LH.
Tel: 01244-380280 Fax: 01244-371273
Web: www.chesterzoo.co.uk
Zoo Director, Prof. G. McGregor Reid

THE WORLD

WORLD GEOGRAPHICAL STATISTICS

THE EARTH

The shape of the Earth is that of an oblate spheroid or solid of revolution whose meridian sections are ellipses, whilst the sections at right angles are circles.

DIMENSIONS
Equatorial diameter = 12,756.27 km (7,926.38 miles)
Polar diameter = 12,713.50 km (7,899.80 miles)
Equatorial circumference = 40,075.01 km (24,901.46 miles)
Polar circumference = 40,007.86 km (24,859.73 miles)
Mass = 5,974,000,000,000,000,000,000 tonnes
(5.879×10^{21} tons)

The equatorial circumference is divided into 360 degrees of longitude, which is measured in degrees, minutes and seconds east or west of the Greenwich meridian (0°) to 180°, the meridian 180° E. coinciding with 180° W. This dateline was internationally ratified on 13 October 1884.

Distance north and south of the Equator is measured in degrees, minutes and seconds of latitude. The Equator is 0°, the North Pole is 90° N. and the South Pole is 90° S. The Tropics lie at 23° 27' N. (Tropic of Cancer) and 23° 27' S. (Tropic of Capricorn). The Arctic Circle lies at 66° 33' N. and the Antarctic Circle at 66° 33' S. (NB The Tropics and the Arctic and Antarctic circles are affected by the slow decrease in obliquity of the ecliptic, of about 0.47 arcseconds per year. The effect of this is that the Arctic and Antarctic circles are currently moving towards their respective poles by about 14 metres per annum, while the Tropics move towards the Equator by the same amount.

AREA, ETC.
The surface area of the Earth is 510,069,120 km² (196,938,800 miles²), of which the water area is 70.92 per cent and the land area is 29.08 per cent.

The radial velocity on the Earth's surface at the Equator is 1,669.79 km per hour (1,037.56 m.p.h.). The Earth's mean velocity in its orbit around the Sun is 107,229 km per hour (66,629 m.p.h.). The Earth's mean distance from the Sun is 149,597,870 km (92,955,807 miles).

OCEANS

AREA
	km²	miles²
Pacific	155,557,000	59,270,000
Atlantic	76,762,000	29,638,000
Indian	68,556,000	26,467,000
Southern	20,327,000	7,848,300
Arctic	14,056,000	5,427,000

The Equator divides the Pacific into the North and South Pacific and the Atlantic into the North and South Atlantic. In 2000 the International Hydrographic Organisation approved the description of the 20,327,000 km²; (7,848,300 miles²) of circum-Antarctic waters up to 60° S. as the Southern Ocean – a seventh ocean.

GREATEST OCEAN DEPTHS
Greatest depth	Location	metres	feet
Mariana Trench*	Pacific	10,924	35,840
Puerto Rico Trench	Atlantic	8,605	28,232
South Sandwich Trench	Southern	7,235	23,737
Java (Sunda) Trench	Indian	7,125	23,376
Molloy Deep	Arctic	5,680	18,400

*A depth here of 11,034 metres/32,300 feet by the Soviet Vityaz is not internationally accepted.

SEAS

AREA
	km²	miles²
South China	2,974,600	1,148,500
Caribbean	2,515,900	971,400
Mediterranean	2,509,900	969,100
Bering	2,261,000	873,000
Gulf of Mexico	1,507,600	582,100
Okhotsk	1,392,000	537,500
Japan	1,012,900	391,100
Hudson Bay	730,100	281,900
East China	664,600	256,600
Andaman	564,880	218,100
Black Sea	507,900	196,100
Red Sea	453,000	174,900
North Sea	427,100	164,900
Baltic Sea	382,000	147,500
Yellow Sea	294,000	113,500
Persian/Arabian Gulf	230,000	88,800

GREATEST DEPTHS OF SEAS LISTED ABOVE
	Maximum depth Metres	feet
Caribbean	8,605	28,232
East China (Ryu Kyu Trench)	7,507	24,629
South China	7,258	23,812
Mediterranean (Ionian Basin)	5,150	16,896
Andaman	4,267	14,000
Bering	3,936	12,913
Gulf of Mexico	3,504	11,496
Okhotsk	3,365	11,040
Japan	3,053	10,016
Red Sea	2,266	7,434
Black Sea	2,212	7,257
North Sea	439	1,440
Hudson Bay	111	364
Baltic Sea	90	295
Persian Gulf	73	240
Yellow Sea	58	190

THE CONTINENTS

There are six geographic continents, although America is often divided politically into North and Central America, and South America, so making seven.

AFRICA is surrounded by sea except for the narrow isthmus of Suez in the north-east, through which was cut the Suez Canal (1869). Its extreme longitudes are 17° 20' W. at Cape Verde, Senegal, and 51° 24' E. at Raas Xaafunn, Somalia. The extreme latitudes are 37° 20' N. at Cape Blanc, Tunisia, and 34° 50' S. at Cape Agulhas, South Africa, about 4,400 miles apart. The Equator passes through the middle of the continent.

NORTH AMERICA, including Mexico, is surrounded by ocean except in the south, where the isthmian states of CENTRAL AMERICA link North America with South America. Its extreme longitudes are 168° 5′ W. at Cape Prince of Wales, Alaska, and 55° 40′ W. at Cape Charles, Newfoundland. The extreme continental latitudes are the tip of the Boothia peninsula, NW Territories, Canada (71° 51′ N.) and 14° 22′ N. in southern Mexico near La Victoria, Guatemala.

SOUTH AMERICA lies mostly in the southern hemisphere; the Equator passing through the north of the continent. It is surrounded by ocean except where it is joined to Central America in the north by the narrow isthmus through which was cut the Panama Canal (1914). Its extreme longitudes are 34° 47′ W. at Cape Branco in Brazil and 81° 20′ W. at Punta Pariña, Peru. The extreme continental latitudes are 12° 25′ N. at Punta Gallinas, Colombia, and 53° 54′ S. at the southernmost tip of Peninsula de Brunswick, Chile. Cape Horn, on Cape Island, Chile, lies in 55° 59′ S.

ANTARCTICA lies almost entirely within the Antarctic Circle (66° 33′ S.) and is the largest of the world's glaciated areas. Ninety-eight per cent of the continent is permanently ice-covered. The ice amounts to some 7.2 million cubic miles (30 million km³) and represents more than 70 per cent of the world's fresh water. The environment is too hostile for unsupported human habitation.

ASIA is the largest continent and occupies 29.6 per cent of the world's land surface. The extreme longitudes are 26° 05′ E. at Baba Buran, Turkey and 169° 40′ W. at Mys Dezhneva (East Cape), Russia, a distance of about 6,000 miles. Its extreme northern latitude is 77° 45′ N. at Mys Chelyuskin, Russia, and it extends over 5,000 miles south to Tanjong Piai, Malaysia.

AUSTRALIA is the smallest of the continents and lies in the southern hemisphere. It is entirely surrounded by ocean. Its extreme longitudes are 113° 11′ E. at Steep Point and 153° 11′ E. at Cape Byron. The extreme latitudes are 10° 42′ S. at Cape York and 39° S. at South East Point, Tasmania. Australia, together with New Zealand (Australasia), Papua New Guinea and the Pacific Islands, comprises Oceania.

EUROPE, including European Russia, is the smallest continent in the northern hemisphere. Its extreme latitudes are 71° 11′ N. at Nord Kapp in Norway, and 36° 23′ N. at Ákra Taínaron (Matapás) in southern Greece, a distance of about 2,400 miles. Its breadth from Cabo Carvoeiro in Portugal (9° 34′ W.) in the west to the Kara River, north of the Urals (66° 30′ E.) in the east is about 3,300 miles. The division between Europe and Asia is generally regarded as the watershed of the Ural Mountains; down the Ural river to Guryev, Kazakhstan; across the Caspian Sea to Apsheronskiy Poluostrov, near Baku; along the watershed of the Caucasus Mountains to Anapa and thence across the Black Sea to the Bosporus in Turkey; across the Sea of Marmara to Çanakkale Boğzi (Dardanelles).

	Area	
	km²	miles²
Asia	43,998,000	16,988,000
*America	41,918,000	16,185,000
Africa	29,800,000	11,506,000
Antarctica	13,209,000	5,100,000
†Europe	9,699,000	3,745,000
Australia	7,618,493	2,941,526

*North and Central America has an area of 24,255,000 km2 (9,365,000 miles²)

†Includes 5,571,000 km² (2,151,000 miles²) of former USSR territory, including the Baltic states, Belarus, Moldova, Ukraine and the part of Russia west of the Ural Mountains and Kazakhstan west of the Ural river. European Turkey (24,378 km²/9,412 miles²) comprises territory to the west and north of the Bosporus and the Dardanelles

GLACIATED AREAS

It is estimated that 15,915,000 km² (6,145,000 miles²) or 10.73 per cent of the world's land surface is permanently covered with ice.

	Area	
	km²	miles²
South Polar regions	13,830,000	5,340,000
North Polar regions (incl. Greenland or Kalaallit Nunaat)	1,965,000	758,500
Alaska-Canada	58,800	22,700
Asia	37,800	14,600
South America	11,900	4,600
Europe	10,700	4,128
New Zealand	1,015	391
Africa	238	92

The largest glacier is the 515 km/320 mile-long Lambert-Fisher Ice Passage, Mac Robertson Land, Eastern Antarctica.

PENINSULAS

	Area	
	km²	miles²
Arabian	3,250,000	1,250,000
Southern Indian	2,072,000	800,000
Alaskan	1,500,000	580,000
Labradorian	1,300,000	500,000
Scandinavian	800,300	309,000
Iberian	584,000	225,500

LARGEST ISLANDS

Island, and Ocean	*Area*	
	km²	miles²
Greenland (Kalaallit Nunaat), Arctic	2,175,500	840,000
New Guinea, Pacific	792,500	306,000
Borneo, Pacific	725,450	280,100
Madagascar, Indian	587,041	226,674
Baffin Island, Arctic	507,451	195,928
Sumatra, Indian	427,350	165,000
Honshu, Pacific	227,413	87,805
*Great Britain, Atlantic	218,077	84,200
Victoria Island, Arctic	217,292	83,897
Ellesmere Island, Arctic	196,236	75,767
Sulawesi (Celebes), Indian	189,036	72,987
South Island, NZ, Pacific	151,213	58,384

Java (Jawa), Indian	126,650	48,900
North Island, NZ, Pacific	114,487	44,204
Cuba, Atlantic	110,862	42,804
Newfoundland, Atlantic	108,855	42,030
Luzon, Pacific	105,360	40,680
Iceland, Atlantic	102,820	39,700
Mindanao, Pacific	95,247	36,775
Ireland, Atlantic	82,462	31,839

*Mainland only

LARGEST DESERTS

	Area (approx) km^2	miles^2
The Sahara, N. Africa	9,000,000	3,500,000
The Gobi, Mongolia/China	1,300,000	500,000
Australian Desert (Great Sandy, Gibson, Simpson and Great Victoria)	1,120,000	460,000
Arabian Desert	1,000,000	385,000
Kalahari Desert, Botswana/ Namibia/S. Africa	570,000	220,000
Taklimakan Shamo, Mongolia/China	320,000	125,000
*Kara Kum, Turkmenistan	310,000	120,000
Thar Desert, India/Pakistan	260,000	100,000
Somali Desert, Somalia	260,000	100,000
Atacama Desert, Chile	180,000	70,000
Sonoran Desert, USA/Mexico	180,000	70,000
Namib, Namibia	135,000	52,000
Dasht-e Lut, Iran	52,000	20,000
Mojave Desert, USA	38,850	15,000

*Together with the Kyzyl Kum (100,000 miles^2) known as the Turkestan Desert

Antarctica is described as a Polar Desert since precipitation is less than 5 cm per annum.

DEEPEST DEPRESSIONS

	Maximum depth below sea level metres	feet
Dead Sea, Jordan/Israel	408	1,338
Lake Assal, Djibouti	156	511
Turfan Depression, Sinkiang, China	153	505
Qattara Depression, Egypt	132	436
Mangyshlak peninsula, Kazakhstan	131	433
Danakil Depression, Ethiopia	116	383
Death Valley, California, USA	86	282
Salton Sink, California, USA	71	235
W. of Ustyurt plateau, Kazakhstan	70	230
Prikaspiyskaya Nizmennost', Russia/Kazakhstan	67	220
Lake Sarykamysh, Uzbekistan/ Turkmenistan	45	148
El Faiyûm, Egypt	44	147
Península Valdés, Chubut, Argentina	40	131
Lake Eyre, South Australia	16	52

The world's largest exposed depression is the Prikaspiyskaya Nizmennost' covering the hinterland of the northern third of the Caspian Sea, which is itself 28 m (92 ft) below sea level.

Western Antarctica and Central Greenland largely comprise crypto-depressions under ice burdens. The Antarctic Bentley subglacial trench has a bedrock 2,538 m (8,326 ft) below sea-level. In Greenland (lat. 73° N., long. 39° W.) the bedrock is 365 m (1,197 ft) below sea-level.

Nearly one quarter of the area of The Netherlands lies marginally below sea-level, an area of more than 10,000^2/3,860 miles^2.

LONGEST MOUNTAIN RANGES

Range, and location	Length km	miles
Cordillera de Los Andes, W. South America	7,200	4,500
Rocky Mountains, W. North America	4,800	3,000
Himalaya-Karakoram-Hindu Kush, S. Central Asia	3,850	2,400
Great Dividing Range, E. Australia	3,620	2,250
Trans-Antarctic Mts, Antarctica	3,540	2,200
Atlantic Coast Range, E. Brazil	3,050	1,900
West Sumatran-Javan Range, Indonesia	2,900	1,800
Aleutian Range, Alaska and NW Pacific	2,650	1,650
Tien Shan, S. Central Asia	2,250	1,400
Central New Guinea Range, Irian Jaya/Papua New Guinea	2,010	1,250

HIGHEST MOUNTAINS

The world's twelve 8,000-metre (26,246 ft) mountains (*with five subsidiary peaks*) are all in the Himalaya-Karakoram-Hindu Kush ranges.

Mountain	Height metres	feet
Mt Everest* (Qomolangma)	8,850	29,035
K2 (Qogir)†	8,611	28,251
Kangchenjunga	8,597	28,208
Lhotse I	*8,510*	*27,923*
Makalu I	8,480	27,824
Lhotse Shar (II)	*8,400*	*27,560*
Dhaulagiri I	8,171	26,810
Manaslu I (Kutang I)	8,156	26,760
Cho Oyu	8,153	26,750
Nanga Parbat (Diamir)	8,125	26,660
Annapurna I	8,078	26,504
Gasherbrum I (Hidden Peak)	8,068	26,470
Broad Peak I	8,046	26,400
Shisham Pangma (Gosainthan)	8,012	26,287
Gasherbrum II	*8,034*	*26,360*
Makalu South-East	*8,010*	*26,280*
Broad Peak Central	*8,000*	*26,246*

*Named after Sir George Everest (1790–1866), Surveyor-General of India 1830–43, in 1863. He pronounced his name Eve-rest

†Formerly named after Col. H. H. Godwin-Austen (1834-1923)

The culminating summits in the other major mountain ranges are:

Mountain, by range or country	Height metres	feet
Pik Pobedy, Tien Shan	7,439	24,406
Cerro Aconcagua, Cordillera de Los Andes	6,960	22,834
Mt McKinley (S. Peak), Alaska Range	6,194	20,320
Kilimanjaro (Kibo), Tanzania	5,894	19,340
Hkakabo Razi, Myanmar	5,881	19,296
El'brus, (W. Peak), Caucasus	5,642	18,510
Citlaltépetl (Orizaba), Sierra Madre Oriental, Mexico	5,655	18,555
Vinson Massif, E. Antarctica	4,897	16,066
Puncak Jaya, Central New Guinea Range	4,884	16,023
Mt Blanc, Alps	4,807	15,771
Klyuchevskaya Sopka, Kamchatka peninsula, Russia	4,750	15,584
Ras Dashan, Ethiopian Highlands	4,620	15,158
Zard Kuh, Zagros Mts, Iran	4,547	14,921
Mt Kirkpatrick, Trans Antarctic	4,527	14,855
Mt Belukha, Altai Mts, Russia/Kazakhstan	4,505	14,783
Mt Elbert, Rocky Mountains	4,400	14,433
Mt Rainier, Cascade Range, N. America	4,392	14,410
Nevado de Colima, Sierra Madre Occidental, Mexico	4,268	14,003
Jebel Toubkal, Atlas Mts, N. Africa	4,165	13,665
Kinabalu, Crocker Range, Borneo	4,101	13,455
Kerinci, West Sumatran-Javan Range, Indonesia	3,800	12,467
Jabal an NabiShu'ayb, N. Tihamat, Yemen	3,760	12,336
Mt Cook (Aorangi), Southern Alps, New Zealand	3,754	12,315
Teotepec, Sierra Madre del Sur, Mexico	3,703	12,149
Thaban Ntlenyana, Drakensberg, South Africa	3,482	11,425
Pico de Bandeira, Atlantic Coast Range	2,890	9,482
Shishaldin, Aleutian Range	2,861	9,387
Kosciusko, Great Dividing Range, Australia	2,228	7,310

HIGHEST ACTIVE VOLCANOES

Volcano (last major eruption), and location	Height metres	feet
Ojos del Salado (1981), Andes, Argentina/Chile	6,880	22,572
Volcán Llullaillaco (1877), Andes, Argentina/Chile	6,723	22,057
Volcán Guallatiri (1960, 1993), Andes, Chile	6,069	19,882
Cotopaxi (1940, 1975), Andes, Ecuador	5,897	19,347
Tupungatito (1986), Andes, Chile	5,640	18,504
Láscar (2000), Andes, Chile	5,591	18,346
Popocatépetl (1999–2003), Mexico	5,465	17,930
Nevado del Ruiz (1845, 1985, 1991), Colombia	5,321	17,457
Sangay (1998, 2002), Andes, Ecuador	5,188	17,021
Irruputuncu (1995), Chile	5,163	16,939
Klyuchevskaya Sopka (2000–3), Kamchatka peninsula, Russia	4,835	15,863
Guagua Pichincha (2001), Andes, Ecuador	4,784	15,696
Puracé (1977), Colombia	4,756	15,601
Wrangell (1907), Alaska, USA	4,316	14,163

Shasta (1786), California, USA	4,316	14,163
Galeras (2000), Colombia	4,275	14,028
Mauna Loa (1984, 1987, 2003), Hawaii Is.	4,170	13,680
Cameroon (2000), Cameroon	4,095	13,435

OTHER NOTABLE VOLCANOES

	Height metres	feet
Erebus (1998, 2001), Ross Island, Antarctica	3,794	12,448
Fuji (1708), Honshu, Japan	3,775	12,388
Santa Maria (2000), Guatemala	3,772	12,375
Semeru (2003), Java, Indonesia	3,675	12,060
Nyiragongo (2002–3), Dem Rep. of Congo	3,474	11,400
Mt Etna (1169, 1669, 1993, 1996–9, 2000-3), Sicily, Italy	3,368	11,053
Raung (2000, 2002), Java, Indonesia	3,322	10,932
Sheveluch (1997, 1999, 2000–1, 2003), Kamchatka, Russia	3,283	10,771
Llaima (1998, 2003), Chile	3,125	10,253
Mt St Helens (1980, 1986, 1991, 1998), Washington State, USA	2,549	8,363
Beerenberg (1985), Jan Mayen Island	2,277	7,470
Pinatubo (1991, 1995, 2002), Luzon, Philippines	1,598	5,249
Hekla (1981, 1991, 2000), Iceland	1,491	4,892
Mt Unzen (1792, 1991, 1996, 2000), Kyushu, Japan	1,360	4,462
Vesuvius (AD 79, 1631, 1944), Italy	1,281	4,203
Kilauea (1996, 1997, 2000–3), Hawaii, USA	1,249	4,009
Soufrière (1902, 1979, 1997), St Vincent	1,178	3,865
Soufrière Hills (1997–2003), Montserrat	914	3,001
Stromboli (1996, 1998, 2000, 2002-3), Lipari Is., Italy	926	3,038
Krakatau (1883, 1995, 1999, 2001), Sunda Strait, Indonesia	813	2,667
Santorini (Thíra) (1628 BC, 1950), Aegean Sea, Greece	564	1,850
Tristan da Cunha (1961), South Atlantic	243	800
Surtsey (1963–7), off Iceland	173	568

LARGEST LAKES

The areas of some of the lakes listed are subject to seasonal variation.

	Area km^2	miles^2	Length km^2	miles^2
Caspian Sea, Iran/ Azerbaijan/Russia/ Turkmenistan/ Kazakhstan	371,000	143,000	1,171	728
*Michigan–Huron, USA/Canada	117,610	45,300	1,010	627
Superior, Canada/USA	82,100	31,700	563	350
Victoria, Uganda/ Tanzania/Kenya	69,500	26,828	362	225
Tanganyika, Dem. Rep. of Congo/ Tanzania/Zambia/ Burundi	32,900	12,665	725	450
Great Bear, Canada	31,328	12,096	309	192
‡Aral Sea, Kazakhstan/ Uzbekistan	30,700	11,850	320	200

Area	km²	Length miles²	km²	miles²
†Baykal (*Baikal*), Russia	30,500	11,776	620	385
Malawi (Nyasa), Tanzania/				
Malawi/Mozambique	28,900	11,150	580	360
Great Slave, Canada	28,570	11,031	480	298
Erie, Canada/USA	25,670	9,910	388	241
Winnipeg, Canada	24,390	9,417	428	266
Ontario, Canada/USA	19,010	7,340	310	193
Balkhash, Kazakhstan	18,427	7,115	605	376
Ladozhskoye (*Ladoga*),				
Russia	17,700	6,835	193	120

*Lakes Michigan and Huron may be regarded as lobes of the same lake. The Michigan lobe has an area of 57,750 km² (22,300 miles²) and the Huron lobe an area of 59,570 km² (23,000 miles²)
†World's deepest lake (1,940 m/6,365 ft)
‡Northern part (Little Aral Sea) dammed off in 1997
The most voluminous lakes are the Caspian Sea (saline) with 78,700 km³ (18, 880 miles³) and Baikal (fresh water) with 23,000 km³ (5,518 miles³).

UNITED KINGDOM, BY COUNTRY

	km²	miles²	km²	miles²
Lough Neagh, Northern Ireland	381.73	147.39	28.90	18.00
Loch Lomond, Scotland	71.12	27.46	36.44	22.64
Windermere, England	14.74	5.69	16.90	10.50
Lake Vyrnwy, Wales (artificial)	4.53	1.75	7.56	4.70
Llyn Tegid (*Bala*), Wales (natural)	4.38	1.69	5.80	3.65

LONGEST RIVERS

River, source and outflow	Length km	miles
Nile (*Bahr-el-Nil*), R. Luvironza, Burundi – E. Mediterranean Sea	6,725	4,180
Amazon (*Amazonas*), Lago Villafro, Peru – S. Atlantic Ocean	6,448	4,007
Yangtze-Kiang (*Chang Jiang*), Kunlun Mts, W. China – Yellow Sea	6,380	3,964
Mississippi-Missouri-Red Rock, Montana – Gulf of Mexico	5,970	3,710
Yenisey-Angara, W. Mongolia – Kara Sea	5,536	3,440
Huang He (*Yellow River*), Bayan Har Shan range, central China – Yellow Sea	5,463	3,395
Ob'-Irtysh, W. Mongolia – Kara Sea	5,410	3,362
Zaïre (*Congo*), R. Lualaba, Dem. Rep. of Congo-Zambia – S. Atlantic Ocean	4,665	2,900
Amur-Argun, R. Argun, Khingan Mts, N. China – Sea of Okhotsk	4,416	2,744
Lena-Kirenga, R. Kirenga, W. of Lake Baykal – Laptev Sea, Arctic Ocean	4,400	2,734
Mekong, Lants'ang, Tibet – South China Sea	4,345	2,700
Mackenzie-Peace, Tatlatui Lake, British Columbia – Beaufort Sea	4,240	2,635
Paraná-Río de la Plata, R. Paranáiba, central Brazil – S. Atlantic Ocean	4,240	2,635
Niger, Loma Mts, Guinea – Gulf of Guinea, E. Atlantic Ocean	4,170	2,590
Murray-Darling, SE Queensland – Lake Alexandrina, S. Australia	3,717	2,310
Volga, Valdai plateau – Caspian Sea	3,685	2,290

OTHER NOTABLE RIVERS

	km	miles
Rio Grande, USA – Mexican border	3,057	1,900
Ganges-Brahmaputra, R. Matsang, SW Tibet – Bay of Bengal	2,900	1,800
Indus, R. Sengge, SW Tibet – N. Arabian Sea	2,897	1,799
Danube (*Donau*), Black Forest, SW Germany – Black Sea	2,856	1,775
Tigris-Euphrates, R. Murat, E. Turkey – Persian Gulf	2,800	1,740
Zambezi, NW Zambia – S. Indian Ocean	2,735	1,700
Irrawaddy, R. Mali Hka, Myanmar – Andaman Sea	2,151	1,337
Don, SE of Novomoskovsk – Sea of Azov	1,969	1,224

BRITISH ISLES

	km	miles
Shannon, Co. Cavan, Rep. of Ireland – Atlantic Ocean	386	240
Severn, Powys, Wales – Bristol Channel	354	220
Thames, Gloucestershire, England – North Sea	346	215
Tay, Perthshire, Scotland – North Sea	188	117
Clyde, Lanarkshire, Scotland – Firth of Clyde	158	98.5
Tweed, Peeblesshire, Scotland – North Sea	155	96.5
Bann (Upper and Lower), Co. Down, N. Ireland – Atlantic Ocean	122	76

GREATEST WATERFALLS – BY HEIGHT

Waterfall, river and location	Total drop metres	feet	Greatest single leap metres	feet
Saltó Angel, Carrao Auyán Tepuí, Venezuela	979	3,212	807	2,648
Tugela, Tugela, Natal, S. Africa (5 leaps)	948	3,110	410	1,350
Utigård, Jostedal Glacier, Norway	800	2,625	600	1,970
Mongefossen, Monge, Norway	774	2,540	–	–
Yosemite, Yosemite Creek, USA	739	2,425	435	1,430
*Østre Mardøla Foss, Mardals, Norway	655	2,149	296	974
*Tyssestrengene, Tysso, Norway	646	2,120	289	948
Cuquenán, Arabopó, Venezuela	610	2,000	–	–
Sutherland, Arthur, NZ	580	1,904	248	815

*Volume much affected by hydroelectric harnessing

BRITISH ISLES, BY COUNTRY

Waterfall, river and location	Total drop metres	feet
Eas a' Chuàl Aluinn, Glas Bheinn, Sutherland, Scotland	200	658
Powerscourt Falls, Dargle, Co. Wicklow, Rep. of Ireland	106	350
Pistyll-y-Llyn, Powys/ Dyfed border, Wales	c.72	c.235 (cascades)
Pistyll Rhyadr, Clwyd/		

Powys border, Wales	71.5	235	(single leap)
Caldron Snout, R. Tees,			
Cumbria/Durham,			
England	61	200	(cascades)

GREATEST WATERFALLS – BY VOLUME

Waterfall, river and location	Mean annual flow	
	m^3/sec	galls/sec
Inga (Congo dam site),		
Livingstone Falls, Dem.		
Rep. of Congo	43,000	9,460,000
Khône, Mekong, Laos	41,000	9,000,000
Boyoma (Stanley), R. Lualaba,		
Dem. Rep. of Congo	c.17,000	c.3,750,000
Guaíra (Sete Quedas), Pavaná,		
Brazil (submerged by Itaipu		
hydroelectric dams, 1982)	13,000	2,860,000
Niagara (Horseshoe), R. Niagara/		
Lake Erie–Lake Ontario	6,000	1,320,000
Paulo Afonso, R. São Francisco,		
Brazil	2,830	622,500
Urubupunga, Alto Paraná, Brazil	2,745	604,000
Cataratas del Iguazú, R. Iguaçu,		
Brazil/Argentina	1,750	380,000
Patos-Maribando, Rio Grande,		
Brazil	1,500	330,000
Churchill, R. Churchill, Canada	1,132	249,000
Victoria (Mosi-oa-tunya),		
R. Zambezi, Zambia/		
Zimbabwe	1,000	222,000

TALLEST DAMS

	metres	feet
*Rogun, R. Vakhsh, Tajikistan	335	1,098
Nurek, R. Vakhsh, Tajikistan (1980)	300	984
Grande Dixence, Switzerland (1961)	285	935
*Longtan, R. Hangshui, China	285	935
Inguri, Georgia (1980)	272	892
Borucu, Costa Rica	267	876
Vaiont, Italy (1980)	262	859
Manuel M. Torres, Chicoasén,		
Mexico (1980)	261	856
Tehri, R. Bhagivathi, India	261	856
*Construction ceased		

The world's most massive dam is the Syncrude Tailings dam in Alberta, Canada, which will have a volume of 540 million cubic metres/706 million cubic yards.

The Three Gorges Chang Jiang (Yangtze) Dam, China, with a crest length of 1,983 m/6,505 ft, is due for completion in 2009 (stage 3).

The Yacyretá-Apipe dam across the River Paraná, Argentina-Paraguay, is being completed to a length of 69,600 m/43.24 miles.

TALLEST INHABITED BUILDINGS

Building and city	Height	
	metres	feet
Petronas Towers I and II, Kuala Lumpur,		
Malaysia (1998) (88 stories)	451.9	1,482
Sears Tower, Chicago[1] (1974), (110 stories)	443	1,454
Jin Mao, Shanghai, China (1998) (86 stories)	420	1,378
International Finance Centre,		
Hong Kong (2003)	412	1,352

CITIC Plaza, Guangzhou, China (1996)	391	1,283
Shun Hing Square, Shenzhen, China (1996)	384	1,260
Empire State Building, New York[2](1931)	381	1,250
Central Plaza, Hong Kong (1992)	373	1,227
Bank of China Tower, Hong Kong (1989)	368	1,209
Emirates Tower One, Dubai (2000)	355	1,165
The Centre, Hong Kong (1998)	350	1,148
Tuntex & Chein-Tai Tower, Taiwan (1998)	347	1,140
Aon Center, Chicago (1973)	346	1,136
Kingdom Centre, Riadh, Saudi Arabia (2001)	345	1,132
John Hancock Center, Chicago (1969)	343	1,127
Baurj al Arab Hotel, Dubai (1999)	321	1,053
Chrysler Building, New York (1930)	318	1,046

[1] With TV antennae, 520 m/1,707 f

[2] With TV tower (added 1950–1), 430.9 m/1,414 ft

Note: The Two World Trade Centre towers, One/North (1972) 110 stories, 415m 1,368ft or 521,m 1,716ft with TV antennae; and Two/South (1973) 110 stories, 415m 1,362ft, were destroyed by two terrorist hijacked aircraft on 11 September 2001.

TALLEST STRUCTURES

Structure and location	Height	
	metres	feet
*Warszawa Radio Mast,		
Konstantynow, Poland (1974)	646	2,120
KVLY (formerly KTHI)-TV Mast,		
Blanchard, North Dakota (guyed) (1963)	629	2,063
Indosat Telkom Tower, Jakarta, Indonesia	558	1,831
CN Tower, Metro Centre, Toronto,		
Canada (1975)	555	1,822
Ostankino Tower, Moscow (1967)	540	1,772

*Collapsed during renovation, August 1991. New structure planned on site at Solkajawski. The USA has 8 other guyed TV towers above 555m (1,822 ft).

LONGEST BRIDGES – BY SPAN

Bridge and location	Length	
	metres	feet
SUSPENSION SPANS		
Akashi-Kaikyo, Shikoku, Japan (1998)	1,990	6,529
Storebaelt East Bridge, Denmark (1998)	1,624	5,328
Humber Estuary, Humberside,		
England (1981)	1,410	4,626
Jiangyin (Yangtze), China (1999)	1,385	4,544
Tsing Ma, Hong Kong, China (1997)	1,377	4,518
Verrazano Narrows, Brooklyn–Staten I,		
USA (1964)	1,298	4,260
Golden Gate, San Francisco Bay,		
USA (1937)	1,280	4,200
Höga Kusten, Sweden (1997)	1,210	3,970
Chesapeake Bay No.2, Virginia,		
USA (1999)	1,158	3,800
Mackinac Straits, Michigan, USA (1957)	1,158	3,800
Minami Bisan-Seto, Japan (1988)	1,100	3,609
Bosporus II Fatih Sultan Mehmet,		
Istanbul, Turkey (1992)	1,090	3,576
Bosporus I, Istanbul, Turkey (1973)	1,074	3,524
George Washington, Hudson River,		
New York City, USA (1931)	1,067	3,500
Kurushima III, Japan (1999)	1,030	3,379
Kurushima II, Japan (1999)	1,020	3,346
Ponte 25 de Abril (Tagus), Lisbon,		
Portugal (1966) (road and rail)	1,013	3,323
Firth of Forth (road), nr Edinburgh,		
Scotland (1964)	1,006	3,300
Kita Bisan-Seto, Japan (1988)	990	3,248

*Severn River, Severn Estuary,
England (1966)   988   3,240
*The main span of the 5.15 km/3.2 mile long Second Severn
bridging, opened in 1996, is 456 m/1,496 ft.

CANTILEVER SPANS
Pont de Québec (rail-road),
St Lawrence, Canada (1917)   548.6 1,800
Ravenswood, W. Virginia, USA   525.1 1,723
Firth of Forth (rail), nr Edinburgh, Scotland
(two spans of 1,710ft each) (1890)   521.2 1,710
Minatō (Nankō), Osaka, Japan (1974)   510.0 1,673
Commodore Barry, Chester, Pennsylvania,
USA (1975)   494.3 1,622
Greater New Orleans, Louisiana,
USA (I 1958, II 1988)   480.0 1,575
Howrah (rail-road), Calcutta,
India (1936–43)   457.2 1,500

STEEL ARCH SPANS
Lupu, Shanghai, China (2003)   550.0 1,804
New River Gorge, Fayetteville,
W. Virginia, USA (1977)   518.0 1,700
Bayonne (Kill van Kull), Bayonne,
NJ – Staten I., USA (1931)   510.5 1,675
Sydney Harbour, Sydney, Australia (1932) 502.9 1,650

The 'floating' bridging at Evergreen Point, Seattle, Washington
State, USA (1963), is 3,839 m/12,596 ft long, of which 2,310
m/7,578 ft floats.
The longest stretch of bridgings of any kind is that carrying the
Interstate 55 and Interstate 10 highways at Manchac, Louisiana
(1979), on twin concrete trestles over 55.21 km/34.31 miles.

LONGEST VEHICULAR TUNNELS

Tunnel and location	Length	
	km	miles
*Seikan (rail), Tsugaru Channel, Japan (1988)	53.85	33.46
*Channel Tunnel, (rail) Cheriton, Kent – Sangatte, Calais (1994)	50.45	31.35
Moscow metro, Belyaevo – Bittsevsky, Moscow, Russia (1979)	37.90	23.50
Northern Line tube, East Finchley – Morden, London (1939)	27.84	17.30
Iwate (rail), Japan (2002)	25.81	16.03
Laerdal-Aurland Road Link (2000)	24.51	15.22
*Oshimizu (rail), Honsh, Japan (1982)	22.17	13.78
Simplon II (rail), Brigue, Switzerland – Iselle, Italy (1922)	19.82	12.31
Simplon I (rail), Brigue, Switzerland – Iselle, Italy (1906)	19.80	12.30
Vereina, Switzerland (1999)	19.06	11.84
*Shin-Kanmon (rail), Kanmon Strait, Japan (1975)	18.68	11.61
Appennino (rail), Vernio, Italy (1934)	18.50	11.50
St Gotthard (road), Göschenen – Airolo, Switzerland (1980, re-opened 2001)	16.91	10.51
*Sub-aqueous		

The longest non-vehicular tunnelling in the world is the
Delaware Aqueduct in New York State, USA, constructed
in 1937–44 to a length of 168.9 km/105 miles.
St Gotthard (rail) tunnel (2010) will be 57.07 km/35.46
miles.

BRITAIN – RAIL TUNNELS

	miles	yards
Severn, Bristol – Newport (1873–86)	4	484
Totley, Manchester – Sheffield	3	950
Standedge, Manchester – Huddersfield	3	66
Sodbury, Swindon – Bristol	2	924
Strood, Medway, Kent	2	426
Disley, Stockport – Sheffield	2	346
Ffestiniog, Llandudno – Blaenau Ffestiniog	2	338
Bramhope, Leeds – Harrogate	2	241
Cowburn, Manchester – Sheffield	2	182

The longest road tunnel in Britain is the Mersey
Queensway Tunnel (1934), 3.42 km/2 miles 228 yards
long. The longest canal tunnel, at Standedge, W. Yorks, is
5.12 km/3 miles 417 yards long; it was completed in
1811, closed in 1944 and reopened in 2001.

LONGEST SHIP CANALS

Canal (opening date)	Length		Min. depth	
	km	miles	metres	feet
White Sea-Baltic (formerly Stalin) (1933), of which Canalised river 51.5 km/32 miles	235	146.02	5.0	16.5
*Suez (1869) Links Red and Mediterranean Seas	162	100.60	12.9	42.3
V. I. Lenin Volga-Don (1952) Links Black and Caspian Seas	100	62.20	n/a	n/a
Kiel (or North Sea) (1895) Links North and Baltic Seas	98	60.90	13.7	45.0
*Houston (1940) Links inland city with sea	91	56.70	10.4	34.0
Alphonse XIII (1926) Gives Seville access to sea	85	53.00	7.6	25.0
Panama (1914) Links Pacific Ocean and Caribbean Sea; lake chain, 78.9 km/49 miles dug	82	50.71	12.5	41.0
Manchester Ship (1894) Links city with Irish Channel	64	39.70	8.5	28.0
Welland (1932) Circumvents Niagara Falls and Rapids	43.5	27.00	8.8	29.0
Brussels (Rupel Sea) (1922) Renders Brussels an inland port	32	19.80	6.4	21.0
*Has no locks				

The first section of China's Grand Canal, running 1,782
km/1,107 miles from Beijing to Hangzhou, was opened
AD 610 and completed in 1283. Today it is limited to
2,000 tonne vessels.
    The St Lawrence Seaway comprises the Beauharnois,
Welland and Welland Bypass and Seaway 54–59 canals,
and allows access to Duluth, Minnesota, USA via the
Great Lakes from the Atlantic end of Canada's Gulf of St
Lawrence, a distance of 3,769 km/2,342 miles. The St
Lawrence Canal, completed in 1959, is 293 km/182
miles long.

DISTANCES FROM LONDON BY AIR

This list details the distances in miles from London, Heathrow, to various cities (airports) abroad.

To	Miles
Abidjan	3,197
Abu Dhabi (International)	3,425
Addis Ababa	3,675
Adelaide (International)	10,111
Aden	3,670
Algiers	1,035
'Amman (Queen Alia)	2,287
Amsterdam (Schiphol)	230
Ankara (Esenboga)	1,770
Athens	1,500
Atlanta	4,198
Auckland	11,404
Baghdad (Saddam)	2,551
Bahrain	3,163
Baku	2,485
Bangkok	5,928
Barbados (Grantley Adams)	4,193
Barcelona (Muntadas)	712
Basel-Mulhouse	447
Beijing (Capital)	5,063
Beirut	2,161
Belfast (Aldergrove)	325
Belgrade	1,056
Berlin (Tegel)	588
Bermuda	3,428
Bern	476
Bogotá	5,262
Bombay (Mumbai)	4,478
Boston	3,255
Brasília	5,452
Bratislava	817
Brisbane (Eagle Farm)	10,273
Brussels	217
Bucharest (Otopeni)	1,307
Budapest (Ferihegy)	923
Buenos Aires	6,915
Cairo (International)	2,194
Calcutta	4,958
Calgary	4,357
Canberra	10,563
Cape Town	6,011
Caracas	4,639
Casablanca (Mohamed V)	1,300
Chicago (O'Hare)	3,941
Cologne	331
Colombo (Katunayake)	5,411
Copenhagen	608
Dakar	2,706
Dallas (Fort Worth)	4,736
Dallas (Lovefield)	4,732
Damascus (International)	2,223
Dar-es-Salaam	4,662
Darwin	8,613
Delhi	4,180
Denver	4,655
Detroit (Metropolitan)	3,754
Dhahran	3,143
Dhaka	4,976
Doha	3,253
Dubai	3,414
Dublin	279
Durban	5,937
Düsseldorf	310
Entebbe	4,033
Frankfurt (Main)	406
Freetown	3,046
Geneva	468
Gibraltar	1,084
Gothenburg (Landvetter)	664
Hamburg (Fuhlsbüttel)	463
Harare	5,156
Havana	4,647
Helsinki (Vantaa)	1,148
Hobart	10,826
Ho Chi Minh City	6,345
Hong Kong	5,990
Honolulu	7,220
Houston (Intercontinental)	4,821
Houston (William P. Hobby)	4,837
Islamabad	3,767
Istanbul (Atatürk)	1,560
Jakarta (Halim Perdanakusuma)	7,295
Jeddah	2,947
Johannesburg	5,634
Kabul	3,558
Karachi	3,935
Kathmandu	4,570
Khartoum	3,071
Kiev (Borispol)	1,357
Kiev (Julyany)	1,337
Kingston, Jamaica	4,668
Kuala Lumpur (Subang)	6,557
Kuwait	2,903
Lagos	3,107
Larnaca	2,036
Lima (Callao)	6,303
Lisbon	972
Lomé	3,129
Los Angeles (International)	5,439
Madras	5,113
Madrid (Barajas)	773
Malta	1,305
Manila (Ninoy Aquino)	6,685
Marseille (Provence)	614
Mauritius	6,075
Melbourne (Essendon)	10,504
Melbourne (Tullamarine)	10,499
Mexico City	5,529
Miami	4,414
Milan (Linate)	609
Minsk	1,176
Montego Bay	4,687
Montevideo	6,841
Montreal (Dorval)	3,241
Moscow (Sheremetievo)	1,557
Munich (Franz Josef Strauss)	584
Muscat	3,621
Nairobi (Jomo Kenyatta)	4,248
Naples	1,011
Nassau	4,333
New York (J. F. Kennedy)	3,440
Nice (Côte d'Azur)	645
Oporto	806
Oslo (Gardermoen)	722
Ottawa	3,321
Palma, Majorca (Son San Juan)	836
Paris (Charles de Gaulle)	215
Paris (Le Bourget)	215
Paris (Orly)	227
Perth, Australia	9,008
Port of Spain	4,404
Prague (Ruzine)	649
Pretoria	5,602
Reykjavík (Domestic)	1,167
Reykjavík (Keflavík)	1,177
Rhodes	1,743
Rio de Janeiro (Galeão)	5,745
Riyadh (King Khaled) International	3,067
Rome (Leonardo da Vinci)	895
St John's, Newfoundland	2,308
St Petersburg	1,314
Salzburg (Mozart)	651
San Francisco	5,351
São Paulo (Guarulhos)	5,892
Sarajevo	1,017
Seoul (Kimpo)	5,507
Shanghai	5,725
Shannon	369
Singapore (Changi)	6,756
Sofia	1,266
Stockholm (Arlanda)	908
Suva	10,119
Sydney (Kingsford Smith)	10,568
Tangier	1,120
Tehran	2,741
Tel Aviv	2,227
Tokyo (Narita)	5,956
Toronto	3,544
Tripoli (International)	1,468
Tunis	1,137
Turin (Caselle)	570
Ulaanbaatar	4,340
Valencia	826
Vancouver	4,707
Venice (Marco Polo)	715
Vienna (Schwechat)	790
Vladivostok	5,298
Warsaw	912
Washington (Dulles)	3,665
Wellington	11,692
Yangon/Rangoon	5,582
Yokohama (Aomori)	5,647
Zagreb	848
Zürich	490

TIME ZONES

Standard time differences from the
Greenwich meridian

+   hours ahead of GMT
−   hours behind GMT
*   may vary from standard time at
    some part of the year (Summer
    Time or Daylight Saving Time)
‡   some areas may keep another
    time zone
h   hours
m   minutes

	h	m
Afghanistan	+ 4	30
* Albania	+ 1	
Algeria	+ 1	
* Andorra	+ 1	
Angola	+ 1	
Anguilla	− 4	
Antigua and Barbuda	− 4	
Argentina	− 3	
* Armenia	+ 4	
Aruba	− 4	
Ascension Island	0	
* Australia		
ACT, NSW (except Broken		
Hill area) Qld, Tas., Vic,		
Whitsunday Islands	+10	
* Broken Hill area (NSW)	+ 9	30
* Lord Howe Island	+10	30
Northern Territory	+ 9	30
* South Australia	+ 9	30
Western Australia	+ 8	
* Austria	+ 1	
* Azerbaijan	+ 4	
* Bahamas	− 5	
Bahrain	+ 3	
Bangladesh	+ 6	
Barbados	− 4	
* Belarus	+ 2	
* Belgium	+ 1	
Belize	− 6	
Benin	+ 1	
* Bermuda	− 4	
Bhutan	+ 6	
Bolivia	− 4	
* Bosnia-Hercegovina	+ 1	
Botswana	+ 2	
Brazil		
western states	− 5	
central states	− 4	
N. and NE coastal states	− 3	
* S. and E. coastal states,		
including Brasília	− 3	
Fernando de Noronha		
Island	− 2	
British Antarctic Territory	− 3	
British Indian Ocean		
Territory	+ 5	
Diego Garcia	+ 6	

	h	m
British Virgin Islands	− 4	
Brunei	+ 8	
* Bulgaria	+ 2	
Burkina Faso	0	
Burundi	+ 2	
Cambodia	+ 7	
Cameroon	+ 1	
Canada		
* Alberta	− 7	
* ‡British Columbia	− 8	
* ‡Labrador	− 4	
* Manitoba	− 6	
* New Brunswick	− 4	
* Newfoundland	− 3	30
* Northwest Territories		
east of 85° W.	− 5	
85° W. 102° W.	− 6	
* Nunavut	− 7	
* Nova Scotia	− 4	
Ontario		
•east of 90° W.	− 5	
west of 90° W.	− 5	
* Prince Edward Island	− 4	
Québec		
east of 63° W	− 4	
* west of 63° W.	− 5	
‡Saskatchewan	− 6	
* Yukon	− 8	
Cape Verde	− 1	
Cayman Islands	− 5	
Central African Republic	+ 1	
Chad	+ 1	
* Chatham Islands	+12	45
* Chile	− 4	
China (inc. Hong Kong		
and Macao)	+ 8	
Christmas Island		
(Indian Ocean)	+ 7	
Cocos (Keeling) Islands	+ 6	30
Colombia	− 5	
Comoros	+ 3	
Congo (Dem. Rep.)		
Haut-Zaïre, Kasai,		
Kivu, Shaba	+ 2	
Kinshasa, Mbandaka	+ 1	
Congo-Brazzaville	+ 1	
Costa Rica	− 6	
Côte d'Ivoire	0	
* Croatia	+ 1	
* Cuba	− 5	
* Cyprus	+ 2	
* Czech Republic	+ 1	
* Denmark	+ 1	
* Færøe Islands	0	
* Greenland	− 3	
Danmarkshavn, Mesters		
Vig	0	
* Scoresby Sound	− 1	
* Thule area	− 4	
Djibouti	+ 3	

	h	m
Dominica	− 4	
Dominican Republic	− 5	
East Timor	+ 9	
Ecuador	− 5	
Galápagos Islands	− 6	
* Egypt	+ 2	
El Salvador	− 6	
Equatorial Guinea	+ 1	
Eritrea	+ 3	
Estonia	+ 2	
Ethiopia	+ 3	
* Falkland Islands	− 4	
Fiji	+12	
* Finland	+ 2	
* France	+ 1	
French Guiana	− 3	
French Polynesia	−10	
Guadeloupe	− 4	
Martinique	− 4	
Réunion	+ 4	
Marquesas Islands	− 9	30
Gabon	+ 1	
The Gambia	0	
* Georgia	+ 3	
* Germany	+ 1	
Ghana	0	
* Gibraltar	+ 1	
* Greece	+ 2	
Grenada	− 4	
Guam	+10	
Guatemala	− 6	
Guinea	0	
Guinea-Bissau	0	
Guyana	− 4	
Haïti	− 5	
Honduras	− 6	
* Hungary	+ 1	
Iceland	0	
India	+ 5	30
Indonesia		
Java, Kalimantan (west		
and central), Madura,		
Sumatra	+ 7	
Bali, Flores, Kalimantan		
(south and east),		
Lombok, Sulawesi,		
Sumbawa, West Timor	+ 8	
Irian Jaya, Maluku	+ 9	
* Iran	+ 3	30
* Iraq	+ 3	
* Ireland, Republic of	0	
* Israel	+ 2	
* Italy	+ 1	
Jamaica	− 5	
Japan	+ 9	
* Jordan	+ 2	
* Kazakhstan		
western	+ 4	
central	+ 5	
eastern	+ 6	

	h	m		h	m		h	m
Kenya	+ 3		Peru	− 5		Uganda	+ 3	
Kiribati	+12		Philippines	+ 8		Ukraine	+ 2	
Line Islands	+14		Poland	+ 1		United Arab Emirates	+ 1	
Phoenix Islands	+13		Portugal	0		United Kingdom	0	
Korea, North	+ 9		Azores	− 1		United States of America		
Korea, South	+ 9		Madeira	0		Alaska	− 9	
Kuwait	+ 3		Puerto Rico	− 4		Aleutian Islands, east of		
Kyrgyzstan	+ 5		Qatar	+ 3		169° 30 ′W.	− 9	
Laos	+ 7		Réunion	+ 4		Aleutian Islands, west of		
Latvia	+ 2		Romania	+ 2		169° 30 ′W.	−10	
Lebanon	+ 2		Russia			eastern time	− 5	
Lesotho	+ 2		Zone 1	+ 2		central time	− 6	
Liberia	0		Zone 2	+ 3		Hawaii	−10	
Libya	+ 2		Zone 3	+ 4		mountain time	− 7	
Liechtenstein	+ 1		Zone 4	+ 5		Pacific time	− 8	
Line Islands not part of			Zone 5	+ 6		Uruguay	− 3	
Kiribati	−10		Zone 6	+ 7		Uzbekistan	+ 5	
Lithuania	+ 2		Zone 7	+ 8		Vanuatu	+ 1	
Luxembourg	+ 1		Zone 8	+ 9		Vatican City State	+ 1	
Macedonia	+ 1		Zone 9	+10		Venezuela	− 4	
Madagascar	+ 3		Zone 10	+11		Vietnam	+ 7	
Malawi	+ 2		Zone 11	+12		Virgin Islands (US)	− 4	
Malaysia	+ 8		Rwanda	+ 2		Yemen	+ 3	
Maldives	+ 5		St Helena	0		Zambia	+ 2	
Mali	0		St Christopher and Nevis	− 4		Zimbabwe	+ 2	
Malta	+ 1		St Lucia	− 4				
Marshall Islands	+12		St Pierre and Miquelon	− 3				
Ebon Atoll	−12		St Vincent and the					
Mauritania	0		Grenadines	− 4				
Mauritius	+ 4		Samoa	−11				
Mexico	− 6		Samoa, American	− 11				
Nayarit, Sinaloa,			San Marino	+ 1				
S. Baja California	− 7		São Tomé and Princípe	0				
Sonora	− 7		Saudi Arabia	+ 3				
N. Baja California	− 8		Senegal	0				
Micronesia			Serbia & Montenegro	+ 1				
Caroline Islands	+10		Seychelles	+ 4				
Kosrae, Pingelap,			Sierra Leone	0				
Pohnpei	+11		Singapore	+ 8				
Moldova	+ 2		Slovakia	+ 1				
Monaco	+ 1		Slovenia	+ 1				
Mongolia	+ 8		Solomon Islands	+11				
Montserrat	− 4		Somalia	+ 3				
Morocco	0		South Africa	+ 2				
Mozambique	+ 2		South Georgia	− 2				
Myanmar	+ 6	30	Spain	+ 1				
Namibia	+ 1		Canary Islands	0				
Nauru	+12		Sri Lanka	+ 6				
Nepal	+ 5	45	Sudan	+ 3				
Netherlands	+ 1		Suriname	− 3				
Netherlands Antilles	− 4		Swaziland	+ 2				
New Caledonia	+11		Sweden	+ 1				
New Zealand	+12		Switzerland	+ 1				
Cook Islands	−10		Syria	+ 2				
Nicaragua	− 6		Taiwan	+ 8				
Niger	+ 1		Tajikistan	+ 5				
Nigeria	+ 1		Tanzania	+ 3				
Niue	− 11		Thailand	+ 7				
Norfolk Island	+11	30	Togo	0				
Northern Mariana Islands	+10		Tonga	+13				
Norway	+ 1		Trinidad and Tobago	− 4				
Oman	+ 4		Tristan da Cunha	0				
Pakistan	+ 5		Tunisia	+ 1				
Palau	+ 9		Turkey	+ 2				
Panama	− 5		Turkmenistan	+ 5				
Papua New Guinea	+10		Turks and Caicos Islands	− 5				
Paraguay	− 4		Tuvalu	+12				

CURRENCIES AND EXCHANGE RATES

COUNTRY/TERRITORY	MONETARY UNIT	AVERAGE RATE TO £ 1 30 August 2002	AVERAGE RATE TO £ 1 29 August 2003
Afghanistan	Afghani (Af) of 100 puls	Af 7270.11	Af 67.87
Albania	Lek (Lk) of 100 qindraka	Lk 214.21	Lk 196.37
Algeria	Algerian dinar (DA) of 100 centimes	DA 121.13	DA 121.55
American Samoa	Currency is that of the USA	US$1.53	US$1.58
Andorra	Euro (€) of 100 cents	€ 1.56	€ 1.45
Angola	Readjusted kwanza (Krzl) of 100 lwei	Kzrl 70.61	Kzrl 125.89
Anguilla	East Caribbean dollar (EC$) of 100 cents	EC$4.13	EC$4.21
Antigua and Barbuda	East Caribbean dollar (EC$) of 100 cents	EC$4.13	EC$4.21
Argentina	Peso of 10,000 australes	Pesos 5.56	Pesos 4.70
Armenia	Dram of 100 louma	Dram 855.58	Dram 880.91
Aruba	Aruban florin	Florins 2.74	Florins 2.83
Ascension Island	Currency is that of St Helena	at parity with £ sterling	
Australia	Australian dollar ($A) of 100 cents	$A2.77	$A2.47
Norfolk Island	Currency is that of Australia	$A2.77	$A2.47
Austria	Euro (€) of 100 cents	€ 1.56	€ 1.45
Azerbaijan	Manat of 100 gopik	Manat 7490.51	Manat 7757.35
The Bahamas	Bahamian dollar (B$) of 100 cents	B$1.53	B$1.58
Bahrain	Bahraini dinar (BD) of 1,000 fils	BD 0.58	BD 0.60
Bangladesh	Taka (Tk) of 100 poisha	Tk 88.24	Tk 92.20
Barbados	Barbados dollar (BD$) of 100 cents	BD$3.05	BD$3.14
Belarus	Belarusian rouble of 100 kopeks	BYR 2839.17	BYR 3311.27
Belgium	Euro (€) of 100 cents	€ 1.56	€ 1.45
Belize	Belize dollar (BZ$) of 100 cents	BZ$3.02	BZ$3.11
Benin	Franc FCA	Francs 1024.57	Francs 949.21
Bermuda	Bermuda dollar of 100 cents	$1.53	$1.58
Bhutan	Ngultrum of 100 chetrum (Indian currency is also legal tender)	Ngultrum 74.20	Ngultrum 72.39
Bolivia	Boliviano ($b) of 100 centavos	$b11.16	$b12.20
Bosnia-Hercegovina	Convertible marka	Marka 3.07	Marka 2.83
Botswana	Pula (P) of 100 thebe	P 9.70	P 7.69
Brazil	Real of 100 centavos	Real 4.71	Real 4.67
Brunei	Brunei dollar (B$) of 100 sen (fully interchangeable with Singapore currency)	$2.67	$2.77
Bulgaria	Lev of 100 stotinki	Leva 3.04	Leva 2.82
Burkina Faso	Franc CFA	Francs 1024.57	Francs 949.21
Burundi	Burundi franc of 100 centimes	Francs 1336.61	Francs 1696.67
Cambodia	Riel of 100 sen	Riel 5869.66	Riel 6052.78
Cameroon	Franc CFA	Francs 1024.57	Francs 949.21
Canada	Canadian dollar (C$) 100 cents	C$2.38	C$2.20
Cape Verde	Escudo Caboverdiano of 100 centavos	Esc 183.36	Esc 171.96
Cayman Islands	Cayman Islands dollar (CI$) of 100 cents	CI$1.26	CI$1.29
Central African Republic	Franc CFA	Francs 1024.57	Francs 949.21
Chad	Franc CFA	Francs 1024.57	Francs 949.21
Chile	Chilean peso of 100 centavos	Pesos 1081.41	Pesos 1104.57
China	Renminbi Yuan of 10 jiao or 100 fen	Yuan 12.67	Yuan 13.06
Hong Kong	Hong Kong (HK$) of 100 cents	HK$ 11.94	HK$12.31
Macao	Pataca of 100 avos	Pataca 12.29	Pataca 12.68
Colombia	Colombian peso of 100 centavos	Pesos 4092.61	Pesos 4493.58
The Comoros	Comorian franc (KMF) of 100 centimes	Francs 777.11	Francs 717.06
Congo, Rep. of	Franc CFA	Francs 1024.57	Francs 949.21
Congo, Dem. Rep. of	Congolese franc	CFr 535.69	CFr 681.83
Costa Rica	Costa Rican colón ₡ of 100 céntimos	₡558.79	₡639.56
Côte d'Ivoire	Franc CFA	Francs 1024.57	Francs 949.21

Country	Currency		
Croatia	Kuna of 100 lipa	Kuna 11.50	Kuna 10.81
Cuba	Cuban peso of 100 centavos	Pesos 32.14	Pesos 33.14
Cyprus	Cyprus pound (C£) of 100 cents	C£ 0.90	C£ 0.85
Czech Republic	Koruna (Kčs) of 100 haléřu	Kčs 47.91	Kčs 46.96
Denmark	Danish krone of 100 øre	Kroner 11.60	Kroner 10.75
Færøe Islands	Currency is that of Denmark	Kroner 11.60	Kroner 10.75
Djibouti	Djibouti franc of 100 centimes	Francs 252.39	Francs 276.20
Dominica	East Caribbean dollar (EC$) of 100 cents	EC$ 4.13	EC$4.21
Dominican Republic	Dominican Republic peso (RD$) of 100 centavos	RD$ 26.17	RD$52.24
East Timor	Currency is that of the USA	US$1.53	US$1.58
Ecuador	Currency is that of the USA (formerly sucre of 100 centavos)	US$1.53	US$1.58
Egypt	Egyptian pound (£E) of 100 piastres or 1,000 millièmes	£E7.09	£E9.71
El Salvador	El Salvador colón (₡) of 100 centavos	₡13.39	₡13.81
Equatorial Guinea	Franc CFA	Francs 1024.57	Francs 949.21
Eritrea	Nakfa	—	—
Estonia	Kroon of 100 sents	Kroons 24.44	Kroons 22.64
Ethiopia	Ethiopian birr (EB) of 100 cents	EB 12.70	EB 13.49
Falkland Islands	Falkland pound of 100 pence	at parity with £ sterling	
Fiji	Fiji dollar (F$) of 100 cents	F$3.30	F$3.03
Finland	Euro (€) of 100 cents	€ 1.56	€ 1.45
France	Euro (€) of 100 cents	€ 1.56	€ 1.45
French Guiana	Euro (€) of 100 cents	€ 1.56	€ 1.45
French Polynesia	Franc CFP	Francs 184.62	Francs 167.95
Gabon	Franc CFA	Francs 1024.57	Francs 949.21
The Gambia	Dalasi (D) of 100 butut	D30.65	D46.56
Georgia	Laria of 100 tetri	Laria 3.34	Laria 3.33
Germany	Euro (€) of 100 cents	€ 1.56	€ 1.45
Ghana	Cedi of 100 pesewas	Cedi 12761.0	Cedi 13739.1
Gibraltar	Gibraltar pound of 100 pence	at parity with £ sterling	
Greece	Euro (€) of 100 cents	€ 1.56	€ 1.45
Greenland	Currency is that of Denmark	Kroner 11.60	Kroner 10.75
Grenada	East Caribbean dollar (EC$) of 100 cents	EC$4.13	EC$4.21
Guadeloupe	Euro (€) of 100 cents	€ 1.56	€ 1.45
Guam	Currency is that of the USA	US$1.53	US$1.58
Guatemala	Quetzal (Q) of 100 centavos	Q12.07	Q12.54
Guinea	Guinea franc of 100 centimes	Francs 3025.13	Francs 3156.60
Guinea-Bissau	Franc CFA	Francs 1024.57	Francs 949.21
Guyana	Guyana dollar (G$) of 100 cents	G$ 276.26	G$ 282.52
Haiti	Gourde of 100 centimes	Gourdes 42.86	Gourdes 60.92
Honduras	Lempira of 100 centavos	Lempiras 25.10	Lempiras 27.45
Hungary	Forint of 100 fillér	Forints 384.04	Forints 371.98
Iceland	Icelandic króna (Kr) of 100 aurar	Kr 1133.42	Kr 126.40
India	Indian rupee (Rs) of 100 paisa	Rs 74.20	Rs 72.39
Indonesia	Rupiah (Rp) of 100 sen	Rp 13602.8	Rp 13439.2
Iran	Rial	Rials 2678.46	Rials 13123.6
Iraq	Iraqi dinar (ID) of 1,000 fils	ID 0.48	ID 0.49
Ireland, Republic of	Euro (€) of 100 cents	€ 1.56	€ 1.45
Israel	Shekel of 100 agora	Shekels 7.14	Shekels 7.03
Italy	Euro (€) of 100 cents	€ 1.56	€ 1.45
Jamaica	Jamaican dollar (J$) of 100 cents	J$73.85	J$92.33
Japan	Yen	Yen 180.89	Yen 185.36
Jordan	Jordanian dinar (JD) of 1,000 fils	JD 1.08	JD 1.12
Kazakhstan	Tenge	Tenge 236.74	Tenge 232.43
Kenya	Kenya shilling (Ksh) of 100 cents	Ksh 120.29	Ksh 121.14
Kiribati	Australian dollar ($A) of 100 cents	$A2.78	$A2.47
Korea, Dem. People's Rep. of	Won of 100 chon	Won 3.37	Won 3.47
Korea, Republic of	Won	Won 1836.43	Won 1860.03
Kuwait	Kuwaiti dinar (KD) of 1,000 fils	KD 0.46	KD 0.47
Kyrgyzstan	Som	Som 70.41	Som 67.23
Laos	Kip (K) of 100 at	K 11632.2	K 11995.1
Latvia	Lats of 100 santims	Lats 0.92	Lats 0.91
Lebanon	Lebanese pound (L£) of 100 piastres	L£ 2314.57	L£ 2389.74

Lesotho	Loti (M) of 100 lisente	M 16.15	M 11.60
Liberia	Liberian dollar (L$) of 100 cents	L$1.53	L$1.58
Libya	Libyan dinar (LD) of 1,000 dirhams	LD 1.19	LD 2.19
Liechtenstein	Swiss franc of 100 rappen (or centimes)	Francs 2.29	Francs 2.23
Lithuania	Litas of 100 centas	Litas 5.39	Litas 4.99
Luxembourg	Euro (€) of 100 cents	€ 1.56	€ 1.45
Macedonia	Denar of 100 deni	Den 95.49	Den 89.23
Madagascar	Franc malgache (FMG) of 100 centimes	FMG 10178.2	FMG 9390.89
Malawi	Kwacha (K) of 100 tambala	MK 116.46	MK 166.51
Malaysia	Malaysian dollar (ringgit) (M$) of 100 sen	M$5.81	M$5.99
Maldives	Rufiyaa of 100 laaris	Rufiyaa 18.01	Rufiyaa 20.20
Mali	Franc CFA	Francs 1024.57	Francs 949.21
Malta	Maltese lira (LM) of 100 cents of 1,000 mils	LM 0.65	LM 0.61
Marshall Islands	Currency is that of the USA	US$1.53	US$1.58
Martinique	Currency is that of France	€ 1.56	€ 1.45
Mauritania	Ouguiya (UM) of 5 khoums	UM 419.22	UM 420.22
Mauritius	Mauritius rupee of 100 cents	Rs 45.56	Rs 45.69
Mayotte	Euro (€) of 100 cents	€ 1.56	€ 1.45
Mexico	Peso of 100 centavos	Pesos 15.08	Pesos 17.35
Micronesia, Federated States of	Currency is that of the USA	US$1.53	US$1.58
Moldova	Moldovan leu of 100 bani	MDL 20.82	MDL 21.94
Monaco	Euro (€) of 100 cents	€ 1.56	€ 1.45
Mongolia	Tugrik of 100 möngö	Tugriks 1694.32	Tugriks 1777.17
Montserrat	East Caribbean dollar (EC$) of 100 cents	EC$4.13	EC$4.21
Morocco	Dirham (DH) of 100 centimes	DH 16.38	DH 15.54
Mozambique	Metical (MT) of 100 centavos	MT 35605.2	MT 36814.6
Myanmar	Kyat (K) of 100 pyas	K9.79	K9.79
Namibia	Namibian dollar of 100 cents	at parity with SA Rand	
Nauru	Australian dollar ($A) of 100 cents	$A2.77	$A2.47
Nepal	Nepalese rupee of 100 paisa	Rs 117.86	Rs 117.74
The Netherlands	Euro (€) of 100 cents	€ 1.56	€ 1.45
Netherlands Antilles	Netherlands Antilles guilder of 100 cents	Guilders 2.72	Guilders 2.81
New Caledonia	Franc CFP	Francs 191.04	Francs 167.95
New Zealand	New Zealand dollar (NZ$) of 100 cents	NZ$3.24	NZ$2.77
Cook Islands	Currency is that of New Zealand	NZ$3.24	NZ$2.77
Niue	Currency is that of New Zealand	NZ$3.24	NZ$2.77
Tokelau	Currency is that of New Zealand	NZ$3.24	NZ$2.77
Nicaragua	Córdoba (C$) of 100 centavos	C$21.96	C$23.94
Niger	Franc CFA	Francs 1024.57	Francs 949.21
Nigeria	Naira (N) of 100 kobo	N 194.76	N 207.23
Northern Mariana Islands	Currency is that of the USA	US$1.53	US$1.58
Norway	Krone of 100 øre	Kroner 11.54	Kroner 11.99
Oman	Rial Omani (OR) of 1,000 baisas	OR 0.59	OR 0.61
Pakistan	Pakistan rupee of 100 paisa	Rs 91.11	Rs 91.08
Palau	Currency is that of the USA	US$1.53	US$1.58
Panama	Balboa of 100 centésimos (US notes are also in circulation)	Balboa 1.53	Balboa 1.58
Papua New Guinea	Kina (K) of 100 toea	K 6.11	K 5.35
Paraguay	Guarani (Gs) of 100 céntimos	Gs 9542.98	Gs 9903.83
Peru	New Sol of 100 cénts	New Sol 5.50	New Sol 5.49
The Philippines	Philippine peso (P) of 100 centavos	P 79.78	P 86.65
Pitcairn Islands	Currency is that of New Zealand	NZ$3.24	NZ$2.77
Poland	Złoty of 100 groszy	Złotych 6.38	Złotych 6.30
Portugal	Euro (€) of 100 cents	€ 1.56	€ 1.45
Puerto Rico	Currency is that of the USA	US$1.53	US$1.58
Qatar	Qatar riyal of 100 dirhams	Riyals 5.57	Riyals 5.75
Réunion	Euro (€) of 100 cents	€ 1.56	€ 1.45
Romania	Leu of 100 bani	Lei 50844.9	Lei 53574.6
Russia	Rouble of 100 kopeks	Rbl 48.34	Rbl 48.13
Rwanda	Rwanda franc of 100 centimes	Francs 713.24	Francs 845.65

St Christopher and Nevis	East Caribbean dollar (EC$) of 100 cents	EC$4.13	EC$4.21
St Helena	St Helena pound (£) of 100 pence	at parity with £ sterling	
St Lucia	East Caribbean dollar (EC$) of 100 cents	EC$4.13	EC$4.21
St Pierre and Miquelon	Euro (€) of 100 cents	€ 1.56	€ 1.45
St Vincent and the Grenadines	East Caribbean dollar (EC$) of 100 cents	EC$4.13	EC$4.21
Samoa	Tala (S$) of 100 sene	S$5.03	S$4.66
San Marino	Euro (€) of 100 cents	€ 1.56	€ 1.45
São Tomé and Princípe	Dobra of 100 centavos	Dobra 13805.1	Dobra 13731.2
Saudi Arabia	Saudi riyal (SR) of 20 qursh or 100 halala	SR 5.74	SR 5.92
Senegal	Franc CFA	Francs 1024.57	Francs 949.21
Serbia and Montenegro (formerly Yugoslavia)	New dinar of 100 paras	New Dinars 96.26	New Dinars 94.88
Seychelles	Seychelles rupee of 100 cents	Rs 8.60	Rs 8.80
Sierra Leone	Leone (Le) of 100 cents	Le 3114.67	Le 3712.95
Singapore	Singapore dollar (S$) of 100 cents	S$2.67	S$2.77
Slovakia	Koruna (Sk) of 100 halierov	Kčs 68.23	Kčs 60.77
Slovenia	Tolar (SIT) of 100 stotin	Tolars 354.16	Tolars 340.22
Solomon Islands	Solomon Islands dollar (SI$) of 100 cents	SI$11.42	SI$11.89
Somalia	Somali shilling of 100 cents	Shillings 4010.04	Shillings 4135.15
South Africa	Rand (R) of 100 cents	R 16.15	R 11.60
Spain	Euro (€) of 100 cents	€ 1.56	€ 1.45
Sri Lanka	Sri Lankan rupee of 100 cents	Rs 147.42	Rs 152.57
Sudan	Sudanese dinar (SD) of 100 piastres	SD 395.95	SD 412.41
Suriname	Surinamese guilder of 100 cents	Guilders 3334.30	Guilders 3969.43
Swaziland	Lilangeni (E) of 100 cents (South African currency is also in circulation)	at parity with SA Rand	
Sweden	Swedish krona of 100 öre	Kronor 14.27	Kronor 13.35
Switzerland	Swiss franc of 100 rappen (or centimes)	Francs 2.29	Francs 2.23
Syria	Syrian pound (S£) of 100 piastres	S£74.77	S£72.60
Taiwan	New Taiwan dollar NT$) of 100 cents	NT$52.39	NT$53.98
Tajikistan	Somoni (TJS) of 100 dirams	—	—
Tanzania	Tanzanian shilling of 100 cents	Shillings 1473.92	Shillings 1650.11
Thailand	Baht of 100 satang	Baht 64.55	Baht 64.95
Togo	Franc CFA	Francs 1024.57	Francs 949.21
Tonga	Pa'anga (T$) of 100 seniti	T$2.77	T$2.47
Trinidad and Tobago	Trinidad and Tobago dollar (TT$) of 100 cents	TT$9.15	TT$9.70
Tristan da Cunha	Currency is that of the UK	—	—
Tunisia	Tunisian dinar of 1,000 millimes	Dinars 2.12	Dinars 2.08
Turkey	Turkish lira (TL) of 100 kurus	TL 2505511	TL 2214355
Turkmenistan	Manat of 100 tenge	—	—
Turks and Caicos Islands	US dollar (US$)	US$1.53	US$1.58
Tuvalu	Australian dollar ($A) of 100 cents	$A2.77	$A2.47
Uganda	Uganda shilling of 100 cents	Shillings 2764.17	Shillings 3154.23
Ukraine	Hryvna of 100 kopiykas	UAH 8.16	UAH 8.42
United Arab Emirates	UAE dirham (Dh) of 100 fils	Dirham 5.62	Dirham 5.80
United States of America	US dollar (US$) of 100 cents	US$1.53	US$1.58
Uruguay	Uruguayan peso of 100 centésimos	Pesos 41.06	Pesos 43.99
Uzbekistan	Sum of 100 tiyin	Sum 1169.51	Sum 1536.46
Vanuatu	Vatu of 100 centimes	Vatu 211.59	Vatu 194.54
Vatican City State	Euro (€) of 100 cents y	€ 1.56	€ 1.45
Venezuela	Bolívar (Bs) of 100 céntimos	Bs 2130.15	Bs 2522.12
Vietnam	Dông of 10 hào or 100 xu	Dông 23471	Dông 24501.5
Virgin Islands, British	US dollar (US$) (£ sterling and EC$ also circulate)	US$1.53	US$1.58
Virgin Islands, US	Currency is that of the USA	US$1.53	US$1.58
Wallis and Futuna Islands	Franc CFP	Francs 191.04	Francs 167.95
Yemen	Riyal of 100 fils	Riyals 269.97	Riyals 280.95
Zambia	Kwacha (K) of 100 ngwee	K 6887.48	K 7346.99
Zimbabwe	Zimbabwe dollar (Z$) of 100 cents	Z$84.87	Z$1300.52

†The euro is also legal tender in Kosovo and Serbia & Montenegro

WORLD AREA AND POPULATION

The total population of the world in mid-2003 was estimated at 6,301 million, compared with 5,292 million in 1990 and 3,019 million in 1960.

Continent, etc.	Area Sq. miles '000	Sq. km '000	Estimated population mid-2003
Africa	11,704	30,313	850,558,000
North America[1]	8,311	21,525	325,698,000
Latin America[2]	7,933	20,547	543,246,000
Asia[3]	10,637[†]	27,549[†]	3,823,390,000[*]
Europe[4]	1,915[†]	4,961[†]	726,338,000[*]
Oceania[5]	3,286	8,510	32,234,000
Former USSR	8,649	22,402	—
TOTAL	52,435	135,807	6,301,463,000

[1] Includes Greenland and Hawaii
[2] Mexico, the Caribbean and the remainder of the Americas south of the USA
[3] Includes European Turkey
[4] Excludes European Turkey
[5] Includes Australia, New Zealand and the islands inhabited by Micronesian, Melanesian and Polynesian peoples
[*] Figure includes some former USSR countries
[†] Figure excludes former USSR countries
Source: UN Population Division; Department of Economic and Social Affairs (2003)

The population forecast for the years 2025 and 2050 is:

Continent, etc.	Estimated population (million) 2025	2050
Africa	1,292,085	1,803,298
North America[1]	394,312	447,931
Latin America[2]	686,857	767,685
Asia	4,742,232	5,222,058
Europe	696,036	631,938
Oceania	39,933	45,815
TOTAL	7,851,455	8,918,725

[1] Includes Bermuda, Greenland, and St Pierre and Miquelon
[2] Mexico, the Caribbean and the remainder of the Americas south of the USA

AREA AND POPULATION BY CONTINENT

No complete survey of many countries has yet been achieved and consequently accurate area figures are not always available. Similarly, many countries have not recently, or have never, taken a census. The areas of countries given below are derived from estimate figures published by the United Nations and other selected sources and so are intended only as a guide. To convert square km to square miles, multiply by 0.3861022. Population figures for countries are derived from the most recent estimates available and sources vary. Accurate and up-to-date data for the populations of capital cities are scarce, and definitions of cities' extent differ. The figures given below are the latest estimates available. For the latest area and population figures, please consult the A–Z country listings starting on page 741.

EXPLANATION OF SYMBOLS AND TERMS USED IN COUNTRIES OF THE WORLD A–Z DATA
1. Ψ seaport.
2. (m) = male; (f) = female
3. Life expectancy figures are an average for males and females
4. Population growth rate figure is for average growth between 1990–2001
5. Paramilitaries are not included in the total military personnel figure for each country
6. For some countries, depending on source, land area excludes area covered by inland water.

COUNTRY/TERRITORY	AREA Sq. Km	POPULATION	CAPITAL	POPULATION OF CAPITAL
AFRICA				
Algeria	2,381,700	30,841,000	ΨAlgiers (El Djazaïr)	1,507,241
Angola	1,246,700	13,527,000	ΨLuanda	1,822,407
Benin	112,622	5,828,000	ΨPorto Novo	232,756
Botswana	566,700	1,680,863	Gaborone	286,779
Burkina Faso	274,000	11,087,000	Ouagadougou	1,000,000
Burundi	27,834	6,194,000	Bujumbura	235,440
Cameroon	465,400	15,203,000	Yaoundé	653,670
Cape Verde	4,033	406,000	ΨPraia	61,644
Central African Republic	622,984	3,245,000	Bangui	473,817
Chad	1,284,000	6,702,000	N'Djaména	530,100
Comoros	2,235	651,000	Moroni	30,365
Congo, Democratic Republic of	2,344,858	48,040,000	Kinshasa	4,655,313
Congo-Brazzaville	342,000	2,745,000	Brazzaville	937,579
Côte D'ivoire	318,000	16,349,000	Yamoussoukro	126,191
Djibouti	23,200	634,000	ΨDjibouti	62,000
Egypt	995,500	69,080,000	Cairo	7,200,000
Equatorial Guinea	28,051	486,060	ΨMalabo	30,418
Eritrea	117,600	4,298,269	Asmara	450,000
Ethiopia	1,127,130	64,459,000	Addis Ababa	2,495,000

COUNTRY/TERRITORY	AREA Sq. Km	POPULATION	CAPITAL	POPULATION OF CAPITAL
Gabon	257,700	1,262,000	ΨLibreville	362,400
Gambia	11,295	1,411,205	ΨBanjul	270,540
Ghana	227,500	19,734,000	ΨAccra	2,909,643
Guinea	245,857	7,613,870	ΨConakry	763,000
Guinea–Bissau	36,125	1,315,822	ΨBissau	109,214
Kenya	569,100	31,293,000	Nairobi	2,000,000
Lesotho	30,355	2,177,062	Maseru	367,000
Liberia	111,369	3,225,837	ΨMonrovia	421,053
Libya	1,759,500	5,408,000	ΨTripoli	1,000,000
Madagascar	587,041	15,982,563	Antananarivo	2,000,000
Malawi	118,484	10,548,250	Lilongwe	505,200
Mali	1,240,192	11,008,518	Bamako	809,552
Mauritania	1,025,520	2,747,312	Nouakchott	850,000
Mauritius	1,864	1,171,000	ΨPort Louis	146,499
Mayotte (Fr.)	372	170,879	Mamoudzou	12,000
Morocco	446,300	30,430,000	ΨRabat	1,385,872
Western Sahara	252,120	244,943	El-Aaiün	139,000
Mozambique	784,100	18,644,000	ΨMaputo	1,039,700
Namibia	823,300	1,788,000	Windhoek	147,056
Niger	1,267,000	10,355,156	Niamey	627,400
Nigeria	910,800	116,929,000	Abuja	378,671
Réunion (Fr.)	2,547	743,981	St Denis	121,999
Rwanda	26,338	7,312,756	Kigali	116,227
Saint Helena (UK)	122	5,157	ΨJamestown	884
Ascension (UK)	88	1,051	ΨGeorgetown	–
Tristan Da Cunha (UK)	98	277	ΨEdinburgh of the Seven Seas	–
São Tomé and Príncipe	964	165,034	ΨSão Tomé	43,420
Senegal	196,722	10,284,929	ΨDakar	1,641,358
Seychelles	455	81,000	ΨVictoria	24,324
Sierra Leone	71,740	5,426,618	ΨFreetown	469,776
Somalia	637,657	7,488,773	ΨMogadishu	230,000
South Africa	1,221,000	43,792,000	Pretoria	1,800,000
			ΨCape Town	3,088,028
			Bloemfontein	467,400
Sudan	2,376,000	31,809,000	Khartoum	947,483
Swaziland	17,364	1,104,343	Mbabane	38,290
Tanzania	883,600	35,965,000	Dodoma	1,502,344
Togo	56,785	5,153,088	ΨLomé	366,476
Tunisia	155,400	9,562,000	ΨTunis	929,500
Uganda	197,100	24,023,000	Kampala	750,000
Zambia	743,400	10,649,000	Lusaka	982,362
Zimbabwe	386,900	12,852,000	Harare	1,189,103

AMERICA

Central America and the West Indies

Anguilla (UK)	96	12,394	The Valley	2,400
Antigua and Barbuda	443	67,000	ΨSt John's	22,342
Aruba (Neth.)	193	70,007	ΨOranjestad	25,000
Bahamas	13,939	308,000	ΨNassau	172,196
Barbados	431	268,000	ΨBridgetown	108,000
Belize	22,800	241,204	Belmopan	8,130
Bermuda (UK)	52	64,000	ΨHamilton	2,277
Cayman Islands (UK)	259	43,000	ΨGeorge Town	20,626
Costa Rica	51,100	4,112,000	San José	1,982,339
Cuba	109,800	11,237,000	ΨHavana	2,184,990
Dominica	750	71,000	ΨRoseau	16,243
Dominican Republic	48,400	8,507,000	ΨSanto Domingo	2,134,779
El Salvador	20,700	6,400,000	San Salvador	1,985,294
Grenada	345	94,000	ΨSt George's	4,788
Guadeloupe (Fr.)	1,780	435,739	ΨBasse Terre	29,522
Guatemala	108,400	11,687,000	Guatemala City	1,675,589
Haïti	27,750	6,964,549	ΨPort-au-Prince	884,472
Honduras	112,088	6,406,052	Tegucigalpa	850,445
Jamaica	10,800	2,598,000	ΨKingston	524,638
Martinique (Fr.)	1,128	422,277	ΨFort de France	133,920

COUNTRY/TERRITORY	AREA Sq. Km	POPULATION	CAPITAL	POPULATION OF CAPITAL
Montserrat (UK)	102	4,500	ΨPlymouth	1,478
Netherlands Antilles (Neth.)	800	255,000	ΨWillemstad	50,000
Nicaragua	130,000	4,918,393	Managua	864,201
Panama	74,400	2,899,000	ΨPanama City	464,928
Puerto Rico (USA)	9,104	3,834,000	ΨSan Juan	1,222,316
Saint Kitts – Nevis	262	38,000	ΨBasseterre	12,200
Saint Lucia	616	149,000	ΨCastries	51,994
Saint Vincent and The Grenadines	388	109,022	ΨKingstown	15,466
Trinidad and Tobago	5,100	1,300,000	ΨPort of Spain	43,396
Turks and Caicos Islands (UK)	497	19,000	ΨGrand Turk	3,691
Virgin Islands, British (UK)	151	21,000	ΨRoad Town	3,983
Virgin Islands, US (USA)	363	123,000	ΨCharlotte Amalie	11,842
North America				
Canada	9,221,000	30,871,957	Ottawa	1,063,664
Greenland (Den.)	2,175,600	56,000	ΨGodthåb (Nuuk)	13,889
Mexico	1,908,700	100,368,000	Mexico City	8,591,309
Saint Pierre and Miquelon (Fr.)	242	6,954	ΨSt Pierre	5,416
United States Of America	9,159,000	285,926,000	Washington DC	4,923,153
South America				
Argentina	2,736,700	37,488,000	ΨBuenos Aires	11,298,030
Bolivia	1,084,400	8,516,000	La Paz	739,453
Brazil	8,456,500	172,559,000	Brasília	1,737,813
Chile	748,800	15,402,000	Santiago	4,640,635
Colombia	1,038,700	42,803,000	Bogotá	6,712,247
Ecuador	276,800	12,156,608	Quito	1,399,814
Falkland Islands (UK)	12,173	2,564	ΨStanley	1,989
French Guiana (Fr.)	83,534	182,333	ΨCayenne	41,164
Guyana	214,969	697,181	ΨGeorgetown	250,000
Paraguay	397,300	5,636,000	Asunción	550,060
Peru	1,280,000	26,093,000	Lima	6,723,130
South Georgia (UK)	4,092	–	–	–
Suriname	163,265	433,998	ΨParamaribo	265,000
Uruguay	175,000	3,361,000	ΨMontevideo	1,303,182
Venezuela	882,100	24,632,000	Caracas	3,435,795

ASIA

Afghanistan	652,090	22,132,000	Kabul	1,424,400
Bahrain	694	652,000	ΨManama	140,401
Bangladesh	130,200	140,369,000	Dhaka	9,912,908
Bhutan	47,000	1,862,000	Thimphu	30,340
Brunei Darussalam	5,300	332,844	Bandar Seri Begawan	46,000
Cambodia	181,035	11,437,656	ΨPhnom Penh	832,000
China*	9,327,400	1,284,972,000	Beijing	7,362,426
Hong Kong (China)	1,092	6,725,000	–	–
Macao (China)	24	453,733	ΨMacao	241,413
East Timor	14,874	952,618	ΨDili	56,000
India	2,973,200	1,027,015,247	New Delhi	301,297
Indonesia	1,811,600	214,840,000	ΨJakarta	9,160,500
Iran	1,622,000	71,369,000	Tehran	6,758,845
Iraq	437,400	23,584,000	Baghdad	3,841,268
Israel†	20,600	6,172,000	Tel Aviv	1,919,700
West Bank And Gaza Strip	6,231	2,920,454	Gaza City	120,000
Japan	364,500	127,335,000	Tokyo	11,880,000
Jordan	88,900	5,051,000	Amman	1,270,000
Kazakhstan	2,699,700	16,095,000	Astana	320,000
Korea, Democratic People's Republic	120,400	22,428,000	Pyongyang	2,741,260
Korea, Republic of	98,700	47,069,000	Seoul	10,321,000
Kuwait	17,800	1,971,000	ΨKuwait City	388,663
Kyrgyzstan	199,900	4,753,003	Bishkek	589,400
Laos	236,800	5,635,967	Vientiane	555,100
Lebanon	10,200	3,556,000	ΨBeirut	1,100,000
Malaysia	328,600	22,633,000	Kuala Lumpur	1,297,526

COUNTRY/TERRITORY	AREA Sq. Km	POPULATION	CAPITAL	POPULATION OF CAPITAL
Maldives	298	310,764	ΨMalé	74,069
Mongolia	1,566,500	2,654,999	Ulaanbaatar	515,100
Myanmar	676,578	41,994,678	ΨRangoon	2,513,023
Nepal	147,181	25,284,463	Kathmandu	535,000
Oman	212,500	2,622,000	ΨMuscat (Masqat)	540,000
Pakistan	770,900	144,971,000	Islamabad	350,000
Philippines	298,200	77,131,000	ΨManila	1,581,082
Qatar	11,000	575,000	ΨDoha	217,294
Saudi Arabia	2,149,700	21,028,000	Riyadh	3,100,000
Singapore	648	4,108,000	–	–
Sri Lanka	64,600	19,104,000	ΨColombo	615,000
Syria	183,800	16,610,000	Damascus	1,549,000
Taiwan	36,175	22,350,000	Taipei	2,646,474
Tajikistan	143,100	6,578,681	Dushanbe	528,600
Thailand	510,900	63,584,000	ΨBangkok	5,882,000
Turkey[‡]	769,600	67,632,000	Ankara	3,258,026
Turkmenistan	488,100	5,500,000	Ashgabat	407,000
United Arab Emirates	83,600	2,654,000	Abu Dhabi	450,000
Uzbekistan	414,200	25,257,000	Tashkent	2,200,000
Vietnam	325,500	79,175,000	Hanoi	1,073,760
Yemen	527,968	18,078,035	Sana'ā'	926,595

[*]Including Tibet
[†]Including East Jerusalem, the Golan Heights and Israeli Citizens on the West Bank
[‡]Including Turkey in Europe

EUROPE

Albania	28,748	3,731,000	Tirana	244,153
Andorra	464	68,400	Andorra la Vella	20,787
Armenia	29,800	3,800,000	Yerevan	1,254,400
Austria	82,700	8,131,953	Vienna	1,550,123
Azerbaijan	86,600	8,100,000	ΨBaku	1,817,900
Belarus	207,500	10,147,000	Minsk	1,725,100
Belgium	30,200	10,309,725	Brussels	953,175
Bosnia-Hercegovina	51,197	3,784,000	Sarajevo	529,021
Bulgaria	110,600	7,973,671	Sofia	1,096,389
Croatia	55,900	4,655,000	Zagreb	691,724
Cyprus	9,200	790,000	Nicosia	193,000
Czech Republic	77,300	10,260,000	Prague	1,178,576
Denmark	42,400	5,333,000	ΨCopenhagen	1,081,673
Faroe Islands	1,414	47,000	ΨTórshavn	16,218
Estonia	42,300	1,377,000	Tallinn	404,000
Finland	304,600	5,178,000	ΨHelsinki	905,555
France	550,100	59,453,000	Paris	9,645,000
Georgia	69,700	5,239,000	Tbilisi	1,253,100
Germany	356,700	82,007,000	Berlin	3,388,434
Gibraltar (UK)	7	28,000	ΨGibraltar	–
Greece	128,900	10,623,835	Athens	3,072,922
Hungary	92,300	10,197,119	Budapest	1,896,507
Iceland	100,300	281,000	ΨReykjavík	111,345
Ireland, Republic of	68,900	3,917,336	ΨDublin	495,101
Italy	294,100	57,503,000	Rome	2,459,776
Latvia	62,100	2,406,000	Riga	764,328
Liechtenstein	160	33,000	Vaduz	5,106
Lithuania	64,800	3,689,000	Vilnius	542,287
Luxembourg	2,586	442,000	Luxembourg	77,400
Macedonia	25,713	2,046,209	Skopje	429,964
Malta	316	392,000	ΨValletta	7,048
Moldova	33,851	4,335,000	Chişinău	655,940
Monaco	2	34,000	Monaco	27,063
Netherlands	33,900	15,930,000	ΨAmsterdam	736,538
Norway[*]	306,800	4,488,000	ΨOslo	499,693
Poland	304,400	38,577,000	Warsaw	1,609,780
Portugal[†]	91,500	10,033,000	ΨLisbon	1,878,006
Romania	230,300	22,388,000	Bucharest	2,066,723

COUNTRY/TERRITORY	AREA Sq. Km	POPULATION	CAPITAL	POPULATION OF CAPITAL
Russia‡	16,888,500	144,664,000	Moscow	8,539,000
San Marino	61	27,336	San Marino	4,357
Serbia and Montenegro§	102,100	10,538,000	Belgrade	1,338,856
Slovakia	48,100	5,403,000	Bratislava	452,278
Slovenia	20,100	1,985,000	Ljubljana	273,000
Spain**	499,400	39,921,000	Madrid	3,084,673
Sweden	411,600	8,833,000	ΨStockholm	1,148,953
Switzerland	39,600	7,170,000	Bern	321,932
Ukraine	579,400	49,112,000	Kiev (Kyiv)	2,630,000
United Kingdom ††	240,900	59,542,000	ΨLondon	7,074,265
England	130,410	48,903,000	–	–
Northern Ireland	14,160	1,649,000	ΨBelfast	297,300
Scotland	78,789	5,137,000	ΨEdinburgh	448,850
Wales	20,758	2,917,000	ΨCardiff (Caerdydd)	315,040
Vatican City State	0.44	890	Vatican City	766

* Excludes Svalbard and Jan Mayen Islands (approx 62,422 sq. km) and 3,000 population
† Includes Madeira and the Azores
‡ Includes Russia in Asia
§ Formally Federal Republic of Yugoslavia
** Includes Balearic Islands, Canary Islands, Ceuta and Melilla
†† Excludes Isle of Man (572 sq. km), 69,788 population, and Channel Islands (194 sq. km), 142,949 population)

OCEANIA

American Samoa (USA)	197	67,000	ΨPago Pago	3,519
Australia	7,682,300	19,338,000	Canberra	313,900
Norfolk Island	36	2,037	ΨKingston	–
Fiji	18,274	844,330	ΨSuva	77,366
French Polynesia (Fr.)	3,887	257,847	ΨPapeete	36,784
Guam (USA)	545	160,000	Agana	1,139
Kiribati	726	94,149	Tarawa	17,921
Marshall Islands	181	70,822	Dalap-Uliga-Darrit	20,000
Micronesia, Federated States of	702	134,597	Palikir	–
Nauru	21	12,088	ΨNauru	–
New Caledonia (Fr.)	18,736	207,858	ΨNoumea	97,581
New Zealand	268,000	3,808,000	ΨWellington	340,719
Cook Islands	236	20,000	Rarotonga	9,281
Niue	260	2,000	Alofi	–
Ross Dependency*	453,248	–	–	–
Tokelau	12	2,000	–	–
Northern Mariana Islands (USA)	477	77,000	Saipan	–
Palau (USA)	458	20,000	Koror	13,303
Papua New Guinea	452,900	4,920,000	ΨPort Moresby	173,500
Pitcairn Islands (UK)	5	54	–	–
Samoa	2,831	179,058	ΨApia	36,000
Solomon Islands	28,896	480,442	ΨHoniara	40,000
Tonga	650	104,227	ΨNuku'alofa	34,000
Tuvalu	26	10,991	ΨFongafale	2,856
Vanuatu	12,189	192,910	ΨPort Vila	26,100
Wallis and Futuna Islands (Fr.)	200	15,585	ΨMata-Utu	–

*Includes permanent ice shelf

The Antarctic is generally defined as the area lying within the Antarctic Convergence, the zone where cold northward-flowing Antarctic sea water sinks below warmer southward-flowing water. This zone is at about latitude 50° S. in the Atlantic Ocean and latitude 55°–62° S. in the Pacific Ocean. The continent itself lies almost entirely within the Antarctic Circle, an area of about 13.66 million sq. km (5.3 million sq. miles), 99.67 per cent of which is permanently ice-covered. The average thickness of the ice is 2,450 m (7,100 ft) but in places exceeds 4,500 m (14,500 ft). Some mountains protrude, the highest being Vinson Massif, 4,897 m (16,067 ft). The lowest point has been recorded as the Bentley Subglacial Trench at −2,540 metres. The ice amounts to some 30 million cubic km (7.2 million cubic miles) and represents more than 90 per cent of the world's fresh water. Much of the sea freezes in winter, forming fast ice which breaks up in summer and drifts north as pack ice.

The most conspicuous physical features of the continent are its high inland plateau (much of it over 3,000 m (10,000 ft)), the Transantarctic Mountains and the mountainous Antarctic Peninsula and off-lying islands which extend northwards towards South America.

CLIMATE

On land, summer temperatures range from just above freezing around the coast to −34° C (about −30° F) on the plateau, and in winter from −20° C (about −4° F) on the coast to −65° C (about −85° F) inland. Over a large area the maxima do not exceed −15° C (+5° F).

Precipitation is scant over the plateau but amounts to 25–76 cm (10–30 in) (water equivalent) along the coast and some scientific stations are permanently buried by snow. Some rain falls over the more northerly areas in summer. Gravity winds on the plateau slopes and cyclonic storms further north can both exceed 160 km/h (100 m.p.h.) and visibility can be reduced to zero in blizzards.

FLORA AND FAUNA

Although a small number of flowering plants, ferns and clubmosses occur on the sub-Antarctic islands, only two (a grass and a pearlwort) extend south of 60° S. Antarctic vegetation is dominated by lichens and mosses, with a few liverworts, algae and fungi. Most of these occur around the coast or on islands.

The only land animals are tiny insects and mites with nematodes, rotifers and tardigrades in the mosses, but large numbers of seals, penguins and other sea-birds go ashore to breed in the summer. The emperor penguin is the only species which breeds ashore throughout the winter. By contrast, the Antarctic seas abound with life, a wide variety of invertebrates (including krill) and fish providing food for the seals, penguins and other birds, and a residual population of whales.

In 1994 the International Whaling Commission agreed to establish a whale sanctuary around Antarctica in which commercial whaling will be banned for ten years.

POTENTIAL RESOURCES

Minerals may be present in great variety but not in commercially exploitable concentrations in accessible localities. There are indications that off-shore hydrocarbons may be present but mostly below great depths of stormy, ice-infested seas. A 50-year ban on Antarctic mineral exploitation came into effect in January 1998.

Currently, the chief interest is in marine protein, including the shrimp-like krill already fished commercially by Japan and Poland. It is estimated that these could sustain a yield equal to the present total annual world fish catch.

THE ANTARCTIC TREATY

The co-operative 12 nations (Argentina, Australia, Belgium, Chile, France, Japan, New Zealand, Norway, South Africa, the Soviet Union, the UK and the USA) pledged themselves to promote scientific and technical co-operation un-hampered by politics, and the Antarctic Treaty was signed by the 12 states in 1959. The signatories agreed to establish free use of the Antarctic continent for peaceful scientific purposes; to freeze all territorial claims and disputes in the Antarctic; to ban all military activities in the area; and to prohibit nuclear explosions and the disposal of radioactive waste. Since then additional agreements have been reached to promote conservation and regulate tourism, waste disposal and pollution.

The Antarctic Treaty was defined as covering areas south of latitude 60° S., excluding the high seas but including the ice shelves, and came into force in 1961. It has since been signed by a further 31 states, 14 of which are active in the Antarctic and have therefore been accorded consultative status, bringing the number of consultative parties to 26. In 1998 an extension to the treaty came into effect, placing a 50-year ban on mining, oil exploration and mineral extraction in Antarctica. Furthermore, all tourists, explorers and expeditions will now need permission to enter the Antarctic.

TERRITORIAL CLAIMS

Under the provisions of the Antarctic Treaty all territorial claims and disputes were frozen without the acceptance or denial of the claims of the various claimants. The US and Soviet governments also made it clear that although they had not made any specific territorial claims, they did not relinquish the right to make such claims.

Seven states have made claims in the Antarctic: Argentina claims the part of Antarctica between 74° W. and 25° W.; Chile that part between 90° W. and 53° W.; Britain claims the British Antarctic Territory, an area of 1,709,340 sq. km (660,000 sq. miles) between 20° and 80° W. longitude; France claims Terre Adélie, 432,000 sq. km (166,800 sq. miles) between 136° and 142° E.; Australia claims the Australian Antarctic Territory, 6,120,000 sq. km (2,320,000 sq. miles) between 160° and 45° E. longitude excluding Terre Adélie; Norway claims Queen Maud Land between 20° W. and 45° E.; and New Zealand claims the Ross Dependency, 450,000 sq. km (175,000 sq. miles) between 160° E. and 150° W. longitude. The Argentinian, British and Chilean claims overlap; the part of the continent between 90° W. and 150° W. is unclaimed by any state.

SCIENTIFIC RESEARCH

There were 37 permanently occupied stations in 2002 operated by the following nations: Argentina (6), Australia (3), Brazil (1), Chile (2), China (2), France (2), Germany (2), India (1), Japan (2), New Zealand (1), Poland (1), Russia (4), South Africa (1), UK (2), Ukraine (1), Uruguay (2), USA (3, including one at the South Pole) and one operated by the environmental organisation Greenpeace.

The staff of these stations and summer field-workers are the only people present on the continent and off-lying islands. There are no indigenous inhabitants.

THE EUROPEAN UNION

MEMBER STATE	ACCESSION DATE	POPULATION (2001)	GNP (US$ MILLION) (2000)	GDP PER CAPITA (US$) (2000)	COUNCIL VOTES	EP SEATS
Austria	1 January 1995	8,131,953	204,525	23,357	4	21
Belgium	1 January 1958*	10,309,725	251,583	22,323	5	25
Denmark	1 January 1973	5,333,000	172,238	30,141	3	16
Finland	1 January 1995	5,178,000	130,106	23,377	3	16
France	1 January 1958*	59,453,000	1,438,293	21,848	10	87
Germany	1 January 1958*†	82,007,000	2,063,734	22,753	10	99
Greece	1 January 1981	10,623,000	126,269	10,680	5	25
Ireland	1 January 1973	3,841,000	85,979	25,066	3	15
Italy	1 January 1958*	57,503,000	1,163,211	18,653	10	87
Luxembourg	1 January 1958*	442,000	18,439	43,372	2	6
Netherlands	1 January 1958*	15,930,000	397,544	23,294	5	31
Portugal	1 January 1986	10,033,000	111,291	10,603	5	25
Spain	1 January 1986	39,921,000	595,255	14,054	8	64
Sweden	1 January 1995	8,833,000	240,707	25,903	4	22
UK	1 January 1973	59,542,000	1,459,500	24,058	10	87
TOTAL		376.53	8,432,823		87	626

* Acceded to the European Coal and Steel Community (ECSC) on its formation in 1952
† Federal Republic of Germany (West) 1952/1958; German Democratic Republic (East) acceded on German reunification (3 October 1990)
EP European Parliament
Note regarding map (above): Cyprus, the Czech Republic, Estonia, Hungary, Latvia, Lithuania, Malta, Poland, Slovakia and Slovenia are timetabled to become member states of the European Union in May 2004

DEVELOPMENT

1950   Robert Schuman (French foreign minister)
        proposes that France and West Germany pool
        their coal and steel industries under a
        supranational authority (Schuman Plan)
1951   Paris Treaty signed by France, West Germany,
        Belgium, Italy, Luxembourg and the
        Netherlands establishes the European Coal and
        Steel Community (ECSC)
1952   ECSC Treaty enters into force
1957   25 March: Treaty of Rome signed by the six
        ECSC member countries, establishes the
        European Economic Community (EEC) and the
        European Atomic Energy Authority
        (EURATOM). Treaty aims to create a customs
        union; remove obstacles to free movement of
        capital, goods, people and services; establish
        common external trade policy and common
        agricultural and fisheries policies; co-ordinate
        economic policies; harmonise social policies;
        promote co-operation in nuclear research
1958   1 January: EEC and EURATOM begin
        operation. Joint Parliament and Court of Justice
        established for all three communities, and the
        Commission, Council of Ministers, Economic
        and Social Committee and Investment Bank for
        the EEC established
1962   Common Agricultural Policy (CAP) agreed
1967   EEC, ECSC and EURATOM merge to form the
        European Communities (EC), with a single
        Council of Ministers and Commission
1968   EEC customs union completed
        Implementation of CAP completed
1974   Regular heads of governments summits begin
1975   'Own resources' funding of EC budget
        introduced
        UK renegotiates its terms of accession
        European Regional Development Fund created
1979   European Monetary System (EMS) comes into
        operation
        First direct elections to European Parliament
        (June)
1984   Fontainebleau summit settles UK annual budget
        rebate and agrees first major CAP reform
1986   Single European Act (SEA) signed
        European Political Co-operation (EPC)
        established
1988   Second major CAP reform
1991   Maastricht Treaty agreed
1992   31 December: Single internal market
        programme completed
1993   September: the exchange rate mechanism (ERM)
        of the EMS effectively suspended
        1 November: The Maastricht Treaty enters into
        force, establishing the European Union (EU)
1994   1 January: European Economic Area (EEA)
        agreement comes into operation
        Norway rejects EU membership in referendum
1997   Amsterdam Treaty agreed
1998   11 states chosen to enter first round of European
        Monetary Union (EMU)
        European Central Bank replaces European
        Monetary Institute
1999   1 January: Euro launched
        March: 'Agenda 2000' financial and policy
        reform agreed
        1 May: The Amsterdam Treaty enters into force

2000   9 December: Treaty of Nice agreed
2001   7 June: Ireland rejects Treaty of Nice in
        referendum
2002   1 January: Euro coins and banknotes enter
        circulation
        23 July: ECSC Treaty expires following transfer
        of coal and steel sectors to the Treaty of Rome

ENLARGEMENT AND EXTERNAL RELATIONS

The procedure for accession to the EU is laid down in the Treaty of Rome; states must be stable European democracies governed by the rule of law with free market economies. A membership application is studied by the Commission, which produces an Opinion. If the Opinion is positive, negotiations may be opened leading to an Accession Treaty which must be approved by all member state governments and parliaments, the European Parliament, and the applicant state's government and parliament.

Applicants: Morocco (applied 1987/rejected 1987), Turkey (applied 1987/negative Opinion 1989/offered accession partnership 1999), Cyprus (applied 1990/negotiations begun 1998), Malta (applied 1990/reapplied following a change of government 1998/negotiations begun 2000), Switzerland (applied 1992/application put on hold 1994), Hungary (applied 1994/negotiations begun 1998), Poland (applied 1994/negotiations begun 1998), Bulgaria (applied 1995/offered partnership 1998/negotiations begun 2000), Estonia (applied 1995/negotiations begun 1998), Latvia (applied 1995/offered partnership 1998/negotiations begun 2000), Lithuania (applied 1995/offered partnership 1998/negotiations begun 2000), Romania (applied 1995/offered partnership 1998/negotiations begun 2000), Slovakia (applied 1995/offered partnership 1998/negotiations begun 2000), the Czech Republic (applied 1996/negotiations begun 1998), Slovenia (applied 1996/negotiations begun 1998).

Apart from the EEA Agreement, the EU has three types of agreements with other European and CIS states. 'Europe' agreements commit the EU and signatory states to long-term political and economic integration, a free trade zone (apart from agriculture and labour movement) and eventual EU membership. Government representatives from the signatory states are entitled to attend one summit and two finance and foreign council meetings a year. Agreements have been signed with Bulgaria (1993), the Czech Republic (1993), Estonia (1995), Hungary (1991), Latvia (1995), Lithuania (1995), Poland (1991), Romania (1993), Slovakia (1993) and Slovenia (1996). Association agreements include a commitment to EU financial aid and to eventual membership; agreements have been signed with Malta (1970), Cyprus (1972) and Turkey (1963). Partnership and co-operation agreements are based on regulating and improving political and economic relations and mutual trade concessions but exclude any possibility of membership. Agreements have been implemented with Russia (1997), Ukraine (1998) and Georgia, Kazakhstan, Kyrgyzstan, Moldova and Uzbekistan (1999). Agreements have been signed with Belarus (1995) and Turkmenistan (1998) but are not yet in force.

Agenda 2000, a document issued by the Commission in 1997, addressed both the challenges posed by further enlargement of the Union, the institutional reforms that would be required to enable the Union to function effectively with additional members, and also evaluated each applicant in relation to the accession criteria, establishing a new financial framework for the period 2000–6.

In March 1998, formal accession negotiations were begun with Hungary, Poland, Estonia, the Czech Republic, Slovenia and Cyprus; they were begun with Bulgaria, Romania, Latvia, Lithuania, Malta and Slovakia in 2000, following the Helsinki summit in December 1999, when it was also agreed that an accession partnership should be offered to Turkey.

The Göteborg summit in June 2001 agreed on a timetable for accession for the first group of countries to complete negotiations. At the Copenhagen summit in December 2002, Cyprus, the Czech Republic, Estonia, Hungary, Latvia, Lithuania, Malta, Poland, Slovakia and Slovenia were invited to join the EU. The ten countries signed the Treaty of Accession in Athens on 16 April 2003 and are timetabled to become members in May 2004.

THE COUNCIL OF THE EUROPEAN UNION

Wetstraat 175, B-1048 Brussels, Belgium

The Council of the European Union (Council of Ministers) formally comprises the foreign ministers of the member states but in practice the ministers attending depend on the subject under discussion. Council decisions are taken by qualified majority vote (in which members' votes are weighted), by a simple majority, or by unanimity. The Council is assisted by a General Secretariat, whose head has since 1999 been the High Representative for the Common Foreign and Security Policy.

Unanimity votes are taken on sensitive issues such as taxation and constitutional matters; in preparation for an expanded Union, the Amsterdam Treaty extended areas where qualified majority votes may be taken, to areas such as Single Market laws and harmonisation, environment policy, health and safety, transport policy, overseas aid, research and development, culture, consumer protection, education and training, the development of a single currency and some aspects of social policy. Member states have weighted votes in the Council loosely proportional to their relative population sizes (see introductory table), with a total of 87 votes. For a proposal from the Commission to be passed, it must receive 62 votes; 26 votes are necessary to block a proposal, and 23 votes constitute a temporary blocking minority. For other proposals to be passed they must receive 62 votes cast by at least ten member states.

The Treaty of Nice, which was agreed on 7–9 December 2000 and signed on 26 February 2001, agreed amendments to the treaties in relation to the size and composition of the European Commission, the weighting of votes and the extension of qualified majority voting in the Council of Ministers and other issues relating to the Treaty of Amsterdam. The extension of qualified majority voting to external border controls, the EU budget, the composition of the European Courts and certain committees, visa rules and, by 2007, structural funds, was also agreed.

The European Council, comprising the heads of state or government of the member states and the President of the European Commission, meets twice a year to provide overall policy direction. The presidency of the EC is held in rotation for six-month periods, setting the agenda for and chairing all Council meetings. The European Council holds a summit in the country holding the presidency at the end of its period in office. The holders of the presidency for the years 2003–5 are:

2003 Greece, Italy
2004 Ireland, Netherlands
2005 Luxembourg, UK

GENERAL SECRETARIAT OF THE COUNCIL OF THE EUROPEAN UNION

Wetstraat 175, B-1048 Brussels, Belgium
Email: public.info@consilium.eu.int
Secretary-General of the Council of the European Union and High Representative for the Common Foreign and Security Policy, Javier Solana Madariaga (Spain)
Deputy Secretary-General of the Council of the European Union, Pierre de Boissieu (France)

OFFICE OF THE UNITED KINGDOM PERMANENT REPRESENTATIVE TO THE EUROPEAN UNION

Oudergemselaan 10, B-1040 Brussels, Belgium
Ambassador and UK Permanent Representative, HE Sir Nigel Sheinwald, KCMG, *apptd* 2000
Deputy Permanent Representative, W. Stow

THE EUROPEAN COMMISSION

Wetstraat 200, B-1049 Brussels, Belgium

The Commission consists of 20 Commissioners, two each from France, Germany, Italy, Spain and the UK, and one each from the remaining member states. The members of the Commission are appointed for five-year renewable terms by the agreement of the member states; the terms run concurrently with the terms of the European Parliament. The President and the other Commissioners are nominated by the governments of the member states, and, under the terms of the Amsterdam Treaty, the appointments are approved by the European Parliament. The Commissioners pledge sole allegiance to the EC. The Commission initiates and implements EC legislation and is the guardian of the EC treaties. It is the exponent of Community-wide interests rather than the national preoccupations of the Council. Each Commissioner is supported by advisers and oversees whichever of the departments, known as Directorates-General (DGs), is assigned to him. Each Directorate-General is headed by a Director-General.

President Romano Prodi was nominated by the governments of the member states on 24 March 1999, and under the terms of the Amsterdam Treaty, his appointment was approved by the European Parliament on 15 September 1999, having already announced his new Commission in June. The previous Commission had resigned *en masse* after a committee of experts appointed by the European Parliament had concluded that lax management had allowed fraud and nepotism in the Commission's services. The new Commission has restructured the Directorates-General to reflect the priorities of the new administration.

The Commission has a total staff of around 16,000 permanent civil servants.

COMMISSIONERS *as at June 2003*
President, Romano Prodi (Italy)
Vice-President for Administrative Reform; Personnel and
  Administration; Linguistic Services, Neil Kinnock (UK)
Vice-President for Relations with the European Parliament, and
  for Transport and Energy, Loyola de Palacio (Spain)

MEMBERS
Agriculture, Rural Development and Fisheries, Franz Fischler
  (Austria)
Budget, Financial Control, European Anti-Fraud Office,
  Michaele Schreyer (Germany)
Competition, Mario Monti (Italy)
Development, Humanitarian Aid, Chief Executive of EuropeAid,
  Poul Nielson (Denmark)
Economic and Monetary Affairs, Pedro Solbes Mira (Spain)
Education and Culture, Viviane Reding (Luxembourg)
Employment and Social Affairs, Anna Diamantopoulou
  (Greece)
Enlargement, Günter Verheugen (Germany)
Enterprise and Information Society, Erkki Liikanen (Finland)
Environment, Margot Wallström (Sweden)
External Relations, Chairman of EuropeAid, Chris Patten (UK)
Internal Market, Taxation and Customs Union, Frits Bolkestein
  (Netherlands)
Justice and Home Affairs, António Vitorino (Portugal)
Public Health, Consumer Protection, David Byrne (Ireland)
Regional Policy and Institutional Reform, Inter-Governmental
  Conference, Michel Barnier (France)
Research, Philippe Busquin (Belgium)
Trade, Pascal Lamy (France)

THE EUROPEAN PARLIAMENT
Email: civis@europarl.eu.int Web: www.europarl.eu.int

The European Parliament (EP) originated as the Common
Assembly of the ECSC; it acquired its present name in
1962. Members (MEPs) were initially appointed from the
membership of national parliaments; direct elections to
the Parliament were first held in 1979 and take place at
five-year intervals. Elections to the Parliament are held on
differing bases throughout the EC; in June 1999, British
MEPs were elected for the first time by a 'regional list'
system of proportional representation. The Parliament
comprises 626 seats. The most recent elections were held
in June 1999 and the next elections are to be held in June
2004. MEPs serve on committees which scrutinise draft
EC legislation and the activities of the Commission. A
minimum of 12 plenary sessions a year are held in
Strasbourg and six additional shorter plenary sessions a
year are held in Brussels, committees meet in Brussels,
and the Secretariat's headquarters is in Luxembourg.
  The EP has gradually expanded its influence within
the EU through the Single European Act, which
introduced the co-operation procedure, the Maastricht
Treaty, which extended the co-operation procedure and
introduced the co-decision procedure (see Legislative
Process), and the Amsterdam Treaty, which effectively
extended co-decision to all areas except economic and
monetary union. It has general powers of supervision
over the Commission, and consultation and co-decision
with the Council; it votes to approve a newly appointed
Commission and can dismiss it at any time by a two-
thirds majority (as it threatened to do in January 1999).
Under the Maastricht Treaty it has the right to be
consulted on the appointment of the new Commission
and can veto its appointment. It can reject the EU budget
as a whole, alter non-compulsory expenditure not
specified in the EU primary legislation, and can question

the Commission's management of the budget and call in
the Court of Auditors. Although the EP cannot directly
initiate legislation, its reports can spur the Commission
into action. In accordance with the Maastricht Treaty the
EP appointed an ombudsman in October 1995, to
provide citizens with redress against maladministration
by EU institutions.
  The Parliament's organisation is deliberately biased in
favour of multinational political groupings, recognition
of a political grouping in the parliament entitling it to
offices, funding, representation on committees and
influence in debates and legislation. A political grouping
must comprise members from more than one member
state; a grouping with members from two countries needs
23 members for recognition, a grouping with members
from three countries needs 18 members, and a grouping
with members from four or more countries needs only 14
members.

PARLIAMENT, Palais de l'Europe, Allée du Printemps, BP
  1024/F, F-67070 Strasbourg Cedex, France. Tel: (00 33) (3)
  8817 4001; Fax: (00 33) (3) 8825 6501; Wiertzstraat,
  Postbus 1047, B-1047 Brussels, Belgium. Tel: (00 32) (2) 284
  2111; Fax: (00 32) (2) 284 9075/9077
SECRETARIAT, Centre Européen, Plateau du Kirchberg,
  BP 1601, L-2929 Luxembourg.
  Tel: (00 352) 43001; Fax: (00 352) 4300 29393/29292
President, Patrick Cox (Ireland)
Ombudsman, Nikiforos Diamandouros (Greece),
  1 avenue du Président Robert Schuman, BP 403,
  F-67001, Strasbourg, France.
  Email: euro-ombudsman@europarl.eu.int
  Web: www.euro-ombudsman.eu.int

THE LEGISLATIVE PROCESS

The core of the EU policymaking process is a dialogue
between the Commission, which initiates and implements
policy, and the Council of Ministers, which takes policy
decisions. An increasing degree of democratic control is
exercised by the European Parliament.
  The original legislative process is known as the
consultative procedure. The Commission drafts a
proposal which it submits to the Council and to the
Parliament. The Council then consults the Economic and
Social Committee (ESC), the Parliament and the
Committee of the Regions; the Parliament may request
that amendments are made. With or without these
amendments, the proposal is then adopted by the Council
and becomes law.
  Under the Single European Act (SEA), the role of the
Parliament was strengthened by the introduction of the
co-operation procedure. The Parliament now has a
second reading of proposals in some fields, and after the
second reading its rejection of a proposal can only be
overturned by a unanimous decision of the Council. The
Maastricht Treaty extended the scope of the co-operation
procedure, which was applied to Single Market laws and
harmonisation, trans-European networks, development
policy, the social fund, and some aspects of transport,
environment, research, social policy and competition
policy.
  The SEA introduced the assent procedure, whereby an
absolute majority of the Parliament must vote to approve
laws in certain fields before they are passed. Issues
covered by the assent procedure include foreign treaties,
accession treaties, international agreements with
budgetary implications, citizenship, residence rights, the
CAP, and regional and structural funds.

The Maastricht Treaty introduced the co-decision procedure; if, after the Parliament's second reading of a proposal, the Council and Parliament fail to agree, a conciliation committee of the two will reach a compromise. If a compromise is not reached, the Parliament can reject the legislation by the vote of an absolute majority of its members. The Amsterdam Treaty extended co-decision to all areas covered by qualified majority voting, with the exception of measures related to European Monetary Union (EMU).

The Council issues the following legislation:
- Regulations, which are binding in their entirety and directly applicable to all member states; they do not need to be incorporated into national law to come into effect
- Directives, which are less specific, binding as to the result to be achieved but leaving the method of implementation open to member states; a directive thus has no force until it is incorporated into national law
- Decisions, which are also binding but are addressed solely to one or more member states or individuals in a member state
- Recommendations
- Opinions, which are merely persuasive

The Council also has certain budgetary powers, including the power to reject the budget as a whole and to increase expenditure or redistribute money within sectors. However, the final decision on whether the budget should be adopted or rejected lies with the Parliament.

The Council may delegate legislative powers to the Commission. These consist of implementing powers and technical updating of existing legislation.

The European Central Bank has legislative powers within its field of competence. The Commission also has limited legislative powers, where it has been delegated the power to implement or revise legislation by the Council.

THE COMMUNITY BUDGET

The principles of funding the European Community budget were established by the Treaty of Rome and remain with modifications to this day. There is a legally binding limit on the overall level of resources (known as 'own resources') that the Community can raise from its member states; this limit is defined as a percentage of gross national product (GNP). Budget revenue and expenditure must balance and there is therefore no deficit financing. The own resources decision, which came into effect in 1975 and has been regularly updated, states that there are four sources of Community funding under which each member state makes contributions: levies charged on agricultural imports into the Community from non-member states; customs duties on imports from non-member states; contributions based on member states' shares of a notional Community harmonised VAT base; and contributions based on member states' shares of Community GNP. The latter is the budget-balancing item and covers the difference between total expenditure and the revenue from the other three sources. Since 1984 the UK has had an annual rebate equivalent to 66 per cent of the difference between what the UK contributes to the budget and what it receives. This was introduced to compensate the UK for disproportionate contributions caused by its high proportion of agricultural and non-agricultural imports from non-member states and its

relatively small receipts from the Common Agricultural Policy, the most important portion of Community expenditure.

BUDGET 2003

	Billion euro*	As % of total
Agriculture	48.4	48.6
Regional and Social	33.8	34.3
External Action	4.8	4.9
Pre-accession Aid	3.3	3.3
Internal policies	6.6	6.6
Administration	5.2	5.3
Reserves	0.7	0.7
TOTAL		100.0

Source: General Budget of the European Union for the Financial Year 2003
* 1 euro = £0.694 as at 1 July 2003

Under the Edinburgh summit agreement (December 1992) the EC budget rose to a maximum of 1.27 per cent of the EU's GNP in 1999. The agreed budget for 2000–6 will keep the 1.27 per cent ceiling, but resources devoted to the existing member states will fall to 0.98 per cent, with the remaining resources devoted to enlargement.

THE COMMON AGRICULTURAL POLICY

The Common Agricultural Policy (CAP) was established to increase agricultural production, provide a fair standard of living for farmers and ensure the availability of food at reasonable prices. This aim was achieved by a number of mechanisms:
- import levies
- intervention purchase
- export subsidies

These measures stimulated production but also placed increasing demands on the EC budget which were exacerbated by the increase in EC members and yields enlarged by technological innovation; CAP now accounts for over 40 per cent of EC expenditure. To surmount these problems reforms were agreed in 1984, 1988, 1992, 1997 and 1999.

REFORMS
The 1984 reforms created the system of co-responsibility levies: farm payments to the EC by volume of product sold. This system was supplemented by national quotas for particular products, such as milk. The 1988 reforms emphasised 'set-aside', whereby farmers are given direct grants to take land out of production as a means of reducing surpluses. The set-aside reforms were extended in 1993 for another five years and to every farm in the EC. The 1999 reforms will further reduce surpluses of cereals, beef and milk by cutting the intervention prices by up to 20 per cent and compensating producers by making area payments. Under the reforms, CAP rules will also be simplified, eliminating inconsistencies between policies.

Under the Uruguay round agreement of GATT concluded in 1993, the EU was required, over a six-year period from 1 January 1995, to reduce its import levies by 36 per cent, reduce its domestic subsidies by 20 per cent, reduce its export subsidies by 36 per cent in value, and reduce its subsidised exports by 21 per cent in volume. Agenda 2000, the programme to overhaul the policies of the EU and prepare it for the accession of new member states, will temporarily increase the cost of the CAP by €1,000 million a year in compensation payments, but leave it broadly stable by the end of the current planning period in 2006.

THE SINGLE MARKET

Even after the removal of tariffs and quotas between member states in the 1970s and 1980s, the EC was still separated into a number of national markets by a series of non-tariff barriers. It was to overcome these internal barriers to trade that the concept of the Single Market was developed. The measures to be undertaken were codified in the Commission's 1985 White Paper on completing the internal market.

The White Paper included articles removing obstacles that distorted the internal market: the elimination of frontier controls; the mutual recognition of professional qualifications; the harmonisation of product specifications, largely by the mutual recognition of national standards; open tendering for public procurement contracts; the free movement of capital; the harmonisation of VAT and excise duties; and the reduction of state aid to particular industries. The target date for the completion of this process was 31 December 1992. The Single European Act aided the completion of the Single Market by changing the legislative process within the EC, particularly with the introduction of qualified majority voting in the Council of Ministers for some policy areas, and the introduction of the assent procedure in the European Parliament. The SEA also extends EC competence into the fields of technology, the environment, regional policy, monetary policy and external policy. The Single Market came into effect on 1 January 1993. The full implementation of the elimination of frontier controls and the harmonisation of taxes have, however, been repeatedly delayed.

THE EUROPEAN ECONOMIC AREA

The EC Single Market programme spurred European non-member states to open negotiations with the EC on preferential access for their goods, services, labour and capital to the Single Market. Principal among these states were European Free Trade Association (EFTA) members who opened negotiations on extending the Single Market to EFTA by the formation of the European Economic Area (EEA) encompassing all 19 EC and EFTA states. Agreement was reached in May 1992 but the operation of the EEA was delayed by its rejection in a Swiss referendum, necessitating an additional protocol agreed by the remaining 18 states. The EEA came into effect on 1 January 1994 after ratification by 17 member states (Liechtenstein joined on 1 May 1995 after adapting its customs union with Switzerland).

Austria, Finland and Sweden joined the EU itself on 1 January 1995, leaving only Norway, Iceland and Liechtenstein as the non-EU EEA members. Under the EEA agreement, the three states are to adopt the EU's *acquis communautaire*, apart from in the fields of agriculture, fisheries, and coal and steel.

The EEA is controlled by regular ministerial meetings and by a joint EU-EFTA committee which extends relevant EU legislation to EEA states. Apart from single market measures, there is co-operation in education, research and development, consumer policy and tourism. An EFTA Court of Justice has been established in Luxembourg and an EFTA Surveillance Authority in Brussels to supervise the implementation of the EEA Agreement.

THE EUROPEAN MONETARY SYSTEM AND THE SINGLE CURRENCY

The European monetary system (EMS) began operation in March 1979 with three main purposes. The first was to establish monetary stability in Europe, initially in exchange rates between EC member state currencies through the exchange rate mechanism (ERM), and in the longer term to be part of a wider stabilisation process, overcoming inflation and budget and trade deficits. The second purpose was to overcome the constraints resulting from the interdependence of EC economies, and the third was to aid the long-term process of European monetary integration.

The Maastricht Treaty set in motion timetables for achieving economic and monetary union (EMU) and a single currency (the euro). At the Brussels summit in May 1998, 11 member states were judged to fulfil or be close to fulfilling the necessary convergence criteria for participation in the first stage of EMU: Austria, Belgium, Finland, France, Germany, Ireland, Italy, Luxembourg, the Netherlands, Portugal and Spain.

The criteria were that:
- the budget deficit should be 3 per cent or less of gross domestic product (GDP)
- total national debt must not exceed 60 per cent of GDP
- inflation should be no more than 1.5 per cent above the average rate of the three best performing economies in the EU
- long-term interest rates should be no more than 2 per cent above the average of the three best performing economies in the EU in the previous 12 months
- applicants must have been members of the ERM for two years without having realigned or devalued their currency

Under the terms of a stability and growth pact agreed in Dublin in December 1996, penalties may be imposed on EMU members with high budget deficits. Governments with deficits exceeding 3 per cent of GDP will receive a warning and will be obliged to pay up to 0.5 per cent of their GDP into a fund after ten months. This will become a fine if the budget deficit is not rectified within two years. A member state with negative growth will be allowed to apply for an exemption from the fine in 'exceptional circumstances', e.g. a recession whereby GDP had fallen by 0.75 per cent or more during one year.

On 1 January 1999, the qualifying member states adopted the euro at irrevocably fixed exchange rates (*see* table below), the European Central Bank (ECB) took charge of the single monetary policy, and the euro replaced the ECU on a one-for-one basis.

On 19 June 2000, Greece was judged to have fulfilled the criteria for participation and adopted the euro on 1 January 2001. A referendum on the adoption of the euro was held in Denmark on 28 September 2000, but participation was rejected by the electorate.

The euro is now the legal currency in the participating states. Euro notes and coins were introduced on 1 January 2002 and circulated alongside national currencies for a period of up to two months, after which time national notes and coins ceased to be legal tender. The Swedish government announced plans to hold a referendum on adoption of the euro on 14 September 2003 and the

Danish government is considering holding a second referendum on the issue. On 10 June 2003 Britain announced that the euro would not be adopted at present on the grounds that the country was not economically ready to join the single currency. A future joining of the euro-zone was not ruled out.

CONVERSION RATES BETWEEN THE EURO AND THE CURRENCIES OF THE MEMBER STATES ADOPTING THE EURO

€ 1 = 13.7603 Austrian Schilling
       40.3399 Belgian Francs
       2.20371 Dutch Gulden
       5.94573 Finnish Markka
       6.55957 French Francs
       1.95583 German Deutsche Mark
       340.750 Greek Drachma
       0.787564 Irish Punts
       1,936.27 Italian Lire
       40.3399 Luxembourg Francs
       200.482 Portuguese Escudos
       166.386 Spanish Pesetas

Source: The Official Journal of the European Communities

The ECB meets every two weeks to set interest rates for the countries participating in the euro. Its governing council has 17 members, being the six members of the ECB's executive board and the 11 governors of the national central banks of the participating states.

With the advent of EMU, the ERM was revised and Denmark became a member of ERM II, which requires it to maintain its currencies within set margins of the euro. Membership of ERM II is voluntary, although all member states outside the euro zone are encouraged to take part. Sweden and the UK are currently not members.

THE MAASTRICHT TREATY

The Treaty on European Union was agreed at a meeting of the European Council in Maastricht, the Netherlands, in December 1991. It came into effect in November 1993 following ratification by the member states.

Three 'pillars' formed the basis of the new treaty:
- the European Community with its established institutions and decision-making processes
- a Common Foreign and Security Policy (*see* below) with the Western European Union as the potential defence component of the EU
- co-operation in justice and home affairs, with the Council of Ministers to co-ordinate policies on asylum, immigration, conditions of entry, cross-border crime, drug trafficking and terrorism

The Treaty established a common European citizenship for nationals of all member states and introduced the principle of subsidiarity whereby decisions are taken at the most appropriate level: national, regional or local. It extended EC competency into the areas of environmental and industrial policies, consumer affairs, health, and education and training, and extended qualified majority voting in the Council of Ministers to some areas which had previously required a unanimous vote. The powers of the European Parliament over the budget and over the Commission were also enhanced and a co-decision procedure enabled the Parliament to override decisions made by the Council of Ministers in certain policy areas. A separate protocol to the Maastricht Treaty on social policy was agreed by 11 states and was incorporated into the Amsterdam Treaty in 1997 following adoption by the UK.

THE AMSTERDAM TREATY

The treaties of Rome and Maastricht were again amended through the Treaty of Amsterdam, which was signed in October 1997 and which came into effect on 1 May 1999. It extends the scope of qualified majority voting and the powers of the European Parliament. It also includes a formal commitment to fundamental human rights, gives additional powers to the European Court of Justice and provides for the appointment of a High Representative for EU Common Foreign and Security Policy.

COMMON FOREIGN AND SECURITY POLICY

The Common Foreign and Security Policy (CFSP) was created as a pillar of the EU by the Maastricht Treaty (see above). It adopted the machinery of the European Political Co-operation (EPC) framework which it replaced and was charged with providing a forum for member states and EU institutions to consult on foreign affairs.

The CFSP system is headed by the Council of the European Union, which provides general lines of policy. Specific policy decisions are taken by the Council of Foreign Ministers, which meets at least four times a year to determine areas for joint action. The High Representative of the CFSP initiates action, manages the CFSP and represents it abroad. The Council of Ministers is supported by the Political Committee which meets monthly, or within 48 hours if there is a crisis, to prepare for ministerial discussions. A group of correspondents, designated diplomats in each member's foreign ministry, provides day-to-day contact.

The Amsterdam Treaty introduced qualified majority voting for foreign affairs and created a high representative on CFSP to act as a spokesperson. It also established a new policy planning and early warning unit to monitor international developments. The unit is to consist of specialists from the member states, the Council and the Commission, as well as from the Western European Union (WEU).

The member states agreed at the Helsinki summit in December 1999 to establish a capability for military crisis-management operations, known as the rapid reaction force, which would be able to undertake peacemaking missions independently of NATO. The force was declared operational at the Laeken summit on 14–15 December 2001.

THE SCHENGEN AGREEMENT

The Schengen Agreement was signed by France, Germany, Belgium, Luxembourg and the Netherlands in 1985. The Agreement committed the five states to abolishing internal border controls and erecting external frontiers against illegal immigrants, drug traffickers, terrorists and organised crime.

Subsequently signed by Spain and Portugal, the Agreement was ratified by the seven signatory states and entered into force in March 1995 with the removal of internal frontier, passport, customs and immigration controls. Italy and Austria became full members in April 1998 and Greece achieved full membership on 1 January 2000. Provisional agreement was reached in June 1995 between the signatory states and the Nordic Union on a merger of the two frontier-free zones, but Denmark,

Finland, Sweden, Iceland and Norway are not yet full members, although all five have signed the Schengen Agreement. The UK and the Republic of Ireland have not signed the Agreement, but have expressed their intention to join in some aspects of its work.

The Schengen Agreement originated as an intergovernmental agreement but became part of the EU following the signing of the Amsterdam Treaty.

THE TREATY OF NICE

The Treaty of Nice aims to enable the EU to accommodate up to 13 new member states. It extends qualified majority voting to 30 further articles of the treaties that previously required unanimity. The weighting of votes in the EU Council is to be altered from 1 January 2005 in preparation for the new member states, whose numbers of votes have been set. To obtain a qualified majority, a decision will require a specified number of votes (to be reviewed following each accession); the decision will have to be approved by a majority of member states and represent at least 62 per cent of the total population of the EU. The Treaty also sets the number of MEPs that both existing and new member states will have following enlargement.

The Treaty of Maastricht had established the right of groups of member states to work together without requiring the participation of all (enhanced co-operation); the Treaty of Nice removes the right of individual member states to veto the launch of enhanced co-operation and establishes a minimum number of eight member states for establishing enhanced co-operation in the field of common foreign and security policy (CFSP).

The European Commission will be limited to one member per member state from 2005, with a maximum of 27 commissioners; a rotation system is to be introduced once EU membership exceeds 27 states.

The Treaty also adds to the powers of the President of the Commission and amends the rules of the operation of the Court of Justice.

The Treaty was rejected by 54 per cent of voters in a referendum in Ireland, the only country to put the issue to its electorate.

THE LAEKEN SUMMIT

At the European Council held in Laeken, Belgium on 14–15 December 2001, a declaration was agreed which established a convention to prepare for treaty reforms at the intergovernmental conference due to be held in 2004. The convention, composed of representatives of national governments (15 members), national parliaments (30), the European Parliament (16), the European Commission (2) and the applicant states (39), started work on 28 February 2002, under the chairmanship of former French president Valérie Giscard d'Estaing.

The convention, established to discuss fundamental issues such as the consolidation and simplification of European treaties, the division of powers between the EU and member states, and how the EU's institutions can be made more relevant to the citizens of the Union, was due to report its recommendations in March 2003.

The Laeken European Council also agreed a common definition of terrorism, decided to institute an EU-wide arrest warrant, creating a single security area and thereby making it no longer necessary to extradite those accused of serious crimes, and established Eurojust to co-ordinate cross-border co-operation in crime investigation.

COURT OF JUSTICE OF THE EUROPEAN COMMUNITIES

Palais de la Cour de justice, Boulevard Konrad Adenauer, Kirchberg, L–2925 Luxembourg
Email: info@curia.eu.int Web: www.curia.eu.int

The Court of Justice is common to the three European Communities. It exists to safeguard the law in the interpretation and application of the Community treaties, to decide on the legality of decisions of the Council of Ministers or the Commission, and to determine infringements of the treaties. Cases may be brought to it by the member states, the Community institutions, firms or individuals. Its decisions are directly binding in the member countries, and the Maastricht Treaty enhanced the Court's powers by permitting it to impose fines on member states. The 15 judges and eight advocates-general of the Court are appointed for renewable six-year terms by the member governments in concert. During 2002, 477 new cases were lodged at the court and 513 cases were concluded.

Composition of the Court, in order of precedence, as at June 2003:

G. C. Rodríguez Iglesias *(President)*; F. Jacobs *(Advocate-General)*; C. G. Gulmann *(Judge)*; D. A. O Edward *(Judge)*; A. M. La Pergola *(Judge)*; J.-P. Puissochet *(Judge)*; P. Léger *(Advocate-General)*; P. Jann *(Judge)*; D. Ruiz-Jarabo Colomer *(Advocate-General)*; M. Wathelet *(Judge)*; R. Schintgen *(Judge)*; S. Alber *(Advocate-General)*; J. Mischo *(Advocate-General)*; V. Skouris *(Judge)*; F. Macken *(Judge)*; N. Colneric *(Judge)*; S. von Bahr *(Judge)*; A. Tizzano *(Advocate-General)*; J. N. da Cunha Rodrigues *(Judge)*; C. Timmermans *(Judge)*; L. A. Geelhoed *(Advocate-General)*; C. Stix-Hackl *(Advocate-General)*; A. Rosas *(Judge)*; R. Grass *(Registrar)*

COURT OF FIRST INSTANCE

Palais de la Cour de justice, Boulevard Konrad Adenauer, Kirchberg, L-2925 Luxembourg
Established under powers conferred by the Single European Act, the Court of First Instance has jurisdiction to hear and determine all actions brought by natural or legal persons. It is composed of 15 judges, appointed for renewable six-year terms by the governments of the member states. During 2002, 411 new cases were lodged at the court and 331 cases were concluded.

Composition of the Court, as at June 2003:

B. Vesterdorf *(President of the Court of First Instance)*; P. Lindh *(Judge)*; J. Azizi *(Judge)*; P. Mengozzi *(Judge)*; A. Meij *(Judge)*; R. García-Valdecasas y Fernández *(Judge)*; K. Lenaerts *(Judge)*; V. Tiili *(Judge)*; H. Legal *(Judge)*; J. Cooke *(Judge)*; M. Jaeger *(Judge)*; J. Pirrung *(Judge)*; M. Vilaras *(Judge)*; N. Forwood *(Judge)*; M. Martins de Nazaré Ribeiro *(Judge)*; H. Jung *(Registrar)*

THE COMMITTEE OF THE REGIONS

Montoyerstraat 92/102, B–1000 Brussels, Belgium
Email: info@cor.eu.int Web: www.cor.eu.int

The Committee of the Regions (COR) is an advisory and consultative body established to redress the lack of a role for regional and local authorities in the EU democratic system. The COR is composed of 222 appointed and indirectly elected members, of whom half are from large regions and half are from small local authorities, who meet five times each year for two days. The COR has eight commissions which deliver opinions on policies

affecting regions, such as trans-border transport links, economic and social cohesion, education and training, social policy, culture and regional policy.
President, Sir Albert Bore (UK)

THE EUROPEAN ECONOMIC AND SOCIAL COMMITTEE

Ravensteinstraat 2, B-1000 Brussels, Belgium
Web: www.esc.eu.int

The European Economic and Social Committee (EESC) is an advisory and consultative body. It has 222 members, nominated by member states, and is divided into three groups: employers, workers, and other interest groups such as consumers, farmers and the self-employed. It issues opinions on draft EC legislation and can bring matters to the attention of the Commission, Council and Parliament. The EESC's competencies have increased as a result of revisions to the Treaty of Rome, and the Treaty of Nice formally recognised the importance of the opinions of the EU's economic and social partners.
President, Roger Briesch (France)

THE EUROPEAN CENTRAL BANK

29 Kaiserstrasse, D-60311 Frankfurt-am-Main, Germany
Email: info@ecb.int Web: www.ecb.int

The European Central Bank (ECB), which superseded the European Monetary Institute, was established on 1 July 1998. Its governing bodies are the Executive Board, the Governing Council and the General Council. The Executive Board consists of the President, the Vice-President and four other members, who are appointed by the governments of the states participating in the single currency, at the level of Heads of State and Government. The Governing Council comprises the six members of the Executive Board and the 12 governors of the national central banks of the participating states; the General Council comprises the President and Vice-President and the 15 governors of the national central banks, the other members of the Executive Board being entitled to participate but not to vote. The ECB is independent of national governments and of all other EU institutions. It became fully operational on 1 January 1999, and defines and implements the single monetary policy necessary for EMU. It operates as part of the European System of Central Banks (ESCB), which consists of the ECB and the national central banks of the EU member states.
President, Willem Duisenberg (Netherlands)
Vice-President, Lucas Papademos (Greece)

THE EUROPEAN COURT OF AUDITORS

12 rue A. De Gasperi, L-1615 Luxembourg
Email: euraud@eca.eu.int Web: www.eca.eu.int

The European Court of Auditors, established in 1977, examines the accounts of all revenue and expenditure of the European Communities and Community bodies and evaluates whether all revenue has been received and all expenditure incurred in a lawful and regular manner and in accordance with the principles of sound financial management. The Court issues an annual report and a statement of assurance as to the reliability of the accounts and the legality and regularity of the underlying transactions. It also publishes special reports on specific topics and delivers opinions on financial matters. The Court has one member from each member state appointed for a six-year term by the Council of Ministers

following consultation with the European Parliament.
President, Juan M. Fabra Vallés (Spain)

THE EUROPEAN INVESTMENT BANK

100 boulevard Konrad Adenauer, L-2950 Luxembourg
Email: info@eib.org Web: www.eib.org

The European Investment Bank (EIB) was set up in 1958 under the terms of the Treaty of Rome to finance capital investment projects promoting the balanced development of the European Community by providing loans for capital investment projects furthering EU policy objectives, in fields such as regional development, transport and communications, security of energy supplies, the environment, international competitiveness, support for small and medium-sized enterprises, health and education investment, and investment to encourage a knowledge-based economy.

Outside the EU, the EIB participates in the implementation of the EU's development policy, through long-term loans from its own resources or subordinated loans and risk capital from EU or member states' budgetary funds, in some 150 non-EU countries: in pre-accession countries and, under the terms of different association or co-operation agreements, with countries in the Mediterranean region, in the Balkans, in Latin America, Asia and South Africa, in Africa, the Caribbean and the Pacific.

The Bank's total financing operations in 2001 amounted to €36.8 billion, of which €31.2 billion was for investment within the EU.

In June 2000, the EIB launched the Innovation 2000 Initiative, under which €12,000–15,000 million would be available over a three-year period to invest in the provision of new technologies in education, co-finance research and development, finance information and communications technology networks, make use of information technology to increase access to public services and assist SMEs to acquire and use information technologies.

The members of the EIB are the 15 member states of the EU, who have all subscribed to the Bank's capital of €100,000 million. The bulk of the funds required by the Bank to carry out its tasks are borrowed on the capital markets of the EU and non-member countries, and on the international market.

As it operates on a non-profit-making basis, the interest rates charged by the EIB reflect the cost of the Bank's borrowings and closely follow conditions in world capital markets.

The Board of Governors of the EIB consists of one government minister nominated by each of the member countries, usually the finance, economic affairs or treasury minister, who lay down general directives on the credit policy of the Bank and appoint members to the Board of Directors (24 nominated by the member states, one by the European Commission), which takes decisions on the granting and raising of loans and the fixing of interest rates. A Management Committee, composed of the Bank's President and seven Vice-Presidents, also appointed by the Board of Governors, is responsible for the day-to-day operations of the Bank. The President and Vice-Presidents also preside as Chairman and Vice-Chairmen at meetings of the Board of Directors.
President, Philippe Maystadt (Belgium)
Vice-Presidents, Wolfgang Roth; Ewald Nowotny; Peter Sedgwick; Isabel Martín Castellá; Michael G. Tutty; Gerlando Genuardi; Philippe de Fontaine Vive Curtaz

THE EUROPEAN POLICE OFFICE

PO Box 90850, NL-2509 LW The Hague, The Netherlands
Email: info@europol.eu.int Web: www.europol.eu.int

The European Police Office (Europol) came into being on 1 October 1998 and assumed its full powers on 1 July 1999. It superseded the Europol Drugs Unit and exists to improve police co-operation between member states and to combat terrorism, illicit traffic in drugs and other serious forms of international crime. It is ultimately responsible to the Council. Each member state has set up a national unit to liaise with Europol, and the units send at least one liaison officer to represent its interests at Europol headquarters. Europol maintains a computerised information system, designed to facilitate the exchange of information between member states; the system is maintained by the national units and may be consulted by Europol agents. The computerised database may contain both personal and non-personal data; individuals are entitled to request access to data concerning themselves. Europol has a Management Board comprising one senior police representative from each member state. All Europol activities are monitored by an independent joint supervisory body, to ensure the rights of the individual are upheld.

Director, Jürgen Storbeck (Germany)
Deputy Directors, Willy Bruggeman (Belgium); Gilles Leclair (France); Emanuele Marotta (Italy); Georges Rauchs (Luxembourg); David Valls-Russell (UK)

Other bodies:
THE EUROPEAN MEDICINE EVALUATION AGENCY (EMEA), 7 Westferry Circus, London E14 4HB.
Email: mail@emea.eudra.org
THE EUROPEAN ENVIRONMENT AGENCY (EEA), Kongens Nytorv 6, DK-1050, København, Denmark.
Email: eea@eea.eu.int
THE EUROPEAN TRAINING FOUNDATION, Villa Gualino, Viale Settimio Severo 65, I-10133 Torn, Italy.
Email: info@etf.eu.int
THE EUROPEAN CENTRE FOR THE DEVELOPMENT OF VOCATIONAL TRAINING (CEDEFOP), PO Box 22427, GR-55102 Thessaloniki (Finikas), Greece.
Email: webmaster@cedefop.gr
THE EUROPEAN MONITORING CENTRE FOR DRUGS AND DRUG ADDICTION, Rua da Cruz de Santa Apolónia 23-25, P-1149-045 Lisboa, Portugal. Email: info@emcdda.org
THE EUROPEAN FOUNDATION FOR THE IMPROVEMENT OF LIVING AND WORKING CONDITIONS, Wyattville Road, Loughlinstown, Co. Dublin, Ireland. Email: postmaster@eurofound.ie
THE OFFICE FOR HARMONISATION IN THE INTERNAL MARKET (OHIM), Avenida de Europa 4, AC 77, E-03080 Alicante, Spain. Email: information@oami.eu.int

THE COMMUNITY PLANT VARIETY RIGHTS OFFICE (CPVO), BP 2141, F- 49021 Angers Cédex 02, France.
Email: cpvo@cpvo.eu.int
THE EUROPEAN AGENCY FOR RECONSTRUCTION (EAR), PO Box 10177, GR-54626 Thessaloniki, Greece. Email: huges.mingarelli@ear.eu.int
THE EUROPEAN AGENCY FOR SAFETY AND HEALTH AT WORK, Gran Ví 33, E-48009 Bilbao, Spain.
Email: information@osha.eu.int
THE TRANSLATION CENTRE FOR BODIES IN THE EUROPEAN UNION, Bâtiment Nouvel Hémicycle, niveau 4, 1 rue du Fort Thüngen, L-1499 Luxembourg.
Email: cdt@eu.int
THE EUROPEAN MONITORING CENTRE ON RACISM AND XENOPHOBIA, Rahlgasse 3, A-1060 Wien, Austria. Email: office@eumc.eu.int

EUROPEAN COMMUNITY INFORMATION

EUROPEAN COMMISSION REPRESENTATION OFFICES

ENGLAND, 8 Storey's Gate, London SW1P 3AT.
   Tel: 020-7973 1992
WALES, 4 Cathedral Road, Cardiff CF11 9SG.
   Tel: 029-2037 1631
SCOTLAND, 9 Alva Street, Edinburgh EH2 4HP.
   Tel: 0131-225 2058
NORTHERN IRELAND, Windsor House,
   9–15 Bedford Street, Belfast BT2 7EG. Tel: 028-9024 0708
REPUBLIC OF IRELAND, 18 Dawson Street, Dublin 2

EUROPEAN COMMISSION DELEGATIONS

AUSTRALIA, 18 Arkana Street, Yarralumla, ACT 2600,
   and a number of other cities
CANADA, Inn of the Provinces, Office Tower (Suite 1110),
   350 Sparks Street, Ottawa, Ontario K1R 7SA
USA, 2300 M Street NW (Suite 707),
   Washington DC 20037; 1 Dag Hammarskjöld Plaza,
   254 East 47th Street, New York, NY 10017

UK OFFICE OF THE EUROPEAN PARLIAMENT

2 Queen Anne's Gate, London SW1H 9AA.
   Tel: 020-7227 4300

There are European Information Centres, set up to give information and advice to small and medium-sized businesses, in 25 British towns and cities. A number of universities maintain European Documentation Centres. Many local authorities also maintain European Public Information Centres, which provide information to the general public.

EUROPEAN PARLIAMENT

POLITICAL GROUPINGS as at June 2003

	PES	EPP-ED	UEN	ELDR	EUL/NGL	GREEN/EFA	EDD	IND.	TOTAL
Austria	7	7	–	–	–	2	–	5	21
Belgium	5	5	–	5	–	7	–	3	25
Denmark	2	1	1	6	3	–	3	–	16
Finland	3	5	–	5	1	2	–	–	16
France	18	21	4	1	15	9	9	10	87
Germany	35	53	–	–	7	4	–	–	99
Greece	9	9	–	–	7	–	–	–	25
Ireland	1	5	6	1	–	2	–	–	15
Italy	16	35	10	8	6	2	–	10	87
Luxembourg	2	2	–	1	–	1	–	–	6
Netherlands	6	9	–	8	1	4	3	–	31
Portugal	12	9	2	–	2	–	–	–	25
Spain	24	28	–	3	4	4	–	1	64
Sweden	6	7	–	4	3	2	–	–	22
UK	29	37	–	11	–	6	3	1	87
TOTAL	175	233	23	53	49	45	18	30	626

PES   Party of European Socialists (including the British, Irish and Dutch Labour Parties, Northern Ireland Social Democratic and Labour Party, Austrian, Danish, Finnish, German, Italian and Swedish Social Democrats, Belgian, French, Greek, Portuguese, and Spanish Socialists, Italian Democratic Left Party, Luxembourg Socialist Workers' Party), Socialist, Social Democratic and Labour parties

EPP-ED   European People's Party and European Democrats (including British and Danish Conservative Parties, Spanish Popular Party, French Nouvelle UDF, RPR and DL, Irish Fine Gael, Swedish Moderate Party, Finnish National Coalition Party, Austrian People's Party, Greek New Democracy, Belgian Christian Socialists, Italian Christian Democrats, Pensioners' Party and People's Party, Luxembourg Christian Socialists, Portuguese Social Democrats), Christian Democrats, Christian Socialists and Conservatives

UEN   Union for a Europe of Nations

ELDR   European Liberal, Democrat and Reform Party (including British Liberal Democrats, Danish Left and Radical Left Parties, Dutch Democrats '66 and People's Party for Freedom and Democracy, Belgian Liberals, Italian and Luxembourg Democrats, Swedish Liberal People's Party, Finnish Swedish People's Party and Centre Party), centre and liberal parties

EUL/ NGL   Confederal Group of the European United Left/Nordic Green Left (French, Greek, Italian and Portuguese Communist Parties, Italian Refounded Communist Party, Danish, Dutch, Swedish, Finnish, Greek and Spanish Socialist/Left parties)

Green/ EFA   Greens/European Free Alliance Group (Austrian, British, Danish, Finnish, French, German, Greek, Irish, Italian, Luxembourgish, Portuguese, Spanish and Swedish Green Parties, Dutch Green Left Party, Belgian Ecological Parties, Plaid Cymru and Scottish National Parties), green and nationalist parties

EDD   Group for a Europe of Democracies and Diversities (French Hunting, Fishing, Nature and Traditions, Dutch Calvinists and Christians, UK Independence Party, Danish June Movement and Movement Against the EU), anti-EU, anti-federalist and religious parties

Ind.   Independents (Austrian Freedom Party, Belgian Flemish Block, French National Front, Italian National Alliance, Northern Ireland Democratic Unionist Party)

INTERNATIONAL ORGANISATIONS

ANDEAN COMMUNITY

General Secretariat, Paseo de la República 3895,
esq. Aramburú, San Isidro, Lima 27, Peru
Tel: (00 51) (1) 411 1400 Fax: (00 51) (1) 221 3329
Email: contacto@comunidadandina.org
Web: www.comunidadandina.org

The Andean Community came into being on 1 August 1997. It facilitates the development of the member countries through economic and social integration and co-operation, acceleration of the economic growth of the Andean countries, the promotion of job creation, furthering the aim of creating a Latin American common market, strengthening the position of the member states in the international economic context, and reducing the differences in development that exist between the member states.

It aims to achieve its objectives by a programme of complete trade liberalisation, a common external tariff, the reduction of border controls, the progressive harmonisation of economic and social policies, the co-ordination of national legislation in relevant fields, promoting industrialisation and agricultural development, and supporting technological development programmes.

It comprises the five member states, Bolivia, Colombia, Ecuador, Peru and Venezuela, and the bodies of the Andean Integration System (AIS). The General Secretariat of the Andean Community is its executive body, which is responsible for administration, ensuring that member states comply with their obligations, and resolving disputes. The General Secretariat is under the direction of the Secretary-General, who is elected by the Andean Council of Foreign Ministers (ACFM). The General Secretariat can propose decisions or suggestions to the ACFM and to the Commission. It also manages the integration process, ensures that Community commitments are fulfilled, and maintains relations with the member countries and the executive bodies of other international bodies.

The Andean Presidential Council is the highest-level body of the AIS and comprises the presidents of the member states; it meets at least once a year and decides on new policies, evaluates the integration process and makes decisions on reports and suggestions from other bodies. The chairmanship is rotated among the members of the council on a calendar year basis. The ACFM co-ordinates the positions of the member states in international issues, signs international agreements on behalf of its member states and can issue decisions that are legally binding in the member states. The Commission of the Andean Community is composed of a plenipotentiary representative from each member state and makes, implements and evaluates policies in the field of trade and investment in the region. The Court of Justice of the Andean Community comprises one judge from each member state. It ensures the uniform implementation of decisions and settles disputes. The Andean Development Corporation aims to support the sustainable development of the member states by promoting trade and investment. The Andean Parliament submits proposals to other bodies and promotes the harmonisation of legislation.

Secretary-General, Guillermo Fernández de Soto

ARAB MAGHREB UNION

27 Avenue Okba, Rabat, Morocco
Tel: (00 212) (7) 777 2668 Fax: (00 212) (7) 777 2693
Email: sg.uma@maghrebarabe.org
Web: www.maghrebarabe.org

The treaty establishing the Arab Maghreb Union (AMU) was signed on 17 February 1989 by the heads of state of the five member states, Algeria, Libya, Mauritania, Morocco and Tunisia. The AMU aims to strengthen ties between the member states, who share strong historical, cultural and linguistic affinities, by developing agriculture and commerce, introducing the free circulation of goods and services, and establishing joint projects and economic co-operation programmes.

Decisions are made by the Council of Heads of State, which meets annually, and must be unanimous. A Council of Foreign Affairs Ministers meets regularly to prepare for the sessions of the Council of Heads of State. The Secretariat is based in Rabat and there is a Consultative Assembly, which consists of 30 representatives from each member state, based in Algiers, and a Court of Justice, with two judges from each country, based in Nouakchott, Mauritania.

Secretary-General, Mohamed Habib Boularès (Tunisia)

ASIAN DEVELOPMENT BANK

PO Box 789, 0980 Manila, Philippines
Tel: (632) 632 444 Fax: (632) 636 2444
Email: information@adb.org
Web: www.adb.org

The Asian Development Bank (ADB) was founded in 1966 and is a multilateral financial institution dedicated to reducing poverty in Asia and the Pacific. The ADB extends loans, equity investments and technical assistance to governments and public and private enterprises in its developing member countries, promotes investment of public and private capital for development and assists in co-ordinating development policies and plans in the developing member countries. The bank's projects and programmes prioritise economic growth, human development, gender and development, good governance, environmental protection, private sector development and regional co-operation.

The ADB raises funds through members' contributions and bond issues on the world's capital markets. In 2001, the ADB provided loans totalling US$5.3 billion and technical assistance costing US$146.4 million.

There are 61 member countries in the Asian and Pacific region and in Western Europe and North America.

The ADB's headquarters is in the Philippines and there are 22 offices around the world.

ASIA-PACIFIC ECONOMIC CO-OPERATION

35 Heng Mui Keng Terrace, Singapore 119616
Tel: (00 65) 6775 6012 Fax: (00 65) 6775 6013
Email: info@mail.apecsec.org.sg
Web: www.apecsec.org.sg

Asia-Pacific Economic Co-operation (APEC) was founded in 1989 in response to the growing interdependence among Asia-Pacific economies. The 1994 Declaration of Common Resolve envisaged a free trade zone, to be established by 2010 by the industrialised countries and by 2020 by the developing member states. There are three pillars of APEC activities: trade and investment liberalisation, business facilitation, and economic and technical co-operation. Members define and fund work programmes for APEC's four committees, 11 working groups and other APEC fora.

The members are: Australia, Brunei, Canada, Chile, China (People's Republic), China (Hong Kong), Indonesia, Japan, Republic of Korea, Malaysia, Mexico, New Zealand, Papua New Guinea, Peru, the Philippines, Russia, Singapore, Chinese Taipei, Thailand, the USA and Vietnam.

The APEC chairman is responsible for hosting the annual ministerial meeting of foreign and economic ministers. The chairmanship rotates annually among member states. Senior officials of the organisation make recommendations to the ministers and carry out their decisions. They oversee and co-ordinate budgets and work programmes. In addition, there are many advisory groups.

There is a permanent secretariat based in Singapore.

ASSOCIATION OF SOUTH EAST ASIAN NATIONS

70A Jalan Sisingamangaraja, Jakarta 12110, Indonesia
Tel: (00 62) (21) 726 2991 Fax: (00 62) (21) 739 8234
Email: public@asean.or.id
Web: www.asean.or.id

The Association of South East Asian Nations (ASEAN) was formed in 1967 with the aims of accelerating economic growth, social progress and cultural development, and ensuring regional stability. The founding members are Indonesia, Malaysia, the Philippines, Singapore and Thailand. Brunei and Vietnam joined in 1984 and 1995 respectively. Laos and Myanmar were admitted in July 1997. Cambodia was admitted on 30 April 1999.

The ASEAN Summit, a meeting of the heads of government, which convenes every three years, is ASEAN's highest authority, but informal summits are held annually. The ASEAN Ministerial Meeting (AMM) is an annual meeting of ASEAN foreign ministers and is responsible for the formulation of policy guidelines and the co-ordination of activities, although other relevant ministers are included in the AMM depending on the subject under discussion. The ASEAN Economic Ministers (AEM) meet annually to co-ordinate economic policy. The AMM and AEM usually hold a joint ministerial meeting before an ASEAN summit.

The 1992 Summit agreed to set up the ASEAN Free Trade Area (AFTA), which was fully implemented in 2003. A common preferential tariff was introduced in 1993. At the annual summit in 1995, a South East Asia nuclear weapon-free zone was declared.

The Secretary-General of ASEAN is appointed on merit by the heads of government and can initiate, advise on, co-ordinate and implement ASEAN activities. In addition to the ASEAN Secretariat based in Jakarta, each member state has a national secretariat in its foreign ministry which organises and implements activities at national level.

Secretary-General, Ong Keng Yong (Singapore)
ASEAN COMMITTEE IN THE UK,
Indonesian Embassy, 38 Grosvenor Square, London W1X 9AD
Tel 020-7499 7661 Fax 020-7491 4993
Chairman, H.E. Nana S. Sutresna

BALTIC ASSEMBLY

Basteja bulvaris 12, LV-1050 Riga, Latvia
Tel: (00 371) 770 1795 Fax: (00 371) 770 1796
Email: baltasam@parks.lv
Web: www.baltasam.org

The Baltic Assembly (BA) is an international organisation for co-operation between the parliaments of Estonia, Latvia and Lithuania, established in November 1991.

The legislature of each member state appoints 20 parliamentarians to the BA, including a head and deputy head of the national delegation. The BA holds two sessions per year, which are held in each of the member states in rotation.

The Presidium of the BA comprises the head and deputy head of each national delegation. It selects a Chairman, who is the head of the delegation of the member state which will host the following session, and the heads of the two other delegations become Deputy Chairmen. The Presidium is responsible for co-ordinating the activities of BA institutions, organises the sessions, supervises the budget and maintains relations with international organisations and the member states' national legislatures. In addition, there are permanent and ad-hoc committees.

The Baltic Assembly meets once a year with the Baltic Council of Ministers, which comprises the heads of government and ministers of the Baltic states and which carries out intergovernmental and regional co-operation between the Baltic States; the joint sessions are known as the Baltic Council.

Chairperson of the Presidium, Giedrė Purvaneckienė (Lithuania)
Deputy Chairmen, Romualds Ražuks (Latvia); Trivimi Velliste (Estonia); Audrius Klišonis (Lithuania); Arnis Razminovičs (Latvia)

BANK FOR INTERNATIONAL SETTLEMENTS

Centralbahnplatz 2 & Aeschenplatz 1, CH-4002
Basel, Switzerland
Tel: (00 41) (61) 280 8080
Fax: (00 41) (61) 280 9100/8100
Telex: 962 487 biz ch
Email: email@bis.org
Web: www.bis.org

The Bank for International Settlements (BIS), which was founded in 1930, fosters international monetary and financial co-operation by acting as a forum to promote discussion and facilitate decision-making processes among central banks and within the international financial community. It also acts as a centre for economic and monetary research and an agent in connection with international financial operations.

The statutory organs of the BIS are the General Meeting and the Board of Directors. There are 50 member central banks. At present, around 130 central banks and international financial institutions place deposits with the BIS. The total of currency deposits placed with the BIS amounted to approximately US$154 billion at the end of March 2002, representing 7.6 per cent of world foreign exchange reserves. Administrative control is vested in the Board of Directors which comprises 17 members including the Governor of the Bank of England.

Chairman of the Board of Directors and President of the Bank for International Settlements, Nout Wellink (Netherlands)

CAB INTERNATIONAL
Wallingford, Oxon OX10 8DE
Tel: 01491-832111 Fax: 01491-833508
Email: cabi@cabi.org
Web: www.cabi.org

CAB International (formerly the Commonwealth Agricultural Bureau) was founded in 1929. It generates, disseminates and applies scientific knowledge in support of sustainable development, with an emphasis on agriculture, forestry and natural resources and the needs of developing countries. The organisation is owned and governed by its 40 member governments, each represented on an Executive Council. A Governing Board provides guidance to management on policy issues.

CABI has two divisions: bioscience and publishing. These undertake research and consultancy aimed at raising agricultural productivity, conserving biological resources, protecting the environment and controlling disease. The organisation publishes books, journals and newsletters and produces bibliographic databases on agriculture, health and allied disciplines. It also undertakes contracted scientific research and provides consultancy services and information support to developing countries.

Director-General, Dr Denis Blight

CARIBBEAN COMMUNITY AND COMMON MARKET
PO Box 10827, Georgetown, Guyana
Tel: (00 592) 226 9281/9 Fax: (00 592) 226 7816
Email: carisec2@caricom.org
Web: www.caricom.org

The Caribbean Community and Common Market (CARICOM) was established in 1973 with the signing of the Treaty of Chaguaramas, which was revised in 2001. The objectives of Caricom are to improve working and living standards, to aim for full employment, to promote economic development and convergence, to expand economic relations with third states, to enhance economic competitiveness and productivity, to co-ordinate member states' foreign and economic policies and enhance functional co-operation in the delivery of common services, including the promotion of activities in the fields of health, education, transport and telecommunications.

The supreme organ is the Conference of Heads of Government, which determines policy, takes strategic decisions and is responsible for resolving conflicts and all matters relating to the founding treaty. The Community Council of Ministers consists of ministers of government responsible for CARICOM affairs and any other ministers designated by member states, and is responsible for strategic planning in the areas of economic integration, functional co-operation and external relations. The principal administrative arm is the Secretariat, based in Guyana. The Bureau of the Conference of Heads of Government is the executive body. It comprises the Chairman of the Conference, the outgoing Chairman and the Secretary-General, who are authorised to initiate proposals and to secure the implementation of CARICOM decisions. In addition, there are four ministerial councils dealing with trade and economic development, foreign and community relations, human and social development, and finance and planning.

The 15 member states are Antigua and Barbuda, the Bahamas (which is not a member of the Common Market), Barbados, Belize, Dominica, Grenada, Guyana, Haiti, Jamaica, Montserrat, St Christopher and Nevis, St Lucia, St Vincent and the Grenadines, Suriname and Trinidad and Tobago. Anguilla, the British Virgin Islands and the Turks and Caicos Islands are associate members. Aruba, Bermuda, the Cayman Islands, Colombia, the Dominican Republic, Mexico, the Netherlands' Antilles, Puerto Rico and Venezuela have observer status.

Secretary-General, Edwin W. Carrington

COMMISSION OF THE AFRICAN UNION
PO Box 3243, Addis Ababa, Ethiopia
Tel: (00 251) (1) 517700 Fax: (00 251) (1) 517844, 518718

The Organisation of African Unity (OAU) was established in 1963 and has 53 members; Morocco suspended its participation in 1985 in protest at the Polisario-proclaimed Saharan Arab Democratic Republic (SADR), representing Western Sahara, being admitted as a member. The OAU aims to further African unity and solidarity, to co-ordinate political, economic, social and defence policies, and to eliminate colonialism in Africa.

The chief organs are the Assembly of heads of state or government, which is the supreme organ of the OAU and meets once a year to consider matters of common African concern and to co-ordinate the Organisation's policies; the Council of foreign ministers, which is the Organisation's executive body responsible for the implementation of the Assembly's policies, and which meets twice a year; and the Commission of Mediation, Conciliation and Arbitration which promotes the peaceful settlement of disputes between member countries. The main administrative body is the General Secretariat, based in Addis Ababa, headed by a Secretary-General who is elected by the Assembly for a four-year term.

Substantial budgetary arrears due to delays in the payment of national contributions has meant that the OAU continually faces difficulties in furthering its aims. Its budget for 2001 was about US$31 million. In June 1991 the Assembly adopted an African Economic Community Treaty which envisages establishment of the Economic Community after ratification by two-thirds of the OAU's membership. In June 1993 a mechanism was created for conflict prevention, management and resolution, and a peace fund was established.

Following an initiative put forward by Libyan leader Col. Muammar al-Gadhafi at a special conference in Sirte, Libya, in September 1999, it was agreed at the 36th summit of the OAU in July 2000 in Lomé, Togo, to establish an African Union.

The creation of the African Union, which is to have its own parliament, central bank and court of justice, was declared at an extraordinary summit meeting in Sirte on

1–2 March 2001, and legally began operations on 26 May 2001 when two-thirds of the member states had ratified the constituent act.

Secretary-General, Amara Essy (Côte d'Ivoire)

THE COMMONWEALTH

The Commonwealth is a voluntary association of 54 sovereign independent states together with their associated states and dependencies. All of the states were formerly parts of the British Empire or League of Nations (later UN) mandated territories, except for Mozambique which was admitted as a unique case because of its history of co-operation with neighbouring Commonwealth nations.

The status and relationship of member nations were first defined by the Inter-Imperial Relations Committee of the 1926 Imperial Conference, when the six existing dominions (Australia, Canada, the Irish Free State, Newfoundland, New Zealand and South Africa) were described as 'autonomous Communities within the British Empire, equal in status, in no way subordinate one to another in any aspect of their domestic or external affairs, though united by a common allegiance to the Crown and freely associated as Members of the British Commonwealth of Nations'. This formula was given legal substance by the Statute of Westminster 1931.

This concept of a group of countries owing allegiance to a single Crown changed in 1949 when India decided to become a republic. Her continued membership of the Commonwealth was agreed by the other members on the basis of her 'acceptance of the monarch as the symbol of the free association of its independent member nations and as such the Head of the Commonwealth'. This paved the way for other republics to join the association in due course. Member nations agreed at the time of the accession of Queen Elizabeth II to recognise Her Majesty as the new Head of the Commonwealth. However, the position is not vested in the British Crown.

THE MODERN COMMONWEALTH

As the UK's former colonies joined, initially with India and Pakistan in 1947, the Commonwealth was transformed from a grouping of all-white dominions into a multiracial association of equal, sovereign nations. It increasingly focused on promoting development and racial equality. South Africa withdrew in 1961 when it became clear that its reapplication for membership on becoming a republic would be rejected over its policy of apartheid.

The new goals of advocating democracy, the rule of law, good government and social justice were enshrined in the Harare Commonwealth Declaration (1991), which formed the basis of new membership guide-lines agreed in Cyprus in 1993. Following the adoption of measures at the New Zealand summit in 1995 against serious or persistent violations of these principles, Nigeria was suspended in 1995 and Sierra Leone was suspended in 1997 for anti-democratic behaviour. Sierra Leone's suspension was revoked in March 1998 when the legitimate government was returned to power. Similarly, Nigeria's suspension was lifted on 29 May 1999, the day a newly elected civilian president took office. The heads of government meeting in Edinburgh in 1997 established a set of economic principles for the Commonwealth, promoting economic growth whilst protecting smaller member states from the negative effects of globalisation.

MEMBERSHIP

Membership of the Commonwealth involves acceptance of the association's basic principles and is subject to the approval of existing members. There are 54 members at present. (The date of joining the Commonwealth is shown in parenthesis.)

*Antigua and Barbuda (1981)	Namibia (1990)
*Australia (1931)	Nauru (1968)
*The Bahamas (1973)	*New Zealand (1931)
Bangladesh (1972)	Nigeria (1960)
*Barbados (1966)	†Pakistan (1947)
*Belize (1981)	*Papua New Guinea (1975)
Botswana (1966)	*St Christopher and Nevis
Brunei (1984)	(1983)
Cameroon (1995)	*St Lucia (1979)
*Canada (1931)	*St Vincent and the
Cyprus (1961)	Grenadines (1979)
Dominica (1978)	Samoa (1970)
Fiji (1970, 1997, 2001)	Seychelles (1976)
The Gambia (1965)	Sierra Leone (1961)
Ghana (1957)	Singapore (1965)
*Grenada (1974)	*Solomon Islands (1978)
Guyana (1966)	South Africa (1931)
India (1947)	Sri Lanka (1948)
*Jamaica (1962)	Swaziland (1968)
Kenya (1963)	Tanzania (1961)
Kiribati (1979)	Tonga (1970)
Lesotho (1966)	Trinidad and Tobago
Malawi (1964)	(1962)
Malaysia (1957)	*Tuvalu (1978)
The Maldives (1982)	Uganda (1962)
Malta (1964)	*United Kingdom
Mauritius (1968)	Vanuatu (1980)
Mozambique (1995)	Zambia (1964)
	‡Zimbabwe (1980)

* Realms of Queen Elizabeth II; † Suspended 18 October 1999; ‡ Suspended

Tuvalu became a full member on 1 September 2000.

Countries which have left the Commonwealth
Fiji (1987, rejoined 1997, suspended 2000, readmitted 21 December 2001)
Republic of Ireland (1949)
Pakistan (1972, rejoined 1989, suspended 1999)
South Africa (1961, rejoined 1994)

Of the 54 member states, 16 have Queen Elizabeth II as head of state, 33 are republics, and five have national monarchies.

In each of the realms where Queen Elizabeth II is head of state (except for the UK), she is personally represented by a Governor-General, who holds in all essential respects the same position in relation to the administration of public affairs in the realm as is held by Her Majesty in Britain. The Governor-General is appointed by The Queen on the advice of the government of the state concerned.

INTERGOVERNMENTAL AND OTHER LINKS

The main forum for consultation is the Commonwealth heads of government meetings held biennially to discuss international developments and to consider co-operation among members. Decisions are reached by consensus, and the views of the meeting are set out in a communiqué. There are also annual meetings of finance ministers and frequent meetings of ministers and officials in other fields, such as education, health, women's affairs, agriculture, and science. Intergovernmental links are complemented by the activities of some 300 Commonwealth non-governmental organisations linking professionals, sportsmen and sportswomen, and interest groups, forming a 'people's Commonwealth'. The Commonwealth Games take place every four years.

Assistance to other Commonwealth countries normally has priority in the bilateral aid programmes of the association's developed members (Australia, Britain, Canada and New Zealand), who direct about 30 per cent of their aid to other member countries. Developing Commonwealth nations also assist their poorer partners, and many Commonwealth voluntary organisations promote development.

COMMONWEALTH SECRETARIAT

The Commonwealth has a secretariat, established in 1965 in London, which is funded by all member governments. This is the main agency for multilateral communication between member governments on issues relating to the Commonwealth as a whole. It promotes consultation and co-operation, disseminates information on matters of common concern, organises meetings including the biennial summits, co-ordinates Commonwealth activities, and provides technical assistance for economic and social development through the Commonwealth Fund for Technical Co-operation.

The Commonwealth Foundation was established by Commonwealth governments in 1966 as an autonomous body with a board of governors representing Commonwealth governments that fund the Foundation. It promotes and funds exchanges and other activities aimed at strengthening the skills and effectiveness of professionals and non-governmental organisations. It also promotes culture, rural development, social welfare and the role of women.

COMMONWEALTH SECRETARIAT, Marlborough House, Pall Mall, London SW1Y 5HX. Tel: 020-7747 6200 Fax: 020-7930 0827 Email: info@commonwealth.int Web: www.thecommonwealth.org
Secretary-General, Rt. Hon. Don McKinnon (New Zealand)
COMMONWEALTH FOUNDATION, Marlborough House, Pall Mall, London SW1Y 5HY. Tel: 020-7930 3783.
Director, Colin Ball (UK)
COMMONWEALTH INSTITUTE, Kensington High Street, London W8 6NQ. Tel: 020-7603 4535.
Director-General, David French

COMMONWEALTH OF INDEPENDENT STATES

Ul. Kirova 17, Minsk, Belarus
Tel: (00 375) (17) 222 3517 Fax: (00 375) (17) 227 2339 Email: webmaster@www.cis.minsk.by
Web: www.cis.minsk.by

The Commonwealth of Independent States (CIS) is a multilateral grouping of 12 sovereign states that were formerly constituent republics of the USSR (Armenia, Azerbaijan, Belarus, Georgia, Kazakhstan, Kyrgyzstan, Moldova, Russia, Tajikistan, Turkmenistan, Ukraine and Uzbekistan). It was formed in 1991. Georgia joined in 1993. The CIS charter, signed in 1993 by seven states (Armenia, Belarus, Kazakhstan, Kyrgyzstan, Russia, Tajikistan, Uzbekistan) and open for signing by the other states, formally established the functions of the organisation and the obligations of its member states.

The CIS acts as a co-ordinating mechanism for foreign, defence and economic policies and is a forum for addressing problems which have arisen from the break-up of the USSR. These matters are addressed in more than 70 inter-state, intergovernmental co-ordinating and consultative statutory bodies. However, member states have criticised the CIS for operating ineffectively and for failing to carry through decisions made by CIS organs.

STRUCTURE

The two supreme CIS bodies are the Council of Heads of State and the Council of Heads of Government. The Council of Heads of State is the highest organ of the CIS and there are various ministerial, parliamentary, banking, economic and security councils. The Executive Committee, based in Minsk and Moscow, provides administrative support.

DEFENCE CO-OPERATION

On becoming members of the CIS, the states agreed to recognise their existing borders, respect one another's territorial integrity and reject the use of military force or other forms of coercion to settle disputes between them.

A Treaty on Collective Security was signed in 1992 by six states and a joint peacemaking force, to intervene in CIS conflicts, was agreed upon by nine states. Russia concluded bilateral and multilateral agreements with other CIS states under the supervision of the Council of Heads of Collective Security (established 1993). These were gradually upgraded into CIS agreements under the umbrella of the Treaty on Collective Security, enabling Russia to station troops in eight of the other 11 CIS states (not Moldova, Turkmenistan or Ukraine), and giving Russian forces de facto control of virtually all of the former USSR's external borders. Only Ukraine and Moldova remained outside the defence co-operation framework and did not sign the Treaty on Collective Security, from which Azerbaijan, Georgia and Uzbekistan withdrew in 1999, forming a new defensive grouping with Moldova and Ukraine. Russian border guards were also withdrawn from Georgia, Kyrgyzstan and Turkmenistan in 1999.

ECONOMIC CO-OPERATION

In 1991, 11 republics signed a treaty forming an economic community. The principles of the treaty were embodied within the CIS and formed the basis of its economic co-operation. Members agreed to refrain from economic actions that would damage each other and to co-ordinate economic and monetary policies. A Co-ordinating Consultative Committee, an economic arbitration court and an inter-state bank were established. A single monetary unit, the rouble, was originally agreed upon by all member states, and the members recognised that the basis of recovery for their economies was private ownership, free enterprise and competition.

The 11 CIS members who signed the Treaty on the Establishment of an Economic Union in September 1993 (Ukraine is an associate member of the economic union) committed themselves to a common economic space with free movement of goods, services, capital and labour. Belarus, Kazakhstan, Kyrgyzstan and Russia signed the Treaty on the Establishment of a Customs Union in March 1996; the treaty was later signed by Tajikistan and on 10 October 2000, the presidents of the five countries approved a treaty establishing the Eurasian Economic Community.
Executive Secretary, Yuri Yarov

CONFERENCE ON INTERACTION AND CONFIDENCE-BUILDING MEASURES IN ASIA

The Conference on Interaction and Confidence-Building Measures in Asia (CICA) aims to create a security framework for Asia along the same lines as the OSCE in Europe. The foreign ministers of the member states signed the Declaration on the Principles Guiding Relations on 14 September 1999, in which the signatories confirmed their determination to uphold the principles of sovereignty, territorial integrity, peaceful settlement of disputes, non-intervention in internal affairs, economic, social and cultural co-operation, and human rights and fundamental freedoms.

The founder members of CICA are Afghanistan, Azerbaijan, China, Egypt, India, Iran, Israel, Kazakhstan, Kyrgyzstan, Pakistan, the Palestinian National Authority, Russia, Tajikistan, Turkey and Uzbekistan. Mongolia joined in June 2001. Observers are Indonesia, Japan, Lebanon, Malaysia, South Korea, Thailand, Ukraine, the USA and Vietnam.

There is at present no permanent secretariat.

CO-OPERATION COUNCIL FOR THE ARAB STATES OF THE GULF

PO Box 7153, Riyadh 11 462, Saudi Arabia
Tel: (00 966) (01) 482 7777 Fax (00 966) (01) 482 9109
Web: www.gcc-sg.org

The Co-operation Council for the Arab States of the Gulf, or Gulf Co-operation Council (GCC), as it is informally known, was established on 25 May 1981 with the objectives of increasing co-ordination and integration between its member states, harmonising economic, commercial, educational and social policies and promoting scientific and technical innovation in key economic areas.

The GCC has six members: Bahrain, Kuwait, Oman, Qatar, Saudi Arabia and the United Arab Emirates.

The highest authority of the GCC is the Supreme Council, whose presidency rotates among members' heads of states based on the (Arabic) alphabetical order of their names. It holds one regular session every year, but extraordinary sessions may be convened if necessary. The meeting of the Supreme Council is considered valid if attended by two-thirds of the member states.

The Ministerial Council, which ordinarily meets every three months, consists of the Foreign Ministers of the member states or other delegated ministers. The presidency of the Ministerial Council is held by the state which last presided over the Supreme Council or, if necessary, the state which is next to preside over the Supreme Council. Disputes at either commission can be referred to an *ad hoc* commission.

Administrative functions are dealt with by a General Secretariat, which is composed of a Secretary-General, Assistant Secretaries-General, and a number of staff.

COUNCIL OF THE BALTIC SEA STATES

Secretariat, Strömsborg, PO Box 2010,
S-103 11 Stockholm, Sweden
Tel: (00 46) (8) 440 1920 Fax: (00 46) (8) 440 1944
Email: cbss@cbss.st
Web: www.cbss.st

The Council of the Baltic Sea States (CBSS) was founded in March 1992 with the aim of creating a regional forum to increase co-operation and co-ordination among the states which border on the Baltic Sea in assisting new democratic institutions, economic and technical development, humanitarian aid and health, energy and environmental issues, cultural programmes, education, tourism, transportation and communication.

There are 12 members: Denmark, Estonia, Finland, Germany, Iceland, Latvia, Lithuania, Norway, Poland, Russia, Sweden and the European Commission.

The Council consists of the foreign ministers of each member state and a member of the European Commission. Chairmanship of the Council rotates on an annual basis, and the annual session is held in the country currently in the chair. The foreign minister of the presiding country is responsible for co-ordinating activities between the sessions.

Chairmanship July 2003-June 2004, Estonia; *July 2004-June 2005*, Poland

THE COUNCIL OF EUROPE

F-67075 Strasbourg, France
Tel: (00 33) (3) 8841 2033 Fax: (00 33) (3) 8841 2745
Email: point_i@coe.int
Web: www.coe.int

The Council of Europe was founded in 1949. Its aim is to achieve greater unity between its members, to safeguard their European heritage and to facilitate their progress in economic, social, cultural, educational, scientific, legal and administrative matters, and in the furtherance of pluralist democracy, human rights and fundamental freedoms.

There are 44 members. The organs are the Committee of Ministers, consisting of the foreign ministers of member countries, who meet twice yearly, and the Parliamentary Assembly of 301 members, elected or chosen by the national parliaments of member countries in proportion to the relative strength of political parties. There is also a Joint Committee of Ministers and Representatives of the Parliamentary Assembly.

The Committee of Ministers is the executive organ. The majority of its conclusions take the form of international agreements (known as European Conventions) or recommendations to governments. Decisions of the Ministers may also be embodied in partial agreements to which a limited number of member governments are party. Member governments accredit Permanent Representatives to the Council in Strasbourg, who are also the Ministers' Deputies. The Committee of Deputies meets every month to transact business and to take decisions on behalf of Ministers.

The Parliamentary Assembly holds three week-long sessions a year. Its 13 permanent committees meet once or twice between each public plenary session of the Assembly. The Congress of Local and Regional Authorities of Europe each year brings together mayors and municipal councillors in the same numbers as the members of the Parliamentary Assembly.

One of the principal achievements of the Council of

Europe is the European Convention on Human Rights (1950) under which was established the European Commission and the European Court of Human Rights, which were merged in 1993. The reorganised European Court of Human Rights sits in chambers of seven judges or exceptionally as a grand chamber of 17 judges. Litigants must exhaust legal processes in their own country before bringing cases before the court.

Among other conventions and agreements are the European Social Charter, the European Cultural Convention, the European Code of Social Security, the European Convention on the Protection of National Minorities, and conventions on extradition, the legal status of migrant workers, torture prevention, conservation and the transfer of sentenced prisoners. Most recently, the specialised bodies of the Venice Commission and Demosthenes have been set up to assist in developing legislative, administrative and constitutional reforms in central and eastern Europe.

Non-member states take part in certain Council of Europe activities on a regular or *ad hoc* basis; thus the Holy See participates in all the educational, cultural and sports activities. The European Youth Centre is an educational residential centre for young people. The European Youth Foundation provides youth organisations with funds for their international activities.

Secretary-General, Walter Schwimmer (Austria)
Permanent UK Representative, HE Stephen Howarth, *apptd* 2003

THE ECONOMIC COMMUNITY OF WEST AFRICAN STATES

Secretariat Building, 60 Yakubu Gowon Crescent,
PMB 401, Abuja, Nigeria
Tel: (00 234) (9) 314 7647 9 Fax: (00 234) (9) 314 3005/6
Email: info@ecowasmail.net
Web: www.ecowas.int

The Economic Community of West African States (ECOWAS) was founded in 1975 and came into operation in 1977. It aims to promote the cultural, economic and social development of West Africa through mutual co-operation. A revised ECOWAS Treaty was signed in 1993 and came into effect in July 1995. It makes the prevention and control of regional conflicts an aim of ECOWAS and provides for the imposition of a community tax and for the establishment of a regional parliament, an economic and social council and a court of justice.

The supreme authority of ECOWAS is vested in the annual summit of heads of government of all 15 member states. A Council of Ministers, two from each member state, meets biannually to monitor the organisation and make recommendations to the summit. ECOWAS operates through a Secretariat, headed by the Executive Secretary. In addition there are four Deputy Executive Secretaries.

The ECOWAS Parliament was inaugurated in November 2000 and justices for the Court of Justice were sworn in in January 2001.

The Fund for Co-operation, Compensation and Development, situated at Lomé, Togo, has been restructured into three funds: the ECOWAS Regional Development Fund, the ECOWAS Bank for Investment and Development and the ECOWAS Regional Investment Bank. The funds finance development projects and provide compensation to member states that have suffered losses as a result of ECOWAS's policies, particularly trade liberalisation.

The members of ECOWAS are: Benin, Burkina Faso, Cape Verde, Côte d'Ivoire, Gambia, Ghana, Guinea, Guinea-Bissau, Liberia, Mali, Niger, Nigeria, Senegal, Sierra Leone and Togo. Mauritania left the organisation in December 2000.

An ECOWAS Monitoring Group (ECOMOG) peacekeeping force has been involved in attempts to restore peace in Liberia (1990–6), in Guinea-Bissau (1998–9) and in Sierra Leone since 1997.

Executive Secretary, Dr Mohammed Ibn Chambas (Ghana)

THE EUROPEAN BANK FOR RECONSTRUCTION AND DEVELOPMENT

One Exchange Square, London EC2A 2JN
Tel: 020-7338 6000 Fax: 020-7338 6100
Web: www.ebrd.com

The European Bank for Reconstruction and Development (EBRD), established in 1991, is an international institution with 62 members (60 countries, the European Community and the European Investment Bank).

The aim of the EBRD is to build market economies and democracies in 27 countries in central and eastern Europe and central Asia.

The EBRD finances projects in both the private and public sectors, providing direct funding for financial institutions, infrastructure and other key sectors. The main forms of EBRD financing are loans, equity investments and guarantees. No more than 40 per cent of the EBRD's investment can be made in state-owned concerns. EBRD is the largest foreign investor in the region's private sector and in addition to its own lending, facilitates significant foreign direct investment. EBRD pays particular attention to strengthening the financial sector and to promoting small and medium-sized enterprises. It works in co-operation with national governments, private companies, and international organisations such as the OECD, the IMF, the World Bank and the UN specialised agencies.

The EBRD has a subscribed capital of € 20 billion. The EBRD is also able to borrow on world capital markets. Its major subscribers are the USA, 10 per cent; Britain, France, Germany, Italy and Japan, 8.5 per cent each. As of 31 December 2002, the EBRD had signed over 900 projects with a total net value of € 21.5 billion.

The highest authority is the Board of Governors; each member appoints one Governor and one Alternate. The Governors delegate most powers to a 23-member Board of Directors; the Directors are responsible for the EBRD's operations and budget, and are elected by the Governors for three-year terms. The Governors also elect the President of the Board of Directors, who acts as the Bank's president for a four-year term.

President of the Board of Directors, Jean Lemierre (France)

EUROPEAN FREE TRADE ASSOCIATION

Headquarters: 9–11 rue de Varembé,
CH-1211 Geneva 20, Switzerland
Tel: (00 41) (22) 749 1111 Fax: (00 41) (22) 733 9291
Web: www.efta.int
EEA matters: Trierstraat 74, B-1040 Brussels, Belgium
Tel: (00 32) (2) 286 1711 Fax: (00 32) (2) 286 1750
Email: mail.bx1@efta.int

The European Free Trade Association (EFTA) was established in 1960 by Austria, Denmark, Norway, Portugal, Sweden, Switzerland and the UK, and was subsequently joined by Finland (associate member 1961, full member 1986), Iceland (1970) and Liechtenstein (1991). Six members have left to join the European Union: Denmark and the UK (1972), Portugal (1985), Austria, Finland and Sweden (1995). The existing members are Iceland, Liechtenstein, Norway and Switzerland.

The first objective of EFTA was to establish free trade in industrial products between members; this was achieved in 1966. Its second objective was the creation of a single market in western Europe and in 1972 EFTA signed free trade agreements with the EC covering trade in industrial goods; the remaining tariffs on industrial products were abolished in 1977 and the Luxembourg Declaration on broader co-operation between EFTA and the European Community was signed in 1984.

An agreement on the creation of the European Economic Area (EEA), an extension of the EC single market to the EFTA states, was signed in 1992 and entered into force on 1 January 1994. Switzerland rejected EEA membership in a referendum in 1992 and Liechtenstein joined on 1 May 1995 after adapting its customs union with Switzerland. The implementation of the agreement is supervised by the EEA Council, composed of EFTA and EU ministers, and the EFTA Surveillance Authority. The three EFTA EEA members also participate in a wide range of other EC programmes including research and development, environmental matters, and education and training.

In June 2002, a free trade agreement between the EFTA states and Singapore was signed in Egilsstaðir (Iceland). It entered into force on 1 January 2003. In March 2003, EFTA initialled a free trade agreement with Chile in Geneva (Switzerland). The agreement with Chile is the second free trade agreement that the EFTA states have concluded with a country in the Americas, after the agreement concluded with Mexico in 2000. With the Chile agreement, the EFTA states will have concluded free trade agreements with 20 states and territories, representing a population of 340 million, in addition to the free trade relations with the European Union, comprising a population of 375 million. Negotiations on free trade agreements with Lebanon, South Africa, Tunisia and Egypt continued during 2003.

The EFTA Council is the principal organ of the Association. It meets regularly at the level of ambassadors to the EFTA Secretariat in Geneva.

Secretary-General, William Rossier (Switzerland)
Deputy Secretary-General (Geneva), Pétur G. Thorsteinsson (Iceland)
Deputy Secretary-General (Brussels), Per Mannes (Norway)

EUROPEAN ORGANISATION FOR NUCLEAR RESEARCH (CERN)
CH-1211 Geneva 23, Switzerland
Tel: (00 41) (22) 767 4101 Fax: (00 41) (22) 785 0247
Web: www.cern.ch

The Convention establishing the European Organisation for Nuclear Research (CERN) came into force in 1954. CERN promotes European collaboration in high energy physics of a scientific, rather than a military nature.

The member countries are Austria, Belgium, Bulgaria, the Czech Republic, Denmark, Finland, France, Germany, Greece, Hungary, Italy, the Netherlands, Norway, Poland, Portugal, Slovakia, Spain, Sweden, Switzerland and the UK. India, Israel, Japan, Russia, Turkey, the USA, the EU Commission and UNESCO have observer status.

The Council is the highest policy-making body and comprises two delegates from each member state. There is also a Committee of the Council comprising a single delegate from each member state (who is also a Council member) and the chairmen of the scientific policy and finance advisory committees. The Council is chaired by the President who is elected by the Council in Session. The Council also elects the Director-General, who is responsible for the internal organisation of CERN. The Director-General heads a workforce of approximately 2,500, including physicists, craftsmen, technicians and administrative staff. At present over 6,500 physicists use CERN's facilities.

The member countries contribute to the budget in proportion to their net national revenue. The 2002 budget was SFr 1,068 million.

President of the Council, Maurice Bourquin (Switzerland)
Director-General (1999–2004), Prof. Luciano Maiani (Italy)

EUROPEAN SPACE AGENCY
8–10 rue Mario Nikis, F-75738 Paris Cedex 15, France
Tel: (00 33) (1) 5369 7654 Fax: (00 33) (1) 5369 7560
Web: www.esa.int

The European Space Agency (ESA) was created in 1975 by the merger of the European Space Research Organisation (ESRO) and the European Launcher Development Organisation (ELDO). Its aims include the advancement of space research and technology and the implementation of a long-term European space policy.

The member countries are Austria, Belgium, Denmark, Finland, France, Germany, Republic of Ireland, Italy, the Netherlands, Norway, Portugal, Spain, Sweden, Switzerland and the UK. Canada is a co-operating state.

The agency is directed by a Council composed of the representatives of the member states; its chief officer is the Director-General.

Director-General, Jean-Jacques Dordain, *apptd* 2003

FOOD AND AGRICULTURE ORGANISATION OF THE UNITED NATIONS
Viale delle Terme di Caracalla, I-00100 Rome, Italy
Tel: (00 39) (06) 57051 Fax: (00 39) (06) 5705 3152
Email: fao-hq@fao.org
Web: www.fao.org

The Food and Agriculture Organisation (FAO) is a specialised UN agency, established in 1945. It assists rural populations by raising levels of nutrition and living standards, and by encouraging greater efficiency in food production and distribution. It analyses and disseminates information on agriculture and natural resources. The FAO also advises governments on national agricultural policy and planning; its Investment Centre, together with the World Bank and other financial institutions, helps to prepare development projects. The FAO's field programme covers a range of activities, including strengthening crop production, rural and livestock development, and conservation.

The FAO's top priorities are sustainable agriculture, rural development and food security. The Organisation attempts to ensure the availability of adequate food supplies, stability in the flow of supplies and the securing of access to food by the poor. The FAO monitors potential famine areas. The Special Relief Operations Service channels emergency aid from governments and other agencies, and assists in rehabilitation. The Technical

Co-operation Programme responds to urgent or unforeseen requests for technical assistance.

The FAO had 184 members (183 states plus the EU) as at November 2001. It is governed by a biennial conference of its members which sets a programme and budget. The budget for 2002–3 was US$651.8 million, funded by member countries in proportion to their gross national products. The FAO is also funded by the UN Development Programme, donor governments and other institutions.

The Conference elects a Director-General and a 49-member Council which governs between conferences. The Regular and Field Programmes are administered by a Secretariat, headed by the Director-General. Five regional, five sub-regional and over 78 national offices help administer the Field Programme.

Director-General, Jacques Diouf (Senegal)

GUUAM

Web: www.guuam.org

GUUAM (Georgia, Ukraine, Uzbekistan, Azerbaijan and Moldova) was founded as a political, economic and strategic alliance designed to strengthen the independence and sovereignty of its members.

GUUAM seeks to promote trade, economic growth, and co-operation between its members primarily through the establishment of a Eurasian-Transcaucasian transportation corridor (TRACECA). GUUAM is also a forum for the discussion of security problems, promoting conflict resolution and a common position in international organisations.

Following growing co-operation between their countries, on 10 October 1997, the presidents of Azerbaijan, Georgia, Moldova and Ukraine declared their mutual interest in promoting co-operation, security, political and economic contacts. Uzbekistan joined the group in April 1999.

It was decided in September 2000 to convene summits of the Heads of State at least once a year, and meetings at the level of Ministers for Foreign Affairs at least twice a year. A Committee of National Co-ordinators meets quarterly.

An information office is to be established in Kyiv, Ukraine.

INTERNATIONAL ATOMIC ENERGY AGENCY

Vienna International Centre, Wagramerstrasse 5,
PO Box 100, A-1400 Vienna, Austria
Tel: (00 43) (1) 26000 Fax: (00 43) (1) 26007
Email: Official.Mail@iaea.org
Web: www.iaea.org/worldatom

The International Atomic Energy Agency (IAEA) was established in 1957. It is an intergovernmental organisation that reports to, but is not a specialised agency of, the UN.

The IAEA aims to enhance the contribution of atomic energy to peace, health and prosperity and to ensure that any assistance that it provides is not used for military purposes. It establishes atomic energy safety standards and offers services to its member states for the safe operation of their nuclear facilities and for radiation protection. It is the focal point for international conventions on the early notification of a nuclear accident, assistance in the case of such an accident, civil liability for nuclear damage, physical protection of nuclear material, nuclear safety and the safety of spent

fuel and radioactive waste management. The IAEA also encourages research and training in nuclear power. It is additionally charged with drawing up safeguards and verifying their use in accordance with the Nuclear Non-Proliferation Treaty (NPT) 1968, the Treaty for the Prohibition of Nuclear Weapons in Latin America (Tlatelolco Treaty) 1968, the Treaty on a South Pacific Nuclear Free Zone (Rarotonga Treaty), the South East Asia Nuclear Weapon-Free Zone Treaty (Bangkok Treaty) and the African Nuclear Weapon-Free Zone Treaty (Pelindaba Treaty) 1996. Together with the Food and Agriculture Organisation and the World Health Organisation, the IAEA established an International Consultative Group on Food Irradiation in 1983.

In October 2002 the USA reported that North Korea had admitted to having a secret nuclear weapons programme in defiance of a 1994 IAEA agreement. On 12 December, North Korea announced its intention to reactivate its nuclear facilities and on 13 December 2002 asked the IAEA to remove surveillance equipment from its Yongbyon power plant. On 22 December 2002 North Korea began cutting seals and disabling surveillance cameras at the plant and on 27 December 2002 expelled IAEA nuclear inspectors from the country. On 6 January 2003 the IAEA Board of Governors adopted a resolution calling on North Korea to co-operate fully and urgently with the Agency. On 10 January 2003, North Korea announced its withdrawal from the NPT and on 12 February 2003 the IAEA declared North Korea to be in further non-compliance with its nuclear safeguards obligations, referring the matter to the UN Security Council. Following consultations on 9 April 2003, the UN Security Council expressed its concern over North Korea's nuclear programme, announcing that it would keep track of developments.

The IAEA had 136 members as at May 2003. A General Conference of all its members meets annually to decide policy, a programme and a budget (2003, US$240 million), as well as electing a Director-General and a 35-member Board of Governors. The Board meets four times a year to formulate policy which is implemented by the Secretariat under a Director-General.

Director-General, Mohamed El Baradei (Egypt)
Permanent UK Representative, Peter Redmond Jenkins,
    Jaurèsgasse 12, A-1030 Vienna, Austria

INTERNATIONAL CIVIL AVIATION ORGANISATION

999 University Street, Montréal, Québec, Canada H3C 5H7
Tel: (00 1) (514) 954 8219 Fax: (00 1) (514) 954 6077
Email: icaohq@icao.int
Web: www.icao.int

The International Civil Aviation Organisation (ICAO) was founded with the signing of the Chicago Convention on International Civil Aviation in 1944, and became a specialised agency of the United Nations in 1947. It sets international technical standards and recommends practices for all areas of civil aviation, including airworthiness, air navigation, air traffic control and pilot licensing. It encourages uniformity and simplicity in ground regulations and operations at international airports, including immigration and customs control. The ICAO also promotes regional air navigation, plans for ground facilities and collects and distributes air transport statistics world-wide. It is dedicated to improving safety and to the orderly development of civil aviation throughout the world.

The ICAO had 188 members as at June 2003. It is

governed by an assembly of its members which meets at least once every three years. A Council of 33 members is elected, which represents leading air transport nations as well as less developed countries. The Council elects the President, appoints the Secretary-General and supervises the organisation through subsidiary committees, serviced by a Secretariat.

President of the Council, Dr Assad Kotaite (Lebanon)
Secretary-General, R. C. Costa Pereira (Brazil)
UK Representative, D. S. Evans, CMG

INTERNATIONAL CONFEDERATION OF FREE TRADE UNIONS
Koning Albert II laan 5, Bus 1, B-1210 Brussels, Belgium
Tel: (00 32) (2) 224 0211 Fax: (00 32) (2) 201 5815
Email: internetpo@icftu.org
Web: www.icftu.org

The International Confederation of Free Trade Unions (ICFTU) was created in 1949. It aims to establish, maintain and promote free trade unions, and to promote peace with economic security and social justice.

Affiliated to the ICFTU are 231 individual unions and representative bodies in 150 countries and territories. There were 158 million members as at June 2003.

The Congress, the supreme authority of the ICFTU, convenes at least every four years. It is composed of delegates from the affiliated trade union organisations. The Congress elects an Executive Board of 53 members, including five nominated by the Women's Committee and one representing young workers, which meets not less than once a year. The Board establishes the budget and receives suggestions and proposals from affiliates as well as acting on behalf of the Confederation. The Congress also elects the General Secretary.

General Secretary, Guy Ryder (UK)
UK AFFILIATE, TUC, Congress House, 23–28 Great Russell Street, London WC1B 3LS. Tel: 020-7636 4030

INTERNATIONAL CRIMINAL POLICE ORGANISATION (INTERPOL)
200 Quai Charles de Gaulle, F-69006 Lyon, France
Tel: (00 33) (4) 7244 7000 Fax: (00 33) (4) 7244 7163
Email: compr@interpol.int Web: www.interpol.int

Interpol was set up in 1923 to establish an international criminal records office and to harmonise extradition procedures. As of July 2003, the organisation comprised 181 member states.

Interpol's aims are to promote co-operation between criminal police authorities, and to support government agencies concerned with combating crime, whilst respecting national sovereignty. It is financed by annual contributions from the governments of member states.

Interpol's policy is decided by the General Assembly which meets annually; it is composed of delegates appointed by the member states. The 13-member Executive Committee is elected by the General Assembly from among the member states' delegates, and is chaired by the President, who has a four-year term of office. The permanent administrative organ is the General Secretariat, headed by the Secretary-General, who is appointed by the General Assembly.

Secretary-General, Ronald Noble (USA)
UK OFFICE, NCIS Interpol, PO Box 8000, London SE11 5EN.
  Tel: 020-7238 8000.
UK Representative, Peter Hampson, QPM

INTERNATIONAL ENERGY AGENCY
9 rue de la Fédération, F-75739 Paris Cedex 15, France
Tel: (00 33) (1) 4057 6551 Fax: (00 33) (1) 4057 6559
Email: info@iea.org
Web: www.iea.org

The International Energy Agency (IEA), founded in 1974, is an autonomous agency within the framework of the Organisation for Economic Co-operation and Development (OECD). The IEA had 26 member countries as at May 2003.

The IEA's objectives include improvement of energy co-operation world-wide, increased efficiency, development of alternative energy sources and the promotion of relations between oil producing and oil consuming countries. The IEA also maintains an emergency system to alleviate the effects of severe oil supply disruptions.

The main decision-making body is the Governing Board, composed of senior energy officials from member countries. Various standing groups and special committees exist to facilitate the work of the Board. The IEA Secretariat, with a staff of energy experts, carries out the work of the Governing Board and its subordinate bodies. The Executive Director is appointed by the Board.

Executive Director, Claude Mandil (France)

INTERNATIONAL FRANCOPHONE ORGANISATION
Cabinet du Secrétaire général, 28 rue de Bourgogne,
F-75007 Paris, France. Tel: (00 33) (1) 44111250
Fax: (00 33) (1) 441112 76 Email: oif@francophonie.org
Web: www.francophonie.org

The International Francophone Organisation (known as La Francophonie) is an intergovernmental organisation founded in 1970 by 21 French-speaking countries. It aims to prevent conflict and promote development and co-operation between the Francophone countries, to represent its member states internationally and to promote French culture and the use of the French language.

The Conference of Heads of State and Heads of Government of Countries using French as a Common Language, also known as the Francophone Summit, takes place biennially. Other institutions include the Ministerial Conference of La Francophonie, the Permanent Council of La Francophonie and the Secretariat.

The Ministerial Conference of La Francophonie, which consists of the foreign minister or the minister responsible for Francophone affairs of each member state, implements decisions made at the summits and makes preparations for the following summit. It also puts forward prospective new members.

The Permanent Council of La Francophonie, which is chaired by the Secretary-General and consists of representatives of the member states, oversees the execution of decisions made by the Ministerial Conference, allocates funds, and reviews and approves projects.

La Francophonie has a current membership of 56 member states and regional governments.

Secretary-General, Abdou Diouf

INTERNATIONAL FUND FOR AGRICULTURAL DEVELOPMENT

107 Via del Serafico, I-00142 Rome, Italy
Tel: (00 39) (6) 54591 Fax: (00 39) (6) 5459 2143
Email: ifad@ifad.org
Web: www.ifad.org

The establishment of the International Fund for Agricultural Development (IFAD) was proposed by the 1974 World Food Conference and IFAD began operations as a UN specialised agency in 1977. Its purpose is to mobilise additional funds for agricultural and rural development projects in developing countries that benefit the poorest rural populations; provide employment and additional income for poor farmers; reduce malnutrition; and improve food distribution systems.

IFAD had 163 members as at May 2003. Membership is divided into three lists: List A (OECD countries), List B (OPEC countries), and List C (developing countries) which is subdivided into C1 (Africa), C2 (Europe, Asia and the Pacific) and C3 (Latin America and the Caribbean). All powers are vested in a Governing Council of all member countries. It elects an 18-member Executive Board (with 18 alternate members) responsible for IFAD's operations. The Council meets annually and elects a President who is also chairman of the Board. The President serves a four-year term that is renewable once and is assisted by a Vice-President and three Assistant Presidents.

Since its establishment, IFAD has committed a total of US$7.7 billion in loans and US$35.4 million in grants for 633 approved projects in 115 countries and territories.

President, Lennart Båge (Sweden), *apptd* 2001

INTERNATIONAL LABOUR ORGANISATION

4 route des Morillons, CH-1211 Geneva 22, Switzerland
Tel: (00 41) (22) 799 6111 Fax: (00 41) (22) 798 8685
Web: www.ilo.org

The International Labour Organisation (ILO) was established in 1919 as an autonomous body of the League of Nations and became the UN's first specialised agency in 1946. The ILO aims to increase employment, improve working conditions, raise living standards and encourage democratic development. It sets minimum international labour standards through the drafting of international conventions. Member countries are obliged to submit these to their domestic authorities for ratification, and thus undertake to bring their domestic legislation in line with the conventions. Members must report to the ILO periodically on how these regulations are being implemented. The ILO plays a major role in helping developing countries achieve economic stability and job expansion through its wide-ranging programme of technical co-operation. The ILO is also the world's principal resource centre for information, analysis and guidance on labour and employment. The organisation aims to improve working and living conditions throughout the world and to support the transition to democracy and market economies under way in many states.

The ILO had 176 members as at May 2003. It is composed of the International Labour Conference, the Governing Body and the International Labour Office. The Conference of members meets annually, and is attended by national delegations comprising two government delegates, one worker delegate and one employer delegate. It formulates international labour conventions and recommendations, provides a forum for discussion of world employment and social issues, and approves the ILO's programme and budget. The programme and budget set out four strategic objectives for the ILO: the promotion of fundamental principles and rights at work; the creation of greater employment and earning opportunities; the enhancement of social protection; and the strengthening of social dialogue.

The 56-member Governing Body, composed of 28 government, 14 worker and 14 employer members, acts as the ILO's executive council. Ten governments, including the UK, hold permanent seats on the Governing Body because of their industrial importance. There are also various regional conferences and advisory committees. The International Labour Office acts as a secretariat and as a centre for operations, publishing and research.

Director-General, Juan Somavia (Chile)
UK OFFICE, Millbank Tower, 21–24 Millbank,
London SW1P 4QP. Tel: 020-7828 6401
Fax: 020-7233-5925 Email: ipu@ilo-london.org.uk

INTERNATIONAL MARITIME ORGANISATION

4 Albert Embankment, London SE1 7SR
Tel: 020-7735 7611 Fax: 020-7587 3210
Email: info@imo.org
Web: www.imo.org

The International Maritime Organisation (IMO) was established as a UN specialised agency in 1948. Owing to delays in treaty ratification it did not commence operations until 1958. Originally it was called the Inter-Governmental Maritime Consultative Organisation (IMCO) but changed its name in 1982.

The IMO fosters intergovernmental co-operation in technical matters relating to international shipping, especially with regard to safety at sea, efficiency in navigation and protecting the marine environment by preventing and controlling marine pollution caused by shipping. The IMO is responsible for convening maritime conferences and drafting marine conventions. It also provides technical aid to countries wishing to develop their activities at sea.

The IMO had 162 members and two associate members as at May 2003. It is governed by an Assembly comprising delegates of all its members. It meets biennially to formulate policy, set a budget (2002–3, £39.5 million), vote on specific recommendations on pollution and maritime safety and elect the Council. The Council, which meets twice a year, fulfils the functions of the Assembly between sessions and appoints the Secretary-General. It consists of 40 members: ten from the world's largest shipping nations, ten from the nations most dependent on seaborne trade, and 20 other members to ensure a fair geographical representation. The Maritime Safety, Marine Environment Protection, Legal, Technical Co-operation and Facilitation Committees make reports and recommendations to the Council and the Assembly. There are a number of other specialist subsidiary committees.

The IMO acts as the secretariat for the London Convention (1972) which regulates the disposal of land-generated waste at sea.

Secretary-General, William A. O'Neil (Canada)

INTERNATIONAL MONETARY FUND

700 19th Street NW, Washington DC 20431, USA
Tel: (00 1) (202) 623 7300 Fax: (00 1) (202) 623 6278
Email: publicaffairs@imf.org
Web: www.imf.org

The International Monetary Fund (IMF) was established in 1944, at the UN Monetary and Financial Conference held at Bretton Woods, New Hampshire. Its Articles of Agreement entered into force in 1945 and it began operations in 1947.

The IMF exists to promote inter-national monetary co-operation, the expansion of world trade, and exchange stability. It advises members on their economic and financial policies; promotes policy co-ordination among the major industrial countries; and gives technical assistance in central banking, balance of payments accounting, taxation, and other financial matters. The IMF serves as a forum for members to discuss important financial and monetary issues and seeks the balanced growth of international trade and, through this, high levels of employment, income and productive capacity. As at May 2003 the IMF had 184 members.

Upon joining the IMF, a member is assigned a 'quota', based on the member's relative standing in the world economy and its balance of payments position, that determines its capital subscription to the Fund, its access to IMF resources, its voting power, and its share in the allocation of Special Drawing Rights (SDRs). Quotas are reviewed every five years and adjusted accordingly. Since the 12th General Review of quotas in 2003, total Fund quotas stand at SDR 213 billion. The SDR, an international reserve asset issued by the IMF, is calculated daily on a basket of usable currencies and is the IMF's unit of account; on 30 May 2003, SDR 1 equalled US$1.41995. SDRs are allocated at intervals to supplement members' reserves and thereby improve international financial liquidity.

IMF financial resources derive primarily from members' capital subscriptions, which are equivalent to their quotas. In addition, the IMF is authorised to borrow from official lenders. It may also draw on a line of credit of SDR 18.5 billion from various countries under the so-called General Arrangements to Borrow (GAB). Periodic charges are also levied on financial assistance. At the end of May 2001, total outstanding IMF credits amounted to SDR 51.5 billion.

The IMF is not a bank and does not lend money; it provides temporary financial assistance by selling a member's SDRs or other members' currencies in exchange for the member's own currency. The member can then use the purchased currency to alleviate its balance of payments difficulties. The IMF's credit under its regular facilities is made available to members in tranches or segments of 25 per cent of quota. For first credit tranche purchases, members are required to demonstrate reasonable efforts to overcome their balance of payments difficulties. There are no performance criteria. Upper credit tranche purchases are normally associated with stand-by arrangements and are aimed at overcoming balance of payment difficulties and are required to meet certain performance criteria. Repurchases are made in three and a quarter to five years.

The IMF supports long-term efforts at economic reform and transformation as well as medium-term programmes under the extended Fund facility, which runs for three to four years and is aimed at overcoming balance of payments difficulties stemming from macroeconomic and structural problems. Members experiencing a temporary balance of payments shortfall have access to the compensatory and contingency financing facility.

The IMF is headed by a Board of Governors, comprising representatives of all members, which meets annually. The Governors delegate powers to 24 Executive Directors, who are appointed or elected by member countries. The Executive Directors operate the Fund on a daily basis under a Managing Director, whom they elect.
Managing Director, Horst Köhler (Germany)
UK Executive Director, Tom Scholar, Room 11-120, IMF, 700 19th Street NW, Washington DC 20431, USA

INTERNATIONAL RED CROSS AND RED CRESCENT MOVEMENT

19 avenue de la Paix, CH-1202 Geneva, Switzerland
Web: www.icrc.org

The International Red Cross and Red Crescent Movement is composed of three elements – the International Committee of the Red Cross, the International Federation of Red Cross and Red Crescent Societies and the national Red Cross and Red Crescent societies.

The International Committee of the Red Cross (ICRC), the organisation's founding body, was formed in 1863. It aims to negotiate between warring factions and to protect and assist victims of armed conflict. It also seeks to ensure the application of the Geneva Conventions with regard to prisoners of war and detainees.

The International Federation of Red Cross and Red Crescent Societies was founded in 1919 to contribute to the development of the humanitarian activities of national societies, to co-ordinate their relief operations for victims of natural disasters, and to care for refugees outside areas of conflict. There are Red Cross and Red Crescent societies in 175 countries, with a total membership of 250 million.

The International Conference of the Red Cross and Red Crescent meets every four years, bringing together delegates of the ICRC, the International Federation and the national societies, as well as representatives of nations bound by the Geneva Conventions.
President of the ICRC, Jakob Kellenberger
BRITISH RED CROSS, 9 Grosvenor Crescent, London SW1X 7EJ. Tel: 020-7235 5454 Fax: 020-7245 6315.
Email: information@redcross.org.uk
Web: www.redcross.org.uk.
Director-General, Sir Nicholas Young

INTERNATIONAL TELECOMMUNICATION UNION

Place des Nations, CH-1211 Geneva 20, Switzerland
Tel: (00 41) (22) 730 5111 Fax: (00 41) (22) 733 7256
Email: itumail@itu.int
Web: www.itu.int

The International Telecommunication Union (ITU) was founded in Paris in 1865 as the International Telegraph Union and became a UN specialised agency in 1947.

ITU is an intergovernmental organisation for the development of telecommunications and the harmonisation of national telecommunication policies. ITU comprises 189 member states and some 700 members who represent public and private organisations involved in telecommunications. ITU's mission is to promote the development of telecommunications and information and communication technologies; to promote and offer technical assistance to developing countries; and to promote at international level the adoption of a broader approach to the issues of telecommunications.

ITU fulfils its mission through initiatives aimed at promoting the growth and expansion of electronic commerce; a programme of strategic workshops; the adoption of international regulations and treaties governing uses of the frequency spectrum; the adoption of technical standards that foster global interconnectivity and interoperability; and the provision of policy advice and technical assistance to developing countries.

ITU also organises world-wide and regional exhibitions and forums to exchange ideas, knowledge and technology.

Secretary-General, Yoshio Utsumi (Japan)

LEAGUE OF ARAB STATES

Maidane Al-Tahrir, Cairo, Egypt
Tel: (00 20) (2) 575 0511 Fax: (00 20) (2) 574 0331
Web: www.leagueofarabstates.org

The purpose of the League of Arab States, founded in 1945, is to ensure co-operation among member states and protect their independence and sovereignty, to supervise the affairs and interests of Arab countries, to control the execution of agreements concluded among the member states, and to promote the process of integration among them. The League considers itself a regional organisation and has observer status at the United Nations.

Member states are Algeria, Bahrain, the Comoros, Djibouti, Egypt, Iraq, Jordan, Kuwait, Lebanon, Libya, Mauritania, Morocco, Oman, Palestine, Qatar, Saudi Arabia, Somalia, Sudan, Syria, Tunisia, the UAE and Yemen.

Member states participate in various specialised agencies of the League whose role is to develop specific areas of co-operation between Arab states. These include: the Arab Organisation for Mineral Resources; the Arab Monetary Fund; the Arab Satellite Communications Organisation; the Arab Academy of Maritime Transport; the Arab Bank for Economic Development in Africa; the Arab League Educational, Cultural and Scientific Organisation and the Council of Arab Economic Unity.

Secretary-General, Amre Moussa (Egypt)
UK OFFICE, 52 Green Street, London W1Y 3RH.
Tel: 020-7629 0044 Fax: 020-7493 7943

MERCOSUR

Luis Piera 1992, piso 1, 11200-Montevideo, Uruguay
Tel: (00 598) (2) 402 9024 Fax: (00 598) (2) 400 0958
Email: secretaria@mercosur.org.uy Web: www.mercosur.org.uy

Brazil and Argentina signed a Treaty for Integration, Co-operation and Development in 1988 which aimed to create a common market between the two countries within ten years, with the elimination of all tariff barriers and harmonisation of macroeconomic policies; the agreement was to be open to other Latin American countries. Paraguay and Uruguay expressed their interest and MERCOSUR (the Southern Common Market) was created by the Treaty of Asunción, which was signed by the four countries on 26 March 1991. Chile became an associate member in 1996 and Bolivia in 1997.

The Common Market Council (CMC) is the highest-level agency of MERCOSUR, with authority to conduct its policy, and responsibility for compliance with the objects and time frames set forth in the Asunción Treaty. It comprises the ministers of foreign affairs and the economy of the member states. Each country presides over the council for a period of six months, in rotating alphabetical order. The CMC meets at least once a year. The presidents of the member states can take part whenever possible.

The Common Market Group (CMG) is the executive body of MERCOSUR and is co-ordinated by the foreign ministries of the member states. Its function is to ensure compliance with the Asunción Treaty and to implement decisions made by the CMC, and where necessary, to help resolve disputes. It can establish work subgroups to work on particular issues. It is composed of four permanent members and four substitutes from each country. It normally meets at least four times a year.

Other bodies include a Joint Parliamentary Committee, a Trade Commission and a Socio-economic Advisory Forum.

NON-ALIGNED MOVEMENT

Permanent Representative to the UN, New York 10 016, USA
Tel: (00 1) (212) 213 5583 Fax: (00 1) (212) 592 2498

The Non-Aligned Movement (NAM) was created following a conference of non-aligned states held in Belgrade, Yugoslavia in September 1961. Members must be committed to the coexistence of states with different political and social systems, they must not be members of multinational military alliances allied to the great powers, and they should support national liberation movements.

NAM was set up to campaign for an end to colonialism, neo-colonialism, racism and occupation, the dissolution of military blocs, national self-determination for all countries and non-interference in internal affairs, north-south dialogue and political-economic co-operation in the third world (south-south relations) and a new world economic mechanism involving military disarmament and the use of the thereby freed means for development projects.

There are 115 members and 17 observers and about 30 further countries have guest status.

The chairmanship of NAM is held by the head of state of the country due to hold the following summit. The chairman is responsible for the promotion of the principles and activities of the movement and the country's ambassador to the UN represents the organisation at UN level.

THE NORDIC COUNCIL

The Nordic Council was established in March 1952 as an advisory body on economic and social co-operation, comprising parliamentary delegates from Denmark, Iceland, Norway and Sweden. It was subsequently joined by Finland (1956), and representatives from the Færøes (1970), the Åland Islands (1970), and Greenland (1984).

Co-operation is regulated by the Treaty of Helsinki signed in 1962. This was amended in 1971 to create the Nordic Council of Ministers, which discusses all matters except defence and foreign affairs. Matters are given preparatory consideration by a Committee of Co-operation Ministers' Deputies and joint committees of officials. Decisions of the Council of Ministers, which are taken by consensus, are binding, although if ratification by member parliaments is required, decisions only become effective following parliamentary approval. The Council of Ministers is advised by the Nordic Council, to which it reports annually. There are Ministers for Nordic Co-operation in every member government.

The Nordic Council, comprising 87 voting delegates nominated from member parliaments and about 80 non-voting government representatives, meets at least once a year in plenary sessions. The full Council chooses a 13-member Praesidium, which conducts business between sessions. A Secretariat, headed by a Secretary-General, liaises with the Council of Ministers and provides administrative support. The Council of Ministers has a separate Secretariat.

SECRETARIAT OF THE NORDIC COUNCIL,
PO Box 3043, DK-1021 Copenhagen K, Denmark.
Tel: (00 45) 3396 0400 Fax: (00 45) 3311 1870
Email: nordisk-rad@norden.org; Web: www.norden.org
Secretary-General, Frida Nokken (Norway)
SECRETARIAT OF THE NORDIC COUNCIL OF
MINISTERS, Store Strandstræde 18, DK-1255 Copenhagen
K, Denmark. Tel: (00 45) 3396 0200 Fax: (00 45) 3396 0202
Web: www.norden.org
Secretary-General, Per Unckel (Sweden)

NORTH AMERICAN FREE TRADE AGREEMENT

NAFTA Secretariat, Canadian Section, 90 Sparks Street,
Suite 705, Ottawa, Ontario K1P 5B4, Canada
Tel: (00 1) (613) 992 9388 Fax: (00 1) (613) 992 9392
NAFTA Secretariat, Mexican Section, Blvd. Adolfo
López Mateos 3025, 2° Piso, Col. Héroes de Padierna,
C.P. 10700, Mexico, D.F.
Tel: (00 52) (5) 629 9630 Fax: (00 52) (5) 629 9637
NAFTA Secretariat, US Section, 14th Street and Constitution
Avenue, NW, Room 2061, Washington DC, 20230, USA
Tel: (00 1) (202) 482 5438 Fax: (00 1) (202) 482 0148
Email: webmaster@nafta-sec-alena.org
Web: www.nafta-sec-alena.org

The leaders of Canada, Mexico and the USA signed the North American Free Trade Agreement (NAFTA) on 17 December 1992 in their respective capitals; it came into force on 1 January 1994 after being ratified by the legislatures of the three member states.

NAFTA aims to eliminate barriers to trade in goods and services, promote fair competition within the free trade area, protect and enforce intellectual property rights and create a framework for further co-operation. To achieve these aims, import tariffs and quotas are being removed, with the aim of achieving a free trade zone by 2008 at the latest.

The NAFTA Secretariat is composed of Canadian, Mexican and US sections. It is responsible for the administration of the dispute settlement provisions of the agreement, provides assistance to the Free Trade Commission and support for various committees and working groups, and facilitates the operation of the agreement.

NORTH ATLANTIC TREATY ORGANISATION

Leopold III laan, Brussels B-1110, Belgium
Tel: (00 32) (2) 707 4111 Fax: (00 32) (2) 707 4579
Email: natodoc@hq.nato.int
Web: www.nato.int

The North Atlantic Treaty (Treaty of Washington) was signed in 1949 by Belgium, Canada, Denmark, France, Iceland, Italy, Luxembourg, the Netherlands, Norway, Portugal, the UK and the USA. Greece and Turkey acceded to the Treaty in 1952, the Federal Republic of Germany in 1955 (the reunited Germany acceded in October 1990), Spain in 1982, and the Czech Republic, Hungary and Poland in 1999. Bulgaria, Estonia, Latvia, Lithuania, Romania, Slovakia and Slovenia signed membership accords on 26 March 2003 and are expected to join NATO in 2004.

The North Atlantic Treaty Organisation (NATO) is the structural framework for a defensive political and military alliance designed to provide common security for its members through co-operation and consultation in political, military and economic as well as scientific and other non-military fields.

STRUCTURE

The North Atlantic Council (NAC), chaired by the Secretary-General, is the highest authority of the Alliance and is composed of permanent representatives of the 19 member countries. It meets at ministerial level (foreign and/or defence ministers) at least twice a year. The permanent representatives (ambassadors) head national delegations of advisers and experts. The Defence Planning Committee (DPC) and the Nuclear Planning Group (NPG) are composed of representatives of all member countries except France (which does not participate in the integrated military structure). Both the DPC and the NPG also meet at ministerial level (defence ministers) at least twice a year. The NATO Secretary-General chairs the Council, the DPC and the NPG.

The senior military authority in NATO, under the Council and DPC, is the Military Committee composed of the Chief of Defence Staffs of each member country except Iceland, which has no military and is represented by a civilian. The Military Committee, which is assisted by an integrated international military staff, also meets in permanent session with permanent military representatives and is responsible for making recommendations to the Council and DPC on measures considered necessary for the common defence of the NATO area and for supplying guidance on military matters to the major NATO commanders. The Chairman of the Military Committee, elected for a period of two to three years, represents the committee on the Council.

The strategic area covered by the North Atlantic Treaty is divided between two major NATO commands (MNCs), European and Atlantic; and three major subordinate commands (MSCs) within Allied Command Europe, South, Central and North-West. There is also a Regional Planning Group (Canada and the United States).

The major NATO commanders are responsible for the development of defence plans for their respective areas, for the determination of force requirements and for the deployment and exercise of the forces under their command. The major NATO commanders report to the Military Committee. The 2002 Prague summit agreed to the reorganisation of NATO's command structure into two strategic commands, the (operational) strategic command Operations (Europe) and the (functional) strategic command for Transformation (United States).

POST-COLD WAR DEVELOPMENTS

The Euro-Atlantic Partnership Council (EAPC) was established in 1997 to develop closer security links with eastern European and former Soviet states. It focuses on defence planning, defence industry conversion, defence management and force structuring, and the democratic concepts of civilian-military relations. Its membership comprises the 19 NATO members and Albania, Armenia, Austria, Azerbaijan, Belarus, Bulgaria, Croatia, Estonia, Finland, Georgia, Ireland, Kazakhstan, Kyrgyzstan, Latvia, Lithuania, Macedonia, Moldova, Romania, Russia, Slovakia, Slovenia, Sweden, Switzerland, Tajikistan, Turkmenistan, Ukraine and Uzbekistan. Partnership for Peace (PfP) is the basis for practical security co-operation between NATO and individual partner countries in the fields of defence planning and budgeting, military exercises and civil emergency operations.

In March 1999, Poland, the Czech Republic and Hungary acceded to the Treaty. In 1997 NATO and Ukraine signed a charter establishing a programme of co-operation and consultation between them. NATO and Russia committed themselves to help build a stable, secure and undivided continent on the basis of partnership and mutual interest, when they signed the 1997 Founding Act on Mutual Relations, Co-operation and Security, which provided for the creation of a Permanent Joint Council, which meets at foreign minister level at least twice a year. In May 2002 agreement was reached on the establishment of the NATO-Russia Council in which Russia and the 19 NATO countries have an equal role in decision-making on policy to counter terrorism and other security threats. The Council meets every month with four ministerial-level meetings each year. The Mediterranean Dialogue, launched in 1994, aims to promote security and stability in the Mediterranean region and involves the NATO members, Algeria, Egypt, Israel, Jordan, Mauritania, Morocco and Tunisia.

The development of a European Security and Defence Identity (ESDI), which would strengthen NATO's European pillar, was agreed at the 1999 Washington summit.

At the Washington summit a Defence Capabilities Initiative (DCI) was launched, which aims to improve defence capabilities and interoperability among Alliance forces to ensure the effectiveness of future multinational operations. A temporary High Level Steering Group (HLSG) was established to oversee the implementation of the DCI.

At the 2002 Prague summit a military concept for defence against terrorism was agreed, initiatives in the area of nuclear, biological and chemical weapons defence were endorsed and decisions were taken to strengthen NATO's defence against cyber attacks and to initiate a missile defence feasibility study.

NATO AND THE FORMER YUGOSLAVIA

In March 1999, NATO began air operations against military and industrial targets in Yugoslavia following the repression and ethnic cleansing of ethnic Albanians in Kosovo. Yugoslavia accepted a peace plan drawn up by NATO and Russia on 3 June 1999 and the withdrawal of Yugoslav forces from Kosovo took place between 10–20 June. On 12 June 1999, the NATO-led security force (KFOR) entered Kosovo to oversee the demilitarisation of the Kosovo Liberation Army (KLA), facilitate the return of over 850,000 refugees and provide humanitarian support. Demilitarisation of the KLA was completed on 20 September. KFOR remains in Kosovo providing assistance to the UN Mission in Kosovo (UNMIK) in creating a secure environment.

Following the brokering of a cease-fire to end fighting between ethnic Albanians and the Macedonian armed forces, NATO launched 'Operation Essential Harvest' on 22 August 2001 at the request of the Macedonian government. On 16 December 2002 'Operation Amber Fox/Task Force Fox' was replaced by 'Operation Allied Harmony', to provide support for international monitors and to assist the Macedonian government in taking ownership of security throughout the country. 'Operation Allied Harmony' was terminated on 31 March 2003 and peacekeeping operations were handed over to the European Union.

THE 11 SEPTEMBER TERRORIST ATTACKS

Following the terrorist attacks on the USA on 11 September 2001, the NATO members immediately declared their solidarity with the USA and on 12 September formally invoked Article 5 of the Washington Treaty (which stipulates that an armed attack against one or more NATO members is to be considered an attack against all), declaring that the terrorist attack on the USA was an attack on the NATO alliance. The EAPC countries also condemned the atrocities and pledged to undertake efforts to combat terrorism.

IRAQ WAR

On 19 February 2003, following a request by Turkey for defensive assistance in the event of a US-led war with Iraq, NATO's Defence and Planning Committee authorised deployment of surveillance aircraft and missile defences to help protect the country in the event of an attack on its territory or population. The deployment began on 20 February and was concluded on 16 April; the last elements of NATO forces deployed to Turkey left the country on 3 May.

Secretary-General and Chairman of the North Atlantic Council, of the DPC and of the NPG, Lord Robertson (UK) (until Dec. 2003)

UK Permanent Representative on the North Atlantic Council, Sir Emyr Jones Parry

Chairman of the Military Committee, Gen. Harald Kujat (Germany)

Supreme Allied Commander, Europe, Gen. James Jones (USA)

Supreme Allied Commander, Atlantic, Adm. Ian Forbes (UK)

ORGANISATION FOR ECONOMIC CO-OPERATION AND DEVELOPMENT

2 rue André-Pascal, F-75775 Paris
Tel: (00 33) (1) 4524 8200 Fax: (00 33) (1) 4524 8500
Email: webmaster@oecd.org
Web: www.oecd.org

The Organisation for Economic Co-operation and Development (OECD) was formed in 1961 to replace the Organisation for European Economic Co-operation. It is the instrument for international co-operation among industrialised member countries on economic and social policies. Its objectives are to assist its member governments in the formulation and co-ordination of policies designed to achieve high, sustained economic growth while maintaining financial stability, to contribute to world trade on a multilateral basis and to stimulate members' aid to developing countries.

The members are Australia, Austria, Belgium, Canada, Czech Republic, Denmark, Finland, France, Germany, Greece, Hungary, Iceland, Republic of Ireland, Italy, Japan, Republic of Korea, Luxembourg, Mexico, the Netherlands, New Zealand, Norway, Poland, Portugal, Slovakia, Spain, Sweden, Switzerland, Turkey, the UK and the USA.

The Council is the supreme body of the organisation. It is composed of one representative for each member country and meets at permanent representative level under the chairmanship of the Secretary-General, and at ministerial level (usually once a year) under the chairmanship of a minister elected annually. Decisions and recommendations are adopted by the unanimous agreement of all members. Most of the OECD's work is undertaken in over 150 specialised committees and working parties. Five autonomous or semi-autonomous bodies are associated in varying degrees to the Organisation: the Nuclear Energy Agency, the International Energy Agency, the Development Centre, the Centre for Educational Research and Innovation, and the European Conference of Ministers of Transport. These bodies, the committees and the Council are serviced by an international Secretariat headed by the Secretary-General.

Secretary-General, Donald J. Johnston (Canada)
UK Permanent Representative, HE Christopher Crabbie,
  19 rue de Franqueville, Paris F-75116

ORGANISATION FOR SECURITY AND CO-OPERATION IN EUROPE

Kärntner Ring 5–7, A-1010 Vienna, Austria
Tel: (00 43) (1) 514 36 180 Fax: (00 43) (1) 514 36 105 Email: info@osce.org Web: www.osce.org

The Organisation for Security and Co-operation in Europe (OSCE) was launched in 1975 (as the Conference on Security and Co-operation in Europe (CSCE)) under the Helsinki Final Act. This established agreements between NATO members, Warsaw Pact members, and neutral and non-aligned European countries covering security, co-operation and human rights.

The Charter of Paris for a New Europe, signed on 21 November 1990, committed members to support multiparty democracy, free-market economics, the rule of law, and human rights. The signatories also agreed to regular meetings of heads of government, ministers and officials. The first institutionalised heads of state and government summit was held in Helsinki in December 1992, at which the Helsinki Document was adopted. This declared the CSCE to be a regional organisation and defined the structures of the organisation. The summit also appointed a High Commissioner on National Minorities. At its December 1994 summit the CSCE was renamed the Organisation for Security and Co-operation in Europe.

Three structures have been established: the Ministerial Council, which comprises the foreign ministers of participating states and is the central decision-making and governing body, and which meets at least once a year; the Senior Council, which prepares work for the Ministerial Council, carries out its decisions and is responsible for the overview, management and co-ordination of OSCE activities and meets at least three times a year; and the Permanent Council, which is responsible for the day-to-day operational tasks of the OSCE and is the regular body for political consultation, meeting weekly. The chairmanship of the Ministerial Council, Senior Council and Permanent Council rotates among participating states with the Senior Council meeting in Prague and the Permanent Council in Vienna.

The OSCE is also underpinned by four permanent institutions: a Secretariat (Vienna); an Office for Democratic Institutions and Human Rights (Warsaw), which is charged with furthering human rights, democracy and the rule of law; an office of the High Commissioner on National Minorities (The Hague), which identifies ethnic tensions that might endanger peace and promotes their resolution; and a Representative on Freedom of the Media (Vienna), which is responsible for assisting governments in the furthering of free, independent and pluralistic media. There is also a documentation and conference centre in Prague, an OSCE Parliamentary Assembly with a secretariat based in Copenhagen, and a Court of Conciliation and Arbitration in Geneva.

The OSCE has monitoring missions in 18 OSCE countries. The OSCE supervised all elections in Bosnia-Hercegovina between 1996 and 2000 and in Kosovo since 2000. A Joint Consultative Group of the OSCE promotes the objectives and implementation of the Conventional Armed Forces in Europe (CFE) Treaty (1990) which limits conventional ground and air forces. In November 1999, the Charter on European Security committed the OSCE to co-operate with other organisations and institutions concerned with the promotion of security within the OSCE area.

The OSCE has 55 participating states.

Chair of the OSCE, Netherlands (2003); Bulgaria (2004)
Secretary-General of the OSCE, Ján Kubiš (Slovakia)
Director of the Office for Democratic Institutions and Human Rights, Christian Strohal (Austria)
OSCE High Commissioner on National Minorities, Rolf Ekeus (Sweden)
Representative on Freedom of the Media, Freimut Duve (Germany)

ORGANISATION OF AMERICAN STATES

17th Street and Constitution Avenue NW,
Washington DC 20006, USA
Tel: (00 1) (202) 458 3000 Fax: (00 1) (202) 458 6421
Email: pi@oas.org
Web: www.oas.org

Originally founded in 1890 for largely commercial purposes, the Organisation of American States (OAS) adopted its present name and charter in 1948. The charter entered into force in 1951 and was amended in 1967, 1985 and 1996; the 1992 Protocol of Washington will enter into force upon ratification by two-thirds of member states.

The OAS aims to strengthen the peace and security of the continent; to promote and consolidate representative democracy with due respect for the principle of non-intervention; to prevent possible causes of difficulties and to ensure the peaceful resolution of disputes arising among its member states; to provide for common action on the part of those states in the event of aggression; to seek the resolution of political, judicial and economic problems that may arise among them; to promote, by co-operative action, their economic, social and cultural development; and to achieve an effective limitation of conventional weapons so that resources can be devoted to economic and social development.

The Declaration of Principles and the Plan of Action resulting from the 1994 Miami summit and signed by all the members except Cuba, envisage the establishment of a free trade area, in which barriers to trade and investment will be progressively eliminated.

Policy is determined by the annual General Assembly, which is the supreme authority and elects the Secretary-General for a five-year term. The Meeting of Consultation of ministers of foreign affairs considers urgent problems on an *ad hoc* basis. The Permanent Council, comprising one representative from each member state, promotes friendly inter-state relations, acts as an intermediary in case of disputes arising between states and oversees the General Secretariat, the main administrative body. The Inter-American Council for Integral Development was created in 1996 by the ratification of the Protocol of Managua to promote sustainable development.

The 35 member states are Antigua and Barbuda, Argentina, the Bahamas, Barbados, Belize, Bolivia, Brazil, Canada, Chile, Colombia, Costa Rica, Cuba, Dominica, Dominican Republic, Ecuador, El Salvador, Grenada, Guatemala, Guyana, Haiti, Honduras, Jamaica, Mexico, Nicaragua, Panama, Paraguay, Peru, St Christopher and Nevis, St Lucia, St Vincent and the Grenadines, Suriname, Trinidad and Tobago, Uruguay, the USA and Venezuela. The European Union and 39 non-American states have permanent observer status.
Secretary-General, Dr César Gaviria Trujillo (Colombia)

ORGANISATION OF ARAB PETROLEUM EXPORTING COUNTRIES
PO Box 20501, Safat 13066, Kuwait
Tel: (00 965) 484 4500 Fax: (00 965) 481 5747
Email: oapec@qualitynet.net
Web: www.oapecorg.org

The Organisation of Arab Petroleum Exporting Countries (OAPEC) was founded in 1968. Its objectives are to promote co-operation in economic activities, to safeguard members' interests, to unite efforts to ensure the flow of oil to consumer markets, and to create a favourable climate for the investment of capital and expertise.

The Ministerial Council is composed of oil ministers from the member countries and meets twice a year to determine policy and to approve the budgets and accounts of the General Secretariat and the Judicial Tribunal. The Judicial Tribunal is composed of seven part-time judges who rule on disputes between member countries and disputes between countries and oil companies. The executive organ of OAPEC is the General Secretariat.

The members are Algeria, Bahrain, Egypt, Iraq, Kuwait, Libya, Qatar, Saudi Arabia, Syria and the United Arab Emirates. Tunisia's membership has been inactive since 1987.
Secretary-General, Abdel-Aziz A. Al-Turki

ORGANISATION OF THE BLACK SEA ECONOMIC CO-OPERATION
Permanent International Secretariat, Istinye Caddesi, Müsir Fuad Pasa Yalisi, Eski Tersane, 34460 Istinye-Istanbul, Turkey
Tel: (00 90) (212) 229 6330/6335 Fax: (00 90) (212) 229 6336
Email: bsec@turk.net
Web: www.bsec-organization.org

The Black Sea Economic Co-operation (BSEC) resulted from the Istanbul Summit Declaration and the adoption of the Bosporus Statement on 25 June 1992. BSEC acquired a permanent secretariat in 1994. Following the Yalta Summit of the Heads of State or Government in June 1998, a charter was drawn up to found the Organisation of the Black Sea Economic Co-operation, which was inaugurated on 1 May 1999.

The organisation aims to promote closer political and economic co-operation in the context of the European integration process between the countries in the Black Sea region and to foster security, regional initiatives, social justice, economic liberty and respect for human rights.

The Council of the Ministers of Foreign Affairs, the highest decision-making authority, meets twice yearly. The meetings rotate among the member states and the chairman is the foreign minister of the state in which the meeting is held. There is also a Committee of Senior Officials and 15 working groups, which deal with specific areas of co-operation.

There are 11 member states: Albania, Armenia, Azerbaijan, Bulgaria, Georgia, Greece, Moldova, Romania, Russia, Turkey and Ukraine.

ORGANISATION OF THE ISLAMIC CONFERENCE
PO Box 178, Jeddah 21411, Saudi Arabia
Tel: (00 966) (2) 680 0800 Fax: (00 966) (2) 687 3568
Email: oiccabinet@oic-un.org
Web: www.oic-oci.org

The Organisation of the Islamic Conference (OIC) was established in 1969 with the purpose of promoting solidarity and co-operation between Islamic countries. It also has the specific aims of co-ordinating efforts to safeguard the Muslim holy places, supporting the formation of a Palestinian state, assisting member states to maintain their independence, co-ordinating the views of member states in international forums such as the UN, and improving co-operation in the economic, cultural and scientific fields.

The OIC has three central organs, supreme among them the Conference of the Heads of State which meets once every three years to discuss issues of importance to Islamic states. The Conference of Foreign Ministers meets annually to prepare reports for the Conference of Heads of State. The General Secretariat carries out administrative tasks. It is headed by a Secretary-General who is elected by the Conference of Foreign Ministers for a non-renewable four-year term.

In addition to this structure, the OIC has several subsidiary bodies, specialised institutions, affiliated bodies and standing committees. These include the Islamic Solidarity Fund, to aid Islamic institutions in member countries, the Islamic Development Bank, to finance development projects in poorer member states and the Islamic Educational, Scientific and Cultural Organisation. The OIC runs various offices to organise the economic boycott of Israel.

The achievement of the OIC's aims has often been prevented by political rivalry and conflicts between member states, such as the Iran-Iraq war and the Iraqi invasion of Kuwait. Egypt's membership was suspended from 1979 to 1984 because of its peace treaty with Israel. Saudi Arabia, the main source of funding, exercises great influence within the OIC. Since 1991 the OIC has become more united and has spoken out against violence against Muslims in India, the Occupied Territories and Bosnia-Hercegovina. From 1993 to 1995 the OIC co-ordinated the offering of troops to the UN by Muslim states to protect Muslim areas of Bosnia-Hercegovina.

The Organisation has 56 members (55 sovereign Muslim states in Africa, the Middle East, central and south-east Asia and Europe, plus the Palestine Liberation

Organisation) and three observers, the Central African Republic, Turkish Northern Cyprus and Côte d'Ivoire. It has an annual budget of US$11 million.

Secretary-General, Dr Abdelouahed Belkeziz (Morocco)

ORGANISATION OF THE PETROLEUM EXPORTING COUNTRIES

Obere Donaustrasse 93, A-1020 Vienna, Austria
Tel: (00 43) (1) 21112 279 Fax: (00 43) (1) 214 9827
Email: prid@opec.org
Web: www.opec.org

The Organisation of the Petroleum Exporting Countries (OPEC) was created in 1960 as a permanent intergovernmental organisation with the principal aims of unifying and co-ordinating the petroleum policies of its members, determining ways of protecting their interests individually and collectively, and ensuring the stabilisation of prices in international oil markets with a view to eliminating unnecessary fluctuations. Since 1982 OPEC has attempted (only partially successfully) to impose overall production limits and production quotas in an attempt to maintain stable oil prices.

The supreme authority is the Conference of Ministers of oil, mines and energy of member countries, which meets at least twice a year to formulate policy. The Board of Governors, nominated by member countries, directs the management of OPEC and implements conference resolutions. The Secretariat carries out executive functions under the direction of the Board of Governors.

The member states are Algeria, Indonesia, Iran, Iraq, Kuwait, Libya, Nigeria, Qatar, Saudi Arabia, the UAE and Venezuela. Ecuador withdrew in 1992 and Gabon in 1995.

OPEC member countries account for about 39 per cent of global crude oil production and 50 per cent of internationally traded crude oil, and have 79 per cent of the world's proven oil reserves. The value of OPEC oil exports in 2002 was US$207 billion.

Secretary-General, HE Dr Alvaro Silva Calderón (Venezuela)

PACIFIC ISLANDS FORUM

Secretariat, Private Mail Bag, Suva, Fiji
Tel: 679 331 2600 Fax: 679 330 5573
Email:info@forumsec.org.fj
Web: www.forumsec.org.fj

The Pacific Islands Forum (PIF) was established in 1971 and represents heads of governments of all the independent and self-governing Pacific Island countries. It aims to foster co-operation between its governments and to represent the interests of the region in international organisations. The PIF meets annually, following which a dialogue is conducted at ministerial level with the Forum dialogue partners (Canada, China, the European Union, France, India, Indonesia, Japan, Korea, Malaysia, the Philippines, the UK and the USA).

The members of the PIF are Australia, the Cook Islands, Micronesia, Fiji, Kiribati, Nauru, New Zealand, Niue, Palau, Papua New Guinea, the Marshall Islands, Samoa, the Solomon Islands, Tonga, Tuvalu and Vanuatu.

The PIF Secretariat comprises divisions dealing with development and economic policy, trade and investment, political and international affairs, and corporate services.

Secretary-General, W. Noel Levi, CBE (Papua New Guinea)

THE SECRETARIAT OF THE PACIFIC COMMUNITY

BP D5, 98848 Nouméa Cedex, New Caledonia
Tel: (00 687) 262000 Fax: (00 687) 263818
Email: spc@spc.int
Web: www.spc.int

The Secretariat of the Pacific Community (formerly the South Pacific Commission) was established in 1947 by Australia, France, the Netherlands, New Zealand, the UK and the USA with the aim of promoting the economic and social stability of the islands in the region. The Community now numbers 27 member states and territories: the five remaining founder states (the Netherlands has withdrawn), in which no programmes are run, and the other 22 states and territories of Melanesia, Micronesia and Polynesia.

The Secretariat of the Pacific Community (SPC) is a technical assistance agency with programmes in marine resources (coastal and oceanic fisheries; maritime programme), land resources (agriculture, animal health and plant protection; forestry) and social resources (community health; socio-economic and statistical services; community education services).

The governing body is the Conference of the Pacific Community, which meets every two years. The Director-General is the chief executive.

Director-General, Lourdes Pangelinan (Guam)

SHANGHAI CO-OPERATION ORGANISATION

The treaty establishing the Shanghai Co-operation Organisation was signed by China, Kazakhstan, Kyrgyzstan, the Russian Federation, Tajikistan and Uzbekistan on 15 June 2001 in Shanghai. The organisation was set up following five years of co-operation between the signatories (with the exception of Uzbekistan), who had been informally called the Shanghai Five. The Shanghai Co-operation Organisation has been established on the basis of the agreements on confidence-building in the military field and on the mutual reduction of armed forces in the border area signed in Shanghai and Moscow in 1996 and 1997 respectively.

The organisation aims to strengthen mutual trust, friendship and good-neighbourliness between the member states; to encourage effective co-operation between them in the political, trade and economic, scientific and technical, cultural, educational, energy, transport, environmental, and other spheres; and to undertake joint efforts for the maintenance of peace, security and stability in the region, and the building of a new, democratic, just and rational international political and economic order. Co-operation within the organisation's framework is already under way in political, trade and economic, cultural, scientific and technical, and other spheres.

The heads of state hold annual official meetings and there are regular meetings of the heads of government, held alternately in each of the member states. There is no permanent secretariat.

SOUTH ASIAN ASSOCIATION FOR REGIONAL CO-OPERATION

PO Box 4222, Kathmandu, Nepal
Tel: (00 977) (1) 221794/221785
Fax: (00 977) (1) 227033/223991
Email: saarc@saarc-sec.org
Web: www.saarc-sec.org

The South Asian Association for Regional Co-operation (SAARC) was established in 1985 by Bangladesh, Bhutan, India, the Maldives, Nepal, Pakistan and Sri Lanka. Its primary objective is the acceleration of the process of economic and social development in member states through collective action in agreed areas of co-operation. These include agriculture and rural development, human resource development, environment, meteorology and forestry, science and technology, transport and communications, energy, and social development.

A SAARC Preferential Trading Arrangement (SAPTA), which is designed to reduce tariffs on trade between SAARC member states, was signed in 1993 and entered into force in December 1995. A committee of experts was established in 1998 to draft a comprehensive treaty to create a South Asian Free Trade Area (SAFTA). Agreement was reached in January 2002 to work towards the establishment of a South Asian economic union.

The highest authority rests with the heads of state or government of each member state. The Council of Ministers, which meets twice a year, is made up of the foreign ministers of the member states; it is responsible for formulating policy and considering new projects. The Standing Committee is composed of the foreign secretaries of the member states and monitors and co-ordinates SAARC programmes; it meets twice a year. Technical committees are responsible for individual areas of SAARC's activities. The Secretariat co-ordinates, monitors, facilitates and promotes SAARC's activities and serves as a channel of communication between the association and other regional and intergovernmental institutions.

Secretary-General, Q. A. M. A. Rahim (Bangladesh)

SOUTHERN AFRICAN DEVELOPMENT COMMUNITY

Private Bag 0095, Gaborone, Botswana
Tel: (00 267) 351 863 Fax: (00 267) 372 848
Email: sadcsec@sadc.int
Web: www.sadc.int

The Southern African Development Community (SADC) was formed in August 1992 by the members of its predecessor, the Southern African Development Co-ordination Conference, founded in 1980 to harmonise economic development among the countries in Southern Africa and reduce their dependence on South Africa. The SADC now comprises 14 countries, including South Africa, and works on a regional basis to increase economic integration and regional security.

It aims to evolve common political values, systems and institutions, to promote development and economic growth, regional security, self-sustaining development and the interdependence of member states, and to maximise production and strengthen and consolidate the historical, social and cultural links among the peoples of the region.

The headquarters of the SADC is in Gaborone, Botswana, but member states each have a responsibility for an area of economic activity.

Executive Secretary, Dr Prega Ramsamy
Chairman, José Eduardo dos Santos (Angola)

THE UNITED NATIONS

UN Plaza, New York, NY 10017, USA
Tel: (00 1) (212) 963 1234
Web: www.un.org

The United Nations (UN) is an intergovernmental organisation of member states, dedicated through signature of the UN Charter to the maintenance of international peace and security and the solution of economic, social and political problems through international co-operation.

The UN was founded as a successor to the League of Nations and inherited many of its procedures and institutions. The name 'United Nations' was first used in the Washington Declaration 1942 to describe the 26 states that had allied to fight the Axis powers. The UN Charter developed from discussions at the Moscow Conference of the foreign ministers of China, the UK, the USA and the Soviet Union in 1943. Further progress was made at Dumbarton Oaks, Washington, in 1944 during talks involving the same states. The role of the Security Council was formulated at the Yalta Conference in 1945. The Charter was formally drawn up by 50 allied nations at the San Francisco Conference between April and 26 June 1945, when it was signed. Following ratification the UN came into effect on 24 October 1945, which is celebrated annually as United Nations Day. The UN flag is light blue with the UN emblem centred in white.

The principal organs of the UN are the General Assembly, the Security Council, the Economic and Social Council, the Trusteeship Council, the Secretariat and the International Court of Justice. The Economic and Social Council and the Trusteeship Council are auxiliaries, charged with assisting and advising the General Assembly and Security Council. The official languages used are Arabic, Chinese, English, French, Russian and Spanish. Deliberations at the International Court of Justice are in English and French only.

A Millennium summit was held in New York on 6–8 September 2000 at which the reform of the UN was debated and an attempt was made to redefine its role.

MEMBERSHIP

Membership is open to all countries which accept the Charter and its principle of peaceful co-existence. New members are admitted by the General Assembly on the recommendation of the Security Council. The original membership of 51 states has grown to 191.

Afghanistan; Albania; Algeria; Andorra; Angola; Antigua and Barbuda; Argentina*; Armenia; Australia*; Austria; Azerbaijan; Bahamas; Bahrain; Bangladesh; Barbados; Belarus*; Belgium*; Belize; Benin; Bhutan; Bolivia*; Bosnia-Hercegovina; Botswana; Brazil*; Brunei Darussalam; Bulgaria; Burkina Faso; Burundi; Cambodia; Cameroon; Canada*; Cape Verde; Central African Republic; Chad; Chile*; China*; Colombia*; Comoros; Congo; Costa Rica*; Côte d'Ivoire; Croatia; Cuba*; Cyprus; Czech Republic; Democratic People's Republic of Korea; Democratic Republic of the Congo; Denmark*; Djibouti; Dominica; Dominican Republic*; Ecuador*; Egypt*; El Salvador*; Equatorial Guinea; Eritrea; Estonia; Ethiopia*; Fiji; Finland; France*; Gabon; Gambia; Georgia; Germany; Ghana; Greece*; Grenada; Guatemala*; Guinea; Guinea-Bissau; Guyana; Haiti*; Honduras*; Hungary; Iceland; India*; Indonesia; Iran*; Iraq*; Ireland; Israel; Italy; Jamaica; Japan; Jordan; Kazakhstan; Kenya; Kiribati; Korea; Kuwait; Kyrgyzstan;

Laos; Latvia; Lebanon*; Lesotho; Liberia*; Libya; Liechtenstein; Lithuania; Luxembourg*; Macedonia; Madagascar; Malawi; Malaysia; Maldives; Mali; Malta; Marshall Islands; Mauritania; Mauritius; Mexico*; Micronesia (Federated States of); Moldova; Monaco; Mongolia; Morocco; Mozambique; Myanmar; Namibia; Nauru; Nepal; Netherlands*; New Zealand*; Nicaragua*; Niger; Nigeria; Norway*; Oman; Pakistan; Palau; Panama*; Papua New Guinea; Paraguay*; Peru*; Philippines*; Poland*; Portugal; Qatar; Romania; Russian Federation*; Rwanda; Saint Christopher and Nevis; Saint Lucia; Saint Vincent and the Grenadines; Samoa; San Marino; São Tomé and Princípe; Saudi Arabia*; Senegal; Serbia and Montenegro; Seychelles; Sierra Leone; Singapore; Slovakia; Slovenia; Solomon Islands; Somalia; South Africa*; Spain; Sri Lanka; Sudan; Suriname; Swaziland; Sweden; Syrian Arab Republic*;Tajikistan; Tanzania; Thailand; Togo; Tonga; Trinidad and Tobago; Tunisia; Turkey*; Turkmenistan; Tuvalu; Uganda; Ukraine*; United Arab Emirates; United Kingdom*; United States of America*; Uruguay*; Uzbekistan; Vanuatu; Venezuela*; Vietnam; Yemen; Zambia; Zimbabwe.

* Original member (i.e. from 1945). Czechoslovakia, Yugoslavia and the USSR were all original members until their dissolution.

OBSERVERS
Permanent observer status is held by the Holy See. The Palestine Liberation Organisation has special observer status.

NON-MEMBERS
A number of countries are not members, including Taiwan, which was replaced by the People's Republic of China in 1971, East Timor and the Holy See.

THE GENERAL ASSEMBLY
UN Plaza, New York, NY 10017, USA

The General Assembly is the main deliberative organ of the UN. It consists of all members, each entitled to five representatives but having only one vote. The annual session begins on the third Tuesday of September, when the President is elected, and usually continues until mid-December. Special sessions are held on specific issues and emergency special sessions can be called within 24 hours.

The Assembly is empowered to discuss any matter within the scope of the Charter, except when it is under consideration by the Security Council, and to make recommendations. Under the 'uniting for peace' resolution, adopted in 1950, the Assembly may also take action to maintain international peace and security when the Security Council fails to do so because of a lack of unanimity of its permanent members. Important decisions, such as those on peace and security, the election of officers, the budget, etc., need a two-thirds majority. Others need a simple majority. The Assembly has effective power only over the internal operations of the UN itself; external recommendations are not legally binding.

The work of the General Assembly is divided among six main committees, on each of which every member has the right to be represented: disarmament and international security; economic and financial; social, humanitarian and cultural; special political issues and decolonisation (including non-self governing territories); administrative and budgetary; and legal. In addition, the General Assembly appoints ad hoc committees to consider special issues, such as human rights, peacekeeping, disarmament and international law. All committees consider items referred to them by the Assembly and recommend draft resolutions to its plenary meeting.

The Assembly is assisted by a number of functional committees. The General Committee co-ordinates its proceedings and operations, while the Credentials Committee verifies the credentials of representatives. There are also two standing committees, the Advisory Committee on Administration and Budgetary Questions and the Committee on Contributions, which suggests the scale of members' payments to the UN.
President of the General Assembly (2003), Julian Hunte (Saint Lucia)

The Assembly has created a large number of specialised bodies over the years, which are supervised jointly with the Economic and Social Council. They are supported by UN and voluntary contributions from governments, non-governmental organisations and individuals. These organisations include:

THE CONFERENCE ON DISARMAMENT (CD)
Palais des Nations, CH-1211 Geneva 10, Switzerland

Established by the UN as the Committee on Disarmament in 1962, the CD is the single multilateral disarmament negotiating forum. The present title of the organisation was adopted in 1984. There are 66 members.

A Chemical Weapons Convention was agreed in Paris in 1993 and came into force in April 1997 after being ratified by 87 countries. It bans the use, production, stockpiling and transfer of all chemical weapons. All US and Russian weapons must be destroyed within 15 years of the Convention entering into force and all other states' weapons must be destroyed within ten years.
Secretary-General, Vladimir Petrovsky (Russia)
UK Representative, David Broucher, 37–39 rue de Vermont, CH-1211 Geneva 20, Switzerland

THE UNITED NATIONS CHILDREN'S FUND (UNICEF)
3 UN Plaza, New York, NY 10017, USA

Established in 1947 to assist children and mothers in the immediate post-war period, UNICEF now concentrates on developing countries. It provides primary healthcare and health education. In particular, it conducts programmes in oral hydration, immunisation against leading diseases, child growth monitoring and the encouragement of breast-feeding. Its operations are often conducted in co-operation with the World Health Organisation (WHO).
Executive Director, Carol Bellamy (USA)

THE UNITED NATIONS DEVELOPMENT PROGRAMME (UNDP)
1 UN Plaza, New York, NY 10017, USA

Established in 1966 from the merger of the UN Expanded Programme of Technical Assistance and the UN Special Fund, UNDP is the central funding agency for economic and social development projects around the world. Much of its annual expenditure is channelled through UN specialised agencies, governments and non-governmental organisations.
Administrator, Mark Malloch-Brown

THE UNITED NATIONS HIGH COMMISSIONER FOR REFUGEES (UNHCR)
94 rue Montbrillant, PO Box 2500, CH-1211
  Geneva 2, Switzerland

Established in 1951 to protect the rights and interests of refugees, UNHCR organises emergency relief and longer-term solutions, such as voluntary repatriation, local integration or resettlement.
High Commissioner, Ruud Lubbers (Netherlands)
UK OFFICE, 21st Floor, Millbank Tower, 21–24 Millbank,
London SW1P 4QH. Tel: 020-7828 9191

THE UN RELIEF AND WORKS AGENCY FOR PALESTINE REFUGEES IN THE NEAR EAST (UNRWA)
Vienna International Centre, Wagramerstrasse 5,
  PO Box 700, A-1400 Vienna, Austria

Established in 1949 to bring relief to the Palestinians displaced by the Arab-Israeli conflict.
Commissioner-General, Peter Hansen (Denmark)

THE UNITED NATIONS HIGH COMMISSIONER FOR HUMAN RIGHTS

Established in 1993 to secure respect for, and prevent violations of human rights by engaging in dialogue with governments and international organisations. Responsible for the co-ordination of all UN human rights activities.
High Commissioner, Sergio Vieira de Mello (Brazil)

THE SECURITY COUNCIL
UN Plaza, New York, NY 10017, USA

The Security Council is the senior arm of the UN and has the primary responsibility for maintaining world peace and security. It consists of 15 members, each with one representative and one vote. There are five permanent members, China, France, Russia, the UK and the USA, and ten non-permanent members. Each of the non-permanent members is elected for a two-year term by a two-thirds majority of the General Assembly and is ineligible for immediate re-election. Five of the elective seats are allocated to Africa and Asia, one to eastern Europe, two to Latin America and two to western Europe and remaining countries. Procedural questions are determined by a majority vote. Other matters require a majority inclusive of the votes of the permanent members; they thus have a right of veto. The abstention of a permanent member does not constitute a veto. The presidency rotates each month by state in (English) alphabetical order. Parties to a dispute, other non-members and individuals can be invited to participate in Security Council debates but are not permitted to vote.

The Security Council is empowered to settle or adjudicate in disputes or situations which threaten international peace and security. It can adopt political, economic and military measures to achieve this end. Any matter considered to be a threat to or breach of the peace or an act of aggression can be brought to the Security Council's attention by any member state or by the Secretary-General. The Charter envisaged members placing at the disposal of the Security Council armed forces and other facilities which would be co-ordinated by the Military Staff Committee, composed of military representatives of the five permanent members. The Security Council is also supported by a Committee of Experts, to advise on procedural and technical matters, and a Committee on Admission of New Members.

Owing to superpower disunity, the Security Council rarely played the decisive role set out in the Charter; the Military Staff Committee was effectively suspended from 1948 until 1990, when a meeting was convened during the Gulf Crisis on the formation and control of UN-supervised armed forces. However, at an extraordinary meeting of the Security Council in January 1992, heads of government laid plans to transform the UN in light of the changed post-Cold War world. The Secretary-General was asked to draw up a report on enhancing the UN's preventive diplomacy, peacemaking and peacekeeping ability. The report, *An Agenda for Peace,* was produced in June 1992 and centred on the establishment of a UN army composed of national contingents on permanent standby, as envisaged at the time of the UN's formation.

PEACEKEEPING FORCES
The Security Council has established a number of peacekeeping forces since its foundation, comprising contingents provided mainly by neutral and non-aligned UN members. Current forces include: the UN Truce Supervision Organisation (UNTSO), Israel, 1948; the UN Military Observer Group in India and Pakistan (UNMOGIP), 1949; the UN Peacekeeping Force in Cyprus (UNFICYP), 1964; the UN Disengagement Observer Force (UNDOF), Golan Heights, Syria, 1974; the UN Interim Force in Lebanon (UNIFIL), 1978; the UN Iraq-Kuwait Observation Mission (UNIKOM), 1991; the UN Mission for the Referendum in Western Sahara (MINURSO), 1991; the UN Observer Mission in Georgia (UNOMIG), 1993; the United Nations Mission in Bosnia and Hercegovina (UNMIBH), 1995; the United Nations Mission of Observers in Prevlaka (UNMDP), 1996; the United Nations Interim Administration Mission in Kosovo (UNMIK), 1999; the United Nations Mission in Sierra Leone (UNAMISIL), 1999; the United Nations Organisation Mission in the Democratic Republic of the Congo (MONUC), 1999; the United Nations Mission in Ethiopia and Eritrea (UNMEE), 2000; the United Nations Mission of Support in East Timor (UNMISET), 2002; the United Nations Mission in Côte d'Ivoire (MINUCI), 2003.

THE ECONOMIC AND SOCIAL COUNCIL
UN Plaza, New York, NY 10017, USA

The Economic and Social Council is responsible under the General Assembly for the economic and social work of the UN and for the co-ordination of the activities of the 15 specialised agencies and other UN bodies. It makes reports and recommendations on economic, social, cultural, educational, health and related matters, often in consultation with non-governmental organisations, passing the reports to the General Assembly and other UN bodies. It also drafts conventions for submission to the Assembly and calls conferences on matters within its remit.

The Council consists of 54 members, 18 of whom are elected annually by the General Assembly for a three-year term. Each has one vote and can be immediately re-elected on retirement. A President is elected annually and is also eligible for re-election. One substantive session is held annually and decisions are reached by simple majority vote of those present.

The Council has established a number of standing committees on particular issues and several commissions. Commissions include: Statistical, Human Rights, Social Development, Sustainable Development, Status of

Women, Crime Prevention and Criminal Justice, Narcotic Drugs, Science and Technology for Development, and Population; and Regional Economic Commissions for Europe, Asia and the Pacific, Western Asia, Latin America and Africa.

THE TRUSTEESHIP COUNCIL
UN Plaza, New York, NY10017, USA

The Trusteeship Council supervised the administration of territories within the UN Trusteeship system inherited from the League of Nations. It consists of the five permanent members of the Security Council. With the independence of the Republic of Palau in October 1994, all eleven trusteeships have now progressed to independence or merged with neighbouring states and the Trusteeship Council suspended its operations on 1 November 1994.

THE SECRETARIAT
UN Plaza, New York, NY 10017, USA

The Secretariat services the other UN organs and is headed by a Secretary-General elected by a majority vote of the General Assembly on the recommendation of the Security Council. He is assisted by an international staff, chosen to represent the international character of the organisation. The Secretary-General is charged with bringing to the attention of the Security Council any matter which he considers poses a threat to international peace and security. He may also bring other matters to the attention of the General Assembly and other UN bodies and may be entrusted by them with additional duties. As chief administrator to the UN, the Secretary-General is present in person or via representatives at all meetings of the other five main organs of the UN. He may also act as an impartial mediator in disputes between member states.

The power and influence of the Secretary-General has been determined largely by the character of the office-holder and by the state of relations between the superpowers. The thaw in these relations since the mid-1980s has increased the effectiveness of the UN, particularly in its attempts to intervene in international disputes. It helped to end the Iran-Iraq war and sponsored peace in Central America. Following Iraq's invasion of Kuwait in 1990 the UN took its first collective security action since the Korean War. Conflicts in Cyprus, East Timor, Libya, Nigeria and Western Sahara have been successfully prevented from escalating or spreading during Kofi Annan's (the seventh occupant of the post of Secretary-General) time in office. In addition to maintenance of international security, ending poverty and inequality, improving education, reducing HIV/AIDS and safeguarding the environment were some of the issues outlined in the UN Millennium Report.
Secretary-General, Kofi Annan, *apptd* 1996 (Ghana)
Deputy Secretary-General, Louise Frechette, *apptd* 1998 (Canada)

FORMER SECRETARIES-GENERAL

1946–53	Trygve Lie (Norway)
1953–61	Dag Hammarskjöld (Sweden)
1961–71	U Thant (Burma)
1971–81	Kurt Waldheim (Austria)
1981–91	Javier Pérez de Cuéllar (Peru)
1991–96	Boutros Boutros-Ghali (Egypt)

INTERNATIONAL COURT OF JUSTICE
The Peace Palace, NL-2517 KJ The Hague, The Netherlands

The International Court of Justice is the principal judicial organ of the UN. The Statute of the Court is an integral part of the Charter and all members of the UN are *ipso facto* parties to it. The Court is composed of 15 judges, elected by both the General Assembly and the Security Council for nine-year terms which are renewable. Judges may deliberate over cases in which their country is involved. If no judge on the bench is from a country which is a party to a dispute under consideration, that party may designate a judge to participate *ad hoc* in that particular deliberation. If any party to a case fails to adhere to the judgement of the Court, the other party may have recourse to the Security Council.
President, Shi Jiuyong (China)
Vice-President, Raymond Ranjeva (Madagascar)
Judges, Rosalyn Higgins (UK); Pieter H. Kooijmans (Netherlands); Abdul G. Koroma (Sierra Leone); Gonzalo Parra-Aranguren (Venezuela); José Francisco Rezek (Brazil); Vladlen S. Vereshchetin (Russia); Awn Shawkat Al-Khasawneh (Jordan); Thomas Buergenthal (USA); Gilbert Guillaume (France); Nabil Elaraby (Egypt); Hisashi Owada (Japan); Bruno Simma (Germany); Peter Tomka (Slovakia)

INTERNATIONAL CRIMINAL TRIBUNAL FOR THE FORMER YUGOSLAVIA
Churchill Plein 1, PO Box 13888, NL-2501 EW
The Hague, The Netherlands
In February 1993, the Security Council voted to establish a war crimes tribunal for the former Yugoslavia to hear cases covering grave breaches of the Geneva Conventions and crimes against humanity. The Court was inaugurated in November 1993 in The Hague with 11 judges elected by the UN General Assembly from 11 states, divided into two trial chambers of three judges each and an appeal chamber of five judges. The court is unable to force suspects to stand trial but is empowered to pass verdicts in the absence of suspects and can put suspects under an 'act of accusation' which prevents them from leaving their own country.

In October 1995, the tribunal formally charged the Bosnian Serb leaders Radovan Karadzić and Gen. Ratko Mladić, and the Croatian Serb President Milan Martić and 21 others with genocide and crimes against humanity. By January 1997 only one of the 75 suspected war criminals to be indicted had been imprisoned. In May 1999, the tribunal formally charged the Yugoslav president Slobodan Milošević, the Serbian president Milan Milutinović, two other Serb politicians and the Yugoslav armed forces chief of staff Dragoljub Ojdanić. As at June 2003, 54 of the 75 indictees were in proceedings before the tribunal and 21 remained at large.
President, Antonio Cassese (Italy)
Chief Prosecutor, Louise Arbour (Canada)

INTERNATIONAL CRIMINAL TRIBUNAL FOR RWANDA
In November 1994, the UN Security Council voted to establish a tribunal to try those responsible for genocide and other violations of international humanitarian law in Rwanda between 1 January and 31 December 1994. The tribunal, based in Arusha, Tanzania, is empowered to try the most senior people responsible for the massacre. It formally opened in November 1995. To date over 70 suspects have been indicted of whom more than 60 have been arrested and transferred to the Tribunal's custody. Of those so far apprehended, the trials of 10 have been completed resulting in nine convictions and one acquittal.
Chief Prosecutor, Carla del Ponte (Switzerland)

UNITED NATIONS MONITORING, VERIFICATION AND INSPECTION COMMISSION
Room S-3120, New York, NY 10017, USA
Tel: (00 1) (212) 963 3017 Fax: (00 1) (212) 963 3922
Web: www.unmovic.org
The United Nations Monitoring, Verification and Inspection Commission (UNMOVIC), was created by UN Security Council Resolution 1284, adopted in December 1999.
UNMOVIC is mandated to verify Iraq's compliance with its obligation not to possess or acquire weapons of mass destruction (biological or chemical weapons of mass destruction, together with ballistic missiles with a target distance of more than 150 km), to destroy all research, development and production facilities and to desist from the future development or acquisition of such weapons and operate a monitoring and verification programme to ensure that prohibited items and programmes are not reactivated.
In January 2003, three months after UN weapon inspectors were re-admitted to Iraq, Dr Blix stated that Iraq had failed to disarm, greatly strengthening the American and British case for war. He insisted, however, that the weapons inspectors be given more time. US president George Bush presented the deadline of 17 March 2003 for Iraq to disarm and the UN removed all their staff from the region. A second UN resolution was not granted and on 19 March 2003 airstrikes led by the USA began against Baghdad without UN backing. In the thirteenth quarterly report of UNMOVIC, covering March to May 2003, Hans Blix stated that the Commission had at no point during the inspections in Iraq found evidence of the continuation or resumption of programmes of weapons of mass destruction or significant quantity of proscribed items – whether pre-1991 or after. He stressed that this did not mean that such items could not exist as there remained long lists of unaccounted items.
In resolution1483 (May 2003) lifting Iraqi economic sanctions, the Security Council declared its intention to revisit the mandate of UNMOVIC, which remains ready to resume its work in Iraq. In July 2003 Kofi Annan announced the appointment of a new Chief Executive to replace Hans Blix.
Executive Chairman, Dimitri Perricos (Greece)

UK MISSION TO THE UNITED NATIONS
1 Dag Hammarskjöld Plaza, 885 Second Avenue,
New York, NY 10017, USA
Tel: (00 1) (212) 745 9250 Fax: (00 1) (212) 745 9316
Email: uk@un.int
Web: www.ukun.org
Permanent Representative to the United Nations and Representative on the Security Council, Sir Jeremy Greenstock, KCMG, *apptd* 1998
Deputy Permanent Representative, Adam Thomson

UK MISSION TO THE OFFICE OF THE UN AND OTHER INTERNATIONAL ORGANISATIONS IN GENEVA
37–39 rue de Vermont, CH-1211 Geneva 20, Switzerland
Tel: (00 41) (22) 918 2300 Fax: (00 41) (22) 918 2333
Email: mission.uk@ties.itu.int
Permanent UK Representative, Nicholas Thorne, CMG, *apptd* 2003
Deputy Permanent Representative, N. M. McMillan, CMG

UK MISSION TO THE UN IN VIENNA
Jaurèsgasse 12, A-1030 Vienna, Austria UK
Permanent Representative, P. R Jenkins, *apptd* 2001
Deputy Permanent Representative, T. J. Andrews

UN OFFICE AND INFORMATION CENTRE
21st Floor, Millbank Tower, 21–24 Millbank,
London, SW1P 4QH
Tel: 020-7630 1981; Fax: 020-7976 6478
Email: info@uniclondon.org
Web: www.unitednations.org.uk

UNITED NATIONS EDUCATIONAL, SCIENTIFIC AND CULTURAL ORGANISATION

7 place de Fontenoy, F-75352 Paris 07 SP, France
Tel: (00 33) (1) 4568 1000 Fax: (00 33) (1) 4567 1690
Email: clearing-house@unesco.org
Web: www.unesco.org

The United Nations Educational, Scientific and Cultural Organisation (UNESCO) was established in 1946. It promotes collaboration among its member states in education, science, culture and communication. It aims to further a universal respect for human rights, justice and the rule of law, without distinction of race, sex, language or religion, in accordance with the UN Charter.
UNESCO runs a number of programmes to improve education and extend access to it. It provides assistance to ensure the free flow of information and its wider and better balanced dissemination without any obstacle to freedom of expression, and to maintain cultural heritage in the face of development. It fosters research and study in all areas of the social and environmental sciences.
UNESCO had 189 member states as at June 2003. The General Conference, consisting of representatives of all the members, meets biennially to decide the programme and the budget (2002–3, US$544,367,250). It elects the 58-member Executive Board, which supervises operations, and appoints a Director-General who heads a Secretariat responsible for carrying out the organisation's programmes. In most member states national commissions liaise with UNESCO to execute its programme.
The UK withdrew from UNESCO in 1985; it rejoined on 1 July 1997.
Director-General, Koïchiro Matsuura (Japan)

UNITED NATIONS INDUSTRIAL DEVELOPMENT ORGANISATION

Vienna International Centre, Wagramerstrasse 5,
PO Box 300, A-1400 Vienna, Austria
Tel: (00 43) (1) 260 260 Fax: (00 43) (1) 269 2669
Email: unido@unido.org
Web: www.unido.org

The United Nations Industrial Development Organisation (UNIDO) was established in 1966 by the UN General Assembly to act as the central co-ordinating body for industrial activities within the UN. It became a UN specialised agency in 1985. UNIDO aims to help developing countries and those with economies in transition to develop sustainable industrialisation by concentrating on economic competitiveness, environmental awareness and employment issues both in the public and private sectors. UNIDO designs and implements programmes to support industrial development in individual member states and offers specialised support for programme development.

UNIDO had 170 members as at January 2003. It is funded by regular and operational budgets, together with contributions for technical co-operation activities. The regular budget is derived from member states' contributions. Technical co-operation is funded mainly through voluntary contributions from donor countries and institutions and by intergovernmental and non-governmental organisations. A General Conference of all the members meets biennially to discuss strategy and policy, approve the budget (2002–3, regular budget € 133.7 million) and elect the Director-General. The Industrial Development Board is composed of members from 53 member states and reviews the work programme and the budget, which is prepared by the Programme and Budget Committee.

Director-General, Carlos Magariños (Argentina)
Permanent UK Representative, Peter Jenkins, British Embassy, Vienna

UNIVERSAL POSTAL UNION

Weltpoststrasse 4, CH-3000 Bern 15, Switzerland
Tel: (00 41) (31) 350 3111 Fax: (00 41) (31) 350 3110
Email: info@upu.int
Web: www.upu.int

The Universal Postal Union (UPU) was established by the Treaty of Bern 1874, taking effect from 1875, and became a UN specialised agency in 1948. The UPU is an intergovernmental organisation that exists to form and regulate a single postal territory of all member countries for the reciprocal exchange of correspondence without discrimination. It also assists and advises on the improvement of postal services.

The UPU had 189 members as at June 2003. A Universal Postal Congress is the UPU's supreme authority and meets every five years. A Council of Administration composed of 41 members meets annually to ensure continuity between congresses, study regulatory developments and broad policies, approve the budget and examine proposed Treaty changes. A Postal Operations Council, composed of 40 members elected by the Congress, meets annually to deal with specific technical and operational issues. The three UPU bodies are served by the International Bureau, a secretariat headed by a Director-General.

Funding is provided by members according to a scale of contributions drawn up by the Congress. The Council

of Administration sets the biennial budget (2003–4, SFr71,400,000).

Director-General, Thomas E. Leavey (USA)

UNREPRESENTED NATIONS AND PEOPLES ORGANISATION

Eisenhowerlaan 136, NL-2517 KN, The Hague, The Netherlands
Tel: (00 31) (70) 360 3318 Fax: (00 31) (70) 360 3346
Email: unponl@unpo.org
Web: www.unpo.org

The Unrepresented Nations and Peoples Organisation (UNPO) was founded in 1991 to offer an international forum for occupied nations, indigenous peoples and national minorities who are not represented in other international organisations.

UNPO does not aim to represent these nations and peoples, but rather to assist and empower them to represent themselves more effectively, and provides professional services and facilities as well as education and training in the fields of diplomacy, international and human rights law, democratic processes, institution building, conflict management and resolution, and environmental protection.

Participation is open to all nations and peoples who are inadequately represented at the United Nations and who declare allegiance to five principles relating to the right of self-determination of all peoples, human rights, democracy, non-violence and the rejection of terrorism, and protection of the natural environment. Applicants must show that they constitute a 'nation or people' and that the organisation applying for membership is representative of that nation or people.

As at June 2003, there were 53 full members and five former members, who have achieved full independence.

Director-General, Karl von Habsburg (Austria)

WESTERN EUROPEAN UNION

Rue de l'Association 15, B-1000 Brussels, Belgium
Tel: (00 32) (2) 500 4412 Fax: (00 32) (2) 500 4470
Email: ueo.secretariatgeneral@skynet.be
Web: www.weu.int

The Western European Union (WEU) originated as the Brussels Treaty Organisation (BTO) established under the Treaty of Brussels, signed in 1948 by Belgium, France, Luxembourg, the Netherlands and the UK, to provide collective self-defence and economic and social collaboration amongst its signatories. The BTO was modified to become the WEU in 1954 with the admission of West Germany and Italy.

From the late 1970s onwards efforts were made to add a security dimension to the EC's European Political Co-operation. Opposition to these efforts from Denmark, Greece and Ireland led the remaining EC countries, all WEU members, to decide to reactivate the Union in 1984. Members committed themselves to harmonising their views on defence and security and developing a European security identity, while bearing in mind the importance of transatlantic relations. Portugal and Spain joined the WEU in 1988, and Greece became a full member in 1995.

In 1991, the EU Maastricht Treaty committed the European Community to the establishment of a Common Foreign and Security Policy (CFSP). The WEU was designated as the future defence component of the European Union and member states of the EU who were not already members of the WEU were invited to join or become observers. In November 1992 the WEU's role as the common security dimension of the EU was enhanced when WEU ministers signed a declaration with remaining European NATO members to give them various forms of WEU membership. Iceland, Norway and Turkey became associate members; the Republic of Ireland, Denmark, Austria, Finland and Sweden became observers. In 1994 the WEU reached agreements with Estonia, Latvia, Lithuania, Poland, the Czech Republic, Slovakia, Hungary, Romania and Bulgaria, under which they all became associate partners; Slovenia became an associate partner in 1996. The Czech Republic, Hungary and Poland, who had been associate partners, became associate members in 1999, following their accession to NATO.

The WEU has worked in close co-operation with the Atlantic Alliance, and relations between the WEU and NATO were developed on the basis of transparency and complementarity. The 1993 Luxembourg Declaration states that the WEU is ready to participate in the future work of the NATO Alliance as its European pillar, and at the Atlantic Alliance summit in January 1994, NATO expressed its readiness to make Alliance assets and capabilities available for WEU operations. In June 1996, NATO foreign and defence ministers approved the Combined Joint Task Force (CJTF) concept and the elaboration of multinational European command arrangements for WEU-led operations.

A Council of Ministers (foreign and defence) has met biannually in the capital of the presiding country; the presidency rotates biannually, and from 1999 the sequence of WEU presidencies has been harmonised with those of the EU Council of Ministers. A Permanent Council of the member states' permanent representatives meets in Brussels. The Permanent Council is chaired by the Secretary-General and serviced by the Secretariat.

In 1999, NATO and the EU decided to establish a direct relationship; the EU committed itself to ensuring that it was able to take decisions on conflict prevention and crisis management and NATO agreed to give the EU access to its collective assets and capabilities for operations in which NATO as a whole was not engaged. The WEU's crisis management functions were transferred to the EU in July 2001. The necessary WEU functions and structures remain in place to enable member states to fulfil commitments arising from the modified Brussels Treaty including those relating to collective defence and institutional relationship with the WEU.

The Assembly of the WEU is composed of 115 parliamentarians of member states and meets twice annually in Paris to debate matters within the scope of the revised Brussels Treaty.

Presidency (2003) Greece, Italy; (2004) Spain, Netherlands

Secretary-General, Javier Solana Madariaga (Spain)

UK Representative on the Permanent Council, David Richmond

ASSEMBLY, 43 avenue du Président Wilson, F-75775 Paris Cedex 16, France

THE WORLD BANK GROUP

1818 H Street NW, Washington 20433, USA
Tel: (00 1) (202) DC 477 1000 Fax: (00 1) (202) 477 6391
Email: feedback@worldbank.org
Web: www.worldbank.org

The World Bank Group was founded in 1944 and is one of the world's largest sources of development assistance.

The Bank has 183 members. Originally directed towards post-war reconstruction in Europe, the Bank subsequently turned towards assisting less-developed countries and is currently working in more than 100 developing countries. The Bank, which provided US$19.5 billion in loans to its client countries in the 2002 financial year, works with government agencies, non-governmental organisations and the private sector to formulate assistance strategies. Its local offices implement the Bank's programme in each country. It has offices in more than 100 countries.

The Bank is owned by the governments of member countries and its capital is subscribed by its members. It finances its lending primarily from borrowing in world capital markets, and derives a substantial contribution to its resources from its retained earnings and the repayment of loans. The interest rate on its loans is calculated in relation to its cost of borrowing. Loans generally have a grace period of five years and are repayable within 20 years.

The World Bank Group consists of five institutions. The International Bank for Reconstruction and Development (IBRD) provides loans and development assistance to middle-income countries and creditworthy poorer countries. The International Finance Corporation (IFC) promotes private sector investment in developing member countries by mobilising domestic and foreign capital. The International Development Association (IDA) performs the same function as the World Bank but primarily to less-developed countries and on terms that bear less heavily on their balance of payments than IBRD loans. The Multilateral Investment Guarantee Agency (MIGA) promotes foreign direct investment in developing states by providing guarantees to potential investors and advisory services to developing member countries. MIGA has a membership of 157 countries. The International Centre for Settlement of Investment Disputes (ICSID) provides facilities for the settlement by conciliation or arbitration of investment disputes between foreign investors and their host countries. ICSID has a membership of 134 countries.

The IBRD and its affiliates are financially and legally distinct but share headquarters. The IBRD is headed by a Board of Governors, consisting of one Governor and one alternate Governor appointed by each member country. Twenty-four Executive Directors exercise all powers of the Bank except those reserved to the Board of Governors. The President, elected by the Executive Directors, conducts the business of the Bank, assisted by an international staff. Membership in both the IFC (175 members) and the IDA (162 members) is open to all IBRD countries. The IDA is administered by the same staff as the Bank; the IFC has its own personnel but draws on the IBRD for administrative and other support. All share the same President.

President, James D. Wolfensohn (USA)

UK Executive Director, Tom Scholar, Room 11-120, IMF, 700 19th Street NW, Washington DC 20431

UK OFFICE, New Zealand House, 15th Floor, Haymarket, London SW1Y 4TQ.
Tel: 020-7930 8511 Fax: 020-7930 8515

WORLD HEALTH ORGANISATION

20 avenue Appia, CH-1211 Geneva 27, Switzerland
Tel: (00 41) (22) 791 2111 Fax: (00 41) (22) 791 0746
Email: info@who.ch
Web: www.who.ch

The UN International Health Conference, held in 1946, established the World Health Organisation (WHO) as a UN specialised agency, with effect from 1948. It is dedicated to attaining the highest possible level of health for all. It collaborates with member governments, UN agencies and other bodies to improve health standards, control communicable diseases and promote all aspects of family and environmental health. It seeks to raise the standards of health teaching and training, and promotes research through collaborating research centres world-wide.

WHO had 192 members as at June 2003. It is governed by the annual World Health Assembly of members which meets to set policy, approve the budget (2002–3, US$2,223 million), appoint a Director-General, and adopt health conventions and regulations. It also elects 32 members who designate one expert to serve on the Executive Board. The Board effects the programme, suggests initiatives and is empowered to deal with emergencies. A Secretariat, headed by the Director-General, supervises the activities of six regional offices.

Director-General, Dr Jong-Wook Lee (Republic of Korea)

WORLD INTELLECTUAL PROPERTY ORGANISATION

34 chemin des Colombettes, CH-1211 Geneva 20, Switzerland
Tel: (00 41) (22) 338 9111 Fax: (00 41) (22) 733 5428
Email: wipo@wipo.int
Web: www.wipo.int

The World Intellectual Property Organisation (WIPO) was established in 1967 by the Stockholm Convention, which entered into force in 1970. In addition to that Convention, WIPO administers 23 treaties, the principal ones being the Paris Convention for the Protection of Industrial Property and the Bern Convention for the Protection of Literary and Artistic Works. WIPO became a UN specialised agency in 1974.

WIPO promotes the protection of intellectual property throughout the world through co-operation among states, and the administration of various 'Unions', each founded on a multilateral treaty and dealing with the legal and administrative aspects of intellectual property.

Intellectual property comprises two main branches: industrial property (inventions, trademarks, industrial designs and appellations of origin); and copyright (literary, musical, photographic, audiovisual and artistic works, etc.). WIPO also assists creative intellectual activity and facilitates technology transfer, particularly to developing countries.

WIPO had 179 members as at June 2003. The biennial session of all its governing bodies sets policy, a programme and a budget (2002–3, SFr678 million).

A separate International Union for the Protection of New Varieties of Plants (UPOV), established by convention in 1961, is linked to WIPO. It has 45 members.

Director-General, Dr Kamil Idris (Sudan)

WORLD METEOROLOGICAL ORGANISATION

7 bis, avenue de la Paix, PO Box 2300, CH-1211
Geneva 2, Switzerland
Tel: (00 41) (22) 730 8111 Fax: (00 41) (22) 730 8181
Email: wmo@gateway.wmo.ch
Web: www.wmo.ch

The World Meteorological Organisation (WMO) was established in 1950 and became a UN specialised agency in 1951, succeeding the International Meteorological Organisation founded in 1873. It facilitates co-operation in the establishment of networks for making meteorological, climatological, hydrological and geophysical observations, as well as their exchange, processing and standardisation, and assists technology transfer, training and research. It also fosters collaboration between meteorological and hydrological services, and furthers the application of meteorology to aviation, shipping, environment, water problems, agriculture and the mitigation of natural disasters.

The WMO had 179 member states and six member territories as at June 2003. Six regional associations are responsible for the co-ordination of activities within their own regions, There are also eight technical commissions, which study meteorological and hydrological problems, establish methodology and procedures, and make recommendations to the Executive Council and the Congress. The supreme authority is the World Meteorological Congress of member states and member territories, which meets every four years to determine general policy, make recommendations and set a budget (2000–3, SFr252.3 million). It also elects 26 members of the 36-member Executive Council, the other members being the President and three Vice-Presidents of the WMO, and the Presidents of the six regional associations, who are ex-officio members. The Council supervises the implementation of Congress decisions, initiates studies and makes recommendations on matters needing international action. The Secretariat is headed by a Secretary-General, appointed by the Congress.

Secretary-General, G. O. P. Obasi (Nigeria)

WORLD TRADE ORGANISATION

Centre William Rappard, 154 rue de Lausanne,
1211 CH-Geneva 21, Switzerland
Tel: (00 41) (22) 739 5111 Fax: (00 41) (22) 739 5458
Email: enquiries@wto.org
Web: www.wto.org

The World Trade Organisation was established on 1 January 1995 as the successor to the General Agreement on Tariffs and Trade (GATT). GATT was established in 1948 as an interim agreement until the charter of a new international trade organisation could be drafted by a committee of the UN Economic and Social Council and ratified by member states. The charter was never ratified and GATT became the only regime for the regulation of world trade, evolving its own rules and procedures.

GATT was dedicated to the expansion of non-discriminatory international trade and progressively extended free trade via 'rounds' of multilateral negotiations. Eight rounds were concluded: Geneva (1947), Annecy (1948), Torquay (1950), Geneva (1956), Dillon (1960–1), Kennedy (1964–7), Tokyo (1973–9) and Uruguay (1986–94). The Final Act of the Uruguay Round was signed by trade ministers from the 128 GATT negotiating states and the EU in Marrakesh, Morocco, on

15 April 1994. It established the World Trade Organisation (WTO) to supersede GATT and implement the Uruguay Round agreements. The implementation of the Uruguay Round measures in 2002 resulted in a reduction on duties on manufactured goods from 40 per cent in the 1940s to 3 per cent. New talks on agriculture and services began in 2000 and were incorporated into a broader agenda launched at the 2001 Ministerial Conference in Doha, Qatar. The current round of negotiations is scheduled to be concluded by 2005.

The WTO is the legal and institutional foundation of the multilateral trading system. It provides the contractual obligations determining how governments frame and implement trade policy and provides the forum for the debate, negotiation and adjudication of trade problems. The WTO's principal aims are to liberalise world trade and place it on a secure basis, and it seeks to achieve this partly by an agreed set of trade rules and market access agreements and partly through further trade liberalisation negotiations. The WTO also administers and implements a further 29 multilateral agreements in fields such as agriculture, textiles and clothing, services, government procurement, rules of origin and intellectual property.

The highest authority of the WTO is the Ministerial Conference composed of all members, which meets at least once every two years. The General Council meets as required and acts on behalf of the Ministerial Conference in regard to the regular working of the WTO. Composed of all members, the General Council also convenes in two particular forms: as the Dispute Settlement Body, dealing with disputes between members arising from the Uruguay Round Final Act; and as the Trade Policy Review Body, conducting regular reviews of the trade policies of members. A secretariat of 500 staff headed by a Director-General services WTO bodies and provides trade performance and trade policy analysis.

As at April 2003 there were 146 WTO members, and a further 30 governments had applied to join. The WTO budget for 2003 was SFr154 million, with members' contributions calculated on the basis of their share of the total trade conducted by WTO members. The official languages of the WTO are English, French and Spanish.

Director-General, Dr Supachai Panitchpakdi

Permanent UK Representative, Simon Fuller, 37–39 rue de Vermont, CH-1211 Geneva 20

COUNTRIES OF THE WORLD A–Z

AFGHANISTAN

Af ğānistān (Pushtu) /
Afqânestân (Dari)
Afghanistan

AREA – 251,773 sq. miles (652,090 sq. km).
  Neighbours: Iran (west), Pakistan (east and south),
  Tajikistan, Uzbekistan and Turkmenistan (north),
  China (north-east)
POPULATION – 22,132,000: Pushtuns (44 per cent)
  predominate in the south and west; Tajiks (25 per
  cent); Hazaras (10 per cent) in the centre; Uzbeks
  (8 per cent) in the north; Aimaqs (4 per cent); Baluchis
  (0.5 per cent). The principal languages are Dari (a form
  of Persian) and Pushtu
CAPITAL – Kabul (population, 1,424,400, 1988)
MAJOR CITIES – Herat (177,300); Jalalabad (55,000);
  Qandahar (225,500); Mazar-e-Sharif (130,600) (1988
  UN estimates)
CURRENCY – Afghani (Af) of 100 puls
NATIONAL ANTHEM – Sorud-e-Melli
NATIONAL DAY – 19 August
NATIONAL FLAG – Three vertical stripes of black, red
  and green with the royal arms and Arabic device
  'There is no God but Allah and Muhammad is His
  Messenger' in the centre
POPULATION GROWTH RATE – 2.7 per cent
POPULATION DENSITY – 34 per sq. km (1999)

Mountains, chief among which are the Hindu Kush,
cover three-quarters of the country. There are three great
river basins, the Oxus, Helmand, and Kabul. The climate
is dry, with extreme temperatures.

HISTORY AND POLITICS
In December 1979 Soviet troops invaded Afghanistan
and installed a pro-Soviet government. Armed Islamic
resistance groups, the mujahidin, fought against Soviet
and Afghan forces until the government collapsed in
April 1992. Mujahidin forces overran Kabul and declared
an Islamic state.

Fighting between factions of the mujahidin resumed in
December 1992. Between 1994–98, divided mujahidin
forces suffered heavy defeats at the hands of the Taliban
(armed Islamic students), which extended its power across
more than 90 per cent of the country. The forces of the
former government were driven northwards. The United
Islamic Front for the Salvation of Afghanistan (UIFSA) or
Northern Alliance was formed by the four main
mujahidin factions. The Taliban, thought to be backed by
Pakistan and Saudi Arabia, imposed strict Shari'ah law.

The United Nations imposed limited sanctions on
Afghanistan on 19 December 2000 for refusing to
extradite Osama bin Laden, an Islamic terrorist.

Following the 11 September 2001 terrorist attacks on
the USA, which had been carried out by bin Laden's
al-Qa'eda (the base) organisation, and Afghanistan's
subsequent refusal to surrender bin Laden and the
al-Qa'eda leadership to the US authorities, US and UK
forces began military operations against al-Qa'eda and

Taliban targets in Afghanistan on 7 October 2001.
Surrounding countries offered their facilities to the US
forces and intensive US air bombardment conducted from
air bases in Uzbekistan, Tajikistan and Pakistan, together
with material and intelligence assistance by US and UK
special services ground troops to Northern Alliance
forces, swiftly caused the Taliban regime to collapse in
the north of the country, which led to defections from the
Taliban in the south and successes for anti-Taliban
Pushtun militias. Mazar-e-Sharif fell to the Northern
Alliance forces on 9 November, Herat on 12 November,
Kabul on 18 November, and Qandahar surrendered to
opposition forces on 6 December.

Moves to form an alternative government from among
the numerous anti-Taliban factions had begun in
September 2001 and leaders met near Bonn, Germany,
where on 5 December 2001 a multiethnic interim
government was named, which was formed of supporters
of the Northern Alliance, Royalists and other opposition
groups. However, attempts to locate and capture bin
Laden and Mullah Omar, the Taliban leader, were
unsuccessful and pockets of al-Qa'eda and Taliban forces
remained in the mountains in the centre of the country
and along its frontier with Pakistan. On 5 September
2002 an assassination attempt was made upon
transitional president Hamid Karzai by a lone gunman.
On 22 December 2002 the Kabul Declaration on Good
Neighbourly Relations was signed between Afghanistan
and its six neighbours. Tensions remained high
throughout the latter part of 2002 and into 2003 and
US-led coalition forces remained in the country. A 5,000-
strong UN-mandated peacekeeping force, the
International Security Assistance Force (ISAF), and 8,000
US troops remain in the country.

POLITICAL SYSTEM
Following the collapse of Taliban rule in December
2001, an interim government was agreed, which was to
hold office for six months pending the holding of a *Loya
Jirga* (tribal council), which would appoint a transitional
government, to be followed by a general election within
two years. On 13 June 2002, following the *Loya Jirga*,
the interim leader, Hamid Karzai, was voted in as

transitional president of the country. On 22 June a new transitional government was sworn in. Elections are due to take place in June 2004 following the approval of a new constitution by a Constitutional *Loya Jirga*.

HEAD OF STATE
Transitional President, Hamid Karzai, *elected* 13 June 2002
Transitional Vice-Presidents, Gen. Mohammad Qasim Fahim Khan *(Defence)*; Hedayat Amin Arsala *(Public Works)*; Karim Khalili; Nematullah Shahrani

TRANSITIONAL GOVERNMENT *as at May 2003*
Agriculture and Livestock, Hussein Anwari
Border Affairs, Aref Khan Nurzai
Civil Aviation and Tourism, Mirwais Sadeq
Commerce, Mustafa Kazemi
Communications, Masum Stanakzai
Education, Minister Adviser in charge of International Security, Mohammad Yunus Qanuni
Endowment and Religious Affairs, Mohammad Amin Naserya
Foreign Affairs, Abdullah Abdullah
Finance, Ashraf Ghani Ahmadzai
Health, Suhaila Seddiqi
Higher Education, Mohammad Sharif Faez
Information and Culture, Rahin Makhdoom
Interior, Ali Ahmad Jalali
Irrigation and Environment, Ahmad Yusof Nurestani
Justice, Abdul Rahmi Karimi
Housing and Town Planning, Mohammad Yusof Pashton
Labour and Social Affairs, Nur Mohammad Qarqin
Light Industries, Mohammad Alem Razm
Martyrs and Disabled, Abdullah Wardak
Mines and Industries, vacant
Minister Advisor in Tribal Affairs, Taj Mohammad Wardak
Planning, Ustad Mohammad Mohaqqeq
Public Works, Abdollah Ali
Reconstruction, Mohammad Amin Farhang
Return of Refugees, Enayatullah Nazeri
Rural Development, Hanef Atmal
Transport, Mohammad Ali Jawid
Water and Electricity, Shaker Kargar
Women's Affairs, Habiba Sorabi

EMBASSY OF AFGHANISTAN
31 Princes Gate, London SW7 1QQ
Tel: 020-7589 8891

BRITISH EMBASSY
Ambassador Extraordinary and Plenipotentiary, HE Ron Nash, LVO

ECONOMY
The economy has been devastated by the political upheavals of the last 20 years. Traditional industries have diminished as the narcotics trade has grown. Opium production, banned under the Taliban, rose from 185 tonnes in 2001 to 2,700 tonnes in 2002. By the end of 2000 one million people were thought to be close to starvation due to continuing fighting and crop failures caused by three successive years of drought. Food shortages, together with the on-going civil war resulted in the flight of more than two million refugees to Iran and Pakistan, and several hundred thousand internal refugees. By 6 October 2002, 1.7 million refugees had returned to Afghanistan.

Agriculture and sheep raising were traditionally the principal industries. Silk, woollen and hair cloths and carpets were manufactured. Salt, silver, copper, coal, iron, lead, rubies, lapis lazuli, gold, chrome, barite, uranium, and talc are found. There are thought to be considerable fuel reserves.

Afghanistan's debts to the Asian Development Bank, the World Bank and the IMF were cleared by the end of February 2003. The repayments were made using grant contributions from Italy, Japan, Norway, Sweden, the UK and the Afghanistan Reconstruction Trust Fund.
GDP – US$11,166 million (1998); US$100 per capita (2000)
ANNUAL AVERAGE GROWTH OF GDP – 6.0 per cent (1998)
INFLATION RATE – 56.7 per cent (1991); estimated to be 400 per cent in 1996

TRADE
In the past, exports have been Persian lambskins (Karakul), dried fruits, nuts, cotton, raw wool, carpets, spice and natural gas, while the imports are chiefly oil, cotton yarn and piece goods, tea, sugar, machinery and transport equipment.

In 1995 imports totalled US$50 million and exports US$26 million.

Trade with UK	2001	2002
Imports from UK	£3,812,000	£2,918,000
Exports to UK	564,000	249,000

COMMUNICATIONS
Main roads run from Kabul to Qandahar, Herat, Meymaneh via Mazar-e-Sharif and Feyzabad. Roads cross the border with Pakistan at Chaman and via the Khyber Pass, and there are roads from Herat to the borders of Turkmenistan and Iran. Much of the country's road system has been damaged during the fighting. On 10 November 2002, the reconstruction of the main highway stretching from Kabul through Kandahar to Herat, officially began, after the United States, Saudi Arabia and Japan pledged $180 million for road improvement projects. There are two international airports at Kabul and Qandahar and about 1,200 km of inland waterways.

EDUCATION
Education is free and nominally compulsory, elementary schools having been established in most centres; there are secondary schools in large urban areas and four universities, in Kabul, Jalalabad, Balkh and Herat. In March 2002, schools opened to 1.5 million children, many of whom had not received schooling for six years under the Taliban. There are four daily newspapers.
ILLITERACY RATE – (m) 48.1 per cent; (f) 78.1 per cent (2000)
ENROLMENT (percentage of age group) – primary 29 per cent (1993); secondary 14 per cent (1993); tertiary 1.8 per cent (1990)

ALBANIA

Republika e Shqipërisë – Republic of Albania

AREA – 11,099 sq. miles (28,748 sq. km). Neighbours: Montenegro (north), Kosovo and Macedonia (east), Greece (south)
POPULATION – 3,731,000. Muslim (70 per cent), Greek

Orthodox (20 per cent), Roman Catholic (10 per cent). The language is Albanian

CAPITAL – Tirana (population, 244,153, 1990)
CURRENCY – Lek (Lk) of 100 qindarka
NATIONAL ANTHEM – Rreth Flamurit Të Për Bashkuar (The Flag That United Us In The Struggle)
NATIONAL DAY – 28 November
NATIONAL FLAG – Black two-headed eagle on a red field
POPULATION GROWTH RATE – 3.7 per cent
POPULATION DENSITY – 108 per sq. km (1999)
ENROLMENT (percentage of age group) – primary 100 per cent (1997); tertiary 12 per cent (1997)

HISTORY AND POLITICS

Albania was under Turkish suzerainty from 1468 until 1912, when independence was declared. After a period of unrest, a republic was declared in 1925 and in 1928 a monarchy. The King went into exile in 1939 when the country was occupied by the Italians; Albania was liberated in November 1944. Elections in 1945 resulted in a Communist-controlled Assembly; the King was deposed in absentia and a republic declared in January 1946.

From 1946 to 1991 Albania was a one-party, Communist state. In March 1991 multiparty elections took place. Rioting broke out in January 1997 following the collapse of several pyramid investment schemes. Anti-government protests, taking the form of armed rebellion, spread throughout the country.

Following the abandonment of the Rambouillet peace talks on the future of Kosovo, NATO commenced air operations against Yugoslavia in March 1999. Yugoslavia responded by actively expelling hundreds of thousands of Kosovar Albanians, with the majority fleeing to Albania. In April 1999, Albania granted NATO unrestricted access to Albania's airspace, ports and military infrastructure. There were several incursions into Albanian territory by Serb troops. By mid-May 1999, over 400,000 Kosovar Albanians had taken refuge in Albania and over 10,000 NATO troops were stationed there. In June 1999 the refugees began returning home following the end of air operations and the entry of NATO forces into Kosovo. By the end of 1999, nearly all of the refugees had left Albania and the number of NATO troops stationed in the country had fallen to 2,000.

The most recent general election took place on 24 June and 8 July 2001 and resulted in the Socialist Party of Albania (SP) winning 70 seats and the Democratic Alliance (DAP) winning 36 seats in the 140-member People's Assembly.

HEAD OF STATE
President, Gen. Alfred Moisiu, *elected by the People's Assembly* 24 June 2002, *took office* 24 July 2002

COUNCIL OF MINISTERS *as at May 2003*
Prime Minister, Fatos Nano (PSS)
Deputy PM, Foreign Affairs, Ilir Meta (PSS)
Agriculture and Food, Agron Duka (PSS)
Culture, Youth and Sport, Arta Dade (PSS)
Defence, Pandeli Majko (PSS)
Economy, Arben Malaj (PSS)
Education and Science, Luan Memushi (PSS)
Environment, Lufter Xhuveli (PA)
Finance, Kastriot Islami (PSS)
Health, Mustafa Xhani (PSS)
Industry and Energy, Viktor Doda (PSS)

Interior, Luan Rama (PSS)
Justice, Spiro Peci (PBDNj)
Labour and Social Issues, Valentina Leskaj (Ind.)
Local Government and Decentralisation, Ben Blushi (PSS)
Ministers of State, Blendi Klosi *(Anti-Corruption)* (PSS); Sokol Nako *(Integration)* (PSS)
Public Works and Tourism, Besnik Dervishi (PSS)
Transport and Telecommunications, Spartak Poci (PSS)

PA Agrarian Party; PBDNJ Union for Human Rights Party; PSS Socialist Party of Albania; Ind. Independent

EMBASSY OF THE REPUBLIC OF ALBANIA
2nd Floor, 24 Buckingham Gate, London SW1E 6LB
Tel: 020-7828 8897
Ambassador Extraordinary and Plenipotentiary, HE Kastriot Robo, apptd 2002

BRITISH EMBASSY
Rruga Skenderbej 12, Tirana
Tel: (00 355) (42) 34973/4/5
Ambassador Extraordinary and Plenipotentiary, HE David Landsman, OBE, apptd 2001

BRITISH COUNCIL DIRECTOR, Michael Moore, MBE, Rr. 'Ded Gjo Luli' 3/1, Tirana Tel: (00 355) (4) 240856/7
Email: info@britishcouncil.org.al

DEFENCE

The Army has 400 main battle tanks and 103 armoured personnel carriers. The Navy has 20 patrol and coastal combatant vessels at four bases. The Air Force has 98 combat aircraft.
MILITARY EXPENDITURE – 2.6 per cent of GDP (2001)
MILITARY PERSONNEL – 27,000: Army 20,000, Navy 2,500, Air Force 4,500

ECONOMY

Much of the country is mountainous and nearly a half is covered by forest. The main crops are wheat, maize, sugar beet, potatoes and fruit. There are large chromium deposits. The principal industries are agricultural product processing, textiles, oil products and cement. Although agriculture accounts for almost half of GDP, production is held back due to frequent droughts and outdated equipment.

Since April 1992, the government has imposed austerity measures in an attempt to reduce the budget deficit and to cut inflation. Up to US$1,200 million worth of personal savings were lost in the collapse of several fraudulent pyramid savings schemes in January 1997 and the value of the lek fell heavily. Albania receives annual remittances from overseas workers (mainly in Greece and Turkey), of $400-600 million.
GNP – US$3,833 million (2000); US$1,120 per capita (2000)
GDP – US$4,114 million (2001); US$1,197 per capita (2000)
ANNUAL AVERAGE GROWTH OF GDP – 8.0 per cent (1998)
INFLATION RATE – 0.1 per cent (2000)
TOTAL EXTERNAL DEBT – US$784 million (2000)

TRADE

Exports include crude oil, minerals (bitumen, chrome, nickel, copper), tobacco, fruit and vegetables. In 2001, imports totalled US$1,331 million and exports US$305 million. In 2001 Albania had a trade deficit of

US$1,027 million and a current account deficit of US$218 million.

Trade with UK	2001	2002
Imports from UK	£21,732,000	£18,905,000
Exports to UK	1,204,000	2,873,000

ALGERIA

Al-Jumhūriyya al-Jazā'iriyya ad-Dimuqratiyya ash-Sha'biyya – People's Democratic Republic of Algeria

AREA – 916,038 sq. miles (2,381,700 sq. km).
   Neighbours: Morocco and Western Sahara (west), Mauritania and Mali (south-west), Niger (south-east), Libya and Tunisia (east)
POPULATION – 30,841,000 (2001). Arabic is the official language although French and Berber languages are also spoken. The state religion is Sunni Islam
CAPITAL – ΨAlgiers (El Djazaïr, Al-Jazàir) (population, 1,507,241, 1987). It is one of the principal ports of the Mediterranean
MAJOR CITIES – ΨAnnaba; ΨBejaia; Blida (El Boulaida); Constantine (Qacentina); ΨMostaganem; ΨOran (Wahran); Setif; Sidi-Bel-Abbès; ΨSkikda; Tizi Ouzou; Tlemcen
CURRENCY – Algerian dinar (DA) of 100 centimes
NATIONAL ANTHEM – Qassaman Bin Nazilat Il-Mahiqat (We Swear By The Lightning That Destroys)
NATIONAL DAY – 1 November
NATIONAL FLAG – Divided vertically green and white with a red crescent and star over all in the centre
LIFE EXPECTANCY (years) – 70 (2001)
POPULATION GROWTH RATE – 2 per cent
POPULATION DENSITY – 13 per sq. km (2001)
ILLITERACY RATE – (m) 21.8 per cent; (f) 42.9 per cent (2000)
ENROLMENT (percentage of age group) – primary 100 per cent (1997); secondary 63 per cent (1997); tertiary 12 per cent (1997)

HISTORY AND POLITICS

Algeria was annexed to France from 1830 until gaining its independence in 1962 following an eight-year armed liberation struggle by the Front de Libération Nationale (FLN). Ben Bella was elected president in 1963, but was deposed in 1965 by Col. Houari Boumediène, who was formally elected president in 1976. Boumediène died in 1978 and was succeeded by Chadli Bendjedid.

A new constitution agreed by referendum in 1988 moved Algeria towards pluralism. However, the 1991 legislative elections were abandoned in anticipation of the success of the opposition Islamic Salvation Front (FIS), which had campaigned on a radical 'Islamist' platform. President Bendjedid resigned and a Higher Committee of State (HCS), headed by former FLN veteran Mohammed Boudiaf, took power. Gen. Liamine Zeroual was elected president for a five-year term in November 1995, but announced his intention to stand down from office in September 1998. Abdelaziz Bouteflika was elected president on 15 April 1999. The other candidates decided to boycott the election some days before it took place, saying that the military had intervened to rig the vote in his favour.

The most recent elections to the National Assembly took place on 30 May 2002 and were won by the FLN, with Ali Benflis as Prime Minister, securing 199 of the 389 seats. Local elections held on 10 October 2002, secured the return of the FLN.

INSURGENCY

Since 1992, the FIS-backed Islamic Salvation Army (AIS) and the more extreme Armed Islamic Group (GIA) have waged an armed campaign against the regime in favour of an Islamic state. The two groups have targeted the military and security forces, their secular supporters in the population, and foreign expatriates, resulting in some 100,000 deaths since 1992. The AIS announced in June 1999 that it was renouncing the armed struggle following negotiations with the government; the resulting peace plan was approved by 98 per cent of the electorate in a referendum which was held on 16 September 1999. On 5 January 2000, the AIS announced that it had agreed to disband, however, attacks have continued.

Rioting broke out in the Berber-populated Kabyle region in April and May 2001, resulting in about 80 deaths. A joint session of the National People's assembly (the bicameral legislature) on 8 April, backed reform to give the Berber language, Tamazight, equal status with Arabic. The reform bill was approved by 482 votes with two abstentions and no opposition. During 2003 there was a resurgence of Islamist violence.

POLITICAL SYSTEM

The legislature is bicameral. The National People's Assembly (the lower chamber) has 389 members, directly elected for a five-year term. The *Majlis al-Umma* (Council of the Nation) is the upper chamber, with a third of its 144 members appointed by the president; two-thirds are indirectly elected for six-year terms, of which half are re-elected every three years.

HEAD OF STATE
President, Abdelaziz Bouteflika, *elected* April 1999

COUNCIL OF MINISTERS *as at May 2003*
Prime Minister, Ali Benflis
Agriculture and Rural Development, Said Barkat
Communications and Culture, Government Spokesperson, Khalida Toumi
Defence, The President
Employment and Solidarity, Tayeb Belayez
Energy and Mines, Chakib Khelil
Finance, Mohamed Terbeche
Fishing and Marine Resources, Smaïl Mimoun
Health, Population and Hospital Reforms, Abdelhamid Aberkane
Higher Education and Scientific Research, Rachid Harraoubia
Housing, Nadir Ahmimid
Industry and Restructuring, Hachemi Djaaboub
Justice, Keeper of the Seals, Mohammed Cherfi
Labour and Social Security, Tayeb Louh
Ministers-delegate, Abdelkader Messahel *(Maghreb and African Affairs);* Fatima Zahra Bouchemla *(National Community Abroad);* Dahou Ould Kablia *(Local Authorities);* Bouthaina Chriet *(Family Affairs and Women's Issues);* Abdelkader Sellat *(Prison Reform);* Rachid Benaissa *(Rural Development);* Leila Hamou Boutlelis *(Scientific Research);* Fatiha Mentouri *(Financial Reform)*
Ministers of State, Abdelaziz Belkhadem *(Foreign Affairs);* Noureddine Zerhouni *(Interior and Local Authorities);* Ahmed Ouyahia *(Personal Representative of the*

President); National Education, Noureddine Salah
Parliamentary Relations, Noureddine Taleb
Participation and Investment Promotion, Abdelhamid
 Temmar
*Postal Services, Information Technology and
 Telecommunications,* Zineddine Youbi
Public Works, Omar Ghoul
Religious Affairs and Endowments, Bouabdellah
 Ghalamallah
Secretary-General, Ahmed Noui
Small and Medium-sized Enterprises and Handicraft,
 Mostafa Benbada
Tourism and Traditional Industries, Lakhdar Dorbani
Trade, Noureddine Boukrouh
Transport, Abdelmalek Sellal
Urban Planning and the Environment, Cherif Rahmani
Vocational Training, Abdelhamid Abbad
War Veterans, Mohamed Cherif Abbas
Water Resources, Adelmadjid Attar
Youth and Sports, Boubeker Benbouzid

ALGERIAN EMBASSY
54 Holland Park, London W11 3RS
Tel: 020-7221 7800
Ambassador Extraordinary and Plenipotentiary, HE Ahmed
 Attaf, apptd 2001

BRITISH EMBASSY
6 Avenue Souidani Boudjemaa
BP08 Alger-Gare 16000, Algiers
Tel: (00 213) (21) 230068
Ambassador Extraordinary and Plenipotentiary,
 HE Graham Hand

BRITISH COUNCIL, c/o The British Embassy
Email: rachida.benyahia@fco.gov.uk

DEFENCE
The Army has 1,089 main battle tanks and 890
armoured personnel carriers. The Navy has two
submarines, three frigates and 17 patrol and coastal
vessels. The Air Force has 222 combat aircraft and 63
armed helicopters.
MILITARY EXPENDITURE – 6.3 per cent of GDP (2001)
MILITARY PERSONNEL – 136,700: Army 120,000,
 Navy 6,700, Air Force 10,000; Paramilitaries 181,200
CONSCRIPTION DURATION – 18 months

ECONOMY
The main industry is hydrocarbons which accounted for
40.8 per cent of GDP in 2000, followed by services
(29.3 per cent), construction (8.6 per cent), agriculture
(8.1 per cent) and non-hydrocarbons manufacturing
(7.3 per cent). Oil and natural gas are pumped from the
Sahara to terminals on the coast before being exported;
the gas is first liquefied at liquefaction plants at Skikda
and Arzew, although pipelines serve Libya and Italy
direct. In November 1996 a 750-mile gas pipeline to
Spain was opened, enabling Algeria to double its gas
exports to Morocco, Spain, Germany and France.
 Other major industries include a steel industry, motor
vehicles, building materials, paper making, chemical
products and metal manufactures. Most major industrial
enterprises are still under state control.
 Prior to 1989 the economy was centrally planned and
state-controlled in most sectors. In 1994 the government
finally accepted full economic reform and liberalisation
under a reform programme agreed with the IMF. The

government has cut the budget deficit, devalued the
currency and freed price controls. Algeria's foreign debt
fell from 71.9 per cent of GDP in 1996 to 40.7 per cent
in 2001. An extensive privatisation programme began in
1997. Following an earthquake on 21 May 2003 in
northern Algeria in which 2,000 people were killed and
more than 9,000 injured, the government approved a
US$1.8 billion package for the reconstruction of housing
and infrastructure that had been destroyed.
GNP – US$47,897 million (2000); US$1,580 per capita
 (2000)
GDP – US$53,009 million (2001); US$1,663 per capita
 (2000)
ANNUAL AVERAGE GROWTH OF GDP – 3.8 per cent
 (1998)
INFLATION RATE – 2.6 per cent (1999)
UNEMPLOYMENT – 29.8 per cent (2000)
TOTAL EXTERNAL DEBT – US$25,002 million (2000)

TRADE
Export earnings come mainly from crude oil and
liquefied natural gas sales. Natural gas and crude and
refined petroleum acounted for 97 per cent of export
value in 2000. Algeria's main trading partners are France,
Italy, USA, Spain and Germany. Dates and wine are
among the main food imports with trade with Italy at
24 per cent, USA at 13 per cent and France at 11 per cent
(In the year 2000).
 In 1996 imports totalled US$8,840 million and exports
US$12,620 million. In the first quarter of 2000, Algeria
recorded a US$1.98 billion surplus in its trade balance.

Trade with UK	2001	2002
Imports from UK	£118,467,000	£131,522,000
Exports to UK	235,294,000	341,690,000

ANDORRA

Principat d'Andorra – Principality of Andorra

AREA – 179 sq. miles (464 sq. km). Neighbours: Spain
 and France
POPULATION – 68,400 (2002 estimate); less than one-
 quarter of the population are native Andorrans. The
 official language is Catalan, but French and Spanish
 (Castilian) are also spoken. The established religion is
 Roman Catholicism
CAPITAL – Andorra la Vella (population, 20,787, 2001)
CURRENCY – Euro (€) of 100 cents
NATIONAL ANTHEM – El Gran Carlemany, Mon Pare
 (Great Charlemagne, My Father)
NATIONAL DAY – 8 September
NATIONAL FLAG – Three vertical bands, blue, yellow,
 red; Andorran coat of arms frequently imposed on
 central (yellow) band but not essential
LIFE EXPECTANCY (years) – 83 (2001)
POPULATION GROWTH RATE – 4.8 per cent
POPULATION DENSITY – 194 per sq. km (2001)
URBAN POPULATION – 92 per cent (2001)

HISTORY AND POLITICS
Andorra is a small, neutral principality formed by a treaty
in 1278. The first elections under the new constitution
were held in December 1993, and on 20 January 1994
the first sovereign government of Andorra took office.
The Liberal Party of Andorra won the legislative
elections of 4 March 2001, gaining 16 of the 28 seats in
the General Council.

POLITICAL SYSTEM

Under a new constitution promulgated in May 1993, Andorra became an independent, democratic parliamentary co-principality, with sovereignty vested in the people rather than in the two co-princes, as had previously been the case. The constitution enables Andorra to establish an independent judiciary and to carry out its own foreign policy, whilst its people may now join trade unions and political parties. The two co-princes, the President of the French Republic and the Spanish Bishop of Urgel, remain heads of state but now only have the power to veto treaties with France and Spain which affect the state's borders and security. The co-princes are represented by Permanent Delegates of whom one is the French Prefect of the Pyrénées Orientales department at Perpignan and the other is the Spanish Vicar-General of the diocese of Urgel.

Andorra has a unicameral legislature of 28 members known as the *Consell General de las Valls d'Andorra* (Valleys of Andorra General Council), elected for a four-year term. Fourteen members are elected on a national list basis and 14 in seven dual-member constituencies based on Andorra's seven parishes. The Council appoints the head of the executive government, who designates the members of his government.

Permanent French Delegate, Philippe Massoni
Permanent Episcopal Delegate, Nemesi Marqués Oste

EXECUTIVE GOVERNMENT *as at July 2003*
President of the Executive Council, Marc Forné Molné
Agriculture and the Environment, Olga Adellach Coma
Culture, Xavier Montané Atero
Economy, Miquel Àlvarez Marfany
Education, Youth and Sports, Pere Cervós Cardona
Finance, Mireia Maestre Cortadella
Foreign Affairs, Juli Minoves Triquell
Health and Welfare, Mònica Codina Tort
Justice and Interior, Jordi Visent Guitart
Presidency, Tourism, Enric Pujal Areny
Secretary-General, Joaquima Sol Ordis
Territorial Development, Jordi Serra Malleu

ANDORRAN EMBASSY
63 Westover Road, London SW18 2RF. Tel: 020-8874 4806
Ambassador Extraordinary and Plenipotentiary, HE Albert Pintat, apptd 2002

BRITISH AMBASSADOR – HE Peter Torry, resident at Madrid, apptd 1998

ECONOMY

Potatoes are produced in the highlands and tobacco in the valleys. The economy is largely based on tourism, banking, commerce, tobacco, construction and forestry; a third of the country is classified as forest. Andorra has negotiated a customs union with the European Union which came into force in 1991. The economy is now diversifying rapidly into offshore financial services.
GDP – US$1,062 million (1998); US$14,054 per capita (2000)
ANNUAL AVERAGE GROWTH OF GDP – 4.0 per cent (1998)

Trade with UK	2001	2002
Imports from UK	£17,185,000	£7,355,000
Exports to UK	86,000	169,000

COMMUNICATIONS

A road into the valleys from Spain is open all year round, and that from France is closed only occasionally in winter. There are two radio stations in Andorra, one privately owned and Radio Andorra, operated by the government, as well as a state-owned television station.

ANGOLA

República de Angola – Republic of Angola

AREA – 479,500 sq. miles (1,246,700 sq. km).
Neighbours: Democratic Republic of Congo (north and east), Zambia (east), Namibia (south). The enclave of Cabinda is separated from the rest of Angola by the Democratic Republic of Congo and also borders on the Republic of Congo–Brazzaville
POPULATION – 13,527,000. Main ethnic groups are Ovimbundu (37 per cent); Kimbundu (25 per cent); Bakongo (13 per cent). The official language is Portuguese
CAPITAL – ΨLuanda (population, 1,822,407, 1993)
CURRENCY – Readjusted kwanza (Kzrl) of 100 lwei
NATIONAL ANTHEM – Angola Avante (Advance Angola)
NATIONAL DAY – 11 November (Independence Day)
NATIONAL FLAG – Red and black with a yellow star, machete and cog-wheel
LIFE EXPECTANCY (years) – 45 (2001)
POPULATION GROWTH RATE – 3.1 per cent
POPULATION DENSITY – 11 per sq. km (2001)
URBAN POPULATION – 35 per cent (2001)
ENROLMENT (percentage of age group) – tertiary 0.7 per cent (1991)

HISTORY AND POLITICS

After a Portuguese presence of five centuries, and an anti-colonial war since 1961, Angola became independent on 11 November 1975 in the midst of civil war. The Popular Movement for the Liberation of Angola (MPLA) took control early in 1976, but remained under pressure from the National Union for the Total Independence of Angola (UNITA). A peace agreement was signed between the government and UNITA in 1991 and multiparty legislative and presidential elections took place in 1992, which were won by the MPLA and its leader, José Eduardo dos Santos. UNITA refused to accept the results and the civil war resumed in 1993.

UNITA and the MPLA government signed a peace agreement (the Lusaka Protocol) in 1994. A government of national reconciliation was formed in April 1997 and 70 UNITA legislators took up their seats in parliament, although UNITA's leader, Dr Jonas Savimbi, rejected an offer of the vice-presidency. UNITA also refused to allow central state administration to be restored in key areas and fighting resumed in May 1997.

On 31 October 1997 the UN Security Council ordered sanctions against UNITA for failing to meet its obligations under the Lusaka Protocol. UNITA returned much of its territory to government control in December, and in March 1998 UNITA became a legitimate political party. Three of its representatives were appointed governors of provinces of Angola.

Fighting continued and the UN Security Council adopted a resolution in September 1998 which urged the rejection of military force by all parties and named UNITA as 'the primary cause of the crisis in Angola'. In February 1999 the UN Security Council voted to withdraw the UN Observer Mission in Angola, the UN

Secretary-General Kofi Annan having declared that the country was on the verge of a catastrophic breakdown and that there was no more peace to keep. The UN Security Council adopted a further resolution on 13 April 2000, which called for an investigation into allegations that several countries had violated sanctions imposed on UNITA. Government forces succeeded in capturing large tracts of UNITA-controlled territory in late 2000. Following the death of UNITA's leader, Dr Jonas Sawimbi in February 2002, UNITA and the government signed a formal ceasefire agreement in Luanda on 4 April 2002 and pledged to adhere to the 1994 peace agreement, the Lusaka protocol. In addition, provision was made for the demobilisation of around 50,000 UNITA fighters, to be monitored by the UN, and the provision of state aid for some 300,000 family members of these soldiers. On 9 December 2002 the UN Security Council unanimously approved Resolution 1448 lifting all remaining economic and financial sanctions imposed on UNITA. Isaias Samakuva was elected leader of UNITA on 27 June 2003.

SECESSION
In the northern enclave of Cabinda, the Front for the Liberation of the Cabinda Enclave (FLEC) fought a 20-year war of independence until the signing of a ceasefire with the government in September 1995, which was followed by the initialling of a peace agreement in April 1996.

POLITICAL SYSTEM
The MPLA, formerly a Marxist-Leninist party, was the sole legal party until early 1991 when a multiparty system was adopted. The constitution declares Angola to be a democratic state and provides for a president, who appoints a Council of Ministers to assist him, and a 223-member National Assembly. In November 1996 the National Assembly adopted a constitutional amendment extending its mandate for between two and four years. The mandate was extended by the National Assembly on 17 October 2000 with no end date set.

HEAD OF STATE
President, José Eduardo dos Santos, *re-elected* 30 September 1992

COUNCIL OF MINISTERS *as at May 2003*
Prime Minister, Interior, Fernando da Piedade Dias dos Santos "Nando" (MPLA)
Deputy Prime Minister, Aguinaldo Jaime (MPLA)
Agriculture and Rural Development, Gilberto Buta Lutukuta (MPLA)
Assistance and Social Reintegration, João Baptista Kussumua (MPLA)
Commerce, Vitorino Domingos Hossi (UNITA)
Culture, Boaventura Cardoso (MPLA)
Defence, Kundi Paihama (MPLA)
Education, António Burity da Silva Neto (MPLA)
Energy and Water, José Maria Botelho de Vasconcelos (MPLA)
Ex-Servicemen and War Veterans, Pedro José Van- Dúnem (MPLA)
Family and Women's Advancement, Cândida Celeste da Silva (MPLA)
Finance, José Pedro de Morais (MPLA)
Fisheries, Salomão Luheto Xirimbimbi (MPLA)
Foreign Affairs, João Bernardo de Miranda (MPLA)
Geology and Mines, Manuel António Africano (UNITA)

Health, Albertina Júlia Hamukuya (UNITA)
Hotel Industry and Tourism, Jorge Alicerces Valentim (UNITA)
Industry, Joaquim Duarte da Costa David (MPLA)
Information, Pedro Hendrik vaal Neto (MPLA)
Interior, Osvaldo de Jesus Serra Van-Dúnem (MPLA)
Justice, Paulo Tjipilica (FDA)
Oil, Desidério da Graça Veríssimo da Costa (MPLA)
Planning, Ana Dias Lourenço (MPLA)
Posts and Telecommunications, Licínio Tavares Ribeiro (MPLA)
Public Administration, Employment and Social Welfare, António Pitra da Costra Neto (MPLA)
Public Works, Francisco Higino Carneiro (MPLA)
Science and Technology, João Baptista Ngandagina (MPLA)
Territorial Administration, Fernando Faustino Muteka (MPLA)
Transport, André Luís Brandão (MPLA)
Urban Affairs and the Environment, Virgílio Ferreira Fontes Pereira (MPLA)
Youth and Sports, José Marcos Barrica (MPLA)

FDA Angolan Democratic Forum; MPLA Popular Movement for the Liberation of Angola; UNITA National Union for the Total Independence of Angola

EMBASSY OF THE REPUBLIC OF ANGOLA
22 Dorset Street, London W1U 3QY
Tel: 020-7299 9850
Ambassador Extraordinary and Plenipotentiary, HE António DaCosta Fernandes, apptd 1993

BRITISH EMBASSY
Rua Diogo Cao 4 (Caixa Postal 1244), Luanda
Tel: (00 244) (2) 334582
Ambassador Extraordinary and Plenipotentiary, HE John Thompson, MBE, apptd 2002

DEFENCE
The Army has 400 main battle tanks and 170 armoured personnel carriers. The Navy has seven patrol vessels. The Air Force has 104 combat aircraft and 40 armed helicopters.
MILITARY EXPENDITURE – 17.0 per cent of GDP (2001)
MILITARY PERSONNEL – 100,000: Army 90,000, Navy 4,000, Air Force 6,000; Paramilitaries 10,000

ECONOMY
Angola has valuable oil and diamond deposits and exports of these two commodities account for over 90 per cent of total exports. Principal agricultural crops are cassava, maize, bananas, coffee, palm oil and kernels, cotton and sisal. Coffee, sisal, maize and palm oil are exported; exports also include mahogany and other hardwoods from the tropical rain forests in the north of the country.
The government is attempting to restructure the socialist economy by free market reforms but is making little progress, with high inflation and a collapsing economy.
The government raised fuel prices by 1,600 per cent in February 2000 in response to IMF demands to remove state subsidies on petroleum products.
GNP – US$3,847 million (2000); US$290 per capita (2000)
GDP – US$9,471 million (2001); US$590 per capita (2000)

ANNUAL AVERAGE GROWTH OF GDP – 1.0 per cent
(1998)
INFLATION RATE – 325.0 per cent (2000)
TOTAL EXTERNAL DEBT – US$10,146 million (2000)

Trade with UK	2001	2002
Imports from UK	£92,898,000	£66,917,000
Exports to UK	72,195,000	26,461,000

ANTIGUA AND BARBUDA

State of Antigua and Barbuda

AREA – 170 sq. miles (443 sq. km); Antigua 108 sq.
miles (279 sq. km); Barbuda 62 sq.miles (160 sq. km);
Redonda 0.5 sq. mile (1.2 sq. km)
POPULATION – 67,000 (2001); the official language is
English
CAPITAL – ΨSt John's (population, 24,226, 2000)
MAJOR TOWNS – The town of Barbuda is Codrington
CURRENCY – East Caribbean dollar (EC$) of 100 cents
NATIONAL ANTHEM – Fair Antigua and Barbuda
NATIONAL DAY – 1 November (Independence Day)
NATIONAL FLAG – Red with an inverted triangle divided
black over blue over white, with a rising gold sun on
the white band
LIFE EXPECTANCY (years) – 71 (2001)
POPULATION GROWTH RATE – 0.3 per cent
POPULATION DENSITY – 147 per sq. km (2001)
URBAN POPULATION – 37 per cent (2001)
MILITARY EXPENDITURE – 0.7 per cent of GDP (2001)
MILITARY PERSONNEL – 170: Army 125, Navy 45

Antigua is part of the Leeward Islands in the eastern
Caribbean. It is distinguished from the rest of the
Leeward group by its absence of high hills and forest,
and a drier climate than most of the West Indies. Barbuda
is very flat with a large lagoon.

HISTORY AND POLITICS
Antigua was first settled by the English in 1632, and was
granted to Lord Willoughby by Charles II. It became
internally self-governing in 1967 and fully independent
on 1 November 1981.
   The Antigua Labour party won the general election of
9 March 1999 and a sixth successive term of office with
12 seats in the House of Representatives compared to
four seats for the United Progressive Party.

POLITICAL SYSTEM
Antigua and Barbuda is a constitutional monarchy with
Queen Elizabeth II as Head of State, represented by the
Governor-General. There is a Senate of 17 appointed
members and a House of Representatives of 17 members
elected every five years. The Attorney-General may be
appointed.
Governor-General, HE Sir James Carlisle, GCMG

CABINET *as at July 2003*
*Prime Minister, Finance, Foreign Affairs, Justice and Legal
   Affairs and National Security*, Lester Bird
*Deputy Prime Minister, Finance, Public Utilities, Housing
   and Aviation*, Robin Yearwood
Agriculture, Land and Fisheries, Vere Bird Jr
Attorney-General, Gertel Thom
Education, Culture and Technology, Rodney Williams
Health, Social Improvement and Community Development,

John St Luce
*Home Affairs, Youth Empowerment, Information and
   Broadcasting*, Longford Jeremy
Labour and Co-operatives, Public Safety, Steadroy
   Benjamin
*Planning, Implementation and Public Service Affairs, Trade
   and Transport*, Gaston Browne
Sport and Carnival, Guy Yearwood
Tourism, Economic Development and Environment, Molwyn
   Joseph

HIGH COMMISSION FOR ANTIGUA AND BARBUDA
15 Thayer Street, London W1U 3JT
Tel: 020-7486 7073
High Commissioner, HE Sir Ronald M. Sanders, KCMG,
   KCN, CMG, apptd 1995

BRITISH HIGH COMMISSION
PO Box 483, 11 Old Parham Road, St John's
Tel: (00 1 268) 462 0008/9
High Commissioner, HE John White, apptd 2001, resident
   at Bridgetown, Barbados

ECONOMY
The economy is largely based on tourism and related
services, and offshore financial services. Agricultural
production includes livestock, sea island cotton, mixed
market gardening and fishing.
   In 2000 Antigua and Barbuda had a trade deficit of
US$299 million and a current account deficit of US$79
million. In 1999, imports totalled US$414 million and
exports US$38 million.
GNP – US$642 million (2000); US$9,440 per capita
   (2000)
GDP – US$666 million (2001); US$10,204 per capita
   (2000)
ANNUAL AVERAGE GROWTH OF GDP – 3.7 per cent
(1999)
INFLATION RATE – 1.6 per cent (1999)

Trade with UK	2001	2002
Imports from UK	£17,282,000	£17,144,000
Exports to UK	3,362,000	1,853,000

ARGENTINA

República Argentina – Argentine Republic

AREA – 1,052,577 sq. miles (2,736,700 sq. km).
   Neighbours: Bolivia (north), Paraguay, Brazil and
   Uruguay (north-east), Chile (west) from which it is
   separated by the Cordillera de los Andes
POPULATION – 36,223,947 (2001 census) The
   language is Spanish
CAPITAL – ΨBuenos Aires (population, 11,453,725,
   2001; metropolitan area 2,768,772)
MAJOR CITIES – Córdoba (1,368,109); ΨLa Plata
   (681,832); ΨMar del Plata (541,857); Mendoza
   (846,904); ΨRosario (1,159,004); San Miguel de
   Tucumán (736,018)
CURRENCY – Peso of 10,000 australes
NATIONAL ANTHEM – Oid Mortales! (Hear, Oh
   Mortals!)
NATIONAL DAY – 25 May
NATIONAL FLAG – Horizontal bands of blue, white, blue;
   gold sun in centre of white band
LIFE EXPECTANCY (years) – 74 (2001)

POPULATION GROWTH RATE – 1.3 per cent
POPULATION DENSITY – 14 per sq. km (2001)
URBAN POPULATION – 88 per cent (2001)

HISTORY AND POLITICS

The estuary of La Plata was discovered in 1515 by Juan Díaz de Solís and the region was subsequently colonised by the Spanish. Spain ruled the territory from the 16th century until 1810. In 1816, after a long campaign of liberation conducted by General José de San Martín, independence was declared by the Congress of Tucumán. The country's constitution was adopted in 1853 followed by a period of national organisation.

President Juan Domingo Perón was overthrown in 1955 and there followed 18 years of instability until 1973 when he was recalled from exile. Perón died within a year and was succeeded by his widow, Vice-President María Estela Martínez de Perón. A coup led to the establishment of a military junta in 1976. Following the Falkland Islands/Malvinas defeat in 1982, the President, Gen. Galtieri, resigned and the Army appointed Gen. Bignone. A civilian president was elected in 1983. In the October 2001 general election the Justicialist Party (PJ) became the largest party in the Chamber of Deputies.

Vice-President Carlos Alvárez resigned in October 2000 in protest at the president's decision not to dismiss two senior officials involved in a bribery allegation. President Fernando de la Rúa resigned on 20 December 2001 in the face of serious unrest caused by the collapsing economy. Following a series of interim presidents, Eduardo Alberto Duhalde was appointed president by Congress on 1 January 2002, to serve for the rest of de la Rúa's term. He resigned before the first round of the presidential elections held on 27 April 2003 in which former president Carlos Menem gained 24.4 per cent of the vote and Néstor Kirchner 22 per cent. Menem withdrew from the second round and Néstor Kirchner became president-elect by default and was sworn in as president on 25 May.

POLITICAL SYSTEM

The 1853 constitution was amended in 1994. Power is vested in the president who appoints the Cabinet and is directly elected for a once-renewable four-year term. A presidential candidate must win at least 45 per cent of the vote, or 40 per cent with a 10 per cent lead over the nearest challenger, to gain victory in the first round of voting; if no candidate meets these criteria, a second round must be held. The legislature consists of a 72-member (three for each province) Senate and a 257-member Chamber of Deputies. Half of the Chamber of Deputies is elected every two years. Deputies serve for a four-year term. Senators have served for a nine-year term, with a third being elected every three years, but the terms of all sitting senators ended in December 2001. In October 2001 the Senate was directly elected by the provinces for a six-year term, with one-third renewable every two years.

FEDERAL STRUCTURE

The republic is divided into 23 provinces, each with an elected Governor and legislature, and one federal district (Buenos Aires), with an elected mayor and autonomous government.

Province	Area (sq. km)	Population (census 2001)	Capital
Buenos Aires	307,571	13,818,677	La Plata
Catamarca	102,602	333,661	San Fernando del Valle de Catamarca
Chaco	99,633	983,087	Resistencia
Chubut	224,686	413,240	Rawson
Córdoba	165,321	3,061,611	Córdoba
Corrientes	88,199	929,236	Corrientes
Entre Rios	78,781	1,156,799	Paraná
Federal Capital	200	2,768,772	Buenos Aires
Formosa	72,066	485,700	Formosa
Jujuy	53,219	611,484	San Salvador de Jujuy
La Pampa	143,440	298,460	Santa Rosa
La Rioja	89,680	289,820	La Rioja
Mendoza	148,827	1,576,585	Mendoza
Misiones	29,801	963,869	Posadas
Nequén	94,078	473,315	Nequén
Rio Negro	203,013	552,677	Viedma
Salta	155,488	1,079,422	Salta
San Juan	89,651	622,094	San Juan
San Luis	76,748	366,900	San Luis
Santa Cruz	243,943	197,191	Río Gallegos
Santa Fé	133,007	2,997,376	Santa Fé
Santiago del Estero	136,351	806,347	Santiago del Estero
Tierra del Fuego	21,571	100,960	Ushuaia
Tucumán	22,524	1,336,664	San Miguel de Tucumán

HEAD OF STATE

President, Néstor Kirchner, *sworn in* 25 May 2003
Vice-President, Daniel Scioli

CABINET *as at July 2003*
Cabinet Chief, Alberto Fernández
Defence, José Pampuro
Economy, Roberto Lavagna
Education, Daniel Filmus
Federal Planning, Public Investment and Services, Julio De Vido
Foreign Relations, International Trade and Worship, Rafael Bielsa
Health, Ginés González Garcia
Interior, Aníbal Fernández
Justice, Security and Human Rights, Gustavo Béliz
Labour, Employment and Social Security, Carlos Tomada
Secretaries of State, Torcuato Di Tella *(Culture);* Carlos Alberto Zannini *(Legal Affairs);* Sergio Acevedo *(State Intelligence);* Germán Luis Pérez *(Tourism and Sport)*
Secretary-General of the Presidency, Oscar Parrilli
Social Development, Alicia Kirchner

EMBASSY OF THE ARGENTINE REPUBLIC
65 Brook Street, London W1K 4AH
Tel: 020-7318 1300
Ambassador Extraordinary and Plenipotentiary, HE Vicente Berasategui, apptd 2000

BRITISH EMBASSY
Dr Luis Agote 2412/52, 1425 Buenos Aires
Tel: (00 54) (11) 4808 2200
Ambassador Extraordinary and Plenipotentiary, HE Sir Robin Christopher, KBE, CMG, apptd 2000
First Secretary (Commercial), Dave Prodger

Cultural Attaché and British Council Director, Paul Dick
Marcelo T. de Alvear 590, C1058AAF Buenos Aires
Tel: (00 54) (11) 4311/9814/7519
Email: info@britishcouncil.org.ar

DEFENCE

The Army has 200 main battle tanks, 105 armoured infantry fighting vehicles, 450 armoured personnel carriers and 59 helicopters. The Navy has three submarines, five destroyers, eight frigates, 14 patrol and coastal vessels, 25 combat aircraft and 23 armed helicopters. The Air Force has 130 combat aircraft and 29 armed helicopters.

MILITARY EXPENDITURE – 1.7 per cent of GDP (2001)
MILITARY PERSONNEL – 69,900: Army 41,400, Navy 16,000, Air Force 12,500; Paramilitaries 31,240

ECONOMY

The principal crops are wheat, maize, oats, barley, rye, linseed, sunflower seed, alfalfa, sugar, fruit and cotton. Argentina is pre-eminent in the production of beef, mutton and wool. There is an oil refinery in San Lorenzo (Santa Fé province). Natural gas is also produced. Coal, lead, zinc, tungsten, iron ore, sulphur, mica and salt are the other chief minerals being exploited. There are small worked deposits of beryllium, manganese, bismuth, uranium, antimony, copper, kaolin, arsenate, gold, silver and tin. Coal is produced at the Río Turbio mine in the province of Santa Cruz.

Meat-packing is one of the principal industries; flour-milling, sugar-refining, and the wine industry are also important. In recent years progress has been made by the textile, plastic and machine tool industries and engineering, especially in the production of motor vehicles and steel manufactures.

Since late 1998 Argentina has been in a recession. In April 2001, measures to reassure international investors that the country would not default on its debt repayments were introduced. In November 2001, the President announced several economy-boosting measures but in December 2001 defaulted on part of its large public debt. A wave of protests took place across the country in the wake of continued economic instability. In January 2003, the IMF made available an eight-month standby credit of approximately US$1.58 billion to cover Argentina's payment obligations to the IMF. It was also agreed that US$2 billion in repayments to the IMF would be postponed by 1 year, enabling Argentina to clear its arrears with the World Bank and the Inter-American Development Bank.

GNP – US$276,228 million (2000); US$7,460 per capita (2000)
GDP – US$268,773 million (2001); US$7,678 per capita (2000)
ANNUAL AVERAGE GROWTH OF GDP – 3.9 per cent (1998)
INFLATION RATE – 0.9 per cent (2000)
UNEMPLOYMENT – 15.0 per cent (2000)
TOTAL EXTERNAL DEBT – US$146,172 million (2000)

TRADE

The chief imports are machinery, industrial and transport equipment, chemicals, metals and plastics. The chief exports are vegetable products, processed foods, minerals, live animals and oils. Argentina's main trading partners are Brazil and the USA.

In 2000 Argentina had a trade surplus of US$2,558 million and a current account deficit of US$8,970 million. In 2001 imports totalled US$20,311 million and exports US$26,655 million.

Trade with UK	2001	2002
Imports from UK	£266,382,000	£127,923,000
Exports to UK	214,033,000	246,502,000

COMMUNICATIONS

The 33,744 miles of railway are state-owned. The combined national and provincial road network totals approximately 215,434 km of which 63,553 miles are surfaced. Investments of US$20 billion for new roads and an upgrade of existing infrastructure for road, rail and air transport are planned for 2000–5. There are two large ports at Ensenada (La Plata) and Buenos Aires.

CULTURE AND EDUCATION

The literature of Spain is part of Argentine culture. There is little indigenous literature before the break from Spain, but all branches have flourished since the latter half of the 19th century. About 450 daily newspapers are published in Argentina, including seven major ones in the city of Buenos Aires.

Education is compulsory and free from the age of six to 15. The total number of universities is over 50 with 24 national, 25 private and a small number of provincial universities.

ILLITERACY RATE – (m) 3.1 per cent; (f) 3.2 per cent (2000)
ENROLMENT (percentage of age group) – primary 100 per cent (1997); secondary 73 per cent (1997); tertiary 36 per cent (1997)

ARMENIA

Hayastani Hanrapetut'yun – Republic of Armenia

AREA – 11,506 sq. miles (29,800 sq. km). Neighbours: Azerbaijan (east and south-west), Georgia (north), Iran (south), Turkey (west)
POPULATION – 3,800,000 (2002 estimate). Armenians 93.8 per cent, Kurds 1.7 per cent and Russians 1.6 per cent. Azeris formed 2.6 per cent of the population, but most fled or were expelled after the outbreak of war with Azerbaijan. There are also Ukrainians, Greeks and Assyrians. The Armenian diaspora numbers some 5,300,000. Armenian is the official language, though Russian is widely spoken and understood. The main religion is Armenian Orthodox Christian (Armenian Church centred in Etchmiadzin). Armenia adopted Christianity as its official religion in AD 301, the first state in the world to do so
CAPITAL – Yerevan (population, 1,254,400, 1996 estimate)
CURRENCY – Dram of 100 louma
NATIONAL ANTHEM – Mer Hayrenik Azat, Ankakh (Land Of Our Fathers)
NATIONAL DAY – 21 September (Independence Day)
NATIONAL FLAG – Three horizontal stripes of red, blue and orange
POPULATION GROWTH RATE – 0.2 per cent
POPULATION DENSITY – 127 per sq. km (1999)

Armenia lies between the Black and Caspian Seas, occupying the south-western part of the Caucasus region of the former Soviet Union. It is very mountainous, consisting of several vast tablelands surrounded by ridges.

The climate is continental, dry and cold, but the Ararat valley has a long, hot and dry summer.

HISTORY AND POLITICS

Armenia was first unified in 95 BC but was divided between the Persian and Byzantine empires in AD 387 and then conquered in the 11th century by the Seljuk Turks and the Mongols. In the 16th century most of Armenia was incorporated into the Ottoman Empire. In 1639 the country was divided again, the easternmost portions, now the republic of Armenia, becoming part of the Persian Empire. In 1828 eastern Armenia became part of the Russian Empire while western Armenia remained under Ottoman rule. The Ottomans launched pogroms against the Armenians from 1894 onwards, and in 1915 to 1918 massacred 1,500,000 Armenians.

Armenia declared its independence on 28 May 1918, but was crushed and divided between Turkish and Soviet forces in 1920, with the area under Soviet control proclaimed a Soviet Socialist Republic on 29 November 1920. The Soviet government was overthrown by a nationalist revolt in 1921 but reinstated by the Red Army a few months later. In early 1922 Armenia acceded to the USSR.

An Armenian nationalist movement swept to power in national elections in mid-1990. In a referendum in 1991, 99 per cent of the electorate voted for independence, which was declared on 21 September 1991. Prime Minister Vazgen Sarkissian and six other politicians were shot dead in the National Assembly during an attempted coup on 27 October 1999.

Elections took place on 19 February 2003. Robert Kocharian was re-elected president following the second round of voting held on 5 March in which he gained 67.5 per cent of the vote.

In the general election held on 25 May 2003 the Republican Party of Armenia (HHK) was the dominant political party winning 31 of the 131 seats in the National Assembly. Other parties gained 60 seats and non-partisans 36 seats.

FOREIGN RELATIONS

The dispute between the (ethnic Armenian) Nagorno-Karabakh forces supported by Armenia and the Azeri government over Nagorny-Karabakh erupted into all-out war in May 1992, when Nagorno-Karabakh forces breached Azerbaijan's defences to form a land bridge to Armenia. By the end of summer 1992 all of Nagorny-Karabakh was under Armenian control, and by the end of 1993 all Azeri territory that separated Nagorny-Karabakh from Armenia and all mountainous Azeri territory around Nagorno-Karabakh was under the control of Nagorno-Karabakh Armenians. Armenia claims this territory as historically Armenian land arbitrarily given to Azerbaijan by Stalin in 1921–2. A cease-fire agreement between Armenia, Azerbaijan and Nagorno-Karabakh was reached in May 1994, and talks mediated by the OSCE continue to seek a peaceful resolution to the dispute.

In August 1997 Armenia and Russia renewed a Treaty of Friendship, Co-operation and Mutual Assistance in effect since 1991.

POLITICAL SYSTEM

There is a 131-member unicameral National Assembly (*Azgayin Joghov*), directly elected every four years. A new constitution was approved by a referendum in July 1995. Constitutional amendments proposed by President Kocharian were rejected in a referendum held on 25 May 2003.

HEAD OF STATE

President, Robert Kocharian, *elected* 30 March 1998, *sworn* in 9 April 1998, *re-elected* 5 March 2003

CABINET *as at July 2003*
Prime Minister, Andranik Markarian
Agriculture, David Lokian
Culture and Youth Affairs, Tamara Poghosian
Defence, Serge Sarkissian
Ecology, Vardan Ayvazian
Education and Science, Sergo Yeritsian
Energy, Armen Movsisian
Finance and Economy, Vardan Khachaturian
Foreign Affairs, Vardan Oskanian
Health, Norair Davidian
Justice, David Harutyunian
National Security, Karlos Petrosian
Social Security, Aghvan Vardanian
State Income, Yervand Zakarian
State Property, David Vardanian
Territorial Administration and Production Infrastructures,
  Hovik Abrahamian
Trade and Economic Development, Karen Chshmaritian
Transport and Communications, Andranik Manukian
Urban Development, Ara Aramian

EMBASSY OF THE REPUBLIC OF ARMENIA
25a Cheniston Gardens, London W8 6TG
Tel: 020-7938 5435
Ambassador Extraordinary and Plenipotentiary, HE Dr
  Vahe Gabrielyan, apptd 2003

BRITISH EMBASSY
34 Baghramian Avenue, Yerevan
Tel: (00 374) (1) 264 301
Ambassador Extraordinary and Plenipotentiary, HE Thorda
  Abbott-Watt

BRITISH COUNCIL DIRECTOR, Roger Budd, c/o The
British Embassy; Tel: (00 374) (55) 99 23/24
Email: info@britishcouncil.am

DEFENCE

The Army has 110 main battle tanks, 110 armoured infantry fighting vehicles and 36 armoured personnel carriers. The Air Force has eight combat aircraft and 13 armed helicopters.

Russia maintains 2,900 army personnel in Armenia. An agreement on military co-operation with Russia was signed in 1996 which paved the way for joint military exercises. A protocol was also signed on the establishment of coalition troops in Transcaucasia and the planned use of Russian and Armenian armed forces as part of coalition troops in cases of mutual interest. On 19 December 2001, Russian President Vladimir Putin signed a federal law "On Ratifying the Agreement between the Russian Federation and the Republic of Armenia on the Joint Planning of the Use of Troops (Forces) in the Interests of Joint Security Provision". This stipulates measures to prevent the use by third countries of the territory of Armenia for purposes that may inflict damage on Russian national interests.

MILITARY EXPENDITURE – 6.5 per cent of GDP (2001)
MILITARY PERSONNEL – 44,610: Army 38,900,
  Air Force 3,160; Paramilitaries 1,000

CONSCRIPTION DURATION – Two years

ECONOMY

The Armenian economy has been badly affected by the Azeri and Turkish economic embargoes which have been in place since 1988.

Armenia has a strong agricultural sector in low-lying areas, where industrial and fruit crops are grown. Grain is grown in the hills and the country is also noted for its wine and brandy. There are large copper ore and molybdenum deposits and other minerals. The country also has developed chemicals, industrial vehicles and textiles industries.

The government introduced a programme of economic reforms in November 1994 with IMF support, including the liberalisation of prices, stabilisation of the currency and privatisation.

In 1999 Armenia had a trade deficit of US$474 million and a current account deficit of US$307 million. In 2001 imports totalled US$874 million and exports US$343 million.

On 10 December 2002, the general council of the World Trade Organisation (WTO) voted to approve Armenia's application for membership.

In February 2003, Russia assumed the management of Armenia's only nuclear power station and main electricity producer in exchange for US$40 million in fuel debts which Armenia owed Russia.

GNP – US$1,991 million (2000); US$520 per capita (2000)

GDP – US$2,012 million (2001); US$506 per capita (2000)

ANNUAL AVERAGE GROWTH OF GDP – 3.3 per cent (1999)

INFLATION RATE – 0.8 per cent (2000)

UNEMPLOYMENT – 9.3 per cent (1998)

TOTAL EXTERNAL DEBT – US$898 million (2000)

Trade with UK	2001	2002
Imports from UK	£7,678,000	£5,155,000
Exports to UK	567,000	332,000

CULTURE AND EDUCATION

The Armenian alphabet was established in AD 405. Major cultural figures include the poets Narekatsi (10th century), Frick (13th century), Nahapet Kuchak (16th century) and Sayat-Nova (18th century), the composer Aram Khachaturian (1903-78), and the film director Sergei Parajanov.

ENROLMENT (percentage of age group) – tertiary 12.0 per cent (1996)

AUSTRALIA

The Commonwealth of Australia

AREA – 2,954,731 sq. miles (7,682,300 sq. km)

POPULATION – 19,338,000 (2001): 410,000 of Aboriginal and Torres Strait Islander origin (2001 estimate). The language is English

CAPITAL – Canberra, in the Australian Capital Territory (population, 313,900, 2001 estimate). It has been the seat of government since 1927

MAJOR CITIES – ΨAdelaide (1,100,100); ΨBrisbane (1,656,700); ΨHobart (194,400); ΨMelbourne (3,522,000); ΨPerth, including Fremantle (1,400,500); ΨSydney (4,140,800), 2001 estimates

CURRENCY – Australian dollar ($A) of 100 cents

NATIONAL ANTHEM – Advance Australia Fair

NATIONAL DAY – 26 January (Australia Day)

NATIONAL FLAG – The British Blue Ensign with five stars of the Southern Cross in the fly and the white Commonwealth Star of seven points beneath the Union Flag

LIFE EXPECTANCY (years) – 79 (2001)

POPULATION GROWTH RATE – 1.2 per cent

POPULATION DENSITY – 3 per sq. km (2001)

URBAN POPULATION – 91 per cent (2001)

HISTORY AND POLITICS

Australia was discovered by Europeans in the 17th century. Its eastern coast was claimed by Capt. James Cook on behalf of Britain in 1770 and became a penal colony; Tasmania, Western Australia, South Australia, Victoria and Queensland were established as colonies between 1825 and 1859. The colonies were federated as the Commonwealth of Australia on 1 January 1901, at which time Australia gained dominion status within the British Empire. Australia became independent within the British Commonwealth by the 1931 Statute of Westminster. Following a referendum in 1967, the Aboriginal population was granted full political rights. In 1986, the Australia Act was passed, which abolished the remaining legislative, executive and judicial links to the UK, while retaining the British monarch as head of state.

On 13 February 1998, the Constitutional Convention voted by 89 votes to 52 to sever constitutional links with the United Kingdom monarchy. A national referendum was held on the issue on 6 November 1999; the proposition to make Australia a republic was defeated, with 45.3 per cent voting in favour and 54.7 per cent against.

The general election on 10 November 2001 was won by the ruling Liberal Party-National Party Coalition.

POLITICAL SYSTEM

The government is that of a federal commonwealth within the Commonwealth, the executive power being vested in the Sovereign (through the Governor-General), assisted by a federal government. Under the constitution the powers of the federal government are defined, and residuary legislative power remains with the states. The right of a state to legislate on any matter is not abrogated except in connection with matters exclusively under federal control, but where a state law is inconsistent with a law of the Commonwealth the latter prevails to the extent of the inconsistency.

Parliament consists of Queen Elizabeth II, the Senate and the House of Representatives. The constitution provides that the number of members of the House of Representatives shall be, as nearly as practicable, twice the number of senators. Members of the Senate are elected for six years by universal suffrage, half the members retiring every third year, except in the Australian Capital Territory and the Northern Territory, where members are elected for a three-year term. Each of the six states returns 12 senators, and the Australian Capital Territory and the Northern Territory two each. The House of Representatives, similarly elected for a maximum of three years, contains members proportionate to the population, with a minimum of five members for each state. There are now 150 members in the House of Representatives, including one member for the Northern Territory and two for the Australian Capital Territory.

The High Court exercises jurisdiction over all matters

arising under the constitution, all matters arising between the states and between residents of different states, matters to which the Commonwealth of Australia is a party, matters arising under any treaty, and matters affecting foreign representatives in Australia. The High Court also hears appeals from the Federal Court and from the Supreme Courts of states and territories.

The Federal Court of Australia has jurisdiction over important industrial and trade practices, intellectual property, administrative law, admiralty law and bankruptcy matters. It also acts as a court of appeal for decisions from the Australian Capital Territory Supreme Court and certain decisions of state Supreme Courts exercising federal jurisdiction. Each state has its own judicature of supreme, superior and minor courts for criminal and civil cases.

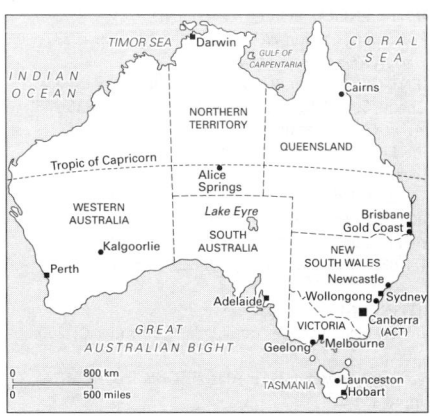

FEDERAL STRUCTURE
In the states, executive authority is vested in a Governor (appointed by the Crown), assisted by a Council of Ministers or Executive Council. Each state has a legislature comprising a Legislative Council and a Legislative Assembly or House of Assembly which are elected for four-year terms, except Queensland, which has a Legislative Assembly only.

The Northern Territory and Australian Capital Territory have a Legislative Assembly only.

GOVERNOR-GENERAL
Governor-General, Maj.-Gen. Michael Jeffery AC, CVO, MC, assumed office 11 August 2003

CABINET *as at May 2003*
Prime Minister, John Howard (LP)
Deputy Prime Minister, Transport and Regional Services, John Anderson (NP)
Agriculture, Fisheries and Forestry, Warren Truss (NP)
Attorney-General, Daryl Williams (LP)
Communications, Information Technology and the Arts, Sen. Richard Alston (LP)
Defence, Robert Hill (LP)
Education, Science and Training, Brendan Nelson (LP)
Employment, Workplace Relations and Small Business, Leader of the House, Tony Abbott (LP)
Environment and Heritage, Leader of the Government in the Senate, David Kemp (LP)
Family and Community Services, Assisting the Prime Minister for the Status of Women, Amanda Vanstone (LP)
Finance and Administration, Nick Minchin (LP)
Foreign Affairs, Alexander Downer (LP)
Health and Aged Care, Kay Patterson (LP)
Immigration and Multicultural Affairs, Aboriginal and Torres Strait Islander Affairs, Philip Ruddock (LP)
Industry, Tourism and Resources, Ian MacFarlane (LP)
Trade, Mark Vaile (NP)
Treasurer, Peter Costello (LP)

LP Liberal Party; NP National Party

AUSTRALIAN HIGH COMMISSION
Australia House, Strand, London WC2B 4LA
Tel: 020-7379 4334
High Commissioner, HE Michael L'Estrange, apptd 2000

NEW SOUTH WALES GOVERNMENT OFFICE,
The Australia Centre, Strand, London WC2B 4LG.
Tel: 020-7887 5871. *Director,* Leanne Grogan

STATES AND TERRITORIES

	Area (sq. km)	Resident population 31 December 2001	Capital	Governor 2003	Premier
Australian Capital Territory (ACT)	2,349	322,600	Canberra	—	Jon Stanhope (Lab)‡
New South Wales (NSW)	801,352	6,642,900	Sydney	HE Prof. Marie Bashir, AO	Robert Carr (Lab)‡
Northern Territory (NT)	1,352,212	199,900	Darwin*	John Anictomatis, OAM†	Clare Martin (Lab)
Queensland (Qld)	1,734,190	3,670,500	Brisbane	HE Maj.-Gen. Peter Arnison, AO	Peter Beattie (Lab)
South Australia (SA)	985,324	1,518,900	Adelaide	Marjorie Jackson-Nelson, AC, MBE	Mike Rann (Lab)
Tasmania (Tas.)	67,914	473,300	Hobart	HE Sir Guy Green, AC, KBE, CVO	Jim Bacon (Lab)
Victoria (Vic.)	227,590	4,854,100	Melbourne	HE John Landy, AC, MBE	Steve Bracks (Lab)
Western Australia (WA)	2,532,422	1,918,800	Perth	HE Lt.-Gen. John M. Sanderson, AC	Dr Geoff Gallop, MLA (Lab)

* Seat of administration
† Administrator
‡ Chief Minister

AGENT-GENERAL FOR QUEENSLAND,
392 Strand, London WC2R 0LZ. Tel: 020-7836 1333.
Agent-General, John Dawson
AGENT-GENERAL FOR SOUTH AUSTRALIA, Australia
Centre, Strand, London WC2B 4LG. Tel: 020-7836 3455.
Agent-General, Maurice de Rohan
AGENT-GENERAL FOR VICTORIA, Victoria House,
Melbourne Place, Strand, London WC2B 4LG.
Tel: 020-7836 2656. *Agent-General,* Peter A. Hansen
AGENT-GENERAL FOR WESTERN AUSTRALIA, Australia
Centre, Melbourne Place, Strand, London WC2B 4LG.
Tel: 020-7240 2881. *Agent-General,* Robert Fisher

BRITISH HIGH COMMISSION
Commonwealth Avenue, Yarralumla, Canberra, ACT 2600
Tel: (00 61) (2) 6270 6666
High Commissioner, HE Sir Alastair Goodlad, KCMG,
apptd 1999
Consuls-General, D. H. Cairns (Brisbane); A. D. Sprake
(Melbourne); H. Dunnachie (Perth); P. Beckingham
(Sydney)

BRITISH COUNCIL DIRECTOR, Simon Gammell
Suite 401, Edgecliff Centre, 203–233 New South Head Road,
Edgecliff, Sydney, NSW 2027
Tel: (00 61) (2) 9326 2022
Email: enquiries@britishcouncil.org.au

DEFENCE

The Army has 71 main battle tanks, 364 armoured
personnel carriers, 111 light assault vehicles, six aircraft
and 104 armed helicopters. The Navy has six submarines,
nine frigates, 15 patrol and coastal vessels and 16 armed
helicopters. There are bases at Sydney, Stirling, Cairns,
Darwin, Flinders, Jervis Bay and Noura. The Air Force
has 156 combat aircraft.
MILITARY EXPENDITURE – 1.9 per cent of GDP (2001)
MILITARY PERSONNEL – 50,920: Army 25,150, Navy
12,570, Air Force 13,200

ECONOMY

The wide range of climatic and soil conditions has
resulted in a diversity of crops. Generally, cereal crops
(excluding rice and sorghum) are widely grown, while
other crops are confined to specific locations in a few
states. However, scant or erratic rainfall, limited potential
for irrigation and unsuitable soils or topography have
restricted intensive agriculture.

Livestock ranching is widespread, primarily cattle and
sheep; meat, meat derivatives, wool and dairy products
are significant agricultural products.

Significant mineral resources include bauxite, coal,
copper, crude petroleum, gems, gold, ilmenite, iron ore,
lead, limestone, manganese, nickel, rutile, salt, silver, tin,
tungsten, uranium, zinc and zircon. In 1999–2000
319,837,000 tonnes of coal, 29,765,000 tonnes of
crude oil, 24,447,000 cubic metres of natural gas,
165,966,000 tonnes of iron ore, 964,000 tonnes of lead,
and 286,359 kilograms of gold were produced.
GNP – US$388,252 million (2000); US$20,240 per
capita (2000)
GDP – US$368,571 million (2001); US$20,298 per
capita (2000)
ANNUAL AVERAGE GROWTH OF GDP – 4.2 per cent
(2000)
INFLATION RATE – 2.9 per cent (2002)
UNEMPLOYMENT – 6.6 per cent (2000)

TRADE

In 2000–1 the main exports were metalliferous ores and
metal scrap (12.3 per cent); coal, coke and briquettes (9.1
per cent); non-ferrous metals (7.9 per cent); gold (4.3 per
cent); and cereals and cereal preparations (4.5 per cent).
The major imports were manufactured articles (11.9 per
cent); motor vehicles and parts (12.1 per cent); computer
technology (7.0 per cent); petroleum and related products
(8.7 per cent); telecommunications equipment (6.7 per
cent); electrical machinery (5.7 per cent); and general
industrial machinery and parts (4.8 per cent).

Australia's main trading partners are Japan, the USA,
New Zealand, China, Korea, Germany, Taiwan,
Singapore and the UK.

In 2001 Australia had a trade surplus of US$2,023
million and a current account deficit of US$9,194
million. Imports totalled US$63,886 million and exports
US$63,387 million.

Trade with UK	2001	2002
Imports from UK	£2,321,828,000	£2,123,928,000
Exports to UK	1,837,977,000	1,774,387,000

COMMUNICATIONS

There are six government-owned railway systems,
operated by the State Rail Authority of NSW, VicRail,
Queensland Government Railways, Western Australian
Government Railways, the State Transport Authority
of Southern Australia, and the National Rail
Corporation (NRC). The NRC incorporates the former
Commonwealth Railways system, and the Tasmanian and
non-metropolitan South Australian railways (urban rail
services in Southern Australia remain the responsibility of
the State Transport Authority). In 1999 there was a total
of 39,930 km of railway track.

The Northern Territory has three main ports: Darwin,
and the private mining ports of Gove and Groote
Eylandt. Most freight in the Territory is moved by road
trains. These are massive trucks hauling two or three
trailers, having a net capacity of about 100 tonnes and
measuring up to 45 metres in length.

EDUCATION

Education is administered by the state governments and is
compulsory between the ages of six and 15 years (16
years in Tasmania). It is available at government schools
controlled by the state education department and at
private or independent schools, some of which are
denominational. Tertiary education is available through
universities and technical and further education colleges.
There are 41 universities in Australia; the Australian
Capital Territory has three universities, New South Wales
13, Queensland nine, Northern Territory one, South
Australia three, Tasmania one, Victoria nine and Western
Australia five.
ENROLMENT (percentage of age group) – primary 100
per cent (1997); secondary 100 per cent (1997);
tertiary 80 per cent (1997)

EXTERNAL TERRITORIES

ASHMORE AND CARTIER ISLANDS

Ashmore Islands (known as Middle, East and West
Islands) and Cartier Island are situated in the Indian
Ocean 850 km and 790 km west of Darwin respectively.
The islands are uninhabited. The territory has been
administered by the Australian Government since 1933.

THE AUSTRALIAN ANTARCTIC TERRITORY

The Australian Antarctic Territory was established in 1933 and comprises all the islands and territories, other than Adélie Land, which are situated south of latitude 60° S. and lying between 160° E. longitude and 45° E. longitude. The territory is administered by the Antarctic Division of the Department of the Environment and Heritage.

CHRISTMAS ISLAND

AREA – 52 sq. miles (135 sq. km)
POPULATION – 1,928 (2001)

Christmas Island is situated in the Indian Ocean about 1,408 km NW of North West Cape in Western Australia. The island became an Australian territory in 1958 and is managed by the Department of Transport and Regional Services. The Shire of Christmas Island (SOCI) has nine elected members. SOCI is responsible for municipal functions and services on the island.
Administrator, W. Taylor

COCOS (KEELING) ISLANDS

AREA – 5.4 sq. miles (14 sq. km)
POPULATION – 600 (2001)

The Cocos (Keeling) Islands are two separate atolls (North Keeling Island and, 24 km to the south, the main atoll) comprising some 27 small coral islands, situated in the Indian Ocean. The main islands of the southern atoll are West Island (about 9 km in length); Home Island, where the Cocos Malay community lives; Direction Island, Horsburgh and South Island.

The islands were declared a British possession in 1857. All land in the islands was granted to George Clunies-Ross and his heirs by Queen Victoria in 1886. In 1978 the Australian Government purchased all Clunies-Ross land and property interests except for the family home and grounds; the last of the remaining grounds were purchased in 1993. Between 1979 and 1984 most of the land was transferred to trusts with the Cocos (Keeling) Islands Council as trustee, the local government body established in 1979 which was replaced by the Shire of the Cocos (Keeling) Islands in July 1992.

On 6 April 1984 the Cocos community, in a UN-supervised Act of Self-Determination, chose to integrate with Australia. The islands are managed by the Australian Government through the Department of Transport and Regional Services.
Administrator, W. Taylor

CORAL SEA ISLANDS TERRITORY

The Coral Sea Islands Territory lies east of Queensland between the Great Barrier Reef and longitude 156° 06'; E., and between latitudes 12° and 24° S. It comprises scattered islands, spread over a sea area of 780,000 sq. km. The islands are formed mainly of coral and sand, and most are extremely small. There is a manned meteorological station in the Willis Group but the remaining islands are uninhabited.

The territory is managed by the Department of Transport and Regional Services.

HEARD ISLAND AND MCDONALD ISLANDS

The Territory of the Heard and McDonald Islands, about 4,100 km south-west of Perth, comprises all the islands and rocks lying between 52° 30'; and 53° 30'; S. latitude and 72° and 74° 30'; E. longitude. The islands are administered by the Antarctic Division of the Department of the Environment and Heritage.

NORFOLK ISLAND

AREA – 13.3 sq. miles (34.5 sq. km)
POPULATION – 2,037 (2001)
SEAT OF GOVERNMENT – Kingston

Norfolk Island is situated in the South Pacific Ocean. It is about 8 km long by 5 km wide. The climate is mild and subtropical.

The island, discovered by Captain Cook in 1774, served as a penal colony from 1788 to 1814 and 1825 to 1855. In 1856, 194 descendants of the Bounty mutineers accepted an invitation to leave Pitcairn and settle on Norfolk Island. Norfolk Island is an Australian external territory.

In 1979 Norfolk Island gained a substantial degree of self-government. Wide powers are exercised by a nine-member Legislative Assembly. The Administrator is responsible to the Australian Minister for Regional Services, Territories and Local Government.
Administrator, A. J. Messner

AUSTRIA

Republik Österreich – Republic of Austria

AREA – 3,108 sq. miles (82,700 sq. km). Neighbours: the Czech Republic and Slovakia (north), Italy and Slovenia (south), Hungary (east), Germany (north-west), Switzerland and Liechtenstein (west)
POPULATION – 8,032,926 (2001 census). The language is German, but the rights of the Slovene, Croat, Hungarian, Czech, Slovak, Roma and Sinti minorities are protected. The predominant religion is Roman Catholicism
CAPITAL – Vienna, on the Danube (population, 1,550,123, 2001 census)
MAJOR CITIES – Graz (226,244); Innsbruck (113,392); Klagenfurt (90,141); Linz (183,904); Salzburg (142,662)
CURRENCY – Euro (€) of 100 cents
NATIONAL ANTHEM – Land Der Berge, Land Am Strome (Land Of Mountains, Land On The River)
NATIONAL DAY – 26 October
NATIONAL FLAG – Three equal horizontal stripes of red, white, red
LIFE EXPECTANCY (years) – 78 (2001)
POPULATION GROWTH RATE – 0.4 per cent
POPULATION DENSITY – 98 per sq. km (2001)

HISTORY AND POLITICS

The Austrian state dates back to the eighth century AD when Emperor Charlemagne conquered the territory and founded the *Ostmark*, the eastern march of the Holy Roman Empire, which had been settled from the sixth century onwards by Bavarian Germans. The Habsburg dynasty established an empire which united much of central Europe, including present-day Austria and Hungary. The Republic of Austria was established in 1918 on the break-up of the Austro-Hungarian Empire. In March 1938 Austria was incorporated into Nazi Germany under the name *Ostmark*. After the liberation of Vienna in 1945, the Republic of Austria was reconstituted within the 1937 frontiers and a freely-elected government took office in December 1945. The country was divided into four zones occupied respectively by the UK, USA, USSR and France, while Vienna was jointly occupied by the four Powers. In 1955 the Austrian State Treaty was signed by the foreign ministers of the four Powers and of Austria. This treaty recognised the re-establishment of Austria as a sovereign, independent and democratic state, having the same frontiers as on 1 January 1938. Austria acceded to the European Union on 1 January 1995.

After the Social Democrats and the Austrian People's Party (ÖVP) failed to form a coalition following the general election of 3 October 1999, a coalition government comprising the ÖVP and the far-right Austrian Freedom Party (FPÖ) (led by Jörg Haider, who had expressed support for some aspects of the wartime Nazi regime) was sworn in on 5 February 2000 after both parties signed a document expressing their commitment to the European Union and aversion to discrimination and intolerance. International opposition to the inclusion of the FPÖ in the government resulted in the suspension of bilateral relations between the governments of the other EU members and Austria. On 1 May, Jörg Haider resigned as leader of the FPÖ in an attempt to calm the situation. The suspension of relations between the EU members and Austria was lifted in September 2000 following an investigation into the Austrian government which cleared it of any wrongdoing. The ÖVP won the legislative elections of 24 November 2002 with 42.3 per cent of the vote. But the Party did not gain enough votes to form a government of its own. After coalition talks with the Social Democrats and Greens failed, ÖVP leader Walter Schüssel announced on 28 February 2003 that he had reformed his previous coalition with the FPÖ and a new cabinet was appointed.

POLITICAL SYSTEM
There is a bicameral national assembly; the lower house *(Nationalrat)* has 183 members and the upper house *(Bundesrat)* has 64 members. There is a 4 per cent qualification for parliamentary representation.

FEDERAL STRUCTURE
There are nine provinces:

Provinces	Area (sq. km)	Population (2001 census)	Capital
Burgenland	3,965	277,569	Eisenstadt
Carinthia	9,533	559,404	Klagenfurt
Lower Austria	19,174	1,545,804	St Pölten
Salzburg	7,154	515,327	Salzburg
Styria	16,388	1,183,303	Graz
Tirol	12,648	673,504	Innsbruck
Upper Austria	11,980	1,376,797	Linz
Vienna	415	1,550,123	Vienna
Vorarlberg	2,601	351,095	Bregenz

HEAD OF STATE
President of the Republic of Austria, Thomas Klestil, *took office* 8 July 1992, *re-elected* 19 April 1998

CABINET *as at July 2003*
Chancellor, Wolfgang Schüssel (ÖVP)
Vice-Chancellor, Social Affairs, Herbert Haupt (FPÖ)
Agriculture and Forestry; Environment and Water Management, Josef Pröll (ÖVP)
Defence, Günther Platter

Economic Affairs and Labour, Martin Bartenstein (ÖVP)
Education, Science and Cultural Affairs, Elisabeth Gehrer (ÖVP)
Finance, Karl-Heinz Grasser (Ind.)
Foreign Affairs, Benita Ferrero-Waldner (ÖVP)
Health, Women's Rights, Maria Rauch-Kallat (ÖVP)
Infrastructure, Hubert Gorbach (FPÖ)
Interior, Ernst Strasser (ÖVP)
Justice, Dieter Böhmdorfer (Ind.)

ÖVP Austrian People's Party; FPÖ Austrian Freedom Party; Ind. Independent

AUSTRIAN EMBASSY
18 Belgrave Mews West, London SW1X 8HU
Tel: 020-7235 3731
Ambassador Extraordinary and Plenipotentiary, HE Alexander Christiani, apptd 2000

BRITISH EMBASSY
Jaurèsgasse 12, 1030 Vienna
Tel: (00 43) (1) 716130
Ambassador Extraordinary and Plenipotentiary, HE John MacGregor, CVO, apptd 2003

BRITISH CONSULAR OFFICES – There is a consular office at Vienna, and Honorary Consulates at Bregenz, Graz, Innsbruck and Salzburg

BRITISH COUNCIL DIRECTOR, Dr Simon Cole
Schenkenstrasse 4, A–1010 Vienna; Tel: (00 43) (1) 533 2616
Email: bc.vienna@britishcouncil.at

DEFENCE
The Army has 274 main battle tanks and 493 armoured personnel carriers. The Air Force has 52 combat aircraft and 11 armed helicopters.

Women were permitted to join the army for the first time in February 1998.
MILITARY EXPENDITURE – 0.8 per cent of GDP (2001)
MILITARY PERSONNEL – Army 34,600, of which Air Force 6,850
CONSCRIPTION DURATION – Eight months, or seven months plus refresher training

ECONOMY
Major industries include iron and steel production, chemicals, electrical goods, mechanical engineering, textiles and paper production. Agricultural products include wheat, rye, barley, oats, maize, potatoes, sugar beet and turnips. Timber forms a valuable source of Austria's indigenous wealth, about 47 per cent of the total land area consisting of forest areas. Strict regulations have preserved Austria's environment. Foreign exchange receipts from tourism are a major contribution to the balance of payments. Austria suffered low economic growth in 2001 and 2002.
GNP – US$204,525 million (2000); US$25,220 per capita (2000)
GDP – US$188,742 million (2001); US$23,357 per capita (2000)
ANNUAL AVERAGE GROWTH OF GDP – 3.3 per cent (2000)
INFLATION RATE – 2.4 per cent (2000)
UNEMPLOYMENT – 3.6 per cent (2000)

TRADE
Main exports are processed goods (iron and steel, other

metal goods, textiles, paper and cardboard products), machinery and transport equipment, other finished goods (including clothing), raw materials, chemical products and foodstuffs. Main imports are machinery and transport equipment, processed goods, chemical products, foodstuffs, fuel and energy. Austria's main trading partners are Germany, Italy, France and Switzerland.

In 2001, Austria had a trade deficit of US$1,328 million and a current account deficit of US$4,103 million. Imports totalled US$70,445 million and exports US$66,671 million.

Trade with UK	2001	2002
Imports from UK	£1,158,500,000	£1,204,200,000
Exports to UK	1,767,000,000	2,177,800,000

COMMUNICATIONS
There is a network of 2,000 km of Autobahn between major cities which also links up with the German and Italian networks. The railways are state-owned and comprised 6,095 km of track in 2001, which includes 3,643 km of electrified track. Of the 425 km of waterways, 351 km are navigable and there is considerable trade through the Danube ports by both local and foreign shipping. There are six commercial airports.

CULTURE AND EDUCATION
In the late 18th and 19th centuries, Vienna became the centre of classical music and the city attracted composers from many countries.

Education is free and compulsory between the ages of six and 15 and there are good facilities for secondary, technical and professional education. There are 14 public, six private and six art universities.

ENROLMENT (percentage of age group) – primary 100 per cent (1997); secondary 100 per cent (1997); tertiary 48 per cent (1997)

AZERBAIJAN

Azərbaycan Respublikasi – Azerbaijani Republic

AREA – 33,436 sq. miles (86,600 sq. km). Neighbours: Iran (south), Armenia (west), Georgia and Russia (north)
POPULATION – 8,100,000 (2002 estimate): 83 per cent Azeri, 6 per cent Russian and 6 per cent Armenian. There are also Kurds, Jews, Georgians and Turks. There are more Azeris in Iran than in Azerbaijan. The population is predominantly Shia Muslim although it was heavily secularised during the Soviet era. The language is Azeri
CAPITAL – ΨBaki (Baku), population, 1,817,900, 2001 estimate
MAJOR CITIES – Gäncä (301,400); Sumqayit (288,400), 2001 estimates
CURRENCY – Manat of 100 gopik
NATIONAL ANTHEM – Azerbaijan! Azerbaijan!
NATIONAL DAY – 28 May (Independence Day)
NATIONAL FLAG – Three horizontal stripes of blue, red and green with a white crescent and eight-pointed star in the centre
POPULATION GROWTH RATE – 1 per cent
POPULATION DENSITY – 92 per sq. km (1999)

Azerbaijan occupies the eastern part of the Caucasus region of the former Soviet Union, on the shore of the Caspian Sea. The north-eastern part of the republic is taken up by the south-eastern end of the main Caucasus ridge, its south-western part by the smaller Caucasus hills and its south-eastern corner by the spurs of the Talysh Ridge. Its central part is a depression irrigated by the River Kura and the lower reaches of its tributary the Araks. Azerbaijan has a continental climate.

HISTORY AND POLITICS
The Turkic Azeri people formed an independent state in the first century BC. Invading Arabs introduced Islam in the seventh century. In the 16th century Azerbaijan was again invaded by Persia and became a Persian province. The country was divided during the Russo-Persian wars of the early 19th century, the northern portion (the present-day Azerbaijan) becoming part of the Russian Empire and the southern portion remaining Persian and subsequently Iranian.

In 1918 the Azerbaijan Democratic Republic was established. It was overthrown by Communists in 1918 and Azerbaijan acceded to the USSR in 1922.

In January 1990, the Azeri Popular Front took power from the local Communist Party and declared independence from the Soviet Union. Soviet troops overthrew the Popular Front and restored the Communist regime, which declared Azerbaijan's independence in August 1991.

Incumbent President Aliyev won the presidential elections of 11 October 1998, with 76.1 per cent of the vote. However, the elections were criticised by the OSCE and other international monitoring groups. A general election was held on 5 November 2000. The New Azerbaijan party, founded by Aliyev, won 62.5 per cent of the vote and 78 seats. The election was boycotted by several parties, who alleged that electoral fraud had been committed; their claims were supported by OSCE observers. Repeat elections were held on 7 January 2001 in 11 districts. Although the president's term of office is five years, non-renewable, in October 2002 Aliyev stated that he would stand again for President in the elections that were due to take place on 15 October 2003.

SECESSION
In 1988 fighting broke out in the predominantly Armenian-populated region of Nagorny-Karabakh between Soviet Azeri forces and ethnic Armenians demanding unification with Armenia. In late 1993 Nagorno-Karabakh forces captured all of the region, together with all Azeri territory separating the region from Armenia (20 per cent of Azeri territory). Azeri forces pushed back the Nagorno-Karabakh forces in early 1994 before a cease-fire agreement was signed in May 1994. The fighting briefly flared up again along the Azeri-Armenian border in April and May 1997. Peace talks, held under the auspices of the OSCE, have yet to yield any significant results, although both sides reaffirmed their commitment to finding a peaceful solution at a meeting in October 1997, in which both sides rejected the idea of full independence for Nagorny-Karabakh as 'unrealistic'. President Aliyev held talks with President Kocharian of Armenia in March and April 2001, but the leaders failed to reach an agreement on the future of Nagorny-Karabakh.

POLITICAL SYSTEM
A new constitution was approved by a referendum in November 1995, which created a presidential republic

with executive power to be exercised by the president and with legislative power vested in the unicameral *Milli Majlis* (National Assembly). The *Milli Majlis* has 125 seats, of which 100 are directly elected and 25 are allocated by proportional representation. The president appoints the prime minister and the Cabinet. Both the president and the National Assembly are directly elected for five-year terms.

HEAD OF STATE
President, Heydar Alirza oglu Aliyev, *assumed office*
   18 June 1993, *elected* 3 October 1993, *re-elected*
   11 October 1998

GOVERNMENT *as at July 2003*
Prime Minister, Artur Rasi-Zade
First Deputy PM, Yagub Abdulla Eyyubov
Deputy Prime Ministers, Abid Sarifov; Ali Gasanov *(Chair
   of State Refugee Committee);* Abbas Abbasov; Elehin
   Efendiyev
Agriculture, Irshad Aliyev
Communications, Nadir Akhmedov
Culture, Polad Bulbuloglu
Defence, Lt.-Gen. Safar Abiyev
Ecology and Natural Resources, Huseyn Bagirov
Economic Development, Farhad Aliyev
Education, Misir Mardanov
Finance, Avaz Alakbarov
Foreign Affairs, Vilayat Mukhtar Guliyev
Fuel and Energy, Mejid Kerimov
Health, Ali Insanov
Interior, Lt.-Gen. Ramil Usubov
Justice, Fikrat Farrukh Mammadov
Labour and Social Security, Ali Nagiyev
National Security, Namiq Abbasov
Taxation, Fazil Mamedov
Transport, Ziya Arzuman Mammadov
Youth and Sports, Abdulfaz Karayev

EMBASSY OF THE AZERBAIJAN REPUBLIC
4 Kensington Court, London W8 5DL
Tel: 020-7938 5482/3412
Ambassador Extraordinary and Plenipotentiary, HE Rafael
   Ibrahimov, apptd 2001

BRITISH EMBASSY
2 Izmir Street, Baku 370065
Tel: (00 994) (12) 975188
Email: offiice@britemb.baku.az
Ambassador Extraordinary and Plenipotentiary, HE
   Andrew Tucker, apptd 2000

BRITISH COUNCIL DIRECTOR, Margaret Jack
1 Vali Mammadov Street, AZ-370004 Baku
Tel: (00 994) (12) 971593 Email: enquiries@britishcouncil.az

DEFENCE
The Army has 220 main battle tanks, 135 armoured infantry fighting vehicles and 381 armoured personnel carriers. The Navy is based at Baku, with a share of the former Soviet Caspian Fleet Flotilla, comprising six patrol and coastal vessels. The Air Force has 48 combat aircraft and 15 attack helicopters.
MILITARY EXPENDITURE – 3.7 per cent of GDP (2001)
MILITARY PERSONNEL – 72,100: Army 62,000, Navy
   2,200, Air Force 7,900; Paramilitaries 15,000
CONSCRIPTION DURATION – 17 months

ECONOMY
Industry is dominated by oil and natural gas extraction and related industries centred on Baku and Sumgait and the large oil deposits in the Caspian Sea, estimated at more than 6,000 million barrels. Natural gas reserves are estimated to be more than 1,200,000 million cubic metres. Five contracts to explore and exploit oilfields in the Caspian Sea have been signed since 1994.

The republic is also rich in mineral resources, with iron, copper, aluminium, lead and zinc, and is important as a cotton-growing area and a silkworm-breeding area.

Around 90 per cent of agricultural land has been privatised. Grapes, cereals (primarily wheat, barley, maize and rice), cotton, vegetables and fruit are the major agricultural products.

The continuing conflict over Nagorny-Karabakh is an obstacle to economic growth and long-term prospects will depend upon global oil prices, new pipelines and and the country's ability to manage its oil wealth.

In 2001 Azerbaijan had a trade surplus of US$614 million and a current account deficit of US$52 million. In 1999 imports totalled US$1,036 million and exports US$929 million.
GNP – US$4,851 million (2000); US$600 per capita
   (2000)
GDP – US$5,692 million (2001); US$655 per capita
   (2000)
ANNUAL AVERAGE GROWTH OF GDP – 11.0 per cent
   (1998)
INFLATION RATE – 1.8 per cent (2000)
UNEMPLOYMENT – 1.2 per cent (1999)
TOTAL EXTERNAL DEBT – US$1,184 million (2000)

Trade with UK	2001	2002
Imports from UK	£36,856,000	£56,260,000
Exports to UK	9,806,000	11,070,000

COMMUNICATIONS
There are 2,200 km of railway track, much of it electrified, and over 25,000 km of roads. There are ferry links to Turkmenistan. Oil pipelines link the Azeri oilfields to the Russian Black Sea port of Novorossiysk and the Georgian port of Supsa. Moscow has agreed to grant $300 million for the construction of the Azeri part of the north-south transport highway linking northern and central Europe with the Gulf countries across Azerbaijan.

CULTURE AND EDUCATION
Azerbaijan was the birthplace of the prophet Zoroaster, who founded one of the first monotheistic religions in the world. The country has witnessed a succession of three religions: Zoroastrianism, Christianity and Islam.

Azeri is one of the Turkic languages. Previously written in the Russian script, Azeri in the Latin script was adopted as the official language in December 1992. In the 18th and 19th centuries Azerbaijani literature produced the poets and dramatists Vagif, Vazekhi, Zakir, Akhundov and Vezirov.

Education up to university level is free. There are several universities and colleges of higher education.

THE BAHAMAS

The Commonwealth of The Bahamas

AREA – 5,361 sq. miles (13,939 sq. km)
POPULATION – 308,000 (2001). The language is
  English
CAPITAL – ΨNassau (population, 172,196, 1996
  estimate)
CURRENCY – Bahamian dollar (B$) of 100 cents
NATIONAL ANTHEM – March On, Bahamaland
NATIONAL DAY – 10 July (Independence Day)
NATIONAL FLAG – Horizontal stripes of aquamarine,
  gold and aquamarine, with a black equilateral triangle
  on the hoist
LIFE EXPECTANCY (years) – 69 (2001)
POPULATION GROWTH RATE – 1.7 per cent
POPULATION DENSITY – 22 per sq. km (2001)

The Bahamas extend from the coast of Florida on the
north-west almost to Hispaniola on the south-east. The
group consists of more than 4,000 islands, islets and cays.
The 14 major islands are inhabited, as are a few of the
smaller islands.

HISTORY AND POLITICS

The Bahamas were settled by the British and became a
Crown colony in 1717. Taken over in 1782 by the
Spanish, the Treaty of Versailles in 1783 restored them to
the British. The Bahamas gained independence on
10 July 1973.
  A general election held in May 2002 was won by the
Progressive Liberal Party which defeated the Free
National Movement Party. The Progressive Liberal Party
holds 29 seats in the House of Assembly, the Free
National Movement seven seats and Independents four
seats.

POLITICAL SYSTEM

The head of state is Queen Elizabeth II who is
represented in the islands by a Governor-General. There
is an appointed Senate of 16 members and an elected
House of Assembly of 40 members.

Governor-General, Dame Ivy Dumont

CABINET *as at July 2003*
Prime Minister, Finance, Perry Christie
Deputy Prime Minister, National Security, Cynthia Pratt
Minister of State for Finance, James Smith
Agriculture, Fisheries and Local Government, V. Alfred Gray
Attorney-General, Education, Alfred Sears
Financial Services and Investments, Allyson Maynard-
  Gibson
Foreign Affairs, Public Service, Fred Mitchell
Health and Environmental Services, Marcus Bethel
Housing and National Insurance, Shane Gibson
Labour and Immigration, Vincent Peet
Social Services and Community Development, Melanie
  Griffin
Tourism, Obediah Wilchcombe
Trade and Industry, Leslie Miller
Transport and Aviation, Glenys Hanna-Martin
Youth, Sports and Culture, Neville Wisdom
Works and Utilities, Bradley Roberts

BAHAMAS HIGH COMMISSION
10 Chesterfiield Street, London W1J 5JL
Tel: 020-7408 4488
High Commissioner, HE Basil O'Brien, CMG, apptd 1999

BRITISH HIGH COMMISSION
Ansbacher House (3rd Floor), East Street
PO Box N-7516, Nassau
Tel: (00 1 242) 325 7471
High Commissioner, HE Rod Gemmell, OBE apptd 2003

DEFENCE

The Navy has seven patrol and coastal vessels, three
harbour patrol units and four light aircraft.
MILITARY EXPENDITURE – 0.6 per cent of GDP (2001)
MILITARY PERSONNEL – Navy 860

ECONOMY

Tourism employs about 40 per cent of the labour force
and provides about half of the country's GDP.
International banking and finance are also important,
accounting for about 15 per cent of GDP. The absence of
direct taxation coupled with internal stability have
enabled the country to become one of the world's
leading offshore financial centres. A securities exchange
was opened in May 2000.
  Manufacturing and agriculture account for less than
10 per cent of GDP. Agricultural production is mainly of
fresh vegetables, fruit, meat and eggs. Crawfish, other
seafood, vegetables, fruit and salt are exported. Reserves
of aragonite and limestone are being commercially
exploited. Freeport is the country's leading industrial
centre, with a pharmaceutical and chemicals plant, an oil
trans-shipment and storage terminal, and port and
bunkering facilities. There are also a brewery and a rum
distillery on New Providence.
GNP – US$4,533 million (2000); US$14,960 per capita
  (2000)
GDP – US$4,818 million (1999); US$14,147 per capita
  (2000)
ANNUAL AVERAGE GROWTH OF GDP – 2.2 per cent
  (1998)
INFLATION RATE – 1.6 per cent (2000)
UNEMPLOYMENT – 7.7 per cent (1998)

TRADE

The imports are chiefly vehicles, manufactured articles,
chemicals and petroleum. The chief exports are
machinery and transport equipment, foodstuffs and
livestock, raw materials, chemicals, manufactured goods,
and beverages and tobacco.
  In 2000 the Bahamas had a trade deficit of US$1,306
million and a current account deficit of US$402 million.
In 2001 imports totalled US$1,891 million and exports
US$649 million.

Trade with UK	2001	2002
Imports from UK	£15,166,000	£36,257,000
Exports to UK	7,108,000	20,676,000

COMMUNICATIONS

The main ports are Nassau (New Providence), Freeport
(Grand Bahama) and Matthew Town (Inagua).
International air services are operated from Abaco,
Bimini, Eleuthera, Exuma, Grand Bahama and New
Providence. More than 60 smaller airports and landing
strips facilitate services between the islands, the services
being mainly provided by Bahamasair, the national

carrier. The Bahamas has some 1,800 km of paved roads. There are no railways.

EDUCATION
Education is compulsory between the ages of five and 16. More than 66,000 students are enrolled in Ministry of Education and independent schools in New Providence and the Family Islands.
ILLITERACY RATE – (m) 5.0 per cent; (f) 3.6 per cent (2000)

BAHRAIN

Dawlat al-Bahrayn – The Kingdom of Bahrain

AREA – 267 sq. miles (694 sq. km)
POPULATION – 650,604 (2001 census); about 70 per cent are Bahraini; about 40 per cent of the Bahrainis are Sunni Muslims, the remaining 60 per cent being Shias; the ruling family and many of the most prominent merchants are Sunnis. The official language is Arabic; English is often used for business, and Farsi, Hindi and Urdu are also spoken
CAPITAL – ΨManama (Al-Manamah) (population, 140,401, 1991 census)
CURRENCY – Bahraini dinar (BD) of 1,000 fils
NATIONAL ANTHEM – Bahrayn Ona, Baladolaman (Our Bahrain, Secure)
NATIONAL DAY – 16 December
NATIONAL FLAG – Red, with vertical serrated white bar next to staff
LIFE EXPECTANCY (years) – 74 (2001)
POPULATION GROWTH RATE – 2.6 per cent
POPULATION DENSITY – 939 per sq. km (2001)
ILLITERACY RATE – (m) 9.0 per cent; (f) 17.4 per cent (2000)

Bahrain consists of a group of low-lying islands situated about half-way down the Gulf, some 20 miles off the east coast of Saudi Arabia. The largest of these, Bahrain Island, is about 30 miles long and 10 miles wide at its broadest, with the capital, Manama, situated on the north shore.

INSURGENCIES
Since 1994 Shi'ite protestors demanding the re-establishment of the National Assembly have regularly clashed with security forces and Shi'ite leaders have been detained. Opponents of the government have engaged in a sustained bombing campaign.

POLITICAL SYSTEM
Bahrain is a constitutional monarchy and has been fully independent since 1971, when British protectorate status was ended. The 1973 constitution provided for a National Assembly but this was dissolved in 1975. A 40-member Consultative Council, the Majlis al-Shura, was appointed in September 1996; it is an advisory body with no legislative powers. A new constitution providing for Bahrain to become a constitutional monarchy with a partially elected parliament was approved on 19 December 2000, endorsed by a referendum, in which women were able to vote for the first time.
   The first legislative elections since 1973 were held on 24 October 2002 when 174 candidates, including eight women, stood for 37 seats in the newly created House of Representatives. Moderate Sunni Islamists and Independents won 21 of the 40 seats, however, the country's main opposition groups boycotted the poll.

HEAD OF STATE
HH The Amir of Bahrain, C.–in –C., Bahrain Defence Force, Shaikh Hamad bin Isa al-Khalifa, KCMG *succeeded* 6 March 1999, *proclaimed king* 14 Feburary 2002
Crown Prince, Chair of the National Economic Development Council, Shaikh Salman bin Hamad al-Khalifa

CABINET *as at July 2003*
Prime Minister, HH Shaikh Khalifa bin Sulman al-Khalifa
Deputy Prime Minister, Foreign Affairs, Shaikh Mohammed bin Mubarak al-Khalifa
Deputy Prime Minister, Islamic Affairs, Shaikh Abdullah bin Khalid al-Khalifa
Commerce, Ali Saleh Abdullah al-Saleh
Defence, Maj.-Gen. Shaikh Khalifa bin Ahmed al-Khalifa
Education, Majed bin Ali al-Nuaimi
Electricity and Water, Shaikh Abdullah bin Sulman al-Khalifa
Finance and National Economy, Abdullah Hassan Seif
Health, Khalil bin Ibrahim Hassan
Industry, Hassan bin Abdullah Fakhroo
Information, Nabil Yacub al-Hamar
Interior, Shaikh Mohammed bin Khalifa al-Khalifa
Justice, Jawad bin Salem al-Orayed
Labour and Social Affairs, Majid bin Muhsen al-Alawi
Minister in the Prime Minister's Office, Shaikh Khalid bin Abdullah al-Khalifa
Ministers of State, Mohammed Ibrahim al-Mutawa *(Cabinet Affairs);* Brig.-Gen. Abdul-Aziz Mohammed al-Fadhil *(Consultative Council Affairs);* Mohammad Abdul Ghaffar Abdullah *(Foreign Affairs);* Abdul Hussain bin Ali Mirza *(Without Portfolio);* Abdulnabi bin Abdullah al-Shola *(Without Portfolio)*
Municipal and Agricultural Affairs, Mohammed Ali bin al-Sheikh Mansur al-Sitri
Oil, Shaikh Isa bin Ali bin Hamad al-Khalifa
Public Works and Housing, Fahmi Ali al-Jouder
Transport and Communications, Shaikh Ali bin Khalifa al Sulman al-Khalifa

EMBASSY OF THE KINGDOM OF BAHRAIN
30 Belgrave Square, London SW1X 8QB
Tel: 020-7201 9170
Ambassador Extraordinary and Plenipotentiary, HE Shaikh Khalid bin Ahmed al Khalifa, apptd 2001

BRITISH EMBASSY
21 Government Avenue, Manama 306, PO Box 114
Tel: (00 973) 534404
Email: britemb@batelco.com.bh
Ambassador Extraordinary and Plenipotentiary, HE Peter Ford, apptd 1999

BRITISH COUNCIL DIRECTOR, Amanda Burrell
AMA Centre, 146 Shaikh Salman Highway, PO Box 452, Manama 356 Tel: (00 973) 261 555
Email: bc.enquiries@britishcouncil.org.bh

DEFENCE
The Army has 140 main battle tanks and 235 armoured personnel carriers. The Navy, based at Mina Salman, has one frigate and 10 patrol and coastal vessels. The Air Force has 34 combat aircraft and 40 armed helicopters.
MILITARY EXPENDITURE – 4.8 per cent of GDP (2001)
MILITARY PERSONNEL – 10,700: Army 8,500, Navy 1,000, Air Force 1,200; Paramilitaries 10,160

ECONOMY

The largest sources of revenue are oil production and refining. The Bahrain field, discovered in 1932, is wholly owned by the Bahrain National Oil Co. The Sitra refinery derives about 70 per cent of its crude oil by submarine pipeline from Saudi Arabia. Bahrain also has a half share with Saudi Arabia in the profits of the offshore Abu Sa'afa field. A reservoir of unassociated gas has recently been developed on Bahrain Island. Petroleum accounted for 70 per cent of total export value in 2000. There is some heavy industry on the islands and a number of small to medium-sized industrial units. The state has developed as a financial centre. Apart from several commercial banks, many international banks have been licensed as offshore banking units; there are also money brokers and merchant banks. Services accounted for 59.8 per cent of GDP in 2000.

GNP – US$6,247 million (1999); US$7,640 per capita (1998)
GDP – US$7,971 million (1999); US$9,939 per capita (2000)
ANNUAL AVERAGE GROWTH OF GDP – 4.0 per cent (1999)
INFLATION RATE – 0.4 per cent (1998)

TRADE

In 2000 the government had a trade surplus of US$1,327 million and a current account surplus of US$113 million. In 2001 imports totalled US$263 million and exports US$5,545 million.

Trade with UK	2001	2002
Imports from UK	£155,920,000	£132,414,000
Exports to UK	101,653,000	77,724,000

COMMUNICATIONS

Bahrain International airport is one of the main air traffic centres of the Gulf; it is the headquarters of Gulf Air, and a stopping point on routes between Europe and Australia and the Far East for other airlines. A causeway links Bahrain to Saudi Arabia. Of the 3,164 km of road, over three quarters is paved. There are no railways.

BANGLADESH

Gaṇ Prajātantrī Bamlādeś – People's Republic of Bangladesh

AREA – 56,977 sq. miles (147,570 sq.km). Neighbours: India (west, north and east), Myanmar (east)
POPULATION – 123,151,246 (2001 census). The state language is Bengali. Use of Bengali is compulsory in all government departments. English is understood and is used widely as an unofficial second language. The faith of 88 per cent of the population is Islam and 10.5 per cent Hinduism. Islam has been declared the state religion
CAPITAL – Dhaka (population, 9,912,908, 2001 census)
CURRENCY – Taka (Tk) of 100 paisa
NATIONAL ANTHEM – Amar Sonar Bangla (My Golden Bengal)
NATIONAL DAY – 26 March (Independence Day)
NATIONAL FLAG – Red circle on a bottle-green ground
LIFE EXPECTANCY (years) – 60 (2001)
POPULATION GROWTH RATE – 2.2 per cent
POPULATION DENSITY – 1,078 per sq. km (2001)
URBAN POPULATION – 26 per cent (2001)

The country is crossed by a network of rivers, including the eastern arms of the Ganges (Padma), the Jamuna (Brahmaputra) and the Meghna, flowing into the Bay of Bengal. The climate is tropical and monsoon; hot and extremely humid during the summer, and mild and dry during the short winter.

HISTORY AND POLITICS

Prior to becoming the eastern province of Pakistan, Bangladesh had been the region of East Bengal and the Sylhet district of Assam of British India. The territory acceded to Pakistan in August 1947, which became a republic on 23 March 1956. Bangladesh achieved its independence from Pakistan on 16 December 1971, following a civil war. Pakistan and Bangladesh accorded one another mutual recognition in 1974.

In 1975 a one-party presidential system was introduced by the ruling Awami League, but this was replaced by a multiparty presidential system of government in 1978 by President Zia Rahman. After President Zia's assassination in 1981, Justice Abdus Sattar became president and was overthrown in a coup led by Army Chief Gen. Ershad in 1982. Following parliamentary elections in 1986, Gen. Ershad was elected president. Popular unrest forced his resignation in December 1990; the Bangladesh Nationalist Party (BNP) won the subsequent parliamentary elections. In August 1991 a constitutional amendment returned Bangladesh to parliamentary rule.

In December 1994, the opposition parties resigned from parliament, demanding fresh elections. Public disorder persisted despite a general election in February 1996 which was won by the BNP, although turnout was a mere five per cent. In March 1996, Prime Minister Zia agreed to new elections; these elections in June 1996 produced a majority for the Awami League under Prime Minister Sheikh Hasina Wajed. In November 1997, the BNP walked out of parliament, accusing the government of repression. They returned in March 1998 after signing a memorandum of understanding with the government.

Border clashes occurred between Bangladeshi and Indian troops on the northern border in April 2001.

In the elections held under a caretaker government on 1 October 2001, the BNP-led four party alliance won more than two-thirds of the seats in Parliament. On 10 October 2001, Khaleda Zia was sworn in as prime minister for a fourth time. President Badruddoza Chowdhury resigned on 21 June 2002 and Jamiruddin Sircar was appointed acting president. Iajuddin Ahmed was elected president on 5 September 2002 and took office on 6 September.

POLITICAL SYSTEM

There is a unicameral parliament *(Jatiya Sangsad)* of 300 directly elected members who can amend the constitution by a two-thirds majority.

HEAD OF STATE

President, Iajuddin Ahmed, *elected by Parliament*
5 September 2002

CABINET *as at July 2003*

Prime Minister, Armed Forces Division, Cabinet Division, Defence, Establishment, Energy and Minerals, Hill Tracts Affairs, Primary and Mass Education, Khaleda Zia
Agriculture, M. K. Anwar
Commerce, Khasru Mahmud Chowdhury
Communications, Nazmul Huda
Disaster Management and Relief, Chowdhury Kamal Ibne Yusuf

Education, Osman Faruque
Environment and Forest, Shahjahan Siraj
Finance and Planning, Saifur Rahman
Fisheries and Livestock, Ukil Abdus Sattar
Food, Abdullah Al Noman
Foreign Affairs, Morshed Khan
Health and Family Welfare, Khondoker Mosharraf
   Hossain
Home Affairs, Altaf Hossain Chowdhury
Housing and Public Works, Mirza Abbas
Industries, Motiur Rahman Nizami
Information, Tariqul Islam
Land, M. Shamsul Islam
Law, Justice and Parliamentary Affairs, Moudud Ahmed
Local Government, Rural Development and Co-operatives,
   Abdul Mannan Bhuiyan
Post and Telecommunications, Mohammad Aminul Hoque
Science and Information and Communications Technology,
   Moyeen Khan
Shipping, Lt-Col. Akbar Hossain
Social Welfare, Ali Ahsan Mojahid
Textiles, Abdul Matin Chowdhury
Water Resources, Hafiz Uddin Ahmed
Women and Children's Affairs, Khurshid Jahan Hoque
BANGLADESH HIGH COMMISSION
28 Queen's Gate, London SW7 5JA
Tel: 020-7584 0081
High Commissioner, HE Sheikh Razzak Ali, apptd 2002

BRITISH HIGH COMMISSION
United Nations Road, Baridhara, Dhaka
PO Box 6079, Dhaka-1212
Tel: (00 880) (2) 882 2705
Email: Dhaka.Press@fco.gov.uk
High Commissioner, HE Dr David Carter, CVO

BRITISH COUNCIL DIRECTOR, Carl Reuter
5 Fuller Road, PO Box 161, Dhaka 1000;
Tel: (00 880) (2) 861 8905/7;
Email: Dhaka.Enquiries@bd.britishcouncil.org.
There is a regional director in Chittagong.

DEFENCE
The army has 200 main battle tanks and 150 armoured
personnel carriers. The Navy has five frigates and
33 patrol and coastal vessels. The Air Force has
83 combat aircraft.
MILITARY EXPENDITURE – 1.4 per cent of GDP (2001)
MILITARY PERSONNEL – 137,000: Army 120,000,
   Navy 10,500, Air Force 6,500; Paramilitaries 63,200

ECONOMY
Bangladesh is self-sufficient in food production.
Agriculture is the primary occupation of 70 per cent of
the population and products include rice, wheat, tobacco,
tea, oil seeds, pulses and sugar cane. The chief industries
are jute, cotton, tea, leather, pharmaceuticals, fertiliser,
sugar, prawn fishing and natural gas. Garment
manufacturing is the main export. Remittances sent home
by Bangladeshis abroad are of considerable significance
to the economy.
   Heavy flooding during the summer of 1998 left 23
million people homeless and killed 1,500; two-thirds of
the country was under water and 800,000 hectares of
farmland was destroyed.
   International donors agreed in April 2000 to provide
around US$2,000 million in additional aid over a
20-year period dependent on the introduction of free-
market economic reforms.

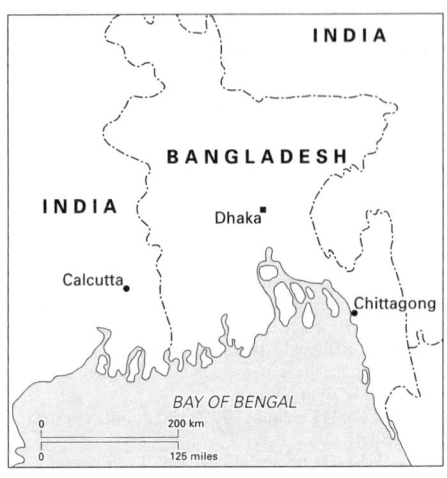

GNP – US$47,864 million (2000); US$370 per capita
   (2000)
GDP – US$46,652 million (2001); US$362 per capita
   (2000)
ANNUAL AVERAGE GROWTH OF GDP – 5.5 per cent
   (2000)
INFLATION RATE – 2.3 per cent (2000)
TOTAL EXTERNAL DEBT – US$15,609 million (2000)

TRADE
In 2000 Bangladesh had a current account deficit of
US$306 million and a trade deficit of US$1,654 million.
In 2001 imports totalled US$8,397 million and exports
US$4,958 million.

Trade with UK	2001	2002
Imports from UK	£67,952,000	£66,185,000
Exports to UK	£455,184,000	481,836,000

COMMUNICATIONS
Principal seaports are Chittagong and Mongla. The
Bangladesh Shipping Corporation was set up by the
Government to operate the Bangladesh merchant fleet.
The principal airports are Dhaka (Zia International) and
Chittagong. The international airline, Bangladesh Biman,
serves Europe, the Middle East, South and South-East
Asia, and an internal network. A railway line links the
Bangladeshi town of Benapol with Petrapol in India and
the country's 36,000 km road network is in good
condition.

EDUCATION
Primary education is compulsory and free. There are
16 public universities, 29 private universities and more
than 600 colleges.
ILLITERACY RATE – (m) 47.7 per cent; (f) 70.1 per cent
   (2000)
ENROLMENT (percentage of age group) – primary 96.6
   per cent (2000); secondary 42.8 per cent (2000);
   tertiary 4.4 per cent (1990)

BARBADOS

AREA – 166 sq. miles (431 sq. km); nearly 21 miles long
   by 14 miles broad
POPULATION – 268,000 (2001). The official language
   is English

CAPITAL – ΨBridgetown in the parish of St Michael (population, 108,000, 1990)
MAJOR TOWNS – Holetown in St James, Oistins in Christ Church and Speightstown in St Peter
CURRENCY – Barbados dollar (BD$) of 100 cents
NATIONAL ANTHEM – In Plenty And In Time Of Need
NATIONAL DAY – 30 November (Independence Day)
NATIONAL FLAG – Three vertical stripes, aquamarine, gold and aquamarine, with a trident head on gold stripe
LIFE EXPECTANCY (years) – 77 (2001)
POPULATION GROWTH RATE – 0.4 per cent
POPULATION DENSITY – 622 per sq. km (2001)
URBAN POPULATION – 51 per cent (2001)
MILITARY EXPENDITURE – 0.5 per cent of GDP (2001)
MILITARY PERSONNEL – 610: Army 500, Navy 110

Barbados is the most easterly of the Caribbean islands. The land rises in a series of terraced tablelands to the highest point, Mt Hillaby (1,116 ft).

HISTORY AND POLITICS
The first inhabitants of Barbados were Arawak Indians but the island was uninhabited when first settled by the British in 1627. It was a Crown Colony from 1652 until it became an independent state within the Commonwealth on 30 November 1966.

In the general election held on 21 May 2003 the governing Barbados Labour Party (BLP) won 23 seats in the 30-seats in the House of Assembly with the Democratic Labour Party gaining seven seats.

POLITICAL SYSTEM
The head of state is the British sovereign whose local representative is the Governor-General. The legislature consists of a Senate and a House of Assembly. The Senate comprises 21 Senators appointed by the Governor-General for a five-year term, of whom 12 are appointed on the advice of the prime minister, two on the advice of the Leader of the Opposition and seven by the Governor-General at his/her discretion to represent religious, economic or social interests. The House of Assembly comprises 30 members elected every five years by adult suffrage.

There are 11 administrative areas (parishes): St Michael, Christ Church, St Andrew, St George, St James, St John, St Joseph, St Lucy, St Peter, St Philip and St Thomas.

Governor-General, HE Sir Clifford Husbands, GCMG, KA, apptd 1996

CABINET *as at July 2003*
Prime Minister, Defence and Security, Finance and Economic Affairs, Owen Arthur
Deputy Prime Minister, Attorney-General, Home Affairs, Mia Mottley
Agriculture and Rural Development, Erskine Griffith
Commerce, Consumer Affairs and Business Development, Ronald Toppin
Education, Youth Affairs and Sports, Reginald Farley
Energy and Public Utilities, Anthony Wood
Foreign Affairs, Foreign Trade, Billie Miller
Health, Jerome Walcott
Housing, Lands and Environment, Elizabeth Thompson
Industry, International Business, Dale Marshall
Labour and Social Security, Rawle Eastmond
Minister of State, Education, Youth Affairs and Sports, Cynthia Forde

Minister of State, Foreign Affairs and Foreign Trade, Kerrie Symmonds
Minister of State, Prime Minister's Office and in the Ministry of the Civil Service, John Williams
Public Works, Gline Clarke
Social Transformation, Hamilton Lashley
Tourism and International Transport, Noel Anderson Lynch

BARBADOS HIGH COMMISSION
1 Great Russell Street, London WC1B 3ND
Tel: 020-7631 4975
High Commissioner, HE Peter Simmons, apptd 1995

BRITISH HIGH COMMISSION
Lower Collymore Rock, PO Box 676, Bridgetown
Tel: (00 1 246) 430 7800
Email: britishhc@sunbeach.net
High Commissioner, HE John White, apptd 2001

ECONOMY
The economy is based on tourism, sugar and light manufacturing. Chief exports are sugar, chemicals, electronic components and clothing.
GNP – US$2,469 million (2000); US$9,250 per capita (2000)
GDP – US$2,600 million (1999); US$9,721 per capita (2000)
ANNUAL AVERAGE GROWTH OF GDP – 2.5 per cent (1999)
INFLATION RATE – 2.4 per cent (2000)
UNEMPLOYMENT – 10.5 per cent (1999)
TOTAL EXTERNAL DEBT – US$589 million (1999)

TRADE
In 2000 Barbados had a current account deficit of US$146 million and a trade deficit of US$744 million. In 2001 exports totalled US$259 million and imports US$1,087 million.

Trade with UK	2001	2002
Imports from UK	£55,734,000	£39,600,000
Exports to UK	40,238,000	25,008,000

COMMUNICATIONS
Barbados has some 965 miles of roads, of which about 917 miles are asphalted. The Grantley Adams International airport is situated at Seawell, 12 miles from Bridgetown. Bridgetown, the only port of entry, has a deep-water harbour with berths for eight ships; oil is pumped ashore at Spring Garden and at an Esso installation on the West Coast.

EDUCATION
Education is free in government schools at primary and secondary levels. There are 104 primary schools, 23 government secondary schools and ten private secondary schools.

BELARUS

Respublika Belarus – Republic of Belarus

AREA – 79,808 sq. miles (207,500 sq. km). Neighbours: Latvia and Lithuania (north), Russia (east), Ukraine (south), Poland (west)
POPULATION – 10,147,000 (2001): 78 per cent Belarusian, 13 per cent Russian, 4 per cent Polish and

3 per cent Ukrainian, with smaller numbers of Jews and Lithuanians. Belarusian and Russian have equal official language status. Most of the population are Belarusian Orthodox with a minority of Roman Catholics

CAPITAL – Minsk (population, 1,725,100); the administrative centre of the CIS

MAJOR CITIES – Brest (300,400); Homyel' (503,700); Hrodna (308,900); Mahilyow (371,300); Vitsyebsk (358,700), 1999 estimates

CURRENCY – Belarusian rouble

NATIONAL ANTHEM – The former Soviet national anthem but with the words omitted

NATIONAL DAY – 3 July (Independence Day)

NATIONAL FLAG – Red with a green strip along the lower edge, and in the hoist a vertical red and white ornamental pattern

LIFE EXPECTANCY (years) – 69 (2001)

POPULATION GROWTH RATE – 0.1 per cent

POPULATION DENSITY – 49 per sq. km (2001)

URBAN POPULATION – 70 per cent (2001)

Belarus is situated in the western part of the European area of the former USSR. The main rivers are the upper reaches of the Dnieper, of the Niemen and of the Western Dvina. Much of the land is a plain, with many lakes, swamps and marshy areas. The climate is continental with mild, humid winters and relatively cool and rainy summers.

HISTORY AND POLITICS

After being absorbed into Lithuania in the 13th and 14th centuries, the Belurusian nationality, language and culture flourished until Belarus came under Polish rule in the mid-16th century. Two hundred years of Polish rule followed until Belarus was re-absorbed into the Russian empire. Belarus was devastated by the German invasion in the Second World War; 25 per cent of the population was killed and thousands deported.

Belarus issued a Declaration of State Sovereignty on 27 July 1990 and declared its independence from the Soviet Union after the failed coup in Moscow in August 1991. Stanislav Shuskevich became Belarusian leader at the head of a coalition of Communists and democrats, but he was forced to resign in January 1994 and was replaced by Gen. Mecheslav Grib who pursued closer political, economic and trade relations with Russia. The presidential election in June 1994 was won by Alyaksandr Lukashenka.

The legislative election held on 15 October 2000, with a second round on 29 October, was condemned as neither free nor fair by opposition groups and international observers from OSCE, the European Parliament and the Council of Europe. Most opposition parties boycotted the election and many opposition candidates were prevented from standing or intimidated into withdrawing by the authorities. Repeat elections were held in 13 of the 110 constituencies of the House of Representatives on 13–18 March 2001, with a second round on 1 April. In the presidential elections held on 9 September 2001 Lukashenka was re-elected with more than 75 per cent of the vote. Observers from the CIS stated that the election was legitimate but observers from the OSCE announced that the election did not comply with OSCE standards. During 2002 the Belarusian authorities refused to renew the visas of OSCE staff but in December 2002 an agreement to open a new office in

Minsk was reached and OSCE staff were readmitted to the country. This led to the lifting in April 2003 of travel bans imposed by the EU and the US in November 2002 on President Lukashenka and seven other senior Belarusian officials because of the country's poor human rights record.

FOREIGN RELATIONS

An agreement was signed with Russia in April 1996 to form a Commonwealth of Independent States (CIS). In April 1997 a treaty of union was signed with Russia. On 8 December 1999, the presidents of Belarus and Russia signed the Treaty on the Creation of a Union State, which committed the two countries to eventually becoming a confederal state.

POLITICAL SYSTEM

The president's term of office is five years, although two referendums in 1996 and 1997 extended Lukashenka's term until 2002; the legitimacy of these extensions was contested by the opposition and a fresh presidential election was held in September 2001. The president has authority to appoint half the members of the constitutional court and the electoral commission. The legislature is the bicameral National Assembly, comprising a 110-member House of Representatives (lower chamber) and a 64-member Council of the Republic (upper chamber). Eight members of the upper chamber are appointed by the president, the rest are indirectly elected by members of the local soviets in each region.

HEAD OF STATE

President, Alyaksandr Lukashenka, *elected* 10 July 1994, *re-elected* 9 September 2001

COUNCIL OF MINISTERS *as at July 2003*
Prime Minister (acting), Sergei Sidorsky
Deputy Prime Ministers, Roman Vnuchko *(Agroindustrial Complex)*; Andrei Kobyakov *(Economics, Trade and International Co-operation)*; Anatoly Tsutsunov *(Energy)*; Vladimir Drazhin *(Labour and Social Security, Social Affairs, Science)*
Agriculture and Food, Zenon Lomat
Architecture and Construction, Gennady Kurochkin
Communications, Vladimir Goncharenko
Culture, Leonid Gulyako
Defence, Col.-Gen. Leonid Maltsev
Education, Pyotr Brigadin
Emergencies, Valery Astapov
Energy, Vladimir Semashko
Finance, Nikolai Korbut
Foreign Affairs, Sergei Martynov
Health, Lyudmila Pastayalka
Housing and Communal Services, Aleksandr Milkota
Industry, Anatoly Kharlap
Information, Mikhail Podgainy
Internal Affairs, Maj.-Gen. Vladimir Naumov
Justice, Viktor Golovanov
Labour and Social Security, Antonina Morova
Natural Resources and Environmental Protection, Leonty Khoruzhik
Revenues, Konstantin Sumar
Sport and Tourism, Yury Sivakou
Statistics and Analysis, Vladimir Zinovsky
Trade, Aleksandr Kulichkov
Transport and Communications, Mikhail Borovoy

EMBASSY OF THE REPUBLIC OF BELARUS
6 Kensington Court, London W8 5DL
Tel: 020-7937 3288
Ambassador Extraordinary and Plenipotentiary,
HE Dr Alyaksei Mazhukhou, apptd 2002

BRITISH EMBASSY
37 Karl Marx Street, 220030 Minsk
Tel: (00 375) (172) 105920
Email: pia@bepost.belpak.minsk.by
Ambassador Extraordinary and Plenipotentiary, HE Brian
Bennett, apptd 2002

DEFENCE

The Army has 1,608 main battle tanks, 1,588 armoured
infantry fighting vehicles and 919 armoured personnel
carriers. The Air Force has 212 combat aircraft and
58 armed helicopters.
MILITARY EXPENDITURE – 2.2 per cent of GDP (2001)
MILITARY PERSONNEL – 79,800: Army 29,300, Central
Units 28,500, Air Force 22,000, of which Air Defence
Force 10,200; Paramilitaries 110,000
CONSCRIPTION DURATION – Nine to 12 months

ECONOMY

As a result of the collapse of the Soviet centrally planned
economic system, the country lost cheap supplies of
energy and raw materials. Energy from Russia is still the
largest import.

In May 1995 a customs union agreement with Russia
took effect. A treaty was signed with Kazakhstan,
Kyrgyzstan and Latvia in March 1996 aimed at the
establishment of a single customs territory.

Industrial output increased by 9.7 per cent in 1999
and GDP growth averaged 6 per cent between 1996 and
2000. The principal industries are transport vehicles,
machine-building, electronics, defence, chemicals and
civil engineering.

During a summit held on 19–20 January 2003
between President Lukashenka and Russian President
Vladimir Putin it was agreed to introduce the Russian
rouble as the single currency of the new Russian Belarus
Union State from 1 January 2005; to form a joint
enterprise to manage the transport of Russian gas to
Europe via Belarus; to complete a joint constitution; and
to unify tariffs, customs and tax systems.

In 2001 Belarus had a trade deficit of US$779 million
and a current account deficit of US$270 million.
Imports totalled US$8,046 million and exports
US$7,525 million.
GNP – US$28,735 million (2000); US$2,870 per capita
(2000)
GDP – US$12,070 million (2001); US$1,022 per capita
(2000)
AVERAGE ANNUAL GROWTH OF GDP – 5.9 per cent
(2000)
INFLATION RATE – 168.6 per cent (2000)
UNEMPLOYMENT – 2.1 per cent (2000)
TOTAL EXTERNAL DEBT – US$851 million (2000)

Trade with UK	2001	2002
Imports from UK	£32,543,000	£34,432,000
Exports to UK	18,003,000	33,838,000

CULTURE AND EDUCATION

Belarusian is an Eastern Slavonic language, closely related
to Russian and Ukrainian and written in the Cyrillic
script.

The national education system comprises pre-school,
general secondary, out-of-school, vocational training
and trade schools, secondary specialised and higher
education. General secondary education begins at the age
of six.
ILLITERACY RATE – (m) 0.3 per cent; (f) 0.6 per cent
(2000)
ENROLMENT (percentage of age group) – primary 98
per cent (1997); tertiary 44.0 per cent (1997)

BELGIUM

*Koninkrijk België / Royaume de Belgique / Königreich Belgien
– Kingdom of Belgium*

AREA – 11,615 sq. miles (30,200 sq. km). Neighbours:
the Netherlands (north), France (south), Germany and
Luxembourg (east)
POPULATION – 10,309,725 (2002). Greater Brussels
978,384; Flanders 5,972,781; Wallonia 3,358,560.
Roman Catholicism is the religion of 86 per cent of
the population. The official languages are Flemish,
French and German
CAPITAL – Brussels (population, 978,384, 2002)
MAJOR CITIES – ΨAntwerp, the chief port (931,718);
Bruges (269,158); Charleroi (424,515); ΨGhent
(493,329); Liège (588,312); Leuven (453,772); Mons
(250,748); Namur (279,675), 1998 estimates
CURRENCY – Euro (€) of 100 cents
NATIONAL ANTHEM – O Vaderland, O Edel Land Der
Belgen (Oh Fatherland, Oh Noble Land Of The
Belgians)
NATIONAL DAY – 21 July (Accession of King Leopold I,
1831)
NATIONAL FLAG – Three vertical bands, black, yellow,
red
LIFE EXPECTANCY (years) – 79 (2001)
POPULATION GROWTH RATE – 0.3 per cent
POPULATION DENSITY – 340 per sq. km (2001)
URBAN POPULATION – 97 per cent (2001)

The Maas and its tributary, the Sambre, divide Belgium
into two distinct regions, that in the west being generally
level and fertile, while the tableland of the Ardennes, in
the east, has mostly poor soil. The polders near the coast,
which are protected by dykes against floods, cover an area
of 193 sq. miles. The principal rivers are the Schelde and
the Maas.

Belgium is divided between those who speak Dutch
(the Flemings) and those who speak French (the
Walloons). Dutch is recognised as the official language in
the northern areas and French in the southern (Walloon)
area and there are guarantees for the respective linguistic
minorities. Brussels is officially bilingual. There is a small
German-speaking area (Eupen and Malmédy) along the
German border, east of Liège.

HISTORY AND POLITICS

The kingdom formed part of the Low Countries
(Netherlands) from 1815 until 14 October 1830, when a
National Congress proclaimed its independence. Belgium
was invaded by Germany in 1914 and Eupen and
Malmédy were ceded to Belgium by Germany under the
Versailles Treaty of 1919. The kingdom was again
invaded by Germany in 1940 and was occupied by Nazi
troops until liberated by the Allies in September 1944. In
1977 Belgium was divided into three administrative
regions: Flanders, Wallonia and Brussels.

A general election was held on 18 May 2003. The results were as follows (seats):

Chamber of Deputies: Flemish Liberals and Democrats (VLD) 25; Socialist Party (PS) (French) 25; Liberal Reform Party (MR) (French) 24; Socialist Party-Spirit (SP.A-Spirit) (Flemish) 23; Flemish Christian Democrats (CD&V) 21; Flemish Bloc (VB) 18; Humanist Democratic Centre (CDH) (French) 8; Ecolo (French Greens) 4; New Flemish Alliance (N-VA) 1; National Front (FN) 1.

Senate: of the 40 seats directly elected, VLD 7; SP.A-Spirit 7; PS 6; CD&V 6; MR 5; VB 5; CDH 2; Ecolo 1; FN 1. A further 31 Senators are indirectly elected or co-opted.

A coalition government of Liberals and Socialists was sworn in on 12 July 2003 with Guy Verhofstadt of the VLD as Prime Minister.

POLITICAL SYSTEM

Belgium is a constitutional representative and hereditary monarchy with a bicameral legislature, consisting of the King, the Senate and the Chamber of Deputies. The parliamentary term is four years. Amendments to the constitution enacted since 1968 have devolved power to the regions. The national government retains competence only in foreign and defence policies, the national budget and monetary policy, social security, and the judicial, legal and penal systems. The Senate has 71 seats, of which 40 are directly elected, 21 indirectly elected and ten co-opted by the Flemish and Francophone Communities. The Chamber of Deputies has 150 seats.

FEDERAL STRUCTURE

There are three communities: Flemish, Francophone, Germanophone. Each community has its own assembly, which elects the community government. At this level, Flanders is covered by the Flemish Community Assembly; most of Wallonia is covered by the Francophone Community Assembly, and the areas of Wallonia in the German-speaking communities of Eupen and Malmédy are covered by the Germanophone Community Assembly; Brussels is covered by a Joint Community Commission of the Flemish and Francophone Community Assemblies.

At regional level, Belgium is divided into the three regions of Wallonia, Brussels and Flanders. Each region has its own assembly and government.

There are ten provinces: five French-speaking in Wallonia (Hainaut, Liège, Luxembourg, Namur and French Brabant); and five Dutch-speaking in Flanders (Antwerp, East Flanders, West Flanders, Limburg and Flemish Brabant). In addition, Belgium has 589 communes as the lowest level of local government.

Minister-President of the Flemish Community and Flemish Region, Bart Somers
Minister-President of the Walloon Region, Jean-Claude Van Cauwenberghe
Minister-President of the French Community, Hervé Hasquin
Minister-President of the German-Speaking Community, Karl-Heinz Lambertz
Minister-President of the Brussels Capital Government, Daniel Ducarme

HEAD OF STATE

HM The King of the Belgians, King Albert II, *born* 6 June 1934; *succeeded* 9 August 1993; *married* 2 July 1959, Donna Paola Ruffo di Calabria, and has *issue* Prince Philippe; Princess Astrid, *b.* 5 June 1962; Prince Laurent, *b.* 19 October 1963
Heir, HRH Prince Philippe Léopold Louis Marie, *born* 15 April 1960; *married* 4 December 1999, Mathilde d'Udekem d'Acoz; has *issue* Princess Elisabeth Thérèse Marie Hélène, *b.* 25 October 2001

CABINET *as at July 2003*

Prime Minister, Guy Verhofstadt
Deputy Prime Minister and Minister for Enlargement and Government Agencies, Johan Vande Lanotte
Deputy Prime Minister and Minister for Foreign Affairs, Louis Michel
Deputy Prime Minister and Minister for Foreign Affairs, Patrick Dewael
Deputy Prime Minister and Minister of Justice, Laurette Onkelinx
Minister for Defence, André Flahaut
Minister for the Civil Service and Modernisation of Public Administration, Luc Van Den Bossche
Minister for the Civil Service, Social Integration and City Administration, Marie Arena
Minister for the Environment, Consumer Affairs and Sustainable Development, Freya Van den Bossche
Minister of Development Co-operation, Marc Verwilghen
Minister of Finance, Didier Reynders
Minister of Labour and Pensions, Frank Vandenbroucke
Minister of Mobility and Social Affairs, Bert Anciaux
Minister of Social Affairs and Public Health, Rudi Demotte
Minister of the Economy, Energy, Foreign Trade and Scientific Research, Fientje Moerman
Minister of the Middle Classes and Agriculture, Sabine Laruelle

Province	Area (sq. km)	Population (2002)	Main Town	Population (2002)
FLANDERS				
Antwerp	2,867	1,652,450	Antwerp	931,718
East Flanders	2,982	1,366,652	Ghent	493,329
Flemish Brabant	2,106	1,022,821	Leuven	453,772
Limburg	2,422	798,583	Hasselt	67,456
West Flanders	3,144	1,132,275	Bruges	269,158
WALLONIA				
Hainaut	3,786	1,281,042	Mons	92,260
Liège	3,862	1,024,130	Liège	588,312
Luxembourg	4,440	250,406	Arlon	15,000
Namur	3,666	447,775	Namur	279,675
Walloon Brabant	1,091	355,207	Wavre	27,000

BELGIAN EMBASSY
103 Eaton Square, London SW1W 9AB
Tel: 020-7470 3700
Ambassador Extraordinary and Plenipotentiary, HE Thierry
de Grüben, apptd 2002

BRITISH EMBASSY
Rue D'Arlon 85, B-1040 Brussels Tel: (00 32) (2) 287 6211
Ambassador Extraordinary and Plenipotentiary, HE Gavin
Hewitt, CMG, apptd 2001

BRITISH COUNCIL DIRECTOR FOR BELGIUM AND
LUXEMBOURG – Stephen Kinnock *(acting)*
Leopold Plaza, Troonstraat 108, B-1050 Brussels
Tel: (00 32) (2) 227 0841 Email: enquiries@britishcouncil.be

DEFENCE
The Army has 132 main battle tanks, 332 armoured
personnel carriers, 218 armoured infantry fighting
vehicles and 74 helicopters. The Navy is based at Ostend
and Zeebrugge and has three frigates. The Air Force has
90 combat aircraft.

The headquarters of NATO, SHAPE and the Western
European Union Military Planning Cell are in Belgium;
1,290 US personnel are stationed in the country.
MILITARY EXPENDITURE – 1.3 per cent of GDP (2001)
MILITARY PERSONNEL – 39,260: Army 26,400, Navy
2,400, Air Force 8,600

ECONOMY
The establishment of the European Commission and
other EU institutions in Belgium in the 1950s brought
multinational companies to the country and promoted
the service sector which accounts for over two-thirds of
Belgium's GDP. With no natural resources except coal,
production of which has now ceased, industry is based
largely on the processing for re-export of imported raw
materials. Principal industries are steel and metal
products, chemicals and petrochemicals, textiles, glass,
and foodstuffs. Industry accounts for approximately
22 per cent of GDP.

Belgium has participated in the European Single
Currency since 1 January 1999.

In 1999 there was a budget deficit of 0.9 per cent
of GDP and public debt was 112.5 per cent of GDP. By
the end of 2001, the debt ratio had been reduced to
103.3 per cent of GDP.
GNP – US$251,583 million (2000); US$24,540
per capita (2000)
GDP – US$227,618 million (2001); US$22,323
per capita (2000)
ANNUAL AVERAGE GROWTH OF GDP – 4.0 per cent
(2000)
INFLATION RATE – 2.5 per cent (2000)
UNEMPLOYMENT – 7.0 per cent (2000)

TRADE
External trade figures relate to Luxembourg as well as
Belgium since the two countries formed an economic
union in 1921. The main trading partners are Germany,
France, the Netherlands and the UK.

In 2001 Belgium and Luxembourg had a trade surplus
of US$3,315 million and a current account surplus of
US$13,037 million. Exports from Belgium totalled
US$189,271 million and imports US$178,468 million.

Trade with UK	2001	2002
Imports from UK	£9,181,600,000	£9,733,000,000
Exports to UK	10,862,800,000	11,317,000,000

COMMUNICATIONS
The rail system is run by the Belgian National Railways
and at 3,471 km the network is one of the densest in the
world. Major ports include Antwerp (the third largest
port in Europe), Zeebrugge, Ghent and Ostend. There are
1,531 km of inland waterways; ship canals link Ghent
with Terneuzen in the Netherlands, Willebroek Rupel
with Brussels, Zeebrugge with Bruges, Liège with
Antwerp and Charleroi with Brussels. The rivers Maas,
Sambre and Schelde form an integral part of the network.
There are nearly 146,000 km of roads, including
1,682 km of motorways.

CULTURE AND EDUCATION
Nursery schools provide free education for children from
two and a half to six years. There are over 4,000 primary
schools (6 to 12 years), more than 1,000 secondary
schools offering a general academic education slightly
over half of which are free institutions (predominantly
Roman Catholic but subsidised by the state) and the
remainder official institutions. The official school-leaving
age is 18.
ENROLMENT (percentage of age group) – primary 100
per cent (1997); secondary 100 per cent (1997);
tertiary 100 per cent (1997)

BELIZE

AREA – 8,769 sq. miles (22,800 sq. km). Neighbours:
Mexico (north and north-west), Guatemala (west and
south)
POPULATION – 241,204, 2000 census: 44 per cent
Mestizo (Maya-Spanish); 26 per cent Creole;
11 per cent Maya; plus a number of East Indian and
Spanish descent. The races are now inter-mixed. The
majority of the population is Christian, about 58 per
cent Catholic and 34 per cent Protestant. The official
language and language of instruction is English.
Spanish is also widely spoken and English Creole is
the vernacular. There are also Garifuna and Maya
speakers
CAPITAL – Belmopan (population, 8,130, 2000 census)
MAJOR CITIES – ΨBelize City (2000 census, 49,050),
the former capital; Corozal (7,888); Dangriga (8,814);
Orange Walk (13,483); San Ignacio (13,260)
CURRENCY – Belize dollar (BZ$) of 100 cents.
The Belize dollar is tied to the US dollar
NATIONAL ANTHEM – Land Of The Free
NATIONAL DAY – 21 September (Independence Day)
NATIONAL FLAG – Blue ground with red band along
top and bottom edges, and in centre a white disc
containing the coat of arms surrounded by a green
garland
LIFE EXPECTANCY (years) – 74 (2001)
POPULATION GROWTH RATE – 2 per cent
POPULATION DENSITY – 10 per sq. km (2001)
URBAN POPULATION – 48 per cent (2001)
MILITARY EXPENDITURE – 2.4 per cent of GDP (2001)
MILITARY PERSONNEL – Army 1,050

HISTORY AND POLITICS
Numerous ruins in the area indicate that Belize was
heavily populated by the Maya Indians. The first British
settlement was established in 1638 but was subject to
repeated attacks by the Spanish, who claimed sovereignty
until defeated by the Royal Navy and settlers in 1798. In
1871 the area was recognised by Britain as a colony and

called British Honduras. The colony became self-governing in 1964, with the UK retaining control of foreign policy, internal security and defence. In 1973 the colony was renamed Belize, and was granted independence on 21 September 1981.

The general election held on 5 March 2003 was won by the ruling People's United Party who took 22 of the 29 seats in the House of Representatives.

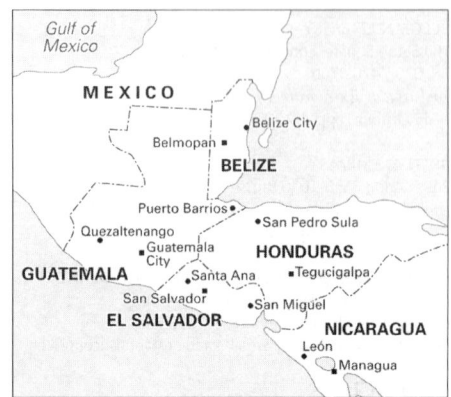

FOREIGN RELATIONS
There has been a longstanding territorial dispute with Guatemala which claims half of the territory of Belize. In September 2002 Belize and Guatemala agreed on a draft settlement to the dispute and on 7 February 2003 confidence-building measures were agreed whereby the Organisation of American States (OAS) would deploy observers in the disputed border area until referendums had been held in both countries on the terms of the September 2002 accord.

POLITICAL SYSTEM
Queen Elizabeth II is head of state, represented in Belize by a Governor-General. There is a National Assembly, comprising a House of Representatives (29 members elected for five years) and a Senate (13 members appointed by the Governor-General, including six on the advice of the prime minister and three on the advice of the opposition leader). Executive power is vested in the Cabinet, which is responsible to the National Assembly.

Governor-General, HE Sir Colville Norbert Young, GCMG, apptd 17 November 1993

CABINET *as at July 2003*
Prime Minister, Education and Public Service, Said Musa
Deputy Prime Minister, Natural Resources, Environment, Commerce and Industry, John Briceño
Agriculture and Fisheries, Servulo Baeza
Attorney-General, Foreign Affairs and Co-operation, Godfrey Smith
Defence and National Emergency Management, Sylvia Flores
Economic Development, Tourism and Culture, Mark Espat
Health, José Coye
Home Affairs, Finance, Budget Management and Investment, Ralph Fonseca
Housing, Cordel Hyde
Human Development, Local Government and Labour, Marcial Mes
Investment and Foreign Trade, Eamon Courtenay
Minister in the Office of the Prime Minister, Francis Fonseca
Ministers of State, Ismael Cal *(Agriculture and Fisheries);* Agripino Cawich *(Finance and Home Affairs);* Ainslie Leslie *(Natural Resources, the Environment, Commerce and Industry);* Dave Burgos *(Public Works, Transport and Communications)*
Public Works, Transport and Communications, Vildo Marin

BELIZE HIGH COMMISSION
22 Harcourt House, 19 Cavendish Square, London W1G 0PL
Tel: 020-7499 9728
High Commissioner, HE Alexis Rosado, apptd 2002

BRITISH HIGH COMMISSION
PO Box 91, Belmopan
Tel: (00 501) (8) 22146
Email: brithicom@btl.net
High Commissioner, HE Philip Priestley, CBE, apptd 2001

ECONOMY
About 30 per cent of the population is engaged in agriculture, which along with fishing accounted for more than 63 per cent of export revenue in 1999. The country is more or less self-sufficient in fresh beef, pork and poultry, but processed meat and dairy products are imported. About 25 per cent of timber production (mostly mahogany) is exported, and there is a large US market for lobster, conch and scale fish. The main export items are sugar, citrus fruits and juice, bananas and marine products. The EU and the US account for almost 90 per cent of export revenue. Tourism is also a valuable source of income.

In 2000 Belize had a trade deficit of US$191 million and a current account deficit of US$139 million. In 2001 imports totalled US$409 million and exports US$166 million.

GNP – US$746 million (2000); US$3,110 per capita (2000)

GDP – US$798 million (2001); US$3,345 per capita (2000)

ANNUAL AVERAGE GROWTH OF GDP – 8.9 per cent (2000)

INFLATION RATE – 0.6 per cent (2000)

TOTAL EXTERNAL DEBT – US$499 million (2000)

Trade with UK	2001	2002
Imports from UK	£13,789,000	£13,710,000
Exports to UK	34,939,000	31,559,000

COMMUNICATIONS
There is a government-operated radio service and three privately owned radio stations. An automatic telephone service, operated by Belize Telecommunications Ltd, covers the whole country.

The principal airport is at Belize City and various airlines operate international flights to the USA and other Central American states. The main port is also Belize City, which has deep water quays. Several inland waterways are also navigable. There are 1,865 miles of road, including four main highways, but there is no railway system.

EDUCATION
Education is compulsory from six to 14 years of age.
ILLITERACY RATE – (m) 6.7 per cent; (f) 6.8 per cent (2000)

BENIN

République du Benin – Republic of Benin

AREA – 43,484 sq. miles (112,622 sq. km). Neighbours: Togo (west), Burkina Faso and Niger (north), Nigeria (east)
POPULATION – 5,828,000. The official language is French
CAPITAL – ΨPorto Novo (population, 232,756, 2000)
MAJOR TOWNS – ΨCotonou (650,660, 2000) is the principal commercial town and port
CURRENCY – Franc CFA of 100 centimes
NATIONAL ANTHEM – L'aube nouvelle (The New Dawn)
NATIONAL DAY – 30 November
NATIONAL FLAG – Two horizontal stripes of yellow over red with a vertical green band in the hoist
POPULATION GROWTH RATE – 2.8 per cent
POPULATION DENSITY – 54 per sq. km (1999)
MILITARY EXPENDITURE – 1.8 per cent of GDP (2001)
MILITARY PERSONNEL – 4,550: Army 4,300, Navy 100, Air Force 150; Paramilitaries 2,500
CONSCRIPTION DURATION – 18 months (selective)
ILLITERACY RATE – (m) 43.1 per cent; (f) 75.3 per cent (2000)
ENROLMENT (percentage of age group) – primary 79 per cent (1997); tertiary 3 per cent (1997)

Benin (formerly known as Dahomey) has a short coastline of 78 miles on the Gulf of Guinea but extends northwards inland for 437 miles.

HISTORY AND POLITICS
Benin was placed under French administration in 1892 and became an independent republic within the French Community in December 1958; full independence outside the Community was proclaimed on 1 August 1960. Between 1963 and 1972 successive governments were overthrown by the military until a coup d'état in 1972 brought to power a Marxist-Leninist military government headed by Lt.-Col. Kérékou.

A pluralistic constitution was adopted in December 1990 and legislative and presidential elections were held in 1991. Nicéphore Soglo was sworn in as president and appointed a Benin Renaissance Party (PRB)-dominated provisional government. He was defeated by Gen. Kérékou in a presidential election in March 1996. In legislative elections held on 30 March 2003 the Presidential Tendency (MP) won and overall parliamentary majority winning 52 of the 83 seats in the National Assembly.

POLITICAL SYSTEM
The president is head of government as well as head of state, and is directly elected for a five-year term, renewable once only. The president appoints and presides over the Council of Ministers. The National Assembly has 83 members, directly elected for a maximum of four years.

HEAD OF STATE
President and Head of the Armed Forces, HE Gen. Mathieu Kérékou, *elected* 1996, *re-elected* 22 March 2001, *sworn in* 3 April 2001

CABINET *as at July 2003*
Agriculture, Husbandry and Fishery, Lazare Sehoueto
Civil Service, Labour and Administrative Reform, Ousmane Batoko

Commerce, Industry, Community Development and Employment Promotion, Fatiou Akplogan
Communications and the Promotion of New Information Technologies, Gaston Zossou
Culture, Handicrafts, Tourism, Frédéric Dohou
Education, Damien Alahassa
Energy, Mining and Water Resources, Kamarou Fassassi
Environment, Housing and Town Planning, Luc-Marie Constant Gnacadja
Family Affairs, Social Welfare and Solidarity: Massiyatou Lauriano
Finance and Economy, Grégoire Laourou
Foreign Affairs and African Integration, Rogatien Biaou
Higher Education and Scientific Research, Kémoko Bagnan
Interior, Security and Territorial Administration, Daniel Tawéma
Justice, Legislation and Human Rights, Dorothée Sossa
Labour, Public Affairs and Administrative Reform, Aboubacar Arouna
Minister of State for National Defence, Pierre Osho
Primary and Secondary Education, Karimou Rafiatou
Public Health, Yvette Celine Seignon
Public Works and Transport, Hamed Akobi
Relations with Institutions, Civilian Society and Benin Nationals Abroad, Alain Adihou
Technical Education and Vocational Training, Léa Hounkpe
Youth, Sports and Leisure, Valentin Aditi Houde

EMBASSY OF THE REPUBLIC OF BENIN
87 Avenue Victor Hugo, F-75116 Paris, France
Tel: (00 33) (1) 4500 9882
Ambassador Extraordinary and Plenipotentiary, vacant
Chargé d'Affaires, Antoine Afouda

BRITISH AMBASSADOR, HE Philip Thomas, CMG, resident at Lagos, Nigeria

ECONOMY
The principal exports are cotton, palm products, groundnuts, shea-nuts, and coffee. Small deposits of gold, iron and chrome have been found. Oil production started in 1983.

In July 2000 the IMF and the International Development Association agreed to a US$460 million debt reduction package for Benin. On 25 March 2003 the IMF announced that Benin had taken the necessary steps to reach its completion point under the enhanced Heavily Indebted Poor Countries (HIPC) initiative.

In 1999 Benin had a trade deficit of US$214 million and a current account deficit of US$191 million. In 2000 imports totalled US$613 million and exports US$392 million.

GNP – US$2,345 million (2000); US$370 per capita (2000)
GDP – US$2,269 million (2001); US$349 per capita (2000)
ANNUAL AVERAGE GROWTH OF GDP – 5.0 per cent (2000)
INFLATION RATE – 4.2 per cent (2000)
TOTAL EXTERNAL DEBT – US$1,599 million (2000)

Trade with UK	2001	2002
Imports from UK	£33,301,000	£43,387,000
Exports to UK	746,000	6,886,000

BHUTAN

Druk Gyal Khab – Kingdom of Bhutan

AREA – 18,147 sq. miles (47,000 sq. km). Neighbours: Tibet (north), India (west, south and east)

POPULATION – 1,862,000: about 80 per cent are Buddhists, the remainder (mostly the Nepali Bhutanese) are Hindu. The official language, for administrative and religious purposes, is Dzongkha, a variant of Tibetan, which functions as a lingua franca amongst a variety of languages and dialects. Nepali remains a recognised language and English remains the medium of instruction and the working language of the administration

CAPITAL – Thimphu (population, 30,340, 1993 estimate)

CURRENCY – Ngultrum of 100 chetrum (Indian currency is also legal tender)

NATIONAL ANTHEM – Druk Tsendhen Koipi Gyelknap Na (In The Thunder Dragon Kingdom)

NATIONAL DAY – 17 December

NATIONAL FLAG – Saffron yellow and orange-red divided diagonally, with dragon device in centre

POPULATION GROWTH RATE – 2.8 per cent

POPULATION DENSITY – 44 per sq. km (1999)

MILITARY EXPENDITURE – 3.8 per cent of GDP (2001)

ILLITERACY RATE – (m) 38.9 per cent; (f) 66.4 per cent (2000)

There is a mountainous northern region which is infertile and sparsely populated, a central zone of upland valleys where most of the population and cultivated land is found, and in the south the densely forested foothills of the Himalayas, which are mainly inhabited by Nepalese settlers and indigenous tribespeople.

INSURGENCIES

In January 1989 the King introduced a code of national etiquette designed to protect the national culture and language from Nepali encroachment. These measures, together with the granting of citizenship only to Nepalis settled in Bhutan before 1958, led to an exodus of ethnic Nepalis to Nepal, where about 96,000 live in camps. In March 2001 Bhutan and Nepal began an agreed process of assessing which refugees were entitled to return to Bhutan. However, a number of Nepalese refugees went on hunger strike in early 2003 in protest against their conditions and the slow progress of the verification and repatriation process.

FOREIGN RELATIONS

Under a 1949 treaty Bhutan is guided by the advice of India in regard to its external relations. It retains its own diplomatic representatives and is a member of the UN. It also receives from India an annual payment of Rs500,000 as compensation for portions of its territory annexed by the British Government in India in 1864.

POLITICAL SYSTEM

Bhutan has a 154-member unicameral *Tshogdu* (National Assembly), 105 of whom are directly elected and serve three-year terms, 12 are representatives of religious bodies and 37 are nominated by the government. The National Assembly meets twice a year. The ten-member Royal Advisory Council, nominated by the King and the National Assembly, acts as a consultative body when the National Assembly is not in session. The King is also assisted by the *Lhengyal Shungtshog* (Cabinet) which is led by an annually rotating chairman. There are no political parties.

In July 1998 the King introduced reforms giving the legislature the right to dismiss the King and to nominate the members of the cabinet, although the King retains the right to assign their portfolios. On 30 November 2001, the process of democratisation was taken further with the inauguration by royal decree of a committee to draft a written constitution.

HEAD OF STATE

HM The King of Bhutan, Jigme Singye Wangchuk, *born* 11 November 1955; *succeeded his father* July 1972; *crowned* 2 June 1974

Heir, Crown Prince Jigme Gesar Namgyal Wangchuk, *designated* 31 October 1988

CABINET *as at July 2003*

Cabinet Chairman, Agriculture, Kinzang Dorji
Chair of the Royal Advisory Council, Rinzin Gyeltshen
Deputy Minister for the Environment, Nado Rinchin
Deputy Minister of Communications, Leki Dorji
Education and Health, Sangay Ngedup
Finance, Yeshey Zimba
Foreign Affairs, Jigme Thinley
Home Affairs, Thinley Gyamtsho
Law, Sonam Tobgye
Trade and Industry, Khandu Wangchuk

ECONOMY

The economy is based on industry, which in 1998 accounted for 35 per cent of GDP, and agriculture (37 per cent of GDP). Agriculture and animal husbandry engage around 94 per cent of the workforce in what is largely a self-sufficient rural society. The principal food crops are rice, wheat, maize and barley. Vegetables and fruit are also produced. Bhutan is the world's largest producer of cardamom, which forms its principal export to countries other than India. Agriculture is, however, limited by the country's mountainous topography and 60 per cent forest cover.

The mountains contain rich deposits of limestone, gypsum, dolomite and graphite and small amounts of coal, which are exported to India. A distillery and cement, chemicals and food-processing plants are in production; a forestry industries complex is being expanded. Tourism and postage stamps are increasingly important sources of foreign exchange.

GNP – US$479 million (2000); US$590 per capita (2000)

GDP – US$533 million (2001); US$232 per capita (2000)

ANNUAL AVERAGE GROWTH OF GDP – 5.8 per cent (1998)

INFLATION RATE – 6.8 per cent (1999)

TOTAL EXTERNAL DEBT – US$198 million (2000)

TRADE

Principal exports are electricity, calcium carbide and timber; main imports are rice, machinery and diesel oil. Bhutan's airline, Druk Air, flies between Paro, New Delhi and Calcutta. In 1999 imports totalled US$182 million and exports US$116 million.

Trade with UK	2001	2002
Imports from UK	£1,644,000	£1,279,000
Exports to UK	2,342,000	640,000

BOLIVIA

República de Bolivia – Republic of Bolivia

AREA – 417,077 sq. miles (1,084,400 sq. km).
  Neighbours: Brazil (north and east), Paraguay and
  Argentina (south), Chile and Peru (west)
POPULATION – 8,516,000 (2001): 12 per cent is of
  white European descent, 30 per cent Mestizo (mixed
  European-Indian), 25 per cent Quechua Indian and
  17 per cent Aymará Indian. The official language is
  Spanish; Quechua and Aymará are also spoken.
  Roman Catholicism was the state religion until
  disestablishment in 1961
CAPITAL – La Paz, the seat of government (population,
  739,453, 1998 estimate)
MAJOR CITIES – Cochabamba (565,395); El Alto
  (534,466); Oruro (223,553); Potosí (140,642); Santa
  Cruz (935,361); Sucre, the legal capital and seat of the
  judiciary (178,426)
CURRENCY – Boliviano ($b) of 100 centavos
NATIONAL ANTHEM – Bolivianos, El Hado Propicio
  (Oh Bolivia, Our Long-Felt Desires)
NATIONAL DAY – 6 August (Independence Day)
NATIONAL FLAG – Three horizontal bands, red, yellow,
  green
LIFE EXPECTANCY (years) – 63 (2001)
POPULATION GROWTH RATE – 2.4 per cent
POPULATION DENSITY – 8 per sq. km (2001)
URBAN POPULATION – 63 per cent (2001)

The chief topographical feature is the great central
plateau over 500 miles in length, at an average altitude of
12,500 feet above sea level, between the two great chains
of the Andes, which traverse the country from south to
north. The total length of the navigable rivers is about
12,000 miles, the principal rivers being the Itenez, Beni,
Mamore and Madre de Dios.

HISTORY AND POLITICS

Bolivia won its independence from Spain in 1825 after a
war of liberation led by Simon Bolivar (1783–1830),
from whom the country derives its name. From 1964 to
1982 Bolivia was ruled by military juntas until civilian
rule was restored.

A wave of protests and strikes took place in September
and October 2000 over economic hardship, but ended
after the government made concessions to public sector
workers and promised investment in areas where coca
was produced. In April 2001 the protestors claimed that
the government had failed to deliver the promised
concessions and recommenced the campaign of
demonstrations and strikes. Presidential and legislative
elections were held on 30 June 2002, but were
inconclusive. Gonzalo Sánchez de Lozada was elected
President in a vote by Congress on 4 August. A state of
national alert was called on 28 March 2003 and on
29 March the government announced that a coup
planned for April had been averted.

POLITICAL SYSTEM

The constitution provides for a directly elected executive
president who appoints the Cabinet. The legislature
(Congress) consists of a 27-member Senate and a
130-member Chamber of Deputies; both chambers are
elected for five-year terms, and the president also for five
years.

HEAD OF STATE

President, Gonzalo Sánchez de Lozada
Vice-President, Carlos D. Mesa Gisbert

CABINET *as at July 2003*
Agriculture, Livestock and Rural Development, Arturo
  Valdiviezo (MIR)
Defence, Freddy Teodovic Ortiz (MNR)
Economic Development, International Trade and Investment,
  Jorge Torres Obleas (MIR)
Education, Culture and Sport, Hugo Carvajal Donoso
  (MIR)
Finance, Comboni Salinas (MNR)
Foreign Affairs and Worship, Carlos Saavedra Bruno (MIR)
Health and Social Protection, Javier Torres Goitia
  Caballero (MNR)
Interior, Yerko Kukoc del Carpio (MNR)
Labour, Micro-enterprises, Juan Walter Subirana Suarez
  (UCS)
Presidency, Justice and Human Rights (acting), José
  Guillermo Justiniano Sandoval (LMNR)
Presidential Delegate for Capitalisation, Juan Carlos
  Virreyra Mendez (MIR)
Public Services, Housing and Infrastructure, Carlos Morales
  Landívar (MNR)
Sustainable Development and Planning, Moira Paz
  Estenssoro (MNR)
Without Portfolio, responsible for Gas and Oil, Jorge
  Berindoague

MIR Revolutionary Leftist Movement; MNR National
Revolutionary Movement; UCS Solidarity Civic Union

BOLIVIAN EMBASSY
106 Eaton Square, London SW1W 9AD
Tel: 020-7235 4248
Ambassador Extraordinary and Plenipotentiary, vacant

BRITISH EMBASSY
Avenida Arce 2732, (Casilla 697) La Paz
Tel: (00 591) (2) 433424
Email: ppa@mail.megalink.com
Ambassador Extraordinary and Plenipotentiary,
  HE William Sinton, OBE, apptd 2001

BRITISH COUNCIL DIRECTOR, Eric Lawrie
Avenida Arce 2708 (esq. Campos), Casilla 15047, La Paz
Tel: (00 591) (2) 2431240
Email: information@britishcouncil.org.bo

DEFENCE

The Army has 72 armoured personnel carriers. The Navy
has 60 patrol vessels. The Air Force has 37 combat
aircraft and 16 armed helicopters.
MILITARY EXPENDITURE – 1.7 per cent of GDP (2001)
MILITARY PERSONNEL – 31,500: Army 25,000, Navy
  3,500, Air Force 3,000; Paramilitaries 37,100
CONSCRIPTION DURATION – 12 months (selective)

ECONOMY

Mining, natural gas, petroleum and agriculture are the
principal industries. The ancient silver mines of Potosí are
now worked chiefly for tin, but gold is obtained on the
Eastern Cordillera of the Andes. Following a decline in
the price of tin, many workers have taken to growing
coca, which has become a significant export. Small
quantities of oil are produced for internal consumption
and gas (currently providing about a quarter of export

income) is piped to Argentina; in December 1997 the World Bank approved financing for the 3,150 km Bolivia-Brazil gas pipeline, which is now in operation. Gas reserves were estimated in 2000 at nearly 40 trillion cubic feet.

In 1996 the government signed an agreement with the South American Common Market (Mercosur) to create a free trade zone within 18 years.

The proposed 2003 budget, submitted to Congress in early February, made provision for expenditure cuts and the imposition of a new 12.5 per cent income tax in order to reduce the primary fiscal deficit. The proposed budget was the cause of major public disturbances in La Paz on 12–13 February in which at least 33 people died. The budget bill was withdrawn from Congress on 12 February amidst fears of a military coup. A new draft budget was submitted on 11 March.

GNP – US$8,206 million (2000); US$990 per capita (2000)

GDP – US$7,960 million (2001); US$995 per capita (2000)

ANNUAL AVERAGE GROWTH OF GDP – 4.7 per cent (1998)

INFLATION RATE – 4.6 per cent (2000)

UNEMPLOYMENT – 7.4 per cent (2000)

TOTAL EXTERNAL DEBT – US$5,762 million (2000)

TRADE

Bolivia's principal exports are natural gas, tin, zinc, silver, gold, coffee and soya beans. The USA and UK are Bolivia's largest export trading partners. The country's low level of industrialisation requires Bolivia to be highly dependent on imports, mainly wheat and flour, iron and steel products, machinery, vehicles and textiles.

In 2000 Bolivia had a trade deficit of US$381 million and a current account deficit of US$464 million. In 2001 imports totalled US$1,724 million and exports US$1,285 million.

Trade with UK	2001	2002
Imports from UK	£10,220,000	£8,111,000
Exports to UK	12,574,000	11,593,000

COMMUNICATIONS

There are 4,300 km of railways in operation, but they are in a state of decay. There are about 49,400 km of roads, of which about 5 per cent are paved. In 1993 Bolivia and Peru signed an agreement granting Bolivia a concession of 162 hectares at the southern Peruvian port of Ilo for 98 years to construct a free trade zone.

EDUCATION

Elementary education is compulsory and free and there are secondary schools in urban centres. Provision is also made for higher education.

ILLITERACY RATE – (m) 7.9 per cent; (f) 20.6 per cent (2000)

BOSNIA-HERCEGOVINA

Republika Bosna i Hercegovina – Republic of Bosnia and Hercegovina

AREA – 19,767 sq. miles (51,197 sq. km). Neighbours: Serbia and Montenegro (east), Croatia (north and west)

POPULATION – 3,784,000; 4.4 million (1991 census): 44 per cent Bosniac, 33 per cent Serbs and 17 per cent Croats. The languages are Bosnian (spoken by Bosniacs and written in the Latin script), Serbian (spoken by Serbs and written in the Cyrillic alphabet) and Croatian (spoken by Croats and written in the Latin script)

CAPITAL – Sarajevo (population, 529,021, 1991 estimate)

MAJOR CITIES – Banja Luka (195,994); Mostar (127,034); Tuzla (131,866); Zenica (145,837)

CURRENCY – Convertible marka

NATIONAL ANTHEM – Jedna Si Jedina (You Are Unique)

NATIONAL DAY – 1 March (anniversary of 1992 declaration of independence)

NATIONAL FLAG – Blue, bearing a yellow triangle above a line of white stars

POPULATION GROWTH RATE – 2.1 per cent (1999)

POPULATION DENSITY – 75 per sq. km (1999)

MILITARY EXPENDITURE – 3.0 per cent of GDP (2001)

MILITARY PERSONNEL – Bosniac Army (VF-B): 9,200; Croat Defence Council (VF-H): 4,000; Bosnian Serb Army (VRS): 6,600

GNP – US$4,899 million (2000); US$1,230 per capita (2000)

GDP – US$4,769 million (2001); US$1,074 per capita (2000)

ANNUAL AVERAGE GROWTH OF GDP – 20 per cent (1998)

TOTAL EXTERNAL DEBT – US$2,828 million (2000)

HISTORY AND POLITICS

The country was settled by Slavs in the seventh century and conquered by the Ottoman Turks in 1463. Ruled by the Turks for over 400 years, the country came under Austro-Hungarian control in 1878. The assassination of the heir to the Austro-Hungarian throne in Sarajevo by an ethnic Serb precipitated the First World War, after which Bosnia-Hercegovina became part of the 'Kingdom of Serbs, Croats and Slovenes' (renamed Yugoslavia in 1929). It was occupied by German and Axis forces between 1941 and 1945. At the end of the war Bosnia-Hercegovina became part of the Socialist Federal Republic of Yugoslavia, which eventually collapsed with the secession of Slovenia and Croatia in 1991.

The Bosnia-Hercegovina government issued a declaration of sovereignty in October 1991 against the wishes of the ethnic Serb Democratic Party. Independence was declared on 1 March 1992 following a referendum which was boycotted by the Bosnian Serbs. Bosnia-Hercegovina was recognised as an independent state by the EC and USA in April 1992 and admitted to UN membership in May 1992.

THE WAR

Fighting broke out in March 1992 between the pro-independence Muslims and Bosnian Serbs who wanted to merge with the Serbian republic to form a Greater Serbia. The Bosnian Serbs, assisted by the Federal Yugoslav Army (JNA), gained control of 70 per cent of Bosnia and in August 1992 declared their own 'Republika Srpska' with its capital at Pale.

The Bosnian government (Muslim) forces formed an alliance with Bosnian Croat and Croat forces in early 1992 which collapsed in 1993. The Muslims then came under fire from both Bosnian Serb and Bosnian Croat forces.

In August 1993 the Bosnian Croats declared a 'Republic of Herceg-Bosna', with its capital in Mostar, and following a cease-fire in February 1994 joined the government forces in a Muslim-Croat Federation.

NATO galvanised the USA, Britain, France, Germany

and Russia to form the Contact Group (CG) to co-ordinate peace efforts. The CG brought about a cease-fire in June 1994 and presented a peace plan, which was rejected by the Bosnian Serbs.

Fighting intensified in 1995, climaxing in a land-grab during the final months of the war. Bosnian Serb forces overran the UN safe areas of Zepa and Srebrenica in July, allegedly massacring thousands of fleeing Muslims, and then laid siege to the Bihać 'safe area' together with Croatian Serbs and rebel Muslims. Bosnian government and Croatian forces lifted the siege of Bihać in August, enabling a joint attack on Serb-held central Bosnia.

The foreign ministers of Bosnia, Croatia and Serbia (rump Yugoslavia) met in Geneva in September 1995 and agreed to a US-sponsored peace accord. A cease-fire agreement was signed on 5 October and observed from 22 October, delayed by a Federation advance in the west and north-west, and Bosnian Serbs overrunning Tuzla. In November 2002, Bosnian Serb Mitar Vasiljevic was sentenced by the International Criminal Tribunal for the Former Yugoslavia in The Hague to 20 years' imprisonment for war crimes. Biljana Plavsic, the former president of the Republika Srpska, was sentenced in February 2003, to 11 years' imprisonment for crimes against humanity.

THE PEACE AGREEMENT

The Dayton Peace Treaty was signed in Paris on 14 December 1995. It was agreed to preserve Bosnia as a single state with a 51:49 division of territory between the Bosnian and Croat Federation and the Republika Srpska (Bosnian Serbs). A Republican (national) government, presidency and democratically elected institutions, based in Federation-controlled Sarajevo, were provided for.

The Dayton agreement provided for the deployment of a NATO-led Peace Implementation Force (IFOR) which took over from UNPROFOR on 20 December 1995 and was mandated until December 1996. IFOR was replaced by a NATO-led Stabilisation Force (SFOR).

Mostar, which had been divided during the war between the Muslims and Croats of the Federation and administered by the EU, held elections in June 1996. The EU withdrew in December 1996, when the Bosnian Croat state of Herceg-Bosna ceased to exist.

There were violent clashes between Croats and SFOR troops in March 2001 after the Croat National Congress resolved to boycott the government and establish institutions in mainly Croat areas.

POLITICAL SYSTEM

Under the Dayton peace agreement, the Bosnian republican (national) government was made responsible for foreign affairs, currency, citizenship and immigration. Executive authority was vested in a democratically elected rotating presidential triumvirate comprising a representative from each community, but in March 2001 the Assembly of Bosnia-Hercegovina nominated two members of a multi-ethnic party.

Legislative authority is vested in a bicameral parliament, the Assembly of Bosnia-Hercegovina, comprising a House of Peoples and a House of Representatives. Both houses have two-year terms. The House of Peoples has 15 members, 10 from the Bosniac-Croat Federation and 5 from the Republika Srpska, who are selected by the House of Representatives. The House of Representatives has 42 members who are directly elected to the two constituent chambers, the Chamber of Deputies of the Federation, which has 28 members, and

the Chamber of Deputies of the Republika Srpska, which has 14 members. Within the Bosniac-Croat Federation there is a 140-member House of Representatives and ten cantonal assemblies; in the Republika Srpska there is an 83-member People's Assembly.

Legislative elections and elections for the collective presidency and the presidency of the Republika Srpska were held on 5 October 2002. The winning parties were: the Bosniac Party of Democratic Action (SDA); the Serb Democratic Party (SDS) and the Croatian Democratic Community (HDZ). Dragan Čavić was elected president of the Republika Srpska and sworn in on 28 November. On 13 January 2003, the all-Bosnian legislature approved the coalition government of Adnan Terzic of the SDA. Mirko Sarović, who was inaugurated as the first chair of the collective presidency on 28 October 2002, resigned on 2 April 2003. Borislav Paravac was elected to replace him and took office on 10 April. The chair of the Presidency rotates among its three members every eight months and Dragan Covic assumed the chair on 27 June 2003.

HEADS OF STATE (FOR ALL BOSNIA)
Chair of the Presidency, Dragan Covic (HDZ)
Presidency Members, Sulejman Tihic (SDA), Borislav Paravac (SDS)

HEAD OF THE FEDERATION
President, Niko Lozancić
Vice-Presidents, Sahbaz Dzikanovic (SbiH); Desnica Radivojevic (SDA)

HEAD OF REPUBLIKA SRPSKA
President, Dragan Čavić (SDS)
Vice-Presidents, Adil Osmanović; Ivan Tomljenovic

COUNCIL OF MINISTERS (FOR ALL BOSNIA)
as at July 2003
Prime Minister, European Integration, Adnan Terzić (SDA)
Civil Works and Communications, Safet Halilović (SBiH)
Finance and Treasury, Ljerka Marić
Foreign Affairs, Mladen Ivanić (PDP)
Foreign Trade and Economic Relations, Mila Gadzić (HDZ)
Human Rights and Refugees, Mirsad Kebo (SDA)
Justice, Slobodan Kovac (SDS)
Security, Barisa Colak (HDZ)
Transport and Communications, Branko Dokić (PDP)
Treasury, Ljerka Marić (HDZ)

FEDERATION CABINET *as at July 2003*
Prime Minister, Ahmet Hadžipašić (SDA)
Deputy PM, Culture and Sport, Gavrilo Grahovac (SBiH)
Deputy PM, Finance, Dragan Vrankić (HDZ)
Agriculture, Marinko Božic (HDZ)
Defence, Miroslav Nikolić (HDZ)
Development and Entrepreneurship, Mladen Čabrilo (SBiH)
Education and Science, Zijad Pašić (SDA)
Health, Tomo Lučić (HDZ)
Industry, Energy and Mining, Izet Žigić (SBiH)
Interior, Mevludin Halilović (SDA)
Justice, Borjana Krišto (HDZ)
Labour and Social Affairs, Radovan Vignjević (SDA)
Refugees and Displaced Persons, Edin Mušić (SDA)
Trade, Maid Ljubović (SBiH)
Transport and Communications, Nedžad Branković (SDA)
Urban Planning and Environment, Ramiz Mehmedagić (SBiH)
War Veterans and Invalids, Ibrahim Nadarevic (SDA)

REPUBLIKA SRPSKA GOVERNMENT *as at July 2003*
Prime Minister, Finance (acting), Dragan Mikerević (PDP)
Administration and Local Government, Slaven Pekić
Agriculture, Forestry and Water Management, Rodoljub
   Trkulja
Defence, Milovan Stanković
Economic Affairs and Co-ordination, Omer Branković
Economy, Energy and Development, Milan Bogicević
Education and Culture, Gojko Savanović
Finance, Branko Krsmanović
Health and Social Care, Marin Kvaternik
Interior, Zoran Djerić
Justice, Saud Filipović
Labour and Veterans, Mico Micić
Refugees and Displaced Persons, Jasmin Samardzić
Science and Technology, Djemal Kolonić
Trade and Tourism, Boris Gaspar
Transport and Communications, Dragan Solaja
Urbanism, Civil Engineering and Ecology, Mensur Sehagić

HDZ Croat Democratic Union; PDP Party for
Democratic Progress; SbiH Party for Bosnia-
Hercegovina; SDA Party for Democratic Action; SDS
Serb Democratic Party

EMBASSY OF BOSNIA HERCEGOVINA
5–7 Lexham Gardens, London W8 5JJ
Tel: 020-7373 0867
Ambassador Extraordinary and Plenipotentiary, HE Elvira
   Begovic, apptd 2001

BRITISH EMBASSY
8 Tina Ujevica, Sarajevo
Tel: (00 387) (33) 444429
Email: britemb@bih.net.ba
Ambassador Extraordinary and Plenipotentiary, HE Ian
   Cliff, OBE, apptd 2001

BRITISH COUNCIL DIRECTOR, Clare Newton
Ljubljanska 9, Sarajevo 71000 Tel: (00 387) (33) 250220
Email: british.council@britishcouncil.ba

ECONOMY

Wheat, maize, potatoes and cabbage are among the major
crops; crude steel and lignite are among the principal
mineral products.

Trade with UK	2001	2002
Imports from UK	£14,713,000	£16,007,000
Exports to UK	2,601,000	3,765,000

BOTSWANA

The Republic of Botswana

AREA – 217,692 sq. miles (566,700 sq. km).
   Neighbours: South Africa (south and east), Zimbabwe
   (north and north-east), Namibia (west), Zambia (north)
POPULATION – 1,680,863 (2001 census): Batswana
   (95 per cent); the remainder are Bakalanga, Basarwa,
   Bakgalagadi, Basubya, Baherero, Bayei, Bambukushu
   and Europeans. The national language is Setswana and
   the official language is English
CAPITAL – Gaborone (population, 186,007, 2001
   census)
MAJOR CITIES – Francistown (83,023); Molepolole
   (54,561); Selebi-Phikwe (49,849)

CURRENCY – Pula (P) of 100 thebe
NATIONAL ANTHEM – Fatshe La Rona (Blessed Be This
   Noble Land)
NATIONAL DAY – 30 September
NATIONAL FLAG – Light blue with a horizontal black
   stripe fimbriated in white across the centre
LIFE EXPECTANCY (years) – 39 (2001)
POPULATION GROWTH RATE – 2.1 per cent
POPULATION DENSITY – 3 per sq. km (2001)
URBAN POPULATION – 49 per cent (2001)

A plateau at a height of about 4,000 feet divides
Botswana into two main topographical regions. To the
east of the plateau streams flow into the Marico, Notwani
and Limpopo rivers; to the west lies a flat region
comprising the Bakgalagadi Desert, the Okavango
Swamps and the Northern State Lands area.

HISTORY AND POLITICS

The Tswana people were dominant in the area now
known as Botswana from the 17th century. In 1885, at
the request of indigenous chiefs fearing invasion by the
Boers, Britain formally took control of Bechuanaland,
and the northern part of the territory was formally
declared a British protectorate, while land to the south of
the Molopo river became British Bechuanaland, which
was later incorporated into the Cape Colony. On
30 September 1966 the British Protectorate of
Bechuanaland became a republic within the
Commonwealth under the name Botswana.
   The last general election on 16 October 1999 was
won by the Botswana Democratic Party with 33 seats
to the Botswana National Front's 7 seats.

POLITICAL SYSTEM

The president is head of state and is elected by an
absolute majority in the National Assembly. He appoints
as vice-president a member of the National Assembly
who is leader of government business in the National
Assembly. The Assembly consists of the president,
40 members elected on a basis of universal adult suffrage,
four co-opted members, and the Attorney-General (non-
voting). Presidential and legislative elections are held
every five years. There is also a 15-member House of
Chiefs which considers legislation affecting the
constitution and chieftaincy matters. In August 1997 the
minimum voting age was lowered from 21 to 18.

HEAD OF STATE

President, C.-in-C. of the Armed Forces, HE Festus Mogae,
   sworn in 2 April 1998
Vice-President, Lt.-Gen. Ian Khama

CABINET *as at July 2003*
Agriculture, Johnnie Swartz
Assistant Ministers, Pelokgale Seloma *(Agriculture);*
   Gladys Kokorwe *(Local Government, Lands and
   Housing)*
Communications, Science and Technology, Lephimotswe
   Boyce Sebetela
Conservation, Tourism and Wildlife, Pelonomi Vensen
Education, George Kgoroba
Finance and Development Planning, Baledzi Gaolathe
Foreign Affairs, Lt.-Gen. Mompati Merafhe
Health, Joy Phumaphi
Labour and Home Affairs, Thebe Mogami
Lands and Housing, Margaret Nasha
Local Government, Michale Tshipinare

Mineral Resources, Energy and Water Affairs, Boometswe
Mokgothu
*Presidential Affairs and Public Administration in the Office
of the President,* Daniel Kwelagobe
Trade and Industry, Jacob Nkate
Works and Transport, Tebelelo Seretse

BOTSWANA HIGH COMMISSION
6 Stratford Place, London W1C 1AY
Tel: 020-7499 0031
High Commissioner, HE Roy Blackbeard, apptd 1998

BRITISH HIGH COMMISSION
Private Bag 0023, Gaborone
Tel: (00 267) 352841
Email: bhc@botsnet.bw
High Commissioner, HE David Merry, CMG, apptd 2001

BRITISH COUNCIL DIRECTOR, David Knox
British High Commission Building, Queen's Road, The Mall,
PO Box 439, Gaborone Tel: (00 267) 3953602
Email: general.enquiries@british council.org.bw

DEFENCE
The Army has 44 armoured personnel carriers. The Air
Wing has 30 combat aircraft.
MILITARY EXPENDITURE – 3.8 per cent of GDP (2001)
MILITARY PERSONNEL – 9,000: Army 8,500, Air Wing
500; Paramilitaries 1,500

ECONOMY
Agriculture is predominantly pastoral and accounts for
around 3 per cent of GDP. Cattle rearing accounts for
about 85 per cent of agricultural output.
Mineral extraction and processing is now the major
source of income following the opening of large mines
for diamonds, copper and nickel. Botswana is one of the
largest producers of diamonds in the world, with
diamonds accounting for 74 per cent of export revenue.
Large deposits of coal have been discovered and are now
being mined.
Service industries account for nearly half of GDP.
Tourism is the third largest industry, generating about
7 per cent of GDP. Main imports are motor vehicles,
machinery and electrical equipment and foodstuffs; main
exports are diamonds, motor vehicles, cupro-nickel and
beef.
In 1999 Botswana had a trade surplus of US$675
million and a current account surplus of US$517 million.
In 2000 imports totalled US$569 million and in 1998
exports US$1,948 million.
GNP – US$5,280 million (2000); US$3,300 per capita
(2000)
GDP – US$5,142 million (2001); US$3,225 per capita
(2000)
ANNUAL AVERAGE GROWTH OF GDP – 7.7 per cent
(2000)
INFLATION RATE – 8.6 per cent (2000)
TOTAL EXTERNAL DEBT – US$413 million (2000)

Trade with UK	2001	2002
Imports from UK	£24,248,000	£16,837,000
Exports to UK	£1,076,865,000	£1,036,914,000

COMMUNICATIONS
The railway from Cape Town to Zimbabwe passes
through eastern Botswana. The main roads are the north-
south road, which closely follows the railway, and the
road running east-west that links Francistown and Maun.

EDUCATION
There are 657 primary schools, 163 community junior
secondary schools, 23 government and government-aided
senior secondary schools and one university.
ILLITERACY RATE – (m) 25.6 per cent; (f) 20.1 per cent
(2000)
ENROLMENT (percentage of age group) – primary 100
per cent (1997); secondary 65 per cent (1997); tertiary
6 per cent (1997)

BRAZIL

*República Federativa do Brasil – Federative Republic of
Brazil*

AREA – 3,252,500 sq. miles (8,456,500 sq. km).
Neighbours: Guyana, Suriname, French Guiana,
Colombia and Venezuela (north), Peru, Bolivia,
Paraguay and Argentina (west), Uruguay (south)
POPULATION – 172,559,000 (2001). Portuguese is the
national language. Spanish and English are widely
spoken
CAPITAL – Brasília (population, 1,737,813, 2000
census)
MAJOR CITIES – Belo Horizonte (2,232,747);
ΨFortaleza (2,138,234); ΨPorto Alegre (1,360,033);
ΨRecife (1,421,993); ΨRio de Janeiro (5,851,914),
the former capital; ΨSalvador (2,440,828);
São Paulo (10,405,867)
CURRENCY – Real of 100 centavos
NATIONAL ANTHEM – Ouviram Do Ipiranga Às
Margens Plácidas (From Peaceful Ypiranga's Banks)
NATIONAL DAY – 7 September (Independence Day)
NATIONAL FLAG – Green with a yellow lozenge
containing a blue sphere studded with white stars, and
crossed by a white band with the motto *Ordem e
Progresso*
LIFE EXPECTANCY (years) – 68 (2001)
POPULATION GROWTH RATE – 1.4 per cent
POPULATION DENSITY – 20 per sq. km (2001)
URBAN POPULATION – 82 per cent (2001)

HISTORY AND POLITICS
Brazil was discovered by the Portuguese navigator Pedro
Álvares Cabral in 1500 and colonised by Portugal in the
early 16th century. In 1822 it became independent under
Dom Pedro I, son of King João VI of Portugal, who had
been forced to flee to Brazil during the Napoleonic Wars.
In 1889, Dom Pedro II was dethroned and a republic was
proclaimed. In 1985 Brazil returned to democratic rule
after two decades of military government.
In the first round of presidential elections held on
6 October 2002 Luis Inácio 'Lula' da Silva of the
Workers' Party (PT) gained 46.4 per cent of the vote. In
the second round vote held on 27 October, da Silva was
elected president with 61.3 per cent of the vote. In
legislative elections held on 6 October 2002 the
Workers' Party became the largest party in the Chamber
of Deputies, winning 91 of the 513 seats, and formed a
coalition government which included six other parties.

POLITICAL SYSTEM
The Federative Republic of Brazil is composed of the
federal district and 26 states. Under the 1988
constitution the president, who heads the executive, is
directly elected for a four-year term; in June 1997
the constitution was amended to allow the president to
stand for a second term. The Congress consists of an
81-member Senate (three senators per state elected for an

eight-year term) and a 513-member Chamber of Deputies which is elected every four years; the number of deputies per state depends upon the state's population. Each state has a Governor, and a Legislative Assembly with a four-year term.

FEDERAL STRUCTURE

Federal Unit	Area (sq. km)	Population (2000 census)	Capital
Central west		11,616,745	
Distrito Federal	5,822	2,043,169	Brasília
Goiás	341,290	4,996,439	Goiânia
Mato Grosso	906,807	2,502,260	Cuiabá
Mato Grosso do Sul	358,159	2,074,877	Campo Grande
North		12,841,299	
Acre	153,150	557,226	Rio Branco
Amapá	143,454	423,581	Macapá
Amazonas	1,577,820	2,813,085	Manaus
Pará	1,253,165	6,189,550	Belém
Rondônia	238,513	1,377,792	Pôrto Velho
Roraima	225,116	324,152	Boa Vista
Tocantins	278,421	1,155,913	Palmas
North-east		47,693,254	
Alagoas	27,933	2,819,172	Maceió
Bahia	567,295	13,066,910	Salvador
Ceará	146,348	7,418,476	Fortaleza
Maranhão	333,366	5,642,960	São Luís
Paraíba	56,585	3,439,344	João Pessoa
Pernambuco	98,938	7,911,937	Recife
Piauí	252,378	2,841,202	Teresina
Rio Grande do Norte	53,307	2,771,538	Natal
Sergipe	22,050	1,781,714	Aracajú
South		25,089,783	
Paraná	199,709	9,558,454	Curitiba
Rio Grande do Sul	282,062	10,181,749	Pôrto Alegre
Santa Catarina	95,443	5,349,580	Florianópolis
South-east		72,297,351	
Espírito Santo	46,184	3,094,390	Vitória
Minas Gerais	588,384	17,866,402	Belo Horizonte
Rio de Janeiro	43,910	14,367,083	Rio de Janeiro
São Paulo	248,809	36,969,476	São Paulo

HEAD OF STATE

President, Luis Inácio 'Lula' da Silva, *sworn in* 1 January 2003
Vice-President, José Alencar

CABINET *as at May 2003*
Chief Minister of the Cabinet, José Dirceu
Chief Minister of the Office for Institutional Security, Jorge Armando Felix
Agrarian Development, Miguel Rossetto
Agriculture, Livestock and Supply, Roberto Rodrigues
Cities, Olívio Dutra
Communications, Miro Teixeira
Culture, Gilberto Gil
Defence, José Viegas Filho
Development, Industry and Foreign Trade, Luiz Fernando Furlan
Education, Cristovam Buarque
Energy and Mines, Dilma Rousseff
Environment, Marina Silva
External Relations, Celso Amorim
Finance, Antonio Palocci

Food Security and Fight Against Hunger, José Graziano da Silva
Health, Humberto Costa
Justice, Márcio Tomaz Bastos
Labour and Employment, Jaques Wagner
National Integration, Ciro Gomes
National Secretary for Human Rights, Nilmario Miranda
Planning, Budget and Management, Guido Mantega
Science and Technology, Roberto Amaral
Secretary-General of the Presidency of the Republic, Luiz Dulci
Secretary of State for Economic and Social Development, Luiz Gushiken
Secretary of State for Fisheries, José Fritsch
Secretary of State for Women's Rights, Emília Fernandes
Social Assistance, Benedita da Silva
Social Welfare, Ricardo Berzoini
Sport, Agnelo Queiroz
Tourism, Walfrido Mares Guia
Transport, Anderson Adauto

BRAZILIAN EMBASSY
32 Green Street, London W1K 7AT
Tel: 020-7499 0877
Ambassador Extraordinary and Plenipotentiary, HE José Mauricio Bustani, apptd 2003

BRITISH EMBASSY
Setor de Embaixadas Sul, Quadra 801, Conjunto K, CEP 70.408–900, Brasília DF
Tel: (00 55) (61) 225 2710
Email: britemb@terra.com.br
Ambassador Extraordinary and Plenipotentiary, HE Sir Roger Bone, KCMG, apptd 1999

BRITISH COUNCIL DIRECTOR, David Cooke
Edifiicio Centro Empresarial Varig, SCN Quadra 04, Bloco B Torre Oeste Conjunto 202, 70710-926 Brasília DF
Tel: (00 55) (61) 327 7230
Email: brasilia@britishcouncil.org.br

DEFENCE

The Army has 178 main battle tanks, 803 armoured personnel carriers and 78 helicopters. The Navy has bases at Rio de Janeiro, Salvador, Recife, Belém, Florianópolis and Ladario. It is equipped with four submarines, one aircraft carrier, 14 frigates and 50 patrol and coastal vessels. Naval aviation has 24 combat aircraft and 54 armed helicopters; the Marines have 33 armoured personnel carriers. The Air Force has 264 combat aircraft and 29 armed helicopters.
MILITARY EXPENDITURE – 2.1 per cent of GDP (2001)
MILITARY PERSONNEL – 287,600: Army 189,000, Navy 48,600, Air Force 50,000; Paramilitaries 385,600
CONSCRIPTION DURATION – 12 months (can be extended to 18)

ECONOMY

There are large mineral deposits including iron ore (hematite), manganese, bauxite, beryllium, chrome, nickel, tungsten, cassiterite, lead, gold, monazite (containing rare earths and thorium) and zirconium. Diamonds and precious and semi-precious stones are also found. Brazil is the world's largest producer of coffee; the other main agricultural products are cassava, maize, soya, rice, wheat, sugar, potatoes, cotton, cocoa, tobacco and peanuts. Tourism is a growing industry; Brazil attracted 5.1 million visitors in 2000. Services generate 60 per cent of GDP.

A new currency, the real, was introduced in 1994 which helped control inflation, doubled interest rates, increased taxes and budget cuts. However, inflation rose to 10.22 per cent in November 2002, the highest level for eight years.

GNP – US$610,058 million (2000); US$3,580 per capita (2000)

GDP – US$502,509 million (2001); US$3,484 per capita (2000)

ANNUAL AVERAGE GROWTH OF GDP – 0.8 per cent (1999)

INFLATION RATE – 10.2 per cent (2002)

UNEMPLOYMENT – 9.6 per cent (1999)

TOTAL EXTERNAL DEBT – US$237,953 million (2000)

TRADE

Principal imports are machinery, fuel and lubricants, mineral products, transport equipment and chemicals. Principal exports are industrial goods, coffee, sugar cane, iron ore, tobacco and soya.

In 2001 Brazil had a trade surplus of US$2,645 million and a current account deficit of US$23,208 million. In 2000 imports totalled US$58,532 million and exports totalled US$55,086 million.

Trade with UK	2001	2002
Imports from UK	£813,401,000	£887,614,000
Exports to UK	1,327,651,000	1,414,884,000

COMMUNICATIONS

There are 1,670,148 km of highways, of which 161,503 km are paved, and the route-length of railways is 30,129 km, of which 2,150 km are electrified. There are ten international airports and internal air services are highly developed. There are 43,000 km of navigable inland waterways. Rio de Janeiro and Santos are the two leading ports. A 3,415 km gas pipeline running from Santa Cruz, Bolivia, to São Paolo, was opened in 2000.

EDUCATION

The education system includes both public and private institutions. Public education is free at all levels.

ILLITERACY RATE – (m) 14.9 per cent; (f) 14.6 per cent (2000)

ENROLMENT (percentage of age group) – primary 100 per cent (1997); secondary 62 per cent (1997); tertiary 15 per cent (1997)

BRUNEI

Negara Brunei Darussalam – State of Brunei Darussalam

AREA – 2,038 sq. miles (5,300 sq. km). Neighbour: Malaysia

POPULATION – 332,844 (2001 census): 66.9 per cent Malay, 15.2 per cent Chinese, 5.9 per cent indigenous races and 12 per cent European, Indian and other races. The majority are Sunni Muslims. The official language is Malay; English and dialects of Chinese are also spoken

CAPITAL – Bandar Seri Begawan (population, 46,000, 2001 estimate)

CURRENCY – Brunei dollar (B$) of 100 sen (fully interchangeable with Singapore currency)

NATIONAL ANTHEM – Allah Peliharakan Sultan (God Bless His Majesty)

NATIONAL DAY – 23 February

NATIONAL FLAG – Yellow with diagonal stripes of white over black and the arms in red all over the centre

LIFE EXPECTANCY (years) – 76 (2001)

POPULATION GROWTH RATE – 2.4 per cent

POPULATION DENSITY – 63 per sq. km (2001)

ILLITERACY RATE – (m) 5.4 per cent; (f) 11.9 per cent (2000)

HISTORY AND POLITICS

Formerly a powerful Muslim sultanate, Brunei was reduced to its present size by the mid-19th century and became a British Protectorate in 1888. In 1959 the Sultan promulgated the first written constitution and on 1 January 1984 Brunei resumed full independence from Britain.

POLITICAL SYSTEM

Supreme executive authority rests with the Sultan, who presides over and is advised by the Privy Council, the Religious Council and the Council of Ministers. The Sultan effectively rules by decree as a state of emergency has been in effect since a revolt in 1962; there are no political parties and no elections.

HEAD OF STATE

HM The Sultan of Brunei, HM Sultan Haji Hassanal Bolkiah Mu'izzaddin Waddaullah, Sultan and Yang Di-Pertuan, GCB, *acceded* 1967, *crowned* 1 August 1968

COUNCIL OF MINISTERS *as at May 2003*

Prime Minister, Defence, Finance, HM The Sultan

Communications, Pehin Dato Zakaria

Development, Pehin Dato Haji Ahmad

Deputy Ministers, Haji ibnu Basith Apong *(Defence);* Pehin Dato Paduka Haji Suyoi *(Education);* Dato Paduka Haji Yakub bin abu Bakar and Pehin Dato Haji Awang Ahmad *(Finance);* Pehin Dato Haji Ali bin Haji Awang *(Foreign Affairs);* Dato Haji Yahya bin Haji Ibrahim *(Religious Affairs)*

Education, Pehin Dato Haji Abdul Aziz

Foreign Affairs, Prince Mohamed Bolkiah

Health, Pehin Dato Haji Abu Bakar Apong

Home Affairs, Special Adviser in the Prime Minister's Office, Pehin Dato Haji Isa Utama

Industry and Primary Resources, Pehin Dato Haji Abdul Rahman Taib

Religious Affairs, Pehin Dato Haji Mohammad Zain

Youth, Sports and Culture, Pehin Dato Haji Awang Hussein

BRUNEI DARUSSALAM HIGH COMMISSION

19–20 Belgrave Square, London SW1X 8PG

Tel: 020-7581 0521

High Commissioner, HE Pengiran Haji Yunus, apptd 2001

BRITISH HIGH COMMISSION

PO Box 2197, Bandar Seri Begawan 8674

Email: brithc@brunet.bn

Tel: (00 673) (2) 222231

High Commissioner, Andrew Caie, apptd 2002

BRITISH COUNCIL DIRECTOR, Amanda Griffiths

Level 2, Block D, Yayasan Sultan Hj Hassanal Bolkiah, Jl Pretty, PO Box 3049, Bandar Seri Begawan BS8675.

Tel: (00 673) (2) 237742

Email: all.enquiries@bn.britishcouncil.org

DEFENCE

The Army has 39 armoured personnel carriers. The Navy, based in Muara, has six patrol and coastal vessels. The Air Force has five armed helicopters. On 9 January 2003 it was agreed by the Sultan and the British prime minister, Tony Blair, that a battalion of the British Brigade of Gurkhas would continue to be stationed in Brunei for a further five years from 29 September 2003.

MILITARY EXPENDITURE – 5.5 per cent of GDP (2001)
MILITARY PERSONNEL – 7,000: Army 4,900, Navy 1,000, Air Force 1,100; Paramilitaries 3,750

ECONOMY

Brunei is the fourth largest world producer of natural gas and in 1999 this was the country's top export. The economy is based on the production of this gas along with oil. Royalties and taxes from these operations form the bulk of government revenue and have enabled the construction of free health, education and welfare services.

In 1998 agriculture accounted for 2.8 per cent of GDP, trade and tourism for 12.6 per cent and finance for 8.3 per cent. Imports cover 80 per cent of domestic food requirements.

GNP – US$7,754 million (1998); US$14,240 per capita (1994)
GDP – US$4,323 million (1998); US$15,345 per capita (2000)
ANNUAL AVERAGE GROWTH OF GDP – 1.0 per cent (1998)

Trade with UK	2001	2002
Imports from UK	£59,666,000	£61,263,000
Exports to UK	34,090,000	36,442,000

COMMUNICATIONS

There are two main ports, at Muara and Kuala Belait, and an international airport at Bandar Seri Begawan. There is a road network of 2,525 km and no rail network.

BULGARIA

Republika Bălgarija – Republic of Bulgaria
AREA – 42,538 sq. miles (110,600 sq. km). Neighbours: Romania (north), Serbia and the Former Yugoslav Republic of Macedonia (west), Greece and Turkey (south)
POPULATION – 7,973,671 (2001 census): 85.7 per cent Bulgarian, 9.4 per cent Turkish, 3.7 per cent Roma, 1.2 per cent others. The language is Bulgarian, a Southern Slavonic tongue closely allied to Serbo-Croat and Russian with local admixtures of modern Greek, Albanian and Turkish words. The alphabet is Cyrillic. The predominant religion is the Bulgarian Orthodox Church (85.7 per cent of the population); Islam is the second largest religion (13.1 per cent).
CAPITAL – Sofia (population, 1,096,389, 2001 census)
MAJOR CITIES – ΨBurgas (193,310); Plovdiv (340,638); ΨVarna (314,539), 2001 census
CURRENCY – Lev of 100 stotinki
NATIONAL ANTHEM – Gorda Stara Planina (Proud And Ancient Mountains)
NATIONAL DAY – 3 March
NATIONAL FLAG – Three horizontal bands, white, green, red
LIFE EXPECTANCY (years) – 71 (2001)
POPULATION DENSITY – 71 per sq. km (2001)
URBAN POPULATION – 68 per cent (2001)

HISTORY AND POLITICS

A principality of Bulgaria was created by the Treaty of Berlin in 1878, and in 1908 the country was declared an independent kingdom. A coup d'état in September 1944 gave power to the Fatherland Front, a coalition of Communists, Agrarians and Social Democrats. In August 1945, the main body of Agrarians and Social Democrats left the government. A referendum in September 1946 led to the abolition of the monarchy and the establishment of a republic.

The Communist Party (BCP) dominated the post-war period. Bulgaria became a multiparty democracy in 1990.

In November 2001 the Bulgarian Socialist Party's (BSP) candidate, Georgi Parvanov, became president. The general election held on 17 June 2001 was won by the National Movement for Simeon II (SND), a movement founded in April 2001 by the former king, which won 43.74 per cent of the vote and 120 of the 240 seats in the legislature. Simeon Saxecoburggotski, the former King, took office as prime minister on 24 July heading a cabinet dominated by the SND.

POLITICAL SYSTEM

A new constitution was adopted in 1991. It provides for a directly-elected president who serves for no more than two five-year terms. The chief executive is the prime minister, who is appointed by the president, and is usually the leader of the largest party in the legislature. There is a unicameral National Assembly of 240 members who are directly elected by proportional representation for four-year terms.

HEAD OF STATE

President, Georgi Parvanov (BSP), *elected* 18 November 2001, *took office* 19 January 2002
Vice-President, Angel Marin (BSP)

COUNCIL OF MINISTERS *as at July 2003*
Prime Minister, Simeon Saxecoburggotski (SND)
Deputy PM, Economy, Nikolay Vassilev Vassilev (SND)
Deputy PM, Labour and Social Policy, Lydia Santova Shouleva (SND)
Agriculture and Forestry, Mekhmed Dikme (MRF)
Civil Service, Dimitar Georgiev Kalchev (BSP)
Culture, Bojidar Zafirov Abrashev (SND)
Defence, Nikolay Avramov Svinarov (SND)
Education and Science, Vladimir Atanassov (SND)
Energy and Energy Resources, Milko Kovachev
Environment and Water, Dolores Borisova Arsenova (SNP)
European Affairs, Meglena Kuneva
Finance, Milen Emilov Velchev (SND)
Foreign Affairs, Solomon Isak Passy (SND)
Health, Bojidar Todorov Finkov (SND)
Internal Affairs, Georgi Petrov Petkanov (SND)
Justice, Anton Iliev Stankov (SND)
Regional Development and Public Works, Valentin Tserovski
Transport and Communications, Plamen Vasilev Petrov (SND)
Without Portfolio, Nezhdet Ismail Mollov (MRF)

BSP Bulgarian Socialist Party; MRF Movement for Rights and Freedoms; SND Simeon II National Movement

EMBASSY OF THE REPUBLIC OF BULGARIA
186–188 Queen's Gate, London SW7 5HL
Tel: 020-7584 9400/9433
Ambassador Extraordinary and Plenipotentiary,
HE Valentin Dobrev, apptd 1998

BRITISH EMBASSY
9 Moskovska Street, Sofiia
Tel: (00 359) (2) 933 9222
Email: britembinf@mail.orbitel.bg
Ambassador Extraordinary and Plenipotentiary,
HE Ian Soutar, apptd 2001

BRITISH COUNCIL DIRECTOR, Ian Stewart
7 Krakra Street, BG-1504 Sofiia. Tel: (00 359) (2) 942 434
Email: bc.sofiia@britishcouncil.bg

DEFENCE

The Army has 1,475 main battle tanks, 214 armoured infantry fighting vehicles and 1,671 armoured personnel carriers. The Navy has one submarine, one frigate, 23 patrol and coastal vessels, and nine armed helicopters. The Air Force has 232 combat aircraft and 43 armed helicopters.
MILITARY EXPENDITURE – 2.8 per cent of GDP (2001)
MILITARY PERSONNEL – 68,450: Army 31,050, Navy 4,370, Air Force 17,780; Paramilitaries 34,000
CONSCRIPTION DURATION – Nine months

ECONOMY

The principal crops are wheat, maize, beet, tomatoes, tobacco, oleaginous seeds, fruit, vegetables and cotton. Around 24 per cent of the population is engaged in agriculture, which accounted for 14 per cent of GDP in 2000. Cadmium, coal, copper, pig iron, kaolin, lead, silver and zinc are produced. Industry accounted for 28 per cent of GDP in 2000.

The government adopted a radical reform package in 1997, including pegging the lev to the Deutsche Mark to stimulate the economy. A US$300 million agreement was negotiated with the IMF at the end of 2001 to promote economic growth.
GNP – US$12,391 million (2000); US$1,520 per capita (2000)
GDP – US$12,714 million (2001); US$1,508 per capita (2000)
ANNUAL AVERAGE GROWTH OF GDP – 3.5 per cent (1998)
INFLATION RATE – 10.3 per cent (2000)
UNEMPLOYMENT – 16.4 per cent (2000)
TOTAL EXTERNAL DEBT – US$10,026 million (2000)

TRADE

Bulgaria is highly dependent on trade and has been a member of the World Trade Organisation since 1996. The principal exports are textiles and clothing, iron and steel products, foodstuffs, beverages, industrial equipment, oil derivatives and non-ferrous metals.

In 2000 Bulgaria had a trade deficit of US$1,176 million and a current account deficit of US$701 million. In 2001 imports totalled US$7,242 million and exports US$5,109 million. The principal trading partners are Russia, Germany and Italy.

Trade with UK	2001	2002
Imports from UK	£121,130,000	£133,712,000
Exports to UK	100,706,000	119,026,000

EDUCATION

Education is free and compulsory for children from six to 16 years inclusive. There are three universities (at Sofia, Plovdiv and Veliko Turnovo), an American University and 21 higher education establishments.
ILLITERACY RATE – (m) 1.0 per cent; (f) 2.1 per cent (2000)
ENROLMENT (percentage of age group) – primary 92 per cent (1996); secondary 74 per cent (1996); tertiary 41.2 per cent (1996)

BURKINA FASO

République Démocratique du Burkina Faso – Democratic Republic of Burkina Faso

AREA – 105,792 sq. miles (274,000 sq. km).
Neighbours: Mali (west), Niger and Benin (east), Togo, Ghana and Côte d'Ivoire (south)
POPULATION – 11,087,000. The official language is French. Mossi, More, Dioula and Gourmantché are indigenous languages
CAPITAL – Ouagadougou (population, 1,000,000, 2000 estimate)
MAJOR CITIES – Bobo-Dioulasso (309,771); Koudougou (72,490), 1996 census
CURRENCY – Franc CFA of 100 centimes
NATIONAL ANTHEM – Ditanyé (Hymn of Victory)
NATIONAL DAY – 11 December
NATIONAL FLAG – Equal bands of red over green, with a yellow star in centre
POPULATION GROWTH RATE – 3 per cent
POPULATION DENSITY – 42 per sq. km (1999)
MILITARY EXPENDITURE – 1.6 per cent of GDP (2001)
MILITARY PERSONNEL – 10,200: Army 5,800, Air Force 200, Paramilitaries 4,200
ILLITERACY RATE – (m) 66.1 per cent; (f) 85.9 per cent (2000)
ENROLMENT (percentage of age group) – primary 40 per cent (1997); tertiary 1 per cent (1997)

Burkina Faso (formerly Upper Volta) is an inland savannah state in West Africa. The largest tribe is the Mossi whose king, the Moro Naba, still wields moral influence.

HISTORY AND POLITICS

Burkina Faso was annexed by France in 1896 and between 1932 and 1947 was administered as part of the Colony of the Ivory Coast. It decided on 11 December 1958 to remain an autonomous republic within the French Community; full independence outside the Community was proclaimed on 5 August 1960.

Following a number of military coups, Capt. Blaise Compaoré seized power in 1987. A new constitution was adopted in 1991. A general election was held in May 2002 and won by the Congress for Democracy and Progress group (CDP). Presidential elections were held in November 1998 and won by Compaoré, the CDP candidate, in the face of a boycott by the opposition parties.

HEAD OF STATE
President, Capt. Blaise Compaoré, *assumed office* October 1987, *elected* December 1991, *re-elected* November 1998

COUNCIL OF MINISTERS *as at July 2003*
Prime Minister, Paramanga Ernest Yonli
Animal Resources, Alphonse Bonou
Basic Education and Literacy, Mathieu Ouedraogo
Civil Service and Administrative Reform, Lassane Savadogo
Culture and Arts, Mahmadoe Ouedraogo
Defence, Kouame Lougue
Economy and Development, Seydou Bouda
Employment, Labour and Youth, Alain Ludovic Tou
Energy, Mines and Quarries, Abdoulaye Abdoukader Cisse
Environment and Quality of Life, Dakar Djiri
Finance and Budget, Jean-Baptiste Compaore
Health, Bedouma Alain Yoda
Human Rights Promotion, Monique Ilbondo
Information, Raymond Edouard Ouedraogo
Infrastructure, Housing and Urban Planning, Hyppolite Lingani
Justice, Keeper of the Seals and Promotion of Human Rights, Boureima Badini
Ministers Delegate, Arsene Armand Hien *(Literacy and Non-formal Education);* Jean de Dieu Somda *(Regional Co-operation);* Patrice Nikiema *(Transport);* Daniel Ouedraogo *(Youth)*
Ministers of State, Salif Diallo *(Agriculture and Water Resources);* Youssouf Ouedraogo *(Foreign Affairs and Regional Co-operation)*
Post and Telecommunications, Justin Tièba Thombiano
Regional Administration and Decentralisation, Moumouni Fabré
Relations with Parliament; Government Spokesman, Adama Fofana
Secondary and Higher Education, Scientific Research, Laya Sawadogo
Security, Djibril Yipene Bassole
Social Affairs and National Solidarity, Mariam Lamizana
Sports and Leisure, Tioundoum Sessouma
Trade, Industry and Crafts, Benoit Ouattara
Women's Promotion, Marie Gisele Guigma

EMBASSY OF THE REPUBLIC OF BURKINA FASO
16 Place Guy d'Arezzo, 1180 Brussels, Belgium
Tel: (00 32) (2) 345 9912
Ambassador Extraordinary and Plenipotentiary, Kadré Désiré Ouédraogo, apptd 2001

BRITISH AMBASSADOR, HE François Gordon, CMG, resident at Abidjan, Côte d'Ivoire

ECONOMY
The principal industry is cattle and sheep rearing. Agriculture employs over 90 per cent of the workforce and contributes 33 per cent of GDP. The chief exports are cotton, livestock and animal feed, and gold. The chief imports are capital goods, foodstuffs and fuel oils.

In 2001 imports totalled US$656 million and exports US$175 million.
GNP – US$2,422 million (2000); US$210 per capita (2000)
GDP – US$2,328 million (2001); US$204 per capita (2000)
ANNUAL AVERAGE GROWTH OF GDP – 2.2 per cent (2000)
INFLATION RATE – 0.3 per cent (2000)
TOTAL EXTERNAL DEBT – US$1,332 million (2000)

Trade with UK	2001	2002
Imports from UK	£7,631,000	£2,553,000
Exports to UK	3,165,000	238,000

COMMUNICATIONS
There are 12,349 km of roads, of which 1,988 km are bituminised. An estimated 60 per cent of the country's villages are further than 3 km from a main road and paths are impassable during the wet season. There are 617 km of railway track in operation. There are two main airports.

BURUNDI

République du Burundi – Republic of Burundi

AREA – 10,747 sq. miles (27,834 sq. km). Neighbours: Rwanda (north), Tanzania (east and south), Democratic Republic of Congo (west)
POPULATION – 6,194,000: 83 per cent Hutu, 15 per cent Tutsi. The official languages are Kirundi, a Bantu language, and French. Kiswahili is also used
CAPITAL – Bujumbura (formerly Usumbura) (population, 235,440, 1990)
MAJOR CITIES – Kitega (18,000)
CURRENCY – Burundi franc of 100 centimes
NATIONAL DAY – 1 July
NATIONAL FLAG – Divided diagonally by a white saltire into red and green triangles; on a white disc in the centre three red six-pointed stars edged in green
NATIONAL ANTHEM – Burundi Bwacu (Dear Burundi)
POPULATION GROWTH RATE – 2 per cent
POPULATION DENSITY – 233 per sq. km (1999)
MILITARY EXPENDITURE – 5.5 per cent of GDP (2001)
MILITARY PERSONNEL – 45,500: Army 40,000, Paramilitaries 5,500
ILLITERACY RATE – (m) 43.4 per cent; (f) 59.3 per cent (2000)
ENROLMENT (percentage of age group) – primary 51 per cent (1997); secondary 7 per cent (1997)

HISTORY AND POLITICS
Formerly a Belgian trusteeship under the United Nations, Burundi became independent as a constitutional monarchy on 1 July 1962. However, the monarchy was overthrown in 1966 and the country became a republic.

Although most of the population is Hutu, political and military power has traditionally rested with the Tutsi minority. Since the 1960s, Hutu attempts to overthrow Tutsi rule have resulted in ethnic massacres. The Tutsi-dominated army attempted a coup in 1993 in which President Melchior Ndadaye was killed. The government regained control in December but two months of inter-racial fighting left more than 50,000 dead and 500,000 refugees.

The Front for Democracy in Burundi (FRODEBU) and the National Unity and Progress Party (UPRONA) agreed to form a coalition government in 1994 with a Tutsi prime minister and Hutu president. However, the government was unable to halt attacks by the Tutsi-dominated army and Hutu militias on each other's communities. The fighting claimed 200,000 lives in 1993–5.

In July 1996 the army again seized power and installed Maj. Buyoya as president. Political parties were banned and the National Assembly was suspended until October 1996 when fewer than half its deputies attended. A multi-ethnic government of national unity was formed in August 1996.

A transitional constitution, designed to provide for a political partnership between Hutus and Tutsis, came into being in June 1998 and a 117-member Transitional

National Assembly was inaugurated in July 1998. An additional 53 members of the National Assembly were elected on 1 January 2002, in accordance with the Arusha peace deal.

In July 2001, Burundi's 19 political parties agreed a peace accord at talks hosted by former South African president, Nelson Mandela. Under the agreement, provision was made for a three-year transitional government to be headed by President Buyoya, a Tutsi, with a Hutu as vice-president – the two switching roles midway through the three-year term. In December 2002 the government signed a cease-fire agreement with the main Hutu rebel group, the National Council for the Defence of Democracy Forces for the Defence of Democracy (CNDD FDD). It was due to become effective on 30 December, but implementation of the cease-fire was delayed indefinitely. As part of the power-sharing agreement President Buyoya handed over the presidency to his Hutu vice-president, Domitien Ndayizeye, who was sworn into office on 30 April 2003 for an initial term of 18 months after which presidential elections would be held. Legislative elections were due to be held in November 2003.

HEAD OF STATE
President, Domitien Ndayizeye, *sworn in* 30 April 2003
Vice-President, Alphonse Marie Kadege

COUNCIL OF MINISTERS *as at July 2003*
Agriculture and Livestock, Pierre Ndikumagenge
Civil Service, Festus Ntanyungu
Communications and Government Spokesman, Albert Mbonerane
Community Development, Casimir Ngendanganya
Defence, Maj.-Gen. Vincent Niyungeko
Development Planning and Reconstruction, Seraphine Wakana
Energy and Mines, Andre Nkundikije
External Relations and Co-operation, Therence Sinunguruza
Finance, Athanase Gahungu
Good Governance and Privatisation, Didace Kiganahe
Handicrafts, Vocational Training and Adult Literacy, Godefroy Hakizimana
Institutional Reforms, Human Rights and Relations with Parliament, Alphonse Barancira
Internal Affairs and Public Security, Salvator Nthabose
Justice, Keeper of the Seals, Fulgence Dwima-Bakana
Labour and Social Security, Dismas Nditabiriye
Minister in the Prime Minister's Office in charge of AIDS Control, Genevieve Sindabizera
Mobilisation for Peace and National Reconciliation, Luc Rukingama
National Education, Prosper Mpawenayo
Public Health, Jean Kamana
Public Works and Equipment, Gaspard Kobako
Reintegration and Resettlement of Displaced Persons and Repatriates, Françoise Ngendahayo
Social Action and Women's Promotion, Marie Goreth Nduwimana
Territorial Development, Environment and Tourism, Barnabe Muteragiranwa
Trade and Industry, Charles Karikurubu
Transport, Posts and Telecommunications, Severin Ndikumugongo
Youth, Culture and Sports, Rodolphe Baranyizigiye

EMBASSY OF THE REPUBLIC OF BURUNDI
46 Sq. Marie Louise, 1000 Brussels, Belgium
Tel: (00 32) (2) 2304535
Ambassador Extraordinary and Plenipotentiary, HE Ferdinand Nyabenda, apptd 2003

BRITISH AMBASSADOR, HE Susan Hogwood, MBE, apptd 2001, resident at Kigali, Rwanda

ECONOMY
The chief crops are coffee and tea, accounting for around 98 per cent of export earnings. Mineral, hide and skin exports are also important. Agriculture accounted for 54 per cent of GDP and employed over 90 per cent of the workforce in 1998. On 9 October 2002 the IMF approved a credit of US$7.3 million in emergency post-conflict assistance to support the country's reconstruction and economic recovery programme.

In 2000 there was a trade deficit of US$59 million and a current account deficit of US$49 million. In 2001 imports totalled US$139 million and exports US$39 million.

GNP – US$732 million (2000); US$110 per capita (2000)
GDP – US$689 million (2001); US$124 per capita (2000)
ANNUAL AVERAGE GROWTH OF GDP – 4.5 per cent (1998)
INFLATION RATE – 24.3 per cent (2000)
TOTAL EXTERNAL DEBT – US$1,100 million (2000)

Trade with UK	2001	2002
Imports from UK	£2,205,000	£1,712,000
Exports to UK	954,000	434,000

CAMBODIA

*Preăh Réachéanachâkr Kâmpuchéa –
The Kingdom of Cambodia*

AREA – 186,160 sq. miles (181,035 sq. km).
  Neighbours: Laos (north), Thailand (north and west), Vietnam (east)
POPULATION – 11,437,656 (1998 census). The official language is Khmer. Chinese, Vietnamese and French are also spoken
CAPITAL – ΨPhnom Penh (population, 832,000, 1998 census)
CURRENCY – Riel of 100 sen
NATIONAL ANTHEM – Nokoreach
NATIONAL DAY – 9 November (Independence Day)
NATIONAL FLAG – Three horizontal stripes of blue, red, blue, with the blue of double width and containing a representation of the temple of Angkor in white
POPULATION GROWTH RATE – 2.7 per cent
POPULATION DENSITY – 60 per sq. km (1999)
ENROLMENT (percentage of age group) – primary 100 per cent (1997); tertiary 24 per cent (1997)

HISTORY AND POLITICS
Cambodia became a French protectorate in 1863 and was granted independence within the French Union as an Associate State in 1949. Full independence was proclaimed in 1953, and Prince Norodom Sihanouk became head of state. In 1970 Prince Sihanouk was deposed and a Khmer Republic was declared.
In 1975, Phnom Penh fell to the North Vietnamese-

backed Khmer Rouge. During Khmer Rouge rule hundreds of thousands of Cambodians fled into exile and an estimated two million were killed.

In 1978, Vietnamese troops invaded Cambodia and the state was renamed the People's Republic of Kampuchea (PRK); in 1989 it became the State of Cambodia (SOC). Following the Vietnamese withdrawal in 1989, the resistance forces regained ground.

In September 1990, the government and the resistance forces established a Supreme National Council and peace agreements were signed in October 1991. In March 1992 the United Nations Transitional Authority for Cambodia (UNTAC) assumed authority from the government in the run-up to the multiparty elections, which were held in May 1993. In September 1993 a new constitution was adopted under which Cambodia became a pluralist liberal democracy with a constitutional monarchy. Prince Sihanouk was elected king and he appointed a new government.

In November 1998 a coalition government was formed with Hun Sen as prime minister and Prince Ranariddh as chairman of the National Assembly. Elections to the National Assembly were held on 27 July 2003. Prime Minister Hun Sen and his Cambodian People's Party won a majority of the votes, though Hun Sen was expected to fall short of the two-thirds majority required to rule in his own right. Full results were expected in September.

INSURGENCIES

The Khmer Rouge was outlawed in 1994 and its leader Pol Pot was captured by a group of defectors in June 1997 and died in captivity on 15 April 1998. The remaining 4,332 Khmer Rouge soldiers surrendered on 9 February 1999.

In 1997 negotiations began between the Royal Government and the UN to set up an international tribunal to prosecute former leaders of the Khmer Rouge regime for atrocities committed during its rule. On 15 January 2001 the Royal Government approved legislation for the creation of the tribunal but in February 2002 the UN broke off negotiations claiming that the planned court did not comply with international standards of justice. Negotiations resumed in November 2002 and on 6 June 2003 an agreement was signed by Cambodia and the UN allowing the majority of tribunal judges to be Cambodian but with a requirement for at least one foreign judge to support a tribunal ruling.

POLITICAL SYSTEM

Legislative power is vested in the National Assembly, which has 122 members elected for five-year terms, and the Senate, which has 61 appointed members and was formed on 25 March 1999, following an amendment to the constitution by the National Assembly. Executive power rests in the Royal Government, with the King having the power only to make appointments and declare a state of emergency, in consultation with the government.

HEAD OF STATE

HM The King of Cambodia, Norodom Sihanouk,
elected by the Council of the Throne 24 September 1993
Chair of the National Assembly, Norodom Ranariddh (F)

ROYAL GOVERNMENT OF CAMBODIA

as at July 2003
Prime Minister, Hun Sen (CPP)
Deputy Prime Minister, Co-Minister of Interior,
Sar Kheng (CPP)

Deputy Prime Minister, Education, Youth and Sports,
Tol Loah (F)
Agriculture, Forestry and Fishing, Personal Advisor to the Prime Minister, Chan Sarun (CCP)
Co-Minister of National Defence,
Prince Sisowath Sereiroat (F)
Commerce, Cham Prasit (CPP)
Culture and Fine Arts, Princess Norodom Bophadevi (F)
Environment, Mok Maret (CPP)
Industry, Mines and Energy, Suy Sem (CPP)
Justice, Neav Sithong (F)
Landscaping, Urbanism and Construction,
Im Chhunlim (CPP)
Planning, Chhay Than (CPP)
Post and Telecommunications, So Khun (CPP)
Public Works and Transport, Khi Tanglim (F)
Relations with National Assembly and Inspection,
Khun Hang (F)
Religious Affairs, Chea Savoeun (F)
Rural Development, Li Thuch (F)
Senior Minister, Co-Minister of Interior, Yu Hokkri (F)
Senior Minister, Co-Minister of National Defence,
Gen. Tie Banh (CPP)
Senior Minister, Economy and Finance, Keat Chhon (CPP)
Senior Minister, Foreign Affairs and International Co-operation, Hor Namhong (F)
Senior Minister, Health, Hong Sun-huot (F)
Senior Minister, Information and Press, Loe Lay-sreng (F)
Senior Minister, Office of the Council of Ministers,
Sok An (CPP)
Social Affairs, Labour, Vocational Training and Youth Rehabilitation, It Sam-heng (CPP)
Tourism, Veng Sereivut (F)
Water Resources, Lim Kean-hao (CPP)
Women's and Veterans' Affairs, Mu Sok-huo (F)

CPP Cambodian People's Party; F United National Front for an Independent, Neutral, Peaceful and Co-operative Cambodia (FUNCINPEC)

ROYAL EMBASSY OF CAMBODIA
4 rue Adolph Yvon, F-75116 Paris, France
Tel: (00 33) (1) 45 03 4720
Ambassador Extraordinary and Plenipotentiary, HE Prak Sokhonn, apptd 1999

BRITISH EMBASSY
29 Street 75, Phnom Penh
Tel: (00 855) (23) 427124/428295
Ambassador Extraordinary and Plenipotentiary,
HE Stephen Bridges, apptd 2001

DEFENCE

The Army has 150 main battle tanks and 190 armoured personnel carriers. The Navy has 4 patrol and coastal vessels. The Air Force has 24 combat aircraft.
MILITARY EXPENDITURE – 5.8 per cent of GDP (2001)
MILITARY PERSONNEL – 125,000: Army 75,000, Navy 3,000, Air Force 2,000, Provincial Forces 45,000; Paramilitaries 67,000

ECONOMY

The economy is largely based on agriculture, fishing and forestry. Agriculture employs over 70 per cent of the workforce and produced 32 per cent of GDP in 2001. In addition to rice, which is the staple crop, the major products are rubber, livestock, maize, timber, pepper, palm sugar, fresh and dried fish, kapok, beans, soya and tobacco. Textiles, leather goods, furnishings, timber and rubber are the main exports; the main imports are cigarettes, gold, diesel and oil.

Extreme drought and flooding in 2002 ruined some US$30 million worth of rice crops. Cambodia's debt to China was written off in November 2002.

In 2000 there was a trade deficit of US$198 million and a current account deficit of US$19 million. Imports totalled US$1,419 million and exports totalled US$1,359 million.

GNP – US$3,150 million (2000); US$260 per capita (2000)

GDP – US$3,384 million (2001); US$237 per capita (2000)

ANNUAL AVERAGE GROWTH OF GDP –1.3 per cent (1998)

INFLATION RATE – 0.8 per cent (2000)

TOTAL EXTERNAL DEBT – US$2,357 million (2000)

Trade with UK	2001	2002
Imports from UK	£3,309,000	£3,871,000
Exports to UK	85,164,000	88,871,000

COMMUNICATIONS

The country has about 34,100 kilometres of roads, although most are now in a state of disrepair. There are two railways, one from Phnom Penh to the Thai border, the other from Phnom Penh to Kampot and Sihanoukville (Kompong Som). Phnom Penh is on a river capable of receiving ships of up to 2,500 tons all the year round. The deep water port at Sihanoukville (Kompong Som) on the Gulf of Thailand can receive ships of up to 10,000 tons. The port is linked to Phnom Penh by a modern highway.

CAMEROON

République du Cameroun – Republic of Cameroon

AREA – 186,160 sq. miles (465,400 sq. km).
  Neighbours: Nigeria (north and west), Chad and Central African Republic (east), Republic of Congo-Brazzaville, Gabon and Equatorial Guinea (south)
POPULATION – 15,203,000. French and English are both official languages and enjoy equal status
CAPITAL – Yaoundé (population, 653,670, 1986 estimate)
MAJOR CITIES – ΨDouala (1,029,731) is the commercial centre
CURRENCY – Franc CFA of 100 centimes
NATIONAL ANTHEM – O Cameroun, Berceau De Nos Ancêtres (O Cameroon, Thou Cradle Of Our Forefathers)
NATIONAL DAY – 20 May
NATIONAL FLAG – Vertical stripes of green, red and yellow with single five-pointed yellow star in centre of red stripe
LIFE EXPECTANCY (years) – 50 (2001)
POPULATION GROWTH RATE – 2.4 per cent
POPULATION DENSITY – 33 per sq. km (2001)
MILITARY EXPENDITURE – 1.3 per cent of GDP (2001)
MILITARY PERSONNEL – 23,100: Army 12,500, Navy 1,300, Air Force 300, Paramilitaries 9,000
ILLITERACY RATE – (m) 17.9 per cent; (f) 30.0 per cent (2000)
ENROLMENT (percentage of age group) – secondary 85 per cent (1997)

HISTORY AND POLITICS

The German colony of the Cameroons, established in 1884, was captured by British and French forces in 1916 and divided into the League of Nations-mandated territories (later UN trusteeships) of East (French) and West (British) Cameroon. On 1 January 1960 East Cameroon became independent as the Republic of Cameroon. This was joined on 1 October 1961 by the southern part of West Cameroon after a plebiscite held under United Nations auspices; the northern part joined Nigeria. Cameroon became a federal republic with separate East and West Cameroon state governments. After a plebiscite held in 1972, Cameroon became a unitary republic and a one-party state.

A coalition government was formed after the multiparty elections of March 1992, following extensive unrest.

The Cameroon People's Democratic Movement (RDCP) retained its overall majority of seats in the National Assembly in the legislative election of 30 June 2002. Opposition groups widespread fraud in the conduct of the elections.

INTERNATIONAL RELATIONS

There have been armed clashes with Nigeria over the disputed Bakassi peninsula. In October 2002 Cameroon was given possession of the peninsula in a ruling by the International Court of Justice. Nigeria was awarded a series of other strategically significant territories near the land border. It was agreed on 15 November 2002 that a UN-led commission would be established to defuse tension in the long-running dispute.

POLITICAL SYSTEM

The president is directly elected for a seven-year term, and appoints the prime minister and Cabinet. The National Assembly comprises 180 members, directly elected for a five-year term. Under the 1995 constitutional amendments a Senate is to be created.

HEAD OF STATE

President and Commander-in-Chief of the Armed Forces,
  Paul Biya, *acceded* 6 November 1982, *elected*
  14 January 1984, *re-elected* 24 April 1988,
  10 October 1992, 12 October 1997

CABINET *as at July 2003*
Prime Minister, Peter Mafany Musonge
Agriculture, Augustin Frederick Kodock
Civil Service and Administrative Reform, René Ze Nguele
Communication, Jacques Famé Ndongo
Culture, Ferdinand Leopold Oyono
Economic Affairs, Planning and Land Management,
  Martin Aristide Okouda
Employment, Robert Nkili
Environment and Forests, Tanyi Mbianyor Oben
Finance, Michel Meva'a M'Eboutou
Foreign Affairs, François-Xavier N'Goubeyou
Higher Education, Maurice Tchuente
Housing, Adji Abdoulaye Haman
Industrial and Commercial Development,
  Bello Bouba Maigari
Interior, Marafa Hamidou Yaya
Justice, Keeper of the Seals, Ali Amadou
Livestock, Fisheries and Animal Industries,
  Hamadjoda Ajoudji
Mines, Water Resources and Energy, Joseph Aoudou
National Education, Joseph Owona
Parliamentary Relations, Grégoire Owona
Post and Telecommunications, Maximin Koué Kongo
Public Health, Urbain Olanguena Awono
Public Works, Dieudonne Ambassa Zang
Science and Technology, Zacharie Perevet

Secretary-General of the Presidency, Jean-Marie
  Atangana Mebara
Social Affairs, Cecile Bomba Nkolo
Technical and Professional Training, Louis Bapes Bapes
Tourism, Pierre Hele
Town Planning, Lekene Donfack
Transport, Ndeh John Begheni
Women's Affairs, Catherine Bakang Mbock
Youth and Sports, Bidoung Mkpatt

HIGH COMMISSION FOR THE REPUBLIC OF
CAMEROON
84 Holland Park, London W11 3SB
Tel: 020-7727 0771
Ambassador Extraordinary and Plenipotentiary,
  HE Samuel Libock-Mbei, apptd 1995

BRITISH HIGH COMMISSION
Avenue Winston Churchill, BP 547 Yaoundé
Tel: (00 237) (2) 220545
High Commissioner, HE Richard Wildash, LVO,
  apptd 2002

BRITISH COUNCIL DIRECTOR, June Rollinson
Avenue Charles de Gaulle, BP 818, Yaoundé.
Tel: (00 237) (2) 211696/203172
Email: bc-yaounde@britishcouncil.cm

ECONOMY

Principal products are cocoa, coffee, bananas, cotton,
timber, groundnuts, aluminium, rubber and palm
products. Crude petroleum is also one of Cameroon's
principal products.

France, Italy, Spain, Belgium and Nigeria are
Cameroon's main trading partners. In 1995 there was a
trade surplus of US$627 million and a current account
surplus of US$90 million. In 1999 exports totalled
US$1,601 million and imports US$1,318 million.

GNP – US$8,644 million (2000); US$580 per capita
  (2000)
GDP – US$8,591 million (2001); US$626 per capita
  (2000)
ANNUAL AVERAGE GROWTH OF GDP –
  5.2 per cent (1998)
INFLATION RATE – 5.3 per cent (1999)
TOTAL EXTERNAL DEBT – US$9,241 million (2000)

Trade with UK	2001	2002
Imports from UK	£35,901,000	£35,739,000
Exports to UK	40,397,000	64,673,000

CANADA

AREA – 3,546,538 sq. miles (9,221,000 sq. km).
  Neighbours: USA (south), Alaska (USA) (west)
POPULATION – 30,871,957 (2001). The languages are
  English and French
CAPITAL – Ottawa (population, 1,063,664, 2001
  census).
MAJOR CITIES – Calgary (951,395); Edmonton
  (937,845); Hamilton (662,401); ΨMontréal
  (3,426,350); Québec (682,757); Toronto (4,682,897);
  ΨVancouver (1,986,965); Winnipeg (671,274),
  2001 census
CURRENCY – Canadian dollar (C$) of 100 cents
NATIONAL ANTHEM – O Canada

NATIONAL DAY – 1 July (Canada Day)
NATIONAL FLAG – Red maple leaf with 11 points on
  white square, flanked by vertical red bars one-half the
  width of the square
LIFE EXPECTANCY (years) – 79 (2001)
POPULATION GROWTH RATE – 1 per cent
POPULATION DENSITY – 3 per sq. km (2001)
URBAN POPULATION – 79 per cent (2001)

Canada occupies the whole of the northern part of the
North American continent, with the exception of Alaska.
In eastern Canada, the southernmost point is Middle
Island in Lake Erie. Canada has six main physiographic
divisions: the Appalachian-Acadian region, the Canadian
shield, which comprises more than half the country, the
St Lawrence-Great Lakes lowland, the interior plains, the
Cordilleran region and the Arctic archipelago.

The climate of the eastern and central portions presents
greater extremes than in corresponding latitudes in
Europe, but in the south-western portion of the prairie
region and the southern portions of the Pacific slope the
climate is milder.

HISTORY AND POLITICS

Canada was originally discovered by Cabot in 1497 and
the French took possession of the country in 1534. The
first permanent settlement at Port Royal (now Annapolis),
Nova Scotia, was founded in 1605, and Québec was
founded in 1608. In 1759 Québec was captured by
British forces under General Wolfe and in 1763 the
whole territory of Canada became a possession of Great
Britain by the Treaty of Paris 1763. Nova Scotia was
ceded in 1713 by the Treaty of Utrecht, the provinces of
New Brunswick and Prince Edward Island being subsequently formed out of it. British Columbia was formed
into a Crown colony in 1858, having previously been a
part of the Hudson Bay Territory, and was united to
Vancouver Island in 1866.

The constitution of Canada has its source in the British
North America Act of 1867 which formed a Dominion,
under the name of Canada, of the four provinces of
Ontario, Québec, New Brunswick and Nova Scotia. To
this federation the other provinces and territories have
subsequently been admitted: Manitoba and Northwest
Territories (1870), British Columbia (1871), Prince
Edward Island (1873), Yukon (1898), Alberta and
Saskatchewan (1905) and Newfoundland (1949). In
1982, the constitution was patriated (severed from the
British parliament) with the approval of all provinces
except Québec. In 1985, the federal prime minister and
the provincial premiers concluded the Meech Lake
Accord which provided for Québec to be recognised as a
distinct society within Canada. However, two provincial
legislatures withheld approval and the accord did not
come into force. In Québec, a referendum calling for
sovereignty and a new political and economic partnership
was defeated in October 1995. In September 1997
Québec was recognised as having a 'unique character' by
leaders of the other provinces and territories. A new
territory, Nunavut, which means 'our land' in the Inuit
language of Inuktitut, was created on 1 April 1999 by
partitioning the Northwest Territories.

In the federal election on 27 November 2000 the
Liberal Party won a third consecutive term of office. The
state of parties in the House of Commons following the
election was Liberals 172, Canadian Alliance 66, Bloc
Québécois 38, New Democrats 13, and Progressive
Conservatives 12.

FEDERAL STRUCTURE

Provinces or Territories (with official contractions)	Area (sq.km)	Population, 1 January 2001	Capital	Lieutenant-Governor	Premier
Alberta (AB)	661,848	3,022,861	Edmonton	Lois Hole	Ralph Klein
British Columbia (BC)	944,735	4,077,369	Victoria	Iona Campagnolo	Gordon Campbell
Manitoba (MB)	647,797	1,149,220	Winnipeg	Peter Liba	Gary Doer
New Brunswick (NB)	72,908	757,267	Fredericton	Marilyn Trenholme Counsell	Bernard Lord
Newfoundland and Labrador (NF)	405,212	537,797	St John's	Arthur House	Roger Grimes
Northwest Territories (NT)	1,346,106	42,105	Yellowknife	†Daniel Joseph Marion	Stephen Kakfwi
Nova Scotia (NS)	55,284	942,322	Halifax	Myra Freeman	John Hamm
Nunavut (NT)§	2,093,190	27,978	Iqaluit	†Peter Irniq	Paul Okalik
Ontario (ON)	1,076,395	11,741,793	Toronto	James Bartleman	Ernie Eves
Prince Edward Island (PE)	5,660	139,078	Charlottetown	J. Léonce Bernard	Patrick Binns
Québec (QC)	1,542,056	7,383,300	Québec	Lise Thibault	Jean Charest
Saskatchewan (SK)	651,036	1,020,650	Regina	Lynda Haverstock	Lorne Calvert
Yukon Territory (YT)	482,443	30,194	Whitehorse	†Judy Gingell	Dennis Fentie

Area figures include land and water area
† Commissioner
§ Nunavut was created in 1999 from the Northwest Territories

POLITICAL SYSTEM

Executive power is vested in a Governor-General appointed by the Sovereign on the advice of the prime minister.

Parliament consists of a Senate and a House of Commons. The Senate consists of 105 members, nominated by the Governor-General on the advice of the prime minister, the seats being distributed between the various provinces. The House of Commons has 301 members directly elected for a five-year term. Representation is proportional to the population of each province.

The judicature is administered by judges following the civil law in Québec province and common law in other provinces. Each province has a Court of Appeal. All superior, county and district court judges are appointed by the Governor General, the others by the Lieutenant-Governors of the provinces.

The highest federal court is the Supreme Court of Canada, which exercises general appellate jurisdiction throughout Canada in civil and criminal cases. There is one other federally constituted court, the Federal Court of Canada, which has jurisdiction on appeals from its trial division, from federal tribunals and reviews of decisions and references by federal boards and commissions.

GOVERNOR-GENERAL
Governor-General and Commander-in-Chief,
HE Adrienne Clarkson

FEDERAL CABINET *as at July 2003*
Prime Minister, Jean Chrétien
Deputy Prime Minister, Finance and National Security,
   John Manley
Agriculture and Agri-Food, Lyle Vanclief
Canadian Wheat Board, Public Works and Government
   Services and Federal Interlocutor for Métis and Non-status
   Indians, Ralph Goodale
Citizenship and Immigration, Denis Coderre
Environment, David Anderson
Fisheries and Oceans, Robert Thibault
Foreign Affairs, William Graham
Health, Anne McLellan
Heritage, Sheila Copps
Human Resources Development, Jane Stewart
Indian Affairs and Northern Development,
   Robert Daniel Nault
Industry and Infrastructure, Allan Rock
Intergovernmental Affairs, President of the Privy Council,
   Stéphane Dion
International Co-operation, Susan Whelan
International Trade, Pierre Pettigrew
Justice and Attorney-General, Martin Cauchon
Labour, Claudette Bradshaw
Leader of the Government in the House of Commons,
   Don Boudria
Leader of the Government in the Senate, Sharon Carstairs
Minister of State (Atlantic Canada Opportunities Agency),
   Gerry Byrne
National Defence, John McCallum
National Revenue, Elinor Caplan
Natural Resources, Herb Dhaliwal
President of the Treasury Board, Lucienne Robillard
Secretaries of State, Paul DeVillers *(Amateur Sport, Deputy*
   Leader of the Government in the House of Commons);
   David Kilgour *(Asia-Pacific);* Gar Knutson
   (Central and Eastern Europe and Middle East);
   Ethel Blondin-Andrews *(Children and Youth);*
   Claude Drouin *(Economic Development Agency of*
   Canada for the Regions of Quebec); Maurizio Bevilacqua
   (International Financial Institutions); Denis Paradis
   (Latin America and Africa, Francophone Affairs);
   Jean Augustine *(Multiculturalism and Status of Women);*
   Andrew Mitchell *(Rural Development);* Stephen Owen
   (Western Economic Diversification, Indian Affairs and
   Northern Development)
Solicitor-General, Wayne Easter
Transport, David Collenette
Veterans' Affairs, Secretary of State for Science, Research and
   Development, Rey Pagtakhan

CANADIAN HIGH COMMISSION
Macdonald House, 1 Grosvenor Square, London W1K 4AB
Tel: 020-7258 6600
Canada House, Pall Mall East, London SW1Y 5BJ
High Commissioner, HE Mel Cappe, apptd 2002

BRITISH HIGH COMMISSION
80 Elgin Street, Ottawa K1P 5K7
Tel: (00 1) (613) 237 1530
High Commissioner, HE Sir Andrew Burns, KCMG,
   apptd 2000

CONSULATES-GENERAL – Montréal,
Toronto, Vancouver
CONSULATES – Halifax/Dartmouth, Québec City,
St John's, Winnipeg

BRITISH COUNCIL DIRECTOR, Peter Chenery
c/o British High Commission; Tel: (00 1) (613) 237 1530;
Email: ottawa.enquiries@ca.britishcouncil.org

BRITISH COUNCIL DIRECTOR IN QUÉBEC,
Sarah Dawbarn, 1000 ouest rue de La Gauchetière, Bureau
4200, Montréal, Québec H3B 4W5. Tel: (00 1) (514) 866 5863
Email: montreal.enquiries@ca.britishcouncil.org

DEFENCE

The Canadian armed forces are unified and organised
into three functional commands: Land Force Command;
Maritime Command; Air Command.

The Army (Land Forces) has 114 main battle tanks and
1,275 armoured personnel carriers. The Navy (Maritime
Forces) has two submarines, four destroyers, 12 frigates
and 14 patrol and coastal vessels. The Air Force has 140
combat aircraft.

MILITARY EXPENDITURE – 1.1 per cent of GDP (2001)
MILITARY PERSONNEL – 52,300: Army 19,300, Navy
   9,000, Air Force 13,500, Paramilitaries 9,350

ECONOMY

About 68 million hectares of land is farmed, around 7.3
per cent of the total land area. Over 60 per cent of this is
under cultivation, the remainder being predominantly
classified as unimproved pasture. More than 80 per cent of
the cultivated land is in the prairie region of western
Canada. The country is one of the world's leading food
producers and in 2000 agriculture accounted for 2.3 per
cent of GDP and employs about 3.7 per cent of the labour
force.

Almost half of Canada's land area is forest, making it
the world's largest exporter of timber, pulp and newsprint.
The fishing industry contributed C$1,657 million in
1998, but Atlantic fish stocks are under restriction orders.

Canada is one of the world's largest producers of
potash and uranium, nickel, asbestos, cadmium, zinc and
elemental sulphur. The country is also rich in gold, copper,
lead, molybdenum, platinum group metals, gypsum,
cobalt, titanium concentrates, and aluminium. The total
value of mineral production in 2000 was C$83,854
million.

Production of gold in 2002 was 4.8 million ounces
(estimate) and production of silver in 2000 was 37.7
million ounces. Uranium production in 2001 was 14,743
tonnes.

The services sector contributed to 67.3 per cent of
GDP in 2000 with finance and real estate generating the
most revenue at 16.1 per cent.

There were 18.8 million foreign tourists in 1998, who
accounted for receipts of C$11.2 billion.

Canada had relatively high growth in GDP during
2002 at 3.3 per cent and this allowed for an increase of
11.5 per cent in federal expenditure for 2003–4.

GNP – US$649,829 million (2000); US$21,130 per
   capita (2000)
GDP – US$677,178 million (2001); US$22,778
   per capita (2000)
ANNUAL AVERAGE GROWTH OF GDP – 3.3 per cent
   (2002)
INFLATION RATE – 2.7 per cent (2000)
UNEMPLOYMENT – 6.8 per cent (2000)

TRADE

The main exports are automotive products, including cars, trucks and parts, machinery and equipment, industrial products and raw materials, forestry products, including wood, wood pulp and paper products, agricultural products (chiefly wheat and meat products), fishery products, and energy products, including crude petroleum and natural gas.

Trade with the USA accounts for about 86 per cent of Canada's exports and 77 per cent of its imports.

In 2001 imports totalled US$227,291 million and exports US$259,858 million. There was a trade surplus of US$41,425 million and a current account surplus of US$19,479 million.

Trade with UK	2001	2002
Imports from UK	£3,251,220,000	£3,152,213,000
Exports to UK	3,787,129,000	3,688,378,000

COMMUNICATIONS

In 1999 there were 901,902 km of roads, of which 318,371 km were paved, including 16,571 km of national highways. The 7,300 km Trans-Canadian Highway links all ten provinces. There are about 50,000 km of railway track in operation.

The bulk of canal shipping in Canada is handled through the two sections of the St Lawrence Seaway, which provide access to the Great Lakes for ocean-going ships.

EDUCATION

Education is under the control of the provincial governments, the cost of the publicly controlled schools being met by local taxation, aided by provincial grants. Education is compulsory between the ages of six or seven and 15 or 16. There are 100 universities and 200 technical institutes and community colleges.

ENROLMENT (percentage of age group) – primary 100 per cent (1997); secondary 100 per cent (1997); tertiary 88 per cent (1997)

CAPE VERDE

República de Cabo Verde – Republic of Cape Verde

AREA – 1,557 sq. miles (4,033 sq. km). Comprising the Windward Islands (Santo Antão, São Vicente, Santa Luzia, São Nicolau, Bõa Vista and Sal) and Leeward Islands (Maio, São Tiago, Fogo and Brava)
POPULATION – 406,000, the majority of whom are Roman Catholic. The official language is Portuguese; a creole is spoken by most of the population
CAPITAL – ΨPraia (population, 61,644, 1995 estimate)
CURRENCY – Escudo Caboverdiano of 100 centavos
NATIONAL ANTHEM – Patria Amada (This Is Our Beloved Country)
NATIONAL DAY – 5 July (Independence Day)
NATIONAL FLAG – Blue with three horizontal stripes of white, red, white near the bottom; over all on these near the hoist a ring of ten yellow stars
POPULATION GROWTH RATE – 2 per cent
POPULATION DENSITY – 104 per sq. km (1999)
MILITARY EXPENDITURE – 1.8 per cent of GDP (2001)
MILITARY PERSONNEL – 1,200: Army 1,000, Air Force 100, Coast Guard 100
CONSCRIPTION DURATION – Selective conscription
ILLITERACY RATE – (m) 15.2 per cent; (f) 33.8 per cent (2000)

ENROLMENT (percentage of age group) – primary 100 per cent (1989); secondary 48 per cent (1997)

HISTORY AND POLITICS

The islands, colonised c.1460, achieved independence from Portugal on 5 July 1975 under the Partido Africano da Independência da Guiné e Cabo Verde (PAIGC). A federation of the islands with Guinea Bissau was planned but this was dropped following the 1980 coup in Guinea Bissau.

The republic was a one-party state under the African Party for the Independence of Cape Verde (PAICV) until the constitution was amended in 1990. Multiparty elections, held in January 1991, were won by the opposition Movement for Democracy (MPD), which was re-elected in December 1995. President António Mascarenhas Monteiro of the MPD was elected in February 1991 and re-elected unopposed in February 1996. The general election held on 14 January 2001 returned the PAICV to power with 40 of the 72 seats in the National Assembly. The MPD won 30 seats and the Democratic Alliance for Change won two seats. Pedro Pires of the PAICV narrowly won the second round of the presidential election held on 25 February 2001 by 164 votes. The MPD candidate, Carlos Veiga, appealed to the Supreme Court, citing irregularities in the conduct of the elections; the court upheld some of the appeals, which reduced Pires's winning margin to just 12 votes.

HEAD OF STATE
President, Pedro Pires, *elected* 25 February 2001, *assumed office* 22 March 2001

COUNCIL OF MINISTERS *as at May 2003*
Prime Minister, José Maria Neves
Deputy Minister for Culture and Sports, Jorge Tolentino
Economy, Growth and Competitiveness, Avelino Bonifacio
Education, Human Resources Development, Victor Borges
Environment, Agriculture and Fisheries, Madalena Neves
Finance, Planning and Regional Development, Carlos Augusto Duarte Burgo
Foreign Affairs and Communities, Fatima Lima Veiga
Justice and Interior, Cristina Fontes
Labour, Employment and Solidarity, Julio Correia
Parliamentary Affairs and Defence, Armindo Cipriano Mauricio
Presidency of the Council of Ministers, Media, Arnaldo Andrade
Senior Minister for Health, Basilio Ramos
Senior Minister for Infrastructure and Transport, Manuel Inocencio Sousa

EMBASSY OF THE REPUBLIC OF CAPE VERDE
Avenue Jeane 29, 1050 Brussels, Belgium
Ambassador Extraordinary and Plenipotentiary, vacant

BRITISH AMBASSADOR, HE Alan Burner, resident at Dakar, Senegal
There is a British Consulate on São Vicente.

ECONOMY

The islands have little rain and agriculture is mostly confined to irrigated inland valleys. The chief products are bananas and coffee (for export), maize, sugar cane and nuts. Fish and shellfish are important exports. Salt is obtained on Sal, Bõa Vista and Maio; volcanic rock is also mined for export.

In 1998 there was a trade deficit of US$186 million and a current account deficit of US$58 million. In 2001 imports totalled US$248 million and exports US$10 million.

The main ports are Praia and Mindelo, and there is an international airport on Sal.

GNP – US$588 million (2000); US$1,330 per capita (2000)

GDP – US$588 million (2001); US$1,299 per capita (2000)

ANNUAL AVERAGE GROWTH OF GDP – 3.0 per cent (1998)

INFLATION RATE – 4.4 per cent (1998)

TOTAL EXTERNAL DEBT – US$327 million (2000)

Trade with UK	2001	2002
Imports from UK	£4,080,000	£5,854,000
Exports to UK	2,877,000	4,069,000

CENTRAL AFRICAN REPUBLIC

République Centrafricaine/Ködrö tî Bê-Afrîka – Central African Republic

AREA – 240,535 sq. miles (622,984 sq. km).
   Neighbours: Chad (north), Sudan (east), Democratic Republic of Congo and Congo-Brazzaville (south), Cameroon (west)

POPULATION – 3,245,000. French is the official language; the national language is Sangho.

CAPITAL – Bangui (population, 473,817, 1984 estimate)

CURRENCY – Franc CFA of 100 centimes

NATIONAL ANTHEM – La Renaissance (The Revival)

NATIONAL DAY – 1 December

NATIONAL FLAG – Four horizontal stripes, blue, white, green, yellow, crossed by central vertical red stripe with a yellow five-pointed star in top left-hand corner

POPULATION GROWTH RATE – 1.9 per cent

POPULATION DENSITY – 6 per sq. km (1999)

MILITARY EXPENDITURE – 1.6 per cent of GDP (2001)

MILITARY PERSONNEL – 2,550: Army 1,400, Air Force 150, Paramilitaries 1,000

CONSCRIPTION DURATION – Two years (selective)

ILLITERACY RATE – (m) 40.2 per cent; (f) 65.1 per cent (2000)

ENROLMENT (percentage of age group) – primary 53 per cent (1990); tertiary 1.4 per cent (1991)

HISTORY AND POLITICS

In December 1958 the French colony of Ubanghi Shari elected to remain within the French Community and adopted the title of the Central African Republic. It became fully independent on 17 August 1960. The first president, David Dacko, was overthrown in 1966 by the then Col. Bokassa, who in 1976 proclaimed himself Emperor and renamed the country the Central African Empire. In 1979 Bokassa was deposed by Dacko in a bloodless coup and the country reverted to a republic. President Dacko surrendered power in 1981 to Gen. André Kolingba, who instituted military rule until 1985, when a civilian-dominated Cabinet was appointed. In November 1986 a referendum was held which approved a new constitution and the establishment of a one-party state.

President Kolingba formed a coalition government in February 1993. Ange-Félix Patassé of the Central African People's Liberation Party (MLPC) won the presidential elections of 1993 and 1999. A multiparty coalition government was formed after the legislative elections of 1998.

A coup took place on 15 March 2003, in which François Bozizé took power, declared himself president, suspended the constitution and dismissed the cabinet. A broad-based transitional government was formed on 31 March. In June, Bozizé stated that his rule would end in January 2005.

POLITICAL SYSTEM

Constitutional reforms were passed in a national referendum in December 1994 which created a constitutional court, introduced elected local assemblies, extended the presidential mandate to a maximum of two six-year terms and subordinated the government to the president.

Following the March 2003 coup, President François Bozizé established a 63-member National Transitional Council to assist the president with legislation, draft a new constitution and prepare for elections in 2004.

HEAD OF STATE
President, Minister of Defence, Gen. François Bozizé, *took* power 15 March 2003

TRANSITIONAL GOVERNMENT *as at May 2003*
Prime Minister; Minister for Economy, Finance, Budget, Planning and International Co-operation, Abel Goumba
Civil Service, Employment and Social Security, Social Integration, Jacques Bothy
Communication, National Reconciliation, Democratic and Civil Culture, Capt. Parfait M'baye
Development, Tourism and Handicrafts, Bruno Dacko
Energy and Mines, Lt. Sylvain N'doutingai
Environment and National Ecology, Joseph Kitiki Kouamba
Equipment and Transport, Pokomandji Sonny
Family and Social Affairs, National Solidarity, Lea Doumta
Foreign Affairs, Regional Integration and Francophone Affairs, Karim Meckassoua
Health and Population, Nestor Mamadou
Interior and Public Security, Lt.-Col. Michel Paulin
Justice and Human Rights, Faustin M'bodou
Livestock Development, Denis Kossi-Bella
Ministers-Delegate, Daniel N'ditifei Boysembe *(Minister-Delegate to the Prime Minister, responsible for Economy, Finance and Budget);* Philippe Ouaradague *(Planning and International Co-operation)*
Modernisation and Development of Agriculture, Pierre Gbianza
National Education, Literacy, Higher Education and Research, Bevarah Lala
Post and Telecommunications, New Technologies, Idriss Salao
Reconstruction of Public Buildings, Town Planning and Housing, Abraham Goto N'goulou
Secretary-General of the Government, Relations with Parliament, Zarambaud Assingambi
Territorial Administration, Marcel Malonga
Trade, Industry and Private Sector Promotion, Hyacinthe Wodobode
Water Resources, Forestry, Hunting and Fisheries, Maurice Yondo
Youth, Sports, Art and Culture, Leon Salam

EMBASSY OF THE CENTRAL AFRICAN REPUBLIC
30 rue des Perchamps, F-75016, Paris
Tel: (00 33) (1) 4224 4256
Ambassador Extraordinary and Plenipotentiary, vacant

BRITISH AMBASSADOR, HE Richard Wildash, LVO, resident at Yaoundé, Cameroon

ECONOMY

Cotton, diamonds, coffee and timber are the major exports. Industrial goods, machinery and transport equipment, foodstuffs and fuels are the main imports.

In 2000 exports totalled US$271 million and imports US$26 million.GNP – US$1,031 million (2000); US$280 per capita (2000)

GDP – US$978 million (2001); US$241 per capita (2000)

ANNUAL AVERAGE GROWTH OF GDP – 5.5 per cent (1998)

INFLATION RATE – 1.5 per cent (1999)

TOTAL EXTERNAL DEBT – US$872 million (2000)

Trade with UK	2001	2002
Imports from UK	£2,095,000	£1,903,000
Exports to UK	228,000	200,000

CHAD

République du Tchad – Republic of Chad

AREA – 495,755 sq. miles (1,284,000 sq. km).
Neighbours: Niger, Nigeria and Cameroon (west), Libya (north), Sudan (east), Central African Republic (south)

POPULATION – 6,702,000; French and Arabic are the official languages; there are more than 50 indigenous languages, of which the most widely spoken is Sara

CAPITAL – N'Djaména (population, 530,100, 1993 census)

CURRENCY – Franc CFA of 100 centimes

NATIONAL ANTHEM – Peuple Tchadien, Debout Et À L'ouvrage (People Of Chad, Arise And To Work)

NATIONAL DAY – 1 December

NATIONAL FLAG – Vertical stripes, blue, yellow and red

POPULATION GROWTH RATE – 2.7 per cent

POPULATION DENSITY – 6 per sq. km (1999)

MILITARY EXPENDITURE – 0.8 per cent of GDP (2001)

MILITARY PERSONNEL – 30,350: Army 25,000, Air Force 350, Republican Guard 5,000; Paramilitaries 4,500

ILLITERACY RATE – (m) 48.4 per cent; (f) 66.0 per cent (2000)

ENROLMENT (percentage of age group) – primary 58 per cent (1997); secondary 10 per cent (1997); tertiary 1 per cent (1997)

HISTORY AND POLITICS

Chad became a member state of the French Community in 1958, and was proclaimed fully independent on 11 August 1960. The constitution was suspended in 1975 when President Tombalbaye was killed in a coup by Gen. Félix Malloum; following a succession of further coups, Idriss Déby came to power in 1990 and announced the adoption of a multiparty system, allowing the legalisation of political parties in 1991 and 1992. A Higher Transitional Council (CST) was elected in 1993 to serve as the transitional legislature and appointed a transitional government in conjunction with President Déby. The CST has twice extended the transitional period by one year to allow sufficient time to organise elections. A new constitution, establishing a unified, democratic state, was confirmed by a referendum held in March 1996. Déby won the first multiparty presidential elections in 1996 and was re-elected in the presidential elections held in May 2001. Elections to the 155-member National Assembly on 21 April 2002 were won by the pro-Déby

Patriotic Salvation Movement (MPS).

INSURGENCIES

Three rebel movements, the Movement for Unity and the Republic (MUR), the Movement for Democracy and Justice in Chad (MDJT), and the Democratic Revolutionary Council (DRC), announced that they had formed an alliance in February 2000.

In January 2002 the government signed a peace accord with the MDJT and on 9 January 2003 an agreement was signed between the government and rebels of the National Resistance Army (ANR), which provided for an immediate cease-fire and a general amnesty. However, the agreement was rejected by at least one of the eight different movements within the ANR.

HEAD OF STATE

President, Idriss Déby, *took power* December 1990, *elected* 3 July 1996, *re-elected* 20 May 2001

GOVERNMENT *as at July 2003*

Prime Minister, Moussa Faki Mahamat
Agriculture, David Houdeingar Ngarimaden
Assistant Secretary-General to the Government, Mahamat Taher Nahar
Civil Service, Labour and Employment, Abakaka Moustapha Lopa
Communications, Government Spokesman, Moktar Wawa Dahab
Culture, Youth and Sport, Dabogo Djimet
Education, Yokabdjim Mandigui
Environment and Water, Djimrangar Dadnadji
Finance and Economy, Idriss Ahmed Idriss
Foreign Affairs and African Integration, Nagoum Yamassoum
Higher Education, Scientific Research and Professional Training, Voksouma Djouma
Industry, Commerce and Handicrafts, Victor Mahamat
Industry, Security, Decentralisation and Immigration, Abderahman Moussa
Justice, Keeper of the Seals, Djimnaye Gaou
Livestock, Adoum Diar
Mines and Energy, Mahamat Taher
Minister-Delegate to the Prime Minister, in charge of Decentralisation, Djimtibaye Lapia Neldjita
Minister Delegate to the Ministry of Economy and Finance, in charge of Budget, Ngoyam Djaibe
National Defence, Veterans and Victims of War, Mahamat Nouri
National Development, Urban Planning and Housing, Brahim Seid
Oil, Ousmane Mahamat Nour Elimi
Planning, Development and Co-operation, Mahamat Hassan
Posts and Telecommunications, Baradine Haroun
Public Health, Aziza Baroud
Public Security and Immigration, Mahamat Ali Abdallah
Public Works and Transport, Adoum Younou
Secretary-General to the Government, in charge of Relations with the Parliament, Abderahim Bireme Hamid
Social Action and Family, Ursule Tourkounda
Territorial Development and Urban Planning, Brahim Said
Tourism, Oumar Boukar

EMBASSY OF THE REPUBLIC OF CHAD
Lambermont 52, 1030 Brussels, Belgium
Tel: (00 32) (2) 215 1975
Ambassador Extraordinary and Plenipotentiary, HE Abderahim Yacoub Ndiaye, apptd 2000

BRITISH AMBASSADOR, HE Richard Wildash, LVO,
resident at Yaoundé, Cameroon
Honorary Consulate, BP1060, N'Djaména

ECONOMY

About 90 per cent of the workforce is occupied in
agriculture, fishing and forestry. There is an oilfield in
Kanem and salt is mined around Lake Chad, but the most
important activities are cotton growing and animal
husbandry. Raw cotton, meat and groundnuts are the
main exports. Chad's main trading partners are France
and Cameroon.

On 7 January 2000 the IMF approved a loan facility of
about US$62 million to support the government's
1999–2002 economic programme. In October 2002
Chad's request for an extension of the commitment
period under the Poverty Reduction and Growth Facility
(PRGF) arrangement was approved by the IMF. As a
result, Chad would be able to draw up to about US$7
million.

In 1994 Chad had a trade deficit of US$77 million
and a current account deficit of US$38 million. In 2001
imports totalled US$632 million and exports US$165
million.

GNP – US$1,541 million (2000); US$200 per capita
(2000)
GDP – US$1,603 million (2001); US$112 per capita
(2000)
ANNUAL AVERAGE GROWTH OF GDP – 6.0 per cent
(1998)
INFLATION RATE – 3.8 per cent (2000)
TOTAL EXTERNAL DEBT – US$1,116 million (2000)

Trade with UK	2001	2002
Imports from UK	£3,664,000	£4,438,000
Exports to UK	39,000	119,000

CHILE

República de Chile – Republic of Chile
AREA – 288,000 sq. miles (748,800 sq. km).
Neighbours: Peru (north), Bolivia and Argentina (east)
POPULATION – 15,402,000. The main groups are:
indigenous Araucanian Indians, Fuegians, Rapanui and
Changos; Spanish settlers and their descendants;
mixed Spanish Indians; and European immigrants.
Because of extensive intermarriage only a few
indigenous Indians are racially separate. The language
is Spanish, with admixtures of local words of Indian
origin. The main religion is Roman Catholicism
CAPITAL – Santiago (population, 4,690,684, 1998 UN
estimate)
MAJOR CITIES – ΨAntofagasta (246,023); Concepción
(368,428); Puente Alto (384,016); ΨValparaíso
(284,086); ΨPunta Arenas (121,533), on the Straits of
Magellan, is the southernmost city in the world (1998
UN estimates)
CURRENCY – Chilean peso of 100 centavos
NATIONAL ANTHEM – Canción Nacional De Chile
(National Anthem Of Chile)
NATIONAL DAY – 18 September (National Anniversary)
NATIONAL FLAG – Two horizontal bands, white, red; in
top sixth a white star on blue square, next staff
LIFE EXPECTANCY (years) – 75 (2001)
POPULATION GROWTH RATE – 1.5 per cent
POPULATION DENSITY – 21 per sq. km (2001)
URBAN POPULATION – 86 per cent (2001)

Chile lies between the Andes (5,000 to 15,000 feet
above sea level) and the shores of the South Pacific,
extending coastwise from the arid north around Arica to
Cape Horn. The extreme length of the country is about
2,800 miles, with an average breadth, north of 41°, of
100 miles.

Island possessions include the Juan Fernández group
(three islands) about 360 miles from Valparaíso; one of
these islands is the reputed scene of Alexander Selkirk's
(Robinson Crusoe) shipwreck. Easter Island, about 2,000
miles away in the South Pacific Ocean, contains stone
platforms and hundreds of stone figures.

HISTORY AND POLITICS

Chile was discovered by Spanish adventurers in the 16th
century and remained under Spanish rule until 1810,
when the first autonomous government was established.
Full independence was consolidated in 1818 after a
revolutionary war.

A Marxist, Salvador Allende, was elected president in
1970, but was overthrown in a military coup in 1973.

Gen. Pinochet, who led the coup, assumed the
presidency until presidential and congressional elections
were held in 1989, beginning the transition to full
democracy.

Gen. Augusto Pinochet was arrested in London on 16
October 1998 following a request by the Spanish
government for his extradition, but extradition
proceedings were dropped on the grounds of poor health
on 2 March 2000, and he was freed and allowed to
return to Chile. The Chilean Supreme Court lifted his
immunity from prosecution in August 2000 and on 1
December he was put under house arrest pending trial on
charges relating to the kidnapping and murder of more
than 70 political opponents. The charges were dismissed
by the Court of Appeals, but formally reinstated on 31
January 2001 after it had been determined that Gen.
Pinochet was fit to stand trial. On 8 March the charges
were reduced to conspiracy to conceal the actions of
military death squads.

Ricardo Lagos Escobar of the Party for Democracy
(PPD) won the presidential election of 16 January 2000.
In the legislative elections held on 16 December 2001,
the Coalition of Parties for Democracy (CPD) remained
the largest group in the Chamber of Deputies but lost its
majority in elections to the Senate.

POLITICAL SYSTEM

Executive power is held by the president. Legislative
power is exercised by a Congress which comprises a
Senate of 47 Senators (38 elected and nine appointed)
and a Chamber of Deputies of 118 elected members.
Senators serve eight-year terms and deputies serve four-
year terms. The presidential term is six years with no
possibility of re-election.

HEAD OF STATE

President of the Republic, Ricardo Lagos Escobar, *elected*
16 January 2000, *sworn in* 11 March 2000

CABINET *as at May 2003*
Agriculture, Jaime Campos
Defence, Michelle Bachelet
Director of the National Women's Secretariat,
Adriana del Piano
Economy and Energy, Jorge Rodríguez Grossi
Education, Mariana Aylwin
Finance, Nicolás Eyzaguirre

Foreign Affairs, María Soledad Alvear
Health, Osvaldo Artaza
Housing, Town Planning and Public Land, Jaime Ravinet
Interior, José Miguel Insulza
Justice, José Antonio Gómez
Labour and Social Security, Ricardo Solari
Mining, Alfonso Dulanto
Minister Secretary-General of the Government,
   Heraldo Muñoz
Minister Secretary-General of the Presidency,
   Mario Fernández
Planning, Cecilia Pérez
Public Works, Transport and Communications,
   Javier Etcheverry

EMBASSY OF CHILE
12 Devonshire Street, London W1G 7DS
Tel: 020-7580 6392
Ambassador Extraordinary and Plenipotentiary,
   HE Mariano Fernández

BRITISH EMBASSY
Avenida El Bosque 0125, Casilla 72-D, Santiago
Tel: (00 56) (2) 370 4100
Email: consulate@fco.gov.uk
Ambassador Extraordinary and Plenipotentiary,
   HE Greg Faulkner, apptd 2000

CONSULAR OFFICES – Punta Arenas, Valparaíso.

BRITISH COUNCIL DIRECTOR, John Knagg, OBE
Eliodoro Yáñez 832, Providencia, Santiago
Tel: (00 56) (2) 410 6900 Email: info@britishcouncil.cl

DEFENCE
The Army has 290 main battle tanks, 20 armoured
infantry fighting vehicles and 908 armoured personnel
carriers. The Navy has three submarines, three destroyers,
three frigates, 27 patrol and coastal vessels, 13 combat
aircraft and 6 armed helicopters. The Air Force has 76
combat aircraft.
MILITARY EXPENDITURE – 4.4 per cent of GDP (2001)
MILITARY PERSONNEL – 80,500: Army 45,000, Navy
   23,000, Air Force 12,500; Paramilitaries 36,800
CONSCRIPTION DURATION – One to 22 months
   (voluntary from 2005)

ECONOMY
Economic reforms during the late 1970s and the 1980s,
with large-scale privatisation and deregulation, have
made Chile one of the most successful economies in Latin
America. Cereals, vegetables, fruit, tobacco, hemp and
vines are grown extensively and livestock accounts for
nearly 40 per cent of agricultural production. Sheep
farming predominates in the extreme south. Agriculture
employs about 12 per cent of the workforce. There are
large timber tracts in the central and southern zones
which produce timber, cellulose and wood for export.
Fishing is also a major industry.
   Chile is rich in copper-ore (around 20 per cent of
global reserves), iron-ore and nitrates, and has the only
commercial production of nitrate of soda (Chile saltpetre)
from natural resources in the world. There are large
deposits of high-grade sulphur. Oil and natural gas are
produced in the Magallanes area, but domestic
production is now declining.
   In 2000 there was a trade surplus of US$1,438 million
and a current account deficit of US$991 million.

GNP – US$69,850 million (2000); US$4,590 per capita
   (2000)
GDP – US$63,545 million (2001); US$4,669 per capita
   (2000)
ANNUAL AVERAGE GROWTH OF GDP – 5.4 per cent
   (2000)
INFLATION RATE – 3.8 per cent (2000)
UNEMPLOYMENT – 8.3 per cent (2000)
TOTAL EXTERNAL DEBT – US$36,978 million (2000)

TRADE
The principal exports are minerals, timber and metal
products, fish products and vegetables. The principal
imports are food products, industrial raw materials,
machinery, and equipment and spares. The main trade
partners are Japan, the USA, Argentina, the UK and
Brazil; in 1996 Chile joined the Mercosur Free Trade
Zone, and in March 1998 signed an extension to a free
trade agreement with Mexico. In December 2002, a Free
Trade Agreement was signed between the United States
and Chile. In 2001 imports totalled US$17,814 million
and exports US$18,505 million.

Trade with UK	2001	2002
Imports from UK	£131,178,000	£116,614,000
Exports to UK	481,785,000	477,977,000

COMMUNICATIONS
With the improvement of the roads an increasing share of
internal transportation is moving by road and rail,
although shipping is still important. The road system is
about 80,000 km in length, of which around 11,000 km
is paved.
   There are 6,782 km of railway track. A railway line
runs from Valparaíso through La Calera and Santiago to
Puerto Montt. With the completion of a section of 435
miles from Corumba, Brazil, to Santa Cruz, Bolivia, the
Trans-Continental Line will link the Chilean Pacific port
of Arica with Rio de Janeiro on the Atlantic. A line runs
from Antofagasta to Salta (Argentina).
   Domestic air traffic is carried by Línea Aérea Nacional
(LAN) and LADECO, which also operate internationally,
and smaller regional carriers.

CULTURE AND EDUCATION
Chilean Nobel Prize winners include the writers Gabriela
Mistral (1945) and Pablo Neruda (1971).
   Elementary education is free and compulsory. There
are 25 state universities and 45 private universities.
ILLITERACY RATE – (m) 4.1 per cent; (f) 4.5 per cent
   (2000)
ENROLMENT (percentage of age group) – primary 100
   per cent (1997); secondary 75 per cent (1997); tertiary
   32 per cent (1997)

CHINA

*Zhonghua Renmin Gongheguo – The People's Republic of
China*

AREA – 3,587,462 sq. miles (9,327,400 sq. km).
   Neighbours: Russia and Mongolia (north), North
   Korea (east), Vietnam, Laos, Myanmar, India, Bhutan
   and Nepal (south), India, Pakistan, Afghanistan,
   Tajikistan, Kyrgyzstan and Kazakhstan (west)
POPULATION – 1,284,972,000. Han Chinese make up
   91.9 per cent of the population and the remainder of
   the population belongs to around 55 ethnic minorities.

Among the largest are the Zhuang of Guangxi, the Hui of Ningxia, the Miao of southern China, the Manchu of Heilongjiang, the Uygurs and Kazakhs of Xinjiang, the Tibetans and the Mongols. The indigenous religions are Confucianism, Taoism and Buddhism. There are also Muslims (officially estimated at about 12 million) and Christians (unofficially estimated at about 50 million). The official language is Mandarin Chinese; of the many local dialects the largest are Cantonese, Fukienese, Xiamenhua and Hakka. The autonomous regions of Mongolia, Tibet and Xinjiang have their own languages

CAPITAL – Beijing (population, 7,362,426, 1990 estimate)

MAJOR CITIES – Chengdu (2,954,872); Chongqing (3,172,178); Dalian (2,483,776); Guangzhou (Canton) (3,935,193); Harbin (2,990,921); Qingdo (2,101,808); ΨShanghai (8,214,384); Shenyang (4,669,737); Tianjin (5,855,044); Wuhan (4,040,113); Wuxi (1,013,606); Yantai (847,285); Zaozhuang (1,793,103)

CURRENCY – Renminbi Yuan of 10 jiao or 100 fen

NATIONAL ANTHEM – Yiyongjun Jinxingqu (March Of The Volunteers)

NATIONAL DAY – 1 October (Founding of People's Republic)

NATIONAL FLAG – Red, with large gold five-point star and four small gold stars in crescent, all in upper quarter next staff

LIFE EXPECTANCY (years) – 71 (2001)

POPULATION GROWTH RATE – 1 per cent

POPULATION DENSITY – 138 per sq. km (2001)

URBAN POPULATION – 37 per cent (2001)

HISTORY AND POLITICS

China was ruled by imperial dynasties for over 20 centuries until revolutionaries led by Sun Yat-sen forced the Emperor to abdicate on 10 October 1911. Neither the new Nationalist Party (Kuomintang (KMT)) government nor the emergent Chinese Communist Party (CCP) were able to unify China, or to agree on the basis for further reform. Warlord infighting rendered China weak, enabling Japan to occupy Manchuria and all the important northern and coastal areas of China by 1939. Japan's occupation was ended by its defeat by the allies in 1945.

The Communists established control over large areas of China in the early 1940s, seizing the territory abandoned by Japan in 1945. Civil war lasted until 1949 when the CCP, led by Mao Zedong (Mao Tse-tung), inaugurated the People's Republic of China (PRC), and the KMT under Chiang Kai-shek went into exile in Taiwan. The USA continued to recognise the Chiang Kai-shek regime as the rightful government of China until 1971, when the PRC took over China's membership of the United Nations from Taiwan.

Under Mao Zedong China was ruled on the basis of four 'cardinal principles': Marxist–Leninist–Maoist thought, the Socialist Road, the dictatorship of the proletariat, and the leadership of the CCP. Mao's 'Great Leap Forward' (1958–61) was an attempt to industrialise rural areas which resulted in a famine in which 30–40 million people died. China was plunged into chaos during the Cultural Revolution (1966–70) when the Red Guards were used to rid the country of 'rightist elements'.

Following the death of Mao Zedong in 1976, the disgraced Deng Xiaoping was recalled. In 1977 he was elected Vice-Chairman of the CCP, becoming the dominant force within the party by eliminating leftist influence, rehabilitating fallen leaders and promoting an 'open door' policy of economic liberalisation. The Congresses of 1982 and 1987 reaffirmed Deng's policies, and in 1987 most of the revolutionary generation was replaced in the top posts by younger, more liberal supporters of reform.

Student-led pro-democracy demonstrations in April and May 1989, centred on Tiananmen Square in Beijing, ended on 3–4 June when the army took control of Beijing, killing thousands of protesters. This strengthened the position of hardliners within the leadership, who re-adopted policies of centralisation based on Marxist ideology. Deng retired from his last official post in November 1989 but retained effective control until late 1994.

At Deng's instigation during 1992 the emphasis switched back to economic reform and the power of the hardliners waned. The 14th Party Congress in 1992 endorsed Deng's calls for faster, bolder economic reforms and his 'socialist market economy'. Deng died on 19 February 1997 and Jiang Zemin assumed the mantle of leader. Jiang continued the economic reforms and also sought to improve China's standing in the international community.

At the 16th Party Congress in November 2002 vice-president Hu Jintao was elected general secretary of the CCP. On 15 March 2003 Hu Jintao was elected by the National People's Congress as the new state president replacing Jiang Zemin who retained his position as head of the Central Military Commission.

INSURGENCIES

Separatists from the Uygur Muslim minority group in Xinjiang Autonomous Region have demonstrated against Han rule. They have claimed responsibility for bomb attacks in the provincial capital, Ürümqi, and in Beijing. Two Muslim separatists were executed in January 1999 as part of an effort to tighten control of the region and in February 2001, the death sentence was passed on the founder of an underground Islamic party.

The government banned the Falun gong cult on 22 July 1999, which had claimed to have 70 million followers; the government had become worried after it was revealed that a large number of Chinese Communist Party officials and senior officers in the People's Liberation Army had joined the cult. Tens of thousands of Falun gong members have been arrested since the ban.

POLITICAL SYSTEM

Under the 1982 constitution, the National People's Congress is the highest organ of state power. It is elected for a term of five years and is supposed to hold one session a year. It is empowered to amend the constitution, make laws, select the president and vice-president and other leading officials of the state, approve the national economic plan, the state budget and the final state accounts, and to decide on questions of war and peace. The State Council is the highest organ of the state administration. It is composed of the Premier, the Vice-Premiers, the State Councillors, heads of Ministries and Commissions, the Auditor-General and the Secretary-General. Command over the armed forces is vested in the Central Military Commission.

Deputies to Congresses at the primary level are 'directly elected' by the voters 'through a secret ballot after democratic consultation'. This is now extended to county level. These Congresses elect the deputies to the Congress at the next higher level. Deputies to the National People's Congress are elected by the People's Congresses of the provinces, autonomous regions and municipalities directly under the central government, and by the armed forces.

Local government is conducted through People's Governments at provincial, municipal and county levels. Autonomous regions, prefectures and counties exist for national minorities and are described as self-governing.

HEAD OF STATE

President of the People's Republic of China, Hu Jintao, *elected* 15 March 2003
Vice-President, Zeng Qinghong
Chairman of the Standing Committee of the National People's Congress, Wu Bangguo
Chairman of the Central Military Committee, Jiang Zemin
Deputy Chairmen of the Central Military Committee, Chi Haotian; Hu Jintao; Zhang Wannian

STATE COUNCIL *as at May 2003*

Premier, Wen Jiabao
Vice-Premiers, Huang Ju; Wu Yi *(Minister of Health);* Zeng Peiyan; Hui Liangyu
State Councillors, Zhou Yongkang; Cao Gangchuan *(Minister for National Defence);* Tang Jiaxuan; Hua Jianmin *(Secretary-General of the State Council);* Chen Zhili

MINISTERS

Agriculture, Du Qinglin
Civil Affairs, Li Xueju
Commerce, Lu Fuyuan
Communications, Zhang Chunxian
Construction, Wang Guangtao
Culture, Sun Jiazheng
Education, Zhou Ji
Finance, Jin Renqing
Foreign Affairs, Li Zhaoxing
Information Industry, Wang Xudong
Justice, Zhang Fusen
Labour and Social Security, Zheng Silin
Land and Natural Resources, Tian Fengshan
Personnel, Zhang Bolin
Public Security, Zhou Yongkang
Railways, Liu Zhijun
Science and Technology, Xu Guanhua
State Security, Xu Yongyue
Supervision, Li Zhilun
Water Resources, Wang Shucheng

MINISTERS IN CHARGE OF STATE COMMISSIONS

Ethnic Affairs, Li Dezhu
Family Planning, Zhang Weiqing
Science, Technology and Industry for National Defence, Zhang Yunchuan
State Development and Reform, Ma Kai

Governor of the People's Bank of China, Zhou Xiaochuan
Auditor-General, Li Jinhua

CHINESE PEOPLE'S POLITICAL CONSULTATIVE CONFERENCE

Chair, Li Ruihuan

THE CHINESE COMMUNIST PARTY
General Secretary, Hu Jintao
Politburo Standing Committee, Hu Jintao; Huang Ju; Jia
    Qinglin; Li Changchun; Luo Gan; Wen Jiabao; Wu
    Bangguo; Wu Guanzheng; Zeng Qinghong
Politburo of the Central Committee, Cao Gangchuan; Chen
    Liangyu; Guo Boxiong; He Guoqiang; Hui Liangya;
    Liu Qi; Liu Yunshan; Wang Lequan; Wang Zhaoguo;
    Wu Yi; Yu Zhengsheng; Zeng Peiyan; Zhang Deijang;
    Zhang Lichang; Zhou Yongkang *(full members)*;
    Wang Gang *(alternate member)*
Secretariat of the Central Committee, He Guoqiang;
    He Yong; Liu Yunshan; Wang Gang; Xu Caihou;
    Zeng Qinghong; Zhou Yongkang

EMBASSY OF THE PEOPLE'S REPUBLIC OF CHINA
49–51 Portland Place, London W1B 1JL
Tel: 020-7299 4049
Ambassador Extraordinary and Plenipotentiary,
    HE Zha Peixin, apptd 2002

BRITISH EMBASSY
11 Guang Hua Lu, Jian Guo Men Wai, Beijing 100600
Tel: (00 86) (10) 6532 1961
Email: consularmail@peking.mail.fco.gov.uk
Ambassador, HE Christopher Hum, CMG, apptd 2002

BRITISH CONSULATES-GENERAL – Chongqing,
Shanghai and Guangzhou

BRITISH COUNCIL DIRECTOR, Michael O'Sullivan
    (Cultural Counsellor), Cultural and Education Section,
    British Embassy, 4/f Landmark Building Tower 1,
    8 North Dongsanhuan Road, Chaoyang District,
    Beijing 100004 Tel: (00 86) (10) 6590 6903
    Email: enquiry@britishcouncil.org.cn. Regional directors
    in Chongqing, Guangzhou and Shanghai

DEFENCE
All three military arms are parts of the People's
Liberation Army (PLA). China has at least 20
intercontinental and 130-150 intermediate range land-
based, and 13 submarine-launched nuclear ballistic
missiles. The Army has some 7,010 main battle tanks and
over 5,000 armoured personnel carriers and armoured
infantry fighting vehicles.

The Navy has 69 submarines, 21 destroyers, 42
frigates, 368 patrol and coastal vessels, 472 combat
aircraft and 45 armed helicopters. The Air Force has more
than 1,900 combat aircraft and some armed helicopters.
MILITARY EXPENDITURE – 4.0 per cent of GDP (2001)
MILITARY PERSONNEL – 2,270,000: Army 1,600,000,
    Navy 250,000, Air Force 420,000, Strategic Missile
    Forces 100,000; Paramilitaries 1,500,000
CONSCRIPTION DURATION – Two years (selective)

ECONOMY
Economic liberalisation in the early 1980s reduced
central planning and broadened the role of the market,
which led to an explosion in manufacturing, concentrated
in China's coastal regions. Foreign direct investment,
especially from Hong Kong and Taiwan, enabled the
construction of a significant industrial base and transport
infrastructure. In the coastal regions the economy has
become a free market in all but name, with several stock
markets and Shanghai's emergence as a financial centre.
Since 1980, special economic zones have been
established in Guangdong, Fujian and Hainan provinces.

In addition, there are free trade and development zones
throughout the country, designed to stimulate both
foreign trade and internal economic development. The
reforms have enabled the economy to grow more than
five-fold since 1980. China has become the third-largest
beneficiary of foreign investment in the world, primarily
into its export industries.

Agriculture remains of great importance, employing
nearly half the working population and accounted for
about 16 per cent of GDP in 2000. Cereals, with peas
and beans, are grown in the northern provinces, and rice,
tea and sugar in the south. Rice is the staple food of the
inhabitants. Cotton (mostly in valleys of the Yangtze and
Yellow Rivers), tea (in the west and south), with hemp,
jute and flax, are the most important crops. Livestock is
raised in large numbers. Sericulture is one of the oldest
industries. Cottons, woollens and silks are manufactured
in large quantities.

Coal, iron ore, tin, antimony, wolfram, bismuth and
molybdenum are abundant. Oil is produced in several
northern provinces, particularly in Heilongjiang and
Shandong. Plans for a 2,400 km oil pipeline from
Russia's east Siberian reserves to Daqing in China were
first announced in July 2001 and although the planning
process for the $1.7 billion project has been making slow
progress, the pipeline is scheduled to open in 2005. In
March 1998, China announced the construction of a
US$2.3 billion 1,875-mile oil pipeline along the Silk
Route to Kazakhstan.

In June 2003 the sluice gates on the Three Gorges dam
above the Yangtse river in central China were closed to
allow the reservoir to fill up and the first generator went
into operation on 10 July. The world's largest
hydroelectric power project, costing US$25 billion, will
supply electricity to power grids in central and eastern
China. More than 600,000 people have been displaced
since construction began in 1993.

Overcapacity in some of the traditional industries is
being tackled, with the closure of 26,000 coal mines and
2,500 steel smelters. There are long-term plans to
privatise all corporations except those in sectors
considered essential to national security. As at mid-2001,
state-owned enterprises accounted for approximately
two-thirds of GDP and employment.

Tourism has become a major industry, with some 89
million foreign visitors in 2002. An outbreak of the
pneumonia-like Severe Acute Respiratory Syndrome
(SARS) virus between November 2002 and June 2003
resulted in a decline in overseas visitors in early 2003.
GNP – US$1,062,919 million (2000); US$840 per
    capita (2000)
GDP – US$1,159,017 million (2001); US$866 per
    capita (2000)
ANNUAL AVERAGE GROWTH OF GDP – 8.0 per cent
    (2000)
INFLATION RATE – 1.4 per cent (2001)
UNEMPLOYMENT – 3.1 per cent (2000)
TOTAL EXTERNAL DEBT – US$149,800 million (2000)

TRADE
Foreign trade and external economic relations have
grown enormously since 1978. In 1995, import tariffs
were cut to an average 23 per cent in line with China's
attempts to join the World Trade Organisation to which
China was formally admitted as a member in November
2001. The principal exports are clothing, electronics,
machine plant, yarns and fabrics, chemicals, footwear,
travel goods, and iron and steel. The principal imports are

machinery, electronics, raw materials, yarns and fabrics, plastics and motor vehicles. The main trading partners are Japan, the USA, Hong Kong, South Korea, Taiwan and Germany.

In 2000 China had a trade surplus of US$34,474 million and a current account surplus of US$20,518 million. In 2001 imports totalled US$243,521 million and exports US$266,620 million.

Trade with UK	2001	2002
Imports from UK	£1,722,272,000	£1,505,238,000
Exports to UK	5,964,414,000	6,972,976,000

COMMUNICATIONS

There are 57,923 km of railway lines, of which 11,783 km are electrified, and approximately 1,278,000 km of highway, of which 9,083 km are motorways. In addition, internal civil aviation has been developed, with routes totalling more than 1,506,000 km. Thirty new airports are due for completion by 2005.

In the past the principal means of communication east to west was by the rivers, the most important of which are the Yangtze (Changjiang) (3,400 miles), the Yellow River (Huanghe) (2,600 miles) and the West River (Xihe) (1,650 miles). These, together with the network of canals connecting them, are still much used but their overall importance has declined. Coastal port facilities are being improved and the merchant fleet expanded.

Postal services and telecommunications have developed in recent years and it is claimed that 95 per cent of all rural townships are on the telephone and that postal routes reach practically every production brigade headquarters.

EDUCATION

Primary education lasts six years and secondary education lasts six years (three years in junior middle school and three years in senior middle school). In 1998 there were 1,022 universities and colleges.
ILLITERACY RATE – (m) 8.3 per cent; (f) 23.7 per cent (2000)
ENROLMENT (percentage of age group) – primary 100 per cent (1997); tertiary 6 per cent (1997)

CULTURE

The Chinese language has many dialects, notably Cantonese, Hakka, Amoy, Foochow, Changsha, Nanchang, Wu (Shanghai) and the northern dialect. The Common Speech or *putonghua* (often referred to as Mandarin) is based on the northern dialect. The Communists have promoted it as the national language and it is taught throughout the country. As *putonghua* encourages the use of the spoken language in writing, the old literary style and ideographic form of writing has fallen into disuse. Since 1956 simplified characters have been introduced to make reading and writing easier. In 1958 the National People's Congress adopted a system of romanisation known as pinyin.

Chinese literature is one of the richest in the world. Paper has been employed for writing and printing for nearly 2,000 years. The Confucian classics which formed the basis of traditional Chinese culture date from the Warring States period (fourth to third centuries BC), as do the earliest texts of Taoism. Histories, philosophical and scientific works, poetry, literary and art criticism, novels and romances survive from most periods.

TIBET

AREA – 463,000 sq. miles (1,199,164 sq. km)
POPULATION – 2,610,000 (2001 estimate)
CAPITAL – Lhasa

Tibet is a plateau seldom lower than 10,000 feet, which forms the northern frontier of India (boundary imperfectly demarcated), from Kashmir to Myanmar, but is separated therefrom by the Himalayas.

From 1911 to 1950, Tibet was virtually an independent country though its status was never officially so recognised. In 1950 Chinese Communist forces invaded eastern Tibet. In 1951 an agreement was reached whereby the Chinese army was allowed entry into Tibet, and a Communist military and administrative headquarters was set up. A series of revolts against Chinese rule culminated in 1959 in a rising in Lhasa, the capital.

In 1964 the Dalai Lama and the Panchen Lama were dismissed, marking the end of co-operation between the Chinese government and the traditional religious authorities. Tibet became an Autonomous Region of China in 1965. Martial law was declared in Tibet in 1989 after serious unrest, and sporadic outbursts of unrest continue.

The Panchen Lama died in 1989. China rejected the Dalai Lama's choice of successor, who is believed to have been executed and enthroned its own candidate.

In December 1997, the International Commission of Jurists issued a report declaring that Tibet was 'under alien subjugation' and called for a UN-managed referendum to decide its future status. China contested that the report failed to acknowledge its historical claims to the region.

The 17th Karmapa Lama, the first reincarnation of a living Buddha to be recognised by both China and the Dalai Lama, defected from Tibet in late December 1999 and fled to India, where he appealed for political asylum. On 16 January 2000, the 7th Reting Lama was ordained in Tibet; the Dalai Lama had refused to recognise him as the reincarnation of the previous Reting Lama. Representatives of the Dalai Lama visited China in September 2002, in an attempt to improve the situation, but relations remain tense.

In May 2001 the government published details of a modernisation programme for Tibet which aimed to improve the low standard of living by promoting market reforms and extensive public construction projects.

SPECIAL ADMINISTRATIVE REGIONS

HONG KONG
AREA – 420 sq. miles (1,092 sq. km)
POPULATION – 6,725,000 (2001)
CURRENCY – Hong Kong dollar (HK$) of 100 cents
FLAG – Red, with a white bauhinia flower of five petals each containing a red star
LIFE EXPECTANCY (years) – 81 (2001)
POPULATION GROWTH RATE – 0.9 per cent
POPULATION DENSITY – 6,158 per sq. km (2001)
URBAN POPULATION – 93.1 per cent (2000 estimate)

Hong Kong, consisting of more than 230 islands and of a portion of the mainland (Kowloon and the New Territories) on the south-east coast of China, is situated at the eastern side of the mouth of the Pearl River. Hong Kong Island is about 11 miles (18 km) long and from two to five miles (three to eight km) broad. It is separated from the mainland by a narrow strait.

The mean monthly temperature ranges from 16° C to 29° C. The average annual rainfall is 2,214 mm, of which nearly 80 per cent falls between May and September.

HISTORY AND POLITICS

Hong Kong Island was first occupied by Great Britain in 1841 and formally ceded by the Treaty of Nanking in 1842. Kowloon was acquired by the Beijing Convention of 1860 and the New Territories, consisting of a peninsula in the southern part of the Guangdong province together with adjacent islands, by a 99-year lease signed on 9 June 1898.

On 19 December 1984 the UK and China signed a Joint Declaration in which it was agreed that China would resume sovereignty over Hong Kong on 1 July 1997. In the run-up to the 1997 handover, the Chinese government's insistence on a greater say in the running of the colony and Governor Patten's plan for an extension of democracy prompted acrimonious disputes. The Chinese government refused to accept the reforms and replaced the Legislative Council.

Hong Kong became, with effect from 1 July 1997, a Special Administrative Region (SAR) of the People's Republic of China.

The Joint Declaration which took effect in May 1985 guarantees: the free movement of goods and capital; the retention of Hong Kong's free port status, separate customs territory and freely convertible currency; the protection of property rights and foreign investment; the right of free movement to and from Hong Kong; Hong Kong's autonomy in the conduct of its external commercial relations and its own monetary and financial policies; and judicial independence. Hong Kong's constitution is the Basic Law, which was passed by China's National People's Congress in 1990 and guarantees that the SAR's social and economic systems will remain unchanged for 50 years.

A Legislative Council election was held on 10 September 2000. The Democratic Party, a pro-democracy opposition party, remained the largest party in the legislature with 12 seats and the pro-China Democratic Alliance for the Betterment of Hong Kong won 11 seats; 20 seats were won by independent candidates.

Following mass pro-democracy demonstrations in July 2003 against a proposed anti-subversion law, the government announced that public consultation on the controvesial bill would re-open in September. Protestors also demanded direct elections for Hong Kong's leader and all members of the Legislative Council.

POLITICAL SYSTEM

Hong Kong is administered by the Hong Kong SAR government, headed by the Chief Executive, who is aided by an Executive Council and a Legislative Council. The Executive Council consists of 14 Principal Officials and five non-officials..

The Legislative Council consists of 60 members, of whom 24 are directly elected. Thirty members are elected by functional constituencies composed of professional and business groups and six are elected by an election committee.

Chief Executive, Tung Chee-hwa, *sworn in* 1 July 1997

EXECUTIVE COUNCIL *as at July 2003*
Non-official Members, Leung Chun-ying; Jasper Tsang; Yok-sing Cheng Yiu-tong; Andrew Liao Cheung-sing
Ex-officio Members, Tung Chee-hwa (plus the 14 heads of government departments listed below)

GOVERNMENT SECRETARIAT *as at July 2003*
Chief Secretary for Administration, Donald Tsang Yam-kuen
Civil Service, Joseph Wong Wing-ping
Commerce, Technology and Industry, Henry Tang Ying-yen
Education and Manpower, Arthur Li Kwok-cheung
Environment, Transport and Works, Sarah Liao Sau-tung
Financial Secretary (acting), Economic Development and Labour, Stephen Ip Shu-kwan
Financial Services and the Treasury, Frederick Ma Si-hang
Health, Welfare and Food, Yeoh Eng-kiong
Home Affairs, Patrick Ho Chi-ping
Housing, Planning and Lands, Michael Suen Ming-yeung
Justice, Elsie Leung Oi-sie
Security, vacant

CONSUL-GENERAL, Sir James Hodge, KCVO, CMG, 1 Supreme Court Road, Central (PO Box 528), Hong Kong. Tel: (00 852) 2901 3000
BRITISH COUNCIL DIRECTOR, Desmond Lauder 3 Supreme Court Road, Admiralty, Hong Kong. Tel: (00 852) 2913 5100 Email: info@britishcouncil.org.hk
HONG KONG ECONOMIC AND TRADE OFFICE, 6 Grafton Street, London W1S 4EQ. Tel: 020-7499 9821. *Director-General,* Andrew Yeung, apptd 2001

ECONOMY

The main economic sector is the services industry, especially financial services. It employed 85 per cent of the workforce and contributed 84.7 per cent of GDP in 1998. Principal exports are clothing, electrical machinery and apparatus, and textiles.

Diversification in terms of products and markets continues to be the main feature of recent industrial development, as are industrial partnerships with overseas companies. The economy is based on export rather than the domestic market. Tourism is very important to the economy; 13.7 million people visited Hong Kong in 2001. The spread of the SARS virus to Hong Kong in March 2003 had a detrimental effect on the economy, especially the tourism industry, with a 65 per cent reduction in the number of visitors in April 2003 compared with the previous year. The World Health Organisation removed Hong Kong from its list of SARS-infected areas on 23 June 2003.

GNP – US$176,157 million (2000); US$24,759 per capita (2001)
GDP – US$161,869 million (2001); US$24,070 per capita (2001)
ANNUAL AVERAGE GROWTH OF GDP – 10.5 per cent (2000)
INFLATION RATE – 3.7 per cent (2000)

TRADE
In 2001 Hong Kong had a trade deficit of US$8,331 million and a current account surplus of US$11,968 million. Imports totalled US$201,076 million and exports US$189,894 million. Hong Kong's principal customers for its domestic products, in order of value of trade, were China, USA and the United Kingdom. China was its principal supplier. About 40 per cent of China's foreign trade passes through Hong Kong.

Trade with UK	2001	2002
Imports from UK	£2,699,380,000	£2,430,799,000
Exports to UK	5,977,696,000	5,766,795,000

COMMUNICATIONS

Hong Kong has one of the world's finest natural harbours, and it is the busiest container port in the world, with eight terminals, as well as large modern cargo and liner terminals. Dockyard facilities include eight floating drydocks, the largest being capable of docking vessels up to 150,000 tonnes deadweight.

An international airport built on reclaimed land at Chek Lap Kok opened in July 1998.

EDUCATION

Free education for children up to the age of 15 is compulsory. Post-secondary education is provided by six universities and one college. The Open Learning Institute of Hong Kong provides university education. There are also seven technical institutes and the Hong Kong Institute of Education.

ILLITERACY RATE – (m) 3.5 per cent; (f) 9.8 per cent (2000)

ENROLMENT (percentage of age group) – primary 98.7 per cent (2001); secondary 91 per cent (2001); tertiary 31.8 per cent (2001)

MACAO (AOMEN)

AREA – 9.2 sq. miles (24 sq. km)

POPULATION – 453,733 (2001 estimate)

CURRENCY – Pataca of 100 avos

FLAG – Green, with a white lotus flower above a white stylised bridge and water, under a large gold five-point star and four gold stars in crescent

Macao, situated at the mouth of the Pearl River, comprises a peninsula and the islands of Coloane and Taipa.

Macao became a Portuguese colony in 1557; in a Sino-Portuguese treaty of 1887 China recognised Portugal's sovereignty over Macao. An agreement to transfer the administration of Macao to the Chinese authorities was signed on 13 April 1987. Macao became the Macao Special Administrative Region (MSAR) of China when power was transferred by the outgoing Portuguese governor Vasco Rocha Vieira to the new chief executive on 19 December 1999. The final session of the Macao SAR Basic Law Drafting Committee had been held in Beijing in January 1993 and had approved the Basic Law which was to serve as Macao's constitution after 1999.

On 10 April 1999, a 200-member committee of Macao residents was established to determine the composition of the first government of the Macao SAR. They elected Edmund Ho Hao Wah to be its first chief executive. The Chief Executive announced in September 1999 that he had appointed the 10 members of his Executive Council, a body intended to assist the chief executive in policy-making. In addition, he appointed seven legislators to the 23-member MSAR First Legislative Council, which included 15 members of the previous 16-member Legislative Assembly; a replacement was chosen for the member who had not wished to continue.

Chief Executive, Edmund Ho Hao Wah

EXECUTIVE COUNCIL SECRETARIAT *as at July 2003*
Administration and Justice, Florinda da Rosa Silva Chan
Economy and Finance, Francis Tam Pak Yuen
Security, Cheong Kuoc Va
Social Affairs and Culture, Fernando Chui Sai On
Transport and Public Works, Ao Man Long

CONSUL-GENERAL, Sir James Hodge, KCVO, CMG, resident at Hong Kong

ECONOMY

Service industries comprise the greatest part of the economy, providing 71.2 per cent of employment in 1997. In 1998, gambling provided 43 per cent of GNP and there were 6.9 million foreign visitors. Gaming taxes account for about 60 per cent of government revenues. In 2001 imports totalled US$2,386 million and exports US$2,299 million.

The main trading partners are the EU, the USA, China, Hong Kong and Japan.

Trade with UK	2001	2002
Imports from UK	£19,647,000	£12,621,000
Exports to UK	39,416,000	31,365,000

COLOMBIA

República de Colombia – Republic of Colombia

AREA – 399,500 sq. miles (1,038,700 sq. km).
　　Neighbours: Venezuela (north and east), Brazil (south-east), Peru (south), Ecuador (south-west), Panama (north-west)

POPULATION – 42,803,000, (2001): 58 per cent mestizo, 20 per cent white, 14 per cent mulatto, 4 per cent black, 3 per cent mixed black-Amerindian, 1 per cent Amerindian. The language is Spanish. Roman Catholicism is the established religion

CAPITAL – Bogotá (population, 6,712,247, 2002 estimate)

MAJOR CITIES – ΨBarranquilla (1,305,334), the major port on the Caribbean; Bucaramanga (549,263); ΨBuenaventura (271,401), the major port on the Pacific; Cali (2,264,256); ΨCartagena (952,523); Medellín (2,026,789)

CURRENCY – Colombian peso of 100 centavos

NATIONAL ANTHEM – Oh Gloria Inmarcesible (Oh Glory Unfading!)

NATIONAL DAY – 20 July (National Independence Day)

NATIONAL FLAG – Broad yellow band in upper half, surmounting equal bands of blue and red

LIFE EXPECTANCY (years) – 71 (2001)

POPULATION GROWTH RATE – 1.8 per cent

POPULATION DENSITY – 41 per sq. km (2001)

URBAN POPULATION – 76 per cent (2001)

Colombia lies in the extreme north-west of South America, having a coastline on both the Caribbean Sea and Pacific Ocean.

The country is divided by the Cordillera de los Andes into a coastal region in the north and west and extensive plains in the east. The eastern range of the Colombian Andes is a series of vast tablelands. This temperate region is the most densely peopled portion of the country. The principal rivers are the Magdalena, Guaviare, Cauca, Atrato, Caquetá, Putumayo and Patia.

HISTORY AND POLITICS

The Colombian coast was visited in 1502 by Columbus, and in 1536 a Spanish expedition penetrated the interior and established a government. The country remained under Spanish rule until 1819 when Simón Bolívar established the Republic of Colombia, consisting of the territories now known as Colombia, Panama, Venezuela and Ecuador. In 1829–30 Venezuela and Ecuador withdrew, and in 1831 the remaining territories formed the Republic of New Granada. The name was changed to the Granadine Confederation in 1858, to the United States of Colombia in 1861 and to the Republic of Colombia in 1866. Panama seceded in 1903.

From 1957 to 1974 the country was governed under the 'National Front' agreement with an alternating presidency and equal numbers of ministerial posts. The alternation of the presidency ended in 1974 and parity in appointments in 1978.

Elections to the legislature took place on 10 March 2002. In the House of Representatives, the Liberal Party (PL) secured 54 seats, while the Social Conservative Party (PSC) won 21, leaving the balance of power in the hands of minor parties. In the Senate, the Liberal Party won 28 seats while some 38 minor parties collectively secured 49 seats. The 2002 presidential election was held on 26 May and was won by Álvaro Uribe Vélez.

INSURGENCIES
Colombia is dogged by insurgency from left-wing guerrillas. The main active guerrilla factions are the Revolutionary Armed Forces of Colombia (FARC) and the National Liberation Army (ELN). Formal peace talks began on 9 November 1998, but fighting continued. The peace process was terminated in February 2002 by president Pastrana Arango after the ELN and FARC carried out joint actions against the right-wing paramilitary United Self-Defence Forces of Colombia (AUC), who had attacked civilians in towns and villages thought to be pro-FARC in December 2000.

FARC explosions in August 2002 prompted a state of emergency, which was extended for a further 90 days in November. An indefinite cease-fire was declared by the AUC in December 2002. There were further FARC bomb attacks in early 2003. In April 2003 Colombia signed agreements with Panama and Venezuela to enhance border security and place tighter controls on drug trafficking. On 30 June 2003 President Uribe unveiled a government security plan to end the civil war and combat the drugs trade. The plan aimed to establish police forces in all parts of the country and to eradicate all drugs crops. On 16 July the government and the AUC agreed to start formal talks aimed at disarming all the paramilitary group's 10,000 gunmen by the end of 2005.

POLITICAL SYSTEM
The Congress is a bicameral legislature. The lower house (the House of Representatives) has 165 members directly elected for a four-year term. The upper house (the Senate) has 102 members, directly elected for four years; two seats are reserved for representatives of indigenous people. The president, who appoints the Cabinet, is directly elected for a single four-year term.

HEAD OF STATE
President, Álvaro Uribe Vélez, *elected* 26 May 2002, *sworn in* 7 August 2003
Vice-President, Defence, Francisco Santos

CABINET *as at July 2003*
Agriculture and Rural Development, Carlos Gustavo Cano
Communications, Marta Pinto De Hart
Culture, María Consuelo Araujo Castro
Defence, Marta Lucía Ramírez
Environment and Development, Cecilia Rodríguez Gonzalez-Rubio
Finance and Public Credit, Alberto Carrasquilla
Foreign Affairs, Carolina Barco

Interior and Justice, Fernando Londoño Hoyos
Mines and Energy, Luis Ernesto Mejía
National Education, Cecilia María Vélez White
Social Protection, Diego Palacio Betancourt
Trade, Industry and Tourism, Jorge Humberto Botero
Transport, Andres Uriel Gallego

EMBASSY OF COLOMBIA
Flat 3A, 3 Hans Crescent, London SW1X 0LN
Tel: 020-7589 9177/5037
Ambassador Extraordinary and Plenipotentiary,
  HE Alfonso Lopez-Caballero, apptd 2002

BRITISH EMBASSY
Edifiicio ING Barings, Carrera 9 No 76-49 Piso 9, Bogotá
Tel: (00 57) (1) 317 6690/6310/6321
Email: britain@cable.net.co
Ambassador Extraordinary and Plenipotentiary,
  HE Tom Duggin, apptd 2001
BRITISH CONSULAR OFFICES – Cali and Medellín

BRITISH COUNCIL DIRECTOR, Joe Docherty
Calle 87 No. 12–79, Bogotá Tel: (00 57) (1) 618 7680
Email: info@britishcouncil.org.co

DEFENCE
The Army has 12 light tanks and 204 armoured personnel carriers. The Navy has four submarines, four corvettes, 27 patrol and coastal vessels, eight aircraft and four helicopters at nine bases. The Air Force has 58 combat aircraft and 23 armed helicopters.
MILITARY EXPENDITURE – 3.5 per cent of GDP (2001)
MILITARY PERSONNEL – 158,000: Army 136,000,
  Navy 15,000, Air Force 7,000; Paramilitaries 104,600
CONSCRIPTION DURATION – 12–18 months

ECONOMY
Coal, natural gas and hydroelectricity resources are largely unexploited, although development of coal is being given priority. The hydrocarbon sector accounts for over half of the mining output, precious metals (gold, platinum and silver) and iron ore accounting for the remainder. Other mineral deposits include nickel, bauxite, copper, gypsum, limestone, phosphates, sulphur and uranium. Colombia is also the world's largest producer of emeralds. Mining generates 5 per cent of GDP.

Major cash crops are coffee, sugar, bananas, cut flowers and cotton. Cattle are raised in large numbers, and meat and cured skins and hides are also exported.

The government has encouraged diversification to reduce dependence on coffee as the major export and this has led to the growth of new export-orientated industries, particularly textiles, paper products and leather goods. Services account for around 63 per cent of GDP, industry 25 per cent and agriculture 12 per cent. The IMF approved a two-year standby facility of US$2.1 billion in January 2003 to underpin government policies designed to reduce the fiscal deficit. Colombia also received a loan of US$3.3 billion over three years from the World Bank for economic reform.

In 2001 there was a trade surplus of US$510 million and a current account deficit of US$1,782 million. In 1996 and 1997 Colombia was blacklisted by the USA for failing to curb levels of drug production sufficiently. These sanctions were ended in March 1998. Under US$7.5 billion 'Plan Colombia', the USA pledged military aid to train Colombian armed forces to control the rebel-dominated coca-growing regions which supply the bulk of the cocaine used in the US.

GNP – US$85,279 million (2000); US$2,020 per capita (2000)

GDP – US$83,432 million (2001); US$1,930 per capita (2000)

ANNUAL AVERAGE GROWTH OF GDP – 2.8 per cent (2000)

INFLATION RATE – 9.5 per cent (2000)

UNEMPLOYMENT – 20.5 per cent (2000)

TOTAL EXTERNAL DEBT – US$34,081 million (2000)

TRADE

Principal exports are petroleum and derivatives, coffee, bananas, cut flowers, clothing and textiles, ferro-nickel and coal. Principal trading partners are the USA, the EU and Latin America.

In 2001 imports totalled US$12,834 million and exports US$12,257 million.

Trade with UK	2001	2002
Imports from UK	£104,929,000	£84,112,000
Exports to UK	320,324,000	218,734,000

COMMUNICATIONS

The Andes make surface transport difficult so air transport is used extensively. There are daily air services between Bogotá and all the principal towns, as well as frequent services to other countries. The road network consists of more than 115,000 km of roads, of which around 14,000 km are paved. The network is poorly maintained. There are 3,380 km of railways and 18,000 km of waterways.

CULTURE AND EDUCATION

There is a flourishing press in urban areas and a national literature supplements the rich inheritance from the time of Spanish colonial rule. Gabriel García Márquez was awarded the Nobel prize for Literature in 1982. State education is free.

ILLITERACY RATE – (m) 8.2 per cent; (f) 8.2 per cent (2000)

ENROLMENT (percentage of age group) – primary 100 per cent (1997); secondary 67 per cent (1997); tertiary 17 per cent (1997)

THE COMOROS

L'Union des Comores – Union of the Comoros

AREA – 863 sq. miles (2,235 sq. km). The Comoro archipelago includes the islands of Ngazidja (formerly Grande Comore), Anjouan, Mayotte and Moheli and certain islets in the Indian Ocean

POPULATION – 651,000, mostly Muslim. French and Arabic are the official languages; the majority of the population speak Comoran, a blend of Arabic and Swahili

CAPITAL – Moroni (population, 30,365, 1991 census), on Ngazidja

CURRENCY – Comorian franc (KMF) of 100 centimes. The Franc CFA of 100 centimes is also used

NATIONAL ANTHEM – Udzima Wa Ya Masiwa (The Union Of The Islands)

NATIONAL DAY – 6 July (Independence Day)

NATIONAL FLAG – Four horizontal stripes – gold, white, red, blue; a green triangle based on the hoist containing a white crescent and four white stars, horns towards the fly

POPULATION GROWTH RATE – 0 per cent

POPULATION DENSITY – 302 per sq. km (1999)

ILLITERACY RATE – (m) 33.5 per cent; (f) 47.2 per cent (2000)

ENROLMENT (percentage of age group) – primary 52 per cent (1993); tertiary 0.6 per cent (1995)

HISTORY AND POLITICS

The islanders voted for independence from France in December 1974 and three islands became independent on 6 July 1975. The island of Mayotte opposed independence and has remained under French administration.

An election in 1993 brought President Djohar's National Rally for Development party (RND) to power. Djohar was temporarily ousted in a coup in 1995 which was thwarted by French troops. While Djohar was abroad for medical attention, Prime Minister Caabiel Yachroutou declared himself interim president and refused to acknowledge Djohar's authority, resulting in the formation of a rival government. Djohar returned to the Comoros in January 1996 but was prohibited from contesting the March 1996 presidential election, which was won by Mohammad Taki Abdoulkarim of the National Union for Democracy in the Comoros. Taki dissolved the National Assembly and legislative elections were held in December 1996 although boycotted by the opposition Forum for National Recovery party (FRN).

President Taki died in office on 6 November 1998 and Tajiddine Ben Said Massonde took over as interim president. His government was deposed in a coup on 30 April 1999 by Col. Assoumani Azali, who was sworn in as president on 6 May. On 2 September 1999, an unsuccessful coup was launched while Col. Azali was overseas. He announced that he would retain power until a presidential election was held, which was due to take place by 14 April 2000. The election did not take place and Col. Azali declared that he would not restore civilian rule due to the issue of Anjouan separatism. However, in March 2001, he announced that the country would be restored to civilian rule in 2002 and that he would not contest the presidential election. However, he resigned as president on 21 January 2002 in order to stand in the April presidential election. The presidential elections were held in 2002 on March 17 and April 14 (Union President); March 31 (local presidents on Anjouan and Moheli); May 12 and 19 (local president for Ngazidja). Elections to the Union parliament were postponed indefinitely in March 2003.

INSURGENCIES

In August 1997 separatists on the islands of Anjouan and Moheli demanded independence from the Comoros and a return to French rule. Following a failed attempt to resolve the situation by force, President Taki assumed absolute power and established a State Transition Commission to function as a Cabinet. In a referendum in October 1997, the inhabitants of Anjouan voted overwhelmingly for independence. Talks mediated by the OAU began in December 1997 and an agreement drawn up with OAU support, which would have given each island considerable autonomy, was signed by Grande Comore and Moheli, but was rejected by Anjouan. Anjouan citizens voted by a large majority against reincorporation into the Comoros in a referendum held on 23 January 2000.

In March 1998, Anjouan's self-proclaimed President Abdallah Ibrahim appointed a prime minister and Cabinet, though their legitimacy has not been recognised internationally. Fighting broke out between President Ibrahim's forces and those of a previous Anjouan prime minister, Chamassi Said Omar, on 5 December 1998. On 1 August 1999, President Ibrahim resigned and transferred most of his powers to Col. Said Abeid. A general election was held in Anjouan in August 1999.

President Azali and the leader of Anjouan, Lt.-Col. Abderemane, signed an agreement on national reconciliation on 17 February 2001, which would have given Anjouan considerable autonomy. The Anjouan government withdrew from the reconciliation process on 15 April, alleging that the conditions of the agreement had not been met. On 14 February 2003, security officials confirmed they had foiled a coup aimed at removing the union government of Assoumani Azali.

POLITICAL SYSTEM
A new constitution which would create a federal structure for Ngazidja, Anjouan and Moheli and give greater autonomy for the islands was approved, in outline, by referendum on 23 December 2001. The final version was accepted by referendum on 17 March 2002 on Moheli and Anjouan but was rejected by the voters of Ngazidja.

HEAD OF STATE
President of the Union, Assoumani Azali, *elected* 14 April 2002, *sworn in* 31 May 2002

COUNCIL OF MINISTERS *as at July 2003*
Vice-President, Finance, Budget, Economy, External Trade, Investment and Privatisation, Caabi El-Yachroutu
Vice-President, Justice, Information, Religious Affairs, Human Rights, and Relations with the Houses of Parliament, Rachid Ben Massoundi
Minister-Delegate at the Ministry of External Relations, in charge of Co-operation, Ali Moumini
Minister of State, Development, Infrastructure, Posts and Telecommunications, International Transport, Government Spokesman, Houmed M'Saidie
Minister of State, External Defence and Territorial Security, Hamada Madi Bolero
Minister of State, Foreign Relations and Co-operation, Francophone Affairs, Environment, Comorans Abroad, Mohamed El-Amine Souef
Minister of State, Social Affairs and Administrative Reforms, Ali Mohamed Soilihi
President of Moheli, Mohamed Said Fazul
President of Anjouan, Col. Mohammed Bacar
President of Ngazidja, Abdou Soule Elbak

EMBASSY OF THE FEDERAL ISLAMIC REPUBLIC OF THE COMOROS
20 rue Marbeau, F-75016 Paris, France
Tel: (00 33) (1) 4067 9054

BRITISH AMBASSADOR, HE Brian Donaldson, resident at Antananarivo, Madagascar

ECONOMY
The most important products are vanilla, copra, cloves and essential oils, which are the principal exports; cacao, sisal and coffee are also cultivated. Ngazidja is well forested and produces some timber. The Comoros are heavily dependent on foreign aid. The islands are a potential haven for tourists but political instability undermines the tourist industry.

GNP – US$212 million (2000); US$380 per capita (2000)

GDP – US$220 million (2001); US$89 per capita (2000)
ANNUAL AVERAGE GROWTH OF GDP – 1.1 per cent (1998)
TOTAL EXTERNAL DEBT – US$232 million (2000)

Trade with UK	2001	2002
Imports from UK	£1,019,000	£743,000
Exports to UK	3,603,000	211,000

DEMOCRATIC REPUBLIC OF CONGO

République Démocratique du Congo – Democratic Republic of Congo

AREA – 905,355 sq. miles (2,344,858 sq. km).
   Neighbours: Central African Republic (north), Sudan (north-east), Uganda, Rwanda, Burundi and Tanzania (east), Zambia (south), Angola (south-west), Republic of Congo-Brazzaville (north-west)
POPULATION – 48,040,000 (1997 UN estimate). The population was 34,671,607 at the 1985 census, composed of Bantu, Hamitic, Nilotic, Sudanese and Pygmoid groups, divided into more than 200 semi-autonomous tribes. More than 400 languages are spoken. Swahili, a Bantu language with an admixture of Arabic, is the nearest approach to a common language in the east and south, while Lingala is the language of a large area along the river and in the north, and Kikongo of the region between Kinshasa and the sea. French is the language of administration. Roman Catholicism is the predominant religion; there are also Protestants, Muslims and Kimbanguists
CAPITAL – Kinshasa (population, 4,655,313, 1994 estimate)
MAJOR CITIES – Kananga (393,030); Kisangani (417,517); Likasi (299,118); Lubumbashi (851,381); ΨMatadi (172,730); Mbandaka (169,841)
CURRENCY – Congolese franc
NATIONAL ANTHEM – Debout Congolais (Stand Up, Congolese)
NATIONAL DAY – 30 June (Independence Day)
NATIONAL FLAG – Blue with a large yellow five-pointed star in the centre and five small yellow five-pointed stars in a vertical line down the hoist
POPULATION GROWTH RATE – 2.6 per cent
POPULATION DENSITY – 21 per sq. km (1999)
MILITARY EXPENDITURE – 8.9 per cent of GDP (2001)
MILITARY PERSONNEL – 81,400: Army 79,000, Navy 900, Air Force 1,500
ILLITERACY RATE – (m) 26.9 per cent; (f) 49.8 per cent (2000)
ENROLMENT (percentage of age group) – primary 72 per cent (1997); secondary 26 per cent (1997); tertiary 2 per cent (1997)

The Democratic Republic of Congo (formerly Zaïre) is Africa's third largest state.

HISTORY AND POLITICS
The state of the Congo, founded in 1885, became a Belgian colony in 1908 and gained its independence in 1960. Mobutu Sésé Seko came to power in a coup in 1965 and was elected president in 1970. Legislative power was vested in a unicameral National Legislative Council, with candidates proposed by the sole legal political party, Mouvement Populaire de la Révolution (MPR).

Political reforms were announced in April 1990 and President Mobutu accepted an opposition-dominated government under Prime Minister Etienne Tshisekedi in October 1991.

In January 1994 President Mobutu dissolved the government and in April promulgated a Transitional Constitutional Act which regulated a period of transition to democracy.

In October 1996 fighting broke out between Zaïrean Tutsis *(Banyamulenge)* and the Zaïrean army in North and South Kivu provinces which had received an influx of Hutu refugees from Rwanda. The pro-Hutu army attempted to expel the Tutsis from the region but found themselves outgunned by the rebels, under the leadership of Laurent Kabila, who were backed by the Rwandan and Ugandan governments. Kabila's Alliance of Democratic Forces for the Liberation of Congo-Zaïre (AFDL) captured Kinshasa in May 1997 and President Mobutu fled. Zaïre was renamed the Democratic Republic of Congo.

A rebellion against the government of Laurent Kabila began in Kivu on 2 August 1998 and by the end of the month the rebels had seized large areas in the east and west of the country. Angola, Chad, Kenya, Namibia and Zimbabwe promised President Kabila military support. The Angolan army quickly recaptured several towns in the south-west, but the rebels maintained their grip on the eastern regions. The rebel movement, the Congolese Democratic Rally (RCD), was supported by Uganda and Rwanda. On 17 May 1999, Ernest Wamba dia Wamba, the RCD leader, was ousted, splitting the movement into two distinct factions, that led by Wamba dia Wamba being called the Congolese Democratic Rally-Liberation Movement (RCD-LM). A cease-fire signed on 31 August 1999 between the government and the two rebel groups has remained largely intact, although localised clashes have been frequent. The main rebel groups, the RCD, the RCD-LM and the Congolese Liberation Movement (MLC) reached agreement on 20 December 1999 to form an umbrella organisation to defeat the government. A new rebel group, the Congolese Democratic Rally-National (RCD-N), was founded in October 2000 and in January 2001, the RCD and the RCD-LM were reunited as the Congolese Liberation Front (FLC).

On 6 December 2000 an agreement between the government and the rebel groups was signed to withdraw troops from the front line and all parties to the civil war had withdrawn their troops 15 km from their frontline positions by 26 March 2001.

President Laurent Désiré Kabila died on 18 January 2001, having been shot by his bodyguard two days previously. His son, Maj.-Gen. Joseph Kabila, was sworn in as president on 26 January. No elections have been held since.

UN-sponsored peace talks began in South Africa in February 2002 and on 16 December the government and the main rebel groups signed a power-sharing agreement. A transitional government including the political opposition as well as representatives of the RCD and FLC was to hold power for two years, after which elections would be held. On 16 March 2003 a draft constitution was agreed whereby incumbent President Joseph Kabila would be supported during the two-year transition period by four vice-presidents. On 7 April Joseph Kabila was sworn in as president of the transitional government and on 2 July he named the transitional government Cabinet. The four vice-presidents were sworn in on 17 July and most of the Cabinet members were sworn in on 18 July. However the ministers representing the RCD and the FLC refused to take the oath of allegiance to President Kabila as head of the transitional government. The last Ugandan troops left eastern Congo in May 2003 but clashes between rival militias led to the deployment of French peacekeepers in Bunia as part of a UN rapid reaction force in June.

POLITICAL SYSTEM

A 300-member Constituent and Legislative Council was established on 21 August 2000 to draft a new constitution, which is to be put to a referendum.

There are 11 regions, each under a Governor and provincial administration: Bas-Zaïre (provincial capital, Matadi); Bandundu (Bandundu); Equateur (Mbandaka); Haut-Zaïre (Kisangani); Kinshasa (Kinshasa); Maniema (Kindu); North Kivu (Goma); South Kivu (Bukavu); Shaba (Katanga) (Lubumbashi); East Kasai (Mbuji-Mayi); West Kasai (Kananga).

HEAD OF STATE

President, Maj.-Gen. Joseph Kabila, *sworn in* 26 January 2001, *sworn in as president of the transitional government* 7 April 2003

Vice-Presidents, Abdoulaye Yerodia *(government);* Z'Ahidi Ngoma *(civilian opposition);* Jean-Pierre Bemba (FLC); Azarias Ruberwa (RCD)

TRANSITIONAL GOVERNMENT *as at July 2003*

Defence, Jean-Pierre Ondekane (RCD)
Economy, Célestin Vunabandi (RCD)
Finance, Mutombo Kyamakosa (government)
Foreign Affairs, Antoine Ghonda Mangalibi (FLC)
Health, Yagi Sitolo (government)
Interior, Théophile Mbemba Fundu (government)
Justice, Kisimba Ngoy (opposition)
Labour and Social Security, Théo Baruti (RCD)
Land Affairs, Venant Tshipasa (opposition)
Mines, Diomi Ndongala (opposition)
Planning, Thamhwe Mwamba (FLC)
Scientific Research, Kamanda wa Kamanda (opposition)
Solidarity and Humanitarian Affairs, Nzuzi wa Mbombo (opposition)
Youth and Sports, Omer Egbake (FLC)

EMBASSY OF THE DEMOCRATIC REPUBLIC OF CONGO
38 Holne Chase, London N2 0QQ
Tel: 020-8458 0254
Ambassador Extraordinary and Plenipotentiary, vacant

BRITISH EMBASSY
83 Avenue du Roi Baudouin, Kinshasa
Tel: (00 243) 98 169 100/111/200
Ambassador Extraordinary and Plenipotentiary,
HE Jim Atkinson, apptd 2000

ECONOMY

Coffee, rubber, cocoa and timber are the most important agricultural exports. The production of cotton, pyrethrum and copal is increasing. Copper is widely exploited, and industrial diamonds and cobalt are also produced. Oil deposits are exploited off the Zaïre estuary and reef-gold is mined in the north-east of the country.

The main industrial products are foodstuffs, beverages, tobacco, textiles, leather, wood products, cement and building materials, metallurgy, small river craft and bicycles. There are reserves of hydroelectric power and the Inga dam on the river Zaïre supplies electricity to

Matadi, Kinshasa and Shaba.

Whilst the country has many natural resources, civil war has led to the collapse of the economy, with total debt amounting to more than twice the GNP.

On 30 July 2003 the IMF announced that US$10 billion of debt relief would be granted to the Democratic Republic of Congo under the Heavily Indebted Poor Countries (HIPC) initiative. On 31 July the World Bank approved a US$120 million loan to boost investment and support public enterprises in key economic sectors.

GNP – US$5,024 million (1998); US$110 per capita (1998)

GDP – US$4,836 million (1998); US$129 per capita (2000)

ANNUAL AVERAGE GROWTH OF GDP – –5.7 per cent (1998)

INFLATION RATE – 175.5 per cent (1997)

TOTAL EXTERNAL DEBT – US$11,645 million (2000)

TRADE

The chief exports are copper, crude oil, coffee, diamonds, rubber, cobalt, gold, zinc and other metals.

Trade with UK	2001	2002
Imports from UK	£9,593,000	£5,591,000
Exports to UK	568,000	942,000

COMMUNICATIONS

There are approximately 145,000 km of roads, of which 20,500 km are earth-surfaced, and 6,000 km of railways. The country has four international and 40 principal airports.

REPUBLIC OF CONGO-BRAZZAVILLE

République du Congo-Brazzaville – Republic of Congo-Brazzaville

AREA – 132,047 sq. miles (342,000 sq. km).
Neighbours: Gabon (west), Cameroon and Central African Republic (north), Angola (Cabinda) (south-west), the Democratic Republic of Congo (east and south)

POPULATION – 2,745,000. The official language is French; Lingala, Monokutuba and Kikongo are widely spoken

CAPITAL – Brazzaville (population, 937,579, 1992 estimate)

MAJOR CITIES – ΨPointe Noire (576,206), the main commercial centre

CURRENCY – Franc CFA of 100 centimes

NATIONAL ANTHEM – La Congolaise

NATIONAL DAY – 15 August

NATIONAL FLAG – Divided diagonally into green, yellow and red bands

POPULATION GROWTH RATE – 2.8 per cent

POPULATION DENSITY – 8 per sq. km (1999)

MILITARY EXPENDITURE – 3.0 per cent of GDP (2001)

MILITARY PERSONNEL – 10,000: Army 8,000, Navy 800, Air Force 1,200; Paramilitaries 2,000

ILLITERACY RATE – (m) 12.5 per cent; (f) 25.6 per cent (2000)

ENROLMENT (percentage of age group) – primary 100 per cent (1997); tertiary 7 per cent (1997)

HISTORY AND POLITICS

Formerly the French colony of Middle Congo, Congo-Brazzaville became a member state of the French Community on 28 November 1958 and fully independent on 17 August 1960.

In 1968, a National Council of army officers took power and created the Parti Congolais du Travail (PCT) and the People's Republic of the Congo. After popular pressure, the PCT abandoned its monopoly of power and renounced Marxism in 1990. In 1992 the country adopted a new multi-party constitution with a directly elected president and a bicameral parliament.

The lack of a parliamentary majority forced President Lissouba to call fresh elections in 1993. These were won by the Pan-African Union for Social Democracy (UPADS) but the results were disputed by opposition groups and violence broke out between rival parties. A new UPADS-dominated government was appointed in January 1995. In June 1997, fighting broke out between forces of President Lissouba and followers of former president Sassou-Nguesso, who was reinstalled as president in October 1997. Elections scheduled for July 1997 were called off and a National Forum for Unity and Democracy was set up to schedule legislative elections. It declared a three-year transition period after which democratic elections would be held. A constitutional committee was inaugurated on 19 November 1998, charged with drafting a constitution to be approved by referendum in 1999.

In April 1999, supporters of former prime minister Bernard Kolelas formed themselves into a political party, the Patriotic Union of Ninja Forces. Following a period of intense fighting, negotiations between the government and the rebels began on 13 November 1999; an accord was reached in which the two sides agreed to an unconditional end to hostilities and the demilitarisation of political parties.

A 'non-exclusive national dialogue' was held between 17 March and 14 April 2001. Rebel leaders and the government adopted a draft constitution, which aimed to establish a directly elected executive presidency and bicameral legislature. The new constitution was approved in a referendum on 20 January 2002. Presidential elections held in March 2002 were won by Denis Sassou-Nguesso who secured nearly 90 per cent of the vote. The Congolese Labour Party (PCT) won an overall majority in elections to the National Assembly held on 26 May and 23 June 2002. There was heavy fighting throughout 2002 but two agreements were signed between the government and the Ninja fighters in March 2003 to end hostilities and restore free movement and the rule of law.

HEAD OF STATE

President, Defence, Denis Sassou-Nguesso, *sworn in* 25 October 1997, *elected* 10 March 2002

CABINET *as at July 2003*
Agriculture, Livestock and Fisheries, Women's Affairs, Jeanne Dambenzet
Civil Service and Administrative Reform, Gabriel Entcha-Ebia
Communications, Relations with Parliament, Government Spokesman, Alain Akoualat
Construction, Town Planning, Housing and Land Reforms, Claude Alphonse
Culture, Arts and Tourism, Jean-Claude Gakosso
Economy, Finance and Budget, Roger Rigobert Andely

Equipment and Public Works, Col. Florent Tsiba
Foreign Affairs, Co-operation and Francophone Affairs,
  Rodolphe Adada
Forestry, Economy and Environment, Henri Djombo
Health and Population, Alain Moka
Higher Education and Scientific Research, Henri Ossebi
*Industrial Development; Small and Medium-sized Enterprises
  and Handicrafts,* Emile Mabonzot
Justice and Human Rights, Keeper of the Seals, Jean-Martin
  M'bemba
Labour, Employment and Social Security, André Okombi
  Salissa
Mines, Energy and Hydraulics, Philippe Mvouo
Minister in the President's Office in charge of State Control,
  Simon Mfoutou
*Minister of State for Transport, Civil Aviation and
  Merchant Navy, Co-ordinator for Government Action,*
  Isidore Mvouba
Ministers-Delegate, Gilbert Ondongo *(Budget Reforms and
  Finance Companies);* Justin Ballay Megot *(Development
  Co-operation and Francophone Affairs);* Lamyr Nguele
  (Land Reform); Brig.-Gen Jacques Yvon Ndolou
  (National Defence); Louis-Marie Nombo Mavoungou
  (Sea Transport and Merchant Marine); Gabriel
  Longombe *(Secretary-General to the Presidency);* Pierre
  Ernest Abandzounou *(Scientific Research);* Jeanne
  Françoise Lekomba *(Women's Affairs)*
Petroleum Affairs, Jean-Baptiste Tati-Loutard
*Planning, Territorial Development and Economic
  Integration,* Pierre Moussa
Posts and Telecommunications, New Technologies, Jean-Felix
  Demba Dello
Primary and Secondary Education, Literacy, Rosalie Kama
Secretary-General to the Government, Thomas Dello
Security and Police, Gen. Pierre Oba
Sports and Youth, Marcel Mbani
*Social Solidarity, Humanitarian Action, Disabled War
  Veterans and Family Affairs,* Emilienne Raoul
Technical Education and Vocational Training, Pierre
  Michel Nguimbi
Territorial Administration and Decentralisation, François
  Ibovi

EMBASSY OF THE REPUBLIC OF CONGO BRAZZAVILLE
37 bis rue Paul Valéry, F-75116 Paris, France
Tel: (00 33) (1) 4500 6057
Ambassador Extraordinary and Plenipotentiary,
  HE Henri Marie Joseph Lopes, apptd 1999

BRITISH AMBASSADOR, HE Jim Atkinson, resident at
  Kinshasa, Democratic Republic of Congo

ECONOMY
Congo-Brazzaville has its own oil deposits, producing
about 9 million tonnes annually. It also produces lead,
zinc and gold. The principal agricultural products are
timber, cassava and yams. Imports are mainly of
machinery. Imports in 2000 totalled US$655 million and
exports US$3,101 million.
GNP – US$1,735 million (2000); US$570 per capita
  (2000)
GDP – US$2,751 million (2001); US$1,005 per capita
  (2000)
ANNUAL AVERAGE GROWTH OF GDP – –1.3 per cent
  (1998)
INFLATION RATE – –0.9 per cent (2000)
TOTAL EXTERNAL DEBT – US$4,887 million (2000)

Trade with UK	2001	2002
Imports from UK	£16,461,000	£16,771,000
Exports to UK	3,421,000	5,844,000

COSTA RICA

República de Costa Rica – Republic of Costa Rica

AREA – 19,654 sq. miles (51,100 sq. km). Neighbours:
  Nicaragua, Panama
POPULATION – 4,112,000 (2001), mainly of European
  origin. The language is Spanish
CAPITAL – San José (population, 1,982,339, 2000
  census)
MAJOR CITIES – Alajuela (223,478); Cartago (132,006),
  2000 census
CURRENCY – Costa Rican colón of 100 céntimos
NATIONAL ANTHEM – Noble Patria, Tu Hermosa
  Bandera (Noble Fatherland, Your Beautiful Flag)
NATIONAL DAY – 15 September
NATIONAL FLAG – Five horizontal bands, blue, white,
  red, white, blue (the red band twice the width of the
  others with emblem near staff)
LIFE EXPECTANCY (years) – 77 (2001)
POPULATION GROWTH RATE – 2.7 per cent
POPULATION DENSITY – 80 per sq. km (2001)
URBAN POPULATION – 60 per cent (2001)
MILITARY EXPENDITURE – 0.5 per cent of GDP (2001)
MILITARY PERSONNEL – 8,400
ILLITERACY RATE – (m) 4.4 per cent; (f) 4.3 per cent
  (2000)
ENROLMENT (percentage of age group) – primary 100
  per cent (1997); secondary 48 per cent (1997); tertiary
  48 per cent (1997)

HISTORY AND POLITICS
For nearly three centuries (1530–1821) Costa Rica was
under Spanish rule. In 1821 the country obtained its
independence, although from 1824 to 1839 it was one
of the United States of Central America.
  In 1948 the Army was abolished, the President
declaring it unnecessary. The main political parties are
the Social Christian Unity Party (PUSC) and the National
Liberation Party (PLN). In the legislative elections held
on 3 February 2002, the PUSC won 19 seats in the
Legislative Assembly, the PLN won 17 seats and the
Citizens' Action Party won 14 seats. The presidential
elections on 3 February and 7 April 2002 were won by
the PUSC candidate, Abel Pacheco.

POLITICAL SYSTEM
Executive power is vested in the president, who is head of
state and government, with legislative power vested
in the 57-member Legislative Assembly. Under the
constitution both the president and the members of the
Legislative Assembly are elected for a single four-year
term and may not be re-elected.

HEAD OF STATE
President, Abel Pacheco, *elected* 7 April 2002
*First Vice-President, Co-ordinator of Social Policy,
  Planning,* Lineth Saborio Chaverri
Second Vice-President (suspended), Luis Fishman
Co-ordinator of the Social Sector, Juan José Trejos

CABINET *as at July 2003*
Agriculture and Livestock, Rodolfo Coto
Children, Rosalia Gil

Culture, Youth and Sport, Guido Saenz Gonzalez
Economy, Industry and Trade, Vilma Villalobos
Environment and Energy, Carlos Manuel Rodriguez
Finance, Alberto Dent
Foreign Affairs and Religion, Roberto Tovar Faja
Foreign Trade, Alberto Trejos
Government Secretary, Maria Lora
Health, Maria del Rocio Saenz
Interior, Police and Public Security, Rogelio Ramos
   Martinez
Justice, Patricia Vega
Labour and Social Security, Ovidio Pacheco Salazar
Planning and Housing, Helio Fallas Venegas
Presidency, Ricardo Toledo
Public Education, Manuel Antonio Bolaños
Public Works and Transport, Javier Chaves Bolanos
Science and Technology, Rogelio Pardo Evans
Tourism, Rodrigo Castro
Women's Affairs, Esmeralda Britton

COSTA RICAN EMBASSY
Flat 1, 14 Lancaster Gate, London W2 3LH
Tel: 020-7706 8844
Ambassador Extraordinary and Plenipotentiary,
   HE Rodolfo Gutiérrez, apptd 1998

BRITISH EMBASSY
Apartado 815, Edifiicio Centro Colón (Eleventh Floor),
San José 1007
Tel: (00 506) 258 2025
Email: britemb@racsa.co.cr
Ambassador Extraordinary and Plenipotentiary and
   Consul-General, Georgina Butler, apptd 2002

ECONOMY

Tourism is the largest single industry, with ecotourism a growing area; one third of the country is national parkland or nature reserve. Abundant flora and fauna, such as macaws, toucans and over 1,000 species of orchid, attract large numbers of visitors. In 2001, there were 1,131,000 tourists. Manufacturing accounts for around 22 per cent of GDP, the principal products being computer components, foodstuffs, textiles, plastic goods and pharmaceuticals. The principal agricultural products are coffee, bananas, sugar and cattle (for meat).
GNP – US$14,510 million (2000); US$3,810 per capita
   (2000)
GDP – US$16,156 million (2001); US$3,964 per capita
   (2000)
ANNUAL AVERAGE GROWTH OF GDP – 1.7 per cent
   (2000)
INFLATION RATE – 11.0 per cent (2000)
UNEMPLOYMENT – 5.2 per cent (2000)
TOTAL EXTERNAL DEBT – US$4,466 million (2000)

TRADE

The chief exports are manufactured goods, bananas, coffee, fish and shellfish, machinery and tropical fruits. The chief imports are raw materials for industry, consumer goods, capital equipment, and fuel and mineral oils. The USA is Costa Rica's largest trading partner and accounts for around 40 per cent of imports and exports. Other major trading partners are Japan, Germany, Mexico and Europe. In 2001 imports totalled US$6,564 million and exports US$5,010 million.

Trade with UK	2001	2002
Imports from UK	£42,964,000	£51,024,000
Exports to UK	135,376,000	317,299,000

COMMUNICATIONS

The chief ports are Limón on the Atlantic coast, through which passes most of the coffee exported, and Caldera on the Pacific coast. LACSA is the national airline, operating flights throughout Central and South America, the Caribbean and the USA, besides internal flights to over 100 local airports by SANSA. There are over 23,000 km of roads, 7,000 km of which are highways. Costa Rica has nine major newspapers, at least 18 television stations and over 35 radio stations.

CÔTE D'IVOIRE

République de la Côte d'Ivoire – Republic of Côte d'Ivoire

AREA – 122,308 sq. miles (318,000 sq. km).
   Neighbours: Guinea and Liberia (west), Mali and
   Burkina Faso (north), Ghana (east)
POPULATION – 16,349,000: 39 per cent Muslim,
   28 per cent Christian (mainly Roman Catholic) and
   17 per cent maintain traditional beliefs. The official
   language is French, but Agni, Baoulé, Dioula, Senoufo
   and Yacouba are spoken
CAPITAL – Yamoussoukro (population, 126,191, 1988),
   the political and administrative capital since 1983
MAJOR CITIES – ΨAbidjan (1,929,079), the economic
   and financial centre
CURRENCY – Franc CFA of 100 centimes
NATIONAL ANTHEM – L'Abidjanaise
NATIONAL DAY – 7 August
NATIONAL FLAG – Three vertical stripes, orange, white
   and green
LIFE EXPECTANCY (years) – 48 (2001)
POPULATION GROWTH RATE – 2.4 per cent
POPULATION DENSITY – 51 per sq. km (2001)
MILITARY EXPENDITURE – 0.9 per cent of GDP (2001)
MILITARY PERSONNEL – 17,050: Army 6,500, Navy
   900, Air Force 700, Paramilitaries 8,950
CONSCRIPTION DURATION – 18 months (selective)
ILLITERACY RATE – (m) 45.1 per cent; (f) 61.2 per cent
   (2000)
ENROLMENT (percentage of age group) – primary
   71 per cent (1997); tertiary 6 per cent (1997)
The climate is equatorial in the south and west, which are mainly forested; tropical in the centre and east, which are savannah regions with trees; dry and tropical in the north, which is a grassy savannah region.

HISTORY AND POLITICS

Although French contact was made in the first half of the 19th century, Côte d'Ivoire became a colony only in 1893 and was finally pacified in 1912. It decided on 5 December 1958 to remain an autonomous republic within the French Community; full independence outside the Community was proclaimed on 7 August 1960.
   After having been president since independence in 1960, President Houphouët-Boigny died in December 1993 and was replaced by the parliamentary speaker Henri Konan-Bédié. The President was deposed by Gen. Robert Guëi in a military coup on 24–25 December 1999, who announced a transitional government on 4 January 2000.

A referendum on a new constitution was held on 23–24 July 2000, which was approved by 86.58 per cent of those who voted.

On 22 October 2000 a presidential election was held. President Guëi dissolved the electoral commission following early results which indicated that Laurent Gbagbo of the Ivorian Popular Front (FPI) was leading, and it was announced that Guëi had won. Demonstrations and mounting violence led to Guëi fleeing the country on 26 October and Gbagbo was inaugurated as president.

In elections to the National Assembly held on 10 December 2000 and 14 January 2001, the FPI won 96 seats and the Democratic Party of Côte d'Ivoire (PDCI) won 94 seats. The election was boycotted by the Rally of Republicans (RDR), the strongest party in the north of the country.

Fighting broke out between government forces and rebel mutineers in September 2002. A short-lived cease-fire in October gave way to further clashes. France deployed hundreds of troops in December after many civilians had been killed. In March 2003 the government and rebels agreed to form a government to include nine members from rebel ranks. A cease-fire was signed between the armed forces and rebel groups in May.

POLITICAL SYSTEM

The Côte d'Ivoire has a presidential system of government and a single-chamber National Assembly of 225 members, directly elected for a five-year term. It has been a multiparty system since 1990. The president's term of office is five years, renewable once only.

HEAD OF STATE

President, Laurent Gbagbo, *elected* 22 October 2000, *sworn in* 26 October 2000

CABINET *as at July 2003*

Prime Minister, Planning and Development, Seydou Diarra (FPI)
Administrative Reform, Eric Kahé (UDCPI)
Animal Production and Marine Resources, Kouassi Adjomani (PDCI)
Culture and Francophone Affairs, Messou Malan (PDCI)
Domestic Trade, Amadou Soumahoro (RDR)
Fight against AIDS, Christine Adjobi (FPI)
Handicrafts and the Informal Sector, Moussa Dosso (MPCI)
Higher Education; Security (interim), Zémogo Fofana (RDR)
Human Rights, Victorine Wodié (PIT)
Industry and Promotion of the Private Sector, Jeannot Ahoussou Kouadio (PDCI)
Labour and Civil Service, Hubert Oulaye (FPI)
Ministers of State, Amadou Gon Coulibaly (RDR) *(Agriculture);* Guillaume Soro (MPCI) *(Communications);* Patrick Achi (PDCI) *(Economic Infrastructure);* Angèle Gnonsoa (PIT) *(Environment);* Bouabre Bohoun (FPI) *(Finance and Economy);* Bamba Mamadou (PDCI) *(Foreign Affairs and Ivorians Abroad);* Toideuse Mabri (UDPCI) *(Health and Population);* Henriette Diabaté (RDR) *(Justice);* Léon-Emmanuel Monnet (FPI) *(Mining and Energy);* Théodore Mel Eg (UDCY) *(Regional Integration and African Unity);* Col.-Maj. Issa Diakité (MPCI) *(Territorial Administration);* Anaky Kobenan (MFA) *(Transport)*
National Education, Michel Amani N'Guessan (FPI)
National Reconciliation, Sébastien Danon Djédjé (FPI)

Planning and Development, Boniface Britto (PDCI)
Relations with Parliament and other Institutions, Alphonse Douaty (FPI)
Religious Affairs, Désiré Gnonkonté (PDCI)
Scientific Research, Mamadou Koné (MPCI)
Small and Medium Enterprises, Roger Banchi (MPIGO)
Solidarity and Social Security, Clotilde Ohouochi (FPI)
Sport and Leisure, Michel Gueu (MPCI)
Technical Education and Professional Training, Youssouf Soumahoro (MJP)
Telecommunications and New Information Technologies, Hamed Bakayoko (RDR)
Tourism, Marcel Tanoh (RDR)
Town Planning and Housing, Raymond N'Dori (FPI)
Victims of War, Refugees and Exiles, Messamba Koné (MPCI)
Water and Forests; Defence (interim), Assoa Adou (FPI)
Women, Family Affairs and Children, Kandia Camara (RDR)
Youth, Employment and Professional Training, Tuo Fozié (MPCI)

FPI Ivorian Popular Front; MFA Movement of the Forces of Hope; MJP Movement for Justice and Peace; MPCI Patriotic Movement of Côte d'Ivoire; MPIGO Ivorian Popular Movement of the Far West; PDCI Democratic Party of Côte d'Ivoire; PIT Ivorian Labour Party; RDR Rally of Republicans; UDCY Democratic Citizen's Union; UDPCI Union for Democracy and Peace in Côte d'Ivoire

EMBASSY OF THE REPUBLIC OF CÔTE D'IVOIRE
2 Upper Belgrave Street, London SW1X 8BJ
Tel: 020-7201 9601
Ambassador Extraordinary and Plenipotentiary,
HE Youssoufou Bamba, apptd 2001

BRITISH EMBASSY
Immeuble 'Bank of Africa', Angle Ave. Terrasson de Fougeres et Rue Gourgas Plateau, BP 2581, Abidjan
Tel: (00 225) (20) 300800
Email: britemb.a@aviso.ci
Ambassador Extraordinary and Plenipotentiary,
HE François Gordon, CMG, apptd 2001

ECONOMY

In the late 1980s the economy contracted considerably as its exports deteriorated in competitiveness and its rivals devalued their currencies while the franc CFA remained pegged to the French franc. An economic reform and stabilisation programme began in 1989 under IMF auspices and has brought down inflation, increased investment and led to GDP growth. The devaluation of the CFA franc in January 1994 has increased exports considerably and restored a trade surplus. In February 1998 a further economic reform programme began.

The principal exports are coffee, cocoa, timber, palm oil, sugar, rubber, pineapples, bananas, and cotton. There are a few deposits of diamonds and minerals including manganese and iron. Oil and gas deposits began to be exploited in 1995.

There was a trade surplus of US$1,797 million in 2000 and a current account deficit of US$13 million. In 2001 imports totalled US$2,545 million and exports US$3,650 million.

GNP – US$9,591 million (2000); US$600 per capita (2000)

GDP – US$10,411 million (2001); US$668 per capita (2000)

ANNUAL AVERAGE GROWTH OF GDP – 5.5 per cent
(1998)
INFLATION RATE – 2.5 per cent (2000)
TOTAL EXTERNAL DEBT – US$12,138 million (2000)

Trade with UK	2001	2002
Imports from UK	£61,044,000	£40,481,000
Exports to UK	84,838,000	92,981,000

CROATIA

Republika Hrvatska – Republic of Croatia

AREA – 21,500 sq. miles (55,900 sq. km). Neighbours:
Slovenia, Hungary (north), Serbia and Montenegro
(east), Bosnia-Hercegovina (south, and east of Adriatic
coastal strip)
POPULATION – 4,655,000: 78 per cent Croat,
12 per cent Serb, 2 per cent Yugoslav; also Hungarians,
Italians, Albanians, Czechs, Ukrainians and Jews.
Roman Catholic 76.5 per cent, Eastern Orthodox
11.1 per cent, Protestant 1.4 per cent, Muslim
1.2 per cent. The language is Croatian in the
Latin script
CAPITAL – Zagreb (population, 867,717, 2001 census)
MAJOR CITIES – Osijek (90,411); Rijeka (143,800);
Split (188,694), 2001 census
CURRENCY – Kuna of 100 lipa
NATIONAL ANTHEM – Lijepa Naša Domovina (Our
Beautiful Homeland)
NATIONAL DAY – 30 May (Statehood Day)
NATIONAL FLAG – Three horizontal stripes of red, white,
blue, with the national arms over all in the centre
LIFE EXPECTANCY (years) – 74 (2001)
POPULATION GROWTH RATE – 0.3 per cent
POPULATION DENSITY – 83 per sq. km (2001)
ILLITERACY RATE – (m) 0.7 per cent; (f) 2.7 per cent
(2000)
ENROLMENT (percentage of age group) – primary
87 per cent (1997); secondary 82 per cent (1997);
tertiary 28 per cent (1997)

Croatia is divided into three major geographic regions:
the Pannonian region in the north, the central mountain
belt, and the Adriatic coast region of Istria and Dalmatia
which has 1,185 islands and islets and 1,104 miles
(1,778 km) of coastline.

HISTORY AND POLITICS
Croatia was part of the Austro-Hungarian Empire from
1526 to 1918. On 29 October 1918 the Croatian
parliament declared Croatia independent and soon after
Croatia joined with Slovenia, Bosnia-Hercegovina, Serbia
and Montenegro to form the 'Kingdom of Serbs, Croats
and Slovenes' (renamed Yugoslavia in 1929). From 1941
to 1945 Yugoslavia was occupied by the Axis powers,
with Italy and Hungary annexing parts of Croatia and a
pro-Nazi Croat puppet state being established in the
remainder of Croatia and Bosnia-Hercegovina. The
armed extremists of this state (Ustaše) engaged in fierce
fighting with Serbian royalists, Communist partisans and
pro-Allied Croat partisans.
At the end of the war Yugoslavia was re-established as
a federal republic under Communist rule but gradually
disintegrated following the death of the wartime partisan
leader Josep Tito in 1980.
In April and May 1990 Croatia's first free, democratic
elections were won by the Croatian Democratic Union

(HDZ) of Dr Franjo Tudjman. War broke out in
September 1991 between Croatia and Serbia after the
ethnic Serb minority in Croatia rejected Croatia's
independence from Yugoslavia, which had been declared
on 30 May. The war in Croatia continued until January
1992 when a cease-fire was declared. The Federal
Yugoslav Army (JNA) and Serb forces had secured control
of virtually all ethnic Serb areas in Croatia.
President Tudjman was re-elected in June 1997, but
was temporarily replaced by Vlatko Pavletić on 26
November 1999 after he fell ill; he died on 10 December.
Stipe Mesić was elected in presidential elections held on
7 February 2000. In the general election held on 3
January 2000, the opposition coalition of the Social
Democratic Party of Croatia (SPH) and the Croatian
Social Liberal Party (HSLS) scored a decisive victory,
winning a total of 68 seats.
Croatia submitted an application for EU membership
in February 2003.

SECESSION
Croatia's ethnic Serbs voted to establish a Republic of
Serbian Krajina (RSK) in 1993.
The Croatian government seized Western Slavonia in
May 1995 and the whole of Krajina in August 1995
prompting the withdrawal of 10,000 UNCRO
peacekeepers and the flight of 150,000 Serbs. The last
Croatian Serb-held area of Eastern Slavonia agreed in
November 1995 to its eventual reintegration into
Croatia, which was achieved on 15 January 1998.

FOREIGN RELATIONS
Croatia was sworn in as a member of the Council of
Europe in November 1996. There has been a dispute
with Yugoslavia spanning around ten years, over the
Prevlaka peninsula, which lies within Croatian territory,
yet controls access to Kotor Bay, Yugoslavia's most
important deep water port. A temporary protocol was
signed between the two governments in December 2002
which gave Croatia full sovereignty, although the area
must remain demilitarised and have joint maritime police
patrols.

POLITICAL SYSTEM
Executive power is vested in a president and government.
The president is directly elected for a five-year term.
Legislative power is vested in the 151-member Chamber
of Representatives, whose members are directly elected
for a four-year term.
The constitution was amended in November 2000 to
reduce the powers of the presidency. A further
amendment was agreed in March 2001, when the
Chamber of Representatives voted to abolish the
Chamber of Counties, the upper house of the legislature.

HEAD OF STATE
President, Stipe Mesić, *elected* 7 February 2000

CABINET *as at July 2003*
Prime Minister, Ivica Račan
Deputy Prime Minister, Goran Granić
Deputy Prime Minister, Slavko Linić
Deputy Prime Minister, Social Affairs, Defence, Željka
Antunović
Deputy Prime Minister, Ante Simonić
Agriculture, Forestry and Fishing, Božidar Pankretić
Crafts, Small and Medium Businesses, Željko Pecek
Croatian Homeland War Veterans, Ivica Pančić
Culture, Antun Vujić

Economy, Ljubo Juršić
Education and Sport, Vladimir Strugar
Environmental Protection and Physical Planning, Ivo Banac
European Integration, Neven Mimica
Finance, Mato Crkvenac
Foreign Affairs, Tonino Picula
Health, Andro Vlahučić
Interior, Šime Lučin
Justice, Administration and Local Self-Government, Ingrid Antičević-Marinović
Labour and Social Welfare, Davorko Vidović
Maritime Affairs, Transport and Communications, Roland Žuvanić
Public Works, Reconstruction and Construction, Radimir Čačić
Science and Technology, Gvozden Flego
Tourism, Pave Župan Rusković
Without Portfolio, Gordana Sobol

HNS Croatian People's Party; HSLS Croatian Social Liberal Party; HSS Croatian Peasants' Party; LS Liberal Party; SPH Social Democratic Party of Croatia

EMBASSY OF THE REPUBLIC OF CROATIA
21 Conway Street, London W1T 6BN
Tel: 020-7387 2022
Ambassador Extraordinary and Plenipotentiary,
  HE Josip Paro, apptd 2002

BRITISH EMBASSY
Ul Ivana Lucica 4, Zagreb Tel: (00 385) (1) 600 9100
Email: british-embassy@zg.tel.hr
Ambassador Extraordinary and Plenipotentiary,
  HE Nicholas Jarrold, apptd 2000

BRITISH COUNCIL DIRECTOR, Roy Cross, Illica 12,
PO Box 55, 10001 Zagreb Tel: (00 385) (1) 4899 500
Email: zagreb.info@britishcouncil.hr

DEFENCE

The Army has 280 main battle tanks, 37 armoured personnel carriers and 106 armoured infantry fighting vehicles. The Air Force has 24 combat aircraft and 22 armed helicopters. The Navy has one submarine and 8 patrol and coastal combatants at five bases.
MILITARY EXPENDITURE – 2.6 per cent of GDP (2001)
MILITARY PERSONNEL – 51,000: Army 45,000, Navy 3,000, Air Force 3,000; Paramilitaries 10,000
CONSCRIPTION DURATION – Six months

ECONOMY

Production was severely hampered during the conflict in 1991–5; the material damage was estimated by the government to be US$27 billion, with the loss of 13,583 lives. Large areas of farmland were destroyed and the tourist industry, which provided one third of total foreign exchange earnings in 1990, was decimated. However, Croatia has seen a rise in tourism since 2000.

Shipbuilding and fishing are major industries on the Adriatic coast. Inland there is a light manufacturing sector, food-processing industries, bauxite deposits, thermal mineral springs, hydroelectric potential, and agriculture based on grain, horticulture, livestock and tobacco. Textiles is one of the most important industries employing more than 17 per cent of the population. In February 2003 the IMF approved a 14-month standby credit of around US$145.5 million to support Croatia's economic and financial programme.

In 2001 Croatia had a trade deficit of US$4,012 million and a current account deficit of US$642 million. Imports totalled US$8,044 million and exports US$4,659 million.
GNP – US$20,240 million (2000); US$4,620 per capita (2000)
GDP – US$19,821 million (2001); US$4,089 per capita (2000)
ANNUAL AVERAGE GROWTH OF GDP – 2.7 per cent (1998)
INFLATION RATE – 5.4 per cent (2000)
UNEMPLOYMENT – 16.1 per cent (2000)
TOTAL EXTERNAL DEBT – US$12,120 million (2000)

Trade with UK	2001	2002
Imports from UK	£88,103,000	£94,486,000
Exports to UK	52,822,000	70,277,000

CUBA

República de Cuba – Republic of Cuba

AREA – 42,231 sq. miles (109,800 sq. km)
POPULATION – 11,237,000. The language is Spanish
CAPITAL – ΨHavana (population, 2,184,990, 1996 UN estimate)
MAJOR CITIES – Camagüey (298,726); Guantánamo (205,078); Holguín (249,492); Santa Clara (207,350); ΨSantiago (433,180), 1996 UN estimates
CURRENCY – Cuban peso of 100 centavos
NATIONAL ANTHEM – Al Combate, Corred Bayameses (To Battle, Men Of Bayamo)
NATIONAL DAY – 1 January (Day of Liberation)
NATIONAL FLAG – Five horizontal bands, blue and white (blue at top and bottom) with red triangle, close to staff, charged with five-point star
LIFE EXPECTANCY (years) – 76 (2001)
POPULATION GROWTH RATE – 0.5 per cent
POPULATION DENSITY – 102 per sq. km (2001)
URBAN POPULATION – 75 per cent (2001)

HISTORY AND POLITICS

The island was visited by Columbus in 1492. Early in the 16th century the island was conquered by the Spanish, and for almost four centuries remained under Spanish rule. Separatist agitation culminated in the closing years of the 19th century in open warfare. In 1898 the USA intervened and demanded the evacuation of Cuba by Spanish forces. The Spanish–American war led to the abandonment of the island, which came under American military rule from 1899 until 1902, when an autonomous government was inaugurated with an elected president, and bicameral legislature.

A revolution led by Dr Fidel Castro overthrew the government of Gen. Batista in 1959. In 1965 the Communist Party of Cuba (PCC) was formed to succeed the United Party of the Socialist Revolution; it is the only authorised political party. A new Socialist constitution came into force in 1976 and indirect elections to the National Assembly of People's Power were subsequently held. The first direct elections to the National Assembly were held in February 1993; all candidates were officially approved by the Communist Party and ran for election unopposed. The 14 provincial assemblies were elected in the same manner. At the election of deputies to the National Assembly held on 19 January 2003, all 609 unopposed PCC candidates received the required 50 per cent of the vote, and on 6 March the National Assembly confirmed Dr Castro as president for a further five-year term.

In June 2003, the European Union imposed restrictions in its political and cultural contacts with Cuba over its poor human rights record.

HEAD OF STATE
President of Council of State and Council of Ministers,
Dr Fidel Castro Ruz, *appointed* 2 November 1976,
re-elected 15 March 1993, 24 February 1998,
6 March 2003

COUNCIL OF STATE *as at July 2003*
President, Dr Fidel Castro Ruz
First Vice-President, Gen. Raúl Castro Ruz
Vice-Presidents, Carlos Lage Dávila; Juan Almeida Bosque;
Abelardo Colomé Ibarra; Esteban Lazo Hernández;
José Ramón Machado Ventura
Secretary, José Miyar Barrueco

COUNCIL OF MINISTERS *as at July 2003*
President, Dr Fidel Castro Ruz
First Vice-President, Revolutionary Armed Forces,
Gen. Raúl Castro Ruz
Vice-Presidents, Osmany Cienfuegos Gorriarán; Gen.
Pedro Miret Prieto; José Ramón Fernández Alvarez;
Adolfo Díaz Suárez; José Luis Rodríguez García
(Economy and Planning)
Secretary, Carlos Lage Dávila
Government Ministers, Ricardo Cabrisas Ruiz;
Wilfredo López Rodríguez
Ministers, Alfredo Jordán Morales *(Agriculture);*
Lina Pedraza Rodríguez *(Auditing and Control);*
Roberto Ignacio González Planas *(Computer Science
and Communications);* Fidel Fernando Figueroa de
la Paz *(Construction);* Abel Prieto Jiménez *(Culture);*
Barbara Castillo Cuesta *(Domestic Trade);* Luis Ignacio
Gómez Gutiérrez *(Education);* Georgina Barreiro
Fajardo *(Finance and Prices);* Alfredo López Valdés
(Fishing Industry); Alejandro Roca Iglesias *(Food
Industry);* Martha Lomas Morales *(Foreign Investment
and Economic Co-operation);* Felipe Pérez Roque
(Foreign Relations); Raúl de la Nuez Ramírez *(Foreign
Trade);* Marcos J. Portal León *(Heavy Industries);*
Fernando Vecino Alegret *(Higher Education);*
Gen. Abelardo Colomé Ibarra *(Interior);* Roberto Díaz
Sotolongo *(Justice);* Alfredo Morales Cartaya *(Labour
and Social Security);* Jesús Pérez Othón *(Light Industry);*
Fernando Acosta Santana *(Metalworking and Electronics
Industry);* Gen. Rogelio Acevedo González *(President of
the Cuban Institute of Civil Aeronautics);* Ernesto López
Domínguez *(President of the Cuban Institute of Radio
and Television);* Francisco Soberón Valdés *(President of
the National Bank of Cuba);* Jorge Luis Aspiolea Roig
(President of the National Institute of Hydrography);
Humberto Rodríguez González *(President of the
National Institute of Sports);* Damodor Peña Pentón
(Public Health); Rosa Eleana Simeón Negrín *(Science,
Technology and Environment);* Div.-Gen. Ulises Rosales
del Toro *(Sugar Industry);* Ibrahim Ferradaz García
(Tourism); Carlos Manuel Pazo Torrado *(Transport);*
Wilfredo López Rodríguez *(Without Portfolio)*

EMBASSY OF THE REPUBLIC OF CUBA
167 High Holborn, London WC1V 6PA
Tel: 020-7240 2488
Ambassador Extraordinary and Plenipotentiary,
HE Dr José Fernández de Cossío, apptd 2000

BRITISH EMBASSY
Calle 34 No. 702/4, entre 7ma Avenida y 17, Miramar, Havana.
Tel: (00 53) (7) 204 1771
Ambassador Extraordinary and Plenipotentiary,
HE Paul Hare, LVO, apptd 2001

BRITISH COUNCIL DIRECTOR, William Edmundson
7ma Avenida, e, Calle 34 y 36, Miramar, Havana
Tel: (00 53) (7) 204 1771/2
Email: information@cu.britishcouncil.org

DEFENCE
The Army has about 900 main battle tanks and 700 armoured personnel carriers. The Navy has five patrol and coastal vessels at seven bases. The Air Force has 130 combat aircraft and 45 armed helicopters.

The last former Soviet combat personnel left Cuba in 1993, but 810 Russian military advisers remained to operate military intelligence facilities. In January 2002 Lourdes, Russia's last military base closed down. The United States has 2,039 personnel at Guantánamo Bay Naval Base, which has been leased since before the 1959 revolution. Suspected al-Qa'eda prisoners taken in the 2001 war in Afghanistan were flown to Guantánamo Bay for interrogation in early 2002.

MILITARY EXPENDITURE – 4.1 per cent of GDP (2001)
MILITARY PERSONNEL – 46,000: Army 35,000, Navy
3,000, Air Force 8,000; Paramilitaries 26,500
CONSCRIPTION DURATION – Two years

ECONOMY
After the revolution virtually all land and industrial and commercial enterprises were nationalised. Following the curtailing of Cuba's privileged trading relationships with the Soviet bloc in 1989, the economy deteriorated sharply and it became necessary to introduce rationing of energy, food and consumer goods. GDP fell by 75 per cent between 1989 and 1994, and the government was forced to introduce reforms. Since 1993, the government has legalised the holding of US dollars by private individuals, permitted private enterprise, cut subsidies to loss-making state industries, allowed prices for some goods and services to rise, and introduced income tax. State farms have been transformed into co-operatives run by private individuals and permitted to sell 20 per cent of produce on the open market, but remain relatively unproductive. In 1995, foreign investors were permitted to buy property and own Cuban-based companies, with British and Canadian firms becoming involved in the oil and mining industries.

Sugar is still the mainstay of the economy and the principal source of foreign exchange; sugar exports generated US$458 million in 1999 and the industry employs some 500,000 workers. Lack of external finance has been a major obstacle to economic recovery, as has the long-standing trade and economic embargo imposed by the USA, which has been criticised repeatedly by the UN and was condemned by the European Parliament in November 1998. In November 2002 the UN General Assembly voted in favour of a non-binding resolution calling for an end to the US trade embargo.

In 2000 1.8 million tourists visited Cuba, generating 43 per cent of income.

GDP – US$23,901 million (1998); US$2,384 per capita (2000)
ANNUAL AVERAGE GROWTH OF GDP – 1.2 per cent (1999)

TRADE

Trade between Cuba and the former socialist economies of Europe has declined since 1989, although Russia remains Cuba's main export partner, taking 23.3 per cent of exports in 2000. The US trade embargo was relaxed in March 1998 to allow food and medicine into the country. Principal exports are sugar, nickel, seafood, citrus fruits, tobacco and rum.

Trade with UK	2001	2002
Imports from UK	£12,965,000	£11,333,000
Exports to UK	11,672,000	8,088,000

COMMUNICATIONS

There are 12,700 km of railway track, of which 5,000 km are in public service. There are about 60,000 km of roads. In March 1998 the ban on direct flights between Cuba and the USA was lifted, although the only air connection with the USA is a weekly charter service between Miami and Havana. Direct telephone links between Cuba and the USA were suspended in December 2000.

EDUCATION

Education is compulsory and free. In 1964 illiteracy was officially declared to be eliminated.
ILLITERACY RATE – (m) 3.2 per cent; (f) 3.4 per cent (2000)
ENROLMENT (percentage of age group) – primary 100 per cent (1997); secondary 81 per cent (1997); tertiary 12 per cent (1997)

CYPRUS

Kypriaki Dimokratía / Kıbrıs Çumhuriyeti – Republic of Cyprus

AREA – 3,538 sq. miles (9,200 sq. km)
POPULATION – 790,000: 85 per cent Greek, 12 per cent Turkish. Greek and Turkish are official languages
CAPITAL – Nicosia (195,300, 2000 estimate)
MAJOR CITIES – ΨFamagusta (34,300); ΨLarnaca (110,900); ΨLimassol (191,500); Paphos (57,400), 1998 estimates
CURRENCY – Cyprus pound (C£) of 100 cents
NATIONAL ANTHEM – Ymnos Eis Tin Eleftherian (Ode To Freedom)
NATIONAL DAY – 1 October (Independence Day)
NATIONAL FLAG – White with a gold map of Cyprus above a wreath of olive
LIFE EXPECTANCY (years) – 78 (2001)
POPULATION GROWTH RATE – 1.3 per cent
POPULATION DENSITY – 86 per sq. km (2001)
URBAN POPULATION – 70 per cent (2001)
ILLITERACY RATE – (m) 1.3 per cent; (f) 4.5 per cent (2000)
ENROLMENT (percentage of age group) – primary 96 per cent (1995); secondary 93 per cent (1995); tertiary 23 per cent (1996)

HISTORY AND POLITICS

Cyprus came under British administration from 1878, and was formally annexed to Britain in 1914 on the outbreak of war with Turkey. From 1925 to 1960 it was a Crown Colony. Following the launching in 1955 of an armed campaign by EOKA in support of union with Greece, a state of emergency was declared which lasted for four years. An agreement was signed on 19 February 1959 between the United Kingdom, Greece, Turkey, and the Greek and Turkish Cypriots which provided that Cyprus would be an independent republic.

The island became independent on 16 August 1960. The constitution provided for a Greek Cypriot president and a Turkish Cypriot vice-president. The constitution proved unworkable and led to intercommunal trouble. The UN Peacekeeping Force in Cyprus (UNFICYP) was set up in 1964.

The Progressive Party of the Working People (AKEL) became the largest party in the House of Representatives following the election of 27 May 2001, winning 20 seats with the Democratic Coalition (DISI). Tassos Papadopoulos of the Democratic Party (DIKO) won the presidential election of 16 February 2003 with 15.5 per cent of the vote.

A peace plan to reunify the island was presented to Cyprus by the UN in November 2002 stipulating a federation with two constituent parts and a rotating presidency. Following four years of accession talks, in December 2002 Cyprus was invited to joint the EU in 2004 providing the two communities agreed to the UN plan by March 2003. The deadline passed without agreement and the EU stated that without reunification only Greek Cyprus would be granted membership. On 30 April the Greek Cypriot Government announced confidence-building measures designed to end the isolation of Turkish Cypriots.

HEAD OF STATE

President, Tassos Papadopoulos, *elected* 16 February 2003, *sworn in* 1 March 2003

COUNCIL OF MINISTERS *as at July 2003*

Agriculture, Environment and Natural Resources, Efthymios Efthymiou
Commerce, Industry and Tourism, Yiorgos Lillikas
Communications and Works, Kiriakos Kazamias
Defence, Kyriakos Mavronicolos
Education and Culture, Pefkios Georgiades
Finance, Markos Kyprianou
Foreign Affairs, George Iacovou
Government Spokesman, Kypros Chrysostomides
Health, Costandia Akkelidou
Interior, Andreas Christou
Justice and Public Order, Doros Theodorou
Labour and Social Insurance, Iaovos Keravnos

CYPRUS HIGH COMMISSION

93 Park Street, London W1K 7ET Tel: 020-7499 8272
High Commissioner, HE Myrna Kleopas, apptd 2000
BRITISH HIGH COMMISSION
Alexander Pallis Street (PO Box 21978), CY-1587 Nicosia
Tel: (00 357) (22) 861100
High Commissioner, HE Lyn Parker, apptd 2001

BRITISH COUNCIL DIRECTOR, Peter Skelton
3 Museum Street, CY-1097 Nicosia
Tel: (00 357) (2) 2665 152
Email: enquiries@britishcouncil.org.cy

BRITISH SOVEREIGN BASE AREAS

The UK retained full sovereignty and jurisdiction over two areas of 99 square miles in all: Akrotiri–Episkopi– Paramali and Dhekelia–Pergamos–Ayios Nicolaos– Xylophagou. The British Administrator of these areas is appointed by The Queen and is responsible to the Secretary of State for Defence. The combined total of

army and RAF personnel stationed in the areas is 3,190.
Administrator of the British Sovereign Base Areas, Air Vice-Marshal T. W. Rimmer, OBE

DEFENCE
The National Guard has 154 main battle tanks, 43 armoured infantry fighting vehicles and 307 armoured personnel carriers. Turkey has about 36,000 troops in northern Cyprus.

In January 1998, a military airfield in Paphos was completed. It is intended to provide a base for Greek military aircraft, as Cyprus does not possess its own air force.

MILITARY EXPENDITURE – 3.6 per cent of GDP (2001)
MILITARY PERSONNEL – National Guard 10,000, Paramilitaries 750; Northern Cyprus Army 5,000, Paramilitaries 150
CONSCRIPTION DURATION – 26 months

ECONOMY
In Greek Cyprus, services accounted for 75.5 per cent of GDP in 2000; industry 13.1 per cent, construction 6.9 per cent and agriculture 4.5 per cent. In Turkish Cyprus, services accounted for about 74 per cent of GDP in 1998. Main products are citrus fruits, grapes and vine products, meat, milk, potatoes and other vegetables. Manufacturing, construction, distribution and other service industries are other major employers. Tourism is the main growth industry. Twenty per cent of the world's ships are Cypriot registered. The accession of Greek Cyprus to the EU in 2004 is expected to have a detrimental effect upon the economic future of the Turkish community.

GNP – US$9,361 million (2000); US$12,370 per capita (2000)
GDP – US$8,698 million (1999); US$11,231 per capita (2000)
ANNUAL AVERAGE GROWTH OF GDP – 4.5 per cent (1999)
INFLATION RATE – 4.1 per cent (2000)
UNEMPLOYMENT – 4.9 per cent (2000)

TRADE
The UK is the main trading partner. In 2000 there was a trade deficit of US$2,606 million and a current account deficit of US$456 million. In 2001 imports totalled US$3,938 million and exports US$976 million.

Trade with UK	2001	2002
Imports from UK	£291,494,000	£272,094,000
Exports to UK	250,115,000	251,678,000

TURKISH REPUBLIC OF NORTHERN CYPRUS
In 1974, mainland Greek officers under instructions from the military junta in Athens launched a coup and installed a former EOKA member, Nikos Sampson, as president. Turkey invaded northern Cyprus and occupied over a third of the island. In 1975 a 'Turkish Federated State of Cyprus' under Rauf Denktaş was declared in this area and in 1983 a 'Declaration of Statehood' was issued which purported to establish the 'Turkish Republic of Northern Cyprus'. The declaration was condemned by the UN Security Council and only Turkey has recognised the new 'state'. In 1985, Denktaş was elected president and a general election was held. Denktaş was re-elected in 1990, 1995 and on 15 April 2000. A UN plan for the

reunification of the island was formally rejected by him on 31 August 1998. On 6 December 1998, elections to the 50-seat Republican Assembly resulted in a coalition government between the National Unity Party, who gained 24 seats, and the Democrat Party, who gained 13 seats. UN-sponsored proximity talks were held on 3–14 December 1999 between representatives of the Greek and Turkish communities, but no agreement was reached. In March 2003 President Dentkaş rejected a UN reunification plan. Confidence-building measures instituted by both governments have improved relations between the two communities.

DE FACTO HEAD OF STATE
President, Rauf Denktaş, *elected* 1985, *re-elected* 1990, 1995, 15 April 2000
Prime Minister, Dervis Eroglu

CZECH REPUBLIC

Česká Republika – Czech Republic

AREA – 29,731 sq. miles (77,300 sq. km). Neighbours: Poland (north-east), Germany (west and north-west), Austria (south), Slovakia (east)
POPULATION – 10,260,000 (2001), 10,302,000 (1991 census): 95 per cent Czech, 3 per cent Slovak. Czech is the official language. The majority of the population is Roman Catholic, with a small Protestant minority
CAPITAL – Prague (Praha) on the Vltava (Moldau) (population, 1,178,576, 2001)
MAJOR CITIES – Brno (Brünn) (379,185); Ostrava (319,293); Plzeň (Pilsen); (166,274), 2001
CURRENCY – Koruna (Kcs) of 100 haléru
NATIONAL ANTHEM – Kde Domov Můj (Where Is My Motherland)
NATIONAL DAY – 28 October
NATIONAL FLAG – White over red horizontally with a blue triangle extending from the hoist to the centre of the flag
LIFE EXPECTANCY (years) – 75 (2001)
POPULATION GROWTH RATE – 0.0 per cent
POPULATION DENSITY – 133 per sq. km (2001)
URBAN POPULATION – 75 per cent (2001)

The Czech Republic is composed of Bohemia and Moravia. Bohemia is surrounded by mountain ranges while Moravian land stretches to the Danubian basin.

HISTORY AND POLITICS
The area came under the rule of the Habsburg dynasty in 1526 and remained part of the Austro-Hungarian Empire until 1918. The rise of Czech nationalism in the late 19th century led to the proclamation of the independence of Czechoslovakia on 28 October 1918 following an amalgamation of Bohemia, Moravia, Slovakia and Ruthenia and was confirmed by the Versailles Peace Conference in 1919.

Czechoslovakia was forced to cede the ethnic German Sudetenland to Nazi Germany in 1938 after the Munich Agreement. German forces invaded the Czech Republic in March 1939 and incorporated it into Germany while Slovakia became a puppet state. The Czech Republic was liberated by Soviet and American forces in May 1945. The pre-war democratic Czechoslovak state was re-established in 1945, having ceded Ruthenia to the Soviet Union. The Communists took power in a coup in 1948 and remained in power until 1989.

In 1968 the Communist Party under Alexander Dubček embarked on a political and economic reform programme (the Prague Spring). The reforms were suppressed following an invasion by Warsaw Pact troops on the night of 20 August 1968, and were abandoned when Gustáv Husák became leader of the Communist Party in 1969.

Mass protests in November 1989 led to the resignation of the Communist Party Central Committee. The Party was forced to concede its monopoly of power and on 10 December a new government was appointed in which only half the ministers were Communists. Husák resigned as president and was replaced by the dissident writer Václav Havel. Free elections were held in June 1990 in which the Communist Party was defeated.

In late 1992 the leaders of the Czech and Slovak republics agreed to dissolve the federation and form two sovereign states; this took effect on 1 January 1993.

The general election in June 2002 produced no outright winner. Vladimír Špidla, leader of the Czech Social Democratic Party (ČSSD) formed a coalition government on 15 July. The ČSSD lost its majority in the Senate following elections held on 26 October and 3 November 2002. President Havel left office on 2 February 2003 but parliament failed to elect a successor and Prime Minister Vladimír Špidla became acting president. On 28 February, Václav Klaus of the Civic Democrat Party (ODS) was elected president and took office on 7 March.

The Czech Republic was invited to join the EU in December 2002 after five years of accession talks and the people voted in favour of joining in 2004 during a referendum held in June 2003.

POLITICAL SYSTEM
The constitution vests legislative power in the bicameral parliament, comprising a 200-member Chamber of Deputies elected for a four-year term and an 81-member Senate elected for a six-year term, one-third being renewed every two years. The president is elected by parliament for a five-year term. Executive power is held by the prime minister and Council of Ministers. A two-thirds majority in parliament is necessary to amend the constitution, and federal laws remain in place unless superseded by Czech ones. A Constitutional Court has been established comprising 15 judges nominated by the president for ten-year terms with Senate approval.

HEAD OF STATE
President, Václav Klaus, *elected by parliament* 28 February 2003, *sworn in* 7 March 2003

COUNCIL OF MINISTERS *as at June 2003*
Prime Minister, Vladimír Špidla (ČSSD)
First Deputy Prime Minister, Interior, Stanislav Gross (ČSSD)
Deputy Prime Minister, Foreign Affairs and Security Policy, Cyril Svoboda (KDU-ČSL)
Deputy Prime Minister, Justice, Pavel Rychetsky (ČSSD)
Deputy Prime Minister, Science, Research and Human Resources, Petr Mareš (US)
Agriculture, Jaroslav Palas (ČSSD)
Culture, Pavel Dostál (ČSSD)
Defence, Miroslav Kostelka (ČSSD)
Education, Youth and Sport, Petra Buzková (ČSSD)
Environment, Libor Ambrozek (KDU-ČSL)
Finance, Bohuslav Sobotka (ČSSD)
Health, Marie Součková (ČSSD)

Industry and Trade, Milan Urban (ČSSD)
Information Technology, Vladimír Mlynář (US)
Labour and Social Affairs, Zdeněk Škromach (ČSSD)
Regional Development, Pavel Němec (US)
Transport and Communications, Milan Šimonovský (KDU-ČSL)

ČSSD Czech Social Democratic Party; KDU-ČSL Christian Democratic Union-Czechoslovak People's Party; US Freedom Union

EMBASSY OF THE CZECH REPUBLIC
26 Kensington Palace Gardens, London W8 4QY
Tel: 020-7243 1115
Ambassador Extraordinary and Plenipotentiary,
  HE Štefan Füle, apptd 2003

BRITISH EMBASSY
Thunovská 14, CZ-11800 Prague 1
Tel: (00 420) (2) 5740 2111
Email: info@britain.cz
Ambassador Extraordinary and Plenipotentiary,
  HE Anne Pringle, apptd 2001

BRITISH COUNCIL DIRECTOR, Paul Docherty *(Cultural Counsellor),* Národní 10, CZ-11000 Prague 1
Tel: (00 420) (2) 2199 1111

DEFENCE
The army has 622 main battle tanks, 879 armoured infantry fighting vehicles and 362 armoured personnel carriers. The Air Force has 44 combat aircraft and 34 attack helicopters. The Czech Republic became a member of NATO on 12 March 1999.

MILITARY EXPENDITURE – 2.2 per cent of GDP (2001)
MILITARY PERSONNEL – 49,450: Army 36,370, Air Force 11,300, Others 1,780; Paramilitaries 5,600
CONSCRIPTION DURATION – 12 months

ECONOMY
Under Communist rule industry and most agricultural land was state-owned. An economic reform programme began in 1990 to produce a free-market economy. This has necessitated a restrictive monetary policy to stem inflation and a restructuring of industry to be competitive, and these were major reasons for the break with Slovakia. As a result, foreign investment (about US$4,500 million in 2000) and private enterprises have grown, over 90 per cent of the economy has been privatised, and reliance on trade with the former Soviet bloc countries has ended. Foreign-owned firms accounted for nearly half of all exports in 2000.

A customs union between the Czech and Slovak Republics is in place but separate currencies were introduced in February 1993 following speculation. The Koruna was made fully convertible in October 1995.

Principal agricultural products are sugar beet, potatoes and cereal crops; the timber industry is also very important. Having been the major industrial area of the Austro-Hungarian Empire, the country has long been industrialised, and machinery, industrial consumer goods and raw materials are major exports. Industry accounts for 36.6 per cent of GDP compared to 5.2 per cent for agriculture. The country's principal trading partner is the EU, which accounts for 69 per cent of exports and 62 per cent of imports.

In 2001 there was a trade deficit of US$3,091 million and a current account deficit of US$2,638 million. In

2000 imports totalled US$33,852 million and exports US$28,996 million.

GNP – US$53,925 million (2000); US$5,250 per capita (2000)

GDP – US$56,424 million (2001); US$4,942 per capita (2000)

ANNUAL AVERAGE GROWTH OF GDP – 2.9 per cent (2000)

INFLATION RATE – 4.1 per cent (2001)

UNEMPLOYMENT – 8.3 per cent (2001)

TOTAL EXTERNAL DEBT – US$21,299 million (2000)

Trade with UK	2001	2002
Imports from UK	£1,078,576,000	£1,030,500,000
Exports to UK	1,124,786,000	1,273,427,000

EDUCATION

Education is compulsory and free for all children from the ages of six to 15. There are nine universities of which the oldest and most famous is Charles University in Prague (founded 1348).

ENROLMENT (percentage of age group) – primary 100 per cent (1997); secondary 99 per cent (1997); tertiary 24 per cent (1997)

DENMARK

Kongeriget Danmark / Kingdom of Denmark

AREA – 16,308 sq. miles (42,400 sq. km). Neighbour: Germany (south)

POPULATION – 5,333,000. The majority of the population is Lutheran. The language is Danish

CAPITAL – ΨCopenhagen (population, 1,081,673, 2001)

MAJOR CITIES – ΨÅlborg (119,996); ΨÅrhus (218,380); ΨOdense (144,849), 2001

CURRENCY – Danish krone of 100 øre

NATIONAL ANTHEMS – Kong Kristian stod ved højen mast (King Christian Stood By The Lofty Mast); Det er et yndigt land (There Is A Lovely Land)

NATIONAL DAY – 5 June (Constitution Day)

NATIONAL FLAG – Red, with white cross

LIFE EXPECTANCY (years) – 76 (2001)

POPULATION GROWTH RATE – 0.3 per cent

POPULATION DENSITY – 126 per sq. km (2001)

HISTORY AND POLITICS

The Danes were at the forefront of Viking expansionism and briefly united England and Scandinavia under Knut (Canute) (995–1035).

The Union of Kalmar (1397) brought Norway and Sweden (including Finland) under Danish rule. Danish power waned during the 16th century, however, enabling Sweden to re-establish its independence in 1523. In the 19th century Norway was ceded to Sweden under the Treaty of Kiel (1814) and both Schleswig and Holstein, which had been subsumed in 1460, were surrendered to Germany.

Denmark remained neutral during the First World War, and in a plebiscite held in accordance with the Versailles Treaty (1919), northern Schleswig voted to return to Danish sovereignty. In 1939 Denmark signed a non-aggression pact with Germany but was invaded on 9 April 1940 and coerced into contributing to the German war effort. Iceland declared its independence from

Denmark in 1944 and the Færøe Islands were granted home rule in 1948. Greenland, which had had the status of a colony, was integrated into Denmark in 1953 and granted home rule in 1979. Social Democrat-led coalitions dominated the post-war era until 1982 when a right-wing government was elected. Denmark joined the European Community in 1973.

A referendum was held on 28 September 2000 on membership of the European single currency. Membership was rejected by 53.1 per cent of those who voted.

The most recent legislative elections were held on 20 November 2001 and the Liberal Party became the largest party in Parliament. A coalition government was formed on 27 November 2001 by Anders Fogh Rasmussen between the Liberal Party and the Conservative People's Party.

POLITICAL SYSTEM

The legislature consists of one chamber, the *Folketing*, of 179 members, including two for the Færøes and two for Greenland, which is elected for a four-year term. The voting age is 18 with voting based on a proportional representation system with a 2 per cent threshold for parliamentary representation.

HEAD OF STATE

HM The Queen of Denmark, Queen Margrethe II, KG, *born* 16 April 1940, *succeeded* 14 January 1972, *married* 10 June 1967, Count Henri de Monpezat (Prince Henrik of Denmark), and *has issue* Crown Prince Frederik (*see* below); Prince Joachim, *born* 7 June 1969, *married* 18 November 1995, Miss Alexandra Manley (Princess Alexandra of Denmark)

Heir, HRH Crown Prince Frederik, *born* 26 May 1968

CABINET *as at July 2003*

Prime Minister, Anders Fogh Rasmussen (V)

Culture, Brian Mikkelsen (KF)

Defence, Svend Aage Jensby (V)

Education, Ulla Toernaes (V)

Ecclesiastical Affairs, Tove Fergo

Economy, Industry, Trade and Nordic Co-operation, Bendt Bendtson (KF)

Employment, Claus Hjort Frederiksen (V)

Environment and Energy, Hans Christian Schmidt (V)

Finance, Thor Pedersen (V)

Food, Agriculture and Fisheries, Mariann Fischer Boel (V)

Foreign Affairs, Per Stig Moeller (KF)

Interior and Health, Lars Loekke Rasmussen (V)

Justice, Lene Espersen (KF)

Refugees, Immigrants and Integration; Minister without portfolio responsible for European Affairs, Bertel Haarder (V)

Science, Technology and Development, Helge Sander (V)

Social Affairs and Equality, Henriette Kjaer (KF)

Taxation, Svend Erik Hovmand (KF)

Transport, Flemming Hansen (KF)

V Liberal Party; KF Conservative People's Party

ROYAL DANISH EMBASSY

55 Sloane Street, London SW1X 9SR

Tel: 020-7333 0200

Ambassador Extraordinary and Plenipotentiary, HE Tom Risdahl Jensen, apptd 2001

BRITISH EMBASSY
36–40 Kastelsvej, DK-2100 Copenhagen Ø
Tel: (00 45) 3544 5200
Email: www.brit-emb@post6.tele.dk
Ambassador Extraordinary and Plenipotentiary, HE Philip
Astley, LVO, apptd 1999

BRITISH COUNCIL DIRECTOR, Dr Michael
Sørensen-Jones, Gammel Mønt 12.3,
DK-1117 Copenhagen K
Tel: (00 45) (33) 369 400
Email: british.council@britishcouncil.dk

DEFENCE

The Army has 248 main battle tanks, 326 armoured
personnel carriers and 12 attack helicopters. The Navy
has four submarines, three offshore patrol frigates and 27
patrol and coastal vessels at three bases. The Air Force has
68 combat aircraft.

MILITARY EXPENDITURE – 1.5 per cent of GDP (2001)
MILITARY PERSONNEL – 22,700: Army 12,800,
Navy 4,000, Air Force 4,500
CONSCRIPTION DURATION – Four to 12 months

ECONOMY

The largest sectors of employment are professional
services and administration; commerce; manufacturing
and agriculture. The chief agricultural products are pigs,
dairy products, poultry and eggs, seeds and cereals;
manufactures are mostly based on imported raw materials
but there are also considerable imports of finished goods.
Denmark is self-sufficient in oil and natural gas and in
2000 became a net energy exporter through exports of
natural gas to Sweden.

GNP – US$172,238 million (2000); US$32,280 per
capita (2000)
GDP – US$162,817 million (2001); US$30,141 per
capita (2000)
ANNUAL AVERAGE GROWTH OF GDP – 2.9 per cent
(2000)
INFLATION RATE – 2.4 per cent (2001)
UNEMPLOYMENT – 4.7 per cent (2001)

TRADE
The principal imports are industrial raw materials,
consumer goods, construction inputs, machinery, raw
materials, vehicles and textile products. The chief exports
are manufactured articles, and agricultural and dairy
products. Germany and Sweden are Denmark's main
trading partners.
In 2001 Denmark had a trade surplus of US$6,960
million and a current account surplus of US$4,142
million. Imports totalled US$43,441 million and exports
US$50,564 million.

Trade with UK	2001	2002
Imports from UK	£2,156,500,000	£2,607,000,000
Exports to UK	2,513,200,000	2,584,000,000

COMMUNICATIONS

In 1996, the Danish mercantile fleet numbered 584 ships
of more than 100 gross tonnage. There are 2,349 km of
railway, of which 600 km are electrified. An additional
network of 526 km is operated by private companies. A
rail tunnel and bridge linking the islands of Sjælland and
Fyn was opened in 1997, and a road and rail tunnel and

bridge across the Øresund, linking Copenhagen with the
Swedish city of Malmö, was opened on 1 July 2000.
Some 38 newspapers are published in Denmark; eight
daily papers are published in Copenhagen. There are
some 250 local commercial and community radio stations
in operation.

CULTURE AND EDUCATION

The Danish language is akin to Swedish and Norwegian.
Education is free and compulsory. Special schools are
numerous, commercial, technical and agricultural
predominating. There are universities at Copenhagen
(founded in 1479), Århus (1928), Odense (1966),
Roskilde (1972) and Ålborg (1974).

ENROLMENT (percentage of age group) – primary 100
per cent (1997); secondary 100 per cent (1997);
tertiary 48 per cent (1997)

THE FÆRØE ISLANDS

AREA – 540 sq. miles (1,399 sq. km)
POPULATION – 46,339 (2001)
CAPITAL – Tórshavn (population, 16,511, 2001)

Since 1948 the Færøes or Sheep Islands have had a
degree of home rule. The islands are governed by a
Løgting of between 27 and 32 members and a *Landsstýri*
of three to six members which deals with special Færøes
affairs, and send two representatives to the *Folketing* at
Copenhagen. The Færøes are not part of the EU. In
elections to the Løgting held on 30 April 2002, Prime
Minister Anfinn Kallsberg's coalition won 16 of the 32
seats, losing his overall majority.

Prime Minister, Anfinn Kallsberg

Trade with UK	2001	2002
Imports from UK	£27,935,000	£6,715,000
Exports to UK	108,873,000	100,816,000

GREENLAND

AREA – 840,004 sq. miles (2,175,600 sq. km) of which
about 16 per cent is ice-free
POPULATION – 56,000 (2002)
CAPITAL – Godthåb (Nuuk) (population, 13,889, 2002)

Greenland attained a status of internal autonomy in May
1979 and a government *(Landsstyret)* was established. It
has a *Landsting* (parliament) of 31 members and sends
two representatives to the *Folketing* at Copenhagen. In
parliamentary elections held on 3 December 2002 the
Forward (Siumut) party won ten seats. Hans Enoksen of
the Forward party became prime minister and formed a
coalition government with the Feeling of Community
(Atássut) party. Greenland negotiated its withdrawal from
the EU, without discontinuing relations with Denmark,
and left on 1 February 1985.
The USA has acquired certain rights to maintain air
bases in Greenland.

Prime Minister, Hans Enoksen

Trade with UK	2001	2002
Imports from UK	£2,994,000	£343,000
Exports to UK	3,220,000	1,137,000

DJIBOUTI

Jumbūriyya Jībūtī/République Djibouti – Republic of Djibouti

AREA – 8,958 sq. miles (23,200 sq. km). Neighbours: Eritrea (north), Ethiopia (west and south), Somalia (south-east)
POPULATION – 634,000, mostly Afar or Issas. The official languages are Arabic and French; Afar and Somali are also spoken
CAPITAL – ΨDjibouti (population, 62,000, 1991)
CURRENCY – Djibouti franc of 100 centimes
NATIONAL ANTHEM – Hinjinne u sara kaca (Arise With Strength)
NATIONAL DAY – 27 June (Independence Day)
NATIONAL FLAG – Blue over green with white triangle in the hoist containing a red star
POPULATION GROWTH RATE – 1.2 per cent
POPULATION DENSITY – 27 per sq. km (1999)
MILITARY EXPENDITURE – 3.9 per cent of GDP (2001)
MILITARY PERSONNEL – 9,850: Army 8,000, Navy 200, Air Force 250, Gendarmerie 1,400; Paramilitaries 2,500
GNP – US$553 million (2000); US$880 per capita (2000)
GDP – US$576 million (2001); US$847 per capita (2000)
ANNUAL AVERAGE GROWTH OF GDP – 2.1 per cent (1998)
TOTAL EXTERNAL DEBT – US$262 million (2000)
ILLITERACY RATE – (m) 24.4 per cent; (f) 45.6 per cent (2000)
ENROLMENT (percentage of age group) – primary 32 per cent (1996); secondary 12 per cent (1996); tertiary 0.3 per cent (1996)

HISTORY AND POLITICS

Formerly French Somaliland and then the French Territory of the Afars and the Issas, the Republic of Djibouti became independent on 27 June 1977. A multiparty constitution was adopted by referendum in 1992 and subsequent multiparty elections held in December 1992 were won by the *Rassemblement populaire pour le Progrès* (RPP, the Popular Rally for Progress). President Aptidon was re-elected for a fourth six-year term in 1993. In December 1997, in the first elections since the 1994 peace accord, the RPP and the Front for the Restoration of Freedom and Democracy (FRUD) formed an alliance and won all 65 seats in the National Assembly. On 9 April 1999, President Ismael Omar Guelleh was elected, gaining approximately three-quarters of the votes cast; about 60 per cent of the electorate were estimated to have voted. On 7 February 2000, the government signed a peace agreement with a breakaway faction of the FRUD, which had continued its armed opposition to the government after the 1994 peace accord.

On 7 December 2000, an attempted coup by a group of police officers was quickly put down by the armed forces.

The In legislative elections held on 10 January 2003, the first elections since independence where the number of parties allowed to contest an election was not limited, the Union for Presidential Majority (UMP), an alliance of parties supporting President Guelleh, won all 65 seats in the National Assembly.

HEAD OF STATE
President, Ismael Omar Guelleh, *elected* 9 April 1999

COUNCIL OF MINISTERS *as at July 2003*
Prime Minister, National and Regional Development, Dilleita Mohamed Dilleita
Agriculture, Livestock and Marine Affairs, Dini Abdallah Bililis
Communication and Culture, Posts and Telecommunications, Government Spokesman, Rifki Abdoulkader Bamakhrama
Defence, Ougoure Kifle Ahmed
Economy, Finance and Privatisation, Yacin Elmi Bouh
Energy and Natural Resources, Muhammad Ali Muhammad
Foreign Affairs and International Co-operation, Relations with Parliament, Ali Abdi Farah
Housing, Town Planning, Environment and Regional Development, Abdallah Abdillahi Miguil
Interior and Decentralisation, Abdoulkadar Doualeh Wais
Justice, Human Rights, Islamic Affairs and Prisons, Ismail Ibrahim Houmed
Labour and Vocational Training, Mohamed Barkat Abdillahi
Ministers-Delegate, Mahamoud Ali Yousouf *(International Co-operation)*; Cheikh Mogueh Dirir Samatar *(Religious Affairs and Muslim Affairs)*; Hawa Ahmed Yousouf *(Women, Families and Social Welfare)*
National Education, Abdi Ibrahim Absieh
Presidential Affairs and Promotion of Investments, Osman Ahmad Moussa
Public Health, Mohamed Ali Kamil
Trade, Industry and Handicrafts, Saleiban Omar Oudine
Transport and Equipment, Elmi Obsieh Wais
Youth, Sport, Leisure and Tourism, Otban Goita Moussa

EMBASSY OF THE REPUBLIC OF DJIBOUTI
26 rue Emile Ménier, F-75116 Paris, France
Tel: (00 33) (1) 4727 4922
Ambassador Extraordinary and Plenipotentiary, HE Mohamed Goumaneh Guirreh, apptd 2002

BRITISH AMBASSADOR, HE Myles Wickstead, apptd 2000, resident at Addis Ababa, Ethiopia

ECONOMY AND TRADE

The economy depends mainly on the operation of the free port, which accounts for about three-quarters of Djibouti's GDP. Agriculture accounts for less than 4 per cent of GDP, but employs three-quarters of the workforce. The main imports are foodstuffs, machinery, clothing, and oil and oil derivatives. The main exports are foodstuffs and livestock. Djibouti's primary trading partners are Ethiopia, Somalia, Yemen and France.

Trade with UK	2001	2002
Imports from UK	£11,609,000	£12,995,000
Exports to UK	123,000	96,000

DOMINICA

The Commonwealth of Dominica

AREA – 288.5 sq. miles (750 sq. km)
POPULATION – 71,000 (2001). English is the official language although Creole French is more commonly used

CAPITAL – ΨRoseau (population, 16,243, 1991)
CURRENCY – East Caribbean dollar (EC$) of 100 cents
NATIONAL ANTHEM – Isle Of Beauty
NATIONAL DAY – 3 November (Independence Day)
NATIONAL FLAG – Green ground with a cross overall of
yellow, black and white stripes, and in the centre a red
disc charged with a Sisserou parrot in natural colours
within a ring of ten green stars
LIFE EXPECTANCY – 74 (2001)
POPULATION GROWTH RATE – 0.1 per cent (1999)
POPULATION DENSITY – 95 per sq. km (2001)

Dominica, in the Lesser Antilles, lies in the Windward
Islands group 95 miles south of Antigua. It is about 29
miles long and 16 miles wide.

HISTORY AND POLITICS

The island was discovered by Columbus in 1493, when it
was a stronghold of the Caribs, who remained virtually
the sole inhabitants until the French established
settlements in the 18th century. It was captured by the
British in 1759 but passed back and forth between
France and Britain until 1805, after which British
possession was not challenged. From 1871 to 1939
Dominica was part of the Leeward Islands Colony, then
from 1940 the island was a unit of the Windward Islands
group. Internal self-government from 1967 was followed
on 3 November 1978 by independence as a republic.

The general election held on 31 January 2000 was
won by the Dominica Labour Party, which gained 10
seats in the House of Assembly, with nine seats going to
the United Workers' Party and two seats to the Dominica
Freedom Party.

Pierre Charles was appointed as prime minister
following the sudden death of his predecessor, Roosevelt
Douglas, on 1 October 2000.

POLITICAL SYSTEM

Executive authority is vested in the president, who is
elected by the House of Assembly for not more than two
terms of five years. Parliament consists of the president
and the House of Assembly (21 representatives elected by
universal adult suffrage for a five-year term) and nine
senators, five of whom are appointed on the advice of the
prime minister and the other four on the advice of the
Leader of the Opposition.

HEAD OF STATE

President, HE Vernon Shaw, *elected* 2 October 1998,
took office 6 October 1998

CABINET *as at July 2003*
Prime Minister, Banana Industry, Finance and Caribbean
Affairs, Labour and Immigration, Pierre Charles (DLP)
Agriculture and the Environment, Vince Henderson (DLP)
Attorney-General, Legal Affairs, Henry Dyer
Communications and Works, Housing and Physical
Planning, Reginald Austrie (DLP)
Community Development and Gender Affairs, Matthew
Walters (DLP)
Foreign Affairs, Trade and Marketing, Osborne Riviere
(DLP)
Health and Social Security, Herbert Sabaroche (DFP)
Tourism, Industry and Enterprise Development, Charles
Savarin (DFP)
Youth and Sports, Education, Science and Technology,
Roosevelt Skerrit (DLP)

DFP Dominica Freedom Party; DLP Dominica Labour
Party

HIGH COMMISSION FOR THE COMMONWEALTH OF
DOMINICA
1 Collingham Gardens, London SW5 0HW
Tel: 020-7370 5194/5
High Commissioner, vacant
BRITISH HIGH COMMISSIONER, HE John White,
resident at Bridgetown, Barbados

BRITISH CONSULATE
PO Box 2269, Roseau
Honorary Consul, Simon Maynard

ECONOMY

Agriculture is the principal occupation, with tropical and
citrus fruits being the main crops. Products for export are
bananas, fruit juices, lime oil, bay oil, copra and rum.
Forestry, fisheries and agro-processing are being
encouraged. The only commercially exploitable mineral is
pumice, used chiefly for building purposes.
Manufacturing consists largely of the processing of
agricultural products although there have been attempts
to diversify into light industry. In 2000 Dominica had a
trade deficit of US$79 million and a current account
deficit of US$69 million. Imports totalled US$147
million and exports US$53 million.
GNP – US$238 million (2000); US$3,260 per capita
(1999)
GDP – US$261 million (2001); US$3,803 per capita
(2000)
ANNUAL AVERAGE GROWTH OF GDP – 2.6 per cent
(1998)
INFLATION RATE – 0.8 per cent (2000)
TOTAL EXTERNAL DEBT – US$108 million (2000)

Trade with UK	2001	2002
Imports from UK	£10,075,000	£9,365,000
Exports to UK	12,048,000	16,112,000

DOMINICAN REPUBLIC

República Dominicana – Dominican Republic

AREA – 18,615 sq. miles (48,400 sq. km). Neighbour:
Haiti (west)
POPULATION – 8,507,000. The language is Spanish
CAPITAL – ΨSanto Domingo (population, 2,134,779,
1993)
MAJOR CITIES – Duarte (272,227); La Vega (335,140);
Puerto Plata (255,061); San Cristóbal (409,381); San
Juan (247,029); Santiago de los Caballeros (690,458),
1993 UN estimates
CURRENCY – Dominican Republic peso (RD$) of 100
centavos
NATIONAL FLAG – Divided into blue and red quarters by
a white cross
NATIONAL ANTHEM – Quisqueyanos Valientes, Alcemos
(Brave Men Of Quisqueya, Let's Raise Our Song)
NATIONAL DAY – 27 February (Independence Day
1844)
LIFE EXPECTANCY (years) – 67 (2001)
POPULATION GROWTH RATE – 1.7 per cent
POPULATION DENSITY – 176 per sq. km (2001)
URBAN POPULATION – 66 per cent (2001)
MILITARY EXPENDITURE – 0.7 per cent of GDP (2001)

MILITARY PERSONNEL – 24,500: Army 15,000, Navy 4,000, Air Force 5,500; Paramilitaries 15,000
ILLITERACY RATE – (m) 16.4 per cent; (f) 16.4 per cent (2000)
ENROLMENT (percentage of age group) – primary 94 per cent (1997); secondary 54 per cent (1997); tertiary 54 per cent (1997)

The Dominican Republic, the eastern part of the island of Hispaniola (Haiti is the western part), is the oldest European settlement in America.

HISTORY AND POLITICS

Santo Domingo was discovered by Columbus in 1492, and was a Spanish colony until 1797, when it passed to France. It was restored to Spanish rule in 1809. Independence was proclaimed in 1821, but in 1822 it was subjugated by the neighbouring Haitians who remained in control until 1844, when the Dominican Republic was proclaimed. The country was occupied by American marines from 1916 until 1924, and ruled by Gen. Rafael Trujillo from 1930 until 1961.

The presidential election on 16 May 2000 was won by Hipólito Mejía, the Dominican Revolutionary Party (PRD) candidate. The general election on 16 May 2002 resulted in the PRD winning 73 seats in the Chamber of Deputies and 29 seats in the Senate.

POLITICAL SYSTEM

Executive power is vested in the president, who is directly elected for a four-year term, renewable once only, and appoints the Cabinet. Legislative power is exercised by the Congress, which has a term of four years. The Congress comprises the Senate of 32 senators, one for each province and one for Santo Domingo, and the 150-member Chamber of Deputies.

HEAD OF STATE

President, Rafael Hipólito Mejía Domingues, *elected* 16 May 2000, *sworn in* 16 August 2000
Vice-President, Minister of Education, Fine Arts and Public Worship, Milagros Ortiz Bosch

CABINET *as at May 2003*

Agriculture, Eligio Jaquez
Attorney-General, Virgilio Bello Rosa
Culture, Tony Raful
Defence, José Miguel Soto Jiménez
Environment, Frank Moya Pons
Finance, José Malkum
Foreign Affairs, Hugo Tolentino Dipp
Health, José Rodríguez Soldevilla
Industry and Commerce, Sonia Gomez
Interior and Police, Pedro Franco Badia
Labour, Milton Ray Guevara
Presidency, Sergio Grullón
Public Works, Miguel Vargas
Sports, Physical Education and Recreation, César Cedeño
Tourism, Rafael Subervi Bonilla
Women, Yadira Henríquez
Youth, Antonio Pena Guaba

EMBASSY OF THE DOMINICAN REPUBLIC
139 Inverness Terrace, London, W2 6JF
Tel: 020-7727 6285
Ambassador Extraordinary and Plenipotentiary,
   HE Rafael Ludovino Fernández, apptd 2000

BRITISH EMBASSY
Edifiicio Corominas Pepín, Ave 27 de Febrero No 233, Sant Domingo
Tel: (00 1 809) 472 7111
Ambassador Extraordinary and Plenipotentiary,
   HE Andrew Ashcroft, apptd 2002

ECONOMY

Sugar, cocoa, coffee, bananas, rice and tobacco are the most important crops. Other products are maize, molasses, beans, tomatoes, cement, ferro-nickel, gold, silver and cattle. Light industry produces beer, tinned foodstuffs, glass products, textiles, soap, cigarettes, construction materials, plastic articles, paint, rum, matches and peanut oil. Tourism is an important part of the economy, with 3 million foreign visitors to the Dominican Republic in 2000, generating US$2.9 billion.
GNP – US$17,847 million (2000); US$2,130 per capita (2000)
GDP – US$21,211 million (2001); US$2,982 per capita (2000)
ANNUAL AVERAGE GROWTH OF GDP – 6.5 per cent (2000)
INFLATION RATE – 6.5 per cent (1999)
TOTAL EXTERNAL DEBT – US$4,598 million (2000)

TRADE

The chief imports are fuel oils, foodstuffs, motor vehicles, pharmaceuticals and machinery components. The chief exports are minerals, sugar and sugar by-products, coffee and cocoa. The USA is the main trading partner.

In 2000 there was a trade deficit of US$3,742 million and a current account deficit of US$1,027 million. Imports totalled US$7,379 million and exports US$966 million.

Trade with UK	2001	2002
Imports from UK	£45,159,000	£50,912,000
Exports to UK	32,137,000	53,447,000

COMMUNICATIONS

There are over 4,000 miles of roads and a direct road from Santo Domingo to Port-au-Prince, the capital of Haiti, but that part of it in the border area has fallen into disuse. The frontier has been closed since 1967, except for the section crossed by the main road linking the two capitals. The construction of a railway between the port of Haina and Santiago is expected to be completed by mid-2004. A telephone system connects all the principal towns. There are more than 90 commercial broadcasting stations and seven television stations.

EAST TIMOR

República Democrática de Timor-Leste/Republik Demokratis Timor Leste/República Demokrátika Timór-Leste – Democratic Republic of East Timor

AREA –5,743 sq. miles (14,874 sq. km). Neighbour: Indonesia (west). The enclave of Oekussi is separated from the rest of East Timor by the Indonesian province of West Timor
POPULATION – 952,618 (2002 estimate): 78 per cent Timorese, 20 per cent Indonesian, 2 per cent Chinese. Tetum is the national language and is spoken by about 60 per cent of the population, although Mambai, Tokodede, Kemak, Galoli, Idate, Waima'a, Naueti, Bunak, Makasae and Fatuluku are also spoken.

Portuguese and Bahasa Indonesian are widely understood. The population is predominantly Roman Catholic

CAPITAL – ΨDili (population, 56,000, 2001 estimate)
MAJOR CITY – Lautem (17,850, 1996 estimate)
CURRENCY – Currency is that of the USA
NATIONAL ANTHEM – Funu Nain Falintil
NATIONAL FLAG – Red with a yellow triangle based on the hoist and surmounted by a black triangle containing a white star
POPULATION DENSITY – 59 per sq. km (1999)
POPULATION GROWTH RATE – 1.7 per cent

HISTORY AND POLITICS

East Timor was a Portuguese colony from 1702 until Portuguese control collapsed following the 1974 coup in Portugal. Local elections were held in early 1975, in which the left-wing, pro-independence Fretilin (Revolutionary Front for an Independent East Timor) emerged as the strongest party. Indonesia had supported Apodeti (Popular Democratic Association of Timor), which urged the integration of the territory into Indonesia. Following its failure to gain a substantial proportion of the vote, Indonesia encouraged the pro-autonomy Democratic Union of Timor (UDT) to attempt a coup in August 1975, but this was convincingly suppressed by the better equipped and disciplined Fretilin. The Portuguese administration withdrew without formally handing over power. Indonesia began to infiltrate the border and attack villages in the frontier regions to create the illusion that the civil war was still continuing in order to justify an invasion. Fretilin proclaimed the Democratic Republic of East Timor on 28 November 1975, which was recognised by Portugal. The following day the leaders of Apodeti and UDT, who had fled to Indonesia following the failed coup, were coerced into signing a request for Indonesian assistance to restore order in East Timor. Indonesian forces began to invade East Timor on 7 December 1975 and declared East Timor Indonesia's 27th province on 17 July 1976 following their establishment of a provisional East Timorese government consisting of Apodeti ministers, which signed a petition requesting integration with Indonesia. Fretilin forces resisted strongly, but by 1979 most of East Timor was under Indonesian control. Resistance and atrocities committed by Indonesian troops left at least 200,000 East Timorese dead, predominantly civilians. About 150,000 Muslims were settled in East Timor alongside the predominantly Roman Catholic population (80 per cent in 1975). The UN did not recognise the annexation.

Following negotiations between Indonesia and Portugal, an agreement was reached to conduct a plebiscite on 30 August 1999, which would offer East Timor autonomy within Indonesia or independence. The plebiscite resulted in a turnout of 98.6 per cent of the electorate, with 78.5 per cent voting for independence for East Timor.

With the agreement of the Indonesian government, the UN sent in peacekeeping troops in September 1999 after civilians were forcibly evacuated from their homes and suffered extensive violence and intimidation at the hands of pro-Indonesian militias and Indonesian troops. Indonesian troops began to withdraw and on 19 October, the Indonesian Consultative Assembly unanimously ratified the result of the referendum on the independence of East Timor. By early October, the UN-established International Force for East Timor (INTERFET) had managed to install its forces on the border with West Timor with the aim of preventing cross-border attacks by pro-Indonesia militias. INTERFET also managed to land troops in the East Timorese enclave of Oekussi. The commander of Indonesian forces in West Timor signed an agreement with INTERFET on the repatriation of refugees on 22 November 1999.

The UN Security Council voted unanimously on 25 October 1999 to replace INTERFET with a UN force of up to 8,950 troops and 1,600 police to support the establishment of a UN Transitional Administration in East Timor (UNTAET). On 27 November, the pro-independence activist José Xanana Gusmão visited Jakarta to establish relations with the Indonesian government. The East Timor National Council (ETNC), which was established to make policy recommendations to UNTAET, held its first meeting on 11 December.

Two reports, published on 31 January 2000, concluded that the Indonesian authorities had co-operated with the pro-Indonesian militias in wide-ranging human rights abuses and called for the establishment of an international war crimes tribunal. UN prosecutors began issuing indictments in December 2000.

The ETNC adopted the US dollar as the country's transitional currency on 24 January 2000.

Indonesia's President Wahid signed a memorandum of understanding with UNTAET on 29 February, to allow the resumption of cross-border trade and transport between East Timor and Indonesia.

José Xanana Gusmão resigned as president of the ETNC on 28 March 2001 and was replaced by Manuel Carrascalão.

East Timor's first presidential elections were held on 14 April 2002 and were won by José Xanana Gusmão with 82.7 per cent of the vote.

Independence was achieved on 20 May 2002 and UNTAET was succeeded by the UN Mission of Support in East Timor (UNMISET) which was due to remain in place until May 2004. On 27 September 2002, East Timor became a member of the UN.

In November 2002 former pro-Jakarta militia leader Eurico Guterres received a UN indictment for crimes against humanity for his role in the 1999 massacre and a further seven senior Indonesian military officers were indicted in February 2003. Indonesia's former military chief in East Timor, Brigadier-General Noer Muis, was sentenced to five years' imprisonment in March 2003 for crimes against humanity.

Serious civil unrest including the looting and burning of shops, offices and the prime minister's home in late 2002 and early 2003, led to the UN Security Council's approval of the strengthening of the 651-member police component of UNMISET in April 2003. On 19 May 2003 the UN Security Council passed a resolution extending UNMISET's mandate until 20 May 2004.

POLITICAL SYSTEM

In October 2000 a 36-member transitional legislative body, the East Timor National Council, was established. It was replaced by an 88-member elected Constituent Assembly which was elected on 30 August 2001 and inaugurated on 15 September.

HEAD OF STATE

President, José Xanana Gusmão, *elected* 14 April 2002, *took office* 20 May 2002

COUNCIL OF MINISTERS *as at July 2003*
Prime Minister, Environment and Development, Mari bin
   Hamud Alkatiri (Fretilin)
Agriculture, Fisheries and Forestry, Estanislau Alexio da
   Silva (Fretilin)
Education, Culture, Youth and Sport, Armindo Maia (Ind.)
Health, Rui María de Araujo (Ind.)
Interior, Rogerio Lobato (Fretilin)
Justice, Domingos Maria Sarmento (Ind.)
Minister of State for Foreign Affairs, José Ramos-Horta
   (Ind.)
Minister of State, Presidency of the Council of Ministers,
   Ana Maria Pessoa Pereira da Silva Pinto (Fretilin)
Planning and Finance, Maria Madalena Brites Boavida
   (Fretilin)
Secretaries of State, Raga Virigilio Smith (Ind.) *(Education,
   Culture, Youth and Sport);* Egidio de Jesus *(Electricity
   and Water);* Arsenio Paixao Bano (Ind.) *(Labour and
   Solidarity);* Roque Felix de Jesus Rodrigues (Ind.)
   (National Defence); Antoninho Bianco (Fretilin)
   (Parliamentary Affairs); João Alves *(Public Works);*
   Gregorio José de Sousa (Fretilin) *(Secretary to the
   Council of Ministers);* Arlindo Rangel da Cruz (Fretilin)
   (Trade and Industry); José Teixeira *(Tourism,
   Environment and Investment)*
Transport, Communications and Public Works, Ovidio de
   Jesus Amaral (Fretilin)

BRITISH EMBASSY
Pantai Kelapa (Avenida de Portugal),
PO Box 194, Dili
Tel: (00 61) 417 841 046
Email: dili.fco@gtnet.gov.uk
Ambassador Extraordinary and Plenipotentiary,
   HE Hamish St Clair Daniel, MBE, apptd 2002

ECONOMY
East Timor's economy has suffered as a result of the
Indonesian withdrawal in 1999. One in three households
live below the poverty line.
   The main commercially grown crops include coffee,
coconuts, cloves and cocoa. There are oil and gas reserves
beneath the sea to the south of the island and under a
deal with Australia negotiated by the UN administration,
East Timor is set to receive the largest proportion of
revenue when gas is shipped to Japan from 2006.

Trade with UK	2002
Imports from UK	£1,586,000
Exports to UK	532,000

COMMUNICATIONS
There is only one major road, which links the main
townships along the northern coast to the east of Dili.
East Timor's national public radio and television services
began broadcasting in May 2002 but public television
broadcasts do not extend much beyond Dili.

ECUADOR

República del Ecuador – Republic of Ecuador

AREA – 106,462 sq. miles (276,800 sq. km).
   Neighbours: Colombia (north), Peru (east and south)
POPULATION – 12,156,608 (2001 census), descendants
   of the Spanish, Amerindians, and mestizos. Spanish is
   the principal language but Quechua is also a
   recognised language and is spoken by most Indians

CAPITAL – Quito (population, 1,399,814, 2001 census)
MAJOR CITIES – Cuenca (276,964); ΨGuayaquil
   (1,952,029), the chief port (2001 census)
CURRENCY – Currency is that of the USA
NATIONAL ANTHEM – Salve, Oh Patria, Mil Veces, Oh
   Patria (Hail, Oh Fatherland, A Thousand Times, Oh
   Fatherland)
NATIONAL DAY – 10 August (Independence Day)
NATIONAL FLAG – Three horizontal bands, yellow, blue
   and red (the yellow band twice the width of the
   others); emblem in centre
LIFE EXPECTANCY (years) – 70 (2001)
POPULATION GROWTH RATE – 2.1 per cent
POPULATION DENSITY – 47 per sq. km (2001)
URBAN POPULATION – 63 per cent (2001)
MILITARY EXPENDITURE – 2.9 per cent of GDP (2001)
MILITARY PERSONNEL – 59,500: Army 50,000, Navy
   5,500, Air Force 4,000; Paramilitaries 270
CONSCRIPTION DURATION – 12 months (selective)

Ecuador is an equatorial state of South America. It
extends across the Western Andes, the highest peaks
being Chimborazo (20,408 ft) and Ilinza (17,405 ft) in
the Western Cordillera; and Cotopaxi (19,612 ft) and
Cayambe (19,160 ft) in the Eastern Cordillera.

HISTORY AND POLITICS
The former kingdom of Quito was conquered by the
Incas of Peru in the 15th century. Early in the 16th
century Pizarro's conquests led to the inclusion of the
present territory of Ecuador in the Spanish viceroyalty of
Quito. Independence was achieved in a revolutionary war
which culminated in the battle of Mount Pichincha
(1822).
   After seven years of military rule, Ecuador returned to
democracy in 1979. In the July 1996 elections the ruling
Social Christian Party (PSC) won a majority of seats but
was replaced as the largest party in the National Congress
by the Popular Democracy Party (DP) in the 1998
elections. Abdala Bucaram was elected president in July
1996, and appointed a coalition government. Bucaram
was ousted by the legislature on the grounds of insanity
and replaced firstly by Vice-President Arteaga and then
by the Speaker of the National Congress, Fabián Alarcón.
   A series of strikes and protests caused disruption
throughout July 1999 and led to mass demonstrations
calling for the removal of the president. Proposed tax
increases led to another wave of protest in November,
which again called for the removal of the president. On
18 January 2000, Quito and most provincial capitals
were occupied by thousands of Indians. President
Mahaud was deposed in a coup by a military junta on 21
January 2000, which was dissolved by the military just
five hours after taking office and Vice-President Noboa
was elevated to the presidency.
   A tax reform bill to reduce the budget deficit, which
would have increased value added tax and fuel costs,
provoked widespread demonstrations and strikes by an
alliance of indigenous farmers and public sector workers
and students in January 2001. The government and the
protestors reached a compromise agreement on 7
February, but on 8 May the National Congress refused to
pass the bill. Further protests took place in February
2002 with the indigenous people's demand that more of
the country's oil revenue be invested in their
communities.
   In legislative elections held on 20 October 2002 the
Social Christian Party (PSC) became the largest party in

the National Congress, with 24 seats. Col. Lucio Guitiérrez, the joint candidate of the Popular Socialist Party (SPS) and the New Country – Pachakutik United Movement (MUPP) was elected president in the second round of voting held on 24 November 2002. Col. Guitiérrez took office on 15 January 2003 and appointed a new Cabinet.

FOREIGN RELATIONS
The border with Peru was demarcated by a 1942 treaty that was partly revoked by Ecuador in 1960 in relation to a disputed 50-mile stretch. An inconclusive four-week border war was fought with Peru in February 1995 until a cease-fire was signed on 1 March 1995. A 54-mile demilitarised zone was agreed in July 1995. An agreement was signed on 26 October 1998 by the presidents of the two countries formally ending the territorial dispute after mediation by Argentina, Brazil, Chile and the USA.

POLITICAL SYSTEM
The 1998 constitution provides for an elected president and vice-president who serve for a single four-year term. There is a unicameral National Congress which meets for two months a year and has 121 members, 20 of whom are elected on a national basis and 101 on a provincial basis, all for four-year terms. Voting is compulsory for all literate and voluntary for all illiterate citizens over the age of 18. The republic is divided into 21 provinces.

HEAD OF STATE
President, Col. Lucio Gutiérrez, *elected* 24 November 2002, *took office* 15 January 2003
Vice-President, Alfredo Palacio

CABINET *as at August 2003*
Agriculture and Livestock, Luis Macas
Education, Culture and Sports, Rosa María Torres
Energy and Mines, Carlos Arboleda
Environment, Edgar Isch
Finance and Economy, Mauricio Pozo
Foreign Relations, Patricio Zuquilanda
Foreign Trade, Industry and Fisheries, Ivonne A-Baki
Government and Police, Luis Felipe Mantilla
Labour and Human Resources, Felipe Mantilla
National Defence, Nelson Herrera
Public Health, Francisco Andino
Public Works and Communications, Estuardo Penaherrera
Secretary-General of the Administration, Patricio Acosta
Secretary-General of Communications, Antonio Tramontana
Social Welfare, Patricio Ortiz
Tourism, Doris Solis
Urban Development and Housing, Nelson Alverez

EMBASSY OF ECUADOR
Flat 3B, 3 Hans Crescent, London SW1X 0LS
Tel: 020-7584 1367/2648/8084
Ambassador Extraordinary and Plenipotentiary, vacant
Chargé d'Affaires Ricardo Falconi-Puig

BRITISH EMBASSY
Citiplaza Building, Av. Naciones Unidas and República de El Salvador, 14th Floor, PO Box 17-17-830, Quito
Tel: (00 593) (2) 2970 800/1
Email: britembq@interactive.net.ec
Ambassador Extraordinary and Plenipotentiary,
   HE Richard Lewington, LVO, apptd 2003

ECONOMY
Agriculture is the most important sector of the economy. The main products for export are fish, bananas, which provide a third of agricultural exports, cocoa and coffee. Other important crops are sugar, soya, rice, cotton, African palm, vegetables, fruit and timber. The main imports are manufactured goods and machinery.

The economy was transformed by the discovery in 1972 of major oil fields in the Oriente area, and oil is now a principal export, accounting for approximately 50 per cent of public-sector revenue and export earnings.

The US dollar was adopted in 1999 in order to stabilise the economy and lower inflation.

In 2000 there was a trade surplus of US$1,395 million and a current account surplus of US$928 million. In 2001 imports totalled US$5,363 million and exports US$4,647 million.

GNP – US$15,256 million (2000); US$1,210 per capita (2000)
GDP – US$17,982 million (2001); US$1,088 per capita (2000)
ANNUAL AVERAGE GROWTH OF GDP – 2.3 per cent (2000)
INFLATION RATE – 96.1 per cent (2000)
UNEMPLOYMENT – 11.5 per cent (1998)
TOTAL EXTERNAL DEBT – US$13,281 million (2000)

Trade with UK	2001	2002
Imports from UK	£34,210,000	£44,312,000
Exports to UK	32,998,000	36,400,000

COMMUNICATIONS
There are 23,256 km of permanent roads and 5,044 km of roads which are only open during the dry season. Ten commercial airlines operate international flights and there are internal services between all important towns.

EDUCATION
Elementary education is free and compulsory. There are ten universities (three at Quito, three at Guayaquil, and one each at Cuenca, Machala, Loja and Portoviejo), polytechnic schools at Quito and Guayaquil and eight technical colleges in other provincial capitals.
ILLITERACY RATE – (m) 6.9 per cent; (f) 10.5 per cent (2000)
ENROLMENT (percentage of age group) – primary 100 per cent (1997); tertiary 20.0 per cent (1990)

GALÁPAGOS ISLANDS
The Galápagos (Giant Tortoise) Islands, forming the province of the Archipelago de Colón, were annexed by Ecuador in 1832. The archipelago lies in the Pacific, about 500 miles from the mainland. There are 12 large and several hundred smaller islands with a total area of about 3,000 sq. miles and an estimated population of 18,640. The capital is Puerto Barquerizo Moreno, on San Cristóbal Island. Although the archipelago lies on the equator, the temperature of the surrounding water is well below equatorial average owing to the Humboldt current. The province consists for the most part of National Park Territory, where unique marine birds, iguanas, and the giant tortoises are conserved. There is some local subsistence farming; the main industry, apart from tourism, is tuna and lobster fishing.

EGYPT

Al-Jumhūriyya al-Miṣriyya al-ʿArabiyya – Arab Republic of Egypt

AREA – 382,885 sq. miles (995,500 sq. km).
Neighbours: Sudan (south), Libya (west), Gaza Strip and Israel (east)

POPULATION – 69,080,000 (2001). The largest, or 'Egyptian' element, is a Hamito-Semite race. A second element is the *Bedouin*, or nomadic Arabs of the Western and Eastern deserts, who are now mainly semi-sedentary tent-dwellers. The third element is the *Nubian* of the Nile Valley of mixed Arab and Negro blood. Over 90 per cent of the population are Muslims of the Sunni denomination, and most of the rest are Coptic Christians. Arabic is the official language

CAPITAL – Cairo (Al-Qāhirah) (population, 7,200,000, 1998 estimate) stands on the Nile about 14 miles from the head of the delta

MAJOR CITIES – ΨAlexandria (Al-Iskandarīya) (3,328,196, 1997 estimate), founded 332 BC by Alexander the Great, was the capital for over 1,000 years; Asyūt (2,802,185); Faiyūm (1,989,881); Ismailia (715,009); ΨPort Said (Būr Saʿīd) (469,533); ΨSuez (As-Suways) (417,610)

CURRENCY – Egyptian pound (£E) of 100 piastres or 1,000 millièmes

NATIONAL ANTHEM – Biladi (My Homeland)

NATIONAL DAY – 23 July (Anniversary of Revolution in 1952)

NATIONAL FLAG – Horizontal bands of red, white and black, with an eagle in the centre of the white band

LIFE EXPECTANCY (years) – 68 (2001)

POPULATION GROWTH RATE – 1.9 per cent

POPULATION DENSITY – 69 per sq. km (2001)

URBAN POPULATION – 43 per cent (2001)

ILLITERACY RATE – (m) 33.3 per cent; (f) 56.1 per cent (2000)

ENROLMENT (percentage of age group) – primary 100 per cent (1997); secondary 78 per cent (1997); tertiary 20 per cent (1997)

The country is mainly flat but there are mountainous areas in the south-west, along the Red Sea coast and in the south of the Sinai peninsula; the highest peak is Mt Catherina (8,668 ft). Most of the land is desert and the Nile valley and delta were the only fertile areas until the opening of the Aswan Dam allowed areas of desert to be reclaimed. West of the Nile Valley is the Western Desert, containing some depressions whose springs irrigate oases. The Eastern Desert between the Nile and the mountains along the Red Sea coast is mostly plateaux dissected by wadis (dry water-courses).

HISTORY AND POLITICS

The unification of the kingdoms of Lower and Upper Egypt under the Pharaohs c.3100 BC marked the establishment of the Egyptian state, with Memphis as its capital. Egypt was ruled for nearly 2,800 years by a succession of 31 Pharaonic dynasties which built the pyramids at Gizeh. A period of Hellenic rule began in 332 BC, followed by a period of rule by Rome (30 BC to AD 324) and then by the Byzantine Empire. In AD 640 Egypt was subjugated by Arab Muslim invaders. In 1517 the country was incorporated in the Ottoman Empire, under which it remained until the early 19th century. A British Protectorate over Egypt lasted from 1914 to

1922, when Sultan Ahmed Fuad was proclaimed King of Egypt. In 1953 the monarchy was deposed and Egypt became a republic.

In 1956 President Nasser seized the assets of the Suez Canal Company. Egyptian occupation of the Canal Zone was used as a pretext for military action by Britain and France in support of their Suez Canal Company interests. A cease-fire and Anglo-French withdrawal were negotiated by the UN.

The Israeli invasion of 1956 overran the Sinai peninsula but six months later Israel withdrew. However, mounting tension culminated in a second invasion of Sinai (the Six Day War in June 1967) and occupation of the peninsula by Israel. Sinai was returned to Egypt in 1982 under the treaty of 1979 which resulted from the Camp David talks and formally terminated a 31-year-old state of war between the two countries.

President Mubarak was nominated by the legislature to run unopposed for a fourth six-year term in June 1999, and was endorsed by a national referendum held on 26 September.

A general election was held in three rounds between 18 October and 15 November 2000. The ruling National Democratic Party (NDP) won 388 of the 444 elective seats, which included some 218 independent candidates who joined the party immediately after the election.

INSURGENCY

Militant Islamist fundamentalists re-emerged in 1992, carrying out attacks on tourists, Coptic Christians, government ministers, civil servants and the security forces. On 27 March 1999, the largest fundamentalist organisation, Gamaat-i-Islamiya, announced that it had given up its violent campaign to overthrow the government. In November 2002, 43 members of the fundamentalist Islamic group Islamic Jihad were arrested for allegedly planning to carry out terrorist attacks against government officials and a foreign establishment.

POLITICAL SYSTEM

The constitution of 1971 provides for an executive president who appoints the Council of Ministers and determines government policy. The president is elected by the legislature every six years. The legislature is the People's Assembly which has 454 members, 444 of whom are elected, the remaining ten nominated by the president. The Shura Council or Consultative Assembly (264 members) has an advisory role. A state of emergency, which was first introduced following the assassination of President Sadat in 1981, remains in force.

HEAD OF STATE

President, Mohammed Hosni Mubarak, *elected* 1981, *re-elected* 1987, 1993, 2 June 1999, *confirmed by national referendum* 26 September 1999

COUNCIL OF MINISTERS *as at July 2003*
Prime Minister, Economy, Atef Mohammad Obeid
Deputy PM, Agriculture and Land Reclamation, Yousef Amin Wali
Communications and Information Technology, Ahmed Muhammad Nazif
Culture, Farouk Hosni Abdel Aziz
Defence and Military Production, Field Marshal Mohammad Hussein Tantawi
Education, Hussein Kamel Bahaeddin
Electricity and Energy, Hassan Ahmed Yunes

Finance, Mohammed Midhat Hasanayn
Foreign Affairs, Ahmed Maher
Foreign Trade, Yussef Boutros Ghali
Health and Population, Mohamed Awad Afifi Tag el-Din
Higher Education, Minister of State for Scientific Research, Mufid Shehab
Information, Muhammad Safwat El-Sherif
Interior, Maj.-Gen. Habib al-Adli
Justice, Farouk Seif El-Nasr
Labour and Emigration, Ahmed al-Amawi
Ministers of State, Mahmoud Zaki Abu Amer
  (Administrative Development); Ahmed Mohamed Shafiq Zaki *(Civil Aviation);* Mamduh Ryad Tadros *(Environment);* Fayza abu al-Nagaa *(Foreign Affairs);* Gen. Sayyid Abduh Mustafa Mash'al *(Military Production);* Kamal Mohammed Al Shazli *(People's National Assembly and Consultative Council Affairs);* Mustafa Abdel Qader *(Rural Development);* Hamdi Abdel-Salaam Mohamed al-Shaib *(Transport)*
Oil and Mineral Resources, Amin Sameh Fahmi
Planning, Minister of State for International Co-operation, Osman Mohamed Osman
Public Enterprise, Mukhtar Khattab
Public Works and Irrigation, Mahmoud Abdul Halim Abu Zaid
Reconstruction, New Urban Zones and Environment, Mohammed Ibrahim Soliman
Religious Affairs and Waqfs (Endowments), Mahmoud Hamdi Zakzouk
Social Insurance and Social Affairs, Amina Hamzah al-Jundi
Supply and Internal Trade, Hassan Ali Khedr
Technological Development and Industry, Ali Fahmi Ibrahim al-Saidi
Tourism, Mamdouh Ahmed Al-Beltagui
Youth, Ali al-Din Hilal al-Dasuqi

EMBASSY OF THE ARAB REPUBLIC OF EGYPT
26 South Street, London W1K 1DW
Tel: 020-7499 2401/3304
Ambassador Extraordinary and Plenipotentiary,
  HE Adel El-Gazzar, apptd 1997

BRITISH EMBASSY
7 Ahmed Ragheb Street, Garden City, Cairo
Tel: (00 20) (2) 794 0850/2/8
Email: info@britishembassy.org.eg
Ambassador Extraordinary and Plenipotentiary,
  HE John Sawers, CMG, apptd 2001

BRITISH COUNCIL DIRECTOR,
Dr John Grote, OBE
(Cultural Counsellor), 192 El Nil Street, Agouza, Cairo
Tel: (00 20) (2) 303 1514
Email: british.council@britishcouncil.org.eg

DEFENCE

The Army has 3,860 main battle tanks, 795 armoured infantry fighting vehicles and 4,267 armoured personnel carriers. The Navy has one destroyer, ten frigates, four submarines, 39 patrol and coastal vessels and 24 armed helicopters at eight bases. The Air Force has 608 combat aircraft and 128 armed helicopters.
MILITARY EXPENDITURE – 4.7 per cent of GDP (2001)
MILITARY PERSONNEL – 443,000: Army 320,000, Navy 19,000, Air Force 29,000, Air Defence Command 75,000; Paramilitaries 325,000
CONSCRIPTION DURATION – 12 months to three years (selective)

ECONOMY

Despite increasing industrialisation, agriculture remains the most important economic activity, employing 35 per cent of the labour force and producing 16 per cent of GDP in 2000–1. Egypt is still a net importer of foodstuffs, especially grain, and a food security programme has been set up with the aim of achieving self-sufficiency. The main cash crop is cotton, of which Egypt is one of the world's main producers. Other important crops are maize, rice, sugar cane, wheat and potatoes. Other fruits and vegetables are also grown.

With its considerable reserves of petroleum and natural gas, and the hydroelectric power produced by the Aswan and High Dams, Egypt is self-sufficient in energy. In 2002 5.2 million foreign tourists visited Egypt.

The government transferred control over exchange rates to the central bank in January 2001. In January 2003 the government allowed the Egyptian pound to free-float against the US dollar in an attempt to pre-empt the detrimental effect the imminent war with Iraq would be likely to have upon the economy.

In 2001 the government had a trade deficit of US$8,321 million and a current account deficit of US$971 million.
GNP – US$95,380 million (2000); US$1,490 per capita (2000)
GDP – US$97,545 million (2001); US$1,355 per capita (2000)
ANNUAL AVERAGE GROWTH OF GDP – 6.4 per cent (2000)
INFLATION RATE – 2.7 per cent (2000)
UNEMPLOYMENT – 8.1 per cent (1999)
TOTAL EXTERNAL DEBT – US$28,957 million (2000)

TRADE
The main imports are wheat, maize, chemicals and motor vehicles and parts. The main exports are crude petroleum, cotton, cotton yarn, oranges, rice and cotton textiles.

In 2001 Egypt's imports totalled US$12,756 million and exports US$4,126 million.

Trade with UK	2001	2002
Imports from UK	£454,844,000	£464,587,000
Exports to UK	420,801,000	432,298,000

COMMUNICATIONS

There are international airports at Cairo and Luxor. The road and rail networks link the Nile valley and delta with the main development areas east and west of the river. Egypt has 3,400 km of waterways, of which half are canals. The Suez Canal was reopened in 1975 and a two-stage development project begun to widen and deepen the canal to allow the passage of larger shipping and to permit two-way traffic. Port Said and Suez have been reconstructed and the port of Alexandria is being improved.

EL SALVADOR

República de El Salvador – Republic of El Salvador

AREA – 7,962 sq. miles (20,700 sq. km). Neighbours: Guatemala (north-west), Honduras (north-east and east)
POPULATION – 6,400,000 (2001): 90 per cent mestizo, 1 per cent Amerindian, 9 per cent European. The language is Spanish
CAPITAL – San Salvador (population, 1,985,294, 2000 estimate)

MAJOR CITIES – San Miguel (239,038); Santa Ana (248,963); 2000 estimates
CURRENCY – US dollar (US$) of 100 cents/El Salvador colón of 100 centavos
NATIONAL ANTHEM – Saludemos La Patria Orgullosos (Let Us Proudly Hail The Fatherland)
NATIONAL DAY – 15 September
NATIONAL FLAG – Three horizontal bands, sky blue, white, sky blue; coat of arms on white band
LIFE EXPECTANCY (years) – 70 (2001)
POPULATION GROWTH RATE – 2 per cent
POPULATION DENSITY – 309 per sq. km (2001)
URBAN POPULATION – 61 per cent (2001)
MILITARY EXPENDITURE – 1.2 per cent of GDP (2001)
MILITARY PERSONNEL – 16,800: Army 15,000, Navy 700, Air Force 1,100; Paramilitaries 12,000
CONSCRIPTION DURATION – 12 months (selective)

El Salvador extends along the Pacific coast of Central America for 160 miles. The surface of the country is very mountainous, many of the peaks being extinct volcanoes. Much of the interior has an average altitude of 2,000 feet.

HISTORY AND POLITICS

El Salvador was conquered in 1526 by Pedro de Alvarado, and formed part of the Spanish viceroyalty of Guatemala until 1821. It is divided into 14 Departments.

Decades of military rule ended in October 1979; a Constituent Assembly was elected in 1982. Subsequent presidential and parliamentary elections were boycotted by the FMLN (Farabundo Martí National Liberation Front) guerrilla movement. Conflict between the guerrillas and the government continued throughout the 1980s until negotiations culminated in a peace plan signed in January 1992. In December 1992 the FMLN disarmed and became a political party.

On 7 March 1999, Francisco Flores of the ruling right-wing National Republican Alliance (ARENA) party won the presidential election; he took office on 1 June. In legislative elections held on 16 March 2003 the FMLN remained the largest party in the Legislative Assembly winning 31 of the 84 seats; ARENA won 27 seats and the National Conciliation Party (PCN) won 16 seats.

HEAD OF STATE
President, Francisco Flores Pérez, elected 7 March 1999, took office 1 June 1999
Vice-President, Minister of the Presidency, Carlos Quintanilla Schmidt

COUNCIL OF STATE as at July 2003
Agriculture and Livestock, Salvador Urrutia Loucel
Defence, Gen. Juan Antonio Martínez Varela
Economy, Miguel Ernesto Lacayo
Education, Rolando Ernesto Marín
Environment and Natural Resources, Walter Jokisch
Foreign Affairs, María Eugenia Brizuela de Avila
Justice, Public Security and Interior, Conrado López Andreu
Labour and Social Security, Jorge Nieto Menéndez
Public Health, José López Beltrán
Public Works, José Angel Quiros
Treasury, Juan José Daboub

EMBASSY OF EL SALVADOR
Mayfair House, 39 Great Portland Street, London W1W 7JZ
Tel: 020-7436 8282
Ambassador Extraordinary and Plenipotentiary,
HE Eduardo Ernesto Vilanova-Molina, apptd 2002

BRITISH AMBASSADOR, HE Richard Lavers, apptd 2003, resident at Guatemala City

ECONOMY

The principal agricultural products are coffee, cotton, sugar cane, maize, shrimps and balsam. In the lower altitudes towards the east, sisal is produced and used in the manufacture of coffee and cereal bags.

The US dollar was adopted on 1 January 2001; the colón remained in use for a transitional period.

Nearly one million people were made homeless and around 20 per cent of the nation's housing was damaged in two major earthquakes in January and February 2001.

GNP – US$12,569 million (2000); US$2,000 per capita (2000)
GDP – US$13,963 million (2001); US$2,103 per capita (2000)
ANNUAL AVERAGE GROWTH OF GDP – 2.0 per cent (2000)
INFLATION RATE – 2.3 per cent (2000)
UNEMPLOYMENT – 7.0 per cent (1999)
TOTAL EXTERNAL DEBT – US$4,023 million (2000)

TRADE
Chief exports are coffee, cotton, sugar, shrimps, sisal, balsam, meat, towels, hides and skins. The chief imports are chemicals, petroleum, manufactured goods, industrial and electronic machinery, pharmaceutical goods, vehicles and consumer goods. The USA is El Salvador's main trading partner.

In 2000 there was a trade deficit of US$1,719 million and a current account deficit of US$418 million. In 2001 imports totalled US$3,866 million and exports US$1,214 million.

Trade with UK	2001	2002
Imports from UK	£17,177,000	£13,045,000
Exports to UK	7,653,000	7,500,000

COMMUNICATIONS

The principal ports are Cutuco, La Unión and Acajutla but ports in Honduras and Guatemala are also used. There are 12,500 km of roads of which 2,000 are paved; there are 602 km of railways. The Pan-American Highway from the Guatemalan frontier passes through San Salvador and Santa Ana, and continues to the Honduran frontier. Comalapa international airport has daily flights to other Central American capitals, Mexico and the USA. There are around 150 broadcasting stations and eight television stations. Four daily newspapers are published in San Salvador.

EDUCATION

Primary education is free and compulsory. There are 38 universities.
ILLITERACY RATE – (m) 18.3 per cent; (f) 23.8 per cent (2000)
ENROLMENT (percentage of age group) – primary 97 per cent (1997); secondary 37 per cent (1997); tertiary 18 per cent (1997)

EQUATORIAL GUINEA

República de Guinea Ecuatorial – Republic of Equatorial Guinea

AREA – 10,831 sq. miles (28,051 sq. km). Neighbours: Cameroon (north), Gabon (east and south)

POPULATION – 486,060 (2001 estimate). The official languages are Spanish and French; Bubi, Fang, Ibo and pidgin English are also spoken

CAPITAL – ΨMalabo on the island of Bioko (population, 30,418, 1983 estimate)

MAJOR TOWN – ΨBata is the principal town and port of Rio Muni

CURRENCY – Franc CFA of 100 centimes

NATIONAL ANTHEM – Caminemos Pisando La Senda De Nuestra Inmensa Felicidad (Let's Walk Down The Path Of Our Immense Happiness)

NATIONAL DAY – 12 October

NATIONAL FLAG – Three horizontal bands, green over white over red; blue triangle next staff; coat of arms in centre of white band

POPULATION GROWTH RATE – 2.5 per cent

POPULATION DENSITY – 16 per sq. km (1999)

MILITARY EXPENDITURE – 0.3 per cent of GDP (2001)

MILITARY PERSONNEL – 1,320: Army 1,100, Navy 120, Air Force 100

ILLITERACY RATE – (m) 7.5 per cent; (f) 25.6 per cent (2000)

HISTORY AND POLITICS

Formerly colonies of Spain, the territories now forming Equatorial Guinea were constituted as two provinces of Metropolitan Spain in 1959, became autonomous in 1963 and fully independent in 1968.

In 1979 President Macias was deposed by a revolutionary military council headed by Col. Obiang Nguema. Constitutional amendments in 1982 provided for legislative elections, which were held in 1983 and 1988, but all candidates were chosen by the president.

A multiparty political system under a new constitution was approved by a referendum in 1991 and ten opposition parties have been legalised, operating alongside the ruling Equatorial Guinea Democratic Party (PDGE). A National Pact was agreed and signed in March 1993 but legislative elections in November, which were won by the PDGE, were boycotted by most of the electorate and opposition parties. In the February 1996 election, the president claimed to have won more than 99 per cent of the vote. Most opposition parties boycotted the ballot. In June 1997 the Progress Party, the largest opposition party, was banned by the government, and in February 1998 opposition party coalitions were deemed illegal. The PDGE won 75 of the 80 seats in the National Assembly elections on 7 March 1999 amid allegations of electoral malpractice.

Prime Minister Angel Serafin Seriche Dougan resigned on 23 February 2001 due to his growing unpopularity. He was replaced by Cándido Muatema Rivas on 26 February. Incumbent President Teodoro Obiang Nguema Mbasogo won the presidential elections of 15 December 2002. Opposition candidates withdrew after voting commenced due to alleged irregularities.

HEAD OF STATE

President of the Supreme Military Council and Minister of Defence, Brig.-Gen. Teodoro Obiang Nguema Mbasogo, *took office* August 1979, *re-elected* June 1989, 25 February 1996, 15 December 2002

COUNCIL OF MINISTERS *as at July 2003*

Prime Minister, Cándido Muatema Rivas (PDGE)

Deputy PM, Interior, Demetrio Elo Ndong Nsefumu (PDGE)

Deputy PM, Social Affairs and Human Rights, Jeremias Ondo Ngomo (UP)

Ministers of State, Francisco Pascual Eyegue Obama (PDGE) *(Agriculture, Animal Husbandry and Rural Development);* Ricardo Mangue Obama Nfube (PDGE) *(Civil Service and Administrative Co-ordination);* Antonio Fernando Nve Ngu (PDGE) *(Education and Science, Government Spokesman);* Carmelo Modu Acuse Bindang (UDS) *(Industry, Commerce and Small Enterprises);* Agustín Nze Nfumu (PDGE) *(Information, Tourism and Culture);* Teodoro Nguema Obiang (PDGE) *(Infrastructure and Forests);* Miguel Abia Biteo Borico (PDGE) *(Presidency, in charge of Relations with Assemblies and Legal Matters);* Alejandro Evuna Owono Asangono (PDGE) *(Presidency, in charge of Special Duties);* Ignacio Milam Tang (PDGE) *(Secretary-General of the Presidency);* Marcelino Oyono Ntutumu (PDGE) *(Transport and Communication);* Lucas Nguema Esono Mbang PDGE) *(Youth and Sports)*

Economic Affairs and Finance, Baltasar Engonga Edjo (PDGE)

Finance and Budget, Marcelino Owono Edu

Fisheries and Environment, Fortunato Ofa Mbo

Foreign Affairs, International Co-operation and Francophone Affairs, Pastor Micha Ondo Bile (PDGE)

Health and Social Welfare, Justino Obama Nve (PDGE)

Interior and Local Corporations, Clemente Engonga Nguema Onguene (PDGE)

Justice and Religion, Rubén Maye Nsue (PDGE)

Labour and Social Security, Miguel Eyanga Djoba Malango

Mines and Energy, Cristóbal Menana Ela (PDGE)

Planning and Economic Development, Antonio Nve Nseng

Social Affairs, Women's Development, Teresa Efua Asangono (PDGE)

PDGE Democratic Party of Equatorial Guinea; UDS Social and Democratic Union; UP Popular Union

EMBASSY OF THE REPUBLIC OF EQUATORIAL GUINEA
6 rue Alfred de Vigny, F-75008 Paris
Tel: (00 33) (1) 4766 4433
Ambassador Extraordinary and Plenipotentiary, vacant
Chargé d'Affaires, Moises Mba Sima Nchama

BRITISH AMBASSADOR, HE Richard Wildash, LVO, resident at Yaoundé, Cameroon

ECONOMY

The chief products are cocoa, coffee and wood. Production has declined and except for cocoa there is little commercial agriculture. The discovery of large oil and gas deposits off Bioko in the 1990s has led to an economic boom. However, the economy is still heavily dependent on outside aid, principally from Spain. Equatorial Guinea entered the 'franc zone' in 1985.

In 1996, there was a trade deficit of US$117 million and a current account deficit of US$344 million. In 2000 imports totalled US$451 million and exports US$1,097 million.

GNP – US$363 million (2000); US$800 per capita (2000)

GDP – US$1,846 million (2001); US$2,628 per capita (2000)

ANNUAL AVERAGE GROWTH OF GDP – 1.4 per cent
(1998)
TOTAL EXTERNAL DEBT – US$248 million (2000)

Trade with UK	2001	2002
Imports from UK	£24,852,000	£36,502,000
Exports to UK	5,696,000	6,737,000

ERITREA

Hagere Eretra/al-Dawla al-Iritra – State of Eritrea

AREA – 45,406 sq. miles (117,600 sq. km). Neighbours:
Sudan (north and north-west), Ethiopia (south and
south-west), Djibouti (south-east)
POPULATION – 4,298,269 (2001 estimate), roughly half
Coptic Christian (mainly highlanders) and half Muslim
(mainly lowlanders). Arabic, Tigrinya and English are
the main working languages. Italian is also widely
spoken. There are nine indigenous language groups:
Afar; Bilen; Hadareb; Kunama; Nara; Rashida; Saho;
Tigre; Tigrinya
CAPITAL – Asmara (population, 450,000, 2001 estimate)
MAJOR TOWNS – ΨAssab; ΨMassawa
CURRENCY – Nakfa
NATIONAL DAY – 24 May (Independence Day)
NATIONAL FLAG – Divided into three triangles; the one
based on the hoist is red and bears a gold olive wreath;
the upper triangle is green and the lower one light
blue
POPULATION GROWTH RATE – 3.9 per cent
POPULATION DENSITY – 32 per sq. km (1999)
ILLITERACY RATE – (m) 32.7 per cent; (f) 55.5 per cent
(2000)
ENROLMENT (percentage of age group) – primary 53
per cent (1997); secondary 20 per cent (1997); tertiary
1 per cent (1997)

HISTORY AND POLITICS
Eritrea was colonised by Italy in the late 19th century
and was the base for the 1936 Italian invasion of
Abyssinia (Ethiopia). After the Italian defeat in East
Africa in 1941 by British and Commonwealth forces,
Eritrea became a British protectorate. This lasted until 15
September 1952 when Eritrea was federated with
Ethiopia. The Ethiopian Emperor Haile Selassie
incorporated Eritrea as a province of Ethiopia in 1962.
An armed campaign for independence began in 1961,
first against Emperor Haile Selassie's forces and from
1974 against the Mengistu regime.
   In 1991 the Mengistu government was overthrown by
the Eritrean People's Liberation Front (EPLF) and the
Ethiopian People's Revolutionary Democratic Front
(EPRDF). The new EPRDF-led government in Ethiopia
agreed to an Eritrean referendum on independence which
was held in April 1993 and recorded a 99.89 per cent
vote in favour. Independence was declared on 24 May
1993.
   On 7 February 2002, the European Parliament
adopted a resolution that expressed concern at increasing
authoritarian tendencies in the country. Legislative
elections scheduled for December 2001 did not take
place and as at the end of July 2003 no new date had
been announced.

FOREIGN RELATIONS
Eritrea had claimed the Hanish and Mohabaka Islands in
the Red Sea, which it seized from Yemen in December
1995; however, on 9 October 1998, the International
Court of Justice ruled that the Hanish Islands belonged to
Yemen and Eritrea formally handed them over to Yemen
on 1 November 1998. The land border with Djibouti is
also disputed.
   In May 1998 sporadic fighting flared up on the border
with Ethiopia, with both countries accusing the other of
sending troops across the border. Proposals for a
resolution of the conflict drawn up by the Organisation
for African Unity (OAU) in November 1998, which
called on Eritrea to hand back the disputed town of
Badme pending adjudication, were rejected by Eritrea.
Full scale fighting broke out on 6 February 1999 and
Ethiopia had captured the town by 28 February. Eritrea
accepted the OAU's proposals on 9 March, but fighting
continued. A further proposal to end the fighting was
brokered by the OAU in July 1999, which envisaged a
return to the original borders and was provisionally
accepted by both sides, but Ethiopia later rejected some
of the provisions. Fighting resumed on 23 February
2000. On 12 May, Ethiopia launched a full-scale
invasion, which ended in early June after Ethiopian forces
had captured much of Eritrea's western lowlands. An
interim peace plan was signed by both countries on 18
June.
   UN observers began to deploy on 15 September 2000.
Direct talks between Eritrea and Ethiopia opened on 23
October and on 12 December a comprehensive peace
agreement was signed in Algeria; UN peacekeeping
troops moved into the buffer zone in April 2001 and on
21 May Eritrea and Ethiopia agreed to set up regional
military commissions to solve local security issues. On 13
April 2002 the independent Eritrea-Ethiopia Boundary
Commission (EEBC), set up to establish a legal
international border, defined the border between the two
countries but its ruling failed to indicate clearly whether
the town of Badme was Eritrean or Ethiopian. On 28
March 2003 the EEBC announced that Badme was on
the Eritrean side of the border. On 4 April the Ethiopian
government declared its opposition to the boundary
ruling and relations between the two countries remain
strained. On 14 March 2003 the UN Security Council
extended the mandate of the UN Mission in Ethiopia and
Eritrea (UNMEE) until 15 September 2003.

POLITICAL SYSTEM
Under the 1997 constitution, the head of state is the
president, elected for a five-year term by the National
Assembly, of which he is chair. The 150-member
unicameral legislature (the Hagerawi Baito) is directly
elected for four years. The president is head of
government and presides over a State Council, which
includes six regional administrators.

HEAD OF STATE
President, Chairman of the National Assembly, Issaias
   Afewerki, *elected by the National Assembly* 22 May 1993

STATE COUNCIL *as at July 2003*
Agriculture, Arefaine Berhe
Commissioner for Eritrean Relief and Refugee Commission,
   Deragon Hailemelekot
Defence, Gen. Sebhat Ephrem

Education, Osman Saleh
Energy and Mines, Tesfai Ghebresselassie
Finance and Development, Berhane Abrehe
Fisheries, Ahmed Hajj Ali
Foreign Affairs, Ali Said Abdellah
Health, Saleh Meki
Industry and Trade, Gergish Teklemikael
Information (acting), Ali Abdu Ahmad
Justice, Fawzia Hashim
Labour and Human Welfare, Askalu Menkerios
Land, Water and Environment, Weldenkiel Ghebremariam
Local Government, vacant
Public Works, Abraha Asfaha
Tourism, Amna Nur Husayn
Transport and Communications, Weldenkiel Abraha

EMBASSY OF THE STATE OF ERITREA
96 White Lion Street, London N1 9PF
Tel: 020-7713 0096.
Ambassador Extraordinary and Plenipotentiary,
HE Negassi Sengal Ghebrezghi, apptd 2003

BRITISH EMBASSY
Emperor Yohannes Avenue, House no 24,
PO Box 5584, Asmara
Tel: (00 291) (1) 120145
Email: alembca@gemel.com.er
Ambassador Extraordinary and Plenipotentiary,
HE Michael Murray, *apptd*

BRITISH COUNCIL DIRECTOR, Dr Negusse Araya
Lorenzo Tazaz Street No 23, PO Box 997, Asmara;
Tel: (00 291) (1) 123415/120529
Email: information@britishcouncil.org.er

DEFENCE
The Army has 100 main battle tanks and 50 armoured infantry fighting vehicles and armoured personnel carriers. The Navy has eight patrol and coastal combatants. The Air Force has 17 combat aircraft.
MILITARY EXPENDITURE – 20.9 per cent of GDP (2001)
MILITARY PERSONNEL – 172,200: Army 170,000, Navy 1,400, Air Force 800
CONSCRIPTION DURATION – 16 months

ECONOMY
Since 1991 the government has attempted to rebuild industry, agriculture and infrastructure which were devastated by the war of independence. The rebuilding programme has focused on the ports of Massawa and Assab, the roads from the ports to Ethiopia, and the railway from Massawa to Sudan via Asmara. The government hopes to base the rebuilding of the economy on the return of well-educated exiles, international aid and investment, the development of tourism along the coast, and the diversification of the economy away from subsistence agriculture which involves around 80 per cent of the population.
GNP – US$696 million (2000); US$170 per capita (2000)
GDP – US$681 million (2001); US$202 per capita (2000)
ANNUAL AVERAGE GROWTH OF GDP – 3.0 per cent (1998)
TOTAL EXTERNAL DEBT – US$311 million (2000)

Trade with UK	2001	2002
Imports from UK	£4,895,000	£3,599,000
Exports to UK	154,000	101,000

ESTONIA

Eesti Vabariik – Republic of Estonia

AREA – 16,269 sq. miles (42,300 sq. km). Neighbours: Russia (east), Latvia (south)
POPULATION – 1,377,000 (2001): 65.3 per cent Estonian, 28.1 per cent Russian, 1.5 per cent Ukrainian, 0.9 per cent Belarusian, 0.9 per cent Finnish. The majority religion is Lutheran, with Russian Orthodox and Baptist minorities. Estonian is the first language of 64.2 per cent and Russian of 28.7 per cent
CAPITAL – Tallinn (population, 404,000, 2000 census)
MAJOR TOWNS AND CITIES – Kohtla-Järve (65,566); Narva (73,295); Pärnu (46,700); Tartu (100,100)
CURRENCY – Kroon of 100 sents
NATIONAL ANTHEM – Mu Isamaa, Mu Õnn Ja Rõõm (My Native Land, My Joy, Delight)
NATIONAL DAY – 24 February (Independence Day)
NATIONAL FLAG – Three horizontal stripes of blue, black, white
LIFE EXPECTANCY (years) – 71 (2001)
POPULATION GROWTH RATE – 1.2 per cent
POPULATION DENSITY – 33 per sq. km (2001)
URBAN POPULATION – 69 per cent (2001)
MILITARY EXPENDITURE – 1.7 per cent of GDP (2001)
MILITARY PERSONNEL – 5,510: Army 2,550, Navy 440, Air Force 220; Paramilitaries 2,600
CONSCRIPTION DURATION – Eight to 11 months

HISTORY AND POLITICS
Estonia, a former province of the Russian Empire, declared its independence on 24 February 1918. A war of independence was fought against the German army until November 1918, and then against Soviet forces until the peace treaty of Tartu was signed in 1920. By this treaty the Soviet Union recognised Estonia's independence.

The Soviet Union annexed Estonia in 1940 under the terms of the Molotov-Ribbentrop pact with Germany. Estonia was occupied when Germany invaded the Soviet Union during the Second World War. In 1944 the Soviet Union recaptured the country from Germany and confirmed its annexation.

The Estonian Supreme Soviet in November 1989 declared the republic to be sovereign and its 1940 annexation by the Soviet Union to be illegal. In February 1990 the leading role of the Communist Party was abolished, and following multiparty elections in March 1990 a period of transition to independence was inaugurated. Independence was declared on 20 August 1991.

Presidential elections held on 27 and 28 August and 21 September 2001 were won by Arnold Rüütel. In legislative elections held on 2 March 2003 the left-wing Centrist Party (KP) and the right-wing Union for the Republic-Res Publica (RP) each won 28 seats in the parliament. On 2 April Juhan Parts of the RP was invited to form a government and a centre-right coalition cabinet comprising the RP, the Reform Party (RE) and the Estonian People's Union (RL) took office on 10 April.

In November 2002 Estonia was formally invited to accession talks with NATO and is expected to join NATO in 2004. In December 2002 Estonia was formally invited to join the EU and a referendum was due to be held in September 2003.

POLITICAL SYSTEM

Legislative power is exercised by the unicameral *Riigikogu* of 101 members elected by proportional representation every four years. The president is elected for a five-year term by the Riigikogu by a two-thirds majority or, if no candidate receives this majority after three rounds of voting, by an electoral assembly composed of Riigikogu members and local government officials. Executive authority is vested in a prime minister who is nominated by the president and who forms a government. Members of the government need not be members of the Riigikogu.

HEAD OF STATE

President, Arnold Rüütel, *elected* by electoral assembly 21 September 2001, *sworn in* 8 October 2001

GOVERNMENT *as at July 2003*
Prime Minister, Juhan Parts (RP)
Agriculture, Tiit Tammsaar (RL)
Culture, Urmas Paet (RE)
Defence, Margus Hanson (RE)
Economic Affairs and Communications, Meelis Atonen (RE)
Education and Science, Toivo Maimets (RP)
Environment, Villu Reiljan (RL)
Finance, Tonis Palts (RP)
Foreign Affairs, Kristiina Ojuland (RE)
Interior, Margus Leivo (RL)
Justice, Ken-Marti Vaher (RP)
Social Affairs, Marko Pomerants (RP)
Without Portfolio, responsible for Ethnic Affairs, Paul-Eerik Rummo (RE)
Without Portfolio, responsible for Regional Affairs, Jaan Ounapuu (RL)
RE Reform Party; RL Estonian People's Union; RP Union for the Republic-Res Publica
EMBASSY OF THE REPUBLIC OF ESTONIA
16 Hyde Park Gate, London SW7 5DG
Tel: 020-7589 3428
Ambassador Extraordinary and Plenipotentiary, HE Kaja Tael, apptd 2001

BRITISH EMBASSY
Wismari 6, EE-10136 Tallinn
Tel: (00 372) 667 4700
Email: information@britishembassy.ee
Ambassador Extraordinary and Plenipotentiary, HE Sarah Squire, *apptd* 2000

BRITISH COUNCIL DIRECTOR, Kyllike Tohver
Resource Centre, Vana Posti 7, EE-10146 Tallinn
Tel: (00 372) 631 4010
Email: british.council@britishcouncil.ee

ECONOMY

Since 1992 the government has introduced free-market reforms, privatisation and restructuring. Estonia is still dependent on Russian natural gas supplies.

Eleven per cent of the workforce is engaged in agriculture, which accounts for 6 per cent of GDP, the main products being rye, oats, barley, flax, potatoes, meat, milk, butter and eggs.

Industry accounts for 20 per cent of employment and 20 per cent of GDP, concentrating on textiles, clothing and footwear, forestry, wood and paper products, and food and fish processing. Some heavy industry exists, mostly chemicals and the manufacture of power equipment.
GNP – US$4,894 million (2000); US$3,580 per capita (2000)
GDP – US$5,281 million (2001); US$3,569 per capita (2000)
ANNUAL AVERAGE GROWTH OF GDP – 6.4 per cent (2000)
INFLATION RATE – 4.0 per cent (2000)
UNEMPLOYMENT – 13.7 per cent (2000)
TOTAL EXTERNAL DEBT – US$3,280 million (2000)

TRADE

Estonia's main trading partners are Finland, Sweden, Germany, Japan and Latvia. The main imports are machinery and equipment, chemicals, clothing and footwear, foodstuffs and vehicles. Exports consist mainly of machinery and equipment, timber and wood products, textiles and clothing, foodstuffs, metals and furniture.

In 2001 there was a trade deficit of US$787 million and a current account deficit of US$339 million. Imports totalled US$4,280 million and exports US$3,274 million.

Trade with UK	2001	2002
Imports from UK	£82,239,000	£98,922,000
Exports to UK	288,422,000	334,768,000

COMMUNICATIONS

Freedom of the press is guaranteed in the constitution, and the state monopoly on television and radio ended soon after independence. All newspapers have been privatised and broadcasting channels are in the process of being privatised. Russian-language news and programmes are provided on Estonian Television.

EDUCATION

Estonia has a three-tier education system, consisting of primary level (four years), secondary level (six years) and university level (four to six years). Primary- and secondary-level education is compulsory from the age of seven to 17, which is due to be extended to 18.

ENROLMENT (percentage of age group) – primary 94 per cent (1997); secondary 100 per cent (1997); tertiary 42 per cent (1997)

ETHIOPIA

Ya'Ityopya Federalawi Dimokrasyawi Repeblik – Federal Democratic Republic of Ethiopia

AREA – 433,512 sq. miles (1,127,130 sq. km). Neighbours: Sudan (west), Kenya (south), Djibouti and Somalia (east), Eritrea (north)
POPULATION – 64,459,000 (2001). About one-third are of Semitic origin (Amharas and Tigreans) and the remainder mainly Oromos (40 per cent), Somalis (6 per cent) and Afar (4 per cent). Amharas, Tigreans and many Oromos are Ethiopian Orthodox Christians. The Afar people in the north and the Somalis in the south-east, as well as some Oromos, are Muslim. Amharic is the most widely used of the 70 languages
CAPITAL – Addis Ababa (population, 2,495,000, 2000 estimate)

MAJOR CITY – Dire Dawa (population, 229,000, 2000 estimate)
CURRENCY – Ethiopian birr (EB) of 100 cents
NATIONAL ANTHEM – Yezeginet Kibir
NATIONAL DAY – 28 May
NATIONAL FLAG – Three horizontal bands: green, yellow, red; in the centre a blue disc, containing a yellow pentagram
LIFE EXPECTANCY (years) – 44 (2001)
POPULATION GROWTH RATE – 2.8 per cent
POPULATION DENSITY – 57 per sq. km (2001)
URBAN POPULATION – 16 per cent (2001)

HISTORY AND POLITICS

The Hamitic culture was heavily influenced by Semitic immigration from Arabia at about the time of Christ. Christianity was introduced in the fourth century. The empire attained its zenith in the sixth century under the Axum rulers but was checked by Islamic expansion from the east. Modern Ethiopia dates from 1855 when Theodros established supremacy over the various tribes. The last emperor was Haile Selassie who reigned from 1930 until 1974, when he was deposed by the armed forces. After ten years of military rule, a Workers' Party on the Soviet model was formed with Lt.-Col. Mengistu Haile Mariam as General Secretary. The People's Democratic Republic of Ethiopia was established under a new constitution in 1987 with Lt.-Col. Mengistu as president. Armed insurgencies by the Eritrean People's Liberation Front (EPLF) and the Ethiopian People's Revolutionary Democratic Front (EPRDF), originating in Tigre, brought down Mengistu's government in May 1991.

A transitional administration comprising the EPRDF and other opposition groups formed a Council of Representatives which governed until 1995 under President Meles Zenawi. In 1994, the Council agreed to a draft federal constitution, which was adopted by an elected Constituent Assembly on 8 December 1994. Multiparty elections in May and June 1995 were won by the EPRDF. The Federal Democratic Republic of Ethiopia was proclaimed on 22 August 1995.

In the general election held on 14 May 2000, the EPRDF won 472 seats. The presidential elections held on 8 October 2001 were won by Lt. Girma Wolde Giorgis.

FOREIGN RELATIONS

Eritrea, which since 1962 had been a province of Ethiopia, seceded and became independent on 24 May 1993. Relations between the two countries had been good until fighting broke out along the border in June 1998, with each side accusing the other of sending troops across the border. Ethiopia launched an attack on Eritrea in May 2000, capturing much of the west of the country. An interim peace plan was signed in June, and a comprehensive peace agreement was signed in December. A new common border was accepted by both countries in April 2002; however both sides lay claim to the town of Badme although an independent boundary commission in April 2003 ruled it lies in Eritrea (see Eritrea).

POLITICAL SYSTEM

The constitution provides for a federal government responsible for foreign affairs, defence and economic policy. The president is elected by both houses of the legislature. The House of People's Representatives (Yehizb Tewokayoch Mekir Bet) has 548 directly elected members who serve a five-year term. The House of Federation

(Yefedereshn Mekir Bet) has 108 members, indirectly elected for a five-year term by the nine regional administrations (Tigre, Afar, Amara, Oromia, Somali, Benshangui, Gambela, Harer and Southern), who have considerable autonomy and the right to secede.

HEAD OF STATE
President, Lt Girma Wolde Giorgis, elected by parliament 8 October 2001

COUNCIL OF MINISTERS as at July 2003
Prime Minister, C.-in-C. of the National Armed Forces, Meles Zenawi
Deputy Prime Minister, Rural Development, Addisu Legesse
Agriculture, Mulatu Teshome
Education, Genet Zewde
Federal Affairs, Abbay Tsehaye
Finance and Economic Development, Sofian Ahmed
Foreign Affairs, Seyoum Mesfin
Health, Kebede Tadesse
Human Resources Development, Tefera Walua
Information, Bereket Simon
Infrastructural Development, Kassu Ilala
Justice, Harka Haroye
Labour and Social Affairs, Hassan Abdella
Mines and Energy, Mohamed Dirir
National Defence, Abbadula Gemeda
Revenue Collection, Getachew Belay
Trade and Industry, Girma Birru
Water Resources, Shiferaw Jarso
Youth, Culture and Sport, Teshome Toga

EMBASSY OF THE FEDERAL DEMOCRATIC REPUBLIC OF ETHIOPIA
17 Princes Gate, London SW7 1PZ
Tel: 020-7589 7212
Email: info@ethioembassy.org.uk
Ambassador Extraordinary and Plenipotentiary, HE Fisseha Adugna, apptd 2002

BRITISH EMBASSY
Fikre Mariam Abatechan Street (PO Box 858), Addis Ababa Tel: (00 251) (1) 612354
Email: britishembassy.addisababa@fco.gov.uk
Ambassador Extraordinary and Plenipotentiary, HE Myles Wickstead

BRITISH COUNCIL DIRECTOR, Rosemary Arnott, OBE
PO Box 1043, Artistic Building, Adwa Avenue, Addis Ababa
Tel: (00 251) (1) 550 022
Email: bc.addisababa@et.britishcouncil.org

DEFENCE

The Army has 300 main battle tanks and 400 armoured infantry fighting vehicles and armoured personnel carriers. The Air Force has 55 combat aircraft and 30 armed helicopters.
MILITARY EXPENDITURE – 9.8 per cent of GDP (2001)
MILITARY PERSONNEL – 252,500: Army 250,000, Air Force 2,500

ECONOMY

The post-Mengistu government implemented a programme of free-market economic reform which reduced government spending and inflation.

Agriculture, hunting, forestry and fishing accounts for approximately 50 per cent of GDP and around 85 per cent of the people are dependent upon the land for a living. The major food crops are teff, maize, barley, sorghum, wheat, pulses and oil seeds. Famine conditions in 1984–5 recurred to a lesser extent in 1992, 1997 and 2000.

The economy deteriorated sharply in 1999 and 2000 as a result of drought, a worsening balance of trade, and war with Eritrea. In April 2001 Ethiopia was permitted to reschedule some two-thirds of its US$430 million debt until 2004 and in January 2003 the USA cancelled a debt of US$30 million owed to it by Ethiopia in January 2003.

Although agricultural liberalisation has led to dramatic progress in food production, in November 2002 Prime Minister Meles Zenawi warned that up to 15 million people could face starvation during 2003. In January 2003 the International Committee of the Red Cross (ICRC) appealed for some US$30 million in international aid to prevent a resurgence of famine during the year.

Ethiopia's largely unexploited, natural resources include gold, platinum, copper and potash. Traces of oil and natural gas have been found.

In 2000 there was a trade deficit of US$645 million and a current account surplus of US$16 million.

GNP – US$6,737 million (2000); US$100 per capita (2000)

GDP – US$6,366 million (2001); US$102 per capita (2000)

ANNUAL AVERAGE GROWTH OF GDP – 0.5 per cent (1998)

INFLATION RATE – 5.9 per cent (1999)

TOTAL EXTERNAL DEBT – US$5,481 million (2000)

TRADE

The chief imports by value are machinery and transport equipment, manufactured goods and chemicals; the principal exports by value are coffee (which normally provides about 60 per cent of Ethiopia's foreign exchange earnings), oil seeds, hides and skins, and pulses. The country's main markets for exports are Germany, Japan, Saudi Arabia, Italy and the USA. In 1999 imports totalled US$1,317 million and in 1998 exports totalled US$561 million.

Trade with UK	2001	2002
Imports from UK	£29,349,000	£40,794,000
Exports to UK	15,262,000	70,405,000

COMMUNICATIONS

A network of roads in rural areas links the major cities with each other, with the Sudanese and Kenyan borders and through Eritrea to the Red Sea coast.

There is a railway link from Addis Ababa to Djibouti. Ethiopian Airlines maintains regular services throughout Africa and to Europe. There are over 50 privately-owned newspapers in addition to the state-owned daily 'Addis Zemen'.

EDUCATION

Elementary and secondary education are provided by government schools in the main centres of population; there are also mission schools. The National University (founded 1961) co-ordinates the institutions of higher education. There are also universities at Alemaya (agricultural), Debub, Mekele, Bashir Dar and Jimma.

ILLITERACY RATE – (m) 56.4 per cent; (f) 66.8 per cent (2000)

ENROLMENT (percentage of age group) – primary 43 per cent (1997); tertiary 1 per cent (1997)

FIJI

Matanitu ko Viti – Republic of the Fiji Islands

AREA – 7,056 sq. miles (18,274 sq. km)

POPULATION – 844,330 (2001 estimate), 44 per cent Indians, 51 per cent Fijians, and 5 per cent other races. Since the 1987 coup many ethnic Indians have left and by 1994 Melanesian Fijians formed the largest population group. The main languages are Fijian and Hindi

CAPITAL – ΨSuva (population, 77,366, 1996), on the island of Viti Levu

CURRENCY – Fiji dollar (F$) of 100 cents

NATIONAL ANTHEM – God Bless Fiji

NATIONAL DAY – 10 October (Fiji Day)

NATIONAL FLAG – Light blue ground with Union flag in top left quarter and the shield of Fiji in the fly

POPULATION GROWTH RATE – 0.3 per cent

POPULATION DENSITY – 44 per sq. km (1999)

MILITARY EXPENDITURE – 1.6 per cent of GDP (2001)

MILITARY PERSONNEL – 3,500: Army 3,200, Navy 300

ILLITERACY RATE – (m) 5.1 per cent; (f) 9.2 per cent (2000)

Fiji is composed of roughly 332 islands (about 100 permanently inhabited) and over 500 islets in the South Pacific, about 1,100 miles north of New Zealand. The group extends 300 miles from east to west and 300 miles north to south. The International Date Line has been diverted to the east of the island group. The largest islands are Viti Levu and Vanua Levu.

HISTORY AND POLITICS

Fiji was a British colony from 1874 until 10 October 1970 when it became an independent state and a member of the Commonwealth. In the general election on 8–15 May 1999, the Fijian Political Party was swept from power by a coalition of parties led by the Fiji Labour Party. Its leader, Mahendra Chaudhry, became Fiji's first ethnic Indian prime minister.

On 19 May 2000 a group of indigenous Fijian rebels

stormed parliament and took the Prime Minister and most of the Cabinet hostage. The army declared martial law on 29 May following the resignation of President Ratu Sir Kamisese Mara. An interim administration was set up on 28 June, following unsuccessful negotiations between the military government and the rebels. The military named an all-indigenous government to replace the multiracial coalition of the deposed premier. The interim government was to rule for two years and prepare for fresh elections. Following the release of the last hostages on 13 July, the Great Council of Chiefs announced the appointment of Ratu Josefa Iloilo as president.

The Fijian High Court ruled on 15 November 2000 that the 1997 Constitution remained in force. Following an appeal by the interim government, the Court of Appeal ruled on 1 March 2001 that the 1997 Constitution was still in force, that the parliament had been suspended rather than dissolved, and that the interim government was not legitimate, but accepted that the then Vice-President Iloilo had the right to exercise presidential powers after the resignation of President Ratu Sir Kamisese Mara. On 7 March the interim government led by Laisenia Qarase offered its collective resignation and Mahendra Chaudhry was reappointed as prime minister, but was dismissed by President Iloilo on 14 March. Qarase was reappointed as interim prime minister the following day. On 8 March 2001 the Great Council of Chiefs rejected the judgement of the Appeal Court and reaffirmed its support for the interim government and again nominated Iloilo as president.

Fiji's membership of the Commonwealth was suspended following the coup but the suspension was revoked in December 2001.

Following legislative elections held in August and September 2001, the United Fiji Party (SDL) became the largest party in the house of representatives with 32 seats.

On 18 July 2003 Fiji's Supreme Court ruled that Prime Minister Laisenia Qarase had breached the power-sharing arrangements of the constitution by excluding members of the FLP from his Cabinet and demanded that the situation be rectified.

HEAD OF STATE

President, Ratu Josefa Iloilo, *appointed* 13 July 2000,
    reappointed 13 March 2001, *sworn in* 15 March 2001
Vice-President, Ratu Jope Naucabalavu Seniloii

CABINET *as at July 2003*

Prime Minister, Minister for Fijian Affairs, Culture and Heritage, National Reconciliation and Unity, Laisenia Qarase (SDL)
Agriculture, Sugar and Land Resettlement, Jonetani Galuinadi (SDL)
Attorney-General, Justice, Qoriniasi Bale (SDL)
Commerce, Business Development and Investment, Tomasi Vuetilovoni (SDL)
Education, Ro Teimumu Kepa (SDL)
Finance and National Planning, Communications, Ratu Jone Kubuabola (SDL)
Fisheries and Forests, Konisi Yabaki (SDL)
Foreign Affairs and External Trade, Kaliopate Tavola (SDL)
Health, Solomone Naivalu (SDL)
Home Affairs and Immigration, Joketani Cokanasiga (SDL)
Information and Media Relations, assisting the Prime Minister for National Reconciliation and Unity, Simione Kaitani

Labour, Industrial Relations and Productivity, Kenneth Zinck (NLUP)
Lands and Mineral Resources, Ratu Naiqama Lalabalavu (MV)
Local Government, Housing and Squatter Settlement and Environment, Mataiasi Ragigia (SDL)
Multi-Ethnic Affairs, George Shiu Raj (SDL)
Public Enterprises and Public Sector Reform, Irami Matiaravula (SDL)
Regional Development, Ilaitia Tuisese (SDL)
Tourism, Pita Nacuva (SDL)
Transport and Civil Aviation, Josefa Vosanibola (SDL)
Women, Social Welfare and Poverty Alleviation, Asenaca Caucau (SDL)
Works and Energy, Savenaca Draunidalo (Ind.)
Youth, Sport and Employment Opportunities, Isireli Leweniqila (MV)

MV Conservative Alliance; NLUP New Labour Unity Party; SDL Fijian People's Party; Ind. Independent

HIGH COMMISSION OF THE REPUBLIC OF FIJI
34 Hyde Park Gate, London SW7 5DN
Tel: 020-7584 3661
High Commissioner, Emitai Lausiki Boladuadua, apptd 2002

BRITISH HIGH COMMISSION
Victoria House, 47 Gladstone Road, PO Box 1355, Suva
Tel: (00 679) 3311033
Email: ukinfo@bhc.org.fj
High Commissioner, HE Charles Mochan, apptd 2002

ECONOMY

Agriculture accounts for 18 per cent of GDP and employed approximately 70 per cent of the workforce in 2001. The principal cash crop is sugar cane, which is the main export, followed by coconuts, ginger and copra. A variety of other fruit, vegetables and root crops are also grown, and self-sufficiency in rice is a major aim. Forestry, fishing and beef production are being encouraged in order to diversify the economy. The processing of agricultural, marine and timber products are the main industries, along with gold mining and textiles.

A cyclone hit Fiji's northern island of Vanua Levu in January 2003 leading to food shortages and outbreaks of disease due to polluted water. The total estimated cost of the damage was F$60 million.

GNP – US$1,480 million (2000); US$1,820 per capita (2000)
GDP – US$1,684 million (2001); US$2,031 per capita (2000)
ANNUAL AVERAGE GROWTH OF GDP – 1.8 per cent (1997)
INFLATION RATE – 1.1 per cent (2000)
UNEMPLOYMENT – 5.4 per cent (1995)
TOTAL EXTERNAL DEBT – US$136 million (2000)

TRADE
The chief imports are foodstuffs, machinery, mineral fuels, chemicals, beverages, tobacco and manufactured articles. Chief exports are sugar, coconut oil, fish, lumber, molasses and ginger.

In 1999 there was a trade deficit of US$116 million and a current account surplus of US$13 million. In 1998 imports totalled US$721 million and exports US$510 million.

Trade with UK	2001	2002
Imports from UK	£3,427,000	£3,110,000
Exports to UK	51,240,000	48,008,000

COMMUNICATIONS
Fiji is one of the main aerial crossroads in the Pacific, providing services to New Zealand, Australia, Tonga, Samoa, Vanuatu, the Solomon Islands, Kiribati, Tuvalu, New Caledonia and American Samoa. Fiji has three ports of entry, at Suva, Lautoka and Levuka. There are 5,100 km of roads.

FINLAND

Suomen Tasavalta/Republiken Finland – Republic of Finland

AREA – 117,154 sq. miles (304,600 sq. km).
   Neighbours: Norway (north-west and north), Russia (east), Sweden (west)
POPULATION – 5,178,000 (2001). Finnish and Swedish are both official languages, 93 per cent speaking Finnish as their first language and 5.6 per cent use Swedish. Sami is spoken by 1,700 of the 6,500-strong Sami population who live in the far north. The population is predominantly Lutheran
CAPITAL – Ψ Helsinki (Helsingfors) (population, 1,163,000, 2000 estimate)
MAJOR CITIES – Espoo (Esbo) (216,836); Ψ Oulu (Uleåborg) (123,274); Tampere (Tammerfors) (197,774); Ψ Turku (Åbo) (173,686); Vantaa (Vanda) (178,856), 2001
CURRENCY – Euro (€) of 100 cents
NATIONAL ANTHEM – Maamme/Vårt Land (Our Land)
NATIONAL DAY – 6 December (Independence Day)
NATIONAL FLAG – White with blue cross
LIFE EXPECTANCY (years) – 78 (2001)
POPULATION GROWTH RATE – 0.3 per cent
POPULATION DENSITY – 17 per sq. km (2001)
URBAN POPULATION – 59 per cent (2001)

HISTORY AND POLITICS
Finland was part of the Swedish Empire from the Middle Ages until it was ceded to Russia in 1809 and became an autonomous grand duchy of the Russian Empire. Finland became independent after the Russian revolution of 1917, but was forced to cede around one-tenth of its land to the Soviet Union and to resettle 10 per cent of its population under the Treaty of Paris (1947). A Soviet-Finnish Co-operation Treaty forced Finland to demilitarise its Soviet border, to enter into a barter trade agreement and to adopt a stance of neutrality. These terms lasted until the demise of the Soviet Union in 1991.

Finland joined the European Union on 1 January 1995 following a referendum in October 1994.

Presidential elections held on 16 January and February 2000 were won by Tarja Halonen of the Finnish Social Democratic Party. Legislative elections held on 16 March 2003 were narrowly won by the centre party (KESK) with 55 seats in parliament. A centre-left coalition comprising KESK, the Finnish Social Democratic Party (SDP) and the Swedish People's Party (SFP) took office on 17 April. On 24 June, Parliament elected Matti Vanhanen of KESK as prime minister.

POLITICAL SYSTEM
Under the constitution there is a unicameral legislature, the *Eduskunta*, composed of 200 members elected by universal suffrage for a four-year term. The highest executive power is held by the president who is directly elected for a period of six years. The first direct elections for the presidency were held in 1994.

HEAD OF STATE
President, Tarja Kaarina Halonen, *elected* 6 February 2000, *inaugurated* 1 March 2000

CABINET *as at July 2003*
Prime Minister, Matti Vanhanen (KESK)
Agriculture and Forestry, Juha Korkäoja (KESK)
Culture, Tanja Karpela (KESK)
Defence, Seppo Kääriäinen (KESK)
Deputy Minister of Finance, Ulla-Maj Wideroos (SFP)
Education, Tuula Haatainen (SDP)
Environment, Jan-Erik Enestam (SFP)
Finance, Antti Kalliomäki (SDP)
Foreign Affairs, Erkki Tuomioja (SDP)
Foreign Trade, Paula Lehtomäki (KESK)
Health and Social Services, Liisa Hyssälä (KESK)
Interior, Kari Rajamäki (SDP)
Justice, Johannes Koskinen (SDP)
Labour, Tarja Filatov (SDP)
Regional and Municipal Affairs, Hannes Manninen (KESK)
Social Affairs and Health, Sinikka Mönkäre (SDP)
Trade and Industry, Mauri Pekkarinen (KESK)
Transport and Communications, Leena Luhtanen (SDP)

KESK Centre Party; SDP Finnish Social Democratic Party; SFP Swedish People's Party

EMBASSY OF FINLAND
38 Chesham Place, London SW1X 8HW
Tel: 020-7838 6200
Ambassador Extraordinary and Plenipotentiary, HE Pertti Salolainen, apptd 1996

BRITISH EMBASSY
Itäinen Puistotie 17, FIN-00140 Helsinki
Tel: (00 358) (9) 2286 5100
Ambassador Extraordinary and Plenipotentiary, HE Matthew Kirk, apptd 2002

BRITISH COUNCIL DIRECTOR, Tuija Talvitie
Hakaniemenkatu 2, FIN-00530 Helsinki
Tel: (00 358) (9) 7743 330
Email: offiice@britishcouncil.fii

DEFENCE
The Army has 268 main battle tanks, 274 armoured infantry fighting vehicles and 1,101 armoured personnel carriers. The Navy has 9 patrol and coastal vessels. The Air Force has 63 combat aircraft.
MILITARY EXPENDITURE – 1.2 per cent of GDP (2001)
MILITARY PERSONNEL – 31,850: Army 24,550, Navy 4,600, Air Force 2,700; Paramilitaries 3,100
CONSCRIPTION DURATION – Six to 12 months

ECONOMY
Important industries are mobile phones, rubber, plastics, chemicals and pharmaceuticals, glass, ceramics, furniture, footwear, foodstuffs and shipbuilding. The euro replaced the Finnish markka in January 2002.

GNP – US$130,106 million (2000); US$25,130 per capita (2000)
GDP – US$121,987 million (2001); US$23,377 per capita (2000)
ANNUAL AVERAGE GROWTH OF GDP – 5.9 per cent (2000)
INFLATION RATE – 3.4 per cent (2000)
UNEMPLOYMENT – 9.7 per cent (2000)

TRADE
The principal imports are raw materials, machinery and manufactured goods. The main exports are electronic and electrical goods, paper and wood pulp, machinery, and metal products. Trade with EU countries accounts for more than half of Finland's total trade.

In 2001 there was a trade surplus of US$12,657 million and a current account surplus of US$8,357 million. Imports totalled US$32,108 million and exports US$42,794 million.

Trade with UK	2001	2002
Imports from UK	£1,544,000,000	£2,668,000,000
Exports to UK	2,834,800,000	1,377,000,000

COMMUNICATIONS
There are 5,859 km of railroad, railway connections with Russia, and passenger boat connections with Sweden, Germany and Estonia. There are also passenger/cargo services between Finland and Britain.

CULTURE AND EDUCATION
Primary education (co-educational comprehensive school) is free and compulsory for children from seven to 16 years.
ENROLMENT (percentage of age group) – primary 99 per cent (1997); secondary 100 per cent (1997); tertiary 74 per cent (1997)

FRANCE

La République française – The French Republic

AREA – 211,577 sq. miles (550,100 sq. km).
  Neighbours: Belgium and Luxembourg (north-east), Germany, Switzerland and Italy (east), Monaco (south), Spain and Andorra (south-west)
POPULATION – 59,453,000 (2001); 57,218,000 (Metropolitan France), and 58,745,000 including overseas departments (1992 official estimate): 72 per cent Catholic, 8 per cent Muslim, 2 per cent Jewish. The language is French; there are several regional languages including Basque, Breton, Catalan, Corsican, Dutch, German and Occitan
CAPITAL – Paris (population, 9,644,507, 1999 census)
MAJOR CITIES – Ψ Bordeaux (753,931); Grenoble (419,334); Lille (1,000,900); Lyon (1,348,832); Ψ Marseille (1,349,772); Nantes (544,932); Nice (888,784); Strasbourg (427,245); Toulon (519,640); Toulouse (761,090). The chief towns of Corsica are Ψ Ajaccio (58,315) and Ψ Bastia (52,446)
CURRENCY – Euro (€) of 100 cents
NATIONAL ANTHEM – La Marseillaise
NATIONAL DAY – 14 July (Bastille Day 1789)
NATIONAL FLAG – The tricolour, three vertical bands, blue, white, red (blue next to flagstaff)
LIFE EXPECTANCY (years) – 79 (2001)
POPULATION GROWTH RATE – 0.4 per cent
POPULATION DENSITY – 108 per sq. km (2001)

HISTORY AND POLITICS
Gaul, the area which is now France, was conquered by Julius Caesar in the 1st century BC and remained a part of the Roman Empire until the Frankish invasions in the 5th and 6th centuries. The Treaty of Verdun (AD 843) divided the Frankish Empire into three parts, of which the western part, *Francia Occidentalis,* became the basis for modern France.

As a result of the French Revolution, a republic was declared in 1792 and the king, Louis XVI, was executed. The republic was overthrown by Napoléon Bonaparte, who established the first French Empire, which ended in 1815. The ensuing Congress of Vienna restored the monarchy, but in 1848 the Second Republic was declared, which lasted only until 1852, when the Second Empire was proclaimed under Napoléon III. He was forced to abdicate after the defeat of France in the Franco-Prussian war (1870–1871) and the Third Republic was established.

In 1940, Germany invaded France, occupying most of the country and establishing a pro-German government in the south. France was liberated in 1944, a provisional government was established under Gen. de Gaulle, and the Fourth Republic was declared in 1946. In 1958, the threat of a military coup following a rebellion in Algeria resulted in the assembly inviting Gen. de Gaulle to return as premier; a new constitution which strengthened the powers of the president was adopted, the Fifth Republic was proclaimed, and Gen. De Gaulle was elected president. France granted its colonies independence between 1954 and 1962.

President Jacques Chirac, the candidate of the Rally for the Republic (RPR), was elected in May 1995.

In the first round of the presidential elections on 21 April 2002, Jacques Chirac won the most votes and National Front leader Jean-Marie Le Pen gained just under 200,000 more votes than Prime Minister Lionel Jospin of the Socialist Party. Jacques Chirac won the second round run-off with Le Pen on 5 May with 82.2 per cent of the vote.

In the elections to the National Assembly held in June 2002 the Union for a Presidential Majority (UMP), an election coalition of the RPR and Liberal Democracy (DL), won an overall majority and a coalition comprising UMP and the Union for French Democracy (UDF) took office on 18 June. In September 2002 the RPR, DL and parts of the UDF merged to form the Union for a Popular Movement (UMP).

A governmental plan for a major decentralisation of power from Paris was launched in October 2002. In March 2003 the Parliament approved constitutional amendments paving the way for the devolution to regions and departments of powers over economic development, transport, tourism, culture and further education.

INSURGENCIES
A desire for greater autonomy and recognition of Corsica's distinctive culture and language led to a campaign of separatist bombings and shootings which began in the mid-1970s. In November 1999, Prime Minister Jospin invited all political groups on the island to engage in dialogue with the French government on the constitutional future of the island. Following discussions, Jospin presented proposals to combine the island's two departments, and give the regional parliament powers over cultural, educational, structural and planning affairs and limited legislative autonomy by 2004 in return for a permanent end to terrorism. The proposals, which were accepted by the Corsican regional parliament on 28 July 2000 and narrowly passed by the National Assembly on 19 December 2001, suffered a setback on 17 January 2002 when the Constitutional Council rejected the legislation as unconstitutional, but allowed provisions permitting the Corsican language to become part of the primary school curriculum. A referendum held on 6 July 2003 narrowly voted against the establishment of a new unified assembly for Corsica with limited powers to raise and spend taxes.

POLITICAL SYSTEM
The head of state is a directly elected president, whose term of office was reduced from seven years to five years, but will be five years with effect from the presidential election held in April and May 2002. The legislature consists of the National Assembly of 577 deputies (555 for Metropolitan France and 22 for the overseas departments and territories) and the Senate of 321 Senators (296 for Metropolitan France, 13 for the overseas departments and territories and 12 for French citizens abroad). Deputies in the National Assembly are directly elected for a five-year term. One-third of the Senate is indirectly elected every three years.

The prime minister is appointed by the president, as is the Council of Ministers on the prime minister's recommendation. They are responsible to the legislature, but as the executive is constitutionally separate from the legislature, ministers may not sit in the legislature and must hand over their seats to a substitute.

HEAD OF STATE
President of the French Republic, Jacques Chirac, elected 7 May 1995, re-elected 5 May 2002

COUNCIL OF MINISTERS *as at July 2003*
Prime Minister, Jean-Pierre Raffarin (UMP)
Administrative Reform, Henri Plagnol (UDF)
Agriculture, Food, Fisheries and Rural Affairs, Hervé Gaymard (UMP)
Capital Works, Transport, Housing, Tourism and the Sea, Gilles de Robien (UDF)
Civil Service, Administrative Reform and Town and Country Planning, Jean-Paul Delevoye (UMP)
Culture and Communications, Jean-Jacques Aillagon (UMP)
Defence, War Veterans, Michèle Alliot-Marie (UMP)
Ecology and Sustainable Development, Roselyne Bachelot-Narquin (UMP)

Economy, Finance and Industry, Francis Mer
Foreign Affairs Co-operation and Francophonie, Dominique de Villepin
Health, the Family and the Disabled, Jean-François Mattéi (UMP)
Interior, Internal Security and Local Freedoms, Nicolas Sarkozy (UMP)
Justice, Keeper of the Seals, Dominique Perben (UMP)
Overseas France, Brigitte Girardin
Social Affairs, Employment and Solidarity, François Fillon (UMP)
Sport, Jean-François Lamour
Youth, National Education and Research, Luc Ferry
UDF Union for French Democracy; UMP Union for a Popular Movement

FRENCH EMBASSY
58 Knightsbridge, London SW1X 7JT
Tel: 020-7073 1000
Ambassador Extraordinary and Plenipotentiary, HE Gérard Errera, apptd 2002

BRITISH EMBASSY
35 rue du Faubourg St Honoré, F-75383 Paris Cedex 08
Tel: (00 33) (1) 4451 3100
Ambassador Extraordinary and Plenipotentiary, HE Sir John Eaton Holmes KBE, CVO, CMG, apptd 2001

BRITISH COUNCIL DIRECTOR, John Tod, OBE
9 rue de Constantine, F-75340 Paris Cédex 07
Tel: (00 33) (1) 4955 7300
Email: information@britishcouncil.fr.

DEFENCE
The Army has 786 main battle tanks, 3,700 armoured personnel carriers, 384 armoured infantry fighting vehicles and 418 helicopters.

The Navy has ten submarines, one aircraft carrier, one cruiser, three destroyers, 30 frigates and 35 patrol and coastal vessels, 58 combat aircraft and 30 armed helicopters. The Navy has four domestic and five overseas bases. The Air Force has 449 combat aircraft.

France deploys 34,981 armed forces personnel abroad; 3,000 in Germany (including members of Eurocorps); 16,900 in French Overseas Departments and Territories; 6,600 in former French colonies in Africa and 8,481 on UN and peacekeeping duties. Compulsory military service was abolished in June 2001.
MILITARY EXPENDITURE – 2.6 per cent of GDP (2001)
MILITARY PERSONNEL – 260,400: Army 137,000, Strategic Nuclear Forces 7,000, Navy 45,600, Air Force 64,000; Paramilitaries (Gendarmerie) 101,399

ECONOMY
Viniculture is extensive, regions famous for their wines including Bordeaux, Burgundy and Champagne. Production of wine in 2000 was 59 million hectolitres. Cognac, liqueurs and cider are also produced. Other important agricultural products include sugar beet, dairy products, cereals and oilseeds. Nearly 55 per cent of the land area of metropolitan France is utilised for agricultural production and a further quarter is accounted for by forests.

Oil is produced from fields in the Landes area, but France is a net importer of crude oil, for processing by its important oil-refining industry. Natural gas is produced in the foothills of the Pyrenees.

Heavy industries include oil-refining and the production of iron and steel, and aluminium. In 2000 production of pig iron was 13.9 million tonnes and steel 21 million tonnes. Other important industries are construction and civil engineering, chemicals, rubber and plastics, pharmaceuticals, vehicle production and telecommunications services.

The Banque de France was made independent of the government in 1994 with the formation of a nine-member monetary policy council to define and implement monetary policy.

France has participated in the European Single Currency since January 1999 and in January 2002 the euro replaced the franc.

Government moves towards privatisation sparked a public sector strike in November 2002 and a series of national strikes took place in May and June 2003 over planned pension reforms.

GNP – US$1,438,293 million (2000); US$24,090 per capita (2000)

GDP – US$1,302,793 million (2001); US$21,848 per capita (2000)

ANNUAL AVERAGE GROWTH OF GDP – 3.3 per cent (2000)

INFLATION RATE – 1.7 per cent (2000)

UNEMPLOYMENT – 10.0 per cent (2000)

TRADE

The principal imports are raw materials for the heavy and manufacturing industries (e.g. oil, minerals, chemicals), machinery and precision instruments, agricultural products, chemicals and vehicles. Agricultural products, chemicals, pharmaceuticals and vehicles are also the principal exports. Most of France's trade is done with other EU countries. There are around 45 million hectares of farmland.

In 2001 there was a trade surplus of US$2,853 million and a current account surplus of US$21,359 million. In 2001 imports totalled US$292,526 million and exports US$294,357 million.

Trade with UK	2001	2002
Imports from UK	£18,394,500,000	£17,844,000,00
Exports to UK	18,222,100,000	17,982,000,000

COMMUNICATIONS

There are approximately 10,000 km of motorways and around 900,000 km of other roads. There are 8,500 km of navigable inland waterways. The railroad system is extensive. The length of the rail network in 2000 was around 26,000 km. The French mercantile marine consisted in 1998 of 210 ships of a total of 4,100,000 tonnes which transported 91,500,000 tonnes of freight.

CULTURE AND EDUCATION

Education is compulsory, free and secular from six to 16. Schools may be single-sex or co-educational. Primary education is given in nursery schools, primary schools and *collèges d'enseignement général* (four-year secondary modern course); secondary education in *collèges d'enseignement technique, collèges d'enseignement secondaire* and *lycées* (seven-year course leading to one of the five *baccalauréats*). Special schools are numerous.

There are many *grandes écoles* in France which award diplomas in many subjects not taught at university, especially applied science and engineering. Most of these are state institutions but have a competitive system of entry, unlike universities. There are universities in 24 towns including 13 in Paris and the immediate area.

ENROLMENT (percentage of age group) – primary 100 per cent (1997); secondary 100 per cent (1997); tertiary 51 per cent (1997)

OVERSEAS DEPARTMENTS

Greater powers of self-government were granted to French Guiana, Guadeloupe, Martinique and Réunion in 1982. These former colonies had enjoyed departmental status since 1946. Their directly elected Assemblies operate in parallel with the existing, indirectly constituted Regional Councils. The French government is represented by a Prefect in each.

FRENCH GUIANA

AREA – 34,749 sq. miles (90,000 sq. km)

POPULATION – 182,333 (2002 estimate)

CAPITAL – Ψ Cayenne (50,675, 1999 census)

Situated on the north-eastern coast of South America, French Guiana is flanked by Suriname on the west and by Brazil on the south and east. Under the administration of French Guiana is a group of islands (St Joseph, Île Royal and Île du Diable), known as Îles du Salut.

Prefect, Ange Mancini

GUADELOUPE

AREA – 658 sq. miles (1,705 sq. km)

POPULATION – 435,739 (2002 estimate)

CAPITAL – Ψ Basse-Terre (12,410, 1999 census) on Guadeloupe

A number of islands in the Leeward Islands group of the West Indies, consisting of the two main islands of Guadeloupe (or Basse-Terre) and Grande-Terre, with the adjacent islands of Marie-Galante, La Désirade and Îles des Saintes, and islands of St-Barthélemy and the part of St-Martin under French administration, which lie over 150 miles to the north-west. The main towns are Ψ Les Abymes (63,054); Ψ St-Martin (29,078); Ψ Pointe-à-Pitre (20,948) in Grande-Terre and Ψ Grand Bourg (5,934) in Marie-Galante.

Prefect, Dominique Vian

MARTINIQUE

AREA – 425 sq. miles (1,102 sq. km)

POPULATION – 422,277 (2002 estimate)

CAPITAL – Ψ Fort-de-France (94,778, 1999 census)

An island situated in the Windward Islands group of the West Indies, between Dominica in the north and St Lucia in the south. The main towns are Ψ Le Lamentin (35,951) and Ψ Schoelcher (20,908).

Prefect, Michel Cadot

RÉUNION

AREA – 969 sq. miles (2,510 sq. km)

POPULATION – 743,981 (2002 estimate)

CAPITAL – St-Denis (158,139, 1999)

Réunion, which became a French possession in 1638, lies in the Indian Ocean, about 569 miles east of Madagascar and 110 miles south-west of Mauritius. Other towns are Saint-Paul (87,712) and Saint-Pierre (129,238). The smaller, uninhabited islands of Bassas da India, Europa, Îles Glorieuses, Juan de Nova and Tromelin are administered from Réunion.

Prefect, Gonthier Friederici

TERRITORIAL COLLECTIVITIES

MAYOTTE
AREA – 144 sq. miles (372 sq. km)
POPULATION – 170,879 (2002 estimate)
CAPITAL – Mamoudzou (32,733, 1997 census)
Part of the Comoros Islands group, Mayotte remained a French dependency when the other three islands became independent as the Comoros Republic in 1975. Since 1976 the island has been a *collectivité territoriale,* an intermediate status between Overseas Department and Overseas Territory.
Prefect, Jean-Jacques Brot

ST PIERRE AND MIQUELON
AREA – 93 sq. miles (242 sq. km)
POPULATION – 6,954 (2002 estimate)
CAPITAL – Ψ St-Pierre (5,618, 1999)
These two small groups of islands off the coast of Newfoundland became a *collectivité territoriale* in 1985.
Prefect, Claude Valleix

OVERSEAS TERRITORIES

FRENCH POLYNESIA
AREA – 1,544 sq. miles (4,000 sq. km)
POPULATION – 257,847 (2002 estimate)
CAPITAL – Ψ Papeete (26,181), in Tahiti
Five archipelagos in the south Pacific, comprising the Society Islands (Windward Islands group includes Tahiti, Moorea, Makatea, Mehetia, Tetiaroa, Tubuai Manu; Leeward Islands group includes Huahine, Raiatea, Tahaa, Bora-Bora, Maupiti), the Tuamotu Islands (Rangiroa, Hao, Turéia, etc.), the Gambier Islands (Mangareva, etc.), the Tubuai Islands (Rimatara, Rurutu, Tubuai, Raivavae, Rapa, etc.) and the Marquesas Islands (Nuku-Hiva, Hiva-Oa, Fatu-Hiva, Tahuata, Ua Huka, etc.).
High Commissioner, Michel Mathieu

NEW CALEDONIA
AREA – 7,172 sq. miles (18,575 sq. km)
POPULATION – 207,858 (2002 estimate)
CAPITAL – Ψ Nouméa (97,581)
New Caledonia is a large island in the western Pacific, 700 miles east of Queensland. Dependencies are the Isles of Pines, the Loyalty Islands (Mahé, Lifou, Urea, etc.), the Bélep Archipelago, the Chesterfield Islands, the Huon Islands and Walpole.
New Caledonia was discovered in 1774 and annexed by France in 1854; from 1871 to 1896 it was a convict settlement. In 1995, the territory was divided into three provinces, each with a provincial assembly which combined to form the Territorial Assembly. In elections in July 1995, Kanaks won majorities in North province and the Loyalty Islands, whereas pro-French settlers won a majority in the South province.
A referendum in 1987 on the question of independence was boycotted by the indigenous Kanaks, and New Caledonia therefore voted to remain French. In April 1998 an agreement was reached between the pro-independence Kanak Socialist National Liberation Front, the anti-independence Rally for Caledonia in the Republic and the French government to hold a referendum on independence in 15-20 years' time, and for greater autonomy for the indigenous people in the intervening period. A referendum on the agreement, the Nouméa Accord, was held on 8 November 1998. It was

supported by 71.9 per cent of voters; more than 74 per cent of registered voters took part.
High Commissioner, Daniel Constantin

SOUTHERN AND ANTARCTIC TERRITORIES
Created in 1955 from former Réunion dependencies, the territory comprises the islands of Amsterdam (25 sq. miles) and St Paul (2.7 sq. miles), the Kerguelen Islands (2,700 sq. miles) and Crozet Islands (116 sq. miles) archipelagos and Adélie Land (116,800 sq. miles) in the Antarctic continent. The only population are members of staff of the scientific stations.
Administrator, François Garde

WALLIS AND FUTUNA ISLANDS
AREA – 77 sq. miles (200 sq. km)
POPULATION – 15,585 (2002 estimate)
CAPITAL – Ψ Mata-Utu on Uvea, the main island of the Wallis group

Two groups of islands (the Wallis Archipelago and the Îles de Hoorn) in the central Pacific, north-east of Fiji.
Administrator, Christian Job

THE FRENCH COMMUNITY
The constitution of the Fifth French Republic, promulgated in 1958, envisaged the establishment of a French Community of States. A number of the former French states in Africa have seceded from the Community but for all practical purposes continue to enjoy the same close links with France as those that remain formally members. Most former French African colonies are closely linked to France by financial, technical and economic agreements.

GABON

République Gabonaise – Gabonese Republic

AREA – 99,115 sq. miles (257,700 sq. km). Neighbours: Equatorial Guinea and Cameroon (north), Republic of Congo-Brazzaville (east and south)
POPULATION – 1,262,000 (2001). The official language is French; Fang is widely spoken
CAPITAL – Ψ Libreville (population, 362,400, 1993)
CURRENCY – Franc CFA of 100 centimes
NATIONAL ANTHEM – La Concorde
NATIONAL DAY – 17 August
NATIONAL FLAG – Horizontal bands, green, yellow and blue
LIFE EXPECTANCY (years) – 53 (2001)
POPULATION GROWTH RATE – 2.7 per cent
POPULATION DENSITY – 5 per sq. km (2001)
MILITARY EXPENDITURE – 2.4 per cent of GDP (2001)
MILITARY PERSONNEL – 4,700: Army 3,200, Navy 500, Air Force 1,000; Paramilitaries 2,000
ILLITERACY RATE – (m) 20.2 per cent; (f) 37.8 per cent (2000)

HISTORY AND POLITICS
The first Europeans to visit the region were the Portuguese in the 15th century, and Dutch, French and English traders arrived over the following decades. In 1849 a slave ship was captured by the French, and the freed slaves formed a settlement which they called Libreville, the current capital. The territory was annexed to French Congo in 1888.

Gabon elected on 28 November 1958 to remain an autonomous republic within the French Community and gained full independence on 17 August 1960.

Multiparty elections held in autumn 1990 were won by the ruling Parti Démocratique Gabonais (PDG), amid allegations of fraud. The PDG formed a coalition government, although the other parties left the government in 1991 in protest at PDG domination. In September 1994, the government and opposition parties signed the Paris Agreement, which provided for a new coalition government and parliamentary elections. The elections, held in December 1996, returned the PDG to power. President Bongo of the PDG, who first took office in 1967, was re-elected for a fifth term of office in December 1998. The latest elections to the National Assembly took place on 9 and 23 December 2001. The government is dominated by the PDG but includes opposition party members from the National Rally of Woodcutters (RNB-RPG) and the Social Democrat Party (PSD).

POLITICAL SYSTEM
The constitution provides for an executive president, directly elected for a seven-year term, who appoints the Council of Ministers. There is a 120-member National Assembly, directly elected for a five-year term, and a 91-member Senate, elected by municipal and regional councillors for a six-year term.

HEAD OF STATE
President, El Hadj Omar Bongo, assumed office December 1967, *re-elected* 1973, 1979, 1986, 1993 and 6 December 1998
Vice-President, Didjob Divungi-di-Ndinge

COUNCIL OF MINISTERS *as at July 2003*
Prime Minister, Jean-François Ntoutoume-Emane (PDG)
Deputy Prime Minister, Human Rights, Agriculture, Livestock and Rural Development, Paul Mba Abessole (RNB-RPG)
Deputy Prime Minister, Town and Country Planning, Emmanuel Ondo Methogo (PDG)
Deputy Prime Minister, Urban Affairs, Antoine de Padoue Mboumbou Miyakou (PDG)
Civil Service, Administrative Reform and Modernisation of the State, Pascal Désiré Missong (PDG)
Commerce and Industrial Development, Regional Integration, Jean-Remy Pendy Bouyiki (PDG)
Communication, Post and Information Technology, Mehdi Teale (PDG)
Culture and Arts, Pierre Amoughe Mba (RNB-RPG)
Defence, Ali Ben Bongo (PDG)
Equipment, Construction and Urban Affairs, Egide Boundono-Simangoye (PDG)
Family and the Advancement of Women, Angélique Ngoma (PDG)
Finance, Economy, Budget and Privatisation, Paul Toungui (PDG)
Foreign Affairs, Co-operation and Francophone Affairs, Jean Ping (PDG)
Higher Education, Scientific Research and Technology, in charge of Relations with Parliament and the Assemblies, Vincent Moulengui Boukoss (RNB-RPG)
Housing, Urban Affairs, Land Survey, Jacques Adiahenot (PDG)
Interior, Public Security, Decentralisation, Gen. Idriss Ngari (PDG)

Justice, Keeper of the Seals, Honorine Dossou Naki (PDG)
Labour and Employment, Clotaire Christian Ivala (PDG)
Merchant Navy, Felix Siby (PDG)
Mines, Energy, Oil and Hydraulic Resources, Richard Onouviet (PDG)
National Education, Daniel Ona-Ondo (PDG)
National Solidarity, Social Affairs and Welfare, Andre Mba Obame (PDG)
Planning and Development Programmes, Casimir Oye Mba (PDG)
Professional Training and Social Rehabilitation, Barnabé Ndaki (PDG)
Public Health, Faustin Boukoubi (PDG)
Relations With Parliament, Government Spokesperson, Rene Ndemezo Obiang (PDG)
Small and Medium Sized Enterprises and Industries, Paul Biyighe-Mba (PDG)
Tourism and Handicrafts, Jean Massima (PDG)
Transport and Civil Aviation, Paulette Missambo (PDG)
Water, Forests, Fishing, Environment and Protection of Nature, Emile Doumba (PDG)
Youth and Sport, Alfred Mabicka (PDG)

PDG Gabonese Democratic Party; RNB-RPG National Rally of Woodcutters

EMBASSY OF THE REPUBLIC OF GABON
27 Elvaston Place, London SW7 5NL
Tel: 020-7823 9986
Ambassador Extraordinary and Plenipotentiary, HE Alain Mensah-Zoguelet, apptd 2003

BRITISH AMBASSADOR, HE Richard Wildash, LVO, resident at Yaoundé, Cameroon

ECONOMY
The economy is heavily dependent on oil, which contributes 40 per cent of GDP and is the leading export, and, to a lesser extent, on other mineral resources, including manganese and uranium. Gabon has considerable timber reserves with 80 per cent of the country still forested, although production has stagnated in recent years.

France and the USA are the main trading partners. In 2000 imports totalled US$994 million and in 1997 exports totalled US$3,024 million.
GNP – US$3,928 million (2000); US$3,190 per capita (2000)
GDP – US$4,334 million (2001); US$3,988 per capita (2000)
ANNUAL AVERAGE GROWTH OF GDP – 4.6 per cent (1997)
INFLATION RATE – 1.5 per cent (2000)
TOTAL EXTERNAL DEBT – US$3,995 million (2000)

Trade with UK	2001	2002
Imports from UK	£34,923,000	£24,625,000
Exports to UK	4,325,000	5,795,000

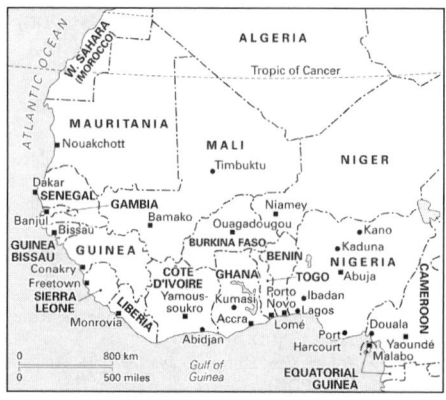

THE GAMBIA

The Republic of the Gambia

AREA – 4,361 sq. miles (11,295 sq. km). Neighbour: Senegal, which surrounds the Gambia except at the coast
POPULATION – 1,411,205 (2001 estimate), mainly Wollof, Mandinka and Fula peoples who originally migrated from the north and east. The official language is English; Fula, Jola, Mandinka, Serahule and Wollof are indigenous languages
CAPITAL – Ψ Banjul (population, 42,407, 1993 census)
CURRENCY – Dalasi (D) of 100 butut
NATIONAL ANTHEM – For The Gambia, Our Homeland
NATIONAL DAY – 18 February (Independence Day)
NATIONAL FLAG – Horizontal stripes of red, blue and green, separated by narrow white stripes
POPULATION GROWTH RATE – 3.3 per cent
POPULATION DENSITY – 112 per sq. km (1999)
MILITARY EXPENDITURE – 0.7 per cent of GDP (2001)
MILITARY PERSONNEL – Army 800

HISTORY AND POLITICS
The Gambia River basin was part of the region dominated in the tenth to 16th centuries by the Songhai and Mali kingdoms centred on the upper Niger. The Portuguese reached the Gambia River in 1447; English merchants began to trade along the river from 1588. Merchants from France, Courland (now Latvia) and the Netherlands also established trading posts. In 1816 the British stationed a garrison on an island at the river mouth which became the capital of a small British-administered colony. In 1889 France agreed that the British rights along the upper river should extend to 10 km from the river on either bank. British administration was extended from the Colony to this Protectorate. The Gambia became independent within the Commonwealth on 18 February 1965, and a republic on 24 April 1970.

In July 1994 junior army officers launched a coup which ousted the president and the government, and a military council was formed. The coup leader, Lt. (later Capt.) Jammeh, assumed the presidency, the constitution was suspended and a civilian-military government was formed to rule in conjunction with the Ruling Military Council. A referendum approved a new constitution in August 1996, Jammeh was elected president the following month and the Ruling Military Council was dissolved. The latest presidential elections were held on

18 October 2001 when Jammeh secured his presidency with 53 per cent of the vote. Legislative elections held on 17 January 2002 were won by The Alliance for Patriotic Reorientation and Construction (APRC). The election was boycotted by opposition parties.

FOREIGN RELATIONS
The relationship with Senegal remains an important factor in political and economic policy. Moves towards a closer association were accelerated after an abortive coup in 1981 was put down with the help of Senegalese troops. In 1982 the Senegambia Confederation was instituted but following disagreements it was dissolved in 1989. A treaty of friendship and co-operation was signed with Senegal in 1991.

POLITICAL SYSTEM
The constitution gives enhanced powers to the president who is elected for an indefinite term. The National Assembly has 53 members, of whom 48 are directly elected, and five appointed by the president, for a five-year term.

HEAD OF STATE
President, Defence, Col. Yahya Jammeh, *took power* 23 July 1994, *elected* 26 September 1996 *re-elected* 18 October 2001
Vice-President, Women and Social Affairs, Isatou Njie-Saidy

CABINET *as at July 2003*
Agriculture, Hassan Sallah
Education, Thérèse Ndong-Jatta
External Affairs, Baboucarr Blaise Jagne
Finance and Economic Affairs, Famara Jatta
Fisheries and Natural Resources, Susan Waffa-Ogooh
Health, Capt.Yankuba Gassama
Interior, Ousman Badjie
Justice, Attorney-General, Joseph Joof
Local Government and Lands, Momodou Nai Ceesay
Public Works, Communications and Information, Presidential Affairs, Capt. Edward Singhateh
Tourism and Culture, Yankuba Touray
Trade, Industry and Employment, Musa Sillah
Youth and Sports, Sarjo Jallow

GAMBIA HIGH COMMISSION
57 Kensington Court, London W8 5DG
Tel: 020-7937 6316/7/8
High Commissioner, HE Gibril Seman Joof, apptd 2000

BRITISH HIGH COMMISSION
48 Atlantic Road, Fajara (PO Box 507), Banjul
Tel: (00 220) 495133/4
Email: bhcbanjul@gamtel.gm
High Commissioner, HE Eric Jenkinson, apptd 2003

ECONOMY
Agriculture accounts for 79.9 per cent of employment and contributes 29.1 per cent of GDP. The chief product, groundnuts, forms over 80 per cent of exports. Other crops are cotton, rice, millet, sorghum and maize. Manufactures are limited to groundnut processing, minor metal fabrications, paints, furniture, soap and bottling. Tourism is developing quickly, providing 16 per cent of GDP. Trade through the Gambia, re-exporting imported goods to neighbouring countries, is an important element in the economy. The main exports are groundnuts,

cotton, and fish and fish products. The main imports are foodstuffs and live animals, industrial goods, machinery and transport equipment, and fuels. In 1997 there was a trade deficit of US$87 million and a current account deficit of US$24 million. Imports in 1999 totalled US$192 million and exports US$7 million.

GNP – US$440 million (2000); US$340 per capita (2000)
GDP – US$405 million (2001); US$311 per capita (2000)
ANNUAL AVERAGE GROWTH OF GDP – 5.4 per cent (1997)
INFLATION RATE – 0.8 per cent (2000)
TOTAL EXTERNAL DEBT – US$471 million (2000)

Trade with UK	2001	2002
Imports from UK	£18,503,000	£16,402,000
Exports to UK	7,726,000	4,805,000

EDUCATION

There are 24 secondary schools (eight high and 16 technical). Two high schools provide A-level education. Gambia College provides post-secondary courses in education, agriculture, public health and nursing. There are seven vocational training institutions. There is one university, based in Serrekunda.
ILLITERACY RATE – (m) 56.0 per cent; (f) 70.6 per cent (2000)
ENROLMENT (percentage of age group) – primary 77 per cent (1997); secondary 25 per cent (1997); tertiary 2 per cent (1997)

GEORGIA

Sak'art'velos Respublikis – Georgia

AREA – 26,808 sq. miles (69,700 sq. km). Neighbours: Russia (north), Azerbaijan (south-east), Armenia (south), Turkey (south-west)
POPULATION – 5,239,000 (2001): 70 per cent Georgian, 8 per cent Armenian, 6 per cent Russian, 6 per cent Azerbaijani, 3 per cent Ossetian and 2 per cent Abkhazian, with smaller groups of Greeks, Ukrainians, Jews and Kurds. Georgian is the sole official language, except in Abkhazia where Abkhazian is also officially recognised. Russian and Armenian are commonly spoken. About 65 per cent of the population are adherents of the Georgian Orthodox Church, 11 per cent are Muslims, 10 per cent are Russian Orthodox and 8 per cent are Armenian Orthodox
CAPITAL – Tbilisi (population, 1,253,100, 1997 estimate)
MAJOR CITIES – Batumi (137,000); Kutaisi (236,000); Rustavi (160,000); Sukhumi (capital of Abkhazia) (122,000), 1990 UN estimates
CURRENCY – Lari of 100 tetri
NATIONAL ANTHEM – Dideba Zetsit Kurtheuls (Praise Be To The Heavenly Bestower Of Blessings)
NATIONAL DAY – 26 May (Independence Day)
NATIONAL FLAG – Cherry red with a canton in the upper hoist divided black over white
LIFE EXPECTANCY (years) – 73 (2001)
POPULATION GROWTH RATE – –0.4 per cent
POPULATION DENSITY – 75 per sq. km (2001)
URBAN POPULATION – 56 per cent (2001)
MILITARY EXPENDITURE – 1.7 per cent of GDP (2001)

MILITARY PERSONNEL – 17,500: Army 8,620, Navy 1,830, Air Force 1,250; Paramilitaries 11,700
CONSCRIPTION DURATION – 18 months
ENROLMENT (percentage of age group) – primary 88 per cent (1997); secondary 77 per cent (1997); tertiary 42 per cent (1997)

Georgia occupies the north-western part of the Caucasus region of the former Soviet Union. It contains the two autonomous republics of Abkhazia and Adjaria and the disputed region of South Ossetia (Tskhinvali).

HISTORY AND POLITICS

The Georgians formed two states, Colchis and Iberia, on the edge of the Black Sea around 1000 BC. After centuries of invasions by Arabs, Turks and Khazars, Georgia entered its 'Golden Age' in the 12th century AD when trade, irrigation and communications were developed. Invasions by the Khazars and Mongols led to the division of Georgia into several states. These struggled against the Turkish and the Persian empires from the 16th to the 18th centuries, gradually turning to the Russian Empire for protection and support. Eastern Georgia signed a treaty of alliance with Russia which recognised Russian supremacy in 1783 and joined the Russian Empire in 1801, followed soon after by Western Georgia.

In the late 19th century, nationalist and Marxist movements competed for limited political influence under autocratic Russian rule. One of the most prominent Marxist activists was Iosif Dzhugashvili (Josef Stalin). After the Russian revolution of 1917, a nationalist government came to power in Georgia supported by allied intervention forces. In 1921 Soviet forces occupied Tbilisi, and in 1922 Georgia joined the Soviet Union as part of the Transcaucasian Soviet Socialist Republic.

In March 1990 the Georgian Supreme Soviet declared illegal the treaties of 1921–2 by which Georgia had joined the Soviet Union. The Communist Party's monopoly on power was abolished and in multiparty elections held in October and November 1990 the nationalist leader Zviad Gamsakhurdia was elected president. Georgia declared its independence from the Soviet Union in May 1991 and was admitted to UN membership on 31 July 1992.

Gamsakhurdia's government faced armed opposition from 1991 onwards. Defeat in the ensuing civil war in Tbilisi led to Gamsakhurdia's overthrow in January 1992, and in March 1992 a state council was appointed with the former Soviet foreign minister Eduard Shevardnadze as chairman. Fighting continued throughout 1992 and 1993. In October 1992 Shevardnadze was elected head of state and Chairman of the Parliament, and a loose alliance of pro-Shevardnadze parties formed a government.

Gamsakhurdia returned to western Georgia in September 1993. President Shevardnadze failed to prevent the advance of Gamsakhurdia's rebels as most government forces were engaged in Abkhazia. Shevardnadze was forced to accept Russian armaments and troops to defeat the rebellion and in return agreed to join the CIS. Georgia rescinded its participation in the CIS Collective Security treaty in February 1999 and Russian troops, who had been guarding Georgia's frontier with Turkey, began to withdraw. The legislative election held on 31 October and 14 November 1999 was won by the Union of the Citizens of Georgia which gained 130 of the 235 seats in the Parliament. In the presidential election held on 9 April

2000, President Shevardnadze was re-elected, gaining 79.8 per cent of the vote. Legislative elections were due to take place on 2 November 2003.

SECESSION
In late 1990 the South Ossetians took up arms against Georgian rule in an attempt to join North Ossetia, itself part of Russia. The South Ossetian provincial parliament voted in November 1992 to secede from Georgia and join Russia. Fighting ceased in June 1992 and a joint Russian-Georgian-Ossetian peacekeeping force was dispatched. Representatives of the South Ossetian and Georgian governments met in April 1996 to agree security and confidence-building measures. Presidential elections in South Ossetia were won by Ludvig Chibirov, the chair of the Supreme Council, in November 1996. Legislative elections were held in May 1999.

In July 1992 the Abkhazian republican parliament declared Abkhazia independent. Fighting broke out between Georgian forces and Abkhazian separatists supported by Russian arms and irregulars; Georgian forces were defeated and were forced to withdraw in September 1993. Negotiations under Russian auspices led to an Abkhaz-Georgian cease-fire and separation of forces agreement being signed in May 1994 and the deployment of 2,500 Russian UN peacekeepers on the Abkhaz-Georgian border. In November 1994 the Abkhaz Supreme Soviet declared Abkhazia's independence again and elected Vladislav Ardzinba as president. Abkhazia was given autonomous republic status under the 1995 constitution; this was rejected by the republican parliament. Elections to the self-declared Abkhaz People's Assembly were held in November 1996. Following a guarantee of security from President Ardzinba, ethnic Georgians who had fled Abkhazia during the fighting began returning in March 1999. A referendum held in Abkhazia in October 1999 approved a new constitution which held Abkhazia to be a sovereign state. On 11 July 2000, Georgia and Abkhazia signed a UN-sponsored protocol on stabilisation measures, agreeing to refrain from the use of force and to establish groups to combat cross-border crime. On 7 March 2003 Russia and Georgia agreed that the CIS collective peacekeeping forces would remain in Abkhazia indefinitely.

FOREIGN RELATIONS
Georgia has signed a Partnership and Co-operation Agreement with the European Union. In May 2002, US military instructors arrived in Tbilisi to train up to 2,000 troops in military strategy and tactics to counter militant activity. A written commitment was issued promising that the troops would not be used against Abkhazia.

Tension grew between Georgia and Russia in September 2002 over Russian accusations that Georgia was harbouring Chechen militants in the Pankisi Gorge in north-east Georgia. Russian President Vladimir Putin warned of military action if Georgia failed to deal with them. Relations improved in October with President Shevardnadze's promise to work with Moscow to counter Chechen rebels and a successful two-month anti-terrorist operation followed.

POLITICAL SYSTEM
The 1995 constitution provides for a federal republic with a unicameral legislature, to become bicameral 'following the creation of appropriate conditions'; and a popularly elected president who serves a maximum of two five-year terms. The present Parliament has 235 members, directly elected for a four-year term.

HEAD OF STATE
President, Eduard Shevardnadze, *elected* 11 October 1992, *re-elected* 1995, 9 April 2000

CABINET *as at July 2003*
Minister of State, Avtandil Jorbenadze
Agriculture, David Kirtvalidze
Culture, Sesili Gogiberidze
Defence, Maj.-Gen. Davit Tevzadze
Economy, Industry and Trade, Giorgi Gachechiladze
Education, Aleksandre Kartozia
Environment, Nino Chkhobadze
Finance and Tax Revenue, Mirian Gogiashvili
Foreign Affairs, Irakli Menagharishvili
Fuel and Energy, David Mirtskulava
Interior, Koba Narchemashvili
Justice, Roland Giligashvili
Labour, Health Care and Social Welfare, Amiran Gamkrelidze
Refugees (acting), Otar Keinashvili
Security, Valeri Khaburzania
State Property, Solomon Pavliashvili
Transport and Communications, Merab Adeishvili
Without Portfolio, Malkhaz Kakabadze

EMBASSY OF GEORGIA
4 Russell Gardens, London W14 8EZ
Tel: 020-7603 7799
Ambassador Extraordinary and Plenipotentiary, HE Teimuraz Mamatsashvili, apptd 1995

BRITISH EMBASSY
Sheraton Metechi Palace Hotel, GE-380003 Tbilisi
Tel: (00 995) (32) 955497
Email: british.embassy@caucasus.net
Ambassador Extraordinary and Plenipotentiary, HE Deborah Barnes-Jones, apptd 2001

BRITISH COUNCIL DIRECTOR, Jo Bakowski
34 Rustaveli Avenue, Tbilisi, GE-380008 Tbilisi
Tel: (00 995) (32) 250407/ 988014
Email: offiice.bc@britishcouncil.org.ge

ECONOMY
The economy was brought to the brink of collapse by civil and secessionist wars and the ending of former Soviet trading relationships. Although Georgia has deposits of coal, they have not been exploited and it is desperately short of energy supplies. In May 2003 work began on the Georgian section of an oil pipeline from Baku, Azerbaijan through Georgia to Ceyhan, Turkey. The only productive sector of the economy is agriculture, which employs 30 per cent of the workforce and generates 38 per cent of GDP, with a concentration on viniculture, tea and tobacco-growing and citrus fruits. The main exports are iron alloys, wine, nuts, chemical fertilisers, and oil and oil products. The main imports are oil and oil products, gas, automobiles, pharmaceuticals and wheat. In January 2001 the IMF approved a three-year loan to Georgia, amounting to some US$141 million. In 1998 exports totalled US$192 million and imports US$887 million.

GNP – US$3,183 million (2000); US$630 per capita (2000)
GDP – US$3,138 million (2001); US$573 per capita (2000)
ANNUAL AVERAGE GROWTH OF GDP – 11.3 per cent (1997)
INFLATION RATE – 19.1 per cent (1999)
UNEMPLOYMENT – 10.8 per cent (2000)
TOTAL EXTERNAL DEBT – US$1,633 million (2000)

Trade with UK	2001	2002
Imports from UK	£19,342,000	£17,165,000
Exports to UK	5,891,000	2,647,000

GERMANY

Bundesrepublik Deutschland – Federal Republic of Germany

AREA – 137,192 sq. miles (356,700 sq. km).
Neighbours: Denmark (north), Poland (east), Czech Republic (east and south-east), Austria (south-east and south), Switzerland (south), France, Luxembourg, Belgium and the Netherlands (west)
POPULATION – 82,007,000 (2001). Approximately 80 per cent of the population live in the former West Germany. 34 per cent of the population are Protestant, 34 per cent Roman Catholic, 28 per cent unaffiliated or of other religions and 4 per cent Muslim. The language is German; there are Danish- and Frisian-speaking minorities in Schleswig-Holstein and a Sorbian-speaking minority in Saxony
CAPITAL – Berlin (population, 3,388,434, 2001 estimate). The seat of government and parliament was transferred from Bonn to Berlin in 2000
MAJOR CITIES – Bremen (540,950); Cologne (967,940); Dortmund (589,240); Dresden (478,631); Duisburg (512,030); Düsseldorf (570,765); Essen (591,889); Frankfurt am Main (641,076); Hamburg (1,726,363); Hannover (516,415); Leipzig (493,052); Munich (1,227,958); Nuremberg (491,307); Stuttgart (587,152), 2001 estimates
CURRENCY – Euro (€) of 100 cents
NATIONAL ANTHEM – Einigkeit Und Recht Und Freiheit (Unity And Right And Freedom)
NATIONAL DAY – 3 October (Anniversary of 1990 Unification)
NATIONAL FLAG – Horizontal bars of black, red and gold
LIFE EXPECTANCY (years) – 78 (2001)
POPULATION GROWTH RATE – 0.3 per cent
POPULATION DENSITY – 230 per sq. km (2001)
URBAN POPULATION – 88 per cent (2001)

HISTORY AND POLITICS

The first German realm was the Holy Roman Empire, established in AD 962 when Otto I of Saxony was crowned Emperor. The Empire endured until 1806, but the achievement of a national state was prevented by fragmentation into small principalities and dukedoms.

The Empire was replaced by a loose association of sovereign states known as the German Confederation, which was dissolved in 1866 and replaced by the Prussian-dominated North German Federation. The south German principalities united with the northern federation to form a second German Empire in 1871 and the King of Prussia was proclaimed Emperor.

Defeat in the First World War led to the abdication of the Emperor, and the country became a republic. The Treaty of Versailles (1919) ceded Alsace-Lorraine to France, and large areas in the east were lost to Poland. The world economic crisis of 1929 contributed to the collapse of the Weimar Republic and the subsequent rise to power of the National Socialist movement of Adolf Hitler, who became Chancellor in 1933.

After concluding a Treaty of Non-Aggression with the Soviet Union in August 1939, Germany invaded Poland (1 September 1939), precipitating the Second World War, which lasted until 1945. Hitler committed suicide on 30 April 1945. On 8 May 1945, Germany unconditionally surrendered.

THE POST-WAR PERIOD

Germany was divided into American, French, British and Soviet zones of occupation. The territories to the east of the Oder and Neisse rivers were placed under Polish and Russian administration and some 7.75 million Germans were deported.

The Federal Republic of Germany (FRG) was created out of the three western zones in 1949. A Communist government was established in the Soviet zone (henceforth the German Democratic Republic (GDR)). In 1961 the Soviet zone of Berlin was sealed off, and the Berlin Wall was built along the zonal boundary, partitioning the western sectors of the city from the eastern.

Soviet-initiated reform in eastern Europe during the late 1980s led to unrest in the GDR, culminating in the opening of the Berlin Wall in November 1989 and the collapse of Communist government. The 'Treaty on the Final Settlement with Respect to Germany' concluded between the FRG, GDR and the four former occupying powers in September 1990, unified Germany with effect from 3 October 1990 as a fully sovereign state. Economic and monetary union preceded formal union on 1 July 1990. Unification is constitutionally the accession of Berlin and the five reformed *Länder* of the GDR to the FRG, which remains in being. Berlin was declared to be the capital of the unified Germany and parliament and government departments were transferred from Bonn.

Presidential elections held on 24 May 1999 were won by Johannes Rau of the Social Democratic Party (SPD). The distribution of seats following the last election for the Bundestag on 22 September 2002 was: SPD 251; Christian Democratic Union (CDU) 190; Christian Social Union (CSU) 58; Greens 55; Free Democratic Party (FDP) 47; Party of Democratic Socialism (PDS) 2. On 22 October Gerhard Schröder of the SPD was re-elected as Federal Chancellor and he formed a coalition government of the SPD and the Greens.

POLITICAL SYSTEM

The Basic Law provides for a president, elected by a Federal Convention (electoral college) for a five-year term, a lower house *(Bundestag)* of 603 members elected by direct universal suffrage for a four-year term of office, and an upper house *(Bundesrat)* composed of 69 members appointed by the governments of the *Länder* in proportion to *Länder* populations, without a fixed term of office.

Judicial authority is exercised by the Federal Constitutional Court, the federal courts provided for in the Basic Law and the courts of the *Länder*.

Economics and Labour, Wolfgang Clement (SPD)
Education and Research, Edelgard Bulmahn (SPD)
Environment, Nature Conservation and Nuclear Safety,
  Jürgen Trittin (Greens)
Family, Senior Citizens, Women and Youth, Renate Schmidt
  (SPD)
Finance, Hans Eichel (SPD)
Health and Social Affairs, Ulla Schmidt (SPD)
Interior, Otto Schily (SPD)
Justice, Brigitte Zypries (SPD)
Ministers of State, Christoph Zöpel (SPD); Ludger Volmer
  (SPD); Hans Martin Bury (SPD); Rolf Schwanitz
  (SPD); Christina Weiss (SPD)
Transport, Construction and Housing, Manfred Stolpe
  (SPD)

SPD Social Democratic Party; Greens, Alliance 90/The
Greens

EMBASSY OF THE FEDERAL REPUBLIC OF GERMANY
23 Belgrave Square/Chesham Place, London SW1X 8PZ
Tel: 020-7824 1300
Ambassador Extraordinary and Plenipotentiary, HE
  Thomas Matussek, apptd 2002

FEDERAL STRUCTURE
Germany is a federal republic composed of 16 states
(Länder) (ten from the former West, five from the former
East, and Berlin). Each Land has its own directly elected
legislature and government led by Minister-Presidents
(prime ministers) or equivalents. The 1949 Basic Law
vests executive power in the Länder governments except
in those areas reserved for the federal government.

HEAD OF STATE
Federal President, Johannes Rau, elected 24 May 1999

CABINET as at July 2003
Federal Chancellor, Gerhard Schröder (SDP)
Head of Chancellory, Frank-Walter Steinmeier (SDP)
Federal Vice-Chancellor, Foreign Affairs, Joschka Fischer
  (Greens)
Consumer Affairs, Food and Agriculture, Renate Künast
  (Greens)
Defence, Peter Struck (SPD)
Economic Co-operation and Development, Heidemarie
  Wieczorek-Zeul (SPD)

BRITISH EMBASSY
Wilhelmstrasse 70, D-10117 Berlin
Tel: (00 49) (30) 204570
Ambassador Extraordinary and Plenipotentiary, HE Sir
  Peter Torry, KCMG, apptd 2003

BRITISH COUNCIL DIRECTOR, Kathryn Board
Hackescher Markt 1, D-10178 Berlin
Tel: (00 49) (30) 311 0990
Email: bc.berlin@britishcouncil.de

DEFENCE
The Army has 2,490 main battle tanks, 3,130 armoured
personnel carriers, 2,243 armoured infantry fighting
vehicles, and 202 attack helicopters. The Navy has 14
submarines, two destroyers, 12 frigates, 25 patrol and
coastal vessels, 66 combat aircraft and 43 armed
helicopters. The Air Force has 446 combat aircraft. There
remain 93,650 NATO personnel in Germany (USA
68,950; UK 17,000; Belgium 2,000; France 3,000;
Netherlands (2,600). Major cuts were made in military
procurement in late 2002.

Land	Area (sq. km)	Population (2001)	Capital	Minister-President (July 2003)
Baden-Württemberg	35,752	10.6m	Stuttgart	Erwin Teufel (CDU)
Bavaria	70,548	12.3m	Munich	Dr Edmund Stoiber (CSU)
Berlin	891	3.4m	–	Klaus Wowereit (SPD)*
Brandenburg	29,476	2.6m	Potsdam	Matthias Platzeck (SPD)
Bremen	404	0.7m	–	Dr Henning Scherf (SPD)*
Hamburg	755	1.7m	–	Ole von Beust (CDU)*
Hesse	21,115	6.1m	Wiesbaden	Roland Koch (CDU)
Lower Saxony	47,613	8.0m	Hannover	Christian Wulff (CDU)
Mecklenburg-Western Pomerania	23,170	1.8m	Schwerin	Dr Harald Ringstorff (SPD)
North Rhine-Westphalia	34,079	18.0m	Düsseldorf	Peter Steinbrueck (SPD)
Rhineland-Palatinate	19,847	4.0m	Mainz	Kurt Beck (SPD)
Saarland	2,570	1.1m	Saarbrücken	Peer Müller (SPD)
Saxony	18,412	4.4m	Dresden	Dr Georg Milbradt (CDU)
Saxony-Anhalt	20,447	2.6m	Magdeburg	Wolfgang Böhmer (CDU)
Schleswig-Holstein	15,770	2.8m	Kiel	Heide Simonis (SPD)
Thuringia	16,172	2.4m	Erfurt	Dieter Althaus (CDU)

*Berlin, Governing Mayor; Bremen, Mayor; Hamburg, First Mayor

MILITARY EXPENDITURE – 1.5 per cent of GDP (2001)
MILITARY PERSONNEL – 296,000: Army 203,200,
Navy 25,500, Air Force 67,300. Under the terms of
the Treaty of Unification, the German armed forces
have been limited to 370,000 active personnel since
the end of 1994
CONSCRIPTION DURATION – Nine months

ECONOMY
Germany has a predominantly industrial economy.
Principal industries are coal mining, iron and steel
production, machine construction, the electrical industry,
the manufacture of steel and metal products, chemicals,
automobile production, electronics, textiles and the
processing of foodstuffs.

The government announced in June 2000 that it was to
abolish all 19 of Germany's nuclear power stations over a
32-year period, which supplied over 30 per cent of the
energy generated in the country.

After a mini-boom generated by new East German
demand in 1990 and 1991, Germany entered its most
severe recession since the war induced by the costs of
reunification. In 1993 a 'Solidarity Pact' was agreed,
which lays down the basis of future funding transfers to
the East based on a 5.5 per cent rise in income taxes,
wage restraint in the West, more private investment in the
East, and the distribution of the funding burden between
the federal and *Länder* governments.

The rate of economic growth increased in 1999 and
2000, aided by the weakness of the euro, but began to
slow in the first quarter of 2001. The euro replaced the
Deutsche Mark in January 2002.

Unemployment rose in 2002 and continued to mount
in early 2003. On 14 March 2003 Chancellor Schröder
set out a major reform package designed to reduce
unemployment and revive the country's economy.

In 2001 there was a trade surplus of US$82,827
million and a current account surplus of US$3,815
million. Imports totalled US$486,294 million and
exports US$570,522 million.

GNP – US$2,063,734 million (2000); US$25,120 per
capita (2000)
GDP – US$1,873,854 million (2001); US$22,753 per
capita (2000)
ANNUAL AVERAGE GROWTH OF GDP – 3.1 per cent
(2000)
INFLATION RATE – 1.9 per cent (2000)
UNEMPLOYMENT – 7.8 per cent (2001)

Trade with UK	2001	2002
Imports from UK	£22,589,100,000	£21,022,600,000
Exports to UK	27,140,300,000	29,381,000,000

COMMUNICATIONS
There was a total road network of around 650,000 km in
2000, comprising 11,500 km of motorways and
230,700 km of other main roads. There are 45,942 km
of railways. Around 20 per cent of domestic freight is
carried on the 7,467 km of inland waterways.

EDUCATION
School attendance is compulsory between the ages of six
and 18 and comprises nine years of full-time education at
primary and main schools and three years of vocational
education on a part-time basis. The secondary school
leaving examination *(Abitur)* entitles the holder to a place
of study at a university or another institution of higher
education.

Children below the age of 18 who are not attending a
general secondary or a full-time vocational school have
compulsory day-release at a vocational school.

There are over 300 higher education institutes and the
largest universities are in Munich, Berlin, Hamburg,
Bonn, Frankfurt and Cologne.

ENROLMENT (percentage of age group) – primary 100
per cent (1997); secondary 100 per cent (1997);
tertiary 47 per cent (1997)

GHANA

The Republic of Ghana

AREA – 87,500 sq. miles (227,500 sq. km). Neighbours:
Burkina Faso (north), Côte d'Ivoire (west), Togo (east)
POPULATION – 19,734,000 (2001); most are Sudanese
Negroes, although Hamitic strains are common in the
north. The official language is English. The principal
indigenous language group is Akan, of which Twi and
Fanti are the most commonly used. Ga, Ewe and
languages of the Mole-Dagbani group are common in
certain regions. Most Ghanaians are Christians,
although there is a substantial Muslim minority in the
north
CAPITAL – Ψ Accra (population, 1,445,515, 1998),
Greater Accra Region (including Tema) 2,909,643
(2000 census)
MAJOR CITIES – Koforidua (81,378); Kumasi (577,878);
Ψ Takoradi (96,897); Tamale (228,827)
CURRENCY – Cedi of 100 pesewas
NATIONAL FLAG – Equal horizontal bands of red over
gold over green; five-point black star on gold stripe
NATIONAL ANTHEM – God Bless Our Homeland Ghana
NATIONAL DAY – 6 March (Independence Day)
LIFE EXPECTANCY (years) – 57 (2001)
POPULATION GROWTH RATE – 2.4 per cent
POPULATION DENSITY – 87 per sq. km (2001)
MILITARY EXPENDITURE – 0.7 per cent of GDP (2001)
MILITARY PERSONNEL – 7,000: Army 5,000, Navy
1,000, Air Force 1,000
ILLITERACY RATE – (m) 19.7 per cent; (f) 37.1 per cent
(2000)
ENROLMENT (percentage of age group) – primary
79 per cent (1997)

HISTORY AND POLITICS
First reached by Europeans in the 15th century, the
constituent parts of Ghana came under British
administration at various times, the original Gold Coast
Colony being constituted in 1874, and Ashanti and the
Northern Territories Protectorate in 1901. Trans-Volta-
Togoland, part of the former German colony of Togo,
was mandated to Britain by the League of Nations after
the First World War and was integrated with the Gold
Coast Colony in 1956 following a plebiscite. The former
Gold Coast Colony and associated territories became the
independent state of Ghana on 6 March 1957 and
became a republic in 1960.

Since 1966, Ghana has experienced long periods of
military rule interspersed with short-lived civilian
governments. A coup in 1979 led to the formation of an
Armed Forces Revolutionary Council chaired by Flt. Lt.
Jerry Rawlings. Civilian rule was restored in 1979 but
another coup in December 1981 brought Rawlings back
to power.

A referendum in 1992 approved a new multiparty constitution and the legalisation of political parties. The National Democratic Congress (NDC) was established as a political party from the ruling Provisional National Defence Council. The presidential and parliamentary elections in late 1992 were won by Rawlings and the NDC.

The NDC lost power in the general election held on 7 December 2000, which was won by the New Patriotic Party (NPP), which obtained 98 seats; the NDC won 93 seats. The presidential election held on 7 and 28 December 2000 was won by John Kufuor of the NPP.

A state of emergency was declared in the Dagbon region of north Ghana after ethnic violence erupted in March 2002. In April 2003 the state of emergency was extended for a further three months.

In May 2002 President Kufuor inaugurated a reconciliation commission to investigate human rights violations during military rule and the commission began hearing testimonies in January 2003.

POLITICAL SYSTEM
The head of state is an executive president elected for a four-year term, renewable only once. The president appoints the Council of Ministers. The unicameral legislature, the Parliament, has 200 members directly elected for a four-year term.

HEAD OF STATE
President, John Kufuor, *elected* 28 December 2000, *sworn in* 7 January 2001
Vice-President, Aliju Mahama

COUNCIL OF MINISTERS *as at July 2003*
Communications and Technology, Albert Kan Dapaah
Defence, Kwame Addo-Kufuor
Education of Girls, Christine Churcher
Education, Youth and Sports, Kwadwo Baah Wiredu
Energy, Paa Kwesi Nduom
Finance and Economic Planning, Yaw Osafo Maado
Food and Agriculture, Maj. Courage Quarshigah
Foreign Affairs, Nana Akufo Addo
Health, Kwaku Afriyie
Information, Nana Akomea
Interior, Hackman Owusu-Agyemang
Justice and Attorney-General, Papa Owusu-Ankomah
Lands and Forestry, Dominic Fobih
Local Government, Kwadwo Agyei-Darko
Manpower Development and Employment, Yaw Barimah
Mines, Cecilia Bannerman
Ministers of State, Rashid Bawa *(Education, Youth and Sports);* Elizabeth Akua Ohene *(Tertiary Education);* Ishmael Ashitey *(Trade, Industry and Presidential Initiatives)*
Parliamentary Affairs, Felix Owusu Agyepong
Ports, Harbours and Railways, Christopher Ameyaw Akumfi
Private Sector Development, Kwamena Bartels
Regional Co-operation NEPAD (New Partnership for Africa's Development), Kofi Konadu Apraku
Roads and Highways, Richard Anane
Science and Environment, Kassim Kassanga
Senior Minister, Chair of the Government Economic Team, Public Sector Reform and National Institutional Renewal Programme, J. H. Mensah
Tourism and Modernisation of the Capital City, Jake Obetsebi Lamptey
Trade, Industry and Special Presidential Initiatives, Allan Kyeremanteng
Women's and Children's Affairs, Gladys Asmah
Works and Housing, Alhaji Mustapha Iddris Ali

OFFICE OF THE HIGH COMMISSION OF GHANA
13 Belgrave Square, London SW1X 8PN
Tel: 020-7235 4142
High Commissioner, HE Isaac Osei, apptd 2001
BRITISH HIGH COMMISSION
PO Box 296, Osu Link, Accra
Tel: (00 233) (21) 221665/7010650
Email: High.Commission@fco.gov.uk
High Commissioner, HE Rod Pullen, apptd 2000

BRITISH COUNCIL DIRECTOR, Terence Humphreys
11 Liberia Road, PO Box GP 771, Accra
Email: infoaccra@gh.britishcouncil.org

ECONOMY
Agriculture is the basis of the economy, generating 37 per cent of GDP. Crops include cocoa, the largest single source of revenue, rice, cassava, plantains, oranges and pineapples, groundnuts, corn, millet, oil palms, yams, maize and vegetables. Livestock is raised in uncultivated areas. Fishing is important in coastal areas and in the Volta lake and river system. Around 57 per cent of the workforce are employed in farming, forestry and fishing.

Manganese production ranks among the world's largest, with 384,173 tonnes of ore being produced in 1998. Gold is the main export; production amounted to 74,315 kg in 1998. Diamonds and bauxite are also produced.

Since 1966 the Volta Dams at Akosombo and Kpong have generated hydroelectric power for the processing of bauxite and fed a power transmission network for most of Ghana, Togo and Benin. There is considerable foreign investment in Ghana, and its economy has grown consistently. In 2000 there was a trade deficit of US$843 million and a current account deficit of US$413 million.
GNP – US$6,594 million (2000); US$340 per capita (2000)
GDP – US$5,301 million (2001); US$251 per capita (2000)
ANNUAL AVERAGE GROWTH OF GDP – 3.8 per cent (1998)
INFLATION RATE – 25.2 per cent (2000)
TOTAL EXTERNAL DEBT – US$6,657 million (2000)

TRADE
Principal exports are gold, cocoa, and timber. Principal imports are capital goods, semi-manufactures, consumables and energy. Imports in 2000 totalled US$2,973 million and in 1998 exports totalled US$1,795 million.

Trade with UK	2001	2002
Imports from UK	£144,909,000	£139,416,000
Exports to UK	134,021,000	121,843,000

GREECE

Elliniki Dimokratia – Hellenic Republic

AREA – 49,577 sq. miles (128,900 sq. km). Neighbours: Albania, Bulgaria and Macedonia (north), Turkey (east)
POPULATION – 10,623,835 (2001): 98 per cent Greek Orthodox, 1 per cent Catholic, 1 per cent Muslim. The language is Greek
CAPITAL – Athens (population 3,072,922, 1991); including Ψ Piraeus and suburbs, 3,096,775 (1991 census)
MAJOR CITIES – Ψ Iráklion (Heraklion) (132,117); Lárisa (113,090); Ψ Pátrai (Patras) (170,452); Ψ Thessaloníki (Salonika) (749,048); Ψ Vólos (116,031), 1991
CURRENCY – Euro (€) of 100 cents
NATIONAL ANTHEM – Imnos Eis Tin Eleftherian (Hymn To Freedom)
NATIONAL DAY – 25 March (Independence Day)
NATIONAL FLAG – Blue and white stripes with a white cross on a blue field in the canton
LIFE EXPECTANCY (years) – 78 (2001)
POPULATION GROWTH RATE – 0.4 per cent
POPULATION DENSITY – 82 per sq. km (2001)
URBAN POPULATION – 60 per cent (2001)

The main areas are: Macedonia, Thrace, Epirus, Thessaly, Continental Greece, Crete and the Peloponnese. The main island groups are the Sporades, the Dodecanese or Southern Sporades, the Cyclades, the Ionian Islands, and the Aegean Islands (Chios, Lesbos, Limnos and Samos).

HISTORY AND POLITICS

Greece was under Turkish rule from the mid-15th century until a war of independence (1821–7) led to the establishment of a Greek kingdom in the Peloponnese in 1829. The remainder of Greece gradually became independent until the Dodecanese were returned by Italy in 1947. After the Nazi German occupation of 1941–4, a civil war between monarchist and Communist groups lasted from 1946 to 1949, and tension between right-wing and radical groups continued after 1949. In 1967 right-wing elements in the army seized power and established a military regime (the 'Greek Colonels'). The King went into voluntary exile in 1967. Unrest in Athens

in 1973–4 intensified after the government was involved in the overthrow of President Makarios of Cyprus in July 1974, and led the Colonels to surrender power. Konstantinos Karamanlis (prime minister 1955–63) returned from exile to form a provisional government, and the first elections for ten years were held in 1974. The restoration of the monarchy was rejected by referendum on 8 December 1974 and Greece became a republic.

A general election was held on 9 April 2000 with the Panhellenic Socialist Party (PASOK) winning 158 seats, the New Democracy Party (Christian Democrats) 125 seats, the Communist Party 11 seats, and the Coalition of the Left and Progress six seats.

POLITICAL SYSTEM

In 1986 most executive power was transferred from the president to the government. The unicameral 300-member Parliament *(Vouli)* is elected for a four-year term by universal adult suffrage under a system of proportional representation, with a 3 per cent threshold for parliamentary representation. The head of state is a president, elected by parliament for a five-year term, renewable once only.

HEAD OF STATE

President of the Hellenic Republic, Constantine Stephanopoulos, *elected by parliament* 1995, *re-elected* 8 February 2000

CABINET *as at July 2003*
Prime Minister, Costas Simitis
Aegean, Nicolaos Sifounakis
Agriculture, Georgios Drys
Alternate Foreign Minister, Anastassios Giannitsis
Culture, Evangelos Venizelos
Development, Apostolos-Athanassios Tsohatzopoulos
Education and Religious Affairs, Petros Ephthimiou
Environment, Town Planning and Public Works, Vasso Papandreou
Foreign Affairs, George Papandreou
Health and Welfare, Constantine Stephanis
Interior, Public Administration and Decentralisation, Costas Skandalidis
Justice, Philippos Petsalnikos
Labour and Social Affairs, Dimitrios Reppas
Macedonia and Thrace, George Paschalidis
Merchant Marine, Georgios Anomeritis
Minister of State, Office of the Prime Minister, Stefanos Manikas
National Defence, Yiannos Papantoniou
National Economy and Finance, Nikolaos Christodoulakis
Press and Media, Christos Protopapas
Public Order, Michalis Chrysohoidis
Transport and Communications, Christos Verelis

EMBASSY OF GREECE
1A Holland Park, London W11 3TP
Tel: 020-7229 3850
Ambassador Extraordinary and Plenipotentiary, HE Alexandros Sandis, apptd 2000

BRITISH EMBASSY
1 Ploutarcou Street, GR-106 75 Athens
Tel: (00 30) (210) 727 2600
Email: britania@hol.gr
Ambassador Extraordinary and Plenipotentiary, HE Sir David C. A. Madden, CMG, apptd 1999

BRITISH COUNCIL DIRECTOR, Chris Hickey
17 Plateia Philikis Etairias, PO Box 3488, GR-10673 Athens
Tel: (00 30) (210) 369 2333
Email: british.council@britishcouncil.gr

DEFENCE
The Army has 1,735 main battle tanks, 1,671 armoured personnel carriers and 501 armoured infantry fighting vehicles. The Navy has eight submarines, two destroyers, 12 frigates, 40 patrol and coastal vessels and 18 armed helicopters. The Air Force has a total of 418 combat aircraft.

Greece maintains 1,250 army personnel in Cyprus. There are 290 US military personnel stationed in Greece.
MILITARY EXPENDITURE – 4.8 per cent of GDP (2001)
MILITARY PERSONNEL – 177,600: Army 114,000, Navy 19,000, Air Force 33,000; Paramilitaries 4,000
CONSCRIPTION DURATION – Up to 19 months

ECONOMY
The principal minerals are nickel, bauxite, iron ore, iron pyrites, manganese magnesite, chrome, lead, zinc and emery. The chief industries are textiles (cotton, woollen and synthetics), chemicals, cement, glass, metallurgy, shipbuilding, domestic electrical equipment and footwear, the production of aluminium, nickel, iron and steel products, tyres, chemicals, fertilisers and sugar (from locally-grown beet). Food processing and ancillary industries are also growing.

In March 2002 Greece and Turkey signed an agreement to build a gas pipeline which will supply Greece with gas from Turkey. Tourism is also a major industry, with an estimated 12.5 million visitors in 2000.

Though there has been substantial industrialisation, agriculture still employs nearly a fifth of the working population and contributes 8.1 per cent of GDP. The most important agricultural products are tobacco, wheat, cotton, sugar, rice, fruit (olives, peaches, vines, oranges, lemons, figs, almonds and currant-vines). Exports of fresh fruit, currants and vegetables are an important contributor to the economy.

In March 1998 the drachma was admitted to the ERM; Greece became a member of EMU on 1 January 2001 since when it has participated in the European Single Currency. The euro replaced the drachma in January 2002.

In 2001 there was a trade deficit of US$19,087 million and a current account deficit of US$9,400 million. In 2001 imports totalled US$29,928 million and exports US$9,483 million.
GNP – US$126,269 million (2000); US$11,960 per capita (2000)
GDP – US$116,347 million (2001); US$10,680 per capita (2000)
ANNUAL AVERAGE GROWTH OF GDP – 4.1 per cent (2000)
INFLATION RATE – 3.2 per cent (2000)
UNEMPLOYMENT – 11.1 per cent (2000)

Trade with UK	2001	2002
Imports from UK	£1,061,900,000	£1,140,800,000
Exports to UK	433,100,100	546,400,000

COMMUNICATIONS
Railways are state-owned, with the exception of the Athens-Piraeus Electric Railway. There are 9,255 km of motorways and 29,350 km of provincial roads.

EDUCATION
Education is free and compulsory from the age of six to 15 and is maintained by state grants. There are eighteen universities and several other institutes of higher learning.
ILLITERACY RATE – (m) 1.5 per cent; (f) 4.0 per cent (2000)
ENROLMENT (percentage of age group) – primary 93 per cent (1997); secondary 95 per cent (1997); tertiary 47 per cent (1997)

CULTURE
Greek civilisation emerged c.1300 BC and the poems of Homer, which were probably current c.800 BC, record the struggle between the Achaeans of Greece and the Phrygians of Troy (1194 to 1184 BC).

The spoken language of modern Greece is descended from the Common Greek of Alexander the Great's empire. Katharevousa, a conservative literary dialect evolved by Adamantios Corais (Diamant Coray) (1748–1833) and used for official and technical matters, has been phased out. Novels and poetry are mostly in Dimotiki, a progressive literary dialect which owes much to John Psycharis (1854–1929). The poets Solomos, Palamas, Cavafy and Sikelianos have won a European reputation. George Seferis (1963) and Odysseus Elytis (1979) have won the Nobel Prize for Literature.

GRENADA

The State of Grenada

AREA – 132 sq. miles (345 sq. km)
POPULATION – 94,000 (2001), of which about 75 per cent are of African descent; there are minorities of Europeans and Indians. The language is English
CAPITAL – Ψ St George's (population, 4,788, 1981)
CURRENCY – East Caribbean dollar (EC$) of 100 cents
NATIONAL ANTHEM – Hail Grenada, Land Of Ours
NATIONAL DAY – 7 February (Independence Day)
NATIONAL FLAG – Divided diagonally into yellow and green triangles within a red border containing six yellow stars, a yellow star on a red disc in the centre and a nutmeg on the green triangle in the hoist
LIFE EXPECTANCY (years) – 65 (2001)
POPULATION GROWTH RATE – 0.3 per cent
POPULATION DENSITY – 272 per sq. km (2001)

HISTORY AND POLITICS
Discovered by Columbus in 1498, and named Concepción, Grenada was originally colonised by France and was ceded to Great Britain by the Treaty of Versailles in 1783. It became a Crown colony in 1877, an Associated State in 1967 and an independent nation within the Commonwealth on 7 February 1974.

The government was overthrown in 1979 by the New Jewel Movement and a People's Revolutionary Government was set up. In October 1983 disagreements within the PRG led to the death of Prime Minister Maurice Bishop, whose government was replaced by a Revolutionary Military Council. These events prompted the intervention of Caribbean and US forces. The Governor-General installed an advisory council to act as an interim government until a general election was held in December 1984. A phased withdrawal of US forces was completed by June 1985.

The general election held on 18 January 1999 was won by the New National Party led by Dr Keith Mitchell. They won all 15 seats in the House of Representatives.

POLITICAL SYSTEM
Queen Elizabeth II is head of state and is represented by a Governor-General. Legislative power is vested in a bicameral parliament consisting of an elected 15-member House of Representatives and a 13-member Senate appointed by the Governor-General.
Governor-General, HE Sir Daniel Williams, GCMG, QC, apptd 1996

CABINET *as at July 2003*
Prime Minister, National Security and Information, Keith Mitchell
Agriculture, Lands, Forestry and Fisheries, Claris Charles
Attorney-General, Raymond Anthony
Communications, Works and Public Utilities, Gregory Bowen
Co-operatives, Housing and Social Services, Cuthbert McQueen
Education, Augustine John
Finance, Trade, Industry and Planning, Anthony Boatswain
Foreign Affairs and International Trade, Legal Affairs, Carriacou and Petit Martinique Affairs, Elvin Nimrod
Health and Environment, Clarice Modeste-Curwen
Implementation, Joslyn Whiteman
Labour and Local Government, Lawrence Joseph
Ministers of State, Laurina Waldron *(Health and Environment);* Mark Isaac *(Information)*
Parliamentary Secretaries, Einstein Louison *(Agriculture, Forestry, Lands and Fisheries);* Eleuthan Noel *(Carriacou and Petit Martinique Affairs);* Richard McPhail *(Communications, Works and Public Utilities);* Yolande Joseph *(Gender and Family Affairs)*
Tourism, Civil Aviation, Culture, Social Security and Gender and Family Affairs, Brenda Hood
Youth, Sports, Community Development, Adrian Mitchell

HIGH COMMISSION FOR GRENADA
5 Chandos Street, London W1G 9DG Tel: 020-7631 4277
Email: grenada@high-commission.demon.co.uk
High Commissioner, HE Ruth Elizabeth Rouse, apptd 1999

BRITISH HIGH COMMISSION
Netherlands Building, Grand Anse, St George's
Tel: (00 1 473) 440 3536/440 3222
Email: bhcgrenada@caribsurf.com
High Commissioner, John White, resident at Bridgetown, Barbados

ECONOMY
Services account for 61 per cent of employment and 71 per cent of GDP. The economy was principally agrarian, but agriculture now employs only 17 per cent of the workforce and produces 10 per cent of GDP. Grenada accounts for about a quarter of world nutmeg production. Cocoa and bananas are also major crops. Manufacturing consists of processing agricultural products and the production of textiles, concrete, aluminium and handicrafts. Tourism is the main foreign exchange earner. In 1998 there were 381,669 tourists.
GNP – US$370 million (2000); US$3,770 per capita (2000)

GDP – US$398 million (2001); US$4,391 per capita (2000)
ANNUAL AVERAGE GROWTH OF GDP – 3.6 per cent (1998)
INFLATION RATE – 2.2 per cent (2000)
UNEMPLOYMENT – 11.0 per cent (2000)
TOTAL EXTERNAL DEBT – US$207 million (2000)

TRADE
The most important exports are nutmegs and cocoa. Imports include machinery and transport equipment, livestock, foodstuffs and beverages, manufactured goods, and fuels. The main trading partners are the USA, the UK and Trinidad and Tobago.
In 2000 there was a trade deficit of US$136 million and there was a current account deficit of US$79 million. In 1998, imports totalled US$200 million and exports US$27 million.

Trade with UK	2001	2002
Imports from UK	£6,955,000	£5,496,000
Exports to UK	829,000	1,307,000

GUATEMALA

República de Guatemala – Republic of Guatemala

AREA – 41,692 sq. miles (108,400 sq. km). Neighbours: Mexico (north and west), El Salvador, Honduras and Belize (east)
POPULATION – 11,687,000 (2001 estimate): 56 per cent mestizo, 44 per cent Amerindian. The language is Spanish, but 40 per cent of the population speak an Indian language
CAPITAL – Guatemala City (population, 1,675,589, 1990 estimate)
MAJOR CITIES – Mazatenango (65,395); Ψ Puerto Barrios (81,078); Quetzaltenango (127,569); Cobán (144,461); Escuintla (119,897), 2002 census
CURRENCY – Quetzal (Q) of 100 centavos
NATIONAL ANTHEM – Guatemala Feliz (Guatemala Be Praised)
NATIONAL DAY – 15 September
NATIONAL FLAG – Three vertical bands, blue, white, blue; coat of arms on white stripe
LIFE EXPECTANCY (years) – 65 (2001)
POPULATION GROWTH RATE – 2.6 per cent
POPULATION DENSITY – 108 per sq. km (2001)
URBAN POPULATION – 40 per cent (2001)
MILITARY EXPENDITURE – 0.9 per cent of GDP (2001)
MILITARY PERSONNEL – 31,400: Army 29,200, Navy 1,500, Air Force 700; Paramilitaries 19,000
CONSCRIPTION DURATION – 30 months (selective)
ILLITERACY RATE – (m) 23.8 per cent; (f) 38.7 per cent (2000)
ENROLMENT (percentage of age group) – primary 88 per cent (1997); secondary 26 per cent (1997); tertiary 9 per cent (1997)

HISTORY AND POLITICS
Guatemala was under Spanish rule from 1524 until gaining independence in 1821. It formed part of the Confederation of Central America from 1823 to 1839.
After a series of military coups, civilian rule was restored with the election of a Constituent Assembly in 1984 and the promulgation of a new constitution in 1985. In May 1993 President Serrano partially

suspended the constitution and attempted to rule by decree but was effectively ousted by the army on 1 June. Ramiro de León Carpio was elected president by Congress to serve out Serrano's term to January 1996.

The legislative election to the National Congress on 7 November 1999 was won by the Guatemalan Republican Front (FRG) which obtained 63 seats; the National Advancement Party (PAN) won 37 seats. The presidential election on 26 December 1999 was won by Alfonso Portillo of the FRG. Legislative elections were scheduled for 9 November and 28 December 2003.

INSURGENCY
Since 1960 the armed forces had been fighting insurgency by the left-wing, mainly Mayan Indian, guerrillas of the Guatemalan Revolutionary National Unity Movement (URNG). Some 200,000 were killed in the fighting. Government-URNG negotiations began in 1991, leading to a reduction in fighting and agreements in 1993. In March 1994 a human rights accord was reached under which a 300-strong UN Observer Mission (MINUGUA) was established in November 1994 to supervise the implementation of government-URNG accords. An accord recognising the rights of the indigenous population was signed in March 1995, but in a referendum held on 16 May 1999, constitutional reforms which would have amended the constitution to allow for the implementation of peace accords were rejected. Representatives of the four rebel groups comprising the URNG signed a peace treaty with the government in December 1996; an independent commission into the 36-year civil war, set up under the 1996 peace treaty, published a report on 25 February 1999 which concluded that the army had committed acts of genocide against the indigenous Mayan population. In August 2000 President Portillo admitted the state's responsibility for atrocities committed during the civil war and vowed that those responsible would be prosecuted. In December 2001 President Portillo paid US$1.8 million in compensation to the families of 226 victims killed by soldiers and paramilitaries in the village of Las Dos Erres in 1982.

POLITICAL SYSTEM
Executive power is vested in the president, who is directly elected for a single four-year term. He appoints the Cabinet. Legislative authority is vested in the National Congress, whose 113 members are directly elected for a four-year term.

HEAD OF STATE
President, Alfonso Portillo Cabrera, elected 26 December 1999, sworn in 14 January 2000
Vice-President, Juan Francisco Reyes López

GOVERNMENT as at July 2003
Agriculture, Livestock and Food, Edin Barrientos
Communications, Transport and Public Works, Flora Marina Escobar Gordillo de Ramos
Culture and Sport, Otilia Lux de Coti
Defence, Gen. Robin Morán Munoz
Economy, Patricia Ramirez
Education, Mario Torres
Energy and Mines, Raúl Archila
Environment and Natural Resources, Sergio Lavarreda
Foreign Affairs, Edgar Gutiérrez Girón

Interior, José Adolfo Reyes Calderon
Labour and Social Security, Victor Moreira
Public Finance, Eduardo Weymann
Public Health and Social Welfare, Julio Molina

EMBASSY OF GUATEMALA
13 Fawcett Street, London SW10 9HN
Tel: 020-7351 3042
Ambassador Extraordinary and Plenipotentiary, HE Alberto Sandoval, apptd 2003

BRITISH EMBASSY
Avenida La Reforma 16-00, Zona 10, Edifiicio Torre Internacional, Nivel 11, Guatemala City
Tel: (00 502) 367 5425/6/7/8/9
Ambassador Extraordinary and Plenipotentiary, Richard D. Lavers

ECONOMY
Agriculture provides one quarter of GDP and employs nearly half of the workforce. The principal export is coffee, other articles being manufactured goods, sugar, bananas and cardamom. The chief imports are raw materials and semi-manufactures, capital goods, consumer goods, and fuel oils. Guatemala has a free trade agreement with El Salvador, Honduras and Mexico; the USA is also one of the country's main trading partners.

On 5 April 2002, the IMF announced that a one-year standby credit of US$67 million had been approved in order to underpin the government's economic policies and the implementation of the 1996 peace accords.

In 2000 there was a trade deficit of US$1,660 million and a current account deficit of US$1,049 million. In 2001 imports totalled US$5,607 million and exports US$2,466 million.
GNP – US$19,164 million (2000); US$1,680 per capita (2000)
GDP – US$20,629 million (2001); US$1,659 per capita (2000)
ANNUAL AVERAGE GROWTH OF GDP – 3.3 per cent (2000)
INFLATION RATE – 6.0 per cent (2000)
TOTAL EXTERNAL DEBT – US$4,622 million (2000)

Trade with UK	2001	2002
Imports from UK	£35,393,000	£33,752,000
Exports to UK	12,892,000	13,756,000

GUINEA

République de Guinée – Republic of Guinea

AREA – 94,926 sq. miles (245,857 sq. km). Neighbours: Guinea-Bissau (west), Senegal and Mali (north), Côte d'Ivoire (east), Sierra Leone and Liberia (south)
POPULATION – 7,613,870 (2001 estimate); the official language is French; Fullah, Malinké and Soussou are indigenous languages
CAPITAL – Ψ Conakry (population, 763,000)
MAJOR CITIES – Kankan; Kindia; Labé; Mamou; N'Zérékoré; Siguiri
CURRENCY – Guinea franc of 100 centimes
NATIONAL ANTHEM – Liberté
NATIONAL DAY – 2 October (Anniversary of the Proclamation of Independence)
NATIONAL FLAG – Three vertical stripes of red, yellow and green

POPULATION DENSITY – 30 per sq. km (1999)
MILITARY EXPENDITURE – 1.5 per cent of GDP (2001)
MILITARY PERSONNEL – 9,700: Army 8,500, Navy
400, Air Force 800; Paramilitaries 2,600
CONSCRIPTION DURATION – Two years
ILLITERACY RATE – (m) 44.9 per cent; (f) 73.0 per cent
(2000)
ENROLMENT (percentage of age group) – primary
54 per cent (1997); secondary 14 per cent (1997);
tertiary 1 per cent (1997)

HISTORY AND POLITICS

Guinea was separated from Senegal in 1891 and
administered by France as a separate colony. On 2
October 1958 Guinea became an independent republic.

Ahmed Sékou Touré assumed office as head of the new
government, and was elected president in 1961. His
death in 1984 was followed by a military coup. Guinea
was ruled by a military government directed by a Military
Committee for National Recovery (CMRN). A new
constitution, providing for the end of military rule, was
approved by referendum in 1990.

In January 1991 the CMRN was dissolved and a
mixed civilian-military Transitional Committee for
National Recovery (CTRN) was established which
appointed a new government. Civil disturbances in 1991
caused the government to introduce a full multiparty
system in April 1992, since when 40 opposition parties
have been legalised. A presidential election held on 14
December 1998 was won by the incumbent President
Lansana Conté with 54 per cent of the vote. Legislative
elections took place on 30 June 2002 and were won by
President Conté's Party of Unity and Progress (PUP),
which gained 85 of the 114 National Assembly seats.
Presidential elections were due to take place in December
2003.

INSURGENCIES

In September 2000, anti-government rebels, believed to
be members of the Guinea Liberation Movement (GLM),
began a series of incursions into Guinea from Liberia and
Sierra Leone. In January 2001 more fighting broke out
after armed groups from Liberia had attacked across the
border.

HEAD OF STATE

President, Maj.-Gen. Lansana Conté, *took power* 3 April
1984, *elected* 19 December 1993, *re-elected*
14 December 1998

COUNCIL OF MINISTERS *as at July 2003*
Prime Minister, Lamine Sidimé
Agriculture and Animal Husbandry, Jean-Paul Sarr
*Commerce, Industry and Small and Medium-sized
Enterprises,* Mariama Dewo Baldé
Communication, Mamady Condé
Defence, Minister at the Presidency, Col. Cande Toure
Economic Affairs, Finance, Sheik Amadou Camara
Employment and Civil Service, Lamine Camara
Fishing and Aquaculture, Oumar Kouyate
Foreign Affairs, Minister at the Presidency, François
Lonseny Fall
Higher Education and Scientific Research, Eugène Camara
Justice, Keeper of the Seals, Mamadou Sylla
Mines, Geology and Environment, Alpha Mady Soumah
Planning, Fassou Niancoye Sagno
Pre-University Teaching and Civil Education, Kalema
Ginavogui

Public Health, Mamadou Saliou Diallo
Public Works, Transport, Cellou Dalein Diallo
Secretary-General to the Government, Ousmane Sanoko
Secretary-General to the President, Fodé Bangoura
Security, Moussa Sampil
Social Affairs, Promotion of Women and Children, Mariama
Aribot
Technical Education and Professional Training, Ibrahima
Souma
Territorial Administration and Decentralisation, Moussa
Solana
Tourism, Hotels and Handicrafts, Sylla Koumba Diakité
Urbanisation and Housing, Blaise Ono Foromo
Water Resources and Energy, Mory Kaba
Youth, Sports and Culture, Abdel Kader Sangaré

EMBASSY OF THE REPUBLIC OF GUINEA
51 rue de la Faisanderie, F-75016 Paris, France
Tel: (00 33) (1) 4704 8148
Ambassador Extraordinary and Plenipotentiary, Ibrahima
Chérif Haidara, apptd 2003

BRITISH CONSULATE GENERAL
BP 834 Conakry, Guinea
Tel: (00 224) 455 807/456 020/452 959
British Ambassador, HE John Mitchiner, resident at
Freetown, Sierra Leone

ECONOMY

The principal products are bauxite, alumina, palm
kernels, millet, cassava, bananas, plantains and rubber.
Deposits of iron ore, gold, diamonds and uranium have
been discovered. Principal imports are cotton goods,
petroleum products, sugar, flour and salt; exports, bauxite,
alumina, iron ore, diamonds, coffee, bananas, palm
kernels and pineapples.

In 1999 there was a trade surplus of US$94 million
and a current account deficit of US$152 million.
GNP – US$3,303 million (2000); US$450 per capita
(2000)
GDP – US$2,885 million (2001); US$397 per capita
(2000)
ANNUAL AVERAGE GROWTH OF GDP – 5.0 per cent
(1998)
TOTAL EXTERNAL DEBT – US$3,388 million (2000)

Trade with UK	2001	2002
Imports from UK	£21,924,000	£26,625,000
Exports to UK	157,000	2,934,000

GUINEA-BISSAU

República da Guiné-Bissau – Republic of Guinea-Bissau

AREA – 13,948 sq. miles (36,125 sq. km). Neighbours:
Senegal (north), Guinea (east and south)
POPULATION – 1,315,822 (2001 estimate). The main
ethnic groups are the Balante, Malinké, Fulani,
Mandjako and Pepel. The official language is
Portuguese; most of the population speak Guinean
Creole
CAPITAL – Ψ Bissau (population, 195,400, 1991)
CURRENCY – Franc CFA
NATIONAL ANTHEM – É Patria Amada (This Is Our
Beloved Country)
NATIONAL DAY – 24 September (Independence Day)

NATIONAL FLAG – Horizontal bands of yellow over green with vertical red band in the hoist charged with a black star
POPULATION GROWTH RATE – 2.2 per cent
POPULATION DENSITY – 33 per sq. km (1999)
MILITARY EXPENDITURE – 1.5 per cent of GDP (2001)
MILITARY PERSONNEL – 9,250: Army 6,800, Navy 350, Air Force 100, Paramilitaries 2,000
CONSCRIPTION DURATION – Selective conscription
ILLITERACY RATE – (m) 40.3 per cent; (f) 81.0 per cent (2000)
ENROLMENT (percentage of age group) – primary 62 per cent (1997)

HISTORY AND POLITICS

Guinea-Bissau, formerly Portuguese Guinea, achieved independence on 24 September 1974. Following a coup led by Maj. (now Brig.-Gen.) Vieira in 1980, a Revolutionary Council was established. The ruling African Party for the Independence of Guinea and Cape Verde (PAIGC) introduced a multiparty system in January 1991. The PAIGC won the election held in June 1994 and Brig.-Gen. Vieira was elected president in August 1994.

In June 1998, fighting broke out in Bissau between troops loyal to President Vieira and supporters of the sacked army chief Ansumane Mane. Guinea and Senegal sent in troops to support Vieira, and a peace agreement was signed on 1 November, which promised legislative and presidential elections in March 1999. A government of national unity was formed in February 1999 and Guinean and Senegalese troops withdrew in March in accordance with the peace agreement, but no elections took place. Fighting resumed in May 1999, and the government was overthrown on 7 May by rebels loyal to Gen. Mane, who appointed the Speaker of the National Assembly as acting president. Legislative elections held on 28 November 1999 resulted in the Social Renewal Party (PRS) gaining 38 seats in the 102-seat National Assembly. The PRS's ally, the Guinea-Bissau Resistance-Batafa Movement (RGB-Batafa), gained 28 seats. In presidential elections, the founder of the PRS, Kumba Yalla, was elected on 16 January 2000. He resigned his chairmanship of the PRS on 11 May 2000. Gen. Ansumane Mane led an attempted coup in November 2000, during which he was killed. The ruling coalition collapsed on 23 January 2001; on 19 March, President Yalla appointed Faustino Imbali to form a new government which was sworn in on 27 March. Imbali was dismissed by President Yalla on 8 December 2001 and replaced by Alamara Nhasse. On 15 December 2002 President Yalla dissolved parliament and dismissed the cabinet, appointing Mario Pires as the new prime minister on 16 November with a Cabinet again dominated by the PRS. Elections due within 90 days of the dissolution of the parliament were postponed until 12 October 2003.

In April 2003 President Yalla announced plans to change the country's capital city from Bissau to the small town of Buba, 200 km south-east of Bissau, once the construction of a deep-water port in Buba and a railway linking it to Mali's capital, Bamako, had been completed.

POLITICAL SYSTEM

A new constitution, which limited the tenure of the presidency to two terms, was adopted in July 1999. Under the constitution, the president is the head of government and appoints the Council of Ministers. There is a unicameral legislature, the Assembleia Nacional Popular (National People's Assembly), composed of 102 members elected by universal suffrage for a four-year term.

HEAD OF STATE

President, Kumba Yalla, *elected* 16 January 2000, *took office* 17 February 2000

COUNCIL OF MINISTERS *as at July 2003*
Prime Minister, Mario Pires
Agriculture, Forestry and Livestock, Daniel Sleimane Embalo
Economy and Finance, Augusto Ussumane So
Education, Antonio Cumba Dias
Foreign Affairs, Fatumata Djau Baldé
Internal Administration, Fernando Correia Landim
Justice, Vesa Gomes Naluak
National Defence, Filomena Mascarenhas Tipote
Presidency, José de Pina
Public Health, Serifo Antonio Embalo
Public Service and Labour, Tibna Sambe Na Wane
Social Infrastructure, Domingos Simoes Perreira
State Minister, Armando Tchoba dos Santos
Trade, Industry and Handicrafts, Botche Cande

EMBASSY OF THE REPUBLIC OF GUINEA-BISSAU
94 rue St Lazare, Paris F-75009, France
Tel: (00 33) (1) 4526 1851
Ambassador Extraordinary and Plenipotentiary, vacant
Chargé d'Affaires, Fali Embalo

BRITISH CONSULATE
Mavegro Int., CP100, Bissau
Tel: (00 245) 201 224/201 216
British Ambassador, HE Alan Burner, resident at Dakar, Senegal

ECONOMY

Guinea-Bissau produces rice, coconuts, groundnuts and plantains. Cattle are raised, and there are bauxite and phosphate deposits. In May 1997 Guinea-Bissau joined the French Franc Zone, and the CFA Franc replaced the peso as currency. In December 2000 an international debt reduction package worth US$790 million for Guinea-Bissau was agreed.

In 1997 there was a trade deficit of US$14 million and a current account deficit of US$30 million. In 2000 imports totalled US$62 million and exports US$62 million.

GNP – US$217 million (2000); US$180 per capita (2000)
GDP – US$205 million (2001); US$279 per capita (2000)
ANNUAL AVERAGE GROWTH OF GDP – 2.4 per cent (1998)
INFLATION RATE – 8.6 per cent (2000)
TOTAL EXTERNAL DEBT – US$942 million (2000)

Trade with UK	2001	2002
Imports from UK	£1,532,000	£1,105,000
Exports to UK	–	1,000

GUYANA

The Co-operative Republic of Guyana

AREA – 83,000 sq. miles (214,969 sq. km). Neighbours: Venezuela (west), Brazil (west and south), Suriname (east)

POPULATION – 697,181 (2001 estimate): 51 per cent East Indian (mainly rural), 30 per cent African (mainly urban), Amerindians, Europeans, Chinese and people of mixed descent; 50 per cent Christian, 35 per cent Hindu, less than 10 per cent Muslim. Guyana is the only English-speaking country in South America

CAPITAL – ΨGeorgetown (population, 250,000)

MAJOR TOWNS – Corriverton (24,000); Linden (35,000); ΨNew Amsterdam (25,000)

CURRENCY – Guyana dollar (G$) of 100 cents

NATIONAL ANTHEM – Dear Land Of Guyana

NATIONAL DAYS – 26 May (Independence Day); 23 February (Republic Day)

NATIONAL FLAG – Green with a yellow, white-bordered triangle based on the hoist and surmounted by a red, black-bordered triangle

POPULATION GROWTH RATE – 0.8 per cent

POPULATION DENSITY – 4 per sq. km (1999)

URBAN POPULATION – 38 per cent (2001)

MILITARY EXPENDITURE – 0.9 per cent of GDP (2001)

MILITARY PERSONNEL – 1,600: Army 1,400, Navy 100, Air Force 100; Paramilitaries 1,500

HISTORY AND POLITICS

Guyana (formerly British Guiana) became independent on 26 May 1966, with a Governor-General appointed by Queen Elizabeth II. It became a republic on 23 February 1970.

In the October 1992 presidential election Dr Cheddi Jagan was elected and his People's Progressive Party (PPP) defeated the People's National Congress (PNC) which had governed since independence. Jagan died in March 1997 and was replaced by former Prime Minister Samuel Hinds. In the December 1997 election, Janet Jagan (who had previously served as prime minister and was the widow of the late president) was elected president and the PPP returned to power. The PNC claimed the result was fixed (in January 2001 a judicial ruling was to declare that the entire election had been null and void). President Janet Jagan resigned on 11 August 1999 on the grounds of ill health and was succeeded by Bharrat Jagdeo, who had previously been the finance minister, but was appointed prime minister just prior to her resignation, the constitution stipulating that if a president left office during his or her term, the prime minister succeeded to the presidency. The general election which was due to be held on 17 January 2001 took place on 19 March 2001; the delay was due to the failure of the National Assembly to pass a bill amending the electoral law. The PPP secured a third consecutive term of office, obtaining 34 seats; the PNC won 27 seats.

POLITICAL SYSTEM

The 1980 constitution provides for an executive president who serves a five-year term, and a National Assembly of 65 members, of which 53 are elected nationally by proportional representation and 12 are regional representatives.

HEAD OF STATE

President, Bharrat Jagdeo, *succeeded* 11 August 1999, *elected* 19 March 2001

CABINET *as at July 2003*

Prime Minister, Public Works, Samuel Hinds

Agriculture, Fisheries, Crops and Livestock, Satyadeow Sawh

Amerindian Affairs, Carolyn Rodrigues

Attorney-General, Legal Affairs, Doodnauth Singh

Culture, Youth and Sports, Gail Teixeira

Education, Henry Jeffrey

Finance, Saisnaraine Kowlessar

Foreign Affairs, Samuel Rudy Insanally

Foreign Trade and International Co-operation, Clement Rohee

Health, Leslie Ramsammy

Home Affairs, Ronald Gajraj

Housing and Water, Shaik Baksh

Human Services, Social Security and Labour, Dale Bisnauth

Local Government and Regional Development, Harripersaud Nokta

Minister in the Ministry of Human Service, Social Security and Labour, Bibi Shadick

Minister in the Ministry of Local Government, Clinton Collymore

Minister in the Office of President, Public Service Management, Jennifer Westford

Trade and Industry, Manzoor Nadir

Transport and Hydraulics, Carl Anthony Xavier

HIGH COMMISSION FOR GUYANA

3 Palace Court, Bayswater Road, London W2 4LP

Tel: 020-7229 7684 Email: ghc.1@ic24.net

High Commissioner, HE Laleshwar Singh, apptd 1993

BRITISH HIGH COMMISSION

44 Main Street (PO Box 10849), Georgetown

Tel: (00 592) (22) 65881/2/3/4

High Commissioner, HE Stephen Hiscock, apptd 2002

ECONOMY

Agriculture is the principal economic activity, accounting for 39 per cent of GDP and employing 19 per cent of the workforce. Main export items include Demerara sugar, gold, rice and bauxite. Diamonds are also mined. There is some cattle ranching in the savanna country, and oil deposits have been found there. Industry is fairly small-scale. Much emphasis is now being placed on eco-tourism. Foreign aid covers much of the government deficit. In December 2002 the Inter-American Development Bank approved US$64 million in interim debt relief for Guyana to be released in stages until 2012.

In 2001 exports totalled US$478 million and imports US$584 million.

GNP – US$652 million (2000); US$860 per capita (2000)

GDP – US$699 million (2001); US$846 per capita (2000)

ANNUAL AVERAGE GROWTH OF GDP – 3.0 per cent (1998)

INFLATION RATE – 6.1 per cent (2000)

TOTAL EXTERNAL DEBT – US$1,455 million (2000)

Trade with UK	2001	2002
Imports from UK	£22,728,000	£18,545,000
Exports to UK	60,600,000	51,451,000

COMMUNICATIONS

Georgetown and New Amsterdam are the principal ports, though bauxite ships also sail to Linden, on the Demerara, and Everton, on the Berbice. The few roads are confined mainly to the coastal areas. Paved roads total about 571 km out of a total network of 7,820 km. Air transport is the easiest form of communication between the coast and the interior. The national airline, Guyana Airways 2000, has been privatised. There is a state-owned radio broadcasting station which operates two channels and a government-owned television service.

EDUCATION

Education is compulsory between the ages of six and 14; nursery, primary and secondary schooling are free. The government assumed total control of the education system in 1976 and made education free, but instituted fees for study at the University of Guyana in 1994.

There are several technical and vocational institutions, as well as some 30 adult education schools. There are also a number of technical and vocational institutions not under the aegis of the Ministry of Education.

ILLITERACY RATE – (m) 1.1 per cent; (f) 1.9 per cent (2000)

ENROLMENT (percentage of age group) – primary 87 per cent (1995); secondary 66 per cent (1995); tertiary 11 per cent (1996)

HAÏTI

République d'Haïti – Republic of Haïti

AREA – 10,714 sq. miles (27,750 sq. km). Neighbour: Dominican Republic (east)

POPULATION – 6,964,549 (2001 estimate) of which 90 per cent are black and 10 per cent mulatto (mixed race). Some 80 per cent of the population are Roman Catholic and 16 per cent Protestant; around half the population also practices Voodoo which was recognised as an official religion in April 2003. Both French and Creole are regarded as official languages. French is the language of government and the press but it is only spoken by the educated mulatto minority. The usual language is Creole

CAPITAL – ΨPort-au-Prince (population, 884,472, 1996 estimate)

MAJOR CITIES – ΨCap Haïtien (102,233); Carrefour (290,204); Delmas (240,429), 1996 UN estimates

CURRENCY – Gourde of 100 centimes

NATIONAL ANTHEM – La Dessalinienne

NATIONAL DAY –1 January

NATIONAL FLAG – Horizontally blue over red

POPULATION GROWTH RATE – 2.1 per cent

POPULATION DENSITY – 281 per sq. km (1999)

URBAN POPULATION – 35.7 per cent (2000)

MILITARY EXPENDITURE – 1.1 per cent of GDP (2001)

ILLITERACY RATE – (m) 48.0 per cent; (f) 52.1 per cent (2000)

ENROLMENT (percentage of age group) – primary 22 per cent (1990)

HISTORY AND POLITICS

Haïti was a French slave colony under the name of Saint-Domingue from 1697 until 1791, when French rule was overthrown in a revolt led by Toussaint L'Ouverture. French rule was restored by Napoleon in 1802 but in 1803 French forces surrendered to a British naval blockade and on 1 January 1804 the colony was declared independent as Haïti by Jean-Jacques Dessalines.

Dessalines became Emperor of Haïti but was assassinated in 1806.

Haïti was under US military occupation from 1915 to 1934. Dr François 'Papa Doc' Duvalier was elected in 1957 and became life president in 1964. He was succeeded in 1971 by his son Jean-Claude 'Baby Doc' Duvalier who fled to France in 1986 in the face of sustained popular unrest. Five years of military government followed until Father Jean-Bertrand Aristide, leader of the National Front for Change and Democracy, won a free presidential election in 1990.

Aristide fled to the USA following a military coup in September 1991. The international community imposed sanctions and in September 1994, an agreement was reached on President Aristide's return and the flight of the military junta members abroad. Aristide returned on 15 October 1994 to appoint a new government.

The presidential election in December 1995 was won by Lavalas Family (FL) candidate René Préval. Following the resignation of Prime Minister Rosny Smarth in October 1997, the President and the legislature were unable to agree on a successor and Haïti had no prime minister until 12 January 1999, when the appointment of Jacques Édouard Alexis was confirmed by a presidential decree, after the Senate but not the Chamber of Deputies had approved the appointment. Elections to the 27-member Senate and 83-member Chamber of Deputies held between 21 May and 30 July 2000 were won by the pro-Aristide FL, winning 18 and 72 seats respectively; there was much international criticism of the manner in which the elections had been conducted.

The presidential election on 26 November 2000 was won by Jean-Bertrand Aristide, who obtained 92 per cent of the vote; the main opposition parties had refused to contest the election, citing irregularities in the earlier legislative election; in response, Aristide promised to hold fresh legislative elections in November 2002, although these did not take place and were scheduled to take place in 2004.

POLITICAL SYSTEM

The head of state is a president, directly elected for a five-year term that may not be renewed immediately. The National Assembly is the bicameral legislature; the lower house, the Chamber of Deputies, has 83 members directly elected for four years. The upper house or Senate has 27 members elected for six years; one third of the senators are elected every two years. The president appoints the prime minister, who must be approved by the National Assembly. The prime minister chooses the Cabinet.

HEAD OF STATE

President, Jean-Bertrand Aristide, *elected* 26 November 2000, *sworn in* 7 February 2001

CABINET *as at July 2003*

Prime Minister, Interior, Territorial Communities, Yvon Neptune

Agriculture, Natural Resources and Rural Development, Sébastien Hilaire

Commerce and Industry, Leslie Gouthier

Culture and Communication, Lilas Desquiron

Economy and Finance, Faubert Gustave

Environment, Webster Pierre

Foreign Affairs, Religious Affairs, Joseph Philippe Antonio

Haïtians Living Abroad, Leslie Voltaire

Interior, Jocelerme Privert

Justice and Public Security, Calixte Delatour
Labour and Social Affairs, Eudes Saint-Preux
National Education, Youth and Sport, Myrtho Celestin Saurel
Planning and External Co-operation, Pierre Duret
Public Health and Population, Henri-Claude Voltaire
Public Works, Transport and Communications, Harry Clinton
Tourism, Martine Deverson
Women's Affairs, Ginette Lubin

BRITISH AMBASSADOR, HE Andrew Ashcroft, apptd 2002, resident at Santo Domingo, Dominican Republic

BRITISH CONSULATE, Hotel Montana (PO Box 1302), Port-au-Prince Tel: (00 509) 257 3969

ECONOMY
Light industrial products account for over 80 per cent of total exports. Coffee is the second largest export earner. Corn, sorghum and rice are also grown. Increased production of tropical fruits and vegetables is being encouraged. Leather goods, textiles, electronic components and sports equipment are manufactured, using imported raw materials, for re-export. Principal imports are foodstuffs, machinery and transport equipment and fuels. In July 2002 Haiti was accepted as the 15th member of the Caribbean Community (Caricom) trade bloc. In 1998 Haïti had a trade deficit of US$341 million and a current account deficit of US$38 million. In 2001 imports totalled US$1,013 million and exports US$274 million.

GNP – US$4,059 million (2000); US$510 per capita (2000)
GDP – US$3,771 million (2001); US$432 per capita (2000)
ANNUAL AVERAGE GROWTH OF GDP – 1.1 per cent (2000)
INFLATION RATE –13.7 per cent (2000)
TOTAL EXTERNAL DEBT – US$1,169 million (2000)

Trade with UK	2001	2002
Imports from UK	£10,509,000	£11,983,000
Exports to UK	391,000	1,008,000

COMMUNICATIONS
There are more than 4,000 km of roads. Air services are maintained between the capital and the principal provincial towns and to the USA and Caribbean and South American countries. The principal towns and villages are connected by telephone and/or telegraph. There are several commercial radio stations and two television stations at Port-au-Prince.

HONDURAS

República de Honduras – Republic of Honduras
AREA – 43,277 sq. miles (112,088 sq. km). Neighbours: Guatemala (north-west), El Salvador (south-west), Nicaragua (south)
POPULATION – 6,406,052 (2001 estimate) of mixed Spanish and Indian blood. The Garifunas in the north are of West Indian origin. The language is Spanish, although English is spoken on the Bay Islands
CAPITAL – Tegucigalpa (population, 850,445, 2001 census)
MAJOR CITIES – Choluteca (120,682); ΨLa Ceiba

(127,476); ΨPuerto Cortés (90,115); San Pedro Sula (513,753); ΨTela (78,537), 2001 census
CURRENCY – Lempira of 100 centavos
NATIONAL ANTHEM – Tu Bandera Es Un Lampo De Cielo (Your Flag Is A Heavenly Light)
NATIONAL DAY – 15 September
NATIONAL FLAG – Three horizontal bands, blue, white, blue (with five blue stars on white band)
POPULATION GROWTH RATE – 3.3 per cent
POPULATION DENSITY –5 7 per sq. km (1999)
MILITARY EXPENDITURE –1 .5 per cent of GDP (2001)
MILITARY PERSONNEL – 8,300: Army 5,500, Navy 1,000, Air Force 1,800; Paramilitaries 6,000

HISTORY AND POLITICS
Discovered and settled by the Spanish in the 16th century, Honduras formed part of the Spanish American dominions until 1821 when independence was proclaimed. Under military government from 1972, Honduras returned to civilian rule in 1981 with an executive presidency, a 128-seat unicameral Congress, and a multi-party system. In October 1997, Congress approved a constitutional amendment reducing the legislature to 80 members. The amendment must also be ratified by the current session of Congress before it becomes law. Legislative elections held on 25 November 2001 were won by the National Party (PNH) who gained 61 seats, with the Liberal Party (PLH) gaining 55 seats. The presidential election held on the same day was won by Ricardo Maduro of the PNH.

HEAD OF STATE
President of the Republic, C-in-C of the Armed Forces, Ricardo Maduro, *elected* 25 November 2001, *took office* 27 January 2002
Vice-Presidents, Vicente Williams; Armida De Lopez; Alberto Diaz

CABINET *as at July 2003*
Agriculture and Livestock, Mariano Jiménez
Culture, Arts and Sports, Mireya Batres
Defence, Federico Breve
Education, Carlos Avila
Finance, Arturo Alvarado
Foreign Relations, Guillermo Pérez
Industry and Commerce, Norman Garcia
Interior and Justice, Jorge Ramón Hernández Alcerro
Labour, Germán Leitzelar
Ministers Without Portfolio, Carlos Vargas *(Health);* Johnny Kafati *(Housing);* Camilo Atala *(Investment Promotion);* Eduardo Kafati *(Public Service);* Ramón Median *(Strategic Affairs and Communication)*
Natural Resources and Environment, Patricia Panting
Presidency, Luis Cosenza
Public Employees' Retirement and Pension, Antonio Rivera Callejas
Public Health, Elias Lizardo
Public Works, Transport and Housing, Jorge Carranza
Security, Juan Angel Arias
Tourism, Thierry De Pierrefeu

EMBASSY OF HONDURAS
115 Gloucester Place, London W1U 6JT
Tel: 020-7486 4880
Ambassador Extraordinary and Plenipotentiary, HE Hernán Antonio Bermúdez, apptd 1999

BRITISH EMBASSY
Edifíco Financiero Banexpo, 3er Piso, Boulevard San Juan
Bosco, Colonia Payaqui, Apartado Postal 290, Tegucigalpa
Tel: (00 504) 232 0612/5144
Ambassador Extraordinary and Plenipotentiary, HE Kay
Coombs, apptd 2002

ECONOMY

Three-quarters of the country is covered by pine forests. Agriculture and cattle raising is mainly confined to the fertile coastal plain on the Caribbean and the extensive valleys in the Comayagua and Olancho regions of the interior. The Mosquitia tropical forest covers the area from the coast to the border with Nicaragua and provides valuable reserves of timber. Lead, zinc and silver are mined on a small scale.

The chief exports are coffee, bananas, frozen meat, shrimps, lobsters and timber, the most important woods being pine, mahogany and cedar. The main imports are machinery and electrical equipment, industrial chemicals and lubricants.

In October 1998 Hurricane Mitch devastated Honduras, killing an estimated 6,500 people and wrecking Tegucigalpa. The cost of repairing the damage was estimated at US$4 billion.

In July 2000, the IMF and the World Bank granted Honduras a debt reduction package worth about US$556 million. An estimated 85 per cent of the population live below the poverty line.

In 2000 Honduras had a trade deficit of US$658 million and a current account deficit of US$510 million. In 2001 imports totalled US$2,918 million and exports US$1,318 million.

GNP – US$5,517 million (2000); US$860 per capita (2000)
GDP – US$6,386 million (2001); US$919 per capita (2000)
ANNUAL AVERAGE GROWTH OF GDP – 4.8 per cent (2000)
INFLATION RATE – 11.1 per cent (2000)
UNEMPLOYMENT – 3.7 per cent (1999)
TOTAL EXTERNAL DEBT – US$5,487 million (2000)

Trade with UK	2001	2002
Imports from UK	£11,415,000	£9,757,000
Exports to UK	31,425,000	19,116,000

COMMUNICATIONS

There are about 595 km of railway in operation, chiefly to serve the banana plantations and the Caribbean ports. There are 15,400 km of roads, of which 3,126 km are paved. There are over 80 smaller airstrips and four international airports, Tegucigalpa, San Pedro Sula, La Ceiba and Roatún (Bay Island).

The chief ports are Puerto Cortés, Tela and Puerto Castilla on the north coast, through which passes the bulk of the trade with the USA and Europe.

EDUCATION

Primary and secondary education is free, primary education being compulsory from the age of seven to 12, and the government has launched a campaign to eradicate illiteracy.

ILLITERACY RATE – (m) 25.6 per cent; (f) 25.2 per cent (2000)
ENROLMENT (percentage of age group) – primary 100 per cent (1997); secondary 21 per cent (1991); tertiary 10.0 per cent (1997)

HUNGARY

Magyar Köztársaság – Republic of Hungary

AREA –35,500 sq. miles (92,300 sq. km). Neighbours: Slovakia (north), Ukraine and Romania (east), Serbia and Montenegro and Croatia (south), Slovenia and Austria (west)
POPULATION – 10,197,119 (2001 census). There are minorities of Romanies (4 per cent), ethnic Germans (3 per cent), Serbs (2 per cent), Romanians (1 per cent) and Slovaks (1 per cent). About two-thirds of the population are Roman Catholic and the remainder mostly Calvinist. The language is Hungarian (Magyar)
CAPITAL – Budapest, (population, 1,775,203, 2001 census)
MAJOR CITIES – Debrecen (211,034); Miskolc (184,125); Pécs (162,498); Szeged (168,372), 2001 census
CURRENCY – Forint of 100 fillér
NATIONAL ANTHEM – Isten Aldd Meg A Magyart (God Bless The Hungarians)
NATIONAL DAYS –1 5 March, 20 August, 23 October
NATIONAL FLAG – Red, white, green (horizontally)
LIFE EXPECTANCY (years) – 72 (2001)
POPULATION GROWTH RATE – 0.4 per cent
POPULATION DENSITY – 107 per sq. km (2001)
URBAN POPULATION – 65 per cent (2001)

HISTORY AND POLITICS

The Hungarians settled the Danube basin in 896 AD and in 1000, King Istvan (Stephen) adopted Roman Catholicism and received a crown from the Pope. The Turks invaded Hungary in 1526; the Austrians finally succeeded in expelling them in 1699. Following nationalist unrest, the *Ausgleich* (compromise) of 1867 created the Dual Monarchy of Austria-Hungary, giving Hungary internal autonomy. The defeat of Austria-Hungary in the First World War led to the declaration of Hungarian independence in November 1918.

Hungary joined the Anti-Comintern Pact in February 1939 and entered the Second World War on the side of Germany in 1941. On 20 January 1945 a Hungarian provisional government of liberation signed an armistice under the terms of which the frontiers of Hungary were withdrawn to the 1937 limits.

After the liberation, a coalition of parties carried out land reform and nationalisation. By 1949 the Communists had succeeded in gaining a monopoly of power and by 1952 practically the entire economy had been 'socialised'.

Divisions within the Communist Party and popular demand for free elections and Soviet troop withdrawals grew. An uprising on 23 October 1956 was quelled by Soviet forces the following morning. But a reformist all-party coalition government under Imre Nagy was formed which declared Hungary's withdrawal from the Warsaw pact. This government was suppressed by a renewed attack by Soviet forces on Budapest on 4 November and a new Communist government under János Kádár was announced the same day.

From 1968 the government gradually introduced economic reforms and some political liberalisation. Kádár was forced to resign in May 1989. In October 1989 the National Assembly *(Országgyülés)* approved an amended constitution which described Hungary as an independent, democratic state. The 386-seat National Assembly is elected on a mixed first past the post and proportional representation basis with a 5 per cent threshold for representation. The first free multiparty elections took place in March and April 1990 and were won by the (conservative) Hungarian Democratic Forum. On 6 June 2000, Ferenc Mádl, an independent candidate, was elected as president.

In the legislative elections in April 2002, no party won an overall majority. The Federation of Young Democrats-Hungarian Civic Party (Fidesz-MPP) won the largest number of seats but Péter Medgyessy of the Hungarian Socialist Party (MSzP), formed a coalition government with the Alliance of Free Democrats (SzDSz). The composition of the National Assembly in May 2002 was: Fidesz-MPP 188, MSzP 178, SzDSz 20.

In December 2002 Hungary was formally invited to join the EU in 2004. A referendum held in April 2003 approved the country's membership.

HEAD OF STATE
President, Ferenc Mádl, *elected* 6 June 2000, *sworn in* 4 August 2000

CABINET *as at July 2003*
Prime Minister, Péter Medgyessy (MSzP)
Prime Minister's Office, in charge of Regional Development, Religious Affairs, Ethnic Hungarians Abroad and Tourism, Peter Kiss (MSzP)
Agriculture and Rural Development, Imre Németh (MSzP)
Defence, Ferenc Juhász (MSzP)
Economy and Transport, István Csillag (SzDSz)
Education, Bálint Magyar (SzDSz)
Environment and Water Management, Miklos Persanyi (SzDSz)
EU Integration, Endre Juhasz
Finance, Csaba László (MSzP)
Foreign Affairs, László Kovács (MSzP)
Health, Social and Family Affairs, Judit Csehák (MSzP)
Information Science and Telecommunications, Kálmán Kovács (SzDSz)
Interior, Mónika Lamperth (MSzP)
Justice, Péter Bárándy (MSzP)
Labour and Employment, Sandor Burany (MSzP)_
National Cultural Heritage, Istvan Hiller (MSzP)
Without Portfolio, in charge of Equal Opportunities, Katalin Levai
Youth and Sports, Ferenc Gyurcsany (MSzP)

MSzP Hungarian Socialist Party; SzDSz Alliance of Free Democrats

EMBASSY OF THE REPUBLIC OF HUNGARY
35 Eaton Place, London SW1X 8BY Tel: 020-7235 5218
Ambassador Extraordinary and Plenipotentiary, HE Béla Szombati, apptd 2002

BRITISH EMBASSY
Harmincad Utca 6, H-1051 Budapest Tel: (00 36) (1) 266 2888
Email: info@britemb.hu
Ambassador Extraordinary and Plenipotentiary, HE John Nichols, apptd 2003

BRITISH COUNCIL DIRECTOR, Dr John Richards, OBE
Benczúr Utca 26, H-1068 Budapest Tel: (00 36) (1) 478 4700
Email: information@britishcouncil.hu

DEFENCE
The Army has 743 main battle tanks, 680 armoured infantry fighting vehicles and 798 armoured personnel carriers. The Air Force has 37 combat aircraft and 49 attack helicopters. Hungary became a member of NATO in March 1999.
MILITARY EXPENDITURE – 1.8 per cent of GDP (2001)
MILITARY PERSONNEL – 33,400: Army 23,600, Army Maritime Wing 270, Air Force 7,700; Paramilitaries 14,000
CONSCRIPTION DURATION – Six months

ECONOMY
Agriculture accounts for around 6 per cent of GDP and employs 7.5 per cent of the workforce. Production is concentrated on maize, wheat, sugar beet, barley, rye and oats.

Industry is mainly based on imported raw materials but Hungary has its own coal, bauxite, considerable deposits of natural gas, some iron ore and oil.

The economy suffered from the loss of export markets in the Soviet Union and the former Yugoslavia, and the transition to a market economy, but now exports the majority of its goods to the countries of the EU. The country has benefited from a strong inflow of foreign direct investment.

The main exports are machinery and equipment, manufactures, foodstuffs, beverages and tobacco products, raw materials and energy transmission equipment.

In 2001 Hungary had a trade deficit of US$2,018 million and a current account deficit of US$1,097 million. Imports totalled US$33,725 million and exports US$30,530 million.
GNP – US$47,249 million (2000); US$4,710 per capita (2000)
GDP – US$52,361 million (2001); US$4,649 per capita (2000)
ANNUAL AVERAGE GROWTH OF GDP – 4.4 per cent (1999)
INFLATION RATE –9.8 per cent (2000)
UNEMPLOYMENT – 6.4 per cent (2000)
TOTAL EXTERNAL DEBT –US$29,415 million (2000)

Trade with UK	2001	2002
Imports from UK	£614,505,000	£748,681,000
Exports to UK	724,445,000	863,120,000

EDUCATION
There are five types of schools under the Ministry of Education: kindergartens for age three to six, general schools for age six to 14 (compulsory), vocational schools (15–18), secondary schools (15–18), universities and adult training schools (over 18).
ILLITERACY RATE – (m) 0.5 per cent; (f) 0.8 per cent (2000)
ENROLMENT (percentage of age group) – primary 100 per cent (1997); secondary 98 per cent (1997); tertiary 24 per cent (1997)

ICELAND

Lýðveldið Ísland – Republic of Iceland
AREA – 38,577 sq. miles (100,300 sq. km)
POPULATION – 281,000 (2001). Some 87.8 per cent of the population are members of the (Lutheran) Church of Iceland. The language is Icelandic
CAPITAL – ΨReykjavík (population, 111,345, 2000)
MAJOR CITIES – Akranes; ΨAkureyri; Egilsstaðir; ΨHafnarfjörður; ΨIsafjörður; Kópavogur; Reykjanesbær; ΨSiglufjörður
CURRENCY – Icelandic króna (Kr) of 100 aurar

NATIONAL ANTHEM – Lofsöngur (Song Of Praise)
NATIONAL DAY –17 June
NATIONAL FLAG –Blue, with white-bordered red cross
LIFE EXPECTANCY (years) – 79 (2001)
POPULATION GROWTH RATE – 0.9 per cent
POPULATION DENSITY – 3 per sq. km (2001)
URBAN POPULATION – 93 per cent (2001)
MILITARY PERSONNEL – Paramilitaries: 120

HISTORY AND POLITICS

Iceland was uninhabited before the ninth century, when settlers came from Norway. For several centuries a form of republican government prevailed, with an annual assembly of leading men called the *Alþingi (Althingi)*, but in 1262 Iceland became subject to Norway, and later to Denmark. During the colonial period, Iceland maintained its cultural integrity but a deterioration in the climate, together with frequent volcanic eruptions and outbreaks of disease, led to a serious drop in living standards and to a decline in the population to little more than 40,000. In the 19th century a struggle for independence led to home rule in 1918 and to independence as a republic in 1944.

On 1 August 2000, President Ólafur Ragnar Grímsson, first elected in June 1996, was re-installed as president for a second term without an election as no other candidate was nominated. The parliamentary (Althingi) elections on 10 May 2003 gave the Independence Party (SSF) 22 seats, Unified Left 20, Progressive Party 12, Left-Green Alliance 5 and Liberals 4. Incumbent Prime Minister David Oddsson of the SSF was sworn into office for a further term on 23 May.

HEAD OF STATE
President, Ólafur Ragnar Grímsson, *elected* 29 June 1996, *re-installed* 1 August 2000

CABINET *as at July 2003*
Prime Minister, Statistical Bureau of Iceland, David Oddsson (SSF)
Agriculture, Gudni Ágústsson (FSF)
Education, Culture and Science, Tomas Ingi Olrich (SSF)
Environment, Siv Fridleifsdóttir (FSF)
Finance, Geir Haarde (SSF)
Fisheries, Árni Mathiesen (SSF)
Foreign Affairs, Halldór Ásgrímsson (FSF)
Health and Social Security, Jón Kristjánsson (FSF)
Justice and Ecclesiastical Affairs, Björn Bjarnason (SSF)
Social Affairs, Arni Magnusson (SSF)
Trade and Industry, Valgerdur Sverrisdóttir (FSF)
Transport, Communications, Sturla Bödvarsson (SSF)

SSF Independence Party; FSF Progressive Party

EMBASSY OF ICELAND
2A Hans Street, London SW1X 0JE
Tel: 020-7259 3999
Ambassador Extraordinary and Plenipotentiary, HE Sverrir Haukur Gunnlaugsson, apptd 2003

BRITISH EMBASSY
Laufásvegur 31, IS-101 Reykjavík
Tel: (00 354) 550 5100
Email: britemb@centrum.is
Ambassador Extraordinary and Plenipotentiary and Consul-General, HE John Culver, LVO, apptd 2000

ECONOMY

Iceland has considerable resources of hydroelectric and geothermal energy. Heavy industry includes an aluminium smelter, a nitrogen fertiliser factory, a cement factory, a diatomite plant and a ferro-silicon plant.

The major sectors of the economy are fishing and fish processing, manufacturing, agriculture, energy production and tourism, which is of growing importance with 302,913 visitors in 2000, accounting for 14 per cent of foreign exchange earnings.

As a member of the European Free Trade Association (EFTA), Iceland has become a member of the European Economic Area (EEA) which extends most of the provisions of the EU's single market to EFTA states.

In 2000 Iceland had a trade deficit of US$474 million and a current account deficit of US$848 million. In 2001 imports totalled US$2,253 million and exports US$2,022 million.
GNP – US$8,540 million (2000); US$30,390 per capita (2000)
GDP – US$7,542 million (2001); US$30,681 per capita (2000)
ANNUAL AVERAGE GROWTH OF GDP – 3.6 per cent (2000)
INFLATION RATE – 5.2 per cent (2000)
UNEMPLOYMENT – 2.3 per cent (2000)

TRADE
The principal exports are fish and fish products, which account for nearly three-quarters of exports, ferro-silicon and aluminium; the chief imports are consumer durables, petroleum products, transport equipment, textiles, foodstuffs, animal feeds and timber. Iceland's main export markets are the UK, Germany, the USA, Spain, Norway, Japan and Switzerland.

Trade with UK	2001	2002
Imports from UK	£157,763,000	£141,621,000
Exports to UK	299,302,000	310,812,000

COMMUNICATIONS

At 1 January 2000, the mercantile marine consisted of 1,067 registered vessels (222,827 gross tons). There are regular shipping services between Reykjavík and Felixstowe, the Humber ports, Europe and the USA.

Road communications are adequate in summer but greatly restricted by snow in winter. Only roads in town centres and key highways are metalled, the rest being of gravel, sand and lava dust. The climate and terrain make first-class surfaces for highways out of the question. There are no railways.

CULTURE

The ancient Norræna (or Northern tongue) has close affinities to Anglo-Saxon and as spoken and written in Iceland today differs little from that introduced into the island in the ninth century. There is a rich literature with two distinct periods of development, from the mid-11th to the late 13th century and from the early 19th century to the present.
ENROLMENT (percentage of age group) – primary 98 per cent (1996); secondary 87 per cent (1995); tertiary 37 per cent (1996)

INDIA

The Republic of India/Bhāratīya Ganarajyă

AREA – 1,143,538 sq. miles (2,973,200 sq. km).
Neighbours: Pakistan (north-west), China, Tibet,
Nepal and Bhutan (north), Myanmar (east),
Bangladesh

POPULATION – 1,027,015,247 (2001): Hindu (81 per
cent), the rest being Muslim (12 per cent), Christian
(2.3 per cent), Sikh (1.9 per cent), Buddhist (0.8 per
cent) and Jain (0.4 per cent). The official languages are
Hindi in the Devanagari script and English, though 17
regional languages are also recognised for adoption as
official state languages

CAPITAL – New Delhi (population, 9,817,439 including
Delhi/Dilli), 2001

MAJOR CITIES – Ahmedabad (3,515,361); Bangalore
(4,292,223); ΨBombay/Mumbai (11,914,398);
ΨCalcutta/Kolkata (4,580,544); Hyderabad
(3,449,878); Kanpur (2,532,138); Lucknow
(2,207,340); ΨMadras/Chennai (4,216,268); Pune
(2,540,069) (2001 figures)

CURRENCY – Indian rupee (Rs) of 100 paise

NATIONAL ANTHEM – Jana-Gana-Mana (Thou Art The
Ruler Of The Minds Of All People)

NATIONAL DAY – 26 January (Republic Day)

NATIONAL FLAG – A horizontal tricolour with bands of
deep saffron, white and dark green in equal
proportions. In the centre of the white band appears
an Asoka wheel in navy blue

LIFE EXPECTANCY (years) – 64 (2001)

POPULATION GROWTH RATE – 1.8 per cent

POPULATION DENSITY – 345 per sq. km (2001)

URBAN POPULATION – 28 per cent (2001)

ILLITERACY RATE – (m) 31.6 per cent; (f) 54.6 per cent
(2000)

ENROLMENT (percentage of age group) – tertiary 7 per
cent (1997)

India has three well-defined regions: the mountain range
of the Himalayas, the Indo-Gangetic plain, and the
southern peninsula. The main mountain ranges are the
Himalayas (over 29,000 feet) and the Western and
Eastern Ghats (over 8,000 feet). Major rivers include the
Ganges, Indus, Krishna, Godavari and Mahanadi.

HISTORY AND POLITICS

The Indus civilisation was fully developed by c.2500 BC
but collapsed c.1750 BC, and was replaced by an Aryan
civilisation from the west. Arab invasions of the north-
west began in the seventh century and Muslim, Hindu
and Buddhist states developed until the establishment of
the Mughal dynasty in 1526. The British East India
Company established settlements throughout the 17th
century; clashes with the French and native princes led to
the British government taking control of the company in
1784 and gradually extending sovereignty over the
whole subcontinent. The separate dominions of India and
Pakistan became independent within the Commonwealth
on 15 August 1947 and India became a republic in 1950.

Between 1947 and 1996, India was ruled by the
Congress (I) Party for all but four years (March
1977–January 1980, November 1989–June 1991).
Congress (I) has been led by members of the Nehru-
Gandhi dynasty for most of the post-independence
period: Prime Ministers Jawaharlal Nehru (1947–64),
Indira Gandhi (1966–1977, 1980–84) and Rajiv

Gandhi (1984–89). Indira Gandhi was assassinated by
Sikh extremists seeking an independent Sikh state in
Punjab; her son Rajiv was assassinated by Sri Lankan
Tamils.

In November 1997, the United Front government (a
coalition of Communist and low-caste parties) collapsed
after Congress (I) withdrew its support. The
parliamentary elections in February 1998 produced no
outright winner; in March 1998, the BJP formed a
coalition government under Atal Bihari Vajpayee, which
collapsed following the loss of a confidence motion on
17 April 1999. The opposition parties were unable to
form a majority government and parliament was
dissolved on 26 April 1999 by President Narayanan. The
BJP-led 24-party National Democratic Alliance won
elections on 3 October 1999 with a majority of 296
seats. A ten-party coalition government was dominated
by the BJP was formed on on 13 October. In the
presidential election held on 15 July 2002, A. P. J. Abdul
Kalam was elected as India's 11th president.

SECESSION

The Hindu Maharaja of Kashmir signed his state's
instrument of accession to India in October 1947, two
months after India and Pakistan became independent.
This was disputed by Pakistan, on the basis that the
majority of the state's population was Muslim. After three
Indian-Pakistani wars, a line of control was agreed under
the 1972 Simla agreement (China has also occupied
some of Kashmir since the 1962 Sino-Indian war).
Kashmir was placed under direct rule in 1990. The
Islamic militant groups Hizbul Mujahidin, Harakat-ul-
Mujahidin and Lashkar-e-Tayyeba continued to launch
attacks on Hindu civilians, government officials and
security forces. The Indian government announced a
unilateral cease-fire during the month of Ramadan,
which began on 28 November 2000 and the cease-fire
was extended until 24 May 2001. In response, Pakistan
announced that its forces would show restraint, but
attacks by Islamic militants continued unabated and
repeated government offers of talks with the militants
were rejected.

FOREIGN RELATIONS

In addition to the territory it won as a result of the Sino-
Indian war in 1962, China claims Arunachal Pradesh and
does not recognise Indian sovereignty over Sikkim. Talks
between India and China in June 2003 resulted in India's
formal recognition of the Tibetan Autonomous Region as
a part of China and a cross-border trade agreement on
Sikkim.

India and Pakistan have fought three major wars since
independence, in 1947–8, 1965 and 1971. Since 1985
they have continued a low-level war at altitude for
control of the Siachen glacier in Kashmir.

In May 1998, India confirmed its nuclear status with
five underground nuclear tests and within three weeks,
Pakistan had followed suit. Both countries' tests sparked
international condemnation.

In May 1999 India launched air attacks on Muslim
insurgents who had occupied mountainous areas within
Indian-controlled Kashmir. Small-scale incidents between
the Indian and Pakistani troops stationed along the line
of control dividing Kashmir continue to occur on a
regular basis. The presidents of India and Pakistan held a
summit in Agra in July 2001, but failed to agree a joint
declaration. A terrorist attack on the federal parliament in
New Delhi on 13 December left 14 people dead. India

held the Islamic separatist organisations Jaish-e-Mohammed (JeM) and Lashkar-e-Tayyeba (LeT) responsible. The Kashmir crisis continued into 2002, amid international fear that the situation could escalate into a nuclear exchange between the two countries. In May, the killing of 34 people at an Indian army camp in Kashmir exacerbated the tensions. There was high-level international diplomatic activity and in June, although the situation was still serious, the threat of war seemed less likely. Tension increased once again in early 2003 with frequent exchanges of fire and shelling between the Indian and Pakistani armies. However, Indian Prime Minister Atal Bihari Vajpayee instigated peaceful dialogue with Pakistan during a visit to Kashmir in April, paving the way for a reduction in tension and the restoration of transport and diplomatic links between the two countries.

POLITICAL SYSTEM
Executive power is vested in the president, elected for a five-year term by an electoral college consisting of the elected members of the Union and State legislatures. The president appoints the prime minister and, on the latter's advice, the ministers, and can dismiss them. The Council of Ministers is collectively responsible to the *Lok Sabha* (lower house). The vice-president is ex-officio chairman of the *Rajya Sabha* (upper house).

Legislative power rests with the president, the Rajya Sabha (245 members serving six-year terms) and the Lok Sabha (545 members). Twelve members of the Rajya Sabha are presidential nominees, the rest are indirectly elected representatives of the State and Union Territories. The 543 members of the Lok Sabha representing the States and Union Territories are directly elected by universal adult franchise for a five-year term, and the two representatives of the Anglo-Indian community are nominated by the president.

FEDERAL STRUCTURE
There are 28 States and seven Union Territories. Each state is headed by a Governor, who is appointed by the president and holds office for five years, and by a Council of Ministers. All states have a Legislative Assembly, and some have also a Legislative Council, elected directly by adult suffrage for a maximum period of five years.

The Union Territories are administered, except where otherwise provided by Parliament, by the president acting through an Administrator or Lieutenant-Governor, or other authority appointed by him.

	Area (sq. km)	Population (2001 census)	Capital
STATES			
Andhra Pradesh	275,069	75,727,541	Hyderabad
Arunachal Pradesh	83,743	1,091,117	Itanagar
Assam	78,438	26,638,407	Dispur
Bihar	94,163	82,878,796	Patna
Chhattisgarh	135,191	20,795,956	Raipur
Goa	3,702	1,343,998	Panaji
Gujarat	196,022	50,596,992	Gandhinagar
Haryana	44,212	21,082,989	Chandigarh
Himachal Pradesh	55,673	6,077,248	Shimla
Jammu and Kashmir	101,387	10,069,917	Srinagar/ Jammu
Jharkhand	79,714	26,909,428	Ranchi
Karnataka	191,791	52,733,958	Bangalore

	Area (sq. km)	Population (2001 census)	Capital
Kerala	38,863	31,838,619	Trivandrum (Thiruvananthapuram)
Madhya Pradesh	308,245	60,385,118	Bhopal Raipur
Maharashtra	307,713	96,752,247	Bombay (Mumbai)
Manipur	22,327	2,388,634	Imphal
Meghalaya	22,429	2,306,069	Shillong
Mizoram	21,081	891,058	Aizawl
Nagaland	16,579	1,988,636	Kohima
Orissa	155,707	36,706,920	Bhubaneswar
Punjab	50,362	24,289,296	Chandigarh
Rajasthan	342,239	56,473,122	Jaipur
Sikkim	7,096	540,493	Gangtok
Tamil Nadu	130,058	62,110,839	Madras (Chennai)
Tripura	10,486	3,191,168	Agartala
Uttar Pradesh	240,928	166,052,859	Lucknow
Uttaranchal	53,483	8,479,562	Dehra Dun
West Bengal	88,752	80,221,171	Calcutta (Kolkata)

UNION TERRITORIES			
Andaman and Nicobar Is.	8,249	356,265	Port Blair
Chandigarh	114	900,914	
Dadra and Nagar Haveli	491	220,451	Silvassa
Daman and Diu	112	158,059	
Delhi/Dilli	1,483	13,782,976	
Lakshadweep	32	60,595	Kavaratti
Pondicherry	480	973,829	

HEAD OF STATE
President of the Republic of India, A. P. J. Abdul Kalam, *elected* 15 July 2002, *took office* 25 July 2002
Vice-President, Bhairon Singh Shekhawat

CABINET *as at July 2003*
Prime Minister, Atomic Energy, Planning, Space, Statistics and Programme Implementation, Atal Bihari Vajpayee (BJP)
Deputy Prime Minister, Home Affairs, Personnel, Public Grievances and Pensions, Lal Krishna Advani (BJP)
Agriculture, Rajnath Singh (BJP)
Chemicals and Fertilisers, Sukhdev Singh Dhindsa (SAD)
Coal and Mines, Kariya Munda
Consumer Affairs, Food and Public Distribution, Sharad Yadav (JD(U))
Culture and Tourism, Jagmohan Malhotra (BJP)
Defence, George Fernandes (SP)
Disinvestment, Communications and Information Technology, Arun Shourie (BJP)
Environment and Forests, T. R. Baalu (DMK)
Foreign Affairs, Yashwant Sinha (BJP)
Finance and Company Affairs, Jaswant Singh (BJP)
Health and Family Welfare, Parliamentary Affairs, Sushma Swaraj (BJP)
Heavy Industry and Public Enterprises, Subodh Mohite (SS)
Human Resource Development, Science and Technology, Ocean Development, Murli Manohar Joshi (BJP)
Labour, Sahib Singh Verma (BJP)

Law and Justice, Commerce and Industry, Arun Jaitley (BJP)
Petroleum and Natural Gas, Ram Naik (BJP)
Railways, Nitish Kumar (SP)
Road Transport and Highways, Maj.-Gen. Bhuwan
   Chandra Khanduri (BJP)
Rural Development, vacant
Shipping, Shatrughan Sinha (BJP)
*Small Scale Industries, Development of North-Eastern
   Region,* C. P. Thakur
Social Justice and Empowerment, Satya Narayan Jatiya (BJP)
Textiles, Kashiram Rana (BJP)
Tribal Affairs, Jual Oram (BJP)
Water Resources, Arjun Charan Sethi (BJD)
Without Portfolio, Murasoli Maran (DMK)
Youth Affairs and Sports, Vikram Verma (BJP)

BJD Biju Janata Dal; BJP Bharatiya Janata Party; DMK
Dravida Munnetra Kazhagam; JD(U) Janata Dal (United);
SAD Shiromani Akali Dal; SP Samata Party; SS Shiv Sena

INDIAN HIGH COMMISSION
India House, Aldwych, London WC2B 4NA
Tel: 020-7836 8484
High Commissioner, HE Shri Ranendra Sen, apptd 2002

BRITISH HIGH COMMISSION
Chanakyapuri, New Delhi 110021
Tel: (00 91) (11) 687 2161
High Commissioner, HE Sir Rob Young, KCMG, apptd
   1998

BRITISH COUNCIL MINISTER – Edmund Marsden
17 Kasturba Gandhi Marg, New Delhi 110 001
Tel: (00 91) (11) 2371 1401
Email: delhi.askaquestion@in.britishcouncil.org

DEFENCE

The Army has 3,898 main battle tanks, 1,500 armoured
infantry fighting vehicles and 317 armoured personnel
carriers. The Navy has 16 submarines, one aircraft carrier,
eight destroyers, 11 frigates, 39 patrol and coastal vessels,
35 combat aircraft and 50 armed helicopters. It has nine
bases including one under construction. The Air Force
has 701 combat aircraft and 22 armed helicopters.
   India exploded its first nuclear weapon in 1974 and is
since believed to have acquired a stockpile of nuclear
arms. It conducted further nuclear tests in May 1998. In
1993–4 India successfully test-fired its intermediate-
range 'Agni' and 'Prithvi' ballistic missiles, and the latter
went into production in September 1997.
MILITARY EXPENDITURE – 2.9 per cent of GDP (2001)
MILITARY PERSONNEL – 1,298,000: Army 1,100,000,
   Navy 53,000, Air Force 145,000; Paramilitaries
   1,089,700

ECONOMY

Agriculture, forestry and fishing supports about 75 per
cent of the population, and contribute 30 per cent of
GDP. Production has grown by 2.67 per cent each year
since 1951, remaining slightly ahead of the 2 per cent
increase necessary to keep pace with the rising
population. Food crops occupy three-quarters of the total
cultivated area. The main food crops are rice, cereals
(principally wheat) and pulses. The major cash crops
include sugar cane, jute, cotton and tea. Other products
include oil seeds, spices, groundnuts, soya bean, tobacco,
rubber and coffee. Livestock is raised, principally for
dairy purposes or for the hides.

Industry is based on the exploitation and processing of
mineral resources, principally coal, oil and iron, and on
the production of textiles.
   The manufacture of paper, cement, pharmaceuticals,
chemicals, fertilisers, petrochemicals, motor vehicles and
commercial vehicles has been expanded. Other principal
manufactures are those derived from agricultural products, textiles, jute goods, sugar and leather, which along
with tea, tobacco, rubber, fish and iron ore are major
exports. India's information technology industry grew
rapidly in the 1990s, reaching sales of $US8.3 billion in
2000 when it comprised 15 per cent of the country's
exports.
   The main exports are textiles, gemstones and jewellery,
chemical products, agricultural produce, engineering
products, leather goods, marine products and ores and
minerals.
   GDP has been rising by about 7 per cent per annum,
but growth has been concentrated in the more prosperous
western and southern states, increasing regional
inequalities.
   In 2000 there was a trade deficit of US$12,193
million and a current account deficit of US$4,198
million. In 2001 imports totalled US$49,618 million
and exports US$43,611 million.
GNP – US$454,800 million (2000); US$450 per capita
   (2000)
GDP – US$477,555 million (2001); US$476 per capita
   (2000)
ANNUAL AVERAGE GROWTH OF GDP – 7.2 per cent
   (1999)
INFLATION RATE – 4.0 per cent (2000)
TOTAL EXTERNAL DEBT – US$99,062 million (2000)

Trade with UK	2001	2002
Imports from UK	£1,782,058,000	£1,768,288,000
Exports to UK	1,884,054,000	1,870,245,000

COMMUNICATIONS

The International Airports Authority manages five
international airports: Indira Gandhi (Delhi/Dilli), Sahar
(Bombay/Mumbai), Dum Dum (Calcutta/Kolkata),
Meenambakkam (Madras/Chennai) and
Triruvananthapuram. The other 88 aerodromes are
controlled and operated by the Civil Aviation
Department of the government. The national airlines are
Indian Airlines (internal) and Air India (international).
   India has the world's most extensive rail network
comprising of some 62,500 km of which 31 per cent is
electrified. The railways are grouped into nine
administrative zones, Southern, Central, Western,
Northern, North-Eastern, North-East Frontier, Eastern,
South-Eastern and South-Central; there is also the
Konkan Railway which links Bombay/Mumbai and
Mangalore. The total length of the road network is about
3,319,644 km of which 1,334,078 km is surfaced. The
national highway system comprises 51,966 km of roads.
   The chief seaports are Bombay/Mumbai, Jawahar Lal
Nehru, Calcutta/Kolkata, Haldia, Madras/Chennai,
Mormugao, Cochin, Visakhapatnam, Kandla, Paradip,
Mangalore, Ennore and Tuticorin.

INDONESIA

Republik Indonesia - Republic of Indonesia

AREA – 696,769 sq. miles (1,811,600 sq. km). Indonesia shares borders with Malaysia (on Borneo) and Papua New Guinea (on New Guinea)

POPULATION – 214,840,000 (2001): 87 per cent Muslim, with Christian, Buddhist, Hindu and Animist minorities. Bahasa Indonesian, a variant of Malay, is the national language, although more than 250 dialects are spoken

CAPITAL – ΨJakarta (population, 8,347,083, 2000 estimate)

MAJOR CITIES – (Java) Bandung (2,136,260), ΨSemarang (1,348,803), ΨSurabaya (2,599,796); (Kalimantan) Banjarmasin (527,415), ΨPontianak (464,534); (Maluku) Ambon (186,911); (Sulawesi) ΨUjung Pandang (1,100,019); (Sumatra) Medan (1,904,273), Palembang (1,451,419), 2000 estimates

CURRENCY – Rupiah (Rp) of 100 sen

NATIONAL ANTHEM – Indonesia Raya (Great Indonesia)

NATIONAL DAY – 17 August (Anniversary of Proclamation of Independence)

NATIONAL FLAG – Equal bands of red over white

LIFE EXPECTANCY (years) – 67 (2001)

POPULATION GROWTH RATE – 1.5 per cent

POPULATION DENSITY – 119 per sq. km (2001)

URBAN POPULATION – 42 per cent (2001)

ILLITERACY RATE – (m) 8.1 per cent; (f) 17.9 per cent (2000)

ENROLMENT (percentage of age group) – primary 100 per cent (1997); secondary 56 per cent (1997); tertiary 56 per cent (1997)

Indonesia comprises the islands of Java, Madura, Sumatra, the Riouw-Lingga archipelago, Bangka and Billiton, part of the island of Borneo (Kalimantan), Sulawesi (formerly Celebes), Maluku (formerly Moluccas), the islands of Bali, Lombok, Sumbawa, Sumba, Flores and others comprising the provinces of East and West Nusa Tenggara and the western half of the islands of New Guinea (Irian Jaya) and Timor.

HISTORY AND POLITICS

From the early part of the 17th century much of the Indonesian archipelago was under Dutch rule. Following the Second World War, during which the archipelago was occupied by the Japanese, a strong nationalistic movement formed and, after sporadic fighting, all the former Dutch East Indies except western New Guinea became independent as Indonesia on 27 December 1949. Western New Guinea became part of Indonesia in 1963 under the name West Irian (now Irian Jaya), this interpretation being confirmed in an 'Act of Free Choice' in July 1969.

Rampant inflation and high food and fuel prices provoked civil unrest during 1997, and by April 1998 riots and protests calling for Gen. Suharto's resignation as president were frequent. On 21 May 1998, he announced he would step down. He was replaced by his deputy B. J. Habibie.

The Golkar Party was defeated in the general election of 7 June 1999, in which the Indonesian Democratic Struggle Party (PDI-P) led by Megawati Sukarnoputri, daughter of Indonesia's first president, gained 37.4 per cent of the vote and won the greatest number of seats. The new government elected Abdurrahman Wahid, the

leader of the National Awakening Party (PKB), as president and Megawati Sukarnoputri was voted vice-president. A coalition government was formed, consisting of the PDI-P, PKB, and the National Mandate Party.

President Wahid was formally censured by the House of Representatives on 1 February 2001 and again on 30 April following a report which had implicated him in two financial scandals. Although he was cleared on 28 May of involvement in the scandals, relations between the president and the legislature had become untenable. On 30 May, the House of Representatives voted overwhelmingly to convene a special session of the People's Consultative Assembly to begin impeachment proceedings against President Wahid; the proceedings began on 20 July and resulted in his dismissal from office on 23 July. Megawati Sukarnoputri, who had been the vice-president, was immediately sworn in as his successor.

On 10 August 2002 the House of Representatives passed amendments to the constitution introducing direct elections for the president and vice-president who had formerly been elected by the People's Consultative Assembly.

FEDERAL STRUCTURE

There are 24 provinces, two special regions and a special capital region.

State	Area (sq. km)	Population (2000 census)	Capital
PROVINCES			
Aceh*	55,392	3,930,905	Banda Aceh
Sumatera Utara	70,787	11,649,655	Medan
Sumatera Barat	49,778	4,248,931	Padang
Riau	94,561	4,957,627	Pakanbaru
Jambi	44,800	2,413,846	Jambi
Sumatera Selatan	103,688	6,899,675	Palembang
Bengkulu	21,168	1,567,432	Bengkulu
Lampung	33,307	6,741,439	Tanjungkarang
Jakarta Raya†	661	8,389,443	Jakarta
Jawa Barat	46,229	35,729,537	Bandung
Jawa Tengah	34,206	31,228,940	Semarang
Yogyakarta*	3,169	3,122,268	Yogyakarta
Jawa Timur	47,921	34,783,640	Surabaya
Bali	5,561	3,151,162	Denpasar
Nusa Tenggara Barat	20,177	4,009,261	Mataram
Nusa Tenggara Timur	47,876	3,952,279	Kupang
Kalimantan Barat	146,760	4,034,198	Pontianak
Kalimantan Tengah	152,600	1,857,000	Palangkaraya
Kalimantan Selatan	37,660	2,985,240	Banjarmasin
Kalimantan Timur	210,985	2,455,120	Samarinda
Sulawesi Utara	19,023	2,012,098	Menado
Sulawesi Tengah	69,726	2,218,435	Palu
Sulawesi Selatan	72,781	8,059,627	Ujung Pandang
Sulawesi Tenggara	27,686	1,821,284	Kendari
Maluku	74,505	1,205,539	Amboina
Irian Jaya	421,981	2,220,934	Jayapura

* Special Region

† Special Capital City Region

INSURGENCIES

In Irian Jaya government forces are fighting the Papua Independent Organisation (OPM) guerrillas who claim the 1969 referendum was rigged and oppose Indonesian settlement. In northern Sumatra the Free Aceh Movement (GAM) is an active, armed organisation. On 7–8 November 1999, a crowd of at least 500,000 people demonstrated in the provincial capital Banda Aceh calling for independence for Aceh. Following a series of violent incidents between separatists and the armed forces, a cease-fire began on 2 June 2000, which lasted until 15 February 2001.

A peace agreement was signed in Geneva on 9 December 2002 between the government and GAM representatives stipulating an internationally monitored cease-fire and providing for autonomy and free elections in Aceh in return for the disarmament of GAM. However, after further violence in early 2003, the peace talks broke down; on 19 May 2003 government forces launched a military offensive in Aceh and martial law was imposed.

Periodic outbursts of violence between Christians and Muslims in Maluku province occurred in 1999 and 2000. The violence intensified in May 2000, following the arrival in Maluku of Laskar Jihad, a group of over 2,000 militant Islamic fighters from other parts of Indonesia. The group disbanded in October 2002.

In Central Kalimantan province, violence occurred in 1999 between indigenous Dayaks and immigrants from the island of Madura. An outbreak of further attacks in 2001 led to the displacement of some 77,000 Madurese.

On 12 February 2002, Christian and Muslim leaders from the eastern Molucca islands (the provinces of Maluku and North Maluku) signed a peace agreement to end three years of sectarian fighting in which 5,000 people had been killed since January 1999.

On 12 October 2002 a terrorist attack on a tourist resort in Bali killed at least 184 people and injured more than 300. The extremist Islamic terror organisation, Jemaah Islamiah alleged to have links with al Qa'eda, was believed to be responsible for the bombings and a number of arrests were made. On 7 August 2003 Amrozi bin Nurhasyim was found guilty of conspiring, planning and carrying out the bombings and sentenced to death.

HEAD OF STATE

President, Megawati Sukarnoputri, *sworn* in 23 July 2001
Vice-President, Hamzah Haz

CABINET *as at July 2003*
Co-ordinating Minister for the Economy, Dorodjatun Kuntjoro Jakti
Co-ordinating Minister for People's Welfare, Yusuf Kalla
Co-ordinating Minister for Political, Social and Security Affairs, Susilo Bambang Yudhoyono
Agriculture, Bungaran Saragih
Defence, Mathori Abdul Djalil
Energy and Mineral Resources, Puronomo Yusgiantoro
Finance, Budiono
Foreign Affairs, Hasan Wirayuda
Forestry, M. Prakosa
Health, Ahmad Sujudi
Home Affairs, Hari Sabarno
Housing and Regional Infrastructure, Soenarno
Industry and Trade, Rini Suwandi
Justice and Human Rights, Yusril Ihza Mahendra
Manpower and Transmigration, Jacob Nuwawea
Maritime Affairs and Fisheries, Rokhmin Dahuri
National Education, Malik Fajar
Religious Affairs, Said Agil Munawar
Social Affairs, Bachtiar Chamsyah
Transport and Telecommunications, Gen. Agum Gumelar

INDONESIAN EMBASSY
38 Grosvenor Square, London W1K 2HW
Tel: 020-7499 7661
Ambassador Extraordinary and Plenipotentiary, vacant
Chargé d'Affaires, Nicholas Tandy Dammen

BRITISH EMBASSY
Jalan M. H. Thamrin 75, Jakarta 10310
Tel: (00 62) (21) 315 6264
Ambassador Extraordinary and Plenipotentiary,
  HE Richard Gozney, CMG, apptd 2000

BRITISH COUNCIL DIRECTOR, Dr Richard Phillips
S. Widjojo Centre, Jalan Jenderal Sudirman Kav 71,
Jakarta 12190. Tel: (00 62) (21) 252 4115
Email: information@britishcouncil.or.id

DEFENCE

The Army has 481 armoured personnel carriers, 11 armoured infantry fighting vehicles and 11 aircraft. The Navy has two submarines, 17 frigates, 36 patrol and coastal vessels and 17 armed helicopters. There are five principal naval bases. The Air Force has 90 combat aircraft.

MILITARY EXPENDITURE – 0.6 per cent of GDP (2001)
MILITARY PERSONNEL – 297,000: Army 230,000, Navy 40,000, Air Force 27,000; Paramilitaries 195,000
CONSCRIPTION DURATION – Two years (selective)

ECONOMY

Oil and liquefied natural gas are the most important assets. Timber is the second largest foreign exchange earner after oil. Indonesia is rich in minerals, particularly tin, of which the country is the world's third biggest producer; coal, nickel and bauxite are the other principal mineral products. There are also considerable deposits of gold, silver, manganese phosphates and sulphur.

Principal exports are petroleum, textiles and clothing, timber, natural gas and rubber. Principal imports are machinery and transport equipment, electrical equipment and chemicals.

Indonesia was one of the countries worst affected by the Asian economic crisis, which began in the latter half of 1997; the ensuing high unemployment and inflation have led to widespread political and inter-ethnic unrest. Tourism is important but separatist violence and terrorist acts such as the Bali bombing have led to a decline in this industry.

In 2000 there was a trade surplus of US$25,040 million and a current account surplus of US$7,985 million. Imports totalled US$33,515 million and exports US$62,124 million.

GNP – US$119,871 million (2000); US$570 per capita (2000)
GDP – US$145,306 million (2001); US$723 per capita (2000)
ANNUAL AVERAGE GROWTH OF GDP – 4.8 per cent (2000)
INFLATION RATE – 3.7 per cent (2000)
UNEMPLOYMENT – 5.5 per cent (1998)
TOTAL EXTERNAL DEBT – US$141,803 million (2000)

Trade with UK	2001	2002
Imports from UK	£311,721,000	£327,163,000
Exports to UK	1,189,763,000	1,076,944,000

COMMUNICATIONS

There are railway systems in Java, Sumatra and Madura linking the main towns. There are about 346,863 km of roads, of which 151,151 km are paved.

Sea communications are maintained by the state-run shipping companies Jakarta-Lloyd (ocean-going) and PELNI (coastal and inter-island) and other small concerns. Transport by small craft on the rivers of the larger islands plays an important part in trade.

Air services are operated by Garuda Indonesian Airways and other local airlines, and Jakarta is served by various international services.

IRAN

Jomhûri-ye-Eslâmi-ye-Îrân - Islamic Republic of Iran

AREA – 623,846 sq. miles (1,622,000 sq. km).
   Neighbours: Armenia, Azerbaijan, Turkmenistan (north), Afghanistan (north-east), Pakistan (south-east), Iraq (south-west), Turkey (north-west)
POPULATION – 71,369,000 (2001): 99 per cent Muslims (Shia 89 per cent and Sunni 10 per cent) with small minorities of Zoroastrians, Jews, and Armenian and Assyrian Christians. The official language is Persian (Farsi). Minority languages are Turkic (26 per cent), Kurdish (9 per cent), Luri (2 per cent), Arabic, Baluchi and Turkish (1 per cent each)
CAPITAL – Tehran (population 6,758,845, 1996 census)
MAJOR CITIES – Ahwaz (804,980); Esfahan (1,266,072); Mashhad (1,887,405); Qom (777,677); Shiraz (1,053,025); Tabriz (1,191,043), 1996 census
CURRENCY – Rial
NATIONAL ANTHEM – Sorûd-E Jomhûri-Ye Eslâmi (Anthem Of The Islamic Republic Of Iran)
NATIONAL DAY – 11 February
NATIONAL FLAG – Three horizontal stripes of green, white, red, with the slogan Allahu Akbar repeated 22 times along the edges of the green and red stripes, and the national emblem in the centre
LIFE EXPECTANCY (years) – 69 (2001)
POPULATION GROWTH RATE – 1.8 per cent
POPULATION DENSITY – 44 per sq. km (2001)
URBAN POPULATION – 65 per cent (2001)

HISTORY AND POLITICS

Iran was ruled from the end of the 18th century by Shahs of the Qajar dynasty. In 1925 the last of the dynasty, Sultan Ahmed Shah, was deposed in his absence by the National Assembly, which handed executive power to Prime Minister Reza Khan. Reza Khan was elected Shah as Reza Shah Pahlavi by the Constituent Assembly in December 1925. In 1941 Reza Shah abdicated in favour of the Crown Prince, who ascended the throne as Mohammed Reza Shah Pahlavi.

In January 1979, the Shah left Iran, handing over power to the Prime Minister, who was ousted by Ayatollah Khomeini, the spiritual leader of the Shia Muslims, on his return from exile. Following a national referendum, an Islamic Republic was declared on 1 April 1979. A new constitution, providing for a president, prime minister, Consultative Assembly, and leadership by Ayatollah Khomeini, was approved by referendum in December 1979. In June 1989 Khomeini died and President Khamenei was appointed Leader of the Islamic Republic. Hojatolislam Ali Akbar Hashemi Rafsanjani was elected president in July 1989, and the post of prime minister was abolished. The 1997 presidential election

was won by Mohammad Khatami, leader of a centre-left coalition. He was seen as a moderate, and since his election has attempted to pursue reformist policies, although these have often been blocked by the conservative clerical establishment. Iran and the UK re-established full diplomatic relations in May 1999. The three rounds of elections to the Majlis held on 18 February, 5 May and 30 May 2000 gave a large majority to reformist candidates. The presidential election on 8 June 2001 resulted in the re-election of Mohammad Khatami, who obtained over 76 per cent of the vote; there were nine other candidates.

FOREIGN RELATIONS

Iran was at war with Iraq following the Iraqi invasion of Iran in September 1980. International efforts to end the fighting resulted in a cease-fire in August 1988. In August 1990 Iraq accepted Iran's conditions for settling the conflict, including a return to the 1975 border, but a formal peace treaty has not been signed.

Relations between Iran and the USA became tense in September 2002 after Russian technicians began the construction of Iran's first nuclear reactor at Bushehr. In December American officials accused Iran of the secret development of two nuclear plants capable of producing nuclear weapons. Iran denied the accusation, but announced in February 2003 that uranium had been discovered and extracted for the production of nuclear energy for peaceful purposes only.

POLITICAL SYSTEM

The leader of the republic is elected by the Council of Experts whose 83 members are popularly elected every eight years. The president, who is the chief executive, is directly elected for a four-year term, renewable once. Ministers are nominated by the president and must obtain a vote of confidence in the Majlis. The Majlis comprises 290 representatives who are directly elected for a four-year term. Laws passed by the Majlis must be approved by the 12-member Guardian Council. In November 1997, President Khatami announced the establishment of the Committee for the Implementation and Supervision of the Constitution, a five-member body to ensure the constitution was abided by and that people's rights were respected.

Spiritual Leader of the Islamic Republic and C.-in-C. of
   Armed Forces, Ayatollah Seyed Ali Khamenei,
   appointed June 1989
President, Seyed Mohammad Khatami, *elected* 23 May
   1997, *re-elected* 8 June 2001
First Vice-President, Mohammad Reza Aref
Vice-Presidents, Mohammad Baqerian; Mohammed Ali
   Najafi *(Advisers to the President);* Gholamreza
   Aqazadeh *(Atomic Energy);* Abdollah Nouri
   (Development and Social Affairs); Masoumeh Ebtekar
   (Environmental Protection); Mohammad Ali Abtahi
   (Legal and Parliamentary Affairs); Mohsen
   Mehrali-Zadeh *(Physical Education)*

COUNCIL OF MINISTERS *as at July 2003*
Administration and Planning, Mohammad Sattarifar
Agricultural Jihad, Mahmoud Hojjati
Commerce, Mohammad Shariatmadari
Co-operatives, Ali Sufi
Culture and Islamic Guidance, Ahmad Masjed-Jame'i
Defence and Logistics, Adm. Ali Shamkhani
Economic Affairs and Finance, Tahmasb Mazaheri
Education, Morteza Haji

Energy, Habibollah Bitaraf
Foreign Affairs, Kamal Kharrazi
Health, Massoud Pezeshkian
Higher Education, Science and Research, Mostafa Moin
Housing and Urban Development, Ali Abol-Alizadeh
Industries and Mines, Es'haq Jahangiri
Information, Ali Yunesi
Information and Communications Technology, Ahmad
  Mo'tamedi
Interior, Chair of State Security Council, Abdulvahed
  Moussavi-Lari
Justice, Hojatolislam Ismail Shostari
Labour and Social Affairs, Safdar Hoseyni
Oil, Bijan Namdar Zanganeh
Roads and Transport, Ahmad Khorram

EMBASSY OF THE ISLAMIC REPUBLIC OF IRAN
16 Prince's Gate, London SW7 1PT
Tel: 020-7225 3000
Ambassador Extraordinary and Plenipotentiary,
  HE Morteza Sarmadi, apptd 2000

BRITISH EMBASSY
143 Ferdowsi Avenue, PO Box 11365–4474, Tehran 11344
Tel: (00 98) (21) 670 5011
Ambassador Extraordinary and Plenipotentiary,
  HE Richard Dalton, CMG, apptd 2002

DEFENCE
The Army has around 1,565 main battle tanks, 590
armoured personnel carriers, 750 armoured infantry
fighting vehicles and 50 attack helicopters. The Navy has
six submarines, three frigates, 56 patrol and coastal
vessels, five combat aircraft and 19 armed helicopters.
There are seven naval bases. The Air Force has some 306
combat aircraft, of which about 60–80 per cent are
serviceable.
MILITARY EXPENDITURE – 5.8 per cent of GDP (2001)
MILITARY PERSONNEL – 520,000: Army 325,000,
  Revolutionary Guard Corps 125,000, Navy 18,000,
  Air Force 52,000; Paramilitaries 40,000
CONSCRIPTION DURATION – 21 months

ECONOMY
Wheat is the principal agricultural crop; other important
crops are barley, rice, cotton, sugar beet, fruit, nuts and
vegetables. Wool is also a major product.
  In addition to oil, the principal industrial products are
carpets, textiles, sugar, cement and other construction
materials, ginned cotton, vegetable oil and other food
products, leather and shoes, metal manufactures,
pharmaceuticals, motor vehicles, fertilisers and plastics.
Privatisation began in 1991.
  It was announced in April 2000 that reserves of gas
had been found in the Gavband region with an estimated
value of US$16,500 million.
  In 2000 there was a trade surplus of US$13,138
million and a current account surplus of US$12,645
million. Imports totalled US$14,296 million and exports
US$28,345 million.
GNP – US$106,707 million (2000); US$1,680 per
  capita (2000)
GDP – US$118,868 million (2001); US$4,690 per
  capita (2000)
ANNUAL AVERAGE GROWTH OF GDP – 2.1 per cent
  (1998)
INFLATION RATE – 14.5 per cent (2000)
TOTAL EXTERNAL DEBT – US$7,953 million (2000)

TRADE
Imports are mainly industrial and agricultural machinery,
motor vehicles and components for assembly, iron and
steel, electrical machinery and goods, foodstuffs and
certain textile fabrics and yarns. The principal exports,
apart from oil and gas, are carpets and fruit. Japan,
Germany, France, the UAE and Italy are Iran's main
trading partners.

Trade with UK	2001	2002
Imports from UK	£430,841,000	£401,728,000
Exports to UK	29,553,000	35,918,000

COMMUNICATIONS
Tehran is the centre of a network of highways linking the
major towns, ports, the Caspian Sea and the national
frontiers; there were 168,000 km of roads in 2001.
  The Trans-Iranian Railway runs from Bandar
Turcoman, on the Caspian Sea, via Tehran to Bandar
Khomeini, on the Persian Gulf. Other lines link Tehran
with Tabriz and Mashhad; Tabriz to Julfa; Zahedan to
Quetta; Ahvaz to Khorramshahr; Qom to Kerman; and
Bandar Turcoman to Gorgan. The rail system is linked to
the Turkish system via Van. A track between Mashhad
and Tedzhen in Turkmenistan, opened in May 1996, has
re-established the ancient Silk Route between China and
the Mediterranean; there were 8,000 km of railway track
in 2001.

EDUCATION AND CULTURE
Since 1943 primary education has been compulsory and
free. There are 48 universities in Iran. The educational
system has been reformed following the revolution.
  Persian or Farsi is an Indo-European language with
many Arabic elements added; the alphabet is mainly
Arabic, with writing from right to left.
ILLITERACY RATE – (m) 16.5 per cent; (f) 30.1 per cent
  (2000)
ENROLMENT (percentage of age group) – primary 98
  per cent (1997); secondary 77 per cent (1997); tertiary
  18 per cent (1997)

IRAQ

Al-Jumhūriyya al-`Irāqiyya – Republic of Iraq

AREA – 168,231 sq. miles (437,400 sq. km).
  Neighbours: Iran (east), Saudi Arabia, Kuwait (south),
  Jordan (west), Syria (north-west), Turkey (north)
POPULATION – 23,584,000 (2001), 16,278,316 (1987
  census). The official language is Arabic. Minority
  languages include Kurdish (about 15 per cent), Turkic
  and Aramaic
CAPITAL – Baghdad (population, 3,841,268, 1987)
MAJOR CITIES – ΨAl-Basra (406,296); Kirkuk
  (418,624); Al-Mawsil (664,221)
CURRENCY – Iraqi dinar (ID) of 1,000 fils
NATIONAL ANTHEM – Land Of Two Rivers
NATIONAL DAY – 9 April (Overthrow of Ba'ath regime
  of Saddam Hussein)
NATIONAL FLAG – Three horizontal stripes of red, white,
  black; on the white stripe three stars and the slogan
  Allahu Akbar all in green
LIFE EXPECTANCY (years) – 63 (2001)
POPULATION GROWTH RATE – 2.8 per cent
POPULATION DENSITY – 54 per sq. km (2001)
URBAN POPULATION – 68 per cent (2001)

ILLITERACY RATE – (m) 34.4 per cent; (f) 54.1 per cent (2000)
ENROLMENT (percentage of age group) – primary 85 per cent (1997); secondary 42 per cent (1997); tertiary 11.2 per cent (1995)

HISTORY AND POLITICS

Iraq is the site of the remains of several ancient civilisations: one site at Tel Hassuna, near Shura, dates back to 5000 BC; Tel Abu Shahrain near 'Ur of the Chaldees' is the site of the Sumerian city of Eridu; the ancient city of Hillah, 70 miles south of Baghdād, is near the site of Babylon and the Tower of Babel. Al-Mawsil governorate covers a great part of the ancient kingdom of Assyria, the ruins of Nineveh, the Assyrian capital, being visible on the banks of the Tigris, opposite Al-Mawsil. Qurna, at the junction of the Tigris and Euphrates, is traditionally supposed to be the site of the Garden of Eden.

Iraq was part of the Ottoman empire from 1534 until it was captured by British forces in 1916. A provisional government was set up in 1920, and in 1921 the Emir Faisal was elected King of Iraq. The country was a monarchy until July 1958, when King Faisal II was assassinated. From 1958 to 2003 Iraq was under the rule of the Ba'ath Party.

FOREIGN RELATIONS

Iraq invaded Iran in September 1980 and was at war until the August 1988 cease-fire. A formal peace treaty has not been signed.

Iraq invaded Kuwait on 2 August 1990 and declared Kuwait a province of Iraq. The UN Security Council declared the annexation void and in January 1991, an alliance of NATO and Middle East countries launched an offensive and liberated Kuwait in February 1991.

A United Nations Special Committee (UNSCOM), charged with securing Iraq's full nuclear, biological and chemical disarmament, was frequently hindered in its task by Iraqi officials.

In December 1999, the UN Security Council created a new weapons inspection body, the UN Monitoring, Verification and Inspection Commission (UNMOVIC), to replace UNSCOM. UNMOVIC was to monitor the elimination of Iraq's nuclear, chemical and biological weapons arsenal and was empowered to suspend all sanctions for four-month renewable phases if the Iraqi authorities co-operated fully with UNMOVIC and the IAEA within a whole 120-day period.

Tensions rose between Iraq and the USA and the UK in September 2002 and in November UN weapons inspectors returned to Iraq backed by a UN resolution warning of consequences if Iraq was found to be in 'material breach' of its terms. Inspections continued into early 2003 and on 7 March UN chief weapons inspector Hans Blix stated that although Iraq was co-operating with the UN, the inspectors needed more time to verify the country's compliance. The situation deteriorated rapidly and on 17 March the UK's ambassador to the UN declared that the diplomatic process on Iraq had ended. On the same day US president George Bush gave Iraqi leader Saddam Hussein 48 hours to leave Iraq with his family and the UN weapons inspectors were evacuated.

A US-led coalition began a bombing campaign against Iraq on 20 March. Baghdad fell to coalition forces on 9 April, Kirkuk on 10 April and the last Ba'athist stronghold of Tikrit on 14 April. On 1 May US President George Bush declared hostilities to be over.

On 22 May the UN Security Council approved a resolution recognising the US-led Coalition Provisional Authority (CPA), headed by Paul Bremner, as the occupying authority in Iraq and economic sanctions were lifted. On 13 July the 25-member Interim Governing Council, appointed by the CPA, met for the first time in Baghdad. Since the end of major combat operations on 1 May 2003 attacks on coalition forces have increased and by 27 August the number of US deaths since the end of hostilities had surpassed the number killed during the war. On 7 August a bomb attack on the Jordanian embassy in Baghdad killed 11 people. A second bomb attack on the UN's headquarters in Baghdad on 19 August killed 20 people including the UN's special envoy to Iraq, Sergio Viera de Mello. A third major attack on a Shiite mosque in Najaf on 29 August killed 85 and injured over 140 people. As at the end of August 2003 the whereabouts of Saddam Hussein remained unknown. (For further updates *see* International Events section.)

INSURGENCIES

Following the allied victory in Kuwait in February 1991, rebellion broke out in the Kurdish north and the Shi'ite south. A UN safe haven in northern Iraq to protect the Kurdish population and air exclusion zones north of the 36th parallel and south of the 33rd parallel were also established. Iraqi aircraft frequently violated the air exclusion zones; allied forces responded by attacking Iraqi air defence installations.

POLITICAL SYSTEM

The Ba'ath Party and institutions of the former regime were abolished by the US administration in May 2003 and a broad-based 25-member Interim Governing Council was appointed by the CPA and inaugurated on 13 July 2003. Its activities include the appointment of interim ministers, working with the CPA on policy and budgets and the establishment of procedures to write a new constitution. Any decisions made by the council are subject to the approval of the US administrator in Iraq. It was decided on 30 July 2003 that the council would have a rotating presidency among nine of its members, with each member serving as president for one month at a time. A constitutional assembly of up to 250 people was expected to be named by late September 2003 to produce a draft constitution, which will then be voted on by Iraqis with elections following some time after that. *Administrator of the Coalition Provisional Authority,*
Paul Bremner, *appointed* 12 May 2003

INTERIM GOVERNING COUNCIL *as at July 2003*
Rotating Presidents: Ibrahim al-Jafari (Shia, Arab, Da'wa); Ahmad Chalabi (Shia, Arab, INC); Muhammad Bahr al-Ulum (Shia, Arab, Ahl al-Bayt); Abd al-Aziz al-Hakim (Shia, Arab, SCIRI); Jalal Talabani (Sunni, Kurd, PUK); Masud Barzani (Sunni, Kurd, KDP); Iyad Alawi (Shia, Arab, INA); Adnan Bajaji (Sunni, Arab, IDM); Muhsin Abd al-Hamid (Sunni, Arab, IIP)
Members: Ahmad Shyaa al-Barak al-Bu Sultan (Shia, Arab, ILU); Nasir Kamil al-Jadurji (Sunni, Arab, NDP); Aqila al-Hashimi (Shia, Arab), Raja Habib al-Khuzai (Shia, Arab); Hamid Majid Musa (Shia, Arab, ICP); Ghazi Mashal Ajil al-Yawir (Sunni, Arab); Samir Shakir Mahmud (Sunni, Arab); Mahmud Ali Uthman (Sunni Kurd); Salah al-Din Muhammad Baha' al Din (Sunni, Kurd, KIU); Younadem Yusif Kana (Assyrian Christian, ADM); Muafak al-Rubiyi (Shia, Arab); Dara Nur Alzin (Sunni, Kurd); Shunkul Habib Umar (Turkoman, IWO);

Wail Abd al-Latif (Shia, Arab); Abd al-Karim Mahmud al Muhammadawi (Shia, Arab, Hizbullah); Izz al-Din Salim (Shia, Arab, IDB)

ADM Assyrian Democratic Movement; ICP Iraqi Communist Party; IDB Islamic Da'wa of Basra; IDM Independent Democrats Movement; IIP Iraqi Islamic Party; ILU Iraqi Lawyers' Union; INA Iraqi National Accord; INC Iraqi National Congress; IWO Iraqi Women's Organisation; KDP Kurdistan Democratic Party; KIU Kurdistan Islamic Union; NDP National Democratic Party; PUK Patriotic Union of Kurdistan; SCIRI Supreme Council of the Islamic Revolution in Iraq.

IRAQI DIPLOMATIC MISSION IN LONDON
Since Iraq's breach of diplomatic relations with Britain in February 1991, the Jordanian Embassy has handled Iraqi interests in the UK.

BRITISH DIPLOMATIC REPRESENTATION
The British Embassy was closed in January 1991. The Russian Embassy has since handled British interests in Iraq.

ECONOMY
Iraq's major industry is oil production which was nationalised in 1972.

Agricultural production is important, with two harvests usually gathered in a year, depending on rainfall. Salinity and soil erosion limit productivity.

The UN imposed economic sanctions and a world-wide ban on Iraqi oil exports in August 1990. In May 1996, Iraq agreed to a UN-proposed 'oil-for-food' deal, permitting the sale of oil to buy food and medicine. Limited oil exports resumed in December 1996. On 14 May 2002, the UN revised the oil-for-food programme, allowing Iraq to import all humanitarian goods apart from those deemed to be of military use. Following the overthrow of Saddam Hussein's regime by US-led coalition in April 2003, UN economic sanctions were lifted on 22 May 2003. An estimated US$30 billion is needed to rebuild Iraqi's shattered infrastructure.
GDP – US$73,848 million (1998); US$3,352 per capita (2000)
ANNUAL AVERAGE GROWTH OF GDP – 15.0 per cent (1998)

TRADE
The principal imports are normally iron and steel, military equipment, building materials, mechanical and electrical machinery, motor vehicles, textiles and clothing, essential foodstuffs and raw industrial materials. The chief exports are normally crude petroleum, dates, raw wool, raw hides and skins and raw cotton.

Free trade agreements have been signed with Egypt, Syria and Tunisia, which were to be put into effect when UN sanctions were lifted.

Trade with UK	2001	2002
Imports from UK	£60,596,000	£47,078,000
Exports to UK	865,000	95,000

COMMUNICATIONS
The port of Al-Baṣra has not been used since the outbreak of hostilities with Iran in 1980. Continuous dredging of the Shatt-al-Arab has also been suspended by hostilities and the channel has seriously silted. The port of Umm Qasr on the Kuwaiti border, which was developed for freight and sulphur handling and includes a container terminal, was opened in late 1993.

Iraqi Republican Railways provided regular passenger and goods services between Al-Baṣra, Baghdad and Al-Mawsil. There is also a metre gauge rail line connecting Baghdad with Khanaqin, Kirkūk and Arbil. Iraqi communications were greatly affected by the Gulf War; large numbers of bridges were destroyed and the railway system extensively disrupted.

IRELAND

Éire / Ireland

AREA – 26,500 sq. miles (68,900 sq. km). Neighbour: Northern Ireland (north)
POPULATION – 3,917,336 (2002 census). In 2000 religious adherence as a percentage of the population was: Roman Catholic 87.2%, Protestant 0.9%, Anglican 3.7%. Irish is the first official language; English is recognised as a second official language, but is more commonly used
CAPITAL – ΨDublin *(Baile Átha Cliath)* (population, 1.122,600, 2002 census)
MAJOR CITIES – ΨCork *(Corcaigh)* (123,338); ΨGalway *(Gaillimh)* (65,774); ΨLimerick *(Luimheach)* (54,058); Waterford *(Port Láirge)* (44,564), 2002 census
CURRENCY – Euro (€) of 100 cents
NATIONAL ANTHEM – Amhrán na bhFiann (The Soldier's Song)
NATIONAL DAY – 17 March (St Patrick's Day)
NATIONAL FLAG – Equal vertical stripes of green, white and orange
LIFE EXPECTANCY (years) – 77 (2001)
POPULATION GROWTH RATE – 0.8 per cent
POPULATION DENSITY – 56 per sq. km (2001)
URBAN POPULATION – 59 per cent (2001)
MILITARY EXPENDITURE – 0.5 per cent of GDP (2001)
MILITARY PERSONNEL – 10,460: Army 8,500, Navy 1,100, Air Force 860

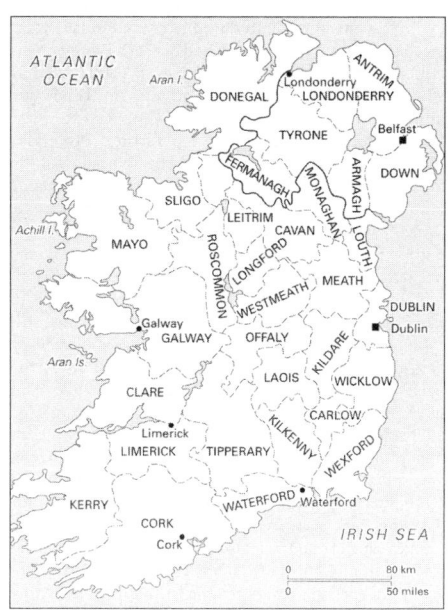

Ireland is separated from Scotland by the North Channel and from England and Wales by the Irish Sea and St George's Channel. The greatest length of the island, from north-east to south-west (Torr Head to Mizen Head), is 302 miles, and the greatest breadth, from east to west (Dundrum Bay to Annagh Head), is 174 miles. On the north coast of Achill Island (Co. Mayo) are the highest cliffs in the British Isles, 2,000 feet sheer above the sea.

The highest point is Carrantuohill (3,414 ft). The principal river is the Shannon (240 miles), which drains the central plain. The Slaney flows into Wexford Harbour, the Liffey to Dublin Bay, the Boyne to Drogheda, the Lee to Cork Harbour, the Blackwater to Youghal Harbour, and the Suir, Barrow and Nore to Waterford Harbour.

The principal hydrographic feature is the loughs; the Shannon chain of Allen, Boderg, Forbes, Ree and Derg, and the Erne chain of Gowna, Oughter, Lower Erne, and Erne; Melvin, Gill, Gara and Conn in the north-west; and Corrib and Mask (joined by a hidden channel) in the west.

The Republic of Ireland is divided into four provinces of 26 counties.

HISTORY AND POLITICS

The first inhabitants of Ireland crossed from Scandinavia to Britain at around 6,000 BC. The settlers were joined by Celts from central Europe from the sixth century BC until about the time of Christ. The introduction of Christianity in the fifth century is traditionally associated with St Patrick and inspired 300 years of rich cultural achievements. The Vikings, who established most of the major towns, including Dublin and Cork, invaded around AD 800 and controlled Ireland until their defeat at the Battle of Clontarf (1014) by Brian Boru, who had become king of all Ireland in 1002.

In the 12th century the Norman English invaded at the invitation of Dermod MacMurrough, the deposed king of Leinster, and established feudal control over most of the island; this lasted for 300 years. King Henry VIII of England reconquered Ireland and in 1541 declared himself king of Ireland, the first English monarch to do so. Protestantism was introduced but failed to take root, except in Ulster where English and Scottish Presbyterians settled during the reign of James I (1603–25). A rebellion initiated by Ulster Catholics in 1641 was ruthlessly crushed by Oliver Cromwell's army. Catholicism was repressed and further Protestant colonisation encouraged. Following the abdication of the Catholic King James II in 1688, Irish Protestants supported William of Orange's accession to the throne. James II was defeated in Ireland, most famously at the Battle of the Boyne (1690), and Protestant ascendancy was restored, enduring throughout the 18th century.

The Irish parliament was granted independence in 1782, although the Dublin administration was still appointed by the king. The parliament was abolished by the Act of Union in 1801 following a rebellion by the Society of the United Irishmen in 1798, and subsequently Irish MPs sat at Westminster. Demands for the restoration of the Irish parliament and home rule for Ireland were successful in 1914, but were delayed when World War I broke out. A rebellion, the Easter Rising of 1916, was suppressed by the British, fuelling support for the Sinn Féin party, which won the 1918 election in Ireland and formed a legislature in Dublin under the leadership of Eamon de Valera. The resulting two-year war of independence between the Irish Republican Army

and British forces ended in a truce, followed by negotiations leading to the signing of the Anglo-Irish Treaty in December 1921. The island was partitioned, the 26 counties of the Irish Free State accepting dominion status within the British Empire, while six of the nine counties of Ulster, where the majority Protestant population opposed home rule, remained part of the United Kingdom, governed by a Northern Ireland parliament.

Civil war broke out between the new Irish government and opponents of the treaty until a truce was reached in May 1923. Constitutional links between the Irish Free State and the UK were gradually removed by the Irish parliament and a new constitution enacted in 1937 declared that 'Ireland is a sovereign, independent, democratic state'. However, it continued in association with the states of the British Commonwealth until 1949, when constitutional links with Britain were severed.

Following the Good Friday Agreement of 10 April 1998, a referendum was held, in which 94 per cent of voters in the Irish Republic and 71 percent of voters in Northern Ireland approved the agreement. The agreement recognises that Northern Ireland remains part of the United Kingdom and shall not cease to be so without the consent of a majority of the people of Northern Ireland. Additionally, a North-South Ministerial Council, comprising officials from both countries, would meet to regulate areas of common interest.

The presidential election in October 1997 was won by Mary McAleese with almost 59 per cent of second-round votes. In the elections to the Dáil Eireann held on 17 May 2002, Fianna Fáil (FF) remained the largest party but without an overall majority. The coalition government, led by Bertie Ahern of FF, includes members of the Progressive Democrats (PD). The composition of the Dáil Eireann as at June 2002 was: FF 80; Fine Gael 31; Labour 21; PD 8; Green Party 6; Sinn Fein 5; Socialist Party 1; Independents 1.

POLITICAL SYSTEM

The president *(Uachtarán na hÉireann)* is directly elected for a term of seven years, and is eligible for a second term. The president is aided and advised by a Council of State.

The National Parliament *(Oireachtas)* consists of the president, House of Representatives *(Dáil Éireann)* and Senate *(Seanad Éireann)*. Dáil Éireann is composed of 166 members elected for a five-year term on a basis of proportional representation by means of the single transferable vote. Seanad Éireann is composed of 60 members, of whom 11 are nominated by the prime minister *(Taoiseach)* and 49 are elected, six by institutions of higher education and 43 from panels of candidates established on a vocational basis.

Executive power is vested in the government subject to the constitution. The government is responsible to the Dáil. The taoiseach is appointed by the president on the nomination of the Dáil. The other members of the government are appointed by the president on the nomination of the taoiseach with the previous approval of the Dáil. The taoiseach appoints a member of the government to be his deputy *(the tánaiste)*.

The judicial system comprises courts of first instance and a court of final appeal called the Supreme Court *(Cúirt Uachtarach)*. The courts of first instance include a High Court *(Ard-Chúirt)* and courts of local and limited jurisdiction, with a right of appeal as determined by law.

The High Court alone has original jurisdiction to consider the question of the validity of any law having regard to the provisions of the constitution. The Supreme Court has appellate jurisdiction from decisions of the High Court.

HEAD OF STATE
President, Mary McAleese, *elected* 30 October 1997, *sworn in* 11 November 1997

CABINET *as at July 2003*
Taoiseach (Prime Minister), Bertie Ahern (FF)
Tánaiste (Deputy PM), Enterprise, Trade and Employment, Mary Harney (PD)
Agriculture and Food, Joe Walsh (FF)
Arts, Sports and Tourism, John O'Donoghue (FF)
Community, Rural and Gaeltacht Affairs, Éamon Ó Cuív (FF)
Defence, Michael Smith (FF)
Education and Science, Noel Dempsey (FF)
Environment and Local Government, Martin Cullen (FF)
Finance, Charlie McCreevy (FF)
Foreign Affairs, Brian Cowen (FF)
Health and Children, Michael Martin (FF)
Justice, Equality and Law Reform, Michael McDowell (FF)
Marine and Natural Resources, Dermot Ahern (FF)
Social and Family Affairs, Mary Coughlan (FF)
Transport, Seamus Brennan (FF)

FF Fianna Fáil; PD Progressive Democrats

IRISH EMBASSY
17 Grosvenor Place, London SW1X 7HR
Tel: 020-7235 2171
Ambassador Extraordinary and Plenipotentiary, HE Dáithí O'Ceallaigh, apptd 2001

BRITISH EMBASSY
29 Merrion Road, Ballsbridge, IE-Dublin 4
Tel: (00 353) (1) 205 3700
Email: bembassy@internet-ireland.ie
Ambassador Extraordinary and Plenipotentiary, HE Stewart Eldon, CMG, OBE, apptd 2003

BRITISH COUNCIL DIRECTOR, Tony Reilly, MBE
Newmount House, 22/24 Lower Mount Street, IE-Dublin 2
Tel: (00 353) (1) 676 4088
Email: helen.jones@ie.britishcouncil.org

ECONOMY

Although industry has expanded greatly since Ireland's entry into the European Community in 1973, agriculture remains important; in 2000, 7.8 per cent of the workforce was employed in agriculture, forestry and fisheries. The main crops are wheat, barley, oats, potatoes and sugar beet. Agriculture has benefited considerably from the EU Common Agricultural Policy and support funds but has suffered from the drift of the rural population to urban areas and abroad.

The traditional brewing, spirits and food-processing sectors have expanded and have been joined by the manufacture of textiles, chemicals, pharmaceuticals, electronics, office machinery and transportation equipment. The services sector is currently the fastest-growing sector of the economy and accounted for 58 per cent of GDP and 63.1 per cent of employment in 1999. Tourism is the most important part of the service sector and in recent years has provided substantial revenue, with 6,416,000 visitors in 2000.

The Kinsale gas field off the south coast provided 28 per cent of Ireland's gas needs in 2000, with 72 per cent coming via an undersea pipeline from Moffat, Scotland. There are five government-funded milled peat power-generating stations. Hydroelectric power from the Shannon barrage and other schemes is also important but Ireland still imports 47 per cent of oil and coal for power generation. Metal content of ores raised (2000) was lead, 86,896 tonnes; zinc, 431,426 tonnes.

Computer equipment and organic chemicals are the main exports. The UK, USA, Germany, France and the Netherlands are Ireland's main trading partners. The euro replaced the punt in January 2002.

In 2001 Ireland had a trade surplus of US$30,003 million and a current account deficit of US$1,043 million. Imports totalled US$51,286 million and exports US$82,976 million.

GNP – US$85,979 million (2000); US$22,660 per capita (2000)
GDP – US$101,185 million (2001); US$25,066 per capita (2000)
ANNUAL AVERAGE GROWTH OF GDP – 8.9 per cent (1998)
INFLATION RATE – 5.6 per cent (2000)
UNEMPLOYMENT – 3.8 per cent (2001)

Trade with UK	2001	2002
Imports from UK	£13,133,800,000	£14,701,800,000
Exports to UK	8,923,600,000	8,998,600,000

COMMUNICATIONS

In 2000 there were 3,314 km of railway operated by Iarnród Eirann. In 1999 the number of ships with cargo which arrived at Irish ports was 17,645 (190,818,000 net registered tons), with a total weight of goods handled of 43,928 million tonnes.

Shannon Airport, Co. Clare, is on the main transatlantic air route. In 2000 the airport handled 2.41 million passengers. Dublin Airport serves the cross-channel and European services operated by the Irish national airline Aer Lingus and other airlines.

EDUCATION

Primary education is directed by the state, with the exception of 37 private primary schools. There were 3,181 state-aided primary schools in 1998–9. In 1998–9 there were 432 recognised secondary schools under private management (mainly religious orders), and 245 vocational schools. There were 16 state comprehensive schools and 66 community schools. Third-level education is catered for by seven university colleges, 13 institutes of technology, seven teacher training colleges and a number of other third-level institutions.

ENROLMENT (percentage of age group) – primary 100 per cent (1997); secondary 100 per cent (1997); tertiary 41 per cent (1997)

ISRAEL

Medinat Yisra'el / Dawlat Isrā'īl – State of Israel

AREA – 7,923 sq. miles (20,600 sq. km). Neighbours: Lebanon (north), Syria (north-east), Jordan and the West Bank (east), the Gaza Strip and the Egyptian province of Sinai (south-west)

POPULATION – 6,172,000 (2001): roughly 82 per cent Jewish, 14 per cent Arab Muslims, 2.5 per cent Christians of which 90 per cent are Arab, and 2 per cent Druze. Since independence Israel has had a policy of granting an immigration visa to every Jew who expresses a desire to settle in Israel. Between 1948 and 1992, 2.3 million immigrants had entered Israel from over 100 different countries. Hebrew and Arabic are the official languages. Arabs are entitled to transact all official business with government departments in Arabic

CAPITAL – Most of the government departments are in Jerusalem, population 758,000 (2001 estimate). A resolution proclaiming Jerusalem as the capital of Israel was adopted by the Knesset in 1950. It is not, however, recognised as the capital by the UN because East Jerusalem is part of the Occupied Territories captured in 1967. The UN and international law continues to reject the Israeli annexation of East Jerusalem and considers the pre-1950 capital Tel Aviv (population, 1,919,700) to be the capital

MAJOR CITIES – Beersheba (and district 172,860); ΨHaifa (and district 942,021); Rishon Le'Zion (202,209), 2000 estimates

CURRENCY – Shekel of 100 agora

NATIONAL ANTHEM – Hatikvah (The Hope)

NATIONAL FLAG – White, with two horizontal blue stripes, the Shield of David in the centre

LIFE EXPECTANCY (years) – 79 (2001)

POPULATION GROWTH RATE – 2.8 per cent

POPULATION DENSITY – 300 per sq. km (2001)

URBAN POPULATION – 92 per cent (2001)

Israel comprises the hill country of Galilee and parts of Judea and Samaria, rising to heights of nearly 4,000 ft; the coastal plain from the Gaza strip to north of Acre, including the plain of Esdraelon running from Haifa Bay to the south-east which divides the hill region; the Negev, a semi-desert triangular-shaped region, extending from a base south of Beersheba, to an apex at the head of the Gulf of Aqaba; and parts of the Jordan valley, including the Hula region, Tiberias and the south-western extremity of the Dead Sea.

The principal river is the Jordan, which rises from three main sources in Israel, Lebanon and Syria, and flows through the Hula valley, Lake Tiberias/Kinneret (Sea of Galilee) and the Jordan Valley into the Dead Sea, falling 1,517 ft from Hulata to the Dead Sea. The other principal rivers are the Yarkon and Kishon. The Dead Sea is a lake (shared between Israel, the West Bank and Jordan), 1,286 ft below sea-level; it has no outlet, the surplus being carried off by evaporation.

HISTORY AND POLITICS

The Ottoman Empire province of Palestine was captured by British forces in 1917, the same year that the British Government issued the Balfour Declaration which was the first significant declaration in favour of a Jewish national home in Palestine. The Balfour Declaration's terms were enshrined in Britain's League of Nations mandate over Palestine, leading to steady Jewish immigration in the inter-war years and a post-1945 flood by Nazi concentration camp survivors. The Arab Palestinian population revolted against Jewish immigration from 1936 onwards, while Jewish groups conducted a terrorist campaign against the British administration from 1945 onwards.

In 1947 Britain announced its withdrawal from Palestine with effect from May 1948, handing over to the UN responsibility for resolving the conflict between Arabs and Jews. Both sides ignored the UN partition plan; on the withdrawal of British forces on 14 May 1948 the State of Israel was proclaimed and the first Arab-Israeli war began. By the time of the January 1949 cease-fire Israeli forces controlled all of the former mandate territory apart from the West Bank (and East Jerusalem) and the Gaza Strip, which had come under Jordanian and Egyptian control respectively.

During the 1967 Six-Day War Israel captured the West Bank and the Gaza Strip, together with Sinai from Egypt and the Golan Heights from Syria, and annexed East Jerusalem. Israel held on to its gains in the 1973 Yom Kippur War. The Golan Heights were annexed in 1981; Sinai was returned to Egypt in 1982 in accordance with the 1979 Israeli–Egyptian peace treaty, and the South Lebanon Security Zone was established after the 1982–5 invasion of Lebanon, but vacated in June 2000. The annexations of East Jerusalem and the Golan Heights remain unrecognised internationally.

President Ezer Weizman announced that he would resign from office on 10 July 2000 following allegations of fraud. On 31 July, Moshe Katsav was elected president. Ehud Barak resigned as prime minister on 9 December 2000 and called a prime ministerial election, which was held on 6 February 2001; it was won by Likud leader Ariel Sharon, who formed a broad-based eight-party coalition which commanded the support of 72 of the 120 members of the Knesset. Saleh Tarif became the first Israeli Arab to be appointed to the cabinet. On 19 August 2001 the Centre Party agreed to join the coalition, bringing its support in the Knesset to 83 members. The Likud-led National Unity government collapsed on

30 October 2002 after the Labour Party withdrew from the coalition in a dispute over the 2003 budget. The general election was brought forward to 28 January 2003 and resulted in a victory for Likud with 37 seats in the Knesset but without an overall majority. A Likud-dominated coalition government was appointed on 27 February 2003 which also included the National Union (NU), the Change-Centre Party (Shinui) and the National Religious Party (NRP). The coalition controls 68 of the 120 seats in the Knesset.

FOREIGN RELATIONS
A peace process, started in October 1991 in Madrid, led to agreements with the Palestine Liberation Organisation, and with Jordan on 14 September 1993. A full peace agreement with Jordan was signed on 26 October 1994.

POLITICAL SYSTEM
Israel is a sovereign democratic republic with executive power vested in a prime minister and Cabinet, and legislative power in a unicameral legislature (Knesset) of 120 members elected by proportional representation for a maximum term of four years. In March 2001 the Knesset passed an amendment to the Basic Law on Government ending the system of separate prime ministerial elections and reverting to the former position where the prime minister is responsible to parliament and formally appointed by the president. The president is head of state and is elected by the Knesset. Previous presidents had been elected for a maximum of two five-year terms, but under a bill approved by the Knesset in December 1998, the president is now elected for a seven-year non-renewable term.

HEAD OF STATE
President of Israel, Moshe Katsav, *elected* 31 July 2000, *sworn in* 1 August 2000

CABINET *as at August 2003*
Prime Minister, Communications and Religious Affairs, Ariel Sharon (L)
Deputy Prime Minister, Foreign Affairs, Sylvan Shalom (L)
Deputy Prime Minister, Justice, Yosef Tommy Lapid (Shinui)
Deputy Prime Minister, Trade and Industry, Ehud Olmert (L)
Agriculture and Rural Development, Yisrael Katz (L)
Defence, Gen. Shaul Mofaz (L)
Education, Culture and Sport, Limor Livnat (L)
Environment, Yehudit Naot (Shinui)
Finance, Binyamin Netanyahu (L)
Health, Danny Naveh (L)
Housing and Construction, Efraim Eitam (NRP)
Immigration Absorption, Tzipi Livni (L)
Interior and Communications, Avraham Poraz (Shinui)
National Infrastructure, Yosef Paritzky (Shinui)
Public Security, Tzahi Hanegbi (L)
Science and Technology, Eliezer Sandberg (Shinui)
Tourism, Binyamin Alon (NU)
Transport, Avigdor Lieberman (NU)
Welfare, Zevekun Orlev (NRP)
Without Portfolio, Meir Sheetrit (L); Uzi Landau (L); Natan Sharansky (L) *(Diaspora Relations);* Gideon Ezra (L) *(Parliamentary Relations)*

L Likud; NRP National Religious Party; NU National Union-Yisrael Beytenu; Shinui Change-Centre Party

EMBASSY OF ISRAEL
2 Palace Green, Kensington, London W8 4QB
Tel: 020-7957 9500
Ambassador Extraordinary and Plenipotentiary, HE Zvi Shtauber, apptd 2001

BRITISH EMBASSY
192 Hayarkon Street, Tel Aviv 63405
Tel: (00 972) (3) 725 1222
Ambassador Extraordinary and Plenipotentiary,
   HE Simon McDonald, CMG, LVO, apptd 2003

BRITISH COUNCIL DIRECTOR, Kevin Lewis
Crystal House, 12 Hahilazon Street, Ramat Gan 52136
Tel Aviv. Tel: (00 972) (3) 611 3600
Email: bcta@britishcouncil.org.il

DEFENCE
Israel is believed to have a nuclear capacity of around 100 warheads which could be delivered by aircraft or Jericho I and II missiles. The Army has 3,750 main battle tanks and around 10,400 armoured personnel carriers. The Navy has three submarines and 48 patrol and coastal vessels at three bases. The Air Force has 454 combat aircraft and 135 armed helicopters.
MILITARY EXPENDITURE – 9.5 per cent of GDP (2001)
MILITARY PERSONNEL – 161,500: Army 120,000, Navy 6,500, Air Force 35,000; Paramilitaries 8,050
CONSCRIPTION DURATION – 24–48 months (Jews and Druze only)

ECONOMY
The country is generally fertile although water supply for irrigation restricts production. Agriculture accounted for 1.8 per cent of GDP in 2000.
   The 'Jaffa' orange is produced in large quantities for export, along with other summer fruits, seasonal vegetables, flowers and glasshouse crops. Olives are cultivated, mainly for the production of oil. The main winter crops are wheat, barley and various kinds of pulses, while in summer sorghum, millet, maize, sesame and summer pulses are grown. Beef, cattle and poultry farming have been developed. Tobacco and cotton are now grown.
   Amongst the most important industries are textiles, foodstuffs and chemicals (mainly fertilisers and pharmaceuticals). Metal-working and science-based industries are sophisticated and technologically advanced and include the aircraft and military industries. Other important manufacturing industries include plastics, rubber, cement, glass, paper and oil refining. Industry accounted for 27 per cent and services for 47 per cent of GDP in 2000.
GNP – US$104,128 million (2000); US$16,710 per capita (2000)
GDP – US$110,386 million (1999); US$19,521 per capita (2000)
ANNUAL AVERAGE GROWTH OF GDP – 5.7 per cent (2000)
INFLATION RATE – 1.1 per cent (2000)
UNEMPLOYMENT – 8.8 per cent (2000)

TRADE
The principal imports are machinery and transport equipment, semi-manufactures, uncut diamonds, chemicals and chemical products, crude oil, and foodstuffs. The principal exports are semi-manufactures, machinery, polished diamonds, chemicals and chemical products, and foodstuffs and uncut diamonds.

In 2001 Israel had a trade deficit of US$3,264 million and a current account deficit of US$1,852 million. Imports totalled US$35,465 million and exports totalled US$29,019 million.

Trade with UK	2001	2002
Imports from UK	£1,365,802,000	£1,440,191,000
Exports to UK	975,348,000	910,853,000

COMMUNICATIONS

Israel State Railways serves Haifa, Tel Aviv, Jerusalem, Lod, Nahariya, Beersheba, Dimona, Ashdod and intermediate stations with a network of 647 km. There were 15,965 km of paved road in 2000. A major road building programme has been under way in the West Bank since 1992. The chief ports are Haifa and Ashdod on the Mediterranean, and Eilat on the Red Sea; Acre has an anchorage for small vessels. The chief international airport is Ben Gurion between Tel Aviv and Jerusalem.

EDUCATION

Education from five to 16 years is free and compulsory. The law also provides for working youths aged 16–18, who for some reason have not completed their education, to be exempted from work in order to do so. There are seven universities including two engineering and technological institutes.

ILLITERACY RATE – (m) 2.1 per cent; (f) 5.8 per cent (2000)

ENROLMENT (percentage of age group) – tertiary 41.1 per cent (1997)

CULTURE

Important historic sites in Israel include: *Jerusalem* – the Church of the Holy Sepulchre, the Al Aqsa Mosque and Dome of the Rock standing on the remains of the Temple Mount of Herod the Great of which the Western (wailing) Wall is a fragment, the Church of the Dormition and the Coenaculum on Mount Zion, Ein Karem, Church of the Visitation, Church of St John the Baptist; *Galilee* – the Sea, Church and Mount of the Beatitudes, ruins of Capernaum and other sites connected with the life of Christ; *Mount Tabor* – Church of the Transfiguration; *Nazareth* – Church of the Annunciation, and other Christian shrines associated with the childhood of Christ; there are also numerous sites dating from biblical and medieval days, such as Ascalon, Caesarea, Atlit, Massada, Megiddo and Hazor.

PALESTINIAN AUTONOMOUS AREAS

AREA – The total area is 2,406 sq. miles (6,231 sq. km). The area which is fully autonomous is 159 sq. miles (412 sq. km), of which the Gaza Strip is 136 sq. miles (352 sq. km) and the Jericho enclave 23 sq. miles (60 sq. km). The partially autonomous area is the remainder of the West Bank, some 2,247 sq. miles (5,819 sq. km). The UN and the international community also recognise East Jerusalem as part of the Occupied Territories

POPULATION – 3,634,585 (2003 estimate), of whom 394,105 live in East Jerusalem. In addition there are 176,000 Jewish settlers in the West Bank and 6,900 in the Gaza Strip (2000 estimate) who remain under Israeli administration and jurisdiction. Some 90 per cent of Palestinians are Muslim (the vast majority Sunni) and 10 per cent are Christians

CAPITAL – Although Palestinians claim East Jerusalem as their capital, the administrative capital has been established in Gaza City (population 460,899)

MAJOR TOWNS – Khan Yunis, Rafah in the Gaza Strip; Nablus, Hebron, Jericho, Ramallah and Bethlehem on the West Bank

FLAG – Three horizontal stripes of black, white, green with a red triangle based on the hoist (the PLO flag)

NATIONAL ANTHEM – Fidai, Fidai (Freedom Fighter, Freedom Fighter)

HISTORY AND POLITICS

Israel captured the Gaza Strip, East Jerusalem and the West Bank during the 1967 Six-Day War and annexed East Jerusalem. After the war the Israeli government began to establish settlements in the Occupied Territories. Palestinian resistance to Israeli rule was led by the Palestine Liberation Organisation (PLO) which was established in 1964. Frustration at continued Israeli occupation led to the start of the intifada, a campaign of sustained unrest, in 1987. When the 1991 Madrid peace process stalled, Israeli and PLO officials engaged in secret negotiations in Norway which led to the signing of the 'Declaration of Principles on Interim Self-Government Arrangements' on 13 September 1993. Under this agreement the PLO renounced terrorism and recognised Israel's right to exist in secure borders, while Israel recognised the PLO as the legitimate representative of the Palestinian people.

The Declaration of Principles established a timetable for progress towards a final settlement: negotiations leading to an Israeli military withdrawal from the Gaza Strip and Jericho by 13 April 1994, when power was to be transferred to a nominated Palestinian National Authority (PNA); elections to a new Palestinian Council, which would also exercise control over six policy areas in the rest of the West Bank (culture, tourism, health, education, social welfare, direct taxation), and the Israeli military administration dissolved by 13 July 1994; negotiations on a permanent settlement, including Jewish settlers and East Jerusalem, to begin by 13 April 1996; and a permanent settlement to be in place by 13 April 1999.

The 'Oslo B' or Taba Accord was signed on 28 September 1995 and provided for Israeli withdrawal from six towns and 85 per cent of Hebron; the extension of self-rule to most of the West Bank by 1998; the release of 5,300 Palestinian prisoners; and the striking out of the demand for Israel's destruction from the PLO's charter. On 29 December 1995 an agreement was reached on the transfer of 17 areas of civilian power to the PNA in Hebron.

Israeli troops left Ramallah, the last of the six West Bank towns, on 27 December 1995 and the inaugural Palestinian National Council meeting on 23 April 1996 voted to amend the PLO charter. The final element of the Declaration of Principles, the 'final status talks' opened in Taba, Egypt, on 5 May 1996 to decide the final status of the West Bank, Gaza and Jerusalem. The election of a Likud-led government opposed to the establishment of a Palestinian state resulted in a deadlock in negotiations in 1997 and delays in the withdrawal of Israeli troops from Hebron.

Legislative elections on 20 January 1996 were won by the mainstream al-Fatah faction of the PLO, with its leader Yasser Arafat winning 88.1 per cent of the vote to become the president of the Palestinian National Authority.

Yasser Arafat had planned to declare an independent Palestinian state on 4 May 1999, the end of the five-year transitional period which had been agreed in the 1993 Oslo peace accords, but the announcement was postponed in the hope that talks with the new Israeli government would lead to a negotiated settlement.

Following a controversial visit in late September 2000 by Likud leader Ariel Sharon to the Temple Mount, a holy site for both Jews and Muslims, a new intifada broke out. Relations between the Israeli government and the PNA deteriorated further after two Israeli soldiers were lynched by Palestinians; on 12 October Israeli forces launched rocket attacks on the residence and offices of Arafat and declared the peace process to be at an end. A summit was held in Sharm el-Shaikh on 17 October and an agreement was reached to end violence and restart negotiations. However, serious clashes resumed in late October. An agreement was reached on 1 November to call a new cease-fire the following day, but it had broken down by the middle of the month. A new round of talks began on 14 December and a US draft accord was discussed, which envisaged a Palestinian state on 95 per cent of the West Bank and the entire Gaza Strip. Agreement could not be reached and the talks broke down on 27 January 2001. Following the election of Ariel Sharon as Israeli prime minister on 6 February, hopes of a peace agreement faded. Relations remained volatile throughout 2001 and 2002 with Palestinian suicide bombings and Israeli retaliation amid cease-fires and intense diplomatic intervention. Renewed violent conflict took place in late 2002–3 and Yasser Arafat underwent a ten-day siege in September 2002 following a fatal suicide bombing in Tel Aviv on 19 September. The siege was lifted on 29 September after a UN Security Council resolution demanded the withdrawal of Israeli forces.

The Palestinian cabinet resigned on 11 September 2002 after the Palestine Legislative Council (PLC) threatened to pass a vote of no confidence in it. On 10 March 2003 the PLC voted to create a new post of prime minister, a move that would curb the powers of President Arafat. Arafat named Mahmoud Abbas as prime minister on 19 March. Abbas's appointment and his cabinet were approved by the PLC on 29 April after extensive negotiation. Abbas resigned on 6 September 2003. For further information *see* Stop Press.

The 'road map' peace plan, set out by the EU, Russia, the UN and the USA was launched on 30 April 2003 and endorsed by the Palestinian and Israeli prime ministers at a summit with US President George Bush on 5 June. The plan is intended to be a phase-by-phase route to ending the violence in the region leading to the establishment of an autonomous Palestinian state by 2005. Although Hamas rejected the 'road map' peace plan, the group, along with Islamic Jihad and Fatah, announced on 30 June that they would observe a three-month truce with Israel. In July Israeli forces withdrew from some key areas in the West Bank and the Gaza Strip.

POLITICAL SYSTEM

The Oslo B accord laid down the political structure of the nascent Palestinian state. Executive authority is vested in the Palestinian National Authority which is headed by a popularly elected leader (rais). Legislative authority is vested in the 88-member Palestinian Legislative Council which is directly elected by means of a first-past-the-post system, and itself elects the four-fifths of the PNA not appointed by the leader.

PALESTINIAN NATIONAL AUTHORITY *as at July 2003*
President, Yasser Arafat
Prime Minister, Interior, vacant
Agriculture, Rafiq al-Natsheh
Cabinet Affairs, Yassir abed Rabbo
Culture, Ziyad Abu-Amr
Economy, Trade and Industry, Mahir al-Masri
Education and Higher Education, Naim Abdul Hummus
Energy, Azzam al-Shawwa
Finance, Salam Fayad
Foreign Affairs, Nabil Sha'ath
Health, Kamal al-Sharafi
Housing and Public Works, Hamdan Ashur
Information, Nabil Amr
Internal Security, Muhammad Dahlan
Justice, Abd-al-Karim Abu-Salah
Labour, Ghassan al-Khatib
Local Government, Jamal al-Shawbaki
Negotiations, vacant
Planning, Nabil Qassis
Prisoners and Detainees, Hisham Abd-al-Raziq
Religious Affairs (Waqf), vacant
Secretary-General of the Government, Hakam Bal'awi
Social Affairs, Intisar al-Wazir
Tourism, Mitri Abu-Aytah
Transport, Sa'adi al-Krunz
Youth and Sport, Abd-al-Fattah Hamayil

PALESTINIAN GENERAL DELEGATION
5 Galena Road, London W6 0LT
Tel: 020-8563 0008
General Delegate, Afif Safieh

BRITISH CONSULATE-GENERAL
19 Nashashibi Street, PO Box 19690, East Jerusalem 97200
Tel: (00 972) (2) 541 4100
Consul-General, John Jenkins, CMG, LVO, apptd 2003

BRITISH COUNCIL DIRECTOR, Sarah Ewans, OBE
31 Nablus Road, PO Box 19136, East Jerusalem
Tel: (00 972) (2) 628 2545.
Email: british.council@ej.britishcouncil.org

Trade with UK	2001	2002
Imports from UK	£240,000	£111,000
Exports to UK	121,000	241,000

ITALY

Repubblica Italiana – Italian Republic

AREA – 113,115 sq. miles (294,100 sq. km).
  Neighbours: Switzerland and Austria (north), Slovenia (east), France (west)
POPULATION – 57,503,000 (2001): 83 per cent Catholic. The language is Italian, a Romance language derived from Latin. There are several regional languages including Sardinian and Catalan in Sardinia, Friulian in Friuli, German and Ladin in the South Tyrol, French in the Valle d'Aosta, and Slovene in parts of Gorizia
CAPITAL – Rome (population, 2,459,776, 2001 census). The Eternal City was founded, according to legend, by Romulus in 753 BC. It was the centre of Latin civilisation and capital of the Roman Republic and Roman Empire

MAJOR CITIES – Bologna (369,955); Florence (352,227); ΨGenoa (603,560); Milan (1,182,693); ΨNaples (993,386); Turin (857,433); Sicily, ΨPalermo (652,640); Sardinia, ΨCagliari (158,351), 2001 census

CURRENCY – Euro (€) of 100 cents

NATIONAL ANTHEM – Inno Di Mameli (Hymn Of Mameli)

NATIONAL DAY – 2 June

NATIONAL FLAG – Vertical stripes of green, white and red

LIFE EXPECTANCY (years) – 79 (2001)

POPULATION GROWTH RATE – 0.1 per cent

POPULATION DENSITY – 196 per sq. km (2001)

URBAN POPULATION – 67 per cent (2001)

Italy consists of a peninsula, the islands of Sicily, Sardinia, Elba and about 70 other small islands. The peninsula is for the most part mountainous, but between the Apennines, which form its spine, and the eastern coastline are two large fertile plains: Emilia-Romagna in the north and Apulia in the south. The Alps divide Italy from France, Switzerland, Austria and Slovenia. Partly within the Italian borders are Monte Rosa (15,217 ft), the Matterhorn (14,780 ft) and several peaks from 12,000 to 14,000 ft. The chief rivers are the Po (405 miles), flowing through Piedmont, Lombardy and the Veneto; the Adige (Trentino and Veneto); the Arno (Florentine plain); and the Tiber (flowing through Rome to Ostia).

HISTORY AND POLITICS

Italian unity was accomplished under the House of Savoy after a struggle from 1848 to 1870 in which Mazzini (1805–72), Garibaldi (1807–82) and Cavour (1810–61) were the principal figures. It was completed when Lombardy was ceded by Austria in 1859 and Venice in 1866, and through the evacuation of Rome by the French in 1870. In 1871 the King of Italy entered Rome, and that city was declared to be the capital.

A fascist regime came to power in 1922 under Benito Mussolini, known as Il Duce (The Leader), who was prime minister from 1922 until 25 July 1943, when the regime was abolished. Mussolini was captured by Italian partisans while attempting to escape across the Swiss frontier and killed on 28 April 1945. Italy became a republic following a referendum on the future of the monarchy in June 1946.

Political instability and corruption led to public disenchantment with the major political parties, whose support collapsed in the 1992 general election. The so-called 'clean hands' investigation into corruption and Mafia links that began in 1992 has led to the arrest by magistrates of thousands of politicians and businessmen.

The general election on 21 April 1996 was won by the left-wing Olive Tree alliance led by the Democratic Party of the Left, whose leader, Romano Prodi, became prime minister. The government collapsed on 9 October 1998 after the Communist Refoundation party, on whose support it had been dependent, refused to vote for the 1999 budget. Massimo D'Alema was invited by the president to form a new government on 20 October. On 19 December 1999, the government collapsed, but Massimo D'Alema was asked to form a new government the following day; he resigned as prime minister on 17 April 2000 following the defeat of his centre-left coalition in regional elections on 16 April. President Ciampi invited Giuliano Amato to form a new

government and Amato was sworn in as prime minister on 26 April 2000.

The general election held on 13 May 2001 was won by the centre-right House of Freedom alliance, which obtained 368 seats. The alliance was led by Forza Italia and also comprised the Christian Democratic Centre, the Christian Democratic Union, the National Alliance, the New Italian Socialist Party and the Northern League. Silvio Berlusconi, the Forza Italia leader, was sworn in as prime minister on 11 June.

On 18 April 2003 the trial of Silvio Berlusconi opened. The prime minister appeared in court on corruption charges relating to the bribery of judges during a business takeover in 1985. Berlusconi denied the charges and in January 2003 stated he would retain his position as prime minister even if found guilty. The trial was halted in June after parliament passed a controversial law granting immunity from prosecution to five holders of key state posts, including the prime minister.

POLITICAL SYSTEM

The constitution provides for the election of the president for a seven-year term by an electoral college which consists of the two houses of the parliament (the Chamber of Deputies and the Senate) sitting in joint session, together with three delegates from each region (one in the case of the Valle d'Aosta). The president, who must be over 50 years of age, has the right to dissolve one or both houses after consultation with the Speakers. Members of both houses were elected wholly by proportional representation until 1993. Now 75 per cent (232) of the 315 elected seats in the Senate are elected on a first-past-the-post basis and the remaining elected seats are filled by proportional representation. There is a variable number of life senators, who are past presidents and senators appointed by incumbent presidents. In the Chamber of Deputies 75 per cent (472) of seats are elected on a first-past-the-post basis, and 25 per cent (158) by proportional representation, with a 4 per cent threshold for parliamentary representation. A referendum on 18 April 1999 on abolishing the seats elected by proportional representation foundered when less than the required 50 per cent of the electorate participated.

HEAD OF STATE

President, Carlo Azeglio Ciampi, elected 13 May 1999, took office 18 May 1999

COUNCIL OF MINISTERS as at July 2003

Prime Minister, Silvio Berlusconi (FI)

Deputy Prime Minister, Gianfranco Fini (AN)

Agriculture and Forestry, Giovanni Alemanno (AN)

Culture, Giuliano Urbani (FI)

Defence, Antonio Martino (FI)

Economy and Finance, Giulio Tremonti (FI)

Education, Higher Education and Scientific Research, Letizia Moratti (Ind.)

Employment and Social Welfare, Roberto Maroni (LN)

Environment, Altero Matteoli (AN)

Foreign Affairs, Franco Frattini (FI)

Health, Gerolamo Sirchia (Ind.)

Industry, Antonio Marzano (FI)

Infrastructure and Transport, Pietro Lunardi (Ind.)

Interior, Giuseppe Pisanu (FI)

Justice, Roberto Castelli (LN)

Telecommunications, Maurizio Gasparri (AN)

AN National Alliance; FI Forza Italia; LN Northern League; Ind. Independent

ITALIAN EMBASSY
14 Three Kings Yard, Davies Street, London W1K 4EH
Tel: 020-7312 2200
Ambassador Extraordinary and Plenipotentiary,
  HE Luigi Amaduzzi, GCVO, apptd 1999

BRITISH EMBASSY
Via XX Settembre 80A, I-00187 Rome
Tel: (00 39) (6) 4220 0001
Ambassador Extraordinary and Plenipotentiary,
  HE Sir Ivor Roberts, KCMG, apptd 2003

BRITISH COUNCIL DIRECTOR, Richard Alford, OBE
Via Quattro Fontane 20, I-00184 Rome
Email: studyandcultureuk@britishcouncil.it

DEFENCE
The Army has 1,018 main battle tanks and 2,937 armoured personnel carriers. The Navy has six submarines, one aircraft carrier, one cruiser, four destroyers, 14 frigates, 16 patrol and coastal vessels, 18 combat aircraft and 79 armed helicopters. There are four naval bases. The Air Force has 261 combat aircraft and six armed helicopters.
MILITARY EXPENDITURE – 2.0 per cent of GDP (2001)
MILITARY PERSONNEL – 216,800: Army 128,000,
  Navy 38,000, Air Force 50,800; Paramilitaries
  254,300
CONSCRIPTION DURATION – Ten months

ECONOMY
Deposits of natural methane gas and oil have been discovered, mainly south of Sicily, and have been rapidly exploited. Production of lignite has also increased. Other minerals include iron ores and pyrites, mercury (over one-quarter of the world production), lead, zinc and aluminium. Rich gold veins were discovered in Sardinia in 1996. Marble is a traditional product of the Massa Carrara district.

Agricultural production is concentrated in Tuscany, Emilia-Romagna, Sicily and the whole of the southern third of the country. The principal products are wine, tobacco, citrus fruits, tomatoes, almonds, sugar beet, wheat and maize.

Tourism is a major contributor to the economy and Italy receives some 57 million visitors a year. The commercial and banking services are concentrated in Rome and in Milan, where the stock market is located.

Industry is centred around Milan (steel, machine tools, motor cars), Turin (motor cars, steel, roller bearings, textiles), Rome (light industries), Venice (shipbuilding, paper, mechanical equipment, electrical goods, woollens), Bologna/Florence (food industry, footwear and textiles, reproduction furniture, glassware, pottery, ceramics), Naples, Bari (valves, vehicle bodies, tyres), Taranto (steel, oil refining), Trieste (shipbuilding) and Cagliari (aluminium production, petrochemicals).

Following a programme of severe austerity measures, Italy satisfied the convergence criteria and participated in the European Single Currency from 1 January 1999. The euro replaced the lira in January 2002.

In 2001 there was a trade surplus of US$15,862 million and a current account deficit of US$163 million. Imports totalled US$232,983 million and exports US$241,729 million.

Italy's chief exports are industrial and agricultural machinery, textiles and clothing, electrical equipment and chemicals. Chief imports are chemicals, motor vehicles and metals. Italy's main trading partners are Germany, France, the UK and the USA.
GNP – US$1,163,211 million (2000); US$20,160 per
  capita (2000)
GDP – US$1,090,910 million (2001); US$18,653 per
  capita (2000)
ANNUAL AVERAGE GROWTH OF GDP – 2.9 per cent
  (2000)
INFLATION RATE – 2.5 per cent (2000)
UNEMPLOYMENT – 10.5 per cent (2000)

Trade with UK	2001	2002
Imports from UK	£8,044,800,000	£8,079,900,000
Exports to UK	9,333,200,000	9,951,500,000

COMMUNICATIONS
The main railway system is state-run by the Ferrovia dello Stato. There are 19,466 km of railway track. A 9,500 km network of motorways (autostrade) covers the country. There are 305,881 km of roads in total. Alitalia is the principal international and domestic airline.

In January 2001, the Italian and French presidents agreed plans to build a 52-km rail tunnel through the Alps as part of a high-speed rail link between Turin and Lyons. Commissioning of the project is scheduled for 2012.

EDUCATION
Education is free and compulsory between the ages of six and 16; this includes five years at primary school and three in 'middle school'. Pupils who obtain the middle school certificate may seek admission to any 'senior secondary school', which may be a lyceum with a classical or scientific or artistic bias, or an institute directed at technology (of which there are eight different types), trade or industry (including vocational schools), or teacher-training. Courses at the lyceums and technical institutes usually last for five years and success in the final examination qualifies for admission to university.

There are 42 state and six private universities, three technical universities and 12 university institutes. The universities at Bologna, Modena, Parma and Padua are of ancient foundation and were started in the 12th century. University education is not free, but entrants with higher qualifications are charged reduced fees according to a sliding scale.
ILLITERACY RATE – (m) 1.1 per cent; (f) 2.0 per cent
  (2000)
ENROLMENT (percentage of age group) – primary 100
  per cent (1997); tertiary 47 per cent (1997)

CULTURE
Florence, the capital of Tuscany, was one of the greatest cities in Europe from the 11th to the 16th centuries, and the cradle of the Renaissance. Under the Medici family in the 15th century flourished many of the greatest names in Italian art, including Filippo Lippi, Botticelli, Donatello and Brunelleschi, and in the 16th century Michelangelo and Leonardo da Vinci.

Italian literature (in addition to Latin literature, which is the common inheritance of western Europe) is one of the richest in Europe, particularly in its golden age (Dante, 1265–1321; Petrarch, 1304–74; Boccaccio, 1313–75) and in the Renaissance (Ariosto, 1474–1533; Machiavelli, 1469–1527; Tasso, 1544–95). Notable in modern Italian literature are Manzoni (1785–1873), Carducci (1835–1907) and Gabriele d'Annunzio (1864–1938).

ISLANDS

CAPRI, in the Bay of Naples; area 4 sq. miles (10 sq. km); population 12,000

EOLIAN ISLANDS, including Lipari; area 45 sq. miles (116 sq. km); population 18,636

FLEGREAN ISLANDS, including Ischia; area 23 sq. miles (60 sq. km); population 51,883

PANTELLERIA ISLAND (part of Trapani Province) in the Sicilian Narrows; area 31 sq. miles (80 sq. km); population 9,601

THE PELAGIAN ISLANDS (Lampedusa, Linosa and Lampione) are part of the province of Agrigento; area 8 sq. miles (21 sq. km); population 4,811

PONTINE ARCHIPELAGO, including Ponza; area 4 sq. miles (10 sq. km); population 2,515

TREMITI ISLANDS; area 1 sq. mile (3 sq. km); population 426

THE TUSCAN ARCHIPELAGO (including Elba); area 113 sq. miles (293 sq. km); population 31,861

JAMAICA

AREA – 4,154 sq. miles (10,800 sq. km)

POPULATION – 2,598,000 (2001). The official language is English; a local patois is also spoken

CAPITAL – ΨKingston (population, 524,638, 1991)

MAJOR CITIES – Mandeville; May Pen; ΨMontego Bay; Ocho Rios; Spanish Town

CURRENCY – Jamaican dollar (J$) of 100 cents

NATIONAL ANTHEM – Jamaica, Land We Love

NATIONAL DAY – 6 August (Independence Day)

NATIONAL FLAG – Gold diagonal cross forming triangles of green at top and bottom, triangles of black at hoist and in fly

LIFE EXPECTANCY (years) – 75 (2001)

POPULATION GROWTH RATE – 0.8 per cent

POPULATION DENSITY – 241 per sq. km (2001)

URBAN POPULATION – 57 per cent (2001)

MILITARY EXPENDITURE – 0.5 per cent of GDP (2001)

MILITARY PERSONNEL – 2,830: Army 2,500, Coast Guard 190, Air Wing 140

ILLITERACY RATE – (m) 17.1 per cent; (f) 9.3 per cent (2000)

ENROLMENT (percentage of age group) – primary 100 per cent (1999); secondary 69 per cent (1999); tertiary 13 per cent (1999)

HISTORY AND POLITICS

The island was discovered by Columbus in 1494, and occupied by Spain from 1509 until 1655 when an English expedition under Admiral Penn and General Venables captured the island. In 1670 it was formally ceded to England by the Treaty of Madrid. Jamaica became an independent state within the Commonwealth on 6 August 1962.

The People's National Party (PNP) has been in power since 1989. At the general election of 16 October 2002, the PNP retained an overall but reduced majority with 34 out of a total of 60 seats, securing a fourth term for the party and a third term for Prime Minister Percival Patterson, who was sworn in on 23 October.

POLITICAL SYSTEM

Queen Elizabeth II is the head of state, represented by the Governor-General. The legislature consists of a Senate of 21 nominated members and a House of Representatives consisting of 60 members elected by universal adult suffrage for a five-year term. The prime minister is the leader of the majority party in the House.

Governor-General, HE Sir Howard Felix Hanlon Cooke, GCMG, GCVO, apptd 1991

CABINET *as at July 2003*

Prime Minister, Defence, Percival J. Patterson, QC

Agriculture, Roger Clarke

Attorney-General, Legal Affairs and Justice, Arnold Nicholson

Commerce, Science and Technology, Phillip Paulwell

Development, Paul Robertson

Education Youth and Culture, Maxine Henry-Wilson

Finance and Planning, Omar Davies

Foreign Affairs and Foreign Trade, Keith Desmond Knight

Health, John Junor

Industry and Tourism, Aloun Angela N'dombet Assamba

Information, Burchell Whiteman

Labour and Social Security, Horace Dalley

Land and Environment, Dean Peart

Local Government, Community Development and Sport, Portia Simpson-Miller

National Security, Peter Phillips

Transport and Works, Robert Pickersgill

Water and Housing, Donald Buchanan

JAMAICAN HIGH COMMISSION
1–2 Prince Consort Road, London SW7 2BZ
Tel: 020-7823 9911
High Commissioner, HE Maxine Roberts, CD, apptd 2002

BRITISH HIGH COMMISSION
PO Box 575, Trafalgar Road, Kingston 10
Tel: (00 1 876) 510 0700
Email: bhckingston@cwjamaica.com
High Commissioner, HE Peter Mathers, LVO, apptd 2002

BRITISH COUNCIL MANAGER, Nicola Johnson
28 Trafalgar Road, Kingston 10
Tel: (00 1 876) 929 7090
Email: bcjamaica@britishcouncil.org.jm

ECONOMY

Alumina, bananas, bauxite and sugar are the main exports. Other exports include garments, processed food products, limestone and horticultural products. A task force was established in January 2001 to foster an increase in sugar production. The country's first gold mine became operational in March 2001.

Since 1989 the PNP government has abolished price subsidies, removed foreign exchange controls and introduced a 10 per cent consumption tax. Jamaica is a popular tourist resort, attracting 1.32 million stopover visitors and almost 908,000 cruise ship passengers in 2000, producing US$1.38 billion in foreign exchange earnings. The economy has faced many problems, including interest repayments on debt which accounted for 41 per cent of government revenue in 1999, low market prices for many of Jamaica's exports and interest rates of over 30 per cent.

In 2000 Jamaica had a trade deficit of US$1,354 million and a current account deficit of US$275 million. In 2001 imports totalled US$3,331 million and exports US$1,225 million.

GNP – US$6,883 million (2000); US$2,610 per capita (2000)
GDP – US$7,784 million (2001); US$2,801 per capita (2000)
ANNUAL AVERAGE GROWTH OF GDP – 0.8 per cent (2000)
INFLATION RATE – 8.2 per cent (2000)
UNEMPLOYMENT – 15.8 per cent (1999)
TOTAL EXTERNAL DEBT – US$4,287 million (2000)

Trade with UK	2001	2002
Imports from UK	£70,674,000	£81,792,000
Exports to UK	117,910,000	106,512,000

COMMUNICATIONS
There are several excellent harbours, Kingston being the principal port. The island has 2,944 miles of main roads and 7,264 miles of subsidiary roads.

JAPAN

Nihon-koku – State of Japan

AREA – 140,192 sq. miles (364,500 sq. km)
POPULATION – 127,335,000 (2001). The principal religions are Mahayana Buddhism and Shinto. About 1 per cent of Japanese are Christians. The language is Japanese
CAPITAL – Tokyo (population, 12,064,101, 2000 census)
MAJOR CITIES – ΨFukuoka (1,341, 489); ΨKobe (1,493,595); Kyoto, the ancient capital (1,467,705); ΨNagoya (2,171,378); ΨOsaka (2,598,589); Sapporo (1,822,300); ΨYokohama (3,426,506), 2000 census
CURRENCY – Yen
NATIONAL ANTHEM – Kimigayo (His Majesty's Reign)
NATIONAL FLAG – White, charged with sun (red)
LIFE EXPECTANCY (years) – 81 (2001)
POPULATION GROWTH RATE – 0.3 per cent
POPULATION DENSITY – 349 per sq. km (2001)
URBAN POPULATION – 79 per cent (2001)

Japan consists of four large islands: *Honshu* (or Mainland) 88,839 sq. miles (230,448 sq. km), *Shikoku*, 7,231 sq. miles (18,757 sq. km), *Kyushu*, 16,170 sq. miles (42,079 sq. km), *Hokkaido*, 30,265 sq. miles (78,508 sq. km), and many small islands (including Okinawa).
The interior is very mountainous, and crossing the mainland from the Sea of Japan to the Pacific is a group of volcanoes, mainly extinct or dormant. Mount Fuji, the most sacred mountain of Japan, is 12,370 ft high and has been dormant since 1707, but volcanoes which are active include Mount Aso in Kyushu.

HISTORY AND POLITICS
According to tradition, Jimmu, the first Emperor of Japan, ascended the throne on 11 February 660 BC. Under the *Meiji* constitution (1889), the monarchy is hereditary in the male heirs of the Imperial house.
After the unconditional surrender to the Allied nations (14 August 1945), Japan was occupied by Allied forces under General MacArthur. A Japanese peace treaty became effective on 28 April 1952. Japan then resumed her status as an independent power.
The (conservative) Liberal Democratic Party (LDP) governed Japan almost without interruption from the Second World War until 1993.
Following the general election held on 25 June 2000,

the Liberal Democratic Party remained the largest party but failed to retain its overall majority, winning 233 seats. The LDP formed a coalition with its previous partners, New Komeito and the New Conservative Party, which accounted for 271 of the 480 seats in the Diet. Prime Minister Yoshiro Mori resigned on 7 April 2001 following mounting criticism of his performance and was replaced by Junichiro Koizumi on 26 April.

POLITICAL SYSTEM
Legislative authority rests with the bicameral Diet (Kokkai), which comprises a 480-member House of Representatives, and a 247-member House of Councillors. The House of Representatives chooses the prime minister from among its ranks, ratifies treaties and passes budget bills. Since January 2000, 180 of its members are elected by proportional representation in 11 regional blocks and 300 in single-member, first-past-the-post constituencies. All members serve four-year terms. The House of Councillors elects half its members every three years for six-year terms. Unlike the lower house it cannot be dissolved by the prime minister. Executive authority is vested in the Cabinet which is responsible to the legislature.

HEAD OF STATE
His Imperial Majesty The Emperor of Japan, Emperor Akihito, *born* 23 December 1933; *succeeded* 8 January 1989; *enthroned* 12 November 1990; *married* 10 April 1959, Miss Michiko Shoda, and has *issue*: the Crown Prince; Prince Fumihito, born 30 November 1965; and Princess Sayako, *born* 18 April 1969
Heir, HRH Crown Prince Naruhito Hironomiya, *born* 23 February 1960, *married* 9 June 1993, Miss Masako Owada

CABINET *as at July 2003*
Prime Minister, Junichiro Koizumi (LDP)
Agriculture, Forestry and Fisheries, Yoshiuki Kamei (LDP)
Economy, Trade and Industry, Takeo Hiranuma (LDP)
Education, Culture, Sports, Science and Technology, Atsuko Toyama (Ind.)
Environment, Shinuchi Suzuki (LDP)
Finance, Masajuro Shiokawa (LDP)
Foreign Affairs, Yoriko Kawaguchi (Ind.)
Health, Labour and Welfare, Chikara Sakaguchi (NK)
Justice, Mayumi Moriyama (LDP)
Land, Infrastructure and Transport, Chikage Ogi (NCP)

Public Management, Home Affairs, Posts and
   Telecommunications, Toranosuke Katayama (LDP)

LDP Liberal Democratic Party; NCP New Conservative
Party; NK New Komeito; Ind. Independent

EMBASSY OF JAPAN
101–104 Piccadilly, London W1J 7JT
Tel: 020-7465 6500
Ambassador Extraordinary and Plenipotentiary,
   HE Masaki Orita, apptd 2001

BRITISH EMBASSY
No. 1 Ichiban-cho, Chiyoda-ku, Tokyo 102-8381
Tel: (00 81) (3) 5211-1100
Email: embassytokyo@fco.gov.uk
Ambassador Extraordinary and Plenipotentiary,
   HE Sir Stephen Gomersall, KCMG, apptd 1999

BRITISH COUNCIL DIRECTOR, *(acting)* Mike Winter
1–2 Kagurazaka, Shinjuku-ku, Tokyo 162-0825.
Tel: (00 81) (3) 3235 8031
Email: bctokyo@britishcouncil.or.jp.
Regional offices in Fukuoka, Kyoto, Nagoya and Osaka

DEFENCE

The constitution prohibits the maintenance of armed
forces, although internal security forces were created in
the 1950s and their mission was extended in 1954 to
include the defence of Japan against aggression. In the
1990s legislation was passed permitting the armed forces
limited participation in UN peacekeeping missions and
allowing them to enter foreign conflicts in order to rescue
Japanese nationals. A revision to the USA–Japan defence
co-operation guidelines agreed in 1997 permits Japan to
play a supporting role in US military operations in areas
surrounding Japan. In July 2003 the Japanese parliament
passed legislation approving the deployment of Japanese
troops in Iraq to assist with post-war reconstruction.

The Ground Self-Defence Force (GSDF) has some
1,040 main battle tanks, around 830 armoured personnel
carriers, 60 infantry fighting vehicles, ten aircraft and 90
attack helicopters. The Maritime Self-Defence Force
(MSDF) has 16 submarines, 44 destroyers, ten frigates,
five patrol and coastal vessels, 80 combat aircraft and 91
armed helicopters at five bases. The Air Self-Defence
Force (ASDF) has 280 combat aircraft.

The USA has 38,450 personnel stationed in Japan.
MILITARY EXPENDITURE – 1.0 per cent of GDP (2001)
MILITARY PERSONNEL – 239,900: Army 148,200,
   Navy 44,400, Air Force 45,600; Paramilitaries 12,250

ECONOMY

Owing to the mountainous nature of the country less
than 20 per cent of its area can be cultivated and only 14
per cent is used for agriculture; 67 per cent is wooded.
The soil is only moderately fertile but intensive
cultivation secures good crops. Tobacco, tea, potatoes,
rice, maize, wheat and other cereals are all cultivated.
Rice is the staple food of the people.

Mineral resources include gold, silver, copper, lead,
zinc, iron chromite, white arsenic, coal, sulphur,
petroleum, salt and uranium. However, iron ore, coal and
crude oil are among the principal imports.

Japan is one of the most highly industrialised nations
in the world, with the whole range of modern light and
heavy industries, including steel, aerospace, computers,
office machinery, motor vehicles, electronics, metals,

machinery, chemicals, textiles (cotton, silk, wool and
synthetics), cement, pottery, glass, rubber, lumber, paper,
oil refining and shipbuilding.

Japan's economy was severely affected by the financial
crisis in Asia during the late 1990s. Its banks had made
loans totalling some US$200 billion to tiger economies,
and following widespread economic collapse in the
region, Japan's financial institutions have suffered.
Emergency measures announced by the government were
perceived by the markets as inadequate. Japan's economy
contracted in 1998; GDP fell by 2.8 per cent.
Unemployment reached 4.8 per cent, the highest level
since the Second World War.

On 21 September 2000 the government unveiled a
Yen 4,000 billion economic stimulus package. A package
of economic reforms was announced on 5 April 2001,
which focused on the structural reform of the financial
industry.

GNP – US$4,519,067 million (2000); US$35,620 per
   capita (2000)
GDP – US$4,245,191 million (2001); US$37,494 per
   capita (2000)
ANNUAL AVERAGE GROWTH OF GDP – 0.5 per cent
   (2000)
INFLATION RATE – –0.1 per cent (2001)
UNEMPLOYMENT – 4.7 per cent (2001)

TRADE

Being deficient in natural resources, Japan has had to
develop a complex foreign trade. Principal imports
include mineral fuels, food, raw materials and metal ores.
Principal exports include machinery, transport
equipment, chemicals, metal products and textiles.

In 2001 Japan had a trade surplus of US$70,214
million and a current account surplus of US$89,280
million. Imports totalled US$349,089 million and
exports US$403,496 million. The USA, China, Australia,
Hong Kong, South Korea, Taiwan and Singapore are
Japan's main trading partners.

Trade with UK	2000	2001
Imports from UK	£3,712,360,000	£3,593,405,000
Exports to UK	9,375,907,000	8,489,641,000

COMMUNICATIONS

There are 23,654 km of railway track and 1,152,207 km
of roads. Shinkansen (bullet train) tracks are currently
being expanded. The Seikan rail tunnel and the Seto
Ohashi rail bridge link the four major islands. There are
six international airports.

EDUCATION

Education at elementary (six-year course) and lower
secondary (three-year course) schools is free, compulsory
and co-educational. The (three-year) upper secondary
schools are attended by 96.7 per cent of the age group.

There are two- or three-year colleges and four-year
universities. Some of the universities have graduate
schools. In 1999 there were 622 universities and
colleges, most of which are privately maintained. The
most prominent universities are the seven state
universities of Tokyo, Kyoto, Tohoku (Sendai), Hokkaido
(Sapporo), Kyushu (Fukuoka), Osaka and Nagoya, and
the two private universities of Keio and Waseda.

ENROLMENT (percentage of age group) – primary 100
   per cent (1997); secondary 100 per cent (1997);
   tertiary 41 per cent (1997)

CULTURE

Japanese is said to be one of the Ural-Altaic group of languages and remained a spoken tongue until the fifth to seventh centuries AD, when Chinese characters came into use. Modern Japanese is written in a mixture of Chinese characters (about 1,800) and also the syllabary characters called Kana.

JORDAN

Al-Mamlaka al-Urdunniyya al-Hashimiyya – Hashemite Kingdom of Jordan

AREA – 34,192 sq. miles (88,900 sq. km). Neighbours: Syria (north), Israel and the West Bank (west), Saudi Arabia (south and east), Iraq (east)

POPULATION – 5,051,000 (2001). The majority are Sunni Muslims and Islam is the religion of the state; however, freedom of belief is guaranteed by the constitution

CAPITAL – Amman (population, 1,270,000, 1997 estimate)

MAJOR CITIES – Irbid (231,511); Az-Zarqa (389,815), 1997 estimates

CURRENCY – Jordanian dinar (JD) of 1,000 fils

NATIONAL ANTHEM - Asha Al Malik (Long Live The King)

NATIONAL DAY – 25 May (Independence Day)

NATIONAL FLAG – Three horizontal stripes of black, white, green and a red triangle based on the hoist, containing a seven-pointed white star

LIFE EXPECTANCY (years) – 71 (2001)

POPULATION GROWTH RATE – 4 per cent

POPULATION DENSITY – 57 per sq. km (2001)

ILLITERACY RATE – (m) 5.2 per cent; (f) 15.7 per cent (2000)

ENROLMENT (percentage of age group) – primary 71 per cent (1997); secondary 57 per cent (1997); tertiary 18 per cent (1997)

HISTORY AND POLITICS

After the defeat of Turkey in the First World War, the Amirate of Transjordan was established in the area east of the River Jordan as a state under British mandate. The mandate was terminated after the Second World War and the Amirate, still ruled by its founder the Amir Abdullah, became the Hashemite Kingdom of Jordan. Following the 1948–9 war between Israel and the Arab states, that part of Palestine remaining in Arab hands (the West Bank and East Jerusalem, but excluding Gaza) was, with Palestinian agreement, incorporated into the Hashemite Kingdom. King Abdullah was assassinated in 1951; his son Talal ruled briefly but abdicated in favour of King Hussein in 1952.

Israel captured the West Bank from Jordan in the 1967 war and annexed East Jerusalem. In 1988 Jordan severed its legal and administrative ties with the occupied West Bank, but did not formally renounce sovereignty over the area.

In 1993, multiparty parliamentary elections were held for the first time since 1956. In elections held on 17 June 2003, independent candidates loyal to King Abdullah won 62 out of 110 seats in the House of Deputies.

FOREIGN RELATIONS

The Middle East peace process begun in 1991, led to Jordan signing an agreement on a 'common agenda' for peace with Israel in 1993. On 25 July 1994 King Hussein and the Israeli Prime Minister signed a framework agreement for peace which ended the state of war existing since 1948. The first Israeli–Jordanian border crossing was opened between Eilat and Aqaba in August 1994. A full peace treaty was signed on 26 October 1994 which established full diplomatic and economic relations between the two states. It included agreements on sharing water from the Jordan and Yarmouk rivers; co-operating in the fields of commerce, transport, tourism, communications, energy and agriculture; and granted King Hussein custodianship of Islamic holy sites in Jerusalem. Israeli forces completed their withdrawal from Jordanian land in the Arava valley on 9 February 1995.

On 25 January 1999, King Hussein signed a decree naming his eldest son, Abdullah ibn al-Hussein, as his new heir, in place of his youngest brother, Prince Hassan; Prince Abdullah became King following the death of King Hussein on 7 February 1999.

Jordan and Kuwait re-established full diplomatic relations on 3 March 1999, which had been broken off following the 1990 Gulf War.

POLITICAL SYSTEM

The constitution provides for a Senate of 40 members (all appointed by the King for a four-year term) and an elected House of Deputies which has 110 members, directly elected for a four-year term.

The King appoints the members of the Council of Ministers. In 1991 a new national charter was formulated which lifted the ban on political parties, imposed in 1957.

HEAD OF STATE

His Majesty The King of the Jordan, Abdullah II, *born* 30 January 1962, *succeeded* 7 February 1999

Crown Prince, Hamzeh ibn al-Hussein, *born* 29 March 1982, son of King Hussein of Jordan

Chief of the Royal Court, Youssef al-Dalabih

COUNCIL OF MINISTERS *as at July 2003*

Prime Minister, Defence, Ali Abu Ragheb

Deputy Prime Minister, Justice and Legal Affairs, Faris al-Nabulsi

Agriculture, Trad al-Fayez

Communications and Information Technology, Fawaz Hatim al-Zu'bi

Culture, Haidar Mahmoud

Education, Khalid Touqan

Energy and Mineral Resources, Muhammad Ali al-Batayinah

Finance, Michel Martu

Foreign Affairs, Marwan Muasher

Health, Walid al-Ma'ani

Higher Education and Scientific Research, Mohammad Hamdan

Industry and Trade, Salaheddine al-Bashir

Interior, Samir Habashneh

Labour, Muzahem al-Muheisin

Ministers of State, Muhammad al-Thneibat *(Administrative Development and Minister for Environment);* Muhammed Samir Tawil *(Economic Affairs);* Shaher Bak *(Foreign Affairs);* Muhammad Affash al-Udwan *(Political Affairs and Information);* Mustafa al-Qaisi *(Prime Ministry Affairs)*

Municipal, Rural, and Environmental Affairs, Abdul
   Razzaq Tbeishat
Planning, Bassem Awadallah
Public Works and Housing, Hosni Abu Gheida
Religious Endowments (Waqfs), Islamic Affairs and Holy
   Places, Ahmad Hilayel
Social Development, Rwaidah al-Ma'aytah
Transport, Tourism and Antiquities, Nadir al-Dhahabi
Water and Irrigation, Hazim al-Nasir

EMBASSY OF THE HASHEMITE KINGDOM OF JORDAN
6 Upper Phillimore Gardens, London W8 7HA
Tel: 020-7937 3685
Ambassador Extraordinary and Plenipotentiary,
   HE Timoor Daghistani, GCVO, apptd 1999

BRITISH EMBASSY
Abdoun (PO Box 87), Amman
Tel: (00 962) (6) 592 3100
Ambassador Extraordinary and Plenipotentiary,
   HE Christopher Prentice, apptd 2002

BRITISH COUNCIL DIRECTOR, Tim Gore
Rainbow Street, PO Box 634, Amman 11118
Tel: (00 962) (6) 463 6147
Email: bcamman@britishcouncil.org.jo

DEFENCE

The Army has 1,179 main battle tanks, 1,500 armoured
personnel carriers and 26 armoured infantry fighting
vehicles. The Navy has three patrol and coastal vessels at
its base at Aqaba. The Air Force has 101 combat aircraft
and 22 armed helicopters.
MILITARY EXPENDITURE – 8.5 per cent of GDP (2001)
MILITARY PERSONNEL – 100,240: Army 84,700,
   Navy 540, Air Force 15,000; Paramilitaries 10,000

ECONOMY

The main agricultural areas are the Jordan valley, the hills
overlooking the valley, and the flatter country to the
south of Amman and around Madaba and Irbid.
However, several large farms, which depend for irrigation
on water pumped from deep aquifers, have been
established in the southern desert area. The rest of the
country is desert and semi-desert. The principal crops are
wheat, barley, vegetables, olives and fruit. Agricultural
production has increased considerably in recent years due
to improvements in production and irrigation techniques.
In September 2002 Jordan and Israel agreed on a plan to
pipe water from the Red Sea to the shrinking Dead Sea.
   Important industrial products are raw phosphates
(1998, 5,925,000 tonnes) and potash (1998, 916,169
tonnes), most of which is exported, together with
fertilisers and pharmaceuticals. The Trans-Arabian oil
pipeline (Tapline) runs through north Jordan from Saudi
Arabia to the Lebanese port of Sidon. A branch pipeline,
together with oil trucked by road from Iraq, feeds a
refinery at Zerqa, which meets most of Jordan's
requirements for refined petroleum products. Sufficient
reserves of natural gas have been discovered in the north-
east to produce electricity for the national grid since
1989.
   In 1999 there was a trade deficit of US$1,460 million
and a current account surplus of US$405 million. In
2001 imports totalled US$4,844 million and exports
US$2,293 million.
GNP – US$8,360 million (2000); US$1,710 per capita
   (2000)

GDP – US$8,829 million (2001); US$1,556 per capita
   (2000)
ANNUAL AVERAGE GROWTH OF GDP – 2.2 per cent
   (1998)
INFLATION RATE – 3.3 per cent (2002)
TOTAL EXTERNAL DEBT – US$8,226 million (2000)

Trade with UK	2001	2002
Imports from UK	£168,910,000	£180,150,000
Exports to UK	16,681,000	31,627,000

COMMUNICATIONS

Amman is linked to Aqaba, Damascus, Baghdad and
Jiddah by roads which are of considerable importance in
the overland trade of the Middle East.
   The former Hejaz Railway runs from Syria through
Jordan, and is used mainly for freight between Amman
and Damascus. The Aqaba railway carries phosphate rock
from the mines of al-Hasa and al-Abiad to Aqaba.

KAZAKHSTAN

Qazaqstan Respūblīkasy – Republic of Kazakhstan

AREA – 1,038,346 sq. miles (2,699,700 sq. km).
   Neighbours: Russia (north and west), Turkmenistan,
   Uzbekistan and Kyrgyzstan (south), China (east)
POPULATION – 16,095,000 (2001): Kazakhs (53 per
   cent), Russians (30 per cent), Ukrainians (4 per cent)
   and ethnic Germans (2 per cent), with smaller numbers
   of Tatars, Uzbeks, Koreans and Belarusians. The
   Russian population is concentrated in the north of the
   country, where it forms a significant majority, and in
   Almaty. The majority of ethnic Kazakhs are Sunni
   Muslims, and this is the main religion of the republic.
   Kazakh (one of the Turkic languages) became the
   official language in 1993; a law passed in July 1997
   decreed Kazakh as the language of state
   administration; Russian has a special status as the
   'social language between peoples'. Otherwise each
   ethnic group uses its own language
CAPITAL – Astana (population, 320,000, 2000 estimate.
   Known as Akmola until May 1998). The capital was
   moved from Alma-Ata (Almaty) in December 1997
MAJOR CITIES – Almaty (1,129,400); Pavlodar
   (300,500); Karaganda (436,900); Shymkent
   (360,100), 1999 estimates
CURRENCY – Tenge
NATIONAL DAY – 25 October (Republic Day)
NATIONAL FLAG – Dark blue with a sun and a soaring
   eagle in the centre all in gold, and a red vertical
   ornamentation stripe near the hoist
LIFE EXPECTANCY (years) – 65 (2001)
POPULATION GROWTH RATE– –0.4 per cent
POPULATION DENSITY – 6 per sq. km (2001)
URBAN POPULATION – 56 per cent (2001)
ENROLMENT (percentage of age group) – tertiary 33 per
   cent (1997)

Kazakhstan occupies the northern part of what was
Soviet Central Asia. It stretches from the Volga and the
Caspian Sea in the west to the Altai and Tienshan
mountains in the east. The country consists of arid
steppes and semi-deserts, flat in the west, hilly in the east
and mountainous in the south-east (Southern Altai and
Tienshan mountains). The main rivers are the Irtysh, the
Ural, the Syr-Darya and the Ili.

HISTORY AND POLITICS

Kazakhstan was inhabited by nomadic tribes before being invaded by Ghenghiz Khan and incorporated into his empire in 1218. After his empire disintegrated, feudal towns emerged based on large oases. These towns affiliated and established a Kazakh state in the late 15th century which engaged in almost continuous warfare with the marauding Khanates on its southern border. After appealing to Russia for aid and protection, in 1731 Kazakhstan acceded to the Russian Empire under a voluntary act of accession.

After the 1917 Russian revolution, Kazakhstan came under the control of White Russian forces until 1919. On 26 August 1920 a constitution was signed under which Kazakhstan became a Soviet Socialist Republic. Under Soviet rule in the 1920s and 1930s there was rapid industrial development and the traditional nomadic way of life disappeared. The Kazakhs suffered greatly in the Stalinist purges, the merchant and religious classes being murdered and thousands dying in the desert on collective farms. Other nationalities, such as Tatars and Germans, were forcibly transported to Kazakhstan by Stalin. Kazakhstan declared its independence on 16 December 1991.

The Communist-derived Congress of People's Unity of Kazakhstan (SNEK) won the March 1994 legislative elections which were ruled invalid by the Constitutional Court. The President responded by dissolving parliament in March 1995. Elections to the new legislature were held in December 1995; the requirement for candidates to achieve an absolute majority made run-offs necessary. A referendum on 29 April 1995 extended President Nazarbayev's term until 2000, but constitutional changes unanimously agreed by parliament brought forward presidential elections to 10 January 1999. Elections to the upper chamber of the legislature were held on 17 September 1999 and to the lower house on 10 and 24 October 1999 and were won by the Fatherland Republican Party. On 12 November 2001, a number of government ministers and officials resigned following a joint statement issued on 16 November claiming that "democratic reforms in Kazakhstan have stopped". On 28 January 2002, Prime Minister Kasymzhomart Tokaev resigned and was replaced by Imangali Tasmagambetov. Prime Minister Tasmagambetov resigned on 11 June 2003 and was replaced with Daniyal Akhmetov on 13 June.

POLITICAL SYSTEM

Executive power is vested in the president and government. The president must be a Kazakh speaker and has the power to appoint the prime minister, other senior ministers and all ambassadors.

A new constitution approved by referendum on 30 August 1995 granted the president the power to dissolve the legislature and to rule by decree. It also nominated Kazakh as the sole official language; prohibited dual citizenship; and created a new bicameral legislature composed of a 39-member Senate, of whom 32 are indirectly elected and seven appointed, and a 77-member directly elected Majlis (lower house of the legislature). The Constitutional Court, which opposed the new constitution, was replaced by a Constitutional Council which was made subject to presidential veto.

HEAD OF STATE

President, Commander-in-Chief of the Armed Forces,
Nursultan Nazarbayev, *elected* 1 December 1991,

confirmed in office by referendum 29 April 1995, *re-elected* 10 January 1999

GOVERNMENT *as at July 2003*
Prime Minister, Daniyal Akhmetov
First Deputy Prime Minister, Alexander Pavlov
Deputy Prime Ministers, Sauat Mynbayev; Akhmetzhan Yesimov *(Agriculture)*
Culture, Information and Social Accord, Mukhtar Kul-Mukhammed
Defence, Gen. Mukhtar Altynbayev
Economy and Budget Planning, Kairat Kelimbetov
Education and Science, Zhaksybek Kulekeyev
Energy and Mineral Resources, Vladimir Shkolnik
Environmental Protection, Aitkul Samakova
Finance and State Revenues, Erbolat Dosayev
Foreign Affairs, Kasymzhomart Tokayev
Industry and Trade, Adilbek Jaksybekov
Interior, Kairbek Suleimenov
Justice, Onalsyn Zhumabekov
Labour and Social Security, Gulzhana Karagusova
Public Health, Zhaksylyk Doskaliyev
Transport and Communications, Kazhmurat Nagmanov

EMBASSY OF THE REPUBLIC OF KAZAKHSTAN
33 Thurloe Square, London SW7 2SD
Tel: 020-7581 4646
Ambassador Extraordinary and Plenipotentiary,
Erlan Idrissov, apptd 2002

BRITISH EMBASSY
Ul. Furmanova 173, Almaty
Tel: (00 7) (3272) 506191/2
Email: british-embassy@kaznet.kz
Ambassador Extraordinary and Plenipotentiary,
HE James Sharp, apptd 2002

BRITISH COUNCIL DIRECTOR, James Kennedy
Republic Square 13, KZ-480013 Almaty
Tel: (00 7) 3272 633339
Email: general@kz.britishcouncil.org

DEFENCE

An agreement signed with Russia in January 1995 provides for eventual reunification of the two states' armed forces. The CIS mutual defence treaty of 1993, to which Kazakhstan is a signatory, retains a common air defence force, while Kazakh forces also take part in the CIS peacekeeping force along the Tajikistan–Afghanistan border. By 1996, all nuclear warheads had been returned to Russia although Kazakhstan retained 48 SS-18 intercontinental ballistic missiles. Kazakhstan participates in the NATO Partnership for Peace programme. The Army has 930 main battle tanks and 1,343 armoured combat vehicles. The Caspian Sea Flotilla, which Kazakhstan shares with Russia and Turkmenistan, operates under Russian command. The Air Force has 164 combat aircraft.
MILITARY EXPENDITURE – 1.3 per cent of GDP (2001)
MILITARY PERSONNEL – 60,000: Army 41,000, Air Force 19,000; Paramilitaries 34,500
CONSCRIPTION DURATION – 31 months

ECONOMY

Kazakhstan is rich in minerals, with copper, lead, gold, uranium, chromium, silver, zinc, iron ore, coal, oil and natural gas. In 1998 production of coal was 68,700,000 tonnes and of iron ore was 18,000,000 tonnes. The oil and gas industry, concentrated in the west of the country, has been expanded by foreign investment, which is also being used to explore the Karachaganak (gas) and Tengiz (oil) fields in the Caspian Sea. Initial exploration of the Kashagan offshore oilfield in 2000 indicated extensive reserves.

Pipelines to Turkey and Russia are in operation and on 27 November 2001, a new pipeline connecting Tengiz to Russia's Novorossiisk was put into operation. Oil production in 1998 was 25.9 million tonnes and gas output was 8.3 billion cubic metres. Industry is dominated by food processing and mining and metals production; textiles, steel and tractors are also produced. The main centres of the metal industry are in the Altai mountains, in Shymkent, north of Lake Balqash and in central Kazakhstan.

Agriculture, including stock-raising, is highly developed, particularly in the central and south-west of the republic. Grain is grown in the north and north-east, and cotton and wool produced in the south and south-east. 12.5 million tonnes of wheat and 3.5 million tonnes of barley were grown in 1999.

A treaty of economic co-operation for 1998–2007 was signed with Russia in October 1998. The tenge was floated on 5 April 1999 in a bid to reduce the trade deficit. Annual trade between Russia and Kazakhstan was maintained at a stable level of $US2.5 billion for several years. In April 2002, this was reported to have exceeded US$4 billion with Kazakhstan being the third main CIS trading partner of Russia.

In 2001 the trade surplus was US$896 million and the current account deficit US$1,749 million. Imports totalled US$6,363 million and exports US$8,647 million.

GNP – US$18,773 million (2000); US$1,260 per capita (2000)
GDP – US$22,635 million (2001); US$1,129 per capita (2000)
ANNUAL AVERAGE GROWTH OF GDP – –2.5 per cent (1998)
INFLATION RATE – 6 per cent (2002)
UNEMPLOYMENT – 13.7 per cent (1998)
TOTAL EXTERNAL DEBT – US$6,664 million (2000)

Trade with UK	2001	2002
Imports from UK	£92,168,000	£91,512,000
Exports to UK	71,052,000	34,333,000

KENYA

Jamhuri ya Kenya – Republic of Kenya

AREA – 218,885 sq. miles (569,100 sq. km).
  Neighbours: Somalia (east), Ethiopia (north), Sudan (north-west), Uganda (west), Tanzania (south)
POPULATION – 31,293,000 (2001). The main tribal groups are the Kikuyu, Luhya, Luo, Kalenjin, Kamba and Masai. The official languages are Swahili, which is generally understood throughout Kenya, and English; numerous indigenous languages are also spoken
CAPITAL – Nairobi (population, 2,143,254, 1999)
MAJOR CITIES – ΨKisumu (322,734); ΨMombasa (665,018); Nakuru (219,366), 1999
CURRENCY – Kenya shilling (Ksh) of 100 cents
NATIONAL ANTHEM – Ee Mungu Nguvu Yetu (Oh God Of All Creation)
NATIONAL DAY – 12 December (Independence Day)

NATIONAL FLAG – Horizontally black, red and green with the red fimbriated in white, and with a shield and crossed spears all over in the centre
LIFE EXPECTANCY (years) – 50 (2001)
POPULATION GROWTH RATE – 2.6 per cent
POPULATION DENSITY – 55 per sq. km (2001)
MILITARY EXPENDITURE – 3.1 per cent of GDP (2001)
MILITARY PERSONNEL – 24,400: Army 20,000, Navy 1,400, Air Force 3,000; Paramilitaries 5,000
ILLITERACY RATE – (m) 11.1 per cent; (f) 24.0 per cent (2000)
ENROLMENT (percentage of age group) – primary 85 per cent (1997)

HISTORY AND POLITICS
Kenya became an independent state and a member of the British Commonwealth on 12 December 1963 and a republic in 1964. In 1982 the government introduced amendments to the constitution making the country a one-party state, with the Kenya African National Union (KANU) as the ruling party. In December 1991, the government yielded to internal and international pressure and introduced a multiparty democracy.

KANU won the elections of 29 December 1997 with 109 out of 210 seats in the National Assembly and President Daniel arap Moi won just over 40 per cent of the vote, securing a fifth term in office. In the legislative elections of 27 December 2002 KANU lost power to the National Rainbow Coalition (NARC) who gained 125 out of 210 seats. Mwai Kibaki of NARC won the simultaneous presidential election with 62.2 per cent of the vote. He took office on 30 December 2002 and the new cabinet was sworn in on 6 January 2003.

POLITICAL SYSTEM
The head of state is a president, directly elected for a five-year term, who is head of government and appoints the Cabinet. The unicameral legislature, the Bunge (National Assembly), has 224 members, of whom 210 are directly elected for a five-year term, 12 appointed by the president, and two ex-officio members, the attorney-general and the speaker. In November 1999, an amendment to the constitution was passed which limited the powers of the president over the National Assembly and affirmed the Bunge's supremacy.

HEAD OF STATE
President and C.-in-C. Armed Forces, Mwai Kibaki (NARC), *elected* 27 December 2002, *took office* 30 December 2002
Vice-President, vacant

CABINET *as at July 2003*
Agriculture, Kipruto Arap Kirwa
Co-operative Development, Peter Njeru Ndwiga
Education, George Saitoti
Energy, Ochilo Ayacko
Environment and Natural Resources, Newton Kulundu
Finance, David Mwiraria
Foreign Affairs and International Co-operation, Kalonzo Musyoka
Gender, Sport and Culture, Najib Balala
Health, Charity Kaluki Ngilu
Home Affairs and National Heritage, Moody Awori
Justice and Constitutional Affairs, Kiraitu Murungi
Labour and Manpower, Chirau Ali Mwakwere
Lands and Settlement, Amos Kimunya
Livestock Development, Joseph Konzolo Munyao

Local Government, Karisa Maitha
Minister of State for National Security and Provincial Administration and National Security (in the Office of the President), Chris Murungaru
Minister of State in the Vice-President's Office, Linah Jebii Kilimo
Planning and National Development, Anyang' Nyong'o
Public Works and Housing, Raila Amolo Odinga
Tourism and Information, Raphael Tuju
Trade and Industry, Mukhisa Kituyi
Transport and Communications, John Njoroge Michuki
Water, Martha Karua

KENYA HIGH COMMISSION
45 Portland Place, London W1B 1AS
Tel: 020-7636 2371
High Commissioner, HE Nancy Kirui, apptd 2000

BRITISH HIGH COMMISSION
Upper Hill Road, PO Box 30465 Nairobi
Tel: (00 254) (2) 714699
Email: consular@nairobi.mail.fco.gov.uk
High Commissioner, HE Edward Clay, CMG, apptd 2001

BRITISH COUNCIL DIRECTOR, Peter Elborn
ICEA Building, Kenyatta Avenue, PO Box 40751, Nairobi.
Tel: (00 254) (2) 334 855/6
Email: information@britishcouncil.or.ke

ECONOMY
Agriculture provides about a quarter of GDP and employs around three-quarters of the workforce. The great variation in altitude and ecology provides conditions under which a wide range of crops can be grown. These include wheat, barley, pyrethrum, coffee, tea, sisal, coconuts, cashew nuts, cotton, maize and a wide variety of tropical and temperate fruits and vegetables.

Mineral production consists of soda ash, salt and limestone. Hydroelectric power has been developed, particularly on the Upper Tana River, and Kenya is now almost self-sufficient in electric power generation.

There has been considerable industrial development over the last 15 years and Kenya has a variety of industries processing agricultural produce and manufacturing products from local and imported raw materials. New industries are steel, textile mills, dehydrated vegetable processing and motor tyre manufacture. Smaller schemes have added to the country's consumer goods manufacturing base. There is an oil refinery in Mombasa supplying both Kenya and Uganda, and a fuel pipeline connects Mombasa and Nairobi.

Tourism generates some US$400 million per year but the industry was adversely affected during 2002 and 2003 by fears of terrorist attacks.

GNP – US$10,610 million (2000); US$350 per capita (2000)
GDP – US$10,419 million (2001); US$342 per capita (2000)
ANNUAL AVERAGE GROWTH OF GDP – 2.7 per cent (1998)
INFLATION RATE – 5.9 per cent (2000)
TOTAL EXTERNAL DEBT – US$6,295 million (2000)

TRADE
Principal exports are coffee and tea, which account for roughly a third of total export earnings. Also exported are fruit, vegetables, and crude animal and vegetable material. Industrial machinery is the largest single import; other imports are transport equipment, petroleum and petroleum products, metals, pharmaceuticals and chemicals.

In 2000 Kenya had a trade deficit of US$1,271 million and a current account deficit of US$238 million. In 2001 imports totalled US$3,192 million and exports US$1,944 million.

Trade with UK	2001	2002
Imports from UK	£172,887,000	£158,864,000
Exports to UK	211,814,000	216,461,000

COMMUNICATIONS
The Kenya Railways Corporation has 2,778 km of railway open to traffic. There are also 67,000 km of road, of which 8,900 km are bitumen surfaced.

The principal port is Mombasa, operated by the Kenya Ports Authority. International air services operate from airports at Nairobi and Mombasa.

KIRIBATI

Ribaberikin Kiribati – Republic of Kiribati

AREA – 280 sq. miles (726 sq. km)
POPULATION – 94,149 (2001 estimate): predominantly Christian. The languages are I-Kiribati and English
CAPITAL – Tarawa (population, 36,717, 2000)
CURRENCY – Australian dollar ($A) of 100 cents
NATIONAL ANTHEM – Teirake Kain Kiribati (Stand Kiribati)
NATIONAL DAY – 12 July (Independence Day)
NATIONAL FLAG – Red, with blue and white wavy lines in base, and in the centre a gold rising sun and a flying frigate bird
POPULATION GROWTH RATE – 1.4 per cent
POPULATION DENSITY – 113 per sq. km (1999)

Kiribati (pronounced Kiribas) comprises 36 islands: the Gilberts Group (17) including Banaba (formerly Ocean Island), the Phoenix Islands (8), and the Line Islands (11), which are situated in the south-west central Pacific around the point at which the International Date Line cuts the Equator. Few of the atolls are more than half a mile in width or more than 12 feet high.

HISTORY AND POLITICS
The Gilbert and Ellice Islands were proclaimed a British protectorate in 1892 and annexed as the Gilbert and Ellice Islands Colony on 10 November 1915 (taking effect 12 January 1916). The Gilbert Islands were occupied by the Japanese army during World War II. Nuclear tests were carried out by the British off Kiritimati (Christmas Island) in 1957. In October 1975 the Ellice Islands seceded to become the independent state of Tuvalu. The Gilbert Islands achieved independence on 12 July 1979 as the Republic of Kiribati.

Teburoro Tito won the presidential election of 1998 and was re-elected in elections held in January and February 2003. However, he was defeated in parliament after a vote of no confidence and resigned in March. Legislative elections were held on 9 and 16 May 2003 with the Maneaban Te Mauri (Protect the Maneaba) gaining 24 seats and Boutokaan Te Koaua (BTK, Pillars of Truth) winning 16 seats in the House of Assembly. Presidential elections took place on 4 July 2003 in which

Anote Tong of the BTK defeated his brother, Harry Tong, with 47.4 per cent of the vote.

POLITICAL SYSTEM

The president is head of state as well as head of government and is directly elected. There is a House of Assembly of 41 members (39 elected members, the Attorney-General and a representative of the Banaban community from Rabi Island). Executive authority is vested in the Cabinet.

HEAD OF STATE

President, Foreign Affairs, Atone Tong, *elected* 4 July 2003, *sworn in* 6 July 2003

COUNCIL OF STATE *as at July 2003*
Chair, Public Service Commissioner, Tion Otang
Speaker of the House of Assembly, Taomati Iuta
Chief Justice, Robin Millhouse

KIRIBATI HIGH COMMISSION
c/o Office of the President, P.O Box 68, Bairiki, Tarawa
High Commissioner, vacant
Acting High Commissioner, David Yeeting

BRITISH HIGH COMMISSIONER, HE Charles Mochan, apptd 2002, resident at Suva, Fiji

ECONOMY

Many people still practise a semi-subsistence economy, the main staples of their diet being coconuts and fish.

The principal imports are foodstuffs, consumer goods, machinery and transport equipment. The principal exports are copra and fish.

In May 2000, Japanese-funded improved port facilities at Betio were opened.

GNP – US$86 million (2000); US$950 per capita (2000)
GDP – US$40 million (2001); US$531 per capita (2000)
ANNUAL AVERAGE GROWTH OF GDP – 2.0 per cent (1998)

Trade with UK	2001	2002
Imports from UK	£74,000	£170,000
Exports to UK	111,000	165,000

COMMUNICATIONS

Air communication exists between most of the islands and is operated by Air Kiribati, a statutory corporation. Air Marshall Islands operates a weekly service between Majuro, Tarawa, Funafuti and Nadi, and Air Nauru between Tarawa, Nauru and Nadi. Inter-island shipping is operated by a statutory corporation, the Shipping Corporation of Kiribati.

EDUCATION

There are 104 primary schools, eight secondary schools and one high school. There is a teacher training college, a technical institute and a marine training centre.

KOREA

Korea's southern and western coasts are fringed with innumerable islands, of which the largest, forming a province of its own, is Cheju. The Korean language is of the Ural-Altaic Group. Its script, Hangul, was invented in the 15th century; prior to this Chinese characters alone were used. Despite the great cultural influence of the Chinese, Koreans have developed and preserved their own cultural heritage.

HISTORY

The Korean peninsula was first unified in AD 668 when Shilla, having emerged as the dominant tribal state, conquered Koguryo and Paekche. The Koryo dynasty ruled from 912 until 1392 and was succeeded by the Choson dynasty, who ruled from 1392 until 1910 when Japan formally annexed Korea. The country remained part of the Japanese Empire until the defeat of Japan in 1945, when it was occupied by troops of the USA and the USSR, the 38th parallel being fixed as the boundary between the two zones of occupation.

The UN in November 1947 resolved that elections should be held for a National Assembly which, when elected, should set up a government. The Soviet government refused to comply and a UN commission was only allowed to operate south of the 38th parallel.

A general election was held on 10 May 1948, and the first National Assembly met in Seoul on 31 May. The Assembly passed a constitution on 12 July and on 15 August 1948 the republic was formally inaugurated and American military government came to an end. Meanwhile, in the Soviet-occupied zone north of the 38th parallel the Democratic People's Republic had been established with its capital at Pyongyang. A Supreme People's Soviet was elected in September 1948, and a Soviet-style constitution adopted.

THE KOREAN WAR

Korea remained divided along the 38th parallel until June 1950, when North Korean forces invaded South Korea. In response to Security Council recommendations, 16 nations, including the USA and the UK, came to the aid of the Republic of Korea. China entered the war on the side of North Korea in November 1950. The fighting was ended by an armistice agreement signed on 27 July 1953. By this agreement (which was not signed by the Republic of Korea), the line of division between North and South Korea remained close to the 38th parallel.

Talks between North and South Korea on the reunification of the country have taken place intermittently. A non-aggression accord was signed between the North and South in 1991 and an agreement on the denuclearisation of the Korean peninsula was reached in 1992. A summit meeting between the presidents of North and South Korea took place on 13–15 June 2000 at which a communiqué was signed agreeing to promote economic co-operation, achieve reconciliation and eventually reunify the two countries.

DEMOCRATIC PEOPLE'S REPUBLIC OF KOREA

Chosun Minchu-chui Inmin Kongwa-guk – Democratic People's Republic of Korea

AREA – 46,308 sq. miles (120,400 sq. km). Neighbours: China, Russia (north), Republic of Korea (south)
POPULATION – 22,428,000 (2001). The language is Korean
CAPITAL – Pyongyang (approximate population, 2,741,260)
CURRENCY – Won of 100 chon
NATIONAL ANTHEM - Aegug-ga (Patriotic Hymn)
NATIONAL DAY – 16 February (Kim Jong-il's birthday)

NATIONAL FLAG – Red with white fimbriations and blue borders at top and bottom; a large red star on a white disc near the hoist
LIFE EXPECTANCY (years) – 65 (2001)
POPULATION GROWTH RATE – 1.1 per cent
POPULATION DENSITY – 186 per sq. km (2001)
URBAN POPULATION – 61 per cent (2001)

FOREIGN RELATIONS
Between 1992 and 1994 North Korea embarked on a clandestine nuclear weapons programme despite being a signatory of the Nuclear Non-Proliferation Treaty (NPT), but halted the programme in November 1994. Tensions began to mount from October 2002 when the USA stated that North Korea had admitted to having continued its nuclear energy programme. Kim Yong-il initially allowed international weapons inspectors into the country, but they were expelled in December after the US halted oil shipments to Pyongyang. North Korea announced that the halting of oil shipments had left the country with no choice but to restart nuclear facilities for energy production. In December, North Korea reactivated its Yongbyon nuclear reactor and UN inspectors were expelled from the country. On 6 January 2003 the International Atomic Energy Agency (IAEA) passed a resolution demanding that North Korea readmit UN inspectors and abandon its nuclear weapons programme within weeks or face possible action by the UN Security Council. On 10 January North Korea announced its withdrawal from the NPT. Relations between the USA and North Korea deteriorated throughout February and March. Talks began in Beijing on 23 April 2003 between delegations from North Korea, the USA and China over North Korea's nuclear ambitions. They were the first international talks since the crisis had erupted in October 2002. The talks ended on 25 April after the USA announced that North Korea had admitted to possessing nuclear weapons. In August, North Korea agreed to talks with South Korea, the USA, Japan, China and Russia on the country's nuclear programme.

POLITICAL SYSTEM
The constitution of the Democratic People's Republic of Korea provides for a Supreme People's Assembly, presently consisting of 687 deputies, which is elected from a single list of candidates every five years by universal suffrage. The Assembly elects a president for a five-year term, and the Central People's Committee. In turn, the Central People's Committee directs the Administrative Council which implements the policy formulated by the Committee. The Administrative Council (36 members), the government of North Korea, includes the prime minister and various ministers. In practice, however, the country is ruled by the Korean Workers' Party which elects a Central Committee; this in turn appoints a Politburo. The senior ministers of the Administrative Council are all members of the Communist Party Central Committee and the majority are also members of the Politburo. Kim Il-sung, who had been head of the state, party and military since the country's inception in 1948, died on 8 July 1994, but was declared the eternal president in September 1998. His son Kim Jong-il, who had been party general secretary since October 1997, became chair of the National Defence Committee, which is now *de facto* the highest office.
   Elections to the Supreme People's Assembly were held on 3 August 2003 in which only the list of the Democratic Front for the Reunification of the Fatherland was allowed to participate.

HEAD OF STATE
Eternal President, Kim Il-sung (deceased)
Chair of the National Defence Commission, Kim Jong-il
Chair of the Standing Committee of the Supreme People's Assembly, Kim Yong-nam

SPA STANDING COMMITTEE
Chairman, Kim Yong-nam
Vice-Chairmen, Yang Hyong-sop; Im Yong-tae
Secretary-General, Kim Yun-hyok
Honorary Vice-Chairmen, Pak Song-chol; Kim Yong-chu; Yi Chong-ok; Chon Mun-sop
Members, Yu Mi-yong; Kang Yong-sop; Yi Kil-song; Yi Chol-pong; Yi Il-hwan; Song Sam-sop

ADMINISTRATIVE COUNCIL *as at July 2003*
Premier, Hong Song-nam
Deputy Premiers, Kwak Pon-ki; Cho Chang-tok; Sin Il-nam
Foreign Affairs, Paek Nam-sun

MINISTERS
Agriculture, Kim Chang-sik
Chair, Physical Culture and Sports Guidance Committee, Pak Myong-chol
Chair, State Planning Committee, Pak Nam-ki
Chemical Industry, Pak Pong-chu
City Management, Choe Chong-kon
Commerce, Yi Yong-son
Construction and Building Materials Industry, Cho Yun-hui
Culture, Kang Nung-su
Director of the Central Statistics Bureau, Kim Chang-su
Director of the Secretariat and State Administration Council, Chong Mun-sang
Education, Kim Yong-chin
Electronics Industry, O Su-yong
Finance, Mun Il-bong
Fisheries, Yi Song-un
Foreign Trade, Ri Kwang-gun
Forestry, Yi Sang-mu
Labour, Yi Won-il
Land and Maritime Transport, Kim Yong-il
Land Environmental Protection, Chang Il-son
Light Industry, Yi Yong-su
Metal and Machine Industry, Chon Sung-hun
Mining Industry, Son Chong-o
People's Armed Forces, Vice-Marshall Kim Il-chol
Posts and Telecommunications, Yi Kun-pom
Power and Coal Industry, Sin Tae-nok
President of the Academy of Sciences, Pyon Yong-nip
President of the Central Bank, Kim Wan-su
Procurement and Food Administration, Choe Nam-kyun
Public Health, Kim Su-hak
Public Security, Choe Yong-su
Railways, Kim Yong-san
State Construction Commission, Pae Tal-chun
State Inspection, Kim Ui-sun

DEFENCE
The Army has about 3,500 main battle tanks and 2,500 armoured personnel carriers. The Navy has 26 submarines, three frigates and about 310 patrol and coastal vessels at 15 bases. The Air Force has 621 combat aircraft and 24 armed helicopters.

MILITARY EXPENDITURE – 11.6 per cent of GDP (2001)

MILITARY PERSONNEL – 1,082,000: Army 950,000, Navy 46,000, Air Force 86,000; Paramilitaries 189,000

CONSCRIPTION DURATION – Three to ten years

ECONOMY

North Korea is rich in minerals and industry was developed, but the economy has stagnated owing to poor planning and a shortage of foreign exchange. The current economic crisis was precipitated by the curtailment of barter trade with the Soviet Union after 1991, and the end of subsidised oil and grain from China. Industrial output has collapsed, with industry operating at one-third of capacity. The economy has been sustained by foreign exchange sent by ethnic Koreans in Japan. In April 1998, South Korea lifted its ban on investment in North Korea, allowing South Koreans to send money to their relatives in the north.

A North Korean survey quoted by South Korean security services stated that up to three million people had died as a result of famine between 1995 and 1998. The USA increased food aid to North Korea in May 1999 but political tension in 2002–3 over North Korea's nuclear programme has led to a reduction in international food and fuel aid.

GDP – US$10,273 million (1998); US$540 per capita (2000)

ANNUAL AVERAGE GROWTH OF GDP– –1.1 per cent (1998)

Trade with UK	2001	2002
Imports from UK	£28,236,000	£16,683,000
Exports to UK	1,423,000	997,000

REPUBLIC OF KOREA

Taehan Min'guk – Republic of Korea

AREA – 37,692 sq. miles (98,700 sq. km). Neighbour: Democratic People's Republic of Korea (north)

POPULATION – 47,069,000 (2001). The largest religions are Buddhism (10.3 million) and Christianity (8.8 million Protestants, 2.9 million Roman Catholics). The language is Korean

CAPITAL – Seoul (population, 10,321,000, 1999 estimate)

MAJOR CITIES – ΨInchon (2,524,000); ΨPusan (3,831,000); Taegu (2,517,000)

CURRENCY – Won

NATIONAL ANTHEM – Aegug-ga (Patriotic Hymn)

NATIONAL DAY – 15 August (Liberation Day)

NATIONAL FLAG – White with a red and blue yin-yang symbol in the centre, surrounded by four black trigrams

LIFE EXPECTANCY (years) – 75 (2001)

POPULATION GROWTH RATE – 0.8 per cent

POPULATION DENSITY – 47,069 per sq. km (2001)

URBAN POPULATION – 82 per cent (2001)

HISTORY AND POLITICS

The most recent elections to the National Assembly in April 2000 produced no outright majority. The Millennium Democratic Party won 115 seats and formed a coalition with the United Liberal Democrats, who won 17 seats; the opposition Grand National Party won 133 seats. In the presidential election of 19 December 2002, Roh Moo-hyun of the Millennium Democratic Party was

elected president with 49 per cent of the vote. He was inaugurated on 25 February 2003.

POLITICAL SYSTEM

A new constitution was adopted in 1988 following a year of political unrest. The president, who is head of state, chief of the executive and commander-in-chief of the armed forces, is directly elected for a single term of five years. He appoints the prime minister with the consent of the National Assembly, and members of the State Council (Cabinet) on the recommendation of the prime minister. The president is also empowered to take wide-ranging measures in an emergency, including the declaration of martial law, but must obtain the agreement of the National Assembly. The National Assembly of 273 members is directly elected for a four-year term.

HEAD OF STATE

President, Roh Moo-hyun, *elected* 19 December 2002, *sworn in* 25 February 2003

CABINET *as at July 2003*
Prime Minister, Goh Kun
Deputy Prime Minister, Education and Human Resources, Yoon Deok-hong
Deputy Prime Minister, Finance and Economy, Kim Jin-pyo
Agriculture and Forestry, Kim Young-jin
Budget, Park Bong-heum
Commerce, Industry and Energy, Yoon Jin-shik
Construction and Transportation, Choi Jong-chan
Culture and Tourism, Lee Chang-dong
Defence, Cho Young-kil
Environment, Han Myung-sook
Foreign Affairs and Trade, Yoon Young-kwan
Gender Equality, Ji Eun-hee
Government Administration and Home Affairs, Kim Doo-kwan
Health and Welfare, Kim Hwa-joong
Information and Communications, Chin Dae-je
Justice, Kang Keum-sil
Labour, Kwon Ki-hong
Maritime Affairs and Fisheries, Huh Sung-kwan
Science and Technology, Park Ho-koon
Unification, Jeong Se-hyun

EMBASSY OF THE REPUBLIC OF KOREA
60 Buckingham Gate, London SW1E 6AJ
Tel: 020-7227 5500/2
Ambassador Extraordinary and Plenipotentiary,
HE Lee Tae-sik, apptd 2003

BRITISH EMBASSY
No. 4, Chung-dong, Chung-Ku, Seoul 100-120
Tel: (00 82) (2) 3210 5500
Email: bembassy@britain.or.kr
Ambassador Extraordinary and Plenipotentiary,
HE Charles Humfrey, CMG, apptd 2000

BRITISH COUNCIL DIRECTOR, Shoba Ponnappa
Joongwhoo Building, 61–21 Taepyungro1-Ka,
Choong-ku, Seoul 100-101
Tel: (0082) (2) 3702 0600
Email: info@britishcouncil.or.kr

DEFENCE

The Army has 2,330 main battle tanks, 2,480 armoured personnel carriers and 117 armed helicopters. The Navy has 20 submarines, six destroyers, nine frigates, 84 patrol and coastal vessels, 16 combat aircraft, 43 armed helicopters and 60 main battle tanks. There are eight naval bases. The Air Force has 538 combat aircraft.

The USA maintains 37,140 personnel in the country.
MILITARY EXPENDITURE – 2.7 per cent of GDP (2001)
MILITARY PERSONNEL – 686,000: Army 560,000,
Navy 63,000, Air Force 63,000; Paramilitaries 4,500
CONSCRIPTION DURATION – 26–30 months; to age 33
(First Combat Forces or Regional Combat Forces)

ECONOMY
Major industries include shipbuilding, construction, iron and steel, textiles, electrical and electronic goods, semiconductors, passenger vehicles and petrochemicals.

The soil is fertile but arable land is limited by the mountainous nature of the country. Staple agricultural products are rice, barley and other cereals, beans and potatoes. Fruit growing, sericulture and the growing of the medicinal root ginseng are also practised. The fishing industry is a major contributor to both food supply and exports.

Korea is deficient in mineral resources, except for deposits of coal on the east coast and tungsten.

Tourism is a growing industry, with 5,320,000 foreign visitors in 2000.

In 2001 there was a trade surplus of US$13,392 million and a current account surplus of US$8,617 million. In 2001 imports totalled US$141,098 million and exports US$150,439 million. The USA, Japan, the EU and China are the main trading partners. Electronic products, machinery, metal goods, passenger vehicles, chemical products and fabric and clothing are the main exports. Electronic products, petroleum, machinery and chemical products are the main imports.
GNP – US$421,069 million (2000); US$8,910 per
capita (2000)
GDP – US$422,167 million (2001); US$9,782 per
capita (2000)
ANNUAL AVERAGE GROWTH OF GDP – 8.8 per cent
(2000)
INFLATION RATE – 4.4 per cent (2001)
UNEMPLOYMENT – 4.2 per cent (2001)
TOTAL EXTERNAL DEBT – US$134,417 million (2000)

Trade with UK	2001	2002
Imports from UK	£1,285,087,000	£1,464,328,000
Exports to UK	2,844,898,000	2,869,107,000

COMMUNICATIONS
In 2000, there were 3,124 km of railway in commercial operation, of which 661 km were electrified. A high-speed railway line is being constructed between Seoul and Pusan and there are plans to build high-speed rail links between Seoul and Mokp'o and Seoul and Kangnung. There were 88,775 km of roads, of which 2,131 km were motorways. There are international airports in Seoul (Kimpo), Kimhae (near Pusan), Taegu and Cheju city. An international airport was opened at Inchon in March 2001. Korean Air and Asiana Airlines operate regular flights to Europe, the USA, the Middle East and south-east Asia. Pusan and Inchon are the major ports with Pusan serving the industrial areas of the south-east. The port of Inchon, 28 miles from Seoul, serves the capital, but development and operation at Inchon are hampered by a tidal variation of 9–10 metres.

EDUCATION
Primary education is compulsory for six years from the age of six. Secondary and higher education is extensive with the option of middle school to age 15 and high school to age 18. In 1997 there were 150 universities and colleges of higher education. There were 888 hospitals. Some 108 daily newspapers are published.
ILLITERACY RATE – (m) 0.9 per cent; (f) 3.6 per cent
(2000)
ENROLMENT (percentage of age group) – primary 94
per cent (1997); secondary 100 per cent (1997);
tertiary 68 per cent (1997)

KUWAIT

Dawlat al-Kuwayt – State of Kuwait

AREA – 6,846 sq. miles (17,800 sq. km). Neighbours:
Iraq (north and west); Saudi Arabia (south and south-west)
POPULATION – 1,971,000 (2001): 41.6 per cent were
Kuwaiti citizens, the remainder being other Arabs,
Iranians, Indians, Pakistanis and Westerners. Islam is
the official religion, though religious freedom is
constitutionally guaranteed. The official language is
–Arabic, and English is widely spoken as a second
language
CAPITAL – ΨKuwait City (Al-Kuwayt) (population,
388,663, 1998)
CURRENCY – Kuwaiti dinar (KD) of 1,000 fils
NATIONAL ANTHEM – Al-Nashīd Al-Watani (National
Anthem)
NATIONAL DAY – 25 February
NATIONAL FLAG – Three horizontal stripes of green,
white and red, with black trapezoid next to staff
LIFE EXPECTANCY (years) – 76 (2001)
POPULATION GROWTH RATE – –0.8 per cent
POPULATION DENSITY – 111 per sq. km (2001)

In 1993 the UN settled the dispute between Kuwait and Iraq, moving the border some few hundred metres northwards. Kuwait has since completed a 130-mile ditch, sand wall and barbed wire system along its border.

HISTORY AND POLITICS
Although Kuwait had been independent for some years, the 'exclusive agreement' of 1899 between the Sheikh of Kuwait and the British government was formally abrogated by an exchange of letters dated 19 June 1961. Iraq invaded Kuwait on 2 August 1990 and it was liberated on 26 February 1991 by an alliance of Western and Arab forces. Iraq built up its armed forces on Kuwait's border in October 1994, until it was deterred by the arrival of US and British forces. Iraq formally recognised the sovereignty and territorial integrity of Kuwait as well as the UN-demarcated border in November 1994. Roughly 600 Kuwaitis are still held in Iraq.

Elections to the National Assembly were held on 5 July 2003 in which Islamists won 21 of the 5 seats, government supporters won 14, Liberals won 3 and Independents won 12. On 13 July the Amir of Kuwait appointed Shaikh Sabah al-Ahmad al-Jaber al-Sabah as prime minister thus separating the post from the role of heir to the throne for the first time since independence.

POLITICAL SYSTEM
Under the constitution legislative power is vested in the Amir and the 50-member National Assembly, and execut-

ive power in the Amir and the Cabinet. Following popular pressure after the liberation, elections for the National Assembly were held in October 1992. The electorate consists of all Kuwaiti male nationals over 21 whose families have lived in the Emirate since before 1921. There are no political parties.

There are six governorates: Capital, Hawalli Ahmai, Al-Jahrah, Al-Farwaniya and Al-Asimah

HEAD OF STATE

HH The Amir of Kuwait, Shaikh Jabir al-Ahmad al-Jabir al-Sabah, *born* 1928, *acceded* 31 December 1977
Crown Prince, HH Shaikh Saad al-Abdullah al-Salim al-Sabah

CABINET *as at July 2003*

Prime Minister, Shaikh Sabah al-Ahmad al-Jaber al-Sabah
Deputy Prime Minister, Cabinet and, National Assembly Affairs, Mohammed Dhaifallah Sharar
Deputy Prime Minister, Defence, Shaikh Jaber Mubarak al-Hamad al-Sabah
Deputy Prime Minister, Interior, Shaikh Nawaf al-Ahmad al-Jaber al-Sabah
Awqaf and Islamic Affairs, Abdullah Maatouq al-Maatouq
Commerce and Industry, Abdullah Abdelrahman al-Taweel
Communications, Planning and Administrative Development, Shaikh Ahmad Abdullah al-Ahmad al-Sabah
Education and Higher Education, Rashid Hamad Muhammad al-Hamad
Energy, Shaikh Ahmad al-Fahad al-Ahmad al-Sabah
Finance, Mahmoud Abdelkhaliq al-Nouri
Foreign Affairs; Social Affairs and Labour (acting), Shaikh Muhammad Sabah al-Salem al-Sabah
Health, Muhammad Ahmad al-Jarallah
Information, Muhammad Abdullah Abu al-Hassan
Justice, Ahmad Yaacoub Baqer al-Abdullah
Public Works and Housing, Bader Nasser al-Humaidi

EMBASSY OF THE STATE OF KUWAIT
2 Albert Gate, London SW1X 7JU
Tel: 020-7590 3400
Ambassador Extraordinary and Plenipotentiary, HE Khaled al-Duwaisan, GCVO, apptd 1993

BRITISH EMBASSY
PO Box 2, Safat, 13001 Kuwait
Tel: (00 965) 240 3334/5/6
Ambassador Extraordinary and Plenipotentiary, HE Christopher Wilton, apptd 2002

BRITISH COUNCIL DIRECTOR, John Gildea
2 Al Arabi Street, Block 2, PO Box 345, 13004 Safat, Mansouriya, Kuwait City Tel: (00 965) 252 0067
Email: bc.kuwait@kw.britishcouncil.org

DEFENCE

The Army has 368 main battle tanks, 151 armoured personnel carriers and 450 armoured infantry fighting vehicles. The Navy has ten patrol and coastal vessels, based at Ras al-Qalaya. The Air Force has 81 combat aircraft and 20 armed helicopters.

The USA and UK station aircraft and support units in the country to patrol the air exclusion zone in southern Iraq.
MILITARY EXPENDITURE – 12.1 per cent of GDP (2001)
MILITARY PERSONNEL – 15,500: Army 11,000, Navy 2,000, Air Force 2,500; Paramilitaries 6,600

ECONOMY

Despite the desert terrain, 8.4 per cent of land is under cultivation; tomatoes, onions, melons and dates are the main crops.

The oil industry is run by the Kuwait Petroleum Corporation. Oil installations were extensively damaged when Iraqi forces set light to oil wells prior to their retreat. Oil production was 107,600,000 tonnes in 1998.

There are four power stations capable of generating almost 7,000 MW of electricity. The country depends on desalination plants for its water supply.

The economy is heavily dependent on foreign labour. In 1998 the workforce comprised 211,559 Kuwaitis and 1,040,437 non-Kuwaitis.
GDP – US$37,783 million (1999); US$19,871 per capita (2000)
ANNUAL AVERAGE GROWTH OF GDP – –13.0 per cent (1998)
INFLATION RATE – 1.8 per cent (2000)

TRADE

Oil is the major export. Non-oil exports, mainly to Asian countries and the Indian sub-continent, have included chemical fertilisers, ammonia and other chemicals, metal pipes and building materials. Re-exports to neighbouring states traditionally accounted for a major proportion of non-oil exports but were brought to a halt by the Iraqi invasion. Major trading partners are Japan, the USA, the UAE, Saudi Arabia and Western Europe.

In 2001 Kuwait had a trade surplus of US$9,241 million and a current account surplus of US$8,566 million. Imports totalled US$7,734 million and exports US$16,139 million.

Trade with UK	2001	2002
Imports from UK	£357,391,000	£310,390,000
Exports to UK	312,498,000	288,275,000

COMMUNICATIONS

There are some 4,741 km of roads. Telecommunications and postal services are conducted by the government.

SOCIAL WELFARE

The government invested its considerable oil revenues in comprehensive social services. Medical services are free to all residents. In 1998 there were 15 hospitals and 70 clinics. Education is free and compulsory from six to 14 years. In 1999 there were 969 schools (608 government-run, 322 private and 39 vocational) and one university.
ILLITERACY RATE – (m) 15.4 per cent; (f) 19.7 per cent (2000)
ENROLMENT (percentage of age group) – primary 77 per cent (1997); secondary 65 per cent (1997); tertiary 19 per cent (1997)

KYRGYZSTAN

Kyrgyz Respublikasy – Kyrgyz Republic

AREA – 77,181 sq. miles (199,900 sq. km). Neighbours: Kazakhstan (north), China (east), Tajikistan (south and south-west), Uzbekistan (west)
POPULATION – 4,753,003 (2001 estimate): 52.4 per cent Kyrgyz (Turkic origin), 21.5 per cent Russian and 12.9 per cent Uzbek, with smaller numbers of Ukrainians, Germans, Tatars and Kazakhs. Islam is the main religion. Kyrgyz, the official language since independence, is a Turkic language, written in the

Roman alphabet since 1992. Russian is an official language having equal rights with Kyrgyz

CAPITAL – Bishkek (population, 589,400, 1997 estimate

CURRENCY – Som of 100 tyin (introduced on 10 May 1993 at rate of 1:200 against the rouble)

NATIONAL ANTHEM – Mamlekettik Gimni (National Anthem)

NATIONAL DAY – 31 August (Independence Day)

NATIONAL FLAG – Red with a rayed sun containing a representation of a yurt, all in gold

POPULATION GROWTH RATE – 1.5 per cent

POPULATION DENSITY – 24 per sq. km (1999)

URBAN POPULATION – 33.3 per cent (2000)

MILITARY EXPENDITURE – 2.0 per cent of GDP (2001)

MILITARY PERSONNEL – 10,900: Army 8,500, Air Force 2,400; Paramilitaries 5,000

CONSCRIPTION DURATION – 18 months

Kyrgyzstan (formerly Kyrgyzia) is mountainous, the major part being covered by the ridge of the Central Tienshan, while the Pamir-Altai system occupies its southern part. There are a number of spacious mountain valleys, the Alai, Susamyr and others.

HISTORY AND POLITICS

The Kyrgyz people were first mentioned in Chinese chronicles in the second millennium BC. They are a merger of two ethnic groups, a Turkic-speaking people driven into the area by the Mongols from the River Yenisei area of Central Asia, and indigenous peoples. After a long period under Mongol, Chinese and Persian rule, the Kyrgyz became part of the Russian Empire in the 1860s and 1870s. Kyrgyzstan became part of the Soviet Union in 1920 and underwent some industrialisation.

Kyrgyzstan declared independence just after the failed Moscow coup on 31 August 1991.

Ethnic tensions between the rural nomadic Kyrgyz, the urban Russians and the wealthy Uzbeks who own many businesses and form the majority in the second largest town of Osh, are never far from the surface.

A referendum on amendments to the constitution was held on 17 October 1998, which introduced private ownership of land.

Legislative elections were held on 20 February and 12 March 2000. The largest opposition parties were not allowed to take part on the grounds of supposed minor infractions of the electoral procedures, a decision which was criticised by observers from the Organisation for Security and Co-operation in Europe; their leaders were allowed to stand as independent candidates. The Communist party and the pro-government Union of Democratic Forces emerged as the largest parties. The results were widely condemned by opposition groups amid allegations of widespread electoral fraud.

The presidential election held on 29 October 2000 was won by the incumbent President Askar Akayev, who obtained 74.3 per cent of the votes cast, but the conduct of the poll was criticised by OSCE observers at the time of the election and later by the EU and the USA.

Following anti-government demonstrations in March 2003 in which five people were killed, Prime Minster Kurmanbek Bakiyev and his government resigned on 22 May. Nikolay Tanayev was confirmed as the new prime minister by parliament on 30 May and his Cabinet was approved on 13 June.

POLITICAL SYSTEM

The head of state is a president directly elected for a five-year term renewable once only. There is a bicameral legislature composed of a 60-member Legislative Assembly and a 45-member People's Assembly, both of which serve for five-year terms. Under amendments to the Constitution approved by a referendum in February 2003, the legislature is to become unilateral. The president appoints the prime minister and the other members of the government. The Assembly of the People of Kyrgyzstan, which comprises the leaders of the republic's ethnic communities, was designated a consultative body in January 1997.

HEAD OF STATE

President, Askar Akayev, *elected* 12 October 1990, *re-elected* 24 December 1995, 29 October 2000

CABINET *as at July 2003*

Prime Minister, Nikolay Tanayev

First Deputy Prime Minister, Justice, Kurmanbek Osmonov

Deputy Prime Minister, Economic Development, Trade and Investments, Dzhoomart Otorbayev

Deputy Prime Minister, Transport and Communications, Kubanychbek Dzhumaliyev

Agriculture and Water Resources, Aleksandr Kostyuk

Chair of the National Security Service, Kalyk Imankulov

Chair of the State Commission for Procurement and Material Reserves, Tashkul Kereksizev

Chair of the State Committee for Management of State Property and Attraction of Direct Investment, Ravshan Dzheyenbekov

Chair of the State Committee for Tourism, Sport and Youth Policy, Okmotbek Almakuchukov

Chief of Staff, Bekbolot Talgarbekov

Defence, Lt.-Gen. Esen Topoyev

Director of the State Agency for Science and Copyright, Roman Umorev

Director of the State Communications Agency, Andrei Titev

Ecology and Emergencies, Satyvaldy Chrymashev

Education, Science and Culture, Ishengul Boldjurova

Finance, Bolot Abildayev

Foreign Affairs, Askar Aitmatov

Health, Mitalip Mamytov

Interior, Bakirdin Subanbekov

Labour and Social Welfare, Roza Aknazarova

Local Government and Regional Development, Director of the State Agency for Registration of Real Estate Rights, Tolebek Umaraliyev

Trade and Industry, Sadriddin Djienbekov

EMBASSY OF THE KYRGYZ REPUBLIC

Ascot House, 119 Crawford Street, London W1U 1BJ

Tel: 020-7935 1462

Ambassador Extraordinary and Plenipotentiary, vacant

BRITISH AMBASSADOR, HE James Sharp, apptd 2002, resident at Almaty, Kazakhstan

BRITISH COUNCIL DIRECTOR, James Kennedy

Republic Square 13, 480013 Almaty Kazakhstan Tel: (00 7) 3272 633339 Email: general@kz.britishcouncil.org

ECONOMY

Agriculture is the main sector of the economy, with sugar beet, grain and sheep the main products. Private ownership of land was legalised in 1997. Industry is concentrated in the food-processing, textiles, timber and mining fields. Since 1992, some 60 per cent of state-owned enterprises have been privatised. Hydroelectric power is abundant and Kyrgyzstan has reserves of gold, coal, mercury and uranium, although only gold has so far been exploited and is the country's largest export.

The president and government have made the Central Bank independent of government and parliamentary control. In March 1996, a treaty was signed with Belarus, Kazakhstan and Russia enhancing economic co-operation and working towards a single customs territory and in December 2000 an agreement was signed with Russia on the joint production of uranium and non-ferrous and precious metals.

In 2000 there was a trade surplus of US$9 million and a current account deficit of US$158 million. In 2001 imports totalled US$468 million and exports US$476 million.

GNP – US$1,345 million (2000); US$270 per capita (2000)

GDP – US$1,525 million (2001); US$265 per capita (2000)

ANNUAL AVERAGE GROWTH OF GDP – 3.6 per cent (1999)

INFLATION RATE – 2.1 per cent (2002)

TOTAL EXTERNAL DEBT – US$1,829 million (2000)

Trade with UK	2001	2002
Imports from UK	£2,559,000	£1,854,000
Exports to UK	163,000	206,000

CULTURE AND EDUCATION

Until the 1930s the Kyrgyz language had an oral tradition of literature which included the epic poem Manas, which tells the history of the Kyrgyz people. Internationally, one of the best-known writers of the former Soviet Union is the Kyrgyz writer Chingiz Aitmatov (1928–).

ENROLMENT (percentage of age group) – primary 100 per cent (1997); tertiary 12 per cent (1997)

LAOS

Satharanarath Pasathipatai Pasason Lao – Lao People's Democratic Republic

AREA – 91,429 sq. miles (236,800 sq. km). Neighbours: China (north), Vietnam (north-east and east), Cambodia (south), Thailand (west), Myanmar (north-west)

POPULATION – 5,635,967 (2001 estimate): 68 per cent Lao Loum (lowland Lao), 22 per cent Lao Theung (upland Lao), 9 per cent Lao Soung (highland Lao, including Hmong and Yau). Lao is the official language; French and English are spoken

CAPITAL – Vientiane (population, 555,100, 1997 estimate)

CURRENCY – Kip (K) of 100 at

NATIONAL ANTHEM – Pheng Xat Lao (Hymn Of The Lao People)

NATIONAL DAY – 2 December

NATIONAL FLAG – Blue background with a central white circle, framed by two horizontal red stripes

POPULATION GROWTH RATE – 2.6 per cent

POPULATION DENSITY – 22 per sq. km (1999)

MILITARY EXPENDITURE – 0.9 per cent of GDP (2001)

MILITARY PERSONNEL – 29,100: Army 25,600, of which Navy 600, Air Force 3,500; Paramilitaries 100,000

CONSCRIPTION DURATION – 18 months minimum

ILLITERACY RATE – (m) 35.9 per cent; (f) 66.8 per cent (2000)

ENROLMENT (percentage of age group) – primary 100 per cent (1997); secondary 29 per cent (1997); tertiary 3 per cent (1997)

HISTORY AND POLITICS

The kingdom of Lane Xang, the Land of a Million Elephants, was founded in the 14th century but broke up at the beginning of the 16th century into the separate kingdoms of Luang Prabang and Vientiane and the principality of Champassac, which together came under French protection in 1893. In 1945 the Japanese staged a coup and suppressed the French administration. In 1947 Laos became a constitutional monarchy under King Sisvang Vong, and an independent sovereign state in 1953.

The Lao People's Democratic Republic was proclaimed in December 1975 following victory by the Pathet Lao and the abdication of the King. A president and Council of Ministers were installed, and a 45-member Supreme People's Council was appointed to draft a constitution, which was approved in 1991. The Lao People's Revo-lutionary Party (LPRP) is the sole legal political organisation. A general election to the enlarged 109-member National Assembly was held on 24 February 2002; all the candidates were approved by the LPRP, which won 108 seats with the remaining seat being won by an approved non-partisan candidate. The president, prime minister and Council of Ministers were confirmed in their posts by the National Assembly on 9 March 2002.

HEAD OF STATE

President, Gen. Khamtay Siphandone, *elected* by the National Assembly 24 February 1998, *re-elected* 9 April 2002

Vice-President, Choummaly Sayasone

COUNCIL OF MINISTERS *as at July 2003*

Prime Minister, Bounnyang Vorachit

Deputy Prime Ministers, Somsavat Lengsavad *(Foreign Affairs);* Thongloun Sisoulit *(State Planning Committee);* Maj.-Gen. Asang Laoly

Agriculture and Forestry, Siene Saphangthong

Communications, Transport, Posts and Construction, Bouathong Vonglokham

Education, Phimmasone Leuangkhamma

Finance, Chansy Phosikham

Industry and Handicrafts, Onneua Phommachanh

Information and Culture, Phandouangchit Vongsa

Interior, Maj.-Gen. Soutchay Thammasith

Justice, Khamouane Boupha

Labour and Social Welfare, Somphan Phengkhammy

Ministers attached to the Prime Minister, Somphavan Inthavong; Somphong Mongkhonvilai; Souly Nanthavong; Bountiam Phitsamai; Saisenglee Tengbliavue

National Defence, Maj.-Gen. Douangchay Phichit

Permanent Secretary of the President's Office, Souban Salitthilat

Public Health, Ponemek Daraloy

Trade and Tourism, Soulivong Daravong

EMBASSY OF THE LAO PEOPLE'S DEMOCRATIC REPUBLIC

74 Avenue Raymond-Poincaré F-75116 Paris

Tel: (00 33) (1) 4553 0298

Ambassador Extraordinary and Plenipotentiary, HE Soutsakhone Pathammavong, apptd 2003

BRITISH EMBASSY

PO Box 6626, Vientiane Tel: (00) (856) (21) 413606

Ambassador Extraordinary and Plenipotentiary, HE Lloyd Smith, CMG, apptd 2002, resident at Bangkok, Thailand

ECONOMY

A 'new economic mechanism' programme was introduced in 1986 which began the liberalisation of the economy. These reforms have produced a market-orientated economic system which has increased growth and reduced inflation. The economy is dominated by the agricultural sector, which employs about three-quarters of the workforce. The seventh congress of the LPRP held in March 2001 defined the principal economic goal to be agricultural development. Although Laos is one of the poorest states in the world, there is potential for increased hydroelectric power exports to Thailand and there are deposits of coal, tin, iron ore, gold, bauxite and lignite. Foreign capital investment in infrastructure began with the 1994 opening of the Friendship Bridge over the Mekong river border with Thailand which links road routes from Singapore to China.

In 1999 Laos had a trade deficit of US$190 million and a current account deficit of US$121 million. In 2001 imports totalled US$551 million and exports US$331 million.

GNP – US$1,519 million (2000); US$290 per capita (2000)

GDP – US$1,712 million (2001); US$324 per capita (2000)

ANNUAL AVERAGE GROWTH OF GDP – 5.7 per cent (2000)

INFLATION RATE – 25.1 per cent (2000)

TOTAL EXTERNAL DEBT – US$2,499 million (2000)

Trade with UK	2001	2002
Imports from UK	£2,316,00	£1,574,000
Exports to UK	7,095,000	10,060,000

LATVIA

Latvijas Republika – Republic of Latvia

AREA – 23,885 sq. miles (62,100 sq. km). Neighbours: Estonia (north), Lithuania and Belarus (south), the Russian Federation (east)

POPULATION – 2,406,000 (2001): 57.7 per cent Latvian, 29.6 per cent Russian, 4.1 per cent Belarusian, with small Ukrainian and Polish minorities. The main religions are Lutheran, Roman Catholic and Russian Orthodox. The official language is Latvian; Russian is also spoken. Education is in Latvian and Russian. Public sector employees must pass language tests in Latvian to a level commensurate with the nature of their employment. The right of minorities to use their mother tongue has been acknowledged

CAPITAL – Riga (population, 747,157, 2002 estimate)

MAJOR CITIES – Daugavpils (113,409); Jelgava (65,927); Jurmala (55,328); Liepaja (87,505); Ventspils (44,004), 2002 estimates

CURRENCY – Lats of 100 santims

NATIONAL ANTHEM – Dievs, Sveti Latviju (God Bless Latvia)

NATIONAL DAY – 18 November (Independence Day 1918)

NATIONAL FLAG – Crimson, with a white horizontal stripe across the centre

LIFE EXPECTANCY (years) – 71 (2001)

POPULATION GROWTH RATE –0.9 per cent

POPULATION DENSITY – 39 per sq. km (2001)

URBAN POPULATION – 96 per cent (2001)

HISTORY AND POLITICS

Latvia came under the control of the German Teutonic Knights at the end of the 13th century. During the next few centuries the country endured sporadic invasions by the Swedes, Poles and Russians. By 1795 Latvia was entirely under Russian control. On 18 November 1918, Latvia declared its independence, but was annexed by the Soviet Union in 1940 under the terms of the Molotov–Ribbentrop pact with Germany. Latvia was invaded and occupied when Germany invaded the Soviet Union during the Second World War but recaptured by the Soviet Union in 1944.

In 1989 the Popular Front of Latvia won the elections to the Supreme Council, and on 4 May 1990 the Supreme Council declared the independent republic of Latvia to be, de jure, still in existence. A national referendum was held in March 1991 in which 73 per cent voted in favour of independence, and this was declared on 21 August 1991. The State Council of the Soviet Union recognised the independence of Latvia on 10 September 1991.

The New Era party (JL) became the largest party in the Saeima in the general election held on 5 October 2002, with 26 out of the 100 seats. JL leader Einars Repse, was nominated prime minister and formed a coalition government led by the JL and including the Greens and Farmers Union (ZZS), For Fatherland and Freedom (TB-LNNK) and the First Party of Latvia (LPP). The prime minister and Cabinet were approved by the Saeima by 21 November.

In November 2002 NATO included Latvia on a list of seven countries invited to join the alliance, Latvia is expected to become a full member of NATO in 2004. In December Latvia was formally invited to join the EU. A referendum on EU membership was scheduled for 20 September 2003.

President Vaira Vike-Freiberga was re-elected by parliament unopposed, on 20 June 2003.

POLITICAL SYSTEM

Executive authority is vested in a prime minister and Cabinet of Ministers. Legislative power is exercised by the unicameral parliament (Saeima), which comprises 100 deputies elected for four-year terms by proportional representation, with a 5 per cent threshold for parliamentary representation. The deputies elect a president of state, serving for four years, who in turn appoints the prime minister. The prime minister appoints, and the Saeima approves, the Cabinet of Ministers.

The electorate and citizenship had been restricted to descendants of Latvian citizens before the 1940 Soviet occupation and to those who could pass the required Latvian language tests, until 1994 when a law was passed enabling naturalisation of long-term residents. In October 1998 a referendum to amend the citizenship law was passed which granted citizenship to those children born in Latvia after Latvian independence if their parents requested it and provided for simpler language tests for older residents.

HEAD OF STATE

President, Vaira Vīķe-Freiberga, *elected* 17 June 1999, *re-elected* 20 June 2003, *sworn in* 8 July 2003

CABINET *as at July 2003*
Prime Minister, Einars Repse (JL)
Deputy Prime Minister, Ainars Slesers (LPP)
Agriculture, Martins Roze (ZZS)
Culture, Inguna Ribena (JL)

Defence, Ģirts Valdis Kristovskis (TB-LNNK)
Economy, Juris Lujans (LPP)
Education and Science, Karlis Sadurskis (JL)
Environmental Protection and Regional Development,
    Raimonds Vejonis (ZZS)
Finance, Valdis Dombrovskis (JL)
Foreign Affairs, Sandra Kalniete (JL)
Health, Ingrida Circene (JL)
Integration Affairs, Nils Muiznieks (Ind.)
Interior, Maris Gulbis (JL)
Justice, Aivars Aksenoks (JL)
*Special Assignments for Affairs of Regional Development and
    Local Governments,* Ivars Gaters (JL)
Special Assignments for Children and Family Affairs, Ainars
    Bastiks (LPP)
Transport, Roberts Zile (TB-LNNK)
Welfare, Dagnija Stake (ZZS)

JL New Era; LPP First Party of Latvia; TB-LNNK For
Fatherland and Freedom; ZZS Greens and Farmers
Union; Ind. Independent

EMBASSY OF THE REPUBLIC OF LATVIA
45 Nottingham Place, London W1U 5LR
Tel: 020-7312 0040
Ambassador Extraordinary and Plenipotentiary, Janis Dripe,
    apptd 2002

BRITISH EMBASSY
5, J. Alunana iela, Riga LV-1010
Tel: (00 371) 777 4700
Email: british.embassy@apollo.lv
Ambassador Extraordinary and Plenipotentiary, HE
    Andrew Tesoriere, apptd 2002

BRITISH COUNCIL DIRECTOR, Chris Edwards
5a Blaumana iela, Riga LV-1011 Tel: (00 371) 728 1730 Email:
mail@britishcouncil.lv

DEFENCE
The Army has three main battle tanks and 13 armoured
personnel carriers, the Navy has four patrol and coastal
vessels and eight defence patrol craft at three bases and
the Air Force has 19 aircraft and five helicopters.
    Russian forces withdrew from Latvia in 1994.
MILITARY EXPENDITURE – 1.2 per cent of GDP (2001)
MILITARY PERSONNEL – 5,500: Army 4,300, Navy
    930, Air Force 270; Paramilitaries 3,200
CONSCRIPTION DURATION – 12 months

ECONOMY
By 2001, 97 per cent of previously state-owned
enterprises had either been privatised or were assigned
for privatisation, and privatised companies accounted for
66 per cent of GDP.
    Latvia is an agricultural exporter, specialising in cattle
and pig breeding, dairy farming and crops, including
sugar beet, flax, cereals and potatoes. In 2001, 13.5 per
cent of the population were employed in agriculture,
which accounted for 4.1 per cent of GDP. Natural
resources include limestone, gypsum, peat and timber.
    Industry is specialised in certain areas including the
production of food and beverages, motor vehicles, textiles
and timber and paper products. Transit, services and
banking are also large sectors with services contributing
70.6 per cent of GDP in 2001.

GNP – US$6,925 million (2000); US$2,920 per capita
    (2000)

GDP – US$7,549 million (2001); US$2,952 per capita
    (2000)
ANNUAL AVERAGE GROWTH OF GDP – 6.6 per cent
    (2000)
INFLATION RATE – 2.7 per cent (2000)
UNEMPLOYMENT – 14.6 per cent (2000)
TOTAL EXTERNAL DEBT – US$3,379 million (2000)

TRADE
In 1996, a free trade regime was agreed with the EU and
EFTA. The main imports are machinery, chemical goods
and transport vehicles, and the main exports are wood
and wood products, textiles and base metals and metallic
products. The most important import partners are
Germany, Russia, Lithuania, Finland and Sweden. The
most important export partners are Germany, the UK,
Sweden, Lithuania and Russia.
    In 2001 there was a trade deficit of US$1,351 million
and a current account deficit of US$758 million. Imports
totalled US$3,504 million and exports US$2,001 million.

Trade with UK	2001	2002
Imports from UK	£86,143,000	£76,802,000
Exports to UK	424,775,000	469,648,000

COMMUNICATIONS
Latvia has 2,413 km of railways and some 20,400 km of
roads. Many of the exports from former CIS states are
transported to Western Europe via Latvia. Latvia is also
being developed as a transportation route from
Scandinavia to central and southern Europe. Several
warm-water ports exist, of which three, Riga, Ventspils
and Liepaja, are developed for commercial transport.

CULTURE AND EDUCATION
The Latvian language belongs to the Baltic branch of the
Indo-European languages. The Latin alphabet is used.
Latvian literature appeared in the 19th century and
played a role in the fight for independence in 1918.
    There are 27 higher education institutions, of which
five are universities.
ILLITERACY RATE – (m) 0.2 per cent; (f) 0.2 per cent
    (2000)
ENROLMENT (percentage of age group) – primary 96
    per cent (1997); secondary 84 per cent (1997); tertiary
    33 per cent (1997)

LEBANON

Al-Jumhūriyya al-Lubnāniyya – Republic of Lebanon

AREA – 3,923 sq. miles (10,200 sq. km). Neighbours:
    Syria (north and east), Israel (south)
POPULATION – 3,556,000 (2001): 32 per cent Shi'ite
    Muslim; 21 per cent Sunni Muslim, 40 per cent
    Christian, 7 per cent Druze. Arabic is the official
    language, and French and English are also widely used
CAPITAL – ΨBeirut (Bayrut) (population, 1,100,000,
    1994)
MAJOR CITIES – ΨSayda (Sidon) (100,000); ΨTarabulus
    (Tripoli) (200,000); ΨSur (Tyre) (70,000)
CURRENCY – Lebanese pound (L£) of 100 piastres
NATIONAL ANTHEM – Kulluna Lil Watan Lil'Ula
    Lil'alam (We All Belong To The Homeland)
NATIONAL DAY – 22 November
NATIONAL FLAG – Horizontal bands of red, white and
    red with a green cedar of Lebanon in the centre of the
    white band

LIFE EXPECTANCY (years) – 73 (2001)
POPULATION GROWTH RATE – 2.5 per cent
POPULATION DENSITY – 349 per sq. km (2001)
URBAN POPULATION – 90 per cent (2001)

HISTORY AND POLITICS

Lebanon became an independent state in 1920, administered under French mandate until 22 November 1943. Powers were transferred to the Lebanese government from January 1944 and French troops were withdrawn in 1946. In 1975, fighting broke out in Beirut between Maronite, Sunni and Shia factions, the latter supported by Palestinian guerrillas based in Lebanon; fighting continued until the end of the civil war in 1990. In 1982 Israeli forces invaded and in 1985 established a buffer zone along the Israeli–Lebanon border controlled by the South Lebanon Army (SLA), a Christian militia. Since 1993 the Lebanese Army has deployed in southern villages alongside UNIFIL forces but has not disarmed Hezbollah forces, who are financed, armed and trained by Syria and Iran.

The Israeli Prime Minister Ehud Barak had committed himself to the withdrawal of Israeli forces from the buffer zone during his election campaign in May 1999 and Israel began its withdrawal in mid-May 2000, initially handing over their positions to the SLA, but a mass movement of exiled civilians, led by Hezbollah forces, effectively routed the SLA. The last Israeli troops left on 24 May 2000 and the SLA troops surrendered to the Lebanese authorities or fled to Israel. Syrian forces remain in west Beirut and in the north and the east of the country.

Parliamentary elections were held in 1992 and local elections were held in 1998. The general election held on 27 August and 3 September 2000 was won by supporters of Rafik Hariri, who had previously been prime minister between 1992 and 1998. Hariri was appointed prime minister by President Lahoud on 23 October 2000 and named his Cabinet, composed equally of Christians and Muslims, on 26 October. Hariri resigned with his entire cabinet on 15 April 2003, although he remained as 'caretaker' prime minister at the request of President Lahoud and was re-appointed on 17 April. A new Cabinet headed by Hariri was approved on 30 April.

FOREIGN RELATIONS

Relations between Lebanon and Israel remain volatile. In March 2001 Lebanon began pumping water from a tributary of the River Jordan to supply a southern border village despite Israeli opposition. Tensions again rose between the two countries in September 2000 over Israeli opposition to Lebanon's plan to divert water from the border River Wazzani which provides 10 per cent of Israel's drinking water.

Following a bomb attack in Beirut on 2 August 2003 which killed a member of Hezbollah and which Lebanon blamed on Israel, an upsurge of fighting between Hezbollah forces and Israeli troops occurred in the disputed border area of Shebaa Farms in southern Lebanon.

POLITICAL SYSTEM

The National Covenant (1943) is characterised by the division of power between the religious communities. The executive comprises the president, prime minister and Cabinet. The president is elected by the National Assembly for a non-renewable term of six years and must be a Maronite Christian. The prime minister is appointed following consultation between the president and National Assembly and must be a Sunni Muslim. The 128-member unicameral National Assembly comprises equal numbers of Christians and Muslims although the speaker must be a Shia Muslim. Political parties are banned.

The constitution was amended on 15 October 1998 to allow the election of Gen. Lahoud as president. Serving state officials had previously been prohibited from standing for the presidency.

HEAD OF STATE
President of the Republic of Lebanon, Gen. Émile Lahoud, elected 15 October 1998, *sworn in* 24 November 1998

CABINET *as at July 2003*
Prime Minister, Rafiq Hariri
Deputy Prime Minister, Issam Fares
Administrative Reforms, Karim Pakradouni
Agriculture, Ali Hassan Khalil
Culture, Ghazi Aridi
Displaced Persons, Abdallah Farhat
Economy and Trade, Marwan Hamadeh
Education and Higher Education, Samir Jisr
Energy and Water Resources, Ayyoub Hamayyed
Environment, Fares Boueiz
Finance, Fouad Siniora
Foreign Affairs and Emigrants, Jean Obeid
Industry, Elie Skaff
Information, Michel Samaha
Interior and Municipal Affairs, Elias Murr
Justice, Bahji Tabbarah
Labour, Assaad Hardane
Ministers of State, Talal Arslan; Khalil Hrawi; Assem
  Kanso; Karam Karam; Abdel Rahim Mrad; Michel
  Musa;
National Defence, Mahmoud Hammud
Post and Telecommunications, Jean-Louis Qordahi
Public Health, Soleiman Franjieh
Public Works and Transport, Najib Miqati
Social Affairs, Assaad Diab
Tourism, Ali Hussein Abdullah
Youth and Sports, Sebouh Hovnanian

LEBANESE EMBASSY
15–21 Palace Gardens Mews, London W8 4QN
Tel: 020-7229 7265/7727 6696
Ambassador Extraordinary and Plenipotentiary, HE Jihad
  Mortada, apptd 1999

BRITISH EMBASSY
Embassies Complex Army Street, Zkak Al-Blat, Serail Hill PO Box
11-471, Beirut Tel: (00 961)-(1) 990 400
Email: britemb@cyberia.net.lb
Ambassador Extraordinary and Plenipotentiary, HE
  Richard Kinchen, apptd 2001

BRITISH COUNCIL DIRECTOR, Dr Ken Churchill, OBE
Sidani Street, Azar Building, Ras Beirut
Tel: (00 961) (1) 740 123
Email: general.enquiries@lb.britishcouncil.org

DEFENCE

The Army has 327 main battle tanks and 1,338 armoured personnel carriers. The Navy has seven patrol and coastal vessels at two bases. There are a 3,638-strong UN peacekeeping force, 18,000 Syrian troops and 150 Iranian Revolutionary Guards operating in Lebanon.
MILITARY EXPENDITURE – 3.5 per cent of GDP (2001)
MILITARY PERSONNEL – 71,830: Army 70,000, Navy
  830, Air Force 1,000; Paramilitaries 13,000
CONSCRIPTION DURATION – 12 months

ECONOMY

Fruits are the most important products. There is some light industry, mostly for the production of con-sumer goods, but most factories are still in need of reconstruction because of the civil war.

A ten-year plan (1993–2002) was initiated to repair war damage and to restore Lebanon's position as a regional financial services and light industrial centre, concentrating on rebuilding housing, transport, services, education and health services, and aiding industry and agriculture.

GNP – US$17,355 million (2000); US$4,010 per capita (2000)

GDP – US$16,709 million (2001); US$4,788 per capita (2000)

ANNUAL AVERAGE GROWTH OF GDP – 5.0 per cent (1998)

INFLATION RATE – 6.8 per cent (1994)

TOTAL EXTERNAL DEBT – US$10,311 million (2000)

TRADE

Principal imports are foodstuffs, machinery and electrical equipment, vehicles, chemical products, mineral ores, and metals and metal products. There is a free trade agreement with Syria. Principal exports include foodstuffs, chemical products, jewellery, machinery and electrical goods, textiles, metals and metal products, paper and paper products, and vehicles. Lebanon is the terminal for two oil pipelines, one formerly belonging to the Iraq Petroleum Company, debouching at Tripoli, the other belonging to the Trans Arabian Pipeline Company, at Sidon. These lines have not functioned for some years.

In 2001 imports totalled US$7,293 million and exports US$870 million.

Trade with UK	2001	2002
Imports from UK	£181,435,000	£158,529,000
Exports to UK	15,996,000	20,084,000

COMMUNICATIONS

There are 7,370 km of roads, of which 6,265 km are paved; there is 222 km of railway track. There is an international airport at Beirut, served by the national carrier Middle East Airlines and other airlines. An internal service operates from Beirut to Tripoli.

EDUCATION

There are 16 universities and colleges of higher education in Lebanon, among them American and French universities, and the Lebanese National University, the Beirut University College, the Kaslik Saint Esprit University and the Arab University in Beirut, with the University of Balamand situated near Tripoli. There is a good provision throughout the country of primary and secondary schools, among which are a great number of private schools.

ILLITERACY RATE – (m) 7.9 per cent; (f) 19.6 per cent (2000)

ENROLMENT (percentage of age group) – primary 100 per cent (1997); tertiary 27 per cent (1997)

LESOTHO

Mmuso wa Lesotho – Kingdom of Lesotho

AREA – 11,720 sq. miles (30,355 sq. km). Neighbour: South Africa, which completely surrounds Lesotho

POPULATION – 2,177,062 (2001 estimate). The languages are Sesotho and English

CAPITAL – Maseru (population, 367,000, 1992 estimate)

CURRENCY – Loti (M) of 100 lisente. The South African rand is also legal tender

NATIONAL ANTHEM – Pina Ea Sechaba

NATIONAL DAY – 4 October (Independence Day)

NATIONAL FLAG – Diagonally white over blue over green with the white of double width, and an assegai and knobkerrie on a Basotho shield in brown in the upper hoist

POPULATION GROWTH RATE – 2.3 per cent

POPULATION DENSITY – 69 per sq. km (1999)

MILITARY EXPENDITURE – 3.1 per cent of GDP (2001)

MILITARY PERSONNEL – Army 2,000

HISTORY AND POLITICS

Lesotho (formerly Basutoland) became a constitutional monarchy within the Commonwealth on 4 October 1966. The constitution was suspended in 1970 and the country was governed by a Council of Ministers until the establishment of a National Assembly in 1974.

Leabua Jonathan's government was overthrown in 1986, and executive and legislative powers were conferred on the King. Elections were held in March 1993 and the Basotho Congress Party (BCP) won all 65 seats in the new National Assembly. A BCP government led by Ntsu Mokhele was formed and King Letsie III swore allegiance to a new multiparty democratic constitution.

On 17 August 1994 King Letsie III and sections of the military mounted a coup attempt, but after mediation, the government, which had refused to leave office, was restored by the King. King Letsie also announced his intention to abdicate in favour of his father, Moshoeshoe II, who was restored on 25 January 1995. When King Moshoeshoe II died in a car crash on 15 January 1996, King Letsie III again ascended to the throne.

At legislative elections held in May 1998, the Lesotho Congress for Democracy won 78 of the 80 seats in the National Assembly. Allegations of electoral fraud, later confirmed by an investigation which said that the election had been marred by irregularities, but that there were insufficient grounds to annul the poll, led to violent protests. There were also reports of an alleged army mutiny. The deteriorating situation led to the intervention of South African and Botswanan military forces on 22 September to restore order after a request by the prime minister, Bethuel Pakalitha Mosisili; they withdrew in May 1999.

The general election that had been due in April 2000, was postponed to 25 May 2002, when the Lesotho Congress for Democracy (LCD) retained its overall majority in the National Assembly.

POLITICAL SYSTEM

In September 1999 it was announced that the first-past-the-post electoral system would be replaced by a new system incorporating a degree of proportional representation and that the number of seats in the National Assembly would be increased by 40 to 120.

HEAD OF STATE

HM The King of Lesotho, King Letsie III, *acceded* February 1996, *crowned* 31 October 1997

COUNCIL OF MINISTERS *as at July 2003*

Prime Minister, Defence, Public Service, Bethuel Pakalitha Mosisili

Agriculture, Co-operatives and Land Reclamation, Vova
   Bulane
Assistant Minister for Finance and Development Planning,
   Popane Lebesa
Assistant Minister of Justice, Human Rights and
   Rehabilitation, Law and Constitutional Affairs, Mpeo
   Mahase
Communications, Information, Broadcasting, Post and
   Telecommunications, Mamphone Khatletla
Education and Manpower Development, Lesao Lehohla
Finance and Development Planning, Timothy Thahane
Foreign Affairs, Mohlabi Kenneth Tsekoa
Gender, Youth and Sports, Mathabiso Lepono
Health and Social Welfare, Motloheloa Phooko
Home Affairs, Motsoahae Thomas Thabane
Industry, Trade and Marketing, Mpho Malie
Justice, Human Rights and Rehabilitation, Law and
   Constitutional Affairs, Refiloe Masemene
Labour and Employment, Sello Machakela
Local Government, Pontso Susan Matimelo Sekatle
Minister in the Prime Minister's Office, Sephiri Motanyane
Natural Resources, Monyane Moleleki
Public Works and Transport, Mofelehetsi Moerane
Tourism, Culture and Environment, Lebohang Ntsinyi

HIGH COMMISSION FOR THE KINGDOM OF LESOTHO
7 Chesham Place, London SW1X 8HN
Tel: 020-7235 5686
Email: lhclesotholondon.org.uk
High Commissioner, HE Lebohang Ramohlanka, apptd
   2000

BRITISH HIGH COMMISSION
PO Box Ms 521, Maseru 100
Tel: (00 266) 2231 3961
Email: hcmaseru@lesoff.co.za
High Commissioner, HE Frank Martin, apptd 2002

ECONOMY
The economy is based on agriculture and animal
husbandry, and the adverse balance of trade (mainly
consumer and capital goods) is offset by the earnings of
the large numbers of the population who work in South
Africa. Apart from some diamonds, Lesotho has few
natural resources. Agriculture contributes 11 per cent of
GDP and the main crops are maize, sorghum and
vegetables. Industry contributes some 42 per cent and
services around 47 per cent of GDP. The Lesotho
National Development Corporation was set up to promote
the development of industry, mining, trade and tourism.
   In 2000 Lesotho had a trade deficit of US$516 million
and a current account deficit of US$151 million. In 1998
imports totalled US$863 million and exports US$194
million.
GNP – US$1,181 million (2000); US$580 per capita
   (2000)
GDP – US$789 million (2001); US$448 per capita
   (2000)
ANNUAL AVERAGE GROWTH OF GDP – –5.5 per cent
   (1998)
INFLATION RATE – 6.1 per cent (2000)
TOTAL EXTERNAL DEBT – US$716 million (2000)

Trade with UK	2001	2002
Imports from UK	£1,941,000	£1,048,000
Exports to UK	1,883,000	1,116,000

COMMUNICATIONS
A tarred road links Maseru to several of the main lowland
towns. The mountainous areas are linked by tarred,
gravelled and earth roads and tracks. Roads link border
towns in South Africa with the main towns in Lesotho.
Maseru is also connected by rail with the main
Bloemfontein–Natal line of the South African Railways.
Scheduled international air services are operated daily
between Maseru and Johannesburg, and other scheduled
international flights are to Gaborone, Harare, Manzini
and Maputo. Internal scheduled services are operated by
the Lesotho Airways Corporation. The telephone
network is fully automated in all urban centres. Radio
telephone communication is used extensively in the
remote rural areas.

EDUCATION
There are over 1,200 primary and over 180 secondary
schools, with emphasis being laid on agricultural and
vocational education. The National University of Lesotho
at Roma was established as a university in 1975.
ILLITERACY RATE – (m) 27.6 per cent; (f) 6.4 per cent
   (2000)
ENROLMENT (percentage of age group) – primary 100
   per cent (1997); secondary 31 per cent (1997); tertiary
   2 per cent (1997)

LIBERIA

Republic of Liberia

AREA – 43,000 sq. miles (111,369 sq. km). Neighbours:
   Guinea (north), Côte d'Ivoire (east), Sierra Leone
   (north-west)
POPULATION – 3,225,837 (2001 estimate). The official
   language is English. The main African languages are
   Bassa, Kpelle and Kru, though some 16 ethnic
   languages are spoken
CAPITAL – ΨMonrovia (population, 421,000, 2000
   estimate
MAJOR CITIES – ΨBuchanan (Grand Bassa);
   ΨGreenville (Sinoe); ΨHarper (Cape Palmas)
CURRENCY – Liberian dollar (L$) of 100 cents
NATIONAL ANTHEM – All Hail, Liberia, Hail
NATIONAL DAY – 26 July
NATIONAL FLAG – Alternate horizontal stripes (five
   white, six red), with five-pointed white star on blue
   field in upper corner next to flagstaff
POPULATION GROWTH RATE – 1.5 per cent
POPULATION DENSITY – 26 per sq. km (1999)
URBAN POPULATION – 44.9 per cent (2000)
MILITARY EXPENDITURE – 5.6 per cent of GDP (2001)
MILITARY PERSONNEL – 15,000 (including militias
   supporting government forces)
ILLITERACY RATE – (m) 29.9 per cent; (f) 62.3 per cent
   (2000)

HISTORY AND POLITICS
Liberia was founded by the American Colonisation
Society in 1822 as a colony for freed American slaves, and
has been recognised since 1847 as an independent state.
   William V. S. Tubman, President since 1944, died in
1971 and was succeeded by Dr Tolbert. The constitution
was suspended following a military coup in 1980 during
which Tolbert was killed. M/Sgt. Samuel Doe assumed
power as chairman of a military council. A new
constitution was endorsed by a referendum in 1984. Doe
and his party, the National Democratic Party of Liberia

(NDPL) won the elections held in 1985. Doe was killed in 1990 and civil war ensued. A cease-fire was declared in August 1993 and a council of state governed the country until a general election was held in July 1997, which was won by the National Patriotic Party (NPP), and Charles Taylor was elected president with 75 per cent of the vote in an election deemed free and fair by international observers.

On 11 August 2003 Charles Taylor resigned as president and went into exile in Nigeria, in a move endeavouring to end civil war and instability in Liberia. Vice-President Moses Blah became interim president until October 2003 when a Transitional Government was due to be set up to rule the country for two years pending elections in 2005. On 20 August 2003 Gyude Bryant of the Liberia Action Party was elected to become Chairman of the Transitional Government by delegates at the Liberian peace talks in Ghana. Wesley Johnson of the opposition United People's Party was elected to become Vice-Chairman of the Transitional Government.

CIVIL WAR
A rebel incursion in 1989 by the National Patriotic Front of Liberia (NPFL) led by Charles Taylor developed into a full-scale civil war in 1990. A five-nation Economic Community of West African States (ECOWAS) peacekeeping force (known as ECOMOG) landed in Monrovia in an effort to end the conflict but in September 1990 President Doe was killed, having refused to step down. The Interim Government of National Unity (IGNU) was formed in August 1990. A peace agreement was signed by the IGNU, NPFL and another rebel group, ULIMO, on 25 July 1993, which brought about a cease-fire on 1 August.

On 7 March 2001 the UN Security Council imposed a diamond embargo on Liberia and accused the country of supporting the Revolutionary United Front, a Sierra Leonean rebel movement.

A state of emergency was declared on 8 February 2002 after Liberians united for Reconciliation and Democracy (LURD) rebels carried out attacks close to the capital. On 29 April 2002 political activity was banned amid a renewed upsurge in fighting. In May 2002, the UN Security Council renewed its sanctions on Liberia, saying the country had not yet severed ties with the rebels. Liberia argued that the arms embargo was preventing the military from fending off rebels in Liberia's north. In September 2002 the state of emergency and a ban on political rallies was lifted by President Taylor, citing a reduced threat from rebels.

In March 2003 fighting flared up again as rebels opened several battlefronts and advanced to within 10 km of Monrovia; tens of thousands of people were displaced by the fighting. Talks in Ghana aimed at ending ongoing rebellion were overshadowed by an indictment accusing President Taylor of war crimes over his alleged backing of rebels in Sierra Leone. The arrest order was not observed and the president returned to Liberia from Ghana. Despite a cease-fire agreed between rebels and government forces on 17 June, fighting intensified in July with rebels battling for control of Monrovia. Nigerian peacekeepers arrived on 4 August 2003; the first contingent of a multinational West African peacekeeping force that will eventually number 3,250. A peace agreement between the Liberian government and two rebel movements was signed in Accra, Ghana, on 18 August.

POLITICAL SYSTEM
The head of state is an executive president, directly elected for a six-year term, who appoints the Cabinet. There is a bicameral legislature consisting of a 64-member lower chamber, the House of Representatives, which is directly elected for a six-year term, and a 26-member Senate, elected for a nine-year term.

HEAD OF STATE
President (interim), Moses Blah *as of* 11 August 2003
Vice-President, vacant

CABINET *as at August 2003*
Agriculture, Othello Brandy
Commerce and Industry, Cora Peabody
Defence, Daniel Chea
Education, Evelyne Kandakai
Finance, Charles Bright
Foreign Affairs, Monie Captan
Gender Development, Musuleng Cooper
Health and Social Welfare, Peter Coleman
Information, Culture and Tourism, Reginald Goodridge
Internal Affairs, Richard Flomo
Justice, Laveli Korboi Johnson
Labour, Christian Herbert
Lands, Mines and Energy, Wisseh McClain *(Planning and Economic Affairs);* Jonathan Taylor *(Presidential Affairs);* Augustine Zayzay *(Without Portfolio)*
Ministers of State, Wisseh McClain *(Planning and Economic Affairs);* Jonathan Taylor *(Presidential Affairs);* Augustine Zayzay *(Without Portfolio)*
National Security, Philip Kamah
Planning and Economic Affairs, Roland Massaquoi
Post and Telecommunications, Melvin Sogbandi
Public Works, Emmet Taylor
Rural Development, Hezekiah Bowen
Transport, Joe W. Mulbah

EMBASSY OF THE REPUBLIC OF LIBERIA
2 Pembridge Place, London W2 4XB
Tel: 020-7221 1036
Ambassador Extraordinary and Plenipotentiary, vacant

BRITISH AMBASSADOR, HE Jean Gordon, CMG, apptd 2001, resident at Abidjan, Côte d'Ivoire

ECONOMY
Before the civil war began principal exports were iron ore, crude rubber, timber, uncut diamonds, palm kernels, cocoa and coffee, but the civil war has resulted in the suspension of most economic activity.
GDP – US$759 million (1998); US$248 per capita (2000)
ANNUAL AVERAGE GROWTH OF GDP – 2.7 per cent (1998)
TOTAL EXTERNAL DEBT – US$2,032 million (2000)

Trade with UK	2001	2002
Imports from UK	£10,410,000	£6,331,000
Exports to UK	12,015,000	3,119,000

COMMUNICATIONS
The artificial harbour and free port of Monrovia was opened in 1948. There are 10,300 km of roads, of which 628 km are paved, and 490 km of railway track. There are nine ports of entry, including three river ports. Robertsfield International Airport and Spriggs Payne airfield are currently being used for flights to other West African countries.

LIBYA

*Al-Jamāhīriyya Al-'Arabiyya
Al-Lībiyya Ash-Sha'biyya Al-Ishtirmākiyya – Great Socialist
People's Libyan Arab Jamahiriya*

AREA – 676,731 sq. miles (1,759,500 sq. km).
  Neighbours: Egypt and Sudan (east), Chad and Niger
  (south), Algeria and Tunisia (west)
POPULATION – 5,408,000 (2001). The people of Libya
  are principally Arab with some Berbers in the west and
  some Tuareg tribesmen in the Fezzan. Islam is the
  official religion. The official language is Arabic
CAPITAL – ΨTripoli (Tarabulus) (population,
  1,000,000, 1991 estimate)
MAJOR CITIES – ΨBangazi (500,000); ΨMisratah
  (200,000); Sirte (100,000)
CURRENCY – Libyan dinar (LD) of 1,000 dirhams
NATIONAL ANTHEM – Allahu Akbar (God Is Great)
NATIONAL DAY – 1 September
NATIONAL FLAG – Libya uses a plain emerald green flag
LIFE EXPECTANCY (years) – 71 (2001)
POPULATION GROWTH RATE – 2.1 per cent
POPULATION DENSITY – 3 per sq. km (2001)
ILLITERACY RATE – (m) 9.2 per cent; (f) 31.7 per cent
  (2000)

The ancient ruins in Cyrenaica, at Cyrene, Ptolemais
(Tolmeta) and Apollonia, are outstanding, as are those at
Leptis Magna, 70 miles east, and at Sabratha, 40 miles
west of Tripoli. An Italian expedition found in the south-
west of the Fezzan a series of rock-paintings more than
5,000 years old.

HISTORY AND POLITICS

From the 16th century Libya was dominated by the
Ottoman Empire, until occupied by Italy in 1911–12 in
the course of the Italo-Turkish War. Under the 1912
Treaty of Ouchy, sovereignty over the province was
transferred by Turkey to Italy, and in 1939 the four
provinces of Libya (Tripoli, Misurata, Bangazi and Derna)
were incorporated in the national territory of Italy as
Libia Italiana. After the Second World War Tripolitania
and Cyrenaica were placed provisionally under British
and the Fezzan under French administration, and in
conformity with a resolution of the UN General
Assembly in 1949, Libya became on 24 December 1951
the first independent state to be created by the UN. The
monarchy was overthrown by a revolution in 1969 and
the country was declared a republic. It was ruled by the
Revolutionary Command Council (RCC) under the
leadership of Col. Muammar al-Gadhafi.

In 1977, a new form of direct democracy, the
'Jamahiriya' (state of the masses) was promulgated and
the official name of the country was changed to Great
Socialist People's Libyan Arab Jamahiriyya. Since a
reorganisation in 1979, neither Col. Gadhafi nor his
former RCC colleagues have held formal posts in the
administration. Gadhafi continues to hold the ceremonial
title 'Leader of the Revolution'.

POLITICAL SYSTEM

At local level authority is vested in about 1,500 Basic and
14 Municipal People's Congresses which appoint Popular
Committees to execute policy. Officials of these
congresses and committees, together with representatives
from unions and other organisations, form the 750-
member General People's Congress, which normally

meets twice each year. In addition, a number of
extraordinary sessions are held throughout the year. This
is the highest policy-making body in the country. The
General People's Congress appoints its own General
Secretariat and the General People's Committee, whose
members head the government departments which
execute policy at national level. The Secretary of the
General People's Committee has functions similar to
those of a prime minister.

*Leader of the Revolution and Supreme Commander of the
  Armed Forces,* Col. Muammar al-Gadhafi

GENERAL PEOPLE'S COMMITTEE *as at July 2003*
Secretary-General (Prime Minister), Shukri Muhammad
  Ghanim
Assistant Secretary-General, Abdullah al-Badri
Deputy Secretary for Production, Al-Baghdadi Ali al-
  Mahmudi
Deputy Secretary for Services, Ma'tuq Muhammad Ma'tuq
Secretary, Economy and Trade, Abd-al-Qadir Umar
  Bilkhayr
Secretary, Finance, Al-Ujayli Abd-al-Salam Burayni
Secretary, Foreign Liaison and International Co-operation,
  Abdel Rahman Muhammad Shalgam
Secretary, Justice and Public Security, Mohammad Ali al-
  Masirati
Secretary, Planning, Al-Taher al-Juhaimi
Secretary, Tourism, Ammar Mabruk al-Lutayyif
*Co-ordinator of the General Provisional Committee for
  Defence,* Abu Bakr Jaber Yunes
Secretary-General of the General People's Congress,
  Mohammad al-Zenati

LIBYAN PEOPLE'S BUREAU
61–62 Ennismore Gardens, London SW7 1NH
Tel 020-7589 6120
Ambassador Extraordinary and Plenipotentiary,
  HE Mohamed Abu Al-Qassim Azwai, apptd 2001

BRITISH EMBASSY
Sharia Uahran 1, PO Box 4206, Tripoli
Tel (00 218) (21) 340 3644/5
Ambassador Extraordinary and Plenipotentiary,
  HE Anthony Layden, apptd 2002

BRITISH COUNCIL DIRECTOR, Tony Jones
British Embassy, 24th Floor, Burj al Fatah, PO Box 4206, Tripoli
Email: info.libya@britishcouncil-ly.org

DEFENCE

The Army has about 985 main battle tanks, 1,000
armoured infantry fighting vehicles and 945 armoured
personnel carriers. The Navy has one submarine, one
frigate, 9 patrol and coastal vessels, and seven armed
helicopters at seven bases. The Air Force has 400 combat
aircraft and 41 armed helicopters.
MILITARY EXPENDITURE – 4.1 per cent of GDP (2001)
MILITARY PERSONNEL – 76,000: Army 45,000, Navy
  8,000, Air Force 23,000
CONSCRIPTION DURATION – One to two years
  (selective)

ECONOMY

Economic sanctions were imposed on Libya in April
1992 by the UN Security Council following Libya's
failure to hand over two suspects in the bombing of Pan-
Am flight 103 over Lockerbie, Scotland, in 1988, in

which 270 people were killed. The UN imposed additional sanctions in December 1993, including freezing assets abroad and restricting imports of spare parts and equipment for the oil and aviation sectors. Some sanctions were suspended in April 1999, following mediation by President Mandela of South Africa in March 1999, which led to the extradition in April of the two Libyan suspects to the Netherlands to stand trial. Following the conviction of one of the two suspects, former Libyan intelligence agent Abdel Baset al-Megrahi, on 31 January 2001, the lifting of the remaining sanctions has been made dependent on Libya accepting responsibility for the Lockerbie bombing and agreeing to pay compensation to the families of the victims. Following months of negotiation, in August 2003 Libya agreed to pay US$2.7 billion in compensation which it hoped would pave the way to a formal end to UN sanctions. On 11 September the United Nations Security Council voted to lift all sanctions against Libya, clearing the way for compensation payments to be made.

The main industry is oil and gas production. There are pipelines from Zaltan to the terminal at al-Burayqah, from Dahra to as-Sidrah, from Amal to Ras Lanuf, and from the Intisar field to az-Zuwaytinah. Cement, construction materials and textiles are also produced. Economic constraints have delayed some projects, particularly since Libya decided in 1983 to go ahead with a major irrigation scheme, the 'Great Man-Made River'. The government is now seeking foreign direct investment for the oil and gas industries and to finance improvements to the country's infrastructure.

In 1999 there was a trade surplus of US$2,762 and a current account surplus of US$1,984.

GDP – US$31,661 million (1998); US$5,667 per capita (2000)

ANNUAL AVERAGE GROWTH OF GDP – 0.6 per cent (1998)

TRADE

Exports are dominated by crude oil, but some wool, cattle, sheep and horses, olive oil, and hides and skins are also exported. Principal imports are machinery and transport equipment, foodstuffs, livestock, and most construction materials and consumer goods.

In 2000 imports totalled US$3,751 and exports US$10,247.

Trade with UK	2001	2002
Imports from UK	£184,424,000	£215,705,000
Exports to UK	189,816,000	167,037,000

COMMUNICATIONS

There are about 19,300 km of roads; the coastal road running from the Tunisian frontier through Tripoli to Bangazi, Tubruq and the Egyptian border serves the main population centres. Main roads also link the provincial centres, and the oil-producing areas of the south with the coastal towns.

LIECHTENSTEIN

Fürstentum Liechtenstein – Principality of Liechtenstein

AREA – 61.5 sq. miles (160 sq. km). Neighbours: Austria, Switzerland

POPULATION – 33,000 (2001). The language of the principality is Standard German. An Alemannic dialect is in general use. About 65.4 per cent of the population are Liechtensteiners, the remainder being mainly Swiss, Austrians and Germans. Roman Catholicism is the religion of 80.4 per cent of the population; there is a Protestant minority

CAPITAL – Vaduz (population, 5,106, 1998)

CURRENCY – Swiss franc of 100 rappen (or centimes)

NATIONAL ANTHEM – Oben Am Jungen Rhein (Up On The Young Rhine)

NATIONAL DAY – 15 August

NATIONAL FLAG – Equal horizontal bands of blue over red; gold crown on blue band near staff

LIFE EXPECTANCY (years) – 79 (2001)

POPULATION GROWTH RATE – 1.2 per cent

POPULATION DENSITY – 206 per sq. km (2001)

HISTORY AND POLITICS

The region was settled in the fifth century AD by the West Germanic Alemanni. The Principality of Liechtenstein was established by Emperor Charles VI in 1719. Following the First World War, Liechtenstein severed its ties with Austria and began its association with Switzerland, taking up the Swiss currency in 1921.

In November 1999, the European Court of Human Rights fined Prince Hans Adam II for abusing his subjects' freedom of speech, a development which prompted a constitutional crisis in the principality.

In February 2000, Prince Hans Adam announced that he wished to hold a referendum on constitutional reform, and threatened to abdicate if the extension of his powers was rejected by the electorate. On 16 March 2003, after intense campaigning both for and against the proposals, the changes to the 1921 constitution were approved in a referendum by 64.3 per cent of the voters of 87.7 per cent turnout.

The Patriotic Union (VU) and the Progressive Citizens' Party (FBP) governed the country in coalition from 1938 until March 1997. The 1997 general election was won by the VU, which lost power to the FBP, who won 13 seats in the general election held on 9 and 11 February 2001. The new government took office on 5 April.

POLITICAL SYSTEM

Liechtenstein is a constitutional monarchy. The Cabinet is appointed by the Prince on the advice of parliament and consists of a head of government and four ministers. The 25-member Landtag, the unicameral parliament, has a four-year term. There is a threshold of 8 per cent for parties to gain representation. The 19 March 2003 referendum approved constitutional reforms which would give the monarch an increase in power including authority to dismiss the government and appoint interim prime ministers. The monarch would also not be subject to the authority of the constitutional court.

HEAD OF STATE
HSH The Prince of Liechtenstein, Hans Adam II, *born* 14 February 1945; *succeeded* 13 November 1989; *married* 30 July 1967, Countess Marie Kinsky; and has *issue*: Prince Alois; Prince Maximilian, *b.* 16 May 1969; Prince Constantin, *b.* 15 March 1972; Princess Tatjana, *b.* 10 April 1973

Heir, HSH Prince Alois, *b.* 11 June 1968, *married* 1993 Duchess Sophie of Bavaria; and has *issue*: Prince Wenzel, *b.* 24 May 1995; Princess Marie, *b.* 17 October 1996; Prince Georg, *b.* 20 April 1999

CABINET *as at July 2003*
Head of Government, Construction, Family Affairs and
   Equal Rights, Finance, General Government Affairs,
   Otmar Hasler
Deputy Head of Government, Education, Justice, Transport,
   Rita Kieber-Beck
Culture and Sports, Environment, Interior, Alois Ospelt
Economy, Health, Social Matters, Hansjörg Frick
Foreign Affairs, Ernst Walch

DIPLOMATIC REPRESENTATION
Liechtenstein is represented in diplomatic and consular
matters in the United Kingdom by the Swiss Embassy.

BRITISH AMBASSADOR, Basil Eastwood, CMG, resident
   at Bern, Switzerland

ECONOMY
The main industries are high and ultra-high vacuum
engineering, the semiconductor industry, roller bearings,
artificial teeth, heating equipment, synthetic fibres,
woollen and homespun fabrics. Following international
accusations that Liechtenstein was a haven for money-
laundering, the country banned anonymous bank
accounts in September 2000.

In 1991 Liechtenstein became a member of the
European Free Trade Association, and joined the
European Economic Area on 1 May 1995.
GDP – US$1,150 million (1998); US$33,394 per capita
   (2000)
ANNUAL AVERAGE GROWTH OF GDP – 2.1 per cent
   (1998)

Trade with UK	2001	2002
Imports from UK	£6,020,000	£4,731,000
Exports to UK	25,010,000	23,799,000

LITHUANIA

Lietuvos Respublika – Republic of Lithuania

AREA – 24,923 sq. miles (64,800 sq. km). Neighbours:
   Latvia (north), Belarus (east and south), Poland and the
   Kaliningrad region of the Russian Federation (south-
   west)
POPULATION – 3,689,000 (2001): 80.6 per cent
   Lithuanian, 8.7 per cent Russian, 7 per cent Polish, 1.6
   per cent Belarusian, 2.1 per cent other. The majority
   are Roman Catholic (79 per cent), with Russian
   Orthodox (4.1 per cent) and Lutheran minorities.
   Lithuanian is the state language
CAPITAL – Vilnius (population, 542,287, 2001 estimate)
MAJOR CITIES – Kaunas (378,943); Klaipeda (192,954),
   2001
CURRENCY – Litas of 100 centas, pegged to the euro,
   €1= 3.45 litas
NATIONAL ANTHEM – Tautiska Giesme (The National
   Song)
NATIONAL DAY – 16 February (Independence Day)
NATIONAL FLAG – Three horizontal stripes of yellow,
   green, red
LIFE EXPECTANCY (years) – 72 (2001)
POPULATION GROWTH RATE –0.2 per cent
POPULATION DENSITY – 57 per sq. km (2001)
URBAN POPULATION – 69 per cent (2001)

Lithuania lies in the middle and lower basin of the river
Nemunas. Along the coast is a lowland plain which rises
inland to form uplands in east and central Lithuania.
These uplands, the Middle Lowlands, give way to the
Baltic Highlands in east and south-east Lithuania; the
highest point is 294 m (965 ft). There is a network of
rivers and over 2,800 lakes, which mainly lie in the east
of the country.

HISTORY AND POLITICS
The first independent Lithuanian state emerged as the
Kingdom of Lithuania in 1251. After forming a joint
Commonwealth and Kingdom with Poland in 1569,
Lithuania was taken over by the Russian Empire in 1795.

Lithuania declared its independence from the Russian
Empire on 16 February 1918 and signed a peace treaty
with the Soviet Union on 12 July 1920. The Soviet
Union annexed Lithuania in 1940 under the terms of the
Molotov–Ribbentrop pact with Germany. Lithuania was
invaded and occupied when Germany invaded the Soviet
Union during the Second World War. In 1944, the Soviet
Union recaptured the country and confirmed its
annexation.

Over 90 per cent of the population voted for
independence in a referendum in February 1991. The
Soviet Union recognised the independence of Lithuania
on 10 September 1991.

The government formed after October 2000 general
election was a minority-centre right coalition led by
Rolandas Paksas. The governing coalition collapsed in
June 2001 and Algirdas Brazauskas of the Social
Democratic Party (SD), who had been Lithuania's last
communist-era ruler and subsequently its president,
formed a coalition government with the New Union
(Social Liberals) (NS(SL)), whose withdrawal from the
previous government had caused it to collapse. The new
government was appointed on 5 July 2001.

On 5 January 2003 former Prime Minister Rolandas
Paksas of LDP was the surprise victor in the second
round of presidential elections. Paksas came second in the
first round in December 2002, when President Valdas
Adamkus fell short of an overall majority. On 26
February 2003 Paksas was inaugurated for a five-year-
term and immediately nominated Brazauskas to be prime
minister again, and his appointment and his new cabinet
were approved by Parliament on 6 March.

FOREIGN RELATIONS
In November 2002 NATO included Latvia on a list of
seven countries invited to join the alliance, Latvia is
expected to become a full member of NATO in 2004.
In December Latvia was formally invited to join the EU.
A referendum held on 10–11 May 2003 resulted in
overwhelming approval for accession.

POLITICAL SYSTEM
Under the 1992 constitution, the head of state is a
directly elected president, whose five-year term of office
is renewable once only. Executive authority is vested
in the government, consisting of the prime minister,
who is appointed by the president with the approval
of the Seimas, and ministers appointed upon the
recommendation of the prime minister. Legislative power
is exercised by the Seimas, a unicameral parliament of
141 members directly elected for four-year terms.
Seventy-one members are elected in first-past-the-post
constituencies and 70 by proportional representation,
with a 5 per cent threshold for representation. The
constitution bans an alignment of Lithuania with any
post-Soviet eastern alliance.

HEAD OF STATE
President, Rolandas Paksas, *elected* 5 January 2003; *sworn in* 26 February 2003

GOVERNMENT *as at July 2003*
Prime Minister, Algirdas Brazauskas (SD)
Agriculture and Forestry, Jeronimas Kraujelis (NS(SL))
Culture, Roma Zakaitiene (SD)
Defence, Linas Linkevicius (ISD)
Economy, Petras Cesna (SD)
Education and Science, Algirdas Monkevicius (NS(SL))
Environment, Arunas Kundrotas (NS(SL))
Finance, Dalia Grybauskaite (SD)
Foreign Affairs, Antanas Valionis (NS(SL))
Health, Juozas Olekas (SD)
Interior, Virgilijus Bulovas
Justice, Vytautas Markevicius (NS(SL))
Social Affairs and Labour, Vilija Blinkeviciute (NS(SL))
Transport, Zigmantas Balcytis (SD)

NS (SL) New Union (Social Liberals); SD Social Democratic Party

EMBASSY OF THE REPUBLIC OF LITHUANIA
84 Gloucester Place, London W1U 6AU
Tel: 020-7486 6401/2
Email: chancery@lithuanianembassy.co.uk
Ambassador Extraordinary and Plenipotentiary,
HE Aurimas Taurantas, apptd 2002

BRITISH EMBASSY
2 Antakalnio, LT-2055 Vilnius
Tel: (00 370) (2) 222 070/1
Ambassador Extraordinary and Plenipotentiary,
HE Jeremy Hill, apptd 2001

BRITISH COUNCIL DIRECTOR, Lina Balenaite
Business Centre 2000, Jogailos 4, LT 2001 Vilnius
Tel: (370) 5 264 4890/1
Email: lina.balenaite@britishcouncil.lt

DEFENCE
The Army has 97 armoured personnel carriers; the Navy has two frigates and five patrol and coastal vessels based at Klaipeda; the Air Force has eight helicopters. The last Russian troops withdrew in 1993.
MILITARY EXPENDITURE – 1.8 per cent of GDP (2001)
MILITARY PERSONNEL – 13,510: Army 8,100, Navy 650, Air Force 1,000; Paramilitaries 13,850
CONSCRIPTION DURATION – 12 months

ECONOMY
The economy was largely agricultural prior to rapid industrialisation during the Soviet era. A privatisation programme began in 1991 and progress in the sale of small enterprises has been quick and successful. In 1997, the privatisation of communication, energy and transport companies was begun.
In 1999, agriculture and forestry accounted for 8.8 per cent of GDP, mining and manufacturing industry 23.3 per cent, construction 8 per cent and transport and communications 11 per cent. The main industries are chemicals and petrochemicals, food processing, wood products, textiles, leather goods, machinery, machine tools and household appliances. Lithuania joined the WTO in 2000.
GNP – US$10,809 million (2000); US$2,930 per capita (2000)

GDP – US$11,834 million (2001); US$3,039 per capita (2000)
ANNUAL AVERAGE GROWTH OF GDP – 5.9 per cent (2001)
INFLATION RATE – 1.3 per cent (2001)
UNEMPLOYMENT – 15.4 per cent (2000)
TOTAL EXTERNAL DEBT – US$4,855 million (2000)

TRADE
Lithuania's main trading partners are Germany, Latvia, Russia, Denmark and Belarus. In January 2001, total foreign investment in Lithuania reached US$2.3 billion.
In 2001 there was a trade deficit of US$1,108 million and a current account deficit of US$574 million. Imports totalled US$6,353 million and exports US$4,583 million.

Trade with UK	2001	2002
Imports from UK	£137,257,000	£149,696,000
Exports to UK	240,897,000	272,102,000

COMMUNICATIONS
There were 71,375 km of roads in 2000; there is a relatively well-developed railway system of 2,898 km running east-west and north-south and linking the major towns with Vilnius and Klaipeda, the main international port. Vilnius has an international airport.

CULTURE AND EDUCATION
Lithuanian culture and literature are closely linked to the national liberation movements of the 19th and early 20th centuries, and the literature of Lithuanians who went into exile during the Soviet era.
Lithuania re-established a national education system in 1990. Education is free and compulsory from seven to 16 years, with the system comprising elementary schools (four years), nine-year schools (five years), and secondary schools (three years). The language of instruction is predominantly Lithuanian, but there are also Russian and Polish schools. There are 105 vocational schools and 65 colleges. Lithuania has eight universities and seven other institutes of higher education. Vilnius University, founded in 1579, is one of the oldest universities in eastern Europe.
ILLITERACY RATE – (m) 0.3 per cent; (f) 0.5 per cent (2000)
ENROLMENT (percentage of age group) – secondary 98 per cent (1997); tertiary 31 per cent (1997)

LUXEMBOURG

Groussherzogtom Lëtzebuerg / Grand-Duché de Luxembourg / Großherzogtum Luxembourg – Grand Duchy of Luxembourg

AREA – 994.6 sq. miles (2,586 sq. km). Neighbours: Germany (east), Belgium (west and north), France (south)
POPULATION – 442,000 (2001), nearly all Roman Catholic. The officially designated 'national language' is Lëtzebuergesch (Luxembourgish), a mainly spoken language. French and German are the official languages for written purposes, and French is the language of administration
CAPITAL – Luxembourg (population, 77,400, 1996)
CURRENCY – Euro (€) of 100 cents
NATIONAL ANTHEM – Ons Hémécht (Our Homeland)
NATIONAL DAY – 23 June

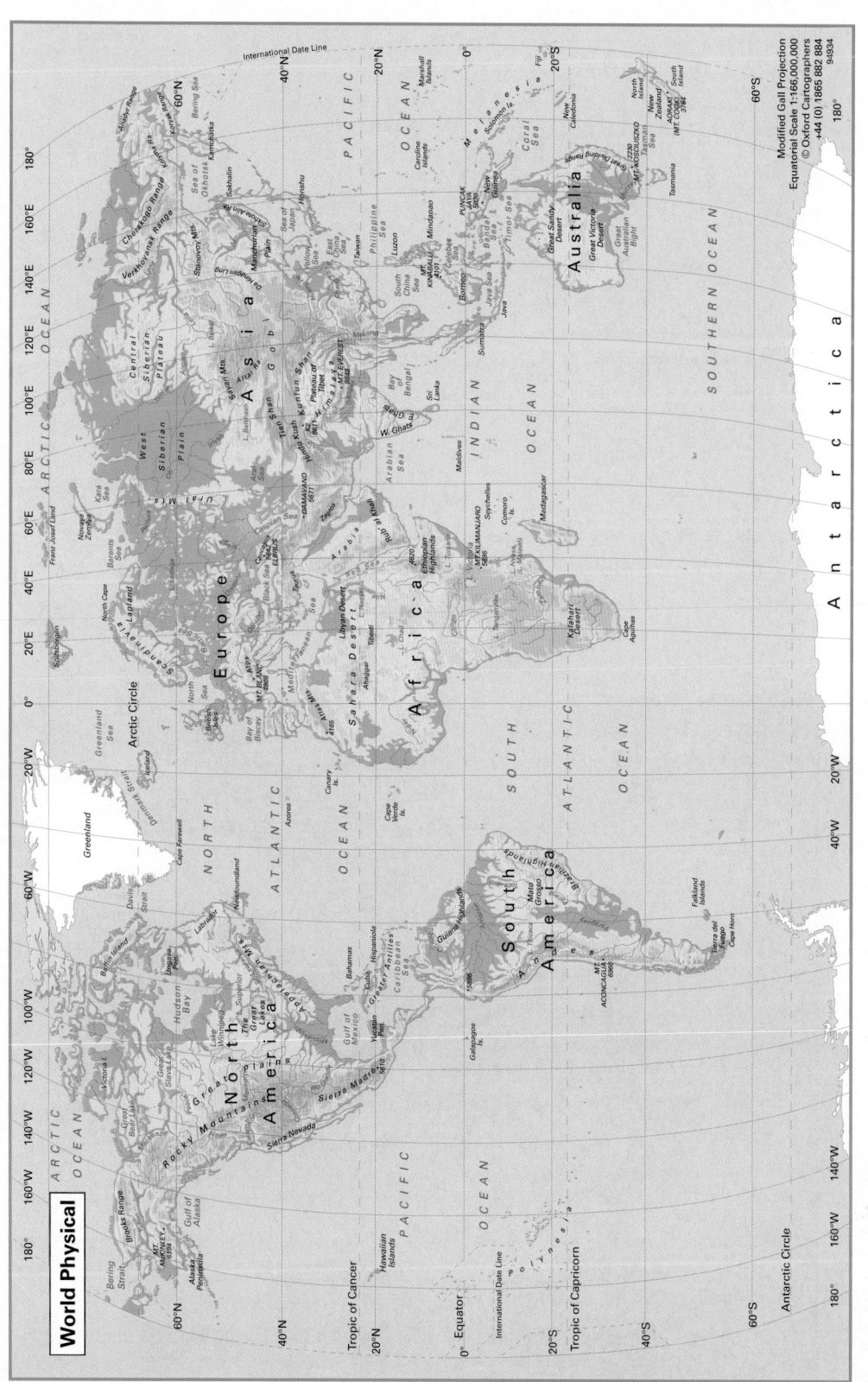

World Physical

Modified Gall Projection
Equatorial Scale 1:166,000,000
© Oxford Cartographers
+44 (0) 1865 882 884
94934

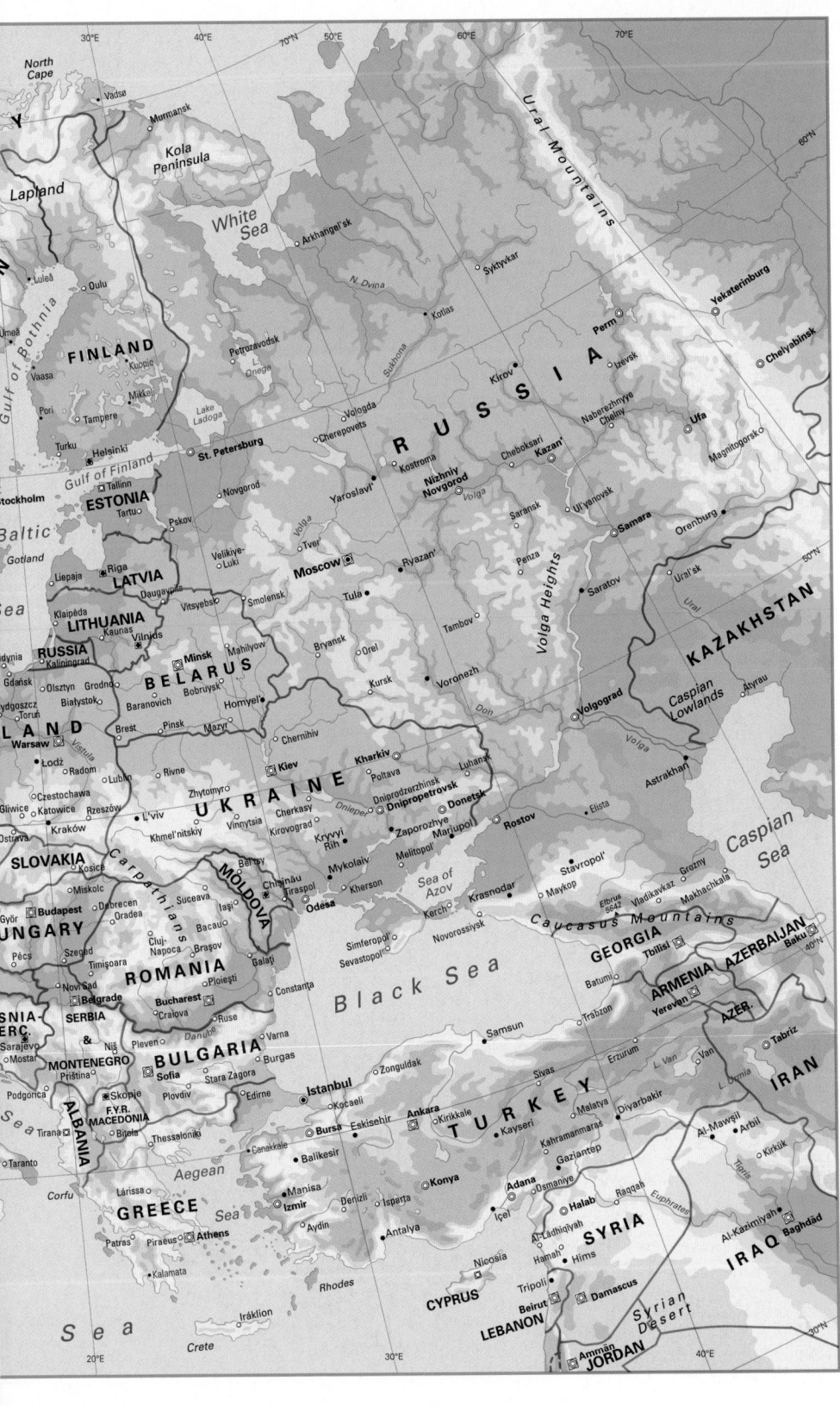

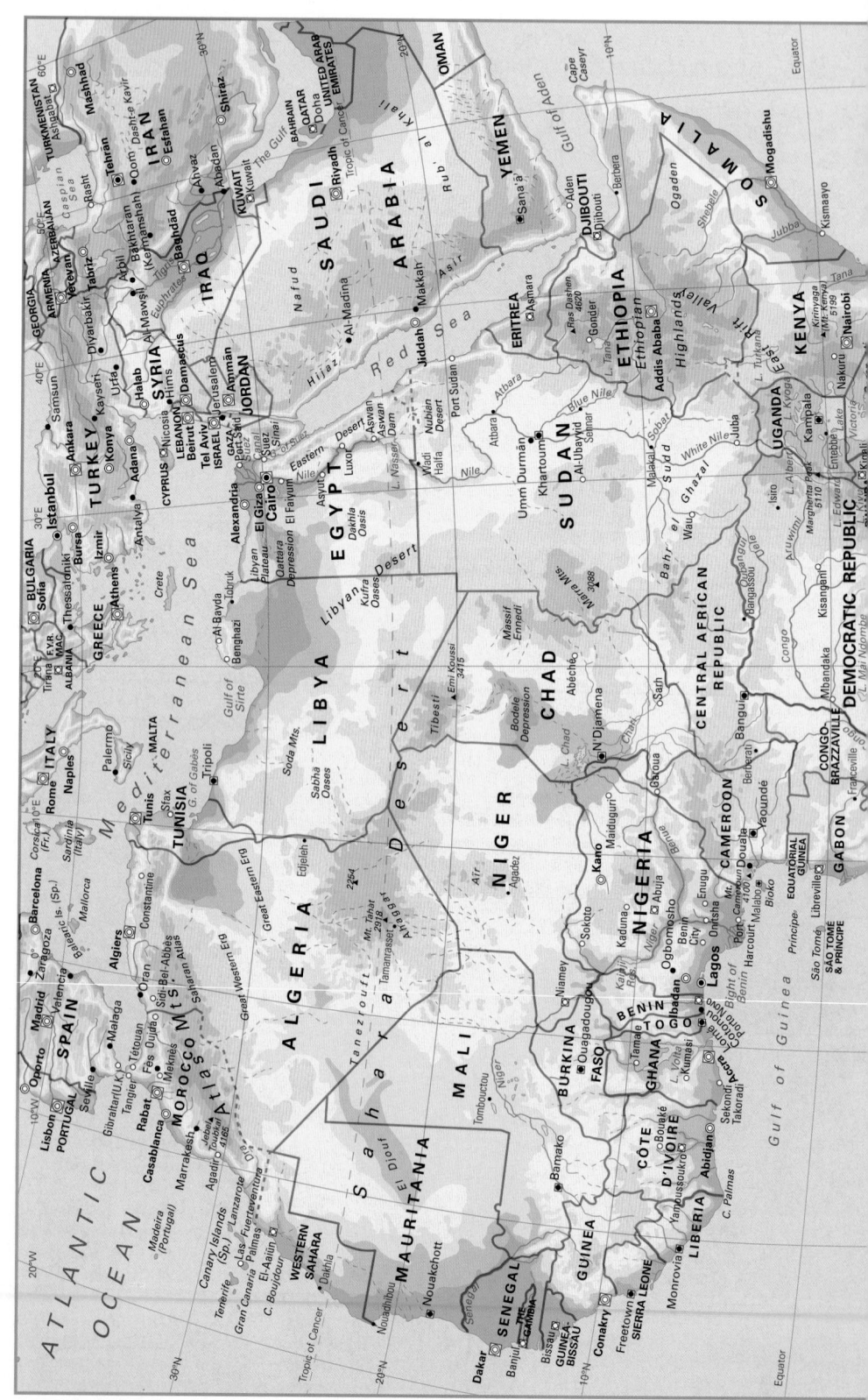

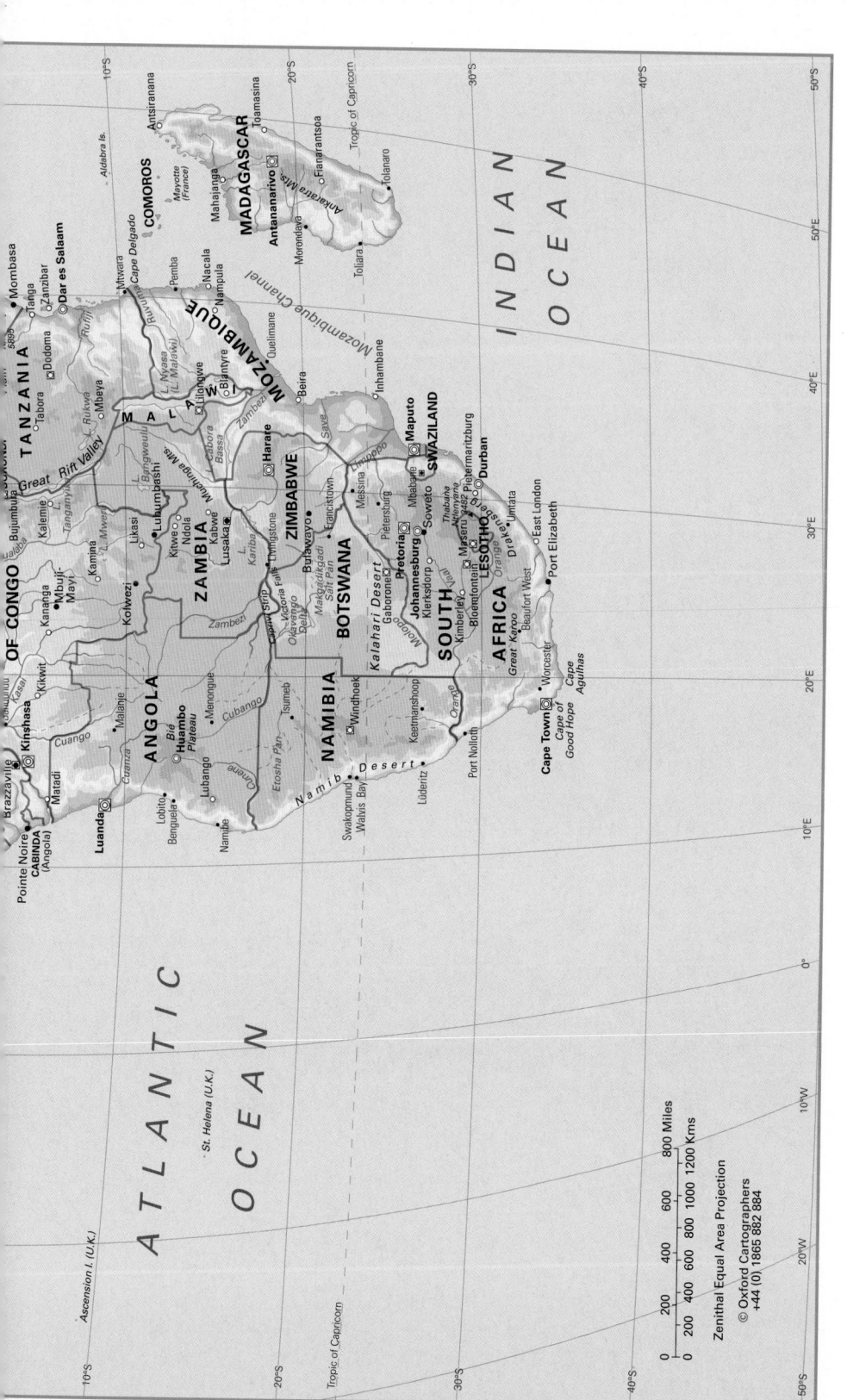

ATLANTIC

OCEAN

Ascension I. (U.K.)

St. Helena (U.K.)

Zenithal Equal Area Projection

© Oxford Cartographers
+44 (0) 1865 882 884

0		200		400		600		800 Miles
0	200	400	600	800	1000	1200 Kms		

Tropic of Capricorn

OF CONGO

Brazzaville
Pointe Noire
CABINDA
(Angola)
Matadi
Kinshasa

Kikwit
Kananga
Mbuji-
Mayi
Kamina

Kwango
Kasai

Luanda

Malanje
Lobito
Benguela
Namibe

Cuango

Bié
Huambo
Plateau
Lubango

ANGOLA

Cuanza

Cubango

Etosha Pan.

Cunene

Menongue

Tsumeb

Windhoek

NAMIBIA

Namib Desert

Swakopmund
Walvis Bay

Lüderitz

Kolwezi
Likasi
Lubumbashi

Bangweulu

Ndola
Kitwe
Kabwe

ZAMBIA

Zambezi

Caprivi Strip

Okavango
Delta

Makgadikgadi
Salt Pan

Maun

Kalahari Desert

BOTSWANA

Gaborone

Keetmanshoop

Port Nolloth

Orange

Cape Town
Cape of
Good Hope

Cape
AguIhas

Worcester

Great Karoo

Bujumbura

Kalemie

Mweru

Tanganyika

Great Rift Valley

TANZANIA

Dodoma
Tabora

Mbeya

Rukwa

L. Nyasa
(L. Malawi)

Mtwara

Pemba

Nacala
Nampula

Mombasa
Tanga
Zanzibar
Dar es Salaam

Rufiji

Ruvuma Cape Delgado

COMOROS

Aldabra Is.

Mayotte
(France)

Mahajanga

Morondava

MADAGASCAR

Antananarivo

Ankaratra Mts.

Fianarantsoa

Toliara

Antsiranana

Toamasina

Tropic of Capricorn

MALAWI

Lilongwe
Blantyre

Cabora
Bassa

Quelimane

Beira

MOZAMBIQUE

Mozambique Channel

INDIAN

OCEAN

Muchinga Mts.

Lusaka

Kariba

Kafue

Livingstone
Victoria Falls

Harare

ZIMBABWE

Bulawayo

Francistown

Limpopo

Save

Inhambane

Messina

Pietersburg

Maputo

SWAZILAND

Mbabane

Pretoria
Johannesburg
Soweto
Klerksdorp

Thabana
Ntlenyana
3482

LESOTHO

Maseru

Drakensberg

Pietermaritzburg

Durban

SOUTH

AFRICA

Kimberley
Bloemfontein

Molopo

Vaal

Orange

Beaufort West

East London

Port Elizabeth

Umtata

0°   10°E   20°E   30°E   40°E   50°E

10°S   20°S   30°S   40°S   50°S

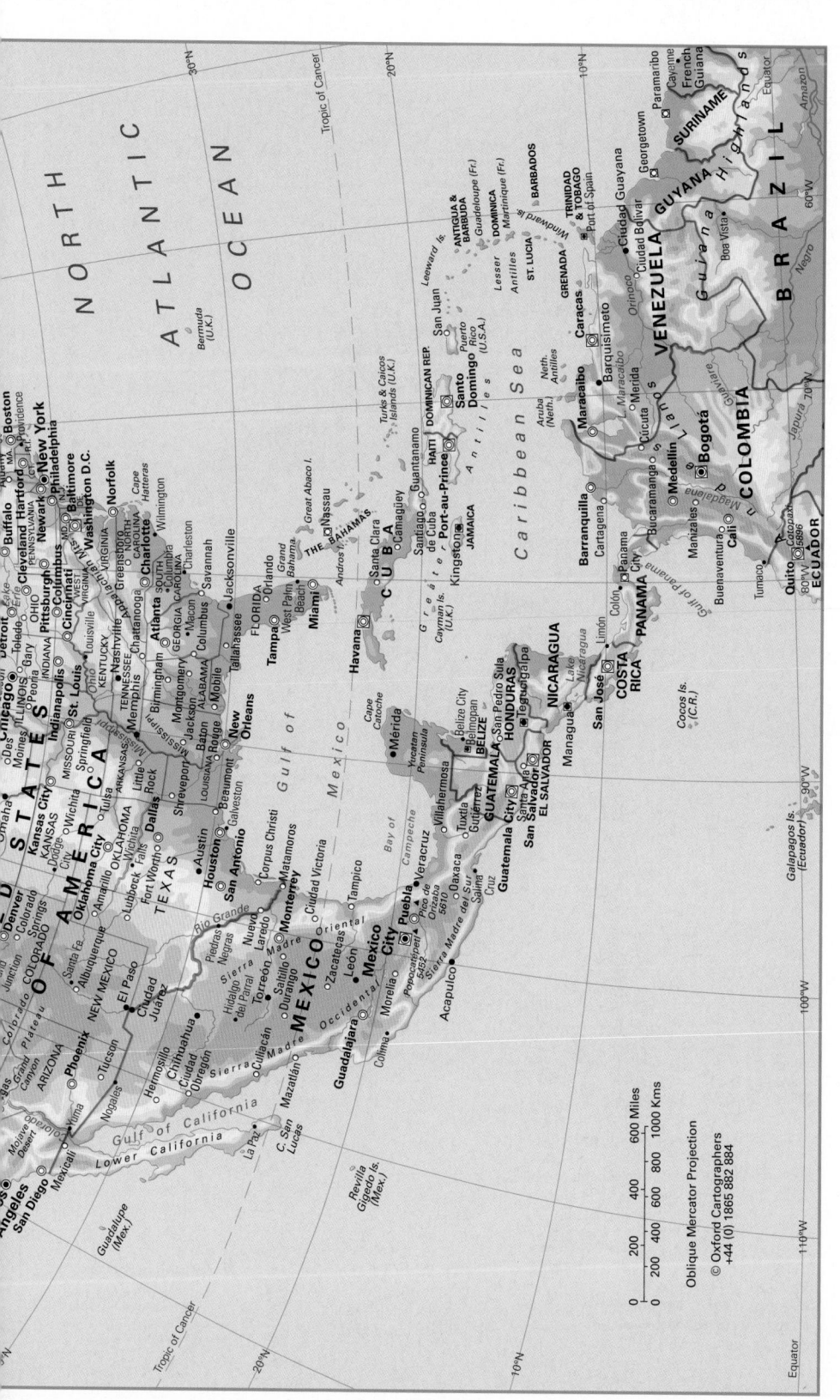

NORTH ATLANTIC OCEAN

UNITED STATES OF AMERICA

Los Angeles
San Diego
Mexicali
Nogales
Tijuana
Mojave Desert
ARIZONA
Tucson
Phoenix
Yuma
NEW MEXICO
Albuquerque
Santa Fe
Colorado Plateau
COLORADO
Denver
Colorado Springs
Grand Canyon
Las Vegas
Lower California
Gulf of California
Guadalupe (Mex.)
C. San Lucas
La Paz
Mazatlán
Culiacán
Ciudad Obregón
Chihuahua
Hermosillo
Ciudad Juárez
El Paso
Sierra Madre Occidental
Hidalgo del Parral
Durango
Torreón
Saltillo
Monterrey
Zacatecas
León
Morelia
Colima
Guadalajara
Aguascalientes
Acapulco
Popocatépetl 5452
MEXICO
Mexico City
Puebla
Pico de Orizaba 5610
Sierra Madre del Sur
Oaxaca
Salina Cruz
Tuxtla Gutiérrez
Villahermosa
Oriental
Ciudad Victoria
Tampico
Matamoros
Nuevo Laredo
Piedras Negras
Rio Grande
Laredo
Corpus Christi
San Antonio
Austin
Houston
Galveston
Beaumont
TEXAS
Fort Worth
Dallas
Oklahoma City
OKLAHOMA
Tulsa
Wichita
Dodge City
KANSAS
Kansas City
Lubbock
Amarillo
Wichita Falls
Little Rock
ARKANSAS
Shreveport
Baton Rouge
LOUISIANA
New Orleans
Mobile
ALABAMA
Jackson
MISSISSIPPI
Montgomery
Memphis
TENNESSEE
Nashville
Chattanooga
Birmingham
GEORGIA
Atlanta
Columbus
Macon
Savannah
FLORIDA
Tallahassee
Jacksonville
Orlando
Tampa
West Palm Beach
Miami
KENTUCKY
Louisville
St. Louis
MISSOURI
Springfield
INDIANA
Indianapolis
Cincinnati
OHIO
Columbus
Pittsburgh
Cleveland
Toledo
Detroit
Gary
Peoria
ILLINOIS
Chicago
Des Moines
Omaha
Columbia
SOUTH CAROLINA
Charleston
NORTH CAROLINA
Charlotte
Greensboro
VIRGINIA
WEST VIRGINIA
Columbus
Washington D.C.
MD.
Baltimore
Philadelphia
DEL.
New York
Newark
Hartford
CONN.
Providence
R.I.
Boston
MA.
Buffalo
Erie
Lake Erie
Cape Hatteras
Wilmington
Norfolk

Gulf of Mexico

Cape Catoche
Yucatan Peninsula
Mérida
Campeche
Bay of Campeche

THE BAHAMAS
Great Abaco I.
Grand Bahama
Nassau
Andros I.
Santa Clara
Camagüey
CUBA
Havana
Guantánamo
Santiago de Cuba
Cayman Is. (U.K.)
JAMAICA
Kingston
Bermuda (U.K.)
Turks & Caicos Islands (U.K.)

Caribbean Sea

DOMINICAN REP.
Santo Domingo
HAITI
Port-au-Prince
Puerto Rico (U.S.A.)
San Juan
Leeward Is.
ANTIGUA & BARBUDA
Guadeloupe (Fr.)
DOMINICA
Martinique (Fr.)
ST. LUCIA
BARBADOS
GRENADA
Lesser Antilles
Windward Is.
TRINIDAD & TOBAGO
Port of Spain

Aruba (Neth.)
Neth. Antilles

BELIZE
Belize City
Belmopan
GUATEMALA
Guatemala City
HONDURAS
San Pedro Sula
Tegucigalpa
EL SALVADOR
San Salvador
Santa Ana
NICARAGUA
Managua
Lake Nicaragua
León
COSTA RICA
San José
Limón
PANAMA
Panama City
Colón
Gulf of Panama

Cocos Is. (C.R.)

Galapagos Is. (Ecuador)

VENEZUELA
Maracaibo
Lake Maracaibo
Barquisimeto
Caracas
Ciudad Bolívar
Ciudad Guayana
Mérida
Cúcuta
Bucaramanga
Barranquilla
Cartagena
COLOMBIA
Medellín
Manizales
Bogotá
Cali
Buenaventura
Tumaco
ECUADOR
Quito
Chimborazo 6896
Llanos
Orinoco
Meta
Guaviare
Japurá
Putumayo
Magdalena

SURINAME
Paramaribo
GUYANA
Georgetown
FRENCH GUIANA
Cayenne
Guiana Highlands
BRAZIL
Boa Vista
Negro
Amazon
Branco
Equator

600 Miles
0 200 400
0 200 400 600 800 1000 Kms

Oblique Mercator Projection

© Oxford Cartographers
+44 (0) 1865 882 884

Tropic of Cancer
30°N
20°N
10°N
Equator
20°N
10°N

110°W
100°W
90°W
80°W
70°W
60°W

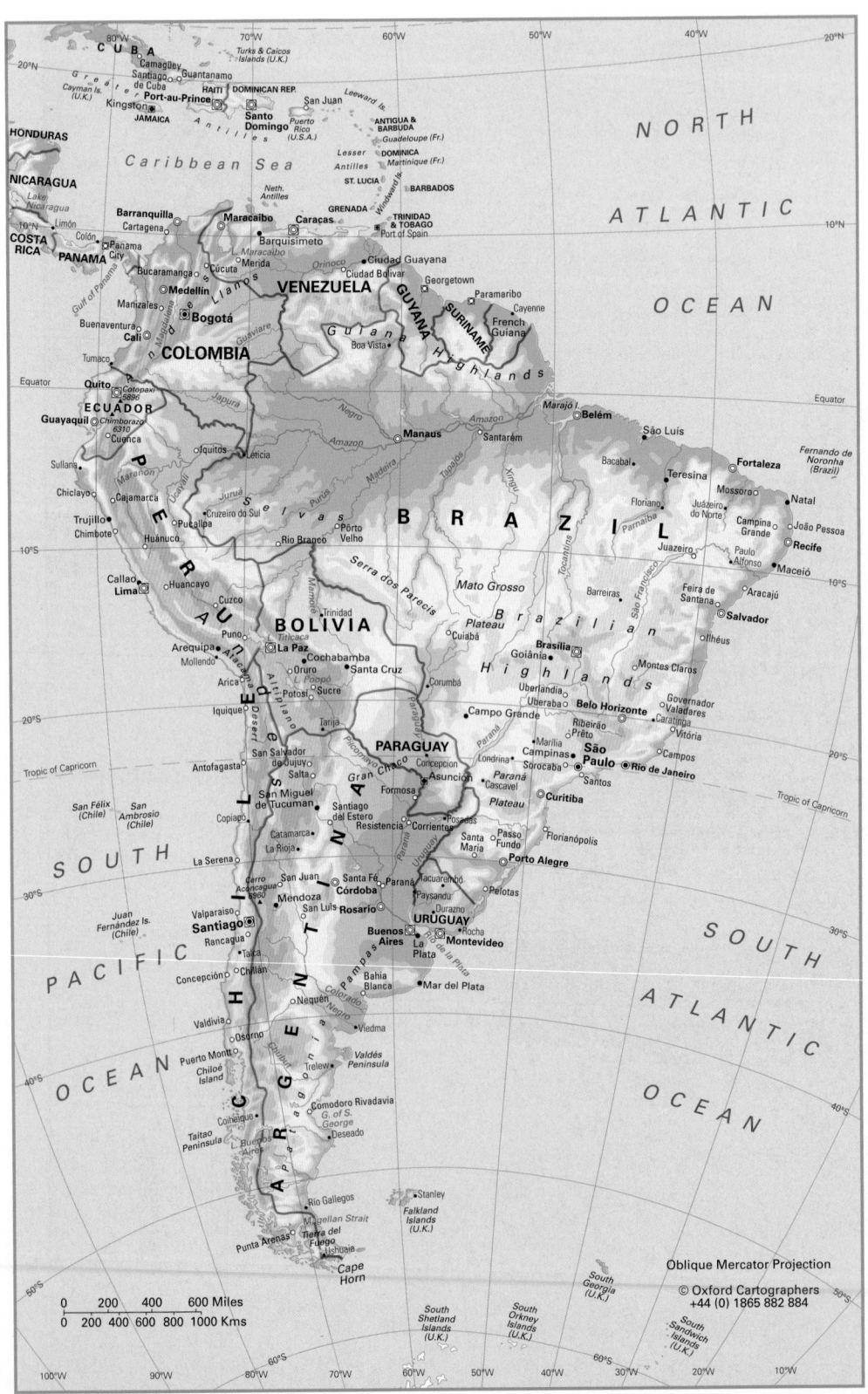

CUBA
80°W
Turks & Caicos
Islands (U.K.)
70°W
60°W
50°W
40°W
30°W
20°N
20°N
Camagüey
Greater
Santiago
de Cuba Guantanamo
Cayman Is.
(U.K.) Kingston
HAITI DOMINICAN REP.
Port-au-Prince
Santo
Domingo
San Juan
Puerto
Rico
(U.S.A.)
Leeward Is.
ANTIGUA &
BARBUDA
Guadeloupe (Fr.)
NORTH
HONDURAS
JAMAICA
Antilles
Caribbean Sea
Lesser
Antilles
DOMINICA
Martinique (Fr.)
ST. LUCIA
ATLANTIC
NICARAGUA
Lake
Nicaragua
Neth.
Antilles
BARBADOS
10°N
COSTA
RICA
Limón
Colón
Panama
City
PANAMA
Barranquilla
Cartagena
GRENADA
TRINIDAD
& TOBAGO
Port of Spain
OCEAN
Maracaibo
Caracas
Barquisimeto
Gulf of Panama
Panama
Maracaibo
Ciudad Guayana
Ciudad Bolívar
Georgetown
Paramaribo
Cayenne
French
Guiana
10°N
Bucaramanga
Cúcuta
Mérida
Orinoco
Llanos
VENEZUELA
GUYANA
SURINAME
Medellín
Buenaventura
Manizales
Bogotá
Guaviare
Boa Vista
Guiana
Highlands
Cali
COLOMBIA
Tumaco
Equator
Quito
Cotopaxi
5896
Japurá
Negro
Amazon
Marajó I.
Belém
São Luís
Equator
ECUADOR
Chimborazo
6310
Guayaquil
Cuenca
Iquitos
Letícia
Manaus
Santarém
Bacabal
Teresina
Fortaleza
Fernando de
Noronha
(Brazil)
Sullana
Marañón
Amazon
Mossoró
Natal
Chiclayo
Cajamarca
Purus
Selvas
Juàzeiro
do Norte
Campina
Grande
João Pessoa
Trujillo
Chimbote
Huánuco
Cruzeiro do Sul
Pucallpa
Juruá
Porto
Velho
Madeira
BRAZIL
Xingu
Tapajós
Parnaíba
Juazeiro
Paulo
Afonso
Recife
Maceió
10°S
Rio Branco
Serra dos Parecis
São Francisco
Feira de
Santana
Aracajú
Salvador
10°S
Callao
Lima
Huancayo
Cuzco
Trinidad
BOLIVIA
Mato Grosso
Barreiras
Ilhéus
Puno
Titicaca
La Paz
Cochabamba
Cuiabá
Plateau
Brasília
Goiânia
Montes Claros
Arequipa
Mollendo
Oruro
Potosí
Poopó
Sucre
Santa Cruz
Corumbá
Campo Grande
Uberlândia
Goiás
Brazilian
Uberaba
Highlands
Governador
Valadares
Caratinga
Vitória
20°S
Arica
Iquique
Tarija
Paraguay
Belo Horizonte
Ribeirão
Prêto
Campos
Antofagasta
San Salvador
de Jujuy
Salta
Pilcomayo
PARAGUAY
Gran Chaco
Concepción
Asunción
Marília
Londrina
Campinas
Sorocaba
São
Paulo
Santos
Rio de Janeiro
20°S
Tropic of Capricorn
San Félix
(Chile)
San
Ambrosio
(Chile)
Copiapó
San Miguel
de Tucumán
Santiago
del Estero
Catamarca
La Rioja
Formosa
Resistencia
Corrientes
Santa
Maria
Paraná
Cascavel
Posadas
Paraná
Passo
Fundo
Florianópolis
Curitiba
Plateau
Tropic of Capricorn
SOUTH
La Serena
Cerro
Aconcagua
6960
San Juan
Mendoza
San Luis
Santa Fé
Paraná
Córdoba
Rosario
Uruguay
Jacuarembó.
Porto Alegre
Pelotas
30°S
Valparaíso
Santiago
Rancagua
Buenos
Aires
La Plata
URUGUAY
Durazno
Paysandú
Rocha
Montevideo
30°S
PACIFIC
Talca
Chillán
Pampas
Bahía
Blanca
Mar del Plata
Juan
Fernández Is.
(Chile)
Concepción
Colorado
Valdivia
Neuquén
Negro
Osorno
Viedma
OCEAN
Puerto Montt
Chiloé
Island
ARGENTINA
Valdés
Peninsula
Trelew
40°S
Patagonia
Taitao
Peninsula
Coihaique
Comodoro Rivadavia
G. of S.
George
Deseado
40°S
Chubut
Buenos
Aires
Río Gallegos
Stanley
Falkland
Islands
(U.K.)
SOUTH
ATLANTIC
Punta Arenas
Magellan Strait
Tierra del
Fuego
Ushuaia
Cape
Horn
Oblique Mercator Projection
OCEAN
© Oxford Cartographers
+44 (0) 1865 882 884
50°S
0   200   400   600 Miles
0   200 400 600 800 1000 Kms
South
Georgia
(U.K.)
South
Shetland
Islands
(U.K.)
South
Orkney
Islands
(U.K.)
South
Sandwich
Islands
(U.K.)
50°S
100°W
90°W
80°W
70°W
60°W
50°W
40°W
30°W
20°W
10°W

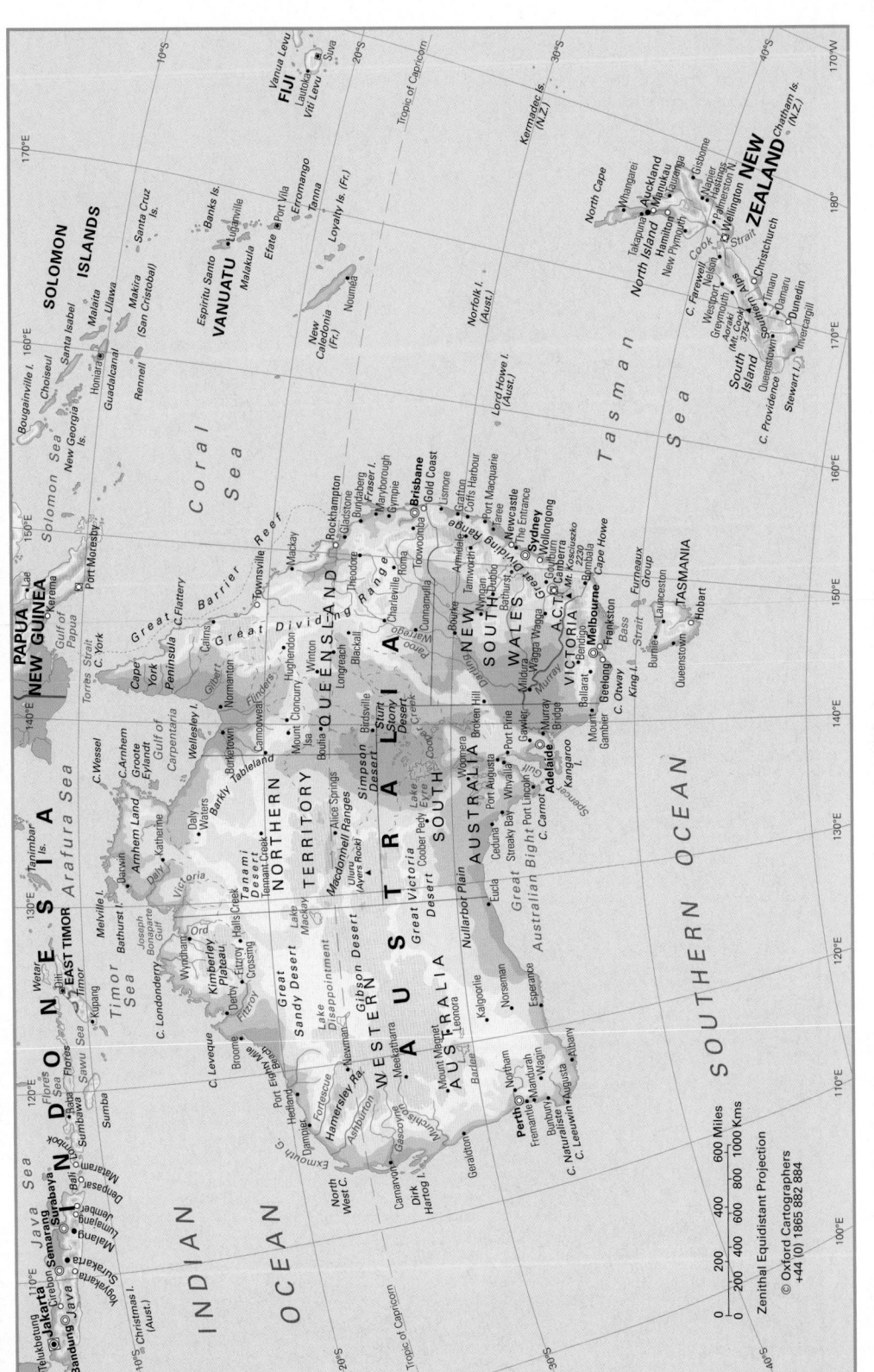

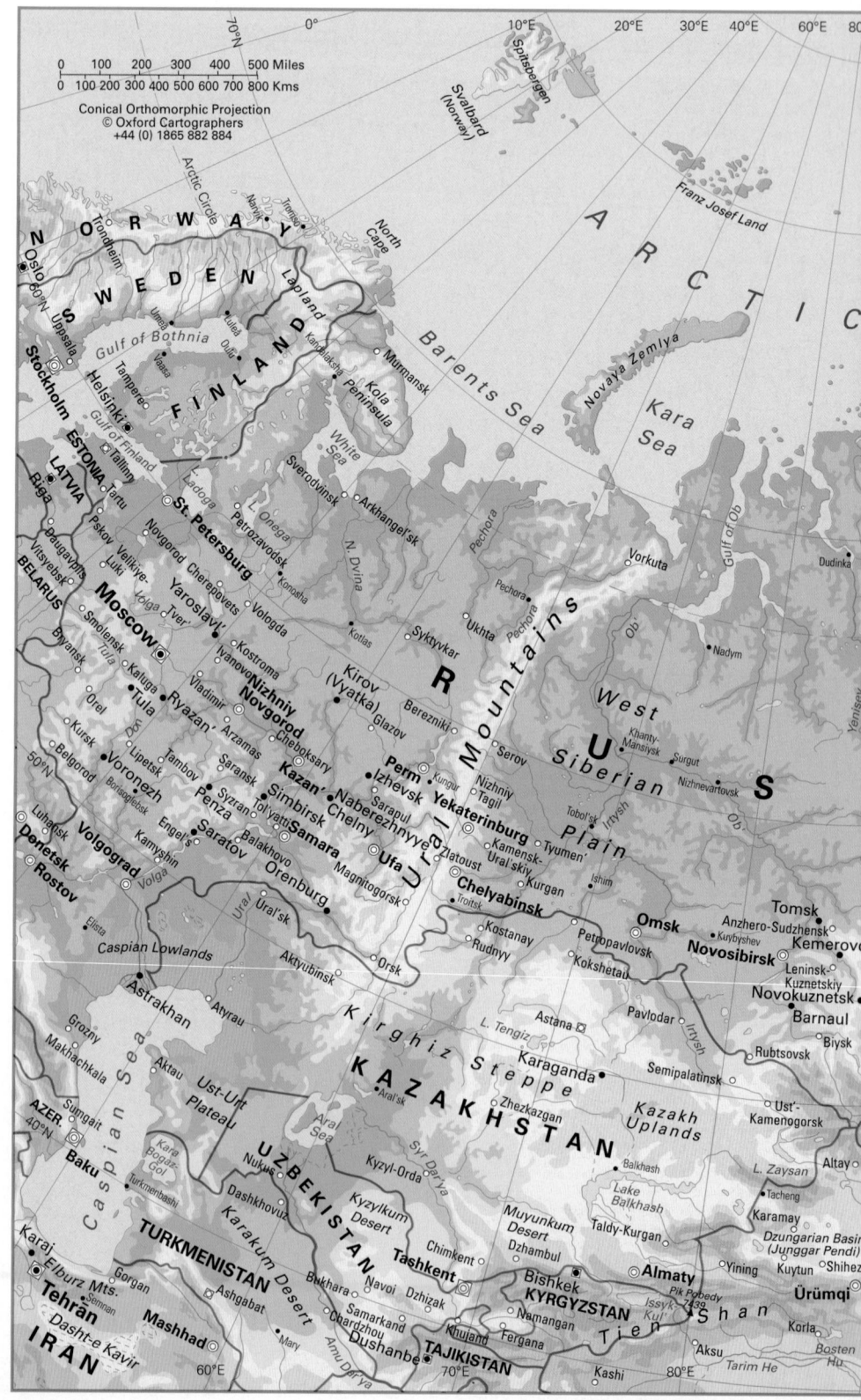

Conical Orthomorphic Projection
© Oxford Cartographers
+44 (0) 1865 882 884

0 100 200 300 400 500 Miles
0 100 200 300 400 500 600 700 800 Kms

70°N   0°   10°E   20°E   30°E 40°E   60°E   80

N O R W A Y
Trondheim   North
                     Cape
Oslo S W E D E N   Lapland   Spitsbergen
60°N Uppsala   Svalbard
Stockholm ESTONIA   Tromsø   (Norway)
                     Murmansk
LATVIA Helsinki F I N L A N D Kola
Riga   Gulf of Bothnia Peninsula   A R C T I C
BELARUS ESTONIA Tartu   Franz Josef Land
        Tallinn   White
        Gulf of Finland Sea
Vilsyebsk St. Petersburg   Novaya Zemlya
BELARUS Pskov Velikiye Cherepovets   Kara
        Luki   Ladoga   Sea
Daugavpils Novgorod Vologda Vorkuta
        Yaroslavl' Kostroma   Gulf of Ob
Smolensk Moscow Tver' Ivanovo Pechora
Bryansk Tula Kaluga Vladimir Nizhniy N. Dvina Dudinka
        Ryazan' Novgorod Kirov Ukhta
Orel Lipetsk Tambov Arzamas (Vyatka) West Nadym
Kursk Voronezh Saransk Cheboksary Glazov Siberian
Belgorod Borisoglebsk Kazan' Perm Serov Khanty- Surgut
        Penza Syzran' Izhevsk Nizhniy Mansiysk Nizhnevartovsk
Luhansk Volgograd Saratov Naberezhnyye Tagil Yekaterinburg Plain
Donetsk Kamyshin Balakhovo Chelny Ufa Kungur Tyumen'
Rostov Engel's Orenburg Zlatoust Kamensk- Tobol'sk Ob Yenisey
        Ural Ural'sk Magnitogorsk Ural skiy Kurgan Ishim
Elista Caspian Lowlands Orsk Troitsk Chelyabinsk Tomsk
Astrakhan Aktyubinsk Kostanay Petropavlovsk Omsk Anzhero-Sudzhensk
Grozny Atyrau Rudnyy Kokshetau Kuybyshev Kemerovo
Makhachkala Ust-Urt K i r g h i z Astana Novosibirsk Leninsk-
        Plateau S t e p p e Pavlodar Kuznetskiy
AZER. Sumgait Aral L. Tengiz K a z a k h Novokuznetsk
40°N Baku Kara Sea Karaganda U p l a n d s Barnaul
        Bogaz Aral'sk Zhezkazgan Biysk
        Gol K A Z A K H S T A N Kazakh Rubtsovsk
Turkmenbashi Nukus Kyzyl-Orda Syr Dar'ya Uplands Ust'-
TURKMENISTAN U Z B E K I S T A N Balkhash Kamenogorsk
Karai Gorgan Dashkhovuz Kyzylkum Lake L. Zaysan Altay
Elburz Mts. Karakum Desert Desert Muyunkum Balkhash Tacheng
Tehran Ashgabat Bukhara Navoi Dzhizak Desert Taldy-Kurgan Karamay Dzungarian Basin
Mashhad Samarkand Tashkent Dzhambul (Junggar Pendi)
Dasht-e Kavir Chardzhou Khujand Almaty Kuytun Shihez
I R A N Mary Dushanbe TAJIKISTAN Bishkek Ürümqi
        Amu Dar'ya Namangan KYRGYZSTAN Pik Pobedy 7439
60°E 70°E Fergana Issyk T i e n   S h a n Korla
        Aksu Kul Bosten
        Kashi 80°E Tarim He Hu

R U S
U r a l   M o u n t a i n s

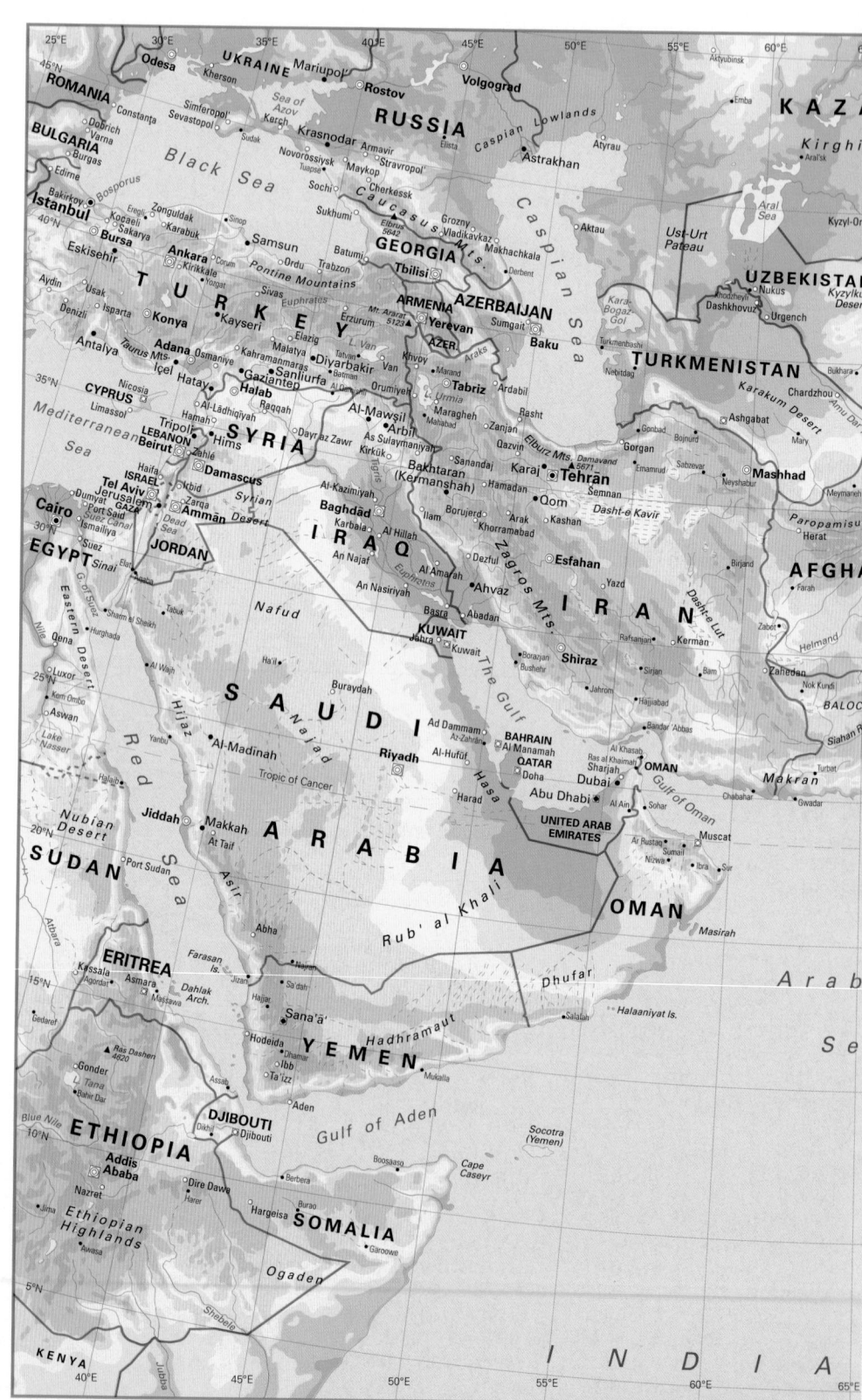

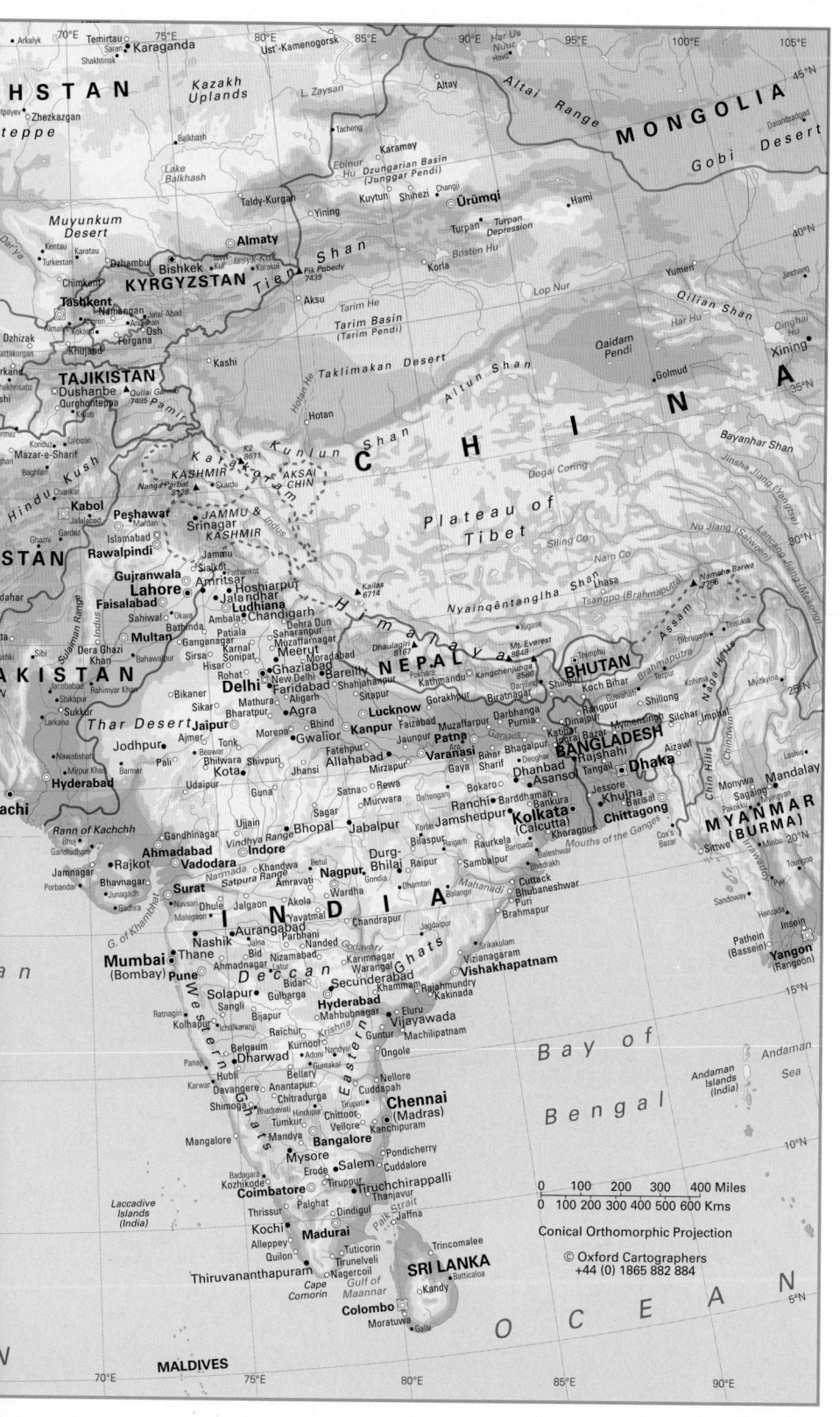

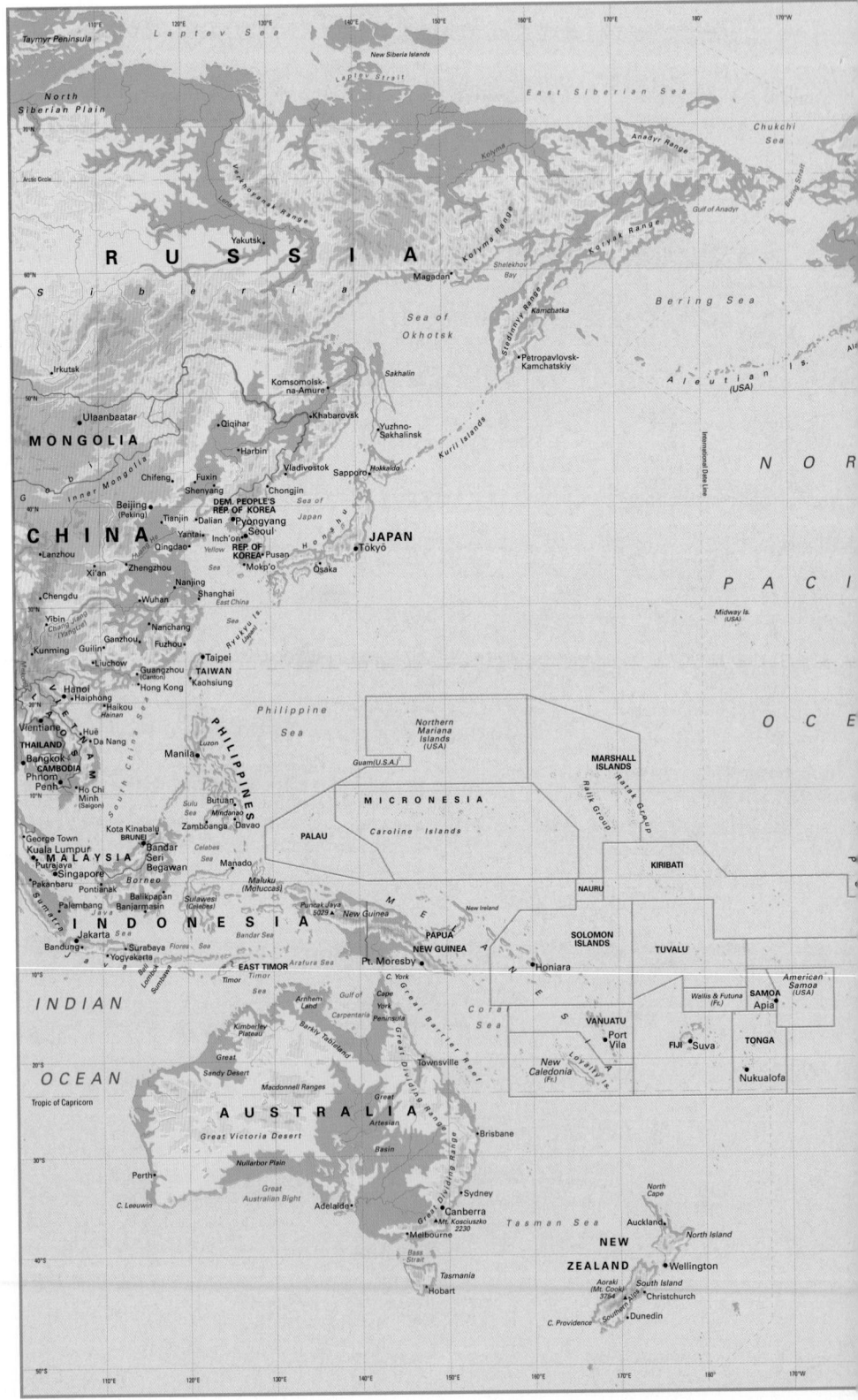

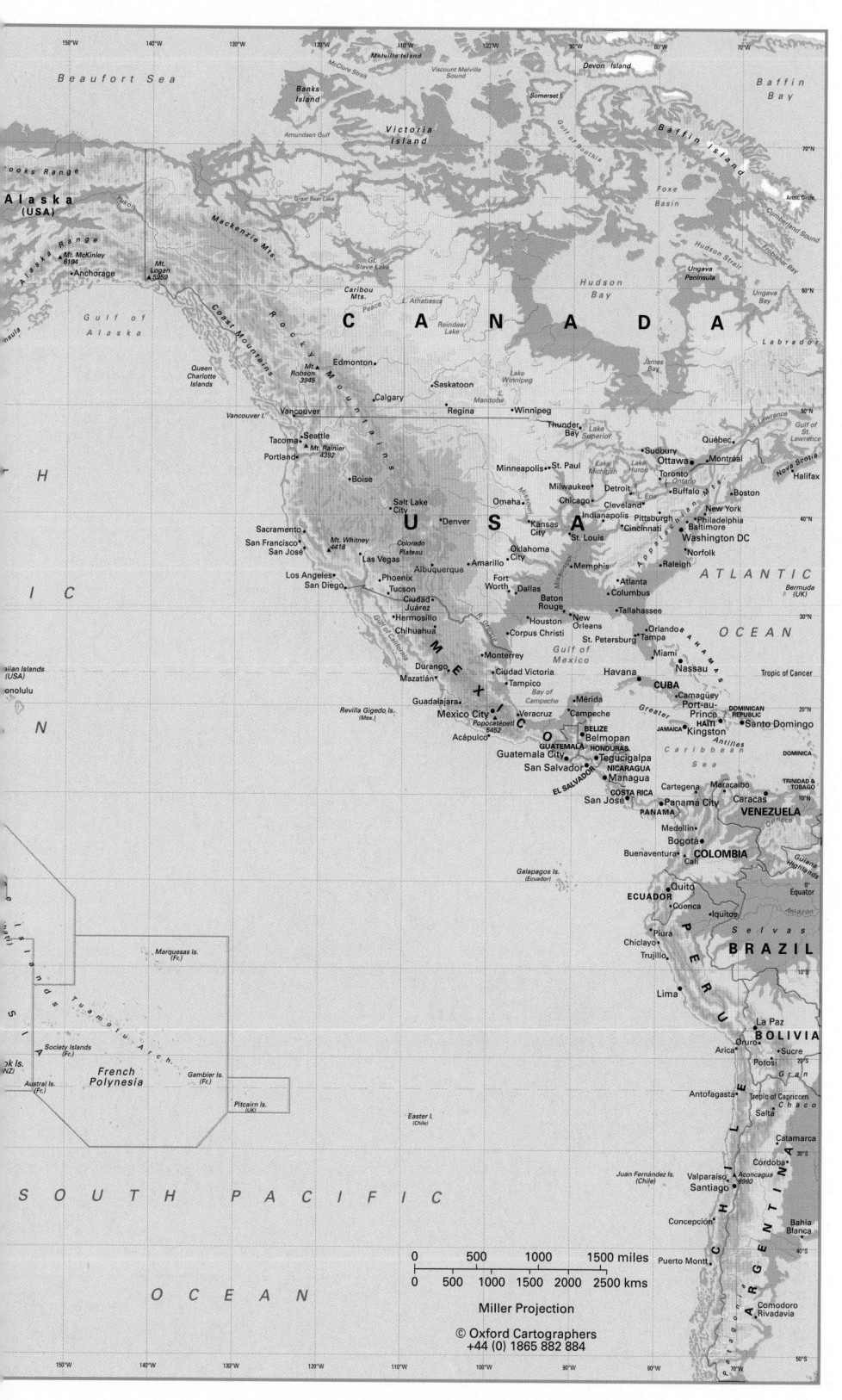

Miller Projection

© Oxford Cartographers
+44 (0) 1865 882 884

0		500		1000		1500 miles
0	500	1000	1500	2000	2500 kms	

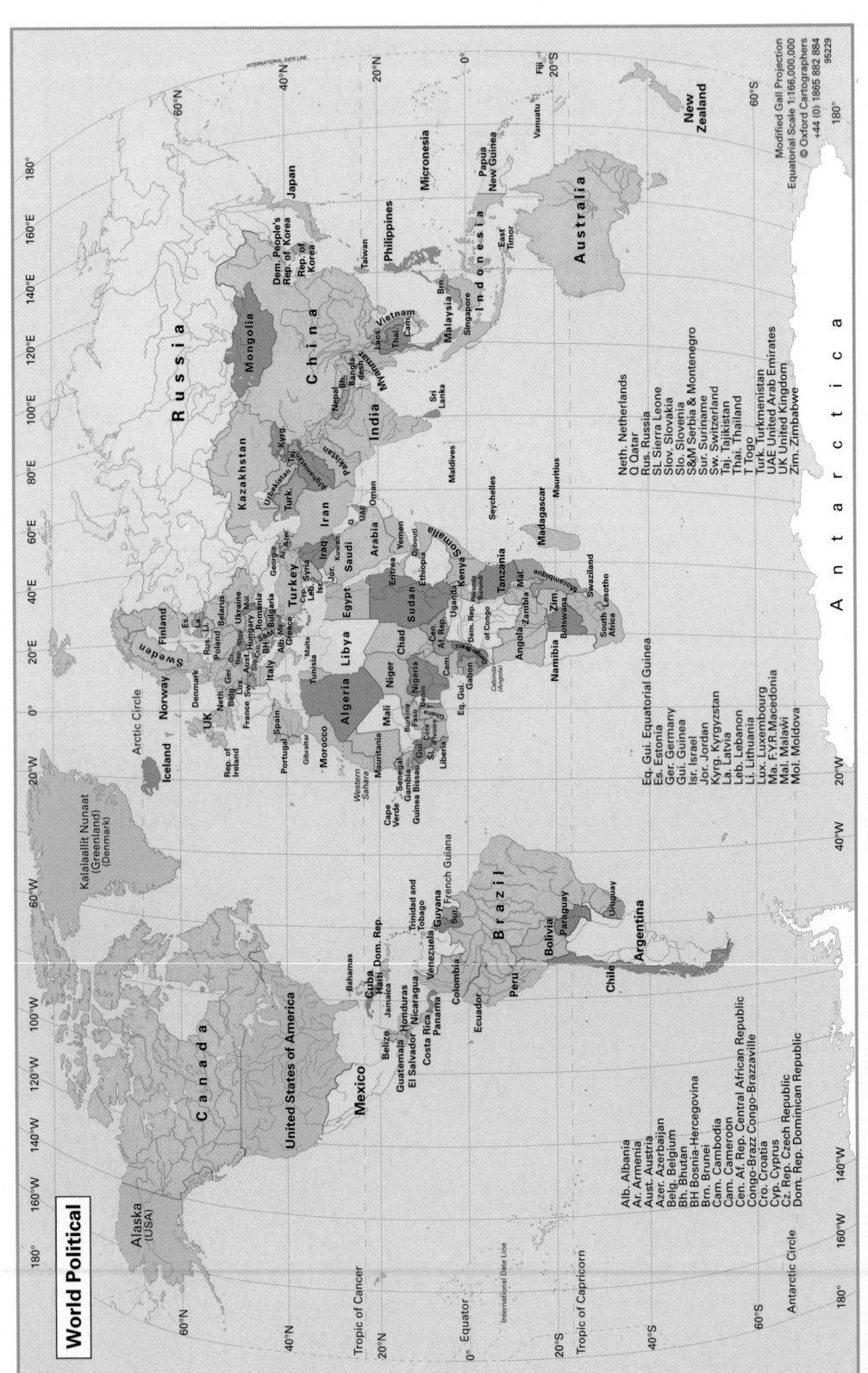

World Political

Modified Gall Projection
Equatorial Scale 1:166,000,000
© Oxford Cartographers
+44 (0) 1865 882 884
95229

Alb. Albania
Ar. Armenia
Aust. Austria
Azer. Azerbaijan
Bel. Belgium
Bh. Bhutan
BH Bosnia-Hercegovina
Brn. Brunei
Cam. Cambodia
Cam. Cameroon
Cen. Af. Rep. Central African Republic
Congo-Brazz Congo-Brazzaville
Cro. Croatia
Cyp. Cyprus
Cz. Rep. Czech Republic
Dom. Rep. Dominican Republic

Eq. Gui. Equatorial Guinea
Es. Estonia
Ger. Germany
Gui. Guinea
Isr. Israel
Jor. Jordan
Kyrg. Kyrgyzstan
La. Latvia
Leb. Lebanon
Li. Lithuania
Lux. Luxembourg
Ma. F.Y.R.Macedonia
Mal. Malawi
Mol. Moldova

Neth. Netherlands
Q Qatar
Rus. Russia
SL Sierra Leone
Slov. Slovakia
Slo. Slovenia
S&M Serbia & Montenegro
Sur. Suriname
Sw. Switzerland
Taj. Tajikistan
Thai. Thailand
T Togo
Turk. Turkmenistan
UAE United Arab Emirates
UK United Kingdom
Zim. Zimbabwe

NATIONAL FLAG – Three horizontal bands, red, white and blue
LIFE EXPECTANCY (years) – 78 (2001)
POPULATION GROWTH RATE – 1.3 per cent
POPULATION DENSITY – 171 per sq. km (2001)
ENROLMENT (percentage of age group) – primary 81 per cent (1985); secondary 64 per cent (1994); tertiary 10 per cent (1996)

HISTORY AND POLITICS
Established as an independent state under the sovereignty of the King of the Netherlands as Grand Duke by the Congress of Vienna in 1815, Luxembourg formed part of the Germanic Confederation from 1815 to 1866, becoming neutral in 1867.

The territory was invaded by Germany in 1914 but was liberated in 1918. By the Treaty of Versailles (1919), Germany renounced its former agreements with Luxembourg and in 1921 an economic union was formed with Belgium. The Grand Duchy was again invaded and occupied by Germany in 1940, and liberated in 1944.

The constitution was modified in 1948 and the stipulation of permanent neutrality was abandoned.

POLITICAL SYSTEM
There is a Chamber of 60 deputies, elected by universal suffrage for five years. Legislation is submitted to the Council of State. The last general election was held on 13 June 1999 and a coalition government was installed. In March 1998, Grand Duke Jean passed certain constitutional powers on to his son and heir, Prince Henri, and announced on 25 December 1999 that he would abdicate in favour of Prince Henri in September 2000.

HEAD OF STATE
HRH The Grand Duke of Luxembourg, HRH Grand Duke Henri, *born* 16 April 1955; *succeeded* (on the abdication of his father) 7 October 2000; *married* 14 February 1981, Maria Teresa Mestre, and has *issue,* Prince Guillaume; Prince Felix, *b.* 3 June 1984; Prince Louis, *b.* 3 August 1986; Princess Alexandra, *b.* 2 February 1991; Prince Sébastien, *b.* 16 April 1992, Princess Gabriella, *b.* 26 March 1994
Heir, HRH Prince Guillaume, *born* 11 November 1981

CABINET *as at July 2003*
Prime Minister, Finance, Jean-Claude Juncker (PCS)
Deputy Prime Minister, Foreign Affairs and Foreign Trade, Civil Service and Administrative Reform, Lydie Polfer (PDL)
Agriculture, Viticulture, Rural Development, Small Businesses, Housing and Tourism, Fernand Boden (PCS)
Culture, Higher Education and Research, Public Works, Erna Hennicot-Schoepges (PCS)
Development Aid and Defence, Environment, Charles Goerens (PDL)
Economy, Transport, Henri Grethen (PDL)
Employment, Religious Affairs, Parliamentary Relations, François Biltgen (PCS)
Family, Social Solidarity and Youth, Advancement of Women, Marie-Josée Jacobs (PCS)
Health and Social Security, Carlo Wagner (PDL)
Home Affairs, Michel Wolter (PCS)
National Education, Vocational Training and Sport, Anne Brasseur (PDL)
Treasury and Budget, Justice, Luc Frieden (PCS)
Secretaries of State, Joseph Schaack (PDL) *(Civil Service*

and Administrative Reform); Eugène Berger (PDL) *(Environment)*

PCS Christian Social Party; PDL Democratic Party

EMBASSY OF LUXEMBOURG
27 Wilton Crescent, London SW1X 8SD
Tel: 020-7235 6961
Ambassador Extraordinary and Plenipotentiary, HE Jean-Louis Wolzfeld, apptd 2002

BRITISH EMBASSY
14 Boulevard Roosevelt, L-2450 Luxembourg
Tel: (00 352) 229864/5/6
Ambassador Extraordinary and Plenipotentiary, HE Gordon Wetherell, apptd 2000

DEFENCE
For legal reasons, NATO's squadron of E-3A Sentry airborne early warning aircraft is registered in Luxembourg.
MILITARY EXPENDITURE – 0.8 per cent of GDP (2001)
MILITARY PERSONNEL – Army 900; Paramilitaries 612

ECONOMY
Luxembourg is a member of the Belgium-Netherlands-Luxembourg Customs Union (Benelux 1960). The country has an important iron and steel industry and is an important financial centre.

The chief exports are metal goods, manufactures, machinery, chemicals, transport equipment, and foodstuffs and livestock. The chief imports are machinery, transport equipment, metal goods, manufactures, chemicals, and foodstuffs and livestock. The euro replaced the Luxembourg franc in January 2002.

In 2001 imports totalled US$10,678 million and exports US$7,918 million.
GNP – US$18,439 million (2000); US$42,060 per capita (2000)
GDP – US$19,802 million (2001); US$43,372 per capita (2000)
ANNUAL AVERAGE GROWTH OF GDP – 7.5 per cent (1999)
INFLATION RATE – 3.1 per cent (2000)
UNEMPLOYMENT – 2.7 per cent (2000)

Trade with UK	2001	2002
Imports from UK	£260,900,000	£346,200,000
Exports to UK	271,600,000	483,500,000

MACEDONIA

Republika Makedonija – Republic of Macedonia

AREA – 9,928 sq. miles (25,713 sq. km). Neighbours: Federal Republic of Yugoslavia (north), Bulgaria (east), Greece (south), Albania (west)
POPULATION – 2,046,209 (2001 estimate); 1,936,877 (1994 census): 66.5 per cent Macedonian, 22.9 per cent Albanian, 4.0 per cent ethnic Turks, 2.3 per cent Romanies, 2.0 per cent Serbs and 0.4 per cent Vlachs. The census results are disputed by the ethnic Albanians and Serbs. Macedonian Orthodox Christianity is the majority religion, with a Muslim minority. The main language is Macedonian (a south Slavic language), which is written in the Cyrillic script
CAPITAL – Skopje (population, 429,964, 1994)

MAJOR CITIES – Bitola (84,002); Kumanovo (69,231); Prilep (70,152)

CURRENCY – Denar of 100 deni

NATIONAL ANTHEM – Denes Nad Makedonija Se Radja Novo Sonce Na Slobodata (Today A New Sun Of Liberty Appears Over Macedonia)

NATIONAL FLAG – Red with an eight-rayed sun displayed over the whole field

POPULATION GROWTH RATE – 0.6 per cent (1999)

POPULATION DENSITY – 78 per sq. km (1999)

URBAN POPULATION – 62 per cent (2000)

MILITARY EXPENDITURE – 2.2 per cent of GDP (2001)

MILITARY PERSONNEL – Army 11,300; Paramilitaries 7,600

CONSCRIPTION DURATION – Nine months

ENROLMENT (percentage of age group) – primary 99 per cent (1997); secondary 63 per cent (1997); tertiary 20 per cent (1997)

HISTORY AND POLITICS

From the ninth to the 14th centuries AD Macedonia was ruled alternately by the Bulgars and the Byzantine Empire. In the middle of the 14th century the area was conquered by the Turks and remained under the Ottoman Empire for over 500 years. After the defeat of Turkey in the two Balkan wars of 1912–13 the geographical area of Macedonia was divided, the major part becoming Serbian (the areas of the present-day Macedonia) and the remainder given to Greece and Bulgaria. In 1918 Serbian Macedonia was incorporated into Serbia as South Serbia. When Yugoslavia was reconstituted in 1944 as a Communist federal republic under President Tito, Macedonia became a constituent republic.

Multiparty elections for the 120-seat assembly held in November and December 1990 produced the first non-Communist government since the Second World War. The electorate overwhelmingly approved Macedonian sovereignty and independence in a referendum and independence was declared on 8 September 1991.

Presidential elections on 14 November and 5 December 1999 were won by Boris Trajkovski of the Internal Macedonian Revolutionary Organisation Democratic Party for Macedonian National Unity (VMRO-DMPNE). The latest elections to the *Sobranie* (National Assembly) were held on 15 September 2002. The largest group in the Assembly was Together for Macedonia (ZMZ), a coalition of the Social Democratic Alliance of Macedonia (SDSM) and the Liberal Democratic Party (LDP), with 59 of the 120 seats. The VMRO-DMPNE won 34 seats A multi-ethnic coalition government, including members of the SDSM, the LDP and the ethnic Albanian Democratic Union for Integration (BDI), was named on 31 October 2002 and took office the following day.

INSURGENCY

Fighting between ethnic Albanian guerrillas belonging to the National Liberation Army (NLA) and Macedonian security forces began on 26 February 2001 in the village of Tanusevci near the border with Kosovo and by mid-March had spread to Tetovo, the largest ethnic Albanian town. The Macedonian government, which included ethnic Albanians, promised to implement reforms to increase minority rights for ethnic Albanians and moderate Albanian parties called on the guerrillas to surrender their arms. The insurgency was condemned by the UN Security Council on 21 March 2001. On 10 April, President Trajkovski announced the establishment

of a commission to investigate discrimination against the Albanian minority.

On 23 May 2001, the two main Albanian parties, the DPA and the PDP, signed an agreement with the NLA, in which the rebels agreed to withdraw in return for an amnesty and NLA participation in discussions with the government. The Macedonian government and international organisations immediately condemned the agreement. President Trajkovski urged the Albanian parties to renounce the agreement, which they refused to do, but it was agreed that discussions should continue in order to preserve the coalition government.

By early June, fighting had become widespread across the north of the country. On 14 June, President Trajkovski made an official request for NATO assistance to disarm the NLA. A cease-fire declared on 12 June ended after only 11 days when Macedonian forces launched an attack on the village of Aracinovo, but halted their offensive when the NLA agreed to withdraw its forces from the village. On 25 June, Macedonian Slavic nationalists stormed parliament in protest against the government's co-operation with NATO in escorting the besieged NLA rebels from Aracinovo to safety.

On 13 August, the leaders of the Macedonian and Albanian parties signed a peace agreement that allowed for increased recruitment of ethnic Albanians into the police force; made Albanian an official language along with Macedonian; gave Christianity and Islam equal status; removed from the constitution any reference to the ethnic background of Macedonian citizens; allowed for a limited amount of devolution; promised human rights, civil liberties, social justice and peaceful co-existence; and cleared the way for the deployment of a NATO disarmament force. Amendments to the constitution were approved by parliament on 15 and 16 November 2001. By August 2002, no further serious fighting had occurred but relations between the country's Macedonian and Albanian populations remained tense. On 31 March 2003 the EU took over peacekeeping duties from NATO with a six-month mandate.

FOREIGN RELATIONS

A new constitution was adopted in November 1991 and then amended at the EC's request to make it clear that Macedonia had no territorial claim on its neighbours. Macedonia applied for EC recognition in December 1991 but was refused because of Greece's objections to the state's name, flag and currency which, according to the Greek government, amounted to a territorial claim on the Greek province of Macedonia. Macedonia gained UN membership on 8 April 1993 following a compromise agreement by which it is referred to formally as the 'Former Yugoslav Republic of Macedonia' (FYROM). A border demarcation agreement was signed with Yugoslavia on 23 February 2001.

HEAD OF STATE

President, Boris Trajkovski, elected 5 December 1999

CABINET *as at July 2003*

Prime Minister, Branko Crvenkovski (SDSM)

Deputy Prime Minister, Finance, Petar Gosev (LPD)

Deputy Prime Ministers, Without Portfolio, Musa Xharferi (BDI), Radmila Secerinska (SDSM)

Agriculture, Forestry and Water Resources Management, Slavko Petrov (LDP)

Culture, Blagoja Stefanovski (SDSM)

Defence, Vlado Buckovski (SDSM)

Economy, Ilija Filipovski (SDSM)
Education and Science, Azis Polozani (BDI)
Environment and Urban Planning, Ljubomir Janev (SDSM)
Foreign Affairs, Ilinka Mitreva (SDSM)
Health, Rexhep Selmani (BDI)
Interior, Hari Kostov (SDSM)
Justice, Ismail Dardhishta (BDI)
Labour and Social Welfare, Jovan Manasievski (LDP)
Local Self-government, Aleksandar Gestakovski (SDSM)
Transport and Communications, Milaim Ajdini (BDI)
Without Portfolio, Vlado Popovski (LDP)

BDI Albanian Democratic Union for Integration; LDP
Liberal Democratic Party; SDSM Social Democratic
Alliance of Macedonia

EMBASSY OF THE REPUBLIC OF MACEDONIA
5th Floor, 25 James Street, London W1U 1DU
Tel: 020 7935 2823
Ambassador Extraordinary and Plenipotentiary,
HE Stevo Crvenkovski, apptd 1997

BRITISH EMBASSY
Dimitrija Chupovski 4/26, Skopje 1000
Tel: (00 389) (2) 3299 299
Ambassador Extraordinary and Plenipotentiary, HE George
Edgar, apptd 2001

BRITISH COUNCIL DIRECTOR, Andrew Hadley
Bulevar Goce Delcev 6, PO Box 562, MK-1000 Skopje
Tel: (00 389) (2) 135 035 Email: info@britishcouncil.org.mk

ECONOMY

The economy was decimated by the UN trade sanctions
against the rump Yugoslavia (from May 1992 until
November 1995), and the Greek economic blockade
(from February 1994 until October 1995). Macedonia is
attempting to transform its economy to a market-
orientated one and to introduce privatisation; by 1997,
45 per cent of the economy was in private hands. In
April 2000, the government sold 65 per cent of
Macedonia's largest bank, the Stopanska bank, and
parliament voted to return property expropriated during
the period under Communist rule. An economic co-
operation agreement was signed by Macedonia and
Albania in July 1999, covering energy, mining and trade.

In 2000 63 per cent of GDP was produced by service
industries, 25 per cent by industry, and 12 per cent by
agriculture.

The main exports are textiles, tobacco, zinc, wine, iron
ore and iron products. The main imports are oil, energy,
telecommunications equipment, metal manufactures,
foodstuffs and medicines.

In 2000 there was a trade deficit of US$558 million
and a current account deficit of US$107 million. In 2001
imports totalled US$1,155 million and exports
US$1,688 million.

GNP – US$3,696 million (2000); US$1,820 per capita
(2000)
GDP – US$3,445 million (2001); US$1,641 per capita
(2000)
ANNUAL AVERAGE GROWTH OF GDP – 2.9 per cent
(1998)
INFLATION RATE – 1.1 per cent (2002)
TOTAL EXTERNAL DEBT – US$1,465 million (2000)

Trade with UK	2001	2002
Imports from UK	£24,560,000	£20,540,000
Exports to UK	17,773,000	17,074,000

MADAGASCAR

*Repoblikan'i Madagasikara / République de Madagascar –
Republic of Madagascar*

AREA – 226,658 sq. miles (587,041 sq. km)
POPULATION – 15,982,563 (2001 estimate). The
people are of mixed Malayo-Polynesian, Arab and
African origin. There are sizeable French, Chinese and
Indian communities. The official languages are
Malagasy and French
CAPITAL – Antananarivo (population, 2,000,000, 1998
estimate)
MAJOR CITIES – ΨAntsiranana (942,410); Fianarantsoa
(2,671,150); ΨMahajanga (100,807); ΨToamasina
(127,441), the chief port
CURRENCY – Franc malgache (FMG) of 100 centimes
NATIONAL ANTHEM – Ry Tanindrazanay Malala O (O,
Our Beloved Country)
NATIONAL DAY – 26 June (Independence Day)
NATIONAL FLAG – Equal horizontal bands of red (above)
and green, with vertical white band by staff
POPULATION GROWTH RATE – 3 per cent
POPULATION DENSITY – 26 per sq. km (1999)
MILITARY EXPENDITURE – 1.0 per cent of GDP (2001)
MILITARY PERSONNEL – 13,500: Army 12,500, Navy
500, Air Force 500; Paramilitaries 8,100
CONSCRIPTION DURATION – 18 months
ILLITERACY RATE – (m) 26.4 per cent; (f) 40.3 per cent
(2000)
ENROLMENT (percentage of age group) – primary 92
per cent (1997); tertiary 2 per cent (1997)

Madagascar lies 240 miles off the east coast of Africa and
is the fourth largest island in the world.

HISTORY AND POLITICS

Madagascar (known from 1958 to 1975 as the Malagasy
Republic) became a French protectorate in 1895, and a
French colony in 1896 when the former queen was
exiled. Republican status was adopted on 14 October
1958, and independence was proclaimed on 26 June
1960.

The post-independence civilian government was
replaced by a military government in 1975 and martial
law was declared. A Supreme Council of the Revolution
under Didier Ratsiraka was established.

In November 1991, President Ratsiraka relinquished
executive power to a new prime minister, Guy
Razanamasy. However, the president retained his official
position and the main opposition grouping, the Forces
Vives, established a rival government led by Albert Zafy.
In December 1991 a transitional government including
Forces Vives and Razanamasy supporters was formed to
draft a new constitution, approved by referendum in
August 1992. In the presidential election held in
November 1992 and February 1993, Albert Zafy became
the first president of the Third Republic, which came into
being at the same time.

President Zafy was defeated in 1996 by former
president Ratsiraka. Following legislative elections held
in May 1998, Ratsiraka's Action de Renouveau de
Madagascar (AREMA) party became the largest party in
the National Assembly. The inconclusive presidential

elections held on 16 December 2001 were followed by violent clashes between supporters of the two main candidates, President Ratsiraka and Marc Ravalomanana, and protests demanding that Ravalomanana be declared president. On 17 April 2002, Madagascar's High Constitutional Court annulled the December election results and ordered a recount. The results of the recount showed that Ravalomanana was the clear winner with 51.5 per cent of the vote against 35.9 per cent for Ratsiraka. Ravalomanana's presidency was legitimised on 6 May when he was sworn into office. Ratsiraka refused to acknowledge this result and fighting between supporters of the two contenders continued until 5 July 2002 when Ratsiraka left the country and the last of his forces surrendered. In elections to the National Assembly held on 15 December 2002, President Ravalomanana's I Love Madagascar party (TIM) won a majority with 103 out of 160 seats. It also has a majority in the Senate. In August 2003 exiled Didier Ratsiraka, who has been accused of embezzling public funds, was sentenced in his absence to 10 years hard labour.

POLITICAL SYSTEM
The president is directly elected and serves a five-year term. The legislature is bicameral. The National Assembly is directly elected and comprises 150 members. The Senate comprises 90 members, of whom two-thirds are elected by an electoral college and one-third are nominated by the president.

HEAD OF STATE
President Marc Ravalomanana, *elected* 29 April 2002, *sworn in* 6 May 2002, *accepted* 5 July 2002.

COUNCIL OF MINISTERS *as at July 2003*
Prime Minister, Jacques Sylla
Deputy Prime Minister, Economic Affairs, Local Government, Public Works and Transport, Zaza Manitranja Ramandimbiarison
Agriculture, Livestock and Fishing, Yvan Randriasandratriniony
Basic and Secondary Education, Dieudonne Michel Razafindrandriantsimaniry
Civil Service, Vola Dieudonne Razafindralambo
Culture, Louise Odette Rahaingosoa
Decentralization and Development of Autonomous Provinces and Communities, Monique Andreas Esoavelomandroso
Defence, Maj.-Gen. Jules Mamizara
Energy and Mines, Jacquis Rabarison
Environment, Water and Forests, Gen. Charles Rabotoarison
Foreign Affairs, Gen. Marcel Ranjeva
Finance and Economy, Andriamparany Radavidson
Health, Andry Rasamindrakotroka
Higher Education and Scientific Research, Jean Theodore Ranjivason
Industrialisation, Commerce and the Private Sector, Mejamirado Razafimihary
Justice, Alice Rajaonah
Labour and Social Legislation, Jean Jacques Rabenirina
Population, Jacob Andriampanjava
Posts and Telecommunications, Hajanirina Razafinjatovo
Public Security, Augustin Amady
Tourism, Roger Mahazoasy
Youth and Sports, Rene Ndalana

EMBASSY OF THE REPUBLIC OF MADAGASCAR
4 avenue Raphael, F- 75016 Paris, France
Tel: (00 33) (1) 4504 6211
Ambassador Plenipotentiary and Extraordinary, vacant

BRITISH EMBASSY
Lot II, 164 Ter Alarobia Ambonilioa,
BP 167, Antananarivo 101
Tel: (00 261) (20) 2249378/9
Ambassador Extraordinary and Plenipotentiary,
HE Brian Donaldson, apptd 2002

ECONOMY
The economy is still largely based on agriculture, which employs more than 80 per cent of the workforce. The main products are rice, cassava, sugar cane, coffee, fish, tropical fruits and sweet potatoes. Development plans have placed emphasis on improving communications, the exploitation of mineral deposits and the creation of small industries. Madagascar was hit by three cyclones in February and April 2000, which caused widespread flooding, resulting in the destruction of much of the rice crop.

In 2000 there was a trade deficit of US$174 million and a current account deficit of US$283 million. In 1999 imports totalled US$378 million and exports US$220 million.

GNP – US$3,869 million (2000); US$250 per capita (2000)
GDP – US$4,566 million (2001); US$249 per capita (2000)
ANNUAL AVERAGE GROWTH OF GDP – 4.8 per cent (2000)
INFLATION RATE – 7.4 per cent (2001)
TOTAL EXTERNAL DEBT – US$4,701 million (2000)

Trade with UK	2001	2002
Imports from UK	£6,651,000	£3,033,000
Exports to UK	24,979,000	17,943,000

MALAWI

Mfuko la Malawi / Republic of Malawi

AREA – 45,747 sq. miles (118,484 sq. km). Neighbours: Tanzania (north-east), Zambia (west), Mozambique (south)
POPULATION – 10,548,250 (2001 estimate). The official languages are Chichewa and English
CAPITAL – Lilongwe (population, 505,200, 2000 estimate)
MAJOR CITIES – Blantyre (502,053), incorporating Blantyre and Limbe, the major commercial and industrial centre; Mzuzu (86,980); Zomba (65,915), the former capital, 1998
CURRENCY – Kwacha (K) of 100 tambala
NATIONAL ANTHEM – O God Bless Our Land Of Malawi
NATIONAL DAY – 6 July (Independence Day)
NATIONAL FLAG – Horizontal stripes of black, red and green, with rising sun in the centre of the black stripe
POPULATION GROWTH RATE – 1.5 per cent
POPULATION DENSITY – 90 per sq. km (1999)
MILITARY EXPENDITURE – 0.3 per cent of GDP (2001)
MILITARY PERSONNEL – Army 5,300; Paramilitaries 1,500

Malawi lies in south-eastern Africa. Much of the eastern border of Malawi is formed by Lake Malawi (formerly Lake Nyasa), which covers nearly half of the north of the country. The valley of the River Shire runs south from the lake, its watershed with the Zambezi lying on the western border with Mozambique and its tributary, the Ruo, with lakes Chiuta and Chirwa, lying on the eastern border with Mozambique. The north and centre are plateaux, and the south highlands. The country is prone to natural disasters, including drought and heavy rainfall.

HISTORY AND POLITICS

Malawi (formerly Nyasaland) assumed internal self-government on 1 February 1963, and became independent on 6 July 1964. It became a republic on 6 July 1966.

In 1991–2 Life President Hastings Banda, who had ruled since independence, came under increasing pressure to introduce a multiparty democratic system of government. In May 1992 aid donors tied new loans to improvements in the human rights record and moves to multiparty democracy. A referendum was held on the adoption of a multiparty democracy in June 1993 and approved by 63 per cent of voters. President Banda and the Malawi Congress Party refused to resign but parliament passed a law to amend the constitution to allow multiparty politics and Banda announced a political amnesty to allow exiles to return. Multiparty presidential and legislative elections held in May 1994 were won by Bakili Muluzi and the United Democratic Front (UDF) respectively. Foreign and multilateral aid has since been restored. Former President Banda died on 25 November 1997. Presidential and legislative elections were due to be held on 25 May 1999, but were delayed until 15 June; they were won by the UDF, who won 93 seats. President Muluzi was also re-elected. On 31 March 2003 Muluzi announced that he would not seek a further term in office during the elections of 2004. He has been accused of corruption and come under international criticism for his efforts to change the Malawian constitution to allow him to stand for a third term.

POLITICAL SYSTEM

There is a Cabinet consisting of the president and ministers. The unicameral National Assembly, which usually meets three times a year, consists of 193 members elected by universal suffrage for a five-year term of office.

HEAD OF STATE

President, Commander-in-Chief of the Armed Forces, Bakili Muluzi, *elected* 17 May 1994, *sworn in* 21 May 1994, *re-elected* 15 June 1999
Vice-President, Privatisation, Justin Malewezi
Second Vice-President, Agriculture, Irrigation and Food Security, Chakufwa Chihana

CABINET *as at July 2003*
Commerce and Industry, Sam Mpasu
Defence, Rodwell Munyenyembe
Disabilities, Susan Chitimbe
Economic Planning and Development, Bingu wa Mutharika
Education, Science and Technology, George Nga Mtafa
Finance, Friday Jumbe
Foreign Affairs and International Co-operation, Lillian Patel
Gender, Youth and Community Services, Alice Sumani
Health and Population, Yusufu Mwawa
HIV/Aids Programmes, Mary Kaphwereza Banda
Home Affairs and Internal Security, Mangeza Maloza

Housing, Samuel Kaliyoma Phumisa
Information, Bernard Chisale
Justice, Paul Maulidi
Labour and Vocational Training, Lee Mulanga
Lands, Physical Planning and Services, Thengo Maloya
Local Government and District Administration, Salim Bagus
Natural Resources and Environmental Affairs, Uladi Mussa
Poverty and Disaster Management, Ludoviko Shati
Presidential Affairs, Ken Lipenga
Special Duties, Patrick Mbewe
Sports, Youth and Culture, Henderson Mabeti
Statutory Corporations, Bob Khamisa
Tourism, National Parks and Wildlife, Wallace Chiume
Transport and Public Works, Clement Stambuli
Without Portfolio, Chipimpha Mughogho

MALAWI HIGH COMMISSION
33 Grosvenor Street, London W1K 4QT
Tel: 020-7491 4172
High Commissioner, HE Bright Msaka, apptd 1998

BRITISH HIGH COMMISSION
PO Box 30042, Lilongwe 3
Tel: (00 265) (1) 772 400
Email: bhclilongwe@fco.gov.uk
High Commissioner, Norman Ling, apptd 2001

BRITISH COUNCIL DIRECTOR, Richard Weyers, Plot No. 13/20 City Centre, PO Box 30222, Lilongwe 3
Tel: (00 265) 773 244 Email: info@britishcouncil.org.mw

ECONOMY

The economy is largely agricultural, providing 90 per cent of export earnings; maize is the main subsistence crop, and tobacco, cassava, millet and rice are the main cash crops and principal exports. There are two sugar mills. A number of light manufacturing industries have been established, mainly in agricultural processing, clothing/textiles and building materials. A prolonged drought caused famine throughout 2002–3.

In 2000 imports totalled US$569 million and exports US$355 million.
GNP – US$1,744 million (2000); US$170 per capita (2000)
GDP – US$1,826 million (2001); US$141 per capita (2000)
ANNUAL AVERAGE GROWTH OF GDP – 2.3 per cent (2000)
INFLATION RATE – 29.5 per cent (2000)
TOTAL EXTERNAL DEBT – US$2,716 million (2000)

Trade with UK	2001	2002
Imports from UK	£8,183,000	£13,506,000
Exports to UK	14,994,000	12,769,000

COMMUNICATIONS

A single-track railway runs from Mchinji on the Zambian border, through Lilongwe and Salima on Lake Malawi (itself served by two passenger and a number of cargo boats) through to Blantyre. The route south to the Mozambique port of Beira was severed by the Mozambican civil war, but the route to Nacala in Mozambique re-opened in September 2002, allowing access to the Indian Ocean coast; there are 797 km of railway track. There are 16,451 km of roads in Malawi of which 3,126 km are bituminised.

EDUCATION

The Ministry of Education and Culture is responsible for secondary schools, technical education and primary teacher training. The University of Malawi was opened in 1965; there are also four colleges and one polytechnic.

ILLITERACY RATE – (m) 25.5 per cent; (f) 53.5 per cent (2000)

ENROLMENT (percentage of age group) –
primary 100 per cent (1997); secondary 17 per cent (1997); tertiary 1 per cent (1997)

MALAYSIA

AREA – 126,385 sq. miles (328,600 sq. km). Thailand borders the Malay peninsula to the north. On Borneo, Malaysia (Sarawak and Sabah) borders Indonesia to the south, and surrounds Brunei to the north

POPULATION – 22,633,000 (2001); Malays (58 per cent), Chinese (27 per cent), and those of Indian and Sri Lankan origin, as well as the indigenous races of Sarawak and Sabah. Bahasa Malaysia (Malay) is the official language, but English, various dialects of Chinese, and Tamil are also widely spoken. There are a few indigenous languages widely spoken in Sabah and Sarawak. Islam is the official religion of Malaysia, each ruler being the head of religion in his state (except in Sabah and Sarawak). The Yang di-Pertuan Agong is the head of religion in Melaka and Penang. The constitution guarantees religious freedom

CAPITAL – Kuala Lumpur (population, 1,297,526, 2000 census); Putrajaya (Administrative Capital) (population 3,000, 1999 estimate)

MAJOR CITIES – Ipoh (566,211); Johore Bharu (384,613); Petaling Jaya (438,084), 2000

CURRENCY – Malaysian dollar (ringgit) (M$) of 100 sen

NATIONAL ANTHEM – Negara-Ku (My Country)

NATIONAL DAY – 31 August (Hari Kebangsaan)

NATIONAL FLAG – Equal horizontal stripes of red (seven) and white (seven); 14-point yellow star and crescent in blue canton

LIFE EXPECTANCY (years) – 73 (2001)

POPULATION GROWTH RATE – 2.2 per cent

POPULATION DENSITY – 1,241 per sq. km (2001)

URBAN POPULATION – 58 per cent (2001)

ILLITERACY RATE – (m) 8.6 per cent; (f) 16.5 per cent (2000)

ENROLMENT (percentage of age group) – primary 100 per cent (1997); tertiary 12 per cent (1997)

Malaysia comprises the 11 states of peninsular Malaya plus Sabah and Sarawak. It occupies two distinct regions, the Malay peninsula which extends from the isthmus of Kra to the Singapore Strait, and the north-western coastal area of the island of Borneo. Each is separated from the other by the South China Sea.

HISTORY AND POLITICS

The Federation of Malaya became an independent country within the Commonwealth on 31 August 1957. On 16 September 1963 the federation was enlarged by the accession of the states of Singapore, Sabah (formerly British North Borneo) and Sarawak, and the name of Malaysia was adopted from that date. On 9 August 1965 Singapore seceded from the federation.

The National Front (Barisan Nasional) Coalition led by Dr Mahathir Mohamed won a fifth term in office in a general election held on 29 November 1999, winning 148 of the 193 seats.

POLITICAL SYSTEM

The constitution provides for a strong federal government and a degree of autonomy for the state governments. It created a constitutional Supreme Head of the Federation (HM the *Yang di-Pertuan Agong*) and a Deputy Supreme Head (HRH *Timbalan Yang di-Pertuan Agong*) to be elected for a term of five years by the rulers from among their number. The Malay rulers are either chosen or succeed to their position in accordance with the custom of the particular state. In other states of Malaysia, choice of the head of state is at the discretion of the Yang di-Pertuan Agong after consultation with the Chief Minister of the state.

The Federal Parliament consists of two houses, the Senate and the House of Representatives. The Senate *(Dewan Negara)* consists of 69 members who serve a six-year term, 26 being elected by the Legislative Assemblies of the states (two from each) and 43 appointed by the Yang di-Pertuan Agong. The House of Representatives (Dewan Rakyat) consists of 193 members elected for a five-year term by universal adult suffrage with a common electoral roll.

FEDERAL STRUCTURE

According to the constitution, each state shall have its own constitution not inconsistent with the federal constitution, with the ruler or governor acting on the advice of an Executive Council appointed on the advice of the Chief Minister and a single-chamber Legislative Assembly. The Legislative Assemblies are fully elected on the same basis as the federal parliament.

Population

State	Area (sq. km)	(2000 census)	Main Town
Johor	18,987	2,565,701	ΨJohor Baharu
Kedah	9,425	1,572,107	Alor Setar
Kelantan	15,024	1,289,199	Kota Baharu
Melaka	1,652	602,867	ΨMelaka
Negeri Sembilan	6,644	830,080	Seremban
Pahang	35,965	1,231,176	ΨKuantan
Penang	1,031	1,225,501	ΨGeorgetown
Perak	21,005	2,030,382	Ipoh
Perlis	795	198,335	Kangar
Sabah	73,619	2,449,389	ΨKota Kinabalu
Sarawak	124,450	2,012,616	ΨKuching
Selangor	7,960	3,947,527	ΨShah Alam
Terengganu	12,955	879,691	ΨKuala Terengganu

Federal Territories

Kuala Lumpur	1,297,526
Labuan	70,517

HEAD OF STATE

Supreme Head of State, HM Tuanku Syed Sirajuddin Putra Jamalullail (Yang di-Pertuan Agong of Perlis), *sworn in* 13 December 2001

CABINET *as at July 2003*

Prime Minister, Finance and Special Functions, Dr Mahathir Mohamed

Deputy Prime Minister, Home Affairs, Abdullah Ahmad Badawi

Agriculture, Effendi Norwani

Culture, Arts and Tourism, Abdul Kadir Sheikh Fadzir

Defence, Najib Tun Razak

Domestic Trade and Consumer Affairs, Muhyiddin Yasin

Education, Musa Mohamad

Energy, Telecommunications and Posts, Leo Moggie Anak Irok
Entrepreneurial Development, Mohamed Nazri Abdul Aziz
Foreign Affairs, Hamid Albar
Health, Chua Jui Meng
Housing and Local Government, Ong Ka Ting
Human Resources, Fong Chan Ong
Information, Mohamad Khalil Yaakob
International Trade and Industry, Rafidah Aziz
Lands and Co-operative Development, Kasitah Gaddam
National Unity and Social Development, Zaharah binti Sulaiman
Primary Industries, Dr Lim Keng Yaik
Prime Minister's Office, Abdul Hamid Zainal Abidin; Bernard Dompok; Pandikar Amin Musa; Rais Yatim
Public Works, Samy Vellu
Rural Development, Azmi Khalid
Science, Technology and Environment, Law Hieng Ding
Second Minister for Finance, Jamaluddin Jarjis
Transport, Chan Kong Choy
Women's Affairs, Shahrizat Abdul Jalil
Youth and Sports, Hishamuddin Tun Hussein

MALAYSIAN HIGH COMMISSION
45 Belgrave Square, London SW1X 8QT
Tel: 020-7235 8033
Email: mwlondon@btinternet.com
High Commissioner, HE Dato Salim bin Hashim, apptd 2001

BRITISH HIGH COMMISSION
185 Jalan Ampang 50450 Kuala Lumpur or PO Box 11030, 50732 Kuala Lumpur
Tel: (00 60) (3) 2170 2200
High Commissioner, HE Bruce Cleghorn, CMG, apptd 2001

BRITISH COUNCIL DIRECTOR, Dr Tom Cameron
Ground Floor, West Block, Wisma Selangor Dredging 142 C
Jalan Ampang 50450 Kuala Lumpur Tel: (00 60) (3) 2723 7900
Email: kualalumpur@britishcouncil.org.my

DEFENCE

The Army has 632 armoured personnel carriers. The Royal Malaysian Navy has four frigates, 41 patrol and coastal vessels and six armed helicopters at four bases. The Royal Malaysian Air Force has 95 combat aircraft. Australia maintains an infantry company and an air force detachment in Malaysia.

MILITARY EXPENDITURE – 3.8 per cent of GDP (2001)
MILITARY PERSONNEL – 100,000: Army 80,000, Navy 12,000, Air Force 8,000; Paramilitaries 20,100

ECONOMY

From being an agriculturally-based economy reliant on raw materials exports at independence, Malaysia has undergone an industrialisation programme and now produces clothing, textiles, rubber goods, electronics, office equipment, cars, household appliances, semi-conductors, food processing and chemicals. There are extensive privatisation programmes involving telecommunications, railways, airports, electricity and shipping. In 2000 42 per cent of GDP was produced by services, 44 per cent by manufacturing and 14 per cent by agriculture.

High government spending and excessive corporate borrowing have contributed to a large domestic debt and a high current account deficit, making the economy vulnerable to international capital fluctuations and forcing the government to adopt austerity measures, including restructuring the financial sector. This facilitated a relatively rapid recovery from the 1997–8 financial crisis.

GNP – US$78,727 million (2000); US$3,380 per capita (2000)
GDP – US$87,540 million (2001); US$4,035 per capita (2000)
ANNUAL AVERAGE GROWTH OF GDP – 8.5 per cent (2000)
INFLATION RATE – 1.5 per cent (2000)
UNEMPLOYMENT – 3.1 per cent (2000)
TOTAL EXTERNAL DEBT – US$41,797 million (2000)

TRADE

Malaysia has had a consistently positive trade balance, helping to underpin the value of its currency. It is the largest exporter of natural rubber, tin, palm oil and tropical hardwoods. Other major export commodities are manufactured and processed products, petroleum, oil and other minerals, palm kernel oil, tea and pepper. Imports consist mainly of machinery and transport equipment, manufactured goods, foods, consumer durables and metal products. Japan, the USA and Singapore are the main trading partners.

In 2000 Malaysia had a trade surplus of US$20,854 million and a current account deficit of US$8,409 million. In 2001 imports totalled US$73,866 million and exports US$88,005 million.

Trade with UK	2001	2002
Imports from UK	£1,033,178,000	£882,248,000
Exports to UK	2,012,187,000	1,796,310,000

MALDIVES

Divehi Rājjē ge Jumhūriyyā – Republic of the Maldives

AREA – 115 sq. miles (298 sq. km)
POPULATION – 310,764 (2001 estimate). The people are Sunni Muslims and the Maldivian (Dhivehi) language is akin to Elu or old Sinhalese
CAPITAL – ΨMalé (population, 74,069, 2000)
CURRENCY – Rufiyaa of 100 laaris
NATIONAL ANTHEM – Gavmi Mi Ekuverikan Mati Tibegen Kurīme Salām (In National Unity We Salute Our Nation)
NATIONAL DAY – 26 July
NATIONAL FLAG – Green field bearing a white crescent, with wide red border
POPULATION GROWTH RATE – 2.7 per cent
POPULATION DENSITY – 931 per sq. km (1999)
MILITARY EXPENDITURE – 6.7 per cent of GDP (2001)
ILLITERACY RATE – (m) 3.7 per cent; (f) 3.6 per cent (2000)

The Maldives are a chain of coral atolls 400 miles to the south-west of Sri Lanka, stretching north for about 600 miles from just south of the Equator. There are about 19 coral atolls comprising over 1,200 islands, 198 of which are inhabited. No point in the entire chain of islands is more than eight feet above sea-level.

HISTORY AND POLITICS

Until 1952 the islands were a sultanate under the protection of the British Crown. Internal self-government was achieved in 1948 and full independence in 1965. The Maldives became a special member of the

Commonwealth in 1982 and a full member in 1985.

The Maldives form a republic which is elective. The legislature, the Citizens' Assembly (Majlis), has 42 representatives elected from all the atolls, and eight appointed by the president, for a five-year term. The government consists of a Cabinet, which is responsible to the Majlis. There are no political parties. Under the 1998 constitution, the president is elected by the Majlis and confirmed by a referendum. The most recent legislative election took place on 19 November 1999. Presidential elections were due to take place in October 2003.

HEAD OF STATE
President, Commander-in-Chief of the Armed Forces, Defence, National Security, Finance and Treasury, HE Maumoon Abdul Gayoom, *elected* 1978, *re-elected* 1983, 1989, 1993, 16 October 1998

CABINET *as at July 2003*
Attorney-General, Mohamed Munnavvar
Communication, Science and Technology, Midhat Hilmy
Construction and Public Works, Umar Zahir
Education, Ismail Shafeeu
Fisheries, Agriculture and Marine Resources, Abdul Rasheed Hussain
Foreign Affairs, Fathullah Jameel
Health, Ahmed Abdulla
Home Affairs, Housing and Environment (acting), Abdul Aziz Yoosuf
Human Resources, Employment and Labour, Abdullah Kamaaludheen
Information, Arts and Culture, Ibrahim Manik
Justice, Ahmed Zahir
Planning and National Development, Ibrahim Hussain Zaki
President's Office, Abdullah Jameel
Tourism, Hassan Sobir
Trade and Industry, Abdulla Yameen
Transport and Civil Aviation, Ilyas Ibrahim
Women's Affairs and Social Welfare, Aneesa Ahmed
Youth and Sports, Mohamed Zahir Hussain
Ministers of State, Maj.-Gen. Anbaree Abdul Sattar
  (Defence and National Security); Mohamed Jaleel
  (Finance and Treasury)

HIGH COMMISSION OF THE REPUBLIC OF MALDIVES
22 Nottingham Place, London W1U 5NJ
Tel: 020-7224 2135
High Commissioner, vacant
Acting High Commissioner, Adam Hassan

BRITISH HIGH COMMISSIONER, HE Stephen Evans, OBE, apptd 2002, resident at Colombo, Sri Lanka

ECONOMY
The vegetation of the islands is coconut palms with some scrub. Hardly any cultivation of crops is possible and nearly all food to supplement the basic fish diet has to be imported. Tourism is expanding rapidly (461,063 visitors in 2001). The principal industry is fishing, which together with tourism accounts for about 30 per cent of GDP. The Maldives National Ship Management Ltd (MNSML) has a fleet of nine merchant ships. There is an international airport at Malé.

In 2000 the Maldives had a trade deficit of US$233 million and a current account deficit of US$53 million. In 2001 imports totalled US$395 million and exports US$76 million.

GNP – US$541 million (2000); US$1,960 per capita (2000)

GDP – US$622 million (2001); US$1,985 per capita (2000)
ANNUAL AVERAGE GROWTH OF GDP – 4.8 per cent (2000)
INFLATION RATE –1.1 per cent (2000)
TOTAL EXTERNAL DEBT – US$207 million (2000)

Trade with UK	2001	2002
Imports from UK	£5,027,000	£3,046,000
Exports to UK	6,447,000	7,216,000

MALI

République du Mali – Republic of Mali

AREA – 478,841 sq. miles (1,240,192 sq. km). Neighbours: Senegal (west), Mauritania (north-west), Algeria (north-east), Niger (east), Burkina Faso and Côte d'Ivoire (south), Guinea (south-west)
POPULATION – 11,008,518 (2001 estimate): 50 per cent Mande (Bambara, Malinke, Sarakole), 17 per cent Peul, 12 per cent Voltaic, 6 per cent Songhai, 10 per cent Tuareg and Moor. The official language is French; Bambara is the largest local language
CAPITAL – Bamako (population, 809,552, 1996 UN estimate)
MAJOR CITIES – Gao; Kayes; Mopti; Ségou; Sikasso; Timbuktu (all regional capitals)
CURRENCY – Franc CFA of 100 centimes
NATIONAL ANTHEM – A Ton Appel, Mali (At Your Call, Mali)
NATIONAL DAY – 22 September
NATIONAL FLAG – Vertical stripes of green (by staff), yellow and red
POPULATION GROWTH RATE – 2.4 per cent
POPULATION DENSITY – 9 per sq. km (1999)
MILITARY EXPENDITURE – 2.5 per cent of GDP (2001)
MILITARY PERSONNEL – Army 7,350; Paramilitaries 4,800
CONSCRIPTION DURATION – Two years (selective)
ILLITERACY RATE – (m) 51.1 per cent; (f) 65.6 per cent (2000)
ENROLMENT (percentage of age group) – primary 49 per cent (1997); secondary 13 per cent (1997); tertiary 1 per cent (1997)

HISTORY AND POLITICS
Formerly the French colony of Soudan, the territory elected on 24 November 1958 to remain an autonomous republic within the French Community. It associated with Senegal in the Federation of Mali, which was granted full independence on 20 June 1960. The Federation was effectively dissolved in August 1960 by the secession of Senegal. The title of the Republic of Mali was adopted in September 1960.

A new constitution establishing a multiparty political system was approved by referendum in January 1992. Alpha Konaré, the Alliance for Democracy in Mali (ADEMA) leader, won the presidential elections in 1992 and was re-elected in 1997. On 14 February 2000, the ADEMA government resigned and a new prime minister and government took office the following day, comprising members of ADEMA and opposition parties. Former military leader and independent candidate Amadou Toumani Touré won the presidential elections held on 12 May 2002. In the legislative elections of

13 July 2002 ADEMA was initially thought to have retained the majority of seats in the Assembly after a low turnout with many void votes; this result was overturned on 10 August by the constitutional court which declared that the Spirit 2002 coalition had won the largest number of seats. The government resigned without explanation on 13 October 2002 and a new 'government of national unity' was sworn in.

HEAD OF STATE
President, Amadou Toumani Touré, *elected* 12 May 2002; *took office* 8 June 2002

CABINET *as at June 2003*
Prime Minister, African Integration, Mohamed Ag Hamani
Agriculture, Livestock and Fishing, Seydou Traoré
Communications and Information Technology, Gaoussou Drabo
Cottage Industry and Tourism, Bah N'diaye
Culture, Sheik Oumar Sissoko
Defence and Veterans, Mahamane Kalil Maïga
Economy and Finance, Bassari Toure
Education, Mamadou Lamine Traoré
Employment and Civil Service, Modibo Diakite
Environment, Nancouma Keita
Equipment and Transport, Ousmane Issoufi Maiga
Foreign Affairs and International Co-operation, Lassine Traoré
Health, Keita Rokiatou N'Diaye
Industry and Commerce, Choguel Kokala Maiga
Justice and Keeper of the Seals, Abdoulaye Garba Tapo
Mines, Energy and Water Resources, Hahmed Diane Semega
Promotion of Women, Children and the Family, Berthe Aissata Bengaly
Secretary-General of the Presidency with the rank of Minister, Maj. Modibo Sidibe
Security and Civil Protection, Col. Souleymane Sidibé
Social Development, Solidarity and the Elderly, N'diayé Fatoumata Coulibaly
State Properties, Lands and Housing, Boubacar Sidiki Touré
Territorial Administration and Local Communities, Gen. Kafougouna Koné
Youth and Sports, Djibril Tangara

EMBASSY OF THE REPUBLIC OF MALI
Avenue Molière 487, B-1060 Brussels, Belgium
Tel: (00 32) (2) 345 7432
Ambassador Extraordinary and Plenipotentiary, Ahmed Mohamed Ag Hamani, apptd 2001

BRITISH EMBASSY
The British Embassy closed on 31 May 2003
All British Embassy staff reside at Dakar

ECONOMY
Mali's principal exports are cotton and gold. Principal imports include machinery and vehicles, petroleum, and foodstuffs. Mali rejoined the CFA Franc Zone in 1984. In September 2002 France stated that it would cancel 40 per cent of Mali's debts owed, amounting to some US$79 million.
GNP – US$2,548 million (2000); US$240 per capita (2000)
GDP – US$2,629 million (2001); US$230 per capita (2000)
ANNUAL AVERAGE GROWTH OF GDP – 5.7 per cent (1998)

INFLATION RATE – –0.7 per cent (2000)
TOTAL EXTERNAL DEBT – US$2,956 million (2000)

Trade with UK	2001	2002
Imports from UK	£17,039,000	£18,946,000
Exports to UK	1,487,000	3,519,000

MALTA

Repubblika ta' Malta / Republic of Malta

AREA – 121.5 sq. miles (316 sq. km)
POPULATION – 392,000 (2001). The Maltese are mainly Roman Catholic. The Maltese language is of Semitic origin and held by some to be derived from the Carthaginian and Phoenician tongues. Maltese and English are the official languages
CAPITAL – ΨValletta (population, 7,048, 2000)
CURRENCY – Maltese lira (LM) of 100 cents or 1,000 mils
NATIONAL ANTHEM – L-Innu Malti (Hymn of Malta)
NATIONAL DAYS – 31 March (Freedom Day); 7 June (Sette Giugno Riots); 8 September (Our Lady of Victories); 21 September (Independence Day); 13 December (Republic Day)
NATIONAL FLAG – Two equal vertical stripes, white at the hoist and red at the fly. A representation of the George Cross is carried edged with red in the canton of the white stripe
LIFE EXPECTANCY (years) – 78 (2001)
POPULATION GROWTH RATE – 1 per cent
POPULATION DENSITY – 1,241 per sq. km (1999)
MILITARY EXPENDITURE – 0.7 per cent of GDP (2001)
MILITARY PERSONNEL – 2,140

HISTORY AND POLITICS
Malta was in turn held by the Phoenicians, Carthaginians, Romans and Arabs. In 1090 it was conquered by Count Roger of Normandy and in 1530 handed over to the Knights of St John. In 1565 it sustained the famous siege, when the Turks were successfully withstood by Grandmaster La Valette. The Knights fortified the islands and built Valletta before being expelled by Napoleon in 1798. The Maltese rose against the French garrison soon afterwards and the island was subsequently blockaded by the British fleet. The Maltese people requested the protection of the British Crown in 1802 on condition that their rights would be respected. The islands were finally annexed to the British Crown by the Treaty of Paris in 1814.
Malta was again besieged during the Second World War. From June 1940 to the end of the war, 432 members of the garrison and 1,540 civilians were killed by enemy aircraft. The island was awarded the George Cross for gallantry on 15 April 1942.
On 21 September 1964 Malta became an independent state within the Commonwealth, and on 13 December 1974 a republic within the Commonwealth.
Elections to the unicameral parliament of 65 members are held every five years by a system of proportional representation; to ensure that a party receiving more than 50 per cent of the votes cast obtains a parliamentary majority, extra seats may be allocated to that party.
In the elections of September 1998 the Nationalist Party (PN) gained victory and Edward Fenech became prime minister. He revived Malta's EU application and in December 2002, Malta was formally invited to join the EU in 2004. In a referendum on EU membership on 8

March 2003, 54 per cent of the electorate voted in favour of accession.

Elections held on 12 April 2003 were again won by the PN with 35 seats; the Labour Party, which opposes EU accession, gained 30 seats. The victory confirmed the pro-EU referendum result; Edward Fenech Adami was again sworn into office with his new cabinet on 15 April 2003.

HEAD OF STATE
President, Guido de Marco, *took office* 4 April 1999

CABINET *as at July 2003*
Prime Minister, Edward Fenech Adami
Deputy Prime Minister, Social Policy, Lawrence Gonzi
Education, Louis Galea
Finance and Economic Affairs, John Dalli
Foreign Affairs, Joe Borg
Gozo, Giovanna Debono
Health, Louis Deguara
IT and Investment, Austin Gatt
Justice and Home Affairs, Tonio Borg
Resources and Infrastructure, Ninu Zammit
Rural Affairs and the Environment, George Pullicino
Tourism, Francis Zammit Dimech
Transport and Telecommunications, Censu Galea
Youth, Sports and Arts, Jesmond Mugliett

MALTA HIGH COMMISSION
Malta House, 36–38 Piccadilly, London W1J 0LE.
Tel: 020-7292 4800
High Commissioner, HE George Bonello DuPuis, apptd 1999

BRITISH HIGH COMMISSION
Whitehall Mansions, Ta'Xbiex Seafront,
Ta'Xbiex MSD 11, Malta GC
Tel: (00 356) 2323 0000
Email: bhccomm@vol.net.mt
High Commissioner, HE Vincent Fean, apptd 2002

BRITISH COUNCIL DIRECTOR, Ronnie Micallef, c/o British High Commission
Email: veronica.attard@britcouncil.org.mt

ECONOMY
Tourism has assumed primary importance, with 1,180,145 tourists visiting the island in 2001.

In 2001 manufacturing employed 21.8 per cent of the workforce and accounted for 22.9 per cent of GDP. Industry is orientated primarily towards exports. Industries include communications equipment, food processing, textiles, footwear and clothing, printing and publishing, plastics and chemical products, electrical machinery, medical equipment and furniture. Value Added Tax was reintroduced in January 1999. Financial services are a growing part of Malta's economy.

In 2001 there was a trade deficit of US$490 million and a current account deficit of US$172 million.
GNP – US$3,559 million (2000); US$9,120 per capita (2000)
GDP – US$3,571 million (2000); US$9,069 per capita (2000)
ANNUAL AVERAGE GROWTH OF GDP – 4.7 per cent (2000)
INFLATION RATE – 2.4 per cent (2000)
UNEMPLOYMENT – 5.3 per cent (1999)
TOTAL EXTERNAL DEBT – US$10,600 million (1999)

TRADE
The principal imports are foodstuffs (mainly wheat, livestock and meats, milk and fruit), fodder, beverages and tobacco, fuels, chemicals, textiles and machinery (industrial, agricultural and transport). The chief exports are processed food, electronics, textiles, and other manufactures. In 2001 imports totalled US$2,592 million and exports US$1,917 million.

Trade with UK	2001	2002
Imports from UK	£217,418,000	£227,041,000
Exports to UK	148,010,000	171,705,000

EDUCATION
Education is compulsory between the ages of five and 16 and is free at all levels. Secondary education in state schools is provided in secondary schools and junior lyceums. There are ten junior lyceums, 18 secondary schools and five centres catering for low achievers. A Junior College, administered by the University of Malta, prepares students specifically for a university course. Tertiary education is available at the University of Malta. The Malta College of Arts, Science and Technology provides technical and vocational courses at post-secondary level.
ILLITERACY RATE – (m) 8.6 per cent; (f) 7.2 per cent (2000)
ENROLMENT (percentage of age group) – primary 100 per cent (1999); secondary 100 per cent (1999); tertiary 21 per cent (1999)

MARSHALL ISLANDS

Republic of the Marshall Islands

AREA – 70 sq. miles (181 sq. km)
POPULATION – 70,822 (2001 estimate): 99 per cent are Micronesian. Almost half the population is under 15. About 60 per cent of the population is concentrated on the two atolls of Majuro and Kwajalein. The population is Christian, primarily Protestant but with a substantial Catholic minority. Marshallese and English are the official languages
CAPITAL – Dalap-Uliga-Darrit, on Majuro Atoll (population, 20,000)
MAJOR TOWN – Ebeye (9,200)
CURRENCY – Currency is that of the USA
NATIONAL ANTHEM – Forever Marshall Islands
NATIONAL DAY – 1 May (Independence Day)
NATIONAL FLAG – Blue with a diagonal ray divided white over orange running from the lower hoist to the upper fly; in the canton a white sun
POPULATION GROWTH RATE – 2.7 per cent
POPULATION DENSITY – 343 per sq. km (1999)

The Republic of the Marshall Islands consists of 29 atolls and five islands in the central Pacific. The islands and atolls form two parallel chains running north-west to south-east: the Ratak (Sunrise) chain and the Ralik (Sunset) chain. The largest atoll is Kwajalein in the Ralik chain.

HISTORY AND POLITICS
The Marshall Islands were claimed by Spain in 1592 but were left undisturbed by the Spanish Empire for 300 years. In 1886 the Marshall Islands formally became a German protectorate. On the outbreak of the First World War in 1914, Japan took control of the islands on behalf

of the Allied powers, and after the war administered the territory as a League of Nations mandate. During the Second World War US armed forces seized the islands from the Japanese after intense fighting. In 1947 the USA entered into agreement with the UN Security Council to administer the Micronesia area, of which the Marshall Islands are a part, as the UN Trust Territory of the Pacific Islands.

The islands became internally self-governing in 1979, and the US Trusteeship administration came to an end on 21 October 1986, when a Compact of Free Association between the USA and the Republic of the Marshall Islands came into effect. By this agreement the USA recognised the Republic of the Marshall Islands as a fully sovereign and independent state. The UN Security Council terminated the UN Trust Territory of the Pacific in relation to the Marshall Islands and recognised its independence in December 1990. A new Compact of Free Association was negotiated in 2003 to replace the original agreement.

FOREIGN RELATIONS
The Republic of the Marshall Islands has no defence forces. The Compact of Free Association places full responsibility for defence of the Marshall Islands on the USA. The US Department of Defense retains control of islands within Kwajalein Atoll where it has a missile test range. In 2000 the government of the Marshall Islands petitioned the USA for US$2.7 billion to fund medical care for victims of radiation from US nuclear tests in the islands in the 1940s and 1950s and to rectify environmental damage.

POLITICAL SYSTEM
The republic is a democracy based on a parliamentary system of government. The executive is headed by the president, who is elected by the Nitijela from among its members. The president serves for a four-year term. The legislature has one chamber, the Nitijela of 33 members and the Council of Chiefs *(Iroij)* of 12 members which has an advisory role.

In the general election which took place on 15 November 1999, the United Democratic Party won 18 seats. Presidential and legislative elections were due in late 2003.

HEAD OF STATE
President, Kessai Note, *elected* 3 January 2000

GOVERNMENT *as at July 2003*
The President
Education, Wilfred Kendall
Finance, Michael Konelious
Foreign Affairs, Gerald Zackios
Health and Environment, Alvin Jacklick
Internal Affairs and Welfare, Nidel Lorak
Justice, Witten Philippo
Minister in Assistance to the President, Tadashi Lometo
Public Works, Rien Morris
Resources and Development, John Silk
Transportation and Communications, Brenson Wase

BRITISH AMBASSADOR, HE Charles Mochan, apptd 2002, resident at Suva, Fiji

ECONOMY
The economy is a mixture of subsistence and a service-based sector. About half the working population is engaged in agriculture and fishing, with coconut oil and copra production comprising 90 per cent of total exports. Imports include oil, food and machinery. The service sector is based in Majuro and Ebeye and concentrated in banking and insurance, construction, transportation and tourism. Direct US aid under the Compact accounts for two-thirds of the islands' budget. The islands charge foreign fishing fleets for licences to fish for tuna in the waters around the islands. The USA, Japan and Australia are the main trading partners.

GNP – US$102 million (2000); US$1,950 per capita (1999)

GDP – US$96 million (2001); US$1,925 per capita (2000)

ANNUAL AVERAGE GROWTH OF GDP – –2.8 per cent (1998)

Trade with UK	2001	2002
Imports from UK	£933,000	£5,076,000
Exports to UK	234,000	824,000

COMMUNICATIONS
Air Marshall Islands provides air services within the islands and to Hawaii. Continental Air Micronesia serves Majuro and Kwajalein with flights to Hawaii and Guam. Majuro also has shipping links to Hawaii, Australia, Japan and throughout the Pacific.

MAURITANIA

Al-Jumhūriyya al-Islāmiyya al-Mawrītāniyya - Islamic Republic of Mauritania

AREA – 395,956 sq. miles (1,025,520 sq. km). Neighbours: Senegal (south-west), Mali (east and south), Algeria and Western Sahara (north)

POPULATION – 2,747,312 (2001 estimate). The official language is Arabic. Pulaar, Soninke, Wolof and French are also spoken

CAPITAL – Nouakchott (population, 850,000)

CURRENCY – Ouguiya (UM) of 5 khoums

NATIONAL DAY – 28 November

NATIONAL FLAG – Yellow star and crescent on green ground

POPULATION GROWTH RATE – 3.2 per cent

POPULATION DENSITY – 3 per sq. km (1999)

MILITARY EXPENDITURE – 2.9 per cent of GDP (2001)

MILITARY PERSONNEL – 15,750: Army 15,000, Navy 500, Air Force 250; Paramilitaries 5,000

CONSCRIPTION DURATION – Two years

ILLITERACY RATE – (m) 47.2 per cent; (f) 67.9 per cent (2000)

ENROLMENT (percentage of age group) – primary 79 per cent (1997); tertiary 4 per cent (1997)

HISTORY AND POLITICS
Mauritania was under French rule from 1814 to 1958, when it elected to remain within the French Community as an autonomous republic. It became fully independent on 28 November 1960. In 1972 Mauritania left the Franc Zone.

Mauritania and Morocco occupied the Western Sahara territory in February 1976 when Spain formally relinquished it and in April 1976 agreed on a new frontier dividing the territory between them. In August 1979, Mauritania relinquished all claim to the southern sector of the Western Sahara after a three-year war against Polisario Front guerrillas.

After a military coup in 1978, Mauritania was ruled by a Military Committee for National Salvation until 1992, when power was transferred to a civilian president and legislature elected under a constitution approved by referendum in July 1991. Multiparty legislative elections in March 1992 were won by the Republican Democratic and Social Party (PRDS) led by President ould Taya. In the presidential election in December 1997, President ould Taya was re-elected following a boycott by opposition parties. The National Assembly election held in October 2001 was won by the PRDS, which gained 64 of the 81. Presidential elections were due in 7 November 2003.

An attempted coup in June 2003 was put down after heavy fighting.

HEAD OF STATE
President, Col. Maaouya ould Sid Ahmed Taya (PRDS), *took power* 12 December 1984, *elected* 17 January 1992, *re-elected* 12 December 1997

COUNCIL OF MINISTERS *as at July 2003*
Prime Minister, Cheik El-Avia ould Mohamed Khouna
Civil Service, Labour, Youth and Sports, Baba ould Sidi
Communications and Relations with Parliament, Government Spokesman, Cheyakh ould Ely
Culture and Islamic Orientation, Lemrabet Ould Mohamed Lemine
Defence, Kaba ould Elewa
Economy and Development, Mohamed ould Nani
Equipment and Transport, Diabira Bakary
Finance, Biodiel ould Houmeid
Fisheries and Marine Economy, Ahmedou ould Ahmedou
Foreign Affairs and Co-operation, Mohamed ould Toulba
Health and Social Affairs, Mohamed Mahmoud ould Jaafar
Interior, Post and Telecommunications, Lemrabet Sidi Mahmoud ould Cheikh Ahmed
Justice, Seghaier ould Mbarek
Mines and Industry, Zidane ould Hamida
National Education, Aboubekrine ould Ahmed
Rural Development and Environment, Boubakar Souly
Trade, Handicrafts and Tourism, Isselmou ould Abdelkader
Water Power and Energy, Kane Moustapha

EMBASSY OF THE ISLAMIC REPUBLIC OF MAURITANIA
8 Carlos Place, London W1K 3AS
Tel: 020-7478 9323
Ambassador Extraordinary and Plenipotentiary,
HE Dr Youssouf Diagana, apptd 1999

BRITISH AMBASSADOR, HE Haydon Warren-Gash, apptd 2002, resident at Rabat, Morocco

ECONOMY
The main source of potential wealth lies in rich deposits of iron ore around Zouérate, in the north of the country, and rich fishing grounds off the coast. In October 2002 the government and the UN issued an urgent appeal for food aid following a severe drought and the sixth poor harvest in a row.

In 1998 Mauritania had a trade surplus of US$40 million and a current account surplus of US$77 million. It was granted US$1,100 million in debt relief in June 2002.

GNP – US$978 million (2000); US$370 per capita (2000)

GDP – US$1,030 million (2001); US$296 per capita (2000)
ANNUAL AVERAGE GROWTH OF GDP – 3.0 per cent (1998)
INFLATION RATE – 3.3 per cent (2000)
TOTAL EXTERNAL DEBT – US$2,500 million (2000)

Trade with UK	2001	2002
Imports from UK	£8,006,000	£14,290,000
Exports to UK	5,809,000	1,636,000

MAURITIUS

Republic of Mauritius

AREA – 788 sq. miles (2,040 sq. km)
POPULATION – 1,171,000 (2001 estimate): Asiatic races (Hindus 51.8 per cent, Muslims 16.5 per cent, Chinese 2.8 per cent), and persons of European (mainly French) extraction, mixed and African descent (28.6 per cent). English is the official language but French may be used in the National Assembly and lower law courts. Creole is the most commonly used language and several Asian languages are also used
CAPITAL – ΨPort Louis (population, 146,499, 2000 estimate)
MAJOR TOWNS – Beau Bassin-Rose Hill (102,770); Curepipe (81,233); Quatre Bornes (78,384); Vacoas-Phoenix (101,000), 2000 estimates
CURRENCY – Mauritius rupee of 100 cents
NATIONAL ANTHEM – Glory To Thee, Motherland
NATIONAL DAY – 12 March
NATIONAL FLAG – Red, blue, yellow and green horizontal stripes
LIFE EXPECTANCY (years) – 72 (2001)
POPULATION GROWTH RATE – 0.9 per cent
POPULATION DENSITY – 628 per sq. km (2001)
URBAN POPULATION – 42 per cent (2001)
MILITARY EXPENDITURE – 0.2 per cent of GDP (2001)
MILITARY PERSONNEL – Paramilitaries 2,000

Mauritius is an island group lying in the Indian Ocean, 550 miles east of Madagascar.

HISTORY AND POLITICS
Mauritius was discovered in 1511 by the Portuguese; the Dutch visited it in 1598 and named it Mauritius after Prince Maurice of Nassau. From 1638 to 1710 it was held as a Dutch colony; the French took possession in 1715 but did not settle until 1721. Mauritius was taken by a British force in 1810 and became a Crown Colony. It became an independent state within the Commonwealth on 12 March 1968 and a republic on 12 March 1992.

The general election held on 11 September 2000 was won by the coalition of the Mauritian Socialist Movement and the Mauritian Militant Movement, who won 54 of the 62 directly elected seats. On 15 February 2002 President Cassam Uteem resigned after refusing to sign a controversial anti-terrorism bill. His successor, acting president Angidi Chettiar, also refused to sign the bill and resigned on 18 February. On 19 February the bill was signed into law by interim president Arianga Pillay, and a presidential election was held on 25 February and won by Karl Offman.

POLITICAL SYSTEM

The president is head of state and is elected by the National Assembly. The prime minister, appointed by the president, is the member of the National Assembly who appears to the president best able to command the support of the majority of members of the Assembly. Other ministers are appointed by the president acting on the advice of the prime minister.

The National Assembly has a five-year term and consists of 62 elected members (the island of Mauritius is divided into 20 three-member constituencies and Rodrigues returns two members), and eight specially elected members. Of the latter, four seats go to the 'best loser' of whichever communities in the island are under-represented in the Assembly after the general election and the four remaining seats are allocated on the basis of both party and community. In November 2001 the National Assembly approved amendments to the constitution giving a considerable degree of autonomy to the island of Rodrigues, including the establishment of an 18-member regional Assembly.

HEAD OF STATE

President, Karl Offmann, *elected* 25 February 2002
Vice-President, Raouf Bundhun

COUNCIL OF MINISTERS *as at July 2003*

Prime Minister, Defence and Home Affairs, Sir Anerood Jugnauth
Deputy Prime Minister, Finance, Paul Bérenger
Agriculture, Pravind Jugnauth
Arts and Culture, Motee Ramdass
Attorney-General, Justice and Human Rights, Emmanuel Leung Shing
Civil Service Affairs and Administrative Reform, Ahmad Sulliman Jeewah
Commerce, Industry and International Trade, Jayen Cuttaree
Co-operatives, Premdut Koonjoo
Education, Louis Steven Obeegadoo
Environment, Rajesh Anand Bhagwan
Financial Services and Corporate Affairs, Sushil Kushiram
Fisheries, Sylvio Michel
Foreign Affairs, Anil Gayan
Health, Ashok Jugnauth
Labour and Industrial Relations, Showkutally Soodhun
Public Infrastructure and Internal Transport, Anil Kumar Bachoo
Public Utilities, Alan Ganoo
Regional Administration of Rodrigues, Urban and Rural Development, Housing and Lands, Joe Lesjongard
Social Security and Reform Institutions, Samioullah Lauthan
Telecommunications and Information Technology, Pradeep Jeeha
Tourism, Nando Bodha
Training, Skills Development and Productivity, Sangeet Fowdar
Women's Rights and Family Welfare, Marie-Arianne Navarre
Youth and Sports, Ravi Yerrigadoo

MAURITIUS HIGH COMMISSION

32–33 Elvaston Place, London SW7 5NW
Tel: 020-7581 0294/5
High Commissioner, HE Mohunlall Goburdhun, apptd 2001

BRITISH HIGH COMMISSION

Les Cascades Building, Edith Cavell Street, Port Louis (PO Box 1063)
Tel: (00 230) 202 9400 Email: bhc@intnet.mu
High Commissioner, HE David Snoxell, apptd 2000

BRITISH COUNCIL DIRECTOR, Rosalind Burford
Royal Road, PO Box 111, Rose Hill.
Email: general.enquiries@mu.britishcouncil.org

ECONOMY

The major cash crop is sugar cane. Tea and tobacco are grown commercially on a smaller scale. Other products include molasses, alcohol, rum, denatured spirits, perfumed spirits and vinegar.

The bulk of the island's requirements in manufactured products still has to be imported. However, the Mauritius Export Processing Zone (MEPZ) Scheme has attracted investment from overseas and the number of export-orientated enterprises had risen from ten in 1971 to 522 in 2001. The biggest firms are in clothing manufacture, particularly woollen knitwear, but the range of goods produced includes toys, plastic products, leather goods, diamond cutting and polishing, watches, television sets and telephones.

Tourism is a major source of income, with an estimated 685,000 tourists in 2002. France is the most important source of tourists, followed closely by the neighbouring French island of Réunion.

GNP – US$4,449 million (2000); US$3,750 per capita (2000)
GDP – US$4,500 million (2001); US$3,886 per capita (2000)
ANNUAL AVERAGE GROWTH OF GDP – 3.4 per cent (1999)
INFLATION RATE – 5.4 per cent (2001)
TOTAL EXTERNAL DEBT – US$2,374 million (2000)

TRADE

Most foodstuffs and raw materials have to be imported from abroad. Apart from local consumption (about 36,500 tonnes a year), the sugar produced is exported, mainly to Britain.

In 2000 Mauritius had a trade deficit of US$394 million and a current account deficit of US$33 million. In 2001 imports totalled US$1,999 million and exports US$1,595 million.

Trade with UK	2001	2002
Imports from UK	£52,293,000	£56,418,000
Exports to UK	337,840,000	337,425,000

COMMUNICATIONS

Port Louis, on the north-west coast, handles the bulk of the island's external trade. A bulk sugar terminal capable of handling the total crop began operating in 1980. The international airport is located at Plaisance, about five miles from Mahébourg. There are five daily newspapers and 15 weeklies, mostly in French.

EDUCATION

Primary and secondary education are free and primary education is compulsory. There are a number of training facilities offering vocational training. The Institute of Education is responsible for training primary and secondary school teachers and for curriculum development.

ILLITERACY RATE – (m) 12.1 per cent; (f) 18.6 per cent (2000)

ENROLMENT (percentage of age group) – primary 100 per cent (1997); tertiary 6 per cent (1997)

RODRIGUES AND DEPENDENCIES

Rodrigues, formerly a dependency but now part of Mauritius, is about 350 miles east of Mauritius, with an area of 40 square miles. Population (2000) 35,776. Cattle, salt fish, sheep, goats, pigs, maize and onions are the principal exports. The island has a degree of self-government, exercised through the Regional Assembly established in October 2002.

Chief Commissioner, Jean Daniel Speville

The islands of Agalega and St Brandon are dependencies of Mauritius. Total population (2000) 170.

MEXICO

Estados Unidos Mexicanos – United Mexican States

AREA – 734,115 sq. miles (1,908,700 sq. km). Neighbours: USA (north), Guatemala and Belize (south-east)

POPULATION – 100,368,000 (2001). Spanish is the official language and is spoken by about 95 per cent of the population. There are five main groups of Indian languages (Náhuatl, Maya, Zapotec, Otomí, Mixtec) and 59 dialects derived from them

CAPITAL – Mexico City (population, 8,591,309, 2000 census)

MAJOR CITIES – Ciudad Juárez (1,217,818); Ecatepec de Morelos (1,647,720); Guadalajara (1,647,720); León (1,133,576); Monterrey (1,108,499); Nezahualcóyotl (1,224,924); Puebla (1,346,176); Tijuana (1,212,232); Toluca (665,617); Torreón (529,093), 2000

CURRENCY – Peso of 100 centavos

NATIONAL ANTHEM – Mexicanos, Al Grito De Guerra (Mexicans, To The War Cry)

NATIONAL DAY – 16 September (Proclamation of Independence)

NATIONAL FLAG – Three vertical bands in green, white, red, with the Mexican emblem (an eagle on a cactus devouring a snake) in the centre

LIFE EXPECTANCY (years) – 73 (2001)

POPULATION GROWTH RATE – 1.7 per cent

POPULATION DENSITY – 53 per sq. km (2001)

URBAN POPULATION – 75 per cent (2001)

ILLITERACY RATE – (m) 6.7 per cent; (f) 10.6 per cent (2000)

ENROLMENT (percentage of age group) – primary 100 per cent (1997); secondary 64 per cent (1997); tertiary 16 per cent (1997)

The Sierra Nevada, known in Mexico as the Sierra Madre, and Rocky Mountains continue south from the northern border with the USA, running parallel to the west and east coasts.

HISTORY AND POLITICS

Present-day Mexico and Guatemala were once the centre of a civilisation which flowered in the periods from AD 500 to 1100 and 1300 to 1500 and collapsed before the Spanish army in the years following 1519. Pre-Columbian Mexico was divided between different Indian cultures, most notably the Mayan, Teotihuacáno, Zapotec, Totonac and Toltec cultures. The last and most famous Indian culture, the Aztec, suffered more than the others at the hands of the Spanish and very few Aztec monuments remain.

After the conquest, the country was largely converted to Christianity and a distinctive colonial civilisation emerged. In 1810 a revolt began against Spanish rule. This was finally successful in 1821, when independence was proclaimed.

Friction with the USA led to the war of 1846–8, at the end of which Mexico was forced to cede the northern provinces of Texas, California and New Mexico. In 1910 began the Mexican Revolution which reformed the social structure and the land system, curbed the power of foreign companies and ushered in the independent industrial Mexico of today.

There are 11 registered political parties; the Partido Revolucionario Institucional (PRI) which constituted the governing party for more than 60 years until its defeat in July 2000, the Partido de Acción Nacional (PAN) and the Partido de la Revolución Democrática (PRD) are the largest.

In presidential and legislative elections on 2 July 2000, Vicente Fox, the PAN candidate, was elected as president and the PAN-led alliance gained 224 seats, the PRI 209 seats and the PRD 67 seats in the Chamber of Deputies.

INSURGENCIES

Two armed revolts of Zapatista peasant Indians in the southern state of Chiapas in January to August 1994 and December 1994 to February 1995 caused a political and economic crisis. Negotiations with the Zapatistas produced a preliminary agreement on indigenous rights in February 1996, but talks broke down and were suspended in September 1996. Further talks took place in November 1998.

Following the inauguration of President Fox on 1 December 2000, the Zapatistas announced that peace talks could be resumed on condition that troops were withdrawn from the Chiapas, a bill of indigenous rights was enacted by Congress and an amnesty was declared for Zapatista rebels held by the authorities. On 24 February 2001, the General Staff, the ruling body of the Zapatistas, began a 3,360-km march from Chiapas to Mexico City in support of the bill. They arrived on 11 March, accompanied by hundreds of supporters, and their leaders addressed parliament on 28 March. Congress enacted a bill of indigenous rights on 1 May, but the Zapatistas broke off negotiations with the government, claiming that the provisions of the bill had been watered down.

POLITICAL SYSTEM

The Congress of the Union consists of a Senate of 128 members, elected for six years, and of a Chamber of Deputies *(Cámara de Diputados)*, at present numbering 500, elected for three years. The head of the government is the president, who is elected for a six-year term and may not be re-elected.

FEDERAL STRUCTURE

The republic is a federal one of 31 states and the federal capital. The states are administered by a governor and their own Chamber of Deputies.

State	Area (sq. km)	Population (2000 census)	Capital
Federal District	1,499	8,605,239	Mexico City
Aguascalientes	5,589	944,285	Aguascalientes
Baja California	70,113	2,487,367	Mexicali
Baja California Sur	73,677	424,041	La Paz
Campeche	51,833	690,689	Campeche
Coahuila	151,571	2,298,070	Saltillo
Colima	5,455	542,627	Colima
Chiapas	73,887	3,920,892	Tuxtla Gutiérrez
Chihuahua	247,087	3,052,907	Chihuahua
Durango	119,648	1,448,661	Victoria de Durango
Guanajuato	30,589	4,663,032	Guanajuato
Guerrero	63,794	3,079,649	Chilpancingo
Hidalgo	20,987	2,235,591	Pachuca de Soto
Jalisco	80,137	6,322,002	Guadalajara
México	21,461	13,096,686	Toluca de Lerdo
Michoacán	59,864	3,985,667	Morelia
Morelos	4,941	1,555,296	Cuernavaca
Nayarit	27,621	920,185	Tepic
Nuevo León	64,555	3,834,141	Monterrey
Oaxaca	95,364	3,438,765	Oaxaca de Juárez
Puebla	33,919	5,076,686	Puebla de Zaragoza
Querétaro	11,769	1,404,306	Querétaro
Quintana Roo	50,350	721,538	Chetumal
San Luis Potosí	62,848	2,299,360	San Luis Potosí
Sinaloa	58,092	2,536,844	Culiacán Rosales
Sonora	184,934	2,216,969	Hermosillo
Tabasco	24,661	1,891,829	Villahermosa
Tamaulipas	79,829	2,753,222	Ciudad Victoria
Tlaxcala	3,914	962,646	Tlaxcala
Veracruz	72,815	6,908,975	Jalapa Enríquez
Yucatán	39,340	1,658,210	Mérida
Zacatecas	75,040	1,353,610	Zacatecas

HEAD OF STATE
President, Vicente Fox, *elected* 2 July 2000, *sworn in* 1 December 2000

CABINET *as at July 2003*
Agrarian Reform, Florencio Salazar
Agriculture, Livestock, Rural Development, Fisheries and Food, Javier Usabiaga Arroyo
Attorney-General, Gen. Rafael Macedo de la Concha
Communications and Transport, Pedro Cerisola Weber
Comptroller-General, Francisco Barrio Terrazas
Defence, Gen. Gerardo Clemente Ricardo Vega
Economy, Fernando Canales Clariond
Education, Reyes Tamez Guerra
Energy, Ernesto Martens Robolledo
Environment and Natural Resources, Victor Lichtinger
Finance and Public Credit, Francisco Gil Diaz
Foreign Affairs, Luis Ernesto Derbez
Health, Julio José Frenk Mora
Interior, Santiago Creel Miranda
Labour and Social Welfare, Carlos Abascal Carranza
Naval Affairs, Adm. Marco Antonio Peyrot Gonzalez
Public Safety and Justice, Alejandro Gertz Manero
Social Development, Josefina Vázquez Mota
Tourism, Leticia Navarro

MEXICAN EMBASSY
42 Hertford Street, London W1J 7JR
Tel: 020-7499 8586
Ambassador Extraordinary and Plenipotentiary, HE Alma Rosa Moreno Razo, apptd 2001

BRITISH EMBASSY
Calle Río Lerma 71, Colonia Cuauhtémoc,
06500 Mexico City Tel: (00 52) (55) 5242 8500
Email: consular.mexico@fco.gov.uk
Ambassador Extraordinary and Plenipotentiary, HE Denise Holt, CMG, apptd 2002

BRITISH COUNCIL DIRECTOR, Clive Bruton
Lope de Vega 316, Col. Chapultepec Morales,
11570 Mexico DF Tel: (00 52) (55) 5263 1900
Email: bcmexico@britishcouncil.org.mx

DEFENCE
The Army has 862 armoured personnel carriers. The Navy has three destroyers, eight frigates, 109 patrol and coastal vessels, and eight combat aircraft. There are 20 naval bases. The Air Force has 107 combat aircraft and 71 armed helicopters.
MILITARY EXPENDITURE – 0.9 per cent of GDP (2001)
MILITARY PERSONNEL – 192,770: Army 144,000, Navy 37,000, Air Force 11,770; Paramilitaries 11,000
CONSCRIPTION DURATION – 12 months (four hours per week) by lottery

ECONOMY
The principal crops are maize, beans, sorghum, rice, wheat, barley, sugar cane, coffee, cotton, tomatoes, chillies, tobacco, chick-peas, groundnuts, cocoa and many kinds of fruit. The maguey, or Mexican cactus, yields several fermented drinks, mezcal and tequila (distilled) and pulque (undistilled). Another species of the plant supplies sisal-hemp (henequen). The forests contain mahogany, rosewood, ebony and chicle trees. Agriculture employs an estimated 20 per cent of the working population.

Until recently, the principal industries were mining and petroleum, but there has been considerable expansion of both light and heavy industries; exports of manufactured goods now average almost 90 per cent of total exports. The steel industry expanded steadily until recently and current production is around 5.8 million tons.

The mineral wealth is great, and the principal minerals are gold, silver, copper, fluorspar, lead, zinc, quicksilver, iron and sulphur. Substantial reserves of uranium have been found. The oil industry is state-owned.

Tariffs on trade between Mexico and the USA and Canada are being reduced and are due to be abolished in 2004 under the North American Free Trade Area agreement.

There is great social inequality; a poverty-alleviation programme guarantees money and food to 2.6 million of the poorest families if they send their children to school.

Mexico joined GATT in 1986 and the OECD in 1994.
GNP – US$497,025 million (2000); US$5,070 per capita (2000)
GDP – US$617,817 million (2001); US$5,805 per capita (2000)
ANNUAL AVERAGE GROWTH OF GDP – 6.9 per cent (2000)
INFLATION RATE – 9.5 per cent (2000)
UNEMPLOYMENT – 1.6 per cent (2000)
TOTAL EXTERNAL DEBT – US$150,288 million (2000)

TRADE

Major imports include computers, auto assembly material, electrical parts, car and truck parts, powdered milk, corn and sorghum, transport, sound-recording and power-generating equipment, chemicals, industrial machinery, pharmaceuticals and specialised appliances. Principal exports include oil, cars, auto engines, fruits and vegetables, shrimps, coffee, computers, cattle, glass, iron and steel pipes, and copper. The main trading partners are the USA, EU, Latin America and Japan.

The North American Free Trade Agreement, to which Mexico is a signatory, came into effect on 1 January 1994; trade between Mexico, Canada and the USA rose by 17 per cent a year. Mexico also has free trade agreements with EFTA, the EU, Bolivia, Chile, Colombia, Costa Rica, El Salvador, Guatemala, Honduras, Israel, Nicaragua and Venezuela.

In 2001 Mexico had a trade deficit of US$9,955 million and a current account deficit of US$17,708 million. In 1999 imports totalled US$182,702 million and exports US$158,547 million.

Trade with UK	2001	2002
Imports from UK	£686,723,000	£708,461,000
Exports to UK	702,499,000	523,329,000

COMMUNICATIONS

Veracruz, Tampico and Coatzacoalcos are the chief ports on the Atlantic, and Guaymas, Mazatlán, Puerto Lázaro Cárdenas and Salina Cruz on the Pacific. Work is proceeding on the reorganisation and re-equipment of the whole rail system. There were 329,532 km of roads in 1999; total track length of the railways was 26,622 km. Mexico City may be reached by at least three highways from the USA, and from the south from Yucatán as well as on two principal highways from the Guatemalan border.

FEDERATED STATES OF MICRONESIA

AREA – 271 sq. miles (702 sq. km)
POPULATION – 134,597 (2001 estimate). The
  population is Micronesian and predominantly
  Christian. English (official) and eight other languages
  are used in different parts of the Federated States:
  Yapese, Ulithian, Woleaian, Pohnpeian, Nukuoran,
  Kapingamarangi, Chuukese and Kosraean
FEDERAL CAPITAL – Palikir, on Pohnpei
CURRENCY – Currency is that of the USA
NATIONAL ANTHEM – Patriots of Micronesia
NATIONAL FLAG – United Nations blue with four white
  stars in the centre
LIFE EXPECTANCY (years) – male 64.4; female 68.8
POPULATION GROWTH RATE – 3.7 per cent
POPULATION DENSITY – 165 per sq. km (1999)

The Federated States of Micronesia comprise more than 600 islands extending 2,900 km (1,800 miles) across the archipelago of the Caroline Islands in the western Pacific Ocean.

HISTORY AND POLITICS

The Spanish Empire claimed sovereignty over the Caroline Islands until 1899, when Spain withdrew from her Pacific territories and sold her possessions in the Caroline Islands to Germany. The Caroline Islands became a German protectorate until the outbreak of the First World War in 1914, when Japan took control of the islands and was given a League of Nations mandate to administer the territory in 1920. During the Second World War, US armed forces took control of the islands from the Japanese. In 1947 the USA entered into agreement with the UN Security Council to administer the Micronesia area, of which the Federated States of Micronesia were a part, as the UN Trust Territory of the Pacific Islands.

The US Trusteeship administration came to an end on 3 November 1986, when a Compact of Free Association between the USA and the Federated States of Micronesia came into effect. By this agreement the USA recognised the Federated States of Micronesia as a fully sovereign and independent state. The independence of the Federated States of Micronesia was recognised by the UN in December 1990.

Legislative elections took place on 4 March 2003 and presidential elections on 10 May 2003.

POLITICAL SYSTEM

The constitution separates the executive, legislative and judicial branches. There is a bill of rights and provision for traditional rights. The executive comprises a federal president and vice-president, both of whom must be chosen from amongst the four nationally elected senators. There is a single-chamber Congress of 14 members, four members elected on a state-wide basis and ten members elected from congressional districts apportioned by population.

The judiciary is headed by the Supreme Court, which is divided into trial and appellate divisions. Below this, each state has its own judicial system.

The Compact of Free Association places full responsibility for the defence of the Federated States of Micronesia on the USA.

FEDERAL STRUCTURE

The Federated States of Micronesia is a federal republic of four constituent states: Chuuk, Kosrae, Pohnpei and Yap. Each of the constituent states has its own government and legislative system.

State	Area (sq. km)	Capital
Chuuk	127	Weno
Kosrae	109	Lelu
Pohnpei	344	Kolonia
Yap	119	Colonia

HEAD OF STATE

President, Joseph J. Urusemal, *elected* 10 May 2003
Vice-President, Redley Killion

CABINET as at July 2003
Economic Affairs, Sebastian Anefal
Finance and Administration, John Ehsa
Foreign Affairs, Ieske Iehsi
Health, Education and Social Services, Eliuel Pretrick
Justice, Paul McIlraith
Public Defender, Beauleen Worswick
Transportation, Communications and Infrastructure,
  Akillino Harris Susaia

BRITISH AMBASSADOR, HE Michael Price, LVO, resident at Suva, Fiji

ECONOMY

The economy is dependent mainly on subsistence agriculture, which employs almost half the population, and foreign aid. Copra and fish are the two main exports. The majority of the working population is engaged in government administration, subsistence farming, fishing, copra production and the tourist industry. Pepper is produced for export on Pohnpei and citrus fruits are commercially grown on Kosrae. The government derives a significant income from licensing fees paid by foreign vessels fishing for tuna and tuna processing plants are being constructed in Pohnpei and Kosrae. In November 2002 the Federated States of Micronesia signed a 20-year funding agreement with the USA under the Compact of Free Association.

GNP – US$250 million (2000); US$2,110 per capita (2000)

GDP – US$237 million (2001); US$1,934 per capita (2000)

Trade with UK	2001	2002
Imports from UK	£7,000	£10,000
Exports to UK	28,000	–

MOLDOVA

Republica Moldova – Republic of Moldova

AREA – 13,012 sq. miles (33,851 sq. km) Neighbours: Ukraine (north, east and south-east), Romania (west)

POPULATION – 4,335,000 (2001 estimate): 65 per cent are Moldovan, 14.2 per cent Ukrainian and 13 per cent Russian, together with smaller numbers of Gagauz (ethnic Turks), Jews and Bulgarians. Most of the population are adherents of the Moldovan Orthodox Church. Moldovan was made the official language (written in the Latin script) in 1989 but the use of Russian in official business is permitted

CAPITAL – Chişinău (population, 655,940, 1997 estimate)

CURRENCY – Moldovan leu of 100 bani (plural lei)

NATIONAL ANTHEM – Lîmbă Noastră (Our Language)

NATIONAL DAY – 27 August (Independence Day)

NATIONAL FLAG – Vertical stripes of blue, yellow, red, with the national arms in the centre

POPULATION GROWTH RATE – –0.2 per cent

POPULATION DENSITY – 129 per sq. km (1999)

MILITARY EXPENDITURE – 1.7 per cent of GDP (2001)

MILITARY PERSONNEL – 7,210: Army 5,560, Air Force 1,400; Paramilitaries 3,400

CONSCRIPTION DURATION – 12 months

ILLITERACY RATE – (m) 0.5 per cent; (f) 1.7 per cent (2000)

ENROLMENT (percentage of age group) – tertiary 27 per cent (1997)

HISTORY AND POLITICS

In the 15th century a Moldovan principality was formed which was absorbed into the Turkish Empire in the 16th century. Moldova was the site of many Russo-Turkish confrontations in the 18th century before the area between the Dniester and Prut rivers (later known as Bessarabia) was annexed to the Russian Empire by the Bucharest Peace Treaty of 1812.

After the Russian Revolution in 1917, an independent Moldovan state was proclaimed in Bessarabia, which came under the control of White Russian forces and was annexed to Romania under the Versailles Peace Treaty (1919). In 1924 the Moldavian Autonomous Soviet Socialist Republic (ASSR) was established on the east bank of the Dniester river as part of Soviet Ukraine. In

August 1940 the Soviet Union forced Romania to cede Bessarabia and the Moldavian Soviet Socialist Republic was formed from the majority of Bessarabia (the southernmost parts were incorporated into the Ukraine) and the Moldavian ASSR.

Moldova (formerly Moldavia) declared its independence from the USSR in August 1991. Reunification with Romania was rejected in a referendum on 6 March 1994, following which the Moldovan parliament voted to join the CIS.

Following the adoption in September 2000 of constitutional changes giving parliament the power to elect the president, a series of parliamentary votes was held in December 2000, in which none of the candidates were able to obtain the support of the required 61 members. In accordance with the constitutional changes, parliament was dissolved on 12 January 2001 and a general election was held on 25 February which was won by the Communist Party of Moldova (PCM), who obtained 71 seats. The new parliament elected the PCM leader, Vladimir Voronin, as president on 4 April 2001 and approved a new government, led by Vasile Tarlev, an independent MP.

INSURGENCIES

After independence was declared in 1991, the majority ethnic Romanian (Moldovan) population expressed a wish to rejoin Romania. This alienated the ethnic Ukrainian and Russian populations who form the majority east of the Dniester, and they declared their independence from Moldova as the Transdniester republic in December 1991. The Moldovan government refused to recognise this and in 1992 a war was waged between government forces and Transdniester forces, who were supported by local Russian soldiers and volunteers.

A mainly Russian CIS peacekeeping force (later changed to a joint Russian-Moldovan-Transdniester force) was deployed in July 1992 and a cease-fire has held since August 1992.

President Voronin and the leader of Transdniester, Igor Smirnov, agreed on 16 May 2001 to co-ordinate their policies on taxation and remove customs posts along the mutual border. In July 2001, a draft treaty on the status of Transdniestria was published. According to this draft, which was prepared with international mediators from Russia, Ukraine and the Organisation for Security and Co-operation in Europe, Moldova is to become a federal state, with each part of the federation having its own constitution. In September 2002 Transdniester authorities agreed to allow the resumption of the Russian withdrawal of weapons in exchange for a Russian promise to cut gas debts. In December 2002 the OSCE extended the deadline for the withdrawal of Russian weapons from Transdniester until the end of 2003. In February 2003 President Voronin called for the establishment of a joint commission with Transdniester to work out a new constitution.

POLITICAL SYSTEM

In July 1994 the Moldovan parliament adopted a new constitution which established a presidential parliamentary republic and provided for autonomous status for the Gagauz region, which was given its own elected National Assembly.

The unicameral Parliament is directly elected for a four-year term. It has 101 members.

The president is elected by parliament and must obtain

the support of at least 61 deputies. If no candidate achieves this, parliament must be dissolved and a general election held.

HEAD OF STATE
President, Vladimir Voronin, *elected by parliament*
 4 April 2001

GOVERNMENT *as at July 2003*
Prime Minister, Vasile Tarlev
First Deputy Prime Minister, Vasile Iovv
Deputy Prime Ministers, Dmitrii Todoroglo *(Agriculture and Food Industry);* Stefan Odagiu *(Economy and Trade);* Valerian Cristea *(Without Portfolio)*
Culture, Vyacheslav Madan
Defence, Victor Gaiciuc
Education and Science, Gheorghe Sima
Energy, Iacob Timciuc
Environment, Construction and Territorial Development, Gheorghe Duca
Finance, Zinaida Greceanii
Foreign Affairs, Nicolae Dudau
Health, Andrei Gherman
Industry and Trade, Mihail Garstea
Interior, Col. Gheorghe Papuc
Justice, Vasile Dulghieru
Labour, Social Protection and Family Affairs, Valerian Revenco
Reintegration, Vasile Sova
Transport and Communications, Vasile Zgardan

EMBASSY OF THE REPUBLIC OF MOLDOVA
Rue Tenbosch 54, Brussels 1050, Belgium
Tel: (00 32) (2) 732 9659
Minister Counsellor and Chargé d'Affaires, Emil Druc

BRITISH AMBASSADOR, HE Bernard Whiteside, CVO, CMG

ECONOMY
The main sector is agriculture, especially viniculture, fruit-growing and market gardening. Industry is small and concentrated east of the Dniester. In 1998, telecommunications, power and heating companies were privatised. Moldova is dependent on Russia for energy supplies and owes approximately US$6,000 million.

In 2001 there was a trade deficit of US$313 million and a current account deficit of US$118 million. In 1998 imports totalled US$1,018 million and exports US$644 million.

GNP – US$1,428 million (2000); US$400 per capita (2000)
GDP – US$1,478 million (2001); US$299 per capita (2000)
ANNUAL AVERAGE GROWTH OF GDP – –8.6 per cent (1998)
INFLATION RATE – 31.3 per cent (2000)
UNEMPLOYMENT – 8.5 per cent (2000)
TOTAL EXTERNAL DEBT – US$1,233 million (2000)

Trade with UK	2001	2002
Imports from UK	£9,195,000	£5,111,000
Exports to UK	4,667,000	2,978,000

MONACO

Principauté de Monaco - Principality of Monaco

AREA – 0.77 sq. miles (2 sq. km). Neighbour: France
POPULATION – 34,000 (2001). Only 7,175 residents have full Monégasque citizenship and thus the right to vote. The official language is French. Monégasque, a mixture of Provençal and Ligurian, is also spoken
CAPITAL – Monaco
CURRENCY – Euro (€) of 100 cents
NATIONAL ANTHEM – Hymne Monégasque (Monegasque Anthem)
NATIONAL DAY – 19 November
NATIONAL FLAG – Two equal horizontal stripes, red over white
LIFE EXPECTANCY (years) – 79 (2001)
POPULATION GROWTH RATE – 1.1 per cent

HISTORY AND POLITICS
The principality, ruled by the Grimaldi family since 1297, was abolished during the French Revolution and re-established in 1815 under the protection of the kingdom of Sardinia. In 1861 Monaco came under French protection.

The 1962 constitution, which can be modified only with the approval of the National Council, maintains the traditional hereditary monarchy and guarantees freedom of association, trade union freedom and the right to strike. Legislative power is held jointly by the Prince and a unicameral, 24-member National Council elected by universal suffrage. Executive power is exercised by the Prince and a four-member Council of Government, headed by a Minister of State, who is nominated by the Prince from a list of three French diplomats submitted by the French government. The judicial code is based on that of France. In the legislative elections of 9 February 2003 the Union for Monaco (UPM) won 21 seats, defeating the National and Democratic Union, which had been in power for most of the previous 40 years.

HEAD OF STATE
HSH The Prince of Monaco, Prince Rainier III Louis-Henri-Maxence Bertrand, *born* 31 May 1923, *succeeded* 9 May 1949; *married* 19 April 1956, Miss Grace Patricia Kelly (died 14 September 1982) and *has issue* Prince Albert; Princess Caroline Louise Marguerite, *born* 23 January 1957; and Princess Stephanie Marie Elisabeth, *born* 1 February 1965
Heir, HRH Prince Albert Alexandre Louis Pierre, *born* 14 March 1958

President of the Crown Council, Charles Ballerio
President of the National Council, Stephane Valeri
Minister of State, Patrick Leclercq
Finance and Economy, Franck Biancheri
Interior, Philippe Deslandes
Public Works and Social Affairs, José Badia

CONSULATE-GENERAL OF MONACO
4 Cromwell Place, London SW7 2JE
Tel: 020-7225 2679
Consul-General, Ivan Bozidar Ivanovic

BRITISH CONSULATE-GENERAL
33 Boulevard Princesse Charlotte, BP 265, MC 98005
Monaco CEDEX
Tel: (00 377) 93 50 99 66
Consul-General, I. Davies

ECONOMY
The whole available ground is built over so that there is no cultivation, though there are some notable public and private gardens. The economy is based on real estate revenues, the financial sector and tourism. There is a small harbour (30 ft alongside quay). Monaco has been in a customs union with the European Union since 1984.
GDP – US$814 million (1998); US$21,848 per capita (2001)
ANNUAL AVERAGE GROWTH OF GDP – 3.3 per cent (1998)

MONGOLIA

Mongol Uls - Mongol State

AREA – 604,829 sq. miles (1,566,500 sq. km).
  Neighbours: Russia (north), China (south)
POPULATION – 2,654,999 (2001 estimate). Mongolians also live in China and in the neighbouring regions of Russia, especially the Mongolian Buryat Autonomous Region. The official language is Khalkha Mongolian
CAPITAL – Ulaanbaatar (population, 515,100, 1998 estimate)
CURRENCY – Tugrik of 100 möngö
NATIONAL ANTHEM – Mongol Ulsiin Teriin Duulal (Mongol National Anthem)
NATIONAL DAY – 11 July
NATIONAL FLAG – Vertical tricolour red, blue, red and in the hoist the traditional Soyombo symbol in gold
POPULATION GROWTH RATE – 3.3 per cent
POPULATION DENSITY – 2 per sq. km (1999)
MILITARY EXPENDITURE – 2.4 per cent of GDP (2001)
MILITARY PERSONNEL – 9,100: Army 7,500, Air Defence 800; Paramilitaries 7,200
CONSCRIPTION DURATION – 12 months
ILLITERACY RATE – (m) 0.8 per cent; (f) 0.7 per cent (2000)
ENROLMENT (percentage of age group) – primary 88 per cent (1997); secondary 56 per cent (1997); tertiary 17.0 per cent (1997)

Mongolia, most of which is at least 1,000 metres above sea level, forms part of the central Asiatic plateau and rises towards the west in the mountains of the Mongolian Altai and Hangai ranges. The Gobi region covers much of the southern half of the country and contains sand deserts interspersed with semi-desert.

HISTORY AND POLITICS
Mongolia, under Genghis Khan the conqueror of China and much of Asia, was for many years a buffer state between Tsarist Russia and China, although it was under general Chinese suzerainty. The Mongolian People's Republic was formally established in 1924. Under the Yalta Agreement, President Chiang Kai-shek of China agreed to a plebiscite, held in 1945, in which the Mongolians declared their desire for independence and this was formally recognised by China.

The Mongolian People's Revolutionary Party (MPRP) was the sole political party from 1924 to 1990. Demonstrations in favour of political and economic reform began in December 1989 and led to changes in the MPRP leadership in March 1990. The MPRP's constitutionally guaranteed monopoly of power was subsequently relinquished, and the introduction of a multiparty system was approved by the Great People's Hural (parliament). The MPRP won the first multiparty elections, held in July 1990. The country's first direct presidential election was held in 1993 and won by the incumbent Punsalmaagiyn Ochirbat, who stood as an opposition candidate after the MPRP refused to endorse him as its candidate; he was ousted in 1997 by the leader of the MPRP, Natsagyn Bagabandi, who won a second term of office in 2001, obtaining 58.13 per cent of the votes cast. The 1996 legislative election was won by the Democratic Union Coalition (Mongolian National Democratic Party and Mongolian Social Democratic Party). The legislative election held in July 2000 resulted in victory for the MPRP, who gained 72 seats.

POLITICAL SYSTEM
A new constitution was approved in January 1992 which established a democratic parliamentary system of government. The president is directly elected for a term of four years. The unicameral legislature is the State Great Hural (Ulsyn Ikh Khural), which has 76 members elected for four-year terms by a simple majority amounting to at least 25 per cent of the votes cast. In July 2000 a constitutional amendment came into force which gives the president the right to dissolve the Great State Hural if it is unable to reach agreement on appointing a prime minister.

HEAD OF STATE
President, Natsagyn Bagabandi, *elected* 18 May 1997, *re-elected* 20 May 2001

CABINET *as at July 2003*
Prime Minister, Nambariyn Enkhbayar
Defence, Jugderdemidyn Gurragchaa
Education, Culture and Science, Ayurzanyn Tsanjid
Environment, Ulambaryn Barsbold
Finance and Economy, Chultemiyn Ulaan
Food and Agriculture, Darjaagyn Nasanjargal
Foreign Affairs, Luvsangyn Erdenechuluun
Government Secretariat, Ulziysaihany Enkhtuvshin
Health, Pagvajavyn Nyamdavaa
Industry and Commerce, Chimidzorigyn Ganzorig
Infrastructure, Byambyn Jigjid
Justice and Internal Affairs, Tsendyn Nyamdorj
Social Welfare and Labour, Shiylegiyn Batbayar

EMBASSY OF MONGOLIA
7 Kensington Court, London W8 5DL
Tel: 020-7937 0150
Ambassador Extraordinary and Plenipotentiary, HE
  Davaasambuu Dalrain, apptd 2001

BRITISH EMBASSY
30 Enkh Taivny Gudamzh (PO Box 703), Ulaanbaatar 13.
Tel: (00 976) (11) 458133
Email: britemb@magicnet.mn
Ambassador Extraordinary and Plenipotentiary, HE Philip
  Rouse, MBE, apptd 2001

ECONOMY
Traditionally the Mongolians led a nomadic life tending flocks of sheep, goats, horses, cows and camels. Collectivisation at the end of the 1950s into huge negdels (co-operatives) and state farms hastened the process of settlement, but within these the herdsmen and their families still move with their traditional gers (circular tents) from pasture to pasture as the seasons change.

The semi-desert areas of the Gobi region provide

pasture for sheep, goats, camels, horses and some cattle. In the steppe areas to the north of the Gobi pasturage is better and livestock more abundant. Even further north, in the better-watered provinces, grain, fodder and vegetable crops are grown.

Although the economy remains predominantly pastoral, factories have started up, coal, copper and molybdenum are mined and the electricity industry has been developed. Ulaanbaatar and Darkhan are the main seats of industry, which includes lime, cement and building materials, a flour mill and a power station. Choibalsan is also being developed industrially.

A prolonged drought and exceptionally severe winters in 1999–2000 and 2001–2 decimated livestock and destroyed the livelihood of thousands of families. In May 2001, international donors promised US$330 million in aid.

A law privatising land ownership came into force on 1 May 2003, with privatisation due to be completed by 28 June 2005.

GNP – US$947 million (2000); US$390 per capita (2000)
GDP – US$1,049 million (2001); US$391 per capita (2000)
ANNUAL AVERAGE GROWTH OF GDP – 3.5 per cent (1998)
INFLATION RATE – 7.6 per cent (1999)
UNEMPLOYMENT – 5.7 per cent (1998)
TOTAL EXTERNAL DEBT – US$859 million (2000)

TRADE
Foreign trade was formerly dominated by the Soviet Union and other Eastern bloc countries, but trade with Western countries, Japan and South Korea is now increasing. Since 1991, trade has been in hard currency, causing particular strain. The principal exports are animal by-products (especially wool, hides and furs) and cattle.

In 1999 there was a trade deficit of US$56 million and a current account deficit of US$112 million. Imports totalled US$426 million and exports US$233 million.

Trade with UK	2001	2002
Imports from UK	£2,405,000	£2,436,000
Exports to UK	8,923,000	3,556,000

MOROCCO

Al-Mamlaka Al-Maghribiyya - Kingdom of Morocco

AREA – 171,654 sq. miles (446,300 sq. km).
   Neighbours: Algeria (east and south-east), Western Sahara (south-west)
POPULATION – 30,430,000 (2001). Standard Arabic is the official language. Maghrebi Arabic and various Berber languages (Tachelhit, Tamazight and Tarafit) are the vernacular. French and Spanish are also spoken, mainly in the towns. Islam is the state religion
CAPITAL – ΨRabat (population, 1,385,872, 1994 census)
MAJOR CITIES – ΨAgadir (923,000); ΨCasablanca (Ad-Dar-el-Beida) (3,100,000); Fez (554,000); Marrakesh (878,000); Meknès (614,000); Oujda (430,000), 1997 estimates
CURRENCY – Dirham (DH) of 100 centimes
NATIONAL ANTHEM – Hymne Cherifien
NATIONAL DAY – 30 July (Anniversary of the Throne)
NATIONAL FLAG – Red, with green pentagram
LIFE EXPECTANCY (years) – 68 (2001)

POPULATION GROWTH RATE – 1.9 per cent
POPULATION DENSITY – 68 per sq. km (2001)
URBAN POPULATION – 33 per cent (2001)

Morocco is traversed in the north by the Rif mountains and, in a south-west to north-east direction, by the Middle Atlas, the High Atlas, the Anti-Atlas and the Sarrho ranges. The north-westerly point of Morocco is the peninsula of Tangier dominated by the Jebel Mousa which, with the rocky eminence of Gibraltar, was known to the ancients as the Pillars of Hercules, the western gateway of the Mediterranean.

HISTORY AND POLITICS
Morocco became an independent sovereign state in 1956, following joint declarations made with France on 2 March 1956 and with Spain on 7 April 1956. The Sultan of Morocco, Sidi Mohammad ben Youssef, adopted the title of King Mohammad V.

Elections to the Chamber of Councillors were held in September 2000. In elections to the House of Representatives on 27 September 2002, the USFP and the Independence Party remained the two largest parties. Driss Jetou was appointed prime minister on 9 October and a coalition government was named on 8 November 2002.

POLITICAL SYSTEM
The King nominates the prime minister and, on the latter's recommendation, appoints the members of the Council of Ministers. The government is responsible both to parliament and to the King. There is a bicameral legislature. The House of Representatives (Majlis al-Nuwab) has 325 members elected for a five-year term by universal suffrage using a first-past-the-post system. The Chamber of Councillors (Majlis al-Mustashareen) has 270 members, 60 per cent of whom are elected by local councils, 20 per cent by employers' associations and 20 per cent by trade unions. One-third of its members are elected every three years.

HEAD OF STATE
HM The King of Morocco, King Mohammed VI (Sidi Mohammed Ben Hassan), *born* 21 August 1963, *acceded* 23 July 1999

COUNCIL OF MINISTERS *as at July 2003*
Prime Minister, Driss Jetou
Agriculture and Rural Development, Mohand Laenser
Communications, Government Spokesman, Nabil Benabdallah
Culture, Mohamed Achaari
Employment, Social Affairs and Solidarity, Mustapha Mansouri
Energy and Mines, Mohammed Boutaleb
Equipment and Transport, Karim Ghellab
Finance and Privatisation, Fathallah Oualaou
Foreign Affairs and Co-operation, Mohamed Ben Aissa
Foreign Trade, Mustapha Mechahouri
General Secretary of the Government, Abdessadek Rabiaa
Handicrafts and Social Economy, Mohamed el-Khalifa
Health, Mohammed Cheikh Biadillah
Higher Education and Scientific Research, Khalid Alioua
Human Rights, Mohamed Aujjar
Industry, Commerce and Telecommunications, Rachid Talbi al-Alami
Interior Affairs, Al Mustapha Sahel
Justice, Mohamed Bouzoubaa

Marine Fisheries, Mohammed Taieb Rhafes
Minister of State, Abbas el-Fassi
Modernisation of the Public Sector, Najib Zerouali
National Education and Youth, Habib el-Malki
Relations with Parliament, Mohammed Saad el-Alami
*Town and Country Planning, Environment and Water
  Resources,* Mohamed el-Yazghi
Tourism, Adil Douiri
Waqf and Islamic Affairs, Ahmed Toufiq

EMBASSY OF THE KINGDOM OF MOROCCO
49 Queen's Gate Gardens, London SW7 5NE
Tel: 020-7581 5001/4
Ambassador Extraordinary and Plenipotentiary, HE
  Mohammed Belmahi, apptd 1999

BRITISH EMBASSY
17 Boulevard de la Tour Hassan (BP 45), Rabat
Tel: (00 212) (0) 37 238600
Email: consular.rabat@fco.gov.uk
Ambassador Extraordinary and Plenipotentiary, HE
  Haydon Warren-Gash, apptd 2002
CONSULATE-GENERAL – Casablanca
CONSULATES – Agadir, Marrakesh, Tangier

BRITISH COUNCIL DIRECTOR, Steve McNulty
BP 427, 36 rue de Tanger, Rabat
Email: britcoun.morocco@britishcouncil.org.ma

DEFENCE

The Army has 744 main battle tanks, 115 armoured
infantry fighting vehicles, and 740 armoured personnel
carriers.

The Navy has two frigates and 27 patrol and coastal
combatant vessels at five bases. The Air Force has 95
combat aircraft and 24 armed helicopters.
MILITARY EXPENDITURE – 4.2 per cent of GDP (2001)
MILITARY PERSONNEL – 196,300: Army 175,000,
  Navy 7,800, Air Force 13,500; Paramilitaries 50,000
CONSCRIPTION DURATION – 18 months

ECONOMY

Morocco's main sources of wealth are agricultural and
mineral. A large-scale privatisation programme has
attracted substantial foreign investment. Agriculture
contributes 17 per cent of GDP and employs 38.5 per
cent of the workforce. The main agricultural exports are
fruit and vegetables, with cereals and sugar beet produced
and sheep reared for domestic consumption. Cork and
wood pulp are the most important commercial forest
products. There is a fishing industry and substantial
quantities of canned fish are exported.

For a developing country Morocco has a large
industrial sector. The main sectors are chemicals, textiles
and leather goods, food processing and cement
production. Manufacturing industries are centred in
Casablanca, Fez, Tangier and Safi.

Morocco's mineral exports are phosphates, fluorite,
barite, manganese, iron ore, lead, zinc, cobalt, copper and
antimony. Morocco possesses nearly three-quarters of the
world's estimated reserves of phosphates. There are oil
refineries at Mohammedia and Sidi Kacem handling
about four million tonnes of crude oil a year.

Morocco has a high proportion of public employees;
the salaries of its 750,000 civil servants consume about
12 per cent of the country's GDP.
GNP – US$33,940 million (2000); US$1,180 per capita
  (2000)

GDP – US$33,733 million (2001); US$1,101 per capita
  (2000)
ANNUAL AVERAGE GROWTH OF GDP – 0.9 per cent
  (2000)
INFLATION RATE – 1.9 per cent (2000)
UNEMPLOYMENT – 22.0 per cent (1999)
TOTAL EXTERNAL DEBT – US$17,944 million (2000)

TRADE
The main imports are petroleum products, machinery,
chemical products, iron and steel, grain and textiles. The
EU, with which an association agreement was signed in
1995, is Morocco's largest trading partner and in 1998
awarded Morocco grants totalling US$98 million. The
main exports are phosphates and phosphoric acid,
textiles and leather, and fish and agricultural products.

In 2000 Morocco had a trade deficit of US$3,235
million and a current account deficit of US$501 million.
In 2001 imports totalled US$10,962 million and exports
US$7,123 million.

Trade with UK	2001	2002
Imports from UK	£370,602,000	£351,019,000
Exports to UK	456,682,000	470,869,000

COMMUNICATIONS

Railroads cover 1,907 km, linking the major towns.
There are 60,449 km of roads; an extensive network of
30,374 km of surfaced roads covers all the main towns.
There are air services between Casablanca, Tangier,
Agadir (seasonal), Marrakesh and London, and also
between Tangier and Gibraltar connecting with London.
Royal Air Maroc is the national airline.

EDUCATION

Education is compulsory between the ages of seven and
16. There are government primary, secondary and
technical schools. At Fez there is a theological university
of great repute in the Muslim world. There is a secular
university at Rabat. Schools for special denominations,
Jewish and Catholic, are permitted and may receive
government grants. American schools operate in Rabat
and Casablanca. There is an English-language university
in Ifrane.
ILLITERACY RATE – (m) 38.1 per cent; (f) 63.9 per cent
  (2000)
ENROLMENT (percentage of age group) – primary
  86 per cent (1997); secondary 39 per cent (1997);
  tertiary 11 per cent (1997)

WESTERN SAHARA

*Al-Jumhūriyya al-'Arabiyya as-Ṣahrāwiyya
ad-Dimuqrātiyya – Sahrawi Arab Democratic Republic*

AREA – 97,344 sq. miles (252,120 sq. km) Neighbours:
  Morocco (north), Algeria (north-east), Mauritania (east
  and south)
POPULATION – 244,943 (2000 estimate). Arabic is the
  official language. Hassaniya and Moroccan Arabic are
  the main spoken languages; Spanish is widely spoken
  in the towns. Almost all the population is Sunni
  Muslim
CAPITAL – El-Aaiūn (population, 139,000, 1990
  estimate)
NATIONAL FLAG – Three horizontal stripes of black,
  white and green with a red crescent and five-pointed
  star in the centre and red triangle based on the hoist

POPULATION GROWTH RATE – 3.4 per cent (1999)
POPULATION DENSITY – 1 per sq. km (1999)

Formerly the Spanish Sahara, the territory was split between Morocco and Mauritania in 1976 after Spain withdrew in December 1975. In 1976 the Polisario Front (Frente Popular para la Liberación de Saguia y Río de Oro) declared Western Sahara to be an independent state, the Sahrawi Arab Democratic Republic, and formed a government which remains in exile. The Polisario Front has been recognised as the legitimate government of Western Sahara by over 70 states and the Organisation of African Unity. In 1979 Mauritania renounced its claim to its share of the territory, which was added by Morocco to its area.

About 167,000 Sahrawis are in exile in Algeria and 15,000 in Mauritania.

In 1988, Morocco and the Polisario Front accepted a UN peace plan under which a cease-fire came into effect in 1991. A referendum to determine the future of the area was to have been held in 1992 but has not yet taken place because the Moroccan government and Polisario have not agreed on the referendum terms or voter eligibility. Voter identification began in 1994 but the failure to agree on eligibility prompted the UN to threaten the suspension of the UN Mission for the Referendum in Western Sahara (MINURSO), which had been deployed since 1991.

In 2000, representatives of the Moroccan government and Polisario held negotiations to discuss differences that prevented the implementation of the UN-mediated referendum. The talks failed when Polisario refused to discuss a Moroccan proposal that the territory accept autonomy status within Morocco. In September 2001, Polisario also rejected a UN peace plan which proposed replacing a referendum by a political arrangement whereby Western Sahara would operate for the following five years as a semi-autonomous territory with Morocco maintaining sovereignty. Legislative elections to the National Assembly were held in 1995; President Mohamed Abdelaziz, who had been elected president since 1982 by the party congress of the Polisario Front, was re-elected by the National Assembly in 1995. Following a vote of no confidence in the previous incumbent, Bouchraya Hamoudi Bayoun was named Prime Minister on 10 February 1999.

The UN has some 231 personnel in Western Sahara pending the referendum (*see* above). The Polisario Front deploys 3,000–6,000 troops in Western Sahara with Algerian-supplied and captured Moroccan tanks, armoured personnel carriers, anti-tank and anti-aircraft weapons.

MOZAMBIQUE

República de Moçambique – Republic of Mozambique

AREA – 301,577 sq. miles (784,100 sq. km).
 Neighbours: Swaziland (south), South Africa (south and west), Zimbabwe (west), Zambia and Malawi (north-west), Tanzania (north)
POPULATION – 18,644,000 (2001). The official language is Portuguese
CAPITAL – ΨMaputo (population, 1,039,700, 1998 census)
MAJOR CITIES – ΨBeira (397,368); ΨMatola (424,662); Nampula (303,346), 1997 census
CURRENCY – Metical (MT) of 100 centavos

NATIONAL ANTHEM – Hino Nacional (National Anthem)
NATIONAL DAY – 25 June (Independence Day)
NATIONAL FLAG – Horizontally green, black, yellow with white fimbriations; a red triangle based on the hoist containing the national emblem
LIFE EXPECTANCY (years) – 39 (2001)
POPULATION GROWTH RATE – 2.8 per cent
POPULATION DENSITY – 24 per sq. km (2001)
MILITARY EXPENDITURE – 1.9 per cent of GDP (2001)
MILITARY PERSONNEL – 11,150: Army 10,000, Navy 150, Air Force 1,000
CONSCRIPTION DURATION – Two years
ILLITERACY RATE – (m) 39.9 per cent; (f) 71.3 per cent (2000)
ENROLMENT (percentage of age group) – primary 60 per cent (1997); secondary 7 per cent (1997); tertiary 1 per cent (1997)

HISTORY AND POLITICS

Mozambique, discovered by Vasco da Gama in 1498 and colonised by Portugal, achieved independence on 25 June 1975. It was a Marxist one-party (Frelimo) state until a multiparty system was adopted in 1990.

The Frelimo government and the rebel Mozambican National Resistance (Renamo) signed a peace agreement in 1992 which ended 16 years of civil war. Demobilisation of government and Renamo troops took place in 1994.

Presidential and legislative elections were held on 3–5 December 1999. The incumbent, Joaquim Chissano of Frelimo, won the presidential election with 52.3 per cent of the vote. Frelimo also won the legislative election, gaining 133 seats to Renamo's 117, amid allegations by Renamo of vote-rigging. No other parties were able to secure the 5 per cent of the total vote necessary to obtain representation.

Mozambique was admitted to the Commonwealth on 12 November 1995 as a special case, because of its close links with Commonwealth countries.

POLITICAL SYSTEM

The president is directly elected and serves a term of five years, which is renewable no more than twice consecutively. The unicameral legislature, the Assembly of the Republic (Assembleia Da Republica), is directly elected for a five-year term and comprises 250 members.

HEAD OF STATE

President, Joaquim Alberto Chissano, *sworn in* November 1986, *elected* 29 October 1994, *re-elected* 5 December 1999

COUNCIL OF MINISTERS *as at July 2003*
Prime Minister, Pascoal Mocumbi
Agriculture and Rural Development, Helder Monteiro Culture,* Miguel Costa Mkaima
Education, Alcido Nguenha
Environmental Action Co-ordination, John Katchamila
Fisheries, Cadmiel Muthemba
Foreign Affairs and Co-operation, Leonardo Simão
Health, Francisco Songane
Higher Education, Science and Technology, Lidia Brito
Independence War Veterans, Gen. (retd) António Hama Thay
Industry and Commerce, Carlos Morgado
Justice, José Abudo
Labour, Mario Sevene

Mineral Resources and Energy, Castigo Langa
Ministers in the President's Office, Almirinho da Cruz
  Manhenje *(Defence, Security Affairs and Interior);*
  Francisco Madeira *(Parliamentary and Diplomatic
  Affairs)*
National Defence, Tobias Dai
Planning and Finance, Luisa Diogo
Public Works and Housing, Roberto White
State Administration, José Ehichana
Tourism, Fernando Sumbane Junior
Transport and Communications, Tomas Salomao
Women's Affairs and Social Welfare Action Co-ordination,
  Virginia Matabele
Youth and Sports, Joel Libombo

HIGH COMMISSION FOR THE REPUBLIC OF
MOZAMBIQUE
21 Fitzroy Square, London W1T 6EL
Tel: 020-7383 3800
High Commissioner, HE Antonio Gumende, apptd 2002

BRITISH HIGH COMMISSION
Av. Vladimir I Lenine 310, Box 55, Maputo
Tel: (00 258) (1) 320111/2/5/6/7
Email: bhc@virconn.com
High Commissioner, HE Robert Dewar, apptd 2000

BRITISH COUNCIL DIRECTOR, Simon Ingram-Hill
Rua John Issa 226, PO Box 4178, Maputo
Tel: (00 258) (1) 310 921
Email: general.enquiries@britishcouncil.org.mz

ECONOMY
The basis of the economy is subsistence agriculture, but
there is an industrial sector based mainly in Beira and
Maputo. There are substantial coal deposits in Tete
province and an offshore gas field at Pande. Economic
subsidies have been removed and an IMF reform
programme is being implemented. The economy is still
heavily dependent on aid. A five-year plan has been
launched with the priorities of rural development,
education, health and land reform.

Severe flooding in February 2000 and again in January
and February 2001 caused widespread devastation,
affecting nearly a quarter of the population and
destroying crops, homes and much of the infrastructure.
Further flooding in January and February 2001 resulted
in some 700,000 people becoming homeless and 35,000
hectares of crops lost. In 2002, a severe drought occurred
in many central and southern parts of the country,
including previously flood-stricken areas.
GNP – US$3,746 million (2000); US$210 per capita
  (2000)
GDP – US$3,561 million (2001); US$195 per capita
  (2000)
ANNUAL AVERAGE GROWTH OF GDP – 9.0 per cent
  (1999)
INFLATION RATE – 15.2 per cent (2002)
TOTAL EXTERNAL DEBT – US$7,135 million (2000)

TRADE
The main exports are shellfish, cotton, sugar, cashew
nuts, copra, tea and sisal. Mozambique's main trading
partners are South Africa, Portugal, Spain and Japan.

In 2000 Mozambique had a trade deficit of US$682
million and a current account deficit of US$764 million.
In 2000 imports totalled US$1,158 million and exports
US$364 million.

Trade with UK	2001	2002
Imports from UK	£12,625,000	£13,671,000
Exports to UK	7,549,000	3,896,000

MYANMAR

Pyidaungsu Myanmar Naingngandaw – Union of Myanmar

AREA – 261,228 sq. miles (676,578 sq. km).
  Neighbours: Bangladesh (west), India (north-west),
  China (north-east), Laos and Thailand (east)
POPULATION – 41,994,678 (2001 estimate). The
  indigenous inhabitants are of similar racial types and
  speak languages of the Tibeto-Burman, Mon-Khmer
  and Thai groups. The three significant non-indigenous
  elements are Indians, Chinese and Bangladeshis.
  Burmese is the official language, but minority
  languages include Bamar, Chin, Kachin, Kayah, Kayin
  (Karen), Mon, Rakhine and Shan. English is spoken in
  educated circles. Buddhism is the religion of 89.3 per
  cent of the people, with 5.6 per cent Christians, 3.8
  per cent Muslims, 0.2 per cent Animists and 0.5 per
  cent Hindus
CAPITAL – ΨRangoon (population, 2,513,023, 1983)
MAJOR CITIES – Mandalay (532,949);
  Mawlamyine/Moulmein (219,961); Pathein/Bassein
  (144,096)
CURRENCY – Kyat (K) of 100 pyas
NATIONAL ANTHEM - Gba Majay Myanmar (We Shall
  Love Myanmar For Ever)
NATIONAL DAY – 4 January
NATIONAL FLAG – Red, with a canton of dark blue,
  inside which are a cogwheel and two rice ears
  surrounded by 14 white stars
POPULATION GROWTH RATE – 1.2 per cent
POPULATION DENSITY – 67 per sq. km (1999)

HISTORY AND POLITICS
The Union of Burma (the name was officially changed to
the Union of Myanmar in 1989) became an independent
republic outside the British Commonwealth on 4 January
1948 and remained a parliamentary democracy for 14
years. In 1962 the army took power, suspended the
parliamentary constitution and instituted a socialist state.

After months of popular demonstrations and a series of
presidents during 1988, Gen. Saw Maung, leader of the
armed forces, assumed power in September 1988. The
People's Assembly, the Council of State and the Council
of Ministers were abolished and replaced by the State
Law and Order Restoration Council (SLORC).

A People's Assembly Election Law was published in
1989 and multiparty elections were held in 1990,
resulting in a majority for the National League for
Democracy (NLD) even though its leader Aung San Suu
Kyi had been under house arrest since July 1989. The
SLORC refused to transfer power to a civilian
government and large numbers of NLD MPs and
supporters were detained or fled to Thailand where an
exile government was set up. The SLORC released Aung
San Suu Kyi (who won the Nobel Peace Prize in 1991) in
1995, although on several occasions subsequently she
was forcibly prevented from attending political meetings
by government troops and was placed under house arrest
a second time from 2000–2. Many other opposition
figures remain in detention or under house arrest. In
1997, the SLORC was renamed the State Peace and
Development Council (SPDC).

The SPDC detained several hundred NLD members in

September 1998 to thwart the NLD's plan to convene a 'People's Parliament' representing the assembly which would have resulted from the 1990 general election. Instead, the NLD set up an interim representation committee to act on behalf of the 'People's Parliament'. UN-brokered talks between Aung San Suu Kyi and the government began in 2000 and since then about 400 dissidents have been released from prison and Aung San Suu Kyi was released from house arrest in May 2002. However, the reconciliation talks have stalled and in May 2003 Aung San Suu Kyi was taken into 'protective custody' following clashes between her supporters and those of the government.

POLITICAL SYSTEM

The constitution was effectively abrogated in 1988 when the executive and legislature were abolished and replaced by the SLORC. There are no permitted political parties.

INSURGENCIES

Since independence in 1948 the government has fought various armed insurgent groups, the largest of which were derived from the Kachin, Kayin (Karen), Karenni, and Wa ethnic groups but the Shan, Mon, Arakan and Chin ethnic minorities have also formed armed groups.

Since 1992, as a result of government offensives, 15 ethnic groups have signed cease-fire agreements with the government. In November 1999, the government launched a military offensive against Kayin (Karen) National Union (KNU) guerrillas and their allies in Karen state.

STATE PEACE AND DEVELOPMENT COUNCIL *as at July 2003*

Chairman, Senior Gen. Than Shwe
Vice-Chairman, Gen. Maung Aye
Members, Rear-Adm. Nyunt Thein; Maj.-Gen. Kyaw Than; Maj.-Gen. Aung Htwe; Maj.-Gen. Ye Myint; Maj.-Gen. Khin Maung Than; Maj.-Gen. Kyaw Win; Maj.-Gen. Thein Sein; Maj.-Gen. Thura Thiha Thura Sit Maung; Brig.-Gen. Thura Shwe Mahn; Brig.-Gen. Myint Aung; Brig.-Gen. Maung Bo; Brig.-Gen. Thiha Thura Tin Aung Myint Oo; Brig.-Gen. Tin Aye
Secretaries, Lt.-Gen. Khin Nyunt, Lt.-Gen. Soe Win

CABINET *as at July 2003*

Prime Minister, Defence, Senior Gen. Than Shwe
Agriculture and Irrigation, Maj.-Gen. Nyunt Tin
Commander in Chief of the Navy, Minister in charge of Political, Economic and Social Tasks within his Command, Vice-Adm. Kyi Min
Commander of Coastal Military Command, Minister in charge of Political, Economic and Social Tasks within his Command, Maj.-Gen. Aye Kywe
Commerce, Brig.-Gen. Pyi Sone
Construction, Maj.-Gen. Saw Tun
Co-operatives, Lt.-Gen. Tin Ngwe
Culture, Maj.-Gen. Kyi Aung
Education, U Than Aung
Electric Power, Maj.-Gen. Tin Htut
Energy, Brig.-Gen. Lun Thi
Finance and Revenue, Maj.-Gen. Hla Tun
First Minister for Industry, Col. U Aung Thaung
Foreign Affairs, U Win Aung
Forestry, U Aung Phone
Health, Kyaw Myint
Home Affairs, Col. Tin Hlaing

Information, Brig.-Gen. Kyaw Hsan
Livestock Breeding and Fisheries, Brig.-Gen. Maung Maung Thein
Mines, Brig.-Gen. Ohn Myint
Minister in the Prime Minister's Office, Labour, U Tin Win
Ministers in the Office of the SPDC Chairman, Lt.-Gen. Min Thein; Brig.-Gen. David Abel
National Planning and Economic Development, U Soe Tha
Prime Minister's Office, Lt.-Col. U Pan Aung; U Than Shwe
Progress of Border Areas and National Races, Development Affairs, Col. Thein Nyunt
Rail Transport, Maj.-Gen. Aung Min
Religious Affairs, Col. U Aung Khin
Second Minister for Industry, Hotels and Tourism, Maj.-Gen. Saw Lwin
Science and Technology, Lt.-Col. U Thaung
Social Welfare, Relief and Resettlement, Immigration and Population, Maj.-Gen. Sein Htwa
Sports, Brig.-Gen. Thura Aye Myint
Telecommunications, Posts and Telegraphs, Brig.-Gen. Thein Zaw
Transport, Maj.-Gen. Hla Myint Swe

EMBASSY OF THE UNION OF MYANMAR

19A Charles Street, Berkeley Square, London W1J 5DX
Tel: 020-7499 8841
Ambassador Extraordinary and Plenipotentiary, HE Dr Kyaw Win, apptd 1999

BRITISH EMBASSY

80 Strand Road (Box No. 638), Rangoon Tel: (00 95) (1) 256918
Ambassador Extraordinary and Plenipotentiary, HE Victoria Bowman, apptd 2002

BRITISH COUNCIL DIRECTOR, Graham Millington *(Cultural Attaché),* 78 Kanna Road, PO Box 638, Rangoon
Email: enquiries@britishcouncil.org.mm

DEFENCE

The Army has some 100 main battle tanks and 270 armoured personnel carriers. The Navy has 73 patrol and coastal vessels at six bases. The Air Force has 113 combat aircraft and 29 armed helicopters.

MILITARY EXPENDITURE – 2.4 per cent of GDP (2001)
MILITARY PERSONNEL – 344,000: Army 325,000, Navy 10,000, Air Force 9,000, Paramilitaries 100,250

ECONOMY

Myanmar is rich in minerals, including petroleum, zinc, nickel, lead, silver, tungsten, wolfram and gemstones. There are refineries at Chauk, the main oilfield, Syriam and Mann. Major reserves of natural gas have been discovered in the Martaban Gulf. However, key industries are controlled by military-run enterprises.

Since 1988, Myanmar has moved from a centrally planned economy to a market-oriented economy and has liberalised domestic and external trade, promoted the development of the private sector and encouraged foreign investment.

Myanmar is thought to be the world's leading producer of heroin, and although the government claims to be attempting to stamp out production, the armed forces are believed to be involved in large-scale trafficking.

The principal exports are agricultural, forestry and fish products, minerals and precious stones. The principal imports are capital goods, chiefly transport equipment, machinery and plant, consumer goods and semi-manufactures.

In July 1997, Myanmar became a member of ASEAN. In 1997 the EU stripped Myanmar of trading privileges and the USA imposed economic sanctions; in July 2003 the USA imposed further sanctions on the Burmese government.

In 2000 there was a trade deficit of US$516 million and a current account deficit of US$243 million. In 2001 imports totalled US$2,767 million and exports US$2,271 million.

GDP – US$12,557 million (1998); US$1,816 per capita (2000)

ANNUAL AVERAGE GROWTH OF GDP – 6.2 per cent (2000)

INFLATION RATE – –0.1 per cent (2000)

TOTAL EXTERNAL DEBT – US$6,046 million (2000)

Trade with UK	2001	2002
Imports from UK	£9,452,000	£7,345,000
Exports to UK	66,634,000	64,337,000

COMMUNICATIONS

The Irrawaddy and its chief tributary, the Chindwin, are important waterways, the main stream being navigable 900 miles from its mouth and carrying much traffic. The chief seaports are Rangoon, Mawlamyine (Moulmein), Akyab (Sittwe) and Pathein (Bassein).

The railway network covers 3,955 km, extending to Myitkyina on the Upper Irrawaddy. There are 2,452 miles of highways and 14,318 miles of other main roads. The airport at Mingaladon, about 13 miles north of Rangoon, handles limited international air traffic.

EDUCATION

Most children attend primary school, and nearly five million are currently enrolled; in middle and high schools, enrolment is over two million. There are 16 universities, nine degree-awarding colleges and 87 other higher education institutions.

Vocational training is provided at 17 teachers' training institutes and schools, 11 technical institutes, 17 technical high schools, 17 agricultural institutes and schools, and 41 vocational schools.

ILLITERACY RATE – (m) 11.0 per cent; (f) 19.4 per cent (2000)

ENROLMENT (percentage of age group) – tertiary 5 per cent (1997)

NAMIBIA

The Republic of Namibia

AREA – 316,654 sq. miles (823,300 sq. km).
Neighbours: Angola (north), South Africa (south), Botswana (east), Zambia and Zimbabwe (north-east)

POPULATION – 1,788,000 (2001). The main population groups include: Ovambo (587,000), Kavango (110,000), Damara (89,000), Herero (89,000), whites (78,000), Nama (57,000), mixed race (48,000), Caprivians (44,000), Rehoboth Baster (29,000), Tswana (7,000). English is the official language, with Afrikaans, German and local languages also in use

CAPITAL – Windhoek (population, 147,056, 1995)

MAJOR TOWNS – Ondangwa (33,000); Oshakati (37,000); Rehoboth (21,500); Swakopmund (18,000); Walvis Bay (50,000), 1995 estimates

CURRENCY – Namibian dollar of 100 cents, at parity to South African rand

NATIONAL ANTHEM - Namibia, Land Of The Brave

NATIONAL DAY – 21 March (Independence Day)

NATIONAL FLAG – Divided diagonally blue, red and green with the red fimbriated in white; a gold twelve-rayed sun in the upper hoist

LIFE EXPECTANCY (years) – 45 (2001)

POPULATION GROWTH RATE – 2.4 per cent

POPULATION DENSITY – 2 per sq. km (2001)

MILITARY EXPENDITURE – 3.1 per cent of GDP (2001)

MILITARY PERSONNEL – 9,200: Army 9,000, Coast Guard 200; Paramilitaries 6,000

ILLITERACY RATE – (m) 17.2 per cent; (f) 18.8 per cent (2000)

ENROLMENT (percentage of age group) – primary 100 per cent (1997); secondary 62 per cent (1997); tertiary 8 per cent (1997)

HISTORY AND POLITICS

The German protectorate of South West Africa from 1884 to 1915, the territory was entrusted to South Africa by the 1919 Treaty of Versailles. The UN terminated South Africa's mandate in 1967.

An administrator-general was appointed in 1977 to govern the territory until independence and a transitional government was installed in 1985. Elections for Namibia's National Assembly took place under UN supervision on 7–11 November 1989 and independence was declared on 21 March 1990. Namibia joined the Commonwealth on independence.

Previously a British and South African colony separate from German South West Africa/Namibia, Walvis Bay was governed from August 1992 by the joint South African-Namibian Walvis Bay Administrative Body until 28 February 1994, when South Africa renounced its claim to sovereignty over the enclave and it became part of Namibia.

Presidential and legislative elections on 30 November to 1 December 1999 were won by the incumbent president, Sam Nujoma, and by the South West Africa People's Organisation of Namibia (SWAPO) respectively. In the 72-seat National Assembly SWAPO has 55 seats, the Congress of Democrats and the Democratic Turnhalle Alliance seven seats each, and other parties three seats. In August 2002, Prime Minister Hage Geingob was replaced by Theo-Ben Gurirab.

INSURGENCIES

Government officials claimed to have uncovered a plot by Mishake Muyongo, a former leader of the opposition Democratic Turnhalle Alliance, and Mishake Boniface Mamili, a Mafwe chief, to launch a secessionist rebellion in the Caprivi strip in 1998. An attempted uprising in August 1999, believed to have been led by the Caprivi Liberation Army, was quickly quashed by government forces and 125 of the leaders of the uprising were put on trial for treason.

POLITICAL SYSTEM

Namibia has an executive president as head of state who exercises the functions of government with the assistance of a Cabinet headed by a prime minister. The president is directly elected for a maximum of two five-year terms; in November 1998, parliament approved an amendment to the constitution allowing President Nujoma to stand for a third term of office in the 1999 elections. There is a bicameral legislature consisting of the 72-member

National Assembly, elected for a five-year term, and the National Council, whose 26 members are indirectly elected by the regional councils from among their own members. The National Council is elected for a six-year term, and its main function is to review and consider legislation from the National Assembly. The constitution can only be changed by a two-thirds majority in the National Assembly.

HEAD OF STATE
President, Dr Sam Nujoma, *elected* 16 February 1990, *re-elected* 8 December 1994, 1 December 1999

CABINET *as at August 2003*
Prime Minister, Theo-Ben Gurirab
Deputy Prime Minister, Revd Hendrik Witbooi
Agriculture, Water and Rural Development, Helmut Angula
Basic Education, Culture and Sport, John Mutorwa
Defence, Erikki Nghimtina
Environment and Tourism, Philemon Malima
Finance, Saarah Kuugongelwa-Amathila
Fisheries and Marine Resources, Abraham Iyambo
Foreign Affairs, Hidipo Hamutenya
Health and Social Services, Libertina Amathila
Higher Education, Training and Employment Creation, Nahas Angula
Home Affairs, Jerry Ekandjo
Information and Broadcasting, Nangolo Mbumba
Justice, Albert Kawana
Labour, Marco Hausiku
Lands, Resettlement, Rehabilitation, Hifikepunye Pohamba
Mines and Energy, Dr Nickey Iyambo
Prisons and Correctional Services, Andimba Toivo ya Toivo
Regional and Local Government and Housing, Joel Kaapanda
Trade and Industry, Jesaya Nyamu
Without Portfolio, Ngarikutuke Tjiriange
Women's Affairs and Child Welfare, Netumbo Nandi-Ndaitwah
Works, Transport and Communication, Moses Amweelo

HIGH COMMISSION OF THE REPUBLIC OF NAMIBIA
6 Chandos Street, London W1G 9LU Tel: 020-7636 6244
Email: namibia-highcomm@btconnect.com
High Commissioner, HE Monica Ndiliawike Nashandi, apptd 1999

BRITISH HIGH COMMISSION
116 Robert Mugabe Avenue, PO Box 22202, Windhoek
Tel: (00 264) (61) 274800 Email: bhc@mweb.com.na
High Commissioner, HE Alasdair MacDermott, apptd 2002

BRITISH COUNCIL OFFICER IN CHARGE,
Patience Mahlalela, 1–5 Fidel Castro Street, Windhoek
Tel: (00 264) (61) 226 776
Email: general.enquiries@britishcouncil.org.na

ECONOMY
Manufacturing contributes around 31 per cent of GDP, with food production, metals and wooden products the most important areas. Around 44 per cent of the population are engaged in agriculture, primarily livestock. Guano is also exported. Deposits of diamonds along the coast and offshore along the seabed are estimated at between 1,500 and 3,000 million carats; Namibia accounts for roughly 8 per cent of world diamond production. Walvis Bay and Lüderitz are the main ports.

There are 62,258 km of roads, of which 5,250 km are surfaced; there are 2,382 km of railway track.

The principal imports are machinery and transport equipment, foodstuffs, beverages and tobacco, and mineral fuels. The principal exports are diamonds and agricultural products.

In 1998 there was a trade deficit of US$173 million and a current account surplus of US$162 million.
GNP – US$3,569 million (2000); US$2,030 per capita (2000)
GDP – US$3,168 million (2001); US$1,981 per capita (2000)
ANNUAL AVERAGE GROWTH OF GDP – 2.4 per cent (1998)
INFLATION RATE – 8 per cent (2001)

Trade with UK	2001	2002
Imports from UK	£12,658,000	£8,366,000
Exports to UK	316,005,000	183,888,000

NAURU

The Republic of Nauru/Naoero

AREA – 8 sq. miles (21 sq. km)
POPULATION – 12,088 (2001). About 43 per cent of Nauruans are adherents of the Nauruan Protestant Church and there is a Roman Catholic mission on the island. The main languages are English and Nauruan
CAPITAL – ΨNauru
CURRENCY – Australian dollar ($A) of 100 cents
NATIONAL ANTHEM – Nauru Bwiema (Nauru, Our Homeland)
NATIONAL DAY – 31 January (Independence Day)
NATIONAL FLAG – Twelve-point star (representing the 12 original Nauruan tribes) below a gold bar (representing the Equator), all on a blue background
POPULATION GROWTH RATE – 0.5 per cent
POPULATION DENSITY – 524 per sq. km (1999)

HISTORY AND POLITICS
From 1888 until the First World War Nauru was administered by Germany. In 1920 it became a British Empire-mandated territory under the League of Nations, administered by Australia. A trusteeship superseding the mandate was approved in 1947 by the UN and Nauru continued to be administered by Australia until it became independent on 31 January 1968. Nauru became a full member of the Commonwealth on 1 May 1999; it had been an associate member since 1968.

President Rene Harris was defeated in a parliamentary vote on 8 January 2003 and was replaced by Bernard Dowiyogo who died on 9 March 2003. Derog Gioura was elected to succeed him on 20 March but following the legislative elections of 3 May 2003, the new parliament elected Ludvig Scotty as president. The new Cabinet was named on 12 June 2003.

POLITICAL SYSTEM
Parliament has 18 members including the Cabinet and Speaker. Voting is compulsory for all Nauruans over 20 years of age, except in certain specified instances. Elections are held every three years. The Cabinet is chosen by the president, who is elected by the parliament from amongst its members, and comprises not fewer than five nor more than six members including the president.

HEAD OF STATE
President, Ludwig Scotty, *elected by parliament* 29 May
2003

CABINET *as at July 2003*
*Civil Aviation, Economic Development, Foreign Affairs,
Public Service, Works and Women's Affairs,* The
President
Education, Youth Affairs, Culture and Tourism, Baron Waca
*Finance, Island Development Industry, Minister assisting the
President, Telecommunications,* David Adeang
Health and Medical Services, Sport and Transport, Kieran
Keke
Justice and Good Governance, Russel Kun
*Works, Housing, Planning and Construction, Fisheries and
Marine Resources,* Dogabe Jeremiah

HONORARY CONSULATE, Romshed Courtyard, Underriver,
Nr. Sevenoaks, Kent TN15 0SD. Tel: 01732-746061
Email: nauru@weald.co.uk
Honorary Consul, Martin Weston

BRITISH HIGH COMMISSIONER, HE Charles Mochan,
resident at Suva, Fiji

ECONOMY

The only fertile areas are in the narrow coastal belt and
local requirements of fruit and vegetables are mostly met
by imports. The economy is heavily dependent on the
extraction of phosphate, of which the island has one of
the world's richest deposits. Considerable investments
have been made abroad with the royalties on phosphate
exports to provide for a time when production declines. A
20-year package of health and education programmes
was agreed with Australia in 1993 as part of a
compensation package for environmental damage caused
by phosphate mining prior to independence. Air Nauru
operates air services throughout the Pacific region and to
Australia, New Zealand, Japan, Singapore and the
Philippines.
GDP – US$32 million (1998); US$2,533 per capita
(2000)
ANNUAL AVERAGE GROWTH OF GDP – 1.9 per cent
(1998)

Trade with UK	2001	2002
Imports from UK	£799,000	£461,000
Exports to UK	4,000	80,000

EDUCATION
Education is compulsory between the ages of six and 17.
There are 10 infant and primary and two secondary
schools on the island with a total enrolment of about
2,707 pupils.

NEPAL

Nepāl Adhirājya / Kingdom of Nepal

AREA – 56,827 sq. miles (147,181 sq. km). Neighbours:
China (north), India (south, west and east)
POPULATION – 25,284,463 (2001 estimate). The
inhabitants are of mixed stock, with Tibetan
characteristics prevailing in the north and Indian in the
south. The official religion is Hinduism; 87 per cent of
the population are Hindus, 8 per cent Buddhist and 3
per cent Muslim. Gautama Buddha was born in Nepal.
The official language is Nepali

CAPITAL – Kathmandu (population, 535,000, 1993)
MAJOR CITIES – Lalitpur (190,000); Biratnagar
(132,000); Bhaktapur (130,000), 1993 estimates
CURRENCY – Nepalese rupee of 100 paisa
NATIONAL ANTHEM - Sri Man Gumbhira Nepali
Prachanda Pratapi Bhupati (May Glory Crown Our
Illustrious Sovereign, The Gallant Nepalese)
NATIONAL DAYS – 18 February (National Democracy
Day); 28 December (The King's Birthday)
NATIONAL FLAG – Double pennant of crimson with blue
border on peaks; white moon with rays in centre of
top peak; white quarter sun, recumbent in centre of
bottom peak
POPULATION GROWTH RATE – 2.4 per cent
POPULATION DENSITY – 152 per sq. km (1999)
MILITARY EXPENDITURE – 2.7 per cent of GDP (2001)
MILITARY PERSONNEL – Army 51,000; Paramilitaries
40,000
ILLITERACY RATE – (m) 40.8 per cent; (f) 76.1 per cent
(2000)
ENROLMENT (percentage of age group) – tertiary 5 per
cent (1997)

Nepal lies between India and the Tibet Autonomous
Region of China on the slopes of the Himalayas, and
includes Mount Everest.

The southern region, the Terai, was covered with
jungle but has been more widely cultivated recently. It
forms about 23 per cent of the total land area and nearly
44 per cent of the population live there. The central belt
is hilly, but with many fertile valleys, leading up to the
snowline at about 16,000 feet. The hills account for 42
per cent of the area and about 48 per cent of the
population. The remainder of the country, the Himalayan
region, consists of high mountains which are sparsely
inhabited.

HISTORY AND POLITICS

Nepal was originally divided into numerous hill clans
and petty principalities but emerged as a nation in the
middle of the 18th century when it was unified by the
warrior Raja of Gorkha, Prithvi Narayan Shah, who
founded the present Nepalese dynasty. In 1846 power
was seized by Jung Bahadur Rana after a massacre of
nobles, and he was the first of a line of hereditary Rana
prime ministers who ruled Nepal for 104 years. During
this time the role of the monarchs was mainly ceremonial.

In 1950–1 a revolutionary movement broke the
hereditary power of the Ranas and restored the
monarchy to its former position. King Mahendra
proscribed all political parties and assumed direct powers
in 1960. In 1962 he introduced a new constitution
embodying a tiered, partyless system of panchyat
(council) democracy.

Mass agitation for political reform led in April 1990 to
the abolition of the panchyat system. A new constitution
was promulgated in November 1990 establishing a
multiparty, parliamentary system of government and a
constitutional monarchy. Elections in May 1991 were
won by the Nepali Congress Party. However, politics is
extremely factionalised and there have been frequent
changes of government over the past decade.

On 1 June 2001, King Birendra, Queen Aishwara and
several other members of the royal family were shot dead
by, Crown Prince Dipendra, who then shot himself, but
survived long enough to be proclaimed king the
following day. King Dipendra was declared dead on 4
June, having never regained consciousness, and Prince

Gyanendra, the brother of the late King Birendra, was crowned as king.

Prime Minister Girija Prasad Koirala resigned on 19 July 2001; he was replaced by former prime minister Sher Bahadur Deuba on 22 July 2001. On 22 May 2002, Deuba asked the King to dissolve parliament and call early elections. In October 2002 Deuba, backed by all the political parties, asked King Gyanendra to delay for a year elections due in November owing to an increase in Maoist violence; the King dismissed Deuba and his cabinet on 7 October and assumed executive powers briefly. Lokendra Bahadur Chand was appointed to head the government and a new cabinet was sworn in on 12 October. Lokendra Bahadur Chand resigned on 30 May 2003 after a failed attempt by politicians to reopen the parliament, dissolved by the King in October 2002. In June 2003 the King appointed Surya Badahur Thapa as prime minister after the political parties failed to agree on a candidate.

INSURGENCIES

Maoist guerrillas from the Communist Party of Nepal, who are opposed to the monarchy, began an armed rebellion in 1996. Their attacks, and the military response to these, have left some 7,000 dead. In 1999, the government offered an amnesty to the guerrillas if they agreed to abandon violence and enter into dialogue with the government. The guerrillas and the government announced a cease-fire on 23 July 2001 and agreed to hold talks but a state of emergency was declared on 26 November 2001 after renewed guerrilla attacks. In August 2002, the state of emergency was lifted. On 30 January 2003 a cease-fire was declared between the Maoists and the government.

POLITICAL SYSTEM

The King retains joint executive power with the Council of Ministers. The bicameral legislature consists of a 205-member House of Representatives, directly elected for a five-year term, and a 60-member National Council, 50 of whom are indirectly elected for a six-year term and ten royal nominees.

HEAD OF STATE

HM The King of Nepal, King Gyanendra Bir Bikram Shah Dev, *acceded* 4 June 2001
Heir, Crown Prince Paras Bir Bikram Shah Dev

COUNCIL OF MINISTERS *as at July 2003*
Prime Minister, Defence and Home Affairs, Foreign Affairs, Surya Bahadur Thapa
Civil Aviation, Culture and Tourism, Sarbendra Nath Shukla
Education and Sports, Hari Bahadur Basnet
Finance, Prakash Chandra Lohani
Information and Communication, Kamal Thapa
Minister of State for Women's and Children's Affairs, Social Welfare, Renu Yadav
Physical Planning and Public Works, Buddhi Man Tamang

ROYAL NEPALESE EMBASSY
12A Kensington Palace Gardens, London W8 4QU
Tel: 020-7229 1594/6231 Email: rnelondon@btconnect.com

BRITISH EMBASSY
Lainchaur Kathmandu, PO Box 106 Tel: (00 977) (1) 4410583
Email: britemb@wlink.com.np
Ambassador Extraordinary and Plenipotentiary, HE Keith Bloomfield, apptd 2002

BRITISH COUNCIL DIRECTOR, Barbara Hewitt
PO Box 640, Lainchaur, Kathmandu Tel: (00 977) (1) 410 798
Email: general.enquiry@britishcouncil.org.np

ECONOMY

The main imports are machinery and transport equipment, and chemical and pharmaceutical products. Tourism is the single largest commercial earner of foreign exchange. Nepal's main trading partners are India, Germany and the USA.

In 2000 Nepal had a trade deficit of US$793 million and a current account deficit of US$277 million. In 2001 imports totalled US$1,473 million and exports US$737 million.

GNP – US$5,584 million (2000); US$240 per capita (2000)
GDP – US$5,525 million (2001); US$230 per capita (2000)
ANNUAL AVERAGE GROWTH OF GDP – 6.0 per cent (2000)
INFLATION RATE – 1.5 per cent (2000)
TOTAL EXTERNAL DEBT – US$2,823 million (2000)

Trade with UK	2001	2002
Imports from UK	£5,932,000	£6,894,000
Exports to UK	9,869,000	8,800,000

COMMUNICATIONS

The total length of roads is 13,223 km, of which 4,073 km are paved. Kathmandu is connected by road with India and Tibet. Internally, the road network links Kathmandu to Kodari and Pokhara, and Pokhara to Sunauli. There are 155 km of railway track.

THE NETHERLANDS

Koninkrijk der Nederlanden – Kingdom of the Netherlands

AREA – 13,039 sq. miles (33,900 sq. km). Neighbours: Belgium (south), Germany (east)
POPULATION – 15,930,000 (2001): 36 per cent Catholic, 27 per cent Reformed Church, 8 per cent Muslim. The language is Dutch, a West Germanic language of Low Franconian origin closely akin to Old English and Low German. It is spoken in the Netherlands and the northern part of Belgium (Flanders). Frisian is spoken in Friesland. Dutch is the official language in the Netherlands Antilles and Aruba; Papiamento, a mixture of Dutch and Spanish, is the vernacular
CAPITAL – ΨAmsterdam (population, 736,538, 2001)
SEAT OF GOVERNMENT – The Hague (Den Haag or, in full, 's-Gravenhage), population 443,745, (2001)
MAJOR CITIES – Eindhoven (203,331); Groningen (173,825); Haarlem (148,779); ΨRotterdam (595,066); Tilburg (195,289); Utrecht (256,202), 2001
CURRENCY – Euro (€) of 100 cents
NATIONAL ANTHEM – Wilhelmus van Nassouwe (William of Nassau)
NATIONAL FLAG – Three horizontal bands of red, white and blue
LIFE EXPECTANCY (years) – 78 (2001)
POPULATION GROWTH RATE – 0.6 per cent
POPULATION DENSITY – 470 per sq. km (2001)
URBAN POPULATION – 90 per cent (2001)

HISTORY AND POLITICS

Following a revolt against Spanish rule under the leadership of William of Orange, the northern provinces were united by the Union of Utrecht (1579) and in 1581 independence was declared. Dutch economic and military power flourished in the 17th and 18th centuries.

The Netherlands were overrun by France in the late 18th century, becoming part of the French Empire until 1814, when the northern and southern Netherlands were united into one kingdom. In 1830 the southern provinces seceded to form Belgium. The Duchy of Luxembourg was made an independent state in 1867.

The Netherlands remained neutral during the First World War but was invaded by Germany during the Second World War and occupied until the war ended. The Netherlands joined the Benelux economic union with Belgium and Luxembourg in 1948 and became a member of NATO in 1949. The Dutch East Indies gained independence as Indonesia in 1949.

On 6 May 2002, right-wing politician Pim Fortuyn, leader of the List Pim Fortuyn (LPF) party, was assassinated, nine days before the general election on 15 May in which the Christian Democratic Appeal (CDA) gained 43 of the 150 seats in the second chamber. A coalition government headed by CDA leader Jan Peter Balkenende and comprising the CDA, LPF and VVD was sworn in on 22 July. Balkenende's government collapsed on 16 October 2002, undermined by in-fighting within the LPF. The general election of 22 January 2003 resulted in a marginal win for the CDA with 23 out of the 75 seats; the PvdA gained 19 seats. After four months of talks a new coalition, comprised of members of the CDA, the VVD and the Democrats 66, led by Balkenende, was sworn into office on 27 May 2003.

POLITICAL SYSTEM

The States-General consists of the *Eerste Kamer* (First Chamber) of 75 members, elected for four years by the Provincial Councillors; and the *Tweede Kamer* (Second Chamber) of 150 members, elected for four years by voters of 18 years and upwards.

HEAD OF STATE

HM The Queen of the Netherlands, Queen Beatrix Wilhelmina Armgard, KG, GCVO, *born* 31 January 1938; *succeeded* 30 April 1980, upon the abdication of her mother Queen Juliana; *married* 10 March 1966, HRH Prince Claus George Willem Otto Frederik Geert of the Netherlands, Jonkheer van Amsberg; and has *issue,* Prince Willem; Prince Johan Friso, *b.* 25 September 1968; Prince Constantijn Christof, *b.* 11 October 1969 *Heir,* HRH Prince Willem Alexander, *b.* 27 April 1967; *married* 2 February 2002, Máxima Zorreguieta

CABINET *as at August 2003*
Prime Minister, General Affairs, Jan Peter Balkenende (CDA)
Deputy Prime Minister, Finance, Gerrit Zalm (VVD)
Deputy Prime Minister, Government Reform and Kingdom Relations, Thom de Graf (D66)
Agriculture, Nature Management and Fisheries, Cornelis Veerman (CDA)
Defence, Henk Kamp (VVD)
Development Co-operation, Agnes van Ardenne-Van der Hoeven (CDA)
Economic Affairs, Laurens Jan Brinkhorst (D66)
Education, Culture and Science, Maria van der Hoevan (CDA)
Foreign Affairs, Jaap de Hoop Scheffer (CDA)
Immigration and Integration, Rita Verdonk (VVD)
Interior and Kingdom Relations, Johan Remkes (VVD)
Justice, Piet Hein Donner (CDA)
Public Health, Welfare and Sport, Hans Hoogervorst (VVD)
Public Housing, Planning and the Environment, Sybilla Dekker (VVD)
Social Affairs and Employment, Aart Jan de Geus (CDA)
Transport, Public Works and Water Management, Karla Peijs (CDA)

CDA Christian Democratic Appeal; D66 Democrats 66; VVD People's Party for Freedom and Democracy

ROYAL NETHERLANDS EMBASSY
38 Hyde Park Gate, London SW7 5DP Tel: 020-7590 3200
Ambassador Extraordinary and Plenipotentiary, HE Count Jan Mark Vladimir Anton de Marchant et d'Ansembourg, apptd 2003

BRITISH EMBASSY
Lange Voorhout 10, The Hague, NL-2514 ED
Tel: (00 31) (0) 70 4270 427
Ambassador Extraordinary and Plenipotentiary, HE Sir Colin Budd, KCMG, apptd 2001

BRITISH COUNCIL DIRECTOR, David Alderdice
Weteringschans 85A, NL-1017 RZ Amsterdam
Tel: (00 31) (0) 20 550 6060
Email: david.alderdice@britcoun.nl

DEFENCE

The Army has 1,598 main battle tanks, 352 armoured infantry fighting vehicles and 316 armoured personnel carriers. The Navy has four submarines, two destroyers, nine frigates, ten combat aircraft and 21 armed helicopters. The Air Force has 143 combat aircraft and 30 armed helicopters.
MILITARY EXPENDITURE – 1.7 per cent of GDP (2001)
MILITARY PERSONNEL – 49,580: Army 23,150, Navy 12,130, Air Force 8,850; Paramilitaries 3,300

ECONOMY

The chief agricultural products are potatoes, wheat, rye, barley, sugar beet, cattle, poultry, pigs, dairy products, vegetables, fruit, flower bulbs, plants and cut flowers and there is an important fishing industry.

Among the principal industries are engineering, electronics, nuclear energy, petrochemicals and plastics, road vehicles, aircraft and defence equipment, shipbuilding repair, steel, textiles of all types, electrical appliances, metal ware, furniture, paper, cigars, sugar, liqueurs, beer and clothing.

The majority of the workforce, 71.8 per cent, are engaged in service industries.
GNP – US$397,544 million (2000); US$24,970 per capita (2000)
GDP – US$374,976 million (2001); US$23,294 per capita (2000)
ANNUAL AVERAGE GROWTH OF GDP – 3.8 per cent (2000)
INFLATION RATE – 2.5 per cent (2000)
UNEMPLOYMENT – 3.3 per cent (2000)

TRADE

Trade, banking and shipping are of particular importance to the economy. The Netherlands is the sixth largest exporter and third largest agricultural exporter in the world. The geographical position of the Netherlands, at the mouths of the Rhine, Maas and Schelde, brings a large volume of transit trade to and from the interior of Europe to Dutch ports. Principal trading partners are Germany, Belgium/Luxembourg, the UK and France.

In 2001 the Netherlands had a trade surplus of US$23,588 million and a current account surplus of US$12,405 million. Imports totalled US$194,400 million and exports US$216,099 million.

Trade with UK	2001	2002
Imports from UK	£13,916,200,000	£13,313,600,000
Exports to UK	14,294,000,000	14,538,400,000

COMMUNICATIONS

There are 58,133 km of inter-urban roads, of which 2,207 km are motorways. The total extent of navigable rivers including canals is 5,046 km. The total length of the railway system is 2,808 km, of which 2,061 km are electrified.

EDUCATION

Primary and secondary education is given in both denominational and state schools and is compulsory.

The principal universities are at Leiden, Utrecht, Groningen, Amsterdam (two), Nijmegen, Maastricht and Rotterdam, and there are technical universities at Delft, Eindhoven, Enschede and Wageningen (agriculture). ENROLMENT (percentage of age group) – primary 100 per cent (1997); secondary 100 per cent (1997); tertiary 47 per cent (1997)

OVERSEAS TERRITORIES

ARUBA

AREA – 75 sq. miles (193 sq. km)
POPULATION – 70,007 (2001 estimate)
CAPITAL – ΨOranjestad (population 25,000); and Sint Nicolaas (17,000)
CURRENCY – Aruban florin

The island of Aruba was from 1828 part of the Dutch West Indies and from 1845 part of the Netherlands Antilles. On 1 January 1986 it became a separate territory within the Kingdom of the Netherlands. The 1983 Constitutional Conference agreed that Aruba's separate status would last for ten years from 1986, after which the island would become fully independent. In 1994 this decision was changed and it was decided that Aruba will retain its separate status within the Kingdom of the Netherlands.
Governor, Olindo Koolman
Prime Minister, Nelson O. Oduber

Trade with UK	2001	2002
Imports from UK	£32,429,000	£27,693,000
Exports to UK	13,778,000	3,848,000

NETHERLANDS ANTILLES

AREA – 309 sq. miles (800 sq. km)
POPULATION – 202,782 (1999), Curaçao 143,387, Bonaire 13,724, St Maarten 41,718, St Eustatius 2,249, Saba 1,704
CAPITAL – ΨWillemstad (on Curaçao) (pop. 50,000)
CURRENCY – Netherlands Antilles guilder of 100 cents

The Netherlands Antilles comprise the islands of Curaçao, Bonaire, part of St Maarten, St Eustatius, and Saba in the West Indies. The Netherlands Antilles, which has a 22-member federal parliament, is largely self-governing under the terms of the Realm Statute which took effect in 1954. The part of St Maarten belonging to the Netherlands voted in a non-binding referendum held in June 2000 to secede from the Netherlands Antilles and become an independent state within the Kingdom of the Netherlands. This was rejected by the government of the Netherlands, which did not believe that St Maarten was large enough to be a viable state, but discussions on its future status continue.
Governor, Frits Goedgedrag
Prime Minister, Etienne Ys

NEW ZEALAND

AREA – 103,077 sq. miles (268,000 sq. km)
POPULATION – 3,808,000 (2001): 79 per cent European stock, 13 per cent Māori, 5 per cent other Pacific islanders. The main religion is Christianity. In 1991 the principal denominations were Anglican 22.1 per cent, Presbyterian 16.3 per cent, Roman Catholic 15 per cent, Methodist 4.2 per cent, Baptist 2.1 per cent. The official languages are English and Maori

Islands	Area (sq. miles)	Population (census 1996)
North Island	44,281	2,749,788
South Island	58,093	930,824
Other islands	1,362	934
Total	103,736	3,681,546

Territories		
Tokelau	5	1,487
Niue	100	1,708*
Cook Islands	93	18,008
Ross Dependency	175,000	–

CAPITAL – ΨWellington (population, 340,719, 2001 census)
MAJOR CITIES – ΨAuckland (1,079,304); ΨChristchurch (340,053); ΨDunedin (109,563); Hamilton (165,576); ΨNapier-Hastings (116,292), 2001 census
CURRENCY – New Zealand dollar (NZ$) of 100 cents
NATIONAL ANTHEM – God Save The Queen/God Defend New Zealand
NATIONAL DAY – 6 February (Waitangi Day)
NATIONAL FLAG – Blue ground, with Union Flag in top left quarter, four five-pointed red stars with white borders on the fly
LIFE EXPECTANCY (years) – 78 (2001)
POPULATION GROWTH RATE – 1.1 per cent
POPULATION DENSITY – 14 per sq. km (2001)
URBAN POPULATION – 86 per cent (2001)

New Zealand consists of a number of islands in the South Pacific Ocean, and also has administrative responsibility for the Ross Dependency in Antarctica. The two larger islands, North Island and South Island, are separated by a relatively narrow strait. The remaining islands are much smaller and widely dispersed.

Much of the North and South Islands is mountainous. The principal range is the Southern Alps, extending the entire length of the South Island and having its culminating point in Mount Cook/Mount Aoraki (3,754 m/12,349 ft). The North Island mountains include several volcanoes, two of which are active. Of the numerous glaciers in the South Island, the Tasman (18 miles long by 1¼ wide), the Franz Josef and the Fox are the best known. The more important rivers include the Waikato (425 km/270 miles in length), Wanganui (180 miles), and Clutha (210 miles) and lakes include Taupo, 234 sq. miles in area; Wakatipu, 113; and Te Anau, 133.

New Zealand includes, in addition to North and South Islands: Chatham Islands (Chatham, Pitt, South East Islands and some rocky islets, combined area, 965 sq. km (373 sq. miles), largely uninhabited); Stewart Island (area 1,746 sq. km (674 sq. miles), largely uninhabited); the Kermadec Group (Raoul or Sunday, Macaulay, Curtis Islands, L'Esperance, and some islets; population 9–10, all government employees at a meteorological station); Campbell Island, used as a weather station; the Three Kings (discovered by Tasman on the Feast of the Epiphany); Auckland Islands; Antipodes Group; Bounty Islands; Snares Islands and Solander.

HISTORY AND POLITICS

The discoverers and first colonists of New Zealand were Polynesians, ancestors of the modern-day Maori, who settled the islands between the ninth and 14th centuries. The Dutch navigator, Abel Tasman, sighted the coast in 1642 but did not land, but the British explorer James Cook circumnavigated New Zealand and landed in 1769. Largely as a result of increased British emigration, the country was annexed by the British government in 1840. The British Lieutenant-Governor, William Hobson, proclaimed sovereignty over the North Island by virtue of the Treaty of Waitangi, signed by him and many Māori chiefs, and over the South Island and Stewart Island by right of discovery.

In 1841 New Zealand was created a separate colony distinct from New South Wales. In 1907 the designation was changed to 'The Dominion of New Zealand'.

Following the general election of 27 July 2002, the state of the parties in the House of Representatives was: Labour Party (LP) 52 seats, National Party 27, New Zealand First 13, ACT New Zealand 9; Green Party 9; United Future 8; Jim Anderton's Progressive Coalition (PC) 2. The Labour Party and the Progressive Coalition formed a minority administration.

POLITICAL SYSTEM

The head of state is the British sovereign, represented by the governor-general who is a New Zealander, appointed on the advice of the New Zealand government. The prime minister and the cabinet are appointed by the governor-general on the advice of the unicameral legislature, the House of Representatives. The House of Representatives has 120 members, elected for a three-year term. A non-binding referendum, held simultaneously with the general election in November 1999, approved a reduction in the number of members to 100 in future parliaments. There is no written constitution.

The judicial system comprises a High Court, a Court of Appeal and district courts having both civil and criminal jurisdiction.

GOVERNOR-GENERAL

Governor-General and Commander-in-Chief, HE Dame Silvia Cartwright, *sworn in* April 2001

THE CABINET *as at August 2003*
Prime Minister, Arts, Culture and Heritage, Helen Clark (LP)
Deputy Prime Minister, Finance and Revenue, Dr Michael Cullen (LP)
ACC, Senior Citizens, Women's Affairs, Ruth Dyson (LP)
Agriculture, Forestry, Biosecurity, and Trade Negotiations, Jim Sutton (LP)
Attorney-General, Labour, in charge of Treaty of Waitangi Negotiations, Margaret Wilson (LP)
Commerce, Immigration, Lianne Dalziel
Conservation, Local Government, Chris Carter (LP)
Customs, Courts, Rick Barker (LP)
Defence, State-owned Enterprises, Tourism, Mark Burton (LP)
Economic Development, Industry and Regional Development, Jim Anderton (PC)
Education, State Services, Sport and Recreation, Trevor Mallard (LP)
Energy, Fisheries, Research, Science and Technology, Crown Research Institutes, Pete Hodgson (LP)
Environment, Disarmament and Arms Control, Marian Hobbs (LP)
Foreign Affairs and Trade, Justice, Pacific Island Affairs, Phil Goff (LP)
Health and Food Safety, Annette King (LP)
Maori Affairs, Parekura Horomia (LP)
Police, Civil Defence, Internal Affairs, Veterans Affairs, George Hawkins (LP)
Social Development, Employment, Broadcasting and Housing, Steve Maharey (LP)
Statistics, Land Information, Youth Affairs, John Tamihere (LP)
Transport, Communications, Corrections and Information Technology, Paul Swain (LP)

NEW ZEALAND HIGH COMMISSION
New Zealand House, 80 The Haymarket, London SW1Y 4TQ
Tel: 020-7930 8422
High Commissioner, HE Russell Marshall, apptd 2002

BRITISH HIGH COMMISSION
44 Hill Street (PO Box 1812), Wellington 1
Tel: (00 64) (4) 924 2888 Email: ppa.mailbox@fco.gov.uk
High Commissioner, HE Richard Fell, CVO, apptd 2001

BRITISH COUNCIL DIRECTOR, Paul Atkins, 44 Hill Street (PO Box 1812) Wellington 1 Tel: (00 64) (4) 495 0987
Email: enquiries@britishcouncil.org.nz

DEFENCE

The Army has 41 armoured personnel carriers. The Navy has three frigates, four patrol and coastal vessels and three armed helicopters. The Air Force has 6 combat aircraft.
MILITARY EXPENDITURE – 1.4 per cent of GDP (2001)
MILITARY PERSONNEL – 8,710: Army 4,530, Navy 1,980, Air Force 2,200

ECONOMY

A programme of privatisation in the 1980s and early 1990s, resulted in only modest economic growth but increased social inequality, and since 1999 the government has ruled out further privatisation, increased the powers of trade unions, renationalised accident insurance and raised the top rate of income tax.

Agricultural production is dominated by cattle- and sheep-rearing, for meat, wool, dairy products and other by-products, such as skins, leather, etc. Timber and wood pulp are also important.

Non-metallic minerals such as coal, clay, limestone and dolomite are more important than metallic ones. Of the metals, the most important are gold and ironsand. Natural gas deposits in the offshore Taranaki Maui field and onshore fields are increasingly being exploited and used for electricity generation and as a premium fuel.

Manufacturing is based on food processing, machinery production, motor vehicle assembly, chemicals, electrical and electronic goods, and paper and printing.

In 2001 New Zealand had a trade surplus of US$1,471 million and a current account deficit of US$1,587 million.

GNP – US$49,750 million (2000); US$12,990 per capita (2000)

GDP – US$48,277 million (2001); US$13,441 per capita (2000)

ANNUAL AVERAGE GROWTH OF GDP – 2.0 per cent (2000)

INFLATION RATE – 2.6 per cent (2000)

UNEMPLOYMENT – 6.0 per cent (1999)

TRADE

New Zealand's largest trading partners are Australia, the USA, Japan and the UK. Main exports include dairy products, meat, timber, fish, fruits and nuts, machinery and aluminium products. Imports include machinery, vehicles, petroleum and petroleum products, textiles, plastics and aircraft. In 2001 imports totalled US$13,347 million and exports US$13,723 million.

Trade with UK	2001*	2002*
Imports from UK	£311,539,000	£311,626,000
Exports to UK	560,459,000	548,625,000

*Includes Niue, Tokelau and Cook Islands

COMMUNICATIONS

The national railway system is owned and operated by the privately-owned Tranz Rail Ltd. There are 4,439 km of railway track. In 1995 there were 2,977 ships registered in New Zealand (gross tonnage 482,180).

There are international airports at Auckland, Christchurch and Wellington. Air New Zealand is the national carrier.

EDUCATION

Schools are free and attendance is compulsory between the ages of six and 15. There are 2,226 state and 56 private primary schools and 320 state and 23 private secondary schools. There are seven universities and 25 polytechnics.

ENROLMENT (percentage of age group) – primary 100 per cent (1997); secondary 100 per cent (1997); tertiary 63 per cent (1997)

TERRITORIES

TOKELAU (OR UNION ISLANDS)

Tokelau is a group of atolls, Fakaofo, Nukunonu and Atafu. It was proclaimed part of New Zealand as from 1 January 1949. The Council of Faipule, composed of one elected representative from each atoll, was established in 1992 to govern Tokelau when the General Fono was not in session. The position of Ulu-o-Tokelau (leader) is rotated among the three Faipule members annually. Administrative responsibility for Tokelau lies with the Administrator but in 1994 his powers were delegated to the General Fono and the Council of Faipule. The General Fono has 48 seats and its numbers are chosen by each atoll's Council of Elders (Taupulega) to serve a three-year term. The Tokelau Amendment Act, passed by the New Zealand Parliament in 1996, conferred legislative power on the General Fono. New Zealand provides substantial aid (NZ$8.5 million in year ended 30 June 2001).

Administrator, Lindsay Watt, apptd 1993

THE ROSS DEPENDENCY

The Ross Dependency, placed under the jurisdiction of New Zealand in 1923, is defined as all the Antarctic islands and territories between 160° E. and 150° W. longitude which are situated south of the 60° S. parallel, including Edward VII Land and portions of Victoria Land. Since 1957 a number of research stations have been established in the Dependency.

ASSOCIATED STATES

COOK ISLANDS

Included in the realm of New Zealand since 1901, the Cook Islands group consists of the islands of Rarotonga, Aitutaki, Mangaia, Atiu, Mauke, Mitiaro, Manuae, Takutea, Palmerston, Penrhyn or Tongareva, Manihiki, Rakahanga, Suwarrow, Pukapuka or Danger, and Nassau. The population is mainly Maori; English and Cook Island Maori are the principal languages spoken.

Queen Elizabeth II has a representative on the islands, and there is a New Zealand High Commissioner. Since 1965 the islands have been in free association with New Zealand and enjoyed complete internal self-government, executive power being in the hands of a Cabinet consisting of a prime minister and five other ministers. There is a 25-member Legislative Assembly. New Zealand has an obligation to assist with foreign affairs and defence if requested. The Cook Islanders are constitutionally guaranteed citizenship both of the Cook Islands and of New Zealand.

Agriculture accounts for 7 per cent of GDP, tourism accounts for 30 per cent and offshore banking and trade are of increasing importance to the economy.

HM Representative, HE Frederick Goodwin
Prime Minister, Dr. Robert Woonton
New Zealand High Commissioner, Kurt Meyer

NIUE

A New Zealand High Commissioner is stationed at Niue, which since 1974 has been self-governing in free association with New Zealand. New Zealand is responsible for external affairs and defence, and continues to give financial aid. Executive power is in the hands of a premier and a Cabinet of three drawn from the Assembly of 20 members. The Assembly is the supreme legislative body.

New Zealand High Commissioner, Sandra Lee

NICARAGUA

República de Nicaragua – Republic of Nicaragua

AREA – 50,193 sq. miles (130,000 sq. km). Neighbours: Honduras (north), Costa Rica (south)
POPULATION – 4,918,393 (2001 estimate): three-quarters are of mixed blood, another 15 per cent are white, mostly of pure Spanish descent, and the remaining 10 per cent are West Indians or Indians. The latter group includes the Misquitos, who live on the Atlantic coast. The official language is Spanish and the majority are Roman Catholic, although the English language and the Moravian Church are widespread on the Atlantic coast
CAPITAL – Managua (population, 864,201, 1995 estimate)
MAJOR CITIES – Chinandega (144,291); Granada (72,640); León (158,577); Masaya (78,308)
CURRENCY – Córdoba (C$) of 100 centavos
NATIONAL ANTHEM – Salve A Tí Nicaragua (Hail, Nicaragua)
NATIONAL DAY – 15 September
NATIONAL FLAG – Horizontal stripes of blue, white and blue, with the Nicaraguan coat of arms in the centre of the white stripe
POPULATION GROWTH RATE – 2.7 per cent
POPULATION DENSITY – 38 per sq. km (1999)
ILLITERACY RATE – (m) 33.1 per cent; (f) 29.8 per cent (2000)
ENROLMENT (percentage of age group) – primary 100 per cent (1997); secondary 55 per cent (1997); tertiary 12 per cent (1997)

HISTORY AND POLITICS
Spanish colonisation of Nicaragua began in 1523. Independence was secured in 1838. Guerrillas of the Sandinista National Liberation Front (FSLN) overthrew the government in 1979, but after ten years in power and a civil war against US-backed Contra guerrillas, the Sandinistas lost their parliamentary majority in elections held in 1990. A coalition of former opposition parties, the Unión Nacional de Oposistora (UNO), formed a government. With the defeat of the Sandinistas, the civil war came to an end.

In presidential and legislative elections held on 4 November 2001, Enrique Bolaños Geyer of the Liberal Constitutionalist Party (PLC) was elected president and the PLC gained 47 seats in the National Assembly, with the FSLN winning 43 seats. The government is formed by a coalition led by the PLC.

FOREIGN RELATIONS
Following a long-running dispute between Nicaragua and Honduras concerning their maritime boundaries, the two countries signed a border accord on 7 March 2000, in which they agreed to conduct joint patrols in the Caribbean and the Gulf of Fonseca, and to withdraw all military forces from their mutual frontier. In February 2001 the Nicaraguan government accused Honduras of failing to withdraw its forces from the mutual border. An agreement was reached on 7 June 2001 which permitted observers from the Organisation of American States to monitor the deployment of land and maritime forces on both sides of the frontier.

POLITICAL SYSTEM
The head of government is the president, elected for a five-year term, not immediately renewable. The president appoints the Cabinet. There is a unicameral legislature, the National Assembly, with 90 members directly elected for a five-year term.

HEAD OF STATE
President, Enrique Bolaños Geyer, *elected* 4 November 2001, *sworn in* 10 January 2002
Vice-President, José Rizo Castellon

CABINET *as at August 2003*
Agriculture and Forests, José Augusto Navarro
Defence, José Adán Guerra
Development, Industry and Commerce, Mario Arana Sevilla
Education, Culture and Sports, Silvio de Franco Montalvan
Environment and Natural Resources, Arturo Harding Lacayo
Family Affairs, Natalia Barillas Cruz
Finance and Public Credit, Eduardo Montealegre Rivas
Foreign Affairs, Norman Caldera Cardinal
Health, José Antonio Alvarado
Interior, Eduardo Urcuyo Llanes
Labour, Virgilio José Gurdián Castellon
Minister President of the Nicaraguan Institute of Municipal Development (INIFOM), Alejandro Fiallos Navarro
Transport and Infrastructure, Pedro Solórzano Castillo

EMBASSY OF NICARAGUA
Suite 31, Vicarage House, 58–60 Kensington Church Street, London W8 4DP Tel: 020-7938 2373
Ambassador Extraordinary and Plenipotentiary, HE Juan B. Sacasa, apptd 2001

BRITISH EMBASSY
Apartado A-169, Plaza Churchill, Reparto 'Los Robles', Managua Tel: (00 505) (2) 780014/780887/674050
Ambassador and Consul-General, HE Tim Brownbill, apptd 2002

DEFENCE
The Army has 127 main battle tanks and 166 armoured personnel carriers. The Navy has five patrol and coastal vessels at three bases. The Air Force has 15 armed helicopters. Full military relations with the USA were restored in 2000 after 21 years.
MILITARY EXPENDITURE – 1.1 per cent of GDP (2001)
MILITARY PERSONNEL – 14,000: Army 12,000, Navy 800, Air Force 1,200
CONSCRIPTION DURATION – 18–36 months

ECONOMY
The country is mainly agricultural. The major crops are maize, sugar cane, rice, sorghum, beans, bananas and coffee; livestock and timber production are also important. Nicaragua possesses deposits of gold and silver.

In December 2002 the IMF approved the release of US$73 million to support the government's economic programme from 2002–5 and the country's debtors cancelled $405 million of its public external debt with immediate effect and rescheduled the remainder.

In 2000 there was a trade deficit of US$995 million and a current account deficit of US$505 million. Imports totalled US$1,776 million and exports US$606 million.
GNP – US$2,053 million (2000); US$400 per capita (2000)
GDP – US$2,125 million (1998); US$478 per capita (2000)

ANNUAL AVERAGE GROWTH OF GDP – 5.0 per cent (1999)
INFLATION RATE – 3.7 per cent (2002)
UNEMPLOYMENT – 9.8 per cent (2000)
TOTAL EXTERNAL DEBT – US$7,019 million (2000)

TRADE
Considerable quantities of foodstuffs are imported as well as cotton goods, jute, iron and steel, machinery and petroleum products. The chief exports are cotton, coffee, beef and sugar.

Trade with UK	2001	2002
Imports from UK	£2,807,000	£4,631,000
Exports to UK	9,469,000	6,071,000

COMMUNICATIONS
The Inter-American Highway runs between the Honduras and the Costa Rican borders; the inter-oceanic highway runs from Corinto on the Pacific coast via Managua to Rama, where there is a natural waterway to Bluefields on the Atlantic; there are 15,478 km of roads. The main airport is at Managua. The chief port is Corinto on the Pacific. There are 252 miles of railway, all on the Pacific side of the country.

NIGER

République du Niger - Republic of Niger

AREA – 489,191 sq. miles (1,267,000 sq. km). Neighbours: Algeria and Libya (north), Chad (east), Nigeria and Benin (south), Mali and Burkina Faso (west). Apart from a small area along the Niger Valley in the south-west near the capital, the country is entirely savannah or desert
POPULATION – 10,355,156 (2001 estimate): Hausa (54 per cent) in the south, Songhai and Djerma in the south-west, Fulani, Beriberi-Manga, and nomadic Tuareg in the north. The main religion is Islam (95 per cent), with Christian and Animist minorities. The official language is French. Hausa, Djerma and Fulani are also spoken
CAPITAL – Niamey (population, 627,400, 1999 estimate)
CURRENCY – Franc CFA of 100 centimes
NATIONAL ANTHEM – Auprès Du Grand Niger Puissant (By The Banks Of The Mighty Great Niger)
NATIONAL DAY – 18 December
NATIONAL FLAG – Three horizontal stripes, orange, white and green with an orange disc in the middle of the white stripe
POPULATION GROWTH RATE – 3.2 per cent
POPULATION DENSITY – 8 per sq. km (1999)
MILITARY EXPENDITURE – 1.8 per cent of GDP (2001)
MILITARY PERSONNEL – 5,300: Army 5,200, Air Force 100; Paramilitaries 5,400
CONSCRIPTION DURATION – Two years (selective)
ILLITERACY RATE – (m) 76.2 per cent; (f) 91.6 per cent (2000)
ENROLMENT (percentage of age group) – primary 29 per cent (1997); secondary 7 per cent (1997); tertiary 0.7 per cent (1991)

HISTORY AND POLITICS
The first French expedition arrived in 1891 and the country was fully occupied by 1914. It decided on 18 December 1958 to remain an autonomous republic within the French Community; full independence outside the Community was proclaimed on 3 August 1960. The president and government were overthrown in a military coup on 27 January 1996 led by Col. Ibrahim Barre Mainassara, who was elected president on 8 July 1996. The pro-Mainassara National Union of Independents for Democratic Renewal won the largest number of seats in legislative elections in 1996, though these were boycotted by main opposition groups. President Mainassara was assassinated on 9 April 1999. On 11 April Major Daouda Mallam Wanke, head of the presidential guard unit responsible for the assassination, was named as the country's new president. In May, President Wanke established a Consultative Council which drafted a new constitution; it was approved by representatives of political groups in June and by a national referendum in July. A presidential election was held in November 1999 and won by Mamadou Tandja of the National Movement for Society in Development (MNSD). In the simultaneous legislative elections the MNSD won an overall majority in the National Assembly.

INSURGENCY
An ethnic Tuareg-based insurgency began in the north of Niger in 1991; a peace accord was signed with the main group, the Front for the Liberation of Aïr and Azawad (FLAA), in 1995 and two splinter groups agreed to a cease-fire in 1997. All rebel groups had been disarmed by 1998.

HEAD OF STATE
President, Mamadou Tandja, *elected* 24 November 1999, *sworn in* 22 December 1999

COUNCIL OF MINISTERS *as at July 2003*
Prime Minister, Hama Amadou
Agricultural Development, Abari Maï Moussa
Animal Resources, Koroné Maoudé
Basic Education and Literacy, Ari Ibrahim
Civil Service, Labour and Government Spokesman, Moussa Saïbou Kassaï
Commerce and Promotion of the Private Sector, Seïni Oumarou
Communications, Government Spokesman, Oumarou Harouna Sidikou
Community Development, Sabiou Daddy Gaoh
Equipment and Territorial Development, Zakaria Mamadou
Finance and Economy, Ali Badjo Gamatié
Foreign Affairs, Co-operation and African Integration, Aissatou Mindaoudou
Interior and Decentralisation, Albade Abouba
Justice, Relations with Parliament, Mati Moussa
Mines and Energy, Rabiou Hassane Yari
Ministers of State, Moumouni Djermakoye Adamou *(African Integration and the New Partnership for Africa's Development);* Abdou Labo *(Sport, Culture and the Francophone Games)*
National Defence, Souley Hassane 'Bonto'
Public Health and the Fight against Endemic Diseases, Mamadou Sourghia
Secondary and Higher Education, Research and Technology, Sala Habi Salissou
Secretaries of State, Karim Fatouma Zara *(Endemic Diseases);* Sani Koini *(Secretary of State for International Co-operation);* Chaibou Mamane *(Fight against Desertification)*
Social Development, Population, Promotion of Women and Protection of Children, Abdoulwahid Halimatou Ousseyni

Tourism and Cottage Industry, Rissa ag Boula
Transport, Souleymane Kane
Urban Affairs, Environment and Public Service, Mamane
Bachir Yahaya
*Water Resources, Environment and the Fight against Desert
Encroachment,* Adamou Namata
Youth and Professional Integration of Youths, Mounkaïla
Sanda

EMBASSY OF THE REPUBLIC OF NIGER
154 rue de Longchamp, F-75116, Paris
Tel: (00 33) (1) 4504 8060
Ambassador Extraordinary and Plenipotentiary, HE
Mariama Hima, apptd 1999

BRITISH AMBASSADOR, HE J. François Gordon, CMG,
resident at Abidjan, Côte d'Ivoire

ECONOMY
The cultivation of groundnuts and the production of
livestock are the main industries and provide two of the
main exports. Other agricultural products include millet,
cassava and sugar cane. There are large uranium deposits
at Arlit and Akouta, and this is the main export. Gold
deposits exist north-west of Niamey. France and Nigeria
are the main trading partners.
In 2000 imports totalled US$372 million and exports
US$283 million.
GNP – US$1,939 million (2000); US$180 per capita
(2000)
GDP – US$1,939 million (2001); US$170 per capita
(2000)
ANNUAL AVERAGE GROWTH OF GDP – 3.4 per cent
(1998)
INFLATION RATE – 2.9 per cent (2000)
TOTAL EXTERNAL DEBT – US$1,638 million (2000)

Trade with UK	2001	2002
Imports from UK	£5,788,000	£6,184,000
Exports to UK	10,228,000	518,000

NIGERIA

Federal Republic of Nigeria

AREA – 356,308 sq. miles (910,800 sq. km).
Neighbours: Benin (west), Niger (north), Chad (north-
east), Cameroon (east)
POPULATION – 116,929,000 (2001) The main ethnic
groups are Hausa/Fulani, Yoruba and Ibo, and the
principal languages are English, Hausa, Yoruba and
Ibo. There are some 373 ethnic groups, who speak
over 500 different languages. The main religions are
Islam (45 per cent, mainly in the north and west) and
Christianity (49 per cent, mainly in the south, the
remainder being Animists
CAPITAL – Abuja (population, 378,671), declared the
federal capital in 1991
MAJOR CITIES – Ibadan (1,295,000); Kaduna
(309,600); Kano (699,900); Lagos, the former capital
(1,347,000); Ogbomosho (660,600); ΨPort Harcourt
(371,000)
CURRENCY – Naira (N) of 100 kobo
NATIONAL ANTHEM – Arise, O Compatriots
NATIONAL DAY – 1 October (Independence Day)
NATIONAL FLAG – Three equal vertical bands, green,
white and green
LIFE EXPECTANCY (years) – 52 (2001)

POPULATION GROWTH RATE – 2.8 per cent
POPULATION DENSITY – 128 per sq. km (2001)
ILLITERACY RATE – (m) 27.6 per cent; (f) 44.2 per cent
(2000)
ENROLMENT (percentage of age group) – tertiary 4.1
per cent (1993)

HISTORY AND POLITICS
The Federation of Nigeria attained independence as a
member of the Commonwealth on 1 October 1960 and
became a republic in 1963. In 1966 the military took
power; in 1979 civil rule was restored after elections at
national and state level. The administration was
overthrown by the military in 1983, and the military
regime itself overthrown in 1985. An Armed Forces
Ruling Council (AFRC) was sworn in and governed until
January 1993, when it was replaced by a National
Defence and Security Council (NDSC) and a civilian
Transitional Council. Full power was handed over to the
Transitional Council in August 1993. Continued
instability led Defence Minister Gen. Sanni Abacha to
launch a military coup in November 1993 and install
himself as head of state.
The military regime vowed to hand over power to an
elected government in October 1998. In June 1998 Gen.
Abacha died of a heart attack and was replaced by Gen.
Abdulsalami Abubakar, who promised to continue with
the handover to civilian rule.
In elections in February 1999 the People's Democratic
Party (PDP) won a majority in both houses of parliament
and Gen. Olusegun Obasanjo, the PDP candidate, was
elected president. President Obasanjo and the civilian
administration took office on 29 May 1999.
In the legislative elections on 12 April 2003 the PDP
retained its majority in both houses of parliament and on
19 April 2003 Gen. Olusegun Obasanjo returned to
office for a second term. The government was dissolved
on 21 May 2003 ahead of the presidential inauguration
and as at 1 July a new government had not been
approved by the Senate; the members of the previous
government remain in post on an interim basis.

POLITICAL SYSTEM
The country is a federal democratic republic. The
president is directly elected for a four-year term,
renewable only once. As head of the government, the
president appoints the Federal Executive Council, which
must be approved by the Senate. The National Assembly
is bicameral; the House of Representatives has 360
members and the Senate has 109 members, both elected
for four-year terms.
Originally comprising three regions, the Federation is
now divided into 36 states and the Federal Capital
Territory.
Several predominantly Muslim northern states
introduced the Islamic Shari'ah legal system during
2000, which President Obasanjo had declared
unconstitutional on 1 November 1999. Bauchi adopted
Shari'ah law in June 2001.

INSURGENCIES
The debate on Shari'ah law has exacerbated divisions
between Muslims and Christians and there have been
sporadic clashes in which hundreds have been killed. A
Yoruba separatist organisation, the Odua People's
Congress, was banned in October 2000 following
clashes between its members and Hausas in Lagos.
Fighting has also occurred between Ijaw and Ilaje

tribesmen in the Niger Delta region and between the Isoko and Oleh tribes in Olomoro.

FEDERAL STRUCTURE

State	Population (1991)	Capital
Sokoto	4,392,391	Sokoto
*Zamfara		Gusau
Kebbi	2,062,226	Birnin-Kebbi
Niger	2,482,367	Minna
Kwara	1,566,469	Ilorin
Kogi	2,099,046	Lokoja
Benue	2,780,398	Makurdi
Plateau	3,283,704	Jos
*Nassarawa		Lafia
Taraba	1,480,590	Jalingo
Adamawa	2,124,049	Yola
Borno	2,596,589	Maiduguri
Yobe	1,411,481	Damaturu
Bauchi	4,294,413	Bauchi
*Gombe		Gombe
Jigawa	2,829,929	Dutse
Kano	5,632,040	Kano
Katsina	3,878,344	Katsina
Kaduna	3,969,252	Kaduna
Federal Capital Territory	378,671	Abuja
Oyo	3,488,789	Ibadan
Osun	2,203,016	Oshogbo
Ogun	2,338,570	Abeokuta
Lagos	5,685,781	Ikeja
Ondo	3,884,485	Akure
*Ekiti		Ado Ekiti
Edo	2,159,848	Benin City
Delta	2,570,181	Asaba
Rivers	3,983,857	Port-Harcourt
*Bayelsa		Yenagoa
Abia	2,297,978	Umuahia
Imo	2,485,499	Owerri
*Ebonyi		Abakaliki
Anambra	2,767,903	Awka
Enugu	3,161,295	Enugu
Cross River	1,865,604	Calabar
Akwa Ibom	2,359,736	Uyo

*State created on 1 October 1996 by dividing state immediately preceding it in list

HEAD OF STATE

President, Olusegun Obasanjo, *elected* 27 February 1999, re-elected 19 April 2003
Vice-President, Atiku Abubakar

FEDERAL EXECUTIVE COUNCIL *as at July 2003*
Agriculture and Rural Development, Mallam Adamu Bello
Aviation, Kema Chikwe
Commerce in Africa, Chief Precious Ngelala
Communications, Bello Haliru Mohammed
Culture and Tourism, Boma Bromillow Jack
Defence, Lt.-Gen. Yakubu Theophilus Danjuma
Education, Babalola Borishade
Environment, Mohammed Kabir Said
Federal Capital Territory, Mohammed Abba-Gana
Finance, Mallam Adamu Ciroma
Foreign Affairs, Sule Lamido
Health, Alphonsus Bosa Nwosu
Industry, Chief Kolawole Jamodu
Information, Jerry Gana
Internal Affairs, Mohammed Sheta
Justice, Attorney-General, Kanu Godwin Agabi

Labour, Employment and Productivity, Musa Gwadabe
Ministers in the Presidency, Chief Bimbola Ogunkelu *(Co-operation and Integration in Africa);* Ibrahim Umar Kida *(Inter-governmental Affairs);* Yomi Edu *(Special Duties)*
Police Affairs, vacant
Power and Steel, Olu Agunloye
Science and Technology, Turner Isoun
Solid Mineral Resources, Dupe Adelja
Sports and Social Development, Steven Ibn Akiga
Transport, Chief Ojo Maduekwe
Water Resources, Muktari Shagari
Women and Youth, Aishat Ismail
Works and Housing, Garba Ali Madaki

NIGERIA HIGH COMMISSION
Nigeria House, 9 Northumberland Avenue, London WC2N 5BX
Tel: 020-7839 1244
High Commissioner, HE Dr Christopher Kolade, apptd 2002

BRITISH HIGH COMMISSION
Shehu Shagari Way (North), Maitama, Abuja
Tel: (00 234) (9) 413 2010/2011/2796/2880
Email: consular.abuja@fco.gov.uk
High Commissioner, HE Philip Thomas, CMG, apptd 2001

BRITISH COUNCIL DIRECTOR, Cathy Stephens
Plot 2935, IBB Way, Maitama, PMB 550, Garki, Abuja
Tel: (00 234) (9) 413 7870-7
Email: maureen.ideozu@ng.britishcouncil.org

DEFENCE
The Army has 200 main battle tanks and 330 armoured personnel carriers. The Navy has one frigate, eight patrol and coastal vessels and two helicopters at three bases. The Air Force has 86 combat aircraft and 16 armed helicopters.
MILITARY EXPENDITURE – 1.3 per cent of GDP (2001)
MILITARY PERSONNEL – 78,500: Army 62,000, Navy 7,000, Air Force 9,500; Paramilitaries 82,000

ECONOMY
Nigeria was a predominantly agricultural country until the early 1970s when oil became the principal source of export revenue (over 90 per cent). Recent governments have attempted to stimulate greater self-reliance by encouraging non-oil exports and the use of local rather than imported raw materials. Much of Nigeria's oil revenue has been squandered on major projects which have failed to generate the predicted returns. Nigeria has also suffered from endemic corruption, especially under Gen. Sani Abacha. Many state and local governments have not published audited accounts for many years. President Obasanjo has attempted to tackle the problem by retiring many army officers suspected of corruption and suspending government contracts signed during the last three months of the previous administration, pending investigations.

Agricultural production has fallen since 1970, largely as a result of a system of marketing boards which fixed prices for agricultural commodities, often setting prices at levels which were too high or low.

Petrol prices are fixed at a level below market rates. These act as a disincentive to producers to refine their oil, which has resulted in widespread fuel shortages.

Three oil refineries are in operation at Port Harcourt, Warri and Kaduna, and steel plants at Warri and Ajaokuta

(non-operational). Other projects include natural gas liquefaction, petrochemicals, fertilisers, power stations and irrigation schemes. Tin and calumbite mining on the Jos plateau, textiles and coal mining are also important.
GNP – US$32,705 million (2000); US$260 per capita (2000)
GDP – US$41,237 million (2001); US$244 per capita (2000)
ANNUAL AVERAGE GROWTH OF GDP – 2.4 per cent (1998)
INFLATION RATE – 14.2 per cent (2002)
TOTAL EXTERNAL DEBT – US$34,134 million (2000)

TRADE
The principal exports are oil, groundnuts, tin, cocoa, rubber, fish and timber. In 1999 there was a trade surplus of US$4,288 million and a current account surplus of US$506 million. In 2000, imports totalled US$8,721 million and exports US$20,975 million.

Trade with UK	2001	2002
Imports from UK	£684,132,000	£716,377,000
Exports to UK	68,249,000	96,807,000

COMMUNICATIONS
There are 194,394 km of roads. The Nigerian railway system, which is controlled by the Nigerian Railway Corporation, has 3,557 route km of lines. The principal international airlines operate from Lagos, Kano and Port Harcourt.

NORWAY

Kongeriket Norge – Kingdom of Norway

AREA – 118,000 sq. miles (306,800 sq. km), of which Svalbard and Jan Mayen have a combined area of 24,355 sq. miles (63,080 sq. km). Neighbours: Sweden, Finland, Russia (east)
POPULATION – 4,488,000 (2001). The language is Norwegian and has two forms: Bokmål and Nynorsk. Sami is spoken in the north of the country. The state religion is Evangelical Lutheran
CAPITAL – ΨOslo (population, 508,726, 2001)
MAJOR CITIES – ΨBergen (230,948); ΨKristiansand (73,087); ΨStavanger (108,848); ΨTrondheim (150,166), 2001 estimates
CURRENCY – Krone of 100 øre
NATIONAL ANTHEM – Ja, Vi Elsker Dette Landet (Yes, We Love This Country)
NATIONAL DAY – 17 May (Constitution Day)
NATIONAL FLAG – Red, with white-bordered blue cross
LIFE EXPECTANCY (years) – 79 (2001)
POPULATION GROWTH RATE – 0.5 per cent
POPULATION DENSITY – 15 per sq. km (2001)

The coastline is deeply indented with numerous fjords and fringed with rocky islands. The surface is mountainous, consisting of elevated and barren tablelands separated by deep and narrow valleys. At the North Cape the sun does not appear to set from about 14 May to 29 July, causing the phenomenon known as the Midnight Sun; conversely, there is no apparent sunrise from about 18 November to 24 January. During the long winter nights the Northern Lights or Aurora Borealis are seen.

HISTORY AND POLITICS
Norway was unified under Harald I Fairhair c.AD 900 and participated in the Viking expansion from the ninth to the 11th centuries. The accession of Magnus VII (1319) unified the Norwegian and Swedish crowns until his son became King Håkon VI of Norway in 1343. The Norwegian and Danish crowns were united in 1380 and confirmed by the Union of Kalmar (1397) which also brought Sweden under the rule of Queen Margrethe of Denmark. Norway remained a Danish province until transferred to Sweden under the Treaty of Kiel (1814). The union with Sweden was dissolved on 7 June 1905 when Norway regained complete independence.
Norway remained neutral during the First World War and on the outbreak of the Second World War but was invaded by Germany in 1940. Neutrality was abandoned when Norway joined NATO in 1949. Norway became a founder member of EFTA in 1960. The Labour Party governed from 1945 to 1965 when the extensive welfare state system was built.
A general election was held on 10 September 2001, in which no party won an outright majority. The Labour Party (DNA) has the largest number of seats (43) but, following a month of talks, three parties, the Conservative Party (H), the Christian Democratic Party (KrF) and the Liberal Party (V), agreed to form a coalition government and on 19 October Kjell Magne Bondevik of the KrF was appointed prime minister.

FOREIGN RELATIONS
Although a referendum in 1972 rejected membership of the EC and the ruling centre-right coalition collapsed in 1990 over the question of EC membership the Storting voted in 1992 to apply to join the EC. Negotiations with the EU concluded on 1 March 1994 with a proposed accession date of 1 January 1995, subject to parliamentary and national referendum ratifications. However, in a national referendum on 28 November 1994 the electorate voted against joining the EU by 52.4 per cent to 47.6 per cent.

POLITICAL SYSTEM
Under the 1814 constitution, the 165-member unicameral legislature, the *Storting,* is directly elected for four years. The Storting elects one-quarter of its members to constitute the *Lagting* (Upper Chamber), the other three-quarters forming the *Odelsting* (Lower Chamber), dividing when legislative matters are under discussion.

HEAD OF STATE
HM The King of Norway, King Harald V, KG, GCVO, *born* 21 February 1937; *succeeded* 17 January 1991, on the death of his father King Olav V; *married* 29 August 1968, Sonja Haraldsen, and has *issue,* Prince Håkon Magnus, and Princess Martha Louise, *born* 22 September 1971
Heir, HRH Crown Prince Håkon Magnus, *born* 20 July 1973, *married* Mette-Marit Tjessem Hoiby

CABINET *as at July 2003*
Prime Minister, Kjell Magne Bondevik (KrF)
Agriculture, Lars Sponheim (V)
Children and Family Affairs, Laila Dåvøy (KrF)
Church and Cultural Affairs, Valgerd Svarstad Haugland (KrF)
Defence, Kristin Krohn Devold (H)
Education and Research, Kristin Clemet (H)
Environment, Børge Brende (H)

Finance, Per-Kristian Foss (H)
Fisheries, Svein Ludvigsen (H)
Foreign Affairs, Jan Petersen (H)
Health, Dagfinn Høybråten (KrF)
Industry and Trade, Ansgar Gabrielsen (H)
International Development, Hilde Frafjord Johnson (KrF)
Justice and Police, Odd Einar Dørum (V)
Labour and Government Administration, Victor Danielsen
  Norman (H)
Local Government and Regional Development, Erna Solberg
  (H)
Petroleum and Energy, Einar Steensnaes (KrF)
Social Affairs, Ingierd Schou (H)
Transport and Communications, Torild Skogsholm (V)

ROYAL NORWEGIAN EMBASSY
25 Belgrave Square, London SW1X 8QD Tel: 020-7591 5500
Ambassador Extraordinary and Plenipotentiary, HE Tarald
  Osnes Brautaset, apptd 2000

BRITISH EMBASSY
Thomas Heftyesgate 8, N-0244 Oslo Tel: (00 47) 2313 2700
Ambassador Extraordinary and Plenipotentiary, HE Alison
  Leslie, apptd 2002

BRITISH COUNCIL DIRECTOR, Joan Barry, Fridtjof
Nansens Plass 5, N-0160 Oslo Tel: (00 47) (22) 396 190
Email: british.council@britishcouncil.no

DEFENCE

Norway is a member of NATO. The Army has 170 main
battle tanks, 157 armoured infantry fighting vehicles and
189 armoured personnel carriers. The Navy has six
submarines, three frigates and 15 patrol and coastal
vessels at three bases. The Air Force has 61 combat
aircraft.
MILITARY EXPENDITURE – 1.8 per cent of GDP (2001)
MILITARY PERSONNEL – Army 14,700, Navy 6,100,
  Air Force 5,000
CONSCRIPTION DURATION – 12 months plus refresher
  training

ECONOMY

The cultivated area is about 10,703 sq. km, 3.5 per cent
of the total surface area. Forests cover 23 per cent; the
rest consists of highland pastures or uninhabitable
mountains. The chief agricultural products are grain,
vegetables, milk, furs and timber.

The Gulf Stream causes the sea temperature to be
higher than average for the latitude, which brings shoals
of herring and cod into the fishing grounds. In 1997 the
catch totalled more than 3 million tonnes. In 1998, dried
cod worth €352 million/US$400 million was produced.

The chief industries are oil production and transport,
construction, electricity supply, manufactures, agriculture
and forestry, fisheries, mining, metal and ferro-alloy
production and shipping. Industries providing both
manufactured products and services for the development
of North Sea energy resources have become increasingly
important. In 1998 150,006,000 tonnes of crude oil
were produced. Norway produces large amounts of
hydroelectric power.
GNP – US$155,064 million (2000); US$34,530 per
  capita (2000)
GDP – US$165,458 million (2001); US$36,198 per
  capita (2000)
ANNUAL AVERAGE GROWTH OF GDP – 2.7 per cent
  (2000)

INFLATION RATE – 1.3 per cent (2001)
UNEMPLOYMENT – 3.4 per cent (2000)

TRADE

The chief imports are motor vehicles, ships and
machinery, clothing, foods and textiles. Exports consist
chiefly of crude oil and gas, machinery and transport
equipment and manufactured goods.

In 2001 Norway had a trade surplus of US$26,018
million and a current account surplus of US$25,960
million. Imports totalled US$32,181 million and exports
US$57,960 million.

Trade with UK	2001	2002
Imports from UK	£1,897,826,000	£1,815,245,000
Exports to UK	5,896,996,000	5,568449,000

COMMUNICATIONS

The total length of railways open at the end of 1999 was
4,021 km, excluding private lines. There are 90,880 km
of public roads in Norway (including urban streets).

CULTURE AND EDUCATION

The Norwegian language in both its present forms is
closely related to other Scandinavian languages.
Independence from Denmark (1814) and resurgent
nationalism led to the development of 'new Norwegian'
based on dialects, which now has equal official standing
with 'bokmål', in which Danish influence is more
obvious. Ludvig Holberg (1684–1754) is regarded as the
father of Norwegian literature, though the modern
period begins with the writings of Henrik Wergeland
(1808–45). Some of the famous names are Henrik Ibsen
(1828–1906), Bjørnstjerne Bjørnson (1832–1910),
Nobel Prizewinner in 1903, and the novelists Jonas Lie
(1833–1908), Alexander Kielland (1849–1906), Knut
Hamsun (1859–1952) and Sigrid Undset (1882–1949),
the latter two also Nobel Prizewinners. Old Norse
literature is among the most ancient and richest in
Europe.

Education from six to 16 is free and compulsory in the
'basic schools', and free from 16 to 19 years. The
majority of pupils receive post-compulsory schooling at
'upper secondary' schools, regional colleges akin to
polytechnics, and 11 universities and other university-
level specialist colleges.
ENROLMENT (percentage of age group) – primary 100
  per cent (1997); secondary 100 per cent (1997);
  tertiary 62 per cent (1997)

TERRITORIES

SVALBARD, area 24,295 sq. miles (62,923 sq. km);
  population 2,332 (2001 estimate); inhabitants mainly
  engaged in coal-mining. The Svalbard archipelago
  consists of the main island, Spitsbergen (15,200 sq.
  miles), North East Land, the Wiche Islands, Barents
  and Edge Islands, Prince Charles Foreland, Hope
  Island, Bear Island and many islands in the
  neighbourhood of the main group. Glaciers cover 60
  per cent of the land area. The sovereignty of Norway
  over the archipelago was recognised by other nations
  in 1920 and in 1925 Norway assumed sovereignty
JAN MAYEN ISLAND was joined to Norway by law in
  1930

NORWEGIAN ANTARCTIC TERRITORIES

BOUVET ISLAND was declared a dependency of Norway in 1930

PETER THE FIRST ISLAND was declared a dependency of Norway in 1931

PRINCESS RAGNHILD LAND has been claimed as Norwegian since 1931

QUEEN MAUD LAND was declared Norwegian territory by the Norwegian government in 1939

OMAN

Saltanat 'Umān - Sultanate of Oman

AREA – 81,731 sq. miles (212,500 sq. km). Neighbours: Yemen, Saudi Arabia and the UAE (west)

POPULATION – 2,622,000 (2001). The official language is Arabic. Islam is the official religion. The majority of the population are Ibadhi Muslims; there is a large Sunni and a small Shia minority. Other religions are tolerated

CAPITAL – ΨMuscat (Masqat) (population, 540,000 2001 estimate)

MAJOR CITIES – ΨBarka; ΨMutrah and Ruwi (the commercial centres); ΨSalalah (the main town of Dhofar); ΨSuhār; ΨSūr

CURRENCY – Rial Omani (OR) of 1,000 baisas

NATIONAL ANTHEM – Ya Rabbana Ifadh Lana Jalalat Al Sultan (O Lord, Protect For Us His Majesty The Sultan)

NATIONAL DAY – 18 November

NATIONAL FLAG – Red with a white panel in the upper fly and a green one in the lower fly; in the canton the national emblem in white

LIFE EXPECTANCY (years) – 71 (2001)

POPULATION GROWTH RATE – 3.5 per cent

POPULATION DENSITY – 12 per sq. km (2001)

Oman lies at the eastern corner of the Arabian peninsula. Sharjah and Fujairah (UAE) separate the main part of Oman from the northernmost part of the state, a peninsula extending into the Strait of Hormuz.

The north and the south of Oman are divided by nearly 400 miles of desert. The Batinah, the coastal plain, is fertile. The Hajjar is a mountain spine running from north-west to south-east and for the most part barren, but valleys penetrate the central massif which are irrigated by wells or a system of underground canals called aflaj which tap the water table. The two plateaus leading from the western slopes of the mountains descend to the Empty Quarter of the Arabian Desert. Dhofar, the southern province, is the only part of the Arabian peninsula to be touched by the south-west monsoon.

HISTORY AND POLITICS

Oman became part of the Islamic empire in the seventh century. From the ninth to 16th centuries the area was governed by a succession of religious leaders, or imams of the Ibadhi branch of Islam. The Portuguese established trading posts on the coast in 1507 but were expelled in 1649.

In 1744 Ahmad bin Said Al bu Said established the current ruling dynasty of sultans. The country was divided between the sultan's stronghold in the coastal Muscat-Matrah region and the imam in the interior. The sultan cultivated close relations with Britain and the Sultanate of Muscat and Oman became a British protectorate in 1798. In the late 19th century Dhofar was annexed.

In the 1950s the imam proclaimed an independent state in a revolt which was put down with British assistance. A seven-year-long Marxist uprising was crushed in 1975. The current sultan ousted his father in a palace coup in 1970 and changed the state's name to the Sultanate of Oman. Dhofar is still governed as a separate province and Muscat has special status.

Legislative elections were scheduled to take place on 2 October 2003.

POLITICAL SYSTEM

In 1996 the sultan issued the Basic Statute of the State which decreed Oman to be a hereditary absolute monarchy. Effective political power remains with the Sultan, who rules by decree and is advised by the Cabinet of Ministers, which he appoints. The sultan is advised by the Council of State (Majlis al-Dawlah), whose 41 members are appointed by him. The 83-member Consultative Council (Majlis ash-Shura) has been directly elected since September 2000. The Council has the right to review legislation, question ministers and make policy proposals. The electorate expanded gradually over the past decade but in November 2002 the Sultan extended voting rights to all citizens over the age of 21, in advance of Shura elections due on 2 October 2003.

HEAD OF STATE

HM The Sultan of Oman, Sultan Qaboos bin Said al-Said, *succeeded* on deposition of Sultan Said bin Taimur, 23 July 1970

COUNCIL OF MINISTERS *as at July 2003*

Prime Minister, Defence, Finance, Foreign Affairs, The Sultan

Personal Representative of The Sultan, HH Sayyid Thuwaini bin Shehab al-Said

Deputy Minister for Cabinet Affairs, HH Sayyid Fahd bin Mamud al-Said

Agriculture and Fisheries, Shaikh Salim bin Halil al-Khalili

Civil Service, Shaikh Abdel Aziz bin Matar al-Azizi

Commerce, Industry and Minerals, Maqbul bin Ali bin Sultan

Defence, Badr bin Saud bin Hareb al-Busaidi

Education and Teaching, Yahia bin Saud Al-Sallimi

Foreign Affairs, Yusuf bin Alawi bin Abdullah

Head of National Authority for Industrial Craftsmanship, Sheika Aisha bint Khalfan bin Jameel al-Sayabiyah

Health, Dr Ali bin Mohammed bin Mousa

Higher Education, Yahya bin Mahfudh al-Mantheri

Housing, Electricity and Water, Shaikh Suhail bin Mustahail bin Salim al-Shamas

Information, Hamad bin Muhammad al-Rashidi

Interior, Saud bin Ibrahim al-Busaidi

Justice, Shaikh Mohammed bin Abdullah bin Zahir al-Hinai

Labour and Training, Jomaa bin Ali bin Jomaa

Minister of State and Governor of Dhofar, Shaikh Mohammad bin Ali al-Qatabi

Minister of State and Governor of Muscat, Mutasim bin Hamad al-Busaidi

Minister of State for Legal Affairs, Mohammed bin Ali bin Nasir al-Alawi

Municipalities, Environment and Water Resources, Khamis bin Mubarak bin Isa al-Alawi

National Economy and Finance, Ahmed bin Abdulnabi Makki

National Heritage and Culture, Haytham bin Tareq al-Said
Palace Affairs, Ali bin Hamud al-Bussaidi
Palace Security, Gen. Ali bin Majed al-Mamari
Petroleum and Gas, Dr Mohammed bin Hamad bin Saif al-Romhi
Religious Property and Affairs, Shaikh Abdallah bin Mahammed al-Salimi
Social Affairs, Shaikh Amer bin Shuwain al-Hosni
Special Advisers to the Sultan, Faisal bin Ali bin Faisal al-Said *(Cultural Affairs);* Shahib ibn Taymur al-Said *(Environment)*
Transport and Telecommunications, Col. Malik bin Sulaiman al-Ma'amari

EMBASSY OF THE SULTANATE OF OMAN
167 Queen's Gate, London SW7 5HE Tel: 020-7225 0001
Ambassador Extraordinary and Plenipotentiary, HE Hussain Ali Abdullatif, apptd 1995

BRITISH EMBASSY
PO Box 185, Mina Al Fahal, Muscat, Postal Code 116
Tel: (00 968) 609 000 Email: becomu@omantel.net.om
Ambassador Extraordinary and Plenipotentiary, HE Stuart Laing, apptd 2002

BRITISH COUNCIL DIRECTOR, Jim Scarth, Road One, Madinat al Sultan, Qaboos West, PO Box 73, Muscat
Tel: (00 968) 600 548
Email: bc.muscat@om.britishcouncil.org

DEFENCE
The Army has 117 main battle tanks and 189 armoured personnel carriers. The Navy has 13 patrol and coastal vessels at six bases. The Air Force has 40 combat aircraft.
MILITARY EXPENDITURE – 14.4 per cent of GDP (2001)
MILITARY PERSONNEL – Army 25,000, Navy 4,200, Air Force 4,100, Royal Household 6,400; Paramilitaries 4,400

ECONOMY
Although there is considerable cultivation in the fertile areas and cattle are raised in the mountains, the backbone of the economy is the oil industry, accounting for about 40 per cent of GDP. Petroleum Development Oman (PDO) (60 per cent owned by the Oman Government) began exporting oil in 1967. Concessions (off and on shore) are held by several major international companies. Production of crude oil and petroleum condensates in 2001 was 349 million barrels and natural gas production was 270.7 million cubic feet.

The government is actively encouraging the diversification of the economy and private sector development. Tourism is also an expanding area.

In 2000 there was a trade surplus of US$6,726 million and a current account deficit of US$3,347 million.
GDP – US$14,162 million (1998); US$7,811 per capita (2000)
ANNUAL AVERAGE GROWTH OF GDP – –1.0 per cent (1999)
INFLATION RATE – –1.1 per cent (2000)
TOTAL EXTERNAL DEBT – US$6,267 million (2000)

TRADE
Trade is mainly with the UAE, UK, Japan, South Korea and China. Chief imports are machinery and transport equipment, industrial goods and foodstuffs. Oil accounts for over 80 per cent of exports.

In 2000 imports totalled US$5,040 million. In 1998 exports US$5,508 totalled million.

Trade with UK	2001	2002
Imports from UK	£302,053,000	£254,951,000
Exports to UK	68,455,000	86,348,000

COMMUNICATIONS
Port Qaboos at Mutrah has eight deep-water berths which have been constructed as part of the harbour facilities. There are some 34,000 km of roads, of which 9,000 km are paved, linking most main population centres of the country with the coast and with the towns of the UAE, though only a trunk road links the north and south of Oman. There are airports at Seeb, Salalah, Sur, Masirah, Khasab and Diba.

SOCIAL WELFARE AND EDUCATION
For many years the Sultanate was a poor country but the advent of oil revenues and the change of regime in 1970 led to a wide-ranging development programme, especially concerned with health, education and communications. There are now 55 hospitals and 118 health centres. Mass immunisation programmes have eradicated poliomyelitis and diphtheria. In 2000 there were 1,008 state schools. There is one state university and several private universities.
ILLITERACY RATE – (m) 19.8 per cent; (f) 38.4 per cent (2000)
ENROLMENT (percentage of age group) – primary 76 per cent (1997); secondary 67 per cent (1997); tertiary 8 per cent (1997)

PAKISTAN

Islāmī Jamhūriya-e-Pākistān - Islamic Republic of Pakistan

AREA – 296,500 sq. miles (770,900 sq. km).
 Neighbours: Iran (west), Afghanistan (north and north-west), China (north-east), the disputed territory of Kashmir, India (east)
POPULATION – 144,971,000 (2001); 95 per cent Muslim, 3.5 per cent Christian, about 1 per cent Hindu, and 0.5 per cent Buddhist. Urdu is the national language, but is only spoken by a small minority of the population. The most widely used language is Punjabi, followed by Sindi and Pushto. English is used in business, government and higher education
CAPITAL – Islamabad (population, 350,000, 1998 census)
MAJOR CITIES – Faisalabad (1,977,246); ΨKarachi (9,269,265); Lahore (5,063,499); Rawalpindi (1,406,214), 1998 census
CURRENCY – Pakistan rupee of 100 paisa
NATIONAL ANTHEM - Pak Sarzamin Shad Bad (Blessed Be The Sacred Land)
NATIONAL DAYS – 23 March (Pakistan Day), 14 August (Independence Day)
NATIONAL FLAG – Green with a white crescent and star, and a white vertical strip in the hoist
LIFE EXPECTANCY (years) – 60 (2001)
POPULATION GROWTH RATE – 2.5 per cent
POPULATION DENSITY – 188 per sq. km (2001)
URBAN POPULATION – 34 per cent (2001)

HISTORY AND POLITICS
Pakistan was constituted as a Dominion under the Indian Independence Act 1947, becoming a republic on

23 March 1956. Until 1972 Pakistan consisted of two geographical units, West and East Pakistan, separated by about 1,100 miles of Indian territory. East Pakistan's insistence on complete autonomy led to civil war in 1971; the independence of East Pakistan as Bangladesh was proclaimed in April 1972.

The government was overthrown on 12 October 1999 by the military under Gen. Pervez Musharraf. Gen. Musharraf declared himself chief executive and dissolved the legislature, but left the president in office.

Pakistan's membership of the Commonwealth was suspended on 18 October 1999.

In 20 June 2001, Gen. Musharraf dismissed the elected president and assumed the presidency himself. The extension of Musharraf's presidency for a further five years was approved by referendum in April 2002. In August 2002 President Musharraf granted himself new powers, including the right to dissolve parliament and dismiss the government.

In the elections to the National Assembly on 10 October 2002, 77 of the 342 seats were won by the Pakistan Muslim League (Qaid-i-Azam-PML-Q), making it the largest single party, and it also gained a majority in the Senate elections in February. Mir Zafarullah Khan Jamali was elected prime minister on 21 November 2002 and both he and the new Cabinet were sworn in on 23 November. Since the 2002 elections, the National Assembly has been unable to function fully because of procedural disruption by members opposed to the president.

On 21 August 2003 the North-West Frontier Province voted to introduce Sharia law.

INSURGENCY

Since early 1994 there has been civil disorder in Sind province, especially in Karachi, in two conflicts: armed militants of the Mohajir Qaumi Movement (MQM) Party, which represents Urdu-speaking Indian Muslims who fled from India at partition and their descendants, are fighting for an autonomous Karachi province; and there is armed conflict between Shia and Sunni fundamentalists. During 2002 there were attacks against Christians and Western groups, which were thought to be the work of Islamic militants opposed to Pakistan's support for the US-led war on Afghanistan.

FOREIGN RELATIONS

There has been a dispute over Kashmir between India and Pakistan since independence in 1947, however, the conflict with India over Kashmir flared up in May 1999 when India launched air attacks on Muslim insurgents who had occupied mountainous regions inside India-controlled Kashmir. Small-scale conflicts continued but in December 2001, India and Pakistan assembled troops along the common border and during May and June 2002 there was concern that the conflict could spiral into a nuclear exchange. Following intense international diplomatic activity, the threat of war receded in July but the situation remained tense into 2003.

POLITICAL SYSTEM

The legislature is bicameral, but was suspended following the coup in October 1999. Under the constitution, the Majlis as-Shoora (National Assembly) has a five-year term and comprises 342 members, of whom 272 are directly elected, 10 represent religious minorities and 60 are co-opted women. The Senate has 100 members. The four provinces each have a provincial assembly and are represented in both legislative chambers.

FEDERAL STRUCTURE

Province	Area (sq. km)	Population (1998 census)	Capital
Baluchistan	347,190	6,511,000	Quetta
Federal Capital Territory Islamabad	906	805,000	–
Federally Administered Tribal Areas	27,220	3,138,000	–
North-West Frontier Province	74,521	17,555,000	Peshawar
Punjab	205,344	72,585,000	Lahore
Sind	140,914	29,991,000	Karachi

HEAD OF STATE

President, Chief of Army Staff, Gen. Pervez Musharraf, *assumed office* 20 June 2001, *confirmed in office by referendum* 30 April 2002

FEDERAL MINISTERS *as at July 2003*

Prime Minister, Mir Zafarullah
Commerce, Hamayoon Akhtar Khan
Communications, Ahmad Ali
Education, Zubaida Jalal
Finance, Revenue, Economic Affairs, Planning, Development and Statistics, Shaukat Aziz
Food, Agriculture and Livestock, Sardar Yar Muhammad Rind
Foreign Affairs, Law, Justice and Human Rights, Mian Khursheed Mehmood Kasuri
Health, Muhammad Nasir Khan
Housing and Works, Syed Safwanullah
Industries and Production, Liaquat Ali Jatoi
Information and Media Development, Sheikh Rasheed Ahmad
Interior and Narcotics Control, Makhdoom Syed Faisal Saleh Hayat
Labour, Manpower and Overseas Pakistanis, Abdus Sattar Laleka
Petroleum and Natural Resources, Chaudhry Nauriz Shakoor Khan
Railways, Ghaus Bakhsh Khan Mahar
Science and Technology, Awais Ahmed Khan Leghari
Senior Federal Minister, Defence, Rao Sikander Iqbal
Water and Power, Interprovincial Co-ordination, Kashmir Affairs, Aftab Ahmad Khan Sherpao

HIGH COMMISSION FOR THE ISLAMIC REPUBLIC OF PAKISTAN

35–36 Lowndes Square, London SW1X 9JN
Tel: 020-7664 9200
High Commissioner, HE Abdul Kader Jaffer, apptd 2000

BRITISH HIGH COMMISSION

Diplomatic Enclave, Ramna 5, PO Box 1122, Islamabad
Tel: (00 92) (51) 2206071/5
Email: bhctrade@isb.comsats.net.pk
High Commissioner, HE Mark Lyall Grant, CMG, apptd 2003

BRITISH COUNCIL DIRECTOR, Andrew Picken, PO Box 1135, Islamabad Tel: (00 92) (51) 111 424 424
Email: bc.islamabad@britishcouncil.org.pk

DEFENCE

In May 1998, Pakistan carried out six underground nuclear tests, less than a month after India had carried out its own nuclear tests. In doing so, it became the world's seventh declared nuclear power.

The Army has some 2,357 main battle tanks, 1,181 armoured personnel carriers and 20 attack helicopters. The Navy has ten submarines, eight frigates, nine patrol and coastal vessels, six combat aircraft and nine armed helicopters based at Karachi. The Air Force has 366 combat aircraft.

MILITARY EXPENDITURE – 4.4 per cent of GDP (2001)
MILITARY PERSONNEL – 620,000: Army 550,000, Navy 25,000, Air Force 45,000; Paramilitaries 29

ECONOMY

Agriculture employs half the workforce and contributes a quarter of GDP. The principal crops are cotton, rice, wheat and sugar cane. Pakistan has one of the longest irrigation systems in the world, irrigating 42.5 million acres. There are large deposits of rock salt.

Pakistan also produces hides and skins, leather, wool, fertilisers, paints and varnishes, soda ash, paper, cement, fish, carpets, sports goods, surgical appliances and engineering goods, including switchgear, transformers, cables and wires.

In 2000 there was a trade deficit of US$1,159 million and a current account deficit of US$96 million.

GNP – US$61,022 million (2000); US$440 per capita (2000)
GDP – US$59,605 million (2001); US$458 per capita (2000)
ANNUAL AVERAGE GROWTH OF GDP – 5.6 per cent (2000)
INFLATION RATE – 4.4 per cent (2000)
UNEMPLOYMENT – 5.9 per cent (1998)
TOTAL EXTERNAL DEBT – US$32,091 million (2000)

TRADE

Principal imports are petroleum products, machinery, fertilisers, transport equipment, edible oils, chemicals and ferrous metals. Principal exports are cotton yarn and cloth, carpets, rice, petroleum products, textiles, leather and fish.

In 2001 imports totalled US$10,191 million and exports US$9,238 million.

Trade with UK	2001	2002
Imports from UK	£229,613,000	£243,643,000
Exports to UK	437,863,000	488,618,000

COMMUNICATIONS

There are major seaports at Karachi and Port Qasim. The main airports are at Karachi, Islamabad, Lahore, Peshawar and Quetta. Pakistan International Airlines operates air services between the principal cities as well as abroad. There are 86,597 km of roads and 7,344 km of rail track.

EDUCATION

Education consists of five years of primary education (five to nine years), three years of middle or lower secondary (general or vocational), two years of upper secondary, two years of higher secondary (intermediate) and two to five years of higher education in colleges and universities. Education is free to upper secondary level.

ILLITERACY RATE – (m) 40.1 per cent; (f) 68.9 per cent (2000)

ENROLMENT (percentage of age group) – tertiary 3.0 per cent (1991)

PALAU

Belu'u era Belau – Republic of Palau

AREA – 176.2 sq. miles (458 sq. km)
POPULATION – 20,000 (2001); 13,900 live on Koror and Babelthaup. The population is Micronesian, and predominantly Roman Catholic with a Protestant minority. Palauan and English are official languages
CAPITAL – Koror (population, 13,303, 2000)
CURRENCY – Currency is that of the USA
NATIONAL FLAG – Light blue with a yellow disc set near the hoist
LIFE EXPECTANCY (years) – 69 (2001)
POPULATION GROWTH RATE – 2.6 per cent
POPULATION DENSITY – 44 per sq. km (2001)

The Republic of Palau consists of 340 islands and islets in the western Pacific Ocean, of which eight are inhabited. Part of the Caroline Islands group, the Palau archipelago stretches over 400 miles (644 km) between 2° and 8°N., and 131° and 138°E. Koror island is about 810 miles (1,300 km) south-west of Guam and about 530 miles (852 km) south-east of Manila.

HISTORY AND POLITICS

Spain acquired sovereignty over the Caroline Islands, of which the Palau archipelago is part, in 1886. After defeat in the Spanish-American war of 1898, Spain sold its remaining Pacific possessions, including Palau, to Germany in 1899. On the outbreak of the First World War in 1914, Japan took control of Palau on behalf of the Allied powers, and Japanese administration was confirmed in a League of Nations mandate in 1921. During the Second World War, Allied forces gained control of the archipelago after intense fighting. In 1947 the USA entered into agreement with the UN Security Council to administer the Micronesia area, including Palau, as the UN Trust Territory of the Pacific Islands.

In 1978, the Palau electorate voted in a referendum not to join the new Federated States of Micronesia and instead became a separate part of the UN Trust Territory. A Compact of Free Association was signed with the USA in 1982 and implemented on 1 October 1994. Under this agreement the USA recognised the Republic of Palau as a fully sovereign and independent state and assumed responsibility for its defence for 50 years.

The last presidential and legislative elections were held on 7 November 2000. Members of both chambers are elected as independents.

POLITICAL SYSTEM

Executive power is vested in the president and vice-president, who are directly elected for four-year terms; the president appoints the Cabinet. There is a bicameral legislature (Olbiil era Kelulau) composed of the 16-member House of Delegates (one member elected from each of the 16 constituent states) and the 14-member Senate. There is also a Council of Chiefs to advise the president on matters concerning traditional law and customs. Each of the 16 component states have their own elected governors and legislatures.

HEAD OF STATE
President, Tommy Remengesau, *elected* 7 November 2000, *took office* 19 January 2001
Vice-President, Health, Sandra Pierantozzi

CABINET *as at July 2003*
Administration, Elbuchel Sadang
Commerce and Trade, Otoichi Besebes
Community and Cultural Affairs, Alexander Merep
Education, Mario Katosang
Justice, Michael Rosenthal
Minister of State, Temmy Shmull
Resources and Development, Fritz Koshiba

BRITISH AMBASSADOR, HE Charles Mochan, resident at Suva, Fiji

ECONOMY
The economy remains heavily dependent on US financial support, which the USA is committed to giving under the Compact of Free Association. Fisheries, tourism, subsistence agriculture and government service are the main areas of employment. Agricultural products include coconuts and copra, and Palau earns significant revenue from the sale of fishing licences to foreign fleets fishing for tuna. The chief exports are fish, mussels, coconuts and copra. There are three airports on Koror, Peleliu and Angaur which have daily flights from Guam operated by Continental Micronesia. There are 61 km of roads, of which 36 km are paved. There is a privately owned television station and a government-operated radio station.
GDP – US$121 million (2001); US$6,163 per capita (2000)
ANNUAL AVERAGE GROWTH OF GDP – –4.0 per cent (1998)

Trade with UK	2001	2002
Imports from UK	£39,000	£51,000
Exports to UK	–	–

EDUCATION AND SOCIAL WELFARE
There is a free public school system which, together with independent missionary schools, provides primary and secondary education. A tertiary technical school has been established on Koror since 1969. General medical and dental care is provided by a public hospital.

PANAMA

República de Panamá - Republic of Panama

AREA – 28,615 sq. miles (74,400 sq. km). Neighbours: Colombia (east), Costa Rica (west)
POPULATION – 2,899,000 (2001): 70 per cent mestizo, 14 per cent mixed Amerindian and black, 10 per cent European, 6 per cent Amerindian. Spanish is the official language
CAPITAL – ΨPanama City (population, 464,928, 2000 census)
CURRENCY – Balboa of 100 centésimos (US notes are also in circulation)
NATIONAL ANTHEM – Alcanzamos Por Fin La Victoria (Victory Is Ours At Last)
NATIONAL DAY – 3 November
NATIONAL FLAG – Four quarters; white with blue star (top, next staff), red (in fly), blue (below, next staff) and white with red star

LIFE EXPECTANCY (years) – 74 (2001)
POPULATION GROWTH RATE – 1.7 per cent
POPULATION DENSITY – 39 per sq. km (2001)
URBAN POPULATION – 57 per cent (2001)
MILITARY EXPENDITURE – 1.3 per cent of GDP (2001)
MILITARY PERSONNEL – Paramilitaries 11,800
ILLITERACY RATE – (m) 7.5 per cent; (f) 8.7 per cent (2000)
ENROLMENT (percentage of age group) – primary 100 per cent (1997); secondary 69 per cent (1997); tertiary 32 per cent (1997)

HISTORY AND POLITICS
After a revolt in 1903, Panama declared its independence from Colombia and established a separate government.
On 25 February 1998, President Delvalle was removed by the National Assembly. Presidential elections were held in May 1989 but Gen. Noriega, the Commander of the Defence Forces, annulled the results and on 15 December he assumed power formally as head of state. On 20 December US troops invaded Panama to oust Noriega. Guillermo Endara, believed to have won the May elections, was installed as president. In 1991 the Legislative Assembly approved a change to the constitution which abolished the armed forces.
The most recent presidential election, on 2 May 1999, was won by Mireya Moscoso of the Arnulfist. Simultaneous legislative elections were won by the coalition with 46 of the 71 contested seats.

POLITICAL SYSTEM
Legislative power is vested in a unicameral Legislative Assembly of 71 members; executive power is held by the president, assisted by two elected vice-presidents and an appointed Cabinet. Elections are held every five years under a system of universal and compulsory adult suffrage.

HEAD OF STATE
President, Mireya Elisa Moscoso de Gruber, *elected* 2 May 1999, *sworn in* 1 September 1999
First Vice-President, Arturo Vallarino
Second Vice-President, Dominador Kaiser Bazán

CABINET *as at July 2003*
Agricultural Development, Lynette Maria Stanziola
Canal Affairs, Jerry Salazar
Commerce and Industry, Joaquín Jácome Diez
Education, Doris Rosas de Mata
Finance and Economy, Norberto Delgado
Foreign Relations, Harmodio Arias
Health, Fernando Gracia García
Housing, Miguel Cárdenas
Interior and Justice, Anibal Raul Salas
Labour and Social Welfare, Jaime Moreno Diez
Presidency, Ivonne Young Valdez
Public Works, Eduardo Quiroz
Women, Youth, Family and Children, Rosabel Verdara

EMBASSY OF THE REPUBLIC OF PANAMA
40 Hertford Street, London W1J 7SH
Tel: 020-7493 4646
Ambassador Extraordinary and Plenipotentiary, HE Ariadne Singares Robinson, apptd 2000

BRITISH EMBASSY
Swiss Tower, Calle 53 (Apartado 889) Zona 1, Panama City
Tel: (00 507) 269 0866 Email: britemb@cwpanama.net
Ambassador Extraordinary and Plenipotentiary, HE Jim
Malcolm, OBE, apptd 2002

ECONOMY

The soil is moderately fertile, but nearly one-half of the
land is uncultivated. The chief crops are bananas, sugar,
coconuts, coffee and cereals. The shrimping industry
plays an important role in the economy. Tourism is the
principal foreign currency earner. There are 547 km of
railway track and 10,792 km of roads.

GNP – US$9,308 million (2000); US$3,260 per capita
(2000)

GDP – US$10,170 million (2001); US$3,508 per capita
(2000)

ANNUAL AVERAGE GROWTH OF GDP – 2.7 per cent
(2000)

INFLATION RATE – 1.4 per cent (2000)

UNEMPLOYMENT – 11.8 per cent (1999)

TOTAL EXTERNAL DEBT – US$7,056 million (2000)

TRADE

Imports are mostly manufactured goods, machinery,
lubricants, chemicals and foodstuffs. Exports are bananas,
petroleum products, shrimps, sugar, meat, coffee and
fishmeal.

In 2001 Panama had a trade deficit of US$499 million
and a current account deficit of US$826 million. Imports
totalled US$2,964 million and exports US$911 million.

Trade with UK†	2001	2002
Imports from UK	£64,523,000	£73,951,000
Exports to UK	10,029,000	11,008,000

†Including Colón Free Zone

THE PANAMA CANAL ZONE

The Panama Canal Zone was created in 1903 by a
contract between Panama and the USA, under which the
USA was given the right to build and operate the canal
and administer the adjacent territory. With effect from 1
October 1979 the Canal Zone (1,142 sq. km/647 sq.
miles) was disestablished, with all areas of land and water
within the Zone reverting to Panama. By the 1977 treaty
with the USA, the USA was allowed the use of operating
bases for the Panama Canal, together with several
military bases, but the Republic of Panama was sovereign
in all such areas. Control of the Canal reverted to Panama
at noon on 31 December 1999.

In the fiscal year 2000, the total number of transits by
ocean-going commercial traffic was 12,303; canal net
tons totalled 229,459,659; cargo tons totalled
193,714,277.

PAPUA NEW GUINEA

*Gau Hedinarai ai Papua-Matamata Guinea – Independent
State of Papua New Guinea*

AREA – 174,192 sq. miles (452,900 sq. km). Neighbour:
Indonesia (west, on New Guinea)

POPULATION – 4,920,000 (2001). English is the official
language; Hiri Motu and Neo-Melanesian are widely
used

CAPITAL – ΨPort Moresby (population, 173,500, 2000
estimate)

MAJOR CITIES – Goroka; Lae; Madang; Mount Hagen;
Rabaul; Wewak

CURRENCY – Kina (K) of 100 toea

NATIONAL ANTHEM – Arise All You Sons

NATIONAL DAY – 16 September (Independence Day)

NATIONAL FLAG – Divided diagonally red (fly) and
black (hoist); on the red a soaring Bird of Paradise in
yellow and on the black five white stars of the
Southern Cross

LIFE EXPECTANCY (years) – 57 (2001)

POPULATION GROWTH RATE – 2.4 per cent

POPULATION DENSITY – 11 per sq. km (2001)

MILITARY EXPENDITURE – 0.9 per cent of GDP (2001)

MILITARY PERSONNEL – 3,100: Army 2,500, Navy
400, Air Force 200

ILLITERACY RATE – (m) 29.4 per cent; (f) 43.2 per cent
(2000)

ENROLMENT (percentage of age group) – tertiary 3 per
cent (1997)

The country has many island groups, principally the
Bismarck Archipelago, a portion of the Solomon Islands,
the Trobriands, the D'Entrecasteaux Islands and the
Louisade Archipelago. The main islands of the Bismarck
Archipelago are New Britain, New Ireland and Manus.
Bougainville is the largest of the Solomon Islands within
Papua New Guinea.

HISTORY AND POLITICS

In 1884 a British protectorate, British New Guinea, was
proclaimed over the southern coast of New Guinea
(Papua) and the adjacent islands, which were annexed
outright in 1888. In 1906 the territory was placed under
the authority of Australia. The northern areas were under
German administration between 1884 and 1914, when
they were occupied by Australian troops and in 1921
became a League of Nations mandate administered by
Australia. The territories were occupied by Japan between
1942 and 1945.

From 1970 there was a gradual assumption of powers
by the Papua New Guinea government, culminating in
formal self-government in December 1973. Papua New
Guinea achieved full independence within the
Commonwealth on 16 September 1975.

Following elections in June 2002, the National
Alliance Party (NAP) was the largest party in Parliament,
and on 5 August 2002, the NAP leader Sir Michael
Somare was elected prime minister for the third time and
formed a coalition cabinet.

INSURGENCIES

From 1989 until 1998 there was a separatist insurrection
in the island of Bougainville, led by the Bougainville
Revolutionary Army (BRA) declared an independent
republic in May 1990. Government forces returned to the
island in October 1992, subsequently capturing 90 per
cent of rebel-held territory.

The cease-fire that came into effect on 30 April 1998
ended nine years of conflict that had caused thousands of
deaths. Autonomy for the island and an interim provincial
government were established under the holoate.
Understanding of March 2000. Agreement was reached
on 26 January 2001 that a referendum on the future of
Bougainville should be held within 15 years. The BRA
surrendered its weapons during May and a formal peace
accord was signed in August 2001.

Border areas are occasionally affected by the overspill
from the separatist struggle in neighbouring Irian Jaya.

POLITICAL SYSTEM
Elections are held every five years. The National
Parliament comprises 109 elected members, 20 from
regional electorates, the remainder from open electorates.
The head of state is the British sovereign, represented by
the Governor-General, who is appointed by parliament
for a six-year term. Provincial governments were
abolished in 1995, and replaced with councils combining
local and national politicians and headed by an appointed
governor.

Governor-General, HE Sir Silas Atopare, GCMG, *apptd*
14 November 1997

NATIONAL EXECUTIVE COUNCIL *as at August 2003*
Prime Minister, Public Service (acting), Sir Michael Somare
Deputy Prime Minister, Trade and Industry, Allan Marat
Agriculture and Livestock, Moses Maladina
Communications and Information (acting), Moses Maladina
Correctional Services, Peter Oresi
Defence, Kappa Yarka
Education, Michael Laimo
Environment and Conservation, Sasa Zibe
Finance and Treasury, Bart Philemon
Fisheries, Andrew Baing
Foreign Affairs and Immigration, Sir Rabbie Namaliu
Forestry, Patrick Pruaitch
Health, Melchior Pep
Housing, Yuntuvi Bao
Inter-government Relations, Sir Peter Barter
Internal Security, Yawa Silupa
Justice, Mark Maipakai
Labour and Industrial Relations, Peter O'Neill
Lands and Physical Planning, Robert Kapaol
Mining, Sam Akoitai
National Planning and Monitoring, Sinai Brown
Petroleum and Energy, Sir Moi Avei
Science and Technology, Alphonse Morial Willie
Transport and Civil Aviation, Don Polye
Welfare and Social Development, Lady Carol Kidu
Works, Gabriel Karpis

PAPUA NEW GUINEA HIGH COMMISSION
3rd Floor, 14 Waterloo Place, London SW1R 4AR
Tel: 020-7930 0922/7
High Commissioner, HE Jean L. Kekedo, OBE, apptd
2002

BRITISH HIGH COMMISSION
PO Box 212, Waigani NCD, Port Moresby
Tel: (00 675) 325 1677 Email: bhcpng@datec.net.pg
High Commissioner, HE Simon Mansfield Scadden, apptd
2000

ECONOMY
A variety of commercial agricultural developments co-
exist with the traditional rural economy. Around 80 per
cent of the population lives in rural areas with few or no
amenities, and is dependent on subsistence agriculture. In
1995, the government initiated an austerity programme
intended to reduce the budget deficit, privatise state
assets and eliminate trade tariffs. However, the
privatisation programme was halted when the current
government came to power. Following prolonged
drought and the financial crisis in south-east Asia, the
country is facing its worst financial crisis since
independence, with debt servicing amounting to a
quarter of government spending.

There are extensive mineral deposits throughout Papua
New Guinea, including copper, gold, silver, nickel,
bauxite and commercial deposits of oil and natural gas,
but exploitation is hampered by the terrain and poor
infrastructure. Industry includes processing of primary
products, and brewing, packaging, paint, plywood, and
metal manufacturing and the construction industries.

In 1999 there was a trade surplus of US$856 million
and a current account surplus of US$95 million. In 2001
imports totalled US$1,073 million and exports
US$1,813 million.

GNP – US$3,607 million (2000); US$700 per capita
(2000)
GDP – US$2,959 million (2001); US$710 per capita
(2000)
ANNUAL AVERAGE GROWTH OF GDP – 3.9 per cent
(1999)
INFLATION RATE – 9.8 per cent (2002)
TOTAL EXTERNAL DEBT – US$2,604 million (2000)

Trade with UK	2001	2002
Imports from UK	£4,319,000	£12,150,000
Exports to UK	41,438,000	49,470,000

COMMUNICATIONS
Air Niugini operates regular air services to other
countries in the region, as well as internal air services.
Several shipping companies operate cargo services to
Australia, Europe, the Far East and USA. There are very
limited cargo and passenger services between the main
ports, outports, plantations and missions. There are
21,433 km of roads, the most important road being that
linking Lae with the populous highlands. Papua New
Guinea is linked by international cable to Australia,
Guam, Hong Kong, the Far East and the USA.

PARAGUAY

República del Paraguay - Republic of Paraguay

AREA – 152,808 sq. miles (397,300 sq. km).
Neighbours: Bolivia (north-west), Brazil (north-east
and east), Argentina (south)
POPULATION – 5,636,000 (2001): 95 per cent mestizo.
Spanish is the official language of the country but
outside the larger towns Guaraní, the language of the
largest single group of Amerindian inhabitants, is
widely spoken, and is also an official language
CAPITAL – Asunción (population, 550,060 1997)
MAJOR CITIES – Ciudad del Este (133,881); San
Lorenzo (133,395)
CURRENCY – Guaraní (Gs) of 100 céntimos
NATIONAL ANTHEM – Paraguayos, República O Muerte
(Paraguayans, Republic Or Death)
NATIONAL DAY – 15 May
NATIONAL FLAG – Three horizontal bands, red, white,
blue with the National seal on the obverse white band
and the Treasury seal on the reverse white band
LIFE EXPECTANCY (years) – 70 (2001)
POPULATION GROWTH RATE – 2.6 per cent
POPULATION DENSITY – 14 per sq. km (2001)
MILITARY EXPENDITURE – 1.1 per cent of GDP (2001)
MILITARY PERSONNEL – 18,600: Army 14,900, Navy
2,000, Air Force 1,700; Paramilitaries 14,800
CONSCRIPTION DURATION – One to two years

Paraguay is an inland subtropical state of South America,
situated between Argentina, Bolivia and Brazil. It is a

country of grassy plains and forested hills. In the angle formed by the Paraná-Paraguay confluence are extensive marshes, one of which, known as Neembucú (or endless) is drained by Lake Ypoa, a large lagoon south-east of the capital. The Chaco, lying between the rivers Paraguay and Pilcomayo and bounded on the north by Bolivia, is a flat plain, rising uniformly towards its western boundary to a height of 1,140 feet.

HISTORY AND POLITICS
Paraguay was settled as a Spanish possession in 1537 and became independent in 1811.

Gen. Alfredo Stroessner, dictator from 1954, was overthrown in February 1989 by Gen. Andrés Rodríguez, who was elected president in May 1989. Elections to the parliament were held in December 1991.

In March 1999 the Chamber of Deputies voted to initiate impeachment proceedings against President Cubas Grau over his alleged involvement in the assassination of the vice-president. He resigned on 28 March and the president of the Senate, Luis González Macchi, was sworn in as the new president.

In the presidential and legislative elections on 27 April 2003, the National Republican Association-Colorado Party (ANR-PC) remained the largest party in Congress, winning 16 out of the 45 seats; its candidate, Nicanor Duarte Frutos, won the presidential election with 37.1 per cent of the vote.

POLITICAL SYSTEM
The constitution provides for a two-chamber legislature consisting of a 45-member Senate and an 80-member Chamber of Deputies, both directly elected for five-year terms. Deputies are elected on a regional basis, the number of seats allocated to each regional department being directly proportional to the department's population. Voting is compulsory for all citizens over 18. The president is elected for a five-year term and may not be re-elected. The vice-president may only contest the presidency if he resigns his post six months before the election. The president appoints the Council of Ministers, which exercises all the functions of government.

HEAD OF STATE
President, Nicanor Duarte Frutos, *elected* 27 April 2002, *sworn in* 15 August 2003
Vice-President, Luis Alberto Castiglioni Soria

CABINET *as at July 2003*
Agriculture and Livestock, Dario Baumgarten
Defence, Adm. Miguel Angel Candia
Education and Culture, Blanca Ovalar de Duarte
Executive Secretary of Technical Secretariat of Planning and Economic and Social Development, Luis Alberto Meyer Jou
Finance and Economy, Alcides Giménez
Foreign Affairs, José Antonio Moreno Ruffinelli
Industry and Commerce, Roberto Fernandez Schroeder
Interior, Osvaldo Benitez
Justice and Labour, José Angel Burro
Public Health and Social Welfare, José Mayans Masi
Public Works and Communications, Antonio Adam Nills
Secretary-General of the Presidency, Stella Samaniego
Women's Affairs, Cristina Muñoz

EMBASSY OF PARAGUAY
344 High Street Kensington, 3rd Floor, London W14 8NS
Tel: 020-7610 4180

Ambassador Extraordinary and Plenipotentiary, Raúl Dos Santos, apptd 1998

BRITISH EMBASSY
Avda. Boggiani 5848, JC/R I6 Boquerón, Asunción
Tel: (00 595) (21) 612611 Email: brembasu@rieder.net.py
Ambassador Extraordinary and Plenipotentiary, HE Anthony Cantor, apptd 2001

ECONOMY
An economic liberalisation programme introduced in 1989 has been continued by subsequent governments. In 2000, Congress approved a privatisation programme. This has reduced foreign debt and attracted foreign investment, notably from Brazil. About half of the population are engaged in agriculture and cattle raising. Cassava, sugar cane, soya, cotton and wheat are the main agricultural products. The forests contain many varieties of timber which find a good market abroad.

Paraguay's rivers give it considerable hydroelectric capacity. There is a hydroelectric power station at Acaray which exports surplus power to Argentina and Brazil. Joint projects have been undertaken with Brazil, on a hydroelectric dam at Itaipú (the largest in the world), and with Argentina, at Yacyretá.

GNP – US$7,933 million (2000); US$1,440 per capita (2000)
GDP – US$6,926 million (2001); US$1,405 per capita (2000)
ANNUAL AVERAGE GROWTH OF GDP – –0.4 per cent (2000)
INFLATION RATE – 9.0 per cent (2000)
TOTAL EXTERNAL DEBT – US$3,091 million (2000)

TRADE
The chief imports are machinery, fuels and lubricants, vehicles, drinks and tobacco. The chief exports are soya, cotton fibres, meat, timber and coffee. The main trading partners are Brazil, Argentina and the USA.

In 2000 Paraguay had a trade deficit of US$532 million and a current account deficit of US$137 million. In 1999 imports totalled US$1,725 million and exports US$741 million.

Trade with UK	2001	2002
Imports from UK	£22,047,000	£13,169,000
Exports to UK	2,176,000	2,117,000

COMMUNICATIONS
There are direct shipping services from Asunción to Europe and the USA, and river steamer services for internal transport. Eight airlines operate services from Asunción. There are 28,900 km of roads in Paraguay, connecting Asunción with São Paulo via the Bridge of Friendship and Foz de Yguazú, and with Buenos Aires via Puerto Pilcomayo. Many earth roads are liable to be closed or to become impassable in wet weather. There are 971 km of railway track. Rail services, with train ferries, provide internal and international links.

EDUCATION
Education is free and compulsory. There are 11 universities and one institute of education.
ILLITERACY RATE – (m) 5.6 per cent; (f) 7.8 per cent (2000)
ENROLMENT (percentage of age group) – primary 100 per cent (1997); secondary 47 per cent (1997); tertiary 10 per cent (1997)

PERU

República del Perú - Republic of Peru

AREA – 492,308 sq. miles (1,280,000 sq. km).
  Neighbours: Ecuador and Colombia (north), Brazil
  and Bolivia (east), Chile (south)
POPULATION – 26,093,000 (2001): 50 per cent
  Amerindian, 40 per cent mestizo, 7 per cent European,
  also Africans, Chinese and Japanese. The official
  languages are Spanish and Quechua. Aymara is also
  widely spoken
CAPITAL – Lima (including ΨCallao, population,
  6,723,130, 2000 estimate)
MAJOR CITIES – Arequipa (762,000); Chiclayo
  (517,000); Chimbote (336,000); Trujillo (652,000)
  2000 estimates
CURRENCY – New Sol of 100 cénts
NATIONAL ANTHEM – Somos Libres, Seámoslo Siempre
  (We Are Free, Let Us Remain So Forever)
NATIONAL DAY – 28 July (Anniversary of Independence)
NATIONAL FLAG – Three vertical stripes of red, white,
  red
LIFE EXPECTANCY (years) – 69 (2001)
POPULATION GROWTH RATE – 1.7 per cent
POPULATION DENSITY – 20 per sq. km (2001)
MILITARY EXPENDITURE - 1.7 per cent of GDP (2001)
MILITARY PERSONNEL - 110,000: Army 70,000, Navy
  25,000, Air Force 15,000; Paramilitaries 77,000
CONSCRIPTION DURATION - Two years (selective)

The country is traversed throughout its length by the
Andes, running parallel to the Pacific coast. There are
three main regions, the Costa, west of the Andes, the
Sierra or mountain ranges of the Andes, which include
the Punas or mountainous wastes below the region of
perpetual snow, and the Montaña or Selva, which is the
vast area of jungle stretching from the eastern foothills of
the Andes to the eastern frontiers of Peru.

HISTORY AND POLITICS
Peru was conquered in the early 16th century by
Francisco Pizarro (1478–1541). He subjugated the Incas
(the ruling caste of the Quechua Indians), who had
started their rise to power some 500 years earlier, and for
nearly three centuries Peru remained under Spanish rule.
A revolutionary war of 1821–4 established its
independence, declared on 28 July 1821. A military junta
ruled Peru from 1968 until 1980 when civilian
government was restored.

In 1992 President Fujimori, faced with increasing
terrorist violence, suspended the constitution, dissolved
Congress and began to govern by decree. In 1992 a
legislative election was held to an 80-seat Democratic
Constituent Congress (CCD) which was installed as an
interim legislature and constituent assembly to write a
new constitution. The new constitution was endorsed in
a national referendum in 1993.

Parliamentary and presidential elections in 1995 were
won by President Fujimori and his Cambio 90-Nueva
Mayoría Party.

The 2000 presidential election returned Fujimori to
office in the simultaneous legislative election, his Peru
2000 alliance won 51 seats, losing its absolute majority.
There were accusations of widespread ballot rigging in
the first round of the presidential election which led an
opposing candidate, Alejandro Toledo, to ask his
supporters to spoil their ballot papers in the second

round. The chief of the Organisation of American States
observer mission concluded that the entire electoral
process had been irregular.

After announcing in September 2000 that he intended
to step down and call a presidential election in which he
would not stand, Fujimori fled to Japan and announced
his resignation on 17 November. Congress voted on 21
November to reject Fujimori's resignation and instead
dismissed him on the grounds of moral incapacity;
Valentín Paniagua of the Popular Action party was sworn
in as interim president the following day.

A general election was held on 8 April 2001 in which
the Peru Possible (PP) party won 43 seats and the
Peruvian Aprista Party (APRA) won 28 seats. The
presidential election was held in two rounds on 8 April
and 3 June and was won by the PP candidate, Alejandro
Toledo, who was sworn in as president on 28 July,
becoming the first Amerindian to hold the position.

A state of emergency was in place from May to June
2003 because of a strike by teachers which attracted
widespread support. The entire cabinet resigned on 23
June 2003 and on 28 June President Toledo appointed
Peru's first female prime minister, Beatriz Merino.

FOREIGN RELATIONS
A 78-km stretch of the border with Ecuador has been in
dispute since 1960. In 1995 an inconclusive border war
was fought between the two countries, and in July 1995
a demilitarised zone was established around the disputed
area. Four guarantor countries (Argentina, Brazil, Chile
and the USA) adjudicated the claims of both countries
and produced an agreement which was signed on 26
October 1998 by the presidents of Ecuador and Peru,
formally ending the dispute.

INSURGENCIES
Since the late 1970s the government has faced violence
from drug organisations and insurgencies from two leftist
guerrilla movements, the Maoist Sendero Luminoso
(Shining Path) and the Movimiento Revolucionario
Túpac Amaru (MRTA); fighting has left 30,000 dead.
Security forces captured the leader of the MRTA in
November 1998 and the leader of Shining Path in
December 1998.

POLITICAL SYSTEM
The constitution, promulgated in December 1993,
provides for the president to be able to serve two terms
rather than one, as previously; a constitutional panel
approved a Bill in August 1996 allowing President
Fujimori to stand for a third term in office. The
unicameral legislature, the Congress of the Republic, has
120 members, directly elected for a five-year term.

HEAD OF STATE
President of the Republic, Alejandro Toledo Manrique,
  elected 3 June 2001, *sworn in* 28 July 2001
First Vice-President, Foreign Trade, Tourism, Raul Diez
  Canseco
Second Vice-President, David Waisman

COUNCIL OF MINISTERS *as at August 2003*
President of the Council of Ministers, Beatriz Merino
Advancement of Women, Social Development, Ana Elena
  Townsend
Agriculture, Francisco Gonzalez
Defence, Aurelio Loret de Mola
Economy and Finance, Javier Silva Reute

Education and Culture, Carlos Malpica
Energy and Mines, Jaime Quijandria
Foreign Affairs, Allan Wagner Tizon
Health, Alvaro Vidal Rivadeneyra
Housing and Construction, Carlos Bruce Montes de Oca
Interior, Alberto Sanabria Ortiz
Justice, Fausto Alvarado Dodero
Labour and Social Promotion, Jesus Alvarado
Production, Javier Reategui Rosello
Transport, Communications and Housing, Eduardo Iriarte
  Jimenez

EMBASSY OF PERU
52 Sloane Street, London SW1X 9SP
Tel: 020-7235 1917/2545/8302
Ambassador Extraordinary and Plenipotentiary, HE
  Armando Lecaros-de-Cossío, apptd 2002

BRITISH EMBASSY
Torre Parque Mar (Piso 22), Avenida José Larco 1301,
Miraflores, Lima
Tel: (00 51) (1) 617 3000 Email: consvisa.lima@fco.gov.uk
Ambassador Extraordinary and Plenipotentiary, HE
  Richard Ralph, CMG, CVO, apptd 2003

BRITISH COUNCIL DIRECTOR, Frank Fitzpatrick
c/o British Embassy, Lima Tel: (00 51) (1) 617 3060
Email: bc.lima@britishcouncil.org.pe

ECONOMY

The chief products of the coastal belt are cotton, sugar
and petroleum. There are large tracts of land suitable for
cultivation and stock-raising (cattle, sheep, llamas, alpacas
and vicuñas) on the eastern slopes of the Andes, and in
the mountain valleys maize, potatoes and wheat are
grown. The jungle area is a source of timber and
petroleum. Other major crops are fruit, vegetables, rice,
barley, grapes and coffee. The mountains contain rich
mineral deposits and mineral exports include lead, zinc,
copper, iron ore and silver. Peru is normally the world's
largest exporter of fishmeal.

Since 1990 the government has launched a radical
free-market restructuring programme which has rebuilt
the foreign exchange reserves, reduced inflation from
7,600 per cent a year in 1990 to four per cent in 1999,
cut subsidies and import tariffs, freed interest rates and
privatised most state firms. Foreign investment has been
encouraged and has grown dramatically. The economic
recovery has increased the gap between rich and poor.
GNP – US$53,392 million (2000); US$2,080 per capita
  (2000)
GDP – US$54,047 million (2001); US$2,085 per capita
  (2000)
ANNUAL AVERAGE GROWTH OF GDP – 3.1 per cent
  (2000)
INFLATION RATE – 3.8 per cent (2000)
UNEMPLOYMENT – 7.4 per cent (2000)
TOTAL EXTERNAL DEBT – US$28,560 million (2000)

TRADE
The principal imports are machinery, chemicals and
pharmaceutical products. The chief exports are minerals
and metals, fishmeal, sugar, cotton and coffee.

In 2000 Peru had a trade deficit of US$323 million
and a current account deficit of US$1,628 million.
Imports totalled US$8,797 million and exports
US$7,028 million.

Trade with UK	2001	2002
Imports from UK	£41,209,000	£43,890,000
Exports to UK	166,553,000	157,588,000

COMMUNICATIONS

There are 73,766 km of roads, of which 16,876 km are
unsurfaced. The Andean Highway forms a link between
the Pacific, the Amazon and the Atlantic. The Pan-
American Highway runs along the Peruvian coast
connecting it with Ecuador and Chile.

The railway is administered by the government. There
are 1,992 km of railway track. There is also steam
navigation on the Ucayali and Huallaga, and in the south
on Lake Titicaca. Air services are maintained throughout
Peru, and there is an international airport at Lima.

EDUCATION

Education is compulsory and free between seven and 16.
There are 51 universities.
ILLITERACY RATE – (m) 5.3 per cent; (f) 14.6 per cent
  (2000)
ENROLMENT (percentage of age group) – primary 100
  per cent (1997); secondary 73 per cent (1997); tertiary
  26 per cent (1997)

THE PHILIPPINES

República ng Pilipinas – Republic of the Philippines

AREA – 114,692 sq. miles (298,200 sq. km)
POPULATION – 77,131,000 (2001). The inhabitants are
of Malay stock, with admixtures of Spanish and
Chinese blood in many localities. The Chinese
minority is estimated at 500,000, with smaller
numbers of Spanish, American and Indian. About 90
per cent are Christian, predominantly Roman
Catholics. Most of the remainder are Muslims or
indigenous animists. The official languages are Filipino
and English. Filipino is based on Tagalog, one of the
Malay–Polynesian languages. English, the language of
government, is spoken by at least 44 per cent of the
population. Spanish is now spoken by a very small
minority
CAPITAL – ΨManila (population, 9,906,048, 2000
census)
MAJOR CITIES – Quezon (2,173,831); ΨCebu
(718,821); ΨDavao (1,147,116); ΨIloilo (365,820);
ΨZamboanga (601,794), 2000 census
CURRENCY – Philippine peso (P) of 100 centavos
NATIONAL ANTHEM – Lupang Hinirang (Beloved Land)
NATIONAL DAY – 12 June (Independence Day 1898)
NATIONAL FLAG – Equal horizontal bands of blue
(above) and red; gold sun with three stars on a white
triangle next staff
LIFE EXPECTANCY (years) – 70 (2001)
POPULATION GROWTH RATE – 2.1 per cent
POPULATION DENSITY – 259 per sq. km (2001)
URBAN POPULATION – 59 per cent (2001)

There are 11 larger islands and 7,079 other islands. The
principal islands (area in sq. km) are: Luzon (104,688);
Mindanao (94,630); Samar (13,080); Negros (12,710);
Palawan (11,785); Panay (11,515); Mindoro (9,735);
Leyte (7,214); Cebu (4,422); Bohol (3,865); Masbate
(3,269). Other groups are the Sulu islands (capital, Jolo),
Babuyanes and Batanes; the Calamian islands; and
Kalayaan Islands.

HISTORY AND POLITICS

The Philippines were conquered by Spain in 1565 and named Filipinas after Philip II of Spain. Independence was declared on 12 June 1898. In the Spanish–American War of 1898, Manila was captured by American troops and remained under US control until 1946. The Republic of the Philippines came into existence on 4 July 1946.

Ferdinand Marcos was president from 1965 to 1986, when he was forced from power by Corazón Aquino, who took over as president and survived seven coup attempts. Fidel Ramos was elected president in May 1992 and was succeeded by Joseph Estrada, the former Vice-President, in May 1998.

The House of Representatives voted on 13 November 2000 to initiate impeachment proceedings against President Estrada, accusing him of corruption. The trial began on 7 December 2000 in the Senate, but foundered on 16 January 2001 after senators refused to consider evidence which allegedly proved Estrada's guilt, and the trial was indefinitely adjourned on the following day. Up to 500,000 demonstrators, led by Vice-President Gloria Macapagal-Arroyo and supported by former presidents Corazón Aquino and Fidel Ramos, gathered in Manila and called on Estrada to resign. On 19 January, the armed forces announced that they had withdrawn their support from the president and on 20 January the Supreme Court ruled that the presidency was vacant, thus allowing Macapagal-Arroyo to be sworn in. Her legitimacy as president was confirmed by the Supreme Court on 2 March.

Elections were held for the House of Representatives and 13 of the 24 Senate seats on 14 May 2001.

INSURGENCIES

On 2 September 1996, the government signed an agreement with the Moro National Liberation Front (MNLF) on the creation of an autonomous Muslim region in Mindanao, Palawan, Sulu and Basilan, ending a 24-year rebellion which had left more than 120,000 people dead. The Moro Islamic Liberation Front (MILF), a radical breakaway group, threatened to disrupt the agreement. The Communist New People's Army (NPA) maintains a presence in eastern Mindanao, Negros, Samar, Bicol, the mountains of northern Luzon and Bataan. The NPA signed a cease-fire agreement with the government in December 1993; peace talks were suspended in February 1999.

The army captured the MILF military headquarters on 9 July 2000, following which MILF withdrew from peace talks scheduled for August. After military action against MILF was formally ended on 6 February 2001, MILF declared a cease-fire on 3 April and negotiations with the government led to a comprehensive peace deal which came into effect on 22 June. Further peace agreements were signed on 6 and 7 May 2002, which dealt with the MILF's co-operation with the armed forces and the police in the areas it controlled and entrusted government funds to the MILF as reparation for areas of Mindanao devastated by the government's military offensives in 2000.

A series of fatal bomb blasts took place in October 2002 which were blamed on Islamic militants.

The cease-fire between government forces and MILF broke down on 11 February 2003 after the army launched an assault involving thousands of troops on one of MILF's biggest camps in North Cotabato province. Heavy fighting between MILF and government forces ensued and spread to the neighbouring provinces of Maguindanao and Sultan Kudara. A cease-fire was signed on 18 July 2003 between the government and MILF ahead of planned peace talks in Malaysia. A state of rebellion was declared on 27 July 2003 when some 300 soldiers staged a 19-hour failed bloodless mutiny in Manila. The state of rebellion was lifted on 11 August 2003 when the government announced that it had contained the conspiracy behind the mutiny.

POLITICAL SYSTEM

A new constitution came into force in July 1987. Legislative authority is vested in a bicameral Congress. The House of Representatives has 250 members, of whom 204 are directly elected and 46 appointed by the President for a three-year term. The Senate has 24 members, of whom 12 are re-elected every three years.

The Autonomous Region of Mindanao consists of four provinces: Sulu, Tawitawi, Lanao del Sur and Maguinadanao. There is a 24-member regional assembly and a governor.

HEAD OF STATE

President, Defence, Gloria Macapagal Arroyo, *assumed office* 20 January 2001
Vice-President, Teofisto Guingona

CABINET *as at August 2003*

Agrarian Reform, Roberto Pagdanganan
Agriculture, Luis Lorenzo
Budget and Management, Emilia Boncodin
Education, Culture and Sport, Edilberto de Jesus
Energy, Vincent Perez
Environment and Natural Resources, Elisea Gozun
Executive Secretary, Alberto Romulo
Finance, José Isidro Camacho
Foreign Affairs, Blas Ople
Health, Manuel Dayrit
Housing, Michael Defensor
Interior and Local Government, José Lina
Justice, Simeon Datumanong
Labour and Employment, Patricia Santo Tomás
Presidential Advisor for Special Concerns, Norberto Gonzales
Press, Hernani Braganza
Public Works and Highways, Bayani Fernando
Science and Technology, Estrella Alabastro
Social Welfare and Development, Corazón Soliman
Socio-economic Planning, Romulo Neri
Tourism, Richard Gordon
Trade and Industry, Manuel Roxas
Transportation and Communications, Gen. Leandro Mendoza

EMBASSY OF THE REPUBLIC OF THE PHILIPPINES
9A Palace Green, London W8 4QE
Tel: 020-7937 1600
Ambassador Extraordinary and Plenipotentiary,
HE Edgardo Espiritu, apptd 2003

BRITISH EMBASSY
Floors 15–17, LV Locsin Building, 6752 Ayala Avenue, Corner of Makati Avenue, 1226 Makati, Manila (PO Box 2927 MCPO)
Tel: (00 63) (2) 816 7116 Email: uk@info.com.ph
Ambassador Extraordinary and Plenipotentiary,
HE Paul Dimond, apptd 2002

BRITISH COUNCIL DIRECTOR, Gill Westaway
10th Floor, Taipan Place, Emerald Avenue, Ortigas Centre, Pasig City 1605 Tel: (00 63) (2) 914 1011
Email: britishcouncil@britishcouncil.org.ph

DEFENCE

The Army has 85 armoured infantry fighting vehicles and 370 armoured personnel carriers. The Navy has one frigate and 58 patrol and coastal vessels at three bases. The Air Force has 49 combat aircraft and 67 armed helicopters.

MILITARY EXPENDITURE – 1.5 per cent of GDP (2001)

MILITARY PERSONNEL – 106,000: Army 66,000, Navy 24,000, Air Force 16,000; Paramilitaries 44,000

ECONOMY

In 1998, 39.8 per cent of the workforce were engaged in agriculture. The chief products are rice, coconuts, sugar cane, bananas, maize and pineapples. There is an increasing number of manufacturing industries and it is the policy of the government to diversify the economy. There are also deposits of copper, coal, gold, silver, chromium, iron and nickel.

Despite an economic reform programme of liberalisation, privatisation and deregulation which led to an increase in export and foreign investment and a reduction in inflation, the Philippines still face a number of economic challenges; the economy is making a slow recovery from the Asian financial crisis of 1997 with lower growth rates than regional competitors.

GNP – US$78,778 million (2000); US$1,040 per capita (2000)

GDP – US$71,438 million (2001); US$988 per capita (2000)

ANNUAL AVERAGE GROWTH OF GDP – 4.0 per cent (2000)

INFLATION RATE – 4.4 per cent (2000)

UNEMPLOYMENT – 10.1 per cent (2000)

TOTAL EXTERNAL DEBT – US$50,063 million (2000)

TRADE

Principal exports are electronic products, machinery and transport equipment, clothing, coconut oil and products, and minerals. Principal imports are fuelstuffs and oils, electronic goods and components, machinery, base metals, transport equipment, textiles and yarns, and cereals. The major trading partners are the USA, Japan, Singapore and Hong Kong.

In 2001 the Philippines had a trade surplus of US$2,746 million and a current account surplus of US$4,503 million. Imports totalled US$31,358 million and exports US$32,664 million.

Trade with UK	2001	2002
Imports from UK	£393,308,000	£353,931,000
Exports to UK	1,198,584,000	979,295,000

COMMUNICATIONS

The highway system covers about 187,000 km. The Philippine National Railway operates 429 km of track. There are 415 ports. There are 82 national airports and 137 privately operated airports. Philippine Airlines has regular flights throughout the Far East, to the USA and Europe, in addition to inter-island services.

EDUCATION

Secondary and higher education is extensive and there are 21 public and 53 private universities recognised by the government, including the Dominican University of Santo Tomás (founded in 1611). There are also 530 other institutions of higher education.

ILLITERACY RATE – (m) 4.5 per cent; (f) 4.8 per cent (2000)

ENROLMENT (percentage of age group) – primary 100 per cent (1997); secondary 78 per cent (1997); tertiary 29 per cent (1997)

POLAND

Rzeczpospolita Polska – Republic of Poland

AREA – 117,077 sq. miles (304,400 sq. km). Neighbours: the Russian Federation (Kaliningrad) (north), Germany (west), the Czech Republic and Slovakia (south), Belarus, Ukraine and Lithuania (east)

POPULATION – 38,577,000 (2001). Roman Catholicism is the religion of 95 per cent of the inhabitants. The language is Polish; there are German, Ukrainian and Belarusian minorities

CAPITAL – Warsaw (population, 1,609,780, 2001 estimate), on the Vistula

MAJOR CITIES – Bydgoszcz (383,213); ΨGdańsk (Danzig) (455,464); Katowice (338,017); Kraków (740,737); Lódź (786,526); Poznań (571,985); ΨSzczecin (Stettin) (415,576); Wroclaw (Breslau) (634,047), 2001 estimates

CURRENCY – Zloty of 100 groszy

NATIONAL ANTHEM – Jeszcze Polska Nie Zginęla (Poland Has Not Yet Perished)

NATIONAL DAY – 3 May

NATIONAL FLAG – Equal horizontal stripes of white (above) and red

LIFE EXPECTANCY (years) – 74 (2001)

POPULATION GROWTH RATE – 0.1 per cent

POPULATION DENSITY – 127 per sq. km (2001)

URBAN POPULATION – 63 per cent (2001)

HISTORY AND POLITICS

The Polish Commonwealth ceased to exist in 1795 after three successive partitions in 1772, 1793 and 1795 in which Prussia, Russia and Austria shared. The Republic of Poland was proclaimed at Warsaw in November 1918, and its independence guaranteed by the signatories of the Treaty of Versailles.

German forces invaded Poland on 1 September 1939; on 17 September, Russian forces invaded eastern Poland, and on 21 September 1939 Poland was declared by Germany and Russia to have ceased to exist. At the end of the war, its frontiers were redrawn; eastern Poland was ceded to the Soviet Union in return for the German territory east of the rivers Oder and Neisse. A coalition government was formed in which the Polish Workers' Party played a large part. In December 1948, the Polish Workers' Party and the Polish Socialist Party merged to form the Polish United Workers' Party (PUWP). A new constitution modelled on the Soviet constitution was adopted in 1952, and was modified in 1976.

Steep price rises in 1980 prompted strikes which forced the government to allow independent trade unions, including 'Solidarity' led by Lech Walesa. The unions agitated for further reforms although their activities were suspended when martial law was in force from December 1981 until July 1983.

A wave of strikes resulted in talks between Walesa and the PUWP early in 1989. Multiparty parliamentary elections were held in the summer of 1989, following which the PUWP ceased to be the ruling party. The post-Communist governments introduced a market economy but economic difficulties and a fragmented parliament led to a succession of short-lived governments.

President Kwasniewski was re-elected for a second term in the first round of the presidential election on 8 October 2000, gaining 53.92 per cent of the vote. Elections held on 23 September 2001 were won by an electoral alliance of the Democratic Left Alliance (SLD) and the Labour Union (UP), which won 216 seats in the *Sejm* and 75 in the senate. A coalition government comprising the SLP, UP and the Polish Peasant Party (PSL) took office on 19 October. The PSL left the ruling coalition in March 2003 over its opposition to government on tax measures.

FOREIGN RELATIONS
Poland became a member of NATO in March 1990. In December 2002, following five years of accession talks, Poland was formally invited to join the EU in 2004. A referendum on EU accession was held on 8 June 2003 in which 77 per cent of voters approved EU membership.

POLITICAL SYSTEM
A new constitution came into effect on 16 October 1997. The President, directly elected for a maximum of two five-year terms, appoints the Prime Minister and has the right to be consulted over the appointment of the foreign, defence and interior ministers. The National Assembly is the bicameral legislature, comprising a 460-member *Sejm* (Diet) and a Senate of 100 members. Both houses have a four-year term. The Senate is elected on a provincial basis.

HEAD OF STATE
President, Aleksander Kwasniewski, *elected* 19 November 1995, *sworn in* 23 December 1995, *re-elected* 8 October 2000

COUNCIL OF MINISTERS *as at July 2003*
Prime Minister, Leszek Miller (SLD)
Deputy Prime Minister, Economy, Labour and Social Policy, Jerzy Hausner (SLD)
Deputy Prime Minister, Infrastructure, Marek Pol (UP)
Agriculture and Rural Development, Wojciech Olejniczak (SLD)
Culture, Waldemar Dabrowski (Ind.)
Defence, Jerzy Szmajdziński (SLD)
Education, Krystyna Lybacka (SLD)
Environment, Czesław Sleziak (SLD)
European Affairs, Danuta Huebner
Foreign Affairs, Wlodzimierz Cimoszewicz (SLD)
Health, Leszek Sikorski (SLD)
Internal Affairs and Administration, Krzysztof Janik (SLD)
Justice, Grzegorz Kurczuk (SLD)
Science, Michal Kleiber (Ind.)
Treasury, Piotr Czyżewski (SLD)
Without Portfolio, Lech Nikolski (SLD)

SLD Democratic Left Alliance; UP Labour Union; Ind. Independent

EMBASSY OF THE REPUBLIC OF POLAND
47 Portland Place, London W1B 1JH
Tel: 0870-774 2700
Ambassador Extraordinary and Plenipotentiary,
HE Stanislaw Komorowski, apptd 1999

BRITISH EMBASSY
Aleje Róz No. 1, PL00-556 Warsaw
Tel: (00 48) (22) 628 1001/5
Email: britemb@it.com.pl

Ambassador Extraordinary and Plenipotentiary,
HE Michael Pakenham, CMG, apptd 2001

CONSULATES – Gdańsk, Katowice, Kraków, Lublin, Poznań, Szczecin, Wroclaw (Breslau)

BRITISH COUNCIL DIRECTOR, Susan Maingay, OBE
Al. Jerozolimskie 59, PL-00–697 Warsaw.
Email: bc.warsaw@britishcouncil.pl.
There is an office in Kraków

DEFENCE
The Army has 1,144 main battle tanks, 1,281 armoured infantry fighting vehicles and 33 armoured personnel carriers. The Navy has four submarines, one destroyer, three frigates, 23 patrol and coastal vessels, 26 combat aircraft and 12 armed helicopters at five bases. The Air Force has 201 combat aircraft.

MILITARY EXPENDITURE – 2.0 per cent of GDP (2001)
MILITARY PERSONNEL – 163,000: Army 104,050, Navy 14,300, Air Force 36,450; Paramilitaries 21,400
CONSCRIPTION DURATION – 12 months

ECONOMY
Poland is well endowed with mineral resources; there are large reserves of brown coal in central and south-western Poland and hard coal in Upper Silesia and the Walbrzych and Lublin regions; sulphur, copper, zinc, lead, natural gas and salt are also produced.

In 1990, the government embarked upon a series of measures designed to introduce a free-market economy.

The transition to a market economy has been painful, with unemployment doubling between 1990 and 1995 and remaining high. Industrial output has improved and the rate of growth of GDP has increased although inflation remains high.

A programme has taken place to modernise the large agricultural sector and adapt it to the EU's common agricultural policy but the sector remains inefficient and future EU subsidy levels have been a major area of controversy.

Poland's major imports are machinery and vehicles, chemical products, leather and textiles, livestock, foodstuffs, luxury goods and metal products. Its major exports are machinery and vehicles, leather and textiles, metal goods, livestock, foodstuffs, luxury goods and chemical products. Germany is Poland's main trading partner.

In 2000 there was a trade deficit of US$12,308 million and a current account deficit of US$9,997 million. In 2001 imports totalled US$50,275 million and exports US$36,092 million.

GNP – US$161,832 million (2000); US$4,190 per capita (2000)
GDP – US$174,597 million (2001); US$4,082 per capita (2000)
ANNUAL AVERAGE GROWTH OF GDP – 4.1 per cent (2000)
INFLATION RATE – 1.9 per cent (2002)
UNEMPLOYMENT – 16.1 per cent (2000)
TOTAL EXTERNAL DEBT – US$63,561 million (2000)

Trade with UK	2001	2002
Imports from UK	£1,299,320,000	£1,316,718,000
Exports to UK	1,192,724,000	1,287,746,000

EDUCATION

Elementary education (ages seven to 15) is compulsory and free. Secondary education is optional and free. There are 179 institutions of higher education, including universities at Krakow, Warsaw, Poznan, Lodz, Wroclaw, Lublin and Torun and a number of other towns.

ILLITERACY RATE – (m) 0.3 per cent; (f) 0.3 per cent (2000)

ENROLMENT (percentage of age group) – primary 96 per cent (1997); secondary 98 per cent (1997); tertiary 25 per cent (1997)

CULTURE

Polish is a western Slavonic tongue, the Latin alphabet being used. Major writers include Henryk Sienkiewicz (1846–1916), Nobel Prize winner for Literature in 1905; Boleslaw Prus (1847–1912); Stanislaw Reymont (1867–1925), Nobel Prize winner in 1924; Czeslaw Milosz, Nobel Prize winner in 1980; and Wislawa Szymborska, Nobel Prize winner in 1996.

PORTUGAL

República Portuguesa – Portuguese Republic

AREA – 35,192 sq. miles (91,500 sq. km). Neighbour: Spain (north and east)

POPULATION – 10,033,000 (2001); 9,833,014 (excluding the Azores and Madeira, 1995). 94 per cent of the population are Catholic. The language is Portuguese

CAPITAL – ΨLisbon (population, 1,878,006, 2000)

MAJOR CITIES – ΨOporto (1,256,633)

CURRENCY – Euro (€) of 100 cents

NATIONAL ANTHEM – A Portuguesa

NATIONAL DAY – 10 June

NATIONAL FLAG – Divided vertically into unequal parts of green and red with the national emblem over all on the line of division

LIFE EXPECTANCY (years) – 76 (2001)

POPULATION GROWTH RATE – 0.1 per cent

POPULATION DENSITY – 110 per sq. km (2001)

URBAN POPULATION – 66 per cent (2001)

HISTORY AND POLITICS

Portugal was a monarchy from the 12th century until 1910, when an armed rising in Lisbon drove King Manuel II into exile and a republic was set up. A period of political instability ensued until the military stepped in and abolished political parties in 1926. The constitution of 1933 gave formal expression to the corporative 'Estado Novo' (New State) which was personified by Dr Antonio Salazar, Prime Minister 1932–68. Dr Caetano succeeded Salazar as Prime Minister in 1968 but his failure to liberalise the regime or to conclude the wars in the African colonies resulted in his government's overthrow by a military coup on 25 April 1974. There was great political turmoil between April 1974 and July 1976, a period in which most of the colonies gained their independence, but with the failure of an attempted coup by the extreme left in November 1975 the situation stabilised. Full civilian government was restored in 1982.

Macao, which had been a Portuguese colony since 1557, was transferred to Chinese sovereignty on 19 December 1999.

In the presidential election held on 14 January 2001, Jorge Sampaio of the Socialist Party was re-elected, gaining 55.8 per cent of the votes cast. In the general election held on 17 March 2002, the Social Democratic Party (PSD) became the largest party in the Assembly winning 102 seats. José Manuel Durão Barroso of the PSD was sworn in as prime minister on 6 April, leading a coalition government of the PSD and the People's Party (PP).

POLITICAL SYSTEM

Under the 1976 constitution, amended in 1982 and 1989, the President is elected for a five-year term by universal adult suffrage. The Prime Minister is designated by the largest party in the legislature. Legislative authority is vested in the 230-member Assembly of the Republic, elected by a system of proportional representation every four years. The President retains certain limited powers to dismiss the government, dissolve the Assembly or veto laws.

HEAD OF STATE

President of the Republic, Jorge Sampaio, *elected* 14 January 1996, *inaugurated* 9 March 1996, *re-elected* 14 January 2001

COUNCIL OF MINISTERS *as at July 2003*

Prime Minister, José Manuel Durão Barroso

Agriculture, Rural Development and Fisheries, Armando José Cordeiro Sevinate Pinto

Assistant to the Prime Minister, José Luis Fazenda Arnaut Duarte

Culture, Pedro Manuel da Cruz Roseta

Economy, Carlos Manuel Tavares da Silva

Education, José David Gomes Justino

Foreign Affairs and Portuguese Communities Abroad, António Manuel de Mendonça Martins da Cruz

Health, Luis Filipe da Conceição Pereira

Internal Administration, António Jorge de Figueiredo Lopes

Justice, Maria Celeste Ferreira Lopes Cardona

Minister of State for Finance, Maria Manuela Dias Ferreira Leite

Minister of State for National Defence, Paulo Sacadura Cabral Portas

Parliamentary Affairs, Luís Manuel Gonçalves Marques Mendes

Presidency, Nuno Albuquerque Morais Sarmento

Public Works, Transport and Housing, António Carmona Rodrigues

Science and Higher Education, Pedro Augusto Lynce de Faria

Social Security and Work, António José de Castro Bagão Félix

Towns, Territorial Planning and Environment, Amílcar Theias

PORTUGUESE EMBASSY

11 Belgrave Square, London SW1X 8PP

Tel: 020-7235 5331

Ambassador Extraordinary and Plenipotentiary, José Gregório Faria, apptd 1997

BRITISH EMBASSY

Rua de São Bernardo 33, P-1249-082 Lisbon

Tel: (00 351) (21) 392 4000

Email: consular@lisbon.mail.fco.gov.uk

Ambassador Extraordinary and Plenipotentiary, HE Dame Glynne Evans, CMG, DBE, apptd 2001

CONSULATES – Oporto, Portimão

HONORARY CONSULATES – Portimão, Funchal (Madeira), Ribeira Grande (Azores)

BRITISH COUNCIL DIRECTOR, Robert Ness
Rua Luís Fernandes, 1-3, P-1249-062 Lisbon.
Tel: (00 351) (21) 321 4500)
Email: lisbon.enquiries@pt.britishcouncil.org
There are also offices at Coimbra, Oporto and Parede

DEFENCE
The Army has 187 main battle tanks and 353 armoured
personnel carriers. The Navy has two submarines, six
frigates and 28 patrol and coastal vessels at four bases.
The Air Force has 50 combat aircraft.
Lisbon is the base of the NATO Iberian Atlantic
Command and the USA maintains 770 personnel in
mainland Portugal and on the Azores.
MILITARY EXPENDITURE – 2.0 per cent of GDP (2001)
MILITARY PERSONNEL – 43,600: Army 25,400, Navy
  10,800, Air Force 7,400; Paramilitaries 46,400
CONSCRIPTION DURATION – Four to 12 months

ECONOMY
The chief agricultural products are wines, dairy products,
potatoes, tomatoes, maize, meat, fruit, olives, wheat, fish,
cork and rice. There are extensive forests of pine, cork,
eucalyptus and chestnut covering about 38 per cent of
the country. Around 13 per cent of the workforce are
engaged in agriculture, the highest percentage in the EU.
The principal mineral products are limestone, granite,
marble, copper, coal, kaolin and wolframite.
The country is moderately industrialised. The principal
manufactures are motor vehicle components, clothing and
footwear, textiles, machinery, pulp and paper,
pharmaceuticals, foodstuffs, chemicals, fertilisers, wood,
cork, furniture, cement, glassware and pottery. There are
a modern steelworks and large shipbuilding and repair
yards at Lisbon and Setúbal, working mainly for foreign
shipowners. There are several hydroelectric power
stations and two thermal power stations.
Portugal has experienced rapid economic growth since
joining the EU in 1986.
Portugal was one of 11 states to adopt the European
single currency on 1 January 1999. The euro replaced the
escudo on 1 January 2002.
During August 2003 forest fires destroyed over
215,000 hectares (531,000 acres) of woodland with
damage estimated at €1 billion.
GNP – US$111,291 million (2000); US$11,120 per
  capita (2000)
GDP – US$108,479 million (2001); US$10,603 per
  capita (2000)
ANNUAL AVERAGE GROWTH OF GDP – 3.3 per cent
  (2000)
INFLATION RATE – 2.9 per cent (2000)
UNEMPLOYMENT – 4.0 per cent (2000)

TRADE
The principal imports are machinery, vehicles, textiles,
agricultural products, chemicals, oil and base metals. The
principal exports are textiles, clothing and shoes,
machinery, automobile parts, wood, pulp, paper and cork,
and minerals.
In 2001 Portugal had a trade deficit of US$12,979
million and a current account deficit of US$9,959
million. Imports totalled US$37,922 million and exports
US$23,902 million.

Trade with UK	2001	2002
Imports from UK	£1,505,000,000	£1,444,000,000
Exports to UK	1,493,500,000	1,596,000,000

COMMUNICATIONS
There are 3,072 km of railway track, of which 461 km
are electrified. There are international airports at Lisbon,
Oporto, Faro and Santa Maria, and Lages (Azores) and
Funchal (Madeira).

EDUCATION
Education is free and compulsory for nine years from the
age of six. Secondary education is mainly conducted in
state general unified schools, lyceums, technical and
professional schools, but there are also private schools.
There are also military, naval, polytechnic and other
special schools. There are 17 public and private
universities including those at Coimbra (founded in
1290), Oporto, Lisbon, Braga, Aveiro, Vila Real, Faro,
Evora and in the Azores.
ILLITERACY RATE – (m) 5.2 per cent; (f) 10.0 per cent
  (2000)
ENROLMENT (percentage of age group) – primary 100
  per cent (1997); secondary 100 per cent (1997);
  tertiary 39 per cent (1997)

AUTONOMOUS REGIONS
Madeira and The Azores are two administratively autonomous regions of Portugal, having locally elected
assemblies and governments.

MADEIRA is a group of islands in the Atlantic Ocean
  about 520 miles south-west of Lisbon, and consists of
  Madeira, Porto, Santo and three uninhabited islands
  (Desertas). Total area is 300 sq. miles (779 sq. km);
  population, 253,482 (2001). ΨFunchal in Madeira,
  the largest island (270 sq. miles), is the capital
  (population 103,961)
THE AZORES are a group of nine islands (Flores, Corvo,
  Terceira, São Jorge, Pico, Faial, Graciosa, São Miguel
  and Santa Maria) in the Atlantic Ocean; area 895 sq.
  miles (2,330 sq. km); population, 243,895 (2001).
  ΨPonta Delgada, on São Miguel, is the capital
  (population, 137,700). Other ports are ΨAngra, in
  Terceira (55,900) and ΨHorta (16,300)

QATAR

Dawlat Qatar – State of Qatar

AREA – 4,231 sq. miles (11,000 sq. km). Neighbours:
  United Arab Emirates (south), Saudi Arabia (south-
  west)
POPULATION – 575,000 (2001). Most of the population
  is concentrated in the urban district of Doha. Arabic is
  the official language. Islam is the religion of 95 per
  cent of the population
CAPITAL – ΨDoha (Ad-Dawhah) (population 285,000
  2001 estimate)
MAJOR CITIES – Ar-Rayyan; Dukhān; ΨMusay'īd;
  Al-Wakrah
CURRENCY – Qatar riyal of 100 dirhams
NATIONAL DAY – 3 September
NATIONAL FLAG – White and maroon, white portion
  nearer the mast; vertical indented line comprising 17
  angles divides the colours
LIFE EXPECTANCY (years) – 70 (2001)
POPULATION GROWTH RATE – 2.2 per cent
POPULATION DENSITY – 52 per sq. km (2001)
MILITARY EXPENDITURE – 7.1 per cent of GDP (2001)
MILITARY PERSONNEL – 12,400: Army 8,500, Navy
  1,800, Air Force 2,100

ILLITERACY RATE – (m) 19.6 per cent; (f) 16.9 per cent (2000)

ENROLMENT (percentage of age group) – primary 80 per cent (1993); secondary 69 per cent (1993); tertiary 27 per cent (1996)

The state of Qatar covers the peninsula of Qatar in the Gulf from approximately the northern shore of Khor al Odaid to the eastern shore of Khor al Salwa.

HISTORY AND POLITICS

Qatar was one of nine independent emirates in the Gulf in special treaty relations with the UK until 1971. On 2 April 1970, a provisional constitution for Qatar was proclaimed, providing for the establishment of a Council of Ministers and for the formation of a Consultative Council to assist the Council of Ministers in running the affairs of the state. There are no political parties or legislature; ministers are chosen by the Amir.

The Amir, who had ruled since 22 February 1972, was overthrown on 27 June 1995 by his son and heir, who assumed power as Amir the same day. A coup attempt was thwarted in February 1996.

Municipal elections were held on 8 March 1999, the first in which women were allowed to vote and contest seats.

In a referendum held on 29 April 2003 voters approved a new constitution, providing for a 45-member Shura (Consultative) Council of which 30 members will be directly elected and 15 appointed by the Amir. The first elections to the council are due to be held in 2004.

On 5 August 2003 the Amir named his younger son, Prince Tamim, as the crown prince to replace Prince Jassim, who had expressed a desire to give up the post.

HEAD OF STATE

HH Amir of Qatar, Minister of Defence and Commander-in-Chief of Armed Forces, Shaikh Hamad bin Khalifa al-Thani, KCMG, *assumed power* 27 June 1995

Crown Prince, HH Shaikh Tamim bin Hamad al-Thani

COUNCIL OF MINISTERS *as at July 2003*

Prime Minister, HH Shaikh Abdulla bin Khalifa al-Thani

Deputy Prime Minister, Shaikh Mohammed bin Khalifa al-Thani

Awqaf (Religious Endowments) and Islamic Affairs, Ahmed Abdulla al-Marri

Civil Service Affairs and Housing, Shaikh Falah bin Jassim al-Thani

Communications and Transport, Shaikh Ahmed bin Nasser al-Thani

Education and Culture, Higher Education, Sheikha bint Ahmed al-Mahmud

Energy and Industry, Abdulla bin Hamad al-Attiyah

Finance, Economy and Trade, Shaikh Hamad bin Faysal al-Thani

Foreign Affairs, Shaikh Hamad bin Jassem bin Jabr al-Thani

Internal Affairs, Shaikh Abdulla bin Khalid al-Thani

Justice, Hassan bin Abdulla al-Ghanem

Municipal Affairs, Agriculture, Ali Mohammed al-Khater

Public Health, Dr Hajr bin Ahmed Hajr

EMBASSY OF THE STATE OF QATAR

1 South Audley Street, London W1K 1NB

Tel: 020-7493 2200

Ambassador Extraordinary and Plenipotentiary, HE Nasser bin Hamid M. Al-Khalifa, apptd 2000

BRITISH EMBASSY

PO Box 3, Doha

Tel: (00 974) 4421991

Email: bembcomm@qatar.net.qa

Ambassador Extraordinary and Plenipotentiary, HE David MacLennan, apptd 1997

BRITISH COUNCIL DIRECTOR, Alan Smart, 93 Al Sadd Street, PO Box 2992, Doha Tel: (00 974) 442 6193/4

Email: alan.smart@qa.britishcouncil.org

ECONOMY

Although Qatar is a desert country, there are gardens and smallholdings near Doha and to the north, and agriculture is being developed, with self-sufficiency an aim.

The Qatar General Petroleum Corporation is the state-owned company controlling Qatar's interests in oil, gas and petrochemicals. The corporation is responsible for Qatar's oil production onshore and offshore. The large reserves of natural gas in the North Field came into production in September 1991.

Current industries include a steel mill, a fertiliser plant, a cement factory, a petrochemical complex and two natural gas liquids plants. With the exception of the cement works at Umm Bāb, all these industries are at Musay'īd, about 30 miles south of Doha. Qatar is also expanding its infrastructure, including electrical generation and water distillation, roads, houses, and government buildings. A drop in demand for crude oil has slowed the economy considerably.

The chief imports are machinery and equipment, manufactures, foodstuffs and livestock, and chemicals.

In 1999 imports totalled US$2,500 million and exports US$7,061 million.

GDP – US$14,473 million (1999); US$29,100 per capita (2000)

ANNUAL AVERAGE GROWTH OF GDP – 4.0 per cent (1998)

INFLATION RATE – 1.9 per cent (2002)

Trade with UK	2001	2002
Imports from UK	£174,811,000	£202,999,000
Exports to UK	32,062,000	28,667,000

COMMUNICATIONS

There are 1,210 km of roads, of which 1,089 km are surfaced. Regular air services provided by Gulf Air and Qatar Airways connect Qatar with the other Gulf states, the Middle East, the Indian sub-continent, Africa and Europe. The Qatar Broadcasting Service transmits on medium wave, shortwave and VHF.

ROMANIA

România – Romania

AREA – 88,577 sq. miles (230,300 sq. km). Neighbours: Ukraine (north and east), Moldova (east), Bulgaria (south), Serbia and Montenegro (south-west), Hungary (north-west)

POPULATION – 21,698,181 (2001 census): 89.4 per cent Romanian, 7.1 per cent Hungarian, 1.7 per cent Roma, 0.5 per cent German, 0.3 per cent Ukrainian, 0.04 per cent Jews and others. Religious affiliation: Orthodox 86.8 per cent, Roman Catholic 5 per cent, Reformed 3.5 per cent, Greek Catholic 1 per cent.

Romanian is a Romance language with many archaic forms and with admixtures of Slavonic, Turkish, Magyar and French words

CAPITAL – Bucharest (population, 2,066,723, 2001 estimate)

MAJOR CITIES – ΨBraşov (324,104); Constanţa (348,985); Cluj-Napoca (321,850); Craiova (303,033); ΨGalaţi (324,234); Iaşi (337,643); Oradea (221,559); Ploieşti (254,304); Timişoara (325,359), 2001 estimates

CURRENCY – Leu (Lei) of 100 bani

NATIONAL ANTHEM – Desteaptă-te, Române, Din Somnul Cel De Moarte (Awake Ye, Romanians, From Your Deadly Slumber)

NATIONAL DAY – 1 December

NATIONAL FLAG – Three vertical bands, blue, yellow, red

LIFE EXPECTANCY (years) – 70 (2001)

POPULATION GROWTH RATE – –0.3 per cent

POPULATION DENSITY – 97 per sq. km (2001)

URBAN POPULATION – 55 per cent (2001)

HISTORY AND POLITICS

Romania has its origin in the union of the Danubian principalities of Wallachia and Moldavia in 1859.

In 1918 Bessarabia, Bukovina, Transylvania and Banat were united with Romania.

In 1947 Romania became 'The Romanian People's Republic' under the leadership of the Romanian Communist Party. A revolution in December 1989 led to the overthrow of Nicolae Ceauşescu, president since 1965. A provisional government abolished the leading role of the Communist Party and held free elections in May 1990.

In the elections held on 26 November 2000 the Social Democratic Party of Romania (PDSR) gained 155 seats in the Chamber of Deputies and 65 seats in the Senate, becoming the largest party in both houses. The PDSR presidential candidate, Ion Iliescu, obtained 36.35 per cent of the vote in the first round of the presidential election. He won the second round, held on 10 December, obtaining 66.83 per cent of the vote. On 27 December, the PDSR reached an agreement with other centre-right parties to enable it to form a workable minority government.

In November 2002 Romania was formally invited to accession talks with NATO and is expected to join in 2004.

POLITICAL SYSTEM

The constitution of 1991 formally makes Romania a multiparty democracy and endorses human rights and a market economy. The parliament comprises the Chamber of Deputies with 345 seats, of which 18 are reserved for ethnic minorities, and the Senate with 140 seats. Both houses are elected for four-year terms.

HEAD OF STATE

President of the Republic, Ion Iliescu, *elected* 10 December 2000

CABINET *as at August 2003*
Prime Minister, Adrian Năstase
Agriculture, Forestry, Water and Environment, Ilie Sârbu
Communications and Information Technology, Dan Nica
Culture and Religious Affairs, Răzvan Theodorescu
Defence, Ioan Mircea Paşcu
Economy and Commerce, Ioan-Dan Popescu
Education, Research and Youth, Alexandru Athanasiu

European Integration, Hildegard Puwak
Foreign Affairs, Mircea Geoană
Health, Mircea Beuran
Interior, Public Administration, Ioan Rus
Justice, Rodica Mihaela Stănoiu
Labour, Social Solidarity and Family, Elena Dumitru
Ministers-Delegate, Vasile Puşcaş *(Chief EU Negotiator);* Ionel Blănculescu *(Co-ordinating the Control Authorities);* Eugen Dijmărescu *(Commerce);* Acsinte Gaspar *(Parliamentary Relations);* Gabriel Oprea *(Public Administration);* Marian Sarbu *(Relations with Social Partners)*
Public Finance, Mihai Tănăsescu
Secretary-General of the Government, Petru Serban Mihailescu
Transport, Construction and Tourism, Miron Tudor Mitrea

EMBASSY OF ROMANIA
Arundel House, 4 Palace Green, London W8 4QD
Tel: 020-7937 9666
Ambassador Extraordinary and Plenipotentiary, HE Dan Ghibernea, apptd 2002

BRITISH EMBASSY
24 Strada Jules Michelet, RO-70154 Bucharest
Tel: (00 40) (21) 201 7200
Ambassador Extraordinary and Plenipotentiary, HE Quinton Quayle, apptd 2002

BRITISH COUNCIL DIRECTOR, Stephan Roman
Calea Dorobantilor 14, RO-71132 Bucharest
Tel: (00 40) (21) 307 9600
Email: bc.romania@britishcouncil.ro

DEFENCE

The Army has 1,258 main battle tanks, 1,786 armoured personnel carriers and 177 armoured infantry fighting vehicles. The Navy has one destroyer, six frigates, 38 patrol and coastal vessels, and seven helicopters at four bases. The Air Force has 202 combat aircraft and 21 attack helicopters.

MILITARY EXPENDITURE – 2.5 per cent of GDP (2001)

MILITARY PERSONNEL – 99,200: Army 66,000, Navy 6,200, Air Force 17,000; Paramilitaries 79,900

CONSCRIPTION DURATION – 12 months

ECONOMY

Agriculture employed 40.8 per cent of the workforce in 2000 and contributed 12.8 per cent of GDP. The principal crops are cereals, vegetables, flax and hemp. Vines and fruits are also grown. The forests of the mountainous regions are extensive, and the timber industry is important.

There are plentiful supplies of natural gas, together with various mineral deposits including coal, iron ore, bauxite, chromium and uranium in quantities which allow a substantial part of the requirements of industry to be met from local resources.

The economy, which was characterised by state-owned and co-operative ownership, excessive centralisation, rigid planning and low efficiency, has been slowly reformed.

Since 1996 the pace of privatisation and restructuring has quickened, subsidies have been reduced and prices liberalised.

An extensive programme of privatisation was announced in March 2002.

GNP – US$37,380 million (2000); US$1,670 per capita (2000)
GDP – US$39,714 million (2001); US$1,635 per capita (2000)
ANNUAL AVERAGE GROWTH OF GDP – 5.3 per cent (2001)
INFLATION RATE – 22.5 per cent (2002)
UNEMPLOYMENT – 7.1 per cent (2000)
TOTAL EXTERNAL DEBT – US$10,224 million (2000)

TRADE
The main imports are machines and equipment, minerals, textiles, chemicals and metallurgical products. The main exports are textiles, metallurgical products, machinery components, minerals, chemicals, shoes and transport equipment. Italy, Germany, Russia, France and the UK are Romania's most important trading partners.

In 2000 Romania had a trade deficit of US$1,684 million and a current account deficit of US$1,359 million. In 2001 imports totalled US$15,561 million and exports US$11,391.

Trade with UK	2001	2002
Imports from UK	£341,709,000	£430,623,000
Exports to UK	458,381,000	531,728,000

COMMUNICATIONS
In 1999 there were 11,376 km of railway track, over a third of which was electrified, and 153,358 km of roads, of which 78,213 km are paved and 113 km are motorway. The main national roads largely follow the railway lines and almost all lead to the capital. The principal ports are Constanţa and Mangalia (on the Black Sea), Sulina (on the Danube Estuary), Galati, Brăila, Giurgiu and Drobeta-Turnu Severin. The Danube and the Black Sea are linked by a canal completed in 1984.

EDUCATION
Education is free and primary and secondary education are compulsory. There are state universities in seven cities, 66 private universities, six polytechnics, two commercial academies, and five agricultural colleges.
ILLITERACY RATE – (m) 1.0 per cent; (f) 2.8 per cent (2000)
ENROLMENT (percentage of age group) – primary 100 per cent (1997); secondary 78 per cent (1997); tertiary 22.5 per cent (1997)

RUSSIA

Rossiiskaya Federatsiya – Russian Federation

AREA – 6,495,577 sq. miles (16,888,500 sq. km). Neighbours: Norway, Finland, Estonia, Latvia, Belarus and Ukraine (west), Georgia, Azerbaijan, Kazakhstan, China, Mongolia and North Korea (south). The Kaliningrad enclave borders Lithuania and Poland
POPULATION – 145,924,900 (2002 estimate): 87.5 per cent Russian, 3.5 per cent Tatar, 2.7 per cent Ukrainian, 1.3 per cent ethnic German, 1.1 per cent Chuvash, 0.9 per cent Bashkir, 0.7 per cent Belarusian and 0.7 per cent Mordovian. There are another six minorities with populations of over half a million and more than 130 nationalities in total. The Russian Orthodox Church is the predominant religion, though the Tatars and many in the north Caucasus are Muslims and there are Jewish communities in Moscow and St Petersburg. The language is Russian

CAPITAL – Moscow (population, 10,101,500, 2002 estimate), founded about 1147, became the centre of the rising Moscow principality and in the 15th century the capital of the whole of Russia (Muscovy). In 1325 it became the seat of the Metropolitan of Russia. In 1703 Peter the Great transferred the capital to St Petersburg, but on 14 March 1918 Moscow was again designated as the capital
MAJOR CITIES – ΨSt Petersburg (4,669,400, 2002 estimate), from 1914 to 1924 Petrograd and from 1924 to 1991 Leningrad. Other cities: Chelyabinsk (1,078,300); Kazan (1,105,300); Nizhny-Novgorod/Gorky (1,311,200); Novosibirsk/Novonikolayevsk (1,425,600); Omsk (1,333,900); Perm/Molotov (1,000,100); Rostov-on-Don (1,070,200); Samara/Kuibyshev (1,158,110); Ufa (1,042,400); Yekaterinburg/Sverdlovsk (1,293,000), 2002 estimates
CURRENCY – Rouble of 100 kopeks
NATIONAL ANTHEM – Russia, Sacred Our Empire (the former Soviet national anthem, with new lyrics)
NATIONAL DAY – 12 June (Independence Day)
NATIONAL FLAG – Three horizontal stripes of white, blue, red
LIFE EXPECTANCY (years) – 66 (2001)
POPULATION GROWTH RATE – –0.2 per cent
POPULATION DENSITY – 9 per sq. km (2001)
URBAN POPULATION – 73 per cent
ILLITERACY RATE – (m) 0.3 per cent; (f) 0.6 per cent (2000)

Russia occupies three-quarters of the land area of the former Soviet Union.

The Russian Federation comprises 89 members: 49 regions *(oblast)* – Amur, Arkhangelsk, Astrakhan, Belgorod, Bryansk, Chelyabinsk, Chita, Irkutsk, Ivanovo, Kaliningrad, Kaluga, Kamchatka, Kemerovo, Kirov, Kostroma, Kurgan, Kursk, Leningrad, Lipetsk, Magadan, Moscow, Murmansk, Nizhny-Novgorod, Novgorod, Novosibirsk, Omsk, Orel, Orenburg, Penza, Perm, Pskov, Rostov, Ryazan, Sakhalin, Samara, Saratov, Smolensk, Sverdlovsk, Tambov, Tomsk, Tula, Tver, Tyumen, Ulyanovsk, Vladimir, Volgograd, Vologda, Voronezh, Yaroslavl; six autonomous territories *(krai)* – Altai, Khabarovsk, Krasnodar, Krasnoyarsk, Primorye, Stavropol; 21 republics – Adygeia, Altai, Bashkortostan, Buryatia, Chechnya, Chuvash, Daghestan, Ingush, Kabardino-Balkar, Kalmykia, Karachai-Cherkessia, Karelia, Khakassia, Komi, Mari-El, Mordovia, North Ossetia (Alania), Sakha, Tatarstan, Tyva, Udmurt; ten autonomous areas – Aga-Buryat, Chuckchi, Evenki, Khanty-Mansi, Komi-Permyak, Koryak, Nenets, Taimyr, Ust-Orda-Buryat, Yamal-Nenets; two cities of federal status – Moscow, St Petersburg; and one autonomous Jewish region, Birobijan.

There are three principal geographic areas: a low-lying flat western area stretching eastwards up to the Yenisei and divided in two by the Ural ridge; the eastern area between the Yenisei and the Pacific, consisting of a number of tablelands and ridges; and a southern mountainous area. Russia has a very long coastline, including the longest Arctic coastline in the world (about 17,000 miles).

The most important rivers are the Volga, the Northern Dvina and the Pechora, the Neva, the Don and the Kuban in the European part, and in the Asiatic part, the Ob, the Irtysh, the Yenisei, the Lena and the Amur, and, further north, Khatanga, Olenek, Yana, Indigirka,

Kolyma and Anadyr. Lake Baikal in eastern Siberia is the deepest lake in the world.

HISTORY AND POLITICS

Russia was formally created from the principality of Muscovy and its territories by Tsar Peter I (The Great) (1682–1725), who initiated its territorial expansion, introduced Western ideas of government and founded St Petersburg.

Discontent caused by autocratic rule, the poor conduct of the military in the First World War and wartime privation led to a revolution which broke out in March 1917. A power struggle ensued between the provisional government and the Bolshevik Party. This led to a second revolution in November 1917 in which the Bolsheviks, led by Lenin, seized power.

Civil war between 'red' Bolshevik forces and 'white' monarchist and anti-Communist forces lasted until the end of 1922. During the civil war, Russia had been declared a Soviet Republic and other Soviet republics had been formed in Ukraine, Belorussia and Transcaucasia. These four republics merged to form the Union of Soviet Socialist Republics (USSR) on 30 December 1922.

Joseph Stalin introduced a policy of rapid industrialisation under a series of five-year plans, brought all sectors of industry under government control, abolished private ownership and enforced the collectivisation of agriculture.

In the Second World War, the USSR lost 27 million combatants and civilians.

Mikhail Gorbachev became Soviet leader in March 1985 and introduced the policies of *perestroika* (complete restructuring) and *glasnost* (openness) in order to revamp the economy, which had stagnated since the 1970s, to root out corruption and inefficiency, and to end the Cold War. The retreat from total control by the Communist Party unleashed ethnic and nationalist tensions.

Following the defeat of an attempted coup by hardline Communists in August 1991, effective political power was now in the hands of the republican leaders, especially Russian President Yeltsin, and the Soviet Union began to break up as the constituent republics declared their independence. Gorbachev resigned as Soviet President on 25 December 1991 and on 26 December 1991 the USSR formally ceased to exist.

Russia was recognised as an independent state by the EC and USA in January 1992; it took over the Soviet Union's seat at the UN in December 1991.

A new Russian Federal Treaty was signed on 13 March 1992 between the central government and the autonomous republics. Tatarstan and Bashkortostan signed the treaty in 1994 after securing considerable legislative and economic autonomy.

The state of the parties in the State *Duma* following the general election on 19 December 1999 was: Communist Party 113 seats; Unity 72; Fatherland-All Russia 67; Union of Rightist Forces 29; Yabloko 21; Zhirinovski's Bloc 17; Our Home is Russia 7; DPA 2; Russian All People Unity 2; others 5.

In the presidential election held on 26 March 2000, Vladimir Putin won 52.94 per cent of the vote, in which the turnout was 68.88 per cent, and was formally inaugurated on 7 May 2000. Elections to the State Duma were scheduled to take place on 7 December 2003.

POLITICAL SYSTEM

The 1993 constitution enshrines the right to private ownership and the freedoms of press, speech, association, worship and travel, and states that Russia is a multiparty democracy. The President is directly elected for a maximum of two four-year terms. The Prime Minister takes over from the President in the event that he is unable to fulfil his duties. Legislative power is vested in the Federal Assembly, comprising the Federation Council (upper house) of 178 members, two elected by each of the 89 members of the Russian Federation; and the State *Duma* (lower house) of 450 members, of which 225 are elected by constituencies on a first-past-the-post basis and 225 by proportional representation, with a five per cent threshold for representation.

The judicial system consists of a Constitutional Court of 19 members appointed for a 12-year term which protects and interprets the constitution and decides if laws are compatible with it. The Supreme Court adjudicates in criminal and civil law cases. The Arbitration Court deals with commercial disputes between companies.

INSURGENCIES

The Chechen republic declared its independence in November 1991 after a nationalist coup in the republic and refused to sign the Russian Federal Treaty in March 1992. Civil war began in early 1994 between the Chechen government and armed opposition forces tacitly supported by the Russian government. The Russian military launched an invasion of Chechnya in December 1994 and captured Grozny in February 1995.

Russian troops were withdrawn in January 1997 when presidential and legislative elections were also held in Chechnya. A treaty renouncing the use of force to resolve Chechnya's status was signed between Presidents Maskhadov and Yeltsin in May 1997.

Following an incursion by Islamic militants into Dagestan on 10 August 1999, Russian forces launched air strikes and Russian ground troops entered the territory. Russian forces captured the Chechen capital, Grozny, on 6 February 2000 and captured the last Chechen-held town on 29 February, but Chechen guerrilla attacks on Russian targets continued. On 8 June 2000, President Putin imposed temporary direct presidential rule on Chechnya.

On 23 October 2002 Chechen separatists seized a Moscow theatre and held some 800 people hostage. The siege ended on 26 October after Russian special forces stormed the building, killing most of the rebels and 119 hostages, most of whom died from the effects of a paralysing gas which had been pumped into the building be the special forces. Sporadic suicide bombings by Chechen rebels against Russian interests continue.

A referendum took place in Chechnya on 23 March 2003 in which the majority voted in favour of a new constitution promising autonomy for the republic but also stating that Chechnya was an integral part of the territory of the Russian Federation.

HEAD OF STATE

President, Vladimir Putin, *elected* 26 March 2000, *inaugurated* 7 May 2000

GOVERNMENT *as at July 2003*

Chair, Academy of Science, Atomic Energy, Central, Customs, Federal Property, Property Relations, Mikhail Kasyanov
Deputy Chairs, Aleksey Gordeyev *(Agriculture and Food, Fisheries, Cartography and Land Survey, Environment);* Alexei Kudrin *(Finance, Economic Development and Trade);* Viktor Khristenko *(Energy, Natural Resources,*

Communications, Railways, Housing and Construction); Boris Alyoshin *(Industrial Policy);* Galina Karelova *(Social Affairs);* Vladimir Yakovlev *(Social and Housing Reforms)*
Anti-Monopoly and Entrepreneurial Affairs, Ilya Yuzhanov
Atomic Energy, Aleksandr Rumyantsev
Culture, Mikhail Shvydkoi
Defence, Sergey Ivanov
Director of the Federal Security Services, Nikolai Patrushev
Economic Development and Trade, German Gref
Education, Vladimir Filippov
Emergencies, Civil Defence, Natural Disasters, Sergei Shoigu
Employment and Social Development, Aleksandr Pochinok
Energy, Igor Yusufov
Foreign Affairs, Igor Ivanov
Head of Government Administration, Igor Shuvalov
Health, Yuri Shevchenko
Interior, Boris Gryzlov
Justice, Yuri Chaika
Nationalities Policy, Vladimir Zorin
Natural Resources, Vitaly Artyukhov
Press, Broadcasting and Mass Communications, Mikhail Lesin
Privatisation, Farid Gazizullin
Railways, Gennady Fadeev
Science, Industry and Technology, Ilya Klebanov
Secretary of the Security Council, Vladimir Rushailo
Social and Economic Development of Chechnya, Stanislav Ilyasov
Tax and Levy Collection, Gennady Bukayev
Telecommunications and Information, Leonid Reyman
Transport, Sergei Frank

EMBASSY OF THE RUSSIAN FEDERATION
13 Kensington Palace Gardens, London W8 4QX
Tel: 020-7229 2666/3628/6412
Ambassador Extraordinary and Plenipotentiary,
HE Grigory B. Karasin, apptd 2000

BRITISH EMBASSY
Smolenskaya Naberezhnaya 10, 121099 Moscow
Tel: (00 7) (095) 956 7200
Email: moscow@britishembassy.ru
Ambassador Extraordinary and Plenipotentiary,
HE Sir Roderic Lyne, KBE, CMG, apptd 1999

CONSULATES-GENERAL – Ekaterinburg, St Petersburg

BRITISH COUNCIL DIRECTOR, Adrian Greer
Ulitsa Nikoloyamskaya 1, RUS-109189 Moscow
Tel: (00 7) (095) 782 0200 Email: bc.moscow@britishcouncil.ru
There are also offices at Ekaterinburg, Nizhni Novgorod, Sochi, St Petersburg and Tomsk

DEFENCE
Since the demise of the Soviet Union the Russian armed forces have been considerably reduced. In November 2000 it was announced that the armed forces would be reduced to 850,000 personnel by 2005. Major army reform is planned for the period 2004–10, including the transition from conscription to voluntary service.

A joint CIS air defence system covers Russia, Armenia, Belarus, Kazakhstan, Kyrgyzstan and Uzbekistan.

The Strategic Nuclear Forces have 13 nuclear-powered ballistic missile submarines with 216 missiles, 735 intercontinental ballistic missiles and 100 anti-ballistic missiles.

The Army has about 21,870 main battle tanks, 25,975 armoured personnel carriers and armoured infantry fighting vehicles, and 1,700 helicopters. The Navy has 53 submarines, one aircraft carrier, seven cruisers, 14 destroyers, ten frigates, 88 patrol and coastal vessels, 217 combat aircraft and 102 armed helicopters. The Air Force has 1,736 combat aircraft.

Russia deploys forces in Armenia (2,900), Georgia (4,000), Moldova (1,000) and Tajikistan (7,800). Russia is the world's third largest contributor to peacekeeping operations. An agreement with Ukraine on the division on the Black Sea Fleet was signed in May 1997.

MILITARY EXPENDITURE – 4.3 per cent of GDP (2001)
MILITARY PERSONNEL – 988,100: Strategic Nuclear Forces 149,000, Army 321,000, Navy 171,500, Air Force 184,600, Paramilitaries 409,100
CONSCRIPTION DURATION – 18–24 months

ECONOMY
Under the Soviet regime, an essentially agrarian economy in 1917 was transformed by the early 1960s into the second strongest industrial power in the world. However, by the early 1970s the concentration of resources on the military-industrial complex was causing the civilian economy to stagnate. Free market reforms were introduced by President Gorbachev, including the legalisation of small private businesses, the reduction of state control over the economy, and denationalisation and privatisation. The first stage of mass privatisation of state industries began in October 1992 and the central distribution system was abolished with effect from 1 January 1993. By February 1996, 80 per cent of the economy had been privatised.

From 1994 to 1996, the economy began to stabilise with economic reforms judged to have become irreversible.

The devaluation of the rouble in 1998 caused the return of growth in the Russian economy in 1999. However, low productivity, overstaffing, and a lack of investment and entrepreneurship remained a problem. In 2001, industrial production grew by more than 5 per cent and investments in basic capital from all sources of financing grew by 8 per cent. GDP rose by 5.1 per cent in 2001 with about 60 per cent of the growth arising from increased consumer demand.

Russia has some of the richest mineral deposits in the world. Coal is mined in the Kuznetsk area, in the Urals, south of Moscow, in the Donets basin and in the Pechora area in the north. Oil is produced in the northern Caucasus, between the Volga and the Urals, and in western Siberia, which also has large deposits of natural gas. A pipeline to bring Caspian oil into Russia via Dagestan and North Ossetia is under construction. Oil production in 2000 was 323.3 million tonnes. Coal and gas deposits in Siberia and the far east (especially Yakutia) are being developed. The Ural mountains contain high-quality iron ore, manganese, copper, aluminium, platinum, precious stones, salt, asbestos, pyrites, coal, oil, etc. Iron ore is also mined near Kursk, Tula, Lipetsk, in several areas in Siberia and in the Kola Peninsula. Non-ferrous metals are found in the Altai, in eastern Siberia, in the northern Caucasus, in the Kuznetsk basin, in the far east and in the far north. 109 tonnes of gold were produced in 2003.

The vast area and the great variety in climatic conditions are reflected in the structure of agriculture. In the far north reindeer breeding, hunting and fishing are predominant. Further south, timber industry is combined with grain growing. In the southern half of the forest zone and in the adjacent forest-steppe zone, the acreage under grain crops is larger and the structure of agriculture more complex. Between the Volga and the Urals cericulture is predominant (particularly summer wheat), followed by cattle breeding. Beyond the Urals is another important grain-growing and stock-breeding area in the southern part of the western Siberian plain. The southern steppe zone is the main wheat granary of Russia, containing also large acreages under barley, maize and sunflowers. In 2001 85 million tons of grain was harvested, an increase of 20 million tons on 2000. In the extreme south cotton is cultivated. Vine, tobacco and other southern crops are grown on the Black Sea shore of the Caucasus.

Moscow and St Petersburg are still the two largest industrial centres in the country, but new industrial areas have been developed in the Urals, the Kuznetsk basin, in Siberia and the far east.

GNP – US$241,027 million (2000); US$1,660 per capita (2000)

GDP – US$309,951 million (2001); US$1,726 per capita (2000)

ANNUAL AVERAGE GROWTH OF GDP – –4.6 per cent (1998)

INFLATION RATE – 20.8 per cent (2000)

UNEMPLOYMENT – 13.4 per cent (1999)

TOTAL EXTERNAL DEBT – US$160,300 million (2000)

TRADE
Russia's main trading partners are Germany, the USA, Italy, China and the former Soviet states. In 2001 there was a trade surplus of US$47,839 million and a current account surplus of US$34,575 million. Imports totalled US$58,992 million and exports US$103,139 million.

Trade with UK	2001	2002
Imports from UK	£898,259,000	£989,683,000
Exports to UK	2,110,905,000	1,995,701,000

COMMUNICATIONS
The European area of Russia is well served by railways, but there are still large areas, notably in the far north and Siberia, with few or no railways. In 2001 there were 149,000 km of railways, of which 86,000 km were used for passenger transport.

The most important ports (Taganrog, Rostov and Novorossiisk) lie around the Black Sea and the Sea of Azov. The northern ports (St Petersburg, Murmansk and Arkhangelsk) are, with the exception of Murmansk, icebound during winter. Several ports have been built along the Arctic Sea route between Murmansk and Vladivostok and are in regular use every summer. The far eastern port of Vladivostok, the Pacific naval base of Russia, is kept open by icebreakers all the year round.

There are 95,900 km of waterways. The great rivers of European Russia flow outwards from the centre, linking all parts of the plain with the chief ports. They are supplemented by a system of canals which provide a through traffic between the White, Baltic, Black and Caspian Seas. The most notable are the White Sea-Baltic Canal, the Moscow-Volga Canal and the Volga-Don Canal linking the Baltic and the White Seas in the north to the Caspian Sea, the Black Sea and the Sea of Azov in the south.

CULTURE
Russian is a branch of the Slavonic family of languages and is written in the Cyrillic script.

Before the westernisation of Russia under Peter the Great (1682–1725), Russian literature consisted mainly of folk ballads *(byliny)*, epic songs, chronicles and works of moral theology. The 18th and 19th centuries saw the development of poetry and fiction. Poetry reached its zenith with Alexander Pushkin (1799–1837), Mikhail Lermontov (1814–41), Alexander Blok (1880–1921), the 1958 Nobel Prize laureate Boris Pasternak (1890–1960), Vladimir Mayakovsky (1893–1930) and Anna Akhmatova (1888–1966). Fiction is associated with the names of Nikolai Gogol (1809–52), Ivan Turgenev (1818–83), Fyodor Dostoevsky (1821–81), Leo Tolstoy (1828–1910), Anton Chekhov (1860–1904), Maxim Gorky (1868–1936), Ivan Bunin (1870–1953), Mikhail Bulgakov (1891–1940), Mikhail Sholokhov (1905–84) and Alexander Solzhenitsyn (b. 1918).

Great names in music include Glinka (1804–57), Borodin (1833–87), Mussorgsky (1839–81), Rimsky-Korsakov (1844–1908), Rubinstein (1829–94), Tchaikovsky (1840–93), Rachmaninov (1873–1943), Skriabin (1872–1915), Prokofiev (1891–1953), Stravinsky (1882–1971), Shostakovich (1906–75), Gubaidulina (b. 1931) and Schnittke (1934–98).

RWANDA

Republika y'u Rwanda/République Rwandaise – Republic of Rwanda

AREA – 10,169 sq. miles (26,338 sq. km). Neighbours: Burundi (south), Democratic Republic of Congo (west), Uganda (north), Tanzania (east)

POPULATION – 8,162,715 (2002 census): Hutus 90 per cent, Tutsis 9 per cent, Twa (pygmy) 1 per cent. Kinyarwanda, French and English are the official languages. Swahili is also spoken

CAPITAL – Kigali (population, 608,141, 2002 census)

CURRENCY – Rwanda franc of 100 centimes

NATIONAL ANTHEM – Rwanda Rwacu, Rwanda Gihugu Cyambyage (My Rwanda, Rwanda Who Gave Me Birth)

NATIONAL DAY – 1 July

NATIONAL FLAG – Broad blue band in upper half, with a sun next fly surmounting equal bands of yellow and green

POPULATION GROWTH RATE – 8 per cent

POPULATION DENSITY – 275 per sq. km (1999)

MILITARY EXPENDITURE – 5.8 per cent of GDP (2001)

MILITARY PERSONNEL – 75,000: Army 64,000, Air Force 1,000, Paramilitaries 10,200

ILLITERACY RATE – (m) 26.4 per cent; (f) 39.8 per cent (2000)

ENROLMENT (percentage of age group) – primary 75 per cent (1991); secondary 8 per cent (1991); tertiary 0.5 per cent (1990)

HISTORY AND POLITICS
The majority Hutu population rebelled against Tutsi feudal rule (under the Belgian colonial authority) in 1959–61, leading to the massacre of thousands of Tutsis. Large numbers fled into exile in Uganda. Rwanda became an independent republic on 1 July 1962.

Armed Tutsi exiles repeatedly attempted to invade Rwanda in the 1960s and 1970s but were defeated by the predominantly Hutu army. Continued Hutu-Tutsi conflict left thousands dead over a period of 30 years. In October 1990 Rwanda was invaded by the Rwandan

Patriotic Front (RPF) of exiled Tutsis and moderate Hutus, who forced the one-party MRND (National Revolutionary Movement for Development) government to introduce a multiparty constitution in 1991. After the government reneged on a 1992 peace agreement, the RPF advanced on Kigali and forced the government to restart negotiations, which led to the August 1993 Arusha peace accord. The accord provided for a transitional period under a broad-based government including the RPF until the 1995 elections, with UN forces in the country throughout the period.

President Habyarimana, who had retained the interim presidency, died on 6 April 1994 in a plane crash widely believed to have been caused by a rocket attack by extremist sections of the Hutu army. The Hutu army and armed militia, the *interahamwe*, then carried out a preplanned act of genocide against the Tutsi minority and moderate Hutus; 800,000 people were massacred in three months. The civil war restarted and the RPF gradually re-established its control over the country, forcing the defeated government forces and two million Hutu refugees into exile. A government report issued in February 2002 revealed that 1,074,017 people, more than 93 per cent of them Tutsis, were killed between 1990 and 1994. On 18 July 1994 the RPF declared victory and established a broad-based government of national unity in which moderate Hutus were given the presidency and premiership and the RPF took eight of the 22 seats.

The 70-member Transitional National Assembly provided for by the Arusha agreement began operation on 12 December 1994 with the extremist Hutu MRND excluded.

Killings by both Hutu militia and government forces continued, and Hutu attacks in central and western Rwanda were frequent in the first half of 1998 and recurred in May and June 2001 in the north west of the country.

At the International Criminal Tribunal for Rwanda (ICTR) in May 1998, former Prime Minister Jean Kambanda pleaded guilty to charges of genocide.

Rwanda has supported a rebellion in the Democratic Republic of Congo led by the Congolese Democratic Rally, a Congolese Tutsi group. Under a peace agreement signed on 30 July 2002 by the presidents of Rwanda and the Democratic Republic of Congo, Rwanda completed the withdrawal of its troops from the Democratic Republic of Congo in October 2002.

The Transitional National Assembly was extended for four further years on 9 June 1999. A new constitution was approved by the Transitional National Assembly on 23 April 2003, supported by 93 per cent of voters in a referendum and came into force on 4 June. The constitution is designed to achieve democracy while preventing another genocide and does not allow any one ethnic group to dominate the government. The first presidential elections since the 1994 genocide took place on 25 August 2003 and were won by the incumbent President Paul Kagame with 95.1 per cent of the vote. Elections to the new parliament were scheduled for 29 September 2003.

POLITICAL SYSTEM

Under the 2003 constitution the President is head of state and is directly elected for a seven-year term, renewable once only. The legislature is bicameral consisting of a National Assembly of 80 members elected by universal suffrage for a five-year term and a 26-member Senate.

HEAD OF STATE

President, Maj-Gen. Paul Kagame, *appointed* 17 April 2000, *sworn in* 22 April 2000, *elected* 25 August 2003

GOVERNMENT *as at August 2003*

Prime Minister, Bernard Makusa (MDR)
Agriculture, Livestock, and Forestry, Ephrem Kabaija
Civil Service, Skills Development, Vocational Training and Labour, André Habib Bumaya
Commerce, Industry and Tourism, Alexandre Byambabaje
Defence and National Security, Maj.-Gen. Marcel Gatsinzi
Education, Science and Technology, Romain Murenzi
Finance and Economic Planning, Donald Kaberuka
Foreign Affairs and Regional Co-operation, Charles Murigande
Gender and Women's Promotion, Marie Mukantabana
Health, Abel Dushimiyimana
Infrastructure, Jean-Damascene Ntawukuriryayo
Internal Affairs, Jean de Dieu Ntiruhungwa
Justice and Institutional Relations, Jean de Dieu Mucyo
Lands, Resettlement and Environmental Protection, Laurent Nkusi
Local Government, Information and Social Affairs, Christophe Bazivamo
Minister in the President's Office, Solina Nyirahabimana
Youth, Culture and Sports, Robert Bayigamba

EMBASSY OF THE REPUBLIC OF RWANDA

Uganda House, 58–59 Trafalgar Square, London WC2N 5DX
Tel: 020-7930 2570
Ambassador Extraordinary and Plenipotentiary,
    HE Rosemary K. Museminali, apptd 2000

BRITISH EMBASSY

Parcelle No. 1131, Blvd de l'Umuganda, Kacyira-Sud,
BP 576 Kigali
Tel: (00 250) 84098/85771/85773
Ambassador Extraordinary and Plenipotentiary,
    HE Susan Elizabeth Hogwood, MBE, apptd 2001

ECONOMY

Coffee, tea and sugar are grown. Tin, hides, bark of quinine and extract of pyrethrum flowers are also exported.

In 2000 there was a trade deficit of US$153 million and a current account deficit of US$7 million. In 2001 imports totalled US$250 million and exports US$85 million.

GNP – US$1,988 million (2000); US$230 per capita (2000)
GDP – US$1,703 million (2001); US$187 per capita (2000)
ANNUAL AVERAGE GROWTH OF GDP – 6.0 per cent (2000)
INFLATION RATE – 4.3 per cent (2000)
TOTAL EXTERNAL DEBT – US$1,271 million (2000)

Trade with UK	2001	2002
Imports from UK	£5,028,000	£3,394,000
Exports to UK	481,000	1,177,000

ST CHRISTOPHER AND NEVIS

The Federation of St Christopher and Nevis

AREA – 100.8 sq. miles (262 sq. km)
POPULATION – 38,000 (2001 estimate). The language is English
CAPITAL – ΨBasseterre (population, 12,200, 1994 estimate)
MAJOR TOWNS – ΨCharlestown (1,700, 1994 estimate), the chief town of Nevis
CURRENCY – East Caribbean dollar (EC$) of 100 cents
NATIONAL ANTHEM – Oh Land Of Beauty
NATIONAL DAY – 19 September (Independence Day)
NATIONAL FLAG – Three diagonal bands, green, black and red; each colour separated by a stripe of yellow. Two white stars on the black band
LIFE EXPECTANCY (years) – 71 (2001)
POPULATION GROWTH RATE – –0.9 per cent
POPULATION DENSITY – 145 per sq. km (2001)

The state of St Christopher and Nevis is located at the northern end of the eastern Caribbean. It comprises the islands of St Christopher (St Kitts) (68 sq. miles) and Nevis (36 sq. miles). The central area of St Christopher is forest-clad and mountainous, rising to the 3,792 ft Mount Liamuiga. Nevis is separated from the southern tip of St Christopher by a strait two miles wide and is dominated by Nevis Peak, 3,232 ft.

HISTORY AND POLITICS

St Christopher was the first island in the British West Indies to be colonised (1623). The Territory of St Christopher and Nevis became a State in Association with Britain in 1967. The State of St Christopher and Nevis became an independent nation on 19 September 1983.

On 10 August 1998 a referendum was held in Nevis on the question of independence from St Christopher; although 61.8 per cent voted in favour of secession, it fell short of the two-thirds majority needed for independence.

In the legislative election held on 6 March 2000, the Labour Party won all eight of the seats on St Christopher. On Nevis, the Concerned Citizens' Movement won two seats and the Nevis Reformation Party one seat.

POLITICAL SYSTEM
Under the constitution, Queen Elizabeth II is Head of State, represented in the islands by the Governor-General. There is a central government with a ministerial system, the head of which is the Prime Minister of St Christopher and Nevis, and a National Assembly located on St Christopher. The National Assembly is composed of the Speaker, three senators (nominated by the Prime Minister and the Leader of the Opposition) and 11 directly elected representatives, who serve a five-year term. On Nevis there is a Nevis Island Administration, the head being styled Premier of Nevis, and a Nevis Island Assembly of five elected and three nominated members.

Governor-General, HE Sir Cuthbert Montraville Sebastian, GCMG, OBE, apptd 1996

CABINET *as at August 2003*
Prime Minister, Finance, National Security, Planning, Development, Denzil Douglas

Deputy Prime Minister, Labour, Social Security, International Trade and Caricom Affairs, Telecommunications and Technology, Sam Condor
Agriculture, Fisheries, Co-operatives, Lands and Housing, Cedric Liburd
Attorney-General, Justice and Legal Affairs, Delano Bart
Foreign Affairs, Education, Timothy Harris
Health, Environment, Earl Asim Martin
Information, Culture, Youth Affairs and Sports, Jacinth Henry-Martin
Public Works, Utilities, Transport and Posts, Halva Hendrickson
Social Development, Community and Gender Affairs, Rupert Herbert
Tourism, Commerce, Consumer Affairs, Dwyer Astaphan

HIGH COMMISSION FOR ST CHRISTOPHER AND NEVIS
2nd Floor, 10 Kensington Court, London W8 5DL
Tel: 020-7460 6500
High Commissioner for St Christopher and Nevis, HE James Ernest Williams, apptd 2001

BRITISH HIGH COMMISSIONER, HE John White, resident at Bridgetown, Barbados

ECONOMY

The economy of the islands has been based on sugar for over three centuries. Tourism and light industry, concentrating on distilling, food processing, clothing and electronics, are now being developed. The economy of Nevis centres on small peasant farmers, but a sea-island cotton industry is being developed for export.

The main exports are sugar, lobsters, beverages and electrical equipment. Foodstuffs, energy, machinery and transport equipment are the main imports.

In 1996 imports totalled US$149 million and exports US$22 million.
GNP – US$269 million (2000); US$6,570 per capita (2000)
GDP – US$343 million (2001); US$8,539 per capita (2000)
ANNUAL AVERAGE GROWTH OF GDP – 2.8 per cent (1999)
INFLATION RATE – 3.9 per cent (1999)
TOTAL EXTERNAL DEBT – US$140 million (2000)

Trade with UK	2001	2002
Imports from UK	£7,469,000	£5,714,000
Exports to UK	7,118,000	3,955,000

COMMUNICATIONS

Basseterre is a port of registry and has deep water harbour facilities. Golden Rock airport, on St Kitts, can take most large jet aircraft; Newcastle airstrip on Nevis can take small aircraft and has night landing facilities. The sea ferry route from Basseterre to Charlestown is 11 miles.

ST LUCIA

AREA – 236.9 sq. miles (616 sq. km)
POPULATION – 149,000 (2001). The official language is English. A French creole is spoken by most of the population
CAPITAL – ΨCastries (population, 62,967, 2000 estimate)
CURRENCY – East Caribbean dollar (EC$) of 100 cents

NATIONAL ANTHEM – Sons And Daughters Of Saint
Lucia
NATIONAL DAY – 22 February (Independence Day)
NATIONAL FLAG – Blue, bearing in centre a device of
yellow over black over white triangles having a
common base
LIFE EXPECTANCY (years) – 74 (2001)
POPULATION GROWTH RATE – 1.2 per cent
POPULATION DENSITY – 242 per sq. km (2001)

St Lucia, the second largest of the Windward group, is 27
miles in length, with an extreme breadth of 14 miles. It is
mountainous, its highest point being Mt Gimie (3,145 ft)
and for the most part it is covered with forest and tropical
vegetation.

HISTORY AND POLITICS
Possession of St Lucia was fiercely disputed and it
constantly changed hands between the British and the
French until 1814 when it was ceded to Britain by the
Treaty of Paris. It became independent within the
Commonwealth on 22 February 1979.

The St Lucia Labour Party maintained its majority in
the House of Assembly in a general election on 3
December 2001, winning 14 seats.

POLITICAL SYSTEM
The Head of State is Queen Elizabeth II, represented on
the island by a St Lucian Governor-General, and there is
a bicameral legislature. The Senate has 11 members, six
appointed by the ruling party, three by the Opposition
and two by the Governor-General. The House of
Assembly, which has a life of five years, has 17 elected
members and a Speaker, who may be appointed from
outside the House.

Governor-General, HE Dame Pearlette Louisy, apptd
1997

CABINET *as at August 2003*
*Prime Minister, Finance, Economic Affairs, Information,
International Financial Services,* Kenny Anthony
Agriculture, Forestry and Fisheries, Calixte George
Attorney-General, Justice, Petrus Compton
Commerce, Tourism, Investment and Consumer Affairs,
Phillip J. Pierre
Communications, Works, Transport and Public Utilities,
Felix Finisterre
Development, Planning, Environment and Housing, Ignatius
Jean
Education, Human Resources Development, Youth and Sport,
Mario Michel
Foreign Affairs, International Trade and Civil Aviation,
Julian Hunte
Health, Human Services, Family Affairs, Damian Greaves
Home Affairs and Gender Relations, Sarah Flood-Beaubrun
Labour Relations, Public Service and Co-operatives, Velon
John
Social Transformation, Culture and Local Government,
Menissa Rambally

HIGH COMMISSION FOR ST LUCIA
1 Collingham Gardens, London SW5 0HW
Tel: 020-7370 7123
High Commissioner for St Lucia, HE Emmanuel Cotter,
MBE, apptd 1998

OFFICE OF THE BRITISH HIGH COMMISSION
Francis Compton Building, 2nd Floor (PO Box 227),
Waterfront, Castries
Tel: (00 1 758) 452 2484/5 Email: britishhc@candw.lc
High Commissioner, HE John White, resident at
Bridgetown, Barbados

ECONOMY
The economy is mainly agrarian, with manufacturing
based on the processing of agricultural products.
Principal crops are bananas, coconuts, cocoa, mangoes,
breadfruit, yams and citrus fruit. Attempts are being made
to increase industrialisation. The currency is tied to the
US dollar at a rate of EC$2.70=US$1.00.

A tropical storm that hit St Lucia in September 2002
destroyed about half of the banana crop.
GNP – US$642 million (2000); US$4,120 per capita
(2000)
GDP – US$689 million (2001); US$4,735 per capita
(2000)
ANNUAL AVERAGE GROWTH OF GDP – 2.8 per cent
(1998)
INFLATION RATE – 1.7 per cent (2001)
TOTAL EXTERNAL DEBT – US$237 million (2000)

TRADE
The principal exports are bananas, coconut products
(copra, edible oils, soap), cardboard boxes, beer, and
textile manufactures. The chief imports are flour, meat,
machinery, building materials, motor vehicles,
manufactured goods, petroleum and fertilisers.

In 2000 St Lucia had a trade deficit of US$253 million
and a current account deficit of US$82 million. In 1997
imports totalled US$332 million and exports US$66
million.

Trade with UK	2001	2002
Imports from UK	£17,004,000	£11,654,000
Exports to UK	16,501,000	23,588,000

ST VINCENT AND THE GRENADINES

AREA – 150 sq. miles (388 sq. km)
POPULATION – 109,022 (2002 estimate). The language
is English
CAPITAL – ΨKingstown (population, 13,857, 2000)
CURRENCY – East Caribbean dollar (EC$) of 100 cents
NATIONAL ANTHEM – St Vincent, Land So Beautiful
NATIONAL DAY – 27 October (Independence Day)
NATIONAL FLAG – Three vertical bands, of blue, yellow
and green, with three green diamonds in the shape of
a 'V' mounted on the yellow band
POPULATION GROWTH RATE – 0.3 per cent
POPULATION DENSITY – 289 per sq. km (1999)

The territory of St Vincent includes certain of the
Grenadines, a chain of small islands stretching 40 miles
across the Caribbean Sea between Grenada and St
Vincent, some of the larger of which are Bequia,
Canouan, Mayreau, Mustique, Union Island, Petit St
Vincent and Prune Island.

HISTORY AND POLITICS
St Vincent was discovered by Christopher Columbus in
1498. It was granted by Charles I to the Earl of Carlisle
in 1627 and after subsequent grants and a series of
occupations alternately by the French and English, it was
finally restored to Britain in 1783. St Vincent achieved

full independence within the Commonwealth as St Vincent and the grenadines on 27 October 1979.

The governing New Democratic party (NDP) won eight seats and the United labour Party (ULP) seven seats at the election held on 15 June 1998. As a consequence of the opposition groups and trade unions pressing for the resignation of the government after it had approved increased benefits for members of the legislature, the government and opposition agreed that the next general election should be held before 31 March 2001. The election took place on 28 March 2001 and was decisively won by the ULP, who obtained 12 seats. The NDP, who had been in power since 1984, won the remaining three seats.

POLITICAL SYSTEM

Queen Elizabeth II is Head of State, represented by a Governor-General. The House of Assembly consists of 15 elected members and four Senators appointed by the government and two by the Opposition. It is presided over by a Speaker elected by the House from within or without it.

Governor-General, Sir Frederic Ballantyne, GCMG, apptd 2002

CABINET *as at July 2003*
Prime Minister, Finance, Planning, Economic Development, Labour, Information, Grenadine Affairs, Legal Affairs, Ralph Gonsalves
Deputy Prime Minister, Foreign Affairs and International Trade, Louis Straker
Agriculture, Lands and Fisheries, Selmon Walters
Education, Youth Affairs, Sport, Mike Browne
Health and the Environment, Douglas Slater
Ministers of State, Montgomery Daniel *(Agriculture, Lands and Fisheries);* Clayton Burgin *(Education, Youth Affairs, Sport);* Conrad Sayers *(Foreign Affairs and International Trade)*
National Security, Public Service, Airport Development, Vincent Beache
Social Development, Family, Gender Affairs, Ecclesiastical Affairs, Girlyn Miguel
Telecommunications, Science, Technology, Industry, Jerrol Thompson
Tourism and Culture, Rene Baptiste
Transport, Works, Housing, Julian Francis

HIGH COMMISSION FOR ST VINCENT AND THE GRENADINES
10 Kensington Court, London W8 5DL
Tel: 020-7565 2874; Email: svghighcom@clara.co.uk
High Commissioner for St Vincent and the Grenadines, HE Cenio E. Lewis, apptd 2001

BRITISH HIGH COMMISSION
Granby Street (PO Box 132), Kingstown
Tel: (00 1 784) 457 1701
Email: bhcsvg@caribsurf.com
High Commissioner, HE John White, resident at Bridgetown, Barbados

ECONOMY

This is based mainly on agriculture but tourism (254,091 visitors in 2001) and manufacturing industries have been expanding. The main products are bananas, arrowroot, coconuts, cocoa, spices and various kinds of food crops. The main imports are foodstuffs, textiles, lumber, chemicals, motor vehicles and fuel. Bananas accounted for 36 per cent of exports in 2000.

In 2000 St Vincent and the Grenadines had a trade deficit of US$91 million and a current account deficit of US$26 million. In 2001 imports totalled US$186 million and exports US$41 million.

GNP – US$313 million (2000); US$2,720 per capita (2000)
GDP – US$338 million (2001); US$3,021 per capita (2000)
ANNUAL AVERAGE GROWTH OF GDP – 5.2 per cent (1998)
INFLATION RATE – 0.2 per cent (2000)
TOTAL EXTERNAL DEBT – US$192 million (2000)

Trade with UK	2001	2002
Imports from UK	£9,223,000	£6,618,000
Exports to UK	13,666,000	14,902,000

SAMOA

Ole Malo Tutoatasi o Samoa / Independent State of Samoa

AREA – 1,093 sq. miles (2,831 sq. km)
POPULATION – 179,058 (2001 estimate), the largest numbers being on Upolu (114,980) and Savai'i (43,150). The Samoans are a Polynesian people, though the population also includes other Pacific Islanders, Euronesians, Chinese and Europeans. The main languages are Samoan and English. The islanders are Christians of different denominations
CAPITAL – ΨApia (population, 38,836, 2001), on Upolu.
CURRENCY – Tala (S$) of 100 sene
NATIONAL ANTHEM – The Banner Of Freedom
NATIONAL DAY – 1 June (Independence Day)
NATIONAL FLAG – Red with a blue canton bearing five white stars of the Southern Cross
POPULATION GROWTH RATE – 0.3 per cent
POPULATION DENSITY – 60 per sq. km (1999)
ILLITERACY RATE – (m) 18.8 per cent; (f) 21.0 per cent (2000)
ENROLMENT (percentage of age group) – primary 96 per cent (1996); secondary 45 per cent (1995)

Samoa consists of the islands of Savai'i, Upolu, Apolima, Manono, Fanuatapu, Namua, Nuutele, Nuulua and Nuusafee. All the islands are mountainous. Upolu, the most fertile, contains the harbours of Apia and Mulifanua, and Savai'i the harbour of Salelologa.

HISTORY AND POLITICS

Formerly administered by New Zealand (latterly with internal self-government), Western Samoa became fully independent on 1 January 1962. The state was treated as a member country of the Commonwealth until its formal admission on 28 August 1970. A constitutional amendment came into effect on 4 July 1997 changing the state's name to the Independent State of Samoa.

Suffrage was made universal following a referendum held in 1990.

In the general election held on 4 March 2001, the Human Rights Protection Party won 23 seats, the Samoan National Development Party won 13 seats and 13 seats were won by independents.

POLITICAL SYSTEM

The 1962 constitution provides for a head of state to be elected by the 49-member legislative assembly, the *Fono*, for a five-year term. Initially two of the four Paramount chiefs jointly held the office of head of state for life. When one of the chiefs died in April 1963, Susuga Malietoa Tanumafili II became head of state for life. The Head of State's functions are analogous to those of a constitutional monarch. Executive government is carried out by a Cabinet of Ministers.

HEAD OF STATE

Head of State for Life, HH Susuga Malietoa Tanumafili II, GCMG, CBE, *since* 15 April 1963

CABINET *as at July 2003*

Prime Minister, Foreign Affairs, Attorney-General, Police and Prisons, Immigration, Public Service Commission, Tuilaepa Sailele Malielegaoi

Deputy Prime Minister, Finance, Misa Telefoni Retzlaff

Agriculture, Forests and Fisheries, Tuisugaletaua Sofara Aveau

Education, Fiame Naomi Mata'afa

Health, Labour, Mulitalo Siafausa

Justice, Seumanu Aita Ah Wa

Public Works, Faumuina Liuga

Revenue, Audit, Ombudsman, Gaina Tino

Tourism, Lands, Survey and Environment, Tuala Sale Tagaloa

Trade and Industry, Hans Joachim Keil

Transport and Shipping, Palusalue Faapo II

Women's Affairs, Internal Affairs, Broadcasting, Tuala Ainiu Iusitino

Youth, Sports and Culture, Ulu Vaomalo Ulu Kini

HIGH COMMISSION FOR THE INDEPENDENT STATE OF SAMOA

Franklin D. Rooseveltlaan 123, B-1050 Brussels

Tel: (00 32) (2) 660 8454

High Commissioner for the Independent State of Samoa, HE Tau'ili'ili'U'ili Meredith, apptd 1998

BRITISH HIGH COMMISSIONER, HE Richard Fell, CVO, apptd 2002, resident at Wellington, New Zealand

HONORARY CONSULATE – PO Box 2029, Apia

ECONOMY

Agriculture is the basis of the economy, employing about two-thirds of the labour force and supplying about 40 per cent of GDP and 90 per cent of exports, the principal cash crops (and exports) being coconuts (copra, oil and cream), cocoa and bananas. Efforts are being made to develop fishing on a commercial scale. Manufacturing is very small in scope and concerned largely with processing agricultural products, but is being encouraged by the government.

Samoa and American Samoa signed a memorandum of understanding on trade, education, health, agriculture and law enforcement in January 2000. In 1999 Samoa had a trade deficit of US$98 million and a current account deficit of US$19 million. In 2001 imports totalled US$130 million and exports US$16 million.

GNP – US$246 million (2000); US$1,450 per capita (2000)

GDP – US$255 million (2001); US$1,419 per capita (2000)

ANNUAL AVERAGE GROWTH OF GDP – 1.1 per cent (1998)

INFLATION RATE – 1.0 per cent (2000)

TOTAL EXTERNAL DEBT – US$197 million (2000)

Trade with UK	2001	2002
Imports from UK	£4,768,000	£1,303,000
Exports to UK	13,000	81,000

SAN MARINO

Repubblica di San Marino – Republic of San Marino

AREA – 24 sq. miles (61 sq. km). Neighbour: Italy

POPULATION – 27,336 (2001 estimate). The official language is Italian and the religion is Roman Catholic

CAPITAL – San Marino (population, 4,357, 1994), on the slope of Monte Titano

CURRENCY – Euro (€) of 100 cents

NATIONAL ANTHEM – Inno Nazionale (National Anthem)

NATIONAL DAY – 3 September

NATIONAL FLAG – Two horizontal bands, white, blue (with coat of arms of the republic in centre)

POPULATION GROWTH RATE – 1 per cent

POPULATION DENSITY – 426 per sq. km (1999)

URBAN POPULATION – 87 per cent (2001)

GDP – US$535 million (1998); US$18,653 per capita (2000)

ANNUAL AVERAGE GROWTH OF GDP – 1.3 per cent (1998)

UNEMPLOYMENT – 3.0 per cent (1999)

HISTORY AND POLITICS

San Marino is a small republic in the hills near Rimini, on the Adriatic, founded, it is said, by a pious stonecutter of Dalmatia in the fourth century. The republic resisted Papal claims and those of neighbouring dukedoms during the 15th to 18th centuries, and its integrity and sovereignty is recognised and respected by Italy.

The principal products are wine, cereals and fruits, and the main industries are tourism, metals, machinery, textiles and food.

San Marino is in a customs union with the European Union.

Following the general election held on 10 June 2001, the number of seats held in the Grand and General Council was as follows: Christian Democratic Party (PDCS) 25, the Socialist Party (PSS) 15, the Progressive Democratic Party (PPDS) 12, others 8.

The PDCS and the PSS formed a coalition government, later joined by the Party of Democrats (PD), which collapsed in June 2002. The PSS, the PD and the Popular Democratic Alliance (APDS) formed a new coalition, which collapsed in December 2002, following which another coalition was formed, which comprises the PSS and the PDCS.

POLITICAL SYSTEM

Executive power is vested in the Congress of State composed of ten ministries under the presidency of the two heads of state, who are elected at six-monthly intervals (every April and October). Legislative power is exercised by the 60-member Great and General Council which is elected for a term of five years. A Council of Twelve forms in certain cases a Supreme Court of Justice.

HEADS OF STATE

Regents, Two 'Capitani Reggenti'

CONGRESS OF STATE *as at July 2003*
Education, University, Cultural Institutions and Social Affairs, Pasquale Valentini (PDCS)
Finance, Budget, Post and Telecommunications, Relations with the Philatelic and Numismatic State Corporations, Pier Marino Mularoni (PDCS)
Foreign and Political Affairs, Fiorenzo Stolfi (PSS)
Health and Social Security, Rosa Zafferani (PDCS)
Industry, Handicrafts, and Relations with the Public Utilities State Corporations, Maurizio Rattini (PSS)
Internal Affairs, Civil Protection, Loris Francini (PDCS)
Justice, Information, Relations with the Castles Councils, Alberto Cecchetti (PSS)
Labour and Co-operation, Gian Carlo Venturini (PDCS)
Territory, Environment, Agriculture and Relations with the Public Works State Corporation, Fabio Berardi (PSS)
Tourism, Commerce, Sport and Transport, Paride Andreoli (PSS)

EMBASSY OF THE REPUBLIC OF SAN MARINO
c/o Consulate of the Republic of San Marino,
Flat 51, 162 Sloane Street, London SW1X 9BS
Tel: 020-7823 4762
Ambassador Extraordinary and Plenipotentiary,
HE Countess Marina Meneghetti de Camillo, apptd 2002, resident at Rome, Italy

BRITISH AMBASSADOR, HE Sir Ivor Roberts, KCMG, apptd 2003, resident at Rome, Italy

BRITISH CONSULATE-GENERAL FOR SAN MARINO
Lungarno Corsini 2, I-50123 Florence, Italy.
Tel: (00 39) (55) 284133
Consul-General, Moira Macfarlane

Trade with UK	2001	2002
Imports from UK	£7,943,000	£7,668,000
Exports to UK	5,377,000	5,675,000

SÃO TOMÉ AND PRÍNCIPE

República Democrática de São Tomé e Príncipe – Democratic Republic of São Tomé and Príncipe

AREA – 372 sq. miles (964 sq. km)
POPULATION – 165,034 (2001 estimate). The official language is Portuguese
CAPITAL – ΨSão Tomé (population, 43,420, 1995 estimate)
CURRENCY – Dobra of 100 centavos
NATIONAL ANTHEM – Independência Total (Total Independence)
NATIONAL DAY – 12 July (Independence Day)
NATIONAL FLAG – Horizontal stripes of green, yellow, green, the yellow of double width and bearing two black stars; and a red triangle in the hoist
POPULATION GROWTH RATE – 3.1 per cent
POPULATION DENSITY – 149 per sq. km (1999)

The islands of São Tomé and Príncipe are situated in the Gulf of Guinea, off the west coast of Africa.

HISTORY AND POLITICS
The islands were first settled by the Portuguese in 1493. In 1951 they became an overseas province of Portugal, and gained full independence on 12 July 1975. A multiparty constitution was approved by referendum in August 1990 under which the president, who is directly elected, serves a five-year term and may stand for a second term. The unicameral Assembleia Nacional (National Assembly) is elected for a four-year term.

In the presidential election which took place on 29 July 2001, Fradique de Menezes of the Independent Democratic Alliance was elected with 56.31 per cent of the vote. Legislative elections were held on 3 March 2002, in which the Movement for the Liberation of São Tomé and Príncipe (MLSTP-PSD) won 24 of the 55 seats in the National Assembly. The Force for Change Democratic Movement-Democratic Convergence Party (MDFM-PCD) won 23 seats and the Ue Kedadji coalition (UK) won 8 seats. Gabriel Costa of the MLSTP-PSD was appointed Prime Minister on 26 March and a government of national unity comprising members of all three parties and independents was sworn in on 8 April. The president dismissed Costa and the entire government on 26 September 2002. A new government was named on 7 October, led by Maria das Neves de Sousa.

On 16 July 2003 the government was toppled during a week-long military coup which took place while the president was visiting Nigeria. De Menezes returned to São Tomé after a democratic rule was reached with the coup leaders; a general amnesty was given to the perpetrators.

HEAD OF STATE
President and Commander-in-Chief of the Armed Forces,
Fradique de Menezes, *elected* 29 July 2001, *sworn in* 3 September 2001

CABINET *as at July 2003*
Prime Minister, Maria das Neves de Sousa (MLSTP-PSD)
Agriculture, Rural Development and Fisheries, Julio Lopes Silva (UK)
Commerce, Industry and Tourism, Arzemiro dos Prazeres (MDFM-PCD)
Defence, Maj. Fernando Danqua (Ind.)
Education and Culture, Fernanda Pontifece Bonfim (MDFM-PCD)
Foreign Affairs and Co-operation, Communities, Mateus Meira Rita (MDFM-PCD)
Health, Claudina Augusto Cruz (MLSTP-PSD)
Infrastructure and Public Works, Joaquim Rafael Branco (MLSTP-PSD)
Justice, State and Administrative Reform, Justino Tavares Viegas (MDFM-PCD)
Labour, Employment and Solidarity, Damião Vaz d'Almeida (MLSTP-PSD)
Planning and Finance, Maria Santos Tebus Torres (MDFM-PCD)
Secretary of State for Environment, Territorial Integrity and Conservation, Arlindo Carvalho (UK)
Secretary of State for State Reforms and Public Administrative Reform, Elsa Teixeira Pinto (MLSTP-PSD)
Youth, Sport and Parliamentary Affairs, José Santiago Viegas (MLSTP-PSD)

MDFM-PCD Force for Change Democratic Movement-Democratic Convergence Party; MLSTP-PSD Movement for the Liberation of São Tomé and Príncipe-Social Democratic Party; UK Ue Kedadji; Ind. Independent

EMBASSY OF THE DEMOCRATIC REPUBLIC OF SÃO
 TOMÉ AND PRÍNCIPE
Square Montgomery, 175 Avenue de Tervuren, B-1150
Brussels Tel: (00 32) (2) 734 8966
Ambassador Extraordinary and Plenipotentiary, vacant
Chargé d'Affaires, Antonio de Lima Veigas

BRITISH CONSULATE
Residencial Avenida, Av. Da Independencia CP 257,
São Tomé Tel: (00 239) (12) 21026/7
British Ambassador, HE John Thompson, MBE

ECONOMY

Agriculture accounts for nearly a quarter of GDP and
employs nearly 40 per cent of the workforce, with cocoa
accounting for 86 per cent of exports in 1997. Drought
and mismanagement have led to declining cocoa
production, which has resulted in balance of payments
deficits.

On 28 April 2000, the IMF approved a three-year
credit of US$8.7 million to support the government's
2000–2 economic programme. A further debt reduction
package worth about US$200 million was agreed by the
IMF and the World Bank on 20 December 2000.

In 1997 imports totalled US$16 million and exports
US$5 million.

GNP – US$43 million (2000); US$290 per capita (2000)
GDP – US$47 million (2001); US$336 per capita (2000)
ANNUAL AVERAGE GROWTH OF GDP – 2.6 per cent
 (1998)
TOTAL EXTERNAL DEBT – US$316 million (2000)

Trade with UK	2001	2002
Imports from UK	£3,353,000	£2,772,000
Exports to UK	132,000	65,000

SAUDI ARABIA

*Al-Mamlaka al-'Arabiyya as-Sa'ūdiyya – Kingdom of
Saudi Arabia*

AREA – 826,808 sq. miles (2,149,700 sq. km).
 Neighbours: UAE and Qatar (east), Jordan, Iraq
 and Kuwait (north), Yemen and Oman (south)
POPULATION – 21,028,000 (2001). Islam is the only
 permitted religion. The language is Arabic
CAPITAL – Riyadh (Ar-Riyad) (population, 4,761,000,
 2001)
MAJOR CITIES – Jiddah (1.5 million); Buraydah;
 Ad-Dammam; Al-Hofuf; Al-Makkah (Mecca);
 Al-Madiinah; Tabuk
CURRENCY – Saudi riyal (SR) of 20 qursh or 100
 halala
NATIONAL ANTHEM – Ash Al-Malik (Long Live Our
 Beloved King)
NATIONAL DAY – 23 September (proclamation and
 unification of the Kingdom, 1932)
NATIONAL FLAG – Green oblong, white Arabic device
 in centre: 'There is no God but God and Muhammad
 is the Prophet of God', and a white scimitar beneath
 the lettering
LIFE EXPECTANCY (years) – 72 (2001)
POPULATION GROWTH RATE – 2.8 per cent
POPULATION DENSITY – 10 per sq. km (2001)

Saudi Arabia comprises most of the Arabian peninsula.
The Nejd ('plateau') extends over the centre of the
peninsula, including the Nafud and Dahna deserts.

The Hejaz ('the boundary') extends along the Red
Sea coast to Asir and contains the holy towns of
Mecca (Al-Makkah) and Medina (Al-Madīnah). Asir
('inaccessible') is so named for its mountainous terrain,
and, with the coastal plain of the Tihama, lies along the
southern Red Sea coast from the Hejaz to the border with
Yemen. It is the only region to enjoy substantial rainfall.
The east and south-east of the country are lower-lying
and largely desert.

Mecca about 60 km east of Jeddah, is the birthplace of
the Prophet Muhammad, and contains the Great Mosque,
within which is the Kaaba *(Ka'abah)* or sacred shrine of
the Muslim religion. This is the focus of the annual Hajj
('pilgrimage'). Medina Al Munawwarah ('The City of
Light'), some 300 km north of Mecca, is celebrated as
the first city to embrace Islam and as the Prophet
Muhammad's burial place.

HISTORY AND POLITICS

In the 18th century Nejd was an independent state
governed from Diriya. It subsequently fell under Turkish
rule; in 1913 Abdul Aziz ibn Saud threw off Turkish rule
and captured the Turkish province of Al Hasa. In 1920
he captured the Asir and in 1921 the Jebel Shammar
territory of the Rashid family. In 1925 he completed the
conquest of the Hejaz. Great Britain recognised Abdul
Aziz ibn Saud as an independent ruler, King of the Hejaz
and of Nejd and its Dependencies, in 1927. The name
was changed to the Kingdom of Saudi Arabia in
September 1932.

POLITICAL SYSTEM

Saudi Arabia is a hereditary monarchy, ruled by the sons
and grandsons of Abdul Aziz ibn Saud, in accordance
with the Islamic Shari'ah law. The line of succession
passes from brother to brother according to age, although
several sons of ibn Saud renounced their right to the
throne. All sons and grandsons of ibn Saud must be
consulted before a new king accedes to the throne.

In 1992 King Fahd announced a new Basic Law for
the system of government based on Shari'ah law and
including rules to protect personal freedoms. The
constitution is defined as the Holy Koran *(Qur'an)* and
the *Sunnah* (the teachings and sayings of the Prophet
Muhammad). The King and the Council of Ministers
(established in 1953) retain executive power. A
consultative council *(Majlis-ash-Shura)* of a chairman and
120 members appointed by the King was set up to share
power with, and question, the government and to make
recommendations to the King. The Majlis-ash-Shura
debates government policy in the areas of the budget,
defence, foreign and social affairs. Members of the ruling
al-Saud family are excluded from membership of the
Council, which has a four-year term and takes decisions
by majority vote. Cabinet ministers have terms of four
years, with the possibility of a two-year extension.

In 1993 the country was reorganised into
13 provinces: Riyadh; Makkah; Al-Madinah; Al Qasim;
Eastern; Asir; Tabuk; Ha'il; Northern Border; Jizan;
Najran; Baha; Al-Jawf. Each province has a governor
appointed by the King and a council of prominent local
citizens to advise the governor on local government,
budgetary and planning issues.

HEAD OF STATE

*Custodian of the Two Holy Mosques and HM The King of
 Saudi Arabia,* King Fahd ibn Abdul Aziz al-Saud, *born
 1923, ascended the throne* 1 June 1982

HRH Crown Prince, Prince Abdullah ibn Abdul Aziz
al-Saud

COUNCIL OF MINISTERS *as at July 2003*
Prime Minister, HM The King
*First Deputy Prime Minister, Commander of the National
Guard,* HRH The Crown Prince
Second Deputy Prime Minister, Defence and Civil Aviation,
HRH Prince Sultan ibn Abdul Aziz al-Saud
Agriculture, Fahd ibn Abd-al-Rahman ibn Sulayman
Balghunaym
Civil Service, Mohammad ibn Ali al-Fayez
Commerce and Industry, Hashem ibn Abdullah ibn
Hashem Yamani
Communications and Information Technology, Muhammad
ibn Jamil ibn Ahmad Mulla
Culture and Information, Fouad ibn Abdul-Salam
Mohammad Farisi
Economy and Planning, Khaled ibn Mohammad
al-Qussaibi
Education, Mohammad ibn Ahmad al-Rashid
Finance, Ibrahim ibn Abdel Aziz al-Assaf
Foreign Affairs, HRH Prince Saud al-Faisal ibn Abdul
Aziz al-Saud
Health, Hamad ibn Abdallah al-Mani
Higher Education, Khalid ibn Muhammad al-Anqari
Interior, HRH Prince Nayef ibn Abdul Aziz al-Saud
Islamic Affairs, Endowments, Call and Guidance, Shaikh
Salah bin Abdel Aziz al-Shaikh
Justice, Abdullah ibn Muhammed ibn Ibrahim al-Shaikh
Labour and Social Affairs, Ali ibn Ibrahim al-Nemla
Ministers of State, Abdallah ibn Ahmad ibn Yusuf Zaynal,
Abdul Aziz ibn Abdullah al-Khuweiter, Musaid ibn
Mohammad al-Eiban, Muttlab ibn Abdullah al-Nafissa
Minister of State, Chief of the Cabinet's Presidency, Prince
Abdul Aziz ibn Fahd ibn Abdul Aziz al-Saud
Municipal and Rural Affairs, Prince Miteb ibn Abdul
Aziz al-Saud
Oil and Mineral Resources, Ali Ibrahim al-Naimi
Pilgrimage Affairs, Ayad ibn Amin Madani
Transport, Jubarah ibn Ayd al-Suraysiri
Water Resources and Electricity, Ghazi Abd-al-Rahman
al-Qusaybi

ROYAL EMBASSY OF SAUDI ARABIA
30 Charles Street, London W1X 7PM
Tel: 020-7917 3000
Ambassador Extraordinary and Plenipotentiary,
HRH Prince Turki Al-Faisal, apptd 2003

BRITISH EMBASSY
PO Box 94351, Riyadh 11693
Tel: (00 966) (1) 488 0077
Ambassador Extraordinary and Plenipotentiary, HE Sir
Derek J. Plumbly, KCMG, apptd 2000

CONSULATE-GENERAL – PO Box 393, Jiddah 21411.
Consul-General, A. Henderson

BRITISH COUNCIL DIRECTOR, Dr David Burton, OBE
Tower B, 2nd Floor, Al-Mousa Centre, Olaya Street,
PO Box 58012, Riyadh 11594
Email: enquiry.riyadh@sa.britishcouncil.org
There are also offices in Jiddah and Ad-Dammam

DEFENCE
The Army has 1,055 main battle tanks, 1,900 armoured
personnel carriers, 970 armoured infantry fighting

vehicles and 12 attack helicopters. The Navy has four
frigates, 26 patrol and coastal vessels and 21 armed
helicopters at six bases. The Air Force has 348 combat
aircraft.
Saudi Arabia is base to the Gulf Co-operational
Council Peninsula Shield Force of 7,000 troops. In April
2003 the US announced that almost all its troops except
some training personnel, would be pulled out of Saudi
Arabia. Leaders of both countries stressed that
co-operation would continue and they would remain
allies.
MILITARY EXPENDITURE – 14.1 per cent of GDP
(2001)
MILITARY PERSONNEL – 124,500: Army 75,000, Navy
15,500, Air Force 18,000, Air Defence Force 16,000;
National Guard 75,000; Paramilitaries 15,500

ECONOMY
Saudi Arabia's economy is susceptible to fluctuation in
world oil prices, which rose sharply in 2000 improving
the country's economic prospects.
The productivity of traditional dryland farming is
supplemented by extensive irrigation, desalination and
use of aquifers. Agriculture accounted for 7 per cent of
GDP in 1998.
The principal industry is oil extraction and processing.
Oil was first found in commercial quantities in 1938.
Proven oil reserves of 259 billion barrels account for
more than one-quarter of the world's proven reserves.
The oil and gas industry contributes around 35–40 per
cent of GDP depending on world prices and the country
is the world's largest oil exporter. Recoverable gas
reserves are estimated at over 220 trillion cubic feet.
Mineral exploitation of gold, silver, copper and other
minerals is also beginning, with gold production of 5.1
tonnes in 1998.
The government, in a series of five-year development
plans begun in 1970, has actively encouraged the
establishment of manufacturing industry. Industries have
developed in the fields of construction materials, metal
fabrication, simple machinery and electrical equipment,
food and beverages, textiles, chemicals and plastics.
The seventh development plan, covering 2000–5, was
approved in September 2000. It aimed to eliminate the
budget and current account deficits, promote economic
growth and diversity and introduce legislation to increase
the proportion of Saudi Arabian citizens in the
workforce.
GNP – US$149,932 million (2000); US$7,230 per
capita (2000)
GDP – US$173,287 million (1999); US$8,309 per
capita (2000)
ANNUAL AVERAGE GROWTH OF GDP – 4.5 per cent
(2000)
INFLATION RATE – –0.8 per cent (2000)

TRADE
Oil remains the main source of receipts in the balance of
payments. The leading suppliers of imports are the USA,
the UK, Germany and Japan, and the chief customers for
exports are Japan, the USA, South Korea and Singapore.
There is a total ban on the importation of alcohol, pork
products, firearms, and items regarded as non-Islamic or
pornographic.
In 2001 there was a trade surplus of US$44,387
million and a current account surplus of US$14,502
million. In 2000 imports totalled US$30,238 million
and exports totalled US$77,583 million.

Trade with UK	2001	2002
Imports from UK	£1,516,348,000	£1,390,713,000
Exports to UK	£991,316,000	£725,222,000

COMMUNICATIONS

There is one railway line from Ad-Dammām to Riyadh, which was opened in 1951 and is operated by the Saudi Government Railway Organisation. The line is being extended to the port of Al-Jubayl on the Gulf. In 1998 the road network totalled 146,524 (of which 48,661 were paved), including an expressway system, connecting all the cities and main towns. Jiddah is the main cargo sea port followed by al-Dammam. The main oil port (the world's largest) is Ras Tanura. The 15.5 mile-long King Fahd Causeway completed in 1986 connects the Eastern Province to the state of Bahrain and is the world's second longest causeway.

There are three international airports at Al-Makkah, Riyadh and Az-Zahran and 22 other commercial airports.

Telecommunications are being rapidly expanded with 3.1 million telephone lines in 1998 and seven earth stations linked to the Intelsat system, allowing direct dialling to 185 countries.

EDUCATION

With the exception of a few schools for expatriate children, all schools are government-supervised and are segregated for boys and girls. There are universities in Jiddah, Al-Makkah, Riyadh (branches in Abha and Qassim), Ad-Dammam (branch at Al-Hufuf) and Az-Zahran, and there are Islamic universities in Al-Madinah and Riyadh together with 83 tertiary colleges. There is great emphasis on vocational training, provided at literacy and artisan skill training centres and more advanced industrial, commercial and agricultural education institutes.

ILLITERACY RATE – (m) 15.9 per cent; (f) 32.8 per cent (2000)

ENROLMENT (percentage of age group) – primary 61 per cent (1996); secondary 42 per cent (1996); tertiary 16.3 per cent (1996)

SENEGAL

République du Sénégal – Republic of Senegal

AREA – 75,955 sq. miles (196,722 sq. km). Neighbours: Mauritania (north), Mali (east), Guinea-Bissau and Guinea (south), the Gambia

POPULATION – 10,284,929 (2001 estimate), 94 per cent Muslim, 4 per cent Christian, 1 per cent Animist. The official language is French; the principal local language is Wolof. Fulani, Serer, Mandinka, Jola and Sarakole are also spoken

CAPITAL – ΨDakar (population, 1,641,358, 1998 UN estimate)

MAJOR CITIES – Rufisque (150,000); Thiés (248,000); ΨZiguinchor (192,000), 1998 UN estimates

CURRENCY – Franc CFA of 100 centimes

NATIONAL ANTHEM – Pincez Tous Vos Koras, Frappez Les Balafons (All Pluck Your Koras, Strike The Balafons)

NATIONAL DAY – 4 April

NATIONAL FLAG – Three vertical bands, green, yellow and red; a green star on the yellow band

POPULATION GROWTH RATE – 2.6 per cent

POPULATION DENSITY – 47 per sq. km (1999)

MILITARY EXPENDITURE – 1.4 per cent of GDP (2001)

MILITARY PERSONNEL – 9,400: Army 8,000, Navy 600, Air Force 800; Paramilitaries 5,800

CONSCRIPTION DURATION – Two years (selective)

ILLITERACY RATE – (m) 52.7 per cent; (f) 72.3 per cent (2000)

ENROLMENT (percentage of age group) – primary 60 per cent (1997)

HISTORY AND POLITICS

Formerly a French colony, Senegal elected in 1958 to remain within the French Community as an autonomous republic. It became independent as part of the Federation of Mali in June 1960 and seceded to form the Republic of Senegal in September 1960.

Abdoulaye Wade, the leader of the Senegalese Democratic Party, was elected in the second round of the presidential election on 19 March 2000 with 58.49 per cent of the vote, thus becoming the first president not to belong to the Socialist Party. The legislative election on 29 April 2001 was won by an alliance of 40 parties, the Sopi (Change) coalition, led by the Senegalese Democratic Party (PDS). Sopi won 89 seats, the Socialist Party (PS), which had been in government, secured only ten seats, and the Alliance of Progress Forces won 11 seats. Abdoulaye Wade dismissed the entire government on 4 November 2002 and Idrissa Seck was named as the new prime minister. The Council of Ministers was appointed on 6 November 2002.

INSURGENCY

A separatist civil war has been fought in the southern Casamance region for the past 17 years. Following a cease-fire in December 1999, a meeting between the two sides in January 2000 agreed to establish a joint body to monitor progress, to withdraw army and rebel forces from occupied villages, and to co-operate on mine clearance and the refugee problem. The government and the MFDC signed a peace agreement on 16 March 2001, but violence in the region increased during the election campaign in April 2001.

POLITICAL SYSTEM

A referendum to approve a new constitution took place on 7 January 2001. The constitution, which was approved by 96 per cent of those voting, dissolved the Senate, reduced the number of MPs in the National Assembly from 140 to 120, shortened the presidential term of office to five years, renewable only once, and guaranteed the right to form political parties. A general election for the National Assembly is held every five years.

HEAD OF STATE

President, Abdoulayé Wade, *elected* 19 March 2000, *sworn in* 1 April 2000

COUNCIL OF MINISTERS *as at July 2003*
Prime Minister, Idrissa Seck
Agriculture and Livestock, Habib Sy
Civil Service, Labour and Employment, Yero Deh
Culture and Communication, Abdou Fall
Decentralised Co-operation and Regional Planning, Soukeyna Ndiaye Ba
Defence, Becaye Diop
Education, Moustapha Sourang

Environment and Protection of Nature, Modou Fada
   Diagne
Family and National Solidarity, Awa Gueye Kebe
Finance and Economy, Abdoulaye Diop
Fisheries, Pape Diouf
Health, Awa Marie Coll Seck
Housing, Madicke Niang
Infrastructure, Equipment and Transport, Mamadou Seck
Interior, Maj.-Gen. Mamadou Niang
Justice, Keeper of the Seals, Serigne Diop
Minister of State for Foreign Affairs and Senegalese Abroad,
   Cheikh Tidiane Gadio
Minister of State for Handicraft and Industry, Landing
   Savane
Minister of State for Mines, Energy and Water Resources,
   Macky Sall
Minister of State for Sport, Youssoupha Ndiaye
Relations with the Assemblies and the African Union,
   Mamadou Diop
Scientific Research and Technology, Christian Sina Diatta
Small and Medium Enterprises and Commerce, Aicha Agne
   Pouye
Social Development, Maimouna Sourang Ndir
Tourism, Ousmane Masseck Ndiaye
Town and Country Planning, Seydou Sy Sall
Women's Enterprises and Micro-credit, Saoudatou
   Ndiaye Seck
Youth, Aliou Sow

EMBASSY OF THE REPUBLIC OF SENEGAL
39 Marloes Road, London W8 6LA
Tel: 020-7938 4048/7937 7237
Ambassador Extraordinary and Plenipotentiary, HE El Hadj
   Amadou Niang, apptd 2001

BRITISH EMBASSY
20 rue du Docteur Guillet (BP 6025), Dakar
Tel: (00 221) 823 7392/9971
Email: britemb@telecomplus.sn
Ambassador Extraordinary and Plenipotentiary, HE E. Alan
   Burner, apptd 1997

BRITISH COUNCIL DIRECTOR, Steve McNulty
34–36 Blvd de la République, BP 6232, Dakar
Tel: (00 221) 822 2015/822 2048
Email: postmaster@britishcouncil.sn

ECONOMY
Around 60 per cent of the workforce are employed in
agriculture. Senegal's principal exports are fish,
groundnuts (raw and processed) and phosphates. Tourism
is also of growing importance as a revenue earner; in
1999 there were some 400,000 overseas visitors.
Principal imports are food, machinery, fuel oils and
transport equipment. Senegal exports fish, furniture,
oilseeds and fruit, rubber, fertilisers and animal fodder to
the UK, and imports foodstuffs, cigarettes, chemicals,
machinery and transport equipment, vegetable fats and
oils, and manufactured goods from the UK.
  In 1999 there was a trade deficit of US$346 million
and a current account deficit of US$320 million. In 2000
imports totalled US$1,521 million and exports US$920
million.
GNP – US$4,714 million (2000); US$490 per capita
   (2000)

GDP – US$4,620 million (2001); US$468 per capita
   (2000)
ANNUAL AVERAGE GROWTH OF GDP – 5.6 per cent
   (1998)
INFLATION RATE – 0.7 per cent (2000)
TOTAL EXTERNAL DEBT – US$3,372 million (2000)

Trade with UK	2001	2002
Imports from UK	£41,168,000	£37,326,000
Exports to UK	10,827,000	10,490,000

SERBIA AND MONTENEGRO

Srbija I Crna Gora

AREA – 392,69 sq. miles (102,100 sq. km). Neighbours:
   Hungary (north), Romania and Bulgaria (east), the
   Former Yugoslav Republic of Macedonia and Albania
   (south), Bosnia-Hercegovina and Croatia (west)
POPULATION – 10,538,000 (2003 estimate): 67.6 per
   cent Serb and Montenegrin, 16.5 per cent Albanian,
   3.2 per cent Muslim Slavs, 3.3 per cent Hungarian,
   with smaller numbers of Romanies, Croats, Slovaks
   and Bulgarians. The majority religion is Serbian
   Orthodox, with significant Muslim and small Roman
   Catholic minorities. The main language is Serbian (74
   per cent), with Albanian and Hungarian minorities.
   Serbian is a South Slav language usually written in the
   Cyrillic script
CAPITAL – Belgrade (population, 1,574,050, 2002
   census)
MAJOR CITIES – Kragujevac (181,061); Niš (250,104);
   Novi Sad (178,896); Podgorica (162,172), the capital
   of Montenegro; Priština (241,565); Subotica
   (146,075), 1997 estimates
CURRENCY – New dinar of 100 paras
NATIONAL ANTHEM – Hej, Sloveni, Jošte Živi Reč Naših
   Dedova (Oh! Slavs, Our Ancestors' Words Still Live)
NATIONAL DAY – 27 April
NATIONAL FLAG – Three horizontal stripes of blue,
   white, red
LIFE EXPECTANCY (years) – 73 (2001)
POPULATION GROWTH RATE – 0.3 per cent
POPULATION DENSITY – 103 per sq. km (2001)
MILITARY EXPENDITURE – 6.3 per cent of GDP (2001)
MILITARY PERSONNEL – 74,500: Army 60,000, Navy
   3,500, Air Force 11,000; Paramilitaries 50,100
CONSCRIPTION DURATION – 12–15 months
ENROLMENT (percentage of age group) – primary 69
   per cent (1997); secondary 62 per cent (1997); tertiary
   22 per cent (1997)

Montenegro and southern Serbia are extremely
mountainous, while the north is dominated by the low-
lying plains of the Danube. The major rivers are: the
Danube, which flows through the north of Serbia to
Romania and Bulgaria; the Sava, which flows eastwards
from Bosnia to join the Danube at Belgrade; the Drina,
which flows along most of the Serbian–Bosnian border
to join the Sava; and the Morava, which flows from the
extreme south to join the Danube in the north.

HISTORY AND POLITICS
Serbia emerged from the rule of the Byzantine Empire in
the 13th century to form a large and prosperous state in
the Balkans. Defeat by the Turks in 1389 led to almost
500 years of Turkish rule. After gaining autonomy within
the Ottoman Empire in 1815, Serbia became fully

independent in 1878 and a kingdom in 1881. Montenegro was part of the Serbian state before it was conquered by the Turks in the fifteenth century; it became independent in 1878. At the end of the First World War Serbia and Montenegro joined with the former Austro-Hungarian provinces of Slovenia, Croatia and Bosnia-Hercegovina to form the 'Kingdom of Serbs, Croats and Slovenes' which was renamed Yugoslavia in 1929. Yugoslavia was occupied by Axis forces in 1941 and reformed as a Communist federal republic under the presidency of partisan leader Josip Tito in 1945.

Tito died in 1980 and was succeeded by a rotating federal presidency which was unable to contain the growing nationalist movements. Efforts by the six republican presidents to negotiate a new federal or confederal structure for the country failed in 1991. On 25 June 1991 Slovenia and Croatia declared their independence from Yugoslavia.

In Croatia the ethnic Serb minority refused to accept Croatia's independence and fighting began in July 1991 between Croat Defence Forces and Serbian guerrillas backed by the Yugoslav National Army (JNA). By September 1991 this had escalated into war between Croatia and Yugoslavia. The war in Croatia continued until January 1992 when the EU and the UN were able to bring about a cease-fire (see Croatia).

Macedonia declared its independence on 18 September 1991.

Bosnia-Hercegovina declared its independence on 1 March 1992. Independence was supported by the Bosniacs (Muslims) and Croats but rejected by the ethnic Serbs and fighting between Bosniacs and Serbs broke out in March 1992. The JNA intervened against the Bosniacs but in May 1992 withdrew to Serbia and Montenegro (see Bosnia-Hercegovina). On 27 April 1992 the two remaining republics of the former Socialist Federal Republic of Yugoslavia, Serbia and Montenegro, announced the formation of a new Yugoslav federation.

Legislative elections were held in Montenegro in May 1998 and were won by reformists led by President Djukanović.

Presidential and legislative elections were held on 24 September 2000, but were largely boycotted in Montenegro on the advice of its government. The Democratic Opposition of Serbia (DOS) became the largest party in both chambers of parliament. In the presidential election, the Federal Election Commission announced that Vojislav Koštunica of the DPS, had won 48.22 per cent, just short of the 50 per cent necessary to win without a second round, although an independent monitoring organisation had given Koštunica a clear majority. Koštunica denounced the official result as fraudulent and refused to participate in the second round, scheduled for 8 October. Tension grew and on 28 September, the Serb Orthodox Church declared that Koštunica was the elected president and the Yugoslav Army guaranteed its neutrality. A general strike began on 2 October. On 5 October, opposition supporters stormed the parliament building and took over the television station and the state news agency and by evening the media organisations were declaring Koštunica to be the elected president. On 7 October Koštunica was sworn in. The DOS and the SPS agreed to dissolve parliament and form a transitional government until a fresh election could be held for the Serbian Parliament. This took place on 23 December 2000 and the DOS won an overwhelming victory, obtaining 176 of the 250 seats.

The SPS won 37, the SRP won 23 and the Party of Serbian Unity won 14.

In Montenegro, which had steadily removed itself from the influence of Serbia, the government coalition collapsed on 29 December 2000. A legislative election was held on 22 April 2001, in which the pro-independence Victory Belongs to Montenegro (VBM) alliance, led by the Democratic Party of Socialists (DPS), won 36 of the 77 seats. The VBM alliance formed a coalition government with the pro-independence Liberal League, which had six seats.

Former President Slobodan Milošević was arrested on 1 April 2001 and on 28 June, he was handed over to the UN International Criminal Tribunal for the Former Yugoslavia, which in May 1999 had indicted him on charges of crimes against humanity. Charges of genocide and ethnic cleansing were later added. The trial opened in The Hague in the Netherlands on 13 February 2002.

On 14 March 2002 the leaders of Serbia, Montenegro and the Federal Republic of Yugoslavia signed an agreement to maintain a joint state and Yugoslavia was re-named Serbia and Montenegro on 4 February 2003.

On 3 March 2003 Svetozvar Marovic was elected president of Serbia and Montenegro by the union parliament.

INSURGENCIES

The province of Kosovo in the south of Serbia is more than 90 per cent ethnically Albanian. In 1989, Slobodan Milošević, then leader of the League of Communists of Serbia, revoked Kosovo's autonomous status, resulting in the progressive exclusion of the Albanian majority from public life. Following clashes between ethnic Albanians and Serbian police in February and March 1998, the Serbian military attacked civilians in the province on the pretext of eliminating support for the Kosovo Liberation Army (KLA), an ethnic Albanian organisation fighting for independence for the province. The international community condemned the brutality of the Serbian forces and a UN arms embargo was imposed on Yugoslavia, but the situation deteriorated with clashes between the KLA and security forces becoming commonplace. Tens of thousands of Kosovar Albanians fled when Yugoslav forces began to attack Kosovar villages. Following warnings to the Yugoslav authorities, NATO commenced air strikes against military targets in Yugoslavia on 24 March 1999. Over eight hundred thousand people fled or were forced to leave their homes and sought refuge in Albania, Macedonia or Montenegro, which, although part of the Yugoslav Federation, had refused to become involved in the fighting; more than five hundred thousand people were displaced within Kosovo. NATO intensified its bombing campaign, now targeting industrial, communications and power links.

On 3 June President Milošević accepted a peace plan agreed by NATO and Russia and the Yugoslav army withdrew to be replaced by the NATO forces. Since the Yugoslav withdrawal, Kosovo has been under the administration of the UN's Interim Administration Mission in Kosovo (UNMIK), who have established the Kosovo Transitional Council composed of four UN and four Kosovar representatives. The NATO-led Kosovo Force (KFOR) has established five command sectors, administered by UK, US, French, German and Italian troops respectively. In addition, parts of the French, German and US sectors are patrolled by Russian troops. KFOR has facilitated the disarming of the KLA and the return of over 850,000 Kosovar Albanian refugees, but at least 200,000 Kosovar Serbs have fled, fearing reprisal attacks, which have frequently occurred.

In May 2001, UNMIK announced that a legislative assembly for Kosovo would be established having powers over health, education, environment and the economy but with UNMIK retaining final authority. Elections to the assembly were held on 17 November 2001 and won by the Democratic league of Kosovo (LDK) who gained 47 of the 120 seats. A power-sharing government was agreed on 28 February 2002 with Bajram Rexhepi of the Democratic Party of Kosovo (PDK) on its head. Ibrahim Rugova of the LDK was elected unopposed as president on 4 March.

Armed fighters belonging to the ethnic Albanian Liberation Army of Preševo, Medvedja and Bujanovac (UCPMB) launched attacks on Serbs in Albanian populated areas of southern Serbia in November 2000. The rebels wanted to annex these areas into Kosovo. A cease-fire was signed on 12 March 2001 after NATO agreed to permit Yugoslav forces to enter the demilitarised buffer zone which had been established on the Serbian side of the border with Kosovo in 1999.

POLITICAL SYSTEM

The federal legislature, the Assembly of Serbia and Montenegro (Skupstina Srbije i Crne Gore), has 126 members elected by the republican assemblies, 91 from Serbia and 35 from Montenegro, for a two-year term. The union government consists of a council of three Serb and two Montenegrin ministers with the president as ex officio chair. The republics each have their own governments, each led by a prime minister. The president of Serbia and Montenegro is elected by the Serbia – Montenegro union parliament.

HEAD OF STATE

President, Chair of the Council of Ministers, Svetozar Marovic, *elected* 3 March 2003

COUNCIL OF MINISTERS *as at July 2003*

Defence, Boris Tadic (Serbia)
Economic Affairs, Branko Lukovac (Montenegro)
Foreign Affairs, Goran Svilanovic (Serbia) (DOS)
Human Rights and Minorities, Rasim Ljajic (Serbia) (DOS)
Trade, Amir Nurkovic (Montenegro)

MONTENEGRO

AREA – 5,331 sq. miles (13,182 sq.km)
POPULATION – 615,000: 62 per cent Montenegrin, 14.5 per cent Bosniac, 6.5 per cent Albanian and 3 per cent Serb

On 20 October 2002 elections to the Montenegrin Republican Assembly took place in which the Democratic Party of Socialists (DPS) won. Filip Vujanovic was nominated to form a new government to present to the new Assembly in early November. Milo Djukanovic resigned as president of Montenegro on 25 November 2002 to become prime minister. Vujanovic, having resigned as prime minister, was elected chair of the parliament and became acting president. On 11 May 2003 Filip Vujanovic was elected Montenegrin president after a third round of elections.

GOVERNMENT OF MONTENEGRO *as at July 2003*

President, Filip Vujanovic
Prime Minister, Milo Djukanovic
Deputy Prime Ministers, Jusuf Kalamperovic; Dragan Djurovic *(Political System);* Branimir Gvozdenovic *(Economic Policy)*
Agriculture, Forestry and Water, Milutin Simovic
Culture, Vesna Kilibarda
Economy, Darko Uskokovic
Education and Science, Slobodan Backovic
Environmental Protection and Urban Planning, Branko Radovic
Finance, Miroslav Ivanisevic
Foreign Affairs, Dragisa Burzan
Foreign Economic Relations, Trade, Slavica Milacic
Health, Miodrag Balicic
Interior and Police, Milan Filipovic
Justice, Zarko Sturanovic
Labour and Welfare, Slavoljub Stijepovic
Maritime Trade and Transport, Andrija Lompar
Protection of National and Ethnic Minorities, Gezim Hajdinaga
Tourism, Predrag Nenezic
Without Portfolio, Suad Numanovic

SERBIA

AREA – 34,175 sq. miles (88,538 sq.km)
POPULATION – 9,300,000, of whom 66 per cent are Serbs

Serbia includes the provinces of Kosovo (population 1.6 million), of great historic importance to Serbs, and Vojvodina (population 2 million): the autonomy of both was ended in September 1990. Vojvodina, with its capital at Novi Sad, has a large Hungarian minority (21 per cent). Kosovo, with its capital at Priština, is predominantly Albanian (90 per cent). Following the conflict in Kosovo, more than 200,000 people have been left homeless and entire villages have been destroyed. The Serbian presidential elections of October and December 2002 were invalidated owing to low turnout of voters. Natasa Micic became acting president in December. The Serbian prime minister, Zoran Djindjic was assassinated on 12 March 2003 and Zoran Zikovic was elected prime minister by parliament on 18 March.

President (acting), Natasa Micic

GOVERNMENT OF SERBIA *as at July 2003*

Prime Minister, Zoran Zivkovic
Deputy Prime Ministers, Nebojsa Covic; Miodrag Isakov; Cedomir Jovanovic; Jozef Kasa; Zarko Korac; Dusan Mihajlovic *(Interior)*
Agriculture, Stojan Jevtic
Construction, Dragoslav Sumarac
Culture, Branislav Lecic

Economy and Finance, Bozidar Djelic
Economy and Privatisation, Aleksandar Vlahovic
Education, Gaso Knezevic
Energy and Mining, Kori Udovicki
Health, Tomica Milosavljevic
International Economic Relations, Goran Pitic
Justice, Vladan Batic
Labour and Employment, Dragan Milovanovic
Local Self-Adminstration, Rodoljub Sabic
President (acting), Natasa Micic
Protection of the Environment, Andjelka Mihajlov
Religious Affairs, Vojo Milovanovic
Science, Technology and Development, Dragan Domazet
Social Policy, Gordana Matkovic
Trade and Tourism, Slobodan Milosavljevic
Transport and Communications, Marija Vukosavljevic

EMBASSY OF THE SERBIA AND MONTENEGRO
28 Belgrave Square, London SW1X 8QB
Tel: 020-7235 9049
Ambassador Extraordinary and Plenipotentiary, HE Dr
  Vladeta Jankovic, apptd 2001

BRITISH EMBASSY
Resavska 46, YU-1100 Belgrade
Tel: (00) (381) (11) 645055
Ambassador Extraordinary and Plenipotentiary, HE Charles
  Crawford, CMG, apptd 2000

BRITISH COUNCIL DIRECTOR, Chris Gibson,
Terazije 8/1, POB 248, YU-11001 Belgrade
Tel: (00 381) (11) 3023 800
Email: info@britcoun.org.yu

ECONOMY
Since 1991 the economy has been devastated by the wars
in Croatia and Bosnia-Hercegovina, by the UN economic
sanctions and trade embargo, and because of the lack of
free-market reforms. Only the country's agricultural self-
sufficiency has kept it afloat. Industrial production
remains extremely low and there is high unemployment,
estimated to be around 30 per cent in 2000.
  Economic sanctions and NATO bombing in 1999
further damaged the already fragile economy. GDP in
2000 was roughly 40 per cent of 1989 levels.
GDP – US$10,883 million (2001); US$1,094 per capita
  (2000)
ANNUAL AVERAGE GROWTH OF GDP – 2.6 per cent
  (1998)
INFLATION RATE – 19 per cent (2002)
TOTAL EXTERNAL DEBT – US$11,960 million (2000)

Trade with UK	2001	2002
Imports from UK	£51,150,000	£61,628,000
Exports to UK	23,955,000	31,402,000

SEYCHELLES

*The Republic of Seychelles/République des Seychelles/
Repiblik Sesel*

AREA – 175 sq. miles (455 sq. km)
POPULATION – 81,000 (2001 estimate). The languages
  are English, French and Créole
CAPITAL – ΨVictoria (population, 71,000, 1998
  estimate), on Mahé
CURRENCY – Seychelles rupee of 100 cents

NATIONAL ANTHEM – Koste Seselwa (Seychellois Unite)
NATIONAL DAY – 18 June
NATIONAL FLAG – Five rays extending from the lower
  hoist over the whole field, coloured blue, yellow,
  green, white and red
LIFE EXPECTANCY (years) – 71 (2001)
POPULATION GROWTH RATE – 1.3 per cent
POPULATION DENSITY – 178 per sq. km (2001)
MILITARY EXPENDITURE – 1.8 per cent of GDP (2001)
MILITARY PERSONNEL – 450: Army 200,
  Paramilitaries 250

Seychelles, in the Indian Ocean, consists of 115 islands
spread over 400,000 sq. miles of ocean. There is a
relatively compact granitic group, 32 islands in all, with
high hills and mountains (highest point about 2,972 ft),
of which Mahé is the largest and most populated (90 per
cent of the population live on Mahé); and the outlying
coralline group, for the most part only a little above sea-
level. Although only 4° S. of the Equator, the climate is
pleasant though tropical.

HISTORY AND POLITICS
Proclaimed French territory in 1756, the Mahé group
was settled as a dependency of Mauritius from 1770, was
captured by a British ship in 1794, and changed hands
several times between 1803 and 1814, when it was
finally assigned to Great Britain. In 1903 these islands,
together with the coralline group, were formed into a
separate colony. On 29 June 1976, the islands became
an independent republic within the Commonwealth. A
coup d'état took place in 1977. Seychelles was a one-
party state from 1979 until 1993, when a multiparty
democratic system was established.
  In presidential elections held from 31 August –
2 September 2001, President René was re-elected with
54 per cent of the vote and in legislative elections held
on 4–6 December 2002, the Seychelles People's
Progressive Front retained its overall majority with
23 out of the 34 seats in the National Assembly.

POLITICAL SYSTEM
Under the constitution adopted in 1993, multiparty
politics was institutionalised, a National Assembly of up
to 34 members (23 elected by constituencies, up to 11 by
proportional representation) was established and the
presidential mandate was set at five years, renewable three
times.

HEAD OF STATE
*President, Head of Government, Defence, Interior and Legal
  Affairs,* France-Albert René, *assumed office* 5 June
  1977; *elected* 1979; *re-elected* 1984, 1989, 1993,
  22 March 1998, 2 September 2001
*Vice-President, Finance, Economic Planning, Information
  Technology and Communications,* James Michel

COUNCIL OF MINISTERS *as at July 2003*
Administration and Manpower Development, Noellie
  Alexander
Agriculture and Marine Resources, William Herminie
Education and Youth, Danny Faure
Employment and Social Affairs, Dolor Ernesta
Environment, Ronald Jumeau
Foreign Affairs, Jérémie Bonnelame
Health, Patrick Pillay
Industry and International Business, Jacquelin Dugasse

Land Use and Habitat, Joseph Belmont
Local Government, Sports and Culture, Sylvette Pool
Tourism and Transport, Simone de Commarmond

SEYCHELLES HIGH COMMISSION
2nd Floor, Eros House, 111 Baker Street, London W1U 6RR
Tel: 020-7224 1660
Email: seyhclon@aol.com
High Commissioner, HE Bertrand Rassool, apptd 1999

BRITISH HIGH COMMISSION
Oliaji Trade Centre, PO Box 161 Victoria, Mahé
Tel: (00 248) 283666
Email: bhcsey@seychelles.net
High Commissioner, HE Fraser Wilson, MBE, apptd 2002

ECONOMY

The economy is based on tourism, fishing, small-scale agriculture and manufacturing, and the re-export of fuel for aircraft and ships. Deep sea tuna fishing by foreign fleets under licence, improved port facilities at Victoria and exports from a tuna canning factory attract growing revenues. The government is attempting to reduce the reliance on tourism, which generates the majority of foreign exchange earnings, by promoting the country as an offshore haven for financial services. There were 129,800 foreign visitors in 2001.

GNP – US$573 million (2000); US$7,050 per capita (2000)
GDP – US$614 million (1999); US$7,272 per capita (2000)
ANNUAL AVERAGE GROWTH OF GDP – 2.9 per cent (1999)
INFLATION RATE – 6.3 per cent (2000)
TOTAL EXTERNAL DEBT – US$163 million (2000)

TRADE
Principal exports are canned tuna, frozen prawns, fish and cinnamon bark. The principal imports were machinery and transport equipment, manufactures, foodstuffs and tobacco, fuel oils and chemicals.

In 1999 there was a trade deficit of US$232 million and a current account deficit of US$114 million. In 1999 imports totalled US$434 million and exports US$145 million.

Trade with UK	2001	2002
Imports from UK	£13,374,000	£13,263,000
Exports to UK	47,857,000	62,151,000

SIERRA LEONE

The Republic of Sierra Leone

AREA – 27,699 sq. miles (71,740 sq. km). Neighbours: Guinea (north, north-east), Liberia (south-east)
POPULATION – 5,426,618 (2001 estimate). The south is inhabited by peoples whose languages fall into the Mende group; the north by the Temne and smaller groups such as the Limba, Loko, Koranko and Susu
CAPITAL – ΨFreetown (population, 469,776, 1985)
CURRENCY – Leone (Le) of 100 cents
NATIONAL ANTHEM – High We Exalt Thee, Realm of the Free
NATIONAL DAY – 27 April (Independence Day)
NATIONAL FLAG – Three horizontal stripes of leaf green, white and cobalt blue
POPULATION GROWTH RATE – 3 per cent
POPULATION DENSITY – 66 per sq. km (1999)

MILITARY EXPENDITURE – 1.7 per cent of GDP (2001)
MILITARY PERSONNEL – Army 14,000: Navy 200

HISTORY AND POLITICS

In the late 18th century a project was begun to settle destitute Africans from England on Freetown peninsula. In 1808 the settlement was declared a Crown colony and became the main base in West Africa for enforcing the 1807 Act outlawing the slave trade. Africans from North America and the West Indies, and Africans rescued from slave ships also settled there. In 1896 a Protectorate was declared over the hinterland.

In 1951 the colony of Freetown and the Protectorate were united and on 27 April 1961 Sierra Leone became a fully independent state within the Commonwealth. The country became a republic in 1971 and a one-party state in 1978, but in September 1991 a new multiparty constitution was adopted and an interim government formed, which was overthrown by a military coup on 29 April 1992. The military government surrendered power to a civilian government on 29 March 1996.

The Sierra Leone People's Party (SLPP) won 27 seats in the 68-member National Assembly and formed a government with the support of the People's Democratic Party and the Democratic Centre Party. The SLPP's candidate, Ahmad Tejan Kabbah, won the presidential contest, attracting 59.4 per cent of the vote.

In May 1997 army officers led by Major Johnny Koroma seized power. President Kabbah fled and a 20-member Armed Forces Revolutionary Council was set up with Koroma as chairman and Revolutionary United Front (RUF) leader Foday Sankoh as Vice-Chairman. In July 1997, a Nigerian-led ECOMOG force was sent to oust Koroma and restore the legitimate government. On 24 October 1997, a peace agreement was reached which provided for Kabbah to return to power within six months and granted immunity from prosecution to Koroma. ECOMOG troops gained control of Freetown on 12 February 1998, and ousted the Koroma regime. President Kabbah returned to Freetown on 10 March 1998.

In the presidential elections held on 14 May 2002, President Kabbah was re-elected with 70 per cent of the vote and the SLPP won 83 of the 112 seats in the parliament in the simultaneous legislative election. A new cabinet, composed of members of the SLPP and independents, was appointed in 21 May.

INSURGENCY
Since May 1991 government forces have been fighting the RUF whose aim is to force all foreigners out of the country and to nationalise the mining sector. Attacks by the RUF intensified in December 1998 and on 6 January 1999 the RUF attacked Freetown. ECOMOG troops launched a counter-attack on 9–10 January, recapturing the city.

President Kabbah and Foday Sankoh signed a cease-fire agreement on 18 May 1999 and it was agreed in July 1999 that Sankoh would be appointed Vice-President and head the Mineral Resources Commission and that the RUF would be given four cabinet posts. A government of national unity was announced on 2 November 1999. Violence continued, despite the efforts of a UN peacekeeping force, the UN Mission to Sierra Leone (UNAMSIL), which officially took over from ECOMOG on 29 April 2000. The cease-fire agreement collapsed when the RUF abducted 500 UNAMSIL peacekeepers between 30 April–6 May, and on 6 May the RUF used captured UNAMSIL weaponry to launch an advance on

Freetown. A temporary British military deployment was despatched to evacuate British, EU and Commonwealth nationals from Freetown. UNAMSIL troops, along with Sierra Leonean Army (SLA) and Nigerian Army troops, went on the offensive and drove the RUF back. RUF leader Foday Sankoh, who had been the Vice-President since November 1999, was arrested on 17 May 2000.

A cease-fire brokered by ECOWAS was signed by the government and the RUF on 11 November 2000, but was never fully implemented. An agreement to end all hostilities was signed by the RUF and the pro-government Civil Defence Forces on 16 May 2001. The state of emergency imposed in 1998 was lifted in March 2002.

In September 2002 the UN decided to extend its military mission within the country for a further eight months and again on 30 March 2003 for a further six months.

On 10 March 2003 the Special Court, established in 2002, approved indictments against seven people for war crimes, crimes against humanity and violations of international law.

HEAD OF STATE
President, Defence, Ahmad Tejan Kabbah, *elected* 15 March 1996, *re-elected* 14 May 2002
Vice-President, Solomon Berewa

CABINET *as at July 2003*
Agriculture and Food Security, Sama Mondeh
Attorney-General, Justice, Eke Halloway
Development and Economic Planning, Mohamed Daramy
Education, Science and Technology, Alpha Wurie
Energy and Power, Emmanuel Grant
Finance, Joseph Bandaba Dauda
Foreign Affairs and International Co-operation, Momodu Koroma
Health and Sanitation, Agnes Taylor-Lewis
Information and Broadcasting, Septimus Kaikai
Labour, Industrial Relations and Social Security, Alpha Timbo
Lands, Country Planning, Forestry and Environment, Alfred Bobson Sesay
Marine Resources, Okere Adams
Mineral Resources, Alhaji Mohamed Deen
Ministers of State, Sahr Randolph Fillie-Faboe *(East);* Dennis Sankoh *(North);* Foday Yumkella *(Presidential Affairs);* S.U.M. Jah *(South)*
Political and Parliamentary Affairs, Internal Affairs (acting), George Banda Thomas
Rural Development and Local Government, Sidikie Brima
Social Welfare, Gender, Children's Affairs, Shirley Gbujama
Trade and Industry, Kadi Sesay
Transport and Communications, Prince A. Harding
Works, Housing and Technical Maintenance, Caiser Boima
Youth and Sports, Dennis Bright

SIERRA LEONE HIGH COMMISSION
1st and 3rd Floors Oxford Circus House, 245 Oxford Street, London W1D 2LX
Tel: 020-7287 9884
High Commissioner, HE Sulaiman Tejan-Jalloh, apptd 2000

BRITISH HIGH COMMISSION
Spur Road, Freetown
Tel: (00 232) (22) 232961/362/563/565
Email: bhc@sierratel.sl
High Commissioner, HE John Mitchiner, apptd 2003

BRITISH COUNCIL DIRECTOR, Rajive Bendre
PO Box 124, Tower Hill, Freetown Tel: (00 232) (22) 222 223
Email: info.enquiry@sl.britishcouncil.org

ECONOMY
On the Freetown peninsula, farming is largely confined to the production of cassava and crops such as maize and vegetables for local consumption. In the hinterland the principal agricultural product is rice, which is the staple food of the country, and cash crops such as cocoa, coffee, palm kernels and ginger. Cattle production is also important.

The economy depends largely on mineral exports, mainly diamonds, gold and bauxite, although mineral production has been disrupted by the insurgency. On 4 December 2002 the UN approved a resolution banning the trade in rough diamonds in areas not controlled by the government.

In 2001 imports totalled US$182 million and exports US$28 million.

GNP – US$647 million (2000); US$130 per capita (2000)
GDP – US$749 million (2001); US$142 per capita (2000)
ANNUAL AVERAGE GROWTH OF GDP – 3.8 per cent (2000)
INFLATION RATE – –0.8 per cent (2000)
TOTAL EXTERNAL DEBT – US$1,273 million (2000)

Trade with UK	2001	2002
Imports from UK	£62,051,000	£32,084,000
Exports to UK	3,046,000	2,656,000

COMMUNICATIONS
Since the phasing out of the railway system in 1974 the road network has been developed considerably; there are now 7,000 miles of roads in the country. A bridge has been constructed over the Mano River linking Sierra Leone and Liberia.

The Freetown international airport is situated at Lungi. The main port is Freetown, which has one of the largest natural harbours in the world. There are smaller ports at Pepel, Bonthe and Niti.

EDUCATION
Technical education is provided in the two government technical institutes, situated in Freetown and Kenema, in two trade centres and in the technical training establishments of the mining companies. Teacher training is carried out at the University of Sierra Leone, six colleges in the provinces and in the Milton Margai Training College near Freetown.
ILLITERACY RATE – (m) 49.3 per cent; (f) 77.4 per cent (2000)
ENROLMENT (percentage of age group) – tertiary 1.3 per cent (1990)

SINGAPORE

Republik Singapura / Xinjiapo Gongheguo / Singapur Kuṭiyaraśu / Republic of Singapore

AREA – 249.2 sq. miles (648 sq. km)

POPULATION – 4,108,000 (2001): Chinese 76.8 per cent, Malays 13.9 per cent, Indians (including those of Pakistani, Bangladeshi and Sri Lankan origin) 7.9 per cent and 1.4 per cent from other ethnic groups. Malay, Mandarin, Tamil and English are the official languages. At least eight Chinese dialects are used. Malay is the national language and English is the language of administration. The religions are Buddhism 42.5 per cent, Islam 14.9 per cent, Christianity 14.6 per cent, Taoism 8.5 per cent, Hinduism 4.0 per cent

CURRENCY – Singapore dollar (S$) of 100 cents

NATIONAL ANTHEM – Majullah Singapura (May Singapore Progress)

NATIONAL DAY – 9 August

NATIONAL FLAG – Horizontal bands of red over white; crescent with five five-point stars on red band near staff

LIFE EXPECTANCY (years) – 78 (2001)

POPULATION GROWTH RATE – 2.8 per cent

POPULATION DENSITY – 6,340 per sq. km (2001)

MILITARY EXPENDITURE – 5.1 per cent of GDP (2001)

MILITARY PERSONNEL – 60,500: Army 50,000, Navy 4,500, Air Force 6,000; Paramilitaries 96,300

CONSCRIPTION DURATION – 24–30 months

ILLITERACY RATE – (m) 3.7 per cent; (f) 11.6 per cent (2000)

ENROLMENT (percentage of age group) – primary 93 per cent (1995); tertiary 38.5 per cent (1996)

Singapore consists of the island of Singapore and 63 islets. Singapore island is 26 miles long and 14 miles in breadth and is situated just north of the Equator off the southern extremity of the Malay peninsula, from which it is separated by the Straits of Johore. A causeway crosses the three-quarters of a mile to the mainland. The climate is hot and humid.

HISTORY AND POLITICS

Singapore, where Sir Stamford Raffles first established a trading post under the East India Company in 1819, was incorporated with Penang and Malacca to form the Straits Settlements in 1826. The Straits Settlements became a Crown colony in 1867. Singapore fell into Japanese hands in 1942 and civil government was not restored until 1946, when it became a separate colony. Internal self-government was introduced in 1959. Singapore became a state of Malaysia in September 1963, but left Malaysia and became an independent sovereign state within the Commonwealth on 9 August 1965. Singapore adopted a republican constitution from that date.

S. R. Nathan became President of Singapore on 1 September 1999; no election was held as he was the sole candidate. After the general election of 3 November 2001 the People's Action Party (PAP) had 82 seats in Parliament.

POLITICAL SYSTEM

The president is directly elected for a six-year term, and can veto government decisions relating to internal security, the budget, financial reserves and the appointment of senior civil servants. The President appoints the Prime Minister and, on his advice, the members of the Cabinet. There is a Parliament of 84 directly elected members, with up to six further non-constituency members from opposition parties (NCMPs), dependent on their share of the vote, directly elected for a five year term. Up to nine members can also be nominated by the government for a two-year term (NMPs). In the present parliament, there are two NCMPs and six NMPs.

HEAD OF STATE

President, Sellapan Rama Nathan, *took office* 1 September 1999

CABINET *as at July 2003*

Prime Minister, Goh Chok Tong

Senior Minister, Prime Minister's Office, Lee Kuan Yew

Deputy Prime Minister, Defence, Tony Tan Kheng Yam

Deputy Prime Minister, Finance, Lee Hsien Loong

Community Development and Sports, Muslim Affairs, Yaacob Ibrahim

Education, Second Minister for Defence, Rear-Adm. Teo Chee Hean

Environment, Lim Swee Say

Foreign Affairs and Law, Shanmugam Jayakumar

Health, Second Minister for Finance, Lim Hng Kiang

Home Affairs, Wong Kan Seng

Information, Communications and the Arts, Lee Boon Yang

Manpower, Minister of State Education, Ng Eng Hen

National Development, Mah Bow Tan

Prime Minister's Office, Second Minister for Foreign Affairs, Lee Yock Suan

Trade and Industry, Brig.-Gen. George Yong Boon Yeo

Transport, Yeo Cheow Tong

Without Portfolio, Prime Minister's Office, Lim Boon Heng

HIGH COMMISSION FOR THE REPUBLIC OF SINGAPORE

9 Wilton Crescent, London SW1X 8SP

Tel: 020-7235 8315

High Commissioner, HE Michael Eng Cheng Teo, apptd 2002

BRITISH HIGH COMMISSION

Tanglin Road, Singapore 247919

Tel: (00 65) 424 4200

Email: commercial.singapore@fco.gov.uk

High Commissioner, HE Alan Collins, CMG, apptd 2003

BRITISH COUNCIL DIRECTOR, Les Dangerfield

30 Napier Road, Singapore 258509 Tel: (00 65) 6473 111

Email: english@britishcouncil.org.sg

ECONOMY

Historically Singapore's economy was based on the sale and distribution of raw materials from surrounding countries and on entrepôt trade in finished products. An industrialisation programme launched in 1968 has established a wide range of manufacturing industries, including shipbuilding, iron and steel, micro-electronics, electrical goods, telecommunications equipment, office machinery, scientific instruments, pharmaceuticals, etc. Singapore has also become an important financial services centre with significant insurance and foreign exchange markets, a stock exchange, 149 commercial banks and 79 merchant banks and an oil-refining centre. In February 1998 the government announced substantial liberalising reforms of the financial sector, aimed at allowing the country to compete more competitively with other financial sectors in the region. Singapore has not been as badly affected as its neighbours by the economic crisis in south-east Asia, due in part to currency reserves estimated at US$118 billion; it was praised by the IMF for its adroit response to the crisis, which included wage cuts.

There were 7,690,000 foreign visitors in 2000.

Singapore's major trading partners are the USA, Malaysia, the EU, Hong Kong and Japan.

In 2000 Singapore had a trade surplus of US$11,400 million and a current account surplus of US$21,797 million. In 2001 imports totalled US$116,000 million and exports US$121,751 million.

GNP – US$99,404 million (2000); US$24,740 per capita (2000)

GDP – US$92,252 million (1999); US$22,959 per capita (2000)

ANNUAL AVERAGE GROWTH OF GDP – 9.9 per cent (2000)

INFLATION RATE – 1.4 per cent (2000)

UNEMPLOYMENT – 4.4 per cent (2000)

Trade with UK	2001	2002
Imports from UK	£1,603,512,000	£1,458,706,000
Exports to UK	2,146,369,000	2,030,952,000

COMMUNICATIONS

Singapore is one of the largest and busiest seaports in the world, with six terminals, deep water wharves and ship repairing facilities. Ships also anchor in the roads, unloading into lighters. In 2000, the total volume of cargo handled was 325,591,100 tonnes. There were 145,383 ship arrivals in 2000.

The international airport is at Changi, in the east of the island, with 64 airlines operating flights to 50 countries and 28,618,200 passengers using the airport in 2000. There are 25.8 km of railway connected to the Malaysian rail system by the causeway across the Straits of Johore, and 3,122 km of roads.

There are 19 radio and four television channels operated by the Singapore Broadcasting Corporation in the four official languages, and three private broadcasting stations.

Singapore's government has prioritised information technology and telecommunications in its programme to transform the country into a knowledge-based economy by 2010.

SLOVAKIA

Slovenská Republika – Slovak Republic

AREA – 18,500 sq. miles (48,100 sq. km). Neighbours: Poland (north), Ukraine (east), Hungary (south), Austria (west), the Czech Republic (north-west)

POPULATION – 5,403,000 (2001): 87.7 per cent are ethnic Slovaks, 10.6 per cent ethnic Hungarians, 1.4 per cent Romany, 1 per cent Czech, with smaller numbers of Ruthenians, Ukrainians and Germans. The population is mainly Christian, some 60 per cent Roman Catholic and 8 per cent Protestant. Slovak is the official language, while Hungarian and Czech are also spoken

CAPITAL – Bratislava (population, 428,672, 2001 census), on the Danube

MAJOR CITIES – Košice (236,093), 2001 census

CURRENCY – Koruna (Sk) of 100 halierov

NATIONAL ANTHEM – Nad Tatrou Sa Blýska (Storm Over The Tatras)

NATIONAL DAYS – 1 January (Establishment of Slovak Republic); 5 July (Day of the Slav Missionaries); 29 August (Slovak National Uprising); 1 September (Constitution Day)

NATIONAL FLAG – Three horizontal stripes of white, blue, red with the arms all over near the hoist

LIFE EXPECTANCY (years) – 73 (2001)

POPULATION GROWTH RATE – 0.3 per cent

POPULATION DENSITY – 112 per sq. km (2001)

URBAN POPULATION – 58 per cent (2001)

ENROLMENT (percentage of age group) – tertiary 22.1 per cent (1996)

The Tatry (Tatras) mountains in the centre and north of Slovakia reach heights of 2,655 m. The major river is the Váh which flows from the Tatry mountains to join the Danube at the Hungarian border.

HISTORY AND POLITICS

At the end of the 11th century Slovakia became part of the Hungarian state when the Magyars gained control of the area. Following the dissolution of the Austro-Hungarian Empire, Slovakia was amalgamated into Czechoslovakia on 28 October 1918, but became independent in March 1939 as a Nazi puppet state when Germany invaded the Czech lands. Slovakia was liberated by Soviet forces in 1945 and returned to Czechoslovakia. The formation of a federal republic between the Czech lands and Slovakia was the only Prague Spring reform to survive the Soviet invasion of 1968. Following the collapse of Communist rule in 1989, the Czech and Slovak republics began to negotiate the dissolution of the federation into two sovereign states in 1992. Dissolution took effect on 1 January 1993.

A coalition government led by the Movement for a Democratic Slovakia (HZDS) was sworn in on 12 January 1993 but was brought down by a no-confidence vote in March 1994. Legislative elections on 30 September and 1 October 1994 returned the HZDS to power at the head of a three-party coalition which took office on 13 December 1994.

Following the legislative elections on 25–26 September 1998, the HZDS remained the largest party, but a four-party coalition government led by the Slovak Democratic Coalition (SDK) was formed.

The March 1998 presidential elections were not contested by the ruling HZDS, who were accused by opposition parties of trying to create a constitutional vacuum as the failure of any candidate to achieve majority support in the legislature by the end of the previous president's term of office led to certain presidential powers being transferred to the prime minister. After the 1998 legislative elections, the National Council voted on 14 January 1999 for direct presidential elections, which were held on 29 May 1999 and won by Rudolf Schuster of the Party of Civil Understanding (SOP).

The HZDS remained the largest party in the National Council after the election of 20–21 September 2002 but it was not included in the government and a new coalition, led by the Slovak Democratic and Christian Union (SDKU), was formed. The number of seats held by each of the parties in the National Council was: HZDS 36; SDKU 28; Hungarian Coalition Party (SMK) 20; Christian Democratic Movement (KDH) 15; New Civic

Alliance (ANO) 15. The new cabinet was named on 16 October 2002.

In November 2002 Slovakia was formally invited to join NATO in 2004 and during an EU summit held in Copenhagen in December 2002 the country was invited to join the union on 1 May 2004. A referendum held on 16–17 May 2003 approved the forthcoming accession.

POLITICAL SYSTEM

The constitution vests legislative power in the National Council of 150 members directly elected for a four-year term by proportional representation with a five per cent threshold for parliamentary representation. The president is elected for a five-year term, renewable only once, by direct election; executive power is held by the prime minister and Cabinet.

HEAD OF STATE

President, Rudolf Schuster, *elected* 29 May 1999, *sworn in* 15 June 1999

CABINET *as at July 2003*

Prime Minister, Mikulas Dzurinda (SDKU)
Deputy Prime Ministers, Pal Csaky (SMK); Robert Nemcsics (ANO) *(Economy)* Ivan Miklos (SDKU) *(Finance);* Daniel Lipsic (KDH) *(Justice)*
Agriculture, Zsolt Simon (SMK)
Construction and Public Works, Laszlo Gyurovsky (SMK)
Culture, Rudolf Chmel (ANO)
Defence, Ivan Simko (SDKU)
Education, Martin Fronc (KDH)
Environment, Laszlo Miklos (SMK)
Foreign Affairs, Eduard Kukan (SDKU)
Health, Rudolf Zajac (ANO)
Interior, Vladimir Palko (KDH)
Labour, Social Affairs and the Family, L'udovit Kanik (SDKU)
Transport, Post and Telecommunication, Pavol Prokopovic (SDKU)

ANO New Civic Alliance; KDH Christian Democratic Movement; SDKU Slovak Democratic and Christian Union; SMK Hungarian Coalition Party

EMBASSY OF THE SLOVAK REPUBLIC
25 Kensington Palace Gardens, London W8 4QY
Tel: 020-7313 6470
Ambassador Extraordinary and Plenipotentiary,
HE František Dlhopolcek, apptd 2000

BRITISH EMBASSY
Panská 16, SK-811 01 Bratislava
Tel: (00 421) (2) 5998 2000
Email: bebra@internet.sk
Ambassador Extraordinary and Plenipotentiary,
HE Roderic Todd, apptd 2002

BRITISH COUNCIL DIRECTOR, Jim McGrath
PO Box 68, Panská 17, SK-814 99 Bratislava
Tel: (00 421) (2) 5443 1074 / 5443 1185
Email: information.centre@britishcouncil.sk.
There are also offices at Banská Bystríca and Košice

DEFENCE

The Army has 272 main battle tanks, 113 armoured personnel carriers and 414 armoured infantry fighting vehicles. The Air Force has 60 combat aircraft and 19 attack helicopters.

MILITARY EXPENDITURE – 2.0 per cent of GDP (2001)
MILITARY PERSONNEL – 26,200: Army 13,000, Air Force 10,200; Paramilitaries 4,700
CONSCRIPTION DURATION – Nine months

ECONOMY

From independence until mid-1994 Slovakia faced economic difficulties because of the structure of its centrally-planned and inefficiently managed economy, reliant on state-subsidised heavy industries with low productivity, and because of the ambivalent attitude to reform of the HZDS government. In mid-1994 the economic situation stabilised as the Moravcik government implemented a second round of privatisation. The election of an HZDS-led government in October 1994 slowed the pace of reform. Following severe depreciation of the Koruna and the failure of the economy to achieve the anticipated growth targets, the SDK-led government introduced a package of austerity measures on 20 May 1999; the basic rate of VAT was raised, there were increases in energy, water, telecommunications and housing prices, and import taxes were reintroduced.

Privatisation has led to an increase in unemployment which stood at around 20 per cent in mid-2003.

Natural resources include brown coal, natural gas, iron ore, antimony, lead, zinc and magnesite.

In 2000 Slovakia had a trade deficit of US$895 million and a current account deficit of US$694 million. Imports totalled US$13,423 million and exports US$11,889 million.

GNP – US$19,969 million (2000); US$3,700 per capita (2000)
GDP – US$20,522 million (2001); US$3,570 per capita (2000)
ANNUAL AVERAGE GROWTH OF GDP – 2.2 per cent (2000)
INFLATION RATE – 12 per cent (2000)
UNEMPLOYMENT – 20 per cent (2003)
TOTAL EXTERNAL DEBT – US$9,462 million (2000)

Trade with UK	2001	2002
Imports from UK	£192,446,000	£200,521,000
Exports to UK	180,559,000	214,996,000

SLOVENIA

Republika Slovenija – Republic of Slovenia

AREA – 7,731 sq. miles (20,100 sq. km). Neighbours: Austria (north), Hungary (north-east), Croatia (east and south), Italy (west)
POPULATION – 1,985,000 (2001). The population is mostly Slovenian. There are small Hungarian (0.5 per cent) and Italian (0.1 per cent) minorities, together with a Romany population. The main religion is Roman Catholicism. Slovene is the official language, together with Hungarian and Italian in ethnically mixed regions
CAPITAL – Ljubljana (population, 257,338, 2002 census)
MAJOR CITIES – Maribor (92,284), 2002 census
CURRENCY – Tolar (SIT) of 100 stotin
NATIONAL ANTHEM – Zdravljica (A Toast)
NATIONAL DAY – 25 June (Statehood Day)
NATIONAL FLAG – Three horizontal stripes of white, blue, red, with the arms in the upper hoist
LIFE EXPECTANCY (years) – 76 (2001)
POPULATION GROWTH RATE – 0.3 per cent

POPULATION DENSITY – 99 per sq. km (2001)
URBAN POPULATION – 49 per cent (2001)
MILITARY EXPENDITURE – 1.5 per cent of GDP (2001)
MILITARY PERSONNEL – Army 9,000; Paramilitaries 4,500
CONSCRIPTION DURATION – Seven months (to end 2004)

Slovenia is a small mountainous state which is the most northerly of the former Yugoslav republics. The two major rivers are the Sava and the Drava. There is a short coastline in the south-west 29 miles (46 km) in length on the Adriatic.

HISTORY AND POLITICS

The area that is now Slovenia came under the control of the Habsburg Empire in the 13th and 14th centuries and remained so until the defeat of the Austro-Hungarian Empire in 1918. On 27 October 1918 Slovenia became part of Yugoslavia. In 1941 German forces invaded Yugoslavia and Slovenia was divided between Germany, Italy and Hungary. Slovenia was reformed as a constituent republic of the federal Yugoslav state in May 1945. After a dispute with Italy and nine years of international administration, the Adriatic coast and hinterland were returned to Slovenia in 1954 and Italy retained Trieste.

Slovenian fears of Serbian dominance led the Slovene Assembly in 1989 to amend the republican constitution to lay the basis of a sovereign state. The first democratic elections, held in April 1990, were won by the pro-independence 'Demos' coalition. In a referendum in December 1990, 88 per cent of the electorate voted for independence, which was declared on 25 June 1991. A ten-day war with the Yugoslav National Army followed before the Army called off hostilities and withdrew under the mediation of the EU.

A coalition led by Liberal Democracy of Slovenia (LDS) formed a government following the 1996 legislative election. President Kučan was re-elected on 23 November 1997.

In the general election which took place on 15 October 2000, the LDS won 34 seats, the Social Democratic Party (SDS) won 14 seats, the United List of Social Democrats (ZLSD) won 11 seats, the Slovene People's Party-Slovene Christian Democrats (SLS-SKD) won 9 seats, New Slovenia won 8 seats, the Democratic Party of Pensioners (DeSUS) won 4 seats and other parties won 10 seats. A coalition government was formed by the LDS, the ZLSD, the SLS-SKD and the DeSUS. Janez Drnovsek was elected president on 1 December 2002 and inaugurated on 22 December.

In November 2002 Slovenia was formally invited to join NATO on 1 May 2004 and during an EU summit held in Copenhagen in December 2002 the country was invited to join the union in 2004. A referendum held on 23 March 2003 overwhelmingly approved the forthcoming accession.

POLITICAL SYSTEM

The head of state is the president, elected for a five-year term. Executive power is vested in the prime minister and Cabinet of Ministers. The lower house of the legislature, the National Assembly, has 90 members directly elected for a four-year term. The upper house, the 40-member National Council, has an advisory role. The National Assembly is elected on a proportional representation basis, with one seat each reserved for the Italian and Hungarian minorities.

HEAD OF STATE
President, Janez Drnovsek (LDS), elected 1 December 2002

EXECUTIVE COUNCIL as at July 2003
President of the Executive Council (Prime Minister), Anton Rop (LDS)
Agriculture, Forestry and Food, Franci But (SLS-SKD)
Culture, Andreja Rihter (ZLSD)
Defence, Anton Grizold (LDS)
Economic Affairs, Tea Petrin (LDS)
Education, Science and Sport, Slavko Gaber
Environment and Physical Planning, Janez Kopac (LDS)
Finance, Dusan Mramor
Foreign Affairs, Dimitrij Rupel (LDS)
Health, Dusan Keber (LDS)
Information and Society, Pavel Gantar (LDS)
Internal Affairs, Rado Bohinc (ZLSD)
Justice, Ivo Bizjak (SLS-SKD)
Labour, Family and Social Affairs, Vlado Dimovski (ZLSD)
Transport, Jakob Presecnik (SLS-SKD)
Without Portfolio, European Affairs, Janez Potocnik
Without Portfolio, Regional Development, Zdenka Kovac

LDS Liberal Democracy of Slovenia; SLS-SKD Slovene People's Party-Slovene Christian Democrats; ZLSD United List of Social Democrats

EMBASSY OF THE REPUBLIC OF SLOVENIA
10 Little College Street, London SW1P 3SH
Tel: 020-7222 5400
Ambassador Extraordinary and Plenipotentiary,
HE Dr Marjan Senjur, apptd 2002

BRITISH EMBASSY
4th Floor, Trg Republike 3, SI-1000 Ljubljana
Tel: (00 386) (1) 200 3910
Email: info@british-embassy.si
Ambassador Extraordinary and Plenipotentiary, HE Hugh Mortimer, LVO, apptd 2000

BRITISH COUNCIL DIRECTOR, Steve Green
Cankarjevo nabrezje 27, SI-1000 Ljubljana
Tel: (00 386) (1) 200 0130 Email: info@britishcouncil.si

ECONOMY

Slovenia's economy has emerged as the most stable of the former Yugoslav economies. It has successfully re-orientated its exports towards Western markets, its main trading partners being Germany, Italy, France, Austria and Croatia. The privatisation process was completed in 1998.

In 1999 agriculture contributed 4 per cent to the total value of GDP, industry 38.5 per cent and services 59.9 per cent. The main agricultural products are potatoes, wheat, corn, sugar beet and wine. The major manufacturing sectors are metalworking, electronics, textiles, automotive parts, chemicals, glass products and food-processing. Tourism and transport are major export earners, with 1,957,000 tourists visiting in 2000.

In 2001 Slovenia had a trade deficit of US$622 million and a current account deficit of US$66 million. Imports totalled US$9,251 million and exports US$10,144 million.
GNP – US$19,979 million (2000); US$10,050 per capita (2000)
GDP – US$18,810 million (2001); US$9,118 per capita (2000)

ANNUAL AVERAGE GROWTH OF GDP – 4.8 per cent (2000)
INFLATION RATE – 7.4 per cent (2002)
UNEMPLOYMENT – 7.4 per cent (1999)
TOTAL EXTERNAL DEBT – US$4,762 million (1997); US$5,491 million (1999 estimate)

Trade with UK	2001	2002
Imports from UK	£157,552,000	£180,859,000
Exports to UK	153,370,000	174,683,000

COMMUNICATIONS
There are 20,128 km of roads and 1,201 km of rail track, of which 499 km is electrified. Important road and rail communications cross the country from west to east (Milan–Ljubljana–Budapest), and north to south (Munich–Ljubljana–Zagreb–Belgrade–Athens). There are international airports at Ljubljana, Maribor and Portorož (Adriatic Coast). Koper is an important shipment point for goods from Austria, Hungary, the Czech Republic and Slovakia.

EDUCATION
Education is compulsory and free between the ages of six and 14. There are 44 colleges and two universities (Ljubljana and Maribor).
ILLITERACY RATE – (m) 0.3 per cent; (f) 0.4 per cent (2000)
ENROLMENT (percentage of age group) – primary 95 per cent (1996); tertiary 36.4 per cent (1996)

SOLOMON ISLANDS

AREA – 11,157 sq. miles (28,896 sq. km)
POPULATION – 480,442 (2001 estimate). English is the official language; there are over 80 local languages
CAPITAL – ΨHoniara (population, 49,107)
CURRENCY – Solomon Islands dollar (SI$) of 100 cents
NATIONAL ANTHEM – God Bless Our Solomon Islands
NATIONAL DAY – 7 July (Independence Day)
NATIONAL FLAG – Blue over green divided by a diagonal yellow band, with five white stars in the top left quarter
POPULATION GROWTH RATE – 3.1 per cent
POPULATION DENSITY – 15 per sq. km (1999)

Forming a scattered archipelago of mountainous islands and low-lying coral atolls, the Solomon Islands stretches about 900 miles in a south-easterly direction from the Shortland Islands to the Santa Cruz islands. The six biggest islands are Choiseul, New Georgia, Santa Isabel, Guadalcanal, Malaita and Makira. They are characterised by thickly-forested mountain ranges intersected by deep, narrow valleys.

HISTORY AND POLITICS
The origin of the present Melanesian inhabitants is uncertain. European interest in the islands began in the mid-16th century and continued intermittently for about 300 years, when the inauguration of sugar plantations in Queensland and Fiji (which created a need for labour) and the arrival of missionaries and traders led to increased European interest in the region. Great Britain declared a Protectorate in 1893 over the Southern Solomons, adding the Santa Cruz group in 1898 and 1899. The islands of the Shortland groups were transferred from Germany to Great Britain by treaty in 1900. The

Solomon Islands achieved internal self-government in 1976, and became independent in July 1978.

In November 2000, a conference of provincial governmental heads called for the introduction of a federal system of government; some of the islands had earlier threatened secession. Legislative elections were held on 5 December 2001 in which the People's Alliance Party gained 20 of the 50 seats in the National Parliament. The party's parliamentary leader, Sir Allan Kemakeza was elected prime minister on 17 December and the new Cabinet was sworn in on 19 December.

INSURGENCY
Following tension between indigenous inhabitants and settlers from other parts of the country, on 28 June 1999, a peace agreement was signed by representatives of the national and provincial governments and the Isatabu Freedom Fighters (IFF), a local militant group, following mediation by the Commonwealth special envoy Sitiveni Rabuka.

Following further tension, on 28 February 2000 the government banned the IFF and their rivals the Malaita Eagles Force (MEF), but lifted the ban on 15 May to facilitate peace talks. MEF guerrillas took Prime Minister Ulufa'alu hostage on 5 June 2000 and took over the capital. The prime minister was freed on 10 June and the MEF and the IMF agreed to a two-week truce to allow mediation by a Commonwealth delegation. A peace deal was signed by the IFF and the MEF on 15 October 2000, agreeing to disarm within 30 days. In response, the National Assembly passed a bill granting an amnesty for those involved in the conflict. A peace deal was signed by the IFF and the Marau Eagles Force, a smaller Malaitan militia, on 7 February 2001. Fighting resumed on 18 March on Guadalcanal.

The economic and social problems escalated during 2002–3 and on 30 June 2003 the Pacific Islands Forum (PIF) endorsed an Australian proposal to send a multinational peacekeeping force to the Solomon Islands to restore law and order and an Australian-led force was deployed in July. On 13 August, IFF leader Harold Keke surrendered to Australian forces.

POLITICAL SYSTEM
The Solomon Islands is a constitutional monarchy. Queen Elizabeth II is represented locally by the Governor-General. Executive authority is exercised by the Cabinet. Legislative power is vested in a unicameral National Parliament of 50 members, elected for a four-year term.

Governor-General, HE John Lapli, GCMG, apptd 1999

CABINET *as at July 2003*
Prime Minister, Sir Allan Kemakesa
Deputy Prime Minister, Finance, Snyder Rini
Agriculture and Primary Industries, Paul Maenu'u
Economic Reform and Structural Adjustment, Daniel Fa'afunua
Fisheries and Marine Resources, Nelson Kile
Foreign Affairs, and Trade Relations, Laurie Hok Si Chan
Forests, Environment and Conservation, David Holosivi
Health and Medical Services, Benjamin Una
Home Affairs, Clement Rojumana
Justice and Legal Affairs, Education and Training (acting), Michael Mainain
Lands and Surveys, Siriako Usa
Mines and Energy, Stephen Paeni
National Planning, Nollen Leni

National Unity, Reconciliation and Peace, Nathaniel
Waena
Police, Augustine Taneko
Provincial Government and Rural Development, Walton
Naezon
Tourism and Aviation, Alex Bartlett
Trade, Industry and Employment, Trevor Olavae
Transport, Works and Communication, Bernard Giro

HIGH COMMISSION OF THE SOLOMON ISLANDS
Avenue Edourd Lacomble 17, B-1040 Brussels.
Tel: (00 32) (2) 2732 7085
Email: siembassy@compuserve.com
High Commissioner, HE Robert Sisilo, apptd 1996

BRITISH HIGH COMMISSION
Telekom House, Mendana Avenue, Honiara.
Tel: (00 677) 21705/6
Email: bhc@solomon.com.sb
High Commissioner, HE Brian Baldwin, apptd 2001

ECONOMY
The main imports are foodstuffs, consumer goods,
machinery and transport materials. Principal exports are
timber, fish, palm oil, copra and cocoa.
  In 1999 there was a trade surplus of US$55 million
and a current account surplus of US$21 million. In 1996
imports totalled US$151 million and exports totalled
US$162 million.
GNP – US$278 million (2000); US$620 per capita
  (2000)
GDP – US$264 million (2001); US$598 per capita
  (2000)
ANNUAL AVERAGE GROWTH OF GDP – –2.2 per cent
  (1998)
INFLATION RATE – 1.8 per cent (2001)
TOTAL EXTERNAL DEBT – US$155 million (2000)

Trade with UK	2001	2002
Imports from UK	£272,000	£393,000
Exports to UK	477,000	20,000

COMMUNICATIONS
Solomon Airlines operates international services to other
Pacific states and Australia. Air Niugini flies from Port
Moresby to Honiara.

SOMALIA

*Jamhuuriyadda Dimoqraadiya Soomaaliya – Somali
Democratic Republic*

AREA – 246,201 sq. miles (637,657 sq. km).
  Neighbours: Djibouti, Ethiopia and Kenya (west)
POPULATION – 7,488,773 (2001 estimate). Somali and
  Arabic are the official languages. English and Italian
  are also spoken
CAPITAL – ΨMogadishu (Muqdisho) (population,
  525,000, 1995 estimate)
MAJOR CITIES – ΨBerbera (15,000); Boroma (65,000);
  Burao (15,000); Hargeysa (20,000); ΨKisimaayo
  (60,000)
CURRENCY – Somali shilling of 100 cents
NATIONAL FLAG – Five-pointed white star on blue
  ground
POPULATION GROWTH RATE – 4.1 per cent
POPULATION DENSITY – 15 per sq. km (1999)

HISTORY AND POLITICS
The British protectorate of Somaliland and the Italian
trust territory of Somalia were joined and became
independent on 1 July 1960. In 1969, the armed forces
seized power and established a ruling Revolutionary
Council under Siad Barre's leadership. Siad Barre was
overthrown by rebels in January 1991, sparking civil war
between rival clan-based movements. The United Somali
Congress (USC) seized control in Mogadishu, while the
Somali National Movement formed a rival administration
in the north. Fighting between the USC and supporters
of the Somali National Alliance (SNA) of Gen.
Mohammed Aideed devastated Mogadishu and large
parts of the south, exacerbating famine conditions. The
UN Operation in Somalia proved ineffective in securing
aid distribution routes and was replaced on 9 December
1992 by a UN-approved, US-led, United Task Force
(UNITAF).
  On 4 May 1993, UNITAF handed over to UNOSOM.
The UN withdrew its troops in March 1995. On 12 June
1995, Gen. Aideed was ousted as SNA leader by a joint
USC-SNA congress which nominated Osman Ali Ato as
its leader. Gen. Aideed responded by declaring himself
president on 15 June 1995, but was shot dead in July
1996 and was replaced as president by his son, Hussein
Aideed.
  A peace plan proposed by Djibouti was
overwhelmingly supported on 16 November 1999 by
representatives of civil society and the armed factions at a
forum in Nairobi. A Somali National Reconciliation
Conference in Djibouti opened on 2 May 2000, which
aimed to lay the foundations of the transitional
institutions of the Somali state, but was opposed by the
Rahawein Resistance Army, the Somali Patriotic
Movement and the leaders of Puntland. The National
Reconciliation Conference appointed a Transitional
National Assembly on 13 August, which on 26 August
appointed Abdiqassim Salad Hassan as president.
President Hassan appointed Ali Khalif Galayadh as prime
minister on 3 October 2000.
  Fighting between pro- and anti-government militias
broke out in the south of the country in July 2001. Prime
Minister Galayadh resigned on 28 October 2001
following a vote of no confidence. Hassan Abshir Farah
was appointed prime minister on 12 November and a
reshuffled cabinet was named on 16 February 2002 and
accepted by the Transitional National Assembly on
6 March.
  In October 2002 internationally backed peace talks
began in Kenya and on 27 October a cease-fire
agreement was signed by 21 warring factions and the
Transitional National Government, under which
hostilities would end for the duration of the talks. The
second phase of the peace talks began in Nairobi in
February 2003 but was plagued by boycotts and disputes.
In early July 2003 an agreement was signed to establish a
federal government and to form a transitional parliament
of 351 members which will appoint the federal president
who, in turn, will name a new prime minister.

INSURGENCIES
With the downfall of Siad Barre, the SNM took control
of the north-west (the former British Somaliland
Protectorate) and in May 1991 declared unilateral
independence as the 'Somaliland Republic'. A
government and legislature was formed which elected
Mohammed Ibrahim Egal as president in May 1993; he
was re-elected in February 1997. A referendum on a new

constitution, which confirmed the independence of Somaliland, was held on 31 May 2001 and was approved by 97.09 per cent of those who voted. Egal died on 3 May 2002 and was succeeded by Vice-President Dahir Riyale Kahin, who was elected president by a narrow margin with 42.1 per cent of the vote on 14 April 2003.

An autonomous administration was proclaimed in north-eastern Somalia on 23 July 1998. Col. Ahmed Abdullahi Yusuf was named as president of the region, calling itself Puntland, and a Cabinet was appointed. On 15 September 1998, a 69-member parliament was inaugurated. On 30 June 2001 Abdullahi was replaced by Yusuf Haji Nur as interim president pending elections held on 14 November in which Jama Ali Jama was elected president. Abdullahi refused to relinquish his claim to the presidency and by May 2002 his supporters had taken control of the whole of the territory.

HEAD OF STATE
Interim President, Abdiqassim Salad Hassan, *sworn in* 27 August 2000

INTERIM CABINET *as at July 2003*
Prime Minister, Hasan Abshir Farah
Constitution and Federalism, vacant
Culture and Heritage, Ali Mursal Muhammad
Defence, Abdiwahab Muhammad Husayn
Disabled and Rehabilitation, Andiqadir Muhammad Abdulle
Diaspora and Refugee Affairs, Ahmad Abdullahi Jama
Education and Training, Husayn Muhammad Usman Jumbur
Environment, Abubakar Abdi Usman
Foreign Affairs, Yusuf Hassan Ibrahim
Health, Usman Muhammad Dufle
Higher Education, Zakariya Mahmud Haji Abdi
Industry, Yusuf Ma'alin Amin 'Badiow'
Information, Abdirahman Adan Ibrahim Ibbi
Internal Affairs, Dahir Sheikh Muhammad Nur
International Co-operation, Husayn Eelaabe Fahiye
Justice and Religious Affairs, Mahmud Umar Farah
Labour, Abdullahi Muhammad Shirwa
Livestock, Husayn Mahmud Shaykh Husayn
Local Government, Muhammad Nur Jiley
Monetary Affairs, Umar Hashi Adan
Ports and Shipping, Abdiweli Jama' Warsameh
Public Works, Muhammad Warsame Ali
Reconciliation and Conflict Resolution, Muhammad Meydane Burale
Reconstruction and Resettlement, Abdiqadir Aw Yusuf Muhammad
Science and Technology, Abdi'aziz Shaykh Muqtar
Sports and Youth Affairs, Abdi'aziz Muqtar Qaridi
Tourism and Wildlife, Hasan Farah Hujaleh
Trade, Muhammad Warsameh Ali
Transport, Abdi Guled Muhammad
Water and Minerals, Ahmad Muhammad Handulle
Women's Affairs, Saynab Aweys Husayn

ECONOMY
Livestock raising is the main occupation and there is a modest export trade in livestock, skins and hides. Italy, the Gulf States and Saudi Arabia import the bulk of the banana crop, the biggest export, which accounts for approximately 40 per cent of exports. The principal imports are machinery and transport equipment, industrial goods and foodstuffs.

GDP – US$1,631 million (1998); US$216 per capita (2000)
ANNUAL AVERAGE GROWTH OF GDP – 2.5 per cent (1998)
TOTAL EXTERNAL DEBT – US$2,562 million (2000)

Trade with UK	2001	2002
Imports from UK	£5,960,000	£9,119,000
Exports to UK	213,000	33,000

SOUTH AFRICA

Republic of South Africa

AREA – 496,915 sq. miles (1,221,000 sq. km). Neighbours: Namibia (north-west), Botswana and Zimbabwe (north), Mozambique and Swaziland (north-east), Lesotho, which is completely surrounded by South Africa
POPULATION – 43,792,000 (2001); 75.2 per cent African, 13.6 per cent white, 8.6 per cent mixed race, 2.6 per cent Indian/Asian. The constitution designates 11 official languages: Afrikaans (spoken by 14.4 per cent as a first language); English (8.6 per cent); IsiNdebele (1.5 per cent); IsiXosa (17.9 per cent), IsiZulu (22.9 per cent); Sepedi (9.2 per cent); Sosetho (7.7 per cent); SiSwati (2.5 per cent); Setswana (8.2 per cent); Tshivenda (2.2 per cent); Xitsonga (4.4 per cent). Afrikaans and English are to remain the languages of record although any citizen may correspond official business in his own language. The majority (68 per cent) of the population is Christian. There are also Hindus (1.5 per cent), Muslims (2 per cent) and Jews (0.4 per cent), as well as native religions (28.5 per cent)
CAPITAL – The seat of the government is Pretoria (population 1,800,000, 1999 estimate); the seat of the legislature is Cape Town (population, 3,088,028, 1999 estimate); the seat of the judiciary is Bloemfontein (467,400, 1999 estimate)
MAJOR CITIES – ΨDurban (2,589,977); ΨEast London (520,008); Johannesburg (3,800,652); Pietermaritzburg (397,086); ΨPort Elizabeth (1,011,378), 1999 estimates
CURRENCY – Rand (R) of 100 cents
NATIONAL ANTHEMS – Nkosi Sikelel' iAfrika (God Bless Africa); Die Stem Van Suid-Afrika (The Call Of South Africa)
NATIONAL DAY – 27 April (Freedom Day)
NATIONAL FLAG – Divided red over blue by a horizontal white-fimbriated green Y; in the hoist a black triangle fimbriated in yellow
LIFE EXPECTANCY (years) – 50 (2001)
POPULATION GROWTH RATE – 1.7 per cent
POPULATION DENSITY – 36 per sq. km (2001)
URBAN POPULATION – 57 per cent (2001)

South Africa occupies the southernmost part of the African continent from the courses of the Limpopo, Marico, Molopo, Nosop and Orange Rivers to the Cape of Good Hope, with the exception of Lesotho, Swaziland and the extreme south of Mozambique. To the west, east and south lie the south Atlantic and southern Indian Oceans. Some 1,192 miles (1,920 km) to the south-east of Cape Town lie Prince Edward and Marion Islands, part of South Africa since 1947.

The Orange, with its tributary the Vaal, is the principal

river, rising in the Drakensberg and flowing into the Atlantic near the border with Namibia. The Limpopo, or Crocodile River, in the north, rises in North-West Province and flows into the Indian Ocean through Mozambique.

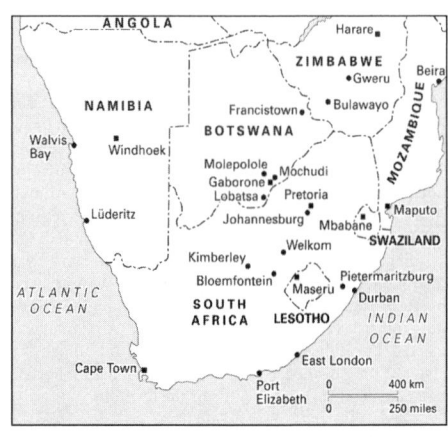

HISTORY AND POLITICS
Hunter-gatherers, the San (Bushmen) and Khoikhoi (Hottentots) inhabited southern Africa from c.8,000 BC. By the eighth century AD, Bantu-speaking peoples had settled the north of the country.

The Portuguese navigator Bartolomeu Días charted the coast in 1488 and the Dutch founded the colony of the Cape of Good Hope in 1652, which was taken by Britain in 1806. The Orange Free State and Transvaal republics were founded by the Boers (the descendants of Dutch settlers) and were recognised by Britain in 1853–4. Natal was annexed to Cape Colony by the British in 1844 and then formed as a separate colony in 1856, to which Zululand was added in 1897 after the British victory in the Zulu wars. Transvaal and the Orange Free State became British colonies after the Boer defeat in the Second Boer War 1899–1902. The self-governing colonies became united in 1910 under the name of the Union of South Africa. Independence within the Commonwealth was gained in 1931 under the Statute of Westminster.

From 1948, when the Afrikaner National Party came to power, South Africa's social and political structure was based on apartheid, a policy of racial segregation. Opposition protests culminated in the Sharpeville massacre in 1960, following which the African National Congress (ANC) and other opposition groups were banned. South Africa left the Commonwealth and became a republic on 31 May 1961, largely as a result of international condemnation.

MOVES TO DEMOCRACY
The first moves to reform apartheid came in 1984, when a new constitution extended the franchise to the mixed race and Indian populations. In 1989, F. W. de Klerk became president of South Africa and lifted the ban on the ANC and restrictions on other anti-apartheid groups and freed Nelson Mandela, the main ANC political detainee. In 1991 the laws implementing apartheid were effectively abolished. In 1992 a referendum amongst the white electorate on continued political reform and a new constitution reached by negotiation was approved.

In 1991 the government, ANC, Inkatha Freedom Party and other civic groups reached agreement on the establishment of an inter-racial administration and the formation of a five-year coalition government following a multiracial election.

In the country's first multiracial general election held on 26–29 April 1994 the ANC gained 252 seats in the 400-seat National Assembly and 60 seats in the 90-seat Senate.

The parliament has passed two significant pieces of legislation to settle the legacy of the apartheid era. In November 1994 parliament passed legislation to restore the rights of those dispossessed of their land. In June 1995 the Truth Commission was established to assess confessions, grant amnesties for political crimes and set compensation for victims.

Following legislative and provincial elections held on 2 June 1999, the ANC gained 266 seats in the National Assembly and, being one seat short of the two-thirds majority required to amend the constitution, entered into

a coalition with the Minority Front, which held just one seat in the National Assembly.

On 14 June 1999 the National Assembly met to select a new president. Thabo Mbeki was elected unopposed and was formally sworn in on 16 June 1999.

POLITICAL SYSTEM
The final constitution came into effect in 1997. Executive power is vested in a president and Cabinet, with the president elected by the National Assembly. Legislative power is vested in a bicameral parliament, a directly elected 400-member National Assembly elected by proportional representation for a five-year term, and an indirectly elected 90-member National Council of Provinces composed of ten members elected by each of the nine regional legislatures for a five-year term.

South Africa is divided into nine regions (Western Cape, Northern Cape, Eastern Cape, Free State, North-West, KwaZulu/Natal, Gauteng, Limpopo, Mpumalanga). Each region has its own premier, a legislature of between 30 and 100 seats elected by proportional representation, and its own constitution.

HEAD OF STATE
President, Commander-in-Chief of the Armed Forces, Thabo Mbeki (ANC), *elected by parliament* 14 June 1999, *sworn in* 16 June 1999
Executive Deputy President, Jacob Zuma (ANC)

CABINET *as at July 2003*
Agriculture and Land Affairs, Angela Didiza (ANC)
Arts, Culture, Science and Technology, Ben Ngubane (IFP)
Communications, Ivy Matsepe-Casaburri (ANC)
Correctional Services, Ben Skosana (IFP)
Defence, Patrick Lekota (ANC)
Education, Kader Asmal (ANC)
Environmental Affairs and Tourism, Mohammed Valli Moosa (ANC)
Finance, Trevor Manuel (ANC)
Foreign Affairs, Nkosazana Dlamini-Zuma (ANC)
Health, Mantombazana Tshabala-Msimang (ANC)
Home Affairs, Chief Mangosuthu Buthelezi (IFP)
Housing, Brigitte Mabandla (ANC)
Intelligence Service, Lindiwe Sisulu-Guma (ANC)
Justice and Constitutional Development, Penuell Maduna (ANC)
Labour, Membathisi Mdladlana (ANC)
Mineral and Energy Affairs, Phumzile Mlambo-Ngcuka (ANC)

Office of the President, Essop Pahad (ANC)
Provincial and Local Government, Sydney Mufamadi (ANC)
Public Enterprises, Jeffrey Radebe (ANC)
Public Service and Administration, Geraldine Fraser-Moleketi (ANC)
Public Works, Stella Sigcau (ANC)
Safety and Security, Charles Nqakula (SACP)
Sports and Recreation, Ngconde Balfour (ANC)
Trade and Industry, Alec Erwin (ANC)
Transport, Dullah Omar (ANC)
Water Affairs and Forestry, Ronnie Kasrils (ANC)
Welfare and Population Development, Zola Skweyiya (ANC)

ANC African National Congress; IFP Inkatha Freedom Party; SACP South African Communist Party

HIGH COMMISSION FOR THE REPUBLIC OF SOUTH AFRICA
South Africa House, Trafalgar Square, London WC2N 5DP.
Tel: 020-7451 7299
High Commissioner, HE Dr Lindiwe Mabuza, apptd 2001

BRITISH HIGH COMMISSION
255 Hill Street, Arcadia 0002 Pretoria
Tel: (00 27) (12) 421 7800
91 Parliament Street, Cape Town, 8001
Tel: (00 27) (21) 405 2400
Email: britain@icon.co.za
High Commissioner (Cape Town), HE Ann Grant, apptd 2001

CONSULATE-GENERAL – Cape Town
CONSULATES – Durban, East London, Port Elizabeth

BRITISH COUNCIL DIRECTOR, Clive Gobby
Ground Floor, Forum 1, Braampark,
33 Hoofd Street, Braamfontein, Johannesburg 2001
Tel: (00 27) (11) 718 4300
Email: information@british council.org.za
There are also offices in Cape Town, Durban and Pretoria

DEFENCE

The new South African National Defence Force (SANDF) was created from the merger of the South African Defence Forces (SADF), the Umkhonto we Sizwe (MK) armed wing of the ANC, the Azanian People's Liberation Army (APLA) of the PAC, and the defence forces of the four former independent homelands.

The Army has 168 main battle tanks, 967 armoured personnel carriers and 1,200 armoured infantry fighting vehicles. The Navy has two submarines and seven patrol and coastal vessels at two bases. The Air Force has 85 combat aircraft and 8 armed helicopters.
MILITARY EXPENDITURE – 1.7 per cent of GDP (2001)
MILITARY PERSONNEL – 60,000: Army 40,250, Navy 5,000, Air Force 9,250

ECONOMY

Mining is of great importance, employing more than 400,000 people in 2000. It is the largest source of foreign exchange. The principal minerals produced are gold, coal, diamonds, copper, iron ore, manganese, lime and limestone, uranium, platinum, fluorspar, andalusite, zinc, zirconium, vanadium, titanium and chrome. South Africa is the world's largest producer of gold, platinum, diamonds, manganese, chrome and vanadium, and has the world's largest reserves of chrome ore, manganese, vanadium and andalusite. In 2000 420 tonnes of gold were produced.

Agriculture, forestry and fishing accounted for 3.2 per cent of GDP in 2000. Over 70 per cent of land is pasture so livestock farming is widespread. Principal crops are maize, sugar cane, fruits and vegetables, wheat, sorghum, sunflower seeds and groundnuts. Cotton is widely grown, and viticulture is also widespread.

Industries, concentrated most heavily around Johannesburg, Pretoria and the major ports, process foodstuffs, metals and non-metallic mineral products, produce oil from coal, and also produce beverages and tobacco, motor vehicles, chemicals and chemical products, machinery, textiles and clothing, and paper and paper products. Industry contributed 30.9 per cent of GDP in 2000.

Energy production is based upon coal and natural gas and the production of synthetic liquid fuel from coal. One nuclear power station is in operation and others are planned. South Africa exports electricity through its electric grid connections to all states in southern Africa.

Tourism accounts for 3.4 per cent of GDP. In 2000 5.9 million foreign tourists visited South Africa.

In 2001 there was a trade surplus of US$4,966 million and a current account deficit of US$166 million. Imports totalled US$28,405 million and exports US$29,284 million.
GNP – US$129,171 million (2000); US$3,020 per capita (2000)
GDP – US$113,274 million (2001); US$2,954 per capita (2000)
ANNUAL AVERAGE GROWTH OF GDP – 3.1 per cent (2000)
INFLATION RATE – 5.3 per cent (2000)
UNEMPLOYMENT – 5.3 per cent (1998)
TOTAL EXTERNAL DEBT – US$24,861 million (2000)

TRADE

Principal exports are gold, base metals and metal products, coal, diamonds, food (especially fruit) and wool. Principal imports are machinery, chemicals, motor vehicles, metals and metal products, food, inedible raw materials and textiles. South Africa's main trading partners are Germany, the USA, the UK, Italy and Japan.

Trade with UK	2001	2002
Imports from UK	£1,547,363,000	£1,609,067,000
Exports to UK	2,953,369,000	2,784,786,000

COMMUNICATIONS

There are international airports at Johannesburg, Durban and Cape Town. South African Airways operates international services to Europe, South America, the Far East, Africa, Australia and the USA, and it is the principal operator of domestic flights. Durban is the largest seaport. Other major ports are Cape Town, Port Elizabeth, East London, Saldanha Mossel Bay and Richards Bay.

CULTURE AND EDUCATION

Higher education is provided at 21 universities and 15 other tertiary-level colleges.
ILLITERACY RATE – (m) 14.0 per cent; (f) 15.4 per cent (2000)

ENROLMENT (percentage of age group) – primary
94 per cent (1996); secondary 51 per cent (1996);
tertiary 19 per cent (1995)

SPAIN

Reino de España – Kingdom of Spain

AREA – 192,078 sq. miles (499,400 sq. km).
Neighbours: Portugal (west), France (north)
POPULATION – 39,921,000 (2001 estimate): 96 per
cent Catholic, 1 per cent Muslim. Castilian Spanish is
the official language, although Basque, Catalan,
Galician and Valencian, a dialect of Catalan, are
spoken and have official status in the autonomous
regions where they are spoken
CAPITAL – Madrid (population, 5,086,635, 2001)
MAJOR CITIES – ΨBarcelona (3,765,994); ΨValencia
(1,397,809); Málaga (775,458); Sevilla (1,180,197);
Zaragoza (638,535), 2001
CURRENCY – Euro (€) of 100 cents
NATIONAL ANTHEM – Marcha Real Española (Spanish
Royal March)
NATIONAL DAY – 12 October
NATIONAL FLAG – Three horizontal stripes of red,
yellow, red, with the yellow of double width
LIFE EXPECTANCY (years) – 79 (2001)
POPULATION GROWTH RATE – 0.1 per cent
POPULATION DENSITY – 80 per sq. km (2001)
URBAN POPULATION – 78 per cent (2001)

The interior of the Iberian peninsula consists of an
elevated tableland surrounded and traversed by mountain
ranges: the Pyrenees, the Cantabrian Mountains, the
Sierra de Guadarrama, Sierra Morena, Sierra Nevada,
Montes de Toledo, etc. The principal rivers are the Duero,
the Tajo, the Guadiana, the Guadalquivir, the Ebro and
the Miño.

HISTORY AND POLITICS

The kingdoms of Castile and Aragón were united in
1479; they captured Granada, the last region of Spain
under Moorish rule, in 1492 and conquered Navarra in
1512. In 1492 Columbus reached the Americas on
behalf of Spain and began the process of colonisation
which led to most of central and south America coming
under Spanish rule until their independence in the 19th
century. A republic was proclaimed in 1931 and in
February 1936 the Popular Front, a left-wing coalition,
was elected. In July 1936 a counter-revolution broke out
in military garrisons in Spanish Morocco and spread
throughout Spain. Civil war ensued until March 1939,
when the Popular Front governments in Madrid and
Barcelona surrendered to the Nationalists (as Gen.
Franco's followers were then named). Gen. Franco
became president and ruled the country until his death in
1975, when, according to his wishes, he was succeeded
as head of state by Prince Juan Carlos of Bourbon
(grandson of Alfonso XIII) and Spain again became a
monarchy. The first free election was held on 15 June
1977.
    The general election of 12 March 2000 was won by
the Popular Party (PP), which won 183 seats in the
Congress of Deputies.

INSURGENCIES

The Basque separatist organisation ETA *(Euzkadi ta
Azkatasuna* – Basque Nation and Liberty) has since its

formation in 1959 carried out a terrorist campaign of
bombings, shootings and kidnappings against the
Spanish state and its security forces in an attempt to gain
independence for the Basque country. ETA rejected
regional autonomy for the Basque country in 1979 as
insufficient and continued its campaign, but increased co-
operation between French and Spanish security forces
had greatly weakened ETA by the early 1990s. On 23
January 2000, over a million people demonstrated in
Madrid against ETA terrorist attacks following a car
bomb explosion in Madrid on 21 January. On 22 March
2002, a local politician from the Socialist Workers' Party
was shot and killed in the Basque town of Orio in what
was thought to be an ETA attack. In August 2002,
Spanish MPs voted to suspend the Basque political party,
Batasuna, because of its links with ETA and on 17 March
2003 the Supreme Court approved a government request
for a permanent ban on Batasuna.

POLITICAL SYSTEM

Under the 1978 constitution there is a bicameral *Cortes
Generales* comprising a 350-member Congress of
Deputies *(Congreso de los Diputados)* elected for a
maximum term of four years, which elects the prime
minister; and a Senate *(Senado)* consisting of 208
directly elected representatives and 51 representatives
appointed by the assemblies of the autonomous regions.
Since the promulgation of the 1978 constitution, 19
autonomous regions have been established, with their
own parliaments and governments. These are Andalucía,
Aragón, Asturias, Balearics, the Basque country, Canaries,
Cantabria, Castilla-La Mancha, Castilla y León,
Catalunya, Ceuta, Extremadura, Galicia, Madrid, Melilla,
Murcia, Navarra, La Rioja and Valencia.

HEAD OF STATE

HM The King of Spain, King Juan Carlos I de Borbón,
    KG, GCVO, *born* 5 January 1938, *acceded to the throne*
    22 November 1975, *married* 14 May 1962, Princess
    Sophie of Greece and *has issue* Príncipe Felipe; Infanta
    Elena Maria Isabel Dominga, *born* 20 December
    1963; and Infanta Cristina Federica Victoria Antonia,
    born 13 June 1965
Heir, HRH The Prince of the Asturias (Príncipe Felipe
    Juan Pablo Alfonso y Todos los Santos), *born*
    30 January 1968

CABINET *as at July 2003*
Prime Minister, José María Aznar López
*First Deputy Prime Minister, Cabinet Office, Government
    Spokesperson,* Mariano Rajoy Brey
Second Deputy Prime Minister, Economy, Rodrigo de Rato
    y Figaredo
Agriculture, Food and Fisheries, Miguel Arias Cañete
Defence, Federico Trillo-Figueroa y Martínez Conde
Development, Francisco Alvárez-Cascos Fernández
Education, Culture and Sport, Pilar del Castillo Vera
Environment, Jaime Matas Palou
Foreign Affairs, Ana de Palacio
Health and Consumer Affairs, Ana María Pastor
Interior, Ángel Acebes Paniagua
Justice, José María Michavila
Labour and Social Affairs, Eduardo Zaplana
Public Administration, Javier Arenas
Science and Technology, Josep Piqué i Camps
Treasury, Cristóbal Montoro Romero

SPANISH EMBASSY
39 Chesham Place, London SW1X 8SB
Tel: 020-7235 5555
Ambassador Extraordinary and Plenipotentiary, HE The
Marqués de Tamarón, apptd 1999

BRITISH EMBASSY
Calle de Fernando el Santo 16, E-28010 Madrid
Tel: (00 34) (91) 700 8200
Ambassador Extraordinary and Plenipotentiary,
HE Stephen Wright, CMG, apptd 2003

CONSULATES-GENERAL – Madrid, Barcelona, Bilbao
CONSULATES – Alicante, Málaga, Palma de Mallorca,
Las Palmas, Santander, Tenerife, Vigo

BRITISH COUNCIL DIRECTOR, Christine Melia
(acting), OBE, Paseo del General Martínez,
Campos 31, E-28010 Madrid
Tel: (00 34) (91) 337 3500 Email:madrid@britishcouncil.es
There are offices in Barcelona, Segovia, Terrassa and
Valencia

DEFENCE
The Army has 682 main battle tanks, 2,023 armoured
personnel carriers and 28 attack helicopters. The Navy
has eight submarines, one aircraft carrier, 15 frigates,
37 patrol and coastal vessels, 17 combat aircraft and
37 armed helicopters at seven bases. The Air Force has
198 combat aircraft. The USA maintains 1,760 naval and
360 air force personnel in Spain.
MILITARY EXPENDITURE – 1.2 per cent of GDP (2001)
MILITARY PERSONNEL – 177,950: Army 118,800,
Navy 26,950, Air Force 22,750; Paramilitaries 73,360

ECONOMY
The expansion of the economy and accession to the EU
have led to reforms in Spanish agriculture, extensive
industrial modernisation and widespread privatisation.
The country is generally fertile and olives, oranges,
lemons, almonds, pomegranates, bananas, apricots,
tomatoes, peppers, cucumbers and grapes are cultivated.
Other agricultural products include wheat, barley, oats,
rice, hemp and flax. The vine is cultivated widely; in the
south-west, around Jerez, sherry and tent wines are
produced. Spain has one of Europe's largest fishing
industries.
Spain's mineral resources of coal, iron, wolfram,
copper, zinc, lead and iron ores are exploited. The
principal industrial goods are cars, steel, ships,
manufactured goods, textiles, chemical products,
footwear and other leather goods. Tourism is a major
industry generating 9 per cent of GDP and employing
11 per cent of the population; some 48 million tourists
visit per year.
Spain successfully met the convergence criteria laid
down for EU economic and monetary union and was a
participant in the European single currency, the euro, on
1 January 1999. The centre-right government has
withdrawn subsidies from uncompetitive industries,
privatised the steel industry and reduced income tax. The
economy has been performing well and unemployment
has been falling steadily. The euro replaced the peseta on
1 January 2002.
In 2001 Spain had a trade deficit of US$31,500
million and a current account deficit of US$15,082
million. Imports totalled US$153,607 million and
exports US$115,155 million.

GNP – US$595,255 million (2000); US$15,080 per
capita (2000)
GDP – US$577,539 million (2001); US$14,054 per
capita (2000)
ANNUAL AVERAGE GROWTH OF GDP – 4.9 per cent
(2000)
INFLATION RATE – 3.4 per cent (2000)
UNEMPLOYMENT – 14.1 per cent (2000)

TRADE
The principal imports are manufactures, military
hardware, semimanufactures, vehicles, consumer
goods, foodstuffs and energy. The principal exports
include manufactures, military hardware, vehicles, semi-
manufactures, foodstuffs, consumer goods and energy.

Trade with UK	2001	2002
Imports from UK	£7,953,300,000	£8,119,300,000
Exports to UK	6,488,500,000	7,842,300,000

EDUCATION
Education is free for those aged six to 18, and
compulsory up to the age of 16. Private schools (30 per
cent of primary and 60 per cent of secondary schools)
have to fulfil certain criteria to receive government
maintenance grants. There are 73 universities, the oldest
of which, Salamanca, was founded in 1218. Other
ancient foundations are Valladolid (1346), Barcelona
(1430), Zaragoza (1474), Santiago (1495), Valencia
(1500), Seville (1505), Madrid (1508), Granada (1531),
Oviedo (1604). Private universities are Deusto in Bilbao,
Navarra in Pamplona, Carlos III in Madrid and one in
Salamanca.
ILLITERACY RATE – (m) 1.4 per cent; (f) 3.2 per cent
(2000)
ENROLMENT (percentage of age group) – primary
100 per cent (1995); secondary 94 per cent (1994);
tertiary 51 per cent (1996)

CULTURE
Castilian is the language of more than three-quarters of
the population of Spain. Basque, said to have been the
original language of Iberia, is spoken in Vizcaya,
Guipúzcoa and Álava. Catalan is spoken in Provençal
Spain, and Galician, spoken in the north-western
provinces, is akin to Portuguese. The governments of
these regions actively encourage use of their local
languages.
The literature of Spain is one of the oldest and richest
in the world, the *Poem of the Cid,* the earliest of the heroic
songs of Spain, having been written about 1140. The
outstanding writings of its golden age are those of
Miguel de Cervantes Saavedra (1547–1616), Lope Felix
de Vega Carpio (1562–1635) and Pedro Calderón de la
Barca (1600–81). The Nobel Prize for Literature has five
times been awarded to Spanish authors: J. Echegaray,
J. Benavente, Juan Ramón Jiménez, Vicente Aleixandre
and Camilo José Cela.

ISLANDS AND ENCLAVES
THE BALEARIC ISLES form an archipelago off the east
coast of Spain. There are four large islands (Majorca,
Minorca, Ibiza and Formentera), and seven smaller
(Aire, Aucanada, Botafoch, Cabrera, Dragonera, Pinto
and El Rey). Area 1,935 sq. miles (5,011 sq. km);
population 841,669. The archipelago forms a province
of Spain, the capital is ΨPalma in Majorca, population
432,113

THE CANARY ISLANDS are an archipelago in the Atlantic, off the African coast, consisting of seven islands and six islets. Area 2,807 sq. miles (7,270 sq. km); population 1,694,477. The Canary Islands form two provinces of Spain: Las Palmas, comprising Gran Canaria, Lanzarote (38,500), Fuerteventura (19,500) and the islets of Alegranza, Roque del Este, Roque del Oeste, Graciosa, Montaña Clara and Lobos, with seat of administration at ΨLas Palmas (587,641) in Gran Canaria; and Santa Cruz de Tenerife, comprising Tenerife, La Palma (76,000), Gomera (31,829), and Hierro (10,000), with seat of administration at ΨSanta Cruz in Tenerife, population estimate 399,104

ISLA DE FAISANES is an uninhabited Franco-Spanish condominium, at the mouth of the Bidassoa in La Higuera bay

ΨCEUTA is a fortified post on the Moroccan coast, opposite Gibraltar. Area 5 sq. miles (13 sq. km); population 71,505

ΨMELILLA is a town on a rocky promontory of the Rif coast, connected with the mainland by a narrow isthmus. Population 66,411. Ceuta and Melilla are autonomous regions of Spain

OVERSEAS TERRITORIES
The following territories are Spanish settlements on the Moroccan seaboard.

PEÑÓN DE ALHUCEMAS is a bay including six islands; population 366

PEÑÓN DE LA GOMERA (or Peñón de Velez) is a fortified rocky islet; population 450

THE CHAFFARINAS (or Zaffarines) is a group of three islands near the Algerian frontier; population 610

SRI LANKA

Śrī Laṅkā Prajātāntrika Samājavādi Janarajaya / Ilaṅkaiś Saṅanāyaka Śośaliśak Kuṭiyaraśa – Democratic Socialist Republic of Sri Lanka

AREA – 24,846 sq. miles (64,600 sq. km)

POPULATION – 19,104,000 (2001): 74 per cent Sinhalese, 12.6 per cent Sri Lankan Tamils, 5.6 per cent Indian Tamils, 7.1 per cent Sri Lankan Moors, 0.7 per cent Burghers, Malays and others. The religion of the majority is Buddhism (69.3 per cent), then Hinduism (15.5 per cent), Islam (7.6 per cent), and Christianity (7.5 per cent). The national languages are Sinhala and Tamil

CAPITAL – ΨColombo (population, 642,163, 2000)

MAJOR CITIES – ΨGalle (971,000); ΨJaffna (879,000); Kandy (1,269,000); ΨTrincomalee (323,000)

CURRENCY – Sri Lankan rupee of 100 cents

NATIONAL ANTHEM – Namo Namo Matha (We All Stand Together)

NATIONAL DAY – 4 February (Independence Day)

NATIONAL FLAG – On a dark red field, within a golden border, a golden lion passant holding a sword in its right paw, and a representation of a *bo*-leaf, issuing from each corner; and to its right, two vertical stripes of saffron and green also placed within a golden border, to represent the minorities of the country

LIFE EXPECTANCY (years) – 72 (2001)

POPULATION GROWTH RATE – 1 per cent

POPULATION DENSITY – 296 per sq. km (2001)

ILLITERACY RATE – (m) 5.6 per cent; (f) 11.0 per cent (2000)

Sri Lanka (formerly Ceylon) is an island in the Indian Ocean, off the southern tip of India and separated from it by the narrow Palk Strait. Forests, jungle and scrub cover the greater part of the island. In areas over 2,000 ft above sea level grasslands *(patanas or talawas)* are found. One of the highest peaks in the central massif is Adam's Peak (7,360 ft), a place of pilgrimage for Buddhists, Hindus and Muslims.

HISTORY AND POLITICS
The Portuguese landed in Ceylon in the early 16th century and founded settlements. The Dutch East India Company controlled the country from 1658 until 1796. The maritime provinces of Ceylon were ceded by the Dutch to the British in 1798, becoming a British Crown Colony in 1802. With the annexation of the Kingdom of Kandy in 1815, all Ceylon came under British rule. Ceylon became a self-governing state and a member of the British Commonwealth on 4 February 1948. A republican constitution was adopted in 1972 and the country was renamed Sri Lanka (meaning 'Resplendent Island').

Eight provincial councils were set up in 1988 under the Indo-Sri Lankan peace accord in an attempt to diffuse ethnic tension. Since then, except for the temporarily merged North-East province, all provinces have had elected provincial councils.

In the presidential election held on 21 December 1999, President Kumaratunga was elected for a second term, gaining 51.37 per cent of the vote. Prime Minister Sirimavo Bandaranaike resigned on 10 August 2000 and was replaced by Ratnasiri Wickremanayake.

In the general election of 5 December 2001, the United National Party (UNP) won 109 seats and the People's Alliance (PA), which had formed the government prior to the election in coalition with other parties, won 77 seats. Ranil Wickremasinghe of the UNP was sworn in as prime minister on 9 December and the new Cabinet was appointed on 12 December.

INSURGENCIES
The Liberation Tigers of Tamil Eelam (LTTE) guerrilla group has been fighting Sri Lankan forces for control of the Tamil majority areas in the north and east of the country since 1983. The LTTE was banned in January 1998 following a truck bomb attack against a Buddhist holy shrine.

A state of war was imposed by President Kumaratunga on 3 May 2000 after LTTE forces captured the Elephant Pass, the only land link to the Jaffna peninsula.

The LTTE declared a month-long unilateral cease-fire on 21 December 2000, to facilitate peace talks. The government rejected the cease-fire and troops launched a fresh offensive in the Jaffna peninsula. The LTTE extended the cease-fire in January 2001, and again in February and March, but the government refused to reciprocate, launching a series of attacks on the Jaffna peninsula. Tensions continued and violence broke out between Hindu and Muslim Tamils in June 2002. The ban on the LTTE was lifted in September 2002 ahead of peace talks which began in Thailand on 16 September. These talks were the first formal negotiations in seven years. A power-sharing agreement was reached during peace talks held in Norway on 2–5 December 2002. The agreement stipulated a federal system of government with substantial regional autonomy for LTTE-held areas in the north and east of the country. Talks on the peace process began in Berlin in February 2003 but in April the LTTE suspended their participation in the talks, stating that they were being marginalised. The rebels affirmed they did not intend to break the cease-fire. Following a government proposal in July for interim administration in north-eastern Sri Lanka, LTTE leaders met in Paris on 21 August to formulate their response to the proposal and it was expected that peace talks would resume by the end of September.

POLITICAL SYSTEM

The 1978 constitution introduced a system of proportional representation. Legislative power is vested in the parliament, whose 225 members are directly elected for a six-year term. Executive power is exercised by the president, elected for six years, and the Cabinet.

HEAD OF STATE

President, Media, Welfare, Chandrika Bandaranaike Kumaratunga, *elected* 9 November 1994, *re-elected* 21 December 1999, *sworn in* 22 December 1999

CABINET *as at July 2003*
Prime Minister, Policy Development, Implementation and Poverty Alleviation, Ranil Wickremasinghe
Agriculture and Livestock, Social Welfare, S. B. Dissanayake
Central Region Development, Tissa Attanayake
Commerce and Consumer Affairs, Ravi Karunanayake
Community Development, P. Chandrasekaran
Co-operatives, Abdul Rahim Mohideen Cader
Defence, Transport, Highways and Aviation, Tilak Marapone
Eastern Region Development and Muslim Religious Affairs, Ports Development and Shipping, Rauf Hakeem
Economic Reforms, Science and Technology, Milinda Moragoda
Employment and Labour, Mahinda Samarasinghe
Enterprise Development, Industrial Policy, Investment Promotion, Constitutional Affairs, G. L. Peiris
Environment and Natural Resources, Rukman Senanayake
Finance, K. N. Choksy
Fisheries and Ocean Resources, Mahinda Wijesekara
Foreign Affairs, Tyronne Fernando
Health, P. Dayaratne
Home Affairs and Local Government, Alik Aluvihare
Housing and Plantation Infrastructure, Arumugam Thondaman
Human Resources Development, Education and Cultural Affairs, Karunasena Kodituwakku
Interior, John Amaratunga
Irrigation and Water Management, Gamini Jayawickrema Perera
Justice, Law Reform and National Reconciliation, W. J. M. Lokubandara
Lands, Rajitha Senaratne
Mass Communication, Imithiyas Bakeer Makar
Plantation Industries, Lakshman Kiriella
Power and Energy, Karu Jayasuriya
Public Administration, Management and Reforms, Vajira Abeywardena
Rural Economy, Bandula Gunawardena
Southern Region Development, Ananda Kularatne
Tourism, Gamini Kulawansa Lokuge
Western Region Development, Mohamad Hanifa Mohamed
Women's Affairs, Amara Piyasiri Ratnayake

HIGH COMMISSION FOR THE DEMOCRATIC SOCIALIST REPUBLIC OF SRI LANKA
13 Hyde Park Gardens, London W2 2LU
Tel: 020-7262 1841/6
Email: mail@slhc.globalnet.co.uk
High Commissioner, HE Faisz Musthapha, apptd 2002

BRITISH HIGH COMMISSION
190 Galle Road, Kollupitiya, PO Box 1433, Colombo 3
Tel: (00 94) (1) 437336/43 Email: bhc@eureka.lk
High Commissioner, HE Stephen Evans, OBE, apptd 2002

BRITISH COUNCIL DIRECTOR, Tony O'Brien
49 Alfred House Gardens, PO Box 753, Colombo 3
Email: enquiries@britishcouncil.lk
There is a regional office in Kandy

DEFENCE

The Army has 62 main battle tanks, 217 armoured personnel carriers and 62 armoured infantry fighting vehicles. The Navy has 61 patrol and coastal vessels at five bases. The Air Force has 22 combat aircraft and 24 armed helicopters.
MILITARY EXPENDITURE – 5.1 per cent of GDP (2001)
MILITARY PERSONNEL – 157,900: Army 118,000, Navy 20,600, Air Force 19,300; Paramilitaries 88,600

ECONOMY

The staple products are tea, rubber, copra, spices and gems. There is increasing emphasis on local production of food, especially rice, and plans for the large-scale production of sugar cane, cotton and citrus fruits.

The principal exports are industrial goods, agricultural products (especially tea), and oil derivatives. Principal imports are manufactures, textiles and clothing, capital goods, consumer goods and oil. Tourism is an important industry, with 400,414 foreign visitors in 2000. In 2000 there was a trade deficit of US$1,044 million and a current account deficit of US$1,042 million. In 2001 imports totalled US$5,925 million and exports US$4,817 million.
GNP – US$16,408 million (2000); US$850 per capita (2000)
GDP – US$16,346 million (2001); US$854 per capita (2000)
ANNUAL AVERAGE GROWTH OF GDP – 6.0 per cent (2000)
INFLATION RATE – 6.2 per cent (2000)
UNEMPLOYMENT – 8.0 per cent (2000)
TOTAL EXTERNAL DEBT – US$9,066 million (2000)

Trade with UK	2001	2002
Imports from UK	£142,372,000	£126,314,000
Exports to UK	400,811,000	421,567,000

COMMUNICATIONS

There are 25,952 km of roads in Sri Lanka, of which 11,077 km are surfaced, and a government-run railway system with 1,459 km of lines. A satellite earth station at Padukka provides telecommunication links world-wide. The principal airport is at Katunayake, north of Colombo.

SUDAN

Al-Jumhūriyya as-Sūdān – Republic of the Sudan

AREA – 913,846 sq. miles (2,376,000 sq. km).
Neighbours: Egypt (north), Eritrea and Ethiopia (east), Kenya, Uganda and the Democratic Republic of Congo (south), Central African Republic, Chad and Libya (west)
POPULATION – 31,809,000 (2001). Arab and Nubian peoples populate the north and centre, Nilotic and Negro peoples the south. Arabic is the official language and Islam the state religion, although the Nilotics of the Bahr el Ghazal and Upper Nile valleys are generally Animists or Christians
CAPITAL – Khartoum (Al-Khartum) (population, 947,483, 1993 census). The combined population of Khartoum, Khartoum North and Umm Durman (excluding refugees and displaced people) is estimated at 3,000,000
MAJOR CITIES – Al-Ubayyid (229,425); Nyala (227,183); ΨPort Sudan (Bur Sudan) (308,195), 1993 census
CURRENCY – Sudanese dinar (SD) of 100 piastres
NATIONAL ANTHEM – Nahnu Djundullah (We Are The Army Of God)
NATIONAL DAY – 1 January (Independence Day)
NATIONAL FLAG – Three horizontal stripes of red, white and black with a green triangle next to the hoist
LIFE EXPECTANCY (years) – 56 (2001)
POPULATION GROWTH RATE – 2.3 per cent
POPULATION DENSITY – 13 per sq. km (2001)
URBAN POPULATION – 37 per cent (2001)
MILITARY EXPENDITURE – 4.3 per cent of GDP (2001)
MILITARY PERSONNEL – 117,000: Army 112,500, Navy 1,500, Air Force 3,000; Paramilitaries 7,000
CONSCRIPTION DURATION – Two years

The White Nile, as the Bahr el Jebel, flows through Sudan from Nimule to Wadi Halfa. The Blue Nile flows from Lake Tana on the Ethiopian plateau through Sudan to join the White Nile at Khartoum. The next confluence of importance is at Atbara where the main Nile is joined by the River Atbara. Between Khartoum and Wadi Halfa lie five of the six cataracts.

HISTORY AND POLITICS

The Anglo-Egyptian Condominium over Sudan was established in 1899 and ended when the Sudan House of Representatives, on 19 December 1955, declared Sudan a fully independent sovereign state. A republic was proclaimed on 1 January 1956, and was recognised by Great Britain and Egypt. Sudan was under military rule from 1958 to 1964, from 1969 to 1986, and from 1989 until presidential and legislative elections were held in March 1996. President al-Bashir was elected with 75.7 per cent of the vote having faced no serious contender. The founding of political parties was legalised on 1 January 1999. In early January 1999, the voting age was lowered to 17 and a new dress code was imposed on women, requiring them to wear headscarves. In December 1999, President al-Bashir suspended the National Assembly and declared a three-month state of emergency, shortly before a vote on constitutional changes, which included the reduction of the powers of the president, was due to be debated. The state of emergency has been repeatedly extended and in December 2001 was extended indefinitely.

Presidential and legislative elections were held on 13–23 December 2000, but were boycotted by most opposition parties. President al-Bashir was re-elected, winning 86.5 per cent of votes cast, and the National Congress won 355 of the 360 seats which were up for election. The civil war prevented balloting in three provinces. On 19 August 2002 President Bashir announced a Cabinet reshuffle which brought members of opposition groups into the Cabinet for the first time.

INSURGENCIES

Nearly 17 years of insurrection in the southern provinces ended in 1972 with the signing of an agreement recognising southern regional autonomy within the Sudanese state. However, insurrection resumed in 1983 and since then there has been civil war in the south of the country between government forces and the Christian and Animist majority in the area, organised into the Sudan People's Liberation Army (SPLA). A peace process begun in September 2000 continued through 2001 and a cease-fire was agreed in January 2002. However in March 2002 the SPLA warned that its attacks on oil installations would continue. The warfare has left an estimated 1.4 million dead, including 300,000 who died in the war-induced famine in 1988 and thousands in a similar situation in 1994. Some three million refugees have fled the fighting, either to the north, to neighbouring states or to the far south near the Ugandan border. The fighting has left large areas of the south desolate and uninhabitable. In July 2002 the government and SPLA signed a framework deal aimed at ending the civil war. The terms of the agreement state that southern Sudan will be able to hold an independence referendum after a six-year power-sharing transition period. Following the rebel capture of the strategically important town of Torit on 30 August 2002, the government suspended peace talks on 1 September. Torit was re-captured by the government on 6 October. Peace talks resumed on 14 October. Several rounds of peace talks took place during 2003 but issues surrounding the sharing of wealth and power during the transitional period of government remained unresolved.

FOREIGN RELATIONS

In 1995 Sudan's relations with its neighbours, notably Egypt, Eritrea and Uganda, deteriorated as they considered that Sudan was arming Islamic and insurgent groups in their states. On 2 May 1999 a peace agreement was signed with Eritrea. Sudan and the UK agreed to resume full diplomatic representation in June 1999. On 8 December 1999, Sudan and Uganda signed an agreement under which they agreed to cease supporting rebel groups in each other's countries, to disarm and disband such groups and to re-establish full diplomatic links. On 24 December, Sudan and Egypt agreed to normalise their relations and seek a solution to their dispute over the Hala'ib region.

HEAD OF STATE

President, Prime Minister, Lt.-Gen. Omar Hassan Ahmad al-Bashir, *appointed* 16 October 1993, *elected* 17 March 1996, *re-elected* 20 December 2000.
First Vice-President, Maj.-Gen. Ali Osman Mohamad Taha
Vice-President, Moses Machar Kashol
Assistant to the President, Mubarek al-Fadil al-Mahdi

CABINET *as at July 2003*
Agriculture and Forestry, Majdhub al-Khalifah Ahmad
Animal Resources, Brig. Galwak Deng
Aviation, Joseph Malwal
Cabinet Affairs, Col.-Maj.-Gen. Tayyar Abdallah Ali Safi al-Nur
Culture, Abd al-Basit Abd al-Majid
Defence, Maj.-Gen. Bakri Hassan Salih
Education and Guidance, Ahmed Babikir Nahar
Electricity, Ali Tamim Fartak
Energy and Mining, Awad Ahmad al-Jaz
Environment and Construction Development, Maj.-Gen. al-Tijani Adam al-Tahir
Finance and National Economy, Ahmad Hasan al-Zubayr
Foreign Affairs, Mustapha Osman Ismail
Foreign Trade, Abdel Hamid Mussa Kasha
Guidance and Awqaf, Isam Ahmad al-Bashir
Health, Ahmad Bilal Uthman
Higher Education, Mubarak Muhammad Ali al-Majdhub
Humanitarian Affairs, Ibrahim Mahmoud Hamid
Industry and Investment, Jalal Yusuf Muhammad al-Dugayr
Information and Communications, Al.-Zahawi Ibrahim Malik
Interior, Maj.-Gen. Abd al-Rahim Muhammad Husayn
International Co-operation, Yusuf Suleiman Takana
Investment, Al-Sherif Ahmed Omar Badr
Irrigation and Water Resources, Kamal Ali Muhammad
Justice, Ali Mohammad Uthman Yassin
Labour and Administrative Reform, Maj.-Gen Allison Manani Magaya
Minister for the Council of Ministers, Karam-al-Din Abd-al-Mawla
Minister in the Federal Administration Office, Nafi Ali Nafi
Presidency, Maj.-Gen. Al-Tayyib Ibrahim Muhammad Khayr
Relations with the National Assembly, Abd al-Basit Salih Sabdarat
Roads and Bridges, Muhammad Tahir Ila
Social Development, Samiyah Ahmad Muhammad
Science and Technology, Zubayr Bashir Taha
Tourism and National Heritage, Abdel Jalil al-Basha Mohamed Ahmed
Transport, Al Sammani al-Sheikh al-Waseilah
Youth and Sport, Hasan Uthman Rizq

EMBASSY OF THE REPUBLIC OF THE SUDAN
3 Cleveland Row, London SW1A 1DD
Tel: 020-7839 8080
Ambassador Extraordinary and Plenipotentiary,
HE Dr Hasan Abdin, apptd 2000

BRITISH EMBASSY
PO Box 801, Khartoum East
Tel: (00 249) (11) 777105
Email: information.khartoum@fco.gov.uk
Ambassador Extraordinary and Plenipotentiary,
HE William Patey, apptd 2002

BRITISH COUNCIL DIRECTOR, Paul Doubleday
14 Abu Sin Street (PO Box 1253), Khartoum
Email: british.council@sd.britishcouncil.org

ECONOMY
Agriculture provides employment for over half the labour force and contributes nearly half of GDP. It is based on large and medium-sized public sector irrigation projects. Mechanised and traditional agriculture is practised in areas of sufficient rainfall. The principal grain crops are *dura* (great millet) and wheat, the staple food of the population. Sesame and groundnuts are other important food crops, which also yield an exportable surplus, and a promising start has been made with castor seed. Sudan still has to achieve self-sufficiency in its production.

In 2001 Sudan had a trade surplus of US$304 million and a current account deficit of US$5,618 million. In 2001 imports totalled US$1,586 million and exports US$1,699 million.

GNP – US$9,599 million (2000); US$310 per capita (2000)
GDP – US$12,560 million (2001); US$353 per capita (2000)
ANNUAL AVERAGE GROWTH OF GDP – 6.0 per cent (1998)
INFLATION RATE – 9.2 per cent (2002)
TOTAL EXTERNAL DEBT – US$15,741 million (2000)

TRADE

Trade with UK	2001	2002
Imports from UK	£80,018,000	£70,807,000
Exports to UK	10,098,000	7,770,000

COMMUNICATIONS
The railway system, adversely affected by the civil war, has a route length of about 5,516 km. There are 11,610 km of roads, of which 4,203 km are paved. Nile river services between Khartoum and Juba have been interrupted by the southern insurrection. Port Sudan is the country's main seaport. Sudan Airways flies services from Khartoum to other parts of Sudan and to other African states, Europe and the Middle East.

EDUCATION
School education is free for most children but not compulsory, beginning with six years of primary education, followed by three years of secondary education at general secondary schools, the more academic higher secondary schools or vocational schools. The medium of instruction is Arabic. English has not been taught in schools since new Arabisation legislation came into effect in 1991.

In addition to 20 universities there are various technical post-secondary institutes as well as professional and vocational training establishments.
ILLITERACY RATE – (m) 30.2 per cent; (f) 53.7 per cent (2000)

SURINAME

Republiek Suriname – Republic of Suriname

AREA – 63,037 sq. miles (163,265 sq. km). Neighbours: French Guiana (east), Brazil (south), Guyana (west)
POPULATION – 433,998 (2001 estimate): 37 per cent Hindustani, 31 per cent Creole, 15 per cent Javanese, 10 per cent African and small numbers of Amerindian, Chinese and Europeans. The official language is Dutch, the native language is Sranang Tongo, and other widely-used languages are Hindustani and Javanese
CAPITAL – ΨParamaribo (population, 213,836, 2000)
CURRENCY – Suriname guilder of 100 cents
NATIONAL ANTHEM – God Zij Met Ons Suriname (God Be With Our Suriname)
NATIONAL DAY – 25 November
NATIONAL FLAG – Horizontal stripes of green, white,

red, white, green, with a five-pointed yellow star in the centre

POPULATION GROWTH RATE – 0.4 per cent

POPULATION DENSITY – 3 per sq. km (1999)

MILITARY EXPENDITURE – 5.3 per cent of GDP (2001)

MILITARY PERSONNEL – 1,840: Army 1,400, Navy 240, Air Force 200

ILLITERACY RATE – (m) 4.1 per cent; (f) 7.4 per cent (2000)

HISTORY AND POLITICS

Formerly known as Dutch Guiana, Suriname remained part of the Netherlands West Indies until 25 November 1975, when it achieved complete independence. The civilian government was ousted in 1980 by the military who appointed a predominantly civilian government in 1982.

The New Front for Democracy, a four-party bloc consisting of the National Party of Suriname (NPS), The Progressive Reform Party, Pertjajah Luhur and the Suriname Labour Party, won 32 of the 51 seats in the elections to the National Assembly on 25 May 2000 and appointed Ronald Venetiaan of the NPS as president on 4 August 2000.

POLITICAL SYSTEM

The unicameral legislature, the National Assembly, has 51 members, directly elected for a five-year term. The president is elected by a two-thirds majority in the National Assembly, or if the required majority cannot be achieved, by a specially convened United Peoples' Conference, including district and local council representatives, for a five-year term of office.

HEAD OF STATE

President, Ronald Venetiaan, *inaugurated* 4 August 2000
Vice-President, Prime Minister, Jules Ajodhia

COUNCIL OF MINISTERS *as at July 2003*
Agriculture, Animal Husbandry and Fisheries, Geeta Gangaram Panday
Defence, Ronald Assen
Education and Community Development, Walter Sandriman
Finance, Humphrey Hildenberg
Foreign Affairs, Marie Levens
Health, Rakieb Khudabux
Internal Affairs, Trade and Industry, Urmila Joella-Sewnundum
Justice and Police, Siegfried Gilds
Labour and Technological Sciences, Clifford Marica
Natural Resources, Rudi Demon
Planning and Development Co-operation, Stanley Raghoebarsingh
Public Works, Dewanand Balesar
Regional Development, Romeo van Russel
Social Affairs and Housing, vacant
Transport, Communication and Tourism, Guno Castelen

EMBASSY OF THE REPUBLIC OF SURINAME
Alexander Gogelweg 2, NL-2517 JH The Hague, The Netherlands
Tel: (00 31) (070) 361 7445
Ambassador Extraordinary and Plenipotentiary, vacant
Chargé d'Affaires, Nell Stadwijk Kappel

BRITISH AMBASSADOR, HE Stephen Hiscock, apptd 2002 resident at Georgetown, Guyana

BRITISH CONSULATE, c/o VSH United Buildings, Van't Hogerhuystraat, 9-11 PO Box 1860, Paramaribo
Tel: (00 (597) 402558 / 402870 Email: united@sr.net

ECONOMY

Suriname has large timber resources. Rice and sugar cane are the main crops. Bauxite is mined, and is the principal export. Principal trading partners are the Netherlands, the USA and Norway.

In 2000 Suriname had a trade surplus of US$153 million and a current account surplus of US$32 million. Imports totalled US$246 million and exports US$399 million.

GNP – US$788 million (2000); US$1,890 per capita (2000)

GDP – US$758 million (2001); US$1,584 per capita (2000)

ANNUAL AVERAGE GROWTH OF GDP – –0.6 per cent (1998)

INFLATION RATE – 64.3 per cent (2000)

Trade with UK	2001	2002
Imports from UK	£8,020,000	£9,133,000
Exports to UK	19,102,000	3,707,000

SWAZILAND

Umbuso we Swatini / Kingdom of Swaziland

AREA – 6,704 sq. miles (17,364 sq. km). Neighbours: South Africa (north, west and south), Mozambique (east)

POPULATION – 1,104,343 (2001 estimate). The languages are English and Swazi

CAPITAL – Mbabane (population, 67,200, 2002 estimate)

MAJOR TOWNS – Manzini (73,000); Hlatikulu; Mhlume; Nhlangano; Pigg's Peak; Siteki

CURRENCY – Lilangeni (E) of 100 cents (South African currency is also in circulation). Swaziland is a member of the Common Monetary Area and its unit of currency *Emalangeni* (singular *Lilangeni*) has a par value with the South African rand

NATIONAL ANTHEM – Ingoma Yesive

NATIONAL DAY – 6 September (Independence Day)

NATIONAL FLAG – Blue with a wide crimson horizontal band bordered in yellow across the centre, bearing a shield and two spears horizontally

POPULATION GROWTH RATE – 0.3 per cent

POPULATION DENSITY – 56 per sq. km (1999)

ILLITERACY RATE – (m) 19.3 per cent; (f) 21.4 per cent (2000)

ENROLMENT (percentage of age group) – primary 91 per cent (1996); secondary 37 per cent (1996); tertiary 6 per cent (1996)

The broken mountainous Highveld along the western border, with an average altitude of 4,000 ft, is densely forested, mainly with conifers and eucalyptus; the Middleveld, averaging about 2,000 ft, is a mixed farming area including cotton and pineapples; and the Lowveld in the east was mainly scrubland until the introduction of large sugar-cane plantations. Four rivers, the Komati, Usutu, Mbuluzi and Ngwavuma, flow from west to east.

HISTORY AND POLITICS

The Kingdom of Swaziland came into being on 25 April 1967 under a self-government constitution and became an independent kingdom, headed by HM Sobhuza II, in membership of the Commonwealth on 6 September 1968.

An illegal general strike was held on 13–14 November 2000 to support a petition demanding the legalisation of political parties, the revocation of restrictive labour laws and the abolition of the right of traditional chiefs to force people to work without pay. The petition had been drawn up by the Swaziland Federation of Trade Unions and a group of illegal political parties. Several trade union and opposition leaders were arrested shortly before the strike took place and during the demonstrations. The findings of a Constitutional Review Commission published in August 2001, demonstrating that a majority of the population wanted to extend the already wide powers of the King, were opposed by pro-democracy groups.

POLITICAL SYSTEM
The King, assisted by his appointed Cabinet, holds considerable executive, legislative and judicial authority. There is a bicameral legislative body comprising a Senate and a House of Assembly. Each of the 55 *Tinkhundla* (administrative districts) directly elects one member to the House of Assembly. The King appoints ten members to the House of Assembly, making 65 in all, who then elect ten members of their own number to the Senate. To these are added 20 senators appointed by the King, bringing the full membership of the Senate to 30. In addition, the King appoints Commissions, who assess public opinion. There are also public gatherings, where any citizen can express an opinion. All political parties are banned.

The draft of a new constitution, which retained the non-party system but increased the protection of human rights, was published on 31 May 2003 as parliament was dissolved ahead of legislative elections due to be held in October 2003.

HEAD OF STATE
King of Swaziland, HM King Mswati III, *inaugurated* 25 April 1986

CABINET *as at July 2003*
Prime Minister, Dr Barnabas Sibusiso Dlamini
Deputy Prime Minister, Arthur Khoza
Agriculture and Co-operatives, Stella Lukhele
Economic Planning and Development, Prince Guduza Dhalamini
Education, Mntonzima Dlamini
Enterprise and Employment, Lufto Dlamini
Finance, Majozi Sithole
Foreign Affairs and Trade, Roy Fanourakis
Health and Social Welfare, Chief Sipho Shongwe
Home Affairs, Prince Sobandla Dlamini
Housing and Urban Development, Albert Shabangu
Justice and Constitutional Development, Ephraim Magwagwa Mdluli
Natural Resources and Energy, Mahlaba Mamba
Public Service and Information, Abedenigo Ntshangase
Public Works and Transport, John Carmichael
Tourism, Environment and Communications, Phetsile Dlamini

KINGDOM OF SWAZILAND HIGH COMMISSION
20 Buckingham Gate, London SW1E 6LB
Tel: 020-7630 6611

High Commissioner, HE Revd Percy Mngomezulu, apptd 1994

BRITISH HIGH COMMISSION
2nd Floor, Lilunga House, Gilfillan Street, Mbabane
Tel: (00 268) 404 2581/2/3/4
Email: enquiries.mbabane@fco.gov.uk
High Commissioner, HE David Reader, apptd 2001

ECONOMY
Manufacturing has replaced agriculture as the dominant sector, with timber, textiles and footwear the main products. Agricultural products include sugar cane and fruit. GDP growth rates have declined in the 1990s, partly as a result of lower growth rates in South Africa, on which the Swazi economy is strongly dependent. South Africa accounts for around 60 per cent of exports from Swaziland and about 85 per cent of imports.

In 2000 Swaziland had a trade deficit of US$111 million and a current account deficit of US$40 million. In 1996 imports totalled US$1,174 million and exports US$893 million.

GNP – US$1,451 million (2000); US$1,390 per capita (2000)
GDP – US$1,255 million (2001); US$1,507 per capita (2000)
ANNUAL AVERAGE GROWTH OF GDP – 3.5 per cent (1999)
INFLATION RATE – 11.8 per cent (2002)
TOTAL EXTERNAL DEBT – US$262 million (2000)

Trade with UK	2001	2002
Imports from UK	£4,314,000	£2,841,000
Exports to UK	33,651,000	34,576,000

COMMUNICATIONS
Swaziland's railway is 297 km long and connects with the Mozambique port of Maputo and the South African railway network to Richards Bay. A rail line to the north-west border provides a link to Komatipoort. There are 3,800 km of roads, of which 1,064 km are paved. Most passenger and goods traffic is carried by privately-owned motor transport services. There is an international airport at Manzini. Royal Swazi National Airways provides scheduled air services to southern and eastern Africa. International telecommunications and television services are provided through a satellite earth station.

SWEDEN

Konungariket Sverige – Kingdom of Sweden

AREA – 158,308 sq. miles (411,600 sq. km).
  Neighbours: Norway (west), Finland (east)
POPULATION – 8,833,000 (2001) The state religion is
  Lutheran Protestant, to which over 95 per cent
  officially adhere. The language is Swedish; in the
  north there are both Finnish- and Lapp-speaking
  communities
CAPITAL – ΨStockholm (population, 1,684,420, 2002
  estimate)
MAJOR CITIES – ΨGothenburg (Göteborg) (474,298);
  ΨMalmö (264,989); Uppsala (192,401), 2002
  estimates
CURRENCY – Swedish krona of 100 öre
NATIONAL ANTHEM – Du Gamla, Du Fria (Thou
  Ancient, Thou Freeborn)
NATIONAL DAY – 6 June (Day of the Swedish Flag)

NATIONAL FLAG — Yellow cross on a blue ground
LIFE EXPECTANCY (years) — 80 (2001)
POPULATION GROWTH RATE — 0.3 per cent
POPULATION DENSITY — 21 per sq. km (2001)

HISTORY AND POLITICS

Sweden takes its name from the Svear people who inhabited the region during the seventh century AD. The Swedes participated in the Viking expansion during the ninth to 11th centuries and established sovereignty over Finland in the 13th century. The Union of Kalmar (1397) brought Sweden and Norway under Danish rule. Northern Sweden regained its independence following a rebellion by noblemen in 1521 which resulted in the election to the Swedish throne of Gustav I of the house of Vasa.

Sweden's power climaxed in the 17th century under Gustavus II Adolf. The Danes were driven out of southern Sweden, the Baltic coast of Russia was seized and the Swedish army pushed into Germany after vanquishing the Catholic League. Swedish power waned in the 17th and 18th centuries. Finland was lost to Russia in 1809; Norway was ceded to Sweden under the Congress of Vienna (1814–15) but seceded in 1905.

Sweden remained neutral during both World Wars. Post-war party politics was dominated by Social Democrat-led coalitions which established a mixed economy and a generous welfare state. Right-wing and centrist parties held power from 1976–82 and 1991–4. Sweden applied for EU membership in July 1991 and acceded to the EU on 1 January 1995.

After the general election of 15 September 2002 the Swedish Social Democratic Labour Party (SAP) remained the largest party in the legislature with 144 seats. Prime Minister Goran Persson was unable to conclude an agreement on a coalition government and again led a minority SAP Cabinet.

POLITICAL SYSTEM

Sweden is a constitutional monarchy, with the monarch retaining purely ceremonial functions as head of state. Under the Act of Succession 1810 (with amendments) the throne is hereditary in the House of Bernadotte. The constitution is based upon the Instrument of Government 1974, which amended the 1810 Act and removed from the monarch the roles of appointing the prime minister and signing parliamentary bills into law. A 1979 amendment vested the succession in the monarch's eldest child irrespective of sex.

Executive power is vested in the prime minister and Council of Ministers. There is a unicameral legislature *(Riksdag)* of 349 members elected by universal suffrage on a proportional representation basis (with a 4 per cent threshold for representation) for four years. The Council of Ministers *(Statsråd)* is responsible to the *Riksdag.* Sweden is divided into 24 counties *(län)* and 288 municipalities *(kommun).*

HEAD OF STATE

HM The King of Sweden, Carl XVI Gustaf, KG, *born* 30 April 1946, *succeeded* 15 September 1973, *married* 19 June 1976 Fräulein Silvia Renate Sommerlath and has *issue,* Crown Princess Victoria; Prince Carl Philip Edmund Bertil, Duke of Värmland, *born* 13 May 1979; Princess Madeleine Thérèse Amelie Josephine, Duchess of Hälsingland and Gästrikland, *born* 10 June 1982

Heir, HRH Crown Princess Victoria Ingrid Alice Désirée, Duchess of Västergötland, *born* 14 July 1977

CABINET *as at July 2003*
Prime Minister, Göran Persson
Deputy Prime Minister, Margareta Winberg
Agriculture, Food and Fisheries, Consumer Equality Affairs, Ann-Christin Nyqvist
Children and Families, Berit Andnor
Co-ordination, Paer Nuder
Culture, Marita Ulvskog
Defence, Leni Björklund
Democracy and Integration, Mona Sahlin
Deputy Ministers, Lena Hallengren *(Education and Science);* Gunnar Lund *(Finance)*
Development Co-operation, Migration and Asylum Policy, Jan Karlsson
Education and Science, Schools and Adult Education, Thomas Östros
Environment, Lena Sommestad
Finance, Bosse Ringholm
Foreign Affairs, vacant
Health and Social Affairs, Lars Engqvist
Industry, Employment and Communications, Leif Pagrotsky
Infrastructure, Ulrica Messing
Justice, Thomas Bodström
Local Government and Housing, Lars-Erik Lövden
Public Health and Social Services, Morgan Johansson
Working Life, Hans Karlsson

EMBASSY OF SWEDEN
11 Montagu Place, London W1H 2AL
Tel: 020-7917 6400
Ambassador Extraordinary and Plenipotentiary, HE Mats Bergquist, CMG, apptd 1997

BRITISH EMBASSY
Skarpögatan 6–8, Box 27819, S-115 93 Stockholm
Tel: (00 46) (8) 671 3000
Ambassador Extraordinary and Plenipotentiary, HE John Grant, CMG, apptd 1999

CONSULATE-GENERAL — Gothenburg
CONSULATES — Malmö, Sundsvall

BRITISH COUNCIL DIRECTOR, Jim Potts
PO Box 27819, S-115 93 Stockholm
Tel: (00 46) (8) 671 3110 Email: info@britishcouncil.se

DEFENCE

The Army has 280 main battle tanks, 650 armoured personnel carriers and 1,189 armoured infantry fighting vehicles. The Navy has seven submarines and 45 patrol and coastal vessels at four bases. The Air Force has 203 combat aircraft.

Sweden has a policy of non-alignment in peace and neutrality in war, and it maintains a 'total defence' which includes peacetime organisations for civil, economic and psychological defence.
MILITARY EXPENDITURE — 1.9 per cent of GDP (2001)
MILITARY PERSONNEL — 33,900: Army 19,100, Navy 7,100, Air Force 7,700; Paramilitaries 600
CONSCRIPTION DURATION — Seven to 15 months

ECONOMY

Less than 10 per cent of the land area is farmland and less than 3 per cent of the labour force is employed in farming, although Sweden is more than 80 per cent self-sufficient in food.

Industrial prosperity is based on natural resources: forests, mineral deposits and water power. The forests cover about half the total land surface and sustain timber, finished wood products, pulp and paper milling industries. The mineral resources include iron ore, lead, zinc, sulphur, granite, marble, precious and heavy metals (the latter not exploited) and extensive deposits of low-grade uranium ore. Industries based on mining are important but it is the general engineering industry that provides 80 per cent of Sweden's exports, especially specialised machinery and systems, motor vehicles, aircraft, electrical and electronic equipment, pharmaceuticals, plastics and chemical industries.

Hydroelectricity supplies 15 per cent of energy needs. Sweden has no significant indigenous resources of conventional hydrocarbon fuels and relies for 50 per cent of its energy needs upon imported oil and coal.

Sweden experienced a deep recession between 1992 and 1994. The centre-right government, elected in 1991, introduced austerity measures and free market economic reforms. In October 1997 Sweden decided not to join European economic and monetary union (EMU) at the first stage; a referendum on EMU membership was held on 14 September 2003 (see Stop Press).

In 2001 there was a trade surplus of US$13,832 million and a current account surplus of US$6,696 million. Imports totalled US$62,670 million and exports US$75,139 million.

GNP – US$240,707 million (2000); US$27,140 per capita (2000)
GDP – US$210,108 million (2001); US$25,903 per capita (2000)
ANNUAL AVERAGE GROWTH OF GDP – 4.6 per cent (2000)
INFLATION RATE – 1 per cent (2000)
UNEMPLOYMENT – 4.7 per cent (2000)

TRADE
About 45 per cent of industrial output is exported, mainly in the form of cars, trucks, machinery, and electrical and communications equipment. Sweden conducts 70 per cent of its trade with EFTA and the rest of the EU.

Trade with UK	2001	2002
Imports from UK	£3,783,600,000	£3,642,700,000
Exports to UK	4,425,100,000	4,102,900,000

COMMUNICATIONS
The total length of railroads is 12,821 km. The road network is about 210,000 km in length. The mercantile marine amounted in 1996 to 2,950,000 gross tonnage. Regular domestic air traffic is maintained by the Scandinavian Airlines System and by Malmö Aviation. Regular European and intercontinental air traffic is maintained by the Scandinavian Airlines System. The Øresund Bridge connects Sweden to Denmark.

EDUCATION
The state system provides nine years' free and compulsory schooling from the age of seven to 16 in the comprehensive elementary schools. Around 95 per cent continue into further education of two to four years' duration in the upper secondary schools and a unified higher education system administered in six regional areas containing one of the universities: Uppsala

(founded 1477); Lund (1668); Stockholm (1878); Gothenburg (1887); Umeå (1963) and Linköping (1967). There are 40 institutions of higher education including three technical universities in Stockholm, Gothenburg and Luleå.
ENROLMENT (percentage of age group) – primary 100 per cent (1996); secondary 99 per cent (1996); tertiary 50 per cent (1996)

CULTURE
Swedish belongs, with Danish and Norwegian, to the North Germanic language group. Swedish literature dates back to King Magnus Eriksson, who codified the old Swedish provincial laws in 1350. With his translation of the Bible, Olaus Petri (1493–1552) formed the basis for the modern Swedish language. Literature flourished during the reign of Gustavus III, who founded the Swedish Academy in 1786. Notable Swedish writers include Almquist (1795–1866), Strindberg (1849–1912) and Lagerlöf (1858–1940), Nobel Prizewinner in 1909. Contemporary authors include Lagerquist (1891–1974), Nobel Laureate in 1951, Martinson (1904–78) and Johnson (1900–76), Nobel Laureates jointly in 1974. The Swedish scientist Alfred Nobel (1833–96) founded the Nobel Prizes for literature, science and peace.

SWITZERLAND

Schweizerische Eidgenossenschaft / Confédération Suisse / Confederazione Svizzera / Confederaziun Svizra – Swiss Confederation

AREA – 15,231 sq. miles (39,600 sq. km). Neighbours: France (west and north-west), Germany (north), Austria and Liechtenstein (east), Italy (south)
POPULATION – 7,170,000 (2001): 46.1 per cent Roman Catholic, 40 per cent Protestant, 5 per cent other religions and 8.9 per cent without religion. The official languages are German (the first language of 63.7 per cent), French (19.2 per cent), Italian (7.6 per cent) and Romansch (0.6 per cent). German is the dominant language in 19 of the 26 cantons; French in Fribourg, Jura, Geneva, Neuchatel, Valais and Vaud; Italian in Ticino; and Romansch in parts of Graubünden
CAPITAL – Bern (population, 317,367, 2001 estimate)
MAJOR CITIES – Basel (402,387); Geneva (452,248); Lausanne (286,106); Lucerne (180,427); Winterthur (118,578); Zurich (935,118), 1998
CURRENCY – Swiss franc of 100 rappen (or centimes)
NATIONAL ANTHEM – Schweizerpsalm (Swiss Psalm)
NATIONAL DAY – 1 August
NATIONAL FLAG – Square and red, bearing a couped white cross
LIFE EXPECTANCY (years) – 79 (2001)
POPULATION GROWTH RATE – 0.4 per cent
POPULATION DENSITY – 181 per sq. km (2001)
URBAN POPULATION – 67 per cent (2001)

Switzerland is the most mountainous country in Europe. The Alps, from 1,700 to 4,634 m (5,000 to 15,217 ft) in height, occupy its southern and eastern frontiers and the chief part of its interior; the Jura mountains rise in the north-west. The Alps occupy 60 per cent, and the Jura mountains 12 per cent of the country. The highest peak, Mont Blanc, Pennine Alps (4,807 m / 15,782 ft) is partly in France and partly in Italy; Monte Rosa (4,634 m/15,217 ft) and Matterhorn (4,478 m/14,780 ft) are partly in Switzerland and partly in Italy. The highest wholly Swiss peaks are Finsteraarhorn (4,274 m/14,026 ft), Aletschhorn (4,195/13,711), Jungfrau (4,158/13,671), Mönch (4,099/13,456), Eiger (3,970/13,040), Schreckhorn (4,078/13,385), and Wetterhorn (3,701/12,150) in the Bernese Alps, and Dom (4,545/14,918), Weisshorn (4,506/14,803) and Breithorn (4,165/13,685). The Swiss lakes include Lakes Maggiore, Zurich, Lucerne, Neuchâtel, Geneva, Constance, Thun, Zug, Lugano, Brienz and the Walensee.

HISTORY AND POLITICS

The Swiss confederation was formed as an alliance of three cantons in 1291 and achieved full independence under the Peace of Westphalia (1648), having been a province of the Holy Roman Empire since 1033. French Revolutionary forces seized Switzerland in 1789 and named it the Helvetic Republic. Independence was not restored until the Congress of Vienna (1815), which also joined Geneva, Neuchatel and Valais to the confederation and instituted perpetual neutrality in foreign affairs. In 1847 a war broke out between the Protestant and Roman Catholic cantons, the latter being defeated. A new constitution was adopted in 1848 which enhanced the powers of the central government.

Proportional representation was introduced in 1919 and ensured coalition governments throughout the 20th century. Women were given the vote in 1971.

On 24 October 1999, the ruling coalition, comprising the Social Democrats, the Swiss People's Party, the Radical Democrats and the Christian Democrats, in power since 1959, was re-elected with 173 of the 200 seats in the National Council. Legislative elections were scheduled for 19 October 2003.

FOREIGN RELATIONS

The Federal Council voted in 1992 to apply for European Community membership. The European Economic Area (EEA) Treaty between the EC and EFTA, which extends the provisions of the EC single internal market to EFTA states, was rejected in a national referendum on 6 December 1992. Switzerland is consequently the only EFTA state outside the EEA. On 21 May 2000, a referendum on seven bilateral agreements with the EU, which would progressively reduce trade barriers and allow the free movement of people between Switzerland and the EU, was passed, with 67.2 per cent of voters in favour.

Following a referendum held on 3 March 2002 Switzerland formally became a full member of the UN on 10 September 2002.

POLITICAL SYSTEM

The federal government consists of the Federal Assembly of two chambers, a National Council *(Nationalrat)* of 200 members, and a States Council *(Ständerat)* of 46 members (two from each canton and one from each demi-canton). Members of the National Council are elected for four years, elections taking place in October. The executive power is in the hands of a Federal Council *(Bundesrat)* of seven members, elected for four years by the Federal Assembly and presided over by the president of the Confederation. Each year the Federal Assembly elects from the Federal Council the president and the vice-president. Not more than one person from the same canton may be elected a member of the Federal Council; however, there is a tradition that Italian- and French-speaking areas should between them be represented on the Federal Council by at least two members.

CONFEDERAL STRUCTURE

There are 23 cantons, three of which are subdivided, making 26 in all. Each canton has its own government. The main language in 19 of the cantons is German; in the others it is French (*) or Italian (†).

Canton	Area (sq. km)	Population (2001)
Aargau	1,404	549,500
Appenzell-Ausserrhoden	243	53,200
Appenzell-Innerrhoden	173	15,100
Basel-Country (Basel-Landschaft)	517	262,300
Basel-Town (Basel-Stadt)	37	187,600
Bern	5,959	946,100
*Fribourg	1,671	239,200
*Geneva	282	413,800
Glarus	685	38,500
Graubünden/Grischun	7,105	187,500
*Jura	838	68,900
Lucerne (Luzern)	1,493	349,600
*Neuchatel	803	166,600
Nidwalden	276	38,400
Obwalden	491	32,700
St Gallen	2,026	452,200
Schaffhausen	299	73,200
Schwyz	908	133,000
Solothurn	791	245,100
Thurgau	991	227,700
†Ticino	2,812	312,200
Uri	1,077	35,000
*Valais	5,225	277,600
*Vaud	3,212	625,000
Zug	239	101,000
Zurich	1,729	1,227,900

FEDERAL COUNCIL *as at July 2003*
President of the Swiss Confederation (2003), Interior, Pascal Couchepin (FDP)
Vice-President (2003), Ruth Metzler-Arnold (CVP)
Federal Chancellor, Annemarie Huber-Hotz (FDP)
Defence, Civil Protection and Sport, Samuel Schmid (SVP)
Finance, Kaspar Villiger (FDP)
Foreign Affairs, Micheline Calmy-Rey (SPS)
Justice and Police, Ruth Metzler-Arnold (CVP)
Public Economy, Joseph Deiss (CVP)
Transport, Communications and Energy, Moritz Leuenberger (SPS)

CVP Christian Democratic People's Party; SPS Social Democratic Party; FDP Radical Democratic Party; SVP Swiss People's Party

EMBASSY OF SWITZERLAND
16–18 Montagu Place, London W1H 2BQ
Tel: 020-7616 6000
Ambassador Extraordinary and Plenipotentiary, HE Bruno Max Spinner, apptd 2000

BRITISH EMBASSY
Thunstrasse 50, CH-3005 Bern
Tel: (00 41) (31) 359 7700
Email: info@britain-in-switzerland.ch
Ambassador Extraordinary and Plenipotentiary, HE Basil Eastwood, CMG, apptd 2001

CONSULATE-GENERAL – Geneva
CONSULAR OFFICES – Basel, Bern (at Embassy),
Lugano, Montreux, Valais, Zurich

BRITISH COUNCIL DIRECTOR, Caroline Morrissey
Sennweg 2, PO Box 532, CH-3000 Bern 9
Tel: (00 31) 301 1473 Email: britishcouncil@britishcouncil.ch

DEFENCE
The Army has 556 main battle tanks, 1,257 armoured
personnel carriers and 435 armoured infantry fighting
vehicles. The Air Force has 138 combat aircraft.
MILITARY EXPENDITURE – 1.2 per cent of GDP (2001)
MILITARY PERSONNEL – 3,500 active (351,200 to be
mobilised: Army 320,400, Air Force 30,600);
Paramilitaries 280,000
CONSCRIPTION DURATION – 15 weeks, then ten
refresher courses

ECONOMY
Agriculture is followed chiefly in the valleys and the
central plateau, where cereals, flax, hemp, wine and
tobacco are produced, and fruits and vegetables are
grown. Dairying and stock-raising are the principal
industries; there are 293,949 hectares of open arable
land, 115,933 hectares of cultivated grassland and
626,799 hectares of natural grassland and pasture. The
forests cover about 30 per cent of the whole surface. The
chief manufacturing industries comprise engineering and
electrical engineering, metalworking, chemicals and
pharmaceuticals, textiles, watchmaking, woodworking,
foodstuffs, publishing and footwear. Banking, insurance
and tourism are major industries.
GNP – US$273,829 million (2000); US$38,140 per
capita (2000)
GDP – US$247,362 million (2001); US$33,394 per
capita (2000)
ANNUAL AVERAGE GROWTH OF GDP – 3.4 per cent
(2000)
INFLATION RATE – 1.6 per cent (2000)
UNEMPLOYMENT – 2.7 per cent (2000)

TRADE
The principal imports are machinery, chemicals, vehicles,
metals, textiles, precision instruments, watches and
jewellery. The principal exports are machinery, chemicals,
precision instruments, watches and jewellery, and metals.
In 2000 Switzerland had a trade surplus of US$389
million and a current account surplus of US$32,542
million. In 2001 imports totalled US$77,070 million
and exports US$78,066 million.

Trade with UK	2001	2002
Imports from UK	£3,761,730,000	£3,303,852,000
Exports to UK	4,830,993,000	4,935,485,000

COMMUNICATIONS
There are 71,086 km of roads, of which 1,613 km are
national highways; a further 200 km of motorway
construction is expected to be completed by 2010.
Railway tracks comprise 2,910 km, almost all of which is
electrified.

EDUCATION
Education is controlled by cantonal and communal
authorities and is free and compulsory from age seven to
16. Special schools make a feature of commercial and
technical instruction. Universities are Basel (founded
1460), Bern (1834), Fribourg (1889), Geneva (1873),

Lausanne (1890), Zürich (1832), and Neuchatel (1909),
the technical universities of Lausanne and Zurich and the
economics university of St Gall.
ENROLMENT (percentage of age group) – primary
97 per cent (1997); secondary 100 per cent (1997);
tertiary 33 per cent (1997)

SYRIA

*Al-Jumhūriyya Al-'Arabiyya as-Sūriyya – Syrian Arab
Republic*

AREA – 70,692 sq. miles (183,800 sq. km). Neighbours:
Lebanon (west), Israel and Jordan (south-west), Iraq
(east), Turkey (north)
POPULATION – 16,610,000 (2001): mostly Muslim.
Arabic is the principal language, but Kurdish, Turkish
and Armenian are spoken among significant minorities
and a few villages still speak Aramaic, the language
spoken by Christ and the Apostles. English has taken
over from French as the main foreign language
CAPITAL – Damascus (Dimashq) (population, 1,549,000,
1994)
MAJOR CITIES – Halab (Aleppo) (1,542,000); Hamah
(273,000); Hims (558,000); ΨAl-Ladhiqiyah, the
principal port (303,000), 1994 estimates
CURRENCY – Syrian pound (S$) of 100 piastres
NATIONAL ANTHEM – Humata Al-Diyari Alaykum
Salaam (Defenders Of The Realm On You Be Peace)
NATIONAL DAY – 17 April
NATIONAL FLAG – Red over white over black horizontal
bands, with two green stars on central white band
LIFE EXPECTANCY (years) – 71 (2001)
POPULATION GROWTH RATE – 2.7 per cent
POPULATION DENSITY – 90 per sq. km (2001)
URBAN POPULATION – 52 per cent (2001)

The Orontes flows northwards from the Lebanon range
across the northern boundary to Antakya (Antioch,
Turkey). The Euphrates crosses the northern boundary
near Jerablus and flows through north-eastern Syria to
the boundary of Iraq.
The region is rich in historical remains. Damascus
(Dimishq ash-Sham) is said to be the oldest continuously
inhabited city in the world (although Halab disputes this
claim), having existed as a city for over 4,000 years. The
city contains the Omayed Mosque, the Tomb of Saladin,
and the 'street which is called Straight' (Acts 9:11), while
to the north-east is the Roman outpost of Dmeir and
further east is Palmyra. On the Mediterranean coast at
Amrit are ruins of the Phoenician town of Marath, and of
Crusaders' fortresses at Markab, Sahyoun, and Krak des
Chevaliers. One of the oldest alphabets in the world has
been discovered at Ugarit (Ras Shamra), a Phoenician
village near Al-Ladhiqiyah. Hittite cities dating from
2000 to 1500 BC, have been explored on the west bank
of the Euphrates at Jerablus and Kadesh.

HISTORY AND POLITICS
Once part of the Ottoman Empire, Syria came under
French mandate after the First World War. Syria became
an independent republic during the Second World War;
the first independently elected parliament met in August
1943, but foreign troops were in occupation until April
1946. Syria remained an independent republic until
1958, when it became part, with Egypt, of the United
Arab Republic. It seceded from the United Arab Republic
in September 1961.
Elections   to   the   250-seat   People's   Council   in

November 1998 resulted in the National Progressive Front retaining all of its 167 seats unchallenged. This seven-party bloc is dominated by the Ba'ath Party, its allies being the Arab Socialist Union, Socialist Unionist Party, Arab Socialist Movement, Syrian Communist Party and Socialist Unionist Democratic Party. Independents won 83 seats. Mahmoud Zubi, who had been prime minister since 1987, resigned on 7 March 2000 and was replaced by Mustafa Mohamad Miro on 13 March. Zubi committed suicide on 21 May following his expulsion from the Ba'ath Party amid allegations of corruption.

President Hafez al-Assad, who had seized power in a military coup in 1970 and been elected president in 1971 and re-elected in 1978, 1985, 1992 and 1999, died on 10 June 2000. On 18 June, his son, Bashar al-Assad, was unanimously elected as leader by the Ba'ath Party; on 27 June the legislature nominated him for the presidency, and on 10 July he was elected president, gaining 97.29 per cent of the votes cast. Legislative elections took place on 5 March 2003, in which the Ba'ath Party and its allies retained its 167 seats and Independents won 83 seats.

POLITICAL SYSTEM

The constitution promulgated in 1973 declares that Syria is a democratic, popular socialist state, and that the Arab Socialist Renaissance (Ba'ath) Party, which has been the ruling party since 1963, is the leading party in the state and society. The president is head of state and is elected by parliament for a seven-year term. The legislature, the *Majlis al-Chaab* (People's Council) has 250 members directly elected for a four-year term. The only candidates permitted for elections are from parties allied with the Ba'ath Party or Independents.

HEAD OF STATE

President, Bashar al-Assad, *elected by parliament* 27 June 2000, *approved by referendum* 10 July 2000
Vice-Presidents, Abdel Halim Khaddam; Zuheir Masharqa

CABINET *as at September 2003*
Prime Minister, Mohammed Naji al-Otari
The cabinet resigned on 10 September 2003.

EMBASSY OF THE SYRIAN ARAB REPUBLIC
8 Belgrave Square, London SW1X 8PH
Tel: 020-7245 9012
Ambassador Extraordinary and Plenipotentiary, Mouafak Nassar, apptd 2002

BRITISH EMBASSY
Kotob Building, 11 Mohammad Kurd Ali Street, Malki, Damascus (PO Box 37)
Tel: (00 963) (11) 373 9241/2/3/7
Ambassador Extraordinary and Plenipotentiary, HE Peter Ford, apptd 2003

BRITISH COUNCIL DIRECTOR, Patrick Brazier
Maysaloun Street, Shalaan, PO Box 33105, Damascus
Tel: (00 963) (11) 331 0631
Email: general.enquiries@sy.britishcouncil.org

DEFENCE

The Army has 4,700 main battle tanks, 1,600 armoured personnel carriers and 2,700 armoured infantry fighting vehicles. The Navy has two frigates, 18 patrol and coastal vessels and 16 armed helicopters at three bases. The Air Force has 611 combat aircraft and 90 armed helicopters.

Syria maintains a force of some 18,000 men in Lebanon; 1,037 UN troops are deployed on the Golan Heights.
MILITARY EXPENDITURE – 10.9 per cent of GDP (2001)
MILITARY PERSONNEL – 319,000: Army 215,000, Navy 4,000, Air Force 40,000, Air Defence Command 60,000; Paramilitaries 108,000
CONSCRIPTION DURATION – 30 months

ECONOMY

Large areas are under cultivation in the north-east of the country as a result of irrigation from the Thawra dam. There are an increasing number of light assembly plants as Syria's industrialisation programme develops. Leather goods, wool and silk, textiles, vegetable oil, soap, sugar, plastics and metal utensils are produced. Oil production is proceeding in the region of Deir ez Zor. A pipeline has been built to the Mediterranean port of Banias, via Hims. Two oil refineries are in production at Hims and Banias. Oil production in 2002 was 28,600,000 tonnes. Syria also has gas reserves, deposits of phosphate and rock salt, and produces asphalt.
GNP – US$15,146 million (2000); US$940 per capita (2000)
GDP – US$17,938 million (2001); US$2,721 per capita (2000)
ANNUAL AVERAGE GROWTH OF GDP – –1.8 per cent (1999)
INFLATION RATE – –0.4 per cent (2000)
TOTAL EXTERNAL DEBT – US$21,657 million (2000)

TRADE

The principal imports are manufactures, metals and metal goods, machinery, foodstuffs and transport equipment. Principal exports include oil and oil derivatives, agricultural products (chiefly fruit and vegetables, cotton and wheat) and textiles.

In 2000 Syria had a trade deficit of US$1,423 million and a current account surplus of US$1,062 million. In 2000 imports totalled US$16,706 million and exports US$19,260 million.

Trade with UK	2001	2002
Imports from UK	£66,695,000	£83,946,000
Exports to UK	88,087,000	117,525,000

COMMUNICATIONS

A railway track has been opened connecting Hims with Damascus and a track links Hims, Hamah, Halab, Deir ez Zor and Qamishliye to the Iraqi frontier. All the principal towns in the country are connected by roads which vary from modern dual carriageways to narrow country lanes. An internal air service operates between all major towns. The main international airport is at Damascus.

EDUCATION

Education is under state control. Elementary education is free at state schools and is compulsory from the age of seven. Secondary education is not compulsory and is free only at the state schools. There are universities at Damascus, Halab, Tishrin, Al-Ladhiqiyah and the Ba'ath University, Hims.
ILLITERACY RATE – (m) 11.7 per cent; (f) 39.5 per cent (2000)
ENROLMENT (percentage of age group) – primary 100 per cent (1997); secondary 43 per cent (1997); tertiary 16 per cent (1997)

TAIWAN

Chung-hua Min-kuo – Republic of China

AREA – 13,914 sq. miles (36,175 sq. km)
POPULATION – 22,350,000 (2001). Mandarin Chinese
  has been the official language since 1949. Now
  Taiwanese, spoken by 85 per cent of the population,
  is growing in importance
CAPITAL – Taipei (population, 2,646,474, 2001
  estimate)
MAJOR CITIES – ΨKaohsiung (1,499,457); Taichung
  (983,694); Tainan (740,846), 2001 estimates
CURRENCY – New Taiwan dollar (NT$) of 100 cents
NATIONAL ANTHEM – San Min Chu I (Our Aim Shall
  Be To Found A Free Land)
NATIONAL DAY – 10 October
NATIONAL FLAG – Red, with blue quarter at top next
  staff, bearing a 12-point white sun
LIFE EXPECTANCY (years) – 77 (2001)
POPULATION GROWTH RATE – 0.8 per cent
POPULATION DENSITY – 618 per sq. km

HISTORY AND POLITICS

Settled for centuries by the Chinese, the island was ceded
by China to Japan in 1895 and remained part of the
Japanese empire until Japan's defeat in 1945. Nationalist
Kuomintang (KMT) leader Gen. Chiang Kai-shek
withdrew to Taiwan in 1949, towards the end of the war
against the Communist regime in mainland China, after
which the territory continued under his presidency until
his death in 1975. He was succeeded as president by his
son Gen. Chiang Ching-kuo who ruled until his death in
1988, when Vice-President Lee Teng-hui was appointed
president. Martial law was lifted in 1987 after 38 years.

In 1991, President Lee announced that the 'period of
Communist rebellion' on the Chinese mainland was over,
recognising *de facto* the People's Republic of China. The
announcement also ended emergency measures which
had frozen political life on Taiwan since 1949. In
1991–2 power shifted away from mainlanders to native
Taiwanese with the forcible retirement of the 'Senior
Parliamentarians' who had retained their seats since
being elected on the mainland in 1948. The new
parliament, the Legislative Yuan, gained control of the
budget, of law-making and of the appointment of the
prime minister.

President Chen Shui-bian of the Democratic
Progressive Party won the presidential election on
18 March 2000 with 39 per cent of the vote, ahead of
two KMT candidates, and took office on 20 May. In the
general election to the Legislative Yuan on 1 December
2001, the Democratic Progressive Party (DPP) won
87 of the 225 seats; the KMT won 68 seats; the People
First Party won 46 seats; the Taiwan Solidarity Union
won 13 seats; independents and minor parties won
11 seats. President Chen Shui-bian named Yu Shyi Kun
as premier and he took office on 1 February 2002.
Efforts to create a coalition government were rebuffed by
the KMT and the Executive Yuan comprises members of
the DPP and independents.

FOREIGN RELATIONS

Taiwan (Republic of China) held China's seat on the UN
Security Council until 25 October 1971 when it was
replaced by the People's Republic of China. The Republic
of China is recognised by less than 30 states.

Direct tourism, trade and communications links
between mainland China and the Taiwanese islands of
Kinmen and Matsu were inaugurated on 2 January 2001,
the first direct links between Taiwan and the People's
Republic of China since 1949.

POLITICAL SYSTEM

The legislature is bicameral. The Legislative Yuan has
225 members, 176 elected and 49 appointed
proportionately by party, and serves a three-year term.
Constitutional reforms passed by the Legislative Yuan in
1994 provide for the president and vice-president to be
directly elected for four-year terms (previously the
president was elected by parliament). The National
Assembly, which had previously been an elected upper
chamber, voted on 24 April 2000 to transform itself into
a largely ceremonial body, to be convened when
necessary to consider constitutional amendments, the
impeachment of a president, or territorial changes.
Members will be appointed proportionally by the parties
in the Legislative Yuan.

HEAD OF STATE

President, Chen Shui-bian, *elected* 18 March 2000,
  sworn in 20 May 2000
Vice-President, Annette Lu

EXECUTIVE YUAN *as at July 2003*

Prime Minister, Yu Shyi-kun
*Deputy Prime Minister, Chair of Council for Economic
  Planning and Development,* Lin Hsin-yi
Administrator, Environmental Protection Administration,
  Hao Lung-bin
Chairs of Commissions, Ouyang Min-shen *(Atomic Energy
  Commission);* Hwang Tzong-leh *(Fair Trade);* Hsu
  Chih-hsiung *(Mongolian and Tibetan Affairs);* Lin
  Feng-mei *(National Youth Commission);* Chang Fu-mei
  (Overseas Chinese Affairs); Lin Chia-cheng *(Research,
  Development and Evaluation);* Teng Tzu-lin *(Veterans'
  Affairs)*
Chairs of Councils, Lee Ching-lung *(Agriculture);* Tchen
  Yu-chiou *(Cultural Affairs);* Yeh Chu-lan *(Hakka
  Affairs);* Chen Chien-nien *(Indigenous People);* Chen
  Chu *(Labour Affairs);* Tsai Ing-wen *(Mainland Affairs);*
  Wei Che-ho *(National Science Council);* Lin Te-fu
  (Physical Fitness and Sports)
*Chair of the Research, Development and Evaluation
  Commission,* Lin Chia-cheng
Directors, Wang Chun *(Coast Guard Administration);* Tu
  Cheng-sheng *(National Palace Museum)*
Directors-General, Hale S. C. Liu *(Budget, Accounting and
  Statistics);* Lee Yi-yang *(Central Personnel
  Administration);* Arthur Iap *(Government Information
  Office)*
Economic Affairs, Lin Yi-fu
Education, Huang Jung-tsun
Finance, Lin Chuan
Foreign Affairs, Eugene Chien
Governor of the Central Bank of China, Perng Fai-nan
Health, Chen Chien-jen
Interior, Yu Cheng-hsien
Justice, Chen Ding-nan
National Defence, Tang Yian-min
Secretary-General of the Executive Yuan, Liu Shyh-fang
Transport and Communications, Lin Ling-san
Without Portfolio, Chen Chi-nan; Hu Sheng-cheng;
  Huang Hwe-chen; Kuo yao-chi *(Chair of Public
  Construction Commission);* Lin Sheng-feng; Tsai
  Ching-yen; Yeh Jiunn-rong

BRITISH COUNCIL DIRECTOR, Susana Galvan *(acting)*
7-F-1, British Trade and Cultural Office, Education and
Cultural Section, 99 Jen Ai Road, Section 2, Taipei 100
Tel: (00 886) (2) 2192 7050
Email: inquiries@britishcouncil.org.tw
There is a regional office in Kaohsiung

DEFENCE
The Army has 926 main battle tanks, 950 armoured
personnel carriers and 225 armoured infantry fighting
vehicles. The Navy has four submarines, 11 destroyers,
21 frigates, 59 patrol and coastal vessels, 32 combat
aircraft and 20 armed helicopters at four bases. The Air
Force has 479 combat aircraft.
MILITARY EXPENDITURE – 3.7 per cent of GDP (2001)
MILITARY PERSONNEL – 370,000: Army 240,000,
   Navy 62,000, Air Force 68,000; Paramilitaries 26,650
CONSCRIPTION DURATION – 22 months

ECONOMY
Taiwan has transformed itself from a mainly agricultural
country to a highly developed industrial economy.
The industrial base has expanded to include steel,
shipbuilding, chemicals, cement, machinery, electrical
equipment and textiles. In 1999 agriculture contributed
2.6 per cent of GDP, industry 33 per cent and services
64 per cent.
   The soil is very fertile, producing sugar, rice, sweet
potatoes, tea, fruit and tobacco. Livestock provided a
third of the value of Taiwan's agricultural produce in
1996. Taiwan produces one-tenth of its coal needs and
some natural gas. The principal seaports are Keelung and
Kaohsiung situated in the north and south of the island
respectively.

TRADE
The principal exports are electronic goods, machinery,
metal goods, textiles, plastic products, and toys and
games. The main imports are oil, chemicals, machinery
and natural resources. The main trading partners are the
USA, Japan, Hong Kong, Germany, and the Republic of
Korea.
   In 2001 imports totalled US$107,274 million and
exports US$122,505 million.

Trade with UK	2001	2002
Imports from UK	£881,251,000	£853,718,000
Exports to UK	2,891,871,000	2,474,824,000

TAJIKISTAN

Çumhurii Toçikiston – Republic of Tajikistan

AREA – 55,251 sq. miles (143,100 sq. km). Neighbours:
   Uzbekistan (north-west), Kyrgyzstan (north-east),
   China (east), Afghanistan (south)
POPULATION – 6,578,681 (2001 estimate): 62 per cent
   Tajik, 23 per cent Uzbek and 8 per cent Russian, with
   smaller numbers of Tatars, Kyrgyz, Germans and
   Ukrainians. The people are predominantly Sunni
   Muslim. The main languages are Tajik, Uzbek and
   Russian. Tajik is close to the Farsi spoken in Iran
CAPITAL – Dushanbe (population, 562,000 2000
   estimate)
CURRENCY – Somoni of 100 dirams
NATIONAL DAY – 9 September (Independence Day)

NATIONAL FLAG – Three horizontal stripes of red, white
   and green with the white of double width and charged
   with a crown and seven stars, all in gold
POPULATION GROWTH RATE – 1.7 per cent
POPULATION DENSITY – 44 per sq. km (1999)
MILITARY EXPENDITURE – 1.7 per cent of GDP (2001)
MILITARY PERSONNEL – Army 6,000; Paramilitaries
   1,200
CONSCRIPTION DURATION – Two years
ILLITERACY RATE – (m) 0.4 per cent; (f) 1.2 per cent
   (2000)
ENROLMENT (percentage of age group) – tertiary
   20 per cent (1997)

HISTORY AND POLITICS
The area that is now Tajikistan was conquered by
Alexander the Great in the fourth century BC and
remained under Greek and Greco-Persian rule for 200
years, until the Kingdom of Kusha was established, based
on Bacharia (Bukhara). Tajikistan was invaded by both
the Arabs and the Samanid Persians between the seventh
and ninth centuries AD. The cities of Bukhara and
Samarkand were two of the most important cultural and
educational centres in the Islamic world. The Tajiks lived
under the control of various feudal emirates until the area
was subsumed within the Russian Empire in 1868. At the
time of the Russian revolution in 1917 the central Asian
emirates attempted to re-establish their independence.
Soviet power was re-established in northern Tajikistan by
1 April 1918, when the Turkestan Soviet Socialist
Republic was formed, and the Bukhara emirate was
overthrown by Soviet forces in 1920. In 1924 the
Tajikistan Autonomous Soviet Socialist Republic was
formed as part of the Uzbek Republic before Tajikistan
was given full republican status within the Soviet Union
in 1929.
   Tajikistan declared independence from the Soviet
Union on 9 September 1991. The Islamic-Democratic
alliance formed a government in September 1992 but
civil war broke out as forces loyal to the former
Communist regime rebelled against the new government.
By early November, pro-Communist forces controlled
virtually all the country and the Supreme Soviet installed
Emomaly Rakhmonov as its Speaker and head of state.
   A cease-fire in October 1994 allowed presidential and
parliamentary elections to be held, which were won by
Emomaly Rakhmonov and the ruling (former
Communist) People's Democratic Party of Tajikistan
(HDKT), although the elections were boycotted by most
opposition groups. Fighting restarted in early 1995. A
peace agreement was signed in December 1996 which
provided for the formation of a National Reconciliation
Commission (NRC), a general amnesty and an exchange
of prisoners. The agreement has held, although there
have been sporadic outbreaks of violence since it was
signed. A referendum was held on constitutional
amendments demanded by the opposition on 26
September 1999 and was approved by the electorate. It
amended the 1994 constitution to create a bicameral
legislature, extended the president's term of office from
five to seven years and allowed the formation of religious
political parties. Legislation to allow the formation of a
bicameral legislature was passed in December 1999.
   Presidential elections which took place on
6 November 1999 resulted in a landslide victory for the
incumbent President Rakhmonov, who gained over
96 per cent of the vote in a poll which the Organisation
for Security and Co-operation in Europe had refused to

monitor due to restrictions imposed on candidates and political parties. Oqil Oqilov was named as prime minister on 20 December when President Rakhmonov announced a new government. Following an election to the Assembly of Representatives on 27 February and 12 March 2000, the HDKT won 30 of the 63 seats, gaining 64.5 per cent of the vote; the Communist Party won 13 seats, the Islamic Renaissance Party won 2 and independent candidates won 15 seats, with three seats remaining vacant.

POLITICAL SYSTEM

Under the 1999 constitutional amendments, the president may serve only a single seven-year term, but further constitutional amendments approve by referendum in June 2003 permit the current incumbent, Emomaly Rakhmonov, to stand for two further terms after his current term finishes in 2006. The new bicameral legislature consists of a 63-seat *Majlisi Mamoyandogan* (Assembly of Representatives), which is directly elected and serves a five-year term, and the *Majlisi Milli* (National Assembly), which has 33 members, 25 of which are elected for a five-year term by five regional assemblies and eight are appointed by the president. Administratively Tajikistan is divided into two regions and one autonomous region.

HEAD OF STATE

President, Emomaly Sharifovich Rakhmonov, *elected by Supreme Soviet* 19 November 1992, *elected* 6 November 1994, *re-elected* 6 November 1999

COUNCIL OF MINISTERS *as at July 2003*

Prime Minister, Akil Akilov

First Deputy Prime Minister, Relations with CIS States, Haji Akbar Turajonzoda

Deputy Prime Ministers, Kozidavlat Koimdodov; Nigina Sharapova; Zokir Vazirov; Maj.-Gen. Saidamir Zuhurov; Asadullo Ghulomov *(Energy)*

Agriculture, Tursun Rahmatov

Chairs of State Committees, Matlubkhon Davlatov *(Administration of Affairs of State);* Ismat Eshmirzoyev *(Construction and Architecture);* Sadullo Khayrulloyev *(Land Resources and Reclamation);* Salomsho Muhabbatov *(Oil and Gas);* Sayfullo Rahimov *(Radio and Television)*

Communications, Said Zuvaidov

Culture, Karomatullo Olimov

Defence, Col.-Gen. Sherali Khayrulloyev

Economics and Trade, Hakim Soliyev

Education, Safarali Radzhabov

Emergency Situations and Civil Defence, Maj.-Gen. Mirzo Zieyev

Energy, Abdullo Yorov

Environmental Protection, Usmonqul Shokirov

Finance, Safarali Najmiddinov

Foreign Affairs, Talbak Nazarov

Grain, Bekmurod Urokov

Health, Nusratullo Faizulloyev

Industry, Zayd Saidov

Interior, Khumdin Sharipov

Justice, Halifabobo Hamidov

Labour, Employment and Social Welfare, Mahmadsho Ilolov

Land Improvement and Water Economy, Abduqohir Nazirov

Security, Khayruddin Abdurahimov

State Revenue and Tax Collection, Ghulomjon Boboyev

Transport and Roads, Abdujalol Salimov

HONORARY CONSULATE

33 Ovington Square, London SW3 1LJ

Honorary Consul, Benjamin Brahms

BRITISH EMBASSY

43 Lufti Street, Dushanbe

Tel: (00) (992) (91) 901 5078

Ambassador Extraordinary and Plenipotentiary, HE Michael Smith, apptd 2001

ECONOMY

In January 1994 Tajikistan entered into a monetary union with Russia. The Tajik rouble replaced the Russian rouble in May 1995. The economy is being reformed and privatisation undertaken in order to attract foreign investment.

Agriculture is the major sector of the economy, concentrating on cotton-growing and cattle-breeding. Tajikistan also has rich mineral deposits of mercury, lead, zinc, oil, gold and uranium. Industry specialises in the production of clothing and textiles.

A new currency, the somoni, was introduced on 30 October 2000, replacing the Tajik rouble.

GNP – US$1,109 million (2000); US$180 per capita (2000)

GDP – US$1,058 million (2001); US$143 per capita (2000)

ANNUAL AVERAGE GROWTH OF GDP – 8.3 per cent (2000)

INFLATION RATE – 12 per cent (2001)

TOTAL EXTERNAL DEBT – US$1,170 million (2000)

Trade with UK	2001	2002
Imports from UK	£619,000	£707,000
Exports to UK	1,226,000	1,581,000

TANZANIA

Jamhuri ya Muungano wa Tanzania/United Republic of Tanzania

AREA – 339,846 sq. miles (883,600 sq. km).
  Neighbours: Kenya and Uganda (north), Mozambique (south), Malawi and Zambia (south-west), Rwanda, Burundi and the Democratic Republic of Congo (west)

POPULATION – 35,965,000 (2001). Africans form a large majority, with European, Asian, and other non-African minorities. The African population consists mostly of tribes of mixed Bantu race. The official languages are Swahili and English

CAPITAL – Dodoma (population, 1,502,344, 1995)

MAJOR CITIES – ΨDar es Salaam (1,360,850), the economic and administrative centre; Mbeya (152,844); Mwanza (223,013); ΨTanga (187,155), 1988 estimates

CURRENCY – Tanzanian shilling of 100 cents

NATIONAL ANTHEM – Mungu Ibariki Afrika (God Bless Africa)

NATIONAL DAY – 26 April (Union Day)

NATIONAL FLAG – Green (above) and blue; divided by diagonal black stripe bordered by gold, running from bottom (next staff) to top (in fly)

LIFE EXPECTANCY (years) – 51 (2001)

POPULATION GROWTH RATE – 2.9 per cent

POPULATION DENSITY – 41 per sq. km (2001)

MILITARY EXPENDITURE – 1.6 per cent of GDP (2001)

MILITARY PERSONNEL – 27,000: Army 23,000, Navy 1,000, Air Force 3,000; Paramilitaries 1,400

CONSCRIPTION DURATION – Two years

HISTORY AND POLITICS

Tanganyika became an independent state and a member of the British Commonwealth on 9 December 1961, and a republic within the Commonwealth on 9 December 1962. Zanzibar, comprising the islands of Zanzibar, Pemba and Mafia, was formerly ruled by the Sultan of Zanzibar and was a British Protectorate until 10 December 1963 when it became an independent state within the Commonwealth. On 26 April 1964 Tanganyika united with Zanzibar to form the United Republic of Tanzania.

The sole legal political party from 1977 to 1992 was the Chama Cha Mapinduzi – the Revolutionary Party of Tanzania (CCM). The constitution was amended in 1992 to allow multiparty politics, with the stipulation that all parties must be active in both the mainland and in Zanzibar and that parties must not be formed on regional, religious, tribal or racial grounds.

The first multiparty presidential and parliamentary elections were held in October and November 1995 and were won by the CCM.

Presidential and general elections were held on 29 October 2000. President Mkapa was re-elected, winning 71.7 per cent of the vote, and the CCM won an overwhelming majority in the National Assembly.

In Zanzibar, Amani Abeid Karume, the CCM candidate, was elected president and the CCM won a majority, but the results were disputed following violent protests and the annulment of the results in 16 of the 50 constituencies by the National Electoral Commission because of irregularities. A re-run was held in the 16 constituencies on 5 November. All 16 seats were won by the CCM. A series of demonstrations in protest at the conduct of the elections was organised by the main opposition party, the Civic United Front, in January 2001.

POLITICAL SYSTEM

The president is directly elected and may serve two five-year terms. The National Assembly contains up to 296 members, of whom 280 are directly elected, five are chosen by the Zanzibar House of Representatives, up to ten members are appointed by the president and one seat is reserved for the Attorney-General. Constituency members are elected at a general election held at a maximum of five-yearly intervals. Although Zanzibar has its own president, government and 60-member House of Representatives, Tanganyika is governed by the government of the Union. The president of Zanzibar is also a member of the Union Cabinet.

HEAD OF STATE

President of the United Republic, Benjamin Mkapa, *elected* 29 October 1995, *re-elected* 5 November 2000
Vice-President, Ali Mohamed Sheni
President of Zanzibar, Amani Abeid Karume

CABINET *as at July 2003*

The President of the United Republic
The Vice-President
The President of Zanzibar
Prime Minister, Frederick Sumaye
Agriculture and Food, Charles Keenja
Attorney-General, Andrew Cheng
Communications and Transport, Mark Mwandosya
Community Development, Women's Affairs and Children, Asha-Rose Migiro
Co-operatives and Marketing, George Kahama
Defence, Philemon Sarungi

Education, James Mungai
Energy and Mineral Resources, Daniel Yona Ndhiwa
Finance, Basil Mramba
Foreign Affairs and International Co-operation, Jakaya Kikwete
Health, Anna Abdallah
Home Affairs, Mohammed Seif Khatib
Justice and Constitutional Affairs, Harith Bakari Mwapachu
Labour, Youth Development and Sport, Juma Athumani Kapuya
Land, Housing and Urban Development, Gideon Cheyo
Ministers of State in the President's Office, Mary Nagu *(Civil Service);* Abdallah Kigoda *(Planning and Privatisation);* Brig.-Gen. Hassan Ngwiliza *(Regional Administration and Local Government);* Wilson Masilingi *(Security)*
Ministers of State in the Prime Minister's Office, William Lukuvi *(Information and Policy);* Ramadhani Mapuri
Ministers of State in the Vice-President's Office, Edgar Maokola Majogo *(Poverty);* Arcado Ntagwiza
Natural Resources, Tourism and Environment, Zakia Meghji
Science, Technology and Higher Education, Pius Ng'wandu
Trade and Industry, Juma Ngasongwa
Water and Livestock Development, Edward Lowassa
Works, John Magufuli

HIGH COMMISSION FOR THE UNITED REPUBLIC OF TANZANIA
43 Hertford Street, London W1Y 8DB
Tel: 020-7499 8951
High Commissioner, HE Hassan Omar Gumbo Kibelloh, apptd 2002

BRITISH HIGH COMMISSION
Umoja House, Garden Avenue (PO Box 9200), Dar es Salaam
Tel: (00 255) (22) 211 0101
High Commissioner, HE Andrew Pocock, apptd 2001

BRITISH COUNCIL DIRECTOR, Tom Cowin
Samora Avenue/Ohio Street, PO Box 9100, Dar es Salaam
Tel: (00 255) (22) 211 6574 Email: info@britishcouncil.or.tz

ECONOMY

The islands of Zanzibar and Pemba produce a large part of the world's supply of cloves and clove oil; coconuts, coconut oil and copra are also produced. Tanzania's chief exports are coffee, cotton and cashew nuts. The chief imports are capital equipment, oil and oil derivatives, and consumer goods. Industry, which accounts for 14 per cent of GDP, is largely concerned with the processing of raw material for export or local consumption.

In 2000 Tanzania had a trade deficit of US$674 million and a current account deficit of US$480 million. In 2001 imports totalled US$1,712 million and exports US$776 million.

GNP – US$9,013 million (2000); US$270 per capita (2000)
GDP – US$9,119 million (2001); US$210 per capita (2000)
ANNUAL AVERAGE GROWTH OF GDP – 3.8 per cent (1998)
INFLATION RATE – 5.9 per cent (2000)
TOTAL EXTERNAL DEBT – US$7,445 million (2000)

Trade with UK	2001	2002
Imports from UK	£65,957,000	£61,343,000
Exports to UK	35,249,000	38,967,000

COMMUNICATIONS

The main ports are Dar es Salaam, Tanga, Mtwara, Zanzibar, Mkoani and Wete, in addition to Mwanza, Musoma and Bukoba on Lake Victoria and Kigoma on Lake Tanganyika. Coastal shipping services connect the mainland to Zanzibar, and lake services are operated on Lake Tanganyika and Lake Malawi with neighbouring countries. The principal international airports are Dar es Salaam, Kilimanjaro and Zanzibar.

EDUCATION

The school system is administered in Swahili but the government is making efforts to improve English standards for the purposes of secondary and higher education. There are three institutes of higher education.
ILLITERACY RATE – (m) 15.3 per cent; (f) 32.9 per cent (2000)
ENROLMENT (percentage of age group) – primary 67 per cent (1997); tertiary 1 per cent (1997)

THAILAND

Prathes Thai – Kingdom of Thailand

AREA – 196,500 sq. miles (510,900 sq. km).
  Neighbours: Malaysia (south), Myanmar (west), Laos and Cambodia (east)
POPULATION – 63,584,000 (2001). The principal language is Thai, a monosyllabic, tonal language of the Indo-Chinese linguistic family, with a vocabulary strongly influenced by Sanskrit and Pali. The principal religion is Buddhism (94.37 per cent), with Muslim and Christian minorities
CAPITAL – ΨBangkok (population, 5,882,000, 1998 estimate)
MAJOR CITIES – Chiang Mai (159,000); Chon Buri (229,400); Nakhon Ratchasima (260,500); Nanthanburi (476,300); Songkhla (288,000), 1998 estimates
CURRENCY – Baht of 100 satang
NATIONAL ANTHEM – Pleng Chart (National Anthem)
NATIONAL DAY – 5 December (The King's Birthday)
NATIONAL FLAG – Five horizontal bands, red, white, dark blue, white, red (the blue band twice the width of the others)
LIFE EXPECTANCY (years) – 70 (2001)
POPULATION GROWTH RATE – 1.4 per cent
POPULATION DENSITY – 124 per sq. km (2001)

Thailand, formerly known as Siam, is divided geographically into four: the centre is a plain; to the north-east there is a plateau area and to the north-west mountains. The south of Thailand consists of a narrow mountainous peninsula. The principal rivers are the Chao Phraya in the central plains, and the Mekong on the northern and north-eastern borders.

HISTORY AND POLITICS

The Thai nation was founded in the 13th century. Although occupied by Burma in the 18th century, Thailand is the only country in the region not to have been colonised by a European power.

Following a revolution in 1932, Thailand became a constitutional monarchy. After a military coup in February 1991, a new constitution was approved under which the military would have significant political power. Parties aligned with the military won the general election in March 1992, but mass demonstrations held in Bangkok, with the help of the King, forced the government from power. Military power was curbed, the 1978 constitution was restored and the interim government sacked military chiefs.

Parliamentary elections in September 1992 resulted in a majority for those parties not allied with the military. The first election to the Senate was held on 4 March 2000. A rerun was held in 78 seats on 29 April following evidence of fraud. Further re-runs were necessary for some seats.

A general election took place on 6 January 2001. The Thai Rak Thai (TRT) party won 248 seats and formed a coalition with the Chart Thai party and the New Aspiration party.

FOREIGN RELATIONS

Laos occupied two Thai islands in the Mekong river on 19 August 2000 and evicted the inhabitants, claiming that it had jurisdiction over all the islands in the Mekong under a 1926 treaty.

On 9–11 February 2001 fighting occurred between the Thai army and Myanmarese troops who had crossed the border in pursuit of rebels in Chiang Rai province. The two countries agreed on 19–20 June to resolve the border tension and co-operate on fighting drug production and smuggling.

POLITICAL SYSTEM

The constitution provides for a National Assembly consisting of a 200-member Senate, directly elected on a non-party basis for a six-year term, and a 500-member House of Representatives elected by universal adult suffrage, 400 elected in single-member constituencies and 100 from party lists, for a term of four years.

HEAD OF STATE

HM The King of Thailand, King Bhumibol Adulyadej, *born* 5 December 1927; *succeeded his brother* 9 June 1946; *married* 28 April 1950 Mom Rajawongse Sirikit Kitiyakara; *crowned* 5 May 1950; *and has issue,* Princess Ubol Ratana, *born* 6 April 1951; Crown Prince Maha Vajiralongkorn; Princess Maha Chakri Sirindhorn, *born* 2 April 1955; Princess Chulabhorn, *born* 4 July 1957
Heir, HRH Crown Prince Maha Vajiralongkorn, *born* 28 July 1952; *married* 3 January 1977 Soamsawali Kitiyakra

CABINET *as at July 2003*
Prime Minister, Thaksin Shinawatra (TRT)
Deputy Prime Ministers, Gen. Chavalit Yongchaiyudh (TRT); Somkid Jatusripitak (TRT) *(Economic Affairs);* Suwit Khunkitti (TRT); Chaturon Chaisang (TRT); Korn Dappharansi; Police Capt. Purachai Piumsombun (TRT); Wissanu Krea-ngam
Agriculture and Co-operatives, Sora-at Klinpratoom
Commerce, Adisai Bodharamik (TRT)
Culture, Uraiwan Thienthong
Defence, Thammarak Isarangura (TRT)
Education, Pongpol Adireksarn
Energy, Prommin Lertsuridej
Finance, Suchart Jaovisidha
Foreign Affairs, Surakiet Sathirathai (TRT)
Industry, Somsak Thepsutin (TRT)
Information and Communications Technology, Surapong Suebwonglee
Interior, Wan Muhamad Noor Matha (NAP)
Justice, Pongthep Thapkanjana (CT)

Labour, Suwat Liptapanlop
Natural Resources and Environment, Prapat Panyachatraksa
Public Health, Sudarat Keyuraphan (TRT)
Science and Technology, Pinij Jaarusombat
Social Development and Human Security, Anurak
  Chureemas
Tourism and Sports, Sonataya Kunplome (CT)
Transport, Suriya Junggrungreangkit (TRT)

CT Chart Thai; NAP New Aspiration Party; TRT
Thai Rak Thai

ROYAL THAI EMBASSY
29–30 Queen's Gate, London SW7 5JB
Tel: 020-7589 2944
Ambassador Extraordinary and Plenipotentiary, HE Vikrom
  Koompirochana, apptd 2003

BRITISH EMBASSY
1031 Wireless Road, Bangkok 10330
Tel: (00 66) (2) 305 8333
Ambassador Extraordinary and Plenipotentiary, HE David
  Fall, apptd 2003

BRITISH COUNCIL DIRECTOR, Peter Upton
254 Chulalongkorn Soi 64, Siam Square, Phayathai Road,
Pathumwan, Bangkok 10330
Tel: (00 66) (2) 652 5480 Email: info@britishcouncil.or.th

DEFENCE
The Army has 333 main battle tanks, 946 armoured
personnel carriers and three attack helicopters. The Navy
has one aircraft carrier, 12 frigates, 88 patrol and coastal
vessels, 44 combat aircraft and eight armed helicopters at
five bases. The Air Force has 194 combat aircraft.
MILITARY EXPENDITURE – 1.7 per cent of GDP (2001)
MILITARY PERSONNEL – 306,000: Army 190,000,
  Navy 68,000, Air Force 48,000; Paramilitaries
  113,000

ECONOMY
Thailand was one of the countries worst affected by the
economic crisis in south-east Asia. In May 1997 the
stock market fell to an eight-year low. In July 1997 the
government allowed the currency to float freely, resulting
in a *de facto* devaluation of 20 per cent and triggering
a currency crisis throughout south-east Asia. On 5 August
1997, an IMF loan of US$16.7 billion was announced,
in return for emergency financial reforms. However, these
reforms were only implemented after a delay and were
seen by the markets as inadequate, further damaging
economic confidence. The government resigned on
3 November 1997, and was replaced by an eight-party
coalition. The Thai economy contracted by about
8 per cent in 1998. In March 1999, the government
announced a package of tax cuts and increased spending
designed to stimulate the economy.
  The agricultural sector employs around half of the
labour force. In 1999 it contributed 13 per cent of GDP.
Rice remains the most important crop; other main crops
are sugar, maize, sorghum, cassava, rubber, tobacco, kenaf
and jute. In recent years fishing and livestock production
have gained importance. There are reserves of oil, natural
gas and lignite; mineral resources include tin, tungsten,
lead and iron.
  Important industrial sectors include textiles,
transportation vehicles and equipment, construction
materials, brewing, petroleum refining, electrical
appliances, plastics, computers and parts, and integrated

circuits. In 1999, industry contributed 40 per cent of
GDP. Since 1982 tourism has been the main foreign
exchange earner. In 1998, there were 7.8 million foreign
visitors.
GNP – US$121,602 million (2000); US$2,000 per
  capita (2000)
GDP – US$114,760 million (2001); US$1,945 per
  capita (2000)
ANNUAL AVERAGE GROWTH OF GDP – 4.4 per cent
  (2000)
INFLATION RATE – 1.5 per cent (2000)
UNEMPLOYMENT – 2.4 per cent (2000)
TOTAL EXTERNAL DEBT – US$79,675 million (2000)

TRADE
Thailand's main exports are computers and parts, cars,
integrated circuit boards, precious stones, rice, maize,
canned sea food, fabrics, sugar and tin. Main imports
are crude oil, chemicals, electrical goods, industrial
machinery, iron, steel and transport equipment.
  In 2001 Thailand had a trade surplus of US$8,582
million and a current account surplus of US$6,227
million. Imports totalled US$62,058 million and exports
US$65,113 million.

Trade with UK	2001	2002
Imports from UK	£595,702,000	£532,348,000
Exports to UK	1,669,135,000	1,608,303,000

COMMUNICATIONS
Navigable waterways have a length of about 1,100 km in
the dry season and 1,600 km in the wet season. There are
4,071 km of railways. Bangkok is the international
airport, though airports at Chiang Mai, Phuket and Hat
Yai also receive international flights. There are two
important ports in the country, Bangkok and Sattahip.
There are 3,999 km of principal waterways.

EDUCATION
Primary education is compulsory and free, and secondary
education in government schools is free. Private
universities and colleges are playing an increasing role in
higher education. There are 62 higher institutes of
learning.
ILLITERACY RATE – (m) 2.8 per cent; (f) 6.1 per cent
  (2000)
ENROLMENT (percentage of age group) – tertiary 22 per
  cent (1997)

TOGO

République Togolaise – Togolese Republic

AREA – 21,925 sq. miles (56,785 sq. km). Neighbours:
  Ghana (west), Burkina Faso (north), Benin (east)
POPULATION – 5,153,088 (2001 estimate). The official
  language is French; Ewe, Watchi and Kabiyé are the
  main indigenous languages
CAPITAL – ΨLomé (population, 700,000, 1997
  estimate)
CURRENCY – Franc CFA of 100 centimes
NATIONAL ANTHEM – Écartons Tous Mauvais Esprit
  Qui Gêne L'Unité Nationale (Let Us Discard All Ill
  Feelings Which Harm National Unity)
NATIONAL DAY – 27 April
NATIONAL FLAG – Five alternating green and yellow
  horizontal stripes; a quarter in red at top next staff
  bearing a white star
POPULATION GROWTH RATE – 2.6 per cent

POPULATION DENSITY – 79 per sq. km (1999)
MILITARY EXPENDITURE – 2.5 per cent of GDP (2001)
MILITARY PERSONNEL – 9,450: Army 9,000, Navy
200, Air Force 250; Paramilitaries 750
CONSCRIPTION DURATION – Two years (selective)
ILLITERACY RATE – (m) 25.5 per cent; (f) 59.2 per cent
(2000)
ENROLMENT (percentage of age group) – primary 100
per cent (1997); secondary 27 per cent (1997); tertiary
4 per cent (1997)

HISTORY AND POLITICS

The first president of Togo, Sylvanus Olympio, was
assassinated in 1963. In 1967, there was an army coup
d'état and the army commander Lt.-Col. (later Gen.)
Eyadéma named himself president. In April 1990,
following increasing popular pressure, the government
was forced to concede a political amnesty, the
introduction of a multiparty constitution and a national
conference. In August 1991 the national conference
stripped President Eyadéma of all powers, banned the
Rassemblement du peuple togolais (RPT), which had been
the sole legal party, and elected Kokou Koffigoh as prime
minister of an interim government. Troops loyal to
President Eyadéma attempted to overthrow Koffigoh
three times (in October, November and December 1991)
but were frustrated by pro-democracy supporters. A new
multiparty constitution was approved by referendum in
September 1992. In November, Eyadéma, who had
regained the position of head of state in August 1992,
ordered the Army to crush civil unrest and a general
strike against his rule. In February 1993, as violence
continued, Koffigoh and Eyadéma agreed on the
formation of a crisis government, which the national
conference and the Collective Democratic Opposition-2
(COD-2) declared illegal.

The presidential election of 21 June 1998 was won by
Gen. Eyadéma. Legislative elections to the national
Assembly were held on 27 October 2002. The elections
had been repeatedly postponed since March 2000. The
main opposition parties boycotted the election and the
RPT retained its overwhelming majority winning 72 of
the 81 seats. In the presidential elections of 1 June 2003
President Eyadéma was re-elected with 57.2 per cent of
the vote. The government resigned on 24 June 2003 after
President Eyadéma's re-inauguration and the president
stated he intended to appoint a new government of
national unity under Koffi Sama who was re-appointed as
prime minister on 1 July. The new cabinet was named on
29 July.

HEAD OF STATE
President, Gen. Gnassingbé Eyadéma, *assumed office*
14 April 1967, *re-elected* 1986, 1993, 21 June 1998,
1 June 2003

GOVERNMENT *as at August 2003*
Prime Minister, Koffi Sama
Agriculture, Livestock and Fisheries, Komikpime Bamnante
Civil Service, Labour and Employment, Rodolphe Osseyi
*Commerce, Industry, Transport and Development of the Free
Zone*, Tankpadja Lalle
Communication and Civic Education, Pitang Tchalla
Culture, Angèle Aguigah
Economic Affairs, Finance and Privatisation, Ayaovi
Debaba Bale
Energy and Water Resources, Issifou Okoulou-Kantchati
Environment and Forest Resources, Gen. Zoumaro Gnofame

Equipment, Mines, Energy, Post and Telecommunications,
Faure Gnassingbé
Foreign Affairs and Co-operation, Kokou Tozoun
Higher Education and Water Resources, Charles Agba
Interior, Security and Decentralisation, Maj. Akila Esso
Bokco
Justice and Keeper of the Seals, Katari Foli-Bazi
*Minister-Delegate at the Prime Minister's Office, in charge of
the Private Sector*, Maria Apoudjak
National Defence and Veterans, Brig.-Gen. Assani Tidjani
Primary and Secondary Education, Komi Klassou
Promotion of Democracy and the Rule of Law, Roland
Kroptsra
Public Health, Suzanne Aho Assouma
Relations with Parliament, Comlangan Mawutoè
d'Almeida
*Secretary of State at the Ministry of Economy, Finance and
Privatisation, in charge of the Budget*, M'ba Legzim
*Social Affairs, Promotion of Women and Protection of
Children*, Sayo Boyoti
Technical Education and Professional Training, Edoh
Kodjo Agbobli
Tourism, Handicrafts and Leisure, Dorothée Iloudjè
Urban Affairs and Housing, Dovi Kavégué
Youth and Sports, Agouta Ouyenga

EMBASSY OF THE REPUBLIC OF TOGO
8 rue Alfred-Roll, F-75017 Paris, France
Tel: (00 33) (1) 4380 1213
Ambassador Extraordinary and Plenipotentiary, HE Sotou
Bere, apptd 2003

BRITISH AMBASSADOR, HE Rod Pullen, resident at
Accra, Ghana

ECONOMY

Although the economy remains largely agricultural,
exports of phosphates have superseded agricultural
products as the main source of export earnings. Other
exports include palm kernels, copra and manioc.

In December 1998 the EU announced that it would
not resume developmental aid to Togo following
irregularities in the country's election process.

In 1999 Togo had a trade deficit of US$98 million and
a current account deficit of US$127 million. In 2001
imports totalled US$355 million and exports US$226
million.

GNP – US$1,318 million (2000); US$290 per capita
(2000)
GDP – US$1,259 million (2001); US$306 per capita
(2000)
ANNUAL AVERAGE GROWTH OF GDP – 6.0 per cent
(1998)
INFLATION RATE – 1.9 per cent (2000)
TOTAL EXTERNAL DEBT – US$1,435 million (2000)

Trade with UK	2001	2002
Imports from UK	£33,871,000	£25,845,000
Exports to UK	1,072,000	1,547,000

TONGA

Pule'anga Tonga / Kingdom of Tonga

AREA – 250 sq. miles (650 sq. km)
POPULATION – 104,227 (2001 estimate). The languages
are Tongan and English
CAPITAL – ΨNuku'alofa (population, 34,000, 1990), on
Tongatapu

CURRENCY – Pa'anga (T$) of 100 seniti
NATIONAL ANTHEM – E, 'Otua Mafimafi (Oh, Almighty God Above)
NATIONAL DAY – 4 June (Emancipation Day)
NATIONAL FLAG – Red with a white canton containing a couped red cross
POPULATION GROWTH RATE – 0.1 per cent
POPULATION DENSITY – 151 per sq. km (1999)

Tonga, or the Friendly Islands, comprises a group of islands situated in the southern Pacific some 450 miles east-south-east of Fiji. The largest island, Tongatapu, was discovered by Tasman in 1643.

HISTORY AND POLITICS

The Kingdom of Tonga is an independent constitutional monarchy within the Commonwealth. Prior to 4 June 1970 it had been a British-protected state for 70 years. The constitution provides for a government consisting of the Sovereign, an appointed privy council which functions as a Cabinet, a legislative assembly and a judiciary. The 30-member legislative assembly comprises the King, the 11-member privy council, nine hereditary nobles elected by their peers, and nine popularly elected representatives who hold office for three years. The most recent election took place on 7 March 2002 when the Human Rights and Democracy Movement won seven of the popularly elected seats in the Legislative Assembly.

HEAD OF STATE

King of Tonga, HM King Taufa'ahau Tupou IV, GCMG, GCVO, KBE, *born* 4 July 1918, *acceded* 16 December 1965
Heir, HRH Crown Prince Tupouto'a

CABINET *as at July 2003*
Prime Minister, Agriculture and Fisheries, Civil Aviation and Communications, Foreign Affairs and Defence, HRH Prince 'Ulukalala Lavaka Ata
Deputy Prime Minister, Works, Marine Affairs and Ports, Environment, Cecil Cocker
Education, Paula Bloomfield
Finance, Siosiua Utoikamanu
Governor of Ha'apai, Malupo
Governor of Vava'u, Capt. S. M. Tuita
Health, Viliami Tangi
Justice and Attorney-General, Aisea Taumoepeau
Labour, Commerce and Industries, Tourism, Paunga Massaso
Lands, Survey, and Natural Resources, Fielakepa
Police, Prisons and Fire Services, Immigration, Clive Edwards

TONGA HIGH COMMISSION
36 Molyneux Street, London W1H 5BQ
Tel: 020-7724 5828
High Commissioner, HE Col. Fetu'utolu Tupou, apptd 2000

BRITISH HIGH COMMISSION
PO Box 56, Nuku'alofa
Tel: (00 676) 24285/24395
Email: britcomt@kalianet.to
High Commissioner, HE Paul Nessling, apptd 2002

ECONOMY

The economy is primarily agricultural; the main crops are coconuts, vanilla, yams, taro, cassava, groundnuts, squash pumpkins and other fruit. Fish is an important staple food, though recent shortfalls have led to canned fish being imported. Industry is based on the processing of agricultural produce, and the manufacture of foodstuffs, clothing and sports equipment.

GNP – US$166 million (2000); US$1,660 per capita (2000)
GDP – US$142 million (2001); US$1,460 per capita (2000)
ANNUAL AVERAGE GROWTH OF GDP – –0.3 per cent (1998)
INFLATION RATE – 5.9 per cent (2000)
TOTAL EXTERNAL DEBT – US$58 million (2000)

TRADE
The principal exports are fish and vanilla. The principal imports are manufactures, foodstuffs, machinery and transport equipment and combustible fuels.
In 1999 imports totalled US$73 million and exports US$12 million.

Trade with UK	2001	2002
Imports from UK	£1,281,000	£810,000
Exports to UK	253,000	29,000

TRINIDAD AND TOBAGO

The Republic of Trinidad and Tobago

AREA – 1,962 sq. miles (5,100 sq. km)
POPULATION – 1,300,000 (2001). The language is English. The main religions are Roman Catholicism (29.4 per cent of the population), Hinduism (23.8 per cent); Anglicanism (10.9 per cent); Islam (5.8 per cent) and Presbyterianism (3.4 per cent)
CAPITAL – ΨPort of Spain (population, 49,031, 2000 census)
MAJOR CITIES – San Fernando (55,419); ΨScarborough, the main town of Tobago
CURRENCY – Trinidad and Tobago dollar (TT$) of 100 cents
NATIONAL ANTHEM – Forged From The Love Of Liberty
NATIONAL DAY – 31 August (Independence Day)
NATIONAL FLAG – Black diagonal stripe bordered with white stripes, running from top by staff, all on a red field
LIFE EXPECTANCY (years) – 75 (2001)
POPULATION GROWTH RATE – 0.6 per cent
POPULATION DENSITY – 255 per sq. km (2001)
MILITARY EXPENDITURE – 0.8 per cent of GDP (2001)
MILITARY PERSONNEL – 2,700: Army 2,000, Coast Guard 700

Trinidad, the most southerly of the West Indian islands, lies seven miles off the north coast of Venezuela. The island is about 50 miles in length by 37 miles in width. Two mountain systems, the Northern and Southern Ranges, stretch across almost its entire width and a third, the Central Range, lies diagonally across its middle portion; otherwise the island is mostly flat. Tobago lies 19 miles north-east of Trinidad.

HISTORY AND POLITICS

Trinidad was discovered by Columbus in 1498, was colonised in 1532 by the Spaniards, capitulated to the British in 1797, and was ceded to Britain under the Treaty of Amiens (1802). Tobago was discovered by Columbus in 1498. Dutch colonists arrived in 1632; Tobago subsequently changed hands numerous times until it was ceded to Britain by France in 1814 and amalgamated with Trinidad in 1888. The Territory of Trinidad and Tobago became an independent state and a member of the British Commonwealth on 31 August 1962, and a republic in 1976.

In the general election held on 10 December 2001 the ruling United National Congress (UNC) and the opposition People's National Movement (PNM) each won 18 of the 36 seats in the House of Representatives. On 24 December President Robinson chose Patrick Manning, leader of PNM, as prime minister. The UNC condemned the president's choice and called for fresh elections. A new Cabinet was sworn into office on 27 December. On 6 April 2002 President Robinson suspended parliament because no speaker had been elected. Fresh elections took place on 7 October 2002 in which the PNM won 20 of the 36 seats, thereby resolving the parliamentary deadlock of the 2001 elections. Patrick Manning was again sworn in as prime minister and named his government on 9 September 2002. George Maxwell Richards was elected president on 14 February 2003 and took office on 17 March.

POLITICAL SYSTEM
The president is elected for five years by all members of the Senate and the House of Representatives. The House of Representatives has 36 members, directly elected for a five-year term, and the Senate has 31, of whom 16 are appointed on the advice of the prime minister, six on the advice of the Leader of the Opposition and nine at the discretion of the president. Legislation was passed in September 1980 which afforded Tobago a degree of self-administration through the 15-member Tobago House of Assembly, of whom 12 are directly elected and three chosen by the House for a four-year term.

HEAD OF STATE
President, George Maxwell Richards, *elected by parliament* 14 February 2003

CABINET *as at July 2003*
Prime Minister, Finance, Patrick Manning
Agriculture, Land and Marine Resources, John Rahael
Attorney-General, Glenda Morean
Community Development and Gender Affairs, Joan Yuille Williams
Culture and Tourism, Penelope Beckles
Education, Hazel Anne Marie Manning
Energy and Energy Industries, Eric Williams
Foreign Affairs, Knowlson Gift
Health, Colm Imbert
Housing, Martin Joseph
Labour, Small and Micro Enterprises, Lawrence Achong
Legal Affairs, Camille Robinson-Regis
Local Government, Jarrette Narine
National Security, Howard Chin Lee
Planning and Development, Keith Rowley
Public Administration and Information, Lenny Saith
Public Utilities and Environment, Rennie Dumas
Science, Technology and Tertiary Education, Danny Montano
Social Development, Mustapha Abdul-Hamid
Sports and Youth Affairs, Roger Boynes
Trade, Industry, Minister in the Ministry of Finance, Kenneth Valley
Ministers in the Ministry of Finance, Conrad Enill; Christine Sahadeo
Minister in the Office of the Prime Minister, Christine Kangaloo

Works and Transport, Franklyn Khan

HIGH COMMISSION OF THE REPUBLIC OF TRINIDAD AND TOBAGO
42 Belgrave Square, London SW1X 8NT
Tel: 020-7245 9351
High Commissioner, vacant
Acting High Commissioner and Counsellor, Sandra McIntyre-Trotman

BRITISH HIGH COMMISSION
19 St Clair Ave, St Clair, Port of Spain
Tel: (00 1 868) 622 2748/8960
Email: csbhc@opus.co.tt
High Commissioner, HE Peter Harborne, apptd 1999

ECONOMY
Trinidad and Tobago's main source of revenue is from oil. Trinidad has large reserves of natural gas, and in March 2000, an agreement was signed to expand significantly the production of liquefied natural gas. In May 2000, it was announced that an additional natural gas deposit of some 56,600 million cubic metres had been discovered and the discovery of a further deposit of some three trillion cubic feet was announced in September. Fertilisers, tyres, clothing, soap, furniture and foodstuffs are manufactured locally while motor vehicles, radios, TV sets, and electro-domestic equipment are assembled from parts, mainly from Japan. The main agricultural products are sugar, cocoa, coffee, horticultural products and teak.

In 1998 Trinidad and Tobago had a trade deficit of US$741 million and a current account deficit of US$644 million. In 2000 imports totalled US$3,308 million and exports US$4,655 million.
GNP – US$6,415 million (2000); US$4,930 per capita (2000)
GDP – US$8,412 million (2001); US$6,239 per capita (2000)
ANNUAL AVERAGE GROWTH OF GDP – 3.3 per cent (1998)
INFLATION RATE – 3.6 per cent (2000)
UNEMPLOYMENT – 13.1 per cent (1999)
TOTAL EXTERNAL DEBT – US$2,467 million (2000)

Trade with UK	2001	2002
Imports from UK	£91,611,000	£81,380,000
Exports to UK	53,927,000	56,963,000

COMMUNICATIONS
The three main ports are Scarborough (Tobago), Port of Spain and Point Lisas where new industries powered by local natural gas are located. The international airport, Piarco, is at Port of Spain.

EDUCATION
Education is free at all state-owned and government-assisted denominational schools and certain faculties at the University of the West Indies. Attendance is compulsory for children aged six to 12 years, after which attendance at free secondary schools is determined by success in the secondary school entrance examination at 11 years. There are three technical institutes, two teacher training colleges, and one of the three branches of the University of West Indies is located in Trinidad.
ILLITERACY RATE – (m) 1.1 per cent; (f) 2.4 per cent (2000)
ENROLMENT (percentage of age group) – primary 99 per cent (1997); secondary 74 per cent (1997); tertiary 8 per cent (1997)

TUNISIA

Al-Jumhūriyya at-Tūnisiyya – Republic of Tunisia

AREA – 59,769 sq. miles (155,400 sq. km). Neighbours: Algeria (west), Libya (south)
POPULATION – 9,562,000 (2001). Arabic is the official language
CAPITAL – ΨTunis (population, 929,500 2001 estimate)
MAJOR CITIES – ΨBizerte (518,500); ΨSfax (808,700); ΨSousse (492,500), 2001 estimates
CURRENCY – Tunisian dinar of 1,000 millimes
NATIONAL ANTHEM – Himat Al Hima (Defenders Of The Homeland)
NATIONAL DAY – 20 March
NATIONAL FLAG – Red with a white disc containing a red crescent and star
LIFE EXPECTANCY (years) – 70 (2001)
POPULATION GROWTH RATE – 1.4 per cent
POPULATION DENSITY – 62 per sq. km (2001)
URBAN POPULATION – 66 per cent (2001)
MILITARY EXPENDITURE – 1.9 per cent of GDP (2001)
MILITARY PERSONNEL – 35,000: Army 27,000, Navy 4,500, Air Force 3,500; Paramilitaries 12,000
CONSCRIPTION DURATION – 12 months (selective)

HISTORY AND POLITICS
A French Protectorate from 1881 to 1956, Tunisia became an independent sovereign state on 20 March 1956. In 1957 the Constituent Assembly abolished the monarchy and elected M. Bourguiba president of the Republic. In March 1975 the National Assembly proclaimed M. Bourguiba as president for life. He was deposed on 7 November 1987 and succeeded by President Zine el-Abidine Ben Ali, who was subsequently elected in 1989 and re-elected in 1994.

President Ben Ali was elected for a third term of office on 24 October 1999, gaining 99.4 per cent of the vote; there were two other candidates. A parallel legislative election was won by the Democratic Constitutional Rally (RCD), who gained 91.6 per cent of the vote, winning 148 of the 182 seats in the National Assembly *(Majlis al-Nuwaab)*. The Movement of Social Democrats (MDS) won 13 seats, the Unionist Democratic Union (UDU) and the Party of People's Unity (PUP) won 7 seats each, the Movement for Renewal (MR) won 5 seats and the Social-Liberal Party won 2 seats.

POLITICAL SYSTEM
The 1959 constitution was amended in 2002 to allow the president to seek a fourth term and to allow the formation of a second parliamentary assembly.

HEAD OF STATE
President, Gen. Zine el-Abidine Ben Ali, *took office* 7 November 1987, *elected* 2 April 1989, *re-elected* 20 March 1994, 24 October 1999

CABINET *as at July 2003*
Prime Minister, Mohammed Ghannouchi
Agriculture, Environment and Land Development, Hydraulic Resources, Habib Haddad
Communication Technologies, Transport, Sadok Rabah
Culture, Youth and Leisure, Abdelbaki Hermassi
Director of the Presidential Office, Ahmed Eyadh Ouederni
Economic Development, International Co-operation, Mohamed Nouri Jouini

Education and Training, Moncer Rouissi
Employment, Chedli Laroussi
Equipment, Housing and Territorial Development, Slaheddine Belaid
Finance, Taoufik Baccar
Foreign Affairs, Habib Ben Yahia
Higher Education, Scientific Research and Technology, Sadok Chaâbane
Industry and Energy, Moncef Ben Abdallah
Interior, Hedi M'henni
Justice, Human Rights, Bechir Tekkari
Minister of State (special advisor to the president), Abdelaziz Ben Dhia
National Defence, Dali Jazi
Public Health, Habib Mbarek
Religious Affairs, Jelloul Jeribi
Secretary-General of the Government, in charge of Relations with Parliament, Mohamed Rachid Kechiche
Social Affairs and Solidarity, Chedli Neffati
Sports, Abderrahim Zouari
State Property and Land Affairs, Ridha Grira
Tourism, Trade and Handicrafts, Mondher Zenaidi
Women, Family and Children's Affairs, Neziha Ben Yedder

TUNISIAN EMBASSY
29 Prince's Gate, London SW7 1QG
Tel: 020-7584 8117
Ambassador Extraordinary and Plenipotentiary, HE Khémaies Jhinaoui, apptd 1999

BRITISH EMBASSY
5 Place de la Victoire, Tunis 1000
Tel: (00 216) (7) 341444
Email: british.emb@planet.tn
Ambassador Extraordinary and Plenipotentiary, HE Robin Kealy, CMG, apptd 2002

ECONOMY
Agriculture and fisheries employed 22 per cent of the workforce in 1999 and accounted for 13 per cent of GDP. The valleys of the northern region support large flocks and herds and contain rich agricultural areas in which cereal crops, citrus fruits, dates, melons, potatoes, peppers and tomatoes are grown. Vines and olives are extensively cultivated. Crude oil production in 2002 was 3.6 million tonnes. Gas has also been discovered off the east coast but is only exploited in small quantities. Tourism is the main foreign exchange earner and there were 5.6 million visitors in 2001.

In 2000 Tunisia had a trade deficit of US$2,252 million and a current account deficit of US$821 million. In 2001 imports totalled US$9,552 million and exports US$6,609 million.
GNP – US$20,057 million (2000); US$2,100 per capita (2000)
GDP – US$20,035 million (2001); US$2,058 per capita (2000)
ANNUAL AVERAGE GROWTH OF GDP – 5.0 per cent (2000)
INFLATION RATE – 2.9 per cent (2000)
UNEMPLOYMENT – 15.6 per cent (2000)
TOTAL EXTERNAL DEBT – US$10,610 million (2000)

TRADE
The chief exports are manufactures, textiles and leather goods, phosphates, mechanical and electronic products, agricultural products and energy. The chief imports are manufactures, raw materials and semi-manufactures,

consumer goods, capital goods, and foodstuffs. France remains the main trading partner. Tunisia became an associate of the EC in 1969. In July 1995 a new EU-Tunisian partnership agreement was signed which aims to modernise Tunisia's economy and improve its competitiveness with a view to creating a free trade zone with the EU by 2008.

Trade with UK	2001	2002
Imports from UK	£141,433,000	£135,170,000
Exports to UK	120,062,000	114,406,000

EDUCATION

There are 141 centres of higher education, of which eight are universities.

ILLITERACY RATE – (m) 18.6 per cent; (f) 39.4 per cent (2000)

ENROLMENT (percentage of age group) – primary 100 per cent (1997); secondary 64 per cent (1997); tertiary 14 per cent (1997)

TURKEY

Türkiye Çumhuriyeti – Republic of Turkey

AREA – 314,508 sq. miles (774,815 sq. km).
  Neighbours: Greece (west), Bulgaria (north), Georgia, Armenia, Azerbaijan and Iran (east), Syria and Iraq (south)

POPULATION – 67,632,000 (2001); Islam ceased to be the state religion in 1928 but 98.99 per cent of the population are Muslim. The main religious minorities, which are concentrated in Istanbul and on the Syrian frontier, are Greek Orthodox, Armenian, Syrian Christian, and Jewish. The language is Turkish; Kurdish is widely spoken in the south-east of the country

CAPITAL – Ankara (Angora), in Asia (population, 3,203,362, 2000 census). Ankara (or Ancyra) was the capital of the Roman Province of *Galatia Prima*, and a marble temple (now in ruins), dedicated to Augustus, contains the *Monumentum (Marmor) Ancyranum*, inscribed with a record of the reign of Augustus Caesar

MAJOR CITIES – Adana (1,682,483); Bursa (1,958,529); Gaziantep (1,127,686); ΨIstanbul (9,198,809); ΨIzmir (3,114,859); Konya (1,931,773), 2000 estimates. Istanbul, in Europe, is the former capital. The Roman city of Byzantium, was selected by Constantine the Great as the capital of the Roman Empire about AD 328 and renamed Constantinople. Istanbul contains the celebrated church of St Sophia, which, after becoming a mosque, was made a museum in 1934. It also contains Topkapi, former palace of the Ottoman Sultans, which is also a museum

CURRENCY – Turkish lira (TL) of 100 kurus

NATIONAL ANTHEM – Istiklal Marsi (The Independence March)

NATIONAL DAY – 29 October (Republic Day)

NATIONAL FLAG – Red, with white crescent and star

LIFE EXPECTANCY (years) – 70 (2001)

POPULATION GROWTH RATE – 1.7 per cent

POPULATION DENSITY – 88 per sq. km (2001)

URBAN POPULATION – 66 per cent (2001)

Turkey in Europe consists of Eastern Thrace, including the cities of Istanbul and Edirne, and is separated from Asia by the Bosporus at Istanbul and by the Dardanelles (about 40 miles in length with a width varying from one to four miles). Turkey in Asia comprises the whole of Asia Minor or Anatolia.

HISTORY AND POLITICS

On 29 October 1923 the National Assembly declared Turkey a republic and elected Gazi Mustafa Kemal (later known as Kemal Atatürk) president. In 1945 a multiparty system was introduced but in 1960 the government was overthrown by the armed forces. A new constitution was adopted in 1961 and a civilian government took office. Civilian governments remained in power until September 1980 with mounting problems with the economy and terrorism led to a military takeover.

Following the general election in November 1983 the military leadership handed over power to a civilian government.

Following elections on 3 November 2002, the Islamic Justice and Development Party (AKP), led by Recep Tayyip Erdogan, won an overall majority with 363 of the 550 seats in the parliament. However Erdogan had been prevented from standing for parliament owing to a past conviction. The deputy leader of the AKP, Abdullah Gul, was therefore appointed prime minister on 16 November 2002 and his cabinet took office on 18 November. In late December the National Assembly overruled the president's veto and voted to amend the law to permit Erdogan to stand for election to parliament. He won a by-election on 9 March 2003 and Prime Minister Gul resigned with his entire government on 11 March. On 14 March Erdogan was appointed prime minister and named his new government.

In June and July 2003 the parliament passed a package of laws easing restrictions on freedom of speech; Kurdish language rights and on reducing the political role of the military as part programme which aims to meet EU preconditions to the commencement of accession negotiations.

INSURGENCIES

Since 1984 Turkey has been fighting armed guerrillas of the Marxist-Leninist Kurdistan Workers' Party (PKK) in the south-east of the country where Kurds are the majority population. The leader of the PKK, Abdullah Öcalan was captured by Turkish authorities in February 1999 in Kenya and returned to Turkey to stand trial, where he was found guilty of treason on 31 May and sentenced to death on 29 June 1999. The Turkish government announced on 12 January 2000 that it would suspend the execution, pending an appeal. The PKK announced on 8 February 2000 that it had renounced violence and removed the word 'Kurdistan', which is illegal in Turkey, from its title.

POLITICAL SYSTEM

A new constitution, extending the powers of the president, was approved in 1982. It provided for the separation of powers between the legislature, executive and judiciary, and the holding of free elections to the unicameral Grand National Assembly, which now has 550 members elected every five years.

HEAD OF STATE

President, Ahmet Necdet Sezer, *elected by parliament for a seven-year term* 5 May 2000, *took office* 16 May 2000

CABINET *as at July 2003*
Prime Minister, Recep Tayyip Erdogan
Deputy Prime Minister, Minister of State and Minister of Foreign Affairs, Abdullah Gul

Deputy Prime Minister, Minister of State, Abdullatif Sener
Deputy Prime Minister, Minister of State, Mehmet Ali Sahin
Agriculture and Village Affairs, Sami Guclu
Culture, Erkan Mumku
National Education, Huseyin Celik
Energy and Natural Resources, Hilmi Guler
Environment and Forestry, Osman Pepe
Finance, Kemal Unakitan
Health, Recep Akdag
Interior, Abdulkadir Aksu
Justice, Government Spokesman, Cemil Cicek
Labour and Social Security, Murat Basesgioglu
Ministers of State, Ali Babacan; Besir Atalay; Kursat Tuzmen; Mehmet Ali Sahin; Mehmet Aydin
National Defence, Vecdi Gonul
Public Works and Housing, Zeki Ergezen
Tourism, Guldal Aksit
Trade and Industry, Ali Coskun
Transport, Binali Yildirim

TURKISH EMBASSY
43 Belgrave Square, London SW1X 8PA
Tel: 020-7393 0202
Ambassador Extraordinary and Plenipotentiary, HE Akin Alptuna, apptd 2000

BRITISH EMBASSY
Sehit Ersan Caddesi 46/A, Çankaya, Ankara
Tel: (00 90) (312) 455 3344
Email: britembinf@turk.net
Ambassador Extraordinary and Plenipotentiary, HE Peter Westmacott, CMQ, LVO apptd 2002

BRITISH COUNCIL DIRECTOR, Ray Thomas
Esat Caddesi No: 41, Kucukesat, TR-06660 Ankara
Tel: (00 90) (312) 424 1644
Email: bc.ankara@britishcouncil.org.tr

DEFENCE

The Army has 4,205 main battle tanks, 3,643 armoured personnel carriers, 650 armoured infantry fighting vehicles and 37 attack helicopters. The Navy has 13 submarines, 19 frigates, 49 patrol and coastal vessels and 16 armed helicopters at twelve bases. The Air Force has 485 combat aircraft. Between 150,000 and 200,000 troops are stationed in the south-east of the country to prevent Kurdish insurgency. Since its invasion of Cyprus in 1974, Turkey has maintained forces in the north of the island and at present has about 36,000 men stationed there.

As a member of NATO, Turkey is host to the Head-quarters Allied Land Forces South-Eastern Europe and the Sixth Allied Tactical Air Force Headquarters. US (2,040 personnel) and UK (160 personnel) air force detachments are based at Incirlik air base in southern Turkey to patrol the air exclusion zone over northern Iraq. In March 2003 the parliament rejected a deal which would have allowed deployment of US forces in preparation for the war in Iraq but it allowed US forces the use of Turkish airspace. The dispatchment of Turkish forces into Kurdish areas of northern Iraq was also authorised.

MILITARY EXPENDITURE – 5.0 per cent of GDP (2001)
MILITARY PERSONNEL – 514,850: Army 402,000, Navy 52,750, Air Force 60,100; Paramilitaries 152,200
CONSCRIPTION DURATION – 18 months

ECONOMY

Agricultural production accounted for 14.4 per cent of GDP in 2000. About 40 per cent of the working population is employed in agriculture. The principal crops are wheat, barley, rice, tobacco, sugar beet, tea, olives, grapes, figs and hazelnuts. Tobacco, sultana and fig cultivation is centred around Izmir, where substantial quantities of cotton are also grown. The main cotton area is in the Cukurova plain around Adana.

The main export minerals are chromite and boron. Tourism is a major industry, with over 7.5 million visitors in 1999.

The bulk of the country's requirements in sugar, cotton, woollen and silk textiles, and cement, is produced locally. Other industries include vehicle assembly, paper, glass and glassware, iron and steel, leather and leather goods, sulphur refining, canning and rubber goods, soaps and cosmetics, pharmaceutical products, and prepared foodstuffs.

Turkey was accepted as a candidate for EU membership in December 1999 and following an EU summit in December 2002, the end of 2004 was set as the earliest possible date for the commencement of accession negotiations provided reforms continue.

After years of economic difficulty, a controversial economic recovery programme was agreed with the IMF in 2002. The government's main priorities are to make progress with tax reforms and privatisation and to reduce employment in the public sector.

GNP – US$202,131 million (2000); US$3,100 per capita (2000)
GDP – US$147,627 million (2001); US$2,998 per capita (2000)
ANNUAL AVERAGE GROWTH OF GDP – 7.5 per cent (2000)
INFLATION RATE – 54.9 per cent (2000)
UNEMPLOYMENT – 7.3 per cent (1999)
TOTAL EXTERNAL DEBT – US$116,209 million (2000)

TRADE

The main imports are machinery, crude oil and petroleum products, iron and steel, vehicles, medicines, chemicals and electrical appliances. Agricultural commodities represented 13.9 per cent of total exports in 2000. Other exports are minerals, textiles, glass and cement. Germany, the USA and Italy are the main trading partners.

In 2001 Turkey had a trade deficit of US$4,537 million and a current account deficit of US$3,396 million. Imports totalled US$53,499 million and exports US$26,572 million.

Trade with UK	2001	2002
Imports from UK	£1,202,014,000	£1,378,933,000
Exports to UK	1,775,821,000	2,314,734,000

EDUCATION

Education is free and secular, and since August 1997, compulsory from the ages of six to 14. There are elementary, secondary and vocational schools.

ILLITERACY RATE – (m) 6.5 per cent; (f) 23.4 per cent (2000)
ENROLMENT (percentage of age group) – primary 107 per cent (1997); secondary 58 per cent (1997); tertiary 21 per cent (1997)

CULTURE

Turkish is a Ural-Altaic language. Turkish was written in Arabic script until 1928 when a version of the Roman alphabet reflecting Turkish phonetics was adopted.

TURKMENISTAN

Turkmenostan Respublikasy – Republic of Turkmenistan

AREA – 188,456 sq. miles (488,100 sq. km).
  Neighbours: Iran and Afghanistan (south), Uzbekistan
  (east and north), Kazakhstan (north-west)
POPULATION – 5,500,000 (2002 estimate); 4,483,000
  (1996 census): 77 per cent Turkmen, 9.2 per cent
  Uzbek, 6.7 per cent Russian, together with smaller
  numbers of Kazakhs, Tatars, Ukrainians and
  Armenians. Most of the population are Sunni Muslims.
  The main languages are Turkmen (72 per cent),
  Russian (9 per cent), Uzbek (9 per cent). Turkmen is
  one of the Turkic languages
CAPITAL – Ashgabat (population, 604,700, 1995)
MAJOR CITIES – Charjou (203,000); Tashauz (165,400),
  1995
CURRENCY – Manat of 100 tenge
NATIONAL ANTHEM – Garashciiz Bitarap
  Turkmenistaniin Devlet Gimni (Independent Neutral
  Turkmenistan State Anthem)
NATIONAL DAY – 27–28 October (Independence Day)
NATIONAL FLAG – Green with a vertical carpet pattern
  near the hoist in black, white, green and wine-red; and
  in the lower part of the carpet design two laurel
  branches; in the upper hoist a crescent and five stars,
  all in white
POPULATION GROWTH RATE – 0.7 per cent
POPULATION DENSITY – 9 per sq. km (1999)
MILITARY EXPENDITURE – 3.2 per cent of GDP (2001)
MILITARY PERSONNEL – 17,500: Army 14,500, Air
  Force 3,000
CONSCRIPTION DURATION – Two years

HISTORY AND POLITICS

Turkmenistan has been invaded and occupied by many
empires: Persian; Greek, under Alexander the Great;
Parthian; Mongol. From the early 19th century until
1886 Turkmenistan was gradually incorporated into the
Russian Empire. Soviet control over Turkmenistan was
established on 30 April 1918 when it became an
Autonomous Soviet Socialist Republic. Turkmenistan
became a full republic of the Soviet Union in February
1925. Turkmenistan declared its independence from the
Soviet Union on 27 October 1991 and gained UN
membership on 2 March 1992.

The autocratic government of President Niyazov has
prevented any effective political opposition or free press
through harassment and authoritarianism. The political
leadership has rejected political pluralism and instead a
cult of personality has developed around President
Niyazov. The Supreme Soviet voted on 30 December
1993 to extend the term of President Niyazov to 2002
and this was confirmed by a 99.99 per cent vote in a
referendum on 15 January 1994. On 28 December
1999, the legislature removed the limit on his term of
office, effectively making him life president. The
Communist Party, renamed the Democratic Party (DP),
remains in power. Legislative elections to the *Khalk
Maslakhaty* held on 5 April 1998 were won by the
Democratic Party. General elections were held on 12
December 1999, in which all 50 seats in the *Majlis* were
won by candidates of the DP, the sole legal party.

FOREIGN RELATIONS

Agreement on dual citizenship for ethnic Russians in
Turkmenistan was reached in 1993. In December 1993

Turkmenistan signed the CIS charter to become a full CIS
member and in January 1994 became a member of the
CIS economic union. On 10 April 2003 the dual
citizenship deal was cancelled by President Niyazov and
those holding dual citizenship were given two months in
which to decide which passport to retain. A diplomatic
row with Russia consequently followed as Turkmenistan
rejected Russian allegations that the move would force
tens of thousands of ethnic Russians with dual citizenship
to leave the country, thereby jeopardising their rights.

POLITICAL SYSTEM

The 1992 constitution declares the president head of
state and government. The legislature is the 50-member
Majlis (formerly the Supreme Soviet). The *Khalk
Maslakhaty* (People's Council) is a supervisory body
with no legislative powers. The *Majlis* approved an
amendment to the constitution on 28 December 1999,
allowing President Niyazov to remain in power
indefinitely.

HEAD OF STATE

*President, Head of Government, Chair of the Council of
  Ministers,* Saparmurad Niyazov, *elected* 27 October
  1990, *re-elected* 21 June 1992, *appointed head of
  government* 18 May 1992, *elected by referendum for an
  eight-year term* 15 January 1994, *term extended
  indefinitely* 28 December 1999

COUNCIL OF MINISTERS *as at July 2003*

Prime Minister, The President
Deputy Prime Ministers, Muhammetnazar Hudaygulyyev
  (Construction and Construction Materials Industry);
  Rejepbay Arazov *(Defence);* Gurbanguli
  Berdymuhamedov *(Health and the Pharmaceutical
  Industry);* Gurbansoltan Handurdyyeva; Rashid
  Meredov *(Foreign Affairs); (Health and the
  Pharmaceutical Industry);* Yolly Gurbanmuradov;
  Seitbay Gandimov *(Interbank Council);* Dortkuly
  Aydogyev *(Textile Industry, Trade and Customs)*
Chair, Committee for Tourism and Sports, Nepesov Arslan
  Sakoyevich
Chair of the State Committee for Land Use and Land Reform,
  Seyitguly Chareyev
Chair of the State Border Service, Tirksih Tyrmyev
Chair of the State Commodity and Raw Materials Exchange,
  Ilyas Mahtumovich Chariyev
Chair of the Supreme Court, Ovezgeldy Atayev
*Agriculture, Director of the State Fund for the Development
  of Agriculture,* Bengench Atamuradov
Communications and Transport, Resulberdi
  Khodzhagurbanov
Culture, Orazgeldi Aydogdiyev
Economy and Finance, Yazguly Kakalyyev
Education, Mammetdurdy Saryhanov
Energy and Industry, Atamurad Berdiyev
General Public Prosecutor, Kurbanbibi Atadjanova
Interior, Ashir Atayev
Justice (acting), Taganmyrat Gocyyev
National Security, Batyr Busakov
Natural Resources and Environmental Protection, Matkarim
  Rajapov
Oil and Gas Industry and Mineral Resources, Tachberdy
  Taggivev
Social Security, Enebay Ataeva
Trade and Foreign Economic Relations, Dortguly
  Aidogdyev
Water Resources, Gurbangeldi Velmyradov

EMBASSY OF TURKMENISTAN
2nd Floor South, St George's House, 14/17 Wells Street,
London W1P 3FP
Tel: 020-7255 1071
Ambassador Extraordinary and Plenipotentiary, vacant
Counsellor, Nurmurat Redjebov

BRITISH EMBASSY
301–308, Office Building, Four Points Ak Altin Hotel, Ashgabat
Tel: (00 993) (12) 363462/363463/363464
Ambassador Extraordinary and Plenipotentiary, HE Paul
   Brummel, apptd 2002

ECONOMY
Revenues from natural gas reserves make the country
economically viable and have enabled the government to
maintain low stable prices for basic commodities and
utilities. The principal industries are cotton cultivation,
stock-raising and mineral extraction, together with
natural gas production and the silk industry. Arable land
is irrigated by the Niyazov canal, which cuts through the
Kara Kum desert. There are estimated reserves of some
700 million tonnes of oil and 8,000,000 million cubic
metres of natural gas. Natural gas is exported by pipeline
to Ukraine and western Europe. An agreement to build
further pipelines under the Caspian Sea, through
Azerbaijan and Georgia, to supply gas to Turkey was
reached in November 1999. In April 2003 agreement
was under which Russia would buy 60 billion cubic
metres of gas from Turkmenistan annually beginning in
2004. In 1997 there was a trade deficit of US$231
million and a current account deficit of US$580 million.
GNP – US$3,886 million (2000); US$750 per capita
   (2000)
GDP – US$5,962 million (2001); US$934 per capita
   (2000)
ANNUAL AVERAGE GROWTH OF GDP – 5.0 per cent
   (1998)
TOTAL EXTERNAL DEBT – US$2,259 million (2000)

Trade with UK	2001	2002
Imports from UK	£6,679,000	£6,909,000
Exports to UK	2,035,000	4,651,000

TUVALU

*Fakavae Aliki-Moloi Tuvalu/Constitutional Monarchy of
Tuvalu*

AREA – 10 sq. miles (26 sq. km)
POPULATION – 10,991 (2001). About 1,500 Tuvaluans
   work overseas, mostly in Nauru, or as seamen. The
   people are almost entirely Polynesian. The principal
   languages are Tuvaluan and English.
CAPITAL – ΨFongafale (population, 2,856)
CURRENCY – The Australian dollar ($A) of 100 cents is
   legal tender. In addition there are Tuvalu dollar and
   cent coins in circulation
NATIONAL ANTHEM – Tuvalu Mo Te Atua (Tuvalu For
   The Almighty)
NATIONAL DAY – 1 October (Independence Day)
NATIONAL FLAG – Light blue ground with Union flag in
   top left quarter and nine five-pointed gold stars in the
   fly
POPULATION GROWTH RATE – 1.8 per cent
POPULATION DENSITY – 423 per sq. km (1999)

Tuvalu comprises nine coral atolls situated in the south-
west Pacific around the point at which the International
Date Line cuts the Equator. Few of the atolls are more
than 12 ft above sea level.

HISTORY AND POLITICS
Tuvalu, formerly the Ellice Islands, formed part of the
Gilbert and Ellice Islands Colony until 1 October 1975,
when separate constitutions came into force. Separation
from the Gilbert Islands was implemented on 1 January
1976. On 1 October 1978 Tuvalu became a fully
independent state within the Commonwealth.
   Following the death of Prime Minister Ionatana
Ionatana on 8 December 2000, Faimalaga Luka was
chosen to replace him on 23 February 2001. Luka's
government lost a vote of no confidence on 7 December
2001 and Koloa Talake was elected prime minister on 13
December. In parliamentary elections held on 25 July
2002 Prime Minister Talake lost his seat. Saufatu
Sopanga was elected prime minister by parliament on
2 August.
   Tuvalu became a full member of the UN on
17 February 2000.

POLITICAL SYSTEM
The constitution provides for a prime minister and four
other ministers, who must be members of the 13-member
parliament, 12 of whom are directly elected. The prime
minister presides at meetings of the Cabinet, which
consists of the five Ministers and is attended by the
Attorney-General.

Governor-General, Sir Tomasi Puapua

CABINET *as at July 2003*
Prime Minister, Foreign Affairs, Labour, Saufatu Sopoanga
*Deputy Prime Minister, Works, Communications and
   Transport,* Maatia Toafa
Finance and Economic Planning, Industry, Bikenibeu
   Paeniu
Health, Education and Sports, Alesana K. Seluka
Home Affairs and Rural Development, Otinielu Tuasi
Natural Resources, Energy and the Environment, Tourism,
   Samuelu P. Teo

HONORARY CONSULATE OF TUVALU
Tuvalu House, 230 Worple Road, London SW20 8RH
Tel: 020-8879 0985
Honorary Consul, Iftikhar Ayaz

BRITISH HIGH COMMISSIONER, HE Charles Mochan,
   apptd 2002, resident at Suva, Fiji

ECONOMY
The main imports are foodstuffs, semi-manufactures,
machinery and transport equipment and fuels. The main
exports are copra and fish, though philatelic sales provide
a major source of revenue and handicraft sales are
increasing. However, Tuvalu is almost entirely dependent
on foreign aid. Funafuti has an airfield from which a
service operates regularly to Fiji and Kiribati, and is also
the only port.
GDP – US$14 million (1998); US$1,491 per capita
   (2000)
ANNUAL AVERAGE GROWTH OF GDP – 2.0 per cent
   (1998)

Trade with UK	2001	2002
Imports from UK	£147,000	£34,000
Exports to UK	167,000	511,000

UGANDA

Republic of Uganda

AREA – 75,808 sq. miles (197,100 sq. km). Neighbours: Democratic Republic of Congo (west), Sudan (north), Kenya (east), Tanzania and Rwanda (south)
POPULATION – 24,023,000 (2001): 17 per cent Baganda, 12 per cent Karamojong; many other ethnic groups including Basoga, Iteso, Langi, Banyarwanda, Bagisu, Acholi, Lugbara, Banyoro and Batoro. The official language is English.
CAPITAL – Kampala (population, 774,241, 1991)
MAJOR CITIES – Jinja (65,169); Masaka (49,585); Mbale (53,987) 1991 census
CURRENCY – Uganda shilling of 100 cents
NATIONAL ANTHEM – Oh Uganda
NATIONAL DAY – 9 October (Independence Day)
NATIONAL FLAG – Six horizontal stripes of black, yellow, red, with a white disc in the centre containing the badge of a crested crane
LIFE EXPECTANCY (years) – 45 (2001)
POPULATION GROWTH RATE – 3 per cent
POPULATION DENSITY – 122 per sq. km (2001)
URBAN POPULATION – 15 per cent (2001)
MILITARY EXPENDITURE – 2.2 per cent of GDP (2001)
MILITARY PERSONNEL – Ugandan People's Defence Force 60,000; Paramilitaries 1,800

HISTORY AND POLITICS

Uganda became an independent state within the Commonwealth on 9 October 1962, after some 70 years of British rule. A republic was instituted in 1967. In 1971 an army coup took place and Maj.-Gen. Idi Amin, the army commander, proclaimed himself head of state. In 1979 President Amin was overthrown. Dr Milton Obote became president in 1980 but was ousted by a military coup in 1985. A military council was installed but the National Resistance Movement led by Yoweri Museveni captured Kampala in January 1986, securing control of the rest of the country in the following few months. Yoweri Museveni was sworn in as president in January 1986. President Museveni won the first direct presidential election on 9 May 1996. Supporters of the president won a majority of seats in legislative elections on 27 June. The suspension of political party activity introduced by President Museveni in 1986, was endorsed in a referendum held on 29 June 2000, in which 90.7 per cent of those voting backed the continuation of the no party 'Movement' system, in which political parties were allowed to exist, but not to contest elections.

President Museveni was re-elected on 12 March 2001, winning 69.3 per cent of the vote. A general election was held on 26 June in which most seats were won by supporters of the no party 'Movement' system.

In February and March 2003 both the courts and the president made moves towards allowing political parties.

INSURGENCIES

When Idi Amin was overthrown in 1979, thousands of his troops fled across the border into Sudan where some joined a rebel group, the Uganda National Rescue Front (UNRF). Over 1,000 rebels made peace after President Yoweri Museveni came to power in 1986, and the remainder, known as UNRF 2 signed a peace deal on 24 December 2002 ending more than five years of negotiations between the government and rebels.

POLITICAL SYSTEM

A new constitution, promulgated on 8 October 1995, endorsed the existing non-party political system. The president, who is head of government, is directly elected for a five-year term. The legislature, the 276-seat National Assembly, is also directly elected for a five-year term; 214 members are elected by constituencies and 62 are elected indirectly to represent particular groups.

HEAD OF STATE

President,Commander-in-Chief, Yoweri Museveni, *sworn in* 29 January 1986, *elected* 9 May 1996, *re-elected* 12 March 2001
Vice-President, Gilbert Balibaseka Bukenya

CABINET *as at July 2003*
The President
The Vice-President
Prime Minister, Apolo Nsibambi
First Deputy Prime Minister, Disaster Preparedness, Brig. Moses Ali
Second Deputy Prime Minister, Foreign Affairs, James Wambogo Wapakhabulo
Third Deputy Prime Minister, Public Service, Henry Muganwa Kajura
Agriculture, Animal Industry and Fisheries, Wilberforce Kisamba Mugwera
Attorney-General, Francis Ayume
Defence, Amama Mbabazi
Education and Sports, Edward Kiddu Makubuya
Energy and Minerals, Ssyda Namirembe Bbumba
Finance, Planning and Economic Development, Gerald Ssendaula
Gender, Zoe Bakoko-Bakoru
Health, Jim Katugugu Muhwezi
Internal Affairs, Ruhakana Rugunda
Justice and Constitutional Affairs, Janet Mukwaya
Local Government, Tarsis Kabwegyere
Parliamentary Affairs, Hope Mwesigye
Presidency, Kirunda Kivejinja
Prime Minister's Office, George Mondo Kagonyera
Public Works, Housing and Communications, John Nassasira
Regional Co-operation, Augustine Nshimye Ssebutulo
Tourism, Trade and Industry, Edward Rugumayo
Water, Lands and Environment, Col. Kahinda Otafiire
Without Portfolio, National Political Commissar, Crispus Kiyonga

UGANDA HIGH COMMISSION
Uganda House, 58–59 Trafalgar Square, London WC2N 5DX
Tel: 020-7839 5783
High Commissioner, HE Prof. George Kirya, apptd 1990

BRITISH HIGH COMMISSION
10–12 Parliament Avenue, PO Box 7070, Kampala
Tel: (00 256) (78) 312000
High Commissioner, HE Adam Wood, apptd 2002

BRITISH COUNCIL DIRECTOR, Philip Goodwin
Rwenzori Courts, Plot 2 and 4a, Nakasero Road, PO Box 7070, Kampala Tel: (00 256) (78) 234 725/730
Email: info@britishcouncil.or.ug

ECONOMY

On 8 February 2000, the IMF pledged US$139 million in debt relief, and the International Development Association (IDA) announced that it would give assistance of US$629 million over 20 years. In March, donor countries pledged at least US$2,000 million over three years to support economic development. The principal export earners are coffee, tobacco, cotton and tea. Hydroelectricity is produced from the Owen Falls power station, some of which is exported to Kenya, Tanzania and Rwanda. The principal food crops are plantains, sugar cane, cassava, maize and sorghum.

In 2001 imports totalled US$1,594 million and exports US$456 million.

GNP – US$6,699 million (2000); US$300 per capita (2000)

GDP – US$5,707 million (2001); US$257 per capita (2000)

ANNUAL AVERAGE GROWTH OF GDP – 1.4 per cent (1998)

INFLATION RATE – 2.8 per cent (2000)

TOTAL EXTERNAL DEBT – US$3,409 million (2000)

Trade with UK	2001	2002
Imports from UK	£34,814,000	£33,666,000
Exports to UK	8,542,000	10,672,000

COMMUNICATIONS

There is an international airport at Entebbe, and eight other airfields around the country. Having no sea coast, Uganda is dependent upon rail and road links to Mombasa and Dar es Salaam for its trade.

EDUCATION

Education is a joint undertaking by the government, local authorities and voluntary agencies. In 1996, the Universal Primary Programme was launched, under which four children per family are entitled to receive free primary education.

ILLITERACY RATE – (m) 22.4 per cent; (f) 43.1 per cent (2000)

ENROLMENT (percentage of age group) – tertiary 2 per cent (1997)

UKRAINE

Ukraina – Ukraine

AREA – 233,846 sq. miles (579,400 sq. km).
Neighbours: Belarus (north), Russia (north and east), Romania and Moldova (south-west), Hungary, Slovakia and Poland (west)

POPULATION – 49,112,000 (2001); 51,471,000 (1989 census): 73 per cent Ukrainian, 22 per cent Russian, with smaller numbers of Jews, Belarusians, Moldovans, Tatars, Poles, Hungarians and Greeks. The majority religion is Orthodox Christianity.

CAPITAL – Kiev (Kyiv) (population, 2,602,000, 2001 census)

MAJOR CITIES – Dnipropetrovsk (1,064,000); Donetsk (1,016,000); Kharkiv (1,470,000); Lviv (732,000), ΨOdesa (1,029,000), Zaporizhzhya (814,000), 2001 census

CURRENCY – Hryvna of 100 kopiykas

NATIONAL ANTHEM – Shche Ne Vmerla, Ukraïna (Thou Hast Not Perished, Ukraine)

NATIONAL DAY – 24 August (Independence Day)

NATIONAL FLAG – Two horizontal stripes of blue over yellow

POPULATION GROWTH RATE – −0.5 per cent

POPULATION DENSITY – 85 per sq. km (2001)

URBAN POPULATION – 68 per cent (2001)

ILLITERACY RATE – (m) 0.3 per cent; (f) 0.5 per cent (2000)

ENROLMENT (percentage of age group) – tertiary 42 per cent (1997)

Ukraine consists of 24 regions and the Autonomous Republic of Crimea. The Carpathian mountains lie in the south-western part of the republic. The main rivers are the Dnieper with its tributaries, the Southern Bug and the Northern Donets (a tributary of the Don).

HISTORY AND POLITICS

The earliest Slavic state was formed in the middle reaches of the Dnieper River with its capital at Kyiv in the ninth century AD. The state lasted until Kyiv fell to the Tatar-Mongols in 1240. For the next four centuries Ukraine was invaded and ruled by Poles and Lithuanians. Kyiv was liberated from the Poles in 1648 and in 1654 Ukraine became a protectorate of Russia.

Ukraine declared its independence in 1918, but was invaded by Poland in 1919 before becoming a constituent republic of the USSR on 30 December 1922.

Ukraine declared itself independent of the Soviet Union on 24 August 1991. Independence was confirmed by a referendum held on 1 December 1991 and Leonid Kravchuk was elected to the presidency. In the June 1994 presidential election Leonid Kuchma defeated President Kravchuk. President Kuchma won a second term of office in a presidential election on 14 November 1999, receiving 56.25 per cent of the vote.

In January 2000, the Supreme Council split into two factions following a failed attempt by the pro-government faction to remove the Speaker, Oleksandr Tkachenko, from office. The minority left-wing faction remained in control of the Supreme Council building until the pro-government majority faction forcibly took control of the Supreme Council building on 8 February 2000.

In legislative elections held on 31 March 2002, the Our Ukraine bloc became the largest party in the parliament winning 112 seats. The For United Ukraine bloc won 102 seats and the Communist Party of Ukraine 66 seats. Following lengthy discussions during the summer of 2002, a coalition comprising supporters of President Kuchma and a number of independents was agreed in late October 2002. The incumbent Prime Minister, Anatoliy Kinakh was dismissed by the president on 16 November 2002 and Viktor Yanukovych, his replacement, was approved by parliament on 21 November.

INSURGENCIES

A pro-Russian majority in the Crimean parliament voted to make Crimea an autonomous republic in September 1991, which was accepted by Ukraine, but then voted for independence, which was not accepted, and the declaration of independence was rescinded in May 1992. Elections to the Crimean parliament in August 1995 saw a dramatic drop in support for pro-Russian parties. Arkady Demydenko was appointed Prime Minister of Crimea on 26 February 1996. A new constitution, which gave Crimea property and budget rights, came into effect in January 1999.

A referendum in June 1994 in the Donbass region of eastern Ukraine in favour of closer economic ties with Russia and making Russian an official language was overwhelmingly passed, as was one in the Crimea in favour of dual Russian-Ukrainian citizenship.

FOREIGN RELATIONS
In May 1997, a treaty of friendship and co-operation was signed with Russia. Agreement was also reached over the division of the former Soviet Black Sea Fleet. In February 1998, a treaty on economic co-operation was signed between Ukraine and Russia which aimed to strengthen industrial and commercial links and move towards the introduction of the free movement of goods, services, capital and labour.

Ukraine signed a partnership and co-operation agreement with the EU in June 1994 and in July 1997 signed the NATO-Ukraine Charter to enhance co-operation on peacekeeping.

POLITICAL SYSTEM
The unicameral Supreme Council has 450 members, who serve a four-year term. Half of the seats in the Supreme Council are elected from single-seat constituencies by a simple majority, and the other 225 are to be filled by proportional representation from party lists, with a 4 per cent threshold for representation. A member may only be elected if the turnout in the electoral district is above 50 per cent.

HEAD OF STATE
President, Leonid Kuchma, *elected* 10 July 1994, *sworn in* 19 July 1994, *re-elected* 14 November 1999

CABINET *as at July 2003*
Prime Minister, Viktor Yanukovych
First Deputy Prime Minister, Finance, Mykola Azarov
Deputy Prime Ministers, Ivan Kirilenko *(Agriculture);* Vitaliy Gaiduk *(Energy);* Dmitro Tabachnik *(Humanitarian Affairs)*
Agroindustrial Policy, Serhiy Ryzhuk
Culture and Art, Yuriy Bohutskiy
Defence, Yevhen Marchuk
Economy and European Integration, Valeriy Khoroshkovskyy
Education and Science, Vasyl Kremen
Emergency Situations, Grygoriy Reva
Energy and Fuel, Serhiy Yermilov
Environment and Natural Resources, vacant
Foreign Affairs, Anatoliy Zlenko
Health Protection, Andriy Pidayev
Industrial Policy, Anatoliy Myalytsa
Interior, Yuriy Smirnov
Justice, Oleksandr Lavrynovych
Labour and Social Policy, Mykhaylo Papiyev
Relations with the Supreme Council, Ivan Thalenko
Transport, Georgiy Kirpa

UKRAINIAN EMBASSY
60 Holland Park, London W11 3SJ
Tel: 020-7727 6312
Ambassador Extraordinary and Plenipotentiary, Ihor Mitiukov, apptd 2002

BRITISH EMBASSY
UA-01025 Kyiv, Desyatinna 9
Tel: (00 380) (44) 462 0011/2/3/4
Ambassador Extraordinary and Plenipotentiary, HE Robert Brinkley, apptd 2002

BRITISH COUNCIL DIRECTOR, Liliana Biglou
4/12 Vul. Hryhoriya Skovorody, UA-04070 Kyiv
Tel: (00 380) (44) 490 5600
Email: enquiry@britishcouncil.org.ua

DEFENCE
The Constitution bans the stationing of foreign troops on Ukrainian soil, but permits Russia to retain naval bases. The Army has 3,905 main battle tanks, 1,682 armoured personnel carriers, 3,043 armoured infantry fighting vehicles and 205 attack helicopters. The Navy has one submarine, three principal surface combat vessels and nine patrol and coastal vessels at six bases. The Air Force has 499 combat aircraft. A detachment of Ukrainian troops was sent to Iraq in August 2003 and as part of a contingent of soldiers which are to be deployed to help restore stability.
MILITARY EXPENDITURE – 2.2 per cent of GDP (2001)
MILITARY PERSONNEL – 302,300: Army 150,700, Navy 13,500, Air Force 49,100; Paramilitaries 112,500
CONSCRIPTION DURATION – 18 months to two years

ECONOMY
The Communist-led government of 1991–4 was characterised by economic mismanagement and opposition to economic reforms. Successive governments were unable to gain consensus for a reform programme, which delayed economic restructuring. Ukraine joined the CIS economic union as an associate member in 1993.

Since his election in 1999, President Kuchma has introduced a wide-ranging economic reform programme. Continuing economic difficulties led to the devaluation of the hryvna in February 1999. In March 2000, the IMF issued an interim statement about the alleged misuse of foreign currency reserves, saying that Ukraine had received IMF funds in 1997–8 that it would not have received had the true state of the country's reserves been known. The IMF subsequently suspended its loan programme to Ukraine.

Metal processing, the manufacture of machinery, and the chemical and petrochemical industries are major contributors to Ukraine's GDP; mining and metallurgy account for more than 40 per cent of exports. The southern part of the country contains a coal-mining and iron and steel industrial area. Ukraine also contains engineering and chemical industries and ship building yards on the Black Sea coast. Ukrainian agricultural production is good with large areas under cultivation with wheat, cotton, flax and sugar beet; stock-raising is very important. There are large deposits of coal and salt, iron ore, manganese and quicksilver.

Russia is the main trading partner, accounting for 24 per cent of exports and 41.7 per cent of imports in 2000. Trade negotiations between Ukraine and Russia in April 2002 included agreements on gas transits and oil pipelines. Turkey, Germany, the USA and Turkmenistan are also major trading partners.

In 2001 there was a trade surplus of US$198 million and a current account surplus of US$1,402 million. In 1999 imports totalled US$11,846 million and exports US$11,582 million.
GNP – US$34,565 million (2000); US$700 per capita (2000)
GDP – US$37,588 million (2001); US$639 per capita (2000)
ANNUAL AVERAGE GROWTH OF GDP – –6 per cent (2000)
INFLATION RATE – 22.7 per cent (1999)

UNEMPLOYMENT – 11.7 per cent (2000)
TOTAL EXTERNAL DEBT – US$12,166 million (2000)

Trade with UK	2001	2002
Imports from UK	£204,461,000	£182,436,000
Exports to UK	72,028,000	148,201,000

UNITED ARAB EMIRATES

*Dawlat Al-Amarat Al-'Arabiyya Al-Muttahida – United
Arab Emirates*

AREA – 32,154 sq. miles (83,600 sq. km) approximately.
    Neighbours: Oman (north-east and east), Saudi Arabia
    (south and west), Qatar (north-west)
POPULATION – 2,654,000 (2001), of which 75 per cent
    are expatriates. The official language is Arabic, and
    English is widely spoken. The established religion is
    Islam
CAPITAL – Abu Dhabi (population, 450,000)
CURRENCY – UAE dirham (Dh) of 100 fils
NATIONAL DAY – 2 December
NATIONAL FLAG – Horizontal stripes of green over
    white over black with vertical red stripe in the hoist
LIFE EXPECTANCY (years) – 78 (2001)
POPULATION GROWTH RATE – 2.5 per cent
POPULATION DENSITY – 32 per sq. km (2001)

The United Arab Emirates is situated in the south-east of
the Arabian peninsula. Six of the emirates lie on the shore
of the Gulf between the Musandam peninsula in the east
and the Qatar peninsula in the west while the seventh,
Fujairah, lies on the Gulf of Oman.

HISTORY AND POLITICS

The United Arab Emirates (formerly the Trucial States) is
composed of seven emirates (Abu Dhabi, Ajman, Dubai,
Fujairah, Ras al-Khaimah, Sharjah and Umm al-Qaiwain)
which came together as an independent state on 2
December 1971 when they ended their individual special
treaty relationships with the British government (Ras al-
Khaimah joined the other six on 10 February 1972). On
independence, the Union Government assumed full
responsibility for all internal and external affairs apart
from some internal matters that remained the prerogative
of the individual emirates.

FOREIGN RELATIONS

Relations with Iran remain strained over Iran's illegal
occupation of three UAE islands in the Gulf (Abu Musa
and the Two Tunbs).

POLITICAL SYSTEM

Overall authority lies with the Supreme Council of the
seven emirate rulers, each of whom also governs in his
own territory. The president and vice-president are
elected every five years by the Supreme Council from
among its members. The president appoints the Council
of Ministers. A 40-member Federal National Council,
comprising eight members each from Abu Dhabi and
Dubai, six each from Sharjah and Ras al-Khaimah and
four each for Fujairah, Umm al-Qaiwain and Ajman,
appointed by the rulers of each emirate, studies draft laws
referred to it by the Council of Ministers.

The legal system consists of both secular and religious
courts guided by the Islamic philosophy of justice.
Individual emirates retain their own penal codes and
courts alongside a federal court system and penal code.

FEDERAL STRUCTURE

Each emirate has its separate government, with Abu
Dhabi having an executive council chaired by the Crown
Prince.

HEAD OF STATE

President, HH Sheikh Zayed bin Sultan al-Nahyan *(Abu
    Dhabi), elected* 1971, *re-elected* 1976, 1981, 1986,
    1991, 1996, December 2001
Vice-President, Prime Minister, HH Sheikh Maktoum bin
    Rashid al-Maktoum *(Dubai)*

SUPREME COUNCIL

The President
The Vice-President
HH Sheikh Sultan bin Mohammed al-Qassimi *(Sharjah)*
HH Sheikh Saqr bin Mohammed al-Qassimi *(Ras
    Al-Khaimah)*
HH Sheikh Hamad bin Mohammed al-Sharqi *(Fujairah)*
HH Sheikh Humaid bin Rashid al-Nuaimi *(Ajman)*
HH Sheikh Rashid bin Ahmad al-Mualla *(Umm
    al-Qaiwain)*

COUNCIL OF MINISTERS *as at July 2003*

The Vice-President
Deputy Prime Minister, Sheikh Sultan bin Zayed
    al-Nahyan
Agriculture and Fisheries, Saeed Mohammed al-Raqabani
Communications, Ahmed Humaid al-Tayir
Defence, HH Gen. Sheikh Mohammed bin Rashid
    al-Maktoum
Economy and Commerce, HH Sheikh Fahim bin Sultan
    al-Qassimi
Education and Youth, Ali Abd al-Aziz al-Sharhan
Electricity and Water, Humaid bin Nasir al-Uways
Finance and Industry, HH Sheikh Hamdan bin Rashid
    al-Maktoum
Foreign Affairs, Rashid Abdullah al-Nuaimi
Health, Hamad Abdul Rahman al-Madfa
Higher Education and Scientific Research, HH Sheikh
    Nahyan bin Mubarak al-Nahyan
Information and Culture, HH Sheikh Abdullah bin Zayed
    al-Nahyan
Interior, Lt.-Gen. Mohammed Saeed al-Badi
Justice, Islamic Affairs and Awqaf (Religious Endowments),
    Mohammed Nakhira al-Dhahiri
Labour and Social Affairs, Matar Humaid al-Tayir
Ministers of State, Saeed Khalfan al-Ghaith *(Cabinet
    Affairs);* Mohammed Khalfan bin Kharbash *(Finance
    and Industrial Affairs);* Sheikh Hamdan bin Zayed
    al-Nahyan *(Foreign Affairs);* Sheikh Majid bin Saeed
    al-Nuaimi *(Supreme Council Affairs)*
Petroleum and Mineral Resources, Ubayd bin Sayf al-Nasiri
Planning, HH Sheikh Humaid bin Ahmed al-Mualla
Public Works and Housing, Rakadh bin Salem al-Rakadh

EMBASSY OF THE UNITED ARAB EMIRATES
30 Princes Gate, London SW7 1PT
Tel 020-7581 1281
Ambassador Extraordinary and Plenipotentiary, HE Easa
    Saleh al-Gurg, CBE, apptd 1991

BRITISH EMBASSIES
PO Box 248, Abu Dhabi
Tel: (00 971) (2) 610 1100
Ambassador Extraordinary and Plenipotentiary, HE Richard
    Makepeace, apptd 2003
PO Box 65, Dubai
Tel: (00 971) (4) 309 4444

BRITISH COUNCIL DIRECTOR, Peter Ellwood, OBE
Villa no. 7, Al-Nasr Street, Khalidiya, PO Box 46523, Abu Dhabi
Tel: (00 971) (2) 665 9300
Email: information@ae.britishcouncil.org

DEFENCE
The Army has 381 main battle tanks, 750 armoured
personnel carriers and 430 armoured infantry fighting
vehicles. The Navy has two frigates and 16 patrol and
coastal vessels. The Air Force has 101 combat aircraft and
49 armed helicopters.
MILITARY EXPENDITURE – 4.6 per cent of GDP (2001)
MILITARY PERSONNEL – 41,500: Army 35,000, Navy
2,500, Air Force 4,000

ECONOMY
The UAE is the Gulf's third largest oil producer after
Saudi Arabia and Iran, with oil reserves of 98,200 million
barrels and gas reserves of 5,800 million cubic metres. Oil
production in 2000 accounted for 33.9 per cent of GDP.
Other important sectors of the economy are
manufacturing (aluminium, cement, chemicals, fertilisers,
pharmaceuticals, ship repair), government services,
construction, transport, communications, financial services
and tourism. Agricultural production has increased due to
large-scale water desalination and irrigation projects.
There is no personal or corporate taxation apart from on
oil companies and foreign banks. There are several free
zones, where overseas companies can trade tax-free.

Oil revenues over the past 30 years have enabled the
government to invest heavily in education, health and
social services, housing, transport and communications
infrastructure, and agriculture, and enabled the UAE's
citizens to have one of the highest GDPs per capita in the
world.
GNP – US$48,673 million (1998); US$17,870 per
capita (1998)
GDP – US$45,899 million (1998); US$20,457 per
capita (2000)
ANNUAL AVERAGE GROWTH OF GDP – –7.0 per cent
(1998)

Trade with UK	2001	2002
Imports from UK	£1,609,622,000	£1,612,780,000
Exports to UK	688,349,000	783,980,000

EDUCATION
In 2000 there were 747 government schools, where
education is free; and 426 private schools. There are five
universities.
ILLITERACY RATE – (m) 25.9 per cent; (f) 21.1 per cent
(2000)
ENROLMENT (percentage of age group) – primary 89 per
cent (1997); secondary 80 per cent (1997); tertiary 12
per cent (1997)

UNITED STATES OF AMERICA

AREA – 3,615,275 sq. miles (9,363,520 sq. km).
Neighbours: Canada (north), Mexico (south)
POPULATION – 281,421,906 (2001). The language is
English. There is a significant Spanish-speaking
minority
CAPITAL – Washington DC (population, 4,923,153,
2000 census). The area of the District of Columbia
(with which the City of Washington is considered
co-extensive) is 61 sq. miles, with a resident population
(2000 census) of 572,059. The District of Columbia is
governed by an elected mayor and City Council

MAJOR CITIES –ΨChicago (2,896,016); Dallas
(1,188,580); ΨDetroit (951,270); ΨHouston
(1,953,631); ΨLos Angeles (3,694,820); ΨNew York
(8,008,278); ΨPhiladelphia (1,517,550); Phoenix
(1,321,045); San Antonio (1,144,646); ΨSan Diego
(1,223,400), 2000 census
CURRENCY – US dollar (US$) of 100 cents
NATIONAL ANTHEM – The Star-Spangled Banner
NATIONAL DAY – 4 July (Independence Day)
NATIONAL FLAG – Thirteen horizontal stripes,
alternately red and white, with blue canton in the hoist
showing 50 white stars in nine horizontal rows of six
and five alternately (known as the Star-Spangled
Banner)
LIFE EXPECTANCY (years) – 77 (2001)
POPULATION GROWTH RATE – 1.0 per cent (2001)
POPULATION DENSITY – 31 per sq. km (2001)
URBAN POPULATION – 77 per cent (2001)

The coastline has a length of about 2,069 miles on the
Atlantic, 7,623 miles on the Pacific, 1,060 miles on the
Arctic, and 1,631 miles on the Gulf of Mexico. The
principal river is the Mississippi-Missouri-Red (3,710 miles
long), traversing the whole country to its mouth in the Gulf
of Mexico. The chain of the Rocky Mountains separates the
western portion of the country from the remainder. West of
these, bordering the Pacific coast, the Cascade Mountains
and Sierra Nevada form the outer edge of a high tableland,
consisting in part of stony and sandy desert and partly of
grazing land and forested mountains, and including the
Great Salt Lake, which extends to the Rocky Mountains. In
the eastern states large forests still exist, the remnants of the
forests which formerly extended over all the Atlantic slope.
The highest point is Mount McKinley (20,320 ft) in Alaska,
and the lowest point of dry land is in Death Valley (Inyo,
California), 282 ft below sea level.

AREA AND POPULATION

	Total land Area (sq. km)	Population census 1990
The United States (a)	9,159,116	248,709,873
Outlying areas under		
US jurisdiction	10,929	3,862,431
Territories	10,888	3,862,238
Puerto Rico	8,875	3,522,037
Guam	544	133,152
US Virgin Islands	346	101,809
American Samoa	200	46,773
Northern Mariana Is.	464	43,345
Other US possessions	41	193
Population abroad (b)	–	925,845
Total	9,170,045	253,498,149

(a) the 50 states and the Federal District of Columbia
(b) excludes US citizens temporarily abroad on business

RESIDENT POPULATION BY RACE 2001 ESTIMATE
(Thousands)

White	211,461
Black	34,658
*American Indian	2,476
Asian	10,242
Native Hawaiian and other Pacific Islanders	399
†Hispanic origin	35,306
Other race	15,359
Two or more races	6,826
Total	316,727

*Includes Eskimo and Aleut
†Persons of Hispanic origin may be of any race

IMMIGRATION
From 1820 to 2000, 666,089,431 immigrants were admitted to the United States. The total number of immigrants in 2000 was 849,807, of which 400,879 came from North and South America (173,919 from Mexico), 265,400 from Asia and 132,480 from Europe.

HISTORY AND POLITICS
The area which is now the USA was first inhabited by nomadic hunters who probably arrived from Asia c.30,000 BC. The first (failed) European colony was founded by Sir Walter Raleigh in 1585. By 1733 there were 13 British colonies, composed largely of religious non-conformists who had left Britain to escape persecution; the French and Spanish had also founded colonies. The War of Independence broke out in 1775 largely because of the colonists' objection to being taxed by, but having no representation in, the British Parliament. The forces of the British government were defeated with French, Spanish and Dutch assistance. The Declaration of Independence which inaugurated the United States of America was signed on 4 July 1776; Britain recognised American sovereignty in 1783. The first federal constitution was drawn up in 1787; ten amendments, termed the Bill of Rights, were added in 1791. The 13 original states of the Union ratified the constitution between 1787 and 1790. Vermont, Kentucky and Tennessee were admitted in the 1790s but most of the states acceded in the 19th century as the opening up of the centre and west led to the creation of new states and European or neighbouring countries ceded or sold their territories to the USA.

The Civil War (1861–5) was fought over the issue of slavery, which was integral to the economy of the southern states but was opposed by the northern states. The northern states defeated the Confederacy of southern states (South Carolina, Georgia, Alabama, Florida, Mississippi, Louisiana).

The USA emerged as a world economic and military superpower in the 20th century and played a decisive role in the two world wars. Its economic and military (including nuclear) supremacy gave the USA a key role in shaping the post-war world.

FOREIGN RELATIONS
Following the terrorist attacks in New York and Washington DC of 11 September 2001, believed to have been carried out by Osama bin Laden's Islamist group, al Qa'eda, the USA led a military operation against al Qa'eda and the Taliban in Afghanistan on 7 October 2001 (see Afghanistan). Attempts to capture bin Laden and the Taliban leader, Mullah Omar, were unsuccessful.

Tensions rose between the USA and Iraq in September 2002 over US concerns that Iraq was developing weapons of mass destruction. UN weapons inspections continued into 2003 but the situation deteriorated and on 20 March 2003 the USA led a military campaign to remove the Iraqi president, Saddam Hussein, from power. US forces advanced into central Baghdad in early April and on 1 May, US President George Bush declared the major part of the war in Iraq to be over. US troops remained in Iraq to stabilise the country. As at September 2003 the whereabouts of Saddam Hussein remained unknown.

A Department of Homeland Security was created in November 2002 in the biggest reorganisation of the federal government for more than 50 years in response to the threat of terrorist attacks on US soil.

POLITICAL SYSTEM
By the constitution of 17 September 1787 (to which amendments were added in 1791, 1798, 1804, 1865, 1868, 1870, 1913, 1920, 1933, 1951, 1961, 1964, 1967, 1971 and 1992), the government of the United States is entrusted to three separate authorities: the executive (the president and Cabinet), the legislature (Congress) and the judicature. The president is indirectly elected by an electoral college every four years. There is also a vice-president, who, should the president die, becomes president for the remainder of the term. The tenure of the presidency is limited to two terms. The president, with the consent of the Senate, appoints the Cabinet officers and all the chief officials. He makes recommendations of a general nature to Congress, and when laws are passed by Congress he may return them to Congress with a veto. But if a measure so vetoed is again passed by both Houses of Congress by two-thirds majority in each House, it becomes law, notwithstanding the objection of the president. The president must be at least 35 years of age and a native citizen of the United States.

PRESIDENTIAL ELECTIONS
Each state elects (on the first Tuesday after the first Monday in November of the year preceding the year in which the presidential term expires) a number of electors (members of the electoral college), equal to the whole number of Senators and Representatives to which the state may be entitled in the Congress. The electors for each state meet in their respective states on the first Monday after the second Wednesday in December following, and vote for a president by ballot. The ballots are then sent to Washington, and opened on 6 January by the President of the Senate in the presence of Congress. The candidate who has received a majority of the whole number of electoral votes cast is declared president for the ensuing term. If no one has a majority, then from the highest on the list (not exceeding three) the House of Representatives elects a president, the votes being taken by states, the representation from each state having one vote. A presidential term begins at noon on 20 January.

HEAD OF STATE
President of the United States, George Walker Bush, *born* 6 July 1946, *elected* 7 November 2000, *sworn in* 20 January 2001. Republican
Vice-President, Richard B. Cheney, *born* 30 January 1941

THE CABINET *as at July 2003*
Agriculture, Ann Veneman
Attorney-General, John Ashcroft
Commerce, Don Evans
Defence, Donald Rumsfeld
Education, Rod Paige
Energy, Spencer Abraham
Health and Human Services, Tommy Thompson
Homeland Security, Tom Ridge
Housing and Urban Development, Mel Martinez
Interior, Gale Norton
Labour, Elaine Chao
Representative for Trade Negotiations, Robert Zoellick
Secretary of State, Colin Powell
Transportation, Norman Mineta
Treasury, John Snow
Veterans' Affairs, Anthony Principi

THE STATES OF THE UNION

The United States of America is a federal republic consisting of 50 states and the federal District of Columbia and of organised territories. Of the present 50 states, 13 are original states, seven were admitted without previous organisation as territories, and 30 were admitted after such organisation.

State (with date and order of admission)	Area sq. km	Population (2002 estimates)	Capital	Governor (end of term in office)	
Alabama (AL) (1819) (22)	133,915	4,486,508	Montgomery	Robert Riley (R)	(2006)
Alaska (AK) (1959) (49)	1,530,694	643,786	Juneau	Frank Murkowski (R)	(2006)
Arizona (AZ) (1912) (48)	295,259	5,456,453	Phoenix	Janet Napolitano (D)	(2006)
Arkansas (AR) (1836) (25)	137,754	2,710,079	Little Rock	Mike Huckabee (R)	(2006)
California (CA) (1850) (31)	411,047	35,116,033	Sacramento	Gray Davis (D)*	(2006)
Colorado (CO) (1876) (38)	269,595	4,506,542	Denver	Bill Owens (R)	(2006)
Connecticut (CT) § (1788) (5)	12,997	3,460,503	Hartford	John Rowland (R)	(2006)
Delaware (DE) § (1787) (1)	5,297	807,385	Dover	Ruth Ann Minner (D)	(2004)
Florida (FL) (1845) (27)	151,939	16,713,149	Tallahassee	Jeb Bush (R)	(2006)
Georgia (GA) § (1788) (4)	152,576	8,560,310	Atlanta	Sonny Perdue (R)	(2006)
Hawaii (HI) (1959) (50)	16,760	1,244,898	Honolulu	Linda Lingle (R)	(2006)
Idaho (ID) (1890) (43)	216,430	1,341,131	Boise	Dirk Kempthorne (R)	(2006)
Illinois (IL) (1818) (21)	145,933	12,600,620	Springfield	Rod Blagojevich (D)	(2006)
Indiana (IN) (1816) (19)	93,719	6,159,068	Indianapolis	Joe Kiernan (D)	(2004)
Iowa (IA) (1846) (29)	145,752	2,936,760	Des Moines	Tom Vilsack (D)	(2006)
Kansas (KS) (1861) (34)	213,097	2,715,884	Topeka	Kathleen Sebelius (D)	(2006)
Kentucky (KY) (1792) (15)	104,661	4,092,891	Frankfort	Paul Patton (D)	(2003)
Louisiana (LA) (1812) (18)	123,677	4,482,646	Baton Rouge	M. J. Mike Foster (R)	(2004)
Maine (ME) (1820) (23)	86,156	1,294,464	Augusta	John Baldacci (D)	(2006)
Maryland (MD) § (1788) (7)	27,091	5,458,137	Annapolis	Robert Ehrlich (D)	(2006)
Massachusetts (MA) § (1788) (6)	21,455	6,427,801	Boston	Mitt Romney (R)	(2006)
Michigan (MI) (1837) (26)	151,584	10,050,446	Lansing	Jennifer Granholme (D)	(2006)
Minnesota (MN) (1858) (32)	218,600	5,019,720	St Paul	Tim Pawlenty (R)	(2006)
Mississippi (MS) (1817) (20)	123,514	2,871,782	Jackson	David Ronald Musgrove (D)	(2004)
Missouri (MO) (1821) (24)	180,514	5,672,579	Jefferson City	Bob Holden (D)	(2004)
Montana (MT) (1889) (41)	380,848	909,453	Helena	Judy Martz (R)	(2004)
Nebraska (NE) (1867) (37)	200,349	1,729,180	Lincoln	Mike Johanns (R)	(2006)
Nevada (NV) (1864) (36)	286,352	2,173,491	Carson City	Kenny Guinn (R)	(2006)
New Hampshire (NH) § (1788) (9)	24,033	1,275,056	Concord	Craig Benson (R)	(2004)
New Jersey (NJ) § (1787) (3)	20,168	8,590,300	Trenton	James McGreevey (D)	(2004)
New Mexico (NM) (1912) (47)	314,925	1,855,059	Santa Fé	Bill Richardson (D)	(2006)
New York (NY) § (1788) (11)	127,189	19,157,532	Albany	George Pataki (R)	(2006)
North Carolina (NC) § (1789) (12)	136,412	8,320,146	Raleigh	Mike Easley (D)	(2004)
North Dakota (ND) (1889) (39)	183,117	634,110	Bismarck	John Hoeven (R)	(2004)
Ohio (OH) (1803) (17)	107,044	11,421,267	Columbus	Bob Taft (R)	(2006)
Oklahoma (OK) (1907) (46)	181,185	3,493,714	Oklahoma City	Brad Henry (D)	(2006)
Oregon (OR) (1859) (33)	251,418	3,521,515	Salem	Ted Kulongoski (D)	(2006)
Pennsylvania (PA) § (1787) (2)	117,347	12,335,091	Harrisburg	Edward Rendell (D)	(2006)
Rhode Island (RI) § (1790) (13)	3,139	1,069,725	Providence	Don Carcieri (R)	(2006)
South Carolina (SC) § (1788) (8)	80,582	4,107,183	Columbia	Mark Sanford (R)	(2006)
South Dakota (SD) (1889) (40)	199,730	761,063	Pierre	Mike Rounds (R)	(2006)
Tennessee (TN) (1796) (16)	109,153	5,797,289	Nashville	Phil Bredesen (D)	(2006)
Texas (TX) (1845) (28)	691,027	21,779,893	Austin	Rick Perry (R)	(2006)
Utah (UT) (1896) (45)	219,888	2,316,256	Salt Lake City	Mike Leavitt (R)	(2004)
Vermont (VT) (1791) (14)	24,900	616,592	Montpelier	James Douglas (R)	(2004)
Virginia (VA) § (1788) (10)	105,586	7,293,542	Richmond	Mark Warner (D)	(2005)
Washington (WA) (1889) (42)	176,479	6,068,996	Olympia	Gary Locke (D)	(2004)
West Virginia (WV) (1863) (35)	62,761	1,801,873	Charleston	Bob Wise (D)	(2004)
Wisconsin (WI) (1848) (30)	145,436	5,441,196	Madison	Jim Doyle (D)	(2006)
Wyoming (WY) (1890) (44)	253,324	498,703	Cheyenne	Dave Freudenthal (D)	(2006)
Dist. of Columbia (DC) (1791)	179	570,898	–	Anthony Williams (D) (Mayor)	

* RECALL ELECTION WAS DUE TO BE HELD IN OCTOBER 2003

OUTLYING TERRITORIES AND POSSESSIONS

	Area sq. km	Population (2002 estimates)	Capital	Governor (end of term in office)	
American Samoa	200	67,084*	Pago Pago	Togiola Tulafono (D)	(2004)
Guam	544	157,557*	Hagatna	Felix Perez Camacho (R)	(2006)
Northern Mariana Islands	464	74,612*	Saipan	Juan N. Babauta (R)	(2005)
Puerto Rico	8,875	3,808,610*	San Juan	Sila María Calderón (D)	(2004)
US Virgin Islands	346	122,211*	Charlotte Amalie	Charles Wesley Turnbull (D)	(2006)

§The 13 original states
D Democratic Party; I Independent; R Republican Party
* 2001 estimates

UNITED STATES EMBASSY
24 Grosvenor Square, London W1A 1AE
Tel: 020-7499 9000
Ambassador Extraordinary and Plenipotentiary, HE William
S. Farish, apptd 2001

BRITISH EMBASSY
3100 Massachusetts Avenue NW, Washington DC 20008
Tel: (00 1) (202) 588 6500
Ambassador Extraordinary and Plenipotentiary, HE David
Manning, KCMG, apptd 2003

BRITISH COUNCIL DIRECTOR, Andy Mackay
(Cultural Attaché), c/o British Embassy
Tel: (001) (202) 588 6500/7830
Email: enquiries@us.britishcouncil.org

THE CONGRESS

Legislative power is vested in two houses, the Senate and the House of Representatives. The Senate has 100 members, two Senators from each state, elected for the term of six years, and each Senator has one vote. The House of Representatives consists of 435 Representatives, directly elected in each state for a two-year term, a resident commissioner from Puerto Rico and a delegate each from American Samoa, the District of Columbia, Guam and the Virgin Islands. Members of the 108th Congress were elected on 5 November 2002. The 108th Congress is constituted as follows:

Senate Republicans 51; Democrats 48; Independent 1;
  total 100
House Republicans 229; Democrats 205; Independent 1;
  total 435
President of the Senate, The Vice-President
Senate Majority Leader, Bill Frist (R), *Tennessee*
Speaker of the House of Representatives, J. Dennis Hastert
  (R), Illinois

THE JUDICATURE

The federal judiciary consists of three sets of federal courts: the Supreme Court at Washington DC, consisting of a Chief Justice and eight Associate Justices, with original jurisdiction in cases where a state is a party to the suit, and with appellate jurisdiction from inferior federal courts and from the judgments of the highest courts of the states; the United States Courts of Appeals, dealing with appeals from district courts and from certain federal administrative agencies, and consisting of 168 circuit judges within 13 circuits and the 94 United States district courts served by 575 district court judges.

DEFENCE

Each military department is separately organised and functions under the direction, authority and control of the Secretary of Defence. The Air Force has primary responsibility for the Department of Defence space development programmes and projects. Under strategic command the USA has 432 submarine-launched ballistic missiles, 550 inter-continental ballistic missiles, 208 heavy nuclear-capable bombers and 60 strategic defence interceptor aircraft together with multiple intelligence satellites, radars and early warning systems throughout the world. The Army has 7,620 main battle tanks, 6,710 armoured infantry fighting vehicles, 15,910 armoured personnel carriers, 282 aircraft and 1,294 armed helicopters.

The Navy has 72 strategic submarines, 54 tactical submarines, 12 aircraft carriers, 27 cruisers, 55 destroyers, 35 frigates, 21 patrol and coastal vessels, 41 amphibious and support ships, 1,705 combat aircraft and 693 armed helicopters. The Marine Corps has 403 main battle tanks and 1,321 amphibious armoured vehicles. The Air Force has 208 long-range strike aircraft, 2,928 tactical combat aircraft and 227 helicopters.

The major deployments of US personnel overseas are: Germany (68,950); South Korea (37,140); Japan (38,450); Italy (10,790); UK (9,400); Turkey (3,860).
MILITARY EXPENDITURE – 3.2 per cent of GDP (2001)
MILITARY PERSONNEL – 1,414,000: Army 485,500, Navy 385,400, Marine Corps 173,400, Air Force 369,700, Coast Guard 40,320, Paramilitaries 53,000

ECONOMY AND FINANCE

In 2000 central government budget receipts totalled US$2,025.0 billion and outlays US$1,788.1 billion. The largest items of expenditure were: defence US$293.9 billion, social security US$409.4 billion, income security US$247.4 billion, debt interest US$223.2 billion. In the year to the end of September 2000, US$58,364 million was spent on education, US$154,215 million on health, US$197,115 million on Medicare, US$247,380 million on income security, US$409,437 million on social security and US$47,084 million on veterans' benefits and services.
GNP – US$9,601,505 million (2000); US$34,100 per
  capita (2000)
GDP – US$10,171,400 million (2000); US$34,637 per
  capita (2000)
ANNUAL AVERAGE GROWTH OF GDP – 5.0 per cent
  (2000)
INFLATION RATE – 3.4 per cent (2000)
UNEMPLOYMENT – 4.0 per cent (2000)

AGRICULTURE

The total number of farms in 2001 was 2,157,780 with a total area of land in farms of 941,210,000 acres, and an average acreage per farm of 436 acres. Principal crops are maize for grain, soybeans, wheat, hay, cotton, tobacco, grain sorghums, potatoes, oranges and barley. Gross income from farming in 2001 was US$247 billion. Cash receipts from all crops in 2001 was US$96 billion and from livestock and livestock products US$106 billion.

MINERALS

The value of non-fuel raw mineral production in 1997 totalled an estimated US$39 billion. Mineral exports in 1997 were valued at US$37 billion, and imports at US$58 billion. In 1998 the following quantities of minerals were produced: iron ore 62,931,000 tonnes; marketable phosphate rock 44,200,000 tonnes; copper 1,858,900 tonnes; zinc 755,000 tonnes; lead 415,000 tonnes.

ENERGY

Production in 2001 was 72.51 quadrillion BTU, principally coal, natural gas and crude oil. Petroleum accounted for almost half of energy exports of 3.91 quadrillion BTU. Net imports were 26.02 quadrillion BTU, of which crude oil was 19.90 quadrillion BTU, to meet consumption of 96.88 quadrillion BTU (quadrillion$=10^{15}$).

TRADE

In 2001 the USA had a trade deficit of US$423,670 million and a current account deficit of US$417,440 million. Imports totalled US$1,180,154 million and exports US$730,803 million.

Trade with UK	2001	2002
Imports from UK	£29,491,125,000	£28,379,876,000
Exports to UK	30,352,892,000	26,040,615,000

COMMUNICATIONS

There are approximately 3.91 million miles of public roads and streets. Surfaced roads and streets account for 61.3 per cent of the total. US domestic and international scheduled airlines in 2000 carried approximately 665,042,490 passengers over 692,008,214,000 revenue passenger miles.

EDUCATION

All the states and the District of Columbia have compulsory school attendance laws. In general, children are obliged to attend school from seven to 16 years of age. Most of the revenue for public elementary and secondary school purposes comes from federal, state, and local governments. Less than three per cent comes from gifts and from tuition and transportation fees.

Among the better-known universities are: Harvard, founded at Cambridge, Mass. in 1636, and named after John Harvard of Emmanuel College, Cambridge, England, who bequeathed to it his library and a sum of money in 1638; Yale, founded at New Haven, Connecticut, in 1701; Princeton, NJ, founded 1746.
ENROLMENT (percentage of age group) – primary 100 per cent (1997); secondary 97 per cent (1997); tertiary 81 per cent (1997)

US TERRITORIES, ETC

Responsibility within the federal government for the United States insular areas other than Puerto Rico and Kingman Reef lies with the United States Department of the Interior, either the Office of Insular Affairs (for American Samoa, Guam, the Northern Mariana Islands, the United States Virgin Islands, Navassa Island (3 sq. miles), Palmyra Atoll (1.56 sq. miles) and Wake Atoll (2.5 sq. miles) (shared with the United States Army Space and Missile Defense Command)) or the United States Fish and Wildlife Service (for Baker Island (0.59 sq. miles), Howland Island (1 sq. mile) and Jarvis Island (1.66 sq. miles), Midway Atoll (2 sq. miles) and Johnston Atoll (0.98 sq. miles) (shared with the Defense Special Weapons Agency)). Four of the eight populated insular areas are represented in the United States House of Representatives, Puerto Rico by a resident commissioner and American Samoa, Guam and the United States Virgin Islands each by a delegate. Although represented in the United States House of Representatives by a delegate, the District of Columbia was an incorporated territory for only three years, from 21 February 1871 to 20 June 1874.

THE COMMONWEALTH OF PUERTO RICO

AREA – 3,427 sq. miles (8,875 sq. km)
POPULATION – 3,885,877 (2003 estimate). The majority of the inhabitants are of Spanish descent, and Spanish and English are the official languages
CAPITAL – ΨSan Juan, population of the municipality (2002 estimate), 433,412. Other major towns are: Bayamón (224,670); Carolina (187.468); ΨPonce (186,112)

Puerto Rico (Rich Port) is an island of the Greater Antilles group in the West Indies and was discovered in 1493 by Columbus. It was a Spanish possession until 1898, when the USA took formal possession as a result of the Spanish-American War. The 1952 constitution establishes the Commonwealth of Puerto Rico with full powers of local government. Residents of Puerto Rico are US citizens.
Governor, Sila María Calderón

Trade with UK	2001	2002
Imports from UK	£276,710,000	£257,605,000
Exports to UK	956,814,000	615,579,000

GUAM

AREA – 212 sq. miles (549 sq. km)
POPULATION – 157,557 (2001 estimate): 43 per cent Chamorro stock mingled with Filipino and Spanish blood. The Chamorro language belongs to the Malayo-Polynesian family, but with considerable admixture of Spanish. Chamorro and English are the official languages; most Chamorro residents are bilingual
CAPITAL – Hagatna. Port of entry, ΨApra

Guam is the largest of the Mariana Islands, in the north Pacific Ocean. Guam was occupied by the Japanese in December 1941 but was recaptured by US forces in 1944. Under the Organic Act of Guam 1950, Guam has statutory powers of self-government, and any person born in Guam is a US citizen.
Governor, Felix Perez Camacho

AMERICAN SAMOA
AREA – 77 sq. miles (199 sq. km)
POPULATION – 63,000 (1997 estimate)
CAPITAL – ΨPago Pago (population, 3,519)

American Samoa consists of the islands of Tutuila, Aunu'u, Ofu, Olesega, Ta'u, Rose and Swains Islands. Tutuila, the largest of the group, has an area of 52 sq. miles and a magnificent harbour at Pago Pago. The remaining islands have an area of about 24 sq. miles. Those born in American Samoa are US non-citizen nationals, but some have acquired citizenship through service in the United States armed forces or other naturalisation procedure.
Governor, Togiola Tulafono

THE UNITED STATES VIRGIN ISLANDS
AREA – 134 sq. miles (347 sq. km)
POPULATION – 114,483 (1997 estimate)
CAPITAL – ΨCharlotte Amalie (population, 12,331, 1990), on St Thomas

The US Virgin Islands were purchased from Denmark and came under US sovereignty in 1917. There are three main islands, St Thomas (28 sq. miles), St Croix (84 sq. miles), St John (20 sq. miles) and about 50 small islets or cays.
Governor, Charles Wesley Turnbull

Trade with UK	2001	2002
Imports from UK	£2,992,000	£5,399,000
Exports to UK	8,933,000	1,800,000

NORTHERN MARIANA ISLANDS
AREA – 179 sq. miles (464 sq. km)
POPULATION – 63,763 (1997 estimate)
SEAT OF GOVERNMENT – Saipan (population, 52,706, 1995 census)

The USA administered the Northern Mariana Islands as part of a UN Trusteeship until the trusteeship agreement was terminated in 1986, bringing fully into effect a 1976 congressional law establishing the Northern Mariana Islands as a Commonwealth under US sovereignty. Most of the then residents became US citizens. Those born subsequently in the Northern Mariana Islands are US citizen nationals.
Governor, Juan N. Babauta

URUGUAY

República Oriental del Uruguay – Eastern Republic of Uruguay

AREA – 67,308 sq. miles (175,000 sq. km). Neighbours: Argentina (west), Brazil (north and east)
POPULATION – 3,361,000 (2001): predominantly of Spanish and Italian descent. Spanish is the official language. Many Uruguayans are Roman Catholics. There is no established church
CAPITAL – ΨMontevideo (population, 1,303,182, 1996)
MAJOR CITIES – Canelones; Melo; Mercedes; Minas; ΨPaysandú; Punta del Este; Rivera; Salto
CURRENCY – Uruguayan peso of 100 centésimos
NATIONAL ANTHEM – Orientales, La Patria O La Tumba (Uruguayans, The Fatherland Or Death)
NATIONAL DAY – 25 August (Declaration of Independence, 1825)

NATIONAL FLAG – Four blue and five white horizontal stripes surcharged with sun on a white ground in the top corner, next flagstaff
LIFE EXPECTANCY (years) – 75 (2001)
POPULATION GROWTH RATE – 0.7 per cent
POPULATION DENSITY – 19 per sq. km (2001)
URBAN POPULATION – 92 per cent (2001)
MILITARY EXPENDITURE – 2.0 per cent of GDP (2001)
MILITARY PERSONNEL – 23,900: Army 15,200, Navy 5,700, Air Force 3,000; Paramilitaries 920

The country consists mainly of undulating grassy plains. The principal river is the Rio Negro (with its tributary the Yi), flowing from north-east to south-west into the Rio Uruguay.

HISTORY AND POLITICS
Uruguay (or the *Banda Oriental,* as the territory lying on the eastern bank of the Uruguay River was then called) formed part of Spanish South America from 1726 to 1814, when it was annexed by the Argentine Confederation and then Portugal, becoming a province of Brazil. In 1825, the country threw off Brazilian rule. Uruguay was declared an independent state in 1828 and was inaugurated as a republic in 1830.

General elections held in 1984 marked the return to civilian rule after 11 years of presidential rule with military support. The first fully free presidential and legislative elections since 1971 were held in 1989, and were won by the National (Blanco) Party (NP).

The presidential election on 31 October and 28 November 1999 was won by Jorge Batlle Ibáñez of the Colorado Party (CP), who gained 51.5 per cent of the vote in the second round of the election. The legislative elections for both houses of the General Assembly, which were held simultaneously with the first round of the presidential election, resulted in the Progressive Encounter-Broad Front (EP-FA) winning 40 seats, the CP 33 seats, the NP 22 seats and the New Space party (NE) four seats in the House of Representatives, with the EP-FA winning 12 seats, the CP ten seats, the NP seven seats and the NE one seat in the Senate. A coalition government of the CP and the NP was formed.

POLITICAL SYSTEM
Under the constitution the president (who may serve only a single term of five years) appoints a council of ministers and a Secretary (Planning and Budget Office), and the vice-president presides over Congress. The Congress consists of a Chamber of 99 deputies and a Senate of 30 members (plus the vice-president), elected for five years by proportional representation. The republic is divided into 19 Departments, each with an elected governor and legislature.

HEAD OF STATE
President, Jorge Batlle Ibáñez, *elected* 28 November 1999, *took office* 1 March 2000
Vice-President, Luis Hierro López

COUNCIL OF MINISTERS *as at August 2003*
The President
Economy and Finance, Isaac Alfie
Education, Culture, Youth and Sport, Leonardo Guzman
Foreign Relations, Didier Opertti
Health, Conrado Bonilla
Housing, Territorial Regulation and Environment, Saul Marva Irureta Saralegui

Industry, Energy, Mines and Tourism, Pedro Bordaberry
Interior, Guillermo Sterling
Labour and Social Security, Santiago Pérez del Castillo
Livestock, Agriculture and Fisheries, Martin Aguirrezalaba
National Defence, Yamandu Fau
Planning and Budget, Ariel Davrieux
Public Health, Alfonso Varela
Transport and Public Works, Lucio Cáceres

EMBASSY OF URUGUAY
2nd Floor, 140 Brompton Road, London SW3 1HY
Tel: 020-7589 8835
Ambassador Extraordinary and Plenipotentiary, HE
   Dr Miguel Jorge Berthet, apptd 2001

BRITISH EMBASSY
Calle Marco Bruto 1073, 11300 Montevideo (PO Box 16024).
Tel: (00 598) (2) 622 3650/3630
Email: bemonte@internet.com.uy
Ambassador Extraordinary and Plenipotentiary, HE John
   Everard, apptd 2001

ECONOMY
Beef, mutton and wool are produced and rice, wheat, barley, linseed and sunflower seed are cultivated. Other foodstuffs (citrus, wine, beer), fishing and textile industries are also of importance. Textiles, tyres, sheet-glass, three-ply wood, cement, leather-curing, beet-sugar, plastics, household consumer goods and edible oils are produced. Exploited minerals include clinker, dolomite, marble and granite. Much of the economy is in the hands of state monopolies and there has been only limited market liberalisation. On 18 March 2003 the IMF extended Uruguay's existing standby credit facility, due to expire in March 2004 to March 2005. Repayments of loans amounting to about US$ 94 million were postponed until 2004.
GNP – US$20,010 million (2000); US$6,000 per capita (2000)
GDP – US$18,429 million (2001); US$6,009 per capita (2000)
ANNUAL AVERAGE GROWTH OF GDP – –1.3 per cent (2000)
INFLATION RATE – 4.8 per cent (2000)
UNEMPLOYMENT – 13.6 per cent (2000)
TOTAL EXTERNAL DEBT – US$8,196 million (2000)

TRADE
The major exports are meat, meat by-products and livestock, agricultural products and textiles. The principal imports are machinery and transport equipment and chemical products. Principal trading partners are Brazil, Argentina, the USA and Germany.
   In 2000 Uruguay had a trade deficit of US$937 million and a current account deficit of US$593 million. In 2001 imports totalled US$3,061 million and exports US$2,060 million.

Trade with UK	2001	2002
Imports from UK	£49,518,000	£31,023,000
Exports to UK	35,330,000	46,490,000

COMMUNICATIONS
There are over 50,000 km of roads, including 12,000 km of national highways, and over 2,000 km of standard gauge railway in use. The international airport of Carrasco lies 12 miles outside Montevideo. The River Uruguay is navigable from its estuary to Salto, 200 miles

north, and the Negro is also navigable as far as Mercedes. In December 1998, the Senate approved the construction of a 45-km bridge across the River Plate, linking Uruguay and Argentina.

EDUCATION
Primary and secondary education is compulsory and free, and technical and trade schools and evening courses for adult education are state controlled. The university at Montevideo (founded in 1849) has ten faculties and a new university has been built at Salto.
ILLITERACY RATE – (m) 2.6 per cent; (f) 1.8 per cent (2000)
ENROLMENT (percentage of age group) – primary 100 per cent (1997); tertiary 30 per cent (1997)

UZBEKISTAN

Üzbekiston Žumhurijati – Republic of Uzbekistan

AREA – 159,308 sq. miles (414,200 sq. km).
   Neighbours: Kazakhstan (north and west), Kyrgyzstan and Tajikistan (east), Afghanistan and Turkmenistan (south)
POPULATION – 25,257,000 (2001): 72 per cent Uzbek, 8 per cent Russian, 5 per cent Tajik and 4 per cent Kazakh, with smaller numbers of Tatars, Kara-Kalpaks, Koreans, Ukrainians and Kyrgyz. The predominant religion is Sunni Muslim. Islam is tolerated within strict bounds; it is allowed to play no part in politics. The official language is Uzbek (72 per cent). Russian (8 per cent), Tajik (5 per cent) and Kazakh (4 per cent) are also spoken
CAPITAL – Tashkent (population, 2,142,700, 1998 estimate)
MAJOR CITIES – Samarkand (362,300), which contains the Gur-Emir (Tamerlane's Mausoleum); Bukhara (237,900), which contains the Samanid Mausoleum and the Ulughbek Madrassah
CURRENCY – Soum of 100 tiyin
NATIONAL DAY – 1 September (Independence Day)
NATIONAL FLAG – Three horizontal stripes of blue, white, green, with the white fimbriated in red; on the blue near the hoist a crescent and twelve stars, all in white
LIFE EXPECTANCY (years) – 69 (2001)
POPULATION GROWTH RATE – 1.9 per cent
POPULATION DENSITY – 61 per sq. km (2001)
URBAN POPULATION – 37 per cent (2001)
MILITARY EXPENDITURE – 2.6 per cent of GDP (2001)
MILITARY PERSONNEL – 55,000: Army 40,000, Air Force 15,000; Paramilitaries 20,000
CONSCRIPTION DURATION – 18 months
ILLITERACY RATE – (m) 6.6 per cent; (f) 15.3 per cent (2000)

Uzbekistan occupies the south-central part of former Soviet Central Asia, lying between the high Tienshan Mountains and the Pamir highlands in the east and south-east and sandy lowlands in the west and north-west, in the basin of the Amudarya and Syrdarya rivers.

HISTORY AND POLITICS
In the 13th century the area that is now Uzbekistan became the centre of a great Muslim empire under Amir Timur (Tamerlane), with its capital at Samarkand. By the beginning of the 19th century three independent

Khanates, Khiva, Kokand and Bukhara, existed in what is now Uzbekistan. These were annexed to the Russian Empire in the second half of the 19th century. In November 1917 a Communist revolution broke out in Tashkent and by 1921, all of Uzbekistan had been absorbed into the Soviet Union. Under Soviet rule a massive land irrigation programme was implemented to allow the cultivation of cotton.

Uzbekistan declared its independence from the Soviet Union on 1 September 1991. Its independence was confirmed in a referendum on 29 December and recognised internationally. Elections to the new *Oliy Majlis* were held on 25 December 1994 and won by the ruling People's Democratic Party (PDP) and its allies.

The government of President Karimov is formed by the People's Democratic Party. Despite the constitutionally guaranteed freedom of religion and thought, and respect for human rights and multiparty democracy, censorship is still widely used and little political opposition is tolerated. In March 1995 President Karimov's term of office was extended to 2000 by a national referendum and he won a further five-year term in a presidential election held on 9 January 2000, gaining 91.9 per cent of the vote. The election result attracted criticism from the Organisation for Security and Co-operation in Europe, who claimed no real opposition candidate had been allowed to stand. Legislative elections were held on 5 and 19 December 1999; the People's Democratic Party and its allies won 123 seats. The remaining seats were won by independent candidates and citizens' groups.

The main opposition parties, Erk (Freedom) and Birlik (Unity) nationalist parties, had been banned since the introduction of the multiparty constitution in December 1992, but Birlik held a congress openly for the first time in ten years in May 2003 and Erk held its first formal meeting for 11 years in June.

INSURGENCIES
The Islamic Movement of Uzbekistan (IMU), which seeks to overthrow the government and establish an Islamic state, was founded in 1996. Whilst they have carried out car bombings in Tashkent, their activities have centred on the Fergana valley and they have clashed with Kyrgyz armed forces.

FOREIGN RELATIONS
Uzbekistan is a member of the UN, OSCE, UNESCO, WHO and many other international organisations. On 22 January 2002, a military agreement was signed with the USA over the anti-terrorist operation in Afghanistan, outlining future co-operation and more frequent contact between the two countries.

A final border agreement demarcating the 2,240 km border with Kazakhstan was signed on 9 September 2002. A previous border agreement signed in November 2001 had left unresolved the issue of a number of settlements in southern Uzbekistan which were populated by significant numbers of Kazakh citizens.

POLITICAL SYSTEM
A referendum held on 27 January 2002 approved constitutional amendments on the extension of the presidential term of office from five to seven years and the creation of a bicameral legislature. The amendments were approved by parliament in early April. The second legislative chamber will be established in 2004 following the end of the 1999–2004 parliamentary term.

HEAD OF STATE
President, Islam Karimov, *elected* 29 December 1991, *elected by referendum for a five-year term* 26 March 1995, *re-elected* 9 January 2000

CABINET *as at July 2003*
Chairman of the Cabinet, The President
Prime Minister, Utkur Sultanov
First Deputy Prime Minister, Kozim Tolaganov
Deputy Prime Ministers, Abdulla Oripov *(Communications and Information Technology);* Rustam Sodiqovich *(Economics);* Elyor Majidovich Ganiev *(Foreign Economic Relations);* Bakhtiyor Alimjanov; Dilbar Ghulomova; Rustam Junusov; Mirabror Usmanov
Agriculture and Water Resources, Abduvohid Jorayev
Chairman, Supreme Council, Erkin Khalilov
Communications, Abduwahid Djurabaev
Cultural Affairs, Bahrom Qurbonov
Defence, Kodir Gulomov
Education, R. Djuraev
Emergencies, Bakhityor Jumaboyevich Subanov
Finance, Mamarizo Normurodov
Foreign Affairs, Sodik Safoyev
Health, Feruz Nazirov
Higher and Secondary Specialised Education, Saidahror Gulamov
Interior, Zakir Almatov
Justice, Abdusamad Polvonzoda
Labour and Social Security, Okiljon Obidov

EMBASSY OF THE REPUBLIC OF UZBEKISTAN
41 Holland Park, London W11 3RP
Tel: 020-7229 7679
Ambassador Extraordinary and Plenipotentiary, vacant
Chargé d'Affaires, Alexandr Aliev

BRITISH EMBASSY
Ul. Gulyamova 67, UZ-700000 Tashkent
Tel: (00 99871) 1206451
Ambassador Extraordinary and Plenipotentiary, HE Craig Murray, apptd 2002

BRITISH COUNCIL DIRECTOR, Neville McBain
11 D. Kounaev Street, Tashkent
Tel: (00 998) (71) 120 6752
Email: bc-tashkent@britishcouncil.uz

ECONOMY
Uzbekistan's economy is based on intensive agricultural production. Cotton production is approximately 4 million tonnes per year, made possible by extensive irrigation schemes. Textile manufacture, silk production and leather goods are also important. Wheat, potatoes and rice are widely grown. In addition there are some agricultural and textile machinery plants and several chemical combines. Uzbekistan possesses a wide range of mineral deposits. Copper, uranium, oil, gold and many other metals are extracted. In 1998 oil output was 8.0 million tonnes, and gas production was 55 billion cubic metres. The Muruntao mine is the largest open-cast gold mine in the world; in 1998, 81 tonnes of gold were produced. Total gold reserves are estimated at more than 5,000 tonnes. Foreign direct investment exceeds US$9 billion. South Korea, the USA, Japan, Turkey and the UK are the main investors. Uzbekistan is a member of the Commonwealth of Independent States economic union.

GNP – US$8,843 million (2000); US$360 per capita (2000)
GDP – US$11,270 million (2001); US$543 per capita (2000)
ANNUAL AVERAGE GROWTH OF GDP – 4.4 per cent (1998)
TOTAL EXTERNAL DEBT – US$4,340 million (2000)

Trade with UK	2001	2002
Imports from UK	£20,401,000	£14,622,000
Exports to UK	26,739,000	22,035,000

VANUATU

Ripablik blong Vanuatu / Republic of Vanuatu / République de Vanuatu

AREA – 4,706 sq. miles (12,189 sq. km)
POPULATION – 192,910 (2001 estimate). About 95 per cent are Melanesian, the rest being mostly Micronesian, Polynesian and European. The national language is Bislama, but English and French are also official languages
CAPITAL – ΨPort Vila (population, 29,356, 1999 census), on Efate
MAJOR TOWN – Luganville (10,738, 1999 census), on Espiritu Santo
CURRENCY – Vatu of 100 centimes
NATIONAL ANTHEM – Nasonal Sing Sing Blong Vanuatu (National Anthem Of Vanuatu)
NATIONAL DAY – 30 July (Independence Day)
NATIONAL FLAG – Red over green with a black triangle in the hoist, the three parts being divided by fimbriations of black and yellow, and in the centre of the black triangle a boar's tusk overlaid by two crossed fern leaves
POPULATION GROWTH RATE – 2.4 per cent
POPULATION DENSITY – 15 per sq. km (1999)

Vanuatu is situated in the South Pacific Ocean. It includes 13 large and some 70 small islands, of coral and volcanic origin, including the Banks and Torres Islands in the north. The principal islands are Vanua Lava, Espiritu Santo, Maewo, Pentecost, Ambae, Malekula, Ambrym, Epi, Efate, Erromango, Tanna and Aneityum. Most islands are mountainous and there are active volcanoes on several.

HISTORY AND POLITICS
Vanuatu, the former Anglo-French Condominium of the New Hebrides, became an independent republic within the Commonwealth on 30 July 1980. Parliament consists of 52 members, directly elected for a term of four years. A Council of Chiefs advises on matters of custom. Executive power is held by the prime minister (elected from and by parliament) and a Council of Ministers who are responsible to parliament. The president is elected for a five-year term by the presidents of the six provincial governments and the members of parliament. The most recent presidential election took place on 24 March 1999 and was won by Fr John Bani.
In the legislative election held on 2 May 2002 the Union of Moderate Parties (UMP) won 15 of the 52 seats in the Parliament and the Vanuaaki Pati (VP) won 14 seats. Edward Natapei of the VP was elected prime minister on 3 June, heading a continued VP/UMP coalition government. On 21 April 2003 the opposition National United Party (NUP) agreed to join the coalition.

HEAD OF STATE
President, HE Fr John Bani, *elected* 24 March 1999

COUNCIL OF MINISTERS *as at July 2003*
Prime Minister, Public Services, Edward Natapei (VP)
Deputy Prime Minister, External Trade and Telecommunications, Rialuth Serge Vohor (UMP)
Agriculture, Livestock, Forestry and Fisheries, Steven Kalsakau (UMP)
Comprehensive Reform Programme, Philip Boedoro (VP)
Education, Jacques Sese (UMP)
Finance and Economic Management, Sela Molisa (VP)
Health, Donald Kalpokas (VP)
Industry and Commerce, Jean-Alain Mahé (UMP)
Infrastructure, Public Utilities, Willy Posen (UMP)
Internal Affairs, Joe Natuman (VP)
Lands and Mineral Resources, Jacklyn Rueben Titek (VP)
Ni-Vanuatu Business Development, Nicholas Brown (Ind.)
Youth and Sports, Raphael Worwor (UMP)

BRITISH HIGH COMMISSION
KPMG House, Rue Pasteur, PO Box 567, Port Vila
Tel: (00 678) 23100
Email: bhcvila@vanuatu.com.vu
High Commissioner, HE Michael Hill, OBE, apptd 2000

ECONOMY
Most of the population is employed on plantations or in subsistence agriculture. Subsistence crops include yams, taro, manioc, sweet potato and breadfruit; principal cash crops are copra, cocoa and coffee. Cattle are kept on the plantations and beef is the second largest export. There is a small light industrial sector. Principal exports are copra, meat (frozen, tinned and chilled), timber and cocoa. The main trading partner is Japan. Tourism is a growing industry and the absence of direct taxation has led to growth in the finance and associated industries. Following a tightening up of the country's tax and regulatory systems in May 2003 the Organisation for Economic Co-operation and Development removed Vanuatu from its list of uncooperative tax havens.
In 1999 Vanuatu had a trade deficit of US$51 million and a current account deficit of US$3 million. Imports totalled US$96 million and exports totalled US$26 million.
GNP – US$226 million (2000); US$1,150 per capita (2000)
GDP – US$213 million (2001); US$1,140 per capita (2000)
ANNUAL AVERAGE GROWTH OF GDP – 2.1 per cent (1998)
INFLATION RATE – 2.0 per cent (1999)
TOTAL EXTERNAL DEBT – US$69 million (2000)

Trade with UK	2001	2002
Imports from UK	£463,000	£389,000
Exports to UK	58,000	188,000

VATICAN CITY STATE

Status Civitatis Vaticanae / Stato della Città del Vaticano – State of the Vatican City

AREA – 0.2 sq. miles (0.44 sq. km). Neighbour: Italy
POPULATION – 911 (2003 estimate). The languages are Latin and Italian
CAPITAL – Vatican City (population, 766, 1988)
CURRENCY – Euro (€) of 100 cents

NATIONAL ANTHEM – Inno E Marcia Pontificale (Hymn And Pontifical March)

NATIONAL DAY – 22 October (Inauguration of present Pontiff)

NATIONAL FLAG – Square flag; equal vertical bands of yellow (next staff), and white; crossed keys and triple crown device on white band

POPULATION DENSITY – 2,273 per sq. km (1997)

GDP – US$10 million (1998); US$20,659 per capita (1998)

ANNUAL AVERAGE GROWTH OF GDP – 1.3 per cent (1998)

The office of the ecclesiastical head of the Roman Catholic Church (Holy See) is vested in the Pope, the Sovereign Pontiff. For many centuries the Sovereign Pontiff exercised temporal power but by 1870 the Papal States had become part of unified Italy. The temporal power of the Pope was in suspense until the treaty of 1929 which recognised the full and independent sovereignty of the Holy See in the City of the Vatican.

Sovereign Pontiff, His Holiness Pope John Paul II (Karol Wojtyła), *born* at Wadowice (Kraków, Poland), 18 May 1920, *elected* Pope in succession to Pope John Paul I, 16 October 1978

SECRETARIAT OF STATE *as at July 2003*
Secretary of State, Cardinal Angelo Sodano, apptd December 1990
Assistant Secretary of State, Archbishop Leonardo Sandri
Secretary for Relations with States, Archbishop Jean-Louis Tauran

APOSTOLIC NUNCIATURE
54 Parkside, London SW19 5NE
Tel: 020-8944 7189
Apostolic Nuncio, HE Archbishop Pablo Puente, apptd 1997

BRITISH EMBASSY TO THE HOLY SEE
91 Via dei Condotti, I–00187 Rome
Tel: (00 39) (06) 6992 3561
Ambassador Extraordinary and Plenipotentiary, HE Kathryn Colvin, apptd 2002

Trade with UK	2001	2002
Imports from UK	£1,328,000	£682,000
Exports to UK	11,000	34,000

VENEZUELA

República Bolivariana de Venezuela – Bolivarian Republic of Venezuela

AREA – 339,269 sq. miles (882,100 sq. km).
Neighbours: Colombia (west), Guyana (east), Brazil (south)

POPULATION – 24,632,000 (2001): 67 per cent mestizo, 21 per cent white, 10 per cent black and 2 per cent Amerindian. The language is Spanish. 93 per cent of the population is Roman Catholic

CAPITAL – Caracas (population, 3,435,795, 2002 estimate)

MAJOR CITIES – Barquisimeto (875,788); ΨMaracaibo (1,372,724); Maracay (459,007); Valencia (832,229), 2000 estimates

CURRENCY – Bolívar (Bs) of 100 céntimos

NATIONAL ANTHEM – Gloria Al Bravo Pueblo (Glory To The Brave People)

NATIONAL DAY – 5 July

NATIONAL FLAG – Three horizontal stripes of yellow, blue, red with an arc of seven white stars on the blue stripe and a coat of arms on the upper hoist.

LIFE EXPECTANCY (years) – 73 (2001)

POPULATION GROWTH RATE – 2.1 per cent

POPULATION DENSITY – 28 per sq. km (2001)

URBAN POPULATION – 87 per cent (2001)

ILLITERACY RATE – (m) 6.9 per cent; (f) 7.8 per cent (2000)

ENROLMENT (percentage of age group) – primary 91 per cent (1997); secondary 40 per cent (1997)

Included in the area of the South American republic of Venezuela are 72 islands off the coast, with a total area of about 14,650 sq. miles, the largest being Margarita (area, about 400 sq. miles). The mountains are the Eastern Andes and Maritime Andes, running south-west to north-east. The main range is known as the Sierra Nevada de Mérida, and contains Pico Bolivar (16,411 ft) and Picacho de la Sierra (15,420 ft). The principal river is the Orinoco.

HISTORY AND POLITICS

The first Spanish settlement was established at Cumaná in 1520. An Act of Independence was signed on 15 July 1811 but was followed by several years of struggle until troops led by Simón Bolivar defeated the Spanish at the battle of Carabobo in 1821. Independence from Great Colombia, into which Venezuela had been incorporated in December 1819, was achieved in January 1830.

On 25 May 1999, a referendum on convening a constituent assembly to rewrite the constitution was passed and an election to decide the members of the constituent assembly was held on 25 July 1999. The new constitution was approved in a referendum held on 15 December and was proclaimed on 20 December. The National Congress was dissolved on 4 January 2000 pending elections to the new National Assembly, which were due to be held on 28 May, but were postponed. In the presidential election held on 30 July 2000, President Chávez was re-elected, winning 59 per cent of the vote. In the simultaneous election for the National Assembly, the Fifth Republic Movement (MVR) won 76 seats, Democratic Action 29 seats, Movement towards Socialism 21 seats, and other parties 39 seats. The National Assembly granted President Chávez Frías the power to rule by decree in industrial and economic policy and matters concerning the civil service for a period of one year on 7 November 2000. An attempted military coup on 12 April 2002 forced President Chávez to resign but he was reinstated with his Cabinet on 14 April after popular protest.

On 29 May 2003 a deal was brokered by the Organisation of American States (OAS) between President Chávez and parts of the extra-parliamentary opposition was finalised. This established the framework for a recall referendum to be held in August 2003 to ask the electorate if they wished to cut short Chávez's presidential term and hold immediate elections. A petition was delivered in August with more than three million signatures in favour of a referendum but was rejected by the electoral body.

POLITICAL SYSTEM

Under the 1999 constitution a unicameral legislature, the National Assembly, was created, and the post of vice-president instituted. The president, who is directly elected, serves a six-year term, which is renewable once only. The vice-president is appointed by the president. Legislative power is exercised by the 165-member *Asamblea Nacional* (National Assembly), which is directly elected for a five-year term.

FEDERAL STRUCTURE

Venezuela is divided into 22 states and two federal districts.

HEAD OF STATE

President, Hugo Chávez Frías, *elected* 6 December 1998, *sworn in* 2 February 1999, re-elected 30 July 2000
Vice-President, José Vicente Rangel

COUNCIL OF MINISTERS *as at July 2003*

Agriculture and Lands, Efren Andrade
Attorney-General, Isaias Rodriguez
Defence, José Luis Prieto
Education, Culture and Sports, Aristobulo Isturiz
Energy and Mines, Rafael Ramirez
Environment and Renewable Natural Resources, Ana Elisa Osorio
Finance, Tobías Nóbrega
Foreign Relations, Roy Chaderton
Health and Social Development, María Lourdes Urbaneja
Higher Education, Hector Navarro
Industry and Commerce, Ramón Rosales
Infrastructure, Diasdado Cabello
Interior and Justice, Gen. Lucas Rincon
Labour, María Cristina Iglesias
Planning and Development, Felipe Pérez Marti
Science and Technology, Marlene Yadira Cordova
Secretary of the Presidency, Rafael Vargas Medina

EMBASSY OF THE BOLIVARIAN REPUBLIC OF VENEZUELA
1 Cromwell Road, London SW7 2HR
Tel: 020-7584 4206
Ambassador Extraordinary and Plenipotentiary, HE Alfredo Toro-Hardy, apptd 2001

BRITISH EMBASSY
Edificio Torre Las Mercedes (Piso 3), Avenida La Estancia, Chuao (Apartado 1246), Caracas 1061
Tel: (00 58) (2) 993 4111/4224
Ambassador Extraordinary and Plenipotentiary, HE Edgar Hughes, apptd 2000

BRITISH COUNCIL DIRECTOR, Jonathan Greenwood
Piso 3, Torre Credicard, Av. Principal El Bosque,
El Bosque, Caracas
Tel: (00 58) (212) 952 9965
Email: bc-venezuela@britishcouncil.org.ve

DEFENCE

The Army has 81 main battle tanks, 290 armoured personnel carriers and seven attack helicopters. The Navy has two submarines, six frigates, six patrol and coastal vessels, three combat aircraft and nine armed helicopters at nine bases. The Air Force has 125 combat aircraft and 31 armed helicopters.

MILITARY EXPENDITURE – 1.5 per cent of GDP (2001)
MILITARY PERSONNEL – 82,300: Army 34,000, Navy 18,300, Air Force 7,000, National Guard 23,000
CONSCRIPTION DURATION – 30 months (selective)

ECONOMY

President Hugo Chávez Frías pledged in December 1998 that his government would cut public spending and tackle tax evasion and corruption. Agriculture comprises large-scale commercial farms together with subsistence farming. Land distribution is uneven, with 1 per cent of farms occupying 46 per cent of arable land and 250,000 smallholdings occupying less that 2 per cent of arable land. Products of the tropical forest region include orchids, wild rubber, timber, mangrove bark, balata gum and tonka beans. Agricultural products include corn, bananas, cocoa beans, coffee, cotton, rice, maize, sugar, sesame, groundnuts, potatoes, tomatoes, other vegetables, sisal and tobacco. There is an extensive beef and dairy farming industry. The principal industry is petroleum and gas, which together account for 78 per cent of exports. There are eight refineries. The Orinoco heavy oil belt is being developed.

Aluminium is abundant. Rich iron ore deposits in eastern Venezuela have been developed. Other industry includes a wide variety of manufacturing and component assembly, principally petrochemicals, gold, diamonds and foodstuffs.

A national strike took place in October 2002 and in December, an opposition strike crippled the oil industry leading to fuel shortages. Shops, factories and universities re-opened in February 2003.

GNP – US$104,065 million (2000); US$4,310 per capita (2000)
GDP – US$124,948 million (2001); US$5,017 per capita (2000)
ANNUAL AVERAGE GROWTH OF GDP – 3.2 per cent (2000)
INFLATION RATE – 16.2 per cent (2000)
UNEMPLOYMENT – 14.9 per cent (1999)
TOTAL EXTERNAL DEBT – US$38,196 million (2000)

TRADE

Apart from oil, the main exports are bauxite, iron ore, agricultural products and basic manufactures. The main imports are machinery and transport equipment, chemicals and foodstuffs. The USA and Colombia are the major trading partners.

In 2001 Venezuela had a trade surplus of US$9,774 million and a current account surplus of US$4,364 million. Imports totalled US$18,022 million and exports US$27,409 million.

Trade with UK	2001	2002
Imports from UK	£313,641,000	£233,242,000
Exports to UK	166,228,000	191,431,000

COMMUNICATIONS

There are 96,155 km of roads, some 32,308 km of them paved. Road and river communications have made railways of negligible importance in Venezuela except for carrying iron ore in the south-east, though the government is expanding the network, and there are now some 682 km of railway lines. The Orinoco is navigable for ocean-going ships (up to 40 ft draught) for 150 miles upstream, by large steamers for 700 miles, and by smaller vessels some 900 miles upstream.

VIETNAM

Công Hòa Xã Hôi Chu Nghĩa Viêt Nam – Socialist Republic of Vietnam

AREA – 125,192 sq. miles (325,500 sq. km). Neighbours: China (north), Laos and Cambodia (west)
POPULATION – 79,175,000 (2001). The language is Vietnamese. French, English and Khmer are also spoken
CAPITAL – Hanoi (population, 1,073,760, 1992 estimate)
MAJOR CITIES – Hai Phong (1,447,523); Ho Chi Minh City (3,924,435)
CURRENCY – Dông of 10 hào or 100 xu
NATIONAL ANTHEM – Tien Quan Ca (The Troops Are Advancing)
NATIONAL DAY – 2 September
NATIONAL FLAG – Red, with yellow five-point star in centre
LIFE EXPECTANCY (years) – 69 (2001)
POPULATION GROWTH RATE – 1.6 per cent
POPULATION DENSITY – 243 per sq. km (2001)
ILLITERACY RATE – (m) 4.5 per cent; (f) 8.6 per cent (2000)
ENROLMENT (percentage of age group) – primary 100 per cent (1997); tertiary 7 per cent (1997)

HISTORY AND POLITICS
Vietnam became a unified state at the end of the 18th century, with the assistance of France, whose influence on the region grew. In 1899 the Indo-Chinese Union was proclaimed, uniting Vietnam with Cambodia and Laos under French rule. Vietnam was under Japanese occupation from 1940–1945; insurrection by Communist, Nationalist and Revolutionary forces led to a French withdrawal in 1954 and the division of the country into Communist North Vietnam and non-communist South Vietnam. War broke out between the two countries in 1961, which lasted until 1975. North and South Vietnam were reunified in 1976 under the name of the Socialist Republic of Vietnam. The national flag, anthem and capital of North Vietnam were adopted, and Saigon was renamed Ho Chi Minh City.

INSURGENCY
On 22 March 2002 the office of the UN High Commissioner for Refugees (UNHCR) withdrew from a programme to repatriate about 1,000 Montagnard refugees to Vietnam from camps in Cambodia, after claiming that the Vietnamese authorities were using unacceptable levels of coercion. However, this claim was rejected by the Vietnamese Foreign Ministry. On 31 March the Cambodian government announced that it would allow more than 900 refugees to be moved from the camps to the USA and on 3 June the first group of 50 refugees left the Cambodian capital Phnom Penh on their way to asylum in the USA.

POLITICAL SYSTEM
Effective power lies with the Vietnamese Communist Party (VCP), its highest executive body being the Central Committee, elected by a Party Congress on a national basis. The Politburo and the Secretariat of the Central Committee exercise the real power. The constitution of 1992 reaffirmed Communist Party rule but also formalised free market economic reforms. A new National Assembly *(Quoc-Hoi)* was elected on 19 May 2002; the

VCP holds 449 of the 500 seats. The president is elected for a five-year term by the members of the National Assembly.

HEAD OF STATE
President, Tran Duc Luong, *elected* 25 September 1997
Vice-President, Truong My Hoa

POLITBURO
Secretary-General of the VCP, Nong Duc Manh
Politburo Standing Board, Le Hong Anh; Le Minh Huong; Nguyen Khoa Diem; Nguyen Minh Triet; Nguyen Phu Trong; Nguyen Tan Dzung; Nong Duc Manh; Phan Van Khai; Nguyen Van An; Pham Van Tra; Phan Dien; Tran Dinh Hoan; Truong Quang Duoc; Truong Tan Sang; Tran Duc Luong

COUNCIL OF MINISTERS *as at July 2003*
Prime Minister, Phan Van Khai
Deputy Prime Ministers, Nguyen Tan Dzung; Vu Khoan; Pham Gia Khiem
Agriculture and Rural Development, Le Huy Ngo
Aquatic Resources, Ta Quang Ngoc
Chair of Committee for Population Activities and Family Planning, Le Thoi Thu
Construction, Nguyen Hong Quan
Culture and Information, Pham Quang Nghi
Education and Training, Nguyen Minh Hien
Ethnic Minorities, Ksor Phuc
Finance, Nguyen Sinh Hung
Foreign Affairs, Nguyen Dy Nien
Government Secretariat, Doan Manh Giao
Governor, State Bank, Le Duc Thuy
Industry, Hoang Trung Hai
Internal Affairs, Do Quang Trung
Justice, Uong Chu Luu
Labour, War Invalids and Social Affairs, Nguen Thi Hang
National Defence, Gen. Pham Van Tra
Natural Resources and Environment, Mai Ai Truc
Physical Training and Sports, Nguyen Danh Thai
Planning and Investment, Vo Hong Phuc
Posts and Telecommunications, Do Trung Ta
Public Health, Tran Tui Trung Chien
Science, Technology and Environment, Hoang Van Phong
State Inspector General, Quach le Than
Trade, Truong Dinh Tuyen
Transport, Dao Dinh Binh

EMBASSY OF THE SOCIALIST REPUBLIC OF VIETNAM
12–14 Victoria Road, London W8 5RD
Tel: 020-7937 1912
Ambassador Extraordinary and Plenipotentiary, HE Vuong Thua Phong, apptd 1998

BRITISH EMBASSY
Central Building, 31 Hai Ba Trung, Hanoi
Tel: (00 84) (4) 936 0500
Email: behanoi@fpt.vn
Ambassador Extraordinary and Plenipotentiary, HE Warwick Morris, apptd 2001

CONSULATE-GENERAL – Ho Chi Minh City

BRITISH COUNCIL DIRECTOR, David Cordingley
(Cultural Attaché), 40 Cat Linh Street, Dong Da, Hanoi Tel: (00 84) (4) 843 6780
Email: bchanoi@britishcouncil.org.vn
There is a regional office in Ho Chi Minh City

DEFENCE
The Army has 1,315 main battle tanks, 1,380 armoured personnel carriers and 300 armoured infantry fighting vehicles. The Navy has two submarines, six frigates and 42 patrol and coastal vessels at seven principal bases. The Air Force has 189 combat aircraft and 26 armed helicopters.

MILITARY EXPENDITURE – 7.2 per cent of GDP (2001)
MILITARY PERSONNEL – 484,000: Army 412,000,
  Navy 42,000, Air Force 30,000; Paramilitaries 40,000
CONSCRIPTION DURATION – Two to three years

ECONOMY
Vietnam experienced economic difficulties following the imposition of socialist reforms in the south after 1975. However, economic reforms, known as 'Doi Moi' liberalisation, were instituted in 1986 and have had significant success. The state's share of control has been greatly reduced in most sectors, leading to significant improvement in agricultural production, with Vietnam becoming a major rice exporter. Industry has grown and now contributes 30 per cent of GDP. Building materials, chemicals, machinery and foodstuffs are the main products.

A stock exchange was opened in July 2000. Oil production has increased and large natural gas reserves have been found offshore, though these are also claimed by China.

A bilateral trade agreement between Vietnam and the USA was signed in July 2000. In June 2001, the World Bank granted Vietnam a US$250 million poverty reduction loan and the EU announced that it would commit €2.6 billion in aid.

GNP – US$30,439 million (2000); US$390 per capita (2000)
GDP – US$32,903 million (2001); US$401 per capita (2000)
ANNUAL AVERAGE GROWTH OF GDP – 5.8 per cent (1998)
TOTAL EXTERNAL DEBT – US$12,787 million (2000)

Trade with UK	2001	2002
Imports from UK	£90,422,000	£79,970,000
Exports to UK	428,097,000	487,880,000

YEMEN

Al-Jumhūriyya Al-Yamaniyya – Republic of Yemen

AREA – 203,850 sq. miles (527,968 sq. km).
  Neighbours: Saudi Arabia (north), Oman (east)
POPULATION – 18,078,035 (2001 estimate). The language is Arabic
CAPITAL – Sana'a' (population, 1,590,624, 2001)
MAJOR CITIES – ΨAden ('Adan) (398,300), the former capital of South Yemen, Al-Hudaydah (298,500); Ta'izz (317,600), 1994 census
CURRENCY – Riyal of 100 fils
NATIONAL ANTHEM – Raddidi Ayyatuha Ad-Dunya Nashidi (Repeat, O World, My Song)
NATIONAL DAY – 22 May
NATIONAL FLAG – Horizontal bands of red, white and black
POPULATION GROWTH RATE – 5.4 per cent
POPULATION DENSITY – 33 per sq. km (1999)
ILLITERACY RATE – (m) 32.5 per cent; (f) 74.8 per cent (2000)
ENROLMENT (percentage of age group) – tertiary 4 per cent (1997)

The border with Saudi Arabia, except for the north-west corner, is unclear and is being delineated following an agreement between the two countries signed on 12 June 2000.

HISTORY AND POLITICS
Turkish occupation of North Yemen (1872–1918) was followed by the rule of the Hamid al-Din dynasty until a revolution in 1962 overthrew the monarchy and the Yemen Arab Republic was declared. The People's Republic of South Yemen was set up in 1967 when the British government ceded power to the National Liberation Front, bringing to an end 129 years of British rule in Aden and some years of protectorate status in the hinterland. Negotiations towards merging the two states began in 1979 and unification was proclaimed on 22 May 1990. The constitution was approved by referendum in May 1991.

A power struggle between the former Northern and Southern Yemen élites in mid-1993 led to civil war on 5 May 1994 between the unmerged Northern and Southern forces. Aden was captured by victorious Northern forces on 7 July, ending the civil war.

After the war a coalition government of the General People's Congress and the Islamic Islah was formed and the constitution amended. Gen. Saleh was elected president by the House of Representatives for a five-year term. Multiparty democracy, a free market economy and Sharia law are enshrined in the constitution.

A general election in April 1997 was won by the ruling General People's Congress (GPC). President Ali Abdullah Saleh was re-elected in the first direct presidential election held on 23 September 1999, winning 96.3 per cent of the vote. Legislative elections took place on 27 April 2003, in which the GPC held on to the presidency and a large majority in the House of Representatives, having won 238 of the 301 seats. Bajammal was re-appointed prime minister on 17 May at the head of a re-shuffled cabinet.

POLITICAL SYSTEM
The 1991 constitution was amended following a referendum on 20 February 2001. The president is directly elected and serves a seven-year term which may be renewed once only. The unicameral legislature, the House of Representatives *(Majlis an-Nowab)*, has 301 directly-elected members, who serve a six-year term. In addition, there is an advisory Shura Council, which is appointed by the president and has 111 members.

HEAD OF STATE
President, Field Marshal Ali Abdullah Saleh, *took office* 22 May 1990, *elected* 1 October 1994, *re-elected* 23 September 1999
Vice-President, Gen. Abd Rabbah Mansur Hadi

COUNCIL OF MINISTERS *as at July 2003*
Prime Minister, Abd al-Qadir Abd al-Rahman Bajammal
Deputy Prime Minister, Finance, Alawi Salih al-Salami
Deputy Prime Minister, Planning and International Co-operation, Ahmad Muhammad Abdallah al-Sufan
Agriculture and Irrigation, Hassan Omar Swuid
Awqaf (Religious Endowments) and Religious Guidance, Hamoud Obad
Civil Service and Pensions, Hamood Khaled al-Sofi
Communications and Information Technology, Abd-al-Malik al-Muallimi
Culture and Tourism, Khaled Al-Rowishan
Defence, Maj.-Gen. Abdallah Ali Alywah

Education, Abdul-Salam al-Jawfi
Electricity, Abdul Rahman Mohamad Tarmoom
Expatriate Affairs, Abduh Ali Qubati
Fisheries, Ali Mugawar
Foreign Affairs, Abu-Bakr Abdallah al-Qirdi
Higher Education and Scientific Research, Abd-al-Wahhab Rawih
Human Rights, Amat Al-Aleem Al-Suswah
Industry, Khaled Rageh Sheikh
Information, Husayn Dayfallah al-Awadi
Interior, Rashad al-Alimi
Justice, Adnan Omar al-Gafri
Legal and Parliamentary Affairs, Rashad Ahmed al-Rassas
Local Administration, Sadiq Amin Abu Ras
Ministers of State, Mohamed Yehia Alsharafy *(Consultative Council and Parliamentary Affairs);* Ahmed Mohammed Al-Kohlani *(Mayor of Sana'a);* Maj.-Gen. Abdallah Husayn al-Bashiri *(Secretary-General for the Presidency);* Kassim Al-Ajam; Mohammed Ali Yaser
Oil and Mineral Resources, Rashid Ba-Rabba'a
Public Health and Population, Mohammed Al-Noami
Public Works and Roads, Abdullah Husayn al-Dafai
Social Affairs and Labour, Abd-al-Karim al-Arhabi
Technical Education and Vocational Training, Ali Mansour Mohamed Safa
Water and the Environment, Mohammed Lutf al-Eryani
Transport, Omar Mohsen Amoud
Youth and Sport, Abd al-Rahman Muhammad al-Akwa

EMBASSY OF THE REPUBLIC OF YEMEN
57 Cromwell Road, London SW7 2ED
Tel: 020-7584 6607
Ambassador Extraordinary and Plenipotentiary, HE Dr Mutahar Abdullah Alsaeede, apptd 2001

BRITISH EMBASSY
129 Haddah Road, PO Box 1287, Sana'a'
Tel: (00 967) (1) 264 081/2/3/4
Ambassador Extraordinary and Plenipotentiary, HE Frances Guy, apptd 2001

BRITISH COUNCIL DIRECTOR, Adrian Chadwick
3rd Floor, Administrative Tower, Sana'a' Trade Centre, Algiers Street, PO Box 2157, Sana'a'
Tel: (00 967) 1448 356/7
Email: britishcouncil@ye.britishcouncil.org

DEFENCE
The Army has 790 main battle tanks, 710 armoured personnel carriers and 200 armoured infantry fighting vehicles. The Navy has 11 patrol and coastal vessels at two bases. The Air Force has 76 combat aircraft and eight attack helicopters.
MILITARY EXPENDITURE – 8.1 per cent of GDP (2001)
MILITARY PERSONNEL – 66,500: Army 60,000, Navy 1,500, Air Force 5,000; Paramilitaries 70,000
CONSCRIPTION DURATION – Two years

ECONOMY
The economy has been seriously damaged by the civil war. However, the war had little effect on oil production. An agreement was signed with the French oil company Total in September 1995 for the exploitation of liquefied natural gas over a 25-year period and the construction of a gas liquefication plant by 2000. The principal imports are machinery and transport equipment, raw materials, and foodstuffs and livestock. Agriculture is the main occupation of the inhabitants. This is largely of a subsistence nature, sorghum, sesame, millet, wheat and barley being the chief crops. Exports include cotton, coffee, fruit, vegetables and hides. Imports include food and animals.

In 2000 Yemen had a trade surplus of US$1,609 million and current account surplus of US$1,862 million. In 2001 imports totalled US$2,310 million and exports US$3,215 million.
GNP – US$6,554 million (2000); US$370 per capita (2000)
GDP – US$9,098 million (2001); US$465 per capita (2000)
ANNUAL AVERAGE GROWTH OF GDP – 3.8 per cent (1999)
INFLATION RATE – 7.9 per cent (1998)
TOTAL EXTERNAL DEBT – US$5,616 million (2000)

Trade with UK	2001	2002
Imports from UK	£73,484,000	£74,044,000
Exports to UK	4,750,000	39,769,000

ZAMBIA

Republic of Zambia

AREA – 285,923 sq. miles (743,400 sq. km). Neighbours: Democratic Republic of Congo and Tanzania (north), Malawi (east), Mozambique, Zimbabwe and Namibia (south), Angola (west)
POPULATION – 10,649,000 (2001). English is the official language; other languages spoken include Bemba, Kaonda, Lozi, Lunda, Luvale, Nyanja and Tonga
CAPITAL – Lusaka (population, 1,269,848, 1999)
MAJOR CITIES – Chingola (211,755); Kabwe (233,197); Kitwe (467,084); Luanshya (186,372); Mufulira (204,104); Ndola (441,624)
CURRENCY – Kwacha (K) of 100 ngwee
NATIONAL ANTHEM – Stand And Sing Of Zambia, Proud And Free
NATIONAL DAY – 24 October (Independence Day)
NATIONAL FLAG – Green with three small vertical stripes, red, black and orange (next fly); eagle device on green above stripes
LIFE EXPECTANCY (years) – 42 (2001)
POPULATION GROWTH RATE – 2.5 per cent
POPULATION DENSITY – 14 per sq. km (2001)
MILITARY EXPENDITURE – 0.8 per cent of GDP (2001)
MILITARY PERSONNEL – 21,600: Army 20,000, Air Force 1,600; Paramilitaries 1,400
ILLITERACY RATE – (m) 14.8 per cent; (f) 28.6 per cent (2000)
ENROLMENT (percentage of age group) – primary 89 per cent (1997); secondary 27 per cent (1997); tertiary 3 per cent (1997)

HISTORY AND POLITICS
Northern Rhodesia came under British rule in 1889. It achieved internal self-government when the Federation of Rhodesia and Nyasaland was dissolved in 1963 and became an independent republic within the Commonwealth on 24 October 1964 under the name of Zambia.

Zambia was a one-party state (the United National Independence Party) from 1973 until 1990, when pressure from opposition groups led to a new constitution (August 1991) and multiparty legislative and presidential elections in October 1991. The Movement for Multiparty Democracy (MMD) won 125 of the 150 seats in parliament, and the MMD candidate Frederick Chiluba defeated Kenneth Kaunda, who had ruled since independence, in the presidential election; Kaunda was later stripped of his Zambian citizenship.

Presidential elections held on 27 December 2001 were won by MMD candidate Levy Mwanawasa with 28.7 per cent of the vote. In simultaneous legislative elections the MMD won 69 of the 150 elected seats in the National Assembly; the United Party for National development (UPND) won 49 seats; and other parties and independents won 32 seats. A new Cabinet composed of the MMD was appointed on 7 January 2002. Vice-President Enoch Kavindele was dismissed on 28 May 2003. Nevers Mumba succeeded him on the same day.

HEAD OF STATE
President, Levy Mwanawasa, *elected* 27 December 2001, *sworn in* 2 January 2002
Vice-President, Nevers Mumba

CABINET *as at July 2003*
Agriculture, Food and Fisheries, In the Office of the Vice-President, Mundia Sikatana
Communications and Transport, Bates Namuyamba
Community Development and Social Services, Marina Nsingo
Defence, Michael Mabenga
Education, Andrew Mulenga
Energy and Water Development, George Mpombo
Foreign Affairs, Kalombo Mwansa
Health, Brig.-Gen. Brian Chituwo
Home Affairs, Ronnie Shikapwasha
Information and Broadcasting; Chief Whip, Newstead Zimba
Labour and Social Security, Mutale Nalumango
Lands, Judith Kapijimpanga
Legal Affairs, Attorney-General, Finance (acting), George Kunda
Local Government and Housing, Sylvia Masebo
Mines and Mineral Developments, Kaunda Lembalemba
Science, Technology and Vocational Training, Abel Chambeshi
Sports and Youth Development, Gladys Nyirongo
Tourism, Environment and Natural Resources, Patrick Kalifungwa
Trade and Industry, Dipak Patel
Works and Supply, Ludwig Sondashi

HIGH COMMISSION FOR THE REPUBLIC OF ZAMBIA
2 Palace Gate, London W8 5NG
Tel: 020-7589 6655
High Commissioner, HE Anderson Chibwa, apptd 2003

BRITISH HIGH COMMISSION
5210 Independence Avenue (PO Box 50050),
15101 Ridgeway, Lusaka
Tel: (00 260) (1) 251133
Email: brithc@zamnet.zm
High Commissioner, HE Timothy David, apptd 2002

BRITISH COUNCIL DIRECTOR, Brendan McSharry
Heroes Place, Cairo Road (PO Box 34571), Lusaka
Tel: (00 260) (1) 223 602/228 332
Email: info@britishcouncil.org.zm

ECONOMY
In 1991, the MMD government began the transition from a state-controlled economy to a free market system.

Privatisation has been encouraged, foreign exchange controls have been removed and the Kwacha has been floated. Price subsidies and tariffs have been lowered or abolished, but increased imports have affected manufacturing. In 1997, 71.1 per cent of the workforce were engaged in agriculture, which accounted for 17 per cent of GDP in 1998. Principal agricultural products are maize, sugar, groundnuts, cotton, livestock, vegetables and tobacco. The principal exports are copper and cobalt. The principal imports are industrial goods, machinery and transport equipment, fuel and foodstuffs.

In 1997 imports totalled US$819 million and exports US$915 million.

GNP – US$3,026 million (2000); US$300 per capita (2000)
GDP – US$3,647 million (2001); US$336 per capita (2000)
ANNUAL AVERAGE GROWTH OF GDP – –2.0 per cent (1998)
INFLATION RATE – 24.8 per cent (1997)
TOTAL EXTERNAL DEBT – US$5,730 million (2000)

Trade with UK	2001	2002
Imports from UK	£23,854,000	£19,075,000
Exports to UK	11,718,000	10,741,000

ZIMBABWE

Republic of Zimbabwe

AREA – 148,808 sq. miles (386,900 sq. km).
  Neighbours: Zambia (north), Mozambique (east), South Africa (south), Botswana and Namibia (west)
POPULATION – 12,852,000 (2001); 77 per cent Shona, 17 per cent Ndebele, 1.4 per cent Europeans. The official language is English, with Shona the largest indigenous language group
CAPITAL – Harare (population, 1,189,103, 1992)
MAJOR CITIES – Bulawayo (621,742), the largest town in Matabeleland; Chitungwiza (274,912)
CURRENCY – Zimbabwe dollar (Z$) of 100 cents
NATIONAL ANTHEM – Ngaikomberarwe Nyika Ye Zimbabwe (Blessed Be The Country Of Zimbabwe)
NATIONAL DAY – 18 April (Independence Day)
NATIONAL FLAG – Seven horizontal stripes of green, yellow, red, black, red, yellow, green; a white, black-bordered, triangle based on the hoist containing the national emblem
LIFE EXPECTANCY (years) – 43 (2001)
POPULATION GROWTH RATE – 2.1 per cent
POPULATION DENSITY – 33 per sq. km (2001)
MILITARY EXPENDITURE – 2.9 per cent of GDP (2001)
MILITARY PERSONNEL – 36,000: Army 32,000, Air Force 4,000; Paramilitaries 21,800

HISTORY AND POLITICS
European colonisation of Zimbabwe began in 1890 when settlers forcibly acquired Shona lands, followed by the seizure of Ndebele lands in 1893. It became a self-governing colony under the name of Southern Rhodesia in 1923. A unilateral declaration of independence on 11 November 1965, which resulted in UN sanctions against the country, was finally terminated on 12 December 1979. Following elections in February 1980 the country became independent on 18 April 1980 as the Republic of Zimbabwe, a member of the British Commonwealth.

The independence constitution was amended in 1987, making the presidency an executive post. The president is popularly elected for a six-year term, appoints the Cabinet and can veto parliamentary bills. The unicameral legislature, the House of Assembly, has 150 members: 120 elected, ten traditional chiefs and 20 others appointed by the president.

The most recent general election was held on 24–25 June 2000. The Zimbabwe African National Union – Patriotic Front (ZANU-PF) won 62 of the 120 elective seats and the Movement for Democratic Change (MDC), a new opposition grouping formed by various civic groups and the Zimbabwe Congress of Trade Unions, won 57 seats. President Mugabe was re-elected for a six-year term in elections held on 9–11 March 2002 with 56.2 per cent of the vote. Morgan Tsvangirai of the MDC gained 42.0 per cent of the vote. However, the integrity of the election was called into question by Tsvangirai who claimed that thousands of opposition supporters had been disenfranchised.

LAND REFORM

By 1997 the state had acquired 3.4 million hectares of land, but either left it fallow or distributed it to members of the government. The 1990 amendments to the 1980 constitution had made provision for the compulsory acquisition of farms, with compensation to be paid to the owners. The occupation of white-owned farms by protestors, led by former veterans of the war against the white minority regime, began in February 2000. On 17 March 2000 the Supreme Court ordered the police to evict the black war veterans who had occupied around 600 white-owned farms. The police ignored the judgement with the support of President Mugabe. On 6 April 2000, the House of Assembly approved the Land Acquisition Act, which amended the constitution to enable the government to take over white-owned farms without compensation and redistribute them to landless blacks. A meeting of representatives of the British and Zimbabwean governments on 27 April 2000 failed to resolve the crisis and on 3 May the UK imposed an embargo on weapons sales to Zimbabwe, making financial support for land reform dependent on an end to the farm occupations.

The Supreme Court ruled on 10 November 2000 that the compulsory land seizures were illegal and ordered the removal of squatters. The government rejected the ruling and accelerated the land acquisition programme. On 21 December, the Supreme Court directed the President to produce a land distribution programme within six months and to protect white farmers whose land had been occupied by squatters. Following a Commonwealth meeting, Zimbabwe agreed to end the illegal land occupations and restore the rule of law in return for international assistance. On 2 October, the Supreme Court, dominated by recent appointees of President Mugabe, issued an interim order reversing all previous rulings in order to allow the government to proceed with its fast-track land reform programme. On 9 November, the government issued a decree that any farm given a 'notice of acquisition' would become state property immediately. The government would then be entitled to move settlers onto the land and the owner would be banned from conducting any farming on it. Mugabe ordered some 2,900 white farmers, whose farms had been earmarked to be seized and given to blacks under the government's 'fast-track land reform' programme, to cease work as of 25 June 2002. On 18 September the House of Assembly passed an amendment to the 1992 Land Acquisition Act reducing the time give to white farmers to vacate before being evicted from 90 to 7 days.

HEAD OF STATE

President, C.-in-C. of the Defence Forces, Transport and Energy, Robert Gabriel Mugabe, *elected* 30 December 1987, *re-elected* March 1990, March 1996, 11 March 2002
Vice-Presidents, Simon Vengesai Muzenda; Joseph Msika

CABINET *as at July 2003*
The President
Defence, Sidney Tigere Sekeramayi
Education, Sport and Culture, Aeneas Chigwedere
Energy and Power Development, Amos Midzi
Environment and Tourism, Francis Nhema
Finance and Economic Development, Herbert Murerwa
Foreign Affairs, Stanislaus Mudenge
Health and Child Welfare, David Parirenyatwa
Home Affairs, Kembo Mohadi
Industry and International Trade, Samuel Mumbengegwi
Justice, Legal and Parliamentary Affairs, Patrick Chinamas
Lands, Agriculture and Resettlement, Joseph Made
Local Government, Public Works, National Housing, Higher Education and Technology, Ignatius Chombo
Mines and Energy, Edward Chindori Chininga
Minister of State for Information and Publicity, Jonathan Moyo
Minister of State for State Enterprises and Parastatals, Paul Mangwana
Minister of State for the Land Reform Programme, Flora Bhuka
Minister of State for Science and Technology Development, Olivia Muchena
National Security, Nicholas Goche
Public Service, Labour and Social Welfare, July Moyo
Rural Resources and Water Development, Joyce Mujuru
Small and Medium Enterprise Development, Sithembiso Nyoni
Special Affairs in the President's Office, John Nkomo
Transport and Communications, Witness Mangwende
Youth Development, Gender, Employment Creation, Elliot Manyika

HIGH COMMISSION OF THE REPUBLIC OF ZIMBABWE
Zimbabwe House, 429 Strand, London WC2R 0JR
Tel: 020-7836 7755
High Commissioner, HE Simbarashe Simbanenduku Mumbengegwi, apptd 1999

BRITISH HIGH COMMISSION
Corner House, Samora Machel Avenue/Leopold Takawira Street (PO Box 4490), Harare
Tel: (00 263) (4) 772990/774700
High Commissioner, HE Brian Donnelly, CMG, apptd 2001

BRITISH COUNCIL DIRECTOR, Dr Marcus Milton
Corner House, Samora Machel Avenue, PO Box 664, Harare
Tel: (00 263) (4) 775 313/4
Email: general.enquiries@britishcouncil.org.zw.

ECONOMY
The economy remains highly regulated and weak, inflation and unemployment remain high and rises in the prices of basic commodities and fuel have resulted in widespread strike action and protests. Agriculture accounted for 28 per cent of GDP in 1998 and two-thirds of the workforce are engaged in agriculture. Tobacco remains the most important crop in terms of export (Zimbabwe is the largest exporter in the world),

and maize the most important for domestic consumption.

The manufacturing sector is very dependent on the agricultural sector for raw materials and on imports e.g. fuel oil, steel products and chemicals, as well as heavy machinery and items of transport. The mining sector, although contributing a relatively small portion to GDP, is important to the economy as a foreign exchange earner. Almost all mineral production is exported. Gold is the most important product; others are asbestos, diamonds, silver, nickel, copper, platinum, chrome ore, tin, iron ore and cobalt. There is a successful ferro-chrome industry and a substantial steel works which has been heavily subsidised by government. The main trading partners are South Africa and the UK.

In 1996 imports totalled US$2,803 million and exports US$2,406 million.

GNP – US$5,851million (2000); US$460 per capita (2000)

GDP – US$9,057 million (2001); US$572 per capita (2000)

ANNUAL AVERAGE GROWTH OF GDP – 1.6 per cent (1999)

INFLATION RATE – 58.5 per cent (1999)

TOTAL EXTERNAL DEBT – US$4,002 million (2000)

Trade with UK	2001	2002
Imports from UK	£36,172,000	£34,146,000
Exports to UK	91,419,000	86,200,000

EDUCATION

Education is compulsory, and the language of instruction is English. Over 80 per cent of schools are government-aided. There are four universities; the University of Zimbabwe was founded in 1955.

ILLITERACY RATE – (m) 7.2 per cent; (f) 15.3 per cent (2000)

ENROLMENT (percentage of age group) – tertiary 7 per cent (1997)

UK OVERSEAS TERRITORIES

ANGUILLA

AREA – 37 sq. miles (96 sq. km)
POPULATION – 12,394 (1998 estimate)
CAPITAL – The Valley (population, 2,400, 1994)
CURRENCY – East Caribbean dollar (EC$) of 100 cents
FLAG – British blue ensign with the coat of arms and three dolphins in the fly
POPULATION GROWTH RATE – 6.7 per cent (1999)
POPULATION DENSITY – 134 per sq. km (1999)

Anguilla is a flat coralline island in the Caribbean, the most northerly of the Leeward islands, about 16 miles in length and three and a half miles in breadth at its widest point. The island is covered with low scrub and fringed with white coral-sand beaches. The climate is pleasant, with temperatures in the range of 24–30°C throughout the year.

HISTORY AND POLITICS
Anguilla has been a British colony since 1650. For much of its history it was linked administratively with St Kitts, but three months after the Associated State of Saint Christopher (St Kitts)-Nevis-Anguilla came into being in 1967, the Anguillans repudiated government from St Kitts. A Commissioner was installed in 1969 and in 1976 Anguilla was given a new status and separate constitution. Final separation from St Kitts and Nevis was effected on 19 December 1980 and Anguilla reverted to a British dependency. A new constitution was introduced in 1982, providing for a Governor, an Executive Council comprising four elected Ministers and two ex-officio members (the Attorney-General and Deputy Governor), and a 12-member legislative House of Assembly, consisting of seven elected members, two nominated members, two ex-officio members (the Attorney-General and Deputy Governor) and presided over by a Speaker. The last general election was held in March 2000.

Governor, HE Peter Johnstone, *apptd* 2000
Deputy Governor, Roger Cousins, OBE, *apptd* 1997

EXECUTIVE COUNCIL *as at May 2003*
Chairman of the Executive Council, The Governor
Chief Minister, Osbourne Fleming
Attorney-General, Ronald Scipio
Communications, Public Utilities and Works, Kenneth Harrigan
Finance, Victor Banks
Social Services, Eric Reid
Member of the Executive Council, The Deputy Governor

ECONOMY
Low rainfall limits agricultural output and export earnings are mainly from sales of fish and lobsters. Tourism has developed rapidly in recent years and accounts for most of the island's economic activity.
GDP – US$95 million (1998); US$11,678 per capita (1998)
ANNUAL AVERAGE GROWTH OF GDP – 4.1 per cent (1998)

Trade with UK	2001	2002
Imports from UK	£1,174,000	£1,924,000
Exports to UK	73,000	37,000

BERMUDA

AREA – 20 sq. miles (52 sq. km)
POPULATION – 63,400 (2002 estimate)
CAPITAL – ψHamilton (population, 2,277, 1994)
CURRENCY – Bermuda dollar of 100 cents
FLAG – British red ensign with the shield of arms in the fly
LIFE EXPECTANCY (years) – 77 (2001)
POPULATION GROWTH RATE – 1.7 per cent (1999)
POPULATION DENSITY – 1,231 per sq. km (2001)
GDP – US$2,457 million (1998); US$44,060 per capita (2000)

The Bermudas, or Somers Islands, are a cluster of about 100 small islands (about 20 of which are inhabited) situated in the west of the Atlantic Ocean, the nearest point of the mainland being Cape Hatteras in North Carolina, about 570 miles distant.

HISTORY AND POLITICS
The colony derives its name from Juan Bermudez, a Spaniard, who sighted it before 1515. No settlement was made until 1609 when Sir George Somers, who was shipwrecked there on his way to Virginia, colonised the islands.

Internal self-government was introduced in 1968. There is a Senate of 11 members and an elected House of Assembly of 40 members. The Governor retains responsibility for external affairs, defence, internal security and the police, although administrative matters for the police service have been delegated to the Minister of Labour, Home Affairs and Public Safety. Independence from the UK was rejected in a referendum in August 1995. The last general election was held on 24 July 2003.

Governor and Commander-in-Chief, HE Sir John Vereker, KCB, *apptd* 2002

CABINET *as at March 2003*
Premier, Minister Responsible for Government Services, Jennifer Smith
Deputy Premier, Minister of Finance, Eugene Cox
Attorney-General, Dame Lois Browne-Evans
Community Affairs and Sport, K. H. Randolph Horton
Education and Development, Paula A. Cox
Environment, Dennis P. Lister
Health and Family Services, Nelson Bascome
Housing, Lt.-Col. David Burch
Labour, Home Affairs and Public Safety, Terry E. Lister
Telecommunications and E-Commerce, M. D. Renee Webb
Transport, Ewart Brown
Without Portfolio, Neletha Butterfield
Works and Engineering, Alex Scott

ECONOMY

The islands' economic structure is based on tourism and international company business, attracted by the low level of taxation and sophisticated telecommunications system.

Locally manufactured concentrates, perfumes, cut flowers and pharmaceuticals are the islands' leading exports. Little food is produced except vegetables and fish, other foodstuffs being imported.

Trade with UK	2001	2002
Imports from UK	£33,952,000	£30,920,000
Exports to UK	45,326,000	18,047,000

COMMUNICATIONS

One daily and two weekly newspapers are published in Bermuda. Three commercial companies operate radio and television services, including a cable-television system. The Bermuda Telephone Company, TeleBermuda, and Cable and Wireless provide telecommunications links to more than 140 countries.

EDUCATION

Free elementary education was introduced in 1949. Free secondary education was introduced in 1965 for those children in the aided and maintained schools who were below the upper limit of the statutory school age of 18.

THE BRITISH ANTARCTIC TERRITORY

AREA – 660,000 sq. miles (1,709,340 sq. km.)
POPULATION – No permanent population
FLAG – British white ensign, without the cross of St George, with the coat of arms of the territory in the fly

The British Antarctic Territory was designated in 1962 and consists of the areas south of 60°S. latitude and bounded by longitudes 20°W. and 80°W. The territory includes the South Orkney Islands, the South Shetland Islands, the mountainous Antarctic Peninsula (highest point Mount Jackson, 10,443 ft above sea level) and all adjacent islands, and the land mass extending to the South Pole. The territory has no indigenous inhabitants and the British population consists of the scientists and technicians at the British Antarctic Survey stations. Argentina, Brazil, Bulgaria, Chile, China, Peru, Poland, Republic of Korea, Russia, Ukraine, Uruguay and the USA also have scientific stations in the territory.

Commissioner (non-resident), Alan Edden Huckle, *apptd* 2001

THE BRITISH INDIAN OCEAN TERRITORY

AREA – 23 sq. miles (59 sq. km.)
POPULATION – No permanent population
FLAG – Divided horizontally into blue and white wavy stripes, with the Union Flag in the canton and a crowned palm-tree over all in the fly

The British Indian Ocean Territory was established by an Order in Council in 1965 and included islands formerly administered from Mauritius and the Seychelles. The islands of Farquhar, Desroches and Aldabra became part of the Seychelles when it became independent in 1976; since then the Territory has consisted of the Chagos Archipelago only. The Chagos Archipelago consists of six

main groups of islands situated on the Great Chagos Bank and covering some 21,000 sq. miles (54,389 sq. km). The largest and most southerly of the Chagos Islands is Diego Garcia, a sand cay with a land area of about 17 sq. miles approximately 1,100 miles east of Mahé, used as a joint naval support facility by Britain and the USA.

The other main island groups of the archipelago, Peros Banhos (29 islands with a total land area of 4 sq. miles) and Salamon (11 islands with a total land area of 2 sq. miles) are uninhabited.

The islands' former inhabitants (the Ilois) were expelled between 1967 and 1973 to allow for the construction of the naval base, most being resettled in Mauritius. Following legal action by representatives of the Ilois, on 3 November 2000 the High Court overturned the ordinance that had required the Ilois to seek permission to visit the territory, effectively granting them the right of return.

Commissioner, Alan Edden Huckle, *apptd* 2001
Administrator, Louise Savill, *apptd* 1996

Trade with UK	2001	2002
Imports from UK	£494,000	£1,739,000
Exports to UK	18,000	15,000

BRITISH VIRGIN ISLANDS

AREA – 58 sq. miles (151 sq. km)
POPULATION – 21,000 (2001 estimate; by island: Tortola 16,630; Virgin Gorda 3,063; Anegada 204; Jost Van Dyke 176; other islands 181)
CAPITAL – ΨRoad Town (population, 3,983, 2001 estimate)
CURRENCY – US dollar (US$)
FLAG – British blue ensign with the shield of arms in the fly
POPULATION GROWTH RATE – 2.9 per cent (1999)
POPULATION DENSITY – 134 per sq. km (2001)
GDP – US$604 million (1998); US$29,795 per capita (1998)
ANNUAL AVERAGE GROWTH OF GDP – 1.3 per cent (1998)

The Virgin Islands, divided between the UK and the USA, are situated at the eastern extremity of the Greater Antilles. Those of the group which are British number 46, of which 11 are inhabited, and have a total area of about 58 sq. miles (151 sq. km). The principal islands are Tortola, the largest (area, 21 sq. miles), Virgin Gorda (8 sq. miles), Anegada (15 sq. miles) and Jost Van Dyke (3.5 sq. miles).

Apart from Anegada, which is a flat coral island, the British Virgin Islands are hilly, being an extension of the Puerto Rico and the US Virgin Islands archipelago. The highest point is Sage Mountain on Tortola which rises to a height of 1,780 feet.

HISTORY AND POLITICS

Under the 1977 constitution the Governor, appointed by the Crown, remains responsible for defence and internal security, external affairs and the civil service but in other matters acts in accordance with the advice of the Executive Council. The Executive Council consists of the Governor as Chairman, one ex-officio member (the Attorney-General), the Chief Minister and four other ministers. The Legislative Council consists of a Speaker chosen from outside the Council, one ex-officio member (the Attorney-General), and 13 elected members returned from ten electoral districts.

Governor, HE Thomas Macan, *apptd* 2002
Deputy Governor, Elton Georges, OBE
Chairman of the Executive Council, The Governor
Chief Minister and Minister of Finance, Ralph O'Neal, OBE
Deputy Chief Minister and Minister of Communications and Works, Julian Fraser
Attorney-General, Cherno Jallow
Education and Culture, Andrew Fahie
Health and Welfare, Ethlyn Smith
Natural Resources and Labour, Reeial George

ECONOMY

Tourism is the main industry but the financial centre is growing steadily in importance. Other industries include a rum distillery, three stone-crushing plants and factories manufacturing concrete blocks and paint. The major export items are fresh fish, gravel, sand, fruit and vegetables; exports are largely confined to the US Virgin Islands. Chief imports are building materials, machinery, cars and beverages.

Trade with UK	2001	2002
Imports from UK	£7,272,000	£25,839,000
Exports to UK	6,836,000	18,871,000

COMMUNICATIONS

The principal airport is on Beef Island, linked by bridge to Tortola, and an extended runway of 3,600 ft enables larger aircraft to call. There is a second airfield on Virgin Gorda and a third on Anegada. There are direct shipping services to the UK and the USA and fast passenger services connect the main islands by ferry.

CAYMAN ISLANDS

AREA – 99.6 sq. miles (259 sq. km)
POPULATION – 43,000 (2000 estimate)
CAPITAL – ψGeorge Town (population, 20,626, 1999 census)
CURRENCY – Cayman Islands dollar (CI$) of 100 cents
FLAG – British blue ensign with the arms on a white disc in the fly
POPULATION GROWTH RATE – 4.5 per cent (1999)
POPULATION DENSITY – 166 per sq. km (2001)
GDP – US$972 million (1998); US$23,809 per capita (1999)
ANNUAL AVERAGE GROWTH OF GDP – 4.5 per cent (2000)

The Cayman Islands consist of three islands, Grand Cayman, Cayman Brac, and Little Cayman. About 150 miles south of Cuba, the islands are divided from Jamaica, 180 miles to the south-east, by the Cayman Trench, the deepest part of the Caribbean. The nearest point on the US mainland is Miami in Florida, 450 miles to the north.

HISTORY AND POLITICS

The colony derives its name from the Carib word for the crocodile, 'caymanas', which appeared in the log of the first English visitor to the islands, Sir Francis Drake.

Although tradition has it that the first settlers arrived in 1658, the first recorded settlers arrived in 1666–71. The first recorded permanent settlers followed the first land grant by Britain in 1734. The islands were placed under direct control of Jamaica in 1863. When Jamaica became independent in 1962, the islands opted to remain under the British Crown.

The constitution provides for a Governor, a Legislative Assembly and an Executive Council, and effectively allows a large measure of self-government. Unless there are exceptional reasons, the Governor accepts the advice of the Executive Council, which comprises three official members and five ministers elected from the 15 elected members of the Assembly. The official members also sit in the Assembly. A constitutional review is currently in progress. The Governor has responsibility for the police, civil service, defence and external affairs. The Governor handed over the presidency of the Legislative Assembly to the Speaker in 1991. The normal life of the Assembly is four years; the most recent general election was held on 8 November 2000.

Governor, HE Bruce Dinwiddy, *apptd* 2002

EXECUTIVE COUNCIL *as at March 2003*
President, The Governor
Chief Secretary, Internal and External Affairs, James Ryan, MBE
Community Services, Women's Affairs, Youth and Sport, Frank McField
Education, Human Resources and Culture, Roy Bodden
Finance and Economic Development, George McCarthy, OBE
Health Services, District Administration and Agriculture, Gilbert McLean
Legal Affairs, Attorney-General, vacant
Planning, Communications, Works and Information Technology, Linford Pierson, OBE
Tourism, Environment, Development and Commerce, McKeeva Bush, OBE

CAYMAN ISLANDS GOVERNMENT OFFICE, 6 Arlington Street, London SW1A 1RE. Tel: 020-7491 7772.
Government Representative, Jennifer Dilbert

ECONOMY

With a complete absence of direct taxation, the Cayman Islands has become successful over the past 30 years as an offshore financial centre. With representation from 61 countries, there were, at the end of 2001, 531 banks and trust companies, of which local offices were maintained by 121. Following accusations of money laundering, an agreement was signed with the USA in November 2001 to share information on bank accounts. In addition, there were 694 licensed insurance companies and 64,495 registered companies. The Cayman Islands stock exchange opened in January 1997. Tourism, with an emphasis on scuba diving, has also been developed successfully. There were 302,797 visitors by air and 1,574,750 cruise ship callers in 2002.

The two industries support a heavy imbalance in trade resulting from the need to import most of what is consumed and used on the islands, and have created a thriving local economy. Import duty and fees from financial centre operations have provided revenue enabling the government to undertake heavy investment in education, health, social programmes and infrastructure.

Trade with UK	2001	2002
Imports from UK	9,734,000	8,969,000
Exports to UK	93,318,000	4,477,000

FALKLAND ISLANDS

AREA – 4,700 sq. miles (12,173 sq. km)
POPULATION – 2,564 (2001 census)
CAPITAL – ψStanley (population, 1,989, 1996 census)
CURRENCY – Falkland pound of 100 pence
FLAG – British blue ensign with the arms on a white disc
in the fly
POPULATION GROWTH RATE – 14 per cent
URBAN POPULATION – 84.0 per cent (2001)

The Falkland Islands, the only considerable group in the South Atlantic, lie about 300 miles east of the Straits of Magellan. They consist of East Falkland (area 2,610 sq. miles; 6,759 sq. km), West Falkland (2,090 sq. miles; 5,413 sq. km) and over 700 small islands. Mount Usborne (E. Falkland), the loftiest peak, rises 2,312 feet above sea level. The islands are chiefly moorland.

HISTORY AND POLITICS
The Falklands were sighted first by Davis in 1592, and then by Hawkins in 1594; the first known landing was by Strong in 1690. A settlement was made by France in 1764; this was subsequently sold to Spain, but the latter country recognised Great Britain's title to a part at least of the group in 1771. The first British settlement was established in 1766. After Argentina declared independence from Spain, the Argentine government in 1820 proclaimed its sovereignty over the Falklands and a settlement was founded in 1826. The settlement was destroyed by the Americans in 1831. In 1833 occupation was resumed by the British for the protection of the seal-fisheries, and the islands were permanently colonised. Argentina continued to claim sovereignty over the islands (known to them as *las Islas Malvinas*), and in pursuance of this claim invaded the islands on 2 April 1982 and also occupied South Georgia. A naval and military force dispatched from Great Britain recaptured South Georgia on 25 April and after landing at San Carlos on 21 May, recaptured the islands from the Argentines, who surrendered on 14 June 1982. A British naval and military garrison of 1,265 personnel remains in the area.

Under the 1985 constitution, the Governor is advised by an Executive Council consisting of three elected members of the Legislative Council and two ex-officio members, the Chief Executive and the Financial Secretary. The Legislative Council consists of eight elected members and the same two ex-officio members.

Governor and Chairman of the Executive Council, HE
Howard Pearce, CVO, *apptd* 2002
Chief Executive, Chris Simpkins
Attorney-General, David G. Lang, CBE, QC
Commander, British Forces, Falkland Islands, Brig. James
Gordon
Financial Secretary, Derek F. Howatt

FALKLAND ISLANDS GOVERNMENT OFFICE,
Falkland House, 14 Broadway, London SW1H 0BH.
Tel: 020-7222 2542.
Government Representative, Miss S. Cameron

ECONOMY
The economy was formerly based solely on agriculture, principally sheep farming with a little dairy farming for domestic requirements and crops for winter fodder. Since the establishment of an interim conservation and management fishing zone around the islands in 1987 and the consequent introduction of a licensing regime for vessels fishing within the 200-mile zone, the economy has diversified. Income from the associated fishing activities, mainly for illex squid, is now the largest source of revenue. The increase in government revenue from fishing licences has led to the establishment of a substantial health, education and welfare system. The islands are now self-financing except for defence. Chief imports are provisions, alcoholic beverages, timber, clothing and hardware. Tourism is a small but expanding industry.

In 1996, the Falkland Islands government awarded seven production licences to search for offshore hydrocarbons in the North Falkland Basin. By the end of 1998, no commercially viable accumulations of oil had been found, but the exploration revealed the presence of organic-rich source rock, indicating the presence of considerable quantities of oil in the North Falkland Basin. Further exploratory searches are planned.

An EU-standard abattoir was opened in 2001, enabling the Falkland Islands to export meat to the European Union.

Trade with UK	2001	2002
Imports from UK	£19,756,000	£17,223,000
Exports to UK	6,873,000	5,454,000

GIBRALTAR

AREA – 2.3 sq. miles (6 sq. km)
POPULATION – 27,649 (2001 estimate)
CAPITAL – ΨGibraltar
CURRENCY – Gibraltar pound of 100 pence
FLAG – White with a red stripe along the lower edge;
over all a red castle with a key hanging from its
gateway
POPULATION GROWTH RATE – 0.6 per cent (2000)
POPULATION DENSITY – 4,159 per sq. km (2000)

Gibraltar is a rocky promontory which juts southwards from the south-east coast of Spain, with which it is connected by a low isthmus. It is about 20 miles (32 km) from the opposite coast of Africa. The town stands at the foot of the promontory on the west side.

HISTORY AND POLITICS
Gibraltar was captured in 1704, during the War of the Spanish Succession, by a combined Dutch and English force, and was ceded to Great Britain by the Treaty of Utrecht (1713). The Treaty of Utrecht stipulates that if Britain ever relinquishes its colonial rights over Gibraltar the colony would return to Spain. In a 1967 referendum on the colony's status, 12,138 people voted to remain a British Dependent Territory and 44 voted to join Spain. Spain closed the border with Gibraltar from 1969 to 1985 and refused to engage in any trade.

The 1969 constitution makes provision for certain domestic matters to devolve on a local government of ministers appointed from among elected members of the House of Assembly. The House of Assembly consists of an independent Speaker, 15 elected members, the

Attorney-General and the Financial and Development Secretary.

The Governor retains responsibility for external affairs, defence, internal security and financial security, while the local government is responsible for other domestic matters. The Gibraltar government has recently been pressing for more local autonomy especially in its relations with the EU, and this has led to tension with the UK and Spanish governments. Gibraltar is part of the EU (with the UK government responsible for enforcing EU directives affecting Gibraltar) but is not a fully-fledged member and is exempt from the Common Customs Tariff and the Common Agricultural Policy. Value added tax is not applied. The Gibraltar Social Democrats won the last election in February 2000.

Talks between the UK and Spain on the future of Gibraltar resumed in July 2001, but were boycotted by the Gibraltarian government which had insisted on the right to veto any proposals on which it disagreed. The latest round of talks held in February 2002 failed to establish an agreement.

Governor and Commander-in-Chief, HE Sir Francis Richards, KCMG, CVO, *apptd* 2003
Commander British Forces, HM Naval Base, Gibraltar, Cdre R. Clapp
Deputy Governor, D. Blunt
Attorney-General, R. Rhoda
Chief Justice, Derek Schofield
Chief Minister, Peter Caruana
Deputy Chief Minister, Trade, Industry and Telecommunication, Keith Azopardi
Education, Training, Culture and Health, Dr Bernard Linares
Employment and Consumer Affairs, Hubert Corby
Housing, Jaime Netto
Public Services, Environment, Sport and Youth, Ernest Britto
Social Affairs, Yvette Del Agua
Speaker, John Alcantara, CBE
Tourism and Transport, Joe Holliday

GOVERNMENT OF GIBRALTAR, Arundel Great Court, 178–179 The Strand, London WC2R 1EL.
Tel: 020-7836 0777.
Government Representative, A. Poggio

ECONOMY

Gibraltar has an extensive shipping trade and is a popular shopping centre and tourist resort. The chief sources of revenue are the port dues, the rent of the Crown estate in the town, and duties on consumer items. The free port tradition of Gibraltar is still reflected in the low rates of import duty. A financial services industry is expanding, based on Gibraltar's status as an offshore financial centre. However, many jobs have been lost as a result of reductions in the British naval and military presence.

Trade with UK	2001	2002
Imports from UK	£127,634,000	£128,339,000
Exports to UK	14,328,000	22,615,000

EDUCATION

Education is compulsory and free for children between the ages of five and 15 whose parents are ordinarily resident in Gibraltar. Scholarships are available for higher education in Britain. The total enrolment in government schools was 5,043 in September 2001.

MONTSERRAT

AREA – 39 sq. miles (102 sq. km)
POPULATION – 4,500 (2001 estimate)
CAPITAL – ψPlymouth
CURRENCY – East Caribbean dollar (EC$) of 100 cents
FLAG – British blue ensign with the shield of arms in the fly
POPULATION GROWTH RATE – 0.5 per cent (1999)
POPULATION DENSITY – 108 per sq. km (1999)
GDP – US$38 million (1998); US$3,570 per capita (1998)

Montserrat is about 11 miles long and seven miles wide. It is volcanic with several hot springs. About two-thirds of the island is mountainous, the rest capable of cultivation but volcanic activity has caused the evacuation of two-thirds of the island.

HISTORY AND POLITICS

Discovered by Columbus in 1493, Montserrat became a British colony in 1632. The first settlers were predominantly Irish indentured servants from St Christopher. Montserrat was captured by the French in 1664, 1667 and 1782 but the island reverted to Britain within a few years on each occasion and was finally assigned to Great Britain in 1783.

A ministerial system was introduced in Montserrat in 1960. The Executive Council is presided over by the Governor and is composed of four elected members (the Chief and three other Ministers) and two ex-officio members (the Attorney-General and the Financial Secretary). The four Ministers are appointed from the members of the political party or coalition holding the majority in the Legislative Council. The Legislative Council consists of the Speaker, two ex-officio members (the Attorney-General and the Financial Secretary) and nine elected members. Following elections in April 2001 the elected element of the legislature comprised the following parties: New People's Liberation Movement 7; National Progressive Party 2.

Governor, HE Anthony Longrigg, CMG, *apptd* 2001

EXECUTIVE COUNCIL *as at March 2003*
President, The Governor
Chief Minister and Minister of Finance and Economic Development, Dr John Osborne
Agriculture, Lands, Housing and the Environment, Margaret Dyer-Howe
Attorney-General, Esco Henry-Greer
Communications and Works, John Wilson
Education, Health and Community Services, Isabelle Meade
Financial Secretary, John Skerritt

ECONOMY

The economy, which consists of tourism, related construction activities, offshore business services and agriculture, has been seriously affected by relocation to the north of the island due to volcanic activity.

Trade with UK	2001	2002
Imports from UK	£1,138,000	£1,337,000
Exports to UK	23,000	18,000

PITCAIRN ISLANDS

AREA – 2 sq. miles (5 sq. km)
POPULATION – 54 (1999). Since 1887 the islanders
  have generally been adherents of the Seventh-day
  Adventist Church
CURRENCY – Currency is that of New Zealand
FLAG – British blue ensign with the arms in the fly

Pitcairn is the chief of a group of islands situated about
midway between New Zealand and Panama in the South
Pacific Ocean. The island rises in cliffs to a height of
1,100 feet and access from the sea is possible only at
Bounty Bay, a small rocky cove, and then only by surf
boats. The other three islands of the group (Henderson,
lying 105 miles east-north-east of Pitcairn, Oeno, lying
75 miles north-west, and Ducie, lying 293 miles east) are
all uninhabited.

HISTORY AND POLITICS
First settled in 1790 by the Bounty mutineers and their
Tahitian companions, Pitcairn was left uninhabited in
1856 when the entire population was resettled on
Norfolk Island. The present community are descendants
of two parties who, not wishing to remain on Norfolk,
returned to Pitcairn in 1859 and 1864 respectively.
  Pitcairn became a British settlement under the British
Settlement Act 1887 and was administered by the
Governor of Fiji from 1952 until 1970, when the
administration was transferred to the British High
Commission in New Zealand and the British High
Commissioner was appointed Governor. The local
Government Ordinance of 1964 provides for a Council
of ten members of whom six are elected.

Governor of Pitcairn, Henderson, Ducie and Oeno Islands,
  HE Richard Fell, CVO *(British High Commissioner to
  New Zealand)*
Island Mayor, Steve Christian

ECONOMY
The islanders live by subsistence gardening and fishing.
Wood carvings and other handicrafts are sold to passing
ships and to a few overseas customers. Other than small
fees charged for gun and driving licences there are no
taxes and government revenue is derived almost solely
from the sale of postage stamps and income from
investments. Communication with the outside world is
maintained by cargo vessels travelling between New
Zealand and Panama which call at irregular intervals, and
by means of a satellite service providing telephone,
email and fax facilities.

Trade with UK	2001	2002
Imports from UK	£892,000	£609,000
Exports to UK	2,000	44,000

EDUCATION
Education is compulsory between the ages of five and 15.
Secondary education in New Zealand is encouraged by
the administration, which provides scholarships and
bursaries. Medical care is provided by a registered nurse
when a doctor is not present.

ST HELENA AND DEPENDENCIES

AREA – 47 sq. miles (122 sq. km)
POPULATION – 5,157 (1998 census)
CAPITAL – ψJamestown (population, 884, 1998)
CURRENCY – St Helena pound (£) of 100 pence
FLAG – British blue ensign with the shield of arms in the
  fly
POPULATION GROWTH RATE – 0.8 per cent (1998)
POPULATION DENSITY – 40 per sq. km (1998)
URBAN POPULATION – 39.2 per cent (1998)
ILLITERACY RATE – 3.6 per cent (1998)

St Helena is situated in the South Atlantic Ocean, 955
miles south of the Equator, 702 miles south-east of
Ascension, 1,140 miles from the nearest point of the
African continent, 1,800 miles from the coast of South
America and 1,694 miles from Cape Town. It is 10.5
miles long and 6.5 wide.
  St Helena is of volcanic origin, and consists of
numerous rugged mountains, the highest rising to 2,700
feet (820 m), interspersed with picturesque ravines.
Although within the tropics, the south-east trade winds
keep the temperature mild and equable.

HISTORY AND POLITICS
St Helena was probably discovered by the Portuguese
navigator João da Nova in 1502. It was used as a port of
call for vessels of all nations trading to the East until it
was annexed by the Dutch in 1633. It was never
occupied by them, however, and the English East India
Company seized it in 1659. From 1815 to 1821 the
island was lent to the British government as a place of
exile for the Emperor Napoleon Bonaparte who died in
St Helena on 5 May 1821, and in 1834 it was annexed
to the British Crown.
  The island was settled by the East India Company in
the 17th and 18th centuries with planters and company
soldiers from England and slaves from the Indian
subcontinent and Madagascar.
  The government of St Helena is administered by a
Governor, with the aid of a Legislative Council,
consisting of a Speaker, three ex-officio members (Chief
Secretary, Financial Secretary and Attorney-General) and
12 elected members. Five committees of the Legislative
Council are responsible for the overseeing of the
activities of the five biggest government departments and
have in addition a wide range of statutory and
administrative functions. The Governor is also assisted by
an Executive Council of the three ex-officio members and
the chairmen of the Council committees.

Governor, HE David Hollamby, *apptd* 1999

EXECUTIVE COUNCIL *as at March 2003*
The Governor
Attorney-General, Kurt De Freitas, OBE
Chief Justice, G. W. Martin, OBE
Chief Engineer, M. Baird
Chief of Police, D. F. Thomas
Chief Secretary, J. M. Styles
Deputy Secretary, E. C. Yon, MBE
Financial Secretary, R. Dolan
Chief Officers: S. I. Ellick *(Administrative Health and Social
  Services)*; W. R. Clingham *(Agriculture and Natural
  Resources)*; M. Stewart *(Chief Auditor)*; Dr C. S. Essex
  (Development); P. M. Lawrence *(Education)*; J. E. Gough
  (Employment and Benefits); D. H. Wade *(Finance)*; B. A.
  George *(Personnel)*; B. J. Francis *(Post Mistress)*

ECONOMY

St Helena was intended as a maritime base, with an economy dedicated to the provision of supplies for shipping and the local garrison, rather than as a self-sufficient colony. St Helena still receives an annual grant from the UK. The only significant export is canned and frozen fish. The other exports are a small amount of high quality coffee and cottage industry products (including lace, decorative woodwork and beadwork). James's Bay, on the north-west of the island, possesses a good anchorage. There is as yet no airport or airstrip.

Trade with UK	2001	2002
Imports from UK	£9,674,000	£12,450,000
Exports to UK	415,000	606,000

ASCENSION ISLAND

AREA – 34 sq. miles (88 sq. km)
POPULATION – 980 (2001 census)
CAPITAL – ψGeorgetown
CURRENCY – Currency is that of St Helena or the UK

The small island of Ascension lies in the South Atlantic some 750 miles north-west of the island of St Helena. It is a rocky peak of purely volcanic origin. The highest point (Green Mountain), some 2,817 ft, is covered with lush vegetation. The island is a breeding area for green turtles and for the sooty tern, or wideawake. Other wildlife includes feral donkeys and sheep, nine varieties of sea birds, including the indigenous Ascension frigate bird, and five land birds.

British forces returned to the island in April 1982 in support of operations in the Falkland Islands. At present there are about 25 RAF personnel on the island together with some 200 civilian workers supporting the air link to the Falklands.

HISTORY AND POLITICS
Ascension is said to have been discovered by João da Nova in 1501 and two years later was visited on Ascension Day by Alphonse d'Albuquerque, who gave the island its present name. It was uninhabited until the arrival of Napoleon in St Helena in 1815 when a small British naval garrison was stationed on the island. As HMS *Ascension* it remained under the supervision of the Board of Admiralty until 1922, when it was made a dependency of St Helena.

The British Foreign Secretary appoints the Administrator who is responsible to the Governor resident in St Helena. There is a small police force, bank and post office. The Ascension Island government is responsible for health and education. The Ascension Island Works and Services Agency operates the port and provides other public services such as road and building maintenance.

Administrator, Andrew Kettlewell, *apptd* 2002

COMMUNICATIONS
Cable and Wireless operates the international and internal telephone service. The BBC opened its Atlantic relay station broadcasting to Africa and South America in 1967. There is a monthly shipping service and a flight every five days by RAF Tristars which transit Ascension en route to the Falkland Islands. US aircraft and ships service the American base.

TRISTAN DA CUNHA

AREA – 38 sq. miles (98 sq. km)
POPULATION – 277 (2003 estimate)
CAPITAL – ψEdinburgh of the Seven Seas
CURRENCY – Currency is that of the UK
FLAG – Tristan da Cunha's own flag was raised on 18 November 2002 and the coat of arms reads: 'Our Faith is our Strength'.

Tristan da Cunha is the chief island of a group of islands in the South Atlantic which lies some 1,260 nautical miles (2,333 km) south-south-west of St Helena.

All the islands are volcanic and steep-sided with cliffs or narrow beaches. Tristan has a volcanic cone rising to 6,760 feet (2,060 m).

The islands have a warm-temperate oceanic climate which is damp and windy. Rainfall averages 66 inches a year on the coast of Tristan da Cunha.

Population is centred in the settlement of Edinburgh on Tristan da Cunha. In addition, there is a meteorological station maintained on Gough Island by the South African government. Inaccessible Island and the Nightingale Islands are uninhabited.

HISTORY AND POLITICS

Tristan da Cunha was discovered in 1506 by the Portuguese admiral Tristão da Cunha. In 1760 a British naval officer visited the islands and gave his name to Nightingale Island. In 1816 the group was annexed to the British Crown and a garrison was placed on Tristan da Cunha, but this force was withdrawn in 1817. Corporal William Glass remained at his own request with his wife and two children. This party, with two others, formed a settlement. In 1827 five women from St Helena, and afterwards others from Cape Colony, joined the party.

Due to its position on a main sailing route the colony thrived, with an economy based on trading with whalers, sealers and other passing ships. However, the replacement of sail by steam and the opening of the Suez Canal in the late 19th century led to decline.

In October 1961 a volcano, believed to have been extinct for thousands of years, erupted and the danger of further volcanic activity led to the evacuation of inhabitants to the UK. An advance party returned to Tristan da Cunha in 1963 and subsequently the main body of the islanders returned to the island.

GOVERNMENT

In 1938 Tristan da Cunha and the neighbouring islands of Inaccessible, Nightingale and Gough were made dependencies of St Helena. They are administered by the Governor of St Helena through a resident Administrator, with headquarters at Edinburgh. Under a constitution introduced in 1985, the Administrator is advised by an Island Council of eight elected members, of whom one must be a woman, and three appointed members. Elections are held every three years.

Administrator, Bill Dickson, *apptd* 2001

ECONOMY

The island is almost financially self-sufficient; UK government aid finances training scholarships and a resident medical officer at the hospital. The main industries are crayfish fishing, fish-processing and agriculture. There are no taxes, income being derived from the royalties from the rock lobster fishery around the islands, interest from the reserve fund, and the sales of stamps and handicrafts, as well as vegetables, to passing ships. Tourism is increasing, the island being on the itinerary of several environmental tours. Apart from the fishing industry, the other main employer is the administration itself. There is a school catering for children up to age 15. Healthcare and education are free for the islanders.

COMMUNICATIONS
Scheduled visits to the island are restricted to about six calls a year by fishing vessels from Cape Town and annual calls of the RMS *St Helena* and the *SA Agulhas*, also from Cape Town. A wireless station on the island is in daily contact with Cape Town and a radio-telephone service was established in 1969, the same year that electricity was introduced to all the islanders' homes. A marine satellite system providing direct dialling telephone, telex and fax facilities was installed in 1992. Since 1998 the island has had internet and email facilities, as well as a public telephone. Satellite television was introduced in 2001.

SOUTH GEORGIA AND THE SOUTH SANDWICH ISLANDS

AREA – 1,580 sq. miles (4,092 sq. km)
POPULATION – No permanent population

South Georgia is an island 800 miles east-south-east of the Falkland group. The population comprises the government's marine officer and the staff of the newly established scientific research station operated by the British Antarctic Survey and the curator of the museum at King Edward Point, and staff of the British Antarctic Survey at Bird Island, to the north-west of South Georgia.

The South Sandwich Islands lie some 470 miles south-east of South Georgia.

The present constitution came into effect in 1985. It provides for a Commissioner who, for the time being, is the officer administering the government of the Falkland Islands.

In 1993 the UK government decreed an extension of Crown sovereignty and jurisdiction from 12 miles around South Georgia and the South Sandwich Islands to 200 miles around each in order to preserve marine stocks.

Commissioner for South Georgia and the South Sandwich Islands, Howard Pearce, CVO, *apptd* 2002

TURKS AND CAICOS ISLANDS

AREA – 191.2 sq. miles (497 sq. km)
POPULATION – 19,000 (1999 estimate)
CAPITAL – ᴪGrand Turk (population, 3,691, 1994)
CURRENCY – US dollar (US$)
FLAG – British blue ensign with the shield of arms in the fly
POPULATION GROWTH RATE – 3.3 per cent
POPULATION DENSITY – 37 per sq. km (2001)

The Turks and Caicos Islands are about 50 miles south-east of the Bahamas of which they are geographically an extension. There are over 30 islands, of which eight are inhabited, covering an estimated area of 166 sq. miles (430 sq. km). The principal island and seat of government is Grand Turk.

HISTORY AND POLITICS
A constitution was introduced in 1988, and amended in 1993, which provides for an Executive Council and a Legislative Council. The Executive Council is presided over by the Governor and comprises the Chief Minister and five elected Ministers, together with the ex-officio Chief Secretary and Attorney-General.

At the general election of 24 April 2003, the People's Democratic Movement won seven seats and the Progressive National Party six seats in the Legislative Council.

Governor, HE Jim Poston, *apptd* 2002

EXECUTIVE COUNCIL *as at March 2003*
President, The Governor
Attorney-General, David Jeremiah
Chief Minister, Commerce and Development, Finance, Derek H. Taylor, OBE
Chief Secretary, Cynthia Astwood, MBE
Communications, Oswald Skippings
Health, Education, Youth, Sports and Women's Affairs, Clarence Selver
Home Affairs, Larry Coalbrooke
Natural Resources and Deputy Chief Minister, Hilly Ewing
Public Works and Utilities, Noel Skippings

ECONOMY
The most important industries are fishing, tourism and offshore finance. The islands were visited by 151,000 tourists in 2000.

Trade with UK	2001	2002
Imports from UK	£779,000	£1,167,000
Exports to UK	151,000	495,000

COMMUNICATIONS
The principal airports are on the islands of Grand Turk and Providenciales. Air services link Providenciales with London, Miami, Fort Lauderdale, Atlanta, Jamaica, the Bahamas, Haiti and the Dominican Republic. An internal air service provides a regular service between the principal islands. There are direct shipping services to the USA (Miami). A comprehensive telephone and telex service is provided by Cable and Wireless (WI) Ltd.

THE YEAR 2002–3

EVENTS OF THE YEAR

1 SEPTEMBER 2002 TO 31 AUGUST 2003

BRITISH AFFAIRS

SEPTEMBER 2002

5. Gas workers discovered a grave containing eight human skeletons under the kitchen floor at the Palace of Holyroodhouse. **16.** The Oxford, Cambridge and RSA Examinations (OCR) exam board formally apologised to an A-level student who was wrongly graded. **19.** The Secretary of State for Transport, Alistair Darling, announced the introduction of a computerised road hazards test in November. **24.** Parliament was recalled from the summer recess to hear a statement from the Prime Minister on Iraq and weapons of mass destruction; the Government published a 50-page dossier detailing the history of Iraq's weapons of mass destruction programme, its breach of UN resolutions and attempts to rebuild that illegal programme. **26.** A private letter from the Prince of Wales to the Prime Minister, in which the Prince supposedly endorsed the view that the rural community was more discriminated against than ethnic minority communities, was proved to be fictitious; the disputed document was revealed to be part of the minutes of a confidential meeting between the Prince and Mr Blair at St James's Palace. **29.** Seventy-nine patients and staff at the Royal Bournemouth Hospital contracted the Norwalk virus. **30.** The Ministry of Defence announced plans to spend £13 billion on two new US F35 Joint Strike Fighter aircraft carriers. A 15-year-old black schoolboy was stabbed in the heart by a group of four youths in what police believe was a racially motivated attack; the victim survived. The initial findings of the 2001 UK population census were published.

OCTOBER 2002

2. Mike Tomlinson, the former chief inspector of schools, called for A-level grades to be reviewed in 27 subjects after accusations that the grades were manipulated. The review affected three examination boards: OCR, Edexcel and the Assessment and Qualifications Alliance (AQA). The French Government announced that it would lift its six-year export ban on British beef. **4.** The Department for Education and Skills announced that over 90,000 A-level exam papers would be remarked in an attempt to establish whether candidates had been downgraded. **7.** The Conservative party conference began in Bournemouth. **9.** The London Underground trade unions, ASLEF and the RMT, called off further industrial action after the Mayor of London, Ken Livingstone, said that he would appoint an independent mediator in the spring and would honour any pay increase recommended by that mediator. **19.** Documents seen by the *Sunday Times* alleged that Jack McConnell, the former First Minister of Scotland, may have broken electoral rules by failing to declare a £4,200 donation to his electoral campaign. **20.** Further financial irregularities were discovered in four Labour constituency parties in Scotland. The Labour party ordered every local branch in Britain to check its accounts. **21.** An earthquake tremor measuring 3.2 on the Richter scale and lasting two

seconds shook Greater Manchester. **22.** The Government announced plans to recruit 50,000 extra classroom assistants by 2006. **23.** Estelle Morris resigned as Secretary of State for Education, citing a lack of confidence in her ability to do the job following a series of difficulties in running the department, including the A-level downgrading controversy; in a Cabinet reshuffle the following day, Charles Clarke was appointed Secretary of State for Education, Peter Hain Secretary of State for Wales, Paul Murphy Secretary of State for Northern Ireland and John Reid was appointed party chairman. **24.** Two hundred prisoners were moved from overcrowded Lincoln prison after a riot in which inmates took control of the buildings for three hours. The Army announced changes to the way that deaths of soldiers will be investigated in the light of concerns raised about the investigations into the deaths of four soldiers at the Royal Logistics Corps headquarters at Deepcut barracks in recent years; in future, the police will decide whether a soldier's death is suspicious. A remembrance service was held at St Paul's Cathedral to commemorate those killed in the terrorist attack in Bali on 12 October 2002. **26.** A report published by the Office for National Statistics found that in 2000 there were 1.75 million one-parent families in Britain, representing a quarter of families with children. **27.** Nine people were killed in severe gales throughout Britain; around 20,000 homes were still without power more than four days later. It was reported that John Hutton, the Minister for Health, had put a contract to tender to obtain sufficient smallpox vaccine to immunise the entire British population in the event of a bio-terrorism attack. **28.** Two earthquake tremors, measuring 2 and 1.7 on the Richter scale, were recorded in Manchester. **29.** MPs agreed revised working hours at Westminster, including extra sittings on three mornings a week, an end to late-night votes, and a shortening of the three-month summer recess. **31.** Hospital consultants rejected a contract offering pay rises of up to 24 per cent in return for more evening and weekend work; Dr Peter Hawker, the chairman of the British Medical Association's consultants' committee, resigned after spending two years negotiating the contract with the Department of Health. Dr George Carey stood down as Archbishop of Canterbury.

NOVEMBER 2002

3. The Ministry of Defence confirmed that two Royal Navy ships had moved to Gibraltar after intelligence indicated a possibility of an al-Qa'eda attack on British and NATO military shipping in the area. **6.** A British banker, Peter Shaw, escaped from his kidnappers after being held hostage in Georgia for five months; he returned to the UK the following day. **7.** The Queen planted a cross in the 'field of remembrance' outside Westminster Abbey, taking on a role that the late Queen Elizabeth the Queen Mother had performed for more than fifty years. The Home Secretary, David Blunkett, issued an assessment of the anti-terrorist measures taken by the Government since 11 September 2001, and warned in the preface about the threat posed by al-Qa'eda. **13.** At the state opening of the 2002-3 session of Parliament, the Queen's Speech mentioned 19 new bills; these included a Criminal Justice Bill to strengthen victims' rights, abolition of the double jeopardy rule to allow retrial where 'new and compelling' evidence emerges, better protection against child abuse on the internet, reformation of licensing hours and legislation to enable NHS hospitals to become foundation trusts. Members of the Fire Brigades Union went on national strike in support of a pay demand; Green Goddess fire engines manned by members of the armed forces provided cover for emergency calls. **14.** The Church of England Synod decided that divorcees with a former spouse still living could remarry in church, subject to meeting certain conditions. **15.** The Moors murderer Myra Hindley died aged 60, following a respiratory infection. **19.** Vandals smashed 24 Victorian stained-glass windows in the cloisters of Gloucester Cathedral, causing damage estimated at £43,000. **22.** An eight-day national fire brigade strike started at 9am after the pay dispute remained unresolved. **23.** An off-duty doctor saved the life of a 21-year-old woman after she was struck by lightning while surfing in Cornwall. **24.** An Oxford University student, Dino Yankov, died after a human catapult stunt went wrong. A man bitten by a bat died after contracting rabies, the first rabies case in Britain for 100 years. London members of the National Union of Teachers and the National Association of Schoolmasters/Union of Women Teachers went on strike over their London living allowance. **27.** It was reported that at least three black widow spiders had been found in bunches of Tesco grapes; a Tesco spokesman said that reduced pesticide levels may have allowed the spiders to hide amongst the fruit without harm and the Food Standards Agency said it would not be taking any action. **28.** The NHS announced a new pay and productivity package for NHS nurses, therapists and support staff, providing a minimum pay rise of 10 per cent plus rewards for extra responsibilities and a minimum wage of £10,100 a year for all NHS staff. **29.** Louise Saunders, a British backpacker missing for three days on an Australian mountain, was found safe only three miles from where she disappeared. **30.** It was claimed that Cherie Blair had been advised by a convicted conman, Peter Foster, over the purchase of two flats in Bristol, one for her son Euan and another as an investment; a Downing Street spokesman denied that Foster had ever acted as a financial advisor to the Blairs.

DECEMBER 2002

2. Ministers ruled out mass immunisation against smallpox as protection against bio-terrorism attacks, although army and RAF personnel who would deal with nuclear, biological or chemical attacks, specialists from the defence medical services and relevant NHS staff would be asked to volunteer for vaccination. Firefighters called off their third eight-day strike and agreed to hold talks with employers through the conciliation service Acas. A pilot scheme to test every newborn baby for deafness was extended nationwide. **3.** A survey by the Food Standards Agency and the Department of Health found that fewer than one in seven people are eating the daily recommended amount of fruit and vegetables. An overhanging branch sliced the top off a double-decker bus in Millbank, London, injuring ten people. **4.** The Prime Minister confirmed that a Government report to be published in January 2003 would propose an increase in university fees but the option of levying an advance tuition fee had been dropped; the confirmation came as

thousands of students marched in London to protest against the proposals. **5.** The first batch of immigrants accepted by the Government under the Anglo-French agreement to close the Sangatte refugee camp arrived in Britain; under the terms of the deal, Britain would take 1,000 Iraqi Kurds and 200 Afghans who have families already settled in Britain. **6.** A Chechen leader, Akhmed Zakayev, who fought as a commander in the Chechen war and is accused by the Russian government of helping to plan the Moscow theatre siege, was released from detention at Heathrow after actress Vanessa Redgrave provided a £50,000 surety. **7.** A blaze destroyed part of Edinburgh's Old Town, causing millions of pounds of damage to the World Heritage Site. The Miss World contest took place at Alexandra Palace, London; it was relocated after riots in Nigeria in protest at aspects of the competition. **8.** Following the trials of royal butlers Paul Burrell and Harold Brown, a St James's Palace spokesman confirmed that the palace was reviewing all 'gifts' made to staff and would pay any associated tax liabilities. **9.** Cherie Blair admitted telephoning Janes, the solicitors for Peter Foster, the convicted conman, in connection with the deportation case against him; Janes confirmed that Mrs Blair had participated in a conference call with Carole Caplin, Mr Foster's girlfriend and her own confidante, but had not tried to influence the proceedings or choice of counsel. **10.** Cherie Blair made a public statement regarding her involvement with Peter Foster, stating that Foster is the boyfriend of her close friend Carole Caplin but that she was not aware of the extent of his criminal convictions; she confirmed that she had consulted him during the process of purchasing two flats in Bristol, but said that he had never acted as her 'financial advisor' and stated that the property was purchased in an entirely lawful and proper way. **13.** A deaf charity worker, Ian Stillman, arrived back in the UK after being freed from prison in India. **14.** Two cargo ships collided in the English Channel in thick fog; the *Tricolor,* which was carrying 2,900 luxury cars, sank. **16.** The Prime Minister welcomed President Assad of Syria to Downing Street to launch a Middle East peace initiative. Despite warning beacons and messages from coastguards, a cargo vessel, the *Nicola,* collided with the *Tricolor* wreck in the English Channel; the *Nicola* docked in Hamburg after being freed by tugs. **18.** The Foreign Secretary, Jack Straw, made a statement declaring that Baghdad's 12,000-page declaration of its weapons programmes was a blatant lie. The Defence Secretary, Geoff Hoon, announced details of 'contingency preparations', including the imminent deployment to the Gulf of a six-strong naval task group and a nuclear submarine. A report was published on the cause of death of two-year-old Ainlee Labonte; the author, Helen Kenward, an independent child protection expert, concluded that although no individual could be held responsible, her death could have been avoided had health authorities, social services and police in Newham, London, worked together. Buckingham Palace announced that The Queen would pay an annual rent of £120,000 for up to seven years on behalf of Prince and Princess Michael of Kent for their apartments at Kensington Palace. **22.** The missing mother of a 12-year-old boy who had been left to fend for himself for 12 days was found at a hotel in Wandsworth; during his mother's absence the boy had continued to attend school, left notes for the milkman and visited a friend without arousing suspicion until the mother's absence was reported to the police by a colleague. **25.** In the 70th royal Christmas broadcast, The Queen expressed her sadness at the death of her mother and sister in 2002, but joy at the success of her golden jubilee celebrations. **26.** An armed siege began when police tried to remove a car in Marvin Street in Hackney, London, for forensic examination. **29.** Part of Brighton's historic west pier collapsed into the sea after severe weather conditions battered the south coast. **30.** Police confirmed that a man was being held hostage in the armed siege in Hackney. **31.** Dozens of roads across the country were impassable and homes flooded after heavy rain and flash floods.

JANUARY 2003

1. A Turkish tanker became stuck on the wreck of the *Tricolor,* the third ship to collide with the vessel; the tanker freed itself on the rising tide. **5.** The man held hostage for 11 days in Hackney escaped. Six Algerian men were arrested after the potentially lethal poison ricin was found by anti-terrorist police in Wood Green, London. **6.** Temperatures in some parts of the country dropped to minus 16°C overnight. **7.** The Defence Secretary ordered the call-up of 1,500 army reservists for possible operations against Iraq, though he said that this did not mean that a decision had been taken to commit British forces to such operations. Mr Hoon also announced that a Royal Navy task group would leave for the Gulf on 11 January; the official purpose of this deployment was to take part in joint naval exercises in the summer but its course would take it to the Gulf region. **8.** The Home Secretary announced that Jamaican citizens travelling to Britain from 10 January would need a visa. Blizzards swept across south and east Britain, forcing the closure of roads, rail links and schools; London had its largest snowfall since February 1991. **9.** The Hackney siege, Britain's longest running siege, ended on its 15th day after police exchanged fire with the gunman and then smashed windows to deal with a fire that broke out on the premises; later that day the gunman, Eli Hall, was found dead. Kenneth Jones, a British climber from Manchester, was found after he had crawled for four days and nights across several miles of the Carpathian mountain range in Romania with a broken leg and pelvis. **13.** The Queen had an operation on her right knee to remove a piece of torn cartilage. **14.** A policeman was stabbed to death and four others injured as they arrested three men in Manchester on an immigration matter; subsequently the suspects were thought to be involved in the production of the poison ricin. **15.** The Strategic Rail Authority announced that it would be cutting the number of services on some lines to improve punctuality and reliability, resulting in 100 trains a day being cut across the network by May 2003. **20.** The Defence Secretary announced the deployment of 30,000 ground troops to the Gulf. Anti-terrorist police raided Finsbury Park mosque in London; seven men were arrested under the Terrorism Act. A British pensioner, Reginald Crew, who was suffering from incurable motor neurone disease, ended his life by assisted suicide in Switzerland, where euthanasia is legal. **21.** Members of the Fire Brigades Union staged another 24-hour strike. The Government announced plans to abolish GCSE and A-level examinations and replace them with a baccalaureate-style qualification. **22.** The Education Secretary published a White Paper on the future of higher education, which included a proposal allowing universities to charge tuition fees of up to £3,000 a year from 2006. **25.** More than 30 people were injured after an underground train derailed on London's Central line; the line was shut for

safety checks. **28.** The Government announced that a bill would be introduced to enable the Government to impose a pay settlement on the striking firefighters. A report by Lord Laming on the state of child protection in Britain, following the inquiry into the murder of eight-year-old Victoria Climbie in February 2000, recommended a complete overhaul of child protection services; the report made 108 recommendations to public services, of which 46 should be implemented within three months. **30.** In south-east England, more than 8 cm of snow fell in two hours, with freezing conditions turning it to ice, as the evening rush hour began; roads came to a standstill, with some drivers forced to spend the night in their car, and mainline and London Underground rail services were also severely disrupted. Stansted airport was closed and Heathrow and Gatwick flights suffered long delays and cancellations. **31.** The Prime Minister and President Bush drew up a timetable for a final warning to Saddam Hussein; Mr Blair urged President Bush to work with the United Nations to disarm Saddam Hussein and to avoid solitary US military action.

FEBRUARY 2003

2. A report by the medical director of the Royal Leicester Infirmary trust stated that Dr Andrew Holton, who worked at the hospital in the 1990s, misdiagnosed a third of the children referred to him with epilepsy. **4.** The recommendations of the joint committee on reform on the House of Lords were debated in both houses of Parliament. **5.** The American Secretary of State, Colin Powell, publicised previously classified information regarding Iraq's plans to build and conceal nuclear, biological and chemical weapons; the Foreign Secretary stated that Mr Powell had presented a 'most powerful and authoritative case' against Saddam. **5.** The House of Bishops announced guidelines for couples wishing to remarry in a Church of England service. **6.** The Government deployed one third of the RAF's aircraft to the Gulf in preparation for war. **9.** Tunnelling work on a section of the Channel Tunnel rail link was suspended indefinitely after a landslide in Stratford in which several back gardens disappeared into a 32-foot hole. **11.** An audiotape believed to be recorded by Osama bin Laden was broadcast on the al-Jazeera satellite television channel. **11.** A suspected al-Qa'eda attack prompted the largest security operation at Heathrow airport for nearly a decade; 450 troops with armoured vehicles and more than 1,300 police officers were deployed the airport and surrounding areas. **13.** A ban on all cigarette advertising, including sponsorship, product placement and direct marketing, came into force at midnight. Gatwick airport's north terminal was closed and evacuated after a live hand grenade was found in the luggage of a man arriving on a flight from Caracas in Venezuela. **14.** An RAF Nimrod aircraft was deployed 44,000 feet over London as a radio communication 'relay system' for police and military operating on the ground. **15.** The biggest-ever public protest took place in London when an estimated 750,000 protestors marched in opposition to war with Iraq, converging with an estimated 250,000 more people for a rally in Hyde Park. **17.** A congestion charge of £5 was introduced for motorists entering central London; the number of cars entering central London dropped by about 30 per cent on the first day of the charge. **19.** The Foreign Office advised Britons to leave Iraq and the Israeli Occupied Territories and avoid 'non-essential' travel to Israel and Kuwait. **20.** The Archbishop of Canterbury, Dr Rowan Williams, and the Archbishop of

Westminster, Cormac Murphy-O'Connor, issued a joint statement outlining their doubts over the 'moral legitimacy' of a conflict with Iraq and their concerns over the 'unpredictable humanitarian consequences'. **22.** The Prime Minister had a private audience with the Pope to discuss the situation in Iraq. **26.** In a House of Commons debate calling for support of the Government's stance on Iraq, 122 Labour MPs and 77 MPs from other parties voted against the motion. **27.** The 104th Archbishop of Canterbury, Dr Rowan Williams, was enthroned at Canterbury Cathedral. A British pensioner, Derek Bond, was released after being detained for 20 days in South Africa on suspicion of being one of the USA's most wanted fugitives; the FBI admitted that it had been a case of mistaken identity. In a House of Commons vote, 199 MPs voted against military action to disarm Saddam Hussein; the opposing MPs included 121 Labour MPs. **28.** Two-year-old Merlin Reid was found unharmed over a mile away from his grandparents' house, from which he had wandered ten hours previously.

MARCH 2003

3. Lady Helen Taylor gave birth to her third child, Eloise Taylor. **5.** An Audit Commission investigation found that only three out of 41 NHS trusts had published accurate waiting list figures. **9.** The International Development Secretary, Clare Short, declared that she would resign from the Government if it sanctioned military action against Iraq without a second United Nations resolution. Eight US B52 bombers arrived at RAF Fairford in Gloucestershire. **12.** St Hilda's College, the last all-female college in Oxford, voted against becoming co-educational. **13.** A report compiled by the Prince of Wales's private secretary, Sir Michael Peat, announced that the Royal Family was to establish a register of private and public gifts to ensure transparency in their financial dealings; the Prince of Wales aide Michael Fawcett resigned following Sir Michael Peat's report and allegations of financial impropriety at St James's Palace. **17.** Britain and the USA decided to abandon diplomatic efforts to obtain UN backing for military action in Iraq. Robin Cook, the Leader of the House of Commons, resigned in protest at the decision. It was announced that Chris Patten, the EU External Relations Commissioner and former Governor of Hong Kong, would become Chancellor of Oxford University. The first known British sufferer from severe acute respiratory syndrome (Sars), a pneumonia-type virus, was admitted to hospital in Manchester after returning from Hong Kong. **18.** The Government secured the support of Parliament for British involvement in war against Iraq when an anti-war motion was defeated in the Commons by 396 votes to 217; the main vote endorsing military action was passed by 412 to 149. **20.** The invasion of Iraq by British and US troops began. Thousands of schoolchildren attended an anti-war demonstration in London and there were also demonstrations in Bristol, Manchester, Sheffield, Bradford and Glasgow. **21.** The Archbishop of Canterbury made a joint statement with the Chief Rabbi and the chairman of the Council of Mosques and Imams that the war in Iraq was not a religious one and that it was only a limited means to an end. **27.** The first British soldiers injured in the Gulf returned home for treatment. **28.** Adam Ingram, the armed forces minister, expressed regret for the words used by the Prime Minister, who claimed that two British soldiers were 'executed', after one of the bereaved families complained and insisted that they had been told by his regiment that he had been killed in action.

APRIL 2003

3. The Boarding Schools Association recommended to 550 independent and state schools that they should consider a ten-day quarantine period for all pupils returning after the Easter holidays from Sars-affected areas such as Hong Kong and China. **5.** Winchester College, one of Britain's top independent schools, was suspended from the Headmasters' and Headmistresses' Conference for matters concerning management and governance at the school. Many British boarding schools remained open for the Easter holidays as some pupils from Sars-affected areas did not return home for the holidays. **6.** New employment legislation was introduced, including the right for parents of young and disabled children to ask employers for flexible working arrangements; paternity leave of up to two weeks; maternity leave extended up to a year and statutory maternity pay increased to £100 a week. **9.** The Chancellor made the annual Budget speech. **11.** The Prime Minister and President Bush broadcast to the Iraqi people from a new television channel, Towards Freedom TV, set up on board an American transport plane. **14.** The Prime Minister declared victory in Iraq in a speech to the House of Commons after US troops captured the centre of Tikrit. **15.** The International Development Secretary, Clare Short, stated that the overthrow of Saddam Hussein's regime in Iraq did not justify the loss of a single life, the rapid collapse of the Iraqi regime had not been prepared for adequately and that any further conflict in the Middle East would be intolerable. The Queen's review of the Queen's Company of the Grenadier Guards was threatened by a swarm of bees on the parade ground; the royal beekeeper and pest controller, Peter Sheppard, managed to remove the swarm 30 minutes before the parade was due to begin. **17.** The Archbishop of Canterbury washed the feet of 12 worshippers in the Maundy Thursday service in Canterbury Cathedral; cathedral archivists said that they could find no records of the ceremony having been carried out at Canterbury before. **18.** The National Union of Teachers announced that thousands of schools would have to cut spending on staff and books for 2003–4 as the Government had miscalculated the national education budget. About 140 pupils returning to British boarding schools from Asia were transferred to the Isle of Wight for a 10-day quarantine period as a precaution against the Sars virus. **20.** Hospitals in Britain were put on alert for a possible outbreak of Sars and contingency plans were put in place. **22.** Documents found by a *Daily Telegraph* journalist in Baghdad suggested that the Labour backbencher George Galloway had received money from Saddam Hussein's regime; Galloway denied the allegations. **23.** The Labour Party chairman Ian McCartney announced an inquiry by the party into the allegations against George Galloway. **24.** The Dean of York Minster announced the introduction of an entry charge for visitors in an attempt to cut its deficit of £600,000. The Charity Commission launched an inquiry into the workings of the Mariam Appeal, the organisation founded by George Galloway to treat sick Iraqi children. **27.** St James's Palace announced that the Prince of Wales and his sons would move into Clarence House, the former home of Queen Elizabeth the Queen Mother. **28.** The Health Secretary, Alan Milburn, announced that foreign recruits to the NHS from Sars-affected areas were to have their start dates deferred. The Chief of Defence Staff, Adm. Sir Michael Boyce (who was to retire on 2 May 2003) stated that the Government should not pursue another war until at least 2005, as forces were overstretched and both troops and equipment needed time to recover from the Iraqi conflict. **30.** Israeli security officials stated that the two suicide bombers of a seafront bar in Tel Aviv on 29 April held British passports.

MAY 2003

1. The local government elections resulted in the Conservative party winning control of 14 more councils, three from Labour and 11 from previously hung councils; the Liberal Democrats secured some 30 per cent of the popular vote, while the British National Party made gains in the north-east and the West Midlands and picked up their first seat in the home counties, winning 11 seats overall. In the regional elections, Labour become the largest party in the Scottish Parliament. **2.** The Education Secretary published spending data showing that local authorities had failed to pass on £590 million in funding to schools; the National Association of Head Teachers and the Local Government Association rejected the Government's explanation of the shortfall in school funding and said that teacher redundancies would be inevitable unless a substantial extra sum was provided. **4.** The Government told schools to go into debt rather than make staff redundant, authorising local authorities to underwrite deficit budgets at schools worst affected by the funding crisis. The Department of Education and Skills issued new rules for childminders in England banning them from smacking children under eight years old in their care, and from smoking in front of children in their care. **5.** The Home Secretary agreed with interior ministers from other industrialised countries at a meeting in Paris to develop the technology that would allow biometric chips to be introduced in British passports. **6.** It was announced that the Countess of Wessex is expecting a baby in December 2003. George Galloway was suspended from the Labour Party pending an internal party investigation into complaints that his opposition to the Iraq war brought the party into disrepute. A preliminary inquiry was also started by the Parliamentary Commissioner for Standards into the allegations that Mr Galloway had received money from the former Iraqi government and had not declared this in the Register of Members' Interests. **9.** The Strategic Rail Authority announced the abolition of price capping on season tickets after Network Rail, the government's not-for-profit replacement for Railtrack, stated that it needed £11 billion extra funding to maintain the railways until 2006. The US Congress bestowed the Congressional Gold Medal on Tony Blair. **12.** Clare Short, the International Development Secretary, resigned from the Cabinet; in her resignation speech, she accused the Prime Minister of ruling by diktat, sidelining the Cabinet and centralising power in his hands and those of a few advisors. Baroness Amos was named as Clare Short's successor and became the first black woman to hold a Cabinet post. **13.** Members of the Manx parliament, the House of Keys, voted 15 to four in favour of a bill to give terminally ill adults the right to choose medical help to die; further research is to take place before the introduction of the legislation. **20.** The Education Secretary admitted that the literacy and numeracy targets in the national tests for 11-year-olds were unachievable for 2004 and extended the target date to 2006. A factory worker from Somerset received £400 worth of tax credits after frustration at the delays in receiving payments under the new tax credit system led him to glue himself to the

enquiries desk in his local tax office. Canon Jeffrey John was nominated as the next suffragan bishop of Reading, the first openly homosexual priest to be nominated for the episcopate. **23.** A 4 foot high wall of concrete was installed outside Parliament as a security measure. **25.** Britain's entry in the Eurovision song contest failed to score any points, the lowest score ever by a British entry. **28.** The Prime Minister flew to the Gulf to visit British troops in Iraq. **29.** A BBC defence correspondent, Andrew Gilligan, claimed on the *Today* programme that the Government had 'sexed up' information about weapons of mass destruction in Iraq in a dossier published in autumn 2002, in order to strengthen its presentation of the case for war on Iraq; he also stated that Alastair Campbell, the Government's director of communications, was responsible for inserting into the 'dodgy' dossier the claim that Iraq could deploy weapons of mass destruction in 45 minutes.

JUNE 2003

1. An intelligence memo revealed that a section of the Government's dossier on weapons of mass destruction had been dropped prior to publication. The Prime Minister, in St Petersburg for the celebrations of the city's 300th anniversary, claimed in a television broadcast to have fresh evidence from Iraqi scientists concerning weapons of mass destruction. **2.** The last village in Britain without mains electricity, Cwm Brefi in Wales, was connected to the National Grid. The Queen celebrated the 50th anniversary of her coronation. **4.** The foreign affairs select committee announced it was going to investigate the Government's presentation of intelligence on Iraq's weapons of mass destruction. **9.** The Chancellor made a statement in the House of Commons on why the UK economy does not meet his five conditions for joining the euro zone. **11.** A cross-party Commons health committee reported that sexual health must be treated as a priority, specifically recommending the immediate introduction of a national screening programme for chlamydia. Five people were killed and three seriously injured when a transporter carrying armoured vehicles jackknifed on the M1 and ploughed through a central reservation. **12.** A Cabinet reshuffle was announced earlier than planned after the Health Secretary, Alan Milburn, resigned; John Reid replaced Alan Milburn, while Peter Hain became Leader of the Commons. The Lord Chancellor, Lord Irvine, stepped down to allow the Lord Chancellor's Department to be abolished and replaced with a new Department of Constitutional Affairs, with Lord Falconer becoming the first Secretary of State for Constitutional Affairs. **16.** The Deputy Prime Minister, John Prescott, announced that referendums would be held in 2004 for three English regions (the north-east, north-west, and Yorkshire and the Humber) to decide whether regional assemblies should be introduced. **19.** BBC defence correspondent Andrew Gilligan gave evidence to the foreign affairs select committee of the House of Commons. **22.** An intruder gained access to the 21st birthday party of Prince William at Windsor Castle and climbed onto a stage beside the prince as he gave a speech; the man, a comedian, was unarmed and the incident was a publicity stunt for his forthcoming one-man show at the Edinburgh Festival. **23.** The Home Secretary called for an immediate investigation into how the intruder had managed to gain access to a party, which was attended by most of the Royal family. **24.** President Putin of Russia began a state visit to the UK, the first by a Russian leader in 129 years. **25.** The Government's director of communications, Alastair Campbell, gave evidence to the foreign affairs select committee; he vigorously denied the BBC's claims regarding the 'dodgy' dossier and demanded an apology from the BBC. **26.** The BBC's director-general, Greg Dyke, refused to withdraw the BBC's allegations about the doctored dossier on Iraq and said the BBC would stand firm against pressure from the Government. **27.** The train operator Connex became the first operator to have its franchise revoked after being accused by the SRA of financial mismanagement and poor service. **28.** Callie Rogers, aged 16, became one of the youngest winners of the National Lottery when she won £1,875,000. **30.** In a House of Commons debate on foxhunting, a majority of 208 MPs voted for an outright ban.

JULY 2003

2. In response to a question in the House of Commons, the Prime Minister stated that the 45-minute deployment claim in the 'dodgy' dossier was present in the first draft of the dossier presented by the Joint Intelligence Committee and had not been inserted by anyone at Downing Street or any minister. The Trade and Industry Secretary announced the introduction of anti-ageism measures to protect employees, expected to come into effect in 2006. **4.** A 12-mile section of the railway between Leyburn and Leeming Bar in North Yorkshire, which closed in 1954, reopened after Wensleydale Railway plc obtained a licence, issued shares and raised £1.2 million from private investors to fund the restoration of the track, stations and trains. **5.** In an interview with *The Observer* newspaper the Prime Minister denied allegations that he had altered the dossier on Iraq, stating that the charge was extremely serious, absurd and fundamentally wrong. **6.** Canon Jeffrey John, whose nomination as the next Bishop of Reading had caused controversy because of his homosexuality, withdrew his acceptance of the post, stating that he was doing so for the sake of Church unity. The BBC board of governors backed the director-general, issuing a statement that rejected claims by the Government that the BBC's coverage of the Iraq war had been biased by its opposition to the conflict. **7.** The foreign affairs select committee published its report on the Government's presentation of the case for war with Iraq; it cleared Mr Campbell of the allegations made against him, but said that 'undue prominence' was given to the 45-minute deployment claim. **9.** The Defence Secretary, Geoff Hoon, named Dr David Kelly, an MOD microbiologist and weapons consultant, in a letter to the BBC, asking the corporation to confirm or deny whether he was the source of Mr Gilligan's story. Six managers and two companies, Railtrack and Balfour Beatty, were charged with manslaughter due to gross negligence in connection with the Hatfield train crash in October 2001. **15.** The foreign affairs select committee reopened its inquiry into the Government's presentation of the case for war with Iraq; it heard Dr David Kelly, an MOD official who admitted briefing Andrew Gilligan, but concluded that Dr Kelly was not the source of Mr Gilligan's story. **17.** Andrew Gilligan gave evidence to the foreign affairs select committee in a private session and was later accused by the committee chairman of changing his story. **18.** Dr David Kelly, believed by the Government to be the source behind the BBC's allegations concerning the doctored dossier on Iraq, was found dead in an Oxfordshire wood close to his home;

the Government announced that Lord Hutton, the former Lord Chief Justice of Northern Ireland, would conduct an inquiry into the circumstances leading to the death of Dr Kelly. Thousands of passengers were stranded at Heathrow airport after an unofficial strike by British Airways staff against a new clocking-on system led to the cancellation of 89 flights. **19.** The Ministry of Defence admitted confirming Dr Kelly's name to three newspapers on 9 July, contradicting claims by the Defence Secretary, Geoff Hoon, that there had been no such breach of confidentiality. **21.** Lord Archer was released from prison after serving half of his four-year sentence for perjury and perverting the course of justice. **23.** The Defence Secretary visited the widow of Dr Kelly. British Airways unions called an official strike ballot over the introduction of a new clocking-on system. Laura Trowbridge, an experienced caver taking part in a television documentary, was successfully rescued by 100 volunteers from Otter Hole, near Chepstow, after falling and becoming trapped for 24 hours with a suspected broken pelvis.

AUGUST 2003

4. The Prince of Wales moved into Clarence House. A heatwave began, with temperatures in London reaching 90°F; rail travel was severely disrupted after rail operators were ordered by Network Rail to observe 60 mph speed restrictions because of fears that the rails could buckle in the heat. Part of the freighter *Tricolor* that sank in the English Channel on 14 December 2002 was raised in the first stage of a £25 million salvage operation. **5.** Canon Gene Robinson became the first openly homosexual bishop in the Anglican Communion after being elected Bishop of New Hampshire by the bishops of the Episcopal Church of the USA. **6.** Clarence House opened to the public for the first time. The funeral of the biological weapons expert Dr David Kelly took place in Oxfordshire. **8.** Six Britons convicted of a bombing campaign in Saudi Arabia in 2000, who claimed that they were tortured and falsely imprisoned, flew home after being pardoned by King Fahd. **10.** Temperatures rose to record levels, with the highest ever temperature of 100.6°F (38.1°C) recorded in the UK, in Gravesend, Kent. **11.** On the first day of the inquiry into the death of Dr David Kelly, Lord Hutton heard that two intelligence officials had formally complained about the wording of the dossier on Iraqi chemical and biological weapons that formed the Government's case for war. The National Grid made an emergency request for extra power supplies after a surge in demand for air-conditioning depleted reserves and demand from Europe increased because the heatwave forced nuclear generators to shut down. **12.** Andrew Gilligan, the BBC journalist who first made the doctored dossier claims on the Radio 4 *Today* programme gave evidence to the Hutton inquiry. **13.** British Airways suspended flights to Saudi Arabia after being warned of suspected terrorist action against one of its aircraft. **19.** The Government director of communications, Alastair Campbell, gave evidence to the Hutton inquiry. A new computer virus, MSBlaster, caused problems for businesses and individuals throughout the UK. **21.** Princess Alice, Duchess of Gloucester, became the oldest ever member of the Royal Family after reaching the age of 101 years and 239 days, a day older than the late Queen Elizabeth the Queen Mother. **27.** The Defence Secretary, Geoff Hoon, gave evidence to the Hutton inquiry. **28.** The Prime Minister gave evidence to the Hutton inquiry. **29.** Alastair Campbell resigned as the

Government's director of communications after nine years in the post; Downing Street announced that a restructured press operation would be headed by David Hill, a former Labour Party press chief. **31.** The Home Secretary announced that he would be using executive powers to extend the Nationality, Immigration and Asylum Act 2002 so that any refugees or asylum seekers in Britain who have previously received a prison sentence of less than two years for serious crimes such as terrorism, rape, murder or kidnapping, could be deported from the country; at present, only those sentenced to more than two years for serious offences can be deported.

NORTHERN IRELAND AFFAIRS

SEPTEMBER 2002

30. Gerry Adams, the president of Sinn Fein, denied allegations in *A Secret History of the IRA* by Ed Moloney, that he was the mastermind behind two IRA units responsible for the disappearance and murder of at least nine people in the 1970s and early 1980s.

OCTOBER 2002

6. Denis Donaldson, Sinn Fein's head of administration, was charged with possessing information likely to be of use to terrorists. **10.** Two Democratic Unionist Party ministers, Peter Robinson and Nigel Dodds, resigned from the Northern Ireland Executive. **21.** Devolution in Northern Ireland was suspended for the fourth time after claims that an IRA spy ring had been uncovered at the Northern Ireland Office; the Northern Ireland Secretary, John Reid, announced the indefinite resumption of direct rule from Westminster. **25.** A bomb for which the Continuity IRA claimed responsibility partially exploded in Belfast city centre; no one was injured. **29.** The Provisional IRA announced that they were ending contacts with the body responsible for overseeing the decommissioning and destruction of arms.

NOVEMBER 2002

3. A Roman Catholic man from west Belfast was taken to hospital with his hands nailed to blocks of wood after being 'crucified' in what was believed to be a punishment beating. **7.** A civil servant who worked for the First Minister and the Deputy First Minister for Northern Ireland was arrested on suspicion of being an IRA spy.

DECEMBER 2002

16. It was announced that community relations groups in Northern Ireland were to receive over £7m in European Union funding as part of the Peace Two programme supporting groups and organisations promoting reconciliation.

JANUARY 2003

6. A pipe bomb was found taped to the front gate of Holy Cross Primary School in north Belfast; the Red Hand Defenders, a cover name used in the past by elements within the Ulster Defence Association, admitted planting the device. **7.** Northern Ireland's First Minister, David Trimble, met the Prime Minister to discuss the restoration of the Northern Ireland Assembly **8.** Gerry Adams met the Prime Minister for talks about restoring the assembly. **9.** A bomb-making factory was discovered by police in Co. Antrim during an operation that was part of an investigation into the feud between rival factions of the paramilitary Ulster Defence Association. **10.** The

loyalist paramilitary leader Johnny Adair returned to Maghaberry prison after having his early release licence revoked by the Secretary of State, Paul Murphy. **14.** At the judicial inquiry into the events of 'Bloody Sunday' in 30 January 1972, Sir Edward Heath, the prime minister of the time, gave evidence concerning the exact instructions he gave army chiefs in the run-up to the day.

FEBRUARY 2003

1. John Gregg, a self-styled 'brigadier' of the Ulster Defence Association, and a colleague were shot dead by gunmen who ambushed their taxi; the gunmen were thought to be members of Johnny Adair's 'C Company'. **2.** Army patrols in Belfast were stepped up in case of reprisals for the murder of John Gregg. **6.** The feud between the UDA and the breakaway 'C Company' faction was resolved, according to the UDA; more than 20 people, including Adair's wife and children, agreed to leave the country under police escort and about 100 'C Company' men accepted an offer to rejoin the UDA. **10.** A bomb allegedly planted by the Continuity IRA exploded in the centre of Enniskillen; no casualties were reported.

MARCH 2003

5. The Prime Minister announced that the Northern Ireland Assembly elections would be postponed until 29 May 2003 in an attempt to resolve the deadlock in the peace process. **24.** The Secretary of State, Paul Murphy, held discussions with the Irish Foreign Minister, Brian Cowen, to finalise the position of the two governments before the announcement of the latest Northern Ireland initiative. **30.** At Sinn Fein's annual conference in Dublin, delegates rejected a motion linking any decision to support the police in Northern Ireland to the end of British jurisdiction in the province; Gerry Adams stated that the terms and context for the party to join the police board were not yet right.

APRIL 2003

2. The report by Sir John Stevens, Commissioner of the Metropolitan Police, on his investigation of allegations of collusion between the British security forces and terrorists in Northern Ireland in the late 1980s and early 1990s was leaked in advance of publication; the leaked text found that a covert army unit colluded with loyalist paramilitaries to target suspected IRA terrorists for assassination and that the unit, known as the Force Research Unit, was responsible for a number of murders in the late 1980s and early 1990s. **7.** Gen. Sir Mike Jackson, now the Chief of the General Staff, told the Bloody Sunday inquiry how he and other paratroopers had come under fire from the IRA; he dismissed suggestions that a shoot-to-kill policy was being followed on the day that troops shot 13 people dead during a civil rights march. **8.** President Bush met the Prime Minister in Belfast and, together with the Irish Prime Minister, Bertie Ahern, called for 'irrevocable' action by terrorist groups in Northern Ireland to consign paramilitary activity to the past. **9.** At the Central Criminal Court in London, five men were convicted of taking part in a Real IRA terror campaign in 2001, causing bomb explosions at the BBC Television Centre on 4 March, at Ealing Broadway, west London, on 2 August, and in Birmingham on 3 November 2001. **10.** The British government suspended publication of a blueprint paving the way for a return to power-sharing in Northern Ireland after the IRA refused to make a public statement announcing the end of its 'war' and military activities, including a visible destruction of its arsenal. **16.** Sir John Stevens published the report of his investigation into collusion between the British security forces and terrorists; it identified Brig. Gordon Kerr, who ran the Force Research Unit, and Brian Nelson, a deceased FRU agent who infiltrated the UDA, as key figures in a 'dirty war' against the IRA. **22.** It was announced that the Royal Irish Regiment would be reduced considerably in size. **27.** In a speech, Gerry Adams said that the IRA was committed to decommissioning weapons and declaring its conflict over; the following day the Prime Minister called on the IRA to clarify its intentions regarding the peace process. **29.** Leaked transcripts of secretly recorded telephone conversations between Martin McGuinness, the former Northern Ireland Education Minister, and Mo Mowlam, the former Northern Ireland Secretary and Jonathan Powell, the Prime Minister's chief of staff, were made public, indicating that MI5 had bugged the offices of senior politicians. **30.** The wife of the loyalist Johnny Adair was the target of a shooting at her home in Bolton, England; the UDA admitted responsibility for the attack on Gina Adair, said to have been ordered to avenge the murder of John Gregg.

MAY 2003

1. The Prime Minister announced that elections to the Northern Ireland Assembly scheduled for 29 May would be postponed until the autumn after the IRA failed to state unequivocally that it would end all paramilitary activities. **5.** A bomb was found in Belfast city centre a few hours before a marathon would have taken runners past the bomb; dissident republicans were blamed for planting the bomb. **7.** The inquiry into the events of Bloody Sunday heard that the head of MI5's Irish anti-terrorist section believed the agent known as 'Infliction' was telling the truth when he said that Martin McGuinness had admitted to him at the time that he had fired the first shot on Bloody Sunday. **9.** Jim Johnston, a loyalist terrorist, was shot dead outside his home in Co. Down. **11.** Britain's most important agent inside the IRA, code-named 'Stakeknife', was named as Alfredo Scappaticci; on 13 May, Scappaticci released a statement in which he denied that he was ever an army spy and claimed that he was a victim of misinformation by security forces. **12.** A letter bomb addressed to David Trimble partially exploded at the party's Belfast headquarters, no one was injured. **17.** Police raided the home of former undercover agent Kevin Fulton; the raid was believed to be in connection with the exposure of Scappaticci. Former army officers threatened to name three British agents working within the IRA in response to Sir John Stevens' conclusions that they had collaborated with loyalist terrorists to murder suspected IRA sympathisers. **26.** Robert Young appeared in court accused of murdering the loyalist paramilitary Jim Johnston; he pleaded not guilty. **27.** It was reported that three home service battalions of the Royal Irish Regiment were to be disbanded in an effort to persuade the IRA to stand down; the General Officer Commanding Northern Ireland, Lt-Gen. Philip Trousdell, issued a statement the following day which said that there was no timetable in place for disbanding the three battalions. **28.** A man and a woman were arrested in Sussex in connection with the murder of the human rights lawyer Pat Finucane in 1989. **29.** Kenneth Barrett was charged with the murder of Pat Finucane, the attempted murder of Thomas McCreery

and Elizabeth McEvoy in 1991, and with membership of the proscribed Ulster Defence Association and Ulster Freedom Fighters. **30.** Police divers searched a reservoir in Belfast for Alan McCullough, an associate of Johnny Adair, after he went missing upon his return to Northern Ireland from England; his body was found on 5 June and responsibility for his murder was claimed by the Ulster Freedom Fighters.

JUNE 2003

2. Northern Ireland Secretary Paul Murphy and Defence Secretary Geoff Hoon met to discuss the future of three home service battalions of the Royal Irish Regiment; on 10 June, Mr Hoon announced that the Royal Irish Regiment would not be disbanded as part of the Northern Ireland peace process. It was revealed in an autobiography by Michael Stone, convicted of the murders of three men and released from prison under the 1998 Good Friday peace accord, that there had been a plot during the mid-1980s by the loyalist Red Hand Commando, a paramilitary group with close ties to the Ulster Volunteer Force, to assassinate the then head of the Greater London Council, Ken Livingstone; Mr Stone claimed that the plot had been called off at the last minute. **12.** A Belfast loyalist, Ihab Shoukri, was charged with the murder of Alan McCullough, and with being a member of the Ulster Freedom Fighters. **15.** Two men were charged with the murder of David Barnes, who was shot in his Belfast flat in March. Police stopped a van in Londonderry, intercepting one of the biggest bombs ever to be found in the UK; the 1,200lb device was believed to have been made by the Real IRA. **17.** Alfredo Scappaticci, named in May as the government's top spy within the IRA, won the right to proceed with his application for a judicial review. **18.** During the trial of alleged Real IRA leader Michael McKevitt on charges of directing terrorism and belonging to an illegal organisation, Dublin's Special Criminal Court heard that McKevitt had told David Rupert, an undercover agent working with the FBI and MI5, that the Real IRA had been responsible for making the bomb that killed 29 people in Omagh in 1998; on 25 June the court heard how the organisation recruited a former French Foreign Legion weapons expert for a plot to assassinate a senior member of the British government, and that McKevitt had revealed to David Rupert plans which included up to six attacks in one year on MI6 headquarters. **23.** Three Ulster Unionist Party MPs resigned the party whip in the House of Commons; Jeffrey Donaldson, Revd Martin Smyth and David Burnside said they were opposed to the UUP's willingness to condone concessions to the IRA; on 27 June they were suspended from the party. **28.** Paul Holland appeared before Belfast magistrates charged with murdering PC Edward Spence in May 1991.

JULY 2003

1. The widow of Pat Finucane was awarded £30,000 in costs and expenses after the European Court of Human Rights ruled that the investigation by the Police Service of Northern Ireland into Mr Finucane's death lacked independence, was ineffective and a breach of human rights. **4.** The Northern Ireland Police Service warned 300 politicians and policemen in Northern Ireland that they could be on a Real IRA hitlist after it was found that a clerk at a Belfast hospital had accessed patient files; the clerk was charged with possessing information likely to be of use to a terrorist organisation. **6.** The annual Orange Order parade at Drumcree, a flashpoint for violence in past years, passed off peacefully. **8.** David Trimble survived a UUP vote of no confidence by 63 per cent to 37 per cent, after he was called to account for his policies by party members opposed to the Good Friday Agreement. **12.** It was revealed that Alfredo Scappaticci, the man named as a British spy in the IRA, had alleged that Northern Ireland's education minister, Martin McGuiness, was involved in the murder of another British informer, Frank Hegarty; Scappaticci's allegations were recorded in 1993 by researchers for the programme *The Cook Report* and were screened on the BBC's *Panorama* programme on 13 July. **13.** A member of the Real IRA allegedly selling bomb-making expertise to Islamic militants was arrested in Ramallah by the Israeli authorities; on 16 July a Belfast journalist, John Morgan, was released by the Israeli after it was found that there was no evidence to tie him to Palestinian terrorist activities. **16.** The security services were cleared of collusion in a break-in by the IRA at Special Branch offices in Belfast in March 2002. **19.** Army bomb experts carried out controlled explosions on a device left on a bus in Belfast by two masked men who had ordered the driver to stop near a police station. **22.** Liam Campbell, a suspected member of the Real IRA, was ordered by the High Court in Dublin to pay one million euros (more than £700,000) following a case brought against him by the Criminal Assets Bureau, set up to seize the assets of criminals and terrorists. **24.** Michael McKevitt, on trial at Dublin's Special Criminal Court, dismissed his legal team after three judges rejected a defence application to stop the trial; the trial ended on 28 July. **26.** Wayne Stephen Dowie was charged with the murder of Jonathan Stewart and remanded in custody by magistrates in Belfast; the murder was said to have been part of a loyalist feud which resulted in five deaths.

AUGUST 2003
2. Kevin Fulton, a former British soldier and undercover agent within the IRA, named a Belfast journalist, Sean Maguire, as a British spy within the IRA. **3.** Police questioned ten men in connection with the discovery of a suspected terrorist training camp, believed by police to be linked to the Continuity IRA. **4.** It was announced that members of the police force in Northern Ireland who are members of the Freemasons, the Catholic Knights of Colmbanus, the Protestant Orange Order or any other organisation that could call into question their impartiality, would be obliged to disclose their involvement to their superiors. **5.** Eight men were charged with membership of the IRA at Dublin's Special Criminal Court following an Irish police operation in Co. Waterford. **6.** Michael McKevitt was found guilty of directing terrorism and of being a member of the Real IRA but refused to enter the courtroom at Dublin's Special Criminal Court to hear the verdict; on 7 August he was sentenced to 20 years' imprisonment for directing terrorism and a six-year sentence, to run concurrently, for being a member of the IRA. **8.** The British government promised £800,000 to the families of the Omagh bombing victims to help with their civil action against five men they believe to be responsible for the atrocity. **10.** Three men were arrested in Britain in connection with the activities of the Continuity IRA after two handguns and a rifle were found at commercial premises in West Yorkshire. **16.** A former soldier in the army's Force Research Unit made the claim to Sir John Stevens that army intelligence officers encouraged former informants in the IRA to return to Northern Ireland

despite the danger this would put them in, in order to save the cost of resettling former informants in safe houses; Thomas McCartney, a 'supergrass' who gave evidence against Northern Ireland paramilitaries, threatened to expose the identities of a dozen undercover officers unless he received a sum of £250,000, claiming that after giving evidence he was only paid £25,000 by the Royal Ulster Constabulary and now lives in poverty in a council house. **17.** Sinn Fein requested that the British and Irish governments erase the criminal records of all 15,000 IRA members to help reintegrate those released under the Good Friday Agreement. Daniel McGurk was shot dead at his home in Belfast in a suspected punishment shooting believed to be ordered by the Real IRA. **18.** Alfredo Scappaticci failed in his request through the High Court that the Government should issue a statement saying that he had not been an army spy within the IRA. **24.** A book by the BBC's Northern Ireland security editor Brian Rowan claimed that the Special Branch and MI5 had secretly copied files stolen by the IRA from government offices in Belfast before returning them to where they had been hidden. **27.** A skeleton was found near Carlingford, Co. Louth; it was subsequently identified as that of Jean McConville, a mother of ten who was allegedly abducted and killed by the IRA in 1972. **31.** Following the death of a 21-year-old soldier at Shackleton Barracks in Ballykelly, a 24-year-old man was charged with murder and was due to appear before Londonderry magistrates on 1 September.

ARTS AND THE MEDIA

SEPTEMBER 2002
24. The football used for the Football Association Cup Final in 1888, in which West Bromwich Albion defeated Preston North End, was sold for £32,900 at a memorabilia auction in London. **25.** English Heritage launched a £7 million plan to turn Hadrian's Wall into a visitor attraction. **26.** The Barbican Centre in London announced plans for a £12.25 million redevelopment to take place between 2003 and 2006. Camelot, the Lotto operator, announced a venture with the French lottery firm Française des Jeux to create a joint game with a £50 million jackpot to start in 2004. **30.** President Ciampi of Italy announced plans to return to Greece a fragment of the Parthenon frieze.

OCTOBER 2002
2. Pop singer Robbie Williams signed a £50 million deal to produce six albums for record company EMI. **9.** The German Beck collection sold at auction at Sotheby's for £14.4 million. **10.** Hungarian author Imre Kertész won the Nobel Prize for Literature. **20.** ITV announced plans to replace its regional onscreen identities with a single ITV1 brand for all national programmes. A bloodstained silk purse and 21 gold coins carried by Adm. Lord Nelson when he died in the battle of Trafalgar were put up for auction at Sotheby's; a Turkish sabre owned by Nelson sold for £2.1 million. **22.** The Canadian author Yann Martel won the Booker Prize for *Life of Pi*. Sotheby's was fined £12 million by the European Commission for colluding with Christie's to rig prices in the art auction market. **30.** The culture minister Kim Howells attacked the Turner Prize entries as 'conceptual bullshit'.

NOVEMBER 2002
3. The National Gallery accused the Duke of Northumberland of acting 'unethically' for signing a provisional deal to sell Raphael's *Madonna of the Pinks* to the Getty Museum in Los Angeles for £35 million before offering it to the National Gallery, where it has hung for a decade. The film *Harry Potter and the Chamber of Secrets* was premiered at the Odeon Cinema, Leicester Square, London. **5.** The National Gallery unveiled plans for the first phase of a £100 million refurbishment. **10.** *This is Another Place,* the first solo Tracey Emin show for five years, opened at the Museum of Modern Art in Oxford. **11.** An exhibition of 40,000 miniature clay figures by the sculptor Anthony Gormley, *Field for the British Isles,* opened at the British Museum. **15.** The National Gallery announced that it would ask the Heritage Lottery Fund for funds to buy Raphael's *Madonna of the Pinks* in a bid to keep the painting in Britain. **18.** The British Library announced it had bought the archive of the Royal Philharmonic Society, the second oldest musical society in the world; founded in 1813, the archive contains more than 250 original scores, including that of Beethoven's Ninth Symphony, Mendelssohn's First Symphony and Elgar's *The Dream of Gerontius.* **25.** The value of a portrait by Van Dyck was put at more than £1.6 million after restorers found the royal cipher of Charles I when they removed the back from the picture; the portrait was bought for £437,587 in 2001. The world's longest running play, *The Mousetrap,* celebrated 50 years on the London stage; the 20,807th performance was attended by The Queen and Prince Philip.

DECEMBER 2002
1. Less than two years after construction began, the 'topping out' party was held to celebrate the completion of Swiss Re, nicknamed the 'Gherkin Tower', designed by Fosters and Partners. **2.** The children's charity Barnardo's won a top prize in the Advertising Effectiveness Awards for its campaign featuring images of child abuse. **8.** Keith Tyson won the 2002 Turner Prize. **12.** A piece of card containing clues to the next Harry Potter novel sold for £28,680 at Sotheby's; the 93-word teaser to *Harry Potter and the Order of the Phoenix,* handwritten by author J. K. Rowling, raised £24,000 for Book Aid International. **16.** New watercolour works by David Hockney were revealed in *The Times.* **18.** Monica Mason, a lifelong member of the Royal Ballet, replaced Ross Stretton as the company's director.

JANUARY 2003
7. A married couple, Michael Frayn and Claire Tomalin, each won their respective categories in the Whitbread Prize (novel and biography); Paul Farley won the poetry category, Hilary McKay the children's category, and Norman Lebrecht the first novel prize. **10.** The film director Anthony Minghella was appointed head of the British Film Institute. Tapes of recordings by the Beatles, allegedly stolen 30 years ago, were recovered by police after being offered for sale to the record company EMI for £270,000; three people in the Netherlands and two people in London were arrested in connection with the sale of the tapes. **13.** A watercolour by Renoir in collaboration with Emile Zola, who signed an inscription at the bottom of the painting, was found in the safe of London diamond brokers Hennig & Co. after missing for decades. **14.** Rebekah Wade, former editor of the *News of the World,* took over from David Yelland as editor of the

Sun, becoming the first female editor of the paper. **20.** The British director Stephen Daldry won two Golden Globes for his second major feature film *The Hours.* **28.** Biographer Claire Tomalin won the £25,000 Whitbread Book of the Year prize for *Samuel Pepys: The Unequalled Self,* defeating her husband, novelist Michael Frayn.

FEBRUARY 2003
5. Kevin Spacey, the Oscar-winning actor, was named as the new artistic director of the Old Vic Theatre in London. **14.** The portraits of Sir William Killigrew (1606–95) and his wife Mary Hill, by Van Dyck, were reunited for the first time at the Tate Britain gallery with the help of funding from the National Art Collections Fund; the pictures were sold separately after the family lost its fortune. Sam Mendes became the first triple winner of Lawrence Olivier awards, winning the best director and best revival awards for *Twelfth Night* and *Uncle Vanya* and a special award in recognition of his ten years as artistic director of the Donmar Warehouse in London. **17.** The first portrait of Lord Irvine of Lairg, Lord Chancellor, was unveiled; commissioned by the Inner Temple, the oil painting was painted by James Lloyd, winner of the BP Portrait Award. **19.** It was reported that a collection of 19 watercolours by William Blake, the English artist and poet, had been sold to an anonymous overseas art collector for more than £5 million; the sale was a huge windfall for Paul Williams and Jeffery Bates, two Yorkshire book dealers who spotted the folio, as well as the previous owners of the Glasgow Bookshop where the watercolours were found in 2001. **19.** An exhibition of Titian's paintings opened at the National Gallery; it included four paintings from *Camerino* which have not hung together since *c.*1598. **23.** At the British Academy Film and Television Awards (BAFTAS) Nicole Kidman won the best actress award for *The Hours* and Daniel Day-Lewis best actor for *Gangs of New York.* **26.** An exhibition entitled *Days Like These* opened at Tate Britain; intended as a showcase for British contemporary art, its centrepiece was Cornelia Parker's *The Distance (A Kiss with added String 2003),* which entwined Rodin's famous sculpture *The Kiss* in string.

MARCH 2003
4. A film poster advertising the 1943 Western *The Outlaw* and depicting the actress Jane Russell sold at auction for £52,875. **11.** *The Times* reported the discovery of a Rembrandt painting that had been hidden for more than 300 years under layers of paint applied by one of Rembrandt's pupils. **31.** *The Times* reported that the war with Iraq had generated increased interest in Iraqi culture; the British Museum, which holds the greatest collection of Mesopotamian art outside Iraq, had seen attendances soar at its Ancient Near East department.

APRIL 2003
1. A pair of previously unpublished Beatrix Potter watercolours of Peter Rabbit and Benjamin Bunny were sold for £40,000 at Bonhams. Almost 300 outfits by the fashion designer Vivienne Westwood were bought by the Victoria and Albert Museum. An exhibition featuring the work of nine artists shortlisted for the £24,000 Beck's Futures award opened in London; many of the exhibits were absent, or in one case replaced by a framed legal document declaring that the artist was keeping her work of art secret. **2.** The decorations and medals of Al Deere, a Battle of Britain fighter, were bought by the RAF

Museum for £138,000. **4.** Seven previously unpublished manuscripts by Virginia Woolf were discovered in a tin trunk which the British Library bought for £100,000. **5.** A man was arrested for allegedly vandalising Cornelia Parker's *The Distance: A Kiss with added String* at Tate Britain; conservators said the work did not appear to have been harmed. **7.** The British Museum announced that an amateur archaeologist, Ken Wallace, had discovered more than 3,000 silver and gold Iron Age coins, the largest number ever found together in Britain. **9.** Lesley Douglas, the head of programmes at BBC Radio 2, told a radio conference that the station would increase the use of album tracks in an effort to help build artists' careers and to break the cycle of record companies pumping resources into pop hits. **10.** The painting *Landscape at Krumau* by Egon Schiele, which was looted by the Nazis, was returned to the heirs of the Jewish collectors from whom it was stolen. **14.** A new art gallery owned by Charles Saatchi opened in the former County Hall on the South Bank; exhibits included Damien Hirst's shark in formaldehyde and Tracey Emin's unmade bed. A ring and a bracelet that once belonged to Marilyn Monroe were stolen from an exhibition about the actress. **16.** Medieval wall paintings were discovered in a Norman parish church in east London; they are thought to be 13th-century decorations by Cistercian monks, and the only examples in London. **22.** The 73-year-old poet Ursula Fanthorpe, who only started writing poetry in her mid fifties, was awarded the 2003 Queen's Gold Medal for Poetry. **27.** Paintings by Picasso, Van Gogh and Gauguin were stolen from the Whitworth Gallery in Manchester; the three paintings were recovered the following day after an anonymous tip-off led police to their location outside a public lavatory, where a note was found which claimed that they had only been stolen to highlight poor security at the gallery. A group of 600 men and women stripped naked in the London department store Selfridges as part of an installation by the American artist Spencer Tunick. John Bayley, widower of the author Iris Murdoch, announced that he would be putting up for sale her working library, a collection of 1,000 books. **28.** Five miniatures dating from the Tudor period were stolen from Hever Castle, Kent, while it was open to the public. **29.** The £24,000 Beck's Futures prize was awarded to Rosalind Nashashibi for her three-minute film *The States of Things* which shows elderly women rummaging through a jumble sale in Glasgow. **30.** A lock of hair belonging to reggae star Bob Marley was sold at Christie's for £2,585.

MAY 2003

1. A 17th-century miniature of Shah Jahan, who built the Taj Mahal, was sold for £574,250; it had been bought in 2002 as part of a lot costing £881 at Sotheby's auction house. **6.** J. K. Rowling, author of the *Harry Potter* books, and her publisher Bloomsbury asked police to investigate the theft of two copies of the latest book in the series, which were found in a field in Suffolk near to the book's printer; on 8 May an employee at the printer was charged with the theft. **7.** Pete Townshend, the former lead guitarist with *The Who*, was placed on the sex offenders register for five years after being cautioned for viewing child pornography on the internet. *Dans les Roses* by Renoir fetched £14.6 million at Sotheby's in New York. **12.** David Gilmour became the first winner of the Elizabeth Longford Prize for Historical Biography for *The Long Recessional: The Imperial Life of Rudyard Kipling*. A collection of guitars belonging to the late John

Entwistle, guitarist with *The Who*, fetched more than £1.1 million at Sotheby's in London. **13.** A 3,000-year-old Egyptian mummy set a world record at auction when it was sold for £883,750 at Christie's in London. Two Italian sisters returned to Sir Paul McCartney a diary belonging to him that they had taken from his house in London 20 years previously. **14.** Michael Morpurgo was named as the new Children's Laureate. **15.** A painting by Mark Rothko, part of the first series of paintings he produced for the Four Seasons Restaurant in New York, sold for the record price of £10 million at Christie's in New York. A small Nottingham museum was awarded the first Gulbenkian Prize for staging mock court trials to teach citizenship; the one-year-old National Centre for Citizenship and the Law is based in a Victorian courthouse and 18th-century prison. **18.** Dia:Beacon, the largest contemporary art museum in the world, opened in New York. **19.** Peter Bellwood was named as one of Scotland Yard's most wanted suspects for the theft of thousands of rare maps throughout Europe. **20.** The Jerwood Painting Prize was won by Australian artist Shani Rys James for *Black Cot*. **22.** The 15-year-old violinist Chlöe Hanslip was named young British performer of the year at the Classical Brit awards. The working manuscript of Beethoven's Ninth Symphony fetched £2.1 million at auction at Sotheby's in London, making it the most expensive single manuscript ever sold. A world record £565,250 was paid at Christie's in London for an 1842 daguerreotype of the remains of the Temple of Olympian Zeus in Athens. **25.** A lost masterpiece by the 16th-century Italian Old Master Annibale Carracci was rediscovered when a man took it to be valued at Sotheby's in London; he was unaware of the importance of the Montalto Madonna, which disappeared 90 years after it was completed. **28.** It was announced that a musical of *The Lord of the Rings* would be produced in the West End, opening in spring 2005. **30.** A man was arrested after throwing red paint over the artist Jake Chapman, one of the nominees for the Turner Prize; the protest was apparently over Chapman's alterations of Goya's masterpieces.

JUNE 2003

1. The Design Museum's £25,000 Designer of the Year award was won by the vice-president of industrial design Jonathan Ive for developing innovative products such as the iMac and iPod MP3 player at Apple. **3.** Valerie Martin, a relatively unknown author from New Orleans, won the Orange Prize for her novel *Property*. **4.** Liverpool was chosen as the 2008 European Capital of Culture. **5.** Christopher Ondaatje, the Sri-Lankan philanthropist, announced that he would be supporting the new Royal Society of Literature Ondaatje Prize, which will reward writing that 'evokes the spirit of a place'. **6.** The biographer Hilary Spurling and Mark Amery, the literary editor of *The Spectator*, were joint winners of the Heywood Hill Literary Prize. A bronze brooch dating from around AD 650 was found in an Anglo-Saxon burial ground at West Hesterton, near Malton in North Yorkshire; it is thought to be inscribed with the oldest form of English writing ever found. **8.** *The Trip*, a film written by Jack Nicholson in 1967 and starring Peter Fonda, was approved by British censors after being banned for 35 years for explicit scenes of drug-taking. **9.** T. J. Binyon's biography of the Russian poet Alexander Pushkin won the Samuel Johnson Prize for Non-Fiction. **10.** The Minister for Arts, Baroness Blackstone, placed a temporary export ban on a

16th-century Italian bronze incense-burner that originally belonged to the Wernher Collection; a two-month deadline was set to raise the £90,000 needed to keep it in Britain. Charlotte Harris, a 21-year-old fine art student, won the BP Portrait Award for her untitled portrait of her 83-year-old grandmother. **17.** Almost 8,000 copies of the fifth Harry Potter novel were stolen from a Merseyside warehouse two days before the book's publication. **21.** *Harry Potter and the Order of the Phoenix,* released at one minute past midnight, became the fastest-selling book ever after selling more than 500 copies a minute during the first hour of its release in Britain. **23.** The painting *Landscape at Krumau* by Egon Schiele was sold at Sotheby's in London for more than £12.6 million. **25.** The Bronze Age Ringlemere gold cup, believed to have been made at the time Stonehenge was built, was bought by the British Museum from Cliff Bradshaw, who found it on farmland in Kent. The Aventis Prize for the best popular science book was won by psychologist Chris McManus for *Right Hand, Left Hand,* his investigation of the asymmetry of the natural world. Alan Davidson, children's author and writer of *Escape from Cold Ditch* – a story about chickens escaping from a chicken farm across a barbed wire fence – initiated legal action against DreamWorks studio and Nick Park, creators of the film *Chicken Run,* which Mr Davidson claims was based on his novel rather than on an original idea by Nick Park. **26.** Jake and Dinos Chapman won the Charles Wollaston Award from the Royal Academy of Art. **30.** The poet Seamus Heaney said that the rap artist Eminem had reignited interest in poetry in the same way that John Lennon and Bob Dylan had in the 1960s and 1970s.

JULY 2003

2. The film director Ken Loach was made a film laureate by the Japanese Praemium Imperiale awards and Bridget Riley won the prize for painting. **3.** The Culture Secretary, Tessa Jowell, announced changes to the National Lottery, including the end of Camelot's monopoly and the introduction of legislation to ensure that the money generated is spent more proportionally throughout the country. The first example of Ice Age cave art, believed to be about 12,000 years old and depicting animals and geometric patterns, went on show at Creswell Crags near Worksop. **8.** A first edition of Jane Austen's *Pride and Prejudice* was sold at auction in Edinburgh for £22,000. **9.** Buckingham Palace announced that the writer and broadcaster William Shawcross had been chosen by The Queen to write the official biography of Queen Elizabeth the Queen Mother. **10.** The BBC won exclusive rights to screen all of England's competitive and friendly football matches for four years starting with the 2004–5 season in a deal costing £330 million. The Press Complaints Commission decided not to censure the *News of the World* for paying £10,000 to a convicted criminal and key witness in a plot to kidnap the singer Victoria Beckham; the newspaper's action had been referred to the Attorney General in June. The Las Vegas casino owner Steve Wynn bought Rembrandt's *Self-Portrait with Shaded Eyes* for almost £7 million. **14.** A retrospective of the work of the 1960s designer Ossie Clark opened at the Victoria and Albert Museum. A former worker in a hostel for the homeless, Ian Duhig, was nominated for the Forward Poetry Prize for *The Lammas Hireling.* **18.** Animal rights protesters protested at an exhibition in Hackney, London, where live cattle had been spray-painted as part of the exhibition. **19.** Pierce Brosnan, the actor who plays

James Bond, was awarded an honorary OBE by The Queen. Egypt demanded that the 2,000 year-old Rosetta Stone be returned to Cairo by the British Museum, where it forms the centrepiece of the Egyptology collection. **22.** Revd Graham Taylor received £314,000 from the Penguin Group USA for his previously self-published children's fantasy book *Shadowmancer;* first editions of the book had been selling on the internet for hundreds of pounds. **24.** The Sutcliffe archive, containing items belonging to Stuart Sutcliffe, the 'fifth' Beatle, went on display before being auctioned at Bonhams on 29 July. **27.** A 3,500-year-old inscription revealing that the Sudanese kingdom of Kush came close to destroying the Egyptian empire was discovered in an ancient tomb at El Kab in Upper Egypt by Egyptologists from the British Museum. **28.** The Press Complaints Commission announced that it would investigate the *Daily Mirror's* decision to pay £125,000 to Tony Martin for the story of his conviction and imprisonment for the manslaughter of Fred Barras. **29.** A £2.65 million Lottery-funded website about migration to Britain was launched; it contains documents, photographs and papers charting the history and family backgrounds of Britain's migrant population since the time of the slave trade. **30.** The band *Radiohead* threatened to take legal action against the BBC for using its track 'There There' for a television licence campaign without permission. **31.** The Australian actress Nicole Kidman received substantial damages and a public apology from the *Daily Mail* after the newspaper published allegations of an affair with her married co-star Jude Law which the paper alleged had led to the breakdown of his marriage to actress Sadie Frost.

AUGUST 2003

2. The director of the British Museum, Neil MacGregor, confirmed that the museum had been in talks with the Greek government about loaning the Elgin marbles to the newly built Acropolis Museum in Athens at the time of the Olympic Games in the city in 2004. **7.** The Government put a temporary export ban on the Jenkins Venus statue after it was sold to a foreign bidder at Christie's for £7.9 million. **10.** The National Portrait Gallery, the National Museums and Galleries of Wales and the Captain Cook Memorial Museum raised the £950,000 needed to keep William Parry's 1775 painting *Omai* in Britain after it was sold to a foreign buyer and was the subject of a temporary export ban. **12.** The Brontë Society received £600,000 from Customs and Excise, representing VAT payments since 1990 from which it should have been exempt, after a ten-year battle over the status of the Brontë Parsonage Museum. **13.** The BBC's board of governors ruled that the *Correspondent* documentary had been wrong to show the dead bodies of two British soldiers killed in Iraq. Robert Dixon, a computer graphics artist, accused the artist Damien Hirst of copying his work after Hirst produced a circular pattern picture for a children's colouring book in *The Guardian* that Mr Dixon claimed was practically identical to a pattern he had produced in 1981. **14.** Animal rights groups objected to *Amazing Revelations,* a piece of art by Damien Hirst which consists of hundreds of butterfly wings and which was part of an exhibition at the White Cube gallery, London. **17.** Salvagers announced plans to salvage gold coins from the wreck of the 19th-century steamship *SS Republic.* **21.** It was revealed that a granite memorial to the former Poet Laureate Ted Hughes had been erected on Dartmoor. **22.** The former Museums and Galleries Commissioner Sir Hugh Leggatt said that the law which forced dealers to pay tax on sales commission in the UK but not abroad should be abolished. **26.** The family of Martin Luther King announced that they were putting up for sale 7,000 documents written in his own hand, including the historic 'I Have A Dream' speech. **27.** Two thieves posing as tourists overpowered a guard at Drumlanrig Castle and stole the *Madonna of the Yarnwinder* by Leonardo da Vinci; a £1 million reward was offered by the insurers for the picture's recovery. **29.** A unique collection of watercolours painted by Beatrix Potter was discovered by BBC Television's *Antiques Roadshow* programme. **31.** Damien Hirst's *Hymn,* a piece replicating a child's plastic anatomy set on a huge scale, was bought by South Korean businessman Ci Kim for more than £1 million.

CRIMES AND LEGAL AFFAIRS

SEPTEMBER 2002
24. Sir John Stevens, the Metropolitan Police Commissioner, and his predecessor Lord Condon went on trial at the Central Criminal Court over alleged breaches of safety in police car chases. **30.** Victims of the Potters Bar rail crash began a group action to establish who was to blame for the disaster.

OCTOBER 2002
2. Lord Archer paid £2.7 million to the *Daily Star* after it was found that he had lied in a libel case against the newspaper in 1997. **8.** Ian Huntley was declared fit to plead and stand trial for the murders of Holly Wells and Jessica Chapman. **9.** A terminally ill man, Brad Stephens, was cleared of possession of cannabis by Carmarthen magistrates on the grounds that it was a medical necessity for him. **10.** The Governor of Lincoln prison imposed an additional six-month suspended penalty on Lord Archer for breaking prison rules by making money through publishing a diary about his prison experiences. **21.** The satellite broadcaster BSkyB was cleared of overcharging ITV for access to the satellite network. **25.** The Court of Appeal overturned a ruling that the detention of terrorist suspects was unlawful. An employment tribunal found that Lady Archer had acted fairly in sacking her personal assistant for breaching a confidentiality agreement. The property tycoon Nicholas van Hoogstraten was jailed for ten years at the Central Criminal Court for the manslaughter of his business associate Mohammed Raja in 1999; on 23 July 2003, the Court of Appeal overturned his conviction. Dulcie Bernard, who is severely disabled, became the first person to win damages under the Human Rights Act when the London Borough of Enfield was ordered to pay her family £10,000 for failing to provide suitable care. **28.** Chris Davies, a Liberal Democrat MEP, was found guilty at Minshull Street County Court of possessing cannabis and fined £100. **29.** Following a pilot scheme of on-the-spot fines for antisocial behaviour, the Government announced plans to extend the scheme to the rest of the country.

NOVEMBER 2002
1. The trial of the former royal butler Paul Burrell collapsed after it emerged that he had told The Queen in 1997 that he had taken items belonging to Diana, Princess of Wales from Kensington Palace to store elsewhere. **4.** The Court of Appeal freed Josephine Smith, jailed in 1993 for shooting dead her abusive husband. **5.** MI5 officer David Shayler was jailed for six months after

being convicted of passing 28 secret documents to the *Mail on Sunday*. The police named the man they believed killed Suzy Lamplugh 16 years ago as John Cannan, a convicted serial rapist and murderer. A Court of Appeal judgement gave same sex couples the same tenancy rights as married couples, allowing homosexual partners to inherit statutory tenancies if the couple have been living together as if they were a married couple. **6.** The Dowager Countess of Cawdor began a civil action to regain possession of Cawdor castle after claiming that the 7th Earl of Cawdor, who had moved into the property while the countess was abroad, was in breach of the lease and was endangering 'priceless' heirlooms. Eleven British planespotters accused of spying were cleared by a Greek court. Glynn Kenyon was sentenced at Bradford Crown Court to 16 life sentences for 43 sex offences and another life sentence for attempted murder; the evidence at the trial was so harrowing that the judge exempted members of the jury from further jury service for 50 years. **7.** Police announced the appointment of an expert in the usage of opiate-based painkiller diamorphine to investigate the deaths of more than 50 elderly patients at the Gosport War Memorial community hospital. **21.** The Princess Royal was found guilty at East Berkshire magistrates' court of offences under the Dangerous Dogs Act 1991 after her English bull terrier bit two boys in Windsor Great Park; she was fined £500. **25.** The law lords ruled that the Home Secretary should play no part in setting the length of prison sentences, bringing England and Wales in line with Scotland and Northern Ireland. Home Secretary David Blunkett announced proposals for new legislation on serious crimes to prevent 'soft sentencing'.

DECEMBER 2002
1. Liam Gallagher, the lead singer of the rock band Oasis, and three band members were charged with grievous bodily harm, trespassing and damaging property after a bar brawl in Munich in which Gallagher lost his front teeth and allegedly kicked a policeman in the chest. **2.** As a result of 'Operation Orb', a suspect was arrested near Maidstone, Kent, in connection with attacks by the 'trophy' rapist; on 5 December Antoni Imiela was charged with nine counts of rape. **3.** The royal butler Harold Brown, accused of stealing from Diana, Princess of Wales, was found not guilty at the Central Criminal Court. **5.** Television presenter John Leslie was arrested after attending a police station in London to answer questions about allegations of rape and indecent assault made by three women; on 18 June he was charged with two offences of indecently assaulting a woman, but he was cleared of these charges at Southwark Crown Court on 31 July after the case against him was dropped. Two pilots, Christopher Barrett-Jolley and Peter Carine, were sentenced to 20 years in prison for bringing £22 million of cocaine into Britain, the largest consignment of the drug known to have been brought into the country by air. **6.** The Government announced plans to allow 'civil partnerships' to be legally registered; this would allow same sex couples equal rights with married couples, such as qualifying for next-of-kin entitlements on inheritance tax, pensions and property; the Government said that it did not intend to extend the arrangement to cohabiting heterosexual couples. **9.** Christopher Allison, a consultant psychiatrist, was found guilty at Winchester Crown Court of two rapes and nine indecent assaults on six women patients during the 1980s and 1990s. **16.** John Allen was found guilty of the murder of his wife and two children

27 years ago after new evidence from his former mistress caused the case to be reopened. **19.** The Lord Chief Justice, Lord Woolf, announced that burglars facing a sentence of up to 18 months should be given a non-custodial sentence supervised by the probation service in a move to reduce the number of prisoners. Stuart Campbell, the uncle of Danielle Jones, was sentenced to life imprisonment and 10 years for kidnapping after being convicted of her murder. **31.** In Birmingham, two teenage girls, Charlene Ellis and Latisha Shakespeare, were killed by sub-machine gun fire at a New Year's Eve party; they were thought to have been caught in the crossfire of two rival gangs.

JANUARY 2003
3. A man was arrested by police after causing an estimated £200,000 worth of damage to Waltham Abbey, Essex, and attacking a man and smashing car windows in a nine-minute rampage with two axes. **5.** Anthony Hardy was arrested after dismembered female remains were discovered in and around his London bedsit; he was charged with the murder of three women. **13.** Pete Townshend, the guitarist and songwriter with *The Who*, was arrested after admitting that he had accessed child pornography websites; his arrest was one of a number in Britain arising from 'Operation Ore' in the US in which the US authorities recovered thousands of credit card details from a US-based child pornography website and passed on a list of 7,272 names to British authorities. **15.** The television presenter Matthew Kelly was arrested as part of an investigation into the abuse of teenage boys in the 1970s; he was released from police bail without charge on 24 February, although he was cautioned for possession of cocaine. **21.** Simon Vallor was jailed for two years for releasing three computer virus programs. **29.** The Appeal Court overturned the conviction of Sally Clark, who had been jailed for life for murdering her two baby sons; the judges ruled that the conviction was unsafe because vital medical evidence had been withheld from the defence team at her trial.

FEBRUARY 2003
3. A woman subsequently identified as Margaret Muller, an American artist studying at the Slade School of Fine Art, was found stabbed to death in Hackney, London; on 6 May a man was arrested on suspicion of her murder. **4.** Marsha McDonnell, a 19-year-old gap-year student, was found with severe head injuries just yards from her home in south-west London; she later died in hospital. **8.** Police announced that they were reinvestigating another attack on a girl which took place on 8 January 2003 in south-west London; the victim had been taken to hospital after being found with head injuries. **24.** A Muslim cleric, Abdullah El-Faisal, who preached the killing of 'unbelievers' including Jews, Hindus and westerners, was convicted on three counts of both soliciting murder and inciting racial hatred under the Offences Against the Person Act, 1861. **25.** An 18-year-old male student was attacked with a blunt object a few hundred yards from where Marsha McDonnell died on 4 February; the police feared her killer might have struck again.

MARCH 2003
4. A 22-year-old policeman who ran away with his 15-year-old girlfriend, prompting a four-day search, was arrested on suspicion of abduction. **7.** Surrey police announced that a year-long enquiry into the deaths of soldiers at the Deepcut army base had not found any

evidence of murder. **11.** Victoria Beckham, a former member of the Spice Girls, agreed to pay damages of £55,000 and formally apologised to the owners of a shop she accused of selling fake autographs of her husband David, the England football captain. Judge Michael Stokes denounced the decision to imprison a woman for failing to ensure that her daughter attended school and ordered her release. **16.** The body of 17-year-old Hannah Foster was found in a country lane; she had been missing since 14 February when she disappeared near her home in Southampton. **25.** Steven Wilson was jailed for life at Birmingham Crown Court for stabbing his two young sons to death; he was also found guilty of causing actual bodily harm to his wife. **28.** Anthony Goodridge, a former policeman involved in the Soham murders investigation in 2002, was jailed for six months after pleading guilty to downloading child pornography onto his home computer; his arrest was a result of Operation Ore.

APRIL 2003
1. Jason Dockrill of Stratford, London, was charged at the Central Criminal Court with the murder of Suvi Aronen, a 23-year-old Finnish student, on 20 March, and with the assault and robbery of two other people. Two Algerian immigrants, Baghdad Meziane and Brahim Benmerzouga, were jailed for 11 years each after raising thousands of pounds through credit card fraud for the al-Qa'eda terrorist network. **2.** Two children who were injured in a machete attack at their nursery school in 1996 were awarded £20,000 compensation after a seven-year case against the Criminal Injuries Compensation Authority. **3.** Robert Ashman was convicted of attempted murder for an attack on Nigel Jones, the MP for Cheltenham, with a Samurai sword in January 2000. **4.** Ian Parr, a former employee of BAE Systems, was jailed for ten years at the Central Criminal Court for planning to sell defence secrets to the Russians. **5.** The Home Secretary announced that he would withdraw the British citizenship of the radical Muslim cleric Sheikh Abu Hamza under new legislation that allows the Government to strip an individual with dual nationality of their British passport if their activities threaten the national interest. **7.** Major Charles Ingram, his wife Diana and Tecwen Whittock were all found guilty of deception for plotting to cheat on the quiz show *Who Wants to be a Millionaire* and, through Whittock coughing to indicate the correct answers, winning the £1 million prize unfairly. **8.** The Court of Appeal ruled that Mr and Mrs Hashmi of Leeds could use embryo selection to ensure that a child they conceived in the future had stem cells compatible with their son four-year-old Zain, who suffers from a rare, inherited blood disorder which prevents him from producing red blood cells; the disorder can be cured using stem cells that match his taken from the umbilical cord of a new baby. **10.** Martin Cattlin was cleared of the rape of a young girl in 1990, and received a public apology from Lord Justice Kay after it was found that two doctors had failed to give evidence at Mr Cattlin's original trial which would have proved he was innocent; he spent almost seven years in prison. **11.** Lea Shakespeare was given ten life sentences after being convicted of rape, arson and theft. **15.** In Seattle, USA, James Ujaama, a former associate of Sheikh Abu Hamza, pleaded guilty to conspiring to help the Taliban, saying that he had been instructed by Hamza to accompany another student, Feroz Abbasi, to an al-Qa'eda camp in Afghanistan in late 2000 'to undergo violent jihad

training'. 16. Ian Huntley and Maxine Carr, the couple accused of the murders of Holly Wells and Jessica Chapman in Soham in August 2002, appeared in court to enter their pleas for a trial scheduled to begin on 6 October; Huntley pleaded not guilty to murder but guilty to the joint charge of conspiracy to pervert the course of justice, while Carr pleaded not guilty to the charge of conspiracy to pervert the course of justice and two charges of assisting an offender. 20. A badly burnt body was identified through dental records as that of music teacher Jane Longhurst, who had gone missing on 14 March; on 25 April Graham Coutts, a 35-year-old musician, was arrested on suspicion of her murder. An investigation was reopened into the murder of 12-year-old Muriel Drinkwater, who was raped, beaten and shot through the heart as she walked home from school in 1946; detectives believed traces of the killer's DNA could still be found on the gun used to murder the girl. 23. Robert Noble was jailed for life for the murder of Alyson Caplan after he pleaded guilty at the Central Criminal Court in London; he claimed he wanted to know 'what it would be like to kill someone'. 26. The Home Office published figures showing that 416 criminals who had been electronically tagged and released from prison early had removed their tags and were 'unlawfully at large'. 28. At Bristol Crown Court, David Carter was sentenced to life imprisonment for the murders of his 15-year-old stepdaughter Joanne Lojko and her 21-year-old boyfriend Garry Crease; he had shot them both after Ms Lojko had discovered him spying on her while she was taking a bath and Mr Crease had confronted him over the matter. 29. The trial began at Reading Crown Court of Trupti Patel on three charges of murder after three of her four children died; she was found not guilty on 11 June.

MAY 2003
1. The body of millionaire businessman Amarjit Chohan was found in the sea near Bournemouth; he, his wife, two young children and mother-in-law were reported missing in mid-February; Peter Rees was charged with the murder of Mr Chohan on 16 May. 5. Police arrested a man on suspicion of the murder of 18-year-old Laura Torn who had been missing from her home in north Lincolnshire since 27 April; her boot was found in the River Trent. 7. The Home Secretary announced new proposals for sentencing guidelines. Police investigating the disappearance of Laura Torn found a body in Nottinghamshire, subsequently identified as that of Ms Torn and on 8 May Guy Beckett was charged with her murder. 9. The jury at an inquest returned the unprecedented verdict of 'suicide by cop' on a man who confronted armed police officers with a gun and was shot dead by them; two suicide notes were later found in the house of Michael Malsbury. 12. The results of a government investigation were published, revealing that thousands of human brains have been illegally retained for research and teaching without the consent of the patients' families. 14. Robert Pearson, the acting head of a Roman Catholic school in Everton, Merseyside, was found to be a member of an internet paedophile ring and was jailed for more than five years at Guildford Crown Court after he pleaded guilty to 26 counts of making and distributing indecent images, conspiracy to distribute, and three counts of indecent assault on a girl under 14 years of age. 15. The Prison Service admitted that the mass murderer Harold Shipman, who is serving a life sentence for murdering at least 215 of his patients during his time as a family doctor, had cared for an elderly

prisoner in his prison's healthcare wing. 16. Rena Salmon was found guilty of the murder of Lorna Stewart and jailed for life; Mrs Salmon shot Ms Stewart on 10 September 2002 because of Ms Stewart's relationship with Mr Salmon. Richard Kemp was jailed for life for the murder of Camilla Petersen, a 15-year-old student from Denmark, while she was staying on the Isle of Wight. Nadine Milroy-Sloan was convicted by a jury at the Central Criminal Court of perverting the course of justice after she lied to police about being raped by the former MP Neil Hamilton and his wife Christine; she was sentenced to three years in prison on 13 June. 19. Margaret Grant won her case to ensure that all parties involved in IVF treatment are informed before an embryo is discarded. 20. The Government announced that an amendment would be made to the Criminal Justice Bill enabling companies to be held liable for a new offence of corporate manslaughter if their managers were found responsible for workplace deaths caused by gross negligence. Leayon Dudley was jailed for life for the murder of PC Bryan Moore and the manslaughter of PC Andrew Munn on 15 August 2002; he had driven into their parked patrol car at 80 mph because they were trying to lay a stinger trap which would have stopped him speeding. Col. Tim Collins of the Royal Irish Regiment was accused of 'serious breaches' of the Geneva Convention, including allegedly punching, kicking and threatening Iraqi prisoners of war; on 25 May, Major Re Biastre, the US officer who had made the accusations, admitted that his claims were based on secondhand information and that he had not witnessed any of the alleged incidents. 21. Mary Bell, who as an 11-year-old had killed two young boys, won a lifelong, worldwide ban on anyone revealing her or her daughter's new identity. An armed robber stole precious gems worth £6 million from Graff's jewellery shop in New Bond Street, London, in a lunchtime raid; Zoltan Valent was charged with the theft at Bow Street Magistrates Court on 27 June. 25. The Government announced plans for legislation that would see men convicted of beating their wives placed on a 'domestic violence register' similar to the sex offenders register. 27. The Commissioner of the Metropolitan Police, Sir John Stevens, was warned that he might face a retrial after a jury at the Central Criminal Court failed to reach a verdict on charges under the 1974 Health and Safety at Work Act brought after two officers who had fallen through roofs in the course of their duties. 28. The mother of Maxine Carr, the woman accused of perverting the course of justice in the Soham murders case, was charged with intimidating a witness in the case. 29. Major Charles Ingram, convicted of deception on the quiz show *Who Wants to be a Millionaire,* pleaded not guilty at Bournemouth Crown Court to five separate charges of insurance fraud. 30. Gary Bartlam of the 1st Battalion of the Royal Regiment was arrested while on a month's leave after staff at a photographic shop alerted the police when they developed images on Bartlam's film apparently showing British troops carrying out sex acts in front of a gagged and bound Iraqi prisoner.

JUNE 2003
1. Two men were arrested on suspicion of desecrating a Muslim woman's body in a mortuary by placing bacon on it; the men were former hospital porters at Hillingdon Hospital, where the incident took place in January 2003. 3. Two sisters from Thailand were jailed for running a prostitution ring; Bupa Savada was jailed for five years for

controlling prostitutes and living off immoral earnings and Monporn Hughes was jailed for three and a half years for living off immoral earnings. **7.** Radio One disc jockey Sara Cox won her privacy case against the *People* newspaper after it printed unauthorised photos of her on her honeymoon; the newspaper was ordered to pay £50,000 damages to Ms Cox. **9.** Ian Huntley, the man accused of the Soham murders, was taken to hospital after he tried to commit suicide by taking an overdose of anti-depressant pills; he was returned to prison on 10 June. Andrew George was charged with the murder of Hilda Murrell, a peace campaigner who was stabbed to death near her home in Shrewsbury in 1984. Four Sri Lankan Tamils were jailed at the Central Criminal Court in London for the murder of Supenthar Ramachandran, whom they set alight in a London park. **10.** George Kelly, who was hanged for the murder of Leonard Thomas in a bungled robbery in Liverpool in March 1949, had his conviction overturned by the Court of Appeal; Lord Justice Rix ruled that he had not received a fair trial after a document revealed that a key prosecution witness had lied in court. **11.** DC John Beresford was jailed for 15 months at Newcastle Crown Court after being found guilty of grievous bodily harm; his assault on Graeme McMillan had left the victim brain-damaged. Police began a search for 16-year-old Kayleigh Quinn who went missing with Steven Barton, a convicted rapist; the pair had left a jointly written note indicating that they planned to commit suicide. Kayleigh Quinn was found near her home in Pulborough; Mr Barton was also found and taken into police custody. **18.** The High Court ruled that JobCentre Plus, an agency of the Department of Work and Pensions, had acted illegally in preventing the Ann Summers company from advertising for staff at job centres; it deemed JobCentre Plus's policy excluding companies involved in selling sex-related products to be 'irrational' and unlawful. **19.** Doraj Miah was sentenced to be held indefinitely at Rampton maximum security hospital after he appeared at the Central Criminal Court in London charged with the rape and murder of art teacher Hazel Prager. Jason Phillips, the member of London rap group So Solid Crew known as 'G-Man', was jailed for four years for carrying a loaded gun. **20.** Lee Craytor pleaded guilty to the murder of his girlfriend's five-year-old daughter, Danielle Reid, at Perth High Court; Danielle's mother, Tracy Reid, admitted to attempting to pervert the course of justice by disposing of the body. **21.** The Police Complaints Authority began an investigation into two police officers following a complaint that the officers had left a body hanging from a tree for three days after it was reported to them by Max Porter; three days after Mr Porter reported finding the body he was walking in the same spot and found that the body was still in the same place. **22.** The Home Secretary demanded an urgent report into how Aaron Barschak, a comedian from north London, managed to penetrate heavy police security to gatecrash Prince William's 21st birthday party at Windsor Castle; Mr Barschak was dressed as Osama bin Laden when he jumped on stage next to the prince. **23.** Robert Dickenson, who was charged with shooting his neighbour, George Wilson, in a row over a garden hedge, was found dead in his cell at Lincoln prison on the day he was due to appear in court. Suryakant Patel was charged with murdering his 13-year-old daughter after she was found drowned in a bath. **25.** Gurdev Mann was found guilty at Leicester Crown Court of murdering his wife, Narinder Kaur Mann, because she did not like the 'stale' food she had cooked for him. **26.**

Former radio and television presenter Chris Evans lost his case for compensation against his former employer Virgin Radio after he was sacked for failing to turn up for work for six days in a row; on 28 July Evans agreed to pay £7 million to Scottish Media Group, the owners of Virgin Radio.

JULY 2003

1. Fourteen-year-old Jodi Jones' body was discovered by family members on a woodland pathway near her home in Midlothian after she failed to return home from her boyfriend's house; it emerged that she had never arrived at his house. The Trade and Industry Secretary announced the introduction of legislation making it unlawful for companies to hire or fire employees on the basis of age. **2.** Recorder Peter Rook criticised two police officers from Forest Gate police station, London, for leaving a Colombian woman alone on a main road at 4 a.m. after they had arrested her boyfriend and taken him to the police station; the woman was raped by Patrick Gallagher and then assaulted by another man. Gallagher was jailed for eight years after admitting raping her. Hundreds of Kenyan women won legal aid for their cases against the Ministry of Defence in pursuit of their claims that they were raped or gang-raped for more than 30 years by British soldiers stationed in Kenya. Richard Markham was jailed for life at Winchester Crown Court for the murder of his friend Tristian Lovelock. **3.** Michael Shirley was cleared by the Court of Appeal and released from prison after serving 16 years for the murder of barmaid Linda Cook. Fifteen-year-old Fahad Javaid was jailed for nine years for raping a woman at knifepoint in a park. **4.** Jeffrey Gafoor was jailed for life for the murder of Lynette White in 1988, after the DNA sample of his nephew led to his arrest; three men had previously been wrongly imprisoned for the crime. **6.** Detectives announced that they were treating as murder the death of Stephen Hilder, who died of multiple injuries after his main and reserve parachutes failed to open during a parachute jump on 4 July; detectives found that the cords on both parachutes had been deliberately cut. After the European Court of Human Rights ruled that the Government's failure to recognise transsexuals' change of sex breached the European Convention of Human Rights, the Government announced legislation giving transsexuals the legal right to marry and to have their gender changed on their birth certificate. A man was shot in the street in the Lozells area of Birmingham. **8.** Randle Williams was jailed for life at Bristol Crown Court after he was found guilty of strangling and drowning his wife, Natalie Williams, shortly after he had taken out extra life insurance and his company had gone into liquidation. The Crown Prosecution Service decided not to bring charges against nine Ministry of Defence scientists after an investigation of experiments at Porton Down between 1939 and 1989 to gauge the military value of certain substances; volunteers who participated in the tests claimed that they were told the tests were intended to find a cure for the common cold. **9.** Six senior managers and their companies, Railtrack and Balfour Beatty, were charged with manslaughter by gross negligence over the Hatfield rail crash, which killed four people and injured more than 100 in October 2001. An official investigation by the Commission for Racial Equality uncovered 20 failures in prison procedures at Feltham Young Offender Institution; the investigation was instigated after an Asian prisoner, Zahid Mubarek, was placed in a cell with a known racist who subsequently beat him to death. On

20 July a solicitor involved in the investigation said that there was no evidence that prison managers at Feltham had discriminated against Mubarek. **15.** The headmistress of a London school, Colleen McCabe, was found guilty of theft and deception by a jury at Southwark Crown Court; she had stolen school funds to pay for foreign holidays and shopping trips. **16.** Stephen Hinchliffe, the former chairman of the Facia retail group, was jailed for 18 months after the Attorney General successfully argued that his original 15-month suspended sentence for conspiracy to defraud Facia had been too lenient. **18.** Ken Williams and his partner Christine Green were jailed for two and four years respectively for child cruelty and neglect after Mr Williams' five-year-old daughter, Annastacia Williams died in September 2002 from head injuries. **21.** PC John Cunningham was critically ill after being shot at close range while on duty at Shettleston police station in Glasgow. The body of Nancy Chohan, wife of the murdered millionaire Amarjit Chohan, was found in the sea off Dorset. Mark Corner was arrested on suspicion of murdering Pauleen Stephen and another unidentified woman after their dismembered bodies were found in bin bags in Everton, Merseyside. **23.** The Mayor of London, Ken Livingstone, was cleared by the Standards Board for England of bringing the office of Mayor of London into disrepute and was exonerated of wrongly spending his budget to defend himself after he was accused of pushing Robin Hedges at a party and causing him head injuries. **24.** Paul Murray was charged with the attempted murder of PC John Cunningham, who was shot while on duty at Shettleston police station on 21 July. Jonathan King, the pop entrepreneur serving a seven-year prison sentence for sex offences, filed an appeal in the European Court of Human Rights on the grounds that damaging publicity had prevented him from receiving a fair trial. A military tribunal ruled that Major Charles Ingram should resign his commission, and he was subsequently ordered to leave the army because of his conviction for deception in April. Five people were arrested over a £6.35 million credit card fraud. **28.** Tony Martin, who was jailed for five years for the manslaughter of burglar Fred Barras, was freed from prison after serving two-thirds of his sentence. Two children, Christopher and Charlie Knight, died in an arson attack on a pub in Stoke Newington, London, and two other children were critically injured. **29.** Twenty-one West African men and women were arrested at nine addresses in London in connection with the murder of a boy, aged between four and seven, whose torso was found in the Thames in September 2001. The former MI5 officer David Shayler, who was given a prison sentence for breaching the Official Secrets Act, was refused permission by the Court of Appeal to challenge his conviction. **30.** Shaied Iqbal was given eight life sentences for murdering eight members of one family by deliberately starting a fire at a terrace house in Huddersfield. **31.** The inquiry under Lord Hutton into the death of the government scientist and chemical weapons expert Dr David Kelly officially opened.

AUGUST 2003

1. Peter Rees, the man charged with killing millionaire businessman Amarjit Chohan, was further charged with the murder of Mr Chohan's wife, mother-in-law and two young children at the Central Criminal Court in London. **4.** Detectives investigating the murders of the Chohan family named Kenneth Regan as a possible second suspect in the case; Mr Regan was arrested in Belgium on 2 August and police started extradition proceedings. Detective Inspector David Smith was suspended from his post after the Shipman inquiry found that the lives of some of Shipman's victims would have been saved had Mr Smith properly directed police action during the time serial killer Harold Shipman was under investigation. **5.** Rana Faruqui was found dead outside her home in Buckinghamshire after making an emergency call to the police 15 minutes earlier; her former boyfriend, Stephen Griffiths, was arrested on 7 August. **6.** Daniel Cummings was jailed for life at London's Central Criminal Court for shooting dead a rival gang member, Adrian Crawford, in December 2002. **10.** A Dorset man from was charged with the murder of Angela Chiu, who was stabbed at her home in Poole. Police announced that they had arrested a man in connection with the disappearance on Boxing Day 1996 of 13-year-old David Spencer and 11-year-old Patrick Warren; the man had sent a letter to police in Birmingham claiming that the two boys were buried in Woodgate Valley, but a police search found nothing. **12.** It was announced that Libya would formally accept responsibility for the Lockerbie bombing, which killed 270 people in 1988, and had agreed to pay up compensation to the families of the victims. **13.** A Briton, Hemant Lakhani, appeared in court in the USA on charges of supporting terrorists by importing a Russian-made anti-aircraft missile into the country. **14.** Alison Welfare was jailed for 12 months for making a false accusation of rape against her boyfriend. A former US Marine, Toby Studabaker, who ran away with a 12-year-old British girl he had befriended on the internet, was arrested in Frankfurt on two charges of abduction and was extradited to Britain. **16.** Robert Naylor, Benjamin Wilson and James Moloney were charged at Bow Street Magistrates Court with offences under the Terrorism Act. The Government announced that it had reached an agreement with the US authorities that the nine Britons being held on terror charges at Guantanamo Bay should serve their sentences in Britain following trials held in Cuba. **18.** Dale Harvey was shot dead in his car by two men on a motorcycle in what appeared to be a contract killing; Harvey was due in court shortly to answer charges of importing cocaine. **20.** DC Brian Stevens, a police family liaison officer attached to the Soham murders investigation, was acquitted of downloading child pornography after it was found that an expert witness had made substantial errors in his analysis of the officer's laptop computer. **21.** Dr Syed Amjad Husain was arrested in Darlington on suspicion of indecently assaulting five women and children at his surgery and making indecent images of children. **22.** Following the acquittal of DC Brian Stevens, a prosecutor halted the trial of a teacher on similar charges in order to ensure the dependability of expert witnesses. **23.** Detectives arrested a man on suspicion of the manslaughter of Rachel Whitear, who was believed to have died of a heroin overdose in May 2000 and whose image was used in an anti-drugs campaign; an inquest into Ms Whitear's death found no definite cause of death and showed that the heroin in her body was not at a fatal level. **25.** Tommy Sheridan, leader of the Scottish Socialist Party, was jailed for seven days after refusing to pay a £200 fine for breaching the peace during an anti-nuclear demonstration in February 2002. **26.** A former soldier at Deepcut barracks, Leslie Skinner, appeared at Guildford magistrates' court on charges of sexually assaulting a 17-year-old male recruit; he denied the allegations. **27.** Police released CCTV footage of a man who raped and beat to death a mother of two in Croydon. **28.** At the Hutton inquiry, the Prime Minister said that he would take full responsibility for the Government's strategy of naming Dr David Kelly. **29.** It was confirmed that British inquests will be held into the deaths of Diana, Princess of Wales and Dodi Fayed. **30.** Three men were held in Dover after attempting to enter Britain with concealed weapons. Businessman Amarjit Singh and his nephew Raginder Singh were shot dead in Forest Gate, London.

ECONOMIC AND BUSINESS AFFAIRS

SEPTEMBER 2002
30. Standard Life, Europe's largest mutual insurer, cut savers' policy bonuses and introduced early exit penalties.

OCTOBER 2002
1. The High Court ruled that Railtrack could be taken out of administration, allowing its return to public ownership as Network Rail. **18.** The mobile phone company Ericsson announced third-quarter losses of around £386 million. **19.** Rolls-Royce announced a £325 million maintenance deal with Virgin Atlantic to maintain the engines of the Airbus A340-600 fleet. **21.** Office for National Statistics showed that £43.7 billion was placed in pension schemes in 2001, not the £86.4 billion announced by government ministers. The life insurer Prudential announced the introduction of penalties for early withdrawals from its with-profits bonds and pension schemes.

NOVEMBER 2002
4. The Royal College of Nursing's annual survey found that almost a third of nurses take a second job to supplement their income, while two-thirds regularly work longer hours than stipulated in their contracts. It emerged that for almost five years the Inland Revenue had been overpaying pension fund rebates to thousands who had opted out of SERPS after its computer system mistakenly counted information twice. **6.** The Strategic Rail Authority announced that train operating companies would have to forfeit 'excessive' profits, which would be reinvested in the rail network. **12.** Vodafone Group reported a 41 per cent rise in profits on turnover that had increased 67 per cent to £14.9 billion. **13.** The Office for National Statistics reported that the number of people out of work and claiming benefit fell by 4,500 in October 2002, taking unemployment to 940,500, the lowest figure for 27 years. **27.** The Chancellor of the Exchequer, Gordon Brown, announced in his pre-Budget speech that the Government would increase borrowing by £20 billion over two years; he cut his growth forecast to 1.6 per cent, and expected inflation to remain close to 2.5 per cent. **28.** In a statement to the Commons, the Trade and Industry Secretary announced a financial rescue package of £650 million for British Energy, to prevent the nuclear generator from going into liquidation; the executive chairman of British Energy, Robin Jeffrey, was made redundant. **29.** The Office for Fair Trading fined Hasbro UK, a leading toy manufacturer, £4.95 million for price-fixing with retailers.

DECEMBER 2002
1. Rolls Royce announced a deal with Lufthansa to maintain the engines of a new fleet of long-haul aircraft. **4.** Abbey Life was fined a record £1 million after a

review of endowment policy sales uncovered a catalogue of compliance failures over more than a decade. **8.** The value of shares in the telecommunications group Cable & Wireless almost halved after the firm had to secure a £1.5 billion loan guarantee following the downgrading of its debt to junk status by the credit rating agency Moodys. **20.** The investment bank Credit Suisse First Boston was fined £4 million for systematically attempting to deceive financial regulators and tax authorities; the penalty, imposed by the Financial Services Authority (FSA), is the highest ever levied by a UK regulator.

JANUARY 2003
6. The value of shares in the life insurer Britannic halved after it issued a profit warning. **7.** Official figures showed that the rate of return on capital invested in UK non-financial companies dropped to 11 per cent in the third quarter of 2002, the lowest since 1993. **23.** The FTSE 100 share index fell by 1.5 per cent, closing at 3,622.2, a seven-year low. **24.** The FTSE 100 index fell further closing at 3,603.7; its lowest level since December 1995. Official figures showed that British economic growth halved to 0.4 per cent in the fourth quarter of 2002. **26.** It was reported that British Energy was close to an agreement on debt repayments which would save it from going into administration. **29.** The Swedish fashion chain Hennes & Mauritz announced that it intended to triple its rate of expansion in the UK after a 50 per cent rise in annual profits. **31.** Ryanair bought the low-fare airline Buzz in a £3 million deal; it paid a total of £15 million for the company, but received £12 million from pre-booked tickets. The FSA relaxed the rules for measuring the solvency of life insurers for the fourth time in 17 months, to help insurers avoid being forced to sell shares in a falling market.

FEBRUARY 2003
1. The mutual life insurer Standard Life announced that it would cut bonuses on with-profits policies by an average of 20 per cent and overall payments by 15 per cent. **2.** The Trade and Industry ministers confirmed that the Government had provided British Energy with £650 million to keep the company afloat, but it did not know how much the company's restructuring would cost overall. **3.** The price of platinum reached $698 an ounce in London, the highest level for almost 23 years. **6.** The Bank of England cut interest rates by 0.25 per cent to 3.75 per cent. **7.** Pay rises for public sector workers were announced; the Lord Chancellor was awarded an increase of 12.6 per cent, teachers received 2.9 per cent, the armed forces 3.7 per cent and MPs 2.25 per cent. **8.** After protests by ministers and Labour backbenchers at the size of the Lord Chancellor's pay increase, his department announced that he would not be taking his 12.6 per cent pay rise, but only 2.25 per cent in line with his Cabinet colleagues. **11.** The music group Boosey & Hawkes agreed to sell its instruments division to Rutland Fund Management for £33.2 million. **12.** Unemployment figures showed a further fall in those out of work and claiming benefit, dropping to 928,500 in January. **13.** The Rail Regulator, Tom Windsor, recommended that Network Rail, the not-for-profit company created by the Government to replace Railtrack, should reduce its over-spending of £1.5 billion a year by cutting some spending on its infrastructure, including basic maintenance, providing this would not compromise safety or the long-term sustainability of the network. The Bank of Scotland was fined £750,000 by the FSA for

failing to administer customer accounts properly. **18.** Figures from the Office for National Statistics showed that the inflation was unchanged, at 2.7 per cent, in January. **19.** Two leading retailers, Littlewoods and Argos, were fined £22.6 million by the Office of Fair Trading for illegal price-fixing on Hasbro toys; their role was revealed by Hasbro after it was fined in November 2002 and agreed to co-operate fully in the investigation. **25.** The pound dropped 0.8 per cent against the euro, closing at 68.4p, a four-year low. **27.** Rachel Lomax, formerly the Permanent Secretary at the Department of Transport, was appointed deputy governor of the Bank of England, the first woman to hold the position, and Richard Lambert, former editor of the *Financial Times,* was appointed to the bank's Monetary Policy Committee.

MARCH 2003
11. Sotheby's and Christie's agreed to pay £12 million damages each to clients who lost money through their collusion over commission rates in auctions outside the USA. The FTSE fell to an eight-year low as fears of war with Iraq increased. **15.** The supermarket group Sainsbury announced that Sir Peter Davis, the current chief executive, would become chairman in March 2004. **17.** Stock markets rose and the price of gold and oil fell for the third day running as war with Iraq seemed more certain. **19.** Official figures showed that inflation had reached its highest level in five years in February 2003, with the underlying rate increasing to 3 per cent. **25.** The Inland Revenue agreed to settle a £1.5 billion tax dispute with the telecommunications group Cable & Wireless; as a result the company's shares rose by 13.25 per cent. **27.** The chemist chain Boots announced the closure of its Wellbeing beauty services operation with the loss of 700 jobs. **31.** The mutual life insurer Equitable Life announced that compensation for 60,000 policyholders with a guaranteed pension had been put on hold pending a new agreement concerning the level of payments; the policyholders had been waiting almost three years to receive redress after a House of Lords ruling in 2000.

APRIL 2003
3. The furniture retailer MFI was presented with a £28.5 million Customs and Excise bill for underpaying tax, but announced that it planned to contest the demand. British Airways announced a sharp drop in passenger traffic for March, which it believed to be caused by the war in Iraq and the outbreak of the Sars virus. **9.** The Chancellor announced the 2003 Budget; new measures included the introduction of child trust funds with an initial endowment of £250 awarded to all children born after September 2002; new tax breaks for small- and medium-sized companies; and the abolition of tax on bingo from 4 August. The Chancellor also announced that £3 billion would be allocated to pay for the cost of the war with Iraq, with £64 million set aside for reconstruction and £70 million added to Britain's contribution to the humanitarian effort. **16.** Lincoln Assurance was fined £485,000 by the FSA for mis-selling endowment savings plans between 1998 and 2000. **20.** The Innovations Catalogue announced that it would close in summer 2003 owing to the drop in demand for its products. **27.** The Selfridges department store chain instructed investment bank Merrill Lynch to start a formal auction process for the group. The Royal Bank of Scotland and the Japanese securities firm Nomura decided to write off the value of their investment in the Meridian Hotels

group and cede control to the lenders, CIBC, Merrill Lynch and Lehman Brothers.

MAY 2003
12. The Chancellor raised the top limit for individual investment in premium bonds from £20,000 to £30,000. **13.** SBC International Cinemas, owner of a handful of screens in Scotland and northern England, became Britain's largest operator of multiplex cinemas after acquiring Warner Village for £250 million. **15.** The Government announced that up to 10 million workers faced a shortfall in their state pension after the Inland Revenue failed to send reminders for the tax years 1997–2001 to people who were not paying enough national insurance. **23.** The Financial Ombudsman Service (FOS) ordered the mutual company Equitable Life to pay compensation for mis-selling to investors who bought policies between September 1998 and February 2002. **28.** Network Rail announced that its debts had risen to £9.4 billion owing to heavy spending on maintenance and rail replacement; it also announced a loss of £290 million compared to a £295 million profit in 2002. **30.** The personal injury claims firm the Accident Group made 2,500 staff redundant after its parent company, Amulet, went into receivership; staff were told of their redundancies via text messages and email.

JUNE 2003
1. British Energy announced losses in excess of £4 billion, mainly caused by a £3.8 billion writedown of its electricity generation assets. **2.** The Rail Regulator said that Network Rail was likely to spend £12 billion more than its budget by April 2006 and that the company's lack of equity shareholders was the main reason for the soaring costs. **4.** Cable & Wireless's new management announced plans to cut 1,500 jobs in the UK, suspend payments to shareholders and dispose of the group's loss-making US operations. **6.** In its half-year report, MyTravel, the package holiday group previously known as Airtours, reported debts of £618 million and said that it would only avoid insolvency if it could agree with bondholders to repay them in December 2006 rather than January 2004. **9.** The Chancellor made a statement in the House of Commons explaining why the UK economy did not meet his five conditions for joining the euro zone. **12.** The Government announced plans to create a pensions protection fund, a compulsory insurance that would pay out to members of final-salary pension schemes if there was not enough money in their fund. The airline BMI announced that it would be cutting 1,500 jobs over the next three years. **16.** Rolls-Royce secured a £600 million contract to supply engines for new aircraft ordered by Emirates, the Dubai-based airline. **17.** The pound jumped to a five-year high against the dollar. **30.** Sir Edward George retired as Governor of the Bank of England and was succeeded by Mervyn King.

JULY 2003
2. HSBC, Britain's largest bank, announced that it was cutting 1,400 jobs. **9.** The Inland Revenue suspended payment of arrears and emergency payments of tax credits to commit more resources to dealing with the backlog of tax credit applications. The Office for National Statistics announced that fraud involving the non-payment of VAT by importers of mobile phones was responsible for a deficit in import figures of about £11.1 billion in 2002. **10.** The Bank of England cut interest

rates to 3.5 per cent. **15.** Aviva, the UK's largest insurer, announced it would be cutting 1,000 jobs at its Norwich Union business.

AUGUST 2003

3. In a preliminary judgement, the European Commission ruled that the Government's financial rescue package for British Energy was unlawful and would have to be repaid to the Exchequer. **7.** Sanderson Wallpapers went into receivership. **11.** The appointment was announced of Alistair Buchanan as the new chief executive of Ofgem, the body which regulates the gas and electricity markets. **12.** BSkyB posted its first annual pre-tax profit of £128 million, compared to a £1.28 billion loss in 2002. **22.** The Association of British Insurers, which represents the UK insurance industry, reported that life and pension savings had fallen from £3 billion in the second quarter of 2002 to £2.4 billion for the same period in 2003.

ENVIRONMENT AND SCIENCE

SEPTEMBER 2002

26. A report by US scientists suggested that consuming two or three Ecstasy pills could cause permanent brain damage.

OCTOBER 2002

2. Scientists announced they had mapped the genetic codes of both the malaria parasite and the mosquito species that transmits it, paving the way for the development of new drugs to combat malaria. **21.** Ministry of Defence scientists produced the first vaccine to protect against bubonic plague. **25.** A report by the Public Health Laboratory Service alleged that eggs from Spain could be to blame for Britain's recent salmonella outbreak, in which 250 people contracted a rare strain of salmonella enteritidis. **29.** Around 50 seabirds died on the Cumbrian coast as a result of an oil leak from a power station in the Isle of Man.

NOVEMBER 2002

8. A project supported by the Environment Agency and English Nature showed that using pheromones as 'sex traps' was a viable method for controlling numbers of the Giant North American Signal Crayfish, which is threatening to wipe out the native crayfish population. **20.** The first public autopsy for 170 years was held in a London art gallery; the autopsy was conducted by Prof. Gunther von Hagens, the doctor behind the Body Worlds exhibition. **18.** A survey for the Wildlife Trusts reported that otters have been recorded in many town and city centres for the first time in decades and in many northern cities for the first time since the Industrial Revolution. **25.** *Nature* magazine reported that a new science called 'metabonomics', developed at Imperial College London, could be used to detect when blood vessels were beginning to clog as a result of coronary artery disease, paving the way for a blood test for heart disease. **27.** Surgeons announced that the technology was theoretically available to carry out human face transplants. **30.** The Nobel prize-winning scientist Prof. Stan Prusiner, who discovered the cause of BSE, suggested that the entire British population should be tested for variant CJD as well as every cow and sheep entering the food chain, as animals infected with BSE were still being sold for human consumption.

DECEMBER 2002

1. A pioneering procedure allowing doctors to implant new pulmonary heart valves without opening up a patient's chest was used successfully to treat four young heart patients. **2.** The Engineering and Physical Sciences Research Council awarded Professor Stephen Salter of Edinburgh University a grant of £105,000 to develop his design for a 'rainmaker'; using wind power to drive a turbine, the rainmaker would suck water out of the sea, creating clouds in desert areas where there is not normally enough moisture vapour to produce rain, and thereby helping to combat drought. **6.** The first elephant to be conceived by artificial insemination was born at Colchester Zoo, Essex. It was reported that hundreds of seabirds smothered in heavy fuel oil were being washed up on the East Anglian coast after a series of unexplained oil slicks.

JANUARY 2003

6. At the American Astronomical Society's annual meeting in Seattle, the first results from the large area surveys of the sky were announced. Findings included the discovery of several hundred million stars surrounding the galaxy's main disc, thought to be the remains of a satellite galaxy, which could hold clues as to how the Milky Way and other galaxies evolved; and the discovery of the most distant known planet closely orbiting a star about 5,000 light years away. Police marksmen were called out to hunt a 'puma-like' animal after a 'big cat' near Llangadog, Wales, killed a farmer's dog; there was a second sighting of the animal on 8 January. **10.** Jonathan Simms, a Belfast teenager dying from variant CJD, was reported to have started treatment using the controversial drug pentosan polysulphate, in the hope that the disease's progression might be slowed; on 12 May it was announced that after regular injections the teenager was no longer deteriorating and had shown small signs of improvement. **22.** The space probe Pioneer 10 sent its last signal home after more than 30 years in space.

FEBRUARY 2003

1. The space shuttle *Columbia* disintegrated as it re-entered the earth's atmosphere; all seven astronauts on board were killed. **14.** The Roslin Institute in Edinburgh announced that six-year-old Dolly the sheep, the first animal to be cloned from an adult cell, had been put down. **20.** The Boomerang Nebula, formed from the gas blown away from a star in the latter stages of its life, was identified by astronomers as the coldest area ever detected in space.

MARCH 2003

7. New images of Jupiter taken by the Cassini space probe led scientists to revise theories about how Jupiter got its belts. **20.** Research published in *Nature* journal announced that scientists at Rockefeller University, USA, had identified the chemical triggers that turn skin into hair, opening up the possibility for treatments for baldness and unwanted bodily hair.

APRIL 2003

2. The World Health Organisation advised travellers to avoid Hong Kong and southern China after an outbreak of severe acute respiratory syndrome (Sars), a serious disease with pneumonia-like symptoms believed to have originated in southern China in November 2002. **6.** A study of global temperature over the past 1,000 years published by Harvard University showed that the world experienced a warm period between the ninth and 14th centuries; the study also identified a 'little ice age' from 1300 to 1900 which may be responsible for exaggerating current global warming trends as the records used by scientists date from a time when the earth was relatively cold. **10.** *The Times* reported that for the first time an airline passenger had been diagnosed and treated for a heart attack at 37,000 feet using new equipment that enables ECG readings to be taken onboard which are then used to seek advice on treatment from doctors on the ground. **13.** Canadian researchers published the genetic sequence of the Sars virus. **15.** It was reported that a German biotechnology company had developed a new high-speed test for Sars. **21.** A grey seal trapped in a shallow stretch of the River Leven, near Balloch, was given an official fishing permit by the local angling association after repeated attempts by marine rescuers failed to capture the seal and return him to the sea. **23.** The World Health Organisation advised travellers to avoid the Canadian city of Toronto after an outbreak there of the Sars virus.

MAY 2003
4. The Food Standards Agency announced that Britons may be risking their health if their intake of vitamins and dietary supplements significantly exceeds the recommended daily allowance, and that those taking large quantities could effectively be poisoning themselves. Two US astronauts and a Russian cosmonaut returned from the international space station Mir, landing in Kazakhstan. **12.** The fourth otter survey of England by the Environment Agency, English Nature and the Wildlife Trusts found signs of a clear recovery of the species, with a 527 per cent increase since the first survey in 1977 in the number of places where otters live. **23.** A healthy 6lb girl was delivered in Cape Town, South Africa, after developing inside her mother's liver; the baby's location was discovered after an ultra-sound scan at 39 weeks found that the mother's womb was empty, and an emergency operation delivered the baby. A 84-mile walk along Hadrian's Wall was opened, allowing the wall to be walked in its entirety for the first time in 1,600 years. **27.** The National Institute for Clinical Excellence recommended that a new 'smart' pill for treating colon and breast cancers (Capecitabine, distributed under the trade name Xeloda) should be made available on the NHS.

JUNE 2003
2. The British space probe Beagle 2 was launched in the nose cone of a European Space Agency rocket from Kazakhstan; it is due to land on Mars on 25 December 2003. **8.** NASA launched the first of two robotic explorers from Cape Canaveral, Florida; Mars Exploration Rover 1, a six-wheeled robot the size of a small car, is due to arrive on Mars in early 2004. **12.** *Nature* journal reported that 160,000 year old fossilised human skulls had been unearthed in Ethiopia. **19.** It was announced that US scientists had mapped the 78 genes that make up the male Y-chromosome. **24.** The World Health Organisation lifted its warning about travel to Beijing, China, after public hygiene measures and warmer temperatures in the region had ended the Sars virus threat. **27.** The *British Medical Journal* heralded the invention of a new 'polypill', thought to have the potential to eliminate 80 per cent of heart attacks and strokes if taken daily.

JULY 2003
3. The discovery of a new species of dinosaur was announced by the Bernard Price Institute for Palaeontological Research in Johannesburg, South Africa; the bones were originally unearthed by Prof. James Kitching in 1973, but were only recently identified as a sauropod dating back some 215 million years. **4.** Kew Gardens was designated as a World Heritage Site. **11.** A campaign was launched at the Royal Botanic Gardens in Kew to create a network of 20 rainforest-canopy observatories around the world. **13.** Scientists from the French National Health and Medical Research Institute announced they had discovered a way to regenerate damaged neurones in the brain and spinal column in mice by genetically eliminating two proteins that cause scar tissue. **14.** The Trade and Industry Secretary announced government plans to set up offshore wind farms in the Thames Estuary, the Wash and off the north-west coast. **22.** Kirsty Brown, a British marine biologist at the Rothera research station, was dragged to her death by a leopard seal during a snorkelling expedition off the Antarctic coast.

AUGUST 2003
8. A study published in the *Lancet* reported that taking hormone replacement therapy (HRT) doubled the risk of breast cancer. **10.** The Atlantic Salmon Trust reported that thousands of grilse (North Atlantic salmon) had failed to return to spawn in the European rivers and were feared dead; the fish normally return between July and early August. **13.** Scientists at King's College London reported that they had successfully grown stem cells from human embryos; stem cells can develop into any tissue in the human body, which should enable them to be used to develop treatments for conditions such as Parkinson's disease, heart disease, diabetes and paralysis. **27.** The Earth and Mars were at their closest for almost 60,000 years.

SPORT

SEPTEMBER 2002
26. The Football Association announced a £757 million scheme to build a national football stadium at Wembley. **27.** Tennis player Tim Henman won the ATP President's Cup; the event organisers cancelled further tournaments due to financial difficulties. **29.** Tony Rickardsson won the speedway grand prix for the fifth time in nine years. The European team won the Ryder Cup golfing tournament. **30.** The International Olympic Committee and the World Anti-Doping Agency banned genetic doping, a means of enhancing an athlete's performance by injecting a muscle-building gene.

OCTOBER 2002
13. Paula Radcliffe won the Chicago Marathon, breaking the world record by 1 minute, 29 seconds. **21.** Tim Don won the duathlon world title in Georgia, USA. **29.** The Jockey Club announced that two jockeys had tested positive for cocaine use in the preceding six months.

NOVEMBER 2002
4. The National Angling Alliance produced a code of conduct for coarse fishing. **11.** At the inquest into the death of the former West Bromwich Albion footballer Jeff Astle, a verdict of death by industrial disease was recorded after the inquest heard that Astle suffered from a brain condition that was likely to have been exacerbated

by heading leather footballs. **14.** The Jockey Club banned jockey Dean Gallagher for 18 months after he tested positive for cocaine on 4 September. **17.** Paula Radcliffe was awarded the women's IAAF World Athlete of the Year award at the World Athletics Gala in Monte Carlo. **24.** Ellen MacArthur won the Route du Rhum single-handed transatlantic yacht race after completing the course in the record-breaking time of 13 days, 13 hours and 47 minutes. **29.** Graham Bradley, a former jump jockey, was banned by the Jockey Club from entering any of their licensed premises after it found him guilty of race-fixing and misleading the Jockey Club committee regarding his relationship with a suspected drug smuggler; he was also fined £2,500 for bringing racing into disrepute and £400 for entering the weighing room without leave.

DECEMBER 2002
3. Aston Villa confirmed that the Football Association was investigating its former manager John Gregory over transfer dealings. An MCC spokesman said that the Ashes were considered too frail to tour Australia for the test series and would remain in the Lord's museum until after Christmas, when restoration work would commence. Be My Royal, ridden by jockey David Casey, won the Hennessy Gold Cup at Newbury despite rupturing a tendon close to the finish line. **4.** Sir Steve Redgrave, a vice-president of the British Olympic Association, appealed to the Government to back London's bid to stage the 2012 Olympic Games. **6.** Two British teenagers, Keri-Anne Payne and Stephanie Proud, won gold medals on the opening day of the junior swimming world cup in Melbourne. **8.** Paula Radcliffe was voted BBC Sports Personality of the Year and George Best was honoured with a lifetime achievement award. **16.** Ronaldo Luis Nazario de Lima was named European Footballer of the year; the following day he was named FIFA World Player of the Year. **19.** Sir Brian Mawhinney, the former Northern Ireland secretary, was appointed as the Football League's new chairman.

JANUARY 2003
5. Kenensia Bekele of Ethiopia won the Great North Cross-Country race; Edith Masai of Kenya won the women's race. England won the fifth test in the Ashes series by 225 runs, although Australia won the series by four matches to five. **11.** Lee Bowyer was given a six-match ban by UEFA for stamping on Malaga midfielder Gerardo during a UEFA Cup tie in December 2002. **13.** Fifteen-year-old Seb Clover from the Isle of Wight became the youngest yachtsman to sail solo across the Atlantic. **14.** The England and Wales Cricket Board (ECB) decided to go ahead with England's world cup fixture against Zimbabwe in Harare in February despite demonstrations from protestors opposed to the Zimbabwe regime. **15.** England cricket players announced their support for the ECB's decision to play the world cup match against Zimbabwe in February. The British Boxing Board of Control, the sport's governing body, warned trainers and boxers that they would have their licences revoked if they became involved in televised fights for charity; the warning came after the televised fight between comedian Ricky Gervais and Grant Bovey, the husband of Anthea Turner, was watched by five million people and raised £5,000 for charity. **22.** In the Australian Open quarter-final, Andy Roddick (USA) and Younes El Aynaoui (Morocco) participated in the longest final set in a tennis grand slam event since

1968; Roddick eventually won the match after a final set lasting 2 hours, 23 minutes. **24.** The International Cricket Council confirmed that England's match against Zimbabwe in Harare on 13 February would go ahead. **27.** Britain's swimming team returned home from the world cup with 21 gold, ten silver and eight bronze medals, and Alison Sheppard won the women's overall world cup prize of $50,000. **26.** Martina Navratilova became the oldest winner of a tennis grand slam title at the age of 46 after winning the Australian Open mixed doubles with Leander Paes. **27.** The England cricket team made an urgent request for their opening world cup match on 13 February to be relocated from Zimbabwe to South Africa, breaking the official line that they supported the ECB's decision to go ahead with the game. **30.** Leeds United announced the sale of player Jonathan Woodgate to Newcastle for £9 million. **31.** Peter Ridsdale, the chairman of Leeds United, was forced to recruit 24-hour protection after receiving menacing calls and threats from Leeds United football fans following his announcement of the sale of Jonathan Woodgate.

FEBRUARY 2003
1. The International Paralympic Committee decided that events for intellectually disabled athletes would not to be included in the 2004 Paralympic Games; the president of the Federation for Intellectually Disabled Athletes in Europe appealed against the decision. Charles Francis, who was given a lifetime suspension by Athletics Canada after admitting encouraging former sprinter Ben Johnson to take banned steriods, confirmed that he was working as a coaching consultant for triple Olympic champion Marion Jones and her boyfriend, the 100 metres world record-holder Tim Montgomery. **4.** The ECB made a formal request for the world cup match in Zimbabwe to be moved to a safer venue in South Africa. **5.** The French rugby union player Pieter de Villiers was dismissed from the French team by coach, Bernard Laporte after it was announced that he had tested positive for ecstasy and cocaine. **6.** The Olympic sprinter Marion Jones announced that she had cut all ties with Canadian coach Charlie Francis after her sponsor Nike advised that her future earnings could be affected if she continued to be coached by him. **8.** The cricket world cup officially opened in Cape Town, South Africa, even though a final decision had not been made as to whether England would play their opening match in Harare on 13 February. **10.** Two Zimbabwean cricketers, Henry Olonga and Andy Flower, refused to remove the black armbands they were wearing during a cricket world cup match as a protest over 'the death of democracy' in their country; on 19 February Olonga was dropped from the Zimbabwe team and the following day he was expelled from his club on the grounds that his actions had brought the game and the club into disrepute. **11.** England cricketers withdrew from their world cup match in Zimbabwe; the International Cricket Council said that the match would not automatically be rescheduled. The England rugby player Nick Duncombe died suddenly, aged 21, during a warm-weather training tour with his club Harlequins. **15.** The ICC announced that Zimbabwe had been awarded all four points from the cancelled fixture against England. Nasser Hussain, the England cricket captain, announced at a press conference that he was considering his future after becoming increasingly isolated in the row with the ICC over the cancelled match in Zimbabwe. David Beckham had two stitches to a cut above his eye after allegedly being hit by a football

boot kicked by his manager, Sir Alex Ferguson, in the Manchester United dressing room. **17.** Sir Alex Ferguson admitted injuring David Beckham, describing the incident as a 'freak act of nature' and apologised to Beckham. **22.** Shoaib Akhtar became the first cricketer to bowl at more than 100 mph while playing for Pakistan against England in a world cup match in Cape Town; his delivery was timed at 100.23 mph, the fastest ball ever recorded with an officially recognised speed gun. **23.** Paula Radcliffe won a 10 km road race in Puerto Rico in a record-breaking 30 minutes, 21 seconds. Mike Tyson knocked out Clifford Etienne in 49 seconds in a boxing match in Memphis, USA. Ellen MacArthur's team had to drop out of the Jules Verne competition for the fastest circumnavigation of the globe after their catamaran *Kingfisher* 2 was dismasted.

MARCH 2003

4. Nasser Hussain resigned as England's captain for one-day matches. **5.** The Prince of Wales was carried through the streets of Ashbourne, Derbyshire, to start the annual Shrovetide football match, played since the 15th century between the 'up'ards' and 'down'ards'. The London Marathon's board of directors announced that they would be keeping men's and women's races separate in the 2003 marathon but would allow men to pace the women's race. **15.** Andy Flower and Henry Olonga, being Zimbabwean cricketers who mounted a protest at cricket world cup match, both announcement their retirement from international cricket; Olonga said that he would remain in South Africa for the immediate future as he did not consider it safe to return to Zimbabwe. In the World Indoor Championships in Birmingham, the sprint hurdles world record holder Colin Jackson failed to win a medal in the last competition of his 18-year career; he retired after the championships. **21.** The chairman of Leeds United FC, Peter Ridsdale, announced that manager Terry Venables; Venables was replaced until the end of the season by Peter Reid. **30.** England beat Ireland to win the rugby union Six Nations Championship with a grand slam. **31.** In a statement released to the Stock Exchange, Peter Ridsdale announced he was standing down as chairman of Leeds United; he was replaced by Prof. John McKenzie.

APRIL 2003

4. During a practice for the 149th Boat Race in London, the London Authority launch *Westbourne* collided with the Cambridge boat, causing one of the rowers to suffer a sprained wrist. **5.** The Grand National was won by Monty's Pass at odds of 16-1; owner Mike Futter collected £800,000 after backing him to win. **6.** In what is thought to be the closest-ever boat race, Oxford beat Cambridge by a distance officially reckoned to be one foot. Daijiro Kato, the former 250cc motorcycling world champion, suffered serious injuries and was taken to hospital in a coma after a crash at the Japanese grand prix at Suzuka; he died on 20 April. **13.** Paula Radcliffe won the women's race in the Flora London Marathon in 2 hours, 15 minutes, 25 seconds, nearly two minutes faster than her 2002 record. Mike Weir became the first Canadian and the first left-hander to win the Masters golf tournament when he defeated Len Mattiace in Augusta, USA. **16.** The Zimbabwean cricketer Andy Flower was formally welcomed as he joined Essex county cricket club. **19.** Michaela Tabb became the first woman to referee a world championship snooker match. The semi-paralysed former boxer Michael Watson completed the

London Marathon after six days; for the last mile he was accompanied by Chris Eubank, his adversary in the fight which put him into a coma for 40 days. **23.** It was reported that the World Boxing Council had declared itself bankrupt. **30.** The 140th edition of *Wisden Cricketers' Almanack* was published, with a change to its cover for the first time since 1938. **29.** The Duke of Kent, president of the All England Lawn Tennis and Croquet Club, announced the end of the tradition that Wimbledon's Centre Court players should bow or curtsey to the royal box; the only exception is if The Queen or the Prince of Wales is present.

MAY 2003

4. Emma Richards aged 28 from Scotland became the youngest competitor to complete the 28,000 mile Around Alone yacht race. **15.** The Government announced a £2.4 billion package of public funding to support London's bid to host the 2012 Olympics. **12.** Denise Lewis, the Olympic heptathlon champion, defended her choice of Dr Ekkhart Arbeit as her coach; Arbeit was the chief athletics coach for the East German team in the 1970s and 1980s, when the state encouraged the use of illegal substances by their athletes. **19.** Pen Hadow became the first man to walk solo and unaided to the North Pole from the Canadian side, reaching the Pole in 64 days; bad weather prevented him from being picked up by plane until 27 May. **21.** Tanni Grey-Thompson, Britain's foremost wheelchair athlete, announced that she would not be competing in the world athletics championships in Paris later in the year because UK Athletics had not told her about the trial for the event. **22.** The Swedish golfer Annika Sorenstram became the first women for 58 years to participate in a men's professional tour event when she teed off at the Bank of America Colonial Tournament in Fort Worth, Texas. **31.** British Formula One driver Jenson Button survived a 180 mph crash in the Monaco grand prix.

JUNE 2003

1. Pablo Montoya won the Monaco grand prix, the first win for the BMW-Williams team in Monte Carlo since 1983. **5.** Chester-le-Street's cricket stadium became the first new test ground in England for 101 years with the start of the second match of England's mini-series against Zimbabwe. Serena Williams, the women's tennis world number one, was booed at the end of her semi-final at the French Open after being beaten by Justine Henin-Hardenne of Belgium. **13.** In The Queen's Birthday Honours, footballer David Beckham was awarded an OBE, and other honours were awarded to cricketer Alec Stewart, jockey Tony McCoy, boxer Joe Calzaghe, hurdler Colin Jackson, swimmer Alison Sheppard and footballer Shaun Goater; David Hemery, the former hurdler who stepped down as president of UK Athletics in November 2002, was awarded a CBE. **20.** The representatives of footballer David Beckham confirmed that he would join the Spanish club Real Madrid after a deal was completed with Manchester United. **22.** Lennox Lewis retained his world heavyweight title after beating Vitali Klitschko in six rounds. **26.** The Cameroon footballer Marc Vivien-Foe collapsed during a Confederations Cup semi-final in Lyons; medical staff were unable to revive him.

JULY 2003

1. Ken Bates announced that he had sold Chelsea Football Club to the Russian billionaire Roman

Abramovich for £59.3 million. **6.** Roger Federer became the first Swiss player to win the men's singles at Wimbledon, beating Australian Mark Philippoussis in straight sets. **12.** England beat South Africa in the Natwest series final at Lord's after bowling the South Africans out for 107 runs in 32.1 overs, the lowest total against England and the worst in a one-day international at Lord's by a side batting first. **14.** Valentino Rossi crossed the finishing line first at the British motorcycle grand prix but was later relegated to third place after he received a 10-second penalty for overtaking while yellow warning flags were displayed. **20.** Ben Curtis was the unexpected winner of the 132nd Open golf championship at Sandwich; ranked number 396 in the world, British bookmakers had given odds of 750-1 against his victory. **21.** British free-diver Tanya Streeter reached a depth of 400 feet in the variable ballast discipline, beating both the women's and men's records. **22.** Alec Stewart announced his retirement from test cricket at the end of the 2003 season. **23.** James Gibson of Great Britain won the gold medal in the 50 metres breaststroke at the world championships in Barcelona. **27.** Lance Armstrong won the Tour de France for the fifth successive year. **28.** Nasser Hussain resigned from his post as captain of the England cricket team. **31.** Michael Vaughan captained the England cricket team for the second test against South Africa at Lord's. Austrian skydiver Felix Baumgartner became the first person to fly across the English Channel without power; he achieved this in 12 minutes, 3 seconds after free-falling at a speed of 220 mph from a height of 30,000 feet above Dover with the aid of a 6 foot carbon-fibre wing.

AUGUST 2003

2. On the third day of the second test at Lord's the South African cricketer, Graeme Smith scored 259 runs, the highest test score by an overseas player at Lord's. **15.** Paula Radcliffe withdrew from Britain's team for the world championships in Paris after deciding that she was not fit enough to run. **16.** Christiano Ronaldo made his debut for Manchester Utd when he was brought on as a substitute in United's first premiership game of the season. **17.** Shaun Micheel, ranked 136th in the world, won the US PGA golf championship. **18.** England won the third test against South Africa at Trent Bridge, with James Kirtley capturing the final South African wicket in his bowling debut for England. **23.** The World Athletics Championships began in Paris. **25.** Jonathan Edwards, the reigning Olympic triple jump champion and world record holder, announced his retirement at the world championships in Paris.

INTERNATIONAL EVENTS

AFRICA

SEPTEMBER 2002

1. The rebel Sudan People's Liberation Movement captured the town of Torit; government forces recaptured the town on 6 October. **13.** An Italian ship ran aground off Cape St Lucia, around 600 km east of Johannesburg, and began leaking oil. mid-September. **17.** Rwandan troops began to withdraw from the Democratic Republic of Congo. **19.** Fighting broke out in Abidjan, Côte d'Ivoire, between government forces and rebel soldiers protesting against plans to force them to retire; a ceasefire was agreed on 3 October. **27.** A ferry sank off the coast of Senegal; the death toll was 1,200.

OCTOBER 2002

10. In a border dispute between Cameroon and Nigeria, the International Court of Justice ruled in favour of Cameroon, giving it possession of the oil-rich Bakassi peninsula. **25.** In the Central African Republic, rebel forces loyal to former chief of general staff François Bozize occupied much of northern Bangui. **27.** In Togo, elections to the National Assembly took place; the ruling Togolese People's Rally won the most seats. **30.** There were nine bomb blasts in Soweto; one person was killed.

NOVEMBER 2002

4. In Senegal, President Wade dismissed the government, apparently because of the ferry disaster in September. **10.** In South Africa, the 'Warriors of the Boer Nation', a right-wing extremist group, claimed responsibility for the bomb explosions in September. **12.** In Zimbabwe, an US aid worker was shot dead at a road block by security forces. **17.** A bomb blast damaged a police station in Cape Town, South Africa; as a result, the hunt was stepped up for Kobus Pretorius and his two brothers, believed to be responsible for other bomb attacks. **19.** Ten people were killed and about 278 injured when riots broke out in Nigeria in protest at the Miss World competition due to be held there in December. **21.** In Algeria, 12 people were killed in three separate attacks by suspected Islamic extremists in Algeria. **22.** There was further rioting in Nigeria in protest at the staging of the 'Miss World' contest; more than 100 people were killed and 500 injured. **23.** The 'Miss World' contestants were flown from Nigeria to England, after the organisers of the competition decided to hold it in England. **24.** In Algeria, a militant group linked to al-Qa'eda killed nine soldiers and four police officers. **26.** Nigeria's Islamic authority issued a 'fatwa' against the journalist who wrote the article about the Miss World contest that sparked the recent riots. **28.** Two synchronised terrorist attacks took place in Kenya, leaving 15 dead; in the first, two surface-to-air missiles were fired at an Israeli plane but missed, while in the second attack a suicide bomber successfully targeted the Israeli-owned 'Paradise Hotel'; 12 suspects were arrested the following day; on 8 December, al-Qa'eda claimed responsibility for the attacks.

DECEMBER 2002

3. The government of Burundi signed a cease fire agreement with the main Hutu rebel group in the hope of ending the nine-year civil war. **7.** Zambia's home affairs minister, Lackson Mapushi, died in a car crash. **17.** The government of the Democratic Republic of Congo and

the country's main rebel groups signed a power-sharing deal in South Africa with the intention of ending the civil conflict. **15.** Presidential elections took place in Equatorial Guinea; the incumbent president Teodoro Obiang Nguena Mbasogo won a landslide victory. **24.** The Ugandan government and the rebel Uganda National Rescue Front signed a peace deal under which the rebels would receive money for resettlement and a number of low-ranking government positions. **29.** The National Rainbow Coalition won landslide victories in Kenya's presidential, parliamentary and local elections.

JANUARY 2003

5. Islamic rebels in Algeria ambushed government forces, killing 43; in a separate attack, rebels killed 13 civilians during a raid on a village in the Zabana region. **7.** In South Africa, five carriages of a passenger train derailed outside Cape Town; at least 11 people died and up to 40 were injured. **8.** United Nations investigators found evidence to support reports that Congolese rebels had killed and eaten pygmies. **10.** Pokot tribesmen crossed the border from Kenya into Uganda and attacked Karamojong herdsmen in the Nakapiripirit district; 52 people were killed. **12.** The Rwandan government was obliged to release from prison the first of some 40,000 genocide suspects because the country's prisons are unable to cope with the number of suspects. **21.** One man died and seven were injured in a firebomb attack on the offices of the ruling Zanu (PF) party in Harare, Zimbabwe; the Movement for Democratic Change was blamed for the attack. **24.** A Kenyan government minister was killed and three other ministers injured when their plane crashed shortly after takeoff. **31.** Mobs attacked French soldiers in Abidjan, Côte d'Ivoire.

FEBRUARY 2003

2. In Nigeria, an explosion in the centre of Lagos killed 30 people. **5.** In the Democratic Republic of Congo, a heavy storm killed 164 people, injured more than 1,700, and destroyed thousands of homes. **10.** Two Zimbabwean cricketers, Henry Olonga and Andy Flower, refused to remove black armbands that they were wearing during a cricket world cup match against Namibia in Harare in protest at 'the death of democracy' in their country; on 19 February Olonga was dropped from the Zimbabwe team and the following day he was expelled from his club on the grounds that his actions had brought the game and the club into disrepute.

MARCH 2003

5. In Nigeria, a leading opposition politician of the All Nigeria People's Party, Harry Marshall, was murdered in what was believed to be a political assassination. **6.** An Air Algérie passenger jet crashed soon after take-off from Tamanrasset in the Sahara desert, killing all but one of the 104 people on board. **17.** The Commonwealth announced that it was extending its suspension of Zimbabwe for a further nine months. **19.** In South Africa, 23 Afrikaaners were indicted for high treason, for their part in a plan to assassinate Nelson Mandela.

APRIL 2003

3. In the Democratic Republic of Congo, at least 1,000 people were murdered in attacks in the Ituri province. **7.** President Joseph Kabila was sworn in as the head of a transitional government in the Democratic Republic of Congo. **23.** Ninety per cent of Zimbabwe's workers went on strike in protest at a 300 per cent fuel price rise. **25.**

Winnie Mandela received a five-year prison sentence for her involvement in an £80,000 bank loan fraud. **28.** Around 70 British and US oil workers were trapped on four oil rigs off Nigeria by a strike.

MAY 2003
9. Floods caused by heavy rains in south-east Ethiopia killed at least 38 and displaced nearly 100,000. **10.** The doors of an aircraft opened in mid-flight over the Democratic Republic of Congo when the pressure system broke down; at least 120 passengers were sucked out of the aircraft to their deaths. **14.** Seventeen European tourists held hostage in the Sahara by a terrorist group were flown home. **15.** Kenyan authorities warned that Fazul Abdallah Mohammed, an al-Qa'eda suspect wanted in connection with the 1998 bombings of US embassies in Nairobi and Dar es Salaam, was believed to be planning another attack. **16.** There were four explosions in Casablanca, Morocco, in what appeared to be a co-ordinated attack on a Jewish centre and tourist targets; 41 people died and 60 were injured. **21.** An earthquake in northern Algeria killed more than 2,000 people and injured around 7,000. **27.** A second earthquake in Algeria left three people dead and 187 injured.

JUNE 2003
1. In Togo, presidential elections resulted in victory for the incumbent, Gnassingbé Eyadema. A 'mass action' began by Harare residents and students demanding President Mugabe's resignation. **3.** In the Democratic Republic of Congo, militia attacked humanitarian workers and their families in Bunia. **4.** President Charles Taylor of Liberia was indicted for crimes against humanity by the UN-backed international war crimes tribunal for Sierra Leone. **8.** Rebels in Mauritania mounted an unsuccessful coup against the president. **22.** In Malawi, five men suspected of helping to channel money to al-Qa'eda were arrested; on 24 June the men were handed over to US officials. Rebels of the Lord's Resistance Army attacked the town of Soroti and abducted over 50 schoolgirls. Four Kenyans were charged with the murder of 10 Kenyans and three Israeli tourists in the hotel bombing in Mombasa in November 2002. **30.** In Algeria, a military aircraft crashed into houses in a town south-west of Algiers, killing 15 people. A general strike in Nigeria, called by the Nigeria Labour Congress to protest at a petrol price increase of more than 50 per cent, paralysed most of the main cities.

JULY 2003
2. Hundreds of Kenyan women who claim they were raped by British soldiers stationed in the country won legal aid to sue the Ministry of Defence. **8.** A plane carrying 117 passengers crashed during an emergency landing in Sudan; the sole survivor was a three-year-old boy. **17.** In the Democratic Republic of Congo, the first power-sharing transitional government, headed by Joseph Kabila, was sworn in. **20.** Liberian rebels reached the outskirts of the capital, Monrovia. **22.** Liberian rebels extended their control over Monrovia as President Taylor vowed to 'fight till the last man'. A plane crashed into Mount Kenya, killing 12 US tourists on board. **25.** President Bush ordered a US amphibious task force to stand by off the coast of Liberia as Liberians pleaded for international help. **26.** The Algerian government offered safe passage to members of an extremist Islamic group if they would free 15 European tourists held in a remote mountain area for more than five months; 14 hostages

were freed on 19 August, amid speculation that Germany had paid a ransom for them. **29.** Nigeria said that it would not send troops to help end the fighting in Liberia unless western countries provided further funding for the operation.

AUGUST 2003
3. Heavy fighting continued in Liberia despite President Taylor's pledge to leave office on 11 August. **5.** The former Zambian president Frederick Chiluba was charged with stealing more than £20 million from public funds and for fraudulent behaviour. **7.** Thousands of Liberians welcomed to Monrovia a convoy of 100 Nigerian peacekeepers sent to police the unstable ceasefire and lift the siege of the city by rebel forces. **13.** US troops were deployed in Liberia to support the peacekeeping operation of West African countries. In Burundi, 200 people were believed to have died in an attack on the capital, Bujumbura, by Hutu rebels. **15.** Libya sent a letter to the UN Security Council admitting responsibility for the Lockerbie bombing in 1988. **18.** In Liberia, a peace agreement was signed by government and rebel forces. **19.** A number of Islamic extremists were convicted of involvement in the suicide attacks in Morocco in May; four men were sentenced to death. Zimbabwe's government banned international relief agencies from distributing food aid and demanded that they hand over their stocks to the government. **20.** Libya began transferring funds to the Bank for International Settlements to compensate families of the Lockerbie bombing victims. **25.** Rwanda's first official presidential election since the 1994 genocide took place; the incumbent president, Paul Kagame, gained more than 95 per cent of the vote. France stated that despite the deaths of two servicemen in Côte d'Ivoire, it was still committed to restoring peace in the country.

THE AMERICAS

SEPTEMBER 2002
11. The anniversary of the terrorist attacks on New York and Washington in 2001 was marked by religious services and other ceremonies throughout the USA. **23.** A contingency plan was issued for vaccinating all US citizens against smallpox within five days in the event of a biological terror attack.

OCTOBER 2002
1. Two people died and dozens were injured after a passenger on a Greyhound bus to San Francisco slashed the driver's throat. **3.** More than 500,000 residents in Louisiana and Texas were evacuated as 'Hurricane Lili' reached the US coast. Six people were killed in a series of random shootings by a gunman in Montgomery County, Washington DC. **4.** John Walker Lindh, a US recruit to the Taliban, was jailed for 20 years for fighting in Afghanistan. A 64-year-old woman with lung cancer was awarded $28 billion in damages against the Philip Morris tobacco company, in the biggest individual damages award in US history. A seventh victim was wounded by the sniper in Montgomery County, Washington. **7.** A 13-year-old boy became the eighth person to be shot by the Washington sniper; he was wounded. **9.** A ninth person was killed by the Washington sniper at a petrol station. **11.** The tenth victim of the sniper was killed near Fredericksburg, Virginia. **14.** The eleventh victim of the sniper was shot dead. **19.** The twelfth sniper victim was

shot dead. **22.** The thirteenth victim of the sniper was shot dead. **24.** Two men believed to have carried out the sniper attacks in Washington DC were arrested in Maryland. **25.** President Bush and President Jiang Zemin of China met at Bush's Texas ranch and stated their united opposition to North Korea's nuclear weapons strategy. A senator and his wife and daughter were killed when their private aircraft crashed. **28.** Luiz Inacio Lula da Silva won the Brazilian presidential election with 46.4 per cent of the vote. A gunmen killed three people in a classroom at the University of Arizona nursing school in Tucson. Rap DJ Jason Mizell, of the group Run DMC, was shot dead by intruders at a recording studio.

NOVEMBER 2002

5. The Republicans won a fifth consecutive majory in the the US mid-term elections to the House of Representatives. **7.** Virginia was chosen as the location for the trial of the two men arrested for the Washington sniper killings. **8.** President Bush issued his strongest threat yet that he was ready to go to war with Iraq if Saddam Hussein refused to comply with new conditions proposed by UN weapons inspectors. Colombia extended the country's state of emergency (declared in August) for a further 90 days. **11.** At least 36 people were killed and hundreds were missing after more than 50 tornados hit eastern America. **14.** Aimal Khan Kasi, who was found guilty of the murder of two CIA employees in Pakistan in 1993, was executed in Virginia. **15.** Colombian security forces rescued a bishop and a priest four days after they were kidnapped by Marxist guerillas. **18.** In Venezuela, three people were killed in Caracas amid violent protests after the army took control of the police force. **19.** Legislation was passed allowing civilian pilots on US airliners flying to Britain to carry guns and to shoot dead terrorists or deranged passengers who try to seize the controls of the aircraft. **23.** The Bolivian president, Gonzálo Sánchez de Lozada, introduced legislation extending state healthcare insurance coverage for women and children. **31.** Following a series of bribery scandals in Chile involving public sector workers and politicians, measures were introduced to increase accountability and transparency in the public sector.

DECEMBER 2002

2. A fire in a crowded basement nightclub in Caracas, Venezuela, killed at least 47 people. **7.** In Caracas, gunmen opened fire in a plaza crowded with opposition demonstrators, killing three people and wounding 28. A man was found guilty of shooting a hole in the trans-Alaska oil pipeline in 2001 while drunk. **11.** The European rocket Ariane-5 crashed into the Atlantic Ocean shortly after take-off from Korou, French Guiana. **13.** Henry Kissinger resigned as chairman of an independent inquiry into the 11 September 2001 attacks. **15.** President Bush expanded the CIA's powers, giving agents the right to kill up to 25 specified suspected terrorists, including Osama bin Laden, without the need for presidential approval. **18.** Some of the world's top architects revealed their plans for the World Trade Center site, after the public rejected the initial redevelopment plans as lacking in grandeur. **29.** The US Secretary of State, Colin Powell, ruled out an attack on North Korea in spite of the country's apparent plans to develop nuclear weapons. The Raelian cult, which had claimed to have created the world's first human clone, came under investigation by the US government. **27.** A month-long general strike that was crippling Venezuela's oil industry forced the country to import food from the Dominican Republic and petrol from Brazil, and to negotiate with Colombia for milk and meat.

JANUARY 2003

3. A man was sentenced to death in California for the kidnap and murder of seven-year-old Danielle van Dam in February 2002. **6.** President Bush announced a series of tax cuts, the aim of which was to aid the faltering US economy. **8.** A man was sentenced to death for his role in forcing seven restaurant staff into a freezer, where five were shot dead and two were wounded. **12.** Leopoldo Galtieri, the Argentine dictator who ordered the invasion of the Falkland Islands, died from a heart attack at the age of 76. The USA announced the deployment of 62,000 troops to the Gulf. **15.** Lucio Gutierrez was sworn in as the new president of Ecuador. **16.** Argentina reached an agreement with the International Monetary Fund to stave off an immediate default on its debts and relieve the pressure on its fragile economy. **17.** Mudslides swept through shantytowns in south-eastern Brazil, leaving at least 14 people dead. **22.** An earthquake, measuring 7.6 on the Richter Scale, in western Mexico killed at least 26 people and injured 400. **24.** A British journalist and her US colleague were kidnapped in Columbia by members of the left-wing rebel group ELN. **30.** Richard Reid, the Briton who tried to blow up a trans-Atlantic jet with explosives hidden in his shoe, was sentenced to life imprisonment by a US court.

FEBRUARY 2003

1. The space shuttle *Columbia* disintegrated on re-entry into the earth's atmosphere, killing all seven astronauts on board; NASA was accused of ignoring warnings from its own technicians and government auditors that a space shuttle disaster was imminent. **2.** The hostages kidnapped in Colombia in January were released. **6.** In Colombia, a car bomb exploded outside a club hosting a children's party and a wedding reception, killing 31 people and injuring 160. **17.** A fight in a nightclub in Chicago caused a stampede for the exit in which 21 people were crushed to death. **21.** A fire in a Rhode Island nightclub killed at least 95 people and more than 160 were injured. On Staten Island, New York, an explosion on a barge containing 100,000 barrels of petrol killed two men and injured another. **28.** Daniel Libeskind was appointed chief architect of the World Trade Center site development in New York.

MARCH 2003

13. Elizabeth Smart, a 15-year-old Mormon girl abducted at knifepoint from her bedroom in June 2002, was found alive and well 12 miles from her home. **16.** Cases of the Sars virus began to be diagnosed in Canada. **24.** US leaders expressed anger at Iraqi television footage showing the bodies of four US soldiers, claiming that the footage broke the Geneva Conventions; the soldiers were believed to have been executed. **25.** President Bush made an emergency request to Congress for some $75 billion additional funding for the war in Iraq. **26.** More than 30,000 US reinforcements were ordered to the Gulf. **27.** Four senior commanders at the USA's leading air force officer training school were dismissed after complaints by women recruits of rape and sexual harassment. **28.** Many hospitals were closed in the Toronto area of Canada in an attempt to prevent the spread of the Sars virus, and those involved in the treatment of Sars patients were asked to go into voluntary quarantine. **31.** In Bolivia, 700 people were missing after a landslide buried 400 houses in the north of the country.

APRIL 2003

2. Cuban authorities thwarted an attempt by five people to hijack a ferry from Havana; three men were executed on 11 April after being convicted of terrorism. **8.** Cuba was severely criticised by other countries after 71 dissidents, democracy activists and journalists were jailed for up to 27 years for treason and collaboration with the USA. **23.** The World Health Organisation warned travellers against visiting the Canadian city of Toronto because of the Sars virus outbreak; the Canadian government reacted with anger to the warning. **28.** Two Canadian Sikhs pleaded not guilty to causing an explosion that destroyed a jumbo jet 18 years ago, killing all 329 passengers flying from Montreal to London.

MAY 2003

5. Tornadoes in the Midwest and southern USA killed 38 people. **8.** In Utah, a climber who had broken his arm and spent five days pinned by a fallen boulder on a narrow ledge in a remote canyon, amputated his arm in order to escape. **14.** Former president Carlos Menem pulled out of the imminent presidential election in Argentina after opinion polls indicated that he had little chance of winning; the election was won by default to Nestor Kirchner. Texan sheriffs discovered the bodies of 17 Mexicans believed to be illegal immigrants after the driver who smuggled them over the border abandoned his cargo. **21.** Legislative elections in Barbados were won by the governing Barbados Labour Party in a landslide victory. A bomb destroyed a classroom at Yale University without harming anyone; no-one claimed responsibility for planting the device. **24.** In Venezuela, clashes occurred as opponents of President Chavez held a protest in a pro-Chavez area in Caracas; one person was shot dead and 22 were injured. **25.** Nestor Kirchner took office as Argentina's sixth president in 18 months.

JUNE 2003

4. Thousands of students, striking government workers and teachers staged protests throughout Peru in defiance of the state of emergency imposed by President Toledo. **5.** Two editors at the *New York Times*, Howell Raines and Gerald Boyes, resigned after a scandal over a young reporter who fabricated stories for years before being exposed. **23.** In Brazil, police began to investigate the deaths of 21 people who died after treatment with an apparently corrupt version of a drug used in X-rays and other radiological examinations. **24.** President Bush pledged to work with Congress to send billions of dollars in aid to Pakistan, half of it for defence, as thanks for the country's support in the war against terrorism.

JULY 2003

2. The US suspended military aid to 35 countries, including South Africa, Colombia and Venezuela, which had not granted US citizens immunity from prosecution by the International Criminal Court. **9.** A 38-year-old man from Arkansas awoke from a 19-year coma. **17.** Honduran police found 2 tonnes of cocaine aboard the British-registered *Board Fire Leader*. **26.** In Brazil, riot police used tear gas to break up a stampede by thousands of people who had been queuing for days in Rio to apply for 2,000 refuse collection jobs. The US Supreme Court overturned a Texan law which outlawed homosexual sex.

AUGUST 2003

5. The first actively homosexual bishop, Canon Gene Robinson, was endorsed as Bishop of New Hampshire by bishops of the Episcopal Church of America. Film actor Arnold Schwarzenegger announced that he would run for the governorship of the state of California in forthcoming elections. **9.** US prosecutors accused al-Qa'eda suspect Zacarias Moussaoui of plotting to hijack a fifth aircraft for an attack on the White House on 11 September 2001. **10.** The first extra-terrestrial wedding took place between a cosmonaut in space and a US woman in Texas; the ceremony was conducted via satellite link. **14.** A massive power cut affected New York, other parts of the US north-east and two Canadian cities. **22.** A Brazilian space rocket exploded at its launch site, killing 19 people. **24.** A Haitian plane crashed on take-off from Cap Haitian, killing all 21 on board. **25.** Colombia's two most powerful rebel groups, FARC and ELN, announced that they would fight together. **27.** A man about to lose his job in Chicago shot dead six of his colleagues before being killed by police. **28.** The USA abandoned its opposition to a multilateral UN force in Iraq, indicating that it was prepared to let its soldiers serve under UN command. **29.** Transcripts of the final telephone calls of people trapped in the World Trade Center when the two towers collapsed on 11 September 2001 were made publicly available, amid some controversy. A teenager from Minnesota was charged with creating and releasing computer viruses that had crippled email systems world-wide.

ASIA

SEPTEMBER 2002

17. The Japanese prime minister made public for the first time that North Korea had abducted a number of Japanese citizens between 1977 and 1983. **23.** Islamic gunmen stormed a crowded Hindu temple in Gujarat, India, killing at least 29 people. **25.** Seven Christian charity workers were murdered in Pakistan by gunmen who raided their office. **25.** In China, 21 children died at a junior school after a staircase bannister rail gave way and they fell; four school officials were arrested. In Burma, four people were sentenced to death by hanging after being found guilty of treason. **30.** A Chinese shopkeeper was sentenced to death for killing at least 38 people and leaving hundreds seriously ill after putting rat poison in snacks sold by a rival.

OCTOBER 2002

2. In Kashmir, at least 13 people were killed in a series of attacks by militant separatists attempting to disrupt elections. **3.** At least ten soldiers and civilians were killed by separatist militants in Kashmir. **9.** The party that had dominated Indian-controlled Kashmir for half a century conceded defeat lost control of the state assembly. **12.** In Bali, a car bomb exploded outside the Sari nightclub; the eventual toll was put at 190 dead and 300 injured, the majority of them young Australian tourists. **17.** In the southern Philippines, six people died and 143 were wounded by bombs in a bazaar in Zamboanga. **22.** An oil tanker sank in the Caspian Sea off the coast of Azerbaijan. **27.** Thirty-six bodies were recovered from a coalmine in Lulinag, northern China after a gas explosion. **28.** Hakusui Ito, a right-wing Japanese politician, was arrested on suspicion of murdering an opposition MP, Kouki Ishii. **29.** In Vietnam, 48 people were killed by a fire in a five-storey building in Ho Chi Minh City.

NOVEMBER 2002

7. An Indonesian man admitted playing a major role in the Bali bombing. **8.** In Thailand, a new law came into force making it illegal to smoke in virtually every indoor public place. **10.** In the Philippines, a plane carrying 34 people crashed into Manila Bay shortly after takeoff; 17 passengers and crew were rescued. In Bali, police announced that the man who bought the van used in the nightclub bombing was a student of Abu Bakar Bashir, associated with the terrorist group Jemaah Islamiah thought to be behind the bombing. **14.** China signalled the identity of a new national leader, by declaring that all other contenders for the job were ineligible; on 15 November Jiang Zemin emerged as the new leader. **15.** A Hindu ceremony took place in Bali for the victims of the Sari club bombing and their families on the site of the club. **17.** North Korea claimed to have developed nuclear weapons. Indonesian police identified Imam Samudra as the mastermind of the Bali bombings; he is believed to have been trained in bomb-making by al-Qa'eda; Imam Samudra was arrested on 21 November as he boarded a ferry on Java and confessed the following day to a role in a series of bombings in 2000 that killed 19 people. **18.** A landmine exploded under a bus in Andhra Pradesh state, India, killing at least 30 people. **21.** In Pakistan, Mir Zafarullah Jamali was elected prime minister. **24.** In Jammu and Kashmir, Indian security forces ended a siege of two Hindu temples by an Islamic suicide group; 12 people died.

DECEMBER 2002

4. East Timor declared a state of emergency after police firing on a student demonstration caused the demonstrators to go on the rampage, looting and setting buildings alight. **5.** In an attempt to the end the civil war, the Sri Lankan government and Tamil rebels agreed to work on a peace deal that would give regional autonomy to rebel-held areas. **7.** In Bangladesh, bombs exploded in four separate cinemas, killing at least 20 people and injuring about 300. **11.** A peace deal was signed between Indonesian diplomats and rebels from the northern province of Aceh. In Japan, Masumi Hayashi was sentenced to death for the murders of four people and injury of 63 others after she served arsenic-laced curry at a summer festival in 1998. **12.** North Korea responded to the USA's halting of its oil aid by stating that it would restart a nuclear power plant suspected of supplying weapons-grade plutonium. **15.** Pakistan said that it had foiled a plot by Islamic militants to kill US diplomats. In India, violence erupted in Gujarat after Hindu nationalists celebrated a landslide victory in the state's elections. **18.** In India, three men were sentenced to death for helping to plan an attack on India's parliament on 13 December 2001. **27.** North Korea ordered UN observers to leave the Yongbyon nuclear power plant. **29.** The temperature in the mountains in western Azerbaijan fell to −28°C, the lowest for 106 years. In the Philippines, a giant concrete bust of former president Ferdinand Marcos carved into a mountainside was blown up by an unidentified man.

JANUARY 2003

10. North Korea withdrew from the global treaty limiting nuclear weapons, which prompted urgent talks between President Bush and the Chinese government.

25. In Afghanistan, the first women for more than a decade took driving tests; under the Taliban regime, driving for women was a crime punishable by death. **26.** The first direct flight from Taiwan to mainland China for more than half a century took off. **31.** US spy satellites detected signs that North Korea was removing its stockpile of spent nuclear fuel rods from storage, giving rise to fears that it was preparing to produce nuclear weapons.

FEBRUARY 2002

5. North Korea claimed to have restarted a nuclear reactor capable of producing weapons-grade plutonium. **6.** North Korea's leadership threatened a pre-emptive strike against the USA as the nuclear weapons crisis and domestic troubles deepened. North Korea warned that a US strike against its nuclear facilities would trigger an attack on South Korea. Indian police arrested a Muslim cleric alleged to have plotted the murder of 58 Hindus, killed when their train was set alight in February 2002. **11.** In China, the outbreak of severe acute respiratory syndrome (Sars), a serious disease with pneumonia-like symptoms believed to have originated in southern China in November 2002, was affecting about 300 people. **12.** The CIA stated that North Korea had nuclear weapons and a missile that could reach the west coast of the USA. Ali Imron confessed to involvement in the Bali bombing in October 2002 and expressed regret for the deaths of non-Americans. **13.** Japan threatened a pre-emptive strike against North Korea if it prepared a ballistic missile attack. **18.** In South Korea, more than 130 people were killed after a man set fire to an underground train in Daegu; he was later identified as a suicidal psychiatric patient who did not want to die alone. **20.** Seventeen people were killed in a plane crash in north-west Pakistan, including Pakistan's air force commander, his wife and several senior officers. **25.** Roh Moo-Hyun was sworn in as the new president of South Korea. **24.** North Korea test-fired a missile into the Sea of Japan. An earthquake in western China measuring 6.8 on the Richter scale killed at least 257 people and injured more than 1,000. **28.** In Pakistan, a gunman shot two policemen dead and wounded five others outside the US consulate in Karachi.

MARCH 2003

1. Khalid Sheikh Mohammed, regarded as the mastermind behind the al-Qa'eda attacks in the USA on 11 September 2001, was captured in Pakistan. **3.** Four North Korean fighter planes intercepted and shadowed a US military plane for 22 minutes over the Sea of Japan. **5.** A bomb believed to be the responsibility of Islamic militants exploded at an airport in Davao in the south Philippines; 20 people were killed and 115 injured. **10.** North Korea fired a second missile into the Sea of Japan. **13.** In India, a bomb exploded on a train in Bombay, killing at least ten people. **17.** The Sars virus outbreak was now affecting China, Vietnam, Singapore, Hong Kong, the Philippines, Indonesia and Thailand. After weekend elections China announced that Wen Jiabao had been elected prime minister and Hu Jintao, the leader of the National People's Congress, had become President, but it was clear that Jiang Zemin would continue to head the military. **26.** China admitted that a Sars outbreak in Guangdong province was much worse than first thought, with 31 out of 792 cases proving fatal; in Singapore, schools were ordered to close for nine days after recording the first fatality from the Sars virus. North Korea stated that it was increasing its military budget in order to put the state's entire population under arms. **28.** Japan launched its first spy satellites to counter the threat from North Korea.

APRIL 2003
1. A bomb in the southern Philippines killed up to 15 people and wounded 44 others as they disembarked from a ferry. The Hong Kong government opened quarantine camps in an attempt to stop the spread of the Sars virus. **2.** In the Philippines, bombs exploded outside three mosques in Davao. **7.** More fatalities in China, Hong Kong and Singapore from the Sars virus put the death toll at 101. **8.** Officials in Hong Kong suggested that the Sars outbreak could have been spread by cockroaches carrying the disease from floor to floor in a single office block. **9.** In Afghanistan, 11 civilians were killed when a US bomb missed its target and landed on a house. **17.** In Pakistan, a man was sentenced to death for shooting dead seven members of his family in a so-called honour killing because his daughter had decided to marry a Christian. **18.** South Korea announced that it had reopened a reprocessing plant capable of producing weapons-grade plutonium within months. **22.** A Pakistani army helicopter crashed in northern Pakistan, killing all on board. **23.** In China, the USA and North Korea held their first talks since the nuclear crisis began; it subsequently emerged that North Korea had offered to scrap its nuclear programme and to allow weapons inspectors back into the country. **24.** The worst storm in north-east India for decades flattened villages in the Dhubri district; at least 38 people were killed, more than 2,000 were injured, and hundreds were missing. **25.** North Korea told the USA that it possessed a nuclear bomb and reportedly threatened to sell weapons-grade plutonium to the highest bidder. In Bangladesh, at least 200 people were killed in fierce storms. **27.** In Indonesia, 11 people were injured when a bomb exploded at an airport outside Jakarta. **28.** Sixteen Chinese officials were dismissed for dereliction of duty during the Sars epidemic as the country continued its struggle to contain the virus. **29.** Thousands of people attacked local government offices outside Beijing and a Sars quarantine centre was set ablaze in civil unrest sparked by the illness.

MAY 2003
1. The Indian prime minister, Atal Behari Vajpayee, announced that India would restore diplomatic respresentation and air links with Pakistan in an attempt to reduce tension between the two nations. **6.** China ordered 10,000 more people into quarantine in Nanjing, after a new outbreak of Sars was suspected. **12.** Amrozi bin Nurhasyim went on trial for his role in the Bali bombing in 2002. **19.** Indonesia mounted a military offensive against separatists in the province of Aceh. Sri Lanka experienced its worst flooding in half a century; some 200 were feared dead. **21.** The Japanese prime minister stated that Japan has the right to make a pre-emptive strike on any country preparing to attack it. **23.** The Everest speed climbing record was broken by a Nepalese Sherpa who reached the summit in 12 hours, 45 minutes. **26.** Two ferries collided at the mouth of Manila Bay, killing 28 of the 1,600 passengers on the two vessels. India announced that it would resume bus links with Pakistan. An earthquake measuring 7.2 on the Richter Scale hit northern Japan; 98 people were injured. **28.** Two men were killed when their helicopter crashed at base camp on Mount Everest.

JUNE 2003
1. China reported that no new deaths from Sars had occurred since mid-April. **2.** In Pakistan, a bill was passed to implement Sharia law in the North-West Frontier province. **5.** It was decided to withdraw US troops from the demilitarised zone between North and South Korea after the US government concluded that they were within easy range of North Korean artillery fire. The Afghan government claimed that more than 40 Taliban rebel fighters had been killed in the heaviest fighting since the Taliban regime was overthrown. **9.** North Korea justified the nation's pursuit of nuclear weapons by stating that it was to reduce the expense of conventional weaponry to defend the country. **10.** Japan detained two North Korean cargo ships in Japanese ports. **11.** The prime minister of Kazakhstan, Imangaly Tasmagambetov, announced his resignation. **12.** In Mongolia, a mass grave dating from the 1930s was discovered in Ulaanbaatar; it contained the remains of about 1,000 victims. **13.** Daniyal Akhmetov was appointed prime minister of Kazakhstan. **15.** North and South Korea reconnected railway tracks in the middle of the demilitarised zone between the two countries. **17.** The WHO lifted its warning against travel to Taiwan, stating that the Taiwanese health authorities had brought the Sars epidemic under control. **23.** In Afghanistan, a US-led assault began against suspected Taliban and al-Qa'eda fighters along the country's border with Pakistan. Hong Kong was removed from the WHO's list of areas affected by Sars. **24.** The WHO lifted its warning against travel to Beijing, China, after the Sars outbreak appeared to be diminishing. **30.** In Pakistan three Islamic militants were sentence to death for planning a suicide bomb attack that killed 11 French engineers in Karachi in 2002.

JULY 2003
4. A suicide bombing at a Shi'ite mosque in Quetta, south-western Pakistan, left at least 44 dead and 65 injured. **8.** Two Iranian sisters joined at the head since birth died after an operation lasting more than 50 hours attempted to separate them. **9.** In Bangladesh at least 400 people drowned when an overcrowded ferry was sucked into a whirlpool. **10.** In Hong Kong 21 passengers died after their bus plunged off a bridge after colliding with a lorry. **20.** US intelligence officials claimed that there was strong evidence that North Korea had built a second secret plant capable of producing weapons grade plutonium. **21.** Hundreds of Taleban fighters crossed into Afghanistan from Pakistan and claimed large areas of the country, according to the US commander of coalition forces in Kabul. **26.** North Korea threatened to conduct underground nuclear tests. Three earthquakes hit north-east Japan; more than 420 people were injured. **27.** Philippine army mutineers who had barricaded themselves into a shopping centre in Manila and packed it with explosives surrendered to loyalist forces.

AUGUST 2003
3. North Korea confirmed that it would hold multilateral talks on its nuclear weapons programme. **4.** More than 10,000 people falsely declared dead in northern India by greedy relatives and corrupt officials wanting to steal their land staged a protest in Lucknow to prove that they were still alive. **5.** In Indonesia a car bomb exploded outside a hotel in Jakarta, killing at least 14 people and injuring about 150; the blast was blamed on the Islamic extremist group Jemaah Islamiyah. **7.** Amrozi bin Nurhasyim was sentenced to death by firing squad for his part in the Bali

bombings of October 2002. **8.** Amrozi bin Nurhasyim announced he wanted to appeal against the death sentence imposed upon him. **13.** In Afghanistan, at least 61 people were killed and dozens injured in the worst outbreak of violence for more than a year. **17.** Indonesian police arrested nine suspects in connection with the Jakarta hotel bombing. **25.** Two huge car bombs exploded in Bombay, killing at least 47 people and injuring about 143. More than 50 Taliban fighters were killed in Kabul in an operation by US and Afghan government forces. **26.** India blamed the Bombay bomb blasts on a Pakistan-backed Muslim insurgent group and accused Pakistan of inciting terrorism in India. **28.** North Korea threatened to test a nuclear weapon and declare itself a nuclear state. **30.** Afghan forces supported by US forces and aircraft killed about 20 militants.

AUSTRALASIA AND THE PACIFIC

SEPTEMBER 2002
6. The Aborigine Mirrar people responded positively to an offer by the Anglo-Australian mining company Rio Tinto to close the Jabiluka uranium mine in Kakadu national park. **12.** The Australian Nuclear Science and Technology Organisation, the government's nuclear safety body, approved the construction of a new nuclear research reactor in a Sydney suburb.

OCTOBER 2002
5. A Queensland senator, Andrew Bartlett, was elected federal party leader of the Australian democrats. **21.** A gunman shot dead two students and wounded five others on a Melbourne campus. **23.** Australia submitted a formal request to the UN Security Council sanctions committee requesting that the Islamist group Jemaah Islamiyh be listed as a terrorist entity. **24.** In Adelaide, a tourist train crashed into a school bus, killing four and injuring 12 others.

NOVEMBER 2002
9. Over 100 bushfires spread across eastern Australia with soaring temperatures and gusting winds sending the blazes out of control, in conditions believed to be the worst for more than 100 years.

DECEMBER 2002
4. Fifty bush fires burned around north and south-west Sydney, some of which appeared to have been started deliberately. **6.** The bush fires intensified and an elderly man was killed.

JANUARY 2003
3. Eighteen people were hurt in Victoria after a chair lift collapsed. **19.** A bush fire that rapidly spread through Canberra's suburbs killed four, injured 260 and destroyed almost 400 homes. **30.** Eight people died and some forty were injured, when a double-decker commuter train derailed south of Sydney. **21.** A man was charged with the murder of Caroline Stuttle, a British packpacker killed in Australia in April 2002.

FEBRUARY 2003
28. It was brought to the attention of the Australian government that 'yellow crazy ants' are threatening to obliterate wildlife, pastureland and remote communities across northern Australia; the ants blind their victims, leaving them vulnerable to attack and starvation.

MARCH 2003
18. Australia confirmed that 2,000 of its troops would take part in a US-led war against Iraq.

APRIL 2003
7. In Pitcairn nine men out of a total population of 45 were charged with sexual offences after allegations of widespread sexual abuse.

MAY 2003
6. Pressure for the removal of Dr Peter Hollingworth as governor-general of Australia grew after an opinon poll found that more than 75 per cent of Australians wanted him to resign; this followed the controversy over a church inquiry which criticised him for allowing a paedophile to continue working as a priest. **8.** Peter Hollingworth was accused of rape and denied the allegation on television. **25.** Peter Hollingworth announced his resignation as governor-general. **29.** A man tried to hijack a domestic flight from Melbourne to Tasmania; two air stewards were injured.

JUNE 2003
22. Maj.-Gen. Michael Jeffery was appointed governor-general of Australia.

JULY 2003
1. A cave containing Aboriginal art believed to be 4,000 years old was found by a bush walker in a remote area of New South Wales. **22.** The Australian prime minister, John Howard, said that many south Pacific island nations are too small to survive and should form a federal state.

AUGUST 2003
13. Australia expressed concern that another 'catastrophic' terrorist attack was only a matter of time. **18.** A father and his baby daughter were badly injured in an attack by youths in a Sydney suburb. **19.** A 30 ft humpback whale leapt from the ocean onto a sailing boat off the coast of Australia, almost killing a family of five. **25.** Australian authorities reopened the investigation into the disappearance of Harold Holt, a former prime minister who vanished in 1967.

EUROPE

SEPTEMBER 2002
16. The Dutch government resigned after three months in office. **23.** In Spain, two people were killed by a bomb explosion in Bilbao; the attack was believed to have been carried out by two Eta terrorists, who were thought to be the only victims. **25.** The remains of 30,000 victims of Stalin's purges were discovered in Toksovo, near St Petersburg. At a meeting in France, the British home secretary and the French interior minister, Nicolas Sarkozy, agreed that the Sangatte refugee camp near Calais would be closed by April 2003. **30.** In Sweden, Kerim Sadok Chatty, arrested on suspicion of attempting to hijack a RyanAir flight in August 2002, was released from custody for lack of evidence; on 8 November, he was charged with illegal possession of firearms. In Germany, kidnappers abducted Jakob von Metzler, the heir to a private banking dynasty, but failed to release the 11-year-old boy even though his father paid the ransom of 1 million euros; his body was found in a lake north of Frankfurt on 1 October.

OCTOBER 2002

8. In Russia, an Azerbaijani man was killed in a racist attack by a group of seven Russian schoolgirls. **10.** In Chechnya, at least 20 Chechen policemen were killed and 20 were buried in rubble following an explosion at a police station in Grozny. **11.** In Slovakia, fighting broke out between football fans on the eve of the Euro 2004 qualifing match between Slovakia and England; two England football fans were shot in Bratislava. In Finland, an explosion at a shopping centre in Helsinki killed six and injured more than 60. **18.** Corsican separatists detonated 14 bombs, as part of their campaign to speed up negotiations for greater autonomy from France; there were no casualties. **22.** An explosion at a steelworks in Liège, Belgium, killed two and injured 27. **23.** In Russia, an estimated 50 Chechen separatists seized a Moscow theatre and took around 700 people hostage; the following day one hostage was shot dead and another was injured as she tried to escape. **25.** President Putin of Russia said that he would not give in to the demands of the Chechen rebels, who threatened to start shooting hostages at regular intervals if their demands for an end to the war in Chechnya were not met. **26.** Special forces ended the Moscow theatre siege by releasing gas into the theatre that caused severe breathing difficulties; 90 hostages and most of the rebels died, and surviving hostages were taken to hospital. There was anger among the relatives of the dead hostages when the Russian government refused to disclose the name of the gas used in the rescue mission. **27.** In Sicily, Mount Etna erupted. **29.** Eurostar rail services closed down after powerlines were short-circuited by salt water blown onshore by heavy storms. **31.** An earthquake struck southern Italy, killing at least 20 people, including 18 children killed when their school collapsed; the village of San Giuliano de Puglia was evacuated on 1 November after two days of further tremors. The Yves Saint Laurent fashion house in Paris, founded in 1961, closed.

NOVEMBER 2002

3. Chechen rebels shot down a Russian helicopter, killing nine. **4.** The Justice and Development Party won the general election in Turkey. **6.** Peter Shaw, a British businessman held hostage in Georgia for four months, escaped during a gun battle between his captors and government troops. In Greece, 11 British plane spotters were cleared of spying by a Greek court. **7.** In a referendum held in Gibraltar, 98.97 per cent of the population voted against co-sovereignty with Spain. **9.** In Italy, 400,000 Europeans took part in a march through Florence in protest at globalisation and possible military action against Iraq. **10.** In France, riot police sealed off a church in Calais after it was occupied by more than 100 asylum seekers who had been refused access to the Red Cross centre at Sangatte; the asylum seekers were forcibly evicted from the church on 14 November. **13.** The Danish prime minister, Anders Fogh Rasmussen, demanded action to halt the African practice of female circumcision in his country. President Lukashenko of Belarus threatened to remove police from the country's borders, thereby flooding Europe with illegal immigrants, if Belarus was refused entry into Nato. **15.** In Belgium, Nizar Trabelsi, a member of al-Qa'eda, confessed that he had planned to bomb a US air force bunker in Belgium believed to contain nuclear warheads. **16.** Abdullah Gul became prime minister of Turkey. **17.** In Italy, an appeals court sentenced Giulio Andreotti, the former prime minister, to 24 years imprisonment for

involvement in the murder of an investigative journalist 23 years previously. In Spain, oil from a stricken tanker threatened a 25-mile stretch of the north-west coast and a rescue operation to save seabirds covered in oil started; the tanker sank on 19 November, leaking more than 4,000 tons of oil into the sea. **20.** In Norway, an investigation was reopened into an air crash in 1982 in which 15 people died, after it was claimed that two British fighter planes were in the same area at the time. **24.** Swiss voters rejected proposals to curb the number of asylum seekers entering the country. **27.** An Italian airliner en route to Paris was diverted to Lyons after a mentally ill passenger attempted to hijack the aircraft.

DECEMBER 2002

4. In Germany, a 25-year-old woman was filmed by fellow art students as she committed suicide by jumping off a building in Berlin. In the Netherlands, bombs were found at Ikea shops in Amsterdam and Sliedrecht; they were detonated in controlled explosions. **8.** In the third presidential election in Serbia in a year, the 32 per cent turnout was too low for the vote to pass the threshold and so no president was elected. **13.** A car bomb in Kosovo injured 32 people. In Chechnya, two Russian soldiers were killed and two injured when a landmine exploded under their vehicle. **16.** In Germany, some public sector workers went on strike in pursuit of a pay rise. **17.** In France, evidence emerged of a plot to launch a chemical attack in Europe after the arrest of four terrorist suspects in Paris. **27.** Turkey's parliament voted to amend the constitution to allow Recep Tayyip Erdogan, the leader of the Justice and Development Party, to fight a by-election. A French scientist and member of the Raelian cult claimed to have created the first cloned baby at an undisclosed location. In Chechnya, more than 60 people were killed in a suicide attack on the headquarters of the pro-Russian Chechen administration in Grozny. Police in France broke up an Islamic fundamentalist cell planning a terrorist attack on the Russian Embassy in Paris in revenge for the death of the Chechen rebels in the Moscow theatre siege. **29.** The term of office of President Milan Milutinovic of Serbia was declared at an end, removing his immunity from facing trial at the UN war crimes tribunal.

JANUARY 2003

1. In Germany, talks began to avert a strike by all public sector workers; workers were protesting at the disparity between salaries in eastern and western Germany. In Austria, a law came into force requiring all foreigners applying to live in the country to prove their proficiency in German. **5.** In Germany, a light aircraft was hijacked by Franz-Stephen Strambach, who intended to crash it into the European Central Bank in Frankfurt; the military authorities succeeded in persuading him to abort the hijacking. **6.** The governor of the Bank of France, who had been expected to become the next chairman of the European Central Bank, went on trial on charges of fraud in relation to the accounts of the Credit Lyonais Bank, which collapsed owing billions of pounds. **7.** President Chirac of France ordered his armed forces to be 'ready for every eventuality' and indicated to the USA that France would be prepared to take part in a war against Iraq. **8.** A civilian airliner crashed in south-east Turkey; 75 people were killed and five survived. **10.** German government and local authority negotiators conceded the pay demands of public sector workers, averting a national strike. **12.** In Russia, two women were killed and nine people were injured when a hand grenade exploded at a Moscow medical academy. **22.** In Italy, five Moroccans were questioned by police after a raid on an abandoned farmhouse near Venice. US military personnel arrived in Turkey to examine military bases and ports for possible use in a war against Iraq despite Turkish opposition to a war. **24.** In Spain, 16 North Africans believed to have links with al-Qa'eda cells in Britain, were detained by police after it was alleged that they were planning to launch a chemical attack against Britain. The Czech Parliament failed in its second attempt to elect a new head of state. **29.** The split in Europe over war with Iraq; Britain, the Czech Republic, Denmark, Hungary, Italy, Poland, Portugal and Spain supported the USA but France and Germany remained critical of what they feared to be a rush to war. **31.** Italian police claimed to have broken up an al-Qa'eda cell after arresting 28 Pakistanis in Naples.

FEBRUARY 2003
1. In Germany, the Social Democrat party suffered defeats in the regional elections. President Vaclav Havel of the Czech Republic left office even though a successor had not been elected. **6.** A French waiter accused of stealing hundreds of works of art from museums throughout Europe was jailed for four years in Switzerland for thefts in that country; he stole 232 works valued at £662 million over seven years. **19.** In Germany, a Moroccan student, Mounir el Motassadeq, was sentenced to 15 years imprisonment for his involvement in the 11 September 2001 attacks in the USA. **20.** Spain closed the only exclusively Basque-language newspaper in the region and arrested ten members of staff on suspicion of connections with the terrorist group Eta. **28.** Vaclav Klaus was elected president of the Czech Republic.

MARCH 2003
10. The prime minister of Malta, Eddie Fenech Adami, called a general election for 12 April, four days before the country was due to sign the accession treaty to the EU. Four Algerian extremists who planned to blow up a Christmas market in Strasbourg in 2000, were jailed for between ten and 12 years in Frankfurt. **12.** The Serbian prime minister Zoran Djindjic was shot dead by a sniper in Belgrade; the government blamed the Zemun Clan, a Belgrade criminal gang. **16.** The Sars virus was diagnosed in Germany. **18.** France promised military assistance for the USA and Britain in the event of a chemical or biological attack by Iraqi forces, even though the French government remained opposed to war on Iraq. **20.** The Turkish parliament backed a resolution authorising US and British military planes to use Turkish airspace during the war with Iraq. In France, powder believed to contain traces of the poison ricin was discovered at a Paris railway station; on 11 April the French authorities announced that the powder was harmless. **27.** A left-wing activist, Volkert van der Graaf, admitted in court that he had killed the Dutch politician Pim Fortuyn in May 2002 with the aim of defending Dutch Muslims from persecution; on 15 April he was sentenced to 18 years in prison. **27.** A mass grave was found in Bosnia; believed to be the largest found to date, experts estimated that up to 600 Muslim victims of the Srebrenica massacre were buried there. **28.** The body of Ivan Stambolic, the former Serb president and Slobodan Milosevic's mentor, was found buried in a wood in Serbia three years after he had disappeared.

APRIL 2003
1. The war memorial to Commonwealth soldiers at Etaples, France, was desecrated and daubed with anti-British slogans in protest at the war with Iraq. **5.** In France, Jews were attacked by Muslim youths during protests against the war in Iraq. In Spain, police hunted a serial murderer nicknamed the 'Playing Card Killer' because he had left a playing card at the site of each of the four murders attributed to him. **7.** Five Chechen police officials died when their car was blown up in Grozny. **9.** The Norwegian parliament voted to ban smoking in bars, restaurants, cafés and nightclubs nationwide from spring 2004. **11.** In Germany, police stormed a bus in Berlin in which hostages had been held for four and a half days. **16.** In Greece, protests at the presence of the British prime minister at an EU accession ceremony in Athens turned violent as rioters fought running battles with police. **17.** In Russia, a leading opposition politician, Sergei Yushenkov, was shot dead in Moscow. **23.** For the first time in three decades, Greek and Turkish Cypriots were able to freely cross the UN 'green line' dividing the island, although they had to return to their homes by midnight.

MAY 2003
1. In south-east Turkey, an earthquake that hit the town of Bingal caused the deaths of 140 schoolchildren. **8.** The skeletons of 41 victims of the massacre of Muslims in Srebrenica during the Bosnian war were found 10 km from the town. **12.** A suicide bombing in a government compound in Chechnya killed over 40 and injured more than 100. **13.** In France, thousands of workers took part in the largest anti-government demonstration for almost ten years, protesting against pension reform plans. **14.** In Chechnya, a female suicide bomber killed at least 14 people in a crowded market square. **18.** A general election took place in Belgium; the centre-left coalition led by Prime Minister Guy Verhofstadt was returned to power. **20.** In Turkey, a bomb exploded in a café in Ankara, killing one person and injuring another. **26.** An aircraft bringing Spanish peacekeeping troops home from Afghanistan crashed in north-east Turkey, killing 74. **30.** The last Air France Concorde flight from Paris took place.

JUNE 2003
1. The Italian Senate voted in favour of a clause granting prime minister Silvio Berlusconi immunity from prosecution for as long as he remains in office. **5.** A Chechen woman blew herself up next to a military bus in southern Russia, killing 18 people and injuring many more. **26.** Jean-Marie Le Pen, leader of the French National Party, lost a libel case against the national newspaper Le Monde which said that he had tortured Algerians while serving with the French Army. **30.** Italy assumed the EU presidency amid controversy surrounding Berlusconi's fitness to lead Europe. In France, several summer art festivals were cancelled or postponed as actors, musicians and stage technicians protested against reforms of the state benefits for 'resting' entertainers.

JULY 2003
2. In Germany, a 16 year-old student opened fire in a classroom and wounded a teacher before shooting himself dead. **3.** Italian Premier, Silvio Berlusconi, caused offence to a German minister after comparing him to a Nazi general. **5.** Two female suicide bombers, believed to

be Chechens, blew themselves up at an rock concert in Moscow, killing over 18 people. **9.** The German Chancellor, Gerhard Schröder, cancelled his summer holiday to Italy as the row between the two countries worsened. **11.** Spain agreed to send troops to Iraq, the country's largest foreign military expedition for over a century. Stefano Stefani, an Italian minister criticised for calling Germans 'hyper-nationalistic blondes' and arrogant beer guzzlers, resigned. **19.** Pierre Robert, a Frenchman accused of masterminding the Casablanca suicide bombings in May 2003, went on trial. **20.** Sixteen people were injured in two bomb blasts in Nice that were blamed on Corsican nationalists. **22.** In Spain, Basque terrorists exploded bombs in Benidorm and Alicante, injuring 13. In France, fire broke out at the top of the Eiffel Tower. **28.** Vandals desecrated 45 graves at a Commonwealth war cemetery in northern France. **29.** There were widespread forest fires in southern France, many believed to have been deliberately started; four tourists died. **31.** A Bosnian Serb doctor who set up concentration camps in Bosnia was jailed for life.

AUGUST 2003
2. A Russian military hospital close to the Chechen border was destroyed when a suicide bomber crashed a lorry laden with explosives into the building; at least 50 died. The French actress Marie Trintigant died five days after falling into a coma following an argument with her boyfriend in a Lithuanian hotel room. **3.** A ninth person died in Portugal's worst forest fires in living memory. **4.** Members of the parliament in Azerbaijan appointed President Aliyev's son Ilham as prime minister. **9.** Victims of the Moscow theatre siege of October 2002 decided to take their fight for compensation to the European Court of Human Rights after Russian authorities rejected claims for damages. German police believed they had foiled a plan by Islamic terrorists to bomb holiday resorts on the Spanish coast popular with British tourists. **12.** In Germany, figures were released that suggested that over 1,000 East Germans were killed as they attempted to reach West Germany in the years that Germany was divided. **18.** In Georgia, electricity and water supplies throughout the country were disrupted in what was believed to be an act of sabotage. **20.** President Chirac of France questioned the government's handling of two weeks of extremely hot weather in France that was believed to have contributed to the deaths of 10,400 elderly people. The remains of more than 190 people were found in a mass grave in eastern Bosnia. In Germany, police found more than 100 lbs of cyanide at the home of a man who had threatened to poison the water supply of Einbeck, western Germany. **28.** The funeral was held in Geneva, Switzerland, of the UN diplomat Sergio Veira de Mello, who was killed in the bombing of the UN headquarters in Baghdad on 19 August.

EUROPEAN UNION

OCTOBER 2002
28. Valéry Giscard d'Estaing, a former president of France and Chairman of the European Convention, backed the proposal by the head of a forum charged with reforming the community, for renaming the EU the United States of Europe. **30.** Brussels claimed that a EU scheme to provide cheap drugs for the sick in the developing world was being exploited by smugglers.

NOVEMBER 2002
7. The EU agreed to ban the use of animals for the testing of certain cosmetic products. **8.** The EU rejected demands for the lifting of sanctions against Zimbabwe. **10.** Talks were held to establish a new strategic partnership between Russia and the EU. **15.** The EU called for a ban to prevent the president of Belarus, Alexander Lukashenka, entering all 15 existing EU member states and those countries negotiating to join the EU. The ban was called for in response to apparent human rights abuses in Belarus. **20.** The EU pledged £75 million in aid to Spanish fisherman to compensate for any losses resulting from an oil slick off the Spanish coast following the sinking of an oil tanker. **25.** A four-day EU summit with developing nations collapsed because of a boycott by scores of countries over an EU ban on Zimbabwe's representatives.

DECEMBER 2002
12. Turkey started negotiations on its entry into the EU for December 2004. **13.** An agreement was made to admit ten new members to the EU in May 2004, the greatest EU enlargement to date.

JANUARY 2003
8. Germany was given less than five months to put its public finances in order or face being fined by the European Commission. **13.** The EU warned Austria, Belgium, Greece, Italy and Portugal to observe the minimum animal welfare standards required under European law for egg-laying hens. **15.** The European Parliament's ban on the use of animals for testing cosmetics came into force.

FEBRUARY 2003
12. President Robert Mugabe was given permission to visit France in violation of a EU travel ban. **17.** After an emergency summit, the EU declared that weapons inspections in Iraq could not be allowed to continue indefinitely, disarmament of Iraq should only be carried out through the United Nations and that force should only be used as a last resort.

MARCH 2003
9. In a referendum, Malta voted to join the EU. **11.** Turkey was given its strongest warning to date that it risks failing to enter the EU if it continues to support the Turkish Cypriot leader Rauf Denktas in his refusal to accept UN plans to reunite Cyprus. **12.** The EU threatened to refuse to make a financial contribution towards the cost of rebuilding Iraq in the event of a war without UN backing. **23.** In a referendum, Slovenia voted to join the EU.

APRIL 2003
9. The European Parliament approved the accession treaties of the ten candidates to join the EU. **16.** A summit was held in Athens to agree formally the future accession of the Czech Republic, Estonia, Hungary, Latvia, Lithuania, Malta, Poland, Slovakia, Slovenia and a divided Cyprus.

MAY 2003
6. The Italian prime minister Silvio Berlusconi and the president of the European Commission, Romano Prodi, traded accusations of corruption. **11.** In a referendum, Lithuania voted to join the EU. **16.** Britain warned other European countries that it would oppose any moves to

strengthen the EU's defence capabilities that would undermine the security commitments provided by Nato. **18.** In a referendum, Slovakia voted to join the EU, although only 52.15 per cent of the electorate voted. **26.** Valéry Giscard d'Estaing was obliged to tone down elements of the initial draft for a European constitution that implied a transfer of more authority from sovereign states to EU institutions.

JUNE 2003
1. At a summit at Evian-les-Bains, EU leaders promised $600 million a year to Africa to help combat Aids and HIV. **4.** Member governments approved plans to send troops to the Democratic Republic of Congo, the first EU peacekeeping mission outside Europe. **16.** The EU urged Iran to give weapons inspectors 'urgent and unconditional' access to its nuclear facilities. **26.** MEPs agreed reforms to the Common Agricultural Policy which guaranteed farmers subsidies until at 2013, even if they do not produce food, in return for better food quality and environmental care.

JULY 2003
3. The European Parliament adopted legislation requiring GM foods to be more clearly labelled. **14.** Cyprus ratified its act of accession to the EU in a referendum. **23.** The European Commission concluded that a British government rescue plan for British Energy breached its rules. **30.** Britain stated that it would reopen attempts to change key sections of the proposed European constitution despite warnings that this risked undoing months of negotiations.

AUGUST 2003
7. The European Commission threatened to take legal action against the German government if it failed to reform its law on tin cans which stipulated that a consumer must return the empty can to the place it was purchased in order to receive back the small deposit on the can. **23.** Italy appealed to the EU for help to stem the flow of immigrants into the country and suggested a pan-European coastguard as well as EU funding for its border security. **27.** France faced being fined for breaching the EU's rules on budget deficits.

INTERNATIONAL RELATIONS

OCTOBER 2002
6. A summit meeting of heads of state and heads of government of the member states of the Commonwealth of Independent States was held in Chisinau, Moldova.

NOVEMBER 2002
10. A more streamlined structure was proposed for Nato. **11.** The United Nations presented a peace plan for Cyprus that will establish a 'Swiss-style' federation in the divided island, and gave Greek and Turkish Cypriots one week to respond in an effort to begin negotiations before the EU summit in December. **17.** The Hungarian defence minister admitted that his country had met less than a third of its commitments since being accepted for Nato membership in 1999. **19.** Nato proposed an increase in its firepower, with 13,000 more tanks, a dozen warships, 500 combat aircraft and a rise of about 227,000 in the total number of troops.

DECEMBER 2002
15. The UN's chief weapons inspector, Hans Blix, gave Iraq two weeks to identify key Iraqi scientists so they could be interviewed by UN experts about Iraq's weapons of mass destruction. **16.** Nato and the EU signed an agreement that would enable European troops to borrow Nato assets to carry out EU peacekeeping operations. **20.** Libya was elected to head the UN Human Rights Commission, which caused outrage among Western nations because of Libya's record of internal repression.

JANUARY 2003
22. A diplomatic rift opened between Britain and France over a possible invitation to President Mugabe of Zimbabwe to attend a Paris summit on Africa in February. **29.** Four Nato members, led by France and Germany, refused to discuss a US proposal to send Nato Patriot missiles and surveillance aircraft to Turkey to protect the country from a possible Iraqi attack. **31.** The British prime minister Tony Blair and US President George Bush drew up a timetable for a final warning to Saddam Hussein; Mr Blair urged President Bush to work with the United Nations to disarm Iraq and to avoid unilateral US military action.

FEBRUARY 2003
9. Belgium, France and Germany vetoed a decision to start making contingency plans to defend Turkey in the event of a war with Iraq, deepening the rift within Nato. **14.** Following Hans Blix's report on Iraq, France, Germany and Russia pressed for the UN weapons inspection teams to be given more time, while Britain and USA made the case for war. **16.** Nato members agreed to preparations to help Turkey in the event of war with Iraq.

MARCH 2003
7. The British foreign secretary, Jack Straw, requested that the UN Security Council agree to a final deadline of 17 March for Saddam Hussein to co-operate fully with the UN disarmament process. **11.** The International Criminal Court, the world's first permanent international criminal court, opened at the Hague in the Netherlands. **15.** The WHO issued an emergency bulletin warning travellers about the dangers of travel to areas affected the Sars virus; on 28 March, the WHO recommended screening measures at airports in Canada, China, Hong Kong, Singapore, Taiwan and Vietnam. **17.** A second UN resolution on war with Iraq was not agreed. The Commonwealth announced that it was extending its suspension of Zimbabwe for a further nine months.

APRIL 2003
16. The Nato rift over Iraq reopened after the USA's allies began to assemble a stabilisation force to support coalition troops but did not include France. **24.** The USA placed a new emphasis on its relations with Spain and Italy, indicated by consulting Madrid and Rome over Nato decision-making, in an attempt to limit France's input. **28.** The WHO announced that the Sars virus appeared to have peaked in all countries except China.

MAY 2003
9. The USA and Britain handed a draft resolution to the UN Security Council which asked it to grant them a mandate to rule Iraq as 'occupying powers' and called for the immediate lifting of sanctions against Iraq and the use of oil revenues to fund reconstruction. **21.** France,

Germany and Russia demonstrated their support for the US campaign to end sanctions against Iraq by pledging to vote at the UN for the new draft resolution that would determine Iraq's future. **22.** The USA and Britain gained international legal backing for their occupation of Iraq in a UN vote which also ended 13 years of sanctions against Iraq. **28.** The French ambassador to the UN announced that a French-led multinational peacekeeping force would be sent to the Democratic Republic of Congo because of the ethnic atrocities that had recently taken place there. **30.** During talks in Moscow, China and Russia agreed to increase military co-operation. The head of the International Atomic Energy Agency, Mohammed Elbaradei, accepted an invitation to visit Iran.

JUNE 2003
2. At the G8 summit in Evian-les-Bains, Iran and North Korea were identified as a 'pre-eminent threat to international security' and were ordered to stop all attempts to acquire weapons of mass destruction. **5.** The UN's chief weapons inspector, Hans Blix, challenged the US and British claim that Saddam Hussein had been stockpiling weapons of mass destruction. **17.** A two-day conference called by the WHO started in Malaysia to review the current state of knowledge about the Sars virus and could be contained. **12.** The UN Security Council adopted resolution 1487, in effect extending immunity for UN peacekeepers from potential prosecution by the UN's International Criminal Court by 12 months. **26.** Leading doctors stated that Unicef's concentration on Aids, malaria and the rights of female children was distracting resources from the wider issues of childhood mortality.

AUGUST 2003
11. Nato took command of the international peacekeeping force in Afghanistan at a time that increasing lawlessness was forcing aid agencies to withdraw. **27.** Diplomats from six countries met in China for discussions about ending North Korea's nuclear weapons programme.

THE MIDDLE EAST

SEPTEMBER 2002
23. Israel mounted a raid on the Gaza Strip in which nine Palestinians were killed. **25.** Two members of the militant Islamic group Hamas were killed and a Hamas bomb maker injured in an Israeli air strike in Gaza. **29.** A German was killed in a car explosion in Riyadh, Saudi Arabia. A gunfight took place outside the British embassy in Yemen as guards fired on tribesmen apparently trying to break through a security road block. In Iran, five men convicted of abducting, raping and robbing women were publicly hanged in Tehran.

OCTOBER 2002
6. An explosion on board a French tanker off the coast of Yemen was believed to be the result of an al-Qa'eda attack. **7.** At least ten people were killed and dozens more injured when the Israeli army fired a rocket into a crowded street. **8.** Two suspected al-Qa'eda gunmen launched an attack on US troops on a live-firing exercise in Kuwait, killing one and wounding another serviceman; the two gunmen were killed by return fire; the following day, Kuwait announced that it had arrested up to 50 people suspected of aiding the two Kuwaiti gunmen. **10.**

An Israeli bus driver held down a Palestinian suicide bomber, preventing him from detonating his explosives, but when the bomber staggered away moments later, he blew himself up, killing a woman and injuring 12 others. **14.** In Iraq, thousands of British graves from the Second World War were desecrated by Iraqis in reaction to the threat of a renewed bombing campaign by British and US forces. **15.** A referendum was held in Iraq on whether Saddam Hussein should remain in power; the President won 100 per cent of the vote. **17.** Eight Palestinians were killed by Israeli tanks in the Gaza Strip. **21.** Two suicide car bombers rammed a bus in northern Israel, killing 14 and injuring more than 40. **24.** In Bahrain, women were given the vote for the first time. **27.** A suicide bomber killed three Israeli soldiers on the West Bank. **28.** A US diplomat, Laurence Foley, was shot dead in Amman, Jordan. **31.** Yemen issued a warning that any boat approaching a commercial vessel in its ports without authorisation would be fired on.

NOVEMBER 2002
5. The prime minister of Israel, Ariel Sharon, called for an early election. **7.** A Palestinian suicide bomber was killed by Israeli troops at a West Bank checkpoint, though he detonated a device that killed another Palestinian. **9.** The head of Islamic Jihad's military wing, Iyad Sawalhe, was shot dead in Jenin by Israeli forces. **10.** Five Israelis were killed when a Palestinian opened fire in a kibbutz in northern Israel. **12.** Iraq's parliament rejected the UN's ultimatum to dismantle its weapons of mass destruction. Israel launched an air attack on Gaza City in revenge for the kibbutz murders. **13.** Saddam Hussein accepted the UN's stringent conditions for the return of UN weapons inspectors to Iraq. **15.** Gunmen killed at least 12 Israelis in an ambush in the West Bank city of Hebron. **17.** An attempted hijack took place aboard an El Al flight from Tel Aviv to Istanbul but the lone terrorist was overpowered by security guards and the flight landed in Turkey as scheduled. The British Embassy in Sana'a, Yemen, was closed to visitors after evidence emerged of an al-Qa'eda plan for attacks on Western targets in the Yemeni capital. **19.** Iran freed 20 Iraqi prisoners of war held since the 1980–8 war between the two countries. **21.** An US nurse was shot dead at a Christian mission in Lebanon. **22.** A British UN engineer was shot dead in a gunfight between Israeli troops and Palestinian gunmen as he worked on the rebuilding of a refugee camp on the West Bank. **27.** A Palestinian car bomber was killed as he attempted to ram an Israeli army post. UN weapons inspectors were admitted into Iraq unhindered.

DECEMBER 2002
6. Israeli troops killed 10 Palestinians during a raid in the Gaza Strip. **7.** Iraq released a 11,807-page dossier to the UN, declaring itself free from weapons of mass destruction. **10.** US weapons specialists boarded a ship off the coast of Yemen after it was found to be carrying Scud-type missiles from North Korea. **12.** Five Palestinians were killed by Israeli soldiers as they tried to infiltrate Israel from Gaza. **13.** The first Israeli female soldier was shot by a Palestinian sniper. **21.** In the United Arab Emirates, a man carrying a suspected bomb was stopped as he tried to board a Royal Jordanian Airlines flight at Abu Dhabi. **29.** Israeli soldiers shot dead an 11-year-old boy on the West Bank.

JANUARY 2003

2. Israeli soldiers killed six Palestinians near Alai Sinai. **5.** A double suicide bombing killed more than 22 people and wounded dozens in Tel Aviv. **13.** The USA attacked an anti-ship missile launcher in southern Iraq that was situated within range of US warships in the Gulf. British troops arrived in Kuwait to prepare for a possible ground invasion of Iraq. **16.** UN weapons inspectors in Iraq discovered empty warheads designed to carry chemical weapons; it was also reported that weapons inspectors had uncovered recent documentation in the homes of two Iraqi nuclear physicists relating to ongoing work to develop nuclear weapons. **18.** UN weapons inspectors in Iraq revealed that they had discovered documents linked to nuclear weapons technology while searching a scientist's house.   **20.** Saddam Hussein promised to increase Iraqi co-operation with UN weapons inspectors, but this pledge was dismissed as worthless by the USA and Britain. **23.** The US deputy defence minister claimed that Saddam Hussein had threatened to kill Iraqi scientists who co-operated with UN weapons inspectors and their families.   **25.** At least 11 Palestinians were killed and more than 40 wounded when Israeli troops attacked Gaza City. **27.** The UN's chief weapons inspector, Hans Blix, stated that Saddam Hussein had failed to disarm, greatly strengthening the US and British case for war. **28.** Ariel Sharon won the Israeli election.

FEBRUARY 2003

10. The USA expressed concern over Iran's plans to enrich plutonium for their nuclear energy programme. **11.** Fourteen people were trampled to death in Saudi Arabia during the Eid al-Adha festival which ends the annual pilgrimage to Mecca. **12.** US aircraft attacked an Iraqi surface-to-surface missile launcher in the air exclusion zone in southern Iraq, according to US officials. UN weapons inspectors in Iraq discovered a banned weapons system in violation of UN restrictions. **11.** Al-Jazeera released an audiotape message believed to be from Osama bin Laden encouraging suicide attacks against the USA and its allies. **15.** Iraq reinforced defences around its northern oilfields and troops were ordered to set light to the oil reserves in the event of a US attack on Iraq. **19.** An Iranian military transport aircraft crashed near the city of Shahdad; there were no survivors. Eleven Palestinians were killed and 19 injured in an Israeli attack in Gaza said to be in retaliation for an attack a week before that had left four Israeli soldiers dead. **26.** Ariel Sharon removed Binyamin Netanyahu from the post of foreign minister in Israel's new coalition government; Netanyahu was offered the position of finance minister.

MARCH 2003

1. Iraq began decommissioning its arsenal of banned al-Samoud missiles. **2.** Three Palestinians were killed by the Israeli army at a refugee camp. **3.** Eight people were killed during an Israeli raid to the south of Gaza City. **5.** Fifteen people were killed and 55 injured when a Palestinian bus passenger blew himself up in Haifa. The US Secretary of State, Colin Powell, claimed that despite destroying some of its existing stocks, Iraq was producing more of the banned al-Samoud missiles in defiance of the UN. **6.** Eight Palestinians were killed during an Israeli raid in Gaza. **7.** The USA and Britain gave Saddam Hussein a deadline of 17 March to disarm or face war. **10.** The Palestinian president Yasser Arafat nominated his deputy, Mahmoud Abbas, as prime minister; the move was denounced as a 'sham' by Israeli officials because of

the limitations of the prime minister's power. **16.** As President Bush and Mr Blair indicated that they were ready to go to war without UN backing, US and British troops in Kuwait moved into their final positions in preparation for military action against Iraq. The USA and Britain gave Saddam Hussein his last warning to leave Iraq and go into exile or face war. **17.** In a televised address, President Bush told the Iraqi people that they were about to be freed and gave Saddam Hussein and his sons 48 hours to leave Iraq. Ten Palestinians were killed during Israeli army raids in the Gaza Strip. A US woman taking part in a protest against Israeli operations in Gaza was killed when a bulldozer ran her over as she sat in the road. **20.** The invasion of Iraq by British and US troops began with an aerial bombardment of the capital Baghdad and the strategically important southern city of Basra. Iraq retaliated by launching missiles over the border into Kuwait. **21.** British and US troops carried out a heavy aerial bombardment of Baghdad throughout the night. A British helicopter crashed accidentally in Iraq, killing all 12 on board. **22.** An ITN journalist, Terry Lloyd, was missing after he and colleagues came under fire near Basra; on 24 March, it was announced that his body had been found in a hospital in Basra. **23.** Ten US marines were killed near Nasariyah by Iraqi soldiers who opened fire after pretending to surrender. A US soldier killed an officer and wounded 16 soldiers in northern Kuwait in what was believed to be a politically motivated attack because he had converted to Islam and did not support the war with Iraq. **25.** US and British forces shelled targets in Basra to support an apparent uprising against the militias controlling Iraq's second city. **26.** Fifteen Iraqis were killed and around 30 injured by allied bombs that fell on a marketplace in Baghdad. Allied forces bombed Iraqi television stations. **28.** More than 50 Iraqis were killed and 49 injured by an allied bomb that fell on a Baghdad marketplace. Hundreds of Iranian demonstrators smashed the windows of the British embassy in Tehran and burned Union Jacks in protest at the war in Iraq. Syria and Iran were warned by the USA to stop helping Iraqi forces or to be held accountable for 'hostile acts'. **29.** Four US soldiers died by a suicide bomber. **30.** Seven Iraqi women and children were killed by allied troops when they opened fire on a van which failed to stop at a checkpoint outside Najaf. British forces launched the battle to take control of Basra with an assault on fortified Iraqi positions in a south-eastern suburb. A Palestinian suicide bomber blew himself up outside a busy café in Natanya, Israel, injuring 56 people.

APRIL 2003

2. A British foreign correspondent, two photographers and a peace activist were released after being detained for eight days in a Baghdad prison. **4.** In Iraq, five people died at a checkpoint in an apparent suicide bombing, including three US soldiers, a pregnant woman and the driver of the vehicle that contained a car bomb. Coalition forces gained control of Baghdad's airport. **6.** Hundreds of Iraqi exiles joined allied forces and assembled themselves under the banner of 'Free Iraqi Force' to help remove Saddam's regime. **6.** The BBC news reporter John Simpson was injured by shrapnel while reporting in northern Iraq when US forces mistakenly bombed a frontline position of their own special forces and allied Kurdish fighters, killing 18 and injuring 45. **7.** Col. Chris Vernon, a British military spokesman, announced that militarily Britain and the USA had won the war in Iraq after successfully taking Basra and Baghdad. **7.** US tanks entered Baghdad and British paratroopers took control of Basra; thousands of Iraqis welcomed British forces in the centre of Basra. Saddam Hussein's secretary-general, Ali Hassin al-Majid was killed when an US bomb hit his compound in Basra. More than 1,000 Iraqi troops were killed by US forces fighting their way into Baghdad. **8.** It was believed that Saddam Hussein survived a second US bombing strike that was designed to kill him and his closest associates. **9.** Baghdad fell to allied forces; a 20-foot statue of Saddam Hussein in the centre of the city was toppled as thousands of jubilant Iraqis destroyed statues and pictures throughout the city and chanted in praise of President Bush and Mr Blair. **10.** A prominent cleric was hacked to death by Shia Muslims days after returning to Iraq from exile. **11.** In Baghdad, the looting of government buildings and hospitals by citizens continued. Ten suspects in the bombing of the USS *Cole* in October 2000 escaped from prison in the Yemeni city of Aden. **11.** President Bush and Mr Blair broadcast to the Iraqi people from a new television channel, Towards Freedom TV, set up on board a US transport plane. **12.** Saddam Hussein's chief scientific adviser surrendered to US forces in Baghdad; Gen. Amer al-Saadi was believed to have been masterminded Iraq's efforts to conceal weapons projects during the run-up to the war. A British student was shot by an Israeli sniper as he tried to help two girls out of danger during a protest in the Gaza Strip. **13.** President Bush accused Syria of having weapons of mass destruction and gave the Syrian government its gravest warning yet to stop harbouring Iraqi officials. **14.** Saddam Hussein's home town of Tikrit fell to coalition forces, ending the last major military operation of the war in Iraq. The USA, with British backing, threatened Syria with economic sanctions should Damascus refuse to hand over Iraqi officials and abandon its suspected chemical weapons programme. **15.** Abu Abbas, the Palestinian terrorist who masterminded the 1985 attack on the Italian cruise ship *Achille Lauro*, was captured by US special forces in Iraq. Three Palestinians and three Israelis were killed in shootings at a crossing point between Gaza and Israel. **16.** In a letter to *The Times*, Queen Rania of Jordan appealed to President Bush and Mr Blair to make Iraq safe enough for aid organisations to enter and for casualties to be immediately evacuated. **24.** The former deputy prime minister of Iraq, Tariq Aziz, was held by US troops after surrendering to allied forces. A suicide bomber blew himself up at a railway station north of Tel Aviv; the bomber and a security guard were killed. **25.** Saddam Hussein's intelligence chief, Farouk Hijazi, was captured by US forces close to Iraq's border with Syria. **26.** At least 12 Iraqis, including several members of the same family, were killed when an arms dump in Baghdad exploded, sending rockets flying into nearby houses. **29.** US forces killed 14 and injured dozens of protesters in the Iraqi town of Fallujah. The British Embassy in Baghdad reopened for the first time in 12 years. A Palestinian suicide bomber blew himself in Tel Aviv, killing at least two people and injuring about 50. The USA announced that its 12-year military presence in Saudi Arabia would end.

MAY 2003

1. An Israeli raid on the Gaza Strip killed 12 Palestinians. **4.** US Secretary of State Colin Powell said that he had given Syria a final warning to stop aiding terrorist groups and cautioned that it would face 'continuing difficulties' with the USA if it failed to do so. **5.** A leading Iraqi

biological weapons scientist, the only woman on the USA's 'most wanted' deck of cards, was in taken into custody by US forces. **12.** There were four co-ordinated suicide bombings in the Saudi capital Riyadh against Western targets, three residential compounds and a jointly owned US-Saudi company. **13.** In Iraq, a mass grave was found south of Baghdad containing the remains of about 3,000 victims of Saddam Hussein's repression. **14.** The USA warned Saudi Arabia to 'crack down' on terrorists and accused it of failing to try to prevent the Riyadh suicide bombings; the mastermind of the attacks claimed that he had received orders from Osama bin Laden. **16.** The Iraqi port of Umm Qasr in southern Iraq was handed back to its municipal council in the first transfer of power to an Iraqi authority since the allied invasion. **18.** Four members of al-Qa'eda were arrested in Saudi Arabia on suspicion of plotting the recent suicide bombings in Riyadh. **19.** A female suicide bomber killed three people in northern Israel shortly after Israeli forces sealed off the West Bank and Gaza Strip. In Iraq, a US transport helicopter crashed southeast of Karbala. **20.** Britain, USA and Germany closed their embassies in Riyadh, Saudi Arabia, after intelligence agencies warned of the possibility of imminent terrorist attacks. **21.** Three men, believed to be Moroccans, were arrested in Saudi Arabia as they were about to hijack an airliner and crash it into a Saudi skyscraper. Many expatriate schools in Saudi Arabia closed for fear of further terrorist attacks. **23.** President Bush agreed to modify the 'roadmap to peace' in order to win a qualified acceptance by Israel. **25.** The Israeli prime minister Ariel Sharon convinced his divided cabinet to endorse the US 'roadmap to peace', committing Israel to the creation of a Palestinian state. **27.** Iraq's acting oil minister announced that Iraq would start exporting oil again within three weeks and targeted an output of 1.4 million barrels a day, compared to a daily 2 million barrels before the war. **28.** Britain again warned Iran against interfering in Iraq and told it to stop supporting terrorist groups and to co-operate with UN nuclear weapons inspectors. The US defence secretary Donald Rumsfeld admitted there was some doubt as to whether weapons of mass destruction would be found in Iraq and that it was possible that they had been destroyed before the war began.

JUNE 2003

2. Iran rejected demands by the USA and other countries that it allow more rigorous inspections of its nuclear programme by the International Atomic Energy Agency. **4.** US forces began an engineering and forensic operation in a house in Baghdad in an attempt to determine whether or not Saddam Hussein was killed during the war; he was believed to have hidden in the house. In Egypt, President Bush met five Arab leaders to discuss the Middle East peace process, and particularly the 'roadmap to peace'. **10.** In Iran, a march by students quickly turned into pro-reform demonstrations. **12.** It was announced that more than half of the 'most wanted' members of the former Iraqi regime had been captured. **15.** British military vehicles were stoned in Basra as 10,000 Iraqis took to the streets to demand self-government. **17.** In Jordan, elections to the enlarged 110-member House of Representatives took place. **25.** Four British soldiers and two Iraqis died in Iraq after a mob, angry at house-to-house searches by British troops, turned on members of the Royal Military Police who were training Iraqi police officers. **26.** Two would-be suicide bombers were shot dead by Israeli police. Ali

Abdul Rachman al-Gamdi, the suspected mastermind of the Riyadh bombings in May, was taken into custody by the Saudi authorities. **27.** An agreement was reached for Israeli forces to begin a withdrawal from the Gaza Strip.

JULY 2003
4. An Arab television station broadcast what appeared to be a call to arms for the Iraqi people from former dictator Saddam Hussein; the authenticity of the tape was unclear. **13.** The Emir of Kuwait issued a decree separating the post of prime minister from that of Crown Prince for the first time since the country's independence. **20.** In Iraq, Shia Muslims held a demonstration in Najaf. **22.** Saddam Hussein's sons, Uday and Qusay, were killed by US troops after a six-hour gun battle in the northern Iraqi city of Mosul; they were buried in Awja on 2 August. **27.** The leader of Islamic militant group Hezbollah warned the USA that US interests around the world would be attacked if the USA attempted to wipe out the group. **29.** Ariel Sharon insisted that Israel would continue to build a security fence to separate Israel from Palestinian areas despite US opposition.

AUGUST 2003
3. Palestinian president Yasser Arafat backed down from a confrontation with militants wanted by Israel after trying to expel them from his headquarters in Ramallah. **7.** In Baghdad a huge bomb at the Jordanian embassy killed at least 12 people and injured 50. **9.** Seven British soldiers and four Iraqi civilians were injured in Basra after the worst rioting in Iraq since the overthrow of Saddam Hussein in April; the rioting was over power and fuel shortages. **10.** In Basra, a former British army Gurkha working for the allied administration in Iraq was killed on the second day of rioting in the city. Israel launched air strikes on southern Lebanon in retaliation for an attack on an Israeli town by Hezbollah. **12.** President Mohammad Khatami of Iran resigned following weeks of violent student protests and attacks by hardline conservative and liberal politicians. **13.** In Iraq, a governing council of 25 members held its first meeting. **16.** Iran admitted that a Canadian journalist was beaten to death after her arrest during a demonstration in June. **19.** A suicide bomber rammed a lorry packed with explosives into the UN headquarters in Baghdad, killing the UN special representative Sergio Vieira de Mello and at least 19 others, and injuring more than 100. A suicide bomber in Jerusalem destroyed one bus and damaged another, killing over 20 people and injuring more than 100. **24.** Four members of Hamas were killed in a helicopter strike in Gaza City. **25.** Israeli police clashed with Muslims on the Temple Mount in Jerusalem after the compound was reopened to Christians and Jews. **27.**The last US military unit in Saudi Arabia left the kingdom. **30.** In Iraq, a car bomb exploded in Najaf and killed over 75 people, including the country's foremost Shia Muslim leader.

PRIME MINISTERS AND LEADERS OF THE OPPOSITION

PRIME MINISTERS

Over the centuries there has been some variation in the determination of the dates of appointment of Prime Ministers. Where possible, the date given is that on which a new Prime Minister kissed the Sovereign's hands and accepted the commission to form a ministry. However, until the middle of the 19th century the dating of a commission or transfer of seals could be the date of taking office. Where the composition of the Government changed, e.g. became a coalition, but the Prime Minister remained the same, the date of the change of government is given.

YEAR APPOINTED

1721	Sir Robert Walpole, Whig
1742	The Earl of Wilmington, Whig
1743	Henry Pelham, Whig
1754	The Duke of Newcastle, Whig
1756	The Duke of Devonshire, Whig
1757	The Duke of Newcastle, Whig
1762	The Earl of Bute, Tory
1763	George Grenville, Whig
1765	The Marquess of Rockingham, Whig
1766	The Earl of Chatham, Whig
1767	The Duke of Grafton, Whig
1770	Lord North, Tory
1782 March	The Marquess of Rockingham, Whig
1782 July	The Earl of Shelburne, Whig
1783 April	The Duke of Portland, Coalition
1783 Dec.	William Pitt, Tory
1801	Henry Addington, Tory
1804	William Pitt, Tory
1806	The Lord Grenville, Whig
1807	The Duke of Portland, Tory
1809	Spencer Perceval, Tory
1812	The Earl of Liverpool, Tory
1827 April	George Canning, Tory
1827 Aug.	Viscount Goderich, Tory
1828	The Duke of Wellington, Tory
1830	The Earl Grey, Whig
1834 July	The Viscount Melbourne, Whig
1834 Nov.	The Duke of Wellington, Tory
1834 Dec.	Sir Robert Peel, Tory
1835	The Viscount of Melbourne, Whig
1841	Sir Robert Peel, Tory
1846	Lord John Russell (later The Earl Russell), Whig
1852 Feb.	The Earl of Derby, Tory
1852 Dec.	The Earl of Aberdeen, Peelite
1855	The Viscount Palmerston, Liberal
1858	The Earl of Derby, Conservative
1859	The Viscount Palmerston, Liberal
1865	The Earl Russell, Liberal
1866	The Earl of Derby, Conservative
1868 Feb.	Benjamin Disraeli, Conservative
1868 Dec.	William Gladstone, Liberal
1874	Benjamin Disraeli, Conservative
1880	William Gladstone, Liberal
1885	The Marquess of Salisbury, Conservative
1886 Feb.	William Gladstone, Liberal
1886 July	The Marquess of Salisbury, Conservative
1892	William Gladstone, Liberal
1894	The Earl of Rosebery, Liberal
1895	The Marquess of Salisbury, Conservative
1902	Arthur Balfour, Conservative
1905	Sir Henry Campbell-Bannerman, Liberal
1908	Herbert Asquith, Liberal
1915	Herbert Asquith, Coalition
1916	David Lloyd-George, Coalition
1922	Andrew Bonar Law, Conservative
1923	Stanley Baldwin, Conservative
1924 Jan.	Ramsay MacDonald, Labour
1924 Nov.	Stanley Baldwin, Conservative
1929	Ramsay MacDonald, Labour
1931	Ramsay MacDonald, Coalition
1935	Stanley Baldwin, Coalition
1937	Neville Chamberlain, Coalition
1940	Winston Churchill, Coalition
1945 May	Winston Churchill, Conservative
1945 July	Clement Attlee, Labour
1951	Sir Winston Churchill, Conservative
1955	Sir Anthony Eden, Conservative
1957	Harold Macmillan, Conservative
1963	Sir Alec Douglas-Home, Conservative
1964	Harold Wilson, Labour
1970	Edward Heath, Conservative
1974	Harold Wilson, Labour
1976	James Callaghan, Labour
1979	Margaret Thatcher, Conservative
1990	John Major, Conservative
1997	Anthony Blair, Labour

LEADERS OF THE OPPOSITION

The office of Leader of the Opposition was officially recognised in 1937 and a salary was assigned to the post.

YEAR APPOINTED

1916	Herbert Asquith, Liberal
1918	William Adamson, Labour
1921	John Clynes, Labour
1922	Ramsay MacDonald, Labour (leader of official Opposition)
1924	Stanley Baldwin, Conservative
1929	Stanley Baldwin, Conservative
1931	Arthur Henderson, Labour (leader of Labour Opposition)
1931	George Lansbury, Labour
1935	Clement Attlee, Labour
1945	Clement Attlee, Labour
1945	Winston Churchill, Conservative
1951	Clement Attlee, Labour
1955	Hugh Gaitskell, Labour
1963	Harold Wilson, Labour
1965	Edward Heath, Conservative
1974	Edward Heath, Conservative
1970	Harold Wilson, Labour
1975	Margaret Thatcher, Conservative
1979	James Callaghan, Labour
1980	Michael Foot, Labour
1983	Neil Kinnock, Labour
1992	John Smith, Labour
1994	Anthony Blair, Labour
1997	William Hague, Conservative
2001	Iain Duncan Smith

OBITUARIES

Aberconway, Lord, industrialist and horticulturist, president of the Royal Horticultural Society (1961–84) and oversaw the running of the Chelsea Flower Show, aged 89 – *d.* 4 February 2003, *b.* 16 April 1913

Agnelli, Giovanni, head of the Fiat car dynasty, aged 81 – *d.* 24 January 2003, *b.* 12 March 1921

Alexander, David, publisher and co-founder of Lion Publishing, aged 64 – *d.* 13 November 2002, *b.* 17 November 1937

Al-Khoei, Abdul Majid, Shia cleric, leading figure in the exiled Iraqi community in Britain, aged 42 – murdered on 10 April in Iraq, *b.* in Najaf, Iraq

Allaun, Frank, Labour MP (1955–83) and founder of the Campaign for Nuclear Disarmament, aged 89 – *d.* 26 November 2002, *b.* 27 February 1913

Amias, The Revd Saul, Anglo-Jewish minister, aged 95 – *d.* 1 December 2002, *b.* 9 March 1907

Amies, Sir Hardy, KCVO, fashion designer and The Queen's official dressmaker (1955–90), aged 93 – *d.* 5 March 2003, *b.* 17 July 1909

Atkins, Dr Robert, nutritionist, founder of the protein-based 'Atkins diet', aged 72 – *d.* 17 April 2003, *b.* 17 October 1930

Balfour (4th), The Earl of, aged 77 – *d.* 27 June 2003, *b.* 23 December 1925

Barrowclough, Sir Anthony, QC, Parliamentary Commissioner for Administration and Health Service Commissioner for England, Wales and Scotland (1985–90) aged 78 – *d.* 3 June 2003, *b.* 24 June 1924

Beach, Capt. Edward L., commanded the nuclear powered submarine, 'Triton' on the first underwater circumnavigation of the globe in 1960, aged 84 – *d.* 1 December 2002, *b.* 20 April 1918

Bedford (13th), The Duke of, owner of Woburn Abbey, aged 85 – *d.* 25 October 2002, *b.* 1917

Bedford (14th), The Duke of, successful stockbroker, inherited the role of custodian of Woburn Abbey in 1974 when he was Marquess of Tavistock, aged 63 – *d.* 13 June 2003, *b.* 21 January 1940

Bennet, Sir Frederick, PC, Conservative MP for Reading North (1951–5), Torquay (1955–74); and Torbay (1974–87), aged 83 – *d.* 14 September 2002, *b.* 2 December 1918

Betts, The Rt. Revd Stanley, CBE, suffragan bishop of Maidstone and bishop to the Armed Forces (1956–66), aged 91 – *d.* 7 June 2003, *b.* 23 March 1912

Black, Sir Douglas, medical scientist and former president of the Royal College of Physicians, aged 89 – *d.* 13 September 2002, *b.* 29 May 1913

Boardman, Lord, MC, TD, Conservative MP for Leicester South West, Minister for Industry (1972–4), Chief Secretary to the Treasury (1974) and chairman of the National Westminster Bank (1983–9), aged 84 – *d.* 10 March 2003, *b.* 12 January 1919

Boosey, Georgina, managing editor of *Vogue* (1978–93), aged 67 – *d.* 5 February 2003, *b.* 3 January 1936

Bradley, Tom, Labour MP for Leicester North East (1962–74), Leicester East (1974–83), party chairman (1975–6), aged 76 – *d.* 9 September 2002, *b.* 13 April 1926

Brasher, Chris, CBE, athlete and founder of the London Marathon, aged 74 – *d.* 28 February 2003, *b.* 21 August 1928

Broom, Air Marshal Sir Ivor, KCB, CBE, DSO, DFC, AFC, wartime bomber pilot and controller, National Air Traffic Services (1974–77), aged 82 – *d.* 24 January 2003, *b.* 2 June 1920

Brown, Dee, librarian and author, aged 94 – *d.* 12 December 2002, *b.* 29 February 1908

Brown, Sir John, CBE, publisher, Oxford University Press (1956–80), aged 86 – *d.* 3 March 2003, *b.* 7 July 1916

Brown, Sir Ralph Kilner, bronze medallist in the 1934 Empire Games and High Court judge, aged 93 – *d.* 15 June 2003, *b.* 28 August 1909

Brunner, Lady Elizabeth, OBE, chairman of the National Federation of Women's Institutes (1951–6) aged 98 – *d.* 5 January 2003, *b.* 14 April 1904

Butterworth, Lord, CBE, vice-chancellor of Warwick University (1963–85), aged 85 – *d.* 19 June 2003, *b.* 13 March 1918

Chadwick, Lynn, CBE, sculptor, won the Venice Biennale in 1956, aged 88 – *d.* 25 April 2003, *b.* 24 November 1914

Clapham, Sir Michael, KBE, director of ICI (1961–74), president of the Confederation of British Industry (1972–4), chairman of BPM Holdings and IMI Ltd (1974–81), director Lloyds Bank (1971–82) and director of Grindlay's Bank (1975–84), aged 90 – *d.* 11 November 2002, *b.* 17 January 1912

Clee, Lord Gladwin of, CBE, trade union leader and life peer, aged 72 – *d.* 10 April 2003, *b.* 6 June 1930

Coburn, James, film actor, starred in *The Magnificent Seven* as the knife-thrower 'Britt', aged 74 – *d.* 18 November 2002, *b.* 31 August 1928

Cohen, Her Hon. Myrella, LLD, QC, longest serving woman judge (1972–95); worked extensively on Jewish divorce laws, aged 74 – *d.* 25 October 2002, *b.* 16 December 1927

Coleridge, Lady Georgina, 2nd daughter of 11th Marquess of Tweeddale, editor of *Homes and Gardens* (1949–63) and publishing director of *Country Life* until 1982, aged 87 – *d.* 25 March 2003, *b.* 19 March 1916

Cooke, Janette, the first thalidomide victim to give birth and chairman of the Thalidomide Society – *d.* 9 November 2002, *b.* 1962

Cookson, William, founder and editor of poetry magazine *Agenda*, aged 63 – *d.* 2 January 2003, *b.* 4 January 2003

Cork, Sir Roger, Lord Mayor of London (1996–7), aged 55 – *d.* 21 October 2002, *b.* 31 March 1947

Coxeter, Donald, FRS, geometer who inspired Buckminster Fuller and the graphic artist M. C. Escher, aged 96 – *d.* 31 March 2003, *b.* 9 February 1907

Craven, Air Marshal Sir Robert, KBE, CB, DFC, aged 87 – d. 20 February 2003, b. 16 January 1916

Crawford, Sir Stewart, GCMG, CVO, aged 89 – d. 11 October 2002, b. 27 August 1913

Crawford, Vice-Admiral Sir William, KBE, CB, DSC, captain of the Royal Naval College, Dartmouth, (1954–6), aged 95 – d. 16 June 2003, b. 14 September 1907

Crookenden, Lt.-Gen. Sir Napier, soldier at the D-Day landings, aged 87 – d. 31 October 2002, b. 31 August 1915

Cross, Air Chief Marshal Sir Kenneth, KCB, CBE, DSO, DFC, fighter pilot who survived more than a week afloat in Arctic waters after the sinking of the aircraft carrier *Glorious* in 1940, aged 91 – d. 18 June 2003, b. 4 October 1911

Daniel, Sir Goronwy, KCVO, CB, civil servant and Permanent Under-Secretary of State Welsh Office, (1964–9); principal of University College of Wales, Aberystwyth (1969–79) and vice-chancellor 1977–9; lord-lieutenant for Dyfed (1978–89), aged 88 – d. 17 January 2003, b. 21 March 1914

Davies, Rear-Admiral Anthony, CB, CVO, warden of St George's House, Windsor Castle (1966–72) aged 90 – d. 14 January 2003, b. in India 13 June 1912

Dillion, Sir Brian, PC, Lord Justice of Appeal (1982–94), aged 77 – d. 22 June 2003, b. 2 October 1925

Djindjic, Zoran, Serbian prime minister, aged 50 – assassinated on 12 March 2003, b. in Bosnia on 2 August 1952

Donegan, Lonnie, skiffle guitarist who achieved 31 Top Ten hits in the 1950s including *My Old Man's a Dustman*, aged 71 – d. 3 November 2002, b. 29 April 1931

Dowling, Dame Jean, DCVO, chief clerk to the Queen (1961–76), aged 86 – d. 22 December 2002, b. 7 November 1916

Duncombe, Nick, England rugby player and Harlequins scrum-half, aged 21 – d. 14 February 2003, b. 21 January 1982

Edwards, Sir George, OM, CBE, FRS, aeronautical engineer, chairman of British Aircraft Corporation, (1963–75), aged 94 – d. 2 March 2003, b. 9 July 1908

Elphick, Michael, actor, aged 55 – d. 7 September 2002, b. 19 September 1946

Erzinçlioğlu, Zakaria, Britain's leading forensic entomologist, aged 50 – d. 26 September 2002, b. 30 December 1951

Faith, Adam, pop-star and actor, aged 62 – d. 8 March 2003, b. 23 June 1940

Flower, Rear-Adm. James, CB, marine engineer, aged 79 – d. 19 December 2002, b. 5 July 1923

Fraser, Sir Ian, CBE, MC, director-general of the Takeover Panel (1968–72) and chairman of Lazards (1980–85), aged 79 – d. 8 May 2003, b. 7 August 1923

French, Francis-Jane, Irish genealogist, contributor to Debrett's and Burke's Peerage, aged 73 – d. 23 October 2002, b. 15 September 1929

French, Sir Christopher, High Court judge (1982–97), aged 77 – d. 14 March 2003, b. 14 October 1925

Galtieri, Gen. Leopoldo, president of Argentina (1976–83), aged 76 – d. 12 January 2003, b. 15 July 1926

Gardiner, Sir George Arthur, Conservative MP for Reigate (1974–97), aged 67 – d. 17 November 2002, b. 3 March 1935

Getty, Sir John Paul, KBE, American-born billionaire philanthropist, aged 70 – d. 17 April 2003, b. 7 September 1932

Gibb, Maurice, bassist, keyboard player and singer with the Bee Gees, aged 53 – d. 12 January 2003, b. 22 December 1949

Glanton, Lord Dacre of, Regius professor of Modern History at Oxford (1957–80), aged 89 – d. 26 January 2003, b. 15 January 1914

Gordon-Creed, Lt.-Col. Geoffrey, DSO, MC, spy and saboteur, aged 82 – d. 26 November 2002, b. 29 January 1920

Gosney, Prof. William Bell, Emeritus professor of Refrigeration Engineering at London University, aged 79 – d. 5 December 2002, b. 9 July 1923

Graham, Winston, OBE, author of the Poldark novels, aged 93 – d. 10 July 2003, b. 30 June 1910

Gray, Lord, Scottish peer, aged 71 – d. 3 July 1931, b. 3 July 1931

Greenhill, Basil, CB, CMG, director of the National Maritime Museum, Greenwich (1967–83), aged 83 – d. 8 April 2003, b. 26 February 1920

Gregorie, Eugene T., yacht and car designer, designed the Lincoln Continental, aged 94 – d. 1 December 2002, b. 12 October 1908

Grenfell-Baines, Sir George, OBE, architect and town planner, aged 95 – d. 9 May 2003, b. 30 April 1908

Grimston of Westbury (2nd), Lord, aged 78 – d. 16 June 2003, b. 14 June 1925

Grimthorpe, Lord, OBE, aged 87 – d. 6 July 2003, b. 16 September 1915

Grimwade, Arthur, director of Christie's (1954–79) and prime warden of the Worshipful Company of Goldsmiths (1984–5), aged 89 – d. 21 November 2002, b. 10 February 1913

Guest, George, CBE, organist and choirmaster of St John's College, Cambridge (1951–91), aged 78 – d. 20 November 2002, b. 9 February 1924

Habakkuk, Sir John, principal of Jesus College, Oxford (1967–84) and vice-chancellor of Oxford University (1973–7), aged 87 – d. 3 November 2002, b. 13 May 1915

Hall, Conrad, Tahiti-born cinematographer, worked on *Butch Cassidy and the Sundance Kid* and more recently *American Beauty*, aged 76 – d. 4 January 2003, b. 1926

Hambro, Charles, Conservative life peer and banker, aged 72 – d. 7 November 2002, b. 24 July 1930

Harris, Richard, actor, aged 72 – d. 25 October 2002, b. 1 October 1930

Harrison, Sir Donald, ear, nose and throat surgeon, developed a procedure allowing throat cancer patients to speak, aged 78 – d. 12 April 2003, b. 9 March 1925

Haslam, Lord, industrialist, chairman of British Steel (1983–6) and British Coal (1986–90), aged 79 – d. 2 November 2002, b. 4 February 1923

Havelock-Allan, Sir Anthony, Bt., film producer, worked on *Brief Encounter* (1946) and *Great Expectations* (1946), aged 98 – d. 11 January 2003, b. 28 February 1904

Hawker, The Rt. Revd Dennis, suffragan bishop of Grantham, (1972–87), aged 81 – d. 31 January 2003, b. 8 February 1921

Hawkins, Sir Paul, Conservative MP for Norfolk South West (1964–87), aged 90 – d. 29 December 2002, b. 7 August 1912

Heath, Henry, CMG, QPM, CPM, commissioner of police in Hong Kong (1959–67), aged 90 – d. 29 July 2002, b. 18 March 1912

Heim, The Most Revd Bruno, first Apostolic Nuncio to Britain, aged 92 – d. 18 March 2003, b. 5 March 1911 in Switzerland

Hepburn, Katherine, American actress, aged 96 – d. 29 June 2003, b. 12 May 1907

Herbert, Jocelyn, set designer at the Royal Court, aged 86 – d. 6 May 2003, b. 22 February 1917

Hibbert, Sir Reginald, GCMG, diplomat, aged 80 – d. 5 October 2002, b. 21 February 1922

Hill, Christopher, FBA, historian and master of Balliol College (1965–78), aged 91 – d. 24 February 2003, b. 6 February 1912

Hiller, Dame Wendy, DBE, actress, aged 90 – d. 14 May 2003, b. 15 August 1912

Hird, Dame Thora, OBE, actress, comedienne and television presenter, aged 91 – d. 15 March 2003, b. 28 May 1911

Hodgson, Sir Derek, judge and law commissioner, aged 85 – d. 10 October 2002, b. 24 May 1917

Hogg, Vice-Admiral Sir Ian, KCB, DSC, vice-chief of the Defence Staff (1967–70), aged 91 – d. 2 March 2003, b. 30 May 1911

Hope, Bob, entertainer, aged 100 – d. 23 July 2003, b. 29 May 1903

Hylton-Foster, Baroness, DBE, life peer, convenor of the Cross-bench peers (1974–95), aged 94 – d. 31 October 2002, b. 19 May 1908

Ienaga, Saburo, Japanese historian, nominated for the Nobel Peace Prize in 2001, aged 89 – d. 1 December 2002, b. 3 September 1913

Jenkins of Hillhead, Lord, OM, PC, life peer, Home Secretary (1965–7) and (1974–6), Chancellor of the Exchequer (1967–70), president of the European Commission (1977–81), one of the founders of the Social Democratic Party and its first leader in 1981, aged 82 – d. 5 January 2002, b. 11 November 1920

Jones, Aubrey, PC, Conservative MP (1950–65), chairman of Labour's National Board for Prices and Incomes (1965–70) and Liberal Party candidate 1983, aged 91 – d. 10 April 2003, b. 20 November 1911

Joy, Thomas, LVO, bookseller at Hatchards in Piccadilly (1965–85), aged 98 – d. 15 April 2003, b. 30 December 1904

Katz, Prof. Sir Bernard, FRS, biophysicist, won the 1970 Nobel Prize for Medicine for his work on neurotransmitters, aged 92 – d. 20 April 2003, b. 26 March 1911 in Leipzig, Germany

Keinosuke Enoeda, chief instructor to the Karate Union of Great Britain (1968–2003), aged 67 – d. 29 March 2003, b. 4 July 1935, in Japan

Keith, Alan, OBE, broadcaster, aged 94 – d. 18 March 2003, b. 19 October 1908

Keith, Stuart, ornithologist, aged 71 – d. 13 February 2003, b. 4 September 1931

Kelly, Dr David, CMG, scientist, UN arms inspector and biological warfare advisor at the Ministry of Defence, aged 59 – d. 18 July 2003, b. 17 May 1944

Kerruish, Sir Charles, OBE, president of Tynwald (1990–2000), aged 86 – d. 23 July 2003, b. 23 July 1917

Khan, Prince Sadruddin Aga, KBE, spiritual leader of the Ismaili Shia Muslims and UN High Commissioner for Refugees (1965–77), aged 70 – d. 12 May 2003, b. 17 January 1933 in Paris

Kilbourn, Annelisa, British veterinarian and wildlife expert in Africa, aged 35 – d. in a plane crash 2 November 2002, b. 27 June 1967

Knight, Sir Arthur, chairman of the textile group Courtaulds (1975–9) and of the National Enterprise Board (1979–80), aged 86 – d. 5 April 2003, b. 29 March 1917

Lasko, Prof. Peter, CBE, director of the Courtauld Institute (1974–85), aged 79 – d. 19 May 2003, b. 5 March 1924

Leckie, Viscount Younger of, KT, KCVO, TD, PC, Secretary of State for Scotland (1979–86), and for Defence (1986–9), aged 71 – d. 26 January 2003, b. 22 September 1931

Lew, Jonathan, chief executive of the United Synagogue (1986–98), aged 65 – d. 26 February 2003, b. 23 November 1937

Lloyd, Terry, ITN reporter, aged 50 – d. near Basra in Iraq whilst reporting on the war 22 March 2003, b. 21 November 1952

Longden, John, jockey, aged 95 – d. 14 February 2003, b. 15 February 1907

Longford, Elizabeth, Countess of, CBE, author, aged 96 – d. 23 October 2002, b. 30 August 1906

MacGregor of MacGregor, Brig. Sir Gregor, Bt., 6th Baronet of Lanrick and Balquhidder, 23rd Chief of Clan Gregor and Grand Master Mason of Scotland (1988–93), aged 77 – d. 30 March 2003, b. 22 December 1925

Maclean, Vice-Adm. Sir Hector, KBE, CB, DSC, chief of Allied Staff, Mediterranean (1959–62), aged 94 – d. 19 February 2003, b. in Bangladore, India, 7 August 1908

MacNaughton, Ian, actor and television director, worked on *Monty Python's Flying Circus*, aged 76 – d. 10 December 2002, b. 30 December 1925

Mann, Herbie, American jazz flautist, aged 73 – d. 2 July 2003 in Pecos, New Mexico, b. 16 April 1930

Margadale, Lord, aged 72 – d. 6 April 2003, b. 17 July 1930

Mathison, Peter, chief executive of the Benefits Agency (1995–2000), aged 57 – d. 21 November 2002, b. 29 March 1945

Matta, Roberto, Chilean surrealist painter, aged 91 – d. 25 November 2002, b. 11 November 1911

McClatchey, Deaconess Diana, campaigner for women's ordination, aged 82 – d. 4 July 2003, b. 10 July 1920

McCowan, Sir Anthony, PC, Lord Justice of Appeal (1989–97), aged 75 – d. 3 July 2003, b. 12 January 1928

McGowan, Lord, aged 64 – d. 6 May 2003, b. 20 July 1938

Menuhin, Lady, ballerina, aged 91 – d. 25 January 2003, b. 12 November 1912

Millichip, Sir Bert, chairman of the Football Association (1981–96), aged 88 – d. 18 December 2002, b. 5 August 1914

Mizell, Jason 'Jam Master Jay', member of influential rap band Run-DMC, aged 37 – shot dead 30 October 2002, b. 21 January 1965

Moiseiwitsch, Tanya, CBE, theatre designer, aged 88 – d. 19 February 2003, b. 3 December 1914

Moore, Lt.-Cdr. Richard Valentine, GC, CBE, awarded the George Cross for defusing unexploded bombs during the Second World War, aged 87 – d. 25 April 2003, b. 14 February 1916

Morgan, Prof. Walter, CBE, FRS, biochemist and one of the first molecular biologists, vice-president of the Royal Society (1961–4), aged 102 – d. 10 February 2003, b. 5 October 1900

Neaman, Yfrah, OBE, Israel-born violinist and teacher, aged 79 – d. 4 January 2003, b. 13 February 1923

Nevill, Maj.-Gen. CB, CBE, DSO, GOC, 2nd infantry division, aged 95 – d. 19 September 2002, b. 14 July 1907

Nicholson, Max, CB, CVO, environmentalist and author, helped to establish the World Wildlife Fund, aged 98 – d. 26 April 2003, b. 12 July 1904

Nixon, Robert, artist, illustrator and cartoonist, best known for his comic strip artwork in *The Beano* and *The Dandy*, aged 63 – d. 22 October 2002, b. 7 July 1939

Ogden, Sir Michael, advocate and chairman of the Criminal Injuries Compensation Board (1975–89), aged 76 – d. 31 January 2003, b. 9 April 1926

Oram, Daphne, composer, pioneer of electronic music, director of BBC's radiophonic workshop, aged 77 – d. 5 January 2003, b. 31 December 1925

Osborne, Adam, entrepreneur, introduced the first portable computer the *Osborne 1* in 1981, aged 64 – d. 18 March 2003, b. 6 March 1939

Oxfuird, 13th Viscount of, CBE, Deputy Speaker House of Lords (1990–2003), aged 68 – d. 3 January 2003, b. 1934

Pain, Sir Peter, High Court judge, aged 89 – d. 16 January 2003, b. 6 September 1913

Paul, Noel, CBE, chief officer of the Press Council (1968–79), aged 87 – d. 5 December 2002, b. 29 December 1914

Peake, Air Cdre. Dame Felicity, DBE, director of the Women's Auxiliary Air Force (WAAF) and later first director of the WRAF, aged 89 – d. 3 November 2002, b. 1 May 1913

Peck, Gregory, actor, aged 87 – d. 12 June 2003, b. 5 April 1916

Pedder, Air Marshal Sir Ian, KCB, OBE, DFC, ground attack specialist and controller, National Air Traffic Services (1981–5), aged 76 – d. 4 December 2002, b. 2 May 1926

Perry of Walton, Lord, OBE, FRS, life peer and vice-chancellor of the Open University (1969–81), aged 82 – d. 18 July 2003, b. 16 June 1921

Persson, Erling, founder of Hennes & Mauritz (H&M), aged 85 – d. 28 October 2002, b. 21 January 1917

Perth, 17th Earl of, PC, aged 95 – d. 25 November 2002, b. 13 May 1907

Poulton, His Hon. William, judge, aged 65 – d. 29 December 2002, b. 15 December 1937

Pounds, Maj.-Gen. Derek, CB, aged 80 – d. 7 November 2002, b. 13 October 1922

Prestwich, John, medieval historian, Fellow of Queen's College, Oxford and member of the Bletchley Park Hut 3 team responsible for decoding Enigma (1941–4), aged 88 – d. 25 January 2003, b. 26 June 1914

Prigogine, Prof. Vicomte Ilya, winner of the Nobel Prize for Chemistry in 1977, aged 86 – d. 28 May 2003, b. 25 January 1917, in Moscow

Rado, Gaby, foreign correspondent at Channel 4 News, aged 48– d. whilst reporting in Iraq 30 March 2003, b. 17 January 1955 in Budapest, Hungary

Redgrave, Lady, actress, aged 92 – d. 23 May 2003, b. 28 May 1910

Reinhardt, Max, publisher, aged 86 – d. 19 November 2002, b. 30 November 2002

Reisz, Karel, Czech-born film and theatre director, directed *Saturday Night and Sunday Morning* (1960) and *The French Lieutenant's Woman* (1981), aged 76 – d. 25 November 2002, b. 21 July 1926

Ritts, Herb, photographer, aged 50 – d. 26 December 2002, b. 1952

Roberts, Percy, chairman and chief executive of Mirror Group Newspapers (1977–80), aged 82 – d. 21 January 2003, b. 30 July 1920

Robertson, Ian, director of the National Army Museum (1988–2003) and archaeology contributor to *Whitaker's Almanack*, aged 60 – d. 1 August 2003, b. 4 April 1943

Robinson, Derek, director of the Euratom/UKAEA Fusion Programme and Culham Science Centre, aged 61 – d. 2 December 2002, b. 27 May 1941

Ross, Sir Keith, Bt., consultant cardiothoracic surgeon and member of the medical team which performed the first UK heart transplant, aged 75 – d. 18 February 2003, b. 9 May 1927

Rothschild, Baroness Eugene de, also known as Miss Jeanne Stuart, actress, aged 94 – d. 12 February 2003, b. 13 August 1908

Rowley, Frank, civil engineer responsible for the Dornoch Firth Bridge and Falkirk Wheel, Scotland, aged 62 – d. 17 March 2003, b. 4 May 1940

Ryder of Eaton Hastings, Lord, life peer and chairman of the National Enterprise Board (1974–7), aged 86 – d. 12 May 2003, b. 16 September 1916

Salisbury (6th), Marquess of, aged 86 – d. 11 July 2003, b. 24 October 1916

Sanyal, B. C., Indian artist, aged 101 – d. 9 January 2003, b. 22 April 1901

Saunders, Sir Peter, theatre manager and producer, staged the West End's longest running play, *The Mousetrap*, aged 91 – d. 6 February 2003, b. 23 November 1911

Schimmel, Prof. Annemarie, German-born Islamic scholar and linguist, aged 80 – d. 26 January 2003, b. 2 April 1922

Schlesinger, John, television and theatre director, aged 77 – d. 25 July 2003, b. 16 February 1926

Serota, Baroness, life peer, Deputy Leader of the House of Lords and social reformer, aged 83 – d. 21 October 2002, b. 15 October 1919

Shawcross, Lord, GBE, PC, QC, life peer and privy counsellor, Attorney-General (1945–51) and chief prosecutor at the Nuremberg War Crimes Tribunal, aged 101 – d. 10 July 2003, b. 4 February 1902

Sheene, Barry, MBE, motorcycling champion, aged 52 – d. 10 March 2003, b. 11 September 1950

Shelton, Sir William, MP for Clapham (1970–4) and Streatham (1974–92), aged 73 – d. 2 January 2003, b. 30 October 1929

Shields, Carol, author, shortlisted for both the Booker and Orange Prizes in 2003, aged 68 – d. 16 July 2003, b. 2 June 1935

Shields, Sir Neil, OBE, MC, chairman of the Commission for New towns (1982–95), aged 83 – d. 12 September 2002, b. 7 September 1919

Shrewsbury, Countess of, aged 90 – d. 19 February 2003, b. 24 January 1913

Simone, Nina, jazz singer, aged 70 – d. 20 April 2003, b. 21 February 1933

Smith, Peter, OBE, chairman of Securicor (1974–89), aged 82 – d. 21 November 2002, b. 18 August 1920

Smith, Prof. Sir John, CBE, QC, FBA, jurist and academic author, aged 81 – d. 14 February 2003, b. 15 January 1922

Stanbridge, Air Vice-Marshal Sir Brian, KCVO, CBE, AFC, aged 78 – d. 12 February 2003, b. 6 July 1924

Stodart of Leaston, Lord, PC, life peer, aged 86 – d. 31 May 2003, b. 6 June 1916

Stokes, Alexander, crystallographer, worked on determining the structure of DNA, aged 83 – d. 5 February 2003, b. 27 June 1919

Strummer, Joe, lead singer of The Clash, aged 50 – d. 22 December 2002, b. 21 August 1952

Stubbins, Albert, footballer, aged 83 – d. 28 December 2002, b. 17 July 1919

Studd, Sir Peter, GBE, KCVO, 643rd Lord Mayor of London (1970–1), aged 86 – d. 22 June 2003, b. 15 September 1916

Sullivan, Johnny, British middleweight boxing champion (1954–5), aged 70 – d. 4 February 2003, b. 19 December 1932

Swanwick, Sir Graham, MBE, QC, High Court judge, aged 96 – d. 23 June 2003, b. 24 August 1906

Thatcher, Sir Dennis, Bt. MBE, TD, businessman and husband of Baroness Margaret Thatcher, aged 88 – d. 26 June 2003, b. 10 May 1915

Thistlewaite, Prof. Frank, CBE, founding vice-chancellor of the University of East Anglia, aged 87 – d. 17 February 2003, b. 24 July 1915

Tidbury, Sir Charles, chairman of Whitbread (1978–84), aged 77 – d. 3 July 2003, b. 26 January 1926

Titman, Sir John, KCVO, secretary of the Lord Chamberlain's Office (1978–91) and serjeant-at-arms to the Queen (1982–91), aged 76 – d. 11 January 2003, b. 28 May 1926

To Huu, 'poet laureate of North Vietnam' and deputy prime minister of reunified Vietnam (1980–6), aged 82 – d. 2002, b. 1920

Todd, Sir Garfield, prime minister of Southern Rhodesia (1953–58), aged 94 – d. 13 October 2002, b. 13 July 1908

Torlonia, Infanta Beatriz, great-granddaughter of Queen Victoria and eldest daughter of King Alfonso and Queen Ena of Spain, aged 93 – d. 23 November 2002, b. 22 June 1909

Turnball, Archie, publisher and director of Edinburgh University Press (1953–87), aged 79 – d. 8 February 2003, b. 7 July 1923

Urbani, Dr Carlo, epidemiologist, president of Médicins Sans Frontières Italy (1999–2003), aged 46 – d. of Sars 29 March 2003 in Bangkok, b. 19 October 1956

Vogelpoel, Pauline, MBE, director of the Contemporary Art Society (1956–82), aged 76 – d. 22 December 2002, b. 24 April 1926

Wainwright, Richard, Liberal MP for Colne Valley (1966–70) and (1974–87), aged 84 – d. 16 January 2003, b. 11 April 1918

Ward, Maj.-Gen. Sir Philip, KCVO, CBE, aged 78 – d. 6 January 2003, b. 10 July 1924

Watson, Graham, head of the literary agency Curtis Brown, aged 89 – d. 14 November 2002, b. 8 June 1913

Welch, Ann, aviatrix, holder of the British women's distance record for gliding and manager of the British gliding team for 20 years, aged 85 – d. 5 December 2002, b. 20 May 1917

Wesley, Mary, prolific author, books include The Camomile Lawn, aged 90 – d. 30 December 2002, b. 24 June 1912

Weston, The Rt. Revd Frank, bishop of Knaresborough, aged 67 – d. 29 April 2003, b. 16 September 1935

White, Barry, American soul singer, aged 58 – d. 4 July 2003, b. 12 September 1944

Wilberforce, Lord, KT, PC, CMG, OBE, Lord of Appeal in Ordinary 1964–82, aged 95 – d. 15 February 2003, b. 11 March 1907

Wilkins, Sir Graham, chairman and chief executive of the Beecham Group (1975–84) and chairman of Thorn EMI (1958–89), aged 79 – d. 2 July 2003, b. 22 January 1924

Williams, Sir Robert, microbiologist and president of the Royal College of Pathologists (1975–8), aged 86 – d. 24 May 2003, b. 30 June 1916

Williamson, Malcolm, CBE, composer and master of the Queen's Music (1975–2003), aged 71 – d. 2 March 2003, b. 21 November 1931

Williamson, David, genealogist and co-editor of Debrett's Peerage and Baronetage (1983–2003), aged 76 – d. 21 April 2003, b. 25 February 1927

Wilson, Sir Charles, chairman of the Committee of Vice-Chancellors and Principals (1964–7), aged 93 – d. 9 November 2002, b. 16 May 1909

Wilson, Sir Robert, CBE, FRS, astrophysicist and space scientist, aged 75 – d. 2 September 2002, b. 16 April 1927

Wright, Lady Beatrice, MBE, American-born MP for Bodmin and vice-president of the Royal National Institute for the Deaf, aged 92 – d. 17 March 2003, b. 17 June 1910

Young, Baroness, PC, leader of the House of Lords (1981–3), aged 75 – d. 6 September 2002, b. 23 October 1926

Zorina, Vera, ballerina, aged 86 – d. 9 April 2003, b. 2 January 1917

ARCHAEOLOGY

BOXGROVE

The majority of sites of archaeological interest that are discovered are destroyed after recording by development or agriculture. However, a small number, especially in urban areas, are back-filled to allow further investigation in years to come. An even smaller minority are so important that they are acquired for permanent preservation. Therefore, English Heritage's purchase of a disused quarry at Boxgrove near Chichester, Sussex, announced in May 2003, is especially noteworthy.

English Heritage concluded the purchase of the 20-acre site (with £100,000 from the Aggregates Levy Sustainability Fund) because it is the most significant Stone Age site in Britain, with potential for further discoveries. Its importance derives from the discovery in 1993 of Boxgrove Man, represented by a shinbone belonging to a hominid, *Homo heidelbergensis,* which is an ancestor of both the Neanderthals and modern man. Two teeth from another individual were found in the same area. These remains date to about half a million years ago. At that time what is now the quarry would have been a raised beach at the foot of a chalk cliff where a spring replenished a small lake that was an important source of water for both the early humans and contemporary animals, including elephants, giant and red deer, rhinoceros, bison and horses. So well are the remains preserved that researchers from University College, London have been able to demonstrate how the hunters were squatting down as they made stone tools to butcher and then eat the carcass. Now that the site is owned by English Heritage, the intention is to make Boxgrove a centre for research into this earliest period of human activity in Britain as well as for education and training.

STONEHENGE CHANGES

Plans for the better management and interpretation of Stonehenge, a World Heritage site, took a step forward in the year under review when English Heritage published details of a £57-million redevelopment scheme. In addition to replacing the facilities for visitors, it hopes to persuade arable farmers to return land to grass within the boundary of the 7,000-acre site, with funding for this aspect from a government-backed grant scheme paying £160 per acre. Of the total cost, £26 million has been pledged by the Heritage Lottery Fund, while English Heritage is providing £11.7 million and the Government £10 million, with the shortfall of £10 million to be raised by an appeal. The target date for the completion of the scheme is 2008, but this will depend on the outcome of public inquiries and the resolution of the two most contentious issues: the new visitor centre, and transportation. It is clear from the vigour of public debate that discussion of these vital issues is far from over.

Andrew Selkirk in *Current Archaeology* (December 2002) highlighted another issue relating to this vast site: 'where is the main access to Stonehenge to be, and what should we tell people about Stonehenge? Here we come to the strange story of Durrington Walls. Durrington Walls is the huge henge monument excavated in the late 1960s in advance of road building by Geoffrey Wainwright, and it is clearly the forerunner of Stonehenge. In the late Neolithic, it must have dominated the landscape. It is a huge site where the whole tribe could have assembled from many miles around for its annual celebration. The story of Stonehenge is of the abandonment of Durrington Walls and its replacement by Stonehenge, of the abandonment of Grooved Ware pottery and its replacement by Beaker pottery, and of the transition from a tribal society to a chieftain society. Durrington at present is left on the edge of the World Heritage site and is neglected. It needs to be brought forward, the story of Stonehenge begins there, and this is where I believe the visit to Stonehenge should also begin. This is the story of Stonehenge that needs to be told: will English Heritage tell it?'

AVEBURY

The press reported in April 2003 that work had begun at the Avebury stone circle in Wiltshire, owned by the National Trust, to straighten two of the 14 foot-high stones which have been leaning perilously out of true. The Avebury stones are substantially larger than those at Stonehenge, and form one of the largest prehistoric stone circles in Europe. As work progressed to straighten the two 50-ton stones, resetting them in the position in which they were erected about 2,500 BC, it is reported that archaeologists discovered another stone which could perhaps weigh as much as 100 tons. This unexpected discovery will require careful evaluation.

AMESBURY BURIAL FINDS

Excavation in advance of development in Amesbury, Wiltshire, discovered the burial of an individual who, because of the arrowheads and wristguards buried with him, came to be known as the 'Amesbury Archer'. In his account of the discovery in *Current Archaeology* (February 2003), Dr Andrew Fitzpatrick summarises the significance of the discovery and that of a nearby grave, known as the archer's companion, as follows: 'The "Amesbury Archer" is not only early (his body is radiocarbon dated to between 2,400–2,200 cal. BC), and his grave the most well-furnished Beaker burial yet found in Britain, but it is one of the "richest" in Europe. In the past Beaker burials have often been considered "rich" if they contain more than a handful of objects, one of which is of copper or bronze, or of gold. It is the number of finds, almost 100 (mainly of flint), their early date within the Bronze Age, the quality of some of them, and above all the associations between them that is particularly important. All the finds are of well-known types within the Beaker cultural "package" that is found across much of central and western Europe in the 3rd millennium BC. The gold "earrings" or perhaps more likely, hair tress ornaments, are rare, with only seven other find spots known in Britain, and are typical of primary Bell Beaker goldwork. The association of three tanged copper knives of slightly different shapes and sizes is without parallel, and their metals are all continental European. The number of beakers from a single burial is also unique. The "all over cord" beaker has the sort of decoration found on the earliest British beakers, although of the others, two are comb decorated and the two by the Archer's face are decorated with virtually identical plaited cord impressions. The arrowheads, "wristguards" or "bracers", and other tools are amongst the largest groups of archery equipment found together. The flints represent materials for most eventualities and appear to have been largely produced by one person. The Archer's burial site lies about 5 km south-east of Stonehenge. It was later in the 3rd millennium BC, on the basis of the radiocarbon dates between 2,400–2,100 cal. BC, that the massive stones were brought to Stonehenge for the stone circles and the avenue leading to or from the River Avon was built. The great temples of Woodhenge and Durrington Walls, both a similar distance away from the burial of the Amesbury Archer and his companion, continue to be used and modified. Can it be a coincidence that the richest Early Bronze Age burial in Britain and his companion should be so close to the great monuments of Durrington Walls, Stonehenge and Woodhenge? ... The discovery of the burial of the Amesbury Archer and his companion shows for the first time that at this date there were individuals and perhaps families of great wealth and status. That this elite had ties across Europe is shown by the discovery that the Archer seems to have come from central Europe.' This latter suggestion derives from oxygen-isotope analysis of the teeth, which indicates 'that the Archer lived as a child in central Europe, perhaps close to the Alps'.

Nor were the discovery of the Amesbury Archer and his companion, with the impressive range of grave goods, the only significant discoveries in the area. *Current Archaeology* (June 2003) reported that only half a mile away at Boscombe were found the remains of six people dating to the Early Bronze Age at around 2,300 BC. 'Preliminary analysis of the bones suggested that there were four adults and two children. The grave contained four pots in the Beaker style, some flint tools, one flint arrowhead and a bone toggle for fastening clothing. The grave is unusual in that it has such a large number of people buried in it.' Dr Andrew Fitzpatrick of Wessex Archaeology is quoted as saying, 'This new find is really unusual. It is exceptionally rare to find the remains of so many people in one grave like this in southern England. The number of beaker pots in the grave, four, is only exceeded by the grave of the Amesbury Archer, where there were five. The grave is fascinating because we are seeing the moment when Britain was moving from the Neolithic into the Bronze Age, around 2,300 BC. The large number of bodies placed in this grave is something more commonly found in the Neolithic, but the Beaker style pottery is found in Bronze Age burials.'

PREHISTORIC LONDON

As a rule, less attention has been given to the archaeology of the London area before the advent of the Romans, so the opening of a new permanent gallery covering this period at the Museum of London in October 2002 is to be welcomed. Of the items on display, two in particular attracted the attention of the media, and not without cause. The first is the reconstruction of the face of Shepperton Woman, so named after the location of her grave. She lived some time during the period 3,640 and 3,100 BC, probably came from Derbyshire or the Mendips judging by the lead deposits on her teeth, and died some time between the ages of 30 and 40. What is of particular interest is the application to this ancient skull of the modern facial reconstruction techniques used by the police. Caroline Wilkinson, a facial anthropologist at Manchester University Medical Faculty, reconstructed the face from the fragments of skull. Modelling clay was used to represent muscle structure and in time the shape of the head emerged, showing that, according to Ms Wilkinson, 'She had quite a heavy brow and strong jaw fairly typical of a lot of the skulls of this age'.

The second skull of interest was one found on the foreshore at Chelsea by Fiona Haughey of the Institute of Archaeology and which was radiocarbon dated to somewhere between 1,750 BC and 1,610 BC in the Middle Bronze Age. It was a male skull with a hole measuring approximately 1¾ inches by 1¼ inches which had been neatly made, suggesting trepanation rather than an attack. Dr Simon Mays of English Heritage said that 'Trepanning is probably the oldest form of surgery we know' and Chelsea Man could have had the operation to cure physical complaints such as headaches or alternatively to release evil spirits that were thought to cause various kinds of mental incapacity. In all, some 40 trepanned skulls have been found in Britain. The operation on Chelsea Man would have been carried out with a flint tool and despite the pain [he would have undoubtedly suffered] there is no evidence of the wound becoming infected; Dr Mays said, 'He would have been walking around happily with this hole in his head for a long period'.

FIRST TB VICTIM

The police have found that there is merit in retaining evidence from the past so that new scientific techniques may be applied to it. This has proved equally the case with the skeleton of a man who died in his 30s in about 300 BC and whose grave was excavated in Tarrant Hinton, Dorset, during the 1970s. The application of DNA tests to the skeletal material suggests that this man was one of the earliest victims of tuberculosis in Britain. Although a respiratory disease, TB also affects the spine, resulting in clear evidence of damage. Dr Simon Mays of English Heritage said, 'This is the earliest case of TB yet found in Britain and it indicates that even in a remote rural settlement the disease was here centuries before the Roman conquest. It could have come over from the Continent, where we know the disease was present in prehistoric times, through trading links with Dorset.'

SUTTON COMMON FORT

As part of the Sutton Common Project, English Heritage has been funding an excavation near Askern, South Yorkshire, which has resulted in the discovery of a most unusual Iron Age site, described in the *English Heritage Conservation Bulletin* (October 2002). Although the site has been known for over 100 years, the Sutton Common Project has revealed something of the nature of the fort at the site. This 'comprises two enormous and enigmatic enclosures, one with a grand entrance, linked by what appears to be a ceremonial walkway'. The director of excavations, Robert Van de Noort of Exeter University, said, 'Within the ramparts we have uncovered the remains of several round houses, boundaries, a well and a wide avenue through the site. But we have found no evidence ... to show that anyone actually lived here. It ... may mean that Sutton Common was primarily a symbolic or ceremonial place, rather than a political or economic centre'. The co-director of the excavations, Henry Chapman of the University of Hull, observed, 'The building techniques and architecture of the ramparts closely resemble those of early Iron Age hill forts elsewhere in England. However, instead of building the fort on a hill, the impassable wetlands were used to create an impregnable site, the biggest marshland fort in England.'

IRON AGE HOARD

A discovery by amateur archaeologists field-walking in east Leicestershire in 2000, followed up by professional excavations in 2001 and 2003, has uncovered the largest hoard of Iron Age gold and silver coins – over 3,000 –

ever found in this country. As Jonathan Williams and Richard Hobbs of the British Museum explain in *Minerva* (July/August 2003), these coins are 'mostly ancient British but many Roman *denarii* as well. The British coins are predominantly of the series attributed to the people known as the *Corieltauvi*, who seem to have inhabited large swathes of the East Midlands and Lincolnshire. This site alone has doubled the total number of coins of this series so far recorded, and has made many types once rare and exciting seem rather ordinary, while also turning up some unusual new pieces. The most intriguing of these is a completely new type of the powerful King Cunobelin, whose capital was at Colchester. This coin names both him and another king, Dubnovellaunos, previously thought perhaps to have been his predecessor. This is the first time their names have ever appeared together on the same coin, and it raises the question of whether they were contemporaries. It reminds us (once again) just how little we actually know about the history of Britain before the Roman invasion. The coins were discovered in over 15 discrete hoards, located close together on a hill-top. The coins are undated, but best estimates put the bulk of them in the early decades of the first century AD, just before the Roman invasion ... Work is still ongoing, but so far no Roman coins later than the reign of Tiberius (AD 14–37) have been discovered within the hoards. This does not mean that they were not buried later, after the Roman invasion in AD 43, but we cannot be certain. Why is this so important? Because up to now we have been unable to show conclusively through archaeology that Roman coins circulated in Britain before the invasion. Many pre-Roman British coin designs were copied from Roman ones, so they must have. But it seemed we could not find them, until this find materialised.'

With the largest group of Iron Age coins was found the remains of a Roman dress, or parade, helmet. A rare find indeed, and the remains are being treated in the conservation department of the British Museum. 'In addition to the coin hoards and helmet fragments, the site has also recently produced a series of shallow pits containing animal bones, including some complete skulls and carcasses. This latest discovery only adds to the "Britishness" of the site. The curious grouping of all those coin-hoards so close to one another, together with the unusual find of the helmet, had already pointed in the direction of ritual activity as the reason behind the deliberate abandonment of all this precious metal in one place. There were too many for it to be a series of emergency concealments. But the proximity of the animal bones is really suggestive of some form of open-air communal religious activity. We know almost nothing for certain about the religion of the ancient Britons (almost everything written about "Celtic" religion, and especially the famous Druids, in ancient Britain is unfounded speculation). There are no sources that can tell us anything about what kind of festival might have involved the slaughter (and eating?) of animals, and the burying of gold and silver ... But at the moment our working hypothesis is that all the finds on this site, both metal and bone, were deposited in the course of ritual activity.'

LONDON INSCRIPTION

Current Archaeology (November 2002) reports that 'The most important Roman inscription to be found for several years was discovered recently in London'. The location of the excavation is Tabard Square in Southwark and the small plaque, only about a foot square, was found by Pre-Construct Archaeology Ltd in a pit. It is reported to be well carved and preserved, although the bottom part is missing. The text has been translated as: 'To the Powers of the Emperors/And to the God Mars Camulus/Tiberinius Celerianus/A citizen of the Bellovaci/Moritix (equals an unknown title)/Of the Londoners ...'. The report notes that the god Camulus is an element in the name for Roman Colchester, *Camulodunum,* which means 'the fortress of Camulos'. The word *Moritix* is a genuine puzzle in that it is 'a word that is unknown except in inscriptions'. It has been interpreted in a number of ways, including 'sea captain' or 'head of a guild'. Perhaps most interesting of all is the Latin word translated as 'Of the Londoners', namely *Londiniensium,* about which it is noted that 'it refers to a people, not a place. It is usual in Latin inscriptions to refer to the full title of a place ... Here Londoners stand alone, with no reference to the *civitas,* or indeed the *vicus* of London. This confirms the suggestion that the status of London was peculiar, and there is an implication that London had no official status – it was neither a *civitas* nor a *vicus:* in other words, London was not a chartered town, but was imperial domain and remained so till the end, when in the fourth century it was renamed Augusta – the emperor's town'.

SHADWELL

During December 2002 and January 2003 the media showed considerable interest in the unexpected discovery of Roman remains in Shadwell, about one and a half miles east of the Roman city of London. The site is described by Alistair Douglas of Pre-Construct Archaeology Ltd in *Minerva* (May/June 2003): 'The discovery of significant Roman remains at Shadwell East, including a bath-house, point to the existence of a settlement of far greater importance than previously appreciated. This extra-mural settlement may be a reflection of a structural shift in the economy of Late Roman London.' The site investigated by Pre-Construct Archaeology was at 172–6 The Highway, Shadwell, London E1, and the archaeological work was undertaken in advance of residential redevelopment by Wimpey Homes. Because of the significance of the finds, the remains have been buried under sand and shingle to enable future generations to reinvestigate the site when the block of flats built there is no longer required.

It is noted that the bath-house had at least 11 rooms, including an apse, and had, as would be expected, a hypocaust underfloor heating system, with an external fire-box adjacent to the north wall providing the heat and the hot air being drawn 'through an arched opening into the building under the floor and channelled up hollow box flue tiles to warm the walls. The fire-box may also have heated a water tank that could have supplied hot water to a plunge pool ... Immediately to the north was an open yard area bounded by a range of clay-and-timber buildings, with hearths and walls with painted plaster. The floor levels produced pottery, coins, hairpins, jewellery, and a fragmentary inscription.' The view is that the bath-house was in operation for some 200 years until it was demolished, apparently deliberately, in about 400 AD. It is observed that: 'Bathing was central to the Roman way of life, not only for the purposes of personal hygiene but also as a focus for social interaction and discourse. A *mansio* or inn with a substantial bath suite attached seems a reasonable interpretation for the remains found at Shadwell. The site's location one and a half miles east of *Londonium,* close by a Roman road, is of major significance. It is immediately to the west of the Roman "tower" excavated in 1974 and 1976 and is opposite and to the east of Tobacco Dock, excavated in 2002. The direction of flow of the Roman ditches suggests there may have been a river channel forming a junction with the Roman road. This would have made a suitable location for a trading settlement'.

INCHMARNOCK

Minerva (March/April 2003) gives an account of excavations undertaken at St Marnock's Chapel on Inchmarnock, off the west coast of Bute, Scotland, by Dr Christopher Lowe of Headland Archaeology Ltd on behalf of the island's owner, Sir Robert Smith. It is noted that these excavations 'have revealed a remarkable number of pieces of inscribed slate. Provisionally dated to the eighth or ninth century AD (possibly continuing later), this is the largest assemblage of such material known from Scotland ... One outstanding piece, with a sketch on one side and practice writing on the other, provides further evidence of literacy at the site, as well as an insight into the dress, weaponry and ship technology of the time ... Incised on one face are four human figures, in profile facing to the right, an oared ship, and a possible letter-form (d?) with a terminal serif. The scene is dominated by a complete figure with long swept-back hair, moustache, whiskers on the chin, and a prominent brow. The neck and body are clothed in a mailshirt. The leg on the left side of the figure is cross-gartered; the other is possibly covered in mail. The shoes are pointed, and a cross-hatched belt or strap hangs between the legs. To his left are the remains of another figure (extant from feet to just below the shoulders), similarly clad in a mailshirt/skirt combination'. Behind this dominant figure is a second shorter figure who appears to be secured to the figure in front by a length of rope or chain. After the detailed description of what is depicted, it is noted that: 'Datable palaeographically to the eighth or possibly the ninth century, this is a find of international importance. It not only provides graphic evidence for the dress, weapons, and ship technology of the time, but may also provide a very personal account by a local, literate individual of a significant event in the island's history. The stone depicts three warrior-like figures, at least one of whom is armed with a spear. The figure on the right, however, is dressed differently; the head is downcast and the hands appear to be shackled. The slight build may suggest a young male or female, or possibly an ecclesiastical figure. The box-like feature around the figure's wrists may represent a padlock and shackle; alternatively, it may represent our earliest depiction of a house-shaped shrine or relic'. Following his description Dr Lowe observes that: 'In conclusion, the stone appears to depict a slave-raiding party and it is, perhaps, tempting to identify the wild-haired warriors as Vikings. But why was the stone carved? The piece may have formed a template for work in another medium, perhaps for a piece of metalwork or tapestry. It may, on the other hand, constitute a devotional piece in its own right, perhaps commemorating a local martyr'.

THE NEWPORT SHIP

The Newport Ship was found during a watching brief in 2002 on the very deep excavations required for the orchestra pit of a new theatre and arts centre commissioned by Newport City Council in Wales. The site is on the west bank of the River Usk and as preservation of the ship where it was found was not practicable, a full programme of excavation was commissioned. This is described by the project officer J. Kate Howell in *Current Archaeology* (February 2003). 'The ship extended for 23 m in length across the coffer

dam, although the bow and stern lay just outside the excavation area. Almost all of the hull was intact, surviving in places up to deck level. The maximum width of the ship as found was 8 m, tapering towards the ends. The vessel lay with the bow inland and the stern towards the river, apparently within an old channel ... The ship was constructed in the northern European "clinker-built" tradition (i.e. with overlapping side planks or strakes), current from the Viking period into the 16th century. Almost all of the structural timbers are oak, although the keel is beech, and some softwood species were used for internal features ... Within the clay filling of the vessel were numerous ship timbers, likely to have come from the vessel itself, but discarded during its subsequent breakup. Many of these were internal structures that rarely survive in ancient shipwrecks, including fragments of decking and rigging. A sample from a dislocated timber – a large structural member known as a "knee" – underwent tree-ring analysis by Nigel Nayling of the University of Wales, Lampeter. The parent tree had been felled between September 1465 and April 1466 ... The ship would certainly have been capable of sea voyages, and almost certainly sailed around the coast of Wales and England. Finds suggest that it travelled to Ireland, France and Portugal. It is likely that the ship was a trading vessel, rather than a military craft, engaging in commerce around north-west Europe. In the turbulent times of the 15th century, however, merchant ships could well have been commandeered for military service.'

It is not clear what happened to the ship on its last voyage, although damage had been repaired so that the ship could sail into Newport and be docked on the west bank of the River Usk. The account notes: 'Artefacts, both organic and inorganic, were well-preserved within the clay that filled the ship. Around 240 shards of pottery were recovered, all Merida ware produced in Portugal throughout the medieval and post-medieval periods. This type of pottery was often used on board ships, and it may be that these pots were used by the crew, rather than being the remains of a cargo. Large quantities of animal and fish bones were recovered, possibly including marine mammal, along with numerous oyster, mussel and limpet shells. The rim of a small glass vessel was found, and several stone cannon shots suggest the presence of at least one gun on board, for signalling purposes and defence.' Of the six coins found on board four were Portuguese, struck in Lisbon and dating to the period between 1433 and 1481.

The archaeological significance of the Newport Ship was clear both to the public, who supported its preservation, and to the National Assembly for Wales, which agreed funding to lift, conserve and display the exposed part of the ship. It is unfortunate, given the undoubted importance of the discovery, that media accounts were preoccupied with the disputes between various parties about precisely how much of the ship should be saved and which organisation owed money to which other.

RIPPING UP HISTORY

In July 2003 English Heritage published a report entitled *Ripping Up History* which warned of the damage done to archaeological sites through modern farming methods. Dr Simon Thurley, the chief executive of English Heritage, observed that intensive ploughing had probably done more damage in 60 years than traditional agriculture had done in the preceding 600. English Heritage called for changes in the law and to the method of farm subsidies, and it may well be that proposed changes to the EU Common Agricultural Policy offer the possibility of a more heritage-focused programme of farming support. It is not simply a matter of attitude but also of the power of modern agricultural machinery; for example, farm tractors are up to ten times more powerful than those in the 1940s and the resultant force exerted during ploughing cannot be withstood by any archaeological site. English Heritage would therefore prefer to see archaeological sites revert to grass or to low-impact cultivation techniques.

This is not the first occasion that attention has been drawn to the damage done by intensive farming. In autumn 2002, Dominic Powlesland of the Landscape Research Centre in the Vale of Pickering, Yorkshire, pointed out the damage being done there by deep ploughing. A particular problem in the Vale of Pickering is the encouragement given to farmers to grow potatoes suitable for chip manufacture. A similar warning had been given by Dr Keith Ray, the country archaeologist for Herefordshire, who also drew attention to changes in potato-growing practices that, according to a media report, 'are completely erasing archaeological sites that otherwise would be safely buried beneath the reach of agricultural cultivation'. The problem would appear to be that over the last 10 to 15 years supermarkets and therefore chip manufacturers have demanded perfectly shaped, unblemished potatoes, which has led farmers to grow potatoes on land previously used for other arable crops in order to avoid pests and diseases. Dr Ray also said, 'It is time for us to put our hands up now and call a stop to our infatuation with the perfect potato if we want to rescue our heritage'. It is reported that the Department for the Environment, Food and Rural Affairs is working on plans for the management of archaeological sites threatened by potato cultivation.

JOHN HURST

The death of John Hurst (1927–2003) has robbed British archaeology of one of its major contributors. After reading archaeology at Cambridge University, he pursued a career as an inspector of ancient monuments in the former Ministry of Works and its successor incarnations. He was one of the founding fathers of medieval and post-medieval archaeology, having a long and continuing interest in the ceramics of those hitherto neglected periods. In addition to his dating and interpretation of ceramic material from excavations and in museum collections, John Hurst will be particularly remembered for his partnership with Maurice Beresford in excavating the deserted medieval village site at Warram Percy in Yorkshire. The excavations there continued for some 40 years and were crucial in the development of open-area excavation. The Deserted Medieval Village Research Group and the Society for Post-Medieval Archaeology were just two of the bodies which he helped to found and through which archaeological complexities became better understood by new generations of archaeologists and the interested public.

ST PANCRAS' CEMETERY

The construction of St Pancras Railway Station in north London in the mid 19th century led to the Midland Railway Company cutting through a graveyard and disturbing some 40,000 graves, to great public disquiet. The same graveyard, Camley Street Cemetery, was back in the news at the end of 2002 as archaeologists excavating some 2,000 graves were instructed to stop work, having completed the investigation of only about 100, and to leave the site on the orders of the Channel

Tunnel Rail Link company. More than 1,000 graves were threatened with destruction by mechanical means without proper recording. The reason this could happen is that the Channel Tunnel Rail Link operates under a special Act of Parliament which allows many of the usual requirements to be overridden in the interest of speed of development. Although the CTRL obtained a Home Office licence to remove the graves, the archaeologists claimed they were given insufficient time to complete a proper investigation.

Although the issue was resolved following an outcry, it is worth explaining the cemetery's significance. It would appear that the most recent of the graves there dates from 1854 and as records exist of the people who were buried there, the potential for a major study of the London population was considerable. David Miles, the chief archaeologist of English Heritage, said, 'The remains are well-preserved. We are dealing with people for whom there is documentary evidence. We know who they were, often what jobs they did, and what they died of. They included rich and poor, immigrants and natives. The bodies already excavated have been showing very interesting pathologies, and we now know that burials like these are enormously important historically.'

MARITIME ARCHAEOLOGY

As a consequence of the National Heritage Act 2002, English Heritage has become the lead agency for the management of England's maritime archaeological heritage, i.e. any relevant site which lies between the low-water line and the edge of the 12-mile limit. While these sites may exceed 40,000 in number, only 51 shipwrecks around the UK have been officially designated by the Advisory Committee on Historic Wreck Sites. Sean Kingsley in *Minerva* (September/October 2002) observes that: 'Several of these shipwrecks contained fascinating hulls and cargoes, which are unique in UK waters and whose study promises access to poorly known trade networks and naval architectural traditions. Henry V's *Grace Dieu* along the Hamble river in Hampshire, for example, was a massive behemoth which pushed available overlapping wooden plank technology (clinker construction) to the limits. Too expensive to use and too prestigious to risk on the high seas once launched in 1420, she was almost immediately mothballed at her mooring and eventually sank in 1436 after being struck by lightning and burnt. The Salcombe Cannon site in south-west England contains Moroccan scrap jewellery and coins dating from 1510–1636, struck in Marrakesh and Fez under the Sa'did Sharifs dynasty. Her study will pioneer knowledge about trade between North Africa and England. A far different site is the *President,* a probable English East Indiaman which sank off Mounts Bay in Cornwall in 1684 whilst on a homeward voyage with an extremely valuable cargo of spices, indigo, drugs, Indian goods, and 100 tons of pepper ... Although the site was salvaged soon after being wrecked, it represents the first English East Indiaman located in UK waters'.

The challenge to English Heritage in its new role is considerable, as is the need for funding, not least to enable publication of the backlog of excavation reports to adequate academic standards. It is reported that: 'Reasonably, English Heritage has not accepted that dissemination of the backlog of unpublished work should be financed from its core funding. However, to its credit it has applied to the DCMS for necessary funding as a one-off measure to oversee a programme of appropriate level of analysis, conservation, and dissemination.'

ARCHITECTURE

BALTIC CENTRE FOR CONTEMPORARY ARTS
Gateshead
Architect: Ellis Williams Architects

In September 1994, Dominic Williams, of architects Ellis Williams, won the competition to design the conversion of the Baltic Flour Mills building on Gateshead's riverside into an international centre for contemporary arts. This began a process of design development, interspersed with various artistic events, fundraising activities and several re-assessments of the brief and concept for the galleries. During this time the concept took root of the centre as an 'art factory', in which the galleries would not be centred about a permanent collection but would provide an environment where artists and public could together engage in a process where 'the edges between learning and leisure, education and entertainment are blurred' and where all these influences are brought to bear on the process of artistic creation. From this it was a short step to utilising the construction of the new centre as the first subject of this ethos. Phases of enabling works, partial demolition and stabilisation, and the insertion of a new interior have all been absorbed into significant artistic and cultural events during the eight years of construction.

The Baltic Flour Mills have long been a monumental presence on the south bank of the River Tyne, just downstream from the famous bridge-scape of the Gateshead-Newcastle river crossing. The building was a disused flour silo, its massive masonry walls enclosing ranks of tall concrete silos, with facades of blank brickwork buttressed visually by towers at the four corners. The new gallery has been created by stripping away the internal complex of silos, removing the short infill brick walls at each end to admit light, and installing an independent internal structure of columns and floors to house the various facilities required for the new galleries.

Entry to the galleries is through a new riverside building accommodating a café, bar, bookshop and riverside terrace. This is separate from the mill structure except for a short glazed link taking the entrance route through to the ground-floor level. It is a low-slung, ground-hugging two-storey structure, deliberately designed so as not to detract from the power and verticality of the main building. It brings the gallery entrance substantially closer to the point where a constant flow of pedestrians arrives on the south bank via the new Millennium Bridge (architects: Wilkinson Eyre), the new icon of Tyneside with its twin cable-strung arches acting in tandem to permit the passage of ships.

Visitors are guided into the centre through two substantial blank piers made from Corten steel, an appropriately robust and industrial finish to reflect the muscularity of the original building. From the entrance, the route passes up short flights of stairs (there is also a lift), and on to the main ground-floor gallery level. Ahead lies a bank of three viewing lifts, but just before entering the mass of the Mill building, the ceiling opens up and through a glazed roof, the newly glazed west elevation is suddenly revealed, capped by the dramatically projecting public viewing box at level 5.

To gain access to the galleries, one passes the bank of three glass-sided lifts to enter the main ground-floor gallery/auditorium. This level provides studio accommodation for a number of resident artists as well as incorporating a large loading bay delivering to an enormous goods lift at the east end of the building. The goods lift serves all main floor levels and enables substantial works of art to be distributed throughout the building.

The glass-sided lifts provide the main vertical circulation to the principal gallery spaces, which are placed on the upper floors. They are set back from the newly glazed infill section to the west facade, leaving a clear void from ground level to level 5 that is roughly the height of the original concrete silos. The principal public art spaces are placed towards the top of the building. Level 3 includes the main 'close control gallery', i.e. an exhibition space subject to a high degree of environmental control that allows very sensitive pieces of art to be displayed. Level 4 features the High Gallery; as its name implies, this is the tallest of the spaces, lit by a high level of natural daylight, which enters through long sloping laylights either side of the soffit of the central band of space that is placed at level 6, the top floor. At the intermediate level 5, the lifts give access to a public viewing platform, expressed as a projecting box with a fully glazed wall, that provides stunning views up the River Tyne.

The structure at roof level is a lightweight construction of steel and glass and currently is laid out as a restaurant. It rises above the parapet level of the original side walls, allowing views over the river and city. The structural design of the restaurant space includes an arched steel roof member welded to vertical columns which stand free in front of the line of the glazed side walls and rise from a projecting beam supporting the floor. They are linked at eaves and floor with further steel beams to form a vierendeel truss running along each side of the space. These in turn are supported back onto the tops of the inset columns rising through the galleries below by means of stainless-steel forked supports picking up each pair of verticals on the vierendeel. The complex geometry of the stainless-steel supports rising and falling diagonally in section and on plan is resolved into special stainless-steel castings stitch-welded to the tubes. This filigree of supports is visible through the rooflights to level 4, helping to reinforce the concept of a roof-top box hovering over the galleries below.

The loads pass down the building on two new rows of columns, each set back from the line of the north and south original walls, which sit on their own foundations. The columns were inserted following the removal of the concrete silo shafts to create the clear internal space. The reinforced concrete silo shafts provided much of the structural stability to the original building, and this had to be compensated for during the demolition and reconstruction phases. It was provided by cocooning the entire building in a space frame restraining the external walls while the silos were carefully removed section by section from the inside.

The original walls have been carefully restored, while the corner towers, which now accommodate staircases, lifts and vertical riser shafts, have each acquired a new Corten steel cap; the colour of the rusting steel faces makes a close match with the rust-red brickwork of the facades.

One concession to the current vogue for hi-tech insertions is made at the east end, where the tall glass walls between the two corner towers can be shaded by a huge PVC-coated polyester sail that slides across the outside of the facade on rails. Above it, reflecting the projecting viewing box on the west elevation, is a slightly smaller projecting box with a fully glazed end wall. This is one of the most eye-popping ladies lavatories in the country, with cubicles tucked into the back wall and a range of free-standing wash-basins lined up in front of the glazing, provided the ladies with extraordinary views over the river valley and city as hands are washed!

The new gallery opened to the public on 13 July 2002, and is already playing an important role in the continuing renaissance of the region. The result of a long and difficult gestation period is a building of monumental scale that can accommodate in its wealth of display and studio spaces all that modern art has to offer, but remains true to its industrial background.

BEDDINGTON ZERO ENERGY DEVELOPMENT
Hackbridge, London
Architect: Bill Dunster Architects

'Sustainable development' is often paid lip service by developers who are either ignorant of the underlying principles of ecologically sustainable building design or simply unwilling to put their money into projects that are seen as risky and unconventional because they are not the norm. The BioRegional Development Group, however, is one developer committed to demonstrating that design of a more sustainable type can provide attractive and affordable living accommodation for the average person and still be commercially viable. Developed in partnership with the Peabody Trust, the design and construction of this 'urban eco-village' in south London is the first major project to be realised by the Group. It demonstrates the practical application of sustainable technologies in energy efficiency, renewable energy sources and water harvesting, coupled with social initiatives including communal car use and the use of local products and materials for construction and energy.

Beddington Zero (fossil) Energy Development, known generally as BedZed, is the first high-density low-rise housing development in the UK to be designed on the basis of 'carbon neutrality', i.e. by generating all its heat and power from renewable sources and avoiding the use of fossil fuels in its energy creation processes, it can claim to have zero net carbon emissions, and to make no contribution to global warming or the greenhouse effect. However, this development is also special in that it extends the sustainable approach right through the life cycle to embrace a total concept of 'green living'.

BedZed comprises 82 homes, plus office space and 23 live-work studio apartments. It achieves a density of 352 habitable rooms per hectare, far higher than current inner London norms. Together with a combined heat and power unit, the accommodation is squeezed onto a 1.65 hectare site formerly occupied by a sewage works. It provides for a wide social mix, with social and affordable housing for key workers and people on low incomes and a proportion for shared ownership and for sale on the open market. Selling prices are comparable with more conventionally designed homes in the area.

The housing units range from one-bedroom flats to four-bedroom town houses, and are arranged in a series of south-facing terraces, separated by narrow mews. The terraces are limited in length to a maximum of six ground-floor units per terrace. Solar orientation was the key determinant of the overall layout, with each terrace adopting a stepped section. This combined typically a two-storey maisonette with a second-floor flat above, all with generous south-facing window walls, sheltering a north-facing live-work/office unit at ground level, with a small mezzanine level lit by an overhead rooflight. The stepped section over the live-work unit provides two small areas of external terrace/gardens. The lower of these is accessed via a bridge crossing the mews from the terrace behind, though access is shared between adjacent flats, generating three bridges per terrace. It is a concept that both visually and physically links the terraces together, though whether physical separation will prove a disincentive to the use of these gardens in the sky remains to be seen.

The south-facing terraces have full-length windows forming the outer wall of a buffer zone or 'sun space', maximising solar heat gain, while north-facing glazing is kept to a minimum. On the north, east and west elevations the windows are triple-glazed units with Krypton gas filling the air spaces, while rooflights are also triple-glazed, with low-e glass.

Walls and roofs have been provided with substantial levels of thermal insulation; the 300 mm depth of Rockwool insulation leading to increased overall wall thicknesses, evident where the smaller windows generate very deep reveals and sills on the inside. Exposed concrete floors have been used for their thermal mass and the regulating effect they have on temperature variations over the course of the day, while the concrete ground slab has also been provided with a 300 mm layer of polystyrene sheet insulation. All these measures are intended to reduce heat loss to the point where satisfactory ambient temperatures can be maintained by little more than body heat, cooking and lighting, eliminating the need for heat input from external sources.

To maximise the energy retention properties of these elements, great attention has been paid to air tightness in the construction and the elimination of unwanted air leaks and draughts. The corollary of these provisions is, of course, that ventilation needs to be carefully controlled and capable of sensitive adjustment to suit occupiers' needs while maintaining a sufficient influx of fresh air. Ventilation at BedZed is achieved through natural means, with wind-driven cowls situated at roof-level over each unit. The distinctive wind-cowls project high above the roof-line and add a note of playfulness with their brightly coloured vanes. They are designed to point into the wind, forcing fresh air down into the rooms below via a duct and wall-mounted delivery grilles. Stale air is drawn out via similar grilles and ducts serving the kitchen, bathrooms and toilets, helping to remove unpleasant odours and excess moisture, by exploiting the negative pressure generated on the downwind side of the wind-cowls. Incoming air is tempered by a heat exchanger located in the cowl, which recovers between 50 per cent and 70 per cent of the heat (or coolness) from the outgoing air and maintains the internal temperature of the rooms.

With the building's heating needs provided by solar and occupant-generated energy, general power requirements are significantly reduced. This has made the implementation of an on-site biofuel heat and power plant a cost-effective, as well as sustainable, option. The plant is fuelled by chipped urban tree waste, a material which local authorities generate in abundance and which is supplied to the development free of charge. The woodchip is delivered to a chip store, from where it is lifted into a gasifier which converts it into wood gas. The gas is used to drive a diesel engine which generates electricity. The plant has been sized so that it will deliver sufficient electricity to run all the low-energy lighting and appliances used in the development. Waste heat from the generation process is used to provide hot water for homes and offices, which is distributed across the site via a heavily insulated district heating system.

Mains water consumption is also greatly reduced by the development's rainwater recovery and grey-water treatment systems. Rainwater is collected from the roofs and gardens and stored in tanks located within the foundations of the terraces. This provides water for flushing toilets and for irrigation of the gardens. Sewage and waste effluent passes through a septic tank and the output is fed through a biological treatment system that restores the waste water to a sufficiently clean standard for it to be returned to the storage tanks and then used for flushing the toilets again. The combination of recovery systems and use of water-efficient appliances, such as dual-flush low-flush toilets, has led to as much as a 40 per cent reduction in mains water usage.

Every aspect of the design and procurement of the BedZed development has been subjected to the same rigorous principles of sustainability and minimum environmental impact. This has extended to the sourcing of materials, which took into account such factors as the benefits of using locally produced materials to minimise transportation and the reuse of salvaged materials, such as reclaimed structural steel, recycled green glass 'sand', reclaimed timber, reused aggregate excavated from the site and incorporated in foundation works and roads, and even recycled crushed concrete. It is also evident in the consideration of transport needs. The development aims to reduce car dependence by fostering a mixed living/working ethic, but also addresses fossil-fuel depletion with the provision of a number of communal, electrically powered cars. These derive their energy from a range of photovoltaic cells installed as part of the south-facing glazed enclosures to the upper-level flats.

Work commenced on site in May 2000 and the residents moved in between March and summer 2002. Despite the usual, inevitable, teething problems, early reports are largely favourable about the living conditions, both environmental and social.

LABAN CENTRE
Deptford, London
Architect: Herzog and de Meuron

This vibrant and complex insertion into the deprived hinterland of Deptford Creek, in south-east London, provides a stunning new home for the Laban Centre, an international school for dance training, health and performance formerly based in New Cross. The school has some 350 students from all over the world, and was founded after the Second World War by Hungarian emigré Rudolf Laban. The £22 million building is intended to act as the vanguard of a programme of regeneration in one of the poorest areas of the UK.

Herzog and de Meuron, winners of a design competition in 1997, have invested an essentially simple shed-like building with considerable subtlety and sophistication. The defining characteristic of the design lies in the complex internal planning, which is opened up to the outside world through a sequence of tapering circulation spaces cutting through the plan and providing visual links to key reference points in the surrounding area.

The building is approached from the west across a garden, which will be landscaped with geometric sculpted grass mounds forming a terrace and amphitheatre in front of the main elevation. The facade facing the garden is a gentle concave curve, the centre recessed so that the building embraces the visitor entering through the garden and up a shallow ramp to the main entrance doors. The first and most striking aspect of the building is its shimmering glazed elevations, which immediately set it apart from its more prosaic neighbours and lend it a slightly surreal air. Predominantly silver grey but highlighted with vertical strips infused with a palette of striking colours, it is mostly translucent, giving hints of the internal spaces and activities. It is formed from clear and coloured polycarbonate sandwich panels; an ultra-violet protective coating on the outer sheet and colour applied to the inner sheet are set in front of an inner translucent glazed facade to create a broad ventilated cavity. The strips rise from ground level to parapet with no apparent supports or fixings, each panel set flush with its neighbour to create an uninterrupted smooth face.

This mysterious curtain of light contrasts with a number of clear glazed windows, which seem to be randomly disposed but are sited where the internal spaces can profit from views to the outside. The window openings are punched through from the inner façade; the sharp rectangular shapes overlay the flush surface and are further accentuated by the crisp white frames of the openings. During the day these appear as an abstract pattern of dark reflective glazed rectangles set against a softly shimmering background. By night the relationship changes dramatically as the clear windows provide views deep into the interior and the translucent polycarbonate screen glows with the lighting of the interior spaces, emphasising the bands of colour.

The distinctive and subtle colouring of the facade anticipates the more intense application of the same palette of colours in the vibrant internal spaces. The architects' desire to give colour a pivotal role in the design of the building led to a collaboration with the artist Michael Craig-Martin. He proposed a limited but vibrant and contrasting range of colours: magenta, lime green and turquoise. As one progresses through the various circulation spaces each colour in turn assumes dominance, with the other two used for doors and secondary elements such as lockers, giving a varied but co-ordinated series of lively and welcoming spaces. Elsewhere the colour range is neutral, with black, grey or white predominant, relieved by the occasional touch of natural wood, as in the dance studio and staircase handrails.

The second unusual aspect of the building becomes apparent on passing through the entrance doors into the lobby. From here, it can be seen that the external ramp is a continuation of large expanses of sloping floor, leading up and down to different levels in the building. The interior of the building has been laid out to suggest an internal 'townscape', with sloping 'streets' and irregular 'urban' spaces, rather than a conventionally ordered interior with corridors.

Immediately upon entering the building one is confronted by a large and dominant spiral staircase in black concrete, spiralling upwards through the space. When it meets the floor, the balustrade wall of the stair extends into a long, gently curving dividing wall between the ramped street to the left, which rises past the entrance to the main auditorium and terminates in a bar area, and another narrower curving passageway to the right which leads down to the lower levels and a rear exit. To the right of this interplay of curves and ramps the two lower storeys are visible through a full-height glazed wall. The upper level contains the library, the lower level a cafeteria and dance health centre. Both the library and cafeteria floors are also ramped, sloping downwards to the rear in the opposite direction to the rising ramp to the left of the spiral stair. The complexity of the changes of level and the juxtaposition of curved and angled planes generates a great sense of movement and drama.

The main auditorium, the focus of the building's primary dance performance activity, sits at the heart of the building and acts as a generator for the open 'townscape' of the upper levels. It is surrounded by 10 of the 13 individual dance studios at the upper level, which are interlinked by a meandering circuit of circulation areas structured around three wedge-shaped corridor spaces. These widen as they approach the exterior and open up the interior to views of the outside world through the clear glazed sections in the external envelope. Two narrow cross-corridors connect these tapering spaces, running past two internal light-wells punched down into the heart of the building and providing a series of visual interconnections through their glazed walls. At one point, part of the floor of one light-well is angled unexpectedly downwards so that it penetrates the upper parts of the ramped entrance lobby below, admitting daylight and offering glimpses of the upper levels.

The irregular geometrical planning resulting from the tapered internal corridors, the curved frontage and the non-parallel sides of the building means that no two internal spaces are the same. The spaces on the first floor are taken up into the gently pitched roof, so each of the dance studios has its particular qualities of plan and section, size, lighting and aspect, giving a great sense of variety and interest, and adding to the complexity of the interior architecture. The studios benefit from a diffused lightness and airiness, with the occasional hints of exotic colour suffused into the translucent facade screen contrasting with the sudden clarity of the punched openings for the clear glazed windows.

After the lightness and intense colour of the studio spaces, the 300-seat theatre comes as a complete contrast. Stained black timber boarding lines the walls and floors, providing a 'black box' in which the curving rows of seating focus the attention onto a proscenium arch stage. Nothing is allowed to detract from the performers on stage.

This is a completely unfussy building – no superfluous detail or decoration; robustness and simplicity characterise the selection of materials and their treatment. Yet its highly developed use of curving, sloping and faceted surfaces, coupled with the interplay between transparency, translucence and reflection, and the carefully controlled use of vibrant colours against a neutral background all contribute to the creation of a wonderfully complex, stylish and invigorating piece of architecture.

The surrounding parts of Deptford are in much need of regeneration and it is no coincidence that the new building seeks to emphasise key features of the neighbourhood; the careful orientation of the primary circulation spaces focus on the nearby spire of St Paul's Church to the west, and the masts and rigging of the *Cutty Sark* in Greenwich to the east. Believed to be the world's largest purpose-built contemporary dance centre, Laban provides an inspiring example of what can be achieved through the rigorous application of innovative conceptual

thinking and a happy collaboration between artist and architect.

NATIONAL MARITIME MUSEUM
Falmouth, Cornwall
Architect: Long and Kentish

Falmouth has always had a close relationship with and dependence on the sea. Boasting one of the finest natural harbours in Europe, it is a favoured port for shipping large and small, and had its own fishing fleet. The town is therefore an appropriate home for a maritime museum, and has acquired an exceptional new building to add Falmouth's name to the growing list of Cornish tourist attractions.

Long and Kentish were appointed architect for the project following a competitive interview process in 1996. A site for a new museum had been identified by the water's edge, on an area of reclaimed land left undeveloped after the abandonment of an earlier scheme for luxury houses around a small marina and club house, which was not fully completed. The undeveloped section of land was purchased by a local consortium, the Port Pendennis Partnership, in conjunction with English Partnerships, with the aim of regenerating the surrounding areas of the town, rather than providing more low-density housing.

The site is located towards the southern end of the town, just behind the docks and boathouses, where a headland juts out into the harbour. It is a prominent position addressing both the busy waters of the harbour and the view back towards the docks and the main body of the town, and plays an important role in mediating between the different scales and characteristics of the large, rugged masses of the working boatsheds and the smaller residential units of the surrounding town. When the proposed development of the area is complete, the museum will form the backdrop to a small square formed with two other new buildings, providing a cinema and shops, together with some residential units. This is a deliberate attempt to create a focal point for events and activities that will help to bring an increased sense of public life and participation to this part of the town.

In responding to a challenging site, the architects have devised a complex building that relates in different ways to the varying nature of its immediate surroundings, and captures the qualities of its maritime setting and function. The key element in the composition is the tower, which pins the various components of the building to the site and provides a point of focus at the point where the building literally puts its feet into the water. The tower is a cross between a fortified lookout post and a traditional lighthouse, and from its observation deck at the top provides panoramic views across the town and the estuary. Equipped with video consoles, telescopes and other instruments, the space has the feel of a ship's bridge.

At the bottom of the tower, the shaft of which houses a lift set inside a broad spiral staircase, one descends below the tidal water line into an underwater observation room, where 5-metre high windows of 80 mm thick laminated glass provide aquarium-like views of the marine life in the harbour as the sea rises and falls.

In between these extremes, the museum offers more conventional displays, centred around its core collection of some 140 small boats (the National Collection of Small Boats) donated by the Maritime Museum in Greenwich, and the pre-existing collection of the Cornwall Maritime Museum, recounting in particular the history of the

Cornish packet ships, which has always been housed in Falmouth. Separate proposals for housing these two collections had been presented to the Heritage Lottery Fund, which provided 75 per cent of the funding following the agreement to merge the two submissions into one project.

An exhibition designer, Land Design Studio, was appointed to develop the fitting-out of the museum's design and construction, in a deliberate attempt to integrate as far as possible the architectural concepts with the techniques of display. Often nowadays this involves controlled 'black box' environments, geared to video and computer-based presentations, without any architectural involvement. However, in the new museum a happy compromise has been reached. The core of the building is divided into two major gallery spaces: a 'black box' gallery, enabling lighting and sound visualisations to recreate the experience of being at sea and using archive film footage to present the boats on display in action; the other gallery, and indeed the remainder of the museum, presents the exhibits in natural light.

The building is entered from the small square to the west, and from the admission foyer one can explore the museum in three different ways. Doors to the right lead into the Dark Gallery, a long rectangular hall three storeys high and traversed by an inclined ramp winding up around the perimeter. To the left, past the shop and admissions counter, is the entrance to the Cornwall Gallery straight ahead, or with a right turn one can enter the main Daylit Gallery. The largest of the gallery spaces, this is an impressively tall, robustly structured space, tapering in plan in response to the overall profile of the site, with a workmanlike feel akin to that of a boatshed. Dividing the Daylit from the Dark Gallery, but visible only from the main hall side, is an enormous curved wall faced in pale birch veneered panels. Light streams down from a rooflight above, giving the impression that the whole of the side wall of the gallery is formed from the hull of an ocean liner. It is an effective backdrop to the flotilla of small boats, mostly suspended within the space, but all aligned in the same direction and tilted off the vertical as though they are battling their way together through an invisible sea.

A staircase at the far end ascends to a balcony and from here further sequences of ramps lead back and forth, up to the upper levels, giving views over the hall. At the second floor, the café projects forwards from the main building façade on the north-east corner, with views overlooking the square, the town and the harbour; it is one of the few places on the external elevations where a range of windows is inserted and the interior engages with the outside world.

The café, with its kitchen and servery, forms the upper part of the third major spatial component of the building. This is a narrow wing parallel to the main hall and connected to it spatially through the openings in the structure and the views either way from the ascending/descending ramped walkways. At ground level, adjacent to the first of the Cornwall Galleries and rising through the full height of the space, is the Waterside Gallery. This features an indoor boating pool complete with artificial wind, where would-be young sailors can try their hand with model sail boats. This wing is capped with a dramatic monopitch roof, whose eaves-level slowly drops along its length, giving the alarming impression from the outside that it is about to slide off its supports into the harbour. The downward slope is terminated by the tower, and at this point the building envelope recedes

dramatically, leaving tall columns descending clear into the water below to create a tidal pool sheltered by the oversailing roof. At high level, under the roof, large wooden shutters can be opened in the summer months to admit the sounds and breezes of the estuary and enhance the exhibition experience.

With the exception of the tower, which is faced in a textured blockwork, the majority of the building is clad externally in timber, primarily green oak; this material reflects not only the traditional material used to construct boats but also the vernacular style of the boatsheds and warehouses of the docks and harbourside. The cladding has been handled in a variety of ways to produce a range of visual effects that help to distinguish the individual components of the building while maintaining a coherent colour and scale throughout that gives the complex forms a unified totality. The material will weather over time to a soft silver grey. The pitched roofs are completed in slate, and the south-east corner features a double-gable roof acting in counterpoint to the vertical tower, the two elements separated by an open balcony at second-floor level.

The building engages actively with its surroundings, particularly on the water frontages, where, as a requirement of the brief, walkways provide public access round the building and connect with the quayside and the mooring pontoons for small craft. This fascinating building, opened to the public in December 2002, has restored some of the traditional heart to Falmouth and deserves to be a resounding success.

ART

In 2002–3, there were fewer futile debates than in previous years about the worthiness of the so-called Brit Art movement, perhaps justifiably, as the Young British Artists reached their collective peak over a decade ago. However, the classical music conductor Simon Rattle did fire off a vitriolic parting shot before moving to Germany to direct the Berlin Philharmonic; in an interview with the *Die Zeit* newspaper just before taking up his new post, he lambasted artists such as Tracey Emin and Damien Hirst for producing what he described as 'biographically-oriented art' that was, he claimed, 'bullshit'. Although he has frequently attacked Britain's lack of financial commitment to the arts, these were Rattle's first public comments specifically about the visual arts and were met with derision by the art world.

The 1990s Young British Artists phenomenon was thrust back into the limelight by the opening of Charles Saatchi's much-delayed museum in County Hall. The Edwardian oak-panelled interior of the former Greater London Council's headquarters was widely regarded as a bizarre environment for the display of this art, especially such famous works as Tracey Emin's unmade bed and Chris Ofili's elephant dung paintings. The opening was a media circus but critical reception was cool.

Damien Hirst had a busy year, with some unusual projects. Venturing into virgin territory for an artist, a small piece of his art went into space on the British space probe *Beagle 2*, heading for Mars, where it is due to arrive on Christmas Day 2003; the work doubles as an artistic statement and a calibration tool for the probe's sensors and cameras. He also collaborated on a theatre adaptation of the social and musical experience of Glastonbury, designing the festival sets, with tents, a totem pole and a car. Hirst was not pleased, however, by Saatchi's display of his works at County Hall; he claimed that his spotted mini car, displayed in the gallery's foyer, was never meant to be exhibited as a work of art in that way.

The 'bad girl' of Young British Art, Tracey Emin, was given a showing of new work at Oxford's museum of modern art, now more catchily titled Modern Art Oxford. The Chapman brothers, Jake and Dinos, were also given a show in Oxford, and were subsequently nominated for the 2003 Turner Prize for this show and for an intriguing installation of faux tribal sculpture at their London gallery White Cube. This sculpture was bought by Saatchi for a reputed £1 million. The Chapmans hit the headlines again in July 2003 when they were 'deselected' as official war artists by the Imperial War Museum because it was believed they would use the position to make a political statement against the Iraq war. In their place, former Turner-prize winner Steve McQueen was to be sent to interpret the aftermath of the conflict.

Anthony Gormley, famous for the *Angel of the North*, returned to the north-east to invite residents of Gateshead to have their bodies cast for an exhibition at the new Baltic Centre for Contemporary Art. The volunteers' plaster-cast moulds became the basis of around 250 abstract stainless steel figures. Gormley also installed an array of metallic figures in the Australian outback in 2002, and took his field of tiny terracotta figures on tour to China.

Another of Britain's most vaunted sculptors, Anish Kapoor, awarded a CBE in the Queen's Birthday Honours, unveiled one of the world's largest works of art at the Tate Modern in autumn 2003. His giant red PVC sculpture stretched the full 155 metres of the Tate's cavernous entrance hall and was called *Marsyas* after the Greek flautist flayed alive by Apollo. However, the work was affectionately likened to another instrument, an ear trumpet.

PRIZES

The 2002 Turner Prize was yet again one of the year's talking points, although not so much for its shortlisted artists – Liam Gillick, Fiona Banner, Catherine Yass and the winner Keith Tyson – but for the scornful attack on it of the then Culture Minister, Kim Howells. He was so outraged at the standard of entries for the £20,000 award that he called it 'cold, mechanical, conceptual bullshit'. He hit out at the wider art establishment for letting British art lose its way, but his attacks fell mainly on deaf ears as he is not known for his taste in art, despite having spent four years at art college and being a painter himself. In fact, the work on show was much more varied and less overtly conceptual than in 2001. The prize-winning works by Keith Tyson, which utilised scientific formulae and random thought generation, were much more generous than those of the previous winner, Martin Creed, whose empty room with the lights going on and off caused such uproar. The shortlist for the 2003 Turner Prize included a potter, Grayson Perry, as well as the Chapman brothers, video artist Willie Doherty and installation artist Anya Gallacio.

In October 2002, the Paul Hamlyn Foundation awarded £30,000 bursaries to five artists, including minimalist Ceal Floyer for her *Rubbish Bag*, a black bin bag filled with air and tied at the top.

The annual £24,000 Beck's Futures prize was awarded to Glasgow-based artist Rosalind Nashashibi for a series of seemingly banal but moving films shot in the Midwest of America and on the west bank in Palestine.

Wales staked its claim to a share of the prize scene by instituting the Artes Mundi; worth £40,000, it is the biggest cash award for an individual artist. The first winner, from a shortlist of 12 international entries, will be announced in March 2004.

There were no surprises in the 2003 Citibank Photography Prize, whose £20,000 prize was won by fashion photographer-turned artist Juergen Teller. The runners-up were Czech-born Jitka Hanzlová, Dutch photographer Bertien van Manen, and Briton Simon Norfolk, who documented war-scarred Afghanistan.

A different kind of judging resulted in the publication of the first of *ArtReview* magazine's listings of the 100 most influential people in the art world. The advertising mogul and art collector Charles Saatchi headed the list, while the top ten also included businessmen and philanthropists, such as Ronald Lauder and François Pinault, as well as a painter, Gerhard Richter, at number four and Tate director Sir Nicholas Serota at number six.

THREATS AND THEFTS

The floods that struck central Europe in August 2002 especially affected the East German city of Dresden, where the River Elbe burst its banks. After water levels dropped, the main concern was for Dresden's numerous cultural monuments, including the 19th-century Semper opera house and baroque palaces such as the Zwinger and the Albertinum, both home to thousands of paintings, antiques and works of art. Although works by Raphael, Titian and Correggio escaped unscathed, many works went to the Royal Academy in London from March to June 2003 while the museums were repaired.

The war in Iraq, and in particular the looting and vandalism in Baghdad after the allied forces took control in April 2003, raised fears for the country's archaeological heritage. Outrage was expressed that 170,000 objects had gone missing and that centuries of Babylonian and Mesopotamian history were being destroyed by looters. But after much hyperbolic posturing in the newspapers about the cradle of Earth's earliest civilisations being laid to waste, and heartfelt messages of support from academics and museum colleagues around the world, it was discovered that many of the artefacts had been kept safely in the basement. Eventually, the number of missing objects was put more conservatively at between 3,000 and 12,000 items, although 32 of these were said to be of great importance.

The most bizarre act of art vandalism was undoubtedly the beheading of a statue of former Prime Minister Margaret Thatcher at the Guildhall Art Gallery in London by theatre producer Paul Kelleher. At his court hearing at Southwark Crown Court, Kelleher claimed in his defence that his attack on the 8 ft marble sculpture with a cricket bat was an act of artistic expression against the ills of the world's political system. Kelleher was sentenced to three months in jail.

August 2002 saw the recovery by police in Dublin of a masterpiece by the Dutch old master Peter Paul Rubens. It was one of three works still missing from the 18 works (including a Vermeer, a Goya and a Gainsborough) stolen in May 1986 from Sir Alfred Beit's private collection at Russborough House in Co. Wicklow. The thief was Martin Cahill, known as 'The General', a legendary figure in Irish crime who was murdered by the IRA in 1994. Rubens was in the headlines for a second time that month when his painting *The Massacre of the Innocents* was auctioned at Sotheby's in London. Despite doubts about the accuracy of the work's attribution, it was bought for an astonishing £49 million by the chairman of the Thomson Corporation.

The British Museum complied with the ruling on a claim that four drawings in its collection had been looted from Czech lawyer Arthur Feldmann by the Gestapo in 1939. The London-based Commission for Looted Art in Europe demonstrated that the works were among 750 collected by Dr Feldmann and ruled that they should be returned to his family. This was the first claim against a British collection that demanded the return of works of art, although the Tate has compensated the children of a Jewish man for a painting stolen by Nazis in 1937.

Two works by J. M. W. Turner from the Tate's collection, stolen while on loan to a German museum in 1994, were recovered and returned in December 2002 after a lengthy investigation. Both works, *Shade and Darkness: The Evening of the Deluge* and *Light and Colour: The Morning after the Deluge – Moses Writing the Book of Genesis*, went back on display at Tate Britain in January 2003.

The theft of Van Gogh, Gauguin and Picasso watercolours from the Whitworth Art Gallery, Manchester, in April 2003 turned out to be a protest against the lax security at many regional museums. The works, valued at £2–4 million but not insured, were found in a public lavatory with a note saying, 'We did not intend to steal these paintings, just to highlight the woeful security'. The paintings were not damaged but had been taken out of their frames and rolled up, prompting the belief that this was actually a heist that turned sour, forcing the burglars to jettison the pictures.

AUCTION UPS AND DOWNS

A record price for a British artist was achieved in the modern and contemporary art sales in New York in November 2002, when David Hockney's *Portrait of Nick Wilder*, a trademark Californian pool painting from the 1960s, fetched £1.8 million at Christie's. This explains why Hockney appeared in a list of the top ten bestselling artists published by *ArtReview* in June 2003. At number one was American painter Jasper Johns, whose works at auction have earned a total of £92.8 million.

The biggest buyer of the year was the Las Vegas tycoon Steve Wynn, who spent more than £25 million in less than 24 hours in May 2003. One of the biggest private art

collectors in the USA, Wynn paid £14.6 million for a large Renoir painting at Sotheby's in New York, before spending almost £10.8 million for a self-portrait by Paul Cézanne at Christie's in New York the following evening. At Sotheby's in London in July, Wynn beat off other bidders to secure a self-portrait by Rembrandt for a record £6.9 million.

In the UK art market, 18th-century art eclipsed the hegemony of Victorian pictures in the June 2003 sales, when a portrait of Mary Wordsworth, Lady Kent by Sir Joshua Reynolds sold for £2.69 million at Sotheby's. Like the Victorian market, the sales of Irish paintings were more subdued in 2002–3; since a number of rich buyers, including newspaper magnate Tony O'Reilly and racehorse owner John Magnier, started paying heady prices for Irish artists such as Orpen, Yeats and Lavery in the late 1990s, the top-quality pictures and their potential buyers have steadily faded.

There was hope that the modern and contemporary markets might start to fill the gap left by the diminishing numbers of Impressionist and early 20th-century masterpieces coming to auction. In June 2003, Sotheby's sold a rare Lucio Fontana, the 1964 *Concetto Spaziale*, for £1.4 million, and at Christie's a work by a lesser-known artist, Nicolas de Staël's 1955 *Ciel*, sold for £1.1 million. These were not the best examples of post-war European art by any means, but the results were encouraging. The market with the greatest scarcity of good paintings coming to auction, the Old Masters, nevertheless managed a reasonable sale total of £9.3 million at Christie's, compared to £14.2 million the previous year.

A record price of £12.6 million for the Austrian painter Egon Schiele was achieved at a June sale at Sotheby's, London. The work, *Landscape at Krumau*, was returned to its owners 65 years after it was looted by the Nazis.

The fallout from the 2002 court case over price-fixing by Sotheby's and Christie's hit Sotheby's the hardest. In October 2002, it was fined around £13 million by the European Commission for colluding with Christie's to rig commission fees, bringing Sotheby's total costs for trials and fines to £247 million.

NEW SPACES

Despite some hyperbole following the July 2002 opening of the Baltic Centre for Contemporary Art in Gateshead – it was even dubbed 'the Tate Modern on the Tyne' – the radical £46 million venue quickly came under pressure as it started to run out of funds. In summer 2003 Sune Nordgren, the Baltic's charismatic director who had been in charge of the building and preparations for six years, left to direct the National Museum for Art, Architecture and Design in Oslo, Norway.

Although *Newsweek* magazine included Newcastle-Gateshead in its September 2002 list of the top eight creative cities of the world and despite being the bookie's favourite, designation as the European Capital Culture of 2008 went to Liverpool, which also beat bids from Birmingham, Cardiff, Oxford and Bristol. The Merseyside city, expected to reap £2 billion-worth of investment as a result, was chosen for its new cultural ventures, such as the FACT (Foundation of Art and Creative Technology) Centre and the Liverpool Biennial of Contemporary Visual Art, as well as the existing museums and galleries, and the distinctive waterfront with its architectural richness. The importance of Liverpool's success was highlighted by a report showing that in 2002 three times more money was spent on arts venues in Manchester and Liverpool than in London. The Northwest Development Agency revealed that almost £100 million was spent in the region, compared with £33.7 million on new or updated facilities in London.

London's open spaces received a revamp when Lord Foster's scheme to redesign Trafalgar Square got under way with the pedestrianisation of the north side, nearest the

National Gallery. Plans to excavate the underground vaults around the square and install a glass pavilion, similar to that at the Louvre in Paris, were put to Westminster Council and await approval and funding. Six artists – Sokari Douglas Camp, Marc Quinn, Stefan Gec, Sarah Lucas, Thomas Schutte and Chris Burden – are competing to fill the empty fourth plinth in Trafalgar Square. One of them will receive the commission to make a work for the plinth, where it will be displayed for 12–18 months.

The first stage of the £30-million Darwin Centre, a low-key extension to the Natural History Museum, opened in September 2002 to show a collection of rare specimens preserved in jars. The second phase of building is scheduled to open in 2007.

The Queen's Gallery, at the Palace of Holyrood in Edinburgh, was opened in November 2002, with a display of 73 drawings by Leonardo da Vinci from the Royal Collection.

FUNDING AND FINDS

In September 2002, the chairman of the Tate empire, David Verey, said that the five Tate museums were heading for a financial crisis and would have to make cuts of £1.5 million to balance the books. The Government's £27.8 million funding for the Tate was deemed insufficient to help buy significant works for the collection and to support and promote British art. The £2 million available for acquisitions in 2002–3 (£0.2 million less than in the 1982 budget) means that the Tate could miss out on important works. A notable example is Joshua Reynold's magnificent *Portrait of Omai*, which was in danger of being sold to a foreign institution or individual, although it was eventually acquired for the nation.

The British Museum was also denied a government package to help clear its £6 million deficit. The lack of a one-off cash injection in addition to its £36 million grant did not dampen the Museum's 250th anniversary exhibitions in 2003, but was a blow to the new director, Neil MacGregor, who inherited the deficit when he moved to the post from the National Gallery.

A rather cruel joke by a *Sunday Times* reporter emphasised the funding crises at many museums and galleries. The journalist pretended to be a wealthy arts patron keen to donate large sums of money to various museums, but prefaced his negotiations by showing museum directors and fundraisers his own hastily daubed abstract self-portrait. The aim of the undercover operation was to see whether cash-strapped institutions such as the Victoria and Albert Museum, the Royal Academy and the British Museum might be willing to make aesthetic compromises to meet the wishes of donors.

The British Museum's 250th anniversary began with an exhibition of assorted artefacts from the collection under the title 'The Museum of the Mind – Art and Memory in World Cultures'. In February 2003, MacGregor grasped the thorny issue of the Elgin Marbles, saying that they would never be returned to Greece because they could be seen in a broader historical context at the British Museum. However, an olive branch was extended to the Greeks in July 2003 with the suggestion that the Parthenon marbles would be repatriated in time for the Athens Olympics in 2004.

In February 2003, the National Gallery unearthed from its vaults a painting by Italian Renaissance artist Sandro Boticelli, estimated to be worth £10 million; the painting was thought to have lain unidentified for 150 years. The eight-year process of cleaning another picture yielded a similar discovery when it revealed a previously unidentified work to be by the Italian master Giovanni Bellini.

More complicated was the case of an old favourite at the National Gallery, Raphael's *Madonna of the Pinks*. The painting has been on show since 1992, when it was revealed to be a real Raphael and not by an assistant.

However, the work was actually owned by the Duke of Northumberland, who approached the Getty Museum in California to buy the picture for £29 million, in order to help pay for refurbishment at Alnwick Castle. The National Gallery mounted a 'Save the Raphael' appeal to keep the painting in Britain and set about raising the required sum. The director of the National Gallery, Charles Saumarez-Smith, succeeded in bargaining the price down by pointing out how enormous the Duke's tax bill would be if he sold the work abroad. In July 2003, £11 million of lottery money plus £9.5 million from the gallery's own fundraising campaign was enough to keep the Raphael in the country.

SHOWS

The National Gallery spent three years gathering important loans from all over the world to put together the exhibition of Titian's work that opened in February 2003. It was Britain's first large-scale display of the Renaissance master, and from London the show travelled to the Museo del Prado in Madrid, itself a significant lender to the exhibition.

The Victoria and Albert Museum staged the first of the year's big fashion exhibitions, dedicated to the Italian designer Gianni Versace, murdered in 1997, whose designs are synonymous with glamour and showmanship. The display of 130 garments was also a celebration of celebrity, which many interpreted as a shamelessly populist ploy to ensure good visitor numbers. The V&A's record visitor numbers were, however, justified for the exhibition 'Art Deco 1910–39', which attracted 360,000 people before it closed in July 2003.

There were also shows of the fashion photographer Guy Bourdin and the British designer Ossie Clark at the Victoria and Albert, and of the shoe designer Manolo Blahnik at the Design Museum. But the biggest fashion entrant onto the museum scene was Zandra Rhodes, who opened her own Fashion and Textile Museum in Bermondsey, south London. The brightly-coloured building, the work of Mexican architect Ricardo Legoretta, cost Rhodes around £4 million for the privilege of being able to show a collection of 3,000 designs, some her own and some by other fashion designers. Other venerable museums followed suit, including the Royal Academy, which announced that an exhibition of Giorgio Armani designs would open its new premises in the former Museum of Mankind in October 2003.

The Royal Academy also courted controversy by putting on a cutting-edge exhibition of work for sale from the best galleries in London, creating the kind of art fair not normally associated with such an august institution. However, it can and has taken risks, putting on the infamous 1998 Sensation exhibition of Young British Art from the Saatchi collection and more recently 'The Galleries Show' precisely because it is not a publicly funded institution like the Tate or the British Museum.

The Royal Academy's most ambitious, and certainly one of its most successful shows to date, 'The Aztecs', opened in October 2002. It brought together 380 artefacts, including sculptures, masks, mosaics and rare gold objects, to create the largest-ever survey of Aztec culture. However, its next big show, of Egyptian art, had to be cancelled owing to political instability in the Middle East, but theatre producer Andrew Lloyd Webber came to the rescue in May 2003. In place of the cancelled exhibition, Lloyd Webber pledged to show his 200-strong collection of Pre-Raphaelite, Italian and French masterpieces in September 2003.

The big shows at the Tate Modern included retrospectives of two American artists: the Abstract Expressionist painter Barnett Newman, whose vertically striped 'zip' paintings pioneered much of Minimal art; and the enigmatic sculptress Eva Hesse, who died in 1970 at the young age of 34. The Tate's first-ever large-scale display of photography headed a summer of photography shows in

2003. The title of the show, 'Cruel and Tender: the Real in Twentieth-Century Photography', referred to a description of Walker Evans's work as 'tender cruelty'.

The Tate Britain's Lucian Freud exhibition, which ended in September 2002, was a great draw, as was an interesting show entitled 'Constable to Delacroix' which surveyed the influence that British Romanticists had on their French counterparts. Tate Britain's second triennial exhibition of contemporary British art included many of the best artists, young and old, but Cornelia Parker's binding of Rodin's *The Kiss* stole most of the headlines. Bridget Riley, the painter that inspired the term 'Op-art' (optical art) and a thousand and one psychedelic patterns of the 1960s, was also given a big show at Tate Britain.

A rare outing for one of the most neglected 20th-century British artists came at the end of February 2003. Landscape painter and portraitist Graham Sutherland was given a timely retrospective at the Olympia Fine Arts Fair, one of the most significant shows since his death in 1980.

Some of the world's best living artists were on show throughout the year in London. One of the most controversial of performance and installation artists, Santiago Sierra, opened a new space for the Lisson Gallery in September 2002 by shuttering off the space with corrugated metal, leaving bemused collectors and critics standing on an empty pavement. He also caused a stir at the Venice Biennale, the art world's most important biennial gathering, by refusing entry to all those without a valid Spanish passport. The British representative in Venice was painter Chris Ofili, whose red, black and green pavilion, co-designed with architect David Adjaye, won much applause but was denied official prizes at the Biennale ceremony, sparking rumours that Britain and the USA were being tacitly shunned because of the war on Iraq.

Perhaps the most audacious and celebrated contemporary artist of the moment, Matthew Barney, received a showing of his full-length art films in London and subsequently in Edinburgh. His cycle of five bizarre but imaginative 'Cremaster' movies was first shown at Brixton's Ritzy Cinema in October 2002, although Britain was denied the full retrospective museum show that toured with much fanfare from Cologne to Paris and then to New York's Guggenheim Museum.

COMINGS AND GOINGS

Pop artist Peter Blake, best known for his collage design for the Beatles' *Sergeant Pepper's Lonely Hearts Club Band* album cover, was knighted in 2002. Two Scottish artists were awarded OBEs in the Queen's 2003 Birthday Honours; Elizabeth Blackadder had already become Scotland's first female 'painter laureate' in 2001, but Jack Vettriano has largely been ignored by the arts establishment because of his commercial success – he produced the UK's best-selling fine art print.

The pioneering French photographer Henri Cartier-Bresson celebrated his 95th birthday in April 2003. A foundation has been set up in Paris in his honour, and various books and exhibitions celebrated his legacy from almost a century of photography.

Glasgow celebrated the centenary of the death of James Abbot McNeill Whistler with various exhibitions dedicated to his life (a small part of which was spent in Glasgow) and his works. Chief among these is the iconic portrait of his mother, or *Arrangement in Grey and Black: Portrait of the Painter's Mother*, which went on display after years of painstaking conservation.

A much-loved curator and museum director, Bryan Robertson, was one of the losses to the art world during the year. Robertson is credited with introducing Britain to the exciting innovations of post-war American art during his tenure at the Whitechapel Art Gallery from 1952 to 1969.

His 'This is Tomorrow' exhibition first coined the term 'Pop art' and showcased new talents such as Richard Hamilton and Bridget Riley.

The sculptor Lynn Chadwick died in April 2003, at the age of 88. He came to prominence by winning the International Prize for Sculpture at the 1956 Venice Biennale, beating no less than Alberto Giacometti. His angular, spiky works in welded iron, steel, brass and copper led the art critic Herbert Read to define a wave of post-war angst in British art as containing a 'geometry of fear'. This label meant that by the 1960s Chadwick's work was seen in Britain as representative of the previous decade and therefore dated. It did not affect his reputation abroad, but for 20 years he was ignored by much of the British art world. It was not until 1992 that Chadwick received a retrospective exhibition at the Yorkshire Sculpture Park and only in 2002 did he become a Royal Academician.

Another artist who came to prominence during the 1950s and 1960s died in May 2003. Painter Alan Green was one of the few British exponents of complete abstraction, the likes of which are more associated with the New York school of Jackson Pollock and Mark Rothko.

Philanthropist billionaire Sir John Paul Getty II, who died in April 2003 aged 70, was a great benefactor to the arts. He lived in the UK and was a self-confessed Anglophile, which helps to explain the enormous sums (estimated at some £100 million) that he generously donated to such British institutions as the National Gallery and the British Film Institute.

Robert Lenkiewicz, who died in August 2002, was an artist routinely described as an outsider or a rebel. Although born and bred in London, he never achieved much recognition in the capital for his dark and sombre portraits, but gained some notoriety after faking his own death in 1981 and for embalming the dead body of one of his most regular sitters, Edward Mackenzie, a down-and-out nicknamed Diogenes after the Greek philosopher, since both had lived in a barrel. A scandal ensued after Lenkiewicz's death when Mackenzie's body was found in his Plymouth studio, having been embalmed some 20 years earlier, apparently a dying wish of the tramp.

An artist of much greater stature passed away in the same month but on the other side of the Atlantic. Larry Rivers helped change the course of American art in the 1950s and 1960s, paving the way in the USA for Pop artists such as Roy Lichtenstein. Like his contemporary Jackson Pollock, Rivers was as well known for his fast living and bad-boy persona as he was for his art, to say nothing of his varied career as a sometime actor, film-maker, sculptor and jazz saxophonist.

The Chilean-born Surrealist painter Roberto Matta died in November 2002 at the age of 91. One of the last surviving members of the movement founded by André Breton, Matta will be remembered also as a forerunner of the American Abstract Expressionist movement.

The much-admired New York dealer and collector Holly Solomon was also mourned in August. She amassed a considerable collection of Pop art and her interest culminated in her being immortalised in one of Warhol's famous 12-panel portraits. Her pioneering support of early 1970s performance art in a Greene Street loft space led to her first commercial gallery on West Broadway and she maintained her dealing activities until her death.

Eduardo Chillida, one of the greatest modern sculptors of stone, died aged 78 in August 2002. He never realised his most ambitious sculptural project, to hollow out a huge chamber in Tindaya Mountain on Fuerteventura, one of the Canary Islands, largely because of environmental protests, but he was awarded the gold medal of the Spanish Royal Academy of Fine Arts and honoured with a museum near his hometown of San Sebastián.

BROADCASTING

TELEVISION

Much of the year's broadcasting was dominated by the Iraq crisis and subsequent war. Elsewhere, the main terrestrial channels battled it out as competition from multi-channel television increased. Just before Easter 2003, for the first time in British television history, multi-channel television claimed a greater share of viewing (26.1 per cent) than either of the main terrestrial networks; BBC1 achieved 23.9 per cent and ITV1 23.8 per cent. Multi-channel was boosted by the heavily publicised 300th edition of *The Simpsons* on Sky One and a key match on Sky Sports involving Manchester United. But for most viewers the main noticeable difference during the year 2002–3 was the domination of soaps (*Coronation Street* had its best year for a long time), reality shows and factual entertainment such as Channel 4's big successes *Jamie's Kitchen*, *Wife Swap* and *Faking It*. Lifestyle shows, especially those with a property theme, also proliferated. These shows are cheaper to make than more traditional genres like drama, but small-screen fiction can still make a big impact, as the success of two very different programmes showed – Stephen Poliakoff's first costume drama *The Lost Prince* on BBC1, and ITV1's edgy *The Second Coming*, set in contemporary Manchester.

WAR GAMES PROVE DEADLY

With opinion polls showing the country divided about going to war with Saddam Hussein, television was inevitably the Prime Minister's chief medium of communication to rally the nation's support. He presented his case in a special edition of BBC2's *Newsnight* hosted by Jeremy Paxman. An invited audience, many of them sceptical about an invasion, quizzed Blair on the Government's foreign policy. The Prime Minister received a more hostile reception when, on 7 March 2003, he defended the imminent war to a live audience of young people on MTV. On ITV1's *Tonight*, an audience of women, unconvinced by his case, slow-handclapped Blair.

When the war started, television offered audiences an unprecedented opportunity to watch events as they unfolded. Reporters and camera crews were 'embedded' with the armed forces, to use the jargon, travelling with troops and stationed on aircraft carriers or at bases. With half the audience connected to multi-channel television, rolling news services like Sky News and BBC News 24 came into their own, providing non-stop coverage. Meanwhile, the main networks interrupted regular schedules for live reporting of events from Iraq at key stages of the conflict. 'War coverage is changed forever,' claimed the BBC's director of news Richard Sambrook.

Never before had audiences been able to see such dramatic, albeit edited, footage of the forces doing the jobs they were trained for. Broadcasters had to follow taste and decency guidelines so pictures of dead bodies or other victims of the war were shown sparingly. But despite so much airtime devoted to the conflict, commentators wondered if viewers were any better informed than in the days before non-stop television news. Opinion formers wanted to know who had the most to gain by having reporters 'embedded' in military units. Was it the public, seeking as true a picture of events as possible, or the Government, keen to put its own spin on events?

Writing in *The Guardian*, BBC presenter and producer Armando Iannucci argued that whereas television coverage of the Gulf War in 1991 resembled a video game because of the hazy computer-generated images of weapons exploding, the present war was more like a perverted form of reality television. 'Rolling news coverage and embedded reporting took us, apparently, right into the heart of the horrific action,' he wrote. 'And yet the coverage of this war was noted for both its inaccuracy and lack of objectivity. If we were getting facts around the clock, why did so many of those facts prove inaccurate?'

Inevitably it was the BBC, legally obliged to be impartial, who received the most intense criticism of its coverage. The anti-war lobby accused the organisation of being 'shackled' by the Government and the military, while the Government and, in some cases, the military, egged on by the *Daily Telegraph*, attacked the BBC for being pro-Iraqi, for giving too much airtime to those who opposed the war and for providing too sceptical a view of events. However, the biggest row over the BBC's reporting came some two months after the fall of Saddam Hussein in the very public and bruising dispute over a report by BBC defence correspondent Andrew Gilligan.

The Government's director of communications, Alastair Campbell, accused the BBC of lying after a report by Andrew Gilligan on the *Today* programme on 29 May. His report claimed that a well-placed source had told him that the Government had deliberately 'sexed up' a dossier on Iraq to show that Saddam could use weapons of mass destruction 'within 45 minutes'. In a subsequent newspaper article, Gilligan named Campbell as the man responsible for exaggerating the threat from Iraq. Campbell denied the charge and later insisted he had been cleared of doctoring the dossier by a House of Commons select committee. The BBC stood by its story. Some observers suggested that the BBC was now more powerful than the Government.

The row took on a new gravity on 18 July when the dead body of Dr David Kelly, the government scientist who turned out to be the source of Gilligan's story, was discovered. His apparant suicide led to calls from MPs for the resignation of BBC chairman Gavyn Davies. Commentators speculated that the row might lead the Government to take revenge on the BBC when the corporation's charter, which guarantees the licence fee, is renewed in 2006.

The star turn of the BBC's Iraqi reporting team was Rageh Omar, based in Baghdad during the war. According to the BBC, nearly 90 per cent of the population watched Omar on BBC News 24 or the main news bulletins. John Simpson, the BBC's veteran world affairs editor, based in the north of Iraq during the hostilities, was less visible than in previous conflicts. Simpson was injured in a 'friendly fire' incident in which the BBC's Kurdish translator, Kamran Abdurrazak Muhammed, was killed by a bomb dropped from a US warplane. Worryingly, the death toll of television news people killed in the war appeared to be higher than in other similar conflicts. For the first time in its history, ITN lost a reporter: Terry Lloyd, a veteran of many wars and one of its most distinguished journalists, was shot dead on 22 March.

Many viewers missed the presence of the BBC's formidable foreign correspondent Kate Adie. In January 2003 the BBC confirmed that Adie had left her post as chief news correspondent. Adie, aged 57, was a frequent critic of what she regarded as the trivialisation of television news, describing herself as a 'terribly old-fashioned old trout' compared with today's reporters and their 'cute faces and cute bottoms, and nothing else in between'. The year saw two other familiar faces from BBC News standing down; Peter Sissons and Michael Buerk were replaced on the *Ten O'Clock News* by Huw Edwards and Fiona Bruce. Youth had apparently triumphed over experience.

It might be crass to talk in terms of any one organisation having 'a good war', but ITV1's decision to move its main evening news bulletin forward an hour to 9 p.m. for the duration of the war proved a ratings winner; seven million people tuned in regularly, double the normal number. Reviewers praised ITV's war reporting, regarding it as a welcome return to form following a generally poor showing by ITV1's main news show *News At Ten*, nicknamed 'News At When' because audiences could no longer be sure what time it would be broadcast. On 24 March, ITV1 achieved 9.3 million viewers – its highest news ratings for five years.

As for the rolling news services, there was a consensus that Sky News had the edge over BBC News 24, while CNN, whose coverage of the first Gulf War was such a triumph, was eclipsed to some extent by the highly patriotic Fox News, owned by Rupert Murdoch's News Corporation. Viewers complained to the Independent Television Commission about Fox's war reporting, but the regulator cleared the channel of breaking codes on impartiality. Speaking at Goldsmith's College, London, in April 2003, the BBC's director-general Greg Dyke attacked Fox, saying: 'Commercial pressures may tempt others to follow the Fox News formula of gung-ho patriotism, but for the BBC this would be a terrible mistake'. However, Sky News's credibility took a knock when in July it was revealed that reporter James Forlong had faked a report during the war; Forlong resigned.

War or no war, the year saw further gains by multi-channel television as the main terrestrial channels defended their audience share in time-honoured fashion. Multi-channel television was boosted further by the successful launch in November 2002 of Freeview, new digital terrestrial service backed by the BBC and Sky which offers up to 30 channels. All that viewers need to watch is a so-called 'digibox', retailing at less than £100, plus a conventional television aerial. No monthly subscription fees are involved. By early summer 2003, research published by the BBC suggested that Freeview was proving even more popular than DVD players; the one million mark was passed in July 2003.

VOTING MANIA HITS TELEVISION

The year's big reality TV hit was ITV1's *I'm A Celebrity ... Get Me Out Of Here!*, presented by Ant and Dec, whose *Saturday Night Takeaway* series also scored during the year. In the show a group of personalities, most past their sell-by date, competed to survive the rigours of life in the Australian rainforest and the verdict of viewers, whose votes decided the eventual winner by a process of elimination. Nearly 11 million viewers tuned in to witness veteran disc jockey Tony Blackburn crowned

king of the jungle in September 2002. Audiences loved seeing B-grade celebrities suffer humiliation; author Philip Hensher wrote: 'I'm absolutely a fan. I love watching these people breaking down before me.' Not everyone agreed. When the second series followed in spring 2003, some opinion formers wondered if *I'm A Celebrity* had gone too far in humiliating the contestants.

One of the year's most engaging television events was BBC2's *Great Britons* initiative, shown in autumn 2002, in which audiences were asked to vote for the greatest Britons ever. Despite alleged attempts at vote-rigging, Winston Churchill won the day, pipping Isambard Kingdom Brunel and Princess Diana. Shakespeare only managed fifth place. However, audience participation by voting was no guarantee of a hit show; BBC1's talent show *Fame Academy* was regarded as a pale copy of ITV's *Pop Idol*. Even Greg Dyke acknowledged that it was derivative.

The year's big comedy hit was BBC2's *The Office*, back for a second series in autumn 2002. Up to five million tuned in to watch this critically acclaimed show, which had a huge impact on public consciousness. Critics compared the central character, the cringe-making Dave Brent, to that other great small-screen anti-hero Basil Fawlty. Some found *The Office* too excruciating to watch; Simon Edge, writing in the *Daily Express*, said: 'There is no denying it is brilliantly scripted, and co-writer Ricky Gervais doubles as one of the cleverest comedy actors on the box; rarely does a performer say so much with a flick of a lip or the glance of an eye. But it was too painful to watch.' A new BBC1 sitcom from Harry Enfield, *Celeb*, in which he played an ageing rock star, flopped, but *My Family*, starring Robert Lindsay and Zoe Wanamaker as the long-suffering parents of the Harper offspring, returned for another successful run.

BBC 2 tickled the nation's funny bone with the successful transfer to television of *Deadringers*, on popular Radio 4 satire show, and new runs of *I'm Alan Partridge, Marion and Geoff* and *The League of Gentlemen*. Further evidence of BBC2's originality in comedy came with *Double Take,* in which doubles of famous people, notably Tony Blair, George Bush, David and Victoria Beckham and the royal family, were filmed in embarrassing situations. *The Evening Standard's* television critic Victor Lewis Smith described the series 'as a gem and the most successful fusion between art and comedy in years'. BBC3, launched in February 2003, struggled to achieve large audiences but the fledgling channel could claim at least one cult hit with the hidden camera comedy show *3 Non-Blondes*.

BIG BROTHER FALTERS

The fourth *Big Brother* series failed to match the impact of the three preceding series. Reviewers agreed that it was not so well-cast as the earlier programmes and had become too politically correct for its own good. Not even the *Sun's* offer of a £50,000 prize to the first (heterosexual) couple to have sex in the Big Brother house could revive interest. About a million fewer viewers watched the 2003 series than had watched in 2002.

Cynics wondered if the saga of Angus Deayton's forced resignation as the host of *Have I Got News For You* in autumn 2002 provided more compelling entertainment than many of the shows that were commissioned to amuse. The tabloids had published new stories about Deayton's serial use of call girls and cocaine. The revelations helped increase the show's ratings as team captains Ian Hislop and Paul Merton teased Deayton on air about his indiscretions. Numerous stand-in presenters were employed to take Deayton's place, perhaps the most hilarious being television veteran Bruce Forsyth.

The year 2002–3 saw the departure of two other television institutions. Michael Aspel and Cilla Black announced they were calling it a day as the hosts, respectively, of *This Is Your Life* and *Blind Date*; Black revealed her decision live on air. Another small-screen entertainment warhorse, *Who Wants To Be A Millionaire*, showed signs of fatigue as ITV showed fewer episodes of the once all-conquering quiz in an attempt to restore ratings. However, a court case involving allegations of cheating by one of the show's contestants, Major Charles Ingram, put the show back on the front pages. Ingram was found guilty of cheating after a member of the audience helped him to the £1 million prize money by coughing when he believed presenter Chris Tarrant was reading out the right answer. A *Tonight* documentary on the incident broadcast on Easter Monday achieved one of ITV's highest audiences of the year, a massive 16.1 million.

Tonight, once derided for its soft approach to current affairs, had another success during the year, although the controversy following the screening of *Living with Michael Jackson*, watched by 15.3 million people, may make it difficult for presenter Martin Bashir to secure another big-name interviewee. Jackson accused Bashir of betraying him and took producers Granada to court to protect his reputation. The film implied that Jackson's relationship with children was not as innocent as the star claimed.

One new television celebrity to emerge during the year was Channel 4 magician Derren Brown, evidence that magic was back in vogue among programme directors. But there were quibbles that the public was being misled as the television station appeared to elevate magic to the status of genuine science.

Lauded by layman and scientist alike, David Attenborough, arguably the BBC's greatest broadcaster, celebrated his half-centenary in broadcasting in autumn 2002 with another natural history blockbuster, *Life of Mammals*. Not every critic was impressed. It was true that the series failed to match the impact of the great man's previous documentary *Blue Planet*. Perhaps Attenborough's paternalistic style and dyed-in-the-wool Reithian values were beginning to look a little old-fashioned. But the BBC honoured its debt to Attenborough with a special film, shown on BBC4, that looked back at his extraordinary career with the corporation.

Television has the ability to change the public's perception of a star virtually overnight. Jamie Oliver was one of those whose credibility soared. His Channel 4 series *Jamie's Kitchen* became compulsive viewing for many in autumn 2002. Mark Lawson noted in *The Guardian*: 'Before the show began, Oliver was derided by pundits as a mockney gobshite ... But after a month of being seen on Tuesday nights cajoling 15 unemployed young people into becoming chefs Oliver has become a media saint.' Nearly seven million tuned in to watch the last episode.

Oliver's series was one of Channel 4's big hits of the year. But as the station tried to restore its credibility as the natural home for small-screen innovation, critics complained that too many of its shows had become indistinguishable from offerings on BBC2 or even Channel 5, relaunched as Five in autumn 2002. Property shows like *A Place in the Sun* and *Relocation, Relocation* were difficult to distinguish from similar programmes broadcast by rivals. However, Channel 4, twenty years

old in November 2002, proved it could still be relied upon to annoy and to screen the unpredictable, with the revisionist history series *Empire*, presented by Niall Ferguson, and *Autopsy*, a broadcast of Britain's first public autopsy for 170 years, performed by Professor Von Hagens at his Body Worlds exhibition in front of a large paying audience.

THE STREET BACK ON FORM

Once the undisputed mainstay of the schedules, drama in general struggled to make a big impact in 2002–3. Excluding the soaps, the main channels' flagship dramas no longer commanded the huge audiences of the 1990s. Perhaps the year's most successful drama was *The Lost Prince*, Stephen Poliakoff's ravishing account of the hidden son of King George V and Queen Mary, starring Michael Gambon, Gina McKee and Miranda Richardson. 'Entrancing stuff,' said Paul Hoggart in *The Times*, 'even to a hardened Poliakoff sceptic'. Another costume drama, ITV1's version of *Dr Zhivago* adapted by the ubiquitous Andrew Davies, failed to impress critics, many of whom felt it could not match David Lean's 1965 classic film starring Julie Christie and Omar Sharif. The *Mail* reckoned it was 'crude, banal and sex-obsessed'. However, there was praise for another Davies screenplay, his version of George Eliot's final novel *Daniel Deronda*, which attracted almost eight million viewers on Saturday nights despite tough competition from ITV1. Generally, BBC1 got the better of ITV1 in the drama stakes. In spring, the political thriller *State of Play* had audiences hooked, while lighter pieces like the Manchester hairdressers' saga *Cutting It* also impressed.

There was controversy over two BBC2 dramas, the Victorian lesbian serial *Tipping the Velvet*, and *Cambridge Spies* starring Tom Hollander, Rupert Perry-Jones, Toby Stephens and Samuel West as the infamous double agents Burgess, MacLean, Philby and Blunt. In spite of an explicit sex scene in which one of the protagonists used a dildo, some reviewers complained that *Tipping the Velvet* had failed to live up its erotic hype. Meanwhile, several newspapers suggested it was wrong for the BBC to present such a sympathetic portrait of a group of traitors, but few could deny that *Cambridge Spies* was well-acted and ambitiously executed.

The ITV1 signature piece *Cold Feet*, making what appeared to be its final bow, signed off with the death of one of its leading characters, Rachel, the victim of a car crash; more than 10 million tuned in. But critics said that *Cold Feet* was past its best. The reviewers had kinder words for a new production from Manchester-based Red Productions, *The Second Coming*, a highly charged story of a man convinced that he was Christ and had returned to 21st century Britain to redeem our sins. Christopher Eccleston was outstanding in the lead role.

After years in the doldrums, *Coronation Street* was back on form. Now effectively running five days a week, the climax of a storyline involving serial murderer Richard Hillman drew an astonishing 19.4 million viewers, a figure unlikely to be beaten during the remainder of 2003. Two decidedly dog-eared soaps, Channel 4's *Brookside* and ITV1's *Crossroads*, were finally laid to rest during the year, reminders, if they were needed, of how successfully Granada had reinvented 'Corrie'.

If many audiences despaired at the sameness of so much television during the year – BBC Television's former programme head Mark Thompson (now running Channel 4) acknowledged the medium was suffering from a 'creative deficit' when speaking at the Edinburgh Television Festival in August 2002 – at least the BBC had finally rediscovered the arts. Alan Yentob's three-part programme depicting the life of Leonardo de Vinci was hailed as a landmark in arts television, though reviewers were less enamoured of his new BBC1 arts series *Imagine*, arguing that it lacked genuine depth.

RADIO

Digital radio finally began its long-heralded breakthrough. As BBC Radio's managing director Jenny Abramsky said towards the end of June 2003, digital radio was 'on its way to becoming a mass-market proposition'. Having launched another three digital stations during the year to add to its two existing ones, the BBC had a vested interest in banging the drum for digital radio. Though with sets retailing at £99, a new generation of portable digital radios poised to arrive on the market, and more and more people tuning in via digital television services such as Sky and Freeview, audiences are beginning to realise the real benefits of greater choice and crystal-clear reception that the new technology offers.

Overall, BBC Radio, marking its 80th birthday with a special concert carried live on 14 November by Radio 3, had another good year. The BBC's audience share stood at 53.5 per cent, up from 52.6 per cent, though this figure was boosted by the inclusion for the first time of the World Service's 1.4 million listeners. The commercial sector was not only struggling still with a difficult advertising market, but at 44.5 per cent its overall audience share represented a further decline.

The commercial stations blamed their relatively poor performance on the war in Iraq, reasoning that during times of crisis the British turn to the BBC. The sombre mood undoubtedly saw record numbers listening for the duration of the conflict to Radio 4's flagship news and current affairs programme *Today*. Not everything went the BBC's way, however, as Radio 1 failed to reverse the downward slide of the previous year. Tough competition, demographic trends that continue to erode its core audience of 15- to 24-year-olds, and more young people spending their leisure time surfing the internet or playing computer games all hurt the station.

While Radio 1 struggled, radio, or rather radio presenters, were never far from the national spotlight. In a sensational court case, the medium's former golden boy, Chris Evans, was forced to pay damages, expected to be around £5 million, after losing a case for unfair dismissal against his former employer, Virgin Radio. When Radio 2's veteran DJ Johnny Walker announced on air that he needed treatment for cancer, the newspapers gave the story extensive coverage.

DIGITAL'S CHRISTMAS CRACKER

By Christmas 2002, the BBC had completed its roll-out of digital stations: 1Xtra, billed as an alternative black music station, launched in late summer 2002; the Asian Network, aimed at young urban British Asians, followed in October; and BBC7, an all-speech station featuring archive drama and comedy plus a daily live children's show, began broadcasting in December. With these new listening opportunities being promoted across other BBC services, it was perhaps not surprising that demand for digital sets surged in the run-up to Christmas. Many customers were disappointed as sets sold out faster than shops could stock them.

Even so, by the time the first official audience figures were published by Rajar (the body that monitors rating listening) in May 2003, it was estimated that fewer than 200,000 homes owned a digital radio. Encouragingly for the broadcasters, the majority of the 1.5 million or so digital radio listeners were tuning in on their digital television sets, via Sky Digital, Freeview or cable. Initial feedback suggested that BBC7 was doing well; the BBC claimed that one in five people bought their sets specifically to listen to the station. More detailed audience figures will be available in autumn 2003.

Serious times demand serious radio and 2002–3 was a year of outstanding achievement for Radio 4. The number of listeners broke through the 10 million barrier; and in another milestone, Radio 4 became London's most popular station, beating Capital FM for the first time. A further first came when the network was named station of the year at the Radio Academy awards, beating both Radio 2 and Classic FM. The judges said the network had 'reassessed itself as the voice of informed debate, drama and comedy of the highest quality'.

Die-hard Radio 4 fans perhaps wondered what all the fuss was about. Radio 4 has always been a byword for quality speech broadcasting. Yet its newly fashionable status, highlighted by a *Radio Times* cover in June depicting a headphone-wearing Stephen Fry wearing an 'I Love Radio 4' lapel badge, did not detract from the station's seriousness or intelligence. It was suggested by Radio 4's controller Helen Boaden that one reason Radio 4 was doing so well, especially in the evenings, was because people were becoming tired of television schedules packed with soaps, lifestyle and reality series. 'People spend more time with BBC Radio than they do with BBC Television,' she claimed. 'It's fantastic that people still find that kind of commitment to what was seen as a fading medium.'

The *Today* programme, despite the departure of its high-profile editor Rod Liddle, added more than 800,000 new listeners during the course of 2002–3. Overall, audiences for news and speech-based radio rose due to the tense international situation. As noted above, *Today's* coverage of the Iraq war and the events that precipitated it placed a great strain on the BBC's relationship with the Government. The programme's willingness to tackle the Government robustly, and the Conservative Party's poor standing in the opinion polls for much of the year, led some observers to remark that *Today* had assumed the role of official opposition to the Government. In the USA, where broadcasters tended to accept the Bush agenda over the Iraq invasion, *Today* won a loyal audience as listeners tuned in over the internet.

It was not only Radio 4's news and current affairs coverage that provoked controversy. A sex-in-the-shower scene in *The Archers* involving Brian, the landlord of The Bull, and his lover Siobhan, the mother of his love child, created a stir amongst those who expected more wholesome fare from Ambridge. The storyline was good for ratings; more than five million tuned in. Other highlights from the drama department were adaptations of Zeitgeist novelists Nick Hornby and Joanna Trollope, Ewan McGregor reading Chekhov's short stories and a serialisation of Philip Pullman's *His Dark Materials* trilogy. In comedy, the surreal *Little Britain* secured a cult following. Meanwhile a celebration of Bob Dylan at 60, a punk retrospective and coverage of the Glastonbury Festival – another first for the network – suggested that Radio 4 was attempting to win younger audiences; research showed that the average listener was still about 53. 'The new Radio 4 listener cannot easily be defined by class, creed or colour,' Ms Boaden declared, perhaps a little too hopefully.

RADIO 2 ROLLS ON

Throughout the period, Radio 2 sustained its performance as Britain's most popular station; around 13 million people tune in every week. The biggest change to the service's schedules during the year under review was the much-trailed departure of Jimmy Young. The 81-year-old DJ vacated his weekday lunchtime show in December 2002, making way for Jeremy Vine, late of *Newsnight*, who took over in January 2003. Station boss James Moir, himself due to retire at the end of 2003, was relieved that Young, whose Radio 2 show had run for almost 30 years, did not use his final programme to launch an attack on the BBC, something of a tradition for radio presenters who feel betrayed by management. Young saved his remarks for a column in the *Sunday Express*, published days after his departure. In it Young questioned the justification for the licence fee that funds the BBC and claimed that his experience at Broadcasting House had been mixed to say the least. 'I was going to write that I enjoyed that relationship (with the BBC),' said Young, 'but that wouldn't be true. Sometimes enjoyable, often not, would be a more accurate description.' But Moir had the last word; figures published in spring 2003 showed that Vine's ratings were as good as Young's.

In March 2003, to listeners' sorrow, the death was announced of Alan Keith, creator and presenter of *Your Hundred Best Tunes*, at the age of 94. Keith had been about to announce his retirement from the show he had hosted for more than 40 years. Two other Radio 2 stalwarts, Terry Wogan and Steve Wright, showed that although the network had succeeded in attracting listeners in their 30s and 40s by hiring younger DJs like Jonathan Ross, there was still support for Radio 2 presenters of a certain age. An extra 600,000 people tuned in to Wogan and Wright's shows. Never lost for words, Wogan, aged 64, said: 'Don't diss us, man, it's a big up from the coffin-dodgers. Grey is the new black.'

Although other BBC national stations generally managed to retain or increase listening levels, Radio 1's ratings crumbled as it attempted to compete with new entrants like Smash Hits and dance-focused Kiss. In the first quarter of 2003, Radio 1's audience dipped below 8 per cent, dangerously near its lowest-ever figure; weekly audiences were down to 10 million. The fall was all the more painful because of attempts to rejuvenate the network by launching new talent and reworked shows. Sarah Cox's breakfast show lost 130,000 listeners. One of the flagging network's few success stories was the newly launched chart show hosted by 24-year-old Wes Butters. He replaced the ageing Mark Goodier, winning 100,000 new listeners in the process.

Radio 1's disappointing ratings were not the only cause of anxiety at the BBC. In January 2003, recording studio boss Neil Fraser, founder of Ariwa Sounds, accused Radio 1 of contributing to the rise in gun crime. 'The producers of BBC Radio 1 ragga and hip hop shows should share some of the guilt every time a black youth dies by the gun in Britain,' he wrote in a letter to the *Daily Telegraph*.

This was not a charge that could be levelled against Radio 3. During 2002–3, this once-staid station made further strides towards broadening its appeal, offering, to quote controller Roger Wright, 'a world that takes you further, instead of giving you what you already know'. In February 2003 the network took on Woody Allen, Jools Holland, André Previn and George Melly as jazz presenters and announced that Andy Kershaw's world music programme was being extended. However, there was criticism later in the year when Wright announced that from September 2003 two of the station's staples, archive shows *Listeners' Choice* and *BBC Legends*, were being axed. Another casualty was *Sunday Live* presented by Stephanie Hughes. In the *Sunday Times*, radio columnist Paul Donovan complained: 'The BBC's vaults contain gems beyond compare. And now is not the time to deprive Radio 3 weekend listeners of any of them.'

NOT SO GOLD FOR CAPITAL

Britain's largest commercial radio group, Capital, had a challenging year. Its flagship station, London's Capital FM, celebrating its 30th anniversary, suffered from the onward march of Radio 4; year-on-year, audiences fell by a fifth. There was some comfort in Chris Tarrant's refashioned breakfast show adding 100,000 listeners, but observers wondered if Capital was becoming too dependent on him. Arch-rival Heart was narrowing the gap with the station; some experts predict that Heart might eventually overtake Capital. The station's chief executive David Mansfield acknowledged there were problems when he said in May 2003: 'We're working hard to put things right and still have a lot to do. If further changes need to be made then we'll make them.' The truth was that in the keenly contested London market, all contemporary music stations – with the exception of Heart – were struggling.

But it was not all bad news in the commercial sector. After several abortive attempts to relaunch its breakfast show, Virgin Radio, celebrating its 10th anniversary in May, finally appears to have got it right. A new format presented by Pete and Geoff, publicised by a £3 million marketing campaign, increased the station's audience share by 12 per cent. It was welcome news for Virgin, struggling to stem the steady loss of listeners since Chris Evans' departure. Another coup for the company came in the summer when Evans lost his case for unfair dismissal; Virgin's owners, the Scottish Media Group, was expected to seek damages of around £5 million. In the seven-week-long case, Mr Justice Lightman described the ex-Virgin DJ as 'a prima donna' and 'a liar'.

Classic FM continued to surge forward, adding around 100,000 new listeners. In the early summer of 2003, many listeners were baffled and angered by the sudden disappearance of breakfast show host Henry Kelly. After 11 years with Classic, he was replaced by Simon Bates. Immediately Classic's fans voiced their anger, posting messages on the network's website. One wrote: 'I am shocked, horrified and disgusted at Henry's dumping – black armbands all round for the demise of our radio station'. New recruits included Mark Goodier, from Radio 1, Aled Jones, and 22-year-old Lisa Duncombe, a recent graduate who was given the job of fronting the weekend lunchtime show.

With the Communications Bill becoming law in July 2003, relaxed rules on media ownership from December will allow foreign media groups to buy British radio stations for the first time. There were fears, expressed in a letter to the *Guardian* signed by performers including Tom Jones and Chrissie Hynde, that if this happens commercial radio as a whole might adopt an even less adventurous playlist policy to please advertisers. One likely predator is the US's Clear Channel, which owns 1,200 radio stations in the USA. Speaking at the Radio Festival in July 2003, David Mansfield of Capital said: 'We at Capital are driven by listeners and not about selling hamburgers and Fords. We will probably have a major cultural clash should Clear Channel make an approach.'

BUSINESS AND FINANCE

Business in the United Kingdom in the last few years has been a case of 'betwixt and between'. The long shadows cast by the dot-com collapse and the attacks of 11 September 2001 in the USA blighted prospects well into 2002. By the time of the first anniversary of 11 September 2001, businessmen and financiers had turned their attention to the Gulf, and the apparent inevitability of US action against Iraq. The months that followed formed a watershed, with uncertainty in the run-up to the Iraq invasion giving way to exuberance that the war proved short and relatively clear-cut. Oil prices, which had peaked, fell back sharply, while stockmarkets rallied, albeit briefly.

The period also saw a marked increase in takeover activity, bringing cheer to the hard-hit UK financial sector. Bankers and support staff had lost their jobs in droves when the dot-com boom turned to bust; the Centre for Economics and Business Research (CEBR), a London-based think-tank, found that 22,000 jobs in banking, insurance and fund management were lost between December 2000, the peak of employment, and September 2002. City jobs peaked at 324,000 in 2000; by the end of 2003, City jobs were forecast to bottom out at 293,000 before slowly picking up again. The downturn bit deeply into firms such as Zurich Financial Services, Europe's third largest insurer, which announced in September 2002 that it was losing 4,500 jobs. Ironically, the move coincided with figures showing that unemployment in Britain was at its lowest level for 27 years, down to 943,300 claimants. Widespread job losses in manufacturing and IT were outweighed by recruitment in the service sector, driven by booming retail sales.

The headlines were dominated by personalities, from Philip Green, the retail billionaire, to Mervyn King, the steady-handed economist chosen to succeed Sir Edward George when he retired as Governor of the Bank of England after a decade-long term. King took office in July 2003 and caught pundits off-guard by cutting interest rates by a quarter point to 3.5 per cent, the lowest level since 1955. The move was welcomed by borrowers, but added to the pressure on pensioners and others relying on income from their savings. King appeared intent on drawing a line under the era of his more reserved predecessor. Unmarried, and an Aston Villa fan, he spoke of his desire to be seen as a 'people's governor', explaining the Bank of England's decisions in different regions of the country each month. He became known for livening up his regular briefings with phrases taken from the football field, and once likened the economy to a disco dancer.

Green, meanwhile, led the way in what proved to be a time of tumultuous change for Britain's retail sector. In autumn 2002, Green added Arcadia, owner of Dorothy Perkins and Top Shop among others, to an empire fronted by the high street store chain Bhs. Green momentarily lost his place in the limelight in early 2003 when Wm Morrison, the northern supermarket group, made a surprise £2.9 billion recommended offer for Safeway. But he soon joined the party with a bid of his own, and within weeks six bids for Safeway were on the table.

In a further reshaping of the retail landscape, Harvey Nichols, the Knightsbridge fashion store, was taken back into private ownership by Dickson Poon, the Hong Kong entrepreneur. Selfridges found itself at the centre of a takeover battle between Galen Weston, a Canadian food and department store billionaire, and Robert Tchenguiz, a London-based property tycoon. Weston's late brother, Garry, was the man behind Associated British Foods, maker of Wagon Wheels; his branch of the family also owned Fortnum & Mason. The bid from the Canadian side of the clan promised to reunite two of London's most prestigious stores.

Hamleys, the Regent Street toyshop, succumbed to a takeover bid from Baugur, an Icelandic retailer. Littlewoods, controlled for years by the reclusive Moores family, was bought by the equally publicity-shy Barclay brothers for £750 million.

Six Continents, formerly Bass, split itself into a hotel arm, InterContinental Hotels Group, and a pubs company, Mitchells & Butlers. Things went less smoothly for Le Meridien, the hotels group whose premier London properties include the Grosvenor House and the Waldorf. A backlog over rents left the group on the brink of administration and spurred a rescue package led by Lehman Brothers, the investment bank.

In January 2003, P&O Princess agreed to a £3.3 billion bid from Carnival Corporation of the US, creating the world's largest cruise operator, with 65 ships and brands including P&O Cruises and Swan Hellenic. Carnival swooped after P&O Princess announced a merger with Royal Caribbean. Uncertainty over the three-way tussle dragged on for more than a year, and ended with Carnival's shares being dual-listed in London and New York, providing liquidity for UK shareholders.

FINANCIAL MARKETS

The pick-up in mergers and acquisitions activity came as a welcome relief to deal-starved corporate financiers. According to Thomson Financial, global mergers and acquisitions activity in 2002 fell to £750 billion, a drop of two-thirds from the peak reached in 2000 at the height of the dot-com frenzy. European deals declined 13 per cent between 2001 and 2002, to their lowest level since 1997.

Concurrently, the FTSE 100 stock market index declined 24.5 per cent in 2002. This was the worst single showing for the index since 1974, when the market fell 55 per cent as a result of the secondary banking crisis and oil price shock. In October 2002, the FTSE touched 3,721, a six-year low, before falling further to hit a seven-year low of 3,287 in March 2003. The index then rallied to settle near 4,000, in a classic 'bear' market.

Although psychologically unsettling for armchair investors despairing at their shrinking savings plans, the fall in share prices made companies cheaper for would-be acquirers. And with interest rates at a near 40-year low of 4 per cent at the beginning of 2003, before falling even further, there was no shortage of cheap money to bankroll company buying sprees.

Fall-out continued throughout the year from the succession of accounting scandals in the USA, which started with Enron, the energy trader, and widened to include companies like WorldCom. Andersen, auditor to both firms, collapsed under pressure from US regulators, who then embarked on reforms to accounting and corporate governance. These threatened to ensnare the UK, which has always seen itself as a cut above the US system.

There was fierce resistance to the USA's Sarbanes-Oxley Act, named for two US senators, which proposed forcing any UK (or indeed non-US) accounting firm involved in auditing US companies to register with a new Public Company Accounting Oversight Board. This brought the prospect of US regulators imposing their will on UK firms. European authorities threatened tit-for-tat retaliation against US firms operating in Europe.

Andersen's demise – it was subsumed in the UK by Deloitte & Touche – saw the affairs of Britain's biggest companies left in the hands of just four accountancy firms. It was suggested that auditors should be forced to rotate clients every few years, but the idea was rejected as impractical. PricewaterhouseCoopers alone audits about half the companies in the FTSE 100, and rotating clients between the 'Big Four' – the only firms big enough to take on the major companies – would have created chaos. Auditors conceded instead that the lead partner on an audit would be replaced every five years, bringing some semblance of independence.

A government inquiry headed by Derek Higgs, an investment banker, published a report in January 2003 calling for major reforms to corporate governance in Britain. A key recommendation was that boards should have more non-executive directors, and no one individual should hold more than one FTSE 100 chairmanship. The Higgs report introduced the notion of a senior independent non-executive director who would become a key point of contact for shareholders, effectively bypassing the chairman. Unsurprisingly, the proposed reforms were greeted with howls of protest. Many chairmen described them as unworkable, with predictions that companies would need to recruit 5,000 new non-executives. A working party was set up to consider some of the more contentious proposals, and a watered-down version of the reforms duly emerged.

Another huge regulatory shake-up began in summer 2003 when the Enterprise Act 2002 came into effect. Company directors convicted of serious market abuses, such as price-fixing, face unlimited fines or up to five years in jail. The Act made operating a cartel a criminal offence, and gave the Office of Fair Trading and the Serious Fraud Office the power to bug directors' homes, offices and cars. Immunity would be granted to cartel members who turned whistle-blower.

Digby Jones, director-general of the Confederation of British Industry (CBI), issued regular warnings that red tape and taxes had 'relentlessly eroded' Britain's competitiveness. The CBI's quarterly industrial trends survey, released soon after the end of hostilities in Iraq, showed total manufacturing orders falling at the fastest rate for four years. The figures suggested that weakness in global trading conditions had spread to the UK. The CBI survey also showed a decline in manufacturers' confidence.

The Chancellor of the Exchequer, Gordon Brown, saw his borrowing projections run wide of the mark. In the year to April 2003, government borrowing was £25.2 billion, £1 billion more than the Chancellor had anticipated. The Centre for Economics and Business Research forecast that the deficit would reach £31.2 billion in 2004–5.

Pensions, a dry subject at the best of times, became exciting in 2002–3 for all the wrong reasons. The Government feared that pensioners were saving far too little for their retirement, while companies admitted that their company pension schemes were massively underfunded. Across UK industry, pension deficits ballooned to £160 billion under FRS17, the accounting rule that requires pension schemes to be valued according to market values. Because pensioners are living longer, and falling stockmarkets had decimated pension funds' value, more and more companies were forced to make one-off payments to make up the deficit in their pension funds.

Companies were expected to spend an extra £8 billion topping up their pension funds in 2003 alone. This figure was set to rise to £12 billion in 2004 and £16 billion in 2005. The CBI warned that the deficit would hit corporate tax receipts and affect UK economic growth.

UK airlines, hard hit by the downturn in travel after 11 September 2001, suffered further knocks. The weak global economy meant that bookings from business travellers remained weak. Bookings suffered from the uncertainty in the run-up to the war in Iraq, then were hit further by the outbreak of the SARS illness. British Airways saw its credit rating cut to 'junk' status by Standard & Poor's and lost its place in the FTSE 100 index. The airline disclosed that war in Iraq and SARS had cost it £200 million in losses in a three-month stretch in 2003. This was followed by a damaging dispute over the introduction of swipe cards for check-in staff that disrupted services and cost BA up to £40 million.

PROPERTY PRICES

The period proved unsettling for Britain's property sector, both commercial and residential. The boom in residential prices continued throughout 2002, with house prices, particularly in London and south-east England, rising by as much as 30 per cent over the year. The market was fuelled by the 'buy to let' trend, in which owners rushed to buy second homes for rental, stirring memories of the boom-bust cycle of the late 1980s and early 1990s.

By spring 2003, house sales had slowed noticeably, although prices remained static or dipped only slightly. Economists said a crash in property prices was unlikely as interest rates were low, making borrowing more affordable. Monthly statistics suggested that homeowners were remortgaging to fund home improvements or consumer spending. The lower level of lending for house purchases suggested that house prices would continue to ease, although annual gains of 12–20 per cent appeared sustainable. Affordability of homes remained an issue for first-time buyers. The average price for a house in the UK as a whole was about £146,000. In London, the average price of a house was in the £240,000–£250,000 range.

In the commercial property sector, observers were reminded that long construction cycles often leave developments out of sync with demand. The City of London skyline was transformed by the Swiss Re tower, the so-called 'erotic gherkin', yet half of the building remained unlet. By the end of 2003, another 1 million square feet of office space became available at Canary Wharf, as much again as the original Canary Wharf tower.

Rents for office space in the City itself were down by as much as 27 per cent year-on-year. In contrast, regional

UK office markets held up reasonably well, with annual rentals up about 1 per cent.

There was a surge in the number of legal actions brought by disgruntled former employees. In a particularly brutal encounter, Steven Horkulak, former head of global interest-rate derivatives at Cantor Fitzgerald, the moneybroker, won nearly £1 million from Cantor after successfully bringing a claim for constructive dismissal. The hearing descended into a slanging match between Horkulak and Lee Amaitis, Cantor's president and chief executive.

Horkulak portrayed Amaitis as a foul-mouthed bully who frequented lap-dancing clubs. Amaitis in turn drew attention to Horkulak's history of problems with alcohol and cocaine abuse. The case opened old wounds from Cantor's 2002 clash with its arch-rival Icap, in which the latter was accused of trying to poach Cantor staff in the aftermath of the 11 September attacks; Cantor lost 658 employees when the World Trade Center towers collapsed.

Louise Barton, a former media analyst, kept up her long-running quest to extract compensation from Investec Henderson Crosthwaite, the South African-owned investment bank. She sued for sex discrimination and unequal pay after discovering that male colleagues were paid twice as much as her. The case threatened to expose the City's male-biased culture.

Such cases can prove highly distasteful. The claimants seek to cause maximum embarrassment to their former employer in the hope that they will cave in and 'settle' before too much dirty linen is aired. One City worker claimed he was asked to dress up in a Nazi uniform as a forfeit for being late for work. A woman at a City bank told how male colleagues had referred to her as a 'tethered goat', i.e. a tasty bit of bait used to entice prospective clients.

In an unusual variation on such cases, 60 former Sainsbury's store managers who had been sacked en masse brought a claim for constructive dismissal. A tribunal in Watford heard that the supermarket group had waited until after the busy Christmas period before sacking them, so as not to disrupt trading at such an important time of the year. The managers, many of them with more than 20 years' service, were given 48 hours to agree to a half-day assessment of their suitability for the job or leave with a severance package. They won their claim on a technicality, and the case left the supermarket group, with its slogan 'Making Life Taste Better', looking like a callous employer.

The surprise event of 2003 was Ken Bates' abrupt exit from Chelsea Village, the quoted company behind Chelsea Football Club. Bates, unpredictable at the best of times, had long been dogged by rumours about Chelsea's finances. The company had run up debts of £90 million redeveloping the Stamford Bridge venue with hotels, a health club, and a new West Stand.

In July 2003, Bates announced that he was selling to a Russian oil magnate, Roman Abramovich. The £150 million deal absorbed Chelsea's debts and left Bates with a personal windfall of about £17.5 million. It was the first agreed takeover bid for a Premier League football club since Rupert Murdoch's blocked £623 million bid for Manchester United in 1999. Chelsea FC was left in the enviable position of having a proprietor with a blank chequebook willing to pay millions of pounds apiece for Europe's best footballers. The deal was overshadowed by a City investigation into share dealings in the days leading up to the bid.

Mohamed Al Fayed, owner of Harrods, and proprietor of Fulham Football Club, quit the UK for Switzerland in March 2003 after the Inland Revenue ended a special arrangement under which he paid a flat £240,000 a year in tax regardless of how much money he brought into Britain. The move limits him to spending no more than 90 days a year in the UK. Al Fayed's departure accompanied continuing speculation about his finances. Harrods, a bell-wether of the health of high street retailers, had lost a succession of top executives, while Fulham FC had proved a drain on cash. Al Fayed insisted throughout that his finances were in good shape.

Fears for UK electricity supply were stirred by events at British Energy, the privatised nuclear power generator. In autumn 2002, the company was forced to turn to the Government for help amid fears that it was about to go bust. The company, which supplies about a fifth of the UK's electricity, had been hit by depressed electricity prices and high fixed costs. The Government threw it a £450 million lifeline.

British Energy admitted racking up losses of £4.3 billion in the year to June 2003, most of it owing to writing down the value of the company's nine power stations. Worryingly, even with the Government's aid, the generator admitted that it could be another year before its future was secure. Advisers were working on a restructuring plan that they hoped to sign off with creditors by autumn 2003, but the plan will then have to receive approval from the European Commission.

In the midst of this, the Government announced plans to tap into wind energy to provide up to 5 per cent of Britain's electricity. The Trade and Industry Secretary, Patricia Hewitt, said she was confident that one in six homes in the UK, or nearly four million households, would switch on to wind power. Potential sites for wind farms include the Thames estuary, the Wash and a stretch of the Irish Sea from Cumbria to north Wales. Hewitt compared the project's potential to the North Sea oil boom in the 1970s, which boosted infrastructure in Scotland and created thousands of jobs. She predicted that the wind farm schemes could support 20,000 jobs by 2010, and help communities blighted by the closures of steelworks and shipbuilding yards.

CORPORATE FRAUD

While America struggled with corporate disasters such as Enron, WorldCom, Tyco and the rest, most of the UK pain was reserved for smaller, more anonymous manufacturers. They were grappling with the usual problems of a strong pound making British goods more expensive, and competition from fleet-footed overseas competitors.

But a handful of cases did make it to court, keeping serious fraud in the headlines. A high-profile case involved former executives of Wickes, the DIY chain, who were accused by the Serious Fraud Office of fraudulently inflating profits at the company in the mid-1990s; bonuses were linked to profits, giving an apparent motive. Those in the dock included Henry Sweetbaum, the former Wickes chairman and chief executive.

The Wickes trial ran for nine months in 2002 and ended, embarrassingly for the SFO, with acquittals all round. A fifth former executive, who was tried separately in 2003, was also cleared. The case, which cost about £20 million, was the first big setback for the SFO since the early 1990s, when it suffered a run of failed prosecutions, including the Maxwell brothers, the financial adviser Roger Levitt and George Walker, the Brent Walker founder.

The SFO enjoyed greater success with Stephen Hinchliffe, the man who built the Facia retail chain in the mid-1990s. Hinchliffe was jailed in 2001 for bribing bank officials to advance huge loans with which to buy store chains like Salisbury and Contessa. He faced a second trial, this time for stealing £1.75 million from Facia, but pleaded guilty and was given a suspended sentence. The SFO protested that this was too lenient and the Court of Appeal agreed; Hinchliffe was returned to prison to begin an 18-month sentence.

The Hinchliffe case was taken as a sign that attitudes were hardening towards white collar crime.

In a rare case, Tim Blackstone, a former City journalist turned PR man, was charged with insider trading. He was PR adviser to Murray Financial, an Edinburgh firm specialising in takeovers of building societies, and bought shares in Murray after being briefed about its secret plans to take over Leek United. He was convicted and fined a token £1,000.

The case was spiced up by the fact that the defendant was the brother of Baroness Blackstone, then Minister for Arts, and had starred, as a young man, in porn films with titles such as *I Am Not Feeling Myself Tonight*.

In August 2002, Colin Skellett, chairman and chief executive of Wessex Water, was arrested on suspicion of accepting a £1 million backhander from YTL, the Malaysian company that had recently acquired Wessex. After months of investigation, the police concluded that the money was in fact a consultancy fee and Skellett had done nothing wrong.

Skellett gave up the non-executive chairmanship of Jarvis, the rail contractor under investigation in connection with the Potters Bar rail crash in May 2002 in which seven people died. The company was the maintenance contractor on the stretch of track where the accident occurred.

Another incident, the Hatfield train crash of October 2001, resulted in manslaughter charges against six managers working for Network Rail, the successor to Railtrack, and Balfour Beatty, the maintenance firm. They were charged in July 2003 with four counts of manslaughter due to gross negligence.

Another six men, including Gerald Corbett, former Railtrack chief executive and then chairman of Woolworths, were summonsed under health and safety legislation.

Britain's media sector endured a rough ride, with advertising sharply down on both sides of the Atlantic. Commentators said they expected little improvement until 2004. The sector's rising stars included Sly Bailey, who quit IPC to become chief executive of Trinity Mirror, publisher of the *Daily Mirror*.

SHAREHOLDERS REVOLT

A familiar refrain during much of 2003 was the cry of 'rewards for failure'. Shareholders and ministers, it seemed, had had enough of 'fat cat' executives who engineered huge pay-offs for themselves despite failing to run their companies successfully. Protests merged with a general disquiet over excessive remuneration.

In May 2003, shareholders in GlaxoSmithKline, the drugs giant, defeated plans to award a £15 million 'golden parachute' to its chief executive, Jean-Pierre Garnier. He stood to receive the pay-off even if ousted for poor performance. The revolt by shareholders was seen as a hardening of attitudes towards boardroom largesse. The Trade and Industry Secretary joined the debate, saying that a combination of improved transparency and increased shareholder activism would ensure that directors' pay was more closely linked to company performance. Ms Hewitt said, 'We have no problem with big rewards for big success, but I do have an issue with rewards for failure'.

The boardroom pay debate subsequently caught up with Sir Martin Sorrell, chief executive of the advertising group WPP. More than a third of WPP shareholders voted against Sir Martin's remuneration package, which put him on a three-year contract. Under a long-term incentive plan, Sir Martin could receive a tranche of shares in 2004 worth £65 million.

Elsewhere, there was an unusual focus on women working at the highest levels in the City and business. Robin Saunders, head of the principal finance unit at WestLB, the German bank, saw her deal-making record come under scrutiny. It emerged that WestLB had unexpectedly made a £360 million provision against a loan to Box Clever, a struggling TV rentals business. Saunders, an American, made her name providing the financial backing for high-profile businesses, including Formula One and the new Wembley stadium.

Another American, Barbara Cassani, who made millions selling the low-cost carrier Go to easyJet, was chosen to lead London's bid to host the 2012 Olympic Games. Plans by Camelot, the lottery operator, to launch a 'penny' lottery to raise funds for the bid (encouraging shoppers to give up their loose change) suggested a typically British approach to the Olympics in a year when pennies were hard to find.

CONSERVATION AND HERITAGE

THE NATURAL ENVIRONMENT

YELLOW PERIL

Ragwort makes a colourful sight along road and motorway verges in late summer, but it is classed as an injurious weed and is poisonous to horses and cattle. Some 4,000 horses are believed to have succumbed to ragwort poisoning in 2002. The Government's response was to introduce a Ragwort Control Bill, enabling the Department for the Environment, Food and Rural Affairs (DEFRA) to take enforcement action against owners who allow their land to become infested with the weed. It will also put an onus on public bodies to control ragwort, especially when it grows close to pastures and hayfields.

Ragwort is difficult to control, and probably impossible to eradicate. Each plant can produce up to 150,000 seeds, which have a high germination rate but may also lie dormant in the soil for up to 20 years. It can be controlled using selective weed-killers, but the most effective, if time-consuming, method is to pull up the young plants by hand before the seeds are ripe. Sheep can also be used to get rid of ragwort by grazing the less poisonous young plants. Critics point out that measures to control ragwort exist in the Weeds Act of 1959, and that, since ragwort is distasteful to horses and cattle, the animals only eat it when they run out of grass. No stockman worth his salt would allow such a situation to arise. However, it is probable that livestock are consuming ragwort in silage or hay.

It will be hard for landowners to control ragwort so long as there are large reservoirs of the plant on motorway verges and railway embankments. On the other hand, the cost of control would run into millions, and involve damage to other, more desirable wild plants by the large-scale use of herbicides. In the meantime, English Nature has published measures to control ragwort by judicious grazing, gleaned from experience on its own nature reserves.

CAIRNGORMS NATIONAL PARK

Britain's latest national park, only the second to be declared in Scotland, 'opened for business' in March 2003, though the formal opening ceremony is scheduled for September. The park, the largest in Britain, extends over 1,466 square miles from Grantown-on-Spey in the north, Ballater and Glenbuchat in the east, and Glen Clova in the south. It incorporates the semi-arctic high tops of Ben Macdui and its neighbouring hills, the highest mountain range in Britain, along with the largest native pine forests and the headwaters of the Spey and the Dee. Parts of the area, including the RSPB's large Abernethy reserve, famous for its ospreys, and the National Trust for Scotland's Mar Lodge estate are already nature reserves. It also includes three ski resorts and several large private estates. The park has been given its own authority, which will employ about 80 staff, with a budget of around £5 million a year.

The national park will build on the co-operation of landowners and users achieved by the informal Cairngorm Partnership of recent years. Its aims are set out in general terms as the conservation of the area's 'natural and cultural heritage', promoting 'public understanding and enjoyment', with what one hopes will be a wise blend of 'sustainable use and economic development'. The test to its effectiveness will be whether national park status helps those involved to get to grips with the long-running problem of over-grazing by red deer and sheep, and enable some natural regeneration in the dwindling natural forests of the region.

The park got off to a slightly sour start over its chosen boundaries, which form a compromise between the smaller park favoured by Government and the much larger one advocated by Scottish Natural Heritage and local pressure groups. The omission of the high hills of Perthshire, which include such popular attractions as Killiecrankie and the Falls of Bruar, was particularly controversial. The Government felt that a larger national park would be unwieldy and too expensive to run, but holds out the possibility of extending it after a trial period. In the meantime, the park's newly appointed board has embarked on a period of public consultation.

THIRD AIRPORT PROTEST

With Heathrow and Gatwick Airports full to capacity and air travel expected to increase, the search is on for a third national airport near London. The option that has received most press coverage – and certainly the most irate protest – is the site near Cliffe on the Thames estuary between Gravesend and the Isle of Grain. The new airport would be twice the size of Heathrow, and some 1,100 homes would have to be destroyed to make way for it. Moreover, it would obliterate the RSPB's Northward Hill nature reserve, which has the largest heronry in Britain, and impinge on mud-flats, salt marshes and wet grassland used by breeding avocets and which teem with shore birds, especially in winter and on passage. The Government's own scientists advised that at this site the risk of bird strikes would be unacceptably high, unless measures were taken to persuade the birds to go somewhere else – like destroying their feeding grounds. To build the airport at Cliffe, the Government would face very strong local resistance, and a certain challenge in the European Court on environmental grounds.

Conservationists are frankly baffled that so unsuitable a site has even been considered. 'It fails spectacularly on environmental, social and economic grounds', wrote Graham Wynne, RSPB's director. 'If a place so rich in wildlife disappears under concrete, then nowhere in this country is safe.' Indeed, the proposal seems so unlikely to succeed that cynics suspect that Cliffe is a red herring, intended to make the alternative sites at Stansted, or by extending Gatwick or Heathrow, or both, seem palatable by comparison.

COD FARMS

The fish-shop cod of the future are likely to come from cages, not the open sea. The predicted imminent collapse of cod stocks in the North Sea led to the imposition of strict quotas for cod catches in 2001 to give the stock time to recover. With stocks still perilously low two years later, the EU has replaced the emergency measures with a long-term recovery plan based on a reduced allowable catch in proportion to the size of each fishing fleet.

With wild cod set to become an expensive luxury, there is much interest in a technique pioneered in Norway to farm cod in a similar way to Atlantic salmon. Britain's first commercial cod-farm has started up at Vidlin Voe in Shetland, and harvested the first of an expected 40 tonnes (about14,000 fish) a year. An application for three large offshore cod-farms off the island of Arran by a Norwegian-based company is under consideration.

Like salmon farms, cod farms will have environmental consequences. The fish will be fed on fish-meal processed from sand-eels and other small fish. Waste and excreta pile up in the sheltered waters below the cages, and have caused disease and plankton blooms as well as effectively sterilizing the nearby seabed. In the case of salmon, the future of wild salmon has been jeopardized by sea-louse infestation and interbreeding with escaped farm fish. According to the World-wide Fund for Nature, wild salmon have declined by 45 per cent since 1983, while Scottish farmed-salmon production has risen to a peak of 150,000 tonnes. The production has been accompanied by an estimated discharge of 7.2 million kilograms of waste; 51 pollution incidents were reported between 1996 and 2002. If past experience is anything to go by, where there is a market, there will be fish-farms. Perhaps the best way the consumer can prevent a repetition of the salmon debacle is to adopt the advice of one butcher on the Isle of Man: 'Make a fish happy – eat a cow'.

WIND ENERGY AND BIRDS
Governments on the windy Atlantic coast of Europe see wind as the energy source of the future. It is clean, relatively cheap and infinitely renewable. The UK Government's White Paper *Low energy future: creating a modern economy,* published in February 2003, sets out its plans to cut Britain's fossil fuel emissions by 60 per cent by 2050. It hopes to double the amount of energy produced by renewable sources by 2020. One consequence is that Government looks favourably on applications for wind farms. For once, it has the enthusiastic support of environmental pressure groups like Friends of the Earth and Greenpeace. The latter would like to see wind turbines providing a quarter of our electricity needs by 2020, which would require 15,000 off-shore turbines costing about £20 billion. At present there are around 1,000 wind turbines in the UK.

Not everyone loves to see steel-clad windmills 300 or 400 feet high overlooking their home or dominating a favourite view. There were many objections to the proposed wind-farms at Cefn Croes in the Cambrian Mountains and on the Island of Lewis in the Outer Hebrides. One of the unanswered questions is whether wind-farms present a threat to birds. The issue has become pressing because of a proposal by National Windpower to build 27 turbines in the heart of Romney Marsh on a bird migration route, and another proposal for 90 turbines in Liverpool Bay, west of Blackpool, where England's largest flock of Common Scoter duck overwinters. In the latter case, permission was granted by the Crown Estates without any serious environmental assessment, causing concern to the RSPB, a supporter of wind-farming in principle. Such evidence as there is comes from northern Spain where a farm of nearly 1,000 turbines has resulted in mass bird casualties, including endangered griffon vultures and eagles. Possible remedies include spacing the turbines more widely or turning them off during migrations, or, better still, not siting wind-farms where birds are likely to crash into them.

GM CROPS DEBATED
The Government published its long-awaited report on GM crops and their impact on public health and the environment in July 2003. The review panel found no scientific case for ruling out GM crops altogether, but neither did it give them the green light. At present, the central issue is their impact on farmland, particularly organic crops, and on wildlife. The crop trials conducted in Britain suggest that the risk of wild contamination is slight, and that there is no likelihood of aggressive 'superweeds' resistant to herbicides developing as a result. However they acknowledge that the risk will grow as GM-based agriculture increases. A second report produced by the Prime Minister's Strategy Unit concludes that in the short term there will be limited economic benefit from GM crops grown in the UK, mainly because of the reluctance of consumers to buy them.

Proponents of GM technology claim that it could be of enormous benefit to wildlife. In theory, a farmer will need to use less weed-killer and sow later, resulting in a harmlessly weedy crop, full of insects for birds to eat. There is some support from UK trials using GM sugar beet, which reduced farming costs substantially and left a weedier environment that would benefit birds like corn bunting. However, experience in the USA, where commercial GM crops have been grown for several years, casts doubt on such claims. According to the Soil Association, the dependency on agrochemicals is as great as ever. Organic growers have faced contamination from GM crops, most notoriously in the Canadian state of Saskatchewan, which lost its entire organic oilseed rape industry to cross-border contamination. The easy way in which oilseed rape escapes from fields and spreads along road verges and traffic islands suggests a similar scenario in Britain. Moreover, GM oilseed rape could interbreed with wild brassicas, thus introducing the gene into the wild.

The Government has also launched a nationwide public debate before deciding whether or not to allow GM crops to be commercially grown here. Parish Councils and other bodies across the country are giving people the opportunity to air their views. DEFRA has promised that there will be 'no snap decisions' and that the findings will be considered carefully. However, Michael Meacher, the former Countryside Minister who resigned over the issue in June 2003, pointed out that Britain may not be in a position to refuse a licence for a GM crop as this may not be an option under EU law. Meanwhile, the USA has decided to use trade agreements to challenge the EU's current stance on GM crops. Many feel that GM technology is inevitable, whether 'we' like it or not.

OTTERS RETURNING
A national survey of otters, the fourth since 1979, has confirmed that the animal is recovering its former ground and, to a lesser extent, its numbers, since the low point in the late 1970s when otters were suffering from the effects of pesticides. The new study, commissioned by the Environment Agency, examined 3,000 'potential otter sites' and found evidence of the animal – mainly their dung (called 'spraints') or paw-marks rather than actual sightings – at 36 per cent of them, compared with 23 per cent in 1994 and only 6 per cent in 1979. In effect, you are five times more likely to see an otter today than you were 20 years ago.

The welcome news is a vindication of the ban on the most harmful pesticides, and perhaps also a sign that water quality has improved. The return of this elusive animal has been strengthened by reintroductions in some areas, and by making river banks more 'otter-friendly' with the provision of artificial holts. Otters are being seen more often in cities with large rivers, and may be more tolerant of humans since otter hunting was banned in 1978. Unfortunately, this also means more otters are becoming road casualties. The animals seem to use road bridges most often at high water, and one solution may be the provision of 'otter ledges' below the arches.

HEDGEHOGS: VICTIMS OR VILLAINS?

Hedgehogs in the Outer Hebrides are harming the prospects of ground-nesting birds by eating their eggs, according to Scottish Natural Heritage (SNH). Hedgehogs were unknown there before being introduced by gardeners to control the slugs. The animals multiplied, and at the same time the breeding success of snipe, dunlin, lapwing and other birds spiralled downwards. The Outer Hebrides have an unusually high nesting density of waders and their breeding performance there is of international significance. After considering the matter, the Scottish Executive gave SNH the go-ahead for a hedgehog eradication programme, starting on the island of North Uist.

The project attracted attention because hedgehog lovers wanted the animals to be repatriated to the mainland, whilst SNH, claiming that most of them would soon die of starvation and might harm the livelihood of resident hedgehogs, thinks it would be kinder to kill the animals by humane injection. The hedgehog party has received support from Dr Pat Morris, an authority on hedgehogs, who says the animals would have a better than 50:50 chance of survival so long as they were relocated to places where there are no badgers.

In the event, only 66 hedgehogs were trapped on North Uist, far fewer than expected. Either the animals are wary of traps or there are fewer of them than was believed. In 2004 the trappers will move to South Uist and Benbecula, where it is believed there are more hedgehogs.

BLUEBELL BLUES

Britain has more bluebell woods than anywhere else in the world. It is partly because our mild, wet climate is just right for the plant, but also because the animals that used to dig up and eat bluebell bulbs, the wild boar and its domestic equivalent the outpastured pig, are no longer around. It is also due to lack of competition: until recently, bluebells did not have to compete for soil and space with another aggressive bulb plant. However, this situation may be changing.

Wild boars, or pig hybrids very like boars, are now established in some areas of south-east England and Dorset after escaping from farms, and will probably spread into neighbouring counties. They will not eat all the bluebells, but will certainly churn up the forest floor and make continuous drifts of the flower less likely. Another threat may be the increasing risk of hybridisation with the garden bluebell, which is a fertile cross between our bluebell and the Spanish bluebell, a less graceful, less fragrant plant with pallid blue flowers. The garden plant seems to be increasing in the wild and is starting to appear in hedge banks and wood borders. In part this is because they are sold to well-meaning local authorities and amenity bodies as native bluebells!

A more insidious threat is climate change. Bluebells develop flower buds during the summer which lie dormant over winter until rising temperatures trigger their growth. This successful strategy could rebound if earlier springs allow competing grasses and cow parsley to shade out the bluebell's foliage before it can build up the necessary energy reserves stored in the bulb. Finally, there is a now illegal trade in bluebell bulbs. In 2003, three men were prosecuted for digging up bluebells in a Norfolk wood, two of them receiving jail sentences.

WILD PLANT ATLAS

A *New Atlas of the British and Irish Flora* was published in September 2002, the first thorough national survey of our wild flora since 1962. The scheme, in which 1,600 (unpaid) botanists took part, mapped some 4,000 species at a scale of 10 by 10 km, and also includes data on change. The atlas reveals a surprisingly unstable flora, with many native or long-established plants in decline, but many others, especially recent introductions, doing extremely well. Essentially, our flora is becoming more cosmopolitan and more metropolitan. The most successful plant in England is the buddleia, which is four times as common now as in 1962. Big plants, including trees and shrubs are doing relatively well, small ones, especially annuals, rather badly. A controversial measure was the categorising of plants formerly regarded as native, like the red poppy, as 'archaeophytes' or ancient introductions, on the grounds that they seem to lack a 'wild' habitat.

The atlas showed the most botanically diverse corner of Britain to be around Wareham in Dorset. Similar studies among animals indicate that the richest place for invertebrates is a patch of rough grassland on Canvey Island in the Thames estuary. The site, described by English Nature as 'a little brown rainforest', is due to be transformed into a business park unless conservation bodies can save it.

RUDDY DUCKS

Few conservation policies have sparked more protest than the Government's decision to wipe out all but a handful of the popular ruddy duck. The cull, which is supported by the RSPB and the Wildfowl and Wetlands Trust, is to safeguard the rare white-headed duck of Spain and prevent interbreeding between the two closely related species. The ruddy duck, a native of America, became established in Britain after escaping from the wildfowl collection at Slimbridge. There are an estimated 6,000 ruddy ducks in Britain, and the drake, with its attractive plumage, bright blue beak and extrovert behaviour during the breeding season, endeared itself to many birdwatchers. Some of the ducks migrate to the continent and will certainly spread in Europe if not culled. Whether the ruddy duck really threatens the survival of the white-headed duck is far from certain, but the latter has already reached dangerously low numbers from the drainage and pollution of its aquatic habitat.

A trial cull starting in 1999 tested different control measures, but it transpired that the only effective measure is to shoot the ducks when they congregate on certain lakes and reservoirs in winter. The trial succeeded, not without difficulty, in killing 2,600 birds. The aim is to reduce the population to 'fewer than 175 individuals' over the next four to ten years, at a cost estimated at £4–6 million.

THE BUILT ENVIRONMENT

The year under review was dominated by the preparation for and, in July 2003, the launch of the most extensive review of the protective regimes for the historic environment since the Second World War. Commissioned by the Secretary of State at the Department for Culture, Media and Sport, Tessa Jowell, the so-called Review of Designations looked at the scope for integration, particularly in listing and scheduling, of the present split of functions between the Secretary of State, English Heritage, regional assemblies and local authorities, and the particular problems posed by 20th-century structures. The consultation paper (deadline for comments, October 2003) will be followed in early 2004 by a White Paper.

The consultation paper contained a number of moderately radical suggestions, the main one being that henceforward the power to list, which has resided with the Secretary of State at the DCMS on the advice of English Heritage, should be passed to the latter. This would make it easier to introduce a formal right of appeal against a decision of English Heritage, to be heard by representatives of the Secretary of State. There were concurrent technical reviews on the unification of consent regimes and another looking at the reconfiguration of Planning Policy Guidance (PPG) 15 and 16 on the historic environment and archaeology respectively. The first considered the possibility of introducing a single global consent; at present, owners may need not only planning permission but also listed building consent, conservation area consent and scheduled monument consent. The PPGs 15 and 16 are the principal means of communicating government policy on architectural conservation and the current regimes of protection. So far, the review is limited to England.

The review is one of the outcomes of the State of the Historic Environment Report 2002 (SHER), launched on 25 November 2002. Compiled by English Heritage, and also limited to England, SHER is the most comprehensive examination of the field for decades. It was awash with facts: only 5 per cent of people whose homes are listed said they would prefer to live in a new building; membership of environmental organisations has grown by 8.5 times since 1971; there are more privately owned historic homes and castles open to the public in England than there are in the care of the National Trust and English Heritage combined; the government department with the greatest direct responsibility for listed buildings and scheduled monuments is the Ministry of Defence; local authority conservation resources have fallen in real terms by 8 per cent between 1996 and 2000; and English Heritage's own grant funding has fell in real terms by some 23 per cent over the five years to 2000. At the launch of SHER, Ms Jowell pledged 'to put the historic environment at the heart of everything we do'.

In December 2002, the organisation Heritage Link was launched, to co-ordinate action between the various elements within the voluntary sector of the conservation movement, both for its own sake and to improve its effectiveness in government lobbying. Another body, Heritage Information, was launched twice in the course of the year, once to the trade and then later to the general public. Originally called the Building Conservation Centre Trust and funded by substantial grant-aid from the Department for Environment, Food and Rural Affairs (£375,000 over three years), the Heritage Lottery Fund (£365,000 over three years), English Heritage (£75,000 over three years), the Architectural Heritage Fund

(£20,000) and £245,000 raised from charitable trusts, livery companies and other organisations, the trust aims to build a website which will provide information on craftsmen, contractors, experts, consultants, academics, training courses, products, books, news and jobs. It hopes to prove the ultimate 'one-stop shop'. The National Heritage Training Group has also been set up with the allied aim of bringing together employers, heritage regulators and grant-giving bodies, trade associations and conservation societies.

November 2002 saw the first National Maintenance Week organised by the Society for the Protection of Ancient Buildings with the help of a grant from English Heritage. Just as the leaves were beginning to fall and the gutters to become clogged, SPAB reminded the nation of the need to unblock the drains, put back the slipped slates and generally practise a 'stitch in time'. It brought the issue to the fore and was a media success, as was the *Restoration* television series in summer 2003. Reaching an audience of millions, *Restoration* had celebrity presenters making the case for the restoration of 30 buildings –including a purpose-built 19th-century coffin factory in Birmingham, a huge Nonconformist chapel in Stoke-on-Trent, a prisoner-of-war camp in the north-east and a lino factory in Belfast – and the audience voted for their favourite cause. Never before had architectural conservation been so dramatically 'put on the map' in media terms.

HERITAGE LOTTERY FUND

Head and shoulders above all other conservation organisations in terms of the funds at its disposal remained The Heritage Lottery Fund. Established in 1995 to disburse the 'heritage' monies generated by the National Lottery, the HLF launched its new strategic plan for the next five years. Building on the success of its first seven years, in which it has committed £2 billion to 10,000 projects, half of which are now complete, HLF proposes to employ up to 40 new staff. This is partly a result of the decision to regionalise but primarily to engender new applications, particularly in the geographical 'cold spots' where applications have been fewer than expected. HLF also widened the definition of 'heritage' to embrace projects where there is no formal designation by statutory authorities but which may nevertheless be valued by the local community. It further extended its remit to embrace oral history and traditions based on language. There was additional stress on training, a new initiative aimed at youth called Young Roots, and a relaxation in the requirements for partnership funding, 10 per cent only being the norm for grants between £50,000 and £1 million and 25 per cent for amounts above that. This was set against the backdrop of a projected decline in income over the five-year period from £300 million in 2002–3 to £262 million in 2006–7.

The most dramatic of all the grants announcements in the year was from the National Heritage Memorial Fund. The grant was for saving Tyntesfield House in Somerset, a fairytale Gothic house with a private chapel of Oxbridge proportions, designed by John Norton for Lord Wraxall. The generosity of the NHMF and of members of the public, who contributed several million pounds, allowed the house and contents to be preserved intact by the the National Trust. This one grant virtually wiped out the reserves of the NHMF but the Heritage Lottery Fund took similar largesse in its stride. In a partnership with English Heritage (the Joint Scheme), the two organisations promised to find £30 million for the conservation of historic places of worship in 2003–4, a considerable increase from the £21 million provided in 2002–3. Similarly, some £30 million a year was channelled through the HLF's Townscape Heritage Initiative, and a panoply of small grants helped many local initiatives, including: £6,000 to collect old recipes of North Yorkshire; some £7,000 to build up an archive about Fontmell Magna in Dorset; and £5,000 to repair the ancient wooden stairway to the bell tower at Wetton in Derbyshire.

However, it is the grand gesture that tends to command the headlines. Grant announcements in the course of the year included those to: De La Warr Pavilion, Bexhill-on-Sea, Sussex (£1,900,000), to create an arts centre in this Modernist icon by Eric Mendelsohn; new museums at Beverley, East Yorkshire (£3,919,000), Lincoln (£5,141,000) and Leeds (£19,063,000); rehousing the greatest collection of architectural drawings in the world, those owned by the RIBA, in the Victoria & Albert Museum (£3,272,000); Hardwick Park, Co. Durham (£4,056,000), the glorious 18th-century park that used to be a byword for local authority neglect; St Francis' Church, Gorton, Manchester (£3,800,000), a great Franciscan church built to serve the slums of east Manchester; the Mary Rose Trust (£4,170,000), for the second phase of the project to conserve the remains of Henry VIII's flagship; the National Waterfront Museum, Swansea (£10,699,000), the largest-ever HLF grant in Wales; Dimbola Lodge, Freshwater, Isle of Wight (£88,100), to improve the museum created in the house of pioneer photographer Julia Margaret Cameron; Oxford Prison (£1.8 million), to create a major visitor attraction in what had hitherto been the city's prison; Stonehenge (£26 million) to improve visitor conditions at Britain's most important pre-Christian site; the Hampshire photographic project (£78,000), to record the historic buildings of the county; Broadwood Piano Archive (£67,300), to repair and rebind the papers of the country's most famous piano manufacturers, dating from the late 18th century onwards; Linthorpe Cemetery, Middlesbrough (£596,500), to conserve a major Victorian cemetery, symbolic of the ability of the HLF's newly expanded Public Parks Initiative, to offer more of a lifeline for historic green spaces than the previous Urban Parks Programme; Hopetoun House, West Lothian (£977,000), to conserve one of the greatest houses, mostly by Robert Adam, in the hinterland of Edinburgh; Birmingham Town Hall (£13.5 million), the largest-ever HLF grant in the West Midlands, going to England's purest homage to the Maison Carree of 1834, closed in 1996 as unsafe; and University College, London (£4.9 million), to build a new panopticon building in Gordon Street, Bloomsbury, to display fully for the first time the Petrie Collection of Egyptology.

Many HLF-funded schemes are now coming to fruition. These include: London's Museum in the Docklands, which opened in May 2003; the Workhouse at Southwell, Nottinghamshire, displayed by the National Trust; St Nicholas, Burnage, Manchester, a 1930s design by Cachemaille-Day saved from almost certain demolition by a grant of £1.1 million; the Anderton Boat Lift at Northwich, Cheshire (£3.3 million), Victorian engineering of 1875 at its most big boned; St Luke's Church, Old Street, Islington, gutted in 1959 but now reroofed to house the London Symphony Orchestra; St Ethelburga's Church in the City of London, blown up by the IRA in 1993 (£243,000); and Oxford Railway Station, a pioneering design of 1851 in structural iron, which is no longer in Oxford but has been re-erected at Quainton, Buckinghamshire, to serve the private railway open to the public in that village.

ENGLISH HERITAGE

English Heritage, under its dynamic new chief executive Dr Simon Thurley, has not allowed what it deems to be a freeze in its grant-in-aid from the Government to stifle initiatives. It now has a new Centre for Archaeology based at Portsmouth which issues regular scholarly and technical reports. EH's archaeological resources have also been boosted by the establishment of the Aggregates Levy Sustainability Fund (ALSF), in effect a tax on aggregates extraction. This has permitted English Heritage, together with the Countryside Agency and English Nature, to distribute £16 million in 2002–3 and £13.5 million in 2003–4 to redress some of the damage caused by quarrying; the measures include extensive schemes of landscape restoration and archaeological recording.

Its publications in the year ranged from major studies of historic paint finishes, the architecture of shops, the investment performance of listed office buildings, a guide to the minefield of the new building regulations as they impact on historic buildings, major research transactions on sandstone and limestone roofing, and its latest Buildings at Risk lists which, outside London, cover Grade II* and Grade I buildings at varying degrees of risk. News on that front was moderately comforting; 114 buildings were removed from the 2002 list, although another 94 were added. Its first-ever survey of local authority conservation officers, written jointly with the Institute of Historic Building Conservation and called *Heritage Under Pressure,* was published in March 2003. This produced the depressing finding that some 15 per cent of local authorities had no conservation officer at all and that where there were officers, they were hopelessly overworked. At least 25 per cent of district councils never kept a register of structures at risk, and many of those compiled had never been updated. Net expenditure on the historic environment and conservation by local planning authorities declined by 8 per cent in real terms between 1998 and 2003, whilst local authority staff costs dropped by 10 per cent in real terms in the same period. English Heritage's chief contribution to study is the National Monuments Record based in Swindon, and further steps towards making its extraordinary photographic collection available to a broader public were taken in March 2003, when 20,000 images showing 300 years of working life in England were made available electronically through 'Viewfinder'.

In Wales, Cadw, the Welsh equivalent of English Heritage, announced a measure of controlled delegation to Welsh planning authorities on applications for listed building consent. The councils will only receive these powers if they are able to demonstrate clear professional competence in conservation work and display 'an effective proven track record of development control, including Enforcement Action'. The toughness of these conditions has meant a low take-up rate. Cadw also issued advice on providing disabled access to historic buildings, and the report of the Historic Buildings Council for Wales for 2001–2, published in 2003, described in some detail many of the remarkable structures which benefited from public grant-aid, particularly the underground rockwork gardens at Dewstow House, Caerwent (1890), and the Eagle

Academy at Cowbridge, Vale of Glamorgan, constructed as an Assembly Room in 1740. In July 2002, the sixth and final volume of the *Register of Parks and Gardens of Special Historic Interest in Wales,* compiled by Cadw and ICOMOS, became available. It covers 64 sites in Carmarthenshire, Ceredigion and Pembrokeshire. In spring 2003, an independent assessment of the protection of the historic environment in Wales compiled on behalf of the Welsh Assembly identified the need for greater co-ordination of activity and found the protection of the 19th-century Welsh heritage particularly in need of improvement.

The activities of Historic Scotland mirrored those of its English and Welsh counterparts. Its outstanding publications record expanded further, with major works on the conservation of plasterwork and of timber, sash and case windows. Its Building at Risk activity was largely concentrated through the publications of the Scottish Civic Trust, the latest report emerging in early 2003.

The National Trust acquired not only Tyntesfield House in Somerset but in early 2003 it also took into its care the iconic Red House at Bexleyheath on the outskirts of London. Commissioned by William Morris from the architect Philip Webb, it is the earliest and most powerful expression of the Arts and Crafts Movement. The trust also announced a project to encourage volunteering in conservation and community projects through corporate and public sector organisations called the Employee Volunteering Project (EVP). Other new attractions to open their doors in 2002–3 included: the Imperial War Museum North in Salford, designed by Daniel Liebeskind; the Macclesfield Silk Museum, rehoused in the former Macclesfield School of Art and Science; the Melton Carnegie Museum at Melton Mowbray, housed in the former library of 1904; the Mayflower Centre in Plymouth, which includes an exhibition on the history of emigration from the city; Urbis in Manchester and FACT in Liverpool, both celebrating urban life; and the Roman amphitheatre in the City of London under the new Guildhall Art Gallery.

LISTING

The bedrock of any conservation policy remains the identification of buildings for protection and the chief vehicle for this is listing. Structures added to the lists in the course of the year included: a remarkable late 19th-century allotment shed in Nottingham; the studio at Chapel House, Horham, Suffolk, built for his own use by Benjamin Britten; the 1914 Rachel Macmillan Nursery School in Greenwich, a pioneering example of the building type; a pit for breeding swans at the Great Hospital, Bishopsgate, Norwich; the Victory or Memorial Arch of 1919–22 at Waterloo Station; and the former Post Office Tower, off London's Tottenham Court Road. Among the upgradings were that of Tickford Bridge of 1810 in Newport Pagnell, Buckinghamshire, moved into Grade I because of its identification as an extremely early example of cast-iron engineering. Sometimes listing proves unnecessary; English Heritage was able to announce an arrangement with the Post Office by which none of its distinctive red cast-iron letterboxes would be replaced other than for exceptional reasons. As there are 85,000, listing each one would have choked the system.

Listing does not preclude applications to demolish, and 137 structures in England and nine in Wales came under threat in 2002 (compared with 212 in 2001). Particularly controversial was the application to demolish completely, and perhaps resite, the Grade I-listed medieval church at Eastwood in Essex to allow Southend Airport to be expanded; the application was refused. The threat to a distinctive Modern Movement villa, Greenside, near Wentworth Golf Course in Surrey led the Twentieth Century Society to consider legal action, which staved off the threat. A Grade II*-listed medieval house at Bryn Parc, Denbigh, North Wales, was severely damaged by fire, and among serious losses was that of the Durnford Street School at Middleton in Manchester, a major work of 1904 by Edgar Wood. There were public inquiries on a restaurant planned for the bailey of Cardiff Castle, and on a scheme for retirement housing near the Governor's House in Berwick-on-Tweed, Northumberland; the latter was rejected in July 2003.

The projected scheme of mass clearance of 19th-century housing at Nelson in Lancashire became symbolic of the threat which much housing of that date faces in the north-west. Some longstanding cases moved closer to satisfactory solutions, with the purchase of the Midland Hotel at Morecambe, one of the most important 1930s buildings in the area, by the developers Urban Splash; the conversion of the Grade I-listed chapel George's Meeting House, Exeter, into a pub; and the serving of a repairs notice by Wolverhampton Council on the long-derelict mid 18th-century Molineux Hotel in the city centre. The battle to maintain the remains of the Baltic Exchange in the City of London, blown up by the IRA in 1992, finally failed when the dismantled remains of the Grade II*-listed building of 1905 were sold off to architectural salvage companies.

Increasing concern was expressed in the course of the year over the fate of historic churches. The Government's decision to extend the repayment of all but 5 per cent of the 17.5 per cent VAT paid on repairs to March 2004 was welcome, but it seemed likely that the rate of redundancy would continue to rise from the comparatively low base of recent years. The chief recipient of outstanding redundant Anglican churches in England is the Churches Conservation Trust, which was able to announce the vesting of the Lumley Chapel at St Dunstan's, Cheam, full of outstanding monuments; St John the Baptist at Stamford, Lincolnshire, a Grade I medieval church; and the continuation of its heroic efforts at St Paul's, Portland Square, Bristol, buoyed up by two substantial grants from the Heritage Lottery Fund totalling some £2.3 million. The Friends of Friendless Churches was able to announce the vesting of outstanding Welsh churches at Brithdir and Ynyscynhaearn in Gwynedd, whilst the Historic Chapels Trust was able to save the 1861 Penrose Methodist Chapel in Cornwall, and open to the public in October 2002 the 1899 Unitarian Chapel at Wallasey, Merseyside, celebrated for its elaborate Arts and Crafts decoration in the chancel.

DANCE

Before the 2002–3 season even began it was overshadowed by the resignation of Ross Stretton, the Royal Ballet's Australian director, after only one year in the job. He expressed a desire to look to the future of the art form, with the implied criticism that the Royal Ballet wished merely to nurture the past. In fact his position had become untenable; he had lost the confidence of the dancers because of his abrasive management style and dubious casting decisions, and his repertoire choices had led to widespread disquiet. After a few months of uncertainty, Monica Mason, the company's former principal dancer and assistant director, was confirmed as director in a effort to restore calm. She became only the second woman to direct the company, the first being its founder Dame Ninette de Valois. In contrast to the Royal Ballet's undignified drama, Rambert Dance Company moved smoothly from the directorship of Christopher Bruce to that of Mark Baldwin, and Scottish Ballet made plans during the season for its new direction under the leadership of former Royal Ballet dancer and choreographer Ashley Page.

MACMILLAN TRIBUTE

The Royal Ballet's 2002–3 season had been designed in part as a tribute to its former director Sir Kenneth MacMillan, to mark the 10th anniversary of his death; MacMillan was also the subject of a conference at the Royal Academy of Dance and an exhibition at the Theatre Museum. The Royal Ballet's season opened with performances of his powerful full-length work *Mayerling*; it was during a performance of this work that he died backstage at the Royal Opera House in 1992. Following her appointment as director, Monica Mason made changes to the planned repertoire to strengthen the tribute, in consultation with MacMillan's widow. A programme to mark the 10th anniversary of the death of Rudolf Nureyev was also inserted into the repertoire in place of some of the works planned by Stretton.

The season produced some outstanding performances, especially in MacMillan works, but was otherwise disappointing, which was perhaps not surprising in the circumstances. The Nureyev tribute included mesmerising film of the dancer projected at the back of the stage, but had the nonsensical idea of allowing dancers to perform at the front of the stage in competition with the filmed images. The inevitable contrast in size, medium and magnetism ensured that the dancers were irrelevant to the proceedings, doing them a grave disservice. The most serious failure of the season was a new production of *The Sleeping Beauty*, mounted by Natalia Makarova with designs by Luisa Spinatelli. It replaced Anthony Dowell's 1994 production which, although choreographically distinguished, had been ruined by its overblown designs. Makarova's production, which premièred in March 2003, had neither choreographic nor scenic virtue, and lost both the poetry and the drama inherent in Tchaikovsky's score. Towards the end of the season, the company's former resident choreographer David Bintley, now director of Birmingham Royal Ballet, returned to mount a new work, *Les Saisons*, to music by Glazunov; this started beautifully but deteriorated into disappointing banality.

More successful were a revival of Ashton's intricate, mysterious *Scènes de Ballet* and the introduction into the repertoire of *Gong*, the first work by the highly popular American choreographer Mark Morris to be danced by the Royal Ballet. MacMillan's *Danses Concertantes* was revived with the original designs by Nicholas Georgiadis reinstated, and the Italian dancer Alessandra Ferri, who had inspired MacMillan when she was a young dancer with the Royal Ballet in the early 1980s, returned to dance Juliet in his production of *Romeo and Juliet* when Darcey Bussell was forced to withdraw because of injury. Great performances by Alina Cojocaru and Johann Kobborg in a string of works, especially *Mayerling* and *Manon*, graced the season, and Tamara Rojo continued to dance with unparalleled power and honesty, most notably in *Song of the Earth*, MacMillan's beautiful and poignant work to Mahler's song cycle. The Royal Ballet still has no music director, but in February 2003 mourned the loss of its former principal conductor and music director John Lanchbery.

CHANGES

Early in 2003 the Royal Opera House announced that Dame Judith Mayhew would become the first woman to chair its board on the retirement of Sir Colin Southgate in August 2003. The Prince of Wales accepted an invitation to succeed his late aunt Princess Margaret as president of the Royal Ballet and Birmingham Royal Ballet. The Royal Ballet School moved during the year into new premises opposite the Royal Opera House in Covent Garden; this will enable future generations of dancers once more to reap the benefits of regular contact with and observation of today's most exciting artists.

One of the Royal Ballet's most popular character dancers, the choreographer Ashley Page, left during the 2002–3 season to take up his new position as artistic director of Scottish Ballet. The Glasgow-based company largely marked time until Page arrived and announced his plans for the future. The company is due to perform Richard Alston's *Dangerous Liaisons* and works by Siobhan Davies, Stephen Petronio and Page himself, followed by a new production of *The Nutcracker* to be mounted by Page. It will be interesting to see if Page can create a coherent new identity for the company in coming years.

The season's other new director, Mark Baldwin, took over the running of Rambert Dance Company in a smooth and well-managed transition. Baldwin was a dancer with Rambert from 1983 to 1992 and has wide experience as a choreographer. His first months with the company saw the introduction into the repertoire of new works by Karol Armitage and Rafael Bonachela (with useful publicity generated by a film featuring Kylie Minogue in Bonachela's work *21*) and Hans Van Manen's beautiful *Visions Fugitives*, performed by Rambert for the first time.

The Rambert company's season at Sadler's Wells in November 2002 marked its farewell to Christopher Bruce after eight and a half years as director. However, his association with Rambert stretches back more than 40 years to when he joined the Rambert school at the age of 13. He joined the then Ballet Rambert in 1963 and was highly successful as a dancer before beginning his choreographic career in 1969. He was Rambert's associate director between 1975 and 1979 and associate choreographer between 1980 and 1987, returning as artistic director in 1994. Among his best-known works are *Cruel Garden* (created in collaboration with Lindsay Kemp), *Ghost Dances*, *Swansong* and *Rooster*. The farewell performance for Bruce at Sadler's Wells on 14 November 2002 was organised by the company's new head of development, the former Royal Ballet principal Bruce Sansom, who has returned to the UK after several years in the USA training in arts administration.

Birmingham Royal Ballet confirmed its identity as a company that gives high-standard performances of works that are both popular and accessible. In October 2002 its director David Bintley created an attractive new work, *Concert Fantasy*, to Tchaikovsky's music, and two significant works were introduced into the repertoire: Jerome Robbins's *Fancy Free* and Balanchine's *Western Symphony*. The company also revived Peter Wright's stylish 1984 production of *The Sleeping Beauty*, providing a real classical challenge to its dancers as well as provoking many favourable comparisons between this production, designed by Philip Prowse, and the Royal Ballet's new staging at Covent Garden.

NEW NUTCRACKER
English National Ballet's season was blighted by a disastrous new production of *The Nutcracker* with designs by the distinguished cartoonist Gerald Scarfe. This was the first time Scarfe had designed for ballet and the results were completely inappropriate for the poetry of Tchaikovsky's music. The sets and costumes were brightly coloured and harsh, with tiresome contemporary references and caricatures in place of characters. Christopher Hampson's attempts to provide new choreography for sections of the ballet were barely noticeable, overwhelmed by the force of the designs. Even Irek Mukhamedov could not create interest in the role of Drosselmeyer, with a ridiculous spiky black wig and a permanent expression of (perhaps understandable) astonishment.

Hampson's choreography to Prokofiev's 'lost' score *Trapèze*, which was premièred at Sadler's Wells in April 2003 (the company's first performances at this venue for 15 years), was much more successful, and was joined on the same programme by a popular if rather hackneyed *pas de deux* for Agnes Oaks and Thomas Edur created by Wayne McGregor and entitled *2 Human*. In autumn 2002 Mark Morris's *Drink To Me Only With Thine Eyes* was introduced into the repertoire to great acclaim, and a revival of MacMillan's *The Rite of Spring* was performed with power and conviction. The company danced for the first time at the Linbury Studio Theatre at the Royal Opera House in May 2003, with Adam Cooper as guest artist in MacMillan's 1988 *Hamlet*-inspired work *Sea of Troubles*. The season ended with a popular season at Sadler's Wells that included the world première of *Melody on the Move*, a witty and enjoyable work by Michael Corder.

The much smaller touring company Northern Ballet Theatre consolidated its reputation for mounting popular story ballets and performing them with great gusto under the artistic direction of David Nixon. Nixon created a vigorous new work, *Wuthering Heights*, for the company in September 2002, and any choreographic deficiencies in the work were compensated for by the conviction and enthusiasm of the dancers. Nixon also mounted his

Beauty and the Beast, created in 1997 when he was director of BalletMet Columbus in USA, and in a brave departure brought Birgit Scherzer's abstract *Requiem!!* into the repertoire. This over-ambitious piece, danced to Mozart's great work, wallowed in often impenetrable symbolism but allowed the dancers to show their versatility and commitment.

LABAN
Laban, the impressive new £22 million building on Deptford Creekside in London, designed by the Swiss architects Herzog & de Meuron, was built to house the Laban Centre for Movement and Dance. It was officially opened in a gala ceremony on 5 February 2003. The principal and chief executive of the centre, Dr Marion North, retired at the end of the 2002–3 academic year after a long and distinguished career in dance education. Laban is said to be the world's largest purpose-built space for contemporary dance, a field which is enjoying increasing popularity, and will provide an enormous boost to the teaching, rehearsal and research facilities in the UK.

Leading figures in contemporary dance, including Richard Alston and Siobhan Davies, presented new works during the year. Alston created *Stampede*, a well-mannered piece set to Italian Renaissance music, in his company's first-ever season at Sadler's Wells Theatre in October 2002. Siobhan Davies created her first work for nearly two years when she mounted *Plants and Ghosts* for her company at Hangar 3022 at the former US airfield at Upper Heyford, Oxfordshire, in September 2002. The work was specially conceived for non-theatre venues, and was set to a 'sound installation' by Max Eastley. It required a high level of nervous energy from its performers but did not add up to a coherent whole from a spectator's point of view. By contrast, Akram Khan continued to excite audiences with *Ronin*, the second part of his dance trilogy of solo Kathak dance shows, presented at the Purcell Room in April 2003.

Matthew Bourne broke away from his original company Adventures in Motion Pictures to form New Adventures, and mounted a critically acclaimed dance drama *Play Without Words*, based on the 1963 film *The Servant*, at the Royal National Theatre in September 2002. He then revived his 1992 *Nutcracker* at Sadler's Wells and enjoyed a huge popular success.

Other notable productions during the year included a new version of *Hamlet* by Kim Brandstrup for his Arc Dance Company, a setting of Purcell's *Dido and Aeneas* by Henri Oguike, and *Critics' Choice* *****, mounted by George Piper Dances, the group founded by ex-Royal Ballet dancers Michael Nunn and William Trevitt. For this piece they invited five leading choreographers – Akram Khan, Christopher Wheeldon, Michael Clark, Russell Maliphant and Matthew Bourne – to create short pieces that were interspersed with filmed sequences showing rehearsals for the works and interviews explaining the choreographers' working methods. The result, shown at the Queen Elizabeth Hall in March 2003 and then on tour, was both intriguing and entertaining.

MIXING GENRES
Michael Clark's new work *Would, Should, Can, Did*, given as part of the Only Connect 'genre-bending' season at the Barbican Centre in April 2003, was billed as seven 'artistic experiments' involving Clark and visual artists, musicians, composers and designers, but it contributed little he has not shown before. Cathy

Marston's ambitious work *Sophie/Stateless* was inspired by the novel *Sophie's Choice* and given at the Linbury Studio Theatre at the Royal Opera House in January 2003. *Sophie* used only two dancers and made heavy use of video sequences played alongside the dance. It was followed by *Stateless*, an abstract work exploring the theme of dispossession.

Musicals with a high dance content continue to flourish in London, with former Royal Ballet dancer Sarah Wildor having a considerable success in Susan Stroman's *Contact*, and her husband Adam Cooper leading the Leicester Haymarket's production of *On Your Toes* at the Royal Festival Hall in the summer of 2003.

Robyn Orlin, the Johannesburg-based choreographer, mounted her successful satirical work *Daddy I've Seen This Piece Six Times Before and I Still Don't Know Why They're Hurting Each Other* at The Pit in London in the summer of 2002. Other notable visitors to the UK in 2002–3 included Merce Cunningham, a group of principals and soloists from New York City Ballet, Garth Fagan Dance, Lyon Opera Ballet, the Royal Ballet of Flanders, Paul Taylor Dance Company, the Kirov, and Twyla Tharp with her new company Twyla Tharp Dance. Two visitors from Germany, Pina Bausch with *Kontakthof* and Sasha Waltz with *Körper*, demonstrated the power of their form of expressionist dance theatre.

Dance Theatre of Harlem returned to London after an absence of 14 years, and the Eifman Ballet Theatre from St Petersburg presented two dramatic works, *Red Giselle* and *Tchaikovsky*, at Sadler's Wells in February 2003. Antonio Gades brought his dance-drama *Fuenteovejuna*, performed by the Spanish National Dance Company, to the same theatre in June 2003. Maurice Béjart's risible *Mother Teresa and the Children of the World* was given at the Peacock Theatre in February 2003. Carlos Acosta, a guest principal with the Royal Ballet, brought a company from his native Cuba to perform his work *Tocororo* at Sadler's Wells in July 2003. The work, based partly on his own remarkable life, was praised for its energy but was considered disappointing.

LOOKING FORWARD
In spring 2003 the Arts Council of England announced that a Youth Dance Agency for England would be set up as part of a wide-ranging scheme to give talented young people wider access to music and dance opportunities at various leading organisations. The agency will be developed over the next three years and will act as a focal point for information and advice while also seeking to raise the profile of all forms of youth dance.

The Arts Council's spending plans for 2003–6 also show significant increases in funding for dance. Ballet received an unexpected fillip during the year when a visit to the Royal Ballet at the Royal Opera House by the England football captain David Beckham and his wife Victoria attracted enormous publicity. But in spite of this endorsement the world of classical ballet is undergoing something of a crisis of confidence, in contrast to the current vigour of the contemporary dance scene. In January 2003 directors of classical ballet companies from around the world gathered at Snape Maltings in Suffolk to discuss the problems facing them: the perceived globalisation of ballet, with shared productions and the watering-down of different national styles; the need to balance box-office needs with artistic experimentation; the lack of creativity among classical choreographers; and the wide-ranging demands made on directors of large classical companies. Another gathering is planned for

2005 and it is hoped that these meetings will help to give directors the impetus to tackle these issues and take the art of ballet forward with renewed confidence.

PRODUCTIONS

ROYAL BALLET
Founded 1931 as the Vic-Wells Ballet
Royal Opera House, Covent Garden, London WC2E 9DD

WORLD PREMIÈRES:
The Sleeping Beauty (Petipa, prod. Natalia Makarova), 8 March 2003. A full-length work. Music, Tchaikovsky; design, Luisa Spinatelli. Cast led by Darcey Bussell, Roberto Bolle and Marianela Nuñez
Memory (Irek Mukhamedov), 5 April 2003. A solo. Music, Skriabin. Danced by Irek Mukhamedov as part of a tribute to Rudolf Nureyev, who danced a solo to the same music choreographed by Frederick Ashton for his debut performance in London in 1961
Les Saisons (David Bintley), 21 May 2003. A one-act work. Music, Glazunov; sets, Peter J. Davison; costumes, Charles Quiggin. Cast led by Jaimie Tapper, Deirdre Chapman, Lauren Cuthbertson, Mara Galeazzi, Marianela Nuñez, Alina Cojocaru, Johan Kobborg, Isabel McMeekan, Jonathan Cope and Martin Harvey

COMPANY PREMIÈRES:
Gong (Mark Morris, 2001), 22 October 2002. A one-act work. Music, Colin McPhee; costumes, Isaac Mizrahi
Sinfonietta (Jiří Kylián, 1978), 13 January 2003. A one-act work. Music, Janáček; design, Walter Nobbe
Surge (formerly named *Lamé*) (Pierre Darde), 5 April 2003. A solo. Music, Franco Donatoni. Dancer, Laurent Hilaire. Also danced as part of the Nureyev tribute
Full-length works from the repertoire: *Mayerling* (MacMillan, 1978), *Swan Lake* (Petipa/Ivanov, prod. Dowell 1987), *The Nutcracker* (Ivanov, prod. Wright 1984 with revisions 1999), *Manon* (MacMillan, 1974), *Romeo and Juliet* (MacMillan, 1965).
One-act works from the repertoire: *Tryst* (Wheeldon, 2002), *Carmen* (Ek, 1992), *Scènes de Ballet* (Ashton, 1944), *Winter Dreams* (MacMillan, 1991), *Apollo* (Balanchine, 1928), *pas de deux* from *In the middle, somewhat elevated* (Forsythe, 1988), *pas de trois* from *Images of Love* (MacMillan, 1964), solo from *Le Corsaire* (after Petipa, 1899), *pas de deux* from *La Sylphide* (Bournonville, 1836), *Raymonda Act III* (Nureyev after Petipa, 1964), *Danses Concertantes* (MacMillan, 1955, with the original designs by Nicholas Georgiadis), *The Judas Tree* (MacMillan, 1992), *Gloria* (MacMillan, 1980), *Song of the Earth* (MacMillan, 1965).
The company toured to Russia (Moscow and St Petersburg) in June–July 2003, performing *Tryst*, extracts from *La Sylphide*, *Le Corsaire* and *Winter Dreams*, *Thaïs pas de deux* (Ashton, 1971), *Swan Lake*, *Mayerling*, *Scènes de Ballet*, *The Judas Tree*, *Gloria*, *Song of the Earth*, *Romeo and Juliet*, *Marguerite and Armand* (Ashton, 1963) and *A Month in the Country* (Ashton, 1976).

BIRMINGHAM ROYAL BALLET
Founded 1946 as the Sadler's Wells Opera Ballet
Birmingham Hippodrome, Thorp Street, Birmingham B5 4AU

WORLD PREMIÈRE:
Concert Fantasy (David Bintley), 2 October 2002. A one-act work. Music, Tchaikovsky. Cast led by Nao Sakuma and Chi Cao

COMPANY PREMIÈRES:
Fancy Free (Jerome Robbins, 1944), 2 October 2002. A one-act work. Music, Leonard Bernstein; sets, Oliver Smith; costumes, Kermit Love. Cast led by Michael Revie, Robert Parker and James Grundy
   Western Symphony (George Balanchine, 1954), 2 October 2002. A one-act work. Music, traditional American melodies arranged by Hershy Kay; sets, John Boyt; costumes, Karinska. Cast led by Andrew Murphy, Monica Zamora, Lucinda Dunn and Asta Bazeviciute
   Full length works from the repertoire: *Far from the Madding Crowd* (Bintley, 1996); *The Nutcracker* (Ivanov, prod. Wright, additional choreography by Redmon, 1990), *Coppélia* (Petipa, Cecchetti and Wright, prod. Wright 1995), *Arthur, Parts 1 and 2* (Bintley, 2000 and 2001), *The Sleeping Beauty* (Petipa, prod. Wright 1984).
   In addition to performances at the newly refurbished Birmingham Hippodrome Theatre and a short season at The Academy at the National Indoor Arena in Birmingham, the company toured to Sunderland (two seasons), Plymouth (three seasons), Bradford, Edinburgh and Salford.

ENGLISH NATIONAL BALLET
Founded 1950 as London Festival Ballet
Markova House, 39 Jay Mews, London SW7 2ES

WORLD PREMIÈRES:
The Nutcracker (Christopher Hampson), 10 October 2002. A full-length work. Music, Tchaikovsky; design, Gerald Scarfe. Cast led by Agnes Oaks, Thomas Edur, Irek Mukhamedov and Erina Takahashi
   Trapèze (Christopher Hampson), 8 April 2003, to open the *Tour de Force* programme. A one-act work. Music, Prokofiev. Cast led by Sarah McIlroy and Jan-Erik Wikström
   2 Human (Wayne McGregor), 8 April 2003, to open the *Tour de Force* programme. A *pas de deux*. Music, J. S. Bach; design, Ursula Bombshell. Dancers, Agnes Oaks and Thomas Edur
   Melody on the Move (Michael Corder), 8 July 2003. A one-act work. Music, British 'light' music of the 1930s, 1940s and 1950s; design, Mark Bailey. Cast led by Agnes Oaks and Thomas Edur

COMPANY PREMIÈRE:
Drink To Me Only With Thine Eyes (Mark Morris, 1988), 12 November 2002. A one-act work. Music, Virgil Thomson; design, Santo Loquasto. Cast led by Erina Takahashi, Cameron McMillan, Jan-Erik Wikström and Gary Avis
   Full-length works from the repertoire: *Swan Lake* (Petipa/Ivanov, prod. Deane 1997), *Coppélia* (Petipa and Cecchetti, prod. Hynd 1985).
   One-act works from the repertoire: *Double Concerto* (Hampson, 2001), *The Rite of Spring* (MacMillan, 1962), *Facing Viv* (Cathy Marston, 2002), *Manoeuvre* (Patrick Lewis, 2002).
   The full company toured to Bristol, Liverpool (two seasons), Southampton (two seasons), Manchester (two

seasons) and London (The Coliseum and two seasons at Sadler's Wells). Dancers from the company participated in a festival of music, words and dance at Westminster Abbey, London on 13 May 2003. The company also performed a programme of new choreography by six dancers from the company and *Sea of Troubles* (MacMillan, 1988) at the Linbury Studio Theatre at the Royal Opera House, London in May 2003 as part of the international celebration of Kenneth MacMillan.
   In April–May 2003 the company split into two groups and went on two small-scale tours (called *Tour de Force*). One group toured *Trapèze, Facing Viv* and the *Grand Pas* from *Paquita* to Swindon, Crawley, Blackpool and Poole. The other toured *Hollywood Smash & Grab* (a new work by Noel Wallace, to music by Brian Eno and with sets by Noel Wallace and costumes by Caroline Harris), *Sideshow* (MacMillan, 1972), *2 Human* and *Manoeuvre* to Brighton, Barnstaple, Malvern and Scunthorpe.
   In July 2003 the company toured to Athens, Greece and performed *Drink To Me Only With Thine Eyes, Double Concerto* and *The Rite of Spring.*

RAMBERT DANCE COMPANY
Founded 1926 as the Marie Rambert Dancers
94 Chiswick High Road, London W4 1SH

WORLD PREMIÈRES:
PreSentient (Wayne McGregor), 9 October 2002. Music, Steve Reich; design, Ursula Bombshell
   21 (Rafael Bonachela), 9 April 2003. Music, Benjamin Wallfisch; creative directors and design, William Baker and Alan Macdonald; incorporating a short projected film featuring Kylie Minogue
   Living Toys (Karole Armitage), 29 May 2003. Music, Thomas Adès; design, Peter Speliopoulos

COMPANY PREMIÈRES:
Study from *Blackbird* (Kylián, 2001), 25 September 2002. Music, traditional Georgian music; design, Joke Visser
   Visions Fugitives (Hans Van Manen, 1990), 27 March 2003. Music, Prokofiev; design, Keso Dekker
   Works from the repertoire: *Hurricane* (Bruce, 2000), *Ground Level Overlay* (Cunningham, 1995), *The Parades Gone By* (Kemp, 1975), *Cheese* (James, 2000), *Grinning in your Face* (Bruce, 2001), *Sounding* (Davies, 1989), *Ghost Dances* (Bruce, 1981).
   The company performed in Salford, Jersey, Edinburgh, Canterbury, London (two seasons at Sadler's Wells), Plymouth, Truro, Snape, Sheffield, Aberdeen, Woking, Newcastle upon Tyne, Mold and Glasgow.
   The company also performed in Biarritz, France on 7 September 2002, with a repertoire of *Ground Level Overlay, Study* from *Blackbird, Hurricane* and *Ghost Dances.* In October 2002 it toured to Basle, Switzerland with a repertoire of *Study* from *Blackbird, Hurricane, PreSentient* and *Ghost Dances.* In July 2003 it visited Berlin, Germany and performed *PreSentient, Ghost Dances* and *Visions Fugitives.*

RICHARD ALSTON DANCE COMPANY
Founded 1994
The Place, 17 Duke's Road, London WC1H 9AB
All works danced by the company are choreographed by Richard Alston.

WORLD PREMIÈRE:
Stampede, 15 October 2002. Music, 14th-century Italian music arranged and played by the Dufay Collective; design, Fotini Dimou

Works from the repertoire: *Rumours, Visions* (1994), *Touch and Go* (2002), *A Sudden Exit* (1999), *Slow Airs (Almost All)* (1999), *Red Run* (1998).

The company performed in High Wycombe, Northampton, London (Sadler's Wells), Brecon, Cambridge, Malvern, Chichester, Edinburgh, Nottingham, Stoke-on-Trent, Norwich, Sheffield, Canterbury, Salford, Glasgow, Liverpool, Brighton, Oxford and Bath. It also appeared at the Sixth European Dance Festival in Cyprus in May 2003, performing *Red Run, A Sudden Exit* and *Touch and Go*.

Dancers from the company performed in a programme of new works by company member Martin Lawrance at The Place, London in June 2003, which also included a solo, *Never Told*, created by Richard Alston.

SCOTTISH BALLET
Founded 1956 as the Western Theatre Ballet
261 West Princes Street, Glasgow G4 9EE

COMPANY PREMIÈRE:
Tzaikerk (Robert Cohan, 1967), 3 September 2002. A dance for six women. Music, Alan Hovhaness

Full-length work from the repertoire: *The Snowman* (North, 1993, expanded 2001).

One-act works from the repertoire: *Light Fandango* (North, 1997), *Five Brahms Waltzes in the Manner of Isadora Duncan* (Ashton, 1976), *pas de deux* from *The Two Pigeons* (Ashton, 1961), *Offenbach in the Underworld* (North, 1995), *pas de deux* from *Flower Festival in Genzano* (Bournonville, 1858), *Troy Game* (North, 1974).

The company performed in Dunfermline, Musselburgh, Oban, Barra, Benbecula, Portree, Ullapool, Stornoway, Dumfries, Galashiels, Montrose, Haddo House, Stranraer, Irvine, Berwick-upon-Tweed, Stirling, Glasgow (two seasons), Edinburgh, Aberdeen, Inverness and Hull.

DANCE AWARDS

CRITICS' CIRCLE NATIONAL DANCE AWARDS 2002
De Valois Award for Outstanding Contribution to Dance – Christopher Bruce (Rambert Dance Company)
Best Male Dancer – Thomas Edur (English National Ballet)
Best Female Dancer – Alina Cojocaru (Royal Ballet)
Best Partnership – Agnes Oaks and Thomas Edur (English National Ballet)
Award for Service to Dance – Dame Beryl Grey, DBE
Best Classical Choreographer – Christopher Hampson (English National Ballet)
Best Modern Choreographer – Mark Morris (Mark Morris Dance Group)
Outstanding Young Female Dancer (Classical) – Marianela Nuñez (Royal Ballet)
Outstanding Young Female Dancer (Modern) – Joanne Fong (Arc Dance Company)
Outstanding Young Male Dancer (Classical) – Ivan Putrov (Royal Ballet)
Outstanding Young Male Dancer (Modern) – Martin Lindinger (Rambert Dance Company)
Company Prize for Outstanding Repertoire (Classical) – Birmingham Royal Ballet
Company Prize for Outstanding Repertoire (Modern) – Rambert Dance Company
Best Foreign Dance Company – Mark Morris Dance Group (USA)

LAURENCE OLIVIER AWARDS 2003 (DANCE)
Best Theatre Choreographer – Matthew Bourne, *Play Without Words,* Lyttelton Theatre
Best New Dance Production – Polyphonia, *Danses Concertantes,* principals and soloists of New York City Ballet at Sadler's Wells
Outstanding Achievement in Dance – Robyn Orlin, *Daddy, I've Seen This Piece Six Times and I Still Don't Know Why They're Hurting Each Other,* The Pit

BARCLAYS THEATRE AWARD FOR OUTSTANDING ACHIEVEMENT IN DANCE 2002
Christopher Hampson, Double Concerto, English National Ballet

ARTS COUNCIL OF ENGLAND DANCE ARTISTS FELLOWSHIPS 2002
(to recognise outstanding contributions to the sector over a number of years)
Mark Baldwin, Matthew Hawkins, Bode Lawal, Liz Aggiss, Pit Fong Loh, Nigel Charnock

JERWOOD CHOREOGRAPHY AWARDS 2002
(to encourage experimentation in choreographic development)
£17,000 Award – Rosemary Butcher
£8,500 Awards – Maresa von Stockert; Ben Wright and Rachel Krische

FILM

'Do I have an original thought in my head?' moans blocked screenwriter Charlie Kaufman (Nicolas Cage) in *Adaptation*. 'Why can't there be a movie simply about flowers?' The question is comic, but serious. In the film, Kaufman has been hired to turn Susan Orlean's non-fiction bestseller *The Orchid Thief* into a Hollywood movie. Not coincidentally, his namesake, the non-fictional screenwriter Charlie Kaufman had been hired to do the very same thing. His solution? To write himself into the script, making his dilemma the dramatic focus of the story: 'I don't want to cram in sex, or guns, or car-chases, or characters learning profound life lessons, or growing, or coming to like each other, or overcoming obstacles to succeed in the end – the book isn't like that and life isn't like that,' affirms his semi-fictional alter-ego.

It is a daring post-modern conceit, but it pays off handsomely in *Adaptation*. Kaufman satirises the crass commercialism of the Hollywood system, its crushing recourse to the three-act structure as propagated by screenwriting gurus like Robert McKee (who agreed to be played by actor Brian Cox in the film); but he also parodies himself, the neurotic intellectual misfit, an artistic snob incapable of normal human relationships. The Hollywood insider jibes cut deeper because Kaufman is obviously ambivalent about his talent and his integrity; hence the inspired invention of his philistine twin Donald (also played by Cage), entirely devoid of Charlie's scruples, inhibitions and wit. But that is not all; interspersing Charlie's travails at the word processor with scenes from his numerous aborted drafts, the film incorporates a good deal of material from *The Orchid Thief*, including scientific and cultural observations, Orlean's growing fascination with an obsessive horticulturalist, and even a brief history of recorded time. It is this formal dexterity and richness, this 'adaptability', which really distinguishes *Adaptation*, the most highly evolved American movie of the year, even if Kaufman and director Spike Jonze (the team behind *Being John Malkovich*) seem at a loss as to how to end it.

MORE OF THE SAME

Elsewhere originality was in very short supply. With few exceptions, the notable films of the year derived from literature, comic books or old movies. In turbulent times – many 2002 and 2003 films went into production in the aftermath of 11 September 2001 and were released as the US launched its second war of the 21st century – studios, film-makers and audiences clung to the tried and tested. Like last year, the global box-office was dominated by *Harry Potter* and *The Lord of the Rings*, each second instalments (with third episodes scheduled for Christmas 2003). Warmly reviewed, these series marry innovative computer-generated imagery with classic, even old-fashioned, story-telling; they are fantastic moral fables aimed at family audiences. *Harry Potter and the Chamber of Secrets* generated $728 million world-wide; *The Lord of the Rings: The Two Towers* trumped that with $916 million. Between them, these two series take four of the top five positions in the chart of UK box-office hits, and helped boost British cinema

admissions to 175.9 million, an increase of 13 per cent on 2001 and of 79.5 per cent on 1992.

The US audience also grew in 2002, but admissions were down in the first half of 2003 as one blockbuster after another failed to meet expectations. Emboldened by the success of the first film on DVD and video (and doubtless by the example of *The Lord of the Rings*), Warner Bros gambled on shooting parts two and three of *The Matrix* back-to-back and scheduled them to open within six months of each other. While world-wide grosses of over $600 million for *Matrix Reloaded* are hardly disastrous, they are well short of the film-makers' billion-dollar projections, and poor word-of-mouth publicity may make *Matrix Revolutions* difficult to sell in November 2003. Ancillaries include *Animatrix*, a straight-to-video/DVD release comprising nine short animated films which form a loose prequel and side-project to the series; a computer game; and an IMAX giant-screen version of the film.

While Miramax announced plans to release Quentin Tarantino's long-awaited *Kill Bill* in two parts, probably a few months apart, in autumn 2003, the diminishing returns for sequels to *The Fast and the Furious*, *X-Men*, *Legally Blonde*, *Men in Black*, *Dumb and Dumber*, *Charlie's Angels*, *Lara Croft: Tomb Raider* and *The Terminator* suggested that the appetite for second and third helpings may be on the wane.

It has become the norm for these blockbusters to rake in the bulk of their revenue over the opening weekend (supported by a blanket release in up to 3,500 cinemas in the US and saturation advertising), and then to see box-office admissions drop by 50 per cent or more in the second week. The most notable victim of the trend was perhaps Ang Lee's disappointingly verbose and humourless *The Hulk*, with revenue down 70 per cent in week two after a colossal $62 million opening weekend. This release pattern mitigates the effect of bad reviews and negative word-of-mouth, but it hardly breeds confidence in the long-term health of the industry. Perhaps sensing that the writing is on the wall, Hollywood studios snapped up remake rights to energetic and imaginative Asian thrillers and horror movies, of which *The Ring* was the first to the screen. Many more are in the pipeline.

Immediate returns are such an integral part of the film business now that the odds are stacked against smaller films which might need time to find their audience, but with the blockbusters falling by the wayside, a few 'sleeper' hits have emerged. The most successful was the ethnic comedy *My Big Fat Greek Wedding*, shot for less than $5 million, which was still opening in new cinemas 40 weeks into release and has taken more than $300 million worldwide. Two British movies also showed that small can be beautiful; Gurinder Chadha's *Bend It Like Beckham* was an unpretentious crowd-pleaser about a British Asian girl who resists family pressure to give up her dream of playing football professionally. It has made $25 million in the USA to date, despite Beckham's very low public profile there, and $70 million worldwide.

Danny Boyle's *28 Days Later* looks set to do similar business. A horror movie heavily derivative of George

Romero's *Dawn of the Dead*, it imagines a handful of human survivors fighting off hordes of zombies on the streets of an eerily deserted London. It was filmed on digital video (DV) cameras and cast unknowns in the leading roles, but tapped into so many topical anxieties – anthrax, chemical weapons, BSE, SARS – that it restored Boyle's commercial clout and critical reputation after the clobbering which greeted *The Beach*. Intriguingly, 28 days into its US release, the studio promoted a new, bleaker ending, tacked on to the original with the caption 'But what if ...'. This may be the first time that an alternate ending has been appended to a film on its cinema release, a marketing coup obviously inspired by the bonus features commonly attached to DVD releases.

DIGITOPIA

A low-cost, high-returns proposition for software suppliers, the phenomenally successful DVD format has provided a welcome boost for studio profit margins. Launched in the UK as recently as 1998, the Digital Versatile Disc has already found a place in over a quarter of UK homes. More than 80 million DVD discs were sold in the UK in 2002 alone. In the USA in 2002, DVD releases earned more than double the revenues from cinema exhibition, and at $20 billion overtook VHS sales and rental to become the most lucrative sector of the movie business. It is projected that DVD will account for nearly three-quarters of the total US home video sales and rental market by the end of 2003.

These figures dwarf the take-up of CDs in the music business two decades ago, and on the face of it can only be a boon to Hollywood. There are concerns, however. The music business is suffering dramatically falling sales, down 10 per cent in 2002, because digitisation has opened the floodgates to piracy, especially over the internet. The film studios, most of them part of the same entertainment conglomerates, are afraid that this could be their fate. It costs less than one dollar to produce a DVD, so the potential for pirates to undercut the market is considerable; and despite a studio's best efforts, black-market discs of even the most closely guarded titles are invariably available within days, or even before, the US cinema release. At present, the market for recordable DVDs is very small, but the hardware is becoming cheaper, and when movies can be streamed down the internet as quickly and smoothly as songs, revenues will become vulnerable. Cassandras can point to Hong Kong, where the industry was decimated in the 1990s by the impact of pirate VCDs, an even cheaper version of DVD technology.

Nevertheless, digital film-making continues to liberate film-makers to produce some of the most risky, challenging, adventurous work around. In 2002 this brought us *Atanarjuat – the Fast Runner*, the first-ever feature from the Inuit. A strange, entrancing film, *Atanarjuat* boasted at least one sequence as exciting and memorable as any this year, the ten-minute pursuit of a naked man across the ice-floes, and reminded us of the movies' roots in oral storytelling and primitive myth. In *Waking Life* and *Tape*, Richard Linklater proved the formal and pragmatic versatility of the new technology; the former is a woozy, philosophical dreamscape of a movie, filmed first on digital with live actors on real locations, then painted over into a pulsing stream-of-unconsciousness by a team of animators using rotoscope software. *Tape*, on the other hand, is filmed theatre, a Pinteresque three-hander which was shot in a couple of days and produced under the auspices of InDigEnt (Independent Digital Entertainment), a remarkably successful outfit which also presented the Sundance 2002 prize-winners *Tadpole* and *Personal Velocity*. While these DV features do not share an aesthetic or artistic agenda, they do allow independent work to reach mainstream audiences by keeping costs to a minimum, and the flexibility inherent in DV can have a political effect. A case in point is Michael Winterbottom's Berlin Silver Bear winner *In This World*, a documentary-style feature inspired by the wave of anti-immigration feeling in Britain, and improvised on the old Silk Road. Beginning in a Peshawar refugee camp on the Pakistan-Afghanistan border, the film follows two young men on the long hard journey through Quetta, Tehran, Istanbul, Paris and Sangatte to London. It is an eloquent, emotionally devastating film which insists simply on the human ties which bind us, and on the physical and economic gulf which keeps us apart. It could never have been made with the expensive apparatus and logistical support that 35 mm film requires.

If *Tadpole* looked cheap and nasty, then *28 Days Later*, Winterbottom's *24-Hour Party People* (a very different, larky project about Factory Records) and Julio Medem's high definition *Sex y Lucia* revealed the eye-catching visual textures that the new medium can throw up. And Alexander Sokurov scored an unexpected London box-office success with *Russian Ark*, an extraordinary magical history tour of the Hermitage museum in St Petersburg, filmed in one flowing, unbroken take lasting more than 90 minutes.

But arguably the most audacious film of the year – shot on DV, almost entirely from two camera positions within a car – was *10*, in which Iranian master Abbas Kiarostami honed minimalism to a point of pure emotion. The title refers to a modern woman's ten car journeys around Tehran. Mania (Mania Akbari) is the mother of a young boy (the first of her passengers) but separated from his father, which is a source of outrage to the vociferously chauvinist child. In other episodes we see her give lifts to an old woman, to her sister and to a prostitute. *10* reflects on the position of women in Iranian society – it has not been shown in Iran itself, where the censors have been so heavy-handed that Kiarostami joked that they would have to rename it *7* – but for such a self-effacing film it is also a radical experimental work about age, intimacy, conversation and communication.

REEL TIME

DV cameras are small, light and unobtrusive; like all video cameras, they can shoot much longer than film cameras before being reloaded. Movies like *10* and *In This World* exploit these attributes to convey a powerful sense of realism, and both features have been mistaken for documentaries. While Hollywood embraces CGI and an ever more synthetic *mise-en-scène*, distributors have identified a new audience for non-fiction films. In part this may reflect a more politically engaged population post-11 September, but it also reflects to some extent the impoverished state of television documentary programming in an era of deregulated broadcasting. And then there was the impact of *Bowling for Columbine*, a critical and commercial hit. Written, directed and presented by Michael Moore, a political agitator who also wrote the bestselling book *Stupid White Men*, *Bowling for Columbine* became the first documentary to screen in competition at Cannes for decades, and went on to make $21 million at the US box office. Setting out to explore why the USA should suffer 11,000 homicides a year –

exemplified by the tragedy at Columbine High School on 20 April 1999 – Moore adopts a scattershot satirical form which is both comic and, at times, horrific. He raises pertinent, uncomfortable questions about gun culture, about the media (which he blames for creating a climate of racist paranoia), and about the poverty trap. Admittedly he is not above rhetorical grandstanding, and his political potshots can be facile (he equates US interventions in Panama and Kosovo, for instance) but at least Moore is holding the establishment and individuals to account, both for their actions and their inactions.

More documentaries than ever before have been released to cinemas this year. Among them were *Capturing the Friedmans, Spellbound, The Kid Stays in the Picture,* and *Winged Migration* in the USA; and in the UK, *Live Forever, Hoover Street Revival* and the French hit *Etre et Avoir (To Be and To Have)*. In a sorely below-par Cannes film festival 2003 ('the worst ever', according to some old enough to know), *Bright Leaves* by Ross McElwee and *The Fog of War* by Errol Morris were both outstanding.

AND THE BAND PLAYED ON

Although the orchestra tried to drown him out after he exceeded his allotted time, Michael Moore berated George W. Bush when he accepted his Oscar for best documentary in March 2003, dragging his fellow nominees on to the platform with him. There was speculation that this year's ceremony would be cancelled because of the Iraq war, but in the event it was show business as usual. A much stronger competition than last year failed to honour such impressive fare as Todd Haynes' superbly appointed Sirkian melodrama *Far From Heaven* (though Julianne Moore was nominated for the best actress award); Steven Soderbergh's heady Tarkovsky remake *Solaris*; Jack Nicholson, nominated but unsuccessfully for the acerbic Midwestern comedy *About Schmidt*; Paul Thomas Anderson's surrealist romantic comedy *Punch Drunk Love*; Peter Mullan's scalding true-life exposé *The Magdalene Sisters* (the Golden Lion winner at Venice); or such foreign language favourites as Almodovar's delicately modulated *Talk to Her*, Alfonso Cuaron's popular Mexican comedy *Y Tu Mama Tambien* (both were nominated in the best director category), and the Brazilian favela drama *City of God*. Even *Adaptation* lost out in everything but the best supporting actor category (Chris Cooper).

British Oscar hopes rested principally on *The Hours*, a florid but moving adaptation by *Billy Elliot* director Steven Daldry of Michael Cunningham's novel. Scripted by David Hare, it featured more great female performances in one movie than the rest of Hollywood could muster in a year's output. There was Nicole Kidman, with a prosthetic nose, as Virginia Woolf in the 1920s, with Miranda Richardson as her sister; Julianne Moore as a suicidal wife and mother in the 1950s, with Toni Colette as her neighbour; and Meryl Streep as a New York literati in the 1990s, with Claire Danes as her daughter. Although these women's relationships trace an emancipatory arc, the film suggests Woolf's insights into the human condition are as pertinent as ever; bookended by suicides, the film is about the transience of happiness, the dissatisfactions as well as the consolations of love, time shared and time lost. Kidman picked up the Oscar for best actress, and asked her co-stars to share it with her.

The biggest loser on Oscar night was Martin Scorsese's *The Gangs of New York*. A project Scorsese has nurtured since the 1970s, and spent two years filming and editing, *Gangs* recreates the lower depths of New York City life in the mid-19th century as recorded in Herbert Asbury's imaginative reportage. Irish immigrants war with rival ethnic gangs in a town where the law keeps its distance. Somewhere between a Western and a gangster movie, this opulently staged epic teems with life, at least until a wan Leonardo DiCaprio romances Cameron Diaz's underwritten pickpocket. Both are over-whelmed by Daniel Day-Lewis, in scene-chomping mode as the ferocious crime-lord Bill the Butcher. Despite a running time only 12 minutes under three hours, the film's relationships all feel malnourished, things getting especially sketchy about two-thirds of the way through; rumours were rife that scissor-happy Miramax producer Harvey Weinstein was to blame.

Weinstein's aggressive Oscar campaign on Scorsese's behalf likewise backfired, when Roman Polanski picked up the statuette (though not in person; he's still a fugitive from US justice on an outstanding charge of statuary rape) for *The Pianist*. Oscars for best actor, best director and best screenplay topped off a remarkable awards season for this true-life Second World War drama. Based on the life of pianist Wladyslaw Szpilman but owing much to the experiences of the film-maker, who lost his own parents to the Nazi genocide, it was also a winner at Cannes in 2002 (the Palme d'Or), the Baftas, and the French César awards. The most telling aspect of Polanski's account of the Holocaust is its simplicity and restraint. If the horrors he himself experienced in the Warsaw ghetto fuelled the clammy expressionism of his earlier work, this dramatic recreation is understated, clean and void of sentimentality.

What Polanski does is bear witness, meticulously tracking the increments to genocide, the noose tightening inexorably as Jewish rights of association and employment are curtailed, identification becomes mandatory and the ghetto is walled in. Each new outrage is dated and debated in the Szpilman household, but the behaviour of Wladyslaw (the plaintive Oscar-winner Adrien Brody) is typical; he keeps his head down and hopes for the best. The film is haunted by the spectre of Jewish resistance, or the lack of it, but there is no mystery to this; ruthless executions keep Jews and their sympathisers in passivity. Wladyslaw is passive by nature, an artist, an observer; for much of the film we watch him watching as the world falls to ruin. Polanski does not give us phoney heroics but a profound helplessness which besets even the survivor, left alone to mourn the dead.

By contrast, there was *Chicago*. A flashy, syncopated jazz-age musical based on the popular Broadway show by John Kanter and Fred Ebb, this lampoons tabloid cynicism, celebrity and corruption, but through such safe, outmoded 1920s caricatures as to be utterly innocuous. Rob Marshall, a choreographer making his first feature as director, stages the film in such as a way as to highlight its theatricality, but there is no sense of real lives going on off-stage, no interest in the way popular myths sustain and constrain societies – nothing to compare with Francis Coppola's maligned *Cotton Club*, for instance. Snappy, Bob Fosse-like choreography and showstopping tunes carry the day. *Chicago* achieved 13 Oscar nominations and won six, including best picture and best supporting actress (Catherine Zeta-Jones). This year, perhaps old fashioned razzmatazz, nostalgia and escapism was all anybody really wanted.

BRITISH ACADEMY OF FILM AND TELEVISION AWARDS 2003

Best Film: *The Pianist*
Outstanding British Film: *The Warrior*
Special Achievement for First Feature Film: Asif Kopadia,
   Director/Co-writer *(The Warrior)*
Achievement in Direction: *The Pianist* (Roman Polanski)
Screenplay (original): *Talk to Her* (Pedro Almodóvar)
Screenplay (adapted): *Adaptation* (Charlie Kaufman/
   Donald Kaufman)
Best Actress: Nicole Kidman *(The Hours)*
Best Actor: Daniel Day-Lewis *(Gangs of New York)*
Best Supporting Actress: Catherine Zeta-Jones *(Chicago)*
Best Supporting Actor: Christopher Walken *(Catch Me If
   You Can)*
Cinematography: *Road to Perdition* (Conrad L. Hall)
Costume Design: *The Lord of the Rings: The Two Towers*

OSCARS 2003
Best Actor: Adrien Brody *(The Pianist)*
Best Supporting Actor: Chris Cooper *(Adaptation)*
Best Actress: Nicole Kidman *(The Hours)*
Best Supporting Actress: Catherine Zeta-Jones *(Chicago)*
Animated Feature Film: *Spirited Away* (Hayao Miyazaki)
Art Direction: *Chicago* (John Myhre; Gordon Sim)
Cinematography: *Road to Perdition* (Conrad L. Hall)
Costume Design: *Chicago*
Directing: *The Pianist* (Roman Polanski)
Documentary Feature: *Bowling for Columbine*
Music (score): *Frida* (Elliot Goldenthal)
Music (song): *Lose Yourself* from *8 Mile*
Best Picture: *Chicago*
Foreign Language Film: *Nowhere in Africa*
Writing (original screenplay): *Talk to Her* (Pedro
   Almodóvar)
Writing (adapted screenplay): *The Pianist* (Ronald
   Harwood)

LITERATURE

The year 2003 was that of The Big Read, an initiative by the BBC modelled on its successful Great Britons project of 2002, in which celebrities argued the merits of national heroes before a nationwide vote elected Winston Churchill the winner. In a 90-minute programme on BBC2 in March 2003, well-known figures talked about their favourite books, in categories including romance, science fiction, humour and children's books. Viewers were given two weeks to nominate their favourites – which did not have to be one of the books discussed – and in April a list of the nation's top 100 books was published. Bookshops promoted these, and increased sales of 'backlist' books; Paulo Coelho's *The Alchemist* and Harper Lee's *To Kill a Mocking Bird* doubled their sales, with Daphne du Maurier's *Rebecca*, Arundhati Roy's *The God of Small Things*, Gabriel Garcia Marquez's *Love In the Time of Cholera*, Jack Kerouac's *On the Road*, Donna Tartt's *A Secret History*, Patrick Susskind's *Perfume* and Arthur Golden's *Memoirs of a Geisha* also conspicuous gainers. The merits of the books were debated off-screen as well as on, including in reading groups and at platform events at the British Library. Bookmaker William Hill made Tolkien's *The Lord of the Rings* the odds-on favourite when the list was announced; Tolkien came out top of book chain Waterstone's 100 Best Books of the Century promotion in 1997. The new list, though, showed how tastes had changed. Novelists who appeared on that earlier list but not in the Big Read included E. M. Forster, Irvine Welsh, Alice Walker, Toni Morrison, A. S. Byatt, Jostein Gaarder, Roddy Doyle, Tom Wolfe and Nicholas Evans. The popularity of D. H. Lawrence and Virginia Woolf had also waned. New favourites included J. K. Rowling and Philip Pullman, Meg Cabot (author of the *Princess Diaries*), Jacqueline Wilson, Terry Pratchett and Helen Fielding. In June the 'Big Read Battle of the Books' television series began on digital station BBC4, and starting in October Clive Anderson will host nine 90-minute BBC2 programmes, the first of which will reveal the top 21 books chosen by the 140,000 votes cast, and the last in December will unveil Britain's favourite book.

Orange, the communications company behind the Orange Prize also instigated a complementary vote – through libraries, shops, websites and mobiles – to find the nation's favourite 40 books by women. Jane Austen's *Pride and Prejudice* came top, and Alice Walker, Toni Morrison and Virginia Woolf all appeared on this list. The Orange Prize itself went to a surprise choice in 2003; *Property*, Valerie Martin's story of slave owners in the Deep South, succeeded over big names on the shortlist that included Carol Shields *(Unless)*, Zadie Smith *(The Autograph Man)* and Donna Tartt *(The Little Friend)*. The sales of Martin's novel increased tenfold after her win.

Granta Magazine undertook for the third decade the exercise of choosing the 20 best British novelists under the age of 40, an idea initiated in 1983 by the Book Marketing Council and repeated in 1993 by the then editor Bill Buford. A panel of five writers and critics chaired by the current editor Ian Jack selected the following authors for the Granta Best of Young British Novelists: Monica Ali, Nicola Barker, Rachel Cusk, Peter Ho Davies, Susan Elderkin, Philip Hensher, A. L.

Kennedy, Hari Kunzru, Toby Litt, David Mitchell, Andrew O'Hagan, David Peace, Dan Rhodes, Ben Rice, Rachel Seiffert, Zadie Smith, Adam Thirlwell, Alan Warner, Sarah Waters and Robert McLiam Wilson. Omissions that were commented upon included Giles Foden, Jon McGregor, Niall Griffiths, Maggie O'Farrell, Zoe Heller and Tobias Hill. The most surprising inclusion was Monica Ali, because at the time she had not been published, but when her novel *Brick Lane* came out shortly after the announcement of the Granta list, this story of a Bangladeshi woman making a new life in London achieved critical acclaim as well as high sales.

The judges of the Man Booker prize in 2002 grumbled about the books publishers submitted and claimed that they were being iconoclastic, but the shortlist contained four previous Booker runners-up as well as the unsuccessful favourite for the 2002 Orange Prize, Sarah Waters's *Fingersmith;* this time the book was the bookmakers' second favourite after William Trevor's *The Story of Lucy Gault.* The winner, though, was a surprise; Canadian Yann Martel's *Life of Pi* is a strange story of a boy adrift with a hyena, a monkey, a zebra and a tiger. Despite missing out on the Orange and Man Booker prizes, Sarah Waters not only made Granta's best young novelists list but also went on to be honoured in the British Book Awards, the trade's celebration of its own, as author of the year, and to be named the Booksellers Association/Nielsen Bookdata author of the year, a double achieved the previous year by Philip Pullman. The British Book Awards also saw *Life of Pi* go head to head against Ian McEwan's *Atonement* and the autobiography of Manchester United footballer Roy Keane as the book of the year. Although these awards are given on the basis of commercial rather than literary criteria, sales beyond expectations qualify, and Martel took the crown.

Michael Moore, author of the bestselling non-fiction work *Stupid White Men,* claimed at the British Book Awards ceremony that he had been the victim of censorship by HarperCollins, and that the company had delayed his book and asked him to tone down his attack on George Bush after 11 September 2001. Moore's book was eventually published by Penguin, and became a bestseller. HarperCollins denied any unwillingness to publish, and was later notable for signing up some of the more radical authors writing after the war in Iraq. These included a deal with Noreena Hertz to publish *IOU: The Story of the Debt,* an attack on the West's handling of debt in the developing world. The Iraqi war inevitably led to related publishing activity, starting with a book rushed out in September 2002, *War on Iraq: What Team Bush Doesn't Want You To Know,* by Scott Ritter, a former UN weapons inspector and leading opponent of war on Iraq. Two anthologies for children were published after the war, *Kids' Night In* and *Lines in the Sand,* and the proceeds are going to charities for children who suffered in war.

PHOENIX FEVER

Harry Potter and the Order of the Phoenix, J. K. Rowling's 766 page-long fifth book, was published at midnight on 21 June 2003. Although taster fragments were strategically released, the strict embargo on the book gave rise to drama, with theft from the printers, and copies mysteriously 'found in a field' that fell into the hands of a tabloid newspaper. Publication was remarkable in many ways: a record 8.5 million copies were shipped in the first print run; and there were queues at bookshops all over Britain, hundreds of which opened specially, with many children waiting over an hour in the middle of the night for their copies. Some booksellers, including online bookseller Amazon, made considerable losses because they offered substantial discounts despite a market that would undoubtedly have paid the recommended price of £16.99. The book broke sales records; 1.7m copies were sold on the first day, more than any recent title has sold in a year. Another million copies sold over the next week.

In the USA, publisher Scholastic reported sales of five million copies on the first day. In Germany, 450,000 copies of the English language edition were sold to fans who could not wait for the German translation in November. The Indigo Chapter chain in Canada sold more than 100,000 copies. Penguin India distributed 100,000 copies within a week. The two leading bookshop chains in South Africa sold 27,000 copies between them. Thousands were sold in Singapore, Hong Kong, Thailand and Taiwan. In Australia, there were sales of 170,000 copies on publication day, and the 100,000 copies shipped to New Zealand sold out.

The one scheduled author event filled the Albert Hall five days after publication, when J. K. Rowling read from the book and was interviewed by Stephen Fry, reader of the British audiotapes of the Harry Potter books, in front of an audience of 4,000 schoolchildren who had won 'Golden Snitch' tickets or whose schools had been drawn in a ballot. Until the Albert Hall event, the identity of the character who dies in the book was a closely guarded secret in the media, so as not to spoil the story for those who had not read it. Fry let it slip to the audience and to all the children watching globally on a live webcast. The book was well-received by reviewers, though there was some debate about the length. What some saw as rich detail for children now eager to submerge themselves in the world of Harry Potter, others saw as *longueurs* that failed to advance the plot. Nevertheless, the book was eagerly devoured by adults and children alike. It introduced a new character, the Defence Against the Dark Arts Teacher Dolores Umbridge, whose attitudes satirised government intervention in the education system. It also featured Harry's first kiss.

The 'Harry Potter effect' continued to bring financial advantages for children's authors. Louisa Young received an advance of nearly £1 million from Puffin Books for a trilogy called *Lionboy*, written with her daughter Isabel Adomakoh Young under the pseudonym of Zouzou Corder, in which the hero speaks the language of cats, while Philip Ardagh, author of the punning and gothic *Awful End* series struck a US deal for a six-figure sum. Garth Nix, whose fantasy novel *Sabriel* was a hit in autumn 2002, also secured a new six-figure deal.

Another conspicuous success in children's books was Graham Taylor's *Shadowmancer*, a tale of 18th-century sorcery that could not find a publisher. The author, a vicar from North Yorkshire, published it himself before getting an agent and a publication deal with Faber. *Shadowmancer* entered the bestseller lists, and earned Taylor a book deal for US rights of more than £300,000.

Harry Potter has not only increased the possibility of big advances for children's literature, it has also furthered the concept of a 'crossover' book read by both adults and children. One book moved this concept forward again:

Mark Haddon's whodunnit narrated by a boy with Asperger's Syndrome, *The Curious Incident of the Dog in the Night-Time*, was published by Cape (adults) and David Fickling Books (children's), different divisions of the same company. It was a bestseller, with more copies sold in the adult edition.

MEMORABLE MEMOIRS

In autumn 2002, former Conservative MP Edwina Currie published her diaries, and with them came the revelation that she had had an affair with former Prime Minister John Major while he was still a junior minister. Little, Brown (publishers in 1987, while the affair was going on, of the Prime Minister's wife Norma Major's biography of Joan Sutherland) had bought Currie's book for about £300,000 without knowing about the affair, and serial rights were sold to the *Times* for a sum which may have been higher had not the insistence on secrecy before publication restricted the number of bidders to one. For most of the previous year, only three people at the publishing house knew of the diaries; they were described in the Little, Brown schedule as 'Liverpool Novel', due out in autumn 2003. Even the company's sales reps knew nothing until they read the news in the Sunday papers. Although the newspapers gave the story blanket coverage, sales of the book itself were disappointing.

Another book to cause controversy was Ulrika Jonsson's autobiography *Honest,* which referred to her rape by an unnamed television presenter. The tabloids concluded that the culprit was John Leslie, and several other accusations against him emerged. It took 10 months to clear his name.

Bristol was the second British city to promote a particular book for World Book Day. In 2002, the inhabitants of Leeds were encouraged to read Patrick Susskind's *Perfume.* As part of its bid to become European City of Culture, Bristol pushed Robert Louis Stevenson's *Treasure Island,* with 8,000 copies donated by the publisher Penguin, because in the book it is in a Bristol pub that Blind Pew passes on the Black Spot. World Book Day was also celebrated with the first WBD Online Festival using the People's Network of computers in UK libraries. Authors appearing online included Nigella Lawson, Meera Syal, Andy McNab, Michael Rosen and John Sergeant. Terry Pratchett took part in a webcast from the spectacular new library in Peckham, South London.

DRILLERS AND THRILLERS

A controversial scheme arose to have prisoners involved in the process by which millions of copies of books are pulped each year by the book industry. Book Industry Communication, the body that orchestrates the trade's returns process, proposed that inmates at the maximum-security Altcourse prison in Liverpool might drill holes in the books before sending them on to be completely destroyed. Resistance to the idea put it on hold.

Novelist Jeffery Archer, who was given a four-year sentence for perjury, enjoyed publication while he was still inside. He produced *A Prison Diary,* as well as a new novel, *Sons of Fortune.*

John Grisham, whose paperbacks regularly sell one million copies and whose legal thrillers have been guaranteed bestsellers every year since the early 1990s, increased his hardback sales with his new novel *The King of Torts.* It sold more than 27,000 copies in its first week on sale. Another big success was popular novelist Martina Cole, who specialises in tough heroines, and rode long in the bestseller lists with *Dangerous Lady*.

A conspicuous commercial success in both the UK and the USA was Allison Pearson's *I Don't Know How She Does It,* which gave rise to the coinage 'Mum Lit'. The story of a successful city banker trying to balance family and children, it originated, like *Bridget Jones' Diary,* from a newspaper column.

The surprise hit of autumn 2002 was *What Not To Wear* by Trinny Woodall and Susannah Constantine. It tied-in to the television series of the same name, in which the authors give the sartorially challenged a dressing-down as they dress them up. The book outsold popular chefs Jamie Oliver and Nigella Lawson.

Trivia also became the rage as *Schott's Original Miscellany* by Ben Schott was the surprise Christmas 2002 bestseller, a collection of trivia in an elegantly packaged small format that came with a choice of only slightly dissimilar jackets in cream or white. It spawned imitations and parodies including *Shite's Unoriginal Miscellany, Fotheringham's Sporting Trivia, Sullivan's Music Trivia,* and *That Book* by Mitch Symons. Schott's own follow-up was *Schott's Food and Drink Miscellany.*

The diet book of the year was the fat-and-protein-based *Atkins Diet* and its spin-offs. This achieved sales of 2 million copies, despite the sudden death of author Robert Atkins – for reasons unrelated to his diet – and despite reservations being expressed about the long-term safety of the diet. The surprise flop of the year was Kylie Mynogue's autobiography, *La La La,* which spent only a week on the bestseller lists.

Claire Tomalin's biography of Pepys, *Samuel Pepys: The Unequalled Self* won the Whitbread prize and became a bestseller. When the book won the biography category of the award (one of five genres judged against each other), the media was tickled by the fact that Tomalin was in contention with her husband Michael Frayn, whose *Spies* had won the novel category.

Novelist Norman Lebrecht struck a blow for writers whose careers start late in life when he won the Whitbread first novel award at the age of 54 for *The Song of Names,* with its insights into the British Jewish community in the 20th century. However, he is a spring chicken compared to Mary Wesley, who died in 2003, and who published her first novel, *Jumping the Queue,* at the age of 70. It was not until her fifth, *Not That Sort of Girl,* that she became one of the nation's bestselling novelists. Before her death she gave her papers and long interviews to Patrick Marnham, biographer of Georges Simenon and Diego Rivera, who will write her life story. The literary world also mourned the novelist Carol Shields, who died of cancer in 2003 shortly after her book *Unless,* the story of a woman writer and translator whose daughter turns her back on society to beg on street corners, had been shortlisted for the Orange Prize.

Children's Laureate Anne Fine brought her two-year appointment to a close with a powerful attack in the pages of the *Guardian* on a children's book. Six weeks before its publication she lambasted Melvin Burgess's teenage novel *Doing It,* of which she said, 'All the publishers who have touched this novel should be deeply ashamed of themselves'. The publicity that ensued prompted the publishers to bring the book out as quickly as possible. Burgess described *Doing It,* an explicit and comic account of the sexual activity and feelings of a group of teenagers, as the 'knobby book for boys' he had long wanted to write. Fine objected to its crudeness and its sexism. Defenders of the book included literary journalist David Sexton and the distinguished children's author Nina Bawden. Michael Morpurgo, who took over from Fine as Children's Laureate, has a different agenda; he feels strongly that literature should be reinstated over government-directed 'literacy' in British schools.

LITERARY AWARDS

NOBEL PRIZE FOR LITERATURE 2002 – Imre Kertesz
BOOKER PRIZE 2002 – Yann Martel, *Life of Pi*
WHITBREAD PRIZE 2002
Novel: *Spies,* Michael Frayn
First novel: *The Song of Names,* Norman Lebrecht
Biography: *Samuel Pepys: The Unequalled Self,*
    Claire Tomalin
Children's book: *Saffy's Angel,* Hilary McKay
Poetry: *The Ice Age,* Paul Farley

CRIME WRITERS ASSOCIATION 2002
Gold Dagger (fiction): Jose Carlos Samoza, *The Athenian
    Murders*
Silver Dagger (fiction): James Crumley, *The Final Country*
Creasey Dagger (first novel): Louise Welsh, *The Cutting
    Room*

SMARTIES PRIZE 2002 (children's books)
Age 0-5: *Jazzy in the Jungle,* Lucy Cousins
Age 6-8: *That Pesky Rat,* Lauren Child
Age 9-11: *Mortal Engines,* Philip Reeve

T. S. ELIOT Poetry Prize 2002 – Alice Oswald, *Dart*

MUSIC

As part of the continuous improvement programme which has already seen the refurbishment of the concert hall, theatre and cinemas, the Corporation of London granted the Barbican Centre full funding for a £12.25 million refurbishment of its foyers, plus the creation of two new entrances fitting for a world-class venue, as part of a £31.23 million investment in the fabric of the building over the next six years.

In 2002 the Barbican inaugurated the new 'Mostly Mozart' summer festival, in conjunction with media sponsors Classic FM. The festival had a great success in its first year, reaching its box office target and, more significantly, attracting a new audience to the Barbican – 60 per cent were newcomers to the centre. The new year at the Barbican started with 'Philip on Film', a major retrospective of Philip Glass' film music, including the UK première of *Shorts*, new films (co-commissioned by the Barbican) by Atom Egoyan, Peter Greenaway, Shirin Neshat, Michal Rovner and Godfrey Reggio. Philip Glass with his ensemble performed the film scores live while the films were screened. 'Great Performers' celebrated American opera for a week in June 2003 with performances of André Previn's opera *A Streetcar Named Desire*, with Renée Fleming, and the British première of John Adams' controversial oratorio *El Niño* (a Barbican co-commission), based on the story of the Nativity. Finnish opera singer Karita Mattila made a welcome return in April to give the British première of *Quatre Instants* by compatriot Kaija Saariaho, also co-commissioned by the Barbican. To mark the 25th anniversary of the Voyager space mission, NASA and the Barbican approached the Kronos Quartet to commission a new work inspired by the sounds of space. In March 2003 Kronos and an 80-strong choir gave the British première of *Sun Rings* by Terry Riley with visuals by Willie Williams (whose previous projects include work with U2 and the Rolling Stones).

Other commendable performances at the Barbican included the San Francisco Symphony Orchestra and Michael Tilson Thomas in May, giving the British première of John Adams' *My Father Knew Charles Ives* (dedicated to Tilson Thomas), the first of three works Adams is to write over the next decade for what is now his hometown orchestra. Mariss Jansons, newly appointed to lead the Concertgebouw Orchestra from 2004, brought his American orchestra, the Pittsburgh Symphony, to the Barbican, performing Bartok's *Music for Strings, Percussion and Celesta* and Shostakovich's 10th Symphony with an almost shocking intensity. The St Petersburg Symphony Orchestra, under conductor Yuri Temirkhanov, marked the 50th anniversary of Prokofiev's death in March with an electrifying concert of Prokofiev's Piano Concerto No. 3 with pianist Nikolai Demidenko and Rachmaninov's forbidding *Symphonic Dances*. The playing was exceptional, superbly controlled and emotionally wide-ranging.

George Benjamin, one of the most prominent composers of his generation, curated a year-long series in 2002–3 with the London Symphony Orchestra at the Barbican Hall, underlining the LSO's commitment to presenting the finest music of the 21st century. The highly successful series included many of Benjamin's own works (some world premières) and music which has inspired and influenced him throughout his life and career, including works by Boulez, Beethoven, Debussy, Goehr, Ives, Knussen, Mahler, Messiaen, Ravel, Sibelius and Stravinsky. Pierre Boulez conducted the LSO in the opening concert of the season, the world première of *Palimpsest II* (winner of the Royal Philharmonic Society Award for large-scale composition), coupled with *Palimpsest I*, which Benjamin wrote for the LSO's world tour with Boulez in 2000. Other memorable performances in the series included Benjamin's *Antara* (an IRCAM commission to commemorate the 10th anniversary of the Pompidou Centre), the first of his solo piano compositions *Shadowlines*, Boulez's *Improvisations sur Mallarmé*, and Messiaen's *Oiseaux Exotiques*.

The London Sinfonietta continued their dynamic programming, bold thinking, and unparalleled commitment to uniting new music and new audiences in their 2002–3 season. As well as its world-class concert series on the South Bank as associate artists of the Royal Festival Hall, concerts around the world, groundbreaking educational work and exciting use of new technologies took the London Sinfonietta's music-making far and wide. In autumn 2002, the Sinfonietta released the first of its own-label CDs, with the aim of making concert performances of new or unrecorded repertoire available to a world-wide audience. 'Blue Touch Paper', also launched in autumn 2002, is a major new London Sinfonietta initiative giving young composers Mary Bellamy, Tansy Davies, Ben Foskett, Dai Fujikura, Bryn Harrison and Ian Vine unparalleled access to London Sinfonietta musicians, conductors, music technology and composer 'mentors', confirming the ensemble's commitment to young composers. In April a concert entitled 'Electronica' explored the relationship between instrumental virtuosity and live electronics. Pieces included Boulez's *Anthèmes 2*, which surrounded solo violinist Clio Gould with an array of sonorities, Jonathan Harvey's *Bird Concerto*, in which Sound Intermedia created customised joysticks to control the interaction between pre-recorded birdsong, piano solo (Joanna MacGregor) and ensemble, and Matthias Pintscher's *Tenebrae*, which mixed solo viola (Paul Silverthorne) against a bank of electronics and ensemble.

The London Philharmonic, under the direction of Kurt Masur, Sir Charles Mackerras, Valery Gergiev and Ingo Metzmacher, enjoyed another safe season of Shostakovich, Wagner, Beethoven, Prokofiev, Kodály, Tchaikovsky and Dvořák. The real highlight, though, was a spine-tingling performance of Janáček's *Taras Bulba*, played with iron control and virtuosity by the entire orchestra, superbly directed by chief conductor Kurt Masur.

Sonic Arts Network and the BBC curated 'Cut & Splice', a series of live performances and panel discussions at the ICA. Offering a broad slice through the history of radical electronic music, the series revealed a cross-section from the clunky sounds of the 1960s to the digital world of today. The eclectic programme included new digital work by Markus Popp's 'Oval' project, a UK première from Montreal sound artist Christian Calon, an extremely rare performance of 1970s spliced tape compositions by 76-year-old Bernard Parmegiani, and a new realisation of John Cage's pre-DJ phono-blitz *Cartridge Music* (1960) by Quartet Electronische. Run over five consecutive Thursday nights in April, 'Cut & Splice' surveyed the diverse range of cutting-edge electroacoustics over the last 40 years. All performances were broadcast on Radio 3's *Hear and Now,* with selected extracts broadcast on John Peel's Radio 1 programme.

OUTSIDE LONDON

The Birmingham Contemporary Music Group (BCMG) began its 2002–3 season with the première of *The torn fields,* a new work by Mark-Anthony Turnage, at the Berlin Festival and continued with concerts in Birmingham and London conducted by Simon Rattle. Other highlights included a tour of India with composer Judith Weir, an all-Turnage concert (as part of the BBC's Composer-in-focus weekend at the Barbican, London), a weekend of electronic music in Birmingham to celebrate the 20th anniversary of BEAST (Birmingham Electro Acoustic Sound Theatre) and the premières of Param Vir's *The Theatre of Magical Beings,* and Simon Holt's *Boots of Lead* for chamber orchestra and mezzo soprano. All three new works (Turnage, Vir and Holt) were commissioned through BCMG's 'Sound Investment' scheme. Param Vir's first commissioned work for BCMG, scored for 24 players, is divided into five movements, each associated with the image of a mythical creature. Holt's *Boots of Lead* is the culmination of a five-part cycle of works inspired by the poetry of Emily Dickinson entitled *The Ribbon of Time.*

BCMG also introduced a new element into its Birmingham programme. 'Creative Exchange' is an ongoing project with composer/conductor Peter Wiegold to assist BCMG players to hone their creative and improvisational skills. Stephen Newbould was appointed artistic director of BCMG in early 2003 following the departure of Simon Clugston. In his previous role as BCMG's development manager, Newbould masterminded the ensemble's enormously successful 'Sound Investment' commissioning scheme as well as broadening BCMG's general funding base.

The BBC Scottish Symphony Orchestra certainly had another successful year. Following in the footsteps of Osmo Vänskä, the new chief conductor, young conductor Ilan Volkov moved into a different sphere, producing from the SSO one of the greatest musical performances of Mahler's Sixth Symphony of recent decades. Also programmed in his inaugural concert with the orchestra was Ligeti's *San Francisco Polyphony.* Volkov gave himself as completely to this music as he did to the Mahler, and the result was a gripping and glittering orchestral showcase.

The BBC National Orchestra of Wales (BBC NOW) has shown new commitment to the performance of contemporary music, highlighted by Michael Berkeley's position as joint composer-in-association with BBC NOW and the Cardiff-based Royal Welsh College of Music and Drama. In its 2002–3 season the orchestra premièred its first commission from Berkeley, as well as works by David Matthews, Ceiri Torjussen and Philip Cashian. The orchestra has gone from strength to strength under its formidable conducting team, which includes Richard Hickox (principal conductor since September 2000), principal guest conductor Joseph Swensen, conductor laureate Tadaaki Otaka and associate guest conductor Grant Llewellyn.

The Royal Liverpool Philharmonic Orchestra celebrated a proud day for Liverpool in June 2003 when the city was designated the European Capital of Culture for 2008, inserting an unscheduled playing of Beethoven's *Ode to Joy* at the start of its concert at the Philharmonic Hall. A fanfare composed by Ian Stephens also featured, followed by a few words from Professor Peter Toyne, chairman of the Liverpool Culture Company, before the concert, celebrating the 50th birthday of the British pianist Peter Donohoe, got underway. The concert was the last in the orchestra's main season, and was conducted by the RLPO's American music director Gerard Schwarz.

FESTIVALS

With around 60 events over 10 days, including 26 world premières, 38 UK premières, 14 festival commissions/co-commissions (Evan Parker, Rolf Hind, Joe Cutler, Arlene Sierra, Jennifer Walshe, Ian Vine, Jonathan Powell, James Saunders, Bryn Harrison, Matthew Wright, Mathew Adkins, Jo Thomas, Gerald Barry) the Huddersfield Contemporary Music Festival was again a remarkable success. Notable highlights included visits of key composers such as Per Nørgård and Christian Wolff, both of whom participated in truly enlightening discussions as well as attending a number of performances of their work. The presence also of Aldo Clementi and Gerald Barry maintained the international perspective of the festival and provided some unforgettable musical experiences.

As ever, the festival balanced its international perspective with opportunities to showcase the best and most creative British and international artists. Many of these composers were from the younger generation, and their fresh outlook on composition was inspiring to all who heard it. In addition, some of the festival's key events involved new technology in various guises, including a visit by IRCAM to give the UK première of Martin Matalon's film score to Buñuel's *L'Age d'Or,* together with the *Percussions de Strasbourg.* Other significant premières were performed by the BBC Scottish Symphony Orchestra, conducted by Martyn Brabbins, including Stuart MacRae's granite-hewn *Ancrene Wisse* and Joe Duddell's accessible but verbose *Not Waving But Drowning.* But the energy and abundance of Rolf Hind's performance of Nørgård's *Concerto in Due Tempi* was unforgettable, and made a fitting climax to the festival's celebration of Nørgård's music. As well as a celebration of Wolff, there were outstanding performances of Morton Feldman's music. Ensemble Recherche's programme of early pieces revealed how Feldman came to terms with Webern's influence in the extreme brevity of sets of pieces for cello and piano. Nicolas Hodges' performance of Feldman's *For Bunita Marcus,* an 80-minute solo piano piece, was an amazing feat of concentration and endlessly varied quietness.

The Edinburgh International Festival 2003 under the direction of Brian McMaster attracted audiences from far and wide with another popular programme of opera, music, theatre and dance. The music programme offered variety and diversity, from the Korean vocal storytelling tradition, Pansori, to large-scale orchestral and choral concerts, and from French baroque music performed by Ian Bostridge and Emmanuelle Haïm to contemporary music influenced by the traditions of China, Korea, India and Japan. Beethoven's Complete String Quartets were performed in order of composition over three days by the Auer String Quartet, the Párkányi String Quartet, the

Petersen String Quartet and the Janáček String Quartet, followed by Elliott Carter's Complete String Quartets performed by the Pacifica String Quartet. The Los Angeles Philharmonic was in residence for a week, and Alfred Brendel, András Schiff, Grigory Sokolov and Thomas Quasthoff all gave recitals.

Throughout the festival there was also the chance to hear some of the most exciting of the new generation of conductors, including Ingo Metzmacher, Ilan Volkov, Jonathan Nott and Garry Walker, alongside established figures such as Bernard Haitink, Sir Charles Mackerras and Esa-Pekka Salonen. The Royal Bank of Scotland's '£5 Turn up and Try It' tickets built on the success of the 2002 Royal Bank '£5 Nights' series of classical music concerts, which attracted large numbers of younger customers who did not book ahead and who were willing to try new experiences. The festival also presented traditional and contemporary classical music from China, Korea, India and Japan, a fascinating insight into the variety and beauty of traditional music, as well as into the influence traditional music from Asia has had on contemporary classical music of today. In a series of late night concerts entitled 'Connecting Cultures', traditional music was juxtaposed with music by composers from the same country working in the western classical idiom. The series featured work by Guo Wenjing, Isang Yun, Nitin Sawhney and Toshio Hoskawa performed by the Paragon Ensemble and the Nieuw Ensemble. Li Xiangting, Tomiyama Seikin and Shiv Kumar Sharma were among the traditional musicians. Bank of Scotland's Fireworks Concert in Princes Street Gardens closed the 2003 festival on 30 August, with Nicholas Kraemer conducting the Scottish Chamber Orchestra and the Scottish Chamber Orchestra Chorus in a feast of Handel, including Music for the Royal Fireworks and excerpts from the Water Music and Zadok the Priest.

The annual season of Promenade Concerts in London, under the directorship of Nicholas Kenyon, remains one of the largest music festivals anywhere, and the 2003 series included 73 consecutive concerts at the Royal Albert Hall and eight Chamber Music Proms concerts at the nearby Victoria and Albert Museum from July to September. As well as being broadcast live on BBC Radio 3 every evening, each concert was audio-streamed onto the internet, and a selection of concerts was shown on BBC Television, on the digital television channel BBC4, and also video-streamed onto an interactive website. Each year the BBC Proms explore a different theme as a way of bringing together music which spans many centuries and different styles. This year's theme was the Greek myths, and the Proms were presented in collaboration with both the National Gallery and the British Museum.

Countless composers have drawn their inspiration from Greek myths, and Berlioz's epic opera The Trojans, under Sir Colin Davies, was the centrepiece of the Proms season, alongside Strauss's Elektra, Tippett's King Priam and Purcell's Dido and Aeneas. Other myth-inspired work included Stravinsky's Apollon musagète, Stravinsky's Perséphone, Nielsen's Helios, Barber's Medea's Meditation and Dance of Vengeance, Britten's Young Apollo, Musgrave's Helios, Stravinsky's Orpheus, Berlioz's La mort d'Orphée, Mendelssohn's Antigone and Stravinsky's Oedipus rex. The Proms marked the bicentenary of Hector Berlioz's birth with performances of his works for voice and orchestra, Les nuits d'été and La mort de Cléopâtre, and Symphonie fantastique was performed by Valery Gergiev and the excellent Rotterdam Philharmonic. There were also performances of his choral

work The Childhood of Christ and the opera Benvenuto Cellini, while his dazzling Roman Carnival Overture kick-started the festivities on the last night. The 50th anniversary of Prokofiev's death was also commemorated this season, with a performance of his oratorio Ivan the Terrible given on the first night, and his popular Peter and the Wolf in the new 'Nation's Favourite' Prom. Various of his concertos and symphonies were performed throughout the season and, more unusually, a semi-staged performance of his opera War and Peace, along with his cantata Alexander Nevsky.

The Proms reached a wider audience with the 'Late Junction' Prom, a wide-ranging musical marathon inspired by Radio 3's eclectic cult programme, and there were guest appearances throughout the season by Sir Simon Rattle and the Berliner Philharmoniker, Mariss Jansons and the Pittsburgh Symphony, Daniel Barenboim and his West-Eastern Divan Youth Orchestra, Bobby McFerrin and the Vienna Philharmonic Orchestra, Valery Gergiev and the Rotterdam Philharmonic Orchestra. New commissions and premières were showcased by Harrison Birtwhistle (The Shadow of Night), Oliver Knussen (Violin Concerto), Judith Weir (The Welcome Arrival of Rain), Philip Cashian (Tableaux), Sally Beamish (Trumpet Concerto), James MacMillan (Symphony No. 3 'Silence'), John Adams (On the Transmigration of Souls), Elliot Carter (Boston Concerto), Heiner Goebbels (Aus einem Tagebuch) and Erkki-Sven Tüür (Violin Concerto).

LOSSES

With the death of composer Luciano Berio on 27 May 2003, aged 77, music lost an intellectual mentor, one of the handful of composers who redrew the landscape of music and wrote some of the most moving and beautiful scores of the post-war period. With Stockhausen and Boulez, he was a pioneer in the exploration of new technical resources and in the extension of Schoenberg's serial principle. With the late Bruno Maderna, he co-directed the new electronic studio at the Italian state radio from 1953 to 1960, and in 1958 produced an acknowledged classic of electronic music in Omaggio A Joyce. Berio's best-known and probably most characteristic work, Sinfonia (1968–9), is a richly complex hour-long collage in which spoken and sung texts in many languages are combined with an orchestral score of huge sophistication. The second movement, O King, is a homage to Martin Luther King Jr., in which the phonemes of King's name provide the text. The central movement is a whirlwind of memories of western music, superimposed on the scherzo of Mahler's Second Symphony. Among the numerous recent premières, Sequenza XIV for solo cello (2001–2) stands out, as this was the last of his long series of pieces for individual instruments which began with Sequenza I, for flute, more than 40 years earlier.

Daphne Blake Oram, composer and inventor, died on 5 January 2003. Her death follows that of the other woman pioneer in the electronic medium, Delia Derbyshire, in July 2001. But unlike Derbyshire, who was able to work in electronic music studios, Oram came from the generation that had founded the studios despite resistance and indifference. Her independent outlook is illustrated in her idiosyncratic, almost mystical book An Individual Note Of Music, Sound and Electronics (1972).

AWARDS

The Royal Philharmonic Society Music Awards were presented in May 2003, honouring achievement and excellence during 2002. Winners included the Nash Ensemble in the chamber ensemble category, 'for its versatile programming, which included the classics, the exploration of neglected repertoire and a strong commitment to new music. The jury was particularly impressed not only by their consistently superb ensemble playing but also by the quality and musicality of the individual members.' The award for chamber-scale composition went to James Dillon for *The Book of Elements, volume 5*, 'a work which redefines the traditional gestures of piano writing and which is also the culmination of a major compositional project. The five volumes of *The Book of Elements* represent one of the most significant contributions to the piano repertoire of recent years. Cast in a single movement, the fifth and final volume is an endlessly fascinating, kaleidoscopic tour de force.' Also commended in this category were Per Nørgård's String Quartet No. 9 and Thomas Adès' Piano Quintet.

The concert series and festivals award went to 'SBC/RAM Signs, Games and Messages – the music of György Kurtág', 'an imaginative collaboration between the South Bank Centre and the Royal Academy of Music which has further developed the annual composition festivals of the RAM and brought them into the international arena. The festival provided a focus on the rich and intricate sound world of György Kurtág and triumphantly fulfilled the three RPS criteria of creativity, excellence and understanding.' The jury identified three other outstanding contenders: the Bromsgrove Concerts Mixing Music Series, Edinburgh International Festival/Royal Bank of Scotland £5 Nights at Usher Hall, and the Britten Sinfonia Norwich and Cambridge series.

The award for best conductor went to Marin Alsop, the new principal conductor of the Bournemouth Symphony Orchestra. During 2002 a series of highly acclaimed concerts with several of the country's leading orchestras consolidated her rapidly growing reputation. The jury commended her for 'her impressive discipline' and 'rich fund of humanity and sensibility that enables her to communicate fresh, stimulating ideas with compelling conviction'. The Society for the Promotion of New Music (SPNM)'s 'Sound Inventors' won the education award for its work in 'giving young composers from 8–18 the invaluable experience of working to high professional levels, guided by distinguished composers, and of hearing their own music performed in public and recorded by leading ensembles. The scope of the scheme – over 700 young people nationally, writing in a wide variety of styles – and the quality of the training, sets this project apart as an example of excellence, in helping to create the next generation of composers'. Other winners included the London Sinfonietta in the large ensemble category, because it 'has pursued its pioneering goals with consistency and success for 35 years in a year when many mainstream orchestras are retreating into the defensive bunker of core repertoire. The year 2002 was particularly rich in achievement and endeavour for the London Sinfonietta and included 36 world or UK premières including one in an underground station and over the internet. The ensemble's playing has long established it in the première league of contemporary music ensembles and the excellence of its education programme is second to none within the orchestral world.'

The jury unanimously gave the large-scale composition award to George Benjamin's *Palimpsests*. 'His new composite score is relatively compact, yet conjures a world of references and memories, strikingly overwritten with the imaginative vision of George Benjamin himself.' The jury were drawn to its 'distinctive instrumentation and the drama and progression of the music, which sounds inevitable yet never predictable – exactly the right notes (and in the right order!) – a genuine "palimpsest" in which familiar ingredients are wonderfully made new'. Paul Lewis won the award for best instrumentalist, both as a soloist and a fine chamber player. The jury was struck by 'his refreshing and deeply considered approach to established repertoire, as well as his exploration of less well-known works. His Schubert Sonata series, presented throughout the UK in 2002, exemplified his innate and most intelligent musicianship.' The best singer award went to Lisa Saffer for her performance of Lulu at English National Opera, which displayed 'consummate musicality, and a beauty of tone rarely heard in this role'. The young artist award went to a performer of 'extraordinary artistry and astounding virtuosity'; Simon Trpčeski, still only 24 years of age, made a huge impact throughout the UK during 2002, giving recital performances as well as releasing his EMI debut disc to critical acclaim. In his capacity as a member of the BBC Radio 3 New Generation Artists Scheme he performed concertos with the BBC Philharmonic and the BBC Scottish Symphony Orchestra as well as with the Bournemouth Symphony Orchestra. His two Wigmore Hall recitals were notable for their bold programming and for the excitement they generated amongst audiences and critics alike.

The audience development award went to Joanna MacGregor and 'recognised innovation in every aspect of the presentation of music to a new audience – from the choice of repertoire to the marketing and the long-term legacy of the chosen approach'. The jury was encouraged to see some excellent initiatives from the larger opera companies and orchestras, but this year the award went to MacGregor whose 'imaginative programming, partnerships, integrity and tireless energy is attracting new audiences across the world and opening up new horizons in music for many people'. The BBC Radio 3 Listeners award went to Angela Hewitt for her performance in Dominic Muldowney's Second Piano Concerto with the BBC Symphony Orchestra.

The Association of British Orchestras Award 2003 was presented at the conclusion of a stunning programme of Brahms given by the London Symphony Orchestra conducted by Bernard Haitink.

OPERA

The Royal Opera's new music director, Antonio Pappano, conducted the new production of *Ariadne auf Naxos* by Richard Strauss that opened the 2002–3 season. Giving evidence of his versatility and wide musical tastes, he also conducted new productions of Berg's *Wozzeck*, Puccini's *Madama Butterfly* and Leoncavallo's *Pagliacci*, as well as a revival of Verdi's *Falstaff* in which the title role was splendidly taken by Welsh baritone Bryn Terfel. *Pagliacci*, directed and designed with great lavishness by Franco Zeffirelli, and given on its own without another opera, starred Placido Domingo, in fine resonant voice, as Canio at some performances. At other performances a completely different cast featured Welsh tenor Dennis O'Neill as Canio, while Domingo conducted. A performance with the first cast was relayed not only to the Covent Garden Piazza, but also to Victoria Park in Tower Hamlets, London, Baltic Square at Gateshead and the Botanical Gardens in Belfast. The total audience was estimated at over 10,000.

The world première of Nicholas Maw's opera *Sophie's Choice* took place in December 2002. Commissioned by BBC Radio 3 and the Royal Opera House, the opera is based on William Styron's 1979 novel, from which Maw himself extracted an excellent libretto. Directed by Trevor Nunn, conducted by Simon Rattle, and with the Austrian soprano Angelika Kirchschlager making her Covent Garden debut in the title role, the production was greatly admired. However, for sheer enjoyment the revivals of Elijah Moshinsky's 1977 production of Wagner's *Lohengrin* and of John Copley's 1982 staging of Handel's *Semele*, both lovingly rehearsed by their original directors, were impossible to beat. *Semele* was conducted by Charles Mackerras, who had been awarded the Companion of Honour in the Queen's Birthday Honours. Mackerras also conducted a fine concert performance of Dvorak's *Rusalka* with American soprano Renée Fleming in the title role.

The financial crisis of English National Opera grew worse in autumn 2002. In December 2002 the company's board presented the Arts Council with a strategy for change in which the permanent company would be reduced from 500 to 400 people and the number of performances from 175 to 150 each season. In February 2003 Sean Doran, the Irish-born director of Australia's Perth Arts Festival, was appointed artistic director of ENO. Later in the month chorus members belonging to Equity voted for industrial action over the reduction of permanent chorus numbers and one performance of *The Capture of Troy* had to be cancelled. On 20 March a deal was struck with Equity and further strikes were averted. The following day the Arts Council announced a subsidy of £13.9 million for 2002–3 and £15 million for 2003–4.

Meanwhile, to mark the bicentenary of the birth of Hector Berlioz in 1803 there were splendid new productions of *The Trojans, Part I: The Capture of Troy* and *Part II: The Trojans at Carthage*, in both of which the chorus was magnificent. The British première of Poul Ruder's *The Handmaid's Tale*, adapted by Paul Bentley from Margaret Atwood's novel, was given in April 2003. The production, originally staged by the Royal Danish Opera in Copenhagen, where the opera was premièred in 2000, was directed by Phyllida Lloyd. The long title role

of Offred was beautifully sung by Canadian mezzo Stephanie Marshall, while the chorus singing was again superb.

Concert performances of Wagner's *The Rhinegold, The Valkyrie* and *Siegfried* were given by ENO at the Barbican. During June 2003 the Barbican also presented the British premières of two operas by American composers. *El Niño*, an updated version of the Nativity by John Adams, starred soprano Dawn Upshaw and bass-baritone Willard White, and was directed by Peter Sellars and conducted by the composer. *A Streetcar Named Desire* by André Previn, based on the play by Tennessee Williams, featured soprano Renée Fleming as Blanche and baritone Rodney Gilfry as Stanley, with Previn as conductor. Only two performances each of these works were given; *Streetcar* would certainly merit a longer run.

Scottish Opera concentrated mainly on getting on stage its production of Wagner's *Der Ring des Nibelungen*, directed by Tim Albery and conducted by music director Richard Armstrong, who has renewed his contract until 2005. *Siegfried* and *Götterdämmerung* were performed in Glasgow during the season, receiving the same praise that the earlier instalments of the gigantic work had done. The complete *Ring* cycle was staged for the first time at the 2003 Edinburgh International Festival. Other operas at the festival, Wagner's *Lohengrin*, Handel's *Amadigi* and *Poro*, Verdi's *Macbeth* and Rossini's *Zelmira*, were all given in concert.

Welsh National Opera opened the season with Johann Strauss' evergreen *Die Fledermaus*, in a new production by Calixto Bieito, whose staging of *A Masked Ball* at English National Opera caused so much outrage. His *Fledermaus*, though highly original, was far less controversial and caused a fair amount of amusement. Revivals of old favourites such as Joachim Herz's production of *Madam Butterfly*, dating from 1978, and Göran Järvefelt's staging of *La Bohème*, first seen in 1989, were greatly enjoyed, as was the double bill of *Cavalleria rusticana* and *Pagliacci*, with tenor Dennis O'Neill singing both Turiddu and Canio.

Die Fledermaus was also one of the three new productions at Glyndebourne Festival Opera in 2003. Conducted by Vladimir Jurowski and directed by Stephen Lawless, this was the first Johann Strauss operetta to be staged at Glyndebourne. Earlier in the season another new departure took place when a Wagner opera, *Tristan und Isolde*, opened the festival. John Christie, who built the original Glyndebourne Theatre in 1934 and whose favourite composer was Wagner, would have been very pleased. The production, directed by Nikolaus Lehnhoff, was not liked by everyone, but the London Philharmonic Orchestra under Jiří Bělohlávek sounded wonderful in the resonant new theatre. The second new production, Mozart's *Idomeneo*, directed by Peter Sellars, was less popular, mainly because of two dancers whose shadowing of two of the singers was most intrusive. But the playing, this time by the Orchestra of the Age of Enlightenment under Simon Rattle, was greatly admired. The opera was given complete, including the final dances.

Moran Caplan, who died in June 2003 aged 87, was general administrator of Glyndebourne from 1948 until his retirement in 1981, having joined the company as assistant manager to Rudolf Bing in 1945. Caplat, who served as a naval officer during the Second World War, ran Glyndebourne with ship-shape efficiency during his tenure. Sesto Bruscantini, the Italian bass-baritone who sang at Glyndebourne from 1951 to 1961, died in May 2003, aged 84. His performances of Mozart, Rossini and Donizetti were appreciated as much for their dramatic as their musical excellence. During the 1970s he appeared at Covent Garden, and also sang the title role of *Falstaff* with Scottish Opera.

SUMMER FESTIVALS

During the summer of 2003, 'country-house opera' continued to flourish. Garsington Opera celebrated its 15th birthday with a rarity by Richard Strauss, *Die schweigsame Frau*, which was given an enjoyable production directed and designed by David Fielding. *La finta giardiniera,* by the 18-year-old Mozart, was also popular in Paul Curran's deft comic staging. At Grange Park Opera, Chabrier's *Le Roi malgré lui,* an even greater rarity, was directed by Simon Callow. Although the opera was warmly welcomed, neither the performance nor the staging was much liked by the critics. Opera Holland Park also included a rarity in its programme, Cilea's *L'Arlesiana;* the opera may have been dismissed as 'preposterous verismo', but the performance and direction were praised.

At the Aldeburgh Festival, two staged concert performances of Britten's *Gloriana* were given at Snape Maltings, with Christine Brewer as Elizabeth I and Tom Randle as the Earl of Essex. There was also a showing of the 1939 film *The Private Lives of Elizabeth and Essex,* starring Bette Davis and Errol Flynn, with a gloriously lush musical score by the Austrian composer Erich Wolfgang Korngold.

The world première of Simon Holt's *Who put Bella in the Wych-elm?* shared a double bill with the British première of Salvatore Sciarrino's *L'infinito nero* at the Jubilee Hall. This double bill was later given in London at the newly refurbished Almeida Theatre. Almeida Opera also gave three world premières in conjunction with the Genesis Opera Project for the discovery of new operatic talent. Nine teams out of 210 applications were selected for development in the first project, and from these, three chamber operas were commissioned and performed: *Sirius on Earth,* by Canadian composer Paul Frehner and librettist Angela Murphy; *Thwaite* (given at The Place), by the Dublin-based composer Jurgen Simpson and librettist Simon Doyle; and *The Eternity Man,* by Australian composer Jonathan Mills and librettist Dorothy Porter.

The Buxton Festival presented *Maria Padilla,* one of Donizetti's unjustly neglected serious operas, in its first fully professional staging in the UK. The festival also included a new, updated production of Handel's *Semele* and *Gwyneth and the Green Knight* by Lynne Plowman with a libretto by Martin Riley. Described as a 'musical adventure for all the family', *Gwyneth and the Green Knight* was given by Music Theatre Wales, which earlier scored a great success with the chamber opera at the Linbury Studio Theatre at the Royal Opera House. The compliments showered by the critics on the hitherto unknown Welsh composer were unprecedented in their unanimity.

The 2003 Promenade Concerts at the Royal Albert Hall included several operas. The Berlioz bicentenary was celebrated with *Benvenuto Cellini,* conducted by Roger Norrington, and the two parts of *Les Troyens,* given as two concerts in the afternoon and evening of one day,

with Canadian tenor Ben Heppner as Aeneas and Colin Davis conducting. There were also performances of Michael Tippett's *King Priam* and Richard Strauss' *Elektra* as well as the Glyndebourne production of *Die Fledermaus* and, to commemorate the 50th anniversary of the death of Prokofiev, ENO's magnificent production (semi-staged) of *War and Peace,* conducted by Paul Daniel.

LOSSES

Malcolm Williamson, the Australian-born composer who became Master of the Queen's Music in 1975, died in March 2003, aged 71. He wrote 11 operas, including *Our Man in Havana* (1963), based on the novel by Graham Greene, *English Eccentrics* (1964), based on the book by Edith Sitwell, and *The Violins of St Jacques* (1966), based on the novel by Patrick Leigh Fermor, as well as several operas for children. *Our Man in Havana* and *The Violins of St Jacques* were performed with great success at Sadler's Wells theatre.

Shirley Chapman, the English mezzo who died in November 2002, sang with Sadler's Wells (which later became ENO) from 1963 until 1978. Among her many roles for the company were Josephine in *The Violins of St Jacques,* the Countess of Essex in Britten's *Gloriana* and Rosalind in Richard Rodney Bennett's *The Mines of Sulphur.*

In December 2002 the English director Anthony Besch died, aged 78. During his career he worked at Glyndebourne, the Wexford Festival and Covent Garden (where his production of *La clemenza di Tito* by Mozart in 1974 was notably successful) and with Welsh National, Scottish and English National Operas and the New Opera Company. He staged many premières, including Harrison Birtwistle's *Punch and Judy* at Aldeburgh in 1968 and Iain Hamilton's *The Catiline Conspiracy* for Scottish Opera in 1974. He also directed the first performances in Britain of Dallapiccola's *Il prigioniero,* Martinů's *Julietta,* Szymanowski's *King Roger,* Shostakovich's *The Nose* and Ginastera's *Bomarzo.* He was especially good at dealing with students and putting them at ease on stage.

John Shaw, the Australian baritone who died in February 2003 aged 78, was a member of the Royal Opera for 16 years. He made his debut at Covent Garden in 1958 as Rigoletto and sang roles in many other Verdi operas, including Amonasro in *Aida,* the title role of *Simon Boccanegra,* Ford in *Falstaff* and Rodrigo in *Don Carlos.* He was also a notably unpleasant Scarpia in *Tosca.*

Dennis Wicks, the English bass who died in June 2003 aged 77, began his long career in 1950 in the chorus at Glyndebourne, where he also sang small roles. In 1962 he was engaged by the Royal Opera, where his roles became larger and included Dansker in Britten's *Billy Budd,* Graf Waldner in Richard Strauss' *Arabella* and Rocco in Beethoven's *Fidelio.* He transferred to ENO in 1971 and took on major roles, such as Baron Ochs in *Der Rosenkavalier,* Sarastro in *The Magic Flute,* the Grand Inquisitor in *Don Carlos,* Daland in *The Flying Dutchman,* Varlaam in *Boris Godunov* and many others. He sang in the British premières of Ginastera's *Bomarzo* and Ligeti's *Le grand macabre* and in the world premières of Iain Hamilton's *The Royal Hunt of the Sun* and David Blake's *Toussaint.* He retired in 1990.

The Swiss tenor Hugues Cuenod, a frequent visitor to Britain, celebrated his 101st birthday on 26 June 2003. At Glyndebourne between 1954 and 1975 he sang more than a dozen roles, beginning with Sellem the Auctioneer, which he had created at the world première

of Stravinsky's *The Rake's Progress* at Venice in 1951.
Other roles at Glyndebourne included Dr Caius in
Falstaff, Don Basilio in *Le nozze di Figaro,* the Dancing
Master in *Ariadne auf Naxos,* Monsieur Taupe the
Prompter in *Capriccio,* Monsieur Triquet in *Eugene Onegin*
and two superbly comic female characters in operas by
Cavalli, Erice in *L'Ormindo* and Linfea in *La Callisto.* He
also appeared at Covent Garden, singing the Astrologer
in *The Golden Cockerel* and Vasek in Smetana's *The
Bartered Bride.*

PRODUCTIONS

In the summaries of company activities shown below, the
dates in brackets indicate the year that the current
productions entered the company's repertory.

ROYAL OPERA
Founded 1946
Royal Opera House, Covent Garden, London WC2E 9DD
Productions from the repertory: *Rigoletto* (2001),
Turandot (1984), *Die Meistersinger von Nurnberg* (1993),
La traviata (1994), *La Cenerentola* (2000), *Falstaff* (1999),
The Cunning Little Vixen (1990), *Lohengrin* (1977), *Semele*
(1982).

NEW PRODUCTIONS:
Ariadne auf Naxos (R. Strauss), 6 September 2002.
Conductor, Antonio Pappano; director, Christof Loy;
designer, Herbert Murauer. Petra Lang (Ariadne), Marlis
Petersen (Zerbinetta), Sophie Koch (The Composer),
Robert Brubaker (Bacchus), Nathan Gunn (Harlequin)
La clemenza di Tito (Mozart), 7 September 2002.
Conductor, Colin Davis; director, Stephen Lawless; set
designer, Benoit Dugardyn; costume designer, Sue
Willmington. Barbara Frittoli (Vitellia), Vesselina
Kasarova (Sesto), Bruce Ford (Tito), Katerina Karnéus
(Annio), Anna Netrebko (Servilia), Brindley Sherratt
(Publio)
I masnadieri (Verdi), 30 September 2002. Conductor,
Edward Downes; director Elijah Moshinsky; designer,
Paul Brown. Paula Delligatti (Amalia), Franco Farina
(Carlo), Dmitri Hvorostovsky (Francesco), René Pape
(Massimiliano)
Wozzeck (Berg), 15 October 2002. Conductor,
Antonio Pappano; director, Keith Warner; set designer,
Stefanos Lazaridis; costume designer, Marie-Jeanne
Lecca. Matthias Goerne (Wozzeck), Katarina Dalayman
(Marie), Graham Clark (Captain), Eric Halfvarson
(Doctor), Kim Begley (Drum Major)
Sophie's Choice (Nicholas Maw). World première, 7
December 2002. Conductor, Simon Rattle; director,
Trevor Nunn; designer, Rob Howell. Angelika
Kirchschlager (Sophie), Dale Duesing (Narrator), Rodney
Gilfry (Nathan), Gordon Gietz (Stingo), Jorma Silvasti
(Rudolph Franz Hoss), Stephanie Friede (Wanda)
Die Zauberflöte (Mozart), 25 January 2003. Conductor,
Colin Davis; director, David McVicar; designer, John
Macfarlane. Will Hartmann (Tamino), Dorothea
Roschmann (Pamina), Diana Damrau (Queen of Night),
Simon Keenlyside (Papageno), Franz-Josef Selig
(Sarastro), Adrian Thompson (Monostatos), Thomas Allen
(Speaker)
Madama Butterfly (Puccini), 18 March 2003.
Conductor, Antonio Pappano; directors, Patrice
Caurier/Moshe Leiser; set designer, Christian Fenouillat;
costume designer, Agostino Cavalca. Cristina Gallardo-
Domas (Butterfly), Marco Berti (Pinkerton), Lucio Gallo

(Sharpless), Enkelejda Shkosa (Suzuki), Peter Hoare
(Goro)
Elektra (R. Strauss), 31 March 2003. Conductor,
Semyon Bychkov; director and set designer, Charles
Edwards; costume designer, Brigitte Reiffenstuel. Lisa
Gasteen (Elektra), Anne Schwanewilms (Chrysothemis),
Felicity Palmer (Klytemnestra), John Tomlinson (Orest),
Siegfried Jerusalem (Aegisthus)
Luisa Miller (Verdi), 22 April 2003. Conductor,
Maurizio Benini; director, Olivier Tambosi; designer,
Roland Aeschlimann. Barbara Frittoli (Luisa), Marcelo
Alvarez (Rodolfo), Carlo Guelfi (Miller), Philip Ens
(Wurm), Ferruccio Furlanetto (Count Walter)
Hamlet (Thomas), 12 May 2003. Conductor, Louis
Langrée; directors, Patrice Caurier/Moshe Leiser; set
designer, Christian Fenouillat; costume designer,
Agostino Cavalca. Simon Keenlyside (Hamlet), Robert
Lloyd (Claudius), Yvonne Naef (Gertrude), Natalie Dessay
(Ophelia), Markus Hollow (Ghost of Hamlet's Father)
Pagliacci (Leoncavallo), 7 July 2003. Conductor,
Antonio Pappano; director and set designer, Franco
Zeffirelli; costume designer, Raimonda Gaetani. Placido
Domingo (Canio), Angela Gheorghiu (Nedda), Lado
Ataneli (Tonio), Dmitri Hvorostovsky (Silvio), Daniil
Shtoda (Beppe)
Rusalka (Dvorak), 14 July 2003, concert performance.
Conductor, Charles Mackerras. Renée Fleming (Rusalka),
Sergei Larin (Prince), Larissa Diadkova (Jezibaba), Eva
Urbanova (Foreign Princess)

ENGLISH NATIONAL OPERA
Founded 1931
London Coliseum, St Martin's Lane, London WC2N 4BS
Productions from the repertory: *The Rhinegold* (concert
performance at the Barbican, 2001), *The Barber of Seville*
(1987), *The Valkyrie* (concert performance at the
Barbican, 2002), *Xerxes* (1985), *Khovanshchina* (1994),
Rigoletto (1982), *Der Rosenkavalier* (1994), *Alcina* (1999),
Tristan and Isolde (1996).

NEW PRODUCTIONS:
Tosca (Puccini), 21 November 2002. Conductor, Mark
Shanahan; director, David McVicar; set designer, Michael
Vale; costume designer, Brigitte Reiffenstuel. Cheryl
Barker (Tosca), John Hudson (Cavaradossi), Peter
Coleman-Wright (Scarpia), Jonathan Veira (Sacristan),
Nicholas Garrett (Angelotti)
Siegfried (Wagner), 10 December 2002. Concert
performance at the Barbican. Conductor, Paul Daniel.
Stephen O'Mara (Siegfried), Kathleen Broderick
(Brünnhilde), Robert Hayward (The Wanderer), John
Graham-Hall (Mime), Alison Roddy (Woodbird), Andrew
Shore (Alberich), Gerard O'Connor (Fafner)
The Trojans, Part I: The Capture of Troy (Berlioz), 27
January 2003. Conductor, Paul Daniel; director, Richard
Jones; designer, Stewart Laing. Susan Bickley (Cassandra),
John Daszak (Aeneas), Robert Poulton (Choroebus),
Victoria Simmonds (Ascanius)
The Handmaid's Tale (Poul Ruders), 3 April 2003,
British première. Conductor, Elgar Howarth; director,
Phyllida Lloyd; designer, Peter McKintosh. Stephanie
Marshall (Offred), Heather Shipp (Offred's double),
Catherine Wyn-Rogers (Serena Joy), Helen Field (Aunt
Lydia), Andrew Rees (Luke), Alison Roddy (Moira),
Richard Coxon (Nick)
The Trojans, Part II: The Trojans in Carthage (Berlioz),
8 May 2003. Conductor, Paul Daniel; director Richard
Jones; designer, John Macfarlane. Susan Parry (Dido),

John Daszak (Aeneas), Anne Marie Gibbons (Anna), Victoria Simmonds (Ascanius), Clive Bayley (Narbal), Christopher Saunders (Hylas), Iain Paterson (Pantheus), Colin Lee (Iopas)

OPERA NORTH
Founded 1978
Grand Theatre, 40 New Briggate, Leeds LS1 6NU
Productions from the repertory: *Jenůfa* (1995), *The Secret Marriage* (1993), *Julietta* (1997), *Troilus and Cressida* (1995).

NEW PRODUCTIONS:
Tosca (Puccini), 13 September 2002. Conductor, Steven Sloane; director, Christopher Alden; set designer, Charles Edwards; costume designer, Jon Morrell. Nina Pavlovski (Tosca), Rafael Rojas (Cavaradossi), Robert McFarland (Scarpia), Clive Bayley (Angelotti)
Der Rosenkavalier (R. Strauss), 12 October 2002. Conductor, Dietfried Bernet; director and designer, David McVicar. Janis Kelly (Marschallin), Deanne Meek (Octavian), Conal Coad (Baron Ochs), Marie Arnet (Sophie), Christopher Purves (Faninal), Philip Sheffield (Valzacchi), Louise Mott (Annina), Richard Coxon (Italian Singer)
Idomeneo (Mozart), 24 January 2003. Conductor, David Parry; director, Tim Albery; designer, Dany Lyne. Paul Nilon (Idomeneo), Paula Hoffman (Idamante), Natasha Marsh (Ilya), Janis Kelly (Elettra), Ryland Davies (Arbace)
The Magic Flute (Mozart), 17 April 2003. Conductor, William Lacey; director Tim Supple; designer, Jean Kalman. Philippe Do (Tamino), Thora Einarsdottir (Pamina), Helen Williams (Queen of Night), Matthew Sharp (Papageno), Mark Coles (Sarastro), Claire Wild (Papagena), Keel Watson (Speaker)
La Damnation de Faust (Berlioz), concert performance, 6 May 2003. Conductor Frederic Chaslin. Stephen O'Mara (Faust), Alastair Miles (Méphistophélès), Lilli Paasikivi (Marguerite)
Performances were given at the Grand Theatre, Leeds and on tour at Nottingham, Hull, Salford Quays, Newcastle-upon-Tyne and Sheffield.

SCOTTISH OPERA
Founded 1962
39 Elmbank Crescent, Glasgow G2 4PT
Productions from the repertory: *Siegfried* (2002), *Die Fledermaus* (1996), *Rigoletto* (1997), *Das Rheingold* (2000), *Die Walküre* (2001)

NEW PRODUCTIONS:
Orfeo ed Euridice (Gluck), 27 November 2002. Conductor, Raymond Leppard; director, Lucinda Childs; designer, Claire Sternberg. Aleka Ponjavic (Orfeo), Rachel Hynes (Euridice), Gillian Keith (Amor)
Götterdämmerung (Wagner), 5 April 2003. Conductor, Richard Armstrong; director, Tim Albery; set designer, Hildegard Bechtler; costume designer, Ana Jebens. Elizabeth Byrne (Brünnhilde), Graham Sanders (Siegfried), Peter Sidhom (Alberich), Mats Almgren (Hagen), Peter Savidge (Gunther), Elaine McKrill (Gutrune), Jane Irwin (Waltraute)
The Magic Flute (Mozart), 16 May 2003. Conductor, Vincent de Kort; director, Jonathan Moore; designer, Rae Smith. Iain Paton (Tamino), Marie Arnet (Pamina), Roland Wood (Papageno), Jennifer Rhys-Davies (Queen of Night), Pauls Putnins (Sarastro), Roderick Williams (Speaker), Gillian Keith (Papagena)

Performances were given at the Theatre Royal, Glasgow and on tour in Edinburgh, Inverness, Aberdeen and Stoke-on-Trent.

WELSH NATIONAL OPERA
Founded 1946
John Street, Cardiff CF1 4SP
Productions from the repertory: *Tosca* (1992), *Madam Butterfly* (1978), *Cavalleria rusticana* and *Pagliacci* (1996), *Jenůfa* (1998), *La Bohème* (1984), *Don Giovanni* (1996).

NEW PRODUCTIONS:
Die Fledermaus (J. Strauss), 14 September 2002. Conductor, Claude Schnitzler; director Calixto Bieito; set designer, Alfons Flores; costume designer, Merce Paloma. Geraldine McGreevy (Rosalinde), Paul Nilon (Eisenstein), Natalie Christie (Adele), Wynne Evans (Alfred), Richard Whitehouse (Falke), Sara Fulgoni (Orlofsky), Donald Maxwell (Frank)
The Elixir of Love (Donizetti), 19 February 2003. Conductor, Julian Smith; director, Daniel Slater; designer, Robert Innes Hopkins. Natalie Christie (Adina), Gwyn Hughes Jones (Nemorino), David Kempster (Belcore), Neal Davies (Dulcamara)
Jephtha (Handel), 17 May 2003. Conductor, Paul McCreesh; director, Katie Mitchell; designer, Vicki Mortimer. Mark Padmore (Jephtha), Christopher Purves (Zebul), Susan Bickley (Storge), Sarah Tynan (Iphis), Daniel Taylor (Hamor), Charlotte Ellett (Angel)

Performances were given at the New Theatre, Cardiff and on tour in Bristol, Liverpool, Birmingham, Oxford, Belfast, Southampton, Swansea, Milton Keynes, Llandudno and Plymouth.

GLYNDEBOURNE FESTIVAL OPERA
Founded 1934
Glyndebourne, Lewes, East Sussex BN8 5UU
The Festival ran from 19 May to 31 August 2003. *La Bohème* (2000), *Le nozze di Figaro* (2000) and *Theodora* (1996) were revived.

NEW PRODUCTIONS:
Tristan und Isolde (Wagner), 19 May 2003. Conductor, Jiří Bělohlávek; director, Nikolaus Lehnhoff; set designer, Roland Aeschlimann; costume designer, Andrea Schmidt-Futterer. Robert Gambill (Tristan), Nina Stemme (Isolde), Yvonne Wiedstruck (Brangäne), Bo Skovhus (Kurwenal), René Pape (King Marke), Richard Decker (Melot)
Idomeneo (Mozart), 10 June 2003. Conductor, Simon Rattle; director, Peter Sellars; set designer, Anish Kapoor; costume designer, Mark Bouman. Philip Langridge (Idomeneo), Magdalena Kožená (Idamante), Christane Oelze (Ilia), Anne Schwanewilms (Elettra), Peter Hoare (Arbace)
Die Fledermaus (Johann Strauss), 27 July 2003. Conductor, Vladimir Jurowski; director, Stephen Lawless; set designer, Benoit Dugardyn; costume designer, Ingeborg Bernerth. Pamela Armstrong (Rosalinde), Thomas Allen (Eisenstein), Lyubov Petrova (Adele), Pär Lindskog (Alfred), Malena Ernman (Prince Orlovsky), Håkon Hagegård (Dr Falke), Artur Korn (Frank), Udo Samel (Frosch)

GLYNDEBOURNE TOURING OPERA
Idomeneo (2003), *La traviata* (1987) and *Theodora* (1996) were performed from 7 October to 13 December 2003 at Glyndebourne, Woking, Milton Keynes, Norwich, Stoke-on-Trent, Plymouth, Oxford and Edinburgh.

GARSINGTON OPERA
Founded 1989
Garsington Manor, Garsington, Oxford OX44 9DH
The season ran from 14 June to 12 July 2003. New productions were:

Die schweigsame Frau (Richard Strauss), 14 June 2003. Conductor, Elgar Howarth; director, David Fielding; designers, David Fielding, Andrew Walsh. Stephen Richardson (Sir Morosus), Rebecca de Pont Davis (Housekeeper), Russell Smythe (The Barber), Jeffrey Lloyd-Roberts (Henry), Christine Buffle (Aminta)

Il barbiere di Siviglia (Rossini), 18 June 2003. Conductor, David Parry; director, Marco Gandini; set designer, Edoardo Sanchi; costume designer, Maurizio Millenotti. Christine Rice (Rosina), Colin Lee (Count Almaviva), Luca Salsi (Figaro), Robert Poulton (Dr Bartolo), Brindley Sherratt (Don Basilio), Lynda Russell (Berta)

La finta giardiniera (Mozart), 26 June 2003. Conductor, Steuart Bedford; director, Paul Curran; designer, Kevin Knight. Lisa Saffer (Sandrina), Majella Cullagh (Arminda), Michelle Walton (Ramiro), Carla Huhtanen (Serpetta), Adrian Thompson (The Mayor), Iain Paton (Count Belfiore), Damian Thantrey (Nardo).

ENGLISH TOURING OPERA
Founded 1980 as Opera 80
The Cunning Little Vixen (Janácek) and *Don Giovanni* (Mozart) were toured to Richmond, Buxton, Wolverhampton and Bath between 23 October and 30 November 2002.

Ariadne on Naxos (Richard Strauss) and *Die Fledermaus* (Johann Strauss) were toured to Truro, Jersey, Exeter, Sheffield, York, Brighton, Coventry, Darlington and Perth between 1 April and 31 May 2003.

PARLIAMENT

In 2002–3, Prime Minister Tony Blair faced his most difficult year since coming to power, with opposition to the war in Iraq and further backbench rebellions over university top-up fees and foundation hospitals that saw his majority of 164 fall to just 35 at one stage. Any relief offered by the rising of Parliament for the summer recess was quickly dispelled by the row over the suicide of one of the Government's leading weapons experts, which led to calls for the immediate recall of Parliament.

It was the Government's close relationship with the USA and their stance on the war on international terrorism in Iraq that caused Mr Blair the greatest headache. On 24 September 2002, Parliament was recalled from the summer recess to hear a statement from Mr Blair on Iraq and weapons of mass destruction, when he published a 50-page dossier detailing the history of 'Iraq's weapons of mass destruction programme, its breach of UN resolutions and current attempts to rebuild that illegal programme'. He concluded, '[in previous conflicts] we proceeded with care, with full debate in this House, and when we took military action, we did so as a last resort. We shall act in the same way now, but I hope we can do so secure in the knowledge that should Saddam continue to defy the will of the international community, this House, as it has in our history so many times before, will not shrink from doing what is necessary and what is right'. The Conservative leader, Iain Duncan Smith, pledged general support for the Government, agreeing that 'war should be a last resort when all other efforts have failed, but Britain should never shy away from its responsibilities in time of international crisis'. Liberal Democrat leader Charles Kennedy was more cautious, asking if the Prime Minister 'truly believes that, on the evidence published today, a sufficient case has now been made that both clarifies Iraq's present capacity as well as its intent', and calling for the full involvement of the United Nations. The statement was followed by a debate on the issue upon a procedural motion on the adjournment of the House, which would not normally be voted on. The Father of the House, Tam Dalyell (Labour), objected to this procedure and the consequent decision by the Speaker not to accept his amendment, which would have allowed a substantive vote on the issue for those opposed to any war.

The Foreign Secretary, Jack Straw, said that 'if there is military action, any participation in it by Her Majesty's Government would be strictly in accordance with our obligations under international law and its purpose would be the disarmament of the Iraqi regime's weapons of mass destruction and an end to its deliberate and persistent flouting of the will of the United Nations ... the choice is Saddam's'. The Shadow Foreign Secretary, Michael Ancram, said, 'We support the Prime Minster's stance today. We share his analysis of the threat ... we accept that military action may well in the end be necessary; and if it is, we will support it'. Liberal Democrat Foreign Affairs spokesman Menzies Campbell was more circumspect: 'I do not shrink from the conclusion that military action may be required, but I am firmly of the view that it must be the last resort. It must be consistent with international law and must be authorised by the United Nations and endorsed by the House of Commons'. The chairman of the select committee on defence, Bruce George (Labour), welcomed the publication of the dossier 'because it goes some way towards convincing the doubters ... that there appears to be substantial grounds for taking firm action, whatever form that might take'. Scottish National Party parliamentary leader Alex Salmond felt that 'at this moment, with so much at stake for all of us, what America desperately needs is a candid friend to tell the truth, not a cheerleader willing to pay a "blood price"'. Amongst the most vocal of the rebels was Scottish Labour MP George Galloway (who was later deprived of the Labour whip for his comments on the war and now sits as an independent): 'The British people instinctively know that adding another war to the Middle East where there are quite enough wars already does not seem like a sensible idea ... does not sound like a recipe for security and peace in the world or like a recipe for the diminution of terrorism'. Chris Smith, the former Labour Culture Secretary, urged the Government 'in a choice between a UN-led, UN-decided process and a decision to deploy force inspired by the US President alone, our cause must surely lie with the international community and the UN'. Support for the government line came from one possibly unexpected source, Labour MP Ann Clwyd (who had been sacked from her front bench position over Iraq in 1995 but who, after the conflict, was appointed as the Prime Minister's special envoy to Iraq): 'I cannot believe that, once it knows all the facts, this House will not add its support to the call'. Labour rebel MPs forced a procedural division at the end of the debate, in which most MPs from all parties did not take part but some 70 MPs (58 Labour, five Scottish Nationalists, four Welsh Nationalists and three Liberal Democrats) registered their disapproval of the Government's position.

On 7 November, the last day before the end of the 2001–2 session of Parliament, Mr Straw reported back to the Commons on negotiations on a UN Security Council resolution on Iraq. He concluded that 'by adopting the resolution, the Security Council will send the clearest possible signal of its determination to uphold the authority of the United Nations ... the choice for Saddam Hussein is to comply with the UN or face the serious consequences'. Backbencher Alice Mahon (Labour) felt that 'this is a war resolution. The United States, with the help of our Government, shamefully, appears to have bullied and intimidated people into coming into line and, perhaps, also promised the spoils of war'.

On 18 December, the Defence Secretary, Geoff Hoon, made a statement on contingency preparations for possible military action against Iraq: 'as long as Saddam's compliance with UNSCR 1441 is in doubt, the threat of force must remain and must be real'. Former Conservative minister Douglas Hogg expressed the misgivings of many backbenchers, 'while a Security Council resolution may make a policy of war legal, it does not make it wise or moral', and veteran Labour backbencher Dennis Skinner felt 'outside this place there is probably a majority of British people who are against a war on Iraq ... vanity is not sufficient reason to spill the blood of innocents'.

On its return from the Christmas recess on 7 January 2003, Mr Hoon updated the House on the contingency preparations for Iraq, making clear the Government's 'commitment to the disarmament of Iraq's weapons of mass destruction and to the United Nations process'. None of the deployments he announced 'mean that the use of force is inevitable ... no decision has been taken to commit those forces to action'. Former Foreign Office minister Tony Lloyd (Labour) asked for 'a national consensus before we can be prepared to commit the men and women serving in our armed forces and put their lives at risk ... a huge number of people believe that Britain is acting not in its own interests or in the interests of Middle East peace but solely in the interests of the relationship with the US'.

On 20 January Mr Hoon announced further deployments to Iraq: 'while we want Saddam to disarm voluntarily, it is evident that we will not achieve that unless we present him with a clear and credible threat of force'. Alice Mahon was concerned: 'Whenever the Government say that no decision has been taken to join Bush in his war against Iraq, many of us remain deeply sceptical ... will he accept that his Government have not made the case for a war against Iraq?' On 21 January Mr Straw reported back on the outcome of the UN Security Council called to discuss the international community's response to global terrorism. Labour backbencher Glenda Jackson wondered why 'there was such a rush to get the weapons inspectors out of Iraq and to make decisions before they have had any chance genuinely to search that country to see whether there are any such weapons'.

On 3 February Mr Blair reported on his visit to Washington for talks with President Bush on the Middle East peace process and developments in Iraq, and on the publication of a second dossier on Saddam's weapons of mass destruction: 'even now, I hope that conflict with Iraq can be avoided. Even now, I hope that Saddam can come to his senses, co-operate fully and disarm peacefully, as the UN has demanded. But if he does not – if he rejects the peaceful route – he must be disarmed by force.' Although supported by the Conservative front bench, Liberal Democrat leader Charles Kennedy felt 'the Government has still to make a credible case. That case, for any fair-minded person viewing it, has to be based on credible evidence, which has not so far been forthcoming.' On 6 February Mr Hoon again updated MPs on contingency preparations, in particular the deployment of air forces: 'It is still possible for Saddam to change his behaviour ... but time is running out'. Former Labour transport minister Gavin Strang wondered 'why the Government cannot keep open an option of an inspection process lasting months rather than weeks'. When pressed on whether MPs would be able to vote on going to war, Mr Hoon was clear that 'our preference is for a vote before any deployment, but, in the circumstances, it may be necessary to delay that until shortly afterwards. That has always been the position.'

On 11 February the Minister of State for Defence, Adam Ingram, answered an Urgent Question from Conservative defence spokesman Bernard Jenkin on the meeting of the North Atlantic Council which included consideration of Turkey's role in any planned military action in Iraq. Questions were also now being raised about the second, so-called 'dodgy', dossier. Glenda Jackson felt 'the Government have markedly failed to convince the British people, most centrally because people have lost trust in that Government ... it was not the dossier that my constituents found dodgy but the attempt by the Government to present it as exclusively the work of British intelligence agencies and as containing up-to-date material'. Just before the half-term recess on 13 February, Mr Straw briefed MPs on the forthcoming UN Security Council meeting in New York, which would receive a report from UN weapons

inspectors. 'Even at this late stage, armed intervention is not inevitable ... full Iraqi compliance with Resolution 1441 will deliver the outcome the entire international community wish to see'. Labour backbencher Gordon Prentice thought 'it would be an absolute outrage if we went to war without a majority of members of the Labour party, the Parliamentary Labour party and the British public endorsing the action'.

BACKBENCH REVOLT ON WAR

On 25 February the Prime Minister made a further statement to the House, reporting that the UK, USA and Spain would delay putting forward a resolution to the UN declaring that Iraq had failed to take the final opportunity to comply with resolution 1441, to give Saddam 'one further final chance to disarm voluntarily'. Liberal Democrat Paul Marsden (who defected from the Labour Party in 2001) wanted 'to give the weapons inspectors many more months to let them do their job properly and bring about a peaceful change, rather than enter into a war'. On 26 February a debate was held calling for support of the Government's stance, and 122 Labour MPs and 77 MPs from other parties voted against the Government in favour of an amendment moved by Chris Smith that 'finds the case for military action against Iraq as yet unproven'. This was, at the time, the largest backbench revolt against any Government. Former Labour minister Peter Kilfoyle urged MPs to vote for the amendment 'to reconnect with the overwhelming consensus of the British people'.

On 10 March Mr Straw reported back on the UN Security Council meeting in New York the previous weekend when the UK, the USA and Spain had proposed a second resolution calling on Iraq for 'full, unconditional and active co-operation'. Former Labour minister Doug Henderson feared that the British public would see that 'we are in favour of the UN when it suits us and not when it does not'.

On 17 March Mr Straw reported to the House that the UK and US governments had 'reluctantly concluded that a UN Security Council consensus on a new resolution would not be possible ... and the Cabinet has decided to ask the House to support the UK's participation in military operations, should they be necessary, with the object of ensuring the disarmament of Iraq's weapons of mass destruction and thereby the maintenance of the authority of the UN'. This was followed by a personal statement from the Leader of the House and former Foreign Secretary Robin Cook on why he had felt it necessary to resign from the Government: 'I cannot support a war without international agreement or domestic support'. On 18 March, a debate was held supporting 'the decision of Her Majesty's Government that the UK should use all means necessary to ensure the destruction of Iraq's weapons of mass destruction'. It was introduced by the Prime Minister, who said, 'it is time for this House to show that we will stand up for what we know to be right; to show that we will confront the tyrannies and dictatorships and terrorists who put our way of life at risk; to show, at the moment of decision, we have the courage to do the right thing'. One hundred and thirty-nine Labour, 16 Conservative and all 53 Liberal Democrat MPs voted against the Government in support of an amendment expressing the view that the case for war 'has not yet been established', although the amendment was defeated by 396 votes to 217, a government majority of 196, and the Government's motion passed by 412 votes to 149. Three Conservative spokesmen (John Baron, Humphrey Malins and John Randall) resigned from their posts over the issue, being unable to support the official Opposition line in favour of military action. During the debate Father of the House Tam Dalyell argued, 'what could be more calculated to act as a recruiting sergeant for a young generation throughout the Islamic and Arabic world than putting 600 cruise missiles on Baghdad?' On 19 March, junior Foreign Office minister Mike O'Brien responded to an Urgent Question from the Conservative international development spokesman Caroline Spelman on humanitarian contingency planning for Iraq, leading many to ask why the Secretary of State for International Affairs (Clare Short), who was known not to favour the military option, or at least her department, were not answering for the Government. On 20 March, Defence Secretary Geoff Hoon reported that military action had begun in Iraq. Labour backbench rebel George Galloway sought assurances that 'British forces will not face prosecution in the International Criminal Court by other countries for the actions that he has ordered them to carry out today'. On 21 March Mr Hoon reported the first British casualties of the conflict.

On 24 March Mr Blair reported on the outcome of the European Council in Brussels and discussion on the conflict. 'It is worth restating our central objectives. They are to remove Saddam from power and to ensure that Iraq is disarmed of all chemical, biological and nuclear weapons programmes.' Clare Short then made a statement about the humanitarian situation and preparations for reconstruction in Iraq. On 26 March Geoff Hoon updated the House on the military action.

On 3 April, Mr Hoon reported on military action two weeks into the campaign, claiming 'remarkable progress, following the main outlines of our military plan ... we are committed to seeing through what we have begun – removing the regime that has terrified the Iraqi people and impoverished the nation for two decades'. On 7 April, Mr Hoon reported the seizure of Baghdad international airport by US soldiers and marines and the deployment of British troops in force in Basra, but said, 'we must be patient as there are many difficult and dangerous challenges lying ahead'. Former Labour sports minister Kate Hoey wondered, 'how does he possibly think we can win over the hearts and minds of the Iraqi civilians by using cluster bombs?'

On 10 April, Foreign Secretary Jack Straw reported progress after 23 days of the conflict: 'in committing our armed forces in this way, we in this House took the most difficult decision that can face any democracy. But we were right to do so and today we are well on the way to achieving the objectives that we in this House set'. Clare Short reported on the humanitarian situation: 'as the military phase of the crisis comes to an end, the priority will be to provide order and humanitarian relief and to establish an Iraqi interim authority so that the long-term reconstruction can begin'.

On 14 April, just before rising for the Easter recess, Mr Blair reported that 'less than four weeks from the commencement of the war, the regime of Saddam is gone, the bulk of Iraq is under coalition control and the vast majority of Iraqis are rejoicing at Saddam's departure ... now there is a heavy responsibility on us to make the peace worth the war ... we shall do so ... with a fixed and steady resolve that the cause was just, the victory right and the future for us to make in a way that will stand the judgement of history.'

Returning from the Easter recess on 28 April, the House heard from Mr Straw that 'large-scale combat operations are now over and the overwhelming majority of the country is under coalition control'. He also expressed support for the US 'road map' for peace in the Middle East.

On 12 May Mr Straw reported on UK and US proposals for UN involvement in the reconstruction of Iraq. Shadow Foreign Secretary Michael Ancram felt the Government 'owe it to our forces and to the people of Iraq to win the peace – they are not making a very good fist of it right now'. This was followed by a personal statement by Clare Short on her decision to resign from the Government. 'I am ashamed that the UK Government has agreed the resolution that has been tabled in New York and shocked by the secrecy and lack of consultation.' She felt that the Prime Minister's political legacy was at risk because he is 'increasingly obsessed with his place in history ... There is no real collective responsibility because there is no collective – just diktats in favour of increasingly badly thought through policy initiatives that come from on high.'

INTELLIGENCE ROW

Following a huge media row over the presentation of the intelligence that led to the vote to go to war, on 4 June a Liberal Democrat motion calling for an independent judicial inquiry into 'the handling of the intelligence received, its assessment and the decisions made by ministers based on it' was defeated by 313 votes to 202, a government majority of 101, with no Labour MPs voting for it.

On 19 June, the BBC's defence correspondent Andrew Gilligan gave evidence to the Foreign Affairs select committee inquiry on the Government's presentation of the case for war in Iraq, regarding his claim that Alastair Campbell, the Prime Minister's director of communications, was responsible for inserting into the 'dodgy' dossier the claim that Iraq could deploy weapons of mass destruction in 45 minutes. On 25 June Alastair Campbell vigorously denied the claims while giving evidence to the committee and demanded an apology from the BBC. On 7 July the committee published its report, clearing Mr Campbell – on the casting vote of the Labour chairman Donald Anderson – but saying 'undue prominence' was given to the 45-minute claim. The select committee reopened its inquiry on 15 July, calling Dr David Kelly, an MOD official who admitted meeting the journalist; the committee concluded that it did not believe Dr Kelly was the source of Mr Gilligan's story and said he had been badly treated by the MOD. On 17 July Mr Gilligan again gave evidence in a private session and was later criticised for not revealing his source to MPs and was accused by Donald Anderson of changing his story. This whole saga, and the row between the BBC and the Government and calls for a judicial inquiry, became the issues dominating politics before the 2003 summer recess.

During Prime Minister's Question Time on 2 July, Charles Kennedy asked Tony Blair to clarify events over the inclusion of the 45-minute claim. Mr Blair replied, 'The clarification is this: in the first draft presented by the Joint Intelligence Committee, the 45-minutes claim was there. The allegation that the claim was inserted by anyone in No. 10 Downing Street or any minister is completely and totally incorrect. If he has evidence to support the claim that we inserted intelligence into the dossier, let him now state the basis for that allegation.' On 9 July the Leader of the Opposition, Iain Duncan Smith, asked the Prime Minister to apologise for misrepresenting the status of the dossier. He replied, 'The Foreign Secretary has already apologised on behalf of the whole Government for the mistake that was made. I do not accept, in any shape or form, that the information in that second briefing was wrong.' On 16 July Mr Blair again restated the Government's case, 'I do not accept that people were misled at all. I stand entirely by what was in the dossier and, in case anyone should doubt that weapons of mass destruction were an issue that did not just preoccupy the British or American Governments, in resolution 1441 the whole of the UN Security Council – not just Britain and America – agreed that they were an issue.'

Late on 24 June, Defence Secretary Geoff Hoon came to the House to report two serious incidents involving British troops in Iraq, when six British personnel were killed. Tam Dalyell felt that 'like it or not, British forces are perceived as less of a liberating force and more an occupying army ... should we not make an urgent approach to the UN?'

On 3 July, the newly appointed Minister of State for International Development, Hilary Benn, made a statement on the humanitarian situation in Iraq: 'the coalition is working urgently to build on the progress achieved so far, and to make real, lasting and visible improvements to the lives of the Iraqi people'.

Before rising for the summer recess, the Foreign Secretary updated the House on the situation in Iraq on 15 July. A sovereign Iraqi government had been established. Reconstruction, in which the whole international community was playing a significant part, was under way. On 16 July the Conservatives instigated a debate calling for a judicial inquiry to establish the facts surrounding the intelligence information published before the war; it was defeated by 299 votes to 200, a government majority of 99, with only six Labour MPs voting with the Opposition but many more abstaining.

LABOUR REBELS ON TOP-UP FEES

Perhaps emboldened by the Iraq issue, Labour backbenchers also expressed their dismay over some of the core elements of the Government's legislative programme in 2002–3. On 22 January 2003, the Education and Skills Secretary, Charles Clarke, published a White Paper on higher education which included the concept of top-up fees of up to £3,000 a year for university students; this coincided with an Early Day Motion signed by some 135 Labour backbench MPs opposing the imposition of such fees. Mr Clarke admitted the measure might be unpopular but argued that 'the British system of student support will remain amongst the most generous in the world'. Conservative education spokesman Damian Green felt the Secretary of State was in the past 'opposed to his own policy as announced today'. Liberal Democrat spokesperson Phil Willis thought 'the Government have not solved the problem, they have added to it'. His party in coalition with Labour in the Scottish Executive had expressly ruled out top-up fees in Scotland. Labour backbenchers lined up to criticise the proposal – former minister Angela Eagle voiced the concern that 'many of us on the Labour benches are very worried about the concept of variable top-up fees and their possible effects on the practical chances of people from poorer backgrounds to aspire to some of the elite universities'. The Labour chairman of the Education select committee, Barry Sheerman, asked for assurances that his committee would be allowed to look in detail at the proposals and 'that notice will be taken of those opinions before a final policy is determined'. During a debate on the issue on 23 June, Higher Education Minister Alan Johnson claimed he would not be advocating plans to allow universities to charge top-up fees if he thought the policy would damage the chances of 'working-class kids', which led former lifelong learning minister George Mudie to ask if Mr Johnson really believed 'the nonsense' he was reading out. Labour backbencher Paul Farrelly referred to the fact that the Government 'could hardly demonstrate a resounding feeling of confidence in the central plank of

their university policy'. In the event, only 10 Labour MPs voted against the Government but with abstentions the government's majority was reduced to only 74 (267 to 193). On 25 June, the Conservatives sought to capitalise on the Government's discomfort by tabling for debate the exact motion opposing top-up fees that, by this time, some 150 Labour MPs had signed, but none of the Labour signatories voted for it when given the chance.

FOUNDATION HOSPITALS

On 11 December 2002, the Health Secretary, Alan Milburn, detailed planned expenditure, resources and responsibilities within the National Health Service, introducing the concept of foundation hospitals: 'for the first time, locally run primary care trusts will receive funding from central Government rather than through health authorities ... it is time not just to invest more resources in front-line services, but to invest power and trust in those services'. Conservative health spokesman Liam Fox gave a cautious welcome to the concept, saying 'it will have the support of Conservative Members', but Liberal Democrat health spokesperson Evan Harris felt the Government 'must go back to the drawing board ... he has pleased no-one and is trying to please everyone and trying to have it both ways. This is typical new Labour.' On 8 January 2003, the Conservatives debated a motion to allow all hospitals to bid for foundation status – this was easily defeated by 381 votes to 144, but the Government's majority fell to just 132 when some 45 backbenchers defied ministers to vote against the substantive motion welcoming the principle of NHS foundation trusts (passed by 282 votes to 150).

The Health and Social Care (Community Health and Standards) Bill was introduced in the Commons on 7 May 2003. Mr Milburn felt the measure was set to 'prove that an NHS based on traditional Labour values can give patients a modern, responsive service ... this is the era of public-service investment. It must also be the era of public-service reform.' Whilst many of the measures included in the bill were welcomed, the issue of foundation hospitals, though supported in principle by the Conservatives, was seen as anathema by many traditional Labour MPs, as it seemed set to create a two-tier health service. Addressing these concerns Mr Milburn said, 'In no way can this bill be reasonably described as privatisation, or a step in that direction – through the front door, through the back door or through the side door ... This is not privatisation. It is democratisation.' Former Labour health secretary Frank Dobson called the proposals 'the very last thing that the NHS needs'. The Labour chairman of the Health select committee, David Hinchliffe, even went as far as moving a reasoned amendment declining to give the bill a second reading: 'because we oppose certain principles in the bill as it relates to foundation trusts, we are forced to put forward this amendment, as it is impossible to amend the bill to address principles that, in our view, are at fault ... the last thing we need is more restructuring. The proposals are not fair, consistent and need to be rethought. It is a departure from our commitment to primary care-led national health service and it resurrects the competitive market ethos, which the Government were elected to get rid of.' Even the independent MP for Wyre Forest, former doctor Richard Taylor, felt that 'instead of rushing this bill through, the Government should concentrate on supporting the existing initiatives, improving morale, management and the relations between managers and clinicians'. In the vote, the reasoned amendment was defeated by 297 votes to 117, a government majority of 180 (65 Labour MPs voted against the Government and the Conservatives, as well as a number of Labour MPs, abstained). The second reading itself was passed by 304 votes to 230, a government majority of 64 (31 Labour MPs voted with both Opposition parties against the Government).

The bill passed through its committee stage without this aspect being amended and returned to the Commons for its remaining stages on 8 July, with the rebels still hoping to force changes during a debate, limited by a timetable motion. David Hinchliffe moved another amendment 'to delete the foundation trust proposals from the bill. I certainly support the remainder of the bill. It could be carried forward without Part 1, which is the controversial element that many Labour members oppose ... I am concerned that the policy is part of a growing trend of policy making on the hoof ... the policy has not been properly thought through and there has been no proper consultation.' Former welfare reform minister Frank Field called on the Government 'to draw back a little in their proposed pace of reform'. Health Minister John Hutton tried to reassure the rebels that 'this is not about competition, privatisation or two tiers: it is about taking forward traditional NHS values and applying them in the new world and new society in which we live'. With all the Opposition parties voting for the amendment, it was only defeated by 286 voted to 251, a government majority of just 35 (62 Labour MPs voted against the Government). The third reading was passed by 306 votes to 57, a government majority of 249.

There was also a row over the 'West Lothian question' – the fact that loyal Scottish and Welsh Labour MPs helped the proposal to go through when the measure did not affect those regions and the Scottish Executive had actually rejected foundation hospitals in favour of an integrated healthcare system. This led Mr Blair to warn Labour backbenchers at a private meeting of the Parliamentary Labour Party the day after the vote not to let their party 'self destruct' through divisions. The health bill is to go to the Lords for consideration in October 2003, where it is likely to receive a rocky ride.

HUNTING BILL

In this session, the Government pressed ahead with the Hunting Bill, seen as a sop to dissident backbenchers. The bill introduced by the Government proposed a ban on some hunts but would allow others to continue under licence. The bill was published with a statement in the House by the Rural Affairs Minister, Alun Michael, on 3 December 2002, when he claimed that 'the two principles of cruelty and utility provide the golden thread that runs from the start to the finish of the process and through the drafting of the bill'. Introducing the second reading in the Commons on 16 December, Mr Michael felt he had presented a bill 'that will prevent cruelty caused by hunting with dogs while dealing with the genuine needs of farmers, gamekeepers and land managers – a bill that will stand the test of time and make good, effective law'. It was passed by 368 votes to 155, a government majority of 213. At the same time, 200 MPs signed a Commons motion saying only a total ban on hunting would be acceptable. The bill completed its tightly timetabled committee stage by the end of February 2003 but then seemed to disappear from the parliamentary timetable. When asked during May whether the Government was to live up to its commitment to ban hunting, the Leader of the House of Commons, John Reid, hinted that the bill could fall victim to pressures on parliamentary time, stressing the 'crowded' nature of the timetable at Westminster. The following month, however, the new Leader of the House, Peter Hain, announced the bill's return for its remaining stages in the Commons on 30 June, a move criticised by

his Conservative shadow Eric Forth as it meant only one day's debate would be held. Prior to the debate some 145 MPs, led by Tony Banks (Labour) tabled an amendment that would ban all hunting, leading Mr Hain to suggest the bill would be delayed if an outright ban were agreed, as he had been advised that the bill would then have to go back into committee, thus delaying its passage to the Lords. In the event, at the end of the debate, to the surprise of everybody, Mr Michael decided at the last minute to withdraw the Government's own amendment (on a partial ban) as an 'act of good faith' once they realised that MPs risked not getting the vote they had been promised on the outright ban proposal if the government amendment were passed. As a result, MPs voted by 362 votes to 154, a majority of 208, for a total ban. Conservative spokesman James Gray wondered 'why the Government are ignoring vital rural issues in favour of a little tokenism on foxhunting'. Mr Banks felt 'hunting is not a matter of class hatred but of principle and morality. We gave an undertaking to ban hunting and we are fulfilling our manifesto commitment'. As forecast, the bill then had to return to committee to ensure that it was in order before coming back to the Commons for its third reading on 9 July, which was passed by 317 votes to 145, but a call from the Conservatives for compensation for those who may lose their livelihoods failed to be added to the bill. This bill will go to the Lords for consideration in September 2003, where it is likely to run into concerted opposition.

LORDS AMENDS COMMUNICATIONS BILL

As ever, the House of Lords made several attempts to amend the Government's legislative programme – in particular inflicting a series of defeats on the Communications Bill, the Licensing Bill and the Sexual Offences Bill (the last two of which were introduced in the Lords).

On the first day of the report stage of the Communications Bill on 23 June 2003, the Lords inflicted two defeats on the Government. They approved by 179 votes to 74 a cross-party amendment moved by Lord Puttnam (Labour) to put 'citizenship' at the heart of the duties of OFCOM, the new communications industry watchdog. Lord Puttnam felt his amendment 'properly redresses the balance that makes communications different and so would make the bill all the better for its insertion'. Then the Lords voted by 113 to 110 in favour of an amendment moved by the Earl of Northesk (Conservative) requiring OFCOM to promote the take-up of high-speed broadband access. On the fourth day of the report stage on 2 July the Government were defeated by 158 votes to 117 on an amendment tabled by Lord Gordon of Strathblane (Labour) intended to prohibit 'offensive' advertisements. In addition, the Conservative culture, media and sport spokesman Baroness Buscombe's amendment overturning the disqualification of religious groups was approved by 115 votes to 99, a majority against the Government of 16. She thought her amendment 'seeks to remedy the blatant injustice found in the face of the bill'. On third reading on 8 July, government plans for a consumer panel to be set up to advise OFCOM and to have a say over broadcast content, a plan strongly supported by consumer organisations, were defeated when an amendment to restrict the panel's rights, tabled by Baroness Buscombe, was voted through by 158 votes to 141. An amendment moved by Lord McNally (Lib. Dem.) and Lord Crickhowell (Conservative), to prevent a national newspaper owner with a national market share of 20 per cent or more from holding a licence for Channel 5 was defeated by 167 votes to 137. These defeats were amended in the

Commons on 14 July and the bill received royal assent on 17 July.

LICENSING AND SEXUAL OFFENCES IN LORDS

On the Licensing Bill (Lords), a series of defeats were inflicted on the Government on the first day of the report stage on 24 February 2003. An amendment moved by Baroness Buscombe to exclude schools from the provisions of the bill was supported 169 votes to 107 – 'the Government have not made the case for having an additional layer of bureaucracy for schools to deal with'. An amendment moved by Lord Redesdale (Lib. Dem.) to exclude most unamplified live music from the new laws was passed by 151 votes to 115 – 'we are not against the bill but we believe that live music is a fundamental right and we have to be proportional'. Another amendment moved by Lord Redesdale, on setting up a central licensing authority or register, was passed by 143 votes to 111 – 'I believe that it would save a great deal of money not just in the short term but in the long term'. And another amendment moved by Baroness Buscombe, to place a new duty on the licensing authority to protect the 'amenity and environment' of local residents, was passed by 135 votes to 99 – 'my amendments seek ... the need for local authorities to make decisions that offer a compromise and a sensible balance'. On the second day of the report stage on 27 February, two further defeats were inflicted. An amendment moved by Lord Redesdale on ownership was passed by 99 votes to 92. An amendment moved by Lord Brooke of Sutton Mandeville (Conservative) on the local democratic accountability of licensing authorities was passed by 98 votes to 97. On the third and final day of the report stage on 4 March, a new clause moved by Baroness Buscombe and supported by the bishops, barring children under 14 from bars, pubs and clubs unless they are with an adult, was approved by 184 votes to 111. At the third reading on 11 March, an amendment moved by Baroness Buscombe exempting small venues from requiring entertainment licences was supported by 150 votes to 120. When the bill moved to the Commons for its second reading on 24 March, the Culture Secretary, Tessa Jowell, said the Government would not try to overturn all the changes made by the Lords. The Government would keep to the 'spirit of amendments' in the Lords by excluding 'incidental live music' from the licensing regime; 'people will not be arrested for singing 'Happy Birthday' in a restaurant and postmen will not need licences to whistle on their rounds'. After the Lords failed to insist on their other amendments on 3 July, the bill received royal assent on 10 July.

The Lords inserted two new clauses in the Sexual Offences Bill (Lords). On first day of the report stage on 2 June 2003, a new clause introduced by Lord Ackner (Cross-bench), on the anonymity of a defendant in a rape charge, was agreed by 109 voted to 105. On the second day of the report stage on 9 June, a new clause introduced by Conservative spokesman Baroness Noakes on sexual activity in a public lavatory was added by 133 vote to 95. She felt, 'It creates places that ordinary people don't want to go to and certainly don't want their children to use'. The bill moved to the Commons just before the summer recess and will go into committee in October 2003.

END OF 2001–2 SESSION

On other issues the Government faced the usual crop of difficulties. On returning after the summer recess on 15 October 2002, the Prime Minister made a statement on the bombings in Bali earlier in the month that had left least 11 British citizens dead. 'An act of pure wickedness

... the war against terrorism is indeed a war, but a different sort to the ones we are used to. Its outcome, however, is as important as any we have fought before'. The Foreign Secretary, Jack Straw, was forced to return to the House on 21 October to defend the Foreign Office from claims that it had not done enough to warn British citizens of the dangers. On 15 October also, the then Northern Ireland Secretary, John Reid, reported to the House that he had made an order under the Northern Ireland Act 2000 to suspend devolved government in Northern Ireland with effect from midnight the previous day. 'It became clear that an impasse had been reached and that decisive action was needed to safeguard the progress made and tackle the remaining challenges ... it creates a breathing space – a chance to gather strength – before the process moves forward once again.' The then Education and Skills Secretary, Estelle Morris, apologised to MPs about confusion over A-level grading and reported on the action the Government had taken to avoid the situation arising again. In an Opposition debate on this subject the next day her shadow, Damian Green, felt that 'Ministers are the problem. Non-stop intervention, meddling, pointless initiatives and meaningless targets have left teachers crying out to be allowed to get on with their job of teaching'. Ms Morris resigned from her post on 23 October, saying the job was too important to have 'second best': 'I am not having second best in a post that is as important as this and that is why I have made the decision'. On 17 October, the Work and Pensions Secretary Andrew Smith announced a consultation to simplify the system of housing benefit.

The dispute over the Fire Service had simmered throughout the summer and on 22 October 2002 the Deputy Prime Minister, John Prescott, told the House of the plans that the Government had put in place to secure public safety in the event of industrial action by the Fire Brigades Union.

On 28 October, Mr Blair reported on the outcome of the European Council meeting in Brussels, which had set the framework for the final stage of enlargement negotiations. 'The way is clear to finish the enlargement negotiations by December ... I hope the House will welcome this important step towards a Europe united, democratic and free'. The Leader of the Opposition, Iain Duncan Smith, felt 'proposals to give away yet more powers from national governments to the Commission have been tabled over British objections'. Liberal Democrat leader Charles Kennedy feared 'are we not in danger of missing the boat in the formative stage of the single currency in the same way as we did at the outset of the establishment of the CAP'.

On 29 October, the House agreed the report of the Modernisation Committee on the procedures of the House by 311 votes to 234. From January 2003, the House would sit early (11.30 a.m.) and rise early (6.30 p.m. or 7.30 p.m.) on Tuesdays, Wednesdays and Thursdays, and Prime Minister's Question Time would therefore be at 12 noon on Wednesdays. A parliamentary calendar would be agreed one year in advance, with changes to the summer recess meaning that the House rose earlier in July but would return for two weeks in September before rising again for the party conference season. A half-term recess in February would be introduced formally, as would an extra constituency week, to be taken with either the Whit or Easter recess. The system of planted Parliamentary Questions would be replaced by formal Written Ministerial statements. Private Notice Questions would be replaced by Urgent Questions. More government bills would be introduced in draft for pre-legislative scrutiny and, with the Houses' agreement, bills could be carried over from one session to the next. The then Leader of the House, Robin Cook, wanted the Commons 'to remain the great forum of our nation ... I want the Commons to derive its authority from the respect and trust of the public ... to remain the crucible in which Governments are forged and are broken. To retain that public support, the Commons must accept reform.' Opposition amendments were tabled, according to Shadow Leader of the House Eric Forth, 'where we think there is yet another step in the diminution of the role of the House and the reduction in the possibility for members to hold the Government to account'; all were rejected.

On 6 November 2002, the Environment, Food and Rural Affairs Secretary, Margaret Beckett, published the Government's response to the foot and mouth inquiry reports, which she felt represented 'a massive programme of work and reform ... to establish more effective safeguards and an even more effective response'. Her Conservative shadow, David Lidington, felt much of what was proposed 'seems sensible and welcome', while Liberal Democrat spokesperson Andrew George regretted the failure to hold a public inquiry. The 2001–2 session of Parliament was prorogued on 7 November 2002.

THE QUEEN'S SPEECH
The Queen's Speech on 13 November 2002, opening the 2002–3 session, contained proposals for 19 bills for the new session and mentioned three bills that would be introduced in draft. The Prime Minister felt it 'continues our programme on the economy, on our public services, on a strong civic society and on a foreign policy that allows us to play our part in Europe properly'. Iain Duncan Smith thought it 'offers more of the same failed policies as before, with more edicts, more targets, more indicators, more centralisation, more spin and more control ... each year the Government promise real reform and each year they fail to deliver'. Charles Kennedy said 'much of the Queen's Speech is sensible, but in its measures on law and order and on crime and punishment, there is also much that is too illiberal'.

On 14 November, John Prescott made a statement on the fire dispute, which the Government believed was 'wrong, unnecessary and unreasonable' and warned the Fire Brigades Union that if the action continued 'the Government may have to review many of the issues which until now we have kept off the table'.

On 18 November, Work and Pensions Secretary Andrew Smith delivered the annual benefits uprating statement (an increase of 1.7 per cent, in line with RPI), with above-inflation increases for pensions and some maternity allowances. On 19 November the Home Secretary, David Blunkett, published a White Paper on sexual offences law reform designed to 'provide confidence and protection, laws that remain true to the time-honoured and accepted parameters of a free and civilised society'.

On 25 November the Prime Minister had to answer an Urgent Question from Iain Duncan Smith on the fire dispute, on the fourth day of an eight-day strike. He reiterated that the dispute 'cannot be justified'. Mr Duncan Smith demanded 'action not words ... the country deserves better from this Government'. Mr Blair also reported on the outcome of the NATO summit in Prague, where seven new members had been welcomed into the alliance. Mr Duncan Smith felt that the summit had not addressed 'the confusion between the EU and NATO, which is already affecting operations'. On 26 November John Prescott outlined the measures the Government were taking to bring an end to the fire dispute: 'we have a once-in-a-generation opportunity to introduce radical change in order to provide a modern

fire service for the 21st century. It is in the interests of everybody to achieve that vision.'

On 27 November, the Chancellor of the Exchequer, Gordon Brown, delivered his annual pre-Budget report, in which he downgraded his hopes for UK economic growth and announced increases in government borrowing to cover extra spending on schools and hospitals: 'We will honour our commitments to invest in public services, to advance enterprise and fairness and to meet and master global challenges.' The Shadow Chancellor, Michael Howard, referred to 'the downgraded forecasts of a downgraded Chancellor' and Liberal Democrat economic spokesperson Matthew Taylor accused Mr Brown of 'running out of money and running out of ideas' and warned that 'the Budget will go bust in the long-term unless you tackle the collapse in British industry and stop relying on an unsustainable boom in consumer debt to keep your growth figures up'.

On 28 November, the Transport Secretary, Alistair Darling, made a statement on the consultation on airport capacity following a court ruling that Gatwick should not have been excluded form the original process. The Trade and Industry Secretary, Patricia Hewitt, made a statement on the future of British Energy's plans for the solvent restructuring of the company: 'I have set out the limits of what the Government are willing to do to support solvent restructuring. It is now up to the company.' Her Conservative shadow, Tim Yeo, accused her of failing to 'address the central absurdity of the Government's policy: the imposition of the climate change levy on British Energy'.

On 2 December, Home Secretary David Blunkett made a statement on his agreement with the French Government to close the Sangatte refugee centre by the end of December, but also warned that he expected 'a step change in the operation, efficiency and competence within the system and how it is handled'. On 3 December, the new Education and Skills Secretary, Charles Clarke, reported on the findings of the Tomlinson inquiry into A-level standards. On 5 December, the Minister for Local Government and the Regions, Nick Raynsford, made the usual statement on the local government financial settlement for 2003–4, announcing an 8 per cent cash increase in the settlement, which he felt 'provides substantial real-terms growth in funding'.

On 9 December, Charles Clarke outlined the Government's education and skills plan for the next three-year period. Improved standards would only be achieved if 'as well as substantial investment, we reform our schools and colleges so that they genuinely fulfil every child's aspirations'. Conservative education spokesman Damian Green thought it appropriate that the statement was being made 'on the day on which the department has been forced to admit that it is missing more than half the targets that it has set itself on school standards'. On 10 December, Alistair Darling detailed the investment strategy for improving Britain's transport infrastructure: 'the Government are spending more on road and rail to tackle congestion, to improve reliability and to make journey's safer ... that investment will be sustained year on year, because it is an essential part of building our economic prosperity and improving our quality of life'. While welcoming the extra investment, the Conservative transport spokesman, Tim Collins, thought 'the ten-year transport plan is now effectively in tatters and few will believe that these projects are certain to happen'. For the Liberal Democrats, transport spokesman Don Foster wondered that 'all we can look forward to now is worsening public transport and longer and wider traffic jams'. On 11 December, the Foreign

Secretary gave an update on the publication of the Intelligence and Security Committee report on the Bali bombing.

On 16 December, Tony Blair reported on the outcome of the EU summit in Copenhagen that had successfully concluded the negotiations to admit to membership Cyprus, Malta and 10 countries from eastern and central Europe: 'it is our job to be part of the new Europe that is developing, to be a leading power within it and to understand the degree to which our national interest is bound up in it'. Iain Duncan Smith felt the Prime Minister had been 'outflanked by France and Germany again'. This was followed by a statement by John Prescott on the publication of the report by Sir George Bain into the fire dispute; the report recommended major structural changes to the service, providing 'a fair deal for the firefighters, a fair deal for other workers and a fair deal for the economy'. On 17 December, Work and Pensions Secretary Andrew Smith published a green paper on occupational and private pensions, *Simplicity, Security and Choice: Working and Saving for Retirement,* pointing out that 'if people want their standards of living to continue to rise in retirement, they must either save more or work longer'. The Conservative pensions spokesman, David Willetts, thought the statement 'simply fails to match the scale of the crisis in the savings of our country'. Liberal Democrat spokesperson Steve Webb called it 'an Arthur Daley scheme'. Following this, Alistair Darling made a statement on progress on the 10-year investment plan for transport, stressing that 'just as elsewhere, with investment must come reform'. On 18 December, the day before rising for the Christmas recess, the Scottish Secretary, Helen Liddell, explained to the House why the reduction in the number of Westminster seats held by Scottish MPs and Holyrood seats held by Scottish MSPs, as promised in the Scotland Act 1998, would not be introduced until June 2006.

On 14 January 2003, junior Trade and Industry minister Nigel Griffiths responded to an Urgent Question from Conservative energy spokesman Crispin Blunt on a security breach by Greenpeace activists at Sizewell nuclear power station; he stressed that at no time did they enter sensitive areas. On 15 January, the Home Secretary made a statement on events in Greater Manchester the previous night which had resulted in the death of a police detective constable while trying to detain two foreign nationals. The Defence Secretary, Geoff Hoon, made a statement on missile defence, saying he was minded to accept the US request to use RAF Fylingdales: 'missile defence is a defensive system that threatens no-one. We see no reason to believe fears that development will be strategically destabilising.' Although the statement was welcomed by the Conservative front bench, the Liberal Democrats were more circumspect and their defence spokesperson Paul Keetch felt 'the House of Commons is being presented with a fait accompli'. Labour backbencher Malcolm Savidge objected to the proposal, which was opposed 'by more than 70 per cent of the British public'.

On 20 January, John Prescott brought the House up-to-date on the firefighters' dispute: 'Further strike action will achieve nothing ... pay and modernisation must go hand in hand'. He promised a White Paper later in the year. His Conservative shadow, David Davis, called for an injunction to stop the planned strikes: 'It is now time to put the public first and politics last'. On 23 January, the Economic Secretary to the Treasury, John Healey, made a statement in response to the Stockade case in the Court of Appeal.

On 27 January, Andrew Smith made a statement on the implementation of the child support reforms, to ensure that more children benefit from regular maintenance, and a new IT system from EDS to deliver it. On 28 January, John Prescott announced that, with the breakdown of the latest talks at ACAS, the Government would be introducing legislation in the public interest to take new powers of direction over the fire service. Alan Milburn announced the publication of the report of the Lamming inquiry into the death of Victoria Climbie: 'we cannot undo the wrongs done to Victoria Climbie. We can, though, seek to put right for others what so fundamentally failed for her'. He promised to publish a green paper before the summer recess. On 29 January, Patricia Hewitt announced the publication of the report of the co-ordinating group on audit and accounting issues and the report of the review of the regulatory regime of the accountancy profession, introducing a overall package of reform that 'is tough when it is needed but measured and proportionate. It will ensure that our corporate governance structures remain amongst the best in the world'. On 30 January Geoff Hoon made a statement on the future aircraft carrier programme, innovatively splitting the contract between the two main bidders, BAE Systems and Thales UK.

LORDS' REFORM

On 4 February 2003, the recommendations of the joint committee on House of Lords reform was debated in both Houses. The House of Commons was entirely unable to decide which of the seven options for reform to adopt, although the House of Lords came down in favour of a fully appointed second chamber. The voting was as follows:

For a fully appointed second chamber:
• House of Lords: 335 in favour, 110 against
• House of Commons: 245 in favour, 323 against
For a fully elected second chamber:
• House of Lords: 106 in favour, 329 against
• House of Commons: 272 in favour, 289 against
For an 80 per cent appointed/20 per cent elected second chamber:
• House of Lords: 39 in favour, 376 against
• House of Commons: rejected without a vote
For an 80 per cent elected/20 per cent appointed second chamber:
• House of Lords: 93 in favour, 339 against
• House of Commons: 281 in favour, 284 against
For a 60 per cent appointed/40 per cent elected second chamber:
• House of Lords: 60 in favour, 359 against
• House of Commons: rejected without a vote
For a 60 per cent elected/40 per cent appointed second chamber:
• House of Lords: 91 in favour, 318 against
• House of Commons: 253 votes in favour, 316 against
For a 50 per cent appointed/50 per cent elected second chamber:
• House of Lords: 84 in favour, 322 against
• House of Commons: rejected without a vote

In the House of Commons an amendment moved by Dennis Skinner (Labour) calling for the abolition of the House of Lords was rejected by 390 votes to 172. The chairman of the joint committee, Jack Cunningham, thought the inconclusive votes meant Parliament was unlikely to agree a way forward for some time.

On 5 February, John Prescott announced the publication of *Sustainable Communities: Building for the Future,* outlining plans making provisions for more affordable housing. On 13 February, David Blunkett responded to an Urgent Question from his Conservative shadow Oliver Letwin on the appearance of tanks to enhance security at Heathrow airport: 'the public must be alert but not alarmed'. Later Conservative backbencher Michael Trend made a personal statement apologising to the House for his 'muddled, naïve and negligent understanding of the additional costs allowance' which had caused the Standards and Privileges committee to recommend he be suspended from the House for two weeks.

On 24 February, Patricia Hewitt published a White Paper on energy, setting out four goals: 'to cut greenhouse gas emissions, to secure reliable energy supplies, to maintain competitive energy markets in the UK and to ensure that every home is adequately and affordably heated'. Tim Yeo thought the White Paper 'full of overblown prime ministerial rhetoric and claims and wholly inadequate to meet the challenges that Britain faces'.

On 12 March, David Blunkett published a White Paper on anti-social behaviour: 'bad behaviour must be dealt with decisively and there is a need to restore pride in our communities'. On 20 March, John Prescott reported that, as a result of the beginning of the conflict in Iraq, the Fire Brigades Union had called off its latest strike but the Government would still be introducing a bill to give the Government power to impose terms and conditions within the fire service and direct the use of fire service assets and facilities. David Davis welcomed the measure as long overdue.

THE BUDGET

Later than usual, on 9 April, Chancellor Gordon Brown presented his seventh Budget Statement (the first to be presented at 12.30 p.m. rather than at 3.30 p.m.), cutting his predictions for UK economic growth and announcing an increase in government borrowing. He announced measures including greater taxes for smokers and drinkers, a new 'baby bond' and increased benefits for pensioners. Mr Brown remained bullish over prospects for the UK economy, saying that Britain was in a much stronger position than other countries amid the global slowdown. He felt this was a 'Budget meeting our responsibilities abroad and at home: steadfast for stability, enterprise and full employment; tackling inequality; building an NHS free at the point of need. A Britain of economic strength and social justice'. Iain Duncan Smith thought the 'Budget message to the British people is clear – higher taxes, that is more pain today. Higher borrowing, that is more pain tomorrow'. Charles Kennedy said the Budget was a combination of 'buck-passing' and 'cross your fingers and hope for the best ... there is a sense of denial about this amazing account the Chancellor has been able to give us'. The Labour chairman of the Treasury select committee, John McFall, agreed that 'this is the time for fiscal loosening ... there is a sound economic case for extra borrowing when the risks are all on the downside'. After a shorter than usual four days of debate on the Budget, Shadow Chancellor Michael Howard accused the Government of being one which 'know only how to tax, how to spend and how to fail', but the Budget was approved by 322 votes to 187. The Finance Bill, containing the Budget proposals, was given a second reading in the Commons on 6 May and completed committee consideration by 17 June (having had two extra days added to the timetable), with the third reading on 1 July. After consideration in the Lords on 3 July, the Finance Act received royal assent on 10 July.

On 14 April, the Northern Ireland Secretary, Paul Murphy, made a statement on recent political developments in the province and the postponement of elections to the Northern Ireland Assembly for a period of four weeks. On 28 April, Alan Milburn detailed the

Government's response to the outbreak of Severe Acute Respiratory Syndrome (SARS) in south-east Asia and the impact on the UK: 'a precautionary but proportionate response'. The Paymaster-General, Dawn Primarolo, reported on the confusion surrounding the new child and working tax credits that had been introduced earlier in the month, apologising for 'the difficulties experienced by individual families'. Michael Howard thought the Chancellor should be accepting 'responsibility and apologising to the hundreds of thousands of families who have needlessly been caused distress and dismay because of his incompetence'. Matthew Taylor knew constituents were 'not getting the payments that they need to pay their bills ... do the Government have a system in place to enable them to prioritise those who are most needy and still missing out?'

On 1 May, Paul Murphy came to the House to report that elections to the Northern Ireland Assembly would now have to be postponed until the autumn and a bill would be introduced to allow for this. The Conservative Northern Ireland spokesman, Quentin Davies, thought 'the Government have shown that they do not take their own constitutional rules seriously and devolution ... is merely the plaything of the Government'. On 15 May, Culture Secretary Tessa Jowell announced that the Government had decided to give their backing to a bid to host the Olympic Games in London in 2012. 'We believe that it should host the greatest games on earth.'

On 20 May, Charles Clarke responded to an Urgent Question from Damian Green on proposed changes to primary school tests and targets which would give schools 'more control of their own improvement and in providing children with a broad, rich curriculum'. Mr Green thought the new strategy was 'a smokescreen designed to hide the central fact that the Government are failing in primary schools'.

On 4 June, Tony Blair reported on the outcome of the G8 summit in France which had covered the Middle East peace process and weapons of mass destruction and had strengthened the New Partnership for Africa's Development.

On 9 June, Gordon Brown made a statement on economic and monetary union (EMU), setting out why the UK economy did not yet meet the conditions to join EMU. The economic case for meeting his five tests for euro entry had to be 'clear and unambiguous' and they had not been met. The Government would report back on progress towards meeting the tests in the 2004 Budget and then decide whether to assess the tests again. A referendum bill would be unveiled in autumn 2003 to pave the way for a possible referendum in 2004. He claimed that the statement had 'strengthened our commitment to and support for the principle of joining the euro and shows that the gains to the country and to our businesses are greater than anticipated'. Michael Howard thought the statement was not the result of any real assessment of Britain's economic interest: 'It is a result of the frantic efforts by the Chancellor and the Prime Minister to cover up their differences'. On 10 June, a motion to carry over the Government's Planning and Compulsory Purchase Bill until the next session of Parliament was passed by 279 votes to 162, despite criticism from the Opposition spokesman Geoffrey Clifton Brown that the Government were 'performing a sheepish and embarrassed U-turn over one of their flagship bills of this session ... smothering under the guise of complex parliamentary procedure the admission that the bill was, from the start, a deeply flawed and poorly drafted measure'. On 11 June, Andrew Smith made a statement on proposed government reform of occupational pensions following the earlier green paper, promising 'a balancing package to reduce costs and complexity of regulation, making it easier for employers to run schemes while ensuring that pensions promised are pensions delivered'. On 12 June, Defence Minister Adam Ingram made a statement on a British contribution to a multinational force for the Democratic Republic of the Congo, a move welcomed by Opposition parties.

On 16 June, John Prescott made a statement on the referendums for establishing regional assemblies in the English regions, which, following consultation, would be held first in the north-east, the north-west and Yorkshire and Humber. David Davis questioned whether the total of only 8,000 replies nationally really justified any referendums. In a protest against the Government's handling of the Licensing Bill, Conservative MPs forced a debate and division on a motion on the Speaker's absence, usually passed on the nod.

CONSTITUTIONAL UPSET IN RESHUFFLE

Following the Government reshuffle, the Speaker of the House, Michael Martin, ordered the Prime Minister to make a statement to the House on 18 June on the changes to government departments that the reshuffle entailed; these included the proposed abolition of the post of Lord Chancellor and the setting up of a supreme court. Mr Blair thought such reforms 'are essential acts of constitutional modernisation' and were, in any case, part of a consultation process. Iain Duncan Smith disagreed: 'last week the Prime Minister ripped up the constitution in a matter of hours, without consultation ... as though our constitution were the Prime Minister's personal plaything and as though only he had the right to make a final decision'. David Blunkett published a consultation paper outlining proposals to help prevent and tackle the consequences of domestic violence, which was welcomed by the Opposition parties. On 19 June, Alistair Darling, Secretary of State for Transport and Scotland following the reshuffle, made a statement on the results of the Strategic Rail Authority's consultation on rail fares, with proposals that would 'reflect a realistic balance between what the travelling public pays and what the taxpayer contributes'. Tim Collins thought that the Government had produced 'later trains, slower trains and now vastly more expensive trains'. Liberal Democrat spokesperson Don Foster wondered how 'he could seriously believe that further fare increases will persuade people to get out of their cars and onto rail'.

On 23 June, Tony Blair reported on the outcome of the European Council in Greece when the Council had received the draft constitutional treaty prepared by the European Convention under Valery Giscard d'Estaing. He believed that 'with Europe at a crucial point of evolution, this nation has to have the confidence to stride forward in Europe, not hang back'. Iain Duncan Smith repeated his call for a referendum on the new European constitution. On 24 June, David Blunkett made a statement on the breach of security at Windsor Castle during a party to celebrate the 21st birthday of Prince William, an incident which was 'wholly unacceptable'. This was followed by a statement by the new Health Secretary, John Reid, on the publication of a White Paper on genetics and health care, welcomed by the Opposition parties. On 26 June, Margaret Beckett reported on the successful outcome of the final negotiations on the reform of the Common Agricultural Policy (CAP), getting 'the best settlement for UK farmers, consumers, taxpayers and the environment and laying the foundations for a successful outcome at the World Trade Organisation negotiations in Mexico later in the year'. David Lidington feared the Government 'have been stitched up yet again by a Franco-German alliance that gives precious little credit for the concessions granted on so many European issues that the Government have been ready to make'.

On 30 June, John Prescott published a White Paper on the fire and rescue service: 'we want to build on what is good and tackle those areas where there are shortcomings, many of which have been exposed in the course of the dispute'.

On 7 July, Chris Mullin, who returned to the Government as a junior Foreign Office minister in the reshuffle, answered an Urgent Question from Douglas Hogg on the detention and trial of two UK nationals held by the USA in Guantanamo Bay; he admitted, 'we have strong reservations about the military commission ... If there were any suggestion that the death penalty might be sought in these cases, we would raise the strongest possible objections'. On 9 July, Charles Clarke published a White Paper on the Government's skills strategy, intended 'finally to tackle the skills weaknesses that have dogged us for so long'. Damian Green called it 'a timid half-hearted disappointment that does not measure up to the importance of the task'. Alistair Darling made a statement about the next stage in implementing the Government's transport investment programme, detailing his decisions on a number of road projects and publishing a consultation document on how to get the best out of existing road space and the possibilities opened up by new technologies.

On 14 July, the Lord Chancellor, Lord Falconer of Thoroton, made a statement in the House of Lords on proposals for constitutional reform, covering judicial appointments, the setting-up of a supreme court and the future of QCs, to 'create a modern legal system which builds on its current independence and quality, ensuring a better justice system serving the public'. The Conservative Leader in the Lords, Lord Strathclyde, feared 'if the result of the most botched reshuffle in living memory were to be botched and hasty legal reform, we shall all regret it for many years indeed'. For the Liberal Democrats, Lord Goodhart felt 'however clumsy and cackhanded the method by which they were introduced ... we must take the view that we support them'.

On 17 July, the last day before the summer recess, Charles Clarke made a statement on the funding of schools for 2004–5 and 2005–6, guaranteeing every school would receive at least a minimum increase in its funding per pupil to ensure no repeat of this year's problems. 'I recognise this has been a difficult year ... I believe the steps I have outlined today provide a realistic framework of stability and certainty for the next two years.' Damian Green felt 'the crisis ... has been both hugely unnecessary and damaging to our schools'. Liberal Democrat spokesperson Phil Willis thought Mr Clarke 'ought to be ashamed of the cowardly way in which he sneaked it out on the very day that schools go into recess for the summer, when they can do nothing about it'. Labour MP Clive Betts then made a personal statement on the report of the Standards and Privileges committee that recommended he be suspended from the House for a week over his 'errors of judgement' in supporting the application of his Brazilian researcher for a visa.

The House of Commons rose for the summer recess on 17 July 2003. Under the new regime, it returned for two weeks' business in September before rising until mid October for the party conference recess. The House of Lords rose on 18 July. The row over the 'dodgy' dossier and the future of Tony Blair, however, showed no sign of abating as the Houses broke for the summer.

PUBLIC ACTS OF PARLIAMENT

This list of Public Acts commences with five Public Acts which received the royal assent before 1 September 2002. Those Public Acts which follow received the royal assent after 31 August 2002. The date stated after each Act is the date on which it came into effect; c. indicates the chapter number of each Act.

Finance Act 2002 c.23, 24 July 2002. Grants certain duties, alters others, and amends the law relating to the national debt and the public revenue, and makes further provision in connection with finance.

Export Control Act 2002 c.28, various dates, to be appointed. Makes provision to enable controls to be imposed on the exportation of goods, the transfer of technology, the provision of technical assistance overseas and activities connected with trade in controlled goods; and for connected purposes.

Proceeds of Crime Act 2002 c.29, various dates, some to be appointed. Establishes the Assets Recovery Agency and makes provision about the appointment of its director and his functions (including Revenue functions); provides for confiscation orders in relation to persons who benefit from criminal conduct and for restraint orders to prohibit dealing with property, allows the recovery of property which is or represents property obtained through unlawful conduct or which is intended to be used in unlawful conduct; makes provision about money laundering, investigations relating to benefit from criminal conduct or to property which is or represents property obtained through unlawful conduct or to money laundering; makes provision to give effect to overseas requests and orders made where property is found or believed to be obtained through criminal conduct; and for connected purposes.

Police Reform Act 2002 c.30, various dates, some to be appointed. Makes new provision about the supervision, administration, functions and conduct of police forces, police officers and other persons serving with, or carrying out functions in relation to, the police; amends police powers and provides for the exercise of police powers by persons who are not police officers; amends the law relating to anti-social behaviour orders, and the law relating to sex offender orders; and for connected purposes.

Education Act 2002 c.32, various dates, some to be appointed. Makes provision about education, training and childcare.

Copyright (Visually Impaired Persons) Act 2002 c.33, various dates, some to be appointed. Permits, without infringement of copyright, the transfer of copyright works to formats accessible to visually impaired persons.

Employee Share Schemes Act 2002 c.34, repealed with effect from income tax year 2003–4 and corporation tax accounting periods after 5 April 2003. Makes provision relating to employee share schemes; and for connected purposes.

Public Trustee (Liability and Fees) Act 2002 c.35, 7 November 2002. Amends the Public Trustee Act 1906 in respect of the liability and fees of the Public Trustee; and for connected purposes.

Tobacco Advertising and Promotion Act 2002 c.36, various dates. Controls the advertising and promotion of tobacco products; and for connected purposes.

Private Hire Vehicles (Carriage of Guide Dogs etc.) Act 2002 c.37, various dates, some to be appointed. Makes provision for the carriage of disabled persons accompanied by guide dogs, hearing dogs or other assistance dogs by drivers and operators of private hire vehicles; and for connected purposes.

Adoption and Children Act 2002 c.38, various dates, some to be appointed. Restates and amends the law relating to adoption; makes further amendments of the law relating to children; amends section 93 of the Local Government Act 2000; and for connected purposes.

Commonwealth Act 2002 c.39, 7 January 2003. Amends the law with respect to the Commonwealth Institute; makes provision in connection with the admission of Cameroon and Mozambique to the Commonwealth; and for connected purposes.

Enterprise Act 2002 c.40, various dates, some to be appointed. Establishes and provides for the functions of the Office of Fair Trading, the Competition Appeal Tribunal and the Competition Service; makes provision about mergers and market structures and conduct; amends the constitution and functions of the Competition Commission; creates an offence for those entering into certain anti-competitive agreements; provides for the disqualification of directors of companies engaging in certain anti-competitive practices; makes other provision about competition law; amends the law relating to the protection of the collective interests of consumers; makes further provision about the disclosure of information obtained under competition and consumer legislation; amends the Insolvency Act 1986 and makes other provision about insolvency; and for connected purposes.

Nationality, Immigration and Asylum Act 2002 c.41, various dates, some to be appointed. Makes provision about nationality, immigration and asylum; creates offences in connection with international traffic in prostitution; makes provision about international projects connected with migration; and for connected purposes.

Animal Health Act 2002 c.42, various dates. Amends the 1981 Act.

Consolidated Fund (No. 2) Act 2002 c.43, 17 December 2002. Authorises the use of resources for the service of the years ending on 31 March 2003 and 2004 and applies certain sums out of the Consolidated Fund to the service of the years ending on 31 March 2003 and 2004.

Appropriation (No. 2) Act 2002 c.44, 17 December 2002. Modifies limits on non-operating appropriations in aid set for the year that ended 31 March 2002.

Income Tax (Earnings and Pensions) Act 2003 c.1, for the purposes of income tax, for the tax year 2003–4 and subsequent tax years, and for the purposes of corporation tax, for accounting periods ending after 5 April 2003. Restates, with minor changes, certain enactments relating to income tax on employment income, pension income and social security income; and for connected purposes.

Consolidated Fund Act 2003 c.2, 20 March 2003. Authorises the use of resources for the service of the years ending on 31 March 2002 and 2003 and applies certain sums out of the Consolidated Fund to the service of the years ending on 31 March 2002 and 2003.

Northern Ireland Assembly Elections Act 2003 c.3, 20 March 2003. Makes provision about the date of the poll for the election of the next Northern Ireland Assembly, and for disregarding certain days for the purposes of the period after a poll within which an Assembly must meet; and for connected purposes.

Health (Wales) Act 2003 c.4, various dates, some to be appointed. Makes provision about community health councils in Wales; establishes and makes provision about the Wales Centre for Health; and makes provision for the establishment of, and otherwise about, Health Professions Wales.

Community Care (Delayed Discharges etc.) Act 2003 c.5, various dates, some to be appointed. Makes provision requiring social services authorities to make payments in cases where the discharge of patients is delayed for reasons relating to the provision of community care services or services for carers; and enables the Secretary of State and the National Assembly for Wales to require certain community care services and services for carers provided by social services authorities to be free of charge to persons receiving those services.

Police (Northern Ireland) Act 2003 c.6, various dates, some to be appointed. Makes provision about policing in Northern Ireland and the exercise of police powers in Northern Ireland by persons who are not police officers; and amends the Police and Criminal Evidence (Northern Ireland) Order 1989.

European Parliament (Representation) Act 2003 c.7, various dates, some to be appointed. Makes provision enabling alterations to be made to the total number of members of the European Parliament to be elected for the United Kingdom and to their distribution between the electoral regions; and for and in connection with the establishment of an electoral region including Gibraltar for the purposes of European Parliamentary elections; and for connected purposes.

National Minimum Wage (Enforcement Notices) Act 2003 c.8, 8 July 2003. Makes provision enabling an enforcement notice under National Minimum Wage Act 1998, s.19 to impose a requirement under s.19(2) in relation to a person, whether or not a requirement under s.19(1) is, or may be, imposed in relation to that or any other person; and to limit the pay reference periods in respect of which a requirement under s.19(2) may be imposed.

Electricity (Miscellaneous Provisions) Act 2003 c.9, 8 May 2003. Makes provision in connection with the provision of financial assistance to, or the acquisition of any securities of or any part of the undertaking or assets of, British Energy plc or any of its subsidiaries; provides for the repeal of Part 2 of the Electricity Act 1989; amends Schedule 12 to that Act and makes provision for undertakings to make grants under that Schedule to be disregarded for tax purposes.

Regional Assemblies (Preparations) Act 2003 c.10, part on 8 May 2003, the remainder on 8 July 2003. Makes provision for the holding of referendums about the establishment of elected assemblies for the regions of England (except London); for reviewing the structure of local government in regions where the holding of a referendum is under consideration; for the holding of referendums about options for implementing the recommendations of such reviews; for implementing the recommendations of such reviews; for the Electoral Commission to give advice in connection with the establishment of assemblies; for payment of grant in connection with the activities of regional chambers; and for incurring expenditure in preparation for assemblies and in connection with the transfer of functions to them.

Industrial Development (Financial Assistance) Act 2003 c.11, 8 May 2003. Amends Industrial Development Act 1982 s.8(5).

Northern Ireland Assembly (Elections and Periods of Suspension) Act 2003 c.12, 15 May 2003. Makes further provision about the election of the next Northern Ireland Assembly; makes further provision about periods when Northern Ireland Act 2000, s.1 is in force; and for connected purposes.

Appropriation Act 2003 c.13, 10 July 2003. Authorises the use of resources for the service of the year ending 31 March 2004 and applies certain sums out of the Consolidated Fund to the service of the year ending 31 March 2004; appropriates the further supply authorised in this session of Parliament; and repeals certain Consolidated Fund and Appropriation Acts.

Finance Act 2003 c.14, 10 July 2003. Grants certain duties, alters others, and amends the law relating to the national debt and the public revenue, and makes further provision in connection with finance.

Co-operatives and Community Benefit Societies Act 2003 c.15, various dates, some to be appointed. Enables the law relating to co-operatives and community benefit societies registered under the Industrial and Provident Societies Act 1965 to be amended so as to bring it into conformity with certain aspects of the law relating to companies; permits a registered society whose business is conducted for the benefit of the community to provide that its assets are dedicated permanently for that purpose; and for connected purposes.

Marine Safety Act 2003 c.16, 10 September 2003. Makes provision about the giving of directions in respect of ships for purposes relating to safety or pollution and about the taking of action to enforce, in connection with, or in lieu of, directions; and about fire-fighting in connection with marine incidents; and for connected purposes.

Licensing Act 2003 c.17, various dates, some to be appointed. Makes provision about the regulation of the sale and supply of alcohol, the provision of entertainment and the provision of late-night refreshment, about offences relating to alcohol and for connected purposes.

Sunday Working (Scotland) Act 2003 c.18, various dates, some to be appointed. Makes provision as to the rights of shop workers and betting workers under the law of Scotland in relation to Sunday working; and for connected purposes.

Aviation (Offences) Act 2003 c.19, 10 September 2003. Makes provision about the enforcement of certain offences connected with aviation.

Railways and Transport Safety Act 2003 c.20, various dates, some to be appointed. Makes provision about railways, including tramways; and about transport safety; and for connected purposes.

Communications Act 2003 c.21, various dates, some to be appointed. Confers functions on the Office of Communications; makes provision about the regulation of the provision of electronic communications, networks and services and of the use of the electro-magnetic spectrum; makes provision about the regulation of broadcasting and of the provision of television and radio services; makes provision about mergers involving newspaper and other media enterprises and, in that connection, amends the Enterprise Act 2002; and for connected purposes.

WHITE PAPERS, REPORTS ETC

This section provides an outline of a selection of White Papers and Reports that have been published in the last year. For further information visit www.official-documents.co.uk or www. parliament.co.uk. Alternatively, visit the websites of individual government departments.

'Protecting the Public: Strengthening Protection against Sex Offenders and Reforming the Law on Sexual Offences' was presented to Parliament in November 2002 by the Secretary of State for the Home Department. This White Paper outlines proposals to strengthen the law on sex offenders and to modernise penalties and the law in this area. It seeks to clarify and revise the laws on indecency, sexual assault and rape and focuses extensively on sexual crimes against children. The paper seeks to reform in particular, the Sexual Offences Act 1956 and to bring it up-to-date so that existing gaps in the law are filled. The paper puts forward proposals to reform certain legislation contained within the 1956 Act, such as the rule against double jeopardy and the law on the admissibility of previous convictions.

'The Future of Higher Education' was presented to Parliament by the Secretary of State for Education and Skills in January 2003. This White Paper sets out the Government's measures to bring major improvements to the funding of research within universities, to improve and reward good teaching, to enable and encourage more people from poorer backgrounds to enter higher education, to restore grants and help with fee costs, to abolish up-front tuition fees for all students, to allow universities to secure a contribution of up to £3,000 per year to the cost of each course, paid when graduates are in secure work, and to help universities build up endowment funds. The paper also outlines the Government's promise to increase spending on research in 2005–6 by £1.25 billion.

'Respect and Responsibility – Taking a Stand Against Anti-Social Behaviour' was presented to Parliament by the Secretary of State for the Home Department in March 2003. This White Paper sets out the Government's next steps for dealing with the problem of anti-social behaviour at all levels within society. Included in the paper are proposals for a cross-section of society from local councils, community support officers and police officers to the general public, to deal with a wide range of anti-social behaviour.

'Safety and Justice: The Government's Proposals on Domestic Violence' was presented to Parliament by the Secretary of State for the Home Department in June 2003. This consultation paper sets out the Government's new strategy for dealing with domestic violence, and builds on the proposals in the 2002 *'Justice for All'* White Paper. The paper looks at the action the Government is taking to educate people about domestic violence and how best to change attitudes; working with agencies to address risk factors and identify victims of abuse at an earlier stage; the provision of information to victims to help them gain access to legal protection and support services; and preventing domestic violence offenders from re-offending.

'Consultation Paper on Proposed Changes to Publicly Funded Immigration and Asylum Work' was issued by the Department for Constitutional Affairs in June 2003. This paper sets out for consultation proposed changes to the way in which publicly funded legal services in the areas of immigration and asylum are delivered. Since the Government is committed to using the resources available for funding this area of legal work economically, the paper outlines two main proposals to enable the government to deliver effective and sustainable services within an agreed budget. These proposals state that each client will receive a unique file number, enabling the monitoring of costs, they will only be allowed up to a set maximum number of hours of legal advice in connection with his or her case, and a system of accreditation will be introduced, ensuring that payment of public funds will only be made to individual advisers who are accredited.

'Command Paper on Draft Civil Contingencies Bill' was launched for consultation on 19 June 2003 by Douglas Alexander, Minister for the Cabinet Office. The draft Bill, with accompanying non-legislative measures, seeks to deliver a single framework for civil protection in the UK. The paper contains proposals which will modernise the legislative tools available to the Government to deal with the most serious emergencies. It proposes a two-tier duty to be introduced at a local level for responders to codify existing best practice, and seeks to introduce a new regional civil protection tier which will work to ensure consistency of activity across and between tiers.

'Consultation Note on Proposals to Amend the National Minimum Wage Act 1998' was issued on 12 August 2003 by the Department for Trade and Industry. This consultation paper puts forward proposals for possible amendments to the National Minimum Wage Act 1998, in anticipation of the forthcoming Employment Relations Bill, scheduled for the 2003–4 Parliamentary session. It presents the Department of Trade and Industry with an opportunity to make some minor amendments to the Act. The paper discusses proposed amendments under Sections 13, 15, 17, 19, and 21 of the National Minimum Wage Act 1998.

SCIENCE AND DISCOVERY

NORTH SEA IMPACT CRATER

Around 160 impact structures, resulting from asteroid or comet collisions, have been identified on Earth's surface. Perhaps best known are Meteor Crater in Arizona, and the 300 km-diameter Chicxulub structure in the Yucatan peninsula; the latter is associated by many with the demise of the dinosaurs 65 million years ago. Discovery of the UK's first impact structure was announced in the journal *Nature* in August 2002 by Simon Stewart and Philip Allen, following examination of three-dimensional seismic reflection data obtained during exploration of the North Sea Trent gas field in the early 1990s.

The data revealed a 3 km-diameter 'bowl' with a central peak, surrounded by two zones of concentric ring structures, giving an overall diameter of 20 km. Located at 54°14′ N., 1°14′ E., 130 km east of the Humber estuary, the structure has been named Silverpit after a nearby sea-floor channel. The crater is buried by between 300 and 1500 metres of sediment, in turn overlain by 40 metres of seawater. Magnetic data rule out a volcanic origin, while seismic studies argue against the structure having been formed by intrusion of a salt dome from below; an impact origin seems most likely.

The Silverpit crater is remarkably well-preserved compared with other, eroded terrestrial impact structures. It is believed that the crater was formed about 60 million years ago as the result of the impact of a 120-metre diameter body into seabed clay. Its unusual state of preservation is due to rapid coverage by sediments. Silverpit bears more similarity to impact formations on Jupiter's icy satellites than to those on Earth's rocky Moon. Further study of Silverpit's geology may afford greater insight into the processes involved in impact crater formation.

DISCOVERIES AT SOLAR SYSTEM FRINGE

The Solar System is thought to be surrounded by a halo of small icy bodies known as the Oort Cloud, out to a distance perhaps one-third of the way to the nearest star. An inwards extension from the Oort Cloud forms a broad disk, called the Kuiper Belt, beyond the orbit of Neptune (30.6 astronomical units from the Sun; one AU is equivalent to Earth's orbital distance of 150 million km). Gravitational perturbation of bodies from this region is believed to be the source of short-period comets.

Since 1992, searches using large telescopes have discovered over 600 bodies orbiting in this region, confirming the belt's existence. In October 2002, Chad Trujillo and Mike Brown of the California Institute of Technology reported their discovery of the largest known Kuiper Belt Object (KBO) so far. Quaoar, named after the creation force worshipped by the Native American tribe which once lived in the Los Angeles area, has a diameter of 1200 km, which is about half the diameter of Pluto and significantly larger than the previous record-holding KBO Varuna (900 km).

The discovery was made using the historic 1.2 metre Oschin Telescope at Mount Palomar on 4 June 2002, and lends further weight to the suggestion that Pluto is simply the largest of a population of several thousand KBOs rather than a planet in its own right. Quaoar takes

288 years to complete its slightly eccentric orbit at a mean distance of 43 AU from the Sun.

The finding that several KBOs possess satellites has presented some interesting challenges for orbital dynamicists. A number of asteroids in the Solar System's Main Belt between Mars and Jupiter are known to have satellites whose presence can be accounted for by gravitational capture following collisions. However, it is more difficult to explain why eight KBOs, including the Pluto-Charon system, have relatively large moons orbiting them.

Two mechanisms have been proposed for the formation of binary KBOs. In the first, two similarly-sized objects may collide under the gravitational influence of a third, merging and becoming bound to this third body as a satellite. Alternatively, transient binding between two bodies may be rendered permanent by loss of energy from the pair to passing smaller objects, a process of 'dynamical friction'. Observation with the Hubble Space Telescope may tell astronomers which mechanism predominates; the first predicts more distant orbits than the second. If the second, energy-loss mechanism is correct, the prediction is that up to 5 per cent of KBOs may have large satellites.

SEA-FLOOR METHANE

Around continental margins, at depths of more than 300 metres, huge gas deposits are found in the form of hydrates, just above and in the upper levels of the sea-floor. The commonest gas hydrate contains methane (a by-product of decay of organic material), forming a lattice-structure material similar to ice. As well as providing a possible energy source, these gas hydrates may be important climatically; methane is a more potent greenhouse gas than carbon dioxide, and according to some researchers, catastrophic release of sea-floor deposits may have contributed to episodes of global warming in Earth's past.

Increasing temperatures at depth impose a lower level to which gas hydrates can form and remain stable in sea-floor sediments. Once thought to be a fairly even layer, this 'base of gas hydrate stability' has been found to be highly structured on the continental shelf of North America. New higher-resolution seismological studies indicate gaps and 'chimney' structures probably associated with geological faults. Gas hydrate material in the vicinity of these chimneys appears to be more susceptible to temperature changes; here, gas may dissociate from water and be rapidly released. Chimneys may act as natural safety valves, preventing pressure build-up and making catastrophic release less likely.

The climatic influence of methane release from sea-floor gas hydrate deposits remains to be determined; much of the methane may be oxidised to carbon dioxide by sea water, with only a small proportion making it to the surface and thence into the atmosphere.

MAPPING THE MOUSE

In recent years, determining the complete DNA sequences of a range of organisms has come to be seen as a key step towards understanding gene function and regulation. Conservation of some genes over the course of evolutionary time can be indicative of common ancestry, while others may be found only in advanced organisms. Sequencing of the entire human DNA complement (the genome) was essentially completed in 2001, but uncovering the precise functions of some of our genes will depend on continued research with simpler animals. To this end, publication in 2002 of the physical map and draft sequence of the mouse genome by collaborating scientists in the UK, USA and Canada represents important progress.

The physical map, showing the order and organisation of genes in the 2,800 million base mouse genome, reveals some interesting data on the similarities between mice and men. *Homo sapiens* and *Mus musculus* show substantial correspondence in the arrangement (synteny) of genes on their chromosomes. In all, about 180 regions have been identified in which the gene order is conserved between mouse and human. This may have implications for sequencing other mammalian genomes; if gene synteny is highly conserved across mammalian species, genomic sequencing may be more readily achievable.

The draft version of the mouse genome sequence indicates that 99 per cent of its 30,000 genes are shared with humans. The fully deciphered mouse genome provides a major leap forward for studies of mammalian gene function. For about 20 years, scientists have been able to create 'knockout' mice, in which particular genes have been disabled; such studies have obvious implications for addressing human genetic disease, and the availability of the complete genome sequence will increase the precision with which knockouts can be engineered. The high degree of conserved synteny between mouse and human could also help close the final few gaps in the human genome.

MALARIA PARASITES AND VECTOR SEQUENCED

Malaria remains a serious cause of disease in sub-Saharan Africa, responsible for 2.7 million deaths a year, a million of them among children. As part of the drive to tackle the disease, a major international effort began in 1996 to obtain the full genome DNA sequence for the protozoan parasite *Plasmodium falciparum* which causes the most severe form of human malaria. Details of the completed sequence were published in *Nature* in October 2002.

Construction of stable templates for sequencing was rendered difficult by the unusually high (80 per cent) A:T richness of *P. falciparum* DNA. The final full sequence (23 million bases of DNA, arranged in 14 chromosomes) was determined from 500,000 individual subfragments. A total of 5,279 postulated genes was identified, 60 per cent of which are of as yet unknown function and appear to be unique to malaria parasites. *P. falciparum* lacks genes coding for the equivalents (homologues) of many metabolic enzymes and membrane-located receptors for uptake of metabolic precursors, consistent with its parasitic lifestyle; nutrients are largely scavenged from infected host cells.

In parallel, the genome sequence of *Plasmodium yoelii yoelii*, which infects rodents and has long been used as a laboratory model, was also published. Studies of the sequence show that the arrangement (synteny) of genes encoding essential 'housekeeping' proteins is highly conserved between *P. yoelii yoelii* and *P. falciparum*, but that the intergenic regions vary considerably.

Comparative genomic studies will be further extended by the ongoing sequencing of *Plasmodium vivax*, which produces a less severe form of human malaria. Lessons from *Plasmodium* species can also be expected to apply to

sequencing of other protozoan parasites, including *Toxoplasma* and *Theilerea*.

Completion of the *P. falciparum* genome sequence, a considerable achievement, may be viewed as a preliminary step in the concerted effort to identify targets for new effective antimalarial drugs and candidate antigens for vaccine production. Meanwhile, the simultaneous announcement in the American journal *Science* of the complete genome sequence of the mosquito *Anopheles gambiae* should further development of more effective strategies for controlling the vector which spreads malaria.

GENOMIC SECRETS OF 'SIMPLER' ORGANISMS UNCOVERED

While publication of genome sequences for the mouse and for the malaria parasite and its insect vector have grabbed the headlines, progress in sequencing less glamorous organisms continues apace. Deciphering the genomes of these ostensibly simpler species plays a vital role in understanding the workings of more highly evolved organisms.

April 2003 saw the publication of the draft genome sequence for the familiar bread mould *Neurospora crassa*, a fungus which in the 1930s was used as a model in studies leading to the recognition that proteins are encoded by genes. *N. crassa* has a total genome of about 42.9 million bases, encoding an estimated 10,000 genes (around twice as many as the yeasts *Saccharomyces cerevisiae* and *Schizosaccharomyces pombe*). Only 1,400 of these have so far been identified as homologues of genes in other eukaryotic (non-bacterial) species.

N. crassa has very little redundancy in its genome; duplicated gene sequences are eliminated by a mechanism of repeat-induced point mutation (RIP), which may be a defence against mobile genetic elements including viruses. Regions where RIP appears to have acted are further 'silenced' by DNA methylation. *Neurospora* shows a circadian growth rhythm; studies of the genome sequence should aid in understanding how this is regulated.

Another long-studied organism, the motile slime mould *Dictyostelium discoideum,* is undergoing sequencing, with preliminary results for one of its six chromosomes reported in July 2002. Also described as a soil amoeba, *Dictyostelium* has an estimated 11,000 genes in 34 million bases of DNA (similar to the genome size in *Neurospora*). Like *Plasmodium, Dictyostelium* shows a high A:T content in its DNA, presenting problems for sequencing. Early indications are that *Dictyostelium* has more in common with higher organisms than it does with, for instance, yeasts, at the gene level.

In December 2002, the draft genome sequence of the sea squirt *Ciona intestalis* was published. Although a simple invertebrate, this organism lies on the vertebrate evolutionary line and it is hoped that its genome will provide clues to the establishment of the more advanced body plan which followed. Sea squirts and vertebrates last shared a common ancestor some 550 million years ago at the time of the so-called Cambrian explosion, when a diverse range of animal species arose. *C. intestalis* has 16,000 genes spanning 160 million bases of DNA – comparable to the fruitfly or nematode worm, but much smaller than the typical 30,000 gene complement of vertebrates. Interestingly, *Ciona* appears to have acquired a bacterial gene – perhaps via a long-lost symbiotic relationship – for production of a cellulose-like component of its tough outer membrane.

ANTHRAX GENOME

Completion of the 5.23 million base genome sequence of *Bacillus anthracis* (from essentially the same strain used in suspected postal bioterrorism attacks in the USA during late 2001) was announced in June 2003. The genome encodes 5,508 predicted open reading frames. Comparison of the completed sequence with those from other *Bacillus* species, including the food-poisoning organism *B. cereus* and *B. thuringiensis* (an insect pathogen used in pesticides) has produced some interesting and unexpected conclusions.

Many of the specific virulence factors in Bacilli have been localised to genes carried on self-replicating extrachromosomal DNA molecules known as plasmids; *B. anthracis* has two such plasmids, pXO1 and pXO2. Genomic studies suggest that a 'pathogenicity island' on pXO1, coupled with a mutation in the gene for a regulatory protein (PlcR) which controls expression of a wide range of other genes, including many involved in virulence, are evolutionarily recent developments which distinguish *B. anthracis* from its close relatives. Perhaps the most surprising finding, however, is that genes for several of the virulence factors are carried on the chromosome. These include haemolysins and phospholipases. The gene repertoire of the *Bacillus* chromosome goes beyond the basic metabolic essentials.

In evolutionary terms, this tends to suggest that *B. anthracis* has an ancestry from a parasitic or saprophytic species – scavenging nutrients from living or dead tissue – rather than being a simple soil-living opportunist. Introduction of further virulence factors via plasmids has allowed exploitation of a wider range of hosts, emphasising once again how easily such traits can be transferred between bacteria by mobile genetic elements such as plasmids.

COMET'S CLOSE SOLAR PASSAGE

Comet scientists have had a mixed year, with the loss of the Contour probe (originally scheduled to visit several comets) during firing of its rocket motor on 15 August 2002, and the postponement of the February 2003 launch of Rosetta following problems with the Ariane 5 launcher. Rosetta will now launch in February 2004, retargeted to meet Comet 67P/Churyomo-Gerasimonko in 2014.

However, the veteran Solar and Heliospheric Observatory (SOHO) spacecraft, stationed around the gravitationally stable L$_1$ Lagrangian point 1.5 million km towards the Sun from Earth, offered spectacular views of Comet 2002V1 NEAT rounding the Sun on 18 February 2003. Discovered in November 2002, the comet was a reasonable binocular-visible object for observers in the northern hemisphere during late January before it moved too close to the Sun for conventional viewing. As seen in the SOHO LASCO C3 coronagraph, Comet NEAT became very bright with a strong, sweeping tail. Its closest passage (perihelion) to the Sun – 15 million km (0.1 AU) – coincided with a dramatic coronal mass ejection in the inner solar atmosphere but this had no obvious effect on the comet, which will return in 37,000 years.

SOHO's coronagraphs have been used to observe comets in the past, the brightest previous example being 96P/Macholz in January 2002. Over 600 small sungrazing comets have now been discovered in the SOHO coronagraphs' fields of view since the spacecraft's 1995 launch. These comets belong to a handful of 'families' resulting from the breakup of larger progenitors

in the distant past, and nearly all appear to be destroyed by the Sun's intense heat during perihelion passage.

Meanwhile, comets 2001Q4 NEAT and 2002V7 LINEAR – further discoveries by automated search telescopes at Mount Palomar and White Sands, New Mexico, respectively – are expected to become bright naked-eye objects in April and May 2004.

EVAPORATING EXOPLANET

Since the first confirmed detection in 1991, astronomers have discovered over a hundred planets orbiting other stars. Most of these extrasolar planets are bigger than Jupiter, the largest of our Sun's family, and have been found by measuring precisely tiny shifts in the spectral patterns of solar-type stars at distances between 20 and 200 light years from Earth.

An alternative detection method, based on observing the very small drop in brightness produced when a planet crosses in front of (transits) the star in line of sight, has turned up a couple of interesting exoplanets. One is a body probably comprised mostly of hydrogen, about a third as large again as Jupiter and containing 0.65 times Jupiter's mass, orbiting a faint star designated HD209458.

HD209458 is a Sun-like star, 150 light years away in the constellation of Pegasus. The planet's transits dim the star's apparent brightness by 1.5 per cent, and its orbital period has been measured as a mere 3.5 days, putting it very close to the primary. Ultraviolet wavelength observations by Alfred Vidal-Mdjar (Institut d'Astrophysique, Paris) and his colleagues, using Hubble Space Telescope, show that the planet is surrounded by a hydrogen atmosphere 600,000 km in diameter, which is being steadily stripped away by HD 209458's stellar wind – rather like a comet losing material from its nucleus into a tail.

Some workers have speculated that 'hot Jupiters' cannot be found within about 7 million km of their host star, since they may rapidly 'evaporate' by a mechanism similar to that which removes material from the HD209458 planet.

DINOSAUR POINTERS ON EARLY FLIGHT

The evolutionary lineage of modern birds can be traced back in the fossil record through the well-known *Archaeopteryx* to the bipedal carnivorous dinosaurs classified as theropods. The evidence suggests that some theropods evolved feathers before the development of flight. How flight was first achieved has been an area of debate among palaeontologists – did the earliest ancestors of modern birds use powered flight (wing beats) from a running start on the ground, or did they glide, launching themselves from high platforms?

Discoveries in Liaoning, China, point strongly to a gliding arboreal lifestyle for an early four-winged species. Chinese scientists analysed fossils of *Microrapter gui*, dated to the early Cretaceous period 124–128 million years ago, and found it had feathers on both its forelimbs and legs. The presence of hindwings appears incompatible with a ground-based lifestyle (the feathers would drag and become fouled) and the forewing structure, while similar to that of *Archaeopteryx*, is not designed for powered flight strokes. Most probably, *M. gui* glided from tree to tree, possibly in a manner similar to modern flying squirrels. The type specimen is small, with a total length of 77 cm and a long tail.

Insights into the lifestyle of a different sort of flying dinosaur, a novel pterosaur species from lower Cretaceous deposits in north-eastern Brazil, have been provided by analysis of its skull. *Thallassodromeus sethi* had an unusually large, essentially hollow bony crest on its skull. Well irrigated with blood vessels, the crest seems to have had a primary function in keeping the body cool. The lower jaw is similar to that of modern skimmer bird species, suggesting that *T. sethi* may have made its living 110 million years ago by skimming fish from just below the surface of a lagoon or the ocean. *Thallassodromeus* accordingly translates as 'sea runner'.

CELLULAR ORGANISATION REVEALED
Existing methods in both light and electron microscopy have long allowed biologists to study whole cells or, via immunofluorescence or fluorescent-tag techniques, the localisation of individual proteins. Obtaining a picture of the distribution and arrangement of small intracellular structures – organelles such as the Golgi body, or actin filaments – in the 5 to 10 nanometre size range has, however, proved more difficult. Part of the problem is that in preparing the samples for study, the cell's native structures, including, for example, membranes to which actin may be anchored, may themselves have to be disrupted, introducing experimental artifacts. The new method of cryo electron tomography (cryo ET), pioneered by Wolfgang Baumeister and colleagues at the Max Planck Institute for Biochemistry in Martinsried, Germany, offers the possibility of examining undisrupted organelle distribution and structure.

Cryo ET relies on rapid vitrification (flash freezing) of the sample, which is examined as thin layers in an electron microscope. The sample is tilted through a range of angles, and successive two-dimensional images at differing presentations to the microscope's electron beam are processed in a computer to produce a three-dimensional reconstruction.

Studies on the slime mould *Dictyostelium discoideum* reveal the power of cryo ET. As a highly motile amoeboid organism, *Dictyostelium* depends on rapid rearrangement of its actin scaffold (cytoskeleton). Cryo ET has shown fine detail of actin filaments and their cross-links with one another and to the cell membrane. The technique resolves ribosomes 'decorating' the endoplasmic reticulum, distributed throughout the cell, at sites of protein synthesis. Also revealed are the protein-degrading proteasomes, elusive structures previously only hinted at in whole-cell electron micrographs. Anticipated further improvements in resolution may allow detailed study of the proteins involved in linking the cytoskeleton to the membrane, and how this effects cell motility.

DISSECTING PROTEASOME FUNCTION
While much work has considered how eukaryotic cells regulate protein synthesis, it is only recently that studies have been carried out on protein degradation. Degradation is an important process, both for removing proteins which are no longer required and for destroying those which may be aberrant. The major cellular machinery for protein degradation is a small structure called the proteasome. Proteasomes are distributed throughout the cell, and may themselves account for as much as 1 per cent of cellular protein; their abundance and widespread distribution in the cell has recently been confirmed by the novel imaging technique of cryo electron tomography.

The proteasome consists of a complex of proteins. Degradation is carried out by enzymes (proteases) which form a cylindrical core; protein digestion occurs on the cylinder's inner surface. At either end of the cylinder is a second complex, whose principal role is regulatory. Recent work has highlighted the nature of some of the regulatory complex 'lid' proteins, including an enzyme critically required for removal of ubiquitin from proteins targeted for degradation.

Ubiquitin is a small protein (76 amino acids) found in all eukaryotic cells. Proteins are commonly regulated by attachment of a single ubiquitin molecule. Those destined for degradation, however, are frequently coupled to chains of several ubiquitin molecules. It is this polyubiquitination signal which is recognised by the proteasome's regulatory complex, leading to the protein being bound, then fed into the core. Before it can enter the proteasome core, the protein must be freed from the polyubiquitin chain. Results published in autumn 2002 show that this vital role is co-ordinated and carried out by a zinc-dependent metalloprotease in the regulatory complex identified as POH1. The protein is encoded by a gene called rpn11 in yeast; genetic analysis shows this to be essential for viability, underlining the importance of deubiquitination for correct degradation of unwanted cellular proteins, and the requirement for ubiquitin recycling. Such studies also re-emphasise the usefulness of yeast genetics as a tool for dissecting protein function at molecular level.

ANCESTRY OF MAN'S BEST FRIEND
While it has long been accepted that the domestic dog originated from the close association of wild wolves with early man, determining when and where the relationship took hold is difficult. Studies of mitochondrial DNA sequences from fossil dog bones, and comparison of these with sequences from wolves and other canine species including coyotes and jackals, indicate that recognisably modern dogs were living with humans in central Europe as far back as 10,000 to 14,000 years ago. The similarities in mitochondrial DNA sequences between dogs and wolves are considerable, but researchers were surprised to find sufficient differences between the two to imply an evolutionary divergence time of 135,000 years. This is clearly incompatible with the established history of mankind, and is taken to indicate that early domesticated dogs continued to interbreed with wild wolf populations.

Other mitochondrial DNA studies place the first domestication of dogs as having occurred in east Asia, and close the divergence time to a still lengthy 110,000 years. The evidence further suggests that New World domestic dogs travelled with the first humans to colonise continental North America across the Bering land bridge 10,000 to 15,000 years ago. Analyses of dog remains from pre-Columbian Peru, Bolivia and Mexico are interpreted as showing five separate dog lineages, all of essentially European origin.

CONTACT LOST WITH *PIONEER 10*
Launched on 2 March 1972, NASA's *Pioneer 10* became the first probe to make a close passage by Jupiter, on 3 December 1973, returning close-up images of the giant planet's atmospheric clouds and valuable data about its magnetosphere and radiation belts. *Pioneer 10* was also the first spacecraft to cross the asteroid belt between Mars and Jupiter, proving that the collision risk on such missions was less than had been feared. Following its Jupiter encounter, *Pioneer 10* continued onwards and out of the Solar System, crossing the orbit of Pluto in 1983, and continuing to send valuable data on the solar wind streaming outwards from the Sun.

Detailed telemetry was received from *Pioneer 10* until 1997 and finally, on 22 January 2003, scientists working at the Jet Propulsion Laboratory's Deep Space Network had their last feeble communication from the probe, by then 82 astronomical units (almost half a light-day) away. No further communication is expected, the thermocouples in the probe's plutonium power source now having failed.

Pioneer 10 will silently continue its long voyage into interstellar space, heading in the general direction of the bright star Aldebaran in Taurus, 68 light years away, a trip which will take about two million years. Both *Pioneer 10* and its sister craft *Pioneer 11* (which stopped communications in 1995) carry message plaques indicating their terrestrial origin.

LONG-LOST ROCKET RECOVERED

While *Pioneer 10* was lost during the year under review, another piece of aged space hardware was recovered on 3 September 2002. Using a 0.45 metre aperture telescope equipped with a sensitive CCD camera, the Arizona-based Canadian astronomer Bill Yeung detected a faint, fast-moving object initially thought to be a near-Earth asteroid. However, analysis of follow-up observations by the Minor Planet Center in Cambridge, Massachusetts, revealed that the object, provisionally designated J002E3, was in fact an elliptical 50-day orbit around Earth. Further calculations showed that J002E3 was probably the discarded third (SIVB) stage from an Apollo lunar mission, almost certainly *Apollo 12* which launched on 14 November 1969; the SIVB stages of subsequent missions were deliberately crashed onto the Moon as part of seismological studies, while those of Apollos 8, 10 and 11 were discarded into Sun-centred (heliocentric) orbits. The brightness and spectrum (characteristic of the titanium oxide paint used on Saturn rockets) of J002E3 further confirm its identity.

J002E3 has an interesting orbital history. After being jettisoned on sending the *Apollo 12* astronauts towards the Moon, the SIVB stage remained in a chaotic orbit around Earth until March 1971, then escaped into a heliocentric orbit. Passage close to the L_1 Lagrangian point, where the gravity of the Sun and Earth roughly balance, led to the object's recapture as a temporary satellite in April 2002.

Projecting its movements forwards showed that J002E3 should return to a heliocentric orbit in June 2003, but will probably be recaptured once more in a further 30 years.

METEORITES FALL ON RUSSIA AND USA

In an event reminiscent of the 1908 Tunguska fireball, albeit on a smaller scale, a large meteorite impact on 25 September 2002 caused devastation over a 100 square kilometre area of Siberia, 1100 km from the city of Irkutsk, and 60 km from the village of Mama. The meteorite appears to have vaporised in the stratosphere at an altitude of 30 km, and the resulting blast caused seismic tremors felt up to 95 km away. Residents in nearby villages witnessed the bright fireball associated with the meteorite's arrival, and this was also recorded by US surveillance satellites. Investigations were hindered by winter snowfall, but in June 2003 the Russian Academy of Sciences announced the identification of the impact site and the recovery of meteorite fragments.

Rather more readily recovered were hundreds of fragments from a car-sized meteorite which came down on the Chicago suburb of Park Forest shortly before midnight local time on 26 March 2003. A bright fireball was seen by hundreds of witnesses across the American Midwest, streaking northwards and ending with its breakup and sonic booms just south of Chicago. At least six houses and three cars were damaged by fragments, weighing up to 3 kg, from the rocky chondrite meteorite, which came down in a 10 km-long elliptical strewn field.

OLDEST *HOMO SAPIENS* REMAINS

The theory that modern *Homo sapiens* first arose in Africa, spreading from there to colonise other parts of the globe, gained important support with the publication in June 2003 of results from studies of three cranial fossils. A team led by Prof. Tim White from the University of California, Berkeley, found the fossil skulls near the village of Herto in the Middle Awash river valley region of Ethiopia. This region has been a rich source of important fossil finds used to trace mankind's ancestry.

The finds, from November 1997, have been accurately dated by radioisotope techniques to between 160,000 and 154,000 years ago, making these the oldest known examples of recognisably modern human remains by some 50,000 years. The skulls are from two adults and a child, and show evidence of mortuary practices, perhaps a funeral ritual.

Related fossil evidence indicates the use of stone tools to butcher bovines and hippopotamuses. These ancient humans evidently inhabited the margin of a freshwater lake. The fossils have been given the name *Homo sapiens idaltu*, 'elder' in the local Afar language. They pre-date European Neanderthals, and also have very distinct cranial features, lending weight to the 'Out of Africa' hypothesis for the origin of modern man; *Homo sapiens* arose as a distinct line in eastern Africa well before the Neanderthals made their appearance further north, ruling out the possibility that the Neanderthals could have been human ancestors.

CERN PRODUCES ANTIHYDROGEN

Understanding the fundamental forces which govern the nature of the Universe and the matter in it depends fundamentally on studies of the particle world. An important component of this is antimatter, essentially a 'mirror' equivalent of the ordinary matter which comprises the bulk of what we see around us. How matter came to predominate over antimatter in our Universe is a key question in theoretical physics; according to the accepted models, matter and antimatter should have been created in equal quantities in the Big Bang. Producing antimatter in quantities sufficient for study to provide insights into its behaviour is a major challenge for atomic physicists.

In summer 2002, the international Athena group, working at the European Centre for Nuclear Research (CERN) at Geneva, Switzerland, reported success in creating cold antihydrogen atoms (consisting of a negatively charged antiproton orbited by a positively charged positron – a mirror version of normal hydrogen's proton and electron). The antiprotons were produced in a particle accelerator, the positrons from decay of a radioactive source. The antihydrogen atoms were formed at extremely low temperatures, and detected by the characteristic signature of secondary particles produced on their annihilation as they collided with the walls of the experimental apparatus. Rather as in neutrino studies, detection is a major hurdle in this work – only 130 out of an estimated 50,000 antihydrogen atoms produced in the experiment could be detected.

The next step in such studies will be to trap antihydrogen atoms, using 'wall free' magnetic constraint at temperatures within a few degrees of absolute zero (–273°C). The low temperatures are necessary to slow movement of the antiparticles, making them less likely to escape confinement.

CERN SEEKS HIGGS BOSON
Construction work has begun on another CERN experiment, the Large Hadron Collider (LHC), which, it is hoped, should give insights into the existence and nature of the Higgs Boson, a theoretically predicted subatomic particle believed to be responsible for imparting mass to matter. Nicknamed the 'God particle', the Higgs Boson, if it can be detected, should hold the key to explaining many fundamental physical properties.

Scheduled to commence operation in 2005, the LHC is a huge collaborative venture involving 6,500 scientists from over 80 countries. With a circumference of 27 km, the LHC is designed to collide protons at high energies in extremely narrow beams about 10 microns, constrained by enormous, powerful magnets using supercooled, superconducting technology. Theory predicts that these beams should yield one Higgs Boson for every 10 trillion proton collisions; even at the expected collision rate of 800 million per second, this corresponds to only a single Higgs Boson per day!

SUNSPOT DETAILS REVEALED
Observatories around the world keep a continuous eye on the activity of our Sun, which is most obviously manifested in the form of dark sunspots whose numbers rise and fall in a roughly 11-year cycle, last reaching a peak in 2000 and 2001. Sunspots provide a unique natural 'laboratory' in which energetic magnetically driven processes can be studied, and scientists would like to learn more about how sunspot activity affects Earth and, possibly, its climate.

Typical well-developed sunspots consist of a darker (cooler) central region, the umbra, surrounded by a radial pattern of lighter filaments, the penumbra, which is still dark by comparison with the adjacent bright surface, the photosphere. Results reported in November 2002 from the Swedish 1-metre Solar Telescope on La Palma in the Canary Islands show unprecedented amounts of detail in the penumbral regions of sunspots.

Opened in May 2002, the telescope uses adaptive optics to counter the distorting effects of Earth's atmospheric turbulence. The light-gathering mirror has 19 independently controlled elements which are constantly adjusted to obtain the clearest possible image. Images from the telescope reveal penumbral filaments 150 to 180 km in width, containing a 90 km-wide dark core whose nature as yet remains uncertain. Filaments contain strong magnetic fields and are associated with gas flow; individual examples have lifetimes of the order of an hour. Where dark cores are seen, these persist for as long as the filament.

The Swedish telescope results pave the way for more detailed examination of the complex magnetohydrodynamic processes associated with sunspots. High spatial resolution coupled to the ability to sample data rapidly across a range of spectral wavelengths is a priority for solar telescopes now under development.

GAMMA-RAY BURST-SUPERNOVA LINK CONFIRMED
Gamma-ray bursts, the most enormous transient outpourings of energy observed in our Universe, have been the subject of much speculation as to their nature and source since the first detections were made in the 1960s. Most of these events are short-lived (between one and 10 seconds), and they appear randomly across the whole sky, indicating an origin beyond our home Milky Way galaxy. The majority of gamma-ray bursts are thought to come from distant galaxies more than 5 billion light years away, which we see – as a result of the long 'look-back' time – in their relative infancy during what may have been a particularly active period in their history.

It had been speculated that supernova explosions could be a source of gamma-ray bursts, and an event on 29 March 2003 has provided confirmation that this is the case. Designated GRB 030329, the event was of unusually long duration, lasting for 50 seconds from the initial detection by instruments aboard NASA's High Energy Transient Explorer 2 (HETE-2) satellite. The gamma-ray burst's long duration allowed its position – in the constellation Leo – to be pinpointed, and astronomers in Australia were soon afterwards able to detect the fading visible-light 'afterglow'. Later, a spectrum was obtained, allowing the red-shift, and therefore the object's distance – a relatively nearby 2 billion light years – to be determined. The afterglow was, in fact, so bright that even amateur astronomers were able to detect it, using CCD equipment.

Subsequent brightening of a supernova (designated 2003dh, and detectable only in large telescopes) at the location of the gamma-ray burst confirmed the link between the two phenomena. The enormous release of gamma rays is a theoretically predicted consequence of the collapse of the core in a massive star, forming a black hole at the same time as its outer layers are blasted apart in a supernova explosion at the end of its lifetime when internal nuclear reactions can no longer support it. GRB 030329/supernova 2003dh appears to have occurred in a dwarf galaxy.

MAPPING THE EARLY UNIVERSE
The remnant radiation from the early Universe has been studied in ever greater detail over the past decade, following the momentous announcement of the detection of 'ripples' (anisotropies) in this cosmic microwave background (CMB) with the COBE satellite in 1992. This radiation, dating to 380,000 years after the Big Bang, comes from the era when the Universe first became transparent, and represents the farthest back in time we can ever hope to see. Studies of the CMB's unevenness allow competing theories on the nature and origin of the Universe to be tested. Balloon-borne experiments and observations from high mountain tops have allowed small areas of the background radiation to be mapped in detail. February 2003 brought a significant step forward with the announcement of a fine-detail all-sky map of the CMB from the Wilkinson Microwave Anisotropy Probe (WMAP).

Launched in June 2001, WMAP operates from a position close to the gravitationally stable Lagrangian L_2 point, 1.5 million km from Earth in the direction away from the Sun. This positioning reduces interfering terrestrial radiation. The probe's instruments are sufficiently sensitive to record differences in the microwave background to the level of one part in 1.5 million, a significant improvement on the COBE data. Inhomogeneities in the background provide the 'seeds' around which large-scale structures in the modern Universe, such as galaxy clusters, first formed.

WMAP's results confirm that the Universe is 'flat', having undergone an extremely rapid expansion phase (referred to by cosmologists as inflation) in the first instants of the Big Bang. The age of the Universe has been refined to 13.7±0.2 billion years. Polarisation of the cosmic microwave background measured by WMAP shows that the first stars formed between 100 million and 400 million years after the Big Bang, earlier than previously suspected. WMAP data show that cold dark matter constitutes 23 per cent of the Universe, compared with 4 per cent visible 'normal' matter. The remaining 73 per cent is comprised of dark energy, an as yet unexplained force which accelerates the Universe's expansion.

Further studies of the CMB's polarisation and a higher resolution map of its anisotropies are major aims for the European Space Agency's Planck spacecraft, scheduled for launch in 2007.

EARTH'S ANCIENT MANTLE MATERIAL

Over geological timescales, Earth's outer layers (the crust and the underlying deeper mantle) are subject to gradual renewal and recycling. Convection brings a steady supply of new crustal material from the mantle to the surface at the mid-ocean ridges, while old crust is subducted back down into the mantle where continental plates meet. The subducted material should eventually re-emerge, but there are uncertainties as to the timescale. Molten mantle material also rises to Earth's surface in plumes, whose positions are marked by island volcanic 'hotspots' like Hawaii and the Azores. Studies of volcanic basalts from the Azores have provided some insights to recycling processes in the mantle.

When mantle material is extruded at mid-oceanic ridges, certain trace elements partition into the crust, leaving the mantle depleted. By measuring the relative abundances of these elements, geologists can detect the signature of ancient recycled mantle material in basalts. Osmium isotope abundances in basalts from the islands of Pico and Faial show the mantle plume under the Azores to contain material which underwent partitioning 2.5 billion years ago, and must therefore have undergone long-term storage in the mantle after being subducted. Most of the convecting mantle turns over on much shorter timescales (ocean floor crust is typically no more than 200 million years old), and this remarkably long residence time suggests that the ancient mantle material now being incorporated into the Azores plume may have been carried down to the boundary plane between the upper and lower mantle at a depth of 660 km. Here, it was isolated from shorter-timescale mixing with the rest of the mantle, preserving the ancient osmium-isotope signature.

The depth of the ancient continental plates – typically more than a billion years old, in contrast to the younger oceanic crust – has been a matter of some conjecture. Past heat-flow and geochemical studies put the 'roots' of the continental shields, which are slowly moved around by convection in the mantle below (continental drift), at either 250 km or 400 km. Work published in April 2003, based on a technique of 'seismic tomography' to measure earthquake shear waves of differing polarisation, shows that the proposed 250 km depth is correct for the solid continental crust. Below this level lies a transition region in which mantle flows become more fluid, meeting the mantle proper at a depth of 400 km.

GENE REGULATION BY RNA INTERFERENCE

The phenomenon of RNA interference (RNAi) has attracted considerable interest in the past few years. First found in the nematode worm *Caeborhabditis elegans*, RNAi has been studied in a range of eukaryotic organisms, including yeasts, *Neurospora*, plants, *Drosophila* and mammals. The mechanism's components are highly conserved between species, perhaps indicating that RNAi was developed early in evolutionary history. Much research centres on how RNAi may serve to regulate gene expression.

Genes coding for proteins in the cell first have to be transcribed from genomic DNA into single-stranded messenger RNA (mRNA). This, in turn, is translated by ribosomes, which assemble amino acid subunits into long chains (polypeptides) in the order determined by the sequence of A, G, C and U nucleotide bases along the mRNA. Until recently, protein synthesis was thought to be regulated solely by induction of transcription, followed by rapid decay of mRNA once it was no longer required. The RNAi phenomenon, however, introduces regulation at another level.

Researchers have found that genes can be silenced by the introduction of double-stranded RNA (dsRNA) versions of their coding sequence. The mechanism involves a number of components, starting with a protein called Dicer. Pairs of Dicer molecules bind to dsRNA and cut it into small pieces, 22 nucleotides long. These small interfering RNA molecules (siRNA) are then delivered to a protein complex known as RISC (RNA-induced silencing complex), which contains RNA-cleaving enzymes, or nucleases. Delivery of siRNA to RISC may be mediated by a third component of the system, Argonaute.

The RNAi mechanism depends on the classical Watson-Crick base-pairing rules (A:U, G:C). siRNA in a RISC complex is unwound, allowing its pairing with the complementary sequence on an mRNA molecule, leading in turn to its nuclease digestion and cessation of protein synthesis.

It has been proposed that the RNAi machinery in eukaryotic cells originally evolved as a defence against RNA viruses. Whatever its origins, it offers researchers a powerful tool for conducting genome-wide knockout analyses. Specifically-tailored dsRNAs, designed to silence cancer or viral genes, are a hoped-for medical application; encouraging results have already been obtained in preventing polio virus and HIV infection in tissue culture cells. Delivery in a therapeutic context, however, is a major problem, and it will be many years yet before clinical trials of RNAi-based treatments can begin. Nonetheless, remarkable progress has been made in understanding RNA interference as a means of gene regulation, given that the phenomenon was barely suspected less than 15 years ago.

RNAi STUDIES SHOW HOW THE WORM TURNS

The nematode worm *Caenorhabditis elegans* has been used as a model in developmental biology since the 1960s. Around a millimetre in length, *C. elegans* has a body made up of 959 cells whose individual lineages can be followed in the microscope through the worm's three-day life cycle. *C. elegans* shows programmed cell death, particularly in its neural system, and observations of its genetics and cell biology offer clues to the workings of higher organisms. Pioneering studies of *C. elegans* by

Sydney Brenner, Sir John Sulston and Robert Horvitz were recognised in their receipt of the 2002 Nobel Prize for Physiology or Medicine.

C. elegans has become the first organism to have its genome explored by systematic silencing using RNAi. Using the known, complete genome sequence, researchers in Cambridge and Salamanca constructed plasmid clones, inducibly producing dsRNA for 16,757 of the worm's 19,427 predicted open reading frames. Introduction of these was relatively straightforward; *E. coli* bacteria containing dsRNA were fed to larval worms, which were then mated. RNAi effects were observed in roughly 10 per cent of the resulting embryos. These ranged from sterility and morphological defects, to unco-ordinated movement (a result of silencing neural genes), aberrant development and lethality.

The genes most prone to showing observable defects on RNAi silencing were those which are highly conserved throughout eukaryotic species. Where genes had become duplicated, silencing of a single copy gave no observable effect. Genes affected by RNAi tend to be clustered in regions up to 1 million bases long, suggestive of co-ordinated regulation.

Significantly, about 50 per cent of the genes in *C. elegans* have human homologues. RNAi studies on these, which include several involved in genetic diseases, could clarify their function.

A parallel study by scientists in Boston, Washington and Cambridge focused on *C. elegans* fat metabolism, identifying 305 genes in which RNAi silencing reduced the accumulation of fat droplets in the worm's intestinal cells. Again, many of these genes have human equivalents and such screens may in future provide clues for treatment of metabolic diseases.

RARE ASTRONOMICAL EVENTS IN UK SKIES

For those fortunate enough to enjoy clear skies, a number of rare astronomical events were visible in 2002–3. The Leonid meteor shower, centre of much attention in recent years, was again forecast to produce high activity in two bursts on the morning of 19 November 2002. Although moonlight swamped much of the spectacle, these materialised roughly as expected, around 04h 10m and 10h 50m GMT. Observers reported rates up to 15–20 per minute in each hour-long burst (from western Europe, including the British Isles, and North America respectively) corresponding, after correction for lunar glare and other factors, to equivalent rates of 3000 per hour. The outbursts came as Earth again encountered debris filaments shed by Comet 55P/Tempel-Tuttle in 1767 and 1866, these having already produced meteor storms a year previously. Occurrence of storm activity as predicted lends further authority to the Leonid meteor stream model originally developed by David Asher and Robert McNaught as a predictive tool. The 2002 storms are likely to have been the last in the current cycle, and Leonid activity of such intensity is unlikely again before 2098.

On the morning of 7 May, conditions were found across much of the British Isles for Mercury's transit in front of the Sun. The innermost planet appeared a tiny, dark circular spot (blacker than a large sunspot near the apparent centre of the Sun's disk at the time), taking five hours to complete its westward passage. Given their short duration, and the fact that they can only occur during brief 'windows' in May or November an average of eight years apart, transits of Mercury are rare at a given location. The previous event visible in the UK, in November 1973, was largely lost to clouds, while the next will not take place until 2016. The event was seen by many as a practice run for the even rarer transit of Venus on 8 June 2004. Care must, of course, be taken when observing these; direct viewing of the Sun through a telescope will damage eyesight and must not be attempted.

Although not as dramatic as the 1999 total eclipse, which drew hundreds of thousands of would-be observers to south-west England, a rare annular eclipse of the Sun close to dawn on 31 May 2003 drew many enthusiasts to north-east Scotland. Annular eclipses occur when the New Moon is close to apogee (farthest in its elliptical orbit from Earth), such that its apparent disk is too small to cover that of the Sun; in popular terms, this leaves a 'ring of fire' at mid-eclipse, which can in its own way be spectacular. Coastal cloud spoiled the view of sunrise over the North Sea for many, but several observers did capture the unusual low reddened 'crescent' Sun and annularity on camera. The next annular eclipse visible from the UK occurs in 2093.

PENGUINS FEEL HEAT

Each winter, continental Antarctica is surrounded by 20 million square kilometres of temporary sea ice. As this melts in the spring, penguins regain access to their rookeries on the beaches of the continent. Around 150 colonies of Adélie penguins, numbering five million individuals, nest on Antarctica. Ecologists studying them have raised concerns that the penguins' breeding pattern may be subject to disruption by changes in the Antarctic sea ice associated with global warming.

Outside the breeding season, the penguins spend their time among the offshore pack ice, building up their fat reserves on a staple diet of krill, a crustacean that feeds on algae thriving on the ice's underside. During breeding, however, the penguins are unable to feed.

Changes in the sea ice around the Antarctic peninsula have been brought about by a rise in winter temperature of up to 3°C in the past 50 years. This has led to a series of winters in which little ice has formed, and has seen a reduction in penguin breeding success in the following summers.

Conversely, on Ross Island on the opposite side of the continent, loss of sea ice has led to an increase in penguin numbers, as access is afforded to rich feeding grounds which were previously out of reach. A downside to this is that the breakup and beaching of very large icebergs can sometimes cut off the breeding rookeries from the sea; seasons of heavy pack ice are disastrous for penguins.

Preserved remains in nesting sites allow reconstruction of penguin breeding history as far back as 6,000 years ago. Interestingly, conditions in the Ross Sea were particularly favourable 3,000 to 4,000 years ago, during a period of cooling. Some scientists are now looking to penguin breeding success as a sensitive 'barometer' of changes brought about by global warming.

THEATRE

London's West End theatres are some of the most delightful buildings in the capital but, dating mostly from the 19th and early 20th centuries, they are beginning to show their age. Unlike the subsidised theatre, they have not benefited from modern design or National Lottery money, and cramped seats, too few toilets and inadequate bars can put people off going to the theatre. Audiences were scarce in any case in 2002–3, as the Iraq war and the SARS illness put people off travelling. In a bid to make theatre-going glamorous again, Sir Cameron Mackintosh announced in June 2003 plans to spend £35m of his own money renovating six of the seven theatres he owns in the West End.

The work will be carried out in phases, beginning with the Prince of Wales theatre, an unlovely but listed theatre built in 1937, with notorious bottlenecks in the bar and auditorium. The architects, Arts Team @ RHWL, will create a grand staircase, multi-level foyers, and a new bar with views looking south towards Trafalgar Square. The theatre will reopen in spring 2004 with *Mamma Mia!* Then work will begin on the Strand, the Albery and Wyndham's Theatre, three theatres designed at the end of the 19th century by W. G. R. Sprague, one of the greatest theatre architects; here an upgrade in comfort is needed rather than any structural changes.

Most radical of all will be the redevelopment of the block that includes the Gielgud and Queens theatres in Shaftesbury Avenue. Work will start in 2005 when the leases currently held by Andrew Lloyd Webber's Really Useful Group run out. The Queens was bombed during the Second World War and is notable for the shiny black façade that replaced the old building. That will be removed and the original design restored. Shops and offices between the two theatres will be cleared out in order to create a single foyer. This foyer will also serve an entirely new theatre, a 500-seater to be called the Sondheim, which will be built within the existing upper circle of the Queens, fulfilling the need for a smaller space to which successes from theatres like the Donmar, Almeida and Cottesloe can easily transfer. Sondheim professed himself delighted with the choice of name, which will no doubt also be popular with American tourists.

Along with these architectural improvements, Mackintosh intends to cut costs by rationalising ticket sales and promises that booking fees will be kept to a minimum, admitting that 'people worry about the added extras of coming to the theatre'. Furthermore, Mackintosh has been an outspoken critic of the West End's grime, traffic congestion, poor public transport and inadequate policing, and recognising Mackintosh's generosity, the leader of Westminster Council, in whose borough most of the West End theatres are situated, has promised to clean up the area and even offered the prospect of alfresco dining in Leicester Square until 1 a.m.

RARE PROGRAMMING

The West End was criticised often during the year as producers resorted to increasingly desperate measures in their efforts to attract new audiences. Although there was some fluff among the pieces on offer, there were also some demanding plays starring big names, but new writing was notably sparse. The Norwegian playwright Ibsen is rarely seen in the commercial sector, but the Royal Shakespeare Company's production of *Brand* came to the Haymarket Theatre Royal with Ralph Fiennes as the uncompromising pastor. Meanwhile, *The Master Builder* played at the Albery where Patrick Stewart – returning to his roots from his television role as Jean-Luc Picard in *Star Trek: The Next Generation* – beamed in from America to play the part of Solness, the architect driven to increasingly reckless behaviour by an admiring young woman. The Swedish playwright Strindberg also got a rare showing when Sean Mathias brought his Broadway production of *Dance of Death* to London, with two blackly comic performances from Ian McKellen and Frances de la Tour as the couple locked in marital combat for over 25 years.

The most daring programming was the RSC season of plays by Shakespeare's contemporaries and successors. First given at the Swan in Stratford under director Gregory Doran, the season consisted of *The Malcontent* by John Marston, *The Island Princess* by John Fletcher, *The Roman Actor* by Philip Massinger, Shakespeare's *Edward III* (the least exciting of the lot), and *Eastward Ho!* by Ben Jonson, John Marston and George Chapman. Some of these plays had not been professionally produced for 400 years. The RSC's financial difficulties meant that initially it was unable to transfer the productions to London when the season proved an unexpected hit. The 28-strong company of actors, led by Sir Antony Sher, and 20 musicians appealed to the producer Thelma Holt who, with impresario Bill Kenwright, moved the plays into the Gielgud theatre for a season at Christmas 2002 when they played to respectable houses.

Such courage was rare and playwright Sir Alan Ayckbourn launched a savage attack on play-it-safe West End theatre producers over their use of American stars, singling out Madonna, seen last year in *Up for Grabs*. Ayckbourn claimed that the stars could not hack it and was angered by the decision of the producers of his trilogy *Damsels in Distress* to increase the number of performances of the most popular comedy in the trilogy to the detriment of the other two. He felt, he said, that his work had been 'condemned to the dustbin' and announced that he would not be seeking to put his plays on in the West End again. He described London's commercial theatre as 'ossified, lethargic and incapable of producing new work'. In spite of this attack, the American stars kept coming, though with rather less success than Kevin Spacey or Gwyneth Paltrow in previous years. Spacey has maintained his connection with London theatre and it was announced that he had taken up the position of artistic director of the Old Vic, although the exact nature of his role is as yet unclear.

Michael Richards, a familiar face from US television's *Seinfeld*, played the outrageous villain in the classic black farce *Arsenic and Old Lace*, a revival in which he was one of the few members of the cast to strike the right note of horror and farce. Matthew Perry, who need never work again after his lengthy stint in *Friends*, was rather more adventurous when he chose to appear with Minnie Driver, Hank Azaria and Kelly Reilly in David Mamet's *Sexual Perversity in Chicago*, a much darker piece than his long-running television sitcom but sharing some similarities in its preoccupation with single life in America. Gillian Anderson, best known for *The X-Files*, made her British debut in *What the Night is For,* as one half of a couple meeting again 11 years after their affair had ended and wondering whether to rekindle the flame.

Not all the stars were American. Dames Judi Dench and Maggie Smith appeared together on stage for the first time in 40 years in David Hare's new play *The Breath of Life,* unusually conventional West End fare for Hare except that it portrays two women in their sixties – one a novelist and the other an art historian – who are both leading active lives. Sean Bean made Shakespeare commercial when he stepped out as a brawny, handsome Macbeth with Samantha Bond as his murderous accomplice in Edward Hall's production of Shakespeare's play. And Kristin Scott Thomas abandoned her home city of Paris to play the restless Masha in Michael Blakemore's production of *Three Sisters* at the Playhouse. Then there were the one-person shows, always cheap to stage, which relied on the fame of the actor or of the person portrayed; Dawn French played a deserted wife in *My Brilliant Divorce;* Jerome Flynn put on a fez and became Tommy Cooper in *Jus' Like That;* and Tom Courtenay explored the complicated world of Philip Larkin in *Pretending to be Me.*

British musicals are renowned the world over but there was nothing to shout about this year. The most ambitious was *Our House,* which drew on the songs of Madness just as *We Will Rock You* drew on the music of Queen and *Mamma Mia!* on the songs of Abba. Tim Firth was given the task of stringing together a story out of such songs as 'Baggy Trousers' and 'It Must Be Love'. He adopted a device used in the film *Sliding Doors,* offering two possible scenarios after the hero, Joe, is involved in a break-in. In the first, Joe honourably confesses and is sent to jail; in the second, he escapes and becomes an evil property developer. The musical had its supporters, especially when Suggs, lead singer of Madness, joined the cast but it was never a commercial hit and closed in less than a year. The disastrous Gallic pop version of *Romeo and Juliet – the Musical,* however, closed in a matter of weeks.

Ragtime is an epic musical, later made into a film, which traces the fortunes of three archetypal American families and was first staged many years ago in New York. The judgement of those who hesitated then to bring it to London proved sound when even the talents of Maria Friedman, as Mother, did not enable it to survive long at the Piccadilly. The most successful musical of all during the year was yet another revival of *Joseph and his Amazing Technicolor Dreamcoat* at the New London theatre.

Musical entertainments seemed to fare better. The legendary Elaine Stritch, dressed in black tights and a white shirt and with just a chair for a set, held court at the Old Vic in *Elaine Stritch at Liberty,* in which she mixed stories from her traumatic life with classic songs. The choreographer and director Susan Stroman brought over her unusual Broadway hit *Contact,* a celebration and exploration of different kinds of dance with a London cast that included Sarah Wildor and Leigh Zimmerman. *The Rat Pack – Live from Las Vegas* proved a popular recreation of Sammy Davis Jr., Dean Martin and Frank Sinatra in one of their Las Vegas shows. It did not win the approval of the critics, but it was not loathed quite as much as *Mum's the Word,* an anecdotal account of motherhood with Jenny Éclair and Imogen Stubbs.

ALL CHANGE AT THE NATIONAL

The National Theatre undoubtedly attracted more attention than any other this year. Several theatres changed their artistic director but nowhere was the changeover more striking than the replacement of Trevor

Nunn by Nicholas Hytner. In his last six months at the National, Nunn embarked on an extraordinary run of productions, beginning with Glenn Close in *A Streetcar Named Desire;* Close made a rather elderly, strident Blanche, her performance recalling Joan Crawford rather than Vivien Leigh. This was followed by productions of *Anything Goes* and *Love's Labour's Lost* performed by the same company of actors. While in charge, Nunn directed a musical at the National every year, in the belief that they have a valid place in the repertoire, and also to provide a fun show at Christmas, all but guaranteed to balance the books. Last year's *South Pacific* was disappointing, but Cole Porter's *Anything Goes* was an inspired production of a gloriously silly account of a transatlantic crossing which includes some of Porter's best songs. A motley crew sail on John Gunter's ocean liner, including celebrity criminals, female evangelists, fortune-hunters and socialites. The songs provided the critics with their punchlines ('It's delightful, it's delicious, it's de-lovely') for a production that will transfer to the Theatre Royal Drury Lane in the autumn.

Love's Labour's Lost, with Joseph Fiennes as Berowne, was also admired for the bitter-sweet mood created onstage. Nunn framed his production with scenes from the Great War in which Berowne, hit by shrapnel, looks back on an Edwardian idyll, a poignant contrast to the horrors of war. It was a typically detailed, almost novelistic concept with a beautiful set, again by John Gunter, dominated by a great leafy tree. There were many tributes to the director, who is a master of his craft and, it turns out, a generous benefactor of the National, paying himself for the creation of the Loft studio there. Nunn was often his worst enemy, however, always quick to point out that his repertoire at the National had consisted of far more than just musicals, and that his record on new plays was not as bad as his critics made out.

Not even Nunn could have directed everything in his last six months and the final show of the 'Transformation' season, designed to draw new audiences into the theatre, was also its biggest hit. Matthew Bourne's *Play Without Words,* inspired by Joseph Losey's 1963 film *The Servant,* was a subversive tale of class and sex which existed on the cusp of dance and theatre; there are plans to revive it in 2004. The touring company Out of Joint docked in the Lyttelton with a double bill that included April de Angelis's imaginative recreation of the theatre of David Garrick, *A Laughing Matter,* and Goldsmith's classic *She Stoops to Conquer,* the comedy that Garrick foolishly turned down. Dame Eileen Atkins distinguished herself as the forsaken novelist wife in the Australian adultery drama *Honour.* The run of *Talking Cure,* Christopher Hampton's fascinating exploration of the relationship between Freud and Jung, with Ralph Fiennes as Jung, never recovered from the death of the actor James Hazeldine just before the play opened.

Few directors have been as successful as Nicholas Hytner in drawing a line between one era and the next when he took over from Nunn at the National. In an effort to lower the average age of audiences and to attract first-timers, he launched a £10 season at the Olivier over the notoriously difficult summer months with the help of a £1 million three-year sponsorship deal with Travelex. Two-thirds of the tickets cost £10 for a season in which costs are kept down by stripping the theatre back to its original amphitheatre and creating a huge metaphorical space. An impressive season was launched with Hytner's own modern dress production of *Henry V;* the scene in which Henry's advisors seek legal justification for his attack on France inevitably struck a contemporary nerve. Adrian Lester's chilly Henry was revealed as a master of spin, very aware of the effect of his words on others, whether face-to-face or to camera. A stark contrast was created between the romantic vision of Penny Downie's Chorus, imagining a country fully behind their leader and eager to join up, and the reality of men who would far rather not be forced to scale the walls of Agincourt again. This classic was followed by John Guare's new stage version of *His Girl Friday*, with Zoe Wanamaker and Alex Jennings as the journalist and her bullying editor, and Kenneth Branagh in David Mamet's *Edmond*. Initial reports indicated that the season had attracted an audience different from the usual NT theatregoers and that it did extremely well at the box office.

But the Lyttelton was no less popular, with the arrival of *Jerry Springer – the Opera*, first developed at BAC before going to the 2002 Edinburgh Festival. Richard Thomas and Stewart Lee's filthy, outrageous satire on confessional TV brilliantly mixes posh singers with the trailer trash guests on Springer's show, including a man wearing a vast diaper. It is surely destined for a long commercial life elsewhere and illustrates Hytner's determination to rub out the borders between different art forms. Then followed a revival of Tom Stoppard's *Jumpers*, a philosophical comedy about the existence of God and the arrival of men on the moon. Simon Russell Beale dominated as the conceited, insecure philosopher clinging to his belief in God and in moral absolutes as his wife, a popular nightclub singer, has a nervous breakdown. David Leveaux's production revealed the bleak undertones to the play's high jinks. Hytner intends to stage only new plays in the Cottesloe and he found two winners in Owen McCafferty's *Scenes from the Big Picture*, a day in the life of 21 Belfast inhabitants, impeccably directed by Peter Gill; and *Elmina's Kitchen* by Kwame Kwei-Armah, a raucous comedy with a serious message about the way in which young black kids are drawn into crime.

UPS AND DOWNS FOR SHAKESPEARE

Another company to get a new boss was the Royal Shakespeare Company, where consolidation rather than fireworks was needed after all the crises of the previous year. Michael Boyd, the new artistic director, has reiterated his belief in the ensemble but is still working on plans for the future. Without a base in London, the company currently lacks a strong identity. An adaptation of Salman Rushdie's *Midnight's Children* at the Barbican struggled with a complicated narrative and proved long and rambling. Touring productions of *Coriolanus* and *The Merry Wives of Windsor* came to the Old Vic, which has been touted, along with the New London, as a possible London home for the company. Greg Hicks proved a fine, samurai Coriolanus in David Farr's Japanese-inspired production.

While the RSC struggled to get back on its feet, Shakespeare's Globe found it hard to repeat the triumphs of 2002. Artistic director Mark Rylance pursued his policy of stretching audiences' imaginations just as Shakespeare had done in his day. The 2003 season was given the topical name of 'Regime Change', and featured an all-male production of *Richard II* with Rylance as the titular king, followed by an all-female production of *Richard III* with Kathryn Hunter as the murderous hunchback. Rylance was reported as saying 'I love actors playing characters they're clearly not and taking the audience with them'. Both he and Hunter won plaudits for their roles, although there were reservations about the productions as a whole.

With new plays in short supply elsewhere, the Royal Court had a crucial role to play, and produced some important works. Stephen Daldry returned to the theatre, fresh from his triumph with his film *The Hours*, to direct Michael Gambon and Daniel Craig in *A Number*, Caryl Churchill's unusual elliptical study of fathers and sons. Rona Munro's *Iron* transferred from the Traverse Theatre in Edinburgh, an astonishingly unclichéd look at a murderess (brilliantly played by Sandy McDade) and her relationship with the daughter who visits her in prison for the first time in 15 years. Then came Terry Johnson's homage to Hitchcock, *Hitchcock Blonde*, which later transferred to the West End. Johnson has portrayed such real-life characters as Einstein, Marilyn Monroe and Barbara Windsor in previous plays. Here he explores the relationship between Hitchcock's films and his erotic obsessions in a play which ambitiously works in three different time periods. William Hootkins achieved an astonishing resemblance to the film director, deftly filleting a Dover sole at one point. Rosamund Pike, hot from the James Bond film *Die Another Day*, appeared as the beautiful woman he auditions to play the body double for the famous shower scene in *Psycho*. Finally came Roy Williams' *Fallout*, which shared with Kwame Kwei-Armah's *Elmina's Kitchen* a concern with the attraction of violence for young black kids in a scenario reminiscent of the circumstances surrounding the death of Damilola Taylor, the young boy who was stabbed in south London in 2000.

NEW BEGINNINGS

Small companies often win as much attention as the larger ones these days, especially the Donmar and the Almeida. They both gained new artistic directors during the year. At the Donmar, Sam Mendes said goodbye after 10 glorious years with illuminating and award-winning productions of *Uncle Vanya* and *Twelfth Night*. Having the same actors in both plays heightened some of the shared themes. Simon Russell Beale headed the company as a self-hating Vanya and a hilarious but heart-wrenching Malvolio. Mendes' productions were melancholic, as befits a farewell, but touched with humanity, especially when Paul Jesson's Toby Belch and David Bradley's Aguecheek sat contentedly farting after a long night's drinking.

Michael Grandage, already part of the team at the Donmar, took over as artistic director in autumn 2002 and launched his tenure with a revival of *The Vortex*, starring rising talent Chiwetel Ejiofor as Nicky and Francesca Annis as his mother. Although audiences have come to accept black actors playing in the classics, the casting of Ejiofor in Coward did ruffle some feathers, but most people admired a production which stripped away the stylistic clichés to expose the bitter feelings beneath.

Grandage's first season has been bold and so far his courage has paid off. He followed *The Vortex* with Dario Fo's political farce *Accidental Death of an Anarchist*, with Rhys Ifans as the lunatic who run rings round the corrupt and stupid coppers. This was followed by a rare revival of Albert Camus' *Caligula* with Michael Sheen as the tragic tyrant. Then Grandage continued the Donmar's tradition of presenting small-scale Sondheim with *Pacific Overtures*, a co-production with the Chicago Shakespeare Theater.

The Almeida had a quieter year as Jonathan Kent and Ian McDiarmid left to pursue their freelance careers and the building closed for refurbishment. Michael Attenborough was appointed as Kent and McDiarmid's successor and he opened his season in spring 2003 with a production of Ibsen's *The Lady from the Sea* directed by

Trevor Nunn immediately after he left the National. Natasha Richardson bravely played Ellida, a part her mother, Vanessa Redgrave, had excelled in many years ago at the Roundhouse. Richardson impressed as the febrile, haunted woman who longs for the sea and feels cursed by her sailor lover. But Nunn's production was most remarkable for the more realistic, less mystical scenes, especially when Claudie Blakley's Bolette agrees to a marriage of convenience with her old tutor. The improvements to the building were admired as much as the production; no more waiting in the rain in the gap between bar and auditorium, proper lavatories, a new bar, and air conditioning. Hidden away backstage are better facilities for the actors.

In Hampstead, a completely new theatre was opened. Costing £15.4 million, it was designed by Bennetts Associates and is situated just round the corner from the old Portakabin. From the outside the new building appears quite simple but the bar is dramatically dominated on one side by a vast zinc drum which forms the back of the auditorium. The first production, Station House Opera's *How to Behave,* provided an opportunity for the audience to explore the whole building, including backstage. Plays by Tim Firth, Stephen Adly Guirgis and Tamsin Oglesby followed. Having settled the theatre in its new home, Jenny Topper, the current artistic director, leaves in autumn 2003, to be replaced by Anthony Clark.

For years people have complained about the demise of regional theatre; most actors now go straight into television rather than beginning their careers in repertory in the regions where they can tackle a wide range of parts. As additional government funds start to flow into theatre, there is a new spirit of pride and aggression abroad and also a large number of new artistic directors. A triumvirate, Ruth Mackenzie, Steven Pimlott and Martin Duncan, took over at Chichester, promising to create a festival atmosphere with a season on a watery, Venetian theme, including productions of *The Merchant of Venice, The Gondoliers,* a Goldoni comedy, and a musical version of *The Water Babies.* In the west, there is hope that the Bristol Old Vic's long decline will be reversed as David Farr and Simon Reade have been appointed as joint artistic directors; their first season included Sam West's production of *Les Liaisons Dangereuses* and Farr's own adaptation of *Great Expectations.* They promise to appeal to a family audience.

Jonathan Church, who took over from Bill Alexander at the Birmingham Repertory Theatre, and Rachel Kavanaugh staged David Hare's trilogy on the state of the nation to great acclaim. Ian Brown at the West Yorkshire Playhouse in Leeds persuaded Christopher Eccleston to attempt Hamlet, his first Shakespearean role, and Michael Grandage continues as associate director at the Crucible in Sheffield as well as running the Donmar. His northern production of *The Tempest* with Derek Jacobi was a triumph and transferred to the Old Vic. Claire Price played Miranda, and later in the year provided fine support to Ralph Fiennes in the London production of *Brand,* proving that the regions are still a good place for young performers to learn their craft.

THEATRE AWARDS

EVENING STANDARD AWARDS
Best Play – Caryl Churchill, *A Number*
Best Actor – Simon Russell Beale, *Twelfth Night/Uncle Vanya*
Best Actress – Clare Higgins, *Vincent in Brixton*

Best Musical – *The Full Monty*
Most Promising Playwright – Vassily Sigarev, *Plasticine*
Best Director – Sam Mendes, *Twelfth Night/Uncle Vanya*
Best Designer – Ian MacNeil, *Plasticine*
Outstanding Newcomer – Jake Gyllenhaal, *This is our Youth*
Special Award – Shakespeare's Globe

CRITICS' CIRCLE AWARDS
Best New Play – Peter Gill, *The York Realist*
Best Musical – *Anything Goes*
Best Director – Sam Mendes, *Twelfth Night/Uncle Vanya*
Best Actress – Clare Higgins, *Vincent in Brixton*
Most Promising Playwright – Charlotte Eilenberg, *The Lucky Ones*
Most Promising Newcomer – Alison Pargeter
Best Shakespearean Performance – Mark Rylance, *Twelfth Night*

LAURENCE OLIVIER AWARDS
Best New Play – Nicholas Wright, *Vincent in Brixton*
Best New Musical – *Our House*
Best Entertainment – *Play Without Words*
Outstanding Musical – *Anything Goes*
Best New Comedy – *The Lieutenant of Inishmore*
Best Revival – *Twelfth Night/Uncle Vanya*
Best Director – Sam Mendes, *Twelfth Night/Uncle Vanya*
Best Designer – Bunny Christie, *A Streetcar Named Desire*
Best Lighting Designer – Peter Mumford, *The Bacchai*
Best Costume Designer – Jenny Tiramani, *Twelfth Night*
Best Actor – Simon Russell Beale, *Uncle Vanya*
Best Actress – Clare Higgins, *Vincent in Brixton*
Best Supporting Performance – Essie Davis, *A Streetcar Named Desire*
Best Actor in a Musical – Alex Jennings, *My Fair Lady*
Best Actress in a Musical – Joanna Riding, *My Fair Lady*
Best Supporting Performance in a Musical – Paul Baker, *Taboo*
Most Promising Performer – Noel Clarke, *Where Do We Live*
Most Promising Playwright – Charlotte Eilenberg, *The Lucky Ones*
Outstanding Achievement of the Year – Gregory Doran and the RSC Swan Ensemble for the Jacobean season at the Gielgud theatre
Special Award – Sam Mendes for 10 years as artistic director of the Donmar Warehouse

BARCLAYS TMA REGIONAL THEATRE AWARDS 2002
Best Actress – Diana Quick, *Ghosts*
Best Actor – Corin Redgrave, *The Browning Version*
Best Actress in a Supporting Role – Mairead McKinley, *The Clearing*
Best Actor in a Supporting Role – Jimmy Chisholm, *Amadeus*
Best Director – Emma Rice, *The Red Shoes*
Best Designer – Simon Higlett, *Elizabeth Rex/Three Sisters*
Best New Play – *Gagarin Way*
Best Touring Production – *Rose Rage*
Best Musical – *Fiddler on the Roof*
Best Show for Children and Young People – *Lifeboat*
Most Welcoming Theatre – Wolverhampton Grand
Special Achievement – mind … the gap
Eclipse Award – Contact Theatre, Manchester

WEATHER

JULY 2002
This was the wettest July since 1988. The 1st to the 12th was unsettled and cool with frequent outbreaks of rain. Most days were wet, especially in central and southern areas of England. Thundery showers also affected a number of places from the 10th to the 12th. From the 13th to the 18th a ridge of high pressure extended from the Azores, bringing mainly dry weather, good sunny periods and very warm conditions at times, especially in the south. There was occasional light rain or showery outbreaks in south-west England on the 13th and in northern parts during the 15th to the 17th. The 19th to the 25th was changeable with southern areas staying mainly dry apart from the odd outbreak of light rain or drizzle. A small active low crossed central Britain on the 19th and 20th bringing heavy rain at times to the Midlands and northern areas. A severe hailstorm was observed at Santon Downham on the 20th, while East Anglia, Lincs and East Kent had thundery showers later. Some hill and coastal fog affected south-western parts during the 25th. It was warm or hot during the 26th to the 31st. Herne Bay, Kent reached 32°C on the 28th, while in East Anglia thunderstorms broke out later. On the 29th, 33°C was touched at Northolt, Middlesex and 32°C in central London making it the hottest July day in the capital since 1989. The 30th saw heavy thunderstorms break out widely over the Midlands, northern England, East Anglia and parts of south-east England giving torrential downpours and local flooding in places. The 31st saw early morning storms in Norfolk petering out but more thundery rain with local downpours developed over central southern England during the day. Heavy rain arrived in south-west England later.

AUGUST 2002
This was the dullest August since 1987. From the 1st to the 9th weak low pressure over or near the region created frequent outbreaks of heavy thundery rain. Much of northern England was very wet on the 1st. Fylingdales had 115mm of rain in 24hrs, the wettest day since 1984. At Leeming 91mm fell in 24hrs, their wettest day since 1971. From the 3rd to the 5th storms affected quite a few areas especially central England, the south-east and East Anglia, with some flash floods in places. During the 7th there were more flash floods in parts of south-east England and the Midlands. Thunderstorms deposited 60mm of rain in an hour at Olney west of Bedford and at Hampstead Heath in London – both one in 200 year events. Hampstead's total was 71mm, with local tube networks disrupted. The 8th and 9th saw more heavy thundery rain breaking out in many areas. From the 10th to the 16th low pressure moved away allowing a weak ridge to extend from the Azores. It was mainly dry with good sunny periods, however there were thundery outbreaks on the 10th and 15th over East Anglia and south-east England. Early on the 10th, Southend had 54mm of rain causing local flooding. The 17th to the 19th was mostly very warm or hot but unsettled as more thundery rain, heavy in places, fell in some parts. Wales and western areas were especially wet on the 17th, while further east some locations touched 31°C. Most thundery activity moved to the Midlands and East Anglia thereafter as weak fronts migrated eastwards. With low pressure close by over the North Sea from the 20th to the 24th,

the pattern stayed unsettled with rain at times. There were some downpours in Kent and London late on the 20th. The north-east was wet on the 22nd and again on the 23rd. Thundery showers also affected south-east and south-west England on the 23rd. Northern England was very wet on the 24th and thundery showers broke out later that day over many southern counties of England. The 25th to the 31st was mainly dry as the Azores high extended its influence over the region. Thundery rain broke out later over the extreme south on the 25th. A low off Northern Ireland gave north-western districts a wet day on the 30th as it moved away to Scandinavia.

SEPTEMBER 2002
This was the sunniest September since 1991. The 1st to the 4th was a mainly dry and sunny start to the month as high pressure drifted east to Russia, with a low forming over the North Sea by the 4th. The 5th to the 9th was changeable to begin with as low pressure south of Iceland moved to the Irish Sea by the 7th. There were occasional outbreaks of rain and showers, especially in the west and north-west. Some heavy thundery rain affected Kent and Sussex overnight from the 6th to the 7th. A depression from Biscay on the 8th passed over the region during the 9th, bringing squally winds and depositing copious amounts of rain over a wide area. The rain was torrential in places causing flooding, especially in the north-west, Midlands and the Swanage area where 121mm fell in 24 hours, a one in 280-year event. Parts of the Isle of Wight were also deluged with up to 75mm of rain in 24 hours. The 10th to the 20th was mostly dry. The high centre later migrated to a position north then north-west of the UK. It was rather cloudy at times in eastern areas but there were often good sunny periods in central and western parts. It was rather cool at times near the east coast but mostly rather warm or warm at times in remaining areas with Exeter reaching 26.5°C on the 13th. Odd spots of rain occasionally broke out over east coast counties and East Anglia from the 16th onwards. Some thundery rain affected south-west England at times during the 19th and 20th. From the 21st to the 30th high pressure continued to dominate the weather, later drifting south then eastwards into the continent. Though mainly dry with lengthy sunny spells there were some scattered light showers in places on the 22nd, and in the east on the 23rd and 24th as weak fronts gyrated round the high. Some showery rain also affected northern and eastern areas early on the 26th with thunder reported in East Anglia. Temperatures were mostly near normal, becoming rather warm at times especially after the 28th as a south-easterly airflow became established. Some places experienced their first ground frosts of autumn. The last day of the month saw showery outbreaks over Wales and south-west England, with a report of thunder in Cornwall.

OCTOBER 2002
This was the first month since December 2001 to be colder than average. From the 1st to the 10th it was warm and mostly dry with sunny spells, especially at first. Prestatyn in Clwyd reached 23.8°C on the 1st, however occasional rain affected some areas during the first few days of the month. Thereafter the weather became mainly dry and sunny. As low pressure moved away to Denmark on the 5th, a weak ridge of high pressure

extending from north Scandinavia settled over the region for a few days. Atlantic fronts brought rain to south-west districts on the 8th and 9th as a low passed close by reaching France by the 10th and bringing chilly east-south-easterly winds to many areas. The 11th to the 15th was unsettled, mostly cold and very wet and windy. A slow moving front gave very heavy rain to the north and north-west during the 11th and 12th. A low crossing southern areas on the 13th deposited copious amounts of rain, especially over south-west England and south Wales, causing serious flooding in places. Pembery Sands near Swansea received 72mm in 12 hrs. Another low gave heavy rain on the 15th in the south-west, Midlands, south-east and eastern counties with some places having their wettest October day on record. Dunkeswell in Devon totalled 120mm in 4 days. A tornado at Torquay on the 15th damaged a church roof and uprooted trees, while others in Essex near Colchester and Maldon caused damage to outhouses. The 16th to the 19th was a quieter interlude after rain cleared from East Anglia early on 16th. Lowestoft had 63mm of rain in 24 hours from some thundery outbreaks. Thereafter it was mainly rather cold and dry with frost at night, apart from a few showers in the extreme south-east on the 17th and 18th. Rain spread back into the south-west later on the 19th. The 20th to the 24th saw a frosty start in the north with Shap in Cumbria falling to minus 6.2°C early on the 20th. More heavy rain caused local flooding in the north on the 20th and 21st as a deep low tracked north-north-east over the UK. It was mostly cold and showery thereafter with some thunder and also some snow falling over the Peak District and Cumbria. The 25th brought gales and squally showers, some with thunder as a vigorous low passed to the north. At Portchester in Hampshire a tornado and whirlwind did much damage to roofs, garages, walls and fences. The 26th was quieter but rain and thunder affected the south-west later. On the 27th a deep depression moved from south-west Ireland to north-east England bringing rain and storm force winds. Mumbles near Swansea had a gust of 84kts. There were some fatalities and widespread damage to trees and power lines brought disruption to road and rail networks. The 28th to the 31st was dry at first and then saw occasional rain with patchy mist. Hill and coastal fog was present from the 29th to the 31st.

NOVEMBER 2002

This was the mildest November since 1994. The 1st to the 2nd saw a mild but very wet and windy start to the month as fronts moved north-east across the region. The 3rd to the 4th was mainly mild and dry after some scattered showers, a number of which were accompanied by thunder. The 5th to the 10th saw Atlantic depressions passing by which brought wet and windy weather but it was mild or very mild. 17.2°C was recorded at Saunton Sands in Devon on the 5th. There were periods of rain and showers, heavy at times, with thunder. The 9th gave a dry interlude before rain spread in during the evening, preceding another mild day with rain at times on the 10th. From the 11th to the 14th a north Atlantic low brought bands of rain and secondary depressions to the region. During the 13th and 14th one such secondary depression migrated northwards from Biscay touching 965mbs. There was 80mm of rain overnight in Penzance with severe flooding there and in St Ives. Much of Devon and Cornwall had heavy thundery rain with many roads impassable due to flooding. A gust of 64kts was recorded at Portland. The 15th to the 20th was rather unsettled with rain at times. A low centre to the south on the 15th and 16th brought rain and thundery showers to many places especially to southern areas. A quieter interlude from the 17th to the 18th allowed fog and overnight

frost to develop, with Redesdale in Northumberland falling to minus 3.1°C. Rain edged slowly into the west on the 19th and 20th. The 21st to the 24th saw low pressure west of Ireland and more bands of rain and showers affected the region. Some were heavy and thundery, especially in the south during the 23rd and 24th. From the 25th to the 26th it was mainly dry but with fairly extensive mist and fog slow to clear in places. Some scattered showers broke out from time to time in extreme southern and western areas. The 27th to the 30th was unsettled and mostly wet again. Atlantic fronts brought yet more rain to south and south-western areas during the 27th and 28th with showers turning thundery in many places. Cornwall saw widespread flooding with some main roads closed. After a brief foggy respite on the 29th more wet weather spread in from the south-west on the 30th. Central London had its wettest November since 1940, while Milford Haven in south-west Wales received 372mm of rain, a record for November from 1964. Birmingham had its first air frost-free November since 1946.

DECEMBER 2002

This was the dullest December since 1989 and the wettest since 1993. From the 1st to the 4th the weather was changeable with rain and showers especially in west and north-west areas, as low pressure and weather fronts moved south-eastwards. It was mainly mild, with some thunder reported on the 4th. A gust of 61kts was recorded at Aberdaron on the Lleyn Peninsula on the 1st. The 5th to the 11th saw the high pressure over Scandinavia bringing cold easterly winds, however it was mostly dry. There were sunny periods at times and some patchy rain or drizzle, mainly in the south. There was some sleet or snow in the north on the 7th, also over Dartmoor and north-east England on the 8th. A depression over Biscay on the 10th strengthened the easterly winds, bringing a little snow to high ground in the West Country. The 12th to the 16th was dry in most places at first. A low moving slowly north-north-east from Biscay reached south-east England by the 15th and brought outbreaks of rain with sleet and snow, mainly over high ground. It was rather cold or cold and very wet on the 14th and 15th. From the 17th to the 19th an anticyclone centred over the Borders then migrated east-south-east to the continent bringing cold easterly winds and some overnight frost especially in the north. There were sunny spells later, with some fog in northern areas. Rain reached Cornwall and Devon later on 19th. Redesdale in Northumberland fell to minus 6.6°C early on the 20th. Many places had a very wet 36 hours from late on the 20th to early on the 22nd causing local flooding. Llanbedr in Gwynedd reached 15.4°C on the 23rd. The 24th to the 27th saw vigorous depressions from the south-west passing close to or over the region, bringing more rain and heavy showers. It stayed mostly very mild, indeed the three-day Christmas period was one of the mildest for at least a decade. Flooding continued to be a problem in many areas. After a mainly dry start on the 28th, more very mild but very wet weather spread north-east during the 29th and 30th as a low and its fronts stalled over the region. During the 30th there were isolated reports of thunder, while at Brighton a section of the West Pier fell into the sea. Central London had its wettest December on record since 1940. Most places began dry and cold on the 31st before further rain spread in from the south-west.

JANUARY 2003

This was the second sunniest January since 1961. From the 1st to the 3rd there were frequent spells of rain as low pressure and associated fronts stalled then drifted south.

There were also some thundery outbreaks over southern counties. It was mild at first but there were wintry showers in the north-east later. A swollen River Thames caused local flooding in the Chertsey and Weybridge areas on the 3rd. The 4th to the 6th was cold with sunny periods and some wintry showers in east coast counties. There was overnight frost and some substantial snow in east Kent later on the 6th. From the 7th to the 10th an anticyclone to the north brought very cold east-north-easterly winds, snow and widespread overnight frost. The Thames at Oxford was reported as being the highest since 1947. The extreme south-east saw 2 to 5cms of snow early on the 7th which brought chaos during rush hour. More snow on the 8th affected Greater London south of the M25, north-west Kent, Essex and parts of Surrey. Between 4 and 8cms fell in most places, with up to 12cms in Essex. In central London it was the heaviest snowfall since February 1991. As the high slipped south the frost and patchy freezing fog was displaced by mainly drier and milder conditions from the 11th to the 14th. The 15th to the 17th saw a deep depression to the north and brought changeable weather and sunny periods. Rain belts affected the region on the 15th and 17th, with thunder in north-western areas on the 17th and a gust of 72kts at Capel Curig. The 18th to the 22nd was very wet in most places as complex low pressure crossed the UK to the North Sea. There were frequent outbreaks of rain and showers, some heavy with thunder, becoming more scattered on the 22nd. The 23rd to 27th was breezy but mostly dry with reasonable sunny spells, although there was some rain in the north on the 24th and 25th. An anticyclone to the south-west brought very mild air to many places on the 26th and 27th. East Malling in Kent reached 17.4°C probably making it the warmest January day in England on record. The 28th to the 31st saw low pressure over the Baltic and high pressure over the North Atlantic and Greenland which fed progressively colder air southwards. Snow showers on the 29th left significant falls over Wales and parts of the south-west and central southern England and some thunder was also reported. Later during the 30th more substantial bands of snow affected east coast counties, East Anglia, Essex, Bedfordshire and Hertfordshire, giving between 5 and 12cms of snowfall in most places. North and north-west suburbs of London also experienced a period of heavy snow. There was major disruption and gridlock on motorways in Essex and Hertfordshire and some tube networks were also affected.

FEBRUARY 2003

This February was the sunniest since 1988, the coldest since 1996 and the driest since 1998. From the 1st to the 7th a deep, complex low moved steadily from Iceland to the Balkans and by the 6th this introduced changeable weather. There was some thunder reported on the 2nd and 3rd. Overnight frost was widespread but it became milder and cloudier during the 6th and 7th with occasional light rain and drizzle. The 8th to the 12th was unsettled and mild or very mild with spells of rain, as Atlantic fronts advanced across the UK. However, the associated weather bands stalled over south-eastern England later on the 11th as pressure rose to the east and over the region. It became murky on the 12th with patchy rain and drizzle and some hill and coastal fog. The 13th to the 19th saw cold, dry anticyclonic weather with widespread frost at night. This was severe in places inland as high pressure settled over south Scandinavia. The dry easterly or south-easterly winds felt very cold at times, however sunshine was plentiful. The temperature fell to minus 10.5°C at Redesdale in Northumberland on the 18th. The 20th to the 26th was more changeable but mainly dry as high pressure slowly receded east into

Russia and fronts made limited progress from the Atlantic. A maximum of 15.7°C was recorded in central London on the 26th. Occasional rain and cloud affected south-west districts from time to time as weather fronts grazed the area, while other parts had patchy mist and fog on occasions during the morning. From the 27th to the 28th low pressure over the north Atlantic became more intense, driving rain belts across the region from the south-west. Patchy mist and fog gave way to bands of rain and showers, heavy at times, especially on the 28th.

MARCH 2003

This month was the sunniest March on record. The 1st to the 6th was a changeable period, mostly warm with sunny spells and some rain at times. Thunder was heard in places on the 1st. A slow moving cold front gave a wet day in most areas on the 5th as a low passed to the north of the UK. Bands of rain and showers, often heavy crossed the region, some places reported thunder later. Thereafter there was rain at times mainly in the north and west, with gusts of 60kts being recorded in exposed spots. It became mainly dry in the south from the 9th and generally warm in most areas. There were some thundery showers in northern districts on the 10th. The 12th to the 19th saw high pressure take up residence over the North Sea. The weather became mainly very warm and sunny by day, especially inland. Dry conditions prevailed apart from some scattered showers in the north-east at first on the 12th and 13th. Fog affected coastal areas adjacent to the North Sea later in the period; this kept the temperature at Walton on the Naze in Essex below 5°C on the 19th. Minus 6.6°C was noted at Redesdale in Northumberland early on the 19th. From the 20th to the 27th the anticyclone migrated to Eastern Europe but maintained its influence over the region. The dry sunny theme continued, interrupted only by some scattered thundery showers in the extreme north and north-west on the 24th. Most days were very warm particularly inland, however the clear skies allowed more sharp drops in temperature after dusk, with fairly widespread overnight frost. Minus 6.6°C was registered at Redhill Airfield in Surrey on the 22nd. Central London's temperature rose to 20.0°C on the 23rd. Coastal fog returned to counties adjacent to the North Sea during the 27th, while thundery rain broke out in the extreme south-west. The 28th to the 31st saw more changeable patterns as weak fronts grazed southern districts at first, introducing a little rain before retreating. Dry sunny warm weather established itself again on the 30th and 31st as a ridge of high pressure rebuilt over the region. North Sea fog continued to plague East Coast counties, which was slow to clear at times.

APRIL 2003

This was the warmest April since 1987 and the sunniest since 1990. The 1st to the 3rd saw an active front which swept south-east bringing sunny spells and blustery thundery showers on the 1st. Thereafter there were sunny periods and it was warmer, with mostly light scattered showers. From the 4th to the 9th it was mainly dry as an anticyclone over the UK migrated north-east to Scandinavia, later extending a tongue south-westwards towards the region. It became sunny and warm or very warm inland during the 4th and 5th but colder after with overnight frost, though still mostly sunny. The 9th saw occasional sleet break out in places. The 10th to the 12th was cold especially at first with widespread overnight frost and a band of light sleet and snow affecting southern England during the 10th. At Hawarden near Chester minus 7.5°C was recorded. It was mostly sunny by the 12th after the clearance of early morning mist and fog patches. From the 13th to the 18th it was mainly dry, sunny and very warm as the Scandinavian high became the dominant feature of the weather. Some light rain in southern areas on the 14th left dust deposits. Southerly winds brought extremely high temperatures inland, with Wolverhampton reaching 27.3°C on the 16th. This was the highest and earliest April temperature in the UK since April 16th 1949. Records were broken in many places. Cardiff Weather Centre also reached 27°C, its highest April value since 1980. Some areas had moorland and heather fires; for example one near Bolton on the 15th, while a stiff easterly breeze from the 17th fanned outbreaks in west Surrey and Hampshire during the 18th. From the 19th to the 23rd the weather was more changeable as a shallow low from the south brought cloud and lower temperatures. Forest and moorland fires affected parts of Wales, Cornwall and Dorset on the 20th. Thundery showers broke out early in the south-east on the 21st, giving a second dust fall in places. Thundery rain also affected Cumbria and north-west England. Dry sunny and warm weather returned on the 22nd and 23rd, however rain moved into the south-west later. The 24th to the 30th was mostly unsettled and sometimes windy as low-pressure systems from the North Atlantic tracked close by or over the UK. Bands of rain and showers often heavy with thunder affected many parts, especially in the west and north-west of the region. Rain on the 25th and a few thundery showers in the south on the 26th was followed by widespread wind and heavy rain later on the 27th and into the 28th. There were locally heavy thundery showers in the north-west on the 29th, while more thundery outbreaks affected western and southern areas during the 30th.

MAY 2003

The 1st to the 4th saw low pressure over or close by the UK. Unsettled and very wet weather prevailed for the first few days with frequent rain and showers often heavy and thundery. It became drier and warmer away from the north-west during the 3rd and 4th. The 5th to the 10th was more changeable and settled away from the west and north-west as weak fronts traversed the region. However there were scattered thundery outbreaks on the 5th. The 9th saw scattered light rain or showers in western areas, while rain and drizzle affected many places on the 10th. From the 11th to the 14th a depression tracking eastwards over northern parts of the UK brought progressively cooler air as winds veered to the north-west. A rather unsettled regime was established with frequent rain and showers, some heavy with thunder and hail, in particular over the south-east and East Anglia. A violent storm struck Abinger Hanger in Surrey on the 13th and a lightning strike in the village caused much local damage. From the 15th to the 21st a complex low-pressure area to the north-west drifted east-north-east to Scandinavia during the period. The 15th started dry after widespread overnight frost, minus 3.4°C being recorded at Bastreet in Cornwall. However rain moved into Devon and Cornwall later as Atlantic fronts pushed in from the south-west. A rather cool unsettled period ensued as bands of rain and showers often heavy with hail and thunder moved across the region. A violent thunderstorm was noted at Coulsdon in Surrey on the 19th. Hill and coastal fog shrouded some southern areas on the 21st as fresh Atlantic fronts moved in. The 22nd to the 25th was mostly unsettled as a low east of Scotland moved south-east. Patchy rain and hill and coastal fog on the 22nd gave way to more showery conditions and sunny periods later. There were some significant thundery outbreaks over the Midlands, the south-east and East Anglia on the 24th, with some downpours reported in places. From the 26th to the 31st an anticyclone over the Azores brought mainly dry, sunny and very warm conditions as it

migrated to south Scandinavia. After the clearance of patchy hill and coastal fog and some light rain or drizzle in south and westerly areas on the 26th and 27th, temperatures steadily rose under the combined effect of prolonged sunshine and warmer air being drawn in from the continent. Sea fog affected places in the south on the 28th, while northern England had some outbreaks of heavy rain at times during the 29th and early on the 30th. Many places became hot during the 30th and 31st, central London recording 29.1°C on the 31st. Thundery showers broke out over the Midlands and north-east England during the evening of the 31st.

JUNE 2003

This month was the warmest June since 1976 and the sunniest since 1996. The 1st to 9th was mostly warm with sunny periods but rather unsettled with rain at times, as weak Atlantic fronts and shallow low pressure centres crossed the region. The Midlands and the south-east had thundery showers on the 1st, with Shepshed in Leicestershire catching 39mm of rain in 1 hour. Widespread storms affected east and south-east England early on the 2nd, with 60mm of rain being reported from St Leonards causing flash flooding in places. Generally, showers and outbreaks of rain affected many parts from time to time. Some showers turned thundery in association with a secondary low which tracked north-east across the region on the 8th. The 10th to the 16th was generally more settled as high pressure dominated. After the clearance of thundery rain from some central and eastern areas on the 10th, and some scattered showers in the north-west on the 11th and 12th, it became mostly sunny, dry and very warm everywhere. An area of thunder affected the Channel Islands and coastal areas of south-west England on the 14th. It became hot in places during the 15th and 16th. Thundery showers broke out in south-west districts later in the evening of the 16th. During the 17th, heavy thunderstorms tracked from the Midlands to Lincolnshire and north-east England, also from south of London to the Essex coast. The rain was torrential in places, with flooding and lightning strikes disrupting railway networks in the north-east, especially the Tyne and Wear Metro. 24mm of rain fell in an hour at Coningsby in Lincolnshire. A breezy few days followed, with rain and drizzle in north-west areas. Mist and coastal fog affected the south-west and south Wales during the 19th and thereafter a ridge of high pressure gave a warm sunny day on the 20th. The 21st to 23rd saw a thundery spell, especially overnight from the 22nd to the 23rd as a low moved eastwards over Scotland. The temperature rose to 30.5°C at Shepshed in Leicestershire on the 22nd, the highest recorded in the UK so far this year. The 24th to the 26th was a relatively quiet period as a weak ridge stretched itself across the region from a high over Scandinavia. Counties bordering the English Channel had the odd thundery outbreak overnight from the 25th to the 26th. The 27th to the 30th saw changeable weather with thundery rain at times. Heavy thundery outbreaks affected much of the north and east of England later on the 27th, followed by two days of very warm sunny conditions. Rain in the south later on the 29th spread north during the 30th delivering copious amounts with thunder, particularly to the Midlands.

AVERAGE AND GENERAL MONTHLY VALUES 2002–3 (JUNE)

	Rainfall (mm)				Temperature (°C)				Bright Sunshine (hrs per day)			
	1961–90	2001	2002	2003	1961–90	2001	2002	2003	1961–90	2001	2002	2003
ENGLAND AND WALES												
January	77	70	90	84	3.8	3.4	5.3	4.2	1.6	2.15	1.42	2.35
February	55	90	129	39	3.8	4.4	6.6	3.7	2.4	3.17	2.71	3.47
March	63	86	49	39	5.6	5.1	7.2	7.2	3.5	2.96	3.60	5.56
April	53	93	54	43	7.7	7.5	8.8	9.3	4.9	4.75	6.35	6.42
May	56	42	92	73	10.9	12.1	11.4	11.6	6.2	7.54	6.04	5.96
June	58	39	55	67	13.9	13.8	13.9	15.5	6.4	6.93	5.77	7.13
July	56	72	82		15.7	16.5	15.4		6.0	6.27	5.51	
August	68	85	67		15.6	16.4	16.5		6.0	5.71	5.29	
September	70	80	35		13.6	13.0	13.9		4.5	3.77	5.43	
October	77	131	134		10.7	13.0	9.8		3.2	3.34	3.16	
November	81	67	150		6.6	7.1	8.2		2.2	2.17	1.91	
December	82	44	131		4.7	3.4	5.4		1.5	2.37	1.16	
YEAR	796	899	1068		9.4	9.6	10.2		4.0	4.26	4.00	
SCOTLAND												
January	117	86	206	167	3.1	1.9	4.3	2.6	1.3	1.75	0.99	1.22
February	78	91	235	57	3.1	2.4	3.6	2.7	2.4	2.70	1.93	3.18
March	94	74	124	86	4.6	2.8	5.0	5.7	3.2	4.08	3.42	4.88
April	60	70	87	58	6.5	5.7	7.0	8.0	4.8	4.81	4.90	5.94
May	67	41	101	139	9.3	10.4	9.5	9.1	5.6	7.11	5.62	4.58
June	67	87	129	79	12.1	11.0	11.8	13.0	5.6	4.77	4.70	5.55
July	74	99	124		13.6	13.2	12.5		4.9	3.86	3.47	
August	92	111	87		13.5	13.0	14.0		4.9	4.10	4.11	
September	111	104	50		11.5	10.7	11.8		3.5	3.11	3.51	
October	120	238	182		9.1	10.7	6.8		2.6	1.98	2.49	
November	118	150	159		5.3	5.9	6.2		1.7	1.18	1.31	
December	115	116	68		3.9	2.5	3.5		1.0	1.25	0.79	
YEAR	1,113	1,267	1,552		7.9	7.5	8.0		3.5	3.39	3.10	

Source: Data provided by the Met Office

WIND FORCE MEASURES

The *Beaufort Scale* of wind force has been accepted internationally and is used in communicating weather conditions. Devised originally by Admiral Sir Francis Beaufort in 1805, it now consists of the numbers 0–17, each representing a certain strength or velocity of wind at 10 m (33 ft) above ground in the open.

Scale no.	Wind Force	mph	knots
0	Calm	1	1
1	Light air	1–3	1–3
2	Slight breeze	4–7	4–6
3	Gentle breeze	8–12	7–10
4	Moderate breeze	13–18	11–16
5	Fresh breeze	19–24	17–21
6	Strong breeze	25–31	22–27
7	High wind	32–38	28–33
8	Gale	39–46	34–40
9	Strong gale	47–54	41–47
10	Whole gale	55–63	48–55
11	Storm	64–72	56–63
12	Hurricane	73–82	64–71
13	–	83–92	72–80
14	–	93–103	81–89
15	–	104–114	90–99
16	–	115–125	100–108
17	–	126–136	109–118

TEMPERATURE, RAINFALL AND SUNSHINE

At selected climatological reporting stations, July 2002 – June 2003 and calendar year 2002

Ht   height (in metres) of station above mean sea level
°C   mean air temperature
Rain   total monthly rainfall
Sun   monthy total (hours)
Source: Data provided by the Met Office

		July 2002			August 2002			September 2002			October 2002		
	Ht		Rain	Sun		Rain	Sun		Rain	Sun		Rain	Sun
	m	°C	mm	hrs	°C	mm	hrs	°C	mm	hrs	°C	mm	hrs
Lerwick	82	12.3	56.2	129.3	13.8	53.7	115.8	11.9	43.7	89.2	7.4	91.2	99.7
Stornoway	15	12.5	100.2	106.4	13.9	44.0	128.1	12.9	38.0	82.4	8.7	91.4	71.7
Dyce	65	14.0	101.4	140.6	15.0	107.8	139.3	12.9	15.6	117.1	8.0	230.4	99.1
Eskdalemuir	242	12.8	109.8	99.4	14.7	129.5	134.1	11.7	60.8	120.9	6.7	230.8	84.9
Aldergrove	68	14.1	102	122.5	15.5	46.4	145.6	13.5	27.2	135.6	9.0	161.8	84.0
Leeds	64	16.6	119.4	119.4	17.9	113.8	112.8	14.9	23.6	108.4	10	101.8	68.8
Valley	10	14.6	60.4	139.4	15.3	85.0	166.2	14.6	21.0	168.7	10.9	161.4	96.8
Coleshill	–	16.2	65.0	–	17.2	44.8	–	14.5	29.2	–	9.9	138.8	–
Skegness	6	16.3	91.8	194.0	17.5	43.0	166.6	14.9	22.5	129.3	10.4	96.0	97.8
Bristol	42	16.2	37.8	158.4	17.5	44.2	154.0	15.3	36.4	159.2	11.1	142.3	98.5
St Mawgan	103	15.1	59.4	210.9	16.0	62.8	193.9	15.0	19.2	213.1	12.1	136.8	112.9
Hastings	45	16.8	65.3	233.1	18.3	20.5	230.2	16.0	60.1	199.5	12.2	62.2	120.6

	November 2002			December 2002			The Year 2002			January 2003			February 2003		
		rain	sun		rain	sun		rain	sun		rain	sun		rain	sun
	°C	mm	hrs	°C	mm	hrs	°C	mm	hrs	°C	mm	hrs	°C	mm	hrs
Lerwick	6.5	140.9	41.4	4.8	116.7	11.3	8.1	93.1	99.1	3.9	204	42.1	4.5	48.5	69.6
Stornoway	8.2	95.4	35.7	5.5	29.8	25.4	9.2	90.95	97.8	4.8	154.2	27.9	5.6	54.4	56.2
Dyce	7.5	185.4	57.5	5.4	111.4	15.9	9.0	90.8	116.4	4.2	91.8	69.2	3.4	11.3	89.6
Eskdalemuir	5.6	197.2	41.5	3.4	129.2	31.7	8.0	175.2	87.5	2.4	164.0	61.7	2.0	68.9	105.1
Aldergrove	8.5	158.2	58.2	5.6	52.2	51.3	9.9	95.4	107.8	4.4	73.8	78.9	4.5	49.8	91.7
Leeds	8.3	92.6	36.5	5.5	116.2	34.1	11.0	88.3	–	5.4	33.2	62.0	4.1	29.6	93.3
Valley	9.8	171.0	66.6	6.4	82.6		10.7	78.6	–	5.7	62.8	85.0	5.4	37.4	108.1
Coleshill	8.5	100.4	–	5.6	93.4	–	10.6	–	–	4.3	60.6	–	3.8	20.2	–
Skegness	8.5	89.0	42.7	6.1	90.5	18.5	–	–	–	4.9	91.5	48.6	4.1	14.2	92.0
Bristol	9.6	104.4	58.3	6.4	95.0	38.8	11.2	74.4	–	4.8	62.2	84.9	4.6	28.5	70.8
St Mawgan	10.7	235.6	81.2	7.7	145.2	52.4	11.3	97.6	119.7	6.2	79.2	94.4	6.1	75.8	119.4
Hastings	10.7	150.0	77.2	7.2	154.1	32.4	–	–	–	5.4	50.7	102.5	4.7	25.7	110.3

	March 2003			April 2003			May 2003			June 2003		
		Rain	Sun		Rain	Sun		Rain	Sun		Rain	Sun
	°C	mm	hrs	°C	mm	hrs	°C	mm	hrs	°C	mm	hrs
Lerwick	6.4	72.0	104.6	6.9	30.7	147.4	8.4	85.3	148.8	11.8	89.7	109.8
Stornoway	7.1	76.0	69.6	9.7	32.2	171.6	9.5	102.6	123.2	13.3	66.2	121.9
Dyce	6.4	17.2	190.5	8.1	55.2	160.4	10.5	86.8	199.1	14.4	20.6	197.8
Eskdalemuir	5.4	109.6	164.1	8.3	65.8	189.1	9.4	127.6	139.1	13.2	57.0	181.3
Aldergrove	7.0	35.2	161.2	9.4	32.4	176.3	10.8	106.8	123.5	14.3	50.4	159.5
Leeds	8.0	23.4	144.8	10.6	40.0	174.0	13.0	85.0	142.5	17.0	96.2	175.4
Valley	7.7	41.6	191.1	10.0	55.0	203.3	11.5	89.0	182.3	14.8	58.6	215.2
Coleshill	7.3	23.6	–	9.5	34.8	–	12.2	51.6	–	16.4	62.8	–
Skegness	7.0	25.0	161.2	8.8	28.0	193.8	12.5	61.4	212.8	–	–	–
Bristol	8.5	27.6	173.5	10.5	34.0	172.9	12.4	68.2	168.6	16.6	46.6	192.9
St Mawgan	9.2	30.2	173.3	10.6	49.4	222.0	11.7	80.6	215.2	14.9	93.0	239.6
Hastings	8.5	24.5	177.72	10.3	23.7	222.2	12.8	43.2	227.9	–	–	–

METEOROLOGICAL OBSERVATIONS LONDON (HEATHROW)

Temperature maxima and minima cover the 24-hour period 9 – 9 h; mean wind speed is 10 m above ground; rainfall is for the 24 hours starting on 9 h on the day of entry; sunshine is for the 24 hours. *Source:* Data provided by the Met Office

JULY 2002

Day	Temperature Max C°	Min C°	Wind knots	Sun hrs	Rain mm
1	18.4	11.7	11.3	4.4	2.4
2	19.0	10.7	10.6	2.0	12.0
3	17.9	11.1	7.4	2.0	5.8
4	19.9	9.9	8.2	7.2	2.8
5	19.8	12.3	7.0	0.9	7.8
6	20.9	13.0	5.5	3.3	0.4
7	20.8	13.6	8.7	2.9	0.6
8	19.0	15.1	9.5	0.0	11.6
9	21.4	15.5	8.7	4.7	1.4
10	19.1	10.7	8.0	10.7	4.6
11	20.1	10.5	7.1	9.8	2.4
12	17.3	10.4	2.6	0.1	Trace
13	22.7	10.9	5.0	14.7	0.0
14	25.0	11.4	3.7	15.2	0.0
15	25.9	13.1	5.0	10.8	0.0
16	25.6	15.9	5.8	10.8	0.0
17	21.9	13.1	6.6	7.9	0.0
18	23.4	14.8	7.2	6.3	0.0
19	24.2	12.9	6.7	12.6	0.0
20	23.2	14.4	6.1	7.5	0.0
21	19.8	11.6	6.3	4.5	0.0
22	22.3	10.5	6.0	6.3	Trace
23	20.4	14.3	9.4	0.5	Trace
24	20.3	14.9	7.3	5.1	0.0
25	21.7	12.2	6.6	3.6	0.0
26	27.6	16.1	7.1	10.6	0.0
27	24.9	15.6	6.9	5.5	0.0
28	29.7	17.0	4.7	13.6	0.0
29	32.5	18.0	5.7	7.6	0.0
30	25.4	18.8	5.5	2.1	4.2
31	21.8	17.6	5.6	0.7	11.2

AUGUST 2002

Day	Temperature Max C°	Min C°	Wind knots	Sun hrs	Rain mm
1	21.1	12.7	3.0	2.7	0.0
2	23.6	12.1	6.6	11.5	0.4
3	19.3	15.3	4.8	2.1	17.6
4	21.8	12.8	5.0	4.9	4.5
5	21.3	12.3	4.8	3.1	1.4
6	24.0	15.1	5.7	5.1	0.0
7	26.7	16.1	4.3	9.0	3.2
8	20.4	15.4	5.1	0.7	5.8
9	19.7	13.9	6.9	2.6	2.4
10	22.1	14.1	5.6	4.5	0.6
11	21.9	13.8	6.1	4.0	0.2
12	22.6	14.9	6.1	6.2	0.0
13	25.6	13.2	5.4	9.4	0.0
14	25.4	15.1	4.8	13.2	0.0
15	28.4	16.7	3.9	7.3	0.0
16	27.1	16.1	5.4	12.1	0.0
17	30.0	15.7	7.2	9.9	0.0
18	25.8	17.1	4.1	4.9	Trace
19	25.5	17.7	4.9	7.4	Trace
20	23.2	16.9	4.8	2.6	Trace
21	23.2	14.3	5.6	11.4	0.0
22	23.5	15.0	4.6	7.6	Trace
23	23.5	14.6	3.0	5.3	Trace
24	23.6	15.1	3.4	7.1	Trace
25	21.7	15.0	7.5	6.1	Trace
26	17.6	12.7	10.0	0.0	Trace
27	22.1	14.7	8.6	4.4	0.0
28	24.0	14.4	4.4	11.2	0.0
29	24.5	14.0	5.2	2.1	Trace
30	22.6	16.1	9.3	1.8	0.2
31	20.9	13.5	7.1	10.2	0.0

SEPTEMBER 2002

Day	Temperature Max C°	Min C°	Wind knots	Sun hrs	Rain mm
1	21.1	9.3	4.9	10.9	0.0
2	22.9	10.2	8.4	10.2	0.0
3	24.0	14.7	7.6	3.1	0.0
4	23.4	11.3	4.0	8.3	0.0
5	23.4	12.7	6.3	7.6	2.0
6	22.7	15.6	11.4	5.0	1.2
7	21.0	13.7	7.4	7.3	0.2
8	20.6	10.1	4.7	6.7	0.2
9	15.6	11.7	7.5	0.0	15.8
10	21.1	10.0	3.4	11.5	0.0
11	22.4	9.9	5.7	9.6	0.0
12	23.5	14.3	8.9	9.2	0.0
13	24.6	13.3	9.0	11.3	0.0
14	19.3	15.0	10.9	2.0	0.0
15	18.3	14.3	9.7	2.8	0.0
16	19.5	10.1	6.8	8.1	0.0
17	19.2	11.8	6.9	2.7	0.0
18	18.7	11.6	7.1	0.0	0.0
19	19.7	12.8	6.4	1.8	0.0
20	18.9	14.2	4.8	0.3	0.0
21	19.1	13.1	5.0	3.9	0.0
22	17.9	12.6	9.6	4.6	0.2
23	19.2	10.5	11.0	8.5	0.0
24	18.1	8.9	8.9	6.9	0.0
25	19.0	7.0	6.5	5.2	0.4
26	18.2	11.0	8.1	8.7	0.0
27	17.2	7.7	3.8	0.0	0.0
28	19.2	8.6	3.3	5.3	Trace
29	20.7	9.2	6.1	9.1	0.0
30	21.4	9.4	5.3	7.6	0.0

OCTOBER 2002

Day	Temperature Max C°	Min C°	Wind knots	Sun hrs	Rain mm
1	21.8	10.3	3.6	2.0	Trace
2	19.9	13.9	5.8	2.8	0.6
3	20.3	13.9	6.5	6.6	0.0
4	18.8	6.8	5.6	7.4	0.0
5	18.8	7.8	7.9	2.4	Trace
6	18.7	11.3	8.9	7.9	0.0
7	17.5	11.4	3.5	1.5	0.0
8	16.4	11.2	8.2	1.5	0.0
9	15.6	8.4	10.6	7.8	0.2
10	16.7	10.8	9.3	4.9	Trace
11	13.7	10.8	7.8	0.0	3.6
12	16.2	9.1	7.9	5.6	0.0
13	11.9	5.4	8.7	0.0	11.8
14	12.2	8.3	8.7	0.1	3.2
15	14.4	9.0	13.4	0.0	10.8
16	11.7	9.3	8.6	0.0	0.0
17	11.9	3.9	6.4	6.9	1.8
18	10.7	2.8	5.5	4.2	1.6
19	11.9	0.9	5.6	7.8	0.0
20	14.1	4.3	8.2	0.0	1.6
21	17.6	7.6	7.4	2.3	7.0
22	16.4	12.9	10.6	1.2	3.8
23	12.1	7.2	13.7	8.8	0.0
24	14.4	2.4	5.8	5.5	3.0
25	16.3	6.9	15.3	3.1	4.4
26	16.1	9.3	14.6	7.3	2.0
27	14.1	11.2	24.8	5.3	0.2
28	13.7	4.9	7.6	5.9	Trace
29	14.2	8.1	7.8	0.2	0.2
30	11.5	9.9	6.0	0.0	5.6
31	13.9	10.1	5.2	0.2	0.2

NOVEMBER 2002

		Temperature Max C°	Min C°	Wind knots	Sun hrs	Rain mm
Day	1	15.2	11.5	8.6	0.0	4.8
	2	15.9	10.1	7.5	0.2	16.0
	3	14.8	10.3	10.9	4.7	1.2
	4	14.2	6.7	6.8	6.7	Trace
	5	14.3	7.7	6.8	0.1	5.2
	6	13.8	11.9	10.0	0.0	13.2
	7	10.9	4.7	10.0	7.4	1.0
	8	13.9	5.0	11.5	0.0	7.6
	9	11.5	7.9	5.7	2.2	8.6
	10	15.4	7.6	8.0	0.0	1.4
	11	14.1	7.3	10.0	6.7	8.8
	12	12.7	9.5	9.3	1.6	13.8
	13	12.2	7.6	8.8	2.6	8.6
	14	13.2	9.3	13.3	4.9	10.0
	15	13.2	6.7	5.8	1.7	1.4
	16	10.4	6.6	4.2	0.4	0.8
	17	9.0	7.3	4.3	0.0	2.8
	18	9.9	0.6	4.1	5.1	0.0
	19	10.3	1.4	8.3	4.0	Trace
	20	11.7	7.2	9.4	0.0	3.8
	21	12.0	8.4	9.5	0.1	12.4
	22	11.2	8.1	9.5	2.2	12.2
	23	12.3	5.7	8.0	3.9	3.2
	24	10.3	4.6	5.3	0.8	7.2
	25	8.7	4.8	4.3	0.2	Trace
	26	12.8	3.5	5.5	5.5	0.0
	27	11.8	4.8	12.2	2.0	1.2
	28	13.3	8.3	7.5	2.6	1.4
	29	9.4	6.5	4.8	0.5	0.0
	30	12.2	7.1	6.0	0.0	4.4

DECEMBER 2002

		Temperature Max C°	Min C°	Wind knots	Sun hrs	Rain mm
Day	1	12.4	7.6	13.1	1.6	2.6
	2	10.9	7.7	14.0	1.4	0.8
	3	10.5	6.8	6.2	1.0	0.8
	4	10.2	5.7	7.4	0.9	3.6
	5	8.8	4.3	9.2	6.5	Trace
	6	8.5	4.9	10.6	0.0	0.2
	7	5.9	4.3	11.6	0.0	0.2
	8	4.0	3.4	10.8	0.0	0.4
	9	5.4	2.5	12.1	6.0	Trace
	10	3.8	1.0	14.1	0.0	Trace
	11	3.8	0.8	13.5	0.0	0.0
	12	5.7	2.5	6.8	0.0	2.0
	13	7.3	2.5	5.9	0.0	0.2
	14	7.6	5.7	9.5	0.0	8.8
	15	7.7	6.0	10.8	0.0	6.6
	16	7.0	5.4	7.5	0.0	0.4
	17	5.6	4.6	8.3	0.0	Trace
	18	7.0	0.2	7.7	6.9	0.0
	19	6.4	1.5	8.0	4.8	0.0
	20	7.3	1.1	3.8	0.0	4.0
	21	12.0	3.1	5.3	0.0	18.0
	22	12.8	6.1	10.0	0.4	Trace
	23	12.4	8.8	7.5	0.0	2.2
	24	13.8	10.3	9.8	1.8	0.4
	25	12.1	9.6	6.6	1.6	4.6
	26	12.6	9.1	11.7	0.1	11.2
	27	12.4	10.1	9.3	0.0	Trace
	28	11.2	5.4	8.3	1.1	10.2
	29	13.4	5.8	10.4	0.0	5.6
	30	11.5	8.2	8.6	0.0	24.4
	31	9.9	4.7	7.0	0.0	11.8

JANUARY 2003

		Temperature Max C°	Min C°	Wind knots	Sun hrs	Rain mm
Day	1	12.9	3.7	9.6	0.0	16.0
	2	11.3	8.6	10.0	0.1	1.8
	3	7.5	5.3	8.7	1.6	0.8
	4	4.1	0.6	7.0	5.1	0.0
	5	4.9	−2.4	2.3	3.9	0.0
	6	3.9	−1.6	6.5	7.2	0.3
	7	1.7	−1.7	7.4	3.2	Trace
	8	1.0	−3.8	5.0	0.0	2.1
	9	3.1	−1.1	9.0	6.8	0.2
	10	5.1	0.4	10.5	1.1	0.2
	11	3.9	−2.1	4.8	7.2	0.0
	12	7.9	−5.1	5.3	6.0	Trace
	13	11.7	−3.2	12.8	3.2	0.0
	14	10.5	7.2	14.7	0.0	0.0
	15	10.4	8.7	13.4	0.5	0.2
	16	10.1	2.7	9.3	4.8	Trace
	17	7.2	4.1	12.2	0.0	0.6
	18	9.7	1.9	9.5	1.1	11.8
	19	10.1	4.5	9.6	2.8	5.6
	20	9.7	5.5	14.0	0.0	5.4
	21	9.4	8.0	10.7	0.1	11.2
	22	9.5	4.8	11.0	1.8	0.2
	23	8.7	5.4	9.2	5.6	0.2
	24	10.3	−0.2	6.5	4.5	1.0
	25	12.9	2.7	10.8	3.1	0.8
	26	12.7	4.4	8.7	0.1	0.4
	27	15.1	6.0	10.4	7.6	0.8
	28	9.4	4.6	17.7	5.0	1.6
	29	6.8	4.7	16.8	3.5	Trace
	30	2.6	0.9	15.4	1.7	4.8
	31	3.5	−2.2	9.8	6.0	7.6

FEBRUARY 2003

		Temperature Max C°	Min C°	Wind knots	Sun hrs	Rain mm
Day	1	8.1	−1.6	7.5	3.5	0.8
	2	8.8	1.5	13.6	2.8	0.6
	3	7.1	3.5	13.7	6.3	Trace
	4	6.2	−1.1	11.8	3.8	0.2
	5	5.0	−0.3	7.3	6.9	0.0
	6	8.1	−3.6	5.8	0.0	0.8
	7	10.8	0.4	7.0	0.5	Trace
	8	10.9	8.1	9.7	0.0	5.2
	9	8.3	7.3	8.9	0.0	1.6
	10	6.8	3.5	5.5	0.0	3.6
	11	6.9	5.0	4.7	0.0	2.8
	12	7.5	5.5	5.6	0.0	0.2
	13	2.7	1.4	7.3	3.5	0.0
	14	4.7	−1.6	7.3	7.0	0.0
	15	4.8	−1.8	8.4	4.0	Trace
	16	4.0	1.0	8.8	3.2	Trace
	17	4.4	−0.3	8.5	7.9	0.0
	18	5.4	−2.9	8.3	9.5	0.0
	19	5.1	−2.8	10.0	6.1	0.0
	20	8.8	0.3	7.1	3.8	0.2
	21	12.9	−0.4	3.5	9.3	0.0
	22	9.5	1.2	7.0	8.0	Trace
	23	13.3	2.5	7.2	2.0	0.2
	24	14.0	4.2	6.5	2.1	0.0
	25	12.7	3.7	8.4	6.4	0.0
	26	14.5	5.1	6.9	2.7	0.0
	27	13.8	5.3	7.0	1.8	0.2
	28	10.6	7.9	11.6	0.1	4.4

MARCH 2003

Day	Temperature Max C°	Min C°	Wind knots	Sun hrs	Rain mm
1	14.3	3.7	8.4	1.0	1.6
2	11.6	5.4	5.9	7.6	0.0
3	9.8	1.0	6.7	0.2	0.8
4	14.2	4.6	9.8	0.5	Trace
5	12.9	9.5	10.1	0.0	7.4
6	12.1	2.5	8.3	9.0	0.0
7	11.3	5.0	13.2	1.4	5.0
8	11.3	5.6	17.4	0.0	0.2
9	13.2	8.1	16.3	3.5	Trace
10	13.2	7.9	12.9	0.8	0.0
11	12.0	8.5	13.5	0.1	Trace
12	9.1	5.6	12.3	1.7	1.0
13	9.4	4.8	9.8	5.9	0.0
14	10.9	1.8	10.2	10.1	0.0
15	10.6	2.4	9.5	10.3	0.2
16	13.7	2.4	6.7	10.4	0.0
17	16.6	0.6	5.2	10.0	0.0
18	12.0	3.6	7.6	8.2	0.0
19	14.8	0.4	3.1	9.4	0.0
20	15.4	0.7	4.8	8.4	0.0
21	9.8	5.0	6.7	1.9	0.2
22	13.5	0.7	6.7	9.8	0.0
23	18.9	1.3	5.7	10.6	0.0
24	17.0	5.9	7.8	7.8	0.0
25	16.9	6.1	3.6	7.3	0.0
26	16.8	5.9	5.8	8.4	0.0
27	17.1	5.5	7.1	8.5	0.0
28	15.3	4.3	6.8	2.0	Trace
29	16.0	5.9	4.8	0.6	0.0
30	16.6	7.7	8.0	10.1	0.0
31	14.2	4.2	5.4	11.4	0.0

APRIL 2003

Day	Temperature Max C°	Min C°	Wind knots	Sun hrs	Rain mm
1	11.8	3.7	12.4	1.8	3.4
2	11.5	4.8	12.0	7.4	0.2
3	13.5	3.3	7.8	8.6	Trace
4	19.7	5.9	8.9	8.7	0.0
5	16.1	7.9	9.6	11.9	0.0
6	9.7	9.0	9.5	0.0	0.0
7	9.5	1.5	8.0	11.2	0.0
8	9.3	−0.5	7.0	10.7	0.0
9	8.1	−0.2	7.6	5.0	Trace
10	8.9	1.2	8.7	3.6	0.4
11	9.8	−0.7	3.8	4.1	0.0
12	14.6	0.5	6.6	7.1	Trace
13	18.6	5.5	10.2	8.3	Trace
14	18.2	11.3	8.8	0.0	Trace
15	23.5	10.5	5.4	7.9	0.0
16	26.0	8.7	6.9	12.9	0.0
17	22.4	10.7	9.6	12.8	0.0
18	21.4	9.7	11.0	12.6	0.0
19	11.0	5.7	13.3	1.4	Trace
20	15.2	6.4	11.2	5.4	2.8
21	15.7	9.2	9.8	8.3	0.0
22	17.7	5.5	4.5	9.1	0.0
23	18.7	6.5	7.8	11.7	0.0
24	16.5	6.4	5.7	2.2	0.2
25	18.9	9.7	7.9	0.3	5.0
26	16.7	7.9	8.8	4.0	0.4
27	17.4	9.7	14.2	5.6	8.0
28	14.9	10.1	12.2	0.1	1.2
29	17.7	8.7	12.3	9.5	0.6
30	17.7	9.9	10.5	5.8	7.8

MAY 2003

Day	Temperature Max C°	Min C°	Wind knots	Sun hrs	Rain mm
1	17.0	8.6	12.5	5.7	3.2
2	14.6	9.5	12.8	1.5	4.0
3	16.9	7.6	13.0	6.1	Trace
4	22.0	7.4	9.8	10.9	Trace
5	17.3	11.6	11.1	9.7	0.0
6	17.6	5.3	7.2	12.9	0.0
7	19.7	6.1	5.4	12.2	0.0
8	15.9	7.5	5.5	2.4	0.0
9	18.1	8.2	7.6	11.8	0.0
10	15.3	6.3	9.3	4.9	Trace
11	17.2	5.7	8.6	6.7	Trace
12	14.6	7.2	10.0	4.8	6.2
13	13.0	3.8	9.0	7.2	4.8
14	15.9	4.4	9.8	7.7	Trace
15	16.8	4.4	5.6	12.0	2.8
16	12.9	8.5	8.6	0.0	2.0
17	16.0	10.6	11.6	2.1	3.4
18	16.7	11.0	14.1	1.6	Trace
19	16.5	10.9	11.5	4.6	8.7
20	15.0	8.0	15.3	2.2	1.4
21	16.6	10.0	10.6	4.8	1.8
22	19.0	13.0	13.3	0.4	0.2
23	18.0	12.5	13.5	3.4	Trace
24	17.8	9.4	6.9	5.5	0.6
25	18.3	8.4	8.3	6.3	Trace
26	19.9	8.3	6.1	12.4	Trace
27	19.3	11.2	5.3	0.1	0.0
28	23.7	11.7	5.1	8.8	0.0
29	25.8	11.9	6.1	12.4	0.0
30	27.2	12.5	4.4	10.4	0.0
31	28.9	15.8	7.9	14.0	Trace

JUNE 2003

Day	Temperature Max C°	Min C°	Wind knots	Sun hrs	Rain mm
1	24.0	14.4	6.3	1.5	1.0
2	22.7	14.7	7.6	5.7	Trace
3	22.5	11.5	7.3	3.3	0.4
4	21.5	13.4	7.1	4.1	2.0
5	21.8	10.5	10.3	13.7	Trace
6	19.1	12.1	9.1	0.1	3.6
7	23.2	15.1	9.8	7.2	7.0
8	21.9	11.9	10.3	7.0	2.8
9	21.0	9.9	7.8	12.4	1.0
10	22.7	14.9	12.0	6.2	Trace
11	21.6	13.6	10.3	10.0	Trace
12	23.5	12.7	7.8	11.2	0.0
13	23.6	10.6	5.3	14.2	Trace
14	24.8	16.0	8.3	12.7	0.0
15	26.5	12.1	4.4	15.0	0.0
16	27.5	14.8	5.8	13.0	0.0
17	26.1	15.7	6.3	3.9	1.0
18	21.1	13.3	11.8	3.7	Trace
19	24.7	16.6	13.2	4.4	0.0
20	22.4	12.0	8.8	15.4	0.0
21	25.3	11.6	6.0	12.3	1.4
22	25.7	14.9	8.1	1.4	18.4
23	23.4	15.8	10.2	8.4	0.0
24	23.6	11.1	5.1	15.4	0.0
25	22.8	13.4	8.8	10.4	Trace
26	24.4	14.9	9.0	7.7	0.0
27	22.3	15.8	6.3	0.1	Trace
28	22.5	10.7	5.5	10.5	0.0
29	26.3	10.9	8.5	11.8	2.2
30	21.2	15.4	9.0	2.8	6.8

SPORTS RESULTS

For 2004 sports fixtures, *see* pages 12–13

ALPINE SKIING

WORLD CUP 2002–3
MEN
Downhill: Stephan Eberharter (Austria), 790 points
Slalom: Kalle Palander (Finland), 658 points
Giant Slalom: Michael von Gruenigen (Switzerland), 542
   points
Super Giant Slalom: Stephan Eberharter (Austria), 356
   points
Overall: Stephan Eberharter (Austria), 1,333 points

WOMEN
Downhill: Michaela Dorfmeister (Austria), 332 points
Slalom: Janica Kostelic (Croatia), 710 points
Giant Slalom: Anja Paerson (Sweden), 514 points
Super Giant Slalom: Carole Montillet (France), 493 points
Overall: Janica Kostelic (Croatia), 1,570 points

WORLD CHAMPIONSHIP 2003
San Moritz, February

MEN
Downhill: Michael Walchhofer (Austria)
Slalom: Ivica Kostelic (Croatia)
Giant Slalom: Bode Miller (USA)
Super Giant Slalom: Stephan Eberharter (Austria)
Combined: Bode Miller (USA)

WOMEN
Downhill: Mélanie Turgeon (Canada)
Slalom: Janica Kostelic (Croatia)
Giant Slalom: Anja Paerson (Sweden)
Super Giant Slalom: Michaela Dorfmeister (Austria)
Combined: Janica Kostelic (Croatia)

AMERICAN FOOTBALL

AFC Championship 2003: Oakland Raiders beat
   Tennessee Titans 41–24
NFC Championship 2003: Tampa Bay Buccaneers beat
   Philadelphia Eagles 27–10
XXXVII American Superbowl 2003 (San Diego, 26
   January 2003): Tampa Bay Buccaneers beat Oakland
   Raiders 48–21

ANGLING

NATIONAL COARSE CHAMPIONSHIPS 2003
Division: 1
Individual Winner: T. Hopley
Team Winners: Bawtry & District A. C.

Division: 2
Individual winner: A. Wright
Team winners: Team Van Den Eyde Wigan

Division: 3
Individual winner: A. Innes
Team winners: Team Daiwa Trentmen

Division: 4
Individual winner: M. Sharpe
Team winners: Slaithwaite & District

Division: 5
Individual winner: C. Lemon
Team winners: Team Mosella Strike

Ladies' Championship
Winner: Helen Dagnell

ASSOCIATION FOOTBALL

LEAGUE COMPETITIONS 2002–3

ENGLAND AND WALES
Premiership
1. Manchester United, 83 points
2. Arsenal, 78 points
Relegated: West Ham United; West Bromwich Albion;
   Sunderland

Division 1
1. Portsmouth, 98 points
2. Leicester City, 92 points
Play-off winner and third promotion place:
   Wolverhampton Wanderers
Relegated: Sheffield Wednesday, Brighton and Hove
   Albion, Grimsby Town

Division 2
1. Wigan Athletic, 100 points
2. Crewe Alexandria, 86 points
Play-off winner and third promotion place: Cardiff City
Relegated: Cheltenham Town, Huddersfield Town,
   Mansfield Town, Northampton Town

Division 3
1. Rushden and Diamonds, 87 points
2. Hartlepool United, 85 points
3. Wrexham, 84 points
Play-off winner and fourth promotion place: Bournemouth
Relegated: Exeter City, Shrewsbury Town

Football Conference
1. Yeovil Town, 95 points
Play-off winner and second promotion place: Doncaster
   Rovers

League of Wales
1. Barry Town, 83 points
2. Llansantffraid, 80 points
3. Bangor City, 71 points

Women's Premier League National Division
1. Fulham, 49 points
2. Doncaster Belles, 41 points
3. Arsenal, 40 points

SCOTLAND
Premier Division
1. Rangers, 97 points (+73 GD)
2. Celtic, 97 points (+72 GD)

Division 1
1. Falkirk, 81 points
2. Clyde, 72 points
Relegated: Arbroath, 15 points

Division 2
1. Raith Rovers, 59 points
2. Brechin City, 55 points
Relegated: Cowdenbeath, 36 points

Division 3
1. Morton, 72 points
2. East Fife, 71 points
Bottom: East Stirlingshire, 13 points

NORTHERN IRELAND
Irish League Premier Division
1. Glentoran, 90 points; 2. Portadown, 80 points;
3. Coleraine; 73 points.

REPUBLIC OF IRELAND
Premier Division 2002–3: 1. Bohemians, 54 points;
2. Shelbourne, 49 points; 3. Shamrock Rovers, 43 points.

FRANCE
French League:
1. Lyon, 68 points; 2. Monaco, 67 points;
3. Marseille, 65 points

GERMANY
German League: 1. Bayern Munich, 75 points; 2. Stuttgart
Kickers, 59 points; 3. Borrusia Dortmund, 58 points

ITALY
Italian League: 1. Juventus, 72 points; 2. Internazionale,
65 points; 3. Milan, 61 points

HOLLAND
Dutch League: 1. PSV Eindhoven, 84 points; 2. Ajax, 83
points; 3. Feyenoord, 80 points

SPAIN
Spanish League: 1. Real Madrid, 78 points; 2.
Real Sociedad, 76 points; 3. Deportivo La Coruña,
72 points

CUP COMPETITIONS

ENGLAND
FA Cup final 2003: Arsenal beat Southampton 1–0
League Cup final 2003: Liverpool beat Manchester United
2–0
LDV Vans Trophy: Bristol City beat Carlisle United 2–0
FA Vase final 2003: Brigg Town beat Sudbury 2–1
FA Trophy final 2003: Burscough beat Tamworth 2–1
Community Shield 2003: Manchester United beat Arsenal
4–3 on penalties *(1–1 after normal time, no extra time
played)*

WOMEN
Women's FA Cup final 2003: Fulham beat Charlton
Athletic 3–0
Women's League Cup Final 2003: Fulham beat Arsenal
3–2 on penalties *(1–1 aet)*
Community Shield: Fulham beat Doncaster Rovers Belles
1–0

WALES
FA Wales Cup final 2003: Barry Town beat Cwmbran
Town 4–3 on penalties *(2–2 aet)*
FA Wales Premier Cup final 2003: Wrexham beat
Newport County 6–1

SCOTLAND
Scottish Cup final 2003: Rangers beat Dundee 1–0
League Cup final 2003: Rangers beat Celtic 2–1

NORTHERN IRELAND
Irish Cup final 2003: Coleraine beat Glentoran 1–0

EUROPE
European Champions' League final 2003: Milan beat
Juventus 3–2 on penalties *(0–0 aet)*
UEFA Cup final 2003: Porto beat Celtic 3–2 *(aet)*
European Super Cup final 2002: Real Madrid beat
Feyenoord 3–1
InterToto Cup winners 2002: Fulham (England); Stuttgart
(Germany); Malaga (Spain)

WORLD FOOTBALLER OF THE YEAR
2002 – Ronaldo (Brazil)
2001 – Luis Figo (Portugal)
2000 – Zinedine Zidane (France)
1999 – Rivaldo (Brazil)
1998 – Zinedine Zidane (France)
1997 – Ronaldo (Brazil)
1996 – Ronaldo (Brazil)
1995 – George Weah (Liberia)
1994 – Romario (Brazil)
1993 – Roberto Baggio (Italy)
1992 – Marco van Basten (Netherlands)

ATHLETICS

RWA WOMEN'S NATIONAL 10KM WALK
Held at Leicester, 1 September 2002

Individual: Estle Viljoen (South Africa) 49min 06sec
Team: Steyning 17pts

RWA MEN'S NATIONAL 50KM WALK
Held at Colchester, 8 September 2002

Individual: Mike Smith (Coventry) 4hr 42min 58sec
Team: Coventry Godiva 293pts

IAAF GRAND PRIX FINAL
Held at Paris, 14 September 2002

MEN		min	sec
100m	Tim Montgomery (USA)		9.78
400m	Michael Blackwood (Jamaica)		44.72
1500m	Hicham El Guerrouj (Morocco)	3	29.27
3000m	Abraham Chebii (Kenya)	8	33.42
400m H	Felix Sanchez (Dominica)		47.62

		metres
High Jump	Stefan Holm (Sweden)	2.31
Pole Vault	Jeff Hartwig (USA)	5.75
Triple Jump	Christian Olsson (Sweden)	17.48
Shot	Adam Nelson (USA)	21.34
Hammer	Koji Murofushi (Japan)	81.14

WOMEN		min	sec
100m	Marion Jones (USA)		10.88
400m	Ana Guevara (Mexico)		49.90
1500m	Yelena Zadorozhnaya (Russia)	4	00.63
3000m	Gabriela Szabo (Romania)	8	56.29
100m H	Gail Devers (USA)		12.51

		metres
Long Jump	Maureen Maggi (Brazil)	7.02
Discus	Natalya Sadova (Russia)	65.79
Javelin	Osleidys Menendez (Cuba)	65.69

Men's Overall Winner: Tim Montgomery (USA)

Women's Overall Winner: Marion Jones (USA)

WORLD CUP
Held at Madrid, 20–21 September 2002

MEN

100m	10.06s	Uchenna Emedolu (Africa/Ngr)
200m	20.18s	Francis Obikwelu (Europe/Por)
400m	44.60s	Michael Blackwood (Americas/Jam)
800m	1:43.83	Antonio Reina (Spain)
1500m	3:31.20	Bernard Lagat (Africa/Ken)
3000m	7:41.37	Craig Mottram (Oceania/Aus)
5000m	13:30.04	Alberto Garcia (Spain)
3000m St	8:25.34	Wilson Boit Kipketer (Africa/Ken)
110m H	13.10	Anier Garcia (Americas/Cub)
400m H	48.27	James Carter (USA)
4 x 100m	37.95	USA
4 x 400m	2:59.19	Americas
High Jump	2.31m	Yaroslav Rykabov (Europe/Rus)
Pole Vault	5.75m	Okkert Brits (Africa/RSA)
Long Jump	8.21m	Savante Stringfellow (USA)
Triple Jump	17.34m	Jonathan Edwards (Great Britain)
Shot	20.80m	Adam Nelson (USA)
Discus	71.25m	Robert Fazekas (Europe/Hun)
Hammer	80.93m	Adrian Annus (Europe/Hun)
Javelin	86.44m	Sergei Makarov (Europe/Rus)

Points: Africa 134; USA 119; Europe 115; Americas 111; Spain 94; Germany 86.5; Great Britain 86; Asia 80; Oceania 62.5

WOMEN

100m	10.90s	Marion Jones (USA)
200m	22.49s	Debbie Ferguson (Americas/Bah)
400m	49.56s	Ana Guevara (Americas/Mex)
800m	1:58.60	Maria Mutola (Africa/Moz)
1500m	4:01.57	Sureyya Ayhan (Europe/Tur)
3000m	8:50.88	Berhane Adere (Africa/Eth)
5000m	15:18.15	Olga Yegorova (Russia)
100m H	12.65	Gail Devers (USA)
400m H	53.74	Yuliya Pechinkina (Russia)
4 x 100m	41.91	Americas
4 x 400m	3:23.53	Americas
High Jump	2.02m	Hestrie Cloete (Africa/RSA)
Pole Vault	4.55m	Annika Becker (Germany)
Long Jump	6.85m	Tatyana Kotova (Russia)
Triple Jump	14.37m	Francoise Mbango (Africa/Cmr)

Shot	20.20m	Irina Korzhanenko (Russia)
Discus	62.47m	Beatrice Faumuina (Oceania/Nzl)
Hammer	70.75m	Gu Yuan (Asia/Chn)
Javelin	64.41m	Osleidys Menendez (Americas/Cub)

Points: Russia 126; Europe 123; Americas 110; USA 105; Africa 99; Germany 79; Asia 75; Spain 74.5; Oceania 59

20th WORLD RACE WALKING CUP
Held in Turin, 12–13 October 2002

MEN

20km	Individual	1:21:26	Jefferson Perez (Ecuador)
	Team	Russia 24 pts	
50km	Individual	3:40:59	Alexei Voyevodin (Russia)
	Team	Russia 7 pts	

WOMEN

20km	Individual	1:28:55	Erica Alridi (Italy)
	Team	Russia 9pts	

EUROPEAN CROSS COUNTRY CHAMPIONSHIPS
Held at Medulin, Croatia, 8 December 2002

SENIOR MEN (9830m)

Individual	Sergei Lebed (Ukraine)	28m 58s
Team	Spain 31pts	

JUNIOR MEN (6170m)

Individual	Yevgeni Rybakov (Russia)	18m 16s
Team	Russia 37pts	

SENIOR WOMEN (6170m)

Individual	Helena Javornik (Slovenia)	20m 16s
Team	Russia 48pts	

JUNIOR WOMEN (3730m)

Individual	Charlotte Dale (Great Britain)	12m 26s
Team	Great Britain 27pts	

EUROPEAN INDOOR CUP
Held at Leipzig, 15 February 2003

MEN

60m	6.55	Jason Gardener (Great Britain)
400m	46.76	Marek Plawgo (Poland)
800m	1:48.65	Rene Herms (Germany)
1500m	3:41.64	Juan Carlos Higuero (Spain)
3000m	8:00.28	Yusef El Nasri (Spain)
60m H	7.68	Mike Fenner (Germany)
High Jump	2.28m	Alessandro Talotti (Italy)
Long Jump	8.09m	Yago Lamela (Spain)
Shot	19.69m	Ralf Bartels (Germany)
Medley Relay	4:14.42	France

Points: Spain 56; Germany 56; France 49; Russia 49; Italy 47; Poland 46; Great Britain 39; Greece 24

WOMEN

60m	7.18	Christine Arron (France)
400m	51.91	Grit Breuer (Germany)
800m	2:03.14	Mayte Martinez (Spain)
1500m	4:08.63	Hayley Tullett (Great Britain)
3000m	8:55.41	Galina Bogomolova (Russia)
60m H	7.94	Glory Alozie (Spain)

Pole Vault	4.65m	Svetlana Feofanova (Russia)	
Triple Jump	14.23m	Adelina Gavrila (Romania)	
Medley Relay	4:41.69		Russia

Points: Russia 60; Germany 49; Great Britain 40; France 40; Poland 40; Spain 37; Greece 32; Romania 31

ENGLISH NATIONAL CROSS COUNTRY CHAMPIONSHIPS

Held at Parliament Hill Fields, London, 22 February 2003

SENIOR MEN (12km)

Individual:	Matt Smith (Tipton)	41m 54s
Team:	Leeds City 181pts	

JUNIOR MEN (10km)

Individual:	Mohamed Farah (WSE Hounslow)	33m 20s
Team:	Aldershot, Farnham & District 59pts	

SENIOR WOMEN (8km)

Individual:	Hayley Yelling (WSE Hounslow)	32m 18s
Team:	Chester-le-Street 48pts	

JUNIOR WOMEN (5km)

Individual:	Louise Damen (Bournemouth)	19m 55s
Team:	Charnwood 123pts	

AAA INDOOR CHAMPIONSHIPS

Held at Birmingham, 1–2 March 2003

MEN

60m	Mark Lewis-Francis (Birchfield)	6.58
200m	Allyn Condon (Sale Manchester)	20.69
400m	Daniel Batman (Australia)	45.93
800m	Neil Speaight (Belgrave)	1:51.99
1500m	James Thie (Cardiff)	3:41.84
3000m	Mohamed Farah (WSE Hounslow)	8:05.58
60m H	Dominic Girdler (Belgrave)	7.78
High Jump	Dalton Grant (Woodford G/Essex L)	2.25m
Pole Vault	Viktor Chistiakov (Australia)	5.60m
Long Jump	Chris Tomlinson (Newham)	7.90m
Triple Jump	Tosin Oke (Woodford G/Essex L)	16.61m
Shot	Scott Rider (Harrow)	17.60m

WOMEN

60m	Joice Maduaka (Woodford G/Essex L)	7.32
200m	Ciara Sheehy (Ireland)	23.17
400m	Jenny Meadows (Wigan)	53.31
800m	Jo Fenn (Woodford G/Essex L)	1:59.74
1500m	Hayley Ovens (Edinburgh)	4:16.53
3000m	Kerry Gillibrand (Sale Manchester)	9:39.56
60m H	Sarah Claxton (Belgrave)	8.12
High Jump	Susan Jones (Trafford)	1.93m
Pole Vault	Tracey Bloomfield (Guildford)	4.00m
Long Jump	Ruth Irving (Edinburgh)	6.24m
Triple Jump	Sandra Swennen (Belgium)	13.51m
Shot	Eva Massey (Belgrave)	16.29m

IAAF WORLD INDOOR CHAMPIONSHIPS

Held at Birmingham, March 14–16 2003

MEN

60m	Justin Gatlin (USA)	6.46
200m	Marlon Devonish (Great Britain)	20.62
400m	Tyree Washington (USA)	45.34
800m	David Krummenacker (USA)	1:45.69
1500m	Driss Maazouzi (France)	3:42.59
3000m	Haile Gebreselassie (Ethiopia)	7:40.97
60m H	Allen Johnson (USA)	7.47
4 x 400m	United States	3:04.09
High Jump	Stefan Holm (Sweden)	2.35m
Pole Vault	Tim Lobinger (Germany)	5.80m
Long Jump	Dwight Phillips (USA)	8.29m
Triple Jump	Christian Olsson (Sweden)	17.70m
Shot	Manuel Martinez (Spain)	21.24m
Heptathlon	Tom Pappas (USA)	6361pts

WOMEN

60m	Zhanna Block (Ukraine)	7.04
200m	Michelle Collins (USA)	22.18
400m	Natalya Nazarova (Russia)	50.83
800m	Maria Mutola (Mozambique)	1:58.94
1500m	Regina Jacobs (USA)	4:01.67
3000m	Berhane Adere (Ethiopia)	8:40.25
60m H	Gail Devers (USA)	7.81
4 x 400m	Russia	3:28.45
High Jump	Kajsa Bergquist (Sweden)	2.01m
Pole Vault	Svetlana Feofanova (Russia)	4.80m
Long Jump	Tatyana Kotova (Russia)	6.84m
Triple Jump	Ashia Hansen (Great Britain)	15.01m
Shot	Irina Korzhanenko (Russia)	20.55m
Pentathlon	Carolina Klüft (Sweden)	4933pts

IAAF WORLD CROSS COUNTRY CHAMPIONSHIPS

Held in Lausanne, Switzerland, March 29–30 2003

SENIOR MEN (12.355km)

Individual:	Kenenisa Bekele (Ethiopia)	35m 56s
Team:	Kenya 17pts	

SENIOR MEN (4.03km)

Individual:	Kenenisa Bekele (Ethiopia)	11m 01s
Team:	Kenya 14pts	

JUNIOR MEN (7.9km)

Individual:	Eliud Kipchoge (Kenya)	2m 47s
Team:	Kenya 15pts	

SENIOR WOMEN (7.9km)

Individual:	Werknesh Kidane (Ethiopia)	25m 53s
Team:	Ethiopia 18pts	

SENIOR WOMEN (4.03km)

Individual:	Edith Masai (Kenya)	12m 43s
Team:	Kenya 18pts	

JUNIOR WOMEN (6km)

Individual:	Tirunesh Dibaba (Ethiopia)	20m 21s
Team:	Ethiopia 14pts	

EUROPEAN CUP SUPER LEAGUE

Held at Florence, Italy, 21–22 June 2003

MEN

		Min	Sec
100m	Mark Lewis-Francis (GBR)		10.22
200m	Konstadinos Kederis (Greece)		20.37
400m	Marc Raquil (France)		44.88
800m	Antonio Reina (Spain)	1	48.13
1500m	Juan Carlos Higuero (Spain)	3	49.16
3000m	Fouad Chouki (France)	8	22.56
5000m	Ismail Sghyr (France)	13	43.70

		Min	Sec
3000m St	Pavel Potpovich (Russia)	8	26.28
110m H	Ladji Doucoure (France)		13.55
400m H	Chris Rawlinson (GBR)		48.45
4 x 100m	Italy		38.42
4 x 400m	Great Britain	3	02.43

		Metres
High Jump	Yaroslva Rybakov (Russia)	2.34
Pole Vault	Romain Mesnil (France)	5.75
Long Jump	Louis Tsatoumas (Greece)	8.06
Triple Jump	Fabrizio Donato (Italy)	17.16
Shot	Manuel Martinez (Spain)	21.08
Discus	Dmitri Shevchenko (Russia)	65.39
Hammer	Karsten Kobs (Germany)	80.63
Javelin	Sergei Makarov (Russia)	85.86

Points: France 109; Germany 100.5; Great Britain 96; Russia 92; Italy 84; Poland 83; Spain 80; Greece 74.5

WOMEN

		Min	Sec
100m	Christine Arron (France)		11.07
200m	Anastasia Kapachinskaya (Russia)		22.71
400m	Svetlana Pospelova (Russia)		50.85
800m	Claudia Gesell (Germany)	2	00.85
1500m	Natalia Rodriguez (Spain)	4	07.18
3000m	Olga Yegorova (Russia)	8	55.73
5000m	Yelena Zadorozhnaya (Russia)	15	34.07
3000m St	Giulnara Samitova (Russia)	9	40.89
100m H	Glory Alozie (Spain)		12.86
400m H	Ionela Tirlea (Romania)		54.47
4 x 100m	France		42.62
4 x 400m	Russia	3	26.02

		Metres
High Jump	Daniela Rath (Germany)	2.00
Pole Vault	Annika Becker (Germany)	4.50
Long Jump	Eunice Barber (France)	6.76
Triple Jump	Anna Pyatykh (Russia)	14.79
Shot	Astrid Kumbernuss (Germany)	19.46
Discus	Ekaterini Voggoli (Greece)	62.11
Hammer	Manuela Montebrun (France)	74.43
Javelin	Steffi Nerius (Germany)	63.30

Points: Russia 130; Germany 103; France 102; Great Britain 83; Spain 82; Greece 78.5; Romania 77.5; Italy 62

AAA CHAMPIONSHIPS
Held at Birmingham, 25–27 July 2003

MEN

100m	Dwain Chambers (Belgrave)	10.08
200m	Julian Golding (Blackheath)	20.37
400m	Daniel Caines (Birchfield)	45.6
800m	Ricky Soos (Mansfield)	1:47.51
1500m	Michael East (Newham)	3:42.29
5000m	Andrew Graffin (Belgrave)	13:56.59
3000m St	Stuart Stokes (Sale Manchester)	8:40.10
5000m Walk	Steve Hollier (Wolverhampton)	20:59.46
110m H	Damien Greaves (Newham)	13.66
400m H	Chris Rawlinson (Trafford)	49.24

		Metres
High Jump	Ben Challenger (Belgrave)	2.24
Pole Vault	Nick Buckfield (Crawley)	5.50
Long Jump	Darren Ritchie (Sale Manchester)	7.74
Triple Jump	Larry Achike (Shaftesbury Barnet)	16.55
Shot	Carl Myerscough (Blackpool)	21.55
Discus	Emeka Udechuku (Woodford Green)	57.26

Hammer	Bill Beauchamp (Newham)	69.33
Javelin	Mick Hill (Leeds)	76.35

Held at Watford, 5 July 2003

10,000m	Fabiano Joseph (Tanzania)	27: 32.81

WOMEN

100m	Joice Maduaka (Woodford Green)	11.31
200m	Abi Oyepitan (Shaftesbury Barnet)	22.95
400m	Helen Karagounis (Birchfield)	52.51
800m	Lucy Vaughan (WSE Hounslow)	2:03.70
1500m	Hayley Tullett (Swansea)	4:08.12
5000m	Hayley Yelling (WSE Hounslow)	15:53.30
2000m St	Tara Krzywicki (Charnwood)	6:28.07
5000m Walk	Lisa Kehler (Wolverhampton)	23:10.15
100m H	Rachel King (Belgrave)	13.07
400m H	Liz Fairs (Trafford)	57.06

		Metres
High Jump	Susan Jones (Trafford)	1.86
Pole Vault	Tracey Bloomfield (Guildford)	4.15
Long Jump	Jade Johnson (Herne Hill)	6.49
Triple Jump	Yamile Aldama (Shaftesbury Barnet)	14.98
Shot	Joanne Duncan (Woodford Green)	16.19
Discus	Shelley Newman (Belgrave)	58.16
Hammer	Lorraine Shaw (Sale Manchester)	65.93
Javelin	Goldie Sayers (Belgrave)	56.29

Held at Watford, 5 July 2003

10,000m	Aniko Kalovics (Hungary)	31: 40.31

WORLD ATHLETICS CHAMPIONSHIPS
Held at Paris, France, 23–31 August 2003

MEN

100m	Kim Collins (St Kitts/Nevis)	10.07
200m	John Capel (USA)	20.30
400m	Jerome Young (USA)	44.50
800m	Djabir Said-Guerni (Algeria)	1: 44.81
1500m	Hicham El Guerrouj (Morocco)	3: 31.77
5000m	Eliud Kipchoge (Kenya)	12: 52.79
10,000m	Kenenisa Bekele (Ethiopia)	26: 49.57
Marathon	Jaouad Gharib (Morocco)	2h 08 31
3000m St	Saif Saaeed Shaheen (Qatar)	8: 04.39
20km Walk	Jefferson Perez (Ecuador)	1h 17 21
50km Walk	Robert Korzeniowski (Poland)	3h 36 03
100m H	Allen Johnson (USA)	13.12
400m H	Felix Sanchez (Dominica)	47.25
4 x 100m	United States	38.06
4 x 400m	United States	2: 58.88

		Metres
High Jump	Jacques Freitag (South Africa)	2.35
Pole Vault	Giuseppe Gibilisco (Italy)	5.90
Long Jump	Dwight Phillips (USA)	8.32
Triple Jump	Christian Olsson (Sweden)	17.72
Shot	Abdrei Mikhnevich (Belarus)	21.69
Discus	Virgilijus Alekna (Lithuania)	69.69
Hammer	Ivan Tikhon (Belarus)	83.05
Javelin	Sergei Makarov (Russia)	85.44
Decathlon	Tom Pappas (USA)	8750pts

WOMEN

100m	Kelli White (USA)	10.85
200m	Kelli White (USA)	22.05
400m	Ana Guevara (Mexico)	48.89
800m	Maria Mutola (Mozambique)	1: 59.89
1500m	Tatyana Tomashova (Russia)	3: 58.52
5000m	Tirunesh Dibaba (Ethiopia)	14: 51.72
10,000m	Berhane Adere (Ethiopia)	30: 04.18
Marathon	Catherine Ndereba (Kenya)	2h 23 55

20km Walk	Yelena Nikolayeva (Russia)	1h 26.52
100m H	Perdita Felicien (Canada)	12.53
400m H	Jana Pittman (Australia)	53.22
4 x 100m	France	41.78
4 x 400m	United States	3: 22.63

		Metres
High Jump	Hestrie Cloete (South Africa)	2.06
Pole Vault	Svetlana Feofanova (Russia)	4.75
Long Jump	Eunice Barber (France)	6.99
Triple Jump	Tatyana Lebedeva (Russia)	15.18
Shot	Svetlana Krivelyova (Russia)	20.63
Discus	Irina Yatchenko (Belarus)	67.32
Hammer	Yipsi Moreno (Cuba)	73.33
Javelin	Mirela Manjani (Greece)	66.52
Heptathlon	Carolina Kluft (Sweden)	7001pts

BADMINTON

WORLD CHAMPIONSHIP 2003
NIA Birmingham, 28 July – 3 August

Men's Singles: Xuanze Xia (China) beat Choong Hann Wong (Malaysia) 2–1
Ladies' Singles: Ning Zhang (China) beat Ruina Gong (China) 2–0
Men's Doubles: Lars Paaske and Jonas Rasmussen (Denmark) beat Sigit Budiarto and Candra Wijaya (Indonesia) 2–1
Ladies' Doubles: Ling Gao and Sui Huang (China) beat Yili Wei and Tingting Zhao (China) 2–0
Mixed Doubles: Dong-Moon Kim and Kyung-Min Ra (Korea) beat Ling Gao and Jun Zhang (China) 4–3

ENGLISH NATIONAL CHAMPIONSHIPS 2003
Burgess Hill, Bournemouth, 31 January–2 February

Men's Singles: Colin Haughton beat Mark Burgess 2–0
Ladies' Singles: Julia Mann beat Tracey Hallam 2–0
Men's Doubles: Anthony Clark and Nathan Robertson beat Simon Archer and Ian Sullivan 2–0
Ladies' Doubles: Gail Emms and Donna Kellogg beat Ella Tripp and Joanne Wright 2–1
Mixed Doubles: Nathan Robertson and Gail Emms beat Robert Blair and Natalie Munt 2–1

SCOTTISH NATIONAL CHAMPIONSHIPS 2003
Perth, 31 January–2 February

Men's Singles: G. Simpson beat C. Robertson 2–1
Ladies' Singles: F. Sneddon beat M. Douglas (walkover)
Men's Doubles: A. Gatt and K. Middlemiss beat C. Hill and B. Hogg 2–0
Ladies' Doubles: K. McEwan and E. Middlemiss beat S. Hughes and F. Sneddon 2–0
Mixed Doubles: R. Hogg and K. McEwan beat C. Robertson and S. Watt 2–0

ALL-ENGLAND CHAMPIONSHIPS 2003
NIA Birmingham, 12–16 February

Men's Singles: Muhammad Hafiz Hashim (Malaysia) beat Hong Chen (China) 2–0
Ladies' Singles: Mi Zhou (China) beat Xingfang Xie (China) 2–0

Men's Doubles: Sigit Budiarto and Candra Wiyaja (Indonesia) beat Dong-Soo Lee and Yong-Sung Yoo (Korea) 2–0
Ladies' Doubles: Ling Gao and Sui Huang (China) beat Wei Yang and Jiewen Zhang (China) 2–0
Mixed Doubles: Jun Zhang and Ling Gao (China) beat Qiqiu Chen and Tingting Zhao (China) 2–0

BASEBALL

American League Championship Series 2002: Anaheim Angels beat Minnesota Twins 4–1
National League Championship Series 2002: San Francisco Giants beat St Louis Cardinals 4–1
World Series 2002: Anaheim Angels beat San Francisco Giants 4–3

BASKETBALL

BRITISH
MEN
BBL Championship Final 2003: Scottish Phoenix Mitsubishi Rocks beat Brighton Bears 83–76
BBL Trophy Final 2003: Chester Jets beat London Towers 84–82
National Cup 2003: Brighton Bears beat Chester Jets 89–79
BBL Champions 2002–3: Westfield Sharks Sheffield, 66 points

WOMEN
WNBL Conference 2002–3: Sheffield Hatters
WNBL Conference Championship 2002–3: Sheffield Hatters
National Cup Final 2002–3: Rhondda Rebels beat Sheffield Hatters 78–73

WORLD CHAMPIONSHIPS 2002
USA, September

Yugoslavia beat Argentina 84–77

NORTH AMERICA – NATIONAL BASKETBALL LEAGUE (NBA)
Eastern Conference final 2003: New Jersey Nets beat Detroit Pistons 4–0 (best of 7 series)
Western Conference final 2003: San Antonio Spurs beat Dallas Mavericks 4–2 (best of 7 series)
NBA final 2003: San Antonio Spurs beat New Jersey Nets 4–2 (best of 7 series)

BOWLS – OUTDOOR

BRITISH ISLES CHAMPIONSHIPS 2003
Ayr, July

Singles: Iain McLean (Scotland) beat Martyn Sekjer (England) 21–20
Pairs: England beat Guernsey 19–17
Triples: Scotland beat England 19–18
Fours: Wales beat Scotland 25–9

ENGLISH NATIONAL CHAMPIONSHIPS 2003
Worthing, August

MEN
Singles: Paul Allenby (Yorkshire 'A') beat Mark Walton
(Yorkshire 'B') 21–13
Pairs: Suffolk 'A' beat Worcestershire 'A' 20–10
Triples: Berkshire 'A' beat Suffolk 'A' 15–13
Fours: Cornwall 'B' beat Lancashire 'A' 20–17
Middleton Cup (Inter-County Championship) final 2003:
Devon beat Lincolnshire 128–122

BOWLS – INDOOR

WORLD CHAMPIONSHIPS 2003
Belfast, April

Men's Singles: Stephen Moran (Ireland) beat Neal Mollet
(Guernsey) 2–1
Women's Singles: Carol Ashby (England) beat Wendy
Jensen (New Zealand) 2–0
Mixed Pairs: Julie Forrest and Mark Johnston (Scotland)
beat Muriel Wilkinson and Jonathan Ross (Ireland)
2–1

BRITISH ISLES INDOOR BOWLS
CHAMPIONSHIPS 2003
Thornaby, March

Singles: Jonathan Ross (Ireland) beat Stuart Cruickshank
(Scotland) 21–11
Pairs: Wales beat England 19–10
Triples: England beat Wales 18–17
Fours: Scotland beat England 18–15

ENGLISH NATIONAL CHAMPIONSHIPS 2003
Melton Mowbray, April

Singles: Billy Jackson beat Mark Bantock 21–8
Pairs: Melton and District beat Stanley 20–10
Triples: Cumbria beat Exonia 19–18
Fours: Exonia beat City of Ely 19–17

Liberty Trophy (Inter-County Championship) final 2003:
Kent beat Essex 126–88
Champion of Champions 2002–3: Nicky Brett (City of
Ely) beat Mark O'Riordan (Thornaby) 21–16

BOXING

PROFESSIONAL BOXING
as at 1 September 2003

WORLD BOXING COUNCIL (WBC) CHAMPIONS
Heavy: Lennox Lewis (GBR)
Cruiser: Wayne Braithwaite (Guyana)
Light-heavy: Antonio Tarver (USA)
Super-middle: Marcus Beyer (Germany)
Middle: Bernard Hopkins (USA)
Super-welter: Oscar de la Hoya (USA)
Welter: Ricardo Mayorga (Nicaragua)
Super-light: Kostya Tszyu (Australia)
Light: Floyd Mayweather (USA)
Super-Feather: Sirimongkol Singmanassak (Thailand)
Feather: Erik Morales (Mexico)
Super-bantam: Oscar Larios (Mexico)
Bantam: Veerophol Sahaprom (Thailand)
Super-fly: Masamori Tokuyama (Japan)

Fly: Pongsaklek Wonjongkam (Thailand)
Light-fly: Jorge Arce (Mexico)
Straw: Jose Antonio Aguirre (Mexico)

WORLD BOXING ASSOCIATION (WBA) CHAMPIONS
Heavy: Roy Jones (USA)
Cruiser: Jean-Marc Mormeck (France)
Light-heavy: Mehdi Sahnoune (France)
Super-middle: Sven Ottke (Germany)
Middle: William Joppy (USA)
Super-welter: Alex Garcia (Mexico)
Welter: Ricardo Mayorga (Nicaragua)
Super-light: Vivian Harris (Guyana)
Light: Leonard Dorin (Romania)
Super-feather: Yodsanan Nanthachaitha (Thailand)
Feather: Derrick Gainer (USA)
Super-bantam: Mahyar Monshipor (France)
Bantam: Johnny Bredahl (Denmark)
Super-fly: Alexander Muñoz (Venezuela)
Fly: Eric Morel (USA)
Light-fly: Rosendo Alverez (Nicaragua)
Straw: Noel Arambulet (Venezuela)

WORLD BOXING ORGANISATION (WBO) CHAMPIONS
Heavy: Corrie Sanders (USA)
Cruiser: Johnny Nelson (England)
Light-heavy: Daruisz Michalczewsky (Germany)
Super-middle: Joe Calzaghe (Wales)
Middle: Harry Simon (Namibia)
Super-welter: Daniel Santos (Puerto Rico)
Welter: Antonio Margarito (Mexico)
Super-light: Zab Judah (USA)
Light: Artur Grigorian (Uzbekistan)
Super-feather: Acelino Freitas (Brazil)
Feather: Manuel Medina (Mexico)
Super-bantam: Joan Guzman (Dominican Republic)
Bantam: Cruz Carbajal (Mexico)
Super-fly: Mark Johnson (USA)
Fly: Omar Narvaez (Argentina)
Light-fly: Nelson Dieppa (Puerto Rico)
Straw: Ivan Calderon (Puerto Rico)

INTERNATIONAL BOXING FEDERATION (IBF)
CHAMPIONS
Heavy: Chris Byrd (USA)
Cruiser: James Toney (USA)
Light-heavy: Antonio Tarver (USA)
Super-middle: Sven Ottke (Germany)
Middle: Bernard Hopkins (USA)
Super-welter: Ronald Wright (USA)
Welter: Cory Spinks (USA)
Super-light: Kostya Tszyu (Australia)
Light: Paul Spadafora (USA)
Super-feather: Carlos Hernandez (USA)
Feather: Juan Manuel Marquez (Mexico)
Super-bantam: Manny Pacquiao (Philippines)
Bantam: Rafael Marquez (Mexico)
Super-fly: Luis Perez (Nicaragua)
Fly: Irene Pacheco (Colombia)
Light-fly: Jose Victor Burgos (Mexico)
Straw: Edgar Cardenas (Mexico)

BRITISH CHAMPIONS
Heavy: Danny Williams
Cruiser: Mark Hobson
Light-heavy: Peter Oboh
Super-middle: Matthew Barney
Middle: Howard Eastman

Junior-middle: Jamie Moore
Welter: David Barnes
Junior-welter: Junior Witter
Light: Graham Earl
Super-feather: Alex Arthur
Feather: Roy Rutherford
Super-bantam: Esham Pickering
Bantam: Nicky Booth
Fly: Jason Booth

CHESS

FIDE World Champion 2002–3: Ruslan Ponomariov
(Ukraine)
British Champion 2003: Abhijit Kunte (India)

CRICKET

TEST SERIES
ENGLAND V. AUSTRALIA
Brisbane (7–10 November 2002): Australia beat England
by 384 runs. Australia 492 and 296–5; England 325
and 79.
Adelaide (21–24 November 2002): Australia beat
England by an innings and 51 runs. England 342 and
159; Australia 552–9.
Perth (29 November–1 December 2002): Australia beat
England by an innings and 48 runs. England 185 and
223; Australia 456.
Melbourne (26–30 December 2002): Australia beat
England by five wickets. Australia 551–6 and 107–5;
England 270 and 387.
Sydney (2–6 January 2003): England beat Australia by
225 runs. England 362 and 452–9; Australia 363 and
226.

ENGLAND V. ZIMBABWE
Lord's (22–26 May): England beat Zimbabwe by an
innings and 92 runs. England 472; Zimbabwe 147
and 233.
Riverside (5–9 June): England beat Zimbabwe by an
innings and 69 runs. England 416; Zimbabwe 94 and
253.

ENGLAND V. SOUTH AFRICA
Edgbaston (24–28 July): England drew with South Africa.
South Africa 594–5 and 134–4; England 408 and
110–1.
Lord's (31 July–4 August): South Africa beat England by
an innings and 92 runs. England 173 and 417; South
Africa 682–6.
Trent Bridge (14–18 August): England beat South Africa
by 70 runs. England 445 and 118; South Africa 362
and 131.
Headingley (21–25 August): South Africa beat England
by 191 runs. South Africa 342 and 365; England 307
and 209.
The Oval (4–8 September): England beat South Africa by
9 wickets. South Africa 484 and 229; England 604
and 110.

ONE-DAY INTERNATIONALS
VB SERIES ONE-DAY INTERNATIONALS
Sydney (13 December 2002): Australia beat England by 7
wickets. England 251–8; Australia 252–3.
Melbourne (15 December 2002): Australia beat England
by 89 runs. England 229; Australia 318–6.
Brisbane (17 December 2002): England beat Sri Lanka
by 43 runs. England 292; Sri Lanka 249–6.

Perth (20 December 2002): England beat Sri Lanka by
95 runs. England 258–9; Sri Lanka 163.
Perth (22 December 2002): Australia beat Sri Lanka by
142 runs. Australia 305–5; Sri Lanka 163.
Sydney (9 January 2003): Sri Lanka beat Australia by 79
runs. Sri Lanka 343–5; Australia 264.
Hobart (11 January 2003): Australia beat England by 7
runs. Australia 271–4; England 264–7.
Sydney (13 January 2003): Sri Lanka beat England by 31
runs. Sri Lanka 284–7; England 253.
Brisbane (15 January 2003): Australia beat Sri Lanka by 4
wickets. Sri Lanka 211–9; Australia 214–6.
Adelaide (17 January 2003): England beat Sri Lanka by
19 runs. England 279–7; Sri Lanka 260.
Adelaide (19 January 2003): Australia beat England by 4
wickets. England 152; Australia 153–6.
Melbourne (21 January 2003): Australia beat Sri Lanka by
9 wickets. Sri Lanka 214–8; Australia 215–1.
Final, first-leg Sydney (23 January 2003): Australia beat
England by 10 wickets. England 117; Australia
118–0.
Final, second-leg Melbourne (25 January 2003): Australia
beat England by 5 runs. Australia 229–7; England
224.

NATWEST CHALLENGE SERIES ONE-DAY
INTERNATIONALS
Old Trafford (17 June 2003): Pakistan beat England by 2
wickets. England 204–9; Pakistan 208–8.
The Oval (20 June 2003): England beat Pakistan by 7
wickets. Pakistan 185; England 189–3.
Lord's (22 June 2003): England beat Pakistan by 4
wickets. Pakistan 229–7; England 231–6.

NATWEST SERIES ONE-DAY INTERNATIONALS
Trent Bridge (26 June 2003): Zimbabwe beat England by
4 wickets. England 191–8; Zimbabwe 195–6.
The Oval (28 June 2003): England beat South Africa by
6 wickets. South Africa 264–6; England 265–4.
Canterbury (29 June 2003): South Africa beat Zimbabwe
by 46 runs. South Africa 272–5; Zimbabwe 226–9.
Headingley (1 July 2003): England v. Zimbabwe No
result.
Old Trafford (3 July 2003): South Africa beat England
by 7 wickets. England 223–7; South Africa 227–3.
Cardiff (5 July 2003): South Africa beat Zimbabwe by 9
wickets. Zimbabwe 174–8; South Africa 175–1.
Bristol (6 July 2003): England beat Zimbabwe by 6
wickets. Zimbabwe 92; England 95–4.
Edgbaston (8 July 2003) England beat South Africa by 4
wickets. South Africa 198–9. England 199–6.
Rose Bowl (10 July 2003) South Africa beat Zimbabwe by
7 wickets. Zimbabwe 173–8; South Africa. 174–3.
Lord's (12 July 2003): England beat South Africa by 7
wickets. South Africa 107; England 111–3.

WORLD CUP
POOL STAGES
POOL A

	P	W	L	NR	T	PTS	NRR
Australia	6	6	-	-	-	24	+2.045
India	6	5	1	-	-	20	+1.108
Zimbabwe	6	3	2	1	-	14	+0.504
England	6	3	3	-	-	12	+0.821
Pakistan	6	2	3	1	-	10	+0.227
Netherlands	6	1	5	-	-	4	-1.454
Namibia	6	-	6	-	-	0	-2.955

POOL B

	P	W	L	NR	T	PTS	NRR
Sri Lanka	6	4	1	-	1	18	+1.204
Kenya	6	4	2	-	-	16	-0.691
New Zealand	6	4	2	-	-	16	+0.990
West Indies	6	3	2	1	-	14	+1.103
South Africa	6	3	2	-	1	14	+1.730
Canada	6	1	5	-	-	4	-1.989
Bangladesh	6	-	5	1	-	2	-2.046

SUPER SIX

	P	W	L	NR	T	PTS	NRR
Australia	5	5	-	-	-	24	+1.854
India	5	4	1	-	-	20	+0.886
Kenya	5	3	2	-	-	14	+0.354
Sri Lanka	5	2	3	-	-	11.5	-0.844
New Zealand	5	1	4	-	-	8	-0.896
Zimbabwe	5	-	5	-	-	3.5	-1.254

SEMI FINALS

Port Elizabeth (18 March 2003): Australia beat Sri Lanka by 48 runs (Duckworth Lewis method). Australia 212–7; Sri Lanka 123–7.

Durban (20 March 2003): India beat Kenya by 91 runs. India 270–4; Kenya 179.

FINAL

Johannesburg (23 March 2003): Australia beat India by 125 runs. Australia 359–2; India 234.

ENGLAND AND WALES DOMESTIC COMPETITIONS

County Championship: see Stop Press
National League: see Stop Press
C & G Trophy final: Gloucestershire beat Worcestershire by 7 wickets. Worcestershire 149; Gloucestershire 150–3.
Twenty 20 Cup final 2003: Surrey beat Warwickshire by 9 wickets. Warwickshire 115; Surrey 119–1.

OTHER INTERNATIONAL DOMESTIC CHAMPIONSHIPS

Australia: Pura Cup 2002–3: New South Wales beat Queensland by 246 runs. New South Wales 282 and 263; Queensland 84 and 215.
Bangladesh: IMT National Cricket League, Final 2002–3: Khulna Division beat Dhaka Division by 3 wickets. Dhaka 362 and 196; Khulna 338 and 223–7. *IMT One Day League:* Dhaka Division beat Khulna Division by 181 runs. Dhaka 236; Khulna 55.
India: Irani Trophy 2002–3: Railways beat Rest of India by 5 wickets. Railways 316 and 244–5; Rest of India 266 and 292. *Ranji Trophy 2002–3:* Mumbai beat Tamil Nadu by 141 runs. Mumbai 260 and 387–7; Tamil Nadu 271 and 235. *Duleep Trophy 2002–3:* Elite C, 21 points. *Deodhar Trophy 2002–3:* North Zone, 13 points.
New Zealand: State Max 2002–3: Cancelled. *State Championship:* Auckland, 34pts; Wellington, 31pts; Otago, 26pts. *State Shield:* Auckland, 27pts; Wellington, 25pts; Northern Districts, 23pts.
Pakistan: Patron's Cup 2002–3: Pakistan International Airlines beat Water and Power Development Authority by 55 runs. Pakistan International Airlines 273–7; Water and Power Development Authority 218–9. *Quaid-e-Azam Trophy 2002–3:* Pakistan International Airlines beat Khan Research Labs by 10 wickets. Khan Research Labs 263 and 214; Pakistan International Airlines 466 and 12–0.

South Africa: SuperSport Series 2002–3: Easterns beat Western Province by 273 runs. Easterns 238 and 472; Western Province 309 and 128. *Standard Bank Cup 2002–3:* Western Province beat Griqualand West by 9 wickets. Griqualand West 125; Western Province 129–1.
Sri Lanka: Premier League Final 2002–3: Moors Sports Club beat Bloomfield Cricket and Athletic Club by 1 wicket. Bloomfield 121 and 172; Moors 188 and 106–9. *Kandos Limited Over Tournament Final 2002–3:* Bloomfield Cricket and Athletic Club beat Galle Cricket Club by 92 runs. Bloomfield 235–5; Galle 143.
West Indies: Carib International Challenge 2002–3: Barbados beat Jamaica by 7 wickets. Barbados 369 and 35–3; Jamaica 184 and 219. *Red Stripe Bowl 2002–03:* Barbados beat Jamaica by 33 runs. Barbados 241–8; Jamaica 208.
Zimbabwe: Logan Cup 2002–3: Mashonaland. *Inter-Provincial One-Day Competition 2002–3:* Mashonaland.

CURLING

EUROPEAN CHAMPIONSHIPS 2002
Grindelwald, Switzerland, December
Men's Champions: Germany
Women's Champions: Sweden

WORLD CHAMPIONSHIPS 2003
Winnipeg, Canada, April

MEN'S FINAL
Canada beat Switzerland 10–6

WOMEN'S FINAL
USA beat Canada 5–3

CYCLING

BRITISH NATIONAL ROAD RACE CHAMPIONSHIPS 2003
Newport, June

MEN
Road race (132 miles): Roger Hammond 5h 21min 15sec

WOMEN
Road race (73.5 miles): Nicole Cooke 3h 32min 45sec

WORLD ROAD CYCLING CHAMPIONSHIPS 2002
Hasselt-Zolder, Belgium

MEN
Elite Time trial: Santiago Botero Echeverry (Spain) 48:08.4
Road race (256 km): Mario Cipollini (Italy) 5 h 30.03

WOMEN
Elite Time trial: Zoulfia Zabirova (Russia) 30:02.6
Road race (128 km): Susanne Ljungskog (Sweden) 2h 59.15

Giro d'Italia 2003: Gilberto Simoni
Tour de France 2003: Lance Armstrong
Tour of Spain 2003: see Stop Press

UCI STANDINGS *at 1 September 2003*
1. Paolo Bettini (Italy)
2. Erik Zabel (Germany)
3. Gilberto Simoni (Italy)

WORLD TRACK CHAMPIONSHIPS 2003
August, Stuttgart, Germany

MEN
1km time trial: Stefan Nimke (Germany) 1:01.225
Scratch Race: Franco Marvulli (Switzerland)
Individual pursuit: Bradley Wiggins (GBR) 4:18.576
Keirin: Laurent Gane (France)
Madison: Switzerland (Bruno Risi, Franco Marvulli)
   13 points
Olympic sprint: Germany (Carsten Bergemann, Jens
   Fiedler, René Wolff) 49.957
Points race: Franz Stocher (Austria) 77 points
Sprint: Laurent Gane (France) Run 1, 10.394; Decider
   10.769
Team pursuit: Australia (Graeme Brown, Brett Lancaster,
   Luke Roberts, Stephen Woodbridge) 3:57.280

WOMEN
500m Time Trial: Natallia Tsylinskaya (Belarus) 34.078
Individual pursuit: Leontien Zijlaard van Moorsel
   (Netherlands) 3:32.657
Keirin: Svetlana Grankovskaya (Russia)
Scratch Race: Olga Slusareva (Russia)
Points race: (24km) Olga Slusareva (Russia) 27 points
Sprint: Svetlana Grankovskaya (Russia) Run 1, 12.558;
   Run 2, 11.798

DARTS

Embassy World Championship 2003: Raymond van
   Barneveld (Netherlands) beat Ritchie Davies (Wales)
   6–3
Ladbrokes World Darts Championship 2003: John Part
   (Canada) beat Phil Taylor (England) 7–6

EQUESTRIANISM

Badminton Horse Trials 2003: Pippa Funnell on Supreme
   Rock
British Open Horse Trials 2003 (Gatcombe Park): William
   Fox-Pitt on Stunning
Burghley Horse Trials 2003: Pippa Funnell (Great Britain)
   on Primmore's Pride

ETON FIVES

Amateur Championship (Kinnaird Cup) final 2003: R. A.
   Mason and T. R. Dunbar beat J. P. Toop and M. C. T.
   Wiseman 3–1
Alan Barber Cup final 2002: Old Salopians beat Old
   Cholmeleians 2–1
County Championship final 2002: Kent beat Warwickshire
   3–0.
Schools' Championship 2003: Eton 1 (C. P. A. Nissen and
   E. F. J. Nissen) beat Harrow 1 (P. R. Dunbar and
   C. Bowen) 12–6, 12–2, 12–5
Preparatory Schools' Tournament 2003: Highgate 1 (J. Ho
   and A. Yanaorski) beat Highgate 2 (J. Meyrick and
   S. Little) 2–0

FENCING

WORLD CHAMPIONSHIPS 2002

MEN
Individual Foil: Simone Vanni (Italy)
Individual Epée: Pavel Kolobkov (Russia)
Individual Sabre: Stanislaw Pozdniakov (Russia)
Team Epée: France
Team Foil: Germany
Team Sabre: Russia

WOMEN
Individual Foil: Svetlana Bojko (Russia)
Individual Epée: Hee Hyun (Korea)
Individual Sabre: Xue Tan (China)
Team Foil: Russia
Team Epée: Hungary
Team Sabre: Russia

BRITISH CHAMPIONSHIPS 2003
MEN
Individual Foil: David Mansour
Individual Epée: Tristan Lane
Individual Sabre: Michael Johnson
Team Foil: Salle Paul 'A'
Team Epée: Haverstock 'A'
Team Sabre: LTFC

WOMEN
Individual Foil: Dominique Stowell
Individual Epée: Georgina Usher
Individual Sabre: Louise Bond-Williams
Team Foil: Salle Paul
Team Epée: Haverstock Mercenaries
Team Sabre: Laszlo's Fencing

CORBLE CUP 2003 (International Sabre World Cup
   Series): *Men,* Keeth Smart (USA); *Women,* Chrystall
   Nicoll (GBR)
IPSWICH CUP 2003 (International Epée World Cup
   Series): Claudia Bokel (Germany)

GOLF (MEN)

THE MAJOR CHAMPIONSHIPS 2003
US Masters (Augusta, Georgia, 10–13 April): Mike Weir
   (USA), 281
US Open (Olympia Fields, Illinois, 12–15 June): Jim
   Furyk (USA), 272
The Open (Royal St George's, 17–20 July): Ben Curtis
   (USA), 283
US PGA Championship (Oak Hill, New York, 14–17
   August): Shaun Micheel (USA), 276

WORLD RANKINGS *(as at 1 September 2003)*
1. Tiger Woods (USA); 2. Ernie Els (South Africa); 3.
   Davis Love III (USA); 4. Vijay Singh (Fiji); 5. Jim
   Furyk (USA)

EUROPEAN TOUR ORDER OF MERIT *(as at 1
September 2003):*
1. Ernie Els (South Africa); 2. Darren Clarke (Northern
   Ireland); 3. Thomas Bjorn (Denmark); 4. Padraig
   Harrington (Ireland); 5. Phillip Price (Wales)

PGA EUROPEAN TOUR 2002
Dunhill Links Championship (St Andrews): Padraig
Harrington (Ireland), 269
Trophée Lancome (Saint-Nom-La-Bretèche): Alex Cejka
(Germany), 272
Cisco World Matchplay Championship (Wentworth): Ernie
Els (South Africa)
Open de Madrid (Club de Campo): Steen Tinning
(Denmark), 265
Italian Open (Olgiata): Ian Poulter (England), 197
Volvo Masters Andalucia (Valderrama): Bernhard Langer
(Germany), 281

PGA EUROPEAN TOUR 2003
Asian Open (Ta Shee, Taiwan): Padraig Harrington
(Ireland), 273
Hong Kong Open (Hong Kong): Fredrik Jacobson
(Sweden), 260
South African Airways Open (Cape Town, South Africa):
Trevor Immelman (South Africa), 274
Dunhill Championship (Johannesburg, South Africa):
Mark Foster (England), 273
Caltex Masters (Singapore): Lian-Wei Zhang (China), 278
Heineken Classic (Melbourne, Australia): Ernie Els (South
Africa), 273
ANZ Championship (Sydney, Australia): Paul Casey
(England), 45
Johnnie Walker Classic (Perth, Australia): Ernie Els (South
Africa), 259
Malaysian Open (Kuala Lumpur): Arjun Atwal (India),
260
WGC Accenture Matchplay (Carlsbad, USA): Tiger Woods
(USA)
Dubai Desert Classic (Emirates GC): Robert-Jan Derksen
(Netherlands), 271
Qatar Masters (Doha): Darren Fichard (South Africa), 275
Madeira Island Open (Santo de Serra, Portugal): Bradley
Dredge (Wales), 272
Open de Portugal (Vale do Lobo): Fredrik Jacobson
(Sweden), 283
Canarias Open de España (Costa Adeje, Spain): Kenneth
Ferrie (England), 266
Italian Open (Brescia): Mathias Groenberg (Sweden), 271
Benson and Hedges International Open (De Vere Belfry,
England): Paul Casey (England), 277
Deutsche Bank SAP Open of Europe (Gut Kaden,
Germany): Padraig Harrington (Ireland), 269
Volvo PGA Championship (Wentworth, England): Ignacio
Garrido (Spain), 270
Celtic Manor Wales Open (Newport): Ian Poulter
(England), 270
British Masters (Forest of Arden, England): Greg Owen
(England), 274
Aa St Omer Open (France): Brett Rumford (Australia), 269
Championship of Gleneagles (Gleneagles, Scotland): Soren
Kjeldsen (Denmark), 279
Open de France (Le Golf National, France): Philip
Golding (England), 273
European Open (The K Club, Ireland): Phillip Price
(Wales), 272
Scottish Open (Loch Lomond): Ernie Els (South Africa),
267
Irish Open (Port Marnoch): Michael Campbell (New
Zealand), 277
Scandinavian Masters (Barsebäck, Sweden): Adam Scott
(Australia), 277
Nordic Open (Simon's Golf Club, Denmark): Ian Poulter
(England), 266

Russian Open (Le Meridien, Moscow): Marcus Fraser
(Australia), 269
WGC NEC Invitational (Firestone CC, USA): Darren
Clarke (Northern Ireland), 268
BMW International Open (Munchen Nord-Eichenried,
Germany): Lee Westwood (England), 269
European Masters (Crans-sur-Sierre, Switzerland): Ernie
Els (South Africa), 267

AMATEUR CHAMPIONSHIPS
British Amateur Championship 2003 (Royal Troon): Gary
Wolstenholme
English Amateur Championship 2003 (Alwoodley): Gary
Lockerbie
Welsh Amateur Championship 2003 (Southerndown):
Stuart Manley
Scottish Amateur Championship 2003 (St Andrews):
Graham Gordon
Brabazon Trophy (English Open Strokeplay) 2003
(Hunstanton): Jonathan Lupton (Middlesbrough Golf
Club), 287
Welsh Open Strokeplay 2002 (Prestatyn): Michael Skelton,
278
Scottish Open Strokeplay 2003 (Turnberry): Gary
Wolstenholme (Kilworth Springs Golf Club), 273
Irish Amateur Open Championship 2003 (Royal Dublin):
Noel Fox, 282
Lytham Trophy 2003 (Royal Lytham Golf Club): Stuart
Wilson, 283
Berkshire Trophy 2003 (The Berkshire): Ross Fisher and
Andrew Blyth, 275
Irish Amateur Close Championship 2003 (Tramore): Mark
O'Sullivan
Walker Cup 2003: Great Britain and Northern Ireland
beat USA by 12½–11½

GOLF (WOMEN)

THE MAJOR CHAMPIONSHIPS 2003

Kraft Nabisco Championship (Mission Hills Country
Club): Patricia Meunier-Lebouc (France), 281
US Women's Open (Pumpkin Ridge Golf Club): Hilary
Lunke (USA), 283
McDonalds LPGA Championship (Dupont Country Club):
Annika Sorenstam (Sweden), 278
Weetabix Women's British Open (Royal Lytham & St.
Annes, England): Annika Sorenstam (Sweden), 278

EUROPEAN TOUR ORDER OF MERIT 2002:
1. Paula Marti (Spain); 2. Maria Hjorth (Sweden); 3.
Sophie Gustafson (Sweden); 4. Iben Tinning
(Denmark); 5. Asa Gottmo (Sweden)

EUROPEAN LPGA TOUR 2002–3
Biarritz Ladies Classic (Biarritz): Sophie Gustafson
(Sweden), 200
ANZ Ladies Masters (Royal Pines, Australia): Laura Davies
(England), 203
AAMI Women's Australian Open (Terrey Hills, Australia):
Mhairi McKay (Scotland), 277
Tenerife Ladies Open (Golf Las Americas, Spain): Elisabeth
Esterl (Germany), 276
La Perla Italian Open (Poggio dei Medici, Italy): Ludivine
Kreutz (France), 282
Lancia Ladies Open of Portugal (Aroeira): Alison Munt
(Australia), 209

Open De España Femenino (Campo De Golf De
Salamanca, Spain): Federica Dassu (Italy), 282
Ladies Irish Open (Killarney): Sophie Gustafson (Sweden),
202
Arras Open De France Dames (Golf D'Arras): Lynnette
Brooky (New Zealand), 274
Evian Masters (Evian, France): Juli Inkster (USA), 267
HP Open (Stockholm): Sophie Gustafson (Sweden), 269
Wales WPGA Championship of Europe (Royal Porthcawl):
Shani Waugh (Australia), 286
Solheim Cup: Europe beat USA 17½–10½

AMATEUR CHAMPIONSHIPS
British Open Championship 2003 (Lindrick Golf Club,
England): Elisa Serramia (Spain)
Scottish Open Strokeplay Championship 2003 (Troon):
Natalie David, 227
Scottish Ladies (Close) Amateur Championship 2003: Anne
Laing
English Close Amateur Championship 2003 (Aldeburgh
Golf Club): Emma Duggleby
English Strokeplay 2003 (Saunton Golf Club): Sophie
Walker, 303
European Amateur Team Championship 2003 (Frankfurter
Golf Club, Germany): Spain

GREYHOUND RACING

2002
The Laurels (Belle Vue): Full Cigar
Milton Keynes Derby (Milton Keynes): El Ronan
Oaks (Wimbledon): Purley Queen
St Leger (Wimbledon): Alibulk Lad
Television Trophy (Wimbledon): Serious Dog

2003
Grand National (Wimbledon): Selby Ben
The Derby (Wimbledon): Droopys Hewitt
Golden Jacket (Crayford): Centour Corker
The Masters (Reading): Blonde Ranger
Pall Mall Stakes (Oxford): Cooly Cheetah
The Regency (Hove): Soviet Gypsy
Select Stakes (Nottingham): Droopys Shearer
The Laurels (Belle Vue): Farloe Verdict

GYMNASTICS

BRITISH WOMEN'S CHAMPIONSHIPS 2003
Guildford, July

Overall Champion: Elizabeth Tweddle (City of Liverpool)
Individual Apparatus Champions
  Floor: Nicola Willis (South Essex)
  Beam: Lizzie Line (Pinewood)
  Vault: Nicola Willis (South Essex)
  Assymetric Bars: Rebecca Mason (Sandbach)

WORLD CHAMPIONSHIPS 2003
Anaheim USA, August

MEN
Overall Champion: Paul Hamm (USA)
Team Champions: China
Individual Apparatus Champions
  Floor: Paul Hamm (USA) tied with Jordan Jovtchev
  (Bulgaria)
  Pommel Horse: Teng Haibin (China) tied with Takehiro
  Kashima (Japan)
  Still Rings: Jordan Jovtchev (Bulgaria) tied with
  Dimosthenis Tampakos (Greece)
  Vault: Li Xiao-Peng (China)
  Parallel bars: Li Xiao-Peng (China)
  High Bar: Takehiro Kashima (Japan)

WOMEN
Overall Champion: Svetlana Khorkina (Russia)
Team Champions: USA
Individual Apparatus Champions
  Floor: Daiane Dos Santos (Brazil)
  Beam: Fan Ye (China)
  Vault: Oksana Chusovitina (Uzbekistan)
  Assymetric Bars: Chellsie Memmel (USA) tied with
  Hollie Vise (USA)

HOCKEY

MEN
English Hockey League 2002-3: Premier Division:
Cannock 48 points; Division One, Old Loughtonians
50 points; Division Two, Bowdon 55 points
English Hockey League Premiership final 2002–3: Reading
beat Loughborough 5–2
English Hockey League Indoor Championship final 2003:
Loughborough Students beat Guildford 6–5
County Championship final 2003: Warwickshire beat Kent
5–4

WOMEN
English Hockey League 2002-3: Premier Division: Slough
43 points; Division One, Doncaster 43 points;
Division Two, Poynton 39 points
English Hockey League Premiership final 2002–3: Slough
beat Canterbury 2–1
English Hockey League Indoor Championship final 2003:
Slough beat Canterbury 7–2
County Championship final 2003: Norfolk beat
Humberside 5–1

HORSE-RACING

THE FLAT
THE CLASSICS
ONE THOUSAND GUINEAS
(1814) Rowley Mile, Newmarket, for three-year-old fillies

Year	Winner	Betting	Owner	Jockey	Trainer	No. of Runners
1999	Wince	4–1	Prince K. Abdulla	K. Fallon	H. Cecil	22
2000	Lahan	14–1	Hamdan Al Maktoum	R. Hills	J. Gosden	18
2001	Ameerat	11–1	Sheikh Ahmed Al Maktoum	P. Robinson	M. A. Jarvis	15
2002	Kazzia	14–1	Godolphin	F. Dettori	Saeed bin Suroor	17
2003	Russian Rhythm	12–1	Cheveley Park Stud	K. Fallon	Sir Michael Stoute	–

TWO THOUSAND GUINEAS
(1809) Rowley Mile, Newmarket, for three-year-olds

Year	Winner	Betting	Owner	Jockey	Trainer	No. of Runners
1999	Island Sands	10–1	Godolphin	F. Dettori	Saeed bin Suroor	16
2000	King's Best	13–2	Saeed Suhail	K. Fallon	Sir Michael Stoute	27
2001	Golan	11–1	Lord Weinstock	K. Fallon	Sir Michael Stoute	18
2002	Rock of Gibraltar	9–1	Sir Alex Ferguson	J. Murtagh	A. O'Brien	22
2003	Refuse To Bend	9–2	Moyglare Stud Farms	P. Smullen	D. Weld	20

THE DERBY
(1780) Epsom, 1 mile and about 4 f, for three-year-olds

The first winner was Sir Charles Bunbury's Diomed in 1780. The owners with the record number of winners are Lord Egremont, who won in 1782, 1804, 1805, 1807, 1826 (also won five Oaks); and the late Aga Khan, who won in 1930, 1935, 1936, 1948, 1952. Other winning owners are: Duke of Grafton (1802, 1809, 1810, 1815); Mr J. Bowes (1835, 1843, 1852, 1853); Sir J. Hawley (1851, 1858, 1859, 1868); the 1st Duke of Westminster (1880, 1882, 1886, 1899); and Sir Victor Sassoon (1953, 1957, 1958, 1960).
The Derby was run at Newmarket in 1915–18 and 1940–5.

Year	Winner	Betting	Owner	Jockey	Trainer	No. of Runners
1999	Oath	13–2	Prince Ahmed Salman	K. Fallon	H. Cecil	16
2000	Sinndar	7–1	Aga Khan	J. Murtagh	J. Oxx	8
2001	Galileo	11–4	Mrs. John Magnier	M. Kinane	A. O'Brien	12
2002	High Chaparral	7–2	Michael Tabor	J. Murtagh	A. O'Brien	12
2003	Kris Kin	6–1	Saeed Suhail	K. Fallon	Sir Michael Stoute	20

THE OAKS
(1779) Epsom, 1 mile and about 4 f, for three-year-old fillies

Year	Winner	Betting	Owner	Jockey	Trainer	No. of Runners
1997	Reams of Verse	5–6	Prince K. Abdulla	K. Fallon	H. Cecil	12
1998	Shahtoush	12–1	Mrs D. Nagle/Mrs J. Magnier	M. Kinane	A. O'Brien	8
1999	Ramruma	3–1	Prince Fahd Salman	K. Fallon	H. Cecil	10
2000	Love Divine	9–4	Lordship Stud	T. Quinn	H. Cecil	18
2001	Imagine	3–1	Mrs. J. Magnier	M. Kinane	–	12
2002	Kazzia	100–30	Godolphin	F. Dettori	S. bin Suroor	14
2003	Casual Look	10–1	W Farish III	M. Dwyer	A. Balding	–

ST LEGER
(1776) Doncaster, 1 mile and about 6 f, for three-year-olds

Year	Winner	Betting	Owner	Jockey	Trainer	No. of Runners
1997	Silver Patriarch	5–4	P. Winfield	P. Eddery	J. Dunlop	10
1998	Nedawi	5–2	Godolphin	J. Reid	Saeed bin Suroor	9
1999	Mutafaweq	11–2	Godolphin	R. Hills	Saeed bin Suroor	9
2000	Goggles	14–1	Mrs J. Powell	C. Rutter	H. Candy	22
2001	Milan	13–8	–	M. Kinane	A. O'Brien	–
2002	Bollin Eric	7–1	Sir Neil and Lady Westbrook	K. Darley	T. Easterby	8
2003	Brian Boru	5–4	Mrs S. Magnier	J. Spencer	A. O'Brien	12

RESULTS

CAMBRIDGESHIRE HANDICAP
(1839) Newmarket, 1 mile

1999	She's Our Mare (6y), F. Norton
2000	Katy Nowaitee (4y), J. Reid
2001	I Cried For You (6y), M. Fenton
2002	Beauchamp Pilot (4y), E. Ahern

PRIX DE L'ARC DE TRIOMPHE
(1920) Longchamp, 1½ miles

1999	Montjeu (3y), M. Kinane
2000	Sinndar (3y), J. P. Murtagh
2001	Sakhee (4y), F. Dettori
2002	Marienbard (5y), F. Dettori

CESAREWITCH
(1839) Newmarket, 2 miles and about 2 f

1999	Top Cees (9y), K. Fallon
2000	Heros Fatal (6y), G. Carter
2001	Distant Prospect, M. Dwyer
2002	Miss Fara, R. Moore

CHAMPION STAKES
(1877) Newmarket, 1 mile, 2 f

1999	Alborada (4y), G. Duffield
2000	Kalanisi (5y), J. Murtagh
2001	Nayef (3y), R. Hills
2002	Storming Home (4y), M. Hills

DUBAI WORLD CUP
(1957) Dubai, 1 mile and 2 f

2001	Captain Steve (4y), J. D. Bailey
2002	Street Cry (4y), J. D. Bailey
2003	Moon Ballad (4y), F. Dettori

LINCOLN HANDICAP
(1965) Doncaster, 1 mile

2000	John Ferneley (5y), F. Fortune
2001	Nimello (5y), J. Fortune
2002	Nimello (6y), J. Fortune
2003	Pablo (4y), M. Hills

JOCKEY CLUB STAKES
(1894) Newmarket, 2 miles, 24 yds

1999	Rainbow High (4y), M. Hills
2000	Millenary (4y), P. Eddery
2002	Marienbard, J. Spencer
2003	Warrsan (5y), P. Robinson

PRIX DU JOCKEY CLUB
(1836) Chantilly, 1½ miles

2000	Volvoreta, T. Thulliez
2001	Anaba Blue, C. Soumillon
2002	Sulamani, T. Thulliez
2003	Dalakhani, C. Soumillon

ASCOT GOLD CUP
(1807) Ascot, 2 miles and about 4 f

2000	Kayf Tara (6y), M. J. Kinane
2001	Royal Rebel (5y), J. P. Murtagh
2002	Royal Rebel (6y), J. P. Murtagh
2003	Mr Dinos (4y), K. Fallon

IRISH DERBY
(1866) Curragh, 1½ miles, for three-year-olds

2000	Sinndar, J. P. Murrtagh
2001	Galileo, M. Kinane
2002	High Chaparral, M. Kinane
2003	Alamshar, J. P. Murtagh

ECLIPSE STAKES
(1886) Sandown, 1 mile and about 2 f

2000	Giant's Causeway (3y), G. Duffield
2001	Medicean, K. Fallon
2002	Hawk Wing (3y), M. J. Kinane
2003	Falbrav (5y), D. Holland

KING GEORGE VI AND QUEEN ELIZABETH DIAMOND STAKES
(1952) Ascot, 1 mile and about 4 f

1999	Daylami (5y), F. Dettori
2000	Montjeu (4yr), M. J. Kinane
2001	Galileo (3y), M. J. Kinane
2002	Golan, K. Fallon
2003	Alamshar (3y), J.P. Murtagh

GOODWOOD CUP
(1812) Goodwood, about 2 miles

1998	Double Trigger (7y), D. Holland
1999	Kayf Tara (5y), L. Dettori
2000	Royal Rebel (4y), M. J. Kinane
2001	Persian Punch (8y), T. Quinn
2002	Jardines Lookout (5y), M. J. Kinane
2003	Persian Punch (10y), M. Dwyer

STATISTICS

WINNING FLAT OWNERS 2002
Hamdan Al Maktoum	£2,160,974
Godolphin	1,548,044
K. Abdulla	1,209,656
M. Tabor and Mrs J. Magnier	1,048,776
Maktoum Al Maktoum	865,949
Mrs J. Magnier	834,229
Exors of the late Lord Weinstock	801,490
Cheveley Park Stud	587,955
Lucayan Stud	505,428
Sir Alex Ferguson and Mrs J. Magnier	495,900

WINNING FLAT TRAINERS 2002
A. P. O'Brien (Ireland)	£2,718,114
Sir Michael Stoute	2,263,315
M. Johnston	2,183,185
R. Hannon	1,627,722
B. W. Hills	1,586,838
Saeed bin Suroor	1,548,044
T. D. Easterby	1,413,223
M. R. Channon	1,402,044
J. L. Dunlop	1,365,216
J. H. M. Gosden	1,265,993

WINNING FLAT SIRES 2002

	Races won	Stakes
Sadler's Wells by Northern Dancer	52	£1,870,900
Danehill by Danzig	57	1,479,807
Selkirk by Sharpen Up	57	1,023,718
Pivotal by Polar Falcon	40	836,959
Green Desert by Danzig	54	796,489
Spectrum by Rainbow Quest	31	793,146
Woodman by Mr Prospector	18	788,838
Machiavellian by Mr Prospector	27	758,826
Grand Lodge by Chief's Crown	62	752,266
Cadeaux Genereux by Young Generation	53	748,150

WINNING FLAT JOCKEYS 2002

	1st	2nd	3rd	Unpl.	Total mts
K. Fallon	149	86	88	487	810
R. Hughes	126	137	92	451	806
S. Sanders	123	97	87	525	832
D. Holland	113	117	98	520	848
K. Darley	113	108	81	497	799
M. Dwyer	104	104	104	646	958
T. Quinn	104	99	100	462	765
S. Drowne	104	85	106	682	977
J. Quinn	101	95	91	820	1107
F. Lynch	100	77	89	490	756

NATIONAL HUNT
HENNESSY GOLD CUP
(1957) Newbury, 3 miles and about 2½ f

1999	Ever Bless (6y), T. J. Murphy
2000	Kings Road (8y), J. Goldstein
2001	What's Up Boys, P. Flynn
2002	*Be My Royal, (8y), D. Casey

Under review (awaiting outcome of legal proceedings for alleged horse doping offence). Second place: Gingembre

KING GEORGE VI CHASE
(1937) Kempton, about 3 miles

1999	See More Business (9y), M. A. Fitzgerald
2000	First Gold, T. Dounan
2001	Florida Pearl (9y), A. Maguire
2002	Best Mate (7y), A.P. McCoy

CHAMPION HURDLE
(1927) Cheltenham, 2 miles and about ½ f

2000	Istabraq (8y), C. Swan
2001	cancelled due to foot and mouth crisis
2002	Hors La Loi III (7y), D. Gallagher
2003	Rooster Booster (9y), R. Johnson

QUEEN MOTHER CHAMPION CHASE
(1959) Cheltenham, about 2 miles

2000	Edredon Bleu (8y), A. P. McCoy
2001	cancelled due to foot and mouth crisis
2002	Flagship Uberalles, R. Johnson
2003	Moscow Flyer (9y), B. Geraghty

CHELTENHAM GOLD CUP
(1924) 3 miles and about 2½ f

2000	Looks Like Trouble (8y), R. Johnson
2001	cancelled due to foot and mouth crisis
2002	Best Mate (7y), J. Culloty
2003	Best Mate (8y), J. Culloty

GRAND NATIONAL
(1837) Liverpool, 4 miles and about 4 f

2000	Papillon (9y), R. Walsh
2001	Red Marauder (11y), R. Guest
2002	Bindaree (8y), J. Culloty
2003	Monty's Pass (10y), B. Geraghty

ATTHERACES GOLD CUP
(*KNOWN AS WHITBREAD GOLD CUP UNTIL 2002)
(1957) Sandown, 3 miles and about 5 f

2000	Beau (7yr), C. Llewellyn
2001	Ad Hoc, (7y), R. Walsh
2002	Bounce Back, A. P. McCoy
2003	Ad Hoc (9y), R. Walsh

STATISTICS
WINNING NATIONAL HUNT TRAINERS 2002–3

M. C. Pipe	£2,491,352
P. F. Nicholls	2,077,046
J. J. O'Neill	1,491,939
P. J. Hobbs	1,416,759
N. J. Henderson	1,008,080
Miss H. C. Knight	858,600
Miss V. Williams	664,880
Mrs S. J. Smith	611,998
Mrs M. Reveley	484,458
Ferdy Murphy	452,253

WINNING NATIONAL HUNT JOCKEYS 2002–3

	1st	2nd	3rd	Unpl.	Total mts
A. P. McCoy	257	132	118	333	840
R. Johnson	147	116	111	351	725
A. Dobbin	109	65	43	261	478
M. A. Fitzgerald	77	71	45	255	448
R. Walsh	77	49	32	137	295
G. Lee	66	60	66	356	548
A. Thornton	62	95	65	299	521
W. Marston	61	39	55	290	445
B. Fenton	60	46	36	217	359
L. Aspell	59	59	64	311	493

The above statistics have been provided by *Timeform*, publishers of the *Racehorses* and *Chasers and Hurdlers* annuals

ICE HOCKEY

MEN'S WORLD CHAMPIONSHIPS 2003
April, Finland
Final: Canada beat Sweden 3–2

WOMEN'S WORLD CHAMPIONSHIPS 2003
April, China
Cancelled due to Sars outbreak

SUPER LEAGUE

Super League Champions 2002–3: Sheffield Steelers
Play-off Champions 2003: Belfast Giants
Challenge Cup 2002–3: Sheffield Steelers beat
  Nottingham Panthers 3–2

NATIONAL HOCKEY LEAGUE
Eastern Conference final 2002: New Jersey Devils beat
  Ottawa Senators 4–3
Western Conference final 2002: Anaheim Mighty Ducks
  beat Minnesota Wild 4–0
Stanley Cup final series 2003: New Jersey beat Anaheim
  4–3

ICE SKATING

BRITISH FIGURE SKATING CHAMPIONSHIPS 2002
Dumfries, December

Men: Matthew Parr
Women: Karla Quinn
Pairs: Daniella Finch and Perry Drake
Ice Dance: Lauren Morris and Daniel Taylor

EUROPEAN CHAMPIONSHIPS 2003
January, Malmo, Sweden

Men: Evgeni Plushenko (Russia)
Women: Irina Slutskaya (Russia)
Pairs: Tatiana Totmianina and Maxim Marinin (Russia)
Ice Dance: Irina Lobacheva and Ilia Averbukh (Russia)

WORLD CHAMPIONSHIPS 2003
March, Washington, USA

Men: Evgeni Plushenko (Russia)
Women: Michelle Kwan (USA)
Pairs: Xue Shen and Hongbo Zhao (China)
Ice Dance: Shae-Lynn Bourne and Victor Kraatz (Canada)

JUDO

EUROPEAN CHAMPIONSHIPS 2003
May 16–19, Dusseldorf

MEN
Open: Tamerlan Tmenov (Russia)
Heavyweight (over 100kg): Alexandre Mikhaylin (Russia)
Light-heavyweight (100kg): Ariel Zeevi (Israel)
Middleweight (90kg): Valentyn Grekov (Ukraine)
Welterweight (81kg): Sergei Aschwanden (Switzerland)
Lightweight (73kg): Gennadiy Bilodid (Ukraine)
Junior lightweight (66kg): Benjamin Darbelet (France)
Bantamweight (60kg): Nestor Khergiani (Georgia)

WOMEN
Open: Katrin Beinroth (Germany)
Heavyweight (over 78kg): Karina Bryant (GBR)
Light-heavyweight (78kg): Lucia Morico (Italy)
Middleweight (70kg): Rasa Sraka (Slovenia)
Welterweight (63kg): Sara Alvarez (Spain)
Lightweight (57kg): Isabel Fernandez (Spain)
Junior lightweight (52kg): Annabelle Euranie (France)
Bantamweight (48kg): Lioubov Brouletova (Russia)

BRITISH OPEN CHAMPIONSHIPS 2003
April 12–13

MEN
Heavyweight (over 100 kg): Ouaqef Ziad (France)
Light-heavyweight (100 kg): Henry Hubert (Germany)
Middleweight (90 kg): Sven Helbing (Germany)
Welter (81 kg): Mathieu Dafreville (France)
Lightweight (73 kg): Jimmy Pedro (USA)
Junior lightweight (66 kg): James Warren (GBR)
Bantamweight (60 kg): Craig Fallon (GBR)

WOMEN
Heavyweight (over 78 kg): Karina Bryant (GBR)
Light-heavyweight (78 kg): Rachel Wilding (GBR)
Middleweight (70 kg): Marie-Hele Chisholme (Canada)
Welter (63 kg): Daniela Krukower (Argentina) (GBR)
Lightweight (57 kg): Deborah Gravenstyn (USA)
Junior lightweight (52 kg): Sanna Askelof (Sweden)
Bantamweight (48 kg): Young Ran Kim (Korea)

MOTOR CYCLING

500CC GRAND PRIX 2002
Pacific (Motegi, Japan): Alex Barros (Brazil), Honda
Malaysian (Sepang): Max Biaggi (Italy), Yamaha
Australian (Phillip Island): Valentino Rossi (Italy), Honda
Valencia (Valencia): Alex Barros (Brazil), Honda

Riders' Championship 2002: 1. Valentino Rossi (Italy),
  Honda, 355 pts; 2. Max Biaggi (Italy), Yamaha, 215
  pts; 3. Tohru Ukawa (Japan), Honda, 209 pts

500CC GRAND PRIX 2003
Japan (Suzuka): Valentino Rossi (Italy), Honda
South Africa (Phakisa): Sete Gibernau (Spain), Honda
Spanish (Jerez): Valentino Rossi (Italy), Honda
French (Le Mans): Sete Gibernau (Spain), Honda
Italian (Mugello): Valentino Rossi (Italy), Honda
Catalunya (Barcelona): Loris Capirossi (Italy), Ducati
Dutch (Assen): Sete Gibernau (Spain), Honda
British (Donington Park): Max Biaggi (Italy), Honda
German (Sachsenring): Sete Gibernau (Spain), Honda
Czech (Brno): Valentino Rossi (Italy), Honda
Portuguese (Estoril): Valentino Rossi (Italy), Honda
Brazilian (Nelson Piquet): Valentino Rossi (Italy), Honda

250CC GRAND PRIX 2002
Pacific (Motegi, Japan): Toni Elias (Spain), Aprilia
Malaysian (Sepang): Fonsi Nieto (Spain), Aprilia
Australian (Phillip Island): Marco Melandri (Italy), Aprilia
Valencia (Valencia): Marco Melandri (Italy), Aprilia

Riders' Championship 2002: 1 Marco Melandri (Italy),
  Aprilia, 298 pts; 2. Fonsi Nieto (Spain), Aprilia, 241
  pts; 3. Roberto Rolfo (Italy), Aprilia, 219 pts

250CC GRAND PRIX 2003
Japan (Suzuka): Manuel Poggiali (San Marino), Aprilia
South Africa (Phakisa): Manuel Poggiali (San Marino),
  Aprilia
Spanish (Jerez): Toni Elias (Spain), Aprilia
French (Le Mans): Toni Elias (Spain), Aprilia
Italian (Mugello): Manuel Poggiali (San Marino), Aprilia
Catalunya (Barcelona): Randy de Puniet (France), Aprilia
Dutch (Assen): Anthony West (Australia), Aprilia
British (Donington Park): Fonsi Nieto (Spain), Aprilia
German (Sachsenring): Roberto Rolfo (Italy), Honda

Czech (Brno): Randy De Puniet (France), Aprilia
Portuguese (Estoril): Tony Elias (Spain), Aprilia
Brazilian Grand Prix (Nelson Piquet): Manuel Poggiali
(San Marino), Aprilia

125CC GRAND PRIX 2002
Pacific (Motegi, Japan): Daniel Pedrosa (Spain), Honda
Malaysian (Sepang): Arnaud Vincent (France), Aprilia
Australian (Phillip Island): Manuel Poggiali (San Marino),
Gilera
Valencia (Valencia): Daniel Pedrosa (Spain), Honda

Riders' Championship 2002: 1 Arnaud Vincent (France),
Aprilia, 273 pts; 2. Manuel Poggiali (Italy), Gilera,
254 pts; , 3. Daniel Pedrosa (Spain), Honda, 243 pts

125CC GRAND PRIX 2003
Japan (Suzuka): Stefano Perugini (Italy), Aprilia
South Africa (Phakisa): Daniel Pedrosa (Spain), Honda
Spanish (Jerez): Lucio Cecchinello (Italy), Aprilia
French (Le Mans): Daniel Pedrosa (Spain), Honda
Italian (Mugello): Lucio Cecchinello (Italy), Aprilia
Catalunya (Barcelona): Daniel Pedrosa (Spain), Honda
Dutch (Assen): Steve Jenkner (Germany), Aprilia
British (Donington Park): Hector Barbera (Spain), Aprilia
German (Sachsenring) Stefano Perugini (Italy), Aprilia
Czech (Brno): Daniel Pedrosa (Spain), Honda
Portuguese (Estoril): Pablo Nieto (Spain), Aprilia
Brazilian (Nelson Piquet): Jorge Lorenzo (Spain), Derbi

Senior TT 2003, Isle of Man: Adrian Archibald
(Northern Ireland), Suzuki
Junior TT 2003, Isle of Man: Bruce Anstey (New
Zealand), Triumph

WORLD SUPERBIKES 2003
Spain (Valencia): Race 1– Neil Hodgson (GB), Ducati;
Race 2– Neil Hodgson (GB), Ducati
Australia (Philip Island): Race 1– Neil Hodgson (GB),
Ducati; Race 2– Neil Hodgson (GB), Ducati
Japan (Sugo): Race 1– Neil Hodgson (GB), Ducati; Race
2– Neil Hodgson (GB), Ducati
Italy (Monza): Race 1– Neil Hodgson (GB), Ducati; Race
2– Neil Hodgson (GB), Ducati
Germany (Oschersleben): Race 1– Neil Hodgson (GB),
Ducati; Race 2– James Toseland (GB), Ducati
Great Britain (Silverstone): Race 1– Neil Hodgson (GB),
Ducati; Race 2– Neil Hodgson (GB), Ducati
San Marino (Misano): Race 1– Ruben Xaus (Spain),
Ducati; Race 2– Ruben Xaus (Spain), Ducati
United States (Laguna Seca): Race 1– Frankie Chili (Italy),
Ducati; Race 2– Ruben Xaus (Spain), Ducati
European (Brands Hatch): Race 1– Shane Byrne (GB),
Ducati; Race 2– Shane Byrne (GB), Ducati
Netherlands (Assen): Race 1– Ruben Xaus (Spain), Ducati;
Race 2– Neil Hodgson (GB), Ducati

MOTOR RACING

FORMULA ONE GRAND PRIX 2002
United States Grand Prix (Indianapolis) (29 September):
Rubens Barrichello (Brazil), Ferrari
Japanese Grand Prix (Suzuka) (13 October): Michael
Schumacher (Germany), Ferrari

Drivers' World Championship 2002: 1. Michael
Schumacher (Germany), Ferrari, 144 points; 2. Rubens
Barrichello (Brazil), Ferrari, 77 points; 3. Juan Pablo
Montoya (Colombia), Williams, 50 points.

Constructors' World Championship 2002: 1. Ferrari, 221
points; 2. Williams-BMW, 92 points; 3. McLaren-
Mercedes, 65 points.

FORMULA ONE GRAND PRIX 2003
Australian (Melbourne, 9 March) David Coulthard
(Scotland), McLaren
Malaysian Grand Prix (Sepang, 23 March) Kimi
Raikkonen (Finland), McLaren
Brazilian Grand Prix (São Paulo, 6 April) Giancarlo
Fisichella (Italy), Jordan
San Marino Grand Prix (Imola, 20 April) Michael
Schumacher (Germany), Ferrari
Spanish Grand Prix (Barcelona, 4 May) Michael
Schumacher (Germany), Ferrari
Austrian Grand Prix (Spielberg, 18 May) Michael
Schumacher (Germany), Ferrari
Monaco Grand Prix (Monte Carlo, 1 June) Juan Pablo
Montoya (Colombia), Williams
Canadian Grand Prix (Montreal, 15 June) Michael
Schumacher (Germany), Ferrari
European Grand Prix (Nurburgring, 29 June) Ralf
Schumacher (Germany), Williams
French Grand Prix (Magny-Cours, 6 July) Ralf
Schumacher (Germany), Williams
British Grand Prix (Silverstone, 20 July) Rubens
Barrichello (Brazil), Ferarri
German Grand Prix (Hockenheim, 3 August) Juan Pablo
Montoya (Colombia), Williams
Hungarian Grand Prix (Hungaroring, 24 August)
Fernando Alonso (Spain), Renault
Italian Grand Prix (Monza, 14 September): Michael
Schumacher (Germany), Ferrari
US Grand Prix (Indianapolis, 28 September): *see* Stop
Press

Indianapolis 500 2003: Gil De Ferran (Brazil), Marlboro
Team Penske
Le Mans 24-hour Race 2003: Tom Kristensen, Rinaldo
Capello and Guy Smith (Bentley)
Arras-Madrid-Dakar Rally 2003: Cars – Hiroshi
Masuoka (Japan), Mitsubishi; Richard Sainct (France)
KTM; Trucks – Vladimir Tchaguine (Russia), Kamaz

MOTOR RALLYING

WORLD RALLY CHAMPIONSHIPS
2002
Italy: G. Panizzi (France), Peugeot
New Zealand: Marcus Grönholm (Finland), Peugeot
Australia: Marcus Grönholm (Finland), Peugeot
Great Britain: Petter Solberg (Norway), Subaru
Driver's World Championship 2002: Marcus Grönholm
(Finland), 77 points
Manufacturers' World Championship 2002: Peugeot, 165
points

2003
Monte Carlo: Sebastien Loeb (France), Citroen
Swedish: Marcus Grönholm (Finland), Peugeot
Turkey: Carlos Sainz (Spain), Ford
New Zealand: Marcus Grönholm (Finland), Peugeot
Argentina: Marcus Grönholm (Finland), Peugeot
Acropolis: Markko Maertin (Estonia), Ford
Cyprus: Petter Solberg (Norway), Subaru
Germany: Sebastien Loeb (France), Citroen
Finland: Markko Maertin (Estonia), Ford
Australia: Petter Solberg (Norway), Subaru

BRITISH RALLY CHAMPIONSHIPS 2003

Pirelli International: Tapio Laukkanen (Finland), Subaru
Rally of Wales: cancelled
Scottish Rally: Jonny Milner (GB), Toyota
Jim Clark Memorial Rally: Andrew Nesbitt (GB), Subaru
Manx International: Jonny Milner (GB), Toyota
Ulster Rally: Tapio Laukkanen (Finland), Subaru
Yorkshire Rally: see Stop Press

NETBALL

Inter-County Championship 2003: Birmingham
National Clubs League Championship 2003: YWCA Bury
English Counties League Championship 2003: Essex
   Metropolitan
Super Cup 2003: Petchey London Tornadoes

WORLD CHAMPIONSHIP
Jamaica, July
Final: New Zealand beat Australia 49–47

NORDIC EVENTS

BIATHLON WORLD CHAMPIONSHIPS
2003
Khanty-Mansiysk, Russia

MEN
10km sprint: Ole Einar Bjoerndalen (Norway) 26min.
   52.1sec.
12.5km pursuit: Ricco Gross (Germany) 37min. 37.46sec.
15km mass start: Ole Einar Bjoerndalen (Norway) 40min.
   49.71sec.
20km individual: Halvard Hanevold (Norway) 53min.
   39.4sec.
4 x 7.5km relay: Germany 1hr. 18min. 38.05sec.

WOMEN
7.5km sprint: Sylvie Becaert (France) 23min. 46.3sec.
10km pursuit: Sandrine Bailly (France) 35min. 15.64sec.
12.5km mass start: Albina Akhatova (Russia) 37min.
   15.88sec.
15km individual: Katerina Holubcova (Czech Republic)
   48min. 28.4sec.
4 x 6km relay: Russia 1hr. 24min. 34.46sec.

BIATHLON WORLD CUP 2002–3

MEN
Overall: Ole Einar Bjoerndalen (Norway)

WOMEN
Overall: Martina Glagow (Germany)

CROSS-COUNTRY WORLD CUP 2002–3

MEN
Mathias Fredriksson (Sweden)

WOMEN
Bente Skari (Norway)

NORDIC-COMBINED WORLD CUP 2002–3
Ronny Ackermann (Germany)

SKI-JUMPING WORLD CUP 2003
Adam Malysz (Poland)

POLO

Prince of Wales Trophy final 2003: Buzzee Bees beat FCT
   11–10
Queen's Cup final 2003: Dubai beat Labegorce 11–10
Warwickshire Cup 2003: FCT beat Foxcote 13–7
Gold Cup (British Open) final 2003: Hildon Sport beat
   Labegorce 6–5
Coronation Cup 2003: England beat Mexico 8–7

RACKETS

Noel Bruce Cup 2002: Wellington 1 beat Harrow 1 4–0
British Professional Singles Championship final 2003: Neil
   Smith beat Mark Hubbard 3–2
British Open Singles Championship final 2003: Guy Smith-
   Bingham beat Harry Foster 4–0
Amateur Singles Championship final 2002: Guy Smith-
   Bingham beat Harry Foster 3–0
Amateur Doubles Championship 2003: Rupert Owen-
   Browne and Tim Cockroft beat Ali Robinson and Guy
   Barker 3–0
The Foster Cup final 2003 (public schools' single
   championship): George Tysoe (Wellington) beat
   Charlie Monbiot (Radley) 3–0
Varsity Match 2003: Oxford beat Cambridge 3–0
World Championship 2003: James Male (GB) beat
   Jonathan Larken (USA) 5–4

REAL TENNIS

British Professional Singles Championship final 2003:
   Robert Fahey beat Chris Bray 3–0
British Professional Doubles Championship final 2003:
   Mike Gooding and Nick Wood beat Steve Virgona and
   Ruaraidh Gunn 3–2
British Open Singles Championship final 2002: Tim
   Chisholm beat Robert Fahey 3–2
British Open Doubles Championship final 2002: Robert
   Fahey and Steve Virgona beat Julian Snow and Tim
   Chisholm 3–1
Henry Leaf Cup final 2003 (public schools' old boys'
   doubles championship): Canford beat Haileybury 2–1
World Singles Championships 2003: Robert Fahey
   (Australia) beat Tim Chisholm (GB) 7–6
National League Final 2002: Holyport beat Cambridge
   3–0
Women's British Open Singles Championship final 2003:
   Charlotte Cornwallis beat Alex Garside 2–0

ROWING

WORLD CHAMPIONSHIPS 2003
Milan, Italy, August

MEN
Coxed pairs: USA 7:10.11
Coxless pairs: Australia 6:19.31
Coxed fours: USA 6:04.68
Coxless fours: Canada 5:52.91
Single sculls: Norway 6:46.15
Double sculls: France 6:13.93
Quad sculls: Germany 6:12.26
Eights: Canada 6:00.44

WOMEN
Coxless pairs: Great Britain 7:04.88
Coxless fours: USA 6:53.08
Single sculls: Bulgaria 7:18.12
Double sculls: New Zealand 6:45.79
Quad sculls: Australia 6:46.52
Eights: Germany 6:41.23

NATIONAL CHAMPIONSHIPS 2003
Motherwell, July

MEN
Coxless pairs: Nautilus 7:32.79
Coxed fours: Nottingham and Union Rowing Club
  7:12.99
Coxless fours: Nautilus Rowing Club 6:47.41
Single sculls: Leander Club 7:59.23
Double sculls: Nottinghamshire County Rowing
  Association 7:26.78
Quad sculls: Nautilus Rowing Club 6:51.65
Eights: Nautilus 6:26.95

WOMEN
Coxless pairs: Kingston Rowing Club 8:18.31
Coxed fours: University of London/Tideway
  Scullers/London RC 7:49.80
Coxless fours: Nottinghamshire County Rowing
  Association/Cambridge University/Durham Amateur
  Rowing Club/John O'Gaunt 8:06.68
Single sculls: Loughborough Boat Club 8:54.86
Double sculls: Nautilus 8:11.18
Quad sculls: Marlow/Northwich/LEH/Wycliffe 7:43.89
Eights: University of London 7:18.44

THE 149TH UNIVERSITY BOAT RACE
Putney–Mortlake, 4 miles 1 f, 180 yd, 30 March 2002

Oxford beat Cambridge by 1 foot; 18 min. 6 sec.

Cambridge have won 77 times, Oxford 71 and there has
been one dead heat. The record time is 16 min. 19 sec.,
rowed by Cambridge in 1998

HENLEY ROYAL REGATTA 2003
Grand Challenge Cup: Victoria City Rowing Club
  (Canada) beat Princeton Training Center (USA) by 2¾
  lengths
Ladies' Challenge Plate: University of Washington (USA)
  beat Rutgers University (USA) by 4¾ lengths
Thames Challenge Cup: Homberger Ruderklub (Germany)
  beat London Rowing Club 'A' by ½ length
Temple Challenge Cup: Princeton University 'A' (USA)
  beat Princeton University 'B' (USA) by 2¼ lengths
Princess Elizabeth Challenge Cup: Pangbourne College
  beat St. Edward's School by ⅔ length
Remenham Challenge Cup: Western R.C. and Victoria
  C.R.C (Canada) beat N.S.W. Institute of Sport and
  Australian Institute of Sport (Australia) by 1¼ lengths
Stewards' Challenge Cup: Victoria City R.C. (Canada) beat
  Gorge Rowing Centre (Canada) by ⅔ length
Prince Philip Challenge Cup: Leander Club beat Molesey
  B.C. and University of London Tyrian Club easily
Queen Mother Challenge Cup: Gdansk and Warszawa,
  (Poland) beat T.S.S.K.A. Ukraine (Ukraine) ½ length
Visitors' Challenge Cup: N.U.I. Galway and Skibbereen
  R.C. (Ireland) beat Cambridge University by 1 length

Wyfold Challenge Cup: Thames Rowing Club 'A' beat
  Army Rowing Club easily
Britannia Challenge Cup: Goldie Boat Club beat
  University of London 'A' by ⅔ length
Fawley Challenge Cup: Marlow and The King's School,
  Worcester beat Malvern Preparatory School (USA)
  easily
Silver Goblets and Nickalls' Challenge Cup: J. E. Cracknell
  and M. C. Pinsent beat J. L. Read and B. D. Volpenhein
  (USA) by ⅓ length
Double Sculls Challenge Cup: B. Mueller and M. Weiss
  (Germany) beat M. S. Inglis and T. Pascall (Australia)
  by 3 lengths
Diamond Challenge Sculls: A. W. Campbell beat B. P.
  Hopkins (Australia) 1½ lengths
Princess Royal Challenge Cup: C. J. Oliver (Australia) beat
  D. R Martin (Australia) by 1½ lengths
Princess Grace Challenge Cup: T. S. S. K. A. Ukraine
  (Ukraine) beat Australian Institute of Sport (Australia)
  by 1 length
Men's Quadruple Sculls: Commercial R.C. (Ireland) beat
  Leander Club 'A' by 1 length

OTHER ROWING EVENTS
Wingfield Sculls 2002: Ian Lawson (Leander)
Oxford Torpids 2003: Men, Oriel; Women, Merton (Final
  day cancelled due to flooding)
Oxford Summer Eights 2003: Men, Pembroke; Women,
  Pembroke
Head of the River 2003: Men, Leander I; Women,
  Imperial College/Kingston Rowing
  Club/Marlow/Oxford Brookes/Thames Rowing Club

RUGBY FIVES

National Open Singles Championship final 2002:
  N. Roberts beat H. Buchanan
National Open Doubles Championship final 2003: J.
  Beswick and N. Roberts beat H. Buchanan and
  R. Perry
National Club Championship final 2003: Alleyn Old Boys
  beat Manchester YMCA
National Schools' Singles Champion 2003: D. Grant
  (Merchant Taylors' School)
National Schools' Doubles Champions 2003: T. Curtin and
  P. Rider (Christ's Hospital)
Varsity Match 2003: Oxford beat Cambridge

RUGBY LEAGUE

Super League Grand Final 2002 (Old Trafford, 19
  October): St Helens beat Bradford Bulls 19–18
World Club Challenge 2003 (Bolton, 14 February):
  Sydney Roosters beat St Helens 38–0
Challenge Cup final 2002 (Cardiff, 26 April): Bradford
  Bulls beat Leeds Rhinos 22-20
Varsity Match 2003 (Richmond, 5 March): Oxford beat
  Cambridge 25–13

AMATEUR RUGBY LEAGUE 2002–3
National Conference League Premier Division Champions:
  Siddal; Division one: Thatto Heath Crusaders;
  Division two: Wath Brow Hornets
National Cup: Oldham St Annes 15 West Hull 14

RUGBY UNION

SIX NATIONS' CHAMPIONSHIP 2003

15 February	Rome	Italy 30, Wales 22
	London	England 25, France 17
16 February	Edinburgh	Scotland 6, Ireland 36
22 February	Rome	Italy 13, Ireland 37
	Cardiff	Wales 9, England 26
23 February	Paris	France 38, Scotland 3
8 March	Dublin	Ireland 15, France 12
	Edinburgh	Scotland 30, Wales 22
9 March	London	England 40, Italy 5
22 March	Cardiff	Wales 24, Ireland 25
	London	England 40, Scotland 9
23 March	Rome	Italy 27, France 53
29 March	Paris	France 33, Wales 5
	Edinburgh	Scotland 33, Italy 25
30 March	Dublin	Ireland 6, England 42

Final standings: 1. England, 10 points; 2. Ireland, 8 points; 3. France, 6 points; 4. Scotland, 4 points; 5. Italy, 2 points; 6. Wales, 0 points

EUROPEAN COMPETITIONS 2002–3
Heineken European Cup final 2003 (Dublin, 24 May): Toulouse beat Perpignan 22–17
Parker Pen Cup 2003 (Madejski Stadium, 25 May): Wasps beat Bath 48–30
Parker Pen Shield 2003 (25 May): Castres beat Caerphilly 40–12

DOMESTIC COMPETITIONS 2002–3
ENGLAND
Zurich Premiership: Gloucester, 82 points
Championship final: Wasps beat Gloucester 39–3
National League: Division 1, Rotherham, 116 points; *Division 2,* Penzance/Newlyn 45 points; *Division 3* (North), Nuneaton, 46 points; (South) Rosslyn Park, 48 points
Powergen Cup final: Gloucester beat Northampton 40–22
Challenge Shield final: Orrell beat Exeter 26–20
Tetley's County Championship final: Lancashire beat Gloucestershire 24–18
Tetley's County Shield: Northumberland beat Oxfordshire 27–8
121st Varsity Match: Cambridge beat Oxford 15–13

CELTIC
Celtic League Final: Munster beat Neath 37–17

SCOTLAND
Scottish Premier League: Division 1, Boroughmuir, 62 points; *Division 2,* Watsonians, 75 points; Division 3, Dundee HSFP, 74 points
Scottish Cup final 2003: Heriot's FP beat Watsonians 25–13

WALES
Welsh Premiership: Bridgend, 42 points
Welsh National League: Division 1, Pontypool, 90 points; *Division 2,* Bedwas 81 points
Principality Cup final (Cardiff, 3 May): Llanelli beat Newport 32–9

IRELAND
All Ireland League: Division 1, Clontarf, 61 points; Division 2, Dolphin, 57 points; Division 3, Waterpark, 60 points

SAILING

AMERICAS CUP
Auckland, February

Alinghi (Swizerland) beat Team New Zealand (New Zealand) 5–0

SHOOTING

134TH NATIONAL RIFLE ASSOCIATION IMPERIAL MEETING
Bisley, July 2003

World Individual Championship: Dr P. M. Patel, 796.100 v-bulls
Queen's Prize: Dr G. C. D. Barnett, 297.34 v-bulls
Grand Aggregate: Dr P. M. Patel, 697.89 v-bulls
Prince of Wales Prize: M. C. Parker, 75.12 v-bulls
St George's Vase: J. A. M. Paton, 149.24 v-bulls
All Comers' Aggregate: Dr G. C. D. Barnett, 373.42 v-bulls
Kolapore Cup: Great Britain, 1195.180 v-bulls
Chancellor's Trophy: Cambridge University, 1170.125 v-bulls
Musketeers Cup: Edinburgh University, 590.69 v-bulls
County Long-Range Championship: Norfolk, 294.27 v-bulls
Mackinnon Challenge Cup: South Africa, 1131.99 v-bulls
The Albert: N. C. M. Fyfe 221.25 v-bulls
Hopton Challenge Cup: J. S. Collings 996.112 v-bulls

SHORT TRACK SPEED SKATING AND SPEED SKATING

EUROPEAN CHAMPIONSHIPS 2003
January, Heerenveen, Netherlands

MEN
500 metres: Aleksandr Kibalko (Russia) 36.40sec.
1,500 metres: Gianni Romme (Netherlands) 1min. 48.35sec.
5,000 metres: Gianni Romme (Netherlands) 6min. 26.72sec.
10,000 metres: Gianni Romme (Netherlands) 13min. 27.68
Overall: Gianni Romme (Netherlands) 153.002 points

WOMEN
500 metres: Anni Friesinger (Germany) 39.39sec.
1,500 metres: Anni Friesinger (Germany) 1min. 57.87sec.
3,000 metres: Anni Friesinger (Germany) 4min. 08.64sec.
5,000 metres: Claudia Pechstein (Germany) 7min. 05.23sec.
Overall: Anni Friesinger (Germany) 162.965 points

WORLD CHAMPIONSHIPS 2003
Gothenberg, Sweden

MEN
500 metres: Ids Postma (Netherlands) 36.89sec.
1,500 metres: Yevgeny Lalenkov (Russia) 1min. 51.70sec.
5,000 metres: Gianni Romme (Netherlands) 6min. 42.67sec.

10,000 metres: Gianni Romme (Netherlands) 14min. 05.04sec.

WOMEN

500 metres: Jennifer Rodriguez (USA) 40.01sec.
1,500 metres: Maki Tabata (Japan) 2min. 04.71sec.
3,000 metres: Claudia Pechstein (Germany) 4min. 19.99sec.
5,000 metres: Clara Hughes (Canada) 7min. 25.88

EUROPEAN SHORT TRACK CHAMPIONSHIPS 2003
St Petersburg, Russia, January

MEN

500 metres: Fabio Carta (Italy) 42.699sec.
1,000 metres: Michele Antonioli (Italy) 1min. 30.928sec.
1,500 metres: Fabio Carta (Italy) 2min. 23.950sec.
3,000 metres: Fabio Carta (Italy) 5min. 09.330sec.
5,000 metres relay: Italy 7min. 00.303sec.
Overall: Fabio Carta (Italy) 115 points

WOMEN

500 metres: Evgenia Radanova (Bulgaria) 45.086sec.
1,000 metres: Evgenia Radanova (Bulgaria) 1min. 43.993sec.
1,500 metres: Evgenia Radanova (Bulgaria) 2min. 34.835sec.
3,000 metres: Evgenia Radanova (Bulgaria) 5min. 30.153sec.
3,000 metres relay: Italy 4 min. 29.255sec.
Overall: Evgenia Radanova (Bulgaria) 136 points

WORLD SHORT TRACK CHAMPIONSHIPS 2003
Warsaw, Poland, March

MEN

500 metres: Jiajun Li (China) 43.210sec.
1,000 metres: Jiajun Li (China) 1min 28.391sec.
1,500 metres: Hyun-Soo Ahn (Korea) 2min. 25.271sec.
3,000 metres: Hyun-Soo Ahn (Korea) 4min. 58.297sec.
5,000 metres relay: Korea 6min. 55.975sec.
Overall: Hyun-Soo Ahn (Korea) 89 points

WOMEN

500 metres: Yang Yang A (China) 44.270sec.
1,000 metres: Evgenia Radanova (Bulgaria) 1min. 31.594sec.
1,500 metres: Eun-Kyung Choi (Korea) 2min. 24.866sec.
3,000 metres: Min-Jee Kim (Korea) 5min. 31.650sec.
3,000 metres relay: China 4min. 22.030sec.
Overall: Eun-Kyung Choi (Korea) 76 points

SNOOKER

2002–3
British Open (Telford): Paul Hunter (England) beat Ian McCulloch (England) 9–4
LG Cup (Preston): Chris Small (Scotland) beat Alan McManus (Scotland) 9–5
Scottish Masters (Glasgow): Ronnie O'Sullivan (England) beat John Higgins (Scotland) 9–4
European Open (Torquay): Ronnie O'Sullivan (England) beat Stephen Hendry (Scotland) 9–6
UK Championships (York): Mark J. Williams (Wales) beat Ken Doherty (Ireland) 10–9
Benson & Hedges Masters (Wembley): Mark J. Williams (Wales) beat Stephen Hendry (Scotland) 10–4

Welsh Open (Cardiff): Stephen Hendry (Scotland) beat Mark J. Williams (Wales) 9–5
Irish Masters (Dublin): Ronnie O'Sullivan (England) beat John Higgins (Scotland) 10–9
Scottish Open (Edinburgh): David Gray (England) beat Mark Selby (England) 9–7
World Championship (Sheffield): Mark J. Williams (Wales) beat Ken Doherty (Ireland) 18–16

WOMEN
World Championship 2003: (Sheffield) Kelly Fisher beat Lisa Quick 4–1

SQUASH RACKETS

MEN
World Open 2002: David Palmer (Australia) beat John White (Scotland) 3–2
European Team Championship final 2003: England drew with France 2–2 (*England win 9–6 on countback*)
British National Championship final 2002: Peter Nicol beat Lee Beachill 3–2

WOMEN
World Open 2002: Sarah Fitz-Gerald (Australia) beat Natalie Pohrer (England) 3–1
World Team Championship final 2002: Australia beat England 2–1
European Team Championship 2003: England beat Holland 2–1
British National Championship 2003: Cassie Jackman beat Rebecca Macree 3–1

SWIMMING

WORLD CHAMPIONSHIPS 2003
Barcelona, July

MEN
50 metres freestyle: Alexander Popov (Russia) 21.92
100 metres freestyle: Alexander Popov (Russia) 48.42
200 metres freestyle: Ian Thorpe (Australia) 1:45.14
400 metres freestyle: Ian Thorpe (Australia) 3:42.58
800 metres freestyle: Grant Hackett (Australia) 7:43.82
1,500 metres freestyle: Grant Hackett (Australia) 14:43.14
50 metres backstroke: Thomas Rupprath (Germany) 24.80
100 metres backstroke: Aaron Peirsol (USA) 53.61
200 metres backstroke: Aaron Peirsol (USA) 1:55.92
50 metres breaststroke: James Gibson (GBR) 27.56
100 metres breaststroke: Kosuke Kitajima (Japan) 59.78
200 metres breaststroke: Kosuke Kitajima (Japan) 2:09.42
50 metres butterfly: Matthew Welsh (Australia) 23.43
100 metres butterfly: Ian Crocker (USA) 50.98
200 metres butterfly: Michael Phelps (USA) 1:54.35
200 metres medley: Michael Phelps (USA) 1:56.04
400 metres medley: Michael Phelps (USA) 4:09.09
4 x 100 metres freestyle relay: Russia 3:14.06
4 x 200 metres freestyle relay: Australia 7:08.58
4 x 100 metres medley relay: USA 3:31.54

WOMEN
50 metres freestyle: Inge De Bruijn (Netherlands) 24.47
100 metres freestyle: Hanna-Maria Seppala (Finland) 54.37
200 metres freestyle: Alena Popchanka (Belarus) 1:58.32
400 metres freestyle: Hannah Stockbauer (Germany) 4:06.75
800 metres freestyle: Hannah Stockbauer (Germany) 8:23.66

1,500 metres freestyle: Hannah Stockbauer (Germany)
  16:00.18
50 metres backstroke: Nina Zhivanevskaya (Spain) 28.48
100 metres backstroke: Antje Buschschulte (Germany)
  1:00.50
200 metres backstroke: Katy Sexton (GBR) 2:08.74
50 metres breaststroke: Xuejuan Luo (China) 30.67
100 metres breaststroke: Xuejuan Luo (China) 1:06.80
200 metres breaststroke: Amanda Beard (USA) 2:22.99
50 metres butterfly: Inge De Bruijn (Netherlands) 25.84
100 metres butterfly: Jenny Thompson (USA) 57.96
200 metres butterfly: Otylia Jedrzejczak (Poland) 2:07.56
200 metres medley: Yana Klochkova (Ukraine) 2:10.75
400 metres medley: Yana Klochkova (Ukraine) 4:36.74
4 x 100 metres freestyle relay: USA 3:38.09
4 x 200 metres freestyle relay: USA 7:55.70
4 x 100 metres medley relay: China 3:59.89

TABLE TENNIS

ENGLISH NATIONAL CHAMPIONSHIPS 2003
Sheffield, March

Men's Singles: Alan Cooke (Derbys) beat Andrew
  Baggaley (Bucks) 4–3
Women's Singles: Andrea Holt (Lancs) beat Helen Lower
  (Staffs) 4–0
Men's Doubles: Alex Perry (Devon) and Terry Young
  (Berks) beat Bryn Drinkhall (Cleveland) and Andrew
  Rushton (Lancs) 3–2
Women's Doubles: Nicola Deaton (Derbys) and Kubrat
  Owolabi (Middx) beat Abigail Embling (Essex) and
  Joanna Parker (Surrey) 3–0
Mixed Doubles: Helen Lower (Staffs) and Alex Perry
  (Devon) beat Kubrat Owolabi (Middx) and Andrew
  Rushton (Lancs) 3–1

EUROPEAN CHAMPIONSHIPS 2003
Courmayeur, Italy, March–April

Men's Singles: Vladimir Samsonov (Belarus) beat Torben
  Wosik (Germany) 4–0
Women's Singles: Otilia Badescu (Romania) beat Wenling
  Tan Monfardini (Italy) 4–3
Men's Doubles: Weixing Chen (Austria) and Evgueny
  Chtchetinine (Belarus) beat Dimitrij Mazunov (Russia)
  and Alexei Smirnov (Russia) 4–0
Women's Doubles: Tamara Boros (Croatia) and Mihaela
  Steff (Romania) beat Csilla Batorfi and Krisztina Toth
  (Hungary) 4–2
Mixed Doubles: Krisztina Toth (Hungary) and Werner
  Schlager (Austria) beat Weixing Chen (Austria) and
  Veronika Pavlovich (Belarus) 4–1
Men's Team: Belarus beat Germany 3–1
Women's Team: Italy beat Croatia 3–1

WORLD CHAMPIONSHIPS 2003
Paris, May

Men's Singles: Werner Schlager (Germany) beat Se Hyuk
  Joo (Korea) 4–2
Women's Singles: Wang Nan (China) beat Yining Zhang
  (China) 4–3
Men's Doubles: Ligin Wang and Sen Yan (China) beat Hao
  Wang and Linghui Kong (China) 4–2
Women's Doubles: Nan Wang and Yining Zhang (China)
  beat Jianfeng Niu and Yue Guo (China) 4–1
Mixed Doubles: Lin Ma and Nan Wang (China) beat
  Guozheng Liu and Yang Bai (China) 4–3

TENNIS

AUSTRALIAN OPEN CHAMPIONSHIPS 2003
Melbourne, 13–26 January

Men's Singles: Andre Agassi (USA) beat Rainer Schuettler
  6–2, 6–2, 6–1
Women's Singles: Serena Williams (USA) beat Venus
  Williams (USA) 7–6 (7–4), 3–6, 6–4
Men's Doubles: Fabrice Santoro and Michael Llodra
  (France) beat Mark Knowles (Bahamas) and Daniel
  Nestor (Canada) 6–4, 3–6, 6–3
Women's Doubles: Venus Williams and Serena Williams
  (USA) beat Virginia Ruano Pascual (Spain) and Paola
  Suarez (Argentina) 4–6, 6–4, 6–3
Mixed Doubles: Martina Navratilova (USA) and Leander
  Paes (India) beat Eleni Daniilidou (Greece) and Todd
  Woodbridge (Australia) 6–4, 7–5

FRENCH OPEN CHAMPIONSHIPS 2003
Paris, 27 May–9 June

Men's Singles: Juan Carlos Fererro (Spain) beat Martin
  Verkerk (Netherlands) 6–1, 6–3, 6–2
Women's Singles: Justine Henin-Hardenne (Belgium) beat
  Kim Clijsters (Belgium) 6–0, 6–4
Men's Doubles: Bob Bryan and Mike Bryan (USA) beat
  Paul Haarhuis (Netherlands) and Yevgeny Kafelnikov
  (Russia) 7–6 (7–3), 6–3
Women's Doubles: Kim Clijsters (Belgium) and Ai
  Sugiyama (Japan) beat Paola Suarez (Argentina) and
  Virginia Ruano Pascual (Spain) 6–7 (5–7), 6–2, 9–7
Mixed Doubles: Lisa Raymond and Mike Bryan (USA)
  beat Elena Likhovtseva (Russia) and Mahesh Bhupathi
  (India) 6–3, 6–4

ALL-ENGLAND CHAMPIONSHIPS 2003
Wimbledon, 23 June–6 July

Men's Singles: Roger Federer (Switzerland) beat Mark
  Philippoussis (Australia) 7–6 (7–5), 6–2, 7–6 (7–3)
Women's Singles: Serena Williams (USA) beat Venus
  Williams (USA) 4–6, 6–4, 6–2
Men's Doubles: Jonas Bjorkman (Sweden) and Todd
  Woodbridge (Australia) beat Mahesh Bhupathi (India)
  and Max Mirnyi (Belarus) 3–6, 6–3, 7–6 (7–4), 6–3
Women's Doubles: Kim Clijsters (Belgium) and Ai
  Sugiyama (Japan) beat Paola Suarez (Argentina) and
  Virginia Ruano Pascual (Spain) 6–4, 6–4
Mixed Doubles: Anastassia Rodionova (Russia) and Andy
  Ram (Israel) beat Martina Navratilova (USA) and
  Leander Paes (India) 6–3, 6–3

US OPEN CHAMPIONSHIPS 2003
New York, 25 August–7 September

Men's Singles: Andy Roddick (USA) beat Juan Carlos
  Fererro (Spain) 6–3, 7–6 (7–2), 6–3
Women's Singles: Justine Henin-Hardenne (Belgium) beat
  Kim Clijsters (Belgium) 7–5, 6–1
Men's Doubles: Jonas Bjorkman (Sweden) and Todd
  Woodbridge (Australia) beat Bob Bryan (USA) and
  Mike Bryan (USA) 5–7, 6–0, 7–5
Women's Doubles: Paola Suarez (Argentina) and Virginia
  Ruano Pascual (Spain) beat Svetlana Kuznetsova
  (Russia) and Martina Navratilova (USA) 6–2, 6–3

Mixed Doubles: Katarina Srebotnik (Slovenia) and Bob Bryan (USA) beat Lina Krasnoroutskaya (Russia) and Daniel Nestor (Canada) 5–7, 7–5, 7–6 (10–5)

TEAM CHAMPIONSHIPS
Davis Cup final 2002: Russia beat France 3–2

VOLLEYBALL

EUROPEAN CHAMPIONSHIP 2003
Italy beat France 3–2

MEN
World League 2002: Brazil beat Serbia and Montenegro 3–2

WOMEN
Grand Prix 2003: China

THE OLYMPIC GAMES

The 28th Olympic Games is due to be held in Athens, Greece on 13 – 29 August 2004. The list below gives the dates of all Games that have taken place since 1896. The first separate winter Games was the 1924 Chamonix-Mont Blanc festival.

1896
(25 March – 3 April 1896 according to the Julian calendar)

1900
Paris, France, 20 May – 28 October 1900

1904
St Louis, USA, 1 July – 23 November 1904

1906
Athens, Greece, 22 April – 2 May 1906

1908
London, England, 27 April – 31 October 1908

1912
Stockholm, Sweden, 5 May – 22 July 1912

1920
Antwerp, Belgium, 20 April – 12 September 1920

1924 (winter)
Chamonix-Mont Blanc, France, 25 January – 4 February 1924

1924 (summer)
Paris, France, 4 May – 27 July 1924

1928 (winter)
St Moritz, Switzerland, 11 – 19 February 1928

1928 (summer)
Amsterdam, Holland, 17 May – 12 August 1928

1932 (winter)
Lake Placid, USA, 4 – 15 February 1932

1932 (summer)
Los Angeles, USA, 30 July – 14 August 1932

1936 (winter)
Garmisch-Partenkirchen, Germany 6 – 16 February 1936

1936 (summer)
Berlin, Germany, 1 – 16 August 1936

1948 (winter)
St Moritz, Switzerland, 30 January – 8 February 1948

1948 (summer)
London, England, 29 July – 14 August 1948

1952 (winter)
Oslo, Norway, 14 – 25 February 1952

1952 (summer)
Helsinki, Finland, 19 July – 3 August 1952

1956 (winter)
Cortina d'Ampezzo, Italy, 26 January – 5 February 1956

1956 (summer)
Melbourne, Australia, 22 November – 8 December 1956 (also in Stockholm, Sweden, 10–17 June 1956)

1960 (winter)
Squaw Valley, USA, 18 – 28 February 1960

1960 (summer)
Rome, Italy, 25 August –11 September 1960

1964 (winter)
Innsbruck, Switzerland, 29 January – 9 February 1964

1964 (summer)
Tokyo, Japan, 10 – 24 October 1964

1968 (winter)
Grenoble, France, 6 – 18 February 1968

1968 (summer)
Mexico City, Mexico, 12 – 27 October 1968

1972 (winter)
Sapporo, Japan, 3 – 13 February 1972

1972 (summer)
Munich, Germany, 26 August – 10 September 1972

1976 (winter)
Innsbruck, Switzerland, 4 – 15 February 1976

1976 (summer)
Montreal, Canada, 17 July – 1 August 1976

1980 (winter)
Lake Placid, USA, 13 – 24 February 1980

1980 (summer)
Moscow, Soviet Union, 19 July – 1 August 1980

1984 (winter)
Sarajevo, Yugoslavia, 8 – 19 February 1984

1984 (summer)
Los Angeles, USA, 28 July – 12 August 1984

1988 (winter)
Calgary, Canada, 13 – 28 February 1988

1988 (summer)
Seoul, Korea, 17 September – 2 October 1988

1992 (winter)
Albertville, France, 8 – 23 February 1992

1992 (summer)
Barcelona, Spain, 25 July – 9 August

1994 (winter)
Lillehammer, Norway, 12 – 27 February 1994

1996 (summer)
Atlanta, USA, 19 July – 4 August 1996

1998 (winter)
Nagano, Japan, 7 – 22 February 1998

2000 (summer)
Sydney, Australia, 15 September – 1 October 2000

2002 (winter)
Salt Lake City, USA, 9 – 24 February 2002

2004 (summer)
Athens, Greece, 13 – 29 August 2004

2008 (winter)
Beijing, China

The following Games were scheduled but did not take place owing to World Wars

1916	Berlin, Germany
1940	Tokyo, Japan; then Helsinki, Finland
1944	London, England

THE COMMONWEALTH GAMES

The Games were originally called the British Empire Games. From 1954 to 1966 the Games were known as the British Empire and Commonwealth Games, and from 1970 to 1974 as the British Commonwealth Games. Since 1978 the Games have been called the Commonwealth Games.

BRITISH EMPIRE GAMES

1930	Hamilton, Canada
1934	London, England
1938	Sydney, Australia
1950	Auckland, New Zealand

BRITISH EMPIRE AND COMMONWEALTH GAMES

1954	Vancouver, Canada
1958	Cardiff, Wales
1962	Perth, Australia
1966	Kingston, Jamaica

BRITISH COMMONWEALTH GAMES

| 1970 | Edinburgh, Scotland |
| 1974 | Christchurch, New Zealand |

COMMONWEALTH GAMES

1978	Edmonton, Canada
1982	Brisbane, Australia
1986	Edinburgh, Scotland
1990	Auckland, New Zealand
1994	Victoria, Canada
1998	Kuala Lumpur, Malaysia
2002	Manchester, England
2006	Melbourne, Australia

FOOTBALL WORLD CUP WINNERS

FIRST HELD 1930

Year	Venue	Winner
1930	Uruguay	Uruguay
1934	Italy	Italy
1938	France	Italy
1950	Brazil	Uruguay
1954	Switzerland	West Germany
1958	Sweden	Brazil
1962	Chile	Brazil
1966	England	England
1970	Mexico	Brazil
1974	West Germany	West Germany
1978	Argentina	Argentina
1982	Spain	Italy
1986	Mexico	Argentina
1990	Italy	West Germany
1994	USA	Brazil
1998	France	France
2002	Korea/Japan	Brazil

FA CUP WINNERS SINCE 1950

FIRST HELD 1872

Year	Winner
1950	Arsenal
1951	Newcastle United
1952	Newcastle United
1953	Blackpool
1954	West Bromwich Albion
1955	Newcastle United
1956	Manchester City
1957	Aston Villa
1958	Bolton Wanderers
1959	Nottingham Forest
1960	Wolverhampton Wanderers
1961	Tottenham Hotspur
1962	Tottenham Hotspur
1963	Manchester United
1964	West Ham United
1965	Liverpool
1966	Everton
1967	Tottenham Hotspur
1968	West Bromwich Albion
1969	Manchester City
1970	Chelsea
1971	Arsenal
1972	Leeds United
1973	Sunderland
1974	Liverpool
1975	West Ham United
1976	Southampton
1977	Manchester United
1978	Ipswich Town
1979	Arsenal
1980	West Ham United
1981	Tottenham Hotspur
1982	Tottenham Hotspur
1983	Manchester United
1984	Everton
1985	Manchester United
1986	Liverpool
1987	Coventry
1988	Wimbledon
1989	Liverpool
1990	Manchester United
1991	Tottenham Hotspur
1992	Liverpool
1993	Arsenal
1994	Manchester United
1995	Everton
1996	Manchester United
1997	Chelsea
1998	Arsenal
1999	Manchester United
2000	Chelsea
2001	Liverpool
2002	Arsenal
2003	Arsenal

SPORTS RECORDS

ATHLETICS WORLD RECORDS
AS AT SEPTEMBER 2003

All the world records given below have been accepted by the International Amateur Athletic Federation except those marked with an asterisk* which are awaiting homologation. Fully automatic timing to 1/100th second is mandatory up to and including 400 metres. For distances up to and including 10,000 metres, records will be accepted to 1/100th second if timed automatically, and to 1/10th if hand timing is used.

MEN'S EVENTS

TRACK EVENTS	hr.	min.	sec.
100 metres			9.78
Tim Montgomery, USA, 2002			
200 metres			19.32
Michael Johnson, USA, 1996			
400 metres			43.18
Michael Johnson, USA, 1999			
800 metres		1	41.11
Wilson Kipketer, Denmark, 1997			
1,000 metres		2	11.96
Noah Ngeny, Kenya, 1999			
1,500 metres		3	26.00
Hicham El Guerrouj, Morocco, 1998			
1 mile		3	43.13
Hicham El Guerrouj, Morocco, 1999			
2,000 metres		4	44.79
Hicham El Guerrouj, Morocco, 1999			
3,000 metres		7	20.67
Daniel Komen, Kenya, 1996			
5,000 metres		12	39.36
Haile Gebreselassie, Ethiopia, 1998			
10,000 metres		26	22.75
Haile Gebreselassie, Ethiopia, 1998			
20,000 metres		56	55.6
Arturo Barrios, Mexico, 1991			
21,101 metres (13 miles 196 yards 1 foot)	1	00	00.00
Arturo Barrios, Mexico, 1991			
25,000 metres	1	13	55.8
Toshihiko Seko, Japan, 1981			
30,000 metres	1	29	18.8
Toshihiko Seko, Japan, 1981			
Marathon	2	05	38.0
Khalid Khannouchi, USA, 2002			
110 metres hurdles (3 ft 6 in)			12.91
Colin Jackson, GB, 1993			
400 metres hurdles (3 ft 0 in)			46.78
Kevin Young, USA, 1992			
3,000 metres steeplechase		7	53.17*
Brahim Boulami, Morocco 2002			

RELAYS		min.	sec.
4 × 100 metres			37.40
USA, 1992, 1993			
4 × 200 metres		1	19.11
Santa Monica TC, 1992			
4 × 400 metres		2	54.20
USA, 1998			
4 × 800 metres		7	03.89
GB, 1982			
4 × 1,500 metres		14	38.80
Federal Republic of Germany, 1977			

FIELD EVENTS	metres	ft	in
High jump	2.45	8	0½
Javier Sotomayor, Cuba, 1993			
Pole vault	6.14	20	1¾
Sergei Bubka, Ukraine, 1994			
Long jump	8.95	29	4½
Mike Powell, USA, 1991			
Triple jump	18.29	60	0¼
Jonathan Edwards, GB, 1995			
Shot	23.12	75	10¼
Randy Barnes, USA, 1990			
Discus	74.08	243	0
Jürgen Schult, GDR, 1986			
Hammer	86.74	284	7
Yuriy Sedykh, USSR, 1986			
Javelin	98.48	323	1
Jan Zelezny, Czech Rep., 1996			
Decathlon†			9,026 points
Roman Sebrle, Czech Rep., 2001			

† Ten events comprising 100 m, long jump, shot, high jump, 400 m, 110 m hurdles, discus, pole vault, javelin, 1500 m

WALKING (TRACK)	hr.	min.	sec.
20,000 metres	1	17	25.6
Bernard Segura, Mexico, 1994			
29,572 metres (18 miles 660 yards)	2	00	00.0
Maurizio Damilano, Italy, 1992			
30,000 metres	2	01	44.1
Maurizio Damilano, Italy, 1992			
50,000 metres	3	40	57.9
Thierry Toutain, France, 1996			

WOMEN'S EVENTS

TRACK EVENTS	hr.	min.	sec.
100 metres			10.49
Florence Griffith-Joyner, USA, 1988			
200 metres			21.34
Florence Griffith-Joyner, USA, 1988			
400 metres			47.60
Marita Koch, GDR, 1985			
800 metres		1	53.28
Jarmila Kratochvilova, Czechoslovakia, 1983			
1,500 metres		3	50.46
Qu Yunxia, China, 1993			
1 mile		4	12.56
Svetlana Masterkova, Russia, 1996			
3,000 metres		8	06.11
Wang Junxia, China, 1993			
5,000 metres		14	28.09
Jiang Bo, China, 1997			
10,000 metres		29	31.78
Wang Junxia, China, 1993			
Marathon	2	15	25.00
Paula Radcliffe, GB, 2003			
100 metres hurdles (2 ft 9 in)			12.21
Yordanka Donkova, Bulgaria, 1988			
400 metres hurdles (2 ft 6 in)			52.34*
Yulia Pechonkina, Russia, 2003			
3,000 metres steeplechase		9	08.35*
Gulnara Samitova, Russia, 2003			

RELAYS		min.	sec.
4 × 100 metres			41.37
GDR, 1985			
4 × 200 metres		1	27.46*
USA, 2000			
4 × 400 metres		3	15.17
USSR, 1988			
4 × 800 metres		7	50.17
USSR, 1984			

FIELD EVENTS	metres	ft	in
High jump	2.09	6	10¼
Stefka Kostadinova, Bulgaria, 1987			
Pole vault	4.82*	15	9¾
Yelena Isinbayeva, Russia, 2003			
Long jump	7.52	24	8¼
Galina Chistiakova, USSR, 1988			
Triple jump	15.50	50	10¼
Inessa Kravets, Ukraine, 1995			
Shot	22.63	74	3
Natalya Lisovskaya, USSR, 1987			
Discus	76.80	252	0
Gabriele Reinsch, GDR, 1988			
Hammer	76.07	249	6
Mihaela Melinte, Romania, 1999			
Javelin (new implement in 1999)	71.54	234	8
Osleidys Menendez, Cuba, 2001			
Heptathlon[†]		7,291 points	
Jackie Joyner-Kersee, USA, 1988			

[†]Seven events comprising 100 m hurdles, shot, high jump, 200 m, long jump, javelin, 800 m

ATHLETICS NATIONAL (UK) RECORDS AS AT SEPTEMBER 2003

Records set anywhere by athletes eligible to represent Great Britain and Northern Ireland

MEN

TRACK EVENTS	hr.	min.	sec.
100 metres			9.87
Linford Christie, 1993 and			
Dwain Chambers, 2002			
200 metres			19.87
John Regis, 1994			
400 metres			44.36
Iwan Thomas, 1997			
800 metres		1	41.73
Sebastian Coe, 1981			
1,000 metres		2	12.18
Sebastian Coe, 1981			
1,500 metres		3	29.67
Sebastian Coe, 1985			
1 mile		3	46.32
Steve Cram, 1985			
2,000 metres		4	51.39
Steve Cram, 1985			
3,000 metres		7	32.79
David Moorcroft, 1982			
5,000 metres		13	00.41
David Moorcroft, 1982			
10,000 metres		27	18.14
Jon Brown, 1998			
20,000 metres		57	28.70
Carl Thackery, 1990			
20,855 metres	1	00	00.00
Carl Thackery, 1990			

	hr.	min.	sec.
25,000 metres	1	15	22.60
Ron Hill, 1965			
30,000 metres	1	31	30.40
Jim Alder, 1970			
Marathon	2	07	13.00
Steve Jones, 1985			
3,000 metres steeplechase		8	07.96
Mark Rowland, 1988			
110 metres hurdles			12.91
Colin Jackson, 1993			
400 metres hurdles			47.82
Kriss Akabusi, 1992			

RELAYS		min.	sec.
4 × 100 metres			37.73
GB team, 1999			
4 × 200 metres		1	21.29
GB team, 1989			
4 × 400 metres		2	56.60
GB team, 1996			
4 × 800 metres		7	03.89
GB team, 1982			

FIELD EVENTS	metres	ft	in
High jump	2.37	7	9¼
Steve Smith, 1993			
Pole vault	5.80	19	0¼
Nick Buckfield, 1998			
Long jump	8.27	27	1¼
Chris Tomlinson, 2002			
Triple jump	18.29	60	0¼
Jonathan Edwards, 1995			
Shot	21.92	71	11
Carl Myerscough, 2003			
Discus	66.64	218	8
Perris Wilkins, 1998			
Hammer	77.54	254	5
Martin Girvan, 1984			
Javelin	91.46	300	1
Steve Backley, 1992			
Decathlon		8,847 points	
Daley Thompson, 1984			

WALKING (TRACK)	hr.	min.	sec.
20,000 metres	1	23	26.5
Ian McCombie, 1990			
30,000 metres	2	19	18.0
Christopher Maddocks, 1984			
50,000 metres	4	05	44.6
Paul Blagg, 1990			
26,037 metres (16 miles 315 yards)	2	00	00.0
Ron Wallwork, 1971			

WOMEN

TRACK EVENTS	hr.	min.	sec.
100 metres			11.10
Kathy Cook, 1981			
200 metres			22.10
Kathy Cook, 1984			
400 metres			49.43
Kathy Cook, 1984			
800 metres		1	56.21
Kelly Holmes, 1995			
1,500 metres		3	58.07
Kelly Holmes, 1997			
1 mile		4	17.57
Zola Budd, 1985			

	hr.	min.	sec.
3,000 metres		8	22.20*
Paula Radcliffe, 2002			
5,000 metres		14	31.42*
Paula Radcliffe, 2002			
10,000 metres		30	01.09*
Paula Radcliffe, 2002			
Marathon			
Paula Radcliffe, 2003	2	15	25.00
100 metres hurdles			12.80
Angela Thorp, 1996			
400 metres hurdles			52.74
Sally Gunnell, 1993			

RELAYS	min.	sec.
4 × 100 metres		42.43
GB team, 1980		
4 × 200 metres	1	31.57
GB team, 1977		
4 × 400 metres	3	22.01
GB team, 1991		
4 × 800 metres	8	23.80
GB team, 1971		

FIELD EVENTS	metres	ft	in
High jump	1.95	6	4¾
Diana Elliott, 1982			
Susan Jones, 2001*			
Pole vault	4.41*	14	5¾
Janine Whitlock, 2002			
Long jump	6.90	22	7¾
Beverley Kinch, 1983			
Triple jump	15.15	49	8½
Ashia Hansen, 1997			
Shot	19.36	63	6¼
Judy Oakes, 1988			
Discus	67.48	221	5
Margaret Ritchie, 1981			
Hammer	68.93	226	1
Lorraine Shaw, 2001			
Javelin (new implement)	64.87*	212	9
Kelly Morgan, 2002			
Heptathlon	6,831 points		
Denise Lewis, 2000			

*Awaiting ratification

SWIMMING WORLD RECORDS
AS AT SEPTEMBER 2003

MEN	min.	sec.
50 metres freestyle		21.64
Alexander Popov, Russia		
100 metres freestyle		47.84
Pieter van den Hoogenband, Netherlands		
200 metres freestyle	1	44.06
Ian Thorpe, Australia		
400 metres freestyle	3	40.08
Ian Thorpe, Australia		
800 metres freestyle	7	39.16
Ian Thorpe, Australia		
1,500 metres freestyle	14	34.56
Grant Hackett, Australia		
100 metres breaststroke		59.78
Kosuke Kitajima, Japan		
50 metres breaststoke		27.18
Oleg Lisogor, Ukraine		
200 metres breaststroke	2	09.42
Kosuke Kitajima, Japan		

	min.	sec.
50 metres butterfly		23.43
Matt Welsh, Australia		
100 metres butterfly		50.98
Ian Crocker, USA		
200 metres butterfly	1	53.93
Michael Phelps, USA		
50 metres backstroke		24.80
Thomas Rupprath, Germany		
100 metres backstroke		53.60
Lenny Krayzelburg, USA		
200 metres backstroke	1	55.15
Aaron Peirsol, USA		
200 metres medley	1	55.94
Michael Phelps, USA		
400 metres medley	4	09.09
Michael Phelps, USA		
4 × 100 metres freestyle relay	3	13.67
Australia		
4 × 200 metres freestyle relay	7	04.66
Australia		
4 × 100 metres medley relay	3	31.54
USA		

WOMEN	min.	sec.
50 metres freestyle		24.13
Inge de Bruin, Netherlands		
100 metres freestyle		53.77
Inge de Bruin, Netherlands		
200 metres freestyle	1	56.64
Franziska van Almsick, Germany		
400 metres freestyle	4	03.85
Janet Evans, USA		
800 metres freestyle	8	16.22
Janet Evans, USA		
1,500 metres freestyle	15	52.10
Janet Evans, USA		
50 metres breaststroke		30.57
Zoe Baker, Great Britain		
100 metres breaststroke	1	06.37
Leisel Jones, Australia		
200 metres breaststroke	2	22.99
Qi Hui, China and Amanda Beard, USA		
50 metres butterfly		25.57
Anna-Karin Kammerling, Sweden		
100 metres butterfly		56.61
Inge de Bruin, Netherlands		
200 metres butterfly	2	05.78
Otylia Jedrejczak, Poland		
50 metres backstroke		28.25
Sandra Volker, Germany		
100 metres backstroke		59.58
Natalie Coughlin, USA		
200 metres backstroke	2	06.62
Krisztina Egerszegi, Hungary		
200 metres medley	2	09.72
Wu Yanyan, China		
400 metres medley	4	33.59
Yana Klochkova, Ukraine		
4 × 100 metres freestyle relay	3	36.00
Germany		
4 × 200 metres freestyle relay	7	55.47
GDR		
4 × 100 metres medley relay	3	58.30
USA		

TIME AND SPACE

ASTRONOMY

TIME MEASUREMENT AND CALENDARS

TIDAL TABLES

ASTRONOMY

The following pages give astronomical data for each month of the year 2004. There are four pages of data for each month. All data are given for 0h Greenwich Mean Time (GMT), i.e. at the midnight at the beginning of the day named. This applies also to data for the months when British Summer Time is in operation (for dates, *see* below).

The astronomical data are given in a form suitable for observation with the naked eye or with a small telescope. These data do not attempt to replace the *Astronomical Almanac* for professional astronomers.

A fuller explanation of how to use the astronomical data is given on page 1255.

CALENDAR FOR EACH MONTH

The calendar for each month comprises dates of general interest plus the dates of birth or death of well-known people. For key religious, civil and legal dates *see* page 9. For details of flag-flying days, *see* page 21. For royal birthdays see pages 21 and 22-3. Public holidays are given in italics. *See* also pages 10 and 11.

Fuller explanations of the various calendars can be found under Time Measurement and Calendars (page 1265).

The zodiacal signs through which the Sun is passing during each month are illustrated. The date of transition from one sign to the next, to the nearest hour, is given under Astronomical Phenomena.

JULIAN DATE

The Julian date on 2004 January 0.0 is 2453004.5. To find the Julian date for any other date in 2004 (at 0h GMT), add the day-of-the-year number on the extreme right of the calendar for each month to the Julian date for January 0.0.

SEASONS

The seasons are defined astronomically as follows:

Spring from the vernal equinox to the summer solstice
Summer from the summer solstice to the autumnal equinox
Autumn from the autumnal equinox to the winter solstice
Winter from the winter solstice to the vernal equinox

The seasons in 2004 are:

Northern hemisphere

Vernal equinox	March 20d 07h GMT
Summer solstice	June 21d 01h GMT
Autumnal equinox	September 22d 16h GMT
Winter solstice	December 21d 13h GMT

Southern hemisphere

Autumnal equinox	March 20d 07h GMT
Winter solstice	June 21d 01h GMT
Vernal equinox	September 22d 16h GMT
Summer solstice	December 21d 13h GMT

The longest day of the year, measured from sunrise to sunset, is at the summer solstice. The longest day in the United Kingdom will fall on 21 June in 2004. *See* also page 1265.

The shortest day of the year is at the winter solstice. The shortest day in the United Kingdom will fall on 21 December in 2004. See also page 1265.

The equinox is the point at which day and night are of equal length all over the world. *See* also page 1265.

In popular parlance, the seasons in the northern hemisphere comprise the following months:

Spring	March, April, May
Summer	June, July, August
Autumn	September, October, November
Winter	December, January, February

BRITISH SUMMER TIME

British Summer Time is the legal time for general purposes during the period in which it is in operation (*see* also page 1257). During this period, clocks are kept one hour ahead of Greenwich Mean Time. The hour of changeover is 01h Greenwich Mean Time. The duration of Summer Time in 2004 is from March 28 01h GMT to October 31 01h GMT.

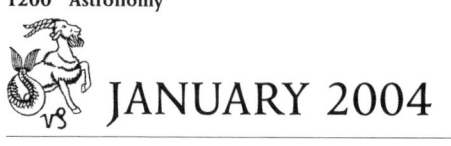

JANUARY 2004

FIRST MONTH, 31 DAYS. *Janus*, god of the portal, facing two ways, past and future

1	*Thursday*	Bank Holiday in UK. The Times first published in 1788	1
2	*Friday*	Isaac Asimov b. 1920. David Bailey b. 1938	2
3	*Saturday*	J. R. R. Tolkein b.1892. Battle of Princeton 1777	3
4	*Sunday*	Augustus John b. 1878. Jacob Grimm b. 1785	4
5	*Monday*	Amy Johnson d. 1941. Sonny Bono d. 1998	week 1 day 5
6	*Tuesday*	Joan of Arc b. 1412. Henry VIII married Anne of Cleves 1540	6
7	*Wednesday*	Millard Fillmore b. 1800. First manned balloon crossing of the English Channel 1785	7
8	*Thursday*	Dennis Wheatley b. 1897. Elvis Presley b. 1935	8
9	*Friday*	Richard Nixon b. 1913. Napoleon Bonaparte d. 1873	9
10	*Saturday*	Dame Barbara Hepworth b. 1903. Coco Chanel d. 1971	10
11	*Sunday*	Thomas Hardy d. 1928. Insulin first administered to a diabetic 1922	11
12	*Monday*	Edmund Burke b. 1729. Agatha Christie d. 1976	week 2 day 12
13	*Tuesday*	Lewis Carroll d. 1898. Stephen Foster d. 1864	13
14	*Wednesday*	Edmund Halley d. 1742. Warren Mitchell b. 1926	14
15	*Thursday*	Ivor Novello b. 1893. British Museum opened 1759	15
16	*Friday*	Andre Michelin b. 1853. John Spenser d. 1599	16
17	*Saturday*	Benjamin Franklin b. 1706. Earl Lloyd-George b. 1863	17
18	*Sunday*	A. A. Milne b. 1882. Captain James Cook discovered the Hawaiian Islands 1778	18
19	*Monday*	James Watt b. 1736. Sir Henry Bessemer b. 1813	week 3 day 19
20	*Tuesday*	George Burns b. 1896. Aristotle Onassis b. 1906	20
21	*Wednesday*	Concorde made the first scheduled supersonic flights 1976	21
22	*Thursday*	Lyndon B. Johnson d. 1973. Queen Victoria d. 1901	22
23	*Friday*	Edouard Manet b. 1832. William Pitt 'the younger' d. 1806	23
24	*Saturday*	Sir Winston Churchill d. 1965. Desmond Morris b. 1928	24
25	*Sunday*	Virginia Woolf b. 1882. Dorothy Wordsworth d. 1855	25
26	*Monday*	Australia Day. Eartha Kitt b. 1928	week 4 day 26
27	*Tuesday*	Wolfgang Amadeus Mozart b. 1756. J. Logie Baird demonstrates television 1926	27
28	*Wednesday*	Henry VII d. 1547. John Baskerville b. 1706	28
29	*Thursday*	Germaine Greer b. 1939. Douglas Haig d. 1928	29
30	*Friday*	Charles I was beheaded 1649. William Jenner b. 1815	30
31	*Saturday*	Guy Fawkes was hanged, drawn and quartered for his part in the Gunpowder Plot 1606	31

ASTRONOMICAL PHENOMENA

d	h	
4	00	Jupiter at stationary point
4	18	Earth at perihelion (147 million km.)
6	14	Mercury at stationary point
7	01	Saturn in conjunction with Moon. Saturn 5°S.
12	13	Jupiter in conjunction with Moon. Jupiter 3°S.
17	09	Mercury at greatest elongation W.24°
20	04	Mercury in conjunction with Moon. Mercury 5°N.
20	18	Sun's longitude 300° ♒
24	19	Venus in conjunction with Moon. Venus 3°N.
28	05	Mars in conjunction with Moon. Mars 2°N.

MINIMA OF ALGOL

d	h	d	h	d	h
3	03.6	14	14.9	26	02.2
6	00.4	17	11.7	28	23.0
8	21.3	20	08.5	31	19.8
11	18.1	23	05.4		

CONSTELLATIONS

The following constellations are near the meridian at

	d	h		d	h
December	1	24	January	16	21
December	16	23	February	1	20
January	1	22	February	15	19

Draco (below the Pole), Ursa Minor (below the Pole), Camelopardus, Perseus, Auriga, Taurus, Orion, Eridanus and Lepdus

THE MOON

Phases, Apsides and Node		d	h	m
○	Full Moon	7	15	40
☾	Last Quarter	15	04	46
●	New Moon	21	21	05
☽	First Quarter	29	06	03
Apogee (405,734 km)		3	20	08
Perigee (362,753 km)		19	19	17
Apogee (404,844 km)		31	13	55

Mean longitude of ascending node on January 1, 48°

THE SUN

s.d. 16′.3

Day	Right Ascension			Dec.		Equation of Time		Rise 52°		Rise 56°		Transit		Set 52°		Set 56°		Sidereal time			Transit of First Point of Aries		
	h	m	s	°	′	m	s	h	m	h	m	h	m	h	m	h	m	h	m	s	h	m	s
1	18	43	03	23	04	− 3	04	8	08	8	31	12	03	15	59	15	35	6	39	59	17	17	11
2	18	47	28	23	00	− 3	32	8	08	8	31	12	04	16	00	15	37	6	43	55	17	13	15
3	18	51	52	22	54	− 4	00	8	08	8	31	12	04	16	01	15	38	6	47	52	17	09	19
4	18	56	16	22	49	− 4	28	8	08	8	30	12	05	16	02	15	39	6	51	49	17	05	23
5	19	00	40	22	42	− 4	55	8	07	8	30	12	05	16	03	15	41	6	55	45	17	01	27
6	19	05	04	22	36	− 5	22	8	07	8	29	12	06	16	04	15	42	6	59	42	16	57	31
7	19	09	27	22	29	− 5	49	8	07	8	29	12	06	16	06	15	43	7	03	38	16	53	35
8	19	13	49	22	21	− 6	15	8	06	8	28	12	06	16	07	15	45	7	07	35	16	49	39
9	19	18	11	22	13	− 6	40	8	06	8	28	12	07	16	08	15	47	7	11	31	16	45	43
10	19	22	33	22	05	− 7	05	8	05	8	27	12	07	16	10	15	48	7	15	28	16	41	48
11	19	26	54	21	56	− 7	29	8	05	8	26	12	08	16	11	15	50	7	19	24	16	37	52
12	19	31	14	21	47	− 7	53	8	04	8	25	12	08	16	13	15	52	7	23	21	16	33	56
13	19	35	34	21	37	− 8	17	8	03	8	24	12	08	16	14	15	53	7	27	18	16	30	00
14	19	39	53	21	27	− 8	39	8	03	8	23	12	09	16	16	15	55	7	31	14	16	26	04
15	19	44	12	21	17	− 9	01	8	02	8	22	12	09	16	17	15	57	7	35	11	16	22	08
16	19	48	30	21	06	− 9	23	8	01	8	21	12	10	16	19	15	59	7	39	07	16	18	12
17	19	52	47	20	55	− 9	44	8	00	8	20	12	10	16	20	16	01	7	43	04	16	14	16
18	19	57	04	20	43	−10	04	7	59	8	18	12	10	16	22	16	03	7	47	00	16	10	20
19	20	01	20	20	31	−10	23	7	58	8	17	12	11	16	24	16	04	7	50	57	16	06	24
20	20	05	35	20	19	−10	42	7	57	8	16	12	11	16	25	16	06	7	54	53	16	02	28
21	20	09	50	20	06	−11	00	7	56	8	14	12	11	16	27	16	08	7	58	50	15	58	33
22	20	14	04	19	52	−11	17	7	55	8	13	12	11	16	29	16	10	8	02	47	15	54	37
23	20	18	17	19	39	−11	34	7	54	8	11	12	12	16	30	16	12	8	06	43	15	50	41
24	20	22	29	19	25	−11	50	7	52	8	10	12	12	16	32	16	15	8	10	40	15	46	45
25	20	26	41	19	11	−12	05	7	51	8	08	12	12	16	34	16	17	8	14	36	15	42	49
26	20	30	51	18	56	−12	19	7	50	8	07	12	12	16	36	16	19	8	18	33	15	38	53
27	20	35	01	18	41	−12	32	7	48	8	05	12	13	16	37	16	21	8	22	29	15	34	57
28	20	39	10	18	26	−12	45	7	47	8	03	12	13	16	39	16	23	8	26	26	15	31	01
29	20	43	19	18	10	−12	56	7	46	8	02	12	13	16	41	16	25	8	30	22	15	27	05
30	20	47	26	17	54	−13	07	7	44	8	00	12	13	16	43	16	27	8	34	19	15	23	09
31	20	51	33	17	37	−13	17	7	43	7	58	12	13	16	45	16	29	8	38	16	15	19	13

DURATION OF TWILIGHT (in minutes)

Latitude	52°	56°	52°	56°	52°	56°	52°	56°
	1 January		11 January		21 January		31 January	
Civil	41	47	40	45	38	43	37	41
Nautical	84	96	82	93	80	90	78	87
Astronomical	125	141	123	138	120	134	117	130

THE NIGHT SKY

Mercury is unsuitably placed for observation for the first few days of the month. For the next fortnight observers in southern England may possibly glimpse the planet as a difficult morning object, very low above the south-eastern horizon at about the time of beginning of morning civil twilight. During this period its magnitude brightens slowly from +0.9 to +0.2. Mercury passes through greatest western elongation (24 degrees) on the 17th.

Venus, magnitude −4.0, is a magnificent evening object in the south-western sky, and by the end of the month can still be seen for as long as three hours after sunset. The waxing crescent Moon, three days old, will be seen passing about 4 degrees south of the planet on the evening of the 24th.

Mars is visible in the southern sky as soon as darkness falls in the early evening, and sets around midnight over the western horizon. During the month its magnitude fades from +0.2 to +0.7, with increasing distance from the Earth. Mars is moving direct in the constellation of Pisces. The Moon, near Last Quarter, passes 3 degrees south of the planet on the 28th.

Jupiter, is a magnificent object in the night sky, now visible well before midnight and is west of the meridian well before dawn. Jupiter's magnitude is −2.3. The planet is in the constellation of Leo and reaches its first stationary point on January 3, before moving slowly retrograde. The gibbous waning Moon will be seen near the planet around the 12th.

Saturn does not come to opposition this year but next does so in January 2005. It was last at opposition on December 31 of last year. This month it is therefore visible for the greater part of the hours of darkness, being seen in the eastern sky as soon as it is dark. Saturn's magnitude is −0.4. It is moving very slowly retrograde in the constellation of Gemini. During the night of January 6-7 the Full Moon passes 4 degrees north of the planet.

THE MOON

Day	RA h m	Dec. °	Hor. par. ′	Semi-diam. ′	Sun's co-long. °	PA of Bright Limb °	Phase %	Age d	Rise 52° h m	Rise 56° h m	Transit h m	Set 52° h m	Set 56° h m
1	1 45	+ 8.8	54.6	14.9	13	248	65	8.6	12 26	12 16	19 38	1 55	2 03
2	2 29	+13.8	54.3	14.8	25	251	74	9.6	12 40	12 26	20 20	3 07	3 20
3	3 15	+18.2	54.1	14.7	37	255	82	10.6	12 58	12 38	21 05	4 18	4 37
4	4 03	+21.9	54.0	14.7	49	260	88	11.6	13 21	12 55	21 53	5 30	5 55
5	4 53	+24.8	54.1	14.7	61	267	94	12.6	13 52	13 21	22 43	6 39	7 09
6	5 45	+26.5	54.3	14.8	73	278	97	13.6	14 34	14 00	23 35	7 42	8 16
7	6 39	+27.0	54.6	14.9	86	302	99	14.6	15 29	14 55	— —	8 35	9 09
8	7 34	+26.2	54.9	15.0	98	50	100	15.6	16 35	16 06	0 27	9 16	9 46
9	8 27	+24.2	55.3	15.1	110	87	98	16.6	17 49	17 26	1 19	9 46	10 11
10	9 20	+20.9	55.7	15.2	122	98	94	17.6	19 07	18 49	2 08	10 09	10 28
11	10 10	+16.6	56.2	15.3	134	105	89	18.6	20 25	20 14	2 56	10 27	10 40
12	10 59	+11.5	56.7	15.5	146	109	82	19.6	21 43	21 38	3 43	10 42	10 49
13	11 47	+ 5.9	57.3	15.6	158	111	73	20.6	23 02	23 02	4 28	10 55	10 57
14	12 35	− 0.2	57.9	15.8	170	112	63	21.6	— —	— —	5 13	11 07	11 05
15	13 23	− 6.3	58.5	15.9	183	112	52	22.6	0 23	0 29	6 00	11 21	11 13
16	14 14	−12.3	59.1	16.1	195	110	41	23.6	1 47	1 59	6 49	11 37	11 24
17	15 09	−17.8	59.6	16.2	207	106	30	24.6	3 15	3 34	7 43	11 59	11 38
18	16 07	−22.3	60.1	16.4	219	100	20	25.6	4 45	5 12	8 41	12 28	12 01
19	17 10	−25.5	60.4	16.4	231	92	12	26.6	6 11	6 45	9 44	13 12	12 38
20	18 15	−27.0	60.4	16.5	243	81	5	27.6	7 25	8 01	10 49	14 14	13 38
21	19 22	−26.5	60.3	16.4	256	62	1	28.6	8 20	8 51	11 53	15 32	15 01
22	20 26	−24.2	59.8	16.3	268	327	0	0.1	8 57	9 22	12 54	17 00	16 36
23	21 26	−20.4	59.2	16.1	280	270	2	1.1	9 23	9 41	13 49	18 28	18 11
24	22 21	−15.5	58.4	15.9	292	258	6	2.1	9 41	9 53	14 40	19 51	19 41
25	23 12	− 9.9	57.6	15.7	304	252	12	3.1	9 56	10 02	15 26	21 11	21 06
26	0 00	− 4.1	56.7	15.5	317	249	20	4.1	10 08	10 10	16 10	22 26	22 27
27	0 45	+ 1.7	55.9	15.2	329	248	29	5.1	10 20	10 17	16 52	23 40	23 46
28	1 30	+ 7.3	55.2	15.1	341	249	38	6.1	10 32	10 24	17 33	— —	— —
29	2 15	+12.5	54.7	14.9	353	251	48	7.1	10 45	10 32	18 16	0 52	1 03
30	3 00	+17.1	54.4	14.8	5	254	57	8.1	11 01	10 43	19 00	2 04	2 21
31	3 48	+21.1	54.2	14.8	17	258	66	9.1	11 22	10 58	19 47	3 16	3 39

MERCURY

Day	RA h m	Dec °	Diam. ″	Phase %	Transit h m	5° high 52° h m	5° high 56° h m
1	17 55	−20.3	10	10	11 11	7 47	8 15
3	17 48	−20.2	9	18	10 58	7 33	8 00
5	17 45	−20.3	9	25	10 47	7 22	7 50
7	17 44	−20.4	8	33	10 39	7 15	7 44
9	17 46	−20.7	8	40	10 33	7 11	7 40
11	17 50	−21.0	8	47	10 30	7 10	7 40
13	17 55	−21.3	7	53	10 27	7 10	7 41
15	18 02	−21.6	7	58	10 27	7 12	7 43
17	18 10	−21.9	7	63	10 27	7 15	7 47
19	18 19	−22.2	6	67	10 28	7 18	7 51
21	18 29	−22.4	6	70	10 30	7 22	7 56
23	18 39	−22.6	6	73	10 33	7 26	8 00
25	18 50	−22.7	6	76	10 36	7 30	8 04
27	19 01	−22.7	6	78	10 40	7 34	8 08
29	19 13	−22.7	6	81	10 44	7 37	8 11
31	19 25	−22.5	6	83	10 48	7 40	8 14

VENUS

Day	RA h m	Dec. °	Diam. ″	Phase %	Transit h m	5° high 52° h m	5° high 56° h m
1	21 05	−18.6	13	83	14 26	18 06	17 42
6	21 29	−16.7	13	82	14 30	18 24	18 03
11	21 53	−14.6	13	81	14 34	18 42	18 24
16	22 17	−12.4	14	80	14 38	18 59	18 44
21	22 39	−10.0	14	78	14 41	19 16	19 04
26	23 02	− 7.6	14	77	14 43	19 33	19 23
31	23 24	− 5.0	15	75	14 46	19 49	19 42

MARS

Day	RA h m	Dec. °	Diam. ″	Phase %	Transit h m	5° high 52° h m	5° high 56° h m
1	0 34	+ 3.7	8	87	17 52	23 40	23 40
6	0 45	+ 5.0	8	87	17 44	23 38	23 39
11	0 56	+ 6.3	8	88	17 35	23 36	23 38
16	1 07	+ 7.6	8	88	17 27	23 34	23 37
21	1 19	+ 8.8	7	88	17 19	23 32	23 36
26	1 31	+10.1	7	88	17 11	23 31	23 36
31	1 42	+11.3	7	89	17 03	23 29	23 36

SUNRISE AND SUNSET

	London 0°05' 51°30'		Bristol 2°35' 51°28'		Birmingham 1°55' 52°28'		Manchester 2°15' 53°28'		Newcastle 1°37' 54°59'		Glasgow 4°14' 55°52'		Belfast 5°56' 54°35'	
	h m	h m	h m	h m	h m	h m	h m	h m	h m	h m	h m	h m	h m	h m
1	8 06	16 01	8 16	16 12	8 18	16 04	8 25	16 00	8 31	15 48	8 47	15 53	8 46	16 08
2	8 06	16 02	8 16	16 13	8 18	16 05	8 25	16 01	8 31	15 50	8 47	15 54	8 46	16 09
3	8 06	16 04	8 16	16 14	8 18	16 06	8 25	16 02	8 31	15 51	8 47	15 56	8 46	16 10
4	8 06	16 05	8 15	16 15	8 18	16 07	8 24	16 03	8 31	15 52	8 47	15 57	8 45	16 12
5	8 05	16 06	8 15	16 16	8 17	16 08	8 24	16 04	8 30	15 53	8 46	15 58	8 45	16 13
6	8 05	16 07	8 15	16 17	8 17	16 10	8 24	16 06	8 30	15 55	8 46	16 00	8 45	16 14
7	8 05	16 08	8 15	16 18	8 17	16 11	8 23	16 07	8 29	15 56	8 45	16 01	8 44	16 16
8	8 04	16 10	8 14	16 20	8 16	16 12	8 23	16 09	8 29	15 58	8 44	16 03	8 44	16 17
9	8 04	16 11	8 14	16 21	8 16	16 14	8 22	16 10	8 28	15 59	8 44	16 04	8 43	16 19
10	8 03	16 12	8 13	16 22	8 15	16 15	8 22	16 11	8 27	16 01	8 43	16 06	8 42	16 20
11	8 03	16 14	8 13	16 24	8 15	16 17	8 21	16 13	8 26	16 02	8 42	16 08	8 41	16 22
12	8 02	16 15	8 12	16 25	8 14	16 18	8 20	16 14	8 26	16 04	8 41	16 09	8 41	16 23
13	8 01	16 17	8 11	16 27	8 13	16 20	8 19	16 16	8 25	16 06	8 40	16 11	8 40	16 25
14	8 01	16 18	8 10	16 28	8 12	16 21	8 18	16 18	8 24	16 07	8 39	16 13	8 39	16 27
15	8 00	16 20	8 10	16 30	8 12	16 23	8 18	16 19	8 23	16 09	8 38	16 15	8 38	16 28
16	7 59	16 21	8 09	16 31	8 11	16 24	8 17	16 21	8 22	16 11	8 37	16 16	8 37	16 30
17	7 58	16 23	8 08	16 33	8 10	16 26	8 16	16 23	8 21	16 13	8 36	16 18	8 36	16 32
18	7 57	16 24	8 07	16 35	8 09	16 28	8 15	16 24	8 19	16 14	8 35	16 20	8 35	16 34
19	7 56	16 26	8 06	16 36	8 08	16 29	8 13	16 26	8 18	16 16	8 33	16 22	8 34	16 36
20	7 55	16 28	8 05	16 38	8 07	16 31	8 12	16 28	8 17	16 18	8 32	16 24	8 32	16 37
21	7 54	16 29	8 04	16 39	8 05	16 33	8 11	16 30	8 16	16 20	8 31	16 26	8 31	16 39
22	7 53	16 31	8 03	16 41	8 04	16 34	8 10	16 31	8 14	16 22	8 29	16 28	8 30	16 41
23	7 52	16 33	8 02	16 43	8 03	16 36	8 09	16 33	8 13	16 24	8 28	16 30	8 28	16 43
24	7 51	16 34	8 01	16 45	8 02	16 38	8 07	16 35	8 12	16 26	8 26	16 32	8 27	16 45
25	7 49	16 36	7 59	16 46	8 01	16 40	8 06	16 37	8 10	16 28	8 25	16 34	8 25	16 47
26	7 48	16 38	7 58	16 48	7 59	16 42	8 05	16 39	8 09	16 30	8 23	16 36	8 24	16 49
27	7 47	16 40	7 57	16 50	7 58	16 43	8 03	16 41	8 07	16 32	8 21	16 38	8 22	16 51
28	7 45	16 41	7 55	16 52	7 56	16 45	8 02	16 43	8 05	16 34	8 20	16 41	8 21	16 53
29	7 44	16 43	7 54	16 53	7 55	16 47	8 00	16 45	8 04	16 36	8 18	16 43	8 19	16 55
30	7 43	16 45	7 53	16 55	7 53	16 49	7 58	16 47	8 02	16 38	8 16	16 45	8 18	16 57
31	7 41	16 47	7 51	16 57	7 52	16 51	7 57	16 49	8 00	16 40	8 14	16 47	8 16	16 59

JUPITER

Day	RA		Dec.		Transit		5° high	
							52°	56°
	h	m	°	'	h	m	h m	h m
1	11	21.0	+5	31	4	40	22 42	22 40
11	11	20.9	+5	35	4	01	22 02	22 00
21	11	19.5	+5	46	3	20	21 20	21 18
31	11	17.1	+6	04	2	38	20 36	20 35

Diameters – equatorial 41" polar 39"

SATURN

Day	RA		Dec.		Transit		5° high	
							52°	56°
	h	m	°	'	h	m	h m	h m
1	6	42.2	+22	25	0	02	7 29	7 46
11	6	38.7	+22	29	23	15	6 47	7 04
21	6	35.4	+22	34	22	33	6 04	6 22
31	6	32.5	+22	37	21	50	5 23	5 40

Diameters – equatorial 20" polar 19"
Rings – major axis 46" minor axis 20"

URANUS

Day	RA		Dec.		Transit		10° high	
							52°	56°
	h	m	°	'	h	m	h m	h m
1	22	09.7	-12	08	15	27	19 09	18 49
11	22	11.4	-11	59	14	50	18 33	18 12
21	22	13.2	-11	48	14	12	17 57	17 36
31	22	15.3	-11	36	13	35	17 21	17 01

Diameter 4"

NEPTUNE

Day	RA		Dec.		Transit		10° high	
							52°	56°
	h	m	°	'	h	m	h m	h m
1	20	56.6	-17	18	14	14	17 18	16 46
11	20	58.0	-17	13	13	36	16 41	16 09
21	20	59.5	-17	07	12	59	16 04	15 33
31	21	01.0	-17	00	12	21	15 27	14 56

Diameter 2"

FEBRUARY 2004

SECOND MONTH, 28 or 29 DAYS. *Februa,* Roman festival of Purification

1	*Sunday*	The first volume of the Oxford English Dictionary published 1884.	32

2	*Monday*	James Joyce b. 1882. Nell Gwyn b. 1650	week 5 day 33
3	*Tuesday*	Walter Bagehot b. 1826. Elizabeth Blackwell b. 1821	34
4	*Wednesday*	Charles Lindbergh b. 1902	35
5	*Thursday*	John Boyd Dunlop b. 1840. Sir Robert Peel b. 1788	36
6	*Friday*	New Zealand Day. Votes for women introduced 1918	37
7	*Saturday*	Charles Dickens b. 1812. Ann Radcliffe d. 1823	38
8	*Sunday*	Jack Lemmon b. 1925. Lana Turner b. 1920	39

9	*Monday*	Yuri Andropov d. 1984. Mia Farrow b. 1945	week 6 day 40
10	*Tuesday*	PAYE introduced 1944. Military conscription introduced in Britain 1916	41
11	*Wednesday*	Mary Quant b. 1934. Rene Descartes d. 1650	42
12	*Thursday*	Lady Jane Grey executed 1554. Charles Darwin b. 1809	43
13	*Friday*	Richard Wagner d. 1883. Massacre of Glencoe 1692	44
14	*Saturday*	St. Valentine's Day. Capt. James Cook killed 1779	45
15	*Sunday*	Jeremy Bentham b. 1748. Introduction of decimal currency in Britain 1971	46

16	*Monday*	Angela Carter d. 1992. John McEnroe b. 1959	week 7 day 47
17	*Tuesday*	Ruth Rendell b.1930. Graham Sutherland d. 1980	48
18	*Wednesday*	Michelangelo d. 1564. Martin Luther d. 1546	49
19	*Thursday*	Lee Marvin b. 1924. Robert Peary d. 1920	50
20	*Friday*	Marie Rambert b. 1888. Adam Black b. 1784	51
21	*Saturday*	Battle of Verdun 1916. Sir Frederick Banting d. 1941	52
22	*Sunday*	Andy Warhol d. 1987. Sir John Mills b. 1908	53

23	*Monday*	John Keats d. 1821. Samuel Pepys b. 1633	week 8 day 54
24	*Tuesday*	Bobby Moore d. 1993. Denis Law b. 1940	55
25	*Wednesday*	Sir David Puttnam b. 1941. Robert Devereux d. 1601	56
26	*Thursday*	Victor Hugo b. 1802. £1 and £2 notes first issued 1797	57
27	*Friday*	Labour Party founded 1900. John Steinbeck b. 1902	58
28	*Saturday*	Charles Blondin b. 1824. Henry James d. 1916	59
29	*Sunday*	Mario Andretti b. 1940. Gioacchino Rossini b. 1792	60

ASTRONOMICAL PHENOMENA

d h
2 09 Neptune in conjunction
3 05 Saturn in conjunction with Moon. Saturn 4°S.
8 16 Jupiter in conjunction with Moon. Jupiter 3°S.
19 08 Sun's longitude 330° ✶
19 14 Mercury in conjunction with Moon.
        Mercury 3°N.
22 02 Uranus in conjunction
23 22 Venus in conjunction with Moon. Venus 3°N.
26 02 Mars in conjunction with Moon. Mars 0°.8N.

MINIMA OF ALGOL

d	h	d	h	d	h
3	16.7	15	03.9	26	15.2
6	13.5	18	00.8	29	12.0
9	10.3	20	21.6		
12	07.1	23	18.4		

CONSTELLATIONS

The following constellations are near the meridian at

	d	h		d	h
January	1	24	February	15	21
January	16	23	March	1	20
February	1	22	March	16	19

Draco (below the Pole), Camelopardus, Auriga, Taurus, Gemini, Orion, Canis Minor, Monoceros, Lepus, Canis Major and Puppis

THE MOON

Phases, Apsides and Node		d	h	m
○	Full Moon	6	08	47
☾	Last Quarter	13	13	40
●	New Moon	20	09	18
☽	First Quarter	28	03	24

	d	h	m
Perigee (368,293 km)	16	07	33
Apogee (404,299 km)	28	10	43

Mean longitude of ascending node on February 1, 46°

THE SUN

s.d. 16'.2

Day	Right Ascension			Dec.		Equation of Time		Rise 52°		Rise 56°		Transit		Set 52°		Set 56°		Sidereal time			Transit of First Point of Aries		
	h	m	s	°	'	m	s	h	m	h	m	h	m	h	m	h	m	h	m	s	h	m	s
1	20	55	38	17	21	−13	26	7	41	7	56	12	14	16	47	16	32	8	42	12	15	15	18
2	20	59	43	17	04	−13	35	7	39	7	54	12	14	16	48	16	34	8	46	09	15	11	22
3	21	03	47	16	47	−13	42	7	38	7	52	12	14	16	50	16	36	8	50	05	15	07	26
4	21	07	51	16	29	−13	49	7	36	7	50	12	14	16	52	16	38	8	54	02	15	03	30
5	21	11	53	16	11	−13	55	7	35	7	48	12	14	16	54	16	40	8	57	58	14	59	34
6	21	15	55	15	53	−14	00	7	33	7	46	12	14	16	56	16	42	9	01	55	14	55	38
7	21	19	55	15	35	−14	04	7	31	7	44	12	14	16	58	16	45	9	05	51	14	51	42
8	21	23	55	15	16	−14	07	7	29	7	42	12	14	17	00	16	47	9	09	48	14	47	46
9	21	27	55	14	57	−14	10	7	28	7	40	12	14	17	01	16	49	9	13	45	14	43	50
10	21	31	53	14	38	−14	12	7	26	7	38	12	14	17	03	16	51	9	17	41	14	39	54
11	21	35	51	14	19	−14	13	7	24	7	36	12	14	17	05	16	53	9	21	38	14	35	58
12	21	39	48	13	59	−14	13	7	22	7	34	12	14	17	07	16	56	9	25	34	14	32	03
13	21	43	44	13	39	−14	13	7	20	7	31	12	14	17	09	16	58	9	29	31	14	28	07
14	21	47	39	13	19	−14	12	7	18	7	29	12	14	17	11	17	00	9	33	27	14	24	11
15	21	51	34	12	59	−14	10	7	16	7	27	12	14	17	13	17	02	9	37	24	14	20	15
16	21	55	28	12	38	−14	08	7	14	7	25	12	14	17	15	17	04	9	41	20	14	16	19
17	21	59	21	12	17	−14	04	7	12	7	22	12	14	17	16	17	07	9	45	17	14	12	23
18	22	03	14	11	56	−14	00	7	10	7	20	12	14	17	18	17	09	9	49	14	14	08	27
19	22	07	06	11	35	−13	56	7	08	7	18	12	14	17	20	17	11	9	53	10	14	04	31
20	22	10	57	11	14	−13	50	7	06	7	15	12	14	17	22	17	13	9	57	07	14	00	35
21	22	14	48	10	53	−13	44	7	04	7	13	12	14	17	24	17	15	10	01	03	13	56	39
22	22	18	37	10	31	−13	38	7	02	7	11	12	14	17	26	17	18	10	05	00	13	52	43
23	22	22	27	10	09	−13	30	7	00	7	08	12	13	17	27	17	20	10	08	56	13	48	48
24	22	26	15	9	47	−13	22	6	58	7	06	12	13	17	29	17	22	10	12	53	13	44	52
25	22	30	03	9	25	−13	14	6	56	7	03	12	13	17	31	17	24	10	16	49	13	40	56
26	22	33	51	9	03	−13	05	6	54	7	01	12	13	17	33	17	26	10	20	46	13	37	00
27	22	37	38	8	40	−12	55	6	52	6	58	12	13	17	35	17	28	10	24	43	13	33	04
28	22	41	24	8	18	−12	45	6	50	6	56	12	13	17	37	17	31	10	28	39	13	29	08
29	22	45	09	7	55	−12	34	6	47	6	53	12	12	17	38	17	33	10	32	36	13	25	12

DURATION OF TWILIGHT (in minutes)

Latitude	52°	56°	52°	56°	52°	56°	52°	56°
	1 February		11 February		21 February		29 February	
Civil	37	41	35	39	34	38	34	37
Nautical	77	86	75	83	74	81	73	80
Astronomical	117	130	114	126	113	124	112	124

THE NIGHT SKY

Mercury is unsuitably placed for observation throughout the month.

Venus continues to be visible as a brilliant evening object, magnitude −4.1, in the south-western sky for several hours after sunset. On the evening of the 23rd the thin crescent Moon, only three days old, passes about 3 degrees south of the planet.

Mars is still visible as an evening object in the south-western sky, its magnitude fading during the month from +0.7 to +1.1. Mars is moving steadily eastwards in the constellation of Aries. Although the planet is moving closer to the Sun, it sets at around the same time each evening during the month, due to its northward motion in declination. The slight reddish tinge of Mars is an aid to its identification. Mars will be seen near the waxing crescent Moon on the evenings of the 25th and 26th.

Jupiter, magnitude −2.5, reaches opposition early next month. It will be seen rising in the eastern sky shortly after sunset, and then will remain visible right through until dawn. Jupiter continues to move retrograde in the constellation of Leo. The gibbous waning Moon passes 2 degrees north of Jupiter on the 8th.

Saturn, magnitude −0.2, is still visible in the south-western quadrant of the sky in the evenings, and may still be seen for several hours after midnight, right through to the end of the month. Saturn is moving slowly retrograde in the constellation of Gemini. The waxing gibbous Moon passes about 4 degrees north of the planet on the 3rd.

Zodiacal Light. The evening cone may be observed stretching up from the western horizon, along the ecliptic, after the end of twilight, from the 8th to the 21st. This faint phenomenon is only visible under good conditions and in the absence of both moonlight and artificial lighting.

THE MOON

Day	RA h m	Dec. °	Hor. par. '	Semi-diam. '	Sun's co-long. °	PA of Bright Limb °	Phase %	Age d	Rise 52° h m	Rise 56° h m	Transit h m	Set 52° h m	Set 56° h m
1	4 37	+24.2	54.2	14.8	30	263	75	10.1	11 50	11 20	20 36	4 27	4 56
2	5 29	+26.2	54.3	14.8	42	269	83	11.1	12 28	11 54	21 27	5 32	6 06
3	6 22	+27.1	54.6	14.9	54	277	89	12.1	13 18	12 44	22 19	6 29	7 04
4	7 17	+26.7	55.0	15.0	66	286	94	13.1	14 21	13 50	23 12	7 14	7 46
5	8 11	+24.9	55.4	15.1	78	299	98	14.1	15 34	15 08	— —	7 48	8 15
6	9 05	+21.9	55.9	15.2	90	336	100	15.1	16 52	16 33	0 03	8 14	8 34
7	9 56	+17.8	56.4	15.4	102	77	99	16.1	18 12	17 59	0 52	8 33	8 48
8	10 46	+12.8	56.9	15.5	115	100	97	17.1	19 31	19 24	1 40	8 48	8 58
9	11 35	+ 7.1	57.4	15.6	127	107	92	18.1	20 51	20 50	2 26	9 02	9 06
10	12 23	+ 1.0	57.9	15.8	139	110	86	19.1	22 12	22 16	3 12	9 15	9 13
11	13 12	- 5.2	58.3	15.9	151	111	77	20.1	23 35	23 45	3 58	9 28	9 21
12	14 02	-11.2	58.6	16.0	163	110	67	21.1	— —	— —	4 46	9 43	9 31
13	14 55	-16.8	59.0	16.1	175	107	57	22.1	1 01	1 18	5 37	10 02	9 43
14	15 51	-21.5	59.2	16.1	187	102	45	23.1	2 29	2 53	6 33	10 27	10 02
15	16 51	-25.0	59.4	16.2	200	96	34	24.1	3 54	4 26	7 32	11 04	10 32
16	17 54	-26.9	59.5	16.2	212	88	24	25.1	5 11	5 47	8 34	11 57	11 21
17	18 58	-27.1	59.5	16.2	224	80	15	26.1	6 11	6 46	9 37	13 07	12 33
18	20 02	-25.4	59.3	16.2	236	71	7	27.1	6 54	7 22	10 38	14 30	14 03
19	21 02	-22.1	59.0	16.1	248	58	3	28.1	7 23	7 45	11 35	15 57	15 37
20	21 59	-17.6	58.5	15.9	261	25	0	29.1	7 44	7 59	12 27	17 23	17 10
21	22 51	-12.2	57.9	15.8	273	278	1	0.6	8 00	8 09	13 16	18 45	18 38
22	23 40	- 6.4	57.2	15.6	285	257	3	1.6	8 13	8 17	14 01	20 03	20 02
23	0 27	- 0.4	56.5	15.4	297	252	8	2.6	8 25	8 24	14 44	21 19	21 23
24	1 13	+ 5.4	55.8	15.2	309	250	14	3.6	8 37	8 31	15 26	22 33	22 43
25	1 58	+10.9	55.2	15.1	322	250	22	4.6	8 50	8 38	16 09	23 47	— —
26	2 44	+15.9	54.8	14.9	334	253	30	5.6	9 04	8 48	16 53	— —	0 02
27	3 31	+20.1	54.4	14.8	346	256	39	6.6	9 23	9 01	17 39	1 00	1 21
28	4 20	+23.5	54.3	14.8	358	260	49	7.6	9 47	9 20	18 27	2 12	2 39
29	5 11	+25.9	54.3	14.8	10	266	58	8.6	10 21	9 48	19 18	3 20	3 53

MERCURY

Day	RA h m	Dec. °	Diam. "	Phase %	Transit h m	5° high 52° h m	5° high 56° h m
1	19 31	-22.5	5	83	10 50	7 41	8 15
3	19 44	-22.2	5	85	10 54	7 44	8 16
5	19 56	-21.9	5	87	10 59	7 46	8 17
7	20 09	-21.5	5	88	11 04	7 47	8 18
9	20 22	-21.0	5	89	11 09	7 48	8 17
11	20 35	-20.4	5	91	11 14	7 48	8 16
13	20 48	-19.7	5	92	11 19	7 48	8 15
15	21 01	-19.0	5	93	11 25	7 48	8 13
17	21 14	-18.1	5	94	11 30	7 47	8 10
19	21 27	-17.2	5	95	11 36	7 46	8 07
21	21 41	-16.1	5	96	11 41	7 44	8 04
23	21 54	-15.0	5	97	11 47	7 42	8 00
25	22 08	-13.8	5	98	11 52	7 40	7 57
27	22 21	-12.5	5	99	11 58	7 38	7 53
29	22 35	-11.1	5	99	12 04	16 34	16 21
31	22 49	- 9.6	5	100	12 10	16 49	16 37

VENUS

Day	RA h m	Dec. °	Diam. "	Phase %	Transit h m	5° high 52° h m	5° high 56° h m
1	23 28	- 4.5	15	75	14 46	19 52	19 45
6	23 49	- 1.9	15	73	14 48	20 08	20 03
11	0 11	+ 0.7	16	72	14 49	20 23	20 20
16	0 32	+ 3.3	16	70	14 50	20 37	20 37
21	0 53	+ 5.9	17	68	14 52	20 52	20 54
26	1 13	+ 8.5	18	66	14 53	21 06	21 10
31	1 34	+10.9	18	64	14 54	21 20	21 26

MARS

Day	RA h m	Dec. °	Diam. "	Phase %	Transit h m	5° high 52° h m	5° high 56° h m
1	1 45	+11.5	7	89	17 02	23 29	23 35
6	1 57	+12.7	7	89	16 54	23 28	23 35
11	2 09	+13.8	6	89	16 46	23 26	23 35
16	2 21	+15.0	6	90	16 39	23 25	23 34
21	2 34	+16.0	6	90	16 32	23 24	23 34
26	2 47	+17.0	6	90	16 25	23 22	23 34
31	2 59	+18.0	6	91	16 18	23 21	23 33

SUNRISE AND SUNSET

	London 0°05′	51°30′	Bristol 2°35′	51°28′	Birmingham 1°55′	52°28′	Manchester 2°15′	53°28′	Newcastle 1°37′	54°59′	Glasgow 4°14′	55°52′	Belfast 5°56′	54°35′
	h m	h m	h m	h m	h m	h m	h m	h m	h m	h m	h m	h m	h m	h m
1	7 40	16 49	7 50	16 59	7 50	16 53	7 55	16 50	7 58	16 42	8 13	16 49	8 14	17 01
2	7 38	16 50	7 48	17 01	7 49	16 55	7 54	16 52	7 57	16 44	8 11	16 51	8 12	17 03
3	7 37	16 52	7 46	17 02	7 47	16 56	7 52	16 54	7 55	16 46	8 09	16 53	8 11	17 05
4	7 35	16 54	7 45	17 04	7 45	16 58	7 50	16 56	7 53	16 48	8 07	16 56	8 09	17 07
5	7 33	16 56	7 43	17 06	7 44	17 00	7 48	16 58	7 51	16 51	8 05	16 58	8 07	17 09
6	7 32	16 58	7 42	17 08	7 42	17 02	7 46	17 00	7 49	16 53	8 03	17 00	8 05	17 11
7	7 30	17 00	7 40	17 10	7 40	17 04	7 45	17 02	7 47	16 55	8 01	17 02	8 03	17 13
8	7 28	17 01	7 38	17 11	7 38	17 06	7 43	17 04	7 45	16 57	7 59	17 04	8 01	17 15
9	7 27	17 03	7 36	17 13	7 37	17 08	7 41	17 06	7 43	16 59	7 57	17 06	7 59	17 18
10	7 25	17 05	7 35	17 15	7 35	17 10	7 39	17 08	7 41	17 01	7 54	17 09	7 57	17 20
11	7 23	17 07	7 33	17 17	7 33	17 12	7 37	17 10	7 39	17 03	7 52	17 11	7 55	17 22
12	7 21	17 09	7 31	17 19	7 31	17 14	7 35	17 12	7 37	17 05	7 50	17 13	7 53	17 24
13	7 19	17 11	7 29	17 21	7 29	17 15	7 33	17 14	7 35	17 07	7 48	17 15	7 51	17 26
14	7 17	17 12	7 27	17 22	7 27	17 17	7 31	17 16	7 33	17 10	7 46	17 17	7 49	17 28
15	7 16	17 14	7 25	17 24	7 25	17 19	7 29	17 18	7 30	17 12	7 43	17 20	7 47	17 30
16	7 14	17 16	7 24	17 26	7 23	17 21	7 27	17 20	7 28	17 14	7 41	17 22	7 44	17 32
17	7 12	17 18	7 22	17 28	7 21	17 23	7 25	17 22	7 26	17 16	7 39	17 24	7 42	17 34
18	7 10	17 20	7 20	17 30	7 19	17 25	7 23	17 24	7 24	17 18	7 37	17 26	7 40	17 36
19	7 08	17 21	7 18	17 32	7 17	17 27	7 21	17 26	7 22	17 20	7 34	17 28	7 38	17 38
20	7 06	17 23	7 16	17 33	7 15	17 29	7 18	17 28	7 19	17 22	7 32	17 31	7 36	17 40
21	7 04	17 25	7 14	17 35	7 13	17 31	7 16	17 30	7 17	17 24	7 29	17 33	7 33	17 42
22	7 02	17 27	7 12	17 37	7 11	17 32	7 14	17 32	7 15	17 26	7 27	17 35	7 31	17 44
23	7 00	17 29	7 10	17 39	7 09	17 34	7 12	17 34	7 12	17 28	7 25	17 37	7 29	17 46
24	6 58	17 30	7 08	17 41	7 07	17 36	7 10	17 36	7 10	17 30	7 22	17 39	7 27	17 48
25	6 56	17 32	7 05	17 42	7 04	17 38	7 07	17 38	7 08	17 32	7 20	17 41	7 24	17 51
26	6 53	17 34	7 03	17 44	7 02	17 40	7 05	17 40	7 05	17 35	7 17	17 43	7 22	17 53
27	6 51	17 36	7 01	17 46	7 00	17 42	7 03	17 42	7 03	17 37	7 15	17 46	7 20	17 55
28	6 49	17 38	6 59	17 48	6 58	17 44	7 01	17 44	7 01	17 39	7 12	17 48	7 17	17 57
29	6 47	17 39	6 57	17 49	6 56	17 45	6 58	17 45	6 58	17 41	7 10	17 50	7 15	17 59

JUPITER

Day	RA		Dec.		Transit		5° high	
							52°	56°
	h	m	°	′	h	m	h m	h m
1	11	16.8	+6	07	2	34	20 32	20 30
11	11	13.2	+6	31	1	51	19 47	19 45
21	11	08.9	+7	00	1	08	19 01	18 58
31	11	04.2	+7	31	0	24	18 14	18 11

Diameters – equatorial 44″ polar 41″

SATURN

Day	RA		Dec.		Transit		5° high	
							52°	56°
	h	m	°	′	h	m	h m	h m
1	6	32.2	+22	38	21	46	5 18	5 36
11	6	29.9	+22	41	21	05	4 37	4 55
21	6	28.3	+22	44	20	24	3 57	4 14
31	6	27.4	+22	46	19	44	3 17	3 34

Diameters – equatorial 20″ polar 18″
Rings – major axis 45″ minor axis 20″

URANUS

Day	RA		Dec.		Transit		10° high	
							52°	56°
	h	m	°	′	h	m	h m	h m
1	22	15.5	−11	35	13	31	17 17	16 57
11	22	17.6	−11	23	12	54	16 41	16 22
21	22	19.8	−11	11	12	17	16 05	15 46
31	22	22.0	−10	58	11	40	15 30	15 11

Diameter 4″

NEPTUNE

Day	RA		Dec.		Transit		10° high	
							52°	56°
	h	m	°	′	h	m	h m	h m
1	21	01.2	−17	00	12	17	9 11	9 42
11	21	02.7	−16	53	11	39	8 32	9 03
21	21	04.2	−16	47	11	01	7 53	8 24
31	21	05.6	−16	41	10	23	7 15	7 45

Diameter 2″

MARCH 2004

THIRD MONTH, 31 DAYS. *Mars,* Roman god of battle

1	*Monday*	St David's Day. Oskar Kokoschka b. 1886	week 9 day 61
2	*Tuesday*	Karen Carpenter b. 1950. D. H. Lawrence d. 1930	62
3	*Wednesday*	Sir Henry Wood b. 1869. Alexander Graham Bell b. 1847	63
4	*Thursday*	Opening of the Forth Railway Bridge 1890	64
5	*Friday*	Josef Stalin d. 1953. William Beveridge b. 1879	65
6	*Saturday*	Elizabeth Barrett Browning b. 1806. Ivor Novello d. 1951	66
7	*Sunday*	Stanley Kubrick d. 2000. Piet Mondrian b. 1872	67
8	*Monday*	Carl Philipp Emanuel Bach b. 1714. Harold Lloyd d. 1971	week 10 day 68
9	*Tuesday*	Ernest Bevin b. 1881. Yuri Gagarin b. 1934	69
10	*Wednesday*	Owen Brannigan b. 1908. Amelia Barr d. 1919	70
11	*Thursday*	First English daily newspaper published 1702. Rupert Murdoch b. 1931	71
12	*Friday*	Liza Minnelli b. 1946. Jack Kerouac b. 1922	72
13	*Saturday*	Sir William Herschel discovered the planet Uranus 1781	73
14	*Sunday*	Albert Einstein b. 1879. Karl Marx d. 1883	74
15	*Monday*	Julius Caesar d. 44 BC. Viscount Melbourne b. 1779	week 11 day 75
16	*Tuesday*	James Madison b. 1751. Leo McKern b. 1920	76
17	*Wednesday*	St Patrick's Day. Christian Doppler d. 1853. Ronnie Kray d. 1995	77
18	*Thursday*	Frederik Willem de Klerk b. 1936. Wilfred Owen b. 1893	78
19	*Friday*	David Livingstone b. 1813. Tommy Cooper b. 1922	79
20	*Saturday*	Henrik Ibsen b. 1828. Sir Isaac Newton d. 1727	80
21	*Sunday*	J. S. Bach b. 1685. Thomas Cranmer d. 1556	81
22	*Monday*	Sir Anthony Van Dyke b. 1599. Marcel Marceau b. 1923	week 12 day 82
23	*Tuesday*	Roger Bannister b. 1929. Joan Crawford b. 1908	83
24	*Wednesday*	Steve McQueen b. 1930. Elizabeth I d. 1603	84
25	*Thursday*	King Faisal of Saudi Arabia d. 1975. Aretha Franklin b. 1942	85
26	*Friday*	Ludwig van Beethoven d. 1827. Leonard Nimoy b. 1931	86
27	*Saturday*	Lord Callaghan b.1912. Dudley Moore d. 2002	87
28	*Sunday*	Dwight Eisenhower d. 1969. Neil Kinnock b. 1942	88
29	*Monday*	John Major b. 1943. Carl Orff d. 1982	week 13 day 89
30	*Tuesday*	Goya b. 1746. Vincent van Gogh b. 1853	90
31	*Wednesday*	Eiffel Tower completed 1889. Robert Bunsen b. 1811	91

ASTRONOMICAL PHENOMENA

d h
1 11 Saturn in conjunction with Moon. Saturn 5°S.
4 02 Mercury in superior conjunction
4 05 Jupiter at opposition
6 18 Jupiter in conjunction with Moon. Jupiter 3°S.
7 17 Saturn at stationary point
20 07 Sun's longitude 0° ♈
22 08 Mercury in conjunction with Moon.
Mercury 3°N.
24 15 Pluto at stationary point
24 22 Venus in conjunction with Moon. Venus 2°N.
26 00 Mars in conjunction with Moon. Mars 0°.8S.
28 20 Saturn in conjunction with Moon. Saturn 5°S.
29 12 Mercury at greatest elongation E.19°
29 17 Venus at greatest elongation E.46°

MINIMA OF ALGOL

d	h	d	h	d	h
3	08.9	14	20.2	26	07.4
6	05.7	17	17.0	29	04.3
9	02.5	20	13.8		
11	23.3	23	10.6		

CONSTELLATIONS

The following constellations are near the meridian at

	d	h		d	h
February	1	24	March	16	21
February	15	23	April	1	20
March	1	21	April	15	19

Cepheus (below the Pole), Camelopardus, Lybx, Gemini, Cancer, Leo, Canis Minor, Hydra, Monoceros, Canis Major and Puppis

THE MOON

Phases, Apsides and Node		d	h	m
○	Full Moon	6	23	14
☾	Last Quarter	13	21	01
●	New Moon	20	22	41
☽	First Quarter	28	23	48

Perigee (369,472 km)	12	04	00
Apogee (404,559 km)	27	07	04

Mean longitude of ascending node on March 1, 45°

THE SUN

s.d. 16'.0

Day	Right Ascension h	m	s	Dec. °	'	Equation of Time m	s	Rise 52° h	m	Rise 56° h	m	Transit h	m	Set 52° h	m	Set 56° h	m	Sidereal time h	m	s	Transit of First Point of Aries h	m	s
1	22	48	55	−7	32	−12	22	6	45	6	51	12	12	17	40	17	35	10	36	32	13	21	16
2	22	52	39	−7	09	−12	10	6	43	6	48	12	12	17	42	17	37	10	40	29	13	17	20
3	22	56	23	−6	47	−11	58	6	41	6	46	12	12	17	44	17	39	10	44	25	13	13	24
4	23	00	07	−6	23	−11	45	6	39	6	43	12	12	17	46	17	41	10	48	22	13	09	28
5	23	03	50	−6	00	−11	32	6	36	6	41	12	11	17	47	17	43	10	52	18	13	05	33
6	23	07	33	−5	37	−11	18	6	34	6	38	12	11	17	49	17	45	10	56	15	13	01	37
7	23	11	15	−5	14	−11	04	6	32	6	36	12	11	17	51	17	47	11	00	12	12	57	41
8	23	14	57	−4	50	−10	49	6	30	6	33	12	11	17	53	17	50	11	04	08	12	53	45
9	23	18	39	−4	27	−10	34	6	27	6	30	12	10	17	54	17	52	11	08	05	12	49	49
10	23	22	20	−4	03	−10	19	6	25	6	28	12	10	17	56	17	54	11	12	01	12	45	53
11	23	26	01	−3	40	−10	03	6	23	6	25	12	10	17	58	17	56	11	15	58	12	41	57
12	23	29	41	−3	16	− 9	47	6	21	6	23	12	10	18	00	17	58	11	19	54	12	38	01
13	23	33	22	−2	53	− 9	31	6	18	6	20	12	09	18	01	18	00	11	23	51	12	34	05
14	23	37	02	−2	29	− 9	14	6	16	6	17	12	09	18	03	18	02	11	27	47	12	30	09
15	23	40	41	−2	05	− 8	57	6	14	6	15	12	09	18	05	18	04	11	31	44	12	26	13
16	23	44	21	−1	42	− 8	41	6	11	6	12	12	09	18	07	18	06	11	35	41	12	22	18
17	23	48	00	−1	18	− 8	23	6	09	6	09	12	08	18	08	18	08	11	39	37	12	18	22
18	23	51	40	−0	54	− 8	06	6	07	6	07	12	08	18	10	18	10	11	43	34	12	14	26
19	23	55	19	−0	30	− 7	49	6	04	6	04	12	08	18	12	18	12	11	47	30	12	10	30
20	23	58	58	−0	07	− 7	31	6	02	6	02	12	07	18	14	18	14	11	51	27	12	06	34
21	0	02	37	+0	17	− 7	13	6	00	5	59	12	07	18	15	18	16	11	55	23	12	02	38
22	0	06	15	+0	41	− 6	55	5	57	5	56	12	07	18	17	18	18	11	59	20	11	58	42
23	0	09	54	+1	04	− 6	37	5	55	5	54	12	06	18	19	18	21	12	03	16	11	54	46
24	0	13	32	+1	28	− 6	19	5	53	5	51	12	06	18	21	18	23	12	07	13	11	50	50
25	0	17	11	+1	52	− 6	01	5	50	5	48	12	06	18	22	18	25	12	11	10	11	46	54
26	0	20	49	+2	15	− 5	43	5	48	5	46	12	06	18	24	18	27	12	15	06	11	42	58
27	0	24	28	+2	39	− 5	25	5	46	5	43	12	05	18	26	18	29	12	19	03	11	39	03
28	0	28	06	+3	02	− 5	07	5	44	5	40	12	05	18	27	18	31	12	22	59	11	35	07
29	0	31	45	+3	26	− 4	49	5	41	5	38	12	05	18	29	18	33	12	26	56	11	31	11
30	0	35	23	+3	49	− 4	31	5	39	5	35	12	04	18	31	18	35	12	30	52	11	27	15
31	0	39	02	+4	12	− 4	13	5	37	5	33	12	04	18	33	18	37	12	34	49	11	23	19

DURATION OF TWILIGHT (in minutes)

Latitude	52°	56°	52°	56°	52°	56°	52°	56°
	1 March		11 March		21 March		31 March	
Civil	34	37	34	37	34	37	34	38
Nautical	73	80	73	80	74	81	75	84
Astronomical	112	124	113	125	115	128	120	135

THE NIGHT SKY

Mercury remains too close to the Sun for the first half of the month but then becomes visible as an evening object, magnitude −1.2 to +0.4, low in the western sky around the time of end of evening civil twilight. This evening apparition of the planet is the most favourable one of the year for observers in the northern hemisphere. Indeed, for those in the latitudes of the British Isles it is the only evening apparition of the year. On the evening of the 22nd the thin crescent Moon, barely 2 days old, could be a useful guide to locating Mercury which may be seen about 5 degrees to the right and 2 degrees below the Moon.

Venus, magnitude −4.3, continues to be visible as a brilliant object in the evenings in the western sky, and attains its greatest eastern elongation (46 degrees) on the 29th. The thin crescent Moon passes 3 degrees south of the planet late on the 24th.

Mars continues to be visible as an evening object in the western sky, setting over the western horizon shortly before midnight. Its magnitude is +1.3. During the month, Mars moves eastwards from Aries into Taurus, passing south of the Pleiades just after the middle of the month. The waxing crescent Moon will be seen approaching the planet during the evening of the 25th. Unfortunately the planet will have set before an actual occultation occurs.

Jupiter, magnitude −2.5, is a magnificent object in the night sky and is visible throughout the hours of darkness as it reaches opposition on the 4th. On the evening of the 6th the Full Moon passes 2 degrees north of the planet.

Saturn continues to be visible as an evening object in the western sky, magnitude 0.0. Saturn is in the constellation of Gemini and reaches its second stationary point on the 7th, resuming its direct motion. On the evening of the 28th the gibbous Moon passes 4 degrees north of the planet.

Zodiacal Light. The evening cone may be observed, stretching up from the western horizon, along the ecliptic, after the end of twilight, from the 9th to the 22nd.

THE MOON

Day	RA		Dec.	Hor. par.	Semi- diam.	Sun's co- long.	PA of Bright Limb	Phase	Age	Rise				Transit		Set			
										52°		56°				52°		56°	
	h	m	°	'	'	°	°	%	d	h	m	h	m	h	m	h	m	h	m
1	6	04	+27.2	54.4	14.8	22	272	67	9.6	11	06	10	30	20	10	4	21	4	56
2	6	58	+27.2	54.8	14.9	35	278	76	10.6	12	04	11	30	21	02	5	10	5	44
3	7	52	+25.8	55.3	15.1	47	285	84	11.6	13	13	12	45	21	53	5	48	6	18
4	8	46	+23.2	55.8	15.2	59	292	90	12.6	14	30	14	08	22	44	6	17	6	40
5	9	39	+19.4	56.5	15.4	71	300	95	13.6	15	50	15	35	23	32	6	38	6	55
6	10	30	+14.6	57.1	15.6	83	313	99	14.6	17	12	17	02	—	—	6	54	7	06
7	11	19	+ 8.9	57.8	15.7	95	29	100	15.6	18	33	18	30	0	20	7	09	7	14
8	12	09	+ 2.8	58.3	15.9	107	99	99	16.6	19	56	19	58	1	06	7	21	7	22
9	12	58	− 3.6	58.8	16.0	120	108	95	17.6	21	21	21	29	1	54	7	34	7	30
10	13	49	− 9.9	59.1	16.1	132	109	89	18.6	22	47	23	02	2	42	7	49	7	38
11	14	42	−15.8	59.3	16.2	144	108	81	19.6	—	—	—	—	3	33	8	06	7	50
12	15	38	−20.8	59.3	16.2	156	104	71	20.6	0	16	0	39	4	28	8	29	8	06
13	16	37	−24.6	59.3	16.2	168	99	60	21.6	1	44	2	14	5	26	9	02	8	31
14	17	39	−26.9	59.2	16.1	180	92	49	22.6	3	04	3	39	6	27	9	49	9	13
15	18	43	−27.4	59.0	16.1	193	85	37	23.6	4	08	4	44	7	29	10	53	10	17
16	19	45	−26.2	58.8	16.0	205	77	27	24.6	4	55	5	26	8	30	12	11	11	41
17	20	45	−23.4	58.4	15.9	217	70	18	25.6	5	27	5	51	9	26	13	36	13	13
18	21	41	−19.2	58.1	15.8	229	64	10	26.6	5	50	6	07	10	19	15	01	14	45
19	22	34	−14.1	57.6	15.7	241	58	4	27.6	6	06	6	18	11	08	16	23	16	13
20	23	23	− 8.5	57.1	15.6	254	47	1	28.6	6	20	6	26	11	53	17	42	17	38
21	0	10	− 2.5	56.6	15.4	266	325	0	0.1	6	32	6	33	12	37	18	58	19	00
22	0	56	+ 3.4	56.0	15.3	278	258	1	1.1	6	43	6	39	13	20	20	14	20	21
23	1	41	+ 9.1	55.5	15.1	290	252	4	2.1	6	55	6	46	14	03	21	28	21	41
24	2	27	+14.3	55.0	15.0	302	252	9	3.1	7	09	6	54	14	46	22	43	23	01
25	3	14	+18.9	54.6	14.9	315	254	16	4.1	7	25	7	05	15	32	23	56	—	—
26	4	03	+22.7	54.3	14.8	327	258	23	5.1	7	47	7	21	16	19	—	—	0	21
27	4	54	+25.5	54.2	14.8	339	262	32	6.1	8	16	7	45	17	09	1	07	1	38
28	5	46	+27.1	54.2	14.8	351	268	41	7.1	8	56	8	20	18	00	2	11	2	46
29	6	39	+27.5	54.4	14.8	3	274	50	8.1	9	48	9	13	18	52	3	05	3	41
30	7	33	+26.7	54.8	14.9	16	280	60	9.1	10	53	10	21	19	43	3	47	4	19
31	8	26	+24.5	55.4	15.1	28	286	69	10.1	12	06	11	40	20	33	4	18	4	45

MERCURY

Day	RA		Dec.	Diam.	Phase	Transit		5° high			
								52°		56°	
	h	m	°	"	%	h	m	h	m	h	m
1	22	42	−10.3	5	100	12	07	16	42	16	29
3	22	56	− 8.8	5	100	12	13	16	57	16	46
5	23	10	− 7.2	5	100	12	19	17	12	17	03
7	23	23	− 5.5	5	100	12	25	17	27	17	20
9	23	37	− 3.8	5	99	12	31	17	43	17	37
11	23	51	− 2.0	5	97	12	37	17	58	17	54
13	0	05	− 0.1	5	95	12	43	18	14	18	11
15	0	19	+ 1.7	5	92	12	49	18	30	18	28
17	0	33	+ 3.6	6	87	12	54	18	45	18	45
19	0	46	+ 5.4	6	82	12	59	18	59	19	01
21	0	58	+ 7.2	6	75	13	04	19	12	19	15
23	1	10	+ 8.8	6	68	13	07	19	24	19	28
25	1	20	+10.3	7	60	13	10	19	33	19	39
27	1	30	+11.7	7	52	13	11	19	41	19	48
29	1	38	+12.8	7	44	13	11	19	46	19	54
31	1	45	+13.7	8	36	13	09	19	49	19	57

VENUS

Day	RA		Dec.	Diam.	Phase	Transit		5° high			
								52°		56°	
	h	m	°	"	%	h	m	h	m	h	m
1	1	30	+10.4	18	65	14	54	21	17	21	23
6	1	51	+12.8	19	63	14	55	21	30	21	38
11	2	11	+15.1	20	60	14	56	21	44	21	53
16	2	32	+17.2	21	58	14	57	21	56	22	08
21	2	53	+19.2	22	56	14	58	22	08	22	22
26	3	13	+21.0	23	53	14	58	22	19	22	35
31	3	34	+22.6	24	50	14	59	22	29	22	47

MARS

Day	RA		Dec.	Diam.	Phase	Transit		5° high			
								52°		56°	
	h	m	°	"	%	h	m	h	m	h	m
1	2	57	+17.8	6	91	16	19	23	21	23	33
6	3	10	+18.7	5	91	16	13	23	19	23	33
11	3	23	+19.6	5	91	16	06	23	18	23	32
16	3	36	+20.4	5	92	16	00	23	16	23	31
21	3	49	+21.2	5	92	15	53	23	14	23	30
26	4	03	+21.8	5	92	15	47	23	12	23	28
31	4	16	+22.5	5	93	15	41	23	09	23	27

SUNRISE AND SUNSET

	London 0°05'	51°30'	Bristol 2°35'	51°28'	Birmingham 1°55'	52°28'	Manchester 2°15'	53°28'	Newcastle 1°37'	54°59'	Glasgow 4°14'	55°52'	Belfast 5°56'	54°35'
	h m	h m	h m	h m	h m	h m	h m	h m	h m	h m	h m	h m	h m	h m
1	6 45	17 41	6 55	17 51	6 53	17 47	6 56	17 47	6 56	17 43	7 07	17 52	7 12	18 01
2	6 43	17 43	6 53	17 53	6 51	17 49	6 54	17 49	6 53	17 45	7 05	17 54	7 10	18 03
3	6 41	17 45	6 51	17 55	6 49	17 51	6 52	17 51	6 51	17 47	7 02	17 56	7 08	18 05
4	6 38	17 46	6 48	17 56	6 47	17 53	6 49	17 53	6 48	17 49	7 00	17 58	7 05	18 07
5	6 36	17 48	6 46	17 58	6 44	17 55	6 47	17 55	6 46	17 51	6 57	18 00	7 03	18 09
6	6 34	17 50	6 44	18 00	6 42	17 56	6 44	17 57	6 43	17 53	6 55	18 02	7 00	18 11
7	6 32	17 52	6 42	18 02	6 40	17 58	6 42	17 59	6 41	17 55	6 52	18 05	6 58	18 13
8	6 30	17 53	6 40	18 03	6 38	18 00	6 40	18 01	6 38	17 57	6 50	18 07	6 55	18 14
9	6 27	17 55	6 37	18 05	6 35	18 02	6 37	18 02	6 36	17 59	6 47	18 09	6 53	18 16
10	6 25	17 57	6 35	18 07	6 33	18 04	6 35	18 04	6 33	18 01	6 45	18 11	6 50	18 18
11	6 23	17 59	6 33	18 09	6 31	18 05	6 33	18 06	6 31	18 03	6 42	18 13	6 48	18 20
12	6 21	18 00	6 31	18 10	6 28	18 07	6 30	18 08	6 28	18 05	6 39	18 15	6 45	18 22
13	6 18	18 02	6 28	18 12	6 26	18 09	6 28	18 10	6 26	18 07	6 37	18 17	6 43	18 24
14	6 16	18 04	6 26	18 14	6 24	18 11	6 25	18 12	6 23	18 09	6 34	18 19	6 41	18 26
15	6 14	18 05	6 24	18 15	6 21	18 13	6 23	18 14	6 21	18 11	6 32	18 21	6 38	18 28
16	6 12	18 07	6 22	18 17	6 19	18 14	6 21	18 16	6 18	18 13	6 29	18 23	6 36	18 30
17	6 09	18 09	6 19	18 19	6 17	18 16	6 18	18 17	6 16	18 15	6 26	18 25	6 33	18 32
18	6 07	18 11	6 17	18 21	6 14	18 18	6 16	18 19	6 13	18 17	6 24	18 27	6 30	18 34
19	6 05	18 12	6 15	18 22	6 12	18 20	6 13	18 21	6 11	18 19	6 21	18 29	6 28	18 36
20	6 02	18 14	6 12	18 24	6 10	18 21	6 11	18 23	6 08	18 21	6 18	18 31	6 25	18 38
21	6 00	18 16	6 10	18 26	6 07	18 23	6 08	18 25	6 06	18 23	6 16	18 33	6 23	18 40
22	5 58	18 17	6 08	18 27	6 05	18 25	6 06	18 27	6 03	18 25	6 13	18 35	6 20	18 42
23	5 56	18 19	6 06	18 29	6 03	18 27	6 04	18 28	6 01	18 27	6 11	18 37	6 18	18 44
24	5 53	18 21	6 03	18 31	6 00	18 28	6 01	18 30	5 58	18 28	6 08	18 39	6 15	18 46
25	5 51	18 22	6 01	18 32	5 58	18 30	5 59	18 32	5 55	18 30	6 05	18 41	6 13	18 47
26	5 49	18 24	5 59	18 34	5 56	18 32	5 56	18 34	5 53	18 32	6 03	18 44	6 10	18 49
27	5 47	18 26	5 57	18 36	5 53	18 34	5 54	18 36	5 50	18 34	6 00	18 46	6 08	18 51
28	5 44	18 27	5 54	18 37	5 51	18 35	5 51	18 38	5 48	18 36	5 57	18 48	6 05	18 53
29	5 42	18 29	5 52	18 39	5 49	18 37	5 49	18 39	5 45	18 38	5 55	18 50	6 03	18 55
30	5 40	18 31	5 50	18 41	5 46	18 39	5 47	18 41	5 43	18 40	5 52	18 52	6 00	18 57
31	5 37	18 32	5 47	18 42	5 44	18 41	5 44	18 43	5 40	18 42	5 50	18 54	5 58	18 59

JUPITER

Day	RA		Dec.		Transit	5° high 52°	56°
	h	m	°	'	h m	h m	h m
1	11	04.7	+7	28	0 28	6 33	6 35
11	10	59.8	+7	58	23 40	5 51	5 54
21	10	55.2	+8	27	22 56	5 10	5 13
31	10	51.1	+8	51	22 12	4 28	4 32

Diameters – equatorial 44" polar 41"

SATURN

Day	RA		Dec.		Transit	5° high 52°	56°
	h	m	°	'	h m	h m	h m
1	6	27.5	+22	46	19 48	3 21	3 38
11	6	27.3	+22	47	19 08	2 41	2 59
21	6	28.0	+22	48	18 30	2 03	2 20
31	6	29.5	+22	49	17 52	1 25	1 43

Diameters – equatorial 19" polar 17"
Rings – major axis 43" minor axis 19"

URANUS

Day	RA		Dec.		Transit	10° high 52°	56°
	h	m	°	'	h m	h m	h m
1	22	21.8	-10	59	11 43	7 54	8 13
11	22	23.9	-10	47	11 06	7 15	7 34
21	22	26.0	-10	35	10 29	6 37	6 55
31	22	27.9	-10	24	9 52	5 58	6 16

Diameter 4"

NEPTUNE

Day	RA		Dec.		Transit	10° high 52°	56°
	h	m	°	'	h m	h m	h m
1	21	05.5	-16	42	10 27	7 19	7 49
11	21	06.8	-16	36	9 49	6 40	7 10
21	21	08.0	-16	31	9 11	6 01	6 31
31	21	09.1	-16	26	8 33	5 22	5 52

Diameter 2"

APRIL 2004

FOURTH MONTH, 30 DAYS. *Aperire*, to open; Earth opens to receive seed

1	*Thursday*	Royal Air Force formed 1918. VAT introduced in Britain 1973	92
2	*Friday*	Hans Christian Andersen b. 1805. Sir Alec Guinness b. 1914	93
3	*Saturday*	Jesse James d. 1882. Helmut Kohl b. 1930	94
4	*Sunday*	Linus Yale b. 1821. Edgar Wallace b. 1875	95

5	*Monday*	Thomas Hobbes b. 1588. Nigel Hawthorne b. 1929	week 14 day 96
6	*Tuesday*	Mormons founded in the US 1830. Isaac Asimov d. 1992	97
7	*Wednesday*	St. Francis Xavier b. 1506. Billie Holiday b. 1915	98
8	*Thursday*	Mary Pickford b. 1893. Pablo Picasso d. 1973	99
9	*Friday*	*Good Friday. Bank Holiday in the UK.* King Edward IV d. 1483	100
10	*Saturday*	Omar Sharif b. 1932. Antonia White d. 1980	101
11	*Sunday*	*Easter Day.* Sir Harry Secombe d. 2001	102

12	*Monday*	*Easter Monday. Bank Holiday in England, Wales and Northern Ireland*	week 15 day 103
13	*Tuesday*	Winfield Woolworth b. 1852. Jean de la Fontaine d. 1695	104
14	*Wednesday*	Abraham Lincoln shot 1865. George Frederick Handel d. 1759	105
15	*Thursday*	John Curry d. 1994. Jean Paul Sartre d. 1980. The Titanic sank 1912	106
16	*Friday*	The Battle of Culloden 1746. Spike Milligan b. 1918	107
17	*Saturday*	Nikita Khrushchev b. 1894. Benjamin Franklin d. 1790	108
18	*Sunday*	Isoroku Yamamoto d. 1941. Albert Einstein d. 1955	109

19	*Monday*	Dudley Moore b. 1935. Pierre Curie d. 1906	week 16 day 110
20	*Tuesday*	Adolf Hitler b. 1889. Benny Hill d. 1992	111
21	*Wednesday*	Norman Parkinson b. 1913. Henry VII d. 1509	112
22	*Thursday*	Vladimir Ilyich Lenin b. 1870. J. Arthur Rank b.1888	113
23	*Friday*	St George's Day. Vladimir Nabokov b. 1899. William Shakespeare b. 1564	114
24	*Saturday*	Wallis Simpson d. 1986. Bill Edrich d. 1986	115
25	*Sunday*	ANZAC landed at Gallipoli 1915. Oliver Cromwell b. 1599	116

26	*Monday*	Rudolf Hess b. 1894. Lady Emma Hamilton b. 1856	week 17 day 117
27	*Tuesday*	Samuel Morse b. 1791. Sergey Prokofiev b. 1891	118
28	*Wednesday*	The mutiny on the Bounty took place 1789. Benito Mussolini d. 1945	119
29	*Thursday*	Edwin Lutyens b. 1869. William Walton b. 1902	120
30	*Friday*	George Washington inaugurated as the first US president 1789. Adolf Hitler d. 1945	121

ASTRONOMICAL PHENOMENA

d h
2 22 Jupiter in conjunction with Moon. Jupiter 3°S.
6 20 Mercury at stationary point
17 01 Mercury in inferior conjunction
19 06 Mercury in conjunction with Moon.
        Mercury 3°N.
19 13 Partial eclipse of Sun
19 18 Sun's longitude 30° ♉
23 11 Venus in conjunction with Moon. Venus 1°N.
23 20 Mars in conjunction with Moon. Mars 2°S.
25 07 Saturn in conjunction with Moon. Saturn 5°S.
30 05 Jupiter in conjunction with Moon. Jupiter 3°S.
30 13 Mercury at stationary point

MINIMA OF ALGOL

d	h	d	h	d	h
1	01.1	12	12.4	23	23.6
3	21.9	15	09.2	26	20.4
6	18.7	18	06.0	29	17.3
9	15.5	21	02.8		

CONSTELLATIONS

The following constellations are near the meridian at

	d	h		d	h
March	1	24	April	15	21
March	16	23	May	1	20
April	1	22	May	16	19

Cepheus (below the Pole), Cassiopeia (below the Pole), Ursa Major, Leo Minor, Leo, Sextans, Hydra and Crater

THE MOON

Phases, Apsides and Node		d	h	m
○	Full Moon	5	11	03
☽	Last Quarter	12	03	46
●	New Moon	19	13	21
☽	First Quarter	27	17	32

Perigee (364,526 km)	8	02	33
Apogee (405,434 km)	24	00	32

Mean longitude of ascending node on April 1, 43°

THE SUN

s.d. 16′.0

Day	Right Ascension			Dec. +		Equation of Time		Rise 52°		Rise 56°		Transit		Set 52°		Set 56°		Sidereal time			Transit of First Point of Aries		
	h	m	s	°	′	m	s	h	m	h	m	h	m	h	m	h	m	h	m	s	h	m	s
1	0	42	40	4	35	−3	55	5	34	5	30	12	04	18	34	18	39	12	38	45	11	19	23
2	0	46	19	4	58	−3	37	5	32	5	27	12	03	18	36	18	41	12	42	42	11	15	27
3	0	49	58	5	21	−3	19	5	30	5	25	12	03	18	38	18	43	12	46	38	11	11	31
4	0	53	37	5	44	−3	02	5	27	5	22	12	03	18	39	18	45	12	50	35	11	07	35
5	0	57	16	6	07	−2	44	5	25	5	19	12	03	18	41	18	47	12	54	32	11	03	39
6	1	00	55	6	30	−2	27	5	23	5	17	12	02	18	43	18	49	12	58	28	10	59	43
7	1	04	35	6	52	−2	10	5	21	5	14	12	02	18	45	18	51	13	02	25	10	55	48
8	1	08	14	7	15	−1	53	5	18	5	12	12	02	18	46	18	53	13	06	21	10	51	52
9	1	11	54	7	37	−1	37	5	16	5	09	12	01	18	48	18	55	13	10	18	10	47	56
10	1	15	35	8	00	−1	20	5	14	5	07	12	01	18	50	18	57	13	14	14	10	44	00
11	1	19	15	8	22	−1	04	5	12	5	04	12	01	18	51	18	59	13	18	11	10	40	04
12	1	22	56	8	44	−0	49	5	09	5	01	12	01	18	53	19	01	13	22	07	10	36	08
13	1	26	37	9	05	−0	33	5	07	4	59	12	00	18	55	19	03	13	26	04	10	32	12
14	1	30	19	9	27	−0	18	5	05	4	56	12	00	18	56	19	05	13	30	01	10	28	16
15	1	34	01	9	49	−0	04	5	03	4	54	12	00	18	58	19	07	13	33	57	10	24	20
16	1	37	43	10	10	+0	11	5	01	4	51	12	00	19	00	19	09	13	37	54	10	20	24
17	1	41	26	10	31	+0	25	4	58	4	49	11	59	19	02	19	11	13	41	50	10	16	28
18	1	45	09	10	52	+0	38	4	56	4	46	11	59	19	03	19	14	13	45	47	10	12	33
19	1	48	52	11	13	+0	51	4	54	4	44	11	59	19	05	19	16	13	49	43	10	08	37
20	1	52	36	11	34	+1	04	4	52	4	41	11	59	19	07	19	18	13	53	40	10	04	41
21	1	56	20	11	54	+1	16	4	50	4	39	11	59	19	08	19	20	13	57	36	10	00	45
22	2	00	05	12	14	+1	28	4	48	4	37	11	58	19	10	19	22	14	01	33	9	56	49
23	2	03	50	12	34	+1	40	4	46	4	34	11	58	19	12	19	24	14	05	30	9	52	53
24	2	07	35	12	54	+1	51	4	44	4	32	11	58	19	14	19	26	14	09	26	9	48	57
25	2	11	22	13	14	+2	01	4	42	4	29	11	58	19	15	19	28	14	13	23	9	45	01
26	2	15	08	13	33	+2	11	4	40	4	27	11	58	19	17	19	30	14	17	19	9	41	05
27	2	18	55	13	53	+2	21	4	38	4	25	11	58	19	19	19	32	14	21	16	9	37	09
28	2	22	43	14	11	+2	30	4	36	4	22	11	57	19	20	19	34	14	25	12	9	33	13
29	2	26	31	14	30	+2	38	4	34	4	20	11	57	19	22	19	36	14	29	09	9	29	18
30	2	30	19	14	49	+2	46	4	32	4	18	11	57	19	24	19	38	14	33	05	9	25	22

DURATION OF TWILIGHT (in minutes)

Latitude	52°	56°	52°	56°	52°	56°	52°	56°
	1 April		11 April		21 April		30 April	
Civil	34	38	35	39	37	42	39	44
Nautical	76	84	79	89	83	96	89	106
Astronomical	120	136	127	147	137	165	152	204

THE NIGHT SKY

Mercury is only likely to be seen in the evenings for the first few days of the month as its magnitude fades from +0.6 to +1.0. It may be glimpsed low in the western sky at the end of evening civil twilight.

Venus continues to be visible as a brilliant evening object, magnitude −4.5. It completely dominates the western sky for several hours after sunset. Venus passes just south of the Pleiades during the first few days of April. On the evenings of the 22nd and 23rd the waxing crescent Moon will be seen in the vicinity of the planet. At the beginning of the month Venus is about 10 degrees further east than Mars but this separation has been almost halved shortly before the end of the month.

Mars is still visible as a evening object, moving eastwards in the constellation of Taurus and passing north of the Hyades early in the month. The bright star in the Hyades, Aldebaran, is about half-a-magnitude brighter than Mars, which has a magnitude of +1.5. The crescent Moon passes 1 degree north of Mars on the evening of the 23rd.

Jupiter, magnitude −2.3, continues to be visible as a brilliant object in the evening sky, in the constellation of Leo. The waxing gibbous Moon passes 2 degrees north of the planet on the night of the 2nd-3rd and again on the 30th.

Saturn, magnitude +0.1, is still visible as an evening object in the south-western quadrant of the sky. By the end of the month it is too low in the west to be seen after midnight. Saturn is in the constellation of Gemini. The crescent Moon passes 4 degrees north of the planet on the 25th. The rings of Saturn present a beautiful spectacle to the observer with a small telescope. Two years ago they were open to their maximum extent and even now the rings extend beyond the polar diameter of the planet.

THE MOON

Day	RA h m	Dec. °	Hor. par. '	Semi-diam. '	Sun's co-long. °	PA of Bright Limb °	Phase %	Age d	Rise 52° h m	Rise 56° h m	Transit h m	Set 52° h m	Set 56° h m
1	9 19	+21.1	56.0	15.3	40	291	78	11.1	13 24	13 05	21 22	4 42	5 02
2	10 10	+16.7	56.8	15.5	52	296	86	12.1	14 45	14 33	22 10	5 00	5 14
3	11 00	+11.3	57.6	15.7	64	300	92	13.1	16 07	16 00	22 57	5 15	5 23
4	11 49	+ 5.3	58.4	15.9	76	304	97	14.1	17 30	17 30	23 44	5 28	5 31
5	12 39	− 1.2	59.1	16.1	89	317	100	15.1	18 55	19 01	— —	5 40	5 38
6	13 30	− 7.7	59.7	16.3	101	101	100	16.1	20 24	20 36	0 33	5 54	5 46
7	14 24	−14.0	60.0	16.4	113	108	97	17.1	21 56	22 15	1 24	6 10	5 56
8	15 20	−19.5	60.1	16.4	125	106	91	18.1	23 27	23 55	2 19	6 31	6 10
9	16 21	−23.8	60.1	16.4	137	102	84	19.1	— —	— —	3 18	7 01	6 32
10	17 24	−26.6	59.8	16.3	150	95	74	20.1	0 53	1 28	4 20	7 44	7 08
11	18 28	−27.6	59.4	16.2	162	88	63	21.1	2 05	2 42	5 23	8 43	8 06
12	19 31	−26.8	58.9	16.1	174	81	52	22.1	2 57	3 30	6 25	9 58	9 26
13	20 32	−24.3	58.4	15.9	186	75	41	23.1	3 32	3 59	7 22	11 22	10 56
14	21 29	−20.4	57.9	15.8	198	69	30	24.1	3 57	4 16	8 16	12 46	12 28
15	22 21	−15.6	57.3	15.6	210	65	21	25.1	4 14	4 28	9 05	14 08	13 56
16	23 10	−10.1	56.8	15.5	223	62	13	26.1	4 28	4 36	9 50	15 27	15 21
17	23 57	− 4.3	56.3	15.3	235	60	7	27.1	4 40	4 43	10 34	16 43	16 42
18	0 42	+ 1.6	55.8	15.2	247	59	2	28.1	4 51	4 49	11 16	17 57	18 02
19	1 27	+ 7.4	55.4	15.1	259	54	0	29.1	5 03	4 55	11 58	19 11	19 22
20	2 13	+12.8	55.0	15.0	272	257	0	0.4	5 15	5 03	12 41	20 26	20 42
21	2 59	+17.6	54.6	14.9	284	252	2	1.4	5 30	5 13	13 26	21 40	22 03
22	3 47	+21.6	54.3	14.8	296	254	6	2.4	5 50	5 26	14 13	22 53	23 22
23	4 37	+24.8	54.2	14.8	308	259	11	3.4	6 15	5 46	15 02	— —	— —
24	5 29	+26.8	54.1	14.7	321	264	17	4.4	6 51	6 16	15 52	0 00	0 34
25	6 22	+27.6	54.2	14.8	333	270	25	5.4	7 38	7 01	16 43	0 58	1 35
26	7 16	+27.2	54.4	14.8	345	276	34	6.4	8 37	8 03	17 34	1 45	2 19
27	8 09	+25.4	54.8	14.9	357	282	43	7.4	9 46	9 18	18 24	2 19	2 49
28	9 00	+22.5	55.3	15.1	9	287	53	8.4	11 01	10 39	19 13	2 45	3 08
29	9 51	+18.5	56.0	15.3	22	291	63	9.4	12 19	12 04	20 00	3 05	3 21
30	10 40	+13.6	56.8	15.5	34	294	72	10.4	13 39	13 30	20 46	3 20	3 31

MERCURY

Day	RA h m	Dec. °	Diam. "	Phase %	Transit h m	5° high 52° h m	5° high 56° h m
1	1 47	+14.1	8	32	13 08	19 49	19 58
3	1 51	+14.7	9	25	13 03	19 47	19 56
5	1 54	+15.1	9	19	12 57	19 42	19 52
7	1 54	+15.2	10	14	12 50	19 35	19 44
9	1 54	+15.0	10	9	12 41	19 24	19 33
11	1 51	+14.6	11	5	12 30	19 11	19 19
13	1 48	+14.0	11	2	12 19	18 55	19 03
15	1 44	+13.2	11	1	12 07	18 39	18 46
17	1 39	+12.3	12	0	11 54	5 25	5 19
19	1 34	+11.3	12	1	11 41	5 18	5 12
21	1 30	+10.3	12	2	11 29	5 11	5 06
23	1 26	+ 9.3	12	4	11 18	5 05	5 01
25	1 23	+ 8.4	12	6	11 07	4 59	4 55
27	1 21	+ 7.6	11	9	10 58	4 53	4 50
29	1 20	+ 7.0	11	13	10 49	4 47	4 45
31	1 21	+ 6.6	11	16	10 42	4 42	4 40

VENUS

Day	RA h m	Dec. °	Diam. "	Phase %	Transit h m	5° high 52° h m	5° high 56° h m
1	3 38	+22.9	24	50	14 59	22 31	22 49
6	3 57	+24.2	26	47	14 59	22 40	23 00
11	4 16	+25.3	27	44	14 58	22 46	23 08
16	4 35	+26.3	29	40	14 57	22 51	23 13
21	4 52	+27.0	31	37	14 54	22 52	23 16
26	5 07	+27.5	33	33	14 49	22 51	23 15
31	5 20	+27.7	36	29	14 42	22 46	23 11

MARS

Day	RA h m	Dec. °	Diam. "	Phase %	Transit h m	5° high 52° h m	5° high 56° h m
1	4 19	+22.6	5	93	15 40	23 09	23 26
6	4 33	+23.1	5	93	15 34	23 06	23 24
11	4 47	+23.6	5	94	15 28	23 03	23 22
16	5 00	+23.9	5	94	15 22	22 59	23 19
21	5 14	+24.2	4	94	15 16	22 56	23 15
26	5 28	+24.5	4	95	15 10	22 51	23 11
31	5 42	+24.6	4	95	15 04	22 46	23 06

SUNRISE AND SUNSET

	London 0°05' 51°30'		Bristol 2°35' 51°28'		Birmingham 1°55' 52°28'		Manchester 2°15' 53°28'		Newcastle 1°37' 54°59'		Glasgow 4°14' 55°52'		Belfast 5°56' 54°35'	
	h m	h m	h m	h m	h m	h m	h m	h m	h m	h m	h m	h m	h m	h m
1	5 35	18 34	5 45	18 44	5 42	18 42	5 42	18 45	5 38	18 44	5 47	18 56	5 55	19 01
2	5 33	18 36	5 43	18 46	5 39	18 44	5 39	18 47	5 35	18 46	5 44	18 58	5 53	19 03
3	5 31	18 37	5 41	18 47	5 37	18 46	5 37	18 49	5 33	18 48	5 42	19 00	5 50	19 05
4	5 28	18 39	5 38	18 49	5 35	18 48	5 35	18 50	5 30	18 50	5 39	19 02	5 48	19 07
5	5 26	18 41	5 36	18 51	5 32	18 49	5 32	18 52	5 27	18 52	5 37	19 04	5 45	19 09
6	5 24	18 42	5 34	18 52	5 30	18 51	5 30	18 54	5 25	18 54	5 34	19 06	5 43	19 10
7	5 22	18 44	5 32	18 54	5 28	18 53	5 27	18 56	5 22	18 56	5 31	19 08	5 40	19 12
8	5 19	18 46	5 29	18 56	5 25	18 55	5 25	18 58	5 20	18 58	5 29	19 10	5 38	19 14
9	5 17	18 47	5 27	18 57	5 23	18 56	5 23	18 59	5 17	19 00	5 26	19 12	5 35	19 16
10	5 15	18 49	5 25	18 59	5 21	18 58	5 20	19 01	5 15	19 02	5 24	19 14	5 33	19 18
11	5 13	18 51	5 23	19 01	5 18	19 00	5 18	19 03	5 13	19 04	5 21	19 16	5 31	19 20
12	5 11	18 52	5 21	19 02	5 16	19 02	5 16	19 05	5 10	19 05	5 19	19 18	5 28	19 22
13	5 08	18 54	5 19	19 04	5 14	19 03	5 13	19 07	5 08	19 07	5 16	19 20	5 26	19 24
14	5 06	18 56	5 16	19 06	5 12	19 05	5 11	19 09	5 05	19 09	5 14	19 22	5 23	19 26
15	5 04	18 58	5 14	19 07	5 09	19 07	5 09	19 10	5 03	19 11	5 11	19 24	5 21	19 28
16	5 02	18 59	5 12	19 09	5 07	19 09	5 06	19 12	5 00	19 13	5 09	19 26	5 19	19 30
17	5 00	19 01	5 10	19 11	5 05	19 10	5 04	19 14	4 58	19 15	5 06	19 28	5 16	19 32
18	4 58	19 03	5 08	19 12	5 03	19 12	5 02	19 16	4 56	19 17	5 04	19 30	5 14	19 33
19	4 56	19 04	5 06	19 14	5 01	19 14	5 00	19 18	4 53	19 19	5 01	19 32	5 11	19 35
20	4 54	19 06	5 04	19 16	4 59	19 16	4 57	19 19	4 51	19 21	4 59	19 34	5 09	19 37
21	4 51	19 08	5 02	19 17	4 56	19 17	4 55	19 21	4 48	19 23	4 56	19 36	5 07	19 39
22	4 49	19 09	4 59	19 19	4 54	19 19	4 53	19 23	4 46	19 25	4 54	19 38	5 05	19 41
23	4 47	19 11	4 57	19 21	4 52	19 21	4 51	19 25	4 44	19 27	4 51	19 40	5 02	19 43
24	4 45	19 13	4 55	19 22	4 50	19 23	4 49	19 27	4 41	19 29	4 49	19 42	5 00	19 45
25	4 43	19 14	4 53	19 24	4 48	19 24	4 46	19 29	4 39	19 31	4 47	19 44	4 58	19 47
26	4 41	19 16	4 51	19 26	4 46	19 26	4 44	19 30	4 37	19 33	4 44	19 46	4 55	19 49
27	4 39	19 18	4 49	19 27	4 44	19 28	4 42	19 32	4 35	19 35	4 42	19 48	4 53	19 51
28	4 37	19 19	4 48	19 29	4 42	19 29	4 40	19 34	4 32	19 37	4 40	19 50	4 51	19 53
29	4 36	19 21	4 46	19 31	4 40	19 31	4 38	19 36	4 30	19 39	4 37	19 52	4 49	19 54
30	4 34	19 22	4 44	19 32	4 38	19 33	4 36	19 38	4 28	19 40	4 35	19 54	4 47	19 56

JUPITER

Day	RA		Dec.		Transit		5° high 52°		56°	
	h	m	°	'	h	m	h	m	h	m
1	10	50.7	+8	53	22	08	4	24	4	28
11	10	47.5	+9	11	21	26	3	43	3	47
21	10	45.3	+9	23	20	44	3	03	3	07
31	10	44.2	+9	28	20	04	2	23	2	27

Diameters – equatorial 42" polar 39"

SATURN

Day	RA		Dec.		Transit		5° high 52°		56°	
	h	m	°	'	h	m	h	m	h	m
1	6	29.7	+22	49	17	48	1	21	1	39
11	6	31.9	+22	48	17	11	0	44	1	02
21	6	34.9	+22	47	16	35	0	08	0	25
31	6	38.4	+22	46	15	59	23	28	23	46

Diameters – equatorial 18" polar 16"
Rings – major axis 40" minor axis 18"

URANUS

Day	RA		Dec.		Transit		10° high 52°		56°	
	h	m	°	'	h	m	h	m	h	m
1	22	28.1	-10	23	9	48	5	54	6	12
11	22	29.9	-10	13	9	10	5	15	5	33
21	22	31.4	-10	05	8	32	4	37	4	54
31	22	32.8	- 9	57	7	54	3	58	4	16

Diameter 4"

NEPTUNE

Day	RA		Dec.		Transit		10° high 52°		56°	
	h	m	°	'	h	m	h	m	h	m
1	21	09.2	-16	26	8	29	5	18	5	48
11	21	10.0	-16	22	7	51	4	39	5	09
21	21	10.7	-16	19	7	12	4	00	4	29
31	21	11.2	-16	17	6	33	3	21	3	50

Diameter 2"

 MAY 2004  Ⅱ

FIFTH MONTH, 31 DAYS. *Maia,* goddess of growth and increase

1	*Saturday*	Great Exhibition opened 1851. Union of England and Scotland proclaimed 1707	122
2	*Sunday*	Dr. Benjamin Spock b. 1903. Jerome K. Jerome b. 1859	123

3	*Monday*	Bank Holiday in the UK. Niccolo Machiavelli b. 1469	week 18 day 124
4	*Tuesday*	Daily Mail first published 1896. Josip Tito d. 1980	125
5	*Wednesday*	Tammy Wynette b. 1942. Karl Marx b. 1818	126
6	*Thursday*	First issue of postage stamps 1840. Tony Blair b. 1953	127
7	*Friday*	Robert Browning b. 1812. Pyotr Tchaikovsky b. 1840	128
8	*Saturday*	Sir David Attenborough b. 1926. Harry Truman b. 1884	129
9	*Sunday*	Alan Bennett b. 1934. Glenda Jackson b. 1936	130

10	*Monday*	Fred Astaire b. 1899. Joan Crawford d. 1977	week 19 day 131
11	*Tuesday*	Paul Nash b. 1889. Irving Berlin b. 1888	132
12	*Wednesday*	Florence Nightingale b. 1820. Sir Charles Barry d. 1860	133
13	*Thursday*	Daphne du Maurier b. 1907. Laurie Lee d. 1997	134
14	*Friday*	Proclamation of the State of Israel 1948. Thomas Gainsborough b. 1727	135
15	*Saturday*	Arthur Schnitzler b. 1862. Joseph Whitaker d. 1895	136
16	*Sunday*	Film Academy Awards first presented 1929. H. E. Bates b. 1905	137

17	*Monday*	Dennis Potter b. 1935. Dennis Hopper b. 1936	week 20 day 138
18	*Tuesday*	Nathaniel Hawthorne d. 1864. George Meredith d. 1909	139
19	*Wednesday*	Anne Boleyn executed 1536. James Boswell d. 1795	140
20	*Thursday*	First Chelsea Flower Show 1913. John Stuart Mill b. 1806	141
21	*Friday*	Manchester Ship Canal opened 1834.	142
22	*Saturday*	Blackwall Tunnel opened 1897. Lord Laurence Olivier b. 1907	143
23	*Sunday*	Henrik Ibsen d. 1906. Carl Linnaeus b. 1707	144

24	*Monday*	Nicolas Copernicus d. 1543. Sir Harold Wilson d. 1995	week 21 day 145
25	*Tuesday*	Sir Ian McKellan b. 1939. Mike Myers b. 1963	146
26	*Wednesday*	Last public hanging in England 1868. Queen Mary b. 1867	147
27	*Thursday*	John Calvin d. 1564. Victor Kiam d. 2001	148
28	*Friday*	Ian Fleming b. 1908. Anne Bronte d. 1849	149
29	*Saturday*	Mount Everest conquered 1953. Erich Honecker d. 1994	150
30	*Sunday*	Christopher Marlowe d. 1593. Alexander Pope d. 1744	151

31	*Monday*	Bank Holiday in the UK. Joseph Grimaldi d. 1837.	week 22 day 152

ASTRONOMICAL PHENOMENA

d h
2 08 Venus at greatest brilliancy
4 21 Total eclipse of Moon
5 03 Jupiter at stationary point
14 20 Mercury at greatest elongation W.26°
16 21 Mercury in conjunction with Moon. Mercury 2°S.
17 12 Neptune at stationary point
17 22 Venus at stationary point
20 17 Sun's longitude 60° Ⅱ
21 12 Venus in conjunction with Moon. Venus 0°.3S.
22 16 Mars in conjunction with Moon. Mars 3°S.
22 19 Saturn in conjunction with Moon. Saturn 5°S.
25 06 Saturn in conjunction with Mars. Saturn 2°S.
27 14 Jupiter in conjunction with Moon. Jupiter 3°S.

MINIMA OF ALGOL

Algol is inconveniently situated for observation during May

CONSTELLATIONS

The following constellations are near the meridian at

	d	h		d	h
April	1	24	May	16	21
April	15	23	June	1	20
May	1	22	June	15	19

Cepheus (below the Pole), Cassiopeia (below the Pole), Ursa Minor, Ursa Major, Canes Venatici, Coma Berenices, Bootes, Leo, Virgo, Crater, Corvus and Hydra

THE MOON

Phases, Apsides and Node		d	h	m
○	Full Moon	4	20	33
☾	Last Quarter	11	11	04
●	New Moon	19	04	52
☽	First Quarter	27	07	57
Perigee (359,799 km)		6	04	39
Apogee (406,281 km)		21	12	13

Mean longitude of ascending node on May 1, 41°

THE SUN

s.d. 16′.0

Day	Right Ascension h	m	s	Dec. + °	′	Equation of Time m	s	Rise 52° h	m	Rise 56° h	m	Transit h	m	Set 52° h	m	Set 56° h	m	Sidereal time h	m	s	Transit of First Point of Aries h	m	s
1	2	34	08	15	07	+2	54	4	30	4	15	11	57	19	25	19	40	14	37	02	9	21	26
2	2	37	58	15	25	+3	01	4	28	4	13	11	57	19	27	19	42	14	40	59	9	17	30
3	2	41	48	15	43	+3	07	4	26	4	11	11	57	19	29	19	44	14	44	55	9	13	34
4	2	45	38	16	00	+3	13	4	24	4	09	11	57	19	30	19	46	14	48	52	9	09	38
5	2	49	29	16	17	+3	19	4	22	4	07	11	57	19	32	19	48	14	52	48	9	05	42
6	2	53	21	16	34	+3	24	4	21	4	05	11	57	19	34	19	50	14	56	45	9	01	46
7	2	57	13	16	51	+3	28	4	19	4	02	11	57	19	35	19	52	15	00	41	8	57	50
8	3	01	06	17	07	+3	32	4	17	4	00	11	56	19	37	19	54	15	04	38	8	53	54
9	3	05	00	17	23	+3	35	4	15	3	58	11	56	19	38	19	56	15	08	34	8	49	58
10	3	08	54	17	39	+3	37	4	14	3	56	11	56	19	40	19	58	15	12	31	8	46	03
11	3	12	48	17	55	+3	39	4	12	3	54	11	56	19	42	20	00	15	16	28	8	42	07
12	3	16	44	18	10	+3	41	4	10	3	52	11	56	19	43	20	02	15	20	24	8	38	11
13	3	20	39	18	25	+3	41	4	09	3	50	11	56	19	45	20	03	15	24	21	8	34	15
14	3	24	36	18	39	+3	41	4	07	3	49	11	56	19	46	20	05	15	28	17	8	30	19
15	3	28	33	18	54	+3	41	4	06	3	47	11	56	19	48	20	07	15	32	14	8	26	23
16	3	32	30	19	08	+3	40	4	04	3	45	11	56	19	49	20	09	15	36	10	8	22	27
17	3	36	28	19	21	+3	38	4	03	3	43	11	56	19	51	20	11	15	40	07	8	18	31
18	3	40	27	19	35	+3	36	4	01	3	41	11	56	19	52	20	13	15	44	03	8	14	35
19	3	44	26	19	48	+3	34	4	00	3	40	11	56	19	54	20	14	15	48	00	8	10	39
20	3	48	26	20	00	+3	30	3	59	3	38	11	57	19	55	20	16	15	51	57	8	06	43
21	3	52	27	20	13	+3	27	3	57	3	36	11	57	19	57	20	18	15	55	53	8	02	48
22	3	56	27	20	25	+3	22	3	56	3	35	11	57	19	58	20	20	15	59	50	7	58	52
23	4	00	29	20	36	+3	17	3	55	3	33	11	57	20	00	20	21	16	03	46	7	54	56
24	4	04	31	20	47	+3	12	3	54	3	32	11	57	20	01	20	23	16	07	43	7	51	00
25	4	08	33	20	58	+3	06	3	52	3	30	11	57	20	02	20	25	16	11	39	7	47	04
26	4	12	36	21	09	+3	00	3	51	3	29	11	57	20	04	20	26	16	15	36	7	43	08
27	4	16	39	21	19	+2	53	3	50	3	28	11	57	20	05	20	28	16	19	32	7	39	12
28	4	20	43	21	29	+2	46	3	49	3	26	11	57	20	06	20	29	16	23	29	7	35	16
29	4	24	47	21	38	+2	38	3	48	3	25	11	57	20	07	20	31	16	27	26	7	31	20
30	4	28	52	21	47	+2	30	3	47	3	24	11	58	20	08	20	32	16	31	22	7	27	24
31	4	32	57	21	56	+2	22	3	47	3	23	11	58	20	10	20	34	16	35	19	7	23	28

DURATION OF TWILIGHT (in minutes)

Latitude	52°	56°	52°	56°	52°	56°	52°	56°
	1 May		11 May		21 May		31 May	
Civil	39	44	41	48	44	53	46	57
Nautical	89	106	97	120	106	141	115	187
Astronomical	152	204	176	TAN	TAN	TAN	TAN	TAN

THE NIGHT SKY

Mercury reaches greatest western elongation on the 14th but the long duration of twilight makes observation impossible from the latitudes of the British Isles.

Venus, magnitude –4.5, attains its greatest brilliancy on the 2nd, and thus continues to dominate the western sky in the evenings for most of the month. However, the time between sunset and Venus setting is decreasing quite markedly and by the end of the month Venus is unlikely to be seen for much more than a quarter of an hour after sunset. Observers with small telescopes will notice a significant change in the apparent shape and size of the planet during May. On the 1st it is about one-third illuminated with a diameter of 36 arcseconds, while on the 31st it is an incredibly thin sliver, only 3% illuminated, but with a diameter of 56 arcseconds. An occultation of Venus by the thin crescent Moon, only 2 days old, occurs during daylight on the morning of the 21st. Last month observers will have noticed the separation between Venus and Mars decreasing but this month sees the separation increasing to over 20 degrees by the end of the month.

Mars, magnitude +1.7, is still visible as an evening object in the western sky, moving from Taurus into Gemini early in the month. Mars is moving steadily towards Saturn, passing 1.6 degrees north of it on May 25, Saturn then being 1.5 magnitudes brighter than Mars.

Jupiter, magnitude –2.1, continues to be visible as a brilliant object in the western sky, in the evenings. On May 5 Jupiter reaches its second stationary point and resumes its direct motion, moving slowly eastwards in Leo. By the end of the month it is not visible for long after midnight. The Moon, at First Quarter, passes 2 degrees north of the planet on the 27th.

Saturn, magnitude +0.2, is coming towards the end of its evening apparition, and can only be seen for a short time after dusk, low in the western sky.

THE MOON

Day	RA h m	Dec. °	Hor. par. '	Semi-diam. '	Sun's co-long. °	PA of Bright Limb °	Phase %	Age d	Rise 52° h m	Rise 56° h m	Transit h m	Set 52° h m	Set 56° h m
1	11 29	+ 7.9	57.8	15.7	46	297	81	11.4	15 00	14 57	21 32	3 34	3 39
2	12 18	+ 1.6	58.7	16.0	58	297	89	12.4	16 24	16 26	22 20	3 46	3 46
3	13 08	− 4.9	59.5	16.2	70	297	95	13.4	17 51	18 00	23 10	3 59	3 54
4	14 01	−11.4	60.2	16.4	82	294	99	14.4	19 23	19 39	— —	4 14	4 03
5	14 57	−17.4	60.7	16.5	95	121	100	15.4	20 57	21 22	0 04	4 32	4 15
6	15 57	−22.3	60.9	16.6	107	108	98	16.4	22 30	23 03	1 03	4 58	4 33
7	17 01	−25.8	60.8	16.6	119	101	93	17.4	23 51	— —	2 06	5 36	5 03
8	18 08	−27.5	60.5	16.5	131	93	86	18.4	— —	0 29	3 11	6 30	5 53
9	19 14	−27.2	59.9	16.3	143	86	77	19.4	0 53	1 28	4 16	7 43	7 08
10	20 17	−25.1	59.2	16.1	156	79	66	20.4	1 35	2 04	5 17	9 06	8 39
11	21 15	−21.4	58.5	15.9	168	73	55	21.4	2 03	2 24	6 12	10 33	10 12
12	22 10	−16.8	57.7	15.7	180	69	44	22.4	2 22	2 37	7 03	11 56	11 43
13	23 00	−11.4	57.0	15.5	192	66	34	23.4	2 37	2 46	7 49	13 16	13 08
14	23 47	− 5.6	56.4	15.4	204	64	24	24.4	2 49	2 53	8 33	14 32	14 30
15	0 32	+ 0.2	55.8	15.2	217	64	16	25.4	3 00	3 00	9 15	15 46	15 49
16	1 16	+ 6.0	55.3	15.1	229	65	9	26.4	3 11	3 06	9 57	16 59	17 08
17	2 01	+11.4	54.9	15.0	241	68	4	27.4	3 23	3 13	10 39	18 13	18 27
18	2 46	+16.3	54.5	14.9	253	74	1	28.4	3 37	3 21	11 23	19 27	19 47
19	3 34	+20.6	54.3	14.8	266	108	0	29.4	3 55	3 33	12 09	20 40	21 07
20	4 23	+24.0	54.1	14.7	278	245	1	0.8	4 18	3 50	12 57	21 50	22 22
21	5 15	+26.3	54.0	14.7	290	256	3	1.8	4 50	4 17	13 47	22 51	23 27
22	6 08	+27.5	54.0	14.7	302	264	7	2.8	5 32	4 56	14 38	23 42	— —
23	7 01	+27.4	54.1	14.7	315	271	13	3.8	6 27	5 52	15 29	— —	0 17
24	7 54	+26.0	54.3	14.8	327	277	20	4.8	7 33	7 02	16 19	0 20	0 51
25	8 45	+23.5	54.7	14.9	339	283	28	5.8	8 45	8 21	17 07	0 49	1 14
26	9 35	+19.8	55.2	15.1	351	287	37	6.8	10 01	9 43	17 53	1 10	1 29
27	10 24	+15.3	55.9	15.2	3	291	47	7.8	11 18	11 06	18 38	1 26	1 39
28	11 11	+ 9.9	56.7	15.5	16	294	57	8.8	12 36	12 30	19 23	1 40	1 48
29	11 59	+ 4.0	57.6	15.7	28	295	67	9.8	13 56	13 55	20 08	1 52	1 55
30	12 47	− 2.3	58.6	16.0	40	295	77	10.8	15 19	15 24	20 56	2 04	2 02
31	13 37	− 8.7	59.5	16.2	52	293	86	11.8	16 46	16 59	21 47	2 17	2 09

MERCURY

Day	RA h m	Dec. °	Diam. "	Phase %	Transit h m	5° high 52° h m	5° high 56° h m
1	1 21	+ 6.6	11	16	10 42	4 42	4 40
3	1 22	+ 6.3	10	20	10 36	4 37	4 35
5	1 25	+ 6.2	10	23	10 31	4 32	4 30
7	1 28	+ 6.3	10	27	10 27	4 28	4 26
9	1 33	+ 6.5	9	31	10 24	4 23	4 21
11	1 38	+ 6.8	9	34	10 21	4 19	4 16
13	1 44	+ 7.3	8	37	10 20	4 15	4 12
15	1 51	+ 7.9	8	41	10 19	4 11	4 07
17	1 59	+ 8.6	8	44	10 19	4 07	4 03
19	2 08	+ 9.5	8	48	10 20	4 03	3 59
21	2 17	+10.3	7	51	10 21	4 00	3 55
23	2 27	+11.3	7	55	10 23	3 57	3 51
25	2 37	+12.3	7	58	10 26	3 54	3 47
27	2 48	+13.4	7	62	10 30	3 52	3 44
29	3 00	+14.5	6	66	10 34	3 50	3 41
31	3 13	+15.7	6	70	10 39	3 49	3 39

VENUS

Day	RA h m	Dec. °	Diam. "	Phase %	Transit h m	5° high 52° h m	5° high 56° h m
1	5 20	+27.7	36	29	14 42	22 46	23 11
6	5 31	+27.8	39	25	14 33	22 36	23 01
11	5 39	+27.7	42	20	14 20	22 22	22 47
16	5 42	+27.4	46	15	14 04	22 03	22 27
21	5 42	+26.8	49	10	13 43	21 38	22 01
26	5 37	+26.0	53	6	13 18	21 07	21 29
31	5 28	+25.0	56	3	12 50	20 31	20 51

MARS

Day	RA h m	Dec. °	Diam. "	Phase %	Transit h m	5° high 52° h m	5° high 56° h m
1	5 42	+24.6	4	95	15 04	22 46	23 06
6	5 56	+24.7	4	95	14 59	22 41	23 01
11	6 10	+24.7	4	96	14 53	22 35	22 55
16	6 24	+24.6	4	96	14 47	22 28	22 48
21	6 38	+24.4	4	96	14 41	22 21	22 41
26	6 52	+24.2	4	97	14 35	22 14	22 33
31	7 06	+23.8	4	97	14 29	22 06	22 25

SUNRISE AND SUNSET

	London 0°05'	51°30'	Bristol 2°35'	51°28'	Birmingham 1°55'	52°28'	Manchester 2°15'	53°28'	Newcastle 1°37'	54°59'	Glasgow 4°14'	55°52'	Belfast 5°56'	54°35'
	h m	h m	h m	h m	h m	h m	h m	h m	h m	h m	h m	h m	h m	h m
1	4 32	19 24	4 42	19 34	4 36	19 35	4 34	19 39	4 26	19 42	4 33	19 56	4 45	19 58
2	4 30	19 26	4 40	19 36	4 34	19 36	4 32	19 41	4 24	19 44	4 31	19 58	4 43	20 00
3	4 28	19 27	4 38	19 37	4 32	19 38	4 30	19 43	4 22	19 46	4 29	20 00	4 40	20 02
4	4 26	19 29	4 36	19 39	4 30	19 40	4 28	19 45	4 20	19 48	4 26	20 02	4 38	20 04
5	4 24	19 31	4 35	19 40	4 28	19 41	4 26	19 46	4 17	19 50	4 24	20 04	4 36	20 06
6	4 23	19 32	4 33	19 42	4 27	19 43	4 24	19 48	4 15	19 52	4 22	20 06	4 34	20 07
7	4 21	19 34	4 31	19 44	4 25	19 45	4 22	19 50	4 13	19 54	4 20	20 08	4 32	20 09
8	4 19	19 35	4 29	19 45	4 23	19 46	4 20	19 52	4 11	19 56	4 18	20 10	4 30	20 11
9	4 18	19 37	4 28	19 47	4 21	19 48	4 19	19 53	4 09	19 57	4 16	20 12	4 29	20 13
10	4 16	19 38	4 26	19 48	4 19	19 50	4 17	19 55	4 08	19 59	4 14	20 14	4 27	20 15
11	4 14	19 40	4 24	19 50	4 18	19 51	4 15	19 57	4 06	20 01	4 12	20 16	4 25	20 17
12	4 13	19 42	4 23	19 51	4 16	19 53	4 13	19 58	4 04	20 03	4 10	20 18	4 23	20 18
13	4 11	19 43	4 21	19 53	4 15	19 54	4 12	20 00	4 02	20 05	4 08	20 20	4 21	20 20
14	4 10	19 45	4 20	19 55	4 13	19 56	4 10	20 02	4 00	20 07	4 06	20 22	4 19	20 22
15	4 08	19 46	4 18	19 56	4 11	19 58	4 08	20 03	3 58	20 08	4 04	20 23	4 18	20 24
16	4 07	19 48	4 17	19 58	4 10	19 59	4 07	20 05	3 57	20 10	4 02	20 25	4 16	20 25
17	4 05	19 49	4 15	19 59	4 08	20 01	4 05	20 07	3 55	20 12	4 01	20 27	4 14	20 27
18	4 04	19 51	4 14	20 00	4 07	20 02	4 04	20 08	3 53	20 14	3 59	20 29	4 13	20 29
19	4 03	19 52	4 13	20 02	4 05	20 04	4 02	20 10	3 52	20 15	3 57	20 31	4 11	20 30
20	4 01	19 53	4 11	20 03	4 04	20 05	4 01	20 11	3 50	20 17	3 56	20 32	4 10	20 32
21	4 00	19 55	4 10	20 05	4 03	20 07	3 59	20 13	3 49	20 19	3 54	20 34	4 08	20 34
22	3 59	19 56	4 09	20 06	4 01	20 08	3 58	20 14	3 47	20 20	3 52	20 36	4 07	20 35
23	3 57	19 58	4 08	20 07	4 00	20 09	3 57	20 16	3 46	20 22	3 51	20 37	4 05	20 37
24	3 56	19 59	4 06	20 09	3 59	20 11	3 55	20 17	3 44	20 23	3 49	20 39	4 04	20 38
25	3 55	20 00	4 05	20 10	3 58	20 12	3 54	20 19	3 43	20 25	3 48	20 41	4 03	20 40
26	3 54	20 01	4 04	20 11	3 57	20 14	3 53	20 20	3 42	20 26	3 47	20 42	4 01	20 41
27	3 53	20 03	4 03	20 12	3 56	20 15	3 52	20 22	3 40	20 28	3 45	20 44	4 00	20 43
28	3 52	20 04	4 02	20 14	3 55	20 16	3 51	20 23	3 39	20 29	3 44	20 45	3 59	20 44
29	3 51	20 05	4 01	20 15	3 54	20 17	3 49	20 24	3 38	20 31	3 43	20 47	3 58	20 45
30	3 50	20 06	4 00	20 16	3 53	20 19	3 48	20 25	3 37	20 32	3 42	20 48	3 57	20 47
31	3 49	20 07	4 00	20 17	3 52	20 20	3 48	20 27	3 36	20 33	3 41	20 50	3 56	20 48

JUPITER

Day	RA		Dec.		Transit		5° high	
							52°	56°
	h	m	°	'	h	m	h m	h m
1	10	44.2	+9	28	20	04	2 23	2 27
11	10	44.3	+9	25	19	25	1 43	1 48
21	10	45.4	+9	16	18	47	1 04	1 09
31	10	47.7	+9	01	18	10	0 26	0 30

Diameters – equatorial 39" polar 36"

SATURN

Day	RA		Dec.		Transit		5° high	
							52°	56°
	h	m	°	'	h	m	h m	h m
1	6	38.4	+22	46	15	59	23 28	23 46
11	6	42.5	+22	43	15	24	22 53	23 10
21	6	47.0	+22	39	14	49	22 17	22 35
31	6	51.9	+22	34	14	15	21 43	22 00

Diameters – equatorial 17" polar 16"
Rings – major axis 39" minor axis 17"

URANUS

Day	RA		Dec.		Transit		10° high	
							52°	56°
	h	m	°	'	h	m	h m	h m
1	22	32.8	−9	57	7	54	3 58	4 16
11	22	33.8	−9	51	7	16	3 19	3 37
21	22	34.6	−9	47	6	38	2 40	2 57
31	22	35.1	−9	45	5	59	2 01	2 18

Diameter 4"

NEPTUNE

Day	RA		Dec.		Transit		10° high	
							52°	56°
	h	m	°	'	h	m	h m	h m
1	21	11.2	−16	17	6	33	3 21	3 50
11	21	11.4	−16	16	5	54	2 42	3 11
21	21	11.5	−16	16	5	15	2 03	2 32
31	21	11.3	−16	17	4	35	1 23	1 52

Diameter 2"

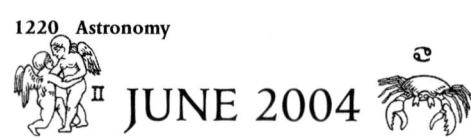

JUNE 2004

SIXTH MONTH, 30 DAYS. *Junius,* Roman gens (family)

1	*Tuesday*	Battle of the Glorious First of June 1794. Marilyn Monroe b. 1926	153
2	*Wednesday*	Coronation of Queen Elizabeth I 1953. Jonny Speight b. 1920	154
3	*Thursday*	Richard Cobden b. 1804. King George III b. 1738	155
4	*Friday*	Kaiser Wilhelm II d. 1941. Lord Thorneycroft d. 1994	156
5	*Saturday*	Robert Kennedy shot 1968. John Maynard Keynes b. 1883	157
6	*Sunday*	Sir John Stainer b. 1840. Carl Jung d. 1961	158
7	*Monday*	Dean Martin b. 1917. Paul Gauguin b. 1848	week 23 day 159
8	*Tuesday*	Frank Lloyd Wright b. 1869. Robert Stevenson b.1772	160
9	*Wednesday*	Charles Dickens d. 1870. Elizabeth Garrett Anderson b. 1836	161
10	*Thursday*	First Oxford and Cambridge Universities Boat Race 1829	162
11	*Friday*	Jacques Cousteau b. 1910. Klemens Metternich d. 1859	163
12	*Saturday*	Anne Frank b. 1929. George Bush Snr. b. 1924	164
13	*Sunday*	Dr. Thomas Arnold b. 1795. Benny Goodman d. 1986	165
14	*Monday*	Argentinians in Falkland Islands surrender 1982. Steffi Graf b. 1969	week 24 day 166
15	*Tuesday*	Magna Carta sealed 1215. Yuri Andropov b. 1914	167
16	*Wednesday*	Valentina Tereshkova became the first woman in space 1963	168
17	*Thursday*	Ken Loach b. 1936. Barry Manilow b. 1946	169
18	*Friday*	Battle of Waterloo 1815. Paul Eddington b. 1927	170
19	*Saturday*	Metropolitan Police founded 1829. Salman Rushdie b. 1947	171
20	*Sunday*	Catherine Cookson b. 1906. Nicole Kidman b. 1967	172
21	*Monday*	Benazir Bhutto b. 1953. Joseph Kesselring b. 1902	week 25 day 173
22	*Tuesday*	Giuseppe Mazzini b. 1805. Fred Astaire d. 1987	174
23	*Wednesday*	Cecil James Sharp d. 1924. David Ogilvy b. 1911	175
24	*Thursday*	Robert Bruce defeated Edward II's army at the Battle of Bannockburn	176
25	*Friday*	Battle of Little Big Horn 1876. Antonio Gaudi b. 1852	177
26	*Saturday*	Laurie Lee b. 1914. Willy Messerschmitt b. 1898	178
27	*Sunday*	Helen Keller b. 1880. Joseph Smith d. 1844	179
28	*Monday*	Treaty of Versailles signed 1919. Richard Rogers b. 1902	week 26 day 180
29	*Tuesday*	Daily Telegraph first published 1855. Lana Turner d. 1995	181
30	*Wednesday*	Tower Bridge opened 1894. Sir Stanley Spencer b. 1891	182

ASTRONOMICAL PHENOMENA

d h
8 09 Venus in inferior conjunction (transit)
10 16 Uranus at stationary point
11 12 Pluto at opposition
12 23 Venus in conjunction with Mercury. Venus 1°S.
16 16 Venus in conjunction with Moon. Venus 5°S.
17 17 Mercury in conjunction with Moon. Mercury 3°S.
18 21 Mercury in superior conjunction
19 08 Saturn in conjunction with Moon. Saturn 5°S.
20 11 Mars in conjunction with Moon. Mars 4°S.
21 01 Sun's longitude 90° ♋
24 02 Jupiter in conjunction with Moon. Jupiter 3°S.
27 00 Saturn in conjunction with Mercury. Saturn 2°S.
29 23 Venus at stationary point

MINIMA OF ALGOL

Algol is inconveniently situated for observation during June

CONSTELLATIONS

The following constellations are near the meridian at

d	h		d	h
May 1	24	June	15	21
May 16	23	July	1	20
June 1	22	July	16	19

Cassiopeia (below the Pole), Ursa Minor, Draco, Ursa Major, Canes Venatici, Bootes, Corona, Serpens, Virgo and Libra

THE MOON

Phases, Apsides and Node	d	h	m
○ Full Moon	3	04	20
☾ Last Quarter	9	20	02
● New Moon	17	20	27
☽ First Quarter	25	19	08
Perigee (357,243 km)	3	13	18
Apogee (406,574 km)	17	16	17

Mean longitude of ascending node on June 1, 40°

THE SUN

s.d. 15′.8

Day	Right Ascension			Dec. +		Equation of Time		Rise 52°		56°		Transit		Set 52°		56°		Sidereal time			Transit of First Point of Aries		
	h	m	s	°	′	m	s	h	m	h	m	h	m	h	m	h	m	h	m	s	h	m	s
1	4	37	02	22	04	+2	13	3	46	3	22	11	58	20	11	20	35	16	39	15	7	19	33
2	4	41	08	22	12	+2	04	3	45	3	21	11	58	20	12	20	36	16	43	12	7	15	37
3	4	45	14	22	20	+1	54	3	44	3	20	11	58	20	13	20	37	16	47	08	7	11	41
4	4	49	21	22	27	+1	44	3	44	3	19	11	58	20	14	20	39	16	51	05	7	07	45
5	4	53	28	22	34	+1	34	3	43	3	18	11	59	20	15	20	40	16	55	02	7	03	49
6	4	57	35	22	40	+1	23	3	42	3	17	11	59	20	16	20	41	16	58	58	6	59	53
7	5	01	43	22	46	+1	12	3	42	3	16	11	59	20	17	20	42	17	02	55	6	55	57
8	5	05	50	22	51	+1	01	3	41	3	16	11	59	20	17	20	43	17	06	51	6	52	01
9	5	09	59	22	57	+0	49	3	41	3	15	11	59	20	18	20	44	17	10	48	6	48	05
10	5	14	07	23	01	+0	37	3	40	3	15	11	59	20	19	20	45	17	14	44	6	44	09
11	5	18	16	23	06	+0	25	3	40	3	14	12	00	20	20	20	46	17	18	41	6	40	13
12	5	22	24	23	10	+0	13	3	40	3	14	12	00	20	20	20	46	17	22	37	6	36	17
13	5	26	33	23	13	+0	01	3	40	3	13	12	00	20	21	20	47	17	26	34	6	32	22
14	5	30	43	23	16	−0	12	3	39	3	13	12	00	20	21	20	48	17	30	31	6	28	26
15	5	34	52	23	19	−0	25	3	39	3	13	12	01	20	22	20	48	17	34	27	6	24	30
16	5	39	02	23	21	−0	38	3	39	3	13	12	01	20	22	20	49	17	38	24	6	20	34
17	5	43	11	23	23	−0	51	3	39	3	13	12	01	20	23	20	49	17	42	20	6	16	38
18	5	47	21	23	25	−1	04	3	39	3	13	12	01	20	23	20	50	17	46	17	6	12	42
19	5	51	31	23	26	−1	17	3	39	3	13	12	01	20	23	20	50	17	50	13	6	08	46
20	5	55	40	23	26	−1	30	3	40	3	13	12	02	20	24	20	50	17	54	10	6	04	50
21	5	59	50	23	26	−1	44	3	40	3	13	12	02	20	24	20	51	17	58	06	6	00	54
22	6	04	00	23	26	−1	57	3	40	3	13	12	02	20	24	20	51	18	02	03	5	56	58
23	6	08	09	23	26	−2	10	3	40	3	14	12	02	20	24	20	51	18	06	00	5	53	02
24	6	12	19	23	25	−2	23	3	41	3	14	12	02	20	24	20	51	18	09	56	5	49	07
25	6	16	28	23	23	−2	35	3	41	3	15	12	03	20	24	20	51	18	13	53	5	45	11
26	6	20	37	23	21	−2	48	3	42	3	15	12	03	20	24	20	50	18	17	49	5	41	15
27	6	24	46	23	19	−3	01	3	42	3	16	12	03	20	24	20	50	18	21	46	5	37	19
28	6	28	55	23	16	−3	13	3	43	3	16	12	03	20	24	20	50	18	25	42	5	33	23
29	6	33	04	23	13	−3	25	3	43	3	17	12	04	20	24	20	50	18	29	39	5	29	27
30	6	37	12	23	10	−3	37	3	44	3	18	12	04	20	23	20	49	18	33	35	5	25	31

DURATION OF TWILIGHT (in minutes)

Latitude	52°	56°	52°	56°	52°	56°	52°	56°
	1 June		11 June		21 June		30 June	
Civil	46	58	48	61	49	63	48	61
Nautical	116	TAN	124	TAN	127	TAN	124	TAN
Astronomical	TAN	TAN	TAN	TAN	TAN	TAN	TAN	TAN

THE NIGHT SKY

Mercury is unsuitably placed for observation throughout the month, superior conjunction occurring on the 18th.

Venus is moving rapidly towards the Sun and is unlikely to be seen after the first couple of days in the month. During that period it will only be visible for a very short time, low above the western horizon just after sunset. Its magnitude then is −4.0. Venus moves quickly through inferior conjunction on the 8th and during the last fortnight of the month it may be seen as a morning object, magnitude −4.3, low above the eastern horizon before dawn. Venus transits the Sun on the 8th and this phenomenon, which last occurred in 1882, will be visible from the British Isles during the morning.

Mars, magnitude +1.8, is no longer a conspicuous object and it will only be possible to detect the planet low above the west-north-western horizon for a short while before observation is inhibited by the gathering twilight. Mars is unlikely to be seen after the middle of the month. If observers can detect a faint point of light in that area it is more likely to be Pollux, which is 0.7 magnitudes brighter than Mars and passes 5 degrees south of the star around June 13-14.

Jupiter, magnitude −1.9, continues to be visible as a brilliant object in the western sky in the evenings. On the night of the 23rd-24th the crescent Moon passes 2 degrees north of the planet.

Saturn, magnitude +0.1, is now coming to the end of its evening apparition, and is disappearing over the western horizon before dark. Observers will need very good conditions to be able to see it even in the first few days of the month.

THE MOON

Day	RA h m	Dec. °	Hor. par. '	Semi-diam. '	Sun's co-long. °	PA of Bright Limb °	Phase %	Age d	Rise 52° h m	Rise 56° h m	Transit h m	Set 52° h m	Set 56° h m
1	14 31	−14.8	60.4	16.4	64	288	93	12.8	18 19	18 39	22 43	2 34	2 19
2	15 30	−20.3	61.0	16.6	77	280	98	13.8	19 55	20 23	23 45	2 55	2 34
3	16 33	−24.5	61.3	16.7	89	234	100	14.8	21 25	22 00	— —	3 26	2 57
4	17 40	−27.0	61.3	16.7	101	109	99	15.8	22 38	23 15	0 51	4 13	3 37
5	18 48	−27.5	61.0	16.6	113	94	95	16.8	23 30	— —	1 58	5 20	4 43
6	19 54	−25.9	60.5	16.5	125	85	88	17.8	— —	0 02	3 03	6 43	6 12
7	20 57	−22.7	59.7	16.3	138	78	80	18.8	0 05	0 29	4 03	8 12	7 49
8	21 54	−18.1	58.8	16.0	150	72	70	19.8	0 28	0 45	4 57	9 40	9 24
9	22 46	−12.8	57.9	15.8	162	69	59	20.8	0 44	0 55	5 47	11 02	10 53
10	23 35	− 7.0	57.0	15.5	174	67	48	21.8	0 58	1 03	6 32	12 21	12 17
11	0 21	− 1.1	56.2	15.3	186	66	38	22.8	1 09	1 10	7 15	13 36	13 38
12	1 06	+ 4.7	55.6	15.1	199	67	29	23.8	1 20	1 16	7 56	14 49	14 57
13	1 50	+10.2	55.0	15.0	211	69	20	24.8	1 31	1 23	8 38	16 03	16 15
14	2 35	+15.3	54.6	14.9	223	72	13	25.8	1 45	1 31	9 21	17 16	17 35
15	3 22	+19.7	54.3	14.8	235	77	7	26.8	2 01	1 41	10 06	18 29	18 54
16	4 11	+23.2	54.1	14.7	248	85	3	27.8	2 22	1 57	10 53	19 40	20 11
17	5 02	+25.8	54.0	14.7	260	102	1	28.8	2 51	2 20	11 43	20 44	21 20
18	5 54	+27.3	53.9	14.7	272	202	0	0.1	3 30	2 55	12 34	21 39	22 14
19	6 48	+27.5	54.0	14.7	284	255	1	1.1	4 21	3 46	13 25	22 21	22 53
20	7 41	+26.4	54.2	14.8	297	269	4	2.1	5 24	4 52	14 15	22 52	23 19
21	8 33	+24.1	54.4	14.8	309	277	9	3.1	6 35	6 09	15 04	23 15	23 36
22	9 23	+20.7	54.8	14.9	321	283	15	4.1	7 49	7 29	15 50	23 32	23 47
23	10 11	+16.4	55.3	15.1	333	288	23	5.1	9 05	8 51	16 35	23 46	23 56
24	10 58	+11.3	55.9	15.2	346	291	32	6.1	10 21	10 13	17 19	23 59	— —
25	11 44	+ 5.7	56.6	15.4	358	293	42	7.1	11 37	11 35	18 02	— —	0 03
26	12 31	− 0.3	57.4	15.7	10	293	52	8.1	12 56	12 59	18 47	0 10	0 10
27	13 19	− 6.5	58.3	15.9	22	292	63	9.1	14 19	14 28	19 35	0 23	0 17
28	14 10	−12.6	59.2	16.1	34	290	73	10.1	15 46	16 03	20 27	0 37	0 25
29	15 05	−18.2	60.1	16.4	47	285	83	11.1	17 19	17 43	21 25	0 55	0 37
30	16 04	−22.9	60.7	16.5	59	278	91	12.1	18 51	19 23	22 28	1 20	0 55

MERCURY

Day	RA h m	Dec. °	Diam. "	Phase %	Transit h m	5° high 52° h m	5° high 56° h m
1	3 20	+16.3	6	72	10 42	3 48	3 38
3	3 34	+17.4	6	76	10 48	3 48	3 36
5	3 48	+18.6	6	81	10 55	3 48	3 35
7	4 04	+19.7	6	85	11 03	3 49	3 35
9	4 20	+20.8	5	89	11 12	3 51	3 36
11	4 37	+21.8	5	93	11 21	3 55	3 38
13	4 55	+22.7	5	96	11 31	3 59	3 42
15	5 14	+23.4	5	98	11 42	4 05	3 47
17	5 33	+24.1	5	100	11 53	4 13	3 53
19	5 52	+24.5	5	100	12 05	19 48	20 09
21	6 11	+24.7	5	99	12 16	20 01	20 21
23	6 30	+24.8	5	98	12 27	20 12	20 32
25	6 49	+24.7	5	96	12 38	20 21	20 41
27	7 07	+24.4	5	93	12 48	20 29	20 49
29	7 25	+23.9	5	90	12 58	20 35	20 54
31	7 42	+23.3	5	86	13 07	20 40	20 58

VENUS

Day	RA h m	Dec. °	Diam. "	Phase %	Transit h m	5° high 52° h m	5° high 56° h m
1	5 26	+24.7	56	2	12 43	5 03	4 43
6	5 14	+23.4	58	0	12 11	4 40	4 21
11	5 01	+21.9	58	0	11 39	4 16	4 00
16	4 49	+20.5	56	2	11 08	3 53	3 39
21	4 40	+19.3	53	6	10 40	3 32	3 19
26	4 35	+18.4	50	10	10 16	3 13	3 00
31	4 35	+17.8	46	14	9 55	2 56	2 44

MARS

Day	RA h m	Dec. °	Diam. "	Phase %	Transit h m	5° high 52° h m	5° high 56° h m
1	7 08	+23.8	4	97	14 28	22 04	22 23
6	7 22	+23.4	4	97	14 22	21 55	22 13
11	7 35	+22.9	4	97	14 16	21 46	22 04
16	7 49	+22.3	4	98	14 10	21 36	21 53
21	8 02	+21.7	4	98	14 03	21 26	21 42
26	8 15	+21.1	4	98	13 57	21 15	21 31
31	8 29	+20.3	4	98	13 50	21 04	21 19

SUNRISE AND SUNSET

	London 0°05' 51°30'		Bristol 2°35' 51°28'		Birmingham 1°55' 52°28'		Manchester 2°15' 53°28'		Newcastle 1°37' 54°59'		Glasgow 4°14' 55°52'		Belfast 5°56' 54°35'	
	h m	h m	h m	h m	h m	h m	h m	h m	h m	h m	h m	h m	h m	h m
1	3 49	20 08	3 59	20 18	3 51	20 21	3 47	20 28	3 35	20 35	3 40	20 51	3 55	20 49
2	3 48	20 09	3 58	20 19	3 50	20 22	3 46	20 29	3 34	20 36	3 39	20 52	3 54	20 51
3	3 47	20 10	3 57	20 20	3 49	20 23	3 45	20 30	3 33	20 37	3 38	20 53	3 53	20 52
4	3 46	20 11	3 57	20 21	3 49	20 24	3 44	20 31	3 32	20 38	3 37	20 55	3 52	20 53
5	3 46	20 12	3 56	20 22	3 48	20 25	3 44	20 32	3 31	20 39	3 36	20 56	3 51	20 54
6	3 45	20 13	3 55	20 23	3 47	20 26	3 43	20 33	3 31	20 40	3 35	20 57	3 51	20 55
7	3 45	20 14	3 55	20 24	3 47	20 27	3 42	20 34	3 30	20 41	3 34	20 58	3 50	20 56
8	3 44	20 15	3 55	20 25	3 46	20 28	3 42	20 35	3 29	20 42	3 34	20 59	3 49	20 57
9	3 44	20 16	3 54	20 26	3 46	20 28	3 41	20 36	3 29	20 43	3 33	21 00	3 49	20 58
10	3 44	20 16	3 54	20 26	3 45	20 29	3 41	20 37	3 28	20 44	3 33	21 01	3 48	20 58
11	3 43	20 17	3 53	20 27	3 45	20 30	3 40	20 37	3 28	20 45	3 32	21 02	3 48	20 59
12	3 43	20 18	3 53	20 28	3 45	20 31	3 40	20 38	3 28	20 45	3 32	21 02	3 48	21 00
13	3 43	20 18	3 53	20 28	3 45	20 31	3 40	20 39	3 27	20 46	3 31	21 03	3 47	21 01
14	3 43	20 19	3 53	20 29	3 44	20 32	3 40	20 39	3 27	20 47	3 31	21 04	3 47	21 01
15	3 43	20 19	3 53	20 29	3 44	20 32	3 40	20 40	3 27	20 47	3 31	21 04	3 47	21 02
16	3 42	20 20	3 53	20 30	3 44	20 33	3 39	20 40	3 27	20 48	3 31	21 05	3 47	21 02
17	3 42	20 20	3 53	20 30	3 44	20 33	3 39	20 41	3 27	20 48	3 31	21 05	3 47	21 03
18	3 43	20 21	3 53	20 30	3 44	20 34	3 39	20 41	3 27	20 49	3 31	21 06	3 47	21 03
19	3 43	20 21	3 53	20 31	3 44	20 34	3 40	20 41	3 27	20 49	3 31	21 06	3 47	21 03
20	3 43	20 21	3 53	20 31	3 45	20 34	3 40	20 42	3 27	20 49	3 31	21 06	3 47	21 04
21	3 43	20 21	3 53	20 31	3 45	20 34	3 40	20 42	3 27	20 49	3 31	21 06	3 47	21 04
22	3 43	20 22	3 53	20 31	3 45	20 34	3 40	20 42	3 27	20 50	3 31	21 07	3 47	21 04
23	3 43	20 22	3 54	20 31	3 45	20 35	3 40	20 42	3 28	20 50	3 32	21 07	3 48	21 04
24	3 44	20 22	3 54	20 31	3 46	20 35	3 41	20 42	3 28	20 50	3 32	21 07	3 48	21 04
25	3 44	20 22	3 54	20 31	3 46	20 35	3 41	20 42	3 29	20 50	3 33	21 07	3 49	21 04
26	3 45	20 22	3 55	20 31	3 46	20 34	3 42	20 42	3 29	20 50	3 33	21 06	3 49	21 04
27	3 45	20 22	3 55	20 31	3 47	20 34	3 42	20 42	3 30	20 49	3 34	21 06	3 50	21 04
28	3 46	20 21	3 56	20 31	3 48	20 34	3 43	20 42	3 30	20 49	3 34	21 06	3 50	21 04
29	3 46	20 21	3 56	20 31	3 48	20 34	3 43	20 41	3 31	20 49	3 35	21 06	3 51	21 03
30	3 47	20 21	3 57	20 31	3 49	20 34	3 44	20 41	3 32	20 48	3 36	21 05	3 52	21 03

JUPITER

Day	RA h m	Dec. ° '	Transit h m	5° high 52° h m	5° high 56° h m
1	10 48.0	+8 59	18 06	0 22	0 26
11	10 51.3	+8 37	17 30	23 40	23 44
21	10 55.5	+8 09	16 55	23 03	23 06
31	11 00.4	+7 37	16 21	22 26	22 29

Diameters – equatorial 35" polar 33"

SATURN

Day	RA h m	Dec. ° '	Transit h m	5° high 52° h m	5° high 56° h m
1	6 52.4	+22 34	14 11	21 39	21 56
11	6 57.6	+22 28	13 37	21 04	21 21
21	7 03.0	+22 21	13 03	20 30	20 47
31	7 08.6	+22 14	12 29	19 55	20 12

Diameters – equatorial 17" polar 15"
Rings – major axis 38" minor axis 16"

URANUS

Day	RA h m	Dec. ° '	Transit h m	10° high 52° h m	10° high 56° h m
1	22 35.1	-9 44	5 55	1 57	2 14
11	22 35.3	-9 44	5 16	1 18	1 35
21	22 35.1	-9 45	4 36	0 39	0 56
31	22 34.7	-9 48	3 56	23 55	0 16

Diameter 4"

NEPTUNE

Day	RA h m	Dec. ° '	Transit h m	10° high 52° h m	10° high 56° h m
1	21 11.3	-16 17	4 31	1 19	1 48
11	21 10.9	-16 19	3 52	0 40	1 09
21	21 10.3	-16 22	3 12	0 00	0 30
31	21 09.5	-16 26	2 32	23 17	23 46

Diameter 2"

JULY 2004

SEVENTH MONTH, 31 DAYS. *Julius* Caesar, formerly Quintilis, fifth month of Roman pre-Julian calendar

1	*Thursday*	Battle of the Boyne 1690 (old calendar). Diana Princess of Wales b. 1961	183
2	*Friday*	Battle of Marston Moor 1644. Ernest Hemingway d. 1961	184
3	*Saturday*	Betty Grable d. 1973. Tom Stoppard b. 1937	185
4	*Sunday*	Louis Armstrong b.1900. Marie Curie d. 1934	186

5	*Monday*	National Health Service started 1948. Cecil Rhodes b. 1853	week 27 day 187
6	*Tuesday*	Aneurin Bevan d. 1960. John Flaxman b. 1755	188
7	*Wednesday*	Sir Arthur Conan Doyle d. 1930. Stephen Runciman b. 1903	189
8	*Thursday*	Vivien Leigh d. 1967. Kim Il-sung d. 1994	190
9	*Friday*	David Hockney b. 1937. Sir Edward Heath b. 1916	191
10	*Saturday*	Camille Pissarro b. 1830. Marcel Proust b. 1871	192
11	*Sunday*	King Robert I b. 1274. Sir Laurence Olivier d. 1989	193

12	*Monday*	*Public holiday Northern Ireland.* Kenneth More d. 1982	week 28 day 194
13	*Tuesday*	Ruth Ellis, the last woman to be executed in Britain, 1955	195
14	*Wednesday*	Jules Mazarin b. 1602. Anne Necker d. 1817	196
15	*Thursday*	Rembrandt van Rijn b. 1606. Iris Murdoch b. 1919	197
16	*Friday*	Sir Joshua Reynolds b. 1723. Queen Anne of Cleves d. 1557	198
17	*Saturday*	James Cagney b. 1899. Adam Smith d. 1790	199
18	*Sunday*	Nelson Mandela b. 1918. Jane Austen d. 1817	200

19	*Monday*	Mary Rose sank 1545. Edgar Degas b. 1834	week 29 day 201
20	*Tuesday*	Neil Armstrong and Edwin Aldrin landed on the moon 1969	202
21	*Wednesday*	Isaac Stern b. 1920. Robin Williams b. 1952	203
22	*Thursday*	Tate Gallery opened 1897. Willem Dafoe b. 1955	204
23	*Friday*	Raymond Chandler b. 1888. Woody Harrelson b. 1961	205
24	*Saturday*	Simón Bolívar b. 1783. Amelia Earhart b. 1897	206
25	*Sunday*	The first test tube baby, Louise Brown, b. 1978	207

26	*Monday*	Mick Jagger b. 1943. Carl Jung b. 1875	week 30 day 208
27	*Tuesday*	Alexandre Dumas b. 1824. James Mason d. 1984	209
28	*Wednesday*	Sir Garfield Sobers b. 1936. Jacqueline Onassis b. 1929	210
29	*Thursday*	Vincent van Gogh d. 1890. Benito Mussolini b. 1883	211
30	*Friday*	England beat Germany 4-2 in the World Cup Final 1966	212
31	*Saturday*	Sir George Oswald Browning Allen b. 1902. John Ericsson b. 1803	213

ASTRONOMICAL PHENOMENA

d	h	
5	10	Earth at aphelion (152 million km.)
8	17	Saturn in conjunction
11	00	Mars in conjunction with Mercury. Mars 0°.2 S.
13	22	Venus in conjunction with Moon. Venus 8°S.
15	00	Venus at greatest brilliancy
16	21	Saturn in conjunction with Moon. Saturn 5°S.
19	04	Mars in conjunction with Moon. Mars 4°S.
19	19	Mercury in conjunction with Moon. Mercury 5°S.
21	16	Jupiter in conjunction with Moon. Jupiter 3°S.
22	12	Sun's longitude 120° ♌
27	03	Mercury at greatest elongation E.27°

MINIMA OF ALGOL

d	h	d	h	d	h
1	19.2	13	06.4	24	17.7
4	16.0	16	03.2	27	14.5
7	12.8	19	00.0	30	11.3
10	09.6	21	20.9		

CONSTELLATIONS

The following constellations are near the meridian at

	d	h		d	h
June	1	24	July	16	21
June	15	23	August	1	20
July	1	22	August	16	19

Ursa Minor, Draco, Coruna, Hercules, Lyra, Serpens, Ophiuchus, Libra, Scorpius and Sagittarius

THE MOON

Phases, Apsides and Node	d	h	m
○ Full Moon	2	11	09
☾ Last Quarter	9	07	34
● New Moon	17	11	24
☽ First Quarter	25	03	37
○ Full Moon	31	18	05

	d	h	m
Perigee (357,452 km)	1	23	03
Apogee (406,173 km)	14	21	19
Perigee (360,336 km)	30	06	28

Mean longitude of ascending node on July 1, 38°

THE SUN

s.d. 15'.8

Day	Right Ascension			Dec. +		Equation of Time		Rise 52°		Rise 56°		Transit		Set 52°		Set 56°		Sidereal time			Transit of First Point of Aries		
	h	m	s	°	'	m	s	h	m	h	m	h	m	h	m	h	m	h	m	s	h	m	s
1	6	41	20	23	06	−3	48	3	44	3	19	12	04	20	23	20	49	18	37	32	5	21	35
2	6	45	28	23	02	−4	00	3	45	3	19	12	04	20	23	20	48	18	41	29	5	17	39
3	6	49	36	22	57	−4	11	3	46	3	20	12	04	20	22	20	48	18	45	25	5	13	43
4	6	53	43	22	52	−4	22	3	47	3	21	12	04	20	22	20	47	18	49	22	5	09	47
5	6	57	50	22	46	−4	32	3	48	3	22	12	05	20	21	20	46	18	53	18	5	05	51
6	7	01	57	22	41	−4	42	3	49	3	23	12	05	20	21	20	45	18	57	15	5	01	56
7	7	06	03	22	34	−4	52	3	49	3	25	12	05	20	20	20	45	19	01	11	4	58	00
8	7	10	09	22	28	−5	01	3	50	3	26	12	05	20	19	20	44	19	05	08	4	54	04
9	7	14	15	22	21	−5	10	3	51	3	27	12	05	20	18	20	43	19	09	05	4	50	08
10	7	18	20	22	13	−5	19	3	52	3	28	12	05	20	18	20	42	19	13	01	4	46	12
11	7	22	25	22	05	−5	27	3	54	3	30	12	06	20	17	20	41	19	16	58	4	42	16
12	7	26	29	21	57	−5	35	3	55	3	31	12	06	20	16	20	40	19	20	54	4	38	20
13	7	30	33	21	49	−5	42	3	56	3	32	12	06	20	15	20	38	19	24	51	4	34	2
14	7	34	37	21	40	−5	49	3	57	3	34	12	06	20	14	20	37	19	28	47	4	30	28
15	7	38	40	21	30	−5	56	3	58	3	35	12	06	20	13	20	36	19	32	44	4	26	32
16	7	42	42	21	21	−6	02	3	59	3	37	12	06	20	12	20	34	19	36	40	4	22	36
17	7	46	44	21	11	−6	07	4	01	3	38	12	06	20	11	20	33	19	40	37	4	18	41
18	7	50	45	21	00	−6	12	4	02	3	40	12	06	20	10	20	32	19	44	34	4	14	45
19	7	54	46	20	49	−6	16	4	03	3	41	12	06	20	08	20	30	19	48	30	4	10	49
20	7	58	47	20	38	−6	20	4	05	3	43	12	06	20	07	20	29	19	52	27	4	06	53
21	8	02	46	20	27	−6	23	4	06	3	45	12	06	20	06	20	27	19	56	23	4	02	57
22	8	06	46	20	15	−6	26	4	07	3	46	12	06	20	05	20	25	20	00	20	3	59	01
23	8	10	44	20	03	−6	28	4	09	3	48	12	06	20	03	20	24	20	04	16	3	55	05
24	8	14	42	19	50	−6	29	4	10	3	50	12	07	20	02	20	22	20	08	13	3	51	09
25	8	18	40	19	38	−6	30	4	12	3	52	12	07	20	00	20	20	20	12	09	3	47	13
26	8	22	36	19	24	−6	30	4	13	3	53	12	07	19	59	20	18	20	16	06	3	43	17
27	8	26	33	19	11	−6	30	4	15	3	55	12	07	19	57	20	17	20	20	03	3	39	21
28	8	30	28	18	57	−6	29	4	16	3	57	12	06	19	56	20	15	20	23	59	3	35	26
29	8	34	23	18	43	−6	27	4	18	3	59	12	06	19	54	20	13	20	27	56	3	31	30
30	8	38	17	18	29	−6	25	4	19	4	01	12	06	19	53	20	11	20	31	52	3	27	34
31	8	42	11	18	14	−6	22	4	21	4	02	12	06	19	51	20	09	20	35	49	3	23	38

DURATION OF TWILIGHT (in minutes)

Latitude	52°	56°	52°	56°	52°	56°	52°	56°
	1 July		11 July		21 July		31 July	
Civil	48	61	47	58	44	53	42	49
Nautical	124	TAN	117	TAN	107	146	98	123
Astronomical	TAN	TAN	TAN	TAN	TAN	TAN	182	TAN

THE NIGHT SKY

Mercury is at greatest eastern elongation on the 27th, but the long duration of twilight makes observation impossible from the latitudes of the British Isles.

Venus, magnitude −4.5, is rapidly moving away from the Sun and is visible as a brilliant morning object, dominating the eastern sky for several hours before dawn. It will attain its greatest brilliancy on the 15th. Locating Venus in daylight is a challenge for keen-sighted naked-eye observers; it will be even more interesting on the mornings of the 13th and 14th, just after sunrise, when Venus is in the same part of the sky as the thin waning crescent Moon. On the first occasion Venus will be about 10 degrees to the left and below the Moon, while on the second occasion it will be about 8 degrees to the right and below.

Mars is unsuitably placed for observation.

Jupiter, magnitude −1.8, is still visible throughout the month as a conspicuous object in the western sky in the evenings. It is nearing the end of its evening apparition and will not be visible for very long after sunset by the end of the month. The four Galilean satellites are readily observable with a small telescope or even a good pair of binoculars provided that they are held rigidly.

Saturn is not suitably placed for observation as it passes through conjunction on the 8th.

Twilight. Reference to the section above shows that astronomical twilight last all night for a period around the summer solstice (i.e. in June and July), even in southern England. Under these conditions the sky never gets completely dark as the Sun is always less than 18 degrees below the horizon.

THE MOON

Day	RA h m	Dec °	Hor. par. '	Semi-diam. '	Sun's co-long °	PA of Bright Limb °	Phase %	Age d	Rise 52° h m	Rise 56° h m	Transit h m	Set 52° h m	Set 56° h m
1	17 09	−26.1	61.2	16.7	71	267	97	13.1	20 14	20 51	23 34	1 58	1 25
2	18 17	−27.5	61.3	16.7	83	237	100	14.1	21 17	21 52	— —	2 54	2 17
3	19 25	−26.8	61.2	16.7	95	113	99	15.1	22 00	22 28	0 42	4 11	3 37
4	20 31	−24.1	60.7	16.5	108	88	96	16.1	22 29	22 49	1 46	5 41	5 14
5	21 32	−19.9	59.9	16.3	120	78	91	17.1	22 49	23 02	2 45	7 13	6 54
6	22 28	−14.6	59.1	16.1	132	72	83	18.1	23 03	23 11	3 38	8 41	8 29
7	23 19	− 8.7	58.1	15.8	144	69	74	19.1	23 16	23 18	4 26	10 04	9 58
8	0 07	− 2.7	57.2	15.6	156	67	64	20.1	23 27	23 25	5 11	11 22	11 22
9	0 53	+ 3.3	56.3	15.3	169	67	53	21.1	23 39	23 31	5 54	12 37	12 43
10	1 38	+ 9.0	55.6	15.1	181	69	43	22.1	23 51	23 39	6 36	13 52	14 02
11	2 23	+14.2	54.9	15.0	193	71	34	23.1	— —	23 49	7 19	15 05	15 22
12	3 10	+18.8	54.5	14.8	205	75	25	24.1	0 07	— —	8 04	16 19	16 42
13	3 58	+22.6	54.2	14.8	218	80	17	25.1	0 26	0 02	8 50	17 31	18 00
14	4 49	+25.4	54.0	14.7	230	87	11	26.1	0 52	0 23	9 39	18 37	19 12
15	5 41	+27.1	54.0	14.7	242	95	6	27.1	1 28	0 54	10 30	19 35	20 11
16	6 34	+27.5	54.0	14.7	254	108	2	28.1	2 16	1 40	11 21	20 21	20 55
17	7 27	+26.7	54.2	14.8	267	141	0	29.1	3 16	2 42	12 12	20 55	21 24
18	8 20	+24.7	54.4	14.8	279	243	0	0.5	4 25	3 57	13 01	21 20	21 43
19	9 11	+21.5	54.8	14.9	291	271	2	1.5	5 39	5 18	13 48	21 39	21 56
20	10 00	+17.3	55.2	15.0	303	282	6	2.5	6 55	6 40	14 34	21 54	22 05
21	10 47	+12.4	55.6	15.2	316	287	12	3.5	8 11	8 01	15 17	22 06	22 12
22	11 33	+ 6.9	56.1	15.3	328	290	19	4.5	9 26	9 23	16 01	22 18	22 19
23	12 19	+ 0.9	56.8	15.5	340	292	28	5.5	10 43	10 45	16 44	22 29	22 25
24	13 06	− 5.1	57.4	15.6	352	292	38	6.5	12 03	12 10	17 30	22 42	22 33
25	13 54	−11.1	58.2	15.8	5	290	48	7.5	13 26	13 39	18 18	22 58	22 43
26	14 46	−16.7	58.9	16.0	17	287	60	8.5	14 53	15 14	19 12	23 19	22 57
27	15 43	−21.6	59.6	16.2	29	282	70	9.5	16 23	16 52	20 10	23 49	23 20
28	16 44	−25.3	60.2	16.4	41	275	80	10.5	17 49	18 25	21 14	— —	23 59
29	17 49	−27.3	60.6	16.5	53	266	89	11.5	19 00	19 38	22 20	0 35	— —
30	18 56	−27.4	60.8	16.6	66	255	95	12.5	19 52	20 24	23 26	1 42	1 05
31	20 03	−25.5	60.8	16.6	78	233	99	13.5	20 27	20 51	— —	3 06	2 35

MERCURY

Day	RA h m	Dec °	Diam. "	Phase %	Transit h m	5° high 52° h m	5° high 56° h m
1	7 42	+23.3	5	86	13 07	20 40	20 58
3	7 58	+22.6	6	83	13 15	20 43	21 00
5	8 13	+21.8	6	80	13 22	20 45	21 00
7	8 28	+20.9	6	76	13 28	20 45	21 00
9	8 42	+19.9	6	73	13 34	20 45	20 59
11	8 55	+18.8	6	70	13 39	20 44	20 56
13	9 07	+17.7	6	67	13 43	20 41	20 53
15	9 18	+16.6	6	64	13 47	20 38	20 49
17	9 29	+15.5	7	61	13 49	20 35	20 44
19	9 39	+14.4	7	58	13 51	20 31	20 39
21	9 49	+13.2	7	55	13 52	20 26	20 33
23	9 57	+12.1	7	52	13 53	20 20	20 26
25	10 05	+11.0	7	49	13 53	20 14	20 19
27	10 12	+ 9.9	8	46	13 52	20 08	20 12
29	10 18	+ 8.9	8	43	13 50	20 01	20 04
31	10 24	+ 8.0	8	40	13 47	19 53	19 56

VENUS

Day	RA h m	Dec °	Diam. "	Phase %	Transit h m	5° high 52° h m	5° high 56° h m
1	4 35	+17.8	46	14	9 55	2 56	2 44
6	4 37	+17.6	43	19	9 39	2 40	2 29
11	4 44	+17.6	39	24	9 26	2 27	2 15
16	4 53	+17.8	36	28	9 16	2 15	2 03
21	5 05	+18.1	34	32	9 08	2 05	1 53
26	5 18	+18.6	31	36	9 02	1 57	1 44
31	5 34	+19.0	29	39	8 58	1 51	1 37

MARS

Day	RA h m	Dec °	Diam. "	Phase %	Transit h m	5° high 52° h m	5° high 56° h m
1	8 29	+20.3	4	98	13 50	21 04	21 19
6	8 42	+19.5	4	99	13 43	20 53	21 07
11	8 54	+18.7	4	99	13 37	20 41	20 54
16	9 07	+17.8	4	99	13 30	20 29	20 41
21	9 20	+16.8	4	99	13 22	20 17	20 27
26	9 32	+15.8	4	99	13 15	20 04	20 14
31	9 44	+14.8	4	99	13 08	19 51	20 00

SUNRISE AND SUNSET

	London 0°05'	51°30'	Bristol 2°35'	51°28'	Birmingham 1°55'	52°28'	Manchester 2°15'	53°28'	Newcastle 1°37'	54°59'	Glasgow 4°14'	55°52'	Belfast 5°56'	54°35'
	h m	h m	h m	h m	h m	h m	h m	h m	h m	h m	h m	h m	h m	h m
1	3 48	20 21	3 58	20 30	3 49	20 33	3 45	20 41	3 32	20 48	3 36	21 05	3 52	21 03
2	3 48	20 20	3 58	20 30	3 50	20 33	3 46	20 40	3 33	20 47	3 37	21 04	3 53	21 02
3	3 49	20 20	3 59	20 30	3 51	20 32	3 46	20 40	3 34	20 47	3 38	21 04	3 54	21 01
4	3 50	20 19	4 00	20 29	3 52	20 32	3 47	20 39	3 35	20 46	3 39	21 03	3 55	21 01
5	3 51	20 19	4 01	20 29	3 53	20 31	3 48	20 39	3 36	20 46	3 40	21 02	3 56	21 00
6	3 52	20 18	4 02	20 28	3 54	20 31	3 49	20 38	3 37	20 45	3 41	21 01	3 57	21 00
7	3 52	20 18	4 03	20 27	3 55	20 30	3 50	20 37	3 38	20 44	3 42	21 01	3 58	20 59
8	3 53	20 17	4 04	20 27	3 56	20 29	3 51	20 36	3 39	20 43	3 44	21 00	3 59	20 58
9	3 54	20 16	4 05	20 26	3 57	20 29	3 52	20 36	3 40	20 42	3 45	20 59	4 00	20 57
10	3 55	20 15	4 06	20 25	3 58	20 28	3 53	20 35	3 41	20 41	3 46	20 58	4 01	20 56
11	3 56	20 15	4 07	20 24	3 59	20 27	3 54	20 34	3 43	20 40	3 47	20 57	4 03	20 55
12	3 58	20 14	4 08	20 24	4 00	20 26	3 56	20 33	3 44	20 39	3 49	20 56	4 04	20 54
13	3 59	20 13	4 09	20 23	4 01	20 25	3 57	20 32	3 45	20 38	3 50	20 54	4 05	20 53
14	4 00	20 12	4 10	20 22	4 02	20 24	3 58	20 31	3 47	20 37	3 52	20 53	4 06	20 52
15	4 01	20 11	4 11	20 21	4 03	20 23	3 59	20 30	3 48	20 36	3 53	20 52	4 08	20 51
16	4 02	20 10	4 12	20 20	4 05	20 22	4 01	20 29	3 50	20 35	3 54	20 50	4 09	20 49
17	4 03	20 09	4 14	20 19	4 06	20 21	4 02	20 27	3 51	20 33	3 56	20 49	4 11	20 48
18	4 05	20 08	4 15	20 17	4 07	20 20	4 04	20 26	3 52	20 32	3 58	20 48	4 12	20 47
19	4 06	20 06	4 16	20 16	4 09	20 18	4 05	20 25	3 54	20 31	3 59	20 46	4 14	20 46
20	4 07	20 05	4 17	20 15	4 10	20 17	4 06	20 23	3 56	20 29	4 01	20 45	4 15	20 44
21	4 09	20 04	4 19	20 14	4 11	20 16	4 08	20 22	3 57	20 28	4 02	20 43	4 17	20 43
22	4 10	20 03	4 20	20 13	4 13	20 14	4 09	20 21	3 59	20 26	4 04	20 41	4 18	20 41
23	4 11	20 01	4 22	20 11	4 14	20 13	4 11	20 19	4 00	20 24	4 06	20 40	4 20	20 40
24	4 13	20 00	4 23	20 10	4 16	20 12	4 12	20 18	4 02	20 23	4 08	20 38	4 21	20 38
25	4 14	19 59	4 24	20 08	4 17	20 10	4 14	20 16	4 04	20 21	4 09	20 36	4 23	20 36
26	4 16	19 57	4 26	20 07	4 19	20 09	4 15	20 15	4 05	20 19	4 11	20 35	4 25	20 35
27	4 17	19 56	4 27	20 06	4 20	20 07	4 17	20 13	4 07	20 18	4 13	20 33	4 26	20 33
28	4 18	19 54	4 29	20 04	4 22	20 06	4 19	20 11	4 09	20 16	4 15	20 31	4 28	20 31
29	4 20	19 53	4 30	20 03	4 23	20 04	4 20	20 10	4 10	20 14	4 16	20 29	4 30	20 29
30	4 21	19 51	4 32	20 01	4 25	20 02	4 22	20 08	4 12	20 12	4 18	20 27	4 31	20 28
31	4 23	19 49	4 33	19 59	4 26	20 01	4 23	20 06	4 14	20 10	4 20	20 10	4 33	20 26

JUPITER

Day	RA		Dec.		Transit		5° high 52°		56°	
	h	m	°	'	h	m	h	m	h	m
1	11	00.4	+7	37	16	21	22	26	22	29
11	11	06.1	+7	01	15	47	21	49	21	52
21	11	12.3	+6	20	15	14	21	13	21	14
31	11	19.0	+5	37	14	41	20	36	20	38

Diameters – equatorial 33" polar 31"

SATURN

Day	RA		Dec.		Transit		5° high 52°		56°	
	h	m	°	'	h	m	h	m	h	m
1	7	08.6	+22	14	12	29	5	03	4	47
11	7	14.1	+22	05	11	55	4	31	4	14
21	7	19.7	+21	56	11	22	3	58	3	41
31	7	25.1	+21	46	10	48	3	25	3	09

Diameters – equatorial 16" polar 15"
Rings – major axis 37" minor axis 15"

URANUS

Day	RA		Dec.		Transit		5° high 52°		56°	
	h	m	°	'	h	m	h	m	h	m
1	22	34.7	− 9	48	3	56	23	55	0	16
11	22	34.0	− 9	53	3	16	23	16	23	33
21	22	33.0	− 9	59	2	36	22	36	22	54
31	22	31.8	−10	06	1	56	21	56	22	14

Diameter 4"

NEPTUNE

Day	RA		Dec.		Transit		5° high 52°		56°	
	h	m	°	'	h	m	h	m	h	m
1	21	09.5	−16	26	2	32	23	17	23	46
11	21	08.6	−16	30	1	51	22	37	23	07
21	21	07.6	−16	34	1	11	21	57	22	27
31	21	06.6	−16	39	0	31	21	18	21	48

Diameter 2"

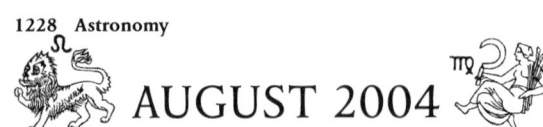

AUGUST 2004

EIGHTH MONTH, 31 DAYS. *Augustus,* formerly *Sextilis,* sixth month of Roman pre-Julian calendar

1	*Sunday*	Francis Scott Key b. 1779. Yves Saint Laurent b. 1936	214

2	*Monday*	*Bank Holiday in Scotland.* Rupert Brooke b. 1887	week 31 day 215
3	*Tuesday*	Discovery of Lake Victoria by John Speke 1858	216
4	*Wednesday*	Britain declares war on Germany 1914	217
5	*Thursday*	Friedrich Engels d. 1895. Neil Armstrong b. 1930	218
6	*Friday*	First atomic bomb dropped, Hiroshima 1945	219
7	*Saturday*	Oliver Hardy d. 1957. Mata Hari b. 1876	220
8	*Sunday*	Great Train Robbery 1963. Russia declared war on Japan 1945	221

9	*Monday*	Second atomic bomb dropped, Nagasaki 1945. John Dryden b. 1631	week 32 day 222
10	*Tuesday*	Greenwich Observatory founded 1675	223
11	*Wednesday*	Jackson Pollock d. 1956. Andrew Carnegie d. 1919	224
12	*Thursday*	George Stephenson d. 1848. Norris McWhirter b. 1925	225
13	*Friday*	Florence Nightingale d. 1910. Fidel Castro b. 1927	226
14	*Saturday*	Enzo Ferarri d. 1988. John Galsworthy b. 1867	227
15	*Sunday*	First ship passed through the Panama Canal 1914	228

16	*Monday*	Madonna Ciccone b. 1958. Georgette Hayer b. 1902	week 33 day 229
17	*Tuesday*	Robert de Niro b. 1943. V. S. Naipaul b. 1932	230
18	*Wednesday*	Roman Polanski b. 1933. Robert Redford b. 1937	231
19	*Thursday*	Bill Clinton b. 1946. Ogden Nash b. 1902	232
20	*Friday*	General William Booth d. 1912. Benjamin Harrison b. 1833	233
21	*Saturday*	Leon Trotsky d. 1940. Count Basie b. 1904	234
22	*Sunday*	Robert Cecil d. 1903. Claude Debussy b. 1862	235

23	*Monday*	Blitz began 1940. King Louis XVI of France b. 1754	week 34 day 236
24	*Tuesday*	Pompeii, Italy, was completely buried following the eruption of Vesuvius AD79	237
25	*Wednesday*	First cross-channel swim by Captain Matthew Webb 1875	238
26	*Thursday*	Guillaume Apollinaire b. 1880. Charles Lindbergh d. 1974	239
27	*Friday*	Charles Stewart Rolls b. 1877. Haile Salassie d. 1975	240
28	*Saturday*	Sir Edward Burne-Jones b. 1833. Leo Tolstoy b. 1828	241
29	*Sunday*	John Locke b. 1632. Richard Attenborough b. 1923	242

30	*Monday*	*Bank Holiday in England, Wales and Northern Ireland*	week 35 day 243
31	*Tuesday*	Charles Baudelaire d. 1867. Henry Moore d. 1986	244

ASTRONOMICAL PHENOMENA

d h
- 6 03 Neptune at opposition
- 10 01 Mercury at stationary point
- 11 23 Venus in conjunction with Moon. Venus 8°S.
- 13 10 Saturn in conjunction with Moon. Saturn 5°S.
- 16 22 Mars in conjunction with Moon. Mars 3°S.
- 17 02 Mercury in conjunction with Moon. Mercury 9°S.
- 17 19 Venus at greatest elongation W.46°
- 18 07 Jupiter in conjunction with Moon. Jupiter 2°S.
- 18 20 Mars in conjunction with Mercury. Mars 6°N.
- 22 19 Sun's longitude 150° ♍
- 23 21 Mercury in inferior conjunction
- 27 19 Uranus at opposition
- 30 19 Pluto at stationary point
- 31 16 Saturn in conjunction with Venus. Saturn 2°N.

MINIMA OF ALGOL

d	h	d	h	d	h
2	08.1	13	19.3	25	06.6
5	04.9	16	16.1	28	03.4
8	01.7	19	12.9	31	00.2
10	22.5	22	09.8		

CONSTELLATIONS

The following constellations are near the meridian at

d	h		d	h
July	1	24	August	16	21
July	16	23	September	1	20
August	1	22	September	15	19

Draco, Hercules, Lyra, Cygnus, Sagitta, Ophiuchus, Serpens, Aquila and Sagittarius

THE MOON

Phases, Apsides and Node	d	h	m
☾ Last Quarter	7	22	01
● New Moon	16	01	24
☽ First Quarter	23	10	12
○ Full Moon	30	02	22

	d	h	m
Apogee (405,260 km)	11	09	40
Perigee (365,128 km)	27	05	46

Mean longitude of ascending node on August 1, 36°

THE SUN

s.d. 16′.1

Day	Right Ascension			Dec. +		Equation of Time		Rise 52°		Rise 56°		Transit		Set 52°		Set 56°		Sidereal time			Transit of First Point of Aries		
	h	m	s	°	′	m	s	h	m	h	m	h	m	h	m	h	m	h	m	s	h	m	s
1	8	46	04	17	59	−6	19	4	22	4	04	12	06	19	49	20	07	20	39	45	3	19	42
2	8	49	57	17	44	−6	15	4	24	4	06	12	06	19	48	20	05	20	43	42	3	15	46
3	8	53	48	17	28	−6	10	4	25	4	08	12	06	19	46	20	03	20	47	38	3	11	50
4	8	57	40	17	12	−6	05	4	27	4	10	12	06	19	44	20	01	20	51	35	3	07	54
5	9	01	30	16	56	−5	59	4	28	4	12	12	06	19	42	19	59	20	55	32	3	03	58
6	9	05	20	16	40	−5	52	4	30	4	14	12	06	19	41	19	56	20	59	28	3	00	02
7	9	09	10	16	23	−5	45	4	31	4	16	12	06	19	39	19	54	21	03	25	2	56	06
8	9	12	59	16	06	−5	38	4	33	4	18	12	06	19	37	19	52	21	07	21	2	52	10
9	9	16	47	15	49	−5	30	4	35	4	20	12	05	19	35	19	50	21	11	18	2	48	15
10	9	20	35	15	32	−5	21	4	36	4	22	12	05	19	33	19	48	21	15	14	2	44	19
11	9	24	22	15	14	−5	12	4	38	4	24	12	05	19	31	19	45	21	19	11	2	40	23
12	9	28	09	14	56	−5	02	4	40	4	25	12	05	19	29	19	43	21	23	07	2	36	27
13	9	31	55	14	38	−4	51	4	41	4	27	12	05	19	27	19	41	21	27	04	2	32	31
14	9	35	41	14	19	−4	40	4	43	4	29	12	05	19	25	19	38	21	31	01	2	28	35
15	9	39	26	14	01	−4	29	4	44	4	31	12	04	19	23	19	36	21	34	57	2	24	39
16	9	43	11	13	42	−4	17	4	46	4	33	12	04	19	21	19	34	21	38	54	2	20	43
17	9	46	55	13	23	−4	04	4	48	4	35	12	04	19	19	19	31	21	42	50	2	16	47
18	9	50	38	13	04	−3	51	4	49	4	37	12	04	19	17	19	29	21	46	47	2	12	51
19	9	54	21	12	44	−3	38	4	51	4	39	12	04	19	15	19	26	21	50	43	2	08	55
20	9	58	04	12	24	−3	24	4	53	4	41	12	03	19	13	19	24	21	54	40	2	05	00
21	10	01	46	12	04	−3	09	4	54	4	43	12	03	19	11	19	22	21	58	36	2	01	04
22	10	05	27	11	44	−2	54	4	56	4	45	12	03	19	09	19	19	22	02	33	1	57	08
23	10	09	08	11	24	−2	39	4	57	4	47	12	03	19	06	19	17	22	06	30	1	53	12
24	10	12	49	11	04	−2	23	4	59	4	49	12	02	19	04	19	14	22	10	26	1	49	16
25	10	16	29	10	43	−2	07	5	01	4	51	12	02	19	02	19	12	22	14	23	1	45	20
26	10	20	09	10	22	−1	50	5	02	4	53	12	02	19	00	19	09	22	18	19	1	41	24
27	10	23	48	10	01	−1	33	5	04	4	55	12	01	18	58	19	07	22	22	16	1	37	28
28	10	27	27	9	40	−1	15	5	06	4	57	12	01	18	56	19	04	22	26	12	1	33	32
29	10	31	06	9	19	−0	57	5	07	4	59	12	01	18	53	19	01	22	30	09	1	29	36
30	10	34	44	8	57	−0	39	5	09	5	01	12	00	18	51	18	59	22	34	05	1	25	40
31	10	38	22	8	36	−0	20	5	10	5	03	12	00	18	49	18	56	22	38	02	1	21	45

DURATION OF TWILIGHT (in minutes)

Latitude	52°	56°	52°	56°	52°	56°	52°	56°
	1 August		11 August		21 August		31 August	
Civil	41	49	39	45	37	42	35	40
Nautical	97	121	90	107	84	97	79	90
Astronomical	179	TAN	154	210	139	168	128	148

THE NIGHT SKY

Mercury is unsuitably placed for observation throughout August, inferior conjunction occurring on the 23rd.

Venus reaches its greatest western elongation (46 degrees) on the 17th and continues to be visible as a magnificent object in the eastern sky in the mornings before sunrise. Its magnitude is −4.3. Saturn, which has been moving outwards from the Sun, passes 2 degrees north of the very much brighter inner planet on the 31st. The waxing crescent Moon is near Venus on the mornings of the 11th and 12th.

Mars is unsuitably placed for observation.

Jupiter, magnitude −1.7, continues to be visible as a bright evening object low in the western sky after sunset, but only for the first few days of the month.

Saturn is slowly emerging from the morning twilight, becoming visible low above the eastern horizon before dawn. It is moving slowly eastwards in the constellation of Gemini. Saturn's magnitude is +0.2.

Uranus is at opposition on the 27th, in the constellation of Aquarius. Uranus is barely visible to the naked eye as its magnitude is +5.7, but it is readily located with only small optical aid.

Neptune is at opposition on the 6th, in the constellation of Capricornus. It is not visible to the naked-eye since its magnitude is +7.8.

Meteors. The maximum of the famous Perseid meteor shower occurs on the morning of the 12th. Conditions are favourable as the old crescent Moon will provide little interference, even though it rises around midnight.

THE MOON

Day	RA h m	Dec. °	Hor. par. '	Semi-diam. '	Sun's co-long. °	PA of Bright Limb °	Phase %	Age d	Rise 52° h m	Rise 56° h m	Transit h m	Set 52° h m	Set 56° h m
1	21 06	−21.8	60.4	16.5	90	128	100	14.5	20 50	21 07	0 27	4 38	4 16
2	22 04	−16.8	59.8	16.3	102	84	98	15.5	21 08	21 18	1 24	6 10	5 55
3	22 58	−11.0	59.0	16.1	114	74	93	16.5	21 21	21 26	2 15	7 38	7 29
4	23 49	− 4.8	58.2	15.8	127	70	86	17.5	21 33	21 32	3 03	9 00	8 58
5	0 36	+ 1.4	57.3	15.6	139	68	78	18.5	21 45	21 39	3 48	10 19	10 22
6	1 23	+ 7.4	56.4	15.4	151	69	69	19.5	21 57	21 46	4 31	11 36	11 45
7	2 09	+12.9	55.6	15.2	163	70	59	20.5	22 11	21 55	5 15	12 51	13 06
8	2 56	+17.7	55.0	15.0	175	73	49	21.5	22 29	22 07	5 59	14 06	14 27
9	3 44	+21.8	54.5	14.9	188	78	40	22.5	22 53	22 25	6 46	15 20	15 47
10	4 34	+24.9	54.3	14.8	200	83	31	23.5	23 25	22 52	7 34	16 29	17 02
11	5 26	+26.9	54.1	14.7	212	89	22	24.5	— —	23 32	8 24	17 30	18 06
12	6 19	+27.7	54.1	14.7	224	96	15	25.5	0 09	— —	9 15	18 19	18 55
13	7 13	+27.2	54.3	14.8	236	104	9	26.5	1 05	0 30	10 06	18 57	19 28
14	8 06	+25.4	54.5	14.9	249	113	4	27.5	2 12	1 42	10 57	19 25	19 49
15	8 57	+22.4	54.9	14.9	261	128	1	28.5	3 26	3 02	11 45	19 45	20 04
16	9 47	+18.4	55.3	15.1	273	192	0	29.5	4 42	4 25	12 31	20 01	20 14
17	10 35	+13.6	55.7	15.2	285	270	1	0.9	5 59	5 48	13 16	20 14	20 22
18	11 22	+ 8.1	56.2	15.3	298	284	4	1.9	7 16	7 11	14 00	20 26	20 28
19	12 08	+ 2.2	56.7	15.4	310	289	9	2.9	8 33	8 33	14 43	20 37	20 35
20	12 55	− 4.0	57.2	15.6	322	291	16	3.9	9 52	9 58	15 28	20 49	20 41
21	13 43	−10.0	57.7	15.7	334	291	24	4.9	11 14	11 25	16 15	21 04	20 50
22	14 33	−15.7	58.3	15.9	347	288	34	5.9	12 39	12 57	17 06	21 22	21 02
23	15 28	−20.7	58.8	16.0	359	284	45	6.9	14 06	14 33	18 01	21 48	21 20
24	16 26	−24.6	59.2	16.1	11	279	57	7.9	15 32	16 06	19 02	22 26	21 51
25	17 28	−27.1	59.6	16.2	23	272	68	8.9	16 47	17 25	20 05	23 22	22 44
26	18 33	−27.8	59.9	16.3	35	264	78	9.9	17 45	18 20	21 09	— —	— —
27	19 39	−26.5	60.0	16.4	48	255	87	10.9	18 25	18 53	22 11	0 38	0 03
28	20 42	−23.5	60.0	16.3	60	246	94	11.9	18 52	19 12	23 09	2 06	1 40
29	21 41	−19.0	59.7	16.3	72	233	98	12.9	19 11	19 25	— —	3 38	3 19
30	22 36	−13.4	59.3	16.2	84	175	100	13.9	19 26	19 33	0 02	5 07	4 56
31	23 28	− 7.3	58.6	16.0	96	83	99	14.9	19 38	19 40	0 52	6 33	6 28

MERCURY

Day	RA h m	Dec. °	Diam. "	Phase %	Transit h m	5° high 52° h m	5° high 56° h m
1	10 26	+ 7.5	8	38	13 45	19 49	19 52
3	10 30	+ 6.7	9	35	13 41	19 41	19 43
5	10 33	+ 5.9	9	31	13 36	19 32	19 33
7	10 35	+ 5.3	9	27	13 30	19 23	19 23
9	10 36	+ 4.9	10	23	13 22	19 13	19 13
11	10 35	+ 4.5	10	19	13 14	19 03	19 03
13	10 34	+ 4.4	10	15	13 04	18 52	18 53
15	10 31	+ 4.5	11	11	12 52	18 42	18 42
17	10 26	+ 4.7	11	8	12 40	18 31	18 32
19	10 21	+ 5.2	11	5	12 27	18 20	18 22
21	10 15	+ 5.8	11	2	12 13	18 10	18 12
23	10 09	+ 6.7	11	1	11 59	5 58	5 56
25	10 03	+ 7.6	11	1	11 45	5 40	5 37
27	9 57	+ 8.6	10	3	11 32	5 22	5 18
29	9 53	+ 9.5	10	5	11 20	5 05	5 00
31	9 50	+10.4	10	10	11 10	4 50	4 45

VENUS

Day	RA h m	Dec. °	Diam. "	Phase %	Transit h m	5° high 52° h m	5° high 56° h m
1	5 37	+19.1	29	40	8 57	1 49	1 36
6	5 55	+19.4	27	43	8 55	1 45	1 31
11	6 13	+19.7	25	46	8 54	1 42	1 28
16	6 33	+19.9	24	49	8 54	1 41	1 27
21	6 53	+19.9	23	52	8 55	1 42	1 28
26	7 15	+19.7	22	55	8 57	1 45	1 31
31	7 36	+19.4	21	57	8 59	1 49	1 35

MARS

Day	RA h m	Dec. °	Diam. "	Phase %	Transit h m	5° high 52° h m	5° high 56° h m
1	9 47	+14.6	4	99	13 06	19 48	19 57
6	9 59	+13.5	4	100	12 59	19 35	19 43
11	10 11	+12.4	4	100	12 51	19 21	19 28
16	10 23	+11.2	4	100	12 44	19 08	19 13
21	10 35	+10.0	4	100	12 36	18 54	18 58
26	10 47	+ 8.8	4	100	12 28	18 40	18 43
31	10 59	+ 7.6	4	100	12 20	18 25	18 28

SUNRISE AND SUNSET

	London 0°05'	51°30'	Bristol 2°35'	51°28'	Birmingham 1°55'	52°28'	Manchester 2°15'	53°28'	Newcastle 1°37'	54°59'	Glasgow 4°14'	55°52'	Belfast 5°56'	54°35'
	h m	h m	h m	h m	h m	h m	h m	h m	h m	h m	h m	h m	h m	h m
1	4 24	19 48	4 35	19 58	4 28	19 59	4 25	20 04	4 16	20 09	4 22	20 23	4 35	20 24
2	4 26	19 46	4 36	19 56	4 29	19 57	4 27	20 03	4 18	20 07	4 24	20 21	4 37	20 22
3	4 27	19 44	4 38	19 54	4 31	19 55	4 28	20 01	4 19	20 05	4 26	20 19	4 38	20 20
4	4 29	19 43	4 39	19 53	4 33	19 54	4 30	19 59	4 21	20 03	4 28	20 17	4 40	20 18
5	4 30	19 41	4 41	19 51	4 34	19 52	4 32	19 57	4 23	20 01	4 29	20 15	4 42	20 16
6	4 32	19 39	4 42	19 49	4 36	19 50	4 33	19 55	4 25	19 59	4 31	20 13	4 44	20 14
7	4 34	19 37	4 44	19 47	4 37	19 48	4 35	19 53	4 27	19 56	4 33	20 11	4 46	20 12
8	4 35	19 36	4 45	19 45	4 39	19 46	4 37	19 51	4 28	19 54	4 35	20 08	4 47	20 10
9	4 37	19 34	4 47	19 44	4 41	19 44	4 39	19 49	4 30	19 52	4 37	20 06	4 49	20 08
10	4 38	19 32	4 48	19 42	4 42	19 42	4 40	19 47	4 32	19 50	4 39	20 04	4 51	20 06
11	4 40	19 30	4 50	19 40	4 44	19 40	4 42	19 45	4 34	19 48	4 41	20 02	4 53	20 04
12	4 41	19 28	4 52	19 38	4 46	19 38	4 44	19 43	4 36	19 46	4 43	19 59	4 55	20 02
13	4 43	19 26	4 53	19 36	4 47	19 36	4 45	19 41	4 38	19 43	4 45	19 57	4 56	19 59
14	4 45	19 24	4 55	19 34	4 49	19 34	4 47	19 39	4 40	19 41	4 47	19 55	4 58	19 57
15	4 46	19 22	4 56	19 32	4 51	19 32	4 49	19 37	4 41	19 39	4 49	19 52	5 00	19 55
16	4 48	19 20	4 58	19 30	4 52	19 30	4 51	19 34	4 43	19 37	4 51	19 50	5 02	19 53
17	4 49	19 18	4 59	19 28	4 54	19 28	4 52	19 32	4 45	19 34	4 53	19 48	5 04	19 50
18	4 51	19 16	5 01	19 26	4 56	19 26	4 54	19 30	4 47	19 32	4 55	19 45	5 06	19 48
19	4 53	19 14	5 03	19 24	4 57	19 24	4 56	19 28	4 49	19 30	4 57	19 43	5 07	19 46
20	4 54	19 12	5 04	19 22	4 59	19 22	4 58	19 26	4 51	19 27	4 59	19 41	5 09	19 44
21	4 56	19 10	5 06	19 20	5 01	19 20	4 59	19 23	4 53	19 25	5 00	19 38	5 11	19 41
22	4 57	19 08	5 07	19 18	5 02	19 17	5 01	19 21	4 54	19 23	5 02	19 36	5 13	19 39
23	4 59	19 06	5 09	19 16	5 04	19 15	5 03	19 19	4 56	19 20	5 04	19 33	5 15	19 36
24	5 00	19 04	5 11	19 13	5 06	19 13	5 05	19 17	4 58	19 18	5 06	19 31	5 17	19 34
25	5 02	19 01	5 12	19 11	5 07	19 11	5 06	19 14	5 00	19 15	5 08	19 28	5 18	19 32
26	5 04	18 59	5 14	19 09	5 09	19 09	5 08	19 12	5 02	19 13	5 10	19 26	5 20	19 29
27	5 05	18 57	5 15	19 07	5 11	19 06	5 10	19 10	5 04	19 11	5 12	19 23	5 22	19 27
28	5 07	18 55	5 17	19 05	5 12	19 04	5 12	19 07	5 06	19 08	5 14	19 21	5 24	19 24
29	5 08	18 53	5 19	19 03	5 14	19 02	5 13	19 05	5 08	19 06	5 16	19 18	5 26	19 22
30	5 10	18 50	5 20	19 00	5 16	19 00	5 15	19 03	5 09	19 03	5 18	19 15	5 28	19 20
31	5 12	18 48	5 22	18 58	5 17	18 57	5 17	19 00	5 11	19 01	5 20	19 13	5 29	19 17

JUPITER

Day	RA		Dec.		Transit		5° high		
							52°		56°
	h	m	°	'	h	m	h m		h m
1	11	19.7	+5	33	14	38	20 33		20 34
11	11	26.8	+4	46	14	06	19 57		19 57
21	11	34.2	+3	58	13	34	19 21		19 20
31	11	41.9	+3	08	13	02	18 45		18 44

Diameters – equatorial 31" polar 29"

SATURN

Day	RA		Dec.		Transit		5° high		
							52°		56°
	h	m	°	'	h	m	h m		h m
1	7	25.6	+21	45	10	44	3 21		3 05
11	7	30.9	+21	34	10	10	2 48		2 32
21	7	35.9	+21	24	9	36	2 15		1 59
31	7	40.5	+21	14	9	01	1 41		1 26

Diameters – equatorial 17" polar 15"
Rings – major axis 38" minor axis 15"

URANUS

Day	RA		Dec.		Transit		10° high		
							52°		56°
	h	m	°	'	h	m	h m		h m
1	22	31.7	−10	07	1	52	21 52		22 10
11	22	30.3	−10	15	1	11	21 12		21 30
21	22	28.9	−10	24	0	30	20 33		20 51
31	22	27.4	−10	32	23	45	19 53		20 11

Diameter 4"

NEPTUNE

Day	RA		Dec.		Transit		10° high		
							52°		56°
	h	m	°	'	h	m	h m		h m
1	21	06.5	−16	39	0	27	3 36		3 06
11	21	05.4	−16	44	23	42	2 55		2 24
21	21	04.3	−16	49	23	02	2 14		1 43
31	21	03.3	−16	53	22	22	1 33		1 02

Diameter 2"

SEPTEMBER 2004

NINTH MONTH, 30 DAYS. *Septem* (seven), seventh month of Roman pre-Julian calendar

1	*Wednesday*	Siegfried Sassoon d. 1967. Englebert Humperdinck b. 1854	245
2	*Thursday*	Fire of London 1666. John Howard b. 1726	246
3	*Friday*	Oliver Cromwell d. 1658. Start of World War II 1939	247
4	*Saturday*	Albert Schweitzer d. 1965. Dawn Fraser b. 1937	248
5	*Sunday*	John Wisden b. 1826. King Louis XIV of France b. 1638	249
6	*Monday*	The Mayflower sailed from Plymouth 1620. John Dalton b. 1766	week 36 day 250
7	*Tuesday*	Buddy Holly b. 1936. Catherine Parr d. 1548	251
8	*Wednesday*	Patsy Cline b. 1932. Michael Frayn b. 1933	252
9	*Thursday*	End of soap rationing 1950. John Curry b. 1949	253
10	*Friday*	Mary Wollstonecraft Godwin d. 1797. Pope Julius III b. 1487	254
11	*Saturday*	D. H. Lawrence b. 1885. Jessica Mitford b. 1917	255
12	*Sunday*	Cleopatra's Needle erected on the Embankment, London 1878	256
13	*Monday*	Arnold Schoenberg b. 1874. General James Wolf d. 1759	week 37 day 257
14	*Tuesday*	Alexander von Humboldt b. 1769. Jan Masaryk b. 1886	258
15	*Wednesday*	Battle of Britain Day. Agatha Christie b. 1890	259
16	*Thursday*	Bonar Law b. 1858. Gabriel Fahrenheit d. 1736	260
17	*Friday*	US Constitution was signed 1787. Sir Francis Chichester b. 1901	261
18	*Saturday*	Greta Garbo b. 1905. Jimi Hendrix d. 1970	262
19	*Sunday*	George Cadbury b. 1839. Sir William Golding b. 1911	263
20	*Monday*	QE2 launched 1966. Sophia Loren b. 1934	week 38 day 264
21	*Tuesday*	John McAdam b. 1756. H. G. Wells b. 1866	265
22	*Wednesday*	Coronation of King George III 1761. Irving Berlin d. 1989	266
23	*Thursday*	Wilkie Collins d. 1889. Michael Faraday b. 1791	267
24	*Friday*	The St Leger horse race was first run at Doncaster 1776. Jim Henson b. 1936	268
25	*Saturday*	Johann Strauss d. 1849. Dmitry Shostakovich b. 1906	269
26	*Sunday*	James Kier Hardie d. 1915. George Gershwin b. 1898	270
27	*Monday*	R. V. Jones b. 1911. Gracie Fields d. 1979	week 39 day 271
28	*Tuesday*	Herman Melville d. 1891. Leslie Crowther d. 1996	272
29	*Wednesday*	Lord Horatio Nelson b. 1758. Trevor Howard b. 1916	273
30	*Thursday*	Marc Bolan b. 1947. Deborah Kerr. b. 1911	274

ASTRONOMICAL PHENOMENA

d	h	
2	13	Mercury at stationary point
9	14	Mercury at greatest elongation W.18
10	00	Saturn in conjunction with Moon. Saturn 5°S.
10	19	Venus in conjunction with Moon. Venus 6°S.
13	04	Mercury in conjunction with Moon. Mercury 3°S.
14	15	Mars in conjunction with Moon. Mars 2°S.
15	01	Jupiter in conjunction with Moon. Jupiter 2°S.
15	13	Mars in conjunction
22	00	Jupiter in conjunction
22	16	Sun's longitude 180° ♎
27	00	Jupiter in conjunction with Mars. Jupiter 0°.2 N.
29	01	Jupiter in conjunction with Mercury. Jupiter 0°.6 S.
29	19	Mars in conjunction with Mercury. Mars 0°.8 S.

MINIMA OF ALGOL

d	h	d	h	d	h
2	21.0	14	08.2	25	19.5
5	17.8	17	05.0	28	16.3
8	14.6	20	01.9		
11	11.4	22	22.7		

CONSTELLATIONS

The following constellations are near the meridian at

	d	h		d	h
August	1	24	September	15	21
August	16	23	October	1	20
September	1	22	October	16	19

Draco, Cepheus, Lyra, Cygnus, Vulpecula, Sagitta, Delphinus, Equuleus, Aquila, Aquarius and Capricornus

THE MOON

Phases, Apsides and Node	d	h	m
☾ Last Quarter	6	15	10
● New Moon	14	14	29
☽ First Quarter	21	15	54
○ Full Moon	28	13	09
Apogee (404,426 km)	8	02	43
Perigee (369,624 km)	22	21	04

Mean longitude of ascending node on September 1, 35°

THE SUN

s.d. 15′.9

Day	Right Ascension			Dec.		Equation of Time		Rise 52°		Rise 56°		Transit		Set 52°		Set 56°		Sidereal time			Transit of First Point of Aries		
	h	m	s	°	′	m	s	h	m	h	m	h	m	h	m	h	m	h	m	s	h	m	s
1	10	42	00	+8	14	−0	01	5	12	5	05	12	00	18	47	18	54	22	41	59	1	17	49
2	10	45	37	+7	52	+0	18	5	14	5	07	12	00	18	44	18	51	22	45	55	1	13	53
3	10	49	14	+7	30	+0	37	5	15	5	09	11	59	18	42	18	49	22	49	52	1	09	57
4	10	52	51	+7	08	+0	57	5	17	5	11	11	59	18	40	18	46	22	53	48	1	06	01
5	10	56	28	+6	46	+1	17	5	19	5	12	11	59	18	37	18	43	22	57	45	1	02	05
6	11	00	04	+6	24	+1	37	5	20	5	14	11	58	18	35	18	41	23	01	41	0	58	09
7	11	03	40	+6	01	+1	58	5	22	5	16	11	58	18	33	18	38	23	05	38	0	54	13
8	11	07	16	+5	39	+2	18	5	23	5	18	11	58	18	30	18	35	23	09	34	0	50	17
9	11	10	52	+5	16	+2	39	5	25	5	20	11	57	18	28	18	33	23	13	31	0	46	21
10	11	14	28	+4	54	+3	00	5	27	5	22	11	57	18	26	18	30	23	17	28	0	42	26
11	11	18	03	+4	31	+3	21	5	28	5	24	11	56	18	24	18	28	23	21	24	0	38	30
12	11	21	39	+4	08	+3	42	5	30	5	26	11	56	18	21	18	25	23	25	21	0	34	34
13	11	25	14	+3	45	+4	03	5	32	5	28	11	56	18	19	18	22	23	29	17	0	30	38
14	11	28	50	+3	22	+4	24	5	33	5	30	11	55	18	17	18	20	23	33	14	0	26	42
15	11	32	25	+2	59	+4	45	5	35	5	32	11	55	18	14	18	17	23	37	10	0	22	46
16	11	36	00	+2	36	+5	07	5	37	5	34	11	55	18	12	18	14	23	41	07	0	18	50
17	11	39	35	+2	13	+5	28	5	38	5	36	11	54	18	10	18	12	23	45	03	0	14	54
18	11	43	11	+1	49	+5	49	5	40	5	38	11	54	18	07	18	09	23	49	00	0	10	58
19	11	46	46	+1	26	+6	11	5	41	5	40	11	54	18	05	18	06	23	52	56	0	07	02
20	11	50	21	+1	03	+6	32	5	43	5	42	11	53	18	02	18	04	23	56	53	0	03	06
21	11	53	56	+0	39	+6	53	5	45	5	44	11	53	18	00	18	01	0	00	50	{23 59 11 / 23 55 15}		
22	11	57	32	+0	16	+7	14	5	46	5	46	11	53	17	58	17	58	0	04	46	23	51	19
23	12	01	07	−0	07	+7	36	5	48	5	48	11	52	17	55	17	56	0	08	43	23	47	23
24	12	04	43	−0	31	+7	56	5	50	5	50	11	52	17	53	17	53	0	12	39	23	43	27
25	12	08	18	−0	54	+8	17	5	51	5	52	11	52	17	51	17	50	0	16	36	23	39	31
26	12	11	54	−1	17	+8	38	5	53	5	54	11	51	17	48	17	48	0	20	32	23	35	35
27	12	15	30	−1	41	+8	59	5	55	5	56	11	51	17	46	17	45	0	24	29	23	31	39
28	12	19	07	−2	04	+9	19	5	56	5	57	11	51	17	44	17	42	0	28	25	23	27	43
29	12	22	43	−2	27	+9	39	5	58	5	59	11	50	17	41	17	40	0	32	22	23	23	47
30	12	26	20	−2	51	+9	59	6	00	6	01	11	50	17	39	17	37	0	36	19	23	19	51

DURATION OF TWILIGHT (in minutes)

Latitude	52°	56°	52°	56°	52°	56°	52°	56°
	1 September		11 September		21 September		30 September	
Civil	35	39	34	38	34	37	34	37
Nautical	79	89	76	85	74	82	73	80
Astronomical	127	147	120	136	116	129	113	125

THE NIGHT SKY

Mercury reaches greatest western elongation (18 degrees) on the 9th. It is therefore visible as a morning object after the first few days of the month and this is the most favourable morning apparition of the year for observers in the British Isles. It may then be seen low above the eastern horizon around the time of beginning of morning civil twilight. During this period its magnitude brightens from +1.2 to −1.2. On the morning of the 10th Mercury passes only 2 arcminutes south of Regulus after sunrise. Earlier, observers may be able to detect Regulus with binoculars, only about 5 arcminutes to the left of the planet. Mercury is nearly 2 magnitudes brighter than Regulus. The planet will be seen about 3 degrees to the right of the old crescent Moon, little more than a day before the New Moon, on the morning of the 13th. Mercury is too close to the Sun to be visible during the last ten days of the month.

Venus, magnitude −4.2, is still visible as a brilliant object in the eastern sky before dawn. The old crescent Moon will be near the planet on the mornings of the 10th and 11th. At the very beginning of the month Venus will be seen passing south of Castor and Pollux.

Mars passes slowly through conjunction on the 15th and therefore remains too close to the Sun for observation.

Jupiter passes through conjunction on the 21st and is therefore too close to the Sun for observation.

Saturn, magnitude +0.2, continues to be visible as a morning object in the eastern sky. It will be rising above the east-north-east horizon before midnight by the end of the month. Early on the 10th the old crescent Moon passes 4 degrees north of the planet.

Zodiacal Light. The morning cone may be seen reaching up from the eastern horizon along the ecliptic, before the beginning of morning twilight, from the 12th to the 26th.

THE MOON

Day	RA h m	Dec. °	Hor. par. '	Semi-diam. '	Sun's co-long. °	PA of Bright Limb °	Phase %	Age d	Rise 52° h m	Rise 56° h m	Transit h m	Set 52° h m	Set 56° h m
1	0 17	− 0.9	57.9	15.8	109	72	95	15.9	19 50	19 47	1 38	7 54	7 55
2	1 05	+ 5.3	57.1	15.6	121	69	90	16.9	20 02	19 53	2 23	9 14	9 20
3	1 52	+11.1	56.3	15.4	133	70	83	17.9	20 15	20 01	3 07	10 31	10 44
4	2 39	+16.4	55.6	15.2	145	72	75	18.9	20 32	20 12	3 52	11 48	12 07
5	3 28	+20.8	55.0	15.0	157	75	66	19.9	20 53	20 27	4 39	13 04	13 29
6	4 18	+24.2	54.6	14.9	169	80	56	20.9	21 22	20 49	5 27	14 16	14 48
7	5 10	+26.6	54.3	14.8	182	85	47	21.9	22 01	21 24	6 17	15 21	15 58
8	6 03	+27.8	54.2	14.8	194	91	37	22.9	22 53	22 16	7 08	16 16	16 53
9	6 56	+27.6	54.3	14.8	206	98	28	23.9	23 56	23 23	7 59	16 58	17 31
10	7 49	+26.2	54.5	14.8	218	104	20	24.9	— —	— —	8 50	17 28	17 56
11	8 41	+23.6	54.9	14.9	231	111	13	25.9	1 08	0 42	9 39	17 51	18 12
12	9 32	+19.9	55.3	15.1	243	117	7	26.9	2 24	2 05	10 26	18 08	18 23
13	10 21	+15.2	55.8	15.2	255	124	3	27.9	3 42	3 29	11 12	18 22	18 31
14	11 08	+ 9.8	56.4	15.4	267	141	1	28.9	5 00	4 53	11 56	18 34	18 38
15	11 55	+ 3.8	57.0	15.5	279	262	0	0.4	6 19	6 17	12 40	18 45	18 44
16	12 42	− 2.4	57.5	15.7	292	287	2	1.4	7 38	7 42	13 25	18 57	18 51
17	13 30	− 8.6	58.0	15.8	304	290	7	2.4	9 00	9 10	14 13	19 10	18 58
18	14 21	−14.5	58.4	15.9	316	289	13	3.4	10 26	10 43	15 03	19 27	19 09
19	15 15	−19.8	58.7	16.0	328	286	22	4.4	11 54	12 18	15 57	19 50	19 25
20	16 12	−24.0	59.0	16.1	341	282	32	5.4	13 21	13 53	16 55	20 24	19 51
21	17 14	−26.8	59.2	16.1	353	275	43	6.4	14 40	15 18	17 57	21 13	20 35
22	18 17	−27.9	59.3	16.2	5	268	54	7.4	15 42	16 19	19 00	22 21	21 44
23	19 21	−27.2	59.3	16.2	17	260	65	8.4	16 26	16 57	20 01	23 44	23 14
24	20 23	−24.7	59.3	16.1	29	253	76	9.4	16 56	17 19	20 59	— —	— —
25	21 22	−20.7	59.1	16.1	42	247	85	10.4	17 17	17 33	21 53	1 13	0 51
26	22 17	−15.5	58.8	16.0	54	242	92	11.4	17 32	17 42	22 42	2 42	2 27
27	23 09	− 9.6	58.4	15.9	66	236	97	12.4	17 45	17 49	23 29	4 07	4 00
28	23 59	− 3.3	57.9	15.8	78	224	100	13.4	17 56	17 55	— —	5 30	5 28
29	0 46	+ 3.0	57.3	15.6	90	85	100	14.4	18 08	18 02	0 14	6 50	6 54
30	1 33	+ 9.0	56.7	15.4	102	71	98	15.4	18 20	18 09	0 59	8 08	8 18

MERCURY

Day	RA h m	Dec. °	Diam. "	Phase %	Transit h m	5° high 52° h m	5° high 56° h m
1	9 50	+10.8	9	13	11 06	4 44	4 38
3	9 50	+11.4	9	19	10 59	4 33	4 27
5	9 52	+11.9	8	26	10 54	4 26	4 19
7	9 57	+12.1	8	35	10 51	4 21	4 15
9	10 04	+12.0	7	44	10 50	4 21	4 14
11	10 12	+11.8	7	52	10 51	4 23	4 17
13	10 22	+11.2	7	61	10 54	4 28	4 22
15	10 33	+10.5	6	69	10 57	4 36	4 31
17	10 46	+ 9.5	6	77	11 02	4 45	4 41
19	10 59	+ 8.4	6	83	11 07	4 56	4 53
21	11 12	+ 7.1	5	88	11 12	5 08	5 06
23	11 25	+ 5.8	5	92	11 18	5 21	5 20
25	11 39	+ 4.3	5	95	11 23	5 34	5 34
27	11 52	+ 2.8	5	97	11 29	5 47	5 49
29	12 05	+ 1.3	5	98	11 34	6 01	6 03
31	12 19	− 0.3	5	99	11 40	6 14	6 18

VENUS

Day	RA h m	Dec. °	Diam. "	Phase %	Transit h m	5° high 52° h m	5° high 56° h m
1	7 41	+19.3	20	57	8 59	1 50	1 36
6	8 03	+18.7	19	60	9 02	1 56	1 43
11	8 26	+17.9	19	62	9 04	2 03	1 51
16	8 48	+16.9	18	64	9 07	2 12	2 01
21	9 11	+15.7	17	66	9 10	2 21	2 12
26	9 34	+14.3	17	68	9 13	2 32	2 24
31	9 56	+12.7	16	70	9 16	2 44	2 36

MARS

Day	RA h m	Dec. °	Diam. "	Phase %	Transit h m	5° high 52° h m	5° high 56° h m
1	11 02	+7.4	4	100	12 19	6 14	6 12
6	11 13	+6.1	4	100	12 11	6 13	6 11
11	11 25	+4.8	4	100	12 03	6 12	6 11
16	11 37	+3.5	4	100	11 55	6 10	6 11
21	11 49	+2.2	4	100	11 47	6 09	6 10
26	12 01	+0.9	4	100	11 39	6 08	6 10
31	12 12	−0.4	4	100	11 31	6 07	6 10

SUNRISE AND SUNSET

	London 0°05' 51°30'		Bristol 2°35' 51°28'		Birmingham 1°55' 52°28'		Manchester 2°15' 53°28'		Newcastle 1°37' 54°59'		Glasgow 4°14' 55°52'		Belfast 5°56' 54°35'	
	h m	h m	h m	h m	h m	h m	h m	h m	h m	h m	h m	h m	h m	h m
1	5 ?	18 46	5 23	18 56	5 19	18 55	5 19	18 58	5 13	18 58	5 22	19 10	5 31	19 15
2	5 1?	18 44	5 25	18 54	5 21	18 53	5 20	18 56	5 15	18 56	5 24	19 08	5 33	19 12
3	5 16	18 42	5 26	18 52	5 22	18 50	5 22	18 53	5 17	18 53	5 26	19 05	5 35	19 10
4	5 18	18 39	5 28	18 49	5 24	18 48	5 24	18 51	5 19	18 51	5 28	19 03	5 37	19 07
5	5 20	18 37	5 30	18 47	5 26	18 46	5 26	18 48	5 21	18 48	5 30	19 00	5 39	19 05
6	5 21	18 35	5 31	18 45	5 27	18 43	5 27	18 46	5 22	18 46	5 32	18 57	5 40	19 02
7	5 23	18 33	5 33	18 42	5 29	18 41	5 29	18 44	5 24	18 43	5 34	18 55	5 42	19 00
8	5 24	18 30	5 34	18 40	5 31	18 39	5 31	18 41	5 26	18 41	5 35	18 52	5 44	18 57
9	5 26	18 28	5 36	18 38	5 32	18 36	5 32	18 39	5 28	18 38	5 37	18 50	5 46	18 55
10	5 28	18 26	5 38	18 36	5 34	18 34	5 34	18 36	5 30	18 35	5 39	18 47	5 48	18 52
11	5 29	18 23	5 39	18 33	5 36	18 32	5 36	18 34	5 32	18 33	5 41	18 44	5 50	18 50
12	5 31	18 21	5 41	18 31	5 37	18 29	5 38	18 31	5 34	18 30	5 43	18 42	5 51	18 47
13	5 32	18 19	5 42	18 29	5 39	18 27	5 39	18 29	5 36	18 28	5 45	18 39	5 53	18 45
14	5 34	18 17	5 44	18 26	5 41	18 25	5 41	18 27	5 37	18 25	5 47	18 36	5 55	18 42
15	5 36	18 14	5 46	18 24	5 42	18 22	5 43	18 24	5 39	18 23	5 49	18 34	5 57	18 40
16	5 37	18 12	5 47	18 22	5 44	18 20	5 45	18 22	5 41	18 20	5 51	18 31	5 59	18 37
17	5 39	18 10	5 49	18 20	5 46	18 17	5 46	18 19	5 43	18 17	5 53	18 28	6 01	18 35
18	5 40	18 07	5 50	18 17	5 47	18 15	5 48	18 17	5 45	18 15	5 55	18 26	6 02	18 32
19	5 42	18 05	5 52	18 15	5 49	18 13	5 50	18 14	5 47	18 12	5 57	18 23	6 04	18 29
20	5 44	18 03	5 54	18 13	5 51	18 10	5 52	18 12	5 49	18 10	5 59	18 20	6 06	18 27
21	5 45	18 00	5 55	18 10	5 52	18 08	5 53	18 09	5 50	18 07	6 01	18 18	6 08	18 24
22	5 47	17 58	5 57	18 08	5 54	18 05	5 55	18 07	5 52	18 05	6 03	18 15	6 10	18 22
23	5 48	17 56	5 58	18 06	5 56	18 03	5 57	18 04	5 54	18 02	6 05	18 13	6 12	18 19
24	5 50	17 53	6 00	18 03	5 57	18 01	5 59	18 02	5 56	17 59	6 07	18 10	6 13	18 17
25	5 52	17 51	6 02	18 01	5 59	17 58	6 00	18 00	5 58	17 57	6 08	18 07	6 15	18 14
26	5 53	17 49	6 03	17 59	6 01	17 56	6 02	17 57	6 00	17 54	6 10	18 05	6 17	18 12
27	5 55	17 47	6 05	17 57	6 02	17 54	6 04	17 55	6 02	17 52	6 12	18 02	6 19	18 09
28	5 56	17 44	6 06	17 54	6 04	17 51	6 06	17 52	6 04	17 49	6 14	17 59	6 21	18 07
29	5 58	17 42	6 08	17 52	6 06	17 49	6 07	17 50	6 06	17 47	6 16	17 57	6 23	18 04
30	6 00	17 40	6 10	17 50	6 07	17 47	6 09	17 47	6 07	17 44	6 18	17 54	6 25	18 02

JUPITER

Day	RA		Dec.		Transit		5° high			
							52°		56°	
	h	m	°	'	h	m	h	m	h	m
1	11	42.7	+3	03	12	59	7	17	7	18
11	11	50.5	+2	12	12	27	6	50	6	51
21	11	58.4	+1	21	11	56	6	23	6	25
31	12	06.4	+0	30	11	25	5	55	5	58

Diameters – equatorial 31″ polar 29″

SATURN

Day	RA		Dec.		Transit		5° high			
							52°		56°	
	h	m	°	'	h	m	h	m	h	m
1	7	40.9	+21	13	8	58	1	38	1	22
11	7	45.1	+21	04	8	22	1	04	0	48
21	7	48.8	+20	55	7	47	0	29	0	14
31	7	51.9	+20	48	7	11	23	50	23	35

Diameters – equatorial 17″ polar 16″
Rings – major axis 39″ minor axis 15″

URANUS

Day	RA		Dec.		Transit		10° high			
							52°		56°	
	h	m	°	'	h	m	h	m	h	m
1	22	27.2	-10	33	23	41	3	38	3	19
11	22	25.7	-10	42	23	00	2	56	2	38
21	22	24.3	-10	50	22	20	2	15	1	56
31	22	23.1	-10	57	21	39	1	33	1	14

Diameter 4″

NEPTUNE

Day	RA		Dec.		Transit		10° high			
							52°		56°	
	h	m	°	'	h	m	h	m	h	m
1	21	03.2	-16	54	22	18	1	29	0	58
11	21	02.3	-16	58	21	37	0	48	0	17
21	21	01.6	-17	01	20	57	0	07	23	32
31	21	01.0	-17	03	20	17	23	23	22	52

Diameter 2″

OCTOBER 2004

TENTH MONTH, 31 DAYS. *Octo* (eighth), eighth month of Roman pre-Julian calendar

1	*Friday*	First issue of News of the World 1843. Julie Andrews b. 1935	275
2	*Saturday*	Dr Marie Stopes d. 1958. Mahatma Gandhi b. 1869	276
3	*Sunday*	James Herriot b. 1916. George Bancroft b. 1800	277
4	*Monday*	Sputnik I launched 1957. Buster Keaton b. 1895	week 40 day 278
5	*Tuesday*	Oxfam founded 1942. Leon Trotsky b. 1879	279
6	*Wednesday*	Britt Ekland b. 1942. Thor Heyerdahl b. 1914	280
7	*Thursday*	Edgar Allan Poe d. 1849. Bishop Desmond Tutu b. 1931	281
8	*Friday*	Great Fire of Chicago 1871. Dame Betty Boothroyd b. 1929	282
9	*Saturday*	Breathalyser testing came into force 1967	283
10	*Sunday*	Harold Pinter b. 1930. David Lee Roth b. 1955	284
11	*Monday*	Donald Dewar d. 2000. Edith Piaf d. 1963	week 41 day 285
12	*Tuesday*	General Robert E. Lee d. 1870. Luciano Pavarotti b. 1935	286
13	*Wednesday*	Margaret Thatcher b. 1925. Beryl Reid d. 1996	287
14	*Thursday*	Battle of Hastings 1066. William Penn b. 1644	288
15	*Friday*	First manned balloon flight 1783. Cole Porter d. 1964	289
16	*Saturday*	Houses of Parliament destroyed by fire 1834. Noah Webster b. 1758	290
17	*Sunday*	Arthur Miller b. 1915. Sir Philip Sidney d. 1586	291
18	*Monday*	Thomas Alva Edison d. 1931. Martina Navratilova b. 1956	week 42 day 292
19	*Tuesday*	Sir Thomas Browne b. 1605. Kenneth Wood d. 1997	293
20	*Wednesday*	Grace Darling d. 1842. Sir Christopher Wren b. 1632	294
21	*Thursday*	Battle of Trafalgar 1805. Sir Alan Cobham d. 1973	295
22	*Friday*	Franz Liszt b. 1811. Joan Fontaine b. 1917	296
23	*Saturday*	Dr. W. G. Grace d. 1915. Theophile Gautier d. 1872	297
24	*Sunday*	United Nations formally came into existence 1945	298
25	*Monday*	Battle of Agincourt 1415. Geoffrey Chaucer d. 1400	week 43 day 299
26	*Tuesday*	Joseph Aloysius Hansom b. 1803. François Mitterand b. 1916	300
27	*Wednesday*	Dylan Thomas b. 1914. Charles Hawtrey d. 1988	301
28	*Thursday*	Statue of Liberty unveiled 1886. Ted Hughes d. 1998	302
29	*Friday*	Wall Street Crash 1929. James Boswell b. 1740	303
30	*Saturday*	Ezra Pound b. 1885. Michael Winner b. 1935	304
31	*Sunday*	Indira Gandhi d. 1984. John Evelyn b. 1620	305

ASTRONOMICAL PHENOMENA

d h
5 18 Mercury in superior conjunction
7 12 Saturn in conjunction with Moon. Saturn 5°S.
10 22 Venus in conjunction with Moon. Venus 4°S.
12 20 Jupiter in conjunction with Moon. Jupiter 1°S.
13 09 Mars in conjunction with Moon. Mars 1°S.
14 03 Partial eclipse of Sun
14 14 Mercury in conjunction with Moon. Mercury 0°.1 S.
23 02 Sun's longitude 210° ♏
24 12 Neptune at stationary point
28 03 Total eclipse of Moon

MINIMA OF ALGOL

d	h	d	h	d	h
1	13.1	13	00.3	24	11.6
4	09.9	15	21.2	27	08.4
7	06.7	18	18.0	30	05.2
10	03.5	21	14.8		

CONSTELLATIONS

The following constellations are near the meridian at

d	h		d	h
September 1	24	October	16	21
September 15	23	November	1	20
October 1	22	November	15	19

Ursa Major (below the Pole), Cepheus, Cassiopeia, Cygnus, Lacerta, Andromeda, Pegasus, Capricornus, Aquarius and Piscis Austrinus

THE MOON

Phases, Apsides and Node	d	h	m
☾ Last Quarter	6	10	12
● New Moon	14	02	48
☽ First Quarter	20	21	59
○ Full Moon	28	03	07
Apogee (404,287 km)	5	22	09
Perigee (367,786 km)	17	23	44

Mean longitude of ascending node on October 1, 33°

THE SUN

s.d. 16'.1

Day	Right Ascension h m s			Dec. ° '		Equation of Time – m s		Rise 52° h m		56° h m		Transit h m		Set 52° h m		56° h m		Sidereal time h m s			Transit of First Point of Aries h m s		
1	12	29	57	3	14	+10	18	6	01	6	03	11	50	17	37	17	35	0	40	15	23	15	56
2	12	33	34	3	37	+10	38	6	03	6	05	11	49	17	35	17	32	0	44	12	23	12	00
3	12	37	12	4	00	+10	57	6	05	6	07	11	49	17	32	17	29	0	48	08	23	08	04
4	12	40	50	4	24	+11	15	6	06	6	09	11	49	17	30	17	27	0	52	05	23	04	08
5	12	44	28	4	47	+11	33	6	08	6	11	11	48	17	28	17	24	0	56	01	23	00	12
6	12	48	07	5	10	+11	51	6	10	6	13	11	48	17	25	17	21	0	59	58	22	56	16
7	12	51	46	5	33	+12	09	6	11	6	15	11	48	17	23	17	19	1	03	54	22	52	20
8	12	55	25	5	56	+12	26	6	13	6	17	11	47	17	21	17	16	1	07	51	22	48	24
9	12	59	05	6	19	+12	42	6	15	6	19	11	47	17	19	17	14	1	11	48	22	44	28
10	13	02	46	6	41	+12	58	6	17	6	22	11	47	17	16	17	11	1	15	44	22	40	32
11	13	06	27	7	04	+13	14	6	18	6	24	11	47	17	14	17	09	1	19	41	22	36	36
12	13	10	08	7	27	+13	29	6	20	6	26	11	46	17	12	17	06	1	23	37	22	32	41
13	13	13	50	7	49	+13	44	6	22	6	28	11	46	17	10	17	04	1	27	34	22	28	45
14	13	17	33	8	11	+13	58	6	23	6	30	11	46	17	08	17	01	1	31	30	22	24	49
15	13	21	16	8	34	+14	11	6	25	6	32	11	46	17	05	16	59	1	35	27	22	20	53
16	13	24	59	8	56	+14	24	6	27	6	34	11	45	17	03	16	56	1	39	23	22	16	57
17	13	28	43	9	18	+14	37	6	29	6	36	11	45	17	01	16	54	1	43	20	22	13	01
18	13	32	28	9	40	+14	48	6	30	6	38	11	45	16	59	16	51	1	47	17	22	09	05
19	13	36	13	10	01	+15	00	6	32	6	40	11	45	16	57	16	49	1	51	13	22	05	09
20	13	39	59	10	23	+15	10	6	34	6	42	11	45	16	55	16	46	1	55	10	22	01	13
21	13	43	46	10	44	+15	20	6	36	6	44	11	45	16	53	16	44	1	59	06	21	57	17
22	13	47	33	11	06	+15	30	6	37	6	46	11	44	16	51	16	42	2	03	03	21	53	21
23	13	51	21	11	27	+15	38	6	39	6	48	11	44	16	49	16	39	2	06	59	21	49	26
24	13	55	10	11	48	+15	46	6	41	6	51	11	44	16	47	16	37	2	10	56	21	45	30
25	13	58	59	12	08	+15	54	6	43	6	53	11	44	16	45	16	35	2	14	52	21	41	34
26	14	02	49	12	29	+16	00	6	45	6	55	11	44	16	43	16	32	2	18	49	21	37	38
27	14	06	39	12	49	+16	06	6	46	6	57	11	44	16	41	16	30	2	22	46	21	33	42
28	14	10	31	13	10	+16	11	6	48	6	59	11	44	16	39	16	28	2	26	42	21	29	46
29	14	14	23	13	29	+16	16	6	50	7	01	11	44	16	37	16	25	2	30	39	21	25	50
30	14	18	16	13	49	+16	19	6	52	7	03	11	44	16	35	16	23	2	34	35	21	21	54
31	14	22	10	14	09	+16	22	6	54	7	05	11	44	16	33	16	21	2	38	32	21	17	58

DURATION OF TWILIGHT (in minutes)

Latitude	52°	56°	52°	56°	52°	56°	52°	56°
	1 October		11 October		21 October		31 October	
Civil	34	37	34	37	34	38	35	39
Nautical	73	80	73	80	74	81	75	83
Astronomical	113	125	112	124	113	124	114	126

THE NIGHT SKY

Mercury passes through superior conjunction on the 5th and is therefore unsuitably placed for observation throughout the month.

Venus, magnitude −4.1, continues to be visible as a brilliant object in the eastern sky in the early mornings before sunrise. The waning crescent Moon is near the planet on the mornings of the 10th and 11th. Venus makes a very close approach to Regulus in Leo on the morning of the 3rd, the minimum separation being only 0.1 degrees.

Mars continues to be too close to the Sun for observation during October but will reappear in the morning skies early next month.

Jupiter emerges from the morning twilight after the first week of the month and can then be seen low above the eastern horizon before dawn. Its magnitude is −1.7. Jupiter is in the constellation of Virgo.

Saturn, magnitude +0.1, although technically a morning object, is now becoming visible in the eastern sky in the late evenings. The Moon, at Last Quarter, passes 5 degrees north of the planet on the 7th. During October Saturn moves from Gemini into Cancer. The observer armed with a small telescope will notice that the rings of Saturn present a beautiful spectacle. The rings were at their maximum opening early in 2003 when the rings extended beyond the polar diameter of Saturn. The diameter of the minor axis is now 15 arcseconds, slightly less than the polar diameter of the planet itself.

THE MOON

Day	RA h m	Dec. °	Hor. par. '	Semi-diam. '	Sun's co-long. °	PA of Bright Limb °	Phase %	Age d	Rise 52° h m	Rise 56° h m	Transit h m	Set 52° h m	Set 56° h m
1	2 21	+14.6	56.0	15.3	115	70	93	16.4	18 35	18 18	1 44	9 27	9 43
2	3 10	+19.4	55.4	15.1	127	73	88	17.4	18 54	18 30	2 30	10 45	11 07
3	4 00	+23.3	54.9	15.0	139	76	81	18.4	19 19	18 49	3 18	12 00	12 29
4	4 52	+26.1	54.5	14.9	151	82	72	19.4	19 54	19 19	4 08	13 09	13 44
5	5 45	+27.7	54.3	14.8	163	87	63	20.4	20 41	20 03	4 59	14 08	14 46
6	6 38	+28.0	54.2	14.8	175	93	54	21.4	21 40	21 04	5 50	14 55	15 31
7	7 31	+27.0	54.3	14.8	188	99	45	22.4	22 48	22 19	6 41	15 30	16 00
8	8 24	+24.8	54.6	14.9	200	105	35	23.4	— —	23 40	7 30	15 55	16 19
9	9 14	+21.4	55.0	15.0	212	110	26	24.4	0 03	— —	8 18	16 14	16 32
10	10 03	+17.1	55.6	15.2	224	114	18	25.4	1 20	1 04	9 04	16 29	16 41
11	10 51	+11.9	56.3	15.3	236	118	11	26.4	2 38	2 27	9 49	16 41	16 48
12	11 38	+ 6.1	57.0	15.5	249	120	5	27.4	3 56	3 52	10 33	16 52	16 54
13	12 25	− 0.2	57.7	15.7	261	123	2	28.4	5 16	5 18	11 18	17 04	17 00
14	13 14	− 6.6	58.4	15.9	273	150	0	29.4	6 39	6 46	12 05	17 17	17 07
15	14 05	−12.8	58.9	16.1	285	290	1	0.9	8 05	8 19	12 56	17 32	17 16
16	14 59	−18.4	59.3	16.2	298	290	5	1.9	9 35	9 57	13 50	17 53	17 30
17	15 57	−23.1	59.5	16.2	310	285	11	2.9	11 06	11 36	14 48	18 23	17 52
18	16 58	−26.4	59.6	16.2	322	279	19	3.9	12 30	13 07	15 50	19 08	18 30
19	18 02	−27.9	59.5	16.2	334	272	29	4.9	13 39	14 17	16 54	20 11	19 33
20	19 07	−27.6	59.4	16.2	346	264	40	5.9	14 28	15 01	17 56	21 30	20 58
21	20 10	−25.5	59.1	16.1	359	258	51	6.9	15 01	15 27	18 54	22 57	22 33
22	21 09	−21.9	58.8	16.0	11	252	62	7.9	15 24	15 42	19 48	— —	— —
23	22 04	−17.0	58.4	15.9	23	247	73	8.9	15 40	15 52	20 38	0 25	0 08
24	22 55	−11.4	58.0	15.8	35	244	82	9.9	15 53	15 59	21 24	1 50	1 40
25	23 44	− 5.3	57.5	15.7	47	242	90	10.9	16 04	16 05	22 09	3 11	3 07
26	0 31	+ 0.9	57.0	15.5	59	242	95	11.9	16 15	16 11	22 53	4 30	4 32
27	1 18	+ 7.0	56.5	15.4	72	243	99	12.9	16 27	16 18	23 37	5 48	5 56
28	2 04	+12.8	56.0	15.3	84	254	100	13.9	16 41	16 26	— —	7 06	7 19
29	2 53	+17.8	55.5	15.1	96	66	99	14.9	16 58	16 37	0 23	8 24	8 44
30	3 42	+22.1	55.1	15.0	108	71	97	15.9	17 20	16 52	1 10	9 41	10 08
31	4 34	+25.3	54.7	14.9	120	76	92	16.9	17 50	17 17	1 59	10 54	11 27

MERCURY

Day	RA h m	Dec. °	Diam. "	Phase %	Transit h m	5° high 52° h m	5° high 56° h m
1	12 19	− 0.3	5	99	11 40	6 14	6 18
3	12 31	− 1.9	5	100	11 45	6 27	6 32
5	12 44	− 3.4	5	100	11 49	6 40	6 47
7	12 57	− 4.9	5	100	11 54	6 53	7 01
9	13 09	− 6.4	5	100	11 59	7 06	7 15
11	13 22	− 7.9	5	99	12 03	16 46	16 35
13	13 34	− 9.3	5	99	12 07	16 42	16 30
15	13 46	−10.7	5	98	12 12	16 38	16 24
17	13 58	−12.1	5	98	12 16	16 34	16 19
19	14 10	−13.4	5	97	12 20	16 31	16 14
21	14 22	−14.6	5	96	12 24	16 27	16 08
23	14 34	−15.8	5	95	12 28	16 23	16 03
25	14 46	−17.0	5	95	12 32	16 19	15 57
27	14 58	−18.1	5	94	12 36	16 16	15 52
29	15 10	−19.1	5	92	12 40	16 13	15 47
31	15 22	−20.1	5	91	12 44	16 09	15 41

VENUS

Day	RA h m	Dec. °	Diam. "	Phase %	Transit h m	5° high 52° h m	5° high 56° h m
1	9 56	+12.7	16	70	9 16	2 44	2 36
6	10 19	+11.0	16	72	9 19	2 56	2 50
11	10 42	+ 9.1	15	74	9 22	3 08	3 04
16	11 04	+ 7.1	15	75	9 25	3 21	3 19
21	11 26	+ 4.9	14	77	9 28	3 35	3 34
26	11 49	+ 2.7	14	78	9 30	3 49	3 50
31	12 11	+ 0.5	14	80	9 33	4 03	4 06

MARS

Day	RA h m	Dec. °	Diam. "	Phase %	Transit h m	5° high 52° h m	5° high 56° h m
1	12 12	−0.4	4	100	11 31	6 07	6 10
6	12 24	−1.7	4	100	11 24	6 06	6 10
11	12 36	−3.0	4	100	11 16	6 05	6 11
16	12 48	−4.3	4	100	11 08	6 04	6 11
21	13 00	−5.6	4	100	11 00	6 03	6 11
26	13 12	−6.9	4	100	10 53	6 03	6 12
31	13 25	−8.1	4	99	10 45	6 02	6 13

SUNRISE AND SUNSET

	London 0°05' / 51°30'		Bristol 2°35' / 51°28'		Birmingham 1°55' / 52°28'		Manchester 2°15' / 53°28'		Newcastle 1°37' / 54°59'		Glasgow 4°14' / 55°52'		Belfast 5°56' / 54°35'	
	h m	h m	h m	h m	h m	h m	h m	h m	h m	h m	h m	h m	h m	h m
1	6 01	17 37	6 11	17 47	6 09	17 44	6 11	17 45	6 09	17 42	6 20	17 52	6 26	17 59
2	6 03	17 35	6 13	17 45	6 11	17 42	6 13	17 43	6 11	17 39	6 22	17 49	6 28	17 57
3	6 05	17 33	6 15	17 43	6 13	17 40	6 15	17 40	6 13	17 37	6 24	17 46	6 30	17 54
4	6 06	17 31	6 16	17 41	6 14	17 37	6 16	17 38	6 15	17 34	6 26	17 44	6 32	17 52
5	6 08	17 28	6 18	17 38	6 16	17 35	6 18	17 35	6 17	17 32	6 28	17 41	6 34	17 49
6	6 10	17 26	6 20	17 36	6 18	17 33	6 20	17 33	6 19	17 29	6 30	17 39	6 36	17 47
7	6 11	17 24	6 21	17 34	6 19	17 30	6 22	17 31	6 21	17 27	6 32	17 36	6 38	17 44
8	6 13	17 22	6 23	17 32	6 21	17 28	6 24	17 28	6 23	17 24	6 34	17 33	6 40	17 42
9	6 15	17 20	6 25	17 30	6 23	17 26	6 25	17 26	6 25	17 22	6 36	17 31	6 41	17 39
10	6 16	17 17	6 26	17 27	6 25	17 23	6 27	17 24	6 27	17 19	6 38	17 28	6 43	17 37
11	6 18	17 15	6 28	17 25	6 26	17 21	6 29	17 21	6 29	17 17	6 40	17 26	6 45	17 34
12	6 20	17 13	6 30	17 23	6 28	17 19	6 31	17 19	6 31	17 14	6 42	17 23	6 47	17 32
13	6 21	17 11	6 31	17 21	6 30	17 17	6 33	17 17	6 33	17 12	6 44	17 21	6 49	17 30
14	6 23	17 09	6 33	17 19	6 32	17 15	6 35	17 14	6 34	17 09	6 46	17 18	6 51	17 27
15	6 25	17 06	6 35	17 17	6 34	17 12	6 36	17 12	6 36	17 07	6 49	17 16	6 53	17 25
16	6 26	17 04	6 36	17 14	6 35	17 10	6 38	17 10	6 38	17 05	6 51	17 13	6 55	17 23
17	6 28	17 02	6 38	17 12	6 37	17 08	6 40	17 08	6 40	17 02	6 53	17 11	6 57	17 20
18	6 30	17 00	6 40	17 10	6 39	17 06	6 42	17 05	6 42	17 00	6 55	17 08	6 59	17 18
19	6 32	16 58	6 42	17 08	6 41	17 04	6 44	17 03	6 44	16 57	6 57	17 06	7 01	17 16
20	6 33	16 56	6 43	17 06	6 42	17 02	6 46	17 01	6 46	16 55	6 59	17 04	7 03	17 13
21	6 35	16 54	6 45	17 04	6 44	16 59	6 48	16 59	6 48	16 53	7 01	17 01	7 05	17 11
22	6 37	16 52	6 47	17 02	6 46	16 57	6 50	16 56	6 50	16 50	7 03	16 59	7 07	17 09
23	6 39	16 50	6 48	17 00	6 48	16 55	6 51	16 54	6 52	16 48	7 05	16 56	7 09	17 06
24	6 40	16 48	6 50	16 58	6 50	16 53	6 53	16 52	6 54	16 46	7 07	16 54	7 11	17 04
25	6 42	16 46	6 52	16 56	6 52	16 51	6 55	16 50	6 56	16 44	7 09	16 52	7 13	17 02
26	6 44	16 44	6 54	16 54	6 53	16 49	6 57	16 48	6 58	16 41	7 11	16 49	7 15	17 00
27	6 46	16 42	6 55	16 52	6 55	16 47	6 59	16 46	7 01	16 39	7 14	16 47	7 17	16 58
28	6 47	16 40	6 57	16 50	6 57	16 45	7 01	16 44	7 03	16 37	7 16	16 45	7 19	16 55
29	6 49	16 38	6 59	16 48	6 59	16 43	7 03	16 42	7 05	16 35	7 18	16 43	7 21	16 53
30	6 51	16 36	7 01	16 47	7 01	16 41	7 05	16 40	7 07	16 33	7 20	16 40	7 23	16 51
31	6 53	16 35	7 02	16 45	7 02	16 39	7 07	16 38	7 09	16 31	7 22	16 38	7 25	16 49

JUPITER

Day	RA		Dec.		Transit		5° high			
							52°		56°	
	h	m	°	'	h	m	h	m	h	m
1	12	06.4	+0	30	11	25	5	55	5	58
11	12	14.2	−0	21	10	53	5	28	5	32
21	12	22.0	−1	11	10	22	5	01	5	05
31	12	29.5	−1	58	9	50	4	33	4	38

Diameters – equatorial 31″ polar 29″

SATURN

Day	RA		Dec.		Transit		5° high			
							52°		56°	
	h	m	°	'	h	m	h	m	h	m
1	7	51.9	+20	48	7	11	23	50	23	35
11	7	54.4	+20	42	6	34	23	14	22	59
21	7	56.2	+20	38	5	56	22	36	22	21
31	7	57.3	+20	36	5	18	21	58	21	43

Diameters – equatorial 18″ polar 17″
Rings – major axis 41″ minor axis 15″

URANUS

Day	RA		Dec.		Transit		10° high			
							52°		56°	
	h	m	°	'	h	m	h	m	h	m
1	22	23.1	−10	57	21	39	1	33	1	14
11	22	22.0	−11	03	20	59	0	52	0	33
21	22	21.2	−11	07	20	19	0	12	23	48
31	22	20.7	−11	09	19	39	23	28	23	08

Diameter 4″

NEPTUNE

Day	RA		Dec.		Transit		10° high			
							52°		56°	
	h	m	°	'	h	m	h	m	h	m
1	21	01.0	−17	03	20	17	23	23	22	52
11	21	00.6	−17	05	19	38	22	43	22	12
21	21	00.4	−17	06	18	58	22	03	21	32
31	21	00.4	−17	06	18	19	21	24	20	53

Diameter 2″

NOVEMBER 2004

ELEVENTH MONTH, 30 DAYS. *Novem* (nine), ninth month of Roman pre-Julian calendar

1	*Monday*	First hydrogen bomb exploded 1952. First premium bonds on sale 1956	week 44 day 306
2	*Tuesday*	First issue of Daily Mirror 1903. Marie Antoinette b. 1755	307
3	*Wednesday*	"Laika" launched into space in Sputnik II 1957. Henri Matisse d. 1954	308
4	*Thursday*	Wilfred Owen d. 1918. Yitzhak Rabin d. 1995	309
5	*Friday*	Guy Fawkes Night. Gunpowder Plot 1605. Lester Piggott b. 1935	310
6	*Saturday*	Abraham Lincoln elected 16th President of the USA 1860	311
7	*Sunday*	Godfrey Kneller d. 1723. Alexander Dubcek d. 1992	312
8	*Monday*	Prof. Christiaan Barnard b. 1922. John Milton d. 1674	week 45 day 313
9	*Tuesday*	Katherine Hepburn b. 1909. Neville Chamberlain d. 1940	314
10	*Wednesday*	Arthur Rimbaud d. 1891. William Hogarth b. 1697	315
11	*Thursday*	Armistice Day 1918. Ned Kelly d. 1880	316
12	*Friday*	General Thomas Fairfax d. 1671. Elizabeth Gaskell d. 1865	317
13	*Saturday*	Robert Louis Stevenson b. 1850. Whoopi Goldberg b. 1949	318
14	*Sunday*	Claude Monet b. 1840. First London to Brighton car run 1896	319
15	*Monday*	William Pitt, Earl of Chatham b. 1708. William Cowper b. 1731	week 46 day 320
16	*Tuesday*	Paul Hindemith b. 1895. George Kaufman b. 1889	321
17	*Wednesday*	Martin Scorcese b. 1942. Auguste Rodin d. 1917	322
18	*Thursday*	Marcel Proust d. 1922. David Wilkie b. 1785	323
19	*Friday*	Gettysburg address 1863. Indira Gandhi b. 1917	324
20	*Saturday*	Fire at Windsor Castle 1992. Edwin Hubble b. 1889	325
21	*Sunday*	Françoise-Marie Voltaire b. 1694. Goldie Hawn b. 1945	326
22	*Monday*	President John F. Kennedy d. 1963. Margaret Thatcher resigned 1990	week 47 day 327
23	*Tuesday*	Boris Karloff b. 1887. Harpo Marx b. 1888	328
24	*Wednesday*	Toulouse Lautrec b. 1864. Robert Erskine Childers d. 1922	329
25	*Thursday*	Lilian Baylis d. 1937. Upton Sinclair d. 1968	330
26	*Friday*	John McAdam d. 1836. Charles M. Schulz b. 1922	331
27	*Saturday*	Anders Celsius b. 1701. Jimi Hendrix b. 1942	332
28	*Sunday*	Sinn Fein founded 1905. Enid Blyton d. 1968	333
29	*Monday*	C. S. Lewis b. 1898. Louisa M. Alcott b. 1832	week 48 day 334
30	*Tuesday*	St Andrews Day. Crystal Palace destroyed by fire 1936	335

ASTRONOMICAL PHENOMENA

d h
3 22 Saturn in conjunction with Moon. Saturn 5°S.
5 02 Jupiter in conjunction with Venus. Jupiter 0°.5 S.
8 07 Saturn at stationary point
9 16 Jupiter in conjunction with Moon. Jupiter 0°.9 S.
10 02 Venus in conjunction with Moon. Venus 0°.2 N.
11 04 Mars in conjunction with Moon. Mars 0°.4 N.
11 19 Uranus at stationary point
14 03 Mercury in conjunction with Moon. Mercury 0°.9 N.
21 01 Mercury at greatest elongation E.22°
21 23 Sun's longitude 240° ♐
30 12 Mercury at stationary point

MINIMA OF ALGOL

d	h	d	h	d	h
2	02.0	13	13.3	25	00.6
4	22.8	16	10.1	27	21.4
7	19.7	19	06.9	30	18.2
10	16.5	22	03.7		

CONSTELLATIONS

The following constellations are near the meridian at

	d	h		d	h
October	1	24	November	15	21
October	16	23	December	1	20
November	1	22	December	16	19

Ursa Major (below the Pole), Cepheus, Cassiopeia, Andromeda, Pegasus, Pisces, Acquaria and Cetus

THE MOON

Phases, Apsides and Node	d	h	m
☾ Last Quarter	5	05	53
● New Moon	12	14	27
☽ First Quarter	19	05	50
○ Full Moon	26	20	07
Apogee (404,962 km)	2	18	04
Perigee (362,328 km)	14	13	47
Apogee (405,928 km)	30	11	14

Mean longitude of ascending node on November 1, 32°

THE SUN

s.d. 16'.2

Day	Right Ascension			Dec.		Equation of Time		Rise 52°		Rise 56°		Transit		Set 52°		Set 56°		Sidereal time			Transit of First Point of Aries		
	h	m	s	°	'	m	s	h	m	h	m	h	m	h	m	h	m	h	m	s	h	m	s
1	14	26	04	14	28	+16	24	6	55	7	08	11	44	16	31	16	19	2	42	28	21	14	02
2	14	29	59	14	47	+16	25	6	57	7	10	11	44	16	29	16	17	2	46	25	21	10	06
3	14	33	56	15	06	+16	26	6	59	7	12	11	44	16	27	16	15	2	50	21	21	06	11
4	14	37	53	15	25	+16	25	7	01	7	14	11	44	16	26	16	12	2	54	18	21	02	15
5	14	41	50	15	43	+16	24	7	03	7	16	11	44	16	24	16	10	2	58	15	20	58	19
6	14	45	49	16	01	+16	22	7	04	7	18	11	44	16	22	16	08	3	02	11	20	54	23
7	14	49	49	16	19	+16	19	7	06	7	20	11	44	16	21	16	06	3	06	08	20	50	27
8	14	53	49	16	36	+16	15	7	08	7	22	11	44	16	19	16	04	3	10	04	20	46	31
9	14	57	50	16	54	+16	11	7	10	7	25	11	44	16	17	16	02	3	14	01	20	42	35
10	15	01	52	17	11	+16	05	7	12	7	27	11	44	16	16	16	01	3	17	57	20	38	39
11	15	05	55	17	27	+15	59	7	13	7	29	11	44	16	14	15	59	3	21	54	20	34	43
12	15	09	59	17	44	+15	51	7	15	7	31	11	44	16	13	15	57	3	25	50	20	30	47
13	15	14	04	18	00	+15	43	7	17	7	33	11	44	16	11	15	55	3	29	47	20	26	51
14	15	18	09	18	15	+15	34	7	19	7	35	11	44	16	10	15	53	3	33	44	20	22	56
15	15	22	16	18	31	+15	25	7	20	7	37	11	45	16	08	15	52	3	37	40	20	19	00
16	15	26	23	18	46	+15	14	7	22	7	39	11	45	16	07	15	50	3	41	37	20	15	04
17	15	30	31	19	01	+15	02	7	24	7	41	11	45	16	06	15	48	3	45	33	20	11	08
18	15	34	40	19	15	+14	50	7	26	7	43	11	45	16	04	15	47	3	49	30	20	07	12
19	15	38	49	19	29	+14	37	7	27	7	45	11	45	16	03	15	45	3	53	26	20	03	16
20	15	43	00	19	43	+14	23	7	29	7	47	11	46	16	02	15	44	3	57	23	19	59	20
21	15	47	11	19	56	+14	09	7	31	7	49	11	46	16	01	15	42	4	01	19	19	55	24
22	15	51	23	20	09	+13	53	7	32	7	51	11	46	16	00	15	41	4	05	16	19	51	28
23	15	55	36	20	22	+13	37	7	34	7	53	11	47	15	59	15	39	4	09	13	19	47	32
24	15	59	49	20	34	+13	20	7	35	7	55	11	47	15	58	15	38	4	13	09	19	43	36
25	16	04	04	20	46	+13	02	7	37	7	57	11	47	15	57	15	37	4	17	06	19	39	41
26	16	08	19	20	58	+12	44	7	39	7	59	11	47	15	56	15	36	4	21	02	19	35	45
27	16	12	34	21	09	+12	24	7	40	8	00	11	48	15	55	15	35	4	24	59	19	31	49
28	16	16	51	21	20	+12	04	7	42	8	02	11	48	15	54	15	34	4	28	55	19	27	53
29	16	21	08	21	30	+11	44	7	43	8	04	11	48	15	53	15	33	4	32	52	19	23	57
30	16	25	26	21	40	+11	22	7	45	8	06	11	49	15	53	15	32	4	36	48	19	20	01

DURATION OF TWILIGHT (in minutes)

Latitude	52°	56°	52°	56°	52°	56°	52°	56°
	1 November		11 November		21 November		30 November	
Civil	36	40	37	41	38	43	40	45
Nautical	75	84	78	87	80	90	82	93
Astronomical	115	127	117	130	120	134	123	138

THE NIGHT SKY

Mercury, despite the fact that it reaches greatest eastern elongation on the 21st, is unsuitably placed for observation during the month.

Venus, magnitude −4.0, continues to be visible as a brilliant object in the eastern morning sky before dawn. The old crescent Moon, only 2 days before New, may be detected nearly 3 degrees below the planet. Venus passes 0.5 degrees north of Jupiter on the 5th and then passes 4 degrees north of Spica on the 16th.

Mars, magnitude +1.7, very slowly becomes a morning object early in the month, low above the south-eastern horizon, by about 06h. The old crescent Moon, only 1 day before New, rises about half-an-hour later than the planet during the early hours of the 11th.

Jupiter continues to be visible in the eastern sky as a brilliant morning object, magnitude −1.7. It is moving outwards from the Sun and is steadily becoming visible for longer and longer each morning. By the end of November it is visible for about four hours before dawn. The old crescent Moon is near the planet on the 9th and 10th.

Saturn, magnitude 0.0, although still technically a morning object, is now appearing in the eastern skies before midnight. Saturn is moving direct in the constellation of Cancer until it reaches its first stationary point on the 8th, when it commences its retrograde motion. The gibbous Moon will be near the planet on the mornings of the 1st and the 28th.

Meteors. Although the Leonids have shown considerable activity in 1999, 2001, and 2002 no major shower is expected in 2004. However, keen observers might like to look out on the morning of the 17th, for an hour or so before dawn, in case they get a pleasant surprise. There will be no interference from moonlight.

THE MOON

Day	RA h m	Dec. °	Hor. par.	Semi-diam.	Sun's co-long. °	PA of Bright Limb °	Phase %	Age d	Rise 52° h m	Rise 56° h m	Transit h m	Set 52° h m	Set 56° h m
1	5 27	+27.3	54.4	14.8	132	82	86	17.9	18 32	17 55	2 50	11 58	12 35
2	6 20	+28.0	54.2	14.8	144	89	79	18.9	19 26	18 49	3 42	12 50	13 27
3	7 14	+27.5	54.1	14.8	157	95	71	19.9	20 31	19 59	4 33	13 29	14 02
4	8 06	+25.7	54.3	14.8	169	101	62	20.9	21 43	21 17	5 22	13 58	14 24
5	8 57	+22.7	54.6	14.9	181	106	52	21.9	22 58	22 39	6 10	14 19	14 39
6	9 45	+18.8	55.0	15.0	193	110	43	22.9	— —	— —	6 56	14 35	14 49
7	10 33	+13.9	55.7	15.2	205	113	33	23.9	0 14	0 01	7 40	14 48	14 56
8	11 19	+ 8.4	56.4	15.4	217	115	24	24.9	1 31	1 24	8 24	14 59	15 03
9	12 06	+ 2.4	57.3	15.6	230	116	16	25.9	2 49	2 47	9 08	15 10	15 09
10	12 53	+ 3.9	58.1	15.8	242	115	9	26.9	4 10	4 14	9 54	15 22	15 15
11	13 43	−10.2	59.0	16.1	254	112	3	27.9	5 35	5 45	10 43	15 36	15 23
12	14 36	−16.2	59.7	16.3	266	102	1	28.9	7 05	7 23	11 36	15 55	15 35
13	15 34	−21.4	60.2	16.4	278	305	0	0.4	8 38	9 04	12 34	16 21	15 53
14	16 36	−25.4	60.5	16.5	291	288	3	1.4	10 09	10 44	13 37	17 00	16 25
15	17 42	−27.6	60.5	16.5	303	278	8	2.4	11 27	12 06	14 43	17 58	17 19
16	18 49	−27.9	60.3	16.4	315	270	16	3.4	12 25	13 01	15 47	19 15	18 40
17	19 54	−26.2	59.9	16.3	327	262	26	4.4	13 04	13 32	16 49	20 42	20 15
18	20 55	−22.8	59.3	16.2	339	255	36	5.4	13 30	13 50	17 45	22 11	21 52
19	21 51	−18.1	58.7	16.0	352	251	47	6.4	13 48	14 02	18 36	23 37	23 25
20	22 44	−12.7	58.1	15.8	4	247	58	7.4	14 02	14 10	19 23	— —	— —
21	23 33	+ 6.7	57.5	15.7	16	245	69	8.4	14 13	14 16	20 07	0 59	0 53
22	0 20	+ 0.5	56.9	15.5	28	245	78	9.4	14 24	14 22	20 51	2 18	2 18
23	1 05	+ 5.5	56.3	15.3	40	246	86	10.4	14 35	14 28	21 34	3 34	3 40
24	1 51	+11.2	55.8	15.2	52	249	92	11.4	14 48	14 35	22 18	4 51	5 02
25	2 38	+16.4	55.4	15.1	65	255	97	12.4	15 03	14 45	23 04	6 08	6 25
26	3 27	+20.9	55.0	15.0	77	268	99	13.4	15 23	14 58	23 53	7 25	7 49
27	4 18	+24.4	54.6	14.9	89	21	100	14.4	15 50	15 19	— —	8 39	9 10
28	5 10	+26.8	54.3	14.8	101	69	99	15.4	16 28	15 52	0 43	9 47	10 23
29	6 04	+27.9	54.1	14.8	113	80	96	16.4	17 18	16 40	1 34	10 44	11 21
30	6 58	+27.7	54.0	14.7	125	89	91	17.4	18 19	17 45	2 26	11 28	12 02

MERCURY

Day	RA h m	Dec. °	Diam. "	Phase %	Transit h m	5° high 52° h m	56° h m
1	15 28	−20.6	5	90	12 46	16 08	15 39
3	15 40	−21.4	5	89	12 51	16 05	15 34
5	15 52	−22.2	5	87	12 55	16 03	15 29
7	16 04	−23.0	5	86	12 59	16 01	15 25
9	16 15	−23.6	5	84	13 03	15 59	15 21
11	16 27	−24.2	6	81	13 06	15 58	15 17
13	16 39	−24.7	6	79	13 10	15 57	15 14
15	16 50	−25.0	6	76	13 13	15 56	15 12
17	17 01	−25.4	6	72	13 16	15 56	15 11
19	17 11	−25.6	6	68	13 18	15 56	15 10
21	17 20	−25.7	7	64	13 19	15 57	15 10
23	17 29	−25.7	7	58	13 20	15 57	15 10
25	17 36	−25.6	7	52	13 18	15 57	15 11
27	17 41	−25.4	8	45	13 15	15 57	15 12
29	17 45	−25.1	8	37	13 10	15 55	15 12
31	17 46	−24.7	8	28	13 02	15 51	15 10

VENUS

Day	RA h m	Dec. °	Diam. "	Phase %	Transit h m	5° high 52° h m	56° h m
1	12 16	0.0	13	80	9 33	4 06	4 10
6	12 38	− 2.3	13	82	9 36	4 21	4 26
11	13 01	− 4.6	13	83	9 39	4 36	4 44
16	13 24	− 6.9	13	84	9 42	4 52	5 01
21	13 47	− 9.1	12	85	9 46	5 08	5 20
26	14 10	−11.3	12	87	9 50	5 24	5 38
31	14 34	−13.3	12	88	9 54	5 41	5 58

MARS

Day	RA h m	Dec. °	Diam. "	Phase %	Transit h m	5° high 52° h m	56° h m
1	13 27	− 8.4	4	99	10 44	6 02	6 13
6	13 39	− 9.6	4	99	10 37	6 02	6 14
11	13 52	−10.8	4	99	10 29	6 02	6 15
16	14 05	−12.0	4	99	10 22	6 02	6 17
21	14 18	−13.2	4	99	10 16	6 02	6 18
26	14 31	−14.3	4	98	10 09	6 02	6 20
31	14 44	−15.4	4	98	10 02	6 03	6 22

SUNRISE AND SUNSET

	London 0°05'	51°30'	Bristol 2°35'	51°28'	Birmingham 1°55'	52°28'	Manchester 2°15'	53°28'	Newcastle 1°37'	54°59'	Glasgow 4°14'	55°52'	Belfast 5°56'	54°35'
	h m	h m	h m	h m	h m	h m	h m	h m	h m	h m	h m	h m	h m	h m
1	6 54	16 33	7 04	16 43	7 04	16 37	7 09	16 36	7 11	16 29	7 24	16 36	7 27	16 47
2	6 56	16 31	7 06	16 41	7 06	16 36	7 10	16 34	7 13	16 27	7 26	16 34	7 29	16 45
3	6 58	16 29	7 08	16 39	7 08	16 34	7 12	16 32	7 15	16 25	7 28	16 32	7 31	16 43
4	7 00	16 28	7 10	16 38	7 10	16 32	7 14	16 30	7 17	16 23	7 30	16 30	7 33	16 41
5	7 01	16 26	7 11	16 36	7 12	16 30	7 16	16 28	7 19	16 21	7 33	16 28	7 35	16 39
6	7 03	16 24	7 13	16 34	7 13	16 28	7 18	16 26	7 21	16 19	7 35	16 26	7 37	16 37
7	7 05	16 23	7 15	16 33	7 15	16 27	7 20	16 25	7 23	16 17	7 37	16 24	7 39	16 35
8	7 07	16 21	7 17	16 31	7 17	16 25	7 22	16 23	7 25	16 15	7 39	16 22	7 41	16 34
9	7 08	16 19	7 18	16 29	7 19	16 23	7 24	16 21	7 27	16 13	7 41	16 20	7 43	16 32
10	7 10	16 18	7 20	16 28	7 21	16 22	7 26	16 20	7 29	16 11	7 43	16 18	7 45	16 30
11	7 12	16 16	7 22	16 26	7 23	16 20	7 28	16 18	7 31	16 09	7 45	16 16	7 47	16 28
12	7 14	16 15	7 24	16 25	7 24	16 19	7 30	16 16	7 33	16 08	7 47	16 14	7 49	16 27
13	7 15	16 13	7 25	16 23	7 26	16 17	7 31	16 15	7 35	16 06	7 49	16 13	7 51	16 25
14	7 17	16 12	7 27	16 22	7 28	16 16	7 33	16 13	7 37	16 04	7 51	16 11	7 53	16 23
15	7 19	16 11	7 29	16 21	7 30	16 14	7 35	16 12	7 39	16 03	7 53	16 09	7 54	16 22
16	7 21	16 09	7 30	16 19	7 32	16 13	7 37	16 10	7 41	16 01	7 55	16 07	7 56	16 20
17	7 22	16 08	7 32	16 18	7 33	16 12	7 39	16 09	7 43	16 00	7 58	16 06	7 58	16 19
18	7 24	16 07	7 34	16 17	7 35	16 10	7 41	16 07	7 45	15 58	8 00	16 04	8 00	16 17
19	7 26	16 06	7 35	16 16	7 37	16 09	7 42	16 06	7 47	15 57	8 02	16 03	8 02	16 16
20	7 27	16 04	7 37	16 14	7 39	16 08	7 44	16 05	7 49	15 55	8 03	16 01	8 04	16 14
21	7 29	16 03	7 39	16 13	7 40	16 07	7 46	16 04	7 51	15 54	8 05	16 00	8 06	16 13
22	7 30	16 02	7 40	16 12	7 42	16 05	7 48	16 02	7 52	15 53	8 07	15 58	8 08	16 12
23	7 32	16 01	7 42	16 11	7 44	16 04	7 49	16 01	7 54	15 51	8 09	15 57	8 09	16 11
24	7 34	16 00	7 44	16 10	7 45	16 03	7 51	16 00	7 56	15 50	8 11	15 56	8 11	16 09
25	7 35	15 59	7 45	16 09	7 47	16 02	7 53	15 59	7 58	15 49	8 13	15 55	8 13	16 08
26	7 37	15 58	7 47	16 08	7 48	16 01	7 54	15 58	8 00	15 48	8 15	15 53	8 15	16 07
27	7 38	15 57	7 48	16 08	7 50	16 00	7 56	15 57	8 01	15 47	8 17	15 52	8 16	16 06
28	7 40	15 57	7 50	16 07	7 51	16 00	7 58	15 56	8 03	15 46	8 18	15 51	8 18	16 05
29	7 41	15 56	7 51	16 06	7 53	15 59	7 59	15 55	8 05	15 45	8 20	15 50	8 20	16 04
30	7 43	15 55	7 52	16 05	7 54	15 58	8 01	15 54	8 06	15 44	8 22	15 49	8 21	16 03

JUPITER

Day	RA		Dec.		Transit		5° high			
							52°		56°	
	h	m	°	'	h	m	h	m	h	m
1	12	30.3	+2	03	9	46	4	30	4	36
11	12	37.5	+2	48	9	14	4	02	4	08
21	12	44.3	+3	30	8	42	3	33	3	40
31	12	50.6	+4	08	8	09	3	04	3	11

Diameters – equatorial 32" polar 30"

SATURN

Day	RA		Dec.		Transit		5° high			
							52°		56°	
	h	m	°	'	h	m	h	m	h	m
1	7	57.3	+20	35	5	14	21	54	21	39
11	7	57.5	+20	36	4	35	21	15	21	00
21	7	56.9	+20	38	3	55	20	35	20	20
31	7	55.6	+20	43	3	14	19	54	19	39

Diameters – equatorial 19" polar 18"
Rings – major axis 44" minor axis 16"

URANUS

Day	RA		Dec.		Transit		10° high			
							52°		56°	
	h	m	°	'	h	m	h	m	h	m
1	22	20.6	−11	10	19	35	23	24	23	04
11	22	20.4	−11	10	18	55	22	44	22	25
21	22	20.6	−11	09	18	16	22	05	21	46
31	22	21.0	−11	06	17	37	21	26	21	07

Diameter 4"

NEPTUNE

Day	RA		Dec.		Transit		10° high			
							52°		56°	
	h	m	°	'	h	m	h	m	h	m
1	21	00.4	−17	06	18	15	21	20	20	49
11	21	00.7	−17	05	17	36	20	42	20	10
21	21	01.2	−17	03	16	57	20	03	19	32
31	21	02.0	−17	00	16	19	19	25	18	54

Diameter 2"

DECEMBER 2004

TWELFTH MONTH, 31 DAYS. *Decem* (ten), tenth month of Roman pre-Julian calendar

1	*Wednesday*	Samuel Courtauld d. 1947. David Ben Gurion d. 1973	336
2	*Thursday*	Opening of St Paul's Cathedral 1697. Napoleon Bonaparte crowned Emperor 1804	337
3	*Friday*	Sir Thomas Beecham b. 1820	338
4	*Saturday*	First publication of The Observer 1791	339
5	*Sunday*	Prohibition repealed in the US 1933. Claude Monet d. 1926	340

6	*Monday*	Anthony Trollope d. 1882. Roy Orbison d. 1988	week 49 day 341
7	*Tuesday*	Battle of Pearl Harbor 1941. Robert Graves d. 1985	342
8	*Wednesday*	Mary, Queen of Scots b. 1542. John Lennon d. 1980	343
9	*Thursday*	Anthony van Dyck d. 1641. Kirk Douglas b. 1918	344
10	*Friday*	Founding of the Royal Academy 1768. Otis Redding d. 1967	345
11	*Saturday*	James II fled from England 1688. Hector Berlioz b. 1803	346
12	*Sunday*	Hovercraft patented 1955. Gustave Flaubert b. 1821	347

13	*Monday*	Abel Tasman discovered New Zealand 1842	week 50 day 348
14	*Tuesday*	Luddite Riots began 1811. Stanley Baldwin d. 1947	349
15	*Wednesday*	Grigori Rasputin d. 1916. Walt Disney d. 1966	350
16	*Thursday*	Boston Tea Party 1773. Wilhelm Grimm d. 1859	351
17	*Friday*	First flight by the Wright Brothers 1903. Sir Humphrey Davy b. 1778	352
18	*Saturday*	Charles Wesley b. 1707. Abolition of Slavery in the US 1865	353
19	*Sunday*	Emily Bronte d. 1848. Edith Piaf b. 1915	354

20	*Monday*	Sir Robert Menzies b. 1894. John Steinbeck d. 1968	week 51 day 355
21	*Tuesday*	Joseph Stalin b. 1879. Benjamin Disraeli b. 1804	356
22	*Wednesday*	George Eliot d. 1880. Sir Henry Cotton d. 1987	357
23	*Thursday*	Richard Arkwright b. 1732. Ronnie Scott d. 1996	358
24	*Friday*	King John b. 1167. George Crabbe b. 1754	359
25	*Saturday*	*Christmas Day.* Sir Isaac Newton b. 1642	360
26	*Sunday*	*Boxing Day.* Radium discovered by the Curies 1898. Henry Miller b. 1891	361

27	*Monday*	*Bank Holiday in the UK.* Charles Lamb d. 1834	week 52 day 362
28	*Tuesday*	*Bank Holiday in the UK.* Maurice Ravel d. 1937	363
29	*Wednesday*	Pablo Casals b. 1876. William Gladstone b. 1809	364
30	*Thursday*	Rudyard Kipling b. 1865. Michael Nesmith b. 1942	365
31	*Friday*	Henri Matisse b. 1869. John Denver b. 1943	366

ASTRONOMICAL PHENOMENA

d	h	
1	04	Saturn in conjunction with Moon. Saturn 5°S.
5	22	Mars in conjunction with Venus. Mars 1°S.
7	11	Jupiter in conjunction with Moon. Jupiter 0°.3 S.
9	23	Mars in conjunction with Moon. Mars 2°N.
10	04	Venus in conjunction with Moon. Venus 3°N.
10	08	Mercury in inferior conjunction
11	20	Mercury in conjunction with Moon. Mercury 6°N.
13	17	Pluto in conjunction
20	07	Mercury at stationary point
21	13	Sun's longitude 270° ♑
28	08	Saturn in conjunction with Moon. Saturn 5°S.
28	18	Venus in conjunction with Mercury. Venus 1°S.
29	20	Mercury at greatest elongation W.22°

MINIMA OF ALGOL

d	h	d	h	d	h
3	15.0	15	02.3	26	13.6
6	11.8	17	23.1	29	10.4
9	08.6	20	19.9		
12	05.5	23	16.7		

CONSTELLATIONS

The following constellations are near the meridian at

d	h		d	h
November	1	24	December	16	21
November	15	23	January	1	20
December	1	22	January	16	19

Ursa Major (below the Pole), Ursa Minor (below the Pole), Cassiopeia, Andromeda, Perseus, Triangulum, Aries, Taurus, Cetus and Eridanus

THE MOON

Phases, Apsides and Node	d	h	m
☾ Last Quarter	5	00	53
● New Moon	12	01	29
☽ First Quarter	18	16	40
○ Full Moon	26	15	06
Perigee (357,991 km)	12	21	20
Apogee (406,480 km)	27	18	59

Mean longitude of ascending node on December 1, 30°

THE SUN

s.d. 16'.3

Day	Right Ascension h m s	Dec. − ° '	Equation of Time m s	Rise 52° h m	Rise 56° h m	Transit h m	Set 52° h m	Set 56° h m	Sidereal time h m s	Transit of First Point of Aries h m s
1	16 29 45	21 49	+11 00	7 46	8 07	11 49	15 52	15 31	4 40 45	19 16 05
2	16 34 04	21 58	+10 38	7 47	8 09	11 50	15 51	15 30	4 44 42	19 12 09
3	16 38 24	22 07	+10 14	7 49	8 10	11 50	15 51	15 29	4 48 38	19 08 13
4	16 42 44	22 15	+ 9 50	7 50	8 12	11 50	15 50	15 28	4 52 35	19 04 17
5	16 47 05	22 23	+ 9 26	7 51	8 14	11 51	15 50	15 28	4 56 31	19 00 21
6	16 51 27	22 30	+ 9 01	7 53	8 15	11 51	15 49	15 27	5 00 28	18 56 25
7	16 55 49	22 37	+ 8 35	7 54	8 16	11 52	15 49	15 27	5 04 24	18 52 30
8	17 00 12	22 44	+ 8 09	7 55	8 18	11 52	15 49	15 26	5 08 21	18 48 34
9	17 04 35	22 50	+ 7 42	7 56	8 19	11 53	15 49	15 26	5 12 18	18 44 38
10	17 08 59	22 55	+ 7 15	7 57	8 20	11 53	15 48	15 25	5 16 14	18 40 42
11	17 13 23	23 00	+ 6 48	7 58	8 21	11 53	15 48	15 25	5 20 11	18 36 46
12	17 17 47	23 05	+ 6 20	7 59	8 23	11 54	15 48	15 25	5 24 07	18 32 50
13	17 22 12	23 09	+ 5 52	8 00	8 24	11 54	15 48	15 25	5 28 04	18 28 54
14	17 26 37	23 13	+ 5 23	8 01	8 25	11 55	15 48	15 25	5 32 00	18 24 58
15	17 31 03	23 16	+ 4 54	8 02	8 26	11 55	15 49	15 25	5 35 57	18 21 02
16	17 35 28	23 19	+ 4 25	8 03	8 26	11 56	15 49	15 25	5 39 53	18 17 06
17	17 39 54	23 22	+ 3 56	8 04	8 27	11 56	15 49	15 25	5 43 50	18 13 10
18	17 44 20	23 24	+ 3 26	8 04	8 28	11 57	15 49	15 26	5 47 47	18 09 15
19	17 48 46	23 25	+ 2 57	8 05	8 29	11 57	15 50	15 26	5 51 43	18 05 19
20	17 53 13	23 26	+ 2 27	8 05	8 29	11 58	15 50	15 26	5 55 40	18 01 23
21	17 57 39	23 26	+ 1 57	8 06	8 30	11 58	15 51	15 27	5 59 36	17 57 27
22	18 02 05	23 26	+ 1 27	8 06	8 30	11 59	15 51	15 27	6 03 33	17 53 31
23	18 06 32	23 26	+ 0 58	8 07	8 31	11 59	15 52	15 28	6 07 29	17 49 35
24	18 10 58	23 25	+ 0 28	8 07	8 31	12 00	15 52	15 29	6 11 26	17 45 39
25	18 15 24	23 24	− 0 02	8 08	8 31	12 00	15 53	15 29	6 15 22	17 41 43
26	18 19 50	23 22	− 0 31	8 08	8 32	12 01	15 54	15 30	6 19 19	17 37 47
27	18 24 17	23 19	− 1 01	8 08	8 32	12 01	15 55	15 31	6 23 16	17 33 51
28	18 28 42	23 17	− 1 30	8 08	8 32	12 02	15 55	15 32	6 27 12	17 29 55
29	18 33 08	23 13	− 1 59	8 08	8 32	12 02	15 56	15 33	6 31 09	17 25 59
30	18 37 34	23 10	− 2 28	8 08	8 32	12 03	15 57	15 34	6 35 05	17 22 04
31	18 41 59	23 05	− 2 57	8 08	8 31	12 03	15 58	15 35	6 39 02	17 18 08

DURATION OF TWILIGHT (in minutes)

Latitude	52°	56°	52°	56°	52°	56°	52°	56°
	1 December		11 December		21 December		31 December	
Civil	40	45	41	47	41	47	41	47
Nautical	82	93	84	96	85	97	84	96
Astronomical	123	138	125	141	126	142	125	141

THE NIGHT SKY

Mercury passes through inferior conjunction on the 10th. It then moves out from the Sun to become visible as a difficult morning object during the second half of the month, its magnitude brightening from +1.1 to −0.3. It becomes visible low in the south-eastern sky around the beginning of morning civil twilight. Greatest western elongation (22 degrees) occurs on the 29th. Venus will be useful in locating Mercury, which is the fainter by 4 magnitudes. On the 19th Mercury is 7 degrees to the left and 3 degrees lower than Venus, while on the 31st Mercury is only 1 degree above Venus.

Venus is still visible as a brilliant object in the south-eastern sky in the mornings before dawn, magnitude −4.0. It is now moving more rapidly towards the Sun and consequently rising later and later until, by the end of December, observers in southern England will not be able to see it before 07h. Because of its southerly declination those in Scotland will have to wait until about 08h. The old crescent Moon, only two days before New, will be seen about 5 degrees north of the planet. Venus passes 1 degree north of Mars on the 5th, and will be of assistance in identifying this much fainter planet. Venus passes 6 degrees north of Antares on the 23rd.

Mars, magnitude +1.6, is visible in the south-eastern sky before the increasing brightness of the pre-dawn sky curtails observation. Mars continues its eastward motion and by the end of the month is within 10 degrees of Antares, in the constellation of Scorpius. Note that Mars is about half a magnitude fainter than the star. The waning crescent Moon, only 2 days before New, will be seen near Mars on the morning of the 10th.

Jupiter continues to be visible as a brilliant morning object in the south-eastern sky, magnitude −1.9. The old crescent Moon is near the planet on the mornings of the 7th and 8th.

Saturn, magnitude −0.2, although it does not reach opposition until next month, is becoming visible for most of the hours of darkness. Saturn is moving slowly retrograde and returns from Cancer into Gemini during the month. On the morning of the 1st the waning gibbous Moon passes 4 degrees north of the planet.

Meteors. The maximum of the well-known Geminid meteor shower occurs on the 13th. Conditions for observation are favourable since there will be no interference from the Moon.

THE MOON

Day	RA h m	Dec. °	Hor. par. ′	Semi-diam. ′	Sun's co-long. °	PA of Bright Limb °	Phase %	Age d	Rise 52° h m	Rise 56° h m	Transit h m	Set 52° h m	Set 56° h m
1	7 50	+26.2	54.0	14.7	137	96	85	18.4	19 28	19 00	3 16	12 00	12 28
2	8 41	+23.6	54.2	14.8	149	102	78	19.4	20 41	20 20	4 04	12 23	12 45
3	9 30	+20.0	54.5	14.8	162	106	69	20.4	21 56	21 40	4 50	12 40	12 57
4	10 17	+15.5	54.9	15.0	174	110	60	21.4	23 10	23 01	5 34	12 54	13 05
5	11 02	+10.3	55.5	15.1	186	113	50	22.4	— —	— —	6 17	13 05	13 11
6	11 48	+ 4.6	56.3	15.3	198	114	40	23.4	0 25	0 21	6 59	13 16	13 17
7	12 33	− 1.4	57.2	15.6	210	114	31	24.4	1 42	1 44	7 43	13 27	13 23
8	13 21	− 7.6	58.1	15.8	222	113	21	25.4	3 03	3 10	8 29	13 40	13 30
9	14 12	−13.7	59.1	16.1	235	109	13	26.4	4 29	4 43	9 19	13 55	13 40
10	15 07	−19.2	60.0	16.3	247	103	6	27.4	6 00	6 22	10 14	14 17	13 54
11	16 07	−23.8	60.7	16.5	259	90	2	28.4	7 34	8 04	11 15	14 50	14 18
12	17 13	−26.8	61.1	16.7	271	18	0	29.4	9 01	9 39	12 21	15 39	15 01
13	18 21	−27.9	61.2	16.7	283	287	2	0.9	10 12	10 49	13 29	16 50	16 12
14	19 29	−26.9	61.1	16.6	296	271	6	1.9	11 00	11 31	14 35	18 17	17 47
15	20 34	−24.0	60.6	16.5	308	261	13	2.9	11 32	11 55	15 35	19 50	19 29
16	21 34	−19.5	59.9	16.3	320	255	22	3.9	11 53	12 09	16 30	21 21	21 07
17	22 30	−14.1	59.1	16.1	332	250	32	4.9	12 09	12 18	17 20	22 46	22 38
18	23 20	− 8.0	58.2	15.9	344	247	43	5.9	12 21	12 25	18 06	— —	— —
19	0 08	− 1.8	57.4	15.6	356	246	53	6.9	12 32	12 31	18 50	0 07	0 05
20	0 55	+ 4.3	56.6	15.4	9	247	64	7.9	12 43	12 37	19 33	1 24	1 28
21	1 40	+10.1	55.9	15.2	21	249	73	8.9	12 55	12 44	20 17	2 41	2 50
22	2 27	+15.4	55.4	15.1	33	252	81	9.9	13 10	12 53	21 02	3 57	4 12
23	3 15	+20.0	54.9	15.0	45	257	88	10.9	13 28	13 05	21 49	5 13	5 35
24	4 05	+23.6	54.5	14.9	57	264	94	11.9	13 53	13 23	22 38	6 28	6 56
25	4 56	+26.3	54.3	14.8	69	275	98	12.9	14 26	13 52	23 29	7 37	8 12
26	5 50	+27.7	54.1	14.7	81	301	100	13.9	15 12	14 35	— —	8 38	9 15
27	6 43	+27.8	54.0	14.7	94	45	100	14.9	16 10	15 35	0 21	9 26	10 01
28	7 36	+26.6	53.9	14.7	106	81	98	15.9	17 17	16 47	1 11	10 01	10 32
29	8 28	+24.3	54.0	14.7	118	94	95	16.9	18 30	18 06	2 00	10 27	10 51
30	9 17	+20.9	54.2	14.8	130	101	90	17.9	19 43	19 26	2 47	10 46	11 04
31	10 04	+16.6	54.5	14.8	142	106	84	18.9	20 57	20 46	3 31	11 00	11 13

MERCURY

Day	RA h m	Dec. °	Diam. ″	Phase %	Transit h m	5° high 52° h m	5° high 56° h m
1	17 46	−24.7	8	28	13 02	15 51	15 10
3	17 43	−24.1	9	20	12 52	15 45	15 07
5	17 38	−23.5	9	11	12 37	15 37	15 01
7	17 30	−22.8	10	5	12 21	15 27	14 54
9	17 19	−21.9	10	1	12 02	15 15	14 44
11	17 07	−21.1	10	0	11 42	8 23	8 53
13	16 56	−20.3	10	4	11 24	7 59	8 27
15	16 47	−19.7	9	9	11 08	7 38	8 05
17	16 41	−19.3	9	17	10 54	7 22	7 48
19	16 38	−19.1	9	26	10 44	7 10	7 36
21	16 37	−19.2	8	34	10 36	7 03	7 28
23	16 39	−19.4	8	42	10 31	6 59	7 25
25	16 44	−19.7	7	50	10 28	6 58	7 25
27	16 50	−20.1	7	56	10 26	7 00	7 27
29	16 57	−20.6	7	62	10 26	7 03	7 32
31	17 06	−21.0	6	66	10 27	7 08	7 38

VENUS

Day	RA h m	Dec. °	Diam. ″	Phase %	Transit h m	5° high 52° h m	5° high 56° h m
1	14 34	−13.3	12	88	9 54	5 41	5 58
6	14 59	−15.3	12	89	9 59	5 58	6 17
11	15 23	−17.1	11	90	10 04	6 15	6 37
16	15 49	−18.7	11	91	10 09	6 32	6 57
21	16 15	−20.1	11	92	10 16	6 49	7 16
26	16 41	−21.2	11	92	10 22	7 04	7 34
31	17 07	−22.1	11	93	10 29	7 18	7 51

MARS

Day	RA h m	Dec. °	Diam. ″	Phase %	Transit h m	5° high 52° h m	5° high 56° h m
1	14 44	−15.4	4	98	10 02	6 03	6 22
6	14 57	−16.4	4	98	9 56	6 03	6 24
11	15 11	−17.4	4	98	9 50	6 04	6 26
16	15 24	−18.3	4	97	9 44	6 04	6 28
21	15 38	−19.2	4	97	9 38	6 05	6 30
26	15 52	−20.0	4	97	9 33	6 05	6 33
31	16 07	−20.7	4	97	9 27	6 06	6 35

SUNRISE AND SUNSET

	London 0°05' 51°30'		Bristol 2°35' 51°28'		Birmingham 1°55' 52°28'		Manchester 2°15' 53°28'		Newcastle 1°37' 54°59'		Glasgow 4°14' 55°52'		Belfast 5°56' 54°35'	
	h m	h m	h m	h m	h m	h m	h m	h m	h m	h m	h m	h m	h m	h m
1	7 44	15 55	7 54	16 05	7 56	15 57	8 02	15 54	8 08	15 43	8 23	15 48	8 23	16 03
2	7 45	15 54	7 55	16 04	7 57	15 57	8 04	15 53	8 09	15 42	8 25	15 48	8 24	16 02
3	7 47	15 54	7 57	16 04	7 59	15 56	8 05	15 52	8 11	15 42	8 27	15 47	8 26	16 01
4	7 48	15 53	7 58	16 03	8 00	15 56	8 07	15 52	8 12	15 41	8 28	15 46	8 27	16 00
5	7 49	15 53	7 59	16 03	8 01	15 55	8 08	15 51	8 14	15 40	8 30	15 45	8 29	16 00
6	7 51	15 52	8 00	16 02	8 03	15 55	8 09	15 51	8 15	15 40	8 31	15 45	8 30	15 59
7	7 52	15 52	8 02	16 02	8 04	15 54	8 10	15 51	8 17	15 39	8 32	15 44	8 31	15 59
8	7 53	15 52	8 03	16 02	8 05	15 54	8 12	15 50	8 18	15 39	8 34	15 44	8 33	15 59
9	7 54	15 51	8 04	16 02	8 06	15 54	8 13	15 50	8 19	15 39	8 35	15 44	8 34	15 58
10	7 55	15 51	8 05	16 01	8 07	15 54	8 14	15 50	8 20	15 38	8 36	15 43	8 35	15 58
11	7 56	15 51	8 06	16 01	8 08	15 54	8 15	15 50	8 21	15 38	8 38	15 43	8 36	15 58
12	7 57	15 51	8 07	16 01	8 09	15 54	8 16	15 49	8 23	15 38	8 39	15 43	8 37	15 58
13	7 58	15 51	8 08	16 01	8 10	15 54	8 17	15 49	8 24	15 38	8 40	15 43	8 38	15 58
14	7 59	15 51	8 09	16 01	8 11	15 54	8 18	15 50	8 25	15 38	8 41	15 43	8 39	15 58
15	8 00	15 51	8 10	16 02	8 12	15 54	8 19	15 50	8 25	15 38	8 42	15 43	8 40	15 58
16	8 01	15 52	8 10	16 02	8 13	15 54	8 20	15 50	8 26	15 38	8 43	15 43	8 41	15 58
17	8 01	15 52	8 11	16 02	8 14	15 54	8 21	15 50	8 27	15 38	8 43	15 43	8 42	15 58
18	8 02	15 52	8 12	16 02	8 14	15 54	8 21	15 50	8 28	15 39	8 44	15 43	8 43	15 58
19	8 03	15 53	8 12	16 03	8 15	15 55	8 22	15 51	8 29	15 39	8 45	15 44	8 43	15 59
20	8 03	15 53	8 13	16 03	8 16	15 55	8 23	15 51	8 29	15 39	8 45	15 44	8 44	15 59
21	8 04	15 53	8 14	16 04	8 16	15 56	8 23	15 52	8 30	15 40	8 46	15 45	8 44	16 00
22	8 04	15 54	8 14	16 04	8 17	15 56	8 23	15 52	8 30	15 40	8 46	15 45	8 45	16 00
23	8 05	15 55	8 15	16 05	8 17	15 57	8 24	15 53	8 31	15 41	8 47	15 46	8 45	16 01
24	8 05	15 55	8 15	16 05	8 17	15 58	8 24	15 53	8 31	15 42	8 47	15 46	8 46	16 01
25	8 05	15 56	8 15	16 06	8 18	15 58	8 25	15 54	8 31	15 42	8 47	15 47	8 46	16 02
26	8 06	15 57	8 15	16 07	8 18	15 59	8 25	15 55	8 31	15 43	8 48	15 48	8 46	16 03
27	8 06	15 57	8 16	16 08	8 18	16 00	8 25	15 56	8 32	15 44	8 48	15 49	8 46	16 04
28	8 06	15 58	8 16	16 08	8 18	16 01	8 25	15 57	8 32	15 45	8 48	15 50	8 46	16 05
29	8 06	15 59	8 16	16 09	8 18	16 02	8 25	15 57	8 32	15 46	8 48	15 51	8 46	16 06
30	8 06	16 00	8 16	16 10	8 18	16 03	8 25	15 58	8 32	15 47	8 48	15 52	8 46	16 07
31	8 06	16 01	8 16	16 11	8 18	16 04	8 25	16 00	8 31	15 48	8 48	15 53	8 46	16 08

JUPITER

Day	RA		Dec.		Transit		5° high 52°		56°	
	h	m	°	'	h	m	h	m	h	m
1	12	50.6	−4	08	8	09	3	04	3	11
11	12	56.3	−4	42	7	35	2	33	2	40
21	13	01.2	−5	10	7	01	2	01	2	09
31	13	05.4	−5	34	6	25	1	28	1	36

Diameters – equatorial 34″ polar 32″

SATURN

Day	RA		Dec.		Transit		5° high 52°		56°	
	h	m	°	'	h	m	h	m	h	m
1	7	55.6	+20	43	3	14	19	54	19	39
11	7	53.5	+20	50	2	33	19	12	18	56
21	7	50.9	+20	58	1	51	18	29	18	13
31	7	47.8	+21	07	1	09	17	45	17	30

Diameters – equatorial 20″ polar 18″
Rings – major axis 46″ minor axis 17″

URANUS

Day	RA		Dec.		Transit		10° high 52°		56°	
	h	m	°	'	h	m	h	m	h	m
1	22	21.0	−11	06	17	37	21	26	21	07
11	22	21.8	−11	01	16	59	20	49	20	29
21	22	22.8	−10	55	16	21	20	11	19	52
31	22	24.2	−10	47	15	43	19	34	19	15

Diameter 4″

NEPTUNE

Day	RA		Dec.		Transit		10° high 52°		56°	
	h	m	°	'	h	m	h	m	h	m
1	21	02.0	−17	00	16	19	19	25	18	54
11	21	02.9	−16	56	15	40	18	47	18	16
21	21	04.0	−16	51	15	02	18	09	17	39
31	21	05.2	−16	46	14	24	17	32	17	02

Diameter 2″

RISING AND SETTING TIMES

TABLE 1. SEMI-DIURNAL ARCS (HOUR ANGLES AT RISING/SETTING)

Dec.	Latitude 0°	10°	20°	30°	40°	45°	50°	52°	54°	56°	58°	60°	Dec.
	h m	h m	h m	h m	h m	h m	h m	h m	h m	h m	h m	h m	
0°	6 00	6 00	6 00	6 00	6 00	6 00	6 00	6 00	6 00	6 00	6 00	6 00	0°
1°	6 00	6 01	6 01	6 02	6 03	6 04	6 05	6 05	6 06	6 06	6 06	6 07	1°
2°	6 00	6 01	6 03	6 05	6 07	6 08	6 10	6 10	6 11	6 12	6 13	6 14	2°
3°	6 00	6 02	6 04	6 07	6 10	6 12	6 14	6 15	6 17	6 18	6 19	6 21	3°
4°	6 00	6 03	6 06	6 09	6 13	6 16	6 19	6 21	6 22	6 24	6 26	6 28	4°
5°	6 00	6 04	6 07	6 12	6 17	6 20	6 24	6 26	6 28	6 30	6 32	6 35	5°
6°	6 00	6 04	6 09	6 14	6 20	6 24	6 29	6 31	6 33	6 36	6 39	6 42	6°
7°	6 00	6 05	6 10	6 16	6 24	6 28	6 34	6 36	6 39	6 42	6 45	6 49	7°
8°	6 00	6 06	6 12	6 19	6 27	6 32	6 39	6 41	6 45	6 48	6 52	6 56	8°
9°	6 00	6 06	6 13	6 21	6 31	6 36	6 44	6 47	6 50	6 54	6 59	7 04	9°
10°	6 00	6 07	6 15	6 23	6 34	6 41	6 49	6 52	6 56	7 01	7 06	7 11	10°
11°	6 00	6 08	6 16	6 26	6 38	6 45	6 54	6 58	7 02	7 07	7 12	7 19	11°
12°	6 00	6 09	6 18	6 28	6 41	6 49	6 59	7 03	7 08	7 13	7 20	7 26	12°
13°	6 00	6 09	6 19	6 31	6 45	6 53	7 04	7 09	7 14	7 20	7 27	7 34	13°
14°	6 00	6 10	6 21	6 33	6 48	6 58	7 09	7 14	7 20	7 27	7 34	7 42	14°
15°	6 00	6 11	6 22	6 36	6 52	7 02	7 14	7 20	7 27	7 34	7 42	7 51	15°
16°	6 00	6 12	6 24	6 38	6 56	7 07	7 20	7 26	7 33	7 41	7 49	7 59	16°
17°	6 00	6 12	6 26	6 41	6 59	7 11	7 25	7 32	7 40	7 48	7 57	8 08	17°
18°	6 00	6 13	6 27	6 43	7 03	7 16	7 31	7 38	7 46	7 55	8 05	8 17	18°
19°	6 00	6 14	6 29	6 46	7 07	7 21	7 37	7 45	7 53	8 03	8 14	8 26	19°
20°	6 00	6 15	6 30	6 49	7 11	7 25	7 43	7 51	8 00	8 11	8 22	8 36	20°
21°	6 00	6 16	6 32	6 51	7 15	7 30	7 49	7 58	8 08	8 19	8 32	8 47	21°
22°	6 00	6 16	6 34	6 54	7 19	7 35	7 55	8 05	8 15	8 27	8 41	8 58	22°
23°	6 00	6 17	6 36	6 57	7 23	7 40	8 02	8 12	8 23	8 36	8 51	9 09	23°
24°	6 00	6 18	6 37	7 00	7 28	7 46	8 08	8 19	8 31	8 45	9 02	9 22	24°
25°	6 00	6 19	6 39	7 02	7 32	7 51	8 15	8 27	8 40	8 55	9 13	9 35	25°
26°	6 00	6 20	6 41	7 05	7 37	7 57	8 22	8 35	8 49	9 05	9 25	9 51	26°
27°	6 00	6 21	6 43	7 08	7 41	8 03	8 30	8 43	8 58	9 16	9 39	10 08	27°
28°	6 00	6 22	6 45	7 12	7 46	8 08	8 37	8 52	9 08	9 28	9 53	10 28	28°
29°	6 00	6 22	6 47	7 15	7 51	8 15	8 45	9 01	9 19	9 41	10 10	10 55	29°
30°	6 00	6 23	6 49	7 18	7 56	8 21	8 54	9 11	9 30	9 55	10 30	12 00	30°
35°	6 00	6 28	6 59	7 35	8 24	8 58	9 46	10 15	10 58	12 00	12 00	12 00	35°
40°	6 00	6 34	7 11	7 56	8 59	9 48	12 00	12 00	12 00	12 00	12 00	12 00	40°
45°	6 00	6 41	7 25	8 21	9 48	12 00	12 00	12 00	12 00	12 00	12 00	12 00	45°
50°	6 00	6 49	7 43	8 54	12 00	12 00	12 00	12 00	12 00	12 00	12 00	12 00	50°
55°	6 00	6 58	8 05	9 42	12 00	12 00	12 00	12 00	12 00	12 00	12 00	12 00	55°
60°	6 00	7 11	8 36	12 00	12 00	12 00	12 00	12 00	12 00	12 00	12 00	12 00	60°
65°	6 00	7 29	9 25	12 00	12 00	12 00	12 00	12 00	12 00	12 00	12 00	12 00	65°
70°	6 00	7 56	12 00	12 00	12 00	12 00	12 00	12 00	12 00	12 00	12 00	12 00	70°
75°	6 00	8 45	12 00	12 00	12 00	12 00	12 00	12 00	12 00	12 00	12 00	12 00	75°
80°	6 00	12 00	12 00	12 00	12 00	12 00	12 00	12 00	12 00	12 00	12 00	12 00	80°

TABLE 2. CORRECTION FOR REFRACTION AND SEMI-DIAMETER

	m	m	m	m	m	m	m	m	m	m	m	m	
0°	3	3	4	4	4	5	5	5	6	6	6	7	0°
10°	3	3	4	4	4	5	5	6	6	6	7	7	10°
20°	4	4	4	4	5	5	6	7	7	8	8	9	20°
25°	4	4	4	4	5	6	7	8	8	9	11	13	25°
30°	4	4	4	5	6	7	8	9	11	14	21	—	30°

NB: Regarding Table 1. If latitude and declination are of the same sign, take out the respondent directly. If they are of opposite signs, subtract the respondent from 12h.

Table 1 gives the complete range of declinations in case any user wishes to calculate semi-diurnal arcs for bodies other than the Sun and Moon.

Example:

Lat.	Dec.	Semi-diurnal arc
+52°	+20°	7h 51m
+52°	-20°	4h 09m

SUNRISE AND SUNSET

The local mean time of sunrise or sunset may be found by obtaining the hour angle from Table 1 and applying it to the time of transit. The hour angle is negative for sunrise and positive for sunset. A small correction to the hour angle, which always has the effect of increasing it numerically, is necessary to allow for the Sun's semi-diameter (16') and for refraction (34'); it is obtained from Table 2. The resulting local mean time may be converted into the standard time of the country by taking the difference between the longitude of the standard meridian of the country and that of the place, adding it to the local mean time if the place is west of the standard meridian, and subtracting it if the place is east.

Example – Required the New Zealand Mean Time (12h fast on GMT) of sunset on May 23 at Auckland, latitude 36° 50' S. (or minus), longitude 11h 39m E. Taking the declination as +20°.6 (page 1217), we find

		h	m
New Zealand Standard Time	+	12	00
Longitude	–	11	39
Longitudinal Correction	+	0	21
Tabular entry for Lat. 30° and Dec. 20°, opposite signs	+	5	11
Proportional part for 6° 50' of Lat.	–		15
Proportional part for 0°.6 of Dec.	–		2
Correction (Table 2)	+		5
Hour angle		4	58
Sun transits (page 1217)		11	57
Longitudinal correction	+		21
New Zealand Mean Time		17	16

MOONRISE AND MOONSET

It is possible to calculate the times of moonrise and moonset using Table 1, though the method is more complicated because the apparent motion of the Moon is much more rapid and also more variable than that of the Sun.

TABLE 3. LONGITUDE CORRECTION

X	40m	45m	50m	55m	60m	65m	70m
A							
h	m	m	m	m	m	m	m
1	2	2	2	2	3	3	3
2	3	4	4	5	5	5	6
3	5	6	6	7	8	8	9
4	7	8	8	9	10	11	12
5	8	9	10	11	13	14	15
6	10	11	13	14	15	16	18
7	12	13	15	16	18	19	20
8	13	15	17	18	20	22	23
9	15	17	19	21	23	24	26
10	17	19	21	23	25	27	29
11	18	21	23	25	28	30	32
12	20	23	25	28	30	33	35
13	22	24	27	30	33	35	38
14	23	26	29	32	35	38	41
15	25	28	31	34	38	41	44
16	27	30	33	37	40	43	47
17	28	32	35	39	43	46	50
18	30	34	38	41	45	49	53
19	32	36	40	44	48	51	55
20	33	38	42	46	50	54	58
21	35	39	44	48	53	57	61
22	37	41	46	50	55	60	64
23	38	43	48	53	58	62	67
24	40	45	50	55	60	65	70

The parallax of the Moon, about 57', is near to the sum of the semi-diameter and refraction but has the opposite effect on these times. It is thus convenient to neglect all three quantities in the method outlined below.

Notation

ϕ	= latitude of observer
λ	= longitude of observer (measured positively towards the west)
T_{-1}	= time of transit of Moon on previous day
T_0	= time of transit of Moon on day in question
T_1	= time of transit of Moon on following day
δ_0	= approximate declination of Moon
δ_R	= declination of Moon at moonrise
δ_S	= declination of Moon at moonset
h_0	= approximate hour angle of Moon
h_R	= hour angle of Moon at moonrise
h_S	= hour angle of Moon at moonset
t_R	= time of moonrise
t_S	= time of moonset

Method

1. With arguments ϕ, δ_0 enter Table 1 on page 1248 to determine h_0 where h_0 is negative for moonrise and positive for moonset.

2. Form approximate times from

$$t_R = T_0 + \lambda + h_0$$
$$t_S = T_0 + \lambda + h_0$$

3. Determine δ_R, δ_S for times t_R, t_S respectively.

4. Re-enter Table 1 on page 1248 with
   (a) arguments ϕ, δ_R to determine h_R
   (b) arguments ϕ, δ_S to determine h_S

5. Form $t_R = T_0 + \lambda + h_R + AX$
             $t_S = T_0 + \lambda + h_S + AX$

where $A = (\lambda + h)$

and $X = (T_0 - T_{-1})$ if $(\lambda + h)$ is negative
           $X = (T_1 - T_0)$ if $(\lambda + h)$ is positive

AX is the respondent in Table 3.

Example – To find the times of moonrise and moonset at Vancouver ($\phi = +49°$, $\lambda = +8h\ 12m$) on 2004 August 8. The starting data (page 1230) are

T_{-1}	= 5h 15m
T_0	= 5h 59m
T_1	= 6h 46m
δ_0	= +18°

1. h_0 = 7h 28m
2. Approximate values
   t_R = 8d 05h 59m + 8h 12m + (–7h 28m)
        = 8d 06h 43m
   t_S = 8d 05h 59m + 8h 12m + (+7h 28m)
        = 8d 21h 39m
3. δ_R = +18°.8
   δ_S = +21°.4
4. h_R = –7h 33m
   h_S = +7h 47m
5. t_R = 8d 05h 59m + 8h 12m + (–7h 33m) + 2m
        = 8d 06h 40m
   t_S = 8d 05h 59m + 8h 12m + (+7h 47m) + 31m
        = 8d 22h 29m

To get the LMT of the phenomenon the longitude is subtracted from the GMT thus:

Moonrise = 8d 06h 40m – 8h 12m = 7d 22h 28m
Moonset = 8d 22h 29m – 8h 12m = 8d 14h 17m

ECLIPSES AND OCCULTATIONS 2004

ECLIPSES

During 2004 there will be four eclipses, two of the Sun and two of the Moon. (Penumbral eclipses are not mentioned in this section as they are so difficult to observe).

1. A partial eclipse of the Sun on 19 April is visible from a small part of Antarctica, the South Atlantic Ocean, southern Africa and Madagascar. The eclipse begins at 11h 30m and ends at 15h 39m.

2. A total eclipse of the Moon on 4 May is visible from Australasia, the western Pacific Ocean, the Indian Ocean, Antarctica, Asia (except the extreme north-east), Europe, Africa, the Atlantic Ocean, Newfoundland and South America. The partial eclipse begins at 18h 48m and ends at 22h 12m. Totality lasts from 19h 52m to 21h 08m.

3. A partial eclipse of the Sun on 14 October is visible from eastern and north-eastern Asia, western Alaska and the north Pacific Ocean, including Hawaii. The eclipse begins at 00h 55m and ends at 05h 04m.

4. A total eclipse of the Moon on 28 October is visible from the western Indian Ocean, western Asia, Africa, Europe, the Atlantic Ocean, Greenland, the Arctic Ocean, extreme north-east Asia, the Americas and the Pacific Ocean. The eclipse begins at 01h 14m and ends at 04h 54m. Totality lasts from 02h 23m to 03h 44m.

TRANSIT

There will be a transit of Venus across the disk of the Sun on 8 June. This will be visible in its entirety from the British Isles. The time of ingress (first contact) is about 5h 20m, and that of second contact 5h 40m. For egress, the corresponding times are 11h 04m and 11h 24m. The position angles are about 119 degrees for ingress and 214 degrees for egress. Transits of Venus are exceedingly rare. The previous one was in 1882 and the next ones after this year are in 2012 and 2117.

LUNAR OCCULTATIONS

Observations of the times of occultations are made by both amateur and professional astronomers. Such observations are later analysed to yield accurate positions of the Moon; this is one method of determining the difference between terrestrial time and universal time.

Many of the observations made by amateurs are obtained with the use of a stop-watch which is compared with a time-signal immediately after the observation. Thus an accuracy of about one-fifth of a second is obtainable, though the observer's personal equation may amount to one-third or one-half of a second.

The list on page 1251 includes most of the occultations visible under favourable conditions in the British Isles. No occultation is included unless the star is at least 10° above the horizon and the Sun sufficiently far below the horizon to permit the star to be seen with the naked eye or with a small telescope. The altitude limit is reduced from 10° to 2° for stars and planets brighter than magnitude 2.0 and such occultations are also predicted in daylight.

The column Phase shows (i) whether a disappearance (D) or reappearance (R) is to be observed; and (ii) whether it is at the dark limb (D) or bright limb (B). The column headed 'El. of Moon' gives the elongation of the Moon from the Sun, in degrees. The elongation increases from 0° at New Moon to 180° at Full Moon and on to 360° (or 0°) at New Moon again. Times and position angles (P), reckoned from the north point in the direction north, east, south, west, are given for Greenwich (lat. 51° 30', long. 0°) and Edinburgh (lat. 56° 00', long. 3° 12' west).

The coefficients a and b are the variations in the GMT for each degree of longitude (positive to the west) and latitude (positive to the north) respectively; they enable approximate times (to within about 1m generally) to be found for any point in the British Isles. If the point of observation is $\Delta\lambda$ degrees west and $\Delta\phi$ degrees north, the approximate time is found by adding $a.\Delta\lambda+b.\Delta\phi$ to the given GMT.

Example: the disappearance of Venus on 21 May at Coventry, found from both Greenwich and Edinburgh.

	Greenwich	Edinburgh
	°	°
Longitude	0.0	+3.2
Long. of Coventry	+1.5	+1.5
$\Delta\lambda$	+1.5	−1.7
Latitude	+51.5	+56.0
Lat. of Coventry	52.4	+52.4
$\Delta\phi$	+0.9	−3.6
	h m	h m
GMT	11 09.9	11 20.0
a.$\Delta\lambda$	−1.1	+0.7
b.$\Delta\phi$	+2.1	−10.8
	11 10.9	11 09.9

If the occultation is given for one station but not the other, the reason for the suppression is given by the following code:

N = star not occulted

A = star's altitude less than 10° (2° for bright stars and planets)

S = Sun not sufficiently below the horizon

G = occultation is of very short duration

In some cases the coefficients a and b are not given; this is because the occultation is so short that prediction for other places by means of these coefficients would not be reliable.

LUNAR OCCULTATIONS 2004

Date		ZC	Mag.	Phase	El. of Moon	GREENWICH UT h	m	a m	b m	P °	EDINBURGH UT h	m	a m	b m	P °
Jan.	3	586	7.0	DD	139	21	17.3	−1.0	+2.8	24	21	34.1	G		354
	5	740	6.3	DD	152	2	23.6	−0.9	−0.3	51	2	20.2	−1.0	+0.3	38
	5	852	5.0	DD	160	20	33.7	−1.4	+1.0	91	20	35.8	−1.0	+1.5	77
	6	900	4.9	DD	164	6	26.7	+0.6	−1.5	111	6	21.4	+0.4	−1.6	107
	14	1821	2.9	DB	256	2	16.1	−1.4	+2.1	77	2	23.6	G		60
	14	1821	2.9	RD	256	3	03.0	−0.2	−1.8	352	2	53.2	G		7
	29	434	6.9	DD	98	23	20.7	−0.3	−2.6	110	23	09.4	−0.5	−2.0	95
	31	660	4.4	DD	117	N					18	15.8	G		148
	31	660	4.4	RD	117	N					18	29.8	G		169
	31	664	5.4	DD	117	18	45.8	G		131	18	35.6	−1.7	+0.1	108
	31	676	7.1	DD	118	20	54.4	−1.4	+1.5	44	20	59.6	−1.1	+2.8	23
Feb.	2	842	6.3	DD	132	A					4	16.6	−0.2	−0.5	38
	24	257	4.5	DD	53	17	58.8	−0.7	+1.7	17	18	10.5	G		348
	25	391	7.4	DD	66	22	16.0	−0.1	−1.3	81	22	10.1	−0.2	−1.1	69
	27	621	6.2	DD	87	N					21	03.9	G		138
	27	630	7.5	DD	88	23	54.5	+0.1	−1.8	101	23	46.6	−0.1	−1.7	93
Mar.	1	912	7.0	DD	110	0	33.6	−0.1	−2.0	112	0	24.1	−0.2	−2.0	106
	1	926	7.0	DD	111	2	17.2	−0.1	−0.9	59	2	12.6	−0.2	−1.0	54
	2	1169	5.4	DD	130	19	30.7	−1.5	+0.8	90	19	31.5	−1.2	+1.5	74
	23	340	7.1	DD	34	A					20	25.6	−0.2	−0.6	49
	24	455	6.1	DD	45	A					21	21.4	−0.2	−0.5	45
	27	849	6.5	DD	78	21	37.8	−1.0	−0.4	52	21	33.7	−1.2	+0.2	40
	28	869	7.2	DD	79	0	19.5	+0.4	−1.6	109	0	13.2	+0.3	−1.7	104
	28	994	6.5	DD	88	19	35.1	−1.1	−3.1	137	S				
	29	1131	7.2	DD	100	22	12.3	−0.8	−1.8	106	22	02.0	−0.9	−1.6	99
	30	1251	5.9	DD	111	22	00.5	G		175	21	42.5	−0.2	−3.5	162
Apr.	1	1393	6.7	DD	125	A					3	25.6	+0.2	−1.6	98
	9	2371	4.9	RD	230	4	08.4	−0.9	−1.2	345	4	01.2	G		347
	22	676	7.1	DD	37	A					21	24.9	+0.6	−2.5	131
	25	1089	6.8	DD	70	22	57.8	+0.4	−2.1	133	22	49.5	+0.3	−2.1	130
	26	1206	5.9	DD	80	21	03.4	−1.8	0.0	52	20	58.9	G		41
	26	1211	6.2	DD	81	21	25.0	−0.5	−2.0	113	21	14.5	−0.6	−1.9	108
	27	1330	7.6	DD	92	21	39.3	−0.6	−2.1	125	21	28.2	−0.7	−2.0	121
	27	1334	7.0	DD	93	23	16.5	+0.1	−2.2	138	23	06.7	−0.1	−2.2	136
	28	1348	7.7	DD	94	A					1	41.2	+0.3	−1.5	95
	29	1544	5.7	DD	114	19	39.1	G		54	N				
	29	1553	7.5	DD	116	23	19.7	0.0	−2.5	166	23	08.7	−0.1	−2.4	165
May	21	VENUS	−4.4	DD	25	11	09.9	−0.7	+2.3	52	11	20.0	−0.4	+3.0	35
	21	VENUS	−4.4	RB	25	12	19.6	−1.6	+0.2	282	12	14.2	−1.6	−0.4	300
	29	1828	6.7	DD	122	23	00.3	−1.0	−1.5	108	22	50.5	−1.0	−1.4	108
Jun.	22	1479	6.3	DD	56	A					22	18.9	+0.4	−2.0	162
Jul.	13	599	4.5	RD	312	2	27.8	+0.3	+1.8	236	2	36.6	+0.2	+1.8	242
Sep.	24	3102	6.9	DD	132	20	03.4	−1.2	+0.9	44	20	03.7	−1.0	+0.8	39
Oct.	5	890	4.5	RD	256	4	10.9	−2.1	−2.1	313	N				
	20	2912	4.6	DD	88	19	04.6	−1.9	−1.0	118	18	55.9	−1.5	−0.5	110
	23	3358	7.2	DD	130	23	59.9	−0.9	−1.2	84	23	52.8	−0.7	−0.8	67
	24	3478	6.5	DD	139	18	36.6	−1.2	+1.4	81	18	40.0	−0.9	+1.5	76
Nov.	17	3010	6.3	DD	70	16	59.2	G		138	A				
	19	3323	7.6	DD	99	22	07.3	−1.6	−3.0	116	21	53.8	−1.0	−1.6	93
	20	3446	7.2	DD	110	19	25.7	−0.7	+1.2	26	19	29.5	−0.4	+1.3	13
	23	155	6.8	DD	137	0	56.6	−1.0	−3.2	113	0	43.3	−0.8	−1.7	91
	23	167	5.7	DD	137	2	41.6	−0.2	+0.5	27	2	45.5	−0.2	+1.8	5
Dec.	17	3392	7.1	DD	78	17	00.7	0.0	+2.0	359	17	15.2	G		334
	17	3409	7.0	DD	80	20	57.8	−0.7	−0.9	73	20	52.4	−0.6	−0.6	57
	18	3535	5.2	DD	92	21	31.3	−0.4	+0.7	26	21	35.5	0.0	+1.7	4
	19	109	6.5	DD	105	23	00.1	−0.6	−0.9	69	22	55.3	−0.6	−0.4	52
	20	214	6.4	DD	114	16	52.6	−0.3	+2.3	20	17	02.3	−0.1	+2.3	9
	22	457	6.5	DD	138	20	09.3	−1.6	+0.8	81	20	09.8	−1.2	+1.3	67
	23	582	5.8	DD	149	19	11.8	−1.3	+1.2	91	19	14.8	−0.9	+1.6	78

MEAN PLACES OF STARS 2004.5

Name	Mag.	RA h	RA m	Dec. °	Dec. '	Spectrum	Name	Mag.	RA h	RA m	Dec. °	Dec. '	Spectrum
α And *Alpheratz*	2.1	0	08.6	+29	07	A0p	γ Corvi	2.6	12	16.0	−17	34	B8
β Cassiopeiae *Caph*	2.3	0	09.4	+59	10	F5	α Crucis	1.0	12	26.9	−63	07	B1
γ Pegasi *Algenib*	2.8	0	13.5	+15	13	B2	γ Crucis	1.6	12	31.4	−57	08	M3
β Mensae	2.9	0	25.9	−77	14	G0	γ Centauri	2.2	12	41.8	−48	59	A0
α Phoenicis	2.4	0	26.5	−42	17	K0	γ Virginis	2.7	12	41.9	− 1	28	F0
α Cassiopeiae *Schedar*	2.2	0	40.8	+56	34	K0	β Crucis	1.3	12	48.0	−59	43	B1
β Ceti *Diphda*	2.0	0	43.8	−17	58	K0	ε Ursae Majoris *Alioth*	1.8	12	54.2	+55	56	A0p
γ Cassiopeiae*	Var.	0	57.0	+60	44	B0p	α Canum *Venaticorum*	2.9	12	56.2	+38	18	A0p
β Andromedae *Mirach*	2.1	1	10.0	+35	39	M0	ζ Ursae Majoris *Mizar*	2.1	13	24.1	+54	54	A2p
δ Cassiopeiae	2.7	1	26.1	+60	16	A5	α Virginis *Spica*	1.0	13	25.4	−11	11	B2
α Eridani *Achernar*	0.5	1	37.9	−57	13	B5	ε Centauri	2.6	13	40.2	−53	29	B1
β Arietis *Sheratan*	2.6	1	54.9	+20	50	A5	η Ursae Majoris *Alkaid*	1.9	13	47.7	+49	17	B3
γ Andromedae *Almak*	2.3	2	04.2	+42	21	K0	β Centauri *Hadar*	0.6	14	04.1	−60	24	B1
α Arietis *Hamal*	2.0	2	07.4	+23	29	K2	θ Centauri	2.1	14	07.0	−36	23	K0
α Ursae Minoris *Polaris*	2.0	2	37.0	+89	17	F8	α Bootis *Arcturus*	0.0	14	15.9	+19	10	K0
β Persei *Algol**	Var.	3	08.5	+40	58	B8	α Centauri *Rigil Kent*	0.1	14	39.9	−60	51	G0
α Persei *Mirfak*	1.8	3	24.6	+49	53	F5	ε Bootis	2.4	14	45.2	+27	03	K0
η Tauri *Alcyone*	2.9	3	47.8	+24	07	B5p	β UMi *Kochab*	2.1	14	50.7	+74	08	K5
α Tauri *Aldebaran*	0.9	4	36.2	+16	31	K5	γ Ursae *Minoris*	3.1	15	20.7	+71	49	A2
β Orionis *Rigel*	0.1	5	14.8	− 8	12	B8p	α CrB *Alphecca*	2.2	15	34.9	+26	42	A0
α Aurigae *Capella*	0.1	5	17.0	+46	00	G0	β Trianguli *Australis*	3.0	15	55.5	−63	27	F0
γ Orionis *Bellatrix*	1.6	5	25.4	+ 6	21	B2	δ Scorpii	2.3	16	00.6	−22	38	B0
β Tauri *Elnath*	1.7	5	26.6	+28	37	B8	β Scorpii	2.6	16	05.7	−19	49	B1
δ Orionis	2.2	5	32.2	− 0	18	B0	α Scorpii *Antares*	1.0	16	29.7	−26	26	M0
α Leporis	2.6	5	32.9	−17	49	F0	α Trianguli *Australis*	1.9	16	49.1	−69	02	K2
ε Orionis	1.7	5	36.4	− 1	12	B0	ε Scorpii	2.3	16	50.5	−34	18	K0
ζ Orionis	1.8	5	41.0	− 1	56	B0	α Herculis†	Var.	17	14.9	+14	23	M3
κ Orionis	2.1	5	48.0	− 9	40	B0	λ Scorpii	1.6	17	33.9	−37	06	B2
α Orionis *Betelgeuse**	Var.	5	55.4	+ 7	24	M0	α Ophiuchi *Rasalhague*	2.1	17	35.1	+12	33	A5
β Aurigae *Menkalinan*	1.9	5	59.9	+44	57	A0p	θ Scorpii	1.9	17	37.6	−43	00	F0
β CMa *Mirzam*	2.0	6	22.9	−17	58	B1	κ Scorpii	2.4	17	42.8	−39	02	B2
α Carinae *Canopus*	−0.7	6	24.1	−52	42	F0	γ Draconis	2.2	17	56.7	+51	29	K5
γ Geminorum *Alhena*	1.9	6	38.0	+16	24	A0	ε Sgr Kaus *Australis*	1.9	18	24.5	−34	23	A0
α Canis Majoris *Sirius*	−1.5	6	45.3	−16	43	A0	α Lyrae *Vega*	0.0	18	37.1	+38	47	A0
ε Canis Majoris	1.5	6	58.8	−28	59	B1	σ Sagittarii	2.0	18	55.5	−26	17	B3
δ Canis Majoris	1.9	7	08.6	−26	24	F8p	β Cygni *Albireo*	3.1	19	30.9	+27	58	K0
α Geminorum *Castor*	1.6	7	34.9	+31	53	A0	α Aquilae *Altair*	0.8	19	51.0	+ 8	53	A5
α CMi *Procyon*	0.4	7	39.5	+ 5	13	F5	α Capricorni	3.8	20	18.3	−12	32	G5
β Geminorum *Pollux*	1.1	7	45.6	+28	01	K0	γ Cygni	2.2	20	22.4	+40	16	F8p
ζ Puppis	2.3	8	03.7	−40	01	Od	α Pavonis	1.9	20	26.0	−56	43	B3
γ Velorum	1.8	8	09.7	−47	21	Oap	α Cygni *Deneb*	1.3	20	41.6	+45	18	A2p
ε Carinae	1.9	8	22.6	−59	31	K0	α Cephei *Alderamin*	2.4	21	18.7	+62	36	A5
δ Velorum	2.0	8	44.8	−54	43	A0	ε Pegasi	2.4	21	44.4	+ 9	54	K0
λ Velorum *Suhail*	2.2	9	08.2	−43	27	K5	δ Capricorni	2.9	21	47.3	−16	06	A5
β Carinae	1.7	9	13.2	−69	44	A0	α Gruis	1.7	22	08.5	−46	56	B5
							δ Cephei†	3.7	22	29.3	+58	26	†
ι Carinae	2.2	9	17.2	−59	18	F0	β Gruis	2.1	22	42.9	−46	52	M3
κ Velorum	2.6	9	22.3	−55	02	B3	α PsA *Fomalhaut*	1.2	22	57.9	−29	36	A3
α Hydrae *Alphard*	2.0	9	27.8	− 8	41	K2	β Pegasi *Scheat*	2.4	23	04.0	+28	06	M0
α Leonis *Regulus*	1.3	10	08.6	+11	57	B8	α Pegasi *Markab*	2.5	23	05.0	+15	14	A0
γ Leonis *Algeiba*	1.9	10	20.2	+19	49	K0							
β Ursae Majoris *Merak*	2.4	11	02.1	+56	21	A0							
α Ursae Majoris *Dubhe*	1.8	11	04.0	+61	44	K0							
δ Leonis	2.6	11	14.3	+20	30	A3							
β Leonis *Denebola*	2.1	11	49.3	+14	33	A2							
γ Ursae Majoris *Phecda*	2.4	11	54.1	+53	40	A0							

*γ Cassiopeiae, 2003 mag. 2.5. β Persei, mag. 2.1 to 3.4.
α Orionis, mag. 0.1 to 1.2.
†α Herculis, mag. 3.1 to 3.9.
δ Cephei, mag. 3.7 to 4.4, spectrum F5 to G0.

The positions of heavenly bodies on the celestial sphere are defined by two co-ordinates, right ascension and declination, which are analogous to longitude and latitude on the surface of the Earth. If we imagine the plane of the terrestrial equator extended indefinitely, it will cut the celestial sphere in a great circle known as the celestial equator. Similarly the plane of the Earth's orbit, when extended, cuts in the great circle called the ecliptic. The two intersections of these circles are known as the First Point of Aries and the First Point of Libra. If from any star a perpendicular is drawn to the celestial equator, the length of this perpendicular is the star's declination. The arc, measured eastwards along the equator from the First Point of Aries to the foot of this perpendicular, is the right ascension. An alternative definition of right ascension is the angle at the celestial pole (where the Earth's axis, if prolonged, would meet the sphere) between the great circles to the First Point of Aries and to the star.

The plane of the Earth's equator has a slow movement, so that our reference system for right ascension and declination is not fixed. The consequent alteration in these quantities from year to year is called precession. In right ascension it is an increase of about 3 seconds a year for equatorial stars, and larger or smaller changes in either direction for stars near the poles, depending on the right ascension of the star. In declination it varies between $+20''$ and $-20''$ according to the right ascension of the star.

A star or other body crosses the meridian when the sidereal time is equal to its right ascension. The altitude is then a maximum, and may be deduced by remembering that the altitude of the elevated pole is numerically equal to the latitude, while that of the equator at its intersection with the meridian is equal to the co-latitude, or complement of the latitude.

Thus in London (lat. 51° 30′) the meridian altitude of Sirius is found as follows:

	°	′
Altitude of equator	38	30
Declination south	16	43
Difference	21	47

The altitude of Capella (Dec. +46° 00′) at lower transit is:

	°	′
Altitude of pole	51	30
Polar distance of star	44	00
Difference	7	30

The brightness of a heavenly body is denoted by its magnitude. Omitting the exceptionally bright stars Sirius and Canopus, the twenty brightest stars are of the first magnitude, while the faintest stars visible to the naked eye are of the sixth magnitude. The magnitude scale is a precise one, as a difference of five magnitudes represents a ratio of 100 to 1 in brightness. Typical second magnitude stars are Polaris and the stars in the belt of Orion. The scale is most easily fixed in memory by comparing the stars with Norton's *Star Atlas*. The stars Sirius and Canopus and the planets Venus and Jupiter are so bright that their magnitudes are expressed by negative numbers. A small telescope will show stars down to the ninth or tenth magnitude, while stars fainter than the twentieth magnitude may be photographed by long exposures with the largest telescopes.

MEAN AND SIDEREAL TIME

Acceleration						Retardation					
h	m	s	m	s	s	h	m	s	m	s	s
1	0	10	0	00	0	1	0	10	0	00	0
2	0	20	3	02	1	2	0	20	3	03	1
3	0	30	9	07	2	3	0	29	9	09	2
4	0	39	15	13	3	4	0	39	15	15	3
5	0	49	21	18	4	5	0	49	21	21	4
6	0	59	27	23	5	6	0	59	27	28	5
7	1	09	33	28	6	7	1	09	33	34	6
8	1	19	39	34	7	8	1	19	39	40	7
9	1	29	45	39	8	9	1	28	45	46	8
10	1	39	51	44	9	10	1	38	51	53	9
11	1	48	57	49	10	11	1	48	57	59	10
12	1	58	60	00		12	1	58	60	00	
13	2	08				13	2	08			
14	2	18				14	2	18			
15	2	28				15	2	27			
16	2	38				16	2	37			
17	2	48				17	2	47			
18	2	57				18	2	57			
19	3	07				19	3	07			
20	3	17				20	3	17			
21	3	27				21	3	26			
22	3	37				22	3	36			
23	3	47				23	3	46			
24	3	57				24	3	56			

The length of a sidereal day in mean time is 23h 56m 04s.09. Hence 1h MT = 1h+9s.86 ST and 1h ST = 1h −9s.83 MT.

To convert an interval of mean time to the corresponding interval of sidereal time, enter the acceleration table with the given mean time (taking the hours and the minutes and seconds separately) and add the acceleration obtained to the given mean time. To convert an interval of sidereal time to the corresponding interval of mean time, take out the retardation for the given sidereal time and subtract.

The columns for the minutes and seconds of the argument are in the form known as critical tables. To use these tables, find in the appropriate left-hand column the two entries between which the given number of minutes and seconds lies; the quantity in the right-hand column between these two entries is the required acceleration or retardation. Thus the acceleration for 11m 26s (which lies between the entries 9m 07s and 15m 13s) is 2s. If the given number of minutes and seconds is a tabular entry, the required acceleration or retardation is the entry in the right-hand column above the given tabular entry, e.g. the retardation for 45m 46s is 7s.

Example – Convert 14h 27m 35s from ST to MT

	h	m	s
Given ST	14	27	35
Retardation for 14h		2	18
Retardation for 27m 35s			5
Corresponding MT	14	25	12

For further explanation, *see* pages 1257–8.

ECLIPSES AND SHADOW TRANSITS OF JUPITER'S SATELLITES 2004

GMT			Sat.	Phen.
d	h	m		
January				
1	05	47	II	Sh.I
3	00	54	II	Ec.D
4	05	58	I	Ec.D
5	03	19	I	Sh.I
5	05	35	I	Sh.E
6	00	26	I	Ec.D
6	01	57	III	Ec.R
7	00	03	I	Sh.E
10	03	28	II	Ec.D
12	00	30	II	Sh.E
12	05	12	I	Sh.I
12	23	24	IV	Ec.R
13	02	19	I	Ec.D
13	02	23	III	Ec.D
13	05	54	III	Ec.R
13	23	40	I	Sh.I
14	01	56	I	Sh.E
17	06	01	II	Ec.D
19	00	14	II	Sh.I
19	03	05	II	Sh.E
19	07	05	I	Sh.I
20	04	13	I	Ec.D
20	06	21	III	Ec.D
21	01	33	I	Sh.I
21	03	49	I	Sh.E
21	05	01	IV	Sh.I
21	22	41	I	Ec.D
23	23	45	III	Sh.E
26	02	49	II	Sh.I
26	05	40	II	Sh.E
27	06	06	I	Ec.D
28	03	26	I	Sh.I
28	05	42	I	Sh.E
29	00	35	I	Ec.D
29	21	55	I	Sh.I
30	00	11	I	Sh.E
31	00	15	III	Sh.I
31	03	42	III	Sh.E
February				
2	05	25	II	Sh.I
4	00	25	II	Ec.D
4	05	20	I	Sh.I
5	02	29	I	Ec.D
5	21	34	II	Sh.E
5	23	48	I	Sh.I
6	02	04	I	Sh.E
6	22	59	IV	Sh.I
7	02	41	IV	Sh.E
7	04	12	III	Sh.I
11	02	59	II	Ec.D
12	04	23	I	Ec.D
12	21	19	II	Sh.I
13	00	10	II	Sh.E
13	01	41	I	Sh.I
13	03	57	I	Sh.E
13	22	51	I	Ec.D
14	22	25	I	Sh.E
17	22	14	III	Ec.D
18	05	32	II	Ec.D
19	06	17	I	Ec.D
19	23	55	II	Sh.I
20	02	46	II	Sh.E
20	03	35	I	Sh.I
20	05	51	I	Sh.E
21	00	45	I	Ec.D
21	22	03	I	Sh.I

GMT			Sat.	Phen.
d	h	m		
22	00	19	I	Sh.E
23	20	34	IV	Sh.E
25	02	13	III	Ec.D
27	02	31	II	Sh.I
27	05	23	II	Sh.E
27	05	28	I	Sh.I
28	02	39	I	Ec.D
28	21	23	II	Ec.D
28	23	57	I	Sh.I
29	02	12	I	Sh.E
29	21	08	I	Ec.D
March				
1	20	41	I	Sh.E
3	01	33	IV	Ec.D
3	05	08	IV	Ec.R
5	05	08	II	Sh.I
6	20	04	III	Sh.I
6	23	29	III	Sh.E
7	01	50	I	Sh.I
7	02	45	II	Ec.R
7	04	06	I	Sh.E
8	01	19	I	Ec.R
8	20	19	I	Sh.I
8	21	17	II	Sh.I
8	22	35	I	Sh.E
9	19	48	I	Ec.R
14	00	03	III	Sh.I
14	03	27	III	Sh.E
14	03	44	I	Sh.I
15	03	14	I	Ec.R
15	21	02	II	Sh.I
15	22	13	I	Sh.I
15	23	53	II	Sh.E
16	00	28	I	Sh.E
16	21	43	I	Ec.R
19	19	36	IV	Ec.D
19	23	03	IV	Ec.R
21	04	01	III	Sh.I
22	23	39	II	Sh.I
23	00	'07	I	Sh.I
23	02	22	I	Sh.E
23	02	30	II	Sh.E
23	23	37	I	Ec.R
24	20	51	I	Sh.I
24	21	10	II	Ec.R
24	21	33	III	Ec.R
30	02	01	I	Sh.I
30	02	16	II	Sh.I
31	01	32	I	Ec.R
31	20	29	I	Sh.I
31	22	45	I	Sh.E
31	23	44	II	Ec.R

GMT			Sat.	Phen.
d	h	m		
April				
1	01	32	III	Ec.R
1	20	01	I	Ec.R
7	22	24	I	Sh.I
8	00	39	I	Sh.E
8	02	18	II	Ec.R
8	21	56	I	Ec.R
9	21	03	II	Sh.E
13	23	01	IV	Sh.E
14	02	12	IV	Sh.E
15	00	18	I	Sh.I
15	02	33	I	Sh.E
15	23	51	I	Ec.R
16	20	50	II	Sh.I
16	21	02	I	Sh.E
16	23	40	II	Sh.E
18	23	16	III	Sh.E
22	02	13	I	Sh.I
23	01	46	I	Ec.R
23	20	41	I	Sh.I
23	22	56	I	Sh.E
23	23	27	II	Sh.I
24	20	14	I	Ec.R
25	20	43	II	Ec.R
25	23	56	III	Sh.I
30	22	36	I	Sh.I
May				
1	00	50	I	Sh.E
1	22	10	I	Ec.R
2	23	18	II	Ec.R
6	21	25	III	Ec.R
8	00	30	I	Sh.I
9	00	05	I	Ec.R
9	21	13	I	Sh.E
11	20	48	II	Sh.E
13	22	04	III	Ec.D
16	20	54	I	Sh.I

GMT			Sat.	Phen.
16	23	08	I	Sh.E
18	23	25	II	Sh.E
22	22	49	I	Sh.I
24	22	24	I	Ec.R
25	22	44	IV	Ec.R
25	23	14	II	Sh.I
31	23	07	III	Sh.E
June				
1	21	26	I	Sh.E
3	22	55	II	Ec.R
16	22	38	I	Ec.R
November				
7	05	20	II	Ec.D
15	06	17	I	Sh.I
16	05	11	II	Sh.E
16	05	33	III	Ec.D
22	05	57	I	Sh.I
23	05	02	II	Sh.I
30	05	02	I	Ec.D
December				
1	04	32	I	Sh.E
4	06	14	III	Sh.E
7	06	54	I	Ec.D
8	04	12	I	Sh.I
8	06	25	I	Sh.E
9	05	01	II	Ec.D
15	06	06	I	Sh.I
18	04	39	II	Sh.E
22	04	15	III	Ec.R
23	05	08	I	Ec.D
24	04	41	I	Sh.E
25	04	31	II	Sh.I
25	07	12	II	Sh.E
29	05	19	III	Ec.D
30	07	01	I	Ec.D
31	04	21	I	Sh.I
31	06	34	I	Sh.E

Jupiter's satellites transit across the disk from east to west, and pass behind the disk from west to east. The shadows that they cast also transit across the disk. With the exception at times of Satellite IV, the satellites also pass through the shadow of the planet, i.e. they are eclipsed. Just before opposition the satellite disappears in the shadow to the west of the planet and reappears from occultation on the east limb. Immediately after opposition the satellite is occulted at the west limb and reappears from eclipse to the east of the planet. At times approximately two to four months before and after opposition, both phases of eclipses of Satellite III may be seen. When Satellite IV is eclipsed, both phases may be seen.

The times given refer to the centre of the satellite. As the satellite is of considerable size, the immersion and emersion phases are not instantaneous. Even when the satellite enters or leaves the shadow along a radius of the shadow, the phase can last for several minutes. With Satellite IV, grazing phenomena can occur so that the light from the satellite may fade and brighten again without a complete eclipse taking place.

The list of phenomena gives most of the eclipses and shadow transits visible in the British Isles under favourable conditions.

Ec.	= Eclipse	R	= Reappearance
Sh.	= Shadow transit	I	= Ingress
D	= Disappearance	E	= Egress

EXPLANATION OF ASTRONOMICAL DATA

Positions of the heavenly bodies are given only to the degree of accuracy required by amateur astronomers for setting telescopes, or for plotting on celestial globes or star atlases. Where intermediate positions are required, linear interpolation may be employed.

Definitions of the terms used cannot be given here. They must be sought in astronomical literature and textbooks.

A special feature has been made of the times when the various heavenly bodies are visible in the British Isles. Since two columns, calculated for latitudes 52° and 56°, are devoted to risings and settings, the range 50° to 58° can be covered by interpolation and extrapolation. The times given in these columns are Greenwich Mean Times for the meridian of Greenwich. An observer west of this meridian must add his/her longitude (in time) and vice versa.

In accordance with the usual convention in astronomy, + and – indicate respectively north and south latitudes or declinations.

All data are, unless otherwise stated, for 0h Greenwich Mean Time (GMT), i.e. at the midnight at the beginning of the day named. Allowance must be made for British Summer Time during the period that this is in operation.

PAGE ONE OF EACH MONTH

The calendar for each month is explained on page 1199.

Under the heading Astronomical Phenomena will be found particulars of the more important conjunctions of the Sun, Moon and planets with each other, and also the dates of other astronomical phenomena of special interest.

Times of Minima of Algol are approximate times of the middle of the period of diminished light.

The Constellations listed each month are those that are near the meridian at the beginning of the month at 22h local mean time. Allowance must be made for British Summer Time if necessary. The fact that any star crosses the meridian 4m earlier each night or 2h earlier each month may be used, in conjunction with the lists given each month, to find what constellations are favourably placed at any moment. The table preceding the list of constellations may be extended indefinitely at the rate just quoted.

The principal phases of the Moon are the GMTs when the difference between the longitude of the Moon and that of the Sun is 0°, 90°, 180° or 270°. The times of perigee and apogee are those when the Moon is nearest to, and farthest from, the Earth, respectively. The nodes or points of intersection of the Moon's orbit and the ecliptic make a complete retrograde circuit of the ecliptic in about 19 years. From a knowledge of the longitude of the ascending node and the inclination, whose value does not vary much from 5°, the path of the Moon among the stars may be plotted on a celestial globe or star atlas.

PAGE TWO OF EACH MONTH

The Sun's semi-diameter, in arc, is given once a month.

The right ascension and declination (Dec.) is that of the true Sun. The right ascension of the mean Sun is obtained by applying the equation of time, with the sign given, to the right ascension of the true Sun, or, more easily, by applying 12h to the Sidereal Time. The direction in which the equation of time has to be applied in different problems is a frequent source of confusion and error. Apparent Solar Time is equal to the Mean Solar Time plus the Equation of Time. For example, at 12h GMT on August 8 the Equation of Time is −5m 34s and thus at 12h Mean Time on that day the Apparent Time is 12h −5m 34s = 11h 54m 26s.

The Greenwich Sidereal Time at 0h and the Transit of the First Point of Aries (which is really the mean time

when the sidereal time is 0h) are used for converting mean time to sidereal time and vice versa.

The GMT of transit of the Sun at Greenwich may also be taken as the local mean time (LMT) of transit in any longitude. It is independent of latitude. The GMT of transit in any longitude is obtained by adding the longitude to the time given if west, and vice versa.

LIGHTING-UP TIME

The legal importance of sunrise and sunset is that the Road Vehicles Lighting Regulations 1989 (SI 1989 No. 1796) make the use of front and rear position lamps on vehicles compulsory during the period between sunset and sunrise. Headlamps on vehicles are required to be used during the hours of darkness on unlit roads or whenever visibility is seriously reduced. The hours of darkness are defined in these regulations as the period between half an hour after sunset and half an hour before sunrise.

In all laws and regulations 'sunset' refers to the local sunset, i.e. the time at which the Sun sets at the place in question. This common-sense interpretation has been upheld by legal tribunals. Thus the necessity for providing for different latitudes and longitudes, as already described, is evident.

SUNRISE AND SUNSET

The times of sunrise and sunset are those when the Sun's upper limb, as affected by refraction, is on the true horizon of an observer at sea-level. Assuming the mean refraction to be 34″, and the Sun's semi-diameter to be 16′, the time given is that when the true zenith distance of the Sun's centre is 90°+34′+16′ or 90° 50′, or, in other words, when the depression of the Sun's centre below the true horizon is 50′. The upper limb is then 34′ below the true horizon, but is brought there by refraction. An observer on a ship might see the Sun for a minute or so longer, because of the dip of the horizon, while another viewing the sunset over hills or mountains would record an earlier time. Nevertheless, the moment when the true zenith distance of the Sun's centre is 90° 50′ is a precise time dependent only on the latitude and longitude of the place, and independent of its altitude above sea-level, the contour of its horizon, the vagaries of refraction or the small seasonal change in the Sun's semi-diameter; this moment is suitable in every way as a definition of sunset (or sunrise) for all statutory purposes. (For further information, see footnote on page 1256.)

TWILIGHT

Light reaches us before sunrise and continues to reach us for some time after sunset. The interval between darkness and sunrise or sunset and darkness is called twilight. Astronomically speaking, twilight is considered to begin or end when the Sun's centre is 18° below the horizon, as no light from the Sun can then reach the observer. As thus defined twilight may last several hours; in high latitudes at the summer solstice the depression of 18° is not reached, and twilight lasts from sunset to sunrise.

The need for some sub-division of twilight is met by dividing the gathering darkness into four stages.

(1) *Sunrise or Sunset*, defined as above
(2) *Civil twilight*, which begins or ends when the Sun's centre is 6° below the horizon. This marks the time when operations requiring daylight may commence or must cease. In England it varies from about 30 to 60 minutes after sunset and the same interval before sunrise

(3) *Nautical twilight*, which begins or ends when the Sun's centre is 12° below the horizon. This marks the time when it is, to all intents and purposes, completely dark

(4) *Astronomical twilight*, which begins or ends when the Sun's centre is 18° below the horizon. This marks theoretical perfect darkness. It is of little practical importance, especially if nautical twilight is tabulated

To assist observers the durations of civil, nautical and astronomical twilights are given at intervals of ten days. The beginning of a particular twilight is found by subtracting the duration from the time of sunrise, while the end is found by adding the duration to the time of sunset. Thus the beginning of astronomical twilight in latitude 52°, on the Greenwich meridian, on March 11 is found as 06h 23m–113m = 04h 30m and similarly the end of civil twilight as 17h 58m+34m = 18h 32m. The letters TAN (twilight all night) are printed when twilight lasts all night.

Under the heading The Night Sky will be found notes describing the position and visibility of the planets and other phenomena.

PAGE THREE OF EACH MONTH

The Moon moves so rapidly among the stars that its position is given only to the degree of accuracy that permits linear interpolation. The right ascension (RA) and declination (Dec.) are geocentric, i.e. for an imaginary observer at the centre of the Earth. To an observer on the surface of the Earth the position is always different, as the altitude is always less on account of parallax, which may reach 1°.

The lunar terminator is the line separating the bright from the dark part of the Moon's disk. Apart from irregularities of the lunar surface, the terminator is elliptical, because it is a circle seen in projection. It becomes the full circle forming the limb, or edge, of the Moon at New and Full Moon. The selenographic longitude of the terminator is measured from the mean centre of the visible disk, which may differ from the visible centre by as much as 8°, because of libration.

Instead of the longitude of the terminator the Sun's selenographic co-longitude (Sun's co-long.) is tabulated. It is numerically equal to the selenographic longitude of the morning terminator, measured eastwards from the mean centre of the disk. Thus its value is approximately 270° at New Moon, 360° at First Quarter, 90° at Full Moon and 180° at Last Quarter.

The Position Angle (PA) of the Bright Limb is the position angle of the midpoint of the illuminated limb, measured eastwards from the north point on the disk. The Phase column shows the percentage of the area of the Moon's disk illuminated; this is also the illuminated percentage of the diameter at right angles to the line of cusps. The terminator is a semi-ellipse whose major axis is the line of cusps, and whose semi-minor axis is determined by the tabulated percentage; from New Moon to Full Moon the east limb is dark, and vice versa.

The times given as moonrise and moonset are those when the upper limb of the Moon is on the horizon of an observer at sea-level. The Sun's horizontal parallax (Hor. par.) is about 9', and is negligible when considering sunrise and sunset, but that of the Moon averages about 57'. Hence the computed time represents the moment when the true zenith distance of the Moon is 90° 50' (as for the Sun) minus the horizontal parallax. The time required for the Sun or Moon to rise or set is about four minutes (except in high latitudes). *See* also page 1249 and footnote below.

The GMT of transit of the Moon over the meridian of Greenwich is given; these times are independent of

latitude but must be corrected for longitude. For places in the British Isles it suffices to add the longitude if west, and vice versa. For other places a further correction is necessary because of the rapid movement of the Moon relative to the stars. The entire correction is conveniently determined by first finding the west longitude λ of the place. If the place is in west longitude, λ is the ordinary west longitude; if the place is in east longitude λ is the complement to 24h (or 360°) of the longitude and will be greater than 12h (or 180°). The correction then consists of two positive portions, namely λ and the fraction $\lambda/24$ (or $\lambda°/360$) multiplied by the difference between consecutive transits. Thus for Christchurch, New Zealand, the longitude is 11h 31m east, so $\lambda=12$h 29m and the fraction $\lambda/24$ is 0.52. The transit on the local date 25 May 2004 is found as follows:

		d	h	m
GMT of transit at Greenwich	May	24	16	19
λ			12	29
0.52 × (17h 07m – 16h 19m)				25
GMT of transit at Christchurch		25	05	13
Corr. to NZ Standard Time			12	00
Local standard time of transit	May	25	17	13

As is evident, for any given place the quantities λ and the correction to local standard time may be combined permanently, being here 24h 29m.

Positions of Mercury are given for every second day, and those of Venus and Mars for every fifth day; they may be interpolated linearly. The diameter (Diam.) is given in seconds of arc. The phase is the illuminated percentage of the disk. In the case of the inner planets this approaches 100 at superior conjunction and 0 at inferior conjunction. When the phase is less than 50 the planet is crescent-shaped or horned; for greater phases it is gibbous. In the case of the exterior planet Mars, the phase approaches 100 at conjunction and opposition, and is a minimum at the quadratures.

Since the planets cannot be seen when on the horizon, the actual times of rising and setting are not given; instead, the time when the planet has an apparent altitude of 5° has been tabulated. If the time of transit is between 00h and 12h the time refers to an altitude of 5° above the eastern horizon; if between 12h and 24h, to the western horizon. The phenomenon tabulated is the one that occurs between sunset and sunrise. The times given may be interpolated for latitude and corrected for longitude, as in the case of the Sun and Moon.

The GMT at which the planet transits the Greenwich meridian is also given. The times of transit are to be corrected to local meridians in the usual way, as already described.

SUNRISE, SUNSET, MOONRISE AND MOONSET

The tables have been constructed for the meridian of Greenwich and for latitudes 52° and 56°. They give Greenwich Mean Time (GMT) throughout the year. To obtain the GMT of the phenomenon as seen from any other latitude and longitude in the British Isles, first interpolate or extrapolate for latitude by the usual rules of proportion. To the time thus found, the longitude (expressed in time) is to be added if west (as it usually is in Great Britain) or subtracted if east. If the longitude is expressed in degrees and minutes of arc, it must be converted to time at the rate of 1° = 4m and 15′ = 1m.

A method of calculating rise and set times for other places in the world is given on pages 1248–9.

PAGE FOUR OF EACH MONTH

The GMTs of sunrise and sunset for seven cities, whose adopted positions in longitude (W.) and latitude (N.) are given immediately below the name, may be used not only for these phenomena, but also for lighting-up times (*see* page 1255 for a fuller explanation).

The particulars for the four outer planets resemble those for the planets on Page Three of each month, except that, under Uranus and Neptune, times when the planet is 10° high instead of 5° high are given; this is because of the inferior brightness of these planets. The diameters given for the rings of Saturn are those of the major axis (in the plane of the planet's equator) and the minor axis respectively. The former has a small seasonal change due to the slightly varying distance of the Earth from Saturn, but the latter varies from zero when the Earth passes through the ring plane every 15 years to a maximum opening half-way between these periods. The rings were last open at their widest extent (and Saturn at its brightest) in 2002; this will occur again in 2017. The Earth passed through the ring plane in 1995–6 and will do so again in 2009.

TIME

From the earliest ages, the natural division of time into recurring periods of day and night has provided the practical time-scale for the everyday activities of the human race. Indeed, if any alternative means of time measurement is adopted, it must be capable of adjustment so as to remain in general agreement with the natural time-scale defined by the diurnal rotation of the Earth on its axis. Ideally the rotation should be measured against a fixed frame of reference; in practice it must be measured against the background provided by the celestial bodies. If the Sun is chosen as the reference point, we obtain Apparent Solar Time, which is the time indicated by a sundial. It is not a uniform time but is subject to variations which amount to as much as a quarter of an hour in each direction. Such wide variations cannot be tolerated in a practical time-scale, and this has led to the concept of Mean Solar Time in which all the days are exactly the same length and equal to the average length of the Apparent Solar Day.

The positions of the stars in the sky are specified in relation to a fictitious reference point in the sky known as the First Point of Aries (or the Vernal Equinox). It is therefore convenient to adopt this same reference point when considering the rotation of the Earth against the background of the stars. The time-scale so obtained is known as Apparent Sidereal Time.

GREENWICH MEAN TIME

The daily rotation of the Earth on its axis causes the Sun and the other heavenly bodies to appear to cross the sky from east to west. It is convenient to represent this relative motion as if the Sun really performed a daily circuit around a fixed Earth. Noon in Apparent Solar Time may then be defined as the time at which the Sun transits across the observer's meridian. In Mean Solar Time, noon is similarly defined by the meridian transit of a fictitious Mean Sun moving uniformly in the sky with the same average speed as the true Sun. Mean Solar Time observed on the meridian of the transit circle telescope of the Royal Observatory at Greenwich is called Greenwich Mean Time (GMT). The mean solar day is divided into 24 hours and, for astronomical and other scientific purposes, these are numbered 0 to 23, commencing at midnight. Civil time is usually reckoned in two periods of 12 hours, designated a.m. (*ante meridiem*, i.e. before noon) and p.m. (*post meridiem*, i.e. after noon), although the 24 hour clock is increasingly being used.

UNIVERSAL TIME

Before 1925 January 1, GMT was reckoned in 24 hours commencing at noon; since that date it has been reckoned from midnight. To avoid confusion in the use of the designation GMT before and after 1925, since 1928 astronomers have tended to use the term Universal Time (UT) or Weltzeit (WZ) to denote GMT measured from Greenwich Mean Midnight.

In precision work it is necessary to take account of small variations in Universal Time. These arise from small irregularities in the rotation of the Earth. Observed astronomical time is designated UT0. Observed time corrected for the effects of the motion of the poles (giving rise to a 'wandering' in longitude) is designated UT1. There is also a seasonal fluctuation in the rate of rotation of the Earth arising from meteorological causes, often called the annual fluctuation. UT1 corrected for this effect is designated UT2 and provides a time-scale free from short-period fluctuations. It is still subject to small secular and irregular changes.

APPARENT SOLAR TIME

As mentioned above, the time shown by a sundial is called Apparent Solar Time. It differs from Mean Solar Time by an amount known as the Equation of Time, which is the total effect of two causes which make the length of the apparent solar day non-uniform. One cause of variation is that the orbit of the Earth is not a circle but an ellipse, having the Sun at one focus. As a consequence, the angular speed of the Earth in its orbit is not constant; it is greatest at the beginning of January when the Earth is nearest the Sun.

The other cause is due to the obliquity of the ecliptic; the plane of the equator (which is at right angles to the axis of rotation of the Earth) does not coincide with the ecliptic (the plane defined by the apparent annual motion of the Sun around the celestial sphere) but is inclined to it at an angle of 23° 26′. As a result, the apparent solar day is shorter than average at the equinoxes and longer at the solstices. From the combined effects of the components due to obliquity and eccentricity, the equation of time reaches its maximum values in February (−14 minutes) and early November (+16 minutes). It has a zero value on four dates during the year, and it is only on these dates (approximately April 15, June 14, September 1 and December 25) that a sundial shows Mean Solar Time.

SIDEREAL TIME

A sidereal day is the duration of a complete rotation of the Earth with reference to the First Point of Aries. The term sidereal (or 'star') time is a little misleading since the time-scale so defined is not exactly the same as that which would be defined by successive transits of a selected star, as there is a small progressive motion between the stars and the First Point of Aries due to the precession of the Earth's axis. This makes the length of the sidereal day shorter than the true period of rotation by 0.008 seconds. Superimposed on this steady precessional motion are small oscillations (nutation), giving rise to fluctuations in apparent sidereal time amounting to as much as 1.2 seconds. It is therefore customary to employ Mean Sidereal Time, from which these fluctuations have been removed. The conversion of GMT to Greenwich sidereal time (GST) may be performed by adding the value of the GST at 0h on the day in question (Page Two of each month) to the GMT converted to sidereal time using the table on page 1253.

Example – To find the GST at August 8d 02h 41m 11s GMT

	h	m	s
GST at 0h	21	07	21
GMT	2	41	11
Acceleration for 2h			20
Acceleration for 41m 11s			7
Sum = GST =	23	48	59

If the observer is not on the Greenwich meridian then his/her longitude, measured positively westwards from Greenwich, must be subtracted from the GST to obtain Local Sidereal Time (LST). Thus, in the above example, an observer 5h east of Greenwich, or 19h west, would find the LST as 4h 48m 59s.

EPHEMERIS TIME

An analysis of observations of the positions of the Sun, Moon and planets taken over an extended period is used in preparing ephemerides. (An ephemeris is a table giving the apparent position of a heavenly body at regular intervals of time, e.g. one day or ten days, and may be used to compare current observations with tabulated positions.) Discrepancies between the positions of heavenly bodies observed over a 300-year period and their predicted positions arose because the time-scale to which the observations were related was based on the assumption that the rate of rotation of the Earth is uniform. It is now known that this rate of rotation is variable. A revised time-scale, Ephemeris Time (ET), was devised to bring the ephemerides into agreement with the observations.

The second of ET is defined in terms of the annual motion of the Earth in its orbit around the Sun (1/31556925.9747 of the tropical year for 1900 January 0d 12h ET). The precise determination of ET from astronomical observations is a lengthy process as the requisite standard of accuracy can only be achieved by averaging over a number of years.

In 1976 the International Astronomical Union adopted Terrestrial Dynamical Time (TDT), a new dynamical time-scale for general use whose scale unit is the SI second (see Atomic Time). TDT was renamed Terrestrial Time (TT) in 1991. ET is now of little more than historical interest.

TERRESTRIAL TIME

The uniform time system used in computing the ephemerides of the solar system is Terrestrial Time (TT), which has replaced ET for this purpose. Except for the most rigorous astronomical calculations, it may be assumed to be the same as ET. During 2004 the estimated difference TT–UT is about 65 seconds.

ATOMIC TIME

The fundamental standards of time and frequency must be defined in terms of a periodic motion adequately uniform, enduring and measurable. Progress has made it possible to use natural standards, such as atomic or molecular oscillations. Continuous oscillations are generated in an electrical circuit, the frequency of which is then compared or brought into coincidence with the frequency characteristic of the absorption or emission by the atoms or molecules when they change between two selected energy levels. The National Physical Laboratory (NPL) routinely uses clocks of high stability produced by locking a quartz oscillator to the frequencies defined by caesium or hydrogen atoms.

International Atomic Time (TAI), established through international collaboration, is formed by combining the readings of many caesium clocks and was set close to the astronomically-based Universal Time (UT) near the beginning of 1958. It was formally recognized in 1971 and since 1988 January 1 has been maintained by the International Bureau of Weights and Measures (BIPM). The second markers are generated according to the International System (SI) definition adopted in 1967 at the 13th General Conference of Weights and Measures: 'The second is the duration of 9 192 631 770 periods of the radiation corresponding to the transition between the two hyperfine levels of the ground state of the caesium-133 atom.'

Civil time in almost all countries is now based on Co-ordinated Universal Time (UTC), which was adopted for scientific purposes on 1972 January 1. UTC differs from TAI by an integer number of seconds (determined from studies of the rate of rotation of the Earth) and was designed to make both atomic time and UT accessible with accuracies appropriate for most users. The UTC time-scale is adjusted by the insertion (or, in principle, omission) of leap seconds in order to keep it within ±0.9 s of UT. These leap seconds are introduced, when necessary, at the same instant throughout the world, either at the end of December or at the end of June. So, for example, the 22nd leap second occurred at 0h UTC on 1999 January 1. All leap seconds so far have been positive, with 61 seconds in the final minute of the UTC month. The time 23h 59m 60s UTC is followed one second later by 0h 0m 00s of the first day of the following month. Notices concerning the insertion of leap seconds are issued by the International Earth Rotation Service (IERS) at the Observatoire de Paris.

RADIO TIME-SIGNALS

UTC is made generally available through time-signals and standard frequency broadcasts such as MSF in the UK, CHU in Canada and WWV and WWVH in the USA. These are based on national time-scales that are maintained in close agreement with UTC and provide traceability to the national time-scale and to UTC. The markers of seconds in the UTC scale coincide with those of TAI.

To disseminate the national time-scale in the UK, special signals are broadcast on behalf of the National Physical Laboratory from the BT radio station at Rugby (call-sign MSF). The signals are controlled from a caesium beam atomic frequency standard and consist of a precise frequency carrier of 60 kHz which is switched off, after being on for at least half a second, to mark every second. The first second of the minute begins with a period of 500 ms with the carrier switched off, to serve as a minute marker. In the other seconds the carrier is always off for at least one tenth of a second at the start and then it carries an on-off code giving the British clock time and date, together with information identifying the start of the next minute. Changes to and from summer time are made following government announcements. Leap seconds are inserted as announced by the IERS and information provided by them on the difference between UTC and UT is also signalled. Other broadcast signals in the UK include the BBC six pips signal, the BT Timeline ('speaking clock'), the NPL Truetime service for computers, and a coded time-signal on the BBC 198 kHz transmitters which is used for timing in the electricity supply industry. From 1972 January 1 the six pips on the BBC have consisted of five short pips from second 55 to second 59 (six pips in the case of a leap second) followed by one lengthened pip, the start of which indicates the exact minute. From 1990 February 5 these signals have been controlled by the BBC with seconds markers referenced to the satellite-based US navigation system GPS (Global Positioning System) and time and day referenced to the MSF transmitter. Formerly they were generated by the Royal Greenwich Observatory. The BT Timeline is compared daily with the National Physical Laboratory caesium beam atomic frequency standard at the Rugby radio station. The NPL Truetime service is directly connected to the national time scale.

Accurate timing may also be obtained from the signals of international navigation systems such as the ground-based Omega, or the satellite-based American GPS or Russian GLONASS systems.

STANDARD TIME

Since 1880 the standard time in Britain has been Greenwich Mean Time (GMT); a statute that year enacted that the word 'time' when used in any legal document relating to Britain meant, unless otherwise specifically stated, the mean time of the Greenwich meridian. Greenwich was adopted as the universal meridian on 13 October 1884. A system of standard time by zones is used world-wide, standard time in each zone differing from that of the Greenwich meridian by an integral number of hours, either fast or slow. The large territories of the USA and Canada are divided into zones approximately 7.5° on either side of central meridians.

Variations from the standard time of some countries occur during part of the year; they are decided annually and are usually referred to as Summer Time or Daylight Saving Time.

At the 180th meridian the time can be either 12 hours fast on Greenwich Mean Time or 12 hours slow, and a change of date occurs. The internationally recognised date or calendar line is a modification of the 180th meridian, drawn so as to include islands of any one group on the same side of the line, or for political reasons. The line is indicated by joining up the following co-ordinates:

Lat.	Long.	Lat.	Long.
60° S.	180°	48° N.	180°
51° S.	180°	53° N.	170° E.
45° S.	172.5° W.	65.5° N.	169° W.
15° S.	172.5° W.	75° N.	180°
5° S.	180°		

Changes to the date line would require an international conference.

BRITISH SUMMER TIME

In 1916 an Act ordained that during a defined period of that year the legal time for general purposes in Great Britain should be one hour in advance of Greenwich Mean Time. The Summer Time Acts 1922 and 1925 defined the period during which Summer Time was to be in force, stabilising practice until the Second World War.

During the war the duration of Summer Time was extended and in the years 1941 to 1945 and in 1947 Double Summer Time (two hours in advance of Greenwich Mean Time) was in force. After the war, Summer Time was extended each year in 1948–52 and 1961–4 by Order in Council.

Between 1968 October 27 and 1971 October 31 clocks were kept one hour ahead of Greenwich Mean Time throughout the year. This was known as British Standard Time.

The most recent legislation is the Summer Time Act 1972, which enacted that 'the period of summer time for the purposes of this Act is the period beginning at two o'clock, Greenwich mean time, in the morning of the day after the third Saturday in March or, if that day is Easter Day, the day after the second Saturday in March, and ending at two o'clock, Greenwich mean time, in the morning of the day after the fourth Saturday in October.'

The duration of Summer Time can be varied by Order in Council and in recent years alterations have been made to bring the operation of Summer Time in Britain closer to similar provisions in other countries of the European Union; for instance, since 1981 the hour of changeover has been 01h Greenwich Mean Time.

The duration of Summer Time in 2004 is:

March 28 01h GMT to October 31 01h GMT

MEAN REFRACTION

Alt.	Ref.		Alt.	Ref.		Alt.	Ref.	
°	′	′	°	′	′	°	′	′
1	20	21	3	12	137	54	6	
1	30	20	3	34	12	9	27	5
1	41	19	4	00	11	11	39	4
1	52	18	4	30	10	15	00	3
2	05	17	5	06	9	20	42	2
2	19	16	5	50	8	32	20	1
2	35	15	6	44	7	62	17	0
2	52	14	7	54		90	00	
3	12							

The refraction table is in the form of a critical table (see page 1253)

ASTRONOMICAL CONSTANTS

Solar parallax	8″.794
Astronomical unit	149597870 km
Precession for the year 2004	50″.291
Precession in right ascension	3s.075
Precession in declination	20″.043
Constant of nutation	9″.202
Constant of aberration	20″.496
Mean obliquity of ecliptic (2004)	23° 26′ 20″
Moon's equatorial hor. parallax	57′ 02″.70
Velocity of light in vacuo per second	299792.5 km
Solar motion per second	20.0 km
Equatorial radius of the Earth	6378.140 km
Polar radius of the Earth	6356.755 km
North galactic pole (IAU standard)	
	RA 12h 49m (1950.0). Dec. +27°.4 N.
Solar apex	RA 18h 06m Dec.+30°

Length of year (in mean solar days)

Tropical	365.24219
Sidereal	365.25636
Anomalistic (perihelion to perihelion)	365.25964
Eclipse	346.62000

Length of month (mean values)	d	h	m	s
New Moon to New	29	12	44	02.9
Sidereal	27	07	43	11.5
Anomalistic (perigee to perigee)	27	13	18	33.2

ELEMENTS OF THE SOLAR SYSTEM

Orb	Mean distance from Sun (Earth = 1)	km 10⁶	Sidereal period days	Synodic period days	Incl. of orbit to ecliptic ° '	Diameter km	Mass (Earth = 1) days	Period of rotation on axis
Sun	—	—	—	—	—	1,392,530	332,946	25–35*
Mercury	0.39	58	88.0	116	7 00	4,879	0.0553	58.646
Venus	0.72	108	224.7	584	3 24	12,104	0.8150	243.019r
Earth	1.00	150	365.3	—	—	12,756e	1.0000	0.997
Mars	1.52	228	687.0	780	1 51	6,794e	0.1074	1.026
Jupiter	5.20	778	4,332.6	399	1 18	{ 142,984e 133,708p	317.89	{ 0.410e
Saturn	9.54	1427	10,759.2	378	2 29	{ 120,536e 108,728p	95.18	{ 0.426e
Uranus	19.18	2870	30,684.6	370	0 46	51,118e	14.54	0.718r
Neptune	30.06	4497	60,191.0	367	1 46	49,528e	17.15	0.671
Pluto	39.80	5954	91,708.2	367	17 09	2,302	0.002	6.387

e equatorial, p polar, r retrograde, * depending on latitude

THE SATELLITES

Name	Star mag.	Mean distance from primary km	Sidereal period of revolution d
EARTH			
I Moon	—	384,400	27.322
MARS			
I Phobos	11	9,378	0.319
II Deimos	12	23,459	1.262
JUPITER			
XVI Metis	17	127,960	0.295
XV Adrastea	19	128,980	0.298
V Amalthea	14	181,300	0.498
XIV Thebe	16	221,900	0.675
I Io	5	421,600	1.769
II Europa	5	670,900	3.552
III Ganymede	5	1,070,000	7.155
IV Callisto	6	1,883,000	16.689
XIII Leda	20	11,094,000	241
VI Himalia	15	11,480,000	251
X Lysithea	18	11,720,000	259
VII Elara	17	11,737,000	260
XII Ananke	19	21,200,000	610
XI Carme	18	22,600,000	702
VIII Pasiphae	17	23,500,000	708
IX Sinope	18	23,700,000	725
SATURN			
XVIII Pan	20	133,583	0.575
XV Atlas	18	137,640	0.602
XVI Prometheus	16	139,353	0.613
XVII Pandora	16	141,700	0.629
XI Epimetheus	15	151,422	0.695
X Janus	14	151,472	0.695
I Mimas	13	185,520	0.942
II Enceladus	12	238,020	1.370
III Tethys	10	294,660	1.888
XIII Telesto	19	294,660	1.888
XIV Calypso	19	294,660	1.888
IV Dione	10	377,400	2.737
XII Helene	18	377,400	2.737
V Rhea	10	527,040	4.518
VI Titan	8	1,221,850	15.945

Name	Star mag.	Mean distance from primary km	Sidereal period of revolution d
SATURN			
VII Hyperion	14	1,481,100	21.277
VIII Iapetus	11	3,561,300	79.330
IX Pheobe	16	12,952,000	550.480
URANUS			
VI Cordelia	24	49,750	0.335
VII Ophelia	24	53,760	0.376
VIII Bianca	23	59,170	0.435
IX Cressida	22	61,780	0.464
X Desdemona	22	62,660	0.474
XI Juliet	21	64,360	0.493
XII Portia	21	66,100	0.513
XIII Rosalind	22	69,930	0.558
XIV Belinda	22	75,260	0.624
XV Puck	20	86,000	0.762
V Miranda	16	129,800	1.413
I Ariel	14	191,200	2.520
II Umbriel	15	266,000	4.144
III Titania	14	435,800	8.706
IV Oberon	14	583,600	13.463
XVI Caliban	–	7,230,000	597.5
XX Stephano	–	7,979,000	673.6
XVII Sycorax	–	12,178,000	1,283.3
XVIII Prospero	–	16,665,000	2,037.1
XIX Setebos	–	17,879,000	2,273.3
NEPTUNE			
III Naiad	25	48,230	0.294
IV Thalassa	24	50,070	0.311
V Despina	23	52,530	0.335
VI Galatea	22	61,950	0.429
VII Larissa	22	73,550	0.555
VIII Proteus	20	117,650	1.122
I Triton	13	354,760	5.877
II Nereid	19	5,513,400	360.136
PLUTO			
I Charon	17	19,600	6.387

During the last few years more small satellites of the outer planets have been discovered. The revised totals are Jupiter 60, Saturn 31, Uranus 21, Neptune 11.

THE EARTH

The shape of the Earth is that of an oblate spheroid or solid of revolution whose meridian sections are ellipses not differing much from circles, whilst the sections at right angles are circles. The length of the equatorial axis is about 12,756 km, and that of the polar axis is 12,714 km. The mean density of the Earth is 5.5 times that of water, although that of the surface layer is less. The Earth and Moon revolve about their common centre of gravity in a lunar month; this centre in turn revolves round the Sun in a plane known as the ecliptic, that passes through the Sun's centre. The Earth's equator is inclined to this plane at an angle of 23.4°. This tilt is the cause of the seasons. In mid-latitudes, and when the Sun is high above the Equator, not only does the high noon altitude make the days longer, but the Sun's rays fall more directly on the Earth's surface; these effects combine to produce summer. In equatorial regions the noon altitude is large throughout the year, and there is little variation in the length of the day. In higher latitudes the noon altitude is lower, and the days in summer are appreciably longer than those in winter.

The average velocity of the Earth in its orbit is 30 km a second. It makes a complete rotation on its axis in about 23h 56m of mean time, which is the sidereal day. Because of its annual revolution round the Sun, the rotation with respect to the Sun, or the solar day, is more than this by about four minutes (see page 1257). The extremity of the axis of rotation, or the North Pole of the Earth, is not rigidly fixed, but wanders over an area roughly 20 metres in diameter.

TERRESTRIAL MAGNETISM

The Earth's main magnetic field corresponds approximately to that of a very strong small bar magnet near the centre of the Earth, but with appreciable smooth spatial departures. The origin of the main field is not fully understood but is generally ascribed to electric currents associated with fluid motions in the Earth's core. As a result not only does the main field vary in strength and direction from place to place, but also with time. Superimposed on the main field are local and regional anomalies whose magnitudes may in places approach that of the main field; these are due to the influence of mineral deposits in the Earth's crust. A small proportion of the field is of external origin, mostly associated with electric currents in the ionosphere. The configuration of the external field and the ionisation of the atmosphere depend on the incident particle and radiation flux from the Sun. There are, therefore, short-term and non-periodic as well as diurnal, 27-day, seasonal and 11-year periodic changes in the magnetic field, dependent upon the position of the Sun and the degree of solar activity.

A magnetic compass points along the horizontal component of a magnetic line of force. These lines of force converge on the 'magnetic dip-poles', the places where the Earth's magnetic field is vertical. These poles move with time, and their present approximate adopted mean positions are 82°.0 N., 113°.1 W. and 64°.5 S., 138°.1 E.

There is also a 'magnetic equator', at all points of which the vertical component of the Earth's magnetic field is zero and a magnetised needle remains horizontal. This line runs between 2° and 12° north of the geographical equator in Asia and Africa, turns sharply south off the west African coast, and crosses South America through Brazil, Bolivia and Peru; it re-crosses the geographical equator in mid-Pacific.

Reference has already been made to secular changes in the Earth's field. The following table indicates the changes in magnetic declination (or variation of the compass). Declination is the angle in the horizontal plane between the direction of true north and that in which a magnetic compass points. Similar, though much smaller, changes have occurred in 'dip' or magnetic inclination. Secular changes differ throughout the world. Although the London observations suggest a cycle with a period of several hundred years, an exact repetition is unlikely.

London			Greenwich		
1580	11°	15′ E.	1900	16°	29′ W.
1622	5°	56′ E.	1925	13°	10′ W.
1665	1°	22′ W.	1950	9°	07′ W.
1730	13°	00′ W.	1975	6°	39′ W.
1773	21°	09′ W.	1998	3°	32′ W.
1850	22°	24′ W.			

In order that up-to-date information on declination may be available, many governments publish magnetic charts on which there are lines (isogonic lines) passing through all places at which specified values of declination will be found at the date of the chart.

In the British Isles, isogonic lines now run approximately north-east to south-west. Though there are considerable local deviations due to geological causes, a rough value of magnetic declination may be obtained by assuming that at 50° N. on the meridian of Greenwich, the value in 2004 is 1° 53′ west and allowing an increase of 15′ for each degree of latitude northwards and one of 27′ for each degree of longitude westwards. For example, at 53° N., 5° W., declination will be about 1° 53′+45′+135′, i.e. 4° 53′ west. The average annual change at the present time is about 10′ decrease.

The number of magnetic observatories is about 180, irregularly distributed over the globe. There are three in Great Britain, run by the British Geological Survey: at Hartland, north Devon; at Eskdalemuir, Dumfries and Galloway; and at Lerwick, Shetland Islands. The following are some recent annual mean values of the magnetic elements for Hartland.

Year	Declination West ° ′	Dip or inclination ° ′	Horizontal force gauss	Vertical force gauss
1960	9 59	66 44	0.1871	0.4350
1965	9 30	66 34	0.1887	0.4354
1970	9 06	66 26	0.1903	0.4364
1975	8 32	66 17	0.1921	0.4373
1980	7 44	66 10	0.1933	0.4377
1985	6 56	66 08	0.1938	0.4380
1990	6 15	66 10	0.1939	0.4388
1995	5 33	66 07	0.1946	0.4395
2000	4 44	66 07	0.1951	0.4405
2002	4 24	66 06	0.1954	0.4410

As well as navigation at sea, in the air and on land by compass the oil industry depends on the Earth's magnetic field as a directional reference. They use magnetic survey tools when drilling well-bores and require accurate estimates of the local magnetic field, taking into account the crustal and external fields.

MAGNETIC STORMS

Occasionally, sometimes with great suddenness, the Earth's magnetic field is subject for several hours to marked disturbance. During a severe storm in 1989 the declination at Lerwick changed by almost 8° in less than an hour. In many instances such disturbances are accompanied by widespread displays of aurorae, marked changes in the incidence of cosmic rays, an increase in the reception of 'noise' from the Sun at radio frequencies, and rapid changes in the ionosphere and induced electric currents within the Earth which adversely affect satellite operations, telecommunications and electric power transmission systems. The disturbances are caused by changes in the stream of ionised particles which emanates from the Sun and through which the Earth is continuously passing. Some of these changes are associated with visible eruptions on the Sun, usually in the region of sun-spots. There is a marked tendency for disturbances to recur after intervals of about 27 days, the apparent period of rotation of the Sun on its axis, which is consistent with the sources being located on particular areas of the Sun.

ARTIFICIAL SATELLITES

Since the beginning of the Space Age, Whitaker's Almanack has given details of every successful satellite launch. This edition gives details of all successful launches that have taken place since the last edition. To consider the orbit of an artificial satellite, it is best to imagine that one is looking at the Earth from a distant point in space. The Earth would then be seen to be rotating about its axis inside the orbit described by the rapidly revolving satellite. The inclination of a satellite orbit to the Earth's equator (which generally remains almost constant throughout the satellite's lifetime) gives at once the maximum range of latitudes over which the satellite passes. Thus a satellite whose orbit has an inclination of 53° will pass overhead all latitudes between 53° S. and 53° N., but would never be seen in the zenith of any place nearer the poles than these latitudes. If we consider a particular place on the earth, whose latitude is less than the inclination of the satellite's orbit, then the Earth's rotation carries this place first under the northbound part of the orbit and then under the southbound part of the orbit, these two occurrences being always less than 12 hours apart for satellites moving in direct orbits (i.e. to the east). (For satellites in retrograde orbits, the words 'northbound' and 'southbound' should be interchanged in the preceding statement.) As the value of the latitude of the observer increases and approaches the value of the inclination of the orbit, so this interval gets shorter until (when the latitude is equal to the inclination) only one overhead passage occurs each day.

OBSERVATION OF SATELLITES

The regression of the orbit around the Earth causes alternate periods of visibility and invisibility, though this is of little concern to the radio or radar observer. To the visual observer the following cycle of events normally occurs (though the cycle may start in any position): invisibility, morning observations before dawn, invisibility, evening observations after dusk, invisibility, morning observations before dawn, and so on. With reasonably high satellites and for observers in high latitudes around the summer solstice, the evening observations follow the morning observations without interruption as sunlight passing over the polar regions can still illuminate satellites which are passing over temperate latitudes at local midnight. At the moment all satellites rely on sunlight to make them visible, though a satellite with a flashing light has been suggested for a future launching. The observer must be in darkness or twilight in order to make any useful observations. (For durations of twilight, and sunrise and sunset times, see Page Two of each month.)

Some of the satellites are visible to the naked eye and much interest has been aroused by the spectacle of a bright satellite disappearing into the Earth's shadow. The event is even more interesting telescopically as the disappearance occurs gradually as the satellite traverses the Earth's penumbral shadow, and during the last few seconds before the eclipse is complete the satellite may change colour (in suitable atmospheric conditions) from yellow to red. This is because the last rays of sunlight are refracted through the denser layers of our atmosphere before striking the satellite.

Some satellites rotate about one or more axes so that a periodic variation in brightness is observed. This was particularly noticeable in several of the Soviet satellites.

Satellite research has provided some interesting results, including a revised value of the Earth's oblateness (1/298.2), and the discovery of the Van Allen radiation belts.

LAUNCHINGS

Apart from their names, e.g. Cosmos 6 Rocket, the satellites are also classified according to their date of launch. Thus 1961 α refers to the first satellite launching of 1961. A number following the Greek letter indicated the relative brightness of the satellites put in orbit. From the beginning of 1963 the Greek letters were replaced by numbers and the numbers by roman letters e.g. 1963–01A. For all satellites successfully injected into orbit the following table gives the designation and names of the main objects, the launch date and some initial orbital data. These are the inclination to the equator (i), the nodal period of revolution (P), and the apogee and perigee heights.

Although most of the satellites launched are injected into orbits less than 1,000 km high, there are an increasing number of satellites in geostationary orbits, i.e. where the orbital inclination is zero, the eccentricity close to zero, and the period of revolution is 1436.1 minutes. Thus the satellite is permanently situated over the equator at one selected longitude at a mean height of 35,786 km. This geostationary band is crowded. In one case there are six television satellites (Astra 2, 5, 6, 7, 1H and 2C) orbiting within a few tens of kilometres of each other. In the sky they appear to be separated by only a few arcminutes.

In 1997 a number of Iridium satellites were launched into high inclination orbits. These are owned by the mobile telephone company Cellnet. For visual observers, these satellites have the interesting characteristic that the large aerials they carry can, when in exactly the right orientation with respect to the Sun and the observer, give off a 'flare' in brightness which can on occasion attain a magnitude of –6, much brighter than Venus. The flare can be visible to the naked eye for nearly a minute.

The Russian Space Station, Mir, 1986—17A, which was launched in 1986 was successfully de-orbited on March 23 2001. The re-entry was carried out in several stages, the first small burn to lower the orbit occurring at 00h 33m. The main de-orbit burn began at 05h 07m, which lowered the perigee height to <80km. At 05h 50m observers in Fiji saw multiple bright re-entry bodies in the sky. The impact area was at about W. 160°, S. 40°. During its 15 years in orbit it had been visited by 111 spacecraft. The record for the longest spaceflight was set by Valeriy Polyakov in 1994-5 who spent 437 days in Mir.

The new International Space Station ISS, 1998—67A, is currently being assembled in an orbit of similar size and inclination to Mir. It will become even brighter as more parts are added to it. When passing over Britain it can appear to be almost as bright as Jupiter on favourable transits, though only visible for four or five minutes on each pass.

ARTIFICIAL SATELLITE LAUNCHES

Desig-nation	Satellite	Launch date	P	i	Apogee	Perigee
2002-			m	°	km	km
011	TDRS9, rocket, rocket	Mar. 8	797.0	17.4	35810	8386
012	GRACE 2, rocket	Mar. 8	94.5	89.0	507	479
013	PROGRESS M1-8, rocket	Mar. 21	92.3	51.6	392	386
014	SZ-3, rocket, module	Mar. 25	91.2	42.4	338	330
015	JCSAT 8, ASTRA 3A, rocket	Mar. 29	632.7	4.0	35716	356
016	INTELSAT 903, rocket	Mar. 30	697.0	25.0	35848	3476
017	COSMOS 2388, rocket, platform	Apr. 1	91.8	62.8	491	231
018	STS 110	Apr. 8	91.6	51.6	402	308
019	NSS 7, rocket	Apr. 16	1436.1	0.0	35797	35777
020	SOYUZ TM-34, rocket	Apr. 25	92.4	51.6	398	386
021	SPOT 5, rocket	May 4	101.1	98.7	815	803
022	AQUA, rocket	May 4	98.3	98.2	681	673
023	DIRECTV 5, rocket, platform, rocket	May 7	759.2	17.7	35809	6569
024	Feng Yung 1D, Hai Yang 1, rocket	May 15	102.2	98.8	872	850
025	OFEQ 5, rocket	May 28	96.0	143.5	766	368
026	COSMOS 2389, rocket	May 28	104.8	83.0	1016	950
027	INTELSAT-905, rocket	Jun. 5	651.8	6.2	35840	1208
028	STS-111	Jun. 5	92.3	51.6	389	381
029	EXPRESS-A4, rocket	Jun. 10	638.3	48.6	36121	239
030	GALAXY 3C, rocket	Jun. 15	748.5	0.0	41467	391
031	IRIDIUM 97 & 98, rocket	Jun. 20	98.0	86.6	669	657
032	NOAA 17	Jun. 24	101.2	98.8	823	807
033	PROGRESS-M 46, rocket	Jun. 26	90.0	51.6	277	269
034	CONTOUR, rocket, rocket	Jul. 3	2423.6	30.5	106689	91
035	STELLAT 5, N STAR C, rocket	Jul. 5	957.5	1.2	35638	15966
036	COSMOS 2390, COSMOS 2391, rocket	Jul. 8	115.7	82.5	1506	1468
037	COSMOS 2392, rocket, platform, rocket	Jul. 25	119.9	63.5	1840	1512
038	HOT BIRD 6, rocket	Aug. 21	834.3	17.7	45635	323
039	ECHOSTAR 8, rocket	Aug. 22	712.8	23.0	35842	4266
040	ATLANTIC BIRD, MSG1, rocket	Aug. 28	640.1	5.5	35861	587
041	INTELSAT 906, rocket	Sep. 6	756.7	3.5	35818	6438
042	USERS, DRTS, rocket, rocket	Sep. 10	93.5	30.4	454	440
043	METSAT 1, rocket	Sep. 12	1399.7	0.5	35634	34508
044	HISPASAT 1D, rocket	Sep. 18	846.4	20.8	46253	269
045	PROGRESS M1-9, rocket	Sep. 25	92.3	51.6	400	376
046	NADEZHDA 7, rocket	Sep. 26	104.9	82.9	1017	965
047	STS 112	Oct. 7	89.0	51.6	239	209
048	INTEGRAL, rocket, rocket	Oct. 17	3936.6	51.8	151581	837
049	JB-3, rocket	Oct. 27	94.1	97.4	483	469
050	SOYUZ TM, rocket	Oct. 30	90.2	51.6	295	277
051	EUTELSAT W5, rocket	Nov. 20	637.5	13.4	35759	557
052	STS-113, UNK	Nov. 24	92.4	51.6	398	386
053	ASTRA 1K, rocket	Nov. 25	90.2	51.6	295	271
054	ALSAT-1, MOZHAYETS, rocket	Nov. 28	99.0	98.2	744	680
055	TDRS 10, rocket	Dec. 5	635.5	26.2	35793	421
056	ADEOS II, FEDSAT, WEOS, MICRO LABSAT, rocket	Dec. 14	101.0	98.7	807	805
057	NSS 6, rocket	Dec. 17	1431.8	0.0	35737	35667
058	RUBIN 2, LATINSAT, SAUDISAT 1C UNISAT 2, TRAILBLAZER, rocket, PLEM COVER, LATINSAT A	Dec. 20	97.9	64.6	678	634
059	COSMOS 2393, rocket, platform rocket	Dec. 24	704.5	62.9	39180	520

ARTIFICIAL SATELLITE LAUNCHES

Desig-nation	Satellite	Launch date	P	i	Apogee	Perigee
2002-			m	°	km	km
060	COSMOS 2394 (GLONASS), 2395, 2396	Dec.25	675.8	64.9	19137	19125
061	SZ-4, rocket, module	Dec. 29	91.2	42.4	337	331
062	NIMIQ-2, rocket	Dec. 29	788.6	16.5	35887	7905
2003-						
001	CORIOLIS, rocket	Jan. 6	95.9	98.7	841	279
002	ICESAT, CHIPSAT, rocket, DPAF	Jan. 13	96.5	94.0	594	586
003	STS 107	Jan. 16	90.1	39.0	287	271
004	SORCE, rocket	Jan. 25	97.3	40.0	649	609
005	NAVSTAR 51 (USA 166), XSS 10, rocket, rocket	Jan. 29	720.7	55.1	20345	20155
006	PROGRESS M-47, rocket	Feb. 2	92.3	51.6	390	382

TIME MEASUREMENT AND CALENDARS

MEASUREMENTS OF TIME

Measurements of time are based on the time taken by the earth to rotate on its axis (day); by the moon to revolve round the earth (month); and by the earth to revolve round the sun (year). From these, which are not commensurable, certain average or mean intervals have been adopted for ordinary use.

THE DAY

The day begins at midnight and is divided into 24 hours of 60 minutes, each of 60 seconds. The hours are counted from midnight up to 12 noon (when the sun crosses the meridian), and these hours are designated a.m. (*ante meridiem*); and again from noon up to 12 midnight, which hours are designated p.m. (*post meridiem*), except when the 24-hour reckoning is employed. The 24-hour reckoning ignores a.m. and p.m., numbering the hours 0 to 23 from midnight.

Colloquially the 24 hours are divided into day and night, day being the time while the sun is above the horizon (including the four stages of twilight defined in the Astronomy section). Day is subdivided into morning, the early part of daytime, ending at noon; afternoon, from noon to about 6 p.m.; and evening, which may be said to extend from 6 p.m. until midnight. Night, the dark period between day and day, begins at the close of astronomical twilight (*see* the Astronomy section) and extends beyond midnight to sunrise the next day.

The names of the days are derived from Old English translations or adaptations of the Roman titles.

Sunday	Sun	Sol
Monday	Moon	Luna
Tuesday	Tiw/Tyr (god of war)	Mars
Wednesday	Woden/Odin	Mercury
Thursday	Thor	Jupiter
Friday	Frigga/Freyja (goddess of love)	Venus
Saturday	Saeternes	Saturn

THE MONTH

The month in the ordinary calendar is approximately the twelfth part of a year, but the lengths of the different months vary from 28 (or 29) days to 31.

THE YEAR

The equinoctial or tropical year is the time that the earth takes to revolve round the sun from equinox to equinox, i.e. 365.24219 mean solar days, or 365 days 5 hours 48 minutes and 45 seconds.

The calendar year usually consists of 365 days but a year containing 366 days is called bissextile (*see* Roman calendar) or leap year, one day being added to the month of February so that a date 'leaps over' a day of the week. In the Roman calendar the day that was repeated was the sixth day before the beginning of March, the equivalent of 24 February.

A year is a leap year if the date of the year is divisible by four without remainder, unless it is the last year of the century. The last year of a century is a leap year only if its number is divisible by 400 without remainder, e.g. the years 1800 and 1900 had only 365 days but the year 2000 has 366 days.

THE SOLSTICE

A solstice is the point in the tropical year at which the sun attains its greatest distance, north or south, from the Equator. In the northern hemisphere the furthest point north of the Equator marks the summer solstice and the furthest point south the winter solstice.

The date of the solstice varies according to locality. For example, if the summer solstice falls on 21 June late in the day by Greenwich time, that day will be the longest of the year at Greenwich though it may be by only a second, but it will fall on 22 June, local date, in Japan, and so 22 June will be the longest day there. The date of the solstice is also affected by the length of the tropical year, which is 365 days 6 hours less about 11 minutes 15 seconds. If a solstice happens late on 21 June in one year, it will be nearly six hours later in the next (unless the next year is a leap year), i.e. early on 22 June, and that will be the longest day.

This delay of the solstice does not continue because the extra day in leap year brings it back a day in the calendar. However, because of the 11 minutes 15 seconds mentioned above, the additional day in leap year brings the solstice back too far by 45 minutes, and the time of the solstice in the calendar is earlier, in a four-year pattern, as the century progresses. The last year of a century is in most cases not a leap year, and the omission of the extra day puts the date of the solstice later by about six hours too much. Compensation for this is made by the fourth centennial year being a leap year. The solstice has become earlier in date throughout the last century and, because the year 2000 was a leap year, the solstice will get earlier still throughout the 21st century.

The date of the winter solstice, the shortest day of the year, is affected by the same factors as the longest day.

At Greenwich the sun sets at its earliest by the clock about ten days before the shortest day. The daily change in the time of sunset is due in the first place to the sun's movement southwards at this time of the year, which diminishes the interval between the sun's transit and its setting. However, the daily decrease of the Equation of Time causes the time of apparent noon to be continuously later day by day, which to some extent counteracts the first effect. The rates of the change of these two quantities are not equal or uniform; their combination causes the date of earliest sunset to be 12 or 13 December at Greenwich. In more southerly latitudes the effect of the movement of the sun is less, and the change in the time of sunset depends on that of the Equation of Time to a greater degree, and the date of earliest sunset is earlier than it is at Greenwich, e.g. on the Equator it is about 1 November.

THE EQUINOX

The equinox is the point at which the sun crosses the Equator and day and night are of equal length all over the world. This occurs in March and September.

DOG DAYS

The days about the heliacal rising of the Dog Star, noted from ancient times as the hottest period of the year in the northern hemisphere, are called the Dog Days. Their incidence has been variously calculated as depending on the Greater or Lesser Dog Star (Sirius or Procyon) and their duration has been reckoned as from 30 to 54 days. A generally accepted period is from 3 July to 15 August.

CHRISTIAN CALENDAR

In the Christian chronological system the years are distinguished by cardinal numbers before or after the birth of Christ, the period being denoted by the letters BC (Before Christ) or, more rarely, AC (*Ante Christum*), and AD (*Anno Domini* – In the Year of Our Lord). The correlative dates of the epoch are the fourth year of the 194th Olympiad, the 753rd year from the foundation of Rome, AM 3761 in Jewish chronology, and the 4714th year of the Julian period. The actual date of the birth of Christ is somewhat uncertain.

The system was introduced into Italy in the sixth century. Though first used in France in the seventh century, it was not universally established there until about the eighth century. It has been said that the system was introduced into England by St Augustine (AD 596), but it was probably not generally used until some centuries later. It was ordered to be used by the Bishops at the Council of Chelsea (AD 816).

THE JULIAN CALENDAR

In the Julian calendar (adopted by the Roman Empire in 45 BC) all the centennial years were leap years, and for this reason towards the close of the 16th century there was a difference of ten days between the tropical and calendar years; the equinox fell on 11 March of the calendar, whereas at the time of the Council of Nicaea (AD 325), it had fallen on 21 March. In 1582 Pope Gregory ordained that 5 October should be called 15 October and that of the end-century years only the fourth should be a leap year.

THE GREGORIAN CALENDAR

The Gregorian calendar was adopted by Italy, France, Spain and Portugal in 1582, by Prussia, the Roman Catholic German states, Switzerland, Holland and Flanders on 1 January 1583, by Poland in 1586, Hungary in 1587, the Protestant German and Netherland states and Denmark in 1700, and by Great Britain and Dominions (including the North American colonies) in 1752, by the omission of eleven days (3 September being reckoned as 14 September). Sweden omitted the leap day in 1700 but observed leap days in 1704 and 1708, and reverted to the Julian calendar by having two leap days in 1712; the Gregorian calendar was adopted in 1753 by the omission of eleven days (18 February being reckoned as 1 March). Japan adopted the calendar in 1872, China in 1912, Bulgaria in 1915, Turkey and Soviet Russia in 1918, Yugoslavia and Romania in 1919, and Greece in 1923.

In the same year that the change was made in England from the Julian to the Gregorian calendar, the beginning of the new year was also changed from 25 March to 1 January.

THE ORTHODOX CHURCHES

Some Orthodox Churches still use the Julian reckoning but the majority of Greek Orthodox Churches and the Romanian Orthodox Church have adopted a modified 'New Calendar', observing the Gregorian calendar for fixed feasts and the Julian for movable feasts.

The Orthodox Church year begins on 1 September. There are four fast periods and, in addition to Pascha (Easter), twelve great feasts, as well as numerous commemorations of the saints of the Old and New Testaments throughout the year.

THE DOMINICAL LETTER

The dominical letter is one of the letters A–G which are used to denote the Sundays in successive years. If the first day of the year is a Sunday the letter is A; if the second, B; the third, C; and so on. A leap year requires two letters, the first for 1 January to 29 February, the second for 1 March to 31 December.

EPIPHANY

The feast of the Epiphany, commemorating the manifestation of Christ, later became associated with the offering of gifts by the Magi. The day was of great importance from the time of the Council of Nicaea (AD 325), as the primate of Alexandria was charged at every Epiphany feast with the announcement in a letter to the churches of the date of the forthcoming Easter. The day was also of importance in Britain as it influenced dates, ecclesiastical and lay, e.g. Plough Monday, when work was resumed in the fields, fell on the Monday in the first full week after Epiphany.

LENT

The Teutonic word *Lent*, which denotes the fast preceding Easter, originally meant no more than the spring season; but from Anglo-Saxon times at least it has been used as the equivalent of the more significant Latin term Quadragesima, meaning the 'forty days' or, more literally, the fortieth day. Ash Wednesday is the first day of Lent, which ends at midnight before Easter Day.

PALM SUNDAY

Palm Sunday, the Sunday before Easter and the beginning of Holy Week, commemorates the triumphal entry of Christ into Jerusalem and is celebrated in Britain (when palm is not available) by branches of willow gathered for use in the decoration of churches on that day.

MAUNDY THURSDAY

Maundy Thursday is the day before Good Friday, the name itself being a corruption of *dies mandati* (day of the mandate) when Christ washed the feet of the disciples and gave them the mandate to love one another.

EASTER DAY

Easter Day is the first Sunday after the full moon which happens on, or next after, the 21st day of March; if the full moon happens on a Sunday, Easter Day is the Sunday after.

This definition is contained in an Act of Parliament (24 Geo. II c. 23) and explanation is given in the preamble to the Act that the day of full moon depends on certain tables that have been prepared. These tables are summarised in the early pages of the Book of Common Prayer. The moon referred to is not the real moon of the heavens, but a hypothetical moon on whose 'full' date of Easter depends, and the lunations of this 'calendar' moon consist of twenty-nine and thirty days alternately, with certain necessary modifications to make the date of its full agree as nearly as possible with that of the real moon, which is known as the Paschal Full Moon.

A FIXED EASTER

In 1928 the House of Commons agreed to a motion for the third reading of a bill proposing that Easter Day shall, in the calendar year next but one after the commencement of the Act and in all subsequent years, be the first Sunday after the second Saturday in April. Easter would thus fall on the second or third Sunday in April, i.e. between 9 and 15 April (inclusive). A clause in the Bill provided that before it shall come into operation, regard shall be had to any opinion expressed officially by the various Christian churches. Efforts by the World Council of Churches to secure a unanimous choice of date for Easter by its member churches have so far been unsuccessful.

ROGATION DAYS

Rogation Days are the Monday, Tuesday and Wednesday preceding Ascension Day and from the fifth century were observed as public fasts with solemn processions and supplications. The processions were discontinued as religious observances at the Reformation, but survive in the ceremony known as 'beating the parish bounds'. Rogation Sunday is the Sunday before Ascension Day.

EMBER DAYS

The Ember Days at the four seasons are the Wednesday, Friday and Saturday (a) before the third Sunday in Advent, (b) before the second Sunday in Lent, and (c) before the Sundays nearest to the festivals of St Peter and of St Michael and All Angels.

TRINITY SUNDAY

Trinity Sunday is eight weeks after Easter Day, on the Sunday following Pentecost (Whit Sunday). Subsequent Sundays are reckoned in the Book of Common Prayer calendar of the Church of England as 'after Trinity'.

Thomas Becket (1118–70) was consecrated Archbishop of Canterbury on the Sunday after Whit Sunday and his first act was to ordain that the day of his consecration should be held as a new festival in honour of the Holy Trinity. This observance spread from Canterbury throughout the whole of Christendom.

MOVABLE FEASTS TO THE YEAR 2035

Year	Ash Wednesday	Easter	Ascension	Pentecost (Whit Sunday)	Advent Sunday
2004	25 February	11 April	20 May	30 May	28 November
2005	9 February	27 March	5 May	15 May	27 November
2006	1 March	16 April	25 May	4 June	3 December
2007	21 February	8 April	17 May	27 May	2 December
2008	6 February	23 March	1 May	11 May	30 November
2009	25 February	12 April	21 May	31 May	29 November
2010	17 February	4 April	13 May	23 May	28 November
2011	9 March	24 April	2 June	12 June	27 November
2012	22 February	8 April	17 May	27 May	2 December
2013	13 February	31 March	9 May	19 May	1 December
2014	5 March	20 April	29 May	8 June	30 November
2015	18 February	5 April	14 May	24 May	29 November
2016	10 February	27 March	5 May	15 May	27 November
2017	1 March	16 April	25 May	4 June	3 December
2018	14 February	1 April	10 May	20 May	2 December
2019	6 March	21 April	30 May	9 June	1 December
2020	26 February	12 April	21 May	31 May	29 November
2021	17 February	4 April	13 May	23 May	28 November
2022	2 March	17 April	26 May	5 June	27 November
2023	22 February	9 April	18 May	28 May	3 December
2024	14 February	31 March	9 May	19 May	1 December
2025	5 March	20 April	29 May	8 June	30 November
2026	18 February	5 April	14 May	24 May	29 November
2027	10 February	28 March	6 May	16 May	28 November
2028	1 March	16 April	25 May	4 June	3 December
2029	14 February	1 April	10 May	20 May	2 December
2030	6 March	21 April	30 May	9 June	1 December
2031	26 February	13 April	22 May	1 June	30 November
2032	11 February	28 March	6 May	16 May	28 November
2033	2 March	17 April	26 May	5 June	27 November
2034	22 February	9 April	18 May	28 May	3 December
2035	7 February	25 March	3 May	13 May	2 December

NOTES

Ash Wednesday (first day in Lent) can fall at earliest on 4 February and at latest on 10 March

Mothering Sunday (fourth Sunday in Lent) can fall at earliest on 1 March and at latest on 4 April

Easter Day can fall at earliest on 22 March and at latest on 25 April

Ascension Day is forty days after Easter Day and can fall at earliest on 30 April and at latest on 3 June

Pentecost (Whit Sunday) is seven weeks after Easter and can fall at earliest on 10 May and at latest on 13 June

Trinity Sunday is the Sunday after Whit Sunday

Corpus Christi falls on the Thursday after Trinity Sunday

Sundays after Pentecost – there are not less than 18 and not more than 23

Advent Sunday is the Sunday nearest to 30 November

EASTER DAYS AND DOMINICAL LETTERS 1500 TO 2035

Dates up to and including 1752 are according to the Julian calendar. For dominical letters in leap years, *see* page below.

		1500–1599	1600–1699	1700–1799	1800–1899	1900–1999	2000–2035
March							
d	22	1573	1668	1761	1818		
e	23	1505/16	1600	1788	1845/56	1913	2008
f	24		1611/95	1706/99		1940	
g	25	1543/54	1627/38/49	1722/33/44	1883/94	1951	2035
A	26	1559/70/81/92	1654/65/76	1749/58/69/80	1815/26/37	1967/78/89	
b	27	1502/13/24/97	1608/87/92	1785/96	1842/53/64	1910/21/32	2005/16
c	28	1529/35/40	1619/24/30	1703/14/25	1869/75/80	1937/48	2027/32
d	29	1551/62	1635/46/57	1719/30/41/52	1807/12/91	1959/64/70	
e	30	1567/78/89	1651/62/73/84	1746/55/66/77	1823/34	1902/75/86/97	
f	31	1510/21/32/83/94	1605/16/78/89	1700/71/82/93	1839/50/61/72	1907/18/29/91	2002/13/24
April							
g	1	1526/37/48	1621/32	1711/16	1804/66/77/88	1923/34/45/56	2018/29
A	2	1553/64	1643/48	1727/38	1809/20/93/99	1961/72	
b	3	1575/80/86	1659/70/81	1743/63/68/74	1825/31/36	1904/83/88/94	
c	4	1507/18/91	1602/13/75/86/97	1708/79/90	1847/58	1915/20/26/99	2010/21
d	5	1523/34/45/56	1607/18/29/40	1702/13/24/95	1801/63/74/85/96	1931/42/53	2015/26
e	6	1539/50/61/72	1634/45/56	1729/35/40/60	1806/17/28/90	1947/58/69/80	
f	7	1504/77/88	1667/72	1751/65/76	1822/33/44	1901/12/85/96	
g	8	1509/15/20/99	1604/10/83/94	1705/87/92/98	1849/55/60	1917/28	2007/12
A	9	1531/42	1615/26/37/99	1710/21/32	1871/82	1939/44/50	2023/34
b	10	1547/58/69	1631/42/53/64	1726/37/48/57	1803/14/87/98	1955/66/77	
c	11	1501/12/63/74/85/96	1658/69/80	1762/73/84	1819/30/41/52	1909/71/82/93	2004
d	12	1506/17/28	1601/12/91/96	1789	1846/57/68	1903/14/25/36/98	2009/20
e	13	1533/44	1623/28	1707/18	1800/73/79/84	1941/52	2031
f	14	1555/60/66	1639/50/61	1723/34/45/54	1805/11/16/95	1963/68/74	
g	15	1571/82/93	1655/66/77/88	1750/59/70/81	1827/38	1900/06/79/90	2001
A	16	1503/14/25/36/87/98	1609/20/82/93	1704/75/86/97	1843/54/65/76	1911/22/33/95	2006/17/28
b	17	1530/41/52	1625/36	1715/20	1808/70/81/92	1927/38/49/60	2022/33
c	18	1557/68	1647/52	1731/42/56	1802/13/24/97	1954/65/76	
d	19	1500/79/84/90	1663/74/85	1747/67/72/78	1829/35/40	1908/81/87/92	
e	20	1511/22/95	1606/17/79/90	1701/12/83/94	1851/62	1919/24/30	2003/14/25
f	21	1527/38/49	1622/33/44	1717/28	1867/78/89	1935/46/57	2019/30
g	22	1565/76	1660	1739/53/64	1810/21/32	1962/73/84	
A	23	1508	1671		1848	1905/16	2000
b	24	1519	1603/14/98	1709/91	1859		2011
c	25	1546	1641	1736	1886	1943	

No dominical letter is placed against intercalary day, February 29, but, since it is still counted as a weekday and given a name, the series of letters moves back one day every leap year after intercalation. Thus, a leap year beginning with the dominical letter C will change to a year with the dominical letter B on March 1

HINDU CALENDAR

The Hindu calendar is a luni-solar calendar of twelve months, each containing 29 days, 12 hours. Each month is divided into a light fortnight (Shukla or Shuddha) and a dark fortnight (Krishna or Vadya) based on the waxing and waning of the moon. In most parts of India the month starts with the light fortnight, i.e. the day after the new moon, although in some regions it begins with the dark fortnight, i.e. the day after the full moon.

The new year begins in the month of Chaitra (March/April) and ends in the month of Phalgun (March). The twelve months, Chaitra, Vaishakh, Jyeshtha, Ashadh, Shravan, Bhadrapad, Ashvin, Kartik, Margashirsh, Paush, Magh and Phalgun, have Sanskrit names derived from twelve asterisms (constellations). There are regional variations to the names of the months but the Sanskrit names are understood throughout India.

Every lunar month must have a solar transit and is termed pure (shuddha). The lunar month without a solar transit is impure (mala) and called an intercalary month. An intercalary month occurs approximately every 32 lunar months, whenever the difference between the Hindu year of 360 lunar days (354 days 8 hours solar time) and the 365 days 6 hours of the solar year reaches

the length of one Hindu lunar month (29 days 12 hours).

The leap month may be added at any point in the Hindu year. The name given to the month varies according to when it occurs but is taken from the month immediately following it. In 2004 the leap month is Shravan.

The days of the week are called Raviwar (Sunday), Somawar (Monday), Mangalwar (Tuesday), Budhawar (Wednesday), Guruwar (Thursday), Shukrawar (Friday) and Shaniwar (Saturday). The names are derived from the Sanskrit names of the Sun, the Moon and five planets, Mars, Mercury, Jupiter, Venus and Saturn.

Most fasts and festivals are based on the lunar calendar but a few are determined by the apparent movement of the Sun, e.g. Sankranti and Pongal (in southern India), which are celebrated on 14/15 January to mark the start of the Sun's apparent journey northwards and a change of season.

Festivals celebrated throughout India are Chaitra (the New Year), Raksha-bandhan (the renewal of the kinship bond between brothers and sisters), Navaratri (a nine-night festival dedicated to the goddess Parvati), Dasara (the victory of Rama over the demon army), Diwali (a festival of lights), Makara Sankranti, Shivaratri (dedicated to Shiva), and Holi (a spring festival).

Regional festivals are Durga-puja (dedicated to the goddess Durga (Parvati)), Sarasvati-puja (dedicated to the goddess Sarasvati), Ganesh Chaturthi (worship of Ganesh on the fourth day (Chaturthi) of the light half of Bhadrapad), Ramanavami (the birth festival of the god Rama) and Janmashtami (the birth festival of the god Krishna).

The main festivals celebrated in Britain are Navaratri, Dasara, Durga-puja, Diwali, Holi, Sarasvati-puja, Ganesh Chaturthi, Raksha-bandhan, Ramanavami and Janmashtami.

For dates of the main festivals in 2004, see page 9.

JEWISH CALENDAR

The story of the Flood in the Book of Genesis indicates the use of a calendar of some kind and that the writers recognised thirty days as the length of a lunation. However, after the diaspora, Jewish communities were left in considerable doubt as to the relation of fasts and festivals. This led to the formation of the Jewish calendar as used today. It is said that this was done in AD 358 by Rabbi Hillel II, though some assert that it did not happen until much later.

The calendar is luni-solar, and is based on the lengths of the lunation and of the tropical year as found by Hipparchus (c.120 BC), which differ little from those adopted at the present day. The year AM 5764 (2003–2004) is the 7th year of the 304th Metonic (Minor or Lunar) cycle of 19 years and the 24th year of the 206th Solar (or Major) cycle of 28 years since the Era of the Creation. Jews hold that the Creation occurred at the time of the autumnal equinox in the year known in the Christian calendar as 3760 BC (954 of the Julian period). The epoch or starting point of Jewish chronology corresponds to 7 October 3761 BC. At the beginning of each solar cycle, the Tekufah of Nisan (the vernal equinox) returns to the same day and to the same hour.

The hour is divided into 1080 minims, and the month between one new moon and the next is reckoned as 29 days, 12 hours, 793 minims. The normal calendar year, called a Regular Common year, consists of 12 months of 30 days and 29 days alternately. Since 12 months such as these comprise only 354 days, in order that each of them shall not diverge greatly from an average place in the solar year, a 13th month is occasionally added after the fifth month of the civil year (which commences on the first day of the month Tishri), or as the penultimate month of the ecclesiastical year (which commences on the first day of the month Nisan). The years when this happens are called Embolismic or leap years.

Of the 19 years that form a Metonic cycle, seven are leap years; they occur at places in the cycle indicated by the numbers 3, 6, 8, 11, 14, 17 and 19, these places being chosen so that the accumulated excesses of the solar years should be as small as possible.

A Jewish year is of one of the following six types:

Minimal Common	353 days
Regular Common	354 days
Full Common	355 days
Minimal Leap	383 days
Regular Leap	384 days
Full Leap	385 days

The Regular year has alternate months of 30 and 29 days. In a Full year, whether common or leap, Marcheshvan, the second month of the civil year, has 30 days instead of 29; in Minimal years Kislev, the third month, has 29 instead of 30. The additional month in leap years is called Adar I and precedes the month called Adar in Common years. Adar II is called Adar Sheni in leap years, and the usual Adar festivals are kept in Adar Sheni. Adar I and Adar II always have 30 days, but neither this, nor the other variations mentioned, is allowed to change the number of days in the other months, which still follow the alternation of the normal twelve.

These are the main features of the Jewish calendar, which must be considered permanent because as a Jewish law it cannot be altered except by a great Sanhedrin.

The Jewish day begins between sunset and nightfall. The time used is that of the meridian of Jerusalem, which is 2h 21m in advance of Greenwich Mean Time. Rules for the beginning of sabbaths and festivals were laid down for the latitude of London in the 18th century and hours for nightfall are now fixed annually by the Chief Rabbi.

JEWISH CALENDAR 5764–5

AM 5764 (764) is a Full Common year of 12 months, 51 sabbaths and 355 days.

Month (first day)	AM 5764	AM 5765
Tishri 1	27 September 2003	16 September 2004
Marcheshvan 1	26 October	15 October
Kislev 1	25 November	14 November
Tebet 1	26 December	13 December
Shebat 1	24 January 2004	
*Adar 1	22 February	
†Adar II	—	
Nisan 1	23 March	
Iyar 1	21 April	
Sivan 1	21 May	
Tammuz 1	19 June	
Ab 1	19 July	
Elul 1	17 August	

*Known as Adar Rishon in leap years
†Known as Adar Sheni in leap years

JEWISH FASTS AND FESTIVALS

For dates of principal festivals in 2004, see page 9.

Tishri 1–2	Rosh Hashanah (New Year)
Tishri 3	*Fast of Gedaliah
Tishri 10	Yom Kippur (Day of Atonement)
Tishri 15–21	Succoth (Feast of Tabernacles)
Tishri 21	Hoshana Rabba
Tishri 22	Shemini Atseret (Solemn Assembly)
Tishri 23	Simchat Torah (Rejoicing of the Law)
Kislev 25	Chanucah (Dedication of the Temple) begins
Tebet 10	Fast of Tebet
†Adar 13	§Fast of Esther
†Adar 14	Purim
†Adar 15	Shushan Purim
Nisan 15–22	Pesach (Passover)
Sivan 6–7	Shavuot (Feast of Weeks)
Tammuz 17	*Fast of Tammuz
Ab 9	*Fast of Ab

*If these dates fall on the sabbath the fast is kept on the following day
† Adar Sheni in leap years
§This fast is observed on Adar 11 (or Adar Sheni 11 in leap years) if Adar 13 falls on a Sabbath

THE MUSLIM CALENDAR

The Muslim era is dated from the *Hijrah*, or flight of the Prophet Muhammad from Mecca to Medina, the corresponding date of which in the Julian calendar is 16 July AD 622. The lunar *hijri* calendar is used principally in Iran, Egypt, Malaysia, Pakistan, Mauritania, various Arab states and certain parts of India. Iran uses the solar *hijri* calendar as well as the lunar *hijri* calendar. The dating system was adopted about AD 639, commencing with the first day of the month Muharram.

The lunar calendar consists of twelve months containing an alternate sequence of 30 and 29 days, with the intercalation of one day at the end of the twelfth month at stated intervals in each cycle of 30 years. The object of the intercalation is to reconcile the date of the first day of the month with the date of the actual new moon.

Some adherents still take the date of the evening of the first physical sighting of the crescent of the new moon as that of the first of the month. If cloud obscures the moon the present month may be extended to 30 days, after which the new month will begin automatically regardless of whether the moon has been seen. (Under religious law a month must have less than 31 days.) This means that the beginning of a new month and the date of religious festivals can vary from the published calendars.

In each cycle of 30 years, 19 years are common and contain 354 days, and 11 years are intercalary (leap years) of 355 days, the latter being called *kabisah*. The mean length of the Hijrah years is 354 days 8 hours 48 minutes and the period of mean lunation is 29 days 12 hours 44 minutes.

To ascertain if a year is common or kabisah, divide it by 30: the quotient gives the number of completed cycles and the remainder shows the place of the year in the current cycle. If the remainder is 2, 5, 7, 10, 13, 16, 18, 21, 24, 26 or 29, the year is kabisah and consists of 355 days.

MUSLIM CALENDAR 1424–25

Hijrah 1424 AH (remainder 14) is a common year, 1425 AH (remainder 15) is a common year. Calendar dates below are estimates based on calculations of moon phases.

Month (Length)	1425 *(1424)* AH
Dhu'l-Qa'da (30)	25 December
Dhu'l-Hijjah (29 or 30)	24 January
Muharram (30)	22 February
Safar (29)	23 March
Rabi' I (30)	21 April
Rabi' II (29)	21 May
Jumada I (30)	19 June
Jumada II (29)	19 July
Rajab (30)	17 August
Sha'ban (29)	16 September
Ramadân (30)	15 October
Shawwâl (29)	14 November

MUSLIM FESTIVALS

Ramadan is a month of fasting for all Muslims because it is the month in which the revelation of the *Qur'an* (Koran) began. During Ramadan Muslims abstain from food, drink and sexual pleasure from dawn until after sunset throughout the month.

The two major festivals are *Id al-Fitr* and *Id al-Adha*. Id al-Fitr marks the end of the Ramadan fast and is celebrated on the day after the sighting of the new moon of the following month. Id al-Adha, the festival of sacrifice (also known as the great festival), celebrates the submission of the Prophet Ibrahim (Abraham) to God. Id al-Adha falls on the tenth day of Dhul-Hijjah, coinciding with the day when those on *hajj* (pilgrimage to Mecca) sacrifice animals.

Other days accorded special recognition are:

Muharram 1	New Year's Day
Muharram 10	Ashura (the day Prophet Noah left the Ark and Prophet Moses was saved from Pharaoh (Sunni), the death of the Prophet's grandson Husain (Shi'ite))
Rabi'u-l-Awwal (Rabi' I) 12	Mawlid al-Nabi (birthday of the Prophet Muhammad)
Rajab 27	Laylat al-Isra' wa'l-Mi'raj (The Night of Journey and Ascension)
Ramadân One of the odd-numbered nights in the last 10 of the month	Laylat al-Qadr (Night of Power)
Dhu'l-Hijjah 10	Id al-Adha (Festival of Sacrifice)

THE SIKH CALENDAR

The Sikh calendar is a lunar calendar of 365 days divided into 12 months. The length of the months varies between 29 and 32 days.

There are no prescribed feast days and no fasting periods. The main celebrations are Baisakhi Mela (the new year and the anniversary of the founding of the Khalsa), Diwali Mela (festival of light), Hola Mohalla Mela (a spring festival held in the Punjab), and the Gurpurbs (anniversaries associated with the ten Gurus).

For dates of the major celebrations in 2004, *see* page 9.

THAI CALENDAR

Thailand adopted the Suriyakati calendar, a modified version of the Gregorian calendar (Suriyakati) during the reign of King Rama V in 1888, using 1 April as the first day of the year. In 1940, the date of the new year was changed to 1 January. The years are counted from the beginning of the Buddhist era (BE), which is calculated to have commenced upon the death of the Lord Buddha, which is taken to have occurred in BC 543, so AD 2004 is BE 2547. The Chinese system of associating years with one of twelve animals is also in use in Thailand. The Chantarakati lunar calendar is used to determine religious holidays; the new year begins on the first day of the waxing moon in November or, if there is a leap month, in December.

CIVIL AND LEGAL CALENDAR

THE HISTORICAL YEAR

Before 1752, two calendar systems were used in England. The civil or legal year began on 25 March and the historical year on 1 January. Thus the civil or legal date 24 March 1658 was the same day as the historical date 24 March 1659; a date in that portion of the year is written as 24 March 165$\frac{8}{9}$, the lower figure showing the historical year.

THE NEW YEAR

In England in the seventh century, and as late as the 13th, the year was reckoned from Christmas Day, but in the 12th century the Church in England began the year with the feast of the Annunciation of the Blessed Virgin ('Lady Day') on 25 March and this practice was adopted generally in the 14th century. The civil or legal year in the British Dominions (exclusive of Scotland) began with Lady Day until 1751. But in and since 1752 the civil year has begun with 1 January. New Year's Day in Scotland was changed from 25 March to 1 January in 1600.

Elsewhere in Europe, 1 January was adopted as the first day of the year by Venice in 1522, German states in 1544, Spain, Portugal and the Roman Catholic Netherlands in 1556, Prussia, Denmark and Sweden in 1559, France in 1564, Lorraine in 1579, the Protestant Netherlands in 1583, Russia in 1725, and Tuscany in 1751.

REGNAL YEARS

Regnal years are the years of a sovereign's reign and each begins on the anniversary of his or her accession, e.g. regnal year 53 of the present Queen begins on 6 February 2004.

The system was used for dating Acts of Parliament until 1962. The Summer Time Act 1925, for example, is quoted as 15 and 16 Geo. V c. 64, because it became law in the parliamentary session which extended over part of both of these regnal years. Acts of a parliamentary session during which a sovereign died were usually given two year numbers, the regnal year of the deceased sovereign and the regnal year of his or her successor, e.g. those passed in 1952 were dated 16 Geo. VI and 1 Elizabeth II. Since 1962 Acts of Parliament have been dated by the calendar year.

QUARTER AND TERM DAYS

Holy days and saints days were the usual means in early times for setting the dates of future and recurrent appointments. The quarter days in England and Wales are the feast of the Nativity (25 December), the feast of the Annunciation (25 March), the feast of St John the Baptist (24 June) and the feast of St Michael and All Angels (29 September).

The term days in Scotland are Candlemas (the feast of the Purification), Whitsunday, Lammas (Loaf Mass), and Martinmas (St Martin's Day). These fell on 2 February, 15 May, 1 August and 11 November respectively. However, by the Term and Quarter Days (Scotland) Act 1990, the dates of the term days were changed to 28 February (Candlemas), 28 May (Whitsunday), 28 August (Lammas) and 28 November (Martinmas).

RED-LETTER DAYS

Red-letter days were originally the holy days and saints days indicated in early ecclesiastical calendars by letters printed in red ink. The days to be distinguished in this way were approved at the Council of Nicaea in AD 325.

These days still have a legal significance, as judges of the Queen's Bench Division wear scarlet robes on red-letter days falling during the law sittings. The days designated as red-letter days for this purpose are:

Holy and saints days

The Conversion of St Paul, the Purification, Ash Wednesday, the Annunciation, the Ascension, the feasts of St Mark, SS Philip and James, St Matthias, St Barnabas, St John the Baptist, St Peter, St Thomas, St James, St Luke, SS Simon and Jude, All Saints, St Andrew.

Civil calendar (for dates, see page 9)

The anniversaries of The Queen's accession, The Queen's birthday and The Queen's coronation, The Queen's official birthday, the birthday of the Duke of Edinburgh, the birthday of the Prince of Wales, St David's Day and Lord Mayor's Day.

PUBLIC HOLIDAYS

Public holidays are divided into two categories, common law and statutory. Common law holidays are holidays 'by habit and custom'; in England, Wales and Northern Ireland these are Good Friday and Christmas Day.

Statutory public holidays, known as bank holidays, were first established by the Bank Holidays Act 1871. They were, literally, days on which the banks (and other public institutions) were closed and financial obligations due on that day were payable the following day. The legislation currently governing public holidays in the UK, which is the Banking and Financial Dealings Act 1971, stipulates the days that are to be public holidays in England, Wales, Scotland and Northern Ireland.

Certain holidays (indicated by * below) are granted annually by royal proclamation, either throughout the UK or in any place in the UK. The public holidays are:

England and Wales
*New Year's Day
Easter Monday
*The first Monday in May
The last Monday in May
The last Monday in August
26 December, if it is not a Sunday
27 December when 25 or 26 December is a Sunday

Scotland
New Year's Day, or if it is a Sunday, 2 January
2 January, or if it is a Sunday, 3 January
Good Friday
The first Monday in May
*The last Monday in May
The first Monday in August
Christmas Day, or if it is a Sunday, 26 December
*Boxing Day – if Christmas Day falls on a Sunday, 26 December is given in lieu and an alternative day is given for Boxing Day

Northern Ireland
*New Year's Day
17 March, or if it is a Sunday, 18 March
Easter Monday
*The first Monday in May
The last Monday in May
*12 July, or if it is a Sunday, 13 July
The last Monday in August
26 December, if it is not a Sunday
27 December if 25 or 26 December is a Sunday

For dates of public holidays in 2004 and 2005, see pages 10–11.

CHRONOLOGICAL CYCLES AND ERAS

SOLAR (OR MAJOR) CYCLE

The solar cycle is a period of twenty-eight years in any corresponding year of which the days of the week recur on the same day of the month.

METONIC (LUNAR, OR MINOR) CYCLE

In 432 BC, Meton, an Athenian astronomer, found that 235 lunations are very nearly, though not exactly, equal in duration to 19 solar years and so after 19 years the phases of the Moon recur on the same days of the month (nearly). The dates of full moon in a cycle of 19 years were inscribed in figures of gold on public monuments in Athens, and the number showing the position of a year in the cycle is called the golden number of that year.

JULIAN PERIOD

The Julian period was proposed by Joseph Scaliger in 1582. The period is 7980 Julian years, and its first year coincides with the year 4713 BC. The figure of 7980 is the product of the number of years in the solar cycle, the Metonic cycle and the cycle of the Roman indiction (28 × 19 × 15).

ROMAN INDICTION

The Roman indiction is a period of fifteen years, instituted for fiscal purposes about AD 300.

EPACT

The epact is the age of the calendar Moon, diminished by one day, on 1 January, in the ecclesiastical lunar calendar.

CHINESE CALENDAR

A lunar calendar was the sole calendar in use in China until 1911, when the government adopted the new (Gregorian) calendar for official and most business activities. The Chinese tend to follow both calendars, the lunar calendar playing an important part in personal life, e.g. birth celebrations, festivals, marriages; and in rural villages the lunar calendar dictates the cycle of activities, denoting the change of weather and farming activities.

The lunar calendar is used in Hong Kong, Singapore, Malaysia, Tibet and elsewhere in south-east Asia. The calendar has a cycle of 60 years. The new year begins at the first new moon after the sun enters the sign of Aquarius, i.e. the new year falls between 21 January and 19 February in the Gregorian calendar.

Each year in the Chinese calendar is associated with one of 12 animals: the rat, the ox, the tiger, the rabbit, the dragon, the snake, the horse, the goat or sheep, the monkey, the chicken or rooster, the dog, and the pig.

The date of the Chinese new year and the astrological sign for the years 2004–2007 are:

2004	22 January	Monkey
2005	9 February	Chicken or Rooster
2006	29 January	Dog
2007	18 February	Pig

COPTIC CALENDAR

In the Coptic calendar, which is used in parts of Egypt and Ethiopia, the year is made up of 12 months of 30 days each, followed, in general, by five complementary days. Every fourth year is an intercalary or leap year and in these years there are six complementary days. The intercalary year of the Coptic calendar immediately precedes the leap year of the Julian calendar. The era is that of Diocletian or the Martyrs, the origin of which is fixed at 29 August AD 284 (Julian date).

INDIAN ERAS

In addition to the Muslim reckoning, other eras are used in India. The Saka era of southern India, dating from 3 March AD 78, was declared the national calendar of the Republic of India with effect from 22 March 1957, to be used concurrently with the Gregorian calendar. As revised, the year of the new Saka era begins at the spring equinox, with five successive months of 31 days and seven of 30 days in ordinary years, and six months of each length in leap years. The year AD 2004 is 1926 of the revised Saka era.

The year AD 2004 corresponds to the following years in other eras:

Year 2061 of the Vikram Samvat era
Year 1411 of the Bengali San era
Year 1180 of the Kollam era
Vedanga Jyotisa year 5 of the five-yearly cycle (386th cycle of Paitamah Siddhanta)
Year 6005 of the Kaliyuga era
Year 2546 of the Buddha Nirvana era

JAPANESE CALENDAR

The Japanese calendar is essentially the same as the Gregorian calendar, the years, months and weeks being of the same length and beginning on the same days as those of the Gregorian calendar. The numeration of the years is different, based on a system of epochs or periods each of which begins at the accession of an Emperor or other important occurrence. The method is not unlike the British system of regnal years, except that each year of a period closes on 31 December. The Japanese chronology begins about AD 650 and the three latest epochs are defined by the reigns of Emperors, whose actual names are not necessarily used:

Epoch
Taishō 1 August 1912 to 25 December 1926
Shōwa 26 December 1926 to 7 January 1989
Heisei 8 January 1989

The year Heisei 16 begins on 1 January 2004.

The months are known as First Month, Second Month, etc., First Month being equivalent to January. The days of the week are Nichiyōbi (Sun-day), Getsuyōbi (Moon-day), Kayōbi (Fire-day), Suiyōbi (Water-day), Mokuyōbi (Wood-day), Kinyōbi (Metal-day), Doyōbi (Earth-day).

THE MASONIC YEAR

Two dates are quoted in warrants, dispensations, etc., issued by the United Grand Lodge of England, those for the current year being expressed as *Anno Domini* 2004 – *Anno Lucis* 6004. This *Anno Lucis* (year of light) is based on the Book of Genesis 1:3, the 4000-year difference being derived, in modified form, from *Ussher's Notation*, published in 1654, which places the Creation of the World in 4004 BC.

OLYMPIADS

Ancient Greek chronology was reckoned in Olympiads, cycles of four years corresponding with the periodic Olympic Games held on the plain of Olympia in Elis once every four years. The intervening years were the first, second, etc., of the Olympiad, which received the name of the victor at the Games. The first recorded Olympiad is that of Choroebus, 776 BC.

ZOROASTRIAN CALENDAR

Zoroastrians, followers of the Iranian prophet Zarathushtra (known to the Greeks as Zoroaster) are mostly to be found in Iran and in India, where they are known as Parsees.

The Zoroastrian era dates from the coronation of the last Zoroastrian Sasanian king in AD 631. The Zoroastrian calendar is divided into twelve months, each comprising 30 days, followed by five holy days of the Gathas at the end of each year to make the year consist of 365 days.

In order to synchronise the calendar with the solar year of 365 days, an extra month was intercalated once every 120 years. However, this intercalation ceased in the 12th century and the New Year, which had fallen in the spring, slipped back to August. Because intercalation ceased at different times in Iran and India, there was one month's difference between the calendar followed in Iran (Kadmi calendar) and that followed by the Parsees (Shenshai calendar). In 1906 a group of Zoroastrians decided to bring the calendar back in line with the seasons again and restore the New Year to 21 March each year (Fasli calendar).

The Shenshai calendar (New Year in August) is mainly used by Parsees. The Fasli calendar (New Year, 21 March) is mainly used by Zoroastrians living in Iran, in the Indian subcontinent, or away from Iran.

THE ROMAN CALENDAR

Roman historians adopted as an epoch the foundation of Rome, which is believed to have happened in the year 753 BC. The ordinal number of the years in Roman reckoning is followed by the letters AUC (*ab urbe condita*), so that the year 2004 is 2757 AUC (MMDCCLVII). The calendar that we know has developed from one said to have been established by Romulus using a year of 304 days divided into ten months, beginning with March. To this Numa added January and February, making the year consist of 12 months of 30 and 29 days alternately, with an additional day so that the total was 355. It is also said that Numa ordered an intercalary month of 22 or 23 days in alternate years, making 90 days in eight years, to be inserted after 23 February.

However, there is some doubt as to the origination and the details of the intercalation in the Roman calendar. It is certain that some scheme of this kind was inaugurated and not fully carried out, for in the year 46 BC Julius Caesar found that the calendar had been allowed to fall into some confusion. He sought the help of the Egyptian astronomer Sosigenes, which led to the construction and adoption (45 BC) of the Julian calendar, and, by a slight alteration, to the Gregorian calendar now in use. The year 46 BC was made to consist of 445 days and is called the Year of Confusion.

In the Roman (Julian) calendar the days of the month were counted backwards from three fixed points, or days, and an intervening day was said to be so many days before the next coming point, the first and last being counted. These three points were the Kalends, the Nones, and the Ides. Their positions in the months and the method of counting from them will be seen in the table below. The year containing 366 days was called *bissextillis annus*, as it had a doubled sixth day (*bissextus dies*) before the March Kalends on 24 February – *ante diem sextum Kalendas Martias*, or a.d. VI Kal. Mart.

Present days of the month	March, May, July, October have thirty-one days		January, August, December have thirty-one days		April, June, September, November have thirty days		February has twenty-eight days, and in leap year twenty-nine	
1	Kalendis		Kalendis		Kalendis		Kalendis	
2	VI		IV ⎱ ante		IV ⎱ ante		IV ⎱ ante	
3	V	ante	III ⎰ Nonas		III ⎰ Nonas		III ⎰ Nonas	
4	IV	Nonas	pridie Nonas		pridie Nonas		pridie Nonas	
5	III		Nonis		Nonis		Nonis	
6	pridie Nonas		VIII		VIII		VIII	
7	Nonis		VII		VII		VII	
8	VIII		VI ⎱ ante		VI ⎱ ante		VI ⎱ ante	
9	VII		V ⎰ Idus		V ⎰ Idus		V ⎰ Idus	
10	VI	ante	IV		IV		IV	
11	V	Idus	III		III		III	
12	IV		pridie Idus		pridie Idus		pridie Idus	
13	III		Idibus		Idibus		Idibus	
14	pridie Idus		XIX		XVIII		XVI	
15	Idibus		XVIII		XVII		XV	
16	XVII		XVII		XVI		XIV	
17	XVI		XVI		XV		XIII	
18	XV		XV		XIV		XII	
19	XIV		XIV		XIII		XI	
20	XIII		XIII		XII	ante Kalendas	X	ante Kalendas
21	XII		XII	ante Kalendas	XI	(of the month	IX	Martias
22	XI	ante Kalendas	XI	(of the month	X	following)	VIII	
23	X	(of the month	X	following)	IX		VII	
24	IX	following)	IX		VIII		*VI	
25	VIII		VIII		VII		V	
26	VII		VII		VI		IV	
27	VI		VI		V		III	
28	V		V		IV		pridie Kalendas
29	IV		IV		III		Martias
30	III		III		pridie Kalendas		
31	pridie Kalendas (Aprilis, Iunias, Sextilis, Novembris)		pridie Kalendas (Februarias, Septembris, Ianuarias)		(Maias, Quinctilis, Octobris, Decembris)		* (repeated in leap year)	

CALENDAR FOR ANY YEAR 1780–2040

To select the correct calendar for any year between 1780 and 2040, consult the index below
*leap year

1780 N*	1813 K	1846 I	1879 G	1912 D*	1945 C	1978 A	2011 M
1781 C	1814 M	1847 K	1880 J*	1913 G	1946 E	1979 C	2012 B*
1782 E	1815 A	1848 N*	1881 M	1914 I	1947 G	1980 F*	2013 E
1783 G	1816 D*	1849 C	1882 A	1915 K	1948 J*	1981 I	2014 G
1784 J*	1817 G	1850 E	1883 C	1916 N*	1949 M	1982 K	2015 I
1785 M	1818 I	1851 G	1884 F*	1917 C	1950 A	1983 M	2016 L*
1786 A	1819 K	1852 J*	1885 I	1918 E	1951 C	1984 B*	2017 A
1787 C	1820 N*	1853 M	1886 K	1919 G	1952 F*	1985 E	2018 C
1788 F*	1821 C	1854 A	1887 M	1920 J*	1953 I	1986 G	2019 E
1789 I	1822 E	1855 C	1888 B*	1921 M	1954 K	1987 I	2020 H*
1790 K	1823 G	1856 F*	1889 E	1922 A	1955 M	1988 L*	2021 K
1791 M	1824 J*	1857 I	1890 G	1923 C	1956 B*	1989 A	2022 M
1792 B*	1825 M	1858 K	1891 I	1924 F*	1957 E	1990 C	2023 A
1793 E	1826 A	1859 M	1892 L*	1925 I	1958 G	1991 E	2024 D*
1794 G	1827 C	1860 B*	1893 A	1926 K	1959 I	1992 H*	2025 G
1795 I	1828 F*	1861 E	1894 C	1927 M	1960 L*	1993 K	2026 I
1796 L*	1829 I	1862 G	1895 E	1928 B*	1961 A	1994 M	2027 K
1797 A	1830 K	1863 I	1896 H*	1929 E	1962 C	1995 A	2028 N*
1798 C	1831 M	1864 L*	1897 K	1930 G	1963 E	1996 D*	2029 C
1799 E	1832 B*	1865 A	1898 M	1931 I	1964 H*	1997 G	2030 E
1800 G	1833 E	1866 C	1899 A	1932 L*	1965 K	1998 I	2031 G
1801 I	1834 G	1867 E	1900 C	1933 A	1966 M	1999 K	2032 J*
1802 K	1835 I	1868 H*	1901 E	1934 C	1967 A	2000 N*	2033 M
1803 M	1836 L*	1869 K	1902 G	1935 E	1968 D*	2001 C	2034 A
1804 B*	1837 A	1870 M	1903 I	1936 H*	1969 G	2002 E	2035 C
1805 E	1838 C	1871 A	1904 L*	1937 K	1970 I	2003 G	2036 F*
1806 G	1839 E	1872 D*	1905 A	1938 M	1971 K	2004 J*	2037 I
1807 I	1840 H*	1873 G	1906 C	1939 A	1972 N*	2005 M	2038 K
1808 L*	1841 K	1874 I	1907 E	1940 D*	1973 C	2006 A	2039 M
1809 A	1842 M	1875 K	1908 H*	1941 G	1974 E	2007 C	2040 B*
1810 C	1843 A	1876 N*	1909 K	1942 I	1975 G	2008 F*	
1811 E	1844 D*	1877 C	1910 M	1943 K	1976 J*	2009 I	
1812 H*	1845 G	1878 E	1911 A	1944 N*	1977 M	2010 K	

A

	January	February	March
Sun.	1 8 15 22 29	5 12 19 26	5 12 19 26
Mon.	2 9 16 23 30	6 13 20 27	6 13 20 27
Tue.	3 10 17 24 31	7 14 21 28	7 14 21 28
Wed.	4 11 18 25	1 8 15 22	1 8 15 22 29
Thur.	5 12 19 26	2 9 16 23	2 9 16 23 30
Fri.	6 13 20 27	3 10 17 24	3 10 17 24 31
Sat.	7 14 21 28	4 11 18 25	4 11 18 25

	April	May	June
Sun.	2 9 16 23 30	7 14 21 28	4 11 18 25
Mon.	3 10 17 24	1 8 15 22 29	5 12 19 26
Tue.	4 11 18 25	2 9 16 23 30	6 13 20 27
Wed.	5 12 19 26	3 10 17 24 31	7 14 21 28
Thur.	6 13 20 27	4 11 18 25	1 8 15 22 29
Fri.	7 14 21 28	5 12 19 26	2 9 16 23 30
Sat.	1 8 15 22 29	6 13 20 27	3 10 17 24

	July	August	September
Sun.	2 9 16 23 30	6 13 20 27	3 10 17 24
Mon.	3 10 17 24 31	7 14 21 28	4 11 18 25
Tue.	4 11 18 25	1 8 15 22 29	5 12 19 26
Wed.	5 12 19 26	2 9 16 23 30	6 13 20 27
Thur.	6 13 20 27	3 10 17 24 31	7 14 21 28
Fri.	7 14 21 28	4 11 18 25	1 8 15 22 29
Sat.	1 8 15 22 29	5 12 19 26	2 9 16 23 30

	October	November	December
Sun.	1 8 15 22 29	5 12 19 26	3 10 17 24 31
Mon.	2 9 16 23 30	6 13 20 27	4 11 18 25
Tue.	3 10 17 24 31	7 14 21 28	5 12 19 26
Wed.	4 11 18 25	1 8 15 22 29	6 13 20 27
Thur.	5 12 19 26	2 9 16 23 30	7 14 21 28
Fri.	6 13 20 27	3 10 17 24	1 8 15 22 29
Sat.	7 14 21 28	4 11 18 25	2 9 16 23 30

EASTER DAYS

March 26	1815, 1826, 1837, 1967, 1978, 1989
April 2	1809, 1893, 1899, 1961
April 9	1871, 1882, 1939, 1950, 2023, 2034
April 16	1786, 1797, 1843, 1854, 1865, 1911, 1922, 1933, 1995, 2006, 2017
April 23	1905

B (LEAP YEAR)

	January	February	March
Sun.	1 8 15 22 29	5 12 19 26	4 11 18 25
Mon.	2 9 16 23 30	6 13 20 27	5 12 19 26
Tue.	3 10 17 24 31	7 14 21 28	6 13 20 27
Wed.	4 11 18 25	1 8 15 22 29	7 14 21 28
Thur.	5 12 19 26	2 9 16 23	1 8 15 22 29
Fri.	6 13 20 27	3 10 17 24	2 9 16 23 30
Sat.	7 14 21 28	4 11 18 25	3 10 17 24 31

	April	May	June
Sun.	1 8 15 22 29	6 13 20 27	3 10 17 24
Mon.	2 9 16 23 30	7 14 21 28	4 11 18 25
Tue.	3 10 17 24	1 8 15 22 29	5 12 19 26
Wed.	4 11 18 25	2 9 16 23 30	6 13 20 27
Thur.	5 12 19 26	3 10 17 24 31	7 14 21 28
Fri.	6 13 20 27	4 11 18 25	1 8 15 22 29
Sat.	7 14 21 28	5 12 19 26	2 9 16 23 30

	July	August	September
Sun.	1 8 15 22 29	5 12 19 26	2 9 16 23 30
Mon.	2 9 16 23 30	6 13 20 27	3 10 17 24
Tue.	3 10 17 24 31	7 14 21 28	4 11 18 25
Wed.	4 11 18 25	1 8 15 22 29	5 12 19 26
Thur.	5 12 19 26	2 9 16 23 30	6 13 20 27
Fri.	6 13 20 27	3 10 17 24 31	7 14 21 28
Sat.	7 14 21 28	4 11 18 25	1 8 15 22 29

	October	November	December
Sun.	7 14 21 28	4 11 18 25	2 9 16 23 30
Mon.	1 8 15 22 29	5 12 19 26	3 10 17 24 31
Tue.	2 9 16 23 30	6 13 20 27	4 11 18 25
Wed.	3 10 17 24 31	7 14 21 28	5 12 19 26
Thur.	4 11 18 25	1 8 15 22 29	6 13 20 27
Fri.	5 12 19 26	2 9 16 23 30	7 14 21 28
Sat.	6 13 20 27	3 10 17 24	1 8 15 22 29

EASTER DAYS

April 1	1804, 1888, 1956, 2040
April 8	1792, 1860, 1928, 2012
April 22	1832, 1984

C

	January	February	March
Sun.	7 14 21 28	4 11 18 25	4 11 18 25
Mon.	1 8 15 22 29	5 12 19 26	5 12 19 26
Tue.	2 9 16 23 30	6 13 20 27	6 13 20 27
Wed.	3 10 17 24 31	7 14 21 28	7 14 21 28
Thur.	4 11 18 25	1 8 15 22	1 8 15 22 29
Fri.	5 12 19 26	2 9 16 23	2 9 16 23 30
Sat.	6 13 20 27	3 10 17 24	3 10 17 24 31

	April	May	June
Sun.	1 8 15 22 29	6 13 20 27	3 10 17 24
Mon.	2 9 16 23 30	7 14 21 28	4 11 18 25
Tue.	3 10 17 24	1 8 15 22 29	5 12 19 26
Wed.	4 11 18 25	2 9 16 23 30	6 13 20 27
Thur.	5 12 19 26	3 10 17 24 31	7 14 21 28
Fri.	6 13 20 27	4 11 18 25	1 8 15 22 29
Sat.	7 14 21 28	5 12 19 26	2 9 16 23 30

	July	August	September
Sun.	1 8 15 22 29	5 12 19 26	2 9 16 23 30
Mon.	2 9 16 23 30	6 13 20 27	3 10 17 24
Tue.	3 10 17 24 31	7 14 21 28	4 11 18 25
Wed.	4 11 18 25	1 8 15 22 29	5 12 19 26
Thur.	5 12 19 26	2 9 16 23 30	6 13 20 27
Fri.	6 13 20 27	3 10 17 24 31	7 14 21 28
Sat.	7 14 21 28	4 11 18 25	1 8 15 22 29

	October	November	December
Sun.	7 14 21 28	4 11 18 25	2 9 16 23 30
Mon.	1 8 15 22 29	5 12 19 26	3 10 17 24 31
Tue.	2 9 16 23 30	6 13 20 27	4 11 18 25
Wed.	3 10 17 24 31	7 14 21 28	5 12 19 26
Thur.	4 11 18 25	1 8 15 22 29	6 13 20 27
Fri.	5 12 19 26	2 9 16 23 30	7 14 21 28
Sat.	6 13 20 27	3 10 17 24	1 8 15 22 29

EASTER DAYS
March 25	1883, 1894, 1951, 2035
April 1	1866, 1877, 1923, 1934, 1945, 2018, 2029
April 8	1787, 1798, 1849, 1855, 1917, 2007
April 15	1781, 1827, 1838, 1900, 1906, 1979, 1990, 2001
April 22	1810, 1821, 1962, 1973

E

	January	February	March
Sun.	6 13 20 27	3 10 17 24	3 10 17 24 31
Mon.	7 14 21 28	4 11 18 25	4 11 18 25
Tue.	1 8 15 22 29	5 12 19 26	5 12 19 26
Wed.	2 9 16 23 30	6 13 20 27	6 13 20 27
Thur.	3 10 17 24 31	7 14 21 28	7 14 21 28
Fri.	4 11 18 25	1 8 15 22	1 8 15 22 29
Sat.	5 12 19 26	2 9 16 23	2 9 16 23 30

	April	May	June
Sun.	7 14 21 28	5 12 19 26	2 9 16 23 30
Mon.	1 8 15 22 29	6 13 20 27	3 10 17 24
Tue.	2 9 16 23 30	7 14 21 28	4 11 18 25
Wed.	3 10 17 24	1 8 15 22 29	5 12 19 26
Thur.	4 11 18 25	2 9 16 23 30	6 13 20 27
Fri.	5 12 19 26	3 10 17 24 31	7 14 21 28
Sat.	6 13 20 27	4 11 18 25	1 8 15 22 29

	July	August	September
Sun.	7 14 21 28	4 11 18 25	1 8 15 22 29
Mon.	1 8 15 22 29	5 12 19 26	2 9 16 23 30
Tue.	2 9 16 23 30	6 13 20 27	3 10 17 24
Wed.	3 10 17 24 31	7 14 21 28	4 11 18 25
Thur.	4 11 18 25	1 8 15 22 29	5 12 19 26
Fri.	5 12 19 26	2 9 16 23 30	6 13 20 27
Sat.	6 13 20 27	3 10 17 24 31	7 14 21 28

	October	November	December
Sun.	6 13 20 27	3 10 17 24	1 8 15 22 29
Mon.	7 14 21 28	4 11 18 25	2 9 16 23 30
Tue.	1 8 15 22 29	5 12 19 26	3 10 17 24 31
Wed.	2 9 16 23 30	6 13 20 27	4 11 18 25
Thur.	3 10 17 24 31	7 14 21 28	5 12 19 26
Fri.	4 11 18 25	1 8 15 22 29	6 13 20 27
Sat.	5 12 19 26	2 9 16 23 30	7 14 21 28

EASTER DAYS
March 24	1799
March 31	1782, 1793, 1839, 1850, 1861, 1907, 1918, 1929, 1991, 2002, 2013
April 7	1822, 1833, 1901, 1985
April 14	1805, 1811, 1895, 1963, 1974
April 21	1867, 1878, 1889, 1935, 1946, 1957, 2019, 2030

D (LEAP YEAR)

	January	February	March
Sun.	7 14 21 28	4 11 18 25	3 10 17 24 31
Mon.	1 8 15 22 29	5 12 19 26	4 11 18 25
Tue.	2 9 16 23 30	6 13 20 27	5 12 19 26
Wed.	3 10 17 24 31	7 14 21 28	6 13 20 27
Thur.	4 11 18 25	1 8 15 22 29	7 14 21 28
Fri.	5 12 19 26	2 9 16 23	1 8 15 22 29
Sat.	6 13 20 27	3 10 17 24	2 9 16 23 30

	April	May	June
Sun.	7 14 21 28	5 12 19 26	2 9 16 23 30
Mon.	1 8 15 22 29	6 13 20 27	3 10 17 24
Tue.	2 9 16 23 30	7 14 21 28	4 11 18 25
Wed.	3 10 17 24	1 8 15 22 29	5 12 19 26
Thur.	4 11 18 25	2 9 16 23 30	6 13 20 27
Fri.	5 12 19 26	3 10 17 24 31	7 14 21 28
Sat.	6 13 20 27	4 11 18 25	1 8 15 22 29

	July	August	September
Sun.	7 14 21 28	4 11 18 25	1 8 15 22 29
Mon.	1 8 15 22 29	5 12 19 26	2 9 16 23 30
Tue.	2 9 16 23 30	6 13 20 27	3 10 17 24
Wed.	3 10 17 24 31	7 14 21 28	4 11 18 25
Thur.	4 11 18 25	1 8 15 22 29	5 12 19 26
Fri.	5 12 19 26	2 9 16 23 30	6 13 20 27
Sat.	6 13 20 27	3 10 17 24 31	7 14 21 28

	October	November	December
Sun.	6 13 20 27	3 10 17 24	1 8 15 22 29
Mon.	7 14 21 28	4 11 18 25	2 9 16 23 30
Tue.	1 8 15 22 29	5 12 19 26	3 10 17 24 31
Wed.	2 9 16 23 30	6 13 20 27	4 11 18 25
Thur.	3 10 17 24 31	7 14 21 28	5 12 19 26
Fri.	4 11 18 25	1 8 15 22 29	6 13 20 27
Sat.	5 12 19 26	2 9 16 23 30	7 14 21 28

EASTER DAYS
March 24	1940
March 31	1872, 2024
April 7	1844, 1912, 1996
April 14	1816, 1968

F (LEAP YEAR)

	January	February	March
Sun.	6 13 20 27	3 10 17 24	2 9 16 23 30
Mon.	7 14 21 28	4 11 18 25	3 10 17 24 31
Tue.	1 8 15 22 29	5 12 19 26	4 11 18 25
Wed.	2 9 16 23 30	6 13 20 27	5 12 19 26
Thur.	3 10 17 24 31	7 14 21 28	6 13 20 27
Fri.	4 11 18 25	1 8 15 22 29	7 14 21 28
Sat.	5 12 19 26	2 9 16 23	1 8 15 22 29

	April	May	June
Sun.	6 13 20 27	4 11 18 25	1 8 15 22 29
Mon.	7 14 21 28	5 12 19 26	2 9 16 23 30
Tue.	1 8 15 22 29	6 13 20 27	3 10 17 24
Wed.	2 9 16 23 30	7 14 21 28	4 11 18 25
Thur.	3 10 17 24	1 8 15 22 29	5 12 19 26
Fri.	4 11 18 25	2 9 16 23 30	6 13 20 27
Sat.	5 12 19 26	3 10 17 24 31	7 14 21 28

	July	August	September
Sun.	6 13 20 27	3 10 17 24 31	7 14 21 28
Mon.	7 14 21 28	4 11 18 25	1 8 15 22 29
Tue.	1 8 15 22 29	5 12 19 26	2 9 16 23 30
Wed.	2 9 16 23 30	6 13 20 27	3 10 17 24
Thur.	3 10 17 24 31	7 14 21 28	4 11 18 25
Fri.	4 11 18 25	1 8 15 22 29	5 12 19 26
Sat.	5 12 19 26	2 9 16 23 30	6 13 20 27

	October	November	December
Sun.	5 12 19 26	2 9 16 23 30	7 14 21 28
Mon.	6 13 20 27	3 10 17 24	1 8 15 22 29
Tue.	7 14 21 28	4 11 18 25	2 9 16 23 30
Wed.	1 8 15 22 29	5 12 19 26	3 10 17 24 31
Thur.	2 9 16 23 30	6 13 20 27	4 11 18 25
Fri.	3 10 17 24 31	7 14 21 28	5 12 19 26
Sat.	4 11 18 25	1 8 15 22 29	6 13 20 27

EASTER DAYS
March 23	1788, 1856, 2008
April 6	1828, 1980
April 13	1884, 1952, 2036
April 20	1924

G

	January	February	March
Sun.	5 12 19 26	2 9 16 23	2 9 16 23 30
Mon.	6 13 20 27	3 10 17 24	3 10 17 24 31
Tue.	7 14 21 28	4 11 18 25	4 11 18 25
Wed.	1 8 15 22 29	5 12 19 26	5 12 19 26
Thur.	2 9 16 23 30	6 13 20 27	6 13 20 27
Fri.	3 10 17 24 31	7 14 21 28	7 14 21 28
Sat.	4 11 18 25	1 8 15 22	1 8 15 22 29

	April	May	June
Sun.	6 13 20 27	4 11 18 25	1 8 15 22 29
Mon.	7 14 21 28	5 12 19 26	2 9 16 23 30
Tue.	1 8 15 22 29	6 13 20 27	3 10 17 24
Wed.	2 9 16 23 30	7 14 21 28	4 11 18 25
Thur.	3 10 17 24	1 8 15 22 29	5 12 19 26
Fri.	4 11 18 25	2 9 16 23 30	6 13 20 27
Sat.	5 12 19 26	3 10 17 24 31	7 14 21 28

	July	August	September
Sun.	6 13 20 27	3 10 17 24 31	7 14 21 28
Mon.	7 14 21 28	4 11 18 25	1 8 15 22 29
Tue.	1 8 15 22 29	5 12 19 26	2 9 16 23 30
Wed.	2 9 16 23 30	6 13 20 27	3 10 17 24
Thur.	3 10 17 24 31	7 14 21 28	4 11 18 25
Fri.	4 11 18 25	1 8 15 22 29	5 12 19 26
Sat.	5 12 19 26	2 9 16 23 30	6 13 20 27

	October	November	December
Sun.	5 12 19 26	2 9 16 23 30	7 14 21 28
Mon.	6 13 20 27	3 10 17 24	1 8 15 22 29
Tue.	7 14 21 28	4 11 18 25	2 9 16 23 30
Wed.	1 8 15 22 29	5 12 19 26	3 10 17 24 31
Thur.	2 9 16 23 30	6 13 20 27	4 11 18 25
Fri.	3 10 17 24 31	7 14 21 28	5 12 19 26
Sat.	4 11 18 25	1 8 15 22 29	6 13 20 27

EASTER DAYS

March 23	1845, 1913
March 30	1823, 1834, 1902, 1975, 1986, 1997
April 6	1806, 1817, 1890, 1947, 1958, 1969
April 13	1800, 1873, 1879, 1941, 2031
April 20	1783, 1794, 1851, 1862, 1919, 1930, 2003, 2014, 2025

I

	January	February	March
Sun.	4 11 18 25	1 8 15 22	1 8 15 22 29
Mon.	5 12 19 26	2 9 16 23	2 9 16 23 30
Tue.	6 13 20 27	3 10 17 24	3 10 17 24 31
Wed.	7 14 21 28	4 11 18 25	4 11 18 25
Thur.	1 8 15 22 29	5 12 19 26	5 12 19 26
Fri.	2 9 16 23 30	6 13 20 27	6 13 20 27
Sat.	3 10 17 24 31	7 14 21 28	7 14 21 28

	April	May	June
Sun.	5 12 19 26	3 10 17 24 31	7 14 21 28
Mon.	6 13 20 27	4 11 18 25	1 8 15 22 29
Tue.	7 14 21 28	5 12 19 26	2 9 16 23 30
Wed.	1 8 15 22 29	6 13 20 27	3 10 17 24
Thur.	2 9 16 23 30	7 14 21 28	4 11 18 25
Fri.	3 10 17 24	1 8 15 22 29	5 12 19 26
Sat.	4 11 18 25	2 9 16 23 30	6 13 20 27

	July	August	September
Sun.	5 12 19 26	2 9 16 23 30	6 13 20 27
Mon.	6 13 20 27	3 10 17 24 31	7 14 21 28
Tue.	7 14 21 28	4 11 18 25	1 8 15 22 29
Wed.	1 8 15 22 29	5 12 19 26	2 9 16 23 30
Thur.	2 9 16 23 30	6 13 20 27	3 10 17 24
Fri.	3 10 17 24 31	7 14 21 28	4 11 18 25
Sat.	4 11 18 25	1 8 15 22 29	5 12 19 26

	October	November	December
Sun.	4 11 18 25	1 8 15 22 29	6 13 20 27
Mon.	5 12 19 26	2 9 16 23 30	7 14 21 28
Tue.	6 13 20 27	3 10 17 24	1 8 15 22 29
Wed.	7 14 21 28	4 11 18 25	2 9 16 23 30
Thur.	1 8 15 22 29	5 12 19 26	3 10 17 24 31
Fri.	2 9 16 23 30	6 13 20 27	4 11 18 25
Sat.	3 10 17 24 31	7 14 21 28	5 12 19 26

EASTER DAYS

March 22	1818
March 29	1807, 1891, 1959, 1970
April 5	1795, 1801, 1863, 1874, 1885, 1931, 1942, 1953, 2015, 2026, 2037
April 12	1789, 1846, 1857, 1903, 1914, 1925, 1998, 2009
April 19	1829, 1835, 1981, 1987

H (LEAP YEAR)

	January	February	March
Sun.	5 12 19 26	2 9 16 23	1 8 15 22 29
Mon.	6 13 20 27	3 10 17 24	2 9 16 23 30
Tue.	7 14 21 28	4 11 18 25	3 10 17 24 31
Wed.	1 8 15 22 29	5 12 19 26	4 11 18 25
Thur.	2 9 16 23 30	6 13 20 27	5 12 19 26
Fri.	3 10 17 24 31	7 14 21 28	6 13 20 27
Sat.	4 11 18 25	1 8 15 22 29	7 14 21 28

	April	May	June
Sun.	5 12 19 26	3 10 17 24 31	7 14 21 28
Mon.	6 13 20 27	4 11 18 25	1 8 15 22 29
Tue.	7 14 21 28	5 12 19 26	2 9 16 23 30
Wed.	1 8 15 22 29	6 13 20 27	3 10 17 24
Thur.	2 9 16 23 30	7 14 21 28	4 11 18 25
Fri.	3 10 17 24	1 8 15 22 29	5 12 19 26
Sat.	4 11 18 25	2 9 16 23 30	6 13 20 27

	July	August	September
Sun.	5 12 19 26	2 9 16 23 30	6 13 20 27
Mon.	6 13 20 27	3 10 17 24 31	7 14 21 28
Tue.	7 14 21 28	4 11 18 25	1 8 15 22 29
Wed.	1 8 15 22 29	5 12 19 26	2 9 16 23 30
Thur.	2 9 16 23 30	6 13 20 27	3 10 17 24
Fri.	3 10 17 24 31	7 14 21 28	4 11 18 25
Sat.	4 11 18 25	1 8 15 22 29	5 12 19 26

	October	November	December
Sun.	4 11 18 25	1 8 15 22 29	6 13 20 27
Mon.	5 12 19 26	2 9 16 23 30	7 14 21 28
Tue.	6 13 20 27	3 10 17 24	1 8 15 22 29
Wed.	7 14 21 28	4 11 18 25	2 9 16 23 30
Thur.	1 8 15 22 29	5 12 19 26	3 10 17 24 31
Fri.	2 9 16 23 30	6 13 20 27	4 11 18 25
Sat.	3 10 17 24 31	7 14 21 28	5 12 19 26

EASTER DAYS

March 29	1812, 1964
April 5	1896
April 12	1868, 1936, 2020
April 19	1840, 1908, 1992

J (LEAP YEAR)

	January	February	March
Sun.	4 11 18 25	1 8 15 22 29	7 14 21 28
Mon.	5 12 19 26	2 9 16 23	1 8 15 22 29
Tue.	6 13 20 27	3 10 17 24	2 9 16 23 30
Wed.	7 14 21 28	4 11 18 25	3 10 17 24 31
Thur.	1 8 15 22 29	5 12 19 26	4 11 18 25
Fri.	2 9 16 23 30	6 13 20 27	5 12 19 26
Sat.	3 10 17 24 31	7 14 21 28	6 13 20 27

	April	May	June
Sun.	4 11 18 25	2 9 16 23 30	6 13 20 27
Mon.	5 12 19 26	3 10 17 24 31	7 14 21 28
Tue.	6 13 20 27	4 11 18 25	1 8 15 22 29
Wed.	7 14 21 28	5 12 19 26	2 9 16 23 30
Thur.	1 8 15 22 29	6 13 20 27	3 10 17 24
Fri.	2 9 16 23 30	7 14 21 28	4 11 18 25
Sat.	3 10 17 24	1 8 15 22 29	5 12 19 26

	July	August	September
Sun.	4 11 18 25	1 8 15 22 29	5 12 19 26
Mon.	5 12 19 26	2 9 16 23 30	6 13 20 27
Tue.	6 13 20 27	3 10 17 24 31	7 14 21 28
Wed.	7 14 21 28	4 11 18 25	1 8 15 22 29
Thur.	1 8 15 22 29	5 12 19 26	2 9 16 23 30
Fri.	2 9 16 23 30	6 13 20 27	3 10 17 24
Sat.	3 10 17 24 31	7 14 21 28	4 11 18 25

	October	November	December
Sun.	3 10 17 24 31	7 14 21 28	5 12 19 26
Mon.	4 11 18 25	1 8 15 22 29	6 13 20 27
Tue.	5 12 19 26	2 9 16 23 30	7 14 21 28
Wed.	6 13 20 27	3 10 17 24	1 8 15 22 29
Thur.	7 14 21 28	4 11 18 25	2 9 16 23 30
Fri.	1 8 15 22 29	5 12 19 26	3 10 17 24 31
Sat.	2 9 16 23 30	6 13 20 27	4 11 18 25

EASTER DAYS

March 28	1880, 1948, 2032
April 4	1920
April 11	1784, 1852, 2004
April 18	1824, 1976

K

	January	February	March
Sun.	3 10 17 24 31	7 14 21 28	7 14 21 28
Mon.	4 11 18 25	1 8 15 22	1 8 15 22 29
Tue.	5 12 19 26	2 9 16 23	2 9 16 23 30
Wed.	6 13 20 27	3 10 17 24	3 10 17 24 31
Thur.	7 14 21 28	4 11 18 25	4 11 18 25
Fri.	1 8 15 22 29	5 12 19 26	5 12 19 26
Sat.	2 9 16 23 30	6 13 20 27	6 13 20 27

	April	May	June
Sun.	4 11 18 25	2 9 16 23 30	6 13 20 27
Mon.	5 12 19 26	3 10 17 24 31	7 14 21 28
Tue.	6 13 20 27	4 11 18 25	1 8 15 22 29
Wed.	7 14 21 28	5 12 19 26	2 9 16 23 30
Thur.	1 8 15 22 29	6 13 20 27	3 10 17 24
Fri.	2 9 16 23 30	7 14 21 28	4 11 18 25
Sat.	3 10 17 24	1 8 15 22 29	5 12 19 26

	July	August	September
Sun.	4 11 18 25	1 8 15 22 29	5 12 19 26
Mon.	5 12 19 26	2 9 16 23 30	6 13 20 27
Tue.	6 13 20 27	3 10 17 24 31	7 14 21 28
Wed.	7 14 21 28	4 11 18 25	1 8 15 22 29
Thur.	1 8 15 22 29	5 12 19 26	2 9 16 23 30
Fri.	2 9 16 23 30	6 13 20 27	3 10 17 24
Sat.	3 10 17 24 31	7 14 21 28	4 11 18 25

	October	November	December
Sun.	3 10 17 24 31	7 14 21 28	5 12 19 26
Mon.	4 11 18 25	1 8 15 22 29	6 13 20 27
Tue.	5 12 19 26	2 9 16 23 30	7 14 21 28
Wed.	6 13 20 27	3 10 17 24	1 8 15 22 29
Thur.	7 14 21 28	4 11 18 25	2 9 16 23 30
Fri.	1 8 15 22 29	5 12 19 26	3 10 17 24 31
Sat.	2 9 16 23 30	6 13 20 27	4 11 18 25

EASTER DAYS

March 28	1869, 1875, 1937, 2027
April 4	1790, 1847, 1858, 1915, 1926, 1999, 2010, 2021
April 11	1819, 1830, 1841, 1909, 1971, 1982, 1993
April 18	1802, 1813, 1897, 1954, 1965
April 25	1886, 1943, 2038

M

	January	February	March
Sun.	2 9 16 23 30	6 13 20 27	6 13 20 27
Mon.	3 10 17 24 31	7 14 21 28	7 14 21 28
Tue.	4 11 18 25	1 8 15 22	1 8 15 22 29
Wed.	5 12 19 26	2 9 16 23	2 9 16 23 30
Thur.	6 13 20 27	3 10 17 24	3 10 17 24 31
Fri.	7 14 21 28	4 11 18 25	4 11 18 25
Sat.	1 8 15 22 29	5 12 19 26	5 12 19 26

	April	May	June
Sun.	3 10 17 24	1 8 15 22 29	5 12 19 26
Mon.	4 11 18 25	2 9 16 23 30	6 13 20 27
Tue.	5 12 19 26	3 10 17 24 31	7 14 21 28
Wed.	6 13 20 27	4 11 18 25	1 8 15 22 29
Thur.	7 14 21 28	5 12 19 26	2 9 16 23 30
Fri.	1 8 15 22 29	6 13 20 27	3 10 17 24
Sat.	2 9 16 23 30	7 14 21 28	4 11 18 25

	July	August	September
Sun.	3 10 17 24 31	7 14 21 28	4 11 18 25
Mon.	4 11 18 25	1 8 15 22 29	5 12 19 26
Tue.	5 12 19 26	2 9 16 23 30	6 13 20 27
Wed.	6 13 20 27	3 10 17 24 31	7 14 21 28
Thur.	7 14 21 28	4 11 18 25	1 8 15 22 29
Fri.	1 8 15 22 29	5 12 19 26	2 9 16 23 30
Sat.	2 9 16 23 30	6 13 20 27	3 10 17 24

	October	November	December
Sun.	2 9 16 23 30	6 13 20 27	4 11 18 25
Mon.	3 10 17 24 31	7 14 21 28	5 12 19 26
Tue.	4 11 18 25	1 8 15 22 29	6 13 20 27
Wed.	5 12 19 26	2 9 16 23 30	7 14 21 28
Thur.	6 13 20 27	3 10 17 24	1 8 15 22 29
Fri.	7 14 21 28	4 11 18 25	2 9 16 23 30
Sat.	1 8 15 22 29	5 12 19 26	3 10 17 24 31

EASTER DAYS

March 27	1785, 1842, 1853, 1910, 1921, 2005
April 3	1825, 1831, 1983, 1994
April 10	1803, 1814, 1887, 1898, 1955, 1966, 1977, 2039
April 17	1870, 1881, 1927, 1938, 1949, 2022, 2033
April 24	1791, 1859, 2011

L (LEAP YEAR)

	January	February	March
Sun.	3 10 17 24 31	7 14 21 28	6 13 20 27
Mon.	4 11 18 25	1 8 15 22 29	7 14 21 28
Tue.	5 12 19 26	2 9 16 23	1 8 15 22 29
Wed.	6 13 20 27	3 10 17 24	2 9 16 23 30
Thur.	7 14 21 28	4 11 18 25	3 10 17 24 31
Fri.	1 8 15 22 29	5 12 19 26	4 11 18 25
Sat.	2 9 16 23 30	6 13 20 27	5 12 19 26

	April	May	June
Sun.	3 10 17 24	1 8 15 22 29	5 12 19 26
Mon.	4 11 18 25	2 9 16 23 30	6 13 20 27
Tue.	5 12 19 26	3 10 17 24 31	7 14 21 28
Wed.	6 13 20 27	4 11 18 25	1 8 15 22 29
Thur.	7 14 21 28	5 12 19 26	2 9 16 23 30
Fri.	1 8 15 22 29	6 13 20 27	3 10 17 24
Sat.	2 9 16 23 30	7 14 21 28	4 11 18 25

	July	August	September
Sun.	3 10 17 24 31	7 14 21 28	4 11 18 25
Mon.	4 11 18 25	1 8 15 22 29	5 12 19 26
Tue.	5 12 19 26	2 9 16 23 30	6 13 20 27
Wed.	6 13 20 27	3 10 17 24 31	7 14 21 28
Thur.	7 14 21 28	4 11 18 25	1 8 15 22 29
Fri.	1 8 15 22 29	5 12 19 26	2 9 16 23 30
Sat.	2 9 16 23 30	6 13 20 27	3 10 17 24

	October	November	December
Sun.	2 9 16 23 30	6 13 20 27	4 11 18 25
Mon.	3 10 17 24 31	7 14 21 28	5 12 19 26
Tue.	4 11 18 25	1 8 15 22 29	6 13 20 27
Wed.	5 12 19 26	2 9 16 23 30	7 14 21 28
Thur.	6 13 20 27	3 10 17 24	1 8 15 22 29
Fri.	7 14 21 28	4 11 18 25	2 9 16 23 30
Sat.	1 8 15 22 29	5 12 19 26	3 10 17 24 31

EASTER DAYS

March 27	1796, 1864, 1932, 2016
April 3	1836, 1904, 1988
April 17	1808, 1892, 1960

N (LEAP YEAR)

	January	February	March
Sun.	2 9 16 23 30	6 13 20 27	5 12 19 26
Mon.	3 10 17 24 31	7 14 21 28	6 13 20 27
Tue.	4 11 18 25	1 8 15 22 29	7 14 21 28
Wed.	5 12 19 26	2 9 16 23	1 8 15 22 29
Thur.	6 13 20 27	3 10 17 24	2 9 16 23 30
Fri.	7 14 21 28	4 11 18 25	3 10 17 24 31
Sat.	1 8 15 22 29	5 12 19 26	4 11 18 25

	April	May	June
Sun.	2 9 16 23 30	7 14 21 28	4 11 18 25
Mon.	3 10 17 24	1 8 15 22 29	5 12 19 26
Tue.	4 11 18 25	2 9 16 23 30	6 13 20 27
Wed.	5 12 19 26	3 10 17 24 31	7 14 21 28
Thur.	6 13 20 27	4 11 18 25	1 8 15 22 29
Fri.	7 14 21 28	5 12 19 26	2 9 16 23 30
Sat.	1 8 15 22 29	6 13 20 27	3 10 17 24

	July	August	September
Sun.	2 9 16 23 30	6 13 20 27	3 10 17 24
Mon.	3 10 17 24 31	7 14 21 28	4 11 18 25
Tue.	4 11 18 25	1 8 15 22 29	5 12 19 26
Wed.	5 12 19 26	2 9 16 23 30	6 13 20 27
Thur.	6 13 20 27	3 10 17 24 31	7 14 21 28
Fri.	7 14 21 28	4 11 18 25	1 8 15 22 29
Sat.	1 8 15 22 29	5 12 19 26	2 9 16 23 30

	October	November	December
Sun.	1 8 15 22 29	5 12 19 26	3 10 17 24 31
Mon.	2 9 16 23 30	6 13 20 27	4 11 18 25
Tue.	3 10 17 24 31	7 14 21 28	5 12 19 26
Wed.	4 11 18 25	1 8 15 22 29	6 13 20 27
Thur.	5 12 19 26	2 9 16 23 30	7 14 21 28
Fri.	6 13 20 27	3 10 17 24	1 8 15 22 29
Sat.	7 14 21 28	4 11 18 25	2 9 16 23 30

EASTER DAYS

March 26	1780
April 2	1820, 1972
April 9	1944
April 16	1876, 2028
April 23	1848, 1916, 2000

GEOLOGICAL TIME

The earth is thought to have come into existence approximately 4,600 million years ago, but for nearly half this time, the Archean era, it was uninhabited. Life is generally believed to have emerged in the succeeding Proterozoic era. The Archean and the Proterozoic eras are often together referred to as the Precambrian.

Although primitive forms of life, e.g. algae and bacteria, existed during the Proterozoic era, it is not until the strata of Palaeozoic rocks is reached that abundant fossilised remains appear.

Since the Precambrian, there have been three great geological eras:

PALAEOZOIC ('ancient life')
c. 550–c. 248 million years ago
Cambrian – Mainly sandstones, slate and shales; limestones in Scotland. Shelled fossils and invertebrates, e.g. trilobites and brachiopods appear as do the earliest known vertebrates (jawless fish)
Ordovician – Mainly shales and mudstones, e.g. in north Wales; limestones in Scotland. First fishes
Silurian – Shales, mudstones and some limestones, found mostly in Wales and southern Scotland
Devonian – Old red sandstone, shale, limestone and slate, e.g. in south Wales and the West Country
Carboniferous – Coal-bearing rocks, millstone grit, limestone and shale. First traces of land-living life
Permian – Marls, sandstones and clays. First reptile fossils

There were two great phases of mountain building in the Palaeozoic era: the Caledonian, characterised in Britain by NE–SW lines of hills and valleys; and the later Hercyian, widespread in west Germany and adjacent areas, and in Britain exemplified in E–W lines of hills and valleys.

The end of the Palaeozoic era was marked by the extensive glaciations of the Permian period in the southern continents and the decline of amphibians. It was succeeded by an era of warm conditions.

MESOZOIC ('middle forms of life')
c. 245–c. 65 million years ago
Triassic – Mostly sandstone, e.g. in the West Midlands; primitive mamals appear
Jurassic – Mainly limestones and clays, typically displayed in the Jura mountains, and in England in a NE–SW belt from Lincolnshire and the Wash to the Severn and the Dorset coast
Cretaceous – Mainly chalk, clay and sands, e.g. in Kent and Sussex

Giant reptiles were dominant during the Mesozoic era, but it was at this time that marsupial mammals first appeared, as well as *Archaeopteryx lithographica,* the earliest known species of bird. Coniferous trees and flowering plants also developed during the era and, with the birds and the mammals, were the main species to survive into the Cenozoic era. The giant reptiles became extinct.

CENOZOIC ('recent life')
from c. 65 million years ago
Palaeocene ⎫ The emergence of new forms of life,
Eocene ⎬ including existing species; primates
⎭ appear
Oligocene – Fossils of a few still existing species
Miocene – Fossil remains show a balance of existing and extinct species

Pliocene – Fossil remains show a majority of still existing species
Pleistocene – The majority of remains are those of still existing species
Holocene – The present, post-glacial period. Existing species only, except for a few exterminated by man.

In the last 25 million years, from the Miocene through the Pliocene periods, the Alpine-Himalayan and the circum-Pacific phases of mountain building reached their climax. During the Pleistocene period ice-sheets repeatedly locked up masses of water as land ice; its weight depressed the land, but the locking-up of the water lowered the sea-level by 100–200 metres. The glaciations and interglacials of the Ice Age are difficult to date and classify, but recent scientific opinion considers the Pleistocene period to have begun approximately 1.64 million years ago. The last glacial retreat, merging into the Holocene period, was 10,000 years ago.

HUMAN DEVELOPMENT

Any consideration of the history of mankind must start with the fact that all members of the human race belong to one species of animal, i.e. *Homo sapiens,* the definition of a species being in biological terms that all its members can interbreed. As a species of mammal it is possible to group man with other similar types, known as the primates. Amongst these is found a sub-group, the apes, which includes, in addition to man, the chimpanzees, gorillas, orang-utans and gibbons. All lack a tail, have shoulder blades at the back, and a Y-shaped chewing pattern on the surface of their molars, as well as showing the more general primate characteristics of four incisors, a thumb which is able to touch the fingers of the same hand, and finger and toe nails instead of claws. The factors available to scientific study suggest that human beings have chimpanzees and gorillas as their nearest relatives in the animal world. However, there remains the possibility that there once lived creatures, now extinct, which were closer to modern man than the chimpanzees and gorillas, and which shared with modern man the characteristics of having flat faces (i.e. the absence of a pronounced muzzle), being bipedal, and possessing large brains.

There are two broad groups of extinct apes recognised by specialists. The ramapithecines, the remains of which, mainly jaw fragments, have been found in east Africa, Asia, and Turkey. They lived about 14 to 8 million years ago, and from the evidence of their teeth it seems they chewed more in the manner of modern man than the other presently living apes. The second group, the australopithecines, have left more numerous remains amongst which sub-groups may be detected, although the geographic spread is limited to south and east Africa. Living between 5 and 1.5 million years ago, they were closer relatives of modern man to the extent that they walked upright, did not have an extensive muzzle and had similar types of pre-molars. The first australopithecine remains were recognised at Taung in South Africa in 1924 and named *Australopithecus africanus,* dating to 2.8–2.3 million years ago. The most impressive discovery was made at Hadar, Ethiopia, in 1974 when about half a skeleton of *Australopithecus afarensis,* known as 'Lucy', was found. Some 3.2 million years ago, Lucy certainly walked upright.

Also in east Africa, especially at Olduvai Gorge in Tanzania, between 1.9 and 1.8 million years ago, lived a hominid group which not only walked upright, had a flat face, and a large brain case, but also made simple pebble

GEOLOGICAL TIME

Era	Period	Epoch	Date began*	Evolutionary stages
Cenozoic	Quaternary	Holocene	0.01	Man
		Pleistocene	1.64	
	Tertiary	Pliocene	5.2	
		Miocene	23.3	
		Oligocene	35.4	
		Eocene	56.5	
		Palaeocene	65.0	
Mesozoic	Cretaceous		145.6	
	Jurassic		208.0	First birds
	Triassic		248.0	First mammals
Palaeozoic	Permian		290.0	First reptiles
	Carboniferous		362.5	First amphibians and insects
	Devonian		408.5	
	Silurian		439.0	
	Ordovician		510.0	First fishes
	Cambrian		550.0	First invertebrates
Precambrian			4,600.0	First primitive life forms e.g. algae and bacteria

* millions of years ago

and flake stone tools. On present evidence these habilines seem to have been the first people to make tools, however crude. This facility is related to the larger brain size and human beings are the only animals to make implements to be used in other processes. These early pebble tool users, because of their distinctive characteristics, have been grouped as a separate sub-species, now extinct, of the genus *Homo* and are known as *Homo habilis*.

The use of fire, again a human characteristic, is associated with another group of extinct hominids whose remains, about a million years old, are found in south and east Africa, China, Indonesia, north Africa and Europe. Mastery of the techniques of making fire probably helped the colonisation of the colder northern areas and in this respect the site of Vertesszollos in Hungary is of particular importance. *Homo ergaster* in Africa and *Homo erectus* in Asia are the names given to this group of fossils and they relate to a number of famous individual discoveries, e.g. Solo Man, Heidelberg Man, and especially Peking Man who lived at the cave site at Choukoutien which has yielded evidence of fire and burnt bone.

The well-known group Neanderthal Man, or *Homo neanderthalensis,* is an extinct form of man who lived between about 230,000 and 28,000 years ago, thus spanning the last Ice Age. Indeed, its ability to adapt to the cold climate on the edge of the ice-sheets is one of its characteristic features, the remains being found only in Europe, Asia and the Middle East. Complete neanderthal skeletons were found during excavations at Tabun in Israel, together with evidence of tool-making and the use of fire. Distinguished by very large brains, it seems that neanderthal man was the first to develop recognisable social customs, especially deliberate burial rites. Why the neanderthals became extinct is not clear but it may be connected with the climatic changes at the end of the Ice Ages, which would have seriously affected their food supplies; possibly they became too specialised for their own good.

The shinbone of Boxgrove Man found in 1993 – *Homo heidelbergensis* – and the Swanscombe skull are the best known human fossil remains found in England. Some specialists see Swanscombe Man (or, more probably, woman) as best grouped together with the Steinheim skull from Germany, seeing both as a separate sub-species. There is too little evidence as yet on which to form a final judgement.

Modern Man, *Homo sapiens,* had evolved to our present physical condition and had colonised much of the world by about 40,000 years ago. There are many previously distinguished individual specimens, e.g. Cromagnon Man, which may now be grouped together as *Homo sapiens*. It was modern man who spread to the American continent by crossing the landbridge between Siberia and Alaska and thence moved south through North America and into South America. Equally it is modern man who over the last 40,000 years has been responsible for the major developments in technology, art and civilisation generally.

One of the problems for those studying fossil man is the lack in many cases of sufficient quantities of fossil bone for analysis. It is important that theories should be tested against evidence, rather than the evidence being made to fit the theory. The Piltdown hoax of 1912 (and not fully exposed until the 1970s) is a well-known example of 'fossils' being forged to fit what was seen in some quarters as the correct theory of man's evolution.

The discovery of the structure of DNA in 1953 has come to have a profound effect upon the study of human evolution. For example it was claimed in 1987 that a common ancestor of all human beings was a person who lived in Africa some 200,000 years ago, thus encouraging the 'out of Africa' theory of hominid migration from east Africa to the Middle East and then throughout the world. There is no doubt that the studies based on DNA have vast potential to elucidate further the course of human evolution.

CULTURAL DEVELOPMENT

The Eurocentric bias of early archaeologists meant that the search for a starting point for the development and transmission of cultural ideas, especially by migration, trade and warfare, concentrated unduly on Europe and the Near East. The Three Age system, whereby pre-history was divided into a Stone Age, a Bronze Age and an Iron Age, was devised by Christian Thomsen, curator of the National Museum of Denmark in the early 19th century, to facilitate the classification of the museum's collections. The descriptive adjectives referred to the materials from which the implements and weapons were made and came to be regarded as the dominant features of the societies to which they related. The refinement of the Three Age system once dominated archaeological thought and remains a generally accepted concept in the popular mind. However, it is now seen by archaeologists as an inadequate model for human development.

Common sense suggests that there were no complete breaks between one so-called Age and another, any more than contemporaries would have regarded 1485 as a complete break between medieval and modern English history. Nor can the Three Age system be applied universally. In some areas it is necessary to insert a Copper Age, while in Africa south of the Sahara there would seem to be no Bronze Age at all; in Australia, Old Stone Age societies survived, while in South America, New Stone Age communities existed into modern times. The civilisations in other parts of the world clearly invalidate a Eurocentric theory of human development.

The concept of the 'Neolithic revolution', associated with the domestication of plants and animals, was a development of particular importance in the human cultural pattern. It reflected change from the primitive hunter/gatherer economies to a more settled agricultural way of life and therefore, so the argument goes, made possible the development of urban civilisation. However, it can no longer be argued that this 'revolution' took place only in one area from which all development stemmed. Though it appears that the cultivation of wheat and barley was first undertaken, together with the domestication of cattle and goats/sheep in the Fertile Crescent (the area bounded by the rivers Tigris and Euphrates), there is evidence that rice was first deliberately planted and pigs domesticated in south-east Asia, maize first cultivated in Central America and llamas first domesticated in South America. It has been recognised in recent years that cultural changes can take place independently of each other in different parts of the world at different rates and different times. There is no need for a general diffusionist theory.

Although scholars will continue to study the particular societies which interest them, it may be possible to obtain a reliable chronological framework, in absolute terms of years, against which the cultural development of any particular area may be set. The development and refinement of radio-carbon dating and other scientific methods of producing absolute chronologies is enabling the cross-referencing of societies to be undertaken. As the techniques of dating become more rigorous in application and the number of scientifically obtained dates increases, the attainment of an absolute chronology for prehistoric societies throughout the world comes closer to being achieved.

TIDAL TABLES

CONSTANTS

The constant tidal difference may be used in conjunction with the time of high water at a standard port shown in the predictions data (below) to find the time of high water at any of the ports or places listed.

These tidal differences are very approximate and should be used only as a guide to the time of high water at the places below. More precise local data should be obtained for navigational and other nautical purposes.

All data allow high water time to be found in Greenwich Mean Time; this applies to data for the months when British Summer Time is in operation and the hour's time difference should be allowed for. Ports marked * are in a different time zone and the standard time zone difference also needs to be added/subtracted to give local time.

EXAMPLE

Required time of high water at Stranraer at 2 January 2004

Appropriate time of high water at Greenock	
Afternoon tide 2 January	2054hrs
Tidal difference	−0020hrs
High water at Stranraer	2034hrs

The columns headed 'Springs' and 'Neaps' show the height, in metres, of the tide above datum for mean high water springs and mean high water neaps respectively.

Port		Diff.		Springs	Neaps
		h	m	m	m
Aberdeen	Leith	−1	19	4.4	3.4
*Antwerp (Prosperpolder)	London	+0	50	5.8	4.8
Ardrossan	Greenock	−0	15	3.2	2.6
Avonmouth	London	−6	45	12.2	9.8
Ayr	Greenock	−0	25	3.0	2.5
Barrow (Docks)	Liverpool	0	00	9.3	7.1
Belfast	London	−2	47	3.5	3.0
Blackpool	Liverpool	−0	10	8.9	7.0
*Boulogne	London	−2	44	8.9	7.2
*Calais	London	−2	04	7.2	5.9
*Cherbourg	London	−6	00	6.4	5.0
Cobh	Liverpool	−5	55	4.2	3.2
Cowes	London	−2	38	4.2	3.5
Dartmouth	London	+4	25	4.9	3.8
*Dieppe	London	−3	03	9.3	7.3
Douglas, IoM	Liverpool	−0	04	6.9	5.4
Dover	London	−2	52	6.7	5.3
Dublin	London	−2	05	4.1	3.4
Dun Loaghaire	London	−2	10	4.1	3.4
*Dunkirk	London	−1	54	6.0	4.9
Fishguard	Liverpool	−4	01	4.8	3.4
Fleetwood	Liverpool	0	00	9.2	7.3
*Flushing	London	−0	15	4.7	3.9
Folkestone	London	−3	04	7.1	5.7
Galway	Liverpool	−6	08	5.1	3.9
Glasgow	Greenock	+0	26	4.7	4.0
Harwich	London	−2	06	4.0	3.4
*Le Havre	London	−3	55	7.9	6.6
Heysham	Liverpool	+0	05	9.4	7.4
Holyhead	Liverpool	−0	50	5.6	4.4
*Hook of Holland	London	−0	01	2.1	1.7
Hull (Albert Dock)	London	−7	40	7.5	5.8
Immingham	London	−8	00	7.3	5.8
Larne	London	−2	40	2.8	2.5
Lerwick	Leith	−3	48	2.2	1.6
Londonderry	London	−5	37	2.7	2.1
Lowestoft	London	−4	25	2.4	2.1
Margate	London	−1	53	4.8	3.9
Milford Haven	Liverpool	−5	08	7.0	5.2
Morecambe	Liverpool	+0	07	9.5	7.4
Newhaven	London	−2	46	6.7	5.1
Oban	Greenock	+5	43	4.0	2.9
*Ostend	London	−1	32	5.1	4.2
Plymouth	London	+4	05	5.5	4.4
Portland	London	+5	09	2.1	1.4
Portsmouth	London	−2	38	4.7	3.8
Ramsgate	London	−2	32	5.2	4.1
Richmond Lock	London	+1	00	4.9	3.7
Rosslare Harbour	Liverpool	−5	24	1.9	1.4
Rosyth	Leith	+0	09	5.8	4.7
*Rotterdam	London	+1	45	2.0	1.7
St Helier	London	+4	48	11.0	8.1
St Malo	London	+4	27	12.2	9.2
St Peter Port	London	+4	54	9.3	7.0
Scrabster	Leith	−6	06	5.0	4.0
Sheerness	London	−1	19	5.8	4.7
Shoreham	London	−2	44	6.3	4.9
Southampton (1st high water)	London	−2	54	4.5	3.7
Spurn Head	London	−8	25	6.9	5.5
Stornoway	Liverpool	−4	16	4.8	3.7
Stranraer	Greenock	−0	20	3.0	2.4
Stromness	Leith	−5	26	3.6	2.7
Swansea	London	−7	35	9.5	7.2
Tees (River Entrance)	Leith	+1	09	5.5	4.3
Tilbury	London	−0	49	6.4	5.4
Tobermory	Liverpool	−5	11	4.4	3.3
Tyne River (North Shields)	London	−10	30	5.0	3.9
Ullapool	Leith	−7	40	5.2	3.9
Walton-on-the-Naze	London	−2	10	4.2	3.4
Wick	Leith	−3	26	3.5	2.8
Zeebrugge	London	−0	55	4.8	3.9

PREDICTIONS

The following data are daily predictions of the time and height of high water at London Bridge, Liverpool, Greenock and Leith. The time of the data is Greenwich Mean Time; this applies also to data for the months when British Summer Time is in operation and the hour's time difference should be allowed for. The datum of predictions for each port shows the difference of height, in metres from Ordnance data (Newlyn).

The tidal information for London Bridge, Liverpool, Greenock and Leith is reproduced with the permission of the UK Hydrographic Office and the Controller of HMSO. Crown copyright reserved.

JANUARY 2004   *High Water*   GMT

	LONDON BRIDGE *Datum of Predictions 3.20m below				LIVERPOOL *Datum of Predictions 4.93m below				GREENOCK *Datum of Predictions 1.62m below				LEITH *Datum of Predictions 2.90m below			
	hr	*m*	*hr*	*ht m*	*hr*	*m*	*hr*	*ht m*	*hr*	*m*	*hr*	*ht m*	*hr*	*m*	*hr*	*ht m*
TH 1	08 27	5.8	21 16	5.9	06 12	7.3	18 36	7.7	07 15	3.0	19 36	3.1	09 55	4.4	22 15	4.6
FR 2	09 34	5.8	22 14	5.9	07 18	7.4	19 40	7.7	08 17	3.0	20 54	3.0	10 55	4.4	23 15	4.5
SA 3	10 35	5.9	23 08	6.0	08 17	7.6	20 37	7.9	09 28	3.0	22 05	3.0	11 54	4.5	—	—
SU 4	11 30	6.1	23 56	6.2	09 06	8.0	21 26	8.1	10 26	3.1	22 59	3.0	00 13	4.6	12 46	4.7
M 5	—	—	12 19	6.3	09 49	8.3	22 09	8.3	11 12	3.2	23 44	3.1	01 04	4.7	13 29	4.9
TU 6	00 41	6.3	13 05	6.4	10 28	8.6	22 48	8.5	11 52	3.4	—	—	01 47	4.9	14 06	5.0
W 7	01 22	6.4	13 47	6.5	11 04	8.8	23 24	8.6	00 24	3.1	12 27	3.4	02 25	5.0	14 41	5.1
TH 8	02 01	6.5	14 27	6.5	11 40	8.9	—	—	01 00	3.1	12 59	3.5	03 01	5.1	15 15	5.2
FR 9	02 38	6.4	15 05	6.5	00 01	8.7	12 17	8.9	01 35	3.0	13 33	3.5	03 36	5.2	15 49	5.2
SA 10	03 14	6.4	15 43	6.6	00 38	8.7	12 54	9.0	02 11	3.0	14 08	3.6	04 12	5.2	16 24	5.2
SU 11	03 49	6.5	16 22	6.6	01 16	8.7	13 32	9.0	02 49	3.0	14 46	3.6	04 49	5.2	16 59	5.2
M 12	04 25	6.5	17 02	6.7	01 55	8.7	14 12	8.9	03 29	3.0	15 25	3.5	05 29	5.1	17 37	5.2
TU 13	05 03	6.5	17 44	6.6	02 36	8.6	14 55	8.8	04 10	3.0	16 06	3.5	06 11	5.0	18 18	5.1
W 14	05 45	6.5	18 30	6.5	03 22	8.4	15 42	8.6	04 52	3.0	16 49	3.4	06 57	4.9	19 05	5.0
TH 15	06 31	6.4	19 21	6.3	04 13	8.1	16 37	8.4	05 38	2.9	17 38	3.3	07 50	4.8	20 00	4.9
FR 16	07 26	6.2	20 20	6.1	05 14	7.9	17 41	8.2	06 30	2.9	18 35	3.2	08 50	4.7	21 10	4.8
SA 17	08 32	6.0	21 30	5.9	06 24	7.8	18 51	8.1	07 34	2.8	19 43	3.1	09 58	4.7	22 27	4.8
SU 18	09 51	6.0	22 43	6.0	07 37	8.0	20 04	8.3	09 03	2.9	21 12	3.1	11 07	4.8	23 40	5.0
M 19	11 07	6.2	23 48	6.2	08 45	8.4	21 13	8.6	10 18	3.0	22 29	3.2	—	—	12 11	5.0
TU 20	—	—	12 13	6.5	09 44	8.9	22 13	9.0	11 15	3.3	23 32	3.3	00 45	5.2	13 09	5.2
W 21	00 46	6.5	13 13	6.8	10 37	9.3	23 06	9.2	—	—	12 04	3.5	01 44	5.4	14 01	5.4
TH 22	01 39	6.7	14 08	7.0	11 26	9.6	23 55	9.4	00 28	3.3	12 51	3.6	02 36	5.6	14 49	5.6
FR 23	02 29	6.9	14 59	7.2	—	—	12 13	9.8	01 22	3.3	13 36	3.7	03 25	5.7	15 36	5.7
SA 24	03 15	6.9	15 46	7.2	00 41	9.4	12 58	9.8	02 10	3.3	14 19	3.8	04 12	5.6	16 22	5.6
SU 25	03 57	6.9	16 30	7.1	01 24	9.2	13 41	9.6	02 54	3.3	15 00	3.8	04 58	5.5	17 07	5.5
M 26	04 36	6.8	17 11	6.9	02 05	9.0	14 22	9.3	03 35	3.3	15 40	3.7	05 42	5.2	17 51	5.4
TU 27	05 12	6.7	17 50	6.6	02 44	8.6	15 02	8.9	04 13	3.3	16 20	3.6	06 27	5.0	18 36	5.1
W 28	05 49	6.5	18 28	6.3	03 23	8.2	15 43	8.4	04 51	3.2	17 00	3.4	07 11	4.7	19 22	4.8
TH 29	06 29	6.3	19 08	6.0	04 06	7.7	16 29	7.9	05 31	3.1	17 43	3.2	07 59	4.5	20 15	4.6
FR 30	07 16	6.0	19 55	5.8	04 58	7.3	17 27	7.4	06 14	3.0	18 30	3.0	08 52	4.3	21 14	4.3
SA 31	08 16	5.7	20 56	5.6	06 05	7.1	18 39	7.2	07 02	2.9	19 27	2.8	09 50	4.2	22 19	4.2

FEBRUARY 2004   *High Water*   GMT

	LONDON BRIDGE				LIVERPOOL				GREENOCK				LEITH			
SU 1	09 32	5.5	22 08	5.6	07 25	7.1	19 58	7.3	08 04	2.8	20 59	2.7	10 56	4.2	23 31	4.3
M 2	10 47	5.6	23 13	5.7	08 35	7.5	21 01	7.6	09 37	2.9	22 40	2.8	—	—	12 07	4.4
TU 3	11 48	5.9	—	—	09 27	7.9	21 51	8.0	10 45	3.0	23 30	2.9	00 39	4.4	13 05	4.6
W 4	00 09	6.0	12 41	6.2	10 11	8.4	22 33	8.4	11 30	3.2	—	—	01 29	4.7	13 48	4.9
TH 5	00 59	6.2	13 29	6.4	10 50	8.7	23 11	8.6	00 12	2.9	12 07	3.3	02 09	4.9	14 25	5.1
FR 6	01 45	6.4	14 12	6.6	11 26	9.0	23 47	8.8	00 51	3.0	12 40	3.4	02 44	5.1	15 00	5.2
SA 7	02 26	6.5	14 52	6.7	—	—	12 02	9.1	01 26	3.0	13 14	3.4	03 19	5.2	15 33	5.4
SU 8	03 04	6.6	15 30	6.8	00 23	9.0	12 38	9.3	02 00	3.0	13 51	3.5	03 53	5.3	16 05	5.4
M 9	03 38	6.6	16 06	6.9	01 00	9.1	13 15	9.4	02 33	3.0	14 28	3.6	04 29	5.4	16 39	5.5
TU 10	04 11	6.7	16 43	6.9	01 37	9.1	13 53	9.4	03 07	3.1	15 06	3.6	05 06	5.3	17 15	5.4
W 11	04 46	6.8	17 22	6.8	02 15	9.0	14 32	9.2	03 41	3.1	15 45	3.6	05 46	5.2	17 54	5.3
TH 12	05 24	6.8	18 04	6.6	02 55	8.8	15 16	8.9	04 17	3.1	16 25	3.5	06 29	5.1	18 39	5.2
FR 13	06 07	6.6	18 50	6.3	03 41	8.4	16 06	8.5	04 55	3.0	17 09	3.3	07 17	4.8	19 31	4.9
SA 14	06 57	6.3	19 44	5.9	04 38	7.9	17 09	8.0	05 40	2.9	18 00	3.1	08 13	4.6	20 40	4.7
SU 15	08 00	5.9	20 55	5.6	05 50	7.6	18 27	7.6	06 37	2.8	19 02	2.9	09 25	4.5	22 09	4.6
M 16	09 26	5.7	22 21	5.6	07 16	7.6	19 57	7.7	08 14	2.7	20 43	2.8	10 44	4.5	23 33	4.7
TU 17	10 57	5.8	23 34	5.9	08 37	8.0	21 13	8.2	10 07	2.9	22 33	2.9	12 00	4.7	—	—
W 18	—	—	12 09	6.2	09 39	8.6	22 11	8.7	11 05	3.2	23 35	3.1	00 46	5.0	13 04	5.0
TH 19	00 35	6.3	13 09	6.7	10 30	9.2	23 00	9.1	11 54	3.4	—	—	01 43	5.3	13 55	5.3
FR 20	01 29	6.6	14 01	7.1	11 16	9.6	23 43	9.3	00 27	3.2	12 40	3.5	02 30	5.5	14 40	5.5
SA 21	02 17	6.9	14 48	7.2	11 58	9.8	—	—	01 15	3.3	13 23	3.6	03 13	5.6	15 21	5.7
SU 22	02 59	7.0	15 30	7.2	00 23	9.4	12 38	9.8	01 57	3.2	14 04	3.7	03 53	5.5	16 01	5.7
M 23	03 37	7.0	16 07	7.1	01 01	9.3	13 16	9.6	02 33	3.3	14 41	3.7	04 32	5.4	16 40	5.6
TU 24	04 11	6.9	16 40	6.9	01 35	9.1	13 51	9.4	03 05	3.3	15 16	3.7	05 10	5.2	17 18	5.4
W 25	04 42	6.8	17 10	6.7	02 09	8.8	14 26	9.0	03 37	3.3	15 50	3.6	05 47	5.0	17 56	5.1
TH 26	05 14	6.7	17 42	6.5	02 42	8.4	15 01	8.5	04 10	3.3	16 25	3.4	06 26	4.7	18 36	4.8
FR 27	05 50	6.5	18 17	6.2	03 17	8.0	15 40	7.9	04 44	3.2	17 02	3.2	07 07	4.5	19 23	4.5
SA 28	06 32	6.1	18 59	5.9	03 59	7.5	16 30	7.3	05 23	3.0	17 45	2.9	07 56	4.3	20 20	4.2
SU 29	07 23	5.8	19 50	5.6	04 57	7.0	17 40	6.8	06 10	2.9	18 38	2.7	08 55	4.1	21 27	4.1

MARCH 2004 *High Water* GMT

	LONDON BRIDGE *Datum of Predictions 3.20m below					LIVERPOOL *Datum of Predictions 4.93m below					GREENOCK *Datum of Predictions 1.62m below					LEITH *Datum of Predictions 2.90m below				
	hr	m	ht	hr	m	ht	hr	m	ht	hr	m	ht	hr	m	ht	hr	m	ht	hr	m	ht
M 1	08 26	5.4	20 56	5.4	06 25	6.8	19 17	6.8	07 08	2.7	19 49	2.5	10 03	4.0	22 44	4.0
TU 2	09 52	5.4	22 26	5.4	08 01	7.1	20 36	7.2	08 25	2.7	22 22	2.6	11 22	4.2	—	—
W 3	11 16	5.6	23 39	5.8	09 02	7.6	21 29	7.8	10 10	2.8	23 12	2.8	00 08	4.3	12 35	4.4
TH 4	—	—	12 16	6.1	09 48	8.2	22 11	8.3	11 02	3.0	23 53	2.9	01 05	4.6	13 23	4.8
FR 5	00 35	6.1	13 06	6.4	10 27	8.7	22 49	8.7	11 39	3.2	—	—	01 46	4.9	14 02	5.1
SA 6	01 23	6.4	13 50	6.7	11 04	9.0	23 25	9.0	00 30	3.0	12 15	3.3	02 21	5.2	14 36	5.3
SU 7	02 05	6.6	14 31	6.9	11 39	9.3	—	—	01 05	3.0	12 51	3.4	02 55	5.4	15 08	5.5
M 8	02 43	6.7	15 09	7.0	00 01	9.2	12 16	9.5	01 37	3.0	13 29	3.5	03 28	5.5	15 40	5.6
TU 9	03 17	6.8	15 45	7.1	00 37	9.4	12 53	9.7	02 08	3.1	14 07	3.6	04 04	5.6	16 15	5.7
W 10	03 51	7.0	16 21	7.0	01 14	9.4	13 31	9.6	02 39	3.2	14 46	3.6	04 41	5.5	16 53	5.6
TH 11	04 27	7.0	16 59	6.9	01 52	9.3	14 11	9.4	03 11	3.2	15 24	3.6	05 21	5.4	17 34	5.5
FR 12	05 05	7.0	17 38	6.6	02 32	9.0	14 54	8.9	03 45	3.2	16 03	3.5	06 03	5.1	18 21	5.2
SA 13	05 48	6.7	18 22	6.2	03 16	8.5	15 44	8.3	04 23	3.1	16 46	3.3	06 50	4.9	19 17	4.9
SU 14	06 39	6.3	19 14	5.7	04 12	7.9	16 50	7.6	05 07	2.9	17 37	3.0	07 47	4.6	20 32	4.6
M 15	07 45	5.8	20 29	5.3	05 31	7.4	18 22	7.2	06 05	2.7	18 43	2.7	09 05	4.3	22 05	4.4
TU 16	09 21	5.5	22 07	5.4	07 08	7.4	20 00	7.5	07 50	2.6	21 18	2.6	10 34	4.4	23 34	4.6
W 17	10 55	5.8	23 22	5.8	08 30	7.9	21 10	8.1	09 56	2.9	22 36	2.8	11 55	4.6	—	—
TH 18	—	—	12 02	6.3	09 29	8.6	22 01	8.6	10 52	3.1	23 29	3.0	00 44	5.0	12 57	5.0
FR 19	00 21	6.3	12 58	6.8	10 16	9.1	22 44	9.1	11 39	3.4	—	—	01 36	5.2	13 43	5.3
SA 20	01 13	6.7	13 46	7.2	10 58	9.5	23 23	9.3	00 15	3.1	12 23	3.5	02 17	5.4	14 23	5.5
SU 21	01 58	7.0	14 29	7.3	11 37	9.6	23 59	9.3	00 56	3.2	13 04	3.5	02 54	5.5	15 01	5.6
M 22	02 37	7.0	15 07	7.2	—	—	12 13	9.6	01 32	3.2	13 42	3.5	03 29	5.4	15 37	5.6
TU 23	03 12	7.0	15 39	7.0	00 31	9.2	12 48	9.4	02 02	3.2	14 17	3.5	04 03	5.3	16 12	5.5
W 24	03 43	6.9	16 06	6.8	01 03	9.0	13 20	9.2	02 31	3.3	14 49	3.5	04 37	5.2	16 48	5.3
TH 25	04 13	6.8	16 33	6.7	01 34	8.8	13 52	8.8	03 01	3.3	15 21	3.4	05 11	5.0	17 24	5.1
FR 26	04 44	6.7	17 02	6.6	02 05	8.5	14 25	8.4	03 32	3.3	15 54	3.2	05 46	4.8	18 03	4.8
SA 27	05 19	6.5	17 37	6.4	02 37	8.1	15 02	7.9	04 05	3.2	16 30	3.0	06 25	4.6	18 47	4.5
SU 28	06 00	6.2	18 19	6.0	03 16	7.7	15 47	7.3	04 42	3.1	17 13	2.8	07 11	4.3	19 40	4.2
M 29	06 48	5.8	19 08	5.7	04 07	7.1	16 51	6.8	05 27	2.9	18 08	2.6	08 08	4.1	20 44	4.0
TU 30	07 47	5.5	20 09	5.4	05 25	6.7	18 32	6.6	06 26	2.7	19 19	2.4	09 18	4.0	21 58	4.0
W 31	09 00	5.4	21 32	5.4	07 15	6.9	20 00	7.0	07 39	2.6	21 30	2.5	10 36	4.1	23 19	4.2

APRIL 2004 *High Water* GMT

	LONDON BRIDGE					LIVERPOOL					GREENOCK					LEITH				
TH 1	10 36	5.6	23 02	5.6	08 25	7.4	20 56	7.7	09 10	2.7	22 39	2.7	11 52	4.4	—	—
FR 2	11 43	6.0	—	—	09 13	8.1	21 39	8.3	10 18	2.9	23 20	2.9	00 25	4.6	12 46	4.7
SA 3	00 02	6.1	12 35	6.5	09 54	8.6	22 18	8.8	11 02	3.1	23 57	3.0	01 11	4.9	13 27	5.1
SU 4	00 51	6.4	13 20	6.8	10 32	9.1	22 55	9.2	11 41	3.3	—	—	01 48	5.2	14 03	5.4
M 5	01 34	6.7	14 02	7.0	11 10	9.4	23 32	9.4	00 32	3.0	12 22	3.4	02 24	5.5	14 37	5.6
TU 6	02 13	6.8	14 42	7.1	11 49	9.7	—	—	01 06	3.1	13 03	3.5	02 59	5.6	15 13	5.7
W 7	02 52	7.0	15 20	7.1	00 10	9.6	12 29	9.8	01 39	3.2	13 45	3.6	03 37	5.7	15 51	5.8
TH 8	03 30	7.1	15 59	7.1	00 50	9.6	13 10	9.6	02 12	3.3	14 25	3.6	04 16	5.6	16 34	5.7
FR 9	04 10	7.1	16 38	6.9	01 31	9.4	13 53	9.3	02 45	3.3	15 06	3.5	04 57	5.4	17 20	5.5
SA 10	04 52	7.0	17 18	6.5	02 13	9.0	14 40	8.8	03 21	3.3	15 48	3.4	05 42	5.2	18 12	5.2
SU 11	05 39	6.7	18 03	6.1	03 01	8.5	15 34	8.1	04 01	3.2	16 34	3.1	06 32	4.9	19 14	4.8
M 12	06 34	6.2	18 58	5.7	04 02	7.9	16 47	7.4	04 47	3.0	17 31	2.8	07 34	4.5	20 34	4.5
TU 13	07 49	5.7	20 23	5.4	05 25	7.4	18 22	7.2	05 51	2.8	19 00	2.6	08 59	4.4	22 01	4.5
W 14	09 24	5.7	21 52	5.5	06 57	7.5	19 47	7.5	08 02	2.7	21 17	2.7	10 25	4.5	23 24	4.7
TH 15	10 41	6.0	23 01	5.9	08 10	8.0	20 49	8.0	09 34	2.9	22 21	2.9	11 39	4.7	—	—
FR 16	11 42	6.5	23 58	6.4	09 06	8.5	21 38	8.5	10 29	3.2	23 09	3.0	00 28	4.9	12 37	5.0
SA 17	—	—	12 35	6.9	09 53	9.0	22 19	8.9	11 16	3.3	23 50	3.1	01 16	5.1	13 22	5.2
SU 18	00 47	6.8	13 22	7.2	10 34	9.2	22 56	9.0	11 58	3.4	—	—	01 55	5.2	14 01	5.4
M 19	01 32	7.0	14 03	7.2	11 11	9.3	23 30	9.1	00 27	3.1	12 39	3.4	02 29	5.3	14 37	5.4
TU 20	02 11	7.0	14 39	7.1	11 46	9.2	—	—	01 00	3.2	13 16	3.3	03 02	5.3	15 12	5.4
W 21	02 46	6.9	15 08	6.9	00 01	9.0	12 19	9.1	01 30	3.2	13 50	3.3	03 35	5.2	15 47	5.3
TH 22	03 17	6.8	15 34	6.7	00 32	8.9	12 50	8.9	01 59	3.3	14 22	3.2	04 07	5.1	16 22	5.1
FR 23	03 47	6.7	16 00	6.6	01 02	8.7	13 22	8.6	02 29	3.3	14 54	3.2	04 40	5.0	16 58	5.0
SA 24	04 19	6.6	16 30	6.5	01 33	8.5	13 56	8.3	02 59	3.3	15 28	3.1	05 14	4.8	17 37	4.8
SU 25	04 55	6.4	17 06	6.3	02 07	8.2	14 33	7.9	03 32	3.3	16 06	2.9	05 52	4.6	18 21	4.5
M 26	05 36	6.2	17 48	6.1	02 46	7.8	15 18	7.4	04 09	3.1	16 51	2.7	06 35	4.4	19 10	4.3
TU 27	06 24	5.9	18 38	5.8	03 35	7.3	16 17	6.9	04 52	2.9	17 48	2.6	07 28	4.2	20 08	4.2
W 28	07 21	5.7	19 37	5.5	04 43	7.0	17 39	6.8	05 50	2.8	18 58	2.5	08 35	4.1	21 16	4.1
TH 29	08 26	5.6	20 48	5.5	06 12	7.0	19 08	7.0	07 01	2.7	20 20	2.5	09 50	4.2	22 28	4.3
FR 30	09 45	5.7	22 11	5.7	07 31	7.4	20 09	7.6	08 18	2.7	21 42	2.7	11 00	4.4	23 33	4.6

MAY 2004   *High Water*   GMT

LONDON BRIDGE — *Datum of Predictions 3.20m below
LIVERPOOL — *Datum of Predictions 4.93m below
GREENOCK — *Datum of Predictions 1.62m below
LEITH — *Datum of Predictions 2.90m below

	LONDON BRIDGE hr m / ht m	/ hr m / ht m	LIVERPOOL hr m / ht m	/ hr m / ht m	GREENOCK hr m / ht m	/ hr m / ht m	LEITH hr m / ht m	/ hr m / ht m
SA 1	10 59 6.1	23 17 6.1	08 26 8.0	20 57 8.2	09 27 2.9	22 35 2.8	11 58 4.7	— —
SU 2	11 56 6.5	— —	09 12 8.6	21 40 8.8	10 21 3.1	23 18 3.0	00 26 4.9	12 45 5.1
M 3	00 10 6.4	12 45 6.8	09 56 9.1	22 21 9.2	11 07 3.3	23 57 3.1	01 10 5.2	13 26 5.4
TU 4	00 57 6.7	13 30 7.1	10 39 9.5	23 03 9.5	11 52 3.4	— —	01 51 5.5	14 06 5.6
W 5	01 42 6.9	14 14 7.1	11 22 9.7	23 45 9.6	00 35 3.2	12 38 3.5	02 30 5.6	14 48 5.8
TH 6	02 27 7.1	14 57 7.1	— —	12 07 9.7	01 13 3.3	13 24 3.5	03 11 5.7	15 32 5.8
FR 7	03 12 7.2	15 39 7.0	00 28 9.6	12 54 9.5	01 50 3.4	14 09 3.5	03 53 5.6	16 20 5.7
SA 8	03 58 7.2	16 22 6.8	01 14 9.4	13 42 9.1	02 27 3.4	14 55 3.4	04 38 5.4	17 11 5.5
SU 9	04 46 7.0	17 06 6.5	02 02 9.0	14 33 8.6	03 07 3.4	15 42 3.2	05 27 5.2	18 08 5.2
M 10	05 38 6.7	17 55 6.2	02 55 8.6	15 32 8.0	03 50 3.3	16 36 3.0	06 22 4.9	19 14 4.9
TU 11	06 38 6.3	18 55 5.8	03 59 8.1	16 44 7.6	04 42 3.1	17 45 2.8	07 30 4.7	20 28 4.7
W 12	07 50 6.0	20 13 5.7	05 14 7.8	18 03 7.4	05 53 2.9	19 17 2.7	08 49 4.6	21 43 4.6
TH 13	09 06 6.0	21 26 5.8	06 30 7.8	19 16 7.6	07 36 2.9	20 46 2.7	10 03 4.6	22 55 4.7
FR 14	10 14 6.2	22 29 6.1	07 37 8.0	20 16 7.9	09 00 3.0	21 47 2.9	11 10 4.8	23 57 4.8
SA 15	11 13 6.6	23 26 6.4	08 33 8.3	21 05 8.3	09 58 3.1	22 35 3.0	— —	12 07 4.9
SU 16	— —	12 05 6.8	09 22 8.6	21 48 8.5	10 47 3.2	23 16 3.0	00 46 4.9	12 55 5.1
M 17	00 16 6.7	12 51 7.0	10 05 8.8	22 26 8.7	11 30 3.2	23 53 3.1	01 27 5.0	13 36 5.1
TU 18	01 02 6.8	13 33 7.0	10 44 8.8	23 00 8.8	— —	12 11 3.2	02 03 5.1	14 14 5.2
W 19	01 43 6.8	14 08 6.9	11 19 8.8	23 32 8.8	00 27 3.1	12 49 3.1	02 36 5.1	14 49 5.1
TH 20	02 21 6.7	14 39 6.7	11 52 8.7	— —	01 00 3.2	13 24 3.1	03 09 5.1	15 25 5.1
FR 21	02 55 6.6	15 06 6.6	00 03 8.7	12 25 8.6	01 31 3.3	13 57 3.0	03 41 5.1	16 01 5.0
SA 22	03 27 6.5	15 34 6.5	00 36 8.6	12 59 8.4	02 02 3.3	14 31 3.0	04 14 5.0	16 38 4.9
SU 23	04 00 6.4	16 07 6.4	01 10 8.5	13 35 8.2	02 34 3.3	15 08 2.9	04 49 4.9	17 17 4.8
M 24	04 38 6.3	16 44 6.3	01 46 8.3	14 14 8.0	03 08 3.3	15 49 2.8	05 27 4.7	17 58 4.6
TU 25	05 19 6.2	17 26 6.1	02 27 8.0	14 58 7.7	03 45 3.2	16 36 2.7	06 09 4.6	18 44 4.5
W 26	06 07 6.1	18 15 5.9	03 14 7.7	15 51 7.4	04 27 3.0	17 32 2.6	06 57 4.4	19 36 4.4
TH 27	06 59 6.0	19 10 5.8	04 12 7.5	16 55 7.2	05 20 2.9	18 33 2.6	07 54 4.4	20 36 4.4
FR 28	07 58 5.9	20 12 5.8	05 20 7.4	18 08 7.3	06 23 2.8	19 36 2.6	09 01 4.4	21 41 4.5
SA 29	09 04 6.0	21 21 5.9	06 29 7.7	19 14 7.7	07 31 2.8	20 42 2.7	10 08 4.5	22 44 4.6
SU 30	10 14 6.2	22 29 6.1	07 33 8.1	20 11 8.2	08 40 2.9	21 45 2.8	11 08 4.8	23 41 4.9
M 31	11 17 6.5	23 30 6.4	08 29 8.6	21 02 8.7	09 42 3.1	22 38 2.9	— —	12 02 5.0

JUNE 2004   *High Water*   GMT

	LONDON BRIDGE hr m / ht m	/ hr m / ht m	LIVERPOOL hr m / ht m	/ hr m / ht m	GREENOCK hr m / ht m	/ hr m / ht m	LEITH hr m / ht m	/ hr m / ht m
TU 1	— —	12 11 6.8	09 21 9.0	21 50 9.1	10 36 3.2	23 25 3.1	00 32 5.2	12 52 5.3
W 2	00 24 6.7	13 02 7.0	10 11 9.3	22 37 9.4	11 27 3.3	— —	01 20 5.4	13 41 5.5
TH 3	01 17 6.9	13 50 7.1	11 01 9.5	23 24 9.5	00 09 3.2	12 17 3.4	02 05 5.5	14 29 5.7
FR 4	02 08 7.1	14 37 7.1	11 51 9.5	— —	00 53 3.3	13 08 3.4	02 50 5.6	15 19 5.7
SA 5	02 59 7.2	15 24 7.0	00 12 9.5	12 43 9.3	01 35 3.4	14 00 3.4	03 36 5.6	16 11 5.7
SU 6	03 50 7.2	16 10 6.9	01 03 9.4	13 35 9.1	02 17 3.5	14 52 3.3	04 25 5.5	17 05 5.5
M 7	04 41 7.1	16 57 6.7	01 54 9.2	14 28 8.7	03 01 3.5	15 45 3.2	05 17 5.3	18 02 5.3
TU 8	05 34 6.9	17 47 6.4	02 48 8.9	15 23 8.3	03 48 3.4	16 43 3.0	06 15 5.1	19 04 5.0
W 9	06 30 6.6	18 43 6.2	03 46 8.5	16 23 7.9	04 40 3.3	17 44 2.9	07 19 5.0	20 07 4.8
TH 10	07 32 6.4	19 45 6.1	04 48 8.2	17 28 7.6	05 43 3.1	18 47 2.8	08 26 4.8	21 11 4.6
FR 11	08 36 6.2	20 50 6.0	05 53 8.0	18 34 7.5	06 55 3.0	19 50 2.8	09 30 4.8	22 14 4.6
SA 12	09 38 6.2	21 51 6.1	06 56 7.9	19 35 7.6	08 13 3.0	20 53 2.8	10 32 4.7	23 15 4.6
SU 13	10 36 6.3	22 49 6.3	07 55 8.0	20 28 7.9	09 20 3.0	21 49 2.9	11 31 4.7	— —
M 14	11 29 6.5	23 42 6.4	08 48 8.1	21 15 8.1	10 15 3.0	22 38 2.9	00 09 4.7	12 24 4.8
TU 15	— —	12 16 6.6	09 35 8.3	21 56 8.3	11 03 3.0	23 21 3.0	00 57 4.8	13 11 4.8
W 16	00 31 6.6	13 00 6.7	10 18 8.4	22 34 8.5	11 47 3.0	23 59 3.1	01 37 4.9	13 53 4.9
TH 17	01 16 6.6	13 39 6.7	10 56 8.4	23 09 8.6	— —	12 27 3.0	02 13 5.0	14 31 4.9
FR 18	01 58 6.6	14 14 6.6	11 32 8.4	23 43 8.6	00 35 3.2	13 04 2.9	02 48 5.0	15 07 5.0
SA 19	02 37 6.5	14 46 6.5	— —	12 07 8.4	01 08 3.2	13 39 2.9	03 21 5.1	15 43 5.0
SU 20	03 13 6.4	15 18 6.4	00 17 8.6	12 43 8.4	01 40 3.3	14 15 2.9	03 55 5.0	16 20 5.0
M 21	03 49 6.3	15 53 6.3	00 54 8.5	13 20 8.3	02 13 3.3	14 54 2.8	04 31 5.0	16 57 4.9
TU 22	04 26 6.3	16 29 6.3	01 31 8.4	13 58 8.2	02 49 3.3	15 36 2.8	05 08 4.9	17 37 4.8
W 23	05 06 6.3	17 09 6.3	02 11 8.3	14 40 8.1	03 27 3.2	16 21 2.8	05 47 4.8	18 19 4.7
TH 24	05 49 6.3	17 53 6.2	02 55 8.2	15 25 7.9	04 07 3.2	17 09 2.7	06 29 4.8	19 06 4.7
FR 25	06 36 6.3	18 41 6.1	03 44 8.1	16 18 7.7	04 53 3.1	17 59 2.7	07 16 4.7	19 58 4.6
SA 26	07 28 6.2	19 36 6.1	04 40 8.0	17 18 7.7	05 46 3.0	18 51 2.7	08 11 4.6	20 56 4.6
SU 27	08 27 6.1	20 38 6.1	05 41 8.0	18 23 7.8	06 46 3.0	19 48 2.7	09 15 4.7	21 59 4.7
M 28	09 34 6.1	21 47 6.1	06 45 8.1	19 28 8.1	07 53 3.0	20 55 2.7	10 23 4.8	23 01 4.8
TU 29	10 42 6.3	22 56 6.3	07 58 8.4	20 29 8.4	09 05 3.0	22 03 2.8	11 27 4.9	— —
W 30	14 43 6.5	23 59 6.5	08 53 8.7	21 26 8.9	10 10 3.1	23 01 3.0	00 00 5.0	12 28 5.2

JULY 2004   *High Water*   GMT

	LONDON BRIDGE *Datum of Predictions 3.20m below				LIVERPOOL *Datum of Predictions 4.93m below				GREENOCK *Datum of Predictions 1.62m below				LEITH *Datum of Predictions 2.90m below			
	hr	ht m	hr	ht m	hr	ht m	hr	ht m	hr	ht m	hr	ht m	hr	ht m	hr	ht m
TH 1	—	—	12 38	6.7	09 52	8.9	22 19	9.2	11 09	3.2	23 51	3.2	00 55	5.2	13 25	5.4
FR 2	00 58	6.8	13 31	6.9	10 48	9.2	23 10	9.5	—	—	12 05	3.3	01 46	5.4	14 19	5.6
SA 3	01 55	7.0	14 22	7.0	11 42	9.3	—	—	00 39	3.3	13 01	3.3	02 36	5.5	15 11	5.7
SU 4	02 49	7.2	15 11	7.0	00 01	9.6	12 35	9.3	01 25	3.5	13 57	3.3	03 25	5.6	16 03	5.7
M 5	03 41	7.2	15 58	7.0	00 52	9.6	13 25	9.2	02 11	3.6	14 51	3.2	04 14	5.6	16 54	5.6
TU 6	04 31	7.2	16 44	6.9	01 42	9.5	14 14	8.9	02 55	3.6	15 41	3.2	05 05	5.5	17 47	5.4
W 7	05 20	7.1	17 29	6.7	02 31	9.2	15 02	8.6	03 40	3.6	16 30	3.1	05 58	5.4	18 40	5.1
TH 8	06 08	6.8	18 15	6.6	03 20	8.9	15 50	8.2	04 27	3.5	17 17	3.1	06 52	5.2	19 34	4.9
FR 9	06 59	6.5	19 05	6.4	04 10	8.5	16 41	7.8	05 16	3.3	18 03	3.0	07 49	5.0	20 28	4.6
SA 10	07 53	6.2	20 01	6.1	05 04	8.0	17 39	7.5	06 09	3.1	18 49	2.9	08 47	4.8	21 25	4.5
SU 11	08 52	6.0	21 04	6.0	06 05	7.7	18 43	7.3	07 08	3.0	19 39	2.8	09 46	4.6	22 23	4.4
M 12	09 52	5.9	22 07	6.0	07 10	7.5	19 47	7.4	08 22	2.8	20 43	2.8	10 47	4.5	23 24	4.4
TU 13	10 48	6.0	23 07	6.1	08 13	7.6	20 43	7.7	09 42	2.8	21 56	2.8	11 50	4.5	—	—
W 14	11 41	6.2	—	—	09 08	7.8	21 31	8.0	10 42	2.8	22 52	3.0	00 23	4.6	12 48	4.6
TH 15	00 01	6.2	12 29	6.4	09 56	8.0	22 14	8.3	11 31	2.9	23 37	3.1	01 13	4.7	13 36	4.7
FR 16	00 52	6.3	13 13	6.5	10 39	8.2	22 52	8.5	—	—	12 14	2.9	01 54	4.9	14 16	4.9
SA 17	01 39	6.4	13 55	6.5	11 17	8.3	23 28	8.7	00 15	3.2	12 54	2.9	02 31	5.0	14 52	5.0
SU 18	02 22	6.5	14 33	6.5	11 54	8.4	—	—	00 50	3.2	13 30	2.8	03 05	5.1	15 26	5.1
M 19	03 01	6.5	15 09	6.4	00 04	8.7	12 29	8.5	01 21	3.3	14 06	2.8	03 39	5.2	16 01	5.1
TU 20	03 37	6.5	15 43	6.4	00 40	8.8	13 05	8.5	01 55	3.3	14 41	2.8	04 13	5.2	16 37	5.1
W 21	04 12	6.5	16 16	6.4	01 15	8.8	13 41	8.5	02 30	3.3	15 18	2.9	04 47	5.2	17 14	5.1
TH 22	04 48	6.6	16 50	6.5	01 52	8.8	14 18	8.5	03 08	3.3	15 56	2.9	05 23	5.1	17 53	5.0
FR 23	05 27	6.6	17 28	6.5	02 32	8.7	14 58	8.4	03 46	3.3	16 35	2.9	06 00	5.1	18 36	4.9
SA 24	06 08	6.5	18 11	6.4	03 15	8.6	15 43	8.2	04 27	3.3	17 16	2.8	06 42	5.0	19 23	4.8
SU 25	06 55	6.3	19 00	6.3	04 04	8.3	16 36	7.9	05 12	3.2	18 01	2.8	07 31	4.9	20 16	4.7
M 26	07 49	6.1	19 59	6.1	05 02	8.1	17 41	7.8	06 04	3.0	18 53	2.7	08 31	4.7	21 19	4.6
TU 27	08 55	5.9	21 10	5.9	06 09	7.9	18 53	7.8	07 08	2.9	20 03	2.7	09 46	4.7	22 28	4.7
W 28	10 11	5.8	22 29	6.0	07 24	7.9	20 07	8.1	08 31	2.9	21 38	2.8	11 04	4.8	23 36	4.8
TH 29	11 21	6.1	23 43	6.2	08 39	8.2	21 13	8.6	09 57	3.0	22 46	3.0	—	—	12 15	5.0
FR 30	—	—	12 22	6.4	09 45	8.6	22 10	9.1	11 04	3.1	23 40	3.2	00 39	5.1	13 18	5.3
SA 31	00 48	6.6	13 18	6.7	10 42	9.0	23 01	9.5	—	—	12 03	3.2	01 36	5.3	14 13	5.6

AUGUST 2004   *High Water*   GMT

	LONDON BRIDGE				LIVERPOOL				GREENOCK				LEITH			
	hr	ht m	hr	ht m	hr	ht m	hr	ht m	hr	ht m	hr	ht m	hr	ht m	hr	ht m
SU 1	01 47	7.0	14 10	7.0	11 34	9.2	23 50	9.7	00 29	3.4	12 59	3.2	02 26	5.6	15 02	5.7
M 2	02 41	7.2	14 57	7.1	—	—	12 22	9.3	01 16	3.5	13 52	3.2	03 13	5.7	15 50	5.7
TU 3	03 29	7.3	15 41	7.1	00 37	9.8	13 08	9.3	02 00	3.6	14 39	3.2	03 59	5.8	16 36	5.6
W 4	04 14	7.3	16 22	7.1	01 22	9.7	13 50	9.1	02 42	3.7	15 22	3.2	04 45	5.7	17 21	5.4
TH 5	04 56	7.2	17 01	7.0	02 04	9.4	14 30	8.8	03 23	3.7	16 00	3.2	05 31	5.5	18 07	5.2
FR 6	05 36	6.9	17 39	6.8	02 45	9.0	15 09	8.4	04 02	3.6	16 37	3.2	06 17	5.3	18 53	4.9
SA 7	06 15	6.5	18 17	6.5	03 27	8.5	15 49	7.9	04 42	3.4	17 14	3.1	07 04	5.0	19 40	4.6
SU 8	06 55	6.2	19 02	6.2	04 11	8.0	16 36	7.5	05 23	3.2	17 54	3.0	07 57	4.7	20 32	4.4
M 9	07 41	5.8	19 58	5.9	05 05	7.5	17 37	7.1	06 10	2.9	18 39	2.9	08 55	4.4	21 29	4.3
TU 10	08 43	5.6	21 12	5.6	06 16	7.1	18 58	7.1	07 06	2.7	19 33	2.8	10 00	4.3	22 33	4.3
W 11	09 59	5.5	22 29	5.7	07 38	7.1	20 14	7.3	08 43	2.6	20 54	2.8	11 13	4.2	23 46	4.4
TH 12	11 04	5.7	23 34	5.9	08 45	7.4	21 11	7.8	10 32	2.7	22 26	2.9	—	—	12 26	4.4
FR 13	12 00	6.0	—	—	09 38	7.8	21 56	8.2	11 21	2.8	23 17	3.1	00 48	4.6	13 19	4.6
SA 14	00 29	6.2	12 51	6.3	10 22	8.1	22 36	8.6	12 02	2.9	23 56	3.2	01 35	4.8	13 59	4.9
SU 15	01 19	6.4	13 36	6.5	11 00	8.4	23 12	8.8	—	—	12 41	2.9	02 12	5.1	14 33	5.1
M 16	02 03	6.6	14 17	6.6	11 36	8.6	23 46	9.0	00 29	3.3	13 17	2.9	02 46	5.2	15 05	5.2
TU 17	02 43	6.7	14 54	6.6	—	—	12 10	8.7	01 01	3.3	13 49	2.9	03 18	5.3	15 38	5.3
W 18	03 18	6.7	15 26	6.6	00 19	9.0	12 44	8.8	01 33	3.4	14 20	3.0	03 50	5.4	16 12	5.3
TH 19	03 52	6.8	15 56	6.6	00 53	9.1	13 17	8.9	02 09	3.4	14 51	3.0	04 22	5.5	16 47	5.3
FR 20	04 25	6.8	16 26	6.7	01 28	9.1	13 52	8.8	02 46	3.5	15 24	3.0	04 56	5.4	17 25	5.3
SA 21	05 00	6.8	17 01	6.7	02 05	9.1	14 29	8.7	03 22	3.5	15 57	3.0	05 33	5.3	18 06	5.1
SU 22	05 38	6.6	17 42	6.6	02 46	8.8	15 11	8.4	04 00	3.4	16 33	3.0	06 15	5.2	18 50	4.9
M 23	06 20	6.3	18 30	6.4	03 33	8.4	16 02	8.0	04 41	3.3	17 14	2.9	07 04	5.0	19 42	4.7
TU 24	07 11	5.9	19 28	6.0	04 32	7.9	17 08	7.6	05 30	3.1	18 05	2.8	08 05	4.7	20 46	4.6
W 25	08 16	5.5	20 43	5.7	05 46	7.5	18 32	7.5	06 32	2.8	19 17	2.7	09 28	4.6	22 06	4.5
TH 26	09 45	5.5	22 17	5.7	07 16	7.5	19 59	7.8	08 12	2.7	21 28	2.8	10 56	4.7	23 25	4.7
FR 27	11 07	5.8	23 39	6.1	08 41	7.9	21 08	8.5	10 05	2.9	22 38	3.1	—	—	12 14	5.0
SA 28	—	—	12 11	6.3	09 44	8.5	22 03	9.1	11 10	3.1	23 30	3.3	00 33	5.0	13 16	5.3
SU 29	00 43	6.6	13 06	6.7	10 35	9.0	22 50	9.6	—	—	12 03	3.2	01 27	5.4	14 05	5.6
M 30	01 39	7.1	13 55	7.0	11 21	9.3	23 34	9.8	00 16	3.5	12 52	3.3	02 13	5.6	14 48	5.7
TU 31	02 27	7.3	14 39	7.2	—	—	12 03	9.4	01 01	3.6	13 36	3.3	02 55	5.8	15 30	5.7

SEPTEMBER 2004 *High Water* GMT

	LONDON BRIDGE *Datum of Predictions 3.20m below				LIVERPOOL *Datum of Predictions 4.93m below				GREENOCK *Datum of Predictions 1.62m below				LEITH *Datum of Predictions 2.90m below			
	hr m	ht m	hr m	ht m	hr m	ht m	hr m	ht m	hr m	ht m	hr m	ht m	hr m	ht m	hr m	ht m
W 1	03 11	7.4	15 19	7.2	00 16	9.9	12 43	9.3	01 43	3.7	14 15	3.3	03 37	5.9	16 10	5.6
TH 2	03 50	7.3	15 55	7.2	00 55	9.7	13 19	9.2	02 22	3.7	14 49	3.3	04 18	5.8	16 50	5.4
FR 3	04 26	7.1	16 28	7.0	01 33	9.4	13 54	8.9	02 58	3.7	15 21	3.3	04 59	5.6	17 30	5.2
SA 4	04 57	6.8	17 01	6.9	02 08	9.0	14 27	8.5	03 32	3.6	15 54	3.3	05 39	5.3	18 10	4.9
SU 5	05 27	6.6	17 36	6.6	02 44	8.5	15 02	8.1	04 07	3.4	16 28	3.3	06 22	5.0	18 52	4.7
M 6	05 59	6.3	18 16	6.3	03 23	7.9	15 42	7.6	04 44	3.2	17 07	3.2	07 11	4.6	19 42	4.4
TU 7	06 37	5.9	19 05	5.8	04 11	7.3	16 36	7.1	05 26	2.9	17 51	3.0	08 08	4.3	20 40	4.2
W 8	07 26	5.6	20 09	5.5	05 21	6.8	18 04	6.8	06 20	2.7	18 46	2.9	09 15	4.1	21 47	4.2
TH 9	08 38	5.3	21 44	5.4	07 06	6.7	19 45	7.1	07 36	2.5	19 56	2.8	10 31	4.1	23 05	4.3
FR 10	10 25	5.4	23 05	5.6	08 23	7.2	20 47	7.6	10 20	2.7	21 52	2.9	11 57	4.3	—	—
SA 11	11 32	5.8	—	—	09 15	7.7	21 33	8.2	11 03	2.9	22 49	3.1	00 18	4.5	12 54	4.6
SU 12	00 03	6.1	12 25	6.2	09 58	8.2	22 11	8.6	11 41	3.0	23 28	3.2	01 07	4.9	13 33	4.9
M 13	00 53	6.4	13 11	6.5	10 35	8.6	22 46	9.0	—	—	12 17	3.1	01 45	5.1	14 06	5.2
TU 14	01 37	6.7	13 51	6.6	11 09	8.8	23 19	9.2	00 00	3.3	12 51	3.1	02 18	5.4	14 38	5.4
W 15	02 15	6.8	14 27	6.7	11 42	9.0	23 52	9.3	00 33	3.4	13 21	3.1	02 50	5.5	15 10	5.5
TH 16	02 51	6.9	14 59	6.7	—	—	12 15	9.1	01 08	3.5	13 50	3.2	03 21	5.6	15 43	5.6
FR 17	03 25	6.9	15 29	6.8	00 26	9.4	12 50	9.2	01 45	3.5	14 19	3.2	03 54	5.7	16 19	5.5
SA 18	03 58	6.9	16 02	6.9	01 03	9.4	13 25	9.1	02 22	3.6	14 50	3.3	04 30	5.6	16 57	5.4
SU 19	04 33	6.8	16 39	6.9	01 41	9.2	14 03	8.9	02 59	3.6	15 23	3.3	05 10	5.5	17 38	5.3
M 20	05 10	6.6	17 21	6.7	02 22	8.9	14 46	8.5	03 37	3.5	15 59	3.2	05 55	5.3	18 23	5.0
TU 21	05 51	6.3	18 10	6.3	03 11	8.3	15 39	8.0	04 18	3.3	16 41	3.1	06 48	5.0	19 17	4.7
W 22	06 39	5.8	19 11	5.8	04 14	7.6	16 50	7.5	05 06	3.0	17 34	2.9	07 56	4.7	20 28	4.5
TH 23	07 45	5.4	20 36	5.5	05 41	7.2	18 27	7.4	06 13	2.8	18 55	2.8	09 27	4.5	21 57	4.5
FR 24	09 32	5.3	22 18	5.7	07 24	7.4	19 56	7.8	08 42	2.7	21 20	2.9	10 56	4.7	23 18	4.8
SA 25	10 56	5.7	23 33	6.2	08 39	8.0	20 59	8.6	10 12	2.9	22 24	3.2	—	—	12 11	5.0
SU 26	11 57	6.3	—	—	09 34	8.6	21 49	9.2	11 05	3.2	23 13	3.5	00 23	5.1	13 06	5.4
M 27	00 31	6.8	12 48	6.8	10 19	9.1	22 32	9.6	11 50	3.3	23 58	3.6	01 13	5.5	13 50	5.6
TU 28	01 22	7.2	13 33	7.1	11 00	9.3	23 13	9.8	—	—	12 32	3.4	01 55	5.7	14 28	5.7
W 29	02 07	7.4	14 14	7.2	11 37	9.4	23 50	9.7	00 40	3.7	13 09	3.4	02 34	5.8	15 05	5.7
TH 30	02 47	7.4	14 52	7.2	—	—	12 12	9.3	01 20	3.7	13 42	3.4	03 12	5.8	15 41	5.6

OCTOBER 2004 *High Water* GMT

	LONDON BRIDGE				LIVERPOOL				GREENOCK				LEITH			
FR 1	03 22	7.2	15 26	7.1	00 26	9.6	12 45	9.1	01 56	3.7	14 13	3.5	03 50	5.7	16 18	5.4
SA 2	03 51	7.0	15 57	7.0	01 00	9.3	13 17	8.9	02 30	3.6	14 44	3.5	04 28	5.5	16 54	5.2
SU 3	04 17	6.8	16 28	6.8	01 33	8.9	13 48	8.6	03 02	3.5	15 16	3.5	05 07	5.2	17 30	5.0
M 4	04 44	6.6	17 02	6.5	02 06	8.4	14 21	8.2	03 36	3.4	15 49	3.5	05 48	4.9	18 10	4.7
TU 5	05 16	6.4	17 42	6.2	02 44	7.9	15 00	7.7	04 12	3.2	16 27	3.3	06 34	4.6	18 57	4.5
W 6	05 54	6.1	18 30	5.8	03 30	7.3	15 50	7.2	04 54	2.9	17 11	3.1	07 28	4.3	19 54	4.3
TH 7	06 40	5.7	19 28	5.5	04 34	6.7	17 06	6.8	05 50	2.7	18 07	3.0	08 33	4.1	21 05	4.2
FR 8	07 41	5.3	20 45	5.3	06 25	6.6	19 04	6.9	07 07	2.6	19 16	2.9	09 45	4.1	22 20	4.3
SA 9	09 24	5.2	22 24	5.5	07 49	7.0	20 11	7.5	09 44	2.7	20 47	2.9	11 05	4.3	23 33	4.5
SU 10	10 54	5.6	23 27	6.0	08 42	7.7	20 58	8.1	10 30	2.9	22 03	3.1	—	—	12 10	4.6
M 11	11 49	6.0	—	—	09 24	8.2	21 37	8.6	11 08	3.1	22 47	3.3	00 27	4.8	12 54	5.0
TU 12	00 17	6.4	12 35	6.4	10 01	8.7	22 12	9.0	11 43	3.2	23 24	3.4	01 08	5.2	13 30	5.3
W 13	01 01	6.7	13 15	6.6	10 35	9.0	22 47	9.3	—	—	12 16	3.2	01 43	5.4	14 04	5.5
TH 14	01 41	6.9	13 52	6.8	11 10	9.3	23 22	9.5	00 01	3.5	12 47	3.3	02 16	5.6	14 39	5.6
FR 15	02 19	7.0	14 28	6.9	11 45	9.4	—	—	00 40	3.6	13 18	3.4	02 51	5.8	15 14	5.7
SA 16	02 56	7.0	15 04	7.0	00 00	9.6	12 23	9.4	01 20	3.6	13 50	3.4	03 28	5.8	15 51	5.7
SU 17	03 33	7.0	15 43	7.0	00 40	9.5	13 02	9.3	02 00	3.7	14 23	3.5	04 08	5.7	16 31	5.5
M 18	04 10	6.8	16 25	6.9	01 22	9.2	13 44	9.0	02 40	3.6	14 59	3.5	04 53	5.6	17 15	5.3
TU 19	04 49	6.6	17 11	6.6	02 08	8.8	14 32	8.6	03 21	3.5	15 37	3.4	05 44	5.3	18 03	5.1
W 20	05 31	6.2	18 05	6.2	03 02	8.2	15 29	8.0	04 05	3.3	16 22	3.3	06 42	5.0	19 02	4.8
TH 21	06 21	5.8	19 12	5.8	04 11	7.5	16 46	7.6	04 59	3.0	17 21	3.1	07 57	4.7	20 21	4.6
FR 22	07 35	5.4	20 42	5.6	05 44	7.2	18 20	7.6	06 27	2.8	19 02	2.9	09 24	4.6	21 49	4.6
SA 23	09 20	5.4	22 07	5.9	07 14	7.5	19 37	8.0	08 47	2.8	20 58	3.1	10 46	4.8	23 04	4.9
SU 24	10 33	5.9	23 13	6.4	08 20	8.1	20 37	8.6	09 55	3.1	22 00	3.4	11 55	5.1	—	—
M 25	11 32	6.4	—	—	09 11	8.6	21 26	9.1	10 44	3.2	22 49	3.5	00 04	5.2	12 47	5.3
TU 26	00 08	6.9	12 22	6.8	09 55	9.0	22 09	9.4	11 25	3.4	23 33	3.6	00 52	5.4	13 28	5.4
W 27	00 57	7.2	13 07	7.1	10 34	9.2	22 48	9.5	—	—	12 03	3.4	01 33	5.6	14 05	5.5
TH 28	01 40	7.3	13 48	7.2	11 09	9.2	23 24	9.4	00 15	3.6	12 38	3.5	02 11	5.6	14 39	5.5
FR 29	02 18	7.2	14 25	7.1	11 42	9.2	23 58	9.3	00 54	3.6	13 09	3.5	02 49	5.6	15 14	5.5
SA 30	02 51	7.0	14 59	7.0	—	—	12 13	9.0	01 30	3.5	13 40	3.6	03 26	5.5	15 48	5.3
SU 31	03 18	6.8	15 30	6.8	00 30	9.0	12 44	8.9	02 03	3.5	14 12	3.6	04 03	5.3	16 22	5.2

NOVEMBER 2004 *High Water* GMT

	LONDON BRIDGE *Datum of Predictions 3.20m below*				LIVERPOOL *Datum of Predictions 4.93m below*				GREENOCK *Datum of Predictions 1.62m below*				LEITH *Datum of Predictions 2.90m below*			
	hr m	ht m	hr m	ht m	hr m	ht m	hr m	ht m	hr m	ht m	hr m	ht m	hr m	ht m	hr m	ht m
M 1	03 42	6.7	16 02	6.6	01 03	8.7	13 17	8.6	02 36	3.4	14 45	3.6	04 42	5.1	16 57	5.0
TU 2	04 10	6.6	16 37	6.4	01 37	8.4	13 52	8.3	03 11	3.3	15 18	3.6	05 22	4.9	17 35	4.8
W 3	04 43	6.4	17 17	6.1	02 16	7.9	14 31	7.9	03 48	3.1	15 55	3.4	06 06	4.6	18 19	4.6
TH 4	05 22	6.1	18 04	5.9	03 01	7.4	15 19	7.5	04 32	2.9	16 38	3.3	06 56	4.4	19 13	4.4
FR 5	06 08	5.8	18 59	5.6	03 59	7.0	16 23	7.1	05 30	2.8	17 32	3.1	07 53	4.3	20 20	4.3
SA 6	07 05	5.5	20 02	5.5	05 20	6.8	17 50	7.1	06 42	2.7	18 38	3.0	08 59	4.2	21 32	4.3
SU 7	08 17	5.4	21 18	5.6	06 53	7.0	19 12	7.4	08 08	2.7	19 50	3.0	10 08	4.4	22 39	4.5
M 8	09 49	5.5	22 33	5.9	07 54	7.6	20 07	8.0	09 32	2.9	21 01	3.1	11 12	4.6	23 36	4.8
TU 9	10 57	5.9	23 31	6.3	08 40	8.1	20 52	8.5	10 22	3.1	21 59	3.3	—	—	12 05	4.9
W 10	11 48	6.3	—	—	09 21	8.7	21 33	9.0	11 02	3.2	22 46	3.4	00 23	5.1	12 49	5.2
TH 11	00 19	6.7	12 34	6.6	09 59	9.1	22 13	9.3	11 39	3.3	23 30	3.5	01 05	5.4	13 29	5.5
FR 12	01 05	6.9	13 17	6.8	10 39	9.4	22 55	9.6	—	—	12 14	3.4	01 44	5.6	14 08	5.6
SA 13	01 48	7.0	14 00	7.0	11 19	9.6	23 38	9.6	00 14	3.6	12 51	3.5	02 25	5.8	14 47	5.7
SU 14	02 30	7.0	14 45	7.1	—	—	12 01	9.6	00 59	3.6	13 28	3.6	03 08	5.8	15 28	5.7
M 15	03 12	7.0	15 31	7.1	00 23	9.5	12 47	9.5	01 44	3.6	14 05	3.7	03 54	5.8	16 11	5.6
TU 16	03 54	6.8	16 19	7.0	01 12	9.2	13 34	9.2	02 29	3.6	14 45	3.7	04 44	5.6	16 59	5.4
W 17	04 38	6.6	17 10	6.7	02 03	8.8	14 27	8.8	03 15	3.4	15 27	3.6	05 38	5.4	17 51	5.2
TH 18	05 24	6.3	18 07	6.4	03 00	8.3	15 26	8.4	04 07	3.2	16 17	3.4	06 39	5.1	18 54	4.9
FR 19	06 17	6.0	19 13	6.1	04 08	7.8	16 37	8.1	05 12	3.0	17 21	3.3	07 52	4.8	20 12	4.8
SA 20	07 31	5.7	20 28	6.0	05 27	7.5	17 54	8.0	06 39	2.9	18 49	3.2	09 07	4.8	21 28	4.8
SU 21	08 52	5.8	21 39	6.1	06 43	7.6	19 04	8.1	08 12	3.0	20 20	3.2	10 20	4.8	22 36	4.9
M 22	10 00	6.0	22 42	6.4	07 48	8.0	20 05	8.5	09 19	3.1	21 27	3.4	11 24	4.9	23 36	5.1
TU 23	10 59	6.4	23 37	6.7	08 41	8.3	20 57	8.8	10 10	3.2	22 20	3.5	—	—	12 18	5.1
W 24	11 51	6.7	—	—	09 27	8.7	21 43	9.0	10 53	3.3	23 07	3.5	00 27	5.2	13 03	5.2
TH 25	00 25	6.9	12 38	6.9	10 07	8.9	22 23	9.0	11 31	3.4	23 51	3.5	01 11	5.3	13 41	5.3
FR 26	01 10	7.0	13 21	7.0	10 43	9.0	23 00	9.0	—	—	12 07	3.5	01 52	5.3	14 17	5.3
SA 27	01 48	6.9	14 01	6.9	11 16	9.0	23 34	8.9	00 31	3.4	12 41	3.5	02 30	5.3	14 51	5.3
SU 28	02 22	6.8	14 37	6.7	11 48	8.9	—	—	01 08	3.4	13 14	3.6	03 08	5.2	15 25	5.3
M 29	02 50	6.6	15 11	6.6	00 07	8.8	12 22	8.8	01 43	3.3	13 47	3.6	03 45	5.2	15 58	5.2
TU 30	03 16	6.5	15 44	6.4	00 42	8.6	12 56	8.7	02 17	3.2	14 20	3.7	04 22	5.0	16 32	5.1

DECEMBER 2004 *High Water* GMT

	LONDON BRIDGE				LIVERPOOL				GREENOCK				LEITH			
W 1	03 46	6.4	16 20	6.3	01 18	8.4	13 33	8.5	02 53	3.2	14 55	3.6	05 01	4.9	17 09	4.9
TH 2	04 21	6.3	17 00	6.2	01 57	8.1	14 13	8.2	03 32	3.1	15 32	3.5	05 42	4.8	17 51	4.8
FR 3	05 00	6.2	17 44	6.1	02 40	7.8	14 57	7.9	04 17	3.0	16 13	3.4	06 26	4.6	18 37	4.6
SA 4	05 44	6.0	18 34	6.0	03 29	7.5	15 50	7.7	05 10	2.9	17 01	3.2	07 16	4.5	19 32	4.5
SU 5	06 35	5.8	19 28	5.9	04 29	7.2	16 51	7.5	06 09	2.8	17 57	3.1	08 12	4.4	20 36	4.5
M 6	07 34	5.7	20 28	5.9	05 38	7.2	17 59	7.6	07 11	2.8	18 57	3.1	09 15	4.4	21 41	4.5
TU 7	08 42	5.7	21 34	6.0	06 47	7.5	19 03	7.9	08 17	2.9	20 03	3.1	10 17	4.6	22 42	4.7
W 8	09 55	5.9	22 41	6.2	07 47	8.0	20 01	8.3	09 23	3.0	21 10	3.2	11 16	4.8	23 38	5.0
TH 9	11 00	6.2	23 40	6.5	08 39	8.5	20 54	8.8	10 18	3.1	22 10	3.3	—	—	12 09	5.1
FR 10	11 56	6.5	—	—	09 27	8.9	21 45	9.2	11 05	3.3	23 03	3.4	00 29	5.2	12 57	5.3
SA 11	00 32	6.7	12 49	6.8	10 13	9.3	22 34	9.4	11 48	3.4	23 54	3.5	01 18	5.4	13 42	5.5
SU 12	01 22	6.9	13 40	7.0	11 00	9.5	23 24	9.5	—	—	12 30	3.5	02 06	5.6	14 26	5.6
M 13	02 10	7.0	14 32	7.1	11 48	9.7	—	—	00 44	3.5	13 13	3.7	02 55	5.8	15 12	5.7
TU 14	02 57	7.0	15 23	7.2	00 14	9.5	12 37	9.6	01 35	3.5	13 56	3.7	03 45	5.8	15 59	5.6
W 15	03 44	6.9	16 14	7.1	01 06	9.3	13 28	9.5	02 26	3.5	14 40	3.8	04 37	5.7	16 48	5.5
TH 16	04 30	6.8	17 06	7.0	01 59	9.0	14 20	9.3	03 18	3.4	15 26	3.7	05 32	5.5	17 42	5.4
FR 17	05 18	6.6	17 59	6.8	02 53	8.6	15 15	9.0	04 12	3.3	16 16	3.6	06 29	5.2	18 41	5.2
SA 18	06 08	6.4	18 56	6.5	03 49	8.2	16 12	8.6	05 10	3.2	17 12	3.5	07 32	5.0	19 47	5.0
SU 19	07 06	6.2	19 58	6.3	04 51	7.9	17 15	8.3	06 11	3.1	18 16	3.4	08 36	4.8	20 55	4.9
M 20	08 12	6.0	21 02	6.2	05 58	7.7	18 20	8.1	07 13	3.0	19 27	3.3	09 40	4.7	21 59	4.9
TU 21	09 19	6.0	22 03	6.2	07 05	7.7	19 26	8.1	08 19	3.0	20 42	3.2	10 43	4.7	23 01	4.8
W 22	10 21	6.2	23 00	6.3	08 05	7.9	20 25	8.2	09 22	3.1	21 48	3.2	11 44	4.7	23 59	4.9
TH 23	11 18	6.3	23 51	6.4	08 57	8.1	21 17	8.3	10 16	3.2	22 44	3.2	—	—	12 34	4.8
FR 24	—	—	12 09	6.5	09 42	8.4	22 02	8.5	11 02	3.3	23 32	3.2	00 51	4.9	13 20	5.0
SA 25	00 38	6.5	12 57	6.6	10 22	8.6	22 43	8.6	11 42	3.4	—	—	01 37	5.0	14 00	5.1
SU 26	01 20	6.6	13 41	6.6	10 59	8.8	23 19	8.6	00 16	3.2	12 21	3.5	02 18	5.0	14 36	5.1
M 27	01 58	6.5	14 21	6.6	11 33	8.8	23 54	8.6	00 56	3.1	12 56	3.5	02 56	5.1	15 09	5.2
TU 28	02 31	6.5	14 58	6.5	—	—	12 08	8.9	01 32	3.1	13 29	3.6	03 31	5.1	15 42	5.2
W 29	03 02	6.4	15 33	6.4	00 29	8.6	12 44	8.8	02 07	3.1	14 02	3.6	04 06	5.1	16 16	5.1
TH 30	03 34	6.3	16 08	6.4	01 05	8.5	13 20	8.7	02 42	3.1	14 37	3.6	04 41	5.0	16 51	5.1
FR 31	04 08	6.3	16 45	6.4	01 42	8.4	13 57	8.6	03 19	3.0	15 13	3.5	05 19	4.9	17 28	5.0

WEIGHTS AND MEASURES

SI UNITS

The Système International d'Unités (SI) is an international and coherent system of units devised to meet all known needs for measurement in science and technology. The system was adopted by the eleventh Conférence Générale des Poids et Mesures (CGPM) in 1960. A comprehensive description of the system is given in *SI The International System of Units* (HMSO). The British Standards describing the essential features of the International System of Units are *Specifications for SI units and recommendations for the use of their multiples and certain other units* (BS 5555:1993) and *Conversion Factors and Tables* (BS 350, Part 1:1974).

The system consists of seven base units and the derived units formed as products or quotients of various powers of the base units. Together the base units and the derived units make up the coherent system of units. In the UK the SI base units, and almost all important derived units, are realised at the National Physical Laboratory and disseminated through the National Measurement System.

BASE UNITS
metre (m) = unit of length
kilogram (kg) = unit of mass
second (s) = unit of time
ampere (A) = unit of electric current
kelvin (K) = unit of thermodynamic temperature
mole (mol) = unit of amount of substance
candela (cd) = unit of luminous intensity

DERIVED UNITS
For some of the derived SI units, special names and symbols exist; those approved by the CGPM are as follows:

hertz (Hz) = unit of frequency
newton (N) = unit of force
pascal (Pa) = unit of pressure, stress
joule (J) = unit of energy, work, quantity of heat
watt (W) = unit of power, radiant flux
coulomb (C) = unit of electric charge, quantity of electricity
volt (V) = unit of electric potential, potential difference, electromotive force
farad (F) = unit of electric capacitance
ohm (Ω) = unit of electric resistance
siemens (S) = unit of electric conductance
weber (Wb) = unit of magnetic flux
tesla (T) = unit of magnetic flux density
henry (H) = unit of inductance
degree Celsius (°C) = unit of Celsius temperature
lumen (lm) = unit of luminous flux
lux (lx) = unit of illuminance
becquerel (Bq) = unit of activity (of a radionuclide)
gray (Gy) = unit of absorbed dose, specific energy imparted, kerma, absorbed dose index
sievert (Sv) = unit of dose equivalent, dose equivalent index
radian (rad) = unit of plane angle
steradian (sr) = unit of solid angle

Other derived units are expressed in terms of base units. Some of the more commonly used derived units are the following:

Unit of area = square metre (m^2)
Unit of volume = cubic metre (m^3)
Unit of velocity = metre per second ($m\ s^{-1}$)
Unit of acceleration = metre per second squared ($m\ s^{-2}$)
Unit of density = kilogram per cubic metre ($kg\ m^{-3}$)
Unit of momentum = kilogram metre per second ($kg\ m\ s^{-1}$)
Unit of magnetic field strength = ampere per metre ($A\ m^{-1}$)
Unit of surface tension = newton per metre ($N\ m^{-1}$)
Unit of dynamic viscosity = pascal second (Pa s)
Unit of heat capacity = joule per kelvin ($J\ K^{-1}$)
Unit of specific heat capacity = joule per kilogram kelvin ($J\ kg^{-1}\ K^{-1}$)
Unit of heat flux density, irradiance = watt per square metre ($W\ m^{-2}$)
Unit of thermal conductivity = watt per metre kelvin ($W\ m^{-1}\ K^{-1}$)
Unit of electric field strength = volt per metre ($V\ m^{-1}$)
Unit of luminance = candela per square metre ($cd\ m^{-2}$)

SI PREFIXES
Decimal multiples and submultiples of the SI units are indicated by SI prefixes. These are as follows:

multiples	submultiples
yotta (Y) x 10^{24}	deci (d) x 10^{-1}
zetta (Z) x 10^{21}	centi (c) x 10^{-2}
exa (E) x 10^{18}	milli (m) x 10^{-3}
peta (P) x 10^{15}	micro (µ) x 10^{-6}
tera (T) x 10^{12}	nano (n) x 10^{-9}
giga (G) x 10^9	pico (p) x 10^{-12}
mega (M) x 10^6	femto (f) x 10^{-15}
kilo (k) x 10^3	atto (a) x 10^{-18}
hecto (h) x 10^2	zepto (z) x 10^{-21}
deca (da) x 10	yocto (y) x 10^{-24}

METRIC UNITS

The metric primary standards are the metre as the unit of measurement of length, and the kilogram as the unit of measurement of mass. Other units of measurement are defined by reference to the primary standards.

MEASUREMENT OF LENGTH
Kilometre (km) = 1000 metres
Metre (m) is the length of the path travelled by light in vacuum during a time interval of 1/299 792 458 of a second
Decimetre (dm) = 1/10 metre
Centimetre (cm) = 1/100 metre
Millimetre (mm) = 1/1000 metre

MEASUREMENT OF AREA
Hectare (ha) = 100 ares
Decare = 10 ares
Are (a) = 100 square metres
Square metre = a superficial area equal to that of a square each side of which measures one metre
Square decimetre = 1/100 square metre

Square centimetre = 1/100 square decimetre
Square millimetre = 1/100 square centimetre

MEASUREMENT OF VOLUME
Cubic metre (m³) = a volume equal to that of a cube each
    edge of which measures one metre
Cubic decimetre = 1/1000 cubic metre
Cubic centimetre (cc) = 1/1000 cubic decimetre
Hectolitre = 100 litres
Litre = a cubic decimetre
Decilitre = 1/10 litre
Centilitre = 1/100 litre
Millilitre = 1/1000 litre

MEASUREMENT OF CAPACITY
Hectolitre (hl) = 100 litres
Litre (l or L) = a cubic decimetre
Decilitre (dl) = 1/10 litre
Centilitre (cl) = 1/100 litre
Millilitre (ml) = 1/1000 litre

MEASUREMENT OF MASS OR WEIGHT
Tonne (t) = 1000 kilograms
Kilogram (kg) is equal to the mass of the international
    prototype of the kilogram
Hectogram (hg) = 1/10 kilogram
Gram (g) = 1/1000 kilogram
*Carat (metric) = 1/5 gram
Milligram (mg) = 1/1000 gram

*Used only for transactions in precious stones or pearls

METRICATION IN THE UK
The European Council Directive 80/181/EEC, as
amended by Council Directive 89/617/EEC, relates to
the use of units of measurement for economic, public
health, public safety or administrative purposes in the
member states of the European Union. The provisions of
the directives were incorporated into British law by the
Weights and Measures Act 1985 (Metrication)
(Amendment) Order 1994 and the Units of Measurement
Regulations 1994; these instruments amended the
Weights and Measures Act 1985. Parallel statutory rules
amending Northern Ireland weights and measures
legislation were made in May 1995.
    The general effect of the 1994 and 1995 legislation is
to end the use of imperial units of measurement for trade,
replacing them with metric units – see below for timetable
for UK metrication. Imperial units can, however, be used
in addition to metric units, as supplementary indications.

IMPERIAL UNITS

The imperial primary standards are the yard as the unit of
measurement of length and the pound as the unit of
measurement of mass. Other units of measurement are
defined by reference to the primary standards. Most of
these units are no longer authorised for use in trade in the
UK — see below.

MEASUREMENT OF LENGTH
Mile = 1760 yards
Furlong = 220 yards
Chain = 22 yards
Yard (yd) = 0.9144 metre
Foot (ft) = 1/3 yard
Inch (in) = 1/36 yard

MEASUREMENT OF AREA
Square mile = 640 acres
Acre = 4840 square yards
Rood = 1210 square yards
Square yard (sq. yd) = a superficial area equal to that of a
    square each side of which measures one yard
Square foot (sq. ft) = 1/9 square yard
Square inch (sq. in) = 1/144 square foot

MEASUREMENT OF VOLUME
Cubic yard = a volume equal to that of a cube each edge
    of which measures one yard
Cubic foot = 1/27 cubic yard
Cubic inch = 1/1728 cubic foot

MEASUREMENT OF CAPACITY
Bushel = 8 gallons
Peck = 2 gallons
Gallon (gal) = 4.54609 cubic decimetres
Quart (qt) = 1/4 gallon
*Pint (pt) = 1/2 quart
Gill = 1/4 pint
*Fluid ounce (fl oz) = 1/20 pint
Fluid drachm = 1/8 fluid ounce
Minim (min) = 1/60 fluid drachm

MEASUREMENT OF MASS OR WEIGHT
Ton = 2240 pounds
Hundredweight (cwt) = 112 pounds
Cental = 100 pounds
Quarter = 28 pounds
Stone = 14 pounds
*Pound (lb) = 0.453 592 37 kilogram
*Ounce (oz) = 1/16 pound
*†Ounce troy (oz tr) = 12/175 pound
Dram (dr) = 1/16 ounce
Grain (gr) = 1/7000 pound
Pennyweight (dwt) = 24 grains
Ounce apothecaries = 480 grains
Drachm (ʒ) = 1/8 ounce apothecaries
Scruple (϶) = 1/3 drachm

*Units of measurement still authorised for use for trade in the
UK
†Used only for transactions in gold, silver or other precious
metals, and articles made therefrom

PHASING-OUT OF IMPERIAL UNITS IN THE UK
Since 1965 the United Kingdom has been adopting
metric weights and measures in response to the adoption
of metric units as the international system of
measurement. Goods sold loose by weight (mainly fresh
foods) are required to be sold in grams and kilograms.
Retailers can continue to display the price per imperial
unit alongside the price per unit in metric unit.
Consumers can continue to express in ounces and pounds
the quantity they wish to buy. Retailers will weigh out
the equivalent quantity in grams and kilograms. The
Weights and Measures Units of Measurement Regulations
1995 (Statutory Instrument 1995 No. 1804) require that
metric units should be used for all economic, public
health, public safety and administrative purposes.

Units of measurement authorised for use in specialised fields are:

Unit	Field of application
fathom	Marine navigation
fluid ounce ⎫	Beer, cider, water, lemonade, fruit
pint ⎬	juice in returnable containers
ounce ⎫	Goods for sale loose from bulk
pound ⎬	
therm	Gas supply

Units of measurement authorised for use in specialised fields from 1 October 1995, without time limit

Unit	Field of application
inch ⎫	
foot ⎬	Road traffic signs, distance and speed
yard ⎬	measurement
mile ⎭	
pint ⎬	Dispense of draught beer or cider
	Milk in returnable containers
acre	Land registration
troy ounce	Transactions in precious metals

MEASUREMENT OF ELECTRICITY

Units of measurement of electricity are defined by the Weights and Measures Act 1985 as follows:

ampere (A) = that constant current which, if maintained in two straight parallel conductors of infinite length, of negligible circular cross-section and placed 1 metre apart in vacuum, would produce between these conductors a force equal to 2×10^7 newton per metre of length

ohm (Ω) = the electric resistance between two points of a conductor when a constant potential difference of 1 volt, applied between the two points, produces in the conductor a current of 1 ampere, the conductor not being the seat of any electromotive force

volt (V) = the difference of electric potential between two points of a conducting wire carrying a constant current of 1 ampere when the power dissipated between these points is equal to 1 watt

watt (W) = the power which in one second gives rise to energy of 1 joule

kilowatt (kW) = 1000 watts

megawatt (MW) = one million watts

WATER AND LIQUOR MEASURES

1 cubic foot = 62.32 lb
1 gallon = 10 lb
1 cubic cm = 1 gram
1000 cubic cm = 1 litre; 1 kilogram
1 cubic metre = 1000 litres; 1000 kg; 1 tonne
An inch of rain on the surface of an acre (43560 sq. ft) = 3630 cubic ft = 100.992 tons
Cisterns: A cistern; 2½ feet and 3 feet deep will hold brimful 186.963 gallons, weighing 1869.63 lb in addition to its own weight

WATER FOR SHIPS
Kilderkin = 18 gallons
Barrel = 36 gallons
Puncheon = 72 gallons
Butt = 110 gallons
Tun = 210 gallons

BOTTLES OF WINE

Traditional equivalents in standard champagne bottles:
Magnum = 2 bottles
Jeroboam = 4 bottles
Rehoboam = 6 bottles
Methuselah = 8 bottles
Salmanazar = 12 bottles
Balthazar = 16 bottles
Nebuchadnezzar = 20 bottles
A quarter of a bottle is known as a *nip*
An eighth of a bottle is known as a *baby*

ANGULAR AND CIRCULAR MEASURES

60 seconds (″) = 1 minute (′)
60 minutes = 1 degree (°)
90 degrees = 1 right angle or quadrant
Diameter of circle × 3.1416 = circumference
Diameter squared × 0.7854 = area of circle
Diameter squared × 3.1416 = surface of sphere
Diameter cubed × 0.523 = solidity of sphere
One degree of circumference × 57.3 = radius*
Diameter of cylinder × 3.1416; product by length or height, gives the surface
Diameter squared × 0.7854; product by length or height, gives solid content

*Or, one radian (the angle subtended at the centre of a circle by an arc of the circumference equal in length to the radius) = 57.3 degrees

MILLION, BILLION, ETC.

Value in the UK		
Million	thousand × thousand	10^6
*Billion	million × million	10^{12}
Trillion	million × billion	10^{18}
Quadrillion	million × trillion	10^{24}

Value in USA		
Million	thousand × thousand	10^6
*Billion	thousand × million	10^9
Trillion	million × million	10^{12}
Quadrillion	million ×x billion US	10^{15}

*The American usage of billion (i.e. 10^9) is increasingly common, and is now universally used by statisticians

NAUTICAL MEASURES

DISTANCE
Distance at sea is measured in nautical miles. The British standard nautical mile was 6080 feet but this measure has been obsolete since 1970 when the international nautical mile of 1852 metres was adopted by the Hydrographic Department of the Ministry of Defence. The cable (600 feet or 100 fathoms) was a measure approximately one-tenth of a nautical mile. Such distances are now expressed in decimal parts of a sea mile or in metres.

Soundings at sea were recorded in fathoms (6 feet). Depths are now expressed in metres on Admiralty charts.

SPEED

Speed is measured in nautical miles per hour, called knots. A ship moving at the rate of 30 nautical miles per hour is said to be doing 30 knots.

knots	m.p.h.	knots	m.p.h.
1	1.1515	9	10.3636
2	2.3030	10	11.5151
3	3.4545	15	17.2727
4	4.6060	20	23.0303
5	5.7575	25	28.7878
6	6.9090	30	34.5454
7	8.0606	35	40.3030
8	9.2121	40	46.0606

TONNAGE

Under the Merchant Shipping Act 1854, the tonnage of UK-registered vessels was measured in tons of 100 cubic feet. The need for a universal method of measurement led to the adoption of the International Convention on Tonnage Measurements of Ships 1969, which measures, in cubic metres, all the internal spaces of a vessel for the gross tonnage and those of the cargo compartments for the net tonnage. The convention has applied since July 1982 to new ships, ships which needed to be remeasured because of substantial alterations, and ships whose owners requested remeasurement. On 18 July 1994 the convention became mandatory and all vessels should have been remeasured by that date; however, there is a backlog and some vessels have not yet been remeasured.

DISTANCE OF THE HORIZON

The limit of distance to which one can see varies with the height of the spectator. The greatest distance at which an object on the surface of the sea, or of a level plain, can be seen by a person whose eyes are at a height of five feet from the same level is nearly three miles. At a height of 20 feet the range is increased to nearly six miles, and an approximate rule for finding the range of vision for small heights is to increase the square root of the number of feet that the eye is above the level surface by a third of itself. The result is the distance of the horizon in miles, but is slightly in excess of that in the table below, which is computed by a more precise formula. The table may be used conversely to show the distance of an object of given height that is just visible from a point on the surface of the earth or sea. Refraction is taken into account both in the approximate rule and in the table.

Height in feet	range in miles
5	2.9
20	5.9
50	9.3
100	13.2
500	29.5
1,000	41.6
2,000	58.9
3,000	72.1
4,000	83.3
5,000	93.1
20,000	186.2

TEMPERATURE SCALES

The SI (International System) unit of temperature is the kelvin, which is defined as the fraction $1/273.16$ of the temperature of the triple point of water (i.e. where ice, water and water vapour are in equilibrium). The zero of the Kelvin scale is absolute zero of temperature. The freezing point of water is 273.15 K and the boiling point (as adopted in the International Temperature Scale of 1990) is 373.124 K.

The Celsius scale (formerly centigrade) is defined by subtracting 273.15 from the Kelvin temperature. The Fahrenheit scale is related to the Celsius scale by the relationships:

temperature °F = (temperature °C x 1.8) + 32
temperature °C = (temperature °F−32) ÷ 1.8

It follows from these definitions that the freezing point of water is 0°C and 32°F. The boiling point is 99.974°C and 211.953°F.

The temperature of the human body varies from person to person and in the same person can be affected by a variety of factors. In most people body temperature varies between 36.5°C and 37.2°C (97.7–98.9°F).

Conversion between scales

°C	°F	°C	°F	°C	°F
100	212	60	140	20	68
99	210.2	59	138.2	19	66.2
98	208.4	58	136.4	18	64.4
97	206.6	57	134.6	17	62.6
96	204.8	56	132.8	16	60.8
95	203	55	131	15	59
94	201.2	54	129.2	14	57.2
93	199.4	53	127.4	13	55.4
92	197.6	52	125.6	12	53.6
91	195.8	51	123.8	11	51.8
90	194	50	122	10	50
89	192.2	49	120.2	9	48.2
88	190.4	48	118.4	8	46.4
87	188.6	47	116.6	7	44.6
86	186.8	46	114.8	6	42.8
85	185	45	113	5	41
84	183.2	44	111.2	4	39.2
83	181.4	43	109.4	3	37.4
82	179.6	42	107.6	2	35.6
81	177.8	41	105.8	1	33.8
80	176	40	104	zero	32
79	174.2	39	102.2	− 1	30.2
78	172.4	38	100.4	− 2	28.4
77	170.6	37	98.6	− 3	26.6
76	168.8	36	96.8	− 4	24.8
75	167	35	95	− 5	23
74	165.2	34	93.2	− 6	21.2
73	163.4	33	91.4	− 7	19.4
72	161.6	32	89.6	− 8	17.6
71	159.8	31	87.8	− 9	15.8
70	158	30	86	−10	14
69	156.2	29	84.2	−11	12.2
68	154.4	28	82.4	−12	10.4
67	152.6	27	80.6	−13	8.6
66	150.8	26	78.8	−14	6.8
65	149	25	77	−15	5
64	147.2	24	75.2	−16	3.2
63	145.4	23	73.4	−17	1.4
62	143.6	22	71.6	−18	0.4
61	141.8	21	69.8	−19	−2.2

PAPER MEASURES

Printing Paper	Writing Paper
516 sheets = 1 ream	480 sheets = 1 ream
2 reams = 1 bundle	20 quires = 1 ream
5 bundles = 1 bale	24 sheets = 1 quire

BROWN PAPERS

	inches		*inches*
Casing	46 x 36	Imperial Cap	29 x 22
Double Imperial	45 x 29	Haven Cap	26 x 21
Elephant	34 x 24	Bag Cap	24 x $19\frac{1}{2}$
Double Four Pound	31 x 21	Kent Cap	21 x 18

PRINTING PAPERS

inches		*inches*	
Foolscap	17 x $13\frac{1}{2}$	Double Large Post	33 x 21
Double Foolscap	27 x 17	Demy	$22\frac{1}{2}$ x $17\frac{1}{2}$
Quad Foolscap	34 x 27	Double Demy	35 x $22\frac{1}{2}$
Crown	20 x 15	Quad Demy	45 x 35
Double Crown	30 x 20	Music Demy	20 x $15\frac{1}{2}$
Quad Crown	40 x 30	Medium	23 x 18
Double Quad Crown	60 x 40	Royal	25 x 20
Post	$19\frac{1}{4}$ x $15\frac{1}{2}$	Super Royal	$27\frac{1}{2}$ x $20\frac{1}{2}$
Double Post	$31\frac{1}{2}$ x $19\frac{1}{2}$	Elephant	28 x 23
		Imperial	30 x 22

WRITING AND DRAWING PAPERS

inches		*inches*	
Emperor	72 x 48	Copy or Draft	20 x 16
Antiquarian	53 x 31	Demy	20 x $15\frac{1}{2}$
Double Elephant	40 x 27	Post	19 x $15\frac{1}{4}$
Grand Eagle	42 x $28\frac{3}{4}$	Pinched Post	18 x $14\frac{3}{4}$
Atlas	34 x 26	Foolscap	17 x $13\frac{1}{2}$
Colombier	$34\frac{1}{2}$ x $23\frac{1}{2}$	Double Foolscap	$26\frac{1}{2}$ x $16\frac{1}{2}$
Imperial	30 x 22	Double Post	$30\frac{1}{2}$ x 19
Elephant	28 x 23	Double Large Post	33 x 21
Cartridge	26 x 21	Double Demy	31 x 20
Super Royal	27 x 19	Brief	16 x $13\frac{1}{4}$
Royal	24 x 19	Pott	15 x $12\frac{1}{2}$
Medium	22 x $17\frac{1}{2}$		
Large Post	21 x $16\frac{1}{2}$		

INTERNATIONAL PAPER SIZES

The basis of the international series of paper sizes is a rectangle having an area of one square metre, the sides of which are in the proportion of $1:\sqrt{2}$. The proportions $1:\sqrt{2}$ have a geometrical relationship, the side and diagonal of any square being in this proportion. The effect of this arrangement is that if the area of the sheet of paper is doubled or halved, the shorter side and the longer side of the new sheet are still in the same proportion $1:\sqrt{2}$. This feature is useful where photographic enlargement or reduction is used, as the proportions remain the same.

Description of the A series is by capital A followed by a figure. The basic size has the description A0 and the higher the figure following the letter, the greater is the number of sub-divisions and therefore the smaller the sheet. Half A0 is A1 and half A1 is A2. Where larger dimensions are required the A is preceded by a figure. Thus 2A means twice the size A0; 4A is four times the size of A0.

SUBSIDIARY SERIES

B sizes are sizes intermediate between any two adjacent sizes of the A series. There is a series of C sizes which is used much less. A is for magazines and books, B for posters, wall charts and other large items, C for envelopes particularly where it is necessary for an envelope (in C series) to fit into another envelope. The size recommended for business correspondence is A4.

Long sizes (DL) are obtainable by dividing any appropriate sizes from the two series above into three, four or eight equal parts parallel with the shorter side in such a manner that the proportion of $1:\sqrt{2}$ is not maintained, the ratio between the longer and the shorter sides being greater than $\sqrt{2}:1$. In practice long sizes should be produced from the A series only.

It is an essential feature of these series that the dimensions are of the trimmed or finished size.

A SERIES

	mm		*mm*
A0	841 x 1189	A6	105 x 148
A1	594 x 841	A7	74 x 105
A2	420 x 594	A8	52 x 74
A3	297 x 420	A9	37 x 52
A4	210 x 297	A10	26 x 37
A5	148 x 210		

B SERIES

	mm		*mm*
B0	1000 x 1414	B6	125 x 176
B1	707 x 1000	B7	88 x 125
B2	500 x 707	B8	62 x 88
B3	353 x 500	B9	44 x 62
B4	250 x 353	B10	31 x 44
B5	176 x 250		

C SERIES		DL	
	mm		*mm*
C4	324 x 229	DL	110 x 220
C5	229 x 162		
C6	114 x 162		

BOUND BOOKS

The book sizes most commonly used are listed below. Approximate centimetre equivalents are also shown. International sizes are converted to their nearest imperial size, e.g. A4 = D4; A5 = D8.

		inches	*cm*
Crown 32mo	C32	$2\frac{1}{2}$ x $3\frac{3}{4}$	6 x 9
Crown 16mo	C16	$3\frac{3}{4}$ x 5	9 x 13
Foolscap 8vo	F8	$4\frac{1}{4}$ x $6\frac{3}{4}$	11 x 17
Demy 16mo	D16	$4\frac{3}{8}$ x $5\frac{5}{8}$	11 x 14
Crown 8vo	C8	5 x $7\frac{1}{2}$	13 x 19
Demy 8vo	D8	$5\frac{5}{8}$ x $8\frac{3}{4}$	14 x 22
Medium 8vo	M8	$5\frac{3}{4}$ x 9	15 x 23
Royal 8vo	R8	$6\frac{1}{4}$ x 10	16 x 25
Super Royal 8vo	suR8	$6\frac{3}{4}$ x 10	17 x 25
Foolscap 4to	F4	$6\frac{3}{4}$ x $8\frac{1}{2}$	17 x 22
Crown 4to	C4	$7\frac{1}{2}$ x 10	19 x 25
Imperial 8vo	Imp8	$7\frac{1}{2}$ x 11	19 x 28
Demy 4to	D4	$8\frac{3}{4}$ x $11\frac{1}{4}$	22 x 29
Royal 4to	R4	10 x $12\frac{1}{2}$	25 x 31
Super Royal 4to	suR4	10 x $13\frac{1}{2}$	25 x 34
Crown Folio	Cfol	10 x 15	25 x 38
Imperial Folio	Impfol	11 x 15	28 x 38

Folio = a sheet folded in half
Quarto (4to) = a sheet folded into four
Octavo (8vo) = a sheet folded into eight
Books are usually bound up in sheets of 16, 32 or 64 pages. Octavo books are generally printed 64 pages at a time, 32 pages on each side of a sheet of quad.

CONVERSION TABLES FOR WEIGHTS AND MEASURES

Bold figures equal units of either of the columns beside them; thus: 1 cm = 0.394 inches and 1 inch = 2.540 cm

LENGTH			AREA			VOLUME			WEIGHT (MASS)		
Centimetres		Inches	Square cm		Square in	Cubic cm		Cubic in	Kilograms		Pounds
2.540	1	0.394	6.452	1	0.155	16.387	1	0.061	0.454	1	2.205
5.080	2	0.787	12.903	2	0.310	32.774	2	0.122	0.907	2	4.409
7.620	3	1.181	19.355	3	0.465	49.161	3	0.183	1.361	3	6.614
10.160	4	1.575	25.806	4	0.620	65.548	4	0.244	1.814	4	8.819
12.700	5	1.969	32.258	5	0.775	81.936	5	0.305	2.268	5	11.023
15.240	6	2.362	38.710	6	0.930	98.323	6	0.366	2.722	6	13.228
17.780	7	2.756	45.161	7	1.085	114.710	7	0.427	3.175	7	15.432
20.320	8	3.150	51.613	8	1.240	131.097	8	0.488	3.629	8	17.637
22.860	9	3.543	58.064	9	1.395	147.484	9	0.549	4.082	9	19.842
25.400	10	3.937	64.516	10	1.550	163.871	10	0.610	4.536	10	22.046
50.800	20	7.874	129.032	20	3.100	327.742	20	1.220	9.072	20	44.092
76.200	30	11.811	193.548	30	4.650	491.613	30	1.831	13.608	30	66.139
101.600	40	15.748	258.064	40	6.200	655.484	40	2.441	18.144	40	88.185
127.000	50	19.685	322.580	50	7.750	819.355	50	3.051	22.680	50	110.231
152.400	60	23.622	387.096	60	9.300	983.226	60	3.661	27.216	60	132.277
177.800	70	27.559	451.612	70	10.850	1147.097	70	4.272	31.752	70	154.324
203.200	80	31.496	516.128	80	12.400	1310.968	80	4.882	36.287	80	176.370
228.600	90	35.433	580.644	90	13.950	1474.839	90	5.492	40.823	90	198.416
254.000	100	39.370	645.160	100	15.500	1638.710	100	6.102	45.359	100	220.464

Metres		Yards	Square m		Square yd	Cubic m		Cubic yd	Metric tonnes		Tons (UK)
0.914	1	1.094	0.836	1	1.196	0.765	1	1.308	1.016	1	0.984
1.829	2	2.187	1.672	2	2.392	1.529	2	2.616	2.032	2	1.968
2.743	3	3.281	2.508	3	3.588	2.294	3	3.924	3.048	3	2.953
3.658	4	4.374	3.345	4	4.784	3.058	4	5.232	4.064	4	3.937
4.572	5	5.468	4.181	5	5.980	3.823	5	6.540	5.080	5	4.921
5.486	6	6.562	5.017	6	7.176	4.587	6	7.848	6.096	6	5.905
6.401	7	7.655	5.853	7	8.372	5.352	7	9.156	7.112	7	6.889
7.315	8	8.749	6.689	8	9.568	6.116	8	10.464	8.128	8	7.874
8.230	9	9.843	7.525	9	10.764	6.881	9	11.772	9.144	9	8.858
9.144	10	10.936	8.361	10	11.960	7.646	10	13.080	10.161	10	9.842
18.288	20	21.872	16.723	20	23.920	15.291	20	26.159	20.321	20	19.684
27.432	30	32.808	25.084	30	35.880	22.937	30	39.239	30.481	30	29.526
36.576	40	43.745	33.445	40	47.840	30.582	40	52.318	40.642	40	39.368
45.720	50	54.681	41.806	50	59.799	38.228	50	65.398	50.802	50	49.210
54.864	60	65.617	50.168	60	71.759	45.873	60	78.477	60.963	60	59.052
64.008	70	76.553	58.529	70	83.719	53.519	70	91.557	71.123	70	68.894
73.152	80	87.489	66.890	80	95.679	61.164	80	104.636	81.284	80	78.737
82.296	90	98.425	75.251	90	107.639	68.810	90	117.716	91.444	90	88.579
91.440	100	109.361	83.613	100	119.599	76.455	100	130.795	101.605	100	98.421

Kilometres		Miles	Hectares		Acres	Litres		Gallons	Metric tonnes		Tons (US)
1.609	1	0.621	0.405	1	2.471	4.546	1	0.220	0.907	1	1.102
3.219	2	1.243	0.809	2	4.942	9.092	2	0.440	1.814	2	2.205
4.828	3	1.864	1.214	3	7.413	13.638	3	0.660	2.722	3	3.305
6.437	4	2.485	1.619	4	9.844	18.184	4	0.880	3.629	4	4.409
8.047	5	3.107	2.023	5	12.355	22.730	5	1.100	4.536	5	5.521
9.656	6	3.728	2.428	6	14.826	27.276	6	1.320	5.443	6	6.614
11.265	7	4.350	2.833	7	17.297	31.822	7	1.540	6.350	7	7.716
12.875	8	4.971	3.327	8	19.769	36.368	8	1.760	7.257	8	8.818
14.484	9	5.592	3.642	9	22.240	40.914	9	1.980	8.165	9	9.921
16.093	10	6.214	4.047	10	24.711	45.460	10	2.200	9.072	10	11.023
32.187	20	12.427	8.094	20	49.421	90.919	20	4.400	18.144	20	22.046
48.280	30	18.641	12.140	30	74.132	136.379	30	6.599	27.216	30	33.069
64.374	40	24.855	16.187	40	98.842	181.839	40	8.799	36.287	40	44.092
80.467	50	31.069	20.234	50	123.555	227.298	50	10.999	45.359	50	55.116
96.561	60	37.282	24.281	60	148.263	272.758	60	13.199	54.431	60	66.139
112.654	70	43.496	28.328	70	172.974	318.217	70	15.398	63.503	70	77.162
128.748	80	49.710	32.375	80	197.684	363.677	80	17.598	72.575	80	88.185
144.841	90	55.923	36.422	90	222.395	409.137	90	19.798	81.647	90	99.208
160.934	100	62.137	40.469	100	247.105	454.596	100	21.998	90.719	100	110.231

ABBREVIATIONS AND ACRONYMS

AA   Alcoholics Anonymous
     Automobile Association
AAA   Amateur Athletic Association
ABA   Amateur Boxing Association
abbr(ev)   abbreviation
ABM   Anti-ballistic missile
abr   abridged
ac   alternating current
a/c   account
AC   (*Ante Christum*) Before Christ
     Companion, Order of
     Australia
ACAS   Advisory, Conciliation and
     Arbitration Service
ACT   Australian Capital Territory
AD   (*Anno Domini*) In the year of
     our Lord
ADB   Asian Development Bank
ADC   Aide-de-Camp
ADC (P)   Personal ADC to The Queen
adj   Adjective
Adj   Adjutant
ad lib   (*ad libitum*) at pleasure
Adm   Admiral
     Admission
adv   Adverb
AE   Air Efficiency Award
AEM   Air Efficiency Medal
AFC   Air Force Cross
AFM   Air Force Medal
AG   Adjutant-General
     Attorney-General
AGM   air-to-ground missile
     annual general meeting
AH   (*Anno Hegirae*) In the year of
     the Hegira
AI   Artificial intelligence
AIDS   Acquired immune deficiency
     syndrome
AIM   Alternative Investment Market
alt   Altitude
am   (*ante meridiem*) before noon
AM   (*Anno mundi*) In the year of the
     world
amp   ampere
     amplifier
AMU   Arab Maghreb Union
ANC   African National Congress
anon   anonymous
ANZAC   Australian and New Zealand
     Army Corps
AO   Air Officer
     Officer, Order of Australia
AOC   Air Officer Commanding
AONB   Area of Outstanding Natural
     Beauty
APEC   Asia Pacific Economic Co-
     operation
APR   annual percentage rate
AS   Anglo-Saxon
ASA   Advertising Standards
     Authority
     Amateur Swimming
     Association
asap   as soon as possible
ASB   Alternative Service Book

ASEAN   Association of South East
     Asian Nations
ASH   Action on Smoking and
     Health
ASLEF   Associated Society of
     Locomotive Engineers and
     Firemen
ASLIB   Association for Information
     Management
ATC   Air Training Corps
AUC   (*ab urbe condita*) In the year
     from the foundation of Rome
     (*anno urbis conditae*) In the year
     of the founding of the city
AUT   Association of University
     Teachers
AV   Audio-visual
     Authorised Version (*of Bible*)
AVR   Army Volunteer Reserve
AWOL   Absent without leave
b   born
     bowled
BA   Bachelor of Arts
BAA   British Airports Authority
     British Astronomical
     Association
BAF   British Athletics Federation
BAFTA   British Academy of Film and
     Television Arts
BAS   Bachelor in Agricultural
     Science
     British Antarctic Survey
BBC   British Broadcasting
     Corporation
BBSRC   Biotechnology and Biological
     Sciences Research Council
BC   Before Christ
     Borough Council
     British Columbia
BCh (D)   Bachelor of (Dental) Surgery
BCL   Bachelor of Civil Law
BCom   Bachelor of Commerce
BD   Bachelor of Divinity
BDA   British Dental Association
BDS   Bachelor of Dental Surgery
BEd   Bachelor of Education
BEM   British Empire Medal
BEng   Bachelor of Engineering
BFI   British Film Institute
BFPO   British Forces Post Office
BLitt   Bachelor of Letters *or* of
     Literature
BM   Bachelor of Medicine
     British Museum
BMA   British Medical Association
BMus   Bachelor of Music
BNFL   British Nuclear Fuels Ltd
BOTB   British Overseas Trade Board
Bp   Bishop
BPharm   Bachelor of Pharmacy
BPhil   Bachelor of Philosophy
bpm   beats per minute
Br(it)   Britain
     British
Brig   Brigadier
BSc   Bachelor of Science

BSE   Bovine spongiform
     encephalopathy
BSI   British Standards Institution
BST   British Summer Time
Bt   Baronet
BTEC   Business and Technology
     Education Council
BTh   Bachelor of Theology
Btu   British thermal unit
BVMS   Bachelor of Veterinary
     Medicine and Surgery
c   (*circa*) about
C   Celsius
     Centigrade
     Conservative
CA   Chartered Accountant
     (*Scotland*)
CAA   Civil Aviation Authority
CAB   Citizens' Advice Bureau
CADW   Ancient Monuments Board for
     Wales
Cantab   (of) Cambridge
Cantuar: of Canterbury (*Archbishop*)
CAP   Common Agricultural Policy
Capt   Captain
Caricom   Caribbean Community and
     Common Market
Carliol: of Carlisle (*Bishop*)
CB   Companion, Order of the
     Bath
CBE   Commander, Order of the
     British Empire
CBI   Confederation of British
     Industry
CBSS   Council of the Baltic Sea
     States
CC   Chamber of Commerce
     Companion, Order of Canada
     City Council
     County Council
     County Court
CCC   County Cricket Club
CCF   Combined Cadet Force
CCTA   City Colleges for Technology
     and the Arts
CChem   Chartered Chemist
CD   Civil Defence
     compact disc
     Corps Diplomatique
Cdr   Commander
Cdre   Commodore
CDS   Chief of the Defence Staff
CE   Christian Era
     Civil Engineer
CEng   Chartered Engineer
CERN   European Organisation for
     Nuclear Research
Cestr: of Chester (*Bishop*)
CET   Central European Time
     Common External Tariff
cf   (*confer*) compare
CF   Chaplain to the Forces
CFC   Chlorofluorocarbon
CGC   Conspicuous Gallantry Cross
Cgeol   Chartered Geologist
CGI   Computer generated imagery

CGM   Conspicuous Gallantry Medal
CGS   Centimetre-gramme-second
       (*system*)
       Chief of General Staff
CH   Companion of Honour
ChB/M Bachelor/Master of Surgery
CI   Channel Islands
       The Imperial Order of the
       Crown of India
CIA   Central Intelligence Agency
CICA   Conference on International
       and Confidence Building
       Measures in Asia
       Criminal Injuries
       Compensation Authority
CICAP Criminal Injuries
       Compensation Appeals Panel
Cicestr: of Chichester (*Bishop*)
CID   Criminal Investigation
       Department
CIE   Companion, Order of the
       Indian Empire
cif   cost, insurance and freight
C-in-C Commander-in-Chief
CIPFA Chartered Institute of Public
       Finance and Accountancy
CIS   Commonwealth of
       Independent States
CJD   Creutzfeld-Jakob disease
CLit   Companion of Literature
CLJ   Commander, Order of St
       Lazarus of Jerusalem
CM   (*Chirurgiae Magister*) Master of
       Surgery
CMG   Companion, Order of
       St Michael and St George
CND   Campaign for Nuclear
       Disarmament
c/o   care of
CO   Commanding Officer
C of E Church of England
COI   Central Office of Information
Col   Colonel
Con   Conservative
cons   consecrated
Cpl   Corporal
CPM   Colonial Police Medal
CPRE   Council for the Protection of
       Rural England
CPS   Crown Prosecution Service
CPVE   Certificate of Pre-Vocational
       Education
CRE   Commission for Racial
       Equality
CSA   Child Support Agency
CSE   Certificate of Secondary
       Education
CSI   Companion, Order of the Star
       of India
CTC   City Technology College
CVO   Commander, Royal Victorian
       Order

d   (*denarius*) penny
DBE   Dame Commander, Order of
       the British Empire
dc   direct current
DC   District Council
       District of Columbia
DCB   Dame Commander, Order of
       the Bath

D Ch   (*Doctor Chirurgiae*) Doctor of
       Surgery
DCL   Doctor of Civil Law
DCM   Distinguished Conduct Medal
DCMG   Dame Commander, Order of
       St Michael and St George
DCMS   Department for Culture,
       Media and Sport
DCVO   Dame Commander, Royal
       Victorian Order
DD   Doctor of Divinity
DDS   Doctor of Dental Surgery
DDT   dichlorodiphenyl
       trichloroethane
del   (*delineavit*) he/she drew it
DEFRA Department of the
       Environment, Food and Rural
       Affairs
DFC   Distinguished Flying Cross
DfES   Department for Education and
       Skills
DFID   Department for International
       Development
DFM   Distinguished Flying Medal
DfT   Department for Transport
DG   (*Dei gratia*) By the grace of
       God
DH   Department of Health
DHA   District Health Authority
Dip Ed Diploma in Education
Dip HE Diploma in Higher Education
Dip Tech Diploma in Technology
DJ   Disc jockey
DL   Deputy Lieutenant
DLitt Doctor of Letters *or* of
       Literature
DM   Deutsche Mark
DMus   Doctor of Music
DNA   deoxyribonucleic acid
DNB   *Dictionary of National
       Biography*
do   (*ditto*) the same
DoH   Department of Health
DOS   Disk operating system
DoT   Department of Transport
DP   Data processing
DPh *or* Doctor of Philosophy
DPhil
DPP   Director of Public
       Prosecutions
Dr   Doctor
DRC   Disability Rights Commission
DSc   Doctor of Science
DSC   Distinguished Service Cross
DSM   Distinguished Service Medal
DSO   Companion, Distinguished
       Service Order
DTI   Department of Trade and
       Industry
DTP   Desk-top publishing
Dunelm: of Durham (*Bishop*)
DV   (*Deo volente*) God willing
DVD   Digital Versatile Disc
DVLA   Driver and Vehicle Licensing
       Agency
DWI   Drinking Water Inspectorate
DWP   Department for Work and
       Pensions

E   East
Ebor: of York (*Archbishop*)

EBRD   European Bank for
       Reconstruction and
       Development
EC   European Community
ECG   Electrocardiogram
ECGD   Export Credits Guarantee
       Department
ECOWAS Economic Community of
       West African States
ECSC   European Coal and Steel
       Community
ECU   European Currency Unit
ED   Efficiency Decoration
EEC   European Economic
       Community
EEG   Electroencephalogram
EFA   European Fighter Aircraft
EFTA   European Free Trade
       Association
eg   (*exempli gratia*) for the sake of
       example
EIB   European Investment Bank
EMS   European Monetary System
EMU   European Monetary Union
EOC   Equal Opportunities
       Commission
EPSRC Engineering and Physical
       Sciences Research Council
ER   (*Elizabetha Regina*) Queen
       Elizabeth
ERM   Exchange Rate Mechanism
ERNIE Electronic random number
       indicator equipment
ESA   European Space Agency
ESP   Extra-sensory perception
ESRC   Economic and Social Research
       Council
ETA   *Euzkadi ta Askatasuna* (Basque
       separatist organisation)
et al (*et alibi*) and elsewhere
       (*et alii*) and others
etc   (*et cetera*) and the other
       things/and so forth
et seq (*et sequentia*) and the following
EU   European Union
Euratom European Atomic Energy
       Commission
Exon: of Exeter (*Bishop*)

f   (*forte*) loud
F   Fahrenheit
       Fellow of
FA   Football Association
FANY   First Aid Nursing Yeomanry
FAO   Food and Agriculture
       Organisation (*UN*)
       For the attention of
FAQ   Frequently asked question
FBA   Fellow, British Academy
FBAA   Fellow, British Association of
       Accountants and Auditors
FBI   Federal Bureau of
       Investigation
FBU   Fire Brigades Union
FCO   Foreign and Commonwealth
       Office
FIMgt Fellow, Institute of
       Management
FBS   Fellow, Botanical Society
FC   Football Club

FCA	Fellow, Institute of Chartered Accountants in England and Wales	FIS	Fellow, Institute of Statisticians	FRICS	Fellow, Royal Institution of Chartered Surveyors
FCCA	Fellow, Chartered Association of Certified Accountants	FJI	Fellow, Institute of Journalists	FRMetS	Fellow, Royal Meteorological Society
FCGI	Fellow, City and Guilds of London Institute	fl	(*floruit*) flourished	FRMS	Fellow, Royal Microscopical Society
FCIA	Fellow, Corporation of Insurance Agents	FLA	Fellow, Library Association	FRNS	Fellow, Royal Numismatic Society
FCIArb	Fellow, Chartered Institute of Arbitrators	FLS	Fellow, Linnaean Society	FRPharmS	Fellow, Royal Pharmaceutical Society
FCIB	Fellow, Chartered Institute of Bankers	FM	Field Marshal frequency modulation	FRPS	Fellow, Royal Photographic Society
	Fellow, Corporation of Insurance Brokers	fo	folio		
FCIBSE	Fellow, Chartered Institution of Building Services Engineers	FO	Flying Officer	FRS	Fellow, Royal Society
		fob	free on board	FRSA	Fellow, Royal Society of Arts
		FPhS	Fellow, Philosophical Society	FRSC	Fellow, Royal Society of Chemistry
FCII	Fellow, Chartered Insurance Institute	FRAD	Fellow, Royal Academy of Dancing	FRSE	Fellow, Royal Society of Edinburgh
FCIPS	Fellow, Chartered Institute of Purchasing and Supply	FRAeS	Fellow, Royal Aeronautical Society	FRSH	Fellow, Royal Society of Health
FCIS	Fellow, Institute of Chartered Secretaries and Administrators	FRAI	Fellow, Royal Anthropological Institute	FRSL	Fellow, Royal Society of Literature
FCIT	Fellow, Chartered Institute of Transport	FRAM	Fellow, Royal Academy of Music	FRTPI	Fellow, Royal Town Planning Institute
FCMA	Fellow, Chartered Institute of Management Accountants	FRAS	Fellow, Royal Asiatic Society Fellow, Royal Astronomical Society	FSA	Fellow, Society of Antiquaries Financial Services Authority Food Standards Agency
FCO	Foreign and Commonwealth Office	FRBS	Fellow, Royal Botanic Society Fellow, Royal Society of British Sculptors	FSS	Fellow, Royal Statistical Society
FCP	Fellow, College of Preceptors	FRCA	Fellow, Royal College of Anaesthetists	FSVA	Fellow, Incorporated Society of Valuers and Auctioneers
FD	(*Fidei Defensor*) Defender of the Faith	FRCGP	Fellow, Royal College of General Practitioners	FT	*Financial Times*
FE	Further Education	FRCM	Fellow, Royal College of Music	FTI	Fellow, Textile Institute
fec	(*fecit*) made this	FRCO	Fellow, Royal College of Organists	FTII	Fellow, Chartered Institute of Taxation
ff	(*fecerunt*) made this (*pl*) folios following	FRCOG	Fellow, Royal College of Obstetricians and Gynaecologists	FZS	Fellow, Zoological Society
ff	(*fortissimo*) very loud	FRCP	Fellow, Royal College of Physicians, London	GATT	General Agreement on Tariffs and Trade
FFA	Fellow, Faculty of Actuaries (*Scotland*)	FRCPath	Fellow, Royal College of Pathologists	GBE	Dame/Knight Grand Cross, Order of the British Empire
	Fellow, Institute of Financial Accountants	FRCPE *or* FRCPEd	Fellow, Royal College of Physicians, Edinburgh	GC	George Cross
FFAS	Fellow, Faculty of Architects and Surveyors	FRCPI	Fellow, Royal College of Physicians, Ireland	GCB	Dame/Knight Grand Cross, Order of the Bath
FFCM	Fellow, Faculty of Community Medicine	FRCPsych	Fellow, Royal College of Psychiatrists	GCC	Gulf Co-operation Council
FFPHM	Fellow, Faculty of Public Health Medicine	FRCR	Fellow, Royal College of Radiologists	GCE	General Certificate of Education
FGS	Fellow, Geological Society	FRCS	Fellow, Royal College of Surgeons of England	GCHQ	Government Communications Headquarters
FHS	Fellow, Heraldry Society	FRCSE *or* FRCSEd	Fellow, Royal College of Surgeons of Edinburgh	GCIE	Knight Grand Commander, Order of the Indian Empire
FHSM	Fellow, Institute of Health Service Management	FRCSGlas	Fellow, Royal College of Physicians and Surgeons of Glasgow	GCLJ	Knight Grand Cross, Order of St Lazarus of Jerusalem
FIA	Fellow, Institute of Actuaries			GCMG	Dame/Knight Grand Cross, Order of St Michael and St George
FIBiol	Fellow, Institute of Biology	FRCSI	Fellow, Royal College of Surgeons in Ireland		
FICE	Fellow, Institution of Civil Engineers	FRCVS	Fellow, Royal College of Veterinary Surgeons	GCSE	General Certificate of Secondary Education
FICS	Fellow, Institution of Chartered Shipbrokers	FREconS	Fellow, Royal Economic Society	GCSI	Knight Grand Commander, Order of the Star of India
FIEE	Fellow, Institution of Electrical Engineers	FREng	Fellow, Royal Academy of Engineering	GCVO	Dame/Knight Grand Cross, Royal Victorian Order
FIERE	Fellow, Institution of Electronic and Radio Engineers	FRGS	Fellow, Royal Geographical Society	GDP	Gross domestic product
				Gen	General
FIFA	International Association Football Federation	FRHistS	Fellow, Royal Historical Society	GHQ	General Headquarters
FIM	Fellow, Institute of Metals			GLA	Greater London Authority
FIMM	Fellow, Institution of Mining and Metallurgy	FRHS	Fellow, Royal Horticultural Society	GM	George Medal genetically modified
FInstF	Fellow, Institute of Fuel	FRIBA	Fellow, Royal Institute of British Architects	GMB	General, Municipal, Boilermakers and Allied Trades Union
FInstP	Fellow, Institute of Physics				
FIQS	Fellow, Institute of Quantity Surveyors			GMT	Greenwich Mean Time

GNP	Gross national product	ICJ	International Court of Justice	KCB	Knight Commander, Order of
GNVQ	General National Vocational	ICRC	International Committee of		the Bath
	Qualification		the Red Cross	KCIE	Knight Commander, Order of
GOC	General Officer Commanding	id	(*idem*) the same		the Indian Empire
GP	General Practitioner	IDA	International Development	KCLJ	Knight Commander, Order of
Gp Capt	Group Captain		Association		St Lazarus of Jerusalem
GSA	Girls' Schools Association	IDD	International direct dialling	KCMG	Knight Commander, Order of
GST	Greenwich Sidereal Time	ie	(*id est*) that is		St Michael and St George
		IEA	International Energy Agency	KCSI	Knight Commander, Order of
HAC	Honourable Artillery	IFA	Independent Financial		the Star of India
	Company		Advisor	KCVO	Knight Commander, Royal
HB	His Beatitude	IFAD	International Fund for		Victorian Order
HBM	Her/His Britannic Majesty('s)		Agricultural Development	KG	Knight of the Garter
HCF	Highest common factor	IFC	International Finance	KGB	(*Komitet Gosudarstvennoi*
	Honorary Chaplain to the		Corporation		*Bezopasnosti*) Committee of
	Forces	IHS	(*Iesus Hominum Salvator*) Jesus		State Security (*USSR*)
HE	Her/His Excellency		the Saviour of Mankind	kHz	kiloHertz
	Higher Education	ILO	International Labour	KLJ	Knight, Order of St Lazarus
	His Eminence		Office/Organisation		of Jerusalem
HGV	Heavy Goods Vehicle	ILR	Independent local radio	ko	knock out (*boxing*)
HH	Her/His Highness	IMF	International Monetary Fund	KP	Knight, Order of St Patrick
	Her/His Honour	IMO	International Maritime	KStJ	Knight, Order of St John of
	His Holiness		Organisation		Jerusalem
HIM	Her/His Imperial Majesty	Inc	Incorporated	Kt	Knight
HIV	Human immunodeficiency	incog	(*incognito*) unknown,	KT	Knight of the Thistle
	virus		unrecognised	kV	Kilovolt
HJS	(*hic jacet sepultus*) here lies	INLA	Irish National Liberation	kW	Kilowatt
	buried		Army	kWh	Kilowatt hour
HM	Her/His Majesty('s)	in loc	(*in loco*) in its place		
HMAS	Her/His Majesty's Australian	Inmarsat	International Maritime	L	Liberal
	Ship		Satellite Organisation	Lab	Labour
HMC	Headmasters' Conference	INRI	(*Iesus Nazarenus Rex*	Lat	Latitude
HMI	Her/His Majesty's Inspector		*Iudaeorum*) Jesus of Nazareth,	lbw	leg before wicket
HML	Her/His Majesty's Lieutenant		King of the Jews	lc	lower case (*printing*)
HMS	Her/His Majesty's Ship	inst	(*instant*) current month	LCJ	Lord Chief Justice
HMSO	Her/His Majesty's Stationery	Intelsat	International	LCM	Least/lowest common
	Office		Telecommunications Satellite		multiple
HNC	Higher National Certificate		Organisation	LD	Liberal Democrat
HND	Higher National Diploma	Interpol	International Criminal Police	LDS	Licentiate in Dental Surgery
HOLMES	Home Office Large Major		Organisation	LEA	Local Education Authority
	Enquiry System	IOC	International Olympic	LHD	(*Literarum Humaniorum Doctor*)
Hon	Honorary		Committee		Doctor of Humane
	Honourable	IOM	Isle of Man		Letters/Literature
hp	horse power	IOU	I owe you	Lib	Liberal
HP	Hire purchase	IOW	Isle of Wight	Lic	(*Licenciado*) lawyer (*Spanish*)
HQ	Headquarters	IQ	Intelligence quotient	Lic Med	Licentiate in Medicine
HR	Human resources	IRA	Irish Republican Army	Lit	Literary
HRH	Her/His Royal Highness	IRC	International Red Cross	Lit Hum	(*Literae Humaniores*) Faculty of
HRT	hormone replacement therapy	Is	Islands		classics and philosophy,
HSE	Health and Safety Executive	ISA	Individual Savings Account		Oxford
	(*hic sepultus est*) here lies buried	ISBN	International Standard Book	Litt D	Doctor of Letters
HSH	Her/His Serene Highness		Number	LJ	Lord Justice
HST	Hubble Space Telescope	ISO	Imperial Service Order	LLB	Bachelor of Laws
HWM	High water mark		International Standards	LLD	Doctor of Laws
			Organisation	LLM	Master of Laws
I	Island	ISSN	International Standard Serial	LM	Licentiate in Midwifery
IAAS	Incorporated Association of		Number	LMS	Local management in schools
	Architects and Surveyors	IT	Information Technology	LMSSA	Licentiate in Medicine and
IAEA	International Atomic Energy	ITC	Independent Television		Surgery, Society of
	Agency		Commission		Apothecaries
IATA	International Air Transport	ITN	Independent Television News	loc cit	(*loco citato*) in the place cited
	Association	ITU	International	log	logarithm
ibid	(*ibidem*) in the same place		Telecommunication Union	Londin:	of London (*Bishop*)
IBRD	International Bank for	ITV	Independent Television	Long	Longitude
	Reconstruction and	IVF	in vitro fertilisation	LRT	London Regional Transport
	Development			LS	(*loco sigilli*) place of the seal
ICAO	International Civil Aviation	J	Judge	LSA	Licentiate of Society of
	Organisation		Justice		Apothecaries
ICBM	Inter-continental ballistic	JP	Justice of the Peace	LSC	Learning and Skills Council
	missile				Legal Services Commission
ICFTU	International Confederation of	KBE	Knight Commander, Order of	Lsd	(*Librae, solidi, denarii*) £,
	Free Trade Unions		the British Empire		shillings and pence

LSE	London School of Economics and Political Science	MV	Merchant Vessel Motor Vessel	OAP OAPEC	old age pension(er) Organisation of Arab Petroleum Exporting Countries
LST	Local Sidereal Time	MVO	Member, Royal Victorian Order		
Lt	Lieutenant				
LTA	Lawn Tennis Association	MW	medium wave	OAS	Organisation of American States
Ltd	Limited (liability)	MWA	Member of the Welsh Assembly		
LTh or				OAU	Organisation of African Unity
L Theol	Licentiate in Theology			Ob or	
LVO	Lieutenant, Royal Victorian Order	N	North	obit	died
		n/a	not applicable	OBE	Officer, Order of the British Empire
LW	long wave		not available		
LWM	Low water mark	NAAFI	Navy, Army and Air Force Institutes	OC	Officer Commanding
				ODA	Overseas Development Administration
M	Member of Monsieur	NAFTA	North American Free Trade Agreement		
				ODPM	Office of the Deputy Prime Minister
MA	Master of Arts	NASA	National Aeronautics and Space Administration		
Maj	Major			OE	Old English
max	maximum	NASUWT	National Association of Schoolmasters/Union of Women Teachers		omissions excepted
MB	Bachelor of Medicine			OECD	Organisation for Economic Co-operation and Development
MBA	Master of Business Administration				
		NATO	North Atlantic Treaty Organisation		
MBC	Metropolitan Borough Council			OED	*Oxford English Dictionary*
		NB	New Brunswick	Ofcom	Office of Communications
MBE	Member, Order of the British Empire		(nota bene) note well	Ofgem	Office of Gas and Electricity Markets
		NCIS	National Criminal Intelligence Service		
MC	Master of Ceremonies Military Cross			OFM	Order of Friars Minor (*Franciscans*)
		NCO	Non-commissioned officer		
MCC	Marylebone Cricket Club	NDPB	Non-departmental public body	Ofreg	Office for the Regulation of Electricity and Gas
MCh(D)	Master of (Dental) Surgery				
MD	Managing Director Doctor of Medicine	NEB	New English Bible	Ofsted	Office for Standards in Education
		nem con	(*nemine contradicente*) no one contradicting		
MDS	Master of Dental Surgery			OFT	Office of Fair Trading
ME	Middle English Myalgic Encephalomyelitis	NERC	Natural Environment Research Council	Oftel	Office of Telecommunications
				Ofwat	Office of Water Services
MEC	Member of Executive Council	nes	not elsewhere specified	OHMS	On Her/His Majesty's Service
MEd	Master of Education	NESTA	National Endowment for Science, Technology and the Arts	ohp	overhead projector
mega	one million times			OIC	Organisation of the Islamic Conference
MEP	Member of the European Parliament				
		NFT	National Film Theatre	OM	Order of Merit
MFH	Master of Foxhounds	NFU	National Farmers' Union	ONO	or near offer
Mgr	Monsignor	NHS	National Health Service	ONS	Office for National Statistics
MI	Military Intelligence	NI	National Insurance Northern Ireland	op	(*opus*) work
micro	one-millionth part			OP	Opposite prompt side (*of theatre*)
milli	one-thousandth part	No	(*numero*) number		
min	minimum	non seq	(*non sequitur*) it does not follow		Order of Preachers (*Dominicans*)
MLA	Member of Legislative Assembly				
		Norvic:	of Norwich (*Bishop*)		out of print (*books*)
MLC	Member of Legislative Council	NP	Notary Public	op cit	(*opere citato*) in the work cited
		NRA	National Rifle Association	OPEC	Organisation of Petroleum Exporting Countries
MLitt	Master of Letters	NS	New Style (*calendar*)		
Mlle	Mademoiselle		Nova Scotia	OPRAF	Office of Passenger Rail Franchising
MLR	Minimum lending rate	NSPCC	National Society for the Prevention of Cruelty to Children		
MM	Military Medal			OPS	Office of Public Service
Mme	Madame			ORR	Office of the Rail Regulator
MN	Merchant Navy	NSW	New South Wales	OS	Old Style (*calendar*) Ordnance Survey
MO	Medical Officer/Orderly	NT	National Theatre		
MoD	Ministry of Defence		National Trust	OSA	Order of St Augustine
MoT	Ministry of Transport		New Testament	OSB	Order of St Benedict
MP	Member of Parliament Military Police		Northern Territory	OSCE	Organisation for Security and Co-operation in Europe
		NUJ	National Union of Journalists		
mph	miles per hour	NUM	National Union of Mineworkers	O St J	Officer, Order of St John of Jerusalem
M Phil	Master of Philosophy				
MR	Master of the Rolls	NUS	National Union of Students	OT	Old Testament
MRC	Medical Research Council	NUT	National Union of Teachers	OTC	Officers' Training Corps
MS	Master of Surgery Manuscript (pl MSS) Multiple Sclerosis	NVQ	National Vocational Qualification	Oxon	(of) Oxford Oxfordshire
		NWT	Northwest Territory		
MSc	Master of Science	NY	New York		
MSP	Member of Scottish Parliament	NZ	New Zealand		
MTh	Master of Theology				
Mus B/D	Bachelor/Doctor of Music				

p page
p (*piano*) softly
PA Personal Assistant
Press Association
Public address (system)
PAYE Pay as You Earn
pc (*per centum*) in the hundred
PC personal computer
Police Constable
politically correct
Privy Counsellor
PCC Press Complaints Commission
PDA Personal digital assistant
PDSA People's Dispensary for Sick Animals
PE Physical Education
Petriburg: of Peterborough (*Bishop*)
PFI Private Finance Initiative
PG Parental Guidance
PGA Professional Golfers Association
PGCE Postgraduate Certificate of Education
PhD Doctor of Philosophy
PHLS Public Health Laboratory Service
PIF Pacific Islands Forum
pl Plural
PLA Port of London Authority
PLC Public Limited Company
PLO Palestine Liberation Organisation
pm (*post meridiem*) after noon
PM Prime Minister
Post mortem
PMRAFNS Princess Mary's Royal Air Force Nursing Service
PO Petty Officer
Pilot Officer
Post Office
postal order
POW Prisoner of War
pp Pages
(*per procurationem*) by proxy
PPARC Particle Physics and Astronomy Research Council
PPS Parliamentary Private Secretary
PR Proportional representation
Public relations
PRA President of the Royal Academy
Pres President
Pro tem (*pro tempore*) for the time being
Prox (*proximo*) next month
PRS President of the Royal Society
PRSE President of the Royal Society of Edinburgh
Ps Psalm
PS (*postscriptum*) postscript
PSBR Public sector borrowing requirement
psc passed Staff College
PSV Public Service Vehicle
PTA Parent-Teacher Association
Pte Private
PTO Please turn over
PVC Polyvinyl chloride

QARANC Queen Alexandra's Royal Army Nursing Corps

QARNNS Queen Alexandra's Royal Naval Nursing Service
QB(D) Queen's Bench (Division)
QC Queen's Counsel
QED (*quod erat demonstrandum*) which was to be proved
QGM Queen's Gallantry Medal
QHC Queen's Honorary Chaplain
QHDS Queen's Honorary Dental Surgeon
QHNS Queen's Honorary Nursing Sister
QHP Queen's Honorary Physician
QHS Queen's Honorary Surgeon
Qld Queensland
QMG Quartermaster General
QPM Queen's Police Medal
QS Quarter Sessions
QSO Quasi-stellar object (quasar)
Queen's Service Order
quango quasi-autonomous non-governmental organisation
qv (*quod vide*) which see

R (*Regina*) Queen
(*Rex*) King
RA Royal Academy/Academician
Royal Artillery
R&B rhythm and blues
R&D research and development
RAC Royal Armoured Corps
Royal Automobile Club
RADA Royal Academy of Dramatic Art
RADC Royal Army Dental Corps
RAE Royal Aerospace Establishment
RAEC Royal Army Educational Corps
RAeS Royal Aeronautical Society
RAF Royal Air Force
RAM Random-access memory
Royal Academy of Music
RAMC Royal Army Medical Corps
RAN Royal Australian Navy
RAOC Royal Army Ordnance Corps
RAPC Royal Army Pay Corps
RAVC Royal Army Veterinary Corps
RBG Royal Botanic Garden
RBS Royal Society of British Sculptors
RC Red Cross
Roman Catholic
RCM Royal College of Music
RCN Royal Canadian Navy
RCT Royal Corps of Transport
RD Refer to drawer (*banking*)
Royal Naval and Royal Marine Forces Reserve Decoration
Rural Dean
RDI Royal Designer for Industry
RE Religious Education
Royal Engineers
REM rapid eye movement
REME Royal Electrical and Mechanical Engineers
Rep Representative
Republican
Rev(d) Reverend
RFU Rugby Football Union
RGN Registered General Nurse

RGS Royal Geographical Society
RHA Regional Health Authority
RHS Royal Horticultural Society
RI Rhode Island
Royal Institute of Painters in Watercolours
Royal Institution
RIBA Royal Institute of British Architects
RIP (*Requiescat in pace*) May he/she rest in peace
RIR Royal Irish Regiment
RL Rugby League
RM Registered Midwife
Royal Marines
RMA Royal Military Academy
RMN Registered Mental Nurse
RMT National Union of Rail, Maritime and Transport Workers
RN Royal Navy
RNIB Royal National Institute for the Blind
RNID Royal National Institute for the Deaf
RNLI Royal National Lifeboat Institution
RNMH Registered Nurse for the Mentally Handicapped
RNR Royal Naval Reserve
RNVR Royal Naval Volunteer Reserve
RNXS Royal Naval Auxiliary Service
RNZN Royal New Zealand Navy
Ro (*Recto*) on the right-hand page
ROC Royal Observer Corps
Roffen: of Rochester (*Bishop*)
ROI Royal Institute of Oil Painters
ROM Read-only memory
RoSPA Royal Society for the Prevention of Accidents
RP Royal Society of Portrait Painters
RPA Rural Payments Agency
rpm revolutions per minute
RRC Lady of Royal Red Cross
RSA Royal Scottish Academician
Royal Society of Arts
RSC Royal Shakespeare Company
RSCN Registered Sick Children's Nurse
RSE Royal Society of Edinburgh
RSM Regimental Sergeant Major
RSPB Royal Society for the Protection of Birds
RSPCA Royal Society for the Prevention of Cruelty to Animals
RSV Revised Standard Version (*of Bible*)
RSVP (Répondez, s'il vous plaît) Please reply
RSW Royal Scottish Society of Painters in Watercolours
Rt Hon Right Honorable
RTPI Royal Town Planning Institute
RU Rugby Union
RUC Royal Ulster Constabulary
RV Revised Version (*of Bible*)
RWS Royal Water Colour Society
RYS Royal Yacht Squadron

s	second	TB	Tuberculosis
	(*solidus*) shilling	TCCB	Test and County Cricket
S	South		Board
SA	Salvation Army	TD	Territorial Efficiency
	South Africa		Decoration
	South America	TEC	Training and Enterprise
	South Australia		Council
SAARC	South Asian Association for	TEFL	Teaching English as a foreign
	Regional		language
	Co-operation	temp	Temperature
SAE	stamped addressed envelope		temporary employee
Salop	Shropshire	TES	*Times Educational Supplement*
SARS	Severe Acute Respiratory	T&G	Transport and General
	Syndrome		Workers' Union
Sarum:	of Salisbury (*Bishop*)	THES	*Times Higher Education*
SAS	Special Air Service Regiment		*Supplement*
SBS	Special Boat Squadron	TLS	*Times Literary Supplement*
	Small Business Service	TNT	trinitrotoluene (*explosive*)
ScD	Doctor of Science	*trans*	Translated
SCM	State Certified Midwife	trs	transpose (*printing*)
SDLP	Social Democratic and Labour	TRH	Their Royal Highnesses
	Party	TT	Tourist Trophy (*motorcycle*
SEAQ	Stock Exchange Automated		*races*)
	Quotations system		Tuberculin tested
SEN	Special Educational Needs	TUC	Trades Union Congress
	State Enrolled Nurse		
SERPS	State Earnings Related	U	Unionist
	Pension Scheme	UAE	United Arab Emirates
SFO	Serious Fraud Office	uc	upper case (*printing*)
SHMIS	Society of Headmasters and	UC	Unitary Council
	Headmistresses of	UCAS	Universities and Colleges
	Independent Schools		Admissions Service
SI	(*Système International d'Unités*)	UCATT	Union of Construction, Allied
	International System of Units		Trades and Technicians
	Statutory Instrument	UCL	University College London
sic	so written	UDA	Ulster Defence Association
Sig	Signature	UDI	Unilateral Declaration of
	Signor		Independence
SJ	Society of Jesus (Jesuits)	UDR	Ulster Defence Regiment
SLD	Social and Liberal Democrats	UEFA	Union of European Football
SMP	Statutory Maternity Pay		Associations
SNP	Scottish National Party	UFF	Ulster Freedom Fighters
SOE	Special Operations Executive	UFO	Unidentified flying object
SOS	Save Our Souls (*distress signal*)	UHF	ultra-high frequency
sp	(*sine prole*) without issue	UK	United Kingdom
spgr	specific gravity	UKAEA	UK Atomic Energy Authority
SRN	State Registered Nurse	UN	United Nations
SRO	Self Regulating Organisations	UNESCO	United Nations Educational,
SS	Saints		Scientific and Cultural
	Schutzstaffel (Nazi paramilitary		Organisation
	organisation)	UNHCR	United Nations High
	Steamship		Commissioner for Refugees
SSC	Solicitor before Supreme	UNICEF	United Nations Children's
	Court (*Scotland*)		Fund
SSN	Standard Serial Number	UNIDO	United Nations Industrial
SSP	Statutory Sick Pay		Development Organisation
SSSI	Site of special scientific	Unita	National Union for the Total
	interest		Independence of Angola
STD	(*Sacrae Theologiae Doctor*)	UNPO	Unrepresented Nations and
	Doctor of Sacred Theology		Peoples Organisation
	Subscriber trunk dialling	UPU	Universal Postal Union
	Sexually transmitted disease	US(A)	United States (of America)
stet	let it stand (*printing*)	USDAW	Union of Shop, Distributive
stp	Standard temperature and		and Allied Workers
	pressure	USM	Unlisted Securities Market
STP	(*Sacrae Theologiae Professor*)	USSR	Union of Soviet Socialist
	Professor of Sacred Theology		Republics
Sub Lt	Sub-Lieutenant	UTC	Co-ordinated Universal Time
SVQ	Scottish Vocational		system
	Qualification	UVF	Ulster Volunteer Force
TA	Territorial Army	v	(*versus*) against

VA	Vicar Apostolic
	Victoria and Albert Order
VAD	Voluntary Aid Detachment
V and A	Victoria and Albert Museum
VAT	Value added tax
VC	Victoria Cross
VCR	video cassette recorder
VD	Venereal disease
	Volunteer Officers' Decoration
VDU	Visual display unit
Ven	Venerable
VHF	very high frequency
VIP	Very important person
Vo	(*Verso*) on the left-hand page
VRD	Royal Naval Volunteer
	Reserve Officers' Decoration
VSO	Voluntary Service Overseas
VTOL	Vertical take-off and landing
	(*aircraft*)
W	West
WCC	World Council of Churches
WEA	Workers' Educational
	Association
WEU	Western European Union
WFTU	World Federation of Trade
	Unions
WHO	World Health Organisation
WI	West Indies
	Women's Institute
Winton:	of Winchester (*Bishop*)
WIPO	World Intellectual Property
	Organisation
WMO	World Meteorological
	Organisation
WO	Warrant Officer
WRAC	Women's Royal Army Corps
WRAF	Women's Royal Air Force
WRNS	Women's Royal Naval Service
WRVS	Women's Royal Voluntary
	Service
WS	Writer to the Signet
WTO	World Trade Organisation
WWW	World Wide Web
YMCA	Young Men's Christian
	Association
YWCA	Young Women's Christian
	Association

INDEX

Hambleton, district council 282, 298
Hamilton
  constituencies
    Scottish Parliament 271
    UK Parliament 174
Hamilton (Bermuda) 1028
Hammersmith, education authority 387
Hammersmith and Fulham
  constituency 153
  London borough council 283, 309
Hampshire
  constituencies 153
  county council 281, 295, 296
  education authority 384
Hampstead & Highgate, constituency 153
Hanoi 1022
Hanover, House of 35
Harare 1025
Harborough
  constituency 153
  district council 282, 298
harbour authorities 461
hardship funds 383
Haringey
  education authority 387
  London borough council 283, 309
Harlow
  constituency 153
  district council 282, 298
Harmonised Index of Consumer Prices (HICP) 563
Harrogate, district council 282, 298
Harrogate & Knaresborough, constituency 154
Harrow
  constituencies 154
  education authority 387
  London borough council 283, 309
Harry, Prince 22
Hart, district council 282, 298
Hartlepool
  constituency 154
  education authority 385
  unitary authority 284, 302
Harwich, constituency 154
Hastings, district council 282, 298
Hastings & Rye, constituency 154
Hatfield train crash 1105
Havana 807
Havant
  constituency 154
  district council 282, 298
Havering
  education authority 387
  London borough council 283, 309
Hawaii 1013
Hayes & Harlington, constituency 154
Hazel Grove, constituency 154
headteachers
  qualifications 376, 377
  salary 377
Health, Department of 193-5
Health Action Zones (HAZs) 429
Health Boards 426
health costs 428

Health Professions Council 406
Health Protection Agency (HPA) 224
Health and Safety Commission 224
Health and Safety Executive 224
Health Service Ombudsman 240, 430
health services, NHS 427-30
Health and Social Services Boards 426
health visitors pay review body 244
Healthy Schools Programme 428-9
Heard Island 755
Heathrow airport 453
Heathrow Express service 455
the Hebrides 314
hedgehogs 1108
Helsinki 830
Hemel Hempstead, constituency 154
Hemsworth, constituency 154
Hendon, constituency 154
Henley, constituency 154
Henry, Prince 22
Her Majesty's Inspectorate for Education and Training in Wales 370
Her Majesty's Stationery Office (HMSO) 182
Heralds' College 214
hereditary peers 41, 42-62
hereditary women peers 41
Hereford
  Bishop 70, 474
  constituency 154
Herefordshire
  education authority 385
  unitary authority 284, 302
Heriot-Watt University 394
heritage see conservation and heritage
Heritage Information 1109
Heritage Link 1109
Heritage Lottery Fund (HLF) 1109-10
Heritage Sites, World 512
Hertford, Bishop Suffragan 477
Hertford & Stortford, constituency 154
Hertfordshire
  constituencies 154
  county council 281, 295, 296
  education authority 384
  university of 395
Hertsmere
  constituency 154
  district council 282, 298
Hexham, constituency 154
Hexham and Newcastle, Bishop (RC) 483
Heywood & Middleton, constituency 154
HFEA (Human Fertilisation and Embryology Authority) 226
HGCA (Home-Grown Cereals Authority) 225
HICP (Harmonised Index of Consumer Prices) 563
HIE (Highlands and Islands Enterprise) 224
Higgs Boson 1152
High Court of Justice
  England and Wales 327, 329-30
  centres 331-4
  Northern Ireland 340

High Court of Justiciary 336, 337-8
High Peak
  constituency 155
  district council 282, 298
High Sheriffs 277
  England 294
  Wales 312
high water 1281-7
higher education 379-83
  admissions 382
  advisory bodies 390
  courses 381-2
  fees 382
    imposition of top-up 1137
  finance 381
  funding councils 391
Higher Education Council 380
Higher Education Funding Councils (HEFCs) 369, 370, 376-7, 380, 383
Higher National Certificates (HNCs) 378, 381
Higher National Course 376
Higher National Diplomas (HNDs) 378, 381
Higher National Qualifications 378
Highland
  education authority 389
  unitary authority 285, 317
Highlands and Islands Enterprise (HIE) 224
Highlands and Islands Scottish Parliament Region 273
highway authorities 456
Highways Agency 203, 456
Hillingdon
  education authority 387
  London borough council 283, 309
Hinckley and Bosworth, district council 282, 298
Hindu calendar 1268-9
  year 2004 9
Hinduism 464-5
  adherents in UK 462
hire-purchase agreements 583
Historic Buildings Council for Wales 225
historic buildings and monuments 517-22
  England 517-21
  Northern Ireland 522
  Scotland 521-2
  Wales 521
  listing of 517, 1109, 1111
  conservation of 1109-11
Historic Buildings and Monuments Commission for England 220
Historic Environment Advisory Council for Scotland 225
Historic Royal Palaces 225
Historic Scotland 1111
  list of properties 521-2
historical year 1270
Hitchin & Harpenden, constituency 155
HLF (Heritage Lottery Fund) 1109-10
HM Coastguard (HMCG) 461
HM Commissary Office 338
HM Customs and Excise 218-19
HM Fleet 360

STOP-PRESS

CHANGES SINCE PAGES WENT TO PRESS

BARONETAGE AND KNIGHTAGE
Died September 2003: Sir Terence Ernest Manitou Frost, Kt., RA; Sir John Walton David Gray, KBE, CMG; Sir Ian Bruce Hope Hunter, Kt., MBE; *Rt. Hon.* Sir Francis Brooks Purchas, Kt; Air Chief Marshal Sir Christopher Neil Foxley-Norris, GCB, DSO, OBE; Col. Sir Allan Macdonald Gilmour, KCVO, OBE, MC; *Hon.* Sir Michael Alexander Geddes Sachs, Kt.

LIFE PEERS
Died September 2003: Lord Blake (cr. 1971)

HEREDITARY PEERS
Died September 2003: Lord Leigh (5th)

PUBLIC BODIES

OFCOM
The Communications Act received Royal Assent on 17 July 2003 granting full regulatory powers to OFCOM, the regulatory body for the UK communications sector. OFCOM will become fully operational by the end of 2003 and replaces the Broadcasting Standards Commission, the Independent Television Commission, the Radio Authority, the Radio Communications Agency and Oftel.

INTERNATIONAL ORGANISATIONS

NATO
On 22 September NATO chief, George Robertson, was succeeded by the Dutch foreign minister, Jaap de Hoop Scheffer.

THE WORLD TRADE ORGANISATION (WTO)
On 12 September, the WTO agreed to admit Cambodia and Nepal as members. The two countries must ratify their accession agreements and membership is likely to take effect in 2004.

COUNTRIES OF THE WORLD

CAMBODIA
On 27 July 2003 the Cambodian People's Party (CPP) won the general election with 69 out of the 123 seats but fell short of the two-thirds majority needed to govern. Opposition parties were expected to boycott the opening of parliament on 27 September.

GUINEA-BISSAU
On 14 September the army launched a bloodless coup and arrested President Kumba Yala. President Yala resigned from his position on 18 September. A committee, led by Bissau Archbishop Jose Camnatne, was set up to propose the structure of the transitional government.

IRAQ
On 1 September Iraq's Governing Council named the 25 ministers of the new cabinet that would form an interim administration.

PALESTINE
On 6 September Mahmoud Abbas resigned from his post of Palestinian prime minister. He listed a number of reasons for his resignation including Israel's unwillingness to adhere to its obligations in the 'road map to peace' process. Ahmed Qureia accepted, in principle, Yasser Arafat's offer of the post of prime minister on 8 September.

SWEDEN
On 14 September a referendum took place on the adoption of the euro; 56.2 per cent of the 81.2% turnout voted against joining the single currency.

BRITISH EVENTS
SEPTEMBER 2003
25. The Hutton inquiry finished after 24 days, Lord Hutton stated he expected to take until December 2003 to write his report.

OBITUARIES
Cash, Johnny, singer and songwriter, aged 71 – *d.* 12 September 2003, *b.* 26 February 1932

Chilcott, Susan, soprano opera singer, aged 40 – *d.* 4 September 2003, *b.* 8 July 1963

Hayter, The 3rd Lord, last family chairman of Chubb & Sons, Locksmiths, aged 92 – *d.* 2 September 2003, *b.* 25 April 1911

Williams of Mostyn, Lord, PC, QC, Lord President of the Privy Council and leader of the House of Lords, aged 62 – *d.* 20 September 2003, *b.* 5 February 1941

SPORTS RESULTS

CRICKET
County Championship Cricket 2003: Division 1, Sussex, 257 points *Relegated,* Essex, 156 points; Nottinghamshire, 132 points; Leicestershire, 125.5 points *Division 2,* Worcestershire, 254.75 points *Promoted,* Northamptonshire, 237 points; Gloucestershire, 190 points
National League 2003: Division 1, Surrey, 50 points *Relegated,* Leicestershire, 28 points; Yorkshire 20 points; Worcestershire, 16 points
Division 2, Lancashire, 58 points *Promoted,* Northamptonshire, 50 points; Hampshire, 44 points

CYCLING
Tour of Spain 2003: Roberto Heras (Spain)

MOTOR RACING
US Grand Prix (Indianapolis, 28 September): Michael Schumacher (Germany), Ferrari

MOTOR RALLYING
British Rally Championships 2003:
Yorkshire Rally, Tapio Laukkanen (Finland), Subaru

PARLIAMENT
On 6 October 2003 Baroness Amos was appointed as leader of the House of Lords, replacing the late Lord Williams of Mostyn. Hilary Benn replaced Baroness Amos as International Development Secretary.